Official SAT Practice

CollegeBoard
+
KHANACADEMY

Start practicing now with Official SAT Practice on Khan Academy.

Benefit from:

Personalized instruction tailored to your strengths and weaknesses.

Practice questions approved by the test maker, and official SAT practice tests.

SAT

Engaging lessons that build familiarity with the SAT format, question styles, and testing experience.

Get started at
satpractice.org

CollegeBoard

2017

College
Handbook

CollegeBoard

2017

College Handbook

Fifty-Fourth Edition
The College Board, New York

About the College Board

The College Board is a mission-driven not-for-profit organization that connects students to college success and opportunity. Founded in 1900, the College Board was created to expand access to higher education. Today, the membership association is made up of over 6,000 of the world's leading educational institutions and is dedicated to promoting excellence and equity in education. Each year, the College Board helps more than seven million students prepare for a successful transition to college through programs and services in college readiness and college success — including the SAT® and the Advanced Placement Program®. The organization also serves the education community through research and advocacy on behalf of students, educators, and schools.

For further information, visit www.collegeboard.org.

Editorial inquiries concerning this book should be directed to Guidance Publications, The College Board, 250 Vesey Street, New York, NY 10281; or telephone 800-323-7155.

Copies of this book are available from your local bookseller or may be ordered from College Board Publications, P.O. Box 7500, London, KY 40742-7500. The book may also be ordered online through the College Board Store at www.collegeboard.org. The price is $31.99.

© 2016 The College Board. College Board, ACCUPLACER, Advanced Placement Program, AP, CLEP, College-Level Examination Program, CSS/Financial Aid PROFILE, SAT, SpringBoard, and the acorn logo are registered trademarks of the College Board. My College QuickStart, MyRoad, My SAT Study Plan, SAT Preparation Booklet, SAT Preparation Center, SAT Reasoning Test, SAT Subject Tests, Score Choice, Skills Insight, The Official SAT Online Course, The Official SAT Question of the Day, The Official SAT Study Guide, and The Official Study Guide for all SAT Subject Tests are trademarks owned by the College Board. PSAT/NMSQT is a registered trademark of the College Board and National Merit Scholarship Corporation. All other products and services may be trademarks of their respective owners. Visit the College Board on the Web: www.collegeboard.org.

ISBN: 978-1-4573-0773-7

Printed in the United States of America

Distributed by Macmillan. For information on bulk purchases, please contact Macmillan Corporate and Premium Sales Department at (800) 221-7945, x5442.

Contents

Preface

When the *College Handbook* first appeared in 1941, students and parents had little access to college information of any kind. Now, in this digital age, many find the amount of available information to be overwhelming.

What's needed is a single, trusted source where the key facts about colleges can be compared and contrasted on a consistent basis. From its inception, the *Handbook* has met this need by providing college-bound students and their advisers with the authoritative, reliable and up-to-date facts necessary to make informed college decisions.

This edition of the *Handbook* presents facts about 3,840 colleges, universities and technical schools. To be included, an institution must be accredited by a national or regional accrediting association recognized by the U.S. Department of Education and offer some undergraduate degree programs — at least an associate degree.

Throughout the *Handbook*, information is presented in accordance with the Common Data Set initiative, in which the College Board has taken a leading role. The goal of this collaborative effort with other publishers and college administrators is to provide students with the most accurate, consistently comparable data available.

The college descriptions are based primarily on information supplied by the colleges themselves in response to the College Board's Annual Survey of Colleges, with some data supplied by federal and state agencies. The survey was completed by participating colleges in spring 2016. Several thousand college administrators across the country participated in this effort. Without their continued cooperation, publication of the *Handbook* would not be possible.

A staff of data editors verified the facts to be certain that all descriptions are as complete and accurate as possible. Although the College Board makes every effort to ensure that the information about colleges is correct and up to date, we urge students to confirm facts with the colleges themselves.

The enormous task of data collection, management and verification was directed by Chris Hagan, with the assistance of Stan Bernstein. Jenny Xie, Randy Peery, Sara Millones, Kayla Tompkins, David Christ, Karen Villa, Jameeka Watkins, Scott Nicoll and Cedric Crawley compiled, edited and verified the data. Technical support was provided by Doris Chow, Assar Tarazi, John Reynolds, Enrique Lara, Wayne Lau, Priyanka Sabapathy and Srinivas Bachu. Thanks also to the staff at DataStream Content Solutions, Inc., who provide the technological savvy that helps us turn our data into books.

We wish to give special acknowledgment to Stan Bernstein, who recently retired. It is with sincere appreciation that we thank him for his many years of yeoman service both to the College Board and to the entire higher education community.

We also thank our readers — you and the many students, parents and counselors whose comments and suggestions over the years have helped to make this the most widely used college directory in the nation. We welcome your suggestions on how the *Handbook* can continue to meet the ever-changing needs of future generations of college-bound students.

Tom Vanderberg
Senior Editor, Guidance Publishing

What's in this book

If you're beginning your college search feeling a bit overwhelmed and intimidated by the sheer number of choices, you're not alone. Just about everyone starts out feeling that way. But even the most daunting job can be easily handled with the right tools and a plan, and the *College Handbook* gives you both.

Getting Started

The *College Handbook* is the best place to begin your college search, and you will no doubt find yourself returning to this source as your search progresses and evolves. You should not, however, rely on this book exclusively. Take advantage of the other resources available to you — the Web, social media, campus visits and interviews, college fairs, your school counselor, family and friends — before you make your final decision. Don't be dismayed if you find that you must change directions more than once as you learn about the colleges. This only means that you are learning more about yourself as well.

The *Handbook* is divided into four major sections. The first (where you are now) contains guidance materials to help you plan for college. Four-year college descriptions are in the second section, two-year college descriptions are in the third, and the last section contains tables and indexes. Margin tabs help you to quickly move from section to section.

Although you might be eager to dive right into the college descriptions, it is far better to start your college search with a basic idea of what you want to look for. Take the time to go through the guidance materials in the first section to get on the right track. Read the articles, ranging from college admission and placement tests to dorm life. The valuable insights you gain will give you confidence as you continue your college search.

Once you can identify your needs and preferences with regard to college size and type and have an idea of what other characteristics are important to you, the indexes at the end of the book will help you locate colleges that fit the bill.

KNOW THE LINGO

You'll find sidebars like this throughout the first part of this book highlighting and defining key terms. There's also a comprehensive glossary beginning on page 39.

For a complete explanation of the various index categories, see "Tables and Indexes" beginning on page 7.

The heart and soul of the *Handbook*, of course, are the descriptions of four-year and two-year colleges. These follow standard formats to make it easy to find a particular item of information in any description and to compare one college with another. Read "The College Descriptions" below to see what the descriptions contain and how the information is presented. If you are not sure of the meaning of a term found in the *Handbook* descriptions or guidance materials, check the glossary beginning on page 39.

The College Descriptions

The college. Each description begins with the college's official name — which isn't always the one in popular use. The heading also includes the college's city, state and website address. You will find college websites to be invaluable resources in your college search. The designation "CB member" after the college's name indicates that the college is a member of the College Board; the four-digit CB code should be used when requesting that SAT® scores or Advanced Placement® (AP®) scores be sent to the college.

Key facts. The bulleted list highlights information that you may want to compare across colleges and that you'll need if you decide to apply. This information includes:

- Type of institution (e.g., liberal arts college, university) and whether it has a religious affiliation.

- Whether the campus is urban, suburban or rural, and whether it is primarily a residential or a commuter campus.

- Total number of undergraduate students; profile of the undergraduate student body (percent part-time, women, minority breakdown, international); total number of graduate students on campus. *Two-year undergraduate data are included under Student Profile.*

- Percentage of applicants admitted to the freshman class, which gives you some idea of how competitive the college is. *Four-year colleges only.*

- Admission requirements for fall 2017: tests, essay, interview (if required of all applicants).

- Percentage of students who graduate within six years (most students take more than four years to earn a bachelor's degree). Caveat: This figure is based on students who enrolled as freshmen and remained to graduate; it does not include students who transferred into or out of the college during that period.

General information. The date the college was founded, the type of institutional accreditation it has, the number and type of degrees awarded in 2014-2015, and whether the college has an ROTC program, will give you a sense of the academic life on campus. Whether the college organizes its calendar on a semester, trimester, quarter or some other schedule indicates the way the college structures its courses.

Pay particular attention to the faculty information. The total number of faculty and its makeup are important to your everyday experience at an institution. Class size information, showing percentages of classes with few or many students, is another indication of a college's learning environment. Colleges were also invited to provide a list of special facilities (from arboretums to zoos) or additional unique information about their institutions in this section.

For two-year colleges only: This is where you will find total enrollment figures for both degree-seeking and non-degree-seeking students, and information about partnerships with other schools or organizations.

Freshman class profile. (*Four-year colleges*) This provides a snapshot of the college's fall 2015 freshman class and is presented in tabular format to make it easily accessible. This is the best source of information about whether your own profile fits in with that of students currently attending the college, and whether you'd be comfortable if admitted.

- Number who applied, were admitted and enrolled.

- Mid-50 percent of enrolled freshmen's SAT/ACT test scores. This is the score range for half the freshman class. (Remember that 25 percent of enrolled freshmen scored below and 25 percent above the reported figures.)

- Information about high school GPA and class rank.

- Percentage who completed the year in good standing and returned as sophomores.

- Percentage who come from out of state, live on campus, are international students, and join fraternities or sororities.

Student profile. (*Two-year colleges*) This is similar to the freshman class profile for four-year colleges, but the data presented covers the entire undergraduate student body.

- Percentage enrolled in transfer or vocational programs. Number admitted and enrolled as first-time, first-year students. Percentage who already have a bachelor's degree or higher. Number who transferred from other institutions.

- Percentage of the total undergraduate student body who are part-time students, live on campus, are women, come from out of state, are minorities and are international students.

Transfer out. (*Two-year colleges*)

- Percentage of students in transfer programs who go on to four-year colleges.

- Colleges to which most students transferred in 2015.

Basis for selection. This is where you can find the details of a college's admission policies, including factors the college considers most important in deciding whether or not to offer you admission. If it says "Open admission," that means the college accepts anyone with a high school or GED diploma, space permitting. Special requirements for homeschooled and learning-disabled students are also reported here.

High school preparation. Almost all colleges listed in the *Handbook* require a high school diploma or its equivalent. Some colleges have very specific requirements in terms of education background and high school courses taken. The required and recommended number of course units that applicants should have taken in high school is listed here. Where a range is given, the lower number represents the required units; the higher number is a recommendation.

2016-17 annual costs. You should estimate the total annual costs for each college you are considering. In doing so, the elements listed below need to be considered. Some colleges were unable to report updated costs at the time this book went to press; for those schools, costs are for the 2015-16 academic year.

- *Tuition/fees* include the cost of instruction and mandated fees for all students. For public colleges, both in-state and out-of-state costs are listed. If the college combines tuition, fees, and room and board expenses, that single figure is given as a comprehensive fee.

- *Room/board* figures are for a student living on campus in a double room with a full meal plan. Single rooms or rooms for three or more could cost a lot more or less than the figure reported here. Many colleges have a range of meal plans with fewer meals per week, which would lower your board cost.

- *Books/supplies* expenses can vary depending on the program you take. Some fields, such as art or architecture, may require more expensive supplies.

- *Personal expenses* include items such as clothing, laundry, entertainment and furnishings. Personal expenses will vary widely depending on your lifestyle. Transportation costs are not included.

- *Per-credit-hour tuition* (two-year colleges only) is of particular interest to students planning to attend college part time.

Financial aid. This information provides a summary of financial aid awarded for the academic year(s) indicated, and describes financial aid award policies for need-based and non-need-based aid. This information will give you an idea of how first-year and undergraduate student assistance has been awarded and will help you compare financial aid policies among the colleges. You should always contact the admission or financial aid office for complete information and for answers to any questions you might have regarding eligibility and award policies.

Application procedures. This is where you can find out about the college's application procedures and deadlines for both admission and financial aid.

- *Admission.* Most colleges require an application fee, noted here, but will waive it for applicants with need. Take note of any "priority dates" — after which qualified applicants are considered on a first-come, first-served basis, and only for as long as slots are available.

- *Financial aid.* Required forms plus priority, closing, notification and reply dates are listed for fall-term financial aid applications. The Free Application for Federal Student Aid (FAFSA) is required by every college offering federal financial aid. If the college requires the CSS/Financial Aid PROFILE® to determine your eligibility for nonfederal funds, it is noted here. "Institutional form" means the college has a form of its own. Pay special attention to priority dates and deadlines; if the college indicates "no deadline" for financial aid, it means it will continue to process requests as long as funds are available. You should always apply as early as possible to obtain the best consideration for financial aid awards.

Academics. Many colleges offer a range of special study options that can enrich or enhance your education experience. Special academic programs are listed in this section. Check the glossary for brief descriptions of each of the programs listed.

College policies on granting credit or advanced placement through the College Board's AP Program, College-Level Examination Program® (CLEP®), SAT Subject Tests™, and/or other placement programs and institutional tests are listed next. Most colleges have a maximum number of credit hours by examination that may be counted toward a degree, which is also listed.

Academic support services list the programs the college provides to assist students in succeeding academically. Preadmission summer programs, special counselors, tutoring, learning disabled programs and study skills assistance are some of the options offered.

Honors college/program. If a college has a separate undergraduate honors college or a program with different admission and academic offerings from those available to regular students, this section will tell you what's available and how to apply.

Majors. Only majors leading to a bachelor's degree (for four-year colleges) or an associate degree (for two-year colleges) are included here. They are listed alphabetically by general category. The majors listed here are based on the U.S. Department of Education's Classification of Instructional Programs; colleges were asked to match the majors they offer to this list. Many colleges additionally offer concentrations within a major, which are not reflected here.

Most popular majors. This will give you an idea of whether a substantial number of students are completing a major in an area that is of interest to you. This list is based on the percentage of students who were awarded degrees in each of the general categories listed in the 2014-15 academic year.

Computing on campus. Whether you bring your own computer to campus, or plan on using college-provided workstations, you'll want to know what technological support the college provides for student use, and whether the college requires you to bring your own PC or laptop. This section lists the number of workstations available for student use and where they're located; whether dorms are wired for high-speed Internet access and/or linked to the campus network; if there is a wireless network; if there's online course registration, an online library or student Web hosting; and whether commuter students can link to the campus network.

Student life. If you attend the college, you will need to know if it requires enrollees to attend freshman orientation, and if it has policies and regulations governing student behavior.

If on-campus housing is available — whether it's in the form of dormitories, apartments, fraternity/sorority housing or cooperative housing — it will be indicated here. Most dormitories today are coeducational, but many colleges offer single-sex accommodations either in separate buildings or separate floors. Some colleges are now also offering "substance-free" or "wellness" dormitories, whose residents pledge not to use alcohol, tobacco or any illegal drugs. This section also indicates if on-campus housing is guaranteed for freshmen, or for all four years; and the policies and deadlines for deposits.

Most colleges have provided a selective list of student activities sponsored by the institution. Read the list carefully to see if it reflects the type of student organizations and opportunities of interest to you.

Athletics. Intercollegiate and intramural sports available at the college are listed here, along with the team name. Sports offered for men or women only are indicated by (M) or (W). The athletic association to which the college belongs also is indicated. If you want to know which colleges play in the NCAA and at what division level, see the index at the back of this book titled "NCAA sports by division," where you'll see each college listed by sport.

Student services. This section lists the college's basic range of services for students. Among these are health, personal counseling, services for adult students, student employment services, placement service for graduates, veterans' counseling and on-campus day care. This section also lists special services/facilities for learning disabled students and those with visual, speech or hearing impairments.

Contact. The last item in each description provides the admission office's address, telephone and fax numbers, the name and/or title of the admission director, and the mailing address of the college office to contact for further information and applications.

Brief Descriptions

The 35 colleges that did not respond to our Annual Survey of Colleges are described in brief with the following information: name, city, state, college type, accreditation, location and calendar. Annual costs and financial aid information are provided, if available. The addresses to contact for further information are also listed.

KNOW THE LINGO

NCAA — The National Collegiate Athletic Association. This is the largest collegiate athletic association, and it oversees the most athletic scholarship money. The NCAA governs league play in 23 championship sports.

NAIA — The National Association of Intercollegiate Athletics. Its members are mostly small colleges, offering 13 sports.

NJCAA — The National Junior College Athletic Association. NJCAA members are all two-year community or junior colleges.

USCAA — United States Collegiate Athletic Association. USCAA's members are primarily very small colleges.

NCCAA — National Christian College Athletic Association. NCCAA sponsors league play among Bible colleges and other Christian-oriented institutions.

Tables and Indexes

The tables and indexes in the back of this book are a useful tool to find colleges quickly and zero in on the schools that interest you.

Early Application and Wait List Outcomes

If you are considering applying to a college early, the Early Decision and Early Action table (that follows the Two-year section) shows application deadlines and notification dates for early application programs, as well as the number of students who applied and were admitted last year under those policies.

If you find that you have been placed on a college's wait list for acceptance, consult the Wait List table that appears next. It will give you a sense of your chances, by showing how many students were placed on the wait list last year, how many accepted their place on the list, and how many were eventually admitted from the list.

College Indexes

You can use the college indexes to quickly find schools that interest you. In most of the indexes, colleges are listed alphabetically by state because, for many students, geographic location is a primary requirement. Colleges that are part of a system are listed alphabetically under the system name.

The following explanation of index terms may help you decide whether a certain type of college or a special program or policy interests you.

College type

Liberal arts. Sometimes known as arts and sciences. The study of liberal arts is intended to develop general knowledge and reasoning ability as opposed to specific preparation for a career. Most liberal arts colleges are privately controlled. They generally don't offer as many majors in the technical or scientific disciplines as comprehensive colleges or universities.

Upper-division. Offer the last two years of undergraduate study (junior and senior courses only), usually in specialized programs leading to the bachelor's degree. Students generally transfer to upper-division colleges after completing an associate degree or after finishing their second year of study at a four-year college.

Specialized. Concentrate their offerings in one or two specific areas, such as business or engineering. Students who enroll at specialized colleges generally have a precise idea of what they want to study.

KNOW THE LINGO

There are so many **types of specialized colleges** that we didn't have room to describe them all here. If you'd like to know more about a specific type of college, see the glossary that begins on page 39.

Special characteristics

Colleges for men/women. Some of these colleges may enroll a few women or men, but their student bodies are predominantly of one sex.

Colleges with religious affiliations. Lists each college under the official name of the denomination with which it is affiliated. Student life at some colleges is greatly influenced by the religious affiliation. At other colleges, the affiliation may be historic only, having little influence on college life.

Historically black colleges. Identifies historically or predominantly black colleges that are committed to educating African American students. The information was obtained from the National Association for Equal Opportunity in Higher Education and the U.S. government.

Hispanic-serving colleges. Identifies colleges where Hispanic students comprise at least 25 percent of the total full-time undergraduate enrollment. The information was obtained from the Hispanic Association of Colleges and Universities (HACU).

Tribal colleges. Identifies colleges committed to serving geographically isolated populations of Native Americans. The information was obtained from the Carnegie Classification of Institutions of Higher Education.

Undergraduate enrollment size

The number of students at a college helps determine its environment.

Very small. Fewer than 750 undergraduates.

Small. 750 to 1,999 undergraduates.

Medium to large. 2,000 to 7,499 undergraduates.

Large. 7,500 to 14,999 undergraduates.

Very large. 15,000 or more undergraduates.

Admission selectivity

Admit under 50%, 50%–75%, over 75%. Colleges in three categories of selectivity that limit admission to applicants who meet specific requirements.

Open admission. Colleges that admit virtually all applicants with a high school diploma or its equivalent, as long as space is available.

Many public institutions offer open admission to state residents but have selective admission requirements for out-of-state students or to selected programs; check the college descriptions to see what applies.

Admission/placement policies

No closing date. These colleges will accept applications up to the time of registration.

SAT Subject Test required/recommended. These two indexes list colleges that require or recommend that applicants take one or more

SAT Subject Tests for admission. The college descriptions provide more detailed information.

Colleges that offer ROTC

The U.S. armed forces offer Reserve Officers' Training Corps programs that prepare candidates for commissions in the Air Force, Army and Navy (Naval ROTC includes the Marine Corps). These programs are offered either at the colleges listed in the index or at cooperating institutions. ROTC programs may take either two or four years to complete. Use this index, organized by branch of service, to find colleges that offer the ROTC program of interest to you.

Colleges with NCAA sports

Lists National Collegiate Athletic Association (NCAA) championship sports by division level and the colleges, state by state, that offer them. Also indicates whether each sport is available for men only or for women only. (Crew is an NCAA sport for women only; use the college search on bigfuture.org to find colleges that offer crew for men.) To be an NCAA member, colleges must offer at least four sports and have at least one in each season (fall, winter and spring).

Alphabetical index of colleges

Lists the name and state abbreviation for every institution in the *Handbook*. If a name has changed, the old name is cross-referenced to the new name.

KEEP IN MIND

The **NCAA sports indexes** only list colleges that offer sports for which the NCAA holds a championship. There are NCAA sports that don't have a championship, such as men's rowing. And remember that many colleges offer sports through a different association (NAIA or NJCAA), or offer intramural play.

About accreditation

Every college and university in this book is accredited by an agency recognized by the U.S. Department of Education. That means you can trust that any of them will give you an education that meets basic standards for college-level study, that your studies will qualify for federal need-based financial aid and/or federal education tax breaks, and that the degree you will earn at the end of your studies will be recognized by future employers.

What Is Accreditation?

Accreditation is a voluntary process of peer review and self-regulation. The standards for each accrediting agency are slightly different but, generally, each agency ensures that its members meet basic standards in their administrative procedures, physical facilities and the quality of their academic programs.

The agencies listed on page 12 are *regional* and *national* agencies that accredit entire institutions. In majors that lead to a professional certification — such as nursing, engineering or teacher education — there may also be *specialized* agencies that accredit just one program, department or school at the college. For example, the Accreditation Board for Engineering and Technology (ABET) accredits engineering and engineering technology programs. In addition to guaranteeing the academic quality of programs, these specialized agencies often have a guidance component that helps university students make the transition to professional careers. You can find more information about specialized accrediting agencies in the College Board's *Book of Majors*, or at the Council for Higher Education Accreditation's website (chea.org).

The agencies listed on page 12

GOOD TO KNOW

Every college contained in the *College Handbook* and bigfuture.org's College Search has been accredited by either a national or regional accrediting agency recognized by the U.S. Department of Education.

What Does Accreditation Mean to Me?

If you attend an accredited college, you can be sure that:

- You will be able to use federal student aid (Title IV money) to help pay for your costs if you qualify based on financial need.

- Your tuition will qualify you for federal income tax deductions and/or credits (if you meet other conditions).

- Academic credits you earn there are eligible to transfer to another accredited college.

- Employers and professional licensing boards will recognize the degree you earn as an academic credential, as will graduate schools and other academic institutions to which you may apply.

You should, however, understand what accreditation *doesn't* mean:

- There's no guarantee that you will receive federal need-based financial aid just by attending any college, even if it's accredited.

- Regional and national accreditation ensures that every academic program at the college meets standards, but that doesn't mean that the quality of every program at the college is equal.

- If you're applying for transfer from one undergraduate institution to another, there's no guarantee that all your credits will count toward the graduation requirements of the college where you plan to finish your degree. If you plan to attend a lower-division college for your first two years of study and then go on to earn a bachelor's degree, be sure to talk to the transfer counselor there before enrolling in courses.

- Similarly, there's no guarantee that graduate schools or employers will see your undergraduate course of study as appropriate preparation for the demands of their program or job requirements.

REGIONAL ACCREDITING ASSOCIATIONS

Middle States Commission on Higher Education
3624 Market Street
Philadelphia, PA 19104
msche.org

Delaware, District of Columbia, Maryland, New Jersey, New York, Pennsylvania, Puerto Rico, Virgin Islands

New England Association of Schools and Colleges
3 Burlington Woods Drive, Suite 100
Burlington, MA 01803-4514
neasc.org

Connecticut, Maine, Massachusetts, New Hampshire, Rhode Island, Vermont

North Central Association of Colleges and Schools
The Higher Learning Commission
230 South LaSalle Street, Suite 7-500
Chicago, IL 60604-1411
ncahlc.org

Arizona, Arkansas, Colorado, Illinois, Indiana, Iowa, Kansas, Michigan, Minnesota, Missouri, Nebraska, New Mexico, North Dakota, Ohio, Oklahoma, South Dakota, West Virginia, Wisconsin, Wyoming

Northwest Commission on Colleges and Universities
8060 165th Avenue N.E., Suite 100
Redmond, WA 98052
nwccu.org

Alaska, Idaho, Montana, Nevada, Oregon, Utah, Washington

Southern Association of Colleges and Schools
1866 Southern Lane
Decatur, GA 30033-4097
sacs.org

Alabama, Florida, Georgia, Kentucky, Louisiana, Mississippi, North Carolina, South Carolina, Tennessee, Texas, Virginia

Western Association of Schools and Colleges
WASC Senior College and University Commission
985 Atlantic Avenue, Suite 100
Alameda, CA 94501
wascsenior.org

Accrediting Commission for Community and Junior Colleges
10 Commercial Boulevard, Suite 204
Novato, CA 94949
accjc.org

American Samoa, California, Guam, Hawaii, Trust Territory of the Pacific

New York Board of Regents
Office of College and University Evaluation
New York State Education Department
89 Washington Avenue
Albany, NY 12234
regents.nysed.gov

NATIONAL ACCREDITING ASSOCIATIONS

ACICS **Accrediting Council for Independent Colleges and Schools**
Washington, DC
acics.org

ACCSC **Accrediting Commission of Career Schools and Colleges**
Arlington, VA
accsc.org

ABHE **Association for Biblical Higher Education**
Orlando, FL
abhe.org

AARTS **Association of Advanced Rabbinical and Talmudic Schools**
11 Broadway, Suite 405
New York, NY 10004

ATS **Association of Theological Schools in the United States and Canada**
Pittsburgh, PA
ats.edu

DETC **Distance Education and Training Council**
Washington, DC
detc.org

TRACS **Transnational Association of Christian Colleges and Schools**
Forest, VA
tracs.org

Selecting colleges

There are more than 3,900 accredited colleges in the United States. This book will help you get an idea of the types of colleges you're interested in attending and learn more about colleges that fall into those categories. From there, you can create a list of colleges you would like to learn more about, and start requesting information from them, visiting their websites, and (if you can) visiting their campuses. By December of your senior year, you should have your choices narrowed down to a final list of four to eight colleges to which you want to apply.

KNOW THE LINGO

"Target" school — a college you'd like to attend that will be somewhat difficult for you to get in. Usually a college where your GPA and standardized test scores would be about average. Most students apply to between two and four target schools.

"Reach" school — a college you'd like to attend, but will be difficult for you to get in. Your GPA and test scores may be below average for this school, but some other aspect of your application may make up for that. You should apply to one or two reach schools.

"Safety" school — a college you'd like to attend that's also sure to accept you. You should apply to at least one safety school.

Finding Your Fit

Every college is unique in some way. And everybody has different interests, ambitions and needs. When investigating colleges, you will probably look for different things than your friends, parents and siblings did when they applied. But there are some "big picture" elements that everyone, including you, should consider.

Colleges fall into broad categories — small and large, liberal arts and professionally oriented, academically selective, and open admission. There are also personal criteria you need to consider, such as whether a college is in your hometown or a thousand miles away.

Type of Institution

This will give you a sense of how the college organizes its academic departments. Different types of institutions include:

Liberal arts colleges offer a broad base of courses in the humanities, social sciences and natural sciences. Most are private and focus mainly on undergraduate students. Classes tend to be small, and personal attention is available. An education at a liberal arts college will prepare you for a broad range of career and graduate school options.

Community and junior colleges offer a degree after the completion of two years of full-time study. They frequently offer technical programs that prepare you for immediate entry into the job market. To learn more about the benefits of attending a community college, read "About Community Colleges" on page 20.

Agricultural colleges, technical schools and professional institutes emphasize preparation for specific careers. Examples include art institutes and music conservatories, Bible colleges, business colleges, schools of health science, seminaries and rabbinical yeshivas, and teachers colleges.

Universities are generally bigger than colleges and offer more majors and research facilities. Classes in introductory subjects may have hundreds of students, and some classes may be taught by graduate students.

Most universities are subdivided into colleges or schools. For example, a state university might have a large college of liberal arts, a school of engineering and applied sciences, a small school of nursing, a teachers college and several graduate schools all on the same campus.

Different universities have different rules for whether you can, for example, take a computer science course offered by the engineering school while enrolled in the liberal arts college. Generally, the different colleges of a university share campus facilities (such as dorms and dining halls) and some research facilities (such as libraries), and a university-wide administration handles admission, financial aid and similar services for the various colleges.

Size of the Student Body and Faculty

Size will affect many of your opportunities and experiences, including:

- the range of academic majors offered;
- the possibilities for extracurricular activities and athletics;
- the amount of personal attention you'll receive from faculty, administrators and other students; and
- the availability and size of academic facilities such as laboratories, libraries and art studios.

When considering size, be sure to look beyond the raw number of students attending. For example, perhaps you're considering a large university, but you'll be applying to its much smaller school of health sciences.

Also remember to investigate not just the number of faculty, but also how accessible faculty members are to students. You can get a rough sense of this from the "class size" entry in the *Handbook* descriptions, but if you are already interested in a particular major or department, it really helps to visit the campus and talk to students who are enrolled in that program.

Location

Do you want to go home frequently, or do you see this as a time to experience a new part of the country? Perhaps you like an urban environment with access to museums, ethnic food or major league ball games. Or maybe you hope for easy access to the outdoors or the serenity of a small town.

Academic Quality

The easiest way to measure a school's quality and the satisfaction of its students is to learn the percentage of students who return after the first year and the percentage of entering students who remain to graduate. Comparatively good retention and graduation rates are indicators that responsible academic, social and financial support systems exist for most students. These figures are reported in the *Handbook* descriptions.

One of the best ways to research a college's reputation is by talking to people who are familiar with colleges or the fields that interest you. Ask your parents if anyone they know went to one of the colleges on your short list. Talk to your school counselor — he or she probably knows quite a bit about local colleges and nationally known universities. Talk to your teachers — they might know the academic reputations of departments that relate to their teaching field. You can also research the reputations of colleges on the Internet, but beware — not everyone on the Internet is an expert, and sometimes rumors get passed along as fact.

If you already know what subjects you want to study, research the strengths of those schools or departments at the colleges and universities in which you're interested. One way to do this is to look at their departmental websites for the following:

- Are there a lot of courses offered, or just a few?

- Do the courses offered concentrate on one subfield within the major? This is not necessarily a bad thing, but it could tell you that the department is strong in some areas and weak in others.

- Do most of the professors have terminal degrees in their field? Usually the Ph.D. is the terminal degree, but in some fields, it's another graduate degree.

- The website may also tell you about research and scholarship that professors are doing, work that undergraduate students are doing, or the careers of recent alumni.

These are general questions that would apply to any department. For questions to ask colleges about a specific major, see the College Board's *Book of Majors*. It contains profiles of undergraduate majors, and each profile has a list of things to look for in a department offering that major.

Campus Life

Consider what your college life will be like beyond the classroom. Aim for a balance between academics, activities and social life. In your research, try to learn the answers to these questions:

- What extracurricular activities, athletics and special activities are available?
- Does the community around the college offer interesting outlets for students?
- Are students welcomed by the surrounding community?
- Is there a congregation of my faith on campus? Are there student groups based around my ethnic group or national culture?
- Is the college religiously affiliated? If so, how does that affiliation affect student life — for example, is attendance at services required?
- How do fraternities and sororities influence campus life?
- Is housing guaranteed? How are dorms assigned? (For more about housing options, see page 37.)

You can learn the answers to many of these questions by reading the college profiles in this book, but for others, you may have to do more in-depth research, such as visiting the college's website or its campus.

Can I Afford This College?

If you only remember one thing from this article, make this it: don't rule out a college that is a great fit because it looks too expensive. The "sticker price" of a college may look scary, but **hardly anyone pays the sticker price because of financial aid**. You won't know how much aid the college will offer you until you apply, so go for it.

The *Handbook* descriptions give you a general idea of the college's cost and its financial aid packages. For a more detailed "financial aid picture" of the colleges and easy, step-by-step instructions for applying for aid, get a copy of the College Board's *Getting Financial Aid* at your library or local bookseller.

Where Can I Get In?

Of course, finding a college that's the right fit for you is only half of the equation. Unless you're applying to a college with an open admission policy, you also have to convince the admission reviewers that you really are a good fit.

What Are Colleges Looking For?

When they review your application, college admission officers want to see, foremost, "students who have challenged themselves academically," says Martha Pitts, the director of admission at the University of Oregon. But they don't just want to see good grades; they also want to make sure that candidates will add something positive to the campus community. Mike Sexton, the

"Students should look at a school because it's the right fit for them academically, socially, spiritually and geographically. **Is cost an important part?** Yes. It's a consideration, but only one among many."

— *Bonnie Lee Behm, Director of Financial Assistance, Villanova University*

Where to Find More Information

Once you've created a list of colleges you'd like to learn more about, you should try to get information from as many sources as possible. Different people will tell you different things about colleges, so the more the merrier!

✔ **Your school counselor** can tell you about colleges and let you know when college fairs or visits from admission recruiters are coming to your school. He or she may also have a file of college course catalogs, viewbooks and other literature.

✔ **Visiting admission staff** who come to your school — either by themselves or as part of a large college fair — can tell you more about the college they represent and its application process.

✔ **College websites and guidebooks** offer a wealth of information about majors offered, activities and life on campus.

✔ **Returning graduates** who went to your school will probably be eager to tell you all about their experiences.

✔ **Campus visits** are a chance to see the campus and its dorms, libraries and other facilities in person; talk to admission officers (whether informally or in an interview); observe classes and talk to students; and much more. Try to visit the campus while classes are in session. For tips on planning a visit, read the articles in the "Find a College" section of bigfuture.org, or get the latest edition of *Campus Visits & College Interviews* by Zola Dincin Schneider (College Board, 2012).

vice president of enrollment management at Santa Clara University, puts it this way: He looks at the applications for "a spark that tells us they'll be good roommates, good lab partners, good to have in class."

One thing you should never do is try to guess what the admission committee is looking for and try to tailor your application to it. Admission officers read thousands of applications every year, and they can almost instantly tell feigned interest in a college or a false presentation of oneself from the real thing.

Your transcript is the most important thing

There it is, in large type, but it bears repeating: Your high school transcript is the most important thing for your application success. Colleges want to see that you've challenged yourself academically throughout high school and that you are willing to put academics first for the next two to four years.

Be aware that admission staff won't just look at the grades on your transcript. They will look at which courses you took, and the grade trend over four years. For example, if you barely passed Intro to Biology as a freshman, but then turned around and got a B in AP Biology as a junior, colleges will consider that a plus. On the other hand, if you've been getting steady C's in English for the last three years, colleges may wonder why you haven't improved.

A related factor that admission officers look for is an upward trend in the difficulty of your course work. Sexton says he becomes concerned when students "start taking a lighter load senior year. I can see why they would do it sometimes, but for some people, it's going to close doors." Don't feel you need to suffocate yourself with too many courses and extracurriculars, but don't try to cruise through your senior year either.

Test scores are just part of the picture

Your scores on the admission tests can be important, but generally they're not as important as your high school transcript. Most often, admission officers will use your test scores to supplement your transcript or help them interpret it.

Although grades earned in high school courses are very important, they don't always mean the same thing. An A earned in the same course taught by different teachers in your school may not represent exactly the same amount of work, the same teaching or the same level of learning. Likewise, an A earned in the same course but in different schools and different parts of the country may not really be the same. That's where standardized tests can help.

If you've already taken an admission test (e.g., the SAT), look at your scores the same way the admission committee will look at them — objectively. They don't represent all that you've achieved or will achieve. The scores are one indicator of how far along you are right now in developing the skills you need for college and a career. In deciding where to apply to college, it's helpful to compare your scores to those of the mid-50 percent score range of freshmen who enrolled the previous year in the colleges you're considering. You'll find this information in the section titled "freshman class profile" of each four-year college description. If your scores compare favorably, you're on your way to finding the right match. But if your scores are higher or lower, it's not necessarily a mismatch. Only 50 out of every 100 freshmen had scores in that range, which means 25 had higher scores and 25 had lower scores. You may be well suited for this college in other important ways. You'll be better able to decide after reading the entire college description, visiting the college's website and (if possible) visiting the campus.

Personality can go a long way

Very few colleges assess applications using just transcripts and test scores. Most will ask for information about your involvement in extracurricular activities, recommendations from your teachers, a recommendation from your counselor, and a brief application essay. Some will ask for an interview as well. A few will ask for recommendations from someone who is not on your school faculty, for example, a minister, employer or friend.

What all of these application components have in common is that they help admission officers look "beyond the numbers" and see what kind of person you are, and how you might contribute to their campus community. They won't be the first, or most important, thing the college looks at, but they can help round out your application and may help the admission committee decide between you and several equally qualified candidates.

Here's a closer look at each of the personal factors colleges usually look at:

Recommendations. Recommendations will give the college a sense of your overall attitude toward learning, your character and the context for the grades on your transcript. Do you have a real passion for mathematics? Did you try really hard and improve over the year to get that "B" in U.S. History? Or could you have been an "A" student if you had taken the class more seriously? For tips on choosing which teachers to ask for recommendations, and how to ask them, see pages 27 and 28.

Extracurriculars. Your involvement in extracurricular activities — whether they're sports, a part-time job, volunteering in your community, the school play, the yearbook or something entirely different — will tell the college about how active you are in your community. From that, they'll have a good picture of your leadership potential and how likely you are to contribute to their own campus community. They'll also have a sense of how much time you spend on nonschool work, which gives them a context for reading your grades. Generally, it's best to dedicate yourself to a few extracurricular activities in which you're really interested. Making minor contributions to 10 different activities doesn't look as impressive as becoming a leader of one club that you're passionate about. Similarly, changing activities every semester makes you look fickle; it's better to show some consistency.

Essays. Admission officers use application essays to learn how creative you are, how well you can write and, sometimes, whether you're truly interested in attending their college. They are the most subjective of all the components of an application, but they are also the one component over which you have total control. For more about how applications are used by admission officials, and tips on writing your essays, read the latest edition of *The College Application Essay* by Sarah Myers McGinty (College Board, 2015).

Interviews. Interviews are rarely required and usually don't carry a great deal of weight in the overall application. If you are asked to come to an interview, you should look at it as an opportunity to put a personal face on your application, tell the college more about yourself, and learn more about whether the college would be a good fit for you. If you are shy, don't worry — no one ever gets rejected by a college because of a bad interview. For more about interviews, including checklists of questions to expect and questions you should ask, read *Campus Visits & College Interviews* by Zola Dincin Schneider (College Board, 2012).

How "interested" are you?

As college admissions have become more competitive, colleges have begun to weigh an additional factor along with the other parts of the application: "demonstrated interest." What this means is that admission officials try to determine whether, if they accept you, you will enroll at their college.

GOOD TO KNOW

You can use the college descriptions in this *Handbook* to learn their high school course requirements and what they recommend beyond these requirements. **This is your best indication of whether you can get in:** Do you have the lab science courses and foreign language study they require? Have you settled for the required minimum of history and social sciences, or have you taken their full recommendation? You can also learn about the high school GPAs of last year's entering class, and how those students were ranked in their high schools.

GOOD TO KNOW

Your school counselor will send the colleges to which you apply a **profile of your high school**, which will list what courses are offered, describe high school diploma requirements and generally give admission officers an overview of the academic program at your school. From this, **colleges will know whether you haven't taken the most rigorous courses available** — or, for that matter, if you've done extremely well despite a gap in your school's academic program.

Interest in a college is not something you should try to fake — if you have to pretend to want to go to a college, you won't be happy going there, so your application is a waste of time. If you really want to go to a college, your interest will show itself naturally, and colleges will be able to tell. That said, here are some things that colleges usually look for when they try to gauge your level of interest:

- Is your application essay customized to the college, or does it seem like a generic essay that you could have sent to any college?

- Did you write the college asking for information about its programs?

- Have you talked to any admission officers from the college — at your high school, via email or when visiting the campus?

- If you interview with the college, do you ask basic questions that you could have answered by reading its website, or do you ask in-depth questions that show that you've already researched the college?

Like the personal factors, your level of interest in the college isn't nearly as important as the courses you've taken, your grades or your test scores. But if the admission committee is trying to decide between you and another equally qualified candidate, it could tip your application one way or the other.

About Community Colleges

Do you want a quick start to a career path? Do you need to cut the cost of a four-year college degree? Do you want to sharpen your study skills before enrolling at a university? Do you need to attend classes at night or on weekends? Do you want to attend a college close to home?

If you said yes to even one question above, check out your options at a community college (CC). You won't be alone — 45 percent of all first-time freshmen go to two-year colleges. One reason: These institutions offer two kinds of learning.

- If your goal is a four-year degree, you can earn a two-year associate degree at a low-cost community college, then transfer to a four-year college as a junior.

- If your goal is career training, you can earn an occupational degree or certificate in two years or less, then start working immediately in many high-demand fields (like health care or computer technology).

Fit Your Education to Your Needs

A community college offers many advantages in terms of academic preparation for upper-division university work.

If you need more academic preparation, a community college can offer a leg up to achieving your goals. New students usually take placement tests in reading, writing and math. Those who need to build skills can take catch-up courses, then — over time — move into a regular academic program.

A STUDENT'S STORY

"I'm getting the basics out of the way at an inexpensive cost," says Samantha Mattioli, a freshman at Westchester Community College in Valhalla, N.Y. Sam, who is majoring in business management, says, **"I won't have a lot of debt** when I finish my associate degree." That will free up funds for her second degree, in massage therapy — step two toward Sam's goal of running her own massage therapy business.

If your high school grades aren't the greatest, but a four-year college is your goal, taking community college courses — and building a record of good grades — can polish your academic record. Then you can transfer. (But don't expect it to be easy — community college courses are no different than four-year college courses.)

If you're achievement oriented, community colleges offer challenging honors courses. Honors programs not only stimulate you but also offer mentoring and networking opportunities. They will also make you a strong candidate for transfer to a four-year college.

If English is your second language, community colleges have special programs that will help you build your English skills.

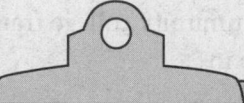

Keep on Track at a Community College

If you go to a community college or junior college, it's important for you to keep your goals in mind as you choose courses.

PLANNING TO TRANSFER TO A FOUR-YEAR COLLEGE?

✔ Talk to advisers at the community college. Most public CCs offer two-year course plans that fulfill requirements at nearby colleges. To transfer without losing credits, follow those plans!

✔ Talk to advisers at the four-year college you hope to attend, too. They may have inside info.

✔ Make sure you've fulfilled requirements to declare a major at the four-year college — not just the general admission requirements. For example, Biology 101 at your CC may transfer, but might not be enough preparation for you to take the junior-level courses in the chemistry major.

✔ Don't self-advise! If you're not sure whether a course will transfer, ask. Wrong courses waste your time and money, and that's discouraging.

✔ Keep going. Don't "gap" your education, taking time out between semesters or colleges. Once you begin, keep at it — that's the path to getting your four-year degree.

TRAINING FOR AN OCCUPATION?

Make sure your degree or certificate can lead to employment.

✔ Talk to advisers at your community college, but don't just accept claims that when you graduate, you'll get a job.

✔ Ask how many students have gone straight from the college to the work-force in recent years, what jobs they got, and with which employers.

✔ Before you enroll, talk to potential employers in the outside world, too.

Learn on Your Schedule

Many CC students have jobs and family responsibilities. Scheduling classes may be a big challenge. So community colleges tend to offer day, night and weekend courses. They have pioneered new teaching methods, too. Many offer online courses (distance learning), combine Internet and classroom learning, give interactive TV courses, condense semester courses into a shorter time frame, and more.

Community College Can Be a Ticket to Hot Job Markets

With two years or less of community college training, you can earn an occupational degree or certificate in

- Fast-growing health fields
- The computer world
- New and emerging fields

A community college may be the best route to many high-demand jobs that require two-year degrees not available at four-year colleges. Look for CC courses in construction technology, culinary arts, law enforcement and biotechnology. With homeland security a constant concern, colleges are training many first responders.

Many community colleges also have certificate options that provide intensive training in a specialized field like computer-assisted drafting, food service technology or paralegal studies. These certificates usually take six months to a year to complete.

CCs often focus on preparing people to work in local industries.

Do you want work in your area? Look for programs like these in local community colleges:

Joliet, Ill. Joliet Junior College is nationally known for its agriculture and horticulture programs. Farming is big business in the Midwest, and Joliet grads have job offers waiting. Students learn at a 100-acre college farm and do paid internships for credit.

Tucson, Ariz. Home to many air-industry businesses, Pima Community College boasts an FAA-certified aviation tech program that prepares students to repair the structure, "airframe" and power plants of commercial jetliners. Pima's job placement record for successful grads of the program is over 95 percent.

Not bad! But also, not the case at every CC or in every field. So research your CC and your local job markets like crazy — just as you'd research a four-year college.

Applying to colleges

After you've gone through some exploration and preliminary research, it's time to sit down and apply! In order to successfully apply, you'll need to budget and manage your time, follow each college's instructions to a tee and, most important, take a good hard look at yourself and your interests.

Managing Your Time

Most deadlines for regular admission applications are due in early January or February, and most early application deadlines are in November. For any application, you'll need to fill out forms and request that your transcript and standardized test scores be sent to the college. For most applications to selective colleges, you'll also need to ask teachers and your counselor for recommendations, write an essay or personal statement, and maybe even schedule an interview with the admission office. You may also want to take the SAT or SAT Subject Tests in November or December. Meanwhile, you'll be in the middle of your senior year, with academic, extracurricular and social commitments all over your calendar.

The first thing you should do once you decide to which colleges you're applying is to make a checklist of all the deadlines and tasks you'll have to accomplish for the applications. Remember to budget time for other people to do things. Teachers won't write recommendations overnight, and testing organizations will need a few weeks to send official score reports to colleges.

For handy checklists, timelines and a college application calendar, grab a copy of *Get It Together for College: A Planner to Help You Get Organized and Get In, 3rd Edition* (College Board, 2015). For more help, use the My Organizer feature of collegeboard.org, which will help you plan and remind you of upcoming deadlines.

JUNIOR YEAR CALENDAR

THE SUMMER BEFORE

- **Read** interesting books — no matter what you select as a major in college, you'll need a good vocabulary and strong reading comprehension skills. Reading is also one of the best ways to get ready.
- **Get a Social Security number** if you don't already have one — you'll need it for your college applications.

- **Think about yourself.** What are you curious about — nature and animals? People and places? Math and science? What do you like to do — working with your hands or with computers? Helping people? Being outdoors? Knowing the basics about yourself will help you make the right college choices.
- **Talk to your family and friends** about college and your goals. They know you best and will have good insights.

SEPTEMBER

- **Meet with your school counselor** to make sure you are taking the courses that colleges look for.
- **Resolve to get the best grades** you can this year. The payoff will be more colleges to choose from, and a better chance for scholarship money.
- **Pick up the *Official Student Guide to the PSAT/NMSQT®*** from your guidance office and take the practice test (you'll take the real test in October).
- Get involved in an **extracurricular activity**.
- Find out if your school will have a **college night**.

OCTOBER

- Take the **PSAT/NMSQT**.
- Don't forget to opt-in to **Student Search Service** to connect with colleges, universities and nonprofit scholarship agencies.
- Attend a **college fair**.
- Begin looking through the *College Handbook* — **start a preliminary list of colleges** that might interest you.
- Start to **learn about financial aid**. Use the College Board's *Getting Financial Aid* to learn how it works, and the financial aid calculators at **bigfuture.org** to estimate how much aid you might receive.

NOVEMBER

- Begin to **research scholarships** — use the College Board's *Scholarship Handbook* to find out about deadlines and eligibility requirements.
- **Learn about the SAT.** Go to sat.org to learn how to get ready and when to register.
- If you are planning to major in the arts (drama, music, fine art), ask your teachers about requirements for a **portfolio or audition**.

DECEMBER

- Review your **PSAT/NMSQT Score Report** with your school counselor. Talk about what courses to take next year, based on your results.
- Spend time over the holidays to **think about what kind of college** you want. Big or small? Far away or close to home? **Make a list** of the college features that are important to you.
- **Begin preparing for the SAT.** Learn about free, personalized practice tools for the SAT from the College Board and Kahn Academy® at **sat.org/practice** and **satpractice.org**.

JANUARY

- **Meet with your school counselor** to talk about the colleges in which you are interested, what entrance exams you should take, and when you should take them.
- If English is not your primary language, decide when to take the **TOEFL** test.
- Start thinking about **what you want to study in college**. Use resources like the College Board's *Book of Majors*.
- **Register for the SAT** if you want to take it in **March**.
- **Begin practicing** for the redesigned SAT by logging on to Khan Academy at **satpractice.org**.
- Learn more about the benefits of opting in to Student Search, which connects you with colleges nationwide.

FEBRUARY

- Think about which teachers you will ask to write **letters of recommendation**.
- **Register for AP Exams** given in May.
- Ask your counselor or teacher about taking the **SAT Subject Tests** in the spring. You should take them while course material is still fresh in your mind.

MARCH

- **Register for the SAT and/or SAT Subject Tests** if you want to take them in **late spring**.
- **Narrow your college list** to a reasonable number. Explore the colleges' websites, read their brochures and catalogs, and talk to your family and friends.
- **Practice the SAT for free**. Go to **satpractice.org**

APRIL

- **Register for the SAT and/or SAT Subject Tests** if you want to take them **before fall**.
- **Plan courses for your senior year.** Make sure you are going to meet the high school course requirements for your top-choice colleges.
- **Plan campus visits.** It's best to go when classes are in session. Start with colleges that are close by.

MAY

- AP Exams are given.
- If you are considering **military academies or ROTC** scholarships, contact your counselor before leaving school for the summer.
- Talk to your counselor about **NCAA requirements** if you want to play Division I or II sports in college.
- Start looking for a **summer job or volunteer work** — the good ones go fast.

SENIOR YEAR CALENDAR

THE SUMMER BEFORE

- **Register for the SAT and/or SAT Subject Tests** if you want to take them in **the fall**.
- If you want to play a NCAA Division I or II sport in college, **register with the NCAA Eligibility Center** at NCAA.org.
- **Visit colleges** on your list. Call ahead for the campus tour schedule.

- Begin working on your **college application essays**.
- Find out about **local scholarships** offered by church groups, civic associations and businesses in your area.
- **Write a résumé** (accomplishments, activities and work experiences) to help you later with your college applications.
- **Request college application forms** if you aren't going to apply online.

SEPTEMBER

- Meet with your school counselor to **finalize your list of colleges**. Be sure your list includes "safety," "reach" and "target" schools.
- **Start a checklist** of all application requirements, deadlines, fees, etc.
- If you can't afford SAT or SAT Subject Test application fees, your counselor can help you request a **fee waiver**.
- Set up **final campus visits and interviews**; attend open houses at colleges that interest you.
- Find out if there will be a **family financial aid night** at your school or elsewhere in your area this fall, and put it on your calendar.
- **Go to FAFSA on the Web** to create an **FSA ID**. You'll need that to access the FAFSA, which you can submit any time after Oct. 1.

OCTOBER

- **Register for the SAT and/or SAT Subject Tests** if you want to take them in **the winter**.
- Opt-in to **Student Search**, which connects you with colleges nationwide.
- If you are going to apply under an **Early Decision or Early Action** plan, get started now.
- **Ask for letters of recommendation** from your counselor, teachers, coaches or employers.
- Write **first drafts of your college essays** and ask your parents and teachers to review them.
- If you need to fill out the **CSS/Financial Aid PROFILE®**, you can do so on collegeboard.org starting Oct. 1.
- **Start working on your FAFSA** and submit it as soon as you can, so you don't miss out on any financial aid. Go to **FAFSA.ed.gov**

NOVEMBER

- **Finish your application essays**. Proofread them rigorously for mistakes.
- **Apply to colleges with rolling admission** (first-come, first-served) as early as possible. Keep hard copies.
- Make sure your **admission test (e.g., SAT) scores** will be sent by the testing agency to each one of your colleges.
- Give your school counselor the proper **forms to send transcripts** to your colleges at least two weeks in advance.

DECEMBER

- Try to **wrap up college applications** before winter break. Make copies for yourself and your school counselor.
- If you applied for **Early Decision**, you should have an answer by Dec. 15. If you are denied or deferred, submit applications now to other colleges.
- **Apply for scholarships** in time to meet application deadlines.
- **Contact the financial aid office** at the colleges on your list to see if they require any **other financial aid forms**.

JANUARY

- **Submit your FAFSA** as soon as you can if you haven't already. Check your college's deadlines and priority dates; some can be as early as Feb. 1.
- **Submit other financial aid forms** that may be required — such as PROFILE or the college's own forms. Keep copies.
- If a college wants to see your **midyear grades**, give the form to your school counselor.
- If you have any **new honors or accomplishments** that were not in your original application, let your colleges know.

FEBRUARY

- **Contact your colleges** to confirm that all application materials have been received.
- Correct or update your **Student Aid Report (SAR)** that follows the FAFSA if necessary.
- If any **special circumstances** affect your family's financial situation, alert each college's financial aid office.
- **File income tax returns early.** Some colleges want copies of your family's returns before finalizing financial aid offers.
- **Register for AP Exams** you want to take. (If you are homeschooled or your school does not offer AP, you must contact AP Services by March 1.)

MARCH

- **Admission decisions start arriving.** Read everything you receive carefully, as some documents may require prompt action on your part.
- **Revisit colleges** that accepted you if it's hard to make a choice.
- **Don't get senioritis!** Colleges want to see strong grades in the second half of your senior year.

APRIL

- **Carefully compare financial aid award letters** from the colleges that accept you — it might not be clear which is the better offer. If you have questions, contact the college's financial aid office or talk to your school counselor.
- **If you don't get enough aid**, consider your options, which include appealing the award.
- Make a final decision, **accept the aid package, and mail a deposit check** to the college you select before May 1 (the acceptance deadline for most schools).
- **Notify the other colleges** that you won't be attending (so another student can have your spot).

MAY

- AP Exams are given. Make sure your **AP score report** is sent to your college. Learn more at apscore.org.
- **Study hard for final exams.** Most admission offers are contingent on your final grades.
- **Thank everyone** who wrote you recommendations or otherwise helped with your college applications.
- If you plan on playing a Division I or II college sport, have your school counselor send your **final transcript to the NCAA Eligibility Center**.
- **If you weren't accepted** anywhere, don't give up — you still have options. Talk to your school counselor about them.

Filling Out the Application

A typical application will ask you to provide some personal information; a list of schools you have attended; brief descriptions of your extracurricular activities, jobs and any academic honors you have earned; and standardized test scores. They will also ask for information about your family and their education background, which colleges may use to determine whether you merit special consideration as a first-generation college student or a "legacy" applicant. Finally, most applications give you the option of affiliating yourself with a race or ethnic group. If you choose to do so, colleges may take that into consideration when reviewing your application; however, your answer won't hurt your chances of admission.

Finally, all applications will ask whether and when you plan to file for financial aid. Checking this box does not mean you have applied for financial aid! It just lets the admission office know that they should coordinate with the financial aid office later on. For more information on financial aid and how to apply for it, read the articles in the "Pay for College" section of bigfuture.org, or get the College Board's book, *Getting Financial Aid*.

What Goes with Your Application

Besides the application form, there are several things that need to be included with your application. You will have to send some of them with the form; others will be sent to the college by other people.

Application fee

The average college application fee is around $25. (Some colleges charge up to $60, while others don't have an application fee at all.) The fee is usually nonrefundable, even if you're not offered admission. Many colleges offer fee waivers for applicants from low-income families. If you need a fee waiver, call the college's admission office for more information.

High school transcript

This form is filled out by an official of your high school. If it comes with your admission materials, you should give it to the guidance office to complete as early as possible. Some colleges send this form directly to your school after receiving your application.

Admission test scores

If you need to submit standardized test scores, you must make sure the testing agency itself sends an official score report. Writing your scores on your application or sending a photocopy of your own personal score report will not suffice. When you take the SAT, you are entitled to four free official score reports, which are sent to the colleges you choose. This service is included in the fee you pay to take the test.

PLANNING AHEAD

In addition to the traditional typed or handwritten application, many schools today accept **online applications** (if they do, it will say so in their *Handbook* description). You may also be able to fill out the **Common Application** and send it to several schools — though you should be aware that some Common Application subscribers also require a supplementary form of their own.

KEEP IN MIND

If you apply online, remember to print your applications and proofread them before you submit them, just as you would with a printed application. Also, be sure to tell your school counselor that you've applied online — your school will still need to send your transcript to the college.

Letters of recommendation

Some colleges ask you to submit one or more letters of recommendation from a teacher, counselor or other adult who knows you well. Usually the person writing the letter will send it directly to the college, though sometimes your school counselor will assemble the letters and send them with your transcript.

Essays short and long

If you're applying to selective colleges, your essay often plays a very important role. Whether you're writing an autobiographical statement or an essay on a specific theme, take the opportunity to express your individuality in a way that sets you apart from other applicants.

Some applications will ask you to attach a separate essay of one or two pages, others will ask you to fill in some one-paragraph short responses directly on the application form, and others will ask for both. Whichever type of question you're answering, give it some thought. Draft, revise and edit your response before putting it with the application, and be sure to type or (if you must) print legibly. (The "fun" fonts that came with your word processor are usually not legible.)

Your parents, school counselors and teachers may have some helpful insights into things you should talk about in your essays. For tips and strategies on how to approach different types of essay questions, general advice on the writing process, and information about how admission officers evaluate essays, obtain a copy of Sarah Myers McGinty's *The College Application Essay* (College Board, 2015).

Interview

An interview is required or recommended by some colleges. Even if it's not required, it's a good idea to set up an interview because it gives you a chance to make a personal connection with someone who will have a voice in deciding whether or not you'll be offered admission. If you're too far away for an on-campus interview, try to arrange to meet with an alumnus in your community.

Try to schedule interviews early in your senior year — if you wait until December you may not have time to make the appointment before the application is due. Also, scheduling an interview late in the year may make the college think that your decision to apply was an afterthought. Many students feel most comfortable scheduling their first interviews with colleges they feel confident about getting into. That way, they can experience interview situations and build their confidence before going to "high stakes" interviews with their "reach" schools.

For tips on preparing for interviews and getting the most out of them, obtain a copy of Zola and Norman Schneider's *Campus Visits & College Interviews* (College Board, 2012), or read the articles in the "Get In" section of bigfuture.org.

How to Ask for Recommendations

The key to getting a great recommendation is to be a great student. But showing good manners helps.

✔ Be sure to *ask* for a recommendation — don't demand one.

✔ Respect the time constraints of those you're asking for this favor. Mary Lee Hoganson, a former counselor at Homewood-Flossmoor High School in Illinois, says that "teachers should always receive a minimum of two weeks' notice."

✔ Provide teachers and counselors with a deadline for each recommendation that you are requesting, especially noting the earliest deadline.

✔ Offer them a "brag sheet" or résumé reminding them of your accomplishments over the years. They might know your work in their classes very well, but they might not remember that you were also responsible for organizing the school talent show your junior year.

✔ Include addressed and stamped envelopes for each school to which you're applying.

✔ On the application form, waive your right to view recommendation letters. This makes the recommendation more credible in the eyes of the college.

✔ Follow up with your recommendation writers a week or so before your first deadline.

✔ Once you have decided which college to attend, write thank-you notes to everyone who provided a recommendation and tell them where you've decided to go to college. Be sure to do this before you leave high school.

Auditions, portfolios and other supplementary materials

If you're applying for a fine or performing arts program in music, studio art or graphic design, you may have to document prior work by auditioning on campus or submitting an audiotape, DVD, slides or some other sample of your work to demonstrate your ability. Talk to a teacher or mentor in your subject for advice on both how to assemble a portfolio and which of your pieces to include. Be sure to check the deadlines for auditions — they are often different from the deadlines for applications.

In some cases, a college will ask all students to submit an academic writing sample, either instead of or in addition to a personal statement. You should send a graded essay, presentation or lab report that you did well on, preferably a copy that has your teacher's comments and the grade you received on it.

Taking college admission and placement tests

In your junior or senior year of high school, you will probably have to take a college admission test to satisfy the admission requirements at the colleges you are considering.

You may also want to take college-level exams in specific subjects in order to strengthen your application portfolio, place out of introductory college courses, get college credit for your high school work, or all three. At the end of this chapter, you'll find an introduction to the two most widely recognized college credit-by-exam programs.

College Admission Tests: Why You Should Take Them

This chapter will give you advice on how to get ready and register for the standardized tests that satisfy the admission requirements at the colleges you are considering. You may also want to take the college-level exams in specific subjects in order to strengthen your application portfolio, place out of introductory college courses, get college credit for your high school work, or all three.

Some colleges also require or recommend one or more SAT Subject Tests. These requirements are all spelled out in the *Handbook* descriptions for each college.

The PSAT/NMSQT®

Taking the PSAT/NMSQT (Preliminary SAT/National Merit Scholarship Qualifying Test) is a great way to practice for the SAT. For many students, the PSAT/NMSQT is also the first step on the road to college. It assesses skills developed through years of study in a wide range of courses. Students taking the test in their junior year also may be eligible to enter National Merit Scholarship Corporation competitions.

If you opt into Student Search Service when you take the test, you might also be eligible for opportunities offered by the American Indian Graduate Center and American Indian Graduate Center Scholars (AIGC and AIGCS), Asian & Pacific Islander American Scholarship Fund (APIASF), Hispanic Scholarship Fund (HSF), the Jack Kent Cooke Foundation (JKCF), and the United Negro College Fund (UNCF).

PLANNING AHEAD

Most students take the SAT in the spring of their junior year and again in the fall of their senior year. Students who take SAT Subject Tests usually do so near the end of the course taken in the subject area for each exam.

Your school counselor can tell you where the SAT will be administered close to your home and school.

The SAT®

The SAT is a globally available test accepted by colleges and universities throughout the United States and in numerous international locations. It is offered at least seven times a year in the United States and U.S. territories, and up to six times a year internationally. The SAT assesses skills in reading, writing and language, and math, while focusing on the knowledge and skills that current research shows are most essential for college and career readiness and success. To learn more about the test, please visit **sat.org**.

Here is an overview of the content and timing of the redesigned SAT, which launched March 2016:

Test Length and Timing: Redesigned SAT

Component	Time allotted (mins.)	Number of questions/tasks
Reading	65	52
Writing and Language	35	44
Essay (optional)	50	1
Math	80	57
Total	180 (230 with Essay)	153 (154 with Essay)

The SAT Subject Tests™

The SAT Subject Tests are one-hour exams that give you the opportunity to demonstrate your knowledge and showcase your achievement in specific subjects. There are 20 SAT Subject Tests, so you can select the tests that best showcase your achievements and interests.

By taking the tests, you can:

- Differentiate yourself by providing a more complete picture of your academic interests.

- Highlight your strength in particular subjects or areas of study, such as science, mathematics, the humanities, or foreign languages.

- Fulfill admission requirements for colleges that require or recommend SAT Subject Tests, especially if you are interested in specific programs or majors.

- Satisfy basic requirements for certain majors or programs of study.

The SAT Subject Tests can also:

- Provide an opportunity for ESL (English as a Second Language) and international students to demonstrate achievement in subject areas that are not as reliant on English language mastery, such as mathematics, science and foreign languages.

- Allow home-schooled students or distance learners to show mastery in specific subjects.

Colleges use SAT Subject Tests to:

- Help put other admission factors, such as grades and course choices, into context.

- Help place students into the right courses, based on how well they've learned the material in specific subjects.

- Connect with or recruit students who are interested in specific majors/programs based on their strengths highlighted by SAT Subject Tests.

Getting Ready for the SAT

The best way to get ready for the SAT is to take challenging courses, study hard and familiarize yourself with the test. College admission staff are more impressed by an academic record that shows real effort and achievement than they are by test scores alone.

Before taking the SAT, you should:

- Take the PSAT/NMSQT.

- Become familiar with the test and Kahn Academy's free practice resources at satpractice.org.

- Review algebra and geometry.

- Read and write as much as possible, in and out of school.

2016-2017 SAT PROGRAM TEST CALENDAR

Test Dates / Registration Deadlines*	Oct. 1	Nov. 5	Dec. 3	Jan. 21	Mar. 11	May 6	June 3
Regular	Sept. 1	Oct. 7	Nov. 3	Dec. 21	Feb. 10	Apr. 7	May 9
Late	Sept. 20	Oct. 25	Nov. 22	Jan. 10	Feb. 28	Apr. 25	May 24
SAT	■	■	■	■	■	■	■
SAT Subject Tests							
Literature	■	■	■	■		■	■
United States (U.S.) History	■	■	■	■		■	■
World History			■				■
Mathematics Level 1†	■	■	■	■		■	■
Mathematics Level 2†	■	■	■	■		■	■
Biology E/M (Ecological/Molecular)	■	■	■	■		■	■
Chemistry	■	■	■	■		■	■
Physics	■	■	■	■		■	■
Languages: Reading Only							
French	■		■	■		■	■
German							■
Modern Hebrew							■
Italian							■
Latin			■				■
Spanish	■		■	■		■	■
Languages: Reading and Listening							
Chinese		■					
French		■					
German		■					
Japanese		■					
Korean		■					
Spanish		■					

*Please note that all registration deadlines are subject to change. Visit sat.org/register for the most up-to-date listings.
†Calculator required.
NOTE: Sunday test dates follow each Saturday test date (except in Oct., when it falls a week later) for students who cannot test on Saturday because of a religious observance.

Services for Students with Disabilities

Students may receive accommodations (extended time, large print, etc.) on College Board exams if they submit an eligibility form and meet the eligibility requirements. All accommodations must be approved by the College Board's Services for Students with Disabilities (SSD). Speak to your school's SSD Coordinator or counselor who can submit an accommodations request for you online, or contact SSD to request a paper Student Eligibility Form.

SSD Contacts
(all College Board programs):
Voice   212-713-8333
TTY   609-882-4118
Fax   866-360-0114
Email   ssd@info.collegeboard.org
collegeboard.org/ssd

Practice Resources

The College Board and Khan Academy have joined in partnership in order to address one of the greatest inequities around college admission exams: the culture of high-priced test preparation. This partnership will level the playing field by providing world-class SAT practice, entirely for free.

Preparing for the SAT

Khan Academy and the College Board have teamed up to provide Official SAT Practice on Khan Academy at satpractice.org. You can use Khan Academy to create a personalized SAT study plan based on your exam results. You can also load your PSAT/NMSQT or PSAT 8/9 scores into Khan Academy to further personalize your practice. These study plans will guide you through an adaptive practice experience that's tailored to your strengths and weaknesses.

These are some of the free resources you can access at satpractice.org:

- Personalized practice recommendations to help you focus on the skills likely to have the biggest impact on your performance
- Thousands of practice problems, reviewed and approved by the College Board
- Four full-length practice tests written by the College Board

Official SAT Practice on Khan Academy links to classroom learning — the best preparation for the SAT.

Practice an SAT question a day with a free mobile app: Daily Practice for the New SAT. You can download it from the App Store or Google Play.

But remember: All of the work you've done in school — including your reading, writing, and math — is what will really help you do your best on the test and to be well-prepared for college.

Test-Taking FAQs

How many times should I take the SAT?

Research shows that many students see modest increases in their score upon taking the test a second time. Taking the test more than twice will probably not lead to significant gains.

Does the SAT have an Essay section?

Yes, but it's optional. If you choose to take that portion of the test, it will come at the end of the exam. You will be asked to write an essay analyzing a source document. The essay prompt is always basically the same; only the passage will change. Many colleges want their applicants to complete the Essay, so be sure to check the requirements of the colleges you are considering before you take the test.

How do I register for the SAT?

The best way to register is online. It's fast and easy, and it helps you avoid late fees or missed postmark deadlines. You can even register for next year's tests over the summer. SAT registration may be completed at sat.org.

To register for the SAT by mail, complete the paper registration form included with the *SAT Registration Guide* and send it with your test fee payment. You can get a *Registration Guide* in your school's guidance office. Registration deadlines are about four and a half weeks before the test date. There are also late registration deadlines, and it's possible to register on a standby basis. Both of these involve an additional fee.

What is Score Choice™?

Score Choice™ is a feature that gives you the option to choose the SAT scores you send to colleges by test date — in accordance with each college's score-use practice. Designed to reduce your stress and improve the test-day experience, Score Choice gives you an opportunity to show colleges the scores you feel best represent your abilities.

Score Choice is optional, so if you don't choose to use it, all of your scores will be sent automatically. Since most colleges only consider your best scores, you should feel comfortable reporting scores from all of your test dates.

Each college and scholarship program has different score-use practices. Our score-reporting process displays score-use practices for each participating institution, but you should also check with colleges to ensure that you are following their requirements. Email reminders will be sent to you if you have not sent SAT scores to any colleges by the usual deadlines.

Remember:

- Scores from an entire SAT test will be sent — scores of individual sections from different test dates cannot be selected independently.

- You can send any or all scores to a college on a single report — it will not cost more to send one, multiple or all test scores. Scores for the optional essay will be sent with all scores from the test date.

- You receive four free score reports with your registration. We continue to recommend that you take full advantage of these reports.

- Score Choice is available via the Web or by calling Customer Service (toll free within the United States).

KNOW THE LINGO

Advanced placement — The ability to skip an introductory course in a subject. Many colleges offer advanced placement in appropriate subjects for AP Exams and/or CLEP Exams. You may also qualify for advanced placement by taking the college's own placement exam.

Credit by exam — College credit earned by achieving a qualifying score on a standardized examination, such as an AP Exam or CLEP exam.

Sophomore standing — If a college grants an incoming student the equivalent of 30 semester hours of credit by exam, they may allow the student to be considered a sophomore for academic purposes, such as when the student registers for courses or can declare a major.

Earning College Credit by Examination

Most colleges allow you to place out of introductory courses in subject areas where you have already done college-level work, either in high school or through your own life experiences. For example, you might be able to skip the first year of college Spanish and go straight to intermediate-level courses. In order to demonstrate your knowledge, the college usually requires you to take either a standardized test, such as an AP Exam, a CLEP exam or an SAT Subject Test, or an exam offered by the college on campus. (You often have a choice of doing either — that is, if you haven't taken the AP Spanish Language and Culture Exam, you can take the college's Spanish placement test as an alternative.)

If you take an AP Exam or CLEP exam, many colleges also allow you to earn credit based on your exam score. To use the same example as above, you wouldn't just place into second-year Spanish; you would also earn credits toward graduation as if you had taken first-year Spanish there on campus. If you have qualifying scores on enough exams, some colleges will even grant you "sophomore standing," meaning you are treated as a sophomore for academic purposes such as when you get to register for courses. (You still have to obey the college's other rules for freshmen, though, so don't expect to be given a single dorm room and a parking permit just because you have sophomore standing through AP.)

AP® Course Calendar

Spring before starting an AP course	Well ahead of time, you need to start thinking about what AP courses you might want to take. Discuss your plans with your parents, teachers and school counselor.
Summer	Some AP teachers require you to complete work (like reading) during the summer months to prepare for their courses. For example, for AP English Literature and Composition you may be given a reading list. Make sure you complete these assignments so that you're up to speed when the class begins.
January	Talk to your AP teachers and/or AP Coordinator about taking the exams. Contact the disabilities (SSD) coordinator at your school if you will need testing accommodations.
February	Deadline for requests for testing accommodations.
March	Deadlines for homeschooled students and students whose schools do not offer AP to arrange for testing at a nearby school.
May 1–5 and May 8–12, 2017	Exam dates.
June 15, 2017	Deadline for receipt of requests for score withholding, score cancellation or a change in a college score report recipient.
July	AP score reports released to designated colleges, and to students and their high schools.

More About AP®

AP offers a wide range of college-level courses that are taught in high schools by high school teachers; a standardized exam is given for each subject every May. AP courses give you a chance to do college-level work while still in high school. Research studies have shown that students with AP experience succeed in college at a higher rate than non-AP students.

In all, there are 38 courses in a wide variety of subject areas. Even if an AP course is not offered at your school, you may still be able to take the exam if you make arrangements with your school's AP Coordinator (usually a school counselor, testing coordinator, or administrator). If your school doesn't offer AP at all, or you are homeschooled, you may be able to make arrangements to take an AP Exam at a nearby school that offers AP.

AP courses are challenging — after all, you're doing college-level work in high school! They can also be very rewarding. If you're not sure whether you should take an AP course, talk to your teachers, your school counselor, and your parents.

More About the College-Level Examination Program® (CLEP®)

CLEP is the most widely accepted college-based credit-by-examination program in the country, serving college students, high school students, military members, veterans, home-schooled students and continuing education students. Over 2,900 accredited colleges and universities award credit for qualifying scores on CLEP exams. You can take a CLEP exam at over 1,800 test centers.

CLEP offers 33 exams in the areas of business, English composition and literature, world languages, history and social sciences, and science and mathematics. You can take a CLEP exam at any time during your college career, and the exams are offered year-round. Find out if your college grants credit for CLEP exams by using the CLEP college search at clep.collegeboard.org/search/colleges.

CLEP is computer based, allowing for instant score reports, so you know that day if you will be awarded credit for your performance. To find out more about CLEP exams, to see a list of suggested textbooks and online resources for each exam, and to download study guides, visit clep.collegeboard.org.

Life on campus

A college isn't just a place where you'll take classes for two or four years. You'll also be spending most of your time there — and, if you're a residential student, you'll even be living there. When you're deciding where to go, academics should come first, but you should also consider how comfortable the campus feels. Some things to take into account are the housing options, local transit, whether the campus feels safe, and the social life of the campus.

Housing Options

At most colleges, you'll have lots of choices about where to live. You may live in an on-campus dorm (usually called a "residence hall"), an off-campus house or apartment building, or a fraternity/sorority house. At some colleges, you won't have as many choices your freshman year, but even then you may have a choice of several freshman dorms.

Typically, after you accept an offer of admission, the college's housing office will ask you to submit a form stating your housing preferences. You can use this form not only to indicate which dorm(s) you prefer, but also to help them match you to a roommate who will be compatible. Are you a quiet person? What times do you usually wake up and go to bed? Are you messy or neat? Do you smoke? The housing office will try to find someone whose answers to those questions were similar to your own.

Living in Dorms

College dormitories have changed a lot over the years. While they were once bare-bones facilities that offered little more than a place to sleep, today most dorms offer a variety of accommodations. It's not uncommon to find study areas, TV lounges, computer labs, small kitchens or even fast-food take-out restaurants built into modern dorms. While some dorms are still built on the traditional floor plan of a hallway of double rooms sharing a bathroom, others are based around suites or apartments.

Some colleges offer theme-related residences, also known as "learning-living communities," that give you the opportunity to live with other students who share similar interests or backgrounds. Students in theme residences not only live together, but also participate in academic and social events related around the dorm's theme. Some theme residences will also have a member of the faculty who lives in the dorm and advises its students. Examples of theme residences include:

- *Diversity programs,* where the residents come from a wide variety of cultural backgrounds

- *Honors residences,* where all the students are on merit scholarships

- *Discipline-based residences,* such as a dorm for engineering and science majors

- *Foreign language immersion dorms,* where all the residents study and speak a particular foreign language

- *Substance-free housing* (a.k.a. "wellness" or "positive choice" housing), where all the residents pledge not to drink, smoke or do drugs

- *Gender-specific housing,* where all residents are the same sex, or *gender-neutral housing,* where residents share rooms with any student regardless of gender, gender identity, or sexual orientation.

Roommate issues

Most roommate situations work out OK; often, freshman roommates become good friends. But there are cases when roommates just don't get along.

The best way to avoid this is to communicate with your roommates. Talk about your habits, preferences, and lifestyles, and how to coordinate sleep time, study time, and having friends over. Remember that communication is a two-way street: try to keep an open mind and listen to what they tell you.

As the semester goes on, be sure to let your roommates know if something is bothering you. Don't ignore problems or obnoxious behavior — they will only get worse if you don't speak up. Similarly, if your roommate complains about your own habits, try to correct them.

If the situation is truly intolerable, the housing office might be able arrange a reassignment midsemester. But because of space issues, this isn't always possible, and when it is possible, it's not always ideal. You might find yourself living in a new dorm, away from friends you've already made, or assigned as a third roommate into a room meant for two.

EXPERT ADVICE

"**Be honest on your housing preferences form.** If you've been pretty quiet throughout high school and always go to bed at 10 p.m., don't say you party a lot and stay up past midnight. Random roommate placement is tricky enough without stacking the deck against yourself."

— *Caitlin, student, Puget Sound University*

Glossary

Definitions of commonly used terms vary from college to college. Consult specific college catalogs or their websites for more detailed information.

Accelerated study. A college program of study completed in less time than is usually required, most often by attending classes in the summer or by taking extra courses during the regular academic terms. Completion of a bachelor's degree program in three years is an example of acceleration.

Accreditation. Recognition by an accrediting organization or agency that a college meets certain standards in its education programs, services and facilities. National or regional accreditation applies to a college as a whole and not to any particular program or course of study. Some programs within colleges, such as an engineering or nursing program, may be accredited by the corresponding professional organizations. See pages 10–12 for more information about accreditation and the names and addresses of the national and regional accrediting associations.

ACT. A college admission examination given at test centers on specified dates. Please visit the organization's website for further information.

Advanced placement. Admission or assignment of a first-year student to an advanced course in a certain subject on the basis of evidence that the student has successfully completed the equivalent of the college's freshman course in that subject.

Advanced Placement Program (AP). An academic program of the College Board that provides high school students with the opportunity to study and learn at the college level. AP offers courses in 38 subjects, each culminating in a rigorous exam. High schools offer the courses and administer the exams to interested students. Most colleges and universities accept qualifying AP Exam scores for credit, advanced placement or both.

Agricultural college. A college or university that primarily trains students in the agricultural sciences and agribusiness operations.

Articulation agreement. A formal agreement between two colleges to facilitate the successful transfer of students from one college to the other without duplication of course work.

Associate degree. A degree granted by a college or university after the satisfactory completion of the equivalent of a two-year, full-time program of study. In general, the associate of arts (A.A.) or associate of science (A.S.) degree is granted after completing a program of study similar to the first two years of a four-year college curriculum. The associate in applied science (A.A.S.) is awarded by many colleges on completion of technological or vocational programs of study.

Bachelor's, or baccalaureate, degree. A degree received after the satisfactory completion of a four- or five-year, full-time program of study (or its part-time equivalent) at a college or university. The bachelor of arts (B.A.), bachelor of science (B.S.) and bachelor of fine arts (B.F.A.) are the most common baccalaureates. Policies concerning their award vary from college to college.

Bible college. An undergraduate institution whose program, in addition to a general education in the liberal arts, includes a significant element of Bible study. Most Bible colleges seek to prepare their students for vocational or lay Christian ministry.

Branch campus. A part of a college, university or community college that is geographically separate from the main campus, has its own faculty and administration, and may have separate admission requirements and degree programs.

Business college. A college that primarily prepares students to work in an office or entrepreneurial setting. The curriculum may focus on management, clerical positions or both.

Campus. The physical location of a college or university. Includes classroom buildings, libraries, research facilities, dormitories, dining halls and administration buildings.

Calendar. The system by which an institution divides its year into shorter periods for instruction and awarding credit. The most common calendars are those based on the semester, trimester, quarter and 4-1-4.

Candidates Reply Date Agreement (CRDA). A college subscribing to this College Board–sponsored agreement will not require any applicants offered admission as freshmen to notify the college of their decision to attend (or to accept an offer of financial aid) before May 1 of the year the applicants apply. The purpose of the agreement is to give applicants time to hear from all the colleges to which they have applied before having to make a commitment to any of them.

CB code. A four-digit College Board code number that students use to designate colleges or scholarship programs to receive their SAT score reports.

Certificate. An award for completing a particular program or course of study, usually given by two-year colleges or vocational or technical schools for nondegree programs of a year or less.

College. The generic term for an institution of higher education. Also a term used to designate divisions within a university.

College-Level Examination Program (CLEP). A program in which students receive college credit by earning a qualifying score in any of 33 examinations in business, composition and literature, world languages, history and social sciences, and science and mathematics. Sponsored by the College Board, exams are administered at over 1,800 test centers. Over 2,900 colleges and universities grant credit for passing a CLEP exam.

College-preparatory subjects. A term used to describe subjects required for admission to, or recommended as preparation for, college. It is usually understood to mean subjects from the fields of English, history and social studies, foreign languages, mathematics, science and the arts.

Combined bachelor's/graduate degree. A program in which students complete a bachelor's degree and a master's degree or first-professional degree in less than the usual amount of time. In most programs, students apply to the graduate program during their first three years of undergraduate study, and begin the graduate program in their fourth year of college. Successful completion results in awarding of both a bachelor's degree and a graduate degree. At some colleges, this option is called a joint degree program.

Common Application. The standard application form distributed by the National Association of Secondary School Principals to colleges who are subscribers to the Common Application Group.

Community/junior college. A college that offers only the first two years of undergraduate study. Community colleges are public institutions, whereas junior colleges are privately operated on a not-for-profit basis. Both usually offer terminal (or "vocational") programs and transfer programs.

Consortium. A group of colleges and universities that share a common geographic location. Consortiums of colleges in the same local area often allow students at one institution to take classes at other consortium colleges and use facilities (such as libraries) at the member colleges. Larger consortiums, on the state or regional level, may allow for "visiting semesters" or offer in-state tuition to out-of-state students.

Cooperative education (co-op). A program that provides for alternative class attendance and employment in business, industry or government. Students are typically paid for their work. Under a cooperative plan, five years are normally required to complete a bachelor's degree, but graduates have the advantage of about a year's practical work experience in addition to their studies.

Cooperative housing. College-owned, operated or affiliated housing in which students share room and board expenses and participate in household chores to reduce their living expenses.

Credit hour. A unit of measure representing an hour (50 minutes) of instruction over a 15-week period in a semester or trimester system, or over a 10-week period in a quarter system. It is applied toward the total number of hours needed for completing the requirements of a degree, diploma, certificate or other formal award.

Credit/placement by examination. Academic credit or placement out of introductory courses granted by a college to entering students who have demonstrated proficiency in college-level studies through examinations such as those administered by the College Board's AP and CLEP programs.

Cross-registration. The practice, through agreements between colleges, of permitting students enrolled at one college or university to enroll in courses at another institution without formally applying for admission to the second institution.

CSS code. A four-digit College Board number that students use to designate colleges or scholarship programs to receive their CSS/Financial Aid PROFILE information. A complete list of all CSS codes can be viewed at the CSS/Financial Aid PROFILE section on collegeboard.org.

CSS/Financial Aid PROFILE®. An application and service offered by the College Board, which is used by some colleges, universities and private scholarship programs to award their own private financial aid funds. Students pay a fee to send reports to institutions and programs that use PROFILE. Students register for PROFILE on collegeboard.org. PROFILE provides a customized application for each registrant based on the individual's information and the requirements of the colleges and programs from which she or he is seeking aid. Students complete and submit the customized application to the College Board for processing and reporting to institutions. The PROFILE is not a federal form and may not be used to apply for federal student aid.

Culinary school. A vocational college that primarily prepares students to work as chefs or caterers.

Deferred admission. The practice of permitting students to postpone enrollment, usually for one year, after acceptance to the college.

Degree. An award given by a college or university certifying that a student has completed a course of study. *See* bachelor's degree, associate degree, graduate degree. *See also* Certificate.

Distance learning. An option for earning course credit off campus via cable television, the Internet, satellite classes, videotapes, correspondence courses or other means. *See also* Virtual university.

Doctoral degree (doctorate). *See* Graduate degree.

Dormitory. *See* Residence hall.

Double major. Any program in which a student concurrently completes the requirements of two majors.

Dual enrollment. The practice of students enrolling in college courses while still in high school.

Early Action (EA). Students who apply under a college's Early Action plan receive a decision earlier than the standard response date but are not required to accept the admission offer or to make a deposit prior to May 1. See the Early Decision/Early Action table for a list of colleges that offer Early Action plans, including application deadlines and notification dates.

Early admission. The policy of some colleges of admitting certain students who have not completed high school — usually students of exceptional ability who have completed their junior year. These students are enrolled full-time in college.

Early Decision (ED). Students who apply under Early Decision make a commitment to enroll at the college if admitted and offered a satisfactory financial aid package. Application deadlines are usually in November or December with a mid-to-late-December notification date. Some colleges have two rounds of Early Decision. See the Early Decision/Early Action table for details.

Engineering college/institute/school. An institution of higher education that primarily prepares students for careers as licensed professional engineers or engineering technologists.

Exchange student program. Any arrangement that permits a student to study for a semester or more at another college in the United States without extending the amount of time required for a degree.

External degree program. A system of study whereby a student earns credit toward a degree through independent study, college courses, proficiency examinations and personal experience. External degree colleges generally have no campus or classroom facilities.

FAFSA. *See* Free Application for Federal Student Aid (FAFSA).

For-profit college. A private institution operated by its owners as a profit-making enterprise.

4-1-4 calendar. A variation of the semester calendar system, the 4-1-4 calendar consists of two terms of about 16 weeks each, separated by a one-month intersession used for intensive short courses, independent study, off-campus work or other types of instruction.

Free Application for Federal Student Aid (FAFSA). A form completed by all applicants for federal student aid. In many states, completion of the FAFSA is also sufficient to establish eligibility for state-sponsored aid programs. There is no charge to students for completing the FAFSA. The online form may be filed any time after Oct. 1 of the year before the year for which one is seeking aid (e.g., after Oct. 1, 2017, for academic year 2018-19 assistance).

General Educational Development (GED). A series of tests that individuals who did not complete high school may take through their state education system to qualify for a high school equivalency certificate.

Grade point average (GPA) or ratio. A system used by many schools for evaluating the overall scholastic performance of students. Grade points are determined by first multiplying the number of hours given for a course by the numerical value of the grade and then dividing the sum of all grade points by the total number of hours carried. The most common system of numerical values for grades is A = 4, B = 3, C = 2, D = 1, and E or F = 0. Also called quality point average or ratio.

Graduate degree. A degree pursued after a student has earned a bachelor's degree. The master's degree, which requires one to three years of study, is usually the degree earned after the bachelor's. The doctoral degree requires further study. First-professional degrees are also graduate degrees.

Health sciences college. An institution of higher education that primarily prepares students to enter work in a clinic, hospital or private medical practice.

Hispanic-serving college. A college where Hispanic students comprise at least 25 percent of the total of full-time undergraduate enrollment.

Historically black college. An institution founded before 1964 whose mission was historically, and remains, the education of African Americans.

Homeschooled. For purposes of the application requirements described in the "basis for selection" entries of the college descriptions, this refers to homeschooling during the four years of secondary school (grades 9–12).

Honors program. Any special program for very able students that offers the opportunity for education enrichment, independent study, acceleration or some combination of these.

Independent student. For financial aid purposes, a student who is not dependent on financial support from his or her parents. Also called a self-supporting student.

Independent study. Academic work chosen or designed by the student under an instructor's supervision. This work is usually undertaken outside of the regular classroom structure.

International Baccalaureate (IB). A high school curriculum offered by some schools in the United States and other countries. Some colleges award credit for completion of this curriculum. Please visit the organization's website for further information.

Internship. A short-term, supervised work experience, usually related to a student's major field, for which the student earns academic credit. The work can be full or part time, on or off campus, paid or unpaid. Student teaching and apprenticeships are examples.

Intersession term. A short term offered between semesters. *See also* 4-1-4 calendar.

Junior college. *See* Community/junior college.

Liberal arts. The study of the humanities (literature, the arts and philosophy), history, foreign languages, social sciences, mathematics and natural sciences. Study of the liberal arts and humanities prepares students to develop general knowledge and reasoning ability rather than specific skills.

Liberal arts/career combination. A program of study in which a student typically completes three years of study in a liberal arts field followed by two years of professional/ technical study (for example, engineering) at the end of which the student is awarded bachelor of arts and bachelor of science degrees. The combination is also referred to as a 3+2 program.

Liberal arts college. A college that emphasizes the liberal arts in its core curriculum and academic offerings and does not offer vocational or professional programs.

Lower division. The freshman and sophomore years of college study.

Major. A student's academic field of specialization. In general, most courses in the major are taken during the junior and senior years.

Maritime college/institute/academy. An institution of higher education that prepares students to operate commercial shipping or fishing vessels. Upon graduation, students of most maritime academies are commissioned as officers in the United States Merchant Marine, and simultaneously commissioned as officers in the U.S. Navy Reserve.

Master's degree. *See* Graduate degree.

Military college/institute/academy. An institution of higher education that prepares students (who are called "cadets" while enrolled) to become active-duty officers in the armed services. The curriculum usually combines a study of the liberal arts, military science and engineering. Cadets usually participate in military training assignments during the summer term in addition to attending the college in the fall and spring semesters.

Minor. Course work that is not as extensive as that in a major but gives students some specialized knowledge of a second field.

NAIA. The National Association of Inter-collegiate Athletics. NAIA members are mostly small colleges. Championships are offered in 13 sports.

NCAA. The National Collegiate Athletic Association. The largest collegiate athletic association, it oversees the most athletic scholarship money. The NCAA governs league play in 23 championship sports.

NCCAA. National Christian College Athletic Association. NCCAA sponsors league play among Bible colleges and other Christian-oriented institutions.

NJCAA. The National Junior College Athletic Association. NJCAA members are two-year junior or community colleges.

Need-based financial aid. Financial aid given to students who have demonstrated financial need, which is calculated by subtracting the student's expected family contribution from a college's total costs. The expected family contribution is derived from a need analysis of the family's overall financial circumstances.

Nondegree study. A college-level course of study that does not lead to a degree. Nondegree study may or may not be part of a program leading to a certificate.

Nursing college. An institution of higher education that primarily prepares students to become registered nurses (RNs) or licensed practical nurses (LPNs).

Open admission. The college admission policy of admitting high school graduates and other adults generally without regard to conventional academic qualifications, such as high school subjects, high school grades and admission test scores. Virtually all applicants with high school diplomas or their equivalent are accepted, space permitting.

Placement by examination. *See* Credit/placement by examination.

Portfolio. A collection of a student's work that demonstrates skills and accomplishments. Portfolios may be physical or electronic. There are academic portfolios that include student written papers and projects, and also portfolios that include created objects, such as art, photography, fashion illustrations, and more.

Private college. Institutions described in this book as "private" are operated on a not-for-profit basis. They may be independent or church affiliated. *See also* Proprietary college.

Professional degree. A degree granted upon completion of academic requirements to become licensed in a recognized profession. The programs of study require at least two years of previous college work for entrance, and at least six years of total college work for completion. The medical doctorate (M.D.) is one kind of first-professional degree.

PROFILE. *See* CSS/Financial Aid PROFILE.

Priority date. The date by which an application, whether for admission, housing or financial aid, must be received to be given the strongest possible consideration. After that date, applicants are considered on a first-come, first-served basis.

Proprietary college. *See* For-profit college.

PSAT/NMSQT (Preliminary SAT/National Merit Scholarship Qualifying Test). A comprehensive program that helps schools put students on the path to college. The PSAT/NMSQT is administered by high schools to sophomores and juniors each year in October and serves as the qualifying test for scholarships awarded by the National Merit Scholarship Corporation.

Public college/university. An institution that is supported by taxes and other public revenue and governed by a county, state or federal government agency.

Quality point average. *See* Grade point average (GPA) or ratio.

Quarter. An academic calendar period of about 12 weeks. Four quarters make up an academic year, but at colleges using the quarter system, students make normal academic progress by attending three quarters each year. In some colleges, students can accelerate their programs by attending all four quarters in one or more years.

Rabbinical college. *See* Seminary/rabbinical college.

Regional accreditation. *See* Accreditation.

Regular admission. Admission during the college's normal calendar for admission, as opposed to Early Decision or Early Action admission.

Reserve Officers' Training Corps (ROTC). Programs conducted by certain colleges in cooperation with the United States Air Force, Army and Navy. Navy ROTC includes the Marine Corps (the Coast Guard and Merchant Marine do not sponsor ROTC programs). Local recruiting offices of the services themselves can supply detailed information about these programs, as can participating colleges.

Residence hall. An on-campus living facility. Also known as a dormitory (or "dorm").

Residency requirement. The minimum number of terms that a student must spend taking courses on campus (as opposed to independent study, transfer credits from other colleges, or credit by examination) to be eligible for graduation. Can also refer to the minimum amount of time a student must have lived in-state in order to qualify for the in-state tuition rate at a public college or university.

Rolling admission. An admission procedure by which the college considers each student's application as soon as all the required credentials, such as school records and test scores, have been received. The college usually notifies an applicant of its decision without delay. At many colleges, rolling admission allows for early notification and works much like nonbinding Early Action programs.

Room and board. The cost of housing and meals for students who reside on campus and/or dine in college-operated meal halls.

SAT. A college admission exam that tests reading, writing and language, and mathematics skills. It is given on specified dates throughout the year at test centers in the United States and other countries. The SAT is used by most colleges and sponsors of financial aid programs.

SAT Subject Tests. Admission tests in specific subjects given at test centers in the United States and other countries on specified dates throughout the year. The tests are used by colleges for help in both evaluating applicants for admission and determining course placement, and exemption of enrolled first-year students. NOTE: SAT Subject Tests have not been redesigned.

Semester. A period of about 16 weeks. Colleges on a semester system offer two semesters of instruction a year; there may be an additional summer session.

Semester at sea. A program for credit, usually for students with majors in oceanography or marine-related fields, in which students live on a ship, frequently a research vessel, for part of a semester. Academic courses are generally taken in conjunction with the sea experience.

Seminary/rabbinical college. An institution that prepares its student for professional religious ministry. Most seminaries are graduate-only institutions that offer first-professional degrees in divinity or rabbinical studies. The seminaries described in this book also offer undergraduate programs in philosophy, theology, Bible studies or other related liberal arts.

Sophomore standing. Consideration of a student as a sophomore for academic purposes such as registering for classes and declaring a major. A college may grant sophomore standing to incoming freshmen if they have enough credits from AP, CLEP or IB exams.

Student Aid Report (SAR). A report produced by the U.S. Department of Education and sent to students in response to their having filed the Free Application for Federal Student Aid (FAFSA). The SAR contains information the student provided on the FAFSA as well as the federally calculated result, which the financial aid office will use in determining the student's eligibility for a Federal Pell Grant and other federal student aid programs.

Student-designed major. An academic program that allows a student to construct a major field of study not formally offered by the college. Often nontraditional and interdisciplinary in nature, the major is developed by the student with the approval of a designated college officer or committee.

Study abroad. Any arrangement by which a student completes part of the college program — typically the junior year but sometimes only a semester or a summer — by studying in another country. A college may operate a campus abroad, or it may have a cooperative agreement with some other U.S. college or an institution of the other country.

Teacher certification. A college program designed to prepare students to meet the requirements for certification as teachers in elementary and secondary schools.

Teachers college. A college that specializes in preparing students to teach in elementary or secondary schools. Most teachers colleges offer a curriculum that combines a study of the liberal arts with the study of pedagogy.

Technical college/school. A college that offers a wide variety of vocational programs to students.

Term. The shorter period into which colleges divide the school year. *See* Calendar.

Terminal degree. The highest degree level attainable in a particular field. For most teaching faculty this is a doctoral degree. In certain fields, however, a master's degree is the highest level.

Terminal program. An education program designed to prepare students for immediate employment. These programs usually can be completed in less than four years beyond high school and are available in most community colleges and vocational-technical institutes.

Test of English as a Foreign Language (TOEFL). A test generally used by international students to demonstrate their English language proficiency at the advanced level required for study at colleges and universities worldwide. Please visit the organization's website for further information.

Transcript. A copy of a student's official academic record listing all courses taken and grades received.

Transfer program. An education program in a two-year college (or a four-year college that offers associate degrees), primarily for students who plan to continue their studies in a four-year college or university.

Transfer student. A student who has attended another college for any period, which may be defined by various colleges as any time from a single term up to three years. A transfer student may receive credit for all or some of the courses successfully completed before the transfer.

Trimester. An academic calendar period of about 15 weeks. Three trimesters make up one year. Students normally progress by attending two of the trimesters each year and in some colleges can accelerate their programs by attending all three trimesters in one or more years.

Tuition. The price of instruction at a college. Tuition may be charged per term or per credit hour.

Two-year college. *See* Community/junior college; Upper-division college.

United Nations semester. A program in which students take courses at a college in New York City while interning at the United Nations.

University. An institution of higher education that is divided into several colleges, schools or institutes. When applying to a university, students typically have to apply for admission to a specific college, which may have its own admission requirements. Not all colleges within a university will admit applicants who are high school graduates — some may be for graduate study only, and some may be upper-division colleges. Generally, university students take classes in the college to which they were accepted, but they may be allowed to take some courses offered by other colleges within the university and can use shared facilities such as libraries and laboratories.

Upper division. The junior and senior years of study.

Upper-division college. A college offering bachelor's degree programs that begin with the junior year. Entering students must have completed their freshman and sophomore years at other colleges.

Urban semester. A program for credit in which students spend a semester in a major city and experience the complexities of an urban center through course work, seminars and/or internships related to their major.

USCAA. United States Collegiate Athletic Association. USCAA's members are primarily very small colleges.

Virtual university. A degree-granting, accredited institution wherein all courses are delivered by distance learning, with no physical campus.

Vocational program. *See* Terminal program.

Wait list. A list of students who meet the admission requirements, but will only be offered a place in the class if space becomes available. See the wait-list table in the back of this book for a list of colleges that placed students on a wait list last year, along with the number of students who were eventually accepted from that list.

Washington semester. A program in which students intern with a government agency or department in the Washington, D.C., metropolitan area. Students earn field service credit for their work and frequently take courses at area colleges.

Weekend college. A program that allows students to take a complete course of study and attend classes only on weekends. These programs are generally restricted to a few areas of study at a college and require more than the traditional number of years to complete.

Work-study. An arrangement by which a student combines employment and college study. The employment may be an integral part of the academic program (as in cooperative education and internships) or simply a means of paying for college (as in the Federal Work-Study Program).

Four-year colleges

Alabama

Alabama Agricultural and Mechanical University

Huntsville, Alabama   CB member
www.aamu.edu   CB code: 1003

- Public 4-year university and agricultural college
- Residential campus in large city
- 4,055 degree-seeking undergraduates
- 969 graduate students
- SAT or ACT (ACT writing optional) required

General. Founded in 1875. Regionally accredited. Campus located near Redstone Arsenal: Defense Research/Space Research Center. **Degrees:** 426 bachelor's awarded; master's, doctoral offered. **ROTC:** Army. **Location:** 2 miles from downtown, 95 miles from Birmingham. **Calendar:** Semester, extensive summer session. **Full-time faculty:** 241 total. **Part-time faculty:** 7 total. **Class size:** 41% < 20, 46% 20-39, 9% 40-49, 3% 50-99, less than 1% >100. **Special facilities:** State black archives research center and museum.

Basis for selection. 2.0 GPA required. Test scores important, but may be waived dependent upon evaluation of GPA and other achievements. Interview, essay recommended. **Home schooled:** Must meet Alabama State Department of Education requirements.

High school preparation. Required units include English 4, mathematics 4 and science 2.

2015-2016 Annual costs. Tuition/fees: $9,214; $16,984 out-of-state. Room/board: $6,340. Books/supplies: $1,500. **Additional information:** Health Insurance for domestic students: $152; Health Insurance for international students: $1,632.

Financial aid. Non-need-based: Scholarships awarded for athletics, minority status.

Application procedures. Admission: Priority date 5/1; deadline 7/15 (receipt date). $25 fee, may be waived for applicants with need. Admission notification on a rolling basis. **Financial aid:** Closing date 3/1. FAFSA, institutional form required. Applicants notified on a rolling basis starting 4/15; must reply within 2 week(s) of notification.

Academics. Bachelor of Technical Studies available to adult learners in nontraditional fields. **Special study options:** Cooperative education, distance learning, double major, dual enrollment of high school students, exchange student, honors, independent study, internships, study abroad, teacher certification program, Washington semester, weekend college. **Credit/placement by examination:** AP, CLEP, SAT, ACT, institutional tests. 9 credit hours maximum toward bachelor's degree. Scores from DANTES, CLEP, ACE, and similar tests, and work experiences considered for credit toward degree.

Support services: Learning center, reduced course load, remedial instruction, study skills assistance, tutoring.

Honors college/program. Second semester freshmen with 20-21 ACT (SAT 1030) may be considered with 3.5 college GPA, 12 credit hours completed at the university, and 3.3 high school GPA.

Majors. Architecture: Urban/community planning. **Biology:** General. **Business:** Accounting, business admin, finance, logistics, marketing. **Communications technology:** Radio/TV. **Computer sciences:** General. **Conservation:** Forestry. **Education:** Art, business, early childhood, elementary, music, physical, school counseling, secondary, special ed, speech impaired. **Engineering:** Civil, electrical, mechanical. **English:** English lit. **Human services:** Social work. **Math:** General. **Physical sciences:** Chemistry, physics. **Protective services:** Law enforcement admin. **Psychology:** General. **Social sciences:** Political science, sociology. **Visual/performing arts:** Art, music. **Work/family studies:** General.

Most popular majors. Biology 10%, business/marketing 15%, education 15%, engineering/engineering technologies 15%, psychology 6%.

Technology on campus. 928 workstations in dormitories, library, computer center, student center. Dormitories linked to campus network. Commuter students can connect to campus network. Helpline available.

Student life. Freshman orientation: Mandatory, $100 fee. Preregistration for classes offered. **Housing:** Guaranteed on-campus for all undergraduates. Single-sex dorms available. $250 deposit, deadline 8/1. **Activities:** Bands, choral groups, dance, drama, literary magazine, music ensembles, radio station, student government, student newspaper, TV station, Christian student organization, honor society, service clubs, NAACP, African-American political club, Baptist student union, Islamic association, Caribbean students association, International Association of Nigerian Students.

Athletics. NCAA. **Intercollegiate:** Baseball M, basketball, bowling W, cross-country, football (tackle) M, golf, soccer W, softball W, tennis, track and field, volleyball W. **Intramural:** Basketball, football (tackle) M, soccer W, softball, volleyball. **Team name:** Bulldogs.

Student services. Adult student services, career counseling, student employment services, health services, personal counseling, placement for graduates, veterans' counselor. **Physically disabled:** Services for visually, speech, hearing impaired.

Contact. E-mail: admissions@aamu.edu
Phone: (256) 372-5245 Toll-free number: (800) 553-0816
Fax: (256) 372-5249
Venita King, Director of Admissions, Alabama Agricultural and Mechanical University, Box 908, Normal, AL 35762

Alabama State University

Montgomery, Alabama
www.alasu.edu   CB code: 1006

- Public 4-year university
- Residential campus in small city
- 4,740 degree-seeking undergraduates: 8% part-time, 61% women
- 613 degree-seeking graduate students
- 48% of applicants admitted
- SAT or ACT (ACT writing optional), interview required
- 32% graduate within 6 years

General. Founded in 1867. Regionally accredited. **Degrees:** 529 bachelor's awarded; master's, professional, doctoral offered. **ROTC:** Army, Air Force. **Location:** 91 miles from Birmingham, 162 miles from Atlanta. **Calendar:** Semester, limited summer session. **Full-time faculty:** 253 total; 65% have terminal degrees, 67% minority, 53% women. **Part-time faculty:** 155 total; 23% have terminal degrees, 75% minority, 56% women. **Class size:** 51% < 20, 48% 20-39, 1% 40-49, less than 1% 50-99, less than 1% >100. **Special facilities:** Black history collection, E. D. Nixon papers from civil rights movement of 1960's.

Freshman class profile. 8,356 applied, 4,004 admitted, 1,019 enrolled.

Mid 50% test scores			
SAT critical reading:	390-470	GPA 2.0-2.99:	46%
SAT math:	380-480	Rank in top quarter:	11%
ACT composite:	15-23	Rank in top tenth:	4%
GPA 3.75 or higher:	4%	Return as sophomores:	61%
GPA 3.50-3.74:	4%	Out-of-state:	42%
GPA 3.0-3.49:	20%	Live on campus:	76%
		International:	1%

Basis for selection. School record and GPA very important; 2.2 GPA from accredited high school required. Interview and essay recommended.

Audition required of music majors. Portfolio recommended for art majors. **Home schooled:** Transcript of courses and grades required. 18 ACT required. **Learning Disabled:** Must submit appropriate documentation in order to be given special consideration.

High school preparation. College-preparatory program recommended. 44 units required. Required units include English 4, mathematics 10, social studies 10 and foreign language 10.

2015-2016 Annual costs. Tuition/fees: $8,720; $15,656 out-of-state. Room/board: $5,422. Books/supplies: $1,600. Personal expenses: $1,380.

2015-2016 Financial aid. Need-based: 797 full-time freshmen applied for aid; 796 deemed to have need; 753 received aid. Average need met was 77%. Average scholarship/grant was $5,621; average loan $3,482. 55% of total undergraduate aid awarded as scholarships/grants, 45% as loans/jobs. **Non-need-based:** Awarded to 2,234 full-time undergraduates, including 264 freshmen. Scholarships awarded for academics, alumni affiliation, art, athletics, job skills, leadership, minority status, music/drama, religious affiliation, ROTC.

Application procedures. Admission: Closing date 7/31 (postmark date). $25 fee, may be waived for applicants with need. Admission notification on a rolling basis. **Financial aid:** Priority date 4/1; no closing date. FAFSA required. Applicants notified on a rolling basis starting 5/1.

Academics. Special study options: Combined bachelor's/graduate degree, cooperative education, cross-registration, distance learning, double major, dual enrollment of high school students, honors, independent study, internships, teacher certification program. Enrollment with Auburn University Montgomery and Troy University Montgomery. **Credit/placement by examination:** AP, CLEP, SAT, ACT, institutional tests. 45 credit hours maximum toward bachelor's degree. Students must have approval of the academic advisor, department head, dean and vice president for academic affairs prior to taking CLEP exam. **Support services:** Learning center, remedial instruction, study skills assistance, tutoring, writing center.

Honors college/program. 3.3 GPA and 24 ACT or 1100 SAT required; 34 freshmen admitted.

Majors. Biology: General. **Business:** Accounting, business admin, finance, marketing. **Communications:** Communications/speech/rhetoric. **Computer sciences:** Computer science. **Education:** Early childhood, elementary, music, physical, secondary, special ed. **Engineering:** Biomedical. **English:** English lit. **Health services:** Health information management. **History:** General. **Human services:** Social work. **Math:** General. **Parks/recreation:** Facilities management. **Physical sciences:** Chemistry, forensic chemistry, physics. **Protective services:** Criminal justice, criminalistics. **Psychology:** General. **Social sciences:** Political science. **Visual/performing arts:** Art, dance, dramatic, music.

Most popular majors. Biology 8%, business/marketing 11%, communications/journalism 7%, computer/information sciences 6%, education 15%, health sciences 10%, security/protective services 13%, visual/performing arts 6%.

Technology on campus. 405 workstations in dormitories, library, computer center, student center. Dormitories wired for high-speed internet access and linked to campus network. Online course registration, online library, helpline, repair service, wireless network available.

Student life. Freshman orientation: Mandatory, $55 fee. Preregistration for classes offered. **Housing:** Coed dorms, single-sex dorms, special housing for disabled, apartments available. $200 fully refundable deposit, deadline 5/31. Living-learning communities available. **Activities:** Bands, campus ministries, choral groups, dance, drama, international student organizations, music ensembles, Model UN, musical theater, radio station, student government, student newspaper, Student Christian Association.

Athletics. NCAA. **Intercollegiate:** Baseball M, basketball, bowling W, cross-country, football (tackle) M, golf, soccer W, softball W, tennis, track and field, volleyball W. **Intramural:** Baseball M, basketball, softball, swimming, tennis, track and field, volleyball W. **Team name:** Hornets.

Student services. Adult student services, alcohol/substance abuse counseling, career counseling, services for economically disadvantaged, student employment services, financial aid counseling, health services, minority student services, personal counseling, placement for graduates, veterans' counselor. **Physically disabled:** Services for visually impaired.

Contact. E-mail: admissions@alasu.edu
Phone: (334) 229-4291 Toll-free number: (800) 253-5037
Fax: (334) 229-4984
William Smith, Director of Admissions and Recruitment, Alabama State University, PO Box 271, Montgomery, AL 36101-0271

Amridge University
Montgomery, Alabama
www.amridgeuniversity.edu   CB code: 7001

- Private 4-year virtual university affiliated with the Church of Christ
- Commuter campus in small city
- 308 degree-seeking undergraduates: 46% part-time, 57% women, 34% African American, 2% Hispanic/Latino
- 310 degree-seeking graduate students

General. Founded in 1967. Regionally accredited. **Degrees:** 50 bachelor's, 3 associate awarded; master's, doctoral offered. **Location:** 100 miles from Birmingham, 150 miles from Atlanta. **Calendar:** Semester, extensive summer session. **Full-time faculty:** 36 total; 83% have terminal degrees. **Part-time faculty:** 28 total; 54% have terminal degrees.

Basis for selection. Open admission, but selective for some programs. Students admitted under conditional admission must earn a 2.0 during the first 24 semester hours attempted. **Home schooled:** Transcript of courses and grades, interview required.

High school preparation. 15 units recommended.

2015-2016 Annual costs. Tuition/fees: $6,900. Books/supplies: $1,500. Personal expenses: $1,750.

2015-2016 Financial aid. Need-based: 4 full-time freshmen applied for aid; 3 deemed to have need; 3 received aid. Average need met was 100%. Average scholarship/grant was $4,120; average loan $3,120. 48% of total undergraduate aid awarded as scholarships/grants, 52% as loans/jobs. **Non-need-based:** Awarded to 156 full-time undergraduates, including 3 freshmen. Scholarships awarded for academics, leadership, religious affiliation.

Application procedures. Admission: No deadline. $50 fee. Application must be submitted online. Admission notification on a rolling basis. **Financial aid:** No deadline. FAFSA, institutional form required. Applicants notified on a rolling basis.

Academics. Special study options: Accelerated study, distance learning, double major, independent study, internships. Participant in the U.S. Department of Education's Distance Education Demonstration Program and in GoArmyEd initiative. **Credit/placement by examination:** AP, CLEP. 36 credit hours maximum toward bachelor's degree. **Support services:** Reduced course load, tutoring, writing center.

Majors. Business: Business admin. **Computer sciences:** General. **Liberal arts:** Arts/sciences. **Theology:** Bible.

Most popular majors. Business/marketing 10%, computer/information sciences 6%, liberal arts 50%, theological studies 34%.

Technology on campus. PC or laptop required. 25 workstations in library, computer center. Online course registration, online library, helpline available.

Student life. Freshman orientation: Available. Preregistration for classes offered. Online orientation available at any time.

Athletics. Team name: Lions.

Student services. Career counseling, financial aid counseling, placement for graduates, veterans' counselor.

Contact. E-mail: admissions@amridgeuniversity.edu
Phone: (334) 387-3877 ext. 1 Toll-free number: (888) 790-8080 ext. 1
Fax: (334) 387-3878
Brooks Housley, Admissions Recruiter, Amridge University, 1200 Taylor Road, Montgomery, AL 36117-3553

Athens State University
Athens, Alabama
www.athens.edu   CB code: 0706

- Public two-year upper-division liberal arts and teachers college
- Commuter campus in large town
- 85% of applicants admitted

General. Founded in 1822. Regionally accredited. **Degrees:** 799 bachelor's awarded. **Articulation:** Agreements with state schools through the Alabama Articulation and General Studies Committee. **Location:** 14 miles from Decatur, 24 miles from Huntsville. **Calendar:** Semester, extensive summer session. **Full-time faculty:** 80 total; 78% have terminal degrees, 16% minority, 52%

women. **Part-time faculty:** 106 total; 18% minority, 61% women. **Class size:** 44% < 20, 44% 20-39, 4% 40-49, 3% 50-99, 5% >100.

Student profile. 2,904 degree-seeking undergraduates. 562 applied as first time-transfer students, 479 admitted, 348 enrolled. 81% transferred from two-year, 19% transferred from four-year institutions.

Women:	65%	Out-of-state:	5%
Part-time:	58%	25 or older:	64%

Basis for selection. College transcript required. Transfer accepted as juniors, seniors.

2015-2016 Annual costs. Tuition/fees: $6,270; $11,790 out-of-state. Books/supplies: $1,000.

Financial aid. Need-based: 1,068 applied for aid; 960 deemed to have need; 958 received aid. Average need met was 2%. 45% of total undergraduate aid awarded as scholarships/grants, 55% as loans/jobs. **Non-need-based:** Awarded to 132 undergraduates. Scholarships awarded for academics, alumni affiliation, art, athletics, leadership, minority status.

Application procedures. Admission: Rolling admission. $30 fee. **Financial aid:** FAFSA required.

Academics. Special study options: Cooperative education, distance learning, double major, dual enrollment of high school students, honors, independent study, internships, liberal arts/career combination, study abroad, teacher certification program, weekend college. **Credit/placement by examination:** AP, CLEP.

Majors. Biology: General. **Business:** Accounting, business admin, human resources, information resources management, logistics, purchasing. **Computer sciences:** General. **Education:** Elementary, kindergarten/preschool, physical, special ed, voc/tech. **English:** English lit. **History:** General. **Liberal arts:** Arts/sciences. **Math:** General. **Parks/recreation:** Sports admin. **Philosophy/religion:** Religion. **Physical sciences:** Chemistry. **Protective services:** Criminal justice. **Psychology:** General. **Social sciences:** Political science, sociology. **Visual/performing arts:** Art.

Most popular majors. Business/marketing 42%, education 28%, liberal arts 6%.

Technology on campus. 341 workstations in library, computer center, student center. Commuter students can connect to campus network. Online library available.

Student life. Activities: Campus ministries, drama, literary magazine, student government, student newspaper, Heritage Reading Council, ASSIST-student United Way, Athenian Ambassadors.

Student services. Career counseling, student employment services, financial aid counseling, minority student services, placement for graduates, veterans' counselor. **Physically disabled:** Services for visually, speech, hearing impaired.

Contact. E-mail: admissions@athens.edu
Phone: (256) 233-8220 Toll-free number: (800) 522-0272
Fax: (256) 233-6565
Necedah Henderson, Coordinator of Admissions, Athens State University, 300 North Beaty Street, Athens, AL 35611

Auburn University
Auburn, Alabama
www.auburn.edu

CB member
CB code: 1005

- Public 4-year university
- Commuter campus in small city
- 21,551 degree-seeking undergraduates: 9% part-time, 49% women, 7% African American, 2% Asian American, 3% Hispanic/Latino, 1% Native American, 1% Multi-racial, non-Hispanic, 1% international
- 5,467 degree-seeking graduate students
- 78% of applicants admitted
- SAT or ACT with writing, application essay required
- 73% graduate within 6 years

General. Founded in 1856. Regionally accredited. **Degrees:** 4,526 bachelor's awarded; master's, professional, doctoral offered. **ROTC:** Army, Naval, Air Force. **Location:** 55 miles from Montgomery, 110 miles from Atlanta. **Calendar:** Semester, extensive summer session. **Full-time faculty:** 1,216 total; 93% have terminal degrees, 18% minority, 38% women. **Part-time faculty:** 183 total; 58% have terminal degrees, 10% minority, 42% women. **Class size:** 33% < 20, 46% 20-39, 7% 40-49, 9% 50-99, 6% >100. **Special**

facilities: Hybridoma facility, herbarium, hypervelocity impact facility, advanced microscopy and imaging laboratory, microelectronics science and technology center, airport with aircraft and flight simulators, governmental services center, pharmacy operations and designs center, drug information and learning resources center, fish molecular genetics and biotechnology laboratory, forest policy center, fusion lab, health behavior assessment center, marriage and family therapy center, microfibrous materials manufacturing center, biomechanics lab, motor behavior center, plasma sciences lab, veterinary medicine radiology clinic, raptor rehabilitation center, animal health clinics, MRI research center.

Freshman class profile. 19,414 applied, 15,077 admitted, 4,902 enrolled.

Mid 50% test scores		Rank in top quarter:	62%
SAT critical reading:	530-630	Rank in top tenth:	31%
SAT math:	540-650	Return as sophomores:	90%
SAT writing:	520-620	Out-of-state:	40%
ACT composite:	24-30	Live on campus:	64%
GPA 3.75 or higher:	60%	International:	1%
GPA 3.50-3.74:	18%	Fraternities:	26%
GPA 3.0-3.49:	20%	Sororities:	51%
GPA 2.0-2.99:	2%		

Basis for selection. Each student evaluated based on combination of standardized test scores, GPA, and additional information required on application.

High school preparation. College-preparatory program required. 12 units required; 15 recommended. Required and recommended units include English 4, mathematics 3, social studies 3-4, science 2 (laboratory 1-2) and foreign language 1. Math must include algebra I, algebra II, and either geometry, trigonometry, calculus or analysis. Science must include biology and a physical science.

2015-2016 Annual costs. Tuition/fees: $10,424; $28,040 out-of-state. Room/board: $12,584. Books/supplies: $1,200. Personal expenses: $2,728.

2014-2015 Financial aid. Need-based: 2,887 full-time freshmen applied for aid; 1,790 deemed to have need; 1,790 received aid. Average need met was 50%. Average scholarship/grant was $8,635; average loan $3,863. 44% of total undergraduate aid awarded as scholarships/grants, 56% as loans/jobs. **Non-need-based:** Awarded to 4,659 full-time undergraduates, including 1,599 freshmen. **Additional information:** State of Alabama has pre-paid college tuition plan for residents.

Application procedures. Admission: Closing date 1/15 (postmark date). $50 fee, may be waived for applicants with need. Admission notification on a rolling basis beginning on or about 10/15. Must reply by May 1 or within 4 week(s) if notified thereafter. **Financial aid:** Priority date 3/1; no closing date. FAFSA required. Applicants notified on a rolling basis starting 10/2.

Academics. Special study options: Accelerated study, cooperative education, distance learning, double major, dual enrollment of high school students, ESL, exchange student, honors, independent study, internships, liberal arts/career combination, study abroad, teacher certification program, Washington semester. DVM-Master's in veterinary specialty, dual option program in education/subject areas. **Credit/placement by examination:** AP, CLEP, institutional tests. **Support services:** Learning center, reduced course load, study skills assistance, tutoring, writing center.

Honors college/program. 29 ACT/1280 SAT (exclusive of Writing) and 3.5 GPA required (3.4 GPA may be considered). Approximately 1000 freshmen accepted last year.

Majors. Architecture: Architecture, environmental design, interior. **Biology:** Bacteriology, biochemistry, biomedical sciences, botany, marine, molecular, zoology. **Business:** Accounting, business admin, entrepreneurial studies, finance, human resources, international, logistics, management information systems, management science, managerial economics, marketing, training/development. **Communications:** Journalism, media studies, public relations, radio/TV. **Computer sciences:** General. **Conservation:** General, environmental science, forest sciences, wildlife/wilderness. **Education:** Agricultural, business, early childhood, early childhood special, elementary, English, foreign languages, French, German, health, mathematics, music, physical, science, social science, Spanish, special ed, voc/tech. **Engineering:** Aerospace, agricultural, architectural, biological, chemical, civil, computer, electrical, manufacturing, materials, mechanical, polymer, software. **English:** English lit. **Foreign languages:** French, German, Spanish. **Health services:** Audiology/speech pathology, clinical lab science, communication disorders, health care admin, nursing (RN), predental, premedicine, prenursing, prepharmacy, preveterinary. **History:** General. **Human services:** General, social work. **Math:** General, applied. **Parks/recreation:** Exercise sciences. **Philosophy/religion:** Philosophy, religion. **Physical sciences:** Chemistry, geology, physics. **Psychology:** General. **Social sciences:** Anthropology, criminology, economics, geography, political science, sociology. **Visual/performing arts:** Art history/conservation, design, dramatic, industrial design, music, studio arts. **Work/family studies:** Apparel marketing, family studies.

Most popular majors. Biology 9%, business/marketing 20%, education 9%, engineering/engineering technologies 17%, health sciences 6%.

Technology on campus. 1,722 workstations in dormitories, library, computer center, student center. Dormitories linked to campus network. Commuter students can connect to campus network. Online course registration, online library, helpline, repair service, wireless network available.

Student life. Freshman orientation: Available, $75 fee. Preregistration for classes offered. **Housing:** Coed dorms, single-sex dorms, special housing for disabled, apartments, fraternity/sorority housing available. $300 partly refundable deposit. Honors housing available. **Activities:** Bands, campus ministries, choral groups, dance, drama, film society, international student organizations, literary magazine, music ensembles, musical theater, opera, radio station, student government, student newspaper, symphony orchestra, TV station, over 300 student organizations.

Athletics. NCAA. **Intercollegiate:** Baseball M, basketball, cross-country, diving, equestrian W, football (tackle) M, golf, gymnastics W, soccer W, softball W, swimming, tennis, track and field, volleyball W. **Intramural:** Badminton, basketball, bowling, cheerleading, football (non-tackle), golf, racquetball, soccer, softball, swimming, table tennis, tennis, track and field, ultimate frisbee, volleyball. **Team name:** Tigers.

Student services. Adult student services, alcohol/substance abuse counseling, career counseling, student employment services, financial aid counseling, health services, minority student services, personal counseling, placement for graduates, veterans' counselor, women's services. **Physically disabled:** Services for visually, speech, hearing impaired.

Contact. E-mail: admissions@auburn.edu
Phone: (334) 844-4080 Toll-free number: (800) 282-8769
Fax: (334) 844-6436
Cindy Singley, Director of University Recruitment, Auburn University, Quad Center, Auburn, AL 36849-5111

Auburn University at Montgomery
Montgomery, Alabama
www.aum.edu   CB code: 1036

- Public 4-year university
- Commuter campus in small city
- 4,142 degree-seeking undergraduates: 26% part-time, 64% women, 35% African American, 2% Asian American, 1% Hispanic/Latino, 1% Native American, 3% Multi-racial, non-Hispanic, 3% international
- 658 degree-seeking graduate students
- 79% of applicants admitted
- SAT or ACT (ACT writing optional) required

General. Founded in 1967. Regionally accredited. **Degrees:** 590 bachelor's awarded; master's, doctoral offered. **ROTC:** Army, Air Force. **Location:** 54 miles from Auburn, 91 miles from Birmingham. **Calendar:** Semester, extensive summer session. **Full-time faculty:** 215 total; 20% minority, 46% women. **Part-time faculty:** 145 total; 14% minority, 64% women. **Class size:** 43% < 20, 54% 20-39, 1% 40-49, 1% 50-99. **Special facilities:** Wellness center, computer lab, geographic information systems and computer cartography lab, tennis courts, athletic fields, learning center and instructional support lab, graphic arts lab, speech and hearing clinic, academic success center.

Freshman class profile. 2,494 applied, 1,963 admitted, 620 enrolled.

Mid 50% test scores			
SAT critical reading:	450-520	End year in good standing:	69%
SAT math:	470-540	Return as sophomores:	64%
ACT composite:	19-23	Out-of-state:	4%
GPA 3.75 or higher:	19%	Live on campus:	34%
GPA 3.50-3.74:	17%	International:	3%
GPA 3.0-3.49:	37%	Fraternities:	3%
GPA 2.0-2.99:	27%	Sororities:	9%
Rank in top quarter:	40%		
Rank in top tenth:	16%		

Basis for selection. GED not accepted. GPA and ACT/SAT scores considered. Provisional admission may be available for students who do not meet requirements for regular admission.

High school preparation. College-preparatory program recommended. 4 units recommended. Recommended units include English 3, mathematics 3, social studies 2, history 2, science 2 (laboratory 2), foreign language 2 and academic electives 2.

2015-2016 Annual costs. Tuition/fees: $9,350; $20,210 out-of-state. Room/board: $5,520.

2015-2016 Financial aid. Need-based: 450 full-time freshmen applied for aid; 395 deemed to have need; 395 received aid. Average scholarship/grant was $4,505; average loan $3,196. 51% of total undergraduate aid awarded as scholarships/grants, 49% as loans/jobs. **Non-need-based:** Awarded to 703 full-time undergraduates, including 199 freshmen.

Application procedures. Admission: Closing date 8/15 (receipt date). No application fee. Admission notification on a rolling basis. **Financial aid:** Priority date 3/1; no closing date. FAFSA required. Applicants notified on a rolling basis starting 4/15.

Academics. Interdisciplinary Master of Liberal Arts available. **Special study options:** Accelerated study, cooperative education, cross-registration, distance learning, double major, dual enrollment of high school students, ESL, honors, independent study, internships, liberal arts/career combination, study abroad, teacher certification program, weekend college. Joint Ph.D. in Public Administration with Auburn University, Joint Masters in Nursing with Auburn University. **Credit/placement by examination:** AP, CLEP, IB, SAT, ACT, institutional tests. 55 credit hours maximum toward bachelor's degree. **Support services:** Learning center, pre-admission summer program, reduced course load, remedial instruction, study skills assistance, tutoring, writing center. Supplemental Instruction.

Majors. Biology: General. **Business:** General, accounting, business admin, finance, human resources, international, management information systems, marketing, organizational leadership. **Communications:** Communications/speech/rhetoric. **Computer sciences:** Computer science. **Education:** Elementary, secondary, special ed. **English:** English lit. **Foreign languages:** General, Spanish. **Health services:** Clinical lab technology, nursing (RN). **History:** General. **Liberal arts:** Arts/sciences. **Math:** General. **Parks/recreation:** Exercise sciences. **Physical sciences:** Chemistry. **Protective services:** Criminal justice. **Psychology:** General. **Social sciences:** Economics, GIS/cartography, political science, sociology. **Visual/performing arts:** Art.

Most popular majors. Biology 6%, business/marketing 25%, communications/journalism 6%, education 9%, health sciences 25%.

Technology on campus. 600 workstations in dormitories, library, computer center, student center. Dormitories wired for high-speed internet access and linked to campus network. Commuter students can connect to campus network. Online course registration, wireless network available.

Student life. Freshman orientation: Mandatory, $125 fee. Preregistration for classes offered. **Housing:** Coed dorms, special housing for disabled, apartments, gender-neutral housing, themed housing available. $100 nonrefundable deposit, deadline 5/1. **Activities:** Campus ministries, drama, international student organizations, literary magazine, music ensembles, musical theater, student government, student newspaper, TV station, Baptist Campus Ministries, Catholic Student Association, NAACP, College Republicans, International Student Association, Chinese Student & Scholar Association, Green Team, Student Council for Exceptional Children, Nonprofit Leadership Alliance, Warhawk Disability Alliance.

Athletics. NAIA. **Intercollegiate:** Baseball M, basketball, cheerleading, cross-country, soccer, softball W, tennis. **Intramural:** Badminton, basketball, football (non-tackle), sand volleyball, soccer, softball, table tennis, ultimate frisbee, volleyball. **Team name:** Warhawks.

Student services. Adult student services, alcohol/substance abuse counseling, career counseling, student employment services, financial aid counseling, health services, personal counseling, placement for graduates, veterans' counselor, women's services. **Physically disabled:** Services for visually, speech, hearing impaired.

Contact. E-mail: admissions@aum.edu
Phone: (334) 244-3615 Toll-free number: (800) 227-2649
Fax: (334) 244-3795
Kate Bartlett, Director of Admissions and Recruiting, Auburn University at Montgomery, PO Box 244023, Montgomery, AL 36124-4023

Birmingham-Southern College
Birmingham, Alabama   CB member
www.bsc.edu   CB code: 1064

- Private 4-year liberal arts college affiliated with the United Methodist Church
- Residential campus in very large city
- 1,346 degree-seeking undergraduates: 1% part-time, 50% women, 11% African American, 5% Asian American, 2% Hispanic/Latino, 1% Native American, 1% Multi-racial, non-Hispanic
- 53% of applicants admitted

▶ SAT or ACT (ACT writing optional), application essay required

▶ 61% graduate within 6 years

General. Founded in 1856. Regionally accredited. **Degrees:** 222 bachelor's awarded. **ROTC:** Army, Air Force. **Location:** 3 miles from downtown. **Calendar:** 4-1-4, limited summer session. **Full-time faculty:** 95 total; 94% have terminal degrees, 5% minority, 42% women. **Part-time faculty:** 36 total; 28% have terminal degrees, 6% minority, 61% women. **Class size:** 65% < 20, 32% 20-39, 1% 40-49, 1% 50-99. **Special facilities:** Southern environmental center and interactive museum, urban environmental park.

Freshman class profile. 3,683 applied, 1,957 admitted, 464 enrolled.

Mid 50% test scores			
SAT critical reading:	480-600	Rank in top quarter:	51%
SAT math:	490-620	Rank in top tenth:	21%
ACT composite:	21-25	Return as sophomores:	86%
GPA 3.75 or higher:	33%	Out-of-state:	45%
GPA 3.50-3.74:	16%	Live on campus:	92%
GPA 3.0-3.49:	29%	Fraternities:	38%
GPA 2.0-2.99:	22%	Sororities:	60%

Basis for selection. High school record most important, followed by test scores, recommendations, and required essay. Interview required for early admission, recommended for borderline applicants. Auditions required for music, theatre, dance majors. **Home schooled:** Interviews recommended.

High school preparation. 16 units required. Required and recommended units include English 4, mathematics 2, social studies 2, history 2, science 2 (laboratory 1), foreign language 2 and academic electives 2.

2015-2016 Annual costs. Tuition/fees: $33,128. Room/board: $11,440. Books/supplies: $1,000.

2015-2016 Financial aid. Need-based: 347 full-time freshmen applied for aid; 288 deemed to have need; 288 received aid. Average need met was 74%. Average scholarship/grant was $5,538; average loan $4,348. 61% of total undergraduate aid awarded as scholarships/grants, 39% as loans/jobs. **Non-need-based:** Awarded to 1,311 full-time undergraduates, including 440 freshmen. Scholarships awarded for academics, alumni affiliation, art, leadership, music/drama, religious affiliation, ROTC, state residency. **Additional information:** Auditions required for music, theatre, dance applicants seeking scholarships. Portfolios required for art applicants seeking scholarships, and essays recommended for all applicants seeking scholarships.

Application procedures. Admission: Priority date 2/1; no deadline. $50 fee, may be waived for applicants with need. Admission notification on a rolling basis beginning on or about 12/1. Must reply by 5/1. **Financial aid:** Priority date 3/1; no closing date. FAFSA required. Applicants notified on a rolling basis starting 3/1; must reply by 5/1.

Academics. Exploration Term program allows students to explore one topic or interest for the month of January. Off-campus opportunities include service learning projects in local, national, or international communities. **Special study options:** Accelerated study, combined bachelor's/graduate degree, cross-registration, double major, exchange student, honors, independent study, internships, semester at sea, student-designed major, study abroad, teacher certification program. 3-2 in nursing with Vanderbilt; 3-2 in engineering with Washington University, Columbia University, University of Alabama, and Auburn University; 3-2 in environment studies with Duke University. **Credit/placement by examination:** AP, CLEP, IB, SAT, ACT, institutional tests. 64 credit hours maximum toward bachelor's degree. **Support services:** Learning center, pre-admission summer program, reduced course load, study skills assistance, tutoring, writing center.

Majors. Biology: General. **Business:** General, accounting, business admin, finance, international, marketing. **Computer sciences:** General, computer science. **Conservation:** Environmental studies. **Education:** General, art, early childhood, elementary, music, secondary, special ed. **English:** English lit. **Foreign languages:** French, German, Spanish. **History:** General. **Math:** General. **Philosophy/religion:** Philosophy, religion. **Physical sciences:** Chemistry, physics. **Psychology:** General. **Social sciences:** Economics, political science, sociology. **Theology:** Sacred music. **Visual/performing arts:** General, art, art history/conservation, dance, dramatic, drawing, music, music history, music theory/composition, painting, photography, piano/keyboard, sculpture, voice/opera.

Most popular majors. Biology 12%, business/marketing 22%, physical sciences 7%, psychology 11%, social sciences 9%, visual/performing arts 10%.

Technology on campus. 252 workstations in dormitories, library, computer center, student center. Dormitories wired for high-speed internet access and linked to campus network. Commuter students can connect to campus network. Online course registration, online library, helpline, student web hosting, wireless network available.

Student life. Freshman orientation: Mandatory. Preregistration for classes offered. One-day mini-session in June and 4-day session prior to beginning of fall classes. **Housing:** Guaranteed on-campus for all undergraduates. Coed dorms, single-sex dorms, special housing for disabled, apartments, fraternity/sorority housing, themed housing available. $300 nonrefundable deposit, deadline 5/1. Handicapped students accommodated on individual basis. **Activities:** Bands, campus ministries, choral groups, drama, international student organizations, literary magazine, music ensembles, Model UN, musical theater, opera, student government, student newspaper, Fellowship of Christian Athletes, Young Republicans, Young Democrats, Black student union, Allies, Students Offering Support, conservancy, Wesley Fellowship, Intervarsity Christian Fellowship.

Athletics. NCAA. **Intercollegiate:** Baseball M, basketball, cheerleading, cross-country, diving, football (tackle) M, golf, lacrosse, soccer, softball W, swimming, tennis, track and field, volleyball W. **Intramural:** Basketball, football (non-tackle), racquetball, soccer, softball, tennis, ultimate frisbee, volleyball, water polo. **Team name:** Panthers.

Student services. Alcohol/substance abuse counseling, chaplain/spiritual director, career counseling, student employment services, financial aid counseling, health services, personal counseling, placement for graduates, veterans' counselor.

Contact. E-mail: admission@bsc.edu
Phone: (205) 226-4696 Toll-free number: (800) 523-5793
Fax: (205) 226-3074
Sheri Salmon, Associate Vice President for Admission, Birmingham-Southern College, 900 Arkadelphia Road, Birmingham, AL 35254

Columbia Southern University
Orange Beach, Alabama
www.columbiasouthern.edu   **CB code: 3878**

▶ For-profit 4-year virtual university

▶ Commuter campus in small town

▶ 24,282 degree-seeking undergraduates: 49% part-time, 35% women, 22% African American, 2% Asian American, 7% Hispanic/Latino, 1% Native American, 3% Multi-racial, non-Hispanic

▶ 8,514 degree-seeking graduate students

General. Accredited by DETC. Columbia Southern University was established to meet the demand for alternatives to the traditional university experience. All degree programs are offered completely online, giving students the flexibility to fit their education around career and family commitments. Degrees are offered in a multitude of areas. **Degrees:** 3,242 bachelor's, 2,064 associate awarded; master's, doctoral offered. **Location:** 60 miles from Mobile, 30 miles from Pensacola, Florida. **Calendar:** Differs by program. **Full-time faculty:** 143 total; 50% have terminal degrees, 16% minority, 43% women. **Part-time faculty:** 369 total; 62% have terminal degrees, 28% minority, 44% women.

Basis for selection. Open admission. **Home schooled:** Transcript of courses and grades required. Required to show proof that they successfully completed their state's requirements for high school graduation. Responsible for compliance with all requirements for their state. An official transcript is required to demonstrate that high school graduation requirements were met.

High school preparation. College-preparatory program recommended.

2016-2017 Annual costs. Tuition/fees (projected): $6,335. Books/supplies: $680. Personal expenses: $3,303.

Application procedures. Admission: No deadline. No application fee. **Financial aid:** No deadline. FAFSA, institutional form required. Applicants notified on a rolling basis.

Academics. Special study options: Distance learning. **Credit/placement by examination:** AP, CLEP. 45 credit hours maximum toward associate degree, 90 toward bachelor's. May transfer CLEP credit up to maximum transfer limit. **Support services:** Learning center, study skills assistance, tutoring, writing center. The Success Center offers academic support in writing, math, and study skills. Specialists offer individual tutoring sessions focused on a student's need or coursework. Academic Advisors offer an initial advising session when the student enrolls into the institution.

Majors. Business: Business admin, human resources, organizational leadership. **Computer sciences:** Information technology, security. **Conservation:** Environmental studies. **Health services:** EMT paramedic, health care admin, mental health services. **Protective services:** Fire services admin, homeland security, police science.

Most popular majors. Business/marketing 53%, engineering/engineering technologies 11%, health sciences 11%, security/protective services 15%.

Technology on campus. PC or laptop required. Commuter students can connect to campus network. Online course registration, online library, helpline available.

Student life. Freshman orientation: Available. Preregistration for classes offered. **Activities:** Student newspaper.

Athletics. Team name: Knights.

Student services. Career counseling, financial aid counseling, veterans' counselor. **Physically disabled:** Services for visually, speech, hearing impaired.

Contact. E-mail: admissions@columbiasouthern.edu
Phone: (800) 977-8449 ext. 1521
Toll-free number: (800) 977-8449 ext. 1521 Fax: (251) 981-3815
Andrew Schneider, Assistant Director of Admissions, Columbia Southern University, 21982 University Lane, Orange Beach, AL 36561

Concordia College
Selma, Alabama
www.ccal.edu   CB code: 1989

- Private 4-year liberal arts college affiliated with the Lutheran Church - Missouri Synod
- Residential campus in large town
- 610 undergraduates

General. Founded in 1922. Regionally accredited. Concordia College is the nation's only Historically Black Lutheran College or University. **Degrees:** 21 bachelor's, 30 associate awarded. **Location:** 50 miles from Montgomery. **Calendar:** Semester, limited summer session. **Full-time faculty:** 23 total. **Part-time faculty:** 24 total.

Basis for selection. Open admission. 2.0 GPA required for unconditional admission. Students who do not fulfill requirements may be admitted on conditional basis.

High school preparation. 20 units recommended. Recommended units include English 4, mathematics 2, social studies 3, science 2 and foreign language 1.

2015-2016 Annual costs. Tuition/fees: $10,120. Room/board: $5,600. Books/supplies: $1,000.

Financial aid. All financial aid based on need.

Application procedures. Admission: Priority date 8/1; deadline 8/15. $10 fee, may be waived for applicants with need. Admission notification on a rolling basis beginning on or about 8/15. **Financial aid:** Priority date 4/1, closing date 4/15. FAFSA, institutional form required. Applicants notified on a rolling basis starting 6/15; must reply within 2 week(s) of notification.

Academics. Special study options: Independent study, liberal arts/career combination. **Credit/placement by examination:** AP, CLEP, institutional tests. **Support services:** Learning center, pre-admission summer program, reduced course load, remedial instruction, tutoring.

Majors. Business: Business admin. **Education:** Early childhood, elementary, kindergarten/preschool.

Most popular majors. Business/marketing 33%, education 67%.

Technology on campus. 30 workstations in library, computer center.

Student life. Freshman orientation: Mandatory. Preregistration for classes offered. **Housing:** Single-sex dorms available. **Activities:** Choral groups, drama, music ensembles, student government, student newspaper, Phi Theta Kappa, Gentlemen Care Group Club, Ambassador's Club, American Red Cross Club.

Athletics. Intercollegiate: Baseball M, basketball, softball W. **Intramural:** Baseball M, basketball, football (tackle) M, softball, table tennis, tennis, volleyball. **Team name:** Hornets.

Student services. Adult student services, career counseling, student employment services, health services, personal counseling, placement for graduates, veterans' counselor.

Contact. E-mail: admissions@ccal.edu
Phone: (334) 874-5700
Gwendolyn Stewart, Director of Admissions, Concordia College, 1712 Broad Street, Selma, AL 36701

Faulkner University
Montgomery, Alabama
www.faulkner.edu   CB code: 1034

- Private 4-year university and liberal arts college affiliated with the Church of Christ
- Commuter campus in large city
- 2,282 degree-seeking undergraduates: 22% part-time, 61% women, 51% African American, 2% Hispanic/Latino, 1% Native American, 2% Multiracial, non-Hispanic, 2% international
- 697 degree-seeking graduate students
- 57% of applicants admitted
- SAT or ACT (ACT writing optional) required
- 30% graduate within 6 years

General. Founded in 1942. Regionally accredited. Additional extended campuses (non-residential) in Birmingham, Huntsville and Mobile. **Degrees:** 513 bachelor's, 21 associate awarded; master's, professional, doctoral offered. **ROTC:** Army, Air Force. **Location:** 10 miles from downtown Montgomery. **Calendar:** Semester, limited summer session. **Full-time faculty:** 120 total; 66% have terminal degrees, 10% minority, 40% women. **Part-time faculty:** 180 total; 36% have terminal degrees, 17% minority, 38% women. **Class size:** 74% < 20, 21% 20-39, 3% 40-49, 1% 50-99. **Special facilities:** Dinner Theatre.

Freshman class profile. 1,712 applied, 981 admitted, 297 enrolled.

Mid 50% test scores			
SAT critical reading:	430-520	GPA 2.0-2.99:	31%
SAT math:	440-510	End year in good standing:	86%
SAT writing:	430-510	Return as sophomores:	57%
ACT composite:	18-24	Out-of-state:	18%
GPA 3.75 or higher:	21%	Live on campus:	72%
GPA 3.50-3.74:	17%	International:	3%
GPA 3.0-3.49:	30%	Fraternities:	14%
		Sororities:	37%

Basis for selection. Academic record, test scores, and personal or career goals most important. Interview and essay strongly recommended. **Home schooled:** Statement describing home school structure and mission, transcript of courses and grades, letter of recommendation (nonparent) required. **Learning Disabled:** After admission, students with disabilities are eligible to apply for services on campus.

High school preparation. College-preparatory program recommended. 15 units required; 18 recommended. Required and recommended units include English 3-4, mathematics 3-4, social studies 2, history 3, science 3-4 (laboratory 1) and foreign language 1.

2015-2016 Annual costs. Tuition/fees: $19,280. Room/board: $7,130. Books/supplies: $1,800. Personal expenses: $1,600. **Additional information:** Required fee includes additional cost per semester for iPad and required software. After 4 semesters and bachelor degree completion, students own the iPad.

2014-2015 Financial aid. Need-based: 348 full-time freshmen applied for aid; 331 deemed to have need; 331 received aid. Average need met was 61%. Average scholarship/grant was $11,419; average loan $3,002. 46% of total undergraduate aid awarded as scholarships/grants, 54% as loans/jobs. **Non-need-based:** Awarded to 330 full-time undergraduates, including 82 freshmen. Scholarships awarded for academics, alumni affiliation, athletics, music/drama, religious affiliation, state residency.

Application procedures. Admission: Priority date 2/15; no deadline. $25 fee, may be waived for applicants with need, free for online applicants. Admission notification on a rolling basis beginning on or about 8/15. **Financial aid:** Priority date 3/15, closing date 8/1. FAFSA, institutional form required. Applicants notified on a rolling basis starting 5/1; must reply within 3 week(s) of notification.

Academics. Full-time students required to take Bible course each semester. **Special study options:** Accelerated study, cross-registration, distance learning, double major, dual enrollment of high school students, honors, independent study, internships, study abroad, teacher certification program, weekend college. **Credit/placement by examination:** AP, CLEP, IB, SAT, ACT, institutional tests. 16 credit hours maximum toward associate degree, 32 toward bachelor's. **Support services:** Learning center, pre-admission summer program, reduced course load, remedial instruction, study skills assistance, tutoring, writing center.

Honors college/program. 27 ACT English/640 SAT verbal and 3.0 GPA required. Students must take five Great Books courses and complete thesis.

Majors. Biology: General, biochemistry. **Business:** General, accounting, business admin, human resources, management information systems, management science. **Computer sciences:** General, computer science, informatics, information technology. **Education:** Biology, drama/dance, early childhood, elementary, English, history, mathematics, music, physical, science, social science. **English:** English lit. **Health services:** Community health services, marriage/family therapy, mental health counseling, predental, premedicine, preoptometry, prephysical therapy, preveterinary. **History:** General. **Liberal arts:** Arts/sciences, humanities. **Math:** General. **Parks/recreation:** Sports admin. **Physical sciences:** Chemistry. **Protective services:** Criminal justice, criminalistics. **Psychology:** Clinical, counseling, forensic, industrial, medical. **Social sciences:** General. **Theology:** Bible, missionary, theology, youth ministry. **Visual/performing arts:** Dramatic, music, musical theater, theater arts management, theater design.

Most popular majors. Business/marketing 60%, security/protective services 16%.

Technology on campus. 275 workstations in dormitories, library, computer center, student center. Dormitories wired for high-speed internet access and linked to campus network. Commuter students can connect to campus network. Online library, helpline, wireless network available.

Student life. Freshman orientation: Mandatory, $150 fee. Preregistration for classes offered. **Policies:** Religious observance required. **Housing:** Guaranteed on-campus for freshmen. Single-sex dorms, special housing for disabled, apartments, wellness housing available. $50 nonrefundable deposit, deadline 7/31. **Activities:** Bands, campus ministries, choral groups, drama, international student organizations, literary magazine, music ensembles, musical theater, student government, student newspaper, minister's club, service organizations, religious organizations.

Athletics. NAIA, NCCAA. **Intercollegiate:** Baseball M, basketball, cheerleading, cross-country, football (tackle) M, golf, softball W, volleyball W. **Intramural:** Badminton, basketball, bowling, football (non-tackle), racquetball, softball, table tennis, tennis, track and field, volleyball. **Team name:** Eagles.

Student services. Adult student services, alcohol/substance abuse counseling, chaplain/spiritual director, career counseling, services for economically disadvantaged, student employment services, financial aid counseling, health services, personal counseling, placement for graduates, veterans' counselor. **Physically disabled:** Services for visually, speech, hearing impaired.

Contact. E-mail: admissions@faulkner.edu
Phone: (334) 386-7200 Toll-free number: (800) 879-9816 ext. 7200
Fax: (334) 386-7137
R. Scott, Director of Admissions, Faulkner University, 5345 Atlanta Highway, Montgomery, AL 36109-3398

Heritage Christian University
Florence, Alabama
www.hcu.edu   CB code: 0805

- Private 4-year virtual Bible college affiliated with the Church of Christ
- Commuter campus in large town
- 60 undergraduates
- 20 graduate students

General. Founded in 1971. Accredited by ABHE. All programs offered via distance education. **Degrees:** 13 bachelor's, 2 associate awarded; master's offered. **Location:** 125 miles from Birmingham, 50 miles from Huntsville. **Calendar:** Semester, limited summer session. **Full-time faculty:** 6 total. **Class size:** 96% < 20, 4% 20-39.

Freshman class profile.

Out-of-state: 40% Live on campus: 10%

Basis for selection. Religious affiliation and recommendations very important, school achievement considered. Interview recommended.

2015-2016 Annual costs. Tuition/fees: $12,030. Room/board: $3,840. Books/supplies: $1,000. Personal expenses: $600.

Application procedures. Admission: Closing date 7/1. $25 fee. Admission notification on a rolling basis. **Financial aid:** Priority date 6/1; no closing date. FAFSA required. Applicants notified on a rolling basis starting 6/1; must reply by 7/28 or within 2 week(s) of notification.

Academics. Special study options: Accelerated study, distance learning, dual enrollment of high school students, independent study, internships. **Credit/placement by examination:** AP, CLEP, institutional tests. 24 credit hours maximum toward associate degree, 24 toward bachelor's. **Support services:** Reduced course load, remedial instruction, study skills assistance, tutoring.

Majors. Theology: Bible.

Technology on campus. 12 workstations in library, computer center. Wireless network available.

Student life. Freshman orientation: Mandatory. Preregistration for classes offered. **Housing:** Guaranteed on-campus for freshmen. Single-sex dorms, apartments, wellness housing available. **Activities:** Student government, Christian service program, mission club.

Student services. Career counseling, student employment services, personal counseling, placement for graduates, veterans' counselor.

Contact. E-mail: hcu@hcu.edu
Phone: (256) 766-6610 Toll-free number: (800) 367-3565
Fax: (256) 766-9289
Jim Collins, Director of Admissions, Heritage Christian University, 3625 Helton Drive, Florence, AL 35630

Herzing University: Birmingham
Birmingham, Alabama
www.herzing.edu   CB code: 2851

- For-profit 4-year business and technical college
- Commuter campus in very large city
- 305 undergraduates

General. Regionally accredited. **Degrees:** 20 bachelor's, 51 associate awarded; master's offered. **Calendar:** Semester, extensive summer session. **Full-time faculty:** 9 total. **Part-time faculty:** 21 total.

Basis for selection. Students must submit high school transcript or GED, interview with admissions representative, pass admissions exam or have 1275 SAT/17 ACT. TEAS test required for nursing applicants.

2015-2016 Annual costs. Certificate programs: $13,670 to $26,820. Associate programs: $26,180 to $53,640. Bachelor's programs: $61,515 to $88,065.

Financial aid. All financial aid based on need.

Application procedures. Admission: No deadline. No application fee. **Financial aid:** FAFSA required.

Academics. Credit/placement by examination: AP, CLEP.

Majors. Business: Business admin. **Computer sciences:** Networking. **Health services:** Health care admin, health information management. **Protective services:** Homeland security. **Visual/performing arts:** Graphic design.

Contact. E-mail: admiss@bhm.herzing.edu
Phone: (205) 916-2800 Toll-free number: (855) 285-3809
Fax: (205) 916-2807
Tommy Dennis, Director of Admissions, Herzing University: Birmingham, 280 West Valley Avenue, Birmingham, AL 35209

Huntingdon College
Montgomery, Alabama
www.huntingdon.edu   CB code: 1303

- Private 4-year liberal arts college affiliated with the United Methodist Church
- Residential campus in small city
- 1,160 degree-seeking undergraduates: 23% part-time, 50% women, 22% African American, 1% Asian American, 3% Hispanic/Latino, 1% Native American, 3% Multi-racial, non-Hispanic
- 58% of applicants admitted
- SAT or ACT (ACT writing optional) required
- 41% graduate within 6 years

General. Founded in 1854. Regionally accredited. Evening studies program offered in Montgomery, Bay Minette, Birmingham, Brewton, Center Point,

Clanton, Daphne, Enterprise, Fairhope, Pell City, Shelby, Opelika, Rainsville, Gadsden and Sumiton. **Degrees:** 231 bachelor's awarded. **ROTC:** Army, Air Force. **Location:** 90 miles from Birmingham, 180 miles from Atlanta. **Calendar:** Semester, limited summer session. **Full-time faculty:** 45 total; 82% have terminal degrees, 4% minority, 49% women. **Part-time faculty:** 77 total; 40% have terminal degrees, 6% minority, 43% women. **Class size:** 58% < 20, 39% 20-39, 2% 40-49, less than 1% 50-99. **Special facilities:** Ecological study center, music facility, center for human performance, archives for the Alabama-West Florida Conference of the United Methodist Church.

Freshman class profile. 1,839 applied, 1,061 admitted, 252 enrolled.

Mid 50% test scores		Rank in top quarter:	29%
SAT critical reading:	440-550	Rank in top tenth:	9%
SAT math:	450-570	End year in good standing:	87%
ACT composite:	19-23	Return as sophomores:	66%
GPA 3.75 or higher:	21%	Out-of-state:	31%
GPA 3.50-3.74:	17%	Live on campus:	81%
GPA 3.0-3.49:	36%	Fraternities:	26%
GPA 2.0-2.99:	26%	Sororities:	48%

Basis for selection. AP, CLEP, IB and dual enrollment credits are considered for acceptance. Important factors in the admission decision are advanced placement or honors courses, evidence of special talent and a leadership record. Interview, campus visit and essay recommended. Audition required of music majors; portfolio recommended for art majors. **Home schooled:** Transcript of courses and grades required. **Learning Disabled:** Student must self-identify to Disabilities Intake Coordinator and provide appropriate and current documentation to verify disability. Documentation should include diagnosis and description of functional limitations that may affect student's academic performance.

High school preparation. College-preparatory program recommended. 17 units recommended. Recommended units include English 4, mathematics 3, social studies 3, history 3, science 2 and foreign language 2.

2015-2016 Annual costs. Tuition/fees: $25,050. Room/board: $8,850.

2015-2016 Financial aid. Need-based: 242 full-time freshmen applied for aid; 209 deemed to have need; 209 received aid. Average need met was 62%. Average scholarship/grant was $15,320; average loan $3,264. 63% of total undergraduate aid awarded as scholarships/grants, 37% as loans/jobs. **Non-need-based:** Awarded to 284 full-time undergraduates, including 63 freshmen. Scholarships awarded for academics, alumni affiliation, leadership, music/drama, religious affiliation, ROTC, state residency.

Application procedures. Admission: No deadline. No application fee. Admission notification on a rolling basis beginning on or about 9/1. May 1st for fall or 30 days after date of acceptance if acceptance issued after 4/1. **Financial aid:** Priority date 3/1; no closing date. FAFSA required. Applicants notified by 3/1; Applicants notified on a rolling basis starting 3/1; must reply by 5/1 or within 2 week(s) of notification.

Academics. Special study options: Cross-registration, distance learning, double major, honors, independent study, internships, liberal arts/career combination, student-designed major, study abroad, teacher certification program. Student exchange program with universities in Ireland; and travel opportunities to all full-time juniors and seniors within regular educational costs or for nominal additional fees. **Credit/placement by examination:** AP, CLEP, IB, SAT, ACT, institutional tests. 30 credit hours maximum toward bachelor's degree. **Support services:** Learning center, reduced course load, study skills assistance, tutoring, writing center.

Majors. Biology: General, biochemistry, cellular/anatomical. **Business:** General, accounting, business admin. **Communications:** General. **Education:** Biology, chemistry, elementary, English, history, mathematics, music, physical, science, social studies. **English:** English lit. **History:** General. **Math:** General. **Parks/recreation:** Exercise sciences, sports admin. **Philosophy/religion:** Religion. **Physical sciences:** Chemistry. **Protective services:** Law enforcement admin. **Psychology:** General. **Social sciences:** Political science. **Theology:** Lay ministry. **Visual/performing arts:** Music performance, studio arts.

Most popular majors. Biology 8%, business/marketing 47%, education 10%, parks/recreation 8%.

Technology on campus. PC or laptop required. 8 workstations in library. Dormitories wired for high-speed internet access and linked to campus network. Commuter students can connect to campus network. Online course registration, online library, repair service, student web hosting, wireless network available.

Student life. Freshman orientation: Mandatory. Preregistration for classes offered. Two day, overnight program where students stay on campus. Generally held in June and July with a one day option in August. **Policies:** Students expected to abide by the Huntingdon College Honor Code. **Housing:** Guaranteed on-campus for all undergraduates. Coed dorms, single-sex dorms,

special housing for disabled, fraternity/sorority housing available. $250 partly refundable deposit, deadline 5/1. Women's housing and men's housing. **Activities:** Bands, campus ministries, choral groups, drama, literary magazine, music ensembles, student government, student newspaper, Huntingdon Hosts/ Huntingdon Ambassadors, campus activities board, commuter student organization, collegiate exchange club, College Republicans, College Democrats, freshman forum, Student Government Association.

Athletics. NCAA. **Intercollegiate:** Baseball M, basketball, football (tackle) M, golf, lacrosse, soccer, softball W, tennis, volleyball W, wrestling M. **Intramural:** Basketball, football (non-tackle), sand volleyball, soccer, softball, table tennis, tennis, volleyball. **Team name:** Hawks.

Student services. Adult student services, chaplain/spiritual director, career counseling, student employment services, financial aid counseling, health services, personal counseling, placement for graduates.

Contact. E-mail: admiss@huntingdon.edu
Phone: (334) 833-4497 Toll-free number: (800) 763-0313
Fax: (334) 833-4347
Laura Duncan, VP for Enrollment Management, Huntingdon College, 1500 East Fairview Avenue, Montgomery, AL 36106-2148

Huntsville Bible College
Huntsville, Alabama
www.hbc1.edu

▶ Private 4-year Bible college
▶ Commuter campus in small city
▶ 74 degree-seeking undergraduates

General. Accredited by ABHE. **Degrees:** 4 bachelor's, 4 associate awarded; master's offered. **Location:** 87 miles from Birmingham; 100 miles from Nashville, TN. **Calendar:** Semester, limited summer session. **Part-time faculty:** 13 total; 15% minority, 23% women.

Basis for selection. Open admission.

2015-2016 Annual costs. Tuition/fees: $5,320. Books/supplies: $200.

Financial aid. All financial aid based on need.

Application procedures. Admission: Closing date 9/1. $25 fee. **Financial aid:** Priority date 4/1, closing date 6/30. FAFSA required. Applicants notified by 8/15; must reply by 9/1.

Academics. Special study options: Distance learning, independent study. **Credit/placement by examination:** AP, CLEP, institutional tests. 63 credit hours maximum toward associate degree, 127 toward bachelor's. **Support services:** Tutoring.

Majors. Theology: Bible, theology.

Technology on campus. 1 workstations in library. Online course registration, online library, wireless network available.

Student life. Freshman orientation: Available. Preregistration for classes offered. **Policies:** Religious observance required. **Activities:** Campus ministries, student government.

Student services. Chaplain/spiritual director, career counseling, financial aid counseling, personal counseling.

Contact. E-mail: huntsvillebiblecollege@gmail.com
Phone: (256) 539-0834 Fax: (256) 539-0854
Belinda Hardin, Dean of Instruction, Huntsville Bible College, 904 Oakwood Avenue, Huntsville, AL 35811-1632

ITT Technical Institute: Birmingham
Bessemer, Alabama
www.itt-tech.edu   CB code: 2696

▶ For-profit 4-year technical college
▶ Commuter campus in very large city
▶ 580 undergraduates
▶ Interview required

General. Accredited by ACICS. **Degrees:** 46 bachelor's, 109 associate awarded. **Calendar:** Quarter, extensive summer session. **Full-time faculty:** 12 total. **Part-time faculty:** 52 total.

Basis for selection. Satisfactory scores from on-site tests in English and mathematics required.

2015-2016 Annual costs. Per-credit-hour charge, $493; academic fee, $200. Some programs require purchase of tools, which could cost an additional $100 to $655. All costs subject to change.

Application procedures. Admission: No deadline. No application fee. Admission notification on a rolling basis. **Financial aid:** No deadline. FAFSA, institutional form required. Applicants notified on a rolling basis.

Academics. Credit/placement by examination: AP, CLEP. **Support services:** Learning center, tutoring.

Majors. Business: Business admin, construction management. **Communications technology:** Animation/special effects. **Computer sciences:** Programming, security. **Protective services:** Law enforcement admin.

Most popular majors. Business/marketing 7%, communication technologies 31%, computer/information sciences 29%, engineering/engineering technologies 16%, security/protective services 16%.

Technology on campus. Online library available.

Student life. Freshman orientation: Available. Preregistration for classes offered.

Student services. Career counseling, student employment services.

Contact. Phone: (205) 991-5410 Toll-free number: (800) 488-7033 Jesse Johnson, Director of Recruitment, ITT Technical Institute: Birmingham, 6270 Park South Drive, Bessemer, AL 35022

Jacksonville State University
Jacksonville, Alabama
www.jsu.edu   CB code: 1736

- Public 4-year university
- Commuter campus in small town
- 6,625 degree-seeking undergraduates: 19% part-time, 57% women
- 931 degree-seeking graduate students
- 67% of applicants admitted
- SAT or ACT (ACT writing optional) required
- 31% graduate within 6 years

General. Founded in 1883. Regionally accredited. **Degrees:** 1,328 bachelor's awarded; master's, doctoral offered. **ROTC:** Army. **Location:** 75 miles from Birmingham, 100 miles from Atlanta. **Calendar:** Semester, extensive summer session. **Full-time faculty:** 317 total; 14% minority, 49% women. **Part-time faculty:** 139 total; 8% minority, 64% women. **Class size:** 40% < 20, 49% 20-39, 4% 40-49, 6% 50-99, less than 1% >100. **Special facilities:** Space observatory, Little River Canyon field school.

Freshman class profile. 3,085 applied, 2,056 admitted, 1,049 enrolled.

Mid 50% test scores			
SAT critical reading:	450-550	Rank in top quarter:	45%
SAT math:	440-550	Rank in top tenth:	20%
ACT composite:	20-26	Return as sophomores:	74%
GPA 3.75 or higher:	27%	Out-of-state:	19%
GPA 3.50-3.74:	19%	Live on campus:	73%
GPA 3.0-3.49:	29%	International:	3%
GPA 2.0-2.99:	25%	Fraternities:	9%
		Sororities:	20%

Basis for selection. High school record and test scores very important. 17 ACT or 830 SAT (exclusive of Writing) required for conditional admission. 20 ACT or 950 SAT (exclusive of Writing) required for unconditional admission. SAT/ACT scores must be submitted by beginning of term.

2015-2016 Annual costs. Tuition/fees: $9,000; $18,000 out-of-state. Room/board: $7,128. Books/supplies: $1,596. Personal expenses: $2,400.

2014-2015 Financial aid. Need-based: 1,108 full-time freshmen applied for aid; 1,083 deemed to have need; 1,083 received aid. Average scholarship/grant was $4,585; average loan $1,000. 65% of total undergraduate aid awarded as scholarships/grants, 35% as loans/jobs. **Non-need-based:** Awarded to 2,483 full-time undergraduates, including 758 freshmen. Scholarships awarded for academics, alumni affiliation, art, athletics, leadership, music/drama, ROTC, state residency.

Application procedures. Admission: No deadline. $35 fee. Admission notification on a rolling basis beginning on or about 9/1. **Financial aid:** Priority date 3/15; no closing date. FAFSA, institutional form required.

Applicants notified on a rolling basis starting 4/16; must reply within 2 week(s) of notification.

Academics. Special study options: Accelerated study, combined bachelor's/graduate degree, cooperative education, cross-registration, distance learning, double major, dual enrollment of high school students, ESL, honors, independent study, internships, liberal arts/career combination, study abroad, teacher certification program, weekend college. **Credit/placement by examination:** AP, CLEP, SAT, ACT, institutional tests. 46 credit hours maximum toward bachelor's degree. Maximum credit hours awarded through CLEP examinations: 31 for general tests, 15 through subject tests. **Support services:** Learning center, pre-admission summer program, remedial instruction, tutoring.

Majors. Biology: General. **Business:** Accounting, business admin, finance, managerial economics, marketing. **Communications:** General, radio/TV. **Computer sciences:** General. **Education:** Early childhood, elementary, health, physical, secondary, special ed. **English:** English lit. **Foreign languages:** General. **Health services:** Nursing (RN), public health nursing. **History:** General. **Human services:** Social work. **Liberal arts:** Arts/sciences. **Math:** General. **Parks/recreation:** General, sports admin. **Physical sciences:** Chemistry, physics. **Protective services:** Criminal justice. **Psychology:** General. **Social sciences:** Economics, geography, political science, sociology. **Visual/performing arts:** Art, dramatic, music. **Work/family studies:** General.

Most popular majors. Business/marketing 13%, education 7%, health sciences 29%, liberal arts 6%, public administration/social services 6%, security/protective services 6%.

Technology on campus. 400 workstations in library, student center. Dormitories linked to campus network. Commuter students can connect to campus network. Online course registration, online library, helpline, wireless network available.

Student life. Freshman orientation: Available, $40 fee. Preregistration for classes offered. **Housing:** Coed dorms, single-sex dorms, special housing for disabled, apartments, fraternity/sorority housing available. $100 fully refundable deposit. **Activities:** Bands, campus ministries, choral groups, dance, drama, film society, international student organizations, literary magazine, music ensembles, Model UN, musical theater, opera, radio station, student government, student newspaper, symphony orchestra, TV station, Panhellenic council, adult learners forum, peer counselors, African American association, book club.

Athletics. NCAA. **Intercollegiate:** Baseball M, basketball, cross-country, football (tackle) M, golf, rifle, soccer W, softball W, tennis, track and field, volleyball W. **Intramural:** Basketball, bowling, football (tackle) M, racquetball, rugby M, softball, tennis, track and field, volleyball. **Team name:** Gamecocks.

Student services. Career counseling, student employment services, financial aid counseling, health services, minority student services, on-campus daycare, personal counseling, placement for graduates, veterans' counselor. **Physically disabled:** Services for visually, speech, hearing impaired.

Contact. E-mail: info@jsu.edu
Phone: (256) 782-5268 Toll-free number: (800) 231-5291
Fax: (256) 782-5953
Andy Green, Director of Admissions, Jacksonville State University, 700 Pelham Road North, Jacksonville, AL 36265-1602

Judson College
Marion, Alabama
www.judson.edu   CB code: 1349

- Private 4-year liberal arts college for women affiliated with the Baptist faith
- Residential campus in small town
- 373 degree-seeking undergraduates
- 63% of applicants admitted
- SAT or ACT (ACT writing optional) required

General. Founded in 1838. Regionally accredited. Men accepted for distance learning program only. **Degrees:** 48 bachelor's, 16 associate awarded. **ROTC:** Army. **Location:** 75 miles from Birmingham and Montgomery. **Calendar:** Semester, limited summer session. **Full-time faculty:** 25 total; 84% have terminal degrees, 4% minority, 44% women. **Part-time faculty:** 14 total; 50% have terminal degrees, 21% minority, 93% women. **Class size:** 81% < 20, 19% 20-39. **Special facilities:** Equine science center, Alabama Women's Hall of Fame, Baptist missionary memorabilia.

Freshman class profile. 329 applied, 207 admitted, 65 enrolled.

Mid 50% test scores			
SAT critical reading:	480-560	GPA 3.0-3.49:	23%
		GPA 2.0-2.99:	18%
SAT math:	400-660	Rank in top quarter:	41%
SAT writing:	510-590	Rank in top tenth:	21%
ACT composite:	19-25	Out-of-state:	19%
GPA 3.75 or higher:	39%	Live on campus:	91%
GPA 3.50-3.74:	20%		

Basis for selection. Academic record, recommendations, test scores considered. Transfer students with official transcripts from regionally accrediited institutions are not required to provide ACT or SAT test scores. Essay required if the file of the applicant is being sent to the Admissions Committee. **Home schooled:** If the diploma is signed by a parent, Judson College requests that the signature be notarized. **Learning Disabled:** Provide current copy of doctor's evaluation containing recommended accommodations.

High school preparation. College-preparatory program recommended. Required and recommended units include English 4, mathematics 2-4, social studies 3-4, science 2-4, foreign language 2 and academic electives 5.

2015-2016 Annual costs. Tuition/fees: $16,850. Room/board: $9,686. Books/supplies: $1,250. Personal expenses: $1,600.

Financial aid. Non-need-based: Scholarships awarded for academics, art, athletics, music/drama, religious affiliation, ROTC, state residency.

Application procedures. Admission: Priority date 8/1; no deadline. $40 fee, may be waived for applicants with need. Admission notification on a rolling basis beginning on or about 8/1. **Financial aid:** Priority date 3/1; no closing date. FAFSA required. Applicants notified on a rolling basis starting 3/1; must reply within 2 week(s) of notification.

Academics. Special study options: Accelerated study, cross-registration, distance learning, double major, dual enrollment of high school students, honors, independent study, internships, student-designed major, study abroad, teacher certification program, Washington semester. **Credit/placement by examination:** AP, CLEP, IB, SAT, ACT, institutional tests. 30 credit hours maximum toward bachelor's degree. No student may receive more than 30 semester hours of non-attendance credit from all sources, or more than six semester hours in any one department. Maximum permitted from CLEP General Examinations is 15 of 30 hours. **Support services:** Reduced course load, remedial instruction, study skills assistance, tutoring, writing center.

Majors. Biology: General. **Business:** Business admin. **Education:** General, elementary, English, mathematics, music, science, social science. **English:** English lit. **Foreign languages:** Spanish. **History:** General. **Human services:** Social work. **Math:** General. **Philosophy/religion:** Religion. **Physical sciences:** Chemistry. **Protective services:** Law enforcement admin. **Psychology:** General. **Visual/performing arts:** Art, music.

Most popular majors. Biology 18%, education 7%, English 9%, history 9%, physical sciences 9%, psychology 18%, security/protective services 7%.

Technology on campus. 52 workstations in library, computer center. Dormitories wired for high-speed internet access. Commuter students can connect to campus network. Online course registration, online library, helpline, wireless network available.

Student life. Freshman orientation: Mandatory, $135 fee. Preregistration for classes offered. **Policies:** Religious observance required. **Housing:** Guaranteed on-campus for all undergraduates. $130 nonrefundable deposit, deadline 8/15. **Activities:** Campus ministries, choral groups, drama, literary magazine, music ensembles, student government, student newspaper, psych-key club, Cahaba River society, Judson Ambassadors, science club, art club, business club, campus ministries council, Quiz Bowl, Voices of Praise, history club.

Athletics. NCCAA. **Intercollegiate:** Basketball W, equestrian W, soccer W, softball W, volleyball W. **Intramural:** Basketball W, field hockey W, soccer W, softball W, tennis W, volleyball W. **Team name:** Eagles.

Student services. Adult student services, alcohol/substance abuse counseling, chaplain/spiritual director, career counseling, student employment services, financial aid counseling, health services, personal counseling. **Physically disabled:** Services for visually impaired.

Contact. E-mail: admissions@judson.edu
Phone: (334) 683-5110 Toll-free number: (800) 447-9472
Fax: (334) 683-5282
Layne Calhoun, Executive Director of Enrollment Services, Judson College, 302 Bibb Street, Marion, AL 36756

Miles College
Birmingham, Alabama   **CB member**
www.miles.edu   **CB code: 1468**

- Private 4-year liberal arts college affiliated with the Christian Methodist Episcopal Church
- Commuter campus in very large city
- 1,690 undergraduates

General. Founded in 1905. Regionally accredited. **Degrees:** 220 bachelor's awarded. **ROTC:** Army, Air Force. **Location:** 6 miles from downtown. **Calendar:** Semester, limited summer session. **Full-time faculty:** 100 total. **Part-time faculty:** 31 total. **Special facilities:** African-American materials center, learning research center, Defense Intelligence Agency Center of Academic Excellence.

Basis for selection. Open admission, but selective for some programs. 3 letters of recommendation required. Admission to education program based on 2.0 GPA, 16 ACT and recommendations.

High school preparation. 20 units recommended. Recommended units include English 4, mathematics 4, social studies 4, history 4 and science 4. 4 units math and science recommended, particularly, for natural science applicants.

2015-2016 Annual costs. Tuition/fees: $11,604. Room/board: $7,042. Books/supplies: $1,200. Personal expenses: $800. **Additional information:** Room and Board cost range between $5,882 and $7,042; depending upon the dormitory to which the individual is assigned.

Financial aid. All financial aid based on need.

Application procedures. Admission: Closing date 7/15. No application fee. Admission notification on a rolling basis. **Financial aid:** Priority date 4/15; no closing date. FAFSA required. Applicants notified on a rolling basis starting 7/15; must reply within 2 week(s) of notification.

Academics. Special study options: Cooperative education, cross-registration, double major, dual enrollment of high school students, exchange student, honors, independent study, internships, teacher certification program. **Credit/placement by examination:** AP, CLEP, institutional tests. **Support services:** Reduced course load, remedial instruction, study skills assistance, tutoring, writing center.

Majors. Biology: General. **Business:** Accounting, business admin, purchasing. **Communications:** Communications/speech/rhetoric. **Computer sciences:** General. **Conservation:** Environmental science. **Education:** Educational technology, elementary, English, mathematics, science, secondary, social science, social studies. **English:** English lit. **History:** General. **Human services:** Social work. **Math:** General. **Physical sciences:** Chemistry. **Social sciences:** Political science. **Visual/performing arts:** Music, music pedagogy, music performance.

Most popular majors. Biology 14%, business/marketing 25%, communications/journalism 10%, computer/information sciences 6%, education 8%, public administration/social services 8%, security/protective services 18%.

Technology on campus. Dormitories linked to campus network. Commuter students can connect to campus network. Online course registration, online library, helpline, wireless network available.

Student life. Freshman orientation: Available, $100 fee. Preregistration for classes offered. Week-long program held week prior to start of classes. **Policies:** Students must maintain 2.0 GPA to participate in student activities that are not co-curricular on campus. **Housing:** Single-sex dorms, apartments, wellness housing available. $150 nonrefundable deposit. **Activities:** Bands, choral groups, dance, drama, music ensembles, Model UN, musical theater, radio station, student government, student newspaper, TV station, interdenominational ministerial association.

Athletics. NCAA. **Intercollegiate:** Baseball M, basketball, cross-country, football (tackle) M, softball W, volleyball. **Intramural:** Badminton, basketball, softball, tennis, volleyball. **Team name:** Golden Bears.

Student services. Adult student services, chaplain/spiritual director, career counseling, services for economically disadvantaged, student employment services, financial aid counseling, health services, personal counseling, placement for graduates.

Contact. E-mail: admissions@miles.edu
Phone: (205) 929-1655 Fax: (205) 923-9292
Christopher Robertson, Director of Admissions and Recruitment, Miles College, 5500 Myron Massey Boulevard, Fairfield, AL 35064

Oakwood University
Huntsville, Alabama
www.oakwood.edu

CB member
CB code: 1586

◆ Private 4-year liberal arts college affiliated with the Seventh-day Adventists
◆ Residential campus in small city
◆ 1,687 degree-seeking undergraduates
◆ 47% of applicants admitted
◆ SAT or ACT (ACT writing optional) required

General. Founded in 1896. Regionally accredited. **Degrees:** 336 bachelor's, 6 associate awarded; master's offered. **Location:** 5 miles from Huntsville. **Calendar:** Semester, limited summer session. **Full-time faculty:** 107 total. **Part-time faculty:** 98 total. **Class size:** 56% < 20, 36% 20-39, 6% 40-49, 3% 50-99.

Freshman class profile. 1,992 applied, 946 admitted, 338 enrolled.

Mid 50% test scores			
SAT critical reading:	410-540	GPA 3.0-3.49:	26%
SAT math:	380-500	GPA 2.0-2.99:	44%
ACT composite:	17-22	Rank in top quarter:	26%
GPA 3.75 or higher:	13%	Rank in top tenth:	8%
GPA 3.50-3.74:	13%	Out-of-state:	89%
		Live on campus:	90%

Basis for selection. 2.0 GPA required. **Home schooled:** Transcript of courses and grades, letter of recommendation (nonparent) required.

High school preparation. College-preparatory program recommended. 18 units recommended. Recommended units include English 4, mathematics 2, social studies 1, history 1, science 2 (laboratory 1) and foreign language 2.

2015-2016 Annual costs. Tuition/fees: $16,720. Room/board: $9,312. Books/supplies: $1,440. Personal expenses: $3,950.

Financial aid. Non-need-based: Scholarships awarded for academics, leadership, religious affiliation, state residency.

Application procedures. Admission: Priority date 6/30; no deadline. $25 fee, may be waived for applicants with need. Admission notification on a rolling basis beginning on or about 12/1. **Financial aid:** Closing date 4/15. FAFSA required. Applicants notified on a rolling basis starting 4/1.

Academics. Special study options: Double major, honors, internships, study abroad, teacher certification program. **Credit/placement by examination:** AP, CLEP, SAT, ACT, institutional tests. **Support services:** Learning center, reduced course load, remedial instruction, study skills assistance, tutoring, writing center.

Majors. Biology: General, biochemistry, biomedical sciences. **Business:** Accounting, business admin, finance, management information systems, marketing, nonprofit/public. **Communications:** Communications/speech/rhetoric, digital media, journalism, media studies, photojournalism, public relations. **Computer sciences:** General, computer science, information technology. **Education:** Biology, business, chemistry, elementary, English, family/consumer sciences, history, mathematics, music, physical, science, social science. **English:** English lit, technical writing. **Foreign languages:** French, Spanish. **Health services:** General, clinical lab science, cytotechnology, dietetics, health care admin, nursing (RN), prephysical therapy. **History:** General. **Human services:** Social work. **Math:** General, applied. **Parks/recreation:** Health/fitness. **Philosophy/religion:** Religion. **Physical sciences:** Chemistry. **Psychology:** General, counseling, industrial. **Social sciences:** International relations, political science. **Theology:** Lay ministry, religious ed, theology. **Visual/performing arts:** Music, music pedagogy, music theory/composition, piano/keyboard, voice/opera. **Work/family studies:** General, family studies, food/nutrition.

Most popular majors. Biology 20%, business/marketing 13%, health sciences 15%, theological studies 8%.

Technology on campus. 300 workstations in dormitories, library. Dormitories wired for high-speed internet access and linked to campus network. Commuter students can connect to campus network. Helpline, wireless network available.

Student life. Freshman orientation: Mandatory, $200 fee. Preregistration for classes offered. **Policies:** Students sit on most faculty and administrative committees. Religious observance required. **Housing:** Single-sex dorms, apartments available. **Activities:** Choral groups, music ensembles, radio station, student government, student newspaper, Outreach, NAACP.

Athletics. Intramural: Baseball M, basketball, golf, gymnastics, soccer, softball, tennis, volleyball. **Team name:** Ambassadors.

Student services. Adult student services, chaplain/spiritual director, career counseling, student employment services, financial aid counseling, health services, on-campus daycare, personal counseling, placement for graduates, veterans' counselor.

Contact. E-mail: admission@oakwood.edu
Phone: (256) 726-7030 Toll-free number: (800) 824-5312
Fax: (256) 726-7154
Nikki Lawson, Director of Admissions, Oakwood University, 7000 Adventist Boulevard, NW, Huntsville, AL 35896

Samford University
Birmingham, Alabama
www.samford.edu

CB member
CB code: 1302

◆ Private 4-year university affiliated with the Baptist faith
◆ Residential campus in small city
◆ 3,145 degree-seeking undergraduates: 3% part-time, 64% women, 7% African American, 1% Asian American, 5% Hispanic/Latino, 2% Multiracial, non-Hispanic, 3% international
◆ 1,980 degree-seeking graduate students
◆ 93% of applicants admitted
◆ SAT or ACT (ACT writing optional), application essay required
◆ 74% graduate within 6 years

General. Founded in 1841. Regionally accredited. **Degrees:** 791 bachelor's awarded; master's, professional, doctoral offered. **ROTC:** Army, Air Force. **Location:** 4 miles from downtown. **Calendar:** 4-1-4, extensive summer session. **Full-time faculty:** 333 total; 89% have terminal degrees, 10% minority, 48% women. **Part-time faculty:** 182 total; 50% have terminal degrees, 10% minority, 57% women. **Class size:** 62% < 20, 34% 20-39, 3% 40-49, 1% 50-99. **Special facilities:** Global center, prayer room, drug information center, human simulation center, medicinal plant conservatory, planetarium, Center for Science and Religion, Law School Moot Courtroom, eDiscovery Institute and Review Center, Business School Investment Trading Room.

Freshman class profile. 3,196 applied, 2,982 admitted, 826 enrolled.

Mid 50% test scores			
SAT critical reading:	500-610	Rank in top quarter:	52%
SAT math:	490-610	Rank in top tenth:	27%
SAT writing:	500-610	End year in good standing:	93%
ACT composite:	23-29	Return as sophomores:	89%
GPA 3.75 or higher:	51%	Out-of-state:	71%
GPA 3.50-3.74:	14%	Live on campus:	96%
GPA 3.0-3.49:	21%	International:	1%
GPA 2.0-2.99:	14%	Fraternities:	40%
		Sororities:	64%

Basis for selection. Rigor of high school record, academic GPA, standardized test scores, application essay, and recommendations considered. Prospective music and theater students are required to participate in an audition and interview process. This audition/interview is used to determine both School of the Arts admission and scholarship eligibility but has no baring on general university admission. **Learning Disabled:** Students with disabilities must meet the admissions requirements as determined by the University and, once accepted into the University, students with disabilities who wish to request accommodations should contact the office of Disability Resources.

High school preparation. College-preparatory program recommended. 13 units required; 16 recommended. Required and recommended units include English 4, mathematics 3-4, history 2-4, science 2 (laboratory 2) and foreign language 2.

2015-2016 Annual costs. Tuition/fees: $28,370. Room/board: $10,234. Books/supplies: $1,000. Personal expenses: $2,938.

2014-2015 Financial aid. Need-based: 576 full-time freshmen applied for aid; 350 deemed to have need; 350 received aid. Average need met was 69%. Average scholarship/grant was $14,744; average loan $3,196. 62% of total undergraduate aid awarded as scholarships/grants, 38% as loans/jobs. **Non-need-based:** Awarded to 1,681 full-time undergraduates, including 439 freshmen. Scholarships awarded for academics, alumni affiliation, art, athletics, leadership, minority status, music/drama, religious affiliation, ROTC, state residency.

Application procedures. Admission: Priority date 4/1; deadline 6/30. $40 fee, may be waived for applicants with need. Admission notification on a rolling basis beginning on or about 11/1. Must reply by 5/1. **Financial aid:** Priority date 3/1; no closing date. FAFSA required. Applicants notified on a rolling basis starting 3/1; must reply by 5/1.

Academics. Special study options: Accelerated study, combined bachelor's/graduate degree, cross-registration, distance learning, double major, dual enrollment of high school students, ESL, honors, independent study, internships, liberal arts/career combination, study abroad, teacher certification program. Undergraduate Dual Degree Engineering Program (3 years at Samford and 2 years at UAB, Auburn, or Mercer) leads to two degrees: B.S. in engineering physics and B.S. of engineering degree from the participating university. **Credit/placement by examination:** AP, CLEP, IB, SAT, ACT, institutional tests. 30 credit hours maximum toward bachelor's degree. **Support services:** Study skills assistance, tutoring, writing center. Offers free tutoring for oral, written, and critical reading assignments.

Honors college/program. The University Fellows Program is limited to 40 students per year. Applicants must have a minimum ACT score of 28 or SAT score of 1260. Successful applicants typically have a minimum ACT score of 30 or SAT score of 1340. Candidates should have a minimum 3.75 overall high school GPA with a strong record in core academic subjects. Preference is given to applicants who have completed rigorous coursework in high school, such as Advanced Placement and International Baccalaureate Programs, as well as students who have distinguished themselves through extracurricular academic experiences.

Majors. Area/ethnic studies: Latin American. **Biology:** General, biochemistry, marine. **Business:** Accounting, business admin, entrepreneurial studies, finance, international, managerial economics, marketing, organizational leadership. **Communications:** Communications/speech/rhetoric, journalism. **Computer sciences:** Computer science. **Conservation:** Environmental science. **Education:** English, history, multi-level teacher, music. **Engineering:** Applied physics. **English:** English lit. **Foreign languages:** General, ancient Greek, classics, French, German, Latin, Spanish. **Health services:** Athletic training, communication disorders, nursing (RN), premedicine. **History:** General. **Human services:** General, youth services. **Math:** General. **Parks/recreation:** Exercise sciences, sports admin. **Philosophy/religion:** Philosophy, religion. **Physical sciences:** Chemistry, physics. **Protective services:** Criminal justice. **Psychology:** General. **Social sciences:** Geography, international relations, political science, sociology. **Theology:** Sacred music. **Visual/performing arts:** Art, dramatic, graphic design, interior design, music, music pedagogy, music performance, music theory/composition, piano/keyboard, voice/opera. **Work/family studies:** Family studies, food/nutrition.

Most popular majors. Business/marketing 16%, communications/journalism 8%, family/consumer sciences 6%, health sciences 30%, parks/recreation 7%.

Technology on campus. 330 workstations in library, computer center, student center. Dormitories wired for high-speed internet access and linked to campus network. Commuter students can connect to campus network. Online course registration, online library, helpline, repair service, wireless network available.

Student life. Freshman orientation: Mandatory, $200 fee. Preregistration for classes offered. Two-day sessions held in the summer. **Policies:** Students are expected to know regulations and policies found in the current catalog and Student Handbook; A Student Code of Values (Samford Community Preamble) is also enforced. **Housing:** Guaranteed on-campus for all undergraduates. Single-sex dorms, fraternity/sorority housing available. $250 non-refundable deposit, deadline 5/1. **Activities:** Bands, campus ministries, choral groups, dance, drama, film society, international student organizations, literary magazine, music ensembles, Model UN, musical theater, opera, radio station, student government, student newspaper, symphony orchestra, Young Life, gospel choir, Nurses Christian Fellowship, College Republicans, College Democrats, Student Government Association, Community Engagement, Black Student Union, Restoring Eden, Global Leadership Council.

Athletics. NCAA. **Intercollegiate:** Baseball M, basketball, cross-country, football (tackle) M, golf, soccer W, softball W, tennis, track and field, volleyball W. **Intramural:** Basketball, bowling, football (non-tackle), racquetball, sand volleyball, soccer, softball, table tennis, tennis, ultimate frisbee, volleyball. **Team name:** Bulldogs.

Student services. Adult student services, alcohol/substance abuse counseling, chaplain/spiritual director, career counseling, student employment services, financial aid counseling, health services, legal services, personal counseling, placement for graduates. **Physically disabled:** Services for visually, speech, hearing impaired.

Contact. E-mail: admission@samford.edu
Phone: (205) 726-3673 Toll-free number: (800) 888-7218
Fax: (205) 726-2171
Jason Black, Dean of Admission, Samford University, 800 Lakeshore Drive, Birmingham, AL 35229

Selma University
Selma, Alabama
www.selmauniversity.org   CB code: 1792

- Private 4-year university affiliated with the Baptist faith
- Large town

- 399 degree-seeking undergraduates
- 22 graduate students

General. Founded in 1878. Regionally accredited; also accredited by ABHE. **Degrees:** 21 bachelor's, 2 associate awarded; master's offered. **Location:** 50 miles from Montgomery. **Calendar:** Semester, limited summer session. **Full-time faculty:** 7 total. **Part-time faculty:** 34 total.

Basis for selection. Open admission. Students with deficient high school record or low test scores must take remedial courses.

2015-2016 Annual costs. Tuition/fees: $6,605. Room/board: $5,000. Books/supplies: $1,000. Personal expenses: $650.

Financial aid. All financial aid based on need.

Application procedures. Admission: No deadline. $20 fee, may be waived for applicants with need. Admission notification on a rolling basis beginning on or about 8/1. **Financial aid:** Priority date 5/1, closing date 6/30. FAFSA, institutional form required. Applicants notified on a rolling basis starting 8/23; must reply within 2 week(s) of notification.

Academics. Credit/placement by examination: AP, CLEP, institutional tests. **Support services:** Reduced course load, remedial instruction, tutoring.

Majors. Business: Business admin. **Philosophy/religion:** Religion.

Most popular majors. Business/marketing 19%, liberal arts 23%, philosophy/religious studies 58%.

Student life. Freshman orientation: Mandatory. Preregistration for classes offered. **Housing:** Single-sex dorms available. **Activities:** Campus ministries, choral groups, music ensembles, student government, Ministerial union.

Athletics. USCAA. **Intercollegiate:** Baseball M. **Team name:** Bulldogs.

Student services. Career counseling, financial aid counseling, personal counseling, veterans' counselor.

Contact. E-mail: info@selmauniversity.org
Phone: (334) 872-2533 ext. 18 Fax: (334) 872-7746
Selma University, 1501 Lapsley Street, Selma, AL 36701

Southeastern Bible College
Birmingham, Alabama
www.sebc.edu   CB code: 1723

- Private 4-year Bible college affiliated with the nondenominational tradition
- Commuter campus in very large city
- 151 undergraduates
- 100% of applicants admitted
- SAT or ACT (ACT writing optional), application essay required

General. Founded in 1935. Accredited by ABHE. **Degrees:** 19 bachelor's, 5 associate awarded. **Calendar:** Semester, limited summer session. **Full-time faculty:** 10 total; 80% have terminal degrees, 20% women. **Part-time faculty:** 20 total; 35% have terminal degrees, 5% minority, 35% women. **Class size:** 92% < 20, 8% 20-39.

Freshman class profile. 18 applied, 18 admitted, 11 enrolled.

Mid 50% test scores		GPA 3.75 or higher:	42%
SAT critical reading:	620-680	GPA 3.50-3.74:	8%
SAT math:	440-630	GPA 3.0-3.49:	9%
SAT writing:	540-580	GPA 2.0-2.99:	33%
ACT composite:	18-25	Return as sophomores:	55%

Basis for selection. High school GPA and SAT or ACT test scores important. Christian character evaluated through 2 recommendations, one from church and the other a personal recommendation. Autobiography and statement of agreement with college's principle doctrines required. Test scores are not required for students out of high school four or more years. **Learning Disabled:** Students should meet with equity coordinator if desired.

High school preparation. College-preparatory program recommended. 24 units recommended. Recommended units include English 4, mathematics 4, social studies 4, science 4 and academic electives 8.

2015-2016 Annual costs. Tuition/fees: $12,600. Room/board: $4,975.

Financial aid. Non-need-based: Scholarships awarded for academics, leadership.

Application procedures. Admission: Priority date 8/1; no deadline. $30 fee, may be waived for applicants with need. Admission notification on a rolling basis. **Financial aid:** Priority date 4/1; no closing date. FAFSA, institutional form required.

Academics. Special study options: Double major, dual enrollment of high school students, internships, study abroad. **Credit/placement by examination:** AP, CLEP, IB, institutional tests. 32 credit hours maximum toward associate degree, 32 toward bachelor's. **Support services:** Learning center, reduced course load, study skills assistance.

Majors. Theology: Bible, lay ministry.

Technology on campus. 25 workstations in library, computer center. Dormitories wired for high-speed internet access. Online library, wireless network available.

Student life. Freshman orientation: Mandatory. Preregistration for classes offered. One-day session held the day before registration. **Policies:** Religious observance required. **Housing:** Single-sex dorms, special housing for disabled available. $200 fully refundable deposit, deadline 8/15. **Activities:** Campus ministries, music ensembles, student government, student missions fellowship.

Athletics. Team name: Sabers.

Student services. Adult student services, chaplain/spiritual director, financial aid counseling, personal counseling. **Physically disabled:** Services for speech, hearing impaired.

Contact. E-mail: info@sebc.edu
Phone: (205) 970-9211 Toll-free number: (800) 749-8878
Fax: (205) 970-9207
Orrett Bailey, Director of Advancement, Southeastern Bible College, 2545 Valleydale Road, Birmingham, AL 35244-2083

Spring Hill College
Mobile, Alabama — **CB member**
www.shc.edu — **CB code: 1733**

▸ Private 4-year liberal arts college affiliated with the Roman Catholic Church
▸ Residential campus in large city
▸ 1,365 degree-seeking undergraduates: 2% part-time, 61% women, 13% African American, 1% Asian American, 4% Hispanic/Latino, 1% Native American, 5% Multi-racial, non-Hispanic, 3% international
▸ 121 degree-seeking graduate students
▸ 41% of applicants admitted
▸ SAT or ACT (ACT writing recommended), application essay required

General. Founded in 1830. Regionally accredited. **Degrees:** 223 bachelor's awarded; master's offered. **ROTC:** Army, Air Force. **Location:** 140 miles from New Orleans. **Calendar:** Semester, limited summer session. **Full-time faculty:** 84 total; 90% have terminal degrees, 12% minority, 50% women. **Part-time faculty:** 51 total; 29% have terminal degrees, 4% minority, 55% women. **Class size:** 56% < 20, 40% 20-39, 4% 40-49, less than 1% 50-99. **Special facilities:** National historic buildings, 450-acre wooded campus, 18-hole golf course.

Freshman class profile. 7,393 applied, 3,055 admitted, 416 enrolled.

Mid 50% test scores			
SAT critical reading:	500-600	Rank in top quarter:	56%
SAT math:	490-610	Rank in top tenth:	26%
ACT composite:	22-27	Return as sophomores:	81%
GPA 3.75 or higher:	47%	Out-of-state:	60%
GPA 3.50-3.74:	16%	Live on campus:	79%
GPA 3.0-3.49:	22%	International:	3%
GPA 2.0-2.99:	14%		

Basis for selection. Grades, scores and achievements/accomplishments outside the classroom considered. Interview recommended; portfolio recommended of art majors. **Home schooled:** Statement describing home school structure and mission, transcript of courses and grades required. Comprehensive portfolio should be submitted and should include thorough explanation of all coursework, how it was graded, comprehensive reading list, documentation of any program affiliation, and personal assessments provided by both the student and the primary teacher. Information on any independent research project, community outreach, or unique experience that enriched the homeschooling experience may be included.

High school preparation. College-preparatory program recommended. 16 units recommended. Recommended units include English 4, mathematics 3, social studies 2, history 1, science 3 (laboratory 1), foreign language 2 and academic electives 1.

2015-2016 Annual costs. Tuition/fees: $34,091. Room/board: $12,090. Books/supplies: $1,500. Personal expenses: $1,770.

2015-2016 Financial aid. Need-based: 371 full-time freshmen applied for aid; 321 deemed to have need; 321 received aid. Average need met was 78%. Average scholarship/grant was $25,257; average loan $3,410. 82% of total undergraduate aid awarded as scholarships/grants, 18% as loans/jobs. **Non-need-based:** Awarded to 1,077 full-time undergraduates, including 296 freshmen. Scholarships awarded for academics, alumni affiliation, art, athletics, job skills, leadership, minority status, ROTC, state residency.

Application procedures. Admission: Priority date 1/15; deadline 7/15 (postmark date). $25 fee, may be waived for applicants with need, free for online applicants. Admission notification on a rolling basis beginning on or about 11/1. Must reply by May 1 or within 2 week(s) if notified thereafter. **Financial aid:** Priority date 3/1; no closing date. FAFSA required. Applicants notified on a rolling basis starting 2/15; must reply by 5/1 or within 2 week(s) of notification.

Academics. Special study options: Accelerated study, distance learning, double major, dual enrollment of high school students, honors, independent study, internships, student-designed major, study abroad, teacher certification program, Washington semester. Marine biology courses at the Dauphin Island Sea Laboratory in conjunction with the Marine Environmental Sciences Consortium; 3-2 engineering with Auburn University, University of Alabama in Birmingham, Marquette University, University of Florida, and Texas A&M University. **Credit/placement by examination:** AP, CLEP, IB, SAT, ACT, institutional tests. 30 credit hours maximum toward bachelor's degree. **Support services:** Learning center, remedial instruction, study skills assistance, tutoring, writing center.

Majors. Biology: General, biochemistry. **Business:** Business admin, organizational leadership. **Communications:** General. **Education:** Biology, early childhood, elementary, English, history, mathematics, social studies, Spanish. **Engineering:** Pre-engineering. **English:** English lit, writing. **Foreign languages:** Spanish. **Health services:** Nursing (RN). **History:** General. **Math:** General. **Philosophy/religion:** Philosophy, religion. **Physical sciences:** Chemistry. **Psychology:** General. **Social sciences:** International relations, political science, sociology. **Visual/performing arts:** Dramatic, graphic design, studio arts, studio arts management.

Most popular majors. Biology 8%, business/marketing 24%, communications/journalism 10%, education 8%, health sciences 6%, liberal arts 6%, psychology 12%, social sciences 7%.

Technology on campus. 200 workstations in library, computer center, student center. Dormitories wired for high-speed internet access and linked to campus network. Commuter students can connect to campus network. Online course registration, online library, helpline, student web hosting, wireless network available.

Student life. Freshman orientation: Mandatory, $275 fee. Preregistration for classes offered. Two-day program held in summer for students and parents. **Housing:** Guaranteed on-campus for all undergraduates. Coed dorms, apartments, themed housing available. $150 fully refundable deposit, deadline 6/1. **Activities:** Jazz band, campus ministries, choral groups, dance, drama, literary magazine, student government, student newspaper, Knights of Columbus, Knights of Columbus Ladies Auxiliary, multicultural student union, political science club, SHAPe, Students for Life, TAG3, French club, Spanish club.

Athletics. NAIA. **Intercollegiate:** Baseball M, basketball, bowling, cross-country, golf, soccer, softball W, tennis, track and field, volleyball W. **Intramural:** Basketball, football (non-tackle), racquetball, soccer, ultimate frisbee, volleyball. **Team name:** Badgers.

Student services. Adult student services, alcohol/substance abuse counseling, chaplain/spiritual director, career counseling, student employment services, financial aid counseling, health services, minority student services, personal counseling, placement for graduates, veterans' counselor.

Contact. E-mail: admit@shc.edu
Phone: (251) 380-3030 Toll-free number: (800) 742-6704
Fax: (251) 460-2186
Robert Stewart, Vice President for Admissions and Financial Aid, Spring Hill College, 4000 Dauphin Street, Mobile, AL 36608-1791

Stillman College
Tuscaloosa, Alabama
www.stillman.edu

CB member
CB code: 1739

- Private 4-year liberal arts college affiliated with the Presbyterian Church (USA)
- Residential campus in small city
- 1,000 undergraduates
- SAT or ACT (ACT writing optional) required

General. Founded in 1876. Regionally accredited. **Degrees:** 122 bachelor's awarded. **ROTC:** Army, Naval, Air Force. **Location:** 60 miles from Birmingham. **Calendar:** Semester, limited summer session. **Full-time faculty:** 53 total. **Class size:** 64% < 20, 24% 20-39, 5% 40-49, 7% 50-99.

Freshman class profile.

GPA 3.75 or higher:	4%	GPA 2.0-2.99:	65%
GPA 3.50-3.74:	6%	Rank in top quarter:	28%
GPA 3.0-3.49:	25%	Rank in top tenth:	8%

Basis for selection. Applicants must submit admissions packet, high school transcript, 2 letters of recommendation, and ACT/SAT. 19 ACT/900 SAT (exclusive of Writing) and 2.5 GPA required. All decisions based on overall admissions file. **Home schooled:** Students unable to present a high school transcript may enroll upon presentation of satisfactory passing score on GED.

High school preparation. 24 units required. Required units include English 4, mathematics 2, social studies 2 and science 1.

2015-2016 Annual costs. Tuition/fees: $15,938. Room/board: $5,952. Books/supplies: $1,220. Personal expenses: $1,300.

Financial aid. All financial aid based on need.

Application procedures. Admission: Priority date 5/1; no deadline. $15 fee, may be waived for applicants with need. Admission notification on a rolling basis. Admitted applicants must reply within 5 days of notification of acceptance. **Financial aid:** Priority date 4/15; no closing date. FAFSA, institutional form required. Applicants notified on a rolling basis; must reply within 4 week(s) of notification.

Academics. Special study options: Combined bachelor's/graduate degree, cooperative education, double major, dual enrollment of high school students, honors, independent study, internships, study abroad, teacher certification program. **Credit/placement by examination:** AP, CLEP, SAT, ACT, institutional tests. 30 credit hours maximum toward bachelor's degree. **Support services:** Learning center, reduced course load, remedial instruction, tutoring, writing center.

Honors college/program. High school average of A-, demonstrated success in arts, 1075 SAT (exclusive of Writing)/23 ACT, demonstrated leadership activity, strong performance in sciences, and original essay required.

Majors. Biology: General. **Business:** Business admin. **Communications:** Journalism. **Education:** Elementary. **English:** English lit. **Health services:** Nursing (RN). **History:** General. **Math:** General. **Parks/recreation:** Health/fitness. **Philosophy/religion:** Religion. **Visual/performing arts:** Art, music.

Most popular majors. Biology 18%, business/marketing 16%, communications/journalism 6%, English 6%, health sciences 14%, history 7%, liberal arts 9%, psychology 12%.

Technology on campus. PC or laptop required. 225 workstations in dormitories, library, computer center, student center. Dormitories wired for high-speed internet access and linked to campus network. Commuter students can connect to campus network. Online course registration, online library, helpline, student web hosting, wireless network available.

Student life. Freshman orientation: Available, $50 fee. Preregistration for classes offered. **Policies:** Religious observance required. **Housing:** Guaranteed on-campus for freshmen. Single-sex dorms available. $200 nonrefundable deposit, deadline 7/1. **Activities:** Bands, choral groups, drama, music ensembles, radio station, student government, student newspaper, Christian Student Association, Chancellorettes, Chancellors.

Athletics. NCAA. **Intercollegiate:** Baseball M, basketball, cross-country, football (tackle) M, softball W, tennis, track and field, volleyball W. **Intramural:** Basketball, softball, track and field W, volleyball. **Team name:** Tigers.

Student services. Chaplain/spiritual director, career counseling, student employment services, financial aid counseling, health services, personal counseling, placement for graduates, veterans' counselor.

Contact. E-mail: vbowen@stillman.edu
Phone: (205) 366-8814 Toll-free number: (800) 841-5722
Fax: (205) 366-8941
Victoria Boman, Director of Admissions, Stillman College, 3601 Stillman Boulevard, Tuscaloosa, AL 35403

Talladega College
Talladega, Alabama
www.talladega.edu

CB code: 1800

- Private 4-year liberal arts college affiliated with the United Church of Christ
- Residential campus in large town
- 1,016 degree-seeking undergraduates
- SAT or ACT, application essay required

General. Founded in 1867. Regionally accredited. **Degrees:** 90 bachelor's awarded. **ROTC:** Army. **Location:** 55 miles from Birmingham, 120 miles from Atlanta. **Calendar:** Semester, limited summer session. **Full-time faculty:** 36 total. **Part-time faculty:** 22 total. **Class size:** 60% < 20, 28% 20-39, 7% 40-49, 4% 50-99, less than 1% >100. **Special facilities:** Amistad murals.

Basis for selection. Open admission, but selective for some programs. A minimum of 2.0 GPA for admissions and SAT/ACT test scores. Audition required of music majors. **Home schooled:** Transcript of courses and grades, state high school equivalency certificate required.

High school preparation. College-preparatory program recommended. 22 units recommended. Recommended units include English 4, mathematics 2, social studies 3, science 2 and academic electives 2. 2 units recommended in health/physical education.

2015-2016 Annual costs. Tuition/fees: $13,828. Room/board: $6,704. Books/supplies: $1,200. Personal expenses: $1,200. **Additional information:** Less than 12 or more than 18 credit hours; $466.33 per credit hour.

Financial aid. All financial aid based on need.

Application procedures. Admission: Priority date 3/1; no deadline. $25 fee, may be waived for applicants with need. Admission notification on a rolling basis. Must reply by 5/1. **Financial aid:** Closing date 3/1. FAFSA, institutional form required. Applicants notified on a rolling basis starting 2/1; must reply within 2 week(s) of notification.

Academics. Special study options: Combined bachelor's/graduate degree, cooperative education, double major, dual enrollment of high school students, independent study, internships, teacher certification program. Dual degree linkage programs with other colleges in nursing, engineering, pharmacy, veterinary sciences, geology, and allied health. **Credit/placement by examination:** AP, CLEP, institutional tests. 12 credit hours maximum toward bachelor's degree. **Support services:** Learning center, pre-admission summer program, reduced course load, remedial instruction, study skills assistance, tutoring, writing center.

Majors. Area/ethnic studies: African-American. **Biology:** General. **Business:** Business admin, marketing. **Communications:** Media studies. **Computer sciences:** General. **Education:** Biology, English, history, mathematics, music. **English:** English lit. **History:** General. **Human services:** General, social work. **Math:** General. **Physical sciences:** Chemistry. **Psychology:** General. **Social sciences:** Sociology. **Visual/performing arts:** Music, studio arts.

Most popular majors. Biology 9%, business/marketing 36%, English 9%, psychology 6%, public administration/social services 17%, social sciences 6%.

Technology on campus. 200 workstations in dormitories, library, computer center. Dormitories wired for high-speed internet access and linked to campus network. Commuter students can connect to campus network. Online course registration, online library, helpline, wireless network available.

Student life. Freshman orientation: Mandatory, $50 fee. Preregistration for classes offered. Held one week prior to school opening. **Housing:** Guaranteed on-campus for freshmen. Single-sex dorms, wellness housing available. $200 nonrefundable deposit. Dorms for honors students, seniors, athletes available. **Activities:** Bands, choral groups, dance, drama, music ensembles, student government, Arna Bontemps Historical Society, biology club, business and economics club, chemistry club, debate club, Faith Outreach campus ministry, foreign language club, math club, National Association of Negro Musicians, psychology club.

Athletics. NAIA. **Intercollegiate:** Baseball M, basketball, cheerleading M, golf M, soccer M, volleyball W. **Intramural:** Football (non-tackle) M, softball W, table tennis, tennis, volleyball W. **Team name:** Tornadoes.

Student services. Alcohol/substance abuse counseling, chaplain/spiritual director, career counseling, student employment services, financial aid counseling, health services, personal counseling, placement for graduates, veterans' counselor. **Physically disabled:** Services for visually, hearing impaired.

Contact. E-mail: admissions@talladega.edu
Phone: (256) 761-6235 Toll-free number: (866) 540-3956
Fax: (256) 362-0274
Brian Gipson, Director of Admissions, Talladega College, 627 West Battle Street, Talladega, AL 35160

Troy University
Troy, Alabama — **CB member**
www.troy.edu — **CB code: 1738**

▶ Public 4-year university
▶ Residential campus in large town
▶ 13,989 degree-seeking undergraduates: 36% part-time, 59% women, 31% African American, 1% Asian American, 4% Hispanic/Latino, 1% Native American, 3% Multi-racial, non-Hispanic, 4% international
▶ 4,357 degree-seeking graduate students
▶ 92% of applicants admitted
▶ SAT or ACT (ACT writing optional) required
▶ 34% graduate within 6 years

General. Founded in 1887. Regionally accredited. **Degrees:** 2,821 bachelor's, 376 associate awarded; master's, professional offered. **ROTC:** Army, Air Force. **Location:** 50 miles from Montgomery. **Calendar:** Semester, extensive summer session. **Full-time faculty:** 543 total; 15% minority, 48% women. **Part-time faculty:** 580 total; 18% minority, 57% women. **Class size:** 60% < 20, 31% 20-39, 5% 40-49, 4% 50-99, less than 1% >100. **Special facilities:** Rosa Parks library and museum, planetarium, performing arts theatre.

Freshman class profile. 5,661 applied, 5,197 admitted, 2,099 enrolled.

GPA 3.75 or higher:	29%	Out-of-state:	28%
GPA 3.50-3.74:	14%	Live on campus:	76%
GPA 3.0-3.49:	27%	International:	5%
GPA 2.0-2.99:	28%	Fraternities:	12%
Return as sophomores:	70%	Sororities:	14%

Basis for selection. Unconditional admission: 2.0 GPA and 20 ACT required. Conditional: GPA less than 2.0 with 20 ACT or 950 SAT; 17-19 ACT or 830-940 SAT with 2.5 GPA; applicants under 25 years of age with state issued GED with score of at least 500 and 17-19 ACT or 830-940 SAT. Audition required of music education majors. **Home schooled:** Students who graduate from home school programs must comply with the same requirements as students graduating from traditional programs. Transcripts and diplomas may be self certified.

High school preparation. 18 units required. Required and recommended units include English 4, mathematics 4, social studies 4, science 4 and foreign language 2.

2015-2016 Annual costs. Tuition/fees: $9,646; $18,256 out-of-state. Room/board: $6,525. Books/supplies: $1,124. Personal expenses: $2,543.

2015-2016 Financial aid. Need-based: Average scholarship/grant was $4,316; average loan $3,412. 19% of total undergraduate aid awarded as scholarships/grants, 81% as loans/jobs. **Non-need-based:** Scholarships awarded for academics, alumni affiliation, art, athletics, leadership, minority status, music/drama, ROTC.

Application procedures. Admission: No deadline. $30 fee. Admission notification on a rolling basis. **Financial aid:** Closing date 5/1. FAFSA, institutional form required. Applicants notified on a rolling basis starting 5/1; must reply within 2 week(s) of notification.

Academics. Special study options: Combined bachelor's/graduate degree, distance learning, double major, dual enrollment of high school students, ESL, external degree, honors, independent study, internships, study abroad, teacher certification program, weekend college. **Credit/placement by examination:** AP, CLEP, SAT, ACT, institutional tests. 45 credit hours maximum toward associate degree, 90 toward bachelor's. **Support services:** Learning center, pre-admission summer program, reduced course load, remedial instruction, study skills assistance, tutoring, writing center.

Majors. Biology: General, biomedical sciences, marine. **Business:** General, accounting, business admin, finance, managerial economics. **Communications:** Communications/speech/rhetoric, journalism, radio/TV. **Computer sciences:** General. **Conservation:** Environmental science. **Education:** Elementary, health, multi-level teacher, secondary. **English:** English lit. **Foreign**

languages: Sign language interpretation, Spanish. **Health services:** Athletic training, nursing (RN). **History:** General. **Human services:** Social work. **Liberal arts:** Arts/sciences. **Math:** General. **Parks/recreation:** Exercise sciences, sports admin. **Physical sciences:** Chemistry, physics. **Protective services:** Criminal justice. **Psychology:** General. **Social sciences:** General, anthropology, economics, political science, sociology. **Visual/performing arts:** Art, dance, music.

Most popular majors. Business/marketing 31%, education 6%, psychology 14%, social sciences 8%.

Technology on campus. 1,945 workstations in library, computer center, student center. Online course registration, online library, helpline available.

Student life. Freshman orientation: Mandatory, $55 fee. Preregistration for classes offered. Two-day sessions held during summer at Troy Campus. Multiple undergraduate orientation dates provided each term during each semester/term at Montgomery Campus. **Housing:** Coed dorms, single-sex dorms, apartments, fraternity/sorority housing, wellness housing available. $100 nonrefundable deposit. Substance-abuse-free housing, honor student housing available. **Activities:** Bands, campus ministries, choral groups, dance, drama, international student organizations, music ensembles, musical theater, opera, radio station, student government, student newspaper, symphony orchestra, TV station, religious organizations, service organizations, professional organizations, honor societies, Young Democrats, Young Republicans.

Athletics. NCAA. **Intercollegiate:** Baseball M, basketball, cheerleading, cross-country, football (tackle) M, golf, rodeo, soccer W, softball W, tennis, track and field, volleyball W. **Intramural:** Basketball, cross-country, diving, field hockey W, golf, softball, swimming, tennis, track and field, volleyball W. **Team name:** Trojans.

Student services. Chaplain/spiritual director, career counseling, student employment services, financial aid counseling, health services, on-campus daycare, personal counseling, placement for graduates, veterans' counselor, women's services. **Physically disabled:** Services for visually, hearing impaired.

Contact. E-mail: bstar@troy.edu
Phone: (334) 670-3179 Toll-free number: (800) 551-9716
Fax: (334) 670-3733
Buddy Starling, Dean of Enrollment Management, Troy University, University Avenue, Adams Administration 111, Troy, AL 36082

Tuskegee University
Tuskegee, Alabama — **CB member**
www.tuskegee.edu — **CB code: 1813**

▶ Private 4-year university
▶ Residential campus in small town
▶ 2,485 degree-seeking undergraduates: 2% part-time, 62% women, 78% African American
▶ 510 degree-seeking graduate students
▶ 53% of applicants admitted
▶ SAT or ACT (ACT writing optional) required
▶ 46% graduate within 6 years; 26% enter graduate study

General. Founded in 1881. Regionally accredited. **Degrees:** 352 bachelor's awarded; master's, professional, doctoral offered. **ROTC:** Army, Naval, Air Force. **Location:** 30 miles from Montgomery, 120 miles from Atlanta. **Calendar:** Semester, limited summer session. **Full-time faculty:** 194 total; 87% have terminal degrees, 84% minority, 32% women. **Part-time faculty:** 13 total; 31% have terminal degrees, 77% minority, 77% women. **Class size:** 57% < 20, 26% 20-39, 7% 40-49, 9% 50-99, less than 1% >100. **Special facilities:** Museums, aerospace science and health education center, bioethics center.

Freshman class profile. 7,529 applied, 3,987 admitted, 595 enrolled.

Mid 50% test scores			
SAT critical reading:	440-510	Rank in top quarter:	60%
SAT math:	420-520	Rank in top tenth:	20%
ACT composite:	18-23	End year in good standing:	73%
GPA 3.75 or higher:	16%	Return as sophomores:	70%
GPA 3.50-3.74:	18%	Out-of-state:	60%
GPA 3.0-3.49:	36%	Live on campus:	98%
GPA 2.0-2.99:	30%	International:	1%

Basis for selection. A student's achievement record and test scores are important. 1000 SAT or 21 ACT are required for engineering, nursing, occupational therapy, and education applicants, preferred for other applicants. National League for Nursing Guidance Examination required of nursing applicants. Essay recommended; interview recommended for veterinary medicine majors. **Home schooled:** Transcript of courses and grades, state high school equivalency certificate required.

High school preparation. College-preparatory program recommended. 16 units required; 26 recommended. Required and recommended units include English 4, mathematics 3-4, social studies 3-4, history 2, science 2-4, foreign language 2, computer science 2 and academic electives 4.

2015-2016 Annual costs. Tuition/fees: $21,535. Room/board: $9,104. Books/supplies: $1,678. Personal expenses: $3,675.

2014-2015 Financial aid. Need-based: 645 full-time freshmen applied for aid; 628 deemed to have need; 628 received aid. Average need met was 70%. Average scholarship/grant was $1,500; average loan $7,500. 19% of total undergraduate aid awarded as scholarships/grants, 81% as loans/jobs. **Non-need-based:** Awarded to 1,037 full-time undergraduates, including 326 freshmen. Scholarships awarded for academics, athletics, ROTC, state residency.

Application procedures. Admission: Priority date 5/1; deadline 7/15 (postmark date). $25 fee. Admission notification on a rolling basis beginning on or about 3/1. Must reply by May 1 or within 2 week(s) if notified thereafter. **Financial aid:** Closing date 3/31. FAFSA, institutional form required. Applicants notified on a rolling basis starting 5/15; must reply within 2 week(s) of notification.

Academics. Special study options: Combined bachelor's/graduate degree, cooperative education, distance learning, double major, honors, independent study, internships, liberal arts/career combination, study abroad, teacher certification program. **Credit/placement by examination:** AP, CLEP, IB, SAT, ACT, institutional tests. Credit-by-examination policies determined individually by dean. **Support services:** Learning center, pre-admission summer program, reduced course load, remedial instruction, study skills assistance, tutoring, writing center.

Majors. Architecture: Architecture. **Biology:** General, ecology. **Business:** Accounting, business admin, finance, hospitality admin, management science. **Communications:** General. **Computer sciences:** General. **Conservation:** General, forestry. **Education:** General, biology, elementary, mathematics, physical, science, voc/tech. **Engineering:** Aerospace, chemical, electrical, mechanical. **English:** English lit. **Health services:** Clinical lab science. **History:** General. **Human services:** Social work. **Math:** General. **Physical sciences:** Chemistry, physics. **Psychology:** General. **Social sciences:** Economics, political science, sociology. **Work/family studies:** Food/nutrition.

Most popular majors. Agriculture 17%, biology 9%, business/marketing 11%, engineering/engineering technologies 18%, health sciences 7%, psychology 15%.

Technology on campus. 1,000 workstations in dormitories, library, computer center, student center. Dormitories wired for high-speed internet access and linked to campus network. Commuter students can connect to campus network. Online course registration, online library, helpline, repair service, wireless network available.

Student life. Freshman orientation: Mandatory. Preregistration for classes offered. **Housing:** Guaranteed on-campus for freshmen. Coed dorms, single-sex dorms, apartments, themed housing available. $500 nonrefundable deposit, deadline 7/15. Honors dormitories available. Freshmen and sophomores not living with parents or guardians required to reside on campus. **Activities:** Bands, campus ministries, choral groups, dance, drama, film society, international student organizations, music ensembles, radio station, student government, student newspaper, symphony orchestra, TV station, President's Men and Women, NAACP, Greek Life, CONSO organizations, college specific organizations, Safe Place, International Student Association.

Athletics. NCAA. **Intercollegiate:** Baseball M, basketball, cross-country, football (tackle) M, softball W, tennis, track and field, volleyball W. **Intramural:** Basketball M, football (non-tackle) M, golf, swimming. **Team name:** Golden Tigers.

Student services. Alcohol/substance abuse counseling, chaplain/spiritual director, career counseling, student employment services, financial aid counseling, health services, minority student services, on-campus daycare, personal counseling, placement for graduates, veterans' counselor. **Physically disabled:** Services for visually, speech, hearing impaired.

Contact. E-mail: admissions@mytu.tuskegee.edu
Phone: (334) 727-8500 Toll-free number: (800) 622-6531
Fax: (334) 727-5750
Courtney Griffin, Executive Director of Enrollment Management, Tuskegee University, Margaret Murray Washington Hall, Tuskegee, AL 36088

United States Sports Academy
Daphne, Alabama
www.ussa.edu

- Private two-year upper-division university
- Large town
- Application essay required

General. Regionally accredited. **Degrees:** 25 bachelor's awarded; master's, doctoral offered. **Articulation:** Agreements with Alabama Southern CC, American River College, Andrew College, Barstow CC, Bishop State CC, Camden County College, City College of San Francisco, Columbus State CC, Consumes River College, Cuyahoga CC, Dakota County Technical College, Dallas County CC, East Mississippi CC, Eastern Iowa CC, Eastern Oklahoma State College, Faulkner State CC, Finger Lakes CC, Gadsden State CC, Hagerstown CC, Herkimer County CC, Hillsborough CC, Hiwassee College, Hudson Valley CC, Jamestown CC, Jones County Junior College, Jefferson Davis CC, Manatee CC, Monroe CC, Northern Virginia CC, Ocean County CC, Pensacola Junior College, Saddleback CC, Suffolk County CC. **Location:** 9 miles from Mobile. **Calendar:** Semester, extensive summer session. **Full-time faculty:** 9 total. **Part-time faculty:** 23 total. **Special facilities:** American Sport Art Museum and Archives.

Student profile. 104 degree-seeking undergraduates, 190 graduate students.

Basis for selection. College transcript, application essay required. Transfer accepted as sophomores, juniors, seniors.

2015-2016 Annual costs. Tuition/fees: $11,800.

Application procedures. Admission: Rolling admission. $50 fee. Application must be submitted online.

Academics. Special study options: Distance learning, internships, student-designed major. **Credit/placement by examination:** AP, CLEP.

Majors. Education: Physical. **Parks/recreation:** Sports admin.

Most popular majors. Education 38%, parks/recreation 62%.

Technology on campus. PC or laptop required. Commuter students can connect to campus network. Online library, wireless network available.

Student services. Adult student services, financial aid counseling. **Physically disabled:** Services for visually, speech, hearing impaired.

Contact. E-mail: admissions@ussa.edu
Phone: (251) 626-3303 Toll-free number: (800) 223-2668
Fax: (251) 625-1035
Tim Foley, Director of Student Services, United States Sports Academy, One Academy Drive, Daphne, AL 36526

University of Alabama
Tuscaloosa, Alabama   CB member
www.ua.edu   CB code: 1830

- Public 4-year university
- Residential campus in small city
- 31,005 degree-seeking undergraduates: 8% part-time, 55% women, 11% African American, 1% Asian American, 4% Hispanic/Latino, 3% Multiracial, non-Hispanic, 2% international
- 5,032 degree-seeking graduate students
- 54% of applicants admitted
- SAT or ACT (ACT writing optional) required
- 67% graduate within 6 years; 26% enter graduate study

General. Founded in 1831. Regionally accredited. **Degrees:** 5,662 bachelor's awarded; master's, professional, doctoral offered. **ROTC:** Army, Air Force. **Location:** 60 miles from Birmingham. **Calendar:** Semester, extensive summer session. **Full-time faculty:** 1,284 total; 81% have terminal degrees, 20% minority, 43% women. **Part-time faculty:** 515 total; 50% have terminal degrees, 15% minority, 52% women. **Class size:** 41% < 20, 33% 20-39, 7% 40-49, 12% 50-99, 7% >100. **Special facilities:** Museum of natural history, arboretum, marine science laboratory, archeological park, observatory, access to CRAY X-UP/24 supercomputer in Huntsville, simulated coal mine setting, concert hall.

Freshman class profile. 36,203 applied, 19,400 admitted, 7,211 enrolled.

Mid 50% test scores			
SAT critical reading:	490-600	Rank in top quarter:	57%
SAT math:	490-610	Rank in top tenth:	37%
SAT writing:	480-600	End year in good standing:	90%
ACT composite:	22-31	Return as sophomores:	87%
GPA 3.75 or higher:	46%	Out-of-state:	65%
GPA 3.50-3.74:	17%	Live on campus:	94%
GPA 3.0-3.49:	24%	International:	1%
GPA 2.0-2.99:	13%	Fraternities:	32%
		Sororities:	50%

Basis for selection. ACT/SAT (Writing essay score reqommended), GPA, and course schedule. Typically, students with 21 ACT or 1000 SAT and 3.0 GPA will be admitted. In most cases, tests are not required of freshman applicants who are 25 years of age or older. Interview required of any student who appeals admission type or rejection. Audition required for some performance programs. **Home schooled:** Statement describing home school structure and mission, state high school equivalency certificate required. Students who do not present certified transcripts must submit GED and meet GED admission policy. **Learning Disabled:** Documentation concerning disability should be submitted to Office of Disability Services upon admission.

High school preparation. College-preparatory program required. 15 units required. Required and recommended units include English 4, mathematics 3, social studies 4, science 3 (laboratory 2), foreign language 1-2 and academic electives 5.

2015-2016 Annual costs. Tuition/fees: $10,170; $25,950 out-of-state. Room/board: $9,030. Books/supplies: $1,200. Personal expenses: $2,366.

2014-2015 Financial aid. Need-based: 4,504 full-time freshmen applied for aid; 3,224 deemed to have need; 3,120 received aid. Average need met was 58%. Average scholarship/grant was $13,123; average loan $3,494. 49% of total undergraduate aid awarded as scholarships/grants, 51% as loans/jobs. **Non-need-based:** Awarded to 12,604 full-time undergraduates, including 3,958 freshmen. Scholarships awarded for academics, alumni affiliation, art, athletics, leadership, minority status, music/drama, ROTC, state residency.

Application procedures. Admission: Priority date 2/1; no deadline. $40 fee, may be waived for applicants with need. Admission notification on a rolling basis. Must reply by 5/1. Freshman enrollment deposit ($200 prepaid tuition) due 5/1. **Financial aid:** Priority date 3/1; no closing date. FAFSA required. Applicants notified on a rolling basis starting 4/1; must reply within 3 week(s) of notification.

Academics. The ENGenuity Lab is open to all students in the College of Engineering to cultivate relationships, explore opportunities and collaborate with peers. **Special study options:** Accelerated study, combined bachelor's/ graduate degree, cooperative education, cross-registration, distance learning, double major, dual enrollment of high school students, ESL, exchange student, external degree, honors, independent study, internships, liberal arts/career combination, student-designed major, study abroad, teacher certification program, Washington semester, weekend college. **Credit/placement by examination:** AP, CLEP, IB, institutional tests. **Support services:** Learning center, pre-admission summer program, remedial instruction, study skills assistance, tutoring, writing center. The Writing Center offers assistance to help students improve various aspects of their writing. The Center for Academic Success offers tutorial services, academic coaching and study skills workshops to enhance learning strategies and improve academic performance.

Honors college/program. Freshmen students with a 3.5 HS GPA and 28 ACT/1250 SAT are eligible to apply. Accepted students must complete 18 hours of Honors-designated courses, which must include at least 6 hours of courses offered directly by the Honors College, and maintain a 3.3 overall GPA. Students work with counselors to identify the most appropriate learning opportunities including: service-learning experiences, intercultural programs, and research opportunities.

Majors. Area/ethnic studies: African-American, American, Latin American. **Biology:** General, marine, microbiology. **Business:** Accounting, business admin, finance, management information systems, management science, managerial economics, marketing, restaurant/food services. **Communications:** Advertising, communications/speech/rhetoric, journalism, public relations, radio/TV. **Computer sciences:** General. **Conservation:** Environmental science. **Education:** Early childhood, elementary, music, physical, secondary, special ed. **Engineering:** Aerospace, architectural, chemical, civil, construction, electrical, environmental, mechanical, metallurgical. **English:** English lit. **Foreign languages:** General, Spanish. **Health services:** Athletic training, audiology/speech pathology, dietetics, facilities admin, nursing (RN). **History:** General. **Human services:** Social work. **Math:** General. **Philosophy/ religion:** Philosophy, religion. **Physical sciences:** Chemistry, geology, physics. **Protective services:** Criminal justice. **Psychology:** General. **Social sciences:** Anthropology, geography, international relations, political science, sociology. **Visual/performing arts:** Art history/conservation, dance, dramatic, interior design, music, studio arts. **Work/family studies:** General, clothing/textiles, family resources, family studies.

Most popular majors. Business/marketing 30%, communications/journalism 10%, education 6%, engineering/engineering technologies 7%, family/ consumer sciences 7%, health sciences 10%.

Technology on campus. 2,500 workstations in dormitories, library, computer center, student center. Dormitories wired for high-speed internet access and linked to campus network. Commuter students can connect to campus network. Online course registration, online library, helpline, repair service, student web hosting, wireless network available.

Student life. Freshman orientation: Mandatory, $120 fee. Preregistration for classes offered. Held from May to August in a one-day and a two-day schedule format. Students admitted for the fall can select from over twenty sessions. **Policies:** Academic integrity policies guided by Capstone Creed and administered through Academic Honors Council. Communinity Living Standards for residential students and a Code of Conduct for all students. **Housing:** Guaranteed on-campus for freshmen. Coed dorms, single-sex dorms, special housing for disabled, apartments, fraternity/sorority housing, themed housing available. $300 partly refundable deposit, deadline 2/13. Apartments for visiting scholars available. **Activities:** Bands, campus ministries, choral groups, dance, drama, film society, international student organizations, literary magazine, music ensembles, Model UN, musical theater, opera, radio station, student government, student newspaper, symphony orchestra, TV station, College Republicans, College Democrats, NAACP, Black Student Union, Baptist Student Association, National Society of Black Engineers, Up til Dawn, International Students Association, Hillel House.

Athletics. NCAA. **Intercollegiate:** Baseball M, basketball, cheerleading, cross-country, diving, football (tackle) M, golf, gymnastics W, rowing (crew) W, soccer W, softball W, swimming, tennis, track and field, volleyball W. **Intramural:** Basketball, football (non-tackle), soccer, tennis, ultimate frisbee, volleyball. **Team name:** Crimson Tide.

Student services. Adult student services, alcohol/substance abuse counseling, chaplain/spiritual director, career counseling, services for economically disadvantaged, student employment services, financial aid counseling, health services, legal services, minority student services, on-campus daycare, personal counseling, placement for graduates, veterans' counselor, women's services. **Physically disabled:** Services for visually, speech, hearing impaired.

Contact. E-mail: admissions@ua.edu
Phone: (205) 348-5666 Toll-free number: (800) 933-2262
Fax: (205) 348-9046
Mary Spiegel, Associate Provost and Executive Director of Enrollment Services, University of Alabama, Box 870132, Tuscaloosa, AL 35487-0132

University of Alabama at Birmingham
Birmingham, Alabama — CB member
www.uab.edu — CB code: 1856

- Public 4-year university
- Residential campus in very large city
- 11,383 degree-seeking undergraduates: 26% part-time, 58% women
- 6,757 degree-seeking graduate students
- SAT or ACT (ACT writing optional) required

General. Founded in 1969. Regionally accredited. **Degrees:** 2,165 bachelor's awarded; master's, professional, doctoral offered. **ROTC:** Army, Air Force. **Location:** Downtown. **Calendar:** Semester, extensive summer session. **Full-time faculty:** 865 total; 86% have terminal degrees, 24% minority, 46% women. **Part-time faculty:** 75 total; 83% have terminal degrees, 8% minority, 48% women. **Class size:** 40% < 20, 37% 20-39, 7% 40-49, 11% 50-99, 5% >100. **Special facilities:** Alabama Museum of Health Sciences.

Freshman class profile.

GPA 3.75 or higher:	43%	Rank in top tenth:	28%
GPA 3.50-3.74:	18%	Out-of-state:	14%
GPA 3.0-3.49:	25%	Live on campus:	68%
GPA 2.0-2.99:	14%	Fraternities:	5%
Rank in top quarter:	55%	Sororities:	7%

Basis for selection. Admissions based on ACT/SAT, GPA, and college preparatory curriculum. Auditions required for music majors. **Home schooled:** Statement describing home school structure and mission, transcript of courses and grades required. Additional documentation may be required depending on the home school laws in the state in which the student lives.

High school preparation. College-preparatory program required. 17 units required. Required units include English 4, mathematics 3, social studies 3, science 3 (laboratory 2), foreign language 1 and academic electives 3.

2015-2016 Annual costs. Tuition/fees: $9,596; $21,956 out-of-state. Room/board: $9,850. Books/supplies: $1,200. Personal expenses: $2,400.

Financial aid. Non-need-based: Scholarships awarded for academics, alumni affiliation, art, athletics, leadership, minority status, music/drama, ROTC.

Application procedures. Admission: Priority date 6/1; no deadline. $30 fee, may be waived for applicants with need. Applicants notified on a rolling basis beginning preceding fall term. **Financial aid:** Priority date 3/1; no closing date. FAFSA required. Applicants notified on a rolling basis starting 3/15; must reply within 4 week(s) of notification.

Academics. Special study options: Accelerated study, combined bachelor's/graduate degree, cooperative education, cross-registration, distance learning, double major, dual enrollment of high school students, ESL, exchange student, honors, independent study, internships, semester at sea, student-designed major, study abroad, teacher certification program. **Credit/placement by examination:** AP, CLEP, IB, SAT, ACT, institutional tests. 45 credit hours maximum toward bachelor's degree. **Support services:** Learning center, reduced course load, remedial instruction, study skills assistance, tutoring, writing center. Academic success center.

Honors college/program. Admitted students with a minimum ACT score of 28 or SAT score of 1260 and a 3.5 GPA will receive an invitation in the mail to join the UAB Honors College. Admitted students who do not meet the standardized test score or GPA requirements must submit an application (including essay, resume, and letter of recommendation) by December 1 in order to be considered for admission.

Majors. Area/ethnic studies: African-American. **Biology:** General, biomedical sciences, neuroscience. **Business:** Accounting, business admin, finance, management information systems, managerial economics, marketing, sales/distribution. **Communications:** Communications/speech/rhetoric. **Computer sciences:** General. **Education:** Early childhood, elementary, health, physical, secondary. **Engineering:** Biomedical, civil, electrical, materials, mechanical. **English:** English lit. **Foreign languages:** General. **Health services:** Clinical lab science, health care admin, health information management, nuclear medical technology, nursing (RN), respiratory therapy technology. **History:** General. **Human services:** Social work. **Math:** General. **Philosophy/religion:** Philosophy. **Physical sciences:** Chemistry, physics. **Protective services:** Criminal justice. **Psychology:** General. **Social sciences:** Anthropology, political science, sociology. **Visual/performing arts:** Art, dramatic, music, musical theater.

Most popular majors. Biology 8%, business/marketing 19%, education 9%, engineering/engineering technologies 6%, health sciences 20%, psychology 8%.

Technology on campus. Dormitories wired for high-speed internet access and linked to campus network. Commuter students can connect to campus network. Online course registration, online library, helpline, student web hosting, wireless network available.

Student life. Freshman orientation: Mandatory, $150 fee. Preregistration for classes offered. Two-day program offered various times between May and August. **Housing:** Coed dorms, special housing for disabled, apartments, themed housing available. $250 fully refundable deposit. **Activities:** Bands, campus ministries, choral groups, dance, drama, international student organizations, literary magazine, music ensembles, musical theater, opera, radio station, student government, student newspaper, Young Democrats, College Republicans, campus civitan club, veterans student organization, Catholic student association, Muslim student association, Chinese student association, African student association.

Athletics. NCAA. **Intercollegiate:** Baseball M, basketball, cross-country W, golf, soccer, softball W, synchronized swimming W, tennis, track and field W, volleyball W. **Intramural:** Badminton, basketball, bowling, football (non-tackle), racquetball, skiing, soccer, softball, squash, swimming, table tennis, tennis, track and field, volleyball, water polo, wrestling M. **Team name:** Blazers.

Student services. Adult student services, career counseling, student employment services, financial aid counseling, health services, minority student services, personal counseling, placement for graduates, veterans' counselor, women's services. **Physically disabled:** Services for visually, speech, hearing impaired.

Contact. E-mail: ChoseUAB@uab.edu
Phone: (205) 934-8221 Toll-free number: (800) 421-8743
Fax: (205) 975-7114
Kirk Kluver, Director of Admissions, University of Alabama at Birmingham, 1720 2nd Avenue South, Birmingham, AL 35294-4600

University of Alabama in Huntsville
Huntsville, Alabama   CB member
www.uah.edu   CB code: 1854

- Public 4-year university
- Commuter campus in small city
- 5,829 degree-seeking undergraduates: 19% part-time, 43% women, 12% African American, 4% Asian American, 4% Hispanic/Latino, 1% Native American, 2% Multi-racial, non-Hispanic, 3% international
- 1,780 degree-seeking graduate students
- 81% of applicants admitted
- SAT or ACT (ACT writing optional) required
- 49% graduate within 6 years

General. Founded in 1950. Regionally accredited. **Degrees:** 1,106 bachelor's awarded; master's, professional, doctoral offered. **ROTC:** Army. **Location:** 100 miles from Birmingham; 100 miles from Nashville, TN. **Calendar:** Semester, extensive summer session. **Full-time faculty:** 319 total; 82% have terminal degrees, 27% minority, 42% women. **Part-time faculty:** 234 total; 6% minority, 47% women. **Class size:** 44% < 20, 37% 20-39, 10% 40-49, 8% 50-99, 1% >100. **Special facilities:** National Space Science and Technology Center located on campus, shared between UAH, NASA and the National Weather Service; optical observatory and radio telescope, rooftop greenhouse used for research and laboratory experiences.

Freshman class profile. 3,308 applied, 2,686 admitted, 1,038 enrolled.

Mid 50% test scores			
SAT critical reading:	520-650	GPA 2.0-2.99:	9%
SAT math:	550-680	Rank in top quarter:	54%
ACT composite:	24-30	Rank in top tenth:	29%
GPA 3.75 or higher:	55%	Return as sophomores:	80%
GPA 3.50-3.74:	17%	Out-of-state:	27%
GPA 3.0-3.49:	19%	Live on campus:	61%
		International:	2%

Basis for selection. School achievement record and test scores are most important. Conditional admission may be available for applicants with evidence of serious commitment to academic pursuits who do not meet requirements for regular admission. Auditions required for majoring or minoring in music. **Home schooled:** Official high school record should contain titles of courses, annotation of general content in academic courses, and textbooks used. Teaching credentials of home school teacher should be included with application.

High school preparation. College-preparatory program required. 20 units required; 26 recommended. Required and recommended units include English 4, mathematics 3-4, social studies 4, science 3-4 (laboratory 2), foreign language 2 and academic electives 6. Social studies requirements may include history. Computer science and visual/performing arts counted in academic electives requirements.

2015-2016 Annual costs. Tuition/fees: $9,128; $20,622 out-of-state. Room/board: $9,205. Books/supplies: $1,639. Personal expenses: $2,110. **Additional information:** Each college has required course fees which vary by college.

2015-2016 Financial aid. Need-based: 1,026 full-time freshmen applied for aid; 555 deemed to have need; 548 received aid. Average need met was 74%. Average scholarship/grant was $10,630; average loan $5,511. 45% of total undergraduate aid awarded as scholarships/grants, 55% as loans/jobs. **Non-need-based:** Awarded to 1,557 full-time undergraduates, including 565 freshmen. Scholarships awarded for academics, art, athletics, leadership, minority status, music/drama, ROTC. **Additional information:** Application deadline for institutional scholarships is December 1.

Application procedures. Admission: Closing date 8/20 (receipt date). $30 fee, may be waived for applicants with need. Admission notification on a rolling basis. Must reply by May 1 or within 3 week(s) if notified thereafter. **Financial aid:** Priority date 4/1, closing date 7/31. FAFSA required. Applicants notified on a rolling basis starting 4/1; must reply within 2 week(s) of notification.

Academics. Special study options: Combined bachelor's/graduate degree, cooperative education, cross-registration, distance learning, double major, dual enrollment of high school students, ESL, honors, independent study, internships, student-designed major, study abroad, teacher certification program. 3-2 program in engineering. Research centers employ undergraduate students on campus and in the community. Co-op program with U.S. Army Redstone Arsenal, NASA Marshall Space Flight Center, U.S. Army Missile Command, over 50 Fortune 500 companies. Intensive Language and Culture (ILC) Program for non-native speakers of English available prior to enrollment in a degree program. Joint Undergraduate Masters program (JUMP). **Credit/placement by examination:** AP, CLEP, IB, SAT, ACT, institutional tests. 32 credit hours maximum toward bachelor's degree. **Support services:**

Learning center, remedial instruction, study skills assistance, tutoring, writing center. Student Success Center provides supplemental instruction for historically difficult classes, tutoring in over 100 subjects, drop-in tutoring for math, academic coaching, grade recovery, and an early alert system. The center also houses career development and experiential learning programs.

Honors college/program. Admission requirements are generally a 3.5 high school GPA (unweighted) and ACT/SAT scores of 28 and 1200. About 120 freshmen admitted. The Honors Diploma consists of 24 credit hours of courses that also count toward a regular undergraduate major.

Majors. Biology: General. **Business:** Accounting, business admin, finance, management information systems, managerial economics, marketing. **Communications:** Communications/speech/rhetoric. **Computer sciences:** General. **Education:** Elementary. **Engineering:** Chemical, civil, computer, electrical, industrial, mechanical. **English:** English lit. **Foreign languages:** General. **Health services:** Nursing (RN). **History:** General. **Math:** General. **Philosophy/religion:** Philosophy. **Physical sciences:** Chemistry, physics. **Psychology:** General. **Social sciences:** Political science, sociology. **Visual/performing arts:** Art, music.

Most popular majors. Biology 7%, business/marketing 21%, engineering/engineering technologies 29%, health sciences 18%.

Technology on campus. 1,227 workstations in dormitories, library, computer center, student center. Dormitories wired for high-speed internet access and linked to campus network. Commuter students can connect to campus network. Online course registration, online library, helpline, repair service, student web hosting, wireless network available.

Student life. Freshman orientation: Mandatory, $150 fee. Preregistration for classes offered. Seven two-day sessions over the course of the summer. **Housing:** Guaranteed on-campus for freshmen. Coed dorms, special housing for disabled, apartments, cooperative housing, fraternity/sorority housing, themed housing available. $150 partly refundable deposit, deadline 6/1. **Activities:** Bands, campus ministries, choral groups, dance, drama, international student organizations, music ensembles, Model UN, musical theater, opera, student government, student newspaper, Black student association, Chinese student & scholar association, Muslim students association, Charger Democrats, College Republicans, Indian student organization, christian Student Org, National Society of Black Engineers, Pink Divas, Baptist Campus Ministries, NAACP, POWER.

Athletics. NCAA. **Intercollegiate:** Baseball M, basketball, cross-country, ice hockey M, soccer, softball W, tennis, track and field, volleyball W. **Intramural:** Basketball, football (non-tackle), racquetball, soccer, softball, tennis, ultimate frisbee, volleyball. **Team name:** Chargers.

Student services. Adult student services, alcohol/substance abuse counseling, career counseling, student employment services, financial aid counseling, health services, minority student services, personal counseling, placement for graduates, veterans' counselor, women's services. **Physically disabled:** Services for visually, speech, hearing impaired.

Contact. E-mail: uahadmissions@uah.edu
Phone: (256) 824-2773 Toll-free number: (800) 824-2255
Fax: (256) 824-4539
Sally Badour, Director of Admissions, University of Alabama in Huntsville, UAH Office of Undergraduate Admissions, Huntsville, AL 35899

University of Mobile
Mobile, Alabama
www.umobile.edu   **CB code: 1515**

- Private 4-year university and liberal arts college affiliated with the Baptist faith
- Commuter campus in small city
- 1,437 degree-seeking undergraduates: 11% part-time, 63% women, 23% African American, 1% Asian American, 2% Hispanic/Latino, 2% Native American, 3% Multi-racial, non-Hispanic, 5% international
- 117 degree-seeking graduate students
- 61% of applicants admitted
- 42% graduate within 6 years

General. Founded in 1961. Regionally accredited. **Degrees:** 317 bachelor's, 13 associate awarded; master's offered. **ROTC:** Army, Air Force. **Location:** 12 miles from downtown, 140 miles from New Orleans. **Calendar:** Semester, limited summer session. **Full-time faculty:** 80 total; 64% have terminal degrees, 9% minority, 59% women. **Part-time faculty:** 90 total; 22% have terminal degrees, 7% minority, 49% women. **Class size:** 52% < 20, 47% 20-39, less than 1% 40-49, less than 1% 50-99. **Special facilities:** Recording

studio, forest resource learning center, nature trails, art building with exhibits, performing arts building.

Freshman class profile. 1,180 applied, 714 admitted, 288 enrolled.

Mid 50% test scores			
		GPA 2.0-2.99:	21%
SAT critical reading:	430-540	Rank in top quarter:	52%
SAT math:	420-580	Rank in top tenth:	23%
ACT composite:	19-25	Return as sophomores:	75%
GPA 3.75 or higher:	28%	Out-of-state:	28%
GPA 3.50-3.74:	17%	Live on campus:	71%
GPA 3.0-3.49:	33%	International:	5%

Basis for selection. Test scores, high school record very important. Interview recommended for nursing majors, audition recommended for music majors, portfolio recommended for art majors. **Home schooled:** Statement describing home school structure and mission required.

High school preparation. 22 units required. Required units include English 4, mathematics 3, social studies 3, history 3, science 3 and foreign language 2.

2015-2016 Annual costs. Tuition/fees: $19,970. Room/board: $9,670. Books/supplies: $1,630. Personal expenses: $1,794.

2015-2016 Financial aid. Need-based: 242 full-time freshmen applied for aid; 214 deemed to have need; 214 received aid. Average need met was 69%. Average scholarship/grant was $5,177; average loan $3,679. 70% of total undergraduate aid awarded as scholarships/grants, 30% as loans/jobs. **Non-need-based:** Awarded to 892 full-time undergraduates, including 247 freshmen. Scholarships awarded for academics, alumni affiliation, athletics, music/drama, religious affiliation.

Application procedures. Admission: No deadline. $25 fee, may be waived for applicants with need. Admission notification on a rolling basis. **Financial aid:** No deadline. FAFSA, institutional form required. Applicants notified on a rolling basis starting 2/1.

Academics. Special study options: Accelerated study, combined bachelor's/graduate degree, distance learning, double major, honors, independent study, internships, teacher certification program. **Credit/placement by examination:** AP, CLEP, IB, SAT, ACT, institutional tests. 30 credit hours maximum toward associate degree, 30 toward bachelor's. **Support services:** Learning center, pre-admission summer program, reduced course load, remedial instruction, study skills assistance, tutoring, writing center.

Majors. Biology: General, marine. **Business:** Accounting, business admin. **Communications:** General. **Computer sciences:** General. **Conservation:** Environmental science. **Education:** Biology, early childhood, elementary, English, history, mathematics, music, physical, social science. **English:** English lit. **Health services:** Athletic training, nursing (RN). **History:** General. **Liberal arts:** Humanities. **Math:** General. **Parks/recreation:** Health/fitness. **Philosophy/religion:** Religion. **Psychology:** General. **Social sciences:** General, political science, sociology. **Theology:** Sacred music. **Visual/performing arts:** Art, music, musical theater, voice/opera.

Most popular majors. Business/marketing 16%, education 22%, health sciences 21%, philosophy/religious studies 6%.

Technology on campus. 120 workstations in dormitories, library, computer center, student center. Dormitories wired for high-speed internet access and linked to campus network. Commuter students can connect to campus network. Online course registration, online library, helpline, wireless network available.

Student life. Freshman orientation: Mandatory. Preregistration for classes offered. **Policies:** Religious observance required. **Housing:** Guaranteed on-campus for freshmen. Single-sex dorms, apartments available. $250 nonrefundable deposit. **Activities:** Bands, campus ministries, choral groups, music ensembles, musical theater, opera, student government, Campus activities board, student government association, ministerial association, honor societies, academic clubs, Fellowship of Christian Athletes.

Athletics. NAIA. **Intercollegiate:** Baseball M, basketball, cheerleading W, cross-country, golf, soccer, softball W, tennis, track and field, volleyball W. **Intramural:** Basketball, football (non-tackle), softball, volleyball. **Team name:** Rams.

Student services. Adult student services, chaplain/spiritual director, career counseling, student employment services, financial aid counseling, health services, personal counseling, placement for graduates, veterans' counselor.

Contact. E-mail: adminfo@umobile.edu
Phone: (251) 442-2273 Toll-free number: (800) 946-7267
Fax: (251) 442-2498
Kim Leousis, Vice President for Enrollment Services and Campus Life, University of Mobile, 5735 College Parkway, Mobile, AL 36613-2842

University of Montevallo
Montevallo, Alabama

CB member
CB code: 1004

www.montevallo.edu

- Public 4-year university and liberal arts college
- Residential campus in small town
- 2,553 degree-seeking undergraduates
- 467 graduate students
- 70% of applicants admitted
- SAT or ACT (ACT writing optional) required

General. Founded in 1896. Regionally accredited. **Degrees:** 300 bachelor's awarded; master's offered. **ROTC:** Army, Air Force. **Location:** 35 miles from Birmingham. **Calendar:** Semester, extensive summer session. **Full-time faculty:** 142 total; 12% minority. **Part-time faculty:** 81 total; 6% minority. **Special facilities:** Ecological preserve, observatory, anagama kiln, speech and hearing center, foreign language laboratory, child development center, mass communication production center, traffic safety center.

Freshman class profile. 2,024 applied, 1,417 admitted, 505 enrolled.

Mid 50% test scores			
		GPA 3.0-3.49:	29%
SAT critical reading:	460-600	GPA 2.0-2.99:	20%
SAT math:	480-580	Out-of-state:	8%
SAT writing:	470-590	Live on campus:	79%
ACT composite:	20-26	Fraternities:	22%
GPA 3.75 or higher:	29%	Sororities:	28%
GPA 3.50-3.74:	22%		

Basis for selection. High school record and test scores essential factors in individual evaluation. Interview recommended. Audition required of music majors; portfolio required of art majors. **Home schooled:** Transcript of courses and grades required. **Learning Disabled:** Conditional admission may be granted if standard requirements not met. Reasonable accommodations will be provided as necessary. Enrolled students needing disability accommodations and services must provide current documentation and make requests through the Services for Students with Disabilities Office.

High school preparation. College-preparatory program recommended. 16 units required. Required and recommended units include English 4, mathematics 2-3, social studies 2, history 2, science 2-3, foreign language 2 and academic electives 4.

2015-2016 Annual costs. Tuition/fees: $11,410; $22,780 out-of-state. Room/board: $6,900. Books/supplies: $2,050. Personal expenses: $2,450.

2015-2016 Financial aid. Need-based: Average need met was 58%. Average scholarship/grant was $9,087; average loan $3,377. 60% of total undergraduate aid awarded as scholarships/grants, 40% as loans/jobs. **Non-need-based:** Scholarships awarded for academics, art, athletics, leadership, minority status, music/drama, religious affiliation, ROTC.

Application procedures. Admission: Closing date 8/20. $30 fee, may be waived for applicants with need. Admission notification on a rolling basis beginning on or about 9/1. **Financial aid:** Priority date 4/1; no closing date. FAFSA required. Applicants notified on a rolling basis starting 4/20; must reply within 2 week(s) of notification.

Academics. Academic support programs available to all first-generation college students from low-income families and students with disabilities through the ASPIRE program. Tutoring, study-skills classes, academic counseling, career exploration, course advisement and registration, computer lab access, computer-assisted instruction, and cultural and social enrichment activities provided. **Special study options:** Accelerated study, cross-registration, double major, dual enrollment of high school students, exchange student, honors, independent study, internships, study abroad, teacher certification program. **Credit/placement by examination:** AP, CLEP, IB, institutional tests. 45 credit hours maximum toward bachelor's degree. **Support services:** Learning center, pre-admission summer program, reduced course load, remedial instruction, study skills assistance, tutoring, writing center.

Majors. Biology: General. **Business:** Accounting, business admin, finance, marketing. **Communications:** Radio/TV. **Education:** Elementary. **English:** English lit, rhetoric/composition. **Foreign languages:** General. **Health services:** Audiology/hearing, speech pathology. **History:** General. **Human services:** Social work. **Math:** General. **Parks/recreation:** Health/fitness. **Physical sciences:** Chemistry. **Psychology:** General. **Social sciences:** General, political science, sociology. **Visual/performing arts:** Art, dramatic, music. **Work/family studies:** General.

Most popular majors. Biology 6%, business/marketing 18%, education 13%, English 8%, family/consumer sciences 7%, history 6%, visual/performing arts 15%.

Technology on campus. 340 workstations in dormitories, library, computer center. Dormitories wired for high-speed internet access and linked to campus network. Commuter students can connect to campus network. Online course registration, online library, helpline, wireless network available.

Student life. Freshman orientation: Mandatory. Preregistration for classes offered. Two preregistration sessions during the summer and orientation immediately prior to beginning of fall semester. **Housing:** Guaranteed on-campus for freshmen. Coed dorms, single-sex dorms, apartments available. $100 fully refundable deposit. Several rooms are handicapped accessible. **Activities:** Bands, campus ministries, choral groups, dance, drama, international student organizations, literary magazine, music ensembles, Model UN, musical theater, student government, student newspaper, TV station, African American Society, Young Republicans, Young Democrats, campus outreach, Episcopal Student Fellowship, Feminine Majority Leadership Alliance.

Athletics. NCAA. **Intercollegiate:** Baseball M, basketball, cross-country, golf, soccer, softball W, tennis W, track and field, volleyball W. **Intramural:** Basketball, soccer, softball, volleyball. **Team name:** Falcons.

Student services. Adult student services, alcohol/substance abuse counseling, chaplain/spiritual director, career counseling, student employment services, financial aid counseling, health services, minority student services, personal counseling, placement for graduates, veterans' counselor. **Physically disabled:** Services for visually, speech, hearing impaired.

Contact. E-mail: admissions@montevallo.edu
Phone: (205) 665-6030 Toll-free number: (800) 292-4349
Fax: (205) 665-6032
Gregory Embry, Director of Admissions, University of Montevallo, Palmer Hall, Station 6030, Montevallo, AL 35115-6000

University of North Alabama
Florence, Alabama

CB member
CB code: 1735

www.una.edu

- Public 4-year university
- Commuter campus in large town
- 5,723 degree-seeking undergraduates: 13% part-time, 58% women, 14% African American, 3% Hispanic/Latino, 1% Native American, 3% Multiracial, non-Hispanic, 4% international
- 964 degree-seeking graduate students
- 58% of applicants admitted
- SAT or ACT (ACT writing optional) required
- 38% graduate within 6 years

General. Founded in 1830. Regionally accredited. **Degrees:** 960 bachelor's awarded; master's offered. **ROTC:** Army. **Location:** 116 miles from Birmingham. **Calendar:** Semester, extensive summer session. **Full-time faculty:** 243 total; 74% have terminal degrees, 14% minority, 50% women. **Part-time faculty:** 118 total; 26% have terminal degrees, 8% minority, 58% women. **Class size:** 44% < 20, 44% 20-39, 7% 40-49, 4% 50-99. **Special facilities:** Planetarium-observatory, laboratory school, entertainment industry center.

Freshman class profile. 3,319 applied, 1,925 admitted, 1,173 enrolled.

Mid 50% test scores			
		End year in good standing:	82%
SAT critical reading:	400-560	Return as sophomores:	76%
SAT math:	410-540	Out-of-state:	15%
ACT composite:	19-25	Live on campus:	66%
GPA 3.75 or higher:	26%	International:	2%
GPA 3.50-3.74:	15%	Fraternities:	13%
GPA 3.0-3.49:	27%	Sororities:	24%
GPA 2.0-2.99:	28%		

Basis for selection. Unconditional admission requires 18 ACT/870 SAT, 2.0 GPA with 13 core units. Conditional admission with 16 ACT/770 SAT and 1.75 GPA with 11 core units. Auditions required of music majors. Interviews recommended for education, nursing, social work, preprofessional programs. Portfolios recommended for art majors.

High school preparation. College-preparatory program recommended. 13 units required. Required units include English 4, mathematics 2, social studies 3, science 2 and academic electives 2. Foreign languages, computer sciences, or any of the courses listed which are not used to meet requirements in those areas.

2015-2016 Annual costs. Tuition/fees: $9,508; $17,128 out-of-state. Room/board: $6,516.

2014-2015 Financial aid. Need-based: 666 full-time freshmen applied for aid; 579 deemed to have need; 567 received aid. Average need met was

56%. Average scholarship/grant was $4,139; average loan $2,889. 49% of total undergraduate aid awarded as scholarships/grants, 51% as loans/jobs. **Non-need-based:** Awarded to 1,610 full-time undergraduates, including 446 freshmen. Scholarships awarded for academics, alumni affiliation, art, athletics, job skills, leadership, minority status, music/drama, religious affiliation, ROTC, state residency.

Application procedures. **Admission:** Priority date 8/1; no deadline. $35 fee, may be waived for applicants with need. Application must be submitted online. Admission notification on a rolling basis beginning on or about 6/15. **Financial aid:** Priority date 6/1; no closing date. FAFSA required. Applicants notified on a rolling basis starting 3/30.

Academics. **Special study options:** Accelerated study, combined bachelor's/graduate degree, cooperative education, distance learning, double major, dual enrollment of high school students, ESL, external degree, honors, independent study, internships, student-designed major, study abroad, teacher certification program, weekend college. **Credit/placement by examination:** AP, CLEP, IB, SAT, ACT, institutional tests. 45 credit hours maximum toward bachelor's degree. **Support services:** Learning center, reduced course load, remedial instruction, study skills assistance, tutoring, writing center. Academic advising, first-year experience, supplemental instruction.

Honors college/program. Admission is selective. The program is open to all students in all majors and consists of 27 credit hours of honors coursework. Students must maintain a 3.25 GPA, adhere to university policies, particpate in program activities, and make satisfactory progress toward completion of the academic requirements.

Majors. **Biology:** General, marine. **Business:** Accounting, business admin, finance, management information systems, managerial economics, marketing. **Communications:** Communications/speech/rhetoric, media studies. **Computer sciences:** General. **Education:** Elementary, multi-level teacher, secondary. **English:** English lit. **Foreign languages:** General, French, German. **Health services:** Nursing (RN). **History:** General. **Human services:** Social work. **Math:** General. **Physical sciences:** Chemistry, physics. **Protective services:** Law enforcement admin. **Psychology:** General. **Social sciences:** General, geography, GIS/cartography, political science, sociology. **Visual/performing arts:** Art, arts management, dramatic, music. **Work/family studies:** General.

Most popular majors. Business/marketing 23%, health sciences 15%, social sciences 6%, visual/performing arts 6%.

Technology on campus. 925 workstations in library, student center. Commuter students can connect to campus network. Online course registration, online library, helpline, wireless network available.

Student life. **Freshman orientation:** Mandatory, $25 fee. Preregistration for classes offered. Two-day sessions in June and July include academic advisement. **Policies:** Freshmen not permitted cars on campus. **Housing:** Coed dorms, single-sex dorms, apartments, fraternity/sorority housing available. $150 nonrefundable deposit. **Activities:** Bands, campus ministries, choral groups, dance, drama, international student organizations, literary magazine, music ensembles, musical theater, opera, radio station, student government, student newspaper, Young Democrats, Young Republicans, Circle-K, Gold Triangle, black student alliance, Christian student fellowship.

Athletics. NCAA. **Intercollegiate:** Baseball M, basketball, cheerleading, cross-country, football (tackle) M, golf M, soccer W, softball W, tennis, volleyball W. **Intramural:** Badminton, baseball M, basketball, bowling, cross-country, football (non-tackle), football (tackle) M, golf M, racquetball, rugby M, softball W, swimming, table tennis, tennis, volleyball. **Team name:** Lions.

Student services. Adult student services, alcohol/substance abuse counseling, chaplain/spiritual director, career counseling, services for economically disadvantaged, student employment services, financial aid counseling, health services, minority student services, on-campus daycare, personal counseling, placement for graduates, veterans' counselor, women's services. **Physically disabled:** Services for visually, speech, hearing impaired.

Contact. E-mail: admissions@una.edu
Phone: (256) 765-4608 Toll-free number: (800) 825-5862
Fax: (256) 765-4329
Julie Taylor, Director of Admissions, University of North Alabama, One Harrison Plaza, UNA Box 5011, Florence, AL 35632-0001

University of Phoenix: Birmingham
Birmingham, Alabama
www.phoenix.edu

- For-profit 4-year university
- Commuter campus in small city

- 198 undergraduates
- 40 graduate students

General. Regionally accredited. **Degrees:** 44 bachelor's awarded; master's offered. **Calendar:** Differs by program. **Full-time faculty:** 7 total. **Part-time faculty:** 66 total.

Basis for selection. Open admission.

2015-2016 Annual costs. Per-credit-hour charge, $410 to $635, depending upon level and course of study. Books, material charges, and other fees vary by course and program. All fees are subject to change.

Application procedures. **Admission:** No deadline. No application fee. **Financial aid:** No deadline.

Academics. Credit/placement by examination: AP, CLEP.

Majors. **Business:** Accounting, accounting/business management, business admin, e-commerce, entrepreneurial studies, finance, human resources, marketing, operations. **Communications:** General. **Computer sciences:** Database management, networking, programming, security, system admin, systems analysis, web page design, webmaster. **Conservation:** Environmental studies. **Health services:** Facilities admin, health information management, long term care admin. **Human services:** General. **Protective services:** Disaster management, law enforcement admin, security management.

Student life. **Freshman orientation:** Mandatory. Preregistration for classes offered.

Contact. Toll-free number: (866) 766-0766
University of Phoenix: Birmingham, 100 Corporate Drive, Birmingham, AL 35242

University of South Alabama
Mobile, Alabama
www.southalabama.edu   **CB code: 1880**

- Public 4-year university
- Commuter campus in small city
- 11,457 degree-seeking undergraduates: 18% part-time, 56% women, 24% African American, 3% Asian American, 3% Hispanic/Latino, 1% Native American, 3% Multi-racial, non-Hispanic, 5% international
- 4,664 degree-seeking graduate students
- 78% of applicants admitted
- 35% graduate within 6 years

General. Founded in 1963. Regionally accredited. **Degrees:** 1,815 bachelor's awarded; master's, professional, doctoral offered. **ROTC:** Army, Air Force. **Location:** 10 miles from downtown, 150 miles from New Orleans. **Calendar:** Semester, extensive summer session. **Full-time faculty:** 568 total; 76% have terminal degrees, 14% minority, 49% women. **Part-time faculty:** 473 total; 12% minority, 64% women. **Class size:** 42% < 20, 37% 20-39, 10% 40-49, 9% 50-99, 2% >100. **Special facilities:** Sea lab.

Freshman class profile. 6,650 applied, 5,203 admitted, 2,105 enrolled.

Mid 50% test scores		GPA 3.0-3.49:	31%
SAT critical reading:	430-560	GPA 2.0-2.99:	17%
SAT math:	430-540	Return as sophomores:	73%
SAT writing:	440-560	Out-of-state:	19%
ACT composite:	20-25	Live on campus:	60%
GPA 3.75 or higher:	35%	International:	5%
GPA 3.50-3.74:	17%		

Basis for selection. School achievement record and test scores are important. Auditions required of music majors. **Learning Disabled:** Students should submit required documentation to special student services office if requesting services.

High school preparation. College-preparatory program recommended. 16 units recommended. Recommended units include English 4, mathematics 3, social studies 3, science 3 (laboratory 2) and academic electives 3.

2015-2016 Annual costs. Tuition/fees: $8,790; $17,580 out-of-state. Room/board: $7,250. Books/supplies: $1,200. Personal expenses: $4,270.

2014-2015 Financial aid. **Need-based:** 1,795 full-time freshmen applied for aid; 1,351 deemed to have need; 1,351 received aid. Average need met was 57%. Average scholarship/grant was $7,057; average loan $3,454. 51% of total undergraduate aid awarded as scholarships/grants, 49% as loans/jobs. **Non-need-based:** Awarded to 6,123 full-time undergraduates, including 1,699 freshmen. Scholarships awarded for academics, alumni affiliation, art, athletics, job skills, leadership, minority status, music/drama, ROTC, state residency.

Application procedures. Admission: Closing date 7/15. $45 fee. Application must be submitted on paper. Admission notification on a rolling basis. **Financial aid:** No deadline. FAFSA, institutional form required.

Academics. Special study options: Accelerated study, combined bachelor's/graduate degree, cooperative education, distance learning, double major, dual enrollment of high school students, ESL, honors, independent study, internships, student-designed major, study abroad, teacher certification program, weekend college. **Credit/placement by examination:** AP, CLEP, IB, SAT, ACT, institutional tests. Maximum of 30 credit hours can be awarded under any combination of AP and CLEP examination credits. **Support services:** Learning center, remedial instruction, study skills assistance, tutoring, writing center.

Majors. Biology: General, biomedical sciences. **Business:** General, accounting, business admin, finance, hospitality admin, marketing. **Communications:** Communications/speech/rhetoric. **Computer sciences:** Computer science, information systems, information technology, security. **Education:** Early childhood, elementary, health, physical, secondary, special ed. **Engineering:** Chemical, civil, computer, electrical, mechanical. **English:** English lit. **Foreign languages:** General. **Health services:** Communication disorders, EMT paramedic, nursing (RN), radiologic technology/medical imaging, respiratory therapy technology. **History:** General. **Human services:** Social work. **Math:** Mathematics/statistics. **Parks/recreation:** General. **Philosophy/religion:** Philosophy. **Physical sciences:** Chemistry, geology, meteorology, physics. **Protective services:** Law enforcement admin. **Psychology:** General. **Social sciences:** Anthropology, geography, political science, sociology. **Visual/performing arts:** Art, dramatic, music.

Most popular majors. Business/marketing 13%, education 11%, engineering/engineering technologies 7%, health sciences 29%.

Technology on campus. PC or laptop required. Dormitories wired for high-speed internet access and linked to campus network. Commuter students can connect to campus network. Online course registration, online library, helpline, wireless network available.

Student life. Freshman orientation: Mandatory, $100 fee. Preregistration for classes offered. **Housing:** Coed dorms, special housing for disabled, apartments, fraternity/sorority housing, themed housing, wellness housing available. $150 partly refundable deposit, deadline 5/1. **Activities:** Bands, campus ministries, choral groups, dance, drama, film society, international student organizations, literary magazine, music ensembles, musical theater, opera, radio station, student government, student newspaper, symphony orchestra, TV station, Baptist Campus Ministries, Campus Outreach, Catholic Student Association, African American Student Association, College Democrats, Indian Student Association, Fellowship of Christian Athletes.

Athletics. NCAA. **Intercollegiate:** Baseball M, basketball, cross-country, football (tackle) M, golf, soccer W, softball W, tennis, track and field, volleyball W. **Intramural:** Basketball, bowling, football (non-tackle), golf, racquetball, soccer, softball, table tennis, tennis, volleyball, water polo. **Team name:** Jaguars.

Student services. Adult student services, alcohol/substance abuse counseling, chaplain/spiritual director, career counseling, services for economically disadvantaged, student employment services, financial aid counseling, health services, minority student services, personal counseling, placement for graduates, veterans' counselor, women's services. **Physically disabled:** Services for visually, speech, hearing impaired.

Contact. E-mail: recruitment@southalabama.edu
Phone: (251) 460-6141 Toll-free number: (800) 872-5247
Fax: (251) 460-7876
Norma Tanner, Director of Admissions, University of South Alabama, Meisler Hall, Suite 2500, Mobile, AL 36688-0002

University of West Alabama
Livingston, Alabama
www.uwa.edu   CB code: 1737

- Public 4-year university
- Residential campus in small town
- 1,913 degree-seeking undergraduates: 11% part-time, 55% women, 40% African American, 2% Hispanic/Latino, 2% Multi-racial, non-Hispanic, 6% international
- 1,841 degree-seeking graduate students
- 73% of applicants admitted

- SAT or ACT (ACT writing optional) required
- 32% graduate within 6 years

General. Founded in 1835. Regionally accredited. **Degrees:** 159 bachelor's, 47 associate awarded; master's offered. **ROTC:** Air Force. **Location:** 60 miles from Tuscaloosa, 35 miles from Meridian, MS. **Calendar:** Semester, limited summer session. **Full-time faculty:** 126 total; 78% have terminal degrees, 18% minority, 56% women. **Part-time faculty:** 124 total; 57% have terminal degrees, 11% minority, 64% women. **Class size:** 53% < 20, 36% 20-39, 9% 40-49, 2% 50-99. **Special facilities:** Nature trail, herbarium, greenhouses, wildflower gardens, bluebird trail, lake, Black Belt museum, university cinema.

Freshman class profile. 1,195 applied, 878 admitted, 420 enrolled.

Mid 50% test scores			
ACT composite:	18-21	Live on campus:	98%
End year in good standing:	59%	International:	2%
Return as sophomores:	64%	Fraternities:	11%
Out-of-state:	18%	Sororities:	16%

Basis for selection. Test scores, alongside previous academic GPA, determine admission. **Home schooled:** Transcript of courses and grades required. Applicants who do not graduate from accredited program must have GED.

High school preparation. 15 units required. Required units include English 3, mathematics 3, social studies 3, science 3 and academic electives 3.

2015-2016 Annual costs. Tuition/fees: $9,062; $16,206 out-of-state. Room/board: $7,480. Books/supplies: $1,200. Personal expenses: $2,694.

2014-2015 Financial aid. Need-based: 312 full-time freshmen applied for aid; 268 deemed to have need; 266 received aid. Average need met was 24%. Average scholarship/grant was $5,170. 48% of total undergraduate aid awarded as scholarships/grants, 52% as loans/jobs. **Non-need-based:** Awarded to 835 full-time undergraduates, including 253 freshmen. Scholarships awarded for academics, alumni affiliation, art, athletics, leadership, music/drama, state residency.

Application procedures. Admission: No deadline. $40 fee. Admission notification on a rolling basis. **Financial aid:** Priority date 3/1; no closing date. FAFSA required. Applicants notified on a rolling basis starting 4/15; must reply within 2 week(s) of notification.

Academics. Special study options: Accelerated study, combined bachelor's/graduate degree, cooperative education, distance learning, double major, dual enrollment of high school students, ESL, honors, independent study, internships, student-designed major, study abroad, teacher certification program. **Credit/placement by examination:** AP, CLEP, IB, SAT, ACT, institutional tests. **Support services:** Remedial instruction, study skills assistance, tutoring, writing center. Math Labs and Peer Tutoring are available through the Counseling Center. Mentors are assigned to all the athletes.

Majors. Biology: General, marine. **Business:** Accounting, business admin, finance, management information systems, marketing. **Education:** Multilevel teacher, physical, special ed. **English:** English lit. **Health services:** Athletic training. **History:** General. **Math:** General. **Parks/recreation:** Exercise sciences. **Physical sciences:** Chemistry. **Psychology:** General. **Social sciences:** Sociology.

Most popular majors. Biology 10%, business/marketing 25%, communications/journalism 7%, education 23%, parks/recreation 6%.

Technology on campus. 400 workstations in dormitories, library, computer center, student center. Dormitories wired for high-speed internet access and linked to campus network. Commuter students can connect to campus network. Online course registration, online library, helpline, wireless network available.

Student life. Freshman orientation: Mandatory, $75 fee. Preregistration for classes offered. Two-day summer session. **Housing:** Guaranteed on-campus for freshmen. Coed dorms, apartments, themed housing, wellness housing available. $140 partly refundable deposit, deadline 5/1. **Activities:** Bands, campus ministries, choral groups, dance, drama, international student organizations, music ensembles, student government, student newspaper, TV station, Baptist Campus Ministries, Wesley Foundation Ministries, Presbyterian Campus Ministries, Black Student Association, PALS Clean Campus Program, Alpha Phi Omega, student government association.

Athletics. NCAA. **Intercollegiate:** Baseball M, basketball, cross-country, football (tackle) M, golf, rodeo, soccer, softball W, tennis, track and field, triathlon W, volleyball W. **Intramural:** Archery, basketball, bowling, football (non-tackle), football (tackle), golf, soccer, softball, table tennis, tennis, ultimate frisbee, volleyball. **Team name:** Tigers.

Student services. Alcohol/substance abuse counseling, career counseling, services for economically disadvantaged, student employment services, financial aid counseling, health services, on-campus daycare, personal counseling, placement for graduates. **Physically disabled:** Services for visually, speech, hearing impaired.

Contact. E-mail: admissions@uwa.edu
Phone: (205) 652-3578 Toll-free number: (888) 636-8800
Fax: (205) 652-3522
C. Bedsole, Director of Admissions, University of West Alabama, Station 4, Livingston, AL 35470

Virginia College in Birmingham
Birmingham, Alabama
www.vc.edu/campus/birmingham-alabama-college.cfm

CB code: 2596

- For-profit 4-year health science and career college
- Commuter campus in very large city
- 2,711 undergraduates
- 180 graduate students
- Interview required

General. Founded in 1975. Regionally accredited; also accredited by ACICS. Birmingham campus includes Culinard: The Culinary Institute of Virginia College, which offers 36-week programs in pastry and culinary arts. **Degrees:** 143 bachelor's, 541 associate awarded; master's offered. **Calendar:** Quarter, extensive summer session. **Full-time faculty:** 78 total. **Part-time faculty:** 296 total. **Special facilities:** Full service restaurant and bakery operated by Culinary Institute.

Basis for selection. Open admission, but selective for some programs. High school record, interview and essay evaluated. **Home schooled:** Diploma and transcript required. **Learning Disabled:** Documentation for untimed testing required.

2015-2016 Annual costs. Personal expenses: $100. **Additional information:** Diploma programs: $13,932-$23,220. Associate degree programs $33,024-$49,059. Bachelor degree programs $70,200-$73,260. Cost of Books and supplies included in program tuition.

Application procedures. Admission: No deadline. $100 fee. Admission notification on a rolling basis. **Financial aid:** No deadline.

Academics. Special study options: Accelerated study, distance learning, independent study, internships. **Credit/placement by examination:** AP, CLEP, institutional tests. 45 credit hours maximum toward associate degree. **Support services:** Learning center, study skills assistance, tutoring.

Majors. Business: Accounting, business admin, human resources, management information systems. **Computer sciences:** LAN/WAN management, networking. **Health services:** Health care admin. **Parks/recreation:** Golf management. **Protective services:** Law enforcement admin. **Visual/performing arts:** Interior design.

Technology on campus. 1,000 workstations in library, computer center. Online library, repair service available.

Student life. Freshman orientation: Mandatory. Preregistration for classes offered.

Student services. Career counseling, student employment services, financial aid counseling, placement for graduates, veterans' counselor.

Contact. Phone: (205) 802-1200 Fax: (205) 271-8225
Bevin Yeskevicz, Director of Admissions, Virginia College in Birmingham, 488 Palisades Blvd., Birmingham, AL 35209

Virginia College in Huntsville
Huntsville, Alabama
www.vc.edu

CB code: 3451

- For-profit 4-year business and technical college
- Commuter campus in small city
- 597 undergraduates

General. Accredited by ACICS. **Degrees:** 7 bachelor's, 71 associate awarded. **Calendar:** Quarter. **Full-time faculty:** 13 total. **Part-time faculty:** 50 total.

Basis for selection. Open admission. Accuplacer or SAT/ACT used for placement. **Home schooled:** Transcript of courses and grades required.

2015-2016 Annual costs. Personal expenses: $2,978. **Additional information:** Diploma programs; $13,392-$23,220. Associate degree programs; $37,152-$40,700. Bachelor degree programs; $69,660-$75,702. Cost of books and supplies included in program tuition. All costs are subject to change.

Application procedures. Admission: No deadline. $100 fee. **Financial aid:** No deadline. FAFSA, institutional form required. Applicants notified on a rolling basis.

Academics. Special study options: Distance learning. **Credit/placement by examination:** AP, CLEP. **Support services:** Learning center, tutoring.

Majors. Computer sciences: LAN/WAN management, modeling/simulation, system admin. **Protective services:** Law enforcement admin.

Contact. E-mail: daryl.coleman@vc.edu
Phone: (256) 533-7387 Fax: (256) 533-7785
Daryl Coleman, Director of Admissions, Virginia College in Huntsville, 2800 Bob Wallace Avenue, Huntsville, AL 35805

Alaska

Alaska Bible College
Palmer, Alaska
www.akbible.edu   CB code: 1237

- Private 4-year Bible college affiliated with the nondenominational tradition
- Residential campus in small town
- 29 degree-seeking undergraduates
- SAT or ACT, application essay required

General. Founded in 1966. Accredited by ABHE. **Degrees:** 2 bachelor's awarded. **Location:** 43 miles from Anchorage, 327 miles from Fairbanks. **Calendar:** Semester. **Full-time faculty:** 20 total. **Special facilities:** Largest theological library collection in Alaska, Alaskan book collection.

Basis for selection. Open admission, but selective for some programs. Applicants are considered on a case-by-case basis. References and indications of religious commitment most important, followed by school grade record. Test scores and extracurricular activities also considered. **Home schooled:** Transcript of courses and grades required. Applicants must have documentation of high school equivalence.

High school preparation. Recommended units include English 4, mathematics 4, social studies 4, history 4, science 4 and foreign language 2.

2015-2016 Annual costs. Tuition/fees: $9,300. Room/board: $5,400. Books/supplies: $300.

Financial aid. Non-need-based: Scholarships awarded for academics.

Application procedures. Admission: Closing date 7/1 (postmark date). $35 fee. Application must be submitted on paper. Admission notification on a rolling basis beginning on or about 7/1. Must reply by 7/15. **Financial aid:** Priority date 5/30; no closing date. FAFSA, institutional form required. Must reply within 2 week(s) of notification.

Academics. Special study options: Double major, dual enrollment of high school students, independent study, internships. **Credit/placement by examination:** AP, CLEP, institutional tests. **Support services:** Reduced course load, remedial instruction, tutoring.

Majors. Theology: Bible, missionary, theology.

Technology on campus. Commuter students can connect to campus network. Online library, repair service, wireless network available.

Student life. Freshman orientation: Mandatory. Preregistration for classes offered. 4-5 day program held immediately before beginning of school year. **Policies:** Religious observance required. **Housing:** Guaranteed on-campus for freshmen. Single-sex dorms, apartments, wellness housing available. $150 fully refundable deposit, deadline 7/1. **Activities:** Campus ministries, radio station, student government.

Student services. Chaplain/spiritual director, financial aid counseling, health services, personal counseling.

Contact. E-mail: info@akbible.edu
Toll-free number: (800) 478-7884
Rebekah Olson, Director of Admissions, Alaska Bible College, 248 East Elmwood Avenue, Palmer, AK 99645

Alaska Pacific University
Anchorage, Alaska
www.alaskapacific.edu   CB code: 4201

- Private 4-year university and liberal arts college affiliated with the United Methodist Church
- Commuter campus in large city
- 291 undergraduates
- 267 graduate students

- 39% of applicants admitted
- SAT or ACT (ACT writing optional), application essay required

General. Founded in 1957. Regionally accredited. **Degrees:** 75 bachelor's, 7 associate awarded; master's, professional offered. **ROTC:** Air Force. **Calendar:** Semester, limited summer session. **Full-time faculty:** 47 total; 92% have terminal degrees, 13% minority, 53% women. **Part-time faculty:** 44 total; 7% have terminal degrees, 2% minority. **Class size:** 96% < 20, 4% 20-39. **Special facilities:** Climbing wall, walking trails, lake for canoeing and kayaking, Alaskan collection.

Freshman class profile. 697 applied, 272 admitted, 49 enrolled.

Out-of-state: 51% **Live on campus:**   95%

Basis for selection. High school record and test scores are required if transferring under 30 credits. **Learning Disabled:** Documentation verifying the disability condition required.

High school preparation. 14 units recommended. Recommended units include English 4, mathematics 3, social studies 1, history 1, science 2 (laboratory 1) and foreign language 2.

2015-2016 Annual costs. Tuition/fees: $19,680. Room/board: $7,000. Books/supplies: $1,200. Personal expenses: $1,400.

Financial aid. Non-need-based: Scholarships awarded for academics, alumni affiliation, art, leadership, music/drama, religious affiliation, state residency.

Application procedures. Admission: Priority date 12/1; deadline 8/15. $25 fee, may be waived for applicants with need. Admission notification on a rolling basis beginning on or about 1/15. **Financial aid:** Priority date 4/15; no closing date. FAFSA required. Applicants notified on a rolling basis starting 2/1; must reply within 4 week(s) of notification.

Academics. Special study options: Accelerated study, combined bachelor's/graduate degree, distance learning, double major, exchange student, independent study, internships, student-designed major, teacher certification program. Eco-League exchange program for Environmental Sciences with Prescott College, Northland College, College of the Atlantic, Antioch College, Green Mountain College. **Credit/placement by examination:** AP, CLEP, IB, SAT, ACT, institutional tests. 22 credit hours maximum toward associate degree, 45 toward bachelor's. Sophomore standing available through AP and IB examinations by earning equivalent of 32 semester hours. **Support services:** Learning center, reduced course load, remedial instruction, study skills assistance, tutoring, writing center.

Majors. Area/ethnic studies: Native American. **Biology:** Marine. **Business:** Business admin. **Conservation:** Environmental science, management/policy. **English:** Creative writing. **Liberal arts:** Arts/sciences. **Parks/recreation:** Facilities management. **Physical sciences:** Geology. **Psychology:** General.

Most popular majors. Biology 21%, business/marketing 22%, education 6%, interdisciplinary studies 7%, liberal arts 6%, natural resources/environmental science 7%, parks/recreation 12%, public administration/social services 7%.

Technology on campus. 85 workstations in dormitories, library, computer center, student center. Dormitories wired for high-speed internet access. Online course registration, online library, helpline, student web hosting, wireless network available.

Student life. Freshman orientation: Mandatory. Preregistration for classes offered. Three days long. **Policies:** Student representation on faculty committees and councils encouraged. **Housing:** Guaranteed on-campus for freshmen. Coed dorms, cooperative housing, themed housing available. $300 deposit, deadline 4/30. **Activities:** Campus ministries, choral groups, drama, international student organizations, literary magazine, music ensembles, student government, student newspaper, art club, business club, environmental club, photography club, psychology club, service club, soccer club, volleyball club.

Athletics. Team name: Moose.

Student services. Chaplain/spiritual director, career counseling, student employment services, financial aid counseling, minority student services, personal counseling.

Contact. E-mail: admissions@alaskapacific.edu
Phone: (907) 564-8248 Toll-free number: (800) 252-7528
Fax: (907) 564-8317
Michelle Wheeler, Director of Enrollment Management, Alaska Pacific University, 4101 University Drive, Anchorage, AK 99508-3051

Charter College
Anchorage, Alaska
www.chartercollege.edu

CB code: 3453

- For-profit 4-year junior and technical college
- Commuter campus in large city
- 3,256 undergraduates

General. Accredited by ACICS. **Degrees:** 59 bachelor's, 300 associate awarded; master's offered. **Calendar:** Differs by program. **Full-time faculty:** 45 total. **Part-time faculty:** 207 total.

Basis for selection. Open admission.

2015-2016 Annual costs. Books/supplies: $700. **Additional information:** Tuition and fees vary depending on program. Examples of Bachelor Degree Programs: Business Management Accounting; $78,800; Criminal Justice; $41,400. Associate Programs: Business Management Practice; $41,370; Paralegal Studies; $41,376. All costs are subject to change.

Application procedures. Admission: No deadline. $20 fee. Admission notification on a rolling basis. **Financial aid:** No deadline. FAFSA required. Applicants notified on a rolling basis; must reply within 5 week(s) of notification.

Academics. Special study options: Double major, internships. **Credit/ placement by examination:** AP, CLEP. Up to 33% of total required credits for associate degree may be earned through examination. **Support services:** Tutoring.

Majors. Business: Accounting/business management, construction management, management information systems. **Computer sciences:** Information technology. **Health services:** Health care admin. **Protective services:** Law enforcement admin.

Most popular majors. Business/marketing 45%, computer/information sciences 28%, security/protective services 26%.

Technology on campus. Online library available.

Student life. Freshman orientation: Available. Preregistration for classes offered.

Student services. Career counseling, student employment services, financial aid counseling.

Contact. E-mail: contact@chartercollege.edu
Phone: (907) 277-1000 Toll-free number: (888) 200-9942
Lily Sirianni, Admissions Director, Charter College, 2221 East Northern Lights Boulevard, Suite 120, Anchorage, AK 99508

University of Alaska Anchorage
Anchorage, Alaska
www.uaa.alaska.edu

CB member
CB code: 4896

- Public 4-year university
- Commuter campus in large city
- 12,352 degree-seeking undergraduates: 45% part-time, 57% women, 4% African American, 8% Asian American, 7% Hispanic/Latino, 6% Native American, 1% Native Hawaiian/Pacific islander, 11% Multi-racial, non-Hispanic, 2% international
- 843 degree-seeking graduate students

General. Founded in 1954. Regionally accredited. **Degrees:** 1,094 bachelor's, 873 associate awarded; master's, doctoral offered. **ROTC:** Army, Air Force. **Location:** 3 miles from downtown. **Calendar:** Semester, extensive summer session. **Full-time faculty:** 648 total; 62% have terminal degrees, 16% minority, 52% women. **Part-time faculty:** 675 total; 5% have terminal degrees, 14% minority, 59% women. **Class size:** 56% < 20, 35% 20-39, 5% 40-49, 3% 50-99, less than 1% >100. **Special facilities:** Small business development center, planetarium and visualization theater, Confucius Institute.

Freshman class profile. 3,775 applied, 2,665 admitted, 1,869 enrolled.

Mid 50% test scores			
SAT critical reading:	440-580	Rank in top quarter:	34%
SAT math:	440-570	Rank in top tenth:	14%
SAT writing:	430-550	End year in good standing:	76%
ACT composite:	17-24	Return as sophomores:	71%
GPA 3.75 or higher:	14%	Out-of-state:	6%
GPA 3.50-3.74:	13%	International:	2%
GPA 3.0-3.49:	28%		
GPA 2.0-2.99:			40%

Basis for selection. Open admission, but selective for some programs. For the bachelor's program, minimum high school GPA of 2.5 and either SAT, ACT or UAA-approved test scores; high school graduates with GPAs between 2.0 and 2.49 admitted on probation. Alternatively, applicants must have successful completion of the GED and either SAT, ACT or UAA-approved test scores. UAA uses ACCUPLACER for adult students who have not taken SAT or ACT. Interview and essay requirements vary according to program. **Home schooled:** Transcript of courses and grades required. **Learning Disabled:** Make an appointment with Disability Support Services, provide current diagnostic and evaluative reports, and request reasonable accommodations that are supported by documentation.

High school preparation. College-preparatory program recommended. Requirements vary by program.

2015-2016 Annual costs. Tuition/fees: $6,414; $20,394 out-of-state. Room/board: $10,254. Books/supplies: $1,591. Personal expenses: $1,607.

2015-2016 Financial aid. Need-based: 1,160 full-time freshmen applied for aid; 784 deemed to have need; 714 received aid. Average need met was 59%. Average scholarship/grant was $3,476; average loan $3,202. 50% of total undergraduate aid awarded as scholarships/grants, 50% as loans/jobs. **Non-need-based:** Scholarships awarded for academics, art, athletics, leadership, minority status, music/drama, ROTC.

Application procedures. Admission: Closing date 6/15. $50 fee, may be waived for applicants with need. Application must be submitted online. Admission notification on a rolling basis. Freshman early admission plan allows students to apply early but wait as long as 2 years to enroll. **Financial aid:** Priority date 4/1; no closing date. FAFSA required. Applicants notified on a rolling basis starting 2/1; must reply within 4 week(s) of notification.

Academics. Special study options: Accelerated study, combined bachelor's/graduate degree, cooperative education, cross-registration, distance learning, double major, dual enrollment of high school students, ESL, exchange student, honors, independent study, internships, liberal arts/career combination, semester at sea, student-designed major, study abroad, teacher certification program, Washington semester. **Credit/placement by examination:** AP, CLEP, IB, SAT, ACT, institutional tests. Credit by examination is considered non-resident credit, and non-resident credit policies apply. **Support services:** Learning center, reduced course load, remedial instruction, study skills assistance, tutoring, writing center. Many programs available to assist non-traditional and/or at-risk students for college success.

Honors college/program. Students must submit a completed University Honors College application, high school transcript, SAT or ACT scores, essay on personal goals, and a completed reference form from two teachers.

Majors. Biology: General. **Business:** Accounting, accounting technology, business admin, construction management, finance, hospitality admin, logistics, management information systems, marketing. **Communications:** Journalism. **Computer sciences:** General. **Conservation:** Environmental studies. **Education:** Early childhood, elementary, kindergarten/preschool, music, physical, secondary. **Engineering:** General, civil, pre-engineering. **English:** English lit. **Foreign languages:** General. **Health services:** Clinical lab science, dental hygiene, dietetics, mental health services, nursing (RN). **History:** General. **Human services:** Social work. **Math:** General. **Philosophy/religion:** Philosophy. **Physical sciences:** Geology. **Psychology:** General. **Social sciences:** Anthropology, economics, political science, sociology. **Visual/performing arts:** Art, music, music performance, theater design. **Work/family studies:** Child care service.

Most popular majors. Business/marketing 19%, engineering/engineering technologies 8%, health sciences 16%, psychology 7%, social sciences 7%.

Technology on campus. Dormitories wired for high-speed internet access and linked to campus network. Commuter students can connect to campus network. Online course registration, online library, helpline, repair service, student web hosting, wireless network available.

Student life. Freshman orientation: Available, $75 fee. Preregistration for classes offered. One-day and evening orientation sessions offered. $25 cost for guests attending with the student. Virtual orientation sessions are also offered for $25. **Housing:** Coed dorms, special housing for disabled, apartments, wellness housing available. $300 fully refundable deposit. Separate floors available for Alaska Natives studying engineering, nursing students, honor students, language and cultures, first-year students under age 20, healthy lifestyle, quiet lifestyle, WWAMI program, and Far East exchange program. **Activities:** Jazz band, campus ministries, choral groups, dance, drama, film society, international student organizations, literary magazine, music ensembles, Model UN, musical theater, opera, radio station, student government, student newspaper, Alaska Native student organization, African American student associations, Baha'i club, College Republicans, Korean Campus Crusade for Christ, Intervarsity Christian Fellowship, Disability Awareness Club, Student Organization Against Racism.

Athletics. NCAA. **Intercollegiate:** Basketball, cross-country, gymnastics W, ice hockey M, skiing, track and field, volleyball W. **Intramural:** Basketball, cheerleading, ice hockey, soccer, volleyball, water polo. **Team name:** Seawolves.

Student services. Adult student services, alcohol/substance abuse counseling, career counseling, services for economically disadvantaged, student employment services, financial aid counseling, health services, legal services, minority student services, on-campus daycare, personal counseling, veterans' counselor. **Physically disabled:** Services for visually, speech, hearing impaired.

Contact. E-mail: enroll@uaa.alaska.edu
Phone: (907) 786-1480 Fax: (907) 786-4888
Eric Pedersen, Associate Vice Chancellor for Enrollment Services, University of Alaska Anchorage, PO Box 141629, Anchorage, AK 99514-1629

University of Alaska Fairbanks
Fairbanks, Alaska   **CB member**
www.uaf.edu   **CB code: 4866**

▶ Public 4-year university
▶ Commuter campus in small city
▶ 5,445 degree-seeking undergraduates: 39% part-time, 55% women, 2% African American, 1% Asian American, 6% Hispanic/Latino, 14% Native American, 4% Multi-racial, non-Hispanic, 1% international
▶ 1,036 degree-seeking graduate students
▶ 42% graduate within 6 years; 21% enter graduate study

General. Founded in 1917. Regionally accredited. University of the Arctic participating institution. **Degrees:** 572 bachelor's, 307 associate awarded; master's, doctoral offered. **ROTC:** Army. **Location:** 4 miles from downtown. **Calendar:** Semester, limited summer session. **Full-time faculty:** 357 total; 76% have terminal degrees, 20% minority, 43% women. **Part-time faculty:** 562 total; 52% have terminal degrees, 13% minority, 46% women. **Class size:** 66% < 20, 27% 20-39, 3% 40-49, 3% 50-99, less than 1% >100. **Special facilities:** Museum of the North, geophysical institute, bioscience library, institute of arctic biology, arctic region supercomputing center, international arctic research center, boreal forest research range, Alaska native language center, institute of marine sciences, institute of northern engineering, rocketry research range, agricultural and forestry experiment station, botanical garden, public broadcasting TV and radio stations, extensive ski and multi-use system.

Freshman class profile. 1,554 applied, 1,136 admitted, 798 enrolled.

Mid 50% test scores			
SAT critical reading:	480-610	GPA 2.0-2.99:	29%
SAT math:	480-610	Rank in top quarter:	38%
SAT writing:	450-570	Rank in top tenth:	18%
ACT composite:	18-26	Return as sophomores:	75%
GPA 3.75 or higher:	23%	Out-of-state:	11%
GPA 3.50-3.74:	18%	Live on campus:	53%
GPA 3.0-3.49:	29%	International:	2%

Basis for selection. Open admission, but selective for some programs. GED not accepted. Minimum 2.5 GPA in 16 core classes; minimum 3.0 overall GPA or at least 2.5 overall GPA and ACT score of at least 18 or SAT score of at least 1290 for bachelor's degree-seeking students. Students with high school GPA below 3.0 and ACT composite score below 18 or total SAT score below 1290 are admitted as pre-majors. Open admissions for certificate and associate degree applicants over age 18. Some students may be required to take ASSET and/or COMPASS tests for additional course placement. Regardless of GPA, ACT and SAT scores are used for placement in English and math classes. **Home schooled:** Transcript of courses and grades, state high school equivalency certificate required. Students who have completed a state-recognized program and have a valid high school diploma may be admitted to a baccalaureate program. All others admitted via individual review by the UAF admissions office. **Learning Disabled:** Disability services program provides assistance for students with documented disabilities.

High school preparation. College-preparatory program required. 16 units required. Required and recommended units include English 4, mathematics 3, social studies 3, science 3 (laboratory 1) and foreign language 2. Mathematics should include 3 from algebra, geometry and trigonometry, precalculus or calculus.

2015-2016 Annual costs. Tuition/fees: $6,804; $20,784 out-of-state. Room/board: $8,380. Books/supplies: $1,400. Personal expenses: $2,250.

2014-2015 Financial aid. Need-based: 682 full-time freshmen applied for aid; 390 deemed to have need; 378 received aid. Average need met was 60%. Average scholarship/grant was $7,188; average loan $2,784. 52% of total undergraduate aid awarded as scholarships/grants, 48% as loans/jobs. **Non-need-based:** Awarded to 750 full-time undergraduates, including 200 freshmen. Scholarships awarded for academics, art, athletics, music/drama, state residency.

Application procedures. Admission: Priority date 2/15; deadline 6/15 (postmark date). $50 fee, may be waived for applicants with need. Admission notification by 9/1. Admission notification on a rolling basis beginning on or about 1/1. Students must have completed 75% of their high school academic core curriculum and have a 3.0 GPA. ACT or SAT (including Writing portions) required prior to enrolling at UAF. Upon receipt of high school diploma, students may change major from General Studies to another program offered at UAF. **Financial aid:** Priority date 2/15, closing date 7/1. FAFSA, institutional form required. Applicants notified on a rolling basis starting 3/1; must reply within 2 week(s) of notification.

Academics. Student support services program (federally funded) for students with qualified at-risk status. **Special study options:** Accelerated study, combined bachelor's/graduate degree, cooperative education, distance learning, double major, dual enrollment of high school students, ESL, exchange student, external degree, honors, independent study, internships, semester at sea, student-designed major, study abroad, teacher certification program. Legislative aide intern program; undergraduate research opportunities. **Credit/placement by examination:** AP, CLEP, IB, institutional tests. Credit by examination is not considered to be a UAF residence credit. A student must have 15 residence credits to earn an associate degree and 30 residence credits to earn a bachelor's degree. Credit by examination is not considered part of semester course load for classification as full-time student. **Support services:** Learning center, pre-admission summer program, remedial instruction, study skills assistance, tutoring, writing center.

Honors college/program. Entering Freshmen must have a cumulative high school GPA of 3.6 and a composite SAT score of 1820 or ACT score of 27. Current UAF students and transfer students must have a combined cumulative GPA of 3.5 that includes at least 24 credits of college courses. Honors students complete honors sections of the core curriculum courses, courses developed specifically for the honors program, and standard courses contracted for honors credit by students with individual professors. Students work with a faculty mentor to complete a capstone project, including a written component and an oral presentation.

Majors. Area/ethnic studies: Native American, Russian/Slavic. **Biology:** General. **Business:** Accounting, business admin, human resources. **Communications:** Communications/speech/rhetoric, journalism. **Computer sciences:** General, computer science. **Conservation:** Fisheries, management/policy, wildlife/wilderness. **Education:** General, elementary, secondary. **Engineering:** General, civil, computer, electrical, geological, mechanical, mining, petroleum. **English:** English lit. **Foreign languages:** General, Japanese, linguistics, Native American. **History:** General. **Human services:** Community org/advocacy, social work. **Liberal arts:** Arts/sciences. **Math:** General. **Philosophy/religion:** Philosophy. **Physical sciences:** Chemistry, geology, physics. **Protective services:** Disaster management. **Psychology:** General. **Social sciences:** Anthropology, economics, geography, political science, sociology. **Visual/performing arts:** Art, film/cinema/video, music, theater design. **Work/family studies:** Child development.

Most popular majors. Biology 9%, business/marketing 10%, engineering/engineering technologies 17%, psychology 6%, public administration/social services 6%, social sciences 7%.

Technology on campus. 125 workstations in dormitories, library, computer center. Dormitories wired for high-speed internet access and linked to campus network. Commuter students can connect to campus network. Online course registration, online library, helpline, repair service, student web hosting, wireless network available.

Student life. Freshman orientation: Mandatory, $35 fee. Preregistration for classes offered. Held over three days immediately before start of classes each fall. **Policies:** Student organizations must be officially recognized on an annual basis by the Student Activities Office. **Housing:** Coed dorms, special housing for disabled, apartments, wellness housing available. $355 partly refundable deposit, deadline 7/1. Alaska native cultural housing available. **Activities:** Jazz band, campus ministries, choral groups, dance, drama, international student organizations, literary magazine, music ensembles, Model UN, radio station, student government, student newspaper, symphony orchestra, Alaskan Academic Association for Students of Color, Alaska Native Social Workers Association, American Indian Science and Engineering Society, Baptist Campus Ministry, Chinese Student Association, Circle K UAF Chapter, Fairbanks Free Thinkers, Gender and Sexuality Alliance, Namaste India Vita: non-denomination campus ministry.

Athletics. NCAA. **Intercollegiate:** Basketball, cross-country, ice hockey M, rifle, skiing, swimming W, volleyball W. **Intramural:** Basketball, football (non-tackle), ice hockey, soccer, ultimate frisbee, volleyball. **Team name:** Nanooks.

Student services. Alcohol/substance abuse counseling, chaplain/spiritual director, career counseling, services for economically disadvantaged, student employment services, financial aid counseling, health services, legal services, minority student services, personal counseling, placement for graduates, women's services. **Physically disabled:** Services for visually, speech, hearing impaired.

Contact. E-mail: admissions@uaf.edu
Phone: (907) 474-7500 Toll-free number: (800) 478-1823
Fax: (907) 474-5379
Mary Kreta, Director of Admissions, University of Alaska Fairbanks, PO Box 757480, Fairbanks, AK 99775-7480

University of Alaska Southeast
Juneau, Alaska — CB member
www.uas.alaska.edu — CB code: 4897

- Public 4-year university and liberal arts college
- Commuter campus in large town
- 1,591 degree-seeking undergraduates
- 353 graduate students

General. Founded in 1972. Regionally accredited. All University of Alaska Southeast campuses (Juneau, Ketchikan, Sitka) are accessible only by ferry or air. **Degrees:** 137 bachelor's, 137 associate awarded; master's offered. **Calendar:** Semester, limited summer session. **Full-time faculty:** 100 total; 50% have terminal degrees, 10% minority, 47% women. **Part-time faculty:** 133 total; 10% have terminal degrees, 11% minority, 54% women. **Class size:** 83% < 20, 15% 20-39, less than 1% 40-49, less than 1% 50-99. **Special facilities:** Ice field, glacier, national forest, raptor center.

Freshman class profile.

GPA 3.75 or higher:	11%	Rank in top quarter:	22%
GPA 3.50-3.74:	10%	Rank in top tenth:	6%
GPA 3.0-3.49:	34%	Out-of-state:	6%
GPA 2.0-2.99:	42%	Live on campus:	26%

Basis for selection. High school record most important. Students not meeting BA requirements counseled to AA or certificate program with possibility of later transfer to BA program. Some BA programs admit students as pre-majors and upon satisfying prerequisites may be admitted to major. Financial statement and immunization records required of international applicants, as well as statement of educational equivalency written in English. **Home schooled:** Student must graduate from accredited home school program or obtain GED.

High school preparation. College-preparatory program recommended.

2015-2016 Annual costs. Tuition/fees: $6,990; $20,970 out-of-state. Room/board: $8,400. Books/supplies: $1,276. Personal expenses: $1,603.

Financial aid. Non-need-based: Scholarships awarded for academics, job skills, leadership, music/drama, state residency. **Additional information:** Transfer, continuing, and freshman scholarship deadline March 1.

Application procedures. Admission: Closing date 8/1 (receipt date). $50 fee, may be waived for applicants with need. Admission notification on a rolling basis beginning on or about 9/1. Housing deposit refundable if letter of cancellation provided prior to July 1. **Financial aid:** Priority date 4/15; no closing date. FAFSA required. Applicants notified on a rolling basis starting 3/1; must reply within 3 week(s) of notification.

Academics. Special study options: Distance learning, double major, dual enrollment of high school students, exchange student, honors, independent study, internships, semester at sea, student-designed major, study abroad, teacher certification program. **Credit/placement by examination:** AP, CLEP, SAT, ACT, institutional tests. 15 credit hours maximum toward associate degree, 30 toward bachelor's. **Support services:** Learning center, pre-admission summer program, remedial instruction, study skills assistance, tutoring, writing center.

Majors. Biology: General, marine. **Business:** General, accounting, management science, marketing. **Communications:** Communications/speech/rhetoric. **Conservation:** Environmental science, environmental studies. **Education:** Elementary. **English:** English lit. **Liberal arts:** Arts/sciences. **Math:** General. **Parks/recreation:** General. **Social sciences:** General, political science. **Visual/performing arts:** Art.

Most popular majors. Biology 18%, business/marketing 43%, interdisciplinary studies 11%, liberal arts 7%, natural resources/environmental science 7%, social sciences 7%.

Technology on campus. 225 workstations in dormitories, library, computer center, student center. Dormitories wired for high-speed internet access and linked to campus network. Commuter students can connect to campus network. Online course registration, online library, helpline, repair service, student web hosting, wireless network available.

Student life. Freshman orientation: Mandatory, $75 fee. Preregistration for classes offered. Three-day program includes outdoor experiences, just before classes start. **Housing:** Coed dorms, special housing for disabled, apartments available. $300 fully refundable deposit, deadline 9/1. **Activities:** Campus ministries, choral groups, dance, drama, international student organizations, music ensembles, radio station, student government, student newspaper, global connections club, Amnesty International, LBGI organization, English club, Wooch Een Native student organization.

Athletics. Intramural: Basketball, softball, tennis, volleyball, weight lifting.

Student services. Adult student services, alcohol/substance abuse counseling, career counseling, student employment services, financial aid counseling, health services, minority student services, personal counseling, placement for graduates, veterans' counselor, women's services. **Physically disabled:** Services for visually, hearing impaired.

Contact. E-mail: admissions@uas.alaska.edu
Phone: (907) 796-6100 Toll-free number: (877) 465-4827
Fax: (907) 796-6365
Joe Nelson, Admissions Director, University of Alaska Southeast, 11120 Glacier Highway, Juneau, AK 99801-8681

Arizona

American Indian College of the Assemblies of God

Phoenix, Arizona
www.aicag.edu   CB code: 2597

▶ Private 4-year Bible and teachers college affiliated with the Assemblies of God
▶ Residential campus in very large city
▶ 91 undergraduates
▶ Application essay required

General. Founded in 1957. Regionally accredited. **Degrees:** 6 bachelor's, 8 associate awarded. **Location:** 15 miles from downtown. **Calendar:** Semester. **Full-time faculty:** 7 total; 29% have terminal degrees, 14% minority, 57% women. **Part-time faculty:** 14 total; 29% minority, 29% women.

Freshman class profile.

GPA 3.0-3.49:	26%	Out-of-state:	13%
GPA 2.0-2.99:	62%	Live on campus:	50%

Basis for selection. Applicants must show Christian commitment, willingness to abide by Student Handbook, favorable reference from home pastor, and ability to complete college-level instruction through SAT/ACT score and transcripts. ACT/SAT requirement may be waived by approval of Academic Dean when other evidence of student ability is available.

2015-2016 Annual costs. Tuition/fees: $19,182. Room/board: $6,202. Books/supplies: $400. Personal expenses: $2,900.

Application procedures. Admission: No deadline. No application fee. Admission notification on a rolling basis. Students admitted with proper paperwork through first week of semester. **Financial aid:** Priority date 4/1; no closing date. FAFSA required. Applicants notified on a rolling basis starting 7/15.

Academics. Special study options: Accelerated study, double major, ESL, independent study, internships, liberal arts/career combination, teacher certification program. **Credit/placement by examination:** AP, CLEP, institutional tests. **Support services:** Learning center, reduced course load, remedial instruction, study skills assistance, tutoring.

Majors. Education: Elementary. **Theology:** Theology.

Most popular majors. Education 34%, theological studies 66%.

Technology on campus. 39 workstations in library, computer center, student center.

Student life. Freshman orientation: Mandatory. Preregistration for classes offered. **Policies:** Religious observance required. **Housing:** Guaranteed on-campus for freshmen. Single-sex dorms, special housing for disabled available. **Activities:** Choral groups, music ensembles, student government, associated student body, campus missions fellowship.

Athletics. Intercollegiate: Basketball. **Intramural:** Basketball. **Team name:** Warriors.

Student services. Adult student services, chaplain/spiritual director, career counseling, student employment services, financial aid counseling, personal counseling, placement for graduates.

Contact. E-mail: aicadm@aicag.edu
Phone: (602) 944-3335 ext. 232
Toll-free number: (800) 933-3828 ext. 232 Fax: (602) 944-8665
Larisa Garman, Director of Enrollment Management, American Indian College of the Assemblies of God, 10020 North 15th Avenue, Phoenix, AZ 85021-2199

Argosy University: Online

Phoenix, Arizona
www.online.argosy.edu

▶ For-profit 4-year virtual university
▶ Very large city
▶ 8,917 degree-seeking undergraduates

General. Regionally accredited. **Degrees:** 671 bachelor's, 376 associate awarded; master's, doctoral offered. **Calendar:** Differs by program. **Full-time faculty:** 88 total. **Part-time faculty:** 1,334 total.

Basis for selection. Open admission.

2015-2016 Annual costs. Tuition/fees: $16,830. **Additional information:** College of Health Sciences programs range $450-$575 per credit-hour-hour. Additional program fees may apply. All costs are subject to change.

Application procedures. Admission: Closing date 9/13. $50 fee. **Financial aid:** No deadline.

Academics. Credit/placement by examination: AP, CLEP.

Majors. Business: Business admin. **Liberal arts:** Arts/sciences. **Protective services:** Law enforcement admin. **Psychology:** General.

Contact. Phone: (866) 427-4679
Matt Gavlik, Senior Director of Admissions, Argosy University: Online, 2233 West Dunlap Avenue, Phoenix, AZ 85021

Argosy University: Phoenix

Phoenix, Arizona
www.argosy.edu/phoenix

▶ For-profit 4-year university
▶ Very large city
▶ 219 degree-seeking undergraduates

General. Regionally accredited. **Degrees:** 28 bachelor's, 2 associate awarded; master's, professional, doctoral offered. **Calendar:** Differs by program. **Full-time faculty:** 25 total. **Part-time faculty:** 58 total.

Basis for selection. Open admission.

2015-2016 Annual costs. Tuition/fees: $16,842. **Additional information:** College of Health Sciences programs range $450-$575 per credit-hour-hour. Additional program fees may apply. All costs are subject to change.

Application procedures. Admission: Closing date 9/13. $50 fee. **Financial aid:** No deadline.

Academics. Credit/placement by examination: AP, CLEP.

Majors. Business: Business admin. **Liberal arts:** Arts/sciences. **Protective services:** Law enforcement admin. **Psychology:** General.

Contact. Phone: (602) 216-2600
Lori Smith, Senior Director of Admissions, Argosy University: Phoenix, 2233 West Dunlap Avenue, Phoenix, AZ 85021

Arizona Christian University

Phoenix, Arizona
www.arizonachristian.edu   CB code: 4736

▶ Private 4-year Bible and liberal arts college affiliated with the nondenominational tradition
▶ Residential campus in very large city
▶ 644 degree-seeking undergraduates: 3% part-time, 39% women, 12% African American, 1% Asian American, 17% Hispanic/Latino, 1% Native American, 1% Native Hawaiian/Pacific islander, 6% Multi-racial, non-Hispanic, 3% international
▶ 51% of applicants admitted
▶ SAT or ACT (ACT writing optional), application essay required
▶ 38% graduate within 6 years

General. Founded in 1960. Regionally accredited. **Degrees:** 100 bachelor's, 1 associate awarded. **ROTC:** Air Force. **Calendar:** Semester, limited summer session. **Full-time faculty:** 14 total. **Part-time faculty:** 83 total. **Class size:** 80% < 20, 14% 20-39, 3% 40-49, 1% 50-99, less than 1% >100.

Freshman class profile. 486 applied, 249 admitted, 121 enrolled.

Mid 50% test scores			
SAT critical reading:	430-560	GPA 3.0-3.49:	31%
SAT math:	470-550	GPA 2.0-2.99:	35%
ACT composite:	19-23	Return as sophomores:	55%
GPA 3.75 or higher:	20%	Out-of-state:	27%
GPA 3.50-3.74:	12%	Live on campus:	54%
		International:	2%

Basis for selection. Written testimony of conversion experience required; school achievement record and recommendations are very important. **Home schooled:** Transcript of courses and grades required. **Learning Disabled:** May be accepted on a provisional status and limited to 12 credit hours per semester.

2016-2017 Annual costs. Tuition/fees (projected): $23,896. Room/board: $9,548. Books/supplies: $1,200. Personal expenses: $2,000.

2014-2015 Financial aid. Need-based: 144 full-time freshmen applied for aid; 123 deemed to have need; 123 received aid. Average need met was 62%. Average scholarship/grant was $3,905; average loan $2,931. 68% of total undergraduate aid awarded as scholarships/grants, 32% as loans/jobs. **Non-need-based:** Awarded to 131 full-time undergraduates, including 63 freshmen. Scholarships awarded for academics, athletics, leadership, music/drama.

Application procedures. Admission: Priority date 4/1; deadline 8/15 (receipt date). $30 fee, may be waived for applicants with need. Application must be submitted online. Admission notification on a rolling basis. **Financial aid:** No deadline. FAFSA required. Applicants notified on a rolling basis.

Academics. Special study options: Distance learning, double major, dual enrollment of high school students, independent study, internships, study abroad, teacher certification program. **Credit/placement by examination:** AP, CLEP, SAT, ACT, institutional tests. 30 credit hours maximum toward bachelor's degree. **Support services:** Remedial instruction, study skills assistance, tutoring.

Majors. Biology: General. **Business:** Business admin. **Communications:** General. **Education:** Biology, business, elementary, English, mathematics, music, science, secondary, social studies. **Psychology:** General, counseling, family. **Social sciences:** U.S. government. **Theology:** Bible, lay ministry, sacred music. **Visual/performing arts:** Voice/opera.

Most popular majors. Business/marketing 21%, communications/journalism 13%, education 16%, psychology 23%, theological studies 19%.

Technology on campus. 35 workstations in dormitories, library, computer center. Dormitories wired for high-speed internet access. Online course registration, online library, wireless network available.

Student life. Freshman orientation: Mandatory. Preregistration for classes offered. Held the beginning of each semester. **Policies:** Religious observance required. **Housing:** Guaranteed on-campus for freshmen. Coed dorms, special housing for disabled available. $200 nonrefundable deposit, deadline 5/1. **Activities:** Jazz band, campus ministries, choral groups, music ensembles, musical theater, Pre-law society, Pre-med club, urban outreach ministries, campus events committee, athletic events committee, intramural sports committee, student life marketing team, missions.

Athletics. NAIA, NCCAA. **Intercollegiate:** Baseball M, basketball, cross-country, football (tackle) M, golf, soccer, softball W, tennis, track and field, volleyball W. **Intramural:** Basketball, football (non-tackle), soccer, table tennis, volleyball. **Team name:** Firestorm.

Student services. Adult student services, chaplain/spiritual director, student employment services, financial aid counseling, personal counseling, veterans' counselor.

Contact. E-mail: admissions@arizonachristian.edu
Phone: (602) 386-4100 Toll-free number: (800) 247-2697
Fax: (602) 404-2159
Lambert Cruz, Registrar & Asst Dir Enrollment Mgmt, Arizona Christian University, 2625 East Cactus Road, Phoenix, AZ 85032-7042

Arizona State University

Tempe, Arizona
www.asu.edu

CB member
CB code: 4007

- Public 4-year university
- Commuter campus in small city

- 41,222 degree-seeking undergraduates: 8% part-time, 43% women, 4% African American, 7% Asian American, 19% Hispanic/Latino, 1% Native American, 4% Multi-racial, non-Hispanic, 11% international
- 9,584 degree-seeking graduate students
- 83% of applicants admitted
- 66% graduate within 6 years; 18% enter graduate study

General. Founded in 1885. Regionally accredited. Additional locations include ASU at the West campus, in northwest Phoenix, welcomes students studying business, education and interdisciplinary arts and sciences. ASU at the Downtown Phoenix campus in metropolitan Phoenix creates strong academic and career connections for students with media, healthcare, corporate and government organizations. ASU at the Polytechnic campus in east Mesa, is home to a tight-knit academic community in the fields of interdisciplinary science, engineering and technology, management and business, education and liberal arts. **Degrees:** 9,053 bachelor's awarded; master's, professional, doctoral offered. **ROTC:** Army, Naval, Air Force. **Location:** ASU at the Tempe campus is 2 miles from Phoenix, within the Phoenix Metropolitan area. **Calendar:** Semester, extensive summer session. **Class size:** 40% < 20, 36% 20-39, 6% 40-49, 12% 50-99, 6% >100. **Special facilities:** Arboretum, art, anthropology, geology, history, and sports museums, herbarium, planetarium, galleries, collections, biodesign institute, global institute of sustainability, creative writing center.

Freshman class profile. 25,380 applied, 21,042 admitted, 8,348 enrolled.

Mid 50% test scores			
SAT critical reading:	510-630	Rank in top quarter:	60%
SAT math:	520-640	Rank in top tenth:	29%
ACT composite:	23-28	End year in good standing:	91%
GPA 3.75 or higher:	32%	Return as sophomores:	86%
GPA 3.50-3.74:	22%	Out-of-state:	37%
GPA 3.0-3.49:	34%	Live on campus:	74%
GPA 2.0-2.99:	12%	International:	13%

Basis for selection. Applicants must meet at least one of the following: Top 25% in high school graduating class, 3.0 GPA in competency courses (4.00 = "A"), ACT 22 (24 nonresidents), SAT Reasoning 1040 (1110 nonresidents). SAT or ACT recommended. SAT/ACT required for honors college and for some majors. Auditions, interviews and/or portfolios required in certain majors. **Home schooled:** Evaluation of laboratory science courses, affidavit of completion of secondary school education, and SAT/ACT required.

High school preparation. College-preparatory program recommended. 16 units required. Required units include English 4, mathematics 4, social studies 1, history 1, science 3 (laboratory 3) and foreign language 2. One unit fine arts required; foreign language units must be from same language. Additional requirements vary by program.

2015-2016 Annual costs. Tuition/fees: $10,156; $25,456 out-of-state. Room/board: $11,061. Books/supplies: $1,081. Personal expenses: $2,028.

2014-2015 Financial aid. Need-based: 6,039 full-time freshmen applied for aid; 4,409 deemed to have need; 4,409 received aid. Average need met was 71%. Average scholarship/grant was $12,181; average loan $3,097. 62% of total undergraduate aid awarded as scholarships/grants, 38% as loans/jobs. **Non-need-based:** Awarded to 9,169 full-time undergraduates, including 2,735 freshmen. Scholarships awarded for academics, art, athletics, leadership, music/drama, state residency.

Application procedures. Admission: $50 fee ($65 out-of-state), may be waived for applicants with need. Admission notification on a rolling basis beginning on or about 9/1. Must reply by May 1 or within 2 week(s) if notified thereafter. **Financial aid:** Priority date 3/1; no closing date. FAFSA required. Applicants notified on a rolling basis starting 3/1.

Academics. Special study options: Accelerated study, combined bachelor's/graduate degree, cooperative education, distance learning, double major, ESL, honors, independent study, internships, liberal arts/career combination, semester at sea, student-designed major, study abroad, teacher certification program, Washington semester. Domestic and international internships, study abroad programs, work-study programs, educational programs. **Credit/placement by examination:** AP, CLEP, IB, SAT, ACT, institutional tests. 60 credit hours maximum toward bachelor's degree. **Support services:** Learning center, study skills assistance, tutoring, writing center.

Honors college/program. Separate application required. GPA (Arizona Board of Regents GPA based on 16 competency courses), class rank, SAT/ACT, essay, two letters of recommendation.

Majors. Architecture: Architecture, environmental design, landscape, urban/community planning. **Area/ethnic studies:** African-American, Asian, Asian-American, Chicano/Hispanic-American/Latino, Native American, women's. **Biology:** General, biochemistry, bioinformatics, biophysics, microbiology, molecular. **Business:** Accounting, actuarial science, business admin, construction management, entrepreneurial studies, finance, management science, marketing, purchasing. **Communications:** Communications/speech/rhetoric. **Computer sciences:** General, computer science, informatics. **Conservation:** Environmental studies. **Education:** Early childhood, elementary, music, secondary, special ed. **Engineering:** Aerospace, biomedical, chemical, civil, computer, construction, electrical, industrial, materials, mechanical. **English:** English lit. **Foreign languages:** East Asian, French, German, Italian, Russian, Spanish. **Health services:** Communication disorders, music therapy. **History:** General. **Math:** General, computational. **Philosophy/religion:** Judaic, philosophy, religion. **Physical sciences:** General, chemistry, geology, physics. **Psychology:** General. **Social sciences:** Anthropology, economics, geography, GIS/cartography, political science, sociology. **Visual/performing arts:** General, art, dance, digital arts, dramatic, graphic design, industrial design, interior design, music, music performance, music theory/composition. **Work/family studies:** Family resources.

Most popular majors. Biology 9%, business/marketing 23%, engineering/engineering technologies 10%, interdisciplinary studies 6%, social sciences 10%, visual/performing arts 8%.

Technology on campus. 2,421 workstations in dormitories, library, computer center, student center. Dormitories wired for high-speed internet access and linked to campus network. Commuter students can connect to campus network. Online course registration, online library, helpline, repair service, student web hosting, wireless network available.

Student life. Freshman orientation: Mandatory. Preregistration for classes offered. One-day programs held between March and July. **Policies:** First-time freshmen expected to live on-campus. **Housing:** Guaranteed on-campus for freshmen. Coed dorms, special housing for disabled, apartments, fraternity/sorority housing available. Honors housing, freshmen housing, residential colleges available. **Activities:** Bands, campus ministries, choral groups, dance, drama, film society, international student organizations, music ensembles, Model UN, musical theater, student government, student newspaper, symphony orchestra, over 850 organizations available.

Athletics. NCAA. **Intercollegiate:** Baseball M, basketball, cross-country, diving, football (tackle) M, golf, gymnastics W, ice hockey M, lacrosse W, sand volleyball W, soccer W, softball W, swimming, tennis W, track and field, volleyball W, water polo W, wrestling M. **Intramural:** Badminton, basketball, football (non-tackle), racquetball, sand volleyball, soccer, softball, table tennis, ultimate frisbee, volleyball. **Team name:** Sun Devils.

Student services. Career counseling, student employment services, financial aid counseling, health services, legal services, minority student services, on-campus daycare, personal counseling, placement for graduates, veterans' counselor. **Physically disabled:** Services for visually, speech, hearing impaired.

Contact. E-mail: admissions@asu.edu
Phone: (480) 965-7788 Fax: (480) 965-3610
Melissa Pizzo, Dean, Admission and Financial Aid Services, Arizona State University, PO Box 870112, Tempe, AZ 85287-0112

Art Institute of Phoenix
Phoenix, Arizona
www.artinstitutes.edu/phoenix   CB code: 4003

- For-profit 3-year culinary school and visual arts college
- Residential campus in very large city
- 1,009 undergraduates
- Application essay, interview required

General. Accredited by ACICS. **Degrees:** 117 bachelor's, 51 associate awarded. **Calendar:** Quarter, extensive summer session. **Full-time faculty:** 43 total. **Part-time faculty:** 68 total. **Special facilities:** Culinary labs, video studio, computer labs, editing suites, sound lab, herb garden.

Basis for selection. High school diploma or GED required; high school GPA considered.

2015-2016 Annual costs. Books/supplies: $2,100. **Additional information:** Diploma programs range from $23,088-$26,455; Associates programs: $43,290; Bachelors programs: $86,580. Books, supplies, fees range depending on program level and course of study. All costs are subject to change.

Application procedures. Admission: Closing date 11/11 (receipt date). $50 fee. Admission notification on a rolling basis. **Financial aid:** No deadline. FAFSA required.

Academics. Special study options: Distance learning, independent study, internships. **Credit/placement by examination:** AP, CLEP, IB, SAT, ACT, institutional tests. **Support services:** Learning center, reduced course load, remedial instruction, study skills assistance, tutoring.

Majors. BACHELOR'S. Business: Apparel. **Communications technology:** Animation/special effects. **Computer sciences:** Computer graphics, web page design, webmaster. **Visual/performing arts:** Cinematography, commercial photography, commercial/advertising art, graphic design, interior design. **ASSOCIATE. Visual/performing arts:** Graphic design.

Most popular majors. Health sciences 92%, personal/culinary services 8%.

Student life. Freshman orientation: Mandatory. Preregistration for classes offered. **Housing:** Apartments available. $150 fully refundable deposit, deadline 10/13. **Activities:** Film society.

Student services. Adult student services, career counseling, student employment services, financial aid counseling, personal counseling, placement for graduates.

Contact. E-mail: aipxadm@aii.edu
Phone: (602) 331-7500 Toll-free number: (800) 474-2479
Fax: (602) 331-5301
Stacey Till, Senior Director of Admissions, Art Institute of Phoenix, 2233 West Dunlap Avenue, Phoenix, AZ 85021-2859

Art Institute of Tucson
Tucson, Arizona
www.artinstitutes.edu/tucson   CB code: 7551

- For-profit 4-year culinary school and visual arts college
- Commuter campus in very large city
- 335 degree-seeking undergraduates
- Application essay, interview required

General. Accredited by ACICS. Selected online courses offered through consortium agreement with the Art Institute of Pittsburgh online division. **Degrees:** 51 bachelor's, 39 associate awarded. **Location:** 115 miles from Phoenix. **Calendar:** Quarter, limited summer session. **Full-time faculty:** 8 total. **Part-time faculty:** 39 total. **Special facilities:** Fully equipped culinary and pastry kitchens, video production room for television, film, animated productions.

Basis for selection. GPA, school record, and talent most important. Applicants to Media Arts & Animation and Game Art & Design bachelor's programs must submit a portfolio. Artwork portfolio required. **Home schooled:** Transcript of courses and grades, interview required.

2015-2016 Annual costs. Tuition/fees: $21,745. Room only: $4,725. Books/supplies: $1,500.

Application procedures. Admission: No deadline. $50 fee. Application must be submitted on paper. Admission notification on a rolling basis.

Academics. Special study options: Accelerated study. **Credit/placement by examination:** AP, CLEP. **Support services:** Tutoring.

Majors. Business: Fashion. **Communications:** Advertising. **Communications technology:** Animation/special effects. **Computer sciences:** Web page design. **Visual/performing arts:** Cinematography, fashion design, graphic design, interior design, photography.

Technology on campus. Online library available.

Student life. Freshman orientation: Mandatory, $100 fee. Preregistration for classes offered. **Housing:** Apartments available. **Activities:** Film society, international student organizations, American Society of Interior Designers student chapter, fashion club.

Student services. Career counseling, student employment services, financial aid counseling, personal counseling, placement for graduates, veterans' counselor.

Contact. Phone: (520) 318-2700 Toll-free number: (866) 690-8850
Fax: (520) 881-4794
Amanda Hosking, Senior Director of Admissions, Art Institute of Tucson, 5099 East Grant Road, #100, Tucson, AZ 85712

Brown Mackie College: Tucson
Tucson, Arizona
www.brownmackie.edu/Tucson   CB code: 3458

- For-profit 4-year career college
- Commuter campus in very large city

- 611 undergraduates
- Interview required

General. Accredited by ACICS. **Degrees:** 19 bachelor's, 135 associate awarded. **Location:** 117 miles from Phoenix. **Calendar:** Differs by program, extensive summer session. **Full-time faculty:** 8 total. **Part-time faculty:** 76 total. **Special facilities:** Labs for medical, surgical technology, computer networking, and occupational therapy assistant programs.

Basis for selection. Open admission, but selective for some programs. Additional admissions criteria for Occupational Therapy Assistant program. **Home schooled:** Transcript of courses and grades, state high school equivalency certificate, interview required.

2015-2016 Annual costs. Tuition/fees: $17,885. Books/supplies: $1,500.

Application procedures. Admission: No deadline. No application fee. Application must be submitted on paper. Admission notification on a rolling basis.

Academics. Special study options: Independent study, internships, liberal arts/career combination. **Credit/placement by examination:** AP, CLEP. **Support services:** Learning center, remedial instruction, study skills assistance, tutoring, writing center.

Majors. Business: Accounting, accounting technology, business admin. **Computer sciences:** Computer science.

Technology on campus. PC or laptop required. 150 workstations in library, computer center. Online library, wireless network available.

Student life. Freshman orientation: Mandatory. Preregistration for classes offered. Conducted prior to first class.

Student services. Career counseling, student employment services, financial aid counseling, personal counseling, placement for graduates, veterans' counselor.

Contact. E-mail: stklein@brownmackie.edu
Phone: (520) 391-3300 Fax: (520) 319-3495
Stacy Klein, Senior Director of Admissions, Brown Mackie College: Tucson, 4585 East Speedway Boulevard, Tucson, AZ 85712

Chamberlain College of Nursing: Phoenix
Phoenix, Arizona
www.chamberlain.edu   CB code: 5768

- For-profit 4-year nursing college
- Large city
- 569 degree-seeking undergraduates
- SAT or ACT required

General. Degrees: 116 bachelor's awarded. **Calendar:** Semester. **Full-time faculty:** 11 total; 100% women. **Part-time faculty:** 49 total; 10% minority, 96% women.

Basis for selection. Test scores, GPA, class rank very important.

2015-2016 Annual costs. Tuition/fees: $18,160. Books/supplies: $1,400. Personal expenses: $2,452.

Application procedures. Admission: No deadline. $95 fee. Admission notification on a rolling basis. **Financial aid:** No deadline.

Academics. Special study options: Accelerated study, distance learning. **Credit/placement by examination:** AP, CLEP.

Majors. Health services: Nursing (RN).

Contact. Chamberlain College of Nursing: Phoenix, 2149 West Dunlap Avenue, Phoenix, AZ 85021

DeVry University: Phoenix
Phoenix, Arizona
www.devry.edu   CB code: 4277

- For-profit 4-year university
- Commuter campus in large city
- 730 degree-seeking undergraduates
- Interview required

General. Founded in 1967. Regionally accredited. Additional locations: Glendale, Mesa, Northeast Phoenix, Henderson (NV). **Degrees:** 180 bachelor's, 23 associate awarded; master's offered. **ROTC:** Air Force. **Calendar:** Semester, extensive summer session. **Full-time faculty:** 32 total; 9% minority, 38% women. **Part-time faculty:** 125 total; 13% minority, 34% women.

Basis for selection. Applicants must have high school diploma or equivalent or a degree from accredited postsecondary institution, demonstrate proficiency in basic college-level skills through SAT or ACT scores or institution-administered placement exams, and be at least 17 years of age on the first day of classes. New students may enter at beginning of any semester. CPT accepted.

High school preparation. College-preparatory program recommended.

2015-2016 Annual costs. Tuition/fees: $17,132. Books/supplies: $1,320. Personal expenses: $2,376.

Financial aid. All financial aid based on need.

Application procedures. Admission: No deadline. $40 fee. Admission notification on a rolling basis. **Financial aid:** No deadline. FAFSA required. Applicants notified on a rolling basis.

Academics. Special study options: Accelerated study, distance learning. **Credit/placement by examination:** AP, CLEP, institutional tests. **Support services:** Learning center, remedial instruction, tutoring.

Majors. Business: Business admin. **Computer sciences:** Networking, systems analysis, web page design. **Engineering:** Software. **Health services:** Clinical lab science.

Most popular majors. Business/marketing 46%, computer/information sciences 19%, engineering/engineering technologies 29%, health sciences 6%.

Technology on campus. 436 workstations in library, computer center. Online course registration, online library, helpline available.

Student life. Freshman orientation: Mandatory. Preregistration for classes offered. **Activities:** Institute of Electrical and Electronics Engineers, Campus Crusaders for Christ, travel club, Sigma Beta Delta, computer society, inventors club, sports compact car club, Tau Alpha Pi, hockey league.

Athletics. Intramural: Field hockey M, golf, softball.

Student services. Career counseling, student employment services, financial aid counseling, placement for graduates, veterans' counselor. **Physically disabled:** Services for visually, hearing impaired.

Contact. E-mail: admissions@phx.devry.edu
Phone: (602) 870-9201 Toll-free number: (800) 528-0250
Fax: (602) 331-1494
Director of Admissions, DeVry University: Phoenix, 2149 West Dunlap Avenue, Phoenix, AZ 85021-2995

Dunlap-Stone University
Phoenix, Arizona
www.dunlap-stone.edu

- For-profit 4-year virtual career college
- Commuter campus in very large city
- 50 degree-seeking undergraduates

General. Accredited by DETC. **Degrees:** 2 associate awarded. **Calendar:** Differs by program, extensive summer session. **Full-time faculty:** 2 total. **Part-time faculty:** 50 total; 20% have terminal degrees.

Basis for selection. Open admission. **Learning Disabled:** Learning disability accommodations reviewed on case by case basis.

2015-2016 Annual costs. Tuition/fees: $9,300. Books/supplies: $450.

Application procedures. Admission: No deadline. $50 fee. Admission notification on a rolling basis.

Academics. Special study options: Accelerated study, distance learning. **Credit/placement by examination:** AP, CLEP, IB. 15 credit hours maximum toward associate degree, 20 toward bachelor's.

Majors. Business: International.

Technology on campus. PC or laptop required. Online library, helpline available.

Student life. Activities: Student newspaper.

Contact. E-mail: info@dunlap-stone.edu
Phone: (602) 648-5750 Toll-free number: (800) 474-8013
Fax: (602) 648-5755
Caulyne Barron, Admissions Director, Dunlap-Stone University, 11225 North 28th Drive Suite B201, Phoenix, AZ 85029

Embry-Riddle Aeronautical University: Prescott Campus

Prescott, Arizona
www.embryriddle.edu

CB member
CB code: 4305

▶ Private 4-year university
▶ Residential campus in large town
▶ 2,193 degree-seeking undergraduates: 5% part-time, 23% women, 2% African American, 5% Asian American, 4% Hispanic/Latino, 1% Native Hawaiian/Pacific islander, 10% Multi-racial, non-Hispanic, 10% international
▶ 60 degree-seeking graduate students
▶ 79% of applicants admitted
▶ 59% graduate within 6 years; 18% enter graduate study

General. Founded in 1978. Regionally accredited. Eastern residential campus in Daytona Beach, Florida. More than 170 continuing education centers located throughout the United States and Europe. **Degrees:** 318 bachelor's awarded; master's offered. **ROTC;** Army, Air Force. **Location:** 100 miles from Phoenix. **Calendar:** Semester, extensive summer session. **Full-time faculty:** 111 total; 76% have terminal degrees, 12% minority, 21% women. **Part-time faculty:** 68 total; 44% have terminal degrees, 10% minority, 32% women. **Special facilities:** Machine vision laboratory, supersonic wind tunnel, fleet of 40 aircraft, engineering and technical center, aviation safety center.

Freshman class profile. 1,908 applied, 1,510 admitted, 1,275 enrolled.

Mid 50% test scores		GPA 2.0-2.99:	9%
SAT critical reading:	490-610	Rank in top quarter:	57%
SAT math:	520-640	Rank in top tenth:	28%
SAT writing:	470-590	Return as sophomores:	77%
ACT composite:	23-28	Out-of-state:	80%
GPA 3.75 or higher:	42%	Live on campus:	91%
GPA 3.50-3.74:	20%	International:	5%
GPA 3.0-3.49:	29%		

Basis for selection. High school GPA, class rank, test scores are most important. Specific requirements vary by degree program. Flight program applicants must pass medical examination for Class I or II Federal Aviation Administration Medical Certificate at least 60 calendar days prior to enrollment. SAT or ACT recommended. Interviews recommended. **Home schooled:** Transcript of courses and grades required.

High school preparation. College-preparatory program required. 13 units required; 15 recommended. Required and recommended units include English 4, mathematics 4, social studies 2, science 2-3 (laboratory 1) and foreign language 1.

2015-2016 Annual costs. Tuition/fees: $33,144. Room/board: $9,990.

Application procedures. Admission: Priority date 1/15; no deadline. $50 fee, may be waived for applicants with need. Admission notification on a rolling basis. Must reply by May 1 or within 4 week(s) if notified thereafter. **Financial aid:** Priority date 3/1; no closing date. FAFSA required. Applicants notified on a rolling basis; must reply within 4 week(s) of notification.

Academics. Special study options: Accelerated study, cooperative education, double major, dual enrollment of high school students, ESL, exchange student, honors, internships, study abroad. **Credit/placement by examination:** AP, CLEP, IB. **Support services:** Remedial instruction, study skills assistance, tutoring, writing center.

Majors. Business: International. **Computer sciences:** Computer science. **Engineering:** Aerospace, computer, electrical, mechanical, software. **Physical sciences:** Astronomy, atmospheric science. **Protective services:** Computer forensics, financial forensics, forensics. **Psychology:** Forensic, industrial. **Social sciences:** International relations.

Most popular majors. Business/marketing 8%, engineering/engineering technologies 43%, social sciences 16%, trade and industry 27%.

Technology on campus. 475 workstations in library, computer center, student center. Dormitories wired for high-speed internet access and linked to campus network. Commuter students can connect to campus network. Online library, helpline, wireless network available.

Student life. Freshman orientation: Mandatory. Preregistration for classes offered. **Housing:** Guaranteed on-campus for freshmen. Coed dorms available. $300 fully refundable deposit, deadline 6/1. **Activities:** Campus ministries, international student organizations, music ensembles, radio station, student government, student newspaper.

Athletics. NAIA. **Intercollegiate:** Basketball M, cross-country, golf, soccer, softball W, volleyball W, wrestling M. **Intramural:** Basketball, bowling, football (non-tackle), racquetball, soccer, softball, table tennis, tennis, volleyball, weight lifting W. **Team name:** Eagles.

Student services. Alcohol/substance abuse counseling, chaplain/spiritual director, career counseling, student employment services, financial aid counseling, health services, minority student services, personal counseling, veterans' counselor, women's services. **Physically disabled:** Services for visually, speech impaired.

Contact. E-mail: Prescott@erau.edu
Phone: (928) 777-6600 Toll-free number: (800) 888-3728
Fax: (928) 777-6606
Sara Bofferding, Director, Admissions-Prescott Campus, Embry-Riddle Aeronautical University: Prescott Campus, 3700 Willow Creek Road, Prescott, AZ 86301-3720

Grand Canyon University

Phoenix, Arizona
www.gcu.edu

CB code: 4331

▶ For-profit 4-year university
▶ Residential campus in very large city
▶ 39,400 undergraduates

General. Founded in 1949. Regionally accredited. **Degrees:** 6,916 bachelor's awarded; master's, doctoral offered. **ROTC:** Army. **Calendar:** Semester, limited summer session. **Full-time faculty:** 210 total. **Part-time faculty:** 2,346 total. **Class size:** 66% < 20, 33% 20-39, less than 1% 40-49, less than 1% 50-99. **Special facilities:** Cadaver laboratory.

Basis for selection. Admissions based on graduation from high school (or GED) and academic potential demonstrated by 2.25 GPA or standardized test scores. Any student willing to uphold the University's vision and mission and who is open to possibility of spiritual as well as intellectual development is encouraged to apply. SAT or ACT recommended. **Home schooled:** Transcript of courses and grades required.

High school preparation. Recommended units include English 4, mathematics 4, social studies 2, science 3 (laboratory 1) and foreign language 1.

2015-2016 Annual costs. Tuition/fees: $17,150. Room/board: $7,900. Books/supplies: $1,200. Personal expenses: $2,400.

Financial aid. Non-need-based: Scholarships awarded for academics, alumni affiliation, art, athletics, leadership, minority status, music/drama, religious affiliation, ROTC, state residency.

Application procedures. Admission: No deadline. No application fee. Admission notification on a rolling basis. **Financial aid:** No deadline. FAFSA required. Applicants notified on a rolling basis.

Academics. Special study options: Accelerated study, combined bachelor's/graduate degree, cooperative education, distance learning, double major, dual enrollment of high school students, exchange student, honors, independent study, internships, liberal arts/career combination, study abroad, teacher certification program. **Credit/placement by examination:** AP, CLEP, IB, institutional tests. 30 credit hours maximum toward bachelor's degree. **Support services:** Learning center, reduced course load, remedial instruction, study skills assistance, tutoring, writing center.

Majors. Biology: General, exercise physiology. **Business:** Accounting, business admin, entrepreneurial studies, finance, information resources management, marketing. **Communications:** Broadcast journalism, communications/speech/rhetoric, journalism. **Education:** Biology, chemistry, drama/dance, early childhood, elementary, English, mathematics, music, physical, secondary, special ed. **English:** English lit. **Health services:** Athletic training, clinical lab science, facilities admin, health care admin, nursing (RN), respiratory therapy technology, substance abuse counseling. **History:** General. **Parks/recreation:** Sports admin. **Philosophy/religion:** Christian. **Protective services:** Disaster management, firefighting, forensics, law enforcement admin. **Social sciences:** Sociology. **Theology:** Bible, pastoral counseling, youth ministry. **Visual/performing arts:** Cinematography, digital arts, dramatic, piano/keyboard, voice/opera.

Most popular majors. Business/marketing 16%, education 11%, health sciences 58%.

Technology on campus. 95 workstations in library, computer center, student center. Dormitories wired for high-speed internet access and linked to campus network. Commuter students can connect to campus network. Online course registration, online library, helpline, wireless network available.

Student life. Freshman orientation: Mandatory. Preregistration for classes offered. Held the week before start of Fall semester. **Policies:** No alcohol, drugs, weapons, drug paraphernalia, spice or candles allowed. Smoking allowed outdoors only. **Housing:** Guaranteed on-campus for all undergraduates. Coed dorms, special housing for disabled, apartments available. **Activities:** Bands, campus ministries, choral groups, dance, drama, international student organizations, literary magazine, music ensembles, musical theater, student government, student newspaper, international student organizations, honors organizations, professional clubs, Christ-purposed relationships, ethnic diversity in Christ, wildlife society, student health advocates, law society, Latino student organization, Adopt-A-Block.

Athletics. NCAA. **Intercollegiate:** Baseball M, basketball, cheerleading, cross-country, diving, golf, soccer, softball W, swimming, tennis, track and field, volleyball, wrestling M. **Intramural:** Basketball, bowling, football (non-tackle), softball, volleyball. **Team name:** Lopes.

Student services. Adult student services, alcohol/substance abuse counseling, chaplain/spiritual director, career counseling, student employment services, financial aid counseling, health services, on-campus daycare, personal counseling, placement for graduates, veterans' counselor, women's services. **Physically disabled:** Services for visually, speech, hearing impaired.

Contact. E-mail: campusadmissions@gcu.edu
Phone: (877) 533-7017 Toll-free number: (888) 261-2393
Fax: (602) 589-2017
Kim Naig, Director of Admissions, Grand Canyon University, 3300 West Camelback Road, Phoenix, AZ 85017-8562

Harrison Middleton University
Tempe, Arizona
www.hmu.edu

♦ For-profit 4-year virtual university
♦ Small city
♦ 17 degree-seeking undergraduates: 29% women
♦ 65 graduate students
♦ Interview required

General. Accredited by DETC. **Degrees:** 2 bachelor's awarded; master's, doctoral offered. **Location:** 12 miles from Phoenix. **Calendar:** Differs by program.

Basis for selection. Open admission. .

2015-2016 Annual costs. Tuition/fees: $9,150.

Application procedures. Admission: No deadline. $50 fee. Application must be submitted on paper. Admission notification on a rolling basis. **Financial aid:** No deadline.

Academics. Special study options: Combined bachelor's/graduate degree, distance learning, student-designed major. **Credit/placement by examination:** AP, CLEP, IB. 15 credit hours maximum toward associate degree, 30 toward bachelor's.

Majors. Liberal arts: Arts/sciences, humanities. **Philosophy/religion:** Philosophy, religion. **Social sciences:** General.

Contact. E-mail: information@hmu.edu
Phone: (877) 248-6724 Toll-free number: (877) 248-6724
Fax: (800) 762-1622
Lauren Guthrie, Registrar, Harrison Middleton University, 1105 East Broadway Road, Tempe, AZ 85282

International Baptist College
Chandler, Arizona
www.ibcs.edu   CB code: 5461

♦ Private 4-year Bible and seminary college affiliated with the Baptist faith
♦ Residential campus in very large city
♦ 32 degree-seeking undergraduates

♦ 12 graduate students
♦ Application essay required

General. Regionally accredited; also accredited by TRACS. **Degrees:** 7 bachelor's, 1 associate awarded; master's, doctoral offered. **Location:** 20 miles from Phoenix. **Calendar:** 4-1-4, limited summer session. **Full-time faculty:** 5 total. **Part-time faculty:** 15 total.

Freshman class profile.

Out-of-state: 80% **Live on campus:**   67%

Basis for selection. Open admission, but selective for some programs.

2015-2016 Annual costs. Tuition/fees: $10,500. Room/board: $5,900. Books/supplies: $1,000.

Application procedures. Admission: No deadline. No application fee. Admission notification on a rolling basis. **Financial aid:** Closing date 8/1.

Academics. Special study options: Distance learning, internships. **Credit/placement by examination:** AP, CLEP.

Majors. Theology: Bible, missionary, pastoral counseling, religious ed, sacred music.

Technology on campus. Dormitories wired for high-speed internet access. Wireless network available.

Student life. Freshman orientation: Mandatory. Preregistration for classes offered. **Policies:** Religious observance required. **Housing:** Single-sex dorms available. **Activities:** Campus ministries, choral groups, drama, music ensembles, student government.

Athletics. Team name: Arrows.

Student services. Student employment services, personal counseling.

Contact. E-mail: info@ibcs.edu
Phone: (480) 245-7970 Toll-free number: (800) 422-4858 ext. 7970
Fax: (480) 245-7909
Lauren Brady, Director of Public Relations and Enrollment, International Baptist College, 2211 West Germann Road, Chandler, AZ 85286

ITT Technical Institute: Tempe
Tempe, Arizona
www.itt-tech.edu

♦ For-profit 4-year technical college
♦ Commuter campus in small city
♦ 445 undergraduates
♦ Interview required

General. Accredited by ACICS. **Degrees:** 55 bachelor's, 137 associate awarded. **Calendar:** Quarter. **Full-time faculty:** 8 total. **Part-time faculty:** 46 total.

Basis for selection. Satisfactory scores from on-site tests in English and math required.

2015-2016 Annual costs. Per-credit-hour charge, $493, will vary depending on program level and course of study. Academic fee, $200. Some programs require purchase of tools, which could cost an additional $500. All costs subject to change.

Application procedures. Admission: No deadline. No application fee. Admission notification on a rolling basis. **Financial aid:** No deadline.

Academics. Credit/placement by examination: AP, CLEP.

Majors. Business: Accounting/business management, business admin, construction management, e-commerce. **Communications technology:** Animation/special effects. **Computer sciences:** Networking, security. **Protective services:** Law enforcement admin.

Contact. Phone: (602) 437-7500 Toll-free number: (800) 879-4881
Fax: (602) 267-8727
Gene McWhorter, Director of Recruitment, ITT Technical Institute: Tempe, 5005 South Wendler Drive, Tempe, AZ 85282

ITT Technical Institute: Tucson
Tucson, Arizona
www.itt-tech.edu   CB code: 3598

▶ For-profit 4-year technical college
▶ Commuter campus in large city
▶ 400 undergraduates
▶ Interview required

General. Founded in 1984. Accredited by ACICS. Classes begin in March, June, September and December. **Degrees:** 43 bachelor's, 95 associate awarded. **Calendar:** Quarter, extensive summer session. **Full-time faculty:** 7 total. **Part-time faculty:** 27 total.

Basis for selection. Satisfactory scores on institutional tests in English and math required.

2015-2016 Annual costs. Per-credit-hour charge, $493, will vary depending on program level and course of study. Academic fee, $200. Some programs require purchase of tools, which could cost an additional $100 to $500. All costs subject to change.

Application procedures. Admission: No deadline. No application fee. Admission notification on a rolling basis. **Financial aid:** No deadline. FAFSA, institutional form required. Applicants notified on a rolling basis.

Academics. Credit/placement by examination: AP, CLEP. **Support services:** Learning center, tutoring.

Majors. Business: Business admin, construction management, e-commerce. **Communications technology:** Animation/special effects. **Computer sciences:** Networking, security. **Protective services:** Law enforcement admin. **Visual/performing arts:** Game design.

Technology on campus. Online library available.

Student life. Freshman orientation: Available. Preregistration for classes offered.

Student services. Career counseling, student employment services, placement for graduates.

Contact. Phone: (520) 408-7488 Toll-free number: (800) 950-2944
Linda Lemken, Director of Recruitment, ITT Technical Institute: Tucson, 1455 West River Road, Tucson, AZ 85704

National Paralegal College
Phoenix, Arizona
www.nationalparalegal.edu

▶ For-profit 4-year virtual career college
▶ Large city
▶ 1,042 degree-seeking undergraduates: 3% part-time, 86% women
▶ 69 degree-seeking graduate students

General. Regionally accredited; also accredited by DETC. **Degrees:** 84 bachelor's, 124 associate awarded. **Calendar:** Differs by program. **Full-time faculty:** 4 total. **Part-time faculty:** 30 total.

Basis for selection. Open admission.

2015-2016 Annual costs. Tuition/fees: $9,945. Books/supplies: $750.

Academics. Credit/placement by examination: AP.

Contact. Phone: (800) 371-6105 ext. 0
Danielle Backman, Admissions Director, National Paralegal College, 717 East Maryland Avenue, Phoenix, AZ 85014-1561

Northcentral University
Prescott Valley, Arizona
www.ncu.edu   CB code: 3883

▶ For-profit two-year upper-division virtual university
▶ Commuter campus in large town

General. Regionally accredited. **Degrees:** 72 bachelor's awarded; master's, doctoral offered. **Articulation:** Agreements with Rio Salado College, Western Governors University. **Location:** 12 miles from Prescott, 92 miles from

Phoenix. **Calendar:** Differs by program, extensive summer session. **Full-time faculty:** 93 total; 100% have terminal degrees. **Part-time faculty:** 418 total; 100% have terminal degrees.

Student profile. 181 degree-seeking undergraduates. 38% entered as juniors, 11% entered as seniors.

Basis for selection. Open admission. High school transcript, college transcript required. A minimum of 60 semester transfer credits or a conferred Associate's degree are required. Official transcripts from a regionally or nationally accredited institution on file for all transfer credit hours accepted by the University.

2015-2016 Annual costs. Bachelor degree programs: range from $10,526-$13,310; Associates programs: $1,296 per credit hour. Books, supplies, fees range depending on program level and course of study. All costs are subject to change.

Application procedures. Admission: Rolling admission. No application fee. Application must be submitted online. **Financial aid:** No deadline. Applicants notified on a rolling basis.

Academics. Regionally accredited; One-to-One faculty mentored approach; No physical residency;100% doctoral faculty; Applied experiential learning; Weekly course starts; Every course can be started any week; and Competitive tuition. **Special study options:** Distance learning, teacher certification program. **Credit/placement by examination:** AP, CLEP, institutional tests.

Majors. Business: General, accounting, business admin, e-commerce, international, management science, marketing. **Computer sciences:** General. **Education:** Multi-level teacher, special ed. **Health services:** Health care admin. **Human services:** General. **Protective services:** Homeland security, law enforcement admin. **Psychology:** General.

Most popular majors. Business/marketing 37%, education 26%, psychology 43%.

Technology on campus. Online course registration, online library, helpline available.

Student life. Activities: Student newspaper.

Student services. Adult student services, financial aid counseling.

Contact. E-mail: admissions@ncu.edu
Phone: (866) 776-0331 Toll-free number: (866) 776-0331
Fax: (928) 541-7817
Don Fisher, Senior Director of Admissions, Northcentral University, 8667 East Hartford Drive, Scottsdale, AZ 85255

Northern Arizona University
Flagstaff, Arizona   CB member
www.nau.edu   CB code: 4006

▶ Public 4-year university
▶ Residential campus in small city
▶ 24,992 degree-seeking undergraduates: 19% part-time, 59% women, 3% African American, 2% Asian American, 22% Hispanic/Latino, 3% Native American, 5% Multi-racial, non-Hispanic, 4% international
▶ 3,761 degree-seeking graduate students
▶ 78% of applicants admitted
▶ 52% graduate within 6 years

General. Founded in 1899. Regionally accredited. **Degrees:** 5,262 bachelor's awarded; master's, professional, doctoral offered. **ROTC:** Army, Air Force. **Location:** 140 miles from Phoenix. **Calendar:** Semester, extensive summer session. **Full-time faculty:** 1,068 total; 3% have terminal degrees, 15% minority, 50% women. **Part-time faculty:** 553 total; less than 1% have terminal degrees, 13% minority, 64% women. **Class size:** 30% < 20, 49% 20-39, 8% 40-49, 10% 50-99, 3% >100. **Special facilities:** 400-acre forest, observatory, skydome.

Freshman class profile. 28,192 applied, 22,025 admitted, 5,218 enrolled.

Mid 50% test scores		GPA 2.0-2.99:	16%
SAT critical reading:	460-580	Rank in top quarter:	53%
SAT math:	460-570	Rank in top tenth:	22%
SAT writing:	450-560	Return as sophomores:	74%
ACT composite:	20-25	Out-of-state:	36%
GPA 3.75 or higher:	37%	Live on campus:	85%
GPA 3.50-3.74:	17%	International:	3%
GPA 3.0-3.49:	30%		

Basis for selection. Applicants will be considered with one of the following: 1) 3.0 GPA or top 25% class rank with no deficiencies in required college preparatory courses; 2) 2.5 core GPA or top 50% class rank with no more than one deficiency in any two subjects in the college preparatory courses. Students with a combination of math and lab science deficiencies are not admissible. Audition required of music, music education majors. **Home schooled:** 22 ACT or 1040 SAT required for Arizona residents. 24 ACT or 1110 SAT required for non-residents. SAT scores are exclusive of writing.

High school preparation. 16 units required. Required units include English 4, mathematics 4, social studies 1, history 1, science 3 (laboratory 3), foreign language 2 and visual/performing arts 1.

2015-2016 Annual costs. Tuition/fees: $10,358; $23,348 out-of-state. Room/board: $9,132. Books/supplies: $1,000. Personal expenses: $2,050.

2014-2015 Financial aid. Need-based: 3,903 full-time freshmen applied for aid; 3,011 deemed to have need; 2,908 received aid. Average need met was 62%. Average scholarship/grant was $6,838; average loan $3,343. 51% of total undergraduate aid awarded as scholarships/grants, 49% as loans/jobs. **Non-need-based:** Awarded to 8,280 full-time undergraduates, including 2,421 freshmen. Scholarships awarded for academics, alumni affiliation, art, athletics, leadership, minority status, music/drama, ROTC, state residency. **Additional information:** Guaranteed fixed tuition for 4 years and guaranteed gift aid for 4 years.

Application procedures. Admission: Priority date 3/1; no deadline. $25 fee, may be waived for applicants with need. Admission notification on a rolling basis. **Financial aid:** Priority date 2/1; no closing date. FAFSA required. Applicants notified on a rolling basis starting 2/1.

Academics. Special study options: Accelerated study, cooperative education, distance learning, double major, dual enrollment of high school students, ESL, exchange student, honors, independent study, internships, study abroad, teacher certification program. **Credit/placement by examination:** AP, CLEP, IB, SAT, ACT, institutional tests. 60 credit hours maximum toward bachelor's degree. **Support services:** Learning center, pre-admission summer program, reduced course load, remedial instruction, study skills assistance, tutoring, writing center.

Honors college/program. 29 ACT or 1290 SAT (exclusive of writing) or rank in top 5% of high school class required.

Majors. Area/ethnic studies: Native American, women's. **Biology:** General, biomedical sciences, microbiology. **Business:** Accounting, business admin, construction management, finance, hospitality admin, management information systems, managerial economics, marketing. **Communications:** Communications/speech/rhetoric, journalism, radio/TV. **Computer sciences:** Computer science, systems analysis. **Conservation:** Environmental science, environmental studies, forest sciences. **Education:** Early childhood, elementary, music, special ed. **Engineering:** Civil, electrical, environmental, mechanical. **English:** English lit. **Foreign languages:** General, Spanish. **Health services:** Dental hygiene, nursing (RN). **History:** General. **Human services:** General, social work. **Liberal arts:** Arts/sciences. **Math:** General. **Parks/recreation:** General, exercise sciences. **Philosophy/religion:** Philosophy. **Physical sciences:** Astronomy, chemistry, geology, physics. **Psychology:** General. **Social sciences:** Anthropology, criminology, geography, international relations, political science, sociology. **Visual/performing arts:** Design, dramatic, interior design, music, music performance, photography, studio arts.

Most popular majors. Biology 6%, business/marketing 19%, education 10%, health sciences 12%, liberal arts 11%, social sciences 8%.

Technology on campus. 1,600 workstations in dormitories, library, computer center, student center. Dormitories wired for high-speed internet access and linked to campus network. Commuter students can connect to campus network. Online course registration, online library, helpline, repair service, student web hosting, wireless network available.

Student life. Freshman orientation: Mandatory. Preregistration for classes offered. Two-day session held in June and July. Enrollment deposit of $325 must be paid prior to registering for orientation session. **Policies:** All new student organizations must submit roster of at least five student members, a full-time faculty or staff member willing to be organization adviser, and organization constitution or governing document. **Housing:** Guaranteed on-campus for freshmen. Coed dorms, single-sex dorms, special housing for disabled, apartments, fraternity/sorority housing, themed housing available. $100 nonrefundable deposit, deadline 5/15. Honor halls, floors for students 21 years of age and older available. **Activities:** Bands, campus ministries, choral groups, dance, drama, international student organizations, literary magazine, music ensembles, Model UN, musical theater, opera, radio station, student government, student newspaper, symphony orchestra, TV station, Catholic Newman Club, Christian Challenge, Native American Church of Northern Arizona University, Younglife, Arizona Students Count, People Representing Individuals and Sexual Minorities, Black Student Union, Chinese Student and Scholar Association, Kayettes, Blue Key Honor Society.

Athletics. NCAA. **Intercollegiate:** Basketball, cross-country, diving W, football (tackle) M, golf W, soccer W, swimming W, tennis, track and field, volleyball W. **Intramural:** Badminton, basketball, football (non-tackle), handball, racquetball, soccer, volleyball, water polo. **Team name:** Lumberjacks.

Student services. Alcohol/substance abuse counseling, chaplain/spiritual director, career counseling, student employment services, financial aid counseling, health services, legal services, minority student services, personal counseling, placement for graduates, veterans' counselor. **Physically disabled:** Services for visually, speech, hearing impaired.

Contact. E-mail: Admissions@nau.edu
Phone: (928) 523-5511 Toll-free number: (888) 628-2968
Fax: (928) 523-0226
Anika Olsen, Director of Admissions, Northern Arizona University, PO Box 4084, Flagstaff, AZ 86011-4084

Prescott College
Prescott, Arizona
www.prescott.edu

CB member
CB code: 0484

- Private 4-year liberal arts college
- Commuter campus in small city
- 395 degree-seeking undergraduates: 24% part-time, 62% women, 3% African American, 2% Asian American, 6% Hispanic/Latino, 4% Native American, 5% Multi-racial, non-Hispanic, 1% international
- 360 degree-seeking graduate students
- 70% of applicants admitted
- SAT or ACT (ACT writing optional), application essay required
- 37% graduate within 6 years

General. Founded in 1966. Regionally accredited. **Degrees:** 110 bachelor's awarded; master's, doctoral offered. **Location:** 100 miles from Phoenix. **Calendar:** Semester, limited summer session. **Full-time faculty:** 36 total; 25% have terminal degrees, 14% minority, 47% women. **Part-time faculty:** 68 total; 16% have terminal degrees, 15% minority, 47% women. **Class size:** 99% < 20, less than 1% 50-99. **Special facilities:** Visual arts center, experimental agroecology farm, field station on the Gulf of California, Natural History Institute.

Freshman class profile. 328 applied, 231 admitted, 35 enrolled.

Mid 50% test scores			
SAT critical reading:	440-580	GPA 3.50-3.74:	5%
SAT math:	460-570	GPA 3.0-3.49:	32%
SAT writing:	430-580	GPA 2.0-2.99:	43%
ACT composite:	19-27	Return as sophomores:	70%
GPA 3.75 or higher:	16%	Out-of-state:	76%
		Live on campus:	94%

Basis for selection. Essay and GPA most important. Letters of recommendation, any personal additions important. College visit, interview recommended. **Home schooled:** Must submit portfolio that includes course titles, course descriptions, and bibliography; minimum length is 5-10 pages.

High school preparation. 16 units recommended. Recommended units include English 4, mathematics 3, social studies 3, science 2, foreign language 1 and visual/performing arts 1.

2015-2016 Annual costs. Tuition/fees: $27,503. Room/board: $7,200. Books/supplies: $2,842. Personal expenses: $818.

2015-2016 Financial aid. Need-based: 28 full-time freshmen applied for aid; 27 deemed to have need; 27 received aid. Average need met was 75%. Average scholarship/grant was $18,461; average loan $3,840. 57% of total undergraduate aid awarded as scholarships/grants, 43% as loans/jobs. **Non-need-based:** Awarded to 86 full-time undergraduates, including 10 freshmen. Scholarships awarded for academics, leadership.

Application procedures. Admission: No deadline. No application fee. Admission notification on a rolling basis beginning on or about 4/1. Must reply by May 1 or within 4 week(s) if notified thereafter. **Financial aid:** Priority date 3/1; no closing date. FAFSA required. Applicants notified on a rolling basis starting 3/15.

Academics. Special study options: Cross-registration, distance learning, double major, exchange student, external degree, independent study, internships, liberal arts/career combination, student-designed major, teacher certification program. Programs also available at center in Tucson. **Credit/placement by examination:** AP, CLEP, IB, institutional tests. 20 credit hours maximum toward bachelor's degree. **Support services:** Learning center, reduced course load, tutoring, writing center.

Majors. Architecture: Environmental design. **Area/ethnic studies:** Latin American, regional, women's. **Biology:** Conservation, ecology, marine, **Conservation:** Environmental studies. **Education:** Early childhood special, elementary, environmental, learning disabled, secondary. **English:** Creative writing. **Health services:** Art therapy, holistic. **Liberal arts:** Humanities. **Psychology:** General, counseling, environmental. **Visual/performing arts:** General, studio arts.

Most popular majors. Education 11%, liberal arts 8%, natural resources/environmental science 18%, parks/recreation 13%, psychology 30%, social sciences 6%.

Technology on campus. 100 workstations in library, computer center, student center. Dormitories wired for high-speed internet access and linked to campus network. Online library, helpline, wireless network available.

Student life. Freshman orientation: Mandatory, $950 fee. Preregistration for classes offered. Wilderness backpacking program offered. Water-based wilderness and community-based programs offered to those who cannot participate in backpacking session. **Housing:** Guaranteed on-campus for freshmen. Coed dorms available. $250 fully refundable deposit, deadline 6/1. **Activities:** Dance, student government, student newspaper, student environmental network, student chapter of Amnesty International, gender and sexuality alliance, peace and justice center, Aztlan center, service learning program, Maasai community project, student arts council, African-inspired dance gatherings.

Student services. Adult student services, career counseling, financial aid counseling, personal counseling, placement for graduates. **Physically disabled:** Services for visually, speech, hearing impaired.

Contact. E-mail: admissions@prescott.edu
Phone: (928) 350-2100 Toll-free number: (877) 350-2100
Fax: (928) 776-5242
Jerri Brown, Director of Admissions, Prescott College, 220 Grove Avenue, Prescott, AZ 86301

Southwest University of Visual Arts
Tucson, Arizona
www.suva.edu   CB code: 3037

- For-profit 4-year visual arts college
- Commuter campus in very large city
- 161 undergraduates
- SAT or ACT with writing, application essay, interview required

General. Degrees: 52 bachelor's awarded; master's offered. **ROTC:** Army. **Calendar:** Semester, extensive summer session. **Full-time faculty:** 28 total. **Part-time faculty:** 19 total. **Class size:** 3% < 20, 97% 20-39.

Basis for selection. High school transcripts, ACT/SAT, essay, interview, personal statement form required. Admissions based on evaluation of strengths, academic preparedness and communication skills. Art work required for illustration, fine arts, animation and graphic design programs.

High school preparation. College-preparatory program recommended.

2015-2016 Annual costs. Tuition/fees: $22,944. Personal expenses: $3,204. **Additional information:** Estimated total costs for books and supplies for each program: $3,900-$4,750.

Financial aid. All financial aid based on need.

Application procedures. Admission: Priority date 5/15; no deadline. $25 fee. Admission notification on a rolling basis. **Financial aid:** No deadline. FAFSA required.

Academics. Special study options: Double major, independent study, internships, liberal arts/career combination. **Credit/placement by examination:** AP, CLEP, IB, SAT, ACT, institutional tests. **Support services:** Learning center, reduced course load, remedial instruction, study skills assistance, tutoring, writing center.

Majors. Architecture: Landscape. **Business:** Marketing. **Communications:** Advertising. **Communications technology:** Animation/special effects. **Visual/performing arts:** Graphic design, illustration, interior design, photography, studio arts.

Technology on campus. 125 workstations in library, computer center, student center. Online course registration, online library, helpline, student web hosting, wireless network available.

Student life. Freshman orientation: Mandatory, $100 fee. Preregistration for classes offered.

Student services. Adult student services, career counseling, student employment services, financial aid counseling, personal counseling, placement for graduates, veterans' counselor.

Contact. E-mail: inquire@suva.edu
Phone: (520) 325-0123 Toll-free number: (800) 825-8753
Fax: (520) 325-5535
Steve Dietzman, Director of Admissions, Southwest University of Visual Arts, 2525 North Country Club Road, Tucson, AZ 85716

University of Advancing Technology
Tempe, Arizona
www.uat.edu   CB code: 3608

- For-profit 4-year university
- Residential campus in small city
- 784 undergraduates
- SAT or ACT (ACT writing optional) required

General. Founded in 1983. Regionally accredited. **Degrees:** 144 bachelor's, 8 associate awarded; master's offered. **Calendar:** Semester, extensive summer session. **Full-time faculty:** 23 total. **Part-time faculty:** 73 total. **Special facilities:** Technology lab, motion capture studio, robotics lab, digital video studio, network security lab, hardware studio, academic excellence in information assurance education center.

Freshman class profile.

GPA 3.75 or higher:	8%	GPA 2.0-2.99:	47%
GPA 3.50-3.74:	11%	Out-of-state:	82%
GPA 3.0-3.49:	29%	Live on campus:	99%

Basis for selection. Academic achievements, leadership experience, career aspirations, hobbies and community and extra-curricular involvement considered. Acceptance based on previous education, ACT/SAT, student's match with university culture and a passion for technology. Test scores considered during admissions process, but not required unless GPA is not satisfactory. **Home schooled:** Transcript of courses and grades, state high school equivalency certificate required.

High school preparation. College-preparatory program recommended.

2015-2016 Annual costs. Tuition/fees: $23,150. Room/board: $7,643. Books/supplies: $500. Personal expenses: $3,000.

Financial aid. Non-need-based: Scholarships awarded for academics, art, leadership.

Application procedures. Admission: No deadline. No application fee. Admission notification on a rolling basis. **Financial aid:** Priority date 4/15; no closing date. FAFSA required. Applicants notified on a rolling basis; must reply within 2 week(s) of notification.

Academics. Special study options: Accelerated study, distance learning, double major, independent study, internships. **Credit/placement by examination:** AP, CLEP. **Support services:** Learning center, tutoring.

Majors. Communications technology: Animation/special effects. **Computer sciences:** Artificial intelligence, LAN/WAN management, networking, security, web page design, webmaster. **Engineering:** Software. **Protective services:** Computer forensics. **Visual/performing arts:** Game design.

Most popular majors. Computer/information sciences 97%.

Technology on campus. 400 workstations in dormitories, library, computer center, student center. Dormitories wired for high-speed internet access and linked to campus network. Commuter students can connect to campus network. Online course registration, online library, helpline, student web hosting, wireless network available.

Student life. Freshman orientation: Mandatory. Preregistration for classes offered. **Housing:** Guaranteed on-campus for freshmen. Coed dorms, special housing for disabled, apartments available. $550 partly refundable deposit. **Activities:** Dance, drama, film society, international student organizations, literary magazine, radio station, student government, student newspaper.

Athletics. Intercollegiate: Fencing.

Student services. Career counseling, student employment services, financial aid counseling, placement for graduates, veterans' counselor.

Contact. E-mail: admissions@uat.edu
Phone: (602) 383-8228 Toll-free number: (800) 658-5744
Fax: (602) 383-8222
Michelle Kable, Manager of Admissions, University of Advancing
Technology, 2625 West Baseline Road, Tempe, AZ 85283-1056

University of Arizona

Tucson, Arizona	CB member
www.arizona.edu	CB code: 4832

- ◆ Public 4-year university
- ◆ Residential campus in very large city
- ◆ 33,364 degree-seeking undergraduates: 11% part-time, 52% women, 4% African American, 6% Asian American, 25% Hispanic/Latino, 1% Native American, 4% Multi-racial, non-Hispanic, 6% international
- ◆ 8,970 degree-seeking graduate students
- ◆ 76% of applicants admitted
- ◆ 61% graduate within 6 years

General. Founded in 1885. Regionally accredited. Sierra Vista campus offers credit-bearing classes in general studies and education. **Degrees:** 6,745 bachelor's awarded; master's, professional, doctoral offered. **ROTC:** Army, Naval, Air Force. **Location:** 111 miles from Phoenix. **Calendar:** Semester, extensive summer session. **Full-time faculty:** 1,614 total; 91% have terminal degrees, 19% minority, 40% women. **Part-time faculty:** 289 total; 62% have terminal degrees, 13% minority, 47% women. **Class size:** 40% < 20, 40% 20-39, 5% 40-49, 8% 50-99, 8% >100. **Special facilities:** Geological museum, state anthropological museum, planetarium, observatory, center for creative photography, wind tunnel, tree ring lab, mirror lab.

Freshman class profile. 35,408 applied, 27,061 admitted, 8,037 enrolled.

Mid 50% test scores			
		GPA 2.0-2.99:	24%
SAT critical reading:	480-600	Rank in top quarter:	54%
SAT math:	480-620	Rank in top tenth:	28%
SAT writing:	470-590	Return as sophomores:	80%
ACT composite:	21-27	Out-of-state:	42%
GPA 3.75 or higher:	21%	Live on campus:	71%
GPA 3.50-3.74:	18%	International:	6%
GPA 3.0-3.49:	37%		

Basis for selection. Applicants must be in top 25% of class or have 3.0 GPA. In-state applicants must have 1040 SAT (exclusive of Writing) or 22 ACT. 1110 SAT (exclusive of Writing) or 24 ACT required of out-of-state applicants. Conditional admission may be offered to in-state applicants who meet 1 or more of the following: top half of class or 2.5 GPA and no more than 1 deficiency in any 2 required subjects. SAT or ACT recommended. Auditions required of applied music and all performance majors. Portfolios required for studio art majors. **Home schooled:** Course work completion information required. **Learning Disabled:** Separate application for fee-based program (SALT).

High school preparation. College-preparatory program recommended. 16 units required. Required units include English 4, mathematics 4, social studies 1, history 1, science 3 (laboratory 3) and foreign language 2. One unit fine arts required.

2015-2016 Annual costs. Tuition/fees: $11,400; $32,600 out-of-state. Room/board: $9,840. Books/supplies: $1,200. Personal expenses: $1,800.

2014-2015 Financial aid. Need-based: 5,183 full-time freshmen applied for aid; 3,837 deemed to have need; 3,691 received aid. Average need met was 59%. Average scholarship/grant was $10,134; average loan $3,299. 59% of total undergraduate aid awarded as scholarships/grants, 41% as loans/jobs. **Non-need-based:** Awarded to 7,538 full-time undergraduates, including 2,399 freshmen. Scholarships awarded for academics, art, athletics, music/drama. **Additional information:** Arizona Assurance Program; provides housing, books, and tuition for all new, incoming resident freshmen; must be Pell-eligible with combined family income less than $42,500; funding provided as grants, scholarships, and federal work-study.

Application procedures. Admission: Closing date 5/1 (postmark date). $50 fee ($75 out-of-state), may be waived for applicants with need. Admission notification on a rolling basis. 2-4 weeks from completion of application. Must reply by May 1 or within 4 week(s) if notified thereafter. **Financial aid:** Priority date 3/1; no closing date. FAFSA required. CSS PROFILE required for some; subset of applicants asked to comply based on FAFSA information. Applicants notified on a rolling basis starting 2/1.

Academics. Special study options: Accelerated study, combined bachelor's/graduate degree, cooperative education, cross-registration, distance learning, double major, dual enrollment of high school students, ESL, exchange student, external degree, honors, independent study, internships, liberal arts/career combination, semester at sea, student-designed major, study abroad, teacher certification program, weekend college. **Credit/placement by examination:** AP, CLEP, IB, SAT, ACT, institutional tests. 60 credit hours maximum toward bachelor's degree. **Support services:** Learning center, pre-admission summer program, reduced course load, study skills assistance, tutoring, writing center.

Majors. Architecture: Architecture, urban/community planning. **Area/ethnic studies:** African-American, Chicano/Hispanic-American/Latino, East Asian, Latin American, Native American, Near/Middle Eastern, women's. **Biology:** General, biochemistry, cellular/molecular, ecology/evolutionary, microbiology, neuroscience, physiology. **Business:** General, accounting, entrepreneurial studies, finance, human resources, management information systems, managerial economics, marketing, operations, retail management. **Communications:** Communications/speech/rhetoric, journalism. **Computer sciences:** General, computer science, web page design. **Conservation:** General, environmental science, environmental studies. **Education:** Art, elementary, kindergarten/preschool, learning sciences, music, special ed. **Engineering:** Aerospace, biological, biomedical, chemical, civil, industrial, mechanical, mining, systems. **English:** Creative writing, English lit. **Foreign languages:** Classics, French, German, Italian, linguistics, Russian, Spanish. **Health services:** Communication disorders, community health services, nursing (RN), preveterinary. **History:** General. **Human services:** General. **Math:** General. **Philosophy/religion:** Judaic, philosophy, religion. **Physical sciences:** Astronomy, chemistry, geology, hydrology, materials science, optics, physics. **Psychology:** General. **Social sciences:** Anthropology, applied economics, economics, geography, GIS/cartography, political science, sociology. **Visual/performing arts:** Art history/conservation, dance, dramatic, film/cinema/video, music, music performance, musical theater, studio arts, theater design. **Work/family studies:** Family studies.

Most popular majors. Biology 10%, business/marketing 16%, engineering/engineering technologies 6%, health sciences 7%, interdisciplinary studies 6%, psychology 7%, social sciences 9%.

Technology on campus. 2,500 workstations in dormitories, library, computer center, student center. Dormitories wired for high-speed internet access and linked to campus network. Commuter students can connect to campus network. Online course registration, online library, helpline, repair service, student web hosting, wireless network available.

Student life. Freshman orientation: Mandatory, $390 fee. Preregistration for classes offered. One-day program offered throughout the summer months. **Housing:** Coed dorms, single-sex dorms, special housing for disabled, apartments, fraternity/sorority housing, themed housing, wellness housing available. $350 partly refundable deposit, deadline 5/1. Special housing for honors students available. **Activities:** Bands, campus ministries, choral groups, dance, drama, international student organizations, literary magazine, music ensembles, Model UN, musical theater, opera, radio station, student government, student newspaper, symphony orchestra, TV station, over 600 clubs and organizations available.

Athletics. NCAA. **Intercollegiate:** Baseball M, basketball, cross-country, diving, football (tackle) M, golf, gymnastics W, soccer W, softball W, swimming, tennis, track and field, volleyball W. **Intramural:** Basketball, football (non-tackle), soccer, softball, tennis, ultimate frisbee, volleyball. **Team name:** Wildcats.

Student services. Adult student services, alcohol/substance abuse counseling, chaplain/spiritual director, career counseling, services for economically disadvantaged, student employment services, financial aid counseling, health services, legal services, minority student services, personal counseling, placement for graduates, veterans' counselor, women's services. **Physically disabled:** Services for visually, speech, hearing impaired.

Contact. E-mail: admissions@arizona.edu
Phone: (520) 621-3237 Fax: (520) 621-9799
Kasey Urquidez, Dean, Undergraduate Admissions, University of Arizona, 1428 East University Boulevard, Tucson, AZ 85721-0040

University of Phoenix: Phoenix-Hohokam

Tempe, Arizona	
www.phoenix.edu	CB code: 1024

- ◆ For-profit 4-year university
- ◆ Small city
- ◆ 3,724 degree-seeking undergraduates

General. Founded in 1976. Regionally accredited. **Degrees:** 19,932 bachelor's, 14,825 associate awarded; master's offered. **Calendar:** Differs by program. **Full-time faculty:** 35 total. **Part-time faculty:** 487 total.

Basis for selection. Open admission, but selective for some programs.

2015-2016 Annual costs. Per-credit-hour charge, $410 to $635, depending upon level and course of study. Books, material charges, and other fees vary by course and program. All fees are subject to change.

Application procedures. Admission: No deadline. No application fee.

Academics. Credit/placement by examination: AP, CLEP.

Majors. Business: Accounting, accounting/business management, business admin, e-commerce, entrepreneurial studies, finance, human resources, marketing, operations. **Communications:** General. **Computer sciences:** General, database management, networking, programming, security, system admin, systems analysis, web page design, webmaster. **Education:** Elementary. **Health services:** Facilities admin, health information management, long term care admin, nursing (RN). **Human services:** General. **Protective services:** Disaster management, law enforcement admin, security management.

Student life. Freshman orientation: Mandatory. Preregistration for classes offered.

Contact. Toll-free number: (866) 766-0766
University of Phoenix: Phoenix-Hohokam, 1625 West Fountainhead Parkway, Tempe, AZ 85282-2371

University of Phoenix: Southern Arizona
Tucson, Arizona
www.phoenix.edu

- For-profit 4-year university
- Very large city
- 1,620 degree-seeking undergraduates

General. Regionally accredited. **Degrees:** 270 bachelor's awarded; master's offered. **Calendar:** Differs by program. **Full-time faculty:** 23 total. **Part-time faculty:** 179 total.

Basis for selection. Open admission, but selective for some programs.

2015-2016 Annual costs. Per-credit-hour charge, $410 to $635, depending upon level and course of study. Books, material charges, and other fees vary by course and program. All fees are subject to change.

Application procedures. Admission: No deadline. No application fee. **Financial aid:** No deadline.

Academics. Credit/placement by examination: AP, CLEP.

Majors. Business: Accounting, accounting/business management, business admin, e-commerce, entrepreneurial studies, finance, human resources, marketing, operations. **Communications:** General. **Computer sciences:** Database management, networking, programming, security, support specialist, system admin, systems analysis, web page design, webmaster. **Conservation:** Environmental studies. **Education:** Elementary. **Health services:** Facilities admin, health information management, long term care admin, nursing (RN). **Human services:** General. **Protective services:** Disaster management, law enforcement admin, security management.

Student life. Freshman orientation: Mandatory. Preregistration for classes offered.

Contact. Toll-free number: (866) 766-0766
University of Phoenix: Southern Arizona, 300 South Craycroft Road, Tucson, AZ 85711-4574

Western International University
Tempe, Arizona
www.west.edu   CB code: 1316

- For-profit 4-year university and business college
- Commuter campus in very large city
- 1,157 degree-seeking undergraduates: 62% women, 15% African American, 1% Asian American, 13% Hispanic/Latino, 2% Native American, 1% Native Hawaiian/Pacific islander, 1% Multi-racial, non-Hispanic
- 493 degree-seeking graduate students

General. Founded in 1978. Regionally accredited. Adult student body. Portfolio evaluation of relevant experience for course credit. **Degrees:** 241 bachelor's, 39 associate awarded; master's offered. **Calendar:** Differs by program, extensive summer session. **Full-time faculty:** 6 total. **Part-time faculty:** 213 total. **Class size:** 94% < 20, 6% 20-39.

Basis for selection. Open admission. **Home schooled:** Student must complete first course with a 2.0 or higher to be accepted into the university.

2015-2016 Annual costs. Personal expenses: $3,736. **Additional information:** $250 per-credit-hour for online undergraduate course; includes books and supplies.

Financial aid. All financial aid based on need.

Application procedures. Admission: No deadline. No application fee. Admission notification on a rolling basis. **Financial aid:** No deadline. FAFSA, institutional form required. Applicants notified on a rolling basis.

Academics. Special study options: Accelerated study, distance learning. Evening courses. **Credit/placement by examination:** AP, CLEP, IB. 24 credit hours maximum toward associate degree, 60 toward bachelor's. Maximum of 60 credits by examination and/or assessment may be counted toward degree; 36 hour residency requirement. **Support services:** Learning center, tutoring, writing center.

Majors. Business: General, accounting, business admin, finance, human resources, management information systems, marketing. **Communications:** Communications/speech/rhetoric. **Computer sciences:** General, information technology. **Liberal arts:** Arts/sciences. **Social sciences:** Criminology.

Most popular majors. Business/marketing 74%, computer/information sciences 8%, liberal arts 22%.

Technology on campus. 195 workstations in library, computer center. Commuter students can connect to campus network. Online course registration, online library, helpline, wireless network available.

Student life. Freshman orientation: Mandatory. Preregistration for classes offered. **Policies:** Cultural activities and special seminars/workshops available. **Activities:** Delta Mu Delta, Upsilon Pi Epsilon, Golden Key honor societies.

Student services. Adult student services, career counseling, financial aid counseling, veterans' counselor.

Contact. Phone: (602) 943-2311 Toll-free number: (866) 948-4636
Fax: (602) 371-8637
Becky Withers, Associate Director of Student Records, Western International University, 1601 West Fountainhead Parkway, Tempe, AZ 85282

Arkansas

Arkansas Baptist College
Little Rock, Arkansas
www.arkansasbaptist.edu   CB code: 7301

- Private 4-year liberal arts college affiliated with the American Baptist Churches in the USA
- Residential campus in small city
- 989 degree-seeking undergraduates

General. Founded in 1884. Regionally accredited. **Degrees:** 40 bachelor's, 103 associate awarded. **Calendar:** Semester, limited summer session. **Full-time faculty:** 27 total. **Part-time faculty:** 21 total. **Class size:** 41% < 20, 56% 20-39, 2% 40-49, 1% 50-99. **Special facilities:** African American leadership institute, literacy writing center.

Basis for selection. Open admission. Applicants with test scores or GPA below our requirement may be admitted provisionally but must earn 2.0 GPA by end of first semester to continue in good academic standing. **Home schooled:** Statement describing home school structure and mission, interview required.

High school preparation. 18 units recommended. Recommended units include English 4, mathematics 4, social studies 1 and science 2. Vocational and agriculture courses also recommended.

2015-2016 Annual costs. Tuition/fees: $8,760. Room/board: $7,826. Books/supplies: $1,325. Personal expenses: $2,600.

Financial aid. All financial aid based on need.

Application procedures. Admission: No deadline. $25 fee, may be waived for applicants with need. Admission notification on a rolling basis beginning on or about 6/30. **Financial aid:** Closing date 4/1. FAFSA required. Applicants notified on a rolling basis starting 6/15.

Academics. Special study options: Double major, independent study, internships. **Credit/placement by examination:** AP, CLEP, institutional tests. **Support services:** Remedial instruction, tutoring, writing center.

Majors. Area/ethnic studies: African-American. **Business:** Accounting, business admin. **Human services:** General. **Philosophy/religion:** Religion. **Protective services:** Corrections. **Theology:** Religious ed.

Most popular majors. Business/marketing 33%, philosophy/religious studies 8%, public administration/social services 39%, security/protective services 14%.

Technology on campus. PC or laptop required. 61 workstations in dormitories, library, computer center. Dormitories wired for high-speed internet access. Commuter students can connect to campus network. Helpline, wireless network available.

Student life. Freshman orientation: Mandatory, $10 fee. Preregistration for classes offered. Held in August and in January each year. **Policies:** Religious observance required. **Housing:** Single-sex dorms available. $150 nonrefundable deposit. **Activities:** Marching band, choral groups, student government, student newspaper, Baptist student union, student teacher organization.

Athletics. NJCAA. **Intercollegiate:** Baseball M, basketball, cheerleading W, football (tackle) M, softball W, track and field, wrestling M. **Team name:** Buffaloes.

Student services. Career counseling, student employment services, health services, on-campus daycare, personal counseling, placement for graduates, veterans' counselor.

Contact. E-mail: admissions@arkansasbaptist.edu
Phone: (501) 244-5186 Toll-free number: (866) 920-4222
Fax: (501) 372-0321
Jocelyn Spriggs, Director of Admissions and Recruitment, Arkansas Baptist College, 1621 Dr. Martin Luther King Drive, Little Rock, AR 72202

Arkansas State University
State University, Arkansas   CB member
www.astate.edu   CB code: 6011

- Public 4-year university
- Commuter campus in small city
- 8,909 degree-seeking undergraduates: 19% part-time, 57% women, 14% African American, 1% Asian American, 2% Hispanic/Latino, 2% Multiracial, non-Hispanic, 6% international
- 3,726 degree-seeking graduate students
- 70% of applicants admitted
- SAT or ACT (ACT writing optional) required
- 39% graduate within 6 years; 25% enter graduate study

General. Founded in 1909. Regionally accredited. **Degrees:** 1,766 bachelor's, 382 associate awarded; master's, professional, doctoral offered. **ROTC:** Army. **Location:** 70 miles from Memphis. **Calendar:** Semester, extensive summer session. **Full-time faculty:** 505 total; 69% have terminal degrees, 16% minority, 53% women. **Part-time faculty:** 206 total; 8% have terminal degrees, 9% minority, 66% women. **Class size:** 49% < 20, 38% 20-39, 8% 40-49, 4% 50-99, 1% >100. **Special facilities:** Environmental ecotoxicology research facility, electron microscope facility, geographic information center facility, equine center, plantation, center for health sciences, museum, Beck PRIDE Center, Regional Center for Disaster Preparedness.

Freshman class profile. 5,346 applied, 3,755 admitted, 1,577 enrolled.

Mid 50% test scores		Rank in top quarter:	49%
SAT critical reading:	400-540	Rank in top tenth:	27%
SAT math:	470-540	End year in good standing:	82%
SAT writing:	420-480	Return as sophomores:	76%
ACT composite:	21-26	Out-of-state:	11%
GPA 3.75 or higher:	37%	Live on campus:	72%
GPA 3.50-3.74:	21%	International:	6%
GPA 3.0-3.49:	28%	Fraternities:	20%
GPA 2.0-2.99:	14%	Sororities:	25%

Basis for selection. 21 ACT and 2.75 H.S. GPA is required. Proof of immunization required. Proof of registration with selective service required for all males 18 to 25. Students without SAT/ACT may submit ASSET or Compass. SAT, SAT Subject Tests, ACT must be received by first day of classes for fall term admission. Auditions required of music majors; portfolios required of art majors.

High school preparation. College-preparatory program recommended. 14 units required. Required and recommended units include English 4, mathematics 4, social studies 1, history 2, science 3 (laboratory 3) and foreign language 2.

2015-2016 Annual costs. Tuition/fees: $8,050; $14,050 out-of-state. Room/board: $8,140. Books/supplies: $1,000. Personal expenses: $4,913. **Additional information:** There is a College Support Assessment Fee, $22 per-credit hour for undergraduate students and $52 per-credit hour for graduate students, for the Colleges of Business, Engineering, Nursing & Health Professions, and Sciences & Mathematics.

2015-2016 Financial aid. Need-based: 1,478 full-time freshmen applied for aid; 1,426 deemed to have need; 1,411 received aid. Average need met was 62%. Average scholarship/grant was $10,000; average loan $6,200. 46% of total undergraduate aid awarded as scholarships/grants, 54% as loans/jobs. **Non-need-based:** Awarded to 4,433 full-time undergraduates, including 955 freshmen. Scholarships awarded for academics, alumni affiliation, art, athletics, leadership, minority status, music/drama, ROTC, state residency.

Application procedures. Admission: Closing date 8/19 (receipt date). $15 fee. Admission notification on a rolling basis. **Financial aid:** Priority date 2/15, closing date 7/1. FAFSA, institutional form required. Applicants notified on a rolling basis starting 6/1; must reply within 2 week(s) of notification.

Academics. Of the first 59 hours completed in college, students allowed to repeat courses with final grade of less than C. No more than 18 semester hours of course work may be repeated. **Special study options:** Accelerated study, distance learning, double major, dual enrollment of high school students, ESL, exchange student, honors, independent study, internships, study abroad, teacher certification program. **Credit/placement by examination:** AP, CLEP, SAT, ACT, institutional tests. 15 credit hours maximum toward associate degree, 30 toward bachelor's. **Support services:** Learning center, reduced course load, remedial instruction, study skills assistance, tutoring.

Honors college/program. 27 ACT or 3.5 GPA required.

Majors. Biology: General. **Business:** Accounting, business admin, finance, international, logistics, managerial economics, marketing. **Communications:**

General. **Computer sciences:** General, data processing. **Conservation:** Wildlife/wilderness. **Education:** Biology, business, chemistry, early childhood, English, foreign languages, mathematics, middle, music, physical, physics, social science, visually handicapped. **Engineering:** General, civil, electrical, mechanical. **English:** English lit. **Foreign languages:** General. **Health services:** Athletic training, audiology/speech pathology, clinical lab science, dietetics, medical radiologic technology/radiation therapy, nursing (RN). **History:** General. **Human services:** Social work. **Math:** General. **Parks/recreation:** Exercise sciences, health/fitness, sports admin. **Philosophy/religion:** Philosophy. **Physical sciences:** Chemistry, physics. **Protective services:** Disaster management. **Psychology:** General. **Social sciences:** Criminology, economics, political science, sociology. **Visual/performing arts:** Art, commercial/advertising art, dramatic, music, music performance.

Most popular majors. Agriculture 6%, business/marketing 14%, education 15%, health sciences 15%, liberal arts 11%, social sciences 6%.

Technology on campus. 600 workstations in dormitories, library, computer center, student center. Dormitories wired for high-speed internet access and linked to campus network. Commuter students can connect to campus network. Online course registration, online library, helpline, wireless network available.

Student life. Freshman orientation: Mandatory. Preregistration for classes offered. All-day session held on various dates. **Policies:** Smoking is prohibited on campus. **Housing:** Coed dorms, single-sex dorms, apartments, fraternity/sorority housing, themed housing, wellness housing available. $100 fully refundable deposit. Honors, STEM, and ROTC living/learning community available. **Activities:** Bands, campus ministries, choral groups, dance, drama, international student organizations, music ensembles, Model UN, musical theater, opera, radio station, student government, student newspaper, symphony orchestra, TV station, Baptist Collegiate Ministries, Catholic Newman Center, Wesley Center, Young Democrats, College Republicans, Habitat for Humanity, Circle K International, Special Olympics College, A-State Rotaract, Students Against Driving Drunk.

Athletics. NCAA. **Intercollegiate:** Baseball M, basketball, bowling W, cross-country, football (tackle) M, golf, soccer W, tennis W, track and field, volleyball W. **Intramural:** Badminton, basketball, bowling, football (non-tackle), handball, lacrosse, racquetball, soccer, softball, table tennis, tennis, ultimate frisbee, volleyball, weight lifting. **Team name:** Red Wolves.

Student services. Adult student services, alcohol/substance abuse counseling, career counseling, student employment services, financial aid counseling, health services, minority student services, on-campus daycare, personal counseling, placement for graduates, veterans' counselor. **Physically disabled:** Services for visually, speech, hearing impaired.

Contact. E-mail: admissions@astate.edu
Phone: (870) 972-2031 Toll-free number: (800) 382-3030
Fax: (870) 972-3406
Tammy Fowler, Director of Recruitment, Arkansas State University, PO Box 1570, State University, AR 72467-1570

Arkansas Tech University
Russellville, Arkansas
www.atu.edu   CB code: 6010

- Public 4-year university and liberal arts college
- Commuter campus in large town
- 8,799 degree-seeking undergraduates: 20% part-time, 55% women, 10% African American, 1% Asian American, 6% Hispanic/Latino, 1% Native American, 3% Multi-racial, non-Hispanic, 4% international
- 842 degree-seeking graduate students
- 89% of applicants admitted
- SAT or ACT (ACT writing optional) required
- 47% graduate within 6 years

General. Founded in 1909. Regionally accredited. **Degrees:** 1,408 bachelor's, 430 associate awarded; master's, doctoral offered. **ROTC:** Army. **Location:** 75 miles from Little Rock, 85 miles from Fort Smith. **Calendar:** Semester, extensive summer session. **Full-time faculty:** 349 total; 62% have terminal degrees, 10% minority, 50% women. **Part-time faculty:** 230 total; 12% have terminal degrees, 9% minority, 64% women. **Class size:** 41% < 20, 46% 20-39, 6% 40-49, 7% 50-99, less than 1% >100. **Special facilities:** Energy center, observatory, technology center.

Freshman class profile. 4,619 applied, 4,116 admitted, 2,013 enrolled.

Mid 50% test scores			
SAT critical reading:	440-530	Rank in top quarter:	34%
SAT math:	440-590	Rank in top tenth:	13%
ACT composite:	18-25	Return as sophomores:	71%
GPA 3.75 or higher:	21%	Out-of-state:	3%
GPA 3.50-3.74:	14%	Live on campus:	63%
GPA 3.0-3.49:	31%	International:	2%
GPA 2.0-2.99:	32%	Fraternities:	8%
		Sororities:	11%

Basis for selection. Secondary school record and standardized test scores very important; class rank considered. **Home schooled:** Documentation of 2.0 GPA and completion of university's secondary school core curriculum, or 450 GED required. 19 ACT, 910 SAT (math and critical reading), or 68 COMPASS also required.

High school preparation. College-preparatory program recommended. 24 units required. Required units include English 4, mathematics 4, social studies 3, history 1, science 3 (laboratory 3), foreign language 2, visual/performing arts .5, academic electives 4.5. Physical education .5, health .5, economics .5, oral communications .5.

2015-2016 Annual costs. Tuition/fees: $7,740; $14,190 out-of-state. Room/board: $6,918. Books/supplies: $1,410. Personal expenses: $1,816.

2014-2015 Financial aid. Need-based: 1,786 full-time freshmen applied for aid; 1,275 deemed to have need; 1,262 received aid. Average need met was 62%. Average scholarship/grant was $4,552; average loan $3,003. 56% of total undergraduate aid awarded as scholarships/grants, 44% as loans/jobs. **Non-need-based:** Awarded to 3,557 full-time undergraduates, including 1,435 freshmen. Scholarships awarded for academics, athletics, leadership, music/drama, ROTC, state residency.

Application procedures. Admission: No deadline. No application fee. Admission notification on a rolling basis. Students can postpone their enrollment for one semester. **Financial aid:** Priority date 3/15; no closing date. FAFSA, institutional form required. Applicants notified on a rolling basis starting 3/15; must reply within 4 week(s) of notification.

Academics. Special study options: Accelerated study, distance learning, double major, dual enrollment of high school students, ESL, honors, independent study, internships, study abroad, teacher certification program, weekend college. **Credit/placement by examination:** AP, CLEP, IB, SAT, ACT, institutional tests. 30 credit hours maximum toward associate degree, 30 toward bachelor's. **Support services:** Learning center, reduced course load, remedial instruction, study skills assistance, tutoring, writing center.

Honors college/program. 3.5 GPA and 28 ACT required.

Majors. Biology: General. **Business:** Accounting, business admin, hospitality admin, managerial economics. **Communications:** Communications/speech/rhetoric, journalism. **Computer sciences:** General, information technology, systems analysis. **Conservation:** Wildlife/wilderness. **Education:** Agricultural, art, biology, business, early childhood, elementary, English, foreign languages, mathematics, middle, music, physical, science, social studies, speech. **Engineering:** Applied physics, electrical, mechanical. **English:** Creative writing, English lit. **Foreign languages:** General. **Health services:** Clinical lab science, health information management, nursing (RN), rehabilitation science. **History:** General, applied. **Math:** General. **Parks/recreation:** Facilities management. **Physical sciences:** General, chemistry, geology, nuclear physics, physics. **Protective services:** Disaster management. **Psychology:** General. **Social sciences:** Political science, sociology. **Visual/performing arts:** Art, graphic design, music.

Most popular majors. Business/marketing 9%, education 17%, health sciences 14%, interdisciplinary studies 21%.

Technology on campus. 1,124 workstations in dormitories, library, computer center, student center. Dormitories wired for high-speed internet access and linked to campus network. Commuter students can connect to campus network. Online course registration, online library, helpline, wireless network available.

Student life. Freshman orientation: Mandatory, $65 fee. Preregistration for classes offered. Two-day on-campus program. Alternatively, students can participate in adventure camp. The $135 fee covers meals, floating, and program materials. Limit of 50 students for each extended session selected on first-come, first-served basis. **Housing:** Guaranteed on-campus for freshmen. Coed dorms, single-sex dorms, special housing for disabled, apartments, cooperative housing, fraternity/sorority housing available. $50 fully refundable deposit, deadline 6/1. **Activities:** Bands, campus ministries, choral groups, dance, drama, international student organizations, literary magazine, music ensembles, Model UN, radio station, student government, student newspaper, symphony orchestra, TV station.

Athletics. NCAA. **Intercollegiate:** Baseball M, basketball, cheerleading, cross-country W, football (tackle) M, golf, softball W, tennis W, volleyball

W. **Intramural:** Basketball, bowling, football (non-tackle), racquetball, sand volleyball, soccer, softball, table tennis, tennis, ultimate frisbee, volleyball. **Team name:** Wonder Boys, Golden Suns.

Student services. Adult student services, alcohol/substance abuse counseling, career counseling, services for economically disadvantaged, student employment services, financial aid counseling, health services, minority student services, personal counseling, placement for graduates, veterans' counselor. **Physically disabled:** Services for visually, speech, hearing impaired.

Contact. E-mail: tech.enroll@atu.edu
Phone: (479) 968-0343 Toll-free number: (800) 582-6953
Fax: (479) 964-0522
Shauna Donnell, Assistant Vice President for Enrollment Management, Arkansas Tech University, 1605 Coliseum Drive, Suite 141, Russellville, AR 72801-2222

Central Baptist College
Conway, Arkansas
www.cbc.edu   **CB code: 0788**

▶ Private 4-year Bible college affiliated with the Baptist faith
▶ Commuter campus in large town
▶ 769 degree-seeking undergraduates: 19% part-time, 47% women
▶ SAT or ACT (ACT writing optional) required

General. Founded in 1952. Regionally accredited. A Bible college with numerous degrees other than ministry available. **Degrees:** 113 bachelor's, 15 associate awarded. **ROTC:** Army. **Location:** 30 miles from Little Rock. **Calendar:** Semester, limited summer session. **Full-time faculty:** 29 total; 48% have terminal degrees, 10% minority, 41% women. **Part-time faculty:** 37 total; 14% have terminal degrees, 16% minority, 43% women.

Freshman class profile.

GPA 3.75 or higher:	22%	GPA 2.0-2.99:	29%
GPA 3.50-3.74:	22%	Out-of-state:	21%
GPA 3.0-3.49:	27%	Live on campus:	83%

Basis for selection. ACT and transfer GPA most important. **Home schooled:** Transcript of courses and grades required.

High school preparation. College-preparatory program recommended. 15 units recommended. Recommended units include English 4, mathematics 2, social studies 2 and science 2.

2015-2016 Annual costs. Tuition/fees: $14,400. Room/board: $7,500. Books/supplies: $1,350. Personal expenses: $1,270.

Financial aid. Non-need-based: Scholarships awarded for academics, alumni affiliation, athletics, leadership, music/drama, religious affiliation.

Application procedures. Admission: Closing date 8/15 (postmark date). No application fee. Application must be submitted online. Admission notification on a rolling basis. **Financial aid:** Priority date 7/1, closing date 8/1. FAFSA, institutional form required. Applicants notified on a rolling basis starting 4/1.

Academics. Special study options: Accelerated study, distance learning, internships, study abroad. **Credit/placement by examination:** AP, CLEP, ACT, institutional tests. 15 credit hours maximum toward associate degree, 30 toward bachelor's. **Support services:** Learning center, reduced course load, remedial instruction, study skills assistance, tutoring.

Majors. Biology: General, biotechnology. **Business:** Accounting, business admin, marketing, organizational behavior. **Communications:** Journalism. **Computer sciences:** Data processing. **Education:** General. **History:** General. **Liberal arts:** Arts/sciences. **Psychology:** General. **Theology:** Bible, sacred music. **Visual/performing arts:** Music.

Most popular majors. Business/marketing 42%, liberal arts 14%, psychology 20%, theological studies 14%.

Technology on campus. 90 workstations in library, computer center. Online library, wireless network available.

Student life. Freshman orientation: Mandatory, $50 fee. Preregistration for classes offered. **Policies:** Religious observance required. **Housing:** Guaranteed on-campus for freshmen. Single-sex dorms, wellness housing available. $100 partly refundable deposit, deadline 8/15. **Activities:** Choral groups, international student organizations, music ensembles, student government, student newspaper, Association of Baptist Students, College Republicans.

Athletics. NAIA, NCCAA. **Intercollegiate:** Baseball M, basketball, golf, soccer, softball W, volleyball W. **Intramural:** Basketball, football (non-tackle), softball, table tennis, tennis, volleyball. **Team name:** Mustangs.

Student services. Career counseling, financial aid counseling, health services, personal counseling, veterans' counselor.

Contact. E-mail: jwilson@cbc.edu
Phone: (501) 205-8889 Fax: (501) 329-2941
Jonathan Wilson, Director of Admissions, Central Baptist College, 1501 College Avenue, Conway, AR 72034

Ecclesia College
Springdale, Arkansas
www.ecollege.edu   **CB code: 6442**

▶ Private 4-year Bible and liberal arts college affiliated with the interdenominational tradition
▶ Residential campus in large town
▶ 193 degree-seeking undergraduates: 12% part-time, 39% women
▶ 2 degree-seeking graduate students
▶ 55% of applicants admitted
▶ SAT or ACT (ACT writing optional), application essay required

General. Accredited by ABHE. Federally recognized work-learning-service college; member Work Colleges Consortium. **Degrees:** 26 bachelor's, 7 associate awarded; master's offered. **Location:** 10 miles from Fayetteville. **Calendar:** Semester, limited summer session. **Full-time faculty:** 15 total; 47% have terminal degrees, 13% minority, 33% women. **Part-time faculty:** 47 total; 32% have terminal degrees, 6% minority, 26% women.

Freshman class profile. 134 applied, 74 admitted, 71 enrolled.

Mid 50% test scores		ACT composite:	17-22
SAT critical reading:	370-480	Out-of-state:	25%
SAT math:	410-510	Live on campus:	70%
SAT writing:	370-530		

Basis for selection. Recommendations and personal character very important. Minimum of 19 ACT or equivalent for standard admissions. **Home schooled:** Interview required.

High school preparation. College-preparatory program recommended. Recommended units include English 4, mathematics 3, social studies 3, science 3 and foreign language 1.

2016-2017 Annual costs. Tuition/fees (projected): $16,090. Room/board: $5,010. Books/supplies: $2,000. Personal expenses: $3,900.

Financial aid. Non-need-based: Scholarships awarded for academics, athletics, job skills, leadership, music/drama.

Application procedures. Admission: Priority date 6/1; deadline 8/24 (receipt date). $35 fee. Admission notification on a rolling basis. **Financial aid:** No deadline. FAFSA required. Applicants notified on a rolling basis starting 7/1.

Academics. Special study options: Distance learning, double major, dual enrollment of high school students, independent study, internships. **Credit/placement by examination:** AP, CLEP, ACT, institutional tests. **Support services:** Remedial instruction, tutoring.

Majors. Business: Business admin. **Communications:** Communications/speech/rhetoric. **Parks/recreation:** Sports admin. **Theology:** Bible, missionary, pastoral counseling, preministerial, religious ed, sacred music, theology, youth ministry.

Most popular majors. Business/marketing 16%, parks/recreation 10%, philosophy/religious studies 53%, theological studies 16%.

Technology on campus. 15 workstations in library, computer center. Dormitories wired for high-speed internet access. Online course registration, online library, wireless network available.

Student life. Freshman orientation: Mandatory. Preregistration for classes offered. **Policies:** All students must sign Code of Honor each semester of enrollment. Religious observance required. **Housing:** Single-sex dorms, apartments, wellness housing available. $100 partly refundable deposit, deadline 6/1. **Activities:** Campus ministries, choral groups, drama, music ensembles, student government.

Athletics. NCCAA. **Intercollegiate:** Baseball M, basketball, cross-country, golf, soccer, softball W. **Intramural:** Sand volleyball, table tennis. **Team name:** Royals.

Student services. Alcohol/substance abuse counseling, chaplain/spiritual director, career counseling, financial aid counseling, personal counseling, placement for graduates. **Physically disabled:** Services for visually impaired.

Contact. E-mail: admissions@ecollege.edu
Phone: (479) 248-7236 ext. 222 Fax: (479) 248-1455
Chad Howard, Director of Admissions, Ecclesia College, 9653 Nations Drive, Springdale, AR 72762

Harding University
Searcy, Arkansas
www.harding.edu   **CB code: 6267**

- Private 4-year university affiliated with the Church of Christ
- Residential campus in large town
- 4,442 degree-seeking undergraduates: 8% part-time, 55% women, 4% African American, 1% Asian American, 3% Hispanic/Latino, 1% Native American, 2% Multi-racial, non-Hispanic, 6% international
- 1,267 degree-seeking graduate students
- 76% of applicants admitted
- SAT or ACT (ACT writing optional) required
- 64% graduate within 6 years; 33% enter graduate study

General. Founded in 1924. Regionally accredited. **Degrees:** 927 bachelor's awarded; master's, professional, doctoral offered. **Location:** 50 miles from Little Rock, 105 miles from Memphis. **Calendar:** Semester, extensive summer session. **Full-time faculty:** 332 total; 67% have terminal degrees, 4% minority, 32% women. **Part-time faculty:** 157 total; 32% have terminal degrees, 7% minority, 46% women. **Class size:** 54% < 20, 30% 20-39, 9% 40-49, 7% 50-99.

Freshman class profile. 2,120 applied, 1,610 admitted, 992 enrolled.

Mid 50% test scores			
SAT critical reading:	490-620	End year in good standing:	95%
SAT math:	480-620	Return as sophomores:	85%
ACT composite:	22-28	Out-of-state:	71%
GPA 3.75 or higher:	50%	Live on campus:	96%
GPA 3.50-3.74:	17%	International:	3%
GPA 3.0-3.49:	22%	Fraternities:	50%
GPA 2.0-2.99:	11%	Sororities:	50%
Rank in top quarter:	51%		
Rank in top tenth:	26%		

Basis for selection. Test scores, academic record, references, interview important. Selective admission with limited openings, students must apply early. Students are encouraged to take rigorous classes in high school. Audition recommended for music majors, portfolio for art majors.

High school preparation. College-preparatory program recommended. 15 units required; 20 recommended. Required and recommended units include English 4, mathematics 3-4, social studies 3-4, science 2-4, foreign language 2 and academic electives 3.

2015-2016 Annual costs. Tuition/fees: $17,670. Room/board: $6,668. Books/supplies: $1,200. Personal expenses: $1,192.

2014-2015 Financial aid. Need-based: 926 full-time freshmen applied for aid; 693 deemed to have need; 689 received aid. Average need met was 81%. Average scholarship/grant was $10,070; average loan $6,799. 52% of total undergraduate aid awarded as scholarships/grants, 48% as loans/jobs. **Non-need-based:** Awarded to 1,083 full-time undergraduates, including 397 freshmen. Scholarships awarded for academics, alumni affiliation, art, athletics, leadership, music/drama, religious affiliation, ROTC, state residency.

Application procedures. Admission: No deadline. $50 fee. Admission notification on a rolling basis. Early application encouraged. **Financial aid:** Priority date 4/15; no closing date. FAFSA required. Applicants notified on a rolling basis starting 2/15; must reply within 2 week(s) of notification.

Academics. Special study options: Accelerated study, combined bachelor's/graduate degree, cooperative education, distance learning, double major, dual enrollment of high school students, ESL, honors, independent study, internships, liberal arts/career combination, student-designed major, study abroad, teacher certification program. **Credit/placement by examination:** AP, CLEP, IB, SAT, ACT, institutional tests. 32 credit hours maximum toward bachelor's degree. **Support services:** Learning center, reduced course load, remedial instruction, study skills assistance, tutoring, writing center.

Honors college/program. ACT score of 27 or higher, or SAT of 1220 (exclusive of Writing) or higher. About 200 students admitted each fall.

Majors. Biology: General, biochemistry, Biochemistry/molecular biology. **Business:** Accounting, business admin, fashion, finance, international, marketing, sales/distribution. **Communications:** Advertising, broadcast journalism, communications/speech/rhetoric, digital media, journalism, public relations. **Computer sciences:** Computer science, information technology, web page design. **Education:** Art, biology, early childhood, early childhood special, elementary, English, family/consumer sciences, French, health, mathematics, middle, multi-level teacher, music, science, social studies, Spanish, special ed, speech. **Engineering:** Biomedical, computer, electrical, mechanical. **English:** English lit. **Foreign languages:** French, Spanish. **Health services:** Athletic training, clinical lab science, communication disorders, dietetics, health care admin, nursing (RN), prepharmacy, speech pathology. **History:** General. **Human services:** General, social work. **Liberal arts:** Humanities. **Math:** General. **Parks/recreation:** Exercise sciences, sports admin. **Physical sciences:** Chemistry, physics. **Protective services:** Criminal justice. **Psychology:** General. **Social sciences:** General, economics, international economic development, political science. **Theology:** Bible, missionary, theology, youth ministry. **Visual/performing arts:** Dramatic, graphic design, interior design, music, painting, studio arts. **Work/family studies:** General, child development, family/community services.

Most popular majors. Business/marketing 16%, computer/information sciences 6%, education 13%, health sciences 14%, liberal arts 8%, parks/recreation 8%.

Technology on campus. 512 workstations in library, computer center, student center. Dormitories wired for high-speed internet access and linked to campus network. Commuter students can connect to campus network. Online course registration, online library, helpline, repair service, wireless network available.

Student life. Freshman orientation: Available, $95 fee. Preregistration for classes offered. Held the 3 days before start of fall semester. Fee includes all activities, meals, t-shirt and academic planner. **Policies:** Religious observance required. **Housing:** Guaranteed on-campus for freshmen. Single-sex dorms, special housing for disabled, apartments, wellness housing available. $130 fully refundable deposit, deadline 5/1. Approved off-campus housing available. **Activities:** Bands, campus ministries, choral groups, drama, film society, international student organizations, music ensembles, musical theater, radio station, student government, student newspaper, symphony orchestra, TV station, College Republicans, College Democrats, Good News Singers, Timothy Club, religious mission campaigns, Multi-cultural Student Action Committee, Harding Athletes as Role Models, Harding in Action.

Athletics. NCAA. **Intercollegiate:** Baseball M, basketball, cheerleading W, cross-country, football (tackle) M, golf, soccer, softball W, tennis, track and field, volleyball W. **Intramural:** Archery M, basketball, cross-country M, football (non-tackle), racquetball M, soccer, softball, swimming, table tennis M, tennis, track and field, volleyball. **Team name:** Bisons.

Student services. Adult student services, alcohol/substance abuse counseling, chaplain/spiritual director, career counseling, student employment services, financial aid counseling, health services, minority student services, personal counseling, placement for graduates. **Physically disabled:** Services for visually, speech, hearing impaired.

Contact. E-mail: admissions@harding.edu
Phone: (501) 279-4407 Toll-free number: (800) 477-4407
Fax: (501) 279-4129
Glenn Dillard, Assistant Vice President for Enrollment Management, Harding University, 915 East Market Avenue, Searcy, AR 72149-2255

Henderson State University
Arkadelphia, Arkansas   **CB member**
www.hsu.edu   **CB code: 6272**

- Public 4-year university and liberal arts college
- Commuter campus in large town
- 3,096 degree-seeking undergraduates: 11% part-time, 57% women, 24% African American, 1% Asian American, 4% Hispanic/Latino, 4% Multi-racial, non-Hispanic, 1% international
- 410 degree-seeking graduate students
- 64% of applicants admitted
- SAT or ACT (ACT writing optional) required
- 34% graduate within 6 years

General. Founded in 1890. Regionally accredited. **Degrees:** 547 bachelor's, 4 associate awarded; master's offered. **ROTC:** Army. **Location:** 67 miles from Little Rock. **Calendar:** Semester, limited summer session. **Full-time faculty:** 178 total; 62% have terminal degrees, 19% minority, 47% women. **Part-time faculty:** 66 total; 21% have terminal degrees, 14% minority, 68%

women. **Class size:** 61% < 20, 34% 20-39, 5% 40-49, less than 1% 50-99, less than 1% >100. **Special facilities:** Planetarium.

Freshman class profile. 3,786 applied, 2,413 admitted, 770 enrolled.

Mid 50% test scores		GPA 2.0-2.99:	31%
SAT critical reading:	430-490	Rank in top quarter:	40%
SAT math:	450-530	Rank in top tenth:	16%
ACT composite:	18-24	Return as sophomores:	58%
GPA 3.75 or higher:	19%	Out-of-state:	16%
GPA 3.50-3.74:	16%	Live on campus:	86%
GPA 3.0-3.49:	32%	International:	1%

Basis for selection. Freshmen with ACT Composite score of 20 will have unconditional admission status. Freshmen with ACT Composite score of 16-19 will be conditionally admitted and required to register with the HSU Advising Center. Institution does not accept recalculated ACT Composite scores for admission. ACT recommended. Test scores must be on file with Admissions prior to registering for classes. Audition recommended for music and theater arts majors. **Home schooled:** Transcript of courses and grades required. 18 ACT required. Completion of college prep curriculum encouraged. **Learning Disabled:** Student Support Disability Services assesses needs of students with learning disabilities.

High school preparation. 14 units required; 22 recommended. Required and recommended units include English 4, mathematics 4, social studies 2, history 1 and science 3. Required: 0.5 oral communications, 0.5 fine art, 6 career focus.

2015-2016 Annual costs. Tuition/fees: $7,809; $14,409 out-of-state. Room/board: $6,500. Books/supplies: $1,600. Personal expenses: $2,200. **Additional information:** Miscellaneous expenses range from $1800 to $2600/year and transportation ranges from $2000 to $3000/year.

2014-2015 Financial aid. Need-based: 679 full-time freshmen applied for aid; 641 deemed to have need; 609 received aid. Average need met was 91%. Average scholarship/grant was $4,641; average loan $3,069. 68% of total undergraduate aid awarded as scholarships/grants, 32% as loans/jobs. **Non-need-based:** Awarded to 1,519 full-time undergraduates, including 650 freshmen. Scholarships awarded for academics, alumni affiliation, art, athletics, job skills, leadership, minority status, music/drama, ROTC, state residency.

Application procedures. Admission: Closing date 7/15 (receipt date). No application fee. Admission notification on a rolling basis. Application closing date 7/15 for applicants with ACT score under 18. **Financial aid:** Priority date 4/15; no closing date. Applicants notified on a rolling basis starting 3/1; must reply within 2 week(s) of notification.

Academics. Special study options: Cross-registration, distance learning, double major, honors, internships, liberal arts/career combination, study abroad, teacher certification program. **Credit/placement by examination:** AP, CLEP, SAT, ACT, institutional tests. 30 credit hours maximum toward bachelor's degree. **Support services:** Learning center, remedial instruction, study skills assistance, tutoring, writing center.

Honors college/program. 26 ACT required; approximately 100 admitted.

Majors. Biology: General. **Business:** General, accounting, management information systems. **Communications:** General, digital media, journalism. **Computer sciences:** General. **Education:** Art, business, early childhood, middle, physical, social science, special ed. **Engineering:** Applied physics. **English:** English lit. **Foreign languages:** Spanish. **Health services:** Athletic training, clinical lab science, nursing (RN), radiologic technology/medical imaging. **History:** General. **Human services:** General, social work. **Math:** General. **Parks/recreation:** Facilities management. **Physical sciences:** Chemistry, physics. **Psychology:** General. **Social sciences:** Political science, sociology. **Visual/performing arts:** Art, dramatic, music, music performance. **Work/family studies:** General, child development.

Most popular majors. Business/marketing 17%, education 14%, health sciences 6%, liberal arts 13%, psychology 9%, visual/performing arts 8%.

Technology on campus. 125 workstations in dormitories, library, computer center, student center. Dormitories linked to campus network. Commuter students can connect to campus network. Online library, helpline, wireless network available.

Student life. Freshman orientation: Mandatory. Preregistration for classes offered. 1.5 day program for students and parents, held several times during July, again in August if necessary. **Housing:** Guaranteed on-campus for freshmen. Coed dorms, single-sex dorms, cooperative housing, themed housing available. $50 nonrefundable deposit. Special hall for Honors College participants, special floor for freshman interest groups available. On-campus apartment for upperclassmen. **Activities:** Bands, campus ministries, choral groups, dance, drama, international student organizations, literary magazine, music ensembles, radio station, student government, student newspaper, TV

station, College Republicans, Young Democrats, Student Foundation, Heart and Key service organization, several religious organizations.

Athletics. NCAA. **Intercollegiate:** Baseball M, basketball, cross-country W, football (tackle) M, golf, softball W, swimming, tennis W, volleyball W. **Team name:** Reddies.

Student services. Career counseling, student employment services, health services, personal counseling, placement for graduates, veterans' counselor. **Physically disabled:** Services for visually, speech, hearing impaired.

Contact. E-mail: admissions@hsu.edu
Phone: (870) 230-5028 Toll-free number: (800) 228-7333
Fax: (870) 230-5066
Vikita Hardwrick, Director of Admissions, Henderson State University, 1100 Henderson Street, Arkadelphia, AR 71999-0001

Hendrix College
Conway, Arkansas
www.hendrix.edu

CB member
CB code: 6273

- Private 4-year liberal arts college affiliated with the United Methodist Church
- Residential campus in small city
- 1,303 degree-seeking undergraduates: 53% women, 5% African American, 5% Asian American, 5% Hispanic/Latino, 1% Native American, 3% Multi-racial, non-Hispanic, 3% international
- 11 degree-seeking graduate students
- 82% of applicants admitted
- SAT or ACT (ACT writing optional), application essay required
- 68% graduate within 6 years; 35% enter graduate study

General. Founded in 1876. Regionally accredited. **Degrees:** 290 bachelor's awarded; master's offered. **ROTC:** Army. **Location:** 30 miles from Little Rock. **Calendar:** Semester. **Full-time faculty:** 107 total; 92% have terminal degrees, 13% minority, 44% women. **Part-time faculty:** 33 total; 42% have terminal degrees, 9% minority, 61% women. **Class size:** 73% < 20, 26% 20-39, 1% 40-49. **Special facilities:** Teaching thrust stage theater with pneumatic lift turn table, wetlands restoration preserve, access to elephant farm for research and volunteer service, ring laser, two pipe organs, institute building for the study of literature and language, nature walk, living learning residential facility, student-run garden.

Freshman class profile. 1,714 applied, 1,412 admitted, 395 enrolled.

Mid 50% test scores		Rank in top quarter:	78%
SAT critical reading:	540-680	Rank in top tenth:	48%
SAT math:	580-660	End year in good standing:	93%
ACT composite:	25-32	Return as sophomores:	79%
GPA 3.75 or higher:	67%	Out-of-state:	48%
GPA 3.50-3.74:	11%	Live on campus:	98%
GPA 3.0-3.49:	19%	International:	2%
GPA 2.0-2.99:	3%		

Basis for selection. Academic competence, scholastic potential, motivation, character, and high school leadership important. High school transcript, application, and school report required. Interview may be required. **Home schooled:** Interview required. Portfolio required.

High school preparation. College-preparatory program required. 14 units recommended. Recommended units include English 4, mathematics 3, social studies 3, science 2 and foreign language 2.

2015-2016 Annual costs. Tuition/fees: $40,870. Room/board: $11,244. Books/supplies: $1,100. Personal expenses: $1,000.

2015-2016 Financial aid. Need-based: 375 full-time freshmen applied for aid; 295 deemed to have need; 295 received aid. Average need met was 89%. Average scholarship/grant was $32,929; average loan $3,245. 85% of total undergraduate aid awarded as scholarships/grants, 15% as loans/jobs. **Non-need-based:** Awarded to 744 full-time undergraduates, including 192 freshmen. Scholarships awarded for academics, art, leadership, music/drama.

Application procedures. Admission: Priority date 2/1; deadline 6/1 (postmark date). $40 fee, may be waived for applicants with need, free for online applicants. Admission notification on a rolling basis beginning on or about 12/15. Must reply by May 1 or within 4 week(s) if notified thereafter. **Financial aid:** Priority date 3/1; no closing date. FAFSA required. Applicants notified on a rolling basis starting 3/1; must reply by 5/1 or within 4 week(s) of notification.

Academics. Special study options: Combined bachelor's/graduate degree, cooperative education, double major, ESL, independent study, internships, student-designed major, study abroad, teacher certification program, Washington semester. Study abroad and multilateral exchange programs with 150 colleges and universities on 6 continents. **Credit/placement by examination:** AP, CLEP, IB, SAT, ACT, institutional tests. 6 credit hours maximum toward bachelor's degree. **Support services:** Pre-admission summer program, study skills assistance, tutoring, writing center.

Majors. Area/ethnic studies: American. **Biology:** General, Biochemistry/molecular biology. **Business:** Accounting. **Computer sciences:** Computer science. **Conservation:** Environmental studies. **Education:** Elementary. **English:** English lit. **Foreign languages:** Classics, French, German, Spanish. **History:** General. **Math:** General. **Philosophy/religion:** Philosophy, religion. **Physical sciences:** Chemical physics, chemistry, physics. **Psychology:** General. **Social sciences:** Anthropology, economics, international relations, political science, sociology. **Visual/performing arts:** Art, dramatic, music.

Most popular majors. Biology 18%, English 9%, foreign language 7%, physical sciences 6%, psychology 10%, social sciences 19%.

Technology on campus. 75 workstations in dormitories, library, computer center, student center. Dormitories wired for high-speed internet access and linked to campus network. Commuter students can connect to campus network. Online course registration, helpline, repair service, student web hosting, wireless network available.

Student life. Freshman orientation: Mandatory. Preregistration for classes offered. 7-day program held prior to fall term. **Housing:** Guaranteed on-campus for freshmen. Coed dorms, single-sex dorms, special housing for disabled, apartments, themed housing, wellness housing available. $350 nonrefundable deposit, deadline 5/1. Suite-style small houses available. **Activities:** Bands, campus ministries, choral groups, dance, drama, film society, international student organizations, literary magazine, music ensembles, Model UN, radio station, student government, student newspaper, Students for Black Culture, Asian cultures club, Friends of India, College Republicans, Volunteer Action Center, Catholic campus ministry, Young Democrats, Habitat for Humanity, Amnesty International.

Athletics. NCAA. **Intercollegiate:** Baseball M, basketball, cross-country, diving, field hockey W, football (tackle) M, golf, lacrosse, soccer, softball W, swimming, tennis, track and field, volleyball W. **Intramural:** Basketball, football (non-tackle), racquetball, soccer, softball, table tennis, tennis. **Team name:** Warriors.

Student services. Alcohol/substance abuse counseling, chaplain/spiritual director, career counseling, student employment services, financial aid counseling, health services, minority student services, personal counseling, placement for graduates. **Physically disabled:** Services for visually impaired.

Contact. E-mail: adm@hendrix.edu
Phone: (501) 450-1362 Toll-free number: (800) 277-9017
Fax: (501) 450-3843
Fred Baker, Director of Admission, Hendrix College, 1600 Washington Avenue, Conway, AR 72032-3080

ITT Technical Institute: Little Rock
Little Rock, Arkansas
www.itt-tech.edu   **CB code: 2721**

- For-profit 4-year technical college
- Commuter campus in small city
- 273 undergraduates
- Interview required

General. Accredited by ACICS. **Degrees:** 12 bachelor's, 69 associate awarded. **Calendar:** Quarter, extensive summer session. **Full-time faculty:** 7 total. **Part-time faculty:** 31 total.

Basis for selection. Satisfactory scores from on-site tests in English and mathematics required.

2015-2016 Annual costs. Per-credit-hour charge, $493; academic fee, $200. Some programs require purchase of tools, which could cost an additional $100 to $500. All costs subject to change.

Application procedures. Admission: No deadline. No application fee. Admission notification on a rolling basis. **Financial aid:** No deadline. FAFSA, institutional form required. Applicants notified on a rolling basis.

Academics. Credit/placement by examination: AP, CLEP. **Support services:** Learning center, tutoring.

Majors. Business: Business admin, construction management. **Communications technology:** Animation/special effects. **Computer sciences:** Security. **Protective services:** Law enforcement admin.

Most popular majors. Communication technologies 46%, computer/information sciences 34%, security/protective services 18%.

Technology on campus. Online library available.

Student life. Freshman orientation: Available. Preregistration for classes offered.

Student services. Career counseling, student employment services, placement for graduates.

Contact. Phone: (501) 565-5550 Toll-free number: (800) 359-4429
Reed Thompson, Director of Recruitment, ITT Technical Institute: Little Rock, 12200 Westhaven Drive, Little Rock, AR 72211

John Brown University
Siloam Springs, Arkansas
www.jbu.edu   **CB code: 6321**

- Private 4-year university and liberal arts college affiliated with the interdenominational tradition
- Residential campus in large town
- 1,685 degree-seeking undergraduates: 9% part-time, 58% women, 2% African American, 2% Asian American, 6% Hispanic/Latino, 2% Native American, 3% Multi-racial, non-Hispanic, 6% international
- 606 degree-seeking graduate students
- 74% of applicants admitted
- Application essay required
- 61% graduate within 6 years

General. Founded in 1919. Regionally accredited. **Degrees:** 534 bachelor's, 1 associate awarded; master's offered. **ROTC:** Army, Air Force. **Location:** 30 miles from Fayetteville, 75 miles from Tulsa, OK. **Calendar:** Semester, limited summer session. **Full-time faculty:** 82 total; 79% have terminal degrees, 10% minority, 28% women. **Part-time faculty:** 120 total; 42% have terminal degrees, 3% minority, 38% women. **Class size:** 52% < 20, 42% 20-39, 6% 40-49, less than 1% 50-99. **Special facilities:** Cadaver lab, outdoor renewable energy lab, indoor high-bay construction management work area, health services training facility, two art galleries, historical cathedral.

Freshman class profile. 1,166 applied, 860 admitted, 360 enrolled.

Mid 50% test scores			
SAT critical reading:	520-660	GPA 2.0-2.99:	2%
SAT math:	510-630	Rank in top quarter:	59%
SAT writing:	480-650	Rank in top tenth:	33%
ACT composite:	24-30	Return as sophomores:	81%
GPA 3.75 or higher:	68%	Out-of-state:	58%
GPA 3.50-3.74:	14%	Live on campus:	90%
GPA 3.0-3.49:	16%	International:	5%

Basis for selection. Test scores, secondary school record, recommendations, essay, interview most important. Special talents, class rank considered. Combined SAT score of 950 (exclusive of Writing), ACT score of 20 or above. Interview recommended. Audition required of music majors; portfolio recommended for art majors. **Home schooled:** Transcript of courses and grades required.

High school preparation. College-preparatory program recommended. Recommended units include English 4, mathematics 3, social studies 2, history 1, science 2 (laboratory 1) and foreign language 2. 4 units of math, 3 science for science and engineering majors; 2 foreign language recommended for home educated students.

2015-2016 Annual costs. Tuition/fees: $24,468. Room/board: $8,664. Books/supplies: $800. Personal expenses: $1,350.

2014-2015 Financial aid. Need-based: 279 full-time freshmen applied for aid; 229 deemed to have need; 229 received aid. Average need met was 77%. Average scholarship/grant was $16,475; average loan $2,874. 70% of total undergraduate aid awarded as scholarships/grants, 30% as loans/jobs. **Non-need-based:** Awarded to 1,203 full-time undergraduates, including 312 freshmen. Scholarships awarded for academics, alumni affiliation, art, athletics, leadership, music/drama, ROTC.

Application procedures. Admission: Priority date 5/1; no deadline. $25 fee, may be waived for applicants with need. Admission notification on a rolling basis beginning on or about 11/1. Must reply by May 1 or within 2 week(s) if notified thereafter. **Financial aid:** Priority date 3/1; no closing date. FAFSA required. Applicants notified on a rolling basis starting 3/1; must reply by 5/1 or within 4 week(s) of notification.

Academics. **Special study options:** Accelerated study, distance learning, double major, dual enrollment of high school students, ESL, exchange student, honors, independent study, internships, liberal arts/career combination, student-designed major, study abroad, teacher certification program, Washington semester. **Credit/placement by examination:** AP, CLEP, IB. 15 credit hours maximum toward associate degree, 30 toward bachelor's. **Support services:** Learning center, reduced course load, remedial instruction, study skills assistance, tutoring, writing center.

Honors college/program. Selected by admissions office/honors committee; based on GPA, SAT/ACT and interview.

Majors. **Biology:** General, biochemistry. **Business:** Accounting, business admin, construction management, international, management information systems, marketing. **Communications:** Broadcast journalism, communications/speech/rhetoric, digital media, journalism, public relations, radio/TV. **Conservation:** Environmental science. **Education:** Early childhood, English, mathematics, middle, music, social studies. **Engineering:** General. **English:** English lit. **Foreign languages:** Spanish. **Health services:** Athletic training. **History:** General. **Math:** General. **Parks/recreation:** Exercise sciences, sports admin. **Physical sciences:** Chemistry. **Psychology:** General. **Social sciences:** Political science. **Theology:** Missionary, sacred music, theology, youth ministry. **Visual/performing arts:** Graphic design, illustration, music, music performance, photography. **Work/family studies:** Family/community services.

Most popular majors. Business/marketing 42%, education 8%, visual/performing arts 10%.

Technology on campus. 200 workstations in dormitories, library, computer center, student center. Dormitories wired for high-speed internet access and linked to campus network. Commuter students can connect to campus network. Online course registration, online library, helpline, wireless network available.

Student life. **Freshman orientation:** Mandatory, $75 fee. Preregistration for classes offered. Held a few days prior to the start of classes each semester. **Policies:** No alcohol, drugs, or tobacco allowed on campus; all applicants required to sign community covenant each year. Religious observance required. **Housing:** Guaranteed on-campus for freshmen. Coed dorms, single-sex dorms, special housing for disabled, apartments available. $100 fully refundable deposit. **Activities:** Bands, campus ministries, choral groups, dance, drama, film society, international student organizations, literary magazine, music ensembles, musical theater, radio station, student government, student newspaper.

Athletics. NAIA. **Intercollegiate:** Basketball, cheerleading, cross-country, golf M, soccer, tennis, volleyball W. **Intramural:** Baseball M, basketball, football (non-tackle), football (tackle) M, racquetball, soccer, softball, tennis, ultimate frisbee, volleyball. **Team name:** Golden Eagles.

Student services. Chaplain/spiritual director, career counseling, student employment services, financial aid counseling, health services, personal counseling, placement for graduates. **Physically disabled:** Services for visually, hearing impaired.

Contact. E-mail: jbuinfo@jbu.edu
Phone: (479) 524-7157 Toll-free number: (877) 528-4636
Fax: (479) 524-4196
Don Crandall, Vice President for Enrollment Management, John Brown University, 2000 West University Street, Siloam Springs, AR 72761-2121

Lyon College
Batesville, Arkansas   **CB member**
www.lyon.edu   **CB code: 6009**

- Private 4-year liberal arts college affiliated with the Presbyterian Church (USA)
- Residential campus in large town
- 676 degree-seeking undergraduates: 47% women, 6% African American, 2% Asian American, 7% Hispanic/Latino, 2% Native American, 2% international
- 59% of applicants admitted
- SAT and SAT Subject Tests or ACT (ACT writing optional) required
- 38% graduate within 6 years

General. Founded in 1872. Regionally accredited. **Degrees:** 121 bachelor's awarded. **Location:** 90 miles from Little Rock. **Calendar:** Semester, limited summer session. **Full-time faculty:** 42 total; 100% have terminal degrees, 14% minority, 29% women. **Part-time faculty:** 40 total; 12% have terminal degrees, 52% women. **Class size:** 62% < 20, 23% 20-39, 5% 40-49, 6% 50-99, 4% >100. **Special facilities:** Ozark Regional Studies Center.

Freshman class profile. 1,607 applied, 950 admitted, 211 enrolled.

Mid 50% test scores		
		GPA 3.0-3.49: 27%
SAT critical reading:	500-600	GPA 2.0-2.99: 8%
SAT math:	490-580	Rank in top quarter: 57%
SAT writing:	460-560	Rank in top tenth: 27%
ACT composite:	22-27	Return as sophomores: 64%
GPA 3.75 or higher:	41%	Out-of-state: 33%
GPA 3.50-3.74:	24%	Live on campus: 85%

Basis for selection. High school academic performance and standardized test scores most important. Personal essays and letters of recommendation considered on case by case basis. Math proficiency and placement judged with ACT math subscores. Auditions or portfolios required for fine arts.

High school preparation. College-preparatory program recommended. 16 units required; 18 recommended. Required and recommended units include English 4, mathematics 3-4, social studies 1, history 2, science 3-4 (laboratory 2), foreign language 2 and academic electives 1.

2015-2016 Annual costs. Tuition/fees: $25,280. Room/board: $8,110. Books/supplies: $1,000. Personal expenses: $1,000.

2015-2016 Financial aid. **Need-based:** Average need met was 73%. Average scholarship/grant was $18,124; average loan $3,400. 73% of total undergraduate aid awarded as scholarships/grants, 27% as loans/jobs. **Non-need-based:** Scholarships awarded for academics, art, athletics, leadership, music/drama, religious affiliation, state residency.

Application procedures. **Admission:** Priority date 1/15; deadline 8/15. $25 fee. Admission notification on a rolling basis. Must reply by May 1 or within 2 week(s) if notified thereafter. **Financial aid:** Priority date 3/15; no closing date. FAFSA required. Applicants notified on a rolling basis starting 3/1; must reply by 8/15.

Academics. Academic honor code administered by peer-elected student honor council. **Special study options:** Combined bachelor's/graduate degree, double major, ESL, independent study, internships, student-designed major, study abroad, teacher certification program, Washington semester. **Credit/placement by examination:** AP, CLEP, IB, ACT, institutional tests. 33 credit hours maximum toward bachelor's degree. **Support services:** Learning center, study skills assistance, tutoring, writing center.

Majors. **Biology:** General. **Business:** Accounting, business admin. **Education:** Early childhood. **English:** English lit. **Foreign languages:** Spanish. **History:** General. **Math:** General. **Philosophy/religion:** Philosophy, religion. **Physical sciences:** Chemistry. **Psychology:** General. **Social sciences:** Economics, political science. **Visual/performing arts:** Art, dramatic, music.

Most popular majors. Biology 22%, business/marketing 16%, English 8%, history 6%, mathematics 7%, psychology 15%, social sciences 10%, visual/performing arts 8%.

Technology on campus. 100 workstations in dormitories, library, computer center, student center. Dormitories wired for high-speed internet access and linked to campus network. Commuter students can connect to campus network. Online course registration, online library, helpline, repair service, wireless network available.

Student life. **Freshman orientation:** Mandatory, $150 fee. Preregistration for classes offered. **Policies:** Social code administered by peer-elected student social council. **Housing:** Guaranteed on-campus for all undergraduates. Coed dorms, apartments available. $100 fully refundable deposit. **Activities:** Bands, campus ministries, choral groups, dance, drama, film society, student government, student newspaper, black student association, Fellowship of Christian Athletes.

Athletics. NAIA. **Intercollegiate:** Baseball M, basketball, cheerleading, cross-country, golf, soccer, softball W, volleyball W. **Intramural:** Badminton, basketball, football (non-tackle), softball, table tennis, tennis, volleyball. **Team name:** Scots.

Student services. Chaplain/spiritual director, career counseling, financial aid counseling, health services, personal counseling, placement for graduates.

Contact. E-mail: admissions@lyon.edu
Phone: (870) 307-7250 Toll-free number: (800) 423-2542
Fax: (870) 307-7542
Donald Taylor, Director of Admissions and Registrar, Lyon College, PO Box 2317, Batesville, AR 72501-2317

Ouachita Baptist University
Arkadelphia, Arkansas
www.obu.edu   **CB code: 6549**

- Private 4-year liberal arts college affiliated with the Baptist faith
- Residential campus in large town

- 1,471 degree-seeking undergraduates: 2% part-time, 52% women, 7% African American, 1% Asian American, 4% Hispanic/Latino, 1% Native American, 2% international
- 60% of applicants admitted
- SAT or ACT (ACT writing optional) required
- 65% graduate within 6 years; 44% enter graduate study

General. Founded in 1886. Regionally accredited. **Degrees:** 338 bachelor's awarded. **ROTC:** Army. **Location:** 65 miles from Little Rock. **Calendar:** Semester, extensive summer session. **Full-time faculty:** 103 total; 87% have terminal degrees, 4% minority, 36% women. **Part-time faculty:** 57 total; 19% have terminal degrees, 58% women. **Class size:** 63% < 20, 34% 20-39, 2% 40-49, less than 1% 50-99.

Freshman class profile. 1,993 applied, 1,200 admitted, 412 enrolled.

Mid 50% test scores			
SAT critical reading:	470-610	Rank in top tenth:	34%
SAT math:	470-630	End year in good standing:	92%
ACT composite:	21-28	Return as sophomores:	76%
GPA 3.75 or higher:	50%	Out-of-state:	33%
GPA 3.50-3.74:	16%	Live on campus:	97%
GPA 3.0-3.49:	24%	International:	1%
GPA 2.0-2.99:	10%	Fraternities:	40%
Rank in top quarter:	59%	Sororities:	45%

Basis for selection. Test scores and school achievement record most important. 2.75 GPA, 20 ACT required. Interview recommended. Portfolio recommended for studio art majors.

High school preparation. College-preparatory program recommended. 15 units required; 19 recommended. Required and recommended units include English 4-6, mathematics 2-3, social studies 1, history 2, science 2-3, foreign language 2 and academic electives 4.

2016-2017 Annual costs. Tuition/fees (projected): $24,940. Room/board: $7,380. Books/supplies: $1,100. Personal expenses: $1,540.

2015-2016 Financial aid. **Need-based:** 376 full-time freshmen applied for aid; 290 deemed to have need; 290 received aid. Average need met was 83%. Average scholarship/grant was $14,052; average loan $2,545. 77% of total undergraduate aid awarded as scholarships/grants, 23% as loans/jobs. **Non-need-based:** Awarded to 838 full-time undergraduates, including 213 freshmen. Scholarships awarded for academics, alumni affiliation, art, athletics, job skills, leadership, minority status, music/drama, religious affiliation, ROTC, state residency.

Application procedures. **Admission:** Priority date 1/15; no deadline. No application fee. Admission notification on a rolling basis. Deferred admission up to one year. **Financial aid:** Priority date 1/15, closing date 6/1. FAFSA required. Applicants notified on a rolling basis starting 11/1; must reply by 6/1.

Academics. International exchange programs in Australia, Austria, China, Costa Rica, England, France, Germany, Hong Kong, Indonesia, Japan, Morocco, New Zealand, Russia, Scotland, and South Africa. **Special study options:** Cross-registration, distance learning, double major, ESL, honors, independent study, internships, study abroad, teacher certification program. Concurrent enrollment. **Credit/placement by examination:** AP, CLEP, IB, ACT, institutional tests. 24 credit hours maximum toward bachelor's degree. **Support services:** Learning center, reduced course load, remedial instruction, study skills assistance, tutoring, writing center.

Majors. **Biology:** General. **Business:** Accounting, business admin. **Communications:** Communications/speech/rhetoric, media studies. **Computer sciences:** Computer science. **Education:** Art, biology, business, chemistry, drama/dance, early childhood, English, foreign languages, French, health, history, mathematics, middle, music, physical, physics, science, secondary, social studies, Spanish, speech. **English:** English lit. **Foreign languages:** Biblical, Spanish. **Health services:** Communication disorders, dietetics, predental, premedicine, prenursing, prepharmacy, prephysical therapy, preveterinary. **History:** General. **Math:** General, applied. **Parks/recreation:** Exercise sciences, health/fitness. **Philosophy/religion:** Philosophy. **Physical sciences:** Chemistry, physics. **Psychology:** General. **Social sciences:** Political science, sociology. **Theology:** Bible, missionary, pastoral counseling, sacred music, theology. **Visual/performing arts:** Dramatic, graphic design, music, music history, music performance, music theory/composition, musical theater, piano/keyboard, studio arts, voice/opera.

Most popular majors. Biology 14%, business/marketing 13%, communications/journalism 8%, education 9%, health sciences 8%, parks/recreation 7%, theological studies 12%, visual/performing arts 11%.

Technology on campus. 275 workstations in dormitories, library, computer center, student center. Dormitories wired for high-speed internet access and linked to campus network. Commuter students can connect to campus network. Online library, helpline, student web hosting, wireless network available.

Student life. **Freshman orientation:** Mandatory. Preregistration for classes offered. Four-day weekend program prior to registration with one session for parents. **Policies:** Students under 22 must live in campus housing unless commuting. Only local fraternities and sororities are permitted. Religious observance required. **Housing:** Guaranteed on-campus for all undergraduates. Single-sex dorms, special housing for disabled, apartments, wellness housing available. $50 fully refundable deposit, deadline 6/1. **Activities:** Bands, campus ministries, choral groups, drama, international student organizations, literary magazine, music ensembles, Model UN, musical theater, opera, student government, student newspaper, Fellowship of Christian Athletes, Ouachita student foundation, Pew College Society, ROMS, Young Democrats, College Republicans.

Athletics. NCAA. **Intercollegiate:** Baseball M, basketball, cheerleading, cross-country W, diving, football (tackle) M, soccer, softball W, swimming, tennis, volleyball W, wrestling M. **Intramural:** Basketball, football (non-tackle), handball, racquetball, soccer, softball, table tennis, volleyball. **Team name:** Tigers.

Student services. Alcohol/substance abuse counseling, chaplain/spiritual director, career counseling, services for economically disadvantaged, student employment services, financial aid counseling, health services, minority student services, personal counseling, placement for graduates, veterans' counselor. **Physically disabled:** Services for visually, speech, hearing impaired.

Contact. E-mail: motll@obu.edu
Phone: (870) 245-5110 Toll-free number: (800) 342-5628
Fax: (870) 245-5500
Lori Motl, Director of Admissions Counseling, Ouachita Baptist University, OBU Box 3776, Arkadelphia, AR 71998-0001

Philander Smith College
Little Rock, Arkansas   **CB member**
www.philander.edu   **CB code: 6578**

- Private 4-year liberal arts college affiliated with the United Methodist Church
- Commuter campus in small city
- 584 degree-seeking undergraduates: 6% part-time, 63% women, 90% African American, 1% Asian American, 1% Hispanic/Latino, 2% Multiracial, non-Hispanic, 5% international
- SAT or ACT (ACT writing optional) required
- 40% graduate within 6 years

General. Founded in 1877. Regionally accredited. **Degrees:** 111 bachelor's awarded. **Calendar:** Semester, limited summer session. **Full-time faculty:** 46 total; 61% have terminal degrees, 52% women. **Part-time faculty:** 10 total; 20% have terminal degrees, 50% women. **Class size:** 83% < 20, 16% 20-39, less than 1% 40-49.

Freshman class profile.

GPA 3.75 or higher:	8%	Rank in top tenth:	15%
GPA 3.50-3.74:	12%	Return as sophomores:	63%
GPA 3.0-3.49:	29%	Out-of-state:	43%
GPA 2.0-2.99:	41%	International:	2%
Rank in top quarter:	32%		

Basis for selection. High school GPA of 2.5 and ACT Composite of 19 along with rigor of high school record for unconditional admission. Students not meeting that criteria can be admitted on probation. Students admitted without ACT scores are administered COMPASS test for placement purposes. Students who score below placement cut-off scores in writing, English, or math also required to take COMPASS test.

High school preparation. College-preparatory program recommended. Recommended units include English 4, mathematics 3, social studies 2, science 2 (laboratory 1), foreign language 2 and academic electives 6.

2015-2016 Annual costs. Tuition/fees: $12,414. Room/board: $8,250. Books/supplies: $1,000. Personal expenses: $1,668.

2014-2015 Financial aid. **Need-based:** 106 full-time freshmen applied for aid; 106 deemed to have need; 106 received aid. Average need met was 59%. Average scholarship/grant was $122,026; average loan $3,075. 53% of total undergraduate aid awarded as scholarships/grants, 47% as loans/jobs. **Non-need-based:** Awarded to 63 full-time undergraduates, including 7 freshmen. Scholarships awarded for academics, athletics, music/drama, religious affiliation.

Application procedures. Admission: Priority date 3/1; deadline 5/1. $25 fee, may be waived for applicants with need. Admission notification on a rolling basis. **Financial aid:** Priority date 3/1; no closing date. FAFSA required. Applicants notified on a rolling basis starting 3/1; must reply within 2 week(s) of notification.

Academics. Special study options: Accelerated study, double major, independent study, internships, study abroad, teacher certification program, weekend college. **Credit/placement by examination:** AP, CLEP, IB, SAT, ACT, institutional tests. 30 credit hours maximum toward bachelor's degree. **Support services:** Learning center, reduced course load, remedial instruction, study skills assistance, tutoring.

Majors. Biology: General. **Business:** Business admin. **Computer sciences:** Computer science. **Education:** Business, early childhood, middle. **English:** English lit. **Human services:** Social work. **Math:** General. **Parks/recreation:** Health/fitness. **Philosophy/religion:** Philosophy. **Physical sciences:** Chemistry. **Psychology:** General. **Social sciences:** Political science, sociology.

Most popular majors. Biology 12%, business/marketing 20%, computer/information sciences 6%, education 7%, English 6%, public administration/social services 12%, social sciences 19%.

Technology on campus. 72 workstations in dormitories, library, computer center. Dormitories wired for high-speed internet access and linked to campus network. Commuter students can connect to campus network. Online library, wireless network available.

Student life. Freshman orientation: Mandatory, $150 fee. Preregistration for classes offered. **Housing:** Coed dorms available. $235 nonrefundable deposit, deadline 5/1. **Activities:** Pep band, campus ministries, choral groups, dance, drama, international student organizations, student government.

Athletics. NAIA. **Intercollegiate:** Basketball, track and field, volleyball W. **Team name:** Panthers.

Student services. Career counseling, student employment services, health services, personal counseling. **Physically disabled:** Services for visually, speech, hearing impaired.

Contact. E-mail: admissions@philander.edu
Phone: (501) 370-5221 Toll-free number: (800) 446-6772
Fax: (501) 370-5225
Damien Williams, Vice-President of Enrollment Management, Philander Smith College, 900 Daisy Bates Drive, Little Rock, AR 72202-3718

Southern Arkansas University
Magnolia, Arkansas
www.saumag.edu   **CB code: 6661**

▶ Public 4-year university
▶ Residential campus in large town
▶ 2,859 degree-seeking undergraduates: 7% part-time, 56% women, 28% African American, 1% Asian American, 3% Hispanic/Latino, 1% Native American, 3% international
▶ 930 degree-seeking graduate students
▶ 67% of applicants admitted
▶ SAT or ACT (ACT writing optional) required
▶ 31% graduate within 6 years

General. Founded in 1909. Regionally accredited. **Degrees:** 440 bachelor's, 149 associate awarded; master's offered. **Location:** 53 miles from Texarkana, TX; 70 miles from Shreveport, LA. **Calendar:** Semester, extensive summer session. **Full-time faculty:** 161 total; 55% have terminal degrees, 14% minority, 45% women. **Part-time faculty:** 119 total; 33% have terminal degrees, 18% minority, 64% women. **Class size:** 43% < 20, 46% 20-39, 8% 40-49, 3% 50-99. **Special facilities:** University farm, natural resource research center, rodeo arena, field station.

Freshman class profile. 2,845 applied, 1,895 admitted, 797 enrolled.

Mid 50% test scores			
SAT critical reading:	390-510	GPA 2.0-2.99:	30%
SAT math:	420-540	Rank in top quarter:	38%
ACT composite:	18-24	Rank in top tenth:	4%
GPA 3.75 or higher:	24%	Return as sophomores:	62%
GPA 3.50-3.74:	14%	Out-of-state:	26%
GPA 3.0-3.49:	31%	Live on campus:	82%
		International:	2%

Basis for selection. For unconditional admission, applicants must have ACT of 19 or higher. ACT of 16 to 18 allows conditional admission. Interview required of nursing majors.

High school preparation. Recommended units include English 4, mathematics 4, social studies 3, science 3 (laboratory 3) and foreign language 2. 0.5 computer science also recommended.

2015-2016 Annual costs. Tuition/fees: $7,881; $11,451 out-of-state. Room/board: $5,704. Books/supplies: $1,600. Personal expenses: $2,528.

2014-2015 Financial aid. Need-based: 669 full-time freshmen applied for aid; 583 deemed to have need; 579 received aid. Average need met was 81%. Average scholarship/grant was $4,732; average loan $2,984. 55% of total undergraduate aid awarded as scholarships/grants, 45% as loans/jobs. **Non-need-based:** Awarded to 1,584 full-time undergraduates, including 565 freshmen. Scholarships awarded for academics, alumni affiliation, art, athletics, leadership, minority status, music/drama, state residency.

Application procedures. Admission: Closing date 8/30 (receipt date). No application fee. Admission notification on a rolling basis. **Financial aid:** Priority date 7/1; no closing date. FAFSA required. Applicants notified on a rolling basis starting 4/15; must reply within 2 week(s) of notification.

Academics. Special study options: Combined bachelor's/graduate degree, cross-registration, distance learning, double major, dual enrollment of high school students, ESL, honors, independent study, internships, study abroad, teacher certification program. **Credit/placement by examination:** AP, CLEP, SAT, ACT. 15 credit hours maximum toward associate degree, 30 toward bachelor's. **Support services:** Learning center, reduced course load, remedial instruction, tutoring, writing center.

Honors college/program. 26 ACT required. Students take up to 18 hours of General Education classes together and 24 hours of honors courses in order to receive an honors degree.

Majors. Biology: General. **Business:** General, accounting. **Communications:** Journalism. **Computer sciences:** General. **Education:** Agricultural, early childhood, middle, music, physical. **English:** English lit. **Foreign languages:** Spanish. **Health services:** Athletic training, clinical lab science, nursing (RN). **History:** General. **Human services:** Community org/advocacy, social work. **Math:** General. **Parks/recreation:** Exercise sciences. **Physical sciences:** Chemistry, physics. **Protective services:** Criminal justice. **Psychology:** General. **Social sciences:** General, political science, sociology. **Visual/performing arts:** Dramatic, game design, music, studio arts.

Most popular majors. Agriculture 6%, biology 8%, business/marketing 19%, education 14%, health sciences 8%, liberal arts 6%, psychology 7%, security/protective services 6%.

Technology on campus. 202 workstations in dormitories, library, computer center. Dormitories wired for high-speed internet access and linked to campus network. Commuter students can connect to campus network. Online library, helpline, wireless network available.

Student life. Freshman orientation: Mandatory, $50 fee. Preregistration for classes offered. Held once a week during summer (students select one session) and the weekend before classes start. **Policies:** Freshmen required to live on campus unless commuting or living with parents. **Housing:** Guaranteed on-campus for all undergraduates. Coed dorms, single-sex dorms, apartments, themed housing, wellness housing available. $100 fully refundable deposit. **Activities:** Bands, choral groups, drama, international student organizations, music ensembles, musical theater, radio station, student government, student newspaper.

Athletics. NCAA. **Intercollegiate:** Baseball M, basketball, cross-country, football (tackle) M, golf, softball W, tennis W, track and field, volleyball W. **Intramural:** Badminton, basketball, football (non-tackle), football (tackle) M, golf, soccer, softball, swimming, table tennis, tennis, ultimate frisbee, volleyball. **Team name:** Muleriders.

Student services. Adult student services, alcohol/substance abuse counseling, career counseling, services for economically disadvantaged, student employment services, financial aid counseling, health services, minority student services, personal counseling, placement for graduates, veterans' counselor, women's services. **Physically disabled:** Services for visually, hearing impaired.

Contact. E-mail: sejennings@saumag.edu
Phone: (870) 235-4040 Toll-free number: (800) 332-7286
Fax: (870) 235-4931
Sarah Jennings, Dean of Enrollment Services, Southern Arkansas University, Box 9382, Magnolia, AR 71754-9382

University of Arkansas
Fayetteville, Arkansas   **CB member**
www.uark.edu   **CB code: 6866**

▶ Public 4-year university
▶ Residential campus in small city

- 21,806 degree-seeking undergraduates: 11% part-time, 52% women, 5% African American, 2% Asian American, 8% Hispanic/Latino, 1% Native American, 3% Multi-racial, non-Hispanic, 3% international
- 4,246 degree-seeking graduate students
- 60% of applicants admitted
- SAT or ACT (ACT writing optional) required
- 62% graduate within 6 years; 32% enter graduate study

General. Founded in 1871. Regionally accredited. **Degrees:** 4,206 bachelor's awarded; master's, professional, doctoral offered. **ROTC:** Army, Air Force. **Location:** 192 miles from Little Rock; 120 miles from Tulsa, OK. **Calendar:** Semester, limited summer session. **Full-time faculty:** 1,137 total; 84% have terminal degrees, 16% minority, 40% women. **Part-time faculty:** 183 total; 38% have terminal degrees, 8% minority, 50% women. **Class size:** 48% < 20, 27% 20-39, 8% 40-49, 12% 50-99, 5% >100. **Special facilities:** Performing arts center, entrepreneurial co-working space, equine pavilion, animal science center, optical network, high performance computing (supercomputing), nanoscale science and engineering building, center for space/planetary sciences, chamber for planetary/asteroid simulation, high density electronics research center, poultry research center.

Freshman class profile. 20,542 applied, 12,337 admitted, 4,915 enrolled.

Mid 50% test scores		Rank in top tenth:	26%
SAT critical reading:	500-600	End year in good standing:	84%
SAT math:	510-620	Return as sophomores:	82%
ACT composite:	23-28	Out-of-state:	50%
GPA 3.75 or higher:	41%	Live on campus:	89%
GPA 3.50-3.74:	24%	International:	2%
GPA 3.0-3.49:	30%	Fraternities:	27%
GPA 2.0-2.99:	5%	Sororities:	50%
Rank in top quarter:	54%		

Basis for selection. Standardized test scores, academic GPA, evidence of commitment to success most important. As mandated by state law, those with ACT scores of 18 or less in English, mathematics or reading are assigned developmental coursework or required to take institutional placement test. Portfolios and/or auditions may be required of applicants who plan to enter the fine arts. **Learning Disabled:** Applicants with autism are strongly encouraged to connect with the University of Arkansas Autism Support Program.

High school preparation. College-preparatory program recommended. 17 units required. Required and recommended units include English 4, mathematics 4, social studies 1, history 2, science 3 (laboratory 1), foreign language 2 and academic electives 2.

2015-2016 Annual costs. Tuition/fees: $8,522; $21,826 out-of-state. Room/board: $9,880.

Application procedures. Admission: Priority date 11/1; deadline 8/1 (receipt date). $40 fee ($50 out-of-state), may be waived for applicants with need. Admission notification on a rolling basis beginning on or about 9/1. **Financial aid:** No deadline. FAFSA required.

Academics. Special study options: Accelerated study, combined bachelor's/graduate degree, cooperative education, cross-registration, distance learning, double major, dual enrollment of high school students, ESL, honors, independent study, internships, liberal arts/career combination, student-designed major, study abroad, teacher certification program, Washington semester. **Credit/placement by examination:** AP, CLEP, IB, SAT, ACT, institutional tests. Do not offer for associate degree, 68 hours of lower level credit allowed for bachelor's degree. **Support services:** Learning center, reduced course load, remedial instruction, study skills assistance, tutoring, writing center. Supplemental Instruction, Academic Coaching.

Honors college/program. Freshman admission requirements: 28 ACT/SAT equivalent, 3.5 GPA required. College of Business requires 28 ACT/SAT equivalent and 3.75 GPA. The Honors College admitted 990 freshman in Fall 2015. Each year the Honors College awards up to 90 freshman fellowships that provide $70,000 over four years, and more than $1 million in study abroad and undergraduate research grants.

Majors. Architecture: Architecture, landscape. **Area/ethnic studies:** American. **Biology:** General. **Business:** General, accounting, business admin, finance, international, logistics, management science, managerial economics, marketing, retail management, training/development. **Communications:** Communications/speech/rhetoric, journalism. **Computer sciences:** General. **Conservation:** Environmental science. **Education:** General, elementary, kindergarten/preschool, special ed, voc/tech. **Engineering:** Agricultural, biological, biomedical, chemical, civil, computer, electrical, industrial, mechanical. **English:** English lit. **Foreign languages:** Classics, French, German, Spanish. **Health services:** Audiology/speech pathology, nursing (RN), premedicine. **History:** General. **Human services:** Social work. **Math:** General. **Parks/recreation:** General, health/fitness. **Philosophy/religion:** Philosophy. **Physical sciences:** Chemistry, geology, physics. **Protective services:** Criminal justice. **Psychology:** General. **Social sciences:** Anthropology, economics,

geography, international relations, political science, sociology. **Visual/performing arts:** Art, dramatic, interior design, music performance. **Work/family studies:** General, clothing/textiles, family studies, food/nutrition.

Most popular majors. Business/marketing 22%, communications/journalism 7%, engineering/engineering technologies 9%, health sciences 8%, social sciences 7%.

Technology on campus. 3,669 workstations in dormitories, library, computer center, student center. Dormitories wired for high-speed internet access and linked to campus network. Commuter students can connect to campus network. Online course registration, online library, helpline, repair service, student web hosting, wireless network available.

Student life. Freshman orientation: Mandatory, $85 fee. Preregistration for classes offered. 2-day or 1-day program held in summer; $50 for guest/parents. **Housing:** Guaranteed on-campus for freshmen. Coed dorms, single-sex dorms, special housing for disabled, apartments, fraternity/sorority housing, themed housing available. $240 partly refundable deposit. Honors, Air Force ROTC housing. **Activities:** Bands, campus ministries, choral groups, dance, drama, international student organizations, music ensembles, Model UN, musical theater, opera, radio station, student government, student newspaper, symphony orchestra, TV station, over 380 organizations available.

Athletics. NCAA. **Intercollegiate:** Baseball M, basketball, cross-country, diving W, football (tackle) M, golf, gymnastics W, soccer W, softball W, swimming W, tennis, track and field, volleyball W. **Intramural:** Badminton, basketball, bowling, football (non-tackle), golf, racquetball, sand volleyball, soccer, softball, table tennis, tennis, volleyball. **Team name:** Razorbacks.

Student services. Adult student services, alcohol/substance abuse counseling, chaplain/spiritual director, career counseling, services for economically disadvantaged, student employment services, financial aid counseling, health services, legal services, minority student services, on-campus daycare, personal counseling, placement for graduates, veterans' counselor, women's services. **Physically disabled:** Services for visually, speech, hearing impaired.

Contact. E-mail: uofa@uark.edu
Phone: (479) 575-5346 Toll-free number: (800) 377-8632
Fax: (479) 575-7515
Suzanne McCray, Vice Provost for Enrollment, University of Arkansas, 232 Silas H. Hunt Hall, Fayetteville, AR 72701

University of Arkansas at Fort Smith
Fort Smith, Arkansas
www.uafs.edu
CB member
CB code: 6220

- Public 4-year university
- Commuter campus in small city
- 5,989 degree-seeking undergraduates

General. Founded in 1928. Regionally accredited. **Degrees:** 784 bachelor's, 335 associate awarded. **ROTC:** Army, Air Force. **Location:** 150 miles from Little Rock; 120 miles from Tulsa, OK. **Calendar:** Semester, limited summer session. **Full-time faculty:** 239 total; 59% have terminal degrees, 18% minority, 50% women. **Part-time faculty:** 201 total; 21% have terminal degrees, 12% minority, 54% women. **Class size:** 39% < 20, 52% 20-39, 3% 40-49, 6% 50-99. **Special facilities:** Arboretum.

Freshman class profile.

GPA 3.75 or higher:	22%	Rank in top tenth:	11%
GPA 3.50-3.74:	15%	Out-of-state:	13%
GPA 3.0-3.49:	27%	Live on campus:	28%
GPA 2.0-2.99:	34%	Fraternities:	5%
Rank in top quarter:	31%	Sororities:	6%

Basis for selection. Open admission, but selective for some programs. Special criteria for health career and education programs. Pre-admission exams are required for all health science programs. Teacher education applicants must take PRAXIS I exam, have grade of C or B in specific English and Rhetoric courses. COMPASS required for placement if ACT/SAT not submitted, or if scores below acceptable minimum (18 on ACT). Interview required of nursing, radiology, surgical technology, paramedic, and dental hygiene majors, as well as teacher education programs. **Home schooled:** 19 ACT or equivalent on SAT or COMPASS required of private school, homeschool, or GED students. **Learning Disabled:** In order to be considered for accommodations, a student must first submit verification of his or her condition based on Student ADA Services' guidelines and meet with the Student ADA Services coordinator to discuss an accommodation request.

High school preparation. College-preparatory program recommended. 14 units recommended. Recommended units include English 4, mathematics 4, social studies 3, science 3 (laboratory 3).

2015-2016 Annual costs. Tuition/fees: $6,322; $14,122 out-of-state. Room/board: $8,068. Books/supplies: $1,264. Personal expenses: $1,980.

Financial aid. Non-need-based: Scholarships awarded for academics, athletics, job skills, leadership, music/drama.

Application procedures. Admission: No deadline. No application fee. Admission notification on a rolling basis. Early applications advised for financial aid. **Financial aid:** Priority date 6/15; no closing date. FAFSA required. Applicants notified on a rolling basis starting 3/1; must reply within 4 week(s) of notification.

Academics. Special study options: Distance learning, double major, dual enrollment of high school students, ESL, external degree, honors, independent study, internships, liberal arts/career combination, student-designed major, study abroad, teacher certification program, weekend college. Associate of Art through distance learning. **Credit/placement by examination:** AP, CLEP, institutional tests. 30 credit hours maximum toward associate degree, 30 toward bachelor's. Prior work/life experience credits awarded for military transcripts only; maximum 30 hours. **Support services:** Learning center, pre-admission summer program, reduced course load, remedial instruction, study skills assistance, tutoring, writing center.

Majors. Biology: General. **Business:** Business admin. **Communications:** General. **Communications technology:** Animation/special effects. **Computer sciences:** General. **Education:** Biology, chemistry, early childhood, English, history, mathematics, middle, music, Spanish. **English:** English lit, technical writing. **Foreign languages:** Spanish. **Health services:** Nursing (RN), radiologic technology/medical imaging. **History:** General. **Math:** General. **Physical sciences:** Chemistry. **Protective services:** Law enforcement admin. **Psychology:** General. **Social sciences:** General. **Visual/performing arts:** Art, dramatic, graphic design, music.

Most popular majors. Biology 6%, business/marketing 16%, computer/information sciences 6%, education 18%, health sciences 12%, interdisciplinary studies 16%, psychology 7%.

Technology on campus. 1,400 workstations in library, computer center, student center. Dormitories wired for high-speed internet access. Online course registration, online library, helpline, repair service, wireless network available.

Student life. Freshman orientation: Available. Preregistration for classes offered. **Housing:** Coed dorms, apartments, wellness housing available. $75 nonrefundable deposit. **Activities:** Bands, campus ministries, choral groups, drama, international student organizations, literary magazine, music ensembles, student government, student newspaper, symphony orchestra, Future Educators Association, math club, drama club, cultural network, Students Together Effectively Progressing (STEP), Sigma Tau Delta, Lions for Christ, Sebastian Commons Organization for Protecting the Environment, transfer student organization, non-traditional students.

Athletics. NCAA. **Intercollegiate:** Baseball M, basketball, cross-country, golf, tennis, volleyball W. **Intramural:** Basketball, football (non-tackle), soccer, softball, ultimate frisbee, volleyball. **Team name:** Lions.

Student services. Adult student services, career counseling, services for economically disadvantaged, student employment services, financial aid counseling, health services, personal counseling, placement for graduates, veterans' counselor. **Physically disabled:** Services for visually, speech, hearing impaired.

Contact. E-mail: information@uafortsmith.edu
Phone: (479) 788-7120 Toll-free number: (888) 512-5466
Fax: (479) 788-7108
University of Arkansas at Fort Smith, PO Box 3649, Fort Smith, AR 72913-3649

University of Arkansas at Little Rock

Little Rock, Arkansas **CB member**
www.ualr.edu **CB code: 6368**

- Public 4-year university
- Commuter campus in small city
- 7,888 degree-seeking undergraduates
- SAT or ACT (ACT writing optional) required

General. Founded in 1927. Regionally accredited. **Degrees:** 1,418 bachelor's, 285 associate awarded; master's, professional, doctoral offered. **ROTC:** Army. **Calendar:** Semester, limited summer session. **Full-time faculty:** 453 total; 53% have terminal degrees, 18% minority, 42% women. **Part-time faculty:** 287 total; 29% have terminal degrees, 14% minority, 50% women. **Class size:** 73% < 20, 20% 20-39, 3% 40-49, 3% 50-99, less than 1%

>100. **Special facilities:** Nanotechnology center, speech and hearing clinic, planetarium, observatory, government documents depository.

Freshman class profile. 859 enrolled.

GPA 3.75 or higher:	20%	Rank in top tenth:	15%
GPA 3.50-3.74:	16%	Out-of-state:	6%
GPA 3.0-3.49:	33%	Fraternities:	6%
GPA 2.0-2.99:	29%	Sororities:	8%
Rank in top quarter:	41%		

Basis for selection. Unconditional admission based on 21 ACT, 990 SAT (exclusive of Writing), 2.5 GPA, and completion of college preparatory curriculum. Students must meet 2 of 3 basic criteria. All students born after January 1, 1957 required to show Arkansas Certificate of Immunization for Institutions of Higher Education. COMPASS or institutional test accepted for admission. Interview recommended for academically weak applicants.

High school preparation. College-preparatory program recommended. 16.5 units recommended. Recommended units include English 4, mathematics 4, social studies 3, science 3, visual/performing arts .5, academic electives 1.5. Communication .5.

2015-2016 Annual costs. Tuition/fees: $8,108; $19,178 out-of-state. Room/board: $7,228. Books/supplies: $1,715. Personal expenses: $1,893.

Financial aid. Non-need-based: Scholarships awarded for academics, art, athletics, leadership, music/drama.

Application procedures. Admission: Closing date 9/1 (postmark date). $40 fee, may be waived for applicants with need. Application must be submitted online. Admission notification on a rolling basis. **Financial aid:** Priority date 3/1; no closing date. FAFSA required. Applicants notified on a rolling basis starting 5/1.

Academics. Special study options: Accelerated study, cooperative education, distance learning, double major, dual enrollment of high school students, ESL, honors, independent study, internships, study abroad, teacher certification program. **Credit/placement by examination:** AP, CLEP, IB, SAT, ACT, institutional tests. 30 credit hours maximum toward associate degree, 30 toward bachelor's. Credit obtained through examination is recorded as approved hours on the official permanent record without grade or grade points. **Support services:** Learning center, reduced course load, remedial instruction, study skills assistance, tutoring, writing center.

Honors college/program. Factors in the selection process are GPA, community involvement, test scores, recommendations, written essays and personal interviews. Although all factors are considered, a student's GPA carries the most weight.

Majors. Biology: General. **Business:** Accounting, business admin, finance, international, management information systems, managerial economics, marketing. **Communications:** Advertising, communications/speech/rhetoric, journalism. **Computer sciences:** General, information systems. **Education:** Early childhood, elementary, middle. **Engineering:** Construction, systems. **English:** English lit, technical writing. **Foreign languages:** French, German, sign language interpretation, Spanish. **Health services:** Audiology/speech pathology, environmental health, nursing (RN). **History:** General. **Human services:** Social work. **Liberal arts:** Arts/sciences, humanities. **Math:** General. **Philosophy/religion:** Philosophy. **Physical sciences:** Chemistry, geology, physics. **Protective services:** Criminal justice. **Psychology:** General. **Social sciences:** Anthropology, economics, international relations, political science, sociology. **Visual/performing arts:** Art, art history/conservation, dance, dramatic, music.

Technology on campus. 500 workstations in dormitories, library, computer center. Dormitories wired for high-speed internet access and linked to campus network. Commuter students can connect to campus network. Online library, wireless network available.

Student life. Freshman orientation: Mandatory. Preregistration for classes offered. **Housing:** Coed dorms, special housing for disabled, apartments, themed housing available. $100 fully refundable deposit, deadline 9/1. **Activities:** Bands, campus ministries, choral groups, dance, drama, international student organizations, literary magazine, music ensembles, Model UN, musical theater, opera, radio station, student government, student newspaper, symphony orchestra, TV station, Baptist student union, University Republicans, Methodist student club, Muslim students association, Young Democrats, Association for Minority Students Education Needs and Development, Advocates for People with Disabilities.

Athletics. NCAA. **Intercollegiate:** Baseball M, basketball, cheerleading W, cross-country, golf, soccer, swimming, tennis, track and field, volleyball W. **Intramural:** Badminton, basketball, bowling, football (tackle) M, golf, softball, swimming, table tennis M, tennis, volleyball. **Team name:** Trojans.

Student services. Adult student services, alcohol/substance abuse counseling, career counseling, services for economically disadvantaged, student

employment services, financial aid counseling, health services, minority student services, personal counseling, placement for graduates, veterans' counselor. **Physically disabled:** Services for visually, speech, hearing impaired.

Contact. E-mail: admissions@ualr.edu
Phone: (501) 569-3127 Toll-free number: (800) 482-8892
Fax: (501) 569-8956
Kathryn Young, Director of Admissions, University of Arkansas at Little Rock, 2801 South University Avenue, Little Rock, AR 72204-1099

University of Arkansas at Monticello
Monticello, Arkansas
www.uamont.edu CB code: 6007

- Public 4-year university and technical college
- Commuter campus in large town
- 3,733 undergraduates
- 160 graduate students

General. Founded in 1909. Regionally accredited. **Degrees:** 325 bachelor's, 355 associate awarded; master's offered. **ROTC:** Army. **Location:** 100 miles from Little Rock, 50 miles from Pine Bluff. **Calendar:** Semester, extensive summer session. **Full-time faculty:** 151 total. **Part-time faculty:** 67 total. **Class size:** 61% < 20, 33% 20-39, 3% 40-49, 3% 50-99, less than 1% >100. **Special facilities:** Museum of natural history, extensive research forest, planetarium, farm.

Freshman class profile.

GPA 3.75 or higher:	6%	Out-of-state:	14%
GPA 3.50-3.74:	7%	Live on campus:	37%
GPA 3.0-3.49:	26%	Fraternities:	9%
GPA 2.0-2.99:	49%	Sororities:	9%

Basis for selection. Open admission, but selective for some programs. ACT, SAT, ASSET, or COMPASS scores may be requested for placement. **Home schooled:** Transcript of courses and grades required. ACT/SAT required for placement.

High school preparation. Recommended units include English 4, mathematics 4, social studies 3, science 3 and foreign language 2.

2015-2016 Annual costs. Tuition/fees: $6,447; $12,297 out-of-state. Room/board: $6,189. Books/supplies: $1,000. Personal expenses: $2,250.

Financial aid. Non-need-based: Scholarships awarded for academics, athletics, job skills, leadership, music/drama, ROTC, state residency.

Application procedures. Admission: Priority date 8/1; no deadline. No application fee. Admission notification on a rolling basis. **Financial aid:** Priority date 5/1; no closing date. FAFSA required. Applicants notified on a rolling basis starting 5/1; must reply within 2 week(s) of notification.

Academics. Special study options: Combined bachelor's/graduate degree, cross-registration, distance learning, double major, dual enrollment of high school students, independent study, internships, liberal arts/career combination, study abroad, teacher certification program. **Credit/placement by examination:** AP, CLEP, IB, institutional tests. 9 credit hours maximum toward bachelor's degree. **Support services:** Learning center, pre-admission summer program, reduced course load, remedial instruction, study skills assistance, tutoring, writing center.

Majors. Biology: General. **Business:** Accounting, business admin, management information systems. **Communications:** Communications/speech/rhetoric, journalism. **Conservation:** Forestry, wildlife/wilderness. **Education:** Kindergarten/preschool, middle, music, physical. **English:** English lit. **Foreign languages:** General. **Health services:** Nursing (RN). **History:** General. **Human services:** Social work. **Math:** General. **Parks/recreation:** Health/fitness. **Physical sciences:** Chemistry. **Protective services:** Criminal justice. **Psychology:** General. **Social sciences:** General, political science. **Visual/performing arts:** Art, music.

Most popular majors. Business/marketing 20%, education 13%, health sciences 9%, liberal arts 8%.

Technology on campus. 400 workstations in dormitories, library, computer center, student center, student center. Dormitories wired for high-speed internet access and linked to campus network. Commuter students can connect to campus network. Online course registration, wireless network available.

Student life. Freshman orientation: Mandatory. Preregistration for classes offered. One-day program held at beginning of semester. **Housing:** Guaranteed on-campus for all undergraduates. Single-sex dorms, special housing for disabled, apartments, wellness housing available. $60 fully

refundable deposit, deadline 8/1. **Activities:** Bands, choral groups, drama, literary magazine, music ensembles, musical theater, student government, student newspaper, Baptist student union, Missionary Baptist student fellowship, Wesley Foundation, Christians in Action, Catholic Weevils, Chi Alpha.

Athletics. NCAA. **Intercollegiate:** Baseball M, basketball, cross-country, football (tackle) M, golf, rodeo, softball W, tennis W, volleyball W. **Intramural:** Archery, badminton, baseball M, basketball, bowling, boxing M, cross-country, football (tackle) M, golf, handball, racquetball, soccer, softball, swimming, table tennis, tennis, track and field, volleyball. **Team name:** Boll Weevils.

Student services. Alcohol/substance abuse counseling, chaplain/spiritual director, career counseling, student employment services, financial aid counseling, health services, personal counseling, placement for graduates, veterans' counselor. **Physically disabled:** Services for visually, speech, hearing impaired.

Contact. E-mail: whitingm@uamont.edu
Phone: (870) 460-1026 Toll-free number: (800) 844-1826
Fax: (870) 460-1926
Mary Whiting, Director of Admissions, University of Arkansas at Monticello, Box 3600, Monticello, AR 71656

University of Arkansas at Pine Bluff
Pine Bluff, Arkansas CB member
www.uapb.edu CB code: 6004

- Public 4-year university
- Commuter campus in small city
- 2,526 degree-seeking undergraduates: 9% part-time, 56% women, 92% African American, 1% Hispanic/Latino, 1% international
- 110 degree-seeking graduate students
- 46% of applicants admitted
- SAT or ACT (ACT writing optional) required

General. Founded in 1873. Regionally accredited. **Degrees:** 359 bachelor's awarded; master's, doctoral offered. **ROTC:** Army. **Location:** 42 miles from Little Rock. **Calendar:** Semester, limited summer session. **Full-time faculty:** 159 total. **Part-time faculty:** 36 total. **Class size:** 42% < 20, 47% 20-39, 6% 40-49, 5% 50-99. **Special facilities:** 220-acre farm, aquaculture fisheries, cultural museum.

Freshman class profile. 4,452 applied, 2,055 admitted, 684 enrolled.

Return as sophomores:	71%	Live on campus:	77%
Out-of-state:	45%	International:	1%

Basis for selection. Admission credentials for entering freshmen must include formal application, high school transcript, ACT test information and scores (SAT is accepted) and immunization record.

High school preparation. 21 units required. Required units include English 4, mathematics 3, social studies 1, history 2, science 3 (laboratory 2), foreign language 2 and academic electives 4.

2015-2016 Annual costs. Tuition/fees: $6,308; $11,978 out-of-state. Room/board: $7,270. Books/supplies: $1,000. Personal expenses: $1,750.

Financial aid. Non-need-based: Scholarships awarded for academics, alumni affiliation, art, athletics, leadership, minority status, music/drama, religious affiliation, ROTC, state residency.

Application procedures. Admission: Priority date 8/1; no deadline. No application fee. Admission notification on a rolling basis. **Financial aid:** Priority date 4/15; no closing date. FAFSA required. Applicants notified on a rolling basis starting 3/1.

Academics. Special study options: Cooperative education, cross-registration, distance learning, double major, dual enrollment of high school students, honors, independent study, internships, study abroad, teacher certification program. **Credit/placement by examination:** AP, CLEP, IB, SAT, ACT. **Support services:** Learning center, pre-admission summer program, reduced course load, remedial instruction, study skills assistance, tutoring, writing center.

Majors. Biology: General. **Business:** Accounting, business admin. **Communications:** Journalism. **Computer sciences:** General. **Conservation:** Fisheries. **Education:** Agricultural, art, business, early childhood, English, family/consumer sciences, mathematics, middle, physical, science, social science, special ed, trade/industrial. **English:** English lit. **Health services:** Nursing (RN). **History:** General. **Human services:** Social work. **Math:**

General. **Physical sciences:** Chemistry, physics. **Protective services:** Criminal justice. **Psychology:** General. **Social sciences:** General. **Visual/performing arts:** Art, music. **Work/family studies:** General, aging.

Most popular majors. Agriculture 6%, biology 10%, business/marketing 14%, education 8%, family/consumer sciences 6%, liberal arts 8%, psychology 7%, security/protective services 13%.

Technology on campus. 1,000 workstations in dormitories, library, computer center, student center. Dormitories linked to campus network. Commuter students can connect to campus network. Online library, helpline, repair service available.

Student life. Freshman orientation: Mandatory. Preregistration for classes offered. **Housing:** Single-sex dorms available. $100 partly refundable deposit. **Activities:** Bands, campus ministries, choral groups, drama, international student organizations, music ensembles, radio station, student government, student newspaper, TV station, Baptist student union, political science/pre-law club, Church of God in Christ, Wesley Foundation, criminal justice club, accounting club, agriculture club, English club, Student Nurses Association, Students in Free Enterprise.

Athletics. NCAA. **Intercollegiate:** Baseball M, basketball, bowling W, cross-country, football (tackle) M, golf, soccer W, softball W, tennis, track and field, volleyball W. **Intramural:** Baseball M, basketball, bowling, cross-country M, football (tackle), golf, gymnastics, handball, racquetball, softball, swimming, table tennis, tennis, volleyball, weight lifting. **Team name:** Golden Lions.

Student services. Adult student services, alcohol/substance abuse counseling, chaplain/spiritual director, career counseling, services for economically disadvantaged, student employment services, financial aid counseling, health services, on-campus daycare, personal counseling, placement for graduates, veterans' counselor.

Contact. E-mail: owasoyop@uapb.edu
Phone: (870) 575-8492 Toll-free number: (800) 264-6585
Fax: (870) 575-4607
Philomena Owasoyo, Director of Admissions, University of Arkansas at Pine Bluff, 1200 North University Drive, Mail Slot 4981, Pine Bluff, AR 71601-2799

University of Arkansas for Medical Sciences
Little Rock, Arkansas
www.uams.edu
CB code: 0424

- Public 4-year university and health science college
- Commuter campus in large city
- 761 degree-seeking undergraduates
- 2,247 graduate students
- SAT or ACT required

General. Founded in 1876. Regionally accredited. University has 5 colleges (medicine, nursing, pharmacy, health-related professions, public health) and graduate school. **Degrees:** 292 bachelor's, 68 associate awarded; master's, professional, doctoral offered. **Location:** 4 miles from downtown. **Calendar:** Semester, limited summer session. **Full-time faculty:** 1,153 total. **Part-time faculty:** 217 total. **Special facilities:** Academic health center.

Basis for selection. Admissions criteria vary according to academic program. Most incoming students must have prior college credit.

High school preparation. College-preparatory program recommended.

2015-2016 Annual costs. Tuition/fees: $7,785; $17,895 out-of-state.

Financial aid. Non-need-based: Scholarships awarded for academics, state residency.

Application procedures. Admission: $50 fee. Admission notification on a rolling basis. Must reply by May 1 or within 2 week(s) if notified thereafter. Application closing dates vary by program. **Financial aid:** No deadline. FAFSA, institutional form required. Applicants notified on a rolling basis starting 5/1; must reply within 4 week(s) of notification.

Academics. Special study options: Accelerated study, combined bachelor's/graduate degree, distance learning, double major, dual enrollment of high school students, honors, independent study, internships, study abroad. **Credit/placement by examination:** AP, CLEP. **Support services:** Learning center, study skills assistance, tutoring.

Majors. Health services: Clinical lab science, cytotechnology, dental hygiene, EMT paramedic, medical radiologic technology/radiation therapy, nuclear medical technology, nursing (RN).

Technology on campus. Dormitories wired for high-speed internet access and linked to campus network. Commuter students can connect to campus network. Online library, helpline, student web hosting, wireless network available.

Student life. Freshman orientation: Mandatory. Preregistration for classes offered. **Housing:** Coed dorms, special housing for disabled, apartments available. **Activities:** Campus ministries, student government.

Student services. Alcohol/substance abuse counseling, chaplain/spiritual director, career counseling, services for economically disadvantaged, financial aid counseling, health services, minority student services, personal counseling. **Physically disabled:** Services for visually, hearing impaired.

Contact. Phone: (501) 686-5000
University of Arkansas for Medical Sciences, 4301 West Markham Street, Little Rock, AR 72205

University of Central Arkansas
Conway, Arkansas
www.uca.edu
CB member
CB code: 6012

- Public 4-year university
- Residential campus in small city
- 9,340 degree-seeking undergraduates: 12% part-time, 59% women, 18% African American, 2% Asian American, 5% Hispanic/Latino, 1% Native American, 4% Multi-racial, non-Hispanic, 4% international
- 1,855 degree-seeking graduate students
- 92% of applicants admitted
- SAT or ACT (ACT writing optional) required
- 45% graduate within 6 years

General. Founded in 1907. Regionally accredited. **Degrees:** 1,420 bachelor's, 109 associate awarded; master's, professional, doctoral offered. **ROTC:** Army. **Location:** 30 miles from Little Rock. **Calendar:** Semester, extensive summer session. **Class size:** 45% < 20, 47% 20-39, 5% 40-49, 3% 50-99, less than 1% >100. **Special facilities:** Observatory, greenhouse, nature reserve, 24-hour study center, human anatomy lab, herbarium, planetarium.

Freshman class profile. 5,063 applied, 4,667 admitted, 2,044 enrolled.

Mid 50% test scores			
SAT critical reading:	440-540	Rank in top quarter:	44%
SAT math:	450-570	Rank in top tenth:	17%
SAT writing:	440-550	Return as sophomores:	72%
ACT composite:	20-26	Out-of-state:	8%
GPA 3.75 or higher:	29%	Live on campus:	86%
GPA 3.50-3.74:	17%	International:	2%
GPA 3.0-3.49:	31%		
GPA 2.0-2.99:	23%		

Basis for selection. Test scores and GPA. **Learning Disabled:** Eligibility for services determined individually based on documentation of need. Prospective students encouraged to meet with DSS staff.

High school preparation. College-preparatory program recommended. Recommended units include English 4, mathematics 4, social studies 1, history 2, science 3 and academic electives 10.

2015-2016 Annual costs. Tuition/fees: $7,889; $13,806 out-of-state. Room/board: $5,982. Books/supplies: $1,200. Personal expenses: $3,449.

Financial aid. Non-need-based: Scholarships awarded for academics, art, athletics, leadership, minority status, music/drama, ROTC, state residency. **Additional information:** Room and board may be paid monthly.

Application procedures. Admission: Priority date 5/1; no deadline. $25 fee, may be waived for applicants with need. Admission notification on a rolling basis. **Financial aid:** Priority date 4/15, closing date 7/1. FAFSA required. Applicants notified on a rolling basis starting 5/4.

Academics. Special study options: Accelerated study, cooperative education, distance learning, double major, dual enrollment of high school students, ESL, honors, independent study, internships, liberal arts/career combination, study abroad, teacher certification program. 5-year professional programs in physical therapy and occupational therapy. **Credit/placement by examination:** AP, CLEP, IB, SAT, ACT, institutional tests. 30 credit hours maximum toward associate degree, 30 toward bachelor's. **Support services:** Learning center, pre-admission summer program, remedial instruction, study skills assistance, tutoring, writing center.

Honors college/program. Special honors courses and minor in interdisciplinary studies offered. 27 ACT and 3.6 GPA minimum.

Majors. Area/ethnic studies: African-American. **Biology:** General. **Business:** General, accounting, business admin, entrepreneurial studies, finance, insurance, management information systems, marketing. **Communications:** Communications/speech/rhetoric, journalism, persuasive communications. **Computer sciences:** General. **Conservation:** Environmental studies. **Education:** Business, family/consumer sciences, kindergarten/preschool, mathematics, middle, physical, science, social studies. **English:** Creative writing, English lit, writing. **Foreign languages:** General, linguistics, Spanish. **Health services:** Athletic training, audiology/speech pathology, clinical lab science, community health services, medical radiologic technology/radiation therapy, nuclear medical technology, nursing (RN), substance abuse counseling. **History:** General. **Human services:** General. **Liberal arts:** Arts/sciences. **Math:** General. **Parks/recreation:** Exercise sciences. **Philosophy/religion:** Philosophy, religion. **Physical sciences:** Chemistry, physics. **Psychology:** General. **Social sciences:** Economics, geography, political science, sociology. **Visual/performing arts:** Art, cinematography, dramatic, interior design, music, music performance. **Work/family studies:** General, food/nutrition.

Most popular majors. Business/marketing 17%, education 11%, family/consumer sciences 7%, health sciences 21%, psychology 6%, social sciences 6%, visual/performing arts 7%.

Technology on campus. 608 workstations in dormitories, library, computer center, student center. Dormitories wired for high-speed internet access and linked to campus network. Commuter students can connect to campus network. Online course registration, online library, helpline, repair service, wireless network available.

Student life. Freshman orientation: Available. Preregistration for classes offered. **Housing:** Guaranteed on-campus for freshmen. Coed dorms, single-sex dorms, special housing for disabled, apartments, fraternity/sorority housing available. $100 fully refundable deposit. **Activities:** Bands, campus ministries, choral groups, dance, drama, film society, international student organizations, literary magazine, music ensembles, Model UN, radio station, student government, student newspaper, symphony orchestra, TV station, Baptist student union, Methodist student union, Newman Club, Young Democrats, College Republicans, Students for Propagation of Black Culture, Association of Baptist Students, Catholic Campus Ministries, ORBIS.

Athletics. NCAA. Intercollegiate: Baseball M, basketball, cross-country, football (tackle) M, golf, soccer, softball W, tennis W, track and field, volleyball W. **Intramural:** Basketball, football (non-tackle), soccer, softball, tennis, volleyball. **Team name:** Bears.

Student services. Alcohol/substance abuse counseling, chaplain/spiritual director, career counseling, student employment services, financial aid counseling, health services, minority student services, personal counseling, placement for graduates, veterans' counselor, women's services. **Physically disabled:** Services for visually, speech, hearing impaired.

Contact. E-mail: admissions@uca.edu
Phone: (501) 450-3128 Toll-free number: (800) 243-8245
Fax: (501) 450-5228
Courtney Mullen, Director of Admissions and Enrollment Services, University of Central Arkansas, 201 Donaghey Avenue, Conway, AR 72035

University of Phoenix: Little Rock
Little Rock, Arkansas
www.phoenix.edu

- For-profit 4-year university
- Commuter campus in small city
- 551 undergraduates
- 70 graduate students

General. Regionally accredited. **Degrees:** 171 bachelor's awarded; master's offered. **Calendar:** Differs by program. **Full-time faculty:** 21 total. **Part-time faculty:** 122 total.

Basis for selection. Open admission, but selective for some programs.

2015-2016 Annual costs. Per-credit-hour charge, $410 to $635, depending upon level and course of study. Books, material charges, and other fees vary by course and program. All fees are subject to change.

Application procedures. Admission: No deadline. No application fee. **Financial aid:** No deadline.

Academics. Credit/placement by examination: AP, CLEP.

Majors. Business: Business admin. **Communications:** General. **Computer sciences:** Programming, security, support specialist, system admin, systems analysis, web page design, webmaster. **Health services:** Facilities admin,

health information management, long term care admin. **Protective services:** Disaster management, law enforcement admin.

Student life. Freshman orientation: Mandatory. Preregistration for classes offered.

Contact. Toll-free number: (866) 766-0766
University of Phoenix: Little Rock, 10800 Financial Center Parkway, Little Rock, AR 72211-3552

University of Phoenix: Northwest Arkansas
Rogers, Arkansas
www.phoenix.edu

- For-profit 4-year university
- Commuter campus in small city
- 530 degree-seeking undergraduates
- 38 graduate students

General. Regionally accredited. **Degrees:** 48 bachelor's awarded; master's offered. **Calendar:** Differs by program. **Full-time faculty:** 7 total. **Part-time faculty:** 81 total.

Basis for selection. Open admission, but selective for some programs.

2015-2016 Annual costs. Per-credit-hour charge, $410 to $635, depending upon level and course of study. Books, material charges, and other fees vary by course and program. All fees are subject to change.

Application procedures. Admission: No deadline. No application fee. **Financial aid:** No deadline.

Academics. Credit/placement by examination: AP, CLEP.

Majors. Business: Business admin, human resources. **Computer sciences:** Programming, security, system admin, systems analysis, web page design, webmaster. **Health services:** Facilities admin, health information management, long term care admin. **Human services:** General. **Protective services:** Disaster management, law enforcement admin.

Student life. Freshman orientation: Mandatory. Preregistration for classes offered.

Contact. Toll-free number: (866) 766-0766
University of Phoenix: Northwest Arkansas, 1625 West Fountainhead Parkway, Tempe, AZ 85282

University of the Ozarks
Clarksville, Arkansas
www.ozarks.edu   CB code: 6111

- Private 4-year university and liberal arts college affiliated with the Presbyterian Church (USA)
- Residential campus in small town
- 640 degree-seeking undergraduates: 1% part-time, 52% women, 6% African American, 10% Hispanic/Latino, 1% Native American, 4% Multi-racial, non-Hispanic, 12% international
- 97% of applicants admitted
- SAT or ACT (ACT writing optional) required
- 43% graduate within 6 years

General. Founded in 1834. Regionally accredited. **Degrees:** 107 bachelor's awarded. **Location:** 100 miles from Little Rock, 65 miles from Fort Smith. **Calendar:** Semester, limited summer session.

Freshman class profile. 744 applied, 720 admitted, 211 enrolled.

Mid 50% test scores			
		ACT composite:	20-25
SAT critical reading:	420-540	Return as sophomores:	75%
SAT math:	430-520	International:	9%
SAT writing:	400-520		

Basis for selection. School achievement record and test scores most important.

High school preparation. College-preparatory program recommended. 18 units recommended. Recommended units include English 4, mathematics 4, social studies 1, history 2, science 3 (laboratory 2) and foreign language 2.

2015-2016 Annual costs. Tuition/fees: $24,350. Room/board: $7,190.

Financial aid. Non-need-based: Scholarships awarded for academics, alumni affiliation, art, leadership, minority status, music/drama, religious affiliation, state residency. **Additional information:** Walton International Scholarship Program provides full scholarships to selected Central American and Mexican residents.

Application procedures. Admission: Priority date 4/1; no deadline. No application fee. Admission notification on a rolling basis. **Financial aid:** Priority date 2/15; no closing date. FAFSA required. Applicants notified on a rolling basis starting 3/1; must reply within 2 week(s) of notification.

Academics. Special study options: Cooperative education, double major, dual enrollment of high school students, independent study, internships, liberal arts/career combination, study abroad, teacher certification program. **Credit/placement by examination:** AP, CLEP, SAT, ACT, institutional tests. 30 credit hours maximum toward bachelor's degree. **Support services:** Learning center, remedial instruction, study skills assistance, tutoring.

Majors. Biology: General. **Business:** Accounting, business admin, marketing. **Communications:** Broadcast journalism, media studies. **Conservation:** Environmental studies. **Education:** Biology, business, early childhood, elementary, middle, physical, science, special ed. **English:** English lit. **Foreign languages:** Spanish. **Health services:** Predental, premedicine, prepharmacy, preveterinary. **History:** General. **Human services:** General. **Math:** General. **Parks/recreation:** Health/fitness. **Philosophy/religion:** Philosophy, religion. **Physical sciences:** Chemistry. **Psychology:** General. **Social sciences:** Economics, political science, sociology. **Visual/performing arts:** Dramatic, music, studio arts.

Technology on campus. Dormitories wired for high-speed internet access and linked to campus network. Commuter students can connect to campus network. Online course registration, online library, helpline, wireless network available.

Student life. Freshman orientation: Mandatory. Preregistration for classes offered. **Housing:** Guaranteed on-campus for freshmen. Coed dorms, single-sex dorms, apartments available. **Activities:** Campus ministries, choral groups, drama, film society, international student organizations, literary magazine, radio station, student government, TV station, Ozarks Area Mission, Alpha & Omega, various religious/ethnic/social service organizations.

Athletics. NCAA. **Intercollegiate:** Baseball M, basketball, cheerleading, cross-country, soccer, softball W, swimming, tennis. **Intramural:** Badminton, basketball, bowling, football (non-tackle), soccer, softball, tennis, volleyball. **Team name:** Eagles.

Student services. Chaplain/spiritual director, career counseling, services for economically disadvantaged, student employment services, financial aid counseling, health services, personal counseling, placement for graduates.

Contact. E-mail: admiss@ozarks.edu
Phone: (479) 979-1227 Toll-free number: (800) 264-8636
Fax: (479) 979-1417
Rick Otto, Director of Institutional Research, University of the Ozarks, 415 North College Avenue, Clarksville, AR 72830-2880

Williams Baptist College
Walnut Ridge, Arkansas
www.wbcoll.edu
CB code: 6658

◊ Private 4-year liberal arts college affiliated with the Southern Baptist Convention

◊ Residential campus in small town

◊ 491 degree-seeking undergraduates: 2% part-time, 49% women

◊ 65% of applicants admitted

◊ SAT or ACT (ACT writing optional) required

General. Founded in 1941. Regionally accredited. **Degrees:** 89 bachelor's, 1 associate awarded. **ROTC:** Army. **Location:** 30 miles from Jonesboro, 100 miles from Memphis. **Calendar:** Semester, limited summer session. **Full-time faculty:** 26 total; 69% have terminal degrees, 42% women. **Part-time faculty:** 24 total; 4% have terminal degrees, 67% women. **Class size:** 52% < 20, 47% 20-39, less than 1% 40-49.

Freshman class profile. 578 applied, 373 admitted, 128 enrolled.

Mid 50% test scores			
ACT composite:	19-24	GPA 2.0-2.99:	31%
		Out-of-state:	34%
GPA 3.75 or higher:	20%	Live on campus:	66%
GPA 3.50-3.74:	15%	International:	2%
GPA 3.0-3.49:	34%		

Basis for selection. 19 ACT and 2.5 GPA required in order to be admitted unconditionally.

High school preparation. College-preparatory program recommended. 19 units recommended. Recommended units include English 4, mathematics 4, social studies 3, science 3 (laboratory 3) and foreign language 2.

2015-2016 Annual costs. Tuition/fees: $16,430. Room/board: $7,000. Books/supplies: $1,200. Personal expenses: $1,500.

2014-2015 Financial aid. Need-based: 127 full-time freshmen applied for aid; 100 deemed to have need; 100 received aid. Average scholarship/grant was $4,276; average loan $2,893. 48% of total undergraduate aid awarded as scholarships/grants, 52% as loans/jobs. **Non-need-based:** Awarded to 594 full-time undergraduates, including 211 freshmen. Scholarships awarded for academics, art, athletics, leadership, minority status, music/drama, religious affiliation, state residency. **Additional information:** Art scholarship applicants must submit portfolio.

Application procedures. Admission: No deadline. No application fee. Admission notification on a rolling basis. **Financial aid:** Priority date 5/1; no closing date. FAFSA required. Applicants notified on a rolling basis starting 4/1; must reply within 2 week(s) of notification.

Academics. Special study options: Double major, dual enrollment of high school students, honors, independent study, internships, study abroad. **Credit/placement by examination:** AP, CLEP, IB, SAT, ACT. 30 credit hours maximum toward bachelor's degree. **Support services:** Learning center, reduced course load, remedial instruction, study skills assistance, tutoring.

Majors. Biology: General. **Business:** Business admin, finance. **Computer sciences:** General. **Education:** General, art, early childhood, elementary, English, music, physical, secondary, social studies. **English:** English lit. **History:** General. **Psychology:** General. **Theology:** Bible, missionary, religious ed, sacred music, theology, youth ministry. **Visual/performing arts:** Studio arts.

Most popular majors. Biology 7%, business/marketing 11%, education 31%, liberal arts 27%, psychology 16%.

Technology on campus. 70 workstations in library, computer center, student center. Dormitories wired for high-speed internet access and linked to campus network. Commuter students can connect to campus network. Online library, wireless network available.

Student life. Freshman orientation: Mandatory, $105 fee. Preregistration for classes offered. Two-day program held at beginning of fall semester. **Policies:** All full-time students under 21 required to live in college housing, unless commuting. Religious observance required. **Housing:** Guaranteed on-campus for all undergraduates. Single-sex dorms, apartments available. $75 partly refundable deposit, deadline 5/1. **Activities:** Campus ministries, choral groups, drama, international student organizations, music ensembles, student government, Fellowship of Christian Athletes, student activities board, student Ambassadors.

Athletics. NAIA. **Intercollegiate:** Baseball M, basketball, cheerleading, cross-country, soccer M, softball W, volleyball W, wrestling M. **Intramural:** Baseball M, basketball, football (non-tackle), softball, volleyball. **Team name:** Eagles.

Student services. Alcohol/substance abuse counseling, chaplain/spiritual director, career counseling, financial aid counseling, health services, personal counseling, veterans' counselor.

Contact. E-mail: admissions@wbcoll.edu
Phone: (870) 759-4121 Toll-free number: (800) 722-4434
Fax: (870) 886-3924
Andrew Watson, Director of Admissions, Williams Baptist College, PO Box 3665, Walnut Ridge, AR 72476

California

Academy of Art University
San Francisco, California
www.academyart.edu
CB code: 1981

- For-profit 4-year university and visual arts college
- Commuter campus in very large city
- 8,969 degree-seeking undergraduates: 41% part-time, 57% women, 7% African American, 8% Asian American, 12% Hispanic/Latino, 1% Native Hawaiian/Pacific islander, 3% Multi-racial, non-Hispanic, 28% international
- 4,674 degree-seeking graduate students
- 31% graduate within 6 years

General. Founded in 1929. **Degrees:** 1,217 bachelor's, 296 associate awarded; master's offered. **Calendar:** Semester, extensive summer session. **Full-time faculty:** 287 total; 16% have terminal degrees, 14% minority, 39% women. **Part-time faculty:** 1,147 total; 19% have terminal degrees, 17% minority, 43% women. **Class size:** 88% < 20, 12% 20-39, less than 1% 50-99. **Special facilities:** 3 nonprofit galleries, photography darkrooms, Bosch Telecen, green screen stage, interior design resource room, foundry, sculpture center, Final Cut Pro, soundstages, Cintiq labs, Media and Avid Express editing stations.

Freshman class profile. 2,732 applied, 2,732 admitted, 992 enrolled.

End year in good standing:	85%	Live on campus:	42%
Return as sophomores:	76%	International:	28%
Out-of-state:	52%		

Basis for selection. Open admission. Continuing education program offered. Interview recommended, and can be in person or over the phone. **Home schooled:** Signed home school program certification form. **Learning Disabled:** Reasonable accommodations made for students with disabilities.

High school preparation. Art and design courses recommended.

2016-2017 Annual costs. Tuition/fees (projected): $26,490. Room/board: $15,250. Books/supplies: $1,764. Personal expenses: $2,434.

2014-2015 Financial aid. Need-based: 366 full-time freshmen applied for aid; 322 deemed to have need; 300 received aid. Average need met was 29%. Average scholarship/grant was $9,290; average loan $3,121. 37% of total undergraduate aid awarded as scholarships/grants, 63% as loans/jobs. **Non-need-based:** Awarded to 291 full-time undergraduates, including 68 freshmen. Scholarships awarded for academics, art, athletics. **Additional information:** Numerous summer grant programs available.

Application procedures. Admission: No deadline. $100 fee. Admission notification on a rolling basis. Accepted applicants may preregister in mid March. **Financial aid:** Priority date 3/1; no closing date. FAFSA, institutional form required. Applicants notified on a rolling basis starting 3/15; must reply within 2 week(s) of notification.

Academics. Special study options: Combined bachelor's/graduate degree, distance learning, ESL, independent study, internships, teacher certification program. Portfolio development, personal enrichment program. **Credit/placement by examination:** AP, CLEP, IB. Interview, essay recommended for placement. Portfolio recommended for bachelor of arts applicants. **Support services:** Learning center, pre-admission summer program, reduced course load, remedial instruction, study skills assistance, tutoring, writing center.

Majors. Architecture: Architecture, landscape. **Business:** Fashion. **Communications:** Advertising, journalism. **Communications technology:** Animation/special effects. **Computer sciences:** Applications programming, web page design. **Education:** Art. **Visual/performing arts:** Acting, art history/conservation, cinematography, costume design, digital arts, fashion design, game design, graphic design, illustration, industrial design, interior design, metal/jewelry, photography, play/screenwriting. **Work/family studies:** Apparel marketing, fashion consultant, merchandising, textile manufacture.

Most popular majors. Communications/journalism 7%, communication technologies 13%, visual/performing arts 72%.

Technology on campus. 900 workstations in dormitories, library, computer center. Dormitories wired for high-speed internet access. Commuter students can connect to campus network. Online course registration, online library, helpline, student web hosting, wireless network available.

Student life. Freshman orientation: Mandatory. Preregistration for classes offered. 5-day session week before start of classes. **Housing:** Guaranteed on-campus for all undergraduates. Coed dorms, single-sex dorms, special housing for disabled, apartments available. $500 nonrefundable deposit. **Activities:** Pep band, choral groups, dance, drama, film society, international student organizations, Model UN, radio station, student government, student newspaper, TV station, Christian Student Fellowship, Permeas Indonesian Association, Indian students association, Black Student Union, Outloud (LGBT Club), veterans club, Chinese student association, Korean student association.

Athletics. NCAA. **Intercollegiate:** Baseball M, basketball, cross-country, golf, soccer, softball W, tennis W, track and field, volleyball W. **Team name:** Urban Knights.

Student services. Career counseling, student employment services, financial aid counseling. **Physically disabled:** Services for visually, speech, hearing impaired.

Contact. E-mail: admissions@academyart.edu
Phone: (415) 274-2200 Toll-free number: (800) 544-2787
Fax: (415) 618-6287
Admissions, Academy of Art University, 79 New Montgomery Street, San Francisco, CA 94105-3410

Academy of Couture Art
Beverly Hills, California
www.academyofcoutureart.edu
CB code: 6454

- Private 4-year institute of couture fashion design
- Commuter campus in very large city
- 17 degree-seeking undergraduates
- Application essay, interview required

General. Regionally accredited; also accredited by ACICS. **Degrees:** 4 bachelor's, 1 associate awarded. **Calendar:** Quarter, extensive summer session.

Basis for selection. Open admission, but selective for some programs. Demonstrated talent, academic accomplishments, and other achievements that indicate success on a college level. A Portfolio is requested only to assess what you love and not your technical skills. Only digitalized portfolio will be considered. It should contain a mood board of all the subjects that inspire you, and sketches that you would love to see realized. If you do not have any art work, please provide pictures of what you consider are the best products of the industry corresponding to your major. **Home schooled:** State high school equivalency certificate required.

High school preparation. College-preparatory program recommended.

2015-2016 Annual costs. Tuition/fees: $22,338. Books/supplies: $2,400.

Financial aid. All financial aid based on need.

Application procedures. Admission: Priority date 7/9; deadline 10/10 (receipt date). $40 fee, may be waived for applicants with need. Admission notification on a rolling basis. Must reply by May 1 or within 2 week(s) if notified thereafter. Fall term applicants who have not yet received a high school diploma are reviewed for conditional acceptance. An application, essay, portfolio, interview(s), and application fee are required for conditional acceptance review. A transcript of current standing is recommended. Should a conditional acceptance be granted, proof of high school diploma will be required before enrollment. Accepted applicants have two quarters to enroll from the date of acceptance. **Financial aid:** Priority date 3/2; no closing date. FAFSA required. Applicants notified on a rolling basis starting 3/2.

Academics. Special study options: Double major, ESL, internships. **Credit/placement by examination:** AP, CLEP, IB, institutional tests. **Support services:** Learning center, pre-admission summer program, reduced course load, remedial instruction, study skills assistance, tutoring, writing center.

Majors. Visual/performing arts: Fashion design. **Work/family studies:** Textile manufacture.

Most popular majors. Family/consumer sciences 50%, visual/performing arts 50%.

Technology on campus. Commuter students can connect to campus network. Repair service, wireless network available.

Student life. Freshman orientation: Mandatory. Preregistration for classes offered. Held two-days before start of classes. **Housing:** Housing, transportation assistance, roommate and ride exchange available. **Activities:** Student government, student newspaper.

Student services. Alcohol/substance abuse counseling, career counseling, student employment services, financial aid counseling, personal counseling, placement for graduates, veterans' counselor, women's services.

Contact. E-mail: info@academyofcoutureart.edu
Phone: (310) 360-8888 ext. 120 Fax: (310) 857-6974
Jennifer Park Zerkel, Director of Admissions, Academy of Couture Art, 8484 Wilshire Boulevard Suite 730, Beverly Hills, CA 90211

Alliant International University
San Diego, California
www.alliant.edu   CB code: 4039

- Private 4-year university
- Commuter campus in very large city
- 675 degree-seeking undergraduates

General. Founded in 1952. Regionally accredited. **Degrees:** 88 bachelor's awarded; master's, professional, doctoral offered. **Location:** 16 miles from downtown. **Calendar:** Semester, limited summer session. **Full-time faculty:** 203 total; 100% have terminal degrees. **Part-time faculty:** 386 total. **Class size:** 99% < 20, less than 1% 20-39.

Basis for selection. Open admission, but selective for some programs. Academic achievement (minimum 2.75 high school GPA), extracurricular activities, enthusiasm for goals and philosophy of institution important. TOEFL (or Alliant English Proficiency Test) required for international students not from countries where English is the official language. **Home schooled:** Applicants must supply the following: certification of completion of a homeschooling program, if available, or documentation of all courses; certificate or diploma from either a homeschool agency, the state department of education, local school district, or regional superintendent of schools; literature describing the homeschool agency (if available).

High school preparation. 16 units recommended. Recommended units include English 4, mathematics 3, social studies 3, history 1, science 2, foreign language 2 and academic electives 1. 12 academic units in last 3 years of high school recommended.

2015-2016 Annual costs. Tuition/fees: $20,740. Room/board: $7,790. Books/supplies: $1,746. Personal expenses: $4,000.

Financial aid. Non-need-based: Scholarships awarded for academics, alumni affiliation, athletics, leadership.

Application procedures. Admission: Priority date 3/2; no deadline. $65 fee, may be waived for applicants with need. Admission notification on a rolling basis beginning on or about 10/1. Must reply by May 1 or within 2 week(s) if notified thereafter. **Financial aid:** Closing date 3/2. FAFSA required. Applicants notified on a rolling basis starting 2/1; must reply within 3 week(s) of notification.

Academics. Special study options: Combined bachelor's/graduate degree, distance learning, ESL, independent study, internships, liberal arts/career combination, study abroad. **Credit/placement by examination:** AP, CLEP, IB, institutional tests. 27 credit hours maximum toward bachelor's degree.

Majors. Business: Business admin. **Education:** ESL. **Liberal arts:** Arts/sciences. **Protective services:** Law enforcement admin. **Psychology:** General, forensic. **Work/family studies:** Child development.

Most popular majors. Business/marketing 68%, psychology 23%, social sciences 9%.

Technology on campus. 304 workstations in library, computer center. Dormitories wired for high-speed internet access and linked to campus network. Commuter students can connect to campus network. Online library, student web hosting available.

Student life. Housing: Guaranteed on-campus for all undergraduates. Coed dorms available. $265 fully refundable deposit. **Activities:** International student organizations, Model UN, student government, student newspaper, Indian student association, Latino student organization, Alliant Turk Society.

Athletics. Intramural: Basketball, bowling, soccer, softball, tennis, volleyball.

Student services. Adult student services, alcohol/substance abuse counseling, career counseling, student employment services, financial aid counseling, health services, personal counseling, placement for graduates, veterans' counselor, women's services. **Physically disabled:** Services for visually, speech, hearing impaired.

Contact. E-mail: admissions@alliant.edu
Phone: (866) 825-5426 Toll-free number: (866) 825-5426
Fax: (858) 635-4555
Kevin McMackin, Undergraduate Recruiter, Alliant International University, 10455 Pomerado Road, San Diego, CA 92131-1799

American Jewish University
Bel-Air, California
www.college.aju.edu   CB code: 4876

- Private 4-year university and liberal arts college affiliated with the Jewish faith
- Residential campus in very large city
- 150 degree-seeking undergraduates
- 40 graduate students
- Application essay required

General. Founded in 1947. Regionally accredited. **Degrees:** 30 bachelor's awarded; master's offered. **Location:** 5 miles from Los Angeles. **Calendar:** Semester. **Full-time faculty:** 8 total; 88% have terminal degrees, 38% women. **Part-time faculty:** 30 total; 40% have terminal degrees, 50% women. **Class size:** 97% < 20, 3% 20-39. **Special facilities:** Sculpture garden, art gallery, synagogue.

Freshman class profile.

GPA 3.50-3.74:	19%	Rank in top quarter:	33%
GPA 3.0-3.49:	45%	Out-of-state:	8%
GPA 2.0-2.99:	36%	Live on campus:	85%

Basis for selection. An applicant's aspirations, goals, personal experience, ability to connect with others, interpersonal skills, and involvement with leadership activities weigh heavily in the application process. On-campus visit highly encouraged. SAT or ACT recommended. Providing test scores can help applicants with less than stellar grades or help applicants' pursuit of merit-based scholarships. Interview recommended. **Home schooled:** Transcript of courses and grades, letter of recommendation (nonparent) required.

High school preparation. College-preparatory program recommended.

2015-2016 Annual costs. Tuition/fees: $29,608. Room/board: $15,170. Books/supplies: $1,710. Personal expenses: $2,277.

Financial aid. Non-need-based: Scholarships awarded for leadership, minority status, music/drama, state residency.

Application procedures. Admission: Priority date 2/15; no deadline. $35 fee, may be waived for applicants with need. Application must be submitted online. Admission notification on a rolling basis beginning on or about 9/15. Varies due to rolling admissions. **Financial aid:** Priority date 3/2; no closing date. FAFSA, institutional form required. Applicants notified on a rolling basis starting 1/1; must reply by 6/30.

Academics. Special study options: Combined bachelor's/graduate degree, cross-registration, double major, independent study, internships, student-designed major, study abroad. **Credit/placement by examination:** AP, CLEP, IB, institutional tests. **Support services:** Reduced course load, study skills assistance, tutoring, writing center.

Majors. Business: General. **Communications:** Media studies. **Health services:** Ethics. **Liberal arts:** Arts/sciences. **Philosophy/religion:** Judaic. **Psychology:** General. **Social sciences:** International relations, political science, U.S. government.

Most popular majors. Business/marketing 23%, communications/journalism 9%, health sciences 32%, philosophy/religious studies 13%, social sciences 18%.

Technology on campus. 38 workstations in dormitories, library, computer center, student center. Dormitories wired for high-speed internet access and linked to campus network. Commuter students can connect to campus network. Online library, helpline, wireless network available.

Student life. Freshman orientation: Mandatory. Preregistration for classes offered. Held 1-2 weeks before the start of the traditional Fall semester. **Housing:** Guaranteed on-campus for all undergraduates. Coed dorms, special housing for disabled, apartments available. $100 nonrefundable deposit.

Activities: Choral groups, dance, drama, literary magazine, student government, student newspaper, TV station, Hillel, Israel Action Committee, National Council for Jewish Women, Giving Tree.

Athletics. Team name: Zion.

Student services. Alcohol/substance abuse counseling, chaplain/spiritual director, career counseling, student employment services, financial aid counseling, health services.

Contact. E-mail: admissions@aju.edu
Phone: (310) 476-9777 ext. 247 Fax: (310) 471-3657
Alvira Chernichovski, Director of Admissions, American Jewish University, Office of Undergraduate Admissions, Bel-Air, CA 90077

Antioch University Los Angeles
Culver City, California
www.antiochla.edu   CB code: 1862

- Private two-year upper-division branch campus and liberal arts college
- Commuter campus in very large city
- 74% of applicants admitted
- Application essay required

General. Founded in 1972. Regionally accredited. Bachelor of Arts Degree Completion program offered on-campus with various attendance options available. **Degrees:** 49 bachelor's awarded; master's offered. **Articulation:** Agreements with UCLA Extension, Santa Monica College, West Los Angeles College, Compton City College. **Location:** 15 miles from Los Angeles. **Calendar:** Quarter, extensive summer session. **Full-time faculty:** 26 total. **Part-time faculty:** 136 total.

Student profile. 954 degree-seeking undergraduates, 3,051 degree-seeking graduate students. 429 applied as first time-transfer students, 318 admitted, 190 enrolled.

Women:	72%	Native American:	1%
African American:	14%	Multi-racial, non-Hispanic:	4%
Asian American:	3%	Part-time:	54%
Hispanic/Latino:	16%	25 or older:	91%

Basis for selection. High school transcript, college transcript, application essay required. Admission decision of full or provisional acceptance made by program chair. Transfer accepted as sophomores, juniors, seniors.

2015-2016 Annual costs. Tuition/fees: $20,670. Books/supplies: $1,746.

Application procedures. Admission: Priority date 7/22; deadline 8/17. $60 fee, may be waived for applicants with need. Must reply by 9/7. AULA does not accept freshman. Applicants are required to have at least 30 quarter/20 semester units of college-level learning from a regionally accredited institution of higher learning. **Financial aid:** FAFSA, institutional form required.

Academics. Prior experiential learning credits. **Special study options:** Accelerated study, combined bachelor's/graduate degree, cooperative education, cross-registration, double major, independent study, internships, liberal arts/career combination, student-designed major, study abroad, teacher certification program, weekend college. **Credit/placement by examination:** AP, CLEP, IB. 40 credit hours maximum toward bachelor's degree. DANTES examinations scores accepted.

Majors. Liberal arts: Arts/sciences.

Technology on campus. 12 workstations in library, computer center. Commuter students can connect to campus network. Online library, helpline, wireless network available.

Student life. Activities: Student government, student newspaper.

Athletics. Team name: Radicals.

Student services. Adult student services, career counseling, student employment services, financial aid counseling, personal counseling, veterans' counselor. **Physically disabled:** Services for visually, speech, hearing impaired.

Contact. E-mail: admissions.aula@antioch.edu
Phone: (310) 578-1080 ext. 100 Toll-free number: (800) 726-8462
Fax: (310) 821-6032
Ercik De La Rosa, Director of Admissions Recruitment, Antioch University Los Angeles, 400 Corporate Pointe, Culver City, CA 90230-7615

Antioch University Santa Barbara
Santa Barbara, California
www.antiochsb.edu   CB code: 3071

- Private two-year upper-division university and liberal arts college
- Commuter campus in small city
- Application essay, interview required

General. Founded in 1852. Regionally accredited. **Degrees:** 171 bachelor's awarded; master's, doctoral offered. **Articulation:** Agreements with Santa Barbara City College, Ventura College, Cuesta College, Allan Hancock Community College, Oxnard College, Moorpark College. **Location:** Downtown. **Calendar:** Continuous, extensive summer session. **Full-time faculty:** 12 total; 83% have terminal degrees, 67% women. **Part-time faculty:** 71 total; 52% have terminal degrees, 59% women.

Student profile. 117 degree-seeking undergraduates, 203 degree-seeking graduate students.

Women:	62%	Part-time:	30%

Basis for selection. Open admission. High school transcript, college transcript, application essay, interview required. Grade averages and the quality and content of previous academic work are evaluated, recognizing that an adult's present capacities may not be reflected in grades earned long before or in fields unrelated to present interests. Transfer accepted as sophomores, juniors, seniors.

2015-2016 Annual costs. Tuition/fees: $18,120. Personal expenses: $2,406.

Financial aid. Need-based: 40% of total undergraduate aid awarded as scholarships/grants, 60% as loans/jobs.

Application procedures. Admission: Rolling admission. $60 fee. **Financial aid:** Priority date 4/1, no deadline. FAFSA required.

Academics. Special study options: Cross-registration, independent study, internships, liberal arts/career combination, teacher certification program. **Credit/placement by examination:** AP, CLEP, IB.

Majors. Liberal arts: Arts/sciences.

Technology on campus. 12 workstations in library. Online library, helpline, wireless network available.

Student life. Activities: Student newspaper.

Student services. Adult student services, financial aid counseling, personal counseling, veterans' counselor.

Contact. E-mail: admissions.ausb@antioch.edu
Phone: (805) 962-8179 Fax: (805) 962-4786
Sharisse Estomo, Director of Admissions, Antioch University Santa Barbara, 602 Anacapa Street, Santa Barbara, CA 93101

Argosy University: Inland Empire
Ontario, California
www.argosy.edu/inlandempire   CB code: 6239

- For-profit 4-year university
- Very large city
- 367 degree-seeking undergraduates: 65% part-time, 72% women
- 277 graduate students

General. Degrees: 38 bachelor's, 3 associate awarded; master's, doctoral offered. **Calendar:** Differs by program. **Full-time faculty:** 4 total. **Part-time faculty:** 63 total.

Basis for selection. Open admission.

2015-2016 Annual costs. Tuition/fees: $16,842. **Additional information:** Tuition indicated is for programs in the College of Arts and Sciences. College of Health Sciences programs are $575 per credit-hour.

Application procedures. Admission: Closing date 9/13. $50 fee. **Financial aid:** No deadline.

Academics. Credit/placement by examination: AP, CLEP.

Majors. Business: Business admin. **Liberal arts:** Arts/sciences. **Protective services:** Police science. **Psychology:** General.

Student life. Freshman orientation: Available. Preregistration for classes offered.

Contact. Phone: (909) 915-3800
Wendy Vasquez-Osborn, Senior Director of Admissions, Argosy University: Inland Empire, 3401 Centre Lake Drive, Suite 200, Ontario, CA 91761

Argosy University: Los Angeles
Los Angeles, California
www.argosy.edu/locations/los-angeles   CB code: 6237

- For-profit 4-year university
- Small city
- 298 degree-seeking undergraduates: 56% part-time, 62% women
- 273 graduate students

General. Regionally accredited. **Degrees:** 26 bachelor's awarded; master's, doctoral offered. **Calendar:** Differs by program. **Full-time faculty:** 3 total. **Part-time faculty:** 56 total.

Basis for selection. Open admission.

2015-2016 Annual costs. Tuition/fees: $16,842. **Additional information:** Tuition indicated is for programs in the College of Arts and Sciences. College of Health Sciences programs are $575 per credit-hour.

Application procedures. Admission: Closing date 9/13. $50 fee. **Financial aid:** No deadline.

Academics. Credit/placement by examination: AP, CLEP.

Majors. Business: Business admin. **Liberal arts:** Arts/sciences. **Protective services:** Police science. **Psychology:** General.

Student life. Freshman orientation: Available. Preregistration for classes offered.

Contact. E-mail: ausmadms@argosy.edu
Daniel Banyai, Senior Director of Admissions, Argosy University: Los Angeles, 5230 Pacific Concourse, Suite 200, Los Angeles, CA 90045

Argosy University: Orange County
Orange, California
www.argosy.edu/orangecounty   CB code: 7910

- For-profit 4-year university
- Very large city
- 222 degree-seeking undergraduates: 59% part-time, 55% women
- 384 graduate students

General. Regionally accredited. **Degrees:** 46 bachelor's awarded; master's, professional, doctoral offered. **Calendar:** Differs by program. **Full-time faculty:** 14 total. **Part-time faculty:** 148 total.

Basis for selection. Open admission.

2015-2016 Annual costs. Tuition/fees: $16,842. **Additional information:** Tuition indicated is for programs in the College of Arts and Sciences. College of Health Sciences programs are $575 per credit-hour.

Application procedures. Admission: Closing date 9/13. $50 fee. **Financial aid:** No deadline.

Academics. Credit/placement by examination: AP, CLEP.

Majors. Business: Business admin. **Liberal arts:** Arts/sciences. **Protective services:** Police science. **Psychology:** General.

Student life. Freshman orientation: Available. Preregistration for classes offered.

Contact. Phone: (714) 620-3715 Toll-free number: (800) 716-9598
Leisa Ruiz, Senior Director of Admissions, Argosy University: Orange County, 601 South Lewis Street, Orange, CA 92868

Argosy University: San Diego
San Diego, California
www.argosy.edu/locations/san-diego

- For-profit 4-year university
- Very large city
- 234 degree-seeking undergraduates: 59% part-time, 54% women
- 204 graduate students

General. Degrees: 32 bachelor's awarded; master's, doctoral offered. **Calendar:** Differs by program. **Full-time faculty:** 3 total. **Part-time faculty:** 57 total.

Basis for selection. Open admission..

2015-2016 Annual costs. Tuition/fees: $16,842. **Additional information:** Tuition indicated is for programs in the College of Arts and Sciences. College of Health Sciences programs are $575 per credit-hour.

Application procedures. Admission: Closing date 9/13. $50 fee. **Financial aid:** No deadline.

Academics. Credit/placement by examination: AP, CLEP.

Majors. Business: Business admin. **Liberal arts:** Arts/sciences. **Protective services:** Police science. **Psychology:** General.

Student life. Freshman orientation: Available. Preregistration for classes offered.

Contact. E-mail: ausdadmissions@argosy.edu
Detroit Whiteside, Senior Director of Admissions, Argosy University: San Diego, 1615 Murray Canyon Road, San Diego, CA 92108

Argosy University: San Francisco Bay Area
Alameda, California
www.argosy.edu/sanfrancisco

- For-profit 4-year university
- Small city
- 139 degree-seeking undergraduates: 73% part-time, 73% women
- 299 graduate students

General. Regionally accredited. **Degrees:** 24 bachelor's awarded; master's, professional, doctoral offered. **Calendar:** Differs by program. **Full-time faculty:** 17 total. **Part-time faculty:** 98 total.

Basis for selection. Open admission.

2015-2016 Annual costs. Tuition/fees: $16,842. **Additional information:** Tuition indicated is for programs in the College of Arts and Sciences. College of Health Sciences programs are $575 per credit-hour.

Application procedures. Admission: Closing date 9/13. $50 fee. **Financial aid:** No deadline.

Academics. Credit/placement by examination: AP, CLEP.

Majors. Business: Business admin. **Liberal arts:** Arts/sciences. **Protective services:** Police science. **Psychology:** General.

Student life. Freshman orientation: Available. Preregistration for classes offered.

Contact. E-mail: ausfadmissions@argosy.edu
Phone: (510) 217-4777
John Stofan, Senior Director of Admissions, Argosy University: San Francisco Bay Area, 1005 Atlantic Avenue, Alameda, CA 94501

Art Center College of Design
Pasadena, California
www.artcenter.edu   CB code: 4009

- Private 4-year visual arts college
- Commuter campus in small city
- 1,890 degree-seeking undergraduates: 16% part-time, 50% women, 1% African American, 36% Asian American, 12% Hispanic/Latino, 4% Multi-racial, non-Hispanic, 27% international

- 209 degree-seeking graduate students
- 80% of applicants admitted
- 68% graduate within 6 years

General. Founded in 1930. Regionally accredited. **Degrees:** 389 bachelor's awarded; master's offered. **Location:** 15 miles from Los Angeles. **Calendar:** Semester, extensive summer session. **Class size:** 94% < 20, 5% 20-39, less than 1% >100. **Special facilities:** Student galleries, technical skill center, color materials and trends exploration lab, photography and film stages.

Freshman class profile. 610 applied, 485 admitted, 180 enrolled.

Return as sophomores:	76%	International:	33%
Out-of-state:	16%		

Basis for selection. Strength of specific portfolio for one major, academic record, standardized test scores. SAT or ACT scores required for students applying while currently enrolled in a U.S. or U.S. sponsored high school. TOEFL or IELTS scores required for international applicants.

High school preparation. College-preparatory program recommended. Art classes recommended.

2015-2016 Annual costs. Tuition/fees: $39,230.

Application procedures. Admission: Priority date 2/15; no deadline. $50 fee, may be waived for applicants with need. Admission notification on a rolling basis beginning on or about 1/1. **Financial aid:** No deadline.

Academics. Special study options: Cross-registration, distance learning, independent study, internships, study abroad. **Credit/placement by examination:** AP, CLEP. **Support services:** Writing center.

Majors. Architecture: Building sciences. **Communications technology:** Animation/special effects. **Visual/performing arts:** Cinematography, commercial/advertising art, graphic design, illustration, photography, studio arts.

Most popular majors. Engineering/engineering technologies 17%, visual/performing arts 74%.

Student life. Freshman orientation: Mandatory. Preregistration for classes offered. **Activities:** Film society, international student organizations, student government.

Contact. E-mail: admissions@artcenter.edu
Phone: (626) 396-2373 Fax: (626) 795-0578
Kit Baron, Vice President, Admissions, Art Center College of Design, 1700 Lida Street, Pasadena, CA 91103

Art Institute of California: Hollywood
North Hollywood, California
www.artinstitutes.edu/hollywood   CB code: 3463

- For-profit 4-year culinary school and visual arts college
- Commuter campus in very large city
- 1,602 undergraduates
- Application essay, interview required

General. Degrees: 213 bachelor's, 124 associate awarded. **Location:** 10 miles from downtown. **Calendar:** Quarter, extensive summer session. **Full-time faculty:** 19 total; 42% have terminal degrees, 10% minority, 53% women. **Part-time faculty:** 108 total; 44% have terminal degrees, 39% minority, 56% women. **Class size:** 71% < 20, 29% 20-39. **Special facilities:** Sewing and construction rooms, interior design resource room, TV studio, video editing labs, photo studio.

Basis for selection. All applicants whose first language is not English must demonstrate competence in the English language. Applicants whose "first" language is English must submit diploma from secondary school (or above) in a system in which English is the official language of instruction.

2015-2016 Annual costs. Books/supplies: $2,199. Personal expenses: $3,096. **Additional information:** Diploma programs range from $25,014-$30,005, books and supplies range from $600-$800, room and board ranges from $14,920-$18,650. Associates programs range from $46,770-$49,438, books and supplies range from $1,050-$1,400, room and board $29,840. Bachelors programs range from from $93,390-$95,070, books and supplies range from $2,450-$2,800, room and board $55,950.

Application procedures. Admission: No deadline. $50 fee. Admission notification on a rolling basis.

Academics. Special study options: Distance learning, internships, weekend college. **Credit/placement by examination:** AP, CLEP, IB, institutional tests. **Support services:** Reduced course load, study skills assistance, tutoring, writing center.

Majors. Business: Fashion. **Communications technology:** Animation/special effects. **Computer sciences:** Web page design. **Visual/performing arts:** Fashion design, graphic design, industrial design, interior design, photography.

Most popular majors. Business/marketing 30%, visual/performing arts 70%.

Technology on campus. 289 workstations in library, computer center. Online course registration, online library, helpline, wireless network available.

Student life. Freshman orientation: Mandatory. Preregistration for classes offered. **Housing:** Single-sex dorms, themed housing available. $250 fully refundable deposit, deadline 10/5. **Activities:** Student newspaper.

Student services. Career counseling, student employment services, financial aid counseling, personal counseling, placement for graduates. **Physically disabled:** Services for hearing impaired.

Contact. E-mail: aicahadm@aii.edu
Phone: (818) 299-5100 Toll-free number: (877) 468-6232
Fax: (877) 299-5151
Melissa Huen, Senior Director of Admissions, Art Institute of California: Hollywood, 5250 Lankershim Boulevard, North Hollywood, CA 91601

Art Institute of California: Inland Empire
San Bernardino, California
www.artinstitutes.edu/inland-empire

- For-profit 4-year culinary school and visual arts college
- Large city
- 2,123 degree-seeking undergraduates

General. Regionally accredited; also accredited by ACCSC. **Degrees:** 157 bachelor's, 278 associate awarded. **Calendar:** Quarter. **Full-time faculty:** 42 total. **Part-time faculty:** 62 total.

Basis for selection. Admission requirements vary by programs.

2015-2016 Annual costs. Books/supplies: $2,203. Personal expenses: $3,096. **Additional information:** Diploma programs range from $24,496-$30,780, books and supplies range from $600-$800, room and board ranges from $11,820. Associates programs range from $47,040-$49,435, books and supplies range from $1,050-$1,400, room and board $23,640. Bachelors programs range from from $93,660-$95,845, books and supplies range from $2,450-$2,800, room and board $44,325.

Application procedures. Admission: $50 fee. **Financial aid:** Closing date 3/2.

Academics. Special study options: Distance learning, internships, study abroad. **Credit/placement by examination:** AP, CLEP.

Majors. Business: Apparel. **Communications technology:** Animation/special effects, recording arts. **Computer sciences:** Computer graphics, web page design. **Visual/performing arts:** Fashion design, graphic design, interior design.

Most popular majors. Communication technologies 10%, computer/information sciences 12%, personal/culinary services 48%, visual/performing arts 30%.

Contact. Toll-free number: (800) 353-0812
Matt Madrid, Senior Director of Admissions, Art Institute of California: Inland Empire, 674 East Brier Drive, San Bernardino, CA 92408-2800

Art Institute of California: Orange County
Santa Ana, California
www.artinstitutes.edu/orangecounty   CB code: 3831

- For-profit 3-year culinary school and visual arts college
- Commuter campus in very large city
- 1,417 degree-seeking undergraduates
- Application essay, interview required

General. **Degrees:** 185 bachelor's, 145 associate awarded. **Location:** 40 miles from Los Angeles, 90 miles from San Diego. **Calendar:** Quarter, extensive summer session. **Full-time faculty:** 51 total. **Part-time faculty:** 61 total. **Special facilities:** 4 professional skills kitchens, 11 computer labs, interior design resource library, interior design studio, industrial design workshop, student dining lab, fashion lab.

Basis for selection. Proof of high school graduation, or equivalent from a foreign institution, required. International students require proof of English proficiency. Acceptance determined by committee of faculty members.

2015-2016 Annual costs. Books/supplies: $2,231. Personal expenses: $3,096. **Additional information:** Diploma programs range from $24,496-$30,778, books and supplies range from $600-$800, room and board ranges from $15,588-$19,485. Associates programs range from $47,055-$49,433, books and supplies range from $1,050-$1,400, room and board range from $23,382-31,176. Bachelors programs range from from $93,6785-$95,843, books and supplies range from $2,450-$2,800, room and board $58,455.

Financial aid. **Non-need-based:** Scholarships awarded for academics, art, minority status.

Application procedures. **Admission:** No deadline. $50 fee. Admission notification on a rolling basis. **Financial aid:** No deadline. FAFSA required. Applicants notified on a rolling basis; must reply within 2 week(s) of notification.

Academics. **Special study options:** Cooperative education, distance learning, internships. Online courses. **Credit/placement by examination:** AP, CLEP, IB, institutional tests. 3 credit hours maximum toward associate degree, 3 toward bachelor's. **Support services:** Learning center, pre-admission summer program, reduced course load, study skills assistance, tutoring.

Majors. **BACHELOR'S.** **Business:** Apparel. **Communications:** Digital media. **Communications technology:** Animation/special effects. **Computer sciences:** Computer graphics, web page design, webmaster. **Visual/performing arts:** Commercial/advertising art, fashion design, graphic design, industrial design, interior design. **ASSOCIATE.** **Communications:** Digital media. **Computer sciences:** Computer graphics, web page design, webmaster. **Visual/performing arts:** Commercial/advertising art, graphic design, interior design.

Technology on campus. 312 workstations in library, computer center, student center. Online course registration, online library, helpline, repair service, wireless network available.

Student life. **Freshman orientation:** Mandatory. Preregistration for classes offered. **Housing:** Special housing for disabled, apartments available. School-sponsored housing available. **Activities:** Film society, student newspaper.

Student services. Career counseling, student employment services, financial aid counseling, personal counseling, placement for graduates, veterans' counselor. **Physically disabled:** Services for visually, speech, hearing impaired.

Contact. E-mail: aicaocadm@aii.edu
Phone: (888) 549-3055 Toll-free number: (888) 549-3055
Fax: (714) 556-1923
Harry Ramos, Senior Director of Admissions, Art Institute of California: Orange County, 3601 West Sunflower Avenue, Santa Ana, CA 92704-7931

Art Institute of California: Sacramento
Sacramento, California
www.artinstitutes.edu/sacramento   CB code: 5737

- For-profit 3-year culinary school and visual arts college
- Large city
- 993 undergraduates

General. Regionally accredited. **Degrees:** 130 bachelor's, 55 associate awarded. **Calendar:** Quarter. **Full-time faculty:** 17 total. **Part-time faculty:** 60 total.

Basis for selection. High school diploma required and GED accepted.

2015-2016 Annual costs. Books/supplies: $2,300. Personal expenses: $3,096. **Additional information:** Diploma programs range from $24,496-$30,782, books and supplies range from $600-$800, room and board $15,375. Associates programs range from $47,077-$49,437, books and supplies range from $1,050-$2,400, room and board $24,600. Bachelors programs range from from $93,6390-$95,847, books and supplies range from $2,450-$2,800, room and board $46,125.

Application procedures. **Admission:** No deadline. $50 fee.

Academics. **Credit/placement by examination:** AP, CLEP.

Majors. **BACHELOR'S.** **Communications technology:** Animation/special effects. **Visual/performing arts:** Cinematography, game design, graphic design, interior design, multimedia. **ASSOCIATE.** **Visual/performing arts:** Graphic design, multimedia.

Student life. **Freshman orientation:** Available, $100 fee. Preregistration for classes offered.

Contact. Phone: (800) 477-1957
Courtney Amos, Director of Admissions, Art Institute of California: Sacramento, 2850 Gateway Oaks Drive, Suite 100, Sacramento, CA 95833

Art Institute of California: San Diego
San Diego, California
www.artinstitutes.edu/sandiego   CB code: 3036

- For-profit 3-year visual arts college
- Residential campus in very large city
- 1,634 undergraduates
- Application essay, interview required

General. Accredited by ACCSC. **Degrees:** 331 bachelor's, 178 associate awarded. **Calendar:** Quarter. **Full-time faculty:** 54 total. **Part-time faculty:** 88 total. **Special facilities:** Dining lab run by culinary students, fashion sewing labs, audio recording studio, motion capture studio.

Basis for selection. Submission of an essay, an official high school transcript with GPA and graduation date as well as an admissions interview are most important. A portfolio and standardized test scores may also be important in the admissions process. **Learning Disabled:** Students requiring assistance should notify Assistant Director of Admissions.

2015-2016 Annual costs. Books/supplies: $2,155. Personal expenses: $3,096. **Additional information:** Diploma programs range from $24,496-$30,778, books and supplies range from $600-$800, room and board ranges from $15,176-$18970. Associates programs range from $47,076-$49,433, books and supplies range from $1,050-$1,400, room and board $30,352. Bachelors programs range from from $93,696-$95,843, books and supplies range from $2,450-$2,800, room and board $56,910.

Application procedures. **Admission:** No deadline. $50 fee. Admission notification on a rolling basis. **Financial aid:** No deadline. FAFSA required.

Academics. **Special study options:** Accelerated study, distance learning, internships. **Credit/placement by examination:** AP, CLEP. **Support services:** Study skills assistance, tutoring.

Majors. **BACHELOR'S.** **Communications:** Advertising. **Computer sciences:** Computer graphics, web page design, webmaster. **Visual/performing arts:** Commercial/advertising art, fashion design, game design, graphic design, interior design, multimedia. **ASSOCIATE.** **Visual/performing arts:** Commercial/advertising art, design, graphic design.

Technology on campus. 300 workstations in library, computer center. Online library, wireless network available.

Student life. **Freshman orientation:** Mandatory. Preregistration for classes offered. **Housing:** Single-sex dorms, apartments available. **Activities:** Student government, student newspaper.

Student services. Alcohol/substance abuse counseling, career counseling, services for economically disadvantaged, student employment services, financial aid counseling, personal counseling. **Physically disabled:** Services for visually, speech, hearing impaired.

Contact. E-mail: aicaadmin@aii.edu
Toll-free number: (866) 275-2422
John Kerns, Director of Admissions, Art Institute of California: San Diego, 7650 Mission Valley Road, San Diego, CA 92108-4423

Art Institute of California: San Francisco
San Francisco, California
www.artinstitutes.edu/sanfrancisco   CB code: 4421

- For-profit 4-year culinary school and visual arts college
- Commuter campus in very large city

- 1,070 degree-seeking undergraduates
- Application essay required

General. Founded in 1939. **Degrees:** 200 bachelor's, 90 associate awarded; master's offered. **Location:** Downtown. **Calendar:** Quarter, extensive summer session. **Full-time faculty:** 23 total. **Part-time faculty:** 93 total.

Basis for selection. High school record and general appropriateness of educational background to specific program applied for most important. Portfolio, interview, standardized test scores also important. Interview and portfolio recommended.

High school preparation. Recommended units include English 1, mathematics 1, social studies 1 and history 1. One art class recommended.

2015-2016 Annual costs. Books/supplies: $2,277. Personal expenses: $2,844. **Additional information:** Diploma programs range from $24,935-$30,784, books and supplies range from $600-$800, room and board ranges from $15,312-$19,140. Associates programs range from $47,057-$49,439, books and supplies range from $1,050-$1,400, room and board $30,624. Bachelors programs range from from $93,677-$95,849, books and supplies range from $2,450-$2,800, room and board $57,420.

Application procedures. Admission: No deadline. $50 fee. Admission notification on a rolling basis. **Financial aid:** No deadline. FAFSA required. Applicants notified on a rolling basis.

Academics. Special study options: Combined bachelor's/graduate degree, distance learning, internships, liberal arts/career combination. **Credit/placement by examination:** AP, CLEP, IB. **Support services:** Reduced course load, remedial instruction, study skills assistance, tutoring. Faculty tutoring, peer tutoring, workshops, college success course.

Majors. Business: Fashion. **Communications technology:** Animation/special effects. **Computer sciences:** Computer graphics, web page design. **Visual/performing arts:** Commercial/advertising art, fashion design, film/cinema/video, graphic design, interior design. **Work/family studies:** Institutional food production.

Technology on campus. 30 workstations in library, computer center. Online library, wireless network available.

Student life. Freshman orientation: Mandatory. Preregistration for classes offered. **Housing:** Coed dorms, apartments available. $300 deposit. **Activities:** International student organizations, Society of Web Architects and Programmers, game art & design club, photo club, Alpha Beta Kappa.

Student services. Career counseling, student employment services, financial aid counseling. **Physically disabled:** Services for hearing impaired.

Contact. E-mail: aisfadm@aii.edu
Phone: (415) 865-0198 Toll-free number: (888) 493-3261
Fax: (415) 863-6344
Jeanne Chang, Senior Director of Admissions, Art Institute of California: San Francisco, 1170 Market Street, San Francisco, CA 94102

Ashford University
San Diego, California — CB member
www.ashford.edu — CB code: 6418

- For-profit 4-year university
- Commuter campus in very large city
- 36,405 degree-seeking undergraduates: 70% women
- 5,381 degree-seeking graduate students

General. Founded in 1918. Regionally accredited. **Degrees:** 10,987 bachelor's, 1,091 associate awarded; master's offered. **Calendar:** Differs by program, extensive summer session.

Basis for selection. Open admission. Must have at least a 2.0 cumulative GPA in high school or prior college coursework. Interviews required for teacher education majors.

High school preparation. College-preparatory program recommended. 20 units recommended. Recommended units include English 4, mathematics 3, social studies 2, history 3, science 3, foreign language 2 and academic electives 3.

2015-2016 Annual costs. Tuition/fees: $10,480. Room/board: $6,300.

Application procedures. Admission: No deadline. No application fee. Admission notification on a rolling basis. **Financial aid:** Priority date 3/1;

no closing date. FAFSA, institutional form required. Applicants notified on a rolling basis starting 2/15; must reply within 2 week(s) of notification.

Academics. Special study options: Distance learning, double major, external degree, honors, independent study, internships, teacher certification program. **Credit/placement by examination:** AP, CLEP, institutional tests. 30 credit hours maximum toward associate degree, 30 toward bachelor's. Awards credit for CLEP exams in accordance with the American Council on Education (ACE) designated passing score and recommended credit. **Support services:** Learning center, reduced course load, tutoring, writing center.

Majors. Biology: General. **Business:** Accounting, business admin, customer service, e-commerce, entrepreneurial studies, finance, human resources, international, logistics, management information systems, managerial economics, operations, organizational leadership, project management, real estate. **Communications:** Communications/speech/rhetoric, journalism. **Computer sciences:** Computer science. **Conservation:** Environmental science, environmental studies. **Education:** General, business, early childhood, educational technology, elementary, foundations, learning sciences, physical. **English:** English lit. **Foreign languages:** Applied linguistics. **Health services:** General, health care admin, health information management, holistic. **History:** General. **Human services:** General. **Liberal arts:** Arts/sciences, library science. **Parks/recreation:** Sports admin. **Protective services:** Criminal justice, law enforcement admin. **Psychology:** General. **Social sciences:** General, cultural anthropology, political science, sociology. **Visual/performing arts:** General, commercial/advertising art. **Work/family studies:** Aging, child development, family resources.

Most popular majors. Business/marketing 34%, education 15%, health sciences 12%, psychology 8%, security/protective services 10%, social sciences 6%.

Technology on campus. PC or laptop required. Online library, helpline available.

Athletics. Intercollegiate: Volleyball W. **Team name:** Saints.

Student services. Adult student services, career counseling, student employment services, financial aid counseling. **Physically disabled:** Services for visually, speech, hearing impaired.

Contact. E-mail: admissions@ashford.edu
Toll-free number: (866) 711-1700
Thad Trapp, Divisional Vice President of Enrollment Services, Ashford University, 8620 Spectrum Center Boulevard, San Diego, CA 92123

Azusa Pacific University
Azusa, California — CB member
www.apu.edu — CB code: 4596

- Private 4-year university affiliated with the interdenominational tradition
- Residential campus in small city
- 5,862 degree-seeking undergraduates: 9% part-time, 65% women, 5% African American, 9% Asian American, 29% Hispanic/Latino, 1% Native Hawaiian/Pacific islander, 8% Multi-racial, non-Hispanic, 2% international
- 3,826 degree-seeking graduate students
- 81% of applicants admitted
- SAT or ACT (ACT writing optional), application essay required
- 68% graduate within 6 years

General. Founded in 1899. Regionally accredited. **Degrees:** 1,783 bachelor's awarded; master's, professional, doctoral offered. **ROTC:** Army, Air Force. **Location:** 30 miles from Los Angeles. **Calendar:** Semester, limited summer session. **Full-time faculty:** 456 total; 64% have terminal degrees, 52% women. **Part-time faculty:** 725 total; 2% have terminal degrees, 60% women. **Class size:** 60% < 20, 36% 20-39, 2% 40-49, 2% 50-99, less than 1% >100.

Freshman class profile. 6,084 applied, 4,922 admitted, 1,192 enrolled.

Mid 50% test scores			
SAT critical reading:	480-590	Rank in top quarter:	55%
SAT math:	470-590	Rank in top tenth:	25%
ACT composite:	21-27	Return as sophomores:	88%
GPA 3.75 or higher:	46%	Out-of-state:	75%
GPA 3.50-3.74:	22%	Live on campus:	97%
GPA 3.0-3.49:	26%	International:	2%
		GPA 2.0-2.99:	6%

Basis for selection. GPA, test scores, references, statement of agreement, essay important. Auditions required for music applicants. Interviews recommended for borderline applicants. **Home schooled:** SAT or ACT and transcript from organization required.

High school preparation. College-preparatory program recommended. Recommended units include English 4, mathematics 3, social studies 1, history 2, science 2 and foreign language 3.

2015-2016 Annual costs. Tuition/fees: $34,754. Room/board: $9,218. Books/supplies: $1,764. Personal expenses: $2,322.

2014-2015 Financial aid. Need-based: 942 full-time freshmen applied for aid; 845 deemed to have need; 844 received aid. Average need met was 35%. Average scholarship/grant was $10,581; average loan $3,712. 73% of total undergraduate aid awarded as scholarships/grants, 27% as loans/jobs. **Non-need-based:** Awarded to 4,220 full-time undergraduates, including 887 freshmen. Scholarships awarded for academics, athletics, leadership, minority status, music/drama, religious affiliation, ROTC.

Application procedures. Admission: Priority date 2/15; deadline 6/1 (postmark date). $45 fee, may be waived for applicants with need. Admission notification by 4/1. Admission notification on a rolling basis beginning on or about 10/1. Must reply by May 1 or within 2 week(s) if notified thereafter. **Financial aid:** Priority date 3/2, closing date 7/1. FAFSA, institutional form required. Applicants notified on a rolling basis starting 3/1; must reply within 3 week(s) of notification.

Academics. Special study options: Accelerated study, cooperative education, distance learning, double major, ESL, exchange student, honors, independent study, internships, study abroad, teacher certification program, urban semester, Washington semester. **Credit/placement by examination:** AP, CLEP, IB, SAT, ACT, institutional tests. Essays required for Analysis and Interpretation of Literature and Freshman College Composition. **Support services:** Learning center, reduced course load, remedial instruction, study skills assistance, tutoring, writing center.

Majors. Biology: General, biochemistry. **Business:** General, accounting, business admin, finance, management information systems, marketing. **Communications:** Communications/speech/rhetoric, journalism. **Computer sciences:** General, computer science. **Education:** Art, business, elementary, middle, multi-level teacher, physical, secondary. **English:** English lit. **Foreign languages:** Spanish. **Health services:** Nurse practitioner, nursing (RN), predental, premedicine. **History:** General. **Human services:** Social work. **Liberal arts:** Arts/sciences. **Math:** General. **Philosophy/religion:** Philosophy, religion. **Physical sciences:** General, chemistry, physics. **Psychology:** General. **Social sciences:** General, international relations, political science, sociology. **Theology:** Bible, religious ed, sacred music, theology. **Visual/performing arts:** Art, dramatic, music, music performance, music theory/composition, studio arts.

Most popular majors. Business/marketing 21%, communications/journalism 6%, health sciences 23%, liberal arts 8%, psychology 10%, visual/performing arts 8%.

Technology on campus. Dormitories wired for high-speed internet access and linked to campus network. Commuter students can connect to campus network. Online course registration, online library, helpline, repair service, wireless network available.

Student life. Freshman orientation: Mandatory. Preregistration for classes offered. Class taken during first semester. **Policies:** Students will refrain from activities which may be spiritually or morally destructive. Religious observance required. **Housing:** Coed dorms, single-sex dorms, apartments, themed housing available. **Activities:** Bands, campus ministries, choral groups, dance, drama, film society, international student organizations, music ensembles, musical theater, opera, radio station, student government, student newspaper, symphony orchestra, TV station, Multi-Ethnic Student Alliance, Japanese Christian Fellowship, Chinese Christian Fellowship.

Athletics. NAIA, NCCAA. **Intercollegiate:** Baseball M, basketball, cross-country, diving W, football (tackle) M, gymnastics W, soccer, softball W, swimming W, tennis, track and field, volleyball W, water polo W. **Intramural:** Basketball, football (tackle) M, skiing, volleyball. **Team name:** Cougars.

Student services. Chaplain/spiritual director, career counseling, student employment services, financial aid counseling, health services, minority student services, personal counseling, placement for graduates, veterans' counselor. **Physically disabled:** Services for visually, speech, hearing impaired.

Contact. E-mail: admissions@apu.edu
Phone: (626) 812-3016 Toll-free number: (800) 825-5278
Fax: (626) 812-3096
Dave Burke, Director of Undergraduate Admissions, Azusa Pacific University, 901 East Alosta Avenue, Azusa, CA 91702-7000

Bergin University of Canine Studies
Rohnert Park, California
www.berginu.edu

- Private 4-year university and career college
- Commuter campus in large town
- 22 degree-seeking undergraduates: 91% women
- 26 degree-seeking graduate students
- Application essay required

General. Regionally accredited; also accredited by ACICS. The first-ever accredited academic institution to offer canine studies degrees. **Degrees:** 5 bachelor's, 15 associate awarded; master's offered. **Location:** 50 miles from San Francisco. **Calendar:** Semester, limited summer session. **Full-time faculty:** 2 total. **Part-time faculty:** 17 total. **Class size:** 100% 20-39.

Basis for selection. Open admission, but selective for some programs. All degree-seeking students must have prior college credits. The Associate's degree requires 24 and the Bachelor's 60. If a candidate has the appropriate transfer credits and submits this along with the following admissions documents, they would be accepted (space allowing). The documents are: verification of high school graduation (copy of transcript, diploma, GED, official college transcripts (unopened and must not indicating issued to student), copy of driver's license (or birth certificate or passport with name and birthdate), a photo is required if a birth certificate is submitted), one-page essay explaining interest/intention to utilize the educational program and two letters of reference. In addition to two letters of recommendation (one personal and one professional), a letter of intent is also required. **Home schooled:** State high school equivalency certificate required. **Learning Disabled:** College needs to be made aware of any special needs due to the type of physical requirements associated with the programs (dog handling).

2016-2017 Annual costs. Tuition/fees (projected): $10,100. Books/supplies: $500.

Application procedures. Admission: Priority date 4/16; deadline 8/16 (receipt date). $50 fee. Admission notification on a rolling basis. **Financial aid:** Closing date 6/30.

Academics. Credit/placement by examination: AP, CLEP.

Technology on campus. 3 workstations in library. Wireless network available.

Contact. E-mail: admissions@berginu.edu
Phone: (707) 545-3647 ext. 21
Connie Van Guilder, Director, Student Services, Bergin University of Canine Studies, 5860 Labath Avenue, Rohnert Park, CA 94928

Bethesda University of California
Anaheim, California
www.buc.edu   CB code: 3895

- Private 4-year university affiliated with the Christian Church
- Commuter campus in large city
- 256 degree-seeking undergraduates
- 95 graduate students
- Application essay, interview required

General. Accredited by ABHE. **Degrees:** 32 bachelor's awarded; master's, doctoral offered. **Location:** 30 miles from Los Angeles. **Calendar:** Semester, limited summer session. **Full-time faculty:** 6 total. **Class size:** 33% < 20, 64% 20-39, 3% 40-49.

Basis for selection. GED not accepted. Admissions decision based on recommendations, essay and interview. Secondary school record also important. ESL placement test not required for students who have TOEFL score 550 or higher or have graduated from English-speaking high school. Auditions required for music majors. Portfolio required for design majors. Christian experience essay required. **Home schooled:** Transcript of courses and grades, state high school equivalency certificate, letter of recommendation (nonparent) required.

High school preparation. College-preparatory program required.

2015-2016 Annual costs. Tuition/fees: $7,930. Books/supplies: $1,000. Personal expenses: $500.

Financial aid. All financial aid based on need.

Application procedures. Admission: Closing date 1/31 (receipt date). $35 fee ($80 out-of-state). Application must be submitted on paper. Admission notification on a rolling basis. **Financial aid:** No deadline. FAFSA, institutional form required. Applicants notified on a rolling basis starting 6/30.

Academics. Special study options: Combined bachelor's/graduate degree, distance learning, dual enrollment of high school students, ESL, external degree, independent study, liberal arts/career combination, study abroad, teacher certification program. **Credit/placement by examination:** AP, CLEP, IB, institutional tests. **Support services:** Reduced course load.

Majors. Computer sciences: Information technology. **Education:** Early childhood. **Foreign languages:** Translation. **Philosophy/religion:** Religion. **Theology:** Bible, missionary, religious ed, sacred music, theology. **Visual/performing arts:** Conducting, design, fashion design, metal/jewelry, music, music management, music performance, music theory/composition, piano/keyboard, stringed instruments, voice/opera.

Technology on campus. PC or laptop required. 30 workstations in dormitories, library, computer center, student center. Dormitories wired for high-speed internet access. Online course registration, helpline, repair service, wireless network available.

Student life. Freshman orientation: Mandatory. Preregistration for classes offered. **Policies:** Religious observance required. **Housing:** Off-campus housing available. **Activities:** Student government.

Athletics. NCCAA. **Team name:** Flames.

Student services. Chaplain/spiritual director, financial aid counseling, personal counseling.

Contact. E-mail: admission@buc.edu
Phone: (800) 960-4583 Fax: (800) 690-4584
Jacqueline Ha, Director of Admissions, Bethesda University of California, 730 North Euclid Street, Anaheim, CA 92801

Biola University
La Mirada, California
www.biola.edu   CB code: 4017

- Private 4-year university and Bible college affiliated with the interdenominational tradition
- Residential campus in large town
- 4,219 degree-seeking undergraduates: 3% part-time, 63% women, 2% African American, 18% Asian American, 19% Hispanic/Latino, 6% Multi-racial, non-Hispanic, 3% international
- 1,997 degree-seeking graduate students
- 73% of applicants admitted
- SAT or ACT (ACT writing optional), application essay required
- 70% graduate within 6 years

General. Founded in 1908. Regionally accredited. Biblically centered Christian institution. Every undergraduate student graduates with Bible minor. **Degrees:** 899 bachelor's awarded; master's, doctoral offered. **ROTC:** Army, Air Force. **Location:** 22 miles from downtown Los Angeles. **Calendar:** 4-1-4, extensive summer session. **Full-time faculty:** 271 total; 83% have terminal degrees, 21% minority, 33% women. **Part-time faculty:** 284 total; 17% minority, 46% women. **Class size:** 47% < 20, 43% 20-39, 5% 40-49, 3% 50-99, 2% >100. **Special facilities:** Concert hall, electron microscope, blackbox theater, recording studio, film studio, MIDI lab for music composition, electronic piano lab, archaeological dig site, art studio, on-campus olive grove, center for multi-ethnic and cross-cultural engagement.

Freshman class profile. 3,701 applied, 2,706 admitted, 829 enrolled.

Mid 50% test scores		
SAT critical reading:	490-620	
SAT math:	490-620	
SAT writing:	490-610	
ACT composite:	21-28	
GPA 3.75 or higher:	34%	
GPA 3.50-3.74:	25%	
GPA 3.0-3.49:	32%	

GPA 2.0-2.99:	9%
Rank in top quarter:	59%
Rank in top tenth:	30%
Return as sophomores:	85%
Out-of-state:	24%
Live on campus:	90%
International:	2%

Basis for selection. Official transcripts, SAT/ACT, application essay/statement of faith. Christian commitment most important; academic record, test scores next in importance. School, community, church activities helpful. Separate application for cinema & media arts program and Torrey Honors program. No exceptions to SAT/ACT requirement. If more than one SAT score is submitted, we take the best scores from each section of all tests submitted and score those. Interview requested of some students. Auditions required for music applicants. Portfolios recommended for art applicants.

Any body of work recommended for cinema & media arts applicants. **Home schooled:** Applicants advised to go through accreditation agency. **Learning Disabled:** Student must request the services of the ODS and provide documentation supporting the nature and limitations of a disability.

High school preparation. College-preparatory program recommended. 16 units required. Required units include English 4, mathematics 3, social studies 1, history 1, science 2 (laboratory 1) and foreign language 4. 1 algebra and 1 chemistry required of nursing applicants. 2 math, 1 physics, 1 chemistry required of biology applicants. Some deficiencies may be satisfied during freshman year.

2015-2016 Annual costs. Tuition/fees: $34,498. Room/board: $9,791.

2014-2015 Financial aid. Need-based: Average need met was 51%. Average scholarship/grant was $15,270; average loan $3,123. 64% of total undergraduate aid awarded as scholarships/grants, 36% as loans/jobs. **Non-need-based:** Scholarships awarded for academics, alumni affiliation, art, athletics, leadership, minority status, music/drama.

Application procedures. Admission: $45 fee, may be waived for applicants with need. Admission notification on a rolling basis beginning on or about 1/15. **Financial aid:** Priority date 3/1; no closing date. FAFSA required. Applicants notified on a rolling basis starting 1/1.

Academics. Special study options: Combined bachelor's/graduate degree, distance learning, double major, ESL, exchange student, honors, internships, New York semester, study abroad, Washington semester. 3-2 program with Los Angeles College of Chiropractic, 3-2 engineering program with University of Southern California. **Credit/placement by examination:** AP, CLEP, IB, SAT, ACT, institutional tests. Maximum of 32 credits from CLEP, AP, and IB can be counted toward degree. **Support services:** Learning center, reduced course load, remedial instruction, study skills assistance, tutoring, writing center. Most departments offer individualized academic help to students, scheduled according to need.

Honors college/program. Admission to the Torrey Honors Program by invitation after application to the university. Students trained in rigorous discussion group format through classical learning style (Socratic Teaching Method), practicing high-level writing and critical thinking skills.

Majors. Biology: General, biochemistry. **Business:** Accounting, business admin, international, management information systems, marketing. **Communications:** Broadcast journalism, communications/speech/rhetoric, journalism, public relations, radio/TV. **Computer sciences:** Computer science. **Education:** General, elementary, music, physical, secondary. **Engineering:** General. **English:** Creative writing, English lit. **Foreign languages:** Spanish. **Health services:** Communication disorders, nursing (RN). **History:** General. **Liberal arts:** Arts/sciences. **Math:** General. **Parks/recreation:** Exercise sciences, health/fitness. **Philosophy/religion:** Philosophy, religion. **Physical sciences:** Chemistry, physics. **Psychology:** General. **Social sciences:** General, anthropology, sociology. **Theology:** Bible, religious ed, theology. **Visual/performing arts:** Art, cinematography, dramatic, drawing, film/cinema/video, multimedia, music, music performance, music theory/composition, painting, photography, sculpture, studio arts, theater arts management.

Most popular majors. Business/marketing 13%, communications/journalism 11%, education 7%, health sciences 8%, psychology 10%, social sciences 9%, theological studies 10%, visual/performing arts 12%.

Technology on campus. 225 workstations in library, computer center. Dormitories wired for high-speed internet access and linked to campus network. Commuter students can connect to campus network. Online course registration, online library, helpline, repair service, student web hosting, wireless network available.

Student life. Freshman orientation: Mandatory. Preregistration for classes offered. Week-long, held week before term begins for both Fall and Spring semesters. Led by current students. Various social activities hosted. **Policies:** Christian service assignment and regular church attendance encouraged. Students adhere to code of conduct and sign contract. Use and possession of drugs and/or alcohol not permitted. Any student under 20 required to live on campus unless living with relatives. Religious observance required. **Housing:** Guaranteed on-campus for freshmen. Coed dorms, single-sex dorms, special housing for disabled, apartments available. $250 partly refundable deposit, deadline 6/1. Flex-style dorms with single sex floors/wings available. **Activities:** Bands, campus ministries, choral groups, drama, film society, international student organizations, music ensembles, musical theater, opera, radio station, student government, student newspaper, symphony orchestra, TV station, Student Missionary Union, Korean student association, evangelism team, International Justice Mission, theology club, Society of Christian Philosophy, Tijuana Ministry, Bas Bleu (women's issues), Naturally Diverse, Revive Prayer Ministry.

Athletics. NAIA. **Intercollegiate:** Baseball M, basketball, cross-country, diving, golf, soccer, softball W, swimming, tennis, track and field, volleyball

W. **Intramural:** Basketball, football (non-tackle), soccer, softball, ultimate frisbee, volleyball. **Team name:** Eagles.

Student services. Alcohol/substance abuse counseling, chaplain/spiritual director, career counseling, student employment services, financial aid counseling, health services, minority student services, personal counseling, placement for graduates, veterans' counselor, women's services. **Physically disabled:** Services for visually, speech, hearing impaired.

Contact. E-mail: admissions@biola.edu
Phone: (562) 903-4752 Toll-free number: (800) 652-4652
Fax: (562) 903-4709
Andre Stephens, Associate Vice President of University Admissions, Biola University, 13800 Biola Avenue, La Mirada, CA 90639-0001

Brandman University
Irvine, California
www.brandman.edu
CB code: 6791

- Private 4-year virtual university
- Commuter campus in large city
- 3,595 degree-seeking undergraduates: 67% part-time, 63% women, 10% African American, 3% Asian American, 30% Hispanic/Latino, 1% Native American, 1% Native Hawaiian/Pacific islander, 4% Multi-racial, non-Hispanic
- 4,079 degree-seeking graduate students
- 74% of applicants admitted

General. 29 campus locations in California and Washington, as well as an online campus that serves students nationally. **Degrees:** 1,139 bachelor's, 83 associate awarded; master's, professional offered. **Location:** 50 miles from Los Angeles, 85 miles from San Diego. **Calendar:** Trimester, extensive summer session. **Full-time faculty:** 73 total; 20% minority, 64% women. **Part-time faculty:** 703 total; 16% minority, 56% women. **Class size:** 90% < 20, 10% 20-39.

Freshman class profile. 50 applied, 37 admitted, 20 enrolled.

Basis for selection. For undergraduate students, admission is based on GPA. Students applying to a baccalaureate program must have a minimum of 2.0 cumulative GPA on all prior college-level coursework. Students applying to the Associate of Arts program must have a minimum high school GPA of 2.0. For graduate students, there are four possible admission options, which are based on 1) GPA, 2) GPA and score on an exam (e.g., GRE), 3) holding a Master's degree or higher, and 4) GPA, score on exam (e.g., GRE), and submission of a portfolio that shows adequate preparation for graduate studies. For undergraduate students, admission is based on GPA. Students applying to the Associate of Arts program must have a minimum high school GPA of 2.0, must have a high school diploma or equivalent, and must pass an admissions test in English and Math. Students applying to a baccalaureate program must have a minimum of 2.0 cumulative GPA on all prior college-level coursework and must have completed at least 12 baccalaureate-level credits. Students are required to submit official transcripts from all colleges and universities attended. Undergraduate students applying for admission to Brandman University through Academic Fresh Start may elect to have all academic coursework, completed at any institution of higher education 10 or more years prior to the time of application, ignored for admission purposes. For graduate students, there are 4 possible admission options, which are based on 1) GPA, 2) GPA and score on an exam (e.g., GRE), 3) holding a Master's degree or higher, and 3) GPA, score on exam (e.g., GRE), and submission of a portfolio that shows adequate preparation for graduate studies.

2015-2016 Annual costs. Books/supplies: $1,752. Personal expenses: $3,800.

Financial aid. Non-need-based: Scholarships awarded for academics.

Application procedures. Admission: No deadline. No application fee. Application must be submitted online. Admission notification on a rolling basis beginning on or about 6/1. **Financial aid:** No deadline. FAFSA required. Applicants notified on a rolling basis starting 6/1.

Academics. Special study options: Distance learning, double major, dual enrollment of high school students, independent study, internships, teacher certification program. **Credit/placement by examination:** AP, CLEP, IB, institutional tests. There is no limit to the number of overall transfer credits accepted as long as students meet residency requirement (15 credits for associate degrees and 30 credits for bachelor's degrees). **Support services:** Learning center, study skills assistance, tutoring, writing center.

Majors. Business: Business admin, organizational leadership. **Communications:** Media studies. **Computer sciences:** Information technology. **Education:** Early childhood. **Health services:** Nursing (RN). **Human services:**

Social work. **Liberal arts:** Arts/sciences. **Protective services:** Criminal justice. **Psychology:** General. **Social sciences:** General, sociology.

Most popular majors. Business/marketing 28%, education 10%, liberal arts 13%, psychology 19%, security/protective services 9%, social sciences 13%.

Technology on campus. 837 workstations in library, computer center. Commuter students can connect to campus network. Online course registration, online library, helpline, wireless network available.

Student life. Freshman orientation: Mandatory. Preregistration for classes offered. Mandatory orientation offered online and on-campus. **Activities:** Business society (Irvine campus), nursing honor society, social work student association.

Student services. Adult student services, career counseling, financial aid counseling, personal counseling, veterans' counselor. **Physically disabled:** Services for visually, speech, hearing impaired.

Contact. E-mail: adminfo@brandman.edu
Phone: (877) 516-4501 Fax: (866) 659-1143
Bethany Tumbleson, Director of Admissions, Brandman University, 16355 Laguna Canyon Road, Irvine, CA 92618

Brooks Institute
Ventura, California
www.brooks.edu
CB code: 4228

- For-profit 3-year visual arts college
- Commuter campus in small city
- 415 degree-seeking undergraduates
- 22 graduate students
- Application essay, interview required

General. Founded in 1945. Accredited by ACICS. Facility in Santa Barbara is phased out and all students now attend their programs in Ventura. **Degrees:** 169 bachelor's awarded; master's offered. **Location:** 90 miles from Los Angeles. **Calendar:** Semester, extensive summer session. **Full-time faculty:** 32 total. **Part-time faculty:** 59 total. **Special facilities:** Digital labs, sounds stages, studio back-lot, prop house.

Basis for selection. School achievement record most important. Photographic experience not required for entrance. Advanced standing may be offered to those with 4X5 view camera experience. Evaluation consists of written examination portfolio and review. TOEFL required of students whose first language is not English. Different standards exist based on paper vs. computer scores and for undergraduate and graduate applicants. At time of matriculation, institution will assess English and math proficiencies for students who have not demonstrated proficiency in both at the college level or by receiving minimum standard scores in national tests. Interviews can be conducted via telephone. Interview and photography portfolio required for advanced standing in core courses. **Home schooled:** GED required if home schooling not recognized by state. **Learning Disabled:** Protocol for students seeking accommodation is mailed to accepted applicants with provisional acceptance letter.

High school preparation. College-preparatory program recommended. Recommended units include English 4, mathematics 2, social studies 1, science 1 and foreign language 2.

2015-2016 Annual costs. Tuition/fees: $20,320. Books/supplies: $2,502. Personal expenses: $1,608.

Application procedures. Admission: No deadline. $50 fee. Admission notification on a rolling basis. Students encouraged to apply at least 6 months in advance. **Financial aid:** Priority date 3/2; no closing date. FAFSA, institutional form required. Applicants notified on a rolling basis starting 5/1.

Academics. Special study options: Accelerated study, combined bachelor's/graduate degree, distance learning, double major, independent study, internships. Documentary courses in foreign countries, travel courses, in-water photography (for upper-division students). **Credit/placement by examination:** AP, CLEP, IB, institutional tests. **Support services:** Remedial instruction, tutoring.

Majors. Communications: Photojournalism. **Visual/performing arts:** Cinematography, film/cinema/video, graphic design, photography.

Technology on campus. 20 workstations in library, computer center. Online library, helpline, wireless network available.

Student life. Freshman orientation: Mandatory. Preregistration for classes offered. Immediately prior to matriculation; normally 2-3 days of activities. **Policies:** Car necessary for travel between campuses and to assignment locations. **Activities:** Student government.

Student services. Career counseling, student employment services, financial aid counseling, personal counseling, placement for graduates.

Contact. E-mail: admissions@brooks.edu
Toll-free number: (888) 304-3456 Fax: (805) 585-8039
Maggie Balderas, Director of Admissions, Brooks Institute, 5301 North Ventura Avenue, Ventura, CA 93001

California Baptist University
Riverside, California — CB member
www.calbaptist.edu — CB code: 4094

- Private 4-year university affiliated with the Southern Baptist Convention
- Commuter campus in large city
- 6,630 degree-seeking undergraduates: 14% part-time, 63% women, 7% African American, 5% Asian American, 34% Hispanic/Latino, 1% Native American, 1% Native Hawaiian/Pacific islander, 6% Multi-racial, non-Hispanic, 2% international
- 1,911 degree-seeking graduate students
- 65% of applicants admitted
- SAT or ACT (ACT writing optional), application essay required
- 55% graduate within 6 years

General. Founded in 1950. Regionally accredited. **Degrees:** 1,284 bachelor's awarded; master's, professional offered. **ROTC:** Army, Air Force. **Location:** 60 miles from Los Angeles. **Calendar:** Semester, extensive summer session. **Full-time faculty:** 290 total; 74% have terminal degrees, 25% minority, 46% women. **Part-time faculty:** 383 total; 18% have terminal degrees, 8% minority, 51% women. **Class size:** 54% < 20, 38% 20-39, 3% 40-49, 4% 50-99, less than 1% >100. **Special facilities:** Music performance and recording studios, aquatic center, Nie Wieder! Holocaust collection, digital design and photography studio, theater arts stage production workshop facility, prayer chapel, hymnology collection, nursing patient simulation laboratory.

Freshman class profile. 4,027 applied, 2,614 admitted, 1,107 enrolled.

Mid 50% test scores		GPA 2.0-2.99:	27%
SAT critical reading:	420-540	Rank in top quarter:	40%
SAT math:	410-540	Rank in top tenth:	12%
SAT writing:	410-530	Return as sophomores:	76%
ACT composite:	17-24	Out-of-state:	8%
GPA 3.75 or higher:	25%	Live on campus:	64%
GPA 3.50-3.74:	14%	International:	3%
GPA 3.0-3.49:	33%		

Basis for selection. School achievement record, test scores, essays, and recommendations are very important in admissions decisions. SAT and SAT Subject Tests or ACT recommended. Interviews recommended. Auditions required for music, drama applicants. **Home schooled:** Transcript of courses and grades, state high school equivalency certificate, letter of recommendation (nonparent) required. Submit an application, $45 application fee, two letters of recommendation, SAT or ACT scores, and one of the following: Official High School Transcripts or General Education Diploma or State Proficiency Exam. **Learning Disabled:** Reasonable accommodations and services provided to eligible students upon review of the following forms: Comprehensive, age-appropriate psycho educational evaluations that are no more than three years old will be accepted. Students must submit the appropriate documentation with the Request for Accommodation Form to the Coordinator of Disabled Student Services a minimum of thirty days prior to the requested services.

High school preparation. College-preparatory program recommended. 15 units required; 24 recommended. Required and recommended units include English 4, mathematics 3-4, social studies 2, history 2, science 2-3 (laboratory 2-3), foreign language 2-3, visual/performing arts 1 and academic electives 3. 2 units of religion, psychology, or sociology.

2015-2016 Annual costs. Tuition/fees: $30,384. Room/board: $9,540. Books/supplies: $1,746. Personal expenses: $3,132.

2015-2016 Financial aid. Need-based: 994 full-time freshmen applied for aid; 898 deemed to have need; 882 received aid. Average need met was 60%. Average scholarship/grant was $16,838; average loan $3,828. 57% of total undergraduate aid awarded as scholarships/grants, 43% as loans/jobs. **Non-need-based:** Awarded to 3,230 full-time undergraduates, including 842 freshmen. Scholarships awarded for academics, art, athletics, music/drama, religious affiliation, ROTC.

Application procedures. Admission: No deadline. $45 fee, may be waived for applicants with need. Application must be submitted online. Admission notification on a rolling basis beginning on or about 11/9. **Financial aid:** Priority date 3/2; no closing date. FAFSA required. Applicants notified on a rolling basis starting 3/2; must reply by 6/1.

Academics. Special study options: Accelerated study, combined bachelor's/graduate degree, distance learning, double major, ESL, exchange student, honors, internships, liberal arts/career combination, study abroad, teacher certification program, Washington semester, weekend college. **Credit/placement by examination:** AP, CLEP, IB, SAT, ACT, institutional tests. 30 credit hours maximum toward bachelor's degree. Portfolio course available to assist students in documenting work that may be counted for credit for prior learning experiences. **Support services:** Learning center, reduced course load, remedial instruction, study skills assistance, tutoring, writing center. Disability support services, online tutoring, workshops (note taking strategies, exam preparation), athletic academic support services.

Majors. Biology: General, exercise physiology. **Business:** General, accounting, marketing, organizational leadership. **Communications:** Communications/speech/rhetoric, journalism, persuasive communications. **Communications technology:** Desktop publishing. **Computer sciences:** Computer science, information technology. **Conservation:** Environmental science. **Education:** Early childhood, mathematics, music. **Engineering:** General, biomedical, chemical, civil, computer, mechanical, software. **English:** English lit. **Foreign languages:** Spanish. **Health services:** Communication disorders, health care admin, international public health, nursing (RN), prephysical therapy, public health ed. **History:** General. **Liberal arts:** Arts/sciences. **Math:** General, statistics. **Parks/recreation:** Exercise sciences. **Philosophy/religion:** Christian, philosophy. **Physical sciences:** Chemistry. **Protective services:** Law enforcement admin. **Psychology:** General. **Social sciences:** Political science, sociology. **Theology:** Bible, missionary. **Visual/performing arts:** General, dramatic, film/cinema/video, music, music performance, music theory/composition, photography, piano/keyboard, voice/opera.

Most popular majors. Business/marketing 17%, communications/journalism 6%, health sciences 17%, liberal arts 7%, parks/recreation 7%, psychology 9%.

Technology on campus. 279 workstations in library, computer center. Dormitories wired for high-speed internet access and linked to campus network. Commuter students can connect to campus network. Online course registration, online library, helpline, wireless network available.

Student life. Freshman orientation: Mandatory, $310 fee. Preregistration for classes offered. Held prior to beginning of semester, for a duration of three days. **Policies:** Students who are under 21 years of age OR who receive more than $8,500 in institutional scholarships per academic year are required to live in student housing. Religious observance required. **Housing:** Guaranteed on-campus for freshmen. Single-sex dorms, apartments, cooperative housing, themed housing available. $100 fully refundable deposit, deadline 8/1. **Activities:** Bands, campus ministries, choral groups, drama, film society, international student organizations, literary magazine, music ensembles, musical theater, student government, student newspaper, symphony orchestra, Fellowship of Christian Athletes, International Service Projects, United States Service Projects, Summer of Service, Caihong Fellowship, FAITH club, International Justice Mission, Third Culture Kollege Students (TCKS), Urban Ministry.

Athletics. NCAA. **Intercollegiate:** Baseball M, basketball, cheerleading W, cross-country, diving, golf, soccer, softball W, swimming, track and field, volleyball, water polo, wrestling M. **Intramural:** Basketball, bowling, football (non-tackle), golf, sand volleyball, soccer, softball W, table tennis, ultimate frisbee. **Team name:** Lancers.

Student services. Adult student services, alcohol/substance abuse counseling, chaplain/spiritual director, career counseling, student employment services, financial aid counseling, health services, personal counseling, placement for graduates, veterans' counselor. **Physically disabled:** Services for visually, speech, hearing impaired.

Contact. E-mail: admissions@calbaptist.edu
Phone: (951) 343-4212 Toll-free number: (877) 228-8866
Fax: (951) 343-4525
Allen Johnson, Dean of Undergraduate Enrollment Services, California Baptist University, 8432 Magnolia Avenue, Riverside, CA 92504-3297

California Christian College
Fresno, California
www.calchristiancollege.edu — CB code: 4123

- Private 4-year Bible college affiliated with the Free Will Baptists
- Residential campus in large city

♦ 18 degree-seeking undergraduates: 39% part-time, 17% women, 22% African American, 56% Hispanic/Latino
♦ Application essay required

General. Regionally accredited; also accredited by TRACS. **Degrees:** 3 bachelor's, 1 associate awarded. **Location:** 200 miles from San Francisco, 220 miles from Los Angeles. **Calendar:** Semester. **Part-time faculty:** 5 total; 40% have terminal degrees, 20% women. **Class size:** 100% < 20. **Special facilities:** Within one hour of three national parks: Yosemite, Kings Canyon, Sequoia.

Freshman class profile. 2 applied, 2 admitted, 1 enrolled.

Basis for selection. Open admission. Required Christian faith commitment. **Home schooled:** Transcript of courses and grades, state high school equivalency certificate, letter of recommendation (nonparent) required.

2016-2017 Annual costs. Tuition/fees (projected): $8,990. Room only: $4,800. Books/supplies: $700. Personal expenses: $2,205.

2015-2016 Financial aid. All financial aid based on need. 1 full-time freshmen applied for aid; 1 deemed to have need; 1 received aid. Average need met was 34%. Average scholarship/grant was $6,275. 44% of total undergraduate aid awarded as scholarships/grants, 56% as loans/jobs.

Application procedures. Admission: No deadline. $40 fee, may be waived for applicants with need. Application must be submitted on paper. Admission notification on a rolling basis. **Financial aid:** Priority date 3/2; no closing date. FAFSA, institutional form required. Applicants notified on a rolling basis starting 5/1.

Academics. Special study options: Honors, independent study, internships, liberal arts/career combination. **Credit/placement by examination:** AP, CLEP, institutional tests. **Support services:** Remedial instruction, study skills assistance, tutoring.

Majors. Theology: Theology.

Technology on campus. 12 workstations in library, computer center. Dormitories wired for high-speed internet access and linked to campus network. Commuter students can connect to campus network. Online course registration, online library, wireless network available.

Student life. Freshman orientation: Mandatory. Preregistration for classes offered. **Policies:** Religious observance required. **Housing:** Single-sex dorms available. **Activities:** Campus ministries, choral groups, music ensembles, student government.

Student services. Chaplain/spiritual director, financial aid counseling, personal counseling.

Contact. E-mail: admissions@calchristiancollege.edu
Phone: (559) 455-5571 Fax: (559) 385-2329
Trent Walley, Director of Admissions, California Christian College, 5364 E. Belmont, Fresno, CA 93727

California Coast University
Santa Ana, California
www.calcoast.edu

♦ For-profit 4-year virtual university
♦ Large city
♦ 5,447 degree-seeking undergraduates

General. Accredited by DETC. **Degrees:** 257 bachelor's, 31 associate awarded; master's, doctoral offered. **Calendar:** Differs by program, extensive summer session. **Part-time faculty:** 26 total.

Basis for selection. Open admission.

2015-2016 Annual costs. Tuition/fees: $4,500. **Additional information:** Active-duty service members and Veterans will receive a 10% tuition discount. Textbooks are not included in tuition fees, but are available from the University's Rental Library at a nominal cost.

Application procedures. Admission: No deadline. $75 fee.

Academics. Special study options: Accelerated study, cross-registration, distance learning, external degree, honors, independent study. **Credit/placement by examination:** AP, CLEP, IB.

Majors. Business: General, business admin. **Health services:** Health care admin. **Psychology:** General. **Social sciences:** Criminology.

Student life. Activities: Student newspaper.

Contact. E-mail: admissions@calcoast.edu
Phone: (714) 547-9625
Damien McMenamin, Admissions Director, California Coast University, 925 North Spurgeon Street, Santa Ana, CA 92701

California College of the Arts
San Francisco, California **CB member**
www.cca.edu **CB code: 4031**

♦ Private 4-year visual arts college
♦ Commuter campus in very large city
♦ 1,504 degree-seeking undergraduates: 5% part-time, 62% women, 4% African American, 16% Asian American, 13% Hispanic/Latino, 1% Native Hawaiian/Pacific islander, 31% international
♦ 455 degree-seeking graduate students
♦ 80% of applicants admitted
♦ Application essay required
♦ 59% graduate within 6 years

General. Founded in 1907. Regionally accredited. 2 campuses located in San Francisco and Oakland. **Degrees:** 264 bachelor's awarded; master's offered. **Location:** 2 miles from downtown. **Calendar:** Semester, limited summer session. **Full-time faculty:** 99 total; 67% have terminal degrees, 20% minority, 50% women. **Part-time faculty:** 400 total; 56% have terminal degrees, 14% minority, 48% women. **Class size:** 95% < 20, 5% 20-39. **Special facilities:** Center for art and public life, contemporary arts, materials resource center.

Freshman class profile. 1,713 applied, 1,364 admitted, 241 enrolled.

Mid 50% test scores			
SAT critical reading:	470-600	GPA 2.0-2.99:	28%
SAT math:	460-640	End year in good standing:	95%
SAT writing:	450-600	Return as sophomores:	82%
ACT composite:	21-28	Out-of-state:	39%
GPA 3.75 or higher:	19%	Live on campus:	84%
GPA 3.50-3.74:	17%	International:	38%
GPA 3.0-3.49:	36%	Fraternities:	1%

Basis for selection. High school achievement as evidenced by grade point average, portfolio of creative work, personal essay/statement of purpose, interview, and 2 letters of recommendation required. The college also reviews art/design activities and interests. SAT or ACT recommended. Test scores are primarily used for placement, but may be considered for admission. SAT or ACT scores with Writing highly recommended and used in English course placement. Portfolio of creative work and statement of artistic and professional goals required. **Home schooled:** Transcript of courses and grades required. Detailed syllabus of courses (equivalent to grades 10-12) and details of curriculum, including community college transcripts (if applicable) required.

High school preparation. College-preparatory program recommended.

2015-2016 Annual costs. Tuition/fees: $43,708. Room only: $9,050. Books/supplies: $1,500. Personal expenses: $2,570.

2014-2015 Financial aid. Need-based: 158 full-time freshmen applied for aid; 146 deemed to have need; 146 received aid. Average need met was 63%. Average scholarship/grant was $25,417; average loan $3,540. 82% of total undergraduate aid awarded as scholarships/grants, 18% as loans/jobs. **Non-need-based:** Awarded to 806 full-time undergraduates, including 215 freshmen. Scholarships awarded for academics, art. **Additional information:** Application deadline for merit scholarships February 1.

Application procedures. Admission: Priority date 2/1; no deadline. $60 fee, may be waived for applicants with need. Admission notification on a rolling basis beginning on or about 12/15. Must reply by May 1 or within 2 week(s) if notified thereafter. Maximum period of postponement is one semester. **Financial aid:** Priority date 2/1; no closing date. FAFSA required. Applicants notified by 4/1.

Academics. Special study options: Combined bachelor's/graduate degree, cross-registration, distance learning, double major, ESL, exchange student, independent study, internships, student-designed major, study abroad. **Credit/placement by examination:** AP, CLEP, IB, SAT, ACT, institutional tests. **Support services:** Learning center, pre-admission summer program, reduced course load, remedial instruction, study skills assistance, tutoring, writing center.

Majors. Architecture: Architecture. **English:** Creative writing. **Visual/performing arts:** Art, ceramics, cinematography, crafts, drawing, fashion design, fiber arts, game design, graphic design, illustration, industrial design, interior design, metal/jewelry, painting, photography, printmaking, sculpture, studio arts.

Most popular majors. Architecture 8%, communication technologies 6%, visual/performing arts 81%.

Technology on campus. PC or laptop required. 420 workstations in dormitories, library, computer center, student center. Dormitories wired for high-speed internet access and linked to campus network. Commuter students can connect to campus network. Online library, helpline, student web hosting, wireless network available.

Student life. Freshman orientation: Mandatory. Preregistration for classes offered. Educational and social programs are offered one week before classes start. **Policies:** Freshmen not permitted cars on campus. **Housing:** Coed dorms, special housing for disabled, apartments available. $600 partly refundable deposit, deadline 5/15. **Activities:** International student organizations, Alliance for Multiculturalism in Architecture, American Institute of Architecture Students, Asian Student Association, Future Action Reclamation Mob, International Interior Design association, CCA/UC Berkeley Queer Straight Alliance, Students of Color Coalition.

Athletics. Team name: Chimera.

Student services. Alcohol/substance abuse counseling, career counseling, student employment services, financial aid counseling, personal counseling, placement for graduates. **Physically disabled:** Services for visually, speech, hearing impaired.

Contact. E-mail: enroll@cca.edu
Phone: (415) 703-9523 Toll-free number: (800) 447-1278
Fax: (415) 703-9539
Arnold Icasiano, Director of Undergraduate Admission, California College of the Arts, 1111 Eighth Street, San Francisco, CA 94107-2247

California College San Diego
San Diego, California
www.cc-sd.edu   CB code: 3354

- Private 4-year business and health science college
- Commuter campus in very large city
- 1,075 degree-seeking undergraduates
- Application essay, interview required

General. Accredited by ACCSC. **Degrees:** 59 bachelor's, 189 associate awarded. **Location:** 5 miles from downtown. **Calendar:** Differs by program, extensive summer session. **Full-time faculty:** 12 total. **Part-time faculty:** 22 total.

Basis for selection. Open admission. **Home schooled:** State high school equivalency certificate required.

2015-2016 Annual costs. 20-month Associate programs: Business Management & Accounting $42,389, Computer Programming $42,273, Computer Technology & Networking $42,408, Graphic Arts $42,387, Medical Specialties $42,411, Respiratory Therapy $49,504. 36-month Bachelor programs: Accounting $74,753, Business Administration $74,620, Computer Science $74,700, Health Information Management $74,700, Healthcare Administration $74,778, Respiratory Therapy $81,719. All fees & books included.

Application procedures. Admission: No deadline. No application fee. Application must be submitted on paper. **Financial aid:** FAFSA, institutional form required.

Academics. Special study options: Combined bachelor's/graduate degree. **Credit/placement by examination:** AP, CLEP. **Support services:** Remedial instruction, tutoring.

Majors. Business: Accounting, business admin. **Computer sciences:** Computer science. **Health services:** Health care admin, respiratory therapy technology.

Most popular majors. Business/marketing 26%, computer/information sciences 13%, health sciences 60%.

Technology on campus. PC or laptop required. Commuter students can connect to campus network. Online library, helpline, repair service, wireless network available.

Student life. Freshman orientation: Mandatory. Preregistration for classes offered.

Athletics. Team name: Bulldogs.

Student services. Adult student services, career counseling, services for economically disadvantaged, student employment services, financial aid counseling, placement for graduates, veterans' counselor.

Contact. Phone: (619) 680-4430 Toll-free number: (800) 622-3188
Fax: (619) 295-7827
Baris Yucelt, Director of Admissions, California College San Diego, 6602 Convoy Court, Suite 100, San Diego, CA 92111

California Institute of Integral Studies
San Francisco, California
www.ciis.edu   CB code: 3609

- Private two-year upper-division university
- Commuter campus in very large city
- 88% of applicants admitted
- Application essay required

General. Regionally accredited. **Degrees:** 65 bachelor's awarded; master's, professional, doctoral offered. **Location:** Downtown. **Calendar:** Semester, extensive summer session. **Class size:** 70% < 20, 30% 20-39. **Special facilities:** Meditation room, Zen roof garden, art galleries in hallways, counseling centers.

Student profile. 102 degree-seeking undergraduates, 1,405 degree-seeking graduate students. 80 applied as first time-transfer students, 70 admitted, 55 enrolled.

Women:	81%	Multi-racial, non-Hispanic:	10%
African American:	8%	International:	3%
Asian American:	5%	Part-time:	15%
Hispanic/Latino:	20%	Out-of-state:	5%
Native American:	1%	25 or older:	95%
Native Hawaiian/Pacific islander:	1%		

Basis for selection. College transcript, application essay required. Transfer accepted as juniors.

2015-2016 Annual costs. Tuition/fees: $18,315. Books/supplies: $1,800. **Additional information:** Above tuition and fees are for fall and spring semesters. Most students also attend in the summer, which would add $8970 in tuition and $215 in fees.

Financial aid. Need-based: 80 applied for aid; 79 deemed to have need; 78 received aid. Average need met was 27%. 39% of total undergraduate aid awarded as scholarships/grants, 61% as loans/jobs. **Non-need-based:** Scholarships awarded for academics, alumni affiliation, art, job skills, leadership, minority status, music/drama, ROTC, state residency.

Application procedures. Admission: Priority date 4/1; deadline 7/1. $65 fee, may be waived for applicants with need. Application priority dates differ by program. **Financial aid:** No deadline.

Academics. Special study options: Distance learning, independent study, internships, study abroad, weekend college. Offers interdisciplinary, cross-cultural, and applied studies in psychology, philosophy, religion, cultural anthropology, transformative studies and leadership, integrative health, women's spirituality, master's in counseling psychology, community mental health, and the arts. **Credit/placement by examination:** AP, CLEP. 30 credit hours maximum toward bachelor's degree. **Support services:** Tutoring, writing center.

Technology on campus. 20 workstations in library, computer center. Commuter students can connect to campus network. Online library, helpline, wireless network available.

Student life. Activities: Dance, drama, international student organizations, student government, People of Color, Queer at CIIS, Student Alliance, Interdisciplinary Dialog Group, UNITE!, AWARE, International Students & Friends, Zen Meditation Group, Theater for Change.

Student services. Career counseling, financial aid counseling, minority student services, personal counseling, placement for graduates.

Contact. E-mail: admissions@ciis.edu
Phone: (415) 575-6150
Wendell Tull, Director of Admissions, California Institute of Integral Studies, 1453 Mission Street, San Francisco, CA 94103

California Institute of Technology

Pasadena, California   **CB member**
www.caltech.edu   **CB code: 4034**

♦ Private 4-year university
♦ Residential campus in small city
♦ 1,001 degree-seeking undergraduates: 39% women, 1% African American, 45% Asian American, 12% Hispanic/Latino, 5% Multi-racial, non-Hispanic, 8% international
♦ 1,254 degree-seeking graduate students
♦ 9% of applicants admitted
♦ SAT or ACT with writing, application essay required
♦ 91% graduate within 6 years; 52% enter graduate study

General. Founded in 1891. Regionally accredited. **Degrees:** 228 bachelor's awarded; master's, doctoral offered. **ROTC:** Army, Air Force. **Location:** 10 miles from downtown Los Angeles. **Calendar:** Quarter. **Full-time faculty:** 330 total; 98% have terminal degrees, 19% minority, 20% women. **Part-time faculty:** 27 total; 56% have terminal degrees, 22% minority, 48% women. **Class size:** 62% < 20, 22% 20-39, 5% 40-49, 7% 50-99, 4% >100. **Special facilities:** Jet Propulsion Laboratory, observatories, wind and water tunnels, radio observatory, seismological laboratory, marine biological laboratory.

Freshman class profile. 6,507 applied, 573 admitted, 241 enrolled.

Mid 50% test scores			
SAT critical reading:	730-800	Rank in top tenth:	99%
SAT math:	770-800	Return as sophomores:	97%
SAT writing:	730-790	Out-of-state:	63%
ACT composite:	34-35	Live on campus:	100%
Rank in top quarter:	100%	International:	7%

Basis for selection. High school preparation and record (particularly in math and science), test scores, extracurricular activities (science and non-science-related), counselors' and teachers' recommendations, and demonstrated interest in math and science are major considerations within a holistic admissions approach. SAT Subject Test requirements: Math level IIC and one science, either biology (environmental or molecular), chemistry, or physics. **Home schooled:** Statement describing home school structure and mission, transcript of courses and grades required.

High school preparation. College-preparatory program required. Required and recommended units include English 3-4, mathematics 4, social studies 1-3, history 1, science 2-4 (laboratory 1) and foreign language 3.

2015-2016 Annual costs. Tuition/fees: $45,390. Room/board: $13,371.

2015-2016 Financial aid. Need-based: 181 full-time freshmen applied for aid; 140 deemed to have need; 140 received aid. Average need met was 100%. Average scholarship/grant was $37,873; average loan $3,349. 90% of total undergraduate aid awarded as scholarships/grants, 10% as loans/jobs. **Non-need-based:** Awarded to 11 full-time undergraduates, including 4 freshmen.

Application procedures. Admission: Closing date 1/3 (postmark date). $75 fee, may be waived for applicants with need. Admission notification by 4/1. Must reply by 5/1. **Financial aid:** Priority date 3/2; no closing date. FAFSA, institutional form, CSS PROFILE required. Applicants notified by 4/15; must reply by 5/1 or within 2 week(s) of notification.

Academics. Special study options: Combined bachelor's/graduate degree, cooperative education, cross-registration, double major, ESL, exchange student, independent study, liberal arts/career combination, student-designed major, study abroad. **Credit/placement by examination:** AP, CLEP, institutional tests. **Support services:** Reduced course load, tutoring, writing center. Although remedial services are not offered formally, remediation is available to students deficient in basic scientific knowledge or technical skills.

Majors. Biology: General. **Business:** Managerial economics. **Computer sciences:** General. **Engineering:** General, applied physics, biomedical, chemical, electrical, environmental, mechanical. **English:** English lit. **History:** General, science/technology. **Math:** General, computational. **Philosophy/religion:** Philosophy. **Physical sciences:** Astrophysics, chemistry, geochemistry, geology, geophysics, physics, planetary. **Social sciences:** General, economics, political science.

Most popular majors. Biology 8%, computer/information sciences 21%, engineering/engineering technologies 35%, mathematics 12%, physical sciences 22%.

Technology on campus. 112 workstations in dormitories, library. Dormitories wired for high-speed internet access and linked to campus network. Commuter students can connect to campus network. Online course registration, online library, helpline, repair service, student web hosting, wireless network available.

Student life. Freshman orientation: Mandatory, $500 fee. Preregistration for classes offered. 3 day Frosh camp. **Policies:** Honor Code: "No member of the Caltech community shall take unfair advantage of any other member of the Caltech community". **Housing:** Guaranteed on-campus for freshmen. Coed dorms, special housing for disabled, apartments available. Pets allowed in dorm rooms. Single family homes available. **Activities:** Bands, choral groups, dance, drama, international student organizations, literary magazine, music ensembles, musical theater, student government, student newspaper, symphony orchestra, Caltech Y, Christian Fellowship, Newman Club, Hillel, Amnesty International, Caltech Center for Diversity.

Athletics. NCAA. **Intercollegiate:** Baseball M, basketball, cross-country, diving, fencing, soccer M, swimming, tennis, track and field, volleyball W, water polo. **Intramural:** Badminton, basketball, football (non-tackle), football (tackle), soccer, softball, ultimate frisbee, volleyball. **Team name:** Beavers.

Student services. Alcohol/substance abuse counseling, career counseling, services for economically disadvantaged, student employment services, financial aid counseling, health services, minority student services, personal counseling, placement for graduates, women's services. **Physically disabled:** Services for visually, speech, hearing impaired.

Contact. E-mail: ugadmissions@caltech.edu
Phone: (626) 395-6341 Fax: (626) 683-3026
Jarrid Whitney, Director of Admissions, California Institute of Technology, 383 South Hill Avenue, Mail Code 10-90, Pasadena, CA 91125

California Institute of the Arts

Valencia, California   **CB member**
www.calarts.edu   **CB code: 4049**

♦ Private 4-year visual arts and performing arts college
♦ Residential campus in small city
♦ 942 degree-seeking undergraduates: 1% part-time, 60% women, 7% African American, 15% Asian American, 15% Hispanic/Latino, 1% Native American, 1% Native Hawaiian/Pacific islander, 6% Multi-racial, non-Hispanic, 7% international
♦ 497 degree-seeking graduate students
♦ 25% of applicants admitted
♦ Application essay required
♦ 57% graduate within 6 years

General. Founded in 1961. Regionally accredited. Single complex of 6 professional schools: art, critical studies, dance, film/video, music and theater. **Degrees:** 290 bachelor's awarded; master's, doctoral offered. **Location:** 30 miles from Los Angeles. **Calendar:** Semester, limited summer session. **Full-time faculty:** 170 total; 61% have terminal degrees, 18% minority, 45% women. **Part-time faculty:** 173 total; 49% have terminal degrees, 17% minority, 40% women. **Class size:** 80% < 20, 18% 20-39, less than 1% 40-49, 2% 50-99. **Special facilities:** Art studios, galleries, animation studios, concert halls, 6 theaters (including a modular theater, a dance theater, and music pavilion).

Freshman class profile. 2,123 applied, 536 admitted, 193 enrolled.

Return as sophomores:	87%	Live on campus:	90%
Out-of-state:	58%		

Basis for selection. Admission is talent based, evaluated by faculty via group review. Portfolio required for art/design, film/video, music composition majors, and theater design and production. Auditions required for acting, dance, music majors. Music applicants may submit audio tape recordings in lieu of live audition for some programs. Interview required for directing/performance/production studies majors. **Home schooled:** Transcript of courses and grades, state high school equivalency certificate, letter of recommendation (nonparent) required.

High school preparation. College-preparatory program recommended. Recommended units include English 4, mathematics 3, social studies 3, history 1, science 3 (laboratory 1), foreign language 2, computer science 1, visual/performing arts 3 and academic electives 2.

2015-2016 Annual costs. Tuition/fees: $43,876. Room/board: $11,165. Books/supplies: $1,545. Personal expenses: $2,400.

2015-2016 Financial aid. Need-based: 150 full-time freshmen applied for aid; 147 deemed to have need; 140 received aid. Average scholarship/

grant was $12,572; average loan $3,506. 62% of total undergraduate aid awarded as scholarships/grants, 38% as loans/jobs. **Non-need-based:** Scholarships awarded for academics, art, minority status, music/drama.

Application procedures. Admission: Priority date 12/1; deadline 1/5 (receipt date). $70 fee, may be waived for applicants with need. Application must be submitted online. Admission notification on a rolling basis beginning on or about 4/1. Must reply by May 1 or within 3 week(s) if notified thereafter. After the regular deadline, applications are continue to be accepted in the order received until programs close. **Financial aid:** Priority date 2/15; no closing date. FAFSA, CSS PROFILE required. Applicants notified on a rolling basis starting 4/1; must reply by 5/1 or within 3 week(s) of notification.

Academics. Special study options: Exchange student, independent study, internships, student-designed major, study abroad. **Credit/placement by examination:** AP, CLEP, institutional tests. **Support services:** Pre-admission summer program, tutoring, writing center.

Majors. Visual/performing arts: Cinematography, dance, design, music performance, music theory/composition, photography, studio arts, theater design.

Technology on campus. 40 workstations in library. Dormitories wired for high-speed internet access. Commuter students can connect to campus network. Online course registration, online library, helpline, repair service, wireless network available.

Student life. Freshman orientation: Available. Preregistration for classes offered. Held the week before classes begin in the fall semester. **Policies:** Student standards of conduct; alcohol and drug policy; exhibition and performance policy; housing policy; pet policy; sexual assault and sexual exploitation policy; student travel policy; vandalism policy. **Housing:** Coed dorms, apartments available. $350 fully refundable deposit, deadline 5/1. **Activities:** Jazz band, dance, drama, film society, literary magazine, music ensembles, musical theater, opera, radio station, student government, student newspaper, TV station, black student union, Latino student union, GLBT student union, Asian club, political issues club, TRTH [Bible] Study, Heart Christian Fellowship.

Student services. Alcohol/substance abuse counseling, career counseling, student employment services, financial aid counseling, health services, personal counseling, placement for graduates. **Physically disabled:** Services for visually, speech, hearing impaired.

Contact. E-mail: admissions@calarts.edu
Phone: (661) 255-1050 ext. 2185 Toll-free number: (800) 545-2787
Fax: (661) 253-7710
Molly Ryan, Director of Admissions, California Institute of the Arts, 24700 McBean Parkway, Valencia, CA 91355

California Lutheran University
Thousand Oaks, California   **CB member**
www.callutheran.edu   **CB code: 4088**

- Private 4-year university and liberal arts college affiliated with the Evangelical Lutheran Church in America
- Residential campus in small city
- 2,802 degree-seeking undergraduates: 5% part-time, 43% women, 4% African American, 6% Asian American, 27% Hispanic/Latino, 1% Native American, 1% Native Hawaiian/Pacific islander, 5% Multi-racial, non-Hispanic, 3% international
- 1,260 degree-seeking graduate students
- 62% of applicants admitted
- SAT or ACT (ACT writing optional), application essay required
- 66% graduate within 6 years; 26% enter graduate study

General. Founded in 1959. Regionally accredited. **Degrees:** 766 bachelor's awarded; master's, professional offered. **ROTC:** Army, Air Force. **Location:** 45 miles from Los Angeles. **Calendar:** Semester, limited summer session. **Full-time faculty:** 193 total; 86% have terminal degrees, 17% minority, 48% women. **Part-time faculty:** 244 total; 36% have terminal degrees, 18% minority, 48% women. **Class size:** 61% < 20, 38% 20-39, less than 1% 40-49, less than 1% 50-99. **Special facilities:** Sports and fitness center with dance studio, Olympic-size pool, television studio with editing room.

Freshman class profile. 6,573 applied, 4,044 admitted, 595 enrolled.

Mid 50% test scores			
SAT critical reading:	500-600	GPA 2.0-2.99:	5%
SAT math:	500-600	Rank in top quarter:	72%
SAT writing:	490-600	Rank in top tenth:	30%
ACT composite:	22-27	End year in good standing:	93%
GPA 3.75 or higher:	45%	Return as sophomores:	84%
GPA 3.50-3.74:	23%	Out-of-state:	16%
GPA 3.0-3.49:	27%	Live on campus:	83%
		International:	2%

Basis for selection. High school achievement record, rank in class, test scores, essay, letters of recommendation very important. Interview recommended. **Home schooled:** Transcript of courses and grades, letter of recommendation (nonparent) required. Encouraged to submit passing score on GED and complete interview with Admission Counselor. Transcript must include: brief description of courses, textbook (title and author) information for each course, how foreign language verbal component and natural science laboratory requirements were met; official transcripts from other school(s) attended. **Learning Disabled:** Meeting with the Accessibility Resource Coordinator is recommended.

High school preparation. College-preparatory program recommended. Required units include English 4, mathematics 3, social studies 2, science 3 (laboratory 2) and foreign language 2. Math must be through algebra II and preferably 4 years; 2 years of foreign language must be same language; highly recommend 3 years of science.

2015-2016 Annual costs. Tuition/fees: $38,430. Room/board: $12,740. Books/supplies: $1,764. Personal expenses: $2,322.

2015-2016 Financial aid. Need-based: 584 full-time freshmen applied for aid; 445 deemed to have need; 445 received aid. Average need met was 73%. Average scholarship/grant was $24,073; average loan $3,450. 76% of total undergraduate aid awarded as scholarships/grants, 24% as loans/jobs. **Non-need-based:** Awarded to 1,657 full-time undergraduates, including 299 freshmen. Scholarships awarded for academics, alumni affiliation, art, leadership, minority status, music/drama, religious affiliation, state residency.

Application procedures. Admission: Priority date 11/1; deadline 1/1 (postmark date). $25 fee, may be waived for applicants with need. Admission notification by 4/15. Admission notification on a rolling basis. Must reply by May 1 or within 2 week(s) if notified thereafter. **Financial aid:** Priority date 3/1, closing date 7/1. FAFSA required. Applicants notified on a rolling basis starting 3/15; must reply within 2 week(s) of notification.

Academics. Special study options: Accelerated study, cooperative education, double major, dual enrollment of high school students, exchange student, honors, independent study, internships, semester at sea, student-designed major, study abroad, teacher certification program, Washington semester. **Credit/placement by examination:** AP, CLEP, IB, SAT, ACT, institutional tests. 32 credit hours maximum toward associate degree, 30 toward bachelor's. **Support services:** Learning center, pre-admission summer program, reduced course load, study skills assistance, tutoring, writing center.

Majors. Biology: General, biochemistry, molecular. **Business:** General, accounting, business admin, finance, management science, managerial economics, marketing. **Communications:** Advertising, broadcast journalism, communications/speech/rhetoric, journalism, public relations. **Computer sciences:** General, computer graphics, computer science, information systems, programming. **Conservation:** Environmental science. **Education:** General, art, early childhood, elementary, English, foreign languages, mathematics, middle, music, physical, reading, science, secondary, social science, social studies, special ed. **English:** English lit, rhetoric/composition. **Foreign languages:** General, French, German, Spanish. **Health services:** Athletic training, predental, premedicine, prepharmacy, preveterinary. **History:** General. **Liberal arts:** Arts/sciences. **Math:** General. **Philosophy/religion:** Philosophy, religion. **Physical sciences:** Chemistry, geology, physics. **Protective services:** Police science. **Psychology:** General. **Social sciences:** Criminology, economics, international relations, political science, sociology. **Theology:** Religious ed, theology, youth ministry. **Visual/performing arts:** General, art, commercial/advertising art, dramatic, music.

Most popular majors. Biology 7%, business/marketing 26%, communications/journalism 14%, parks/recreation 6%, psychology 12%, security/protective services 6%, social sciences 7%.

Technology on campus. 334 workstations in dormitories, library, computer center, student center. Dormitories wired for high-speed internet access and linked to campus network. Commuter students can connect to campus network. Online course registration, online library, helpline, wireless network available.

Student life. Freshman orientation: Mandatory. Preregistration for classes offered. 4-day session held the weekend before classes begin. **Policies:** No alcohol on campus except in the chapel for communion, drug free campus. **Housing:** Coed dorms, special housing for disabled available. $400 fully refundable deposit, deadline 5/1. On campus houses available. **Activities:**

Bands, campus ministries, choral groups, dance, drama, international student organizations, literary magazine, music ensembles, Model UN, musical theater, radio station, student government, student newspaper, symphony orchestra, TV station, Lutheran Church congregation, multicultural and international clubs and organizations, Hillel, Habitat for Humanity.

Athletics. NCAA. **Intercollegiate:** Baseball M, basketball, cross-country, diving, football (tackle) M, golf, soccer, softball W, swimming, tennis, track and field, volleyball, water polo. **Intramural:** Basketball, cheerleading, football (non-tackle), golf, handball, soccer, softball, tennis W, volleyball, water polo. **Team name:** Kingsmen/Regals.

Student services. Adult student services, alcohol/substance abuse counseling, chaplain/spiritual director, career counseling, services for economically disadvantaged, student employment services, financial aid counseling, health services, minority student services, personal counseling, placement for graduates, veterans' counselor, women's services. **Physically disabled:** Services for visually, speech, hearing impaired.

Contact. E-mail: admissions@callutheran.edu
Phone: (805) 493-3135 Toll-free number: (877) 258-3678
Fax: (805) 493-3114
Michael Elgarico, Director of Undergraduate Admission, California Lutheran University, 60 West Olsen Road #1350, Thousand Oaks, CA 91360-2787

California Maritime Academy
Vallejo, California
www.csum.edu

CB member
CB code: 4035

- Public 4-year university and maritime college
- Residential campus in small city
- 1,072 degree-seeking undergraduates: 3% part-time, 15% women, 2% African American, 10% Asian American, 17% Hispanic/Latino, 11% Multi-racial, non-Hispanic, 1% international
- 74 degree-seeking graduate students
- 82% of applicants admitted
- 54% graduate within 6 years

General. Founded in 1929. Regionally accredited. All students participate in at least one 2-month training cruise around Pacific Ocean, or an international experience geared toward their major. **Degrees:** 185 bachelor's awarded; master's offered. **ROTC:** Naval, Air Force. **Location:** 30 miles from San Francisco. **Calendar:** Semester, limited summer session. **Full-time faculty:** 64 total; 62% have terminal degrees, 6% minority, 20% women. **Part-time faculty:** 26 total; 62% have terminal degrees, 12% minority, 35% women. **Class size:** 22% < 20, 56% 20-39, 17% 40-49, 5% 50-99. **Special facilities:** 500-foot training ship, computer-aided radar simulators, bridge simulator, steam simulator.

Freshman class profile. 1,206 applied, 983 admitted, 223 enrolled.

Mid 50% test scores			
SAT critical reading:	490-600	GPA 3.50-3.74:	16%
SAT math:	510-610	GPA 3.0-3.49:	48%
SAT writing:	470-570	GPA 2.0-2.99:	22%
ACT composite:	21-27	Return as sophomores:	82%
GPA 3.75 or higher:	14%	Out-of-state:	15%
		International:	1%

Basis for selection. Applicants must meet California State University Eligibility Index requirements and have strong grades in mathematics and sciences. All accepted students must pass physical examination.

High school preparation. College-preparatory program recommended. 17 units required; 18 recommended. Required and recommended units include English 4, mathematics 3-4, social studies 1, history 1, science 2-3 (laboratory 2-3), foreign language 2, visual/performing arts 1 and academic electives 1. One additional mathematics course recommended for mechanical engineering applicants. Chemistry or physics required. One visual or performing arts elective required.

2015-2016 Annual costs. Tuition/fees: $6,536; $17,696 out-of-state. Room/board: $11,756. Books/supplies: $1,636. Personal expenses: $1,392.

2015-2016 Financial aid. All financial aid based on need. 122 full-time freshmen applied for aid; 122 deemed to have need; 122 received aid. Average scholarship/grant was $7,379; average loan $4,053. 68% of total undergraduate aid awarded as scholarships/grants, 32% as loans/jobs. **Additional information:** US Maritime Administration provides annual incentive payment of $3,000 per student, with certain conditions. Tuition waiver for children of deceased or disabled California veterans.

Application procedures. Admission: Closing date 11/30 (postmark date). $55 fee, may be waived for applicants with need. Admission notification on a rolling basis beginning on or about 2/1. Must reply by May 1 or within 2 week(s) if notified thereafter. **Financial aid:** Priority date 3/2; no closing date. FAFSA required. Applicants notified on a rolling basis starting 4/1.

Academics. Special study options: Cooperative education, double major, honors, internships, semester at sea. International training cruise onboard ship "Golden Bear". **Credit/placement by examination:** AP, CLEP, IB, SAT, ACT. 24 credit hours maximum toward bachelor's degree. **Support services:** Learning center, remedial instruction, study skills assistance, tutoring. Center for Engagement, Teaching and Learning provides free tutoring/workshops hosted by professors.

Majors. Business: Business admin, logistics. **Engineering:** Mechanical.

Most popular majors. Business/marketing 11%, engineering/engineering technologies 39%, interdisciplinary studies 11%, trade and industry 37%.

Technology on campus. PC or laptop required. 85 workstations in dormitories, library, computer center, student center. Dormitories wired for high-speed internet access and linked to campus network. Commuter students can connect to campus network. Online course registration, online library, helpline, wireless network available.

Student life. Freshman orientation: Mandatory, $350 fee. Preregistration for classes offered. Held last week of August. **Policies:** Students required to live on campus except those married or with children. Freshmen not permitted cars on campus. **Housing:** Guaranteed on-campus for all undergraduates. Coed dorms, themed housing available. $500 nonrefundable deposit, deadline 5/1. **Activities:** Choral groups, student government, Asian Pacific Islanders club, student veterans association, Jewish club, Latino club, Society of Women Engineers, American Society of Mechanical Engineers, International Society of Automation, Society of Naval Architects and Marine Engineers, Anchor club, drama club.

Athletics. NAIA. **Intercollegiate:** Basketball, rowing (crew), rugby M, sailing, soccer, water polo. **Intramural:** Badminton, baseball M, basketball, boxing M, golf, racquetball, rowing (crew), rugby M, sailing, softball, tennis, volleyball, water polo. **Team name:** Keelhaulers.

Student services. Career counseling, student employment services, financial aid counseling, health services, minority student services, personal counseling, placement for graduates, veterans' counselor.

Contact. E-mail: admission@csum.edu
Phone: (707) 654-1330 Fax: (707) 654-1336
Marc McGee, Director of Admission, California Maritime Academy, 200 Maritime Academy Drive, Vallejo, CA 94590

California Miramar University
San Diego, California
www.calmu.edu

CB code: 6458

- Private 3-year university and business college
- Commuter campus in very large city
- 361 degree-seeking undergraduates

General. Regionally accredited; also accredited by ACICS, DETC. **Degrees:** 1 bachelor's, 2 associate awarded; master's, professional offered. **Calendar:** Semester, extensive summer session. **Full-time faculty:** 6 total. **Part-time faculty:** 30 total.

Basis for selection. Open admission. Application fees for masters and doctorate degree programs are $40 and $60 respectively.

2015-2016 Annual costs. Tuition/fees: $9,750. Books/supplies: $600.

Application procedures. Admission: $25 fee, may be waived for applicants with need. Application must be submitted online.

Academics. Credit/placement by examination: AP, CLEP. **Support services:** Learning center, study skills assistance, tutoring, writing center.

Majors. BACHELOR'S. Business: Business admin. **Human services:** General. **ASSOCIATE. Business:** Business admin.

Technology on campus. PC or laptop required.

Student services. Career counseling, financial aid counseling, veterans' counselor.

Contact. E-mail: admissions@calmu.edu
Phone: (858) 653-3000
Jean Foster, Director of Admissions, California Miramar University, 9750
Miramar Road, Suite 180, San Diego, CA 92126

California National University for Advanced Studies
Torrance, California
www.cnuas.edu   CB code: 3894

- For-profit 4-year virtual university
- Small city
- 59 degree-seeking undergraduates

General. Accredited by DETC. 100% distance learning university. **Degrees:**
13 bachelor's awarded; master's offered. **Calendar:** Differs by program. **Part-
time faculty:** 60 total.

Basis for selection. Application/portfolio important. **Home schooled:**
Statement describing home school structure and mission, letter of recommendation (nonparent) required.

2015-2016 Annual costs. Tuition is based on individual 15 week trimesters; with the recommendation students take two courses per trimester. Tuition
is charged by the unit. US & Canadian Residents $300/unit, non-US &
Canadian Residents $330/unit. Human Resource certificate program per
course: $930. QAS 301 Six Sigma Green Belt certificate program: $1,285.
QAS 401 Six Sigma Black Belt certificate program: $1,985. Application fee:
US & Canadian $75, non-US & Canadian $100. Registration fee $75. Books
and supplies cost varies by program.

Application procedures. Admission: No deadline. $75 fee. **Financial
aid:** No deadline.

Academics. Special study options: Distance learning. **Credit/placement
by examination:** AP, CLEP.

Majors. Business: Business admin. **Computer sciences:** Computer science.
Engineering: General.

Student life. Freshman orientation: Available. Preregistration for
classes offered.

Contact. E-mail: cnuadms@mail.cnuas.edu
Phone: (818) 830-2411 Toll-free number: (800) 782-2422
Fax: (310) 371-7072
Cynthia Speed, Director of Admissions, California National University for
Advanced Studies, 18520 Hawthorne Blvd, Torrance, CA 90504

California Polytechnic State University: San Luis Obispo
San Luis Obispo, California   CB member
www.calpoly.edu   CB code: 4038

- Public 4-year university
- Residential campus in large town
- 19,971 degree-seeking undergraduates: 4% part-time, 47% women, 1%
  African American, 12% Asian American, 16% Hispanic/Latino, 7%
  Multi-racial, non-Hispanic, 2% international
- 760 degree-seeking graduate students
- 31% of applicants admitted
- SAT or ACT (ACT writing optional) required
- 79% graduate within 6 years

General. Founded in 1901. Regionally accredited. **Degrees:** 4,167 bachelor's awarded; master's offered. **ROTC:** Army. **Location:** 200 miles from
Los Angeles, 230 miles from San Francisco. **Calendar:** Quarter. **Full-time
faculty:** 889 total; 75% have terminal degrees, 36% women. **Part-time
faculty:** 522 total; 28% have terminal degrees, 49% women. **Class size:**
16% < 20, 58% 20-39, 13% 40-49, 8% 50-99, 5% >100. **Special facilities:**
Printing press museum, university farm, dairy products technical center,
architectural design institute.

Freshman class profile. 46,820 applied, 14,651 admitted, 4,943 enrolled.

Mid 50% test scores			
SAT critical reading:	550-650	Rank in top quarter:	84%
SAT math:	580-690	Rank in top tenth:	49%
ACT composite:	26-31	Return as sophomores:	93%
GPA 3.75 or higher:	72%	Out-of-state:	19%
GPA 3.50-3.74:	17%	Live on campus:	99%
GPA 3.0-3.49:	10%	International:	2%
GPA 2.0-2.99:	1%		

Basis for selection. Course work, high school GPA, test scores most
important. Extracurricular activities considered. Portfolio required for art and
design majors; audition required for music majors; portfolio required for
architecture transfer applicants.

High school preparation. College-preparatory program required. 15 units
required; 22 recommended. Required and recommended units include English
4-5, mathematics 3-5, social studies 1, history 1, science 2-4 (laboratory 2),
foreign language 2-4, visual/performing arts 1-2 and academic electives 1.
History must be U.S. history/government.

2015-2016 Annual costs. Tuition/fees: $9,000; $20,160 out-of-state.
Room/board: $12,009. Books/supplies: $1,812. Personal expenses: $1,392.
Additional information: International Student Fee of $300 per quarter.

2014-2015 Financial aid. Need-based: 3,619 full-time freshmen applied
for aid; 1,954 deemed to have need; 1,885 received aid. Average need met
was 56%. Average scholarship/grant was $3,177; average loan $3,276. 63%
of total undergraduate aid awarded as scholarships/grants, 37% as loans/jobs.
Non-need-based: Awarded to 2,524 full-time undergraduates, including 833
freshmen. Scholarships awarded for academics, alumni affiliation, art, athletics, job skills, leadership, music/drama, ROTC, state residency. **Additional
information:** College-administered financial aid is not available for undergraduate international students.

Application procedures. Admission: Closing date 11/30 (postmark
date). $55 fee, may be waived for applicants with need. Application must
be submitted online. Admission notification by 4/1. Must reply by 5/1.
Housing deposit due on first-come, first-served basis. **Financial aid:** Priority
date 3/2; no closing date. FAFSA required. Applicants notified on a rolling
basis starting 4/1.

Academics. Special study options: Cooperative education, distance learning, double major, exchange student, honors, independent study, internships,
liberal arts/career combination, semester at sea, study abroad, teacher certification program. **Credit/placement by examination:** AP, CLEP, IB, SAT,
ACT, institutional tests. 45 credit hours maximum toward bachelor's degree.
Support services: Learning center, pre-admission summer program, reduced
course load, remedial instruction, study skills assistance, tutoring, writing
center.

Majors. Architecture: Architecture, landscape, urban/community planning.
Biology: General, bacteriology, biochemistry. **Business:** Business admin.
Communications: Communications/speech/rhetoric, journalism. **Communications technology:** Graphics. **Computer sciences:** Computer science, systems analysis. **Conservation:** Forestry. **Education:** Agricultural, kindergar-
ten/preschool. **Engineering:** Aerospace, agricultural, architectural, biomedical, civil, computer, electrical, engineering science, environmental, industrial,
manufacturing, materials, mechanical. **English:** English lit. **Foreign languages:** General. **Health services:** Dietetics. **History:** General. **Liberal arts:**
Arts/sciences. **Math:** General, statistics. **Parks/recreation:** General, health/
fitness. **Philosophy/religion:** Philosophy. **Physical sciences:** Chemistry,
geology, physics. **Psychology:** General. **Social sciences:** Economics, political
science, sociology. **Visual/performing arts:** Dramatic, music, studio arts.

Most popular majors. Agriculture 13%, biology 6%, business/marketing
15%, engineering/engineering technologies 24%, social sciences 6%.

Technology on campus. 600 workstations in library, computer center,
student center. Dormitories wired for high-speed internet access and linked
to campus network. Commuter students can connect to campus network.
Online course registration, online library, helpline, student web hosting,
wireless network available.

Student life. Freshman orientation: Mandatory. Preregistration for
classes offered. Multiple sessions held during the months of July and August.
Housing: Coed dorms, special housing for disabled, apartments, gender-
neutral housing, themed housing available. $1,125 fully refundable deposit.
Activities: Bands, campus ministries, choral groups, dance, drama, international student organizations, literary magazine, music ensembles, Model UN,
musical theater, opera, radio station, student government, student newspaper,
symphony orchestra, TV station, American Indian Science & Engineering
Society, Armenian Students Association, Japanese Student Association, Pili-
pino Cultural Exchange, Queer Student Union, Society of Black Engineers
and Scientists, Society of Hispanic Professional Engineers, International club,
Hillel of San Luis Obispo, Movimiento Estudiantil Xicano de Aztlan.

Athletics. NCAA. **Intercollegiate:** Baseball M, basketball, cross-country, football (tackle) M, golf, sand volleyball W, soccer, softball W, swimming, tennis, track and field, volleyball W, wrestling M. **Intramural:** Basketball, football (non-tackle) M, racquetball, sand volleyball, soccer, softball, tennis, volleyball. **Team name:** Mustangs.

Student services. Adult student services, alcohol/substance abuse counseling, career counseling, student employment services, financial aid counseling, health services, minority student services, on-campus daycare, personal counseling, placement for graduates, women's services. **Physically disabled:** Services for visually, speech, hearing impaired.

Contact. E-mail: admissions@calpoly.edu
Phone: (805) 756-2311 Fax: (805) 756-5400
James Maraviglia, Associate Vice Provost for Marketing & Enrollment Development, California Polytechnic State University: San Luis Obispo, Admissions Office, Cal Poly, San Luis Obispo, CA 93407-0031

California State Polytechnic University: Pomona

Pomona, California	**CB member**
www.cpp.edu	**CB code: 4082**

- Public 4-year university
- Commuter campus in small city
- 22,034 degree-seeking undergraduates: 11% part-time, 44% women, 3% African American, 24% Asian American, 40% Hispanic/Latino, 4% Multi-racial, non-Hispanic, 5% international
- 1,553 degree-seeking graduate students
- 39% of applicants admitted
- SAT or ACT (ACT writing optional) required
- 63% graduate within 6 years

General. Founded in 1938. Regionally accredited. **Degrees:** 4,203 bachelor's awarded; master's, professional offered. **ROTC:** Army. **Location:** 30 miles from downtown Los Angeles. **Calendar:** Quarter, extensive summer session. **Full-time faculty:** 573 total; 82% have terminal degrees, 36% minority, 44% women. **Part-time faculty:** 652 total; 30% have terminal degrees, 32% minority, 38% women. **Class size:** 15% < 20, 56% 20-39, 17% 40-49, 11% 50-99, 2% >100. **Special facilities:** Electron microscope center, international center, small ruminant center, Arabian horse center, equine research center, land laboratory, ecological reserve, center for regenerative studies, center for community affairs.

Freshman class profile. 33,857 applied, 13,307 admitted, 2,707 enrolled.

Mid 50% test scores		GPA 3.0-3.49:	34%
SAT critical reading:	450-570	GPA 2.0-2.99:	12%
SAT math:	470-610	Return as sophomores:	91%
ACT composite:	20-27	Out-of-state:	2%
GPA 3.75 or higher:	31%	Live on campus:	48%
GPA 3.50-3.74:	23%	International:	5%

Basis for selection. High school GPA, courses, and test scores important.

High school preparation. College-preparatory program required. 15 units required. Required and recommended units include English 4, mathematics 3-4, social studies 1, history 1, science 2 (laboratory 2), foreign language 2, visual/performing arts 1 and academic electives 1.

2015-2016 Annual costs. Tuition/fees: $6,976; $18,136 out-of-state. Room/board: $15,238. Books/supplies: $1,650. Personal expenses: $1,392. **Additional information:** Published fees may increase when public funding in inadequate. All CSU fees should be regarded as estimates, subject to change upon approval by The Board of Trustees.

2015-2016 Financial aid. **Need-based:** 2,265 full-time freshmen applied for aid; 1,795 deemed to have need; 1,680 received aid. Average need met was 58%. Average scholarship/grant was $10,396; average loan $3,443. 80% of total undergraduate aid awarded as scholarships/grants, 20% as loans/jobs. **Non-need-based:** Awarded to 2,771 full-time undergraduates, including 442 freshmen. Scholarships awarded for academics, alumni affiliation, athletics, leadership, state residency.

Application procedures. **Admission:** Priority date 11/30; deadline 5/1 (postmark date). $55 fee, may be waived for applicants with need. Admission notification on a rolling basis beginning on or about 10/2. Must reply by May 1 or within 3 week(s) if notified thereafter. Applications for first time freshmen accepted October 1 through November 30. **Financial aid:** Priority date 3/2; no closing date. FAFSA required. Applicants notified on a rolling basis starting 4/1; must reply within 2 week(s) of notification.

Academics. **Special study options:** Cooperative education, cross-registration, distance learning, double major, dual enrollment of high school students, ESL, exchange student, external degree, honors, internships, study abroad, teacher certification program. Ocean studies institute, desert studies consortium. **Credit/placement by examination:** AP, CLEP, IB, SAT, ACT, institutional tests. 36 credit hours maximum toward bachelor's degree. **Support services:** Learning center, pre-admission summer program, remedial instruction, study skills assistance, tutoring, writing center.

Honors college/program. Incoming freshmen invited to apply to Honors College if they have scores of 550 or higher on both Math and Critical Reading SAT tests and GPA of 3.5 or higher. Incoming transfer students must have GPA of at least 3.5 at previous institution.

Majors. **Architecture:** Architecture, landscape, urban/community planning. **Area/ethnic studies:** American. **Biology:** General, biotechnology, environmental. **Business:** Business admin, hospitality admin. **Communications:** Communications/speech/rhetoric. **Computer sciences:** Computer science. **Education:** Agricultural. **Engineering:** Aerospace, chemical, civil, computer, electrical, industrial, manufacturing, mechanical. **English:** English lit. **Foreign languages:** Spanish. **Health services:** Dietetics. **History:** General. **Liberal arts:** Arts/sciences, humanities. **Math:** General. **Parks/recreation:** Health/fitness. **Philosophy/religion:** Philosophy. **Physical sciences:** Chemistry, geology, physics. **Psychology:** General. **Social sciences:** Anthropology, economics, geography, political science, sociology. **Visual/performing arts:** Art, art history/conservation, dramatic, graphic design, music. **Work/family studies:** General, clothing/textiles.

Most popular majors. Biology 6%, business/marketing 30%, engineering/engineering technologies 20%.

Technology on campus. 1,800 workstations in library, computer center. Dormitories wired for high-speed internet access and linked to campus network. Commuter students can connect to campus network. Online course registration, helpline, student web hosting, wireless network available.

Student life. **Freshman orientation:** Mandatory, $40 fee. Preregistration for classes offered. Held between June to September (Freshman 3 days, 2 nights). **Housing:** Coed dorms, apartments available. $50 fully refundable deposit. **Activities:** Bands, campus ministries, choral groups, dance, drama, international student organizations, literary magazine, music ensembles, Model UN, musical theater, opera, student government, student newspaper, symphony orchestra, Black Student Union, Queer Student and Allies For Equality, Barkada - Filipino-American Student Association, MEChA, Rose Float club, Hillel, acts2fellowship Christian Fellowship, Muslim Student Association, Inter-Tribal Student Leadership Council, Ahimsa club.

Athletics. NCAA. **Intercollegiate:** Baseball M, basketball, cross-country, soccer, track and field, volleyball W. **Intramural:** Badminton, basketball, football (non-tackle) M, golf, racquetball, soccer, softball, swimming, table tennis, track and field, volleyball. **Team name:** Broncos.

Student services. Adult student services, career counseling, services for economically disadvantaged, student employment services, financial aid counseling, health services, on-campus daycare, personal counseling, placement for graduates, veterans' counselor, women's services. **Physically disabled:** Services for visually, speech, hearing impaired.

Contact. E-mail: admissions@cpp.edu
Phone: (909) 869-5299 Fax: (909) 869-4848
Andrew Wright, Director of Admissions, California State Polytechnic University: Pomona, 3801 West Temple Avenue, Pomona, CA 91768-4019

California State University: Bakersfield

Bakersfield, California	**CB member**
www.csub.edu	**CB code: 4110**

- Public 4-year university and liberal arts college
- Commuter campus in small city
- 7,985 degree-seeking undergraduates: 17% part-time, 61% women, 7% African American, 7% Asian American, 55% Hispanic/Latino, 1% Native American, 3% Multi-racial, non-Hispanic, 4% international
- 801 degree-seeking graduate students
- 100% of applicants admitted
- 41% graduate within 6 years

General. Founded in 1965. Regionally accredited. **Degrees:** 1,492 bachelor's awarded; master's offered. **Location:** 112 miles from Los Angeles. **Calendar:** Quarter, limited summer session. **Full-time faculty:** 272 total; 72% have terminal degrees, 31% minority, 48% women. **Part-time faculty:** 201 total; 14% have terminal degrees, 27% minority, 59% women. **Class size:** 26% < 20, 50% 20-39, 12% 40-49, 9% 50-99, 2% >100. **Special facilities:**

40-acre facility for wild animal care, archaeological information center, center for business and economic research, center for economic education, well-sample repository, center for physiological research.

Freshman class profile. 5,796 applied, 5,796 admitted, 1,462 enrolled.

Mid 50% test scores				
		Return as sophomores:		77%
SAT critical reading:	400-500	Out-of-state:		1%
SAT math:	400-510	International:		4%
ACT composite:	16-22			

Basis for selection. GED not accepted. GPA, test scores, and certain honors courses must place applicant in upper third of California high school graduates (upper sixth for out-of-state applicants) using eligibility index table. Minimum test scores slightly higher for out-of-state students.

High school preparation. College-preparatory program required. 15 units required. Required and recommended units include English 4, mathematics 3-4, social studies 1, history 1, science 2 (laboratory 2), foreign language 2, visual/performing arts 1 and academic electives 1. Foreign language must be in same language; math must include algebra, geometry, and intermediate algebra; science must include biology and a physical science.

2015-2016 Annual costs. Tuition/fees: $6,811; $17,971 out-of-state. Room/board: $12,561. Books/supplies: $1,827. Personal expenses: $1,365.

2014-2015 Financial aid. All financial aid based on need. Average need met was 21%. Average scholarship/grant was $4,128; average loan $1,100. 73% of total undergraduate aid awarded as scholarships/grants, 27% as loans/jobs.

Application procedures. Admission: Priority date 10/1; deadline 3/1. $55 fee, may be waived for applicants with need. Admission notification on a rolling basis beginning on or about 10/1. Financial aid: Priority date 3/2; no closing date. FAFSA required. Applicants notified on a rolling basis starting 4/15; must reply within 3 week(s) of notification.

Academics. Most courses are 5 quarter units. Students enrolled in 3 courses are carrying full unit load. **Special study options:** Accelerated study, cross-registration, distance learning, double major, dual enrollment of high school students, ESL, exchange student, external degree, honors, independent study, internships, liberal arts/career combination, student-designed major, study abroad, teacher certification program. 2+2 at specified locations for liberal studies (teaching) majors. **Credit/placement by examination:** AP, CLEP, SAT, ACT, institutional tests. Unlimited number of hours of credit by examination may be counted toward degree. **Support services:** Learning center, pre-admission summer program, reduced course load, remedial instruction, study skills assistance, tutoring.

Majors. **Biology:** General. **Business:** Business admin. **Communications:** Communications/speech/rhetoric. **Computer sciences:** Computer science. **Conservation:** Land use planning. **Education:** Early childhood. **English:** American lit, English lit. **Foreign languages:** Spanish. **Health services:** Nursing (RN). **History:** General. **Human services:** General. **Liberal arts:** Arts/sciences. **Math:** General. **Philosophy/religion:** Philosophy, religion. **Physical sciences:** Chemistry, geology, physics. **Protective services:** Criminal justice. **Psychology:** General. **Social sciences:** Anthropology, criminology, economics, political science, sociology. **Visual/performing arts:** General, art, dramatic, music.

Most popular majors. Business/marketing 6%, education 8%, liberal arts 29%, mathematics 7%, physical sciences 6%, psychology 9%, social sciences 8%.

Technology on campus. 600 workstations in library, computer center, student center. Dormitories linked to campus network. Commuter students can connect to campus network. Online course registration, online library, helpline, student web hosting available.

Student life. Freshman orientation: Available, $35 fee. Preregistration for classes offered. Housing: Guaranteed on-campus for all undergraduates. Coed dorms, special housing for disabled, themed housing available. Nursing floor and first year housing available. **Activities:** Bands, choral groups, drama, international student organizations, literary magazine, music ensembles, musical theater, opera, student government, student newspaper, Black student union, Movimiento Estudiantil Chicano de Aztlan, Christian union, student nursing association, Circle-K, Latinos United for Education.

Athletics. NCAA. **Intercollegiate:** Basketball, cheerleading, cross-country W, golf M, soccer, softball W, swimming, tennis W, track and field, volleyball W, water polo W, wrestling M. **Intramural:** Badminton, basketball, golf, handball, racquetball, soccer, softball, tennis, volleyball. **Team name:** Road-runners.

Student services. Adult student services, alcohol/substance abuse counseling, career counseling, services for economically disadvantaged, student

employment services, financial aid counseling, health services, minority student services, on-campus daycare, personal counseling, placement for graduates, veterans' counselor. **Physically disabled:** Services for visually, speech, hearing impaired.

Contact. E-mail: admissions@csub.edu
Phone: (661) 654-3036 Toll-free number: (800) 788-2782
Fax: (661) 654-3389
Jacqueline Mimms, Director of Admissions, California State University: Bakersfield, 9001 Stockdale Highway, Bakersfield, CA 93311-1099

California State University: Channel Islands
Camarillo, California — CB member
www.csuci.edu — CB code: 4128

- Public 4-year university
- Commuter campus in small city
- 5,625 degree-seeking undergraduates

General. Regionally accredited. **Degrees:** 1,060 bachelor's awarded; master's offered. **Calendar:** Semester. **Full-time faculty:** 176 total; 67% have terminal degrees, 24% minority. **Part-time faculty:** 210 total; 35% have terminal degrees, 28% minority. **Class size:** 22% < 20, 66% 20-39, 6% 40-49, 5% 50-99, less than 1% >100.

Freshman class profile.

GPA 3.75 or higher:	8%	GPA 2.0-2.99:	36%
GPA 3.50-3.74:	12%	Live on campus:	61%
GPA 3.0-3.49:	44%		

Basis for selection. Priority is given to students with a minimum 3.0 GPA who have also completed A-G courses. Test scores required for students with less than 3.0 GPA.

High school preparation. College-preparatory program required. 15 units required. Required units include English 4, mathematics 3, social studies 1, history 1, science 2 (laboratory 2), foreign language 2, visual/performing arts 1 and academic electives 1.

2015-2016 Annual costs. Tuition/fees: $6,532; $17,692 out-of-state. Room/board: $14,858. Books/supplies: $1,826. Personal expenses: $3,096.

Financial aid. Non-need-based: Scholarships awarded for academics, leadership, state residency.

Application procedures. Admission: Priority date 11/30; deadline 1/15 (receipt date). $55 fee, may be waived for applicants with need. Admission notification on a rolling basis beginning on or about 1/2. Must reply by 5/1. **Financial aid:** Priority date 3/2; no closing date. FAFSA required. Applicants notified by 4/7.

Academics. **Special study options:** Distance learning, double major, independent study, study abroad, teacher certification program. **Credit/placement by examination:** AP, CLEP, SAT, ACT, institutional tests. **Support services:** Pre-admission summer program, remedial instruction, tutoring, writing center.

Majors. **Area/ethnic studies:** Chicano/Hispanic-American/Latino. **Biology:** General, biotechnology. **Business:** General. **Communications:** Communications/speech/rhetoric. **Computer sciences:** General, computer science. **Conservation:** Environmental science, management/policy. **Education:** Early childhood. **English:** English lit. **Foreign languages:** Spanish. **Health services:** Prenursing. **History:** General. **Liberal arts:** Arts/sciences. **Math:** General. **Physical sciences:** Chemistry, physics. **Psychology:** General. **Social sciences:** Anthropology, economics, political science, sociology. **Visual/performing arts:** General, art.

Most popular majors. Biology 7%, business/marketing 15%, communications/journalism 7%, liberal arts 11%, psychology 15%, social sciences 12%, visual/performing arts 7%.

Technology on campus. Dormitories wired for high-speed internet access. Commuter students can connect to campus network. Online course registration, online library, helpline, wireless network available.

Student life. Freshman orientation: Mandatory, $120 fee. Preregistration for classes offered. Two-day session in July. Housing: Coed dorms, special housing for disabled, apartments, wellness housing available. $1,000 fully refundable deposit, deadline 6/1. **Activities:** Choral groups, student government, student newspaper.

Student services. Alcohol/substance abuse counseling, career counseling, services for economically disadvantaged, student employment services, financial aid counseling, health services, personal counseling, veterans' counselor, women's services. **Physically disabled:** Services for visually, speech, hearing impaired.

Contact. E-mail: admissionsandrecords@csuci.edu
Phone: (805) 437-8400
Ginger Reyes, AVP, California State University: Channel Islands, One University Drive, Camarillo, CA 93012

California State University: Chico
Chico, California — **CB member**
www.csuchico.edu — **CB code: 4048**

- Public 4-year university and liberal arts college
- Residential campus in small city
- 16,127 degree-seeking undergraduates: 10% part-time, 52% women, 2% African American, 6% Asian American, 29% Hispanic/Latino, 1% Native American, 5% Multi-racial, non-Hispanic, 4% international
- 760 degree-seeking graduate students
- 65% of applicants admitted
- SAT or ACT (ACT writing optional) required

General. Founded in 1887. Regionally accredited. 119-acre campus, University Farm 800 acres, Ecological Reserves 2,330 acres. **Degrees:** 3,456 bachelor's awarded; master's offered. **Location:** 90 miles from Sacramento, 175 miles from San Francisco. **Calendar:** Semester, limited summer session. **Full-time faculty:** 479 total; 86% have terminal degrees, 16% minority, 46% women. **Part-time faculty:** 503 total; 30% have terminal degrees, 11% minority, 53% women. **Class size:** 26% < 20, 44% 20-39, 16% 40-49, 10% 50-99, 4% >100. **Special facilities:** 1,000-acre farm, planetarium, instructional media center, biology field station, anthropology museum, intercultural studies center, computer graphics lab, assistive technology center, media prep lab, recording arts studio, hydrotherapy pool, echocardiography system, gas displacement chamber, two ecological preserves with nearly 4,100 acres, forensics lab, archaeology lab and research center, gateway science museum.

Freshman class profile. 22,321 applied, 14,441 admitted, 2,699 enrolled.

Mid 50% test scores			
SAT critical reading:	440-550	GPA 2.0-2.99:	15%
SAT math:	450-560	Rank in top quarter:	76%
ACT composite:	19-25	Rank in top tenth:	35%
GPA 3.75 or higher:	14%	Return as sophomores:	85%
GPA 3.50-3.74:	18%	Out-of-state:	1%
GPA 3.0-3.49:	53%	Live on campus:	62%
		International:	3%

Basis for selection. High school GPA and test scores. First-time freshmen applicants rank order based on characteristics of applicant pool. GPA determined from 10th, and 11th grade college prep courses only, excluding physical education. Nursing program open only to state residents. All freshmen applicants must submit SAT or ACT test scores regardless of high school GPA. SAT or ACT must be taken by the December test date for admission consideration. Portfolio required for fine arts and design majors. **Home schooled:** Transcript of courses and grades required. Must be able to verify completion of required college preparatory subject requirements and meet institutional eligibility index. **Learning Disabled:** Students must meet established admission criteria.

High school preparation. College-preparatory program required. 15 units required. Required units include English 4, mathematics 3, social studies 2, science 2 (laboratory 2), foreign language 2, visual/performing arts 1 and academic electives 1.

2015-2016 Annual costs. Tuition/fees: $7,026; $18,182 out-of-state. Room/board: $12,234. Books/supplies: $1,719. Personal expenses: $1,364.

2014-2015 Financial aid. Need-based: 2,493 full-time freshmen applied for aid; 1,982 deemed to have need; 1,945 received aid. Average need met was 68%. Average scholarship/grant was $10,486; average loan $3,431. 54% of total undergraduate aid awarded as scholarships/grants, 46% as loans/jobs. **Non-need-based:** Awarded to 1,130 full-time undergraduates, including 364 freshmen. Scholarships awarded for academics, art, athletics, leadership, minority status, music/drama, religious affiliation.

Application procedures. Admission: Priority date 10/1; deadline 11/30 (postmark date). $55 fee, may be waived for applicants with need. Admission notification on a rolling basis beginning on or about 12/1. Must reply by May 1 or within 2 week(s) if notified thereafter. Applications for the following majors must be made during priority periods of October and August: nursing, media arts, graphic design, recording arts, and interior architecture. All first time freshmen fall applicants should apply between October 1 and November 30. **Financial aid:** Priority date 3/2; no closing date. FAFSA required. Applicants notified on a rolling basis starting 3/2.

Academics. Special study options: Cooperative education, cross-registration, distance learning, double major, dual enrollment of high school students, ESL, exchange student, external degree, honors, independent study, internships, student-designed major, study abroad, teacher certification program. **Credit/placement by examination:** AP, CLEP, IB, SAT, ACT, institutional tests. 30 credit hours maximum toward bachelor's degree. 6 semester hours awarded for each International Baccalaureate higher level exam passed with score of 4 to 7. **Support services:** Learning center, pre-admission summer program, reduced course load, remedial instruction, study skills assistance, tutoring, writing center. Academic advising, cultural enrichment, leadership development, grant aid, graduate advising, financial literacy.

Majors. Area/ethnic studies: Asian, Latin American. **Biology:** General, biochemistry, microbiology. **Business:** Business admin. **Communications:** Journalism. **Computer sciences:** Computer graphics, computer science, information technology. **Conservation:** Environmental science. **Education:** Early childhood. **Engineering:** Civil, computer, electrical, mechanical. **English:** English lit. **Foreign languages:** French, German, Spanish. **Health services:** Communication disorders, dietetics, nursing (RN), recreational therapy. **History:** General. **Human services:** General, social work. **Liberal arts:** Arts/sciences, humanities. **Math:** General. **Parks/recreation:** General, exercise sciences, health/fitness. **Philosophy/religion:** Philosophy, religion. **Physical sciences:** Chemistry, geology, physics. **Protective services:** Criminal justice. **Psychology:** General. **Social sciences:** General, anthropology, economics, geography, international relations, political science, sociology. **Visual/performing arts:** Art, design, dramatic, music, music theory/composition, musical theater, studio arts.

Most popular majors. Business/marketing 16%, engineering/engineering technologies 7%, health sciences 10%, parks/recreation 8%, psychology 7%, social sciences 10%, visual/performing arts 6%.

Technology on campus. 1,212 workstations in dormitories, library, student center. Dormitories wired for high-speed internet access and linked to campus network. Commuter students can connect to campus network. Online course registration, online library, helpline, repair service, student web hosting, wireless network available.

Student life. Freshman orientation: Available, $60 fee. Preregistration for classes offered. Held in June and July. Additional 2-hour mini session and an online informational session without early registration options available in July. **Housing:** Coed dorms, special housing for disabled, apartments, fraternity/sorority housing, themed housing available. $1,000 fully refundable deposit, deadline 4/7. **Activities:** Bands, choral groups, dance, drama, film society, international student organizations, literary magazine, music ensembles, Model UN, musical theater, opera, radio station, student government, student newspaper, symphony orchestra, over 249 student religious, political, ethnic, and social service organizations available.

Athletics. NCAA. **Intercollegiate:** Baseball M, basketball, cross-country, golf, soccer, softball W, track and field, volleyball W. **Intramural:** Badminton, basketball, football (non-tackle), soccer, softball, table tennis, volleyball, water polo. **Team name:** Wildcats.

Student services. Adult student services, alcohol/substance abuse counseling, career counseling, services for economically disadvantaged, student employment services, financial aid counseling, health services, legal services, minority student services, on-campus daycare, personal counseling, placement for graduates, veterans' counselor, women's services. **Physically disabled:** Services for visually, speech, hearing impaired.

Contact. E-mail: info@csuchico.edu
Phone: (530) 898-4428 Toll-free number: (800) 542-4426
Fax: (530) 898-6456
Adam Stoltz, Director, California State University: Chico, 400 West First Street, Chico, CA 95929-0722

California State University: Dominguez Hills
Carson, California — **CB member**
www.csudh.edu — **CB code: 4098**

- Public 4-year university
- Commuter campus in small city
- 12,526 degree-seeking undergraduates: 27% part-time, 63% women, 13% African American, 9% Asian American, 59% Hispanic/Latino, 3% Multi-racial, non-Hispanic, 3% international
- 1,431 degree-seeking graduate students
- 58% of applicants admitted
- 33% graduate within 6 years

General. Founded in 1960. Regionally accredited. **Degrees:** 2,580 bachelor's awarded; master's offered. **ROTC:** Army, Air Force. **Location:** 13 miles from Los Angeles. **Calendar:** Semester, extensive summer session. **Full-time faculty:** 289 total; 68% have terminal degrees, 10% minority, 54% women. **Part-time faculty:** 677 total; 34% have terminal degrees, 12% minority, 56% women. **Class size:** 23% < 20, 54% 20-39, 14% 40-49, 8% 50-99, 1% >100. **Special facilities:** Nature preserve, greenhouse, observatory, urban community research center, Japanese garden, and theater complex.

Freshman class profile. 4,615 applied, 2,672 admitted, 1,305 enrolled.

Mid 50% test scores		GPA 3.0-3.49:	48%
SAT critical reading:	380-470	GPA 2.0-2.99:	37%
SAT math:	370-470	End year in good standing:	81%
SAT writing:	380-470	Return as sophomores:	82%
ACT composite:	15-20	Live on campus:	15%
GPA 3.75 or higher:	5%	International:	5%
GPA 3.50-3.74:	10%		

Basis for selection. Academic record and test scores most important. SAT/ACT required of applicants who do not meet minimum requirement based on admissions eligibility index. Interview required of Educational Opportunity Program applicants. **Home schooled:** Statement describing home school structure and mission, transcript of courses and grades, state high school equivalency certificate required. **Learning Disabled:** Student must show proof of learning disability to Office of Disability Services.

High school preparation. College-preparatory program required. 15 units required. Required units include English 4, mathematics 3, social studies 1, history 1, science 2 (laboratory 2), foreign language 2, visual/performing arts 1 and academic electives 1.

2015-2016 Annual costs. Tuition/fees: $6,278; $17,438 out-of-state. Room/board: $12,790. Books/supplies: $1,746. Personal expenses: $1,365.

2014-2015 Financial aid. **Need-based:** 1,248 full-time freshmen applied for aid; 1,156 deemed to have need; 1,142 received aid. Average need met was 36%. Average scholarship/grant was $5,320; average loan $1,551. 72% of total undergraduate aid awarded as scholarships/grants, 28% as loans/jobs. **Non-need-based:** Awarded to 1,949 full-time undergraduates, including 276 freshmen. Scholarships awarded for academics, alumni affiliation, art, athletics, leadership, music/drama.

Application procedures. **Admission:** Priority date 11/30; no deadline. $55 fee, may be waived for applicants with need. Application must be submitted online. Admission notification on a rolling basis beginning on or about 10/15. Must reply by May 1 or within 2 week(s) if notified thereafter. **Financial aid:** Priority date 3/2; no closing date. FAFSA required. Applicants notified on a rolling basis starting 2/28.

Academics. **Special study options:** Accelerated study, cross-registration, distance learning, double major, dual enrollment of high school students, external degree, honors, independent study, internships, student-designed major, study abroad, teacher certification program, weekend college. **Credit/placement by examination:** AP, CLEP, IB, SAT, ACT, institutional tests. **Support services:** Learning center, pre-admission summer program, reduced course load, remedial instruction, study skills assistance, tutoring, writing center.

Majors. **Area/ethnic studies:** African-American, Chicano/Hispanic-American/Latino. **Biology:** General, biochemistry, cell/histology, ecology, microbiology. **Business:** General, accounting, business admin, entrepreneurial studies, finance, human resources, international, labor studies, logistics, marketing, operations, real estate. **Communications:** Communications/speech/rhetoric, digital media, journalism, persuasive communications, public relations. **Computer sciences:** Computer science, information technology. **Education:** Business, early childhood. **English:** English lit. **Foreign languages:** Linguistics, Spanish. **Health services:** Clinical lab science, health care admin, nursing (RN), physics/radiologic health. **History:** General. **Human services:** General. **Liberal arts:** Arts/sciences. **Math:** General. **Parks/recreation:** Health/fitness. **Philosophy/religion:** Philosophy. **Physical sciences:** Chemistry, geology, physics. **Protective services:** Criminal justice. **Psychology:** General. **Social sciences:** Anthropology, geography, political science, sociology, urban studies. **Visual/performing arts:** Art, art history/conservation, dramatic, graphic design, music.

Most popular majors. Business/marketing 19%, communications/journalism 6%, health sciences 14%, liberal arts 7%, psychology 11%, public administration/social services 6%, security/protective services 7%, social sciences 10%.

Technology on campus. 282 workstations in dormitories, library, computer center. Dormitories wired for high-speed internet access and linked to campus network. Commuter students can connect to campus network. Online course registration, online library, helpline, student web hosting, wireless network available.

Student life. **Freshman orientation:** Available, $87 fee. Preregistration for classes offered. Offered to incoming admitted freshmen and transfer students. **Housing:** Special housing for disabled, apartments available. $300

fully refundable deposit. **Activities:** Bands, choral groups, dance, drama, international student organizations, literary magazine, music ensembles, musical theater, radio station, student government, student newspaper, TV station, L.I.F.E. on campus, Labor and Social Justice club, MECha, Africana Studies, Public Relations Student Society of America, Students for a Quality Education, Student Veterans Alliance, Young Americans for Liberty, Women Success Alliance, Male Success Alliance.

Athletics. NCAA. **Intercollegiate:** Baseball M, basketball, cross-country W, golf M, soccer, softball W, track and field W, volleyball W. **Intramural:** Basketball, cross-country, football (non-tackle), golf, soccer, softball, swimming, tennis, track and field, volleyball, water polo, weight lifting. **Team name:** Toros.

Student services. Career counseling, services for economically disadvantaged, student employment services, financial aid counseling, health services, on-campus daycare, personal counseling, placement for graduates, veterans' counselor, women's services. **Physically disabled:** Services for visually, speech, hearing impaired.

Contact. E-mail: info@csudh.edu
Phone: (310) 243-3645 Fax: (310) 516-3609
Brandy McLelland, Associate VP, Enrollment Management, California State University: Dominguez Hills, 1000 East Victoria Street, Carson, CA 90747

California State University: East Bay

Hayward, California   **CB member**
www.csueastbay.edu   **CB code: 4011**

- Public 4-year university
- Commuter campus in small city
- 12,924 degree-seeking undergraduates: 14% part-time, 62% women, 11% African American, 24% Asian American, 32% Hispanic/Latino, 1% Native Hawaiian/Pacific islander, 6% Multi-racial, non-Hispanic, 6% international
- 2,209 degree-seeking graduate students
- 74% of applicants admitted
- 45% graduate within 6 years

General. Founded in 1957. Regionally accredited. Branch campus in Concord and extensive online courses offered. **Degrees:** 3,057 bachelor's awarded; master's, doctoral offered. **Location:** 30 miles from San Francisco, 30 miles from San Jose. **Calendar:** Quarter, limited summer session. **Full-time faculty:** 354 total; 34% minority, 49% women. **Part-time faculty:** 485 total; 25% minority, 58% women. **Class size:** 15% < 20, 55% 20-39, 11% 40-49, 18% 50-99, 1% >100. **Special facilities:** Ecological field station, museum of anthropology, marine laboratory, geology summer field camp.

Freshman class profile. 14,776 applied, 10,938 admitted, 1,787 enrolled.

Mid 50% test scores		GPA 3.50-3.74:	11%
SAT critical reading:	390-490	GPA 3.0-3.49:	43%
SAT math:	400-510	GPA 2.0-2.99:	39%
SAT writing:	400-490	Return as sophomores:	80%
ACT composite:	16-21	Out-of-state:	1%
GPA 3.75 or higher:	7%	International:	8%

Basis for selection. Eligibility index based on GPA, test results, and 15 units of subject requirements to yield students in top third of California high school graduates. Out-of-state applicants should be in top sixth of high school class. Test scores not required for residents with high school GPA above 3.0, nonresidents with high school GPA above 3.61.

High school preparation. College-preparatory program required. 15 units required. Required units include English 4, mathematics 3, history 2, science 2 (laboratory 2), foreign language 2 and academic electives 1. One visual and performing arts. Math must be algebra, geometry, and intermediate algebra. Science must be biology and a physical science. Foreign language units must be in same language.

2015-2016 Annual costs. Tuition/fees: $6,564; $17,724 out-of-state. Room/board: $12,849. Books/supplies: $1,500. Personal expenses: $1,338.

Financial aid. **Non-need-based:** Scholarships awarded for academics, athletics, music/drama.

Application procedures. **Admission:** Closing date 8/31 (postmark date). $55 fee, may be waived for applicants with need. Admission notification on a rolling basis beginning on or about 10/1. **Financial aid:** Priority date 3/2; no closing date. FAFSA required. Applicants notified on a rolling basis starting 3/30; must reply within 3 week(s) of notification.

Academics. **Special study options:** Accelerated study, cooperative education, cross-registration, distance learning, double major, dual enrollment of high school students, ESL, exchange student, honors, independent study, internships, liberal arts/career combination, student-designed major, study abroad, teacher certification program. **Credit/placement by examination:** AP, CLEP, IB, institutional tests. 45 credit hours maximum toward bachelor's degree. 45-unit limitation excludes Advanced Placement. **Support services:** Learning center, pre-admission summer program, reduced course load, remedial instruction, study skills assistance, tutoring.

Majors. **Area/ethnic studies:** African-American, Asian-American, Chicano/Hispanic-American/Latino, Latin American, Native American. **Biology:** General, biochemistry, biomedical sciences. **Business:** General, accounting, business admin, entrepreneurial studies, finance, human resources, management information systems, managerial economics, marketing, purchasing, real estate. **Communications:** Advertising, broadcast journalism, communications/speech/rhetoric, journalism, public relations. **Computer sciences:** General, computer science, information systems, networking. **Conservation:** General, environmental studies. **Education:** Mathematics, physical, speech. **Engineering:** Software. **English:** American lit, British lit, English lit, rhetoric/composition. **Foreign languages:** French, Spanish. **Health services:** Athletic training, audiology/speech pathology, clinical lab technology, environmental health, prenursing, recreational therapy. **History:** General. **Human services:** General, public policy, social work. **Liberal arts:** Arts/sciences. **Math:** General, applied, statistics. **Parks/recreation:** General, exercise sciences, facilities management, health/fitness. **Philosophy/religion:** Philosophy, religion. **Physical sciences:** Chemistry, geology, physics. **Protective services:** Corrections, law enforcement admin. **Psychology:** General. **Social sciences:** Anthropology, archaeology, economics, geography, political science, sociology. **Visual/performing arts:** Art, art history/conservation, ceramics, commercial/advertising art, dance, dramatic, drawing, music, painting, photography, printmaking, sculpture, studio arts, studio arts management, theater design.

Most popular majors. Business/marketing 21%, health sciences 18%, psychology 7%, public administration/social services 7%, social sciences 9%.

Technology on campus. 1,062 workstations in dormitories, library, computer center. Dormitories wired for high-speed internet access and linked to campus network. Commuter students can connect to campus network. Online course registration, helpline, student web hosting available.

Student life. **Freshman orientation:** Mandatory, $80 fee. Preregistration for classes offered. 2 day program with overnight lodging on campus optional. **Policies:** Community and campus-based volunteer programs available. **Housing:** Apartments available. $900 deposit, deadline 5/1. Private coeducational dormitory adjacent to campus. **Activities:** Bands, choral groups, dance, drama, literary magazine, music ensembles, musical theater, opera, radio station, student government, student newspaper, symphony orchestra, TV station, 90 campus organizations.

Athletics. NAIA, NCAA. **Intercollegiate:** Baseball M, basketball, cross-country, golf, soccer, softball W, swimming W, track and field, volleyball W, water polo W. **Intramural:** Badminton, basketball, golf, gymnastics M, racquetball, soccer, softball, swimming, tennis, volleyball. **Team name:** Pioneers.

Student services. Adult student services, career counseling, services for economically disadvantaged, student employment services, financial aid counseling, health services, legal services, minority student services, on-campus daycare, personal counseling, placement for graduates, veterans' counselor. **Physically disabled:** Services for visually, speech, hearing impaired.

Contact. E-mail: admissions@csueastbay.edu
Phone: (510) 885-2784 Fax: (510) 885-4059
John Pliska, Executive Director, Admissions, California State University: East Bay, 25800 Carlos Bee Boulevard, Hayward, CA 94542-3095

California State University: Fresno

Fresno, California   CB member
www.csufresno.edu   CB code: 4312

- Public 4-year university
- Commuter campus in very large city
- 21,076 degree-seeking undergraduates: 16% part-time, 58% women, 3% African American, 15% Asian American, 48% Hispanic/Latino, 3% Multi-racial, non-Hispanic, 5% international
- 2,651 degree-seeking graduate students
- 52% of applicants admitted
- SAT or ACT (ACT writing optional) required
- 58% graduate within 6 years

General. Founded in 1911. Regionally accredited. **Degrees:** 3,878 bachelor's awarded; master's, doctoral offered. **ROTC:** Army, Air Force. **Location:** 217 miles from Los Angeles, 192 miles from San Francisco. **Calendar:** Semester, limited summer session. **Full-time faculty:** 657 total; 31% minority, 44% women. **Part-time faculty:** 650 total; 60% minority, 55% women. **Class size:** 18% < 20, 49% 20-39, 22% 40-49, 8% 50-99, 3% >100. **Special facilities:** 1,190-acre university farm, planetarium, agricultural research center.

Freshman class profile. 19,935 applied, 10,404 admitted, 3,566 enrolled.

Mid 50% test scores		Rank in top quarter:	80%
SAT critical reading:	390-500	Rank in top tenth:	15%
SAT math:	400-510	End year in good standing:	83%
SAT writing:	390-490	Return as sophomores:	83%
ACT composite:	16-21	Out-of-state:	1%
GPA 3.75 or higher:	21%	Live on campus:	15%
GPA 3.50-3.74:	15%	International:	5%
GPA 3.0-3.49:	42%	Fraternities:	2%
GPA 2.0-2.99:	22%	Sororities:	4%

Basis for selection. Academic GPA, standardized test scores, and rigor of secondary school record are very important. Tests recommended, but not required, if student has a high school GPA of 3.0 or higher. **Home schooled:** Transcript of courses and grades required. **Learning Disabled:** Contact Services for Students with Disabilities after submitting application for consideration.

High school preparation. College-preparatory program required. 15 units required. Required units include English 4, mathematics 3, social studies 1, history 1, science 1 (laboratory 1), foreign language 2, visual/performing arts 1 and academic electives 1.

2015-2016 Annual costs. Tuition/fees: $6,298; $17,458 out-of-state. Room/board: $10,604. Books/supplies: $1,794. Personal expenses: $1,390.

2015-2016 Financial aid. **Need-based:** Average need met was 70%. Average scholarship/grant was $9,984; average loan $3,115. 84% of total undergraduate aid awarded as scholarships/grants, 16% as loans/jobs. **Non-need-based:** Scholarships awarded for academics, art, athletics, leadership, music/drama, ROTC, state residency.

Application procedures. **Admission:** Closing date 11/30 (receipt date). $55 fee, may be waived for applicants with need. Application must be submitted online. Admission notification on a rolling basis. **Financial aid:** Priority date 3/2; no closing date. FAFSA required. Applicants notified on a rolling basis starting 4/1; must reply within 3 week(s) of notification.

Academics. **Special study options:** Accelerated study, combined bachelor's/graduate degree, cooperative education, cross-registration, distance learning, double major, dual enrollment of high school students, ESL, exchange student, honors, independent study, internships, student-designed major, study abroad, teacher certification program. **Credit/placement by examination:** AP, CLEP, IB, institutional tests. 30 credit hours maximum toward bachelor's degree. **Support services:** Learning center, pre-admission summer program, reduced course load, remedial instruction, study skills assistance, tutoring, writing center.

Honors college/program. Admits 50-100 students each year. Criteria include intellectual/creative potential, SAT of 1800, top 10% of graduating class, or minimum GPA of 3.6 through end of junior year. Students participate in 2 general education honors courses and honors colloquium each semester during first 2 years; 3 upper division honors courses during junior and senior years. 30 hours of community service required freshmen year with yearly requirement thereafter.

Majors. **Area/ethnic studies:** African-American, Chicano/Hispanic-American/Latino, Latin American, women's. **Biology:** General. **Business:** Accounting, business admin, finance, human resources, international, logistics, marketing, real estate. **Communications:** Communications/speech/rhetoric, media studies. **Computer sciences:** Computer science, information technology. **Conservation:** Environmental science. **Education:** General, agricultural, early childhood, music. **Engineering:** General, civil, computer, electrical, environmental, mechanical. **English:** English lit. **Foreign languages:** French, linguistics, Spanish. **Health services:** Athletic training, communication disorders, community health services, environmental health, nursing (RN), prenursing. **History:** General. **Human services:** General, social work. **Liberal arts:** Arts/sciences. **Math:** General. **Parks/recreation:** General, exercise sciences, health/fitness, sports studies. **Philosophy/religion:** Philosophy, religion. **Physical sciences:** General, chemistry, geology, physics. **Protective services:** Corrections, criminal justice. **Psychology:** General. **Social sciences:** Anthropology, criminology, economics, geography, political science, sociology. **Visual/performing arts:** Art, dramatic, graphic design, interior design, music, music performance. **Work/family studies:** General.

Most popular majors. Agriculture 6%, business/marketing 14%, health sciences 13%, liberal arts 8%, parks/recreation 6%, psychology 7%, security/protective services 7%, social sciences 6%.

Technology on campus. 1,500 workstations in dormitories, library, computer center, student center. Dormitories linked to campus network. Commuter students can connect to campus network. Online course registration, online library, helpline, repair service, student web hosting, wireless network available.

Student life. Freshman orientation: Mandatory, $55 fee. Preregistration for classes offered. One day program held during June and July for fall semester; November and December for spring semester. **Housing:** Coed dorms, single-sex dorms, fraternity/sorority housing available. $150 partly refundable deposit, deadline 4/1. **Activities:** Bands, choral groups, dance, drama, international student organizations, literary magazine, music ensembles, musical theater, radio station, student government, student newspaper, symphony orchestra, TV station, over 250 student organizations including religious and ethnic groups.

Athletics. NCAA. **Intercollegiate:** Baseball M, basketball, cross-country, diving W, equestrian W, football (tackle) M, golf, lacrosse W, soccer W, softball W, swimming W, tennis, track and field, volleyball W. **Intramural:** Basketball, football (non-tackle), racquetball, soccer, softball, tennis, volleyball. **Team name:** Bulldogs.

Student services. Adult student services, career counseling, services for economically disadvantaged, student employment services, financial aid counseling, health services, minority student services, on-campus daycare, personal counseling, placement for graduates, veterans' counselor, women's services. **Physically disabled:** Services for visually, speech, hearing impaired.

Contact. E-mail: admissions@csufresno.edu
Phone: (559) 278-2261 Fax: (559) 278-4812
Tina Beddall, Director, California State University: Fresno, 5150 North Maple Avenue, M/S JA 57, Fresno, CA 93740-8026

California State University: Fullerton

Fullerton, California	CB member
www.fullerton.edu	CB code: 4589

- Public 4-year university
- Commuter campus in small city
- 33,009 degree-seeking undergraduates: 18% part-time, 55% women, 2% African American, 22% Asian American, 40% Hispanic/Latino, 4% Multi-racial, non-Hispanic, 6% international
- 5,792 degree-seeking graduate students
- 42% of applicants admitted
- SAT or ACT (ACT writing recommended) required
- 62% graduate within 6 years

General. Founded in 1957. Regionally accredited. **Degrees:** 7,725 bachelor's awarded; master's, professional, doctoral offered. **ROTC:** Army. **Location:** 30 miles from Los Angeles. **Calendar:** Semester, limited summer session. **Full-time faculty:** 944 total; 5% have terminal degrees, 29% minority, 49% women. **Part-time faculty:** 1,100 total; less than 1% have terminal degrees, 26% minority, 52% women. **Class size:** 25% < 20, 54% 20-39, 12% 40-49, 7% 50-99, 2% >100. **Special facilities:** Molecular structure center, anthropology museum, arboretum, grand central art center, herbarium, speech, language/hearing clinic, foreign language laboratory, sport and movement institute, institute of gerontology, institute for molecular biology and nutrition, demographic research center, social science research center, CA public archeology center.

Freshman class profile. 41,841 applied, 17,515 admitted, 4,401 enrolled.

Mid 50% test scores		Rank in top tenth:	24%
SAT critical reading:	460-560	End year in good standing:	87%
SAT math:	470-570	Return as sophomores:	88%
ACT composite:	19-24	Out-of-state:	1%
GPA 3.75 or higher:	25%	Live on campus:	28%
GPA 3.50-3.74:	31%	International:	6%
GPA 3.0-3.49:	40%	Fraternities:	2%
GPA 2.0-2.99:	4%	Sororities:	7%
Rank in top quarter:	66%		

Basis for selection. Eligibility index consisting of combination of high school GPA and SAT or ACT score. SAT or ACT required for all first time freshman applicants. Audition required of music majors.

High school preparation. College-preparatory program required. 15 units required; 16 recommended. Required and recommended units include English 4, mathematics 3-4, social studies 1, history 1, science 2 (laboratory 2), foreign language 2-3, visual/performing arts 1 and academic electives 1. 1 unit U.S. history/government required.

2015-2016 Annual costs. Tuition/fees: $6,436; $17,596 out-of-state. Room/board: $14,574. Books/supplies: $1,806. Personal expenses: $1,364.

Financial aid. Non-need-based: Scholarships awarded for academics, art, athletics, leadership, music/drama. **Additional information:** Fee waiver for children of veterans killed in action or with service-connected disability whose annual income is $5,000 or less.

Application procedures. Admission: Priority date 10/30; deadline 11/30 (postmark date). $55 fee, may be waived for applicants with need. Application must be submitted online. Admission notification on a rolling basis beginning on or about 1/1. Must reply by 5/15. Reply date given on notification letter. **Financial aid:** Priority date 3/2, closing date 6/6. FAFSA required. Applicants notified on a rolling basis; must reply within 4 week(s) of notification.

Academics. Special study options: Cooperative education, distance learning, double major, honors, independent study, internships, study abroad, teacher certification program. Service learning. **Credit/placement by examination:** AP, CLEP, IB, SAT, ACT, institutional tests. 30 credit hours maximum toward bachelor's degree. **Support services:** Learning center, preadmission summer program, reduced course load, remedial instruction, study skills assistance, tutoring, writing center.

Majors. Area/ethnic studies: African-American, American, Asian-American, Chicano/Hispanic-American/Latino, European, Latin American, women's. **Biology:** General, biochemistry. **Business:** Accounting, business admin, entrepreneurial studies, finance, international, management science, managerial economics, marketing. **Communications:** Advertising, communications/speech/rhetoric, journalism, public relations, radio/TV. **Computer sciences:** Computer science, information technology. **Education:** Early childhood, music. **Engineering:** General, civil, computer, electrical, mechanical, operations research. **English:** English lit. **Foreign languages:** Comparative lit, French, Japanese, linguistics, Spanish. **Health services:** Athletic training, communication disorders, nursing (RN), prenursing. **History:** General. **Human services:** General. **Liberal arts:** Arts/sciences. **Math:** General, applied, statistics. **Parks/recreation:** Health/fitness. **Philosophy/religion:** Philosophy, religion. **Physical sciences:** Chemistry, geology, physics. **Protective services:** Criminal justice. **Psychology:** General. **Social sciences:** Anthropology, economics, geography, political science, sociology. **Visual/performing arts:** Art, art history/conservation, dance, dramatic, music, music performance, studio arts.

Most popular majors. Business/marketing 24%, communications/journalism 13%, health sciences 10%, parks/recreation 6%, psychology 7%, social sciences 7%, visual/performing arts 6%.

Technology on campus. 2,000 workstations in dormitories, library, computer center, student center. Dormitories wired for high-speed internet access and linked to campus network. Commuter students can connect to campus network. Online course registration, online library, helpline, repair service, wireless network available.

Student life. Freshman orientation: Mandatory. Preregistration for classes offered. **Housing:** Apartments, fraternity/sorority housing available. $350 fully refundable deposit, deadline 4/24. **Activities:** Bands, choral groups, dance, drama, international student organizations, music ensembles, Model UN, musical theater, radio station, student government, student newspaper, symphony orchestra, Chinese Christian Fellowship, Christian student association, disabled student association, Fellowship of Christian Athletes, Human Services Student Association, Movimiento Estudiantil Chicano de Atlan, New Democratic Movement, Political Science Student Association.

Athletics. NCAA. **Intercollegiate:** Baseball M, basketball, cross-country, golf, soccer, softball W, tennis W, track and field, volleyball W. **Intramural:** Badminton, basketball, bowling, football (non-tackle), racquetball, rugby M, skiing, soccer M, softball, swimming, table tennis, volleyball. **Team name:** Titans.

Student services. Adult student services, career counseling, services for economically disadvantaged, student employment services, financial aid counseling, health services, legal services, minority student services, on-campus daycare, personal counseling, placement for graduates, veterans' counselor, women's services. **Physically disabled:** Services for visually, speech, hearing impaired.

Contact. E-mail: admissions@fullerton.edu
Phone: (657) 278-7788 Fax: (657) 278-7699
Jessica Wagoner, Director of Admissions, California State University: Fullerton, P.O. Box 6900, Fullerton, CA 92834-6900

California State University: Long Beach

Long Beach, California	CB member
www.csulb.edu	CB code: 4389

- Public 4-year university
- Commuter campus in large city

♦ 32,079 degree-seeking undergraduates: 17% part-time, 56% women, 4% African American, 23% Asian American, 39% Hispanic/Latino, 5% Multi-racial, non-Hispanic, 7% international

♦ 4,178 degree-seeking graduate students

♦ 34% of applicants admitted

♦ SAT or ACT (ACT writing optional) required

General. Founded in 1949. Regionally accredited. **Degrees:** 7,481 bachelor's awarded; master's, doctoral offered. **ROTC:** Army. **Location:** 25 miles from Los Angeles. **Calendar:** Semester, extensive summer session. **Full-time faculty:** 960 total; 85% have terminal degrees, 34% minority, 48% women. **Part-time faculty:** 1,290 total; 35% have terminal degrees, 31% minority, 53% women. **Special facilities:** Japanese garden, performing arts center, media center.

Freshman class profile. 56,975 applied, 19,650 admitted, 4,506 enrolled.

Mid 50% test scores		GPA 3.0-3.49:	36%
SAT critical reading:	460-570	GPA 2.0-2.99:	7%
SAT math:	470-600	Return as sophomores:	91%
GPA 3.75 or higher:	30%	International:	5%
GPA 3.50-3.74:	27%		

Basis for selection. Admission based on secondary school record and standardized test scores. Audition required of dance, music majors. Portfolio required of art, design majors.

High school preparation. College-preparatory program required. 15 units required. Required units include English 4, mathematics 3, social studies 1, history 1, science 2 (laboratory 2), foreign language 2 and academic electives 1. 1 unit fine arts required.

2015-2016 Annual costs. Tuition/fees: $6,452; $17,612 out-of-state. Room/board: $11,880. Books/supplies: $1,898. Personal expenses: $708.

2015-2016 Financial aid. **Need-based:** Average need met was 81%. Average scholarship/grant was $7,786; average loan $3,366. 72% of total undergraduate aid awarded as scholarships/grants, 28% as loans/jobs. **Non-need-based:** Scholarships awarded for academics, art, athletics, job skills, leadership, music/drama, state residency.

Application procedures. Admission: Closing date 11/30 (postmark date). $55 fee, may be waived for applicants with need. Admission notification on a rolling basis beginning on or about 12/1. **Financial aid:** Priority date 3/2; no closing date. FAFSA required. Applicants notified on a rolling basis starting 3/25; must reply within 3 week(s) of notification.

Academics. Special study options: Accelerated study, cross-registration, distance learning, double major, dual enrollment of high school students, ESL, honors, independent study, internships, student-designed major, study abroad, teacher certification program, Washington semester. Concurrent enrollment at other CSU campuses. **Credit/placement by examination:** AP, CLEP, IB, SAT, ACT, institutional tests. **Support services:** Learning center, pre-admission summer program, reduced course load, remedial instruction, study skills assistance, tutoring, writing center.

Majors. Architecture: Interior. **Area/ethnic studies:** African-American, Asian, Chicano/Hispanic-American/Latino, women's. **Biology:** General, bacteriology, biochemistry, botany, cell/histology, molecular. **Business:** General, accounting, fashion, finance, human resources, international, management science, managerial economics, operations, real estate. **Communications:** Broadcast journalism, journalism, public relations. **Computer sciences:** General, computer science, information systems. **Education:** Art, bilingual, elementary, English, family/consumer sciences, foreign languages, physical, science, social science. **Engineering:** General, aerospace, biomedical, chemical, civil, computer, electrical, materials, mechanical. **English:** Creative writing, English lit, rhetoric/composition, writing. **Foreign languages:** Classics, comparative lit, French, German, Japanese, Spanish. **Health services:** Medical illustrating, medical radiologic technology/radiation therapy, nursing (RN), public health ed. **History:** General. **Human services:** Social work. **Liberal arts:** Arts/sciences. **Math:** General, applied, statistics. **Parks/recreation:** Facilities management. **Philosophy/religion:** Philosophy, religion. **Physical sciences:** Chemistry, geology, physics. **Protective services:** Criminal justice. **Psychology:** General. **Social sciences:** Anthropology, economics, geography, sociology. **Visual/performing arts:** Art, art history/conservation, ceramics, cinematography, commercial/advertising art, conducting, dance, design, dramatic, drawing, fiber arts, industrial design, interior design, jazz, metal/jewelry, music, music history, music performance, painting, photography, piano/keyboard, printmaking, sculpture, studio arts, theater design, voice/opera. **Work/family studies:** General, clothing/textiles, food/nutrition.

Most popular majors. Business/marketing 14%, communications/journalism 9%, engineering/engineering technologies 8%, family/consumer sciences 8%, health sciences 11%, psychology 6%, social sciences 10%, visual/performing arts 9%.

Technology on campus. 1,200 workstations in dormitories, library, computer center. Dormitories linked to campus network. Commuter students can connect to campus network. Online course registration available.

Student life. Freshman orientation: Available, $45 fee. Preregistration for classes offered. One-day pre-semester session. **Housing:** Coed dorms available. **Activities:** Bands, choral groups, dance, drama, film society, literary magazine, music ensembles, musical theater, opera, radio station, student government, student newspaper, symphony orchestra, TV station, more than 150 political, ethnic, and social service organizations.

Athletics. NCAA. **Intercollegiate:** Baseball M, basketball, cross-country, golf, soccer W, softball, tennis W, track and field, volleyball, water polo. **Intramural:** Basketball, handball, racquetball, rugby M, soccer, softball, tennis, volleyball. **Team name:** Forty-Niners.

Student services. Adult student services, alcohol/substance abuse counseling, chaplain/spiritual director, career counseling, services for economically disadvantaged, student employment services, financial aid counseling, health services, minority student services, on-campus daycare, personal counseling, placement for graduates, veterans' counselor, women's services. **Physically disabled:** Services for visually, speech, hearing impaired.

Contact. E-mail: eslb@csulb.edu
Phone: (562) 985-5471 Fax: (562) 985-4973
Thomas Enders, Associate Vice President for Enrollment Services, California State University: Long Beach, 1250 Bellflower Boulevard, Long Beach, CA 90840-0106

California State University: Los Angeles
Los Angeles, California   **CB member**
www.calstatela.edu   **CB code: 4399**

♦ Public 4-year university

♦ Commuter campus in very large city

♦ 23,405 degree-seeking undergraduates: 13% part-time, 58% women, 4% African American, 15% Asian American, 63% Hispanic/Latino, 2% Multi-racial, non-Hispanic, 6% international

♦ 4,237 degree-seeking graduate students

♦ 68% of applicants admitted

♦ 45% graduate within 6 years

General. Founded in 1947. Regionally accredited. **Degrees:** 3,755 bachelor's awarded; master's, professional, doctoral offered. **ROTC:** Army, Air Force. **Location:** 5 miles from downtown. **Calendar:** Quarter, extensive summer session. **Full-time faculty:** 574 total; 4% have terminal degrees, 46% minority, 50% women. **Part-time faculty:** 942 total; 6% have terminal degrees, 50% minority, 48% women. **Class size:** 26% < 20, 56% 20-39, 11% 40-49, 5% 50-99, 2% >100. **Special facilities:** Baroque pipe organ, 4 megavolt Van de Graaff accelerator.

Freshman class profile. 31,855 applied, 21,704 admitted, 3,862 enrolled.

Mid 50% test scores		GPA 3.50-3.74:	13%
SAT critical reading:	390-490	GPA 3.0-3.49:	52%
SAT math:	390-500	GPA 2.0-2.99:	28%
SAT writing:	390-480	Out-of-state:	2%
ACT composite:	15-20	Live on campus:	10%
GPA 3.75 or higher:	6%	International:	6%

Basis for selection. Secondary school record and standardized test scores important. SAT/ACT not required if GPA is 3.0 or above. EPT/ELM required for placement; may be waived based on SAT score. **Home schooled:** Syllabi and written evaluation of courses completed may be required. **Learning Disabled:** Applicants with disabilities are encouraged to complete college preparatory course requirements if possible. If judged unable to fulfill a specific course requirement because of disability, students may substitute alternative college preparatory courses for specific subject requirements.

High school preparation. College-preparatory program required. 15 units required. Required units include English 4, mathematics 3, social studies 1, history 1, science 2 (laboratory 2), foreign language 2, visual/performing arts 1 and academic electives 1.

2015-2016 Annual costs. Tuition/fees: $6,344; $15,272 out-of-state. Room/board: $12,834. Books/supplies: $1,809. Personal expenses: $1,335.

2015-2016 Financial aid. **Need-based:** 2,383 full-time freshmen applied for aid; 2,210 deemed to have need; 2,142 received aid. Average need met was 69%. Average scholarship/grant was $9,713; average loan $3,193. 73% of total undergraduate aid awarded as scholarships/grants, 27% as loans/jobs. **Non-need-based:** Awarded to 252 full-time undergraduates, including 58 freshmen.

Application procedures. Admission: Closing date 11/30 (postmark date). $55 fee, may be waived for applicants with need. Admission notification on a rolling basis beginning on or about 11/1. **Financial aid:** Priority date 3/2; no closing date. FAFSA required. Applicants notified on a rolling basis starting 4/1; must reply within 3 week(s) of notification.

Academics. Special study options: Accelerated study, combined bachelor's/graduate degree, cooperative education, cross-registration, distance learning, double major, dual enrollment of high school students, ESL, honors, independent study, internships, student-designed major, study abroad, teacher certification program. **Credit/placement by examination:** AP, CLEP, SAT, ACT, institutional tests. **Support services:** Learning center, pre-admission summer program, reduced course load, remedial instruction, study skills assistance, tutoring, writing center.

Majors. Area/ethnic studies: African, African-American, American, Chicano/Hispanic-American/Latino, Latin American. **Biology:** General, biochemistry, microbiology. **Business:** Business admin. **Communications:** Communications/speech/rhetoric, journalism, radio/TV. **Computer sciences:** General. **Conservation:** Environmental science. **Education:** Kindergarten/preschool, physical, technology/industrial arts, trade/industrial. **Engineering:** General, civil, electrical, mechanical. **English:** English lit. **Foreign languages:** Chinese, French, Japanese, Spanish. **Health services:** Communication disorders, dietetics, environmental health, nursing (RN), prenursing, vocational rehab counseling. **History:** General. **Human services:** Social work. **Liberal arts:** Arts/sciences. **Math:** General. **Parks/recreation:** Health/fitness. **Philosophy/religion:** Philosophy. **Physical sciences:** Chemistry, geology, physics. **Protective services:** Fire services admin, law enforcement admin. **Psychology:** General. **Social sciences:** Anthropology, economics, geography, political science, sociology. **Visual/performing arts:** Art, commercial/advertising art, dramatic, music, music performance. **Work/family studies:** Food/nutrition.

Most popular majors. Business/marketing 20%, communications/journalism 7%, engineering/engineering technologies 6%, health sciences 12%, psychology 6%, security/protective services 6%, social sciences 13%.

Technology on campus. 1,500 workstations in dormitories, library, computer center, student center. Commuter students can connect to campus network. Online library, helpline, repair service, student web hosting, wireless network available.

Student life. Freshman orientation: Mandatory, $70 fee. Preregistration for classes offered. **Housing:** Coed dorms, special housing for disabled, apartments available. $100 fully refundable deposit, deadline 7/2. **Activities:** Bands, choral groups, dance, drama, film society, international student organizations, literary magazine, music ensembles, opera, radio station, student government, student newspaper, symphony orchestra, TV station, Chicanos for Creative Medicine, Hispanic business society, society of women engineers, Movimiento Estudiantil Chicanos de Aetlar, Asian student union, black student association, Sisters of the African Star, Vietnamese student association, Latin American society, Chinese American service club.

Athletics. NCAA. **Intercollegiate:** Baseball M, basketball, cross-country W, soccer, tennis W, track and field, volleyball W. **Intramural:** Basketball, bowling, gymnastics, handball, judo, racquetball, skiing, soccer, softball, swimming, synchronized swimming, tennis, track and field, volleyball, water polo, wrestling M. **Team name:** Golden Eagles.

Student services. Career counseling, student employment services, health services, on-campus daycare, personal counseling, placement for graduates, veterans' counselor. **Physically disabled:** Services for visually, speech, hearing impaired.

Contact. E-mail: admission@calstatela.edu
Phone: (323) 343-3901 Fax: (323) 343-6306
Chuck Mancillas, University Registrar, California State University: Los Angeles, 5151 State University Drive SA101, Los Angeles, CA 90032

California State University: Monterey Bay
Seaside, California CB member
www.csumb.edu CB code: 1945

- Public 4-year liberal arts and teachers college
- Residential campus in large town
- 6,657 degree-seeking undergraduates: 7% part-time, 62% women, 7% African American, 6% Asian American, 36% Hispanic/Latino, 1% Native American, 1% Native Hawaiian/Pacific islander, 7% Multi-racial, non-Hispanic, 4% international
- 284 degree-seeking graduate students
- 49% of applicants admitted

- SAT or ACT (ACT writing optional) required
- 53% graduate within 6 years

General. Founded in 1995. Regionally accredited. Dedicated to serving low-income, adult learner, first-generation, and underrepresented populations. **Degrees:** 1,202 bachelor's awarded; master's offered. **Location:** 108 miles from San Francisco, 68 miles from San Jose. **Calendar:** Semester, limited summer session. **Full-time faculty:** 152 total; 91% have terminal degrees, 44% minority, 50% women. **Part-time faculty:** 345 total; 30% have terminal degrees, 22% minority, 58% women. **Class size:** 17% < 20, 71% 20-39, 5% 40-49, 6% 50-99, 1% >100. **Special facilities:** Watershed facilities, seafloor mapping lab.

Freshman class profile. 15,561 applied, 7,576 admitted, 1,052 enrolled.

Mid 50% test scores			
SAT critical reading:	430-550	Rank in top quarter:	51%
SAT math:	420-550	Rank in top tenth:	15%
SAT writing:	420-530	Return as sophomores:	82%
ACT composite:	17-23	Out-of-state:	2%
GPA 3.75 or higher:	16%	Live on campus:	84%
GPA 3.50-3.74:	20%	International:	3%
GPA 3.0-3.49:	42%	Fraternities:	2%
GPA 2.0-2.99:	22%	Sororities:	2%

Basis for selection. Students must be high school graduates or GED equivalents, complete 15-unit "a-g" course pattern of college preparatory study with grades of C or better and earn qualifying eligibility index. Minimum qualifying eligibility index is a combination of high school course completion (a-g), GPA calculated based on the a-g courses in grades 10-12, and SAT and/or ACT scores. SAT/ACT required for all freshmen applicants. TOEFL/IELTS for English Proficiency required for international students. **Home schooled:** Applicants may be asked to provide supplemental information to document completion of CSU eligibility requirements. **Learning Disabled:** Reviewed case-by-case by Student Disability Resources department.

High school preparation. College-preparatory program required. 15 units required. Required units include English 4, mathematics 3, social studies 1, history 1, science 2 (laboratory 2), foreign language 2, visual/performing arts 1 and academic electives 1. Science lab units must include 1 biological, 1 physical. Language must be the same language both years. History must include U.S. History.

2015-2016 Annual costs. Tuition/fees: $6,119; $17,279 out-of-state. Room/board: $10,542. Books/supplies: $1,311. Personal expenses: $1,392.

2015-2016 Financial aid. Need-based: 932 full-time freshmen applied for aid; 738 deemed to have need; 666 received aid. Average need met was 65%. Average scholarship/grant was $10,558; average loan $3,327. 74% of total undergraduate aid awarded as scholarships/grants, 26% as loans/jobs. **Non-need-based:** Awarded to 474 full-time undergraduates, including 131 freshmen. Scholarships awarded for academics, athletics, leadership, state residency.

Application procedures. Admission: Closing date 11/30 (receipt date). $55 fee, may be waived for applicants with need. Admission notification by 4/30. Admission notification on a rolling basis beginning on or about 1/1. Must reply by 5/1. $100 confirmation fee required. **Financial aid:** Priority date 3/2, closing date 5/20. FAFSA required. Applicants notified on a rolling basis starting 4/1.

Academics. Special study options: Accelerated study, cross-registration, distance learning, double major, ESL, exchange student, independent study, internships, semester at sea, student-designed major, study abroad, teacher certification program. Service learning. **Credit/placement by examination:** AP, CLEP, IB, SAT, ACT, institutional tests. 30 credit hours maximum toward bachelor's degree. **Support services:** Learning center, reduced course load, remedial instruction, study skills assistance, tutoring, writing center.

Majors. Biology: General. **Business:** Business admin. **Communications:** Radio/TV. **Conservation:** Environmental science, environmental studies. **Foreign languages:** Japanese, linguistics, Spanish. **Health services:** Nursing (RN). **Liberal arts:** Arts/sciences, humanities. **Math:** General. **Parks/recreation:** Health/fitness. **Psychology:** General. **Social sciences:** General, international relations. **Visual/performing arts:** Art, design, music.

Most popular majors. Business/marketing 16%, liberal arts 17%, parks/recreation 11%, psychology 12%, public administration/social services 6%.

Technology on campus. 994 workstations in library, computer center, student center. Dormitories wired for high-speed internet access and linked to campus network. Commuter students can connect to campus network. Online course registration, online library, helpline, student web hosting, wireless network available.

Student life. Freshman orientation: Mandatory, $65 fee. Preregistration for classes offered. **Housing:** Guaranteed on-campus for freshmen. Coed dorms, special housing for disabled, apartments, themed housing, wellness housing available. $250 fully refundable deposit, deadline 5/9. Six-person suite-style living with living areas and kitchenette, substance-free residence hall available. **Activities:** Bands, campus ministries, choral groups, dance, drama, film society, international student organizations, music ensembles, musical theater, radio station, student government, student newspaper, business club, Black Students United, M.E.Ch.A., CAMPers club, media arts club, Otter Movement.

Athletics. NCAA. **Intercollegiate:** Baseball M, basketball, cross-country, golf, soccer, softball W, volleyball W, water polo W. **Intramural:** Basketball, football (non-tackle), soccer, softball. **Team name:** Otters.

Student services. Adult student services, alcohol/substance abuse counseling, chaplain/spiritual director, career counseling, services for economically disadvantaged, student employment services, financial aid counseling, health services, minority student services, on-campus daycare, personal counseling, placement for graduates, veterans' counselor, women's services. **Physically disabled:** Services for visually, speech, hearing impaired.

Contact. E-mail: admissions@csumb.edu
Phone: (831) 582-3738 Fax: (831) 582-3783
David Linnevers, Director of Admissions, California State University: Monterey Bay, 100 Campus Center, Student Services Building, Seaside, CA 93955-8001

California State University: Northridge

Northridge, California — CB member
www.csun.edu — CB code: 4707

▶ Public 4-year university
▶ Commuter campus in very large city
▶ 36,917 degree-seeking undergraduates: 18% part-time, 54% women
▶ 4,631 degree-seeking graduate students
▶ 46% of applicants admitted
▶ SAT or ACT (ACT writing recommended) required

General. Founded in 1958. Regionally accredited. University center in Ventura. **Degrees:** 7,231 bachelor's awarded; master's, doctoral offered. **ROTC:** Army, Air Force. **Location:** 20 miles from Los Angeles. **Calendar:** Semester, limited summer session. **Full-time faculty:** 853 total; 33% minority, 49% women. **Part-time faculty:** 1,172 total; 22% minority, 53% women. **Class size:** 10% < 20, 58% 20-39, 16% 40-49, 11% 50-99, 5% >100. **Special facilities:** Anthropology museum, art botanical gardens, urban archives center, observatory, map library, center for the study of cancer and developmental biology, National Center on Deafness, planetarium.

Freshman class profile. 34,444 applied, 15,706 admitted, 5,637 enrolled.

GPA 3.0-3.49:	70%	Out-of-state:	1%
GPA 2.0-2.99:	30%		

Basis for selection. Index using high school GPA and test scores, and completion of subject requirements. In-state applicants should rank in top third of class; out-of-state in the top sixth. Business administration, economics, engineering, computer science, and physical therapy programs open to California residents only. SAT scores can be used to meet English/Math proficiency requirements. Audition required of music majors.

High school preparation. College-preparatory program required. 15 units required. Required units include English 4, mathematics 3, social studies 1, history 1, science 2 (laboratory 2), foreign language 2, visual/performing arts 1 and academic electives 1.

2015-2016 Annual costs. Tuition/fees: $6,549; $17,709 out-of-state. Room/board: $10,981. Books/supplies: $1,826. Personal expenses: $2,754.

2014-2015 Financial aid. Need-based: 4,814 full-time freshmen applied for aid; 4,629 deemed to have need; 4,629 received aid. Average scholarship/grant was $10,904; average loan $4,675. 81% of total undergraduate aid awarded as scholarships/grants, 19% as loans/jobs. **Non-need-based:** Awarded to 10,387 full-time undergraduates, including 1,632 freshmen. Scholarships awarded for academics, athletics, state residency.

Application procedures. Admission: Closing date 11/30. $55 fee, may be waived for applicants with need. Admission notification on a rolling basis beginning on or about 3/1. Must reply by May 1 or within 2 week(s) if notified thereafter. Applications must be completed by November 30 for business administration, economics and physical therapy programs. **Financial aid:** Priority date 3/2; no closing date. FAFSA required. Applicants notified on a rolling basis starting 4/1.

Academics. Special study options: Cross-registration, distance learning, double major, dual enrollment of high school students, ESL, exchange student,

independent study, internships, student-designed major, study abroad, teacher certification program. Evening degree program, Saturday classes, extended studies, open university, Program for Adult College Education (PACE) available. **Credit/placement by examination:** AP, CLEP, SAT, ACT, institutional tests. **Support services:** Learning center, pre-admission summer program, remedial instruction, tutoring.

Majors. Area/ethnic studies: African-American, Chicano/Hispanic-American/Latino. **Biology:** General, bacteriology, biochemistry, cell/histology, molecular. **Business:** Banking/financial services, business admin, human resources, management information systems, management science, managerial economics, real estate. **Communications:** Broadcast journalism, journalism. **Computer sciences:** General. **Education:** Art, business, English, family/consumer sciences, foreign languages, health, mathematics, music, physical, social science, social studies, speech impaired. **Engineering:** General, chemical, civil, computer, electrical, engineering mechanics, materials, mechanical. **English:** British lit, creative writing, English lit, rhetoric/composition. **Foreign languages:** Comparative lit, French, German, linguistics, Spanish. **Health services:** Nursing (RN), speech pathology. **History:** General. **Liberal arts:** Arts/sciences. **Math:** General, applied, statistics. **Parks/recreation:** General. **Philosophy/religion:** Philosophy, religion. **Physical sciences:** Chemistry, geology, geophysics, physics, planetary. **Psychology:** General. **Social sciences:** Anthropology, economics, geography, political science, sociology, urban studies. **Visual/performing arts:** Art, art history/conservation, ceramics, commercial/advertising art, crafts, dance, dramatic, drawing, metal/jewelry, music, music history, music performance, music theory/composition, painting, printmaking, sculpture. **Work/family studies:** General, business, child care management, clothing/textiles, family studies, family/community services, food/nutrition, housing.

Most popular majors. Business/marketing 18%, communication technologies 9%, English 7%, health sciences 7%, psychology 10%, social sciences 14%, visual/performing arts 6%.

Technology on campus. 723 workstations in library, computer center. Dormitories wired for high-speed internet access and linked to campus network. Commuter students can connect to campus network. Online course registration, online library, helpline, student web hosting, wireless network available.

Student life. Freshman orientation: Mandatory. Preregistration for classes offered. **Housing:** Apartments, fraternity/sorority housing available. Off campus housing choices available. **Activities:** Bands, choral groups, dance, drama, music ensembles, musical theater, radio station, student government, student newspaper, women's center, communities, various clubs and organizations.

Athletics. NCAA. **Intercollegiate:** Baseball M, basketball, cross-country, diving, golf, soccer, softball W, swimming, tennis W, track and field, volleyball, water polo W. **Intramural:** Badminton, baseball M, basketball, bowling, cross-country, diving, handball, ice hockey M, racquetball, rugby, sailing, skiing, soccer, softball, swimming, table tennis, tennis, track and field, volleyball. **Team name:** Matadors.

Student services. Adult student services, alcohol/substance abuse counseling, career counseling, services for economically disadvantaged, student employment services, financial aid counseling, health services, minority student services, on-campus daycare, personal counseling, placement for graduates, veterans' counselor, women's services. **Physically disabled:** Services for visually, speech, hearing impaired.

Contact. E-mail: admissions.records@csun.edu
Phone: (818) 677-3700 Fax: (818) 677-3766
Patricia Lord, Director of Admissions and Records, California State University: Northridge, 18111 Nordhoff Street, Northridge, CA 91330-8207

California State University: Sacramento

Sacramento, California — CB member
www.csus.edu — CB code: 4671

▶ Public 4-year university
▶ Commuter campus in very large city
▶ 27,244 degree-seeking undergraduates: 19% part-time, 56% women, 6% African American, 21% Asian American, 29% Hispanic/Latino, 1% Native Hawaiian/Pacific islander, 6% Multi-racial, non-Hispanic, 3% international
▶ 2,603 degree-seeking graduate students
▶ 67% of applicants admitted
▶ 46% graduate within 6 years

General. Founded in 1947. Regionally accredited. **Degrees:** 5,690 bachelor's awarded; master's, doctoral offered. **ROTC:** Army, Air Force. **Location:**

100 miles from San Francisco. **Calendar:** Semester, extensive summer session. **Full-time faculty:** 646 total; 91% have terminal degrees, 30% minority, 45% women. **Part-time faculty:** 890 total; 26% have terminal degrees, 20% minority, 51% women. **Class size:** 19% < 20, 47% 20-39, 14% 40-49, 12% 50-99, 7% >100. **Special facilities:** Aquatic center, anthropology museum, Hellenic collection.

Freshman class profile. 22,863 applied, 15,377 admitted, 3,781 enrolled.

Mid 50% test scores		GPA 3.0-3.49:	41%
SAT critical reading:	420-520	GPA 2.0-2.99:	24%
SAT math:	420-540	Return as sophomores:	80%
ACT composite:	17-23	Out-of-state:	1%
GPA 3.75 or higher:	16%	Live on campus:	27%
GPA 3.50-3.74:	19%	International:	3%

Basis for selection. Admission requirements vary by programs. If high school GPA is 3.00+, test scores are not required to make an admission decision; if high school GPA is >3.00, either ACT or SAT (exclusive of Writing) is required. ACT and SAT are only used to exempt students from required placement tests in English and Math.

High school preparation. College-preparatory program required. 15 units required. Required units include English 4, mathematics 3, history 2, science 2 (laboratory 2), foreign language 2, visual/performing arts 1 and academic electives 1. History must be U.S. history/government.

2015-2016 Annual costs. Tuition/fees: $6,872; $18,032 out-of-state. Room/board: $13,460. Books/supplies: $1,764. Personal expenses: $2,256.

2014-2015 Financial aid. Need-based: 3,128 full-time freshmen applied for aid; 2,649 deemed to have need; 2,582 received aid. Average need met was 63%. Average scholarship/grant was $8,522; average loan $3,119. 79% of total undergraduate aid awarded as scholarships/grants, 21% as loans/jobs. **Non-need-based:** Awarded to 1,260 full-time undergraduates, including 373 freshmen.

Application procedures. Admission: Priority date 10/1; deadline 11/30 (receipt date). $55 fee, may be waived for applicants with need. Admission notification on a rolling basis beginning on or about 3/1. Must reply by May 1 or within 2 week(s) if notified thereafter. **Financial aid:** No deadline. FAFSA required. Applicants notified on a rolling basis starting 4/23; must reply within 4 week(s) of notification.

Academics. Special study options: Accelerated study, cooperative education, cross-registration, distance learning, double major, dual enrollment of high school students, ESL, honors, independent study, internships, student-designed major, study abroad, teacher certification program. **Credit/placement by examination:** AP, CLEP, IB, SAT, ACT, institutional tests. SAT/ACT may be used to exempt students from English/math placement tests. **Support services:** Learning center, remedial instruction, study skills assistance, tutoring, writing center.

Majors. Architecture: Interior. **Area/ethnic studies:** Asian. **Biology:** General, bacteriology, molecular. **Business:** Accounting, business admin, finance, human resources, insurance, international, marketing, operations, real estate. **Communications:** Communications/speech/rhetoric, journalism. **Computer sciences:** General, information systems. **Conservation:** General, environmental studies. **Education:** General, kindergarten/preschool, mathematics. **Engineering:** Civil, computer, electrical, mechanical. **English:** English lit. **Foreign languages:** American Sign Language, French, Spanish. **Health services:** Audiology/speech pathology, clinical lab technology, nursing (RN), prenursing. **History:** General. **Human services:** Social work. **Liberal arts:** Arts/sciences, humanities. **Math:** General. **Parks/recreation:** General, health/fitness. **Philosophy/religion:** Philosophy, religion. **Physical sciences:** General, chemistry, geology, physics. **Protective services:** Corrections, law enforcement admin. **Psychology:** General. **Social sciences:** General, anthropology, economics, geography, political science, sociology. **Visual/performing arts:** Art, cinematography, commercial/advertising art, dramatic, music, music management, music performance, music theory/composition, photography, voice/opera. **Work/family studies:** General.

Most popular majors. Business/marketing 15%, communications/journalism 9%, engineering/engineering technologies 6%, health sciences 6%, parks/recreation 8%, psychology 6%, security/protective services 8%, social sciences 11%.

Technology on campus. 700 workstations in dormitories, library, computer center, student center. Dormitories wired for high-speed internet access and linked to campus network. Commuter students can connect to campus network. Online course registration, online library, helpline, repair service, student web hosting, wireless network available.

Student life. Freshman orientation: Mandatory, $50 fee. Preregistration for classes offered. **Housing:** Coed dorms, special housing for disabled, apartments, themed housing available. $175 deposit, deadline 6/23. Suite style housing available. **Activities:** Bands, dance, drama, film society, international student organizations, literary magazine, music ensembles, musical theater,

opera, radio station, student government, student newspaper, symphony orchestra, more than 250 clubs, organizations and special interest groups.

Athletics. NCAA. **Intercollegiate:** Baseball M, basketball, cross-country, football (tackle) M, golf, gymnastics W, rowing (crew) W, soccer, softball W, tennis, track and field, volleyball W. **Intramural:** Badminton, basketball, bowling, football (non-tackle), golf, racquetball, skiing, soccer, tennis, volleyball. **Team name:** Hornets.

Student services. Adult student services, alcohol/substance abuse counseling, career counseling, services for economically disadvantaged, student employment services, financial aid counseling, health services, legal services, on-campus daycare, personal counseling, placement for graduates, veterans' counselor, women's services. **Physically disabled:** Services for visually, speech, hearing impaired.

Contact. E-mail: outreach@csus.edu
Phone: (916) 278-7766 Fax: (916) 278-5603
Emiliano Diaz, Director of Outreach, Admissions & Records, California State University: Sacramento, 6000 J Street, Sacramento, CA 95819-6048

California State University: San Bernardino

San Bernardino, California	CB member
www.csusb.edu	CB code: 4099

- Public 4-year university and liberal arts college
- Commuter campus in small city
- 17,721 degree-seeking undergraduates: 11% part-time, 60% women, 6% African American, 6% Asian American, 60% Hispanic/Latino, 3% Multiracial, non-Hispanic, 7% international
- 1,878 degree-seeking graduate students
- 65% of applicants admitted
- SAT or ACT (ACT writing optional) required
- 51% graduate within 6 years

General. Founded in 1962. Regionally accredited. Palm Desert satellite campus offers day and evening courses in degree and credential programs. **Degrees:** 3,155 bachelor's awarded; master's, doctoral offered. **ROTC:** Army, Air Force. **Location:** 60 miles from Los Angeles. **Calendar:** Quarter, limited summer session. **Full-time faculty:** 441 total; 77% have terminal degrees, 31% minority, 47% women. **Part-time faculty:** 545 total; 21% have terminal degrees, 30% minority, 55% women. **Class size:** 23% < 20, 49% 20-39, 8% 40-49, 13% 50-99, 6% >100. **Special facilities:** Animal house, greenhouse, desert studies center, college-operated museum.

Freshman class profile. 13,804 applied, 8,916 admitted, 3,005 enrolled.

Mid 50% test scores		GPA 3.0-3.49:	49%
SAT critical reading:	400-490	GPA 2.0-2.99:	28%
SAT math:	400-500	Return as sophomores:	87%
SAT writing:	390-480	Live on campus:	16%
ACT composite:	16-20	International:	5%
GPA 3.75 or higher:	9%	Fraternities:	7%
GPA 3.50-3.74:	14%	Sororities:	7%

Basis for selection. High school GPA and test scores most important. SAT/ACT not required if high school GPA is 3.0 or higher. Entering undergraduates, except those who qualify for exemption, must take CSU entry-level mathematics (ELM) examination and CSU English placement test (EPT) after admission and before enrolling in classes.

High school preparation. College-preparatory program recommended. 15 units required. Required units include English 4, mathematics 3, social studies 1, history 1, science 2 (laboratory 2), foreign language 2, visual/performing arts 1 and academic electives 1. One visual and performing arts unit also required. Students with disabilities may substitute alternate courses for specific subject requirements.

2015-2016 Annual costs. Tuition/fees: $6,579; $17,739 out-of-state. Room/board: $10,023. Books/supplies: $1,764. Personal expenses: $1,392.

2015-2016 Financial aid. Need-based: 2,757 full-time freshmen applied for aid; 2,527 deemed to have need; 2,466 received aid. Average need met was 65%. Average scholarship/grant was $8,696; average loan $3,260. 78% of total undergraduate aid awarded as scholarships/grants, 22% as loans/jobs. **Non-need-based:** Awarded to 4,824 full-time undergraduates, including 1,506 freshmen.

Application procedures. Admission: Priority date 11/30; no deadline. $55 fee, may be waived for applicants with need. Admission notification on a rolling basis. Students may apply as late as 3 weeks into quarter. **Financial aid:** Priority date 3/2; no closing date. FAFSA required. Applicants notified on a rolling basis starting 4/1.

Academics. **Special study options:** Accelerated study, cooperative education, cross-registration, distance learning, double major, dual enrollment of high school students, exchange student, external degree, honors, independent study, internships, student-designed major, study abroad, teacher certification program. **Credit/placement by examination:** AP, CLEP, IB, SAT, ACT, institutional tests. 40 credit hours maximum toward bachelor's degree. **Support services:** Learning center, pre-admission summer program, remedial instruction, study skills assistance, tutoring, writing center.

Majors. **Area/ethnic studies:** African-American, American, Chicano/Hispanic-American/Latino. **Biology:** General, biochemistry. **Business:** Accounting, business admin, finance, human resources, international, management information systems, managerial economics, marketing, operations, organizational behavior, real estate. **Communications:** Communications/speech/rhetoric, radio/TV. **Computer sciences:** Computer science, systems analysis. **Conservation:** Environmental studies. **Education:** Physical, trade/industrial. **English:** Creative writing, English lit. **Foreign languages:** French, Spanish. **Health services:** Environmental health, kinesiotherapy, nursing (RN), premedicine. **History:** General. **Human services:** General, social work. **Liberal arts:** Arts/sciences, humanities. **Math:** General. **Parks/recreation:** Exercise sciences. **Philosophy/religion:** Philosophy. **Physical sciences:** Chemistry, geology, physics. **Protective services:** Law enforcement admin. **Psychology:** General. **Social sciences:** General, anthropology, economics, geography, political science, sociology. **Visual/performing arts:** Art, art history/conservation, commercial/advertising art, dramatic, music, music history, music performance, musicology, studio arts, theater design, theater history. **Work/family studies:** Child development, family studies, food/nutrition.

Most popular majors. Business/marketing 23%, health sciences 9%, psychology 14%, security/protective services 7%, social sciences 10%.

Technology on campus. 600 workstations in dormitories, library, computer center, student center. Dormitories wired for high-speed internet access and linked to campus network. Commuter students can connect to campus network. Online course registration, online library, helpline, repair service, wireless network available.

Student life. **Freshman orientation:** Mandatory. Preregistration for classes offered. **Housing:** Coed dorms, single-sex dorms, apartments, themed housing available. **Activities:** Jazz band, campus ministries, choral groups, dance, drama, international student organizations, music ensembles, Model UN, musical theater, radio station, student government, student newspaper, symphony orchestra, TV station, more than 80 clubs and organizations.

Athletics. NCAA. **Intercollegiate:** Baseball M, basketball, cross-country W, golf M, soccer, softball W, swimming, tennis W, volleyball W, water polo. **Intramural:** Basketball, field hockey W, soccer, softball M, volleyball. **Team name:** Coyotes.

Student services. Adult student services, career counseling, services for economically disadvantaged, student employment services, financial aid counseling, health services, legal services, minority student services, on-campus daycare, personal counseling, placement for graduates, veterans' counselor, women's services. **Physically disabled:** Services for visually, speech, hearing impaired.

Contact. E-mail: moreinfo@mail.csusb.edu
Phone: (909) 537-5188
Olivia Rosas, Associate Vice President, Enrollment Management, California State University: San Bernardino, 5500 University Parkway, San Bernardino, CA 92407-2397

California State University: San Marcos

San Marcos, California **CB member**
www.csusm.edu **CB code: 5677**

▶ Public 4-year university
▶ Commuter campus in large town
▶ 12,096 degree-seeking undergraduates: 21% part-time, 61% women, 3% African American, 10% Asian American, 42% Hispanic/Latino, 6% Multi-racial, non-Hispanic, 2% international
▶ 375 degree-seeking graduate students
▶ 67% of applicants admitted
▶ SAT or ACT (ACT writing optional) required
▶ 53% graduate within 6 years

General. Founded in 1989. Regionally accredited. **Degrees:** 2,204 bachelor's awarded; master's offered. **ROTC:** Army, Naval, Air Force. **Location:** 30 miles from San Diego. **Calendar:** Semester, limited summer session. **Full-time faculty:** 244 total; 34% minority, 52% women. **Part-time faculty:** 503 total. **Class size:** 15% < 20, 56% 20-39, 22% 40-49, 5% 50-99, 2% >100.

Freshman class profile. 11,560 applied, 7,746 admitted, 2,202 enrolled.

Mid 50% test scores			
SAT critical reading:	420-520	GPA 3.0-3.49:	46%
SAT math:	430-530	GPA 2.0-2.99:	24%
SAT writing:	860-1,040	Return as sophomores:	82%
GPA 3.75 or higher:	13%	Out-of-state:	1%
GPA 3.50-3.74:	17%	International:	2%

Basis for selection. Student eligibility index calculated on GPA and test score combination. **Learning Disabled:** C or better grades in all college preparatory classes. Minimum 2.0 GPA.

High school preparation. College-preparatory program required. 15 units required; 16 recommended. Required and recommended units include English 4, mathematics 3-4, social studies 1, history 1, science 2 (laboratory 2), foreign language 1-2, visual/performing arts 1 and academic electives 1.

2015-2016 Annual costs. Tuition/fees: $7,264; $18,424 out-of-state. Room only: $7,800. Books/supplies: $1,764. Personal expenses: $1,476.

Financial aid. **Non-need-based:** Scholarships awarded for academics, athletics, leadership, state residency.

Application procedures. **Admission:** Closing date 11/30. $55 fee, may be waived for applicants with need. Admission notification on a rolling basis beginning on or about 11/9. Must reply by May 1 or within 4 week(s) if notified thereafter. **Financial aid:** Priority date 3/2; no closing date. FAFSA required. Applicants notified by 4/16.

Academics. **Special study options:** Accelerated study, cross-registration, distance learning, double major, dual enrollment of high school students, ESL, independent study, internships, student-designed major, study abroad, teacher certification program, weekend college. Evening degree program, Saturday classes, ROTC, extended learning, open university, special sessions. **Credit/placement by examination:** AP, CLEP, IB, SAT, ACT, institutional tests. 30 credit hours maximum toward bachelor's degree. **Support services:** Learning center, pre-admission summer program, study skills assistance, tutoring, writing center.

Majors. **Area/ethnic studies:** Women's. **Biology:** General, biochemistry, biotechnology. **Business:** Business admin. **Communications:** Communications/speech/rhetoric. **Computer sciences:** General, computer science. **Engineering:** Applied physics. **English:** English lit. **Foreign languages:** Spanish. **History:** General. **Liberal arts:** Arts/sciences. **Math:** General. **Physical sciences:** Chemistry, physics. **Psychology:** General. **Social sciences:** General, economics, political science, sociology. **Visual/performing arts:** General. **Work/family studies:** Family studies.

Most popular majors. Business/marketing 17%, communications/journalism 7%, family/consumer sciences 10%, health sciences 9%, liberal arts 6%, parks/recreation 7%, psychology 7%, social sciences 19%.

Technology on campus. 1,400 workstations in library, computer center. Dormitories wired for high-speed internet access and linked to campus network. Commuter students can connect to campus network. Online course registration, helpline, wireless network available.

Student life. **Freshman orientation:** Mandatory, $70 fee. Preregistration for classes offered. One-day program. **Housing:** Apartments available. **Activities:** Dance, music ensembles, student newspaper, American Indian Science Engineering Society, Circle K, InterVarsity Christian Fellowship, Latter-day Saints student association, accounting society, Black Men on Campus, College Democrats, pre-health society, student housing association.

Athletics. NAIA. **Intercollegiate:** Baseball M, basketball, cross-country, golf, soccer, softball W, track and field, volleyball W. **Team name:** Cougars.

Student services. Adult student services, alcohol/substance abuse counseling, career counseling, services for economically disadvantaged, student employment services, financial aid counseling, health services, on-campus daycare, personal counseling, placement for graduates, veterans' counselor. **Physically disabled:** Services for visually, speech, hearing impaired.

Contact. E-mail: apply@csusm.edu
Phone: (760) 750-4848 Fax: (760) 750-3248
Scott Hagg, Director of Admissions and Recruitment, California State University: San Marcos, 333 South Twin Oaks Valley Road, San Marcos, CA 92096-0001

California State University: Stanislaus

Turlock, California **CB member**
www.csustan.edu **CB code: 4713**

▶ Public 4-year business and liberal arts college
▶ Commuter campus in small city

- 8,093 degree-seeking undergraduates: 16% part-time, 64% women, 2% African American, 11% Asian American, 49% Hispanic/Latino, 1% Native Hawaiian/Pacific islander, 4% Multi-racial, non-Hispanic, 3% international
- 741 degree-seeking graduate students
- 71% of applicants admitted
- 55% graduate within 6 years

General. Founded in 1957. Regionally accredited. **Degrees:** 1,591 bachelor's awarded; master's, doctoral offered. **Location:** 15 miles from Modesto. **Calendar:** Semester, extensive summer session. **Full-time faculty:** 269 total; 86% have terminal degrees, 30% minority, 47% women. **Part-time faculty:** 280 total; 23% have terminal degrees, 22% minority, 56% women. **Class size:** 19% < 20, 65% 20-39, 10% 40-49, 5% 50-99, less than 1% >100. **Special facilities:** Observatory, interactive television classrooms, laser laboratory, marine sciences station, greenhouse, mainstage theater.

Freshman class profile. 7,080 applied, 5,001 admitted, 1,270 enrolled.

Mid 50% test scores		GPA 2.0-2.99:	22%
SAT critical reading:	400-500	Return as sophomores:	82%
SAT math:	400-510	Out-of-state:	1%
SAT writing:	400-500	Live on campus:	26%
ACT composite:	16-22	International:	5%
GPA 3.75 or higher:	17%	Fraternities:	5%
GPA 3.50-3.74:	17%	Sororities:	7%
GPA 3.0-3.49:	44%		

Basis for selection. High school GPA, courses taken, and test scores. Special consideration for veterans, low-income, and minority applicants. For non-native English speakers, ELPT can be substituted for TOEFL for placement. Exemptions result from scoring well on other specified tests or completion of appropriate courses. Applicants with a minimum high school GPA of 3.0 (3.4 for nonresidents) are exempt from test score requirements. Interview recommended for theatre arts and music majors. Audition recommended for music majors. Portfolio recommended for art majors. **Home schooled:** Transcript of courses and grades required. Applicant must submit SAT or ACT scores. **Learning Disabled:** Students with diagnosed learning disability or neurological disorder that significantly impairs academic performance in specified area may be eligible for waiver of General Education Breadth (GEB) requirement. Additional coursework required in lieu of GEB. Contact Disabled Student Services or submit documentation of disability.

High school preparation. College-preparatory program required. 15 units required. Required units include English 4, mathematics 3, social studies 1, history 1, science 2 (laboratory 2), foreign language 2, visual/performing arts 1 and academic electives 1. History units include history/social studies.

2015-2016 Annual costs. Tuition/fees: $6,700; $17,860 out-of-state. Room/board: $10,090. Books/supplies: $1,780. Personal expenses: $1,392.

Financial aid. Non-need-based: Scholarships awarded for academics, alumni affiliation, art, athletics, leadership, minority status, music/drama, state residency.

Application procedures. Admission: Closing date 11/30 (receipt date). $55 fee, may be waived for applicants with need. Admission notification on a rolling basis beginning on or about 11/1. Must reply by 5/1. **Financial aid:** Priority date 3/2; no closing date. FAFSA required. Applicants notified on a rolling basis starting 3/15; must reply within 3 week(s) of notification.

Academics. First Year Programs, lecture series and cultural offerings, study abroad opportunities, University Honors Program, intensive learning experiences, ESL, community service and service learning opportunities, variety of internships, Cooperative Learning Program. **Special study options:** Accelerated study, cooperative education, cross-registration, distance learning, double major, dual enrollment of high school students, ESL, external degree, honors, independent study, internships, liberal arts/career combination, student-designed major, study abroad, teacher certification program. Additional course offerings developed specifically for learners seeking professional or personal development are available through University Extended Education. **Credit/placement by examination:** AP, CLEP, IB, SAT, ACT, institutional tests. 24 credit hours maximum toward bachelor's degree. Credit by examination does not count toward residency requirement. **Support services:** Learning center, reduced course load, remedial instruction, study skills assistance, tutoring, writing center.

Majors. Area/ethnic studies: General. **Biology:** General. **Business:** Business admin. **Communications:** Communications/speech/rhetoric. **Computer sciences:** Computer science. **Education:** Early childhood, ESL. **English:** English lit. **Foreign languages:** Spanish. **History:** General. **Liberal arts:** Arts/sciences. **Math:** General. **Parks/recreation:** General, health/fitness. **Philosophy/religion:** Philosophy. **Physical sciences:** General, chemistry, geology, physics. **Protective services:** Corrections, criminal justice. **Psychology:** General, cognitive. **Social sciences:** General, anthropology, economics,

geography, political science, sociology. **Visual/performing arts:** Art, dramatic, music, music performance, studio arts.

Most popular majors. Biology 6%, business/marketing 20%, health sciences 7%, liberal arts 8%, psychology 14%, security/protective services 9%, social sciences 12%.

Technology on campus. 250 workstations in dormitories, library, computer center. Dormitories wired for high-speed internet access and linked to campus network. Commuter students can connect to campus network. Online course registration, online library, helpline, wireless network available.

Student life. Freshman orientation: Available. Preregistration for classes offered. Held year-round. **Housing:** Coed dorms, themed housing available. $200 partly refundable deposit. Most housing units are ADA compliant; housing available in summer months. **Activities:** Campus ministries, choral groups, drama, film society, international student organizations, music ensembles, Model UN, musical theater, opera, radio station, student government, student newspaper, symphony orchestra, Over 90 clubs and organizations that range from political, pre-professional, social, fraternities & sororities, cultural, and religious available on campus.

Athletics. NCAA. **Intercollegiate:** Baseball M, basketball, cross-country, golf M, soccer, softball W, tennis W, track and field, volleyball W. **Intramural:** Basketball, cheerleading, football (non-tackle), football (tackle), soccer, ultimate frisbee, volleyball. **Team name:** Warriors.

Student services. Adult student services, alcohol/substance abuse counseling, career counseling, services for economically disadvantaged, student employment services, financial aid counseling, health services, minority student services, on-campus daycare, personal counseling, placement for graduates, veterans' counselor, women's services. **Physically disabled:** Services for visually, speech, hearing impaired.

Contact. E-mail: outreach_help_desk@csustan.edu
Phone: (209) 667-3070 Toll-free number: (800) 300-7420
Fax: (209) 667-3394
Noelia Gonzalez, Director of Admissions, California State University: Stanislaus, One University Circle, Turlock, CA 95382-0256

California University of Management and Sciences
Anaheim, California
www.calums.edu

- Private 4-year university and business college
- Commuter campus in very large city
- 39 degree-seeking undergraduates: 26% women, 3% African American, 5% Asian American, 90% international
- 492 degree-seeking graduate students
- Application essay, interview required

General. Regionally accredited; also accredited by ACICS. **Degrees:** 4 bachelor's awarded; master's offered. **Location:** Approximately 3 miles from Downtown Anaheim. **Calendar:** Quarter. **Full-time faculty:** 7 total; 100% have terminal degrees, 14% women. **Part-time faculty:** 22 total; 68% have terminal degrees, 18% women. **Class size:** 100% < 20.

Basis for selection. School record, GPA, interview most important followed by class rank, test scores, essay and recommendations. TOEFL, EPAT, and Wonderlic used for admission.

High school preparation. College-preparatory program recommended. 26 units required. Required units include English 4, mathematics 4, social studies 2, history 1, science 4 (laboratory 6), foreign language 1, computer science 2, visual/performing arts 1 and academic electives 1.

2015-2016 Annual costs. Tuition/fees: $9,570. Books/supplies: $1,500.

2014-2015 Financial aid. All financial aid based on need. 34% of total undergraduate aid awarded as scholarships/grants, 66% as loans/jobs.

Application procedures. Admission: Priority date 8/15; deadline 9/15 (receipt date). $100 fee. **Financial aid:** Priority date 9/1, closing date 9/15. FAFSA, institutional form required. Applicants notified on a rolling basis; must reply within 2 week(s) of notification.

Academics. Special study options: ESL. **Credit/placement by examination:** AP, CLEP, institutional tests. **Support services:** Remedial instruction, tutoring.

Majors. Business: Business admin. **Parks/recreation:** Sports admin.

Technology on campus. 20 workstations in library, computer center. Online library, wireless network available.

Student life. Freshman orientation: Mandatory. Preregistration for classes offered. **Activities:** Student government, student newspaper.

Student services. Career counseling, financial aid counseling.

Contact. E-mail: lisa@calums.edu
Phone: (714) 533-3946 Fax: (714) 533-7778
Lisa Lee, Director of Admissions, California University of Management and Sciences, 721 North Euclid Streeet, Anaheim, CA 92801-4116

Chapman University
Orange, California   **CB member**
www.chapman.edu   **CB code: 4047**

- Private 4-year university and liberal arts college affiliated with the Christian Church (Disciples of Christ)
- Residential campus in very large city
- 6,281 degree-seeking undergraduates: 4% part-time, 60% women, 1% African American, 10% Asian American, 14% Hispanic/Latino, 6% Multi-racial, non-Hispanic, 4% international
- 1,939 degree-seeking graduate students
- 48% of applicants admitted
- SAT or ACT with writing, application essay required
- 79% graduate within 6 years

General. Founded in 1861. Regionally accredited. **Degrees:** 1,568 bachelor's awarded; master's, professional, doctoral offered. **ROTC:** Army, Air Force. **Location:** 35 miles from Los Angeles, 60 miles from San Diego. **Calendar:** 4-1-4, limited summer session. **Full-time faculty:** 417 total; 87% have terminal degrees, 12% minority, 41% women. **Part-time faculty:** 534 total; 48% women. **Class size:** 45% < 20, 49% 20-39, 3% 40-49, 3% 50-99, less than 1% >100.

Freshman class profile. 13,670 applied, 6,504 admitted, 1,426 enrolled.

Mid 50% test scores			
SAT critical reading:	550-640	Rank in top quarter:	79%
SAT math:	550-650	Rank in top tenth:	39%
SAT writing:	560-660	Return as sophomores:	90%
ACT composite:	25-30	Out-of-state:	36%
GPA 3.75 or higher:	48%	Live on campus:	90%
GPA 3.50-3.74:	23%	International:	3%
GPA 3.0-3.49:	25%	Fraternities:	16%
GPA 2.0-2.99:	4%	Sororities:	39%

Basis for selection. Academic course work plus GPA and test scores most important. Recommendations, essay, extracurricular activities also considered. SAT Subject Tests recommended. Audition required for music, dance, and theater majors. Portfolio required for art and film majors. Supplemental application required for all talent-based majors. **Home schooled:** Statement describing home school structure and mission, transcript of courses and grades, state high school equivalency certificate required.

High school preparation. College-preparatory program recommended. 11 units required; 20 recommended. Required and recommended units include English 2-4, mathematics 2-4, social studies 3-4, science 2-4 (laboratory 1-2) and foreign language 2-4.

2016-2017 Annual costs. Tuition/fees: $48,710. Room/board: $14,368. Books/supplies: $1,560. Personal expenses: $1,600.

2014-2015 Financial aid. Need-based: 1,080 full-time freshmen applied for aid; 870 deemed to have need; 870 received aid. Average need met was 77%. Average scholarship/grant was $16,998; average loan $3,851. 69% of total undergraduate aid awarded as scholarships/grants, 31% as loans/jobs. **Non-need-based:** Awarded to 3,674 full-time undergraduates, including 966 freshmen. Scholarships awarded for academics, alumni affiliation, art, music/drama, religious affiliation.

Application procedures. Admission: Closing date 1/15 (postmark date). $65 fee, may be waived for applicants with need. Application must be submitted online. Admission notification on a rolling basis beginning on or about 3/15. Must reply by May 1 or within 2 week(s) if notified thereafter. **Financial aid:** Priority date 3/2; no closing date. FAFSA required. Applicants notified on a rolling basis starting 3/15; must reply within 3 week(s) of notification.

Academics. Special study options: Combined bachelor's/graduate degree, distance learning, double major, honors, independent study, internships, liberal arts/career combination, semester at sea, student designed major, study

abroad, teacher certification program, Washington semester. **Credit/placement by examination:** AP, CLEP, IB, SAT, ACT, institutional tests. 32 credit hours maximum toward bachelor's degree. **Support services:** Learning center, reduced course load, remedial instruction, study skills assistance, tutoring, writing center.

Majors. Biology: General, biochemistry. **Business:** Accounting, business admin, managerial economics. **Communications:** Broadcast journalism, communications/speech/rhetoric, public relations. **Computer sciences:** General, computer science. **Conservation:** Management/policy. **Education:** General, music. **Engineering:** Software. **English:** Creative writing, English lit. **Foreign languages:** French, Spanish. **Health services:** Athletic training, health services admin, predental, premedicine, preveterinary. **History:** General. **Human services:** Social work. **Math:** General. **Philosophy/religion:** Philosophy, religion. **Physical sciences:** Chemistry, theoretical physics. **Psychology:** General. **Social sciences:** Political science, sociology. **Visual/performing arts:** Acting, art, art history/conservation, cinematography, conducting, dance, dramatic, film/cinema/video, graphic design, music, music performance, music theory/composition, piano/keyboard, play/screenwriting, studio arts, voice/opera.

Most popular majors. Business/marketing 25%, communications/journalism 15%, psychology 8%, visual/performing arts 23%.

Technology on campus. Dormitories wired for high-speed internet access and linked to campus network. Commuter students can connect to campus network. Online course registration, online library, helpline, repair service, student web hosting, wireless network available.

Student life. Freshman orientation: Mandatory. Preregistration for classes offered. 5-day summer program for new students and their parents immediately preceding the start of semester. **Housing:** Guaranteed on-campus for freshmen. Coed dorms, special housing for disabled, apartments, wellness housing available. $600 partly refundable deposit, deadline 5/1. Housing for students with dependents available. **Activities:** Bands, campus ministries, choral groups, dance, drama, film society, international student organizations, literary magazine, music ensembles, Model UN, musical theater, opera, radio station, student government, student newspaper, symphony orchestra.

Athletics. NCAA. **Intercollegiate:** Baseball M, basketball, cross-country, diving, football (tackle) M, golf M, lacrosse W, soccer, softball W, swimming, tennis, track and field, volleyball W, water polo. **Intramural:** Basketball, soccer, ultimate frisbee, volleyball. **Team name:** Panthers.

Student services. Adult student services, alcohol/substance abuse counseling, chaplain/spiritual director, career counseling, student employment services, financial aid counseling, health services, personal counseling, placement for graduates, veterans' counselor. **Physically disabled:** Services for visually, speech, hearing impaired.

Contact. E-mail: admit@chapman.edu
Phone: (714) 997-6711 Toll-free number: (888) 282-7759
Fax: (714) 997-6713
Marcela Mejia-Martinez, Director of Undergraduate Admission, Chapman University, Admission Office, Orange, CA 92866

Charles Drew University of Medicine and Science
Los Angeles, California
www.cdrewu.edu   **CB code: 4982**

- Private 4-year university and health science college
- Commuter campus in very large city
- 85 degree-seeking undergraduates: 38% part-time, 46% women, 39% African American, 9% Asian American, 13% Hispanic/Latino, 1% Native Hawaiian/Pacific islander, 25% Multi-racial, non-Hispanic
- 352 degree-seeking graduate students
- 100% graduate within 6 years

General. Regionally accredited. Charter member of the Hispanic Serving Health Professions Schools. **Degrees:** 3 bachelor's, 22 associate awarded; master's offered. **Location:** Downtown. **Calendar:** Semester, limited summer session. **Full-time faculty:** 52 total; 71% have terminal degrees, 40% minority, 56% women. **Part-time faculty:** 42 total; 83% have terminal degrees, 29% minority, 60% women. **Class size:** 42% < 20, 56% 20-39, 3% 40-49. **Special facilities:** Clinical simulation centers, health sciences library, clinical and population-based research facilities.

Basis for selection. Official transcripts of all schools attended, personal goal statement, three recommendations, SAT scores, evidence of prerequisite courses (if applicable), and participation in an interview with the admissions selection committee required. **Home schooled:** Transcript of courses and grades required.

High school preparation. College-preparatory program required. Required and recommended units include English 3-4, mathematics 3-4, social studies 1, history 1, science 2-3 (laboratory 2), foreign language 2 and visual/performing arts 1.

2015-2016 Annual costs. Tuition/fees: $16,150. Books/supplies: $1,736. Personal expenses: $4,231.

2014-2015 Financial aid. Need-based: 28% of total undergraduate aid awarded as scholarships/grants, 72% as loans/jobs. **Non-need-based:** Scholarships awarded for academics, leadership.

Application procedures. Admission: Priority date 12/1; deadline 3/1 (postmark date). $35 fee, may be waived for applicants with need. Admission notification by 8/1. Admission notification on a rolling basis beginning on or about 1/1. Must reply by May 1 or within 2 week(s) if notified thereafter. Application deadlines vary by program. **Financial aid:** No deadline. FAFSA required. Applicants notified on a rolling basis.

Academics. Special study options: Cross-registration, distance learning, dual enrollment of high school students, independent study. **Credit/placement by examination:** AP, CLEP, IB, SAT, ACT, institutional tests. **Support services:** Learning center, tutoring.

Technology on campus. 100 workstations in library, computer center. Commuter students can connect to campus network. Online library, wireless network available.

Student life. Freshman orientation: Mandatory. Preregistration for classes offered. Held approximately 2 weeks prior to the start of the semester, and run for approximately 2-3 days. **Activities:** Student government.

Student services. Financial aid counseling.

Contact. E-mail: admissionsinfo@cdrewu.edu
Phone: (323) 563-4838 Fax: (323) 569-0597
Amin Maghsoodi, Director of Admissions, Charles Drew University of Medicine and Science, 1731 East 120th Street, Los Angeles, CA 90059

Claremont McKenna College

Claremont, California	**CB member**
www.cmc.edu	**CB code: 4054**

- Private 4-year liberal arts college
- Residential campus in large town
- 1,325 degree-seeking undergraduates: 49% women, 4% African American, 10% Asian American, 14% Hispanic/Latino, 7% Multi-racial, non-Hispanic, 17% international
- 21 degree-seeking graduate students
- 11% of applicants admitted
- SAT or ACT with writing, application essay required
- 92% graduate within 6 years

General. Founded in 1946. Regionally accredited. One of seven members of The Claremont Colleges, which includes five undergraduate liberal arts colleges (Claremont McKenna, Harvey Mudd, Pitzer, Pomona, and Scripps) and two graduate institutions (Claremont Graduate University and the Keck Graduate Institute for Applied Life Sciences). The campuses share some facilities and cross-enrollment is readily available. **Degrees:** 319 bachelor's awarded; master's offered. **ROTC:** Army, Air Force. **Location:** 35 miles from downtown Los Angeles. **Calendar:** Semester. **Full-time faculty:** 150 total; 99% have terminal degrees, 19% minority, 31% women. **Part-time faculty:** 15 total; 93% have terminal degrees, 27% minority, 33% women. **Class size:** 83% < 20, 13% 20-39, 2% 40-49, less than 1% 50-99, less than 1% >100. **Special facilities:** 10 research institutes, athenaeum.

Freshman class profile. 7,156 applied, 784 admitted, 343 enrolled.

Mid 50% test scores		Rank in top tenth:	73%
SAT critical reading:	670-750	Return as sophomores:	95%
SAT math:	670-780	Out-of-state:	54%
SAT writing:	690-760	Live on campus:	100%
ACT composite:	29-33	International:	17%
Rank in top quarter:	98%		

Basis for selection. Applications are reviewed on a holistic basis, taking into account academic and personal achievement in the context of each student's educational and home environment. SAT Subject Tests are only required for home schooled applicants; they will not be considered, even if submitted, for all other applicants. **Home schooled:** Interview, letter of recommendation (nonparent) required. In addition to the components of an application that are required of all students, home-schooled students must also submit the results from an SAT Subject Test in mathematics and an SAT Subject Test in one other field. An extracurricular evaluation is also required and an interview is strongly recommended.

High school preparation. College-preparatory program required. 14 units required; 16 recommended. Required and recommended units include English 4, mathematics 3-4, social studies 1, history 1, science 2-3 (laboratory 2-3) and foreign language 3.

2015-2016 Annual costs. Tuition/fees: $49,045. Room/board: $15,280. Books/supplies: $900.

2015-2016 Financial aid. Need-based: 190 full-time freshmen applied for aid; 141 deemed to have need; 141 received aid. Average need met was 100%. Average scholarship/grant was $39,775; average loan $3,987. 91% of total undergraduate aid awarded as scholarships/grants, 9% as loans/jobs. **Non-need-based:** Awarded to 322 full-time undergraduates, including 80 freshmen. Scholarships awarded for academics, leadership, ROTC.

Application procedures. Admission: Closing date 1/1 (receipt date). $70 fee, may be waived for applicants with need. Application must be submitted online. Admission notification by 4/1. Must reply by 5/1. **Financial aid:** Priority date 1/1, closing date 2/1. FAFSA, CSS PROFILE required. Applicants notified by 4/1; must reply by 5/1.

Academics. Special study options: Combined bachelor's/graduate degree, cross-registration, double major, exchange student, honors, independent study, internships, student-designed major, study abroad, Washington semester. **Credit/placement by examination:** AP, CLEP, IB, institutional tests. 16 credit hours maximum toward bachelor's degree. **Support services:** Tutoring, writing center.

Majors. Area/ethnic studies: African, African-American, American, Asian, Asian-American, Chicano/Hispanic-American/Latino, European, gay/lesbian, Latin American, Near/Middle Eastern, Pacific, regional, South Asian, Southeast Asian, Spanish/Iberian, Western European, women's. **Biology:** General, biochemistry, biophysics, molecular, neuroscience. **Business:** Accounting. **Communications:** Media studies. **Computer sciences:** Computer science. **Conservation:** Environmental science, environmental studies. **English:** English lit. **Foreign languages:** Chinese, classics, French, German, Italian, Japanese, Russian, Spanish. **History:** General. **Math:** General. **Philosophy/religion:** Philosophy, religion. **Physical sciences:** Chemistry, physics. **Psychology:** General. **Social sciences:** Economics, international relations, political science. **Visual/performing arts:** Art, dance, dramatic, film/cinema/video, music.

Most popular majors. Biology 9%, business/marketing 8%, interdisciplinary studies 14%, psychology 8%, social sciences 38%.

Technology on campus. Dormitories wired for high-speed internet access and linked to campus network. Commuter students can connect to campus network. Online course registration, online library, helpline, student web hosting, wireless network available.

Student life. Freshman orientation: Mandatory. Preregistration for classes offered. **Policies:** Freshmen not permitted cars on campus. **Housing:** Guaranteed on-campus for all undergraduates. Coed dorms, special housing for disabled, apartments, wellness housing available. $200 nonrefundable deposit, deadline 7/1. **Activities:** Bands, campus ministries, choral groups, dance, drama, film society, international student organizations, literary magazine, music ensembles, Model UN, musical theater, radio station, student government, student newspaper, symphony orchestra.

Athletics. NCAA. **Intercollegiate:** Baseball M, basketball, cross-country, diving, football (tackle) M, golf, lacrosse W, soccer, softball W, swimming, tennis, track and field, volleyball W, water polo. **Intramural:** Basketball, bowling, rugby, soccer, softball, swimming, volleyball. **Team name:** Stags (M), Athenas (W).

Student services. Alcohol/substance abuse counseling, chaplain/spiritual director, career counseling, student employment services, financial aid counseling, health services, minority student services, personal counseling, placement for graduates, women's services.

Contact. E-mail: admission@cmc.edu
Phone: (909) 621-8088 Fax: (909) 621-8516
Georgette DeVeres, Associate Vice President and Dean of Admission and Financial Aid, Claremont McKenna College, 888 Columbia Avenue, Claremont, CA 91711

Cogswell Polytechnical College
San Jose, California
www.cogswell.edu — CB code: 4057

- For-profit 4-year business and engineering college
- Commuter campus in small city
- 630 degree-seeking undergraduates: 16% part-time, 27% women, 4% African American, 16% Asian American, 18% Hispanic/Latino, 1% Native American, 2% Native Hawaiian/Pacific islander, 9% Multi-racial, non-Hispanic, 1% international
- 61% of applicants admitted
- Application essay, interview required
- 33% graduate within 6 years

General. Founded in 1887. Regionally accredited. Program fusion of art and engineering. Project-based learning. **Degrees:** 57 bachelor's awarded; master's offered. **Location:** 45 miles from San Francisco, 4 miles from San Jose. **Calendar:** Semester, extensive summer session. **Full-time faculty:** 17 total; 24% have terminal degrees, 24% women. **Part-time faculty:** 74 total; 11% have terminal degrees, 23% women. **Class size:** 84% < 20, 16% 20-39. **Special facilities:** Electronic music laboratories, sound/recording studio, video studio, editing studio, computer imaging laboratories, SGI laboratory, MIDI laboratory, 2D and 3D animation laboratories.

Freshman class profile. 349 applied, 212 admitted, 110 enrolled.

Mid 50% test scores		GPA 3.50-3.74:	11%
SAT critical reading:	490-610	GPA 3.0-3.49:	30%
SAT math:	520-610	GPA 2.0-2.99:	52%
SAT writing:	490-580	End year in good standing:	75%
ACT composite:	20-27	Return as sophomores:	78%
GPA 3.75 or higher:	6%	Out-of-state:	8%

Basis for selection. Motivation, 2.7 GPA in academic subjects is recommended, test scores most important. Recommendations, art portfolio required for art programs, personal essay. SAT or ACT recommended. Portfolio required for all digital art programs. **Home schooled:** Transcript of courses and grades, state high school equivalency certificate, interview, letter of recommendation (nonparent) required. **Learning Disabled:** Must be documented by medical/psychological professional; before admission decision is made.

High school preparation. College-preparatory program recommended. 7 units required. Required and recommended units include English 3, mathematics 3, science 1 (laboratory 1), computer science 1 and visual/performing arts 1. 1 algebra, 1 geometry, 1 trigonometry required for engineering program; 1 algebra, 1 geometry required for art programs.

2015-2016 Annual costs. Tuition/fees: $16,640. Room only: $8,000. Books/supplies: $1,764. Personal expenses: $2,322.

2015-2016 Financial aid. Need-based: 50% of total undergraduate aid awarded as scholarships/grants, 50% as loans/jobs. **Non-need-based:** Scholarships awarded for academics.

Application procedures. Admission: No deadline. No application fee. Admission notification on a rolling basis. **Financial aid:** Priority date 3/1; no closing date. FAFSA required. Applicants notified on a rolling basis starting 4/30; must reply within 4 week(s) of notification.

Academics. Special study options: Distance learning, double major, independent study, internships. **Credit/placement by examination:** AP, CLEP, IB, SAT, ACT, institutional tests. 18 credit hours maximum toward bachelor's degree. **Support services:** Pre-admission summer program, reduced course load, remedial instruction, study skills assistance, tutoring.

Most popular majors. Engineering/engineering technologies 11%, security/protective services 11%, visual/performing arts 77%.

Technology on campus. 164 workstations in library, computer center. Commuter students can connect to campus network. Online course registration, online library, helpline, wireless network available.

Student life. Freshman orientation: Mandatory. Preregistration for classes offered. **Housing:** Apartments, gender-neutral housing available. $300 fully refundable deposit, deadline 7/1. **Activities:** Concert band, student government.

Student services. Alcohol/substance abuse counseling, career counseling, student employment services, financial aid counseling, personal counseling, placement for graduates.

Contact. E-mail: admissions@cogswell.edu
Phone: (408) 498-5160 Toll-free number: (855) 264-7935
Fax: (408) 877-7373
Aaron Kark, Executive Director of Enrollment Services, Cogswell Polytechnical College, 191 Baypointe Parkway, San Jose, CA 95134

Coleman University
San Diego, California
www.coleman.edu — CB code: 0955

- Private 4-year university and technical college
- Commuter campus in very large city
- 364 degree-seeking undergraduates: 16% part-time, 10% women, 9% African American, 15% Asian American, 16% Hispanic/Latino, 1% Native American, 2% Native Hawaiian/Pacific islander, 1% Multi-racial, non-Hispanic
- 53 degree-seeking graduate students
- Interview required

General. Founded in 1963. Accredited by ACICS. **Degrees:** 89 bachelor's, 94 associate awarded; master's offered. **Location:** 11 miles from San Diego. **Calendar:** Differs by program. **Full-time faculty:** 13 total; 69% minority, 38% women. **Part-time faculty:** 107 total; 12% have terminal degrees, 29% minority, 29% women. **Class size:** 97% < 20, 3% 20-39.

Freshman class profile. 36 applied, 36 admitted, 36 enrolled.

End year in good standing: 52% **Return as sophomores:** 53%

Basis for selection. Open admission, but selective for some programs. In addition to the HS diploma or GED, applicants are required to take a cognitive ability test. Test scores recommended for placement and credit. Institutionally administered aptitude test required. Cognitive ability test given during interview.

2016-2017 Annual costs. Tuition/fees: $20,725. Personal expenses: $3,159.

Financial aid. All financial aid based on need.

Application procedures. Admission: No deadline. $25 fee. Admission notification on a rolling basis. **Financial aid:** No deadline. FAFSA, institutional form required. Applicants notified on a rolling basis starting 1/4; must reply within 1 week(s) of notification.

Academics. Coleman University's inverted curriculum, or "major first" approach to education allows students to take the technical courses in their major first, as part of their specialized Associate Degree program. **Special study options:** Accelerated study, combined bachelor's/graduate degree, cooperative education, distance learning, double major. **Credit/placement by examination:** AP, CLEP. 36 credit hours maximum toward associate degree, 88 toward bachelor's. **Support services:** Learning center, reduced course load, study skills assistance, tutoring, writing center.

Majors. Computer sciences: Computer graphics, networking, programming, security, web page design.

Technology on campus. 390 workstations in library, computer center. Helpline, wireless network available.

Student life. Freshman orientation: Available. Preregistration for classes offered. Two sessions held before classes start for new students and international students. **Activities:** International student organizations, student activities committee, National Technical Honor Society (NTHS), Business Professionals of America (BPA).

Student services. Career counseling, financial aid counseling, personal counseling, placement for graduates, veterans' counselor. **Physically disabled:** Services for visually impaired.

Contact. E-mail: admis@coleman.edu
Phone: (858) 499-0202 Toll-free number: (800) 430-2030
Fax: (858) 499-0233
Brandi Landrum, Director of Admissions, Coleman University, 8888 Balboa Avenue, San Diego, CA 92123

Columbia College Hollywood
Tarzana, California — CB member
www.columbiacollege.edu — CB code: 1247

- Private 4-year visual arts college
- Commuter campus in very large city

♦ 330 degree-seeking undergraduates
♦ Application essay, interview required

General. Founded in 1952. **Degrees:** 58 bachelor's, 1 associate awarded. **Location:** 15 miles from downtown Los Angeles. **Calendar:** Quarter, limited summer session. **Part-time faculty:** 73 total; 22% have terminal degrees, 23% minority, 25% women.

Freshman class profile.

GPA 3.75 or higher:	12%	GPA 3.0-3.49:	29%
GPA 3.50-3.74:	9%	GPA 2.0-2.99:	49%

Basis for selection. Open admission, but selective for some programs. **Home schooled:** Transcript of courses and grades required.

2015-2016 Annual costs. Tuition/fees: $21,200. Room/board: $11,970. Books/supplies: $273. Personal expenses: $2,898.

Financial aid. All financial aid based on need.

Application procedures. Admission: Priority date 1/5; deadline 2/28 (postmark date). $25 fee, may be waived for applicants with need. Admission notification on a rolling basis. Must reply by 5/1. **Financial aid:** Priority date 3/2, closing date 5/30. FAFSA required. Applicants notified on a rolling basis starting 3/30; must reply within 2 week(s) of notification.

Academics. Special study options: Independent study, internships, weekend college. **Credit/placement by examination:** AP, CLEP, IB, institutional tests. **Support services:** Learning center, reduced course load, remedial instruction, study skills assistance, tutoring.

Majors. Visual/performing arts: Cinematography, film/cinema/video.

Technology on campus. 14 workstations in library. Online course registration, wireless network available.

Student life. Freshman orientation: Mandatory. Preregistration for classes offered. **Housing:** Apartments available. $490 nonrefundable deposit. Pets allowed in dorm rooms. **Activities:** Film society, student government.

Student services. Adult student services, career counseling, student employment services, financial aid counseling, minority student services, personal counseling, placement for graduates, veterans' counselor, women's services.

Contact. E-mail: admissions@columbiacollege.edu
Phone: (818) 345-8414 Toll-free number: (800) 785-0585
Fax: (818) 345-9053
Carmen Munoz, Director of Admissions, Columbia College Hollywood, 18618 Oxnard Street, Tarzana, CA 91356

Concordia University Irvine
Irvine, California CB member
www.cui.edu CB code: 4069

♦ Private 4-year university and liberal arts college affiliated with the Lutheran Church - Missouri Synod
♦ Residential campus in small city
♦ 1,853 degree-seeking undergraduates: 7% part-time, 64% women
♦ 2,474 degree-seeking graduate students
♦ 59% of applicants admitted
♦ SAT or ACT (ACT writing optional) required
♦ 61% graduate within 6 years

General. Founded in 1972. Regionally accredited. **Degrees:** 476 bachelor's awarded; master's, doctoral offered. **Location:** 40 miles from Los Angeles, 80 miles from San Diego. **Calendar:** Semester, limited summer session. **Full-time faculty:** 113 total; 66% have terminal degrees, 16% minority, 48% women. **Part-time faculty:** 305 total; 28% have terminal degrees, 16% minority, 50% women. **Class size:** 53% < 20, 45% 20-39, 2% 40-49, less than 1% 50-99. **Special facilities:** Spectroscopy lab.

Freshman class profile. 3,135 applied, 1,855 admitted, 334 enrolled.

Mid 50% test scores		GPA 3.0-3.49:	37%
SAT critical reading:	440-560	GPA 2.0-2.99:	16%
SAT math:	460-570	End year in good standing:	85%
SAT writing:	440-550	Return as sophomores:	72%
ACT composite:	20-25	Out-of-state:	24%
GPA 3.75 or higher:	28%	Live on campus:	86%
GPA 3.50-3.74:	19%	International:	5%

Basis for selection. Official secondary school transcript and standardized test scores are most important. Recommendations, involvement, and character/personal qualities are also important. Test scores (Dantes, AP, CLEP) are not used for placement but upon review may be accepted for credit. Interview required for Wings program. **Home schooled:** Each file reviewed on individual basis. Some documentation of home school structure, courses and grades, state high school equivalency, and/or personal recommendations may be requested.

High school preparation. College-preparatory program recommended. 12 units required; 18 recommended. Required and recommended units include English 4, mathematics 3, social studies 2, history 2, science 3 (laboratory 2) and foreign language 4. Algebra I and II and geometry specifically required.

2015-2016 Annual costs. Tuition/fees: $31,690. Room/board: $9,890. Books/supplies: $1,700. Personal expenses: $2,500.

2015-2016 Financial aid. Need-based: 296 full-time freshmen applied for aid; 258 deemed to have need; 258 received aid. Average need met was 72%. Average scholarship/grant was $20,127; average loan $3,421. 78% of total undergraduate aid awarded as scholarships/grants, 22% as loans/jobs. **Non-need-based:** Awarded to 491 full-time undergraduates, including 107 freshmen. Scholarships awarded for academics, athletics, music/drama, religious affiliation.

Application procedures. Admission: Priority date 12/1; no deadline. $50 fee, may be waived for applicants with need, free for online applicants. Admission notification on a rolling basis beginning on or about 12/15. Must reply by May 1 or within 4 week(s) if notified thereafter. **Financial aid:** Closing date 3/2. FAFSA required. Applicants notified on a rolling basis starting 3/15; must reply within 4 week(s) of notification.

Academics. Special study options: Accelerated study, distance learning, double major, ESL, exchange student, honors, independent study, internships, student-designed major, study abroad, teacher certification program. **Credit/placement by examination:** AP, CLEP, IB. 32 credit hours maximum toward bachelor's degree. **Support services:** Learning center, pre-admission summer program, reduced course load, study skills assistance, tutoring, writing center.

Majors. Biology: General. **Business:** Business admin. **Communications:** General. **English:** English lit. **Foreign languages:** Biblical. **Health services:** Athletic training, health care admin, nursing (RN). **History:** General. **Liberal arts:** Arts/sciences, humanities. **Math:** General. **Parks/recreation:** Health/fitness. **Philosophy/religion:** Religion. **Physical sciences:** Chemistry, physics. **Psychology:** General, industrial. **Social sciences:** Economics, political science. **Theology:** Religious ed, theology. **Visual/performing arts:** Art, dramatic, graphic design, music.

Most popular majors. Business/marketing 19%, communications/journalism 7%, health sciences 21%, liberal arts 10%, parks/recreation 9%, psychology 10%.

Technology on campus. 100 workstations in dormitories, library, computer center, student center. Dormitories wired for high-speed internet access and linked to campus network. Commuter students can connect to campus network. Online course registration, online library, helpline, wireless network available.

Student life. Freshman orientation: Mandatory, $100 fee. Preregistration for classes offered. Held in summer and fall before start of classes. **Policies:** Freshmen not permitted cars on campus. **Housing:** Guaranteed on-campus for freshmen. Coed dorms, special housing for disabled, themed housing, wellness housing available. $300 nonrefundable deposit, deadline 6/30. **Activities:** Bands, campus ministries, choral groups, drama, international student organizations, literary magazine, music ensembles, musical theater, student government, student newspaper, Nuestra Voz, Improv Club, Republican Club, math club, sports medicine club, Fellowship of Christian Athletes, ethics club, Cross Cultural Link.

Athletics. NAIA. **Intercollegiate:** Baseball M, basketball, cross-country, soccer, softball W, swimming, tennis, track and field, volleyball, water polo. **Intramural:** Basketball, bowling, football (non-tackle), soccer, softball, track and field, ultimate frisbee, volleyball. **Team name:** Eagles.

Student services. Adult student services, alcohol/substance abuse counseling, chaplain/spiritual director, career counseling, financial aid counseling, health services, minority student services, personal counseling.

Contact. E-mail: admission@cui.edu
Phone: (949) 214-3010 Toll-free number: (800) 229-1200 ext. 3010
Fax: (949) 214-3520
Doug Wible, Director of Undergraduate Admissions, Concordia University Irvine, 1530 Concordia West, Irvine, CA 92612-3203

Design Institute of San Diego
San Diego, California
www.disd.edu   CB code: 3492

- For-profit 4-year career college
- Commuter campus in very large city
- 148 degree-seeking undergraduates: 44% part-time, 93% women, 7% African American, 9% Asian American, 17% Hispanic/Latino, 1% Native American, 1% Native Hawaiian/Pacific islander, 7% international
- Application essay, interview required
- 83% graduate within 6 years

General. Accredited by ACICS. **Degrees:** 40 bachelor's awarded. **Calendar:** Semester, limited summer session. **Full-time faculty:** 5 total. **Part-time faculty:** 20 total. **Class size:** 94% < 20, 6% 20-39. **Special facilities:** Full working computer labs, full scale on-site plotters.

Freshman class profile.

End year in good standing: 83%   **Return as sophomores:**   67%

Basis for selection. Official transcripts of all high school and college grades, 2 professional references, and 2 brief essays required. **Home schooled:** Transcript of courses and grades required. **Learning Disabled:** Reasonable accommodation to students with disabilities provided in compliance with state and federal legislation including Sections 504 and 508 of the Rehabilitation Act of 1973 and the Americans with Disabilities Act (ADA). Students who feel they qualify for accommodation should contact Tena Moiola, Director of Student Services, tmoiola@disd.edu, for a full copy of the policy and for assistance in submitting the required written and professional documentation of a disability along with written and official professional documentation of required accommodations.

2015-2016 Annual costs. Tuition/fees: $18,664. Room/board: $11,268. Books/supplies: $1,229.

Financial aid. **Additional information:** Financial aid is available for those who qualify. A free Preliminary Financial Aid Profile will be done for anyone who has applied to the college. This profile is an estimate of financial aid eligibility for grants and loans.

Application procedures. **Admission:** No deadline. $25 fee. Admission notification on a rolling basis. **Financial aid:** No deadline. Applicants notified on a rolling basis.

Academics. **Special study options:** Internships. **Credit/placement by examination:** AP, CLEP, IB. **Support services:** Study skills assistance, tutoring.

Majors. **Visual/performing arts:** Interior design.

Technology on campus. 70 workstations in library, computer center. Commuter students can connect to campus network. Online library, helpline, wireless network available.

Student life. **Freshman orientation:** Mandatory. Preregistration for classes offered. 1-1.5 hour session required for all new students. Books and supplies may be purchased during this time as well as during the first week of classes.

Student services. Career counseling, student employment services, financial aid counseling, personal counseling, placement for graduates, veterans' counselor.

Contact. E-mail: admissions@disd.edu
Phone: (858) 566-1200 Toll-free number: (800) 619-4337
Fax: (858) 566-2711
Liz Barry, Admissions, Design Institute of San Diego, 8555 Commerce Avenue, San Diego, CA 92121

DeVry University: Pomona
Pomona, California
www.devry.edu   CB code: 4214

- For-profit 4-year university
- Commuter campus in small city
- 1,501 degree-seeking undergraduates
- Interview required

General. Founded in 1983. Regionally accredited. Additional locations: Colton, Alhambra, Long Beach, Anaheim, Irvine, Sherman Oaks, Palmdale, Fremont, Daly City, Oakland City, San Jose, Fresno, Bakersfield, Sacramento, San Diego. **Degrees:** 1,255 bachelor's, 185 associate awarded; master's offered. **Location:** 13 miles from Los Angeles. **Calendar:** Semester, extensive summer session. **Full-time faculty:** 21 total; 38% minority, 10% women. **Part-time faculty:** 77 total; 38% minority, 43% women.

Basis for selection. Applicant must have high school diploma or equivalent, degree from an accredited postsecondary institution, or submit acceptable test scores and be at least 17 years of age on the first day of classes.

High school preparation. College-preparatory program recommended.

2015-2016 Annual costs. Tuition/fees: $17,132. Books/supplies: $1,320. Personal expenses: $2,376.

Financial aid. All financial aid based on need.

Application procedures. **Admission:** No deadline. $40 fee. Admission notification on a rolling basis. **Financial aid:** No deadline. FAFSA required. Applicants notified on a rolling basis.

Academics. **Special study options:** Accelerated study, distance learning, study abroad. **Credit/placement by examination:** AP, CLEP, institutional tests. **Support services:** Learning center, remedial instruction, tutoring.

Majors. **Business:** General, accounting, business admin. **Computer sciences:** General, networking, systems analysis, web page design. **Engineering:** Software. **Health services:** Health care admin. **Visual/performing arts:** Game design.

Most popular majors. Business/marketing 66%, computer/information sciences 16%, engineering/engineering technologies 18%.

Technology on campus. 517 workstations in library, computer center. Online course registration, online library, helpline available.

Student life. **Freshman orientation:** Mandatory. Preregistration for classes offered. **Housing:** Private apartments, student-plan housing, private rooms available. **Activities:** Gaming association, Institute for Electrical and Electronic Engineers, Living in Truth, National Society of Black Engineers, Phi Beta Lambda, Society of Hispanic Professional Engineers, networking professional association, Toastmasters.

Student services. Career counseling, student employment services, financial aid counseling, placement for graduates, veterans' counselor. **Physically disabled:** Services for visually, hearing impaired.

Contact. Phone: (909) 622-8866
DeVry University: Pomona, 901 Corporate Center Drive, Pomona, CA 91768-2642

Dominican University of California
San Rafael, California
www.dominican.edu   CB code: 4284

- Private 4-year university
- Residential campus in small city
- 1,358 degree-seeking undergraduates: 14% part-time, 72% women, 5% African American, 22% Asian American, 20% Hispanic/Latino, 1% Native American, 1% Native Hawaiian/Pacific islander, 6% Multi-racial, non-Hispanic, 2% international
- 463 degree-seeking graduate students
- 79% of applicants admitted
- SAT or ACT with writing, application essay required
- 66% graduate within 6 years

General. Founded in 1890. Regionally accredited. Common academic first-year experience focused on Big History; BFA in dance program affiliated with major ballet company; partnership with Buck Institute for Age Research. **Degrees:** 385 bachelor's awarded; master's offered. **ROTC:** Air Force. **Location:** 12 miles from San Francisco. **Calendar:** Semester, limited summer session. **Full-time faculty:** 111 total; 68% have terminal degrees, 19% minority, 60% women. **Part-time faculty:** 174 total; 21% have terminal degrees, 16% minority, 68% women. **Class size:** 66% < 20, 34% 20-39, less than 1% 40-49. **Special facilities:** Heritage and alumni house, NORS-DUC (National Ornamental Research Site at Dominican University of California).

Freshman class profile. 2,178 applied, 1,717 admitted, 255 enrolled.

Mid 50% test scores		GPA 3.0-3.49:	29%
SAT critical reading:	480-560	GPA 2.0-2.99:	13%
SAT math:	470-580	Rank in top quarter:	55%
SAT writing:	470-580	Rank in top tenth:	24%
ACT composite:	21-25	Return as sophomores:	82%
GPA 3.75 or higher:	36%	Out-of-state:	14%
GPA 3.50-3.74:	22%	Live on campus:	92%

Basis for selection. School achievement record, test scores, rigor of secondary school record, character/qualities most important. Interview recommended for borderline applicants. Audition recommended for music majors. Portfolio recommended for art majors. Interview recommended for borderline applicants. Audition recommended for music majors. Portfolio recommended for art majors. **Home schooled:** State high school equivalency certificate required.

High school preparation. College-preparatory program recommended. 11 units required; 18 recommended. Required and recommended units include English 4, mathematics 2-3, social studies 1, history 1-2, science 1-2 (laboratory 1), foreign language 2, computer science 1 and visual/performing arts 1.

2015-2016 Annual costs. Tuition/fees: $42,550. Room/board: $13,940. Books/supplies: $1,746. Personal expenses: $2,296.

2014-2015 Financial aid. **Need-based:** 237 full-time freshmen applied for aid; 213 deemed to have need; 213 received aid. Average need met was 71%. Average scholarship/grant was $24,442; average loan $3,362. 67% of total undergraduate aid awarded as scholarships/grants, 33% as loans/jobs. **Non-need-based:** Awarded to 173 full-time undergraduates, including 58 freshmen. Scholarships awarded for academics, alumni affiliation, athletics, leadership, minority status, music/drama. **Additional information:** 4-year guarantee program.

Application procedures. **Admission:** Priority date 2/1; no deadline. No application fee. Admission notification on a rolling basis beginning on or about 10/15. Must reply by May 1 or within 4 week(s) if notified thereafter. **Financial aid:** Priority date 3/2; no closing date. FAFSA, institutional form required. Applicants notified on a rolling basis starting 3/15; must reply within 2 week(s) of notification.

Academics. **Special study options:** Accelerated study, combined bachelor's/graduate degree, cross-registration, distance learning, double major, dual enrollment of high school students, exchange student, honors, independent study, internships, student-designed major, study abroad, teacher certification program, weekend college. Pathways program (evening/weekend degree program for working adults), semester available at Aquinas College (MI), St. Thomas Aquinas College (NY), Barry University (FL), cross-registration with University of California, Berkeley, (4+1 humanities, occupational therapy, BA - MBA), liberal studies + multiple subject credential. **Credit/placement by examination:** AP, CLEP, IB, SAT, ACT, institutional tests. No more than 30 units from one of the following sources: CLEP/Regents College Exams, ACE/PONSI review courses, experiential learning portfolios. No more than 12 units from challenging courses. No more than 38 units from NLN exams. **Support services:** Learning center, reduced course load, remedial instruction, study skills assistance, tutoring, writing center.

Majors. **Area/ethnic studies:** Women's. **Biology:** General. **Business:** Business admin. **Communications:** Communications/speech/rhetoric. **English:** Creative writing, English lit. **Health services:** Nursing (RN). **History:** General. **Liberal arts:** Arts/sciences, humanities. **Philosophy/religion:** Religion. **Physical sciences:** Chemistry. **Psychology:** General. **Social sciences:** Political science. **Visual/performing arts:** Art, art history/conservation, dance, graphic design, music.

Most popular majors. Biology 12%, business/marketing 17%, health sciences 36%, psychology 8%, social sciences 8%.

Technology on campus. 260 workstations in library, computer center, student center. Dormitories wired for high-speed internet access and linked to campus network. Commuter students can connect to campus network. Helpline, repair service, wireless network available.

Student life. **Freshman orientation:** Available. Preregistration for classes offered. Fall program held week prior to start of classes. **Housing:** Coed dorms available. $500 fully refundable deposit, deadline 5/1. **Activities:** Jazz band, campus ministries, choral groups, dance, drama, international student organizations, literary magazine, music ensembles, radio station, student government, student newspaper, STAND, Dominican Republican Women, ASDU, black student union, Latinos of the Americas, Men's Bible Study, BASIC, Women's Bible Study.

Athletics. NCAA. **Intercollegiate:** Basketball, cross-country M, golf, lacrosse M, soccer, softball W, tennis W, volleyball W. **Intramural:** Cheerleading W. **Team name:** Penguins.

Student services. Adult student services, alcohol/substance abuse counseling, chaplain/spiritual director, career counseling, student employment services, financial aid counseling, health services, personal counseling, veterans' counselor, women's services. **Physically disabled:** Services for visually impaired.

Contact. E-mail: enroll@dominican.edu
Phone: (415) 485-3204 Toll-free number: (888) 323-6763
Fax: (415) 485-3214
Rebecca Finn Kenney, Assistant Vice President Undergraduate
Admissions, Dominican University of California, 50 Acacia Avenue, San Rafael, CA 94901-2298

Ex'pression College
Emeryville, California
www.expression.edu

◆ For-profit 4-year visual arts and technical college
◆ Commuter campus in large town
◆ 445 undergraduates

General. Accredited by ACCSC. The Ex'pression bachelor's degree is accelerated, and may be earned in 2 and a half years. **Degrees:** 147 bachelor's awarded. **Location:** 10 miles from San Francisco. **Calendar:** Semester, extensive summer session. **Full-time faculty:** 48 total. **Part-time faculty:** 58 total. **Special facilities:** 100,000 square foot facility of professional-grade equipment and studios.

Basis for selection. Personal essay, proof of graduation from high school (or an approved equivalent), placement exams in Math and/or English (some exemptions apply), and, if required by the academic program, a portfolio or drawing test. Once an application has been submitted, an entrance interview will be scheduled.

2015-2016 Annual costs. Bachelor's degree programs - $92,429, books and supplies included.

Application procedures. **Admission:** No deadline. $60 fee. **Financial aid:** No deadline.

Academics. **Special study options:** Accelerated study, liberal arts/career combination. **Credit/placement by examination:** AP, CLEP. **Support services:** Pre-admission summer program, study skills assistance, tutoring.

Majors. **Communications technology:** Animation/special effects, graphics, photo/film/video. **Computer sciences:** Computer graphics, modeling/simulation, web page design. **Visual/performing arts:** Cinematography, digital arts, game design, graphic design.

Technology on campus. Student web hosting available.

Student life. **Freshman orientation:** Mandatory. Preregistration for classes offered. Held 2 days before classes begin. **Housing:** Apartments available. **Activities:** Radio station, student government, student newspaper.

Student services. Career counseling, financial aid counseling, personal counseling. **Physically disabled:** Services for hearing impaired.

Contact. E-mail: admissions@expression.edu
Phone: (510) 654-2934 Toll-free number: (877) 833-8800
Tiffany Hartsinck, Director of Admissions, Ex'pression College, 6601 Shellmound Street, Emeryville, CA 94608

Fresno Pacific University
Fresno, California — CB member
www.fresno.edu — CB code: 4616

◆ Private 4-year university and liberal arts college affiliated with the Mennonite Brethren Church
◆ Commuter campus in large city
◆ 2,570 degree-seeking undergraduates
◆ SAT and SAT Subject Tests or ACT (ACT writing optional) required

General. Founded in 1944. Regionally accredited. **Degrees:** 625 bachelor's awarded; master's offered. **Location:** 150 miles from San Francisco. **Calendar:** Semester, limited summer session. **Full-time faculty:** 106 total; 53% have terminal degrees, 13% minority, 43% women. **Part-time faculty:** 19 total; 16% minority, 53% women. **Class size:** 68% < 20, 25% 20-39, 4% 40-49, 3% 50-99. **Special facilities:** Mennonite Brethren studies center, conflict studies and peacemaking center.

Freshman class profile.

GPA 3.75 or higher:	42%	Rank in top quarter:	66%
GPA 3.50-3.74:	18%	Rank in top tenth:	31%
GPA 3.0-3.49:	33%	Out-of-state:	5%
GPA 2.0-2.99:	7%	Live on campus:	66%

Basis for selection. School achievement record and test scores very important, minimum 3.1 high school GPA. Recommendations and autobiography also considered. Interview recommended for academically weak applicants. Auditions for music, English (with drama emphasis) majors.

High school preparation. 13 units required. Required units include English 4, mathematics 3, social studies 2, science 1 (laboratory 1) and foreign language 2. One year of visual or performing arts.

2015-2016 Annual costs. Tuition/fees: $27,854. Room/board: $7,690. Books/supplies: $1,746. Personal expenses: $1,765.

Financial aid. Non-need-based: Scholarships awarded for academics, athletics, leadership, music/drama, religious affiliation.

Application procedures. Admission: Priority date 12/1; deadline 7/31 (postmark date). $40 fee, may be waived for applicants with need. Admission notification on a rolling basis beginning on or about 12/1. **Financial aid:** Closing date 3/2. FAFSA required. Applicants notified on a rolling basis starting 3/2; must reply by 7/30 or within 3 week(s) of notification.

Academics. Special study options: Accelerated study, distance learning, double major, dual enrollment of high school students, ESL, exchange student, independent study, internships, student-designed major, study abroad, teacher certification program, Washington semester. **Credit/placement by examination:** AP, CLEP, IB. 30 credit hours maximum toward associate degree, 30 toward bachelor's. **Support services:** Learning center, pre-admission summer program, reduced course load, remedial instruction, study skills assistance, tutoring, writing center.

Majors. Biology: General. **Business:** General, accounting, business admin, human resources, international, management information systems, marketing, nonprofit/public, organizational behavior. **Communications:** Communications/speech/rhetoric. **Conservation:** Environmental science, environmental studies. **Education:** Biology, business, elementary, English, mathematics, music, physical, science, social science. **English:** Creative writing. **Foreign languages:** Spanish. **Health services:** Athletic training, premedicine. **History:** General. **Human services:** Social work. **Liberal arts:** Arts/sciences. **Math:** General, applied. **Parks/recreation:** Health/fitness, sports admin. **Philosophy/religion:** Philosophy. **Physical sciences:** Chemistry. **Protective services:** Criminalistics. **Psychology:** General. **Social sciences:** General, political science, sociology. **Theology:** Bible. **Visual/performing arts:** Art, dramatic, music, music performance, music theory/composition.

Most popular majors. Business/marketing 26%, education 23%, family/consumer sciences 17%, social sciences 9%.

Technology on campus. 90 workstations in dormitories, library, computer center, student center. Dormitories wired for high-speed internet access and linked to campus network. Commuter students can connect to campus network. Online course registration, online library, helpline, student web hosting, wireless network available.

Student life. Freshman orientation: Mandatory, $25 fee. Preregistration for classes offered. 2-day fall program, 1-day spring. **Housing:** Single-sex dorms, special housing for disabled, apartments, wellness housing available. $200 nonrefundable deposit, deadline 6/1. Several college-rented apartments available nearby. Resident freshmen under age 23 required to live on campus. **Activities:** Bands, campus ministries, choral groups, dance, drama, international student organizations, music ensembles, student government, student newspaper, Amigos Unidos, social work club, Sunbird Conservatives, International Cultural Awareness, Multicultural Scholars, DREAM club, Asian club, Catholic club, missions club, psychology club.

Athletics. NCAA, NCCAA. **Intercollegiate:** Baseball M, basketball, cross-country, soccer, swimming, tennis, track and field, volleyball W, water polo. **Intramural:** Basketball, bowling, football (non-tackle), racquetball, soccer, table tennis, volleyball. **Team name:** Sunbirds.

Student services. Adult student services, alcohol/substance abuse counseling, chaplain/spiritual director, career counseling, student employment services, financial aid counseling, health services, minority student services, personal counseling, placement for graduates, veterans' counselor. **Physically disabled:** Services for visually, hearing impaired.

Contact. E-mail: ugadmis@fresno.edu
Phone: (559) 453-2039 Toll-free number: (800) 660-6089
Fax: (559) 453-2007
Andy Johnson, Director of Undergraduate Admissions, Fresno Pacific University, 1717 South Chestnut Avenue, Fresno, CA 93702-4709

Golden Gate University
San Francisco, California
www.ggu.edu   CB code: 4329

- Private 4-year university
- Commuter campus in very large city
- 435 degree-seeking undergraduates
- 2,292 graduate students

General. Founded in 1853. Regionally accredited. Evening and weekend degree programs available in San Francisco, Silicon Valley, Los Angeles, and Seattle. Program length differs by location. **Degrees:** 136 bachelor's awarded; master's, professional, doctoral offered. **Calendar:** Trimester, extensive summer session. **Full-time faculty:** 71 total; 35% women. **Part-time faculty:** 313 total; 27% women. **Class size:** 96% < 20, 4% 20-39.

Basis for selection. School achievement record most important. Work history or military service factor in determining admission of adult students. SAT recommended. Interviews recommended for undecided major applicants.

High school preparation. 14 units recommended. Recommended units include English 4, mathematics 3, social studies 1, history 1, science 2 (laboratory 1) and foreign language 2.

2015-2016 Annual costs. Tuition/fees: $18,300.

Financial aid. All financial aid based on need.

Application procedures. Admission: Priority date 7/1; no deadline. $55 fee. Admission notification on a rolling basis. Students may be admitted up to 1 year (3 trimesters) before they intend to enroll. **Financial aid:** Priority date 1/2; no closing date. FAFSA, institutional form required. Applicants notified on a rolling basis; must reply within 3 week(s) of notification.

Academics. Professional degree, certification, and lifelong learning programs in business, law, tax, technology and related professions. **Special study options:** Accelerated study, distance learning, ESL, independent study, internships, study abroad. **Credit/placement by examination:** AP, CLEP, IB, institutional tests. **Support services:** Reduced course load, tutoring, writing center.

Majors. Business: Accounting, business admin, finance, human resources, information resources management, international, marketing, operations. **Computer sciences:** Information technology.

Technology on campus. 300 workstations in library, computer center. Commuter students can connect to campus network. Online course registration, online library, wireless network available.

Student life. Activities: Student government, student newspaper, Phi Alpha Delta law fraternity, Chi Pi Alpha, Indonesian students organization, Malayan students association, Chinese students club, Indian student association, Korean student association, American Marketing Association, Toastmasters.

Student services. Adult student services, career counseling, student employment services, personal counseling, veterans' counselor. **Physically disabled:** Services for visually, speech, hearing impaired.

Contact. E-mail: info@ggu.edu
Phone: (415) 442-7800 Fax: (415) 442-7807
Louis Riccardi, Director of Enrollment Services, Golden Gate University, 536 Mission Street, San Francisco, CA 94105-2968

Harvey Mudd College
Claremont, California   CB member
https://www.hmc.edu/admission/   CB code: 4341

- Private 4-year engineering and liberal arts college
- Residential campus in small city
- 812 degree-seeking undergraduates: 47% women, 2% African American, 20% Asian American, 13% Hispanic/Latino, 8% Multi-racial, non-Hispanic, 13% international
- 13% of applicants admitted
- SAT or ACT (ACT writing optional), SAT Subject Tests, application essay required
- 92% graduate within 6 years

General. Founded in 1955. Regionally accredited. Member of consortium of 5 undergraduate and 2 graduate schools on adjoining campuses. Campuses share facilities and cross enrollment is available within the 5 undergraduate colleges, which include Claremont McKenna, Harvey Mudd, Pitzer, Pomona, and Scripps Colleges. **Degrees:** 184 bachelor's awarded. **ROTC:** Army, Air Force. **Location:** 33 miles from Los Angeles. **Calendar:** Semester, limited summer session. **Full-time faculty:** 101 total; 100% have terminal degrees, 27% minority, 40% women. **Part-time faculty:** 13 total; 100% have terminal degrees, 31% minority, 62% women. **Class size:** 59% < 20, 28% 20-39, 3% 40-49, 5% 50-99, 4% >100. **Special facilities:** Observatory, biological field station, high performance parallel processor.

Freshman class profile. 4,119 applied, 534 admitted, 214 enrolled.

Mid 50% test scores		Rank in top tenth:	93%
SAT critical reading:	670-760	Return as sophomores:	96%
SAT math:	730-800	Out-of-state:	48%
SAT writing:	680-760	Live on campus:	100%
ACT composite:	33-35	International:	12%
Rank in top quarter:	98%		

Basis for selection. School record, academic grades, recommendations, essays are most important, test scores, and class rank. Test scores for SAT or ACT, Math 2 subject test, an additional subject test of their choice required for all first year applicants. An additional essay and short answer response required as part of Common Application. Interviews highly recommended, but not required for application and/or admission.

High school preparation. College-preparatory program required. Required and recommended units include English 4, mathematics 4, social studies 2, history 1-2, science 3-4 (laboratory 2), foreign language 2 and academic electives 2. 1 year of Calculus, 1 year of Chemistry, 1 year of Physics are required.

2016-2017 Annual costs. Tuition/fees (projected): $50,749. Room/board: $16,506. Books/supplies: $800. Personal expenses: $1,400.

2014-2015 Financial aid. Need-based: 134 full-time freshmen applied for aid; 103 deemed to have need; 103 received aid. Average need met was 100%. Average scholarship/grant was $41,635; average loan $3,742. 85% of total undergraduate aid awarded as scholarships/grants, 15% as loans/jobs. **Non-need-based:** Awarded to 237 full-time undergraduates, including 62 freshmen. Scholarships awarded for academics. **Additional information:** Students can use 100% of their outside awards toward first reducing the need-based portion of their student loans and/or Federal Work Study award. Once need-based student loans and/or Federal Work Study award have been completely eliminated, any additional outside scholarships may reduce need-based Harvey Mudd Scholarship only. However, to maximize financial aid eligibility, students may retain need-based student loans and/or Federal Work Study award up to their federal need.

Application procedures. Admission: Closing date 1/5 (postmark date). $70 fee, may be waived for applicants with need. Application must be submitted online. Admission notification by 4/1. Must reply by May 1 or within 2 week(s) if notified thereafter. **Financial aid:** Priority date 2/1, closing date 2/1. FAFSA, CSS PROFILE required. Applicants notified by 4/1; must reply by 5/1 or within 2 week(s) of notification.

Academics. Course work is divided equally between a technical core, major, and humanities, social sciences, and arts. **Special study options:** Cross-registration, double major, dual enrollment of high school students, exchange student, independent study, internships, student-designed major, study abroad. Innovative client-sponsored design projects (Clinic Program). **Credit/placement by examination:** AP, CLEP, institutional tests. **Support services:** Learning center, reduced course load, study skills assistance, tutoring, writing center.

Majors. Biology: General. **Computer sciences:** Computer science. **Engineering:** General. **Math:** General. **Physical sciences:** Chemistry, physics.

Most popular majors. Biology 6%, computer/information sciences 30%, engineering/engineering technologies 29%, interdisciplinary studies 15%, mathematics 6%, physical sciences 12%.

Technology on campus. Dormitories wired for high-speed internet access and linked to campus network. Commuter students can connect to campus network. Online course registration, online library, helpline, repair service, student web hosting, wireless network available.

Student life. Freshman orientation: Mandatory. Preregistration for classes offered. Six-day student-led program immediately before the fall semester. **Policies:** Student-directed honor code governs academic and non-academic life on campus. Freshmen not permitted cars on campus. **Housing:** Guaranteed on-campus for freshmen. Coed dorms, apartments, gender-neutral housing available. $150 partly refundable deposit, deadline 5/1. Pets allowed in dorm rooms. **Activities:** Bands, campus ministries, choral groups, dance, drama, international student organizations, literary magazine, music ensembles, radio station, student government, student newspaper, symphony orchestra, Society of Women Engineers (SWE), Asian Pacific Islander Support Program at Mudd (API SPAM), Black Lives and Allies at Mudd (BLAM), Society of Professional Latinos in STEMS (SPLS), Exploring Pan-Asian

Identity and Culture (EPAIC), PRISM, 3-C Intervarsity Christian Fellowship, Hillel, 5C Muslim Student Association, Mudders Making A Difference.

Athletics. NCAA. **Intercollegiate:** Baseball M, basketball, cross-country, diving, football (tackle) M, golf, lacrosse W, soccer, softball W, swimming, tennis, track and field, volleyball W, water polo. **Intramural:** Basketball, bowling, football (non-tackle), soccer, volleyball, water polo.

Student services. Alcohol/substance abuse counseling, chaplain/spiritual director, career counseling, student employment services, financial aid counseling, health services, minority student services, personal counseling, placement for graduates, women's services.

Contact. E-mail: admission@hmc.edu
Phone: (909) 621-8011 Fax: (909) 607-7046
Peter Osgood, Director of Admission, Harvey Mudd College, 301 Platt Boulevard, Claremont, CA 91711-5901

Holy Names University
Oakland, California
www.hnu.edu

CB member
CB code: 4059

▶ Private 4-year university affiliated with the Roman Catholic Church
▶ Commuter campus in large city
▶ 624 degree-seeking undergraduates: 17% part-time, 64% women, 18% African American, 13% Asian American, 37% Hispanic/Latino, 3% Native Hawaiian/Pacific islander, 2% Multi-racial, non-Hispanic, 4% international
▶ 393 degree-seeking graduate students
▶ 44% of applicants admitted
▶ SAT or ACT (ACT writing optional), application essay required
▶ 40% graduate within 6 years

General. Founded in 1868. Regionally accredited. **Degrees:** 184 bachelor's awarded; master's offered. **ROTC:** Army, Air Force. **Location:** 14 miles from San Francisco. **Calendar:** Semester, limited summer session. **Full-time faculty:** 47 total; 83% have terminal degrees, 19% minority, 26% women. **Part-time faculty:** 148 total; 22% minority, 74% women. **Class size:** 75% < 20, 25% 20-39. **Special facilities:** Folk music collection, institute for learning disabled.

Freshman class profile. 854 applied, 375 admitted, 119 enrolled.

Mid 50% test scores		GPA 3.0-3.49:	42%
SAT critical reading:	390-470	GPA 2.0-2.99:	32%
SAT math:	380-470	Return as sophomores:	68%
SAT writing:	390-460	Out-of-state:	9%
ACT composite:	15-21	Live on campus:	63%
GPA 3.75 or higher:	11%	International:	2%
GPA 3.50-3.74:	15%		

Basis for selection. Overall strength of high school preparation, SAT or ACT scores, personal essay, letter of recommendation, extracurricular activities and individual talents and achievements. For non-native English speakers, ESL Center proficiency report certifying completion of Level 107 or higher may be substituted for TOEFL. Proficiency exams in theory, sight-singing, dictation and piano are required of all students entering the music program. Exams offered during week prior to beginning of each semester. Music major applicant must also audition for faculty jury. **Home schooled:** Transcript of courses and grades, letter of recommendation (nonparent) required. Transcript demonstrating completion of basic credit hours for high school along with short evaluation from primary instructor. May require additional portfolio or performance-based assessments to document competency.

High school preparation. College-preparatory program recommended. 15 units required. Required and recommended units include English 4, mathematics 3, history 1-2, science 1-2 (laboratory 1), foreign language 2-3 and academic electives 3. U.S. history or government required, plus 1 additional year of math, foreign language, or lab science.

2015-2016 Annual costs. Tuition/fees: $35,666. Room/board: $12,072. Books/supplies: $1,764. Personal expenses: $2,322.

Financial aid. Non-need-based: Scholarships awarded for academics, athletics, leadership, music/drama, religious affiliation, state residency.

Application procedures. Admission: Priority date 3/2; deadline 8/15 (postmark date). $20 fee, may be waived for applicants with need. Admission notification on a rolling basis beginning on or about 10/1. Must reply by May 1 or within 2 week(s) if notified thereafter. **Financial aid:** Priority date 3/2; no closing date. FAFSA required. Applicants notified on a rolling basis starting 9/1; must reply by 8/26 or within 2 week(s) of notification.

Academics. All undergraduate students must satisfy general education requirements. First component is Foundation in Critical Thinking and Communication. Remaining components use thematic and disciplinary approaches to learning. **Special study options:** Accelerated study, combined bachelor's/graduate degree, cross-registration, distance learning, double major, ESL, exchange student, independent study, internships, liberal arts/career combination, student-designed major, study abroad, teacher certification program, weekend college. **Credit/placement by examination:** AP, CLEP, IB, institutional tests. 6 credit hours maximum toward bachelor's degree. Maximum of 6 credit hours per general exam awarded. **Support services:** Learning center, reduced course load, remedial instruction, study skills assistance, tutoring, writing center.

Majors. Biology: General. **Business:** Accounting, business admin, communications, human resources, international, marketing. **Communications:** Digital media. **English:** English lit. **Foreign languages:** Spanish. **Health services:** Nursing (RN). **History:** General. **Liberal arts:** Arts/sciences, humanities. **Parks/recreation:** Sports admin. **Philosophy/religion:** Philosophy, religion. **Psychology:** General, psychobiology. **Social sciences:** Criminology, international relations, sociology. **Visual/performing arts:** Music, music pedagogy, music performance.

Most popular majors. Business/marketing 15%, health sciences 31%, liberal arts 6%, parks/recreation 9%, psychology 12%, social sciences 11%.

Technology on campus. 100 workstations in dormitories, library, computer center, student center, student center. Dormitories wired for high-speed internet access and linked to campus network. Commuter students can connect to campus network. Online course registration, online library, helpline, wireless network available.

Student life. Freshman orientation: Mandatory. Preregistration for classes offered. 2-3 day weekend event prior to start of term. **Housing:** Guaranteed on-campus for freshmen. Coed dorms, themed housing, wellness housing available. $100 fully refundable deposit, deadline 8/18. **Activities:** Campus ministries, choral groups, drama, film society, music ensembles, Model UN, student government, student newspaper, symphony orchestra, Asian Pacific International, Black Student Union, drama club, speech and debate team, Holy Names Construction, Global Outlook, International Village, Latinos Unidos, social justice club.

Athletics. NCAA. **Intercollegiate:** Baseball M, basketball, cross-country, golf, soccer, softball W, tennis, volleyball. **Team name:** Hawks.

Student services. Adult student services, chaplain/spiritual director, career counseling, student employment services, financial aid counseling, personal counseling. **Physically disabled:** Services for visually impaired.

Contact. E-mail: admission@hnu.edu
Phone: (510) 436-1351 Toll-free number: (800) 430-1321
Fax: (510) 436-1325
Jose Rocha, Associate Dean of Admissions, Holy Names University, 3500 Mountain Boulevard, Oakland, CA 94619-1699

Hope International University
Fullerton, California
www.hiu.edu   CB code: 4614

- Private 4-year university and liberal arts college affiliated with the Christian Church
- Residential campus in small city
- 843 degree-seeking undergraduates: 25% part-time, 54% women, 7% African American, 3% Asian American, 21% Hispanic/Latino, 1% Native American, 1% Native Hawaiian/Pacific islander, 11% Multiracial, non-Hispanic
- 411 degree-seeking graduate students
- 34% of applicants admitted
- SAT or ACT (ACT writing optional), application essay required
- 42% graduate within 6 years

General. Founded in 1928. Regionally accredited; also accredited by ABHE. Extension site in Everett, Washington and over 200 classes offered online. **Degrees:** 156 bachelor's, 12 associate awarded; master's offered. **ROTC:** Army. **Location:** 35 miles from Los Angeles. **Calendar:** 4-1-4, limited summer session. **Full-time faculty:** 42 total; 74% have terminal degrees, 14% minority, 45% women. **Part-time faculty:** 210 total; 26% have terminal degrees, 26% minority, 39% women.

Freshman class profile. 1,051 applied, 360 admitted, 124 enrolled.

Mid 50% test scores			
SAT critical reading:	390-510	GPA 3.0-3.49:	30%
SAT math:	400-520	GPA 2.0-2.99:	42%
SAT writing:	410-510	Rank in top quarter:	36%
ACT composite:	16-22	Rank in top tenth:	12%
GPA 3.75 or higher:	14%	Return as sophomores:	78%
GPA 3.50-3.74:	12%	Live on campus:	58%

Basis for selection. Prior academic achievement, standardized test scores, statement of purpose essays, commitment to the mission of the institution and recommendations are important. Extracurricular activities are also considered along with all other factors bearing on potential success. Interviews recommended for academically borderline applicants. **Home schooled:** If schooled under the auspices of an organization that can offer transcripts, the university will accept these transcripts and SAT/ACT scores. If not, a GED score and SAT/ACT scores are required. **Learning Disabled:** All documentation must be recent, within the past three years of enrollment, and must have been completed by an appropriate professional, e.g., State licensed psychologist or school psychologist. Documentation shall include both appropriate tests of learning abilities as well as interview material.

High school preparation. College-preparatory program recommended. 14 units recommended. Recommended units include English 4, mathematics 3, history 3, science 2 (laboratory 2) and foreign language 2. One half-unit speech and one half-unit computer science or literacy is recommended.

2015-2016 Annual costs. Tuition/fees: $28,550. Room/board: $9,050. Books/supplies: $1,764. Personal expenses: $3,159.

2014-2015 Financial aid. Need-based: 78 full-time freshmen applied for aid; 72 deemed to have need; 72 received aid. Average need met was 42%. Average scholarship/grant was $15,468; average loan $3,372. 53% of total undergraduate aid awarded as scholarships/grants, 47% as loans/jobs. **Non-need-based:** Awarded to 377 full-time undergraduates, including 98 freshmen. Scholarships awarded for academics, athletics, leadership, music/drama.

Application procedures. Admission: Priority date 12/1; deadline 7/1. $40 fee, may be waived for applicants with need. Admission notification on a rolling basis. Must reply by May 1 or within 2 week(s) if notified thereafter. **Financial aid:** Priority date 3/2; no closing date. FAFSA, institutional form required. Applicants notified on a rolling basis starting 2/15; must reply within 2 week(s) of notification.

Academics. Emphasis on field-based interactive learning combined with direct professional involvement with students. **Special study options:** Combined bachelor's/graduate degree, distance learning, ESL, independent study, internships, liberal arts/career combination, study abroad, teacher certification program, urban semester, Washington semester. Contract program option available in collaboration with Cal State University, Fullerton. **Credit/placement by examination:** AP, CLEP, IB, institutional tests. The amount of credit for examinations depends upon the applicability of the exam(s) to the specific degree program requirements. **Support services:** Reduced course load, remedial instruction, study skills assistance, tutoring.

Majors. Business: Business admin. **Education:** Elementary, music, social science. **English:** English lit. **Psychology:** General. **Social sciences:** General. **Theology:** Bible, missionary, sacred music, theology, youth ministry. **Work/family studies:** Family studies.

Most popular majors. Business/marketing 20%, education 10%, family/consumer sciences 13%, liberal arts 7%, psychology 13%, social sciences 8%, theological studies 25%.

Technology on campus. 53 workstations in library, computer center. Dormitories wired for high-speed internet access. Online library, helpline, repair service, wireless network available.

Student life. Freshman orientation: Mandatory, $75 fee. Preregistration for classes offered. Held 3 days before beginning of term. **Policies:** Single students required to live on campus until age 21 or reaching junior standing, unless living at home or given special approval. No alcohol permitted, smoking discouraged. Religious observance required. **Housing:** Guaranteed on-campus for freshmen. Single-sex dorms, wellness housing available. $325 partly refundable deposit, deadline 7/1. **Activities:** Jazz band, campus ministries, choral groups, international student organizations, music ensembles, Model UN, musical theater, student government, student newspaper, school outreach, minority students association, business club.

Athletics. NAIA, NCCAA. **Intercollegiate:** Baseball M, basketball, cheerleading, cross-country, golf, soccer, softball W, tennis, track and field, volleyball. **Intramural:** Basketball, football (non-tackle), soccer, volleyball. **Team name:** Royals.

Student services. Adult student services, chaplain/spiritual director, career counseling, student employment services, financial aid counseling, health services, personal counseling, veterans' counselor.

Contact. E-mail: hiuadmissions@hiu.edu
Phone: (714) 879-3901 ext. 2213 Toll-free number: (866) 722-4673
Fax: (714) 681-7224
Dionne Gutierrez, Director of Traditional Undergraduate Admissions,
Hope International University, 2500 East Nutwood Avenue, Fullerton, CA
92831-3199

Horizon University
San Diego, California
www.horizonuniversity.edu

◗ Private 4-year Bible and liberal arts college affiliated with the nondenominational tradition
◗ Commuter campus in very large city
◗ 48 degree-seeking undergraduates

General. Regionally accredited; also accredited by ABHE. Christ-centered instruction. ADA approved single-story campus. **Degrees:** 7 bachelor's, 1 associate awarded. **Calendar:** Semester, limited summer session. **Part-time faculty:** 11 total; 73% have terminal degrees, 36% minority, 18% women.

Basis for selection. Open admission, but selective for some programs.

2015-2016 Annual costs. Books/supplies: $500.

Application procedures. Admission: $100 fee.

Academics. Special study options: Distance learning. **Credit/placement by examination:** AP, CLEP.

Majors. Theology: Bible.

Technology on campus. 2 workstations in library. Wireless network available.

Student life. Freshman orientation: Mandatory. Preregistration for classes offered. **Policies:** Religious observance required. **Activities:** Campus ministries.

Student services. Financial aid counseling, personal counseling.

Contact. E-mail: info@horizoncollege.org
Phone: (858) 695-8587 Fax: (858) 695-9527
Horizon University, 5331 Mount Alifan Drive, San Diego, CA 92111

Humboldt State University
Arcata, California
www.humboldt.edu
CB member
CB code: 4345

◗ Public 4-year university and liberal arts college
◗ Residential campus in large town
◗ 8,210 degree-seeking undergraduates: 6% part-time, 56% women, 4% African American, 3% Asian American, 33% Hispanic/Latino, 1% Native American, 7% Multi-racial, non-Hispanic, 2% international
◗ 540 degree-seeking graduate students
◗ 75% of applicants admitted
◗ 46% graduate within 6 years

General. Founded in 1913. Regionally accredited. **Degrees:** 1,934 bachelor's awarded; master's offered. **Location:** 275 miles from San Francisco. **Calendar:** Semester, limited summer session. **Full-time faculty:** 226 total; 99% have terminal degrees, 16% minority, 44% women. **Part-time faculty:** 340 total; 24% have terminal degrees, 15% minority, 59% women. **Class size:** 27% < 20, 49% 20-39, 10% 40-49, 10% 50-99, 4% >100. **Special facilities:** Marine lab, observatory, marsh and wildlife sanctuary, small lakes and ponds, 280-acre sand dune preserve, research vessel, freshwater fish hatchery, small-game animal pen, fungal genetic stock center, 360-acre experimental forest, 170,000 specimen herbarium, center for appropriate technology, energy research center.

Freshman class profile. 13,017 applied, 9,765 admitted, 1,420 enrolled.

Mid 50% test scores			
SAT critical reading:	440-560	Rank in top quarter:	46%
SAT math:	430-550	Rank in top tenth:	13%
SAT writing:	430-540	End year in good standing:	86%
ACT composite:	18-24	Return as sophomores:	75%
GPA 3.75 or higher:	12%	Out-of-state:	7%
GPA 3.50-3.74:	14%	Live on campus:	88%
GPA 3.0-3.49:	49%	International:	1%
GPA 2.0-2.99:	25%	Fraternities:	1%
		Sororities:	1%

Basis for selection. State residency, high school GPA and test scores most important. In-state residents with high school GPA of 3.0 or higher or out-of-state applicants with high school GPA over 3.61 do not have to submit test scores for admission. Essay recommended for academically weak, special consideration applicants. **Home schooled:** Transcript of courses and grades required.

High school preparation. College-preparatory program required. 15 units required. Required units include English 4, mathematics 3, social studies 1, history 1, science 2 (laboratory 2), foreign language 2, visual/performing arts 1 and academic electives 1.

2015-2016 Annual costs. Tuition/fees: $7,196; $18,356 out-of-state. Room/board: $12,380. Books/supplies: $1,628. Personal expenses: $1,378.

2014-2015 Financial aid. Need-based: 1,248 full-time freshmen applied for aid; 1,038 deemed to have need; 1,004 received aid. Average need met was 71%. Average scholarship/grant was $9,236; average loan $5,580. 63% of total undergraduate aid awarded as scholarships/grants, 37% as loans/jobs. **Non-need-based:** Awarded to 288 full-time undergraduates, including 74 freshmen. Scholarships awarded for academics, alumni affiliation, athletics, minority status, state residency.

Application procedures. Admission: Priority date 10/31; deadline 11/30 (postmark date). $55 fee, may be waived for applicants with need. Admission notification on a rolling basis beginning on or about 12/1. Must reply by 5/1. **Financial aid:** Priority date 3/1; no closing date. FAFSA required. Applicants notified on a rolling basis starting 4/1; must reply within 4 week(s) of notification.

Academics. Special study options: Combined bachelor's/graduate degree, cross-registration, distance learning, double major, dual enrollment of high school students, ESL, exchange student, independent study, internships, liberal arts/career combination, study abroad, teacher certification program. **Credit/placement by examination:** AP, CLEP, IB, SAT, ACT, institutional tests. 30 credit hours maximum toward bachelor's degree. Humboldt grants undergraduate degree credit for successful completion of non-collegiate instruction, either military or civilian, appropriate to the baccalaureate degree. Credit must be recommended by the Commission on Educational Credit and Credentials of the American Council on Education. **Support services:** Learning center, pre-admission summer program, reduced course load, remedial instruction, study skills assistance, tutoring, writing center.

Majors. Area/ethnic studies: Native American, women's. **Biology:** General, botany, zoology. **Business:** General, business admin. **Communications:** Communications/speech/rhetoric, journalism. **Computer sciences:** Computer science. **Conservation:** Environmental studies, fisheries, forestry, wildlife/wilderness. **Education:** Early childhood, elementary, physical. **Engineering:** Environmental. **English:** English lit, writing. **Foreign languages:** French, Spanish. **Health services:** Kinesiotherapy. **History:** General. **Human services:** Social work. **Liberal arts:** Arts/sciences. **Math:** General. **Parks/recreation:** Health/fitness. **Philosophy/religion:** Philosophy, religion. **Physical sciences:** Chemistry, geology, oceanography, physics. **Psychology:** General. **Social sciences:** General, anthropology, economics, geography, political science, sociology. **Visual/performing arts:** Art, dance, dramatic, music.

Most popular majors. Biology 10%, business/marketing 8%, liberal arts 7%, natural resources/environmental science 15%, psychology 7%, social sciences 10%, visual/performing arts 9%.

Technology on campus. 1,098 workstations in dormitories, library, computer center, student center. Dormitories wired for high-speed internet access and linked to campus network. Commuter students can connect to campus network. Online course registration, online library, helpline, student web hosting, wireless network available.

Student life. Freshman orientation: Mandatory, $50 fee. Preregistration for classes offered. Student-directed program held in August. **Housing:** Coed dorms, single-sex dorms, themed housing, wellness housing available. $500 partly refundable deposit, deadline 4/16. Academic Intensive, The Art Colony, Eco Living, gender neutral, veterans housing available. **Activities:** Bands, campus ministries, choral groups, dance, drama, film society, international student organizations, literary magazine, music ensembles, Model UN, musical theater, radio station, student government, student newspaper, symphony orchestra, Newman Club, Campus Crusade for Christ, Youth Educational Services, black student union, MECHA, Gay, Lesbian and Bisexual Students Association, Native American club, Jewish student union, multicultural center, veterans organization.

Athletics. NCAA. **Intercollegiate:** Basketball, cross-country, football (tackle) M, rowing (crew) W, soccer, softball W, track and field, volleyball W. **Intramural:** Badminton, basketball, football (tackle) M, soccer, softball, volleyball. **Team name:** Lumberjacks.

Student services. Adult student services, alcohol/substance abuse counseling, career counseling, student employment services, financial aid counseling, health services, minority student services, on-campus daycare, personal counseling, placement for graduates, veterans' counselor, women's services. **Physically disabled:** Services for visually, speech, hearing impaired.

Contact. E-mail: hsuinfo@humboldt.edu
Phone: (707) 826-4402 Toll-free number: (866) 850-9556
Fax: (707) 826-6190
Steve Ladwig, Director of Admissions, Humboldt State University, One Harpst Street, Arcata, CA 95521-8299

Humphreys College
Stockton, California
www.humphreys.edu
CB code: 4346

- Private 4-year business, liberal arts and teachers college
- Residential campus in large city
- 617 degree-seeking undergraduates
- Interview required

General. Founded in 1896. Regionally accredited. **Degrees:** 171 bachelor's, 49 associate awarded; master's, professional offered. **Location:** 35 miles from Sacramento, California. **Calendar:** Quarter, extensive summer session. **Full-time faculty:** 69 total. **Part-time faculty:** 121 total. **Class size:** 80% < 20, 20% 20-39.

Freshman class profile.

Out-of-state: 3% **Live on campus:**   25%

Basis for selection. High school diploma or GED required. ACT used for placement only. **Home schooled:** State high school equivalency certificate required.

2015-2016 Annual costs. Tuition/fees: $13,212. Books/supplies: $1,764. Personal expenses: $3,159.

Financial aid. Non-need-based: Scholarships awarded for academics.

Application procedures. Admission: No deadline. $40 fee, may be waived for applicants with need. Application must be submitted on paper. Admission notification on a rolling basis. **Financial aid:** No deadline. FAFSA required. Applicants notified on a rolling basis starting 8/15; must reply within 2 week(s) of notification.

Academics. Special study options: Combined bachelor's/graduate degree, cooperative education, cross-registration, double major, honors, independent study, internships. **Credit/placement by examination:** AP, CLEP, IB, institutional tests. 4 credit hours maximum toward associate degree, 45 toward bachelor's. **Support services:** Learning center, pre-admission summer program, remedial instruction, tutoring, writing center.

Majors. Business: General, accounting, administrative services, business admin, office technology, office/clerical. **Computer sciences:** General. **Education:** General. **Health services:** Medical secretary. **Human services:** Community org/advocacy. **Liberal arts:** Arts/sciences. **Social sciences:** General.

Technology on campus. 25 workstations in library, computer center. Online library, helpline, wireless network available.

Student life. Freshman orientation: Available. Preregistration for classes offered. Held on campus the first week of each academic term. **Housing:** Apartments available. $200 partly refundable deposit, deadline 8/20. **Activities:** Student government, student newspaper, business club.

Student services. Career counseling, student employment services, financial aid counseling, on-campus daycare, personal counseling, placement for graduates, veterans' counselor.

Contact. E-mail: ugadmission@humphreys.edu
Phone: (209) 478-0800 Fax: (209) 478-8721
Santa Lopez-Minarte, Admissions Director, Humphreys College, 6650 Inglewood Avenue, Stockton, CA 95207-3896

Interior Designers Institute
Newport Beach, California
www.idi.edu
CB code: 2318

- For-profit 4-year visual arts college
- Commuter campus in large city
- 202 degree-seeking undergraduates

General. Accredited by ACCSC. **Degrees:** 23 bachelor's, 45 associate awarded; master's offered. **Calendar:** Quarter. **Part-time faculty:** 30 total.

Basis for selection. Open admission.

2015-2016 Annual costs. Books/supplies: $1,500. **Additional information:** 12-week certificate program: $2,200. 2-year associate degree program: $35,900. Bachelor's degree program: $19,950. Tuition does not include $95 Registration Fee.

Application procedures. Admission: No deadline. $95 fee. Application must be submitted on paper.

Academics. Credit/placement by examination: AP, CLEP.

Majors. Visual/performing arts: Interior design.

Contact. E-mail: contact@idi.edu
Phone: (949) 675-4451 Fax: (949) 759-0667
Interior Designers Institute, 1061 Camelback Road, Newport Beach, CA 92660-3228

International Academy of Design and Technology: Sacramento
Sacramento, California
www.iadtsacramento.com

- For-profit 4-year technical and career college
- Commuter campus in very large city
- 60 undergraduates
- Application essay, interview required

General. Regionally accredited; also accredited by ACICS. Small classes offered. **Degrees:** 31 bachelor's, 16 associate awarded. **Calendar:** Quarter, extensive summer session. **Full-time faculty:** 4 total; 50% minority, 50% women. **Part-time faculty:** 28 total; 18% have terminal degrees, 14% minority, 64% women. **Class size:** 94% < 20, 6% 20-39.

Basis for selection. Open admission. Wonderlic entrance exam required.

2015-2016 Annual costs. Personal expenses: $335. **Additional information:** Associate programs: $32,800. Bachelor's programs: $64,800.

Application procedures. Admission: No deadline. $50 fee. Admission notification on a rolling basis. **Financial aid:** No deadline. FAFSA required.

Academics. Special study options: Distance learning, independent study, internships, study abroad. **Credit/placement by examination:** AP, CLEP. **Support services:** Learning center, reduced course load, remedial instruction, study skills assistance, tutoring, writing center.

Majors. Visual/performing arts: Fashion design, interior design.

Student life. Freshman orientation: Mandatory. Preregistration for classes offered. **Activities:** Student government.

Student services. Adult student services, career counseling, services for economically disadvantaged, student employment services, financial aid counseling, placement for graduates.

Contact. Phone: (916) 285-9468 Fax: (916) 285-6986
Sherwyn Flores, Director of Admissions, International Academy of Design and Technology: Sacramento, 2450 Del Paso Road, Sacramento, CA 95834

ITT Technical Institute: Lathrop
Lathrop, California
www.itt-tech.edu
CB code: 2720

- For-profit 4-year technical college
- Commuter campus in small town
- 471 undergraduates
- Interview required

General. Accredited by ACICS. **Degrees:** 52 bachelor's, 125 associate awarded. **Calendar:** Quarter, extensive summer session. **Full-time faculty:** 13 total. **Part-time faculty:** 49 total.

Basis for selection. Satisfactory scores from on-site tests in English and mathematics required.

2015-2016 Annual costs. Per-credit-hour charge, $493, will vary depending on program level and course of study. Academic fee, $200. Some programs require purchase of tools, which could cost an additional $500. All costs subject to change.

Application procedures. Admission: No deadline. No application fee. Admission notification on a rolling basis. **Financial aid:** No deadline. FAFSA, institutional form required. Applicants notified on a rolling basis.

Academics. Credit/placement by examination: AP, CLEP. **Support services:** Learning center, tutoring.

Majors. Business: Business admin, construction management, project management. **Communications technology:** Animation/special effects. **Computer sciences:** Security, system admin. **Protective services:** Law enforcement admin.

Technology on campus. Online library available.

Student life. Freshman orientation: Available. Preregistration for classes offered.

Student services. Career counseling, student employment services, placement for graduates.

Contact. Phone: (209) 858-0077 Toll-free number: (800) 346-1786 Kathy Paradis, Director of Recruitment, ITT Technical Institute: Lathrop, 16916 South Harlan Road, Lathrop, CA 95330

ITT Technical Institute: National City
National City, California
www.itt-tech.edu   CB code: 0206

- For-profit 4-year technical college
- Commuter campus in very large city
- 999 undergraduates
- Interview required

General. Founded in 1981. Accredited by ACICS. **Degrees:** 111 bachelor's, 309 associate awarded. **Calendar:** Quarter, extensive summer session. **Full-time faculty:** 15 total. **Part-time faculty:** 94 total.

Basis for selection. Satisfactory scores from on-site English and mathematics tests required.

2015-2016 Annual costs. Per-credit-hour charge, $493, will vary depending on program level and course of study. Academic fee, $200. Some programs require purchase of tools, which could cost an additional $500. All costs subject to change.

Application procedures. Admission: No deadline. No application fee. Admission notification on a rolling basis. **Financial aid:** No deadline. FAFSA, institutional form required. Applicants notified on a rolling basis.

Academics. Credit/placement by examination: AP, CLEP. **Support services:** Learning center, tutoring.

Majors. Business: Business admin, construction management, project management. **Communications technology:** Animation/special effects. **Computer sciences:** Security. **Protective services:** Law enforcement admin.

Technology on campus. Online library available.

Student life. Freshman orientation: Available. Preregistration for classes offered.

Student services. Career counseling, student employment services, placement for graduates.

Contact. Phone: (858) 571-8500 Toll-free number: (800) 883-0380 Robert Dutton, Director of Recruitment, ITT Technical Institute: National City, 401 Mile of Cars Way, National City, CA 91950

ITT Technical Institute: Oxnard
Oxnard, California
www.itt-tech.edu   CB code: 2744

- For-profit 4-year technical college
- Commuter campus in small city
- 291 undergraduates
- Interview required

General. Accredited by ACICS. **Degrees:** 30 bachelor's, 48 associate awarded. **Location:** 34 miles from Santa Barbara, 52 miles from Los Angeles. **Calendar:** Quarter, extensive summer session. **Full-time faculty:** 11 total. **Part-time faculty:** 30 total.

Basis for selection. Satisfactory scores from on-site tests in English and mathematics required.

2015-2016 Annual costs. Per-credit-hour charge, $493, will vary depending on program level and course of study. Academic fee, $200. Some programs require purchase of tools, which could cost an additional $500. All costs subject to change.

Application procedures. Admission: No deadline. No application fee. Admission notification on a rolling basis. **Financial aid:** No deadline. FAFSA, institutional form required. Applicants notified on a rolling basis.

Academics. Credit/placement by examination: AP, CLEP. **Support services:** Learning center, tutoring.

Majors. Business: Business admin, construction management, e-commerce, project management. **Communications technology:** Animation/special effects. **Computer sciences:** Security. **Protective services:** Law enforcement admin.

Technology on campus. Online library available.

Student life. Freshman orientation: Available. Preregistration for classes offered.

Student services. Career counseling, student employment services, placement for graduates.

Contact. Phone: (805) 988-0143 Toll-free number: (800) 530-1582 Claudia Wilroy, Director of Recruitment, ITT Technical Institute: Oxnard, 2051 Solar Drive, Suite 150, Oxnard, CA 93036

ITT Technical Institute: Rancho Cordova
Rancho Cordova, California
www.itt-tech.edu   CB code: 3597

- For-profit 4-year technical college
- Commuter campus in large city
- 500 undergraduates
- Interview required

General. Founded in 1954. Accredited by ACICS. **Degrees:** 53 bachelor's, 147 associate awarded. **Location:** 11 miles from Sacramento, 87 miles from San Francisco. **Calendar:** Quarter, extensive summer session. **Full-time faculty:** 14 total. **Part-time faculty:** 61 total.

Basis for selection. Satisfactory scores from on-site tests in English and mathematics required.

2015-2016 Annual costs. Per-credit-hour charge, $518, will vary depending on program level and course of study. Academic fee, $200. Some programs require purchase of tools, which could cost an additional $500 to $655. All costs subject to change.

Application procedures. Admission: No deadline. No application fee. Admission notification on a rolling basis. **Financial aid:** No deadline. FAFSA, institutional form required. Applicants notified on a rolling basis.

Academics. Credit/placement by examination: AP, CLEP. **Support services:** Learning center, tutoring.

Majors. Business: Business admin, construction management, project management. **Communications technology:** Animation/special effects. **Computer sciences:** Security, system admin. **Protective services:** Law enforcement admin.

Technology on campus. Online library available.

Student life. Freshman orientation: Available. Preregistration for classes offered.

Student services. Career counseling, student employment services, placement for graduates.

Contact. Phone: (916) 366-3900 Toll-free number: (800) 488-8466 Bob Menszer, Director of Recruitment, ITT Technical Institute: Rancho Cordova, 10863 Gold Center Drive, Rancho Cordova, CA 95670

ITT Technical Institute: San Bernardino
San Bernardino, California
www.itt-tech.edu   CB code: 7103

- For-profit 4-year technical college
- Commuter campus in very large city
- 686 undergraduates
- Interview required

General. Accredited by ACICS. **Degrees:** 86 bachelor's, 209 associate awarded. **Location:** 60 miles from Los Angeles. **Calendar:** Quarter, extensive summer session. **Full-time faculty:** 22 total. **Part-time faculty:** 66 total.

Basis for selection. Satisfactory scores from on-site tests in English and mathematics required.

2015-2016 Annual costs. Per-credit-hour charge, $493, will vary depending on program level and course of study. Academic fee, $200. Some programs require purchase of tools, which could cost an additional $500. All costs subject to change.

Application procedures. Admission: No deadline. No application fee. Admission notification on a rolling basis. **Financial aid:** No deadline. FAFSA, institutional form required. Applicants notified on a rolling basis.

Academics. Credit/placement by examination: AP, CLEP. **Support services:** Learning center, tutoring.

Majors. Business: Business admin, construction management, project management. **Communications technology:** Animation/special effects. **Computer sciences:** Security, system admin. **Protective services:** Law enforcement admin.

Technology on campus. Online library available.

Student life. Freshman orientation: Available. Preregistration for classes offered.

Student services. Career counseling, student employment services, placement for graduates.

Contact. Phone: (800) 888-3801 Fax: (909) 888-6970 Tyron Cooley, Director of Recruitment, ITT Technical Institute: San Bernardino, 670 East Carnegie Drive, San Bernardino, CA 92408-2800

ITT Technical Institute: Sylmar
Sylmar, California
www.itt-tech.edu   CB code: 3571

- For-profit 4-year technical college
- Commuter campus in very large city
- 607 undergraduates
- Interview required

General. Founded in 1982. Accredited by ACICS. **Degrees:** 78 bachelor's, 154 associate awarded. **Calendar:** Quarter, extensive summer session. **Full-time faculty:** 15 total. **Part-time faculty:** 50 total.

Basis for selection. Satisfactory scores from on-site English and mathematics tests required.

2015-2016 Annual costs. Per-credit-hour charge, $493, will vary depending on program level and course of study. Academic fee, $200. Some programs require purchase of tools, which could cost an additional $500. All costs subject to change.

Application procedures. Admission: No deadline. No application fee. Admission notification on a rolling basis. **Financial aid:** No deadline. FAFSA, institutional form required. Applicants notified on a rolling basis.

Academics. Credit/placement by examination: AP, CLEP. **Support services:** Learning center, tutoring.

Majors. Business: Business admin, construction management, project management. **Communications technology:** Animation/special effects. **Computer sciences:** Programming, security, system admin. **Protective services:** Law enforcement admin.

Technology on campus. Online library available.

Student life. Freshman orientation: Available. Preregistration for classes offered.

Student services. Career counseling, student employment services, placement for graduates.

Contact. Phone: (818) 364-5151 Toll-free number: (800) 363-2086 Fax: (818) 364-5150 Kelly Christensen, Director of Recruitment, ITT Technical Institute: Sylmar, 12669 Encinitas Avenue, Sylmar, CA 91342-3664

ITT Technical Institute: Torrance
Torrance, California
www.itt-tech.edu   CB code: 7104

- For-profit 4-year technical college
- Commuter campus in small city
- 453 undergraduates
- Interview required

General. Accredited by ACICS. **Degrees:** 58 bachelor's, 133 associate awarded. **Calendar:** Quarter, extensive summer session. **Full-time faculty:** 11 total. **Part-time faculty:** 52 total.

Basis for selection. Satisfactory from on-site tests in English and mathematics required.

2015-2016 Annual costs. Per-credit-hour charge, $493, will vary depending on program level and course of study. Academic fee, $200. Some programs require purchase of tools, which could cost an additional $500. All costs subject to change.

Application procedures. Admission: No deadline. No application fee. Admission notification on a rolling basis. **Financial aid:** No deadline. FAFSA, institutional form required. Applicants notified on a rolling basis.

Academics. Credit/placement by examination: AP, CLEP. **Support services:** Learning center, tutoring.

Majors. Business: Business admin, construction management, project management. **Communications technology:** Animation/special effects. **Computer sciences:** Security, system admin. **Protective services:** Law enforcement admin.

Technology on campus. Online library available.

Student services. Career counseling, student employment services, placement for graduates.

Contact. Phone: (310) 380-1555 Freddie Polk, Director of Recruitment, ITT Technical Institute: Torrance, 20050 South Vermont Avenue, Torrance, CA 90502

John F. Kennedy University
Pleasant Hill, California
www.jfku.edu   CB code: 1362

- Private two-year upper-division university
- Commuter campus in large town
- Interview required

General. Founded in 1964. Regionally accredited. Undergraduate and graduate degree Linking program. **Degrees:** 63 bachelor's awarded; master's, professional, doctoral offered. **Articulation:** Agreements with all California community colleges. **Location:** 35 miles from San Francisco. **Calendar:** Quarter, limited summer session. **Full-time faculty:** 49 total. **Part-time faculty:** 184 total. **Class size:** 81% < 20, 19% 20-39.

Student profile. 251 degree-seeking undergraduates, 979 graduate students.

Out-of-state:	5%	25 or older:	90%

Basis for selection. Open admission. College transcript, interview required. Deadlines for response to admissions decisions vary with programs. Interview required. Applicants must have 45 quarter hours. Transfer accepted as sophomores, juniors, seniors.

2015-2016 Annual costs. Tuition/fees: $17,469.

Application procedures. Admission: Rolling admission. $65 fee. **Financial aid:** Priority date 4/1. FAFSA, institutional form required.

Academics. Special study options: Accelerated study, combined bachelor's/graduate degree, cross-registration, distance learning, independent study, internships. **Credit/placement by examination:** AP, CLEP. 105 credit hours maximum toward bachelor's degree. Maximum of 105 units through combination of CLEP, DANTES, 2-year schools, and military training. **Support services:** Learning center, study skills assistance, writing center.

Majors. Business: Accounting, business admin. **Communications:** Journalism. **History:** Military. **Liberal arts:** Arts/sciences. **Protective services:** Law enforcement admin. **Psychology:** General. **Visual/performing arts:** Studio arts.

Most popular majors. Business/marketing 27%, health sciences 15%, legal studies 27%, liberal arts 6%, psychology 27%.

Technology on campus. 25 workstations in library, computer center. Commuter students can connect to campus network.

Student life. Activities: Student government, student newspaper.

Student services. Adult student services, career counseling, student employment services, legal services, veterans' counselor. **Physically disabled:** Services for visually, speech, hearing impaired.

Contact. E-mail: proginfo@jfku.edu
Phone: (925) 969-3535 Toll-free number: (800) 696-5358
Fax: (925) 969-3331
Dorian Roberts, Director of Admissions, John F. Kennedy University, 100 Ellinwood Way, Pleasant Hill, CA 94523-4817

John Paul the Great Catholic University
Escondido, California
www.jpcatholic.com   **CB code: 4576**

- Private 4-year university affiliated with the Roman Catholic Church
- Residential campus in small city
- 206 degree-seeking undergraduates: 6% part-time, 43% women, 2% African American, 4% Asian American, 23% Hispanic/Latino, 1% Native Hawaiian/Pacific islander, 3% Multi-racial, non-Hispanic
- 110 degree-seeking graduate students
- 93% of applicants admitted
- Application essay, interview required
- 67% graduate within 6 years

General. Candidate for regional accreditation. **Degrees:** 27 bachelor's awarded; master's offered. **Location:** 30 miles from San Diego. **Calendar:** Quarter, extensive summer session. **Full-time faculty:** 6 total; 33% have terminal degrees. **Part-time faculty:** 21 total; 19% have terminal degrees, 5% minority, 33% women. **Class size:** 47% < 20, 22% 20-39, 9% 40-49, 22% 50-99.

Freshman class profile. 140 applied, 130 admitted, 63 enrolled.

Mid 50% test scores			
		GPA 3.50-3.74:	7%
SAT critical reading:	490-640	GPA 3.0-3.49:	24%
SAT math:	470-600	GPA 2.0-2.99:	21%
SAT writing:	480-630	Return as sophomores:	69%
ACT composite:	22-28	Out-of-state:	49%
GPA 3.75 or higher:	48%	Live on campus:	86%

Basis for selection. Academic GPA and application essay very important. Recommendations and standardized test scores are important. Test scores are not required if an applicant has over 25 credits of college work or has over a 3.5 high school GPA.

High school preparation. College-preparatory program recommended. Recommended units include English 4, mathematics 3, social studies 2, science 3 and foreign language 3.

2015-2016 Annual costs. Tuition/fees: $24,900. Room only: $8,100.

2014-2015 Financial aid. Need-based: 46 full-time freshmen applied for aid; 46 deemed to have need; 46 received aid. Average need met was 45%. Average scholarship/grant was $9,391; average loan $3,111. 64% of total undergraduate aid awarded as scholarships/grants, 36% as loans/jobs. **Non-need-based:** Awarded to 39 full-time undergraduates, including 3 freshmen. Scholarships awarded for academics, leadership.

Application procedures. Admission: Priority date 11/1; no deadline. $50 fee, may be waived for applicants with need. Admission notification on a rolling basis beginning on or about 9/1. Must reply by May 1 or within 4 week(s) if notified thereafter. **Financial aid:** Closing date 4/15. FAFSA, institutional form required. Applicants notified on a rolling basis starting 12/1; must reply by 5/1 or within 2 week(s) of notification.

Academics. Special study options: Distance learning, independent study, internships, study abroad. **Credit/placement by examination:** AP, CLEP, institutional tests. **Support services:** Tutoring, writing center.

Majors. Business: Entrepreneurial studies. **Visual/performing arts:** Cinematography.

Most popular majors. Business/marketing 19%, visual/performing arts 81%.

Technology on campus. PC or laptop required. Commuter students can connect to campus network. Online library, wireless network available.

Student life. Freshman orientation: Mandatory. Preregistration for classes offered. **Housing:** Single-sex dorms, apartments available. $500 non-refundable deposit, deadline 8/1. **Activities:** Campus ministries, choral groups, film society, student government.

Student services. Chaplain/spiritual director, career counseling, financial aid counseling, personal counseling.

Contact. E-mail: mharold@jpcatholic.com
Phone: (858) 653-6740 ext. 1111
Martin Harold, Director of Admission, John Paul the Great Catholic University, 220 West Grand Avenue, Escondido, CA 92025

La Sierra University
Riverside, California   **CB member**
www.lasierra.edu   **CB code: 4380**

- Private 4-year university, Bible and liberal arts college affiliated with the Seventh-day Adventists
- Residential campus in large city
- 2,020 degree-seeking undergraduates: 9% part-time, 59% women, 6% African American, 16% Asian American, 48% Hispanic/Latino, 2% Native Hawaiian/Pacific islander, 4% Multi-racial, non-Hispanic, 11% international
- 365 degree-seeking graduate students
- 45% of applicants admitted
- SAT or ACT (ACT writing optional), application essay required

General. Founded in 1922. Regionally accredited. Additional program offerings include Business, Criminal Justice, Education, and Religion. Affiliated with the Seventh-day Adventist Church. **Degrees:** 304 bachelor's awarded; master's, doctoral offered. **Location:** 55 miles from Los Angeles. **Calendar:** Quarter, limited summer session. **Full-time faculty:** 102 total; 85% have terminal degrees, 32% minority, 42% women. **Part-time faculty:** 186 total; 8% have terminal degrees, 40% minority, 37% women. **Class size:** 69% < 20, 24% 20-39, 4% 40-49, 3% 50-99, less than 1% >100. **Special facilities:** World museum of natural history, mineral spheres collection, arboretum, observatory, woman's resource center, archaeology center.

Freshman class profile. 4,328 applied, 1,931 admitted, 435 enrolled.

Mid 50% test scores			
		GPA 3.0-3.49:	43%
SAT critical reading:	420-510	GPA 2.0-2.99:	18%
SAT math:	420-520	Rank in top quarter:	42%
SAT writing:	420-510	Rank in top tenth:	13%
ACT composite:	16-22	Out-of-state:	6%
GPA 3.75 or higher:	24%	Live on campus:	45%
GPA 3.50-3.74:	15%	International:	8%

Basis for selection. Secondary school record and GPA, test scores, and religious affiliation or commitment important. **Home schooled:** Transcript of courses and grades required. **Learning Disabled:** Applicants and parents are highly encouraged to attend orientation program; incentives given to students who attend.

High school preparation. 15 units required. Required and recommended units include English 4, mathematics 3-4, social studies 2, science 2-3 (laboratory 2-3), foreign language 2-3, visual/performing arts 1 and academic electives 1.

2015-2016 Annual costs. Tuition/fees: $30,471. Room/board: $7,800. Books/supplies: $1,746. Personal expenses: $2,874.

Financial aid. Non-need-based: Scholarships awarded for academics, art, athletics, leadership, music/drama, religious affiliation.

Application procedures. Admission: Closing date 2/1 (postmark date). $30 fee, may be waived for applicants with need. Admission notification by 9/20. Admission notification on a rolling basis beginning on or about 2/1. Must reply by 9/20. **Financial aid:** Priority date 3/2, closing date 8/15. FAFSA required. Applicants notified on a rolling basis starting 4/15; must reply by 8/5 or within 2 week(s) of notification.

Academics. Special study options: Accelerated study, combined bachelor's/graduate degree, cross-registration, distance learning, double major, dual enrollment of high school students, ESL, honors, independent study, internships, student-designed major, study abroad, teacher certification program. **Credit/placement by examination:** AP, CLEP, IB, institutional tests. 24 credit hours maximum toward bachelor's degree. **Support services:** Learning center, pre-admission summer program, reduced course load, remedial instruction, study skills assistance, tutoring, writing center.

Honors college/program. High school GPA above 3.25 and ACT above 60th percentile. 25 freshmen admitted per year. Offers chance to study in special classroom settings, travel internationally, and engage in advanced research. Honors scholarship also available.

Majors. Biology: General, biochemistry, biomedical sciences, biophysics. **Business:** Accounting, business admin, finance, human resources, marketing. **Communications:** Advertising, communications/speech/rhetoric, persuasive communications. **Computer sciences:** Computer science, information systems. **Conservation:** Environmental science. **English:** English lit, writing. **Foreign languages:** Spanish. **History:** General. **Human services:** Social work. **Liberal arts:** Arts/sciences, humanities. **Math:** General. **Parks/recreation:** Exercise sciences, health/fitness. **Philosophy/religion:** Religion. **Physical sciences:** General, chemistry, physics. **Protective services:** Law enforcement admin. **Psychology:** General, psychobiology. **Social sciences:** Political economy, sociology. **Visual/performing arts:** Art, film/cinema/video, graphic design, music, music performance, music technology, studio arts, studio arts management.

Most popular majors. Biology 17%, business/marketing 16%, health sciences 15%, psychology 9%, security/protective services 8%.

Technology on campus. PC or laptop required. 300 workstations in dormitories, library, computer center, student center. Dormitories wired for high-speed internet access and linked to campus network. Commuter students can connect to campus network. Online course registration, online library, helpline, repair service, wireless network available.

Student life. Freshman orientation: Mandatory. Preregistration for classes offered. $200 credit is given to all the freshmen for attending orientation in summer. **Policies:** Smoke, drug, and alcohol free campus. Religious observance required. **Housing:** Guaranteed on-campus for all undergraduates. Single-sex dorms, apartments, wellness housing available. $100 fully refundable deposit, deadline 9/20. Honors residence hall available. **Activities:** Bands, campus ministries, choral groups, drama, international student organizations, literary magazine, music ensembles, student government, student newspaper, symphony orchestra, Accounting and Finance Society, Active Minds at LSU, Amnesty International, Best Buddies International, biology club, biophysics club, black student association, business club, Chemistry Society, Chinese cultural club.

Athletics. NAIA. **Intercollegiate:** Baseball M, basketball, soccer M, softball W, volleyball W. **Intramural:** Basketball, softball W, volleyball W. **Team name:** Golden Eagles.

Student services. Adult student services, alcohol/substance abuse counseling, chaplain/spiritual director, career counseling, student employment services, financial aid counseling, health services, personal counseling, placement for graduates, women's services.

Contact. E-mail: admissions@lasierra.edu
Phone: (951) 785-2176 Toll-free number: (800) 874-5587
Fax: (951) 785-2477
Ivy Tejeda, Associate Director of Admissions, La Sierra University, 4500 Riverwalk Parkway, Riverside, CA 92515-8247

Laguna College of Art and Design
Laguna Beach, California
www.lcad.edu   CB code: 7248

- Private 4-year visual arts college
- Commuter campus in small city
- 567 degree-seeking undergraduates: 10% part-time, 61% women, 2% African American, 16% Asian American, 19% Hispanic/Latino, 1% Native American, 2% Multi-racial, non-Hispanic, 3% international
- 36 degree-seeking graduate students
- 24% of applicants admitted

- Application essay required
- 66% graduate within 6 years

General. Founded in 1961. Regionally accredited. **Degrees:** 76 bachelor's awarded; master's offered. **Location:** 50 miles from Los Angeles, 75 miles from San Diego. **Calendar:** Semester. **Full-time faculty:** 15 total; 13% have terminal degrees, 27% women. **Part-time faculty:** 74 total; 5% have terminal degrees, 31% women. **Class size:** 90% < 20, 10% 20-39, less than 1% 40-49.

Freshman class profile. 549 applied, 131 admitted, 85 enrolled.

Basis for selection. Academic record and overall merit of portfolio. Applicants should contact their admissions counselor or visit our website for major-specific portfolio guidelines. Application fee waived for online applications. Portfolios required. Essay required of all BFA applicants. **Home schooled:** Transcript of courses and grades, state high school equivalency certificate required.

High school preparation. 14 units recommended. Recommended units include English 2, mathematics 2, social studies 2, history 2, science 2, foreign language 2 and academic electives 2. 3 units of studio art, drawing and painting recommended.

2016-2017 Annual costs. Tuition/fees (projected): $28,950. Room only: $9,400. Books/supplies: $1,792. Personal expenses: $6,538.

2014-2015 Financial aid. Need-based: 47 full-time freshmen applied for aid; 47 deemed to have need; 47 received aid. Average scholarship/grant was $6,000; average loan $3,350. 60% of total undergraduate aid awarded as scholarships/grants, 40% as loans/jobs. **Non-need-based:** Scholarships awarded for art. **Additional information:** Need and merit-based scholarship deadline June 1st.

Application procedures. Admission: Priority date 2/2; deadline 8/1 (receipt date). No application fee. Admission notification on a rolling basis. **Financial aid:** No deadline. FAFSA, institutional form required. Applicants notified on a rolling basis; must reply within 2 week(s) of notification.

Academics. Special study options: Cooperative education, double major, exchange student, independent study, internships, study abroad. **Credit/placement by examination:** AP, CLEP. **Support services:** Pre-admission summer program, reduced course load, remedial instruction, tutoring, writing center.

Majors. Visual/performing arts: General, commercial/advertising art, design, digital arts, drawing, game design, graphic design, illustration, painting, studio arts.

Technology on campus. PC or laptop required. 26 workstations in library, computer center, student center. Dormitories wired for high-speed internet access and linked to campus network. Commuter students can connect to campus network. Online course registration, online library, repair service, wireless network available.

Student life. Freshman orientation: Mandatory. Preregistration for classes offered. **Policies:** Very strong student government promoting activities on and off campus. Many art-related social gatherings. **Housing:** Coed dorms available. $600 partly refundable deposit, deadline 4/16. **Activities:** Student government, foreign student organization, cultural diversity organization.

Student services. Career counseling, student employment services, financial aid counseling, personal counseling, placement for graduates, veterans' counselor.

Contact. E-mail: admissions@lcad.edu
Phone: (949) 376-6000 Toll-free number: (800) 255-0762
Fax: (949) 715-8084
Christopher Brown, Admission and Financial Aid Director, Laguna College of Art and Design, 2222 Laguna Canyon Road, Laguna Beach, CA 92651-1136

Life Pacific College
San Dimas, California
www.lifepacific.edu   CB code: 4264

- Private 4-year Bible college affiliated with the Christian Church
- Residential campus in large town
- 520 degree-seeking undergraduates
- SAT or ACT with writing, application essay required

General. Founded in 1925. Regionally accredited; also accredited by ABHE. **Degrees:** 78 bachelor's, 23 associate awarded; master's offered. **Location:** 30 miles from Los Angeles. **Calendar:** Continuous, limited summer session. **Full-time faculty:** 11 total; 73% have terminal degrees, 27% minority, 27% women. **Part-time faculty:** 40 total; 58% have terminal degrees.

Freshman class profile.

Out-of-state: 26% Live on campus: 84%

Basis for selection. Christian character, ministry motivation, and ability to accord with college's program. Cumulative GPA in last school attended and SAT or ACT scores also considered. **Home schooled:** Must present official transcript with graduation date. SAT or ACT required. **Learning Disabled:** The LIFE Challenges Program is available to students with documented learning disabilities.

2015-2016 Annual costs. Tuition/fees: $13,320. Room/board: $7,246. Books/supplies: $1,710. Personal expenses: $2,377.

Financial aid. Non-need-based: Scholarships awarded for academics.

Application procedures. Admission: Priority date 4/1; deadline 5/3 (postmark date). $35 fee. Application must be submitted on paper. Admission notification on a rolling basis. **Financial aid:** No deadline. FAFSA required. Applicants notified on a rolling basis starting 6/1.

Academics. Special study options: Distance learning, dual enrollment of high school students, external degree, internships, study abroad. **Credit/placement by examination:** AP, CLEP, SAT, ACT, institutional tests. 16 credit hours maximum toward associate degree, 32 toward bachelor's. Credit limited by the number of subjects accepted, course by course basis. **Support services:** Reduced course load, remedial instruction, study skills assistance, writing center.

Majors. Theology: Bible, pastoral counseling.

Technology on campus. 20 workstations in dormitories, library. Dormitories wired for high-speed internet access and linked to campus network. Online course registration, online library, wireless network available.

Student life. Freshman orientation: Mandatory, $100 fee. Preregistration for classes offered. One full day (meal provided), includes testing. **Policies:** Chapel attendance twice per week. Religious observance required. **Housing:** Guaranteed on-campus for freshmen. Single-sex dorms, wellness housing available. $200 nonrefundable deposit, deadline 6/1. **Activities:** Campus ministries, drama, music ensembles, student government.

Athletics. Team name: Warriors.

Student services. Adult student services, chaplain/spiritual director, career counseling, student employment services, financial aid counseling, personal counseling, placement for graduates. **Physically disabled:** Services for speech, hearing impaired.

Contact. E-mail: admissions@lifepacific.edu
Phone: (909) 599-5433 ext. 314
Toll-free number: (877) 886-5433 ext. 314 Fax: (909) 706-3070
Judi Csonka, Admissions Director, Life Pacific College, Attn: Admissions, San Dimas, CA 91773

Lincoln University
Oakland, California
www.lincolnuca.edu   CB code: 4386

- Private 4-year university and business college
- Commuter campus in very large city
- 162 degree-seeking undergraduates
- 555 graduate students

General. Founded in 1919. Accredited by ACICS. Institution primarily serves international students. **Degrees:** 18 bachelor's, 4 associate awarded; master's, professional offered. **Location:** 12 miles from San Francisco. **Calendar:** Semester, limited summer session. **Full-time faculty:** 9 total; 33% women. **Part-time faculty:** 24 total.

Basis for selection. High school achievement record is most important. Prior to enrollment, students take following tests and procedures in English placement: 1) Michigan Test of English Language Proficiency (MTELP), 2) Comprehensive English Language Test Structure (CELT-SA), 3) Comprehensive English Language Test Listening (CELT-LA), 4) a writing sample, and 5) a personal interview. Interview recommended and personal statements encouraged. **Home schooled:** Transcript of courses and grades, state high school equivalency certificate required.

2015-2016 Annual costs. Tuition/fees: $10,200. Books/supplies: $1,005. Personal expenses: $2,520.

Financial aid. All financial aid based on need.

Application procedures. Admission: No deadline. $75 fee. Admission notification on a rolling basis. **Financial aid:** Priority date 3/22, closing date 8/22. FAFSA required. Applicants notified by 12/1; must reply by 1/2.

Academics. Special study options: Cross-registration, double major, ESL, internships. **Credit/placement by examination:** AP, CLEP. **Support services:** Reduced course load, tutoring.

Majors. Business: Business admin, entrepreneurial studies, international, management information systems. **Health services:** Sonography.

Technology on campus. 34 workstations in library, computer center. Online library, repair service, wireless network available.

Student life. Freshman orientation: Mandatory. Preregistration for classes offered. One hour discussion of procedures, event announcements. Student government provides information on banking, transportation and other related materials. **Activities:** Student government.

Student services. Career counseling, financial aid counseling, personal counseling.

Contact. E-mail: admissions@lincolnuca.edu
Phone: (510) 628-8010 Toll-free number: (888) 810-9998
Fax: (510) 628-8012
Peggy Au, Director of Admissions and Records, Lincoln University, 401 15th Street, Oakland, CA 94612

Loma Linda University
Loma Linda, California
www.llu.edu   CB code: 4062

- Private 3-year university and health science college affiliated with the Seventh-day Adventists
- Commuter campus in large town
- 1,071 degree-seeking undergraduates

General. Founded in 1905. Regionally accredited. Two undergraduate schools: School of Allied Health and School of Nursing, offering sophomore, junior, senior year study. All LLU programs require previous college credit, thus no first-time freshman applicants accepted. **Degrees:** 340 bachelor's, 87 associate awarded; master's, professional, doctoral offered. **Location:** 60 miles from Los Angeles, 50 miles from Palm Springs. **Calendar:** Quarter, limited summer session. **Full-time faculty:** 353 total; 35% minority, 53% women. **Part-time faculty:** 57 total; 28% minority, 40% women. **Class size:** 59% < 20, 18% 20-39, 15% 40-49, 8% 50-99.

Basis for selection. No first-time freshman accepted, only transfer students. All programs require prior college credits for admission, which varies by program; typically minimum of 48 credit units. Application is made to specific programs, rather than to the University in general. Some programs require interviews or essays.

2015-2016 Annual costs. Tuition/fees: $32,572. Room only: $2,910. Books/supplies: $2,250.

Application procedures. Admission: No deadline. $60 fee. Application must be submitted online. Admission notification on a rolling basis. Varies by program. Each program is applied to separately and has its own requirements and dates. Student must give at least a two-week notice prior to housing entry date in order to receive a full refund; otherwise no refund will be given. **Financial aid:** FAFSA required.

Academics. Special study options: Combined bachelor's/graduate degree, distance learning, double major, independent study, internships. **Credit/placement by examination:** AP, CLEP. **Support services:** Study skills assistance.

Majors. BACHELOR'S. Conservation: Environmental science. **Health services:** Clinical lab science, cytotechnology, dental hygiene, dietetics, EMT paramedic, health care admin, health information management, nursing (RN), radiologic technology/medical imaging, respiratory therapy technology, speech pathology. **Physical sciences:** Geology. **ASSOCIATE. Health services:** Dental hygiene, medical radiologic technology/radiation therapy, physical therapy assistant.

Technology on campus. 482 workstations in library, computer center, student center. Dormitories wired for high-speed internet access and linked to campus network. Commuter students can connect to campus network. Online library, helpline, wireless network available.

Student life. Policies: Students are not allowed to smoke, use alcohol or drugs. Religious observance required. **Housing:** Guaranteed on-campus for all undergraduates. Single-sex dorms, apartments, wellness housing available. $145 fully refundable deposit. **Activities:** Campus ministries, choral groups, international student organizations, music ensembles, student government, student newspaper, Black Health Professional Student Association, Association of Latin American Students, Social Action Corps, Students for International Mission Service.

Athletics. Intramural: Basketball, football (non-tackle), soccer M, softball, tennis, volleyball.

Student services. Alcohol/substance abuse counseling, chaplain/spiritual director, financial aid counseling, health services, on-campus daycare, personal counseling. **Physically disabled:** Services for hearing impaired.

Contact. E-mail: admissions.app@llu.edu
Phone: (909) 651-5029 Toll-free number: (800) 422-4558
Fax: (909) 558-4879
Loma Linda University, Admissions Processing, Loma Linda, CA 92350

Loyola Marymount University
Los Angeles, California — **CB member**
www.lmu.edu — **CB code: 4403**

- Private 4-year university affiliated with the Roman Catholic Church
- Residential campus in very large city
- 6,162 degree-seeking undergraduates: 2% part-time, 56% women, 6% African American, 11% Asian American, 21% Hispanic/Latino, 8% Multi-racial, non-Hispanic, 9% international
- 2,716 degree-seeking graduate students
- 51% of applicants admitted
- SAT or ACT (ACT writing recommended), application essay required

General. Founded in 1911. Regionally accredited. **Degrees:** 1,554 bachelor's awarded; master's, professional, doctoral offered. **ROTC:** Army, Naval, Air Force. **Location:** 15 miles from downtown. **Calendar:** Semester, extensive summer session. **Class size:** 53% < 20, 45% 20-39, less than 1% 40-49, less than 1% 50-99, less than 1% >100. **Special facilities:** Fine arts complex with recital hall and recording arts facilities, marine station, new life sciences building with green roof.

Freshman class profile. 13,288 applied, 6,748 admitted, 1,354 enrolled.

Mid 50% test scores			
SAT critical reading:	550-640	GPA 2.0-2.99:	3%
SAT math:	560-660	End year in good standing:	95%
SAT writing:	550-650	Return as sophomores:	91%
ACT composite:	25-30	Out-of-state:	31%
GPA 3.75 or higher:	51%	Live on campus:	94%
GPA 3.50-3.74:	25%	International:	7%
GPA 3.0-3.49:	21%	Fraternities:	12%
		Sororities:	38%

Basis for selection. High school GPA, curriculum, test scores, recommendations, essays, activities important. Portfolio required for some arts majors.

High school preparation. College-preparatory program required. 18 units recommended. Recommended units include English 4, mathematics 3, social studies 3, science 2, foreign language 3 and academic electives 1.

2015-2016 Annual costs. Tuition/fees: $42,794. Room/board: $13,630.

2014-2015 Financial aid. Need-based: 1,067 full-time freshmen applied for aid; 757 deemed to have need; 757 received aid. Average need met was 68%. Average scholarship/grant was $20,271; average loan $5,220. 72% of total undergraduate aid awarded as scholarships/grants, 28% as loans/jobs. **Non-need-based:** Awarded to 2,008 full-time undergraduates, including 596 freshmen. Scholarships awarded for academics, alumni affiliation, art, music/drama, religious affiliation, ROTC.

Application procedures. Admission: Closing date 1/15. $60 fee, may be waived for applicants with need. Admission notification on a rolling basis beginning on or about 11/1. Must reply by 5/1. Applicants who desire housing or financial aid should apply by January 15. **Financial aid:** Priority date 2/1, closing date 5/30. FAFSA required. Must reply by 5/1 or within 4 week(s) of notification.

Academics. Special study options: Accelerated study, combined bachelor's/graduate degree, cross-registration, distance learning, double major, dual enrollment of high school students, ESL, exchange student, honors, independent study, internships, liberal arts/career combination, student-designed major, study abroad, teacher certification program, Washington semester, weekend college. **Credit/placement by examination:** AP, CLEP, IB, institutional

tests. **Support services:** Learning center, reduced course load, study skills assistance, tutoring, writing center.

Majors. Area/ethnic studies: African-American, Asian, Chicano/Hispanic-American/Latino, European, women's. **Biology:** General, biochemistry. **Business:** Accounting, entrepreneurial studies, finance, management information systems, marketing. **Communications:** Communications/speech/rhetoric. **Communications technology:** Animation/special effects, recording arts. **Computer sciences:** General. **Conservation:** Environmental science. **Engineering:** Applied physics, civil, electrical, mechanical. **English:** English lit. **Foreign languages:** Classics, French, Romance, Spanish. **History:** General. **Liberal arts:** Arts/sciences, humanities. **Math:** General, applied. **Philosophy/religion:** Philosophy. **Physical sciences:** Chemistry, physics. **Psychology:** General. **Social sciences:** Economics, political science, sociology, urban studies. **Theology:** Theology. **Visual/performing arts:** Art history/conservation, cinematography, dance, dramatic, music, play/screenwriting, studio arts.

Most popular majors. Business/marketing 23%, communications/journalism 10%, English 6%, psychology 7%, social sciences 14%, visual/performing arts 14%.

Technology on campus. 820 workstations in dormitories, library, computer center, student center. Dormitories wired for high-speed internet access and linked to campus network. Commuter students can connect to campus network. Online course registration, online library, helpline, repair service, student web hosting, wireless network available.

Student life. Freshman orientation: Mandatory, $225 fee. Preregistration for classes offered. Held in June, a two part program begins with an overnight stay. In August, students participate in a three day program. **Housing:** Guaranteed on-campus for freshmen. Coed dorms, single-sex dorms, special housing for disabled, apartments, themed housing available. $400 nonrefundable deposit. **Activities:** Pep band, campus ministries, choral groups, dance, drama, film society, international student organizations, literary magazine, music ensembles, radio station, student government, student newspaper, TV station, more than 130 student organizations, clubs, and associations.

Athletics. NCAA. **Intercollegiate:** Baseball M, basketball, cross-country, golf M, rowing (crew) W, soccer, softball W, swimming W, tennis, track and field, volleyball W, water polo. **Intramural:** Basketball, football (non-tackle), soccer, tennis, volleyball. **Team name:** Lions.

Student services. Adult student services, alcohol/substance abuse counseling, chaplain/spiritual director, career counseling, services for economically disadvantaged, student employment services, financial aid counseling, health services, minority student services, on-campus daycare, personal counseling, placement for graduates, veterans' counselor. **Physically disabled:** Services for visually, speech, hearing impaired.

Contact. E-mail: admssions@lmu.edu
Phone: (310) 338-2750 Toll-free number: (800) 568-4696
Fax: (310) 338-2750
Matthew Fissinger, Director of Undergraduate Admissions, Loyola Marymount University, 1 LMU Drive, Los Angeles, CA 90045-2659

Marymount California University
Rancho Palos Verdes, California — **CB member**
www.marymountcalifornia.edu — **CB code: 4515**

- Private 4-year liberal arts college affiliated with the Roman Catholic Church
- Residential campus in large town
- 1,059 degree-seeking undergraduates: 4% part-time, 54% women, 9% African American, 5% Asian American, 37% Hispanic/Latino, 1% Native Hawaiian/Pacific islander, 3% Multi-racial, non-Hispanic, 19% international
- 40 degree-seeking graduate students
- 60% of applicants admitted
- 39% graduate within 6 years

General. Founded in 1933. Regionally accredited. **Degrees:** 125 bachelor's, 45 associate awarded; master's offered. **Location:** 30 miles from Los Angeles. **Calendar:** Semester, limited summer session. **Full-time faculty:** 32 total; 50% have terminal degrees, 25% minority, 50% women. **Part-time faculty:** 82 total; 37% have terminal degrees, 26% minority, 51% women. **Class size:** 59% < 20, 41% 20-39.

Freshman class profile. 1,483 applied, 886 admitted, 257 enrolled.

Mid 50% test scores			
SAT critical reading:	400-520	GPA 3.0-3.49:	35%
SAT math:	400-510	GPA 2.0-2.99:	40%
SAT writing:	410-510	Return as sophomores:	58%
ACT composite:	17-22	Out-of-state:	13%
GPA 3.75 or higher:	9%	Live on campus:	68%
GPA 3.50-3.74:	15%	International:	19%

Basis for selection. High school record, quality of academic preparation, recommendations, student's personal statement, standardized test scores all considered. SAT or ACT recommended. SAT and ACT scores are used for initial math and English placement. Students have to option to take placement tests instead. Interview and essay recommended. **Home schooled:** Transcript of courses and grades, letter of recommendation (nonparent) required. General syllabus of all coursework completed or private tutoring received, statement explaining why family chose home schooling and its advantages and disadvantages, required. SAT or ACT scores and state HS equivalency certificate recommended.

High school preparation. Recommended units include English 4, mathematics 3, social studies 2, history 2, science 2, foreign language 2 and academic electives 1.

2015-2016 Annual costs. Tuition/fees: $34,130. Room/board: $13,780.

2014-2015 Financial aid. Need-based: 146 full-time freshmen applied for aid; 144 deemed to have need; 144 received aid. Average need met was 86%. Average scholarship/grant was $25,010; average loan $3,500. 84% of total undergraduate aid awarded as scholarships/grants, 16% as loans/jobs. **Non-need-based:** Awarded to 714 full-time undergraduates, including 172 freshmen. Scholarships awarded for art, athletics, music/drama.

Application procedures. Admission: Priority date 2/1; no deadline. $50 fee, may be waived for applicants with need. Admission notification on a rolling basis beginning on or about 12/1. Must reply by May 1 or within 2 week(s) if notified thereafter. **Financial aid:** Priority date 3/2, closing date 2/15. FAFSA required. Applicants notified by 3/1.

Academics. Special study options: Distance learning, double major, dual enrollment of high school students, ESL, honors, internships, liberal arts/career combination, study abroad, urban semester. **Credit/placement by examination:** AP, CLEP, IB, SAT, ACT, institutional tests. 15 credit hours maximum toward associate degree. **Support services:** Learning center, pre-admission summer program, reduced course load, remedial instruction, study skills assistance, tutoring.

Honors college/program. Average GPA is 3.3; SAT or ACT scores highly recommended. Approximately 30 students admitted each year. Students may earn their way into the Honors program based on academic success in their first year of college. Honors courses are designated each year. Successful Honors students may join Phi Theta Kappa Honor Society; graduates may secure PTK scholarships upon transfer.

Majors. Business: Business admin, entrepreneurial studies, international. **Communications:** Digital media, media studies. **Liberal arts:** Arts/sciences. **Psychology:** General.

Most popular majors. Business/marketing 40%, liberal arts 27%, psychology 25%, visual/performing arts 8%.

Technology on campus. 77 workstations in library, computer center. Dormitories wired for high-speed internet access and linked to campus network. Commuter students can connect to campus network. Online library, helpline, repair service, wireless network available.

Student life. Freshman orientation: Mandatory, $150 fee. Preregistration for classes offered. **Housing:** Coed dorms, special housing for disabled, apartments available. $150 nonrefundable deposit, deadline 7/1. Housing available through volunteers in the community. **Activities:** Jazz band, campus ministries, choral groups, drama, film society, international student organizations, literary magazine, music ensembles, radio station, student government, volunteer club, philosophy discussion club, pre-med club, student integrity council, Phi Theta Kappa, Latinos Unidos, Black Student Union, International Peers, Jewish club, campus ministry leadership team.

Athletics. NJCAA. **Intercollegiate:** Soccer. **Intramural:** Basketball, football (non-tackle), golf, softball. **Team name:** Mariners.

Student services. Adult student services, alcohol/substance abuse counseling, chaplain/spiritual director, career counseling, student employment services, financial aid counseling, health services, personal counseling. **Physically disabled:** Services for visually, hearing impaired.

Contact. E-mail: admissions@marymountcalifornia.edu
Phone: (310) 303-7311 Fax: (310) 265-0962
Barbara Layne, Dean of Enrollment Management, Marymount California University, 30800 Palos Verdes Drive East, Rancho Palos Verdes, CA 90275-6299

The Master's College
Santa Clarita, California
www.masters.edu
CB code: 4411

◗ Private 4-year liberal arts and seminary college affiliated with the non-denominational tradition

◗ Residential campus in small city

◗ 1,133 degree-seeking undergraduates: 14% part-time, 46% women, 4% African American, 6% Asian American, 10% Hispanic/Latino, 1% Native Hawaiian/Pacific islander, 7% Multi-racial, non-Hispanic, 6% international

◗ 465 degree-seeking graduate students

◗ 95% of applicants admitted

◗ SAT or ACT (ACT writing optional), application essay required

◗ 68% graduate within 6 years

General. Founded in 1927. Regionally accredited. Study abroad campus in Israel; summer global missions program. **Degrees:** 277 bachelor's awarded; master's, professional, doctoral offered. **ROTC:** Army, Air Force. **Location:** 40 miles from Los Angeles. **Calendar:** Semester, limited summer session. **Full-time faculty:** 67 total; 75% have terminal degrees, 8% minority, 15% women. **Part-time faculty:** 171 total; 24% have terminal degrees, 10% minority, 30% women. **Class size:** 71% < 20, 20% 20-39, 5% 40-49, 4% 50-99, 1% >100. **Special facilities:** Professional orchestra size audio recording studio.

Freshman class profile. 490 applied, 464 admitted, 201 enrolled.

Mid 50% test scores			
SAT critical reading:	480-620	GPA 2.0-2.99:	8%
SAT math:	480-590	Rank in top quarter:	52%
SAT writing:	480-600	Rank in top tenth:	29%
ACT composite:	21-27	Return as sophomores:	85%
GPA 3.75 or higher:	59%	Out-of-state:	34%
GPA 3.50-3.74:	17%	Live on campus:	90%
GPA 3.0-3.49:	16%	International:	2%

Basis for selection. School achievement record, references, religious commitment most important. Applications from all individuals who have placed their faith in Jesus Christ as Lord and Savior are welcome. **Home schooled:** Transcript of courses and grades, letter of recommendation (nonparent) required.

High school preparation. College-preparatory program recommended. Required and recommended units include English 4, mathematics 3, history 2, science 2 and academic electives 3.

2016-2017 Annual costs. Tuition/fees (projected): $31,970. Room/board: $10,300. Books/supplies: $1,791. Personal expenses: $2,331.

2014-2015 Financial aid. Need-based: 184 full-time freshmen applied for aid; 166 deemed to have need; 166 received aid. Average need met was 71%. Average scholarship/grant was $19,919; average loan $3,214. 68% of total undergraduate aid awarded as scholarships/grants, 32% as loans/jobs. **Non-need-based:** Awarded to 272 full-time undergraduates, including 60 freshmen. Scholarships awarded for academics, alumni affiliation, art, athletics, leadership, music/drama.

Application procedures. Admission: Priority date 3/2; no deadline. $40 fee, may be waived for applicants with need. Admission notification on a rolling basis beginning on or about 11/1. Must reply by May 1 or within 2 week(s) if notified thereafter. **Financial aid:** Priority date 3/2; no closing date. FAFSA, institutional form required. Applicants notified on a rolling basis starting 2/18; must reply by 5/1 or within 2 week(s) of notification.

Academics. Special study options: Accelerated study, distance learning, double major, dual enrollment of high school students, independent study, internships, liberal arts/career combination, study abroad, teacher certification program. Israel semester. **Credit/placement by examination:** AP, CLEP, IB, SAT, ACT, institutional tests. 32 credit hours maximum toward bachelor's degree. **Support services:** Reduced course load, remedial instruction, study skills assistance, tutoring, writing center.

Majors. Biology: General, cellular/molecular, environmental, zoology. **Business:** Accounting, accounting/business management, business admin, finance, international, management information systems, marketing, non-profit/public, organizational leadership. **Communications:** General, communications/speech/rhetoric, digital media, journalism, media studies, persuasive communications, public relations. **Computer sciences:** General, information technology. **Education:** General, elementary, middle, secondary. **English:** English lit. **History:** General. **Liberal arts:** Arts/sciences. **Math:** General, applied. **Social sciences:** Political science, U.S. government. **Theology:** Bible, missionary, pastoral counseling, preministerial, religious ed, sacred music, theology, youth ministry. **Visual/performing arts:** Brass instruments, music, music management, music pedagogy, music performance, music technology, music theory/composition, percussion instruments, piano/keyboard, stringed instruments, voice/opera, woodwind instruments. **Work/family studies:** General, child development, clothing/textiles, communication, food/nutrition, human nutrition.

Most popular majors. Biology 7%, business/marketing 22%, communications/journalism 11%, liberal arts 14%, theological studies 24%.

Technology on campus. PC or laptop required. 60 workstations in library, computer center. Dormitories wired for high-speed internet access and linked to campus network. Commuter students can connect to campus network. Online course registration, online library, helpline, repair service, wireless network available.

Student life. Freshman orientation: Mandatory. Preregistration for classes offered. 5-day program before start of classes; held on campus. **Policies:** Student code of conduct and community covenant based on distinctives of divine authority, heart transformation, sanctifying relationships, and gospel witness. Religious observance required. **Housing:** Single-sex dorms, apartments available. $200 fully refundable deposit, deadline 5/1. **Activities:** Bands, campus ministries, choral groups, drama, international student organizations, music ensembles, opera, student government, student newspaper, Summer global missions teams, outreach week teams, International Justice Mission, Evangelism Society, C3 Unity.

Athletics. NAIA, NCCAA. **Intercollegiate:** Baseball M, basketball, cross-country, golf M, soccer, track and field, volleyball W. **Intramural:** Basketball, football (non-tackle), soccer, softball, table tennis, ultimate frisbee, volleyball. **Team name:** Mustangs.

Student services. Adult student services, chaplain/spiritual director, career counseling, student employment services, financial aid counseling, health services, minority student services, personal counseling, placement for graduates, veterans' counselor. **Physically disabled:** Services for visually, speech impaired.

Contact. E-mail: admissions@masters.edu
Phone: (661) 259-3540 Toll-free number: (800) 568-6248
Fax: (661) 362-2718
Hollie Jackson, Director of Enrollment, The Master's College, Office of Admissions, Santa Clarita, CA 91321-1200

Menlo College
Atherton, California   **CB member**
www.menlo.edu   **CB code: 4483**

▶ Private 4-year business and liberal arts college
▶ Residential campus in small city
▶ 765 degree-seeking undergraduates: 3% part-time, 45% women, 6% African American, 10% Asian American, 22% Hispanic/Latino, 1% Native American, 2% Native Hawaiian/Pacific islander, 7% Multi-racial, non-Hispanic, 14% international
▶ 38% of applicants admitted
▶ SAT or ACT (ACT writing optional), application essay required
▶ 48% graduate within 6 years

General. Founded in 1927. Regionally accredited. A newly established required internship for all business majors affords the opportunity for students to take full advantage of the school location in the heart of the Silicon Valley. **Degrees:** 171 bachelor's awarded. **ROTC:** Air Force. **Location:** 30 miles from San Francisco, 30 miles from San Jose. **Calendar:** Semester, limited summer session. **Full-time faculty:** 29 total; 90% have terminal degrees, 34% minority, 52% women. **Part-time faculty:** 72 total; 42% have terminal degrees, 33% minority, 43% women. **Class size:** 50% < 20, 50% 20-39.

Freshman class profile. 2,445 applied, 931 admitted, 150 enrolled.

Mid 50% test scores			
SAT critical reading:	450-550	GPA 3.0-3.49:	37%
SAT math:	470-560	GPA 2.0-2.99:	29%
SAT writing:	450-530	End year in good standing:	94%
ACT composite:	19-25	Return as sophomores:	71%
GPA 3.75 or higher:	21%	Out-of-state:	37%
GPA 3.50-3.74:	13%	Live on campus:	86%
		International:	17%

Basis for selection. Minimum recalculated academic high school GPA of 2.5 (grades 10th-12th); minimum 1200 SAT or 16 ACT; one recommendation letter; one personal statement; admissions committee reviews candidates based on a combination of GPA and test scores; depth of achievement in co-curricular activities considered. **Home schooled:** Statement describing home school structure and mission, transcript of courses and grades, state high school equivalency certificate, letter of recommendation (nonparent) required.

High school preparation. College-preparatory program recommended. 15 units required; 24 recommended. Required and recommended units include English 4, mathematics 3, social studies 3, science 3 and foreign language 2.

2016-2017 Annual costs. Tuition/fees: $39,950. Room/board: $13,150. Books/supplies: $1,791. Personal expenses: $2,331.

2015-2016 Financial aid. Need-based: 140 full-time freshmen applied for aid; 131 deemed to have need; 131 received aid. Average need met was 70%. Average scholarship/grant was $28,530; average loan $3,159. 71% of total undergraduate aid awarded as scholarships/grants, 29% as loans/jobs. **Non-need-based:** Awarded to 351 full-time undergraduates, including 132 freshmen. Scholarships awarded for academics, athletics.

Application procedures. Admission: Priority date 2/1; deadline 4/1 (receipt date). $40 fee, may be waived for applicants with need. Admission notification on a rolling basis. **Financial aid:** Priority date 3/2, closing date 8/1. FAFSA required. Applicants notified on a rolling basis starting 12/15; must reply by 5/1 or within 2 week(s) of notification.

Academics. Special study options: Accelerated study, combined bachelor's/graduate degree, double major, ESL, independent study, internships, student-designed major, study abroad. **Credit/placement by examination:** AP, CLEP, IB, institutional tests. 30 credit hours maximum toward bachelor's degree. **Support services:** Learning center, reduced course load, remedial instruction, study skills assistance, tutoring, writing center.

Majors. Business: Accounting, business admin, entrepreneurial studies, finance, international, management information systems, marketing, real estate. **Psychology:** General.

Most popular majors. Business/marketing 91%, psychology 9%.

Technology on campus. 220 workstations in library, computer center. Dormitories wired for high-speed internet access and linked to campus network. Commuter students can connect to campus network. Online course registration, online library, helpline, wireless network available.

Student life. Freshman orientation: Mandatory. Preregistration for classes offered. Held 4-5 days before classes begin. Workshops for both parents and students. Off campus trip. **Policies:** Freshmen not permitted cars on campus. **Housing:** Guaranteed on-campus for freshmen. Coed dorms, single-sex dorms, special housing for disabled available. $300 fully refundable deposit, deadline 7/1. **Activities:** Dance, film society, international student organizations, student government, student newspaper, African-American Student Union, Latino Student Union, Venture Christian Club, Rotaract, Chinese culture research club, Women's club, Alpha Chi Honor Society, Delta Mu Delta Honor Society, Gay Straight Alliance.

Athletics. NAIA. **Intercollegiate:** Baseball M, basketball, cross-country, golf, soccer, softball W, track and field, volleyball W, wrestling. **Intramural:** Basketball M. **Team name:** Oaks.

Student services. Adult student services, career counseling, student employment services, financial aid counseling, minority student services, personal counseling, placement for graduates. **Physically disabled:** Services for visually, hearing impaired.

Contact. E-mail: admissions@menlo.edu
Phone: (650) 543-3753 Toll-free number: (800) 556-3656
Fax: (650) 543-4496
Priscila De Souza, Dean of Enrollment Management, Menlo College, 1000 El Camino Real, Atherton, CA 94027

Mills College
Oakland, California   **CB member**
www.mills.edu   **CB code: 4485**

▶ Private 4-year liberal arts college for women
▶ Residential campus in large city
▶ 852 degree-seeking undergraduates: 5% part-time, 100% women, 7% African American, 9% Asian American, 23% Hispanic/Latino, 1% Native American, 10% Multi-racial, non-Hispanic, 1% international
▶ 538 degree-seeking graduate students
▶ 76% of applicants admitted

◆ Application essay required

◆ 70% graduate within 6 years; 28% enter graduate study

General. Founded in 1852. Regionally accredited. Cross registration at University of California-Berkeley and California College of the Arts, and many local community colleges. Institutional emphasis on social justice and "green" practices. **Degrees:** 237 bachelor's awarded; master's, doctoral offered. **ROTC:** Army. **Location:** 18 miles from San Francisco, 8 miles from Berkeley. **Calendar:** Semester, limited summer session. **Full-time faculty:** 99 total; 94% have terminal degrees, 33% minority, 68% women. **Part-time faculty:** 103 total; 62% have terminal degrees, 34% minority, 73% women. **Class size:** 73% < 20, 25% 20-39, 1% 40-49, less than 1% >100. **Special facilities:** Art museum, electronic collaborative learning center, center for contemporary music, laboratory children's school for student teachers, institute for civic leadership, center for the book, botanic garden, organic farm.

Freshman class profile. 839 applied, 639 admitted, 140 enrolled.

Mid 50% test scores		GPA 2.0-2.99:	1%
SAT critical reading:	530-670	Rank in top quarter:	68%
SAT math:	500-620	Rank in top tenth:	28%
SAT writing:	530-650	End year in good standing:	89%
ACT composite:	24-30	Return as sophomores:	81%
GPA 3.75 or higher:	47%	Out-of-state:	32%
GPA 3.50-3.74:	28%	Live on campus:	93%
GPA 3.0-3.49:	24%	International:	4%

Basis for selection. Minimum 3.0 GPA required, school achievement record most important. All credentials considered. SAT or ACT, SAT Subject Tests recommended. Interview recommended. **Home schooled:** Statement describing home school structure and mission, state high school equivalency certificate, letter of recommendation (nonparent) required. Must submit SAT Reasoning Test and two Subject Tests, or ACT.

High school preparation. College-preparatory program recommended. Required and recommended units include English 4, mathematics 3-4, social studies 2-4, history 2-4, science 2-4 (laboratory 2), foreign language 2-4 and visual/performing arts 2.

2015-2016 Annual costs. Tuition/fees: $44,258. Room/board: $12,390. Books/supplies: $1,514. Personal expenses: $2,020.

2015-2016 Financial aid. Need-based: 133 full-time freshmen applied for aid; 113 deemed to have need; 110 received aid. Average need met was 94%. Average scholarship/grant was $36,050; average loan $4,815. 77% of total undergraduate aid awarded as scholarships/grants, 23% as loans/jobs. **Non-need-based:** Awarded to 734 full-time undergraduates, including 142 freshmen. Scholarships awarded for academics, leadership, music/drama.

Application procedures. Admission: Priority date 1/15; no deadline. $50 fee, may be waived for applicants with need. Admission notification on a rolling basis beginning on or about 11/15. Must reply by May 1 or within 2 week(s) if notified thereafter. **Financial aid:** Priority date 2/1, closing date 2/15. FAFSA required. Applicants notified on a rolling basis starting 3/1; must reply by 5/1 or within 2 week(s) of notification.

Academics. Cooperative bachelor of science in nursing program with Samuel Merritt College; pre-nursing students in this program receive a pre-nursing certificate from Mills upon completion of two years of study. Certificate pre-medicine program available to postbaccalaureate students. BA/MA in Infant Mental Health, BA/Teaching Credential/MA, BA/MBA and BA/MPP (Public Policy) are offered. Combination Masters degrees are also offered: MBA/MA in Educational Leadership; MBA/MPP. **Special study options:** Accelerated study, combined bachelor's/graduate degree, cross-registration, double major, exchange student, external degree, independent study, internships, liberal arts/career combination, student-designed major, study abroad, teacher certification program, Washington semester. **Credit/placement by examination:** AP, CLEP, IB, institutional tests. 9 credit hours maximum toward bachelor's degree. **Support services:** Learning center, pre-admission summer program, reduced course load, remedial instruction, study skills assistance, tutoring, writing center.

Majors. Area/ethnic studies: General, American, Chicano/Hispanic-American/Latino, French, gay/lesbian, Latin American, women's. **Biology:** General, biochemistry, molecular biochemistry. **Business:** Managerial economics. **Computer sciences:** General, computer science. **Conservation:** Environmental science, environmental studies. **Engineering:** General. **English:** British lit, creative writing, English lit. **Foreign languages:** French, Spanish. **History:** General, American. **Human services:** Public policy. **Math:** General. **Philosophy/religion:** Philosophy. **Physical sciences:** Chemistry. **Psychology:** General. **Social sciences:** General, anthropology, economics, international relations, political science, sociology, U.S. government. **Visual/performing arts:** Art, art history/conservation, dance, dramatic, multimedia, music, studio arts. **Work/family studies:** Child development.

Most popular majors. Area/ethnic studies 8%, biology 8%, English 15%, interdisciplinary studies 6%, psychology 10%, social sciences 21%, visual/performing arts 11%.

Technology on campus. 299 workstations in dormitories, library, computer center, student center. Dormitories wired for high-speed internet access and linked to campus network. Commuter students can connect to campus network. Online course registration, online library, helpline, student web hosting, wireless network available.

Student life. Freshman orientation: Mandatory. Preregistration for classes offered. 5 days prior to the start of classes in fall. **Policies:** Individual integrity and mutual respect form the foundation of Mills' learning community. It is the responsibility of every student to know and abide by the Honor Code, which obliges students to report any violations of its standards. **Housing:** Guaranteed on-campus for all undergraduates. Special housing for disabled, apartments, cooperative housing, gender-neutral housing, themed housing, wellness housing available. $250 nonrefundable deposit, deadline 5/15. **Activities:** Campus ministries, choral groups, dance, drama, international student organizations, literary magazine, music ensembles, Model UN, student government, student newspaper, Black Women's Collective, Mujeres Unidas, Asian Pacific Islander Sisterhood Alliance, Muslim Student Association, Indigenous Women's Alliance, Pagan Alliance, Workers of Faith, Jewish Student Collective, Feminist Democrats, Earth CORPS.

Athletics. NCAA. **Intercollegiate:** Cross-country W, rowing (crew) W, soccer W, swimming W, tennis W, volleyball W. **Team name:** Cyclones.

Student services. Adult student services, alcohol/substance abuse counseling, chaplain/spiritual director, career counseling, student employment services, financial aid counseling, health services, minority student services, personal counseling, placement for graduates, women's services. **Physically disabled:** Services for visually, speech, hearing impaired.

Contact. E-mail: admission@mills.edu
Phone: (510) 430-2135 Toll-free number: (800) 876-4557
Fax: (510) 430-3314
Robynne Royster, Director of Undergraduate Admission, Mills College, 5000 MacArthur Boulevard, Oakland, CA 94613

Mount Saint Mary's University

Los Angeles, California — CB member
www.msmu.edu — CB code: 4493

◆ Private 4-year university and liberal arts college for women affiliated with the Roman Catholic Church

◆ Residential campus in very large city

◆ 2,779 degree-seeking undergraduates: 23% part-time, 93% women

◆ 686 degree-seeking graduate students

◆ 77% of applicants admitted

◆ SAT or ACT (ACT writing optional), application essay required

◆ 62% graduate within 6 years

General. Founded in 1925. Regionally accredited. Primarily a women's college at the undergraduate level, although men are admitted to undergraduate nursing and music programs, undergraduate degree programs offered online or weekends and evenings, and all graduate programs. **Degrees:** 548 bachelor's, 200 associate awarded; master's, professional offered. **Location:** 2 miles from Los Angeles. **Calendar:** Semester, limited summer session. **Full-time faculty:** 117 total; 68% have terminal degrees, 26% minority. **Part-time faculty:** 382 total; 27% have terminal degrees, 32% minority. **Class size:** 63% < 20, 37% 20-39, less than 1% 40-49. **Special facilities:** Nuclear magnetic resonance (NMR) spectrometer, water jacketed laboratory CO_2 incubator, lab rotator, geneamp thermal cycler, microcentrifuge.

Freshman class profile. 2,407 applied, 1,842 admitted, 551 enrolled.

Mid 50% test scores		GPA 3.0-3.49:	34%
SAT critical reading:	410-510	GPA 2.0-2.99:	21%
SAT math:	420-510	Rank in top quarter:	52%
SAT writing:	400-500	Rank in top tenth:	19%
ACT composite:	16-21	Return as sophomores:	79%
GPA 3.75 or higher:	28%	Out-of-state:	3%
GPA 3.50-3.74:	17%	Live on campus:	43%

Basis for selection. Primary emphasis on school academic record, then test scores, essay, and letters of recommendation. School and community activities also considered. Interview important. Admission requirements considered very competitive in baccalaureate program. Interviews recommended. Auditions recommended of music majors. Portfolios recommended of art majors. **Home schooled:** Statement describing home school structure and mission, transcript of courses and grades, state high school equivalency certificate, letter of recommendation (nonparent) required. **Learning Disabled:** Documentation of learning disability required.

High school preparation. College-preparatory program recommended. Recommended units include English 4, mathematics 3, social studies 3, history 2, science 2 (laboratory 1), foreign language 2 and academic electives 1. For associate degree applicants, required courses include algebra, geometry, American history/government, and 4 units English.

2015-2016 Annual costs. Tuition/fees: $35,944. Room/board: $11,117. Books/supplies: $1,826. Personal expenses: $3,420.

2015-2016 Financial aid. Need-based: 513 full-time freshmen applied for aid; 503 deemed to have need; 502 received aid. Average need met was 73%. Average scholarship/grant was $20,134; average loan $3,656. 80% of total undergraduate aid awarded as scholarships/grants, 20% as loans/jobs. **Non-need-based:** Awarded to 1,926 full-time undergraduates, including 525 freshmen. Scholarships awarded for academics, alumni affiliation, music/drama.

Application procedures. Admission: Priority date 12/1; deadline 2/15 (postmark date). $50 fee, may be waived for applicants with need. Admission notification on a rolling basis beginning on or about 11/1. Must reply by May 1 or within 2 week(s) if notified thereafter. **Financial aid:** Priority date 3/1; no closing date. FAFSA required. Applicants notified on a rolling basis starting 3/1; must reply by 5/1.

Academics. Special study options: Accelerated study, cooperative education, cross-registration, double major, exchange student, honors, independent study, internships, student-designed major, study abroad, teacher certification program, United Nations semester, Washington semester, weekend college. **Credit/placement by examination:** AP, CLEP, IB, SAT, ACT, institutional tests. 24 credit hours maximum toward associate degree, 30 toward bachelor's. **Support services:** Learning center, pre-admission summer program, reduced course load, remedial instruction, study skills assistance, tutoring, writing center.

Majors. Area/ethnic studies: American. **Biology:** General, biochemistry. **Business:** General, accounting, business admin, international. **Communications:** Journalism. **Education:** General. **English:** English lit. **Foreign languages:** French, Spanish. **Health services:** Health care admin, nursing (RN), predental, premedicine, preveterinary. **History:** General. **Human services:** Health policy, social work. **Liberal arts:** Arts/sciences. **Math:** General, applied. **Philosophy/religion:** Philosophy, professional ethics, religion. **Physical sciences:** Chemistry. **Psychology:** General, applied, developmental. **Social sciences:** General, criminology, political science, sociology. **Theology:** Sacred music. **Visual/performing arts:** Art, cinematography, documentaries, music, music performance, music theory/composition, studio arts. **Work/family studies:** Child development.

Most popular majors. Business/marketing 11%, health sciences 39%, psychology 12%, social sciences 12%.

Technology on campus. 170 workstations in dormitories, library, computer center, student center. Dormitories wired for high-speed internet access and linked to campus network. Commuter students can connect to campus network. Online course registration, online library, helpline, student web hosting, wireless network available.

Student life. Freshman orientation: Available. Preregistration for classes offered. Occurs during a weekend, typically in late June. **Policies:** Student resident life largely self-regulated under direction of Residence Council. **Housing:** Guaranteed on-campus for freshmen. Themed housing available. $200 fully refundable deposit, deadline 5/1. **Activities:** Campus ministries, choral groups, dance, film society, music ensembles, student government, symphony orchestra, various academic, service, cultural and Greek organizations and student clubs available.

Athletics. Intramural: Basketball, soccer, softball, swimming, tennis, volleyball. **Team name:** Athenians.

Student services. Adult student services, chaplain/spiritual director, career counseling, student employment services, financial aid counseling, health services, personal counseling, placement for graduates.

Contact. E-mail: admissions@msmu.edu
Phone: (310) 954-4250 Toll-free number: (800) 999-9893
Fax: (310) 954-4259
Renee Rouzan-Kay, Director of Admissions, Mount Saint Mary's University, 12001 Chalon Road, Los Angeles, CA 90049

Mt. Sierra College
Monrovia, California
www.mtsierra.edu   CB code: 3090

- For-profit 3-year visual arts and business college
- Commuter campus in large city
- 530 undergraduates
- Application essay, interview required

General. Accredited by ACCSC. **Degrees:** 70 bachelor's awarded. **Location:** 20 miles from Los Angeles. **Calendar:** Quarter, extensive summer session. **Class size:** 98% < 20, 2% 20-39. **Special facilities:** Green-screen room for special effects video, sound room, mac and game arts computer labs.

Basis for selection. Must have high school diploma or equivalent and take a basic writing, math, online assessments. High school and/or college GPA are also considered. **Home schooled:** Transcript of courses and grades, state high school equivalency certificate, interview required. **Learning Disabled:** Mt. Sierra College makes reasonable accommodations with proper documentation and complies with ADA regulations.

2015-2016 Annual costs. Tuition/fees: $15,588. Books/supplies: $2,100. Personal expenses: $3,159. **Additional information:** Mandatory California State STRF fee, currently $0, laptop expense $500-$1,600, depending on program.

Application procedures. Admission: No deadline. $50 fee, may be waived for applicants with need. Admission notification on a rolling basis. **Financial aid:** No deadline. FAFSA required.

Academics. Special study options: Accelerated study, distance learning, internships, weekend college. **Credit/placement by examination:** AP, CLEP, IB, institutional tests. 12 credit hours maximum toward bachelor's degree. **Support services:** Learning center, study skills assistance, tutoring.

Majors. Business: Business admin, entrepreneurial studies. **Computer sciences:** General, information technology, networking, security, web page design. **Visual/performing arts:** Digital arts, game design, graphic design, multimedia.

Most popular majors. Business/marketing 14%, computer/information sciences 39%, visual/performing arts 47%.

Technology on campus. PC or laptop required. 40 workstations in library, computer center. Commuter students can connect to campus network. Online library, wireless network available.

Student life. Freshman orientation: Available. Preregistration for classes offered. Held prior to class start dates. Date of orientations are announced. **Activities:** Student newspaper.

Student services. Student employment services, financial aid counseling, placement for graduates.

Contact. E-mail: hwhitaker@mtsierra.edu
Phone: (626) 873-2100 Toll-free number: (888) 828-8800
Fax: (626) 359-1378
Herman Whitaker, Senior Director of Admissions and Marketing, Mt. Sierra College, 101 East Huntington Drive, Monrovia, CA 91016

National University
La Jolla, California   CB member
www.nu.edu   CB code: 0470

- Private 4-year university
- Commuter campus in very large city
- 8,555 degree-seeking undergraduates: 62% part-time, 57% women, 11% African American, 10% Asian American, 26% Hispanic/Latino, 1% Native American, 2% Native Hawaiian/Pacific islander, 5% Multi-racial, non-Hispanic, 1% international
- 7,458 degree-seeking graduate students
- Interview required
- 30% graduate within 6 years

General. Founded in 1971. Regionally accredited. Campuses in 11 major cities throughout California; courses offered both on-site and online. Main campuses in San Diego (with 27 campuses in CA, 1 in NV, as well as 9 military bases throughout southern CA). **Degrees:** 1,888 bachelor's, 152 associate awarded; master's offered. **ROTC:** Army, Naval, Air Force. **Calendar:** Differs by program, limited summer session. **Full-time faculty:** 278

total; 74% have terminal degrees, 18% minority, 51% women. **Part-time faculty:** 1,115 total; 29% have terminal degrees, 16% minority, 53% women. **Class size:** 72% < 20, 28% 20-39, less than 1% 40-49. **Special facilities:** Nursing labs, forensics labs, e-book collection, online information centers.

Freshman class profile.

Out-of-state: 15% **International:** 5%

Basis for selection. Open admission, but selective for some programs. Interview, previous business and work experience, academic record considered. **Home schooled:** Undergraduate students who indicate they received their secondary school instruction through home schooling will be required to submit an official high school transcript with the following information: student's name, a list and description of courses completed, grades earned for the courses completed, number of credits earned for each course, names of textbooks utilized in courses, signed by person who administered curriculum, graduation date (if applicable). Courses must be broken down by grade level. Students must also provide a letter from their state Department of Education or local school district confirming home school registration. If the student's home state requires that individuals who were home schooled through secondary school take the GED to show high school completion, the student must submit official GED test scores to the Office of the Registrar. The student will not be required to submit an official high school transcript if providing official GED test scores. Students will be considered to be provisionally accepted until receipt of the required documentation. Students may be allowed to take courses but should note that final verification of high school completion will be made by the Office of the Registrar at the time official high school transcripts are received. Students who are deemed to not have met the high school completion requirement will be required to submit official GED test scores prior to continued enrollment.

2015-2016 Annual costs. Tuition/fees: $12,744. Books/supplies: $1,568. Personal expenses: $2,808.

2015-2016 Financial aid. Need-based: 26% of total undergraduate aid awarded as scholarships/grants, 74% as loans/jobs.

Application procedures. Admission: No deadline. $60 fee. Admission notification on a rolling basis. **Financial aid:** No deadline. FAFSA, institutional form required. Applicants notified on a rolling basis.

Academics. Special study options: Accelerated study, combined bachelor's/graduate degree, cross-registration, distance learning, double major, dual enrollment of high school students, ESL, honors, independent study, internships, study abroad, teacher certification program. **Credit/placement by examination:** AP, CLEP, IB, institutional tests. 14 credit hours maximum toward associate degree, 23 toward bachelor's. **Support services:** Learning center, remedial instruction, tutoring, writing center.

Majors. Biology: General, biostatistics. **Business:** Accounting, business admin, casino management, communications, construction management, finance, management information systems, marketing, office management, organizational behavior, organizational leadership. **Communications:** Digital media, persuasive communications. **Computer sciences:** Computer science, IT project management. **Conservation:** Environmental science. **Education:** Early childhood, elementary, English, health occupations, mathematics, physical, secondary, special ed. **Engineering:** Biomedical, construction, electrical, manufacturing, software. **English:** English lit. **Foreign languages:** Arabic, Chinese, comparative lit, Iranian, Spanish. **Health services:** General, clinical lab science, community health, health care admin, licensed practical nurse, medical radiologic technology/radiation therapy, nursing (RN), prenursing. **History:** General. **Human services:** General. **Liberal arts:** Arts/sciences. **Math:** General. **Parks/recreation:** Sports studies. **Physical sciences:** Geology. **Protective services:** Homeland security, law enforcement admin. **Psychology:** General. **Social sciences:** General, political science, sociology. **Visual/performing arts:** Arts management.

Most popular majors. Business/marketing 29%, health sciences 22%, psychology 10%, security/protective services 9%.

Technology on campus. 3,100 workstations in library, computer center, student center. Commuter students can connect to campus network. Online course registration, online library, helpline, wireless network available.

Student life. Freshman orientation: Available. Preregistration for classes offered.

Student services. Adult student services, career counseling, services for economically disadvantaged, student employment services, financial aid counseling, minority student services, veterans' counselor. **Physically disabled:** Services for visually, speech, hearing impaired.

Contact. E-mail: advisor@nu.edu
Phone: (800) 628-8648 Toll-free number: (800) 628-8648
Fax: (858) 541-7792
Stephanie Thompson, Dir, Operation ASCS, National University, 11255 North Torrey Pines Road, La Jolla, CA 92037-1011

New Charter University
San Francisco, California
www.new.edu CB code: 3877

- For-profit 4-year virtual liberal arts college
- Very large city

General. Accredited by DETC. **Calendar:** Differs by program.

Annual costs/financial aid. Tuition is fixed and flat-rate. Associate Degrees are $5000, Bachelor Degrees are $10,000, and Masters Degrees are $12,000. Undergraduate courses are $250 each. Graduate courses are $1000 per course.

Contact. Director of Admissions, 543 Howard Street, San Francisco, CA 94105

NewSchool of Architecture & Design
San Diego, California
www.newschoolarch.edu CB code: 2419

- For-profit 5-year visual arts and liberal arts college
- Commuter campus in very large city
- 403 degree-seeking undergraduates: 10% part-time, 31% women, 3% African American, 8% Asian American, 36% Hispanic/Latino, 2% Multiracial, non-Hispanic, 22% international
- 107 degree-seeking graduate students
- Application essay required

General. Founded in 1980. Accredited by ACICS. **Degrees:** 66 bachelor's awarded; master's offered. **Location:** Downtown. **Calendar:** Quarter, extensive summer session. **Full-time faculty:** 23 total; 35% women. **Part-time faculty:** 90 total; 24% women. **Special facilities:** Materials lab with 3D printing capability.

Basis for selection. Admission decisions are reached based on combinations of the following: GPA, letters of recommendation, statement of purpose, and portfolio (if required for the program). **Home schooled:** Transcript of courses and grades required. Verification required with nearest school district.

2016-2017 Annual costs. Tuition/fees (projected): $26,463. Books/supplies: $2,775. Personal expenses: $3,132.

2015-2016 Financial aid. Need-based: Average need met was 31%. Average scholarship/grant was $11,013; average loan $4,161. 48% of total undergraduate aid awarded as scholarships/grants, 52% as loans/jobs.

Application procedures. Admission: No deadline. $75 fee, may be waived for applicants with need. Admission notification on a rolling basis.

Academics. Special study options: Accelerated study, distance learning, dual enrollment of high school students, exchange student, independent study, study abroad. **Credit/placement by examination:** AP, CLEP. **Support services:** Learning center, reduced course load, tutoring, writing center.

Majors. Architecture: Architecture. **Business:** Construction management. **Visual/performing arts:** Digital arts.

Most popular majors. Architecture 91%.

Technology on campus. Online course registration, online library, wireless network available.

Student life. Freshman orientation: Available. Preregistration for classes offered. Held the week prior to the start of each quarter. **Housing:** Apartments available. **Activities:** Student government, American Institute of Architects student chapter, Construction Management Student Association, Alpha Rho Chi Professional Co-Ed Fraternity.

Athletics. Intramural: Basketball, soccer.

Student services. Career counseling, student employment services, financial aid counseling, personal counseling, placement for graduates. **Physically disabled:** Services for visually, hearing impaired.

Contact. E-mail: newschooladmissions@newschoolarch.edu
Phone: (619) 684-8841
Johntay Cokley, Admissions Manager, NewSchool of Architecture & Design, 1249 F Street, San Diego, CA 92101

Northwestern Polytechnic University
Fremont, California
www.npu.edu   CB code: 4335

♦ Private 4-year business and engineering college
♦ Commuter campus in small city
♦ 52 degree-seeking undergraduates

General. Accredited by ACICS. **Degrees:** 71 bachelor's awarded; master's, professional offered. **Location:** 42 miles from San Francisco, 7 miles from San Jose. **Calendar:** Trimester, extensive summer session. **Full-time faculty:** 19 total. **Part-time faculty:** 58 total. **Class size:** 62% < 20, 38% 20-39.

Basis for selection. High school record, pre-calculus required. Recommendations and test scores as reference. Interview recommended. English placement exams are given to international students who do not provide standardized English test scores. On-campus English placement exam may replace TOEFL; on-campus freshman exam may replace SAT. Standardized test administered by ETS or on-campus equivalent assessment test acceptable. The test score does not affect the student's admission to the program.

High school preparation. College-preparatory program required. Required and recommended units include English 3, mathematics 2, social studies 1 and science 1. 1 math required for business programs.

2015-2016 Annual costs. Tuition/fees: $10,700. Books/supplies: $800.

Financial aid. Additional information: Work-study, co-op program, internships available. Employment opportunities with local firms help defray costs.

Application procedures. Admission: Priority date 8/1; deadline 8/29 (postmark date). $60 fee. Admission notification on a rolling basis. Must reply by 9/7.

Academics. Curricula designed to meet needs of high-tech industries and global businesses. **Special study options:** ESL. **Credit/placement by examination:** AP, CLEP, IB, institutional tests. 15 credit hours maximum toward bachelor's degree. **Support services:** Learning center, tutoring.

Majors. Business: Business admin. **Engineering:** Electrical, software, systems.

Most popular majors. Business/marketing 63%, engineering/engineering technologies 37%.

Technology on campus. 250 workstations in library, computer center, student center. Dormitories wired for high-speed internet access. Commuter students can connect to campus network. Online library, helpline, repair service, student web hosting, wireless network available.

Student life. Freshman orientation: Mandatory. Preregistration for classes offered. One-day program before the semester start date. **Policies:** Students are required to join student association, and encouraged to join student clubs. **Housing:** Apartments, wellness housing available. $300 fully refundable deposit, deadline 8/1. **Activities:** Dance, international student organizations, literary magazine, music ensembles, Model UN, student government, student newspaper.

Athletics. Intercollegiate: Table tennis. **Intramural:** Table tennis.

Student services. Adult student services, career counseling, services for economically disadvantaged, student employment services, personal counseling, placement for graduates, veterans' counselor.

Contact. E-mail: admission@npu.edu
Phone: (510) 592-9688 ext. 8 Fax: (510) 657-8975
Monica Sinha, Director of Admission, Northwestern Polytechnic University, 47671 Westinghouse Drive, Fremont, CA 94539

Notre Dame de Namur University
Belmont, California   CB member
www.ndnu.edu   CB code: 4063

♦ Private 4-year university and liberal arts college affiliated with the Roman Catholic Church
♦ Residential campus in large town
♦ 1,097 degree-seeking undergraduates
♦ SAT or ACT (ACT writing optional), application essay required

General. Founded in 1851. Regionally accredited. **Degrees:** 273 bachelor's awarded; master's, doctoral offered. **ROTC:** Air Force. **Location:** 19 miles from San Francisco. **Calendar:** Semester, limited summer session. **Full-time faculty:** 60 total; 95% have terminal degrees, 22% minority, 55% women. **Part-time faculty:** 186 total; 37% have terminal degrees, 22% minority, 63% women. **Class size:** 67% < 20, 33% 20-39.

Freshman class profile.

GPA 3.75 or higher:	13%	Rank in top quarter:	35%
GPA 3.50-3.74:	14%	Rank in top tenth:	13%
GPA 3.0-3.49:	36%	Out-of-state:	15%
GPA 2.0-2.99:	37%	Live on campus:	85%

Basis for selection. High school record and GPA most important; test scores also important. Essay, recommendation, and school and community activities considered. Audition for music students. SAT recommended. Audition required for music programs. **Home schooled:** Statement describing home school structure and mission, transcript of courses and grades, state high school equivalency certificate, interview, letter of recommendation (non-parent) required.

High school preparation. College-preparatory program recommended. 15 units required; 18 recommended. Required and recommended units include English 4, mathematics 2-3, social studies 2, history 1, science 1-2 (laboratory 1), foreign language 2-3 and academic electives 3. Electives: 3 units from fine arts, advanced laboratory science, advanced mathematics, advanced social science, computer science, or advanced foreign language recommended.

2015-2016 Annual costs. Tuition/fees: $32,608. Room/board: $13,006. Books/supplies: $1,746. Personal expenses: $3,150.

Financial aid. Non-need-based: Scholarships awarded for academics, art, athletics, leadership, music/drama, religious affiliation, ROTC.

Application procedures. Admission: Priority date 2/1; no deadline. $50 fee, may be waived for applicants with need. Admission notification on a rolling basis beginning on or about 12/1. Must reply by May 1 or within 3 week(s) if notified thereafter. **Financial aid:** Priority date 3/2; no closing date. FAFSA required. CSS PROFILE accepted but not required. Applicants notified on a rolling basis starting 2/15; must reply by 5/1 or within 2 week(s) of notification.

Academics. Special study options: Accelerated study, double major, dual enrollment of high school students, ESL, exchange student, external degree, independent study, internships, student-designed major, study abroad, teacher certification program. **Credit/placement by examination:** AP, CLEP, IB, institutional tests. Units earned by examination cannot be used in satisfying the 30-unit residency requirement. **Support services:** Learning center, reduced course load, remedial instruction, study skills assistance, tutoring, writing center. Coaching, mentoring, Gen 1 Program.

Majors. Biology: General, biochemistry, exercise physiology. **Business:** Business admin. **Communications:** Communications/speech/rhetoric. **Computer sciences:** General. **English:** English lit. **Health services:** Premedicine, prenursing. **History:** General. **Liberal arts:** Arts/sciences. **Philosophy/religion:** Philosophy, religion. **Psychology:** General. **Social sciences:** Political science, sociology. **Visual/performing arts:** Art, dramatic, graphic design, music, music performance, studio arts, voice/opera.

Most popular majors. Biology 14%, business/marketing 20%, communications/journalism 7%, liberal arts 6%, psychology 16%, public administration/social services 12%, social sciences 10%, visual/performing arts 6%.

Technology on campus. 100 workstations in library, computer center. Dormitories wired for high-speed internet access and linked to campus network. Commuter students can connect to campus network. Online library, helpline, wireless network available.

Student life. Freshman orientation: Mandatory, $175 fee. Preregistration for classes offered. Day session offered in summer, week-of-welcome before classes begin in fall. **Policies:** Freshmen not permitted cars on campus. **Housing:** Guaranteed on-campus for freshmen. Coed dorms, themed housing, wellness housing available. $200 nonrefundable deposit, deadline 6/1. **Activities:** Campus ministries, dance, drama, international student organizations, musical theater, student government, student newspaper, Isang Lahi, Latino Unidos, business/career club, black student union, Roteract, Toastmasters, Students for Sustainability, Amnesty International, science and medical careers club.

Athletics. NCAA. **Intercollegiate:** Basketball, cross-country, golf M, lacrosse M, soccer, softball W, tennis W, volleyball W. **Team name:** Argonauts.

Student services. Adult student services, alcohol/substance abuse counseling, chaplain/spiritual director, career counseling, student employment services, financial aid counseling, health services, minority student services, personal counseling, placement for graduates.

Contact. E-mail: admiss@ndnu.edu
Phone: (650) 508-3600 Toll-free number: (800) 263-0545
Fax: (650) 508-3426
Jason Murray, Dean of Enrollment Management, Notre Dame de Namur University, 1500 Ralston Avenue, Belmont, CA 94002-1908

Occidental College
Los Angeles, California

CB member
www.oxy.edu
CB code: 4581

- Private 4-year liberal arts college affiliated with the nondenominational tradition
- Residential campus in very large city
- 2,088 degree-seeking undergraduates: 1% part-time, 57% women, 5% African American, 13% Asian American, 15% Hispanic/Latino, 9% Multi-racial, non-Hispanic, 5% international
- 2 graduate students
- 45% of applicants admitted
- SAT or ACT (ACT writing recommended), application essay required
- 87% graduate within 6 years; 21% enter graduate study

General. Founded in 1887. Regionally accredited. **Degrees:** 462 bachelor's awarded; master's offered. **ROTC:** Army, Air Force. **Location:** 5 miles from downtown. **Calendar:** Semester. **Full-time faculty:** 172 total; 96% have terminal degrees, 27% minority, 50% women. **Part-time faculty:** 88 total; 31% minority, 50% women. **Class size:** 64% < 20, 36% 20-39, less than 1% 40-49, less than 1% 50-99. **Special facilities:** Marine biology program with scuba access, plasma physics and fluid dynamics labs, paleomagnetic lab, dark matter detector, geochemical/environmental lab, ornithology collection, geological collection, shell collection, vivarium, print studio, book arts program, film lab, student garden, student-run coffee lounge.

Freshman class profile. 5,911 applied, 2,652 admitted, 518 enrolled.

Mid 50% test scores			
SAT critical reading:	600-690	**Rank in top quarter:**	90%
SAT math:	600-690	**Rank in top tenth:**	55%
SAT writing:	605-690	**End year in good standing:**	98%
ACT composite:	28-31	**Return as sophomores:**	93%
GPA 3.75 or higher:	43%	**Out-of-state:**	57%
GPA 3.50-3.74:	27%	**Live on campus:**	100%
GPA 3.0-3.49:	28%	**International:**	6%
GPA 2.0-2.99:	2%		

Basis for selection. Primary consideration given to academic credentials and holistic qualities such as intellectual curiosity, out-of-class interests, and personal character. SAT subject tests may be used for some foreign language placement. SAT and SAT Subject Tests or ACT recommended. Interview recommended. **Home schooled:** Statement describing home school structure and mission, transcript of courses and grades, state high school equivalency certificate, letter of recommendation (nonparent) required. At least 2 SAT Subject Tests recommended.

High school preparation. College-preparatory program recommended. 20 units recommended. Recommended units include English 4, mathematics 4, social studies 2, history 2, science 3 (laboratory 2), foreign language 3 and academic electives 2.

2015-2016 Annual costs. Tuition/fees: $49,248. Room/board: $13,946.

2014-2015 Financial aid. Need-based: 374 full-time freshmen applied for aid; 311 deemed to have need; 310 received aid. Average need met was 100%. Average scholarship/grant was $37,998; average loan $4,635. 82% of total undergraduate aid awarded as scholarships/grants, 18% as loans/jobs. **Non-need-based:** Awarded to 714 full-time undergraduates, including 164 freshmen. Scholarships awarded for academics, leadership, music/drama, state residency. **Additional information:** Work-study programs are available during the day when students are not in class.

Application procedures. Admission: Closing date 1/15 (postmark date). $60 fee, may be waived for applicants with need. Application must be submitted online. Admission notification by 4/1. Must reply by May 1 or within 2 week(s) if notified thereafter. **Financial aid:** Priority date 2/1, closing date 2/1. FAFSA, CSS PROFILE required. Applicants notified by 4/1; must reply by 5/1.

Academics. Special study options: Combined bachelor's/graduate degree, cross-registration, double major, dual enrollment of high school students, honors, independent study, internships, student-designed major, study abroad, United Nations semester, Washington semester. Richter Fellowships for funded international research, summer research program, endowment investment management program (Blyth Fund), paid internships. **Credit/placement**

by examination: AP, CLEP, IB, institutional tests. **Support services:** Learning center, pre-admission summer program, study skills assistance, tutoring, writing center.

Majors. Area/ethnic studies: American, East Asian, Latin American. **Biology:** General, biochemistry. **English:** English lit. **Foreign languages:** General, French, Spanish. **History:** General. **Math:** General. **Parks/recreation:** Exercise sciences. **Philosophy/religion:** Philosophy, religion. **Physical sciences:** Chemistry, geology, geophysics, physics. **Psychology:** General. **Social sciences:** Economics, international relations, political science, sociology. **Visual/performing arts:** Art, art history/conservation, dramatic, music.

Most popular majors. Biology 12%, foreign language 7%, parks/recreation 6%, physical sciences 8%, psychology 7%, social sciences 33%, visual/performing arts 8%.

Technology on campus. 300 workstations in library, computer center, student center. Commuter students can connect to campus network. Online course registration, online library, helpline, wireless network available.

Student life. Freshman orientation: Mandatory. Preregistration for classes offered. Held one week in August before the start of classes. Prior to orientation, students can participate in a wilderness trip, community service work, or an arts and culture experience. **Policies:** All residence halls student-run; freshmen, sophomores and juniors are required to live on campus. **Housing:** Guaranteed on-campus for freshmen. Coed dorms, single-sex dorms, fraternity/sorority housing, themed housing, wellness housing available. **Activities:** Bands, campus ministries, choral groups, dance, drama, film society, international student organizations, literary magazine, music ensembles, musical theater, radio station, student government, student newspaper, symphony orchestra, Chinese culture club, Hawai'i club, Queer Student Alliance, South Asian student association, Black Student Alliance, Hillel, La Raza Coalition, InterVarsity Christian Fellowship, Newman Catholic Community, Muslim Student Association.

Athletics. NCAA. **Intercollegiate:** Baseball M, basketball, cross-country, diving, football (tackle) M, golf, lacrosse W, soccer, softball W, swimming, tennis, track and field, volleyball W, water polo. **Intramural:** Basketball, football (non-tackle), soccer, volleyball. **Team name:** Tigers.

Student services. Alcohol/substance abuse counseling, chaplain/spiritual director, career counseling, services for economically disadvantaged, financial aid counseling, health services, minority student services, on-campus daycare, personal counseling, women's services. **Physically disabled:** Services for hearing impaired.

Contact. E-mail: admission@oxy.edu
Phone: (323) 259-2700 Toll-free number: (800) 825-5262
Fax: (323) 341-4875
Vince Cuseo, Vice President for Admission & Financial Aid, Occidental College, 1600 Campus Road, Los Angeles, CA 90041

Otis College of Art and Design
Los Angeles, California

CB member
www.otis.edu
CB code: 4394

- Private 4-year visual arts college
- Commuter campus in very large city
- 1,088 degree-seeking undergraduates
- 53 graduate students
- SAT or ACT (ACT writing optional), application essay required

General. Founded in 1918. Regionally accredited. **Degrees:** 238 bachelor's awarded; master's offered. **Calendar:** Semester, limited summer session. **Full-time faculty:** 55 total; 53% have terminal degrees, 20% minority, 54% women. **Part-time faculty:** 217 total; 39% have terminal degrees, 20% minority, 46% women. **Class size:** 67% < 20, 32% 20-39, less than 1% 40-49. **Special facilities:** Rare art books collection, full foundry and casting facilities, photographic darkroom, fully equipped printmaking studio, fine art book press room, wood and metal working shops, toy design department, digital imaging studio.

Freshman class profile.

GPA 3.75 or higher:	16%	GPA 2.0-2.99:	28%
GPA 3.50-3.74:	15%	Out-of-state:	43%
GPA 3.0-3.49:	41%	Live on campus:	30%

Basis for selection. Portfolio most important, followed by school achievement record, essay and test scores. Activities, leadership, motivation also considered. Portfolio required. Interview recommended. **Home schooled:** Documentation that student has solid academic foundation, is socially and intellectually mature, and has passion for the arts.

High school preparation. College-preparatory program recommended. Required and recommended units include English 4, mathematics 3-4, social studies 1-2, history 2-3, science 2-4 (laboratory 1-4) and foreign language 2. Drawing and as much art as possible recommended.

2015-2016 Annual costs. Tuition/fees: $40,504. Books/supplies: $1,400. Personal expenses: $3,700.

Financial aid. Non-need-based: Scholarships awarded for academics, art.

Application procedures. Admission: Priority date 2/15; no deadline. $60 fee, may be waived for applicants with need. Admission notification on a rolling basis beginning on or about 12/1. Must reply by May 1 or within 2 week(s) if notified thereafter. **Financial aid:** Priority date 2/15; no closing date. FAFSA required. Applicants notified on a rolling basis starting 3/1; must reply within 2 week(s) of notification.

Academics. Approximately one-third of curriculum consists of liberal arts classes. **Special study options:** Cooperative education, ESL, exchange student, honors, internships, study abroad, teacher certification program. **Credit/placement by examination:** AP, CLEP, IB, institutional tests. **Support services:** Learning center, pre-admission summer program, reduced course load, remedial instruction, study skills assistance, tutoring.

Majors. Architecture: Architecture, environmental design, interior, landscape. **Communications technology:** Animation/special effects. **Visual/performing arts:** Art, design, fashion design, graphic design, illustration, industrial design, interior design, multimedia, painting, photography, sculpture, studio arts.

Most popular majors. Visual/performing arts 95%.

Technology on campus. 450 workstations in library, computer center. Helpline, wireless network available.

Student life. Freshman orientation: Mandatory. Preregistration for classes offered. Held in January, July and August. **Housing:** Apartments available. $550 nonrefundable deposit, deadline 6/1. Otis sponsored off-campus apartments available. **Activities:** International student organizations, student government, literary organization, Campus Crusade.

Student services. Adult student services, alcohol/substance abuse counseling, career counseling, student employment services, financial aid counseling, personal counseling, placement for graduates, veterans' counselor. **Physically disabled:** Services for hearing impaired.

Contact. E-mail: admissions@otis.edu
Phone: (310) 665-6820 Toll-free number: (800) 527-6847
Fax: (310) 665-6821
Brooke Randolph, Director of Admissions, Otis College of Art and Design, 9045 Lincoln Boulevard, Los Angeles, CA 90045-9785

Pacific Oaks College
Pasadena, California
www.pacificoaks.edu   **CB code: 0482**

▶ Private two-year upper-division teachers college
▶ Commuter campus in small city
▶ Application essay required

General. Founded in 1951. Regionally accredited. College and children's school founded by Quaker families as community education center. **Degrees:** 196 bachelor's awarded; master's offered. **Articulation:** Agreements with De Anza College, Glendale City College, College of the Canyons, Pasadena City College, Rio Hondo College, Santa Monica College, Santa Barbara College, East Los Angeles College, El Camino College, Mt. San Antonio College, Citrus College. **Location:** 10 miles from downtown Los Angeles. **Calendar:** Semester, limited summer session. **Full-time faculty:** 11 total. **Part-time faculty:** 100 total. **Class size:** 72% < 20, 28% 20-39.

Student profile. 543 degree-seeking undergraduates.

Out-of-state: 19% **25 or older:**   94%

Basis for selection. College transcript, application essay required. Must have completed equivalent of GED. Transfer accepted as juniors, seniors.

2015-2016 Annual costs. Tuition/fees: $22,740. Books/supplies: $1,710. Personal expenses: $3,096.

Application procedures. Admission: Priority date 4/15; deadline 6/1. $55 fee, may be waived for applicants with need. Application must be submitted on paper.

Academics. Special study options: Accelerated study, distance learning, independent study, internships, teacher certification program, weekend college. **Credit/placement by examination:** AP, CLEP. 30 credit hours maximum toward bachelor's degree. Students age 30-35 without a bachelor's degree may earn credit based on life experience.

Majors. Work/family studies: Family studies.

Technology on campus. 17 workstations in library, computer center. Online library available.

Student life. Activities: Teacher education student association; marriage, family therapy student association.

Student services. Adult student services, career counseling, financial aid counseling. **Physically disabled:** Services for visually, speech, hearing impaired.

Contact. E-mail: admissions@pacificoaks.edu
Phone: (626) 529-8061 Toll-free number: (800) 684-0900
Fax: (626) 529-8075
Crystal Miller, Director of Admissions, Pacific Oaks College, 55 Eureka Street, Pasadena, CA 91103

Pacific States University
Los Angeles, California
www.psuca.edu   **CB code: 3547**

▶ Private 4-year university
▶ Commuter campus in very large city
▶ .14 degree-seeking undergraduates

General. Accredited by ACICS. **Degrees:** 3 bachelor's awarded; master's, doctoral offered. **Location:** 5 miles from downtown. **Calendar:** Quarter, limited summer session. **Full-time faculty:** 7 total; 57% have terminal degrees, 100% minority, 14% women. **Part-time faculty:** 23 total; 44% have terminal degrees, 100% minority, 17% women.

Basis for selection. Open admission, but selective for some programs. High school diploma and English proficiency required. TOEFL required of students whose native language is not English. **Home schooled:** Transcript of courses and grades, state high school equivalency certificate required.

2015-2016 Annual costs. Tuition/fees: $16,005. Books/supplies: $2,160.

Financial aid. Non-need-based: Scholarships awarded for academics.

Application procedures. Admission: No deadline. $100 fee. Application must be submitted on paper. Admission notification on a rolling basis. **Financial aid:** No deadline. FAFSA, institutional form required.

Academics. Special study options: Combined bachelor's/graduate degree, distance learning, double major, ESL. **Credit/placement by examination:** AP, CLEP, IB. 8 credit hours maximum toward bachelor's degree.

Majors. Business: Accounting, management information systems, marketing. **Computer sciences:** General.

Technology on campus. 40 workstations in dormitories, library, computer center. Online course registration, online library, wireless network available.

Student life. Freshman orientation: Available. Preregistration for classes offered. Held 2 weeks after each quarter starts, lasting 2 hours. **Housing:** Guaranteed on-campus for all undergraduates. Coed dorms, wellness housing available. $600 fully refundable deposit. **Activities:** Literary magazine, TV station.

Student services. Student employment services, financial aid counseling, personal counseling.

Contact. E-mail: admissions@psuca.edu
Phone: (323) 731-2383 ext. 210 Fax: (323) 731-7276
Maawiya Aeyva, Director of Admissions, Pacific States University, 3424 Wilshire Boulevard 12th floor, Los Angeles, CA 90010

Pacific Union College
Angwin, California
www.puc.edu   **CB code: 4600**

▶ Private 4-year liberal arts college affiliated with the Seventh-day Adventists
▶ Residential campus in small town

- 1,507 degree-seeking undergraduates: 10% part-time, 58% women, 9% African American, 20% Asian American, 28% Hispanic/Latino, 2% Native Hawaiian/Pacific islander, 7% Multi-racial, non-Hispanic, 3% international
- 5 degree-seeking graduate students
- 45% of applicants admitted
- SAT or ACT (ACT writing optional) required
- 44% graduate within 6 years

General. Founded in 1882. Regionally accredited. **Degrees:** 226 bachelor's, 146 associate awarded; master's offered. **Location:** 30 miles from Napa, 75 miles from San Francisco. **Calendar:** Quarter, limited summer session. **Full-time faculty:** 97 total; 52% have terminal degrees, 27% minority, 47% women. **Part-time faculty:** 46 total; 24% have terminal degrees, 22% minority, 56% women. **Class size:** 64% < 20, 28% 20-39, 4% 40-49, 4% 50-99. **Special facilities:** Airport/flight training, 1500-acre nature preserve, art gallery, observatory, biology museum, Pitcairn Island study center.

Freshman class profile. 2,041 applied, 923 admitted, 251 enrolled.

Mid 50% test scores			
		GPA 3.0-3.49:	31%
SAT critical reading:	420-560	GPA 2.0-2.99:	26%
SAT math:	430-570	End year in good standing:	89%
SAT writing:	420-540	Return as sophomores:	76%
ACT composite:	18-23	Out-of-state:	14%
GPA 3.75 or higher:	24%	Live on campus:	96%
GPA 3.50-3.74:	19%	International:	4%

Basis for selection. Minimum GPA of 2.3 in required subjects plus acceptable recommendations. **Home schooled:** Transcript of courses and grades, state high school equivalency certificate, letter of recommendation (nonparent) required. **Learning Disabled:** Documentation if available.

High school preparation. College-preparatory program recommended. 10 units required. Required and recommended units include English 4, mathematics 2-3, history 2, science 2-3 (laboratory 3), foreign language 2 and computer science 1. Religion (if offered).

2016-2017 Annual costs. Tuition/fees: $28,329. Room/board: $7,920. Books/supplies: $1,791. Personal expenses: $2,331. **Additional information:** Student Health Plan $750/year.

2015-2016 Financial aid. **Need-based:** 250 full-time freshmen applied for aid; 201 deemed to have need; 201 received aid. Average need met was 60%. Average scholarship/grant was $18,417; average loan $2,828. 81% of total undergraduate aid awarded as scholarships/grants, 19% as loans/jobs. **Non-need-based:** Awarded to 685 full-time undergraduates, including 128 freshmen. Scholarships awarded for academics, alumni affiliation, art, athletics, leadership, music/drama, religious affiliation.

Application procedures. **Admission:** No deadline. $30 fee, may be waived for applicants with need, free for online applicants. Admission notification on a rolling basis beginning on or about 1/15. Early admission review with 2.75 or higher GPA on three complete years of high school. **Financial aid:** Priority date 3/2; no closing date. FAFSA, institutional form required. Applicants notified on a rolling basis starting 4/1; must reply within 3 week(s) of notification.

Academics. **Special study options:** Cooperative education, distance learning, double major, honors, independent study, internships, liberal arts/career combination, study abroad, teacher certification program. **Credit/placement by examination:** AP, CLEP, IB, SAT, ACT, institutional tests. 24 credit hours maximum toward associate degree, 45 toward bachelor's. **Support services:** Learning center, reduced course load, remedial instruction, study skills assistance, tutoring, writing center.

Majors. Biology: General, biochemistry, biophysics. **Business:** General. **Communications:** Advertising, communications/speech/rhetoric, health, intercultural, journalism. **Computer sciences:** Computer science. **Conservation:** Environmental studies. **Education:** Early childhood, elementary, music, physical, social science. **English:** English lit. **Foreign languages:** Spanish. **Health services:** EMT paramedic, nursing (RN), prechiropractic, predental, premedicine, preoptometry, prepharmacy, preveterinary. **History:** General. **Human services:** Social work. **Math:** General. **Parks/recreation:** Health/fitness. **Philosophy/religion:** Religion. **Physical sciences:** Chemistry, physics. **Psychology:** General. **Social sciences:** Political science. **Theology:** Theology. **Visual/performing arts:** Cinematography, graphic design, music, music performance, photography, studio arts.

Most popular majors. Biology 12%, business/marketing 14%, communications/journalism 8%, health sciences 19%, visual/performing arts 8%.

Technology on campus. 228 workstations in library. Dormitories wired for high-speed internet access and linked to campus network. Commuter students can connect to campus network. Online course registration, online library, helpline, repair service, wireless network available.

Student life. Freshman orientation: Mandatory. Preregistration for classes offered. 4-day event held on-campus and at Albion Field Station from Wednesday night of the last week before the Fall quarter starts to Sunday night of the first week of school. **Policies:** Service animals and emotional support pets allowed according to policy. Religious observance required. **Housing:** Guaranteed on-campus for freshmen. Single-sex dorms, apartments, wellness housing available. $200 nonrefundable deposit, deadline 5/1. **Activities:** Bands, campus ministries, choral groups, drama, film society, literary magazine, music ensembles, student government, student newspaper, symphony orchestra, Service, Service Learning, Amnesty, Black Student Forum, SOL club (Student Organization of Latinos) Asian Student Association, Hawaiian club, social work club, Homeless Ministries.

Athletics. NAIA. **Intercollegiate:** Basketball, cross-country, soccer M, volleyball W. **Intramural:** Badminton, baseball, basketball, football (nontackle), golf, handball, ice hockey, soccer, softball, triathlon, ultimate frisbee, volleyball, water polo. **Team name:** Pioneers.

Student services. Adult student services, alcohol/substance abuse counseling, chaplain/spiritual director, career counseling, student employment services, financial aid counseling, health services, on-campus daycare, personal counseling, placement for graduates. **Physically disabled:** Services for visually, speech, hearing impaired.

Contact. E-mail: enroll@puc.edu
Phone: (707) 965-6336 Toll-free number: (800) 862-7080
Fax: (707) 965-6671
Craig Philpott, Director, Admissions, Pacific Union College, One Angwin Avenue, Angwin, CA 94508-9707

Patten University
Oakland, California   CB member
www.patten.edu   CB code: 4620

- Private 4-year university and liberal arts college affiliated with the interdenominational tradition
- Commuter campus in large city
- 1,492 degree-seeking undergraduates
- 204 graduate students
- Application essay, interview required

General. Founded in 1944. Regionally accredited. **Degrees:** 37 bachelor's, 9 associate awarded; master's offered. **Location:** 18 miles from San Francisco, 30 miles from San Jose. **Calendar:** Trimester, limited summer session. **Full-time faculty:** 9 total; 67% have terminal degrees, 22% minority. **Part-time faculty:** 23 total; 13% have terminal degrees, 22% minority.

Basis for selection. Open admission, but selective for some programs. High school record, interview, essay, test scores important.

High school preparation. 22 units required. Required units include English 4, mathematics 2, social studies 4, history 2, science 2 (laboratory 1), foreign language 1 and academic electives 6.

2015-2016 Annual costs. Tuition/fees: $3,432.

Application procedures. **Admission:** Priority date 3/31; deadline 7/31. $30 fee, may be waived for applicants with need. Admission notification on a rolling basis. **Financial aid:** No deadline. Institutional form required.

Academics. **Special study options:** Accelerated study, combined bachelor's/graduate degree, double major, dual enrollment of high school students, independent study, teacher certification program, weekend college. **Credit/placement by examination:** AP, CLEP, institutional tests. **Support services:** Learning center.

Majors. Business: Business admin. **Education:** Adult/continuing, early childhood. **Liberal arts:** Arts/sciences. **Psychology:** General.

Most popular majors. Business/marketing 39%, liberal arts 12%, psychology 39%, theological studies 17%.

Technology on campus. 30 workstations in library, computer center. Online library, wireless network available.

Student life. Freshman orientation: Mandatory. Preregistration for classes offered. 3-day overview held week before start of classes. **Activities:** Community of Faith groups, prison ministry.

Student services. Adult student services, career counseling, student employment services, personal counseling, placement for graduates, veterans' counselor.

Contact. E-mail: admissions@patten.edu
Phone: (510) 261-8500 ext. 7764 Toll-free number: (877) 472-8836
Fax: (510) 534-4344
Cindi Hogeboom, Director of Admissions, Patten University, 2433
Coolidge Avenue, Oakland, CA 94601-2699

Pepperdine University
Malibu, California — **CB member**
www.pepperdine.edu — **CB code: 4630**

- Private 4-year university and liberal arts college affiliated with the Church of Christ
- Residential campus in small city
- 3,514 degree-seeking undergraduates: 8% part-time, 59% women, 6% African American, 12% Asian American, 16% Hispanic/Latino, 5% Multi-racial, non-Hispanic, 10% international
- 4,068 degree-seeking graduate students
- 38% of applicants admitted
- SAT or ACT (ACT writing optional), application essay required
- 84% graduate within 6 years

General. Founded in 1937. Regionally accredited. Education, psychology, business graduate campuses in Los Angeles. Educational centers in Long Beach, Irvine, Encino, West Los Angeles, Westlake Village. **Degrees:** 910 bachelor's awarded; master's, professional, doctoral offered. **ROTC:** Army, Air Force. **Location:** 14 miles from Santa Monica, 30 miles from Los Angeles. **Calendar:** Semester, limited summer session. **Full-time faculty:** 381 total; 88% have terminal degrees, 19% minority, 39% women. **Part-time faculty:** 324 total; 55% have terminal degrees, 20% minority, 52% women. **Class size:** 69% < 20, 27% 20-39, 2% 40-49, less than 1% 50-99, 1% >100.

Freshman class profile. 9,923 applied, 3,781 admitted, 745 enrolled.

Mid 50% test scores		Rank in top quarter:	80%
SAT critical reading:	550-650	Rank in top tenth:	48%
SAT math:	550-670	Return as sophomores:	94%
SAT writing:	550-650	Out-of-state:	51%
ACT composite:	25-30	Live on campus:	98%
GPA 3.75 or higher:	39%	International:	10%
GPA 3.50-3.74:	24%	Fraternities:	23%
GPA 3.0-3.49:	34%	Sororities:	34%
GPA 2.0-2.99:	3%		

Basis for selection. School achievement record and test scores most important. Special talents, school and community activities, letters of recommendation, personal qualities also considered. Audition required for music, theater majors. Portfolio recommended for art majors. **Home schooled:** Transcript of courses and grades, state high school equivalency certificate required. **Learning Disabled:** Proper documentation from doctor diagnosing learning disability required.

High school preparation. College-preparatory program recommended.

2015-2016 Annual costs. Tuition/fees: $48,342. Room/board: $13,810. Books/supplies: $1,500. Personal expenses: $1,500.

2015-2016 Financial aid. Need-based: 736 full-time freshmen applied for aid; 405 deemed to have need; 401 received aid. Average need met was 73%. Average scholarship/grant was $32,440; average loan $5,774. 82% of total undergraduate aid awarded as scholarships/grants, 18% as loans/jobs. **Non-need-based:** Awarded to 764 full-time undergraduates, including 218 freshmen. Scholarships awarded for academics, art, athletics, leadership, music/drama, religious affiliation.

Application procedures. Admission: Closing date 1/5 (postmark date). $65 fee, may be waived for applicants with need. Admission notification by 4/1. Must reply by 5/1. **Financial aid:** Closing date 2/15. FAFSA required. Applicants notified by 4/15; must reply by 5/1.

Academics. Great books colloquium, freshman seminars and first year faculty mentor program for all students. **Special study options:** Combined bachelor's/graduate degree, distance learning, double major, honors, independent study, internships, student-designed major, study abroad, teacher certification program, Washington semester. 3/2 Engineering program with University of Southern California School of Engineering, or Washington University School of Engineering in St. Louis. 5-year BS/MBA program which allows select Seaver College business majors to earn their bachelor's and MBA or International MBA degrees in five years. Academic Year residential program offered in Heidelberg, Germany; London, United Kingdom; Florence, Italy; Buenos Aires, Argentina; Lausanne, Switzerland; and Shanghai, China. Part-time, evening, weekend classes for business undergrad programs. **Credit/placement by examination:** AP, CLEP, IB, SAT, ACT, institutional tests. 32 credit hours maximum toward bachelor's degree. IB credit

awarded for higher level exams only: 4 credits for each score of 5 and above; maximum 16. **Support services:** Pre-admission summer program, remedial instruction, tutoring, writing center.

Majors. Area/ethnic studies: Asian, Chicano/Hispanic-American/Latino, European, Latin American. **Biology:** General. **Business:** Accounting, business admin, finance, international, marketing. **Communications:** General, advertising, communications/speech/rhetoric, intercultural, journalism, organizational, persuasive communications, radio/TV. **Computer sciences:** Webmaster. **Education:** Chemistry, English, mathematics, music. **English:** Creative writing, English lit. **Foreign languages:** French, German, Italian, Semitic, Spanish. **History:** General. **Liberal arts:** Arts/sciences. **Math:** General. **Parks/recreation:** Exercise sciences, health/fitness, physical fitness technician, sports admin. **Philosophy/religion:** Philosophy, religion. **Physical sciences:** Chemistry, physics. **Psychology:** General. **Social sciences:** Economics, political science, sociology. **Visual/performing arts:** Acting, art, art history/conservation, directing/producing, film/cinema/video, music, music theory/composition, theater design.

Most popular majors. Business/marketing 29%, communications/journalism 18%, interdisciplinary studies 7%, psychology 8%, social sciences 12%, visual/performing arts 6%.

Technology on campus. 292 workstations in dormitories, library, computer center, student center. Dormitories wired for high-speed internet access and linked to campus network. Commuter students can connect to campus network. Online library, helpline, repair service, wireless network available.

Student life. Freshman orientation: Mandatory. Preregistration for classes offered. Held week before start of fall semester. **Policies:** Students required to attend weekly convocation. Freshmen and sophomores live on campus or at home with parent or guardian if single and under 21. **Housing:** Guaranteed on-campus for freshmen. Single-sex dorms, special housing for disabled, apartments available. **Activities:** Bands, campus ministries, choral groups, dance, drama, film society, international student organizations, literary magazine, music ensembles, Model UN, musical theater, opera, radio station, student government, student newspaper, symphony orchestra, TV station, Campus Crusade for Christ, College Republicans, Young Democrats, volunteer center, Black student union, Latin student association, Hawaiian club, Korean student association, Japan club.

Athletics. NCAA. **Intercollegiate:** Baseball M, basketball, cross-country, golf, sand volleyball W, soccer W, swimming W, tennis, track and field, volleyball, water polo M. **Intramural:** Basketball, football (non-tackle), handball, soccer, swimming, volleyball. **Team name:** Waves.

Student services. Alcohol/substance abuse counseling, chaplain/spiritual director, career counseling, student employment services, financial aid counseling, health services, personal counseling, placement for graduates, veterans' counselor. **Physically disabled:** Services for visually, hearing impaired.

Contact. E-mail: admission-seaver@pepperdine.edu
Phone: (310) 506-4392 Fax: (310) 506-4861
Kristin Collins, Dean of Enrollment Managment, Pepperdine University, 24255 Pacific Coast Highway, Malibu, CA 90263-4392

Pitzer College
Claremont, California — **CB member**
www.pitzer.edu — **CB code: 4619**

- Private 4-year liberal arts college
- Residential campus in large town
- 1,067 degree-seeking undergraduates: 3% part-time, 57% women, 5% African American, 9% Asian American, 15% Hispanic/Latino, 9% Multi-racial, non-Hispanic, 7% international
- 13% of applicants admitted
- Application essay required
- 89% graduate within 6 years

General. Founded in 1963. Regionally accredited. One of 5 undergraduate and 2 graduate institutions on adjoining campuses which share facilities. Cross-enrollment available at Claremont-McKenna, Harvey Mudd, Pitzer, Pomona, and Scripps. Interdisciplinary curriculum with social responsibility requirement, intercultural education objective; no academic departments. **Degrees:** 263 bachelor's awarded. **ROTC:** Army, Air Force. **Location:** 35 miles from Los Angeles. **Calendar:** Semester, limited summer session. **Full-time faculty:** 96 total; 100% have terminal degrees, 31% minority, 58% women. **Part-time faculty:** 20 total; 100% have terminal degrees, 30% minority, 55% women. **Class size:** 73% < 20, 26% 20-39, 1% 40-49. **Special facilities:** Ecology center, nature reserve, arboretum, organic garden, women's studies center, restored arts and crafts home with poetry reading room.

Freshman class profile. 4,149 applied, 559 admitted, 267 enrolled.

Mid 50% test scores			
SAT critical reading:	620-720	**GPA 3.0-3.49:**	18%
SAT math:	630-720	**Return as sophomores:**	93%
ACT composite:	29-32	**Out-of-state:**	57%
GPA 3.75 or higher:	60%	**Live on campus:**	100%
GPA 3.50-3.74:	22%	**International:**	5%

Basis for selection. School record, essays, 3 recommendations, test scores, leadership, community service, work experience, talent, involvement in sports considered. SAT/ACT not required of students graduating in top 10% of class, or those with unweighted cumulative GPA of 3.50 or higher in academic subjects. Otherwise, 1 of the following required: ACT or SAT scores; 2 SAT Subject Tests (1 in math); 2 or more AP test scores of at least 4 (1 English or English Language and 1 math or science); 2 International Baccalaureate exams (English 1A and math); or 1 recent junior or senior year graded analytical writing sample from humanities or social science course and 1 recent graded exam from advanced math course. Samples must include teacher's comments, grades, and the assignment. Interview recommended.

High school preparation. College-preparatory program recommended. 21 units required. Required units include English 4, mathematics 3, social studies 3, history 1, science 3 (laboratory 3), foreign language 3 and visual/performing arts 1.

2015-2016 Annual costs. Tuition/fees: $48,670. Room/board: $15,210. Books/supplies: $1,000. Personal expenses: $1,000.

2015-2016 Financial aid. Need-based: 149 full-time freshmen applied for aid; 109 deemed to have need; 109 received aid. Average need met was 100%. Average scholarship/grant was $42,479; average loan $2,631. 89% of total undergraduate aid awarded as scholarships/grants, 11% as loans/jobs. **Non-need-based:** Awarded to 39 full-time undergraduates, including 11 freshmen. Scholarships awarded for academics, leadership, ROTC.

Application procedures. Admission: Closing date 1/1 (postmark date). $70 fee, may be waived for applicants with need. Admission notification by 4/1. Must reply by May 1 or within 1 week(s) if notified thereafter. **Financial aid:** Closing date 2/1. FAFSA, CSS PROFILE required. Applicants notified by 4/1; must reply by 5/1.

Academics. Students may take up to one-third of courses at other Claremont campuses (and more for shared majors) and must take 32 courses for graduation. Can create independent study courses and special majors. **Special study options:** Combined bachelor's/graduate degree, cooperative education, cross-registration, double major, ESL, exchange student, honors, independent study, internships, liberal arts/career combination, student-designed major, study abroad, urban semester. New Resources (for students over age 25 and nontraditional students), joint science program, joint BA/DO program. **Credit/placement by examination:** AP, CLEP, IB. **Support services:** Tutoring, writing center.

Majors. Area/ethnic studies: African-American, American, Asian, Asian-American, Caribbean, Chicano/Hispanic-American/Latino, European, Latin American, women's. **Biology:** General, biochemistry, biophysics, microbiology, neuroscience. **Business:** Organizational behavior. **Conservation:** Environmental science, environmental studies. **English:** Creative writing, English lit. **Foreign languages:** General, Chinese, classics, French, German, Italian, Japanese, linguistics, Russian, Spanish. **History:** General, American, European. **Math:** General. **Philosophy/religion:** Philosophy, religion. **Physical sciences:** Chemistry, organic chemistry, physics. **Psychology:** General. **Social sciences:** General, anthropology, economics, international relations, political science, sociology. **Visual/performing arts:** Art, art history/conservation, cinematography, dance, dramatic, film/cinema/video, studio arts.

Most popular majors. Biology 9%, interdisciplinary studies 12%, natural resources/environmental science 11%, psychology 11%, social sciences 19%.

Technology on campus. 100 workstations in dormitories, library, computer center, student center. Dormitories wired for high-speed internet access and linked to campus network. Commuter students can connect to campus network. Online course registration, online library, helpline, student web hosting, wireless network available.

Student life. Freshman orientation: Mandatory. Preregistration for classes offered. Held the week prior to start of fall semester. **Policies:** Strong philosophical framework of social responsibility and self-governance. Freshmen not permitted cars on campus. **Housing:** Guaranteed on-campus for freshmen. Coed dorms, special housing for disabled available. Green housing available. **Activities:** Campus ministries, choral groups, dance, drama, film society, international student organizations, literary magazine, music ensembles, Model UN, musical theater, radio station, student government, student newspaper, symphony orchestra, over 75 social service, religious, political, and ethnic organizations.

Athletics. NCAA. **Intercollegiate:** Badminton, baseball M, basketball, cross-country, diving, football (tackle) M, golf, lacrosse, soccer, softball W, swimming, tennis, track and field, volleyball W, water polo. **Intramural:** Archery, badminton, basketball, golf, racquetball, sailing, soccer, softball W, squash, tennis. **Team name:** Sagehens.

Student services. Adult student services, alcohol/substance abuse counseling, chaplain/spiritual director, career counseling, student employment services, financial aid counseling, health services, minority student services, personal counseling, women's services. **Physically disabled:** Services for visually, speech, hearing impaired.

Contact. E-mail: admission@pitzer.edu
Phone: (909) 621-8129 Toll-free number: (800) 748-9371
Fax: (909) 621-8770
Angel Perez, Vice President of Admission and Financial Aid, Pitzer College, 1050 North Mills Avenue, Claremont, CA 91711-6101

Platt College: Ontario
Ontario, California
www.plattcollege.edu   CB code: 3015

- For-profit 4-year branch campus and technical college
- Commuter campus in small city
- 431 undergraduates
- Application essay, interview required

General. Accredited by ACCSC. Branch of Los Angeles campus. **Degrees:** 67 bachelor's, 218 associate awarded. **Location:** 20 miles from Los Angeles. **Calendar:** Differs by program. **Full-time faculty:** 20 total; 20% have terminal degrees, 15% minority. **Part-time faculty:** 18 total; 56% have terminal degrees, 67% minority. **Class size:** 71% < 20, 29% 20-39. **Special facilities:** Motion capture lab.

Basis for selection. Students admitted based on interview, high school diploma or GED, entrance test and essay, and completion of the admissions process. Math and English workshops available to students upon entrance if desired or recommended. **Learning Disabled:** Students with learning disabilities may request consideration for extra time to complete entrance test.

2015-2016 Annual costs. Personal expenses: $2,348. **Additional information:** Medical Sciences: certificate $1,795-$31,941; associate $26,913.50-$45,798; bachelor's $24,867.50-$66,858.50. Legal Studies: certificate/diploma $26,981-$31,515.50; associate $31,816-$37,919; Bachelor's $72,936.50-$78,939.50.

Application procedures. Admission: No deadline. $75 fee. Admission notification on a rolling basis. **Financial aid:** Priority date 3/2; no closing date. FAFSA, institutional form required. Applicants notified on a rolling basis starting 1/1.

Academics. Special study options: Accelerated study, cooperative education, internships. **Credit/placement by examination:** AP, CLEP. 48 credit hours maximum toward associate degree, 48 toward bachelor's. **Support services:** Tutoring.

Majors. Communications technology: Animation/special effects, graphics. **Computer sciences:** Computer graphics, web page design. **Visual/performing arts:** General, commercial/advertising art, design.

Technology on campus. 12 workstations in library.

Student life. Freshman orientation: Mandatory. Preregistration for classes offered. Held on first day of classes. **Activities:** Various student clubs and activities available.

Student services. Adult student services, career counseling, student employment services, financial aid counseling, placement for graduates.

Contact. Phone: (909) 941-9410 Toll-free number: (866) 752-8846
Fax: (909) 941-9660
Admissions Director, Platt College: Ontario, 3700 Inland Empire Boulevard, Ontario, CA 91764

Platt College: San Diego
San Diego, California
www.platt.edu   CB code: 3020

- For-profit 4-year visual arts and technical college
- Commuter campus in very large city

◆ 369 degree-seeking undergraduates: 27% women
◆ Application essay, interview required

General. Accredited by ACCSC. **Degrees:** 93 bachelor's, 66 associate awarded. **Calendar:** Differs by program. **Full-time faculty:** 6 total. **Part-time faculty:** 23 total; 26% have terminal degrees, 17% minority, 39% women. **Class size:** 91% < 20, 9% 20-39.

Freshman class profile. 17 applied, 17 admitted, 17 enrolled.

Basis for selection. Open admission, but selective for some programs and for out-of-state students. Aptitude test used to measure academic preparedness to undertake college-level courses; SAT considered in lieu of test. **Learning Disabled:** Documentation of the disability required to ensure reasonable accommodation.

2015-2016 Annual costs. Books/supplies: $1,870. Personal expenses: $4,468. **Additional information:** Medical Sciences: certificate $1,795-$31,941; associate $26,913.50-$45,798; bachelor's $24,867.50-$66,858.50. Legal Studies: certificate/diploma $26,981-$31,515.50; associate $31,816-$37,919; Bachelor's $72,936.50-$78,939.50.

Application procedures. Admission: No deadline. No application fee. Application must be submitted on paper. **Financial aid:** Closing date 3/2. FAFSA, institutional form required. Applicants notified on a rolling basis; must reply within 1 week(s) of notification.

Academics. Special study options: Accelerated study, internships, liberal arts/career combination. **Credit/placement by examination:** AP, CLEP, institutional tests. **Support services:** Study skills assistance, tutoring.

Majors. Visual/performing arts: General, commercial/advertising art.

Technology on campus. 200 workstations in library, computer center. Online library available.

Student life. Freshman orientation: Mandatory. Preregistration for classes offered.

Student services. Career counseling, services for economically disadvantaged, student employment services, financial aid counseling, personal counseling, placement for graduates.

Contact. E-mail: info@platt.edu
Phone: (619) 265-0107 Toll-free number: (866) 752-8826
Fax: (619) 308-0570
Meg Leiker, President, Platt College: San Diego, 6250 El Cajon Boulevard, San Diego, CA 92115

Point Loma Nazarene University

San Diego, California   **CB member**
www.pointloma.edu   **CB code: 4605**

◆ Private 4-year university and liberal arts college affiliated with the Church of the Nazarene
◆ Residential campus in very large city
◆ 2,760 degree-seeking undergraduates: 6% part-time, 64% women, 2% African American, 5% Asian American, 23% Hispanic/Latino, 1% Native American, 1% Native Hawaiian/Pacific islander, 8% Multi-racial, non-Hispanic, 1% international
◆ 822 degree-seeking graduate students
◆ 71% of applicants admitted
◆ SAT or ACT (ACT writing recommended), application essay required
◆ 75% graduate within 6 years

General. Founded in 1902. Regionally accredited. Located on a coastal clifftop overlooking the Pacific Ocean. **Degrees:** 548 bachelor's awarded; master's offered. **ROTC:** Army, Naval, Air Force. **Location:** 5 miles from downtown. **Calendar:** Semester, limited summer session. **Full-time faculty:** 136 total; 85% have terminal degrees, 16% minority, 44% women. **Part-time faculty:** 236 total; 25% have terminal degrees, 14% minority, 59% women. **Class size:** 40% < 20, 44% 20-39, 13% 40-49, 3% 50-99. **Special facilities:** Historical Greek amphitheater.

Freshman class profile. 2,809 applied, 2,004 admitted, 599 enrolled.

Mid 50% test scores			
SAT critical reading:	510-620	GPA 2.0-2.99:	3%
SAT math:	510-630	Rank in top quarter:	63%
SAT writing:	510-610	Rank in top tenth:	33%
ACT composite:	23-28	Return as sophomores:	85%
GPA 3.75 or higher:	59%	Out-of-state:	21%
GPA 3.50-3.74:	17%	Live on campus:	93%
GPA 3.0-3.49:	21%	International:	1%

Basis for selection. Moral character, maturity, intellectual ability, and academic achievement important. Preference given to self-directed applicants who appear to share ideals and objectives of college.

High school preparation. College-preparatory program required. 18 units recommended. Recommended units include English 4, mathematics 3, social studies 2, history 1, science 3 (laboratory 2) and foreign language 2.

2015-2016 Annual costs. Tuition/fees: $32,400. Room/board: $9,800. Books/supplies: $1,764. Personal expenses: $2,322.

2014-2015 Financial aid. Need-based: 515 full-time freshmen applied for aid; 421 deemed to have need; 421 received aid. Average need met was 64%. Average scholarship/grant was $16,970; average loan $3,611. 61% of total undergraduate aid awarded as scholarships/grants, 39% as loans/jobs. **Non-need-based:** Awarded to 686 full-time undergraduates, including 177 freshmen. Scholarships awarded for academics, art, athletics, music/drama, religious affiliation, ROTC.

Application procedures. Admission: Priority date 2/15; deadline 4/1 (receipt date). $55 fee, may be waived for applicants with need. Admission notification on a rolling basis beginning on or about 4/1. Must reply by May 1 or within 2 week(s) if notified thereafter. **Financial aid:** Priority date 3/2; no closing date. FAFSA required. Applicants notified on a rolling basis starting 12/15; must reply by 5/15.

Academics. Special study options: Accelerated study, distance learning, double major, honors, independent study, internships, semester at sea, study abroad, teacher certification program, United Nations semester, Washington semester. **Credit/placement by examination:** AP, CLEP, IB, SAT, ACT, institutional tests. 32 credit hours maximum toward bachelor's degree. Some restrictions apply in special majors. **Support services:** Learning center, reduced course load, remedial instruction, study skills assistance, tutoring, writing center.

Majors. Biology: General, biochemistry. **Business:** Accounting, business admin, communications, entrepreneurial studies, finance, management information systems, management science, managerial economics, marketing, nonprofit/public. **Communications:** Broadcast journalism, communications/speech/rhetoric, journalism, media studies. **Conservation:** Environmental science. **Education:** Art, elementary, music. **Engineering:** Applied physics, software. **English:** English lit, writing. **Foreign languages:** French, Spanish. **Health services:** General, athletic training, dietetics, nursing (RN). **History:** General. **Human services:** Social work. **Liberal arts:** Arts/sciences. **Math:** General. **Parks/recreation:** Exercise sciences. **Philosophy/religion:** Philosophy. **Physical sciences:** Chemistry, physics. **Psychology:** General. **Social sciences:** General, international economic development, political science, sociology. **Theology:** Bible, preministerial, sacred music. **Visual/performing arts:** General, graphic design, music, music performance, music theory/composition, piano/keyboard, voice/opera. **Work/family studies:** Child development, food/nutrition, institutional food production.

Most popular majors. Biology 8%, business/marketing 19%, communications/journalism 6%, health sciences 21%, psychology 9%, visual/performing arts 6%.

Technology on campus. 520 workstations in dormitories, library, computer center, student center. Dormitories wired for high-speed internet access and linked to campus network. Commuter students can connect to campus network. Online course registration, online library, helpline, repair service, wireless network available.

Student life. Freshman orientation: Mandatory. Preregistration for classes offered. Held Friday through Sunday before classes begin. **Policies:** Students are expected to exercise self-discipline, sound judgment and manage conduct both on and off campus consistent with agreements made upon application and with University catalog and Student Handbook. Religious observance required. Freshmen not permitted cars on campus. **Housing:** Guaranteed on-campus for freshmen. Single-sex dorms, special housing for disabled, apartments available. **Activities:** Bands, campus ministries, choral groups, drama, film society, international student organizations, literary magazine, music ensembles, musical theater, opera, radio station, student government, student newspaper, symphony orchestra, TV station, Students for Social Justice, social work club, College Democrats, College Republicans, Brothers and Sisters United, Association of Latin American Students, Asian student union, black student union.

Athletics. NCAA, NCCAA. **Intercollegiate:** Baseball M, basketball, cross-country W, golf W, soccer, tennis, track and field W, volleyball W. **Intramural:** Basketball, football (non-tackle), soccer, softball, tennis, volleyball. **Team name:** Sea Lions.

Student services. Chaplain/spiritual director, career counseling, student employment services, financial aid counseling, health services, minority student services, on-campus daycare, personal counseling, veterans' counselor. **Physically disabled:** Services for visually, speech, hearing impaired.

Contact. E-mail: admissions@pointloma.edu
Phone: (800) 733-7779 Toll-free number: (800) 733-7770
Fax: (619) 849-2601
Shannon Hutchison, Director of Undergraduate Admissions, Point Loma
Nazarene University, 3900 Lomaland Drive, San Diego, CA 92106-2899

Pomona College
Claremont, California
www.pomona.edu

CB member
CB code: 4607

- Private 4-year liberal arts college
- Residential campus in large town
- 1,640 degree-seeking undergraduates
- SAT and SAT Subject Tests or ACT (ACT writing recommended), application essay required

General. Founded in 1887. Regionally accredited. One of 5 undergraduate and 2 graduate schools on adjoining campuses. Campuses share facilities. Cross-enrollment available at any of the 5 undergraduate colleges, which, in addition to Pomona College, include Claremont McKenna College, Harvey Mudd College, Pitzer College, and Scripps College. Extensive overseas studies. **Degrees:** 392 bachelor's awarded. **ROTC:** Army, Air Force. **Location:** 35 miles from Los Angeles, 20 miles from Pasadena. **Calendar:** Semester. **Full-time faculty:** 188 total; 2% have terminal degrees, 31% minority, 44% women. **Part-time faculty:** 44 total; 25% minority, 50% women. **Class size:** 69% < 20, 27% 20-39, 2% 40-49, 1% 50-99. **Special facilities:** Science center, center for modern language and international relations, observatory, biological field station, ecological preserve, botanic garden, social sciences center, Greek theater, multimedia labs, foreign language resource center, college-operated museum.

Freshman class profile.

Rank in top quarter:	99%	Out-of-state:	72%
Rank in top tenth:	91%	Live on campus:	99%

Basis for selection. School achievement record, test scores, essays, 3 recommendations most important. Special skills in music, art, drama, or athletics; leadership, motivation, and diversity of background also important. Some preference to children of alumni; special consideration for underrepresented groups. School and community activities also considered. The two SAT subject tests should be in different academic areas and, in cases where multiple levels are offered (Math I and Math II) the higher level exam should be pursued. Interviews recommended for all; expected of Southern California applicants. Students interested in the fine and performing arts can submit arts portfolios for faculty evaluation. Students with extensive research backgrounds can submit research portfolios. **Home schooled:** Statement describing home school structure and mission, transcript of courses and grades required. SAT and at least four SAT Subject Tests required, more recommended. Detailed description of curriculum required.

High school preparation. College-preparatory program required. 20 units required. Required and recommended units include English 4, mathematics 4, social studies 2-4, science 2-4 (laboratory 2-3) and foreign language 3-4. 3-4 laboratory sciences recommended for science applicants. Mathematics through calculus recommended for all applicants.

2015-2016 Annual costs. Tuition/fees: $47,620. Room/board: $15,150. Books/supplies: $900.

Financial aid. All financial aid based on need. **Additional information:** Financial aid awards loan-free for all eligible students.

Application procedures. Admission: Closing date 1/1 (receipt date). $70 fee, may be waived for applicants with need. Admission notification by 4/1. Must reply by May 1 or within 1 week(s) if notified thereafter. **Financial aid:** Priority date 3/1, closing date 3/1. FAFSA, CSS PROFILE required. Applicants notified by 4/1; must reply by 5/1.

Academics. Special study options: Combined bachelor's/graduate degree, cross-registration, double major, exchange student, independent study, internships, student-designed major, study abroad, Washington semester. 3-2 program in engineering with Washington University in St Louis, California Institute of Technology, and Dartmouth College. **Credit/placement by examination:** AP, CLEP, IB, institutional tests. 8 credit hours maximum toward bachelor's degree. **Support services:** Tutoring, writing center. Quantitative skills center.

Majors. Area/ethnic studies: African-American, American, Asian, Asian-American, Chicano/Hispanic-American/Latino, German, Latin American, Russian/Eastern European/Eurasian, women's. **Biology:** General, molecular, neuroscience. **Communications:** Media studies. **Computer sciences:** Computer science. **Conservation:** Environmental studies. **English:** English lit. **Foreign languages:** Chinese, classics, French, Japanese, linguistics,

Romance, Russian, Spanish. **History:** General. **Human services:** Public policy. **Math:** General. **Philosophy/religion:** Philosophy, religion. **Physical sciences:** Astronomy, chemistry, geology, physics. **Psychology:** General. **Social sciences:** Anthropology, economics, international relations, political science, sociology. **Visual/performing arts:** Art history/conservation, dance, dramatic, music, studio arts.

Most popular majors. Biology 11%, interdisciplinary studies 9%, mathematics 10%, natural resources/environmental science 6%, physical sciences 8%, social sciences 18%, visual/performing arts 7%.

Technology on campus. 180 workstations in dormitories, library, computer center, student center. Dormitories wired for high-speed internet access and linked to campus network. Commuter students can connect to campus network. Online course registration, online library, helpline, repair service, wireless network available.

Student life. Freshman orientation: Mandatory. Preregistration for classes offered. Held immediately prior to fall semester. **Policies:** Freshmen not permitted cars on campus. **Housing:** Guaranteed on-campus for all undergraduates. Coed dorms, themed housing available. $500 nonrefundable deposit, deadline 5/1. **Activities:** Bands, campus ministries, choral groups, dance, drama, film society, international student organizations, literary magazine, music ensembles, Model UN, musical theater, radio station, student government, student newspaper, symphony orchestra, TV station, center for religious activities, international peace, Asian students association, Mortar Board (service organization), women's coalition, Queer Resource Center, Office of Black Student Affairs, Chicano/Latino Student Association.

Athletics. NCAA. **Intercollegiate:** Baseball M, basketball, cross-country, diving, football (tackle) M, golf, lacrosse W, soccer, softball W, swimming, tennis, track and field, volleyball W, water polo. **Intramural:** Badminton, basketball, equestrian, handball, racquetball, skiing, soccer, softball, squash, table tennis, track and field, volleyball, water polo. **Team name:** Sagehens.

Student services. Chaplain/spiritual director, career counseling, student employment services, financial aid counseling, health services, minority student services, personal counseling, placement for graduates. **Physically disabled:** Services for visually, hearing impaired.

Contact. E-mail: admissions@pomona.edu
Phone: (909) 621-8134 Fax: (909) 621-8952
Art Rodriguez, Director of Admissions, Pomona College, 333 North College Way, Claremont, CA 91711-6312

Providence Christian College
Pasadena, California
www.providencecc.edu

CB code: 7893

- Private 4-year liberal arts college affiliated with the nondenominational tradition
- Residential campus in large city
- 145 degree-seeking undergraduates: 50% women
- SAT or ACT (ACT writing optional), application essay, interview required
- 67% graduate within 6 years

General. Regionally accredited. **Degrees:** 14 bachelor's awarded. **Calendar:** Semester. **Full-time faculty:** 6 total; 83% have terminal degrees, 33% women. **Part-time faculty:** 17 total; 29% have terminal degrees, 35% women. **Class size:** 83% < 20, 17% 20-39.

Freshman class profile. 53 enrolled.

GPA 3.75 or higher:	17%	Return as sophomores:	77%
GPA 3.50-3.74:	16%	Out-of-state:	65%
GPA 3.0-3.49:	17%	Live on campus:	6%
GPA 2.0-2.99:	50%		

Basis for selection. Admission is granted to applicants who provide evidence of qualities of mind and purpose required for a liberal arts college education, and whose personal qualifications provide assurance they will be responsible and contributing members of a college community committed to the lordship of Jesus Christ. Qualities of mind are demonstrated by breadth and quality of high school preparation. Among considerations are the application essay and/or an interview. **Home schooled:** Transcript of courses and grades required.

High school preparation. College-preparatory program recommended. 16 units required. Required units include English 3, mathematics 3, social studies 1, history 2, science 2 (laboratory 1) and foreign language 2.

2015-2016 Annual costs. Tuition/fees: $27,173. Room/board: $8,213. Personal expenses: $3,584.

Financial aid. Non-need-based: Scholarships awarded for academics, leadership, music/drama, religious affiliation.

Application procedures. Admission: No deadline. $25 fee. Admission notification on a rolling basis. **Financial aid:** Closing date 3/1. FAFSA, institutional form required. Applicants notified on a rolling basis starting 3/5; must reply by 5/1 or within 3 week(s) of notification.

Academics. Special study options: Dual enrollment of high school students, internships. **Credit/placement by examination:** AP, CLEP. **Support services:** Learning center, reduced course load, remedial instruction, study skills assistance, tutoring, writing center.

Majors. Liberal arts: Arts/sciences.

Technology on campus. PC or laptop required. Commuter students can connect to campus network. Online course registration, helpline, wireless network available.

Student life. Freshman orientation: Mandatory, $200 fee. Preregistration for classes offered. **Policies:** Religious observance required. **Housing:** Guaranteed on-campus for all undergraduates. Single-sex dorms available. $200 nonrefundable deposit, deadline 5/1. **Activities:** Campus ministries, choral groups, dance, drama, literary magazine, student government, student newspaper.

Athletics. Intercollegiate: Baseball M, cross-country. **Intramural:** Basketball M, soccer. **Team name:** Sea Beggars.

Student services. Chaplain/spiritual director, career counseling, student employment services, financial aid counseling.

Contact. E-mail: admissions@providencecc.edu
Phone: (626) 696-4000
Larissa Kamps, Director of Admissions, Providence Christian College, 1539 East Howard Street, Pasadena, CA 91104

Samuel Merritt University
Oakland, California
www.samuelmerritt.edu
CB member
CB code: 4750

- Private two-year upper-division health science and nursing college
- Commuter campus in large city
- Application essay required

General. Founded in 1909. Regionally accredited. Part of Alta Bates Summit Medical Center, a nonprofit, community-based health care organization. **Degrees:** 381 bachelor's awarded; master's, professional, doctoral offered. **ROTC:** Army, Naval, Air Force. **Location:** 15 miles from San Francisco. **Calendar:** Continuous, limited summer session. **Full-time faculty:** 88 total; 72% have terminal degrees, 26% minority. **Part-time faculty:** 141 total; 16% have terminal degrees, 28% minority. **Class size:** 8% < 20, 62% 20-39, 30% 40-49. **Special facilities:** Nursing resource laboratory, health education center, health science library, anatomy laboratory, therapeutic exercise laboratory, living skills laboratory, human occupations laboratory, health sciences simulation lab.

Student profile. 584 undergraduates. 3% entered as juniors. 100% transferred from two-year institutions.

Out-of-state:	2%	25 or older:	65%

Basis for selection. College transcript, application essay required. Must have UC transferable college-level coursework in chemistry, anatomy, physiology, multicultural psychology, English (2) and humanities (2). Letter of recommendation and experience in health care environment required. Transfer accepted as juniors.

2015-2016 Annual costs. Tuition/fees: $44,166. Books/supplies: $1,370.

Financial aid. Non-need-based: Scholarships awarded for academics, leadership, minority status. **Additional information:** Ongoing private scholarships available. Students eligible to work in Medical Center (associated with college).

Application procedures. Admission: Priority date 3/1. $50 fee, may be waived for applicants with need. Application must be submitted on paper. Admission notification 4/1. Must reply by 5/1. **Financial aid:** Priority date 3/2, no deadline. Applicants notified on a rolling basis; must reply within 3 weeks of notification.

Academics. Special study options: Accelerated study, combined bachelor's/graduate degree, cooperative education, cross-registration, distance learning, ESL, independent study, internships, liberal arts/career combination.

Credit/placement by examination: AP, CLEP. 80 credit hours maximum toward bachelor's degree.

Majors. Health services: Nursing (RN).

Technology on campus. 78 workstations in library, computer center. Online course registration, online library, helpline, wireless network available.

Student life. Activities: Student government, student newspaper, multicultural committee, American Physical Therapy Association, California Nursing Students Association, Christian Fellowship, American Occupational Therapy Association, Chi Eta Phi, gay, lesbian, bisexual and transgender group.

Student services. Career counseling, financial aid counseling, health services, personal counseling. **Physically disabled:** Services for visually, speech, hearing impaired.

Contact. E-mail: admission@samuelmerritt.edu
Phone: (510) 869-6576 Toll-free number: (800) 607-6377
Fax: (510) 869-6525
Anne Seed, Director of Admissions, Samuel Merritt University, 370 Hawthorne Avenue, Oakland, CA 94609-9954

San Diego Christian College
Santee, California
www.sdcc.edu
CB code: 4150

- Private 4-year liberal arts college affiliated with the nondenominational tradition
- Residential campus in small city
- 878 degree-seeking undergraduates: 19% part-time, 54% women, 12% African American, 3% Asian American, 21% Hispanic/Latino, 1% Native American, 1% Native Hawaiian/Pacific islander, 5% Multi-racial, non-Hispanic, 1% international
- 36 degree-seeking graduate students
- 52% of applicants admitted
- Application essay required
- 33% graduate within 6 years

General. Founded in 1970. Regionally accredited. **Degrees:** 148 bachelor's, 35 associate awarded; master's offered. **ROTC:** Army, Air Force. **Location:** 15 miles from downtown San Diego. **Calendar:** Continuous, limited summer session. **Full-time faculty:** 21 total; 43% have terminal degrees, 10% minority, 48% women. **Part-time faculty:** 76 total; 46% women. **Class size:** 79% < 20, 19% 20-39, 1% 40-49, less than 1% 50-99. **Special facilities:** Flight simulator and flight school, museum supporting creationist view.

Freshman class profile. 433 applied, 224 admitted, 110 enrolled.

GPA 3.75 or higher:	22%	Return as sophomores:	66%
GPA 3.50-3.74:	13%	Out-of-state:	22%
GPA 3.0-3.49:	27%	Live on campus:	58%
GPA 2.0-2.99:	36%	International:	1%
End year in good standing:	88%		

Basis for selection. Academic abilities as indicated by school achievement record and test scores. Personal and spiritual qualities as indicated by essays and recommendations.

High school preparation. College-preparatory program recommended. 15 units recommended. Recommended units include English 4, mathematics 3, social studies 3, science 3 and foreign language 2.

2016-2017 Annual costs. Tuition/fees (projected): $29,550. Room/board: $10,974. Books/supplies: $1,791. Personal expenses: $2,331.

2014-2015 Financial aid. Need-based: 96% of total undergraduate aid awarded as scholarships/grants, 4% as loans/jobs. **Non-need-based:** Scholarships awarded for academics, alumni affiliation, athletics, leadership, music/drama, state residency.

Application procedures. Admission: Priority date 7/1; no deadline. $25 fee, may be waived for applicants with need, free for online applicants. Admission notification on a rolling basis. **Financial aid:** Priority date 3/2, closing date 7/15. FAFSA, institutional form required. Applicants notified on a rolling basis starting 4/1; must reply by 5/1 or within 4 week(s) of notification.

Academics. Special study options: Accelerated study, distance learning, double major, dual enrollment of high school students, honors, independent study, internships, liberal arts/career combination, study abroad, teacher certification program. **Credit/placement by examination:** AP, CLEP, IB, SAT,

ACT, institutional tests. 15 credit hours maximum toward associate degree, 30 toward bachelor's. **Support services:** Reduced course load, remedial instruction, study skills assistance, tutoring. Online academic support resources in multiple subject areas with video tutorials, self-assessment tools. All students are assigned a Student Success/Graduation Coach to provide them with a single point of contact to help navigate the transition into college.

Majors. Biology: General. **Business:** Business admin. **Communications:** Communications/speech/rhetoric. **Education:** General, biology, elementary, English, history, middle, multi-level teacher, music, physical, secondary, social science. **English:** English lit. **History:** General. **Liberal arts:** Arts/ sciences. **Parks/recreation:** Exercise sciences. **Protective services:** Law enforcement admin. **Psychology:** General. **Theology:** Bible, missionary, youth ministry. **Visual/performing arts:** Dramatic, music, music performance. **Work/family studies:** Family studies.

Most popular majors. Business/marketing 18%, family/consumer sciences 12%, interdisciplinary studies 13%, parks/recreation 9%, psychology 9%, theological studies 20%.

Technology on campus. 50 workstations in library, computer center. Commuter students can connect to campus network. Online library, helpline, wireless network available.

Student life. Freshman orientation: Mandatory, $100 fee. Preregistration for classes offered. Held 2 weeks prior to start of classes. **Policies:** All on-campus undergraduates are required to attend chapel twice a week and complete student ministry/service hours each semester. Religious observance required. **Housing:** Guaranteed on-campus for freshmen. Single-sex dorms available. $250 fully refundable deposit. Campus dorm housing is in apartments. **Activities:** Campus ministries, choral groups, drama, music ensembles, musical theater, student government, ASB, flight team, debate team, missions teams, ministry teams, art club, music teams.

Athletics. NAIA. **Intercollegiate:** Baseball M, basketball, cross-country, soccer, softball W, tennis, volleyball W. **Team name:** Hawks.

Student services. Adult student services, chaplain/spiritual director, career counseling, student employment services, financial aid counseling, health services, personal counseling, placement for graduates, veterans' counselor.

Contact. E-mail: admissions@sdcc.edu
Phone: (619) 201-8787 Toll-free number: (800) 676-2242
Fax: (619) 201-8749
Christine Roberts, Admissions Manager, San Diego Christian College, 200 Riverview Parkway, Santee, CA 92071-5822

San Diego State University
San Diego, California
www.sdsu.edu

CB member
CB code: 4682

- Public 4-year university
- Commuter campus in very large city
- 29,234 degree-seeking undergraduates: 11% part-time, 54% women, 4% African American, 14% Asian American, 31% Hispanic/Latino, 6% Multi-racial, non-Hispanic, 6% international
- 5,020 degree-seeking graduate students
- 34% of applicants admitted
- SAT or ACT (ACT writing optional) required
- 69% graduate within 6 years

General. Founded in 1897. Regionally accredited. Branch campus at Calexico in Imperial Valley. **Degrees:** 6,714 bachelor's awarded; master's, doctoral offered. **ROTC:** Army, Naval, Air Force. **Location:** 8 miles from downtown. **Calendar:** Semester, extensive summer session. **Full-time faculty:** 809 total; 89% have terminal degrees, 27% minority, 47% women. **Part-time faculty:** 893 total; 36% have terminal degrees, 28% minority, 55% women. **Class size:** 28% < 20, 40% 20-39, 7% 40-49, 16% 50-99, 9% >100. **Special facilities:** Observatory, electron microscope facility, open-air theater, aquatic center, international student center, American Language Institute, recital hall, field studies stations (off-campus), multimedia interactive fine arts lab.

Freshman class profile. 58,970 applied, 20,238 admitted, 5,229 enrolled.

Mid 50% test scores			
SAT critical reading:	500-600	Rank in top quarter:	73%
SAT math:	510-630	Rank in top tenth:	33%
SAT writing:	490-590	Return as sophomores:	90%
ACT composite:	22-28	Out-of-state:	13%
GPA 3.75 or higher:	49%	Live on campus:	71%
GPA 3.50-3.74:	26%	International:	7%
GPA 3.0-3.49:	23%	Fraternities:	11%
GPA 2.0-2.99:	2%	Sororities:	14%

Basis for selection. Rigor of secondary school record, Class rank, and Academic GPA very important. **Home schooled:** Transcript of courses and grades required. In cases where the Lab Science courses are not completed at regular high school or community college, course descriptions requested to ensure lab component meets CSU requirement for admission.

High school preparation. College-preparatory program required. 15 units required. Required and recommended units include English 4, mathematics 3-4, social studies 1, history 1, science 2 (laboratory 2), foreign language 2, visual/performing arts 1 and academic electives 1. History must be US history or US government. Science must be 1 biological science and 1 physical science.

2015-2016 Annual costs. Tuition/fees: $6,976; $18,136 out-of-state. Room/board: $15,826. Books/supplies: $1,804. Personal expenses: $1,392.

2015-2016 Financial aid. Need-based: 3,700 full-time freshmen applied for aid; 2,600 deemed to have need; 2,500 received aid. Average need met was 66%. Average scholarship/grant was $10,000; average loan $3,200. 57% of total undergraduate aid awarded as scholarships/grants, 43% as loans/ jobs. **Non-need-based:** Awarded to 7,400 full-time undergraduates, including 1,700 freshmen. Scholarships awarded for academics, alumni affiliation, art, athletics, leadership, music/drama, ROTC, state residency.

Application procedures. Admission: Closing date 11/30. $55 fee, may be waived for applicants with need. Application must be submitted online. Admission notification by 3/1. Must reply by 5/1. **Financial aid:** Priority date 4/1, closing date 3/2. FAFSA required. Applicants notified on a rolling basis starting 3/15.

Academics. Special study options: Combined bachelor's/graduate degree, cross-registration, distance learning, double major, ESL, exchange student, external degree, honors, independent study, internships, liberal arts/career combination, semester at sea, student-designed major, study abroad, teacher certification program. **Credit/placement by examination:** AP, CLEP, IB, SAT, ACT, institutional tests. 30 credit hours maximum toward bachelor's degree. Must be registered in at least 1 course, matriculated and in good standing. Approval of department chair and dean of college required. Restricted to regular undergraduate courses. Does not count toward 30-unit minimum residency requirement. **Support services:** Pre-admission summer program, reduced course load, remedial instruction, tutoring, writing center.

Majors. Area/ethnic studies: African-American, Asian, Chicano/Hispanic-American/Latino, European, Latin American, Native American, Russian/ Eastern European/Eurasian, women's. **Biology:** General, ecology, microbiology, zoology. **Business:** Accounting, business admin, finance, financial planning, hospitality admin, human resources, international, marketing, operations, real estate. **Communications:** Advertising, communications/speech/ rhetoric, digital media, health, journalism, public relations, radio/TV. **Computer sciences:** Computer science, information technology. **Conservation:** Environmental science, environmental studies. **Education:** Early childhood, music. **Engineering:** General, aerospace, civil, computer, electrical, environmental, mechanical. **English:** English lit, writing. **Foreign languages:** Classics, comparative lit, French, German, Japanese, linguistics, Russian, Spanish. **Health services:** Athletic training, communication disorders, dietetics, nursing (RN), speech pathology. **History:** General. **Human services:** General, social work. **Liberal arts:** Arts/sciences, humanities. **Math:** General, applied, statistics. **Parks/recreation:** General, exercise sciences, health/fitness. **Philosophy/religion:** Judaic, philosophy, religion. **Physical sciences:** General, astronomy, chemistry, geology, molecular physics, physics. **Protective services:** Criminal justice. **Psychology:** General. **Social sciences:** General, anthropology, economics, geography, international relations, political science, sociology, urban studies. **Visual/performing arts:** Art, art history/ conservation, dance, dramatic, graphic design, interior design, music, music performance, studio arts.

Most popular majors. Business/marketing 20%, engineering/engineering technologies 7%, health sciences 8%, psychology 8%, security/protective services 6%, social sciences 12%.

Technology on campus. 2,000 workstations in dormitories, library, computer center, student center. Dormitories wired for high-speed internet access and linked to campus network. Commuter students can connect to campus network. Online course registration, online library, helpline, repair service, student web hosting, wireless network available.

Student life. Freshman orientation: Mandatory. Preregistration for classes offered. One-day programs held in July. **Housing:** Coed dorms, special housing for disabled, apartments, fraternity/sorority housing, gender-neutral housing, themed housing, wellness housing available. $375 nonrefundable deposit, deadline 5/1. Quiet study environment, living/learning center available. **Activities:** Bands, campus ministries, choral groups, dance, drama, film society, international student organizations, literary magazine, music ensembles, musical theater, opera, radio station, student government, student newspaper, symphony orchestra, TV station, 289 academic, recreational, sports, ethnic, political, honor, service clubs on campus.

Athletics. NCAA. **Intercollegiate:** Baseball M, basketball, cross-country W, diving W, football (tackle) M, golf, lacrosse W, rowing (crew) W, soccer, softball W, swimming W, tennis, track and field W, volleyball W, water polo W. **Intramural:** Basketball, bowling, football (non-tackle), racquetball, soccer, softball, tennis, volleyball. **Team name:** Aztecs.

Student services. Alcohol/substance abuse counseling, career counseling, services for economically disadvantaged, student employment services, financial aid counseling, health services, minority student services, on-campus daycare, personal counseling, placement for graduates, veterans' counselor, women's services. **Physically disabled:** Services for visually, speech, hearing impaired.

Contact. E-mail: admissions@sdsu.edu
Phone: (619) 594-6336 Toll-free number: (855) 594-6336
Sabrina Cortell, Director of Admissions, San Diego State University, 5500 Campanile Drive, San Diego, CA 92182-7455

San Francisco Art Institute
San Francisco, California
www.sfai.edu   CB code: 4036

- Private 4-year visual arts college
- Commuter campus in very large city
- 404 degree-seeking undergraduates: 6% part-time, 59% women, 4% African American, 4% Asian American, 17% Hispanic/Latino, 1% Native American, 8% Multi-racial, non-Hispanic, 17% international
- 177 degree-seeking graduate students
- 65% of applicants admitted
- Application essay required
- 38% graduate within 6 years

General. Founded in 1871. Regionally accredited. **Degrees:** 118 bachelor's awarded; master's offered. **Location:** 1 mile from downtown. **Calendar:** Semester, limited summer session. **Full-time faculty:** 23 total; 74% have terminal degrees, 26% minority, 44% women. **Part-time faculty:** 109 total; 77% have terminal degrees, 18% minority, 53% women. **Class size:** 93% < 20, 6% 20-39, less than 1% 50-99, less than 1% >100. **Special facilities:** Art galleries; production facilities for photography, printmaking, time-based media, digital imaging and sound; collection of rare books, periodicals, and limited-edition artists' books.

Freshman class profile. 563 applied, 368 admitted, 86 enrolled.

Mid 50% test scores			
SAT critical reading:	480-620	GPA 3.0-3.49:	37%
SAT math:	470-570	GPA 2.0-2.99:	29%
SAT writing:	480-600	Return as sophomores:	54%
ACT composite:	19-25	Out-of-state:	42%
GPA 3.75 or higher:	19%	Live on campus:	83%
GPA 3.50-3.74:	15%	International:	19%

Basis for selection. Evaluation of portfolio (BFA) or critical essay (BA), academic credentials based on transcripts and standardized test scores, letters of recommendation, and personal statement required. SAT or ACT recommended. Portfolio of artwork required for BFA programs; critical essay required for BA programs. Interviews recommended, but not required. **Home schooled:** State high school equivalency certificate, letter of recommendation (nonparent) required.

High school preparation. College-preparatory program recommended. 19 units recommended. Recommended units include English 4, mathematics 2, social studies 3, history 2, science 2, foreign language 2 and visual/performing arts 4. A strong background in English, humanities, and social sciences is recommended along with an extensive high school or extracurricular art education.

2015-2016 Annual costs. Tuition/fees: $41,272. Room/board: $15,666.

2015-2016 Financial aid. **Need-based:** 57 full-time freshmen applied for aid; 50 deemed to have need; 50 received aid. Average need met was 50%. Average scholarship/grant was $5,060; average loan $1,730. 69% of total undergraduate aid awarded as scholarships/grants, 31% as loans/jobs. **Non-need-based:** Awarded to 365 full-time undergraduates, including 78 freshmen. Scholarships awarded for academics, alumni affiliation, art.

Application procedures. Admission: Priority date 2/15; no deadline. $75 fee, may be waived for applicants with need. Admission notification on a rolling basis. Must reply by May 1 or within 3 week(s) if notified thereafter. **Financial aid:** Priority date 3/1; no closing date. FAFSA required. Applicants notified on a rolling basis starting 3/1; must reply within 2 week(s) of notification.

Academics. Special study options: Double major, ESL, exchange student, honors, independent study, internships, study abroad. **Credit/placement by examination:** AP, CLEP, IB, institutional tests. 30 credit hours maximum toward bachelor's degree. **Support services:** Learning center, remedial instruction, study skills assistance, tutoring, writing center.

Majors. Social sciences: Urban studies. **Visual/performing arts:** Art history/conservation, cinematography, design, painting, photography, printmaking, sculpture.

Most popular majors. Visual/performing arts 98%.

Technology on campus. 90 workstations in library, computer center. Online library, helpline, student web hosting, wireless network available.

Student life. Freshman orientation: Mandatory. Preregistration for classes offered. Held one week prior to the start of fall and spring semesters; includes overview of services and resources available, and planned social events. **Housing:** Coed dorms available. $450 nonrefundable deposit, deadline 6/1. **Activities:** Film society, literary magazine, music ensembles, radio station, student government, Indigenous Arts Coalition.

Student services. Career counseling, student employment services, financial aid counseling, personal counseling, placement for graduates, veterans' counselor. **Physically disabled:** Services for visually, speech, hearing impaired.

Contact. E-mail: admissions@sfai.edu
Phone: (415) 749-4500 Toll-free number: (800) 345-7324
Fax: (415) 749-4592
Elizabeth O'Brien, Vice President for Enrollment, San Francisco Art Institute, SFAI - Admissions Office, San Francisco, CA 94133

San Francisco Conservatory of Music
San Francisco, California
www.sfcm.edu   CB code: 4744

- Private 4-year music college
- Commuter campus in very large city
- 157 degree-seeking undergraduates: 1% part-time, 44% women, 3% African American, 11% Asian American, 6% Hispanic/Latino, 1% Native American, 1% Native Hawaiian/Pacific islander, 11% Multi-racial, non-Hispanic, 25% international
- 221 degree-seeking graduate students
- 47% of applicants admitted
- Application essay required
- 65% graduate within 6 years

General. Founded in 1917. Regionally accredited. **Degrees:** 29 bachelor's awarded; master's offered. **Location:** Downtown. **Calendar:** Semester. **Full-time faculty:** 28 total; 36% have terminal degrees, 25% minority, 29% women. **Part-time faculty:** 96 total; 16% have terminal degrees, 8% minority, 31% women. **Class size:** 79% < 20, 19% 20-39, 2% 50-99. **Special facilities:** Three concert performance halls, recording studios, listening lab, music library, soundproof practice rooms, percussion suite, reed-making room, baroque studio, electronic music studio.

Freshman class profile. 362 applied, 169 admitted, 33 enrolled.

End year in good standing:	90%	Live on campus:	94%
Return as sophomores:	73%	International:	30%
Out-of-state:	54%		

Basis for selection. Most important factor is music audition, followed by school achievement record, letters of recommendation and test scores. Musical needs of institution also influence admission decisions. Music audition required. **Home schooled:** Transcript of courses and grades, state high school equivalency certificate, letter of recommendation (nonparent) required. SAT or ACT recommended.

High school preparation. Recommended units include English 3 and foreign language 3.

2015-2016 Annual costs. Tuition/fees: $42,210. Room only: $11,900. **Additional information:** Municipal Transportation Fee is now included within the Comprehensive fee, included within the Required Fees.

2015-2016 Financial aid. Need-based: 32 full-time freshmen applied for aid; 31 deemed to have need; 31 received aid. Average need met was 47%. Average scholarship/grant was $21,500; average loan $5,508. 87% of total undergraduate aid awarded as scholarships/grants, 13% as loans/jobs. **Non-need-based:** Awarded to 50 full-time undergraduates, including 16 freshmen. Scholarships awarded for music/drama.

Application procedures. Admission: Closing date 12/1 (receipt date). $110 fee. Application must be submitted online. Admission notification by 4/1. Admission notification on a rolling basis beginning on or about 3/15. Must reply by May 1 or within 2 week(s) if notified thereafter. **Financial aid:** Priority date 2/15, closing date 3/1. FAFSA required. CSS/Financial Aid PROFILE required of international applicants for any need-based scholarship funding. The school code for this is: 4744. Applicants notified on a rolling basis starting 4/1; must reply within 2 week(s) of notification.

Academics. Special study options: ESL, independent study, internships. **Credit/placement by examination:** AP, CLEP, institutional tests. **Support services:** Remedial instruction, study skills assistance, tutoring. Student Academic Enrichment Center.

Majors. Visual/performing arts: Brass instruments, music technology, music theory/composition, percussion instruments, piano/keyboard, stringed instruments, voice/opera, woodwind instruments.

Technology on campus. 25 workstations in library, computer center. Dormitories wired for high-speed internet access. Online course registration, online library, student web hosting, wireless network available.

Student life. Freshman orientation: Mandatory. Preregistration for classes offered. 1.5-week session held in August prior to registration. **Housing:** Coed dorms, apartments available. $450 nonrefundable deposit, deadline 7/1. **Activities:** Choral groups, music ensembles, musical theater, opera, student government, symphony orchestra.

Student services. Career counseling, student employment services, financial aid counseling, health services, personal counseling.

Contact. E-mail: admit@sfcm.edu
Phone: (415) 503-6231 Toll-free number: (800) 899-7326
Fax: (415) 503-6299
Melissa Cocco-Mitten, Director of Admission, San Francisco Conservatory of Music, 50 Oak Street, San Francisco, CA 94102

San Francisco State University

San Francisco, California   **CB member**
www.sfsu.edu   **CB code: 4684**

- Public 4-year university
- Commuter campus in very large city
- 25,867 degree-seeking undergraduates: 15% part-time, 56% women, 5% African American, 28% Asian American, 29% Hispanic/Latino, 6% Multi-racial, non-Hispanic, 6% international
- 3,082 degree-seeking graduate students
- 68% of applicants admitted
- SAT or ACT (ACT writing optional) required
- 51% graduate within 6 years

General. Founded in 1899. Regionally accredited. **Degrees:** 5,828 bachelor's awarded; master's, professional, doctoral offered. **ROTC:** Army, Air Force. **Location:** 10 miles from downtown. **Calendar:** Semester, limited summer session. **Full-time faculty:** 766 total; 80% have terminal degrees, 35% minority, 49% women. **Part-time faculty:** 913 total; 23% have terminal degrees, 25% minority, 57% women. **Class size:** 23% < 20, 48% 20-39, 12% 40-49, 12% 50-99, 4% >100. **Special facilities:** Marine laboratories, environmental studies center, Sierra Nevada field campus, anthropology museum, astronomy facility.

Freshman class profile. 35,122 applied, 23,841 admitted, 4,276 enrolled.

Mid 50% test scores			
SAT critical reading:	430-540	GPA 3.0-3.49:	47%
SAT math:	430-550	GPA 2.0-2.99:	26%
ACT composite:	18-24	Return as sophomores:	82%
GPA 3.75 or higher:	10%	Out-of-state:	1%
GPA 3.50-3.74:	17%	Live on campus:	49%
		International:	5%

Basis for selection. School achievement record and score on SAT or ACT most important. Students with GPA over 3.0 may be exempted from SAT/ACT. SAT or ACT scores required if high school GPA does not reach a standard of 3.0 for California residents or 3.61 for non-residents. All applicants for admission are urged to take the SAT or ACT. **Home schooled:** Local school district verification of completion of secondary schooling; SAT or ACT scores.

High school preparation. College-preparatory program required. 15 units required; 16 recommended. Required and recommended units include English 4, mathematics 3-4, social studies 1, history 1, science 2 (laboratory 2), foreign language 2, visual/performing arts 1 and academic electives 1.

2015-2016 Annual costs. Tuition/fees: $6,476; $17,636 out-of-state. Room/board: $13,434. Books/supplies: $1,860. Personal expenses: $1,392. **Additional information:** Excluded from the required fees is an optional fee of $2.00 (Student Involvement and Representation Fee). For 2015-2016: Room Only (on campus): $8,090; Board Only (On campus meal plan): $4,144 for all undergraduates, including first-time freshmen.

2015-2016 Financial aid. All financial aid based on need. 3,478 full-time freshmen applied for aid; 2,897 deemed to have need; 2,742 received aid. Average need met was 76%. Average scholarship/grant was $9,203; average loan $3,331. 68% of total undergraduate aid awarded as scholarships/grants, 32% as loans/jobs.

Application procedures. Admission: Priority date 10/1; deadline 11/30. $55 fee, may be waived for applicants with need. Admission notification on a rolling basis beginning on or about 10/1. Must reply by May 1 or within 2 week(s) if notified thereafter. **Financial aid:** Priority date 3/2; no closing date. FAFSA required. Applicants notified on a rolling basis starting 4/15; must reply by 4/15 or within 2 week(s) of notification.

Academics. Special study options: Accelerated study, cooperative education, cross-registration, distance learning, double major, dual enrollment of high school students, ESL, exchange student, honors, independent study, internships, liberal arts/career combination, student-designed major, study abroad, teacher certification program, Washington semester. Community service learning. **Credit/placement by examination:** AP, CLEP, IB, SAT, ACT, institutional tests. 30 credit hours maximum toward bachelor's degree. **Support services:** Learning center, pre-admission summer program, remedial instruction, study skills assistance, tutoring, writing center.

Majors. Area/ethnic studies: African-American, American, Asian-American, Chicano/Hispanic-American/Latino, Native American, women's. **Biology:** General, biochemistry. **Business:** Business admin, hospitality admin, labor studies. **Communications:** Journalism, radio/TV. **Computer sciences:** Computer science. **Conservation:** Environmental studies. **Education:** Early childhood. **Engineering:** Civil, computer, electrical, mechanical. **English:** English lit, rhetoric/composition, technical writing. **Foreign languages:** Chinese, classics, comparative lit, French, German, Italian, Japanese, Spanish. **Health services:** Communication disorders, dietetics, nursing (RN), public health ed. **History:** General. **Human services:** Social work. **Liberal arts:** Arts/sciences, humanities. **Math:** General, applied, statistics. **Parks/recreation:** Exercise sciences, facilities management. **Philosophy/religion:** Judaic, philosophy. **Physical sciences:** Atmospheric science, chemistry, geology, physics. **Protective services:** Criminal justice. **Psychology:** General. **Social sciences:** Anthropology, economics, geography, international relations, political science, sociology, urban studies. **Visual/performing arts:** Art, dance, design, dramatic, film/cinema/video, industrial design, interior design, music, music performance. **Work/family studies:** General, clothing/textiles.

Most popular majors. Biology 7%, business/marketing 24%, communications/journalism 9%, health sciences 9%, social sciences 10%, visual/performing arts 7%.

Technology on campus. 2,800 workstations in library, computer center. Dormitories wired for high-speed internet access and linked to campus network. Online course registration, online library, helpline, repair service, student web hosting, wireless network available.

Student life. Freshman orientation: Mandatory, $35 fee. Preregistration for classes offered. **Housing:** Coed dorms, single-sex dorms, special housing for disabled, apartments, themed housing, wellness housing available. $200 fully refundable deposit, deadline 7/18. Women-only floors available. **Activities:** Concert band, choral groups, dance, drama, film society, international student organizations, literary magazine, music ensembles, Model UN, musical theater, opera, radio station, student government, student newspaper, symphony orchestra, TV station, College Democrats, College Republicans, Muslim Student Association, Hillel, Korean Student Association, Filipino American Collegiate Endeavor, Environmentally Concerned Organization of Students.

Athletics. NCAA. **Intercollegiate:** Baseball M, basketball, cross-country, soccer, softball W, track and field W, volleyball W, wrestling M. **Intramural:** Basketball, soccer, volleyball. **Team name:** Gators.

Student services. Adult student services, alcohol/substance abuse counseling, career counseling, services for economically disadvantaged, student employment services, financial aid counseling, health services, legal services, minority student services, on-campus daycare, personal counseling, placement for graduates, veterans' counselor, women's services. **Physically disabled:** Services for visually, speech, hearing impaired.

Contact. E-mail: ugadmit@sfsu.edu
Phone: (415) 338-6486 Fax: (415) 338-3880
Edward Carrigan, Director, Undergraduate Admissions, San Francisco State University, 1600 Holloway Avenue, San Francisco, CA 94132

San Jose State University

San Jose, California **CB member**
www.sjsu.edu **CB code: 4687**

- Public 4-year university and liberal arts college
- Commuter campus in very large city
- 26,822 degree-seeking undergraduates: 19% part-time, 48% women, 3% African American, 36% Asian American, 26% Hispanic/Latino, 5% Multi-racial, non-Hispanic, 6% international
- 5,951 degree-seeking graduate students
- 55% of applicants admitted
- SAT or ACT (ACT writing optional) required
- 50% graduate within 6 years

General. Founded in 1857. Regionally accredited. **Degrees:** 5,281 bachelor's awarded; master's offered. **ROTC:** Army, Air Force. **Location:** 50 miles from San Francisco. **Calendar:** Semester, limited summer session. **Full-time faculty:** 687 total; 10% minority, 50% women. **Part-time faculty:** 1,068 total; 10% minority, 52% women. **Class size:** 19% < 20, 49% 20-39, 17% 40-49, 7% 50-99, 8% >100. **Special facilities:** Marine laboratory, natural history living museum, nuclear science lab, center for Beethoven studies, Chicano resource center, art metal foundry, deep-sea research ship, electro-acoustic and recording studio.

Freshman class profile. 30,583 applied, 16,890 admitted, 3,461 enrolled.

Mid 50% test scores			
SAT critical reading:	450-570	GPA 3.0-3.49:	44%
SAT math:	470-610	GPA 2.0-2.99:	14%
SAT writing:	450-560	Return as sophomores:	81%
ACT composite:	20-26	Out-of-state:	2.14%
GPA 3.75 or higher:	20%	Live on campus:	56%
GPA 3.50-3.74:	22%	International:	6%

Basis for selection. High school record and test scores most important. SAT or ACT required for applicants with less than 3.0 GPA.

High school preparation. College-preparatory program required. 15 units required. Required units include English 4, mathematics 3, social studies 1, history 1, science 2 (laboratory 2), foreign language 2 and visual/performing arts 1. History is 2 units in history/social science.

2015-2016 Annual costs. Tuition/fees: $7,378; $18,538 out-of-state. Room/board: $14,217. Books/supplies: $1,860. Personal expenses: $1,392.

2014-2015 Financial aid. All financial aid based on need. 2,757 full-time freshmen applied for aid; 2,347 deemed to have need; 2,255 received aid. Average need met was 88%. Average scholarship/grant was $9,354; average loan $7,595. 70% of total undergraduate aid awarded as scholarships/grants, 30% as loans/jobs.

Application procedures. Admission: Closing date 11/30. $55 fee, may be waived for applicants with need. Application must be submitted online. Admission notification on a rolling basis beginning on or about 2/25. Must reply by 5/1. **Financial aid:** Priority date 3/2, closing date 6/15. FAFSA required.

Academics. Special study options: Cooperative education, cross-registration, distance learning, double major, dual enrollment of high school students, honors, independent study, internships, liberal arts/career combination, student-designed major, study abroad, teacher certification program. **Credit/placement by examination:** AP, CLEP. **Support services:** Learning center, pre-admission summer program, remedial instruction, study skills assistance, tutoring, writing center.

Majors. Area/ethnic studies: African-American. **Biology:** General, bacteriology, biochemistry, conservation, marine, microbiology, molecular, physiology. **Business:** Accounting, business admin, finance, hospitality admin, human resources, international, management information systems, marketing. **Communications:** Advertising, journalism, public relations, radio/TV. **Computer sciences:** Computer science. **Conservation:** Environmental studies. **Education:** Early childhood. **Engineering:** General, aerospace, biomedical, chemical, civil, computer, electrical, industrial, materials, mechanical, software. **English:** English lit. **Foreign languages:** Chinese, French, German, Japanese, linguistics, Spanish. **Health services:** Communication disorders, dietetics, health care admin, nursing (RN). **History:** General. **Human services:** Social work. **Liberal arts:** Arts/sciences, humanities. **Math:** General, applied. **Parks/recreation:** General, health/fitness. **Philosophy/religion:** Philosophy, religion. **Physical sciences:** Chemistry, geology, physics. **Protective services:** Criminal justice. **Psychology:** General. **Social sciences:** General, anthropology, economics, geography, political science, sociology. **Visual/performing arts:** General, art, art history/conservation, dance, dramatic, graphic design, industrial design, interior design, jazz, music, music performance, studio arts. **Work/family studies:** Child development.

Most popular majors. Business/marketing 23%, engineering/engineering technologies 10%, health sciences 9%, psychology 6%, social sciences 6%, visual/performing arts 8%.

Technology on campus. Dormitories wired for high-speed internet access and linked to campus network. Commuter students can connect to campus network. Online course registration, online library, helpline, repair service, wireless network available.

Student life. Freshman orientation: Mandatory, $130 fee. Preregistration for classes offered. Mandatory overnight program for all first-time freshmen. **Housing:** Coed dorms, single-sex dorms, apartments, fraternity/sorority housing available. $600 fully refundable deposit, deadline 5/1. **Activities:** Bands, campus ministries, choral groups, dance, drama, film society, international student organizations, literary magazine, music ensembles, Model UN, musical theater, radio station, student government, student newspaper, symphony orchestra.

Athletics. NCAA. **Intercollegiate:** Baseball M, basketball, cross-country, football (tackle) M, golf, sand volleyball W, soccer, softball W, swimming W, tennis W, track and field W, volleyball W, water polo. **Team name:** Spartans.

Student services. Adult student services, alcohol/substance abuse counseling, chaplain/spiritual director, career counseling, services for economically disadvantaged, student employment services, financial aid counseling, health services, legal services, minority student services, on-campus daycare, personal counseling, placement for graduates, veterans' counselor, women's services. **Physically disabled:** Services for visually, speech, hearing impaired.

Contact. E-mail: admissions@sjsu.edu
Phone: (408) 283-7500 Fax: (408) 924-2050
Deanna Gonzales, Director of Undergraduate/Graduate Admissions
Manager, San Jose State University, One Washington Square, San Jose, CA 95192-0016

Santa Clara University

Santa Clara, California **CB member**
www.scu.edu **CB code: 4851**

- Private 4-year university affiliated with the Roman Catholic Church
- Residential campus in small city
- 5,344 degree-seeking undergraduates: 1% part-time, 49% women, 3% African American, 16% Asian American, 17% Hispanic/Latino, 7% Multi-racial, non-Hispanic, 3% international
- 3,219 degree-seeking graduate students
- 49% of applicants admitted
- SAT or ACT (ACT writing optional), application essay required
- 84% graduate within 6 years; 28% enter graduate study

General. Founded in 1851. Regionally accredited. **Degrees:** 1,403 bachelor's awarded; master's, professional, doctoral offered. **ROTC:** Army, Air Force. **Location:** 40 miles from San Francisco; 2 miles from San Jose. **Calendar:** Continuous, limited summer session. **Full-time faculty:** 539 total; 93% have terminal degrees, 27% minority, 45% women. **Part-time faculty:** 395 total; 61% have terminal degrees, 22% minority, 46% women. **Class size:** 46% < 20, 50% 20-39, 2% 40-49, less than 1% 50-99. **Special facilities:** Archeology lab, center for nanostructures, robotics systems lab, satellite mission control room, center for science, technology, and society, Ignatian center for Jesuit education, center for applied ethics, centers of academic outreach in the business and legal disciplines.

Freshman class profile. 14,899 applied, 7,270 admitted, 1,261 enrolled.

Mid 50% test scores			
SAT critical reading:	590-690	GPA 2.0-2.99:	1%
SAT math:	620-710	Rank in top quarter:	83%
ACT composite:	27-32	Rank in top tenth:	50%
GPA 3.75 or higher:	43%	End year in good standing:	97%
GPA 3.50-3.74:	37%	Out-of-state:	42%
GPA 3.0-3.49:	19%	Live on campus:	94%
		International:	3%

Basis for selection. Rigor of high school curriculum, GPA and test scores most important, followed by recommendation, personal essay, and class rank. Extracurricular activities, ethnicity and alumni affiliations given special consideration. Audition recommended for music, theater arts majors. **Home schooled:** Statement describing home school structure and mission required. **Learning Disabled:** Need-blind admissions policy.

High school preparation. College-preparatory program required. 15 units required; 19 recommended. Required and recommended units include English 4, mathematics 3-4, social studies 3, science 2-4 (laboratory 2-3), foreign language 2-4, visual/performing arts 1 and academic electives 1. Social studies includes history units.

2015-2016 Annual costs. Tuition/fees: $45,300. Room/board: $13,425. Books/supplies: $1,764. Personal expenses: $2,322.

2015-2016 Financial aid. Need-based: 761 full-time freshmen applied for aid; 515 deemed to have need; 494 received aid. Average need met was 81%. Average scholarship/grant was $26,964; average loan $3,394. 83% of total undergraduate aid awarded as scholarships/grants, 17% as loans/jobs. **Non-need-based:** Awarded to 2,433 full-time undergraduates, including 588 freshmen. Scholarships awarded for academics, athletics, music/drama, ROTC.

Application procedures. Admission: Closing date 1/7 (postmark date). $60 fee, may be waived for applicants with need. Application must be submitted online. Admission notification by 4/1. Must reply by 5/1. **Financial aid:** Priority date 2/1; no closing date. FAFSA, CSS PROFILE required. Applicants notified by 4/1; must reply by 5/1 or within 2 week(s) of notification.

Academics. Special study options: Combined bachelor's/graduate degree, cooperative education, double major, honors, independent study, internships, liberal arts/career combination, student-designed major, study abroad, Washington semester. **Credit/placement by examination:** AP, CLEP, IB, institutional tests. **Support services:** Learning center, study skills assistance, tutoring, writing center.

Majors. Area/ethnic studies: Women's. **Biology:** General, biochemistry. **Business:** Accounting, accounting/business management, finance, management information systems, managerial economics, marketing, organizational behavior. **Communications:** Communications/speech/rhetoric. **Computer sciences:** Web page design. **Conservation:** Environmental science, environmental studies. **Engineering:** General, applied physics, biomedical, civil, computer, electrical, mechanical. **English:** English lit. **Foreign languages:** Ancient Greek, classics, French, German, Italian, Latin, Spanish. **History:** General. **Liberal arts:** Arts/sciences. **Math:** General. **Philosophy/religion:** Philosophy, religion. **Physical sciences:** Chemistry, physics. **Psychology:** General. **Social sciences:** Anthropology, economics, political science, sociology. **Visual/performing arts:** Art history/conservation, dramatic, music, studio arts.

Most popular majors. Biology 6%, business/marketing 26%, communications/journalism 8%, engineering/engineering technologies 12%, psychology 7%, social sciences 16%.

Technology on campus. 824 workstations in dormitories, library, computer center, student center. Dormitories wired for high-speed internet access and linked to campus network. Commuter students can connect to campus network. Online course registration, online library, helpline, repair service, student web hosting, wireless network available.

Student life. Freshman orientation: Mandatory, $295 fee. Preregistration for classes offered. 2-day session in summer and 2-day session on weekend before school starts. Parents attend separate program. **Policies:** Policies in academic, health, personal safety, wellness needs. Freshmen not permitted cars on campus. **Housing:** Guaranteed on-campus for freshmen. Coed dorms, special housing for disabled, apartments, themed housing available. $250 fully refundable deposit, deadline 5/1. 100% of Freshmen participate in Residential Learning Communities. **Activities:** Bands, campus ministries, choral groups, dance, drama, international student organizations, literary magazine, music ensembles, Model UN, musical theater, opera, radio station, student government, student newspaper, symphony orchestra, Asian Pacific Student Union, Ka Mana'o O Hawaii, community action program, Barkada, MECHA, Chinese student association, CORE Christian Fellowship, Engineers Without Borders, political science student association.

Athletics. NCAA. **Intercollegiate:** Baseball M, basketball, cross-country, golf, rowing (crew), soccer, softball W, tennis, track and field, volleyball W, water polo. **Intramural:** Badminton, basketball, football (non-tackle), soccer, softball, table tennis, tennis, volleyball. **Team name:** Broncos.

Student services. Alcohol/substance abuse counseling, chaplain/spiritual director, career counseling, student employment services, financial aid counseling, health services, legal services, minority student services, on-campus daycare, personal counseling, veterans' counselor. **Physically disabled:** Services for visually, speech, hearing impaired.

Contact. E-mail: Admission@scu.edu
Phone: (408) 554-4700 Fax: (408) 554-5255
Eva Blanco, Dean of Undergraduate Admissions, Santa Clara University, 500 El Camino Real, Santa Clara, CA 95053

Scripps College
Claremont, California
www.scrippscollege.edu

CB member
CB code: 4693

- Private 4-year liberal arts college for women
- Residential campus in large town

- 968 degree-seeking undergraduates: 100% women, 4% African American, 16% Asian American, 11% Hispanic/Latino, 8% Multi-racial, non-Hispanic, 4% international
- 16 graduate students
- 28% of applicants admitted
- SAT or ACT (ACT writing optional), application essay required
- 92% graduate within 6 years

General. Founded in 1926. Regionally accredited. One of cluster of 5 undergraduate and 2 graduate schools on adjoining campuses. Campuses share facilities. Cross-enrollment available at any of the Claremont colleges: Claremont-McKenna, Harvey Mudd, Pitzer, Pomona, and Scripps. **Degrees:** 244 bachelor's awarded. **ROTC:** Army, Air Force. **Location:** 35 miles from Los Angeles. **Calendar:** Semester, limited summer session. **Full-time faculty:** 88 total; 97% have terminal degrees, 31% minority, 58% women. **Part-time faculty:** 34 total; 85% have terminal degrees, 6% minority, 71% women. **Class size:** 83% < 20, 16% 20-39, less than 1% 40-49, less than 1% >100. **Special facilities:** Art slide library, biological field station, humanities museum.

Freshman class profile. 2,613 applied, 729 admitted, 277 enrolled.

Mid 50% test scores			
SAT critical reading:	650-730	Rank in top quarter:	95%
SAT math:	630-720	Rank in top tenth:	72%
SAT writing:	650-730	Return as sophomores:	93%
ACT composite:	29-32	Out-of-state:	55%
GPA 3.75 or higher:	80%	Live on campus:	100%
GPA 3.50-3.74:	11%	International:	6%
GPA 3.0-3.49:	8%		
GPA 2.0-2.99:	1%		

Basis for selection. Rigor of high school curriculum, GPA, class rank, aptitude as reflected in standardized testing most important. Essays, recommendations, required graded writing assignment significant. Interviews recommended. Audition recommended for music, dance majors. Portfolio recommended for art majors. **Home schooled:** Statement describing home school structure and mission, transcript of courses and grades, letter of recommendation (nonparent) required. Interview highly recommended. **Learning Disabled:** Documentation of learning disability required.

High school preparation. College-preparatory program recommended. 16 units required. Required units include English 4, mathematics 3, social studies 3, science 3 and foreign language 3.

2015-2016 Annual costs. Tuition/fees: $49,152. Room/board: $15,108. Books/supplies: $800. Personal expenses: $1,000.

2014-2015 Financial aid. Need-based: 141 full-time freshmen applied for aid; 88 deemed to have need; 88 received aid. Average need met was 100%. Average scholarship/grant was $37,042; average loan $3,060. 85% of total undergraduate aid awarded as scholarships/grants, 15% as loans/jobs. **Non-need-based:** Awarded to 166 full-time undergraduates, including 56 freshmen. Scholarships awarded for academics, leadership.

Application procedures. Admission: Closing date 1/1 (postmark date). $60 fee, may be waived for applicants with need. Admission notification by 4/1. Must reply by 5/1. **Financial aid:** Priority date 2/1, closing date 2/1. FAFSA, CSS PROFILE required. Applicants notified by 4/1; must reply by 5/1.

Academics. Almost half of junior class elects to study abroad for semester or year. **Special study options:** Accelerated study, combined bachelor's/graduate degree, cross-registration, double major, independent study, internships, student-designed major, study abroad, Washington semester. Postbaccalaureate pre-medical certificate program, humanities internship program, 3-2 engineering program with Harvey Mudd College. **Credit/placement by examination:** AP, CLEP, IB, institutional tests. 16 credit hours maximum toward bachelor's degree. SAT Subject Test in foreign languages may meet foreign language graduation requirement. **Support services:** Reduced course load, tutoring, writing center.

Majors. Area/ethnic studies: African-American, American, Asian, Asian-American, Chicano/Hispanic-American/Latino, European, French, German, Italian, Latin American, Near/Middle Eastern, Russian/Eastern European/Eurasian, Spanish/Iberian, women's. **Biology:** General, biochemistry, molecular, neuroscience. **Business:** Accounting, organizational behavior. **Communications:** Media studies. **Computer sciences:** Computer science. **English:** English lit. **Foreign languages:** General, Chinese, classics, French, German, Italian, Japanese, linguistics, Russian, Spanish. **History:** General. **Human services:** Public policy. **Liberal arts:** Humanities. **Math:** General. **Philosophy/religion:** Judaic, philosophy, religion. **Physical sciences:** Chemistry, geology, physics. **Psychology:** General. **Social sciences:** Anthropology, econometrics, economics, political science, sociology. **Visual/performing arts:** Art history/conservation, dance, dramatic, music, studio arts.

Most popular majors. Area/ethnic studies 11%, biology 11%, communications/journalism 7%, interdisciplinary studies 9%, psychology 10%, social sciences 14%, visual/performing arts 8%.

Technology on campus. 151 workstations in dormitories, library, computer center, student center. Dormitories wired for high-speed internet access and linked to campus network. Commuter students can connect to campus network. Online course registration, online library, helpline, repair service, student web hosting, wireless network available.

Student life. Freshman orientation: Mandatory. Preregistration for classes offered. 5-day program begins last Thursday in August. **Housing:** Guaranteed on-campus for freshmen. Special housing for disabled, apartments available. Small college owned houses available. **Activities:** Campus ministries, choral groups, dance, drama, international student organizations, literary magazine, music ensembles, Model UN, radio station, student government, student newspaper, symphony orchestra, Asian American student union, Cafe Con Leche, Wanawake Weusi, Criminal Justice Network, Economic Society, international club, Office of Black Student Affairs, On The Loose, Chicano/Latino Student Affairs.

Athletics. NCAA. **Intercollegiate:** Basketball W, cross-country W, diving W, golf W, lacrosse W, soccer W, softball W, swimming W, tennis W, track and field W, volleyball W, water polo W. **Intramural:** Baseball W, basketball W, cross-country W, diving W, football (tackle) W, golf W, lacrosse W, soccer W, softball W, swimming W, tennis W, track and field W, volleyball W, water polo W. **Team name:** Athenas.

Student services. Adult student services, alcohol/substance abuse counseling, chaplain/spiritual director, career counseling, student employment services, financial aid counseling, health services, minority student services, personal counseling, placement for graduates, women's services. **Physically disabled:** Services for visually, hearing impaired.

Contact. E-mail: admission@scrippscollege.edu
Phone: (909) 621-8149 Toll-free number: (800) 770-1333
Fax: (909) 607-7508
Laura Stratton, Director of Admission, Scripps College, 1030 Columbia Avenue, Claremont, CA 91711-3905

Shasta Bible College and Graduate School
Redding, California
www.shasta.edu | CB code: 4717

- Private 4-year Bible and seminary college affiliated with the Baptist faith
- Residential campus in small city
- 51 undergraduates
- Application essay required

General. Regionally accredited; also accredited by TRACS. A strong emphasis on inductive Bible Study, hermeneutics (Bible Interpretation), biblical languages, evangelism, apologetics, and homiletics (preaching and teaching), along with general education requirements. **Degrees:** 7 bachelor's, 1 associate offered; master's offered. **Calendar:** Semester, limited summer session. **Full-time faculty:** 7 total. **Part-time faculty:** 31 total. **Special facilities:** Vernal pool containing a variety of endangered species, creation museum.

Freshman class profile.

Out-of-state: 10% **Live on campus:** 90%

Basis for selection. An application that includes personal information, educational background, doctrinal statement and lifestyle policies, autobiography, and 4 references required. All applicable transcripts from high school and colleges attended required. **Home schooled:** Transcript of courses and grades required.

2015-2016 Annual costs. Tuition/fees: $11,260. Room only: $2,800. Books/supplies: $3,240.

Financial aid. Non-need-based: Scholarships awarded for music/drama.

Application procedures. Admission: No deadline. $50 fee. Admission notification on a rolling basis. **Financial aid:** Closing date 8/1. FAFSA required. Applicants notified on a rolling basis.

Academics. Special study options: Distance learning, dual enrollment of high school students, independent study, teacher certification program. Association of Christian Schools International certificates, standard and temporary. **Credit/placement by examination:** AP, CLEP, institutional tests. 30 credit hours maximum toward associate degree, 30 toward bachelor's.

Majors. Theology: Theology.

Technology on campus. 10 workstations in library. Dormitories wired for high-speed internet access and linked to campus network. Commuter students can connect to campus network. Online course registration, online library, wireless network available.

Student life. Freshman orientation: Mandatory. Preregistration for classes offered. **Policies:** Lifestyle commitment must be signed annually by each student. Dress code. Religious observance required. **Housing:** Single-sex dorms available. $100 nonrefundable deposit. **Activities:** Campus ministries, choral groups, student government.

Student services. Chaplain/spiritual director, career counseling, financial aid counseling, personal counseling.

Contact. E-mail: admissions@shasta.edu
Phone: (530) 221-4275 Toll-free number: (800) 800-4722
Fax: (530) 221-6929
George Gunn, Dean of Admissions, Shasta Bible College and Graduate School, 2951 Goodwater Avenue, Redding, CA 96002

Silicon Valley University
San Jose, California
www.svuca.edu | CB code: 3600

- Private 4-year business and engineering college
- Commuter campus in very large city
- 206 degree-seeking undergraduates

General. Accredited by ACICS. **Degrees:** 45 bachelor's awarded; master's, doctoral offered. **Calendar:** Trimester. **Full-time faculty:** 2 total. **Part-time faculty:** 27 total.

Basis for selection. Admission requirements vary by programs. **Home schooled:** Transcript of courses and grades, state high school equivalency certificate, interview, letter of recommendation (nonparent) required.

High school preparation. College-preparatory program recommended.

2015-2016 Annual costs. Tuition/fees: $9,750. Books/supplies: $700. **Additional information:** Health Insurance (per trimester) $235 or more. Registration Fee $75 per trimester.

Application procedures. Admission: Closing date 7/1. $75 fee. Application must be submitted online.

Academics. Special study options: Accelerated study, ESL, independent study, internships, weekend college. **Credit/placement by examination:** AP, CLEP.

Majors. Business: Business admin. **Computer sciences:** Computer science.

Technology on campus. 12 workstations in library, computer center. Commuter students can connect to campus network. Online library, wireless network available.

Student life. Freshman orientation: Mandatory. Preregistration for classes offered. **Activities:** International student organizations, student government.

Student services. Minority student services, personal counseling.

Contact. E-mail: studentoffice@svuca.edu
Phone: (408) 435-8989 ext. 106
Seiko Cheng, Admissions Director, Silicon Valley University, 2160 Lundy Avenue Suite #110, San Jose, CA 95131

Simpson University
Redding, California
www.simpsonu.edu | CB code: 4698

- Private 4-year university affiliated with the Christian and Missionary Alliance
- Residential campus in small city
- 959 degree-seeking undergraduates: 3% part-time, 64% women, 4% African American, 4% Asian American, 12% Hispanic/Latino, 4% Native American, 3% Multi-racial, non-Hispanic, 2% international
- 112 degree-seeking graduate students
- 52% of applicants admitted

- SAT or ACT (ACT writing optional), application essay required
- 49% graduate within 6 years

General. Founded in 1921. Regionally accredited. Christ-centered educational community. **Degrees:** 320 bachelor's awarded; master's offered. **Location:** 170 miles from Sacramento. **Calendar:** Semester, limited summer session. **Full-time faculty:** 51 total; 59% have terminal degrees, 16% minority, 39% women. **Part-time faculty:** 195 total; 28% have terminal degrees, 7% minority, 50% women. **Class size:** 78% < 20, 19% 20-39, less than 1% 40-49, 2% 50-99.

Freshman class profile. 620 applied, 321 admitted, 88 enrolled.

Mid 50% test scores			
SAT critical reading:	450-560	GPA 3.0-3.49:	35%
SAT math:	440-560	GPA 2.0-2.99:	14%
SAT writing:	430-530	Rank in top quarter:	28%
ACT composite:	18-24	Rank in top tenth:	16%
GPA 3.75 or higher:	27%	Return as sophomores:	74%
GPA 3.50-3.74:	24%	Out-of-state:	19%
		Live on campus:	85%

Basis for selection. Commitment to Jesus Christ as reflected in personal statement and required references, academic achievement, other recommendations, and standardized test scores important. SAT and SAT Subject Tests or ACT recommended. **Home schooled:** Transcript of courses and grades required.

High school preparation. College-preparatory program recommended. 15 units recommended. Recommended units include English 4, mathematics 2, social studies 2, history 1, science 3, foreign language 2 and visual/performing arts 1. College-preparatory program highly recommended.

2015-2016 Annual costs. Tuition/fees: $25,200. Room/board: $8,050. Books/supplies: $1,552. Personal expenses: $2,258.

2015-2016 Financial aid. Need-based: 88 full-time freshmen applied for aid; 77 deemed to have need; 77 received aid. Average need met was 73%. Average scholarship/grant was $17,794; average loan $3,392. 56% of total undergraduate aid awarded as scholarships/grants, 44% as loans/jobs. **Non-need-based:** Scholarships awarded for academics, alumni affiliation, athletics, leadership, minority status, music/drama, religious affiliation, state residency. **Additional information:** Work-study programs available.

Application procedures. Admission: No deadline. $35 fee, may be waived for applicants with need. Admission notification on a rolling basis. **Financial aid:** Priority date 3/2; no closing date. FAFSA required. Applicants notified on a rolling basis starting 3/2.

Academics. 34-semester-hour teacher credential program permits students to earn California Clear Credential for grades K-8 (multiple subjects) or for grades 7-12 (single subject). **Special study options:** Distance learning, double major, honors, independent study, internships, student-designed major, study abroad, teacher certification program, Washington semester, weekend college. **Credit/placement by examination:** AP, CLEP, SAT, ACT, institutional tests. 30 credit hours maximum toward bachelor's degree. Credit by examination granted only to enrolled students. Students may take challenge exam for particular course only once. **Support services:** Reduced course load, remedial instruction, study skills assistance, tutoring, writing center.

Majors. Biology: General. **Business:** Accounting, business admin, organizational behavior. **Communications:** Communications/speech/rhetoric. **Education:** English, mathematics, music, social science. **English:** English lit. **Foreign languages:** Spanish. **Health services:** Health care admin, nursing practice. **History:** General. **Liberal arts:** Arts/sciences. **Math:** General. **Parks/recreation:** General. **Philosophy/religion:** Christian, religion. **Psychology:** General. **Social sciences:** General. **Theology:** Bible, missionary, pastoral counseling, theology, youth ministry. **Visual/performing arts:** Music.

Most popular majors. Business/marketing 27%, health sciences 18%, liberal arts 9%, psychology 23%, theological studies 8%.

Technology on campus. 50 workstations in library, computer center. Dormitories wired for high-speed internet access and linked to campus network. Commuter students can connect to campus network. Online course registration, online library, helpline, repair service, wireless network available.

Student life. Freshman orientation: Mandatory, $100 fee. Preregistration for classes offered. Sessions include placement tests. **Policies:** All single undergraduates under 22 required to live on campus. Request for off-campus living must be approved by Vice President for Student Development. Religious observance required. **Housing:** Guaranteed on-campus for all undergraduates. Single-sex dorms, special housing for disabled, wellness housing available. $100 partly refundable deposit. **Activities:** Campus ministries, choral groups, dance, drama, film society, international student organizations, music ensembles, student government, student newspaper, Asian Fellowship,

Hispanic Fellowship, summer missions teams, chapel worship team, spiritual action committee, psychology club, Missionary Kids Association, commuter student association.

Athletics. NAIA, NCCAA. **Intercollegiate:** Baseball M, basketball, cross-country, golf, soccer, softball W, volleyball W, wrestling M. **Intramural:** Basketball, football (non-tackle), soccer, ultimate frisbee. **Team name:** Red Hawks.

Student services. Adult student services, alcohol/substance abuse counseling, chaplain/spiritual director, career counseling, student employment services, financial aid counseling, health services, minority student services, personal counseling, veterans' counselor. **Physically disabled:** Services for visually, speech, hearing impaired.

Contact. E-mail: admissions@simpsonu.edu
Phone: (530) 226-4600 Toll-free number: (888) 974-6776
Fax: (530) 226-4851
Dustin Lowe, Director of Admissions, Simpson University, 2211 College View Drive, Redding, CA 96003-8606

Soka University of America
Aliso Viejo, California   **CB member**
www.soka.edu   **CB code: 4066**

- Private 4-year university and liberal arts college
- Residential campus in large town
- 433 degree-seeking undergraduates: 62% women, 4% African American, 17% Asian American, 10% Hispanic/Latino, 4% Multi-racial, non-Hispanic, 39% international
- 12 degree-seeking graduate students
- 46% of applicants admitted
- SAT or ACT with writing, application essay required
- 86% graduate within 6 years; 31% enter graduate study

General. Degrees: 100 bachelor's awarded; master's offered. **Location:** 70 miles from Los Angeles, 75 miles from San Diego. **Calendar:** Semester. **Full-time faculty:** 46 total; 98% have terminal degrees, 37% minority, 41% women. **Part-time faculty:** 25 total; 52% have terminal degrees, 52% minority, 60% women. **Class size:** 96% < 20, 4% 20-39. **Special facilities:** Performing arts center complex, black box theater, dance studio, writing center, language lab, darkroom, aquatic center.

Freshman class profile. 451 applied, 208 admitted, 127 enrolled.

Mid 50% test scores			
SAT critical reading:	490-650	GPA 2.0-2.99:	1%
SAT math:	580-740	Rank in top quarter:	88%
SAT writing:	560-640	Rank in top tenth:	33%
ACT composite:	24-30	End year in good standing:	100%
GPA 3.75 or higher:	67%	Return as sophomores:	94%
GPA 3.50-3.74:	23%	Out-of-state:	38%
GPA 3.0-3.49:	9%	Live on campus:	100%
		International:	40%

Basis for selection. High school curriculum, test scores, essays, and recommendations are very important. Commitment to service, active leadership, and extracurricular activities are also considered during the reading and selection review period. SAT/ACT results must be sent directly by the testing agency. Applicants with prior college experience are also required to submit SAT/ACT with Writing regardless of how many college credits a student may have earned. SAT Subject Tests not required. **Home schooled:** Statement describing home school structure and mission, transcript of courses and grades, state high school equivalency certificate, letter of recommendation (nonparent) required. Program must be accredited by regional, state, or national agency. **Learning Disabled:** Special needs discussed only after student has been admitted and has identified need.

High school preparation. 16 units recommended. Recommended units include English 4, mathematics 3, social studies 1, history 2, science 2 (laboratory 2) and foreign language 2.

2016-2017 Annual costs. Tuition/fees (projected): $29,372. Room/board: $11,812. Books/supplies: $1,592. Personal expenses: $2,072.

2015-2016 Financial aid. Need-based: 127 full-time freshmen applied for aid; 112 deemed to have need; 112 received aid. Average need met was 100%. Average scholarship/grant was $24,750; average loan $5,369. 90% of total undergraduate aid awarded as scholarships/grants, 10% as loans/jobs. **Non-need-based:** Awarded to 427 full-time undergraduates, including 126 freshmen. Scholarships awarded for academics, athletics, leadership, minority status. **Additional information:** All admitted students whose annual family income is $60,000 or less qualify for Soka Opportunity Scholarship, which covers full tuition. All admitted students to the BA in Liberal Arts program will be considered for additional scholarship opportunities for higher income levels. 100% of continuing students who were eligible for need-based financial assistance received a need-based scholarship or grant.

Application procedures. Admission: Closing date 1/15 (receipt date). $45 fee, may be waived for applicants with need. Admission notification by 3/1. Must reply by 5/1. Applications will be evaluated only when all required materials have been received. It is the student's responsibility to ensure that all of the required documents have been requested of the school they are attending and submitted on time. Faxes, emails, or copies of official documents are not accepted. **Financial aid:** Priority date 2/15, closing date 3/2. FAFSA required. Applicants notified on a rolling basis starting 3/15; must reply by 5/1 or within 4 week(s) of notification.

Academics. Learning Clusters occur in 3.5-week block periods provide for field and service learning, traveling to places such as South Africa, China, the Amazon, Panama and India. All students must spend one half of their junior year studying abroad. This requirement is to be fulfilled in a country where the principal language corresponds to a student's language of study. **Special study options:** ESL, independent study, internships, liberal arts/career combination, study abroad. All students must declare an area of concentration in either Environmental Studies, Humanities, International Studies, or Social and Behavioral Sciences. Students who wish to complete a Double Concentration must satisfy specific conditions and academic requirements. **Credit/placement by examination:** AP, CLEP. **Support services:** Study skills assistance, tutoring, writing center.

Majors. Liberal arts: Arts/sciences.

Technology on campus. PC or laptop required. 100 workstations in dormitories, library, computer center, student center. Dormitories wired for high-speed internet access and linked to campus network. Commuter students can connect to campus network. Online course registration, online library, helpline, repair service, wireless network available.

Student life. Freshman orientation: Mandatory. Preregistration for classes offered. 4-day session held before upperclassmen arrive. **Policies:** Students required to live on campus. **Housing:** Guaranteed on-campus for all undergraduates. Coed dorms, single-sex dorms, special housing for disabled, themed housing, wellness housing available. **Activities:** Bands, choral groups, dance, film society, international student organizations, literary magazine, music ensembles, Model UN, student government, student newspaper, symphony orchestra, Amnesty International, Global Brigades, Chinese club, Green Planet, Humanism in Action, Orchestra club, Activist Collective, French club, Ohana Volleyball club, Hip Hop Congress.

Athletics. NAIA. **Intercollegiate:** Cross-country, diving, golf W, soccer, swimming, track and field. **Intramural:** Badminton, basketball, football (non-tackle), handball, racquetball, soccer, softball, tennis, volleyball, weight lifting. **Team name:** Lions.

Student services. Alcohol/substance abuse counseling, career counseling, services for economically disadvantaged, student employment services, financial aid counseling, health services, personal counseling, placement for graduates, veterans' counselor, women's services. **Physically disabled:** Services for visually, hearing impaired.

Contact. E-mail: admission@soka.edu
Phone: (949) 480-4150 Toll-free number: (888) 600-7652
Fax: (949) 480-4151
Andrew Woolsey, Director of Enrollment Services, Soka University of America, One University Drive, Aliso Viejo, CA 92656-8081

Sonoma State University
Rohnert Park, California
www.sonoma.edu

CB code: 4723

- Public 4-year university and liberal arts college
- Commuter campus in large town
- 8,550 degree-seeking undergraduates: 14% part-time, 62% women, 2% African American, 5% Asian American, 29% Hispanic/Latino, 1% Native American, 7% Multi-racial, non-Hispanic, 2% international
- 496 degree-seeking graduate students
- SAT or ACT (ACT writing optional) required

General. Founded in 1960. Regionally accredited. **Degrees:** 1,911 bachelor's awarded; master's offered. **ROTC:** Army, Naval, Air Force. **Location:** 50 miles from San Francisco, 10 miles from Santa Rosa. **Calendar:** Semester, limited summer session. **Full-time faculty:** 231 total; 92% have terminal degrees, 19% minority, 48% women. **Part-time faculty:** 293 total; 34% have terminal degrees, 13% minority, 59% women. **Class size:** 40% < 20, 43% 20-39, 8% 40-49, 6% 50-99, 3% >100. **Special facilities:** Green music

center, observatory, performing arts center, nature preserves, information technology center.

Freshman class profile.

GPA 3.75 or higher:	10%	Live on campus:	90%
GPA 3.50-3.74:	15%	International:	2%
GPA 3.0-3.49:	44%	Fraternities:	16%
GPA 2.0-2.99:	31%	Sororities:	22%
Out-of-state:	1%		

Basis for selection. School GPA and test scores most important. SAT, ACT, SAT Subject Tests must be received before start of term. Audition required of music majors. Portfolio required of art majors. RN required for graduate nursing. **Learning Disabled:** Applicants with disabilities strongly encouraged to complete college preparatory course requirements if at all possible. If applicant judged unable to fulfill specific course requirement because of disability, alternative college preparatory courses may be substituted for specific subject requirements.

High school preparation. College-preparatory program required. 15 units required. Required units include English 4, mathematics 3, history 2, science 2 (laboratory 1), foreign language 2, visual/performing arts 1 and academic electives 1. One visual and performing arts, US government required.

2015-2016 Annual costs. Tuition/fees: $7,324; $18,484 out-of-state. Room/board: $12,814. Books/supplies: $1,826. Personal expenses: $1,364.

Financial aid. Non-need-based: Scholarships awarded for academics, alumni affiliation, art, athletics, leadership, minority status, music/drama. **Additional information:** Pell Grant recipients see no increase in their fees, students with family incomes of $75,000 or less will pay no fees at all.

Application procedures. Admission: Closing date 11/30 (postmark date). $55 fee, may be waived for applicants with need. Admission notification by 3/1. Admission notification on a rolling basis. Must reply by 5/1. **Financial aid:** Priority date 1/31; no closing date. FAFSA required. Applicants notified on a rolling basis starting 3/25; must reply within 2 week(s) of notification.

Academics. Special study options: Accelerated study, combined bachelor's/graduate degree, cross-registration, distance learning, double major, dual enrollment of high school students, ESL, exchange student, external degree, honors, independent study, internships, liberal arts/career combination, New York semester, semester at sea, student-designed major, study abroad, teacher certification program, United Nations semester, urban semester, Washington semester. Combined degree programs: bachelor's/MBA; bachelor's/MPA. **Credit/placement by examination:** AP, CLEP, SAT, ACT, institutional tests. 30 credit hours maximum toward bachelor's degree. **Support services:** Learning center, pre-admission summer program, reduced course load, remedial instruction, study skills assistance, tutoring, writing center.

Majors. Area/ethnic studies: African-American, Chicano/Hispanic-American/Latino, women's. **Biology:** General, biochemistry. **Business:** Business admin. **Communications:** Communications/speech/rhetoric. **Computer sciences:** Computer science, programming. **Conservation:** General, environmental studies. **Engineering:** Computer. **English:** English lit. **Foreign languages:** French, German, Spanish. **Health services:** Nursing (RN). **History:** General. **Liberal arts:** Arts/sciences. **Math:** General. **Philosophy/religion:** Philosophy. **Physical sciences:** Chemistry, geology, physics. **Protective services:** Law enforcement admin. **Psychology:** General. **Social sciences:** Anthropology, economics, geography, political science, sociology. **Visual/performing arts:** General, art history/conservation, dramatic, music, studio arts. **Work/family studies:** Family studies.

Most popular majors. Business/marketing 22%, liberal arts 9%, physical sciences 6%, psychology 12%, social sciences 9%.

Technology on campus. PC or laptop required. 400 workstations in library, computer center. Dormitories wired for high-speed internet access and linked to campus network. Commuter students can connect to campus network. Online course registration, online library, helpline, student web hosting, wireless network available.

Student life. Freshman orientation: Available. Preregistration for classes offered. 2-day residential program in June. Parents invited. **Housing:** Guaranteed on-campus for freshmen. Coed dorms, apartments, wellness housing available. $1,000 partly refundable deposit. Focus learning communities, freshman seminar, women in math/science dorms available. **Activities:** Jazz band, choral groups, dance, drama, literary magazine, music ensembles, Model UN, musical theater, opera, radio station, student government, student newspaper, symphony orchestra, Student Advocates for Education, College Republicans, Asian Pacific Islander Organization, Raza Native American Council, El Movimiento Estudiantil Chicano/a de Aztlán, InterVarsity Christian Fellowship, Hillel, Best Buddies, Student Ambassadors.

Athletics. NCAA. **Intercollegiate:** Baseball M, basketball, golf, soccer, softball W, tennis, track and field W, volleyball W, water polo W. **Intramural:** Basketball, football (non-tackle), soccer, softball, volleyball. **Team name:** Sea Wolves.

Student services. Adult student services, alcohol/substance abuse counseling, career counseling, services for economically disadvantaged, student employment services, financial aid counseling, health services, minority student services, on-campus daycare, personal counseling, placement for graduates, veterans' counselor, women's services. **Physically disabled:** Services for visually, speech, hearing impaired.

Contact. Phone: (707) 664-2778 Fax: (707) 664-2060
Gustavo Flores, Director, Admissions, Sonoma State University, 1801 East Cotati Avenue, Rohnert Park, CA 94928-3609

Southern California Institute of Architecture
Los Angeles, California
www.sciarc.edu   CB code: 1575

- Private 5-year visual arts college
- Commuter campus in very large city
- 255 degree-seeking undergraduates: 37% women, 1% African American, 18% Asian American, 14% Hispanic/Latino, 2% Multi-racial, non-Hispanic, 51% international
- 247 degree-seeking graduate students
- 73% of applicants admitted
- SAT or ACT with writing, application essay required
- 54% graduate within 6 years

General. Founded in 1972. Regionally accredited. **Degrees:** 52 bachelor's awarded; master's offered. **Location:** Downtown Los Angeles. **Calendar:** Semester, limited summer session. **Full-time faculty:** 29 total; 66% have terminal degrees, 24% minority, 24% women. **Part-time faculty:** 39 total; 59% have terminal degrees, 26% minority, 26% women. **Special facilities:** Wood and metal shop, on-site print center, robotics lab, supply store, digital fabrication lab.

Freshman class profile. 214 applied, 157 admitted, 31 enrolled.

Mid 50% test scores			
		GPA 3.50-3.74:	19%
SAT critical reading:	440-570	GPA 3.0-3.49:	44%
SAT math:	540-690	GPA 2.0-2.99:	18%
SAT writing:	470-570	End year in good standing:	88%
ACT composite:	25-29	Return as sophomores:	94%
GPA 3.75 or higher:	19%	Out-of-state:	22%

Basis for selection. Portfolio of work (creative and/or architectural work), personal statement, resume, 3 letters of recommendation, academic transcripts and test scores are required. Applicants that have completed previous architectural design studios are eligible to apply for advanced placement. Applicants that have no previous architectural design studio work must apply for first year placement. Portfolio of visual creative work is required of all applicants. **Home schooled:** Transcript of courses and grades, state high school equivalency certificate required.

High school preparation. Art, design or architecture courses are recommended.

2015-2016 Annual costs. Tuition/fees: $42,220. Books/supplies: $8,076.

2014-2015 Financial aid. **Need-based:** 8 full-time freshmen applied for aid; 8 deemed to have need; 8 received aid. Average need met was 5%. Average scholarship/grant was $13,294. 36% of total undergraduate aid awarded as scholarships/grants, 64% as loans/jobs. **Non-need-based:** Awarded to 101 full-time undergraduates, including 5 freshmen. Scholarships awarded for academics, state residency.

Application procedures. **Admission:** Closing date 1/15 (receipt date). $85 fee, may be waived for applicants with need. Application must be submitted online. Admission notification on a rolling basis beginning on or about 4/1. Must reply by 4/25. **Financial aid:** Closing date 3/2. FAFSA, institutional form required. Applicants notified on a rolling basis starting 3/15; must reply within 3 week(s) of notification.

Academics. **Special study options:** Exchange student, independent study, internships, study abroad. Exchange programs offered in Austria, Australia, Netherlands, Mexico and the United Kingdom. **Credit/placement by examination:** AP, CLEP, IB. Students can transfer in a maximum of 18 credit hours/units from AP or IB examinations. **Support services:** Pre-admission summer program, reduced course load. ESL summer workshop.

Majors. Architecture: Architecture.

Technology on campus. PC or laptop required. 85 workstations in library, computer center. Commuter students can connect to campus network. Online course registration, online library, wireless network available.

Student life. Freshman orientation: Mandatory. Preregistration for classes offered. Held for the three consecutive days prior to the first day of classes; opportunity to visit alumni architectural firms on last day of orientation. **Policies:** Informal weekly gathering of entire school sponsored by student government. **Activities:** Student government.

Student services. Student employment services, financial aid counseling, personal counseling, veterans' counselor. **Physically disabled:** Services for speech, hearing impaired.

Contact. E-mail: admissions@sciarc.edu
Phone: (213) 356-5320 Fax: (213) 613-2260
Sandy Frigo, Director of Admissions, Southern California Institute of Architecture, 960 E 3rd Street, Los Angeles, CA 90013

Southern California Institute of Technology
Anaheim, California
www.scitech.edu   CB code: 3034

- For-profit 4-year business and engineering college
- Commuter campus in large city
- 335 degree-seeking undergraduates: 4% women
- Interview required

General. Accredited by ACCSC. **Degrees:** 44 bachelor's, 1 associate awarded. **Calendar:** Differs by program, extensive summer session. **Full-time faculty:** 16 total. **Special facilities:** Residential wiring lab, commercial wiring lab, programmable logic controller lab, electric motors lab, robotics and automation lab, biomedical instrumentations lab, electronic circuits lab, digital and analog electronics lab, engineering design projects lab, solar power lab, pneumatics lab, computer networking lab.

Basis for selection. Open admission, but selective for some programs. Interview, high school diploma, GED, official transcripts from other schools attended, standardized entrance exam required. **Home schooled:** Transcript of courses and grades, interview required.

2015-2016 Annual costs. Tuition/fees: $9,720. Books/supplies: $2,500.

Application procedures. **Admission:** No deadline. $100 fee. Application must be submitted on paper. **Financial aid:** FAFSA required.

Academics. **Special study options:** Accelerated study, combined bachelor's/graduate degree, cooperative education, double major, ESL, liberal arts/career combination. **Credit/placement by examination:** AP, CLEP. **Support services:** Tutoring.

Majors. Business: Business admin. **Computer sciences:** Computer science. **Engineering:** Electrical.

Most popular majors. Computer/information sciences 7%, engineering/engineering technologies 93%.

Technology on campus. Wireless network available.

Student life. Freshman orientation: Available. Preregistration for classes offered.

Student services. Adult student services, career counseling, student employment services, financial aid counseling, placement for graduates.

Contact. E-mail: admissions@scitech.edu
Phone: (714) 300-0300 Fax: (714) 300-0311
Parviz Shams, School Director, Southern California Institute of Technology, 525 North Muller Street, Anaheim, CA 92801

Southern California Seminary
El Cajon, California
www.socalsem.edu

- Private 4-year Bible and seminary college
- Commuter campus in small city
- 62 degree-seeking undergraduates: 69% part-time, 32% women
- 177 degree-seeking graduate students
- Application essay, interview required

General. Regionally accredited; also accredited by TRACS. **Degrees:** 13 bachelor's awarded; master's, professional offered. **Location:** 20 miles from San Diego. **Calendar:** Trimester, extensive summer session. **Full-time faculty:** 12 total; 58% have terminal degrees, 25% minority, 42% women. **Part-time faculty:** 34 total; 79% have terminal degrees, 24% minority, 21% women. **Class size:** 100% < 20.

Basis for selection. Open admission, but selective for some programs. Application requirements include a standard background check. MMPI (Minnesota Multiphasic Personality Inventory) and interview required of MA in Counseling Psychology and PsyD degree programs applicants. **Home schooled:** Transcript of courses and grades, state high school equivalency certificate, letter of recommendation (nonparent) required. 2 essays on specific content.

High school preparation. College-preparatory program recommended.

2015-2016 Annual costs. Tuition/fees: $14,409. Room only: $5,495. Books/supplies: $1,746. Personal expenses: $2,295.

Application procedures. Admission: No deadline. $34 fee. **Financial aid:** Closing date 3/2.

Academics. Special study options: Distance learning. **Credit/placement by examination:** AP, CLEP, institutional tests.

Majors. Theology: Bible.

Technology on campus. Commuter students can connect to campus network. Online library, helpline, wireless network available.

Student life. Freshman orientation: Mandatory. Preregistration for classes offered. **Housing:** Coed dorms, apartments available.

Student services. Chaplain/spiritual director, financial aid counseling, personal counseling, veterans' counselor.

Contact. E-mail: admissions@socalsem.edu
Phone: (619) 201-8959 Toll-free number: (888) 389-7244
Fax: (619) 201-8975
William George, Vice President of Development, Southern California Seminary, 2075 East Madison Avenue, El Cajon, CA 92019

St. Mary's College of California
Moraga, California
www.stmarys-ca.edu

CB member
CB code: 4675

- Private 4-year liberal arts college affiliated with the Roman Catholic Church
- Residential campus in large town
- 2,916 degree-seeking undergraduates: 9% part-time, 60% women, 4% African American, 10% Asian American, 25% Hispanic/Latino, 1% Native Hawaiian/Pacific islander, 7% Multi-racial, non-Hispanic, 2% international
- 1,090 degree-seeking graduate students
- 76% of applicants admitted
- SAT or ACT (ACT writing optional), application essay required
- 71% graduate within 6 years

General. Founded in 1863. Regionally accredited. **Degrees:** 759 bachelor's awarded; master's, doctoral offered. **ROTC:** Army, Air Force. **Location:** 20 miles from San Francisco. **Calendar:** 4-1-4, limited summer session. **Full-time faculty:** 219 total; 10% minority, 53% women. **Part-time faculty:** 287 total; 11% minority, 62% women. **Class size:** 52% < 20, 48% 20-39, less than 1% 40-49, less than 1% 50-99. **Special facilities:** Observatory, college-operated museum.

Freshman class profile. 4,852 applied, 3,681 admitted, 648 enrolled.

Mid 50% test scores			
SAT critical reading:	510-620	GPA 3.0-3.49:	35%
SAT math:	530-630	GPA 2.0-2.99:	2%
ACT composite:	22-27	Return as sophomores:	88%
GPA 3.75 or higher:	41%	Out-of-state:	16%
GPA 3.50-3.74:	22%	Live on campus:	99%
		International:	2%

Basis for selection. School achievement record most important. Interview recommended. **Home schooled:** Transcript of courses and grades, letter of recommendation (nonparent) required.

High school preparation. College-preparatory program recommended. 16 units required; 19 recommended. Required and recommended units include

English 4, mathematics 3-4, social studies 1, history 1, science 2-3 (laboratory 1), foreign language 2-3 and academic electives 2. One unit each of chemistry, physics, advanced algebra and trigonometry required for math or science majors.

2016-2017 Annual costs. Tuition/fees: $44,360. Room/board: $14,880. Books/supplies: $1,107. Personal expenses: $1,800.

2015-2016 Financial aid. Need-based: 547 full-time freshmen applied for aid; 470 deemed to have need; 469 received aid. Average need met was 72%. Average scholarship/grant was $28,521; average loan $3,769. 72% of total undergraduate aid awarded as scholarships/grants, 28% as loans/jobs. **Non-need-based:** Awarded to 981 full-time undergraduates, including 335 freshmen. Scholarships awarded for academics, athletics, leadership, music/drama, religious affiliation.

Application procedures. Admission: Priority date 11/15; deadline 2/1 (postmark date). $55 fee, may be waived for applicants with need. Admission notification by 3/15. Must reply by May 1 or within 2 week(s) if notified thereafter. **Financial aid:** Priority date 2/15; no closing date. FAFSA required. Applicants notified by 2/15; Applicants notified on a rolling basis starting 2/1; must reply by 5/1.

Academics. Academic support services are available on Sunday evenings or by appointment. **Special study options:** Combined bachelor's/graduate degree, cross-registration, double major, exchange student, honors, independent study, internships, liberal arts/career combination, student-designed major, study abroad, teacher certification program. 4-year interdisciplinary program with Great Books orientation. **Credit/placement by examination:** AP, CLEP, IB, SAT, ACT, institutional tests. 30 credit hours maximum toward bachelor's degree. **Support services:** Learning center, study skills assistance, tutoring, writing center.

Majors. Area/ethnic studies: European, Latin American, women's. **Biology:** General, biochemistry. **Business:** General, accounting, business admin, finance, international. **Communications:** Communications/speech/rhetoric. **Conservation:** Environmental science, environmental studies. **English:** English lit. **Foreign languages:** General, classics, French, German, Italian, Japanese, Spanish. **Health services:** Health care admin. **History:** General. **Liberal arts:** Arts/sciences. **Math:** General. **Parks/recreation:** Exercise sciences, health/fitness, sports admin. **Philosophy/religion:** Philosophy, religion. **Physical sciences:** Chemistry, physics. **Psychology:** General, developmental, experimental, industrial, social. **Social sciences:** Anthropology, archaeology, economics, political science, sociology. **Visual/performing arts:** General, art, dance, dramatic, music.

Most popular majors. Biology 6%, business/marketing 32%, communications/journalism 8%, liberal arts 9%, parks/recreation 6%, social sciences 10%.

Technology on campus. 244 workstations in computer center. Dormitories wired for high-speed internet access and linked to campus network. Commuter students can connect to campus network. Online course registration, online library, helpline, repair service, student web hosting, wireless network available.

Student life. Freshman orientation: Mandatory, $250 fee. Preregistration for classes offered. 4 sessions plus separate transfer session. Freshmen attend 1 session plus 4-day welcome weekend. **Housing:** Guaranteed on-campus for freshmen. Coed dorms, apartments, themed housing available. $350 nonrefundable deposit, deadline 5/1. Honors, Science, Lasallian Community, Santiago Community housing available. **Activities:** Bands, campus ministries, choral groups, dance, drama, international student organizations, literary magazine, music ensembles, musical theater, radio station, student government, student newspaper, TV station, Catholic Institute for Lasallian Social Action, Habitat for Humanity, Amnesty International, Lasallian Collegians, Asian Pacific American Student Association, Black Student Union, Dante, Gay Straight Alliance, Hermanas Unidas, Humans Actively Practicing Aloha Club.

Athletics. NCAA. **Intercollegiate:** Baseball M, basketball, cheerleading W, cross-country, golf M, lacrosse W, rowing (crew) W, soccer, softball W, tennis, track and field, volleyball W. **Intramural:** Badminton, basketball, football (non-tackle), skiing, soccer, softball, volleyball. **Team name:** Gaels.

Student services. Alcohol/substance abuse counseling, chaplain/spiritual director, career counseling, services for economically disadvantaged, student employment services, financial aid counseling, health services, minority student services, personal counseling, placement for graduates, veterans' counselor, women's services. **Physically disabled:** Services for visually, speech, hearing impaired.

Contact. E-mail: smcadmit@stmarys-ca.edu
Phone: (925) 631-4224 Toll-free number: (800) 800-4762
Fax: (925) 376-7193
Michael McKeon, Dean of Admissions, St. Mary's College of California, Box 4800, Moraga, CA 94575-4800

Stanbridge College
Irvine, California
www.stanbridge.edu

- For-profit 4-year health science and technical college
- Large city
- 926 degree-seeking undergraduates
- 164 graduate students

General. Regionally accredited; also accredited by ACCSC. **Degrees:** 20 bachelor's, 133 associate awarded; master's offered. **Calendar:** Quarter, extensive summer session. **Full-time faculty:** 7 total. **Part-time faculty:** 76 total.

Basis for selection. Open admission, but selective for some programs. Applicants are required to complete an admission's assessment and participate in an interview prior to being considered for admissions.

2015-2016 Annual costs. Comprehensive fee: $34,995. Books/supplies: $2,100. Personal expenses: $900.

Financial aid. All financial aid based on need.

Application procedures. Admission: No application fee. **Financial aid:** Closing date 3/2. FAFSA, institutional form required. Applicants notified on a rolling basis starting 1/1; must reply by 2/15 or within 6 week(s) of notification.

Academics. Credit/placement by examination: AP, CLEP. **Support services:** Learning center, remedial instruction, study skills assistance, tutoring.

Majors. Computer sciences: Information technology.

Technology on campus. Online library, helpline, repair service available.

Student life. Freshman orientation: Mandatory. Preregistration for classes offered.

Student services. Adult student services, career counseling, student employment services, financial aid counseling, personal counseling, placement for graduates.

Contact. E-mail: info@stanbridge.edu
Phone: (949) 794-9090 ext. 5116 Fax: (949) 794-9094
Edward Riepma, Director of Admissions, Stanbridge College, 2041 Business Center Drive, Suite 107, Irvine, CA 92612

Stanford University
Stanford, California   **CB member**
www.stanford.edu   **CB code: 4704**

- Private 4-year university and liberal arts college
- Residential campus in small city
- 6,994 degree-seeking undergraduates: 48% women, 6% African American, 20% Asian American, 15% Hispanic/Latino, 1% Native American, 10% Multi-racial, non-Hispanic, 9% international
- 9,196 degree-seeking graduate students
- 9% of applicants admitted
- SAT or ACT with writing, application essay required
- 95% graduate within 6 years

General. Founded in 1885. Regionally accredited. Stanford is a research university with seven schools: Business, Earth Sciences, Education, Engineering, Humanities and Sciences, Law and Medicine. **Degrees:** 1,671 bachelor's awarded; master's, professional, doctoral offered. **ROTC:** Army, Naval, Air Force. **Location:** 29 miles from San Francisco, 22 miles from San Jose. **Calendar:** Quarter, extensive summer session. **Full-time faculty:** 1,589 total; 99% have terminal degrees, 23% minority, 26% women. **Part-time faculty:** 26 total; 92% have terminal degrees, 12% minority, 27% women. **Class size:** 71% < 20, 13% 20-39, 5% 40-49, 8% 50-99, 4% >100. **Special facilities:** Linear accelerator, nature preserve, marine research center, Rodin sculpture garden, medical center, concert hall, three art museums, two observatories.

Freshman class profile. 24,797 applied, 2,140 admitted, 1,720 enrolled.

Mid 50% test scores		GPA 3.0-3.49:	1%
SAT critical reading:	690-780	Rank in top quarter:	99%
SAT math:	700-800	Rank in top tenth:	96%
SAT writing:	690-780	Return as sophomores:	98%
ACT composite:	31-35	Out-of-state:	63%
GPA 3.75 or higher:	95%	Live on campus:	100%
GPA 3.50-3.74:	4%	International:	10%

Basis for selection. Academic excellence is the primary criterion. Prospective students should have challenged themselves throughout high school and done very well. Transcript and recommendations are very important, as are personal qualities. SAT Subject Tests recommended. SAT Subject Tests are recommended but not required. AP examination scores are recommended but not required. If English is not your native language, we recommend, but do not require, the Test of English as a Foreign Language (TOEFL). Arts students may submit supplementary materials for review. Submissions should have previously received significant recognition at regional, state, national or international level. Students who submit an Arts Supplement are not required to major in the arts at Stanford. Similarly, students who do not submit an Arts Supplement may still study or participate in the arts at Stanford. **Home schooled:** Statement describing home school structure and mission required. **Learning Disabled:** Prospective students with disabilities are encouraged to meet with the Office of Accessible Education.

High school preparation. College-preparatory program recommended. 20 units recommended. Recommended units include English 4, mathematics 4, social studies 3, history 3, science 3 (laboratory 3) and foreign language 3.

2015-2016 Annual costs. Tuition/fees: $46,320. Room/board: $14,107. Books/supplies: $1,425. Personal expenses: $2,625.

2014-2015 Financial aid. Need-based: 997 full-time freshmen applied for aid; 811 deemed to have need; 790 received aid. Average need met was 100%. Average scholarship/grant was $43,291; average loan $2,580. 95% of total undergraduate aid awarded as scholarships/grants, 5% as loans/jobs. **Non-need-based:** Awarded to 579 full-time undergraduates, including 136 freshmen. Scholarships awarded for athletics. **Additional information:** For parents with total annual income below $65,000 and typical assets for this income range, parent contribution toward educational costs not expected. Students will still be expected to contribute from their income and savings. For parents with total annual income below $125,000 and typical assets for this income range, the expected parent contribution will be low enough to ensure that all tuition charges are covered with need-based scholarship, federal and state grants, and/or outside scholarship funds. Families with incomes at higher levels (typically up to $200,000) may also qualify for assistance, especially if more than one family member is enrolled in college.

Application procedures. Admission: Closing date 1/3 (postmark date). $90 fee, may be waived for applicants with need. Application must be submitted online. Admission notification by 4/1. Must reply by 5/1. Restrictive Early Action is a non-binding early application option for students who select Stanford as their first choice. **Financial aid:** Priority date 2/15; no closing date. FAFSA, CSS PROFILE required. Applicants notified on a rolling basis starting 4/1; must reply by 5/1.

Academics. Undergraduates interact closely with faculty members in small-group learning situations and by access to research opportunities. **Special study options:** Combined bachelor's/graduate degree, distance learning, double major, exchange student, honors, independent study, internships, New York semester, semester at sea, student-designed major, study abroad, Washington semester. **Credit/placement by examination:** AP, CLEP, IB, institutional tests. 45 Advanced Placement units allowed. **Support services:** Learning center, pre-admission summer program, reduced course load, study skills assistance, tutoring, writing center. Support for research, fellowships and independent projects; pre-professional advising; pre-major advising, tutoring, Hume Center for Writing and Speaking, academic skills coaching.

Majors. Area/ethnic studies: African, African-American, American, Asian-American, Chicano/Hispanic-American/Latino, East Asian, German, Native American, Slavic, Spanish/Iberian, women's. **Biology:** General. **Communications:** General. **Computer sciences:** General, computer science. **Conservation:** Environmental science. **Engineering:** General, aerospace, biomedical, chemical, civil, electrical, environmental, materials, mechanical, petroleum. **English:** English lit, writing. **Foreign languages:** Chinese, classics, comparative lit, French, German, Italian, Japanese, linguistics, Slavic, Spanish. **History:** General. **Human services:** Public policy. **Math:** General. **Philosophy/religion:** Philosophy, religion. **Physical sciences:** Chemistry, geology, geophysics, materials science, physics. **Psychology:** General. **Social sciences:** Anthropology, archaeology, economics, international relations, political science, sociology, urban studies. **Visual/performing arts:** Art, dramatic, music, studio arts.

Most popular majors. Biology 6%, computer/information sciences 13%, engineering/engineering technologies 23%, interdisciplinary studies 19%, social sciences 14%.

Technology on campus. 1,000 workstations in dormitories, library, computer center, student center. Dormitories wired for high-speed internet access and linked to campus network. Commuter students can connect to campus network. Online course registration, online library, helpline, repair service, student web hosting, wireless network available.

Student life. Freshman orientation: Mandatory, $688 fee. Preregistration for classes offered. 6-day academically oriented program held in late September. **Policies:** Students are expected to abide by the Fundamental Standard and the Honor Code. Freshmen not permitted cars on campus. **Housing:** Guaranteed on-campus for all undergraduates. Coed dorms, single-sex dorms, special housing for disabled, apartments, cooperative housing, fraternity/sorority housing, themed housing available. Student-managed housing and substance-free housing available. **Activities:** Bands, campus ministries, choral groups, dance, drama, film society, international student organizations, literary magazine, music ensembles, Model UN, musical theater, opera, radio station, student government, student newspaper, symphony orchestra, TV station, Stanford Daily, Stanford Debate Society, Stanford Solar Car Project, Business Association of Stanford Engineering Students, Ballet Folklorico, 6th Man Club, Black Student Union, Stanford Concert Network, Asian American Theater Project, Ram's Head Theatrical Society.

Athletics. NCAA. **Intercollegiate:** Baseball M, basketball, cross-country, diving, fencing, field hockey W, football (tackle) M, golf, gymnastics, lacrosse W, rowing (crew), sailing, soccer, softball W, squash W, swimming, synchronized swimming W, tennis, track and field, volleyball, water polo, wrestling M. **Intramural:** Badminton, basketball, football (non-tackle), golf, racquetball, rugby, sand volleyball, soccer, softball, squash, table tennis, tennis, ultimate frisbee, volleyball. **Team name:** Cardinal.

Student services. Alcohol/substance abuse counseling, chaplain/spiritual director, career counseling, student employment services, financial aid counseling, health services, legal services, minority student services, on-campus daycare, personal counseling, placement for graduates, veterans' counselor, women's services. **Physically disabled:** Services for visually, speech, hearing impaired.

Contact. E-mail: admission@stanford.edu
Phone: (650) 723-2091 Fax: (650) 723-6050
Colleen Lim, Dean of Undergraduate Admission and Financial Aid, Stanford University, Montag Hall, Stanford, CA 94305-6106

SUM Bible College & Theological Seminary
Oakland, California
www.sum.edu

- Private 4-year Bible and seminary college affiliated with the Assemblies of God
- Residential campus in very large city
- 446 degree-seeking undergraduates: 15% part-time, 44% women
- 47 degree-seeking graduate students
- Application essay, interview required

General. Regionally accredited; also accredited by ABHE. **Degrees:** 60 bachelor's awarded; master's offered. **Location:** Downtown. **Calendar:** Trimester, limited summer session. **Full-time faculty:** 7 total; 29% have terminal degrees. **Part-time faculty:** 26 total; 12% have terminal degrees. **Class size:** 37% < 20, 63% 20-39.

Basis for selection. Open admission, but selective for some programs. Recommendations, interview, character/personal qualities are very important. 2 1-page essays, academic transcripts, and a photo are required. Pastor's recommendation and one general recommendation required. **Home schooled:** Transcript of courses and grades, state high school equivalency certificate, letter of recommendation (nonparent) required.

High school preparation. Required and recommended units include English 4, mathematics 3-4, history 2, science 2-3, foreign language 2-3, visual/performing arts 1 and academic electives 1. No academic requirement for high school diploma. Minimum 2.0 GPA preferred. If student is below 2.0, the student may be enrolled but with academic probation.

2015-2016 Annual costs. Tuition/fees: $8,400. Room only: $2,400. Books/supplies: $1,500. Personal expenses: $4,743. **Additional information:** Additional $520 charge for those required to attend the Mardi Gras practicum. Board plan not available.

Financial aid. Non-need-based: Scholarships awarded for academics, leadership, religious affiliation.

Application procedures. Admission: Closing date 8/8. $20 fee. Application must be submitted on paper. Admission notification on a rolling basis beginning on or about 1/1. **Financial aid:** No deadline. FAFSA required.

Academics. Extensive hands-on ministry training (8 hours per week). **Special study options:** Distance learning. **Credit/placement by examination:** AP, CLEP. No credit for life experience in the academic courses. Field ministry credits can be considered life experience. **Support services:** Reduced course load, remedial instruction, tutoring.

Majors. Theology: Bible.

Technology on campus. 5 workstations in library. Dormitories wired for high-speed internet access and linked to campus network. Online course registration, online library, wireless network available.

Student life. Freshman orientation: Mandatory. Preregistration for classes offered. **Policies:** 2 hours of Christian service required per week. Religious observance required. **Housing:** Guaranteed on-campus for all undergraduates. Single-sex dorms, apartments available. **Activities:** Campus ministries, student government.

Student services. Chaplain/spiritual director, financial aid counseling, health services, personal counseling.

Contact. E-mail: admissions@sum.edu
Phone: (510) 567-6174 Toll-free number: (888) 567-6171
Fax: (510) 568-1024
SUM Bible College & Theological Seminary, 735 105th Avenue, Oakland, CA 94603

Thomas Aquinas College
Santa Paula, California   **CB member**
www.thomasaquinas.edu   **CB code: 4828**

- Private 4-year liberal arts college affiliated with the Roman Catholic Church
- Residential campus in rural community
- 377 degree-seeking undergraduates: 50% women, 1% Asian American, 15% Hispanic/Latino, 7% Multi-racial, non-Hispanic, 3% international
- 75% of applicants admitted
- SAT or ACT (ACT writing optional), application essay required
- 87% graduate within 6 years

General. Founded in 1971. Regionally accredited. **Degrees:** 81 bachelor's awarded. **Location:** 5 miles from Santa Paula, 12 miles from Ojai. **Calendar:** Semester. **Full-time faculty:** 32 total; 88% have terminal degrees, 12% women. **Part-time faculty:** 4 total; 75% have terminal degrees. **Class size:** 100% < 20.

Freshman class profile. 189 applied, 142 admitted, 82 enrolled.

Mid 50% test scores			
SAT critical reading:	610-730	GPA 2.0-2.99:	2%
SAT math:	550-650	Rank in top quarter:	50%
SAT writing:	590-700	Rank in top tenth:	44%
ACT composite:	26-30	Return as sophomores:	94%
GPA 3.75 or higher:	73%	Out-of-state:	64%
GPA 3.50-3.74:	14%	Live on campus:	100%
GPA 3.0-3.49:	11%	International:	1%

Basis for selection. Application essays, 3 letters of reference, academic records, and test scores required. Test scores are accepted on a rolling basis throughout the year. Interview recommended for applicants whose academic preparation is non-traditional, and for those out of high school for significant period of time. **Home schooled:** Those applicants who are not home schooled through formal programs must provide written records of all their studies from grades 9 through 12.

High school preparation. College-preparatory program required. 13 units required; 18 recommended. Required and recommended units include English 4, mathematics 3-4, history 2, science 2-3 (laboratory 2), foreign language 2 and academic electives 3.

2016-2017 Annual costs. Tuition/fees (projected): $24,500. Room/board: $7,950. Books/supplies: $50. Personal expenses: $2,330.

2015-2016 Financial aid. All financial aid based on need. 67 full-time freshmen applied for aid; 62 deemed to have need; 62 received aid. Average need met was 100%. Average scholarship/grant was $14,711; average loan $3,233. 63% of total undergraduate aid awarded as scholarships/grants, 37% as loans/jobs.

Application procedures. Admission: No deadline. No application fee. Admission notification on a rolling basis beginning on or about 10/1. Must reply by May 1 or within 1 week(s) if notified thereafter. **Financial aid:** Closing date 3/2. FAFSA, institutional form required. Applicants notified on a rolling basis starting 2/1; must reply by 5/1 or within 2 week(s) of notification.

Academics. Special study options: Sole academic program offered is an interdisciplinary, liberal arts curriculum leading to a classical, Catholic liberal education. **Credit/placement by examination:** AP, CLEP. **Support services:** Tutoring.

Majors. Liberal arts: Arts/sciences.

Technology on campus. PC or laptop required. 19 workstations in dormitories, library, computer center, student center. Dormitories linked to campus network. Helpline available.

Student life. Freshman orientation: Mandatory. Preregistration for classes offered. 2-day program immediately before classes begin. **Housing:** Guaranteed on-campus for all undergraduates. Single-sex dorms available. **Activities:** Campus ministries, choral groups, dance, drama, literary magazine, music ensembles, musical theater, Medical Society, Pro-life group, Legion of Mary, Third Order Dominican, Tocqueville Political Forum.

Athletics. Intramural: Basketball, football (non-tackle) M, soccer, softball, table tennis, tennis, ultimate frisbee, volleyball.

Student services. Alcohol/substance abuse counseling, chaplain/spiritual director, career counseling, student employment services, financial aid counseling, health services, personal counseling, placement for graduates.

Contact. E-mail: admissions@thomasaquinas.edu
Phone: (805) 525-4417 Toll-free number: (800) 634-9797
Fax: (805) 421-5905
Jonathan Daly, Director of Admissions, Thomas Aquinas College, 10000 Ojai Road, Santa Paula, CA 93060-9621

Touro University Worldwide
Los Alamitos, California
www.tuw.edu   CB code: 4753

▸ Private 4-year business and health science college
▸ Large city
▸ 304 degree-seeking undergraduates: 45% part-time, 69% women
▸ 473 degree-seeking graduate students

General. Regionally accredited. **Degrees:** 4 bachelor's, 1 associate awarded; master's, professional offered. **Location:** Downtown. **Calendar:** Differs by program, limited summer session. **Full-time faculty:** 4 total; 100% have terminal degrees, 50% women. **Part-time faculty:** 12 total; 67% have terminal degrees, 42% women.

Basis for selection. Admission requirements vary by programs. SAT or ACT recommended.

2015-2016 Annual costs. Tuition/fees: $16,900. Books/supplies: $1,072. Personal expenses: $2,542.

Application procedures. Admission: Closing date 5/15. $50 fee. Admission notification on a rolling basis. **Financial aid:** Priority date 5/15, closing date 6/1. FAFSA required. Applicants notified by 8/15.

Academics. Special study options: Distance learning, dual enrollment of high school students, internships, study abroad, **Credit/placement by examination:** AP, CLEP.

Majors. Business: General. **Philosophy/religion:** Judaic. **Psychology:** General.

Most popular majors. Business/marketing 47%, psychology 53%.

Student life. Freshman orientation: Mandatory. Preregistration for classes offered.

Contact. Phone: (818) 575-6800 Fax: (818) 688-3244
Leah Mizrahi, Director of Admissions, Touro University Worldwide, 10601 Calle Lee, #179, Los Alamitos, CA 90720

Trident University International
Cypress, California
www.trident.edu   CB code: 6332

▸ For-profit 4-year virtual university
▸ Very large city
▸ 4,760 undergraduates
▸ Interview required

General. Regionally accredited. **Degrees:** 986 bachelor's awarded; master's, doctoral offered. **Location:** 30 Miles from Los Angeles. **Calendar:** Differs by program, extensive summer session. **Full-time faculty:** 44 total; 30% minority, 41% women. **Part-time faculty:** 435 total; 10% minority, 40% women.

Basis for selection. Open admission. **Home schooled:** Transcript of courses and grades required. Transcripts from State Department of Education or local school board.

2015-2016 Annual costs. Personal expenses: $1,925. **Additional information:** The tuition cost for the Bachelors program (100-400 level courses) is $375 per semester credit hour or $1,500 per course (All Trident courses are 4 semester credit hours). The tuition cost for Retired Military or Veterans of the military or Partnerships in the Bachelors program (100-400 level courses) is $300 per semester credit hour or $1,200 per course. The tuition cost for military students using Military Tuition Assistance; military spouses or Partnerships in the Bachelors program (100-400 level courses) is $250 per semester credit hour or $1,000 per course.

Application procedures. Admission: No deadline. No application fee. **Financial aid:** No deadline. FAFSA, institutional form required.

Academics. Special study options: Distance learning, double major, independent study. **Credit/placement by examination:** AP, CLEP.

Majors. Business: Business admin. **Computer sciences:** General, information technology. **Conservation:** Environmental science. **Health services:** Health care admin.

Most popular majors. Business/marketing 48%, computer/information sciences 9%, health sciences 41%.

Technology on campus. PC or laptop required. Online course registration, online library available.

Student life. Freshman orientation: Available. Preregistration for classes offered. **Activities:** Student newspaper.

Student services. Financial aid counseling, veterans' counselor.

Contact. E-mail: admissions@trident.edu
Phone: (800) 579-3170 Fax: (800) 403-9024
Robert Givenrod, Director of Admissions, Trident University International, Attn: Office of the Registrar, Cypress, CA 90630

University of California: Berkeley
Berkeley, California   CB member
www.berkeley.edu   CB code: 4833

▸ Public 4-year university
▸ Residential campus in small city
▸ 27,496 undergraduates
▸ 10,708 graduate students
▸ 15% of applicants admitted
▸ SAT or ACT with writing, application essay required
▸ 91% graduate within 6 years

General. Founded in 1868. Regionally accredited. **Degrees:** 7,647 bachelor's awarded; master's, professional, doctoral offered. **ROTC:** Army, Naval, Air Force. **Location:** 10 miles from San Francisco. **Calendar:** Semester, extensive summer session. **Special facilities:** Museums of art, anthropology, archaeology, paleontology and vertebrate zoology, film archive, science museum and research center for K-12 education, botanical garden, libraries of rare books, Western and Latin Americana, seismographic station, performing arts facilities.

Freshman class profile. 77,660 applied, 11,891 admitted, 5,546 enrolled.

Mid 50% test scores			
SAT critical reading:	610-730	GPA 3.50-3.74:	11%
SAT math:	640-770	GPA 3.0-3.49:	4%
SAT writing:	620-750	Rank in top quarter:	100%
ACT composite:	29-34	Rank in top tenth:	98%
GPA 3.75 or higher:	85%	Out-of-state:	23%
		Live on campus:	95%

Basis for selection. Thorough review of academic performance; likely contribution to intellectual and cultural vitality of the campus; diversity in personal background and experience; demonstrated qualities in leadership, motivation, concern for others and community; non-academic achievement in the performing arts, athletics or employment; demonstrated interest in major. SAT Subject Tests recommended. SAT Subject Tests recommended only for applicants to Colleges of Chemistry or Engineering.

High school preparation. College-preparatory program required. 15 units required; 18 recommended. Required and recommended units include English 4, mathematics 3-4, history 2, science 2-3 (laboratory 2-3), foreign language 2-3, visual/performing arts 1 and academic electives 1. 2 units in history or social sciences are required.

2015-2016 Annual costs. Tuition/fees: $13,431; $38,139 out-of-state. Room/board: $15,562. Books/supplies: $1,240. Personal expenses: $4,598.

Financial aid. Non-need-based: Scholarships awarded for academics, athletics, leadership. **Additional information:** For resident families whose gross income ranges from $80,000 to $150,000 annually and who have typical assets, parents' contribution capped at maximum of 15% of total income. Tuition and registration fee for low-income California residents covered under the Blue and Gold Opportunity Plan.

Application procedures. Admission: Closing date 11/30. $70 fee, may be waived for applicants with need. Admission notification by 3/31. Must reply by 5/1. **Financial aid:** Priority date 3/2, closing date 3/2. FAFSA required. Applicants notified by 4/15; must reply by 5/1.

Academics. All students required to pass one American cultures class. **Special study options:** Accelerated study, cross-registration, double major, dual enrollment of high school students, ESL, exchange student, honors, independent study, internships, student-designed major, study abroad. Freshman seminar, undergraduate research apprenticeship, university research expeditions. **Credit/placement by examination:** AP, CLEP, institutional tests. **Support services:** Learning center, pre-admission summer program, reduced course load, study skills assistance, tutoring.

Majors. Architecture: Architecture, landscape. **Area/ethnic studies:** African-American, American, Asian, Asian-American, Chicano/Hispanic-American/Latino, Latin American, Native American, Near/Middle Eastern, Southeast Asian, women's. **Biology:** General, botany, cellular/molecular, microbiology, toxicology. **Business:** Business admin. **Communications:** Media studies. **Computer sciences:** Computer science. **Conservation:** General, environmental studies, forest management, forestry. **Engineering:** Applied physics, biomedical, chemical, civil, electrical, engineering science, environmental, geological, manufacturing, mechanical, nuclear, operations research. **English:** English lit, rhetoric/composition. **Foreign languages:** Ancient Greek, Celtic, Chinese, classics, comparative lit, Dutch/Flemish, French, German, Italian, Japanese, Latin, linguistics, Scandinavian, Slavic, Spanish. **History:** General. **Human services:** Social work. **Math:** General, applied, statistics. **Philosophy/religion:** Philosophy. **Physical sciences:** Astrophysics, atmospheric science, chemistry, geology, geophysics, materials science, oceanography, physics. **Psychology:** General. **Social sciences:** Anthropology, economics, geography, political science, sociology, urban studies. **Visual/performing arts:** Art, art history/conservation, dance, dramatic, film/cinema/video, music.

Most popular majors. Biology 12%, engineering/engineering technologies 12%, social sciences 20%.

Technology on campus. Dormitories wired for high-speed internet access and linked to campus network. Commuter students can connect to campus network. Online course registration, online library, helpline, repair service, wireless network available.

Student life. Freshman orientation: Available, $295 fee. Preregistration for classes offered. Cost varies by term and entry status. **Housing:** Guaranteed on-campus for freshmen. Coed dorms, single-sex dorms, special housing for disabled, apartments, cooperative housing, fraternity/sorority housing, themed housing available. $300 partly refundable deposit, deadline 5/25. Apartments for students with children available. **Activities:** Bands, choral groups, dance, drama, film society, international student organizations, literary magazine, music ensembles, Model UN, musical theater, radio station, student government, student newspaper, symphony orchestra, TV station, Asian American Christian fellowship, black recruitment and retention center, hiking and outdoor society, Americorps, forensics, Chabad, Lesbian and Gay alliance, Raza recruitment and retention center, College Democrats, College Republicans.

Athletics. NCAA. **Intercollegiate:** Baseball M, basketball, cross-country, diving, field hockey W, football (tackle) M, golf, gymnastics, rowing (crew), rugby M, soccer, softball W, swimming, tennis, track and field, volleyball W, water polo. **Intramural:** Basketball, bowling, fencing, field hockey M, football (tackle), handball, ice hockey, lacrosse, racquetball, rowing (crew), sailing, skiing, soccer, softball, squash, tennis, volleyball M. **Team name:** Bears.

Student services. Adult student services, alcohol/substance abuse counseling, chaplain/spiritual director, career counseling, services for economically disadvantaged, student employment services, financial aid counseling, health services, legal services, minority student services, on-campus daycare, personal counseling, placement for graduates, veterans' counselor, women's services. **Physically disabled:** Services for visually, speech, hearing impaired.

Contact. Phone: (510) 642-6000
Amy Jarich, Director of Undergraduate Admissions, University of California: Berkeley, 110 Sproul Hall, #5800, Berkeley, CA 94720-5800

University of California: Davis
Davis, California   CB member
www.ucdavis.edu   CB code: 4834

- Public 4-year university
- Residential campus in small city
- 28,239 degree-seeking undergraduates: 1% part-time, 59% women, 2% African American, 32% Asian American, 19% Hispanic/Latino, 5% Multi-racial, non-Hispanic, 11% international
- 6,802 degree-seeking graduate students
- 38% of applicants admitted
- SAT or ACT with writing, application essay required
- 83% graduate within 6 years

General. Founded in 1905. Regionally accredited. **Degrees:** 7,120 bachelor's awarded; master's, professional, doctoral offered. **ROTC:** Army, Naval, Air Force. **Location:** 15 miles from Sacramento, 72 miles from San Francisco. **Calendar:** Quarter, extensive summer session. **Full-time faculty:** 1,652 total; 98% have terminal degrees, 25% minority, 38% women. **Part-time faculty:** 178 total; 98% have terminal degrees, 25% minority, 48% women. **Class size:** 35% < 20, 33% 20-39, 6% 40-49, 11% 50-99, 16% >100. **Special facilities:** Arboretum, equestrian center, craft center, marine laboratory, nuclear laboratory, primate research center, natural reserves, raptor center, veterinary school, center for the performing arts, museum of art.

Freshman class profile. 64,510 applied, 24,614 admitted, 5,369 enrolled.

Mid 50% test scores			
SAT critical reading:	510-630	GPA 3.0-3.49:	22%
SAT math:	560-710	GPA 2.0-2.99:	2%
SAT writing:	530-660	Return as sophomores:	92%
ACT composite:	24-30	Out-of-state:	8%
GPA 3.75 or higher:	62%	Live on campus:	93%
GPA 3.50-3.74:	14%	International:	19%

Basis for selection. Scholastic achievement most important, followed by school and community activities, academic interests, special circumstances, special achievements and awards. Two SAT Subject Tests in different subject areas of student's choice required: history/social science, English literature, mathematics (Level 2), laboratory science or language other than English.

High school preparation. College-preparatory program recommended. 15 units required; 18 recommended. Required and recommended units include English 4, mathematics 3-4, social studies 1, history 1, science 2-3 (laboratory 2-3), foreign language 2-3 and visual/performing arts 1.

2015-2016 Annual costs. Tuition/fees: $13,951; $38,659 out-of-state. Room/board: $14,517. Books/supplies: $1,576. Personal expenses: $3,653.

Financial aid. All financial aid based on need.

Application procedures. Admission: Closing date 11/30. $70 fee, may be waived for applicants with need. Admission notification by 3/31. Must reply by May 1 or within 1 week(s) if notified thereafter. **Financial aid:** Priority date 3/2; no closing date. FAFSA required. Applicants notified on a rolling basis starting 3/16.

Academics. Special study options: Accelerated study, cross-registration, double major, dual enrollment of high school students, ESL, honors, independent study, internships, student-designed major, study abroad, teacher certification program, Washington semester. **Credit/placement by examination:** AP, CLEP, SAT, ACT.

Majors. Architecture: Landscape, urban/community planning. **Area/ethnic studies:** African, African-American, American, Asian-American, Chicano/Hispanic-American/Latino, East Asian, Native American, women's. **Biology:** General, biotechnology, botany, cell/histology, entomology, environmental toxicology, evolutionary, exercise physiology, genetics, microbiology, molecular biochemistry, neurobiology/anatomy, zoology. **Communications:** Communications/speech/rhetoric. **Computer sciences:** Computer science. **Conservation:** General, environmental studies, urban forestry. **Engineering:** Aerospace, applied physics, biomedical, chemical, civil, computer, electrical, materials, mechanical. **English:** English lit. **Foreign languages:** Chinese, comparative lit, French, German, Italian, Japanese, linguistics, Russian, Spanish. **History:** General. **Math:** General, applied, computational, statistics. **Philosophy/religion:** Philosophy, religion. **Physical sciences:** Atmospheric science, chemistry, geology, hydrology, physics. **Psychology:** General. **Social sciences:** Anthropology, economics, international relations, political science, sociology. **Visual/performing arts:** Art history/conservation, design, dramatic, film/cinema/video, music, studio arts. **Work/family studies:** Clothing/textiles, family studies.

Most popular majors. Agriculture 6%, biology 20%, engineering/engineering technologies 11%, psychology 13%, social sciences 19%.

Student life. Freshman orientation: Available. Preregistration for classes offered. **Policies:** Residents and visitors must abide by state and university alcohol regulations. No Alcohol delivery by outside vendors permitted. Behavioral problems while under the influence of alcohol may be subject to disciplinary action. Tobacco use is prohibited on University property. **Housing:** Guaranteed on-campus for freshmen. Coed dorms, single-sex dorms, special housing for disabled, apartments, cooperative housing, themed housing, wellness housing available. $500 fully refundable deposit. Special interest housing available. **Activities:** Bands, campus ministries, choral groups, dance, drama, film society, international student organizations, literary magazine, music ensembles, Model UN, musical theater, radio station, student government, student newspaper, symphony orchestra, TV station.

Athletics. NCAA. **Intercollegiate:** Baseball M, basketball, cross-country, diving W, field hockey W, football (tackle) M, golf, gymnastics W, lacrosse W, soccer, softball W, swimming W, tennis, track and field, volleyball W, water polo. **Intramural:** Badminton, basketball, bowling, golf, racquetball, soccer, softball, squash, table tennis, tennis, volleyball, water polo. **Team name:** Aggies.

Student services. Adult student services, alcohol/substance abuse counseling, chaplain/spiritual director, career counseling, services for economically disadvantaged, student employment services, financial aid counseling, health services, legal services, minority student services, on-campus daycare, personal counseling, placement for graduates, veterans' counselor, women's services. **Physically disabled:** Services for visually, speech, hearing impaired.

Contact. E-mail: undergraduateadmissions@ucdavis.edu
Phone: (530) 752-2971 Fax: (530) 752-1280
Walter Robinson, Director, University of California: Davis, 178 Mrak Hall, One Shields Ave, Davis, CA 95616

University of California: Irvine

Irvine, California	CB member
www.uci.edu	CB code: 4859

- Public 4-year university
- Residential campus in small city
- 25,256 degree-seeking undergraduates: 2% part-time, 54% women, 2% African American, 37% Asian American, 25% Hispanic/Latino, 4% Multi-racial, non-Hispanic, 16% international
- 5,484 degree-seeking graduate students
- 39% of applicants admitted
- SAT or ACT with writing, application essay required
- 88% graduate within 6 years; 14% enter graduate study

General. Founded in 1965. Regionally accredited. **Degrees:** 6,768 bachelor's awarded; master's, professional, doctoral offered. **ROTC:** Army, Air Force. **Location:** 40 miles from Los Angeles. **Calendar:** Quarter, extensive summer session. **Full-time faculty:** 1,203 total; 98% have terminal degrees, 28% minority, 36% women. **Part-time faculty:** 307 total; 98% have terminal degrees, 29% minority, 49% women. **Class size:** 58% < 20, 17% 20-39, 4% 40-49, 8% 50-99, 12% >100. **Special facilities:** Outdoor laboratory, ecological preserve, freshwater marsh reserve, arboretum, center for art and technology, observatory, stem cell research center.

Freshman class profile. 71,768 applied, 27,764 admitted, 5,756 enrolled.

Mid 50% test scores		Rank in top tenth:	96%
SAT critical reading:	490-620	End year in good standing:	97%
SAT math:	550-690	Return as sophomores:	93%
SAT writing:	510-620	Out-of-state:	5%
GPA 3.75 or higher:	81%	Live on campus:	79%
GPA 3.50-3.74:	13%	International:	23%
GPA 3.0-3.49:	6%	Fraternities:	4%
Rank in top quarter:	100%	Sororities:	4%

Basis for selection. Demonstrated record of academic preparation, educational engagement, talent and skills important. SAT Subject Tests recommended. Students need only submit scores for the ACT With Writing or SAT. SAT Subject Test scores no longer required. However, submission of SAT Subject Test scores may add positively to review of student's application.

High school preparation. College-preparatory program required. 15 units required; 18 recommended. Required and recommended units include English 4, mathematics 3-4, social studies 2, science 2-3 (laboratory 2-3), foreign language 2-3 and visual/performing arts 1.

2015-2016 Annual costs. Tuition/fees: $14,750; $39,458 out-of-state. Room/board: $12,947. Books/supplies: $1,749. Personal expenses: $1,840. **Additional information:** Required fees include $1,497 for our student health insurance plan. Although this is a mandatory fee, if a student is covered through private insurance, he or she can waive out.

2014-2015 Financial aid. Need-based: 4,320 full-time freshmen applied for aid; 3,646 deemed to have need; 3,575 received aid. Average need met was 85%. Average scholarship/grant was $18,619; average loan $6,384. 81% of total undergraduate aid awarded as scholarships/grants, 19% as loans/jobs. **Non-need-based:** Awarded to 754 full-time undergraduates, including 124 freshmen. **Additional information:** UC Blue & Gold Opportunity Plan guarantees that needy in-state students from families earning less than $80,000/yr have system-wide tuition and fees paid through scholarships and grants.

Application procedures. Admission: Closing date 11/30 (receipt date). $70 fee, may be waived for applicants with need. Application must be submitted online. Admission notification by 3/31. Must reply by 5/1. **Financial aid:** Priority date 3/3, closing date 6/20. FAFSA required. Applicants notified on a rolling basis starting 4/1.

Academics. Special study options: Accelerated study, cross-registration, distance learning, double major, dual enrollment of high school students, ESL, honors, independent study, internships, semester at sea, study abroad, teacher certification program, Washington semester. **Credit/placement by examination:** AP, CLEP, IB, SAT, ACT, institutional tests. **Support services:** Learning center, pre-admission summer program, reduced course load, remedial instruction, study skills assistance, tutoring, writing center.

Majors. Area/ethnic studies: African-American, Asian-American, Chicano/Hispanic-American/Latino, Chinese, East Asian, European, German. **Biology:** General, Biochemistry/molecular biology, bioinformatics, botany, cellular/molecular, ecology/evolutionary, exercise physiology, genetics, microbiology/immunology, neurobiology/anatomy. **Business:** Business admin, information resources management, managerial economics. **Computer sciences:** General, computer science, informatics. **Conservation:** Environmental science, environmental studies. **Education:** General, biology. **Engineering:** General, aerospace, biomedical, chemical, civil, computer, electrical, environmental, materials, mechanical, software. **English:** English lit. **Foreign languages:** Classics, comparative lit, French, Japanese, Korean, Spanish. **Health services:** Pharmaceutical sciences. **History:** General. **Liberal arts:** Humanities. **Math:** General. **Philosophy/religion:** Philosophy, religion. **Physical sciences:** Chemistry, geology, physics. **Psychology:** General, social. **Social sciences:** General, anthropology, criminology, econometrics, economics, political science, sociology, urban studies. **Visual/performing arts:** General, art history/conservation, dance, dramatic, film/cinema/video, game design, music, music performance, musical theater, studio arts.

Most popular majors. Biology 11%, business/marketing 9%, engineering/engineering technologies 10%, health sciences 11%, psychology 12%, social sciences 19%, visual/performing arts 6%.

Technology on campus. 1,500 workstations in dormitories, library, computer center, student center, student center. Dormitories wired for high-speed internet access and linked to campus network. Commuter students can connect to campus network. Online course registration, online library, helpline, repair service, student web hosting, wireless network available.

Student life. Freshman orientation: Mandatory, $230 fee. Preregistration for classes offered. Two-day program held during summer. **Housing:** Guaranteed on-campus for freshmen. Coed dorms, single-sex dorms, special housing for disabled, apartments, fraternity/sorority housing, themed housing available. $350 partly refundable deposit. **Activities:** Bands, campus ministries, choral groups, dance, drama, film society, international student organizations, literary magazine, music ensembles, Model UN, musical theater, opera, radio station, student government, student newspaper, symphony orchestra.

Athletics. NCAA. **Intercollegiate:** Baseball M, basketball, cross-country, golf, soccer, tennis, track and field, volleyball, water polo. **Intramural:** Basketball, bowling, football (non-tackle), racquetball, soccer, softball, swimming, tennis, track and field, ultimate frisbee, volleyball, water polo, wrestling. **Team name:** Anteaters.

Student services. Adult student services, alcohol/substance abuse counseling, career counseling, services for economically disadvantaged, student employment services, financial aid counseling, health services, minority student services, on-campus daycare, personal counseling, placement for graduates, veterans' counselor, women's services. **Physically disabled:** Services for visually, speech, hearing impaired.

Contact. E-mail: admissions@uci.edu
Phone: (949) 824-6703 Fax: (949) 824-2951
Patricia Morales, Director, Admission & Relations with Schools, University of California: Irvine, 260 Aldrich Hall, Irvine, CA 92697-1075

University of California: Los Angeles

Los Angeles, California	CB member
www.ucla.edu	CB code: 4837

- Public 4-year university
- Residential campus in very large city

Four-Year Colleges

- 29,575 degree-seeking undergraduates: 2% part-time, 56% women, 3% African American, 29% Asian American, 21% Hispanic/Latino, 5% Multi-racial, non-Hispanic, 13% international
- 12,323 degree-seeking graduate students
- 17% of applicants admitted
- SAT or ACT with writing, application essay required
- 91% graduate within 6 years

General. Founded in 1919. Regionally accredited. **Degrees:** 7,959 bachelor's awarded; master's, professional, doctoral offered. **ROTC:** Army, Naval, Air Force. **Location:** 10 miles from downtown Los Angeles. **Calendar:** Quarter, extensive summer session. **Full-time faculty:** 1,931 total; 98% have terminal degrees, 27% minority, 34% women. **Part-time faculty:** 611 total; 98% have terminal degrees, 24% minority, 39% women. **Class size:** 51% < 20, 23% 20-39, 4% 40-49, 11% 50-99, 12% >100. **Special facilities:** Museums with specialized collections, film and television archive, graphic and animation labs, ethnomusicology archive, high power auroral simulation observatory, ranch for ecological studies, lab for embedded collaborative systems, centers for cancer research, plasma physics research labs, research centers for molecular and neuroscience, nanoscience research labs and centers, cell mimetic space exploration center, particle beam physics lab, particle center.

Freshman class profile. 92,698 applied, 16,016 admitted, 5,679 enrolled.

Mid 50% test scores		Rank in top quarter:	100%
SAT critical reading:	570-700	Rank in top tenth:	97%
SAT math:	600-750	Return as sophomores:	96%
SAT writing:	580-720	Out-of-state:	17%
ACT composite:	25-33	Live on campus:	98%
GPA 3.75 or higher:	95%	International:	11%
GPA 3.50-3.74:	3%	Fraternities:	15%
GPA 3.0-3.49:	2%	Sororities:	15%

Basis for selection. GPA, test scores, course work, number of and performance in honors and AP courses most important. Essay considered. Strong senior program important. Extracurricular activities, honors and awards also reviewed. SAT Subject Tests not required but reviewed if submitted; certain SAT Subject Tests may be recommended for some majors. Either the SAT or ACT with Writing examination is required. Audition required of music, dance, theater majors. Portfolio required of art majors.

High school preparation. College-preparatory program required. 15 units required; 18 recommended. Required and recommended units include English 4, mathematics 3-4, history 2, science 2-3 (laboratory 2-3), foreign language 2-3, visual/performing arts 1 and academic electives 1.

2015-2016 Annual costs. Tuition/fees: $12,753; $35,631 out-of-state. Room/board: $13,452. Books/supplies: $1,383. Personal expenses: $3,102.

2014-2015 Financial aid. Need-based: Average need met was 83%. Average scholarship/grant was $20,255; average loan $7,168. 83% of total undergraduate aid awarded as scholarships/grants, 17% as loans/jobs. **Non-need-based:** Awarded to 1,348 full-time undergraduates, including 177 freshmen. Scholarships awarded for academics, art, job skills, ROTC.

Application procedures. Admission: Closing date 11/30 (postmark date). $70 fee, may be waived for applicants with need. Application must be submitted online. Admission notification by 3/31. Must reply by 5/1. **Financial aid:** Priority date 3/2; no closing date. FAFSA required. Applicants notified on a rolling basis starting 3/15.

Academics. All students are required to complete some coursework in English prior to graduation. **Special study options:** Accelerated study, double major, honors, independent study, internships, student-designed major, study abroad, urban semester, Washington semester. **Credit/placement by examination:** AP, CLEP. **Support services:** Learning center, study skills assistance, tutoring, writing center.

Majors. Architecture: Architecture. **Area/ethnic studies:** African-American, Asian, Asian-American, Chicano/Hispanic-American/Latino, East Asian, European, Latin American, Native American, Near/Middle Eastern, Russian/Slavic, Scandinavian. **Biology:** General, biochemistry, biophysics, cellular/molecular, ecology, marine, neuroscience, physiology. **Business:** Managerial economics. **Computer sciences:** General. **Conservation:** Environmental science. **Engineering:** Aerospace, agricultural, chemical, civil, computer, electrical, geological, materials, mechanical. **English:** American lit, English lit. **Foreign languages:** African, ancient Greek, Arabic, Chinese, comparative lit, French, German, Hebrew, Italian, Japanese, Korean, Latin, linguistics, Portuguese, Russian, Scandinavian, Slavic, Spanish. **History:** General. **Math:** General, applied, computational, financial, statistics. **Philosophy/religion:** Judaic, philosophy, religion. **Physical sciences:** Astrophysics, chemistry, geology, geophysics, materials science, physics. **Psychology:** General, psychobiology. **Social sciences:** Anthropology, economics, geography,

international economic development, international economics, political science, sociology. **Visual/performing arts:** Art, art history/conservation, dance, dramatic, film/cinema/video, music, music history, musicology.

Most popular majors. Biology 13%, engineering/engineering technologies 8%, interdisciplinary studies 6%, psychology 10%, social sciences 23%.

Technology on campus. 5,000 workstations in dormitories, library, computer center, student center. Dormitories wired for high-speed internet access and linked to campus network. Commuter students can connect to campus network. Online course registration, online library, helpline, repair service, student web hosting, wireless network available.

Student life. Freshman orientation: Available, $375 fee. Preregistration for classes offered. 3-day, 2-night program. **Housing:** Guaranteed on-campus for freshmen. Coed dorms, special housing for disabled, apartments, cooperative housing, fraternity/sorority housing, themed housing, wellness housing available. **Activities:** Bands, campus ministries, choral groups, dance, drama, film society, international student organizations, literary magazine, music ensembles, Model UN, musical theater, opera, radio station, student government, student newspaper, symphony orchestra, TV station.

Athletics. NCAA. **Intercollegiate:** Baseball M, basketball, cross-country, diving W, football (tackle) M, golf, gymnastics W, rowing (crew) W, soccer, softball W, swimming W, tennis, track and field, volleyball, water polo. **Intramural:** Badminton, basketball, football (non-tackle), golf, racquetball, soccer, squash, swimming, table tennis, tennis, track and field, volleyball. **Team name:** Bruins.

Student services. Alcohol/substance abuse counseling, chaplain/spiritual director, career counseling, services for economically disadvantaged, student employment services, financial aid counseling, health services, legal services, minority student services, on-campus daycare, personal counseling, placement for graduates, veterans' counselor, women's services. **Physically disabled:** Services for visually, speech, hearing impaired.

Contact. E-mail: ugadm@saonet.ucla.edu
Phone: (310) 825-3101 Fax: (310) 206-1206
Gary Clark, Director, Undergraduate Admission, University of California: Los Angeles, 1147 Murphy Hall, Los Angeles, CA 90095-1436

University of California: Merced

Merced, California   **CB member**
www.ucmerced.edu   **CB code: 4129**

- Public 4-year university
- Commuter campus in small city
- 6,237 degree-seeking undergraduates: 1% part-time, 52% women, 5% African American, 23% Asian American, 48% Hispanic/Latino, 1% Native Hawaiian/Pacific islander, 4% Multi-racial, non-Hispanic, 5% international
- 448 degree-seeking graduate students
- 61% of applicants admitted
- SAT or ACT with writing, application essay required
- 66% graduate within 6 years; 23% enter graduate study

General. Regionally accredited. **Degrees:** 1,057 bachelor's awarded; master's, doctoral offered. **Location:** 120 miles from San Francisco, 60 miles from Fresno. **Calendar:** Semester, limited summer session. **Full-time faculty:** 315 total; 82% have terminal degrees, 31% minority, 42% women. **Part-time faculty:** 58 total; 48% have terminal degrees, 33% minority, 47% women. **Class size:** 30% < 20, 38% 20-39, 6% 40-49, 15% 50-99, 11% >100. **Special facilities:** National park research station, energy research institute, center for computational biology, health sciences research institute, stem cell research consortium, genome center, advanced solar technologies institute.

Freshman class profile. 18,620 applied, 11,288 admitted, 1,803 enrolled.

Mid 50% test scores		GPA 3.0-3.49:	43%
SAT critical reading:	440-550	End year in good standing:	77%
SAT math:	460-570	Return as sophomores:	84%
SAT writing:	440-540	Live on campus:	79%
GPA 3.75 or higher:	29%	International:	7%
GPA 3.50-3.74:	28%		

Basis for selection. Academic record and test scores determine eligibility. **Home schooled:** If school is not accredited by a regional association, student must meet eligibility by examination alone.

High school preparation. College-preparatory program required. 15 units required; 18 recommended. Required and recommended units include English 4, mathematics 3-4, history 2, science 2-3 (laboratory 2-3), foreign language

2-3, visual/performing arts 1 and academic electives 1. History is 2 units in history/social science.

2015-2016 Annual costs. Tuition/fees: $13,208; $37,913 out-of-state. Room/board: $15,646. Books/supplies: $1,429. Personal expenses: $4,124.

2014-2015 Financial aid. **Need-based:** 1,496 full-time freshmen applied for aid; 1,389 deemed to have need; 1,381 received aid. Average need met was 88%. Average scholarship/grant was $21,477; average loan $4,771. 80% of total undergraduate aid awarded as scholarships/grants, 20% as loans/jobs. **Non-need-based:** Awarded to 82 full-time undergraduates, including 14 freshmen. Scholarships awarded for academics, leadership.

Application procedures. **Admission:** Closing date 11/30 (postmark date). $70 fee, may be waived for applicants with need. Admission notification on a rolling basis beginning on or about 3/1. Must reply by 5/1. **Financial aid:** Closing date 3/2. FAFSA required. Applicants notified on a rolling basis starting 4/1; must reply by 6/1.

Academics. **Special study options:** Accelerated study, double major, independent study, internships, study abroad, Washington semester. Research opportunities and internships at Lawrence Livermore National Laboratories and Yosemite National Park. **Credit/placement by examination:** AP, CLEP, IB, institutional tests. Credit by examination with the approval of instructor giving examination and dean of school involved. Some courses may not be deemed appropriate for obtaining credit by examination. **Support services:** Learning center, study skills assistance, tutoring, writing center.

Majors. **Biology:** General. **Business:** Business admin. **Engineering:** Biomedical, computer, environmental, materials, mechanical. **English:** English lit. **Foreign languages:** Comparative lit, Hispanic and Latin American. **History:** General. **Math:** Applied. **Physical sciences:** Chemistry, geology, physics. **Psychology:** General. **Social sciences:** Anthropology, economics, political science, sociology.

Most popular majors. Biology 20%, business/marketing 12%, engineering/engineering technologies 15%, interdisciplinary studies 6%, psychology 20%, social sciences 16%.

Technology on campus. 230 workstations in dormitories, library, computer center. Dormitories wired for high-speed internet access and linked to campus network. Commuter students can connect to campus network. Online course registration, online library, helpline, wireless network available.

Student life. **Freshman orientation:** Mandatory, $90 fee. Preregistration for classes offered. 1-day event held before Spring and Fall classes start. Parents and other guests may also register to attend, at a cost of $80. **Policies:** Freshmen not permitted cars on campus. **Housing:** Guaranteed on-campus for freshmen. Coed dorms, special housing for disabled, wellness housing available. $300 partly refundable deposit, deadline 5/3. **Activities:** Pep band, campus ministries, choral groups, dance, film society, radio station, student government, student newspaper, African American Student Union, Liberal Activism Club, Student Government Advisory Committee, Latino Students Alliance, Filipino Student Alliance, Circle K International, American Red Cross Club, Jewish Student Union.

Athletics. NAIA. **Intercollegiate:** Basketball, cross-country, soccer, volleyball. **Intramural:** Archery, basketball, football (non-tackle), soccer, softball, table tennis, volleyball. **Team name:** Golden Bobcats.

Student services. Alcohol/substance abuse counseling, career counseling, services for economically disadvantaged, student employment services, financial aid counseling, health services, minority student services, on-campus daycare, personal counseling, veterans' counselor, women's services. **Physically disabled:** Services for visually, hearing impaired.

Contact. E-mail: admissions@ucmerced.edu
Phone: (209) 228-7178 Toll-free number: (866) 270-7301
Fax: (209) 228-4244
Encarnacion Ruiz, Director, Admissions and Outreach, University of California: Merced, 5200 North Lake Road, Merced, CA 95343-5603

University of California: Riverside
Riverside, California
www.ucr.edu

CB member
CB code: 4839

- Public 4-year university
- Residential campus in large city
- 18,598 degree-seeking undergraduates: 4% African American, 36% Asian American, 38% Hispanic/Latino, 5% Multi-racial, non-Hispanic, 3% international
- 56% of applicants admitted
- SAT or ACT with writing, application essay required
- 73% graduate within 6 years

General. Founded in 1954. Regionally accredited. **Degrees:** 4,718 bachelor's awarded; master's, professional, doctoral offered. **ROTC:** Army, Air Force. **Location:** 60 miles from Los Angeles. **Calendar:** Quarter, limited summer session. **Full-time faculty:** 883 total; 98% have terminal degrees, 40% minority, 34% women. **Part-time faculty:** 166 total; 98% have terminal degrees, 46% minority, 45% women. **Class size:** 29% < 20, 40% 20-39, 3% 40-49, 15% 50-99, 13% >100. **Special facilities:** Botanical gardens, air pollution research center, photography museum, 8 nature preserves, citrus research center and agricultural experiment station, institute of geophysics and planetary physics, water resources center, salinity lab.

Freshman class profile. 38,505 applied, 21,608 admitted, 4,029 enrolled.

Mid 50% test scores			
SAT critical reading:	500-600	GPA 3.0-3.49:	25%
SAT math:	520-650	Rank in top quarter:	100%
SAT writing:	500-610	Rank in top tenth:	94%
ACT composite:	22-28	Return as sophomores:	91%
GPA 3.75 or higher:	45%	Out-of-state:	1%
GPA 3.50-3.74:	30%	Live on campus:	73%
		International:	2%

Basis for selection. A fixed weight point system comprehensive review model that culminates in an Academic Index Score to determine admission for incoming freshmen. Students must take tests by December of their senior year. Official test scores must be received by our office no later than 7/15. **Home schooled:** Portfolio of courses and course descriptions recommended. **Learning Disabled:** Undergraduate Admissions works with Office of Student Special Services on a case by case basis.

High school preparation. College-preparatory program required. Required and recommended units include English 4, mathematics 3-4, history 2, science 2-3 (laboratory 2-3), foreign language 2-3, visual/performing arts 1 and academic electives 1.

2015-2016 Annual costs. Tuition/fees: $13,527; $38,235 out-of-state. Room/board: $15,700. Books/supplies: $1,700. Personal expenses: $1,950.

2014-2015 Financial aid. **Need-based:** 3,667 full-time freshmen applied for aid; 3,167 deemed to have need; 3,117 received aid. Average need met was 85%. Average scholarship/grant was $20,872; average loan $6,116. 63% of total undergraduate aid awarded as scholarships/grants, 37% as loans/jobs. **Non-need-based:** Awarded to 366 full-time undergraduates, including 138 freshmen. Scholarships awarded for academics, alumni affiliation, art, athletics, leadership, music/drama, state residency.

Application procedures. **Admission:** Closing date 11/30 (receipt date). $70 fee ($80 out-of-state), may be waived for applicants with need. Application must be submitted online. Admission notification by 3/31. Admission notification on a rolling basis beginning on or about 2/1. Must reply by 5/1. **Financial aid:** Priority date 3/2, closing date 6/15. FAFSA required. Applicants notified by 3/1; Applicants notified on a rolling basis starting 3/1; must reply by 5/1 or within 3 week(s) of notification.

Academics. **Special study options:** Accelerated study, combined bachelor's/graduate degree, cross-registration, double major, ESL, honors, independent study, internships, study abroad, teacher certification program, Washington semester. **Credit/placement by examination:** AP, CLEP, IB, SAT, ACT, institutional tests. **Support services:** Learning center, pre-admission summer program, reduced course load, study skills assistance, tutoring, writing center.

Majors. **Area/ethnic studies:** General, African-American, Asian, Asian-American, Chicano/Hispanic-American/Latino, German, Latin American, Native American, Russian/Slavic, women's. **Biology:** General, biochemistry, botany, entomology, neuroscience. **Business:** Business admin, managerial economics. **Computer sciences:** Computer science. **Conservation:** Environmental science. **Engineering:** Biomedical, chemical, computer, electrical, environmental, materials, mechanical. **English:** Creative writing, English lit. **Foreign languages:** General, Chinese, classics, comparative lit, French, German, Japanese, linguistics, Russian, Spanish. **History:** General. **Human services:** Public policy. **Liberal arts:** Arts/sciences, humanities. **Math:** General, applied, statistics. **Philosophy/religion:** Philosophy, religion. **Physical sciences:** General, chemistry, geology, geophysics, materials science, physics. **Psychology:** General. **Social sciences:** Anthropology, economics, political science, sociology. **Visual/performing arts:** Art, art history/conservation, dramatic, music, studio arts.

Most popular majors. Biology 13%, business/marketing 16%, engineering/engineering technologies 8%, psychology 9%, social sciences 22%.

Technology on campus. 694 workstations in dormitories, library, computer center, student center. Dormitories wired for high-speed internet access and linked to campus network. Commuter students can connect to campus

network. Online course registration, online library, helpline, repair service, student web hosting, wireless network available.

Student life. Freshman orientation: Mandatory, $250 fee. Preregistration for classes offered. **Housing:** Guaranteed on-campus for freshmen. Coed dorms, special housing for disabled, apartments, themed housing available. $250 partly refundable deposit, deadline 5/10. **Activities:** Bands, campus ministries, choral groups, dance, drama, film society, international student organizations, literary magazine, music ensembles, musical theater, radio station, student government, student newspaper, 350 clubs and organizations available.

Athletics. NCAA. **Intercollegiate:** Baseball M, basketball, cross-country, golf, soccer, softball W, tennis, track and field, volleyball W. **Intramural:** Badminton, basketball, football (non-tackle), racquetball, soccer, softball, table tennis, tennis, ultimate frisbee W, volleyball. **Team name:** Highlanders.

Student services. Adult student services, alcohol/substance abuse counseling, career counseling, student employment services, financial aid counseling, health services, minority student services, on-campus daycare, personal counseling, placement for graduates, veterans' counselor, women's services. **Physically disabled:** Services for visually, speech, hearing impaired.

Contact. E-mail: admissions@ucr.edu
Phone: (951) 827-3411 Fax: (951) 827-6344
Emily Engelschall, Director of Undergraduate Admissions, University of California: Riverside, Undergraduate Admissions, Riverside, CA 92521

University of California: San Diego
La Jolla, California   **CB member**
www.ucsd.edu   **CB code: 4836**

- Public 4-year university
- Residential campus in large town
- 23,850 degree-seeking undergraduates
- SAT or ACT with writing, application essay required

General. Founded in 1959. Regionally accredited. Includes 6 undergraduate colleges, each with different housing and general education requirements. **Degrees:** 5,600 bachelor's awarded; master's, doctoral offered. **Location:** 12 miles from San Diego. **Calendar:** Quarter, extensive summer session. **Full-time faculty:** 943 total; 98% have terminal degrees, 24% minority. **Part-time faculty:** 219 total; 100% have terminal degrees, 17% minority. **Class size:** 44% < 20, 22% 20-39, 4% 40-49, 11% 50-99, 20% >100. **Special facilities:** Performing arts centers, student-run co-ops, supercomputer center, nature preserves, electron beam lithography facility, center for music experiment, structural engineering lab, aquarium, additional specialty research centers.

Freshman class profile.

GPA 3.75 or higher:	80%	Out-of-state:	4%
GPA 3.50-3.74:	16%	Live on campus:	92%
GPA 3.0-3.49:	4%	Fraternities:	10%
Rank in top quarter:	100%	Sororities:	10%
Rank in top tenth:	100%		

Basis for selection. High school course pattern, GPA, essay and test scores most important. Admission for out-of-state applicants more selective than for residents. If not native English speaker, one of following is required: Test of English as a Foreign Language (TOEFL) examination, International English Language Testing System (IELTS) examination (academic modules).

High school preparation. College-preparatory program required. 17 units required. Required and recommended units include English 4, mathematics 3-4, history 2, science 2-3 (laboratory 2-3), foreign language 2-3, visual/performing arts 1 and academic electives 1. History is 2 units in history/social science.

2015-2016 Annual costs. Tuition/fees: $13,557; $38,265 out-of-state. Room/board: $12,071. Books/supplies: $1,502. Personal expenses: $3,434.

Financial aid. Non-need-based: Scholarships awarded for academics, art, athletics, leadership, minority status, music/drama.

Application procedures. Admission: Closing date 11/30 (postmark date). $70 fee, may be waived for applicants with need. Application must be submitted online. Admission notification by 3/31. Admission notification on a rolling basis. Must reply by 5/1. **Financial aid:** Priority date 3/2, closing date 6/1. FAFSA required. Applicants notified on a rolling basis starting 3/15; must reply within 3 week(s) of notification.

Academics. Special study options: Combined bachelor's/graduate degree, cross-registration, double major, dual enrollment of high school students,

ESL, exchange student, honors, independent study, internships, liberal arts/career combination, semester at sea, student-designed major, study abroad, teacher certification program, Washington semester. In-depth academic assignments working in small groups or one-to-one with faculty; research programs. **Credit/placement by examination:** AP, CLEP, IB, SAT, institutional tests. **Support services:** Learning center, pre-admission summer program, reduced course load, study skills assistance, tutoring, writing center.

Majors. Architecture: Urban/community planning. **Area/ethnic studies:** Chinese, German, Italian, Japanese, Latin American, Russian/Slavic, women's. **Biology:** General, animal physiology, bacteriology, biochemistry, bioinformatics, biophysics, biotechnology, cell/histology, ecology, evolutionary, molecular, neuroscience. **Business:** Management science. **Communications:** Communications/speech/rhetoric, digital media. **Computer sciences:** General, computer science, information systems, systems analysis. **Conservation:** Environmental science, environmental studies. **Engineering:** Aerospace, applied physics, biomedical, chemical, computer, electrical, engineering mechanics, engineering science, mechanical, structural, systems. **English:** American lit, British lit, English lit, writing. **Foreign languages:** General, classics, French, German, Italian, Japanese, linguistics, Russian, Spanish. **History:** General. **Human services:** Public policy. **Math:** General, applied. **Philosophy/religion:** Judaic, philosophy, religion. **Physical sciences:** Chemical physics, chemistry, molecular physics, physics, planetary. **Psychology:** General. **Social sciences:** Anthropology, archaeology, economics, political science, sociology, U.S. government, urban studies. **Visual/performing arts:** Art history/conservation, dance, dramatic, music, studio arts. **Work/family studies:** Family studies.

Most popular majors. Biology 17%, engineering/engineering technologies 14%, psychology 8%, social sciences 32%.

Technology on campus. 1,500 workstations in library, computer center, student center. Dormitories wired for high-speed internet access and linked to campus network. Commuter students can connect to campus network. Online course registration, online library, helpline, repair service, student web hosting, wireless network available.

Student life. Freshman orientation: Mandatory, $170 fee. Preregistration for classes offered. One to two-day programs for freshmen and transfers; additional one-day program for international students. **Housing:** Guaranteed on-campus for freshmen. Coed dorms, single-sex dorms, special housing for disabled, apartments, cooperative housing, fraternity/sorority housing available. $650 fully refundable deposit, deadline 6/30. Language, cultural interest and international houses available. **Activities:** Bands, campus ministries, choral groups, dance, drama, film society, international student organizations, literary magazine, music ensembles, Model UN, musical theater, opera, radio station, student government, student newspaper, symphony orchestra, TV station, 550 student organizations available.

Athletics. NCAA. **Intercollegiate:** Baseball M, basketball, cross-country, diving, fencing, golf M, rowing (crew), soccer, softball W, swimming, tennis, track and field, volleyball, water polo. **Intramural:** Basketball, bowling, football (non-tackle), football (tackle), soccer, softball, tennis, volleyball, water polo. **Team name:** Tritons.

Student services. Alcohol/substance abuse counseling, career counseling, services for economically disadvantaged, student employment services, financial aid counseling, health services, legal services, minority student services, on-campus daycare, personal counseling, placement for graduates, veterans' counselor, women's services. **Physically disabled:** Services for visually, speech, hearing impaired.

Contact. E-mail: admissionsreply@ucsd.edu
Phone: (858) 534-4831 Fax: (858) 534-5629
Mara Affre, Assistant Vice Chancellor and Director of Admissions, University of California: San Diego, 9500 Gilman Drive, 0021, La Jolla, CA 92093-0021

University of California: Santa Barbara
Santa Barbara, California   **CB member**
www.ucsb.edu   **CB code: 4835**

- Public 4-year university
- Residential campus in small city
- 20,606 degree-seeking undergraduates: 2% part-time, 53% women, 2% African American, 19% Asian American, 26% Hispanic/Latino, 8% Multi-racial, non-Hispanic, 7% international
- 2,890 degree-seeking graduate students
- 33% of applicants admitted
- SAT or ACT with writing, application essay required
- 81% graduate within 6 years

General. Founded in 1909. Regionally accredited. **Degrees:** 5,360 bachelor's awarded; master's, doctoral offered. **ROTC:** Army, Air Force. **Location:** 10 miles from downtown, 100 miles from Los Angeles. **Calendar:** Quarter, extensive summer session. **Full-time faculty:** 911 total; 100% have terminal degrees, 20% minority, 37% women. **Part-time faculty:** 168 total; 100% have terminal degrees, 10% minority, 43% women. **Class size:** 49% < 20, 29% 20-39, 4% 40-49, 9% 50-99, 9% >100. **Special facilities:** Nature preserves with research facilities, seawater laboratories, robotics laboratory, free electron laser laboratory, institutes for polymers and organic solids, neuroscience research, quantum, nuclear particle astrophysics and cosmology, marine science, theoretical physics.

Freshman class profile. 70,444 applied, 23,020 admitted, 4,473 enrolled.

Mid 50% test scores		Rank in top quarter:	100%
SAT critical reading:	550-670	Rank in top tenth:	100%
SAT math:	580-700	Return as sophomores:	93%
SAT writing:	560-680	Out-of-state:	5%
ACT composite:	24-30	Live on campus:	95%
GPA 3.75 or higher:	86%	International:	8%
GPA 3.50-3.74:	11%	Fraternities:	5%
GPA 3.0-3.49:	3%	Sororities:	13%

Basis for selection. Eligibility established by high school GPA, course requirement, and SAT scores. Special consideration for disadvantaged students. SAT Subject Tests recommended. SAT subject tests not required, certain programs recommend them. Subject tests may satisfy some high school course requirements. College of Engineering recommends applicants take the Math 2 subject test. Audition required of music, dance, drama majors. Portfolio required of art majors.

High school preparation. College-preparatory program required. Required and recommended units include English 4, mathematics 3-4, history 2, (laboratory 2-3), foreign language 2-3, visual/performing arts 1 and academic electives 1.

2015-2016 Annual costs. Tuition/fees: $13,865; $38,573 out-of-state. Room/board: $14,192. Books/supplies: $1,403. Personal expenses: $1,713.

2014-2015 Financial aid. **Need-based:** 3,872 full-time freshmen applied for aid; 3,053 deemed to have need; 2,959 received aid. Average need met was 83%. Average scholarship/grant was $20,515; average loan $6,130. 80% of total undergraduate aid awarded as scholarships/grants, 20% as loans/jobs. **Non-need-based:** Awarded to 657 full-time undergraduates, including 133 freshmen. Scholarships awarded for academics, alumni affiliation, athletics, ROTC.

Application procedures. **Admission:** Closing date 11/30 (postmark date). $70 fee, may be waived for applicants with need. Admission notification by 3/31. Must reply by 5/1. **Financial aid:** Priority date 3/2, closing date 5/31. FAFSA required. Must reply within 2 week(s) of notification.

Academics. **Special study options:** Accelerated study, combined bachelor's/graduate degree, cross-registration, double major, dual enrollment of high school students, ESL, exchange student, honors, independent study, internships, student-designed major, study abroad, teacher certification program, Washington semester. Graduate-level classes, off-campus study, freshman seminars, pre-professional programs and advising, academic minors, and undergraduate research, professional studies in school of environmental science and management and school of education. **Credit/placement by examination:** AP, CLEP, IB, institutional tests. Limits on credits by examination determined by department. A maximum of 8 units EACH in art studio, English, mathematics, and physics is allowed. **Support services:** Learning center, pre-admission summer program, reduced course load, study skills assistance, tutoring, writing center.

Majors. **Area/ethnic studies:** African-American, Asian, Chicano/Hispanic-American/Latino, Latin American, women's. **Biology:** General, aquatic, bacteriology, biochemistry, cell/histology, ecology, marine, molecular, pharmacology, zoology. **Communications:** Communications/speech/rhetoric. **Computer sciences:** General. **Conservation:** Environmental studies. **Engineering:** Chemical, computer, electrical, mechanical. **English:** English lit. **Foreign languages:** Chinese, classics, comparative lit, French, German, Italian, Japanese, linguistics, Portuguese, Slavic, Spanish. **History:** General. **Math:** General, statistics. **Philosophy/religion:** Philosophy, religion. **Physical sciences:** Chemistry, geology, geophysics, physics. **Psychology:** General. **Social sciences:** Anthropology, econometrics, economics, geography, political science, sociology. **Visual/performing arts:** General, art, art history/conservation, cinematography, dance, dramatic, film/cinema/video, music, studio arts.

Most popular majors. Biology 8%, communications/journalism 7%, interdisciplinary studies 9%, psychology 10%, social sciences 26%, visual/performing arts 7%.

Technology on campus. 400 workstations in dormitories, library, computer center, student center. Dormitories wired for high-speed internet access and linked to campus network. Commuter students can connect to campus network. Online course registration, online library, repair service, student web hosting, wireless network available.

Student life. **Freshman orientation:** Available. Preregistration for classes offered. Two-day program; includes sessions for parents. **Housing:** Guaranteed on-campus for freshmen. Coed dorms, apartments, cooperative housing, fraternity/sorority housing, themed housing, wellness housing available. **Activities:** Bands, campus ministries, choral groups, dance, drama, film society, international student organizations, literary magazine, music ensembles, Model UN, musical theater, opera, radio station, student government, student newspaper, symphony orchestra, TV station, Hillel, Catholic Student Organization, Democratic and Republican student organizations, El Congreso, Persian Student Association, Habitat for Humanity.

Athletics. NCAA. **Intercollegiate:** Baseball M, basketball, cross-country, golf M, gymnastics, soccer, softball W, swimming, tennis, track and field, volleyball, water polo. **Intramural:** Badminton, basketball, bowling, cross-country, football (non-tackle), golf, gymnastics, racquetball, rowing (crew), soccer, softball, squash, tennis, volleyball, water polo. **Team name:** Gauchos.

Student services. Adult student services, alcohol/substance abuse counseling, career counseling, services for economically disadvantaged, student employment services, financial aid counseling, health services, minority student services, on-campus daycare, personal counseling, placement for graduates, veterans' counselor, women's services. **Physically disabled:** Services for visually, speech, hearing impaired.

Contact. E-mail: admissions@sa.ucsb.edu
Phone: (805) 893-2881 Fax: (805) 893-2676
Lisa Przekop, Director of Admissions, University of California: Santa Barbara, 1210 Cheadle Hall, Santa Barbara, CA 93106-2014

University of California: Santa Cruz
Santa Cruz, California   **CB member**
www.ucsc.edu   **CB code: 4860**

- Public 4-year university
- Residential campus in small city
- 16,231 degree-seeking undergraduates: 3% part-time, 53% women, 2% African American, 21% Asian American, 31% Hispanic/Latino, 7% Multi-racial, non-Hispanic, 4% international
- 1,637 degree-seeking graduate students
- 51% of applicants admitted
- SAT or ACT with writing, application essay required
- 78% graduate within 6 years

General. Founded in 1965. Regionally accredited. **Degrees:** 4,227 bachelor's awarded; master's, doctoral offered. **ROTC:** Army, Naval, Air Force. **Location:** 75 miles from San Francisco, 30 miles from San Jose. **Calendar:** Quarter, limited summer session. **Special facilities:** Observatories, arboretum, agroecology farm, campus preserve, nonlinear science center, music center, bilingual research center, institutes of marine sciences, ocean health center, tectonics, particle physics institute, center for adaptive optics, Silicon Valley Center Affiliated Research Center, biomedical research program.

Freshman class profile. 44,871 applied, 23,022 admitted, 3,570 enrolled.

Mid 50% test scores		Rank in top quarter:	100%
SAT critical reading:	520-640	Rank in top tenth:	96%
SAT math:	550-670	Return as sophomores:	87%
SAT writing:	520-640	Out-of-state:	5%
ACT composite:	23-29	Live on campus:	98%
GPA 3.75 or higher:	55%	International:	7%
GPA 3.50-3.74:	35%	Fraternities:	1%
GPA 3.0-3.49:	10%	Sororities:	2%

Basis for selection. Test scores, GPA in required subjects most important. Personal statement very important. All applicants must take 2 SAT Subject Tests in different subject areas. Math SAT Subject Test must be Level 2. SAT Subject Tests not required for admission, but may be required for specific majors. Audition required for music majors. Portfolio recommended for art majors. **Home schooled:** Eligibility appraised on basis of entrance examination or previous college-level work. **Learning Disabled:** Any extenuating circumstances should be included in the personal statement.

High school preparation. College-preparatory program required. 15 units required; 18 recommended. Required and recommended units include English 4, mathematics 3-4, social studies 1, history 1, science 2-3 (laboratory 2-3), foreign language 2-3, visual/performing arts 1 and academic electives 1. History is 2 units in history/social science. 2 semesters of approved arts courses from single visual and performing arts discipline: dance, drama/theater, music, or visual art. Required elective includes 2 semesters from following areas: visual and performing arts, history, social science, English, advanced mathematics, laboratory science, foreign language.

2015-2016 Annual costs. Tuition/fees: $13,446; $36,582 out-of-state. Room/board: $14,730.

2014-2015 Financial aid. **Need-based:** 3,368 full-time freshmen applied for aid; 2,772 deemed to have need; 2,685 received aid. Average need met was 81%. Average scholarship/grant was $19,339; average loan $6,477. 78% of total undergraduate aid awarded as scholarships/grants, 22% as loans/jobs. **Non-need-based:** Awarded to 796 full-time undergraduates, including 368 freshmen. Scholarships awarded for academics, alumni affiliation, art, leadership, music/drama. **Additional information:** Blue and Gold Opportunity Plan covers the educational and student services fees for CA residents whose family earns less than $80,000 a year. Blue and Gold students with sufficient financial need can qualify for more grant aid to reduce the cost of attendance.

Application procedures. **Admission:** Closing date 11/30 (postmark date). $70 fee, may be waived for applicants with need. Admission notification by 3/31. Admission notification on a rolling basis beginning on or about 3/15. Must reply by 5/1. **Financial aid:** Closing date 3/2. FAFSA required. Applicants notified on a rolling basis starting 4/1; must reply within 4 week(s) of notification.

Academics. **Special study options:** Combined bachelor's/graduate degree, double major, exchange student, honors, independent study, internships, student-designed major, study abroad, teacher certification program, Washington semester. **Credit/placement by examination:** AP, CLEP, IB, SAT, ACT, institutional tests. **Support services:** Learning center, reduced course load, remedial instruction, study skills assistance, tutoring, writing center.

Majors. **Area/ethnic studies:** American, German, Italian, women's. **Biology:** General, bioinformatics, cellular/molecular, ecology, marine, molecular biochemistry, neuroscience. **Business:** Managerial economics. **Computer sciences:** General, web page design. **Conservation:** Environmental studies. **Engineering:** Biomedical, computer, electrical. **English:** English lit. **Foreign languages:** General, classics, linguistics. **History:** General. **Human services:** Community org/advocacy. **Math:** General. **Philosophy/religion:** Judaic, philosophy. **Physical sciences:** Astrophysics, chemistry, geology, physics. **Psychology:** General, cognitive. **Social sciences:** Anthropology, economics, political science, sociology. **Visual/performing arts:** Art, art history/conservation, dramatic, game design, music.

Most popular majors. Biology 17%, business/marketing 6%, computer/information sciences 6%, psychology 13%, social sciences 15%, visual/performing arts 9%.

Technology on campus. Dormitories wired for high-speed internet access and linked to campus network. Commuter students can connect to campus network. Online course registration, online library, helpline, repair service, student web hosting, wireless network available.

Student life. **Freshman orientation:** Available, $130 fee. Preregistration for classes offered. One-day or overnight sessions held during summer. **Policies:** Student Organization Advising and Resources (SOAR) helps students create their own organizations. Freshmen not permitted cars on campus. **Housing:** Guaranteed on-campus for freshmen. Coed dorms, single-sex dorms, apartments, gender-neutral housing, themed housing, wellness housing available. $150 partly refundable deposit, deadline 5/1. Camper park. **Activities:** Jazz band, campus ministries, choral groups, dance, drama, film society, international student organizations, literary magazine, music ensembles, Model UN, musical theater, opera, radio station, student government, student newspaper, symphony orchestra, TV station, more than 150 student organizations available.

Athletics. NCAA. **Intercollegiate:** Basketball, cross-country, diving, golf W, soccer, swimming, tennis, volleyball. **Intramural:** Basketball, football (non-tackle), soccer, softball, ultimate frisbee, volleyball, water polo. **Team name:** Banana Slugs.

Student services. Adult student services, alcohol/substance abuse counseling, career counseling, services for economically disadvantaged, student employment services, financial aid counseling, health services, minority student services, on-campus daycare, personal counseling, veterans' counselor, women's services. **Physically disabled:** Services for visually, speech, hearing impaired.

Contact. E-mail: admissions@ucsc.edu
Phone: (831) 459-4008 Fax: (831) 459-4452
Michael McCawley, Director of Admissions, University of California: Santa Cruz, Cook House, 1156 High Street, Santa Cruz, CA 95064

University of La Verne
La Verne, California   **CB member**
www.laverne.edu   **CB code: 4381**

- Private 4-year university
- Commuter campus in large town
- 2,859 degree-seeking undergraduates: 3% part-time, 59% women, 5% African American, 6% Asian American, 51% Hispanic/Latino, 1% Native Hawaiian/Pacific islander, 5% Multi-racial, non-Hispanic, 5% international
- 2,010 degree-seeking graduate students
- 47% of applicants admitted
- SAT or ACT with writing, application essay required
- 64% graduate within 6 years

General. Founded in 1891. Regionally accredited. Online programs are available. Regional campuses throughout California provide undergraduate, graduate, and professional programs to adult students. **Degrees:** 549 bachelor's awarded; master's, professional, doctoral offered. **ROTC:** Army. **Location:** 35 miles from Los Angeles. **Calendar:** 4-1-4, limited summer session. **Full-time faculty:** 233 total. **Part-time faculty:** 245 total. **Class size:** 65% < 20, 34% 20-39, less than 1% 40-49, less than 1% 50-99. **Special facilities:** Multiple art and photo galleries, theater, television station, campus radio station, natural science field station, green house, student microscopy and imaging center, teaching museum.

Freshman class profile. 8,179 applied, 3,859 admitted, 724 enrolled.

Mid 50% test scores			
SAT critical reading:	470-560	GPA 2.0-2.99:	9%
SAT math:	470-570	Rank in top quarter:	54%
SAT writing:	460-560	Rank in top tenth:	18%
ACT composite:	20-24	Return as sophomores:	85%
GPA 3.75 or higher:	27%	Out-of-state:	4%
GPA 3.50-3.74:	25%	Live on campus:	51%
GPA 3.0-3.49:	39%	International:	3%

Basis for selection. Secondary school record, academic GPA, standardized test scores, application essay, recommendations, extracurricular activities, and character or personal qualities very important. Class rank also important. Interview, special talents or abilities, first generation, alumni relationships, volunteer work, work experience, and level of applicants interest may also be considered.

High school preparation. College-preparatory program recommended. 14 units required; 19 recommended. Required and recommended units include English 4, mathematics 3-4, social studies 2, history 3, science 2 (laboratory 1-2) and foreign language 2.

2016-2017 Annual costs. Tuition/fees (projected): $40,063. Room/board: $12,710. Books/supplies: $1,791. Personal expenses: $2,431.

2015-2016 Financial aid. **Need-based:** 665 full-time freshmen applied for aid; 624 deemed to have need; 624 received aid. Average need met was 31%. Average scholarship/grant was $11,116; average loan $3,749. 78% of total undergraduate aid awarded as scholarships/grants, 22% as loans/jobs. **Non-need-based:** Awarded to 2,670 full-time undergraduates, including 711 freshmen. Scholarships awarded for academics, alumni affiliation, art, leadership, minority status, music/drama, religious affiliation.

Application procedures. **Admission:** Priority date 2/1; no deadline. $50 fee, may be waived for applicants with need. Admission notification on a rolling basis beginning on or about 12/1. Must reply by May 1 or within 2 week(s) if notified thereafter. **Financial aid:** Priority date 3/2; no closing date. FAFSA required. Applicants notified on a rolling basis starting 3/1; must reply within 2 week(s) of notification.

Academics. Main Campus offers a traditional-age undergraduate program and an accelerated program for adults. Off-campus centers available for degree-seeking students in selected majors. **Special study options:** Distance learning, double major, exchange student, honors, independent study, internships, liberal arts/career combination, semester at sea, student-designed major, study abroad, teacher certification program, weekend college. **Credit/placement by examination:** AP, CLEP, SAT, institutional tests. 44 credit hours maximum toward bachelor's degree. **Support services:** Learning center, remedial instruction, study skills assistance, tutoring, writing center.

Majors. **Biology:** General, environmental. **Business:** Accounting, business admin, e-commerce, international, managerial economics. **Communications:** Communications/speech/rhetoric, journalism, radio/TV. **Computer sciences:** General. **Conservation:** Environmental science. **Education:** General, early childhood, elementary, physical, secondary. **English:** English lit. **Foreign languages:** Comparative lit, French, German, Spanish. **Health services:** Athletic training, health care admin. **History:** General. **Human services:**

General. **Liberal arts:** Arts/sciences. **Math:** General. **Philosophy/religion:** Philosophy, religion. **Physical sciences:** Chemistry, physics. **Psychology:** General. **Social sciences:** General, anthropology, criminology, economics, international relations, political science, sociology. **Visual/performing arts:** Art, art history/conservation, dramatic, music, photography. **Work/family studies:** Child care management.

Most popular majors. Biology 7%, business/marketing 21%, communications/journalism 12%, education 8%, psychology 14%, social sciences 16%.

Technology on campus. 520 workstations in dormitories, library, computer center. Dormitories wired for high-speed internet access and linked to campus network. Commuter students can connect to campus network. Online course registration, online library, helpline, student web hosting, wireless network available.

Student life. Freshman orientation: Available. Preregistration for classes offered. All-day events for both students and parents. Held primarily in August. **Policies:** Students must be in good academic standing to participate in clubs or organizations, including fraternities/sororities. Freshmen not permitted to join fraternities during the Fall term. **Housing:** Coed dorms, single-sex dorms, themed housing available. $300 nonrefundable deposit, deadline 5/1. **Activities:** Pep band, campus ministries, choral groups, dance, drama, international student organizations, literary magazine, music ensembles, Model UN, musical theater, radio station, student government, student newspaper, TV station, Black Student Union, Latino Student Forum, Chinese Students & Scholars Association, Gay-Straight Alliance, Hillel, Reaching Out for Animal Rights, Renew Christian Club, ULV College Democrats, ULV College Republicans.

Athletics. NCAA. **Intercollegiate:** Baseball M, basketball, cross-country, diving, football (tackle) M, golf M, soccer, softball W, swimming, tennis W, track and field, volleyball W, water polo. **Intramural:** Basketball, soccer, softball, table tennis, volleyball. **Team name:** Leopards.

Student services. Adult student services, alcohol/substance abuse counseling, chaplain/spiritual director, career counseling, services for economically disadvantaged, student employment services, financial aid counseling, health services, minority student services, personal counseling, placement for graduates, veterans' counselor. **Physically disabled:** Services for visually, speech, hearing impaired.

Contact. E-mail: admission@laverne.edu
Toll-free number: (800) 876-4858 Fax: (909) 392-2714
Chris Krzak, Dean of Admissions, University of La Verne, 1950 Third Street, La Verne, CA 91750

University of Phoenix: Bay Area
San Jose, California
www.phoenix.edu

- For-profit 4-year career college
- Very large city
- 1,659 undergraduates

General. Regionally accredited. **Degrees:** 205 bachelor's awarded; master's offered. **Calendar:** Differs by program. **Full-time faculty:** 26 total. **Part-time faculty:** 239 total.

Basis for selection. Open admission, but selective for some programs.

2015-2016 Annual costs. Per-credit-hour charge, $XXX to $XXX, depending upon level and course of study. Books, material charges, and other fees vary by course and program. All fees are subject to change.

Application procedures. Admission: No deadline. No application fee. **Financial aid:** No deadline.

Academics. Credit/placement by examination: AP, CLEP.

Majors. Business: Accounting, accounting/business management, business admin, e-commerce, entrepreneurial studies, finance, human resources, marketing, operations. **Communications:** General. **Computer sciences:** Database management, networking, programming, security, system admin, systems analysis, web page design, webmaster. **Conservation:** Environmental studies. **Education:** Elementary. **English:** English lit. **Health services:** Facilities admin, health information management, long term care admin, nursing (RN). **Human services:** General. **Protective services:** Disaster management, law enforcement admin, security management.

Student life. Freshman orientation: Mandatory. Preregistration for classes offered.

Contact. Toll-free number: (866) 766-0766
University of Phoenix: Bay Area, 3590 North First Street, San Jose, CA 95134-1805

University of Phoenix: Central Valley
Fresno, California
www.phoenix.edu

- For-profit 4-year career college
- Large city
- 2,375 undergraduates

General. Regionally accredited. **Degrees:** 323 bachelor's awarded; master's offered. **Calendar:** Differs by program. **Full-time faculty:** 44 total. **Part-time faculty:** 251 total.

Basis for selection. Open admission, but selective for some programs.

2015-2016 Annual costs. Per-credit-hour charge, $XXX to $XXX, depending upon level and course of study. Books, material charges, and other fees vary by course and program. All fees are subject to change.

Application procedures. Admission: No deadline. No application fee. **Financial aid:** No deadline.

Academics. Credit/placement by examination: AP, CLEP.

Majors. Business: Accounting, accounting/business management, business admin, e-commerce, entrepreneurial studies, finance, human resources, marketing, operations. **Communications:** General. **Computer sciences:** Database management, networking, programming, security, system admin, systems analysis, web page design, webmaster. **Education:** Elementary. **English:** English lit. **Health services:** Facilities admin, health information management, long term care admin, nursing (RN). **Human services:** General. **Protective services:** Disaster management, law enforcement admin, security management.

Student life. Freshman orientation: Mandatory. Preregistration for classes offered.

Contact. Toll-free number: (866) 766-0766
University of Phoenix: Central Valley, 45 River Park Place West, Fresno, CA 93720-1552

University of Phoenix: Sacramento Valley
Sacramento, California
www.phoenix.edu

- For-profit 4-year career college
- Large city
- 3,190 undergraduates

General. Regionally accredited. **Degrees:** 481 bachelor's awarded; master's offered. **Calendar:** Differs by program.

Basis for selection. Open admission, but selective for some programs.

2015-2016 Annual costs. Per-credit-hour charge, $410 to $635, depending upon level and course of study. Books, material charges, and other fees vary by course and program. All fees are subject to change.

Application procedures. Admission: No deadline. No application fee. **Financial aid:** No deadline.

Academics. Credit/placement by examination: AP, CLEP.

Majors. Business: Accounting, accounting/business management, business admin, e-commerce, entrepreneurial studies, finance, human resources, marketing, operations. **Communications:** General. **Computer sciences:** General, database management, networking, programming, security, support specialist, system admin, systems analysis, web page design, webmaster. **Conservation:** Environmental studies. **Education:** Elementary. **English:** English lit. **Health services:** Facilities admin, health information management, long term care admin, nursing (RN). **Human services:** General. **Protective services:** Disaster management, law enforcement admin, security management.

Student life. Freshman orientation: Mandatory. Preregistration for classes offered.

Contact. Toll-free number: (866) 766-0766
University of Phoenix: Sacramento Valley, 2860 Gateway Oaks Drive, Sacramento, CA 95833-4334

University of Phoenix: San Diego
San Diego, California
www.phoenix.edu

- For-profit 4-year university
- Very large city
- 5,885 undergraduates

General. Regionally accredited. **Degrees:** 861 bachelor's, 1 associate awarded; master's offered. **Calendar:** Differs by program. **Full-time faculty:** 51 total. **Part-time faculty:** 466 total.

Basis for selection. Open admission, but selective for some programs.

2015-2016 Annual costs. Per-credit-hour charge, $410 to $635, depending upon level and course of study. Books, material charges, and other fees vary by course and program. All fees are subject to change.

Application procedures. **Admission:** No deadline. No application fee. **Financial aid:** No deadline.

Academics. Credit/placement by examination: AP, CLEP.

Majors. Business: Accounting, accounting/business management, business admin, finance, human resources, marketing. **Communications:** General. **Computer sciences:** Database management, networking, programming, security, systems analysis. **Conservation:** Environmental studies. **Education:** Elementary. **English:** English lit. **Health services:** Facilities admin, health information management, long term care admin, nursing (RN). **Human services:** General. **Protective services:** Disaster management, law enforcement admin, security management.

Student life. Freshman orientation: Mandatory. Preregistration for classes offered.

Contact. Toll-free number: (866) 766-0766
University of Phoenix: San Diego, 9645 Granite Ridge Drive, San Diego, CA 92123-2658

University of Phoenix: Southern California
Costa Mesa, California
www.phoenix.edu

- For-profit 4-year career college
- Small city
- 19,688 undergraduates

General. Regionally accredited. **Degrees:** 1,714 bachelor's awarded; master's offered. **Calendar:** Differs by program. **Full-time faculty:** 76 total. **Part-time faculty:** 874 total.

Basis for selection. Open admission, but selective for some programs.

2015-2016 Annual costs. Per-credit-hour charge, $410 to $635, depending upon level and course of study. Books, material charges, and other fees vary by course and program. All fees are subject to change.

Application procedures. Admission: No deadline. No application fee. **Financial aid:** No deadline.

Academics. Credit/placement by examination: AP, CLEP.

Majors. Business: Accounting, accounting/business management, business admin, e-commerce, entrepreneurial studies, finance, human resources, marketing, operations. **Communications:** General. **Computer sciences:** General, database management, networking, programming, security, system admin, systems analysis, web page design, webmaster. **Conservation:** Environmental studies. **Education:** Elementary. **Health services:** Facilities admin, long term care admin, nursing (RN). **Human services:** General. **Protective services:** Disaster management, law enforcement admin, security management.

Student life. Freshman orientation: Mandatory. Preregistration for classes offered.

Contact. Toll-free number: (866) 766-0766
University of Phoenix: Southern California, 3100 Bristol Street, Costa Mesa, CA 92626-3099

University of Redlands
Redlands, California   CB member
www.redlands.edu   CB code: 4848

- Private 4-year university and liberal arts college
- Residential campus in small city
- 3,452 degree-seeking undergraduates: 22% part-time, 56% women, 5% African American, 6% Asian American, 27% Hispanic/Latino, 1% Native American, 1% Native Hawaiian/Pacific islander, 5% Multi-racial, non-Hispanic, 1% international
- 1,722 degree-seeking graduate students
- 68% of applicants admitted
- SAT or ACT (ACT writing optional), application essay required
- 72% graduate within 6 years

General. Founded in 1907. Regionally accredited. NASM accredited School of Music within College of Arts & Sciences. **Degrees:** 859 bachelor's awarded; master's, doctoral offered. **ROTC:** Army, Naval, Air Force. **Location:** 65 miles from Los Angeles, 40 miles from Palm Springs. **Calendar:** 4-1-4, limited summer session. **Full-time faculty:** 199 total; 88% have terminal degrees, 19% minority, 47% women. **Part-time faculty:** 325 total. **Class size:** 65% < 20, 34% 20-39, 1% 40-49, less than 1% 50-99, less than 1% >100. **Special facilities:** Center for the arts, black box theater, community garden.

Freshman class profile. 4,790 applied, 3,234 admitted, 533 enrolled.

Mid 50% test scores			
SAT critical reading:	510-610	Rank in top quarter:	68%
SAT math:	510-610	Rank in top tenth:	38%
ACT composite:	22-28	Return as sophomores:	85%
GPA 3.75 or higher:	41%	Out-of-state:	29%
GPA 3.50-3.74:	20%	Live on campus:	92%
GPA 3.0-3.49:	30%	International:	2%
GPA 2.0-2.99:	9%		

Basis for selection. Course selection and grades important. Recommendations, test scores, essays, extracurricular activities are also considered. Audition required of music majors. Portfolio recommended for art and creative writing majors. **Home schooled:** Statement describing home school structure and mission required. Common application homeschool supplement required.

High school preparation. College-preparatory program required. 13 units required; 16 recommended. Required and recommended units include English 4, mathematics 3, social studies 2-3, science 2-3 (laboratory 2) and foreign language 2-3.

2015-2016 Annual costs. Tuition/fees: $44,900. Room/board: $13,090. Books/supplies: $1,764. Personal expenses: $3,177.

Financial aid. Non-need-based: Scholarships awarded for academics, art, music/drama.

Application procedures. Admission: Priority date 11/15; deadline 1/15 (postmark date). $30 fee, may be waived for applicants with need. Admission notification on a rolling basis beginning on or about 1/10. Must reply by May 1 or within 2 week(s) if notified thereafter. **Financial aid:** Closing date 3/2. FAFSA required. Applicants notified on a rolling basis starting 2/28; must reply by 6/1.

Academics. Special study options: Cross-registration, double major, exchange student, honors, independent study, internships, liberal arts/career combination, New York semester, student-designed major, study abroad, teacher certification program, United Nations semester, Washington semester. Nontraditional study programs available through Johnston Center for Integrated Studies and Schools of Business and Education. **Credit/placement by examination:** AP, CLEP, IB, SAT, ACT, institutional tests. 16 credit hours maximum toward bachelor's degree. **Support services:** Learning center, pre-admission summer program, reduced course load, study skills assistance, tutoring, writing center.

Majors. Area/ethnic studies: Asian, Latin American, women's. **Biology:** General, biochemistry. **Business:** General, accounting, business admin, management information systems, managerial economics. **Conservation:** Environmental science, environmental studies, management/policy. **Education:** Elementary, middle, music, secondary, speech impaired. **English:** Creative writing, English lit. **Foreign languages:** French, German, Spanish. **Health services:** Audiology/speech pathology. **History:** General. **Human services:** Public policy. **Liberal arts:** Arts/sciences. **Math:** General. **Philosophy/religion:** Philosophy, religion. **Physical sciences:** Chemistry, physics. **Psychology:** General. **Social sciences:** Anthropology, economics, international relations, political science, sociology. **Visual/performing arts:** Art, art history/conservation, design, dramatic, music, music history, music performance, music theory/composition, studio arts.

Most popular majors. Biology 6%, business/marketing 42%, health sciences 6%, liberal arts 6%, natural resources/environmental science 6%, psychology 7%, social sciences 9%.

Technology on campus. PC or laptop required. 723 workstations in dormitories, library, computer center, student center. Dormitories wired for high-speed internet access and linked to campus network. Commuter students can connect to campus network. Online library, helpline, repair service, student web hosting, wireless network available.

Student life. Freshman orientation: Mandatory. Preregistration for classes offered. One full week preceding academic school year. **Housing:** Guaranteed on-campus for freshmen. Coed dorms, single-sex dorms, special housing for disabled, apartments, fraternity/sorority housing, themed housing, wellness housing available. **Activities:** Bands, choral groups, dance, drama, literary magazine, music ensembles, musical theater, opera, radio station, student government, student newspaper, symphony orchestra, Associated Students, Intervarsity Christian Fellowship, African American association, Gay, Lesbian, Bisexual student union, women's center, College Republicans, College Democrats, Asian Pacific Islander Association, Theater Association, Students for Environmental Action.

Athletics. NCAA. Intercollegiate: Baseball M, basketball, cross-country, diving, football (tackle) M, golf, lacrosse W, soccer, softball W, swimming, tennis, track and field, volleyball W, water polo. **Intramural:** Basketball, football (non-tackle), racquetball, soccer, softball, table tennis, tennis, ultimate frisbee, volleyball, water polo. **Team name:** Bulldogs.

Student services. Adult student services, alcohol/substance abuse counseling, chaplain/spiritual director, career counseling, student employment services, financial aid counseling, health services, minority student services, personal counseling, placement for graduates, veterans' counselor, women's services. **Physically disabled:** Services for visually, speech, hearing impaired.

Contact. E-mail: admissions@redlands.edu
Phone: (909) 748-8074 Toll-free number: (800) 455-5064
Fax: (909) 335-4089
Phil Moreno, Director of Admissions, University of Redlands, 1200 East Colton Avenue, Redlands, CA 92373-0999

University of San Diego
San Diego, California   **CB member**
www.sandiego.edu   **CB code: 4849**

▸ Private 4-year university affiliated with the Roman Catholic Church
▸ Residential campus in very large city
▸ 5,551 degree-seeking undergraduates: 3% part-time, 54% women, 3% African American, 7% Asian American, 19% Hispanic/Latino, 6% Multiracial, non-Hispanic, 7% international
▸ 2,561 degree-seeking graduate students
▸ 52% of applicants admitted
▸ SAT or ACT with writing, application essay required
▸ 79% graduate within 6 years; 11% enter graduate study

General. Founded in 1949. Regionally accredited. **Degrees:** 1,421 bachelor's awarded; master's, professional, doctoral offered. **ROTC:** Army, Naval, Air Force. **Location:** 5 miles from downtown. **Calendar:** 4-1-4, extensive summer session. **Full-time faculty:** 427 total; 95% have terminal degrees, 21% minority, 47% women. **Part-time faculty:** 436 total; 62% have terminal degrees, 20% minority, 51% women. **Class size:** 40% < 20, 57% 20-39, 3% 40-49, less than 1% 50-99.

Freshman class profile. 13,675 applied, 7,067 admitted, 1,105 enrolled.

Mid 50% test scores		GPA 2.0-2.99:	2%
SAT critical reading:	550-640	Rank in top quarter:	71%
SAT math:	560-670	Rank in top tenth:	36%
SAT writing:	540-650	End year in good standing:	93%
ACT composite:	26-30	Return as sophomores:	87%
GPA 3.75 or higher:	62%	Out-of-state:	42%
GPA 3.50-3.74:	19%	Live on campus:	95%
GPA 3.0-3.49:	17%	International:	6%

Basis for selection. School achievement record, test scores, recommendations, and extracurricular activities are important. Out-of-state and international applicants encouraged. SAT/ACT scores are not required for International applicants unless the International applicant wishes to be considered for merit scholarships. Audition required of choral scholarship applicants. **Home schooled:** Letter of recommendation (nonparent) required. **Learning Disabled:** Must contact Director of Disability Services.

High school preparation. College-preparatory program recommended. 15 units required; 19 recommended. Required and recommended units include English 4, mathematics 3-4, social studies 2-3, science 3-4 (laboratory 2-3) and foreign language 3-4.

2015-2016 Annual costs. Tuition/fees: $44,586. Room/board: $12,042. Books/supplies: $1,764. Personal expenses: $2,322.

2014-2015 Financial aid. Need-based: 826 full-time freshmen applied for aid; 642 deemed to have need; 634 received aid. Average need met was 73%. Average scholarship/grant was $25,383; average loan $5,937. 76% of total undergraduate aid awarded as scholarships/grants, 24% as loans/jobs. **Non-need-based:** Awarded to 2,453 full-time undergraduates, including 754 freshmen. Scholarships awarded for academics, athletics, leadership, music/drama, religious affiliation, ROTC.

Application procedures. Admission: Closing date 12/15 (postmark date). $55 fee, may be waived for applicants with need. Admission notification on a rolling basis beginning on or about 2/25. Must reply by May 1 or within 2 week(s) if notified thereafter. **Financial aid:** Priority date 3/2; no closing date. FAFSA required. Applicants notified on a rolling basis starting 3/1; must reply by 5/1 or within 3 week(s) of notification.

Academics. Special study options: Double major, ESL, honors, independent study, internships, liberal arts/career combination, semester at sea, study abroad, teacher certification program, Washington semester. **Credit/placement by examination:** AP, CLEP, IB, institutional tests. **Support services:** Pre-admission summer program, reduced course load, study skills assistance, tutoring, writing center.

Majors. Architecture: History/criticism. **Area/ethnic studies:** General, Italian. **Biology:** General, biochemistry, biophysics, marine, neuroscience. **Business:** Accounting, business admin, finance, international, managerial economics, marketing, real estate. **Communications:** General. **Computer sciences:** Computer science. **Conservation:** Environmental studies. **Engineering:** Electrical, industrial, mechanical. **English:** English lit. **Foreign languages:** French, Spanish. **History:** General. **Liberal arts:** Arts/sciences, humanities. **Math:** General. **Philosophy/religion:** Philosophy, religion. **Physical sciences:** Chemistry, physics. **Psychology:** General. **Social sciences:** Anthropology, economics, international relations, political science, sociology. **Visual/performing arts:** Art, art history/conservation, dramatic, music.

Most popular majors. Biology 11%, business/marketing 43%, communications/journalism 10%, social sciences 11%.

Technology on campus. 946 workstations in dormitories, library, computer center, student center. Dormitories wired for high-speed internet access and linked to campus network. Commuter students can connect to campus network. Online course registration, online library, helpline, repair service, student web hosting, wireless network available.

Student life. Freshman orientation: Mandatory. Preregistration for classes offered. 4-day program that starts at the beginning of the semester. **Policies:** First and second year students who are under 20 years of age are required to live on campus unless living with parents. **Housing:** Guaranteed on-campus for freshmen. Coed dorms, single-sex dorms, special housing for disabled, apartments, themed housing available. $200 partly refundable deposit, deadline 5/1. **Activities:** Bands, campus ministries, choral groups, dance, drama, international student organizations, music ensembles, Model UN, musical theater, opera, radio station, student government, student newspaper, TV station, Engineers without Borders, Intervarsity Christian Fellowship, Jewish Student Union, marine science club, Muslim Student Association, National Society of Collegiate Scholars, Nonprofit Leadership Organization, Rotaract club, Society of Women Engineers, Student Veterans Organization.

Athletics. NCAA. Intercollegiate: Baseball M, basketball, cross-country, diving W, football (tackle) M, golf M, rowing (crew), soccer, softball W, swimming W, tennis, track and field W, volleyball W. **Intramural:** Basketball, football (non-tackle), soccer, softball, tennis, ultimate frisbee, volleyball. **Team name:** Toreros.

Student services. Alcohol/substance abuse counseling, chaplain/spiritual director, career counseling, services for economically disadvantaged, student employment services, financial aid counseling, health services, legal services, minority student services, on-campus daycare, personal counseling, placement for graduates, veterans' counselor, women's services. **Physically disabled:** Services for visually, speech, hearing impaired.

Contact. E-mail: admissions@sandiego.edu
Phone: (619) 260-4506 Toll-free number: (800) 248-4873
Fax: (619) 260-6836
Minh-Ha Hoang, Director of Admissions and Enrollment, University of San Diego, 5998 Alcala Park, San Diego, CA 92110-2492

University of San Francisco
San Francisco, California · CB member
www.usfca.edu · CB code: 4850

- Private 4-year university affiliated with the Roman Catholic Church
- Residential campus in very large city
- 6,682 degree-seeking undergraduates: 4% part-time, 62% women, 3% African American, 21% Asian American, 20% Hispanic/Latino, 1% Native Hawaiian/Pacific islander, 7% Multi-racial, non-Hispanic, 19% international
- 3,988 degree-seeking graduate students
- 64% of applicants admitted
- SAT or ACT with writing, application essay required
- 71% graduate within 6 years

General. Founded in 1855. Regionally accredited. **Degrees:** 1,612 bachelor's awarded; master's, professional, doctoral offered. **ROTC:** Army, Air Force. **Location:** 3 miles from downtown. **Calendar:** 4-1-4, extensive summer session. **Full-time faculty:** 430 total; 86% have terminal degrees, 24% minority, 48% women. **Part-time faculty:** 613 total; 46% have terminal degrees, 20% minority, 57% women. **Class size:** 48% < 20, 45% 20-39, 6% 40-49, 2% 50-99, less than 1% >100. **Special facilities:** Rare book room, institute for Chinese Western cultural history, electron microscope, law library, center for science and innovation.

Freshman class profile. 15,462 applied, 9,951 admitted, 1,267 enrolled.

Mid 50% test scores			
SAT critical reading:	530-620	Rank in top quarter:	67%
SAT math:	540-640	Rank in top tenth:	25%
SAT writing:	520-620	Return as sophomores:	83%
ACT composite:	24-28	Out-of-state:	26%
GPA 3.75 or higher:	40%	Live on campus:	94%
GPA 3.50-3.74:	24%	International:	20%
GPA 3.0-3.49:	34%	Fraternities:	2%
GPA 2.0-2.99:	2%	Sororities:	1%

Basis for selection. Rigor of secondary school record, academic GPA, standardized test scores, letter of recommendation, and application essay for first-year students. Academic GPA, letter of recommendation for transfer students. Require TOEFL for non-native speakers of English. **Home schooled:** Statement describing home school structure and mission, letter of recommendation (nonparent) required. Statement from parents on curriculum required if student not evaluated through high school homeschooling program or agency that evaluates home school programs. **Learning Disabled:** After acceptance, students with disabilities must contact Office of Disability Related Services to request accommodations.

High school preparation. College-preparatory program recommended. 20 units required. Required units include English 4, mathematics 3, social studies 3, science 2 (laboratory 2), foreign language 2 and academic electives 6. One chemistry and 1 biology or physics required of nursing and science applicants.

2016-2017 Annual costs. Tuition/fees: $44,494. Room/board: $13,990. Books/supplies: $1,600. Personal expenses: $2,600.

2015-2016 Financial aid. **Need-based:** 866 full-time freshmen applied for aid; 715 deemed to have need; 706 received aid. Average scholarship/grant was $23,776; average loan $3,496. 69% of total undergraduate aid awarded as scholarships/grants, 31% as loans/jobs. **Non-need-based:** Awarded to 4,813 full-time undergraduates, including 1,421 freshmen. Scholarships awarded for academics, athletics, ROTC. **Additional information:** Most aid to international students is for athletics.

Application procedures. **Admission:** Priority date 1/15; no deadline. $65 fee, may be waived for applicants with need. Notified on a rolling basis beginning in late January. All first-year applicants notified by April 1st. Must reply by May 1 or within 2 week(s) if notified thereafter. **Financial aid:** Priority date 1/15; no closing date. FAFSA, CSS PROFILE required. Applicants notified on a rolling basis starting 4/1; must reply within 4 week(s) of notification.

Academics. **Special study options:** Combined bachelor's/graduate degree, cooperative education, cross-registration, distance learning, double major, ESL, exchange student, external degree, honors, independent study, internships, liberal arts/career combination, study abroad, teacher certification program, Washington semester. Cooperative work study in computer science courses. **Credit/placement by examination:** AP, CLEP, IB, SAT, ACT, institutional tests. 30 credit hours maximum toward bachelor's degree. Credit for experiential learning limited to maximum of 30 undergraduate semester

units for Degree Completion students in the School of Management's undergraduate McLaren School of Management. **Support services:** Learning center, pre-admission summer program, reduced course load, study skills assistance, tutoring, writing center.

Majors. Architecture: Architecture. **Area/ethnic studies:** American, Asian, Latin American. **Biology:** General. **Business:** Accounting, business admin, entrepreneurial studies, finance, hospitality admin, international, managerial economics, marketing, organizational behavior. **Communications:** Advertising, communications/speech/rhetoric, media studies. **Computer sciences:** General, computer science, information systems, information technology. **Conservation:** Environmental science, environmental studies. **English:** English lit. **Foreign languages:** Comparative lit, French, Japanese, Spanish. **Health services:** Health services admin, nursing (RN). **History:** General. **Human services:** General. **Math:** General. **Parks/recreation:** Exercise sciences. **Philosophy/religion:** Philosophy. **Physical sciences:** Chemistry, physics. **Psychology:** General. **Social sciences:** Applied economics, economics, international economic development, international relations, political science, sociology. **Theology:** Theology. **Visual/performing arts:** General, art history/conservation, commercial/advertising art, design, graphic design, studio arts.

Most popular majors. Business/marketing 35%, communications/journalism 10%, health sciences 12%, psychology 7%, social sciences 11%.

Technology on campus. 273 workstations in dormitories, library, computer center, student center. Dormitories wired for high-speed internet access and linked to campus network. Commuter students can connect to campus network. Online course registration, online library, helpline, student web hosting, wireless network available.

Student life. Freshman orientation: Mandatory. Preregistration for classes offered. Two-day session on the days preceding the start of classes. **Policies:** Freshman and sophomores under 21 required to live in residence halls unless they have permanent address within 40-mile radius of campus. **Housing:** Guaranteed on-campus for freshmen. Coed dorms, single-sex dorms, special housing for disabled, apartments, themed housing available. $300 nonrefundable deposit, deadline 5/1. **Activities:** Bands, campus ministries, choral groups, dance, drama, international student organizations, literary magazine, music ensembles, musical theater, radio station, student government, student newspaper, TV station, St. Ignatius Institute, People Advocating Cultural Endeavors, Phelan multicultural community, Martin-Baro Living Learning Community, Erasmus Community.

Athletics. NCAA. **Intercollegiate:** Baseball M, basketball, cross-country, golf, soccer, tennis, track and field, volleyball W. **Intramural:** Basketball, football (non-tackle), racquetball, soccer, softball, swimming, table tennis, tennis, volleyball. **Team name:** Dons.

Student services. Adult student services, alcohol/substance abuse counseling, chaplain/spiritual director, career counseling, student employment services, financial aid counseling, health services, minority student services, personal counseling, placement for graduates. **Physically disabled:** Services for visually, speech, hearing impaired.

Contact. E-mail: admissions@usfca.edu
Phone: (415) 422-6563 Toll-free number: (800) 225-5873
Fax: (415) 422-2217
Michael Hughes, Director of Admissions, University of San Francisco, 2130 Fulton Street, San Francisco, CA 94117-1080

University of Southern California
Los Angeles, California · CB member
www.usc.edu · CB code: 4852

- Private 4-year university
- Residential campus in very large city
- 18,518 degree-seeking undergraduates: 3% part-time, 51% women, 4% African American, 22% Asian American, 14% Hispanic/Latino, 5% Multi-racial, non-Hispanic, 13% international
- 23,409 degree-seeking graduate students
- 18% of applicants admitted
- SAT or ACT (ACT writing optional), application essay required
- 92% graduate within 6 years

General. Founded in 1880. Regionally accredited. Permanent facilities for study in Sacramento available. **Degrees:** 4,932 bachelor's awarded; master's, professional, doctoral offered. **ROTC:** Army, Naval, Air Force. **Location:** 3 miles from downtown. **Calendar:** Semester, limited summer session. **Full-time faculty:** 1,981 total; 90% have terminal degrees, 30% minority, 39% women. **Part-time faculty:** 1,365 total; 63% have terminal degrees, 29% minority, 47% women. **Class size:** 61% < 20, 20% 20-39, 7% 40-49, 8%

50-99, 3% >100. **Special facilities:** 3 art/architecture galleries, 2 museums, 2 sculpture gardens, marine science center, Gamble House (designed by Greene and Greene), Freeman House (designed by Frank Lloyd Wright), technical theater laboratory, recording studio, cinematic arts complex, integrated media systems center, center for digital arts, engineering undergraduate fabrication laboratory, image processing and informatics laboratory, sun- and wind-simulation labs, rocket propulsion laboratory, geographic information systems laboratory, cognitive neuroscience imaging center.

Freshman class profile. 51,924 applied, 9,181 admitted, 2,949 enrolled.

Mid 50% test scores		Rank in top quarter:	97%
SAT critical reading:	620-730	Rank in top tenth:	88%
SAT math:	650-770	Return as sophomores:	96%
SAT writing:	650-750	Out-of-state:	42%
ACT composite:	30-33	Live on campus:	98%
GPA 3.75 or higher:	59%	International:	15%
GPA 3.50-3.74:	25%	Fraternities:	27%
GPA 3.0-3.49:	14%	Sororities:	24%
GPA 2.0-2.99:	2%		

Basis for selection. GED not accepted. Academic achievement, curriculum and test scores most important. Recommendations, activities, essays/writing samples are also very important. Audition required of music and theater majors. Portfolio required of fine arts and architecture majors. **Home schooled:** 3 SAT Subject tests (1 must be in math) and detailed syllabi of courses, names of textbooks, names and applicable credentials of instructors, details of assistance received or curriculum followed through any public or private agency, and any additional information that may be helpful.

High school preparation. College-preparatory program required. 16 units required; 20 recommended. Required and recommended units include English 4, mathematics 3-4, social studies 2-3, science 2-3 (laboratory 2-3), foreign language 2-3 and academic electives 3.

2016-2017 Annual costs. Tuition/fees (projected): $50,210. Room/board: $13,855. Books/supplies: $1,500. Personal expenses: $1,000.

2014-2015 Financial aid. **Need-based:** 1,786 full-time freshmen applied for aid; 1,031 deemed to have need; 1,030 received aid. Average need met was 100%. Average scholarship/grant was $34,948; average loan $5,195. 81% of total undergraduate aid awarded as scholarships/grants, 19% as loans/jobs. **Non-need-based:** Awarded to 6,928 full-time undergraduates, including 1,408 freshmen. Scholarships awarded for academics, alumni affiliation, art, athletics, leadership, music/drama, ROTC.

Application procedures. Admission: Priority date 12/1; deadline 1/15 (postmark date). $80 fee, may be waived for applicants with need. Admission notification by 4/1. Must reply by 5/1. Students may defer admission for up to one year. **Financial aid:** Priority date 2/16; no closing date. FAFSA, CSS PROFILE required. Applicants notified by 4/1; must reply by 5/1.

Academics. Special study options: Combined bachelor's/graduate degree, cooperative education, distance learning, double major, ESL, exchange student, honors, independent study, internships, liberal arts/career combination, student-designed major, study abroad, Washington semester. Learning communities, thematic option, undergraduate research, freshman seminars. **Credit/placement by examination:** AP, CLEP, IB, institutional tests. 32 credit hours maximum toward bachelor's degree. **Support services:** Learning center, reduced course load, study skills assistance, tutoring, writing center.

Majors. Architecture: Architecture, landscape, real estate development, urban/community planning. **Area/ethnic studies:** African-American, American, Asian-American, Chicano/Hispanic-American/Latino, East Asian, Near/Middle Eastern, Russian/Eastern European/Eurasian. **Biology:** General, biochemistry, biophysics, neuroscience. **Business:** Accounting, business admin. **Communications:** Broadcast journalism, communications/speech/rhetoric, journalism, public relations. **Computer sciences:** Computer science. **Conservation:** Environmental science, environmental studies. **Engineering:** Aerospace, biomedical, chemical, civil, computer, electrical, environmental, industrial, mechanical, structural. **English:** Creative writing, English lit. **Foreign languages:** Classics, comparative lit, East Asian, French, German, Italian, linguistics, Russian, Spanish. **Health services:** Dental hygiene, environmental health, health behavior, international public health, occupational therapy. **History:** General. **Human services:** General. **Math:** General, applied, computational/applied, financial. **Parks/recreation:** Exercise sciences. **Philosophy/religion:** Judaic, philosophy, religion. **Physical sciences:** General, astronomy, chemistry, geology, physics. **Psychology:** General. **Social sciences:** General, anthropology, archaeology, economics, geography, international relations, political economy, political science, sociology. **Visual/performing arts:** General, acting, art, art history/conservation, brass instruments, cinematography, digital arts, dramatic, film/cinema/video, game design, jazz, music, music management, music performance, music theory/composition, percussion instruments, piano/keyboard, play/screenwriting, stringed instruments, studio arts, theater design, voice/opera, woodwind instruments.

Most popular majors. Biology 6%, business/marketing 24%, communications/journalism 10%, engineering/engineering technologies 10%, social sciences 14%, visual/performing arts 12%.

Technology on campus. 2,000 workstations in dormitories, library, computer center, student center. Dormitories wired for high-speed internet access and linked to campus network. Commuter students can connect to campus network. Online course registration, online library, helpline, repair service, student web hosting, wireless network available.

Student life. Freshman orientation: Available. Preregistration for classes offered. **Policies:** Every incoming student required to take online alcohol education course and pass final exam. **Housing:** Guaranteed on-campus for freshmen. Coed dorms, special housing for disabled, apartments, fraternity/sorority housing, themed housing, wellness housing available. $400 fully refundable deposit. Special interest floors available. **Activities:** Bands, campus ministries, choral groups, dance, drama, film society, international student organizations, literary magazine, music ensembles, Model UN, musical theater, opera, radio station, student government, student newspaper, symphony orchestra, TV station, academic honors assembly, emerging leaders program, minority consortium, religious council, residential community council, student program board, student volunteer center.

Athletics. NCAA. **Intercollegiate:** Baseball M, basketball, cross-country W, diving, football (tackle) M, golf, lacrosse W, rowing (crew) W, soccer W, swimming, tennis, track and field, volleyball, water polo. **Intramural:** Badminton, basketball, cross-country, football (non-tackle), golf, racquetball, soccer, softball, tennis, ultimate frisbee, volleyball. **Team name:** Trojans.

Student services. Alcohol/substance abuse counseling, chaplain/spiritual director, career counseling, services for economically disadvantaged, student employment services, financial aid counseling, health services, legal services, minority student services, on-campus daycare, personal counseling, placement for graduates, veterans' counselor, women's services. **Physically disabled:** Services for visually, speech, hearing impaired.

Contact. E-mail: admitusc@usc.edu
Phone: (213) 740-1111 Fax: (213) 821-0200
Timothy Brunold, Dean of Admission, University of Southern California, Office of Admission, Los Angeles, CA 90089-0911

University of the Pacific
Stockton, California **CB member**
www.pacific.edu **CB code: 4065**

- Private 4-year university
- Residential campus in large city
- 3,720 degree-seeking undergraduates: 2% part-time, 52% women, 3% African American, 35% Asian American, 18% Hispanic/Latino, 1% Native Hawaiian/Pacific islander, 6% Multi-racial, non-Hispanic, 7% international
- 2,542 degree-seeking graduate students
- 65% of applicants admitted
- SAT or ACT (ACT writing optional), application essay required
- 70% graduate within 6 years

General. Founded in 1851. Regionally accredited. School of Dentistry in San Francisco. McGeorge School of Law in Sacramento. **Degrees:** 920 bachelor's awarded; master's, professional, doctoral offered. **ROTC:** Air Force. **Location:** 80 miles from San Francisco, 40 miles from Sacramento. **Calendar:** Continuous, limited summer session. **Full-time faculty:** 436 total; 93% have terminal degrees, 21% minority, 43% women. **Part-time faculty:** 332 total; 51% have terminal degrees, 32% minority, 45% women. **Class size:** 56% < 20, 34% 20-39, 5% 40-49, 4% 50-99, less than 1% >100. **Special facilities:** Recital facilities, center for western studies, John Muir papers collection, music conservatory.

Freshman class profile. 14,449 applied, 9,328 admitted, 937 enrolled.

Mid 50% test scores		GPA 2.0-2.99:	13%
SAT critical reading:	490-620	Rank in top quarter:	66%
SAT math:	520-660	Rank in top tenth:	33%
SAT writing:	490-630	Return as sophomores:	85%
ACT composite:	22-29	Out-of-state:	7%
GPA 3.75 or higher:	28%	Live on campus:	77%
GPA 3.50-3.74:	23%	International:	6%
GPA 3.0-3.49:	36%		

Basis for selection. Secondary school record, standardized test scores, recommendations, essay, extracurricular activities important. SAT and SAT Subject Tests or ACT recommended. A chemistry placement is required for majors in Pre-Dentistry, Pre-pharmacy, Biological Sciences, Chemistry, Biochemistry, Chemistry-Biology, Environmental Science, Natural Science

Exploratory or Physics. If you are an Engineering or Health and Exercise Science major a placement is strongly encouraged. Audition required of music/conservatory majors. **Home schooled:** Standardized test scores weighted heavily.

High school preparation. College-preparatory program recommended. 16 units required. Required and recommended units include English 4, mathematics 3, social studies 2, history 1, (laboratory 2), foreign language 2, visual/performing arts 1 and academic electives 1. 1 fine/performing arts required. Lab unit requirement only for science majors.

2015-2016 Annual costs. Tuition/fees: $42,934. Room/board: $12,858. Books/supplies: $1,764. Personal expenses: $2,322.

2015-2016 Financial aid. Need-based: 762 full-time freshmen applied for aid; 667 deemed to have need; 667 received aid. Average scholarship/grant was $24,608; average loan $7,061. 70% of total undergraduate aid awarded as scholarships/grants, 30% as loans/jobs. **Non-need-based:** Awarded to 705 full-time undergraduates, including 217 freshmen. Scholarships awarded for academics, athletics, leadership, music/drama, religious affiliation.

Application procedures. Admission: Priority date 11/15; deadline 1/15. $35 fee, may be waived for applicants with need. Admission notification on a rolling basis beginning on or about 11/1. Must reply by 5/1. Housing deposit refundable if canceled by May 1. **Financial aid:** Priority date 2/15; no closing date. FAFSA required. Applicants notified on a rolling basis starting 3/1.

Academics. Special study options: Accelerated study, combined bachelor's/graduate degree, cooperative education, distance learning, double major, dual enrollment of high school students, ESL, external degree, honors, independent study, internships, liberal arts/career combination, student-designed major, study abroad, teacher certification program, United Nations semester, Washington semester. Practicum, minors, undergraduate research, combination, ethnic studies, environmental science, thematic minors, gender studies, service learning. **Credit/placement by examination:** AP, CLEP, IB, SAT, ACT, institutional tests. 20 credit hours maximum toward bachelor's degree. **Support services:** Learning center, pre-admission summer program, reduced course load, remedial instruction, tutoring, writing center.

Majors. Area/ethnic studies: Asian. **Biology:** General, biochemistry. **Business:** Business admin, organizational behavior. **Communications:** Communications/speech/rhetoric. **Computer sciences:** Computer science, information systems. **Conservation:** Environmental science, environmental studies. **Education:** General, music. **Engineering:** General, applied physics, biomedical, civil, computer, electrical, mechanical. **English:** English lit. **Foreign languages:** French, Spanish. **Health services:** Athletic training, dental hygiene, music therapy, speech pathology. **History:** General. **Liberal arts:** Arts/sciences. **Math:** General, applied. **Philosophy/religion:** Philosophy, religion. **Physical sciences:** Chemistry, geology, physics. **Psychology:** General. **Social sciences:** General, economics, international relations, political science, sociology. **Visual/performing arts:** Art, commercial/advertising art, dramatic, graphic design, jazz, music, music history, music management, music performance, music theory/composition, piano/keyboard, studio arts, voice/opera.

Most popular majors. Biology 13%, business/marketing 19%, education 6%, engineering/engineering technologies 11%, health sciences 7%, parks/recreation 6%, social sciences 6%.

Technology on campus. 325 workstations in dormitories, library, computer center. Dormitories wired for high-speed internet access and linked to campus network. Commuter students can connect to campus network. Online course registration, online library, helpline, wireless network available.

Student life. Freshman orientation: Mandatory, $120 fee. Preregistration for classes offered. Offered in January, June, July & August, 2-4 days each. **Policies:** Freshmen and sophomores required to live on campus unless living with parents. **Housing:** Guaranteed on-campus for freshmen. Coed dorms, apartments, fraternity/sorority housing available. $200 fully refundable deposit. **Activities:** Bands, campus ministries, choral groups, dance, drama, film society, international student organizations, literary magazine, music ensembles, Model UN, musical theater, opera, radio station, student government, student newspaper, 100 student organizations and clubs.

Athletics. NCAA. **Intercollegiate:** Baseball M, basketball, cross-country W, field hockey W, golf M, soccer W, softball W, swimming, tennis, volleyball, water polo. **Intramural:** Badminton, basketball, bowling, football (tackle), golf, racquetball, soccer, softball, swimming, tennis, volleyball, water polo. **Team name:** Tigers.

Student services. Adult student services, alcohol/substance abuse counseling, chaplain/spiritual director, career counseling, services for economically disadvantaged, student employment services, financial aid counseling, health services, personal counseling, placement for graduates, veterans' counselor. **Physically disabled:** Services for visually, speech, hearing impaired.

Contact. E-mail: admissions@pacific.edu
Phone: (209) 946-2211 Toll-free number: (800) 959-2867
Fax: (209) 946-4213
Rich Toledo, Director of Admissions, University of the Pacific, 3601 Pacific Avenue, Stockton, CA 95211-0197

University of the West
Rosemead, California
www.uwest.edu

- Private 4-year business and liberal arts college affiliated with the Buddhist faith
- Commuter campus in small city
- 99 degree-seeking undergraduates
- Application essay required

General. Buddhist-founded institution, whole-person education that values diversity. **Degrees:** 10 bachelor's awarded; master's, doctoral offered. **Location:** 5 miles from Pasadena, 10 miles from Los Angeles. **Calendar:** Semester, extensive summer session. **Full-time faculty:** 17 total; 94% have terminal degrees, 71% minority, 24% women. **Part-time faculty:** 41 total; 42% minority, 32% women. **Class size:** 97% < 20, 3% 20-39. **Special facilities:** Investment lab, meditation hall, career services, yoga, writing center, academic adviser, peer mentor program.

Freshman class profile.

GPA 3.50-3.74:	4%	GPA 2.0-2.99:	71%
GPA 3.0-3.49:	17%	Live on campus:	24%

Basis for selection. Standardized tests not required, but English placement tests administered. Admission decision based on recommendation of department chair after transcript review. SAT scores are not required for admission, however a score does help in consideration for admission and for determination of scholarship awards. **Home schooled:** Handled on case-by-case basis.

High school preparation. College-preparatory program recommended.

2015-2016 Annual costs. Tuition/fees: $13,110. Room/board: $6,920. Books/supplies: $873. Personal expenses: $1,413.

Financial aid. Non-need-based: Scholarships awarded for academics, leadership.

Application procedures. Admission: Closing date 6/14 (postmark date). $75 fee, may be waived for applicants with need. Application must be submitted on paper. Admission notification on a rolling basis. **Financial aid:** No deadline. FAFSA, institutional form required.

Academics. Special study options: Combined bachelor's/graduate degree, double major, dual enrollment of high school students, ESL, exchange student, independent study, internships, study abroad. **Credit/placement by examination:** AP, CLEP. 15 credit hours maximum toward bachelor's degree. **Support services:** Learning center, pre-admission summer program, remedial instruction, study skills assistance, tutoring, writing center.

Majors. Business: Accounting, international. **English:** English lit. **Psychology:** General.

Technology on campus. 30 workstations in dormitories, library, computer center, student center. Dormitories wired for high-speed internet access and linked to campus network. Commuter students can connect to campus network. Online course registration, online library, student web hosting, wireless network available.

Student life. Freshman orientation: Mandatory. Preregistration for classes offered. **Housing:** Guaranteed on-campus for all undergraduates. Coed dorms, apartments available. $200 fully refundable deposit. **Activities:** Concert band, campus ministries, dance, international student organizations, literary magazine, student government.

Student services. Chaplain/spiritual director, career counseling, financial aid counseling.

Contact. E-mail: admission@uwest.edu
Phone: (626) 571-8811 ext. 311 Toll-free number: (855) 468-9378
Fax: (626) 571-1413
Grace Hsiao, Admissions Officer, University of the West, 1409 North Walnut Grove Avenue, Rosemead, CA 91770

Vanguard University of Southern California
Costa Mesa, California　　　　　　　　CB member
www.vanguard.edu　　　　　　　　　　　CB code: 4701

- Private 4-year university and liberal arts college affiliated with the Assemblies of God
- Residential campus in small city
- 1,941 degree-seeking undergraduates
- 268 graduate students
- SAT or ACT (ACT writing optional), application essay required

General. Founded in 1920. Regionally accredited. **Degrees:** 534 bachelor's, 5 associate awarded; master's offered. **ROTC:** Army, Air Force. **Location:** 45 miles from Los Angeles, 70 miles from San Diego. **Calendar:** Semester, limited summer session. **Full-time faculty:** 63 total; 84% have terminal degrees, 19% minority. **Part-time faculty:** 140 total; 18% have terminal degrees, 16% minority. **Class size:** 57% < 20, 34% 20-39, 4% 40-49, 5% 50-99, less than 1% >100.

Basis for selection. Recommended core GPA of 2.8 for freshmen and 2.5 for transfers. For freshman, recommended SAT (CR + M) of 910 and ACT of 21. Christian experience statement, pastoral reference, and transcript request form must be submitted. Applications from Christian students who desire an education that integrates Christian faith with learning and living encouraged.

High school preparation. Recommended units include English 4, mathematics 2, social studies 3 and science 2.

2015-2016 Annual costs. Tuition/fees: $30,050. Room/board: $9,150. Books/supplies: $1,764. Personal expenses: $2,320.

Financial aid. **Non-need-based:** Scholarships awarded for academics, athletics, music/drama, religious affiliation.

Application procedures. **Admission:** Priority date 12/1; deadline 3/2. $45 fee, may be waived for applicants with need. Admission notification on a rolling basis beginning on or about 1/15. Must reply by May 1 or within 3 week(s) if notified thereafter. **Financial aid:** Closing date 3/2. FAFSA required. Applicants notified on a rolling basis starting 4/1; must reply within 3 week(s) of notification.

Academics. **Special study options:** Accelerated study, combined bachelor's/graduate degree, double major, internships, study abroad, teacher certification program. Accelerated bachelor's program through Professional Studies. **Credit/placement by examination:** AP, CLEP, IB, SAT, ACT. 24 credit hours maximum toward bachelor's degree. **Support services:** Learning center, reduced course load, study skills assistance, tutoring, writing center.

Majors. **Biology:** General, biochemistry. **Business:** General, accounting, business admin, finance, international, marketing. **Communications:** Communications/speech/rhetoric, digital media. **Computer sciences:** Information technology. **Education:** Music, physical. **English:** English lit. **Health services:** Athletic training, nursing (RN), premedicine. **History:** General. **Liberal arts:** Arts/sciences. **Math:** General. **Parks/recreation:** Exercise sciences, health/fitness. **Philosophy/religion:** Christian, religion. **Physical sciences:** Chemistry. **Psychology:** General. **Social sciences:** General, anthropology, political science, sociology. **Theology:** Bible, missionary, pastoral counseling, religious ed, theology, youth ministry. **Visual/performing arts:** Cinematography, dramatic, music, music history, music performance, theater design. **Work/family studies:** Family studies.

Most popular majors. Business/marketing 24%, communications/journalism 16%, education 8%, psychology 13%, social sciences 6%, visual/performing arts 10%.

Technology on campus. Dormitories wired for high-speed internet access and linked to campus network. Commuter students can connect to campus network. Online course registration, online library, helpline, wireless network available.

Student life. **Freshman orientation:** Mandatory, $125 fee. Preregistration for classes offered. 4-day program prior to first day of fall semester. **Policies:** Students must be in good standing to live on campus. Religious observance required. **Housing:** Guaranteed on-campus for all undergraduates. Coed dorms, single-sex dorms, apartments, wellness housing available. $400 deposit, deadline 5/1. **Activities:** Bands, campus ministries, choral groups, drama, film society, international student organizations, literary magazine, music ensembles, musical theater, student government, student newspaper, Students for Social Action, Live 2 Free, Club Mosaic, El Puente, Students in Free Enterprise, Invisible Children Club, Acting on AIDS, Prayer Movement, Hands Across the Border.

Athletics. NAIA. **Intercollegiate:** Baseball M, basketball, cross-country, soccer, softball W, swimming, track and field, volleyball W. **Intramural:** Basketball. **Team name:** Lions.

Student services. Adult student services, alcohol/substance abuse counseling, chaplain/spiritual director, career counseling, student employment services, financial aid counseling, health services, minority student services, personal counseling, placement for graduates, veterans' counselor, women's services.

Contact. E-mail: admissions@vanguard.edu
Phone: (714) 966-5496 Toll-free number: (800) 722-6279
Fax: (714) 966-5471
Susan Park, Director of Undergraduate Admissions, Vanguard University of Southern California, 55 Fair Drive, Costa Mesa, CA 92626-9601

West Coast University: Los Angeles
North Hollywood, California
www.westcoastuniversity.edu　　　　　CB code: 6184

- For-profit 4-year health science and nursing college
- Commuter campus in very large city
- 1,435 degree-seeking undergraduates
- Interview required

General. Regionally accredited. **Degrees:** 405 bachelor's awarded; master's offered. **Location:** Downtown. **Calendar:** Semester, extensive summer session. **Full-time faculty:** 48 total. **Part-time faculty:** 50 total. **Class size:** 67% < 20, 21% 20-39, 5% 40-49, 7% 50-99, less than 1% >100. **Special facilities:** Simulation labs.

Basis for selection. Incoming students must pass entrance exams for any program where it is required for entry. Academic record is important but not definitive. Interview with admissions and academic dean is required. **Home schooled:** Evidence that Home School meets State Home School Requirements. **Learning Disabled:** Students with disabilities should request accommodations through Student Services Department.

2015-2016 Annual costs. Tuition/fees: $33,731. Personal expenses: $6,060.

Financial aid. **Non-need-based:** Scholarships awarded for academics.

Application procedures. **Admission:** No deadline. No application fee. Application must be submitted on paper. **Financial aid:** Closing date 6/30. FAFSA, institutional form required. Applicants notified on a rolling basis.

Academics. **Special study options:** Accelerated study, distance learning, internships, study abroad, weekend college. **Credit/placement by examination:** AP, CLEP, institutional tests. May challenge test-out of 12 semester credits, maximum. Must achieve score of 75% or higher, one attempt only. Must be taken before enrolling in the course in which equivalency is sought. **Support services:** Study skills assistance, tutoring.

Majors. **Health services:** Nursing (RN).

Technology on campus. 327 workstations in library, computer center. Commuter students can connect to campus network. Online library, helpline, wireless network available.

Student life. **Freshman orientation:** Mandatory. Preregistration for classes offered. **Activities:** Student government.

Student services. Adult student services, career counseling, services for economically disadvantaged, student employment services, financial aid counseling, placement for graduates.

Contact. Phone: (877) 505-4928 Toll-free number: (877) 505-4928
Fax: (818) 299-5545
Herman Whitaker, Director of Admissions, West Coast University: Los Angeles, 12215 Victory Boulevard, North Hollywood, CA 91606

West Coast University: Ontario
Ontario, California
www.westcoastuniversity.edu　　　　　CB code: 7977

- For-profit 4-year branch campus and nursing college
- Commuter campus in small city
- 1,061 undergraduates
- Interview required

General. Regionally accredited. **Degrees:** 252 bachelor's awarded. **Calendar:** Semester. **Full-time faculty:** 24 total. **Part-time faculty:** 69 total. **Class size:** 57% < 20, 34% 20-39, 6% 40-49, 3% 50-99. **Special facilities:** Simulation labs.

Basis for selection. Open admission, but selective for some programs. **Home schooled:** Evidence that home school meets state home school requirements. **Learning Disabled:** Students with disabilities should request accommodations through Student Services Department.

2015-2016 Annual costs. Tuition/fees: $33,731. Books/supplies: $1,906. Personal expenses: $6,060.

Financial aid. Non-need-based: Scholarships awarded for academics.

Application procedures. Admission: No deadline. No application fee. Application must be submitted on paper. **Financial aid:** Closing date 6/30. FAFSA, institutional form required. Applicants notified on a rolling basis.

Academics. Special study options: Accelerated study, distance learning, internships, study abroad, weekend college. **Credit/placement by examination:** AP, CLEP, institutional tests. May challenge test-out of 12 semester credits, maximum. Must achieve score of 75% or higher, one attempt only. Must be taken before enrolling in the course in which equivalency is sought. **Support services:** Study skills assistance, tutoring.

Majors. Health services: Nursing (RN).

Technology on campus. 274 workstations in library, computer center. Commuter students can connect to campus network. Online library, helpline, wireless network available.

Student life. Freshman orientation: Mandatory. Preregistration for classes offered. **Activities:** Student government.

Student services. Adult student services, career counseling, services for economically disadvantaged, student employment services, financial aid counseling, placement for graduates.

Contact. Phone: (909) 467-6100
Tony Kim, Director of Admissions, West Coast University: Ontario, 2855 East Guasti Road, Ontario, CA 91761

West Coast University: Orange County
Anaheim, California
www.westcoastuniversity.edu   CB code: 7976

‣ For-profit 4-year branch campus and nursing college
‣ Commuter campus in large city
‣ 1,477 undergraduates
‣ Interview required

General. Regionally accredited. **Degrees:** 418 bachelor's awarded. **ROTC:** Air Force. **Calendar:** Semester, extensive summer session. **Full-time faculty:** 31 total. **Part-time faculty:** 79 total. **Class size:** 58% < 20, 32% 20-39, 6% 40-49, 3% 50-99, less than 1% >100. **Special facilities:** Simulation labs.

Basis for selection. Open admission, but selective for some programs. **Home schooled:** Evidence that home school meets state home school requirements. **Learning Disabled:** Students with disabilities should request accommodations through student services department.

2015-2016 Annual costs. Tuition/fees: $33,175. Personal expenses: $6,060.

Financial aid. Non-need-based: Scholarships awarded for academics.

Application procedures. Admission: No deadline. No application fee. Application must be submitted on paper. **Financial aid:** Closing date 6/30. FAFSA, institutional form required. Applicants notified on a rolling basis.

Academics. Special study options: Accelerated study, distance learning, internships, study abroad, weekend college. **Credit/placement by examination:** AP, CLEP, institutional tests. May challenge test-out of 12 semester credits, maximum. Must achieve score of 75% or higher, one attempt only. Must be taken before enrolling in the course in which equivalency is sought. **Support services:** Study skills assistance, tutoring.

Majors. Health services: Dental hygiene, health care admin, nursing (RN).

Technology on campus. 91 workstations in library, computer center. Commuter students can connect to campus network. Online library, helpline, wireless network available.

Student life. Freshman orientation: Mandatory. Preregistration for classes offered. **Activities:** Student government.

Student services. Adult student services, career counseling, services for economically disadvantaged, student employment services, financial aid counseling, placement for graduates.

Contact. Phone: (714) 782-1700 Fax: (714) 533-8742
Christina Downey, Director of Admissions, West Coast University: Orange County, 1477 South Manchester Avenue, Anaheim, CA 92802

Westmont College
Santa Barbara, California   CB member
www.westmont.edu   CB code: 4950

‣ Private 4-year liberal arts college affiliated with the nondenominational tradition
‣ Residential campus in small city
‣ 1,284 degree-seeking undergraduates: 60% women, 1% African American, 7% Asian American, 15% Hispanic/Latino, 7% Multi-racial, non-Hispanic, 1% international
‣ 81% of applicants admitted
‣ SAT or ACT (ACT writing recommended), application essay required
‣ 77% graduate within 6 years

General. Founded in 1937. Regionally accredited. **Degrees:** 314 bachelor's awarded. **ROTC:** Army, Air Force. **Location:** 90 miles from Los Angeles. **Calendar:** Semester, limited summer session. **Full-time faculty:** 93 total; 89% have terminal degrees, 12% minority, 41% women. **Part-time faculty:** 54 total; 33% have terminal degrees, 17% minority, 46% women. **Class size:** 65% < 20, 27% 20-39, 6% 40-49, 2% 50-99. **Special facilities:** Visual arts building with gallery, theater, observatory, electronic music lab, physiology lab, organic garden, Cosmic Muon Detector Array, vivarium.

Freshman class profile. 2,077 applied, 1,687 admitted, 338 enrolled.

Mid 50% test scores		GPA 2.0-2.99:	15%
SAT critical reading:	520-650	Rank in top quarter:	64%
SAT math:	530-650	Rank in top tenth:	37%
SAT writing:	520-640	Return as sophomores:	82%
ACT composite:	23-29	Out-of-state:	29%
GPA 3.75 or higher:	32%	Live on campus:	100%
GPA 3.50-3.74:	19%	International:	1%
GPA 3.0-3.49:	34%		

Basis for selection. Personal Christian statement, college preparatory high school curriculum, high school rank, test scores, 1 academic recommendation, and essay required. Personal interview, teacher, pastor, and other recommendations optional. Test scores must be received by November 1 for Early Action applicants. Personal interviews recommended. **Home schooled:** Applicants encouraged. Evaluation based on individual merit as well as high school achievement. Greater emphasis may be given to SAT or ACT scores.

High school preparation. College-preparatory program required. 16 units required. Required and recommended units include English 4, mathematics 3, social studies 1, history 1, science 3 (laboratory 2), foreign language 2-3 and academic electives 2-4. Three math credits required, one of which must include Algebra 2.

2015-2016 Annual costs. Tuition/fees: $41,360. Room/board: $13,040. Books/supplies: $1,600. Personal expenses: $1,400.

2015-2016 Financial aid. Need-based: 287 full-time freshmen applied for aid; 230 deemed to have need; 230 received aid. Average need met was 81%. Average scholarship/grant was $25,289; average loan $4,510. 73% of total undergraduate aid awarded as scholarships/grants, 27% as loans/jobs. **Non-need-based:** Awarded to 472 full-time undergraduates, including 135 freshmen. Scholarships awarded for academics, art, athletics, leadership, minority status, music/drama.

Application procedures. Admission: Priority date 2/15; no deadline. $40 fee, may be waived for applicants with need. Admission notification on a rolling basis beginning on or about 3/1. Must reply by May 1 or within 2 week(s) if notified thereafter. **Financial aid:** Priority date 3/1; no closing date. FAFSA, institutional form required. PROFILE accepted but not required. Applicants notified on a rolling basis starting 2/1; must reply by 5/1 or within 2 week(s) of notification.

Academics. Special study options: Accelerated study, cross-registration, double major, exchange student, honors, independent study, internships, liberal arts/career combination, New York semester, semester at sea, student-designed major, study abroad, teacher certification program, urban semester, Washington semester. Cross-cultural studies in Western and Eastern Europe,

England, Africa, East Asia, South America and Egypt; semester study available in San Francisco, Los Angeles, Mexico and at one of 12 other member colleges of the Christian College Consortium. **Credit/placement by examination:** AP, CLEP, IB, institutional tests. 32 credit hours maximum toward bachelor's degree. **Support services:** Learning center, pre-admission summer program, study skills assistance, tutoring, writing center.

Majors. **Area/ethnic studies:** European. **Biology:** General. **Business:** General. **Communications:** Communications/speech/rhetoric. **Computer sciences:** Computer science. **Education:** General. **Engineering:** Applied physics. **English:** English lit. **Foreign languages:** French, Spanish. **Health services:** Predental, premedicine, prenursing, prepharmacy, preveterinary. **History:** General. **Math:** General. **Parks/recreation:** Exercise sciences. **Philosophy/religion:** Philosophy, religion. **Physical sciences:** Chemistry, physics. **Psychology:** General. **Social sciences:** General, anthropology, economics, political science, sociology. **Visual/performing arts:** Art, dramatic, music.

Most popular majors. Biology 8%, business/marketing 14%, communications/journalism 8%, English 8%, parks/recreation 15%, psychology 7%, social sciences 10%, visual/performing arts 6%.

Technology on campus. 100 workstations in library, computer center. Dormitories wired for high-speed internet access and linked to campus network. Commuter students can connect to campus network. Online course registration, online library, helpline, repair service, student web hosting, wireless network available.

Student life. **Freshman orientation:** Mandatory. Preregistration for classes offered. Held 4 days before Fall semester begins. **Policies:** Chapel attendance required on Mondays, Wednesdays, and Fridays. Dry, tobacco-free campus. Men and women do not share hallways and bathrooms in dorms. Selected visiting hours for members of opposite sex. Religious observance required. **Housing:** Guaranteed on-campus for all undergraduates. Coed dorms, apartments available. $500 nonrefundable deposit, deadline 5/1. **Activities:** Bands, campus ministries, choral groups, dance, drama, international student organizations, literary magazine, music ensembles, Model UN, musical theater, student government, student newspaper, symphony orchestra, Amnesty International, Habitat for Humanity, Leadership Development Program, political organizations, Fellowship of Christian Athletes, community service organizations.

Athletics. NAIA. **Intercollegiate:** Baseball M, basketball, cross-country, soccer, tennis, track and field, volleyball W. **Intramural:** Badminton, basketball, football (non-tackle), golf, lacrosse, racquetball, soccer, swimming, table tennis, tennis, volleyball. **Team name:** Warriors.

Student services. Alcohol/substance abuse counseling, chaplain/spiritual director, career counseling, student employment services, financial aid counseling, health services, minority student services, personal counseling, placement for graduates. **Physically disabled:** Services for visually, speech, hearing impaired.

Contact. E-mail: admissions@westmont.edu
Phone: (805) 565-6200 Toll-free number: (800) 777-9011
Fax: (805) 565-6234
Silvio Vazquez, Dean of Admission, Westmont College, 955 La Paz Road, Santa Barbara, CA 93108-1089

Westwood College: Anaheim
Anaheim, California
www.westwood.edu/locations/california/anaheim-campus

- For-profit 4-year technical and career college
- Very large city
- 772 degree-seeking undergraduates
- SAT or ACT, interview required

General. Regionally accredited; also accredited by ACICS. This Westwood College campus offers a unique hands-on, career-focused curriculum providing associate degrees that can be earned in as little as three months and bachelor's degrees that can be earned in as little as three years. Degree programs are available in the fields of technology, healthcare, business, design and justice. **Degrees:** 199 bachelor's, 88 associate awarded. **Calendar:** Differs by program. **Full-time faculty:** 15 total. **Part-time faculty:** 58 total.

Basis for selection. Admissions decisions based on assessment test and interview.

2015-2016 Annual costs. Books/supplies: $1,106. **Additional information:** Information Technology: AOS $34,825. Business Administration: AAS $36,428. Computer Aided Design/Architectural Drafting: AAS $38,367. Construction Management: AAS $36,428. Criminal Justice: AAS $38,717. Graphic Design: AAS $40,278. Health Information Technology: AAS

$35,259. Healthcare Office Administration: AAS $35,259. Medical Assisting: AAS $27,251. Paralegal: AAS $33,250. Business Administration: Major in Healthcare Management: BS $72,856. Business Administration: Major in Management: BS $72,856. Business Administration: Major in Marketing Management: BS $72,856. Construction Management: BS $72,856. Criminal Justice: Major in Administration: BS $77,434. Graphic Design: Major in Visual Communications: BS $76,720. Information & Network Technologies: Major in Network Management: BS $69,650. Software Development: Major in Game Software Development: BS $69,650. Medical Assisting: DP $19,465. Additional costs and fees such as books, tool kits, lab fee and online fees may apply.

Application procedures. **Admission:** No deadline. No application fee. Admission notification on a rolling basis. **Financial aid:** FAFSA required. Applicants notified on a rolling basis.

Academics. **Credit/placement by examination:** AP, CLEP.

Majors. **Business:** Accounting/business management, business admin, construction management, marketing. **Computer sciences:** LAN/WAN management. **Health services:** Health care admin. **Protective services:** Law enforcement admin. **Visual/performing arts:** Design.

Contact. E-mail: AdmissionsRepresentativesWW-Campus@westwood.edu
Phone: (714) 704-2720 ext. 60100 Toll-free number: (877) 840-8999
Wes Camp, Director of Admissions, Westwood College: Anaheim, 1551 South Douglass Road, Anaheim, CA 92806

Westwood College: Inland Empire
Upland, California
www.westwood.edu/locations/california/inland-empire-campus

- For-profit 3-year career college
- Commuter campus in small city
- 1,644 degree-seeking undergraduates
- Interview required

General. Regionally accredited; also accredited by ACICS. **Degrees:** 210 bachelor's, 155 associate awarded. **Location:** 45 miles from Los Angeles, 22 miles from Riverside. **Calendar:** Differs by program. **Full-time faculty:** 8 total. **Part-time faculty:** 35 total. **Class size:** 64% < 20, 36% 20-39.

Basis for selection. Interview required, documentation of prior education and proficiency in basic college-level skills required, English language proficiency required for applicants whose native language is not English. Institutional test (ACCUPLACER) and interview most important. Developmental courses may be required for those who do not pass entrance examination. SAT or ACT recommended. If SAT or ACT scores are not submitted or do not meet minimum requirements, students must take campus-administered ACCUPLACER placement exam.

2015-2016 Annual costs. Electronics Technology: AOS $34,825. Information Technology: AOS $34,825. Business Administration: AAS $36,428. Computer Aided Design/Architectural Drafting: AAS $38,367. Construction Management: AAS $36,428. Criminal Justice: AAS $38,717. Graphic Design: AAS $40,278. Health Information Technology: AAS $40,296. Healthcare Office Administration: AAS $35,259. Medical Assisting: AAS $27,251. Medical Insurance Coding & Billing: AAS $35,259. Paralegal: AAS $33,250. Business Administration: Major in Healthcare Management: BS $72,856. Business Administration: Major in Management: BS $72,856. Business Administration: Major in Marketing Management: BS $72,856. Construction Management: BS $72,856. Criminal Justice: Major in Administration: BS $77,434. Graphic Design: Major in Visual Communications: BS $76,720. Information & Network Technologies: Major in Network Management: BS $69,650. Medical Assisting: DP $19,465. Additional costs and fees such as books, tool kits, lab fee and online fees may apply.

Application procedures. **Admission:** No deadline. No application fee. Admission notification on a rolling basis. **Financial aid:** No deadline. FAFSA, institutional form required. Must reply within 1 week(s) of notification.

Academics. **Special study options:** Cooperative education, distance learning, honors, independent study, liberal arts/career combination. Hybrid schedules: combination of both campus and online courses. **Credit/placement by examination:** AP, CLEP, IB, institutional tests. Students may test out of required courses by passing proficiency exams. **Support services:** Learning center, reduced course load, remedial instruction, study skills assistance, tutoring.

Majors. **BACHELOR'S.** **Business:** Accounting/business management, business admin, construction management, marketing. **Computer sciences:**

LAN/WAN management. **Health services:** Health care admin. **Protective services:** Law enforcement admin. **Visual/performing arts:** Design. **ASSOCIATE. Business:** Business admin, construction management. **Computer sciences:** Networking. **Health services:** Health information technology, insurance coding, medical assistant, office admin. **Protective services:** Law enforcement admin. **Visual/performing arts:** Graphic design.

Technology on campus. 50 workstations in library. Online library available.

Student life. Freshman orientation: Mandatory. Preregistration for classes offered. **Activities:** Student government, student newspaper.

Student services. Career counseling, services for economically disadvantaged, student employment services, financial aid counseling, placement for graduates, veterans' counselor.

Contact. E-mail: laiinternet@westwood.edu
Phone: (909) 931-7550 Toll-free number: (866) 221-5632
Fax: (909) 931-5962
David Vopat, Director of Admissions, Westwood College: Inland Empire, 20 West Seventh Street, Upland, CA 91786

Westwood College: South Bay
Torrance, California
www.westwood.edu/locations/california/south-bay-campus

▸ For-profit 4-year technical college
▸ Large city
▸ 906 degree-seeking undergraduates

General. Regionally accredited; also accredited by ACICS. This Westwood College campus offers a unique hands-on, career-focused curriculum providing associate degrees that can be earned in as little as three months and bachelor's degrees that can be earned in as little as three years. Degree programs are available in the fields of technology, healthcare, business, design and justice. **Degrees:** 142 bachelor's, 80 associate awarded. **Calendar:** Differs by program. **Full-time faculty:** 8 total. **Part-time faculty:** 35 total.

Basis for selection. High school record and institutional assessment exam most important. Institutional test (ACCUPLACER) and interview most important. Developmental courses may be required for those who do not pass entrance examination. Institutional assessment exam required if ACT/SAT not submitted.

2015-2016 Annual costs. Books/supplies: $1,106. **Additional information:** Information Technology: AOS $34,825. Business Administration: AS $36,428. Computer Aided Design/Architectural Drafting: AS $38,367. Construction Management: AS $36,428. Criminal Justice: AS $38,717. Dental Assisting: AS $29,897. Graphic Design: AS $40,278. Healthcare Office Administration: AS $35,259. Medical Assisting: AS $27,251. Medical Insurance Coding & Billing: AS $35,259. Business Administration: Major in Healthcare Management: BS $72,856. Business Administration: Major in Management: BS $72,856. Business Administration: Major in Marketing Management: BS $72,856. Construction Management: BS $72,856. Criminal Justice: Major in Administration: BS $77,434. Graphic Design: Major in Visual Communications: $76,720. Information & Network Technologies: Major in Network Management: BS $69,650. Medical Assisting: DP $19,465. Additional costs and fees such as books, tool kits, lab fee and online fees may apply.

Application procedures. Admission: No deadline. No application fee. Admission notification on a rolling basis.

Academics. Credit/placement by examination: AP, CLEP, institutional tests.

Majors. Business: Accounting/business management, business admin, construction management, marketing. **Computer sciences:** LAN/WAN management. **Health services:** Health care admin. **Protective services:** Law enforcement admin. **Visual/performing arts:** Design.

Contact. E-mail: AdmissionsRepresentativesWW-Campus@westwood.edu
Phone: (310) 965-0888 Toll-free number: (888) 403-3308
Fax: (310) 516-8232
Paul Sallenbach, Admissions Director, Westwood College: South Bay, 19700 South Vermont Avenue #100, Torrance, CA 90502

Whittier College
Whittier, California   **CB member**
www.whittier.edu   **CB code: 4952**

▸ Private 4-year liberal arts college
▸ Residential campus in small city
▸ 1,645 degree-seeking undergraduates: 2% part-time, 56% women, 5% African American, 10% Asian American, 44% Hispanic/Latino, 4% Multi-racial, non-Hispanic, 3% international
▸ 485 degree-seeking graduate students
▸ 63% of applicants admitted
▸ SAT or ACT with writing, application essay required
▸ 66% graduate within 6 years; 22% enter graduate study

General. Founded in 1887. Regionally accredited. Historic affiliation with the Quakers. **Degrees:** 383 bachelor's awarded; master's, professional offered. **ROTC:** Army. **Location:** 18 miles from Los Angeles. **Calendar:** 4-1-4, limited summer session. **Full-time faculty:** 116 total; 95% have terminal degrees, 27% minority, 50% women. **Part-time faculty:** 72 total; 29% have terminal degrees, 42% minority, 57% women. **Class size:** 55% < 20, 43% 20-39, less than 1% 40-49, less than 1% 50-99, less than 1% >100. **Special facilities:** Quaker books and materials collection, Keck image processing laboratory, physics and astronomy research lab, environmental science lab, sustainable urban farm learning lab, digital music lab, Richard M. Nixon historical materials special collection, Institute for Baseball Studies, Broadoaks Children's School.

Freshman class profile. 5,192 applied, 3,251 admitted, 445 enrolled.

Mid 50% test scores			
SAT critical reading:	470-580	GPA 2.0-2.99:	10%
SAT math:	470-590	Rank in top quarter:	39%
SAT writing:	450-560	Rank in top tenth:	25%
ACT composite:	20-26	Return as sophomores:	81%
GPA 3.75 or higher:	30%	Out-of-state:	24%
GPA 3.50-3.74:	28%	Live on campus:	70%
GPA 3.0-3.49:	32%	International:	2%

Basis for selection. GPA, course selection, and class rank most important followed by essays, references, interviews, test scores, activities, and geographic considerations. Interview recommended. **Home schooled:** Statement describing home school structure and mission, transcript of courses and grades, letter of recommendation (nonparent) required.

High school preparation. College-preparatory program required. Required and recommended units include English 3-4, mathematics 2-3, social studies 1-2, science 1-2 (laboratory 1) and foreign language 2-3.

2015-2016 Annual costs. Tuition/fees: $43,080. Room/board: $12,672.

2015-2016 Financial aid. Need-based: 402 full-time freshmen applied for aid; 358 deemed to have need; 358 received aid. Average need met was 79%. Average scholarship/grant was $33,748; average loan $4,772. 78% of total undergraduate aid awarded as scholarships/grants, 22% as loans/jobs. **Non-need-based:** Awarded to 426 full-time undergraduates, including 123 freshmen. Scholarships awarded for academics, alumni affiliation, art, minority status, music/drama. **Additional information:** Auditions required for talent scholarship applicants in art, music, and theater.

Application procedures. Admission: Priority date 2/1; no deadline. $50 fee, may be waived for applicants with need. Admission notification on a rolling basis beginning on or about 12/30. Must reply by May 1 or within 2 week(s) if notified thereafter. **Financial aid:** Priority date 3/1, closing date 6/30. FAFSA required. Applicants notified on a rolling basis starting 2/15; must reply within 2 week(s) of notification.

Academics. Special study options: Combined bachelor's/graduate degree, double major, independent study, internships, liberal arts/career combination, semester at sea, student-designed major, study abroad, teacher certification program, United Nations semester, Washington semester. **Credit/placement by examination:** AP, CLEP, IB, SAT, ACT, institutional tests. 30 credit hours maximum toward bachelor's degree. **Support services:** Learning center, study skills assistance, tutoring, writing center.

Majors. Area/ethnic studies: Latin American. **Biology:** General, biochemistry. **Business:** Business admin. **Conservation:** General. **Education:** General, early childhood. **Engineering:** Applied physics. **English:** American lit, British lit, English lit. **Foreign languages:** Chinese, comparative lit, French, Spanish. **Health services:** Predental, premedicine, prepharmacy, preveterinary. **History:** General. **Human services:** Social work. **Liberal arts:** Arts/sciences. **Math:** General. **Parks/recreation:** Exercise sciences. **Philosophy/**

religion: Philosophy, religion. **Physical sciences:** Chemistry, physics. **Psychology:** General. **Social sciences:** General, anthropology, economics, international relations, political science, sociology, urban studies. **Visual/performing arts:** Art, art history/conservation, dramatic, music, music history, theater history.

Most popular majors. Biology 6%, business/marketing 18%, English 7%, foreign language 7%, parks/recreation 9%, psychology 8%, social sciences 18%.

Technology on campus. 175 workstations in library, computer center. Dormitories wired for high-speed internet access and linked to campus network. Commuter students can connect to campus network. Online course registration, online library, helpline, repair service, wireless network available.

Student life. Freshman orientation: Mandatory, $200 fee. Preregistration for classes offered. Begins over Labor Day weekend. **Policies:** "Think About It" online alcohol and sexual assault education course is required of all incoming students. **Housing:** Guaranteed on-campus for freshmen. Coed dorms, special housing for disabled, themed housing available. **Activities:** Jazz band, campus ministries, choral groups, dance, drama, film society, international student organizations, literary magazine, music ensembles, Model UN, musical theater, radio station, student government, student newspaper, TV station, Asian Student Association, Black Student Union, Hawaiian Islanders club, Mid-East Connection, Movimiento Estudiantil Chicano de Aztlan (MEChA), Transgender, Other-identified, Bisexual, Gay, Lesbian & Allies for Diversity, Students for Education Reform, Circle K, Raising Awareness for the Environment, urban agriculture club.

Athletics. NCAA. **Intercollegiate:** Baseball M, basketball, cross-country, diving, football (tackle) M, golf, lacrosse, soccer, softball W, swimming, tennis, track and field, volleyball W, water polo. **Intramural:** Basketball, softball, volleyball. **Team name:** Poets.

Student services. Career counseling, student employment services, financial aid counseling, health services, minority student services, on-campus daycare, personal counseling, placement for graduates. **Physically disabled:** Services for visually, hearing impaired.

Contact. E-mail: admission@whittier.edu
Phone: (562) 907-4238 Toll-free number: (888) 200-0369
Fax: (562) 907-4870
Kieron Miller, Director of Admission, Whittier College, 13406 East Philadelphia Street, Whittier, CA 90608-0634

William Jessup University
Rocklin, California
www.jessup.edu　　　　　　　　　　**CB code: 4756**

- Private 4-year university, Bible and liberal arts college affiliated with the nondenominational tradition
- Residential campus in small city
- 1,093 degree-seeking undergraduates: 17% part-time, 58% women, 5% African American, 4% Asian American, 19% Hispanic/Latino, 1% Native American, 1% Native Hawaiian/Pacific islander, 2% Multi-racial, non-Hispanic
- 64 degree-seeking graduate students
- 76% of applicants admitted
- SAT or ACT (ACT writing recommended) required
- 55% graduate within 6 years

General. Founded in 1939. Regionally accredited; also accredited by ABHE. **Degrees:** 267 bachelor's, 1 associate awarded; master's offered. **ROTC:** Air Force. **Location:** 25 miles from Sacramento. **Calendar:** Semester, limited summer session. **Full-time faculty:** 38 total; 76% have terminal degrees, 18% minority, 32% women. **Part-time faculty:** 162 total; 26% have terminal degrees, 18% minority, 43% women. **Class size:** 70% < 20, 29% 20-39, less than 1% 40-49, less than 1% 50-99.

Freshman class profile. 522 applied, 397 admitted, 147 enrolled.

Mid 50% test scores			
SAT critical reading:	450-580	GPA 3.0-3.49:	22%
SAT math:	440-560	GPA 2.0-2.99:	28%
SAT writing:	440-550	Rank in top quarter:	41%
ACT composite:	18-25	Rank in top tenth:	16%
GPA 3.75 or higher:	32%	Return as sophomores:	74%
GPA 3.50-3.74:	18%	Out-of-state:	7%
		Live on campus:	82%

Basis for selection. Academic records, supporting documents, moral character, willingness to comply with standards and values of university

strongly considered. Interview and personal statement/essay strongly recommended, and may be required. Audition required for music performance and theater scholarship. Portfolio required for art scholarship. **Home schooled:** Professional/third-party home educators transcript provider preferred over in-home development of transcripts. **Learning Disabled:** Once voluntarily disclosed, student is asked to provide documentation of learning disability and to meet with academic support advisor regularly.

High school preparation. College-preparatory program recommended. 16 units required; 23 recommended. Required and recommended units include English 4, mathematics 3-4, social studies 1, history 2, science 3-4 (laboratory 2), foreign language 2-3, computer science 1, visual/performing arts 2 and academic electives 1-3. Religion taken for credit at regionally accredited parochial/Christian high school may be given academic consideration.

2015-2016 Annual costs. Tuition/fees: $26,480. Room/board: $10,278. Books/supplies: $1,791. Personal expenses: $2,331.

2015-2016 Financial aid. Need-based: 140 full-time freshmen applied for aid; 126 deemed to have need; 126 received aid. Average need met was 71%. Average scholarship/grant was $19,174; average loan $3,424. 78% of total undergraduate aid awarded as scholarships/grants, 22% as loans/jobs. **Non-need-based:** Awarded to 212 full-time undergraduates, including 38 freshmen. Scholarships awarded for academics, art, athletics, leadership, minority status, music/drama, religious affiliation, state residency.

Application procedures. Admission: Priority date 4/1; deadline 8/15 (postmark date). $45 fee, may be waived for applicants with need. Admission notification on a rolling basis beginning on or about 10/1. Must reply by June 1 or by date in acceptance letter thereafter. **Financial aid:** Priority date 3/2; no closing date. FAFSA required. Applicants notified on a rolling basis starting 3/2; must reply within 3 week(s) of notification.

Academics. All church vocation/ministry-based degrees offer dual major in Bible & Theology. Emphasis placed on pastoral training, missions, youth ministry, and family & children ministry. **Special study options:** Accelerated study, distance learning, double major, dual enrollment of high school students, independent study, internships, study abroad, teacher certification program, urban semester, Washington semester. School of Professional Studies (adult degree completion program). **Credit/placement by examination:** AP, CLEP, IB, SAT, ACT, institutional tests. 16 credit hours maximum toward associate degree, 16 toward bachelor's. A maximum of 30 units will be awarded for AP, IB, or CLEP. **Support services:** Learning center, reduced course load, study skills assistance, tutoring, writing center.

Majors. Biology: General. **Business:** Business admin. **Computer sciences:** General. **Conservation:** Environmental science. **Education:** Elementary. **English:** English lit. **History:** General. **Math:** General. **Parks/recreation:** Exercise sciences. **Psychology:** General. **Theology:** Bible, theology, youth ministry. **Visual/performing arts:** Music.

Most popular majors. Business/marketing 24%, education 10%, English 7%, psychology 32%, theological studies 16%.

Technology on campus. 53 workstations in library, computer center. Dormitories wired for high-speed internet access and linked to campus network. Commuter students can connect to campus network. Online course registration, online library, helpline, repair service, wireless network available.

Student life. Freshman orientation: Mandatory. Preregistration for classes offered. 4-day program leading up to first day of classes in August. **Policies:** Dry campus. Quiet hours, but no curfew. No formal dress code, but appropriate dress recommended. Chapel attendance required. Religious observance required. **Housing:** Guaranteed on-campus for freshmen. Single-sex dorms, apartments available. **Activities:** Jazz band, campus ministries, choral groups, drama, literary magazine, music ensembles, musical theater, student government, symphony orchestra, spiritual formation groups, chapel services.

Athletics. NAIA. **Intercollegiate:** Baseball M, basketball, cross-country, golf M, soccer, softball W, track and field, volleyball W. **Intramural:** Basketball, soccer, ultimate frisbee, volleyball. **Team name:** Warriors.

Student services. Adult student services, alcohol/substance abuse counseling, chaplain/spiritual director, career counseling, student employment services, financial aid counseling, health services, personal counseling, placement for graduates. **Physically disabled:** Services for visually, hearing impaired.

Contact. E-mail: admissions@jessup.edu
Phone: (916) 577-2222 Fax: (916) 577-2220
Vance Pascua, Dean of Admission & Financial Aid, William Jessup University, 2121 University Ave, Rocklin, CA 95765

Woodbury University
Burbank, California
www.woodbury.edu

CB member
CB code: 4955

- Private 4-year university
- Commuter campus in very large city
- 1,245 degree-seeking undergraduates: 13% part-time, 49% women, 4% African American, 10% Asian American, 27% Hispanic/Latino, 25% international
- 212 degree-seeking graduate students
- 58% of applicants admitted
- SAT or ACT (ACT writing optional), application essay required
- 46% graduate within 6 years

General. Founded in 1884. Regionally accredited. **Degrees:** 318 bachelor's awarded; master's offered. **Location:** 15 miles from downtown Los Angeles. **Calendar:** Semester, limited summer session. **Full-time faculty:** 86 total; 74% have terminal degrees, 16% minority, 44% women. **Part-time faculty:** 212 total; 27% have terminal degrees, 16% minority, 41% women. **Class size:** 82% < 20, 18% 20-39. **Special facilities:** Design galleries, screening room, sound stage.

Freshman class profile. 1,342 applied, 773 admitted, 117 enrolled.

Mid 50% test scores			
SAT critical reading:	430-540	Return as sophomores:	82%
SAT math:	430-520	Out-of-state:	14%
ACT composite:	16-21	Live on campus:	56%
GPA 3.75 or higher:	19%	International:	21%
GPA 3.50-3.74:	18%	Fraternities:	18%
GPA 3.0-3.49:	45%	Sororities:	16%
GPA 2.0-2.99:	18%		

Basis for selection. Primary emphasis placed on applicant's prior academic record and standardized test scores. Interview recommended. **Home schooled:** State high school equivalency certificate required.

High school preparation. College-preparatory program recommended. 23 units recommended. Recommended units include English 4, mathematics 4, social studies 2, history 2, science 4 (laboratory 1), foreign language 2, computer science 1, visual/performing arts 1 and academic electives 2.

2015-2016 Annual costs. Tuition/fees: $36,408. Room/board: $10,668.

2015-2016 Financial aid. Need-based: 115 full-time freshmen applied for aid; 106 deemed to have need; 105 received aid. Average need met was 53%. Average scholarship/grant was $19,891; average loan $3,605. 66% of total undergraduate aid awarded as scholarships/grants, 34% as loans/jobs. **Non-need-based:** Awarded to 121 full-time undergraduates, including 33 freshmen. Scholarships awarded for academics.

Application procedures. Admission: Priority date 3/1; no deadline. $50 fee, may be waived for applicants with need. Admission notification on a rolling basis beginning on or about 10/1. **Financial aid:** Priority date 11/15, closing date 2/1. FAFSA, institutional form, CSS PROFILE required. Applicants notified on a rolling basis starting 11/30.

Academics. Combines professional programs in design, architecture, and business with liberal arts components. **Special study options:** Double major, ESL, independent study, internships, student-designed major, study abroad. **Credit/placement by examination:** AP, CLEP, IB, institutional tests. Institutional/departmental examinations used for placement or counseling. **Support services:** Learning center, reduced course load, remedial instruction, tutoring, writing center.

Majors. Architecture: Architecture, interior. **Business:** Accounting, business admin, fashion, marketing, organizational behavior. **Communications:** Media studies. **Psychology:** General. **Visual/performing arts:** Commercial/advertising art, fashion design, graphic design.

Most popular majors. Architecture 38%, business/marketing 35%, visual/performing arts 15%.

Technology on campus. 239 workstations in library, computer center. Dormitories wired for high-speed internet access. Online library, helpline, wireless network available.

Student life. Freshman orientation: Mandatory, $75 fee. Preregistration for classes offered. **Housing:** Coed dorms available. $250 fully refundable deposit, deadline 5/1. Pets allowed in dorm rooms. Quiet study wing available. **Activities:** Film society, international student organizations, student government, Armenian Student Association, La Voz Unida.

Student services. Career counseling, student employment services, financial aid counseling, health services, personal counseling, placement for graduates. **Physically disabled:** Services for visually, speech, hearing impaired.

Contact. E-mail: admissions@woodbury.edu
Phone: (818) 767-0888 ext. 221 Toll-free number: (800) 784-9663
Fax: (818) 767-7520
Ashraf Zawaideh, Director of Admissions, Woodbury University, 7500 Glenoaks Boulevard, Burbank, CA 91504-1052

World Mission University
Los Angeles, California
www.wmu.edu

- Private 4-year Bible and seminary college affiliated with the nondenominational tradition
- Very large city
- 142 degree-seeking undergraduates

General. Accredited by ABHE. All programs taught in Korean language. **Degrees:** 19 bachelor's awarded; master's, professional offered. **Location:** Downtown. **Calendar:** Semester, limited summer session. **Full-time faculty:** 3 total. **Part-time faculty:** 5 total.

Basis for selection. Admissions criteria include sense of calling for Christian ministry, participation in church community, academic performance, test results, recommendations. Audition and additional supplementary application required for music programs. **Home schooled:** Statement describing home school structure and mission, transcript of courses and grades, letter of recommendation (nonparent) required.

2015-2016 Annual costs. Tuition/fees: $6,600. Books/supplies: $600.

Application procedures. Admission: No deadline. $100 fee. Application must be submitted on paper. Admission notification on a rolling basis.

Academics. Special study options: Distance learning, dual enrollment of high school students, ESL. **Credit/placement by examination:** AP, CLEP, IB, institutional tests.

Majors. Theology: Bible. **Visual/performing arts:** Music.

Technology on campus. Online library, wireless network available.

Student life. Freshman orientation: Mandatory. Preregistration for classes offered.

Contact. E-mail: wmuoffice@gmail.com
Phone: (213) 385-2322 Fax: (213) 385-2332
John Park, Admissions Director, World Mission University, 500 Shatto Place, Los Angeles, CA 90020

Yeshiva Ohr Elchonon Chabad/West Coast Talmudical Seminary
Los Angeles, California
yoec@yoec.edu

CB code: 1331

- Private 4-year rabbinical and seminary college for men affiliated with the Jewish faith
- Residential campus in very large city
- 160 degree-seeking undergraduates: 4% international
- 63% of applicants admitted
- Interview required

General. Founded in 1953. Accredited by AARTS. Ordination available. **Degrees:** 25 bachelor's awarded. **Calendar:** Semester, limited summer session. **Full-time faculty:** 6 total; 100% have terminal degrees. **Part-time faculty:** 4 total.

Freshman class profile. 94 applied, 59 admitted, 59 enrolled.

Out-of-state:	49%	International:	5%
Live on campus:	100%		

Basis for selection. Interview, recommendations, religious affiliation or commitment, and test scores most important. Priority given to California residents. **Home schooled:** Statement describing home school structure and mission, interview, letter of recommendation (nonparent) required.

High school preparation. Recommended units include English 3, mathematics 3, social studies 3, history 2, science 3 and foreign language 2.

2015-2016 Annual costs. Tuition/fees: $13,900. Room/board: $7,350. Books/supplies: $200. Personal expenses: $100.

Financial aid. All financial aid based on need.

Application procedures. Admission: No deadline. No application fee. Admission notification on a rolling basis. **Financial aid:** Priority date 1/15, closing date 6/30. FAFSA, institutional form required. Applicants notified by 5/1; must reply by 7/1.

Academics. Credit/placement by examination: AP, CLEP, institutional tests. 60 credit hours maximum toward bachelor's degree. For transfer students. **Support services:** Pre-admission summer program, remedial instruction, tutoring.

Majors. Theology: Religious ed, Talmudic.

Most popular majors. Liberal arts 50%, theological studies 50%.

Technology on campus. 18 workstations in dormitories, computer center.

Student life. Freshman orientation: Available. Preregistration for classes offered. **Policies:** Religious observance required. Freshmen not permitted cars on campus. **Housing:** Guaranteed on-campus for all undergraduates. $300 fully refundable deposit. **Activities:** Literary magazine, student government, student newspaper.

Student services. Chaplain/spiritual director, career counseling, services for economically disadvantaged, financial aid counseling, minority student services, personal counseling. **Physically disabled:** Services for visually, speech impaired.

Contact. E-mail: MSpalter@yoec.edu
Phone: (323) 937-3763 Fax: (323) 937-9456
Rabbi Chaim Citron, Director of Admissions, Yeshiva Ohr Elchonon Chabad/West Coast Talmudical Seminary, 7215 Waring Avenue, Los Angeles, CA 90046

Colorado

Adams State University
Alamosa, Colorado
www.adams.edu
CB code: 4001

- Public 4-year liberal arts college
- Residential campus in small town
- 2,169 degree-seeking undergraduates: 20% part-time, 47% women, 7% African American, 1% Asian American, 32% Hispanic/Latino, 1% Native American, 4% Multi-racial, non-Hispanic
- 1,279 degree-seeking graduate students
- SAT or ACT (ACT writing optional) required

General. Founded in 1921. Regionally accredited. Hispanic-serving institution. **Degrees:** 374 bachelor's, 297 associate awarded; master's, professional offered. **Location:** 225 miles from Denver; 200 miles from Albuquerque, New Mexico. **Calendar:** Semester, limited summer session. **Full-time faculty:** 113 total; 63% have terminal degrees, 23% minority, 42% women. **Part-time faculty:** 126 total; 10% have terminal degrees, 10% minority, 66% women. **Class size:** 72% < 20, 22% 20-39, 5% 40-49, 1% 50-99. **Special facilities:** Observatory, planetarium, natural history museum, geology museum.

Freshman class profile.

Mid 50% test scores			
SAT critical reading:	430-530	GPA 2.0-2.99:	35%
SAT math:	470-530	Rank in top quarter:	25%
ACT composite:	17-22	Rank in top tenth:	6%
GPA 3.75 or higher:	16%	Return as sophomores:	58%
GPA 3.50-3.74:	13%	Out-of-state:	31%
GPA 3.0-3.49:	34%	Live on campus:	80%

Basis for selection. Open admissions for associate degree programs only. Bachelor's degree candidates must have either 2.0 GPA, or rank in top two-thirds of class with average or above average score on ACT or SAT. ACCUPLACER tests for math and English required if SAT or ACT not available. Audition required of music majors. Portfolio required of art majors. **Home schooled:** Transcript of courses and grades required.

High school preparation. College-preparatory program recommended. 17 units required. Required and recommended units include English 4, mathematics 4, social studies 2, history 1, science 3 (laboratory 2), foreign language 1 and academic electives 2. Computer applications: 0.5 units recommended. Math should include Algebra I and one advanced math course.

2015-2016 Annual costs. Tuition/fees: $8,574; $19,086 out-of-state. Room/board: $7,900. Books/supplies: $1,350. Personal expenses: $1,314.

2015-2016 Financial aid. Need-based: 411 full-time freshmen applied for aid; 331 deemed to have need; 330 received aid. Average need met was 56%. Average scholarship/grant was $7,876; average loan $3,149. 69% of total undergraduate aid awarded as scholarships/grants, 31% as loans/jobs. **Non-need-based:** Scholarships awarded for academics, alumni affiliation, art, athletics, leadership, minority status, music/drama, state residency.

Application procedures. Admission: Priority date 8/1; no deadline. $30 fee, may be waived for applicants with need. Admission notification on a rolling basis. **Financial aid:** No deadline. FAFSA required. Applicants notified on a rolling basis starting 4/30.

Academics. Special study options: Accelerated study, distance learning, double major, dual enrollment of high school students, exchange student, independent study, internships, study abroad, teacher certification program, weekend college. **Credit/placement by examination:** AP, CLEP, IB, SAT, ACT, institutional tests. 15 credit hours maximum toward associate degree, 30 toward bachelor's. **Support services:** Learning center, pre-admission summer program, remedial instruction, study skills assistance, tutoring, writing center.

Majors. Biology: General, bacteriology, biochemistry, cellular/molecular, wildlife. **Business:** General, accounting, business admin, finance, international, management information systems, marketing, small business admin. **Communications:** Advertising, media studies. **Computer sciences:** Computer science. **Conservation:** Management/policy. **Education:** General, art, biology, business, chemistry, drama/dance, elementary, English, history, mathematics, middle, multi-level teacher, music, physical, science, secondary, social science, social studies, Spanish, special ed, speech. **Engineering:** Applied physics. **English:** Creative writing, English lit. **Foreign languages:** Spanish. **Health services:** Health care admin, nursing (RN), predental, premedicine, prenursing, prepharmacy, preveterinary. **History:** General. **Human services:** Social work. **Liberal arts:** Arts/sciences. **Math:** General. **Parks/recreation:** Exercise sciences, health/fitness. **Physical sciences:** Chemical physics, chemistry, geology, physics. **Psychology:** General. **Social sciences:** Criminology, economics, sociology. **Visual/performing arts:** Art, ceramics, dramatic, drawing, metal/jewelry, music, music performance, music theory/composition, painting, photography, printmaking, sculpture, studio arts, voice/opera.

Most popular majors. Business/marketing 33%, health sciences 6%, liberal arts 17%, parks/recreation 8%, psychology 6%, social sciences 11%, visual/performing arts 7%.

Technology on campus. 336 workstations in library, student center. Dormitories wired for high-speed internet access and linked to campus network. Commuter students can connect to campus network. Online course registration, online library, helpline, repair service, student web hosting, wireless network available.

Student life. Freshman orientation: Mandatory, $50 fee. Preregistration for classes offered. Program held weekend before start of semester. **Housing:** Guaranteed on-campus for freshmen. Coed dorms, single-sex dorms, apartments available. $150 partly refundable deposit. Learning community house, freshman interest-group housing, outdoor adventure community, making the grade community (must maintain 3.5 GPA). **Activities:** Bands, campus ministries, choral groups, dance, drama, international student organizations, literary magazine, music ensembles, Model UN, musical theater, radio station, student government, student newspaper, Circle K, College Republicans, Newman club, student ambassadors, teacher education association, associated students and faculty, gay straight alliance, Semillas de la Tierra, El Parnaso.

Athletics. NCAA. **Intercollegiate:** Baseball M, basketball, cross-country, football (tackle) M, golf, lacrosse, soccer, softball W, swimming, track and field, volleyball W, wrestling M. **Intramural:** Basketball, bowling, football (non-tackle), racquetball, skiing, soccer, softball, volleyball, water polo. **Team name:** Grizzlies.

Student services. Adult student services, alcohol/substance abuse counseling, chaplain/spiritual director, career counseling, services for economically disadvantaged, student employment services, financial aid counseling, health services, minority student services, on-campus daycare, personal counseling, veterans' counselor. **Physically disabled:** Services for visually, hearing impaired.

Contact. E-mail: admissions@adams.edu
Phone: (719) 587-7712 Toll-free number: (800) 824-6494
Fax: (719) 587-7522
Eric Carpio, Assistant Vice President for Enrollment Management, Adams State University, 208 Edgemont Boulevard, Alamosa, CO 81101

American Sentinel University
Aurora, Colorado
www.americansentinel.edu
CB code: 3806

- For-profit 4-year virtual university
- Commuter campus in very large city
- 1,712 undergraduates

General. Accredited by DETC. **Degrees:** 842 bachelor's, 6 associate awarded; master's, professional, doctoral offered. **Calendar:** Differs by program, extensive summer session. **Full-time faculty:** 22 total.

Basis for selection. Open admission.

Application procedures. Admission: No deadline. No application fee. Admission notification on a rolling basis. **Financial aid:** No deadline.

Academics. Special study options: Accelerated study, combined bachelor's/graduate degree, distance learning, honors, independent study, liberal arts/career combination. **Credit/placement by examination:** AP, CLEP. 45 credit hours maximum toward associate degree, 90 toward bachelor's. **Support services:** Learning center, reduced course load, study skills assistance, tutoring, writing center.

Majors. Health services: Nursing (RN).

Technology on campus. PC or laptop required.

Student life. Freshman orientation: Mandatory. Preregistration for classes offered. **Activities:** Student newspaper.

Student services. Adult student services, career counseling, financial aid counseling.

Contact. E-mail: admissions@americansentinel.edu
Toll-free number: (866) 922-5690 Fax: (866) 505-2450
Natalie Nixon, Vice President, Admissions, American Sentinel University, 2260 South Xanadu Way, Suite 310, Aurora, CO 80014

Argosy University: Denver
Denver, Colorado
www.argosy.edu/locations/denver

- For-profit 4-year university
- Very large city
- 129 degree-seeking undergraduates: 72% part-time, 72% women
- 288 graduate students

General. Degrees: 22 bachelor's, 1 associate awarded; master's, professional, doctoral offered. **Calendar:** Differs by program. **Full-time faculty:** 8 total. **Part-time faculty:** 79 total.

Basis for selection. Open admission.

2015-2016 Annual costs. Tuition/fees: $16,842. **Additional information:** Tuition indicated is for programs in the College of Arts and Sciences. College of Health Sciences programs are $575 per credit-hour.

Application procedures. Admission: Closing date 9/13. $50 fee. **Financial aid:** No deadline.

Academics. Credit/placement by examination: AP, CLEP.

Majors. Business: Business admin. **Liberal arts:** Arts/sciences. **Protective services:** Law enforcement admin. **Psychology:** General.

Contact. Phone: (303) 923-4110
Diane Rotondo, Senior Director of Admissions, Argosy University: Denver, 7600 East Eastman Avenue, Denver, CO 80231

Aspen University
Denver, Colorado
www.aspen.edu   CB code: 7359

- For-profit 4-year virtual university
- Very large city
- 231 undergraduates
- Application essay required

General. Accredited by DETC. **Degrees:** 40 bachelor's, 2 associate awarded; master's, doctoral offered. **Calendar:** Differs by program, extensive summer session. **Part-time faculty:** 91 total.

Basis for selection. Open admission, but selective for some programs. **Home schooled:** State high school equivalency certificate required.

2015-2016 Annual costs. Associate and bachelor's programs, $150 per credit hour. Required technology fee of $150 per year. Estimated cost for books and supplies is $150 per course.

Application procedures. Admission: No deadline. No application fee. Admission notification on a rolling basis. **Financial aid:** No deadline.

Academics. Special study options: Accelerated study, distance learning. **Credit/placement by examination:** AP, CLEP. **Support services:** Reduced course load, remedial instruction.

Majors. Business: Business admin, restaurant/food services. **Education:** Early childhood. **Protective services:** Law enforcement admin.

Technology on campus. PC or laptop required. Online library available.

Contact. E-mail: admissions@aspen.edu
Phone: (303) 333-4224 Toll-free number: (800) 441-4746
Fax: (303) 336-1144
Angela Siegel, Executive Vice President, Marketing & Enrollment, Aspen University, 720 South Colorado Boulevard, Suite 1150N, Denver, CO 80246

CollegeAmerica: Colorado Springs
Colorado Springs, Colorado
www.collegeamerica.edu

- Private 4-year career college
- Commuter campus in large city
- 430 undergraduates
- Application essay, interview required

General. Accredited by ACCSC. **Degrees:** 22 bachelor's, 82 associate awarded. **Calendar:** Differs by program. **Full-time faculty:** 11 total. **Class size:** 14% < 20, 71% 20-39, 14% 40-49. **Special facilities:** Computer labs.

Basis for selection. Open admission. **Home schooled:** Transcript of courses and grades required.

2015-2016 Annual costs. Tuition varies by program. Associate's programs range from $34,390 to $48,251 for the complete program. Bachelor's programs range from $55,800 to $74,753 for the complete program.

Application procedures. Admission: No deadline. No application fee. Admission notification on a rolling basis. **Financial aid:** No deadline. FAFSA, institutional form required.

Academics. Special study options: Combined bachelor's/graduate degree, distance learning. **Credit/placement by examination:** AP, CLEP. **Support services:** Tutoring.

Majors. Business: Accounting, business admin. **Computer sciences:** Computer graphics, computer science. **Health services:** Health care admin.

Technology on campus. 25 workstations in library, computer center. Online library, wireless network available.

Student life. Freshman orientation: Mandatory. Preregistration for classes offered.

Student services. Placement for graduates.

Contact. E-mail: crenya@collegeamerica.edu
Phone: (719) 637-0600 Toll-free number: (800) 622-2894
Kiersten Murdoch, Director of Admissions, CollegeAmerica: Colorado Springs, 3645 Citadel Drive South, Colorado Springs, CO 80909

CollegeAmerica: Fort Collins
Fort Collins, Colorado
www.collegeamerica.edu

- Private 4-year health science and technical college
- Commuter campus in small city
- 230 undergraduates

General. Accredited by ACCSC. **Degrees:** 6 bachelor's, 30 associate awarded. **Calendar:** Differs by program, extensive summer session. **Full-time faculty:** 5 total. **Part-time faculty:** 14 total.

Basis for selection. Open admission. **Home schooled:** Transcript of courses and grades required.

2015-2016 Annual costs. Tuition varies by program. Associate's programs range from $34,390 to $48,251 for the complete program. Bachelor's programs range from $55,800 to $74,753 for the complete program.

Application procedures. Admission: No deadline. No application fee. **Financial aid:** No deadline.

Academics. Special study options: Accelerated study, combined bachelor's/graduate degree, distance learning, independent study. **Credit/placement by examination:** AP, CLEP. **Support services:** Learning center, remedial instruction, study skills assistance, tutoring.

Majors. Business: General, accounting. **Computer sciences:** General.

Technology on campus. 50 workstations in library, computer center, student center. Online library, helpline, repair service, wireless network available.

Student life. Freshman orientation: Mandatory. Preregistration for classes offered. **Activities:** Student government.

Student services. Adult student services, career counseling, services for economically disadvantaged, student employment services, financial aid counseling, personal counseling, placement for graduates, veterans' counselor.

Contact. Phone: (970) 223-6060 Toll-free number: (800) 622-2894 Kristy McNear, Director of Admissions, CollegeAmerica: Fort Collins, 4601 South Mason Street, Fort Collins, CO 80525

Colorado Christian University
Lakewood, Colorado — CB member
www.ccu.edu — CB code: 4659

- Private 4-year university and liberal arts college affiliated with the non-denominational tradition
- Residential campus in large city
- 3,862 degree-seeking undergraduates
- SAT or ACT (ACT writing optional), application essay required

General. Founded in 1914. Regionally accredited. Adult and graduate programs available online and at Colorado Springs, Grand Junction, Loveland, Northglenn, Sterling, Denver (multiple locations), and Lakewood campuses. **Degrees:** 605 bachelor's, 71 associate awarded; master's offered. **ROTC:** Army, Air Force. **Location:** 10 miles from Denver. **Calendar:** Semester, extensive summer session.

Freshman class profile.

GPA 3.75 or higher:	43%	GPA 2.0-2.99:	12%
GPA 3.50-3.74:	20%	Rank in top quarter:	49%
GPA 3.0-3.49:	25%	Rank in top tenth:	21%

Basis for selection. Traditional undergraduate applicants should exemplify vital Christian experience. Decisions based on high academic ability, personal integrity, and desire for Christ-centered community. Applicant's course selection, academic performance, test scores, essays, spiritual recommendation, activities, and work experience carefully considered. Audition required of music and theater majors.

High school preparation. College-preparatory program recommended. 19 units recommended. Recommended units include English 4, mathematics 3, social studies 3, history 2, science 2 (laboratory 2) and foreign language 2. Recommend 1 unit of computer science.

2015-2016 Annual costs. Tuition/fees: $27,986. Room/board: $10,580. Books/supplies: $1,000. Personal expenses: $797.

Financial aid. **Non-need-based:** Scholarships awarded for academics, athletics, leadership, music/drama.

Application procedures. Admission: Priority date 3/1; deadline 9/1 (receipt date). $30 fee, may be waived for applicants with need. Application must be submitted online. Admission notification on a rolling basis beginning on or about 11/1. **Financial aid:** Priority date 3/15; no closing date. FAFSA required. Applicants notified on a rolling basis starting 4/1; must reply by 5/1 or within 4 week(s) of notification.

Academics. Special study options: Accelerated study, combined bachelor's/graduate degree, cooperative education, distance learning, double major, dual enrollment of high school students, honors, independent study, internships, semester at sea, student-designed major, study abroad, teacher certification program, urban semester, Washington semester, weekend college. American studies program (Washington, DC), host university for Institute for Family Studies; China studies program at various sites in China, Latin American program (Costa Rica), Los Angeles film studies center, Middle East studies (Cairo, Egypt), Oxford honors program (University of Oxford, England), Russian studies program at various sites in Russia, Summer Institute of Journalism (Washington, DC). **Credit/placement by examination:** AP, CLEP, IB, SAT, ACT, institutional tests. 15 credit hours maximum toward associate degree, 45 toward bachelor's. **Support services:** Learning center, reduced course load, remedial instruction, study skills assistance, tutoring, writing center.

Majors. Biology: General. **Business:** Accounting, business admin, human resources, management information systems, management science, organizational behavior. **Communications:** Communications/speech/rhetoric. **Computer sciences:** General. **Education:** General, adult/continuing, early childhood, elementary, English, history, mathematics, music, science, secondary. **English:** English lit. **Health services:** Health care admin, nursing (RN). **History:** General. **Liberal arts:** Arts/sciences. **Math:** General. **Protective services:** Law enforcement admin. **Psychology:** General, psychobiology. **Social sciences:** General. **Theology:** Bible, sacred music, theology, youth ministry. **Visual/performing arts:** Music, music performance, studio arts.

Most popular majors. Business/marketing 43%, education 17%, psychology 9%, theological studies 6%.

Technology on campus. 186 workstations in dormitories, library, computer center, student center. Dormitories wired for high-speed internet access and linked to campus network. Commuter students can connect to campus network. Online course registration, online library, helpline, wireless network available.

Student life. Freshman orientation: Mandatory. Preregistration for classes offered. Seminars for students and parents held 4 days prior to beginning of classes. **Policies:** Use of alcoholic beverages, illegal drugs, and tobacco prohibited on campus and at college-sponsored activities. Premarital sexual relationships prohibited. Religious observance required. **Housing:** Guaranteed on-campus for freshmen. Coed dorms, single-sex dorms, special housing for disabled, apartments, themed housing, wellness housing available. $200 nonrefundable deposit, deadline 9/1. **Activities:** Bands, campus ministries, choral groups, drama, literary magazine, music ensembles, musical theater, student government, student newspaper, symphony orchestra, world missions, discipleship groups, Fat Boys, Footprints, prayer ministry, refugee family ministry, SALT, Snappers, Westside.

Athletics. NCAA, NCCAA. **Intercollegiate:** Baseball M, basketball, cross-country, golf, soccer, softball W, tennis, volleyball W. **Intramural:** Basketball, football (non-tackle), soccer, softball, tennis, volleyball. **Team name:** Cougars.

Student services. Adult student services, chaplain/spiritual director, career counseling, student employment services, financial aid counseling, health services, personal counseling, placement for graduates, veterans' counselor. **Physically disabled:** Services for visually, speech, hearing impaired.

Contact. E-mail: admissions@ccu.edu
Phone: (303) 963-3200 Toll-free number: (800) 443-2484
Fax: (303) 963-3201
Derry Ebert, Dean of Enrollment, Colorado Christian University, 8787 West Alameda Avenue, Lakewood, CO 80226

Colorado College
Colorado Springs, Colorado — CB member
www.coloradocollege.edu — CB code: 4072

- Private 4-year liberal arts college
- Residential campus in large city
- 2,096 degree-seeking undergraduates: 54% women, 3% African American, 5% Asian American, 9% Hispanic/Latino, 9% Multi-racial, non-Hispanic, 7% international
- 11 degree-seeking graduate students
- 17% of applicants admitted
- Application essay required
- 87% graduate within 6 years

General. Founded in 1874. Regionally accredited. Block Plan allows students to take a different subject every three and a half weeks rather than balancing several throughout a semester. Students take one course at a time with each block covering the same amount of material as a semester system. Mountain cabin located about 35 minutes from campus for class and retreat use. Baca campus in Southern Colorado available for intensive study. **Degrees:** 513 bachelor's awarded; master's offered. **ROTC:** Army. **Location:** 70 miles from Denver. **Calendar:** Semester, extensive summer session. **Full-time faculty:** 181 total; 99% have terminal degrees, 23% minority, 46% women. **Part-time faculty:** 31 total. **Class size:** 71% < 20, 29% 20-39, less than 1% 40-49. **Special facilities:** Electronic music studio, telescope dome, multimedia computer lab, press, herbarium, environmental science van equipped for field research, petrographic microscopes, X-ray diffractometer, Fourier transform nuclear magnetic resonance spectrometer, sedimentology lab, metabolic equipment, hydrostatic weighing equipment, cadaver study in sports science, scanning electron microscope, transmission electron microscope.

Freshman class profile. 8,060 applied, 1,381 admitted, 583 enrolled.

Mid 50% test scores			
		Rank in top tenth:	68%
SAT critical reading:	630-710	Return as sophomores:	96%
SAT math:	620-710	Out-of-state:	85%
SAT writing:	620-700	Live on campus:	100%
ACT composite:	28-32	International:	8%
Rank in top quarter:	91%		

Basis for selection. Personal essays, school achievement record most important. Counselor and teacher recommendations, extracurricular activities and test scores also important. Special talents, cultural, socioeconomic, ethnic diversity considered. Challenging curriculum, including honors, AP, IB, recommended when available. Institutional exams used for placement in foreign languages. College has a flexible testing policy. SAT or ACT or 3 exams of student's choice required. Choice of exams must include one quantitative test, one verbal or writing test, and a third test of the student's choice; required exams selected from SAT and/or ACT subsections, Advanced Placement exams, SAT Subject Tests, and/or International Baccalaureate exams. Interview optional. **Home schooled:** Letter of recommendation (nonparent) required. Three letters of recommendation from outside the family required. Reading lists, curriculum information, teacher narratives about courses of study, and copies of papers or projects can be used in place of traditional transcript.

High school preparation. College-preparatory program recommended. 16 units required; 20 recommended. Required and recommended units include English 4.

2015-2016 Annual costs. Tuition/fees: $48,996. Room/board: $11,215. Books/supplies: $1,248. Personal expenses: $1,405.

2015-2016 Financial aid. Need-based: 290 full-time freshmen applied for aid; 226 deemed to have need; 226 received aid. Average need met was 100%. Average scholarship/grant was $45,232; average loan $2,563. 91% of total undergraduate aid awarded as scholarships/grants, 9% as loans/jobs. **Non-need-based:** Awarded to 339 full-time undergraduates, including 129 freshmen. Scholarships awarded for academics, athletics, leadership.

Application procedures. Admission: Closing date 1/15 (postmark date). $60 fee, may be waived for applicants with need. Admission notification by 4/1. Must reply by May 1 or within 2 week(s) if notified thereafter. Campus visit recommended. **Financial aid:** Closing date 2/15. FAFSA, CSS PROFILE required. Applicants notified by 3/15; must reply by 5/1.

Academics. Special study options: Combined bachelor's/graduate degree, double major, ESL, independent study, internships, liberal arts/career combination, semester at sea, student-designed major, study abroad, teacher certification program, urban semester, Washington semester. Teacher licensure program, urban studies, urban arts and urban education (Chicago); science semester (Oak Ridge, Tennessee); tropical field research (Costa Rica); wilderness field station (Wisconsin); ACM London-Florence program; ACM program in Tanzania and Zimbabwe. **Credit/placement by examination:** AP, CLEP, IB, institutional tests. 8 credit hours maximum toward bachelor's degree. Credit awarded for approved Advanced Placement tests (AP), International Baccalaureate (IB) work and college courses. No credit is awarded for CLEP tests. Advanced standing credit can be used to satisfy general education requirements where appropriate, to satisfy major requirements where the department allows, and to accelerate graduation. The college will award up to eight total units (sophomore standing) in transfer credit to students whose scores meet the criteria. **Support services:** Learning center, preadmission summer program, study skills assistance, tutoring, writing center. ESL adjunct courses.

Majors. Area/ethnic studies: Asian, Chicano/Hispanic-American/Latino, French, Italian, regional, Russian/Slavic, women's. **Biology:** Biochemistry, cellular/molecular, ecology/evolutionary, neuroscience. **Computer sciences:** Computer science. **Conservation:** Environmental science, environmental studies. **Education:** General. **English:** Creative writing, English lit. **Foreign languages:** Classics, comparative lit, French, German, Italian, Russian, Spanish. **History:** General. **Liberal arts:** Arts/sciences. **Math:** General. **Philosophy/religion:** Philosophy, religion. **Physical sciences:** Chemistry, geology, physics. **Psychology:** General. **Social sciences:** Anthropology, econometrics, economics, international economics, political science, sociology. **Visual/performing arts:** Art history/conservation, dance, dramatic, film/cinema/video, music, studio arts.

Most popular majors. Biology 14%, English 6%, natural resources/environmental science 8%, physical sciences 8%, social sciences 30%, visual/performing arts 7%.

Technology on campus. 400 workstations in dormitories, library, computer center, student center. Dormitories wired for high-speed internet access and linked to campus network. Commuter students can connect to campus network. Online course registration, helpline, repair service, wireless network available.

Student life. Freshman orientation: Mandatory. Preregistration for classes offered. One-week program held prior to beginning of fall classes; includes service trip. Parents welcome for first 3 days. **Policies:** Fish/crustaceans that live in water at all times are the only pets permitted in dorm rooms. Exceptions made for service animals. Freshmen not permitted cars on campus. **Housing:** Guaranteed on-campus for all undergraduates. Coed dorms, single-sex dorms, apartments, fraternity/sorority housing, themed housing, wellness housing available. Pets allowed in dorm rooms. College-owned cottages available; Greek housing available for fraternities only. **Activities:** Bands, campus ministries, choral groups, dance, drama, film

society, international student organizations, literary magazine, music ensembles, musical theater, opera, radio station, student government, student newspaper, symphony orchestra, Asian American students union, black student union, Chaverim/Hillel, gay/lesbian/bisexual alliance, environmental action, chapel council, Chicano/Latino organization, victim's assistance team.

Athletics. NCAA. **Intercollegiate:** Basketball, cross-country, ice hockey M, lacrosse, soccer, swimming, tennis, track and field, volleyball W. **Intramural:** Basketball, football (non-tackle), ice hockey, soccer, softball, squash, ultimate frisbee, volleyball, water polo. **Team name:** Tigers.

Student services. Alcohol/substance abuse counseling, chaplain/spiritual director, career counseling, financial aid counseling, health services, minority student services, on-campus daycare, personal counseling, women's services. **Physically disabled:** Services for visually, speech, hearing impaired.

Contact. E-mail: admission@coloradocollege.edu
Phone: (719) 389-6344 Toll-free number: (800) 542-7214
Fax: (719) 389-6816
Carlos Jiminez, Director of Admission, Outreach & Recruitment, Colorado College, 14 East Cache La Poudre Street, Colorado Springs, CO 80903-9854

Colorado Heights University
Denver, Colorado
www.chu.edu   CB code: 4878

▸ Private 4-year business and liberal arts college
▸ Residential campus in very large city
▸ 107 degree-seeking undergraduates
▸ Application essay required

General. Accredited by ACICS. Member of the Teikyo University Group of 50 campuses in Asia, Europe, and North America; all students complete part of their studies abroad. **Degrees:** 16 bachelor's awarded; master's offered. **Calendar:** Semester, limited summer session. **Full-time faculty:** 1 total. **Part-time faculty:** 32 total.

Basis for selection. 18 ACT/720 SAT and 2.5 GPA required. Provisional admission may be granted to students who do not meet requirements.

2015-2016 Annual costs. Tuition/fees: $8,796. Room only: $1,750. Books/supplies: $305. Personal expenses: $1,384.

Financial aid. All financial aid based on need.

Application procedures. Admission: No deadline. $50 fee, may be waived for applicants with need, free for online applicants. Admission notification on a rolling basis. **Financial aid:** No deadline. FAFSA required. Applicants notified on a rolling basis.

Academics. Special study options: Combined bachelor's/graduate degree, double major, dual enrollment of high school students, ESL, independent study, internships, liberal arts/career combination, study abroad. **Credit/placement by examination:** AP, CLEP, IB.

Majors. Business: International.

Technology on campus. PC or laptop required. Dormitories wired for high-speed internet access and linked to campus network. Online library available.

Student life. Freshman orientation: Available. Preregistration for classes offered. **Policies:** Students under 21 required to live in dorms; exceptions may be made if living with a family member and for those who live on-campus for 1 year and then meet the waiver requirements to move off-campus. **Housing:** Guaranteed on-campus for all undergraduates. Coed dorms available. $230 nonrefundable deposit.

Athletics. Team name: Voyagers.

Student services. Career counseling, student employment services, financial aid counseling, placement for graduates.

Contact. E-mail: admissions@chu.edu
Phone: (303) 937-4280 Fax: (303) 937-4224
Jason Johnson, Assistant Director of Recruiting, Colorado Heights University, 3001 South Federal Boulevard, Denver, CO 80236

Colorado Mesa University
Grand Junction, Colorado
www.coloradomesa.edu   **CB code: 4484**

▶ Public 4-year community and liberal arts college

▶ Commuter campus in small city

▶ 8,628 degree-seeking undergraduates: 17% part-time, 53% women, 3% African American, 2% Asian American, 17% Hispanic/Latino, 1% Native American, 1% Native Hawaiian/Pacific islander, 4% Multi-racial, non-Hispanic, 1% international

▶ 151 degree-seeking graduate students

▶ 83% of applicants admitted

▶ SAT or ACT (ACT writing optional) required

▶ 37% graduate within 6 years

General. Founded in 1925. Regionally accredited. **Degrees:** 974 bachelor's, 246 associate awarded; master's, professional offered. **Location:** 250 miles from Denver, 300 miles from Salt Lake City. **Calendar:** Semester, limited summer session. **Full-time faculty:** 236 total. **Part-time faculty:** 303 total. **Class size:** 46% < 20, 42% 20-39, 5% 40-49, 6% 50-99, less than 1% >100. **Special facilities:** Electron microscope laboratory, herbarium, computer-aided drafting laboratory, technical training facility, environmental restoration laboratory.

Freshman class profile. 6,667 applied, 5,538 admitted, 2,120 enrolled.

Mid 50% test scores		GPA 2.0-2.99:	40%
SAT critical reading:	430-540	Rank in top quarter:	26%
SAT math:	430-540	Rank in top tenth:	10%
ACT composite:	17-23	Return as sophomores:	70%
GPA 3.75 or higher:	18%	Out-of-state:	17%
GPA 3.50-3.74:	11%	Live on campus:	62%
GPA 3.0-3.49:	27%	International:	1%

Basis for selection. GPA, ACT/SAT, class rank and satisfaction of HEAR requirements. Open admissions to most technical, associates and certificate programs. Audition required of music, music theater, and theater majors. Interview recommended for nursing, allied health, teacher certification majors. **Home schooled:** Statement describing home school structure and mission, transcript of courses and grades required.

High school preparation. College-preparatory program recommended. 17 units required. Required units include English 4, mathematics 4, social studies 2, history 1, science 3 (laboratory 2), foreign language 1 and academic electives 2.

2015-2016 Annual costs. Tuition/fees: $8,008; $19,363 out-of-state. Room/board: $10,526. Books/supplies: $1,200. Personal expenses: $1,330.

Financial aid. Non-need-based: Scholarships awarded for academics, alumni affiliation, art, athletics, leadership, music/drama.

Application procedures. Admission: No deadline. $30 fee, may be waived for applicants with need. Admission notification on a rolling basis beginning on or about 9/1. **Financial aid:** No deadline. FAFSA required. Applicants notified on a rolling basis starting 4/1; must reply within 2 week(s) of notification.

Academics. Special study options: Accelerated study, combined bachelor's/graduate degree, distance learning, double major, dual enrollment of high school students, exchange student, honors, independent study, internships, study abroad, teacher certification program. Area vocational school provides training in technical skills. **Credit/placement by examination:** AP, CLEP, IB, SAT, ACT, institutional tests. 12 credit hours maximum toward associate degree, 20 toward bachelor's. **Support services:** Learning center, pre-admission summer program, reduced course load, remedial instruction, study skills assistance, tutoring, writing center.

Majors. Biology: General. **Business:** General, accounting, hospitality admin, management information systems. **Communications:** Media studies. **Computer sciences:** General. **Conservation:** Environmental science. **English:** English lit. **Foreign languages:** Spanish. **Health services:** Athletic training, nursing (RN), radiologic technology/medical imaging. **History:** General. **Human services:** General, social work. **Liberal arts:** Arts/sciences. **Math:** General. **Parks/recreation:** Exercise sciences, sports admin. **Physical sciences:** General, chemistry, geology, physics. **Protective services:** Criminal justice, police science. **Psychology:** General. **Social sciences:** General, political science, sociology. **Visual/performing arts:** Art, dramatic, graphic design, music.

Most popular majors. Biology 6%, business/marketing 17%, health sciences 13%, parks/recreation 15%, psychology 6%, security/protective services 8%, visual/performing arts 7%.

Technology on campus. 625 workstations in dormitories, library, computer center, student center. Dormitories wired for high-speed internet access and linked to campus network. Commuter students can connect to campus network. Online course registration, online library, helpline, student web hosting, wireless network available.

Student life. Freshman orientation: Available, $15 fee. Preregistration for classes offered. **Housing:** Guaranteed on-campus for freshmen. Coed dorms, special housing for disabled, apartments, wellness housing available. $150 partly refundable deposit. **Activities:** Bands, campus ministries, choral groups, dance, drama, international student organizations, literary magazine, music ensembles, musical theater, radio station, student government, student newspaper, symphony orchestra, TV station, black student alliance, La Raza, Christian student fellowship, Native American student council, Polynesian club, cultural diversity board, dance society, drama society, sustainability council.

Athletics. NCAA. **Intercollegiate:** Baseball M, basketball, cross-country, football (tackle) M, golf, lacrosse, sand volleyball W, soccer, softball W, swimming, tennis, track and field, volleyball W, wrestling M. **Intramural:** Basketball, football (non-tackle), soccer, softball, volleyball. **Team name:** Mavericks.

Student services. Adult student services, alcohol/substance abuse counseling, chaplain/spiritual director, career counseling, services for economically disadvantaged, student employment services, financial aid counseling, health services, minority student services, on-campus daycare, personal counseling, veterans' counselor. **Physically disabled:** Services for visually, speech, hearing impaired.

Contact. E-mail: admissions@coloradomesa.edu
Phone: (970) 248-1875 Toll-free number: (800) 982-6372
Fax: (970) 248-1973
Jared Meier, Director of Admissions, Colorado Mesa University, 1100 North Avenue, Grand Junction, CO 81501-3122

Colorado School of Mines
Golden, Colorado   **CB member**
www.mines.edu   **CB code: 4073**

▶ Public 4-year university and engineering college

▶ Residential campus in large town

▶ 4,533 degree-seeking undergraduates: 4% part-time, 28% women, 1% African American, 5% Asian American, 7% Hispanic/Latino, 5% Multi-racial, non-Hispanic, 6% international

▶ 1,261 degree-seeking graduate students

▶ 38% of applicants admitted

▶ SAT or ACT (ACT writing recommended) required

▶ 77% graduate within 6 years; 19% enter graduate study

General. Founded in 1874. Regionally accredited. **Degrees:** 917 bachelor's awarded; master's, doctoral offered. **ROTC:** Army, Air Force. **Location:** 20 miles from Denver. **Calendar:** Semester, limited summer session. **Full-time faculty:** 278 total; 84% have terminal degrees, 18% minority, 27% women. **Part-time faculty:** 238 total; 13% have terminal degrees, 12% minority, 36% women. **Class size:** 25% < 20, 45% 20-39, 9% 40-49, 15% 50-99, 6% >100. **Special facilities:** Geology museum, Colorado Geological Survey, U.S. Geological Survey (USGS) and earthquake center, experimental mine, graduate research laboratory, center for technology and learning media.

Freshman class profile. 11,752 applied, 4,427 admitted, 1,003 enrolled.

Mid 50% test scores		Rank in top tenth:	56%
SAT critical reading:	600-690	End year in good standing:	99%
SAT math:	650-730	Return as sophomores:	94%
SAT writing:	560-650	Out-of-state:	46%
ACT composite:	28-32	Live on campus:	93%
GPA 3.75 or higher:	66%	International:	5%
GPA 3.50-3.74:	25%	Fraternities:	16%
GPA 3.0-3.49:	9%	Sororities:	35%
Rank in top quarter:	90%		

Basis for selection. Applicants should rank in upper quartile of class. Both test scores and academic record considered. Rigor of coursework and strong and consistent results in all coursework important. Admission is competitive. Applicants encouraged to apply early in fall of senior year and take ACT and/or SAT by September or October of senior year. All ACT and SAT exam results must be submitted by Feb. 1 for consideration in merit scholarship review. **Home schooled:** Transcript of courses and grades required. More weight given to SAT/ACT. Students must complete the same level of course rigor including science requirements with laboratory.

High school preparation. College-preparatory program required. 17 units required. Required units include English 4, mathematics 4, social studies 3, science 3 (laboratory 3), foreign language 1 and academic electives 2. Math units should include at a minimum 2 algebra, 1 geometry, 1 advanced math (including trigonometry). Science units should include 1 chemistry and/or physics with laboratory. Where available, it is highly recommended that students take both chemistry and physics.

2015-2016 Annual costs. Tuition/fees: $17,353; $34,828 out-of-state. Room/board: $11,008. Books/supplies: $1,500. Personal expenses: $1,215.

2014-2015 Financial aid. Need-based: 829 full-time freshmen applied for aid; 522 deemed to have need; 522 received aid. Average need met was 62%. Average scholarship/grant was $4,347; average loan $3,599. 51% of total undergraduate aid awarded as scholarships/grants, 49% as loans/jobs. **Non-need-based:** Awarded to 2,822 full-time undergraduates, including 778 freshmen. Scholarships awarded for academics, alumni affiliation, athletics, music/drama, ROTC.

Application procedures. Admission: Priority date 11/15; deadline 3/1 (receipt date). $45 fee, may be waived for applicants with need, free for online applicants. Admission notification on a rolling basis beginning on or about 10/1. Must reply by May 1 or within 2 week(s) if notified thereafter. Submission and completion of admission application early in fall of senior year (early September to mid-November) is very important as admissions waiting list is frequently activated early in the new year. **Financial aid:** Priority date 3/1, closing date 10/1. FAFSA required. Applicants notified by 3/15; Applicants notified on a rolling basis starting 3/1; must reply by 5/1.

Academics. Curriculum and research program geared towards responsible stewardship of the earth and its resources; broad expertise in resource exploration, extraction, production and utilization. **Special study options:** Combined bachelor's/graduate degree, cooperative education, double major, dual enrollment of high school students, honors, independent study, internships, study abroad, teacher certification program. Teacher certification is in collaboration with University of Northern Colorado. **Credit/placement by examination:** AP, CLEP, IB, institutional tests. Students who receive qualifying exam results on some AP and IB exams will be invited to take challenge exams in some core freshman coursework. **Support services:** Pre-admission summer program, reduced course load, study skills assistance, tutoring, writing center. Center for Academic Services and Advising (CASA) connects student with the tools they need to be successful by providing a variety of academic support and advising services, most of which are free to Mines students.

Majors. Computer sciences: Computer science. **Conservation:** Environmental science. **Engineering:** General, applied physics, biochemical, chemical, civil, electrical, environmental, geological, mechanical, metallurgical, mining, petroleum. **Math:** Applied, probability, statistics. **Physical sciences:** Chemistry, geology, geophysics, physics. **Social sciences:** Economics.

Most popular majors. Engineering/engineering technologies 87%.

Technology on campus. 525 workstations in dormitories, library, computer center, student center. Dormitories wired for high-speed internet access and linked to campus network. Commuter students can connect to campus network. Online course registration, online library, helpline, student web hosting, wireless network available.

Student life. Freshman orientation: Mandatory, $150 fee. Preregistration for classes offered. Held weekend prior to start of fall semester; optional parent/student summer orientation offered early in summer. **Policies:** First-year students required to live on campus for first two semesters. **Housing:** Guaranteed on-campus for freshmen. Coed dorms, apartments, fraternity/sorority housing, gender-neutral housing, themed housing, wellness housing available. **Activities:** Bands, campus ministries, choral groups, dance, drama, international student organizations, literary magazine, music ensembles, musical theater, radio station, student government, student newspaper, symphony orchestra, Society of Women Engineers, American Indian Science and Engineering Society, Professional Asian Society of Engineers and Scientists, National Society of Black Engineers, Society of Hispanic Professional Engineers, Blue Key, Alpha Phi Omega, Circle K International, Engineers Without Borders.

Athletics. NCAA. **Intercollegiate:** Baseball M, basketball, cross-country, diving, football (tackle) M, golf M, soccer, softball W, swimming, track and field, volleyball W, wrestling M. **Intramural:** Badminton, basketball, bowling, cross-country, diving, equestrian, field hockey, football (non-tackle), golf, handball, lacrosse, racquetball, rugby M, skiing, soccer, softball, swimming, table tennis, tennis, track and field, ultimate frisbee, volleyball, water polo, wrestling M. **Team name:** Orediggers.

Student services. Alcohol/substance abuse counseling, career counseling, student employment services, financial aid counseling, health services, minority student services, personal counseling, placement for graduates, veterans' counselor, women's services. **Physically disabled:** Services for visually, hearing impaired.

Contact. E-mail: admit@mines.edu
Phone: (303) 273-3220 Toll-free number: (888) 446-9489
Fax: (303) 273-3509
Director of Admissions, Colorado School of Mines, Undergraduate Admissions Office, Golden, CO 80401-6114

Colorado State University
Fort Collins, Colorado   CB member
www.colostate.edu   CB code: 4075

- Public 4-year university
- Residential campus in small city
- 23,009 degree-seeking undergraduates: 7% part-time, 51% women, 2% African American, 2% Asian American, 11% Hispanic/Latino, 1% Native American, 2% Multi-racial, non-Hispanic, 4% international
- 4,557 degree-seeking graduate students
- 81% of applicants admitted
- SAT or ACT (ACT writing optional), application essay required
- 68% graduate within 6 years; 21% enter graduate study

General. Founded in 1870. Regionally accredited. Colorado State University is a Land Grant University, one of 68 land-grant colleges established under the Morrill Act of 1862. **Degrees:** 5,049 bachelor's awarded; master's, professional, doctoral offered. **ROTC:** Army, Air Force. **Location:** 65 miles from Denver. **Calendar:** Semester, extensive summer session. **Full-time faculty:** 1,009 total; 100% have terminal degrees, 17% minority, 37% women. **Part-time faculty:** 19 total; 100% have terminal degrees, 5% minority, 16% women. **Class size:** 35% < 20, 38% 20-39, 8% 40-49, 11% 50-99, 8% >100. **Special facilities:** Concert hall, thrust theater, music hall, art museum, engineering research center, equine center, veterinary teaching hospital, environmental learning center, plant environmental research center, behavioral science building.

Freshman class profile. 18,556 applied, 14,997 admitted, 4,737 enrolled.

Mid 50% test scores		
SAT critical reading:	520-620	
SAT math:	520-630	
ACT composite:	22-28	
GPA 3.75 or higher:	38%	
GPA 3.50-3.74:	23%	
GPA 3.0-3.49:	31%	
GPA 2.0-2.99:	8%	
Rank in top quarter:	48%	

Rank in top tenth:	19%
End year in good standing:	84%
Return as sophomores:	87%
Out-of-state:	29%
Live on campus:	95%
International:	2%
Fraternities:	7%
Sororities:	11%

Basis for selection. Each application given a careful, individual, holistic review. Priority consideration given to applicants with 3.25 GPA with no D/F grades and who will have successfully satisfied academic course work standards. Applicants with GPA below 3.25, occasional D/F grades, and/or fewer than the 18 recommended high school units encouraged to apply, since many factors are considered in the holistic review process. Letter of recommendation required (preferably from teacher or school-based official).

High school preparation. College-preparatory program required. 17 units required; 18 recommended. Required and recommended units include English 4-4, mathematics 4-4, social studies 2-2, history 1-1, science 3-3 (laboratory 2-2), foreign language 1-2 and academic electives 2-2. Individual programs may have additional requirements.

2015-2016 Annual costs. Tuition/fees: $10,558; $27,267 out-of-state. Room/board: $10,794. Books/supplies: $1,140. Personal expenses: $1,360.

2014-2015 Financial aid. Need-based: 3,520 full-time freshmen applied for aid; 2,181 deemed to have need; 1,990 received aid. Average need met was 64%. Average scholarship/grant was $7,274; average loan $5,099. 54% of total undergraduate aid awarded as scholarships/grants, 46% as loans/jobs. **Non-need-based:** Awarded to 5,481 full-time undergraduates, including 1,473 freshmen. Scholarships awarded for academics, alumni affiliation, art, athletics, leadership, music/drama, state residency. **Additional information:** Colorado students who have a family Adjusted Gross Income (AGI) on their federal income tax return(s) of $57,000 or less (and who meet other eligibility requirements) given grants to cover at least one-half the cost of tuition. Students who are eligible for a federal Pell Grant receive 100% of base tuition and standard fees.

Application procedures. Admission: Closing date 2/1 (receipt date). $50 fee, may be waived for applicants with need. Admission notification on a rolling basis beginning on or about 10/1. Must reply by May 1 or within 2 week(s) if notified thereafter. Early application (once 6th semester transcript is available) encouraged. **Financial aid:** Priority date 3/1; no closing date. FAFSA required. CSS PROFILE required for first-time domestic applicants. Applicants notified on a rolling basis starting 3/1.

Academics. **Special study options:** Accelerated study, combined bachelor's/graduate degree, cooperative education, distance learning, double major, dual enrollment of high school students, ESL, honors, independent study, internships, liberal arts/career combination, semester at sea, study abroad, teacher certification program. **Credit/placement by examination:** AP, CLEP, IB, SAT, ACT, institutional tests. **Support services:** Learning center, study skills assistance, tutoring, writing center.

Majors. **Architecture:** Landscape. **Area/ethnic studies:** General. **Biology:** General, biochemistry, biomedical sciences, ecology, microbiology, wildlife, zoology. **Business:** Accounting, business admin, construction management, finance, management information systems, marketing, real estate, restaurant/food services. **Communications:** Communications/speech/rhetoric, journalism. **Computer sciences:** General, information systems, information technology. **Conservation:** General, forest sciences, water/wetlands/marine, wildlife/wilderness. **Education:** General, agricultural, art, biology, business, chemistry, drama/dance, early childhood, English, family/consumer sciences, French, German, mathematics, music, physics, sales/marketing, science, social studies, Spanish, speech, technology/industrial arts, trade/industrial. **Engineering:** Applied physics, biomedical, chemical, civil, computer, electrical, engineering science, environmental, mechanical. **English:** Creative writing, English lit. **Foreign languages:** General, French, German, Spanish. **Health services:** Athletic training, environmental health, music therapy. **History:** General. **Human services:** Social work. **Liberal arts:** Arts/sciences. **Math:** General. **Parks/recreation:** Exercise sciences, facilities management. **Philosophy/religion:** Philosophy. **Physical sciences:** Chemistry, geology, physics. **Protective services:** Fire services admin. **Psychology:** General. **Social sciences:** Anthropology, economics, political science, sociology. **Visual/performing arts:** Art, conducting, dance, dramatic, graphic design, interior design, music, music performance, music theory/composition, studio arts. **Work/family studies:** General, apparel marketing, family studies, food/nutrition, human nutrition.

Most popular majors. Agriculture 6%, biology 9%, business/marketing 15%, communications/journalism 6%, engineering/engineering technologies 9%, family/consumer sciences 8%, parks/recreation 7%, social sciences 9%.

Technology on campus. 2,000 workstations in dormitories, library, student center. Dormitories wired for high-speed internet access and linked to campus network. Commuter students can connect to campus network. Online course registration, online library, helpline, repair service, student web hosting, wireless network available.

Student life. **Freshman orientation:** Mandatory. Preregistration for classes offered. 19 sessions offered from mid-June to mid-July for freshmen, family members, and guests. Lodging provided for student. **Housing:** Guaranteed on-campus for freshmen. Coed dorms, special housing for disabled, apartments, fraternity/sorority housing, themed housing, wellness housing available. $150 partly refundable deposit. Special interest floors, residential learning communities (curricular, academic, themed) available. **Activities:** Bands, campus ministries, choral groups, dance, drama, international student organizations, literary magazine, music ensembles, musical theater, opera, radio station, student government, student newspaper, symphony orchestra, TV station, Asian/American student services, Black student services, El Centro student services, GLBT student services, Native American student services, Campus Crusade for Christ, Chabad Jewish student alliance, Habitat for Humanity, College Republicans, Young Democrats.

Athletics. NCAA. **Intercollegiate:** Basketball, cross-country, diving W, football (tackle) M, golf, soccer W, softball W, swimming W, tennis W, track and field, volleyball W. **Intramural:** Basketball, bowling, football (non-tackle), golf, racquetball, soccer, softball, table tennis, tennis, ultimate frisbee, volleyball, water polo. **Team name:** Rams.

Student services. Adult student services, alcohol/substance abuse counseling, chaplain/spiritual director, career counseling, services for economically disadvantaged, student employment services, financial aid counseling, health services, legal services, minority student services, on-campus daycare, personal counseling, placement for graduates, veterans' counselor, women's services. **Physically disabled:** Services for visually, speech, hearing impaired.

Contact. E-mail: admissions@colostate.edu
Phone: (970) 491-6909 Fax: (970) 491-7799
Bryan Whish, Director of Undergraduate Admissions, Colorado State University, Office of Admissions/Colorado State University, Fort Collins, CO 80523-1062

Colorado State University: Pueblo
Pueblo, Colorado
www.csupueblo.edu   CB code: 4611

- Public 4-year university
- Commuter campus in small city
- 4,227 degree-seeking undergraduates: 15% part-time, 52% women

- 249 degree-seeking graduate students
- SAT or ACT (ACT writing optional) required

General. Founded in 1933. Regionally accredited. **Degrees:** 842 bachelor's awarded; master's offered. **ROTC:** Army. **Location:** 42 miles from Colorado Springs, 100 miles from Denver. **Calendar:** Semester, extensive summer session. **Full-time faculty:** 172 total; 22% minority, 44% women. **Part-time faculty:** 200 total; 16% minority, 58% women. **Class size:** 48% < 20, 39% 20-39, 7% 40-49, 5% 50-99, less than 1% >100. **Special facilities:** 3 electron microscopes, golf course, river trail system, automotive service, ropes course, music amphitheater, 1+ megawatt solar system, 6 kilowatt solar system.

Freshman class profile.

GPA 3.75 or higher:	20%	Rank in top tenth:	10%
GPA 3.50-3.74:	14%	Out-of-state:	8%
GPA 3.0-3.49:	27%	Live on campus:	54%
GPA 2.0-2.99:	39%	Fraternities:	1%
Rank in top quarter:	31%	Sororities:	1%

Basis for selection. High school achievement record and test scores most important. Auditions for music, portfolios for art required for scholarships.

High school preparation. College-preparatory program required. 17 units required. Required units include English 4, mathematics 4, social studies 2, history 1, science 3 (laboratory 2), foreign language 1 and academic electives 2.

2015-2016 Annual costs. Tuition/fees: $8,281; $19,851 out-of-state. Room/board: $9,636. Books/supplies: $1,200. Personal expenses: $2,260.

Financial aid. **Non-need-based:** Scholarships awarded for academics, alumni affiliation, art, athletics, job skills, leadership, minority status, music/drama, ROTC, state residency.

Application procedures. **Admission:** Closing date 8/1 (receipt date). $25 fee, may be waived for applicants with need. Admission notification on a rolling basis beginning on or about 9/15. **Financial aid:** Closing date 3/1. FAFSA required. Applicants notified on a rolling basis starting 3/15; must reply within 3 week(s) of notification.

Academics. Tutoring center provides face-to-face tutoring for all general education courses and skill-building math courses. **Special study options:** Accelerated study, combined bachelor's/graduate degree, distance learning, double major, dual enrollment of high school students, ESL, exchange student, external degree, honors, independent study, internships, semester at sea, study abroad, teacher certification program, weekend college. **Credit/placement by examination:** AP, CLEP, IB, SAT, ACT, institutional tests. 30 credit hours maximum toward bachelor's degree. **Support services:** Learning center, reduced course load, remedial instruction, study skills assistance, tutoring, writing center.

Majors. **Biology:** General. **Business:** Accounting, managerial economics. **Communications:** Media studies. **Computer sciences:** Information systems. **Engineering:** General, industrial. **English:** English lit. **Foreign languages:** General. **Health services:** Nursing (RN). **History:** General. **Human services:** Social work. **Liberal arts:** Arts/sciences. **Math:** General. **Parks/recreation:** Exercise sciences. **Physical sciences:** Chemistry, physics. **Psychology:** General. **Social sciences:** Political science, sociology. **Visual/performing arts:** Music, studio arts.

Most popular majors. Business/marketing 14%, health sciences 10%, parks/recreation 10%, psychology 8%, public administration/social services 7%, social sciences 14%.

Technology on campus. 700 workstations in dormitories, library, computer center, student center. Dormitories wired for high-speed internet access. Commuter students can connect to campus network. Online course registration, online library, helpline, student web hosting, wireless network available.

Student life. **Freshman orientation:** Mandatory, $20 fee. Preregistration for classes offered. One-day programs held in summer. **Housing:** Guaranteed on-campus for all undergraduates. Coed dorms, special housing for disabled available. $250 fully refundable deposit, deadline 7/1. One traditional style residence hall and 3 suite style residence halls. **Activities:** Bands, campus ministries, choral groups, international student organizations, literary magazine, music ensembles, radio station, student government, student newspaper, symphony orchestra, TV station, Black Student Organization, Bold And Beautiful Educated Sisters, Lambda Theta Nu Sorority, Inc., Alpha Kappa Alpha Sorority, Inc., Campus Crusade for Christ, Christian Challenge, Fellowship of Christian Athletes, Movimiento Estudiantil Chicano de Aztln, PRIZM.

Athletics. NCAA. **Intercollegiate:** Baseball M, basketball, cross-country, diving W, football (tackle) M, golf, lacrosse, soccer, softball W, swimming W, tennis, track and field, volleyball W, wrestling M. **Intramural:** Basketball, football (non-tackle), football (tackle), golf, soccer, softball, volleyball. **Team name:** Thunderwolves.

Student services. Alcohol/substance abuse counseling, career counseling, services for economically disadvantaged, student employment services, financial aid counseling, health services, minority student services, on-campus daycare, personal counseling, placement for graduates, veterans' counselor. **Physically disabled:** Services for visually, speech, hearing impaired.

Contact. E-mail: info@csupueblo.edu
Phone: (719) 549-2461 Fax: (719) 549-2419
Sean McGivney, Director of Admissions & Financial Aid, Colorado State University: Pueblo, 2200 Bonforte Boulevard, Pueblo, CO 81001-4901

Colorado Technical University
Colorado Springs, Colorado
www.coloradotech.edu   **CB code: 4133**

- For-profit 4-year university and technical college
- Commuter campus in large city
- 1,144 undergraduates
- 902 graduate students
- Interview required

General. Founded in 1965. Regionally accredited. **Degrees:** 206 bachelor's, 68 associate awarded; master's, doctoral offered. **ROTC:** Army. **Location:** 63 miles from Denver. **Calendar:** Quarter, extensive summer session. **Full-time faculty:** 24 total. **Part-time faculty:** 248 total. **Class size:** 69% < 20, 31% 20-39. **Special facilities:** Extensive laboratories and computer facilities.

Basis for selection. Open admission, but selective for some programs. Certain programs require successful performance on one or more entrance assessments.

2015-2016 Annual costs. Books/supplies: $1,300. Personal expenses: $1,215. **Additional information:** Associate programs: $30,225-$30,387.50. Bachelor's programs: $58,500-$60,450. Technology fee: $125 per term.

Financial aid. Non-need-based: Scholarships awarded for academics, ROTC.

Application procedures. Admission: No deadline. $50 fee. Admission notification on a rolling basis. **Financial aid:** No deadline. FAFSA required. Applicants notified on a rolling basis starting 6/30.

Academics. Special study options: Accelerated study, cooperative education, distance learning, double major, internships, weekend college. **Credit/placement by examination:** AP, CLEP, institutional tests. 30 credit hours maximum toward associate degree, 60 toward bachelor's. Course challenge test offered. Credit for life experience based on evaluation by faculty. **Support services:** Learning center, reduced course load, remedial instruction, tutoring.

Majors. Business: Business admin, e-commerce, human resources, information resources management, logistics, management information systems. **Computer sciences:** General, computer science, information systems, information technology, system admin, systems analysis. **Engineering:** Computer, electrical, software.

Most popular majors. Business/marketing 34%, computer/information sciences 32%, engineering/engineering technologies 34%.

Technology on campus. 154 workstations in library, computer center. Commuter students can connect to campus network. Online library, helpline, wireless network available.

Student life. Freshman orientation: Mandatory. Preregistration for classes offered. **Policies:** Students must comply with university's standards of conduct. **Housing:** Apartments available. **Activities:** Student government.

Student services. Career counseling, student employment services, financial aid counseling, personal counseling, placement for graduates, veterans' counselor.

Contact. E-mail: cosadmissions@coloradotech.edu
Phone: (719) 598-0200 Toll-free number: (800) 599-9287
Fax: (719) 598-3740
Beth Braaten, Vice President of Admissions, Colorado Technical University, 4435 North Chestnut Street, Colorado Springs, CO 80907

Denver School of Nursing
Denver, Colorado
www.denverschoolofnursing.edu   **CB code: 7419**

- For-profit 4-year nursing college
- Very large city
- 653 full-time, degree-seeking undergraduates

General. Regionally accredited. **Degrees:** 295 bachelor's, 51 associate awarded. **Calendar:** Quarter. **Full-time faculty:** 20 total. **Part-time faculty:** 72 total.

Basis for selection. Admissions based on number of factors including personal statement, previous health care and or volunteer experience and cumulative/science GPA. BSN applicants who appear best qualified for the program will receive invitation for application interview. SAT or ACT recommended.

2015-2016 Annual costs. Total tuition and fees for Bachelor of Science in Nursing Completion program, $54,923. Total Tuition and fees for the Associate Degree in Nursing Completion Program is $43,837.

Financial aid. All financial aid based on need.

Application procedures. Admission: Closing date 4/1. $100 fee. Application must be submitted on paper. Admission notification on a rolling basis. **Financial aid:** No deadline. FAFSA required.

Academics. Credit/placement by examination: AP, CLEP.

Majors. Health services: Nursing (RN).

Technology on campus. 46 workstations in library, computer center. Online library, wireless network available.

Contact. E-mail: jjohnson@denverschoolofnursing.edu
Phone: (303) 292-0015
Jeff Johnson, Director of Admissions, Denver School of Nursing, 1401 19th Street, Denver, CO 80202

DeVry University: Westminster
Westminster, Colorado
www.devry.edu   **CB code: 1327**

- For-profit 4-year university
- Commuter campus in very large city
- 409 degree-seeking undergraduates
- Interview required

General. Founded in 1945. Regionally accredited. Additional locations: Colorado Springs, Denver South, Sandy (UT). **Degrees:** 141 bachelor's, 31 associate awarded; master's offered. **Calendar:** Semester, extensive summer session. **Full-time faculty:** 12 total; 8% minority, 25% women. **Part-time faculty:** 60 total; 8% minority, 40% women.

Basis for selection. Applicants must have high school diploma or equivalent or a degree from an accredited postsecondary institution, demonstrate proficiency in basic college-level skills through SAT or ACT scores or institutional-administered placement exams, and be at least 17 years of age.

High school preparation. College-preparatory program recommended. Math unit must be algebra or higher.

2015-2016 Annual costs. Tuition/fees: $17,132. Books/supplies: $1,320. Personal expenses: $2,376.

Financial aid. All financial aid based on need.

Application procedures. Admission: No deadline. $40 fee. Admission notification on a rolling basis. **Financial aid:** No deadline. FAFSA required. Applicants notified on a rolling basis.

Academics. Special study options: Accelerated study, distance learning. **Credit/placement by examination:** AP, CLEP, institutional tests. **Support services:** Learning center, tutoring.

Majors. Business: Business admin. **Computer sciences:** Networking, systems analysis, web page design. **Engineering:** Software.

Most popular majors. Business/marketing 61%, engineering/engineering technologies 11%, personal/culinary services 28%.

Technology on campus. 308 workstations in library, computer center. Online course registration, online library, helpline available.

Student life. Freshman orientation: Mandatory. Preregistration for classes offered.

Athletics. Intramural: Basketball, volleyball.

Student services. Career counseling, student employment services, financial aid counseling, placement for graduates, veterans' counselor.

Contact. E-mail: denver-admissions@den.devry.edu
Phone: (303) 280-7400 Toll-free number: (888) 212-1857
Fax: (303) 280-7606
DeVry University: Westminster, 1870 West 122nd Avenue, Westminster,
CO 80234-2010

Fort Lewis College
Durango, Colorado
www.fortlewis.edu

CB member
CB code: 4310

- Public 4-year business and liberal arts college
- Residential campus in large town
- 3,570 degree-seeking undergraduates: 6% part-time, 51% women, 1% African American, 1% Asian American, 11% Hispanic/Latino, 25% Native American, 7% Multi-racial, non-Hispanic, 1% international
- 12 degree-seeking graduate students
- 86% of applicants admitted
- SAT or ACT (ACT writing optional) required
- 40% graduate within 6 years; 14% enter graduate study

General. Regionally accredited. **Degrees:** 649 bachelor's awarded; master's offered. **Location:** 220 miles from Albuquerque, NM, 340 miles from Denver. **Calendar:** Semester, limited summer session. **Full-time faculty:** 174 total; 87% have terminal degrees, 9% minority, 51% women. **Part-time faculty:** 78 total; 35% have terminal degrees, 5% minority, 47% women. **Class size:** 42% < 20, 50% 20-39, 5% 40-49, 3% 50-99. **Special facilities:** Southwest studies center, nuclear magnetic resonance spectrometer, archaeological dig site, community concert hall, separations and spectroscopy lab, mass spectrometer facilities, tissue culture facility, atomic force microscope.

Freshman class profile. 3,105 applied, 2,669 admitted, 814 enrolled.

Mid 50% test scores		GPA 2.0-2.99:	27%
SAT critical reading:	460-550	Rank in top quarter:	33%
SAT math:	460-580	Rank in top tenth:	11%
SAT writing:	400-530	End year in good standing:	68%
ACT composite:	19-24	Return as sophomores:	63%
GPA 3.75 or higher:	18%	Out-of-state:	53%
GPA 3.50-3.74:	16%	Live on campus:	93%
GPA 3.0-3.49:	39%	International:	1%

Basis for selection. Colorado Commission on Higher Education index score comprised of high school GPA and test scores utilized as part of admission criteria. Essay recommended. **Home schooled:** Official copy of high school completion records; 1010 SAT (exclusive of Writing), 22 ACT.

High school preparation. College-preparatory program required. 17 units required. Required units include English 4, mathematics 4, social studies 2, history 1, science 3 (laboratory 2), foreign language 1 and academic electives 2.

2015-2016 Annual costs. Tuition/fees: $7,601; $17,817 out-of-state. Room/board: $9,130. Books/supplies: $1,208. Personal expenses: $3,648.

2014-2015 Financial aid. Need-based: 656 full-time freshmen applied for aid; 523 deemed to have need; 522 received aid. Average need met was 90%. Average scholarship/grant was $4,902; average loan $3,325. 55% of total undergraduate aid awarded as scholarships/grants, 45% as loans/jobs. **Non-need-based:** Awarded to 993 full-time undergraduates, including 264 freshmen. Scholarships awarded for academics, alumni affiliation, art, athletics, leadership, music/drama, state residency. **Additional information:** Tuition waived for Native Americans of federally recognized tribes; census number and Certificate of Indian Blood must accompany application.

Application procedures. Admission: Closing date 8/1. $40 fee, may be waived for applicants with need. Admission notification on a rolling basis beginning on or about 10/18. **Financial aid:** Priority date 2/15; no closing date. FAFSA required. Applicants notified by 3/1; Applicants notified on a rolling basis; must reply by 9/16.

Academics. Special study options: Accelerated study, cooperative education, distance learning, double major, dual enrollment of high school students, ESL, exchange student, honors, independent study, internships, liberal arts/career combination, semester at sea, student-designed major, study abroad, teacher certification program. **Credit/placement by examination:** AP, CLEP, IB, SAT, ACT, institutional tests. 24 credit hours maximum toward bachelor's degree. Up to 24 credits may be granted based on CLEP general exam scores. IB diploma holders will receive a minimum of 24 semester credits. **Support services:** Learning center, remedial instruction, study skills assistance, tutoring, writing center.

Majors. Area/ethnic studies: Chicano/Hispanic-American/Latino, Native American, women's. **Biology:** General, ecology. **Business:** General, accounting, business admin, marketing, operations. **Conservation:** Environmental studies. **Education:** Multicultural. **Engineering:** General, applied physics. **English:** English lit. **Foreign languages:** Spanish. **Health services:** Athletic training. **History:** General. **Liberal arts:** Arts/sciences, humanities. **Math:** General. **Parks/recreation:** General, exercise sciences. **Philosophy/religion:** Philosophy. **Physical sciences:** Chemistry, geology, physics. **Psychology:** General, counseling, industrial. **Social sciences:** Anthropology, economics, political science, sociology. **Visual/performing arts:** Dramatic, music, studio arts.

Most popular majors. Biology 8%, business/marketing 17%, natural resources/environmental science 6%, parks/recreation 10%, physical sciences 8%, psychology 7%, social sciences 13%, visual/performing arts 8%.

Technology on campus. 797 workstations in dormitories, library. Dormitories wired for high-speed internet access and linked to campus network. Commuter students can connect to campus network. Online course registration, online library, helpline, student web hosting, wireless network available.

Student life. Freshman orientation: Mandatory. Preregistration for classes offered. **Housing:** Guaranteed on-campus for all undergraduates. Coed dorms, special housing for disabled, apartments, themed housing available. $150 partly refundable deposit, deadline 7/15. **Activities:** Bands, campus ministries, choral groups, dance, drama, literary magazine, musical theater, radio station, student government, student newspaper, Newman club, business club, American Indian business leaders, American Indian science and engineering society, sociology club, Native American club, Habitat for Humanity.

Athletics. NCAA. **Intercollegiate:** Basketball, cross-country, football (tackle) M, golf M, soccer, softball W, volleyball W. **Intramural:** Badminton, basketball, football (non-tackle), football (tackle), racquetball, soccer, softball, tennis, ultimate frisbee, volleyball. **Team name:** Skyhawks.

Student services. Adult student services, alcohol/substance abuse counseling, chaplain/spiritual director, career counseling, services for economically disadvantaged, student employment services, financial aid counseling, health services, legal services, minority student services, on-campus daycare, personal counseling, placement for graduates, veterans' counselor, women's services. **Physically disabled:** Services for visually, speech, hearing impaired.

Contact. E-mail: admission@fortlewis.edu
Phone: (970) 247-7180 Toll-free number: (877) 352-2656
Fax: (970) 247-7179
Andrew Burns, Director of Admission, Fort Lewis College, 1000 Rim Drive, Durango, CO 81301-3999

ITT Technical Institute: Westminster
Westminster, Colorado
www.itt-tech.edu

CB code: 3605

- For-profit 4-year technical college
- Commuter campus in large city
- 212 undergraduates
- Interview required

General. Founded in 1984. Accredited by ACICS. **Degrees:** 10 bachelor's, 46 associate awarded. **Calendar:** Quarter, extensive summer session. **Full-time faculty:** 5 total. **Part-time faculty:** 30 total.

Basis for selection. Satisfactory scores from on-site tests in English and math required.

2015-2016 Annual costs. Per-credit-hour charge, $493; academic fee, $200. Certain programs require purchase of tools, which could cost an additional $150 to $500. All costs are subject to change.

Application procedures. Admission: No deadline. No application fee. Admission notification on a rolling basis. **Financial aid:** No deadline. FAFSA, institutional form required. Applicants notified on a rolling basis.

Academics. Credit/placement by examination: AP, CLEP. **Support services:** Learning center, tutoring.

Majors. Business: Business admin, construction management. **Computer sciences:** Programming, security. **Protective services:** Law enforcement admin.

Technology on campus. Online library available.

Student life. Freshman orientation: Available. Preregistration for classes offered.

Student services. Career counseling, student employment services, placement for graduates.

Contact. Phone: (303) 288-4488 Toll-free number: (800) 395-4488 Niki Donahue, Director of Recruitment, ITT Technical Institute: Westminster, 8620 Wolff Court, Suite 100, Westminster, CO 80031

Johnson & Wales University: Denver
Denver, Colorado
www.jwu.edu — CB code: 3567

- Private 4-year college
- Residential campus in large city
- 1,356 degree-seeking undergraduates: 10% part-time, 59% women, 9% African American, 2% Asian American, 19% Hispanic/Latino, 8% Multiracial, non-Hispanic, 1% international
- 32 degree-seeking graduate students
- 81% of applicants admitted
- 53% graduate within 6 years

General. Regionally accredited. **Degrees:** 238 bachelor's, 245 associate awarded; master's offered. **ROTC:** Army. **Calendar:** Trimester, limited summer session. **Full-time faculty:** 52 total. **Part-time faculty:** 75 total. **Class size:** 61% < 20, 34% 20-39, 5% 40-49. **Special facilities:** Community leadership institute.

Freshman class profile. 2,319 applied, 1,883 admitted, 339 enrolled.

GPA 3.75 or higher:	17%	Return as sophomores:	75%
GPA 3.50-3.74:	16%	Out-of-state:	66%
GPA 3.0-3.49:	35%	Live on campus:	79%
GPA 2.0-2.99:	32%	International:	1%

Basis for selection. Academic record important, including secondary school curriculum, GPA, class rank, test scores. Student motivation and interest given strong consideration. **Home schooled:** Transcript of courses and grades, state high school equivalency certificate required. SAT or ACT required.

High school preparation. College-preparatory program recommended. Required units include English 4, mathematics 3, social studies 2 and science 3.

2015-2016 Annual costs. Tuition/fees: $30,681. Room/board: $11,499. Books/supplies: $1,500. Personal expenses: $1,409.

2015-2016 Financial aid. Need-based: 325 full-time freshmen applied for aid; 281 deemed to have need; 281 received aid. Average need met was 74%. Average scholarship/grant was $9,346; average loan $3,390. 62% of total undergraduate aid awarded as scholarships/grants, 38% as loans/jobs. **Non-need-based:** Awarded to 1,080 full-time undergraduates, including 317 freshmen. Scholarships awarded for academics, alumni affiliation, job skills, leadership, state residency.

Application procedures. Admission: No deadline. No application fee. Admission notification by 11/1. Admission notification on a rolling basis. Must reply by May 1 or within 2 week(s) if notified thereafter. **Financial aid:** No deadline. FAFSA required. Applicants notified on a rolling basis starting 3/1; must reply within 2 week(s) of notification.

Academics. Special study options: Accelerated study, cooperative education, dual enrollment of high school students, ESL, exchange student, honors, independent study, internships, study abroad. **Credit/placement by examination:** AP, CLEP, institutional tests. **Support services:** Learning center, remedial instruction, study skills assistance, tutoring, writing center.

Majors. Business: General, apparel, business admin, entrepreneurial studies, event planning, fashion, hospitality admin, hospitality/recreation, hotel/motel admin, hotel/motel/restaurant management, market research, marketing, merchandising, personal/financial services, resort management, restaurant/food services, retail management, retailing. **Communications:** Media studies, persuasive communications, public relations. **English:** American lit, English lit, writing. **Health services:** Mental health counseling. **Liberal arts:** Arts/sciences. **Protective services:** Law enforcement admin. **Psychology:** General, counseling. **Social sciences:** Sociology. **Work/family studies:** Apparel marketing, business, clothing/textiles, fashion consultant, food/nutrition, human nutrition, institutional food production.

Most popular majors. Business/marketing 29%, family/consumer sciences 36%, parks/recreation 11%, personal/culinary services 17%, security/protective services 8%.

Technology on campus. Dormitories wired for high-speed internet access and linked to campus network. Commuter students can connect to campus network. Online course registration, online library, helpline, repair service, wireless network available.

Student life. Freshman orientation: Mandatory, $300 fee. Preregistration for classes offered. **Housing:** Coed dorms, special housing for disabled, apartments, wellness housing available. $300 deposit, deadline 5/1. **Activities:** Campus ministries, dance, international student organizations, student government, student newspaper.

Athletics. NAIA. **Intercollegiate:** Basketball, cross-country, lacrosse, softball, volleyball W. **Intramural:** Basketball, football (non-tackle), volleyball. **Team name:** Wildcats.

Student services. Adult student services, alcohol/substance abuse counseling, career counseling, student employment services, financial aid counseling, health services, minority student services, personal counseling, placement for graduates. **Physically disabled:** Services for visually, speech, hearing impaired.

Contact. E-mail: den@admissions.jwu.edu
Phone: (303) 256-9311 Toll-free number: (877) 598-3368
Fax: (303) 256-9333
Mike Rusk, Director of Admissions, Johnson & Wales University: Denver, 7150 Montview Boulevard, Denver, CO 80220

Metropolitan State University of Denver
Denver, Colorado — CB member
www.msudenver.edu — CB code: 4505

- Public 4-year liberal arts college
- Commuter campus in very large city
- 20,584 degree-seeking undergraduates
- SAT or ACT (ACT writing optional) required

General. Founded in 1963. Regionally accredited. Library, student center, physical education facilities, child care center shared with Community College of Denver and University of Colorado at Denver. Degree completion programs offered at off-campus sites in North Glen and Englewood. **Degrees:** 3,276 bachelor's awarded; master's offered. **ROTC:** Army, Air Force. **Location:** Downtown. **Calendar:** Semester, extensive summer session. **Full-time faculty:** 547 total; 22% minority, 49% women. **Part-time faculty:** 902 total; 16% minority, 47% women. **Class size:** 34% < 20, 59% 20-39, 6% 40-49, 1% 50-99. **Special facilities:** Art galleries, CAD/CAM laboratory, world indoor airport.

Freshman class profile.

GPA 3.75 or higher:	8%	Rank in top quarter:	22%
GPA 3.50-3.74:	9%	Rank in top tenth:	6%
GPA 3.0-3.49:	29%	Out-of-state:	7%
GPA 2.0-2.99:	53%		

Basis for selection. ACT/SAT, GPA, and class rank important. ACT/SAT not required of those submitting GED. Open admission for applicants 20 years of age and older who are high school graduates, have GED, or have 30 transferable credits. Students 19 years of age or younger with a CCHE index score between 76-91 must apply by April 6.

High school preparation. College-preparatory program recommended. 17 units recommended. Recommended units include English 4, mathematics 4, social studies 3, science 3, foreign language 1 and academic electives 2.

2015-2016 Annual costs. Tuition/fees: $6,420; $19,257 out-of-state. Books/supplies: $1,200. Personal expenses: $4,306.

Application procedures. Admission: Closing date 7/1 (receipt date). $25 fee, may be waived for applicants with need. Admission notification on a rolling basis. **Financial aid:** No deadline. FAFSA required. Applicants notified on a rolling basis starting 3/15.

Academics. Special study options: Accelerated study, cooperative education, cross-registration, distance learning, double major, dual enrollment of high school students, honors, independent study, internships, liberal arts/career combination, student-designed major, study abroad, teacher certification program, Washington semester. **Credit/placement by examination:** AP, CLEP, IB, SAT, ACT. 64 credit hours maximum toward bachelor's degree. **Support services:** Pre-admission summer program, study skills assistance, tutoring, writing center.

Majors. Area/ethnic studies: African-American, Chicano/Hispanic-American/Latino, women's. **Biology:** General. **Business:** Accounting, business admin, finance, hospitality admin, management information systems, marketing. **Communications:** Communications/speech/rhetoric, journalism. **Computer sciences:** Computer science. **Conservation:** General, environmental studies, land use planning. **Education:** Music, special ed. **English:** English lit, rhetoric/composition. **Foreign languages:** General, linguistics. **Health services:** Athletic training, communication disorders, health care admin, nursing (RN). **History:** General. **Human services:** Social work. **Math:** General. **Parks/recreation:** General, exercise sciences. **Philosophy/ religion:** Philosophy. **Physical sciences:** Atmospheric science, chemistry, physics. **Protective services:** Criminal justice, law enforcement admin. **Psychology:** General, developmental. **Social sciences:** Anthropology, economics, political science, sociology. **Visual/performing arts:** General, art, art history/conservation, dramatic, industrial design, music, studio arts.

Most popular majors. Business/marketing 21%, English 7%, health sciences 6%, interdisciplinary studies 9%, psychology 8%, security/protective services 6%.

Technology on campus. 700 workstations in library, computer center, student center. Commuter students can connect to campus network. Online course registration, online library, helpline, repair service, wireless network available.

Student life. Freshman orientation: Mandatory. Preregistration for classes offered. Several sessions held preceding each semester. **Housing:** Off-campus apartments in area. **Activities:** Bands, choral groups, dance, drama, international student organizations, literary magazine, music ensembles, musical theater, radio station, student government, student newspaper, TV station, approximately 100 student organizations and clubs available.

Athletics. NCAA. **Intercollegiate:** Baseball M, basketball, cross-country, diving, golf W, soccer, softball W, tennis, volleyball W. **Intramural:** Basketball, cheerleading W, handball, lacrosse M, racquetball, rugby M, skiing, softball W, tennis, volleyball. **Team name:** Roadrunners.

Student services. Adult student services, alcohol/substance abuse counseling, chaplain/spiritual director, career counseling, services for economically disadvantaged, student employment services, financial aid counseling, health services, legal services, on-campus daycare, personal counseling, placement for graduates, veterans' counselor, women's services. **Physically disabled:** Services for visually, speech, hearing impaired.

Contact. E-mail: askmetro@mscd.edu
Phone: (303) 556-3058 Fax: (303) 556-6345
Vaughn Toland, Director of Admissions, Metropolitan State University of Denver, Campus Box 16, Denver, CO 80217

Naropa University
Boulder, Colorado   **CB member**
www.naropa.edu   **CB code: 0908**

- Private 4-year university and liberal arts college
- Commuter campus in small city
- 396 degree-seeking undergraduates: 7% part-time, 64% women, 2% African American, 1% Asian American, 10% Hispanic/Latino, 1% Native American, 10% Multi-racial, non-Hispanic, 2% international
- 545 degree-seeking graduate students
- 80% of applicants admitted
- Application essay required
- 31% graduate within 6 years

General. Founded in 1974. Regionally accredited. Pedagogy based on contemplative education. **Degrees:** 102 bachelor's awarded; master's offered. **Location:** 35 miles from Denver. **Calendar:** Semester, limited summer session. **Full-time faculty:** 46 total; 83% have terminal degrees, 22% minority, 50% women. **Part-time faculty:** 117 total; 43% have terminal degrees, 14% minority, 74% women. **Class size:** 86% < 20, 13% 20-39, less than 1% 40-49, less than 1% 50-99. **Special facilities:** Meditation halls, writing center, community arts center, career and community engagement center, greenhouse, tea house, art, dance, music and performance studios, recording studio, media lab.

Freshman class profile. 181 applied, 144 admitted, 45 enrolled.

Return as sophomores:	78%	Live on campus:	84%
Out-of-state:	56%	International:	2%

Basis for selection. The ability to succeed in a challenging, highly experiential, personalized academic environment. Academic history, activities, recommendations, awards, and writing ability are considered, as well as a demonstrated ability to cope independently with rigor, conflict, and challenge, as well as the life skills to seek out and to ask for academic or personal support. Applicants should have an understanding of and/or an openness to the concept of contemplative education, involvement with their larger

community, engagement with the arts, and a commitment to issues of diversity through formal or informal volunteer activities or community work. Creative work such as creative writing samples, art slides, music, etc. are optional. **Home schooled:** Portfolio of work completed during high school required, including subjects studied and modes of learning for each subject; extracurricular/community activities; academic achievements that support academic preparedness for college, such as internship positions; parent or teacher narrative; self-evaluation of work and how it contributed to intellectual growth; and transcripts from high schools or colleges.

High school preparation. College-preparatory program recommended. 23 units recommended. Recommended units include English 4, mathematics 3, social studies 3, history 3, science 3 (laboratory 2) and foreign language 3. Art, dance, theater and/or creative writing recommended.

2015-2016 Annual costs. Tuition/fees: $30,940. Room/board: $9,604. Books/supplies: $1,256. Personal expenses: $5,670.

2015-2016 Financial aid. All financial aid based on need. 40 full-time freshmen applied for aid; 36 deemed to have need; 36 received aid. Average need met was 68%. Average scholarship/grant was $18,092; average loan $5,620. 66% of total undergraduate aid awarded as scholarships/grants, 34% as loans/jobs.

Application procedures. Admission: Priority date 2/15; no deadline. $50 fee, may be waived for applicants with need. Admission notification on a rolling basis beginning on or about 9/1. Must reply by May 1 or within 3 week(s) if notified thereafter. **Financial aid:** Priority date 3/1; no closing date. FAFSA required. Applicants notified on a rolling basis starting 3/1; must reply within 4 week(s) of notification.

Academics. Special study options: Double major, independent study, internships, student-designed major, study abroad. Consortium agreement with University of Colorado allows degree-seeking students to take courses at University of Colorado at the in-state tuition rate. **Credit/placement by examination:** AP, CLEP, IB. 30 credit hours maximum toward bachelor's degree. **Support services:** Learning center, reduced course load, study skills assistance, tutoring, writing center. Academic coaching.

Majors. Conservation: Environmental studies. **Education:** Early childhood. **English:** English lit. **Philosophy/religion:** Religion. **Psychology:** General. **Visual/performing arts:** General, music, studio arts.

Most popular majors. Education 6%, English 7%, interdisciplinary studies 9%, parks/recreation 13%, psychology 40%, visual/performing arts 11%.

Technology on campus. 48 workstations in library, computer center. Dormitories wired for high-speed internet access. Commuter students can connect to campus network. Online course registration, online library, helpline, student web hosting, wireless network available.

Student life. Freshman orientation: Mandatory. Preregistration for classes offered. Two-day program. **Policies:** Community code of conduct, and policies on academic dishonesty, alcohol and other drugs, cultural appropriation, dual relationships, non-discrimination and prohibition of harassment. **Housing:** Guaranteed on-campus for freshmen. Apartments available. $300 nonrefundable deposit, deadline 7/1. **Activities:** Dance, drama, international student organizations, literary magazine, music ensembles, student government, Community of Color & Allies, International Students Group, Reconnecting on Outdoor Terrain, Naropa Zazen, Awakening Goddesses, Students for a Sensible Drug Policy, Theatre of the Oppressed at Naropa, Naropa Student Veterans.

Student services. Alcohol/substance abuse counseling, chaplain/spiritual director, career counseling, financial aid counseling, minority student services, personal counseling. **Physically disabled:** Services for visually, hearing impaired.

Contact. E-mail: admissions@naropa.edu
Phone: (303) 546-3572 Toll-free number: (800) 772-6951
Fax: (303) 546-3536
Janet Erickson, Dean of Admissions, Naropa University, 2130 Arapahoe Avenue, Boulder, CO 80302-6697

National American University: Denver
Denver, Colorado
www.national.edu   **CB code: 5354**

- For-profit 4-year university and branch campus college
- Commuter campus in very large city
- 218 undergraduates

General. Founded in 1941. Regionally accredited. **Degrees:** 3 bachelor's, 34 associate awarded. **Calendar:** Quarter, extensive summer session. **Full-time faculty:** 10 total. **Part-time faculty:** 21 total. **Class size:** 92% < 20, 8% 20-39.

Basis for selection. Open admission, but selective for some programs. Selective admissions to nursing program.

2015-2016 Annual costs. Tuition/fees: $16,020. Books/supplies: $1,350. **Additional information:** Additional fees may apply.

Application procedures. Admission: No deadline. $25 fee. Admission notification on a rolling basis. **Financial aid:** No deadline. Applicants notified on a rolling basis.

Academics. Special study options: Accelerated study, cooperative education, distance learning, double major, ESL, external degree, independent study, internships, liberal arts/career combination, weekend college. **Credit/placement by examination:** AP, CLEP, institutional tests. 48 credit hours maximum toward bachelor's degree. **Support services:** Remedial instruction.

Majors. Business: Accounting, business admin, management information systems, management science. **Computer sciences:** Applications programming, information systems, LAN/WAN management, system admin. **Health services:** Facilities admin, health care admin, health services admin.

Technology on campus. Online library available.

Student life. Activities: Student government, Phi Beta Lamda, data processing management association.

Athletics. Team name: Mavericks.

Student services. Career counseling, placement for graduates.

Contact. E-mail: sthompson@national.edu
Phone: (303) 876-7100 Fax: (303) 876-7105
Samantha Thompson, Director of Admissions, National American University: Denver, 1325 South Colorado Boulevard, Suite 100, Denver, CO 80222-3308

Nazarene Bible College
Colorado Springs, Colorado
www.nbc.edu   CB code: 0476

- Private 4-year Bible college affiliated with the Church of the Nazarene
- Commuter campus in very large city
- 760 degree-seeking undergraduates: 85% part-time, 39% women

General. Founded in 1964. Accredited by ABHE. Extensive online program for most majors. **Degrees:** 56 bachelor's, 10 associate awarded. **Location:** 60 miles from Denver. **Calendar:** Trimester, limited summer session. **Full-time faculty:** 9 total; 67% have terminal degrees, 11% women. **Part-time faculty:** 140 total; 33% have terminal degrees, 28% women. **Class size:** 100% < 20.

Freshman class profile.

Return as sophomores: 49% **Out-of-state:**   89%

Basis for selection. Open admission. **Home schooled:** Transcript of courses and grades required.

2015-2016 Annual costs. Tuition/fees: $14,250. Books/supplies: $1,500. Personal expenses: $4,000.

Financial aid. Non-need-based: Scholarships awarded for academics, minority status, religious affiliation.

Application procedures. Admission: No deadline. No application fee. Admission notification on a rolling basis. **Financial aid:** No deadline. FAFSA required. Applicants notified on a rolling basis starting 8/1.

Academics. Full programs offered in evening classes, cater to adult students. Extensive online degree programs offered. Degree completion program offered online and on campus. **Special study options:** Accelerated study, cooperative education, cross-registration, distance learning, double major, dual enrollment of high school students, independent study, internships. **Credit/placement by examination:** AP, CLEP, IB, institutional tests. 24 credit hours maximum toward associate degree, 24 toward bachelor's. **Support services:** Learning center, reduced course load, remedial instruction, study skills assistance, tutoring.

Majors. Philosophy/religion: Professional ethics. **Theology:** Bible, pastoral counseling, religious ed.

Most popular majors. Education 10%, philosophy/religious studies 13%, theological studies 79%.

Technology on campus. 20 workstations in library. Online library, wireless network available.

Student life. Freshman orientation: Mandatory, $60 fee. Preregistration for classes offered. **Policies:** Religious observance required. **Activities:** Campus ministries.

Student services. Adult student services, alcohol/substance abuse counseling, chaplain/spiritual director, career counseling, services for economically disadvantaged, student employment services, financial aid counseling, personal counseling, placement for graduates, women's services. **Physically disabled:** Services for visually, hearing impaired.

Contact. E-mail: admissions@nbc.edu
Phone: (719) 884-5062 Toll-free number: (800) 873-3873 ext. 5062
Fax: (719) 884-5199
Scott McConnaughey, Director of Admissions and Marketing, Nazarene Bible College, 1111 Academy Park Loop, Colorado Springs, CO 80910-3704

Platt College: Aurora
Aurora, Colorado
www.plattcolorado.edu   CB code: 3012

- For-profit 4-year nursing college
- Commuter campus in very large city
- 198 degree-seeking undergraduates
- Application essay, interview required

General. Accredited by ACCSC. **Degrees:** 69 bachelor's awarded. **Calendar:** Quarter. **Full-time faculty:** 12 total. **Part-time faculty:** 28 total.

Basis for selection. Open admission, but selective for some programs. Background check, letter of recommendation, Test of Essential Academic Skills (TEAS) required for nursing applicants. **Home schooled:** State high school equivalency certificate required.

High school preparation. College-preparatory program recommended.

2015-2016 Annual costs. Tuition/fees: $19,786. Books/supplies: $2,150. Personal expenses: $1,700. **Additional information:** Additiona fees may apply.

Financial aid. All financial aid based on need.

Application procedures. Admission: No deadline. $75 fee. Admission notification on a rolling basis. **Financial aid:** No deadline. FAFSA, institutional form required. Applicants notified on a rolling basis.

Academics. Credit/placement by examination: AP, CLEP. **Support services:** Learning center, study skills assistance, tutoring, writing center.

Majors. Health services: Nursing (RN).

Technology on campus. PC or laptop required. Wireless network available.

Student life. Freshman orientation: Mandatory. Preregistration for classes offered.

Contact. E-mail: admissions@plattcolorado.edu
Phone: (303) 369-5151 Toll-free number: (877) 369-5151
Fax: (303) 745-1433
Hollie Caldwell, Dean of Nursing, Platt College: Aurora, 3100 South Parker Road, Aurora, CO 80014-3141

Regis University
Denver, Colorado   CB member
www.regis.edu   CB code: 4656

- Private 4-year university and liberal arts college affiliated with the Roman Catholic Church
- Residential campus in very large city

- 4,414 degree-seeking undergraduates: 45% part-time, 61% women, 5% African American, 5% Asian American, 19% Hispanic/Latino, 1% Native American, 4% Multi-racial, non-Hispanic, 1% international
- 3,654 degree-seeking graduate students
- 66% of applicants admitted
- SAT or ACT (ACT writing optional), application essay required
- 73% graduate within 6 years

General. Founded in 1877. Regionally accredited. **Degrees:** 1,387 bachelor's awarded; master's, professional offered. **ROTC:** Army, Naval, Air Force. **Location:** 10 miles from downtown. **Calendar:** Semester, extensive summer session. **Full-time faculty:** 274 total; 82% have terminal degrees, 11% minority, 59% women. **Part-time faculty:** 529 total; 37% have terminal degrees, 12% minority, 57% women. **Class size:** 64% < 20, 33% 20-39, 2% 40-49, less than 1% 50-99. **Special facilities:** Arboretum, Santos collection (Hispanic religious art), center for the study of war experience, recorder music center.

Freshman class profile. 5,493 applied, 3,609 admitted, 545 enrolled.

Mid 50% test scores		GPA 3.0-3.49:	29%
SAT critical reading:	480-580	GPA 2.0-2.99:	18%
SAT math:	470-590	Rank in top quarter:	50%
SAT writing:	480-570	Rank in top tenth:	21%
ACT composite:	21-27	Return as sophomores:	79%
GPA 3.75 or higher:	38%	Out-of-state:	46%
GPA 3.50-3.74:	15%	International:	1%

Basis for selection. High school record, test scores, recommendations, essay, character and personal qualities are important. Admission polices may vary between Regis College, the College for Professional Studies, and Rueckert-Hartman College for Health Professions. Students advised to take certain courses based on their SAT or ACT results and performance in high school courses to ensure that they are academically prepared. Campus visit recommended. Audition recommended of music majors. **Learning Disabled:** After admission, students requesting accommodations must submit in-depth documentation of a disability.

High school preparation. College-preparatory program required. 15 units required. Required and recommended units include English 4, mathematics 3, social studies 2, science 2 (laboratory 1), foreign language 2 and academic electives 1.

2016-2017 Annual costs. Tuition/fees: $33,935. Room/board: $10,040. Books/supplies: $1,800. Personal expenses: $1,712.

2014-2015 Financial aid. Need-based: 384 full-time freshmen applied for aid; 334 deemed to have need; 334 received aid. Average need met was 83%. Average scholarship/grant was $21,173; average loan $3,634. 55% of total undergraduate aid awarded as scholarships/grants, 45% as loans/jobs. **Non-need-based:** Awarded to 792 full-time undergraduates, including 212 freshmen. Scholarships awarded for academics, athletics, leadership, music/drama, religious affiliation, ROTC, state residency.

Application procedures. Admission: Priority date 4/15; deadline 8/1 (postmark date). No application fee. Admission notification on a rolling basis beginning on or about 9/15. Must reply by May 1 or within 2 week(s) if notified thereafter. **Financial aid:** Priority date 5/31; no closing date. FAFSA required. Applicants notified on a rolling basis starting 3/15.

Academics. Special study options: Accelerated study, combined bachelor's/graduate degree, distance learning, double major, dual enrollment of high school students, honors, independent study, internships, liberal arts/career combination, student-designed major, study abroad, teacher certification program, Washington semester, weekend college. **Credit/placement by examination:** AP, CLEP, IB, SAT, ACT, institutional tests. Regis, CLEP, DANTES, Challenge exams offered. Hours of credit by examination that may be counted toward a bachelor's degree differ by program. **Support services:** Learning center, pre-admission summer program, reduced course load, remedial instruction, study skills assistance, tutoring, writing center.

Majors. Area/ethnic studies: Women's. **Biology:** General, biochemistry, neuroscience. **Business:** Accounting, business admin, finance, human resources, marketing. **Communications:** Communications/speech/rhetoric. **Computer sciences:** General, computer science, system admin. **Conservation:** Environmental science, environmental studies. **Education:** Elementary. **English:** English lit. **Foreign languages:** French, Spanish. **Health services:** Health care admin, health information management, nursing (RN). **History:** General. **Human services:** General. **Liberal arts:** Arts/sciences. **Math:** General. **Parks/recreation:** Exercise sciences. **Philosophy/religion:** Philosophy, religion. **Physical sciences:** Chemistry, physics. **Psychology:** General. **Social sciences:** General, criminology, economics, political science, sociology. **Visual/performing arts:** Art, art history/conservation, music.

Most popular majors. Business/marketing 27%, computer/information sciences 6%, health sciences 33%.

Technology on campus. 547 workstations in dormitories, library, computer center, student center. Dormitories wired for high-speed internet access and linked to campus network. Commuter students can connect to campus network. Online course registration, online library, helpline, wireless network available.

Student life. Freshman orientation: Mandatory, $200 fee. Preregistration for classes offered. Held weekend before classes begin. **Policies:** Freshmen required to live on campus unless residing with parent, guardian or spouse in Denver metropolitan area. **Housing:** Guaranteed on-campus for freshmen. Coed dorms, special housing for disabled, apartments, themed housing, wellness housing available. $150 nonrefundable deposit, deadline 5/1. Romero House for students focusing on social justice. **Activities:** Bands, campus ministries, choral groups, dance, drama, international student organizations, literary magazine, music ensembles, musical theater, radio station, student government, student newspaper, Peer Education, Environmental Action Program, Christian Fellowship, Jewish student group, Asian Awareness Association, Black Student Alliance, Mi Gente, Multicultural Awareness Committee, Romero House, Young Democrats and Republicans.

Athletics. NCAA. **Intercollegiate:** Baseball M, basketball, cross-country, golf, lacrosse W, soccer, softball W, volleyball W. **Team name:** Rangers.

Student services. Adult student services, alcohol/substance abuse counseling, chaplain/spiritual director, career counseling, student employment services, financial aid counseling, health services, minority student services, personal counseling, placement for graduates, veterans' counselor. **Physically disabled:** Services for visually, speech, hearing impaired.

Contact. E-mail: regisadm@regis.edu
Phone: (303) 458-4900 Toll-free number: (800) 944-7667 ext. 4900
Fax: (303) 964-5534
Sarah Engel, Director of Admissions, Regis University, 3333 Regis Boulevard, Mail Code A12, Denver, CO 80221-1099

Rocky Mountain College of Art & Design
Denver, Colorado
www.rmcad.edu   **CB code: 1943**

- For-profit 4-year visual arts college
- Commuter campus in very large city
- 1,074 degree-seeking undergraduates: 36% part-time, 65% women
- 17 degree-seeking graduate students
- Interview required

General. Founded in 1963. Regionally accredited. **Degrees:** 106 bachelor's awarded; master's offered. **Location:** 5 miles from downtown Denver. **Calendar:** Semester, extensive summer session. **Full-time faculty:** 38 total; 34% have terminal degrees, 5% minority, 55% women. **Part-time faculty:** 167 total; 34% have terminal degrees, 14% minority, 55% women. **Class size:** 94% < 20, 6% 20-39. **Special facilities:** Fine arts center, exhibition space, outdoor exhibition space, photography lab and darkroom, documentation room for digitally recording student work for portfolios and assessment.

Freshman class profile. 102 enrolled.

GPA 3.75 or higher:	22%	GPA 2.0-2.99:	43%
GPA 3.50-3.74:	9%	Out-of-state:	65%
GPA 3.0-3.49:	21%		

Basis for selection. Open admission. **Home schooled:** State high school equivalency certificate required.

2016-2017 Annual costs. Tuition/fees (projected): $15,870. Books/supplies: $1,045. Personal expenses: $2,730.

2014-2015 Financial aid. Need-based: 37% of total undergraduate aid awarded as scholarships/grants, 63% as loans/jobs. **Non-need-based:** Scholarships awarded for academics, art, state residency.

Application procedures. Admission: No deadline. $50 fee, may be waived for applicants with need. Admission notification on a rolling basis beginning on or about 9/1. **Financial aid:** Priority date 3/15; no closing date. FAFSA required. Applicants notified on a rolling basis starting 4/1; must reply within 2 week(s) of notification.

Academics. Special study options: Accelerated study, distance learning, dual enrollment of high school students, independent study, internships, teacher certification program. **Credit/placement by examination:** AP, CLEP, IB, SAT, ACT. **Support services:** Learning center, reduced course load, remedial instruction, study skills assistance, tutoring, writing center.

Majors. Communications technology: Animation/special effects. **Computer sciences:** Computer graphics. **Education:** Art. **Visual/performing**

arts: Arts management, commercial photography, fashion design, game design, graphic design, illustration, interior design, studio arts.

Most popular majors. Communication technologies 7%, computer/information sciences 22%, visual/performing arts 67%.

Technology on campus. PC or laptop required. 286 workstations in library, computer center. Online course registration, online library, helpline, repair service, wireless network available.

Student life. Freshman orientation: Mandatory. Preregistration for classes offered. One-day program held before start of term. **Housing:** Coed dorms available. **Activities:** Dance, student government.

Student services. Alcohol/substance abuse counseling, career counseling, student employment services, financial aid counseling, personal counseling, placement for graduates, veterans' counselor. **Physically disabled:** Services for visually, speech, hearing impaired.

Contact. E-mail: admissions@rmcad.edu
Phone: (303) 753-6046 Toll-free number: (800) 888-2787
Fax: (303) 759-4970
Marc Abraham, Director of Admissions, Rocky Mountain College of Art & Design, 1600 Pierce Street, Denver, CO 80214

United States Air Force Academy

USAF Academy, Colorado — CB member
www.academyadmissions.com — CB code: 4830

- Public 4-year liberal arts and military college
- Residential campus in large city
- 4,111 degree-seeking undergraduates: 23% women, 6% African American, 5% Asian American, 10% Hispanic/Latino, 1% Native Hawaiian/Pacific islander, 7% Multi-racial, non-Hispanic, 1% international
- 17% of applicants admitted
- SAT or ACT (ACT writing optional), application essay, interview required
- 80% graduate within 6 years; 12% enter graduate study

General. Founded in 1954. Regionally accredited. **Degrees:** 849 bachelor's awarded. **Location:** 8 miles from Colorado Springs, 60 miles from Denver. **Calendar:** Semester, limited summer session. **Full-time faculty:** 500 total; 60% have terminal degrees, 7% minority, 20% women. **Part-time faculty:** 6 total; 50% have terminal degrees, 67% women. **Class size:** 66% < 20, 34% 20-39, less than 1% 40-49. **Special facilities:** 2 airfields, tri-sonic wind tunnel, aeronautics lab, instrumentation lab, research lab, radio-frequency systems lab, training facility, meteorology lab, engineering mechanics lab, laser optics center, 32 research centers.

Freshman class profile. 9,122 applied, 1,559 admitted, 1,242 enrolled.

Mid 50% test scores			
SAT critical reading:	600-690	Rank in top quarter:	81%
SAT math:	630-710	Rank in top tenth:	52%
ACT composite:	29-32	End year in good standing:	95%
GPA 3.75 or higher:	78%	Return as sophomores:	93%
GPA 3.50-3.74:	13%	Out-of-state:	94%
GPA 3.0-3.49:	8%	Live on campus:	100%
GPA 2.0-2.99:	1%	International:	1%

Basis for selection. Must be a citizen of the United States, unmarried with no dependents, between the ages of 17 and not past the 23rd birthday on July 1 of the year of entry, and of good moral character. Legal nomination from member of Congress, US President or Vice President or other selected sources required. Secondary school record, test scores, leadership ability, extracurricular activities and character are most important. Satisfactory completion of medical exam and fitness test, and personal interview required. Admissions counselors available to assist in the admission process.

High school preparation. College-preparatory program recommended. 25 units recommended. Recommended units include English 4, mathematics 4, social studies 3, history 3, science 4 (laboratory 4), foreign language 2 and computer science 1. English should include college preparatory composition and speech courses. Math should include algebra, geometry, trigonometry, calculus, and functional analysis (if available). Science should include biology, chemistry, physics, computers, and additional science courses. Foreign language instruction should be in a modern language.

2016-2017 Annual costs. All cadet expenses, including tuition, room and board and supplies are paid for by the federal government.

Application procedures. Admission: Closing date 12/31 (postmark date). No application fee. Application must be submitted online. Admission notification on a rolling basis beginning on or about 10/15. Must reply by 5/1. Several stages of application process; applicants should begin process during junior year of high school. **Financial aid:** No deadline.

Academics. Special study options: Double major, ESL, exchange student, honors, independent study, internships, study abroad. Academically at-risk, hospital instruction, extra instruction, and summer programs available. **Credit/placement by examination:** AP, CLEP, IB, institutional tests. Cadets can earn credit by exams (validation) for their courses. The departments plan and offer validation exams and determine how many credits can be offered for placement exams, transfer credit, and AP scores. **Support services:** Learning center, reduced course load, study skills assistance, tutoring, writing center.

Honors college/program. Admission based on incoming academic qualifications, as well as academic performance during the first semester. Approximately 5% of cadets per class year are invited. Cadets who participate enroll in special "Scholars" sections of core courses.

Majors. Biology: General. **Business:** Business admin. **Computer sciences:** Computer science. **Engineering:** General, aerospace, civil, computer, electrical, engineering mechanics, environmental, mechanical, operations research, systems. **English:** English lit. **History:** General. **Liberal arts:** Humanities. **Math:** General. **Physical sciences:** Atmospheric science, chemistry, physics. **Social sciences:** General, economics, geography, political science.

Most popular majors. Biology 7%, business/marketing 21%, engineering/engineering technologies 32%, interdisciplinary studies 9%, social sciences 16%.

Technology on campus. PC or laptop required. 120 workstations in computer center. Dormitories wired for high-speed internet access and linked to campus network. Commuter students can connect to campus network. Online library, helpline, repair service, wireless network available.

Student life. Policies: USAFA is a military training environment producing officers of character to lead the Air Force and nation. All students are active duty military members, bound by the Uniform Code of Military Justice and adhere to the Cadet Honor Code. Freshmen not permitted cars on campus. **Housing:** Guaranteed on-campus for all undergraduates. Coed dorms available. **Activities:** Bands, campus ministries, choral groups, dance, drama, international student organizations, literary magazine, music ensembles, Model UN, musical theater, radio station, student government, symphony orchestra, multicultural council, women's forums, women's aircrew issues, cultural clubs/organizations, Way of Life committee, Native American heritage committee, international club, Tuskegee airmen club, interfaith council.

Athletics. NCAA. **Intercollegiate:** Baseball M, basketball, boxing M, cheerleading, cross-country, diving, fencing, football (tackle) M, golf M, gymnastics, ice hockey M, lacrosse M, rifle, soccer, swimming, tennis, track and field, volleyball W, water polo M, wrestling M. **Intramural:** Basketball, boxing M, cross-country, football (non-tackle), handball, rugby M, soccer, softball, tennis, ultimate frisbee, volleyball. **Team name:** Falcons.

Student services. Alcohol/substance abuse counseling, chaplain/spiritual director, career counseling, health services, legal services, personal counseling, placement for graduates, women's services.

Contact. E-mail: rr_webmail@usafa.edu
Toll-free number: (800) 443-9266 Fax: (719) 333-3012
Col. Carolyn Benyshek, Director of Admissions, United States Air Force Academy, HQ USAFA/RR 2304 Cadet Drive, Suite 2400, USAF Academy, CO 80840-5025

University of Colorado Boulder

Boulder, Colorado — CB member
www.colorado.edu — CB code: 4841

- Public 4-year university
- Residential campus in small city
- 26,491 degree-seeking undergraduates: 6% part-time, 45% women, 2% African American, 5% Asian American, 11% Hispanic/Latino, 5% Multi-racial, non-Hispanic, 6% international
- 5,477 degree-seeking graduate students
- 80% of applicants admitted
- SAT or ACT (ACT writing optional), application essay required
- 71% graduate within 6 years; 20% enter graduate study

General. Founded in 1876. Regionally accredited. **Degrees:** 5,289 bachelor's awarded; master's, professional, doctoral offered. **ROTC:** Army, Naval, Air Force. **Location:** 30 miles from Denver. **Calendar:** Semester, extensive summer session. **Full-time faculty:** 1,499 total; 92% have terminal degrees,

19% minority, 38% women. **Part-time faculty:** 554 total; 43% have terminal degrees, 14% minority, 43% women. **Class size:** 47% < 20, 32% 20-39, 6% 40-49, 9% 50-99, 7% >100. **Special facilities:** Natural history museum, art museum and galleries, heritage center, observatory, planetarium and science center, electron microscopes, outdoor theater, video interactive foreign language laboratory, mountain research station, centrifuge laboratory, engineering lab, multipurpose conference center, concert hall, multi-disciplinary information technology center.

Freshman class profile. 31,291 applied, 24,933 admitted, 6,208 enrolled.

Mid 50% test scores			
SAT critical reading:	530-640	Rank in top tenth:	28%
SAT math:	540-660	End year in good standing:	89%
ACT composite:	24-30	Return as sophomores:	86%
GPA 3.75 or higher:	44%	Out-of-state:	47%
GPA 3.50-3.74:	18%	Live on campus:	95%
GPA 3.0-3.49:	33%	International:	7%
GPA 2.0-2.99:	5%	Fraternities:	12%
Rank in top quarter:	57%	Sororities:	25%

Basis for selection. Rigor of secondary school record, GPA, class rank, test scores most important; personal statement, talents, abilities, recommendations important. One academic letter of recommendation is required. Audition required of music majors. **Home schooled:** Applicants will receive individual consideration and are encouraged to apply.

High school preparation. College-preparatory program recommended. 17 units required. Required units include English 4, mathematics 4, social studies 3, science 3 (laboratory 2) and foreign language 3. One elective required for Program in Environmental Design; one elective (in the arts) required for College of Music. Specific requirements vary by school or college, e.g., English must include 2 of composition for College of Arts & Sciences; College of Media, Communication and Information; and School of Business; 3 single foreign language required for College of Arts and Sciences, College of Engineering, School of Business; 2 single foreign language required for Colleges of Music and Program in Environmental Design.

2015-2016 Annual costs. Tuition/fees: $11,091; $34,125 out-of-state. Room/board: $13,194. Books/supplies: $1,800. Personal expenses: $1,358.

2015-2016 Financial aid. Need-based: 4,134 full-time freshmen applied for aid; 2,616 deemed to have need; 2,526 received aid. Average need met was 81%. Average scholarship/grant was $10,283; average loan $5,354. 57% of total undergraduate aid awarded as scholarships/grants, 43% as loans/jobs. **Non-need-based:** Awarded to 6,966 full-time undergraduates, including 2,153 freshmen. Scholarships awarded for academics, alumni affiliation, art, athletics, leadership, music/drama, ROTC, state residency.

Application procedures. Admission: Priority date 11/15; deadline 1/15 (postmark date). $50 fee, may be waived for applicants with need. Admission notification by 4/1. Must reply by May 1 or within 2 week(s) if notified thereafter. **Financial aid:** Priority date 3/1; no closing date. FAFSA required. PROFILE accepted but not required. Applicants notified on a rolling basis starting 3/15; must reply within 3 week(s) of notification.

Academics. Residential academic programs offered in leadership, natural and environmental sciences, humanities and cultural studies, the arts, honors, international and global affairs, communication and society, the health professions, business, engineering, environmental sustainability, and history, culture, and society. **Special study options:** Accelerated study, combined bachelor's/graduate degree, cooperative education, cross-registration, distance learning, double major, dual enrollment of high school students, ESL, exchange student, honors, independent study, internships, liberal arts/career combination, semester at sea, student-designed major, study abroad, teacher certification program. Undergraduate research opportunities, concurrent bachelor's/master's programs, small group academic programs. **Credit/placement by examination:** AP, CLEP, IB, institutional tests. Policies vary by academic department. **Support services:** Learning center, pre-admission summer program, study skills assistance, tutoring, writing center.

Majors. Architecture: Environmental design. **Area/ethnic studies:** General, Asian, Russian/Slavic, women's. **Biology:** Biochemistry, cellular/molecular, ecology/evolutionary, neuroscience, physiology. **Business:** Accounting, business admin, finance, management information systems, marketing. **Communications:** Communications/speech/rhetoric, journalism, media studies, persuasive communications. **Computer sciences:** Computer science, information systems. **Conservation:** Environmental studies. **Education:** Music. **Engineering:** Aerospace, applied physics, architectural, biochemical, chemical, civil, computer, electrical, environmental, mechanical. **English:** English lit. **Foreign languages:** Chinese, classics, French, Germanic, Italian, Japanese, linguistics, Spanish. **Health services:** Communication disorders. **History:** General. **Liberal arts:** Humanities. **Math:** General, applied. **Philosophy/religion:** Judaic, philosophy, religion. **Physical sciences:** Astronomy, chemistry, geology, physics. **Psychology:** General. **Social sciences:** Anthropology, economics, geography, political science, sociology. **Visual/performing arts:** Art history/conservation, dance, dramatic, film/cinema/video, music, music performance, studio arts.

Most popular majors. Biology 14%, business/marketing 12%, communications/journalism 9%, engineering/engineering technologies 11%, psychology 8%, social sciences 15%.

Technology on campus. 1,804 workstations in dormitories, library, computer center, student center. Dormitories wired for high-speed internet access and linked to campus network. Commuter students can connect to campus network. Online course registration, online library, helpline, repair service, student web hosting, wireless network available.

Student life. Freshman orientation: Mandatory. Preregistration for classes offered. Online experience. **Policies:** Student honor code, student conduct code, sexual misconduct policy, discrimination and harassment policy, campus no smoking policy. **Housing:** Guaranteed on-campus for freshmen. Coed dorms, special housing for disabled, apartments, fraternity/sorority housing, themed housing available. $300 nonrefundable deposit. Residential academic programs within specific dorms. **Activities:** Bands, campus ministries, choral groups, dance, drama, film society, international student organizations, literary magazine, music ensembles, Model UN, musical theater, opera, radio station, student government, student newspaper, symphony orchestra, volunteer resource center, Rocky Mountain Rescue Group student chapter, Multicultural Business Students, Engineers Without Borders, religious campus organizations, Gay-Straight Alliance, student veterans association, College Democrats, College Republicans, Students for Education, Medicine and Services,.

Athletics. NCAA. **Intercollegiate:** Basketball, cheerleading, cross-country, football (tackle) M, golf, lacrosse W, skiing, soccer W, tennis W, track and field, volleyball W. **Intramural:** Basketball, football (non-tackle), ice hockey, soccer, table tennis, tennis, ultimate frisbee, volleyball, water polo. **Team name:** Colorado Buffaloes.

Student services. Adult student services, alcohol/substance abuse counseling, chaplain/spiritual director, career counseling, services for economically disadvantaged, student employment services, financial aid counseling, health services, legal services, minority student services, on-campus daycare, personal counseling, placement for graduates, veterans' counselor, women's services. **Physically disabled:** Services for visually, speech, hearing impaired.

Contact. E-mail: apply@colorado.edu
Phone: (303) 492-6301 Fax: (303) 735-2501
Kevin MacLennan, Director of Admissions, University of Colorado Boulder, Regent Administrative Center 125, Boulder, CO 80309-0552

University of Colorado Colorado Springs
Colorado Springs, Colorado
www.uccs.edu

CB code: 4874

- Public 4-year university
- Commuter campus in large city
- 9,480 degree-seeking undergraduates: 22% part-time, 52% women, 4% African American, 3% Asian American, 16% Hispanic/Latino, 7% Multiracial, non-Hispanic, 1% international
- 1,705 degree-seeking graduate students
- 91% of applicants admitted
- 44% graduate within 6 years

General. Founded in 1965. Regionally accredited. **Degrees:** 1,564 bachelor's awarded; master's, professional, doctoral offered. **ROTC:** Army. **Calendar:** Semester, extensive summer session. **Full-time faculty:** 406 total; 13% minority, 52% women. **Part-time faculty:** 327 total; 10% minority, 56% women. **Class size:** 43% < 20, 37% 20-39, 12% 40-49, 6% 50-99, 2% >100. **Special facilities:** Contemporary art gallery, family development center, student military and veteran affairs center.

Freshman class profile. 7,168 applied, 6,510 admitted, 1,636 enrolled.

Mid 50% test scores			
SAT critical reading:	490-600	GPA 2.0-2.99:	25%
SAT math:	470-590	Rank in top quarter:	37%
ACT composite:	21-26	Rank in top tenth:	11%
GPA 3.75 or higher:	27%	Return as sophomores:	67%
GPA 3.50-3.74:	18%	Out-of-state:	17%
GPA 3.0-3.49:	30%	Live on campus:	54%
		International:	1%

Basis for selection. A combination of ACT or SAT scores, high school GPA or rank percentile, transfer GPA, and completed coursework from high school or other institutions when applicable. **Home schooled:** Transcript of courses and grades, state high school equivalency certificate required. **Learning Disabled:** Students with disabilities may register with the Disability Services Office for assistance with accommodations.

High school preparation. College-preparatory program recommended. 17 units required. Required units include English 4, mathematics 4, social studies 3, history 1, science 3 (laboratory 2), foreign language 1 and academic electives 2.

2015-2016 Annual costs. Tuition/fees: $9,428; $22,298 out-of-state. Room/board: $9,500. Books/supplies: $1,800. Personal expenses: $3,100. **Additional information:** Students in the Western Undergraduate Exchange program pay 150% of in-state tuition rather than the full out-of-state tuition. Also, most students affiliated with the military are eligible for in-state tuition rates.

2014-2015 Financial aid. **Need-based:** 1,494 full-time freshmen applied for aid; 1,090 deemed to have need; 979 received aid. Average need met was 52%. Average scholarship/grant was $5,657; average loan $3,289. 41% of total undergraduate aid awarded as scholarships/grants, 59% as loans/jobs. **Non-need-based:** Awarded to 1,570 full-time undergraduates, including 692 freshmen. Scholarships awarded for academics, alumni affiliation, athletics, leadership, ROTC, state residency.

Application procedures. **Admission:** No deadline. $50 fee. Admission notification on a rolling basis. Students may enroll in a variety of concurrent credit-bearing programs prior to finishing high school but are not considered first-year freshman until the first semester of enrollment in college after graduating from high school. **Financial aid:** Priority date 3/1; no closing date. FAFSA required. Applicants notified on a rolling basis starting 4/15.

Academics. **Special study options:** Accelerated study, cross-registration, distance learning, double major, dual enrollment of high school students, ESL, exchange student, honors, independent study, internships, student-designed major, study abroad, teacher certification program, weekend college. **Credit/placement by examination:** AP, CLEP, IB, SAT, ACT, institutional tests. **Support services:** Learning center, reduced course load, remedial instruction, study skills assistance, tutoring, writing center.

Majors. **Biology:** General, biochemistry, exercise physiology. **Business:** Business admin. **Communications:** General. **Computer sciences:** General, modeling/simulation, security. **Education:** Early childhood. **Engineering:** General, computer, electrical, mechanical. **English:** English lit. **Foreign languages:** Spanish. **Health services:** Nursing (RN). **History:** General. **Math:** General. **Philosophy/religion:** Philosophy. **Physical sciences:** Chemistry, physics. **Protective services:** Law enforcement admin. **Psychology:** General. **Social sciences:** Anthropology, economics, geography, political science, sociology. **Visual/performing arts:** General.

Most popular majors. Biology 7%, business/marketing 17%, communications/journalism 9%, engineering/engineering technologies 6%, health sciences 15%, psychology 8%, security/protective services 6%, social sciences 13%.

Technology on campus. Dormitories wired for high-speed internet access and linked to campus network. Commuter students can connect to campus network. Online course registration, online library, helpline, repair service, wireless network available.

Student life. **Freshman orientation:** Mandatory, $50 fee. Preregistration for classes offered. **Housing:** Coed dorms, single-sex dorms, special housing for disabled, apartments, themed housing available. $600 partly refundable deposit. **Activities:** Pep band, choral groups, dance, drama, international student organizations, literary magazine, radio station, student government, student newspaper, TV station, Asian Pacific Islander Student Union, Black Student Union, Latino Student Union, Society of Native American Peoples, SPECTRUM student diversity council, American Sign Language club, Circulo de Español, United Language and Cultures Association.

Athletics. NCAA. **Intercollegiate:** Baseball M, basketball, cross-country, golf, lacrosse W, soccer, softball W, track and field, volleyball W. **Intramural:** Basketball, football (non-tackle), soccer, volleyball. **Team name:** Mountain Lions.

Student services. Adult student services, alcohol/substance abuse counseling, career counseling, financial aid counseling, health services, minority student services, on-campus daycare, personal counseling, veterans' counselor. **Physically disabled:** Services for visually, speech, hearing impaired.

Contact. E-mail: go@uccs.edu
Phone: (719) 255-3084 Toll-free number: (800) 990-8227 ext. 3383
Fax: (719) 255-3116
Mathew Cox, Director-Enrollment Management, University of Colorado Colorado Springs, 1420 Austin Bluffs Parkway, Colorado Springs, CO 80918

University of Colorado Denver
Denver, Colorado
www.ucdenver.edu   CB code: 4875

- Public 4-year university
- Commuter campus in very large city
- 10,786 degree-seeking undergraduates: 26% part-time, 53% women, 5% African American, 10% Asian American, 17% Hispanic/Latino, 4% Multi-racial, non-Hispanic, 10% international
- 8,385 degree-seeking graduate students
- 73% of applicants admitted
- SAT or ACT (ACT writing optional) required
- 46% graduate within 6 years

General. Founded in 1912. Regionally accredited. Library, student center, and classrooms shared with Metropolitan State University of Denver and Community College of Denver. **Degrees:** 2,435 bachelor's awarded; master's, professional, doctoral offered. **ROTC:** Army, Air Force. **Location:** Downtown Denver. **Calendar:** Semester, extensive summer session. **Full-time faculty:** 3,288 total; 73% have terminal degrees, 14% minority, 54% women. **Part-time faculty:** 528 total; 48% have terminal degrees, 16% minority, 51% women. **Class size:** 35% < 20, 48% 20-39, 9% 40-49, 8% 50-99. **Special facilities:** Computational math centers, applied psychology center, environmental science center, transportation research center, Fourth World center for study of indigenous law and politics, center for media forensics.

Freshman class profile. 7,220 applied, 5,270 admitted, 1,349 enrolled.

Mid 50% test scores			
SAT critical reading:	490-600	GPA 2.0-2.99:	23%
SAT math:	490-610	Rank in top quarter:	47%
ACT composite:	20-25	Rank in top tenth:	18%
GPA 3.75 or higher:	27%	Return as sophomores:	72%
GPA 3.50-3.74:	18%	Out-of-state:	11%
GPA 3.0-3.49:	32%	International:	2%

Basis for selection. Previous academic performance including high school course work and GPA; evidence of academic ability and accomplishments as indicated by test scores; and evidence of maturity, motivation, potential for academic success most important. Audition required of music majors. **Home schooled:** Transcript of courses and grades required.

High school preparation. College-preparatory program recommended. 18 units required; 19 recommended. Required and recommended units include English 4, mathematics 4, social studies 3, history 1, science 3 (laboratory 2), foreign language 1-2 and computer science 2.

2015-2016 Annual costs. Tuition/fees: $10,389; $29,319 out-of-state. Room/board: $9,603. Books/supplies: $1,800.

2014-2015 Financial aid. **Need-based:** 1,080 full-time freshmen applied for aid; 867 deemed to have need; 792 received aid. Average need met was 45%. Average scholarship/grant was $6,559; average loan $2,840. 48% of total undergraduate aid awarded as scholarships/grants, 52% as loans/jobs. **Non-need-based:** Awarded to 596 full-time undergraduates, including 83 freshmen. Scholarships awarded for academics, art, leadership, music/drama, state residency. **Additional information:** Pell eligible, full-time students receive a financial aid package that includes a combination of grants, scholarships, and a work-study award sufficient to fund the student's share of tuition, fees, and estimated book expenses. An eligible student may remain in the program for up to 10 semesters or completion of a bachelor's degree.

Application procedures. **Admission:** Priority date 7/22; no deadline. $50 fee, may be waived for applicants with need. Admission notification on a rolling basis. Must reply before first day of classes. **Financial aid:** No deadline. FAFSA required. Applicants notified on a rolling basis starting 3/24.

Academics. Learning opportunities through center for internships and cooperative education. **Special study options:** Accelerated study, combined bachelor's/graduate degree, cooperative education, cross-registration, distance learning, double major, dual enrollment of high school students, ESL, honors, independent study, internships, student-designed major, study abroad, teacher certification program. **Credit/placement by examination:** AP, CLEP, IB, SAT, ACT, institutional tests. 30 credit hours maximum toward bachelor's degree. **Support services:** Learning center, study skills assistance, tutoring, writing center.

Majors. **Architecture:** Architecture. **Area/ethnic studies:** General. **Biology:** General, biomedical sciences. **Business:** Business admin. **Communications:** Communications/speech/rhetoric. **Computer sciences:** General. **Education:** General. **Engineering:** General, biomedical, civil, electrical, mechanical. **English:** English lit, writing. **Foreign languages:** French, Spanish. **Health services:** Nursing (RN). **History:** General. **Math:** General. **Philosophy/religion:** Philosophy. **Physical sciences:** Chemistry, physics. **Protective**

services: Law enforcement admin. **Psychology:** General, psychobiology. **Social sciences:** Anthropology, economics, geography, political science, sociology. **Visual/performing arts:** Dramatic, music, studio arts.

Most popular majors. Biology 10%, business/marketing 16%, communications/journalism 6%, health sciences 14%, psychology 9%, social sciences 14%, visual/performing arts 9%.

Technology on campus. 205 workstations in library, computer center, student center. Commuter students can connect to campus network. Online course registration, online library, helpline, student web hosting, wireless network available.

Student life. Freshman orientation: Mandatory. Preregistration for classes offered. **Activities:** Jazz band, campus ministries, choral groups, dance, drama, film society, international student organizations, music ensembles, musical theater, student government, student newspaper, over 100 student organizations available.

Athletics. Intramural: Ultimate frisbee. **Team name:** Lynx.

Student services. Alcohol/substance abuse counseling, career counseling, student employment services, financial aid counseling, health services, minority student services, on-campus daycare, personal counseling, placement for graduates, veterans' counselor, women's services. **Physically disabled:** Services for visually, speech, hearing impaired.

Contact. E-mail: admissions@ucdenver.edu
Phone: (303) 315-2601 Fax: (303) 315-2610
Chris Dowen, Director of Admissions, University of Colorado Denver, Box 173364, Campus Box 167, Denver, CO 80217-3364

University of Denver	
Denver, Colorado	**CB member**
www.du.edu	**CB code: 4842**

▶ Private 4-year university
▶ Residential campus in very large city
▶ 5,739 degree-seeking undergraduates: 5% part-time, 54% women, 2% African American, 4% Asian American, 10% Hispanic/Latino, 4% Multiracial, non-Hispanic, 9% international
▶ 5,872 degree-seeking graduate students
▶ 73% of applicants admitted
▶ SAT or ACT (ACT writing optional), application essay required
▶ 77% graduate within 6 years

General. Founded in 1864. Regionally accredited. **Degrees:** 1,285 bachelor's awarded; master's, professional, doctoral offered. **ROTC:** Army, Air Force. **Location:** 8 miles from downtown. **Calendar:** Quarter, limited summer session. **Full-time faculty:** 701 total; 90% have terminal degrees, 16% minority, 44% women. **Part-time faculty:** 578 total; 24% have terminal degrees, 8% minority, 52% women. **Class size:** 53% < 20, 37% 20-39, 3% 40-49, 6% 50-99, less than 1% >100. **Special facilities:** Observatory, high-altitude research laboratory, mechanical engineering testing facility, early learning center, center for gifted children.

Freshman class profile. 15,036 applied, 10,938 admitted, 1,424 enrolled.

Mid 50% test scores			
SAT critical reading:	550-660	Rank in top quarter:	80%
SAT math:	560-660	Rank in top tenth:	45%
SAT writing:	530-630	Return as sophomores:	86%
ACT composite:	23-30	Out-of-state:	66%
GPA 3.75 or higher:	59%	Live on campus:	93%
GPA 3.50-3.74:	16%	International:	6%
GPA 3.0-3.49:	20%	Fraternities:	21%
GPA 2.0-2.99:	5%	Sororities:	19%

Basis for selection. GPA, test scores and strength of curriculum most important. Academic maturity, contributions to school and community activities, leadership also important. Recommendations from teacher and counselor, and personal essay considered. Audition required of music majors. Portfolio recommended of art majors. **Home schooled:** Letter of recommendation (nonparent) required.

High school preparation. College-preparatory program recommended. Recommended units include English 4, mathematics 3, social studies 3, science 3 (laboratory 2) and foreign language 3.

2015-2016 Annual costs. Tuition/fees: $44,178. Room/board: $11,498. Books/supplies: $1,800. Personal expenses: $1,359.

2015-2016 Financial aid. Need-based: 935 full-time freshmen applied for aid; 657 deemed to have need; 657 received aid. Average need met was 82%. Average scholarship/grant was $30,860; average loan $3,357. 85% of total undergraduate aid awarded as scholarships/grants, 15% as loans/jobs. **Non-need-based:** Awarded to 2,810 full-time undergraduates, including 702 freshmen. Scholarships awarded for academics, art, athletics, leadership, music/drama.

Application procedures. Admission: Closing date 1/15 (postmark date). $65 fee, may be waived for applicants with need. Admission notification by 3/15. Must reply by 5/1. **Financial aid:** Priority date 2/15; no closing date. FAFSA, CSS PROFILE required. Applicants notified by 3/22; must reply by 5/1.

Academics. Special 3-week inter-term courses available for focused concentration. **Special study options:** Accelerated study, combined bachelor's/graduate degree, cooperative education, distance learning, double major, dual enrollment of high school students, ESL, honors, independent study, internships, semester at sea, student-designed major, study abroad, teacher certification program, Washington semester, weekend college. Learning disability services. **Credit/placement by examination:** AP, CLEP, IB, institutional tests. 45 credit hours maximum toward bachelor's degree. **Support services:** Learning center, pre-admission summer program, reduced course load, study skills assistance, tutoring, writing center.

Majors. Area/ethnic studies: Asian-American, women's. **Biology:** General, biochemistry, ecology, molecular. **Business:** General, accounting, business admin, construction management, finance, hospitality admin, international, management information systems, managerial economics, marketing, organizational behavior, real estate, statistics. **Communications:** Communications/speech/rhetoric, digital media, journalism, media studies. **Computer sciences:** Computer science, information technology, systems analysis. **Conservation:** Environmental science, environmental studies. **Engineering:** General, computer, electrical, mechanical. **English:** English lit. **Foreign languages:** French, German, Italian, Russian, Spanish. **History:** General. **Human services:** Public policy. **Liberal arts:** Arts/sciences. **Math:** General. **Philosophy/religion:** Philosophy, religion. **Physical sciences:** General, chemistry, environmental chemistry, physics. **Psychology:** General. **Social sciences:** General, anthropology, criminology, economics, geography, international relations, political science, sociology. **Visual/performing arts:** Art, art history/conservation, dramatic, film/cinema/video, graphic design, music, music performance, music technology, musicology.

Most popular majors. Biology 7%, business/marketing 32%, communications/journalism 8%, psychology 8%, social sciences 18%, visual/performing arts 6%.

Technology on campus. PC or laptop required. 200 workstations in dormitories, library, computer center, student center. Dormitories wired for high-speed internet access and linked to campus network. Commuter students can connect to campus network. Online course registration, online library, helpline, repair service, student web hosting, wireless network available.

Student life. Freshman orientation: Mandatory. Preregistration for classes offered. Held first week of September for 5 days; includes programs for parents/families. **Policies:** Code of conduct, honor code in effect. **Housing:** Guaranteed on-campus for freshmen. Coed dorms, apartments, fraternity/sorority housing, themed housing, wellness housing available. $200 nonrefundable deposit, deadline 5/1. **Activities:** Bands, campus ministries, choral groups, dance, drama, film society, international student organizations, literary magazine, music ensembles, Model UN, musical theater, opera, radio station, student government, student newspaper, symphony orchestra, Campus Crusade for Christ, Chabad, Fellowship of Catholic University Students, Hillel, College Democrats, College Republicans, Students for a Democratic Society, Students for a Free Tibet, environmental team, volunteer club.

Athletics. NCAA. **Intercollegiate:** Basketball, diving, golf, gymnastics W, ice hockey M, lacrosse, skiing, soccer, swimming, tennis, volleyball W. **Intramural:** Basketball, football (non-tackle), ice hockey M, soccer, softball. **Team name:** Pioneers.

Student services. Adult student services, alcohol/substance abuse counseling, chaplain/spiritual director, career counseling, student employment services, financial aid counseling, health services, minority student services, personal counseling, placement for graduates, veterans' counselor, women's services. **Physically disabled:** Services for visually, speech, hearing impaired.

Contact. E-mail: admission@du.edu
Phone: (303) 871-2036 Toll-free number: (800) 525-9495
Fax: (303) 871-3301
Todd Rinehart, Director of Admission, University of Denver, 2197 South University Boulevard, Denver, CO 80208

University of Northern Colorado

Greeley, Colorado
www.unco.edu

CB member

CB code: 4074

♦ Public 4-year university
♦ Residential campus in small city
♦ 9,108 degree-seeking undergraduates
♦ 2,360 graduate students

General. Founded in 1889. Regionally accredited. **Degrees:** 2,088 bachelor's awarded; master's, doctoral offered. **ROTC:** Army, Air Force. **Location:** 50 miles from Denver; 50 miles from Cheyenne, Wyoming. **Calendar:** Semester, extensive summer session. **Full-time faculty:** 490 total; 12% minority, 50% women. **Part-time faculty:** 280 total; 8% minority, 71% women. **Class size:** 28% < 20, 51% 20-39, 8% 40-49, 11% 50-99, 1% >100. **Special facilities:** African-American cultural center, Hispanic cultural center, Native American and Asian Pacific cultural center.

Freshman class profile.

GPA 3.75 or higher:	23%	Rank in top quarter:	35%
GPA 3.50-3.74:	15%	Rank in top tenth:	12%
GPA 3.0-3.49:	34%	Out-of-state:	12%
GPA 2.0-2.99:	28%	Live on campus:	89%

Basis for selection. High school cumulative GPA and ACT/SAT scores. The middle range is 3.0 - 3.75 GPA and 21-25 ACT or 970-1170 SAT. Admission decision for transfer students are based on cumulative college GPA with a minimum of 2.4 for strong consideration. High school information is considered when transfer students have fewer than 30 credit hours. SAT or ACT recommended.

High school preparation. College-preparatory program recommended. 19 units recommended. Recommended units include English 4, mathematics 4, social studies 2, history 1, science 3 (laboratory 2), foreign language 1 and academic electives 2.

2015-2016 Annual costs. Tuition/fees: $8,166; $19,752 out-of-state. Room/board: $10,360. Books/supplies: $1,350. Personal expenses: $1,642. **Additional information:** Costs reflect student share of tuition after the Colorado College Opportunity Fund.

Financial aid. **Non-need-based:** Scholarships awarded for academics, athletics, music/drama.

Application procedures. **Admission:** Closing date 8/1 (receipt date). $45 fee, may be waived for applicants with need. Admission notification on a rolling basis. **Financial aid:** Priority date 3/1; no closing date. FAFSA required. Applicants notified on a rolling basis starting 3/1; must reply within 4 week(s) of notification.

Academics. **Special study options:** Cooperative education, cross-registration, distance learning, double major, dual enrollment of high school students, ESL, exchange student, external degree, honors, independent study, internships, semester at sea, student-designed major, study abroad, teacher certification program, urban semester. **Credit/placement by examination:** AP, CLEP, IB, SAT, ACT, institutional tests. 30 credit hours maximum toward bachelor's degree. **Support services:** Learning center, reduced course load, remedial instruction, study skills assistance, tutoring, writing center.

Majors. **Area/ethnic studies:** African-American, Asian, Chicano/Hispanic-American/Latino. **Biology:** General. **Business:** Business admin. **Communications:** Communications/speech/rhetoric, journalism. **Conservation:** Environmental studies. **Education:** Elementary, music, social studies, special ed. **Engineering:** Software. **English:** English lit. **Foreign languages:** General, sign language interpretation, Spanish. **Health services:** Athletic training, audiology/hearing, audiology/speech pathology, dietetics, health care admin, nurse practitioner, public health ed, speech pathology, vocational rehab counseling. **History:** General. **Math:** General. **Parks/recreation:** Exercise sciences, facilities management. **Philosophy/religion:** Philosophy. **Physical sciences:** Chemistry, geology, physics. **Protective services:** Criminal justice. **Psychology:** General. **Social sciences:** General, anthropology, economics, geography, political science, sociology. **Visual/performing arts:** Dramatic, music, music management, musical theater, studio arts. **Work/family studies:** Aging.

Most popular majors. Business/marketing 8%, communications/journalism 7%, health sciences 16%, interdisciplinary studies 16%, parks/recreation 8%, psychology 7%, social sciences 7%, visual/performing arts 6%.

Technology on campus. 1,719 workstations in dormitories, library, computer center, student center. Dormitories wired for high-speed internet access and linked to campus network. Commuter students can connect to campus network. Online course registration, online library, helpline, repair service, wireless network available.

Student life. **Freshman orientation:** Mandatory. Preregistration for classes offered. Two-day sessions that correspond with intended major. **Housing:** Guaranteed on-campus for freshmen. Coed dorms, single-sex dorms, special housing for disabled, apartments, fraternity/sorority housing, wellness housing available. **Activities:** Bands, campus ministries, choral groups, dance, drama, film society, international student organizations, literary magazine, music ensembles, musical theater, opera, radio station, student government, student newspaper, symphony orchestra, TV station, African-American student union, Hispanic students organization, Native American student services, Asian/Pacific American student services.

Athletics. NCAA. **Intercollegiate:** Baseball M, basketball, cross-country W, diving W, football (tackle) M, golf, soccer W, softball W, swimming W, tennis, track and field, volleyball W, wrestling M. **Intramural:** Basketball, football (non-tackle), golf, racquetball, soccer, softball, table tennis, tennis, volleyball, water polo. **Team name:** Bears.

Student services. Adult student services, alcohol/substance abuse counseling, chaplain/spiritual director, career counseling, student employment services, financial aid counseling, health services, legal services, minority student services, personal counseling, placement for graduates, veterans' counselor, women's services. **Physically disabled:** Services for visually, speech, hearing impaired.

Contact. E-mail: admissions@unco.edu
Phone: (970) 351-2881 Toll-free number: (888) 700-4862
Fax: (970) 351-2984
Sean Broghammer, Director of Admissions, University of Northern Colorado, 501 20th Street, Campus Box 10, Greeley, CO 80639

University of Phoenix: Denver

Lone Tree, Colorado
www.phoenix.edu

♦ For-profit 4-year university
♦ Commuter campus in large town
♦ 1,240 degree-seeking undergraduates
♦ 464 graduate students

General. Regionally accredited. **Degrees:** 186 bachelor's awarded; master's offered. **Calendar:** Differs by program. **Full-time faculty:** 31 total. **Part-time faculty:** 174 total.

Basis for selection. Open admission, but selective for some programs.

2015-2016 Annual costs. Per-credit-hour charge, $410 to $635, depending upon level and course of study; electronic course materials fee, $95, if applicable. Book and material charges may vary by course and program. All fees are subject to change.

Application procedures. **Admission:** No deadline. No application fee. **Financial aid:** No deadline.

Academics. **Credit/placement by examination:** AP, CLEP.

Majors. **Business:** Accounting, accounting/business management, business admin, e-commerce, entrepreneurial studies, finance, human resources, marketing, operations. **Communications:** General. **Computer sciences:** Database management, networking, programming, security, system admin, systems analysis, web page design, webmaster. **Conservation:** Environmental studies. **Education:** Elementary. **English:** English lit. **Health services:** Facilities admin, health information management, long term care admin, nursing (RN). **Human services:** General. **Protective services:** Disaster management, law enforcement admin, security management.

Student life. **Freshman orientation:** Mandatory. Preregistration for classes offered.

Contact. Toll-free number: (866) 766-0766
University of Phoenix: Denver, 10004 Park Meadows Drive, Lone Tree, CO 80124-5453

University of Phoenix: Southern Colorado

Colorado Springs, Colorado
www.phoenix.edu

♦ For-profit 4-year university
♦ Commuter campus in large city
♦ 600 degree-seeking undergraduates
♦ 159 graduate students

General. Regionally accredited. **Degrees:** 76 bachelor's awarded; master's offered. **Calendar:** Differs by program. **Full-time faculty:** 14 total. **Part-time faculty:** 57 total.

Basis for selection. Open admission, but selective for some programs.

2015-2016 Annual costs. Per-credit-hour charge, $395 to $635, depending upon level and course of study; electronic course materials fee, $95, if applicable. Book and material charges may vary by course and program. All fees are subject to change.

Application procedures. Admission: No deadline. No application fee. **Financial aid:** No deadline.

Academics. Credit/placement by examination: AP, CLEP.

Majors. Business: Accounting, accounting/business management, business admin, finance, human resources, marketing. **Communications:** General. **Computer sciences:** Database management, networking, programming, security, systems analysis, web page design, webmaster. **Education:** Elementary. **Health services:** Facilities admin, health information management, long term care admin. **Human services:** General. **Protective services:** Disaster management, law enforcement admin, security management.

Student life. Freshman orientation: Mandatory. Preregistration for classes offered.

Contact. Toll-free number: (866) 766-0766
University of Phoenix: Southern Colorado, 5725 Mark Dabling Boulevard, Colorado Springs, CO 80919-2221

Western State Colorado University
Gunnison, Colorado
www.western.edu   **CB code: 4946**

- Public 4-year university and liberal arts college
- Residential campus in small town
- 1,951 degree-seeking undergraduates: 6% part-time, 40% women, 3% African American, 1% Asian American, 10% Hispanic/Latino, 1% Native American, 1% Multi-racial, non-Hispanic
- 235 degree-seeking graduate students
- 98% of applicants admitted
- SAT or ACT (ACT writing optional), application essay required
- 42% graduate within 6 years

General. Founded in 1901. Regionally accredited. College-based mountain search and rescue team. **Degrees:** 391 bachelor's awarded; master's offered. **Location:** 200 miles from Denver. **Calendar:** Semester, limited summer session. **Full-time faculty:** 117 total; 80% have terminal degrees, 3% minority, 39% women. **Part-time faculty:** 47 total; 47% have terminal degrees, 2% minority, 49% women. **Class size:** 59% < 20, 39% 20-39, 2% 40-49, less than 1% 50-99, less than 1% >100. **Special facilities:** Botanical gardens, archaeological site, dinosaur reconstruction lab.

Freshman class profile. 1,631 applied, 1,592 admitted, 467 enrolled.

Mid 50% test scores			
SAT critical reading:	460-580	GPA 3.0-3.49:	30%
SAT math:	450-560	GPA 2.0-2.99:	39%
ACT composite:	17-23	Return as sophomores:	69%
GPA 3.75 or higher:	15%	Out-of-state:	67%
GPA 3.50-3.74:	15%	Live on campus:	89%
		International:	1%

Basis for selection. School achievement record, test scores very important; recommendations considered. Interview recommended for academically weak applicants.

High school preparation. College-preparatory program required. 19 units required. Required and recommended units include English 4, mathematics 4, social studies 3, history 1, science 3 (laboratory 2), foreign language 1-2 and academic electives 2.

2015-2016 Annual costs. Tuition/fees: $8,451; $19,455 out-of-state. Room/board: $9,307.

2015-2016 Financial aid. Need-based: 433 full-time freshmen applied for aid; 263 deemed to have need; 263 received aid. Average need met was 58%. Average scholarship/grant was $7,409; average loan $3,112. 48% of total undergraduate aid awarded as scholarships/grants, 52% as loans/jobs. **Non-need-based:** Awarded to 1,063 full-time undergraduates, including 315 freshmen. Scholarships awarded for academics, alumni affiliation, art, athletics, leadership, music/drama.

Application procedures. Admission: Priority date 6/1; no deadline. $30 fee, may be waived for applicants with need. Admission notification by 10/21. Admission notification on a rolling basis. Must reply by May 1 or within 2 week(s) if notified thereafter. **Financial aid:** Priority date 4/1; no closing date. FAFSA required. Applicants notified on a rolling basis starting 4/1; must reply by 5/1 or within 4 week(s) of notification.

Academics. Special study options: Combined bachelor's/graduate degree, distance learning, double major, dual enrollment of high school students, exchange student, honors, independent study, internships, liberal arts/career combination, semester at sea, study abroad, teacher certification program. **Credit/placement by examination:** AP, CLEP, IB, SAT, ACT, institutional tests. 30 credit hours maximum toward bachelor's degree. **Support services:** Remedial instruction, study skills assistance, tutoring, writing center.

Majors. Biology: General. **Business:** Accounting, business admin, management information systems, resort management. **Communications:** Communications/speech/rhetoric. **Conservation:** Environmental studies. **Education:** Art, English, foreign languages, mathematics, music, physical, science, social science, social studies. **English:** English lit. **Foreign languages:** Spanish. **History:** General. **Math:** General. **Parks/recreation:** Exercise sciences. **Physical sciences:** Chemistry, geology. **Protective services:** Criminal justice, police science. **Psychology:** General. **Social sciences:** Anthropology, economics, political science, sociology. **Visual/performing arts:** Art, music, music management, studio arts.

Most popular majors. Biology 9%, business/marketing 21%, education 6%, parks/recreation 12%, psychology 9%, social sciences 12%, visual/performing arts 7%.

Technology on campus. 200 workstations in dormitories, library, student center. Dormitories wired for high-speed internet access and linked to campus network. Commuter students can connect to campus network. Online course registration, online library, helpline, repair service, wireless network available.

Student life. Freshman orientation: Mandatory, $65 fee. Preregistration for classes offered. Wilderness-based program available. **Housing:** Guaranteed on-campus for freshmen. Coed dorms, special housing for disabled, apartments, themed housing available. $100 fully refundable deposit, deadline 4/9. **Activities:** Bands, campus ministries, choral groups, dance, drama, international student organizations, literary magazine, music ensembles, Model UN, radio station, student government, student newspaper, symphony orchestra, TV station, Hillel, black student alliance, Amigos, Campus Crusade, Hui-O-Ka-Aina, lesbian-gay-bisexual alliance, Newman club, Baptist student union, Christian athletes fellowship, women's action coalition.

Athletics. NCAA. **Intercollegiate:** Basketball, cross-country, diving W, football (tackle) M, skiing, soccer W, swimming W, track and field, volleyball W, wrestling M. **Intramural:** Baseball M, basketball, golf, ice hockey M, lacrosse, rugby, skiing, soccer, softball, swimming, tennis, track and field, volleyball, wrestling M. **Team name:** Mountaineers.

Student services. Adult student services, career counseling, health services, on-campus daycare, personal counseling, veterans' counselor. **Physically disabled:** Services for visually, hearing impaired.

Contact. E-mail: discover@western.edu
Phone: (970) 943-2119 Toll-free number: (800) 876-5309
Fax: (970) 943-2363
Paul Fitzgerald, Director of Recruiting, Western State Colorado University, 600 North Adams Street, Gunnison, CO 81231

Westwood College: Aurora
Aurora, Colorado
www.westwood.edu/locations/colorado/denver-south-campus

- For-profit 4-year career college
- Commuter campus in very large city
- 276 degree-seeking undergraduates
- Interview required

General. Regionally accredited; also accredited by ACICS. This Westwood College campus offers a unique hands-on, career-focused curriculum providing associate degrees that can be earned in as little as three months and bachelor's degrees that can be earned in as little as three years. Degree programs are available in the fields of technology, healthcare, business, design and justice. **Degrees:** 32 bachelor's, 74 associate awarded. **Calendar:** Differs by program. **Full-time faculty:** 3 total. **Part-time faculty:** 32 total.

Basis for selection. Institutional test (ACCUPLACER) and interview most important. Developmental courses may be required for those who do not pass entrance examination. Institutional test (ACCUPLACER) and interview most important. Developmental courses may be required for those who do not pass entrance examination.

2015-2016 Annual costs. Books/supplies: $1,106. Personal expenses: $2,534. **Additional information:** Business Administration: AAS $35,686. Computer Aided Design/Architectural Drafting: AAS $38,367. Construction Management: AAS $35,686. Criminal Justice: AAS $38,717. Graphic Design: AAS $40,278. Healthcare Office Administration: AAS $33,586. Medical Assisting: AAS $33,586. Information Technology: AOS $34,825. Business Administration: Major in Management: BS $71,372. Construction Management: BS $71,372. Criminal Justice: Major in Administration: BS $77,434. Medical Assisting: DP $23,990. Additional costs and fees such as books, tool kits, lab fee and online fees may apply.

Application procedures. Admission: No deadline. No application fee. Admission notification on a rolling basis. **Financial aid:** No deadline. FAFSA, institutional form required. Applicants notified on a rolling basis; must reply within 2 week(s) of notification.

Academics. Special study options: Accelerated study, distance learning, independent study, weekend college. **Credit/placement by examination:** AP, CLEP, institutional tests. 67 credit hours maximum toward associate degree, 135 toward bachelor's. **Support services:** Reduced course load, remedial instruction, study skills assistance, tutoring, writing center.

Majors. Business: Business admin, construction management. **Protective services:** Law enforcement admin.

Technology on campus. 300 workstations in library, computer center, student center. Commuter students can connect to campus network. Online course registration, online library, wireless network available.

Student life. Freshman orientation: Mandatory. Preregistration for classes offered.

Student services. Adult student services, career counseling, student employment services, financial aid counseling, placement for graduates.

Contact. E-mail: AdmissionsRepresentativesWW-Campus@westwood.edu
Phone: (303) 934-1122 Fax: (303) 934-2583
Joshua Rushman, Director of Admissions, Westwood College: Aurora, 350 Blackhawk Street, Aurora, CO 80011

Westwood College: Denver North
Denver, Colorado
www.westwood.edu/locations/colorado/denver-north-campus
CB code: 3948

- For-profit 4-year career college
- Commuter campus in very large city
- 863 degree-seeking undergraduates
- Interview required

General. Founded in 1953. Regionally accredited; also accredited by ACICS. 17-month associate degree programs offered. **Degrees:** 24 bachelor's, 111 associate awarded. **Location:** 5 miles from downtown. **Calendar:** Differs by program. **Full-time faculty:** 4 total. **Part-time faculty:** 37 total.

Basis for selection. SAT/ACT, institutional exam and interview most important. SAT or ACT recommended. ACCUPLACER institutional exam waived for students with sufficient SAT/ACT scores.

High school preparation. At least 1 algebra required for electronics, drafting and surveying programs. General math required for all other programs.

2015-2016 Annual costs. Books/supplies: $1,106. Personal expenses: $2,000. **Additional information:** Business Administration: AAS $35,686. Computer Aided Design/Architectural Drafting: AAS $38,367. Construction Management: AAS $35,686. Criminal Justice: AAS $38,717. Dental Assisting: AAS $29,897. Graphic Design: AAS $40,278. Health Information Technology: AAS $38,384. Healthcare Office Administration: AAS $33,586. Medical Assisting: AAS $33,586. Paralegal: AAS $33,250. Automotive Technology: AOS $36,533. Information Technology: AOS $34,825. Business Administration: Major in Management: BS $71,372. Construction Management: BS $71,372. Criminal Justice: Major in Administration: BS $77,434. Information & Network Technologies: Major in CISCO Network Systems: BS $69,650. Medical Assisting: DP $23,990. Additional costs and fees such as books, tool kits, lab fee and online fees may apply.

Financial aid. Non-need-based: Scholarships awarded for academics, state residency.

Application procedures. Admission: No deadline. No application fee. Admission notification on a rolling basis. **Financial aid:** No deadline. FAFSA, institutional form required. Applicants notified on a rolling basis starting 1/1; must reply within 2 week(s) of notification.

Academics. Instruction and emphasis on laboratory work and practical application. **Special study options:** Accelerated study, cooperative education, distance learning, independent study, internships, liberal arts/career combination. **Credit/placement by examination:** AP, CLEP, institutional tests. 69 credit hours maximum toward associate degree, 140 toward bachelor's. **Support services:** Learning center, remedial instruction, study skills assistance, tutoring.

Majors. Business: Business admin, construction management. **Computer sciences:** Applications programming, networking. **Protective services:** Law enforcement admin.

Most popular majors. Business/marketing 20%, computer/information sciences 44%, engineering/engineering technologies 15%, visual/performing arts 21%.

Technology on campus. 50 workstations in library, computer center. Online library available.

Student life. Freshman orientation: Mandatory. Preregistration for classes offered. **Policies:** No-tolerance drug/alcohol policy.

Student services. Career counseling, student employment services, financial aid counseling, placement for graduates, veterans' counselor. **Physically disabled:** Services for visually impaired.

Contact. E-mail: rdejong@westwood.edu
Phone: (303) 650-5050 Fax: (303) 487-0214
Ron DeJong, Director of Admissions, Westwood College: Denver North, 7350 North Broadway, Denver, CO 80221

Westwood College: Online
Broomfield, Colorado
www.westwood.edu/online-learning

- For-profit 3-year virtual career college
- Very large city
- 676 degree-seeking undergraduates

General. Regionally accredited; also accredited by ACICS. This Westwood College campus offers a unique hands-on, career-focused curriculum providing associate degrees that can be earned in as little as three months and bachelor's degrees that can be earned in as little as three years. Degree programs are available in the fields of technology, healthcare, business, design and justice. **Degrees:** 395 bachelor's, 176 associate awarded; master's offered. **Calendar:** Differs by program.

Basis for selection. Institutional test (ACCUPLACER) and interview most important. Developmental courses may be required for those who do not pass entrance examination. Institutional Exam ACCUPLACER waived for students with sufficient SAT/ACT scores. **Home schooled:** Interview required.

2015-2016 Annual costs. Business Administration: AAS $32,165. Computer Aided Design/Architectural Drafting: AAS $33,565. Criminal Justice: AAS $35,679. Graphic Design: AAS $33,565. Healthcare Office Administration: AAS $34,524. Information Technology: AAS $34,825. Medical Insurance Coding & Billing: AAS $34,524. Paralegal: AAS $33,250. Information Technology: AOS $34,825. Business Administration: Major in Management: BS $64,330. Business Administration: Major in Marketing Management: BS $64,330. Criminal Justice: Major in Administration: BS $71,358. Graphic Design: Major in Visual Communications: BS $63,938. Information Technology: Major in Network Management: BS $69,650. Master of Business Administration: MBA $27,354. Additional costs and fees such as books, tool kits, lab fee and online fees may apply.

Application procedures. Admission: No deadline. No application fee. Admission notification on a rolling basis. **Financial aid:** FAFSA, institutional form required.

Academics. Credit/placement by examination: AP, CLEP, institutional tests.

Majors. BACHELOR'S. Business: Business admin, marketing. **Computer sciences:** LAN/WAN management. **Protective services:** Law enforcement admin. **Visual/performing arts:** Design. **ASSOCIATE. Business:** Business admin. **Computer sciences:** Networking. **Health services:** Insurance coding, office admin. **Protective services:** Law enforcement admin. **Visual/performing arts:** Graphic design.

Student life. Freshman orientation: Available. Preregistration for classes offered.

Contact. E-mail: admissionsrepresentativeswol-all@westwood.edu
Phone: (800) 281-2978
Kim Beckman, Vice President of Admissions, Westwood College: Online,
10249 Church Ranch Way, Broomfield, CO 80021

Connecticut

Albertus Magnus College

New Haven, Connecticut
www.albertus.edu

CB member
CB code: 3001

- Private 4-year liberal arts college affiliated with the Roman Catholic Church
- Residential campus in small city
- 1,188 degree-seeking undergraduates: 14% part-time, 66% women, 32% African American, 17% Hispanic/Latino, 1% Multi-racial, non-Hispanic, 2% international
- 318 degree-seeking graduate students
- 87% of applicants admitted
- SAT or ACT (ACT writing optional), application essay required
- 56% graduate within 6 years

General. Founded in 1925. Regionally accredited. Majority of students enrolled in adult education and graduate programs. Approximately 500 undergraduates are traditional age and are able to live on campus. **Degrees:** 347 bachelor's, 53 associate awarded; master's offered. **Location:** 90 miles from New York City. **Calendar:** Semester, limited summer session. **Full-time faculty:** 48 total. **Part-time faculty:** 180 total. **Class size:** 90% < 20, 10% 20-39.

Freshman class profile. 589 applied, 515 admitted, 145 enrolled.

Mid 50% test scores			
SAT critical reading:	440-490	**Out-of-state:**	8%
SAT math:	420-460	**Live on campus:**	44%
SAT writing:	430-490	**International:**	2%

Basis for selection. School achievement record most important. Recommendations, test scores, interview, school and community activities also considered. **Home schooled:** Letter of recommendation (nonparent) required. GED preferred.

High school preparation. 16 units required. Required and recommended units include English 4, mathematics 2-3, social studies 2-3, science 2-3 (laboratory 1) and foreign language 3.

2015-2016 Annual costs. Tuition/fees: $29,650. Room/board: $13,608. Books/supplies: $900. Personal expenses: $3,514.

2014-2015 Financial aid. Need-based: 71% of total undergraduate aid awarded as scholarships/grants, 29% as loans/jobs. **Non-need-based:** Scholarships awarded for academics, state residency.

Application procedures. Admission: No deadline. $35 fee, may be waived for applicants with need. Admission notification on a rolling basis beginning on or about 12/1. Must reply by May 1 or within 4 week(s) if notified thereafter. **Financial aid:** Priority date 3/15; no closing date. FAFSA required. Applicants notified on a rolling basis starting 4/15; must reply within 2 week(s) of notification.

Academics. Special study options: Accelerated study, combined bachelor's/graduate degree, double major, honors, independent study, internships, liberal arts/career combination, student-designed major, teacher certification program. **Credit/placement by examination:** AP, CLEP, SAT, ACT, institutional tests. 21 credit hours maximum toward associate degree, 45 toward bachelor's. **Support services:** Learning center, reduced course load, study skills assistance, tutoring, writing center.

Majors. Biology: General. **Business:** Accounting, business admin, finance, international, management information systems, managerial economics. **Communications:** Advertising, communications/speech/rhetoric, media studies, sports. **Computer sciences:** Information systems. **Education:** General, art, biology, business, chemistry, English, history, mathematics, middle, science, secondary, social studies, Spanish. **English:** British lit, creative writing, English lit. **Foreign languages:** Spanish. **Health services:** Art therapy, premedicine. **History:** General. **Liberal arts:** Arts/sciences. **Math:** General. **Parks/recreation:** Sports admin. **Philosophy/religion:** Philosophy, religion. **Physical sciences:** Chemistry. **Protective services:** Criminal justice. **Psychology:** General. **Social sciences:** General, political science, sociology. **Visual/performing arts:** General, art, art history/conservation, commercial/advertising art, studio arts.

Most popular majors. Business/marketing 55%, psychology 8%, security/protective services 8%, social sciences 11%.

Technology on campus. 146 workstations in library, computer center, student center. Dormitories wired for high-speed internet access and linked to campus network. Commuter students can connect to campus network. Helpline, repair service, wireless network available.

Student life. Freshman orientation: Mandatory. Preregistration for classes offered. **Housing:** Coed dorms, single-sex dorms, wellness housing available. $400 nonrefundable deposit, deadline 7/1. **Activities:** Campus ministries, choral groups, dance, drama, literary magazine, musical theater, student government, Students United for a Better World.

Athletics. NCAA. **Intercollegiate:** Baseball M, basketball, cross-country, lacrosse, soccer, softball W, tennis, volleyball. **Intramural:** Basketball, racquetball, soccer, table tennis. **Team name:** Falcons.

Student services. Adult student services, chaplain/spiritual director, career counseling, student employment services, financial aid counseling, health services, personal counseling, placement for graduates, veterans' counselor.

Contact. E-mail: admissions@albertus.edu
Phone: (203) 773-8501 Toll-free number: (800) 578-9160
Fax: (203) 773-5248
Melissa Ulery, Dean of Admissions, Albertus Magnus College, 700 Prospect Street, New Haven, CT 06511-1189

Central Connecticut State University

New Britain, Connecticut
www.ccsu.edu

CB member
CB code: 3898

- Public 4-year university
- Commuter campus in small city
- 9,693 degree-seeking undergraduates: 20% part-time, 47% women, 12% African American, 4% Asian American, 13% Hispanic/Latino, 3% Multiracial, non-Hispanic, 1% international
- 1,970 degree-seeking graduate students
- 59% of applicants admitted
- SAT or ACT with writing, application essay required
- 57% graduate within 6 years

General. Founded in 1849. Regionally accredited. **Degrees:** 1,996 bachelor's awarded; master's, doctoral offered. **ROTC:** Army, Air Force. **Location:** 9 miles from Hartford. **Calendar:** Semester, extensive summer session. **Full-time faculty:** 450 total; 84% have terminal degrees, 21% minority, 42% women. **Part-time faculty:** 499 total; 25% have terminal degrees, 15% minority, 47% women. **Class size:** 41% < 20, 55% 20-39, 1% 40-49, 2% 50-99, less than 1% >100. **Special facilities:** Observatory, planetarium.

Freshman class profile. 8,686 applied, 5,096 admitted, 1,363 enrolled.

Mid 50% test scores			
SAT critical reading:	460-550	**GPA 2.0-2.99:**	41%
SAT math:	460-550	**Rank in top quarter:**	28%
SAT writing:	460-550	**Rank in top tenth:**	10%
ACT composite:	20-24	**Return as sophomores:**	78%
GPA 3.75 or higher:	7%	**Out-of-state:**	6%
GPA 3.50-3.74:	12%	**Live on campus:**	64%
GPA 3.0-3.49:	39%	**International:**	1%

Basis for selection. High school record, class rank, SAT scores most important. Letters of recommendation, optional student essay, and resume of activities to assess applicant's attitude toward future success considered. School of Business, social work program, communication program, and School of Education programs require acceptance into majors after admission to the university. Interview optional but would be considered. Audition required for music. **Home schooled:** Statement describing home school structure and mission, transcript of courses and grades, state high school equivalency certificate required.

High school preparation. College-preparatory program required. 13 units required. Required and recommended units include English 4, mathematics 3, social studies 2, history 1, science 2 (laboratory 1) and foreign language 3. Social science should include US history; math should include algebra I and II and geometry.

2015-2016 Annual costs. Tuition/fees: $10,460; $21,570 out-of-state. Room/board: $11,134. Books/supplies: $1,300. Personal expenses: $1,927.

2015-2016 Financial aid. Need-based: 55% of total undergraduate aid awarded as scholarships/grants, 45% as loans/jobs. **Non-need-based:** Scholarships awarded for academics, athletics, minority status.

Application procedures. Admission: Priority date 10/15; deadline 6/1 (receipt date). $50 fee, may be waived for applicants with need. Admission notification on a rolling basis beginning on or about 10/15. Must reply by May 1 or within 2 week(s) if notified thereafter. **Financial aid:** Priority date 3/1, closing date 9/15. FAFSA required. Applicants notified on a rolling basis starting 4/1; must reply within 2 week(s) of notification.

Academics. Special study options: Cooperative education, cross-registration, distance learning, double major, dual enrollment of high school students, ESL, exchange student, honors, independent study, internships, student-designed major, study abroad, teacher certification program. Undergrads may take graduate classes. **Credit/placement by examination:** AP, CLEP, IB, SAT, ACT, institutional tests. 30 credit hours maximum toward bachelor's degree. **Support services:** Learning center, pre-admission summer program, reduced course load, remedial instruction, study skills assistance, tutoring, writing center.

Majors. Biology: General, biochemistry, molecular. **Business:** Accounting, business admin, construction management, finance, management information systems, marketing, travel services. **Communications:** Journalism, media studies, persuasive communications. **Computer sciences:** General, system admin, web page design. **Education:** Art, drama/dance, elementary, kindergarten/preschool, music, physical, technology/industrial arts. **Engineering:** Civil, mechanical. **English:** English lit. **Foreign languages:** French, German, Italian, Spanish. **Health services:** Athletic training, nursing (RN). **History:** General. **Human services:** Social work. **Math:** General. **Parks/recreation:** Exercise sciences. **Philosophy/religion:** Philosophy. **Physical sciences:** Chemistry, geology, physics. **Psychology:** General. **Social sciences:** General, anthropology, criminology, economics, geography, political science, sociology. **Visual/performing arts:** Art, design, dramatic, music.

Most popular majors. Business/marketing 26%, communications/journalism 6%, education 8%, engineering/engineering technologies 8%, psychology 8%, social sciences 12%.

Technology on campus. 400 workstations in dormitories, library, computer center, student center. Dormitories wired for high-speed internet access and linked to campus network. Commuter students can connect to campus network. Online course registration, online library, helpline, repair service, wireless network available.

Student life. Freshman orientation: Mandatory. Preregistration for classes offered. Three-day program held at the end of August. **Housing:** Coed dorms, single-sex dorms, special housing for disabled, gender-neutral housing, themed housing, wellness housing available. $250 nonrefundable deposit, deadline 5/1. First-year experience housing, academic living learning community. **Activities:** Bands, campus ministries, choral groups, dance, drama, film society, international student organizations, literary magazine, music ensembles, musical theater, radio station, student government, student newspaper, TV station, Newman club, Union of Jewish Students, Christian Fellowship, Christian Science organization, Afro-American and African students, Latin American student association.

Athletics. NCAA. **Intercollegiate:** Baseball M, basketball, cross-country, football (tackle) M, golf, lacrosse W, soccer, softball W, swimming W, track and field, volleyball W. **Intramural:** Badminton, basketball, field hockey W, football (tackle) M, gymnastics W, lacrosse M, rugby, soccer, softball W, tennis, volleyball, water polo M. **Team name:** Blue Devils.

Student services. Adult student services, alcohol/substance abuse counseling, chaplain/spiritual director, career counseling, student employment services, financial aid counseling, health services, minority student services, on-campus daycare, personal counseling, placement for graduates, veterans' counselor, women's services. **Physically disabled:** Services for visually, speech, hearing impaired.

Contact. E-mail: admissions@ccsu.edu
Phone: (860) 832-2278 Toll-free number: (888) 733-2278
Fax: (860) 832-2295
Lawrence Hall, Director of Admissions, Central Connecticut State University, 1615 Stanley Street, New Britain, CT 06050

Charter Oak State College
New Britain, Connecticut
www.charteroak.edu

CB member
CB code: 0870

▶ Public 4-year virtual career college
▶ Commuter campus in small city
▶ 1,634 degree-seeking undergraduates: 80% part-time, 67% women, 17% African American, 1% Asian American, 14% Hispanic/Latino, 2% Multi-racial, non-Hispanic, 1% international

---

General. Founded in 1973. Regionally accredited. **Degrees:** 454 bachelor's, 81 associate awarded. **Location:** 10 miles from Hartford. **Calendar:** Semester, extensive summer session. **Part-time faculty:** 173 total; 49% have terminal degrees, 17% minority, 58% women. **Class size:** 79% < 20, 21% 20-39.

Basis for selection. Applicants must be at least 16 years old with at least 9 college-level credits.

High school preparation. College-preparatory program recommended.

2015-2016 Annual costs. Tuition/fees: $9,009; $11,619 out-of-state. Books/supplies: $1,000.

2014-2015 Financial aid. Need-based: 37% of total undergraduate aid awarded as scholarships/grants, 63% as loans/jobs.

Application procedures. Admission: No deadline. $75 fee, may be waived for applicants with need. Admission notification on a rolling basis. **Financial aid:** Priority date 4/15; no closing date. FAFSA required. Applicants notified on a rolling basis.

Academics. Special study options: Accelerated study, distance learning, dual enrollment of high school students, external degree, independent study, liberal arts/career combination, student-designed major, teacher certification program. Students can take courses at any regionally accredited institution. **Credit/placement by examination:** AP, CLEP. **Support services:** Reduced course load, tutoring, writing center. Free tutoring and writing center available to students online.

Majors. Business: Business admin. **Computer sciences:** Security. **Health services:** Health care admin, health information management. **Liberal arts:** Arts/sciences. **Psychology:** General.

Most popular majors. Health sciences 7%, liberal arts 93%.

Technology on campus. Commuter students can connect to campus network. Online course registration, online library, helpline available.

Student life. Freshman orientation: Available. Preregistration for classes offered. **Activities:** Student government.

Student services. Adult student services, financial aid counseling, veterans' counselor.

Contact. E-mail: admissions@charteroak.edu
Phone: (860) 515-3800
Lori Pendleton, Director of Admission, Charter Oak State College, 55 Paul Manafort Drive, New Britain, CT 06053

Connecticut College
New London, Connecticut
www.conncoll.edu

CB member
CB code: 3284

▶ Private 4-year liberal arts college
▶ Residential campus in large town
▶ 1,854 degree-seeking undergraduates: 63% women, 4% African American, 4% Asian American, 9% Hispanic/Latino, 3% Multi-racial, non-Hispanic, 6% international
▶ 4 degree-seeking graduate students
▶ 40% of applicants admitted
▶ Application essay required
▶ 83% graduate within 6 years; 13% enter graduate study

General. Founded in 1911. Regionally accredited. **Degrees:** 444 bachelor's awarded; master's offered. **Location:** 105 miles from Boston, 124 miles from New York City. **Calendar:** Semester. **Full-time faculty:** 180 total; 94% have terminal degrees, 16% minority, 52% women. **Part-time faculty:** 81 total; 47% have terminal degrees, 7% minority, 42% women. **Class size:** 69% < 20, 27% 20-39, 2% 40-49, 2% 50-99, less than 1% >100. **Special facilities:** 750-acre arboretum, greenhouse, language and culture media center, academic resource center, ion accelerator, refracting telescope and observatory, scanning and transmission electron microscopes, nuclear magnetic resonance spectrometer, tunable diode laser spectroscopy laboratory, center for electronic and digital sound, neuroscience and animal behavior laboratories, clinical and social psychology research observation suites.

Freshman class profile. 5,182 applied, 2,071 admitted, 482 enrolled.

Mid 50% test scores		Rank in top tenth:	49%
SAT critical reading:	610-700	Return as sophomores:	90%
SAT math:	610-700	Out-of-state:	83%
SAT writing:	610-700	Live on campus:	100%
ACT composite:	28-31	International:	6%
Rank in top quarter:	79%		

Basis for selection. Rigor of high school program most important. Essay, recommendations, extracurricular activities, and interview also considered. First-year applicants are not required to submit standardized tests, but may choose to submit the results of either SAT Reasoning, 2 Subject Tests, or the ACT. TOEFL or an equivalent exam is required if English is not the first language of the applicant. Interview recommended; arts portfolio optional. **Home schooled:** Statement describing home school structure and mission, transcript of courses and grades required. Interview recommended but not required.

High school preparation. College-preparatory program recommended.

2015-2016 Annual costs. Tuition/fees: $49,350. Room/board: $13,615.

2015-2016 Financial aid. All financial aid based on need. 309 full-time freshmen applied for aid; 284 deemed to have need; 284 received aid. Average need met was 100%. Average scholarship/grant was $37,224; average loan $3,314. 87% of total undergraduate aid awarded as scholarships/grants, 13% as loans/jobs.

Application procedures. Admission: Closing date 1/1. $60 fee, may be waived for applicants with need. Admission notification by 3/31. Must reply by 5/1. **Financial aid:** Priority date 2/1; no closing date. FAFSA, CSS PROFILE required. Applicants notified by 4/1; must reply by 5/1.

Academics. Special study options: Accelerated study, cross-registration, double major, exchange student, independent study, internships, student-designed major, study abroad, teacher certification program, Washington semester. In addition to their major(s), students can earn a certificate from one of our four interdisciplinary centers. **Credit/placement by examination:** AP, CLEP, IB, institutional tests. **Support services:** Learning center, study skills assistance, tutoring, writing center.

Majors. Architecture: Architecture. **Area/ethnic studies:** African, American, Chicano/Hispanic-American/Latino, East Asian, Latin American, women's. **Biology:** General, biochemistry, botany, cellular/molecular, neuroscience. **Computer sciences:** Computer science. **Conservation:** Environmental studies. **English:** English lit. **Foreign languages:** Chinese, classics, French, German, Italian, Japanese, Slavic. **History:** General. **Math:** General. **Philosophy/religion:** Philosophy, religion. **Physical sciences:** Chemistry, physics. **Psychology:** General. **Social sciences:** Anthropology, economics, international relations, political science, sociology, urban studies. **Visual/performing arts:** Art history/conservation, dance, dramatic, film/cinema/video, music, studio arts. **Work/family studies:** Family studies.

Most popular majors. Area/ethnic studies 6%, biology 16%, foreign language 6%, psychology 9%, social sciences 32%, visual/performing arts 10%.

Technology on campus. Commuter students can connect to campus network. Online course registration, helpline, repair service, wireless network available.

Student life. Freshman orientation: Mandatory. Preregistration for classes offered. **Policies:** Honor Code. Freshmen not permitted cars on campus. **Housing:** Guaranteed on-campus for all undergraduates. Coed dorms, gender-neutral housing, themed housing, wellness housing available. Quiet housing, foreign-language housing available. **Activities:** Bands, campus ministries, choral groups, dance, drama, film society, international student organizations, literary magazine, music ensembles, musical theater, radio station, student government, student newspaper, symphony orchestra.

Athletics. NCAA. **Intercollegiate:** Basketball, cross-country, diving, field hockey W, ice hockey, lacrosse, rowing (crew), sailing, soccer, squash, swimming, tennis, track and field, volleyball W, water polo. **Intramural:** Baseball M, basketball, football (non-tackle) M, racquetball, soccer, softball, squash, tennis, volleyball. **Team name:** Camels.

Student services. Adult student services, alcohol/substance abuse counseling, chaplain/spiritual director, career counseling, student employment services, financial aid counseling, health services, minority student services, on-campus daycare, personal counseling, women's services. **Physically disabled:** Services for visually, hearing impaired.

Contact. E-mail: admission@conncoll.edu
Phone: (860) 439-2200 Fax: (860) 439-4301
Andrew Strickler, Dean of Admission and Financial Aid, Connecticut College, 270 Mohegan Avenue, New London, CT 06320

Eastern Connecticut State University
Willimantic, Connecticut
www.easternct.edu

CB member
CB code: 3966

- Public 4-year university and liberal arts college
- Residential campus in large town

- 4,767 degree-seeking undergraduates: 10% part-time, 54% women, 7% African American, 3% Asian American, 10% Hispanic/Latino, 3% Multiracial, non-Hispanic, 1% international
- 145 degree-seeking graduate students
- 64% of applicants admitted
- 56% graduate within 6 years

General. Founded in 1889. Regionally accredited. **Degrees:** 1,042 bachelor's, 9 associate awarded; master's offered. **ROTC:** Army, Air Force. **Location:** 30 miles from Hartford, 90 miles from Boston. **Calendar:** Semester, extensive summer session. **Full-time faculty:** 193 total; 97% have terminal degrees, 22% minority, 46% women. **Part-time faculty:** 276 total; 34% have terminal degrees, 10% minority, 46% women. **Class size:** 37% < 20, 56% 20-39, 6% 40-49, less than 1% 50-99. **Special facilities:** Child and family development complex, sustainable energy institute, free enterprise institute, arboretum, planetarium, farm, 2 electron microscopes.

Freshman class profile. 5,370 applied, 3,413 admitted, 985 enrolled.

Mid 50% test scores				
		GPA 2.0-2.99:		37%
SAT critical reading:	480-570	Rank in top quarter:		31%
SAT math:	470-570	Rank in top tenth:		11%
SAT writing:	480-570	Return as sophomores:		73%
GPA 3.75 or higher:	9%	Out-of-state:		8%
GPA 3.50-3.74:	13%	Live on campus:		89%
GPA 3.0-3.49:	40%	International:		1%

Basis for selection. Applicants should be in top half of class and recommended by high school. Quality of course work very important; 2.5 GPA in college preparatory program required. SAT score also important. Extracurricular activities considered. Interview and essay recommended.

High school preparation. College-preparatory program recommended. Recommended units include English 4, mathematics 4, social studies 2, science 2 and foreign language 2.

2015-2016 Annual costs. Tuition/fees: $10,016; $22,286 out-of-state. Room/board: $12,108. Books/supplies: $1,000. Personal expenses: $1,440.

2014-2015 Financial aid. Need-based: 790 full-time freshmen applied for aid; 577 deemed to have need; 550 received aid.

Application procedures. Admission: Priority date 5/1; no deadline. $50 fee, may be waived for applicants with need. Admission notification on a rolling basis beginning on or about 12/1. Must reply by May 1 or within 2 week(s) if notified thereafter. **Financial aid:** Priority date 3/1; no closing date. FAFSA required. Applicants notified on a rolling basis starting 3/1; must reply by 5/1.

Academics. Special study options: Accelerated study, cooperative education, cross-registration, distance learning, double major, dual enrollment of high school students, exchange student, external degree, honors, independent study, internships, student-designed major, study abroad, teacher certification program. **Credit/placement by examination:** AP, CLEP, SAT, institutional tests. 30 credit hours maximum toward associate degree, 60 toward bachelor's. Institutional placement test required for all entering freshmen. **Support services:** Learning center, pre-admission summer program, reduced course load, remedial instruction, study skills assistance, tutoring, writing center.

Majors. Biology: General, biochemistry. **Business:** Accounting, business admin, management information systems. **Communications:** Communications/speech/rhetoric. **Computer sciences:** General. **Conservation:** Environmental science. **Education:** Early childhood, elementary, middle, physical, secondary. **English:** English lit. **Foreign languages:** Spanish. **History:** General. **Human services:** Social work. **Math:** General. **Parks/recreation:** Sports admin. **Psychology:** General. **Social sciences:** Economics, political science, sociology. **Visual/performing arts:** General, studio arts.

Most popular majors. Business/marketing 17%, communications/journalism 8%, education 7%, English 6%, liberal arts 10%, psychology 10%, social sciences 16%.

Technology on campus. Dormitories wired for high-speed internet access and linked to campus network. Commuter students can connect to campus network. Online library, helpline, repair service, student web hosting, wireless network available.

Student life. Freshman orientation: Mandatory. Preregistration for classes offered. **Policies:** No alcohol permitted on campus; all halls are smoke-free; sign-in guest policy for all first-year halls from 7pm-12am. **Housing:** Coed dorms, apartments available. $250 nonrefundable deposit. **Activities:** Bands, campus ministries, choral groups, dance, drama, international student organizations, literary magazine, music ensembles, musical theater, radio station, student government, student newspaper, TV station, more than 70 clubs and organizations.

Athletics. NCAA. **Intercollegiate:** Baseball M, basketball, cheerleading W, cross-country, field hockey W, lacrosse, soccer, softball W, swimming W, track and field, volleyball W. **Intramural:** Badminton, basketball, bowling, cross-country, football (tackle) M, gymnastics W, racquetball, rugby, skiing, soccer, softball, swimming, tennis, track and field, volleyball, water polo. **Team name:** Warriors.

Student services. Adult student services, alcohol/substance abuse counseling, chaplain/spiritual director, career counseling, services for economically disadvantaged, student employment services, financial aid counseling, health services, minority student services, on-campus daycare, personal counseling, placement for graduates, veterans' counselor, women's services. **Physically disabled:** Services for visually, speech, hearing impaired.

Contact. E-mail: admissions@easternct.edu
Phone: (860) 465-5286 Toll-free number: (877) 353-3278
Fax: (860) 465-5544
Edwin Harris, Director of Enrollment Management, Eastern Connecticut State University, 83 Windham Street, Willimantic, CT 06226-2295

Fairfield University
Fairfield, Connecticut   **CB member**
www.fairfield.edu   **CB code: 3390**

- Private 4-year university affiliated with the Roman Catholic Church
- Residential campus in small city
- 3,863 degree-seeking undergraduates: 4% part-time, 60% women, 2% African American, 2% Asian American, 7% Hispanic/Latino, 1% Multiracial, non-Hispanic, 2% international
- 1,151 degree-seeking graduate students
- 65% of applicants admitted
- Application essay required
- 82% graduate within 6 years; 19% enter graduate study

General. Founded in 1942. Regionally accredited. **Degrees:** 880 bachelor's, 1 associate awarded; master's, professional offered. **ROTC:** Army, Air Force. **Location:** 60 miles from New York City. **Calendar:** Semester, limited summer session. **Full-time faculty:** 266 total; 94% have terminal degrees, 12% minority, 56% women. **Part-time faculty:** 312 total; 44% have terminal degrees, 7% minority, 53% women. **Class size:** 43% < 20, 55% 20-39, 1% 40-49, less than 1% 50-99. **Special facilities:** Media center, 750-seat concert hall/theater, rehearsal and improvisation theater, language learning lab, business education simulation training (BEST) classroom, SIM/simulated hospital environment and human patient simulators in the nursing facility, art gallery and art museum, model interactive high technology classrooms, resource center for core science.

Freshman class profile. 10,767 applied, 6,995 admitted, 966 enrolled.

Mid 50% test scores			
SAT critical reading:	540-630	**GPA 2.0-2.99:**	18%
SAT math:	560-640	**Rank in top quarter:**	69%
SAT writing:	550-640	**Rank in top tenth:**	31%
ACT composite:	25-29	**End year in good standing:**	92%
GPA 3.75 or higher:	25%	**Return as sophomores:**	89%
GPA 3.50-3.74:	19%	**Out-of-state:**	78%
GPA 3.0-3.49:	38%	**Live on campus:**	95%
		International:	2%

Basis for selection. School achievement record, recommendations, school activities, and personal statement are important. Special consideration is given to children/siblings of alumni and students with special talents, diverse or unique backgrounds. Submission of test scores is optional. Fairfield has a test optional policy. Students may choose whether or not to submit their standardized test scores. Interview recommended. Portfolio highly recommended for music majors, resume for theater majors. **Home schooled:** Statement describing home school structure and mission, transcript of courses and grades, state high school equivalency certificate, interview, letter of recommendation (nonparent) required. SAT/ACT required.

High school preparation. College-preparatory program required. 16 units required; 20 recommended. Required and recommended units include English 4, mathematics 3-4, social studies 2, history 2, science 3-4 (laboratory 2) and foreign language 2-4. 1 additional math and 2 science recommended for math, business and science majors.

2015-2016 Annual costs. Tuition/fees: $44,875. Room/board: $13,520. Books/supplies: $1,150. Personal expenses: $930.

2015-2016 Financial aid. Need-based: 718 full-time freshmen applied for aid; 483 deemed to have need; 483 received aid. Average need met was 80%. Average scholarship/grant was $25,764; average loan $3,773. 84% of total undergraduate aid awarded as scholarships/grants, 16% as loans/jobs. **Non-need-based:** Awarded to 1,774 full-time undergraduates, including 502

freshmen. Scholarships awarded for academics, alumni affiliation, art, athletics, leadership, music/drama. **Additional information:** Veteran's Pride Program provides tuition discounts for children of qualified veterans. Bridgeport Tuition Program provides free tuition to qualified students from City of Bridgeport with family income under $50,000.

Application procedures. Admission: Priority date 11/15; deadline 1/15 (postmark date). $60 fee, may be waived for applicants with need. Admission notification by 4/1. Must reply by 5/1. **Financial aid:** Closing date 2/15. FAFSA, CSS PROFILE required. Applicants notified by 4/1; must reply by 5/1.

Academics. Special study options: Accelerated study, combined bachelor's/graduate degree, cross-registration, distance learning, double major, exchange student, honors, independent study, internships, liberal arts/career combination, student-designed major, study abroad, teacher certification program, Washington semester. **Credit/placement by examination:** AP, CLEP, IB, SAT, ACT, institutional tests. 15 credit hours maximum toward bachelor's degree. **Support services:** Pre-admission summer program, reduced course load, study skills assistance, tutoring, writing center, Math lab.

Majors. Area/ethnic studies: American. **Biology:** General, biochemistry. **Business:** Accounting, business admin, finance, international, management information systems, marketing. **Communications:** Communications/speech/rhetoric. **Computer sciences:** General. **Conservation:** Environmental studies. **Engineering:** Biomedical, computer, electrical, mechanical, software. **English:** English lit. **Foreign languages:** French, German, Italian, Spanish. **Health services:** Nursing (RN). **History:** General. **Math:** General. **Philosophy/religion:** Philosophy, religion. **Physical sciences:** Chemistry, physics. **Psychology:** General. **Social sciences:** Economics, international relations, political science, sociology, sociology/anthropology. **Visual/performing arts:** Art history/conservation, dramatic, music, studio arts.

Most popular majors. Business/marketing 33%, communications/journalism 9%, English 7%, health sciences 13%, psychology 7%, social sciences 12%.

Technology on campus. 131 workstations in library, student center. Dormitories wired for high-speed internet access and linked to campus network. Commuter students can connect to campus network. Online course registration, online library, helpline, repair service, student web hosting, wireless network available.

Student life. Freshman orientation: Available, $230 fee. Preregistration for classes offered. Held for two days in late June. **Policies:** Freshmen not permitted cars on campus. **Housing:** Guaranteed on-campus for all undergraduates. Coed dorms, special housing for disabled, apartments, gender-neutral housing, themed housing, wellness housing available. $400 nonrefundable deposit, deadline 5/1. All rooms, apartments, and townhouses are single sex. In the traditional halls they are single sex by wing or floor. **Activities:** Bands, campus ministries, choral groups, dance, drama, international student organizations, literary magazine, music ensembles, Model UN, musical theater, radio station, student government, student newspaper, symphony orchestra, TV station, Fairfield University Student Association, Asian Students Association, South Asian Student Association, Spanish-American & Latino Student Organization, Fairfield Alliance, Students 4 Social Justice, Muslim Student Association, Kadima, Umoja (African American & Carribean Student Association), Model UN.

Athletics. NCAA. **Intercollegiate:** Baseball M, basketball, cross-country, diving, field hockey W, golf, lacrosse, rowing (crew), soccer, softball W, swimming, tennis, volleyball W. **Intramural:** Basketball, football (non-tackle) M, golf, soccer, softball, table tennis, tennis, volleyball. **Team name:** Stags.

Student services. Adult student services, alcohol/substance abuse counseling, chaplain/spiritual director, career counseling, services for economically disadvantaged, student employment services, financial aid counseling, health services, minority student services, on-campus daycare, personal counseling, placement for graduates, veterans' counselor, women's services. **Physically disabled:** Services for visually, speech, hearing impaired.

Contact. E-mail: admis@fairfield.edu
Phone: (203) 254-4100 Fax: (203) 254-4199
Karen Pellegrino, Associate Vice President and Dean of Enrollment, Fairfield University, 1073 North Benson Road, Fairfield, CT 06824

Holy Apostles College and Seminary
Cromwell, Connecticut
www.holyapostles.edu   **CB code: 0921**

- Private 4-year liberal arts and seminary college affiliated with the Roman Catholic Church
- Commuter campus in large town

- 95 degree-seeking undergraduates: 33% part-time, 48% women
- 308 degree-seeking graduate students
- 100% of applicants admitted
- Application essay, interview required

General. Founded in 1956. Regionally accredited. 75% of students are lay students, 25% are seminarians. **Degrees:** 18 bachelor's, 1 associate awarded; master's offered. **Location:** 15 miles from Hartford. **Calendar:** Semester, extensive summer session. **Full-time faculty:** 13 total; 85% have terminal degrees, 23% minority, 46% women. **Part-time faculty:** 54 total; 57% have terminal degrees, 7% minority, 18% women. **Class size:** 97% < 20, 3% 20-39. **Special facilities:** Chapel.

Freshman class profile. 12 applied, 12 admitted, 12 enrolled.

Return as sophomores:	100%	International:	8%
Out-of-state:	25%		

Basis for selection. Interview, level of interest and recommendations most important. 1050 SAT and 3.0 GPA in core courses recommended. SAT recommended. **Home schooled:** State high school equivalency certificate, interview, letter of recommendation (nonparent) required.

2015-2016 Annual costs. Tuition/fees: $9,670. Books/supplies: $750. Personal expenses: $600. **Additional information:** All courses, all degree programs, now $320 per credit hour.

2014-2015 Financial aid. All financial aid based on need. 32% of total undergraduate aid awarded as scholarships/grants, 68% as loans/jobs.

Application procedures. Admission: Priority date 8/15; no deadline. $50 fee, may be waived for applicants with need. Admission notification on a rolling basis. Applications accepted up to one week before beginning of semester. **Financial aid:** Closing date 6/30. FAFSA required. Applicants notified on a rolling basis starting 8/25; must reply within 2 week(s) of notification.

Academics. 85-credit core curriculum required of all undergraduates. **Special study options:** Combined bachelor's/graduate degree, distance learning, double major, ESL, independent study. **Credit/placement by examination:** AP, CLEP, IB, institutional tests. 30 credit hours maximum toward bachelor's degree. **Support services:** Reduced course load, remedial instruction, study skills assistance, tutoring, writing center.

Majors. Liberal arts: Humanities. **Philosophy/religion:** Philosophy, religion. **Social sciences:** General. **Theology:** Theology.

Most popular majors. English 22%, philosophy/religious studies 56%, social sciences 6%, theological studies 17%.

Technology on campus. 10 workstations in library.

Student life. Freshman orientation: Available. Preregistration for classes offered. **Policies:** Men's dorms for seminarians only; other students must commute. Religious observance required. **Activities:** Choral groups, Life League.

Student services. Chaplain/spiritual director, financial aid counseling, personal counseling.

Contact. E-mail: admissions@holyapostles.edu
Phone: (860) 632-3033 Toll-free number: (800) 330-7272
Fax: (860) 632-3075
Elizabeth Rex, Director of Admissions, Holy Apostles College and Seminary, 33 Prospect Hill Road, Cromwell, CT 06416-2005

Lyme Academy College of Fine Arts
Old Lyme, Connecticut
www.lymeacademy.edu   CB code: 1791

- Private 4-year visual arts college
- Residential campus in small town
- 78 degree-seeking undergraduates
- SAT or ACT (ACT writing recommended), application essay, interview required

General. Founded in 1976. Regionally accredited. **Degrees:** 21 bachelor's awarded. **Location:** 40 miles from Hartford, 20 miles from New London. **Calendar:** Semester, limited summer session. **Full-time faculty:** 7 total. **Part-time faculty:** 11 total. **Class size:** 89% < 20, 11% 20-39.

Freshman class profile.

GPA 3.75 or higher:	11%	GPA 2.0-2.99:	23%
GPA 3.50-3.74:	33%	Out-of-state:	56%
GPA 3.0-3.49:	33%		

Basis for selection. Admissions based on portfolio, interview, essay, GPA. SAT/ACT used primarily for placement. Portfolio, campus visit highly recommended. **Home schooled:** Statement describing home school structure and mission, transcript of courses and grades, state high school equivalency certificate, interview, letter of recommendation (nonparent) required. **Learning Disabled:** Students should disclose their disabilities to Student Services so that modifications and assistance can be offered.

2015-2016 Annual costs. Tuition/fees: $31,360. Room only: $7,000. Books/supplies: $2,000. Personal expenses: $500.

Financial aid. Non-need-based: Scholarships awarded for academics, art, leadership.

Application procedures. Admission: Priority date 2/15; no deadline. $55 fee, may be waived for applicants with need. Admission notification on a rolling basis beginning on or about 2/15. Must reply by May 1 or within 2 week(s) if notified thereafter. **Financial aid:** Priority date 2/15, closing date 4/15. FAFSA required. Applicants notified on a rolling basis starting 3/1; must reply by 5/1 or within 2 week(s) of notification.

Academics. Special study options: Cross-registration, independent study. Student/alumni mentorship program. **Credit/placement by examination:** AP, CLEP, SAT, ACT. **Support services:** Pre-admission summer program, reduced course load, remedial instruction, study skills assistance, tutoring.

Majors. Visual/performing arts: Drawing, illustration, painting, sculpture.

Technology on campus. 6 workstations in library. Online library, wireless network available.

Student life. Freshman orientation: Mandatory. Preregistration for classes offered. Usually held several days before start of fall classes. **Activities:** Student government.

Student services. Alcohol/substance abuse counseling, career counseling, financial aid counseling, personal counseling, veterans' counselor, women's services.

Contact. E-mail: admissions@lymeacademy.edu
Phone: (860) 434-5232 ext. 120 Fax: (860) 434-8725
Sarah Churchill, Assistant Dean of Admissions, Lyme Academy College of Fine Arts, 84 Lyme Street, Old Lyme, CT 06371

Mitchell College
New London, Connecticut   **CB member**
www.mitchell.edu   **CB code: 3528**

- Private 4-year liberal arts college
- Residential campus in small city
- 659 degree-seeking undergraduates
- Application essay, interview required

General. Founded in 1938. Regionally accredited. **Degrees:** 160 bachelor's, 14 associate awarded. **Location:** 100 miles from New York City and Boston. **Calendar:** Semester, limited summer session. **Full-time faculty:** 23 total. **Part-time faculty:** 73 total. **Class size:** 77% < 20, 23% 20-39, less than 1% 40-49. **Special facilities:** Two beaches, dock with sailboat fleet, learning resource center for students with learning disabilities, hiking trails, nature preserve.

Freshman class profile.

GPA 3.75 or higher:	1%	GPA 2.0-2.99:	53%
GPA 3.50-3.74:	5%	Out-of-state:	43%
GPA 3.0-3.49:	31%	Live on campus:	80%

Basis for selection. High school achievement, recommendations, motivation and interview very important. **Learning Disabled:** Students applying to Learning Resource Center should submit results of complete psycho-educational evaluation, testing accommodation recommendations made by professional who completed the evaluation, definitive diagnosis of learning disability or ADHD, and standardized achievement testing (reading, writing and math). All documentation should be less than 3 years old; testing must be administered by certified or licensed psychologist.

High school preparation. College-preparatory program recommended. 16 units required. Required units include English 4, mathematics 3, social studies 2, history 1, science 2 (laboratory 1) and academic electives 3.

2015-2016 Annual costs. Tuition/fees: $31,000. Room/board: $12,500. Books/supplies: $1,700. Personal expenses: $1,300.

Financial aid. Non-need-based: Scholarships awarded for academics, alumni affiliation, art, leadership.

Application procedures. Admission: Priority date 4/1; no deadline. $30 fee, may be waived for applicants with need, free for online applicants. Admission notification on a rolling basis beginning on or about 12/15. Must reply by May 1 or within 2 week(s) if notified thereafter. **Financial aid:** Priority date 3/1; no closing date. FAFSA, CSS PROFILE required. Applicants notified on a rolling basis starting 2/15; must reply within 3 week(s) of notification.

Academics. Free professional tutoring offered in most disciplines. **Special study options:** Independent study, internships, liberal arts/career combination, student-designed major, teacher certification program. **Credit/placement by examination:** AP, CLEP, institutional tests. 30 credit hours maximum toward associate degree. **Support services:** Learning center, preadmission summer program, reduced course load, study skills assistance, tutoring, writing center.

Majors. Biology: Environmental. **Business:** Accounting/business management, business admin, hospitality admin, hotel/motel admin, restaurant/food services, small business admin, tourism/travel. **Communications:** Broadcast journalism, digital media, journalism, media studies, organizational, public relations, radio/TV. **Communications technology:** Graphics. **Conservation:** Environmental studies. **Education:** Early childhood, kindergarten/preschool. **Liberal arts:** Arts/sciences, humanities. **Math:** General. **Parks/recreation:** Sports admin. **Protective services:** Criminal justice, homeland security, juvenile corrections. **Psychology:** General, community, developmental. **Social sciences:** Criminology, international economic development. **Visual/performing arts:** Graphic design. **Work/family studies:** Family studies.

Most popular majors. Business/marketing 22%, communications/journalism 7%, education 6%, liberal arts 23%, parks/recreation 13%, psychology 6%, security/protective services 18%.

Technology on campus. Dormitories wired for high-speed internet access and linked to campus network. Commuter students can connect to campus network. Helpline, repair service, wireless network available.

Student life. Freshman orientation: Available. Preregistration for classes offered. Held in September prior to start of classes; concurrent program specific to parent issues. **Housing:** Guaranteed on-campus for all undergraduates. Coed dorms, special housing for disabled, apartments, themed housing available. **Activities:** Dance, drama, radio station, student government, multicultural club, Hillel, spirituality club, African American alliance, communication club, improve club, Bible study club, peer educators, gay straight alliance.

Athletics. NCAA. **Intercollegiate:** Baseball M, basketball, cross-country, golf, lacrosse M, sailing, soccer, softball W, tennis, volleyball W. **Intramural:** Basketball, sailing, soccer, softball, tennis, volleyball. **Team name:** Mariners.

Student services. Adult student services, career counseling, services for economically disadvantaged, student employment services, financial aid counseling, health services, minority student services, personal counseling, veterans' counselor. **Physically disabled:** Services for visually, speech, hearing impaired.

Contact. E-mail: admissions@mitchell.edu
Phone: (860) 701-5037 Toll-free number: (800) 443-2811
Fax: (860) 444-1209
Susan Bibeau, Director of Admissions, Mitchell College, 437 Pequot Avenue, New London, CT 06320-4498

Paier College of Art
Hamden, Connecticut
www.paiercollegeofart.edu   CB code: 3699

- For-profit 4-year visual arts college
- Commuter campus in small city
- 112 degree-seeking undergraduates: 23% part-time, 69% women, 7% African American, 3% Asian American, 11% Hispanic/Latino, 1% Multiracial, non-Hispanic, 1% international
- 80% of applicants admitted
- SAT or ACT, interview required
- 65% graduate within 6 years

General. Founded in 1946. Accredited by ACCSC. **Degrees:** 38 bachelor's, 3 associate awarded. **Location:** 2 miles from New Haven, 30 miles from Hartford. **Calendar:** Semester. **Full-time faculty:** 8 total; 50% have terminal

---

degrees, 12% women. **Part-time faculty:** 26 total; 69% have terminal degrees, 27% women. **Class size:** 99% < 20, 1% 20-39.

Freshman class profile. 25 applied, 20 admitted, 9 enrolled.

Mid 50% test scores			
SAT critical reading:	400-540	GPA 3.0-3.49:	35%
SAT math:	410-560	GPA 2.0-2.99:	22%
GPA 3.75 or higher:	9%	Rank in top quarter:	19%
GPA 3.50-3.74:	34%	End year in good standing:	88%
		Return as sophomores:	89%

Basis for selection. Artistic ability, interest, and potential, as demonstrated in admission interview and portfolio review most important elements. Portfolio of 8 to 10 works of art required; essay recommended. **Home schooled:** Statement describing home school structure and mission, transcript of courses and grades, interview, letter of recommendation (nonparent) required. Notification from school district required stating that student is being home schooled.

High school preparation. 21 units required. Required and recommended units include English 4, mathematics 3, social studies 3, history 1, science 2, computer science 1 and visual/performing arts 2-4. Art classes recommended. All students must pass all state requirements.

2015-2016 Annual costs. Tuition/fees: $15,445. Books/supplies: $2,700. Personal expenses: $1,800.

2014-2015 Financial aid. Need-based: 9 full-time freshmen applied for aid; 6 deemed to have need; 6 received aid. Average need met was 83%. Average scholarship/grant was $7,880; average loan $3,374. 48% of total undergraduate aid awarded as scholarships/grants, 52% as loans/jobs.

Application procedures. Admission: No deadline. $25 fee, may be waived for applicants with need. Application must be submitted on paper. Admission notification on a rolling basis beginning on or about 2/15. **Financial aid:** Priority date 4/16, closing date 8/1. FAFSA required. Applicants notified on a rolling basis starting 6/1; must reply within 3 week(s) of notification.

Academics. Academics required for BFA degrees include: 4 art histories, English I and II, 1 requirement each in the humanities, math, physical and social sciences, and 1 academic elective. **Special study options:** Independent study, internships. **Credit/placement by examination:** AP, CLEP, IB, SAT, ACT. 6 credit hours maximum toward associate degree, 12 toward bachelor's. **Support services:** Reduced course load, remedial instruction, study skills assistance, tutoring.

Majors. Visual/performing arts: Graphic design, illustration, interior design, photography, studio arts.

Technology on campus. 75 workstations in library, computer center. Wireless network available.

Student life. Freshman orientation: Available. Preregistration for classes offered. Open to incoming students and their parents/guardians. Separate 1-hour library orientation. **Activities:** Student government, student newspaper.

Student services. Career counseling, student employment services, financial aid counseling, placement for graduates, veterans' counselor.

Contact. E-mail: paier.admission@snet.net
Phone: (203) 287-3031 Fax: (203) 287-3021
Daniel Paier, Dean of Admissions, Paier College of Art, 20 Gorham Avenue, Hamden, CT 06514-3902

Post University
Waterbury, Connecticut   CB member
www.post.edu   CB code: 3698

- For-profit 4-year university and business college
- Residential campus in small city
- 720 degree-seeking undergraduates: 2% part-time, 45% women, 14% African American, 2% Asian American, 7% Hispanic/Latino, 2% Multiracial, non-Hispanic, 2% international
- 47% of applicants admitted
- SAT or ACT with writing required

General. Founded in 1890. Regionally accredited. **Degrees:** 133 bachelor's, 2 associate awarded; master's offered. **Location:** 32 miles from Hartford, 80 miles from New York City. **Calendar:** Semester, limited summer session. **Full-time faculty:** 30 total; 60% have terminal degrees, 7% minority, 53% women. **Part-time faculty:** 101 total; 36% have terminal degrees, 10% minority, 57% women. **Class size:** 80% < 20, 20% 20-39.

Freshman class profile. 1,244 applied, 586 admitted, 197 enrolled.

Mid 50% test scores			
SAT critical reading:	390-500	GPA 3.0-3.49:	21%
SAT math:	380-510	GPA 2.0-2.99:	68%
SAT writing:	380-510	End year in good standing:	84%
ACT composite:	17-21	Return as sophomores:	38%
GPA 3.75 or higher:	2%	Out-of-state:	36%
GPA 3.50-3.74:	7%	Live on campus:	67%
		International:	1%

Basis for selection. Secondary school transcript, results of SAT/ACT most important. Guidance counselor's recommendation required. School and community activities and test scores also reviewed and considered. Interview recommended. **Home schooled:** Statement describing home school structure and mission, transcript of courses and grades, state high school equivalency certificate, interview, letter of recommendation (nonparent) required. **Learning Disabled:** Students must submit documentation once enrolled to receive services; documentation not used for admissions.

High school preparation. College-preparatory program required. 13 units required. Required and recommended units include English 4, mathematics 3, social studies 1, history 2, science 3 (laboratory 1) and foreign language 2.

2015-2016 Annual costs. Tuition/fees: $27,350. Room/board: $10,500. Books/supplies: $1,500. Personal expenses: $1,200.

2014-2015 Financial aid. Need-based: 178 full-time freshmen applied for aid; 172 deemed to have need; 172 received aid. Average need met was 55%. Average scholarship/grant was $16,655; average loan $364. 80% of total undergraduate aid awarded as scholarships/grants, 20% as loans/jobs. **Non-need-based:** Awarded to 354 full-time undergraduates, including 94 freshmen.

Application procedures. Admission: Priority date 3/1; no deadline. No application fee. Admission notification on a rolling basis beginning on or about 10/1. Must reply by May 1 or within 2 week(s) if notified thereafter. **Financial aid:** Priority date 3/15; no closing date. FAFSA required. Applicants notified on a rolling basis starting 4/15; must reply by 5/1 or within 3 week(s) of notification.

Academics. Special study options: Accelerated study, distance learning, double major, dual enrollment of high school students, ESL, honors, independent study, internships, study abroad. **Credit/placement by examination:** AP, CLEP, IB, SAT, ACT, institutional tests. 15 credit hours maximum toward associate degree, 30 toward bachelor's. Life experience credit offered 15 credits associate degree, 30 for bachelor's. Students should consult with Advising regarding any restrictions. **Support services:** Learning center, study skills assistance, tutoring, writing center. Library Tutorials available.

Majors. Biology: General. **Business:** Accounting, business admin, finance, international, management information systems, marketing. **Communications:** General. **Computer sciences:** General. **Conservation:** Environmental studies. **Parks/recreation:** Sports admin. **Protective services:** Criminal justice, disaster management. **Psychology:** General. **Social sciences:** Sociology. **Work/family studies:** Child development.

Most popular majors. Biology 6%, business/marketing 26%, parks/recreation 9%, public administration/social services 21%, security/protective services 17%.

Technology on campus. 150 workstations in library, computer center. Dormitories wired for high-speed internet access and linked to campus network. Commuter students can connect to campus network. Online course registration, online library, helpline, repair service, wireless network available.

Student life. Freshman orientation: Mandatory. Preregistration for classes offered. Held 2 days prior for U.S. students, and one-week prior to the start of the semester for international students. **Housing:** Guaranteed on-campus for all undergraduates. Coed dorms, apartments, themed housing available. $150 nonrefundable deposit, deadline 5/1. Honors Program housing available. **Activities:** Campus ministries, choral groups, dance, drama, literary magazine, music ensembles, musical theater, student government, Phi Theta Kappa, student ambassadors, peer mentors, peer health educators, Newman club.

Athletics. NCAA. **Intercollegiate:** Baseball M, basketball, bowling W, cross-country, football (tackle) M, golf, lacrosse, soccer, softball W, tennis, track and field, volleyball W. **Intramural:** Basketball. **Team name:** Eagles.

Student services. Adult student services, alcohol/substance abuse counseling, career counseling, student employment services, financial aid counseling, health services, minority student services, personal counseling, placement for graduates, veterans' counselor. **Physically disabled:** Services for visually impaired.

Contact. E-mail: admissions@post.edu
Phone: (203) 596-4520 Toll-free number: (800) 582-8250
Fax: (203) 841-1163
Kathryn Reilly, Director of Admissions, Post University, 800 Country Club Road, Waterbury, CT 06723-2540

Quinnipiac University
Hamden, Connecticut   CB member
www.quinnipiac.edu   CB code: 3712

- Private 4-year university
- Residential campus in small city
- 6,931 degree-seeking undergraduates: 3% part-time, 61% women, 5% African American, 3% Asian American, 9% Hispanic/Latino, 2% Multiracial, non-Hispanic, 2% international
- 2,662 degree-seeking graduate students
- 74% of applicants admitted
- SAT or ACT (ACT writing optional), application essay required
- 76% graduate within 6 years; 39% enter graduate study

General. Founded in 1929. Regionally accredited. **Degrees:** 1,441 bachelor's awarded; master's, professional offered. **ROTC:** Army, Air Force. **Location:** 8 miles from New Haven, 30 miles from Hartford. **Calendar:** Semester, extensive summer session. **Full-time faculty:** 399 total; 86% have terminal degrees, 17% minority, 53% women. **Part-time faculty:** 572 total; 34% have terminal degrees, 8% minority, 58% women. **Class size:** 38% < 20, 56% 20-39, 3% 40-49, 3% 50-99, less than 1% >100. **Special facilities:** Financial technology center, center for entrepreneurship, Quinnipiac polling institute, community health education institute, diagnostic imaging suite, critical care simulation laboratories for neonatal/pediatric and adult patients, motion analysis laboratory, the Irish Famine museum, production TV studio, audio production studio, news technology center, human anatomy lab.

Freshman class profile. 22,745 applied, 16,765 admitted, 1,904 enrolled.

Mid 50% test scores			
SAT critical reading:	490-580	Rank in top quarter:	69%
SAT math:	500-600	Rank in top tenth:	27%
SAT writing:	490-590	End year in good standing:	93%
ACT composite:	22-27	Return as sophomores:	87%
GPA 3.75 or higher:	17%	Out-of-state:	78%
GPA 3.50-3.74:	23%	Live on campus:	95%
GPA 3.0-3.49:	39%	International:	2%
GPA 2.0-2.99:	21%	Fraternities:	20%
		Sororities:	22%

Basis for selection. Primary emphasis placed on high school transcript, grades, grade pattern, level of difficulty. Test scores, essay and recommendation(s) also important. Interview recommended, extracurricular activities, evidence of leadership, and employment also considered. Must send official test scores for all SAT and/or ACT tests taken. Highest SAT (critical reading and math) or ACT (composite) scores used when reviewing applications for admission and for scholarships. University does not 'mix' the old and new SAT individual scores and will not super score the ACT. Campus visit, interview recommended. **Home schooled:** Statement describing home school structure and mission, transcript of courses and grades, letter of recommendation (nonparent) required. Evaluation of completed education required.

High school preparation. College-preparatory program required. 16 units required. Required and recommended units include English 4, mathematics 3, social studies 2, science 3 (laboratory 2), foreign language 2-3 and academic electives 2. 4 lab science and 4 math required for students applying to physical therapy, occupational therapy, nursing, physician assistant and engineering programs. Physics highly recommended for physical therapy and engineering applicants.

2016-2017 Annual costs. Tuition/fees: $43,640. Room/board: $15,170. Books/supplies: $800. Personal expenses: $1,200. **Additional information:** Technology and lab fee $300.

2015-2016 Financial aid. Need-based: 1,548 full-time freshmen applied for aid; 1,222 deemed to have need; 1,215 received aid. Average need met was 67%. Average scholarship/grant was $21,166; average loan $3,550. 65% of total undergraduate aid awarded as scholarships/grants, 35% as loans/jobs. **Non-need-based:** Awarded to 4,535 full-time undergraduates, including 1,558 freshmen. Scholarships awarded for academics, athletics.

Application procedures. Admission: Priority date 11/15; deadline 2/1 (receipt date). $65 fee, may be waived for applicants with need. Application must be submitted online. Admission notification on a rolling basis beginning on or about 12/1. Must reply by May 1 or within 2 week(s) if notified thereafter. Students encouraged to apply early in the fall since applications reviewed in order received. Students applying for Nursing, BS/MOT, BS/DPT in Physical Therapy or BS/MHS in Physician Assistant programs should apply by 11/15. **Financial aid:** Priority date 3/1; no closing date. FAFSA, CSS PROFILE required. Applicants notified on a rolling basis starting 2/15; must reply by 5/1 or within 2 week(s) of notification.

Academics. Special study options: Accelerated study, combined bachelor's/graduate degree, distance learning, double major, honors, independent study, internships, liberal arts/career combination, semester at sea, student-designed major, study abroad, teacher certification program, Washington semester. **Credit/placement by examination:** AP, CLEP, IB, institutional tests. 32 credit hours maximum toward bachelor's degree. **Support services:** Learning center, study skills assistance, tutoring. Veteran's Center.

Majors. Biology: General, biochemistry, biomedical sciences, biotechnology, molecular, neuroscience. **Business:** General, accounting, business admin, communications, entrepreneurial studies, finance, human resources, international, international marketing, management information systems, management science, managerial economics, marketing, nonprofit/public, office management. **Communications:** Advertising, broadcast journalism, communications/speech/rhetoric, digital media, journalism, public relations. **Computer sciences:** General, applications programming, computer graphics, computer science. **Education:** Biology, chemistry, elementary, English, foreign languages, history, mathematics, middle, multi-level teacher, science, secondary, social studies, Spanish. **Engineering:** Civil, industrial, mechanical, software. **English:** English lit, writing. **Foreign languages:** Spanish. **Health services:** Athletic training, health care admin, nursing (RN), predental, premedicine, preveterinary, radiologic technology/medical imaging. **History:** General. **Math:** General. **Physical sciences:** Chemistry. **Protective services:** Criminal justice. **Psychology:** General. **Social sciences:** General, criminology, economics, political science, sociology. **Visual/performing arts:** Dramatic, game design.

Most popular majors. Business/marketing 22%, communications/journalism 16%, health sciences 35%, psychology 6%.

Technology on campus. PC or laptop required. 500 workstations in library, computer center. Dormitories wired for high-speed internet access and linked to campus network. Commuter students can connect to campus network. Online course registration, online library, helpline, repair service, student web hosting, wireless network available.

Student life. Freshman orientation: Mandatory. Preregistration for classes offered. 2-day sessions offered in June and prior to start of fall classes. **Policies:** Freshmen not permitted cars on campus. **Housing:** Guaranteed on-campus for all undergraduates. Coed dorms, apartments, themed housing, wellness housing available. $350 partly refundable deposit, deadline 5/1. **Activities:** Pep band, campus ministries, choral groups, dance, drama, international student organizations, literary magazine, radio station, student government, student newspaper, TV station, Jewish student organization, Catholic services, black student union, Latino cultural society, Greenpeace, Amnesty International, SADD, women's center, Asian and Pacific Islander club, Christian Fellowship.

Athletics. NCAA. **Intercollegiate:** Baseball M, basketball, cross-country, field hockey W, golf W, ice hockey, lacrosse, rugby W, soccer, softball W, tennis, track and field W, volleyball W. **Intramural:** Archery, badminton, baseball M, basketball, bowling, field hockey W, soccer, softball, tennis, volleyball. **Team name:** Bobcats.

Student services. Adult student services, alcohol/substance abuse counseling, chaplain/spiritual director, career counseling, student employment services, financial aid counseling, health services, minority student services, personal counseling, placement for graduates, veterans' counselor.

Contact. E-mail: admissions@quinnipiac.edu
Phone: (203) 582-8600 Toll-free number: (800) 462-1944
Fax: (203) 582-8906
Carla Knowlton, Director of Admissions, Quinnipiac University, 275 Mount Carmel Avenue, Hamden, CT 06518-1908

Sacred Heart University
Fairfield, Connecticut
www.sacredheart.edu

CB member
CB code: 3780

♦ Private 4-year university affiliated with the Roman Catholic Church
♦ Residential campus in large town
♦ 5,109 degree-seeking undergraduates: 13% part-time, 64% women, 4% African American, 2% Asian American, 8% Hispanic/Latino, 2% Multi-racial, non-Hispanic, 1% international
♦ 2,957 degree-seeking graduate students
♦ 59% of applicants admitted
♦ Application essay required
♦ 63% graduate within 6 years

General. Founded in 1963. Regionally accredited. **Degrees:** 977 bachelor's, 4 associate awarded; master's, professional offered. **ROTC:** Air Force. **Location:** 55 miles from New York City. **Calendar:** Semester, extensive summer session. **Full-time faculty:** 263 total; 78% have terminal degrees, 12% minority, 54% women. **Part-time faculty:** 499 total; 26% have terminal degrees, 9% minority, 56% women. **Class size:** 39% < 20, 59% 20-39, less than 1% 40-49, 1% 50-99, less than 1% >100. **Special facilities:** Performing arts center, multipurpose communication studios, 36-hole golf course, rehabilitation clinics for occupational and physical therapies, fashion design studio, chapel.

Freshman class profile. 9,257 applied, 5,460 admitted, 1,290 enrolled.

Mid 50% test scores			
SAT critical reading:	480-610	Rank in top quarter:	35%
SAT math:	480-630	Rank in top tenth:	10%
SAT writing:	470-630	Return as sophomores:	83%
ACT composite:	21-33	Out-of-state:	73%
GPA 3.75 or higher:	29%	Live on campus:	90%
GPA 3.50-3.74:	18%	International:	1%
GPA 3.0-3.49:	40%	Fraternities:	12%
GPA 2.0-2.99:	13%	Sororities:	26%

Basis for selection. High school record and college preparatory curriculum most important. Interview required for early decision candidates, recommended for all others. **Home schooled:** Statement describing home school structure and mission, transcript of courses and grades required. SAT/ACT required.

High school preparation. College-preparatory program required. 22 units required; 30 recommended. Required and recommended units include English 4, mathematics 3-4, social studies 3-4, history 3-4, science 3-4 (laboratory 1-2), foreign language 2-4 and academic electives 3-4.

2015-2016 Annual costs. Tuition/fees: $37,170. Room/board: $14,140. Books/supplies: $1,200. Personal expenses: $1,570.

2015-2016 Financial aid. Need-based: 1,152 full-time freshmen applied for aid; 908 deemed to have need; 908 received aid. Average need met was 57%. Average scholarship/grant was $15,547; average loan $4,065. 65% of total undergraduate aid awarded as scholarships/grants, 35% as loans/jobs. **Non-need-based:** Awarded to 1,936 full-time undergraduates, including 572 freshmen. Scholarships awarded for academics, alumni affiliation, art, athletics, leadership, music/drama, religious affiliation, state residency.

Application procedures. Admission: Priority date 2/15; no deadline. $50 fee. Application must be submitted online. Admission notification on a rolling basis beginning on or about 4/1. Must reply by May 1 or within 2 week(s) if notified thereafter. **Financial aid:** Priority date 2/15; no closing date. FAFSA, CSS PROFILE required. Applicants notified on a rolling basis starting 3/1; must reply within 2 week(s) of notification.

Academics. Special study options: Accelerated study, combined bachelor's/graduate degree, distance learning, double major, dual enrollment of high school students, ESL, honors, independent study, internships, liberal arts/career combination, student-designed major, study abroad, teacher certification program, United Nations semester, Washington semester, weekend college. Service-learning. **Credit/placement by examination:** AP, CLEP, IB, SAT, ACT, institutional tests. 30 credit hours maximum toward bachelor's degree. **Support services:** Learning center, study skills assistance, tutoring, writing center.

Majors. Biology: General. **Business:** Accounting, business admin, marketing. **Communications:** General, communications/speech/rhetoric. **Computer sciences:** General. **English:** English lit. **Foreign languages:** Spanish. **Health services:** Athletic training, nursing (RN). **History:** General. **Human services:** Social work. **Liberal arts:** Arts/sciences. **Math:** General. **Philosophy/religion:** Philosophy, religion. **Physical sciences:** Chemistry. **Protective services:** Criminal justice. **Psychology:** General. **Social sciences:** Economics, political science, sociology. **Visual/performing arts:** Art, dramatic.

Most popular majors. Business/marketing 27%, health sciences 25%, psychology 11%.

Technology on campus. PC or laptop required. Dormitories wired for high-speed internet access and linked to campus network. Commuter students can connect to campus network. Online course registration, online library, helpline, repair service, wireless network available.

Student life. Freshman orientation: Mandatory. Preregistration for classes offered. Two-day program in June for parents and students. **Policies:** Freshman Convocation required for all first-year students; held in September. Freshmen not permitted cars on campus. **Housing:** Guaranteed on-campus for all undergraduates. Coed dorms, special housing for disabled, apartments, wellness housing available. $1,500 nonrefundable deposit, deadline 5/1. **Activities:** Bands, campus ministries, choral groups, dance, drama, film society, international student organizations, literary magazine, music ensembles, Model UN, musical theater, radio station, student government, student newspaper, TV station, College Democrats, College Republicans, green club, Habitat for Humanity, peace by justice, La Hispanidad, Are You Autism Aware, United Campus Alliance.

Athletics. NCAA. **Intercollegiate:** Baseball M, basketball, bowling W, cross-country, equestrian W, fencing, field hockey W, football (tackle) M, golf, ice hockey, lacrosse, rowing (crew) W, soccer, softball W, swimming W, tennis, track and field, volleyball, wrestling M. **Intramural:** Basketball, soccer, softball, tennis, volleyball. **Team name:** Pioneers.

Student services. Adult student services, alcohol/substance abuse counseling, chaplain/spiritual director, career counseling, services for economically disadvantaged, student employment services, financial aid counseling, health services, minority student services, personal counseling, placement for graduates, women's services. **Physically disabled:** Services for visually, speech, hearing impaired.

Contact. E-mail: enroll@sacredheart.edu
Phone: (203) 371-7880 Fax: (203) 365-7607
Kevin O'Sullivan, Executive Director, Undergraduate Admissions, Sacred Heart University, 5151 Park Avenue, Fairfield, CT 06825

Southern Connecticut State University
New Haven, Connecticut **CB member**
www.southernct.edu **CB code: 3662**

- Public 4-year university
- Commuter campus in small city
- 8,106 degree-seeking undergraduates: 15% part-time, 61% women, 17% African American, 3% Asian American, 13% Hispanic/Latino, 2% Multiracial, non-Hispanic, 1% international
- 2,367 degree-seeking graduate students
- 65% of applicants admitted
- SAT or ACT with writing, application essay required
- 52% graduate within 6 years

General. Founded in 1893. Regionally accredited. **Degrees:** 1,577 bachelor's awarded; master's, doctoral offered. **ROTC:** Army, Air Force. **Location:** 75 miles from New York City. **Calendar:** Semester, extensive summer session. **Full-time faculty:** 440 total; 86% have terminal degrees, 19% minority, 51% women. **Part-time faculty:** 520 total; 17% have terminal degrees, 14% minority, 57% women. **Class size:** 44% < 20, 53% 20-39, 2% 40-49, 1% 50-99, less than 1% >100. **Special facilities:** Planetarium, photonics laboratory, geospatial technology laboratory.

Freshman class profile. 8,113 applied, 5,241 admitted, 1,408 enrolled.

Mid 50% test scores		GPA 2.0-2.99:	50%
SAT critical reading:	410-510	Rank in top quarter:	10%
SAT math:	410-500	Rank in top tenth:	1%
SAT writing:	420-520	Return as sophomores:	75%
ACT composite:	18-22	Out-of-state:	7%
GPA 3.75 or higher:	6%	Live on campus:	68%
GPA 3.50-3.74:	11%	Fraternities:	1%
GPA 3.0-3.49:	31%	Sororities:	1%

Basis for selection. School achievement record, test scores most important. Special consideration to culturally disadvantaged students. **Home schooled:** Statement describing home school structure and mission, transcript of courses and grades, letter of recommendation (nonparent) required.

High school preparation. College-preparatory program recommended. 16 units required; 21 recommended. Required and recommended units include English 4, mathematics 3-4, social studies 2-3, history 2-3, science 2-3 (laboratory 1) and foreign language 2-4. One unit of algebra II required.

2015-2016 Annual costs. Tuition/fees: $9,600; $21,870 out-of-state. Room/board: $11,614. Books/supplies: $1,400. Personal expenses: $798.

2015-2016 Financial aid. **Need-based:** 1,146 full-time freshmen applied for aid; 968 deemed to have need; 968 received aid. Average need met was 67%. Average scholarship/grant was $5,583; average loan $3,676. 55% of total undergraduate aid awarded as scholarships/grants, 45% as loans/jobs. **Non-need-based:** Awarded to 1,106 full-time undergraduates, including 298 freshmen. Scholarships awarded for academics, alumni affiliation, athletics, job skills, ROTC, state residency.

Application procedures. **Admission:** No deadline. $50 fee, may be waived for applicants with need. Admission notification on a rolling basis beginning on or about 12/1. Must reply by May 1 or within 2 week(s) if notified thereafter. **Financial aid:** Priority date 3/5, closing date 3/9. FAFSA required. Applicants notified on a rolling basis starting 4/11; must reply within 2 week(s) of notification.

Academics. **Special study options:** Accelerated study, cooperative education, cross-registration, distance learning, double major, dual enrollment of high school students, exchange student, external degree, honors, independent study, internships, liberal arts/career combination, student-designed major, study abroad, teacher certification program. **Credit/placement by examination:** AP, CLEP, SAT, institutional tests. 30 credit hours maximum toward bachelor's degree. **Support services:** Learning center, pre-admission summer program, reduced course load, remedial instruction, study skills assistance, tutoring, writing center.

Majors. **Biology:** General. **Business:** Business admin. **Communications:** Communications/speech/rhetoric, journalism, media studies. **Computer sciences:** General. **Education:** Art, early childhood, elementary, physical, special ed. **English:** English lit. **Foreign languages:** French, German, Italian, Spanish. **Health services:** Athletic training, audiology/speech pathology, nursing (RN). **History:** General. **Human services:** Social work. **Liberal arts:** Arts/sciences, library science. **Math:** General. **Parks/recreation:** General. **Philosophy/religion:** Philosophy. **Physical sciences:** Chemistry, geology, physics. **Psychology:** General. **Social sciences:** Anthropology, economics, geography, political science, sociology. **Visual/performing arts:** Art history/conservation, dramatic, music, studio arts.

Most popular majors. Business/marketing 14%, communications/journalism 6%, education 8%, health sciences 15%, liberal arts 14%, psychology 9%.

Technology on campus. 750 workstations in dormitories, library, computer center, student center. Dormitories wired for high-speed internet access and linked to campus network. Commuter students can connect to campus network. Online course registration, online library, helpline, student web hosting, wireless network available.

Student life. **Freshman orientation:** Mandatory. Preregistration for classes offered. **Policies:** Freshmen not permitted cars on campus. **Housing:** Coed dorms, special housing for disabled, apartments, themed housing available. $250 nonrefundable deposit. **Activities:** Pep band, campus ministries, choral groups, dance, drama, international student organizations, literary magazine, music ensembles, musical theater, radio station, student government, student newspaper, TV station, Christian Fellowship, Newman club, Latin American students organization, black student union, People to People, Students for Disability Rights, veterans club.

Athletics. NCAA. **Intercollegiate:** Baseball M, basketball, cross-country, field hockey W, football (tackle) M, gymnastics W, lacrosse W, soccer, softball W, swimming, track and field, volleyball M. **Intramural:** Basketball, football (non-tackle), soccer, softball, tennis, volleyball. **Team name:** Owls.

Student services. Adult student services, alcohol/substance abuse counseling, chaplain/spiritual director, career counseling, student employment services, financial aid counseling, health services, personal counseling, placement for graduates, veterans' counselor, women's services. **Physically disabled:** Services for visually, speech, hearing impaired.

Contact. E-mail: information@southernct.edu
Phone: (203) 392-5656 Toll-free number: (888) 500-7278
Fax: (203) 392-5727
Kimberly Crone, Associate Vice President for Academic Student Services, Southern Connecticut State University, 131 Farnham Avenue, New Haven, CT 06515-1202

Trinity College
Hartford, Connecticut **CB member**
www.trincoll.edu **CB code: 3899**

- Private 4-year liberal arts college
- Residential campus in large city
- 2,251 degree-seeking undergraduates
- 33% of applicants admitted
- Application essay required

General. Founded in 1823. Regionally accredited. House system based on the British model. **Degrees:** 518 bachelor's awarded; master's offered. **ROTC:** Army. **Location:** 125 miles from New York City, 100 miles from Boston. **Calendar:** Semester, limited summer session. **Full-time faculty:** 193 total; 93% have terminal degrees, 21% minority, 48% women. **Part-time faculty:** 102 total; 62% have terminal degrees, 14% minority, 49% women. **Class size:** 62% < 20, 33% 20-39, 3% 40-49, 2% 50-99. **Special facilities:** Library collections on Native Americans, maritime history, early American texts, nuclear magnetic spectrometer, mass spectrometer, electronic microscope, plasma spectrometer, optical diagnostics and communications laboratory, natural science field station.

Freshman class profile. 7,569 applied, 2,529 admitted, 559 enrolled.

Mid 50% test scores		Rank in top quarter:	80%
SAT critical reading:	540-670	Rank in top tenth:	43%
SAT math:	570-700	Out-of-state:	84%
SAT writing:	550-680	Live on campus:	100%
ACT composite:	26-31		

Basis for selection. School record and recommendations most important. Test scores used for math and writing placement. One of the following required: SAT, ACT, or 2 SAT Subject Tests. Interview recommended.

High school preparation. College-preparatory program recommended. 16 units required. Required units include English 4, mathematics 3, history 2, science 2 (laboratory 2) and foreign language 3.

2015-2016 Annual costs. Tuition/fees: $50,776. Room/board: $13,144. Books/supplies: $1,000. Personal expenses: $1,000.

Financial aid. Non-need-based: Scholarships awarded for academics, leadership.

Application procedures. Admission: Closing date 1/1 (postmark date). $60 fee, may be waived for applicants with need. Admission notification by 4/1. Must reply by May 1 or within 2 week(s) if notified thereafter. **Financial aid:** Priority date 2/1, closing date 3/1. FAFSA, CSS PROFILE required. Applicants notified by 4/1; must reply by 5/1 or within 2 week(s) of notification.

Academics. Math center available. **Special study options:** Accelerated study, combined bachelor's/graduate degree, cross-registration, double major, exchange student, honors, independent study, internships, liberal arts/career combination, New York semester, semester at sea, student-designed major, study abroad, teacher certification program, United Nations semester, urban semester, Washington semester. Community Learning Initiative (courses with community-based components) available. **Credit/placement by examination:** AP, CLEP, IB, institutional tests. **Support services:** Study skills assistance, tutoring, writing center.

Majors. Area/ethnic studies: African, African-American, American, Asian, gay/lesbian, Latin American, Near/Middle Eastern, Russian/Slavic, women's. **Biology:** General, biochemistry, neuroscience. **Computer sciences:** General, computer science. **Conservation:** Environmental science. **Education:** General. **Engineering:** General, biomedical, electrical, mechanical. **English:** Creative writing, English lit. **Foreign languages:** General, Chinese, classics, comparative lit, French, German, Italian, Japanese, Russian, Spanish. **Health services:** Premedicine. **History:** General. **Human services:** Public policy. **Math:** General. **Philosophy/religion:** Judaic, philosophy, religion. **Physical sciences:** Chemistry, physics. **Psychology:** General. **Social sciences:** General, anthropology, economics, international relations, political science, sociology, urban studies. **Visual/performing arts:** General, art, art history/conservation, dance, dramatic, film/cinema/video, music, studio arts.

Most popular majors. Area/ethnic studies 10%, biology 8%, English 7%, psychology 8%, social sciences 27%, visual/performing arts 7%.

Technology on campus. 327 workstations in library, computer center. Dormitories wired for high-speed internet access and linked to campus network. Commuter students can connect to campus network. Online course registration, online library, helpline, student web hosting, wireless network available.

Student life. Freshman orientation: Available. Preregistration for classes offered. 4-day session beginning Thursday before Labor Day. Advising days held in June to begin registration process; optional outdoor challenge program in early August. **Policies:** All dorms are non-smoking. Freshmen not permitted cars on campus. **Housing:** Guaranteed on-campus for freshmen. Coed dorms, fraternity/sorority housing, themed housing available. $500 deposit, deadline 5/1. Community service dorm, quiet dorm, alternative social programming dorm, cooking units available. **Activities:** Jazz band, campus ministries, choral groups, dance, drama, film society, international student organizations, literary magazine, music ensembles, Model UN, musical theater, radio station, student government, student newspaper, TV station, Asian-American student association, Intervarsity Christian Fellowship, Encouraging Respect of Sexualities, Friends Active in Civic Engagement and Service, Hillel, Imani, La Voz Latina, Promoting Healthy Awareness of the Body, Promoting Respect for Inclusive Diversity in Education, black women's organization.

Athletics. NCAA. **Intercollegiate:** Baseball M, basketball, cross-country, diving, field hockey W, football (tackle) M, golf M, ice hockey, lacrosse, rowing (crew), soccer, softball W, squash, swimming, tennis, track and field, volleyball W, wrestling M. **Intramural:** Badminton, basketball, football (non-tackle), ice hockey, soccer, softball, squash, tennis. **Team name:** Bantams.

Student services. Adult student services, alcohol/substance abuse counseling, chaplain/spiritual director, career counseling, services for economically disadvantaged, student employment services, financial aid counseling, health services, minority student services, on-campus daycare, personal counseling, placement for graduates, women's services.

Contact. E-mail: admissions.office@trincoll.edu
Phone: (860) 297-2180 Fax: (860) 297-2287
Angel Perez, Dean of Admissions and Financial Aid, Trinity College, 300 Summit Street, Hartford, CT 06106

United States Coast Guard Academy
New London, Connecticut   **CB member**
www.uscga.edu   **CB code: 5807**

- Public 4-year engineering and military college
- Residential campus in small city
- 898 degree-seeking undergraduates: 35% women, 4% African American, 7% Asian American, 10% Hispanic/Latino, 8% Multi-racial, non-Hispanic, 2% international
- 18% of applicants admitted
- SAT or ACT with writing, application essay required
- 85% graduate within 6 years

General. Founded in 1876. Regionally accredited. Cadets devote themselves to honor concept and go directly into leadership positions in the United States Coast Guard upon graduation. As a federal military service academy, the Coast Guard Academy is a tuition-free degree-granting institution. All students earn a modest stipend while enrolled and receive medical and dental benefits at no charge. Upon graduation from the Academy, there is a five year commitment to serve as a commissioned Coast Guard officer. Approximately 80% of Academy graduates go to sea after graduation, although some go to marine safety offices, ashore operations, or flight training. **Degrees:** 223 bachelor's awarded. **Location:** 120 miles from New York City, 110 miles from Boston. **Calendar:** Semester, limited summer session. **Full-time faculty:** 115 total; 56% have terminal degrees, 12% minority, 28% women. **Part-time faculty:** 14 total; 50% have terminal degrees, 29% women. **Class size:** 78% < 20, 22% 20-39. **Special facilities:** Museum, 295-foot Barque Eagle, ship navigation simulation facilities with bridge simulator, 10,000 gallon circulating water channel, ship model towing tank, observatory with reflector telescope.

Freshman class profile. 2,214 applied, 388 admitted, 291 enrolled.

Mid 50% test scores		GPA 2.0-2.99:	1%
SAT critical reading:	570-660	Rank in top quarter:	79%
SAT math:	610-690	Rank in top tenth:	45%
SAT writing:	560-650	End year in good standing:	94%
ACT composite:	26-31	Return as sophomores:	90%
GPA 3.75 or higher:	65%	Out-of-state:	96%
GPA 3.50-3.74:	20%	Live on campus:	100%
GPA 3.0-3.49:	14%	International:	1%

Basis for selection. Test scores, high school class rank, recommendations, essay, leadership potential as demonstrated by extracurricular activities, athletics, community affairs, and part-time employment considered. Congressional nomination not required. Applicants required to pass medical and physical fitness exams. SAT/ACT must be taken without accommodations. Interview recommended. **Home schooled:** It is recommended that applicants submit scores from AP and/or SAT Subject Tests and a detailed account of curriculum and course content. Applicants are advised to take courses in math and science at a local college and have their professors submit the required academic letters of recommendation. Obtaining academic letters of recommendation from instructors or tutors, other than parents, is recommended. Personal statements should include reasons for undertaking homeschooling, benefits realized, and why the applicant believes their experiences have prepared them to succeed in college.

High school preparation. College-preparatory program recommended. 11 units required. Required and recommended units include English 4, mathematics 4, science 3-4 (laboratory 3). Math units should include algebra, quadratics, plane or coordinate geometry, or equivalent. Calculus and precalculus recommended. Sciences should include chemistry and physics.

2016-2017 Annual costs. Tuition/fees (projected): $978. **Additional information:** For US Citizens, room, tuition, and board at the Coast Guard Academy are paid for by the government. In addition, all US Cadets receive pay totaling $12,324.00 per year. Cadet pay is furnished by the government for uniforms, equipment, textbooks, and other expenses incidental to training.

Application procedures. Admission: Priority date 11/15; deadline 2/1 (postmark date). No application fee. Application must be submitted online. Admission notification by 4/15. Admission notification on a rolling basis beginning on or about 11/15. Must reply by May 1 or within 2 week(s) if notified thereafter. **Financial aid:** No deadline.

Academics. Each student issued a laptop computer. Summers involve introductory and advanced Coast Guard/professional training including opportunities to sail aboard Eagle, fly Coast Guard aircraft, become small arms qualified (rifle and pistol), learn basic shipboard fire fighting and flooding control, and perform actual search and rescue coordination at Coast Guard units. Summer between junior and senior years typically involves piloting and navigation of Coast Guard Cutters and integration into all aspects of operational afloat Coast Guard missions. All graduates commissioned as officers in U.S. Coast Guard with a 5-year obligatory military service after graduation. Approximately 80% of Academy graduates go to sea after graduation, although some go to marine safety offices, ashore operations, or flight training. **Special study options:** Cross-registration, double major, ESL, exchange student, honors, independent study, internships. **Credit/placement by examination:** AP, CLEP, SAT, ACT, institutional tests. **Support services:** Learning center, pre-admission summer program, reduced course load, remedial instruction, study skills assistance, tutoring, writing center.

Majors. Business: Business admin. **Engineering:** Civil, electrical, marine, mechanical. **Physical sciences:** Oceanography. **Social sciences:** Political science.

Most popular majors. Biology 17%, business/marketing 19%, engineering/engineering technologies 37%, mathematics 6%, social sciences 20%.

Technology on campus. PC or laptop required. 280 workstations in dormitories, library, computer center. Dormitories wired for high-speed internet access and linked to campus network. Online course registration, online library, helpline, repair service, student web hosting, wireless network available.

Student life. Freshman orientation: Mandatory. Preregistration for classes offered. 7-week military orientation, including one week onboard the Coast Guard Cutter Eagle. **Policies:** Students part of corps of cadets. On-campus residence mandatory. Cadets cannot be married. Freshmen not permitted cars on campus. **Housing:** Guaranteed on-campus for all undergraduates. Coed dorms, wellness housing available. **Activities:** Bands, campus ministries, choral groups, dance, drama, international student organizations, music ensembles, Model UN, musical theater, student government, Officers Christian Fellowship, multicultural club, Fellowship of Christian Athletes, Spectrum Council (LGBT), Genesis club, women's leadership council, Hillel Jewish club, Compass (Catholic Youth Group), Sustainable living/ Environmental club, International Council club.

Athletics. NCAA. **Intercollegiate:** Baseball M, basketball, cheerleading W, cross-country, diving, football (tackle) M, lacrosse, rifle, rowing (crew), sailing, soccer, softball W, swimming, tennis, track and field, volleyball, wrestling M. **Intramural:** Basketball, bowling, football (non-tackle), golf, racquetball, soccer, softball, tennis, ultimate frisbee, volleyball. **Team name:** Bears.

Student services. Alcohol/substance abuse counseling, chaplain/spiritual director, career counseling, health services, legal services, minority student services, on-campus daycare, personal counseling, placement for graduates, veterans' counselor.

Contact. E-mail: uscga.admissions@uscga.edu
Phone: (860) 444-8500 Toll-free number: (800) 883-8724
Fax: (860) 701-6700
Capt. Robert McKenna, Director of Admissions, United States Coast Guard Academy, 31 Mohegan Avenue, New London, CT 06320

University of Bridgeport
Bridgeport, Connecticut
www.bridgeport.edu   CB code: 3914

- Private 4-year university
- Residential campus in small city
- 2,897 degree-seeking undergraduates: 27% part-time, 64% women, 36% African American, 3% Asian American, 18% Hispanic/Latino, 1% Native American, 2% Multi-racial, non-Hispanic, 16% international
- 2,536 degree-seeking graduate students
- 53% of applicants admitted
- SAT or ACT (ACT writing optional), application essay required

General. Founded in 1927. Regionally accredited. Off-campus facilities in Stamford and Waterbury. **Degrees:** 509 bachelor's, 60 associate awarded; master's, professional, doctoral offered. **ROTC:** Army. **Location:** 60 miles from New York City. **Calendar:** Semester, extensive summer session. **Full-time faculty:** 127 total; 72% have terminal degrees, 19% minority, 42% women. **Part-time faculty:** 407 total; 21% minority, 47% women. **Class size:** 69% < 20, 29% 20-39, less than 1% 40-49, less than 1% 50-99. **Special facilities:** Theater, recital halls, studios, exhibit rooms.

Freshman class profile. 6,599 applied, 3,466 admitted, 412 enrolled.

Mid 50% test scores			
SAT critical reading:	410-510	Rank in top quarter:	30%
SAT math:	420-500	Rank in top tenth:	10%
SAT writing:	410-490	End year in good standing:	67%
ACT composite:	17-23	Return as sophomores:	56%
GPA 3.75 or higher:	12%	Out-of-state:	69%
GPA 3.50-3.74:	12%	Live on campus:	66%
GPA 3.0-3.49:	28%	International:	13%
GPA 2.0-2.99:	48%	Fraternities:	1%
		Sororities:	1%

Basis for selection. School achievement record most important, followed by test scores, activities, trend of grades and curriculum in high school. Audition required of music majors. Portfolio required of fine and applied arts majors. Interview recommended of dental hygiene, basic studies majors.

High school preparation. College-preparatory program recommended. 16 units required. Required units include English 4, mathematics 3, social studies 2, science 2 (laboratory 2) and academic electives 5. 4 math required for math, science, computer science and engineering applicants. Chemistry required for dental hygiene.

2015-2016 Annual costs. Tuition/fees: $30,850. Room/board: $12,990. Books/supplies: $1,500. Personal expenses: $5,000.

Financial aid. Non-need-based: Scholarships awarded for academics, art, athletics, leadership, music/drama.

Application procedures. Admission: Priority date 4/1; no deadline. $25 fee, may be waived for applicants with need. Admission notification on a rolling basis. Must reply by May 1 or within 2 week(s) if notified thereafter. **Financial aid:** Priority date 3/1; no closing date. FAFSA required. Applicants notified on a rolling basis starting 4/1; must reply within 4 week(s) of notification.

Academics. Special study options: Accelerated study, combined bachelor's/graduate degree, cooperative education, cross-registration, distance learning, double major, dual enrollment of high school students, ESL, exchange student, honors, independent study, internships, liberal arts/career combination, New York semester, semester at sea, student-designed major, study abroad, teacher certification program, United Nations semester, Washington semester, weekend college. **Credit/placement by examination:** AP, CLEP, IB, SAT, ACT, institutional tests. 30 credit hours maximum toward associate degree, 30 toward bachelor's. **Support services:** Learning center, pre-admission summer program, reduced course load, remedial instruction, study skills assistance, tutoring, writing center.

Majors. Area/ethnic studies: East Asian. **Biology:** General. **Business:** General, accounting, fashion, finance, international, labor relations, management information systems, marketing. **Communications:** Advertising, communications/speech/rhetoric, journalism, media studies, public relations. **Computer sciences:** General. **Engineering:** Computer. **English:** Creative writing, English lit. **Health services:** Clinical lab science, dental hygiene, nursing (RN). **Human services:** Community org/advocacy. **Liberal arts:** Arts/sciences, humanities. **Math:** General. **Philosophy/religion:** Religion. **Protective services:** Criminal justice. **Psychology:** General. **Social sciences:** General, criminology, international relations, political science, sociology. **Visual/performing arts:** Graphic design, illustration, industrial design, interior design, music.

Most popular majors. Business/marketing 20%, health sciences 14%, liberal arts 14%, psychology 15%, public administration/social services 9%, visual/performing arts 7%.

Technology on campus. 200 workstations in dormitories, library, computer center, student center. Dormitories wired for high-speed internet access and linked to campus network. Commuter students can connect to campus network. Online course registration, online library, helpline, repair service, student web hosting, wireless network available.

Student life. Freshman orientation: Mandatory, $150 fee. Preregistration for classes offered. Held during the summer with final program just prior to class. **Policies:** Student and dormitory governments plan student life activities. **Housing:** Guaranteed on-campus for all undergraduates. Coed dorms, apartments, wellness housing available. $200 nonrefundable deposit, deadline 5/1. Dormitories have special facilities. **Activities:** Choral groups, film society, international student organizations, literary magazine, music ensembles, Model UN, student government, student newspaper, interfaith center, black student alliance, social service sorority, Protestant fellowship, community service project.

Athletics. NCAA. **Intercollegiate:** Baseball M, basketball, cross-country, gymnastics W, lacrosse W, soccer, softball W, swimming, volleyball W. **Intramural:** Basketball, racquetball, soccer, softball, tennis, volleyball. **Team name:** Purple Knights.

Student services. Adult student services, alcohol/substance abuse counseling, chaplain/spiritual director, career counseling, services for economically disadvantaged, student employment services, financial aid counseling, health services, minority student services, personal counseling, placement for graduates, veterans' counselor. **Physically disabled:** Services for visually, speech, hearing impaired.

Contact. E-mail: admit@bridgeport.edu
Phone: (203) 576-4552 Toll-free number: (800) 392-3582
Fax: (203) 576-4941
Karissa Peckham, Dean of Admissions, University of Bridgeport, 126 Park Avenue, Bridgeport, CT 06604

University of Connecticut
Storrs, Connecticut
www.uconn.edu

CB member
CB code: 3915

- Public 4-year university
- Residential campus in large town
- 18,451 degree-seeking undergraduates: 3% part-time, 50% women, 5% African American, 10% Asian American, 9% Hispanic/Latino, 3% Multiracial, non-Hispanic, 5% international
- 7,795 degree-seeking graduate students
- 53% of applicants admitted
- SAT or ACT (ACT writing optional), application essay required
- 83% graduate within 6 years

General. Founded in 1881. Regionally accredited. Students may take courses at nonresidential campuses in Groton, Hartford, Stamford, Waterbury, and Torrington. **Degrees:** 5,320 bachelor's, 20 associate awarded; master's, professional, doctoral offered. **ROTC:** Army, Air Force. **Location:** 26 miles from Hartford, 80 miles from Boston. **Calendar:** Semester, extensive summer session. **Full-time faculty:** 1,209 total; 93% have terminal degrees, 24% minority, 40% women. **Part-time faculty:** 331 total; 17% have terminal degrees, 6% minority, 51% women. **Class size:** 53% < 20, 26% 20-39, 5% 40-49, 8% 50-99, 8% >100. **Special facilities:** Archaeology center, natural history museum, sports museum, conservatory, greenhouses, horse barn, art museum, performing arts center, repertory theater, puppetry museum, nature preserve.

Freshman class profile. 34,978 applied, 18,598 admitted, 3,774 enrolled.

Mid 50% test scores			
SAT critical reading:	550-650	Return as sophomores:	92%
SAT math:	580-690	Out-of-state:	37%
SAT writing:	550-650	Live on campus:	97%
ACT composite:	26-31	International:	9%
Rank in top quarter:	85%	Fraternities:	6%
Rank in top tenth:	50%	Sororities:	10%

Basis for selection. Curriculum, grades, rank in class most important, followed by test scores. Particular consideration given to first generation college and/or socio-economically disadvantaged applicants and applicants with special talents. Audition required of music, acting, puppetry majors. Portfolio required for art major. Interview required for design/technical theater and theater studies majors. **Home schooled:** Statement describing home school structure and mission, transcript of courses and grades required. **Learning Disabled:** Students may submit disability documentation to Center for Students with Disabilities upon admission.

High school preparation. College-preparatory program required. 16 units required. Required and recommended units include English 4, mathematics 3, social studies 2, science 2 (laboratory 2), foreign language 2-3 and academic electives 3. Some programs may require additional units.

2016-2017 Annual costs. Tuition/fees (projected): $13,366; $34,908 out-of-state. Room/board: $12,436. Books/supplies: $850. Personal expenses: $1,650.

2015-2016 Financial aid. **Need-based:** 2,986 full-time freshmen applied for aid; 2,028 deemed to have need; 1,984 received aid. Average need met was 58%. Average scholarship/grant was $13,096; average loan $3,420. 53% of total undergraduate aid awarded as scholarships/grants, 47% as loans/jobs. **Non-need-based:** Awarded to 5,512 full-time undergraduates, including 1,483 freshmen. Scholarships awarded for academics, art, athletics, leadership, minority status, music/drama. **Additional information:** Institution offers variety of need-based financial aid programs. Financial assistance packages may include grants, loans and work-study awards.

Application procedures. Admission: Closing date 1/15. $70 fee, may be waived for applicants with need. Admission notification on a rolling basis beginning on or about 3/1. Must reply by May 1 or within 2 week(s) if notified thereafter. **Financial aid:** Priority date 3/1; no closing date. FAFSA required. Applicants notified on a rolling basis starting 3/1; must reply within 4 week(s) of notification.

Academics. 5-year Eurotech program combining engineering and German language, including 6-month internship in Germany. **Special study options:** Accelerated study, combined bachelor's/graduate degree, cooperative education, distance learning, double major, dual enrollment of high school students, ESL, exchange student, external degree, honors, independent study, internships, liberal arts/career combination, New York semester, semester at sea, student-designed major, study abroad, teacher certification program, urban semester, Washington semester. Winter inter-session, summer session, urban semester. **Credit/placement by examination:** AP, CLEP, IB, institutional tests. 30 credit hours maximum toward bachelor's degree. **Support services:** Learning center, pre-admission summer program, study skills assistance, tutoring, writing center.

Majors. Architecture: Landscape. **Area/ethnic studies:** African-American, American, Latin American, women's. **Biology:** General, animal physiology, biophysics, cellular/molecular, ecology, marine, pathology. **Business:** General, accounting, actuarial science, business admin, finance, financial planning, management information systems, marketing, real estate. **Communications:** Communications/speech/rhetoric, digital media, journalism. **Computer sciences:** Computer science. **Conservation:** General, environmental science, environmental studies. **Education:** Agricultural, elementary, music, physical, science, special ed. **Engineering:** Applied physics, biomedical, chemical, civil, computer, electrical, environmental, industrial, materials, mechanical. **English:** English lit. **Foreign languages:** Chinese, classics, French, German, Italian, linguistics, Spanish. **Health services:** Athletic training, clinical lab science, cytotechnology, dietetics, gene therapy, health care admin, nursing (RN). **History:** General. **Human services:** International policy. **Liberal arts:** Arts/sciences. **Math:** General, applied, statistics. **Parks/recreation:** Sports admin. **Philosophy/religion:** Philosophy. **Physical sciences:** Chemistry, geology, physics. **Psychology:** General, cognitive. **Social sciences:** Anthropology, economics, geography, political science, sociology, urban studies. **Visual/performing arts:** Acting, art history/conservation, dramatic, music, studio arts, theater design. **Work/family studies:** Family studies, family systems.

Most popular majors. Biology 9%, business/marketing 13%, communications/journalism 7%, engineering/engineering technologies 9%, health sciences 12%, psychology 8%, social sciences 11%.

Technology on campus. 1,318 workstations in dormitories, library, computer center, student center. Dormitories wired for high-speed internet access and linked to campus network. Commuter students can connect to campus network. Online course registration, online library, helpline, repair service, wireless network available.

Student life. Freshman orientation: Available, $60 fee. Preregistration for classes offered. Twelve 2-day sessions extending from late May to early July. **Policies:** Freshmen not permitted cars on campus. **Housing:** Coed dorms, single-sex dorms, special housing for disabled, apartments, fraternity/sorority housing, themed housing, wellness housing available. $150 nonrefundable deposit, deadline 5/1. Several Living and Learning Communities including Business Connections, EcoHouse., Global House, Honors, Humanities House, Public Health House, and Women in Math, Science and Engineering. **Activities:** Bands, campus ministries, choral groups, dance, drama, film society, international student organizations, literary magazine, music ensembles, Model UN, musical theater, opera, radio station, student government, student newspaper, symphony orchestra, TV station, over 400 organizations available.

Athletics. NCAA. **Intercollegiate:** Baseball M, basketball, cross-country, diving, field hockey W, football (tackle) M, golf M, ice hockey, lacrosse W, rowing (crew) W, soccer, softball W, swimming, tennis, track and field, volleyball W. **Intramural:** Badminton, baseball M, basketball, bowling, cross-country, diving, equestrian, fencing, football (non-tackle), football (tackle) M, ice hockey, lacrosse, racquetball, rowing (crew), rugby, sailing, skiing, soccer, softball, squash, swimming, table tennis, tennis, track and field, volleyball, water polo, weight lifting M. **Team name:** Huskies.

Student services. Adult student services, alcohol/substance abuse counseling, chaplain/spiritual director, career counseling, student employment services, financial aid counseling, health services, minority student services, on-campus daycare, personal counseling, placement for graduates, veterans' counselor, women's services. **Physically disabled:** Services for visually, speech, hearing impaired.

Contact. E-mail: beahusky@uconn.edu
Phone: (860) 486-3137 Fax: (860) 486-1476
Nathan Fuerst, Director of Undergraduate Admissions, University of Connecticut, 2131 Hillside Road, Unit 3088, Storrs, CT 06269-3088

University of Hartford
West Hartford, Connecticut
www.hartford.edu

CB member
CB code: 3436

- Private 4-year university
- Residential campus in small city
- 5,028 degree-seeking undergraduates: 10% part-time, 51% women, 16% African American, 3% Asian American, 12% Hispanic/Latino, 3% Multiracial, non-Hispanic, 6% international
- 1,613 degree-seeking graduate students
- 63% of applicants admitted
- SAT or ACT (ACT writing optional) required
- 60% graduate within 6 years

General. Founded in 1877. Regionally accredited. **Degrees:** 1,019 bachelor's, 149 associate awarded; master's, professional, doctoral offered. **ROTC:** Army, Air Force. **Location:** 4 miles from downtown. **Calendar:** Semester, extensive summer session. **Full-time faculty:** 354 total; 16% minority, 40% women. **Part-time faculty:** 498 total. **Class size:** 70% < 20, 28% 20-39, less than 1% 40-49, less than 1% 50-99, less than 1% >100. **Special facilities:** Engineering applications center, humanities center, performing arts center, center for professional development, entrepreneurial center, construction institute.

Freshman class profile. 15,125 applied, 9,581 admitted, 1,451 enrolled.

Mid 50% test scores			
SAT critical reading:	470-580	Return as sophomores:	74%
SAT math:	470-580	Out-of-state:	59%
ACT composite:	20-25	Live on campus:	84%
		International:	3%

Basis for selection. Quality of academic program, school achievement record, class rank important. Test scores secondary. Employment, extracurricular activities, and community service considered. Writing samples and interview also considered. Admission committee can offer admission to alternative program. Interview and essay recommended. Audition required of music, dance, acting majors. Portfolio required of art majors. **Home schooled:** Statement describing home school structure and mission, transcript of courses and grades required.

High school preparation. College-preparatory program required. 16 units required. Required and recommended units include English 4, mathematics 2-3, social studies 2, history 2, science 2-3, foreign language 2 and academic electives 4. Physics, chemistry, and 3.5 math (including trigonometry) recommended for engineering and science applicants.

2016-2017 Annual costs. Tuition/fees (projected): $37,790. Room/board: $11,986. Books/supplies: $800. Personal expenses: $1,562.

2015-2016 Financial aid. **Need-based:** 1,269 full-time freshmen applied for aid; 1,115 deemed to have need; 1,112 received aid. Average need met was 68%. Average scholarship/grant was $21,295; average loan $3,528. 68% of total undergraduate aid awarded as scholarships/grants, 32% as loans/jobs. **Non-need-based:** Awarded to 1,174 full-time undergraduates, including 389 freshmen. Scholarships awarded for academics, alumni affiliation, art, athletics, job skills, leadership, minority status, music/drama.

Application procedures. Admission: No deadline. $40 fee, may be waived for applicants with need. Admission notification on a rolling basis beginning on or about 10/1. Must reply by May 1 or within 2 week(s) if notified thereafter. **Financial aid:** Priority date 2/1; no closing date. FAFSA required. Applicants notified on a rolling basis starting 3/1; must reply by 5/1 or within 2 week(s) of notification.

Academics. Special study options: Combined bachelor's/graduate degree, cross-registration, distance learning, double major, dual enrollment of high school students, ESL, exchange student, honors, independent study, internships, liberal arts/career combination, student-designed major, study abroad, teacher certification program, Washington semester, weekend college. Saturday term. **Credit/placement by examination:** AP, CLEP, SAT, ACT, institutional tests. 30 credit hours maximum toward associate degree, 60 toward bachelor's. **Support services:** Learning center, reduced course load, tutoring, writing center.

Majors. Area/ethnic studies: Women's. **Biology:** General. **Business:** Accounting, business admin, entrepreneurial studies, finance, insurance, management information systems, marketing. **Communications:** Communications/speech/rhetoric. **Computer sciences:** General, information systems. **Education:** Early childhood, elementary, music, secondary, special ed. **Engineering:** General, civil, computer, electrical, mechanical. **English:** English lit, technical writing. **Foreign languages:** General. **Health services:** Clinical lab science, medical radiologic technology/radiation therapy, nursing (RN), respiratory therapy technology. **History:** General. **Human services:** Community org/advocacy. **Liberal arts:** Arts/sciences. **Math:** General. **Philosophy/religion:** Judaic, philosophy. **Physical sciences:** Chemistry, physics. **Protective services:** Police science. **Psychology:** General. **Social sciences:** Economics, international relations, political science, sociology. **Visual/performing arts:** General, acting, art history/conservation, ceramics, cinematography, commercial/advertising art, dance, design, dramatic, drawing, film/cinema/video, jazz, music, music history, music management, music performance, music theory/composition, painting, photography, printmaking, sculpture.

Most popular majors. Business/marketing 13%, engineering/engineering technologies 18%, health sciences 15%, visual/performing arts 22%.

Technology on campus. 300 workstations in dormitories, library, computer center. Dormitories wired for high-speed internet access and linked to campus network. Commuter students can connect to campus network. Online course registration, online library, helpline, repair service, student web hosting, wireless network available.

Student life. Freshman orientation: Mandatory. Preregistration for classes offered. **Housing:** Guaranteed on-campus for freshmen. Coed dorms, single-sex dorms, special housing for disabled, apartments, themed housing, wellness housing available. $200 deposit, deadline 5/1. Dormitories with resident faculty members, international residential college, residential college for the arts available. **Activities:** Bands, campus ministries, choral groups, dance, drama, international student organizations, literary magazine, music ensembles, musical theater, opera, radio station, student government, student newspaper, symphony orchestra, TV station, Hillel, Protestant student organization, Newman club, African American students association, academic department clubs, prelaw and premedical societies, Brothers and Sisters United, Global Friends Association, Malaysian student association, Turkish student association.

Athletics. NCAA. **Intercollegiate:** Baseball M, basketball, cross-country, golf, lacrosse M, soccer, softball W, tennis, track and field, volleyball W. **Intramural:** Badminton, basketball, football (non-tackle), handball, racquetball, soccer, softball, squash, tennis, ultimate frisbee, volleyball. **Team name:** Hawks.

Student services. Alcohol/substance abuse counseling, chaplain/spiritual director, career counseling, student employment services, financial aid counseling, health services, minority student services, personal counseling, placement for graduates, veterans' counselor.

Contact. E-mail: admission@hartford.edu
Phone: (860) 768-4296 Fax: (860) 768-4961
Richard Zeiser, Dean of Admission, University of Hartford, Bates House, West Hartford, CT 06117-1599

University of New Haven
West Haven, Connecticut
www.newhaven.edu

CB member
CB code: 3663

- Private 4-year university
- Residential campus in small city
- 4,942 degree-seeking undergraduates: 7% part-time, 50% women, 9% African American, 3% Asian American, 11% Hispanic/Latino, 2% Multiracial, non-Hispanic, 8% international
- 1,732 degree-seeking graduate students
- 82% of applicants admitted
- SAT or ACT (ACT writing optional), application essay required
- 54% graduate within 6 years

General. Founded in 1920. Regionally accredited. Experiential learning emphasized. **Degrees:** 1,218 bachelor's, 38 associate awarded; master's, doctoral offered. **ROTC:** Army, Air Force. **Location:** 3 miles from downtown New Haven, 75 miles from New York City. **Calendar:** 4-1-4, limited summer session. **Full-time faculty:** 268 total; 83% have terminal degrees, 26% minority, 34% women. **Part-time faculty:** 367 total; 43% have terminal degrees, 13% minority, 37% women. **Class size:** 48% < 20, 47% 20-39, 2% 40-49, 3% 50-99, less than 1% >100. **Special facilities:** Theater, music and sound recording studio, shoreline environmental study preserve, institute of forensic science, learning center for finance and technology.

Freshman class profile. 10,748 applied, 8,826 admitted, 1,244 enrolled.

Mid 50% test scores			
		GPA 2.0-2.99:	15%
SAT critical reading:	480-580	Rank in top quarter:	40%
SAT math:	480-580	Rank in top tenth:	16%
SAT writing:	470-570	Return as sophomores:	79%
ACT composite:	21-26	Out-of-state:	64%
GPA 3.75 or higher:	21%	Live on campus:	79%
GPA 3.50-3.74:	31%	International:	4%
GPA 3.0-3.49:	33%		

Basis for selection. Academic record, letters of recommendation, test scores, personal essay, advanced placement or honor courses, and extracurricular activities are reviewed. **Learning Disabled:** Students required to meet with Disability Services Office to receive accommodations and/or services.

High school preparation. College-preparatory program recommended. 17 units recommended. Recommended units include English 4, mathematics 3, social studies 3, science 3 (laboratory 2) and foreign language 2.

2015-2016 Annual costs. Tuition/fees: $35,650. Room/board: $14,720. Books/supplies: $1,000. Personal expenses: $1,000.

2015-2016 Financial aid. Need-based: 1,073 full-time freshmen applied for aid; 973 deemed to have need; 973 received aid. Average need met was 61%. Average scholarship/grant was $19,888; average loan $3,467. 68% of total undergraduate aid awarded as scholarships/grants, 32% as loans/jobs. **Non-need-based:** Awarded to 1,066 full-time undergraduates, including 289 freshmen. Scholarships awarded for academics, art, athletics.

Application procedures. Admission: Priority date 3/1; no deadline. $50 fee, may be waived for applicants with need. Admission notification on a rolling basis beginning on or about 9/1. Must reply by May 1 or within 2 week(s) if notified thereafter. Applications considered into the first week of classes providing there is room for the class and/or major. **Financial aid:** Closing date 3/1. FAFSA required. Applicants notified on a rolling basis starting 3/1; must reply within 2 week(s) of notification.

Academics. Special study options: Accelerated study, combined bachelor's/graduate degree, cooperative education, cross-registration, distance learning, double major, dual enrollment of high school students, ESL, exchange student, honors, independent study, internships, liberal arts/career combination, study abroad, teacher certification program. **Credit/placement by examination:** AP, CLEP, IB, SAT, institutional tests. **Support services:** Learning center, reduced course load, remedial instruction, study skills assistance, tutoring, writing center.

Majors. Architecture: Interior. **Biology:** General, marine. **Business:** Accounting, business admin, finance, hospitality admin, hotel/motel admin, marketing. **Communications:** Communications/speech/rhetoric. **Computer sciences:** General, computer science, information systems. **Conservation:** Environmental science, management/policy. **Engineering:** General, chemical, civil, computer, electrical, industrial, mechanical. **English:** English lit. **Health services:** Dental hygiene, dietetics, EMT paramedic. **History:** General. **Human services:** General. **Liberal arts:** Arts/sciences. **Math:** General, applied. **Parks/recreation:** Sports admin. **Physical sciences:** Chemistry. **Protective services:** Fire safety technology, firefighting, forensics, law enforcement admin. **Psychology:** General, community, forensic. **Social sciences:** Economics, national security policy, political science. **Visual/performing arts:** General, commercial/advertising art, drawing, graphic design, illustration, music, music management, music technology, painting, sculpture, studio arts, theater arts management.

Most popular majors. Biology 7%, business/marketing 11%, engineering/engineering technologies 8%, psychology 7%, security/protective services 40%, visual/performing arts 9%.

Technology on campus. Dormitories wired for high-speed internet access and linked to campus network. Online course registration, helpline, repair service, wireless network available.

Student life. Freshman orientation: Mandatory. Preregistration for classes offered. **Policies:** Freshmen not permitted cars on campus. **Housing:** Coed dorms, special housing for disabled, apartments, themed housing, wellness housing available. $200 nonrefundable deposit, deadline 5/1. Living/learning communities available for freshmen majoring in business, engineering, forensic science, or music. Some dorm rooms are handicap accessible. **Activities:** Bands, campus ministries, dance, film society, international student organizations, literary magazine, music ensembles, Model UN, radio station, student government, student newspaper, TV station.

Athletics. NCAA. **Intercollegiate:** Baseball M, basketball, cross-country, football (tackle) M, lacrosse W, soccer, softball W, tennis W, track and field, volleyball W. **Intramural:** Basketball, football (non-tackle), handball, racquetball, soccer, softball, tennis, volleyball, weight lifting. **Team name:** Chargers.

Student services. Alcohol/substance abuse counseling, career counseling, student employment services, financial aid counseling, health services, minority student services, personal counseling, placement for graduates, veterans' counselor, women's services. **Physically disabled:** Services for visually, speech, hearing impaired.

Contact. E-mail: admissions@newhaven.edu
Phone: (203) 932-7319 Toll-free number: (800) 342-5864 ext. 7319
Fax: (203) 931-6093
Kevin Phillips, Associate Vice President for Enrollment Management,
University of New Haven, 300 Boston Post Road, West Haven, CT
06516-1916

University of Saint Joseph
West Hartford, Connecticut
www.usj.edu

CB member
CB code: 3754

- Private 4-year liberal arts college for women affiliated with the Roman Catholic Church
- Residential campus in small city
- 904 degree-seeking undergraduates: 15% part-time, 98% women, 16% African American, 4% Asian American, 17% Hispanic/Latino, 2% Multiracial, non-Hispanic
- 1,576 degree-seeking graduate students
- 93% of applicants admitted
- Application essay required
- 53% graduate within 6 years

General. Founded in 1932. Regionally accredited. Coeducational programs available for adults seeking to complete a bachelor's degree. **Degrees:** 236 bachelor's awarded; master's, professional offered. **Location:** 3 miles from Hartford. **Calendar:** Semester, limited summer session. **Full-time faculty:** 131 total; 87% have terminal degrees, 24% minority, 70% women. **Part-time faculty:** 161 total; 11% minority, 66% women. **Class size:** 73% < 20, 24% 20-39, 2% 40-49. **Special facilities:** Art gallery, athenaeum.

Freshman class profile. 751 applied, 697 admitted, 213 enrolled.

Mid 50% test scores			
SAT critical reading:	410-530	GPA 2.0-2.99:	30%
SAT math:	410-520	Rank in top quarter:	47%
ACT composite:	16-22	Rank in top tenth:	16%
GPA 3.75 or higher:	21%	Return as sophomores:	68%
GPA 3.50-3.74:	13%	Out-of-state:	7%
GPA 3.0-3.49:	35%	Live on campus:	54%
		International:	1%

Basis for selection. Academic record, standardized test scores (test optional), and supplemental application materials should display evidence of sufficient college-level ability and potential. Test optional; however some academic programs do require test scores as part of the application process. **Home schooled:** Statement describing home school structure and mission, transcript of courses and grades, state high school equivalency certificate, interview, letter of recommendation (nonparent) required.

High school preparation. College-preparatory program required. 16 units required. Required and recommended units include English 4, mathematics 4, social studies 3, science 3 and foreign language 2. 16 units required; 18 units required for students who select to be test optional.

2015-2016 Annual costs. Tuition/fees: $36,140. Room/board: $14,850. Books/supplies: $1,100. Personal expenses: $930.

Financial aid. Non-need-based: Scholarships awarded for academics, leadership, minority status.

Application procedures. Admission: No deadline. $50 fee, may be waived for applicants with need, free for online applicants. Admission notification on a rolling basis beginning on or about 10/1. Must reply by May 1 or within the official acceptance letter's stated time frame. **Financial aid:** No deadline. FAFSA required. Applicants notified on a rolling basis starting 2/15.

Academics. Special study options: Accelerated study, combined bachelor's/graduate degree, cross-registration, distance learning, double major, honors, independent study, internships, liberal arts/career combination, student-designed major, study abroad, teacher certification program, weekend college. **Credit/placement by examination:** AP, CLEP, institutional tests. **Support services:** Learning center, reduced course load, study skills assistance, tutoring, writing center.

Majors. Area/ethnic studies: Women's. **Biology:** General, biochemistry. **Business:** Accounting, business admin. **Education:** Special ed. **English:** English lit. **Foreign languages:** Spanish. **Health services:** Nursing (RN). **History:** General. **Human services:** Public policy, social work. **Math:** General. **Philosophy/religion:** Philosophy, religion. **Physical sciences:** Chemistry. **Psychology:** General. **Visual/performing arts:** Art history/conservation. **Work/family studies:** General, child development, food/nutrition.

Most popular majors. Biology 9%, business/marketing 6%, education 6%, family/consumer sciences 11%, health sciences 33%, psychology 9%, public administration/social services 16%.

Technology on campus. Dormitories wired for high-speed internet access and linked to campus network. Commuter students can connect to campus network. Online course registration, online library, helpline, wireless network available.

Student life. Freshman orientation: Mandatory, $30 fee. Preregistration for classes offered. **Housing:** Special housing for disabled, apartments, themed housing available. $250 nonrefundable deposit, deadline 6/1. Single rooms available for nontraditional students. Medical singles with private bathrooms available on a limited basis. Suite-style rooms also available. **Activities:** Campus ministries, choral groups, dance, drama, international student organizations, literary magazine, music ensembles, student government.

Athletics. NCAA. **Intercollegiate:** Basketball W, cross-country W, diving W, lacrosse W, soccer W, softball W, swimming W, tennis W, volleyball W. **Team name:** Blue Jays.

Student services. Adult student services, alcohol/substance abuse counseling, chaplain/spiritual director, career counseling, student employment services, financial aid counseling, health services, personal counseling, placement for graduates, women's services. **Physically disabled:** Services for visually, hearing impaired.

Contact. E-mail: admissions@usj.edu
Phone: (860) 231-5216 Toll-free number: (866) 442-8752
Fax: (860) 231-5744
Samantha Powers, Associate Director of Admissions, University of Saint Joseph, 1678 Asylum Avenue, West Hartford, CT 06117

Wesleyan University
Middletown, Connecticut   **CB member**
www.wesleyan.edu   **CB code: 3959**

- Private 4-year university and liberal arts college
- Residential campus in large town
- 2,819 degree-seeking undergraduates: 54% women, 7% African American, 8% Asian American, 11% Hispanic/Latino, 6% Multi-racial, non-Hispanic, 9% international
- 196 degree-seeking graduate students
- 22% of applicants admitted
- Application essay required
- 94% graduate within 6 years

General. Founded in 1831. Regionally accredited. **Degrees:** 800 bachelor's awarded; master's, doctoral offered. **ROTC:** Air Force. **Location:** 15 miles from Hartford, 25 miles from New Haven. **Calendar:** Semester, limited summer session. **Full-time faculty:** 369 total; 93% have terminal degrees, 20% minority, 46% women. **Part-time faculty:** 76 total; 51% have terminal degrees, 21% minority, 49% women. **Class size:** 72% < 20, 21% 20-39, 4% 40-49, 2% 50-99, 1% >100. **Special facilities:** 11-building arts center, observatory, science center with electron microscopes and nuclear magnetic resonance spectrometers, film studies center, center for humanities, East Asian studies center, African-American studies center.

Freshman class profile. 9,822 applied, 2,180 admitted, 757 enrolled.

Mid 50% test scores			
SAT critical reading:	620-730	Rank in top tenth:	72%
SAT math:	630-740	Return as sophomores:	95%
SAT writing:	630-750	Out-of-state:	94%
ACT composite:	29-33	Live on campus:	100%
GPA 3.75 or higher:	59%	International:	10%
GPA 3.50-3.74:	26%	Fraternities:	9%
GPA 3.0-3.49:	14%	Sororities:	4%
GPA 2.0-2.99:	1%		

Basis for selection. Test scores optional, high school transcript, class rank, extracurricular activities, 2 teacher evaluations, personal statement, and other evidence of outstanding accomplishments are considered. Test scores are optional. Interview recommended. **Home schooled:** Campus interview, statement describing home school structure and mission, transcript of courses and grades, third-party recommendation, and home-school instructor recommendation strongly recommended. Financial aid applicants should be prepared to submit GED.

High school preparation. College-preparatory program recommended. Recommended units include English 4, mathematics 4, social studies 4, history 4, science 4 (laboratory 3) and foreign language 4.

2015-2016 Annual costs. Tuition/fees: $49,274. Room/board: $13,504. Books/supplies: $1,333. Personal expenses: $1,332. **Additional information:** Comprehensive residential fee for juniors & seniors is $15,350.

2015-2016 Financial aid. All financial aid based on need. 390 full-time freshmen applied for aid; 372 deemed to have need; 372 received aid. Average need met was 100%. Average scholarship/grant was $43,059; average loan $3,068. 89% of total undergraduate aid awarded as scholarships/grants, 11% as loans/jobs. **Additional information:** Most families whose income is below

$60,000 will not be packaged with loans; grant aid will replace the standard loan in the package. Other students demonstrating significant need will graduate with 4-year packaged loan debt of $10,000 or $14,000 depending on need level. All other students will have their 4-year packaged loan debt reduced by about 30%.

Application procedures. Admission: Closing date 1/1 (postmark date). $55 fee, may be waived for applicants with need. Application must be submitted online. Admission notification by 4/1. Must reply by May 1 or within 2 week(s) if notified thereafter. **Financial aid:** Closing date 2/15. FAFSA, CSS PROFILE required. Applicants notified by 4/1; must reply by 5/1.

Academics. Students expected to complete 3 classes in each of following areas before graduation: natural sciences and math, arts and humanities, social and behavioral sciences. **Special study options:** Accelerated study, combined bachelor's/graduate degree, cross-registration, double major, dual enrollment of high school students, exchange student, honors, independent study, internships, semester at sea, student-designed major, study abroad, urban semester, Washington semester. **Credit/placement by examination:** AP, CLEP, IB, institutional tests. 2 credit hours maximum toward bachelor's degree. **Support services:** Reduced course load, tutoring, writing center.

Majors. Area/ethnic studies: African-American, American, East Asian, French, gay/lesbian, German, Latin American, Russian/Eastern European/Eurasian, Russian/Slavic. **Biology:** General, biochemistry, molecular, molecular biochemistry, neuroscience. **Computer sciences:** General. **Conservation:** Environmental science. **English:** English lit. **Foreign languages:** Chinese, classics, East Asian, French, German, Italian, Japanese, Romance, Russian, Spanish. **History:** General. **Liberal arts:** Arts/sciences. **Math:** General. **Philosophy/religion:** Philosophy, religion. **Physical sciences:** Astronomy, chemistry, geology, physics, planetary. **Psychology:** General. **Social sciences:** Anthropology, archaeology, economics, political science, sociology. **Visual/performing arts:** Art history/conservation, dance, dramatic, film/cinema/video, music, studio arts.

Most popular majors. Biology 7%, English 6%, interdisciplinary studies 6%, physical sciences 6%, psychology 13%, social sciences 21%, visual/performing arts 28%.

Technology on campus. 300 workstations in library, computer center, student center. Dormitories wired for high-speed internet access and linked to campus network. Commuter students can connect to campus network. Online course registration, online library, helpline, repair service, student web hosting, wireless network available.

Student life. Freshman orientation: Mandatory. Preregistration for classes offered. Held one week before start of fall classes. **Housing:** Guaranteed on-campus for all undergraduates. Coed dorms, single-sex dorms, special housing for disabled, apartments, fraternity/sorority housing, themed housing, wellness housing available. **Activities:** Bands, campus ministries, choral groups, dance, drama, film society, international student organizations, literary magazine, music ensembles, Model UN, musical theater, radio station, student government, student newspaper, symphony orchestra, more than 230 organizations.

Athletics. NCAA. **Intercollegiate:** Baseball M, basketball, cross-country, diving, field hockey W, football (tackle) M, golf M, ice hockey, lacrosse, rowing (crew), soccer, softball W, squash, swimming, tennis, track and field, volleyball W, wrestling M. **Intramural:** Basketball, ice hockey M, soccer, softball, squash, volleyball. **Team name:** Cardinals.

Student services. Adult student services, alcohol/substance abuse counseling, chaplain/spiritual director, career counseling, student employment services, financial aid counseling, health services, minority student services, on-campus daycare, personal counseling, placement for graduates, women's services. **Physically disabled:** Services for visually, speech, hearing impaired.

Contact. E-mail: admissions@wesleyan.edu
Phone: (860) 685-3000 Fax: (860) 685-3001
Nancy Meislahn, Dean of Admission and Financial Aid, Wesleyan University, 70 Wyllys Avenue, Middletown, CT 06459-0260

Western Connecticut State University
Danbury, Connecticut   **CB member**
www.wcsu.edu   **CB code: 3350**

- Public 4-year university
- Commuter campus in small city
- 5,081 degree-seeking undergraduates: 16% part-time, 54% women, 12% African American, 4% Asian American, 18% Hispanic/Latino, 1% Multi-racial, non-Hispanic
- 437 degree-seeking graduate students

♦ 57% of applicants admitted
♦ 47% graduate within 6 years

General. Founded in 1903. Regionally accredited. **Degrees:** 973 bachelor's, 11 associate awarded; master's, professional offered. **ROTC:** Army, Air Force. **Location:** 65 miles from New York City, 50 miles from Hartford. **Calendar:** Semester, extensive summer session. **Full-time faculty:** 205 total; 43% have terminal degrees. **Part-time faculty:** 388 total. **Class size:** 35% < 20, 64% 20-39, less than 1% 40-49, less than 1% 50-99, less than 1% >100. **Special facilities:** Weather station, observatory, nature preserve, concert park, visual performing arts building.

Freshman class profile. 5,235 applied, 2,999 admitted, 680 enrolled.

Mid 50% test scores		End year in good standing:	82%
SAT critical reading:	450-550	Return as sophomores:	76%
SAT math:	450-540	Out-of-state:	8%
SAT writing:	450-560	Live on campus:	57%
Rank in top quarter:	24%	Fraternities:	5%
Rank in top tenth:	7%	Sororities:	9%

Basis for selection. Limited freshman class spaces given to students with strongest academic and extracurricular backgrounds, including test results. SAT or ACT recommended. Essay and interview recommended. Audition required of music majors. Portfolio recommended of graphic design majors. **Home schooled:** Transcript of courses and grades required. **Learning Disabled:** To receive services or accommodations, students must provide appropriate documentation by contacting the coordinator of Access Ability Services.

High school preparation. College-preparatory program required. 13 units required. Required units include English 4, mathematics 3, social studies 1, history 1, science 2 (laboratory 2) and foreign language 2. Additional credits in fine arts and computer science recommended. Academic course work in computer science, visual arts, theater, music or dance may be substituted for one of the required areas.

2015-2016 Annual costs. Tuition/fees: $9,516; $21,786 out-of-state. Room/board: $11,738. Books/supplies: $1,300. Personal expenses: $2,920.

2014-2015 Financial aid. Need-based: 659 full-time freshmen applied for aid; 543 deemed to have need; 536 received aid. Average need met was 50%. Average scholarship/grant was $6,050; average loan $3,550. 39% of total undergraduate aid awarded as scholarships/grants, 61% as loans/jobs. **Non-need-based:** Awarded to 146 full-time undergraduates, including 29 freshmen. Scholarships awarded for academics, art, minority status, music/drama.

Application procedures. Admission: Priority date 4/1; no deadline. $50 fee, may be waived for applicants with need. Admission notification on a rolling basis beginning on or about 12/1. Must reply by May 1 or within 2 week(s) if notified thereafter. **Financial aid:** Priority date 3/15; no closing date. FAFSA, institutional form required. Applicants notified on a rolling basis starting 4/15; must reply by 5/1 or within 2 week(s) of notification.

Academics. Special study options: Cooperative education, cross-registration, distance learning, dual enrollment of high school students, honors, independent study, internships, student-designed major, study abroad, teacher certification program. **Credit/placement by examination:** AP, CLEP, IB, SAT, institutional tests. 30 credit hours maximum toward associate degree, 60 toward bachelor's. **Support services:** Learning center, pre-admission summer program, reduced course load, study skills assistance, tutoring, writing center.

Majors. Area/ethnic studies: American. **Biology:** General. **Business:** Accounting, business admin, finance, management information systems, marketing. **Communications:** Communications/speech/rhetoric, media studies. **Computer sciences:** General. **Education:** Elementary, health, music, secondary. **English:** Creative writing, English lit, writing. **Foreign languages:** Spanish. **Health services:** Clinical lab science, community health services, nursing (RN). **History:** General. **Human services:** Social work. **Liberal arts:** Arts/sciences. **Math:** General. **Physical sciences:** Atmospheric science, chemistry, geology. **Protective services:** Police science. **Psychology:** General. **Social sciences:** General, economics, political science, sociology. **Visual/performing arts:** Art, dramatic, music, music theory/composition.

Most popular majors. Business/marketing 25%, communications/journalism 8%, health sciences 11%, psychology 10%, security/protective services 11%, visual/performing arts 8%.

Technology on campus. 1,021 workstations in dormitories, library, computer center, student center. Dormitories wired for high-speed internet access and linked to campus network. Commuter students can connect to campus network. Online course registration, online library, helpline, student web hosting, wireless network available.

Student life. Freshman orientation: Available. Preregistration for classes offered. Two-day program for students and parents held the weekend before classes start, 1-day program in June. **Policies:** Hazing and smoking inside all buildings prohibited. Honor code applies. **Housing:** Coed dorms, apartments available. $250 nonrefundable deposit. Honors dorm available. **Activities:** Bands, campus ministries, choral groups, dance, drama, international student organizations, literary magazine, music ensembles, musical theater, opera, radio station, student government, student newspaper, symphony orchestra, Black student alliance, Habitat for Humanity, justice and law club, Newman club.

Athletics. NCAA. **Intercollegiate:** Baseball M, basketball, field hockey W, football (tackle) M, lacrosse, soccer, softball W, swimming W, tennis, volleyball W. **Intramural:** Basketball M, football (non-tackle) M, soccer, softball W. **Team name:** Colonials.

Student services. Adult student services, alcohol/substance abuse counseling, chaplain/spiritual director, career counseling, student employment services, financial aid counseling, health services, minority student services, on-campus daycare, personal counseling, veterans' counselor, women's services. **Physically disabled:** Services for visually, speech, hearing impaired.

Contact. E-mail: admissions@wcsu.edu
Phone: (203) 837-9000 Toll-free number: (877) 837-9278
Fax: (203) 837-8338
Jay Murray, Director, Admissions, Western Connecticut State University, 181 White Street, Danbury, CT 06810-6826

Yale University
New Haven, Connecticut **CB member**
www.yale.edu **CB code: 3987**

♦ Private 4-year university
♦ Residential campus in small city
♦ 5,528 degree-seeking undergraduates: 49% women, 7% African American, 17% Asian American, 11% Hispanic/Latino, 1% Native American, 6% Multi-racial, non-Hispanic, 11% international
♦ 6,779 degree-seeking graduate students
♦ 7% of applicants admitted
♦ SAT or ACT with writing, application essay required
♦ 97% graduate within 6 years

General. Founded in 1701. Regionally accredited. **Degrees:** 1,327 bachelor's awarded; master's, professional, doctoral offered. **ROTC:** Army, Naval, Air Force. **Location:** 75 miles from New York City. **Calendar:** Semester, limited summer session. **Full-time faculty:** 1,159 total; 28% minority, 36% women. **Part-time faculty:** 483 total; 35% minority, 39% women. **Class size:** 74% < 20, 15% 20-39, 2% 40-49, 6% 50-99, 3% >100. **Special facilities:** Yale Art Gallery, British art museum, Peabody Museum of Natural History, institute for global affairs, Center for Engineering Innovation and Design, clean room, wind tunnel, engine testing facility, graphic workstations, robotics labs, nuclear accelerators, nuclear magnetic resonance spectrometers, optical spectroscopy instruments, high-resolution mass spectrometer, x-ray diffraction instruments, scanning electron microscopes, observatories, biospheric studies institute.

Freshman class profile. 30,236 applied, 2,034 admitted, 1,364 enrolled.

Mid 50% test scores		Rank in top tenth:	97%
SAT critical reading:	710-800	Return as sophomores:	99%
SAT math:	710-800	Out-of-state:	92%
SAT writing:	700-790	Live on campus:	100%
ACT composite:	31-35	International:	11%
Rank in top quarter:	99%		

Basis for selection. Honors work at secondary level, standardized test scores, and high degree of accomplishment in one or more nonacademic areas important, followed by diversity of interests, background and special talents. SAT Subject Tests recommended. Yale strongly recommends the Test of English as a Foreign Language (TOEFL) for any applicant whose first language is not English and who has not received at least two years of his or her secondary education in an English-medium curriculum. Students may submit the IELTS (International English Language Testing System) in lieu of the TOEFL (a minimum score of 7 is required) or the Pearson Test of English (a minimum score of 70 is required). Interview recommended. Music, art, dance and film submissions accepted digitally via web portal within the Common Application. **Home schooled:** Letter of recommendation (nonparent) required. Require 2 recommendations from teachers of courses taken outside the home, such as community college courses or courses at local high school.

High school preparation. College-preparatory program recommended. Students recommended to take richest possible mix of demanding academic offerings.

2015-2016 Annual costs. Tuition/fees: $47,600. Room/board: $14,600. Books/supplies: $3,525.

Financial aid. All financial aid based on need. **Additional information:** All scholarships based on demonstrated need.

Application procedures. Admission: Closing date 1/1 (postmark date). $80 fee, may be waived for applicants with need. Admission notification by 4/1. Must reply by 5/1. **Financial aid:** Priority date 3/1, closing date 3/1. FAFSA, CSS PROFILE required. Applicants notified by 4/1; must reply by 5/1.

Academics. Special study options: Accelerated study, combined bachelor's/graduate degree, double major, ESL, honors, independent study, internships, liberal arts/career combination, student-designed major, study abroad. **Credit/placement by examination:** AP, CLEP, IB, institutional tests. **Support services:** Study skills assistance, tutoring, writing center.

Majors. Architecture: Architecture. **Area/ethnic studies:** African, African-American, American, East Asian, European, German, Latin American, Near/Middle Eastern, Russian/Slavic, women's. **Biology:** General, biochemistry, Biochemistry/molecular biology, molecular. **Computer sciences:** General, applications programming. **Conservation:** Environmental studies. **Engineering:** Applied physics, biomedical, chemical, electrical, engineering science, environmental, mechanical. **English:** English lit, general lit. **Foreign languages:** Ancient Greek, Biblical, Chinese, classics, French, German, Italian, Japanese, Latin, linguistics, Portuguese, Russian, Spanish. **History:** General. **Liberal arts:** Humanities. **Math:** General, applied, statistics. **Philosophy/religion:** Judaic, philosophy, religion. **Physical sciences:** Astronomy, astrophysics, chemistry, geology, physics. **Psychology:** General. **Social sciences:** Anthropology, archaeology, economics, international relations, political science, sociology. **Visual/performing arts:** Art, art history/conservation, dramatic, film/cinema/video, music.

Most popular majors. Area/ethnic studies 7%, biology 10%, engineering/engineering technologies 6%, history 7%, interdisciplinary studies 7%, social sciences 29%, visual/performing arts 6%.

Technology on campus. 400 workstations in dormitories, library, computer center, student center. Dormitories wired for high-speed internet access and linked to campus network. Commuter students can connect to campus network. Online course registration, online library, helpline, repair service, student web hosting, wireless network available.

Student life. Freshman orientation: Mandatory. Preregistration for classes offered. **Housing:** Guaranteed on-campus for freshmen. Coed dorms, special housing for disabled available. Students are randomly assigned to one of 12 residential colleges where they live, eat, socialize and pursue various academic and extracurricular activities. All undergraduate housing is provided through the residential college system. **Activities:** Bands, choral groups, dance, drama, film society, literary magazine, music ensembles, musical theater, opera, radio station, student government, student newspaper, symphony orchestra, TV station, over 150 organizations available.

Athletics. NCAA. **Intercollegiate:** Baseball M, basketball, cross-country, diving, fencing, field hockey W, football (tackle) M, golf, gymnastics W, ice hockey, lacrosse, rowing (crew), sailing, soccer, softball W, squash, swimming, tennis, track and field, volleyball W. **Intramural:** Badminton, baseball M, basketball, bowling, cross-country, field hockey W, football (tackle), golf, ice hockey, racquetball, rowing (crew), soccer, softball, squash, swimming, table tennis, tennis, ultimate frisbee, volleyball, water polo, wrestling M. **Team name:** Bulldogs.

Student services. Alcohol/substance abuse counseling, chaplain/spiritual director, career counseling, student employment services, financial aid counseling, health services, minority student services, personal counseling, placement for graduates, women's services. **Physically disabled:** Services for visually, speech, hearing impaired.

Contact. E-mail: student.questions@yale.edu
Phone: (203) 432-9300 Fax: (203) 432-9392
Jeremiah Quinlan, Dean of Undergraduate Admissions, Yale University, Yale Undergraduate Admissions, New Haven, CT 06520-8234

Delaware

Delaware State University

Dover, Delaware

CB member

www.desu.edu

CB code: 5153

- Public 4-year university
- Residential campus in large town
- 3,654 degree-seeking undergraduates
- 385 graduate students
- SAT or ACT with writing required

General. Founded in 1891. Regionally accredited. University has its own fleet of planes. **Degrees:** 533 bachelor's awarded; master's, doctoral offered. **ROTC:** Army, Air Force. **Location:** 46 miles from Wilmington, 100 miles from Washington DC. **Calendar:** Semester, extensive summer session. **Full-time faculty:** 211 total; 93% have terminal degrees, 59% minority, 40% women. **Part-time faculty:** 146 total; 52% minority, 49% women. **Class size:** 48% < 20, 44% 20-39, 4% 40-49, 3% 50-99. **Special facilities:** Science center, observatory, herbarium.

Freshman class profile.

GPA 3.75 or higher:	14%	Rank in top quarter:	27%
GPA 3.50-3.74:	11%	Rank in top tenth:	9%
GPA 3.0-3.49:	28%	Out-of-state:	62%
GPA 2.0-2.99:	47%	Live on campus:	81%

Basis for selection. High school curriculum and GPA most important. Test scores only used in conjunction with GPA. Class rank considered.

High school preparation. College-preparatory program required. 19 units required. Required and recommended units include English 4, mathematics 3, social studies 1, history 2, science 3-4 (laboratory 3), foreign language 2 and academic electives 4. Math units must include 2 algebra and 1 geometry.

2015-2016 Annual costs. Tuition/fees: $7,532; $16,138 out-of-state. Room/board: $10,820. Books/supplies: $1,700. Personal expenses: $1,600.

Financial aid. All financial aid based on need. **Additional information:** Students must file FAFSA by 3/15 every year.

Application procedures. Admission: Priority date 4/1; no deadline. $35 fee, may be waived for applicants with need. Admission notification on a rolling basis beginning on or about 9/1. **Financial aid:** Priority date 3/15, closing date 7/1. FAFSA required. Applicants notified by 3/1; Applicants notified on a rolling basis starting 4/1; must reply by 7/10.

Academics. Special study options: Accelerated study, cooperative education, distance learning, double major, dual enrollment of high school students, ESL, honors, independent study, internships, liberal arts/career combination, semester at sea, study abroad, teacher certification program. **Credit/placement by examination:** AP, CLEP, IB, institutional tests. 30 credit hours maximum toward bachelor's degree. **Support services:** Learning center, preadmission summer program, reduced course load, remedial instruction, study skills assistance, tutoring, writing center.

Majors. Biology: General, biotechnology. **Business:** Accounting, business admin, entrepreneurial studies, finance, hospitality admin, management science, managerial economics, marketing, nonprofit/public. **Communications:** Broadcast journalism, journalism, media studies, radio/TV. **Computer sciences:** Computer science, data processing. **Conservation:** Environmental science, fisheries, forestry, management/policy, wildlife/wilderness. **Education:** General, agricultural, art, biology, business, chemistry, early childhood, elementary, English, French, German, gifted/talented, health, mathematics, middle, music, physical, physics, science, social science, Spanish, special ed, trade/industrial. **Engineering:** Aerospace, applied physics, biomedical, civil, electrical, laser/optical, mining. **English:** English lit. **Foreign languages:** French, German, Spanish. **Health services:** Clinical lab technology, nursing (RN), prenursing, preveterinary. **History:** General. **Human services:** Social work. **Math:** General. **Parks/recreation:** Health/fitness, sports admin. **Philosophy/religion:** Philosophy. **Physical sciences:** Chemistry, forensic chemistry, physics. **Protective services:** Criminal justice, fire safety technology. **Psychology:** General. **Social sciences:** Criminology, political science, sociology, urban studies. **Visual/performing arts:** General, art, music, studio arts, studio arts management. **Work/family studies:** Clothing/textiles, consumer economics, food/nutrition.

Most popular majors. Business/marketing 13%, communications/journalism 8%, education 6%, health sciences 8%, parks/recreation 11%, psychology 10%, public administration/social services 6%, social sciences 12%.

Technology on campus. 400 workstations in library, computer center, student center. Dormitories wired for high-speed internet access and linked to campus network. Online course registration, online library, helpline, wireless network available.

Student life. Freshman orientation: Mandatory, $150 fee. Preregistration for classes offered. Two-day program during June, July and August. **Policies:** First-time, first-year freshmen must submit written request for parking permit. **Housing:** Guaranteed on-campus for freshmen. Coed dorms, single-sex dorms, special housing for disabled, apartments available. $200 nonrefundable deposit, deadline 4/15. Suite style accommodations available for upper class students and honor students; residence hall available for honors students. **Activities:** Bands, campus ministries, choral groups, dance, drama, international student organizations, radio station, student government, student newspaper, TV station, Wesley Foundation, commuters club, NAACP, black studies club, honor societies, Greek letter organizations, student ambassadors.

Athletics. NCAA. **Intercollegiate:** Baseball M, basketball, bowling W, cheerleading, cross-country, equestrian W, football (tackle) M, soccer W, softball W, tennis W, track and field, volleyball W. **Intramural:** Basketball, football (non-tackle), soccer, softball, swimming, table tennis, tennis, track and field, volleyball. **Team name:** Hornets.

Student services. Adult student services, alcohol/substance abuse counseling, chaplain/spiritual director, career counseling, student employment services, financial aid counseling, health services, on-campus daycare, personal counseling, placement for graduates, veterans' counselor. **Physically disabled:** Services for visually, speech, hearing impaired.

Contact. E-mail: admissions@desu.edu
Phone: (302) 857-6351 Toll-free number: (800) 845-2544
Fax: (302) 857-6352
Erin Hill, Executive Director of Admissions, Delaware State University, 1200 North DuPont Highway, Dover, DE 19901

Goldey-Beacom College

Wilmington, Delaware

CB member

www.gbc.edu

CB code: 5255

- Private 4-year business college
- Commuter campus in small city
- 620 degree-seeking undergraduates
- 730 graduate students
- SAT required

General. Founded in 1886. Regionally accredited. **Degrees:** 136 bachelor's, 22 associate awarded; master's offered. **Location:** 8 miles from Wilmington, 36 miles from Philadelphia. **Calendar:** Semester, extensive summer session. **Full-time faculty:** 18 total; 100% have terminal degrees, 17% minority, 39% women. **Part-time faculty:** 64 total; 20% have terminal degrees, 20% minority, 42% women. **Class size:** 50% < 20, 41% 20-39, 9% 40-49. **Special facilities:** Non-denominational chapel, athletic facilities and fields, fitness center, computer lab.

Basis for selection. Bachelor degree candidates must submit SAT scores and official transcripts from high school(s) and or college(s) attended. High school performance is evaluated. When necessary, interviews are requested. Interview recommended. **Home schooled:** Statement describing home school structure and mission, transcript of courses and grades, state high school equivalency certificate, interview required. **Learning Disabled:** Evaluation of disability and submission of documentation regarding disability.

High school preparation. 16 units recommended. Recommended units include English 4, mathematics 3 and science 3. 3 math units required for bachelor's degree applicants.

2015-2016 Annual costs. Tuition/fees: $22,950. Room only: $5,800. Books/supplies: $1,005. Personal expenses: $4,405.

Financial aid. Non-need-based: Scholarships awarded for academics, athletics.

Application procedures. Admission: No deadline. No application fee. Admission notification on a rolling basis. **Financial aid:** Priority date 4/15, closing date 7/15. FAFSA required. Applicants notified on a rolling basis starting 3/1; must reply within 2 week(s) of notification.

Academics. Special study options: Accelerated study, combined bachelor's/graduate degree, cooperative education, double major, dual enrollment

Four-Year Colleges

of high school students, honors, internships. **Credit/placement by examination:** AP, CLEP, SAT, ACT, institutional tests. **Support services:** Learning center, pre-admission summer program, reduced course load, remedial instruction, study skills assistance, tutoring, writing center.

Majors. Business: General, accounting, business admin, finance, international, management information systems, management science, marketing. **English:** English lit. **Psychology:** General. **Social sciences:** Economics.

Most popular majors. Business/marketing 92%.

Technology on campus. 159 workstations in library, computer center, student center. Dormitories linked to campus network. Commuter students can connect to campus network. Online library, wireless network available.

Student life. Freshman orientation: Mandatory. Preregistration for classes offered. **Housing:** Coed dorms, special housing for disabled, apartments, wellness housing available. $400 fully refundable deposit. Apartment-style residence halls available. **Activities:** Drama, international student organizations, student government, student newspaper.

Athletics. NCAA. **Intercollegiate:** Basketball, cross-country, golf M, soccer, softball W, tennis W, volleyball W. **Team name:** Lightning.

Student services. Career counseling, student employment services, financial aid counseling, placement for graduates. **Physically disabled:** Services for visually, speech, hearing impaired.

Contact. E-mail: admissions@gbc.edu
Phone: (302) 225-6248 Toll-free number: (800) 833-4877
Fax: (302) 996-5408
Larry Eby, Director of Admissions, Goldey-Beacom College, 4701 Limestone Road, Wilmington, DE 19808

University of Delaware

Newark, Delaware	
	CB member
www.udel.edu	**CB code: 5811**

- Public 4-year university
- Residential campus in large town
- 17,575 degree-seeking undergraduates: 4% part-time, 58% women, 5% African American, 5% Asian American, 7% Hispanic/Latino, 3% Multiracial, non-Hispanic, 4% international
- 3,694 degree-seeking graduate students
- 63% of applicants admitted
- SAT or ACT with writing, application essay required
- 81% graduate within 6 years

General. Founded in 1743. Regionally accredited. **Degrees:** 4,077 bachelor's, 325 associate awarded; master's, professional, doctoral offered. **ROTC:** Army, Air Force. **Location:** 12 miles from Wilmington, 30 miles from Philadelphia. **Calendar:** 4-1-4, limited summer session. **Full-time faculty:** 1,181 total; 90% have terminal degrees, 20% minority, 41% women. **Part-time faculty:** 474 total; 43% have terminal degrees, 12% minority, 50% women. **Class size:** 31% < 20, 44% 20-39, 9% 40-49, 11% 50-99, 5% >100. **Special facilities:** Science development center, human performance laboratory, greenhouse, preschool lab, nutrition clinic, engineering research centers, 400-acre agriculture research complex, center for composites manufacturing and research, apparel design laboratory, simulated hospital rooms for nursing, physical therapy clinic, applied coastal research, Delaware biotechnology institute.

Freshman class profile. 24,881 applied, 15,567 admitted, 4,098 enrolled.

Mid 50% test scores			
SAT critical reading:	550-650	Rank in top quarter:	68%
SAT math:	560-660	Rank in top tenth:	33%
SAT writing:	550-650	Return as sophomores:	92%
ACT composite:	25-29	Out-of-state:	69%
GPA 3.75 or higher:	50%	Live on campus:	94%
GPA 3.50-3.74:	21%	International:	3%
GPA 3.0-3.49:	24%		
GPA 2.0-2.99:	5%		

Basis for selection. High school record, program of study, test scores most important. References, essay, extracurricular accomplishments considered. SAT Subject Tests recommended. SAT Subject scores required for home-schooled applicants and strongly recommended for applicants to Honors Program. Audition or portfolio required for music or art. **Home schooled:** Transcript of courses and grades required. Students should provide reading lists for courses they have completed. Sample portfolio of work or sample research paper recommended. Applicants should submit at least 2 SAT Subject Tests of their choice.

High school preparation. College-preparatory program required. 18 units required; 22 recommended. Required and recommended units include English 4, mathematics 3-4, social studies 2, history 2, science 3-4 (laboratory 2-3), foreign language 2-4 and academic electives 2. 4 math strongly recommended for engineering, business, science or math applicants. 4 laboratory science strongly recommended for science, nursing, and engineering applicants.

2015-2016 Annual costs. Tuition/fees: $12,520; $31,420 out-of-state. Room/board: $12,146. Books/supplies: $800. Personal expenses: $1,500.

2015-2016 Financial aid. All financial aid based on need. 3,694 full-time freshmen applied for aid; 2,348 deemed to have need; 2,234 received aid. Average need met was 76%. Average scholarship/grant was $9,756; average loan $6,605. 54% of total undergraduate aid awarded as scholarships/grants, 46% as loans/jobs. **Additional information:** 12/15 application deadline to receive scholarship consideration. Sibling/parent tuition credit plan. Senior citizen tuition credit for state residents over 60.

Application procedures. Admission: Closing date 1/15 (postmark date). $75 fee, may be waived for applicants with need. Admission notification on a rolling basis beginning on or about 11/1. Must reply by May 1 or within 3 week(s) if notified thereafter. **Financial aid:** Priority date 2/1, closing date 3/15. FAFSA required. Applicants notified on a rolling basis starting 3/15; must reply by 5/1 or within 3 week(s) of notification.

Academics. Special study options: Accelerated study, cooperative education, distance learning, double major, dual enrollment of high school students, ESL, honors, independent study, internships, liberal arts/career combination, student-designed major, study abroad, teacher certification program, Washington semester. Research program, minors in 68 disciplines, five-year engineering/liberal arts option. **Credit/placement by examination:** AP, CLEP, IB, SAT, institutional tests. For credit/placement to be awarded for International Baccalaureate, applicant must have taken higher level courses and have minimum score of 4 on exams. **Support services:** Pre-admission summer program, reduced course load, remedial instruction, study skills assistance, tutoring, writing center.

Honors college/program. Program emphasizes small classes, undergraduate research, honors housing, special scholarship opportunities. Special application required. SAT Subject scores strongly recommended.

Majors. Area/ethnic studies: Latin American, women's. **Biology:** General, biochemistry, biotechnology, entomology, plant pathology. **Business:** Accounting, business admin, fashion, finance, management information systems, operations. **Communications:** Communications/speech/rhetoric, journalism. **Computer sciences:** General. **Conservation:** General, wildlife/wilderness. **Education:** General, agricultural, biology, chemistry, early childhood, elementary, English, ESL, family/consumer sciences, foreign languages, French, geography, German, health, history, mathematics, middle, music, physical, physics, psychology, science, secondary, social science, Spanish, special ed. **Engineering:** Aerospace, agricultural, biomedical, chemical, civil, computer, electrical, environmental, mechanical, operations research. **English:** English lit. **Foreign languages:** General, Biblical, classics, comparative lit, French, German, Italian, Latin, Russian, Spanish. **Health services:** Athletic training, clinical lab science, clinical lab technology, nursing (RN), predental, premedicine, prepharmacy, preveterinary. **History:** General. **Liberal arts:** Arts/sciences. **Math:** General, statistics. **Parks/recreation:** Exercise sciences, facilities management, health/fitness, sports admin. **Philosophy/religion:** Philosophy. **Physical sciences:** Astronomy, chemistry, geology, geophysics, physics, planetary. **Protective services:** Criminal justice. **Psychology:** General. **Social sciences:** Anthropology, economics, geography, international relations, political science, sociology. **Visual/performing arts:** Art, art history/conservation, commercial/advertising art, fashion design, music, music performance, music theory/composition, piano/keyboard, studio arts, theater design, theater history, voice/opera. **Work/family studies:** General, child care management, family studies, family/community services, food/nutrition.

Most popular majors. Business/marketing 20%, education 7%, engineering/engineering technologies 11%, health sciences 10%, social sciences 11%.

Technology on campus. 900 workstations in dormitories, library, computer center. Dormitories wired for high-speed internet access and linked to campus network. Commuter students can connect to campus network. Online course registration, online library, helpline, repair service, student web hosting, wireless network available.

Student life. Freshman orientation: Mandatory, $120 fee. Preregistration for classes offered. One-day summer program, plus 3-day program before start of classes. **Housing:** Guaranteed on-campus for all undergraduates. Coed dorms, single-sex dorms, special housing for disabled, apartments, fraternity/sorority housing available. $200 partly refundable deposit, deadline 5/1. Living learning communities, substance free, upper division honors, executive apartments in traditional residence halls. **Activities:** Bands, campus ministries, choral groups, dance, drama, film society, international student organizations, literary magazine, music ensembles, Model UN, musical theater, opera, radio station, student government, student newspaper, symphony orchestra, TV station, black student union, Asian student association, Cosmopolitan Club, Hillel, Hispanic student association, Indian student association, lesbian/gay/bisexual student union, returning adult student association.

Athletics. NCAA. **Intercollegiate:** Baseball M, basketball, cheerleading, cross-country W, diving, field hockey W, football (tackle) M, golf M, lacrosse, rowing (crew) W, soccer, softball W, swimming, tennis, track and field W, volleyball W. **Intramural:** Badminton, basketball, cross-country, fencing, field hockey W, golf, lacrosse, racquetball, soccer, softball, table tennis, tennis, volleyball, water polo M. **Team name:** Fightin' Blue Hens.

Student services. Adult student services, alcohol/substance abuse counseling, chaplain/spiritual director, career counseling, services for economically disadvantaged, student employment services, financial aid counseling, health services, minority student services, personal counseling, placement for graduates, veterans' counselor, women's services. **Physically disabled:** Services for visually, speech, hearing impaired.

Contact. E-mail: admissions@udel.edu
Phone: (302) 831-8123 Fax: (302) 831-6905
Jose Aviles, Director of Admission, University of Delaware, 210 South College Avenue, Newark, DE 19716

Wesley College
Dover, Delaware — CB member
www.wesley.edu — CB code: 5894

- Private 4-year liberal arts college affiliated with the United Methodist Church
- Residential campus in large town
- 1,457 full-time, degree-seeking undergraduates
- SAT or ACT (ACT writing optional) required

General. Founded in 1873. Regionally accredited. **Degrees:** 176 bachelor's, 4 associate awarded; master's offered. **ROTC:** Army. **Location:** 75 miles from Philadelphia. **Calendar:** Semester, limited summer session. **Full-time faculty:** 71 total. **Part-time faculty:** 91 total. **Class size:** 55% < 20, 43% 20-39, less than 1% 40-49, 1% 50-99.

Freshman class profile.

GPA 3.75 or higher:	6%	Rank in top tenth:	24%
GPA 3.50-3.74:	9%	Out-of-state:	70%
GPA 3.0-3.49:	27%	Live on campus:	87%
GPA 2.0-2.99:	58%	Sororities:	6%
Rank in top quarter:	56%		

Basis for selection. High school performance most important. Campus interview very important. Extracurricular activities important.

High school preparation. 20 units recommended. Recommended units include English 4, mathematics 4, social studies 2, history 2, science 4, foreign language 2 and academic electives 2.

2015-2016 Annual costs. Tuition/fees: $25,020. Room/board: $10,970. Books/supplies: $2,000. Personal expenses: $1,400.

Financial aid. All financial aid based on need.

Application procedures. Admission: Priority date 4/1; no deadline. $25 fee. Admission notification on a rolling basis. Must reply by May 1 or within 4 week(s) if notified thereafter. **Financial aid:** Priority date 2/1; no closing date. FAFSA, institutional form required. Applicants notified on a rolling basis starting 1/1; must reply within 2 week(s) of notification.

Academics. Credit requirement for bachelor's degree varies according to program. **Special study options:** Double major, ESL, exchange student, honors, independent study, internships, liberal arts/career combination, study abroad, teacher certification program. **Credit/placement by examination:** AP, CLEP, SAT, ACT, institutional tests. 15 credit hours maximum toward associate degree, 33 toward bachelor's. **Support services:** Learning center, reduced course load, remedial instruction, study skills assistance, tutoring, writing center.

Majors. Area/ethnic studies: American. **Biology:** General, Biochemistry/molecular biology. **Business:** Accounting, business admin. **Communications:** Digital media. **Conservation:** Environmental studies. **Education:** Elementary, physical, secondary. **English:** English lit. **Health services:** Clinical lab science, nursing (RN). **History:** General. **Liberal arts:** Arts/sciences. **Math:** General. **Parks/recreation:** Exercise sciences, sports admin. **Philosophy/religion:** General. **Psychology:** General. **Social sciences:** Political science. **Visual/performing arts:** Music.

Most popular majors. Business/marketing 28%, education 11%, health sciences 17%, liberal arts 6%, parks/recreation 8%, psychology 8%.

Technology on campus. 225 workstations in library. Dormitories wired for high-speed internet access and linked to campus network. Commuter students can connect to campus network. Online course registration, online library, helpline, repair service, wireless network available.

Student life. Freshman orientation: Mandatory. Preregistration for classes offered. **Housing:** Coed dorms, single-sex dorms, apartments, wellness housing available. $250 fully refundable deposit, deadline 5/1. Floors in coed dorms are single-sex. **Activities:** Jazz band, choral groups, drama, literary magazine, music ensembles, student government, student newspaper, TV station, community action, Christian student associations, student activity board, National Coed Community Service Organization, black student union.

Athletics. NCAA. **Intercollegiate:** Baseball M, basketball, cheerleading, cross-country, field hockey W, football (tackle) M, golf, lacrosse, soccer, softball W, tennis, volleyball W. **Intramural:** Basketball, cross-country, soccer M, volleyball. **Team name:** Wolverines.

Student services. Chaplain/spiritual director, career counseling, student employment services, financial aid counseling, health services, personal counseling, placement for graduates. **Physically disabled:** Services for speech impaired.

Contact. E-mail: admissions@wesley.edu
Phone: (302) 736-2400 Toll-free number: (800) 937-5398
Fax: (302) 736-2382
Howard Ballentine, Dean of Enrollment Management, Wesley College, 120 North State Street, Dover, DE 19901-3875

Wilmington University
New Castle, Delaware — CB member
www.wilmu.edu — CB code: 5925

- Private 4-year liberal arts college
- Commuter campus in large town
- 9,238 degree-seeking undergraduates: 57% part-time, 65% women, 26% African American, 2% Asian American, 4% Hispanic/Latino, 1% Native American, 2% international
- 6,210 degree-seeking graduate students

General. Founded in 1967. Regionally accredited. Two 7-week sessions within each trimester in addition to regular trimester sessions and weekend modules. **Degrees:** 2,063 bachelor's, 46 associate awarded; master's, doctoral offered. **ROTC:** Army, Air Force. **Location:** 7 miles from Wilmington. **Calendar:** Trimester, limited summer session. **Full-time faculty:** 104 total. **Part-time faculty:** 1,479 total. **Class size:** 83% < 20, 17% 20-39.

Freshman class profile.

Out-of-state:	15%	International:	2%

Basis for selection. Open admission. Interview recommended. **Home schooled:** GED recommended for non accredited programs.

2015-2016 Annual costs. Tuition/fees: $10,430. Books/supplies: $1,000. Personal expenses: $165.

Financial aid. Non-need-based: Scholarships awarded for academics, athletics.

Application procedures. Admission: No deadline. $35 fee, may be waived for applicants with need. Admission notification on a rolling basis. **Financial aid:** Priority date 4/30; no closing date. FAFSA required. Applicants notified on a rolling basis starting 8/5; must reply within 2 week(s) of notification.

Academics. Mentoring program for all interested incoming freshmen. **Special study options:** Accelerated study, cooperative education, distance learning, double major, dual enrollment of high school students, ESL, honors, independent study, internships, liberal arts/career combination, teacher certification program, weekend college. **Credit/placement by examination:** AP, CLEP, institutional tests. 15 credit hours maximum toward associate degree, 15 toward bachelor's. **Support services:** Learning center, remedial instruction, tutoring, writing center.

Majors. Business: Accounting, finance, human resources, information resources management, marketing, organizational behavior. **Communications:** Digital media, persuasive communications. **Communications technology:** Desktop publishing, photo/film/video, radio/TV. **Computer sciences:** General, information technology, programming, web page design. **Education:** General, early childhood, elementary, English, mathematics, middle, science, social science. **Health services:** Preop/surgical nursing. **Liberal arts:** Arts/sciences. **Parks/recreation:** Sports admin. **Protective services:** Criminal justice. **Psychology:** General. **Social sciences:** Political science. **Visual/performing arts:** Game design.

Most popular majors. Business/marketing 28%, computer/information sciences 6%, education 10%, health sciences 23%, interdisciplinary studies 12%, psychology 6%, security/protective services 7%.

Technology on campus. 516 workstations in library, computer center.

Student life. Freshman orientation: Available. Preregistration for classes offered. Videotaped program distributed to all new students. Two new student programs offered in the fall. **Policies:** Adherence to student handbook expected. **Activities:** Student government, professional fraternities/organizations, Sigma Theta Tau Nursing Society, Business Professionals of America, Alpha Delta Chi, criminal justice club.

Athletics. NCAA. **Intercollegiate:** Baseball M, basketball, cross-country, golf M, lacrosse W, soccer, softball W, volleyball W. **Team name:** Wildcats.

Student services. Career counseling, student employment services, financial aid counseling, placement for graduates.

Contact. E-mail: infocenter@wilmu.edu
Phone: (302) 356-4636 Toll-free number: (877) 967-5464
Fax: (302) 328-5902
Laura Morris, Director of Admissions, Wilmington University, 320 N Dupont Highway, New Castle, DE 19720

District of Columbia

American University

Washington, District of Columbia — CB member
www.american.edu — CB code: 5007

- Private 4-year university affiliated with the United Methodist Church
- Residential campus in very large city
- 7,300 degree-seeking undergraduates: 4% part-time, 63% women, 7% African American, 7% Asian American, 12% Hispanic/Latino, 5% Multiracial, non-Hispanic, 7% international
- 5,168 degree-seeking graduate students
- 35% of applicants admitted
- Application essay required
- 81% graduate within 6 years

General. Founded in 1893. Regionally accredited. **Degrees:** 1,697 bachelor's awarded; master's, professional, doctoral offered. **ROTC:** Army, Air Force. **Location:** 2 miles from downtown. **Calendar:** Semester, extensive summer session. **Class size:** 49% < 20, 47% 20-39, 3% 40-49, 1% 50-99, less than 1% >100. **Special facilities:** Arts center, museum, spiritual life center, arboretum, National Public Radio (NPR) station, game lab, community garden, farmer's market.

Freshman class profile. 16,735 applied, 5,860 admitted, 1,787 enrolled.

Mid 50% test scores			
SAT critical reading:	590-690	GPA 3.50-3.74:	24%
SAT math:	560-650	GPA 3.0-3.49:	28%
SAT writing:	570-670	GPA 2.0-2.99:	5%
ACT composite:	26-30	Return as sophomores:	88%
GPA 3.75 or higher:	43%	Out-of-state:	87%
		International:	4%

Basis for selection. High school record, high school GPA, test scores, writing sample, recommendations, rigor of secondary school record very important. Extracurricular activities and leadership roles considered. Prospective students may apply to university through Early or Regular Decision Plan without submitting standardized test scores. Students who do not wish to submit standardized test scores may do so provided they choose the "No, do not consider my SAT/ACT score for admission to AU" when responding to the "Preferred testing plan" question on the General section of the Common Application. If student will be graduating from a secondary school located outside the United States, please note that neither the SAT or ACT is required for admission. Interview optional, non-evaluative and informational in scope. Audition/interview required of music and music theater majors. **Home schooled:** Statement describing home school structure and mission, transcript of courses and grades required. At least two SAT Subject Tests are recommended but not required. An additional letter of recommendation is recommended but not required. All applicants to AU are required to submit two letters of recommendation. Home-schooled applicants are recommended to submit a third letter of recommendation. **Learning Disabled:** Supplementary application, diagnostic reports, and high school transcript required for freshman learning services program.

High school preparation. College-preparatory program recommended. 16 units required; 18 recommended. Required and recommended units include English 4, mathematics 3-4, social studies 2-4, science 3-4 (laboratory 2), foreign language 2-3 and academic electives 3-4.

2016-2017 Annual costs. Tuition/fees (projected): $44,593. Room/board: $14,526. Books/supplies: $800. Personal expenses: $481.

2015-2016 Financial aid. All financial aid based on need. Average need met was 91%. Average scholarship/grant was $27,104; average loan $3,684. 83% of total undergraduate aid awarded as scholarships/grants, 17% as loans/jobs. **Additional information:** Early decision applicants must submit estimated AU institutional financial aid application by 11/15 and a FASFA as soon as possible after Jan 1.

Application procedures. Admission: Closing date 1/15 (postmark date). $70 fee, may be waived for applicants with need. Admission notification by 4/1. Must reply by May 1 or within 4 week(s) if notified thereafter. **Financial aid:** Closing date 2/15. FAFSA required. CSS Profile and FAFSA must be completed by freshmen who are seeking need-based aid. Applicants notified by 4/1; must reply by 5/1 or within 4 week(s) of notification.

Academics. Three-year scholars programs, University College, Honors Program. **Special study options:** Accelerated study, combined bachelor's/graduate degree, distance learning, double major, ESL, honors, independent study, internships, liberal arts/career combination, student-designed major, study abroad, teacher certification program, Washington semester, weekend college. Three 3-year bachelor degree programs are available. One semester, full-year and alternative break and language immersion programs are available. **Credit/placement by examination:** AP, CLEP, IB, institutional tests. 30 credit hours maximum toward bachelor's degree. **Support services:** Learning center, pre-admission summer program, reduced course load, remedial instruction, study skills assistance, tutoring, writing center. Academic Support, Access Center.

Majors. Area/ethnic studies: American, Asian, French, German, Latin American, Near/Middle Eastern, Russian/Slavic, women's. **Biology:** General, biochemistry. **Business:** Accounting, business admin, finance, management information systems. **Communications:** Journalism, media studies, public relations. **Communications technology:** Recording arts. **Computer sciences:** General. **Conservation:** Environmental science, environmental studies. **Education:** Elementary, secondary. **English:** General lit. **Foreign languages:** Arabic, French, German, Russian, Spanish. **Health services:** Public health ed. **History:** General. **Liberal arts:** Arts/sciences. **Math:** General, applied, computational, financial, statistics. **Philosophy/religion:** Judaic, philosophy, religion. **Physical sciences:** Chemistry, physics. **Protective services:** Criminal justice. **Psychology:** General. **Social sciences:** Anthropology, econometrics, economics, international relations, political science, sociology. **Visual/performing arts:** General, art, art history/conservation, cinematography, design, dramatic, film/cinema/video, graphic design, multimedia, music, music history, music performance, music theory/composition, musical theater, studio arts, theater history.

Most popular majors. Business/marketing 16%, communications/journalism 11%, social sciences 40%.

Technology on campus. 700 workstations in dormitories, library, computer center, student center. Dormitories wired for high-speed internet access and linked to campus network. Commuter students can connect to campus network. Online course registration, online library, helpline, repair service, student web hosting, wireless network available.

Student life. Freshman orientation: Available, $160 fee. Preregistration for classes offered. Two-day sessions held in June and July for fall admits and in January for spring admits. **Policies:** Freshmen not permitted cars on campus. **Housing:** Guaranteed on-campus for freshmen. Coed dorms, special housing for disabled, themed housing available. $200 nonrefundable deposit, deadline 5/1. Honors housing, learning communities housing, community service housing, and housing for students with disabilities (which is handed on an individual basis.). **Activities:** Bands, campus ministries, choral groups, dance, drama, film society, international student organizations, literary magazine, music ensembles, Model UN, musical theater, opera, radio station, student government, student newspaper, symphony orchestra, TV station, Kennedy Political Union, Amnesty International, Habitat for Humanity, various ethnic/cultural student associations, Colleges Against Cancer, Operation Smile,Thirst Project @AU-P, various religious associations, Fair Trade Student Association, AU Vets.

Athletics. NCAA. **Intercollegiate:** Basketball, cross-country, diving, field hockey W, lacrosse W, soccer, swimming, track and field, volleyball W, wrestling M. **Intramural:** Basketball, soccer, softball, tennis, ultimate frisbee, volleyball, weight lifting. **Team name:** Eagles.

Student services. Alcohol/substance abuse counseling, chaplain/spiritual director, career counseling, student employment services, financial aid counseling, health services, minority student services, on-campus daycare, personal counseling, placement for graduates, veterans' counselor, women's services. **Physically disabled:** Services for visually, hearing impaired.

Contact. E-mail: admissions@american.edu
Phone: (202) 885-6000 Fax: (202) 885-1025
Greg Grauman, Assistant Vice Provost, Undergraduate Admissions, American University, 4400 Massachusetts Avenue NW, Washington, DC 20016-8001

Catholic University of America

Washington, District of Columbia — CB member
www.cua.edu — CB code: 5104

- Private 4-year university affiliated with the Roman Catholic Church
- Residential campus in very large city
- 3,462 degree-seeking undergraduates: 4% part-time, 53% women, 5% African American, 3% Asian American, 13% Hispanic/Latino, 5% Multiracial, non-Hispanic, 5% international
- 2,948 degree-seeking graduate students

◗ 79% of applicants admitted

◗ Application essay required

◗ 69% graduate within 6 years; 34% enter graduate study

General. Founded in 1887. Regionally accredited. **Degrees:** 823 bachelor's, 5 associate awarded; master's, professional, doctoral offered. **ROTC:** Army, Naval, Air Force. **Location:** Downtown. **Calendar:** Semester, extensive summer session. **Full-time faculty:** 399 total; 94% have terminal degrees, 12% minority, 38% women. **Part-time faculty:** 367 total; 2% have terminal degrees, 10% minority, 44% women. **Class size:** 58% < 20, 34% 20-39, 4% 40-49, 4% 50-99, less than 1% >100. **Special facilities:** Vitreous State Laboratory, rare book collection.

Freshman class profile. 5,991 applied, 4,707 admitted, 908 enrolled.

Mid 50% test scores			
SAT critical reading:	510-620	GPA 2.0-2.99:	20%
SAT math:	510-610	Return as sophomores:	86%
ACT composite:	22-28	Out-of-state:	98%
GPA 3.75 or higher:	28%	Live on campus:	92%
GPA 3.50-3.74:	21%	International:	3%
GPA 3.0-3.49:	31%	Fraternities:	1%
		Sororities:	1%

Basis for selection. Academic GPA, record of achievement, recommendations very important. Essay, extracurricular activities important. test scores, class rank, interview considered. Students admitted to School of Arts and Sciences or School of Philosophy are recommended to submit SAT Subject Test scores in foreign languages for placement purposes. Audition required for music. **Home schooled:** Statement describing home school structure and mission, transcript of courses and grades, state high school equivalency certificate, letter of recommendation (nonparent) required. **Learning Disabled:** Submit documentation to Office of Disability Support Services.

High school preparation. College-preparatory program required. 17 units recommended. Recommended units include English 4, mathematics 3, social studies 4, science 3 (laboratory 1) and foreign language 3. 1 fine arts or humanities recommended.

2015-2016 Annual costs. Tuition/fees: $40,932. Room/board: $13,356. Books/supplies: $838. Personal expenses: $2,070.

2015-2016 Financial aid. **Need-based:** Average need met was 79%. Average scholarship/grant was $24,379; average loan $4,161. 71% of total undergraduate aid awarded as scholarships/grants, 29% as loans/jobs. **Non-need-based:** Scholarships awarded for academics, alumni affiliation, music/drama, religious affiliation.

Application procedures. **Admission:** Closing date 1/15 (postmark date). $55 fee, may be waived for applicants with need. Admission notification on a rolling basis beginning on or about 3/15. Must reply by May 1 or within 2 week(s) if notified thereafter. **Financial aid:** Priority date 2/1, closing date 4/10. FAFSA, CSS PROFILE required. Applicants notified on a rolling basis starting 3/20; must reply by 5/1 or within 2 week(s) of notification.

Academics. **Special study options:** Accelerated study, combined bachelor's/graduate degree, cross-registration, distance learning, double major, dual enrollment of high school students, ESL, honors, independent study, internships, study abroad, teacher certification program, Washington semester. Internship and study opportunities with Congress, federal agencies, and international embassies. **Credit/placement by examination:** AP, CLEP, IB, institutional tests. All credit-by-examination awarded on case-by-case basis. No credit by outside examination given to matriculated students. **Support services:** Learning center, pre-admission summer program, reduced course load, remedial instruction, study skills assistance, tutoring, writing center.

Honors college/program. Applicants with a combined SAT score of 1300 and a high school GPA of 3.5 or above are offered admission; students not meeting these requirements may petition for admission after they matriculate. About 1 in 10 accepted.

Majors. **Architecture:** Architecture. **Biology:** General, biochemistry. **Business:** General, accounting, finance, human resources, international, international finance, management science. **Communications:** Communications/speech/rhetoric. **Computer sciences:** General. **Education:** General, early childhood, elementary, English, ESL, French, German, history, secondary, Spanish. **Engineering:** General, biomedical, civil, electrical, mechanical. **English:** English lit. **Foreign languages:** Classics, French, German, Latin, Spanish. **Health services:** Clinical lab science, nursing (RN). **History:** General. **Human services:** Social work. **Liberal arts:** Arts/sciences. **Math:** General. **Philosophy/religion:** Philosophy, religion. **Physical sciences:** Chemistry, physics. **Psychology:** General. **Social sciences:** Anthropology, economics, political science, sociology. **Visual/performing arts:** Art, art history/conservation, dramatic, music, music history, music performance, music theory/composition, piano/keyboard, voice/opera.

Most popular majors. Architecture 8%, business/marketing 13%, engineering/engineering technologies 8%, health sciences 9%, philosophy/religious studies 6%, psychology 9%, social sciences 14%, visual/performing arts 8%.

Technology on campus. 366 workstations in library, computer center, student center. Dormitories wired for high-speed internet access and linked to campus network. Commuter students can connect to campus network. Online course registration, online library, helpline, student web hosting, wireless network available.

Student life. **Freshman orientation:** Available. Preregistration for classes offered. Held Thursday-Sunday before start of fall semester. **Policies:** Code of Student Conduct is the guiding behavioral document; medical insurance is required for all full-time students and all full and part-time international students; immunization requirement for students under 26 years of age. Freshmen not permitted cars on campus. **Housing:** Guaranteed on-campus for freshmen. Single-sex dorms, apartments, themed housing available. $500 nonrefundable deposit, deadline 5/1. **Activities:** Bands, campus ministries, choral groups, dance, drama, film society, international student organizations, literary magazine, music ensembles, Model UN, musical theater, opera, radio station, student government, student newspaper, symphony orchestra, College Republicans, College Democrats, Filipino Organization of Catholic University Students, Alpha Phi Omega service fraternity, Habitat for Humanity, Student Organization of Latinos, Black Student Alliance, Knights of Columbus, Colleges Against Cancer.

Athletics. NCAA. **Intercollegiate:** Baseball M, basketball, cross-country, diving, field hockey W, football (tackle) M, lacrosse, soccer, softball W, swimming, tennis, track and field, volleyball W. **Intramural:** Basketball, football (non-tackle), racquetball, soccer, softball, tennis, volleyball. **Team name:** Cardinals.

Student services. Adult student services, alcohol/substance abuse counseling, chaplain/spiritual director, career counseling, student employment services, financial aid counseling, health services, legal services, minority student services, personal counseling, placement for graduates, veterans' counselor. **Physically disabled:** Services for visually, speech, hearing impaired.

Contact. E-mail: cua-admissions@cua.edu
Phone: (202) 319-5305 Toll-free number: (800) 673-2772
Fax: (202) 319-6533
Christopher Lydon, VP, Enrollment Management & Marketing, Catholic University of America, 102 Father O'Connell Hall, Washington, DC 20064

Gallaudet University
Washington, District of Columbia
www.gallaudet.edu   **CB code: 5240**

◗ Private 4-year university and liberal arts college

◗ Residential campus in very large city

◗ 989 degree-seeking undergraduates: 3% part-time, 51% women, 13% African American, 3% Asian American, 12% Hispanic/Latino, 1% Native American, 11% Multi-racial, non-Hispanic, 8% international

◗ 444 degree-seeking graduate students

◗ 62% of applicants admitted

◗ SAT or ACT (ACT writing optional), application essay required

◗ 46% graduate within 6 years

General. Founded in 1857. Regionally accredited. Only liberal arts university in the world designed exclusively for deaf and hard of hearing students. Bilingual (English/American Sign Language), multicultural environment, assistive devices (TTY's or campus phones, closed captioned television and campus films), specially-designed classrooms and dormitories available. **Degrees:** 201 bachelor's awarded; master's, doctoral offered. **Location:** Downtown. **Calendar:** Semester, limited summer session. **Full-time faculty:** 181 total; 6% have terminal degrees, 27% minority, 60% women. **Part-time faculty:** 117 total; 16% minority, 62% women. **Class size:** 96% < 20, 4% 20-39. **Special facilities:** Gallaudet Interpreting Services provides interpreters for university-related events.

Freshman class profile. 407 applied, 252 admitted, 178 enrolled.

Mid 50% test scores			
SAT critical reading:	340-420	GPA 3.0-3.49:	37%
SAT math:	390-510	GPA 2.0-2.99:	36%
ACT composite:	16-21	Out-of-state:	98%
GPA 3.75 or higher:	10%	Live on campus:	98%
GPA 3.50-3.74:	16%	International:	7%

Basis for selection. Applicants with hearing loss who show evidence of academic ability and motivation considered. Test scores, grades, class rank, essay, recommendation important. ACT recommended. Interview recommended. **Learning Disabled:** Untimed tests, psychological evaluations confirming disabilities required.

High school preparation. Recommended units include English 4, mathematics 3, social studies 2, science 2, foreign language 2 and visual/performing arts 1.

2015-2016 Annual costs. Tuition/fees: $15,604. Room/board: $12,630. Books/supplies: $1,800. Personal expenses: $3,758.

2014-2015 Financial aid. Need-based: 151 full-time freshmen applied for aid; 142 deemed to have need; 141 received aid. Average need met was 70%. Average scholarship/grant was $19,278; average loan $3,072. 84% of total undergraduate aid awarded as scholarships/grants, 16% as loans/jobs. **Non-need-based:** Awarded to 172 full-time undergraduates, including 36 freshmen. Scholarships awarded for leadership. **Additional information:** Institution receives substantial aid from state vocational rehabilitation agencies, supplemented by institutional grants when needed.

Application procedures. Admission: $50 fee, may be waived for applicants with need. Admission notification on a rolling basis. **Financial aid:** No deadline. FAFSA required. Applicants notified on a rolling basis starting 3/1.

Academics. Undergraduate degree program open to deaf and hard of hearing students and a limited number of hearing students; visiting and exchange student programs available to any qualified student. **Special study options:** Cross-registration, distance learning, double major, ESL, honors, independent study, internships, student-designed major, study abroad, teacher certification program. **Credit/placement by examination:** AP, CLEP, institutional tests. **Support services:** Learning center, pre-admission summer program, reduced course load, remedial instruction, study skills assistance, tutoring, writing center.

Majors. Biology: General. **Business:** Accounting, business admin. **Communications:** Communications/speech/rhetoric. **Computer sciences:** General, information systems. **Education:** General, Deaf/hearing impaired, early childhood, elementary, secondary. **English:** English lit. **Foreign languages:** American Sign Language, sign language interpretation, Spanish. **History:** General. **Human services:** Social work. **Math:** General. **Parks/recreation:** General, health/fitness. **Philosophy/religion:** Philosophy. **Physical sciences:** Chemistry, physics. **Psychology:** General. **Social sciences:** Criminology, political science, sociology. **Visual/performing arts:** General, dramatic.

Most popular majors. Area/ethnic studies 11%, biology 6%, business/marketing 10%, communications/journalism 9%, foreign language 9%, parks/recreation 10%, psychology 8%, public administration/social services 9%, visual/performing arts 7%.

Technology on campus. 352 workstations in dormitories, library, computer center, student center. Dormitories wired for high-speed internet access and linked to campus network. Commuter students can connect to campus network. Online course registration, online library, helpline, repair service, student web hosting, wireless network available.

Student life. Freshman orientation: Mandatory. Preregistration for classes offered. Held 1 week before beginning of semester. **Policies:** No alcohol allowed in freshman dorms; no smoking in residence halls. Only full-time students may reside in dorms. All dormitories equipped for deaf and hard of hearing students. **Housing:** Guaranteed on-campus for freshmen. Coed dorms, special housing for disabled, apartments available. $200 fully refundable deposit. Faculty row housing available; a living learning community led by faculty-in-residence. **Activities:** Campus ministries, dance, drama, film society, international student organizations, literary magazine, student government, student newspaper, TV station, Asian Pacific association, Black deaf student union, Hispanic student association, literary society.

Athletics. NCAA. **Intercollegiate:** Baseball M, basketball, cross-country, diving, football (tackle) M, soccer, softball W, swimming, track and field, volleyball W. **Intramural:** Basketball, football (non-tackle), soccer, table tennis, ultimate frisbee, volleyball. **Team name:** Bisons.

Student services. Adult student services, alcohol/substance abuse counseling, chaplain/spiritual director, career counseling, student employment services, financial aid counseling, health services, minority student services, on-campus daycare, personal counseling, placement for graduates. **Physically disabled:** Services for visually, speech, hearing impaired.

Contact. E-mail: admissions.office@gallaudet.edu
Phone: (202) 651-5750 Toll-free number: (800) 995-0550
Fax: (202) 651-5744
YoungHae Park, Associate Director of Admissions, Gallaudet University, 800 Florida Avenue, NE, Washington, DC 20002

George Washington University
Washington, District of Columbia — CB member
www.gwu.edu/explore — CB code: 5246

- Private 4-year university
- Residential campus in very large city
- 10,901 degree-seeking undergraduates: 8% part-time, 56% women, 6% African American, 10% Asian American, 8% Hispanic/Latino, 4% Multiracial, non-Hispanic, 10% international
- 15,055 graduate students
- 46% of applicants admitted
- SAT or ACT (ACT writing optional), application essay required
- 83% graduate within 6 years

General. Founded in 1821. Regionally accredited. **Degrees:** 2,311 bachelor's, 205 associate awarded; master's, professional, doctoral offered. **ROTC:** Army, Naval, Air Force. **Calendar:** Semester, extensive summer session. **Class size:** 55% < 20, 27% 20-39, 8% 40-49, 6% 50-99, 3% >100. **Special facilities:** Observatory.

Freshman class profile. 19,837 applied, 9,216 admitted, 2,589 enrolled.

Mid 50% test scores			
SAT critical reading:	590-690	Rank in top tenth:	56%
SAT math:	600-700	Out-of-state:	97%
SAT writing:	600-690	Live on campus:	98%
ACT composite:	27-31	International:	10%
Rank in top quarter:	86%	Fraternities:	17%
		Sororities:	29%

Basis for selection. Strong college-preparatory program, 3.0 GPA and class rank in top third important. Teacher and counselor recommendation and personal statement required. SAT Subject Tests required for applicants to 7-year BA/MD and integrated engineering/MD programs (any math and any science); early admission applicants (any math, student's choice); and recommended for all for admission and placement. Interview recommended for all, required of early admission applicants. Audition required of bachelor of music applicants.

High school preparation. College-preparatory program required. Required and recommended units include English 4, mathematics 2-4, social studies 2-4, science 2-4 (laboratory 1) and foreign language 2-4. One physics, 1 chemistry, and additional 1 unit in math required for School of Engineering and Applied Science.

2015-2016 Annual costs. Tuition/fees: $50,435. Room/board: $12,050. Books/supplies: $1,275. Personal expenses: $1,500.

2014-2015 Financial aid. Need-based: 1,530 full-time freshmen applied for aid; 1,116 deemed to have need; 1,105 received aid. Average need met was 89%. Average scholarship/grant was $27,843; average loan $5,006. 81% of total undergraduate aid awarded as scholarships/grants, 19% as loans/jobs. **Non-need-based:** Awarded to 3,960 full-time undergraduates, including 1,479 freshmen. Scholarships awarded for academics, art, athletics, music/drama, ROTC. **Additional information:** Auditions required for performing arts scholarships.

Application procedures. Admission: Priority date 12/1; deadline 1/1. $75 fee, may be waived for applicants with need. Admission notification by 4/1. Admission notification on a rolling basis. Must reply by May 1 or within 2 week(s) if notified thereafter. Applications received after 2/1 reviewed on space-available basis. Supplemental applications required for honors program, 7-year integrated engineering/law program, integrated engineering/MD program. **Financial aid:** Closing date 2/1. FAFSA, CSS PROFILE required. Applicants notified on a rolling basis starting 3/24; must reply by 5/1.

Academics. Special study options: Accelerated study, cooperative education, cross-registration, distance learning, double major, dual enrollment of high school students, exchange student, honors, independent study, internships, liberal arts/career combination, student-designed major, study abroad. 7-year integrated BA/MD liberal arts program, 8-year integrated engineering/JD and engineering/MD programs. **Credit/placement by examination:** AP, CLEP, IB, institutional tests. 30 credit hours maximum toward bachelor's degree. **Support services:** Pre-admission summer program, reduced course load, tutoring.

Majors. Area/ethnic studies: American, European, Latin American, Near/Middle Eastern. **Biology:** General, biomedical sciences, biophysics, pharmacology. **Business:** Accounting, business admin, finance, international, management information systems, tourism promotion. **Communications:** Communications/speech/rhetoric, journalism, political. **Computer sciences:** General, information systems. **Conservation:** General, environmental studies. **Education:** Physical. **Engineering:** General, biomedical, civil, computer, electrical, mechanical. **English:** English lit. **Foreign languages:** General, Arabic, Chinese, classics, French, German, Hebrew, Italian, Japanese, Latin,

Portuguese, Romance, Russian, Spanish. **Health services:** Audiology/speech pathology, clinical lab technology, cytotechnology, physician assistant, sonography. **History:** General. **Human services:** Public policy. **Liberal arts:** Arts/sciences. **Math:** General, applied, statistics. **Parks/recreation:** Exercise sciences. **Philosophy/religion:** Judaic, philosophy, religion. **Physical sciences:** Chemistry, geology, physics. **Protective services:** Criminal justice, police science. **Psychology:** General. **Social sciences:** Anthropology, archaeology, economics, geography, international relations, political science, sociology. **Visual/performing arts:** General, art history/conservation, dance, dramatic, interior design, music, studio arts, theater history.

Most popular majors. Business/marketing 18%, health sciences 9%, psychology 6%, social sciences 34%.

Technology on campus. 600 workstations in dormitories, library, computer center, student center, student center. Dormitories linked to campus network. Commuter students can connect to campus network. Repair service available.

Student life. Housing: Guaranteed on-campus for freshmen. Coed dorms, single-sex dorms, apartments, fraternity/sorority housing, themed housing available. $800 nonrefundable deposit, deadline 5/1. **Activities:** Bands, choral groups, dance, drama, film society, international student organizations, literary magazine, music ensembles, Model UN, musical theater, radio station, student government, student newspaper, symphony orchestra, TV station, religious groups, national political party organizations, ethnic, social action, public affairs groups.

Athletics. NCAA. **Intercollegiate:** Baseball M, basketball, cross-country, diving, golf M, gymnastics W, lacrosse W, rowing (crew), soccer, softball W, squash, swimming, tennis, volleyball W, water polo. **Intramural:** Basketball, football (tackle) M, golf, racquetball, soccer, softball, table tennis, tennis, volleyball. **Team name:** Colonials.

Student services. Alcohol/substance abuse counseling, career counseling, student employment services, financial aid counseling, health services, on-campus daycare, personal counseling, placement for graduates, veterans' counselor. **Physically disabled:** Services for visually, speech, hearing impaired.

Contact. E-mail: gwadm@gwu.edu
Phone: (202) 994-6040 Fax: (202) 994-0325
Karen Felton, Director of Undergraduate Admissions, George Washington University, 2121 I Street NW, Suite 201, Washington, DC 20052

Georgetown University
Washington, District of Columbia CB member
www.georgetown.edu CB code: 5244

- Private 4-year university affiliated with the Roman Catholic Church
- Residential campus in very large city
- 7,168 degree-seeking undergraduates: 3% part-time, 55% women, 6% African American, 10% Asian American, 8% Hispanic/Latino, 5% Multiracial, non-Hispanic, 12% international
- 10,640 degree-seeking graduate students
- 17% of applicants admitted
- SAT or ACT (ACT writing optional), application essay, interview required
- 95% graduate within 6 years

General. Founded in 1789. Regionally accredited. **Degrees:** 1,830 bachelor's awarded; master's, professional, doctoral offered. **ROTC:** Army, Naval, Air Force. **Location:** 1.5 miles from downtown. **Calendar:** Semester, extensive summer session. **Full-time faculty:** 975 total. **Part-time faculty:** 831 total. **Class size:** 60% < 20, 26% 20-39, 8% 40-49, 5% 50-99, 2% >100. **Special facilities:** Observatory, language learning technology lab with satellite link, library with special collections including archives, rare books, prints, manuscripts dealing with medieval and early modern periods, and American history.

Freshman class profile. 19,478 applied, 3,358 admitted, 1,567 enrolled.

Mid 50% test scores			
SAT critical reading:	660-750	Rank in top tenth:	89%
SAT math:	660-750	Return as sophomores:	96%
ACT composite:	30-34	Out-of-state:	99%
Rank in top quarter:	98%	Live on campus:	100%
		International:	10%

Basis for selection. School academic record most important, in addition to test scores, essays, extracurricular activities, interview, and recommendations. Special consideration given to qualified minorities, athletes, internationals, and alumni relatives. SAT Subject Tests recommended. Interview required unless not possible to assign based on geographic area; portfolio recommended for fine arts majors.

High school preparation. College-preparatory program required. Required units include English 4, mathematics 2, social studies 2, history 2, science 1 and foreign language 2. Additional units in science, math, and foreign language recommended for some programs.

2015-2016 Annual costs. Tuition/fees: $48,611. Room/board: $15,160. Books/supplies: $1,200. Personal expenses: $1,936.

2015-2016 Financial aid. Need-based: 1,031 full-time freshmen applied for aid; 632 deemed to have need; 632 received aid. Average need met was 100%. Average scholarship/grant was $42,794; average loan $2,845. 87% of total undergraduate aid awarded as scholarships/grants, 13% as loans/jobs. **Non-need-based:** Awarded to 1,101 full-time undergraduates, including 342 freshmen. Scholarships awarded for athletics.

Application procedures. Admission: Closing date 1/10 (receipt date). $75 fee, may be waived for applicants with need. Admission notification by 4/1. Must reply by May 1 or within 2 week(s) if notified thereafter. Early Action plan limits students from applying to binding Early Decision programs. **Financial aid:** Priority date 2/1; no closing date. FAFSA, CSS PROFILE required. Applicants notified by 4/1; must reply by 5/1 or within 2 week(s) of notification.

Academics. Early assurance program to university's medical and law schools. **Special study options:** Combined bachelor's/graduate degree, cross-registration, distance learning, double major, ESL, honors, independent study, internships, student-designed major, study abroad, Washington semester. **Credit/placement by examination:** AP, CLEP, IB, institutional tests. **Support services:** Learning center, pre-admission summer program, study skills assistance, tutoring, writing center.

Majors. Area/ethnic studies: American, women's. **Biology:** General, biochemistry, biomedical sciences, biophysics, environmental, neurobiology/anatomy. **Business:** Accounting, business admin, finance, information resources management, international, marketing. **Computer sciences:** Computer science. **English:** English lit. **Foreign languages:** Arabic, Chinese, classics, comparative lit, French, German, Italian, Japanese, linguistics, Portuguese, Russian, Spanish. **Health services:** Health care admin, international public health, nursing (RN). **History:** General. **Liberal arts:** Arts/sciences, humanities. **Math:** General. **Philosophy/religion:** Philosophy, religion. **Physical sciences:** Chemistry, physics. **Psychology:** General. **Social sciences:** Anthropology, economics, international economics, international relations, political economy, political science, sociology. **Visual/performing arts:** Art, art history/conservation, dramatic, film/cinema/video, music.

Most popular majors. Business/marketing 23%, English 6%, health sciences 7%, social sciences 33%.

Technology on campus. Dormitories wired for high-speed internet access and linked to campus network. Commuter students can connect to campus network. Online course registration, online library, helpline, repair service, student web hosting, wireless network available.

Student life. Freshman orientation: Mandatory, $210 fee. Preregistration for classes offered. Student volunteer-led program. **Policies:** Freshmen and sophomores required to live on campus. Upperclass students obtain housing via lottery process. Freshmen not permitted cars on campus. **Housing:** Guaranteed on-campus for freshmen. Coed dorms, special housing for disabled, apartments, wellness housing available. Pets allowed in dorm rooms. **Activities:** Bands, campus ministries, choral groups, dance, drama, film society, international student organizations, literary magazine, music ensembles, Model UN, musical theater, radio station, student government, student newspaper, symphony orchestra, TV station, over 170 student organizations available.

Athletics. NCAA. **Intercollegiate:** Baseball M, basketball, cross-country, diving, field hockey W, football (tackle) M, golf, lacrosse, rowing (crew), sailing, soccer, softball W, swimming, tennis, track and field, volleyball W. **Intramural:** Basketball, cross-country, football (non-tackle), golf, handball, racquetball, skiing, soccer, softball, squash, table tennis, tennis, volleyball. **Team name:** Hoyas.

Student services. Alcohol/substance abuse counseling, chaplain/spiritual director, career counseling, student employment services, financial aid counseling, health services, minority student services, on-campus daycare, personal counseling, placement for graduates, women's services. **Physically disabled:** Services for visually, hearing impaired.

Contact. E-mail: guadmiss@georgetown.edu
Phone: (202) 687-3600 Fax: (202) 687-5084
Charles Deacon, Dean of Admissions, Georgetown University, Room 103 White Gravenor Hall, Washington, DC 20057

Howard University
Washington, District of Columbia

www.howard.edu

CB member

CB code: 5297

- Private 4-year university
- Residential campus in very large city
- 6,796 degree-seeking undergraduates: 6% part-time, 68% women, 91% African American, 1% Asian American, 1% Native American, 5% international
- 3,093 degree-seeking graduate students
- 49% of applicants admitted
- SAT or ACT with writing required
- 59% graduate within 6 years; 54% enter graduate study

General. Founded in 1867. Regionally accredited. **Degrees:** 1,350 bachelor's awarded; master's, professional, doctoral offered. **ROTC:** Army, Air Force. **Location:** Downtown. **Calendar:** Semester, extensive summer session. **Full-time faculty:** 1,094 total; 42% women. **Class size:** 57% < 20, 35% 20-39, 4% 40-49, 4% 50-99, less than 1% >100. **Special facilities:** Collections on Africa and persons of African descent, Observatory and Planetarium, Moorland-Spingarn Research Center, Ralph J Bunche Center, Afro-American Resource Center, Patent/TM Resource Center, Channing Pollock Theater Collection.

Freshman class profile. 15,163 applied, 7,436 admitted, 1,676 enrolled.

Mid 50% test scores			
SAT critical reading:	500-610	**GPA 2.0-2.99:**	19%
SAT math:	490-610	**Rank in top quarter:**	52%
SAT writing:	500-600	**Rank in top tenth:**	24%
ACT composite:	21-27	**End year in good standing:**	92%
GPA 3.75 or higher:	16%	**Return as sophomores:**	89%
GPA 3.50-3.74:	22%	**Out-of-state:**	98%
GPA 3.0-3.49:	43%	**Live on campus:**	97%
		International:	7%

Basis for selection. High school achievement record, test scores most important. Requirements vary from college to college. SAT Subject Tests recommended. Dental Hygiene Aptitude Test required of Dental Hygiene applicants. Essay recommended; required of Early Action applicants. Audition required of music, and drama majors. Portfolio required of art, and architecture majors. Interview recommended for pharmacy and pharmaceutical programs, as well as, physician assistant majors. **Home schooled:** Must have GED.

High school preparation. 17 units required. Required units include English 4, mathematics 3, social studies 2, science 2 (laboratory 2), foreign language 2 and academic electives 4. Academic electives must count toward graduation.

2015-2016 Annual costs. Tuition/fees: $23,970. Room/board: $10,740. Books/supplies: $3,000. Personal expenses: $2,500.

2014-2015 Financial aid. **Need-based:** 1,433 full-time freshmen applied for aid; 1,334 deemed to have need; 1,313 received aid. Average need met was 75%. Average scholarship/grant was $6,623; average loan $4,076. 93% of total undergraduate aid awarded as scholarships/grants, 7% as loans/jobs. **Non-need-based:** Awarded to 3,108 full-time undergraduates, including 1,050 freshmen. Scholarships awarded for academics, alumni affiliation, art, athletics, leadership, music/drama, religious affiliation, ROTC.

Application procedures. **Admission:** Closing date 2/15 (receipt date). $45 fee. Application must be submitted online. Admission notification on a rolling basis beginning on or about 12/20. Must reply by May 1 or within 4 week(s) if notified thereafter. **Financial aid:** Priority date 2/1, closing date 5/1. FAFSA required. Applicants notified on a rolling basis starting 2/16; must reply by 2/16 or within 3 week(s) of notification.

Academics. **Special study options:** Accelerated study, combined bachelor's/graduate degree, cooperative education, cross-registration, distance learning, double major, dual enrollment of high school students, exchange student, honors, independent study, internships, student-designed major, study abroad, teacher certification program. **Credit/placement by examination:** AP, CLEP, IB, SAT, ACT, institutional tests. 60 credit hours maximum toward bachelor's degree. **Support services:** Learning center, pre-admission summer program, reduced course load, remedial instruction, study skills assistance, tutoring, writing center.

Majors. **Architecture:** Architecture. **Area/ethnic studies:** African, African-American. **Biology:** General. **Business:** Accounting, business admin, fashion, finance, hospitality admin, hospitality/recreation, insurance, international, management information systems, market research. **Communications:** Broadcast journalism, communications/speech/rhetoric, journalism, radio/TV. **Computer sciences:** Computer science, information systems. **Education:** Art, English, health, music, physical. **Engineering:** Chemical, civil, computer, electrical, mechanical, systems. **English:** English lit. **Foreign languages:** Ancient Greek, classics, French, German, modern Greek, Russian, Spanish. **Health services:** Clinical lab science, medical radiologic technology/radiation therapy, music therapy, physician assistant, recreational therapy. **History:** General. **Math:** General. **Parks/recreation:** General. **Philosophy/religion:** Philosophy. **Physical sciences:** Chemistry, physics. **Psychology:** General. **Social sciences:** Anthropology, economics, political science, sociology. **Visual/performing arts:** General, art, art history/conservation, conducting, dance, design, interior design, jazz, music history, music management, music theory/composition, piano/keyboard, studio arts management, theater arts management, theater design, theater history, voice/opera.

Most popular majors. Biology 9%, business/marketing 14%, communications/journalism 12%, communication technologies 6%, health sciences 7%, physical sciences 11%, psychology 7%, social sciences 11%.

Technology on campus. 7,006 workstations in dormitories, library, computer center, student center. Dormitories wired for high-speed internet access and linked to campus network. Commuter students can connect to campus network. Online course registration, online library, helpline, wireless network available.

Student life. **Freshman orientation:** Mandatory. Preregistration for classes offered. Held during the summer. **Housing:** Guaranteed on-campus for freshmen. Coed dorms, single-sex dorms, apartments, wellness housing available. $200 nonrefundable deposit, deadline 4/1. **Activities:** Bands, campus ministries, choral groups, dance, drama, film society, international student organizations, literary magazine, music ensembles, musical theater, opera, radio station, student government, student newspaper, symphony orchestra, TV station, Absalom Jones Student Association, Adventist Committee, Baptist Student Union, Christian Science Organization, Christian Fellowship-Igbimo Otito, Lutheran Student Organization, Muslim Students, Wesley Foundation Methodist Fellowship, William J. Seymour Pentecostal Fellowship, Academic Honorary Societies.

Athletics. NCAA. **Intercollegiate:** Basketball, bowling W, cross-country, diving, football (tackle) M, lacrosse W, soccer, softball W, swimming, tennis, track and field, volleyball W. **Intramural:** Basketball, soccer, softball W. **Team name:** Bison.

Student services. Alcohol/substance abuse counseling, chaplain/spiritual director, career counseling, student employment services, financial aid counseling, health services, on-campus daycare, personal counseling, placement for graduates, veterans' counselor, women's services. **Physically disabled:** Services for visually, speech impaired.

Contact. E-mail: admission@howard.edu
Phone: (202) 806-2755 Toll-free number: (800) 282-6363
Fax: (202) 806-4465
LaTrice Byam, Director of Admission & University Registrar, Howard University, 2400 Sixth Street NW, Washington, DC 20059

Strayer University
Washington, District of Columbia

www.strayer.edu

CB code: 5632

- For-profit 4-year university
- Commuter campus in very large city
- 1,192 undergraduates

General. Founded in 1892. Regionally accredited. Additional campuses in 14 states. **Degrees:** 105 bachelor's, 36 associate awarded; master's offered. **Location:** Downtown. **Calendar:** Quarter, extensive summer session. **Full-time faculty:** 287 total. **Part-time faculty:** 1,635 total. **Class size:** 48% < 20, 51% 20-39, less than 1% 40-49.

Basis for selection. Institutional placement tests required. Students with SAT scores of 400 or above in verbal and/or mathematics or who have prior college level mathematics/English credits, can waive placement tests. Interview recommended.

High school preparation. College-preparatory program required. 14 units recommended. Recommended units include English 3, mathematics 3, social studies 1, history 1, foreign language 2 and academic electives 4. 1 unit of sociology or psychology recommended; 3 units of art, music, or literature recommended.

2015-2016 Annual costs. Tuition/fees: $42,730. Books/supplies: $1,200.

Application procedures. **Admission:** No deadline. $50 fee. Admission notification on a rolling basis. **Financial aid:** No deadline. FAFSA required. Applicants notified on a rolling basis; must reply within 2 week(s) of notification.

Academics. **Special study options:** Distance learning. **Credit/placement by examination:** AP, CLEP, IB, institutional tests. 63 credit hours maximum toward associate degree, 126 toward bachelor's. **Support services:** Learning center, remedial instruction, tutoring.

Majors. **Business:** General, accounting, accounting/business management, business admin, international. **Computer sciences:** Information systems, information technology. **Protective services:** Law enforcement admin. **Social sciences:** Economics.

Most popular majors. Business/marketing 75%, computer/information sciences 81%.

Technology on campus. 760 workstations in library, computer center. Online course registration, online library, helpline available.

Student life. **Activities:** Student newspaper, accounting club, international club, data processing management association, business administration club, marketing club, human resource management club, Alpha Chi National Honor Society, Alpha Sigma Lambda National Honor Society, Sigma Gamma Rho Sorority, Thai Student Association.

Student services. Adult student services, career counseling, student employment services, financial aid counseling, health services, placement for graduates, veterans' counselor. **Physically disabled:** Services for visually, hearing impaired.

Contact. E-mail: washington@strayer.edu
Phone: (202) 408-2400 Toll-free number: (888) 478-7293
Fax: (202) 419-1425
Reginald Rainey, Vice President, Strayer University, 1133 15th Sreet NW, Washington, DC 20005

Trinity Washington University
Washington, District of Columbia
www.trinitydc.edu

CB member
CB code: 5796

- Private 4-year liberal arts college affiliated with the Roman Catholic Church
- Commuter campus in very large city
- 2,129 degree-seeking undergraduates
- 653 graduate students
- Application essay required

General. Founded in 1897. Regionally accredited. **Degrees:** 225 bachelor's, 30 associate awarded; master's offered. **ROTC:** Army, Air Force. **Calendar:** Semester, extensive summer session. **Full-time faculty:** 77 total. **Part-time faculty:** 191 total. **Class size:** 67% < 20, 33% 20-39.

Freshman class profile.

GPA 3.75 or higher:	4%	GPA 2.0-2.99:	62%
GPA 3.50-3.74:	5%	Out-of-state:	40%
GPA 3.0-3.49:	21%	Live on campus:	40%

Basis for selection. School achievement record, essay, recommendations, interview, school and community activities important. 3.0 GPA preferred. Test scores considered. SAT or ACT recommended. Interview recommended. **Home schooled:** Statement describing home school structure and mission, transcript of courses and grades, interview, letter of recommendation (nonparent) required.

High school preparation. College-preparatory program required. 16 units required. Required and recommended units include English 4, mathematics 3-4, social studies 3-4, history 2, science 2-3 (laboratory 1-2) and foreign language 2.

2015-2016 Annual costs. Tuition/fees: $22,780. Room/board: $10,080. Books/supplies: $1,040. Personal expenses: $1,620.

Financial aid. **Non-need-based:** Scholarships awarded for academics, alumni affiliation, leadership.

Application procedures. **Admission:** Priority date 2/1; deadline 9/1 (receipt date). $40 fee, may be waived for applicants with need, free for online applicants. Admission notification by 9/1. Admission notification on a rolling basis. Must reply by May 1 or within 3 week(s) if notified thereafter. After August 1, must reply within 1 week. **Financial aid:** Priority date 3/1, closing date 4/1. FAFSA required. Applicants notified on a rolling basis starting 2/1; must reply within 2 week(s) of notification.

Academics. **Special study options:** Accelerated study, cross-registration, distance learning, double major, dual enrollment of high school students, honors, independent study, internships, student-designed major, study abroad,

---

teacher certification program, weekend college. **Credit/placement by examination:** AP, CLEP, IB, institutional tests. **Support services:** Reduced course load, remedial instruction, study skills assistance, tutoring, writing center.

Honors college/program. Students are placed in the Honors program based upon assessment scores.

Majors. **Area/ethnic studies:** Women's. **Biology:** General, biochemistry. **Business:** Business admin. **Communications:** Communications/speech/rhetoric. **Education:** General, elementary, English, mathematics, science, social studies. **English:** English lit. **Health services:** General, occupational therapy. **History:** General. **Math:** General. **Philosophy/religion:** Philosophy. **Physical sciences:** Chemistry. **Protective services:** Law enforcement admin. **Psychology:** General. **Social sciences:** Economics, international relations, political science, sociology. **Visual/performing arts:** Studio arts.

Most popular majors. Business/marketing 11%, communications/journalism 6%, health sciences 29%, psychology 25%, security/protective services 10%, social sciences 10%.

Technology on campus. 40 workstations in library, computer center, student center. Dormitories wired for high-speed internet access and linked to campus network. Online course registration, online library, wireless network available.

Student life. **Freshman orientation:** Mandatory. Preregistration for classes offered. **Policies:** Student Code of Responsible Conduct; Honor System; Responsible Student Code of Conduct; Student Financial Responsibility, Harassment Policy; Residence Life Policy. **Housing:** Single-sex dorms, themed housing available. $100 nonrefundable deposit. **Activities:** Campus ministries, choral groups, dance, drama, international student organizations, literary magazine, Model UN, student government, Young Democrats, Republicans, Black Student Alliance, Inter-American club, peer ministry, African student union, business and economics club, communications club, criminal justice club, Hearts and Crafts club, Lasies F.I.R.S.T. club, Muslim student association, Step Sisters, Women's student action coalition.

Athletics. NCAA. **Intercollegiate:** Basketball W, lacrosse W, soccer W, softball W, tennis W, volleyball W. **Team name:** Tigers.

Student services. Adult student services, alcohol/substance abuse counseling, chaplain/spiritual director, career counseling, services for economically disadvantaged, student employment services, financial aid counseling, health services, personal counseling, placement for graduates, veterans' counselor, women's services. **Physically disabled:** Services for visually, speech, hearing impaired.

Contact. E-mail: admissions@trinitydc.edu
Phone: (202) 884-9400 Toll-free number: (800) 492-6882
Fax: (202) 884-9403
Kelly Gosnell, Director of Admissions, Trinity Washington University, 125 Michigan Avenue, NE, Washington, DC 20017

University of Phoenix: Washington DC
Washington, District of Columbia
www.phoenix.edu

- For-profit 4-year university
- Very large city
- 210 degree-seeking undergraduates

General. Regionally accredited. **Degrees:** 23 bachelor's awarded; master's offered. **Calendar:** Differs by program. **Full-time faculty:** 5 total. **Part-time faculty:** 25 total.

Basis for selection. Open admission, but selective for some programs.

2015-2016 Annual costs. Per-credit-hour charge, $395 to $635, depending upon level and course of study. Books, material charges, and other fees vary by course and program. All fees are subject to change.

Application procedures. **Admission:** No deadline. No application fee. **Financial aid:** No deadline.

Academics. **Credit/placement by examination:** AP, CLEP.

Majors. **Business:** Accounting/business management, business admin, e-commerce, finance, human resources, marketing. **Communications:** General. **Computer sciences:** Database management, networking, programming, security, system admin, systems analysis, web page design, webmaster. **Health services:** Facilities admin, health information management, long term care admin, nursing (RN). **Human services:** General. **Protective services:** Disaster management, law enforcement admin, security management.

Student life. Freshman orientation: Mandatory. Preregistration for classes offered.

Contact. Toll-free number: (866) 766-0766
University of Phoenix: Washington DC, 25 Massachusetts Avenue NW, Washington, DC 20001-1431

University of the District of Columbia
Washington, District of Columbia   **CB member**
www.udc.edu   **CB code: 5929**

- Public 4-year university and liberal arts college
- Commuter campus in very large city
- 4,463 degree-seeking undergraduates
- 320 graduate students
- 37% of applicants admitted

General. Founded in 1976. Regionally accredited. **Degrees:** 392 bachelor's, 296 associate awarded; master's offered. **ROTC:** Army, Naval, Air Force. **Location:** Downtown. **Calendar:** Semester, limited summer session. **Full-time faculty:** 287 total.

Freshman class profile. 3,352 applied, 1,250 admitted, 731 enrolled.

Basis for selection. Special requirements for nursing, art, and music programs. Interview recommended for nursing majors. Audition recommended for music majors. Portfolio recommended for art majors. **Home schooled:** Transcript of courses and grades, state high school equivalency certificate required.

High school preparation. College-preparatory program required. Recommended units include English 4, mathematics 2, social studies 2, history 1, science 2, foreign language 2 and academic electives 3.

2015-2016 Annual costs. Tuition/fees: $7,421. Room/board: $13,200. Books/supplies: $1,400. Personal expenses: $1,900.

Financial aid. All financial aid based on need.

Application procedures. Admission: Priority date 5/15; deadline 7/31 (postmark date). $35 fee. Admission notification on a rolling basis. **Financial aid:** No deadline. FAFSA required. Applicants notified on a rolling basis starting 6/1; must reply by 8/28 or within 2 week(s) of notification.

Academics. Special study options: Combined bachelor's/graduate degree, cooperative education, cross-registration, double major, dual enrollment of high school students, ESL, honors, independent study, internships, teacher certification program, weekend college. **Credit/placement by examination:** AP, CLEP, IB, institutional tests. Upon successful completion of the examination, the credit must be approved by the department chairperson and the dean. Credit earned by examination will appear on the students' transcripts as 'CR' and will not be included in computing the grade point average. **Support services:** Learning center, pre-admission summer program, remedial instruction, study skills assistance, tutoring, writing center.

Majors. Architecture: Architecture, urban/community planning. **Biology:** General. **Business:** Accounting, administrative services, business admin, finance, office management, purchasing. **Communications technology:** Graphic/printing. **Computer sciences:** General, computer science, information systems. **Conservation:** General. **Education:** Art, business, early childhood, elementary, health, physical. **Engineering:** Civil, electrical, mechanical. **English:** English lit. **Foreign languages:** French, Spanish. **Health services:** Nursing (RN), nursing education, respiratory therapy technology, speech pathology. **History:** General. **Human services:** Social work. **Math:** General. **Philosophy/religion:** Philosophy. **Physical sciences:** General, chemistry, physics. **Protective services:** Fire services admin. **Psychology:** General. **Social sciences:** Anthropology, economics, political science, sociology, urban studies. **Visual/performing arts:** Dramatic, music, studio arts. **Work/family studies:** General, family studies, food/nutrition.

Most popular majors. Business/marketing 8%, visual/performing arts 14%.

Technology on campus. 2 workstations in library, computer center. Commuter students can connect to campus network. Online course registration, helpline, wireless network available.

Student life. Freshman orientation: Mandatory. Preregistration for classes offered. **Activities:** Bands, choral groups, dance, drama, music ensembles, student government, student newspaper, symphony orchestra, TV station.

Athletics. NCAA. **Intercollegiate:** Basketball, cross-country, soccer, tennis, track and field, volleyball W. **Intramural:** Basketball, softball, swimming, tennis, volleyball W. **Team name:** Firebirds.

Student services. Career counseling, student employment services, financial aid counseling, health services, on-campus daycare, personal counseling, placement for graduates, veterans' counselor. **Physically disabled:** Services for visually, speech, hearing impaired.

Contact. E-mail: UDCadmissions@udc.edu
Phone: (202) 274-6110 Fax: (202) 274-5552
University of the District of Columbia, 4200 Connecticut Avenue NW, Washington, DC 20008

University of the Potomac
Washington, District of Columbia
www.potomac.edu   **CB code: 3569**

- For-profit 3-year business college
- Commuter campus in very large city
- 341 degree-seeking undergraduates
- Interview required

General. Regionally accredited. Additional campus in Tysons, VA. **Degrees:** 48 bachelor's, 23 associate awarded; master's offered. **Location:** Downtown. **Calendar:** Differs by program, extensive summer session. **Full-time faculty:** 4 total. **Part-time faculty:** 62 total.

Basis for selection. Open admission.

2015-2016 Annual costs. Books/supplies: $650. **Additional information:** Bacholer degree program: $541; Associate degree programs: $541; certificates: $250. Books and supplies range depending on program level and course of study. All costs are subject to change.

Application procedures. Admission: No deadline. No application fee. Admission notification on a rolling basis beginning on or about 2/1. **Financial aid:** No deadline. FAFSA, institutional form required. Applicants notified on a rolling basis; must reply within 4 week(s) of notification.

Academics. Credit earned for work-related research projects. **Special study options:** Accelerated study, distance learning, independent study, internships, weekend college. **Credit/placement by examination:** AP, CLEP, institutional tests. 15 credit hours maximum toward associate degree, 30 toward bachelor's. **Support services:** Learning center, remedial instruction, tutoring.

Majors. BACHELOR'S. Business: Accounting, accounting/business management, business admin, international, management information systems, purchasing. **Computer sciences:** General, LAN/WAN management, security. **Protective services:** Computer forensics. **ASSOCIATE. Business:** Accounting technology, information resources management, international, operations. **Computer sciences:** LAN/WAN management, security.

Most popular majors. Business/marketing 78%, computer/information sciences 22%.

Technology on campus. 30 workstations in library, computer center, student center. Online library, wireless network available.

Student life. Freshman orientation: Mandatory. Preregistration for classes offered. **Activities:** Student government.

Student services. Adult student services, financial aid counseling.

Contact. E-mail: admissions@potomac.edu
Phone: (202) 686-0876 Fax: (202) 686-0818
Niambi Green, Director of Admissions, University of the Potomac, 4000 Chesapeake Street NW, Washington, DC 20016

Florida

Adventist University of Health Sciences
Orlando, Florida
www.adu.edu   CB code: 3614

- Private 4-year university and health science college affiliated with the Seventh-day Adventists
- Commuter campus in large city
- 1,704 degree-seeking undergraduates: 63% part-time, 81% women, 14% African American, 7% Asian American, 23% Hispanic/Latino, 1% Native Hawaiian/Pacific islander, 2% Multi-racial, non-Hispanic
- 178 graduate students
- 60% of applicants admitted

General. Regionally accredited. Affiliated with Florida Hospital. **Degrees:** 380 bachelor's, 77 associate awarded; master's, professional offered. **Calendar:** Trimester, limited summer session. **Full-time faculty:** 87 total; 38% have terminal degrees, 33% minority, 70% women. **Part-time faculty:** 179 total; 20% have terminal degrees, 37% minority, 67% women. **Special facilities:** Human patient simulators.

Freshman class profile. 189 applied, 114 admitted, 81 enrolled.

Mid 50% test scores		Return as sophomores:	56%
SAT critical reading:	430-520	Out-of-state:	22%
SAT math:	400-500	International:	1%
ACT composite:	18-21		

Basis for selection. Standard high school diploma from regionally-accredited school required. 2.5 GPA, ACT/SAT and satisfactory recommendations required for general college admission. Professional program admission requirements vary and require essay explaining student's career choice. **Home schooled:** Transcript of courses and grades, state high school equivalency certificate required. Curriculums must be regionally accredited. Applicants who have completed non-regionally accredited home school programs may submit passing GED scores or complete 12 hours of credit from regionally accredited college with 2.5 GPA.

High school preparation. 21 units recommended. Recommended units include English 4, mathematics 3, social studies 3, history 3, science 3 (laboratory 3) and foreign language 2.

2016-2017 Annual costs. Tuition/fees (projected): $13,480. Room/board: $4,200. Books/supplies: $1,600. Personal expenses: $1,512.

2014-2015 Financial aid. **Need-based:** 83 full-time freshmen applied for aid; 76 deemed to have need; 71 received aid. Average need met was 26%. Average scholarship/grant was $5,846; average loan $2,871. 41% of total undergraduate aid awarded as scholarships/grants, 59% as loans/jobs. **Non-need-based:** Awarded to 24 full-time undergraduates, including 10 freshmen. Scholarships awarded for state residency.

Application procedures. **Admission:** Closing date 7/1 (postmark date). $20 fee, may be waived for applicants with need. Application must be submitted online. Admission notification by 8/1. Admission notification on a rolling basis beginning on or about 9/15. Students accepted to professional programs have reply dates in order to claim program seat. **Financial aid:** Priority date 4/10; no closing date. FAFSA, institutional form required. Applicants notified on a rolling basis starting 3/1.

Academics. **Special study options:** Distance learning, double major, dual enrollment of high school students, independent study. **Credit/placement by examination:** AP, CLEP, IB, SAT, ACT, institutional tests. No limit, but are focused on type of exam, course trying to meet, and residency requirement. Credit by examination does not contribute to residency hours. **Support services:** Learning center, remedial instruction, study skills assistance, tutoring, writing center.

Majors. **Biology:** Biomedical sciences. **Health services:** Health care admin, nuclear medical technology, nursing (RN), radiologic technology/medical imaging, sonography.

Technology on campus. PC or laptop required. 40 workstations in dormitories, library. Commuter students can connect to campus network. Online course registration, online library, helpline, repair service, wireless network available.

Student life. **Freshman orientation:** Mandatory. Preregistration for classes offered. One-day program. **Policies:** No-use policy for alcohol, drugs, smoking, and illegal substances. Strong Christian Mission. **Housing:** Apartments, wellness housing available. $200 fully refundable deposit, deadline 8/4. **Activities:** Campus ministries, drama, Student Spiritual Leaders, Club SOTA, nursing club, radiography club, Young Alumni Association, service learning, and mission trip.

Athletics. **Intramural:** Baseball, basketball, soccer.

Student services. Adult student services, alcohol/substance abuse counseling, chaplain/spiritual director, career counseling, student employment services, financial aid counseling, personal counseling, veterans' counselor.

Contact. Phone: (407) 303-7742 Toll-free number: (800) 500-7747 Fax: (407) 303-9408
Katie Shaw, Director of Enrollment Services, Adventist University of Health Sciences, 671 Winyah Drive, Orlando, FL 32803

Argosy University: Sarasota
Sarasota, Florida
www.argosy.edu/locations/sarasota

- For-profit 4-year university
- Small city
- 145 degree-seeking undergraduates: 94% part-time, 71% women
- 541 graduate students

General. Regionally accredited. **Degrees:** 13 bachelor's, 3 associate awarded; master's, professional, doctoral offered. **Calendar:** Differs by program. **Full-time faculty:** 17 total. **Part-time faculty:** 90 total.

Basis for selection. Open admission.

2015-2016 Annual costs. Tuition/fees: $16,842. **Additional information:** Tuition indicated is for programs in the College of Arts and Sciences. College of Health Sciences programs are $575 per credit-hour.

Application procedures. **Admission:** Closing date 9/13. $50 fee. **Financial aid:** No deadline.

Academics. **Credit/placement by examination:** AP, CLEP.

Majors. **Business:** Business admin. **Computer sciences:** Information technology. **Liberal arts:** Arts/sciences. **Protective services:** Police science. **Psychology:** General.

Contact. E-mail: ausradmissions@argosy.edu
Phone: (877) 331-4480 Toll-free number: (800) 331-5995
Rachel Malone, Senior Director of Admissions, Argosy University: Sarasota, 5250 17th Street, Sarasota, FL 34235

Argosy University: Tampa
Tampa, Florida
www.argosy.edu/tampa

- For-profit 4-year university
- Large city
- 132 degree-seeking undergraduates: 75% part-time, 64% women
- 376 graduate students

General. Regionally accredited. **Degrees:** 18 bachelor's awarded; master's, professional, doctoral offered. **Calendar:** Differs by program. **Full-time faculty:** 15 total. **Part-time faculty:** 77 total.

Basis for selection. Open admission.

2015-2016 Annual costs. Tuition/fees: $16,842. **Additional information:** Tuition indicated is for programs in the College of Arts and Sciences. College of Health Sciences programs are $575 per credit-hour.

Application procedures. **Admission:** Closing date 9/13. $50 fee. **Financial aid:** No deadline.

Academics. **Credit/placement by examination:** AP, CLEP.

Majors. **Business:** Business admin. **Liberal arts:** Arts/sciences. **Protective services:** Police science. **Psychology:** General.

Contact. E-mail: autaadmis@argosy.edu
Phone: (866) 357-4426 Toll-free number: (800) 850-6488
Ken Jaco, Senior Director of Admissions, Argosy University: Tampa,
1403 North Howard Avenue, Tampa, FL 33607

Art Institute of Fort Lauderdale
Fort Lauderdale, Florida
www.aifl.edu   **CB code: 5040**

- For-profit 4-year visual arts and technical college
- Commuter campus in large city
- 1,514 undergraduates
- Application essay, interview required

General. Founded in 1968. Accredited by ACICS. **Degrees:** 174 bachelor's,
199 associate awarded. **Location:** 25 miles from Miami, 30 miles from
West Palm Beach. **Calendar:** Quarter, extensive summer session. **Full-time
faculty:** 47 total. **Part-time faculty:** 77 total. **Special facilities:** Broadcasting
studio, full culinary kitchens, full service print center, visual effects studio,
iMac labs.

Freshman class profile.

Out-of-state:	10%	Live on campus:	9%

Basis for selection. Interview, essay important. Portfolio recommended;
required for game art design and illustration majors. **Home schooled:** State
high school equivalency certificate required. **Learning Disabled:** Documentation must be submitted if student needs accommodations.

2015-2016 Annual costs. Tuition/fees: $22,105. Room only: $6,345.
Books/supplies: $1,275. Personal expenses: $1,980.

Financial aid. Non-need-based: Scholarships awarded for academics.
Additional information: Internal scholarships available. Financial planning
program allows personalized service to budget and meet college costs through
individualized payment plans.

Application procedures. Admission: No deadline. $50 fee. Admission
notification on a rolling basis. **Financial aid:** No deadline. FAFSA required.

Academics. Academic program designed to simulate working environment. After completion of associate degree, students may continue to earn
bachelor of science. **Special study options:** Distance learning, ESL, honors,
independent study, internships, study abroad. **Credit/placement by examination:** AP, CLEP, IB, SAT, ACT. SAT/ACT preferred for placement but
ACCUPLACER accepted. **Support services:** Remedial instruction, tutoring,
writing center.

Majors. Business: Fashion. **Communications:** Advertising. **Communications technology:** Animation/special effects. **Computer sciences:** Computer
graphics, web page design. **Visual/performing arts:** Cinematography, commercial photography, fashion design, game design, graphic design, illustration, industrial design, interior design.

Most popular majors. Business/marketing 12%, computer/information
sciences 12%, visual/performing arts 65%.

Technology on campus. Dormitories wired for high-speed internet
access and linked to campus network. Online course registration, online
library, helpline, repair service, student web hosting, wireless network available.

Student life. Freshman orientation: Mandatory. Preregistration for
classes offered. Held at the beginning of each quarter and midquarter. **Housing:** Guaranteed on-campus for all undergraduates. Coed dorms, special
housing for disabled available. $275 deposit. **Activities:** Drama, film society,
international student organizations, music ensembles, radio station, student
government, culinary club, Industrial Design Society of America, American
Society of Interior Design, fashion club, Future Video Producers and Broad-
casters, illustration club, Toastmasters International, actor's club, music club.

Student services. Adult student services, alcohol/substance abuse counseling, career counseling, services for economically disadvantaged, student
employment services, financial aid counseling, personal counseling, placement for graduates, veterans' counselor. **Physically disabled:** Services for
visually, speech, hearing impaired.

Contact. Phone: (954) 463-3000 ext. 2434
Toll-free number: (800) 275-7603 ext. 2434 Fax: (954) 728-8637
Claude Toland, President, Art Institute of Fort Lauderdale, 1799 SE 17th
Street, Fort Lauderdale, FL 33316

Ave Maria University
Ave Maria, Florida
www.avemaria.edu   **CB code: 4249**

- Private 4-year university and liberal arts college affiliated with the Roman
  Catholic Church
- Residential campus in small town
- 1,061 degree-seeking undergraduates: 1% part-time, 51% women, 5%
  African American, 3% Asian American, 15% Hispanic/Latino, 1%
  Native American, 2% international
- 40 degree-seeking graduate students
- 43% of applicants admitted
- SAT or ACT (ACT writing optional), application essay required
- 49% graduate within 6 years

General. Regionally accredited. **Degrees:** 229 bachelor's awarded; master's,
doctoral offered. **Location:** 20 miles from Naples. **Calendar:** Semester,
limited summer session. **Full-time faculty:** 67 total; 85% have terminal
degrees, 18% minority, 28% women. **Part-time faculty:** 26 total; 65% have
terminal degrees, 42% women. **Class size:** 61% < 20, 37% 20-39, 1% 40-
49, less than 1% 50-99.

Freshman class profile. 2,703 applied, 1,171 admitted, 392 enrolled.

GPA 3.75 or higher:	39%	Return as sophomores:	72%
GPA 3.50-3.74:	16%	Out-of-state:	55%
GPA 3.0-3.49:	32%	Live on campus:	92%
GPA 2.0-2.99:	12%	International:	1%

Basis for selection. For regular admission, 2.8 GPA and 1410 SAT/20
ACT required. Students who do not meet all requirements may attain admission by special recommendation of the Admissions Committee. **Home
schooled:** Transcript of courses and grades required.

High school preparation. College-preparatory program recommended.
15 units required; 22 recommended. Required and recommended units include
English 3-4, mathematics 3-4, social studies 1-3, history 1, science 3 (laboratory 3), foreign language 2, visual/performing arts 1-2 and academic electives
1-3.

2015-2016 Annual costs. Tuition/fees: $19,430. Room/board: $10,233.
Books/supplies: $1,000. Personal expenses: $1,000.

Financial aid. Non-need-based: Scholarships awarded for academics, athletics, leadership, music/drama, religious affiliation, state residency.

Application procedures. Admission: No deadline. No application fee.
Admission notification on a rolling basis. **Financial aid:** Priority date 4/1;
no closing date. FAFSA required. Applicants notified on a rolling basis
starting 10/1.

Academics. Special study options: Double major, dual enrollment of high
school students, honors, independent study, internships, study abroad. **Credit/
placement by examination:** AP, CLEP, IB, SAT, ACT, institutional tests.
Support services: Pre-admission summer program, reduced course load,
study skills assistance, tutoring, writing center.

Honors college/program. Priority consideration given to applicants with
3.6 GPA, 1860 SAT/27 ACT.

Majors. Biology: General, biochemistry. **Business:** Business admin,
finance. **Conservation:** Environmental science. **English:** English lit, general
lit. **Foreign languages:** Classics, modern Greek. **Health services:** Health
care admin. **History:** General. **Liberal arts:** Arts/sciences. **Math:** General.
Parks/recreation: Exercise sciences. **Philosophy/religion:** Philosophy.
Physical sciences: Physics. **Psychology:** General. **Social sciences:** Economics, political economy, political science, U.S. government. **Theology:** Sacred
music, theology. **Visual/performing arts:** Music.

Most popular majors. Biology 15%, business/marketing 19%, psychology
14%, social sciences 15%, theological studies 10%.

Technology on campus. 150 workstations in dormitories, library, computer center, student center. Dormitories wired for high-speed internet access
and linked to campus network. Commuter students can connect to campus
network. Online library, helpline, wireless network available.

Student life. Freshman orientation: Mandatory. Preregistration for
classes offered. Three-day program held at beginning of semester. **Policies:**
Policies and procedures aligned with Catholic moral teaching. Students
required to live on campus unless living with a parent or legal guardian, are
23 years of age or older, or receive special permission in certain unusual
cases. **Housing:** Guaranteed on-campus for all undergraduates. Single-sex
dorms, apartments available. $300 nonrefundable deposit. **Activities:** Bands,

campus ministries, choral groups, dance, drama, film society, international student organizations, music ensembles, Model UN, musical theater, radio station, student government, student newspaper, Knights of Columbus, College Republicans, Global Awareness and Activism in Politics, World Youth Alliance, Students for Life, Faith in Action Today, Chastity Team, Communion and Liberation University.

Athletics. NAIA. **Intercollegiate:** Baseball M, basketball, cross-country, football (tackle) M, golf, rowing (crew) W, soccer, softball W, tennis, track and field, volleyball W. **Intramural:** Basketball, football (non-tackle), soccer, ultimate frisbee, volleyball. **Team name:** Gyrene.

Student services. Alcohol/substance abuse counseling, chaplain/spiritual director, career counseling, student employment services, financial aid counseling, health services, personal counseling, veterans' counselor. **Physically disabled:** Services for visually, hearing impaired.

Contact. E-mail: admissions@avemaria.edu
Phone: (239) 280-2556 Toll-free number: (877) 283-8648
Fax: (239) 280-2559
Billee Silva, Director of Admissions, Ave Maria University, 5050 Ave Maria Boulevard, Ave Maria, FL 34142-9505

Baptist College of Florida
Graceville, Florida
www.baptistcollege.edu   CB code: 5209

▶ Private 4-year Bible and teachers college affiliated with the Southern Baptist Convention

▶ Residential campus in small town

▶ 460 degree-seeking undergraduates: 28% part-time, 37% women, 7% African American, 5% Hispanic/Latino, 1% Native American, 4% Multiracial, non-Hispanic

▶ 21 degree-seeking graduate students

▶ 52% of applicants admitted

▶ SAT or ACT (ACT writing optional), application essay required

▶ 47% graduate within 6 years

General. Founded in 1943. Regionally accredited. **Degrees:** 95 bachelor's, 5 associate awarded; master's offered. **Location:** 90 miles from Tallahassee, 60 miles from Panama City. **Calendar:** Semester, limited summer session. **Full-time faculty:** 26 total; 65% have terminal degrees, 23% women. **Part-time faculty:** 48 total; 35% have terminal degrees, 8% minority, 29% women. **Class size:** 88% < 20, 10% 20-39, 1% 40-49, less than 1% 50-99.

Freshman class profile. 138 applied, 72 admitted, 39 enrolled.

Mid 50% test scores		
SAT critical reading:	450-640	**Return as sophomores:** 72%
SAT math:	390-540	**Out-of-state:** 31%
ACT composite:	17-22	**Live on campus:** 69%

Basis for selection. Applicant must be member in good standing of church affiliated with Southern Baptist Convention or other evangelical body. Recommendations very important. Audition required of music applicants. Interview recommended. **Home schooled:** Transcript of courses and grades required. 2.5 GPA; 20 academic units with at least 14 units from fields of English, math, social and natural sciences required.

High school preparation. Recommended units include English 4, mathematics 4, social studies 1, history 2 and science 3.

2016-2017 Annual costs. Tuition/fees (projected): $10,000. Room/board: $4,888. Books/supplies: $950. Personal expenses: $2,000.

2015-2016 Financial aid. **Need-based:** Average need met was 30%. Average scholarship/grant was $5,687; average loan $3,131. 60% of total undergraduate aid awarded as scholarships/grants, 40% as loans/jobs. **Non-need-based:** Scholarships awarded for academics, minority status, music/drama, religious affiliation.

Application procedures. **Admission:** Closing date 8/15 (receipt date). $25 fee, may be waived for applicants with need. Admission notification on a rolling basis. **Financial aid:** Priority date 4/1, closing date 4/15. FAFSA, institutional form required. Applicants notified on a rolling basis starting 6/15; must reply within 4 week(s) of notification.

Academics. **Special study options:** Distance learning, double major, dual enrollment of high school students, independent study, internships, liberal arts/career combination, teacher certification program. **Credit/placement by examination:** AP, CLEP, IB, SAT, ACT, institutional tests. **Support services:** Learning center, reduced course load, remedial instruction, study skills assistance, tutoring, writing center.

Majors. **Business:** Business admin. **Education:** Elementary, history, music. **English:** English lit. **Philosophy/religion:** Religion. **Theology:** Bible, pastoral counseling, religious ed, sacred music, theology. **Visual/performing arts:** Music, music performance.

Most popular majors. Education 14%, psychology 12%, theological studies 55%, visual/performing arts 9%.

Technology on campus. 25 workstations in library, computer center. Commuter students can connect to campus network. Online course registration, online library, wireless network available.

Student life. **Freshman orientation:** Mandatory. Preregistration for classes offered. Held week before classes begin for 1-2 days depending on major. **Policies:** Religious observance required. **Housing:** Single-sex dorms, special housing for disabled, apartments available. $100 fully refundable deposit. **Activities:** Bands, campus ministries, choral groups, drama, music ensembles, musical theater, radio station, Baptist Collegiate Ministry.

Athletics. **Intramural:** Basketball, fencing, football (non-tackle), soccer, ultimate frisbee, volleyball. **Team name:** Eagles.

Student services. Career counseling, student employment services, financial aid counseling, personal counseling, veterans' counselor. **Physically disabled:** Services for visually, speech, hearing impaired.

Contact. E-mail: admissions@baptistcollege.edu
Phone: (850) 263-3261 ext. 460
Toll-free number: (800) 328-2660 ext. 460 Fax: (850) 263-9026
Sandra Richards, Director of Marketing, Baptist College of Florida, 5400 College Drive, Graceville, FL 32440-3306

Barry University
Miami Shores, Florida   CB member
www.barry.edu   CB code: 5053

▶ Private 4-year university affiliated with the Roman Catholic Church

▶ Residential campus in large town

▶ 3,703 degree-seeking undergraduates: 15% part-time, 61% women, 33% African American, 1% Asian American, 31% Hispanic/Latino, 2% Multiracial, non-Hispanic, 8% international

▶ 4,105 degree-seeking graduate students

▶ 55% of applicants admitted

▶ SAT or ACT (ACT writing optional) required

▶ 34% graduate within 6 years

General. Founded in 1940. Regionally accredited. 22 off-campus sites for adult and continuing education and some graduate degrees. **Degrees:** 943 bachelor's awarded; master's, professional, doctoral offered. **ROTC:** Army, Air Force. **Location:** 14 miles from Fort Lauderdale, 7 miles from Miami. **Calendar:** Semester, limited summer session. **Full-time faculty:** 356 total; 35% minority, 55% women. **Part-time faculty:** 484 total; 38% minority, 51% women. **Class size:** 68% < 20, 31% 20-39, less than 1% 40-49, less than 1% 50-99, less than 1% >100. **Special facilities:** Human performance laboratory, athletic training room, cell biology/biotechnology lab, classroom of tomorrow, photography facilities, lighting studio, dark room, imaging lab, performing arts center, biomechanics lab, Center for Dominican Studies.

Freshman class profile. 3,755 applied, 2,071 admitted, 433 enrolled.

Mid 50% test scores			
SAT critical reading:	430-510	**GPA 3.0-3.49:**	37%
SAT math:	420-510	**GPA 2.0-2.99:**	46%
ACT composite:	17-21	**End year in good standing:**	79%
GPA 3.75 or higher:	4%	**Return as sophomores:**	65%
GPA 3.50-3.74:	13%	**International:**	9%

Basis for selection. Test scores and school record important. Higher test score, GPA, and course requirements for certain majors. Interviews highly recommended. **Home schooled:** Statement describing home school structure and mission, transcript of courses and grades, state high school equivalency certificate required. Academic portfolio or GED, copy of home school rules of the state which home school is chartered required. **Learning Disabled:** Students must apply directly to comprehensive service program.

High school preparation. 13 units required; 16 recommended. Required and recommended units include English 4, mathematics 3, social studies 3 and science 3. For nursing program, 1 chemistry, 1 biology, algebra II required. For biology and allied health programs, 2 laboratory science including biology and chemistry, 3.5 math required. For math program, 4 math including algebra, geometry, trigonometry, required. For chemistry program, 3 math, 1 chemistry with lab required.

2015-2016 Annual costs. Tuition/fees: $28,800. Room/board: $10,600. Books/supplies: $1,500. Personal expenses: $2,500.

2015-2016 Financial aid. Need-based: 372 full-time freshmen applied for aid; 355 deemed to have need; 354 received aid. Average need met was 66%. Average scholarship/grant was $11,272; average loan $3,210. 61% of total undergraduate aid awarded as scholarships/grants, 39% as loans/jobs. **Non-need-based:** Awarded to 2,683 full-time undergraduates, including 391 freshmen. Scholarships awarded for academics, art, athletics, music/drama.

Application procedures. Admission: No deadline. No application fee. Admission notification on a rolling basis beginning on or about 9/8. **Financial aid:** No deadline. FAFSA required. Applicants notified on a rolling basis starting 1/25.

Academics. Special study options: Accelerated study, combined bachelor's/graduate degree, double major, ESL, honors, internships, study abroad, teacher certification program. **Credit/placement by examination:** AP, CLEP, IB, SAT, ACT, institutional tests. 30 credit hours maximum toward bachelor's degree. All credit by examination should be completed prior to junior status. **Support services:** Learning center, reduced course load, remedial instruction, study skills assistance, tutoring, writing center.

Majors. Biology: General. **Business:** Accounting, business admin, finance, international, marketing. **Communications:** Advertising, communications/speech/rhetoric, public relations, radio/TV. **Computer sciences:** General, computer science, information technology. **Education:** Early childhood, elementary, physical, special ed. **English:** English lit. **Foreign languages:** French, Spanish. **Health services:** Athletic training, cardiovascular technology, clinical lab science, cytotechnology, health care admin, nuclear medical technology, nursing (RN), predental, premedicine, prepharmacy, preveterinary, sonography. **History:** General. **Human services:** General, social work. **Liberal arts:** Arts/sciences. **Math:** General. **Parks/recreation:** Exercise sciences, health/fitness, sports admin. **Philosophy/religion:** Philosophy. **Physical sciences:** Chemistry. **Psychology:** General. **Social sciences:** Criminology, political science, sociology. **Theology:** Theology. **Visual/performing arts:** Art, dramatic, music, photography.

Most popular majors. Computer/information sciences 9%, health sciences 44%, public administration/social services 18%.

Technology on campus. 165 workstations in dormitories, library, computer center, student center. Dormitories wired for high-speed internet access and linked to campus network. Commuter students can connect to campus network. Online library, helpline, repair service, wireless network available.

Student life. Freshman orientation: Mandatory. Preregistration for classes offered. **Housing:** Coed dorms, single-sex dorms, special housing for disabled available. $200 nonrefundable deposit. **Activities:** Choral groups, dance, drama, literary magazine, music ensembles, musical theater, radio station, student government, student newspaper, TV station, Jamaican association, black student union, Habitat for Humanity, Caribbean student organization, Haitian intercultural association, Jewish/Christian/Muslim interfaith group, Latter-Day Saints student association, Best Buddies, Spanish club, Baptist dialogue group.

Athletics. NCAA. **Intercollegiate:** Baseball M, basketball, golf, rowing (crew) W, soccer, softball W, tennis, volleyball W. **Intramural:** Basketball, football (non-tackle), golf, skin diving, soccer, softball, volleyball. **Team name:** Buccaneers.

Student services. Adult student services, alcohol/substance abuse counseling, chaplain/spiritual director, career counseling, student employment services, financial aid counseling, health services, personal counseling, placement for graduates. **Physically disabled:** Services for visually, speech, hearing impaired.

Contact. E-mail: admissions@mail.barry.edu
Phone: (305) 899-3100 Toll-free number: (800) 695-2279
Fax: (305) 899-2971
Sarah Riley, Associate Director of Undergraduate Admissions, Barry University, 11300 NE Second Avenue, Miami Shores, FL 33161-6695

Beacon College
Leesburg, Florida
www.beaconcollege.edu

CB member
CB code: 3611

- Private 4-year liberal arts college
- Residential campus in large town
- 274 degree-seeking undergraduates: 3% part-time, 40% women, 15% African American, 3% Asian American, 4% Hispanic/Latino, 4% Multiracial, non-Hispanic, 3% international

- 57% of applicants admitted
- 52% graduate within 6 years; 10% enter graduate study

General. Regionally accredited. College is exclusively for students with learning disabilities, learning differences, and/or ADHD. **Degrees:** 36 bachelor's, 23 associate awarded. **Location:** 50 miles from Orlando, 80 miles from Tampa. **Calendar:** Semester, limited summer session. **Full-time faculty:** 21 total; 67% have terminal degrees, 5% minority, 52% women. **Part-time faculty:** 10 total; 30% have terminal degrees, 10% minority, 50% women. **Class size:** 100% < 20.

Freshman class profile. 205 applied, 116 admitted, 62 enrolled.

GPA 3.75 or higher:	9%	Out-of-state:	78%
GPA 3.50-3.74:	7%	Live on campus:	87%
GPA 3.0-3.49:	34%	International:	5%
GPA 2.0-2.99:	41%	Fraternities:	21%
End year in good standing:	92%	Sororities:	8%
Return as sophomores:	76%		

Basis for selection. Must have documented learning disability or ADHD. Recommendations, interview, character, level of interest very important; followed by rigor of secondary school record, GPA, test scores, extracurricular activities, ability, volunteer work. Class rank, work experience considered. Official high school transcripts or GED, recent (within 3 years) psychoeducational evaluation required. Interview may be required but not mandatory. **Home schooled:** State high school equivalency certificate required.

High school preparation. College-preparatory program recommended. 17 units required. Required units include English 4, mathematics 3, social studies 3, history 1, science 3 and academic electives 3.

2015-2016 Annual costs. Tuition/fees: $34,680. Room/board: $10,250. Books/supplies: $1,000. Personal expenses: $4,060.

2014-2015 Financial aid. Need-based: 36 full-time freshmen applied for aid; 12 deemed to have need; 12 received aid. Average need met was 75%. Average scholarship/grant was $7,000; average loan $5,500. 50% of total undergraduate aid awarded as scholarships/grants, 50% as loans/jobs. **Non-need-based:** Awarded to 26 full-time undergraduates, including 18 freshmen. Scholarships awarded for academics, leadership, state residency. **Additional information:** Work-study programs offered based on financial need.

Application procedures. Admission: No deadline. $50 fee, may be waived for applicants with need. Application must be submitted on paper. Admission notification on a rolling basis. Must reply by May 1 or within 2 week(s) if notified thereafter. **Financial aid:** Priority date 4/1; no closing date. FAFSA required. Applicants notified on a rolling basis starting 5/1; must reply within 2 week(s) of notification.

Academics. Provides remedial coursework in writing and math. **Special study options:** Double major, independent study, internships, liberal arts/career combination. **Credit/placement by examination:** AP, CLEP, institutional tests. 9 credit hours maximum toward associate degree, 9 toward bachelor's. **Support services:** Learning center, reduced course load, remedial instruction, study skills assistance, tutoring, writing center. Enrolls students exclusively with learning disabilities, learning differences, and/ or ADHD. Students must have documented evidence of one of these to be considered for admission.

Majors. Business: Business admin, hospitality admin. **Computer sciences:** General. **Liberal arts:** Arts/sciences. **Psychology:** General. **Visual/performing arts:** Studio arts.

Most popular majors. Business/marketing 14%, computer/information sciences 33%, interdisciplinary studies 11%, public administration/social services 36%.

Technology on campus. 120 workstations in library, computer center, student center. Dormitories wired for high-speed internet access and linked to campus network. Commuter students can connect to campus network. Online library, helpline, repair service, student web hosting, wireless network available.

Student life. Freshman orientation: Mandatory, $275 fee. Preregistration for classes offered. Two-day session held in August before 1st day of school. **Policies:** Counseling and life coaching services available to all students. Off-campus activities available; transportation provided at no extra charge. Alcohol- and drug-free campus. **Housing:** Guaranteed on-campus for all undergraduates. Apartments, wellness housing available. **Activities:** Dance, drama, international student organizations, literary magazine, student government, student newspaper, Human Services Ambassadors, Florida Christian Athletes, Active Minds, Gamma Beta Phi Society, Lambda Epsilon Omega Fraternity, Pi Psi Phi Sorority.

Athletics. Team name: Navigators.

Student services. Alcohol/substance abuse counseling, career counseling, student employment services, financial aid counseling, health services, personal counseling, placement for graduates. **Physically disabled:** Services for visually, speech, hearing impaired.

Contact. E-mail: admissions@beaconcollege.edu
Phone: (352) 638-9731 Toll-free number: (855) 220-5376
Fax: (352) 787-0796
Dale Herold, Dean of Admissions & Enrollment Management, Beacon College, 105 East Main Street, Leesburg, FL 34748

Bethune-Cookman University
Daytona Beach, Florida   **CB member**
www.cookman.edu   **CB code: 5061**

▸ Private 4-year liberal arts college affiliated with the United Methodist Church
▸ Residential campus in small city
▸ 3,666 degree-seeking undergraduates: 5% part-time, 58% women, 80% African American, 3% Hispanic/Latino, 2% Multi-racial, non-Hispanic, 2% international
▸ 152 degree-seeking graduate students
▸ 54% of applicants admitted
▸ SAT or ACT (ACT writing optional), application essay required
▸ 30% graduate within 6 years; 26% enter graduate study

General. Founded in 1904. Regionally accredited. **Degrees:** 506 bachelor's awarded; master's offered. **ROTC:** Army, Air Force. **Location:** 60 miles from Orlando. **Calendar:** Semester, limited summer session. **Full-time faculty:** 197 total; 52% have terminal degrees, 53% minority, 49% women. **Part-time faculty:** 95 total; 1% have terminal degrees, 44% minority, 67% women. **Class size:** 44% < 20, 53% 20-39, 1% 40-49, 1% 50-99, less than 1% >100. **Special facilities:** Art gallery/studio, audiologic recording studio, observatory.

Freshman class profile. 8,766 applied, 4,693 admitted, 905 enrolled.

Mid 50% test scores			
SAT critical reading:	360-440	GPA 2.0-2.99:	51%
SAT math:	350-430	Rank in top quarter:	33%
SAT writing:	350-430	Rank in top tenth:	13%
ACT composite:	15-18	Return as sophomores:	61%
GPA 3.75 or higher:	11%	Out-of-state:	26%
GPA 3.50-3.74:	12%	Live on campus:	90%
GPA 3.0-3.49:	26%	International:	1%

Basis for selection. School achievement record most important. Test scores and letters of recommendation important. Interview required of music majors.

High school preparation. 19 units required. Required and recommended units include English 4, mathematics 3, social studies 1, history 2, science 3 (laboratory 1), foreign language 2 and academic electives 6. 1 unit computer literacy.

2015-2016 Annual costs. Tuition/fees: $14,410. Room/board: $8,710. Books/supplies: $1,450. Personal expenses: $3,330.

2014-2015 Financial aid. All financial aid based on need. 927 full-time freshmen applied for aid; 902 deemed to have need; 902 received aid. Average need met was 52%. Average scholarship/grant was $10,571; average loan $3,633. 52% of total undergraduate aid awarded as scholarships/grants, 48% as loans/jobs.

Application procedures. Admission: Priority date 6/30; no deadline. $25 fee, may be waived for applicants with need. Application must be submitted on paper. Admission notification on a rolling basis. **Financial aid:** Priority date 4/1; no closing date. FAFSA required. Applicants notified on a rolling basis starting 4/1; must reply within 3 week(s) of notification.

Academics. Special study options: Accelerated study, combined bachelor's/graduate degree, cooperative education, distance learning, double major, dual enrollment of high school students, honors, independent study, internships, liberal arts/career combination, study abroad, teacher certification program, weekend college. **Credit/placement by examination:** AP, CLEP, IB, SAT, ACT, institutional tests. 30 credit hours maximum toward bachelor's degree. **Support services:** Learning center, reduced course load, remedial instruction, study skills assistance, tutoring, writing center.

Majors. Biology: General. **Business:** Accounting, business admin, finance, hotel/motel admin, international. **Communications:** Communications/speech/rhetoric, media studies. **Computer sciences:** Computer science, information systems. **Conservation:** Environmental science. **Education:** Biology,

business, chemistry, elementary, English, learning disabled, music, physical, social studies. **Engineering:** Computer. **English:** English lit. **Health services:** Clinical lab science, nursing (RN). **History:** General. **Liberal arts:** Arts/sciences. **Math:** General. **Parks/recreation:** General. **Philosophy/religion:** General. **Physical sciences:** Chemistry. **Protective services:** Law enforcement admin. **Psychology:** General. **Social sciences:** International relations, political science, sociology. **Visual/performing arts:** Music technology.

Most popular majors. Business/marketing 16%, communications/journalism 10%, health sciences 7%, liberal arts 14%, psychology 9%, security/protective services 17%.

Technology on campus. 611 workstations in dormitories, library, computer center, student center. Dormitories wired for high-speed internet access and linked to campus network. Commuter students can connect to campus network. Online course registration, online library, helpline, wireless network available.

Student life. Freshman orientation: Mandatory. Preregistration for classes offered. One-week program in beginning of fall and spring semester. **Housing:** Guaranteed on-campus for freshmen. Coed dorms, single-sex dorms, wellness housing available. $200 nonrefundable deposit, deadline 8/15. Scholarship housing available for honor students. **Activities:** Bands, choral groups, dance, drama, international student organizations, music ensembles, Model UN, radio station, student government, student newspaper, YM/YWCA, Religious Life fellowship, pre-seminarian club, Greek letter organization, Gamma Sigma Sigma national service sorority, Kappa Kappa Psi national band fraternity, Alpha Chi honor sorority, Alpha Kappa Mu honor sorority.

Athletics. NCAA. **Intercollegiate:** Baseball M, basketball, bowling W, cross-country, football (tackle) M, golf, softball W, tennis, track and field, volleyball W. **Intramural:** Basketball, football (tackle) M. **Team name:** Wildcats.

Student services. Adult student services, chaplain/spiritual director, career counseling, student employment services, financial aid counseling, health services, personal counseling, placement for graduates, veterans' counselor.

Contact. E-mail: admissions@cookman.edu
Phone: (386) 481-2600 Toll-free number: (800) 448-0228
Fax: (386) 481-2601
Manicia Finch, Director of Admissions, Bethune-Cookman University, 640 Dr. Mary McLeod Bethune Boulevard, Daytona Beach, FL 32114-3099

Carlos Albizu University
Miami, Florida
www.albizu.edu   **CB code: 2102**

▸ Private 4-year university
▸ Commuter campus in very large city
▸ 262 degree-seeking undergraduates: 51% part-time, 74% women
▸ 681 degree-seeking graduate students
▸ Application essay, interview required

General. Founded in 1980. Regionally accredited. **Degrees:** 86 bachelor's awarded; master's, professional offered. **Calendar:** Semester, extensive summer session. **Full-time faculty:** 6 total. **Part-time faculty:** 35 total. **Class size:** 39% < 20, 61% 20-39.

Basis for selection. 2.0 GPA required. **Home schooled:** State high school equivalency certificate required. **Learning Disabled:** Students requiring special accommodation must submit written request to Director of Student Affairs and attach documentary support.

2015-2016 Annual costs. Tuition/fees: $10,194. Books/supplies: $970. Personal expenses: $1,800.

Financial aid. All financial aid based on need.

Application procedures. Admission: No deadline. $25 fee, may be waived for applicants with need. Admission notification on a rolling basis. **Financial aid:** Priority date 6/1; no closing date. FAFSA, institutional form required. Applicants notified on a rolling basis starting 2/1.

Academics. Special study options: Accelerated study, cooperative education, cross-registration, distance learning, double major, dual enrollment of high school students, ESL, honors, independent study, internships, study abroad, teacher certification program, weekend college. **Credit/placement by examination:** AP, CLEP, IB, institutional tests. 12 credit hours maximum toward bachelor's degree. 6 for foreign language, 6 for other foundation courses. **Support services:** Learning center, remedial instruction, study skills assistance, tutoring, writing center.

Majors. Business: General. **Education:** Elementary. **Psychology:** General.

Technology on campus. 50 workstations in library, computer center, student center. Commuter students can connect to campus network. Online course registration, online library, wireless network available.

Student life. Freshman orientation: Mandatory. Preregistration for classes offered. Two-hour program held before session. **Activities:** Student government, student newspaper.

Student services. Adult student services, career counseling, services for economically disadvantaged, student employment services, financial aid counseling, minority student services, placement for graduates.

Contact. E-mail: webmaster@albizu.edu
Phone: (305) 593-1223 ext. 137 Toll-free number: (888) 468-6228
Fax: (305) 593-1854
Gabriela Fontan, Director, Carlos Albizu University, 2173 NW 99th Avenue, Miami, FL 33172

Chamberlain College of Nursing: Jacksonville
Jacksonville, Florida
www.chamberlain.edu   CB code: 5968

▶ For-profit 4-year nursing college
▶ Commuter campus in small city
▶ 356 degree-seeking undergraduates

General. Regionally accredited. **Degrees:** 237 bachelor's awarded. **Calendar:** Semester. **Full-time faculty:** 11 total; 18% minority, 91% women. **Part-time faculty:** 22 total; 18% minority, 96% women.

Basis for selection. Rigor of secondary school record, class rank, GPA, and recommendations very important.

2015-2016 Annual costs. Tuition/fees: $18,160. Books/supplies: $1,400. Personal expenses: $2,452.

Application procedures. Admission: No deadline. $95 fee. Admission notification on a rolling basis. **Financial aid:** No deadline.

Academics. Special study options: Accelerated study, distance learning. **Credit/placement by examination:** AP, CLEP.

Majors. Health services: Nursing (RN).

Contact. Chamberlain College of Nursing: Jacksonville, 5200 Belfort Road, Jacksonville, FL 32256

Chamberlain College of Nursing: Miramar
Miramar, Florida
www.chamberlain.edu   CB code: 7752

▶ For-profit 4-year nursing college
▶ Large town
▶ 497 degree-seeking undergraduates

General. Regionally accredited. **Degrees:** 237 bachelor's awarded. **Calendar:** Semester. **Full-time faculty:** 6 total; 100% women. **Part-time faculty:** 15 total; 27% minority, 93% women.

Basis for selection. GPA, secondary school record very important; standardized test scores recommended.

2015-2016 Annual costs. Tuition/fees: $18,160. Books/supplies: $1,400. Personal expenses: $2,452.

Application procedures. Admission: No deadline. $95 fee. Admission notification on a rolling basis. **Financial aid:** No deadline.

Academics. Credit/placement by examination: AP, CLEP.

Majors. Health services: Nursing (RN).

Contact. Chamberlain College of Nursing: Miramar, 2300 Southwest 145th Avenue, Miramar, FL 33027

City College: Fort Lauderdale
Fort Lauderdale, Florida
www.citycollege.edu   CB code: 3578

▶ Private 4-year business and technical college
▶ Commuter campus in very large city
▶ 750 undergraduates
▶ Application essay, interview required

General. Accredited by ACICS. **Degrees:** 40 bachelor's, 141 associate awarded. **Calendar:** Quarter. **Full-time faculty:** 14 total. **Part-time faculty:** 103 total.

Basis for selection. Open admission, but selective for some programs. **Home schooled:** Statement describing home school structure and mission, transcript of courses and grades required.

2015-2016 Annual costs. Tuition/fees: $14,550. Books/supplies: $1,044. Personal expenses: $2,931. **Additional information:** Additional program fees are charged per credit hour or per course.

Application procedures. Admission: No deadline. $40 fee, may be waived for applicants with need. Admission notification on a rolling basis. **Financial aid:** No deadline.

Academics. Special study options: Distance learning, independent study, internships. **Credit/placement by examination:** AP, CLEP, IB, institutional tests. 15 credit hours maximum toward associate degree, 30 toward bachelor's. **Support services:** Remedial instruction, tutoring.

Majors. Business: Business admin.

Technology on campus. 70 workstations in library. Online library available.

Student life. Freshman orientation: Mandatory. Preregistration for classes offered.

Student services. Adult student services, alcohol/substance abuse counseling, career counseling, student employment services, financial aid counseling, personal counseling, placement for graduates.

Contact. Phone: (954) 492-5353 Fax: (954) 491-1965
Thomas Carpenter, Director of Admissions, City College: Fort Lauderdale, 2000 West Commercial Boulevard, Fort Lauderdale, FL 33309

DeVry University: Miramar
Miramar, Florida
www.devry.edu   CB code: 4134

▶ For-profit 4-year university
▶ Commuter campus in large town
▶ 503 degree-seeking undergraduates
▶ Interview required

General. Additional locations: Fort Lauderdale, Miami. **Degrees:** 448 bachelor's, 59 associate awarded; master's offered. **Calendar:** Semester, extensive summer session. **Full-time faculty:** 18 total; 22% minority, 17% women. **Part-time faculty:** 43 total; 14% minority, 44% women.

Basis for selection. Applicants must have high school diploma or equivalent, or degree from accredited postsecondary institution; demonstrate proficiency in basic college-level skills through SAT, ACT or institution-administered placement exams; and be at least 17. New students may enter at beginning of any semester.

2015-2016 Annual costs. Tuition/fees: $17,132. Books/supplies: $1,320. Personal expenses: $2,376.

Financial aid. All financial aid based on need.

Application procedures. Admission: No deadline. $30 fee. Admission notification on a rolling basis. **Financial aid:** No deadline. FAFSA required. Applicants notified on a rolling basis.

Academics. Special study options: Accelerated study, distance learning. **Credit/placement by examination:** AP, CLEP. **Support services:** Learning center, remedial instruction, tutoring.

Majors. Business: General, accounting, business admin. **Computer sciences:** Networking, systems analysis, web page design.

Most popular majors. Business/marketing 72%, computer/information sciences 19%, engineering/engineering technologies 9%.

Technology on campus. Online course registration, online library, helpline available.

Student life. **Activities:** Student government, student newspaper.

Student services. Career counseling, student employment services, financial aid counseling, placement for graduates, veterans' counselor. **Physically disabled:** Services for visually, hearing impaired.

Contact. E-mail: openhouse@mir.devry.edu
Phone: (954) 499-9700 Toll-free number: (866) 793-3879
Fax: (954) 499-9723
Director of Admission, DeVry University: Miramar, 2300 SW 145th Avenue, Miramar, FL 33027

DeVry University: Orlando
Orlando, Florida
www.devry.edu
CB code: 2881

- For-profit 4-year university
- Commuter campus in very large city
- 914 degree-seeking undergraduates
- Interview required

General. Regionally accredited. Additional locations: Orlando North, Jacksonville, Tampa Bay, Tampa East. **Degrees:** 245 bachelor's, 22 associate awarded; master's offered. **Calendar:** Semester, extensive summer session. **Full-time faculty:** 25 total; 4% minority, 32% women. **Part-time faculty:** 73 total; 10% minority, 51% women.

Basis for selection. Applicants must have high school diploma or equivalent, or degree from an accredited postsecondary institution. New students may enter at the beginning of any semester. SAT/ACT or institution-administered placement examination used to determine proficiency in basic college-level skills.

High school preparation. Required units include mathematics 1. Math unit must be algebra or higher.

2015-2016 Annual costs. Tuition/fees: $17,132. Books/supplies: $1,320. Personal expenses: $2,376.

Financial aid. All financial aid based on need.

Application procedures. **Admission:** No deadline. $30 fee. Admission notification on a rolling basis. **Financial aid:** No deadline. FAFSA required. Applicants notified on a rolling basis.

Academics. **Special study options:** Accelerated study, distance learning, study abroad. **Credit/placement by examination:** AP, CLEP, institutional tests. **Support services:** Learning center, remedial instruction, tutoring.

Majors. **Business:** Business admin. **Computer sciences:** Networking, systems analysis, web page design. **Engineering:** Software.

Most popular majors. Business/marketing 63%, computer/information sciences 20%, engineering/engineering technologies 17%.

Technology on campus. 303 workstations in library, computer center. Online course registration, online library, helpline available.

Student life. **Freshman orientation:** Mandatory. Preregistration for classes offered. **Activities:** Student newspaper, student activities council, National Society of Black Engineers, association for IT professionals, chess club, technology forum, Millennia Engineering Students Association.

Student services. Career counseling, student employment services, financial aid counseling, placement for graduates, veterans' counselor. **Physically disabled:** Services for visually, hearing impaired.

Contact. Phone: (407) 370-3131 Toll-free number: (866) 353-3879
Fax: (407) 370-3198
Director of Admissions, DeVry University: Orlando, 4000 Millennia Boulevard, Orlando, FL 32839-2426

Digital Media Arts College
Boca Raton, Florida
www.dmac.edu
CB code: 5295

- For-profit 3-year visual arts college
- Commuter campus in large city
- 300 degree-seeking undergraduates
- 15 graduate students
- Application essay required

General. Regionally accredited; also accredited by ACICS. **Degrees:** 39 bachelor's, 3 associate awarded; master's offered. **Calendar:** Semester, extensive summer session. **Full-time faculty:** 11 total. **Part-time faculty:** 21 total. **Class size:** 92% < 20, 8% 20-39. **Special facilities:** Green screen room, motion capture studio, houdini software.

Basis for selection. Open admission. Portfolio submission allows a student to potentially qualify for additional scholarships. **Home schooled:** Transcript of courses and grades required. **Learning Disabled:** Students must request ADA accommodations through the Student Services department. Medical documentation will be required.

2015-2016 Annual costs. Tuition/fees: $17,610. Books/supplies: $815.

Financial aid. **Non-need-based:** Scholarships awarded for art.

Application procedures. **Admission:** No deadline. $50 fee, may be waived for applicants with need. Admission notification on a rolling basis. Students who have yet to graduate high school may enroll as non-degree seeking students and have those courses apply to a program once they meet the admissions requirements of that program. **Financial aid:** No deadline. FAFSA required. Applicants notified on a rolling basis starting 1/1; must reply within 4 week(s) of notification.

Academics. **Special study options:** Combined bachelor's/graduate degree, internships. **Credit/placement by examination:** AP, CLEP, IB, institutional tests. 30 credit hours maximum toward associate degree, 66 toward bachelor's. Credit by examination scores of 70 or higher must be achieved to receive advanced standing credit. Credit by examination tests should be scheduled and completed prior to the end of the students' first semester's drop/add period. **Support services:** Reduced course load, tutoring.

Majors. **Computer sciences:** Computer graphics. **Visual/performing arts:** Graphic design.

Technology on campus. PC or laptop required. 77 workstations in library, computer center, student center. Online library, helpline, repair service, wireless network available.

Student life. **Freshman orientation:** Mandatory. Preregistration for classes offered. One-day program typically held on the third day of class. **Activities:** Student government.

Student services. Career counseling, financial aid counseling, placement for graduates.

Contact. E-mail: admissions@dmac.edu
Phone: (866) 255-3622
Aylin Tito, Director of Admissions, Digital Media Arts College, 5400 Broken Sound Boulevard, Boca Raton, FL 33487

Eckerd College
St. Petersburg, Florida
CB member
www.eckerd.edu
CB code: 5223

- Private 4-year liberal arts college affiliated with the Presbyterian Church (USA)
- Residential campus in large city
- 1,779 degree-seeking undergraduates: 2% part-time, 62% women, 3% African American, 2% Asian American, 9% Hispanic/Latino, 3% Multiracial, non-Hispanic, 5% international
- 73% of applicants admitted
- SAT or ACT (ACT writing optional), application essay required
- 64% graduate within 6 years

General. Founded in 1958. Regionally accredited. **Degrees:** 404 bachelor's awarded. **ROTC:** Army, Air Force. **Location:** 25 miles from Tampa. **Calendar:** 4-1-4, limited summer session. **Full-time faculty:** 115 total; 94% have terminal degrees, 15% minority, 43% women. **Part-time faculty:** 53 total; 53% have terminal degrees, 4% minority, 57% women. **Class size:** 52%

< 20, 47% 20-39, 1% 40-49. **Special facilities:** Marine science laboratory, molecular and life sciences building, waterfront dockside facilities.

Freshman class profile. 4,135 applied, 3,016 admitted, 488 enrolled.

Mid 50% test scores			
SAT critical reading:	500-610	GPA 3.0-3.49:	42%
SAT math:	500-600	GPA 2.0-2.99:	17%
ACT composite:	23-28	Return as sophomores:	81%
GPA 3.75 or higher:	18%	Out-of-state:	78%
GPA 3.50-3.74:	23%	Live on campus:	97%
		International:	4%

Basis for selection. School achievement record, school/community involvement, essay, student's character, test scores most important. **Home schooled:** Statement describing home school structure and mission, transcript of courses and grades, state high school equivalency certificate, letter of recommendation (nonparent) required. **Learning Disabled:** Students should provide proper documentation for any disability.

High school preparation. College-preparatory program recommended. 18 units recommended. Recommended units include English 4, mathematics 3, social studies 2, history 1, science 3 (laboratory 2), foreign language 2 and academic electives 3.

2015-2016 Annual costs. Tuition/fees: $40,020. Room/board: $10,920. Books/supplies: $1,200. Personal expenses: $1,440.

2014-2015 Financial aid. Need-based: 448 full-time freshmen applied for aid; 368 deemed to have need; 368 received aid. Average need met was 88%. Average scholarship/grant was $22,273; average loan $3,328. 72% of total undergraduate aid awarded as scholarships/grants, 28% as loans/jobs. **Non-need-based:** Awarded to 670 full-time undergraduates, including 185 freshmen. Scholarships awarded for academics, art, athletics, music/drama, state residency.

Application procedures. Admission: No deadline. $40 fee, may be waived for applicants with need. Admission notification on a rolling basis beginning on or about 10/1. Must reply by May 1 or within 2 week(s) if notified thereafter. **Financial aid:** Priority date 3/1; no closing date. FAFSA required. Applicants notified on a rolling basis starting 2/20.

Academics. Special study options: Accelerated study, combined bachelor's/graduate degree, double major, ESL, honors, independent study, internships, liberal arts/career combination, semester at sea, student-designed major, study abroad. Semester, full year, and winter term international study programs, 3-2 (dual program) in engineering with Columbia University, Washington University (MO), 3-3 accelerated law program with Florida State University. **Credit/placement by examination:** AP, CLEP, IB, institutional tests. 32 credit hours maximum toward bachelor's degree. **Support services:** Reduced course load, study skills assistance, tutoring, writing center.

Majors. Area/ethnic studies: American, East Asian, women's. **Biology:** General, biochemistry, marine. **Business:** Business admin, international, management science. **Communications:** General. **Computer sciences:** General. **Conservation:** Environmental studies. **English:** Creative writing, English lit. **Foreign languages:** Comparative lit, French, Spanish. **History:** General. **Liberal arts:** Humanities. **Math:** General. **Philosophy/religion:** Philosophy, religion. **Physical sciences:** Chemistry, physics. **Psychology:** General. **Social sciences:** Anthropology, economics, international relations, political science, sociology. **Visual/performing arts:** Dramatic, film/cinema/video, music, studio arts.

Most popular majors. Biology 22%, business/marketing 11%, natural resources/environmental science 14%, psychology 11%, social sciences 14%.

Technology on campus. 300 workstations in dormitories, library, computer center, student center. Dormitories wired for high-speed internet access and linked to campus network. Commuter students can connect to campus network. Online course registration, online library, helpline, repair service, student web hosting, wireless network available.

Student life. Freshman orientation: Mandatory. Preregistration for classes offered. 3-week (Autumn Term) session held in fall. **Housing:** Guaranteed on-campus for freshmen. Coed dorms, single-sex dorms, special housing for disabled, apartments, themed housing, wellness housing available. Pets allowed in dorm rooms. Suite-style dorms, substance-free housing, pet dorms, community service dorms available. **Activities:** Concert band, campus ministries, choral groups, dance, drama, international student organizations, literary magazine, music ensembles, Model UN, radio station, student government, student newspaper, TV station, Phi Beta Kappa, Afro-American society, Search and Rescue team, Circle-K, honor societies, Earth society.

Athletics. NCAA. **Intercollegiate:** Baseball M, basketball, golf, sailing, soccer, softball W, tennis, volleyball W. **Intramural:** Baseball M, basketball, bowling, sailing, soccer, softball, swimming, table tennis, tennis, volleyball. **Team name:** Tritons.

Student services. Adult student services, alcohol/substance abuse counseling, chaplain/spiritual director, career counseling, student employment services, financial aid counseling, health services, minority student services, personal counseling, placement for graduates, veterans' counselor, women's services.

Contact. E-mail: admissions@eckerd.edu
Phone: (727) 864-8331 Toll-free number: (800) 456-9009
Fax: (727) 866-2304
John Sullivan, Vice President of Enrollment Management, Eckerd College, 4200 54th Avenue South, St. Petersburg, FL 33711

Edward Waters College
Jacksonville, Florida
www.ewc.edu

CB member
CB code: 5182

▸ Private 4-year liberal arts college affiliated with the African Methodist Episcopal Church
▸ Residential campus in very large city
▸ 933 undergraduates
▸ SAT or ACT (ACT writing optional) required

General. Founded in 1866. Regionally accredited. **Degrees:** 125 bachelor's awarded. **Location:** 134 miles from Orlando. **Calendar:** Semester, limited summer session. **Class size:** 54% < 20, 46% 20-39. **Special facilities:** African art collection, community resource center, community medical center.

Basis for selection. GPA and recommendations very important. ACCUPLACER used for placement only. **Home schooled:** Statement describing home school structure and mission, transcript of courses and grades, state high school equivalency certificate, letter of recommendation (nonparent) required.

High school preparation. College-preparatory program recommended. 13 units recommended. Recommended units include English 4, mathematics 3, social studies 3 and science 3.

2015-2016 Annual costs. Tuition/fees: $12,525. Room/board: $7,282. Books/supplies: $500. Personal expenses: $750.

Application procedures. Admission: Priority date 4/15; no deadline. $25 fee. Admission notification on a rolling basis. Must reply by May 1 or within 4 week(s) if notified thereafter. **Financial aid:** Closing date 4/15. FAFSA required. Applicants notified on a rolling basis starting 5/1; must reply within 2 week(s) of notification.

Academics. Special study options: Accelerated study, cooperative education, cross-registration, double major, dual enrollment of high school students, independent study, internships, liberal arts/career combination, teacher certification program. **Credit/placement by examination:** AP, CLEP, institutional tests. 30 credit hours maximum toward bachelor's degree. **Support services:** Learning center, pre-admission summer program, remedial instruction, study skills assistance, tutoring.

Majors. Biology: General. **Business:** Business admin. **Communications:** Communications/speech/rhetoric. **Education:** General, multi-level teacher, physical. **Math:** General. **Protective services:** Law enforcement admin. **Psychology:** General. **Visual/performing arts:** Music.

Technology on campus. 120 workstations in dormitories, library, computer center. Dormitories wired for high-speed internet access and linked to campus network. Online library, repair service, wireless network available.

Student life. Freshman orientation: Mandatory. Preregistration for classes offered. **Policies:** Smoke-free campus. Religious observance required. **Housing:** Guaranteed on-campus for freshmen. Coed dorms, single-sex dorms, wellness housing available. $100 deposit, deadline 7/31. **Activities:** Bands, campus ministries, choral groups, international student organizations, music ensembles, student government, NAACP, ministerial alliance, debate club, Circle K.

Athletics. NAIA. **Intercollegiate:** Baseball M, basketball, cheerleading, cross-country M, football (tackle) M, golf, softball W, track and field M, volleyball W. **Intramural:** Table tennis, volleyball. **Team name:** Fighting Tigers.

Student services. Adult student services, career counseling, student employment services, financial aid counseling, health services, personal counseling, placement for graduates, veterans' counselor.

Contact. E-mail: admissions@ewc.edu
Phone: (904) 470-8000 Toll-free number: (888) 898-3191
Fax: (904) 470-8041
Joel Walker, Director of Admissions, Edward Waters College, 1658 Kings
Road, Jacksonville, FL 32209

Embry-Riddle Aeronautical University
Daytona Beach, Florida
www.embryriddle.edu

CB member
CB code: 5190

- Private 4-year university
- Residential campus in small city
- 5,247 degree-seeking undergraduates: 7% part-time, 19% women, 6% African American, 4% Asian American, 4% Hispanic/Latino, 8% Multiracial, non-Hispanic, 14% international
- 527 degree-seeking graduate students
- 69% of applicants admitted
- 55% graduate within 6 years; 25% enter graduate study

General. Founded in 1926. Regionally accredited. **Degrees:** 842 bachelor's, 42 associate awarded; master's, doctoral offered. **ROTC:** Army, Naval, Air Force. **Location:** 50 miles from Orlando. **Calendar:** Semester, extensive summer session. **Full-time faculty:** 323 total; 69% have terminal degrees, 13% minority, 24% women. **Part-time faculty:** 126 total; 45% have terminal degrees, 14% minority, 41% women. **Special facilities:** Aviation complex, air traffic control labs, airway science simulation lab, advanced research lab, advanced vehicle green garage, FAA testing center, meteorology labs, weather center, observatory.

Freshman class profile. 4,588 applied, 3,160 admitted, 1,275 enrolled.

Mid 50% test scores			
SAT critical reading:	490-600	**GPA 2.0-2.99:**	12%
SAT math:	520-640	**Rank in top quarter:**	53%
SAT writing:	470-580	**Rank in top tenth:**	22%
ACT composite:	22-28	**Return as sophomores:**	77%
GPA 3.75 or higher:	42%	**Out-of-state:**	37%
GPA 3.50-3.74:	19%	**Live on campus:**	90%
GPA 3.0-3.49:	27%	**International:**	10%

Basis for selection. GPA, class rank, and test scores important. Specific requirements vary by degree program. SAT or ACT recommended. Interview and essay recommended.

High school preparation. College-preparatory program recommended. 14 units required; 15 recommended. Required and recommended units include English 4, mathematics 4, social studies 3, science 2-3 (laboratory 1) and foreign language 1.

2015-2016 Annual costs. Tuition/fees: $33,218. Room/board: $10,382.

Application procedures. Admission: Priority date 3/1; no deadline. $50 fee, may be waived for applicants with need. Admission notification on a rolling basis. Must reply by May 1 or within 4 week(s) if notified thereafter. Early application encouraged since available facilities limit enrollment in some programs. **Financial aid:** Priority date 3/1; no closing date. FAFSA required. Applicants notified on a rolling basis starting 3/1; must reply within 4 week(s) of notification.

Academics. Special study options: Accelerated study, combined bachelor's/graduate degree, cooperative education, double major, dual enrollment of high school students, ESL, exchange student, honors, internships, study abroad. **Credit/placement by examination:** AP, CLEP, IB, institutional tests. 15 credit hours maximum toward bachelor's degree. Course equivalency examinations must be completed prior to the time the student reaches the last 30 credits for bachelor's degree. **Support services:** Pre-admission summer program, remedial instruction, study skills assistance, tutoring, writing center.

Majors. Communications: Communications/speech/rhetoric. **Computer sciences:** Computer science, programming. **Engineering:** Aerospace, applied physics, computer, electrical, mechanical, software. **Math:** Computational. **Military:** Air and space ops. **Physical sciences:** Atmospheric science. **Protective services:** Homeland security. **Psychology:** Environmental.

Most popular majors. Business/marketing 6%, engineering/engineering technologies 36%, security/protective services 6%, trade and industry 44%.

Technology on campus. 1,049 workstations in library, computer center. Dormitories wired for high-speed internet access and linked to campus network. Commuter students can connect to campus network. Online course registration, online library, helpline, student web hosting, wireless network available.

Student life. Freshman orientation: Mandatory. Preregistration for classes offered. **Housing:** Guaranteed on-campus for freshmen. Coed dorms available. $300 fully refundable deposit, deadline 6/1. **Activities:** Campus ministries, film society, international student organizations, music ensembles, radio station, student government, student newspaper, more than 150 clubs and organizations available.

Athletics. NAIA. **Intercollegiate:** Baseball M, basketball, cheerleading, cross-country, golf, soccer, softball W, tennis, track and field, volleyball W. **Intramural:** Basketball, bowling, football (non-tackle), golf, racquetball, soccer, softball, table tennis, tennis, ultimate frisbee, volleyball. **Team name:** Eagles.

Student services. Alcohol/substance abuse counseling, chaplain/spiritual director, career counseling, student employment services, financial aid counseling, health services, minority student services, personal counseling, veterans' counselor, women's services. **Physically disabled:** Services for visually, speech, hearing impaired.

Contact. E-mail: DaytonaBeach@erau.edu
Phone: (386) 226-6100 Toll-free number: (800) 862-2416
Fax: (386) 226-7070
Pablo Alvarez, Director of Admissions, Embry-Riddle Aeronautical University, 600 South Clyde Morris Boulevard, Daytona Beach, FL 32114-3900

Embry-Riddle Aeronautical University: Worldwide Campus
Daytona Beach, Florida
www.embryriddle.edu

CB code: 5036

- Private 4-year virtual university
- Commuter campus in small city
- 10,478 degree-seeking undergraduates: 71% part-time, 11% women
- 4,154 degree-seeking graduate students
- 66% of applicants admitted

General. Regionally accredited. **Degrees:** 1,683 bachelor's, 580 associate awarded; master's, doctoral offered. **Location:** 50 miles from Orlando. **Calendar:** Differs by program, extensive summer session. **Full-time faculty:** 101 total; 80% have terminal degrees, 10% minority, 37% women. **Part-time faculty:** 1,149 total; 62% have terminal degrees, 12% minority, 28% women. **Special facilities:** Virtual crash lab.

Freshman class profile. 942 applied, 619 admitted, 469 enrolled.

Basis for selection. Specific requirements vary by degree program.

High school preparation. College-preparatory program recommended. 12 units recommended. Recommended units include English 4, mathematics 3, social studies 2, science 2 (laboratory 1).

2015-2016 Annual costs. Tuition/fees: $8,520. **Additional information:** Undergraduate tuition is $355 per credit hour. Discounted Tuition rates are available for Active Duty Military Personnel. Embry-Riddle Worldwide does not offer housing.

Application procedures. Admission: No deadline. $50 fee, may be waived for applicants with need. Admission notification on a rolling basis. Must reply by May 1 or within 4 week(s) if notified thereafter. **Financial aid:** Priority date 4/15; no closing date. FAFSA required. Applicants notified on a rolling basis starting 3/1; must reply within 4 week(s) of notification.

Academics. Special study options: Accelerated study, cooperative education, distance learning, double major, dual enrollment of high school students, internships, study abroad. **Credit/placement by examination:** AP, CLEP, institutional tests.

Majors. Business: Business admin, logistics, transportation. **Communications:** Communications/speech/rhetoric. **Protective services:** Disaster management, firefighting, security operations.

Most popular majors. Business/marketing 29%, trade and industry 71%.

Technology on campus. Online library available.

Student life. Freshman orientation: Available. Preregistration for classes offered. Orientation is available online.

Student services. Financial aid counseling, veterans' counselor.

Contact. E-mail: worldwide@erau.edu
Toll-free number: (800) 522-6787 Fax: (386) 226-6984
Valerie Kisseloff, Director of Admissions, Worldwide Campus, Embry-Riddle Aeronautical University: Worldwide Campus, Attn: Worldwide Imaging, Daytona Beach, FL 32114-3900

Everest University: Orange Park
Orange Park, Florida
www.everest.edu

▸ For-profit 4-year business college
▸ Commuter campus in small city
▸ 558 undergraduates

General. Regionally accredited; also accredited by ACICS. **Degrees:** 28 bachelor's, 41 associate awarded. **Calendar:** Quarter. **Full-time faculty:** 20 total. **Part-time faculty:** 28 total.

Basis for selection. Open admission.

2015-2016 Annual costs. Certificate programs: $12,578-$16,434, books and supplies $1,001-$2,400. Associate programs: $38,880, books and supplies $3,300. Bachelor's programs: $70,200, books and supplies $5,100.

Application procedures. Admission: No deadline. **Financial aid:** No deadline.

Academics. Credit/placement by examination: AP, CLEP.

Majors. Business: Business admin. **Protective services:** Criminal justice, law enforcement admin, security management.

Contact. Phone: (904) 264-9122 Toll-free number: (888) 741-4270 Everest University: Orange Park, 805 Wells Road, Orange Park, FL 32073

Everglades University: Boca Raton
Boca Raton, Florida
www.evergladesuniversity.edu   CB code: 3191

▸ Private 4-year university
▸ Commuter campus in small city
▸ 192 degree-seeking undergraduates: 50% women
▸ 38 degree-seeking graduate students
▸ 98% of applicants admitted

General. Regionally accredited. **Degrees:** 23 bachelor's awarded; master's offered. **Calendar:** Semester, extensive summer session. **Full-time faculty:** 19 total; 74% have terminal degrees, 16% minority, 37% women. **Part-time faculty:** 22 total; 59% have terminal degrees, 27% minority, 41% women. **Class size:** 94% < 20, 6% 20-39.

Freshman class profile. 47 applied, 46 admitted, 26 enrolled.

End year in good standing: 83% **Return as sophomores:** 67%

Basis for selection. Test scores important. Any student with a college degree is not required to take an entrance examination. Applicants should complete the University's entrance examination (the Wonderlic) with a score of 15 or higher. Applicants with a score of 1200 on the SAT or with a composite score of 17 or higher on the ACT are not required to complete the University's entrance examination. Florida's CLAST exam is also acceptable with passing or exempt scores (997,998, 999) in computation or reading. **Home schooled:** State high school equivalency certificate required. **Learning Disabled:** Students with disabilities are encouraged to confidentially self-disclose their disabilities to the Campus Vice President, who will provide these students with the University Disability Support Services Manual, and review the necessary documents and process for students to receive reasonable accommodations.

2016-2017 Annual costs. Tuition/fees (projected): $15,993. Books/supplies: $1,200. Personal expenses: $2,208. **Additional information:** Tuition for each undergraduate semester of 12 credits is $7,524. Education fees are $400 per semester for on-campus students. First-time students pay a one-time $145 registration fee upon initial enrollment. Online students pay $800 per semester in education fees.

2015-2016 Financial aid. Need-based: 57% of total undergraduate aid awarded as scholarships/grants, 43% as loans/jobs.

Application procedures. Admission: No deadline. $50 fee. Admission notification on a rolling basis. **Financial aid:** No deadline. FAFSA, institutional form required. Applicants notified on a rolling basis.

Academics. Special study options: Distance learning, weekend college. Programs offered 100% online. The Orlando campus offers class scheduling that allows students to attend at night and on weekends. **Credit/placement by examination:** AP, CLEP. 18 credit hours maximum toward bachelor's degree. **Support services:** Study skills assistance, tutoring.

Majors. Business: Business admin, construction management, hospitality admin, international. **Conservation:** General, land use planning. **Human services:** General.

Most popular majors. Business/marketing 39%, health sciences 43%, trade and industry 17%.

Technology on campus. 25 workstations in library, computer center. Online library, wireless network available.

Student life. Freshman orientation: Mandatory. Preregistration for classes offered. **Housing:** Student Services Department assists students in locating housing. **Activities:** Student government.

Student services. Career counseling, student employment services, financial aid counseling, placement for graduates, veterans' counselor.

Contact. E-mail: admissionsEUB@evergladesuniversity.edu
Phone: (561) 912-1211 Toll-free number: (888) 772-6077
Fax: (561) 912-1191
Debra Rodrigues, Director of Admissions, Everglades University: Boca Raton, 5002 T-REX Avenue, Suite 100, Boca Raton, FL 33431

Everglades University: Orlando
Maitland, Florida
www.evergladesuniversity.edu   CB code: 7399

▸ Private 4-year university and branch campus college
▸ Commuter campus in large city
▸ 135 degree-seeking undergraduates: 67% women
▸ 30 degree-seeking graduate students
▸ 100% of applicants admitted
▸ 66% graduate within 6 years

General. Regionally accredited. **Degrees:** 34 bachelor's awarded; master's offered. **Location:** 8 miles from Orlando. **Calendar:** Semester, extensive summer session. **Full-time faculty:** 7 total; 71% have terminal degrees, 71% minority, 14% women. **Part-time faculty:** 17 total; 53% have terminal degrees, 29% minority, 53% women. **Class size:** 100% < 20.

Freshman class profile. 35 applied, 35 admitted, 28 enrolled.

End year in good standing: 100% **Out-of-state:** 8%
Return as sophomores: 60%

Basis for selection. Test scores important. Any student entering the University with a college degree is not required to take an entrance examination. Applicants should complete the University's entrance examination (the Wonderlic) with a score of 15 or higher. Applicants with a score of 1200 on the SAT or with a composite score of 17 or higher on the ACT are not required to complete the University's entrance examination. Florida's CLAST exam is also acceptable with passing or exempt scores (997, 998, 999) in computation or reading. **Home schooled:** State high school equivalency certificate required. **Learning Disabled:** Students with disabilities are encouraged to confidentially self-disclose their disabilities to the Campus Vice President, who will provide these students with the University Disability Support Services Manual, and review the necessary documents and process for students to receive reasonable accommodations.

2016-2017 Annual costs. Tuition/fees (projected): $15,993. Books/supplies: $1,200. Personal expenses: $2,208. **Additional information:** Tuition for each undergraduate semester of 12 credits is $7,524. Education fees are $400 per semester for on-campus students. First-time students pay a one-time $145 registration fee upon initial enrollment. Online students pay $800 per semester in education fees.

2015-2016 Financial aid. Need-based: 64% of total undergraduate aid awarded as scholarships/grants, 36% as loans/jobs.

Application procedures. Admission: No deadline. $50 fee. Admission notification on a rolling basis. **Financial aid:** No deadline. FAFSA, institutional form required.

Academics. Special study options: Distance learning, weekend college. Programs offered 100% online. The Orlando campus offers class scheduling that allows students to attend at night and on weekends. **Credit/placement by examination:** AP, CLEP. 18 credit hours maximum toward bachelor's degree. **Support services:** Study skills assistance, tutoring.

Majors. Business: Business admin, construction management, hospitality admin, international. **Conservation:** General, land use planning. **Human services:** General.

Most popular majors. Business/marketing 27%, health sciences 58%, trade and industry 15%.

Technology on campus. 20 workstations in library, computer center. Online library, wireless network available.

Student life. Freshman orientation: Mandatory. Preregistration for classes offered. **Activities:** Student government.

Student services. Career counseling, student employment services, financial aid counseling, placement for graduates, veterans' counselor.

Contact. E-mail: admissions-orl@evergladesuniversity.edu
Phone: (407) 277-0311 Toll-free number: (866) 289-1078
Maria Contreras, Director of Admissions-Orlando Campus, Everglades University: Orlando, 850 Trafalgar Court Suite 100, Maitland, FL 32751

Flagler College
Saint Augustine, Florida　　　　　　　　**CB member**
www.flagler.edu　　　　　　　　　　　**CB code: 5235**

◆ Private 4-year liberal arts college
◆ Commuter campus in large town
◆ 2,702 degree-seeking undergraduates: 4% part-time, 61% women, 4% African American, 1% Asian American, 5% Hispanic/Latino, 3% Multiracial, non-Hispanic, 3% international
◆ 50% of applicants admitted
◆ SAT or ACT (ACT writing recommended), application essay required
◆ 61% graduate within 6 years; 17% enter graduate study

General. Founded in 1968. Regionally accredited. Historic St. Augustine Research Institute is a joint partnership of St. Augustine Foundation, Flagler College, and the University of Florida. **Degrees:** 562 bachelor's awarded. **Location:** 35 miles from Jacksonville. **Calendar:** Semester, limited summer session. **Full-time faculty:** 112 total; 70% have terminal degrees, 8% minority, 51% women. **Part-time faculty:** 125 total; 27% have terminal degrees, 8% minority, 46% women. **Class size:** 54% < 20, 46% 20-39. **Special facilities:** Art museum.

Freshman class profile. 5,260 applied, 2,655 admitted, 620 enrolled.

Mid 50% test scores			
SAT critical reading:	490-590	Rank in top quarter:	38%
SAT math:	470-560	Rank in top tenth:	10%
SAT writing:	480-570	End year in good standing:	92%
ACT composite:	21-26	Return as sophomores:	72%
GPA 3.75 or higher:	38%	Out-of-state:	46%
GPA 3.50-3.74:	12%	Live on campus:	91%
GPA 3.0-3.49:	28%	International:	1%
GPA 2.0-2.99:	22%		

Basis for selection. Academic record, including pattern of courses most important, followed by test scores. Extracurricular activities, recommendations, and intended major also considered. Education applicants must have a combined score (critical reading plus mathematics) of at least 1010 on a single administration of the SAT or a composite score of at least 21 on the ACT. Coastal environmental science majors must have an SAT math score of 500 or higher or an ACT math score of 21 or higher. Interview required for early admission applicants. **Home schooled:** Letter of recommendation (nonparent) required.

High school preparation. College-preparatory program required. 16 units required; 24 recommended. Required and recommended units include English 4, mathematics 3-4, social studies 3-4, history 1-4, science 2-4 (laboratory 1-2), foreign language 2 and academic electives 2.

2015-2016 Annual costs. Tuition/fees: $16,900. Room/board: $9,350. Books/supplies: $1,000. Personal expenses: $2,000.

2015-2016 Financial aid. Need-based: 531 full-time freshmen applied for aid; 399 deemed to have need; 399 received aid. Average need met was 58%. Average scholarship/grant was $9,324; average loan $3,153. 53% of total undergraduate aid awarded as scholarships/grants, 47% as loans/jobs. **Non-need-based:** Awarded to 552 full-time undergraduates, including 193

freshmen. Scholarships awarded for academics, art, athletics, job skills, leadership, minority status, music/drama, religious affiliation, state residency.

Application procedures. Admission: Priority date 11/1; deadline 3/1 (postmark date). $50 fee, may be waived for applicants with need. Admission notification by 3/31. Must reply by May 1 or within 3 week(s) if notified thereafter. **Financial aid:** Priority date 3/1; no closing date. FAFSA required. Applicants notified on a rolling basis starting 3/1; must reply within 2 week(s) of notification.

Academics. Special study options: Distance learning, double major, independent study, internships, teacher certification program. **Credit/placement by examination:** AP, CLEP, IB, SAT, ACT, institutional tests. 30 credit hours maximum toward bachelor's degree. **Support services:** Learning center, pre-admission summer program, reduced course load, remedial instruction, study skills assistance, tutoring, writing center. Natural sciences tutoring, Spanish language tutoring, accounting tutoring, mathematics tutoring.

Majors. Area/ethnic studies: Latin American. **Business:** Accounting, business admin, hospitality admin. **Communications:** Journalism, media studies, persuasive communications. **Conservation:** Environmental science. **Education:** Art, Deaf/hearing impaired, elementary, English, social science, special ed. **English:** English lit. **Foreign languages:** Spanish. **History:** General. **Human services:** General. **Liberal arts:** Arts/sciences. **Parks/recreation:** Sports admin. **Philosophy/religion:** General. **Psychology:** General. **Social sciences:** Criminology, economics, political science, sociology. **Visual/performing arts:** Art history/conservation, dramatic, graphic design, studio arts.

Most popular majors. Business/marketing 18%, communications/journalism 14%, education 7%, English 6%, psychology 11%, public administration/social services 6%, social sciences 12%, visual/performing arts 13%.

Technology on campus. 343 workstations in library, computer center, student center. Dormitories wired for high-speed internet access and linked to campus network. Commuter students can connect to campus network. Online course registration, online library, helpline, wireless network available.

Student life. Freshman orientation: Mandatory. Preregistration for classes offered. Three-day program held each semester prior to classes; additional optional summer session. **Policies:** Inter-hall visitation is allowed during specified hours. Alcohol prohibited on campus. No smoking in buildings, including residence halls. **Housing:** Guaranteed on-campus for freshmen. Single-sex dorms available. $200 nonrefundable deposit, deadline 5/1. **Activities:** Campus ministries, choral groups, dance, drama, international student organizations, literary magazine, Model UN, radio station, student government, student newspaper, TV station, Rotaract, Intervarsity Christian Fellowship, Catholic College Fellowship, Society for Advancement of Management, ENACTUS, Deaf Awareness Club, Sport Management Club, Club Unity.

Athletics. NCAA. **Intercollegiate:** Baseball M, basketball, cross-country, golf, soccer, softball W, tennis, track and field, volleyball W. **Intramural:** Badminton, basketball, bowling, football (non-tackle), golf, sand volleyball, soccer, softball, table tennis, tennis, volleyball, weight lifting. **Team name:** Saints.

Student services. Adult student services, alcohol/substance abuse counseling, career counseling, services for economically disadvantaged, student employment services, financial aid counseling, health services, minority student services, personal counseling, placement for graduates, veterans' counselor, women's services. **Physically disabled:** Services for visually, speech, hearing impaired.

Contact. E-mail: admissions@flagler.edu
Phone: (904) 819-6220 Toll-free number: (800) 304-4208
Fax: (904) 819-6466
Rachel Branch, Director of Admission, Flagler College, 74 King Street, St. Augustine, FL 32084

Florida Agricultural and Mechanical University
Tallahassee, Florida　　　　　　　　**CB member**
www.famu.edu　　　　　　　　　　　**CB code: 5215**

◆ Public 4-year university
◆ Residential campus in small city
◆ 7,705 degree-seeking undergraduates: 10% part-time, 64% women, 91% African American, 1% Asian American, 2% Hispanic/Latino, 2% Multiracial, non-Hispanic, 1% international
◆ 1,756 degree-seeking graduate students
◆ 51% of applicants admitted
◆ SAT or ACT with writing, application essay required
◆ 39% graduate within 6 years; 33% enter graduate study

General. Founded in 1887. Regionally accredited. **Degrees:** 1,512 bachelor's, 67 associate awarded; master's, professional, doctoral offered. **ROTC:** Army, Naval, Air Force. **Location:** 169 miles from Jacksonville. **Calendar:** Semester, limited summer session. **Full-time faculty:** 545 total; 74% have terminal degrees, 81% minority, 46% women. **Part-time faculty:** 183 total; 2% have terminal degrees, 80% minority, 56% women. **Class size:** 33% < 20, 48% 20-39, 7% 40-49, 11% 50-99, 1% >100. **Special facilities:** Black archives research center, observatory, fine arts gallery, teaching gymnasium.

Freshman class profile. 5,832 applied, 2,998 admitted, 1,485 enrolled.

Mid 50% test scores			
		GPA 3.0-3.49:	47%
SAT critical reading:	420-540	GPA 2.0-2.99:	18%
SAT math:	420-530	Rank in top quarter:	40%
SAT writing:	400-510	Rank in top tenth:	14%
ACT composite:	18-23	End year in good standing:	76%
GPA 3.75 or higher:	18%	Return as sophomores:	85%
GPA 3.50-3.74:	17%	Out-of-state:	16%

Basis for selection. School achievement record, test scores, recommendations, and essay are very important. Audition required of music major applicants. **Home schooled:** Statement describing home school structure and mission, transcript of courses and grades, letter of recommendation (nonparent) required. Applicant may be asked to complete GED. If educational program is not measured in Carnegie Units, 1010 SAT (exclusive of Writing), 1450 SAT (with Writing), or 21 ACT required. **Learning Disabled:** May seek admission under alternate criteria by requesting it in writing when applying. Current and appropriate documentation required.

High school preparation. College-preparatory program required. 18 units required. Required units include English 4, mathematics 4, social studies 3, science 3 (laboratory 2), foreign language 2 and academic electives 2.

2015-2016 Annual costs. Tuition/fees: $5,785; $17,725 out-of-state. Room/board: $10,100. Books/supplies: $1,138. Personal expenses: $2,124.

2014-2015 Financial aid. **Need-based:** 1,369 full-time freshmen applied for aid; 1,226 deemed to have need; 1,225 received aid. Average need met was 77%. Average scholarship/grant was $7,619; average loan $3,466. 62% of total undergraduate aid awarded as scholarships/grants, 38% as loans/jobs. **Non-need-based:** Awarded to 1,932 full-time undergraduates, including 556 freshmen. Scholarships awarded for academics, art, athletics, leadership, music/drama, ROTC.

Application procedures. **Admission:** Closing date 5/15 (receipt date). $30 fee. Admission notification on a rolling basis. **Financial aid:** Priority date 3/1; no closing date. FAFSA required. Applicants notified on a rolling basis starting 4/15.

Academics. **Special study options:** Accelerated study, combined bachelor's/graduate degree, cooperative education, distance learning, double major, dual enrollment of high school students, honors, independent study, internships, study abroad, teacher certification program, weekend college. **Credit/placement by examination:** AP, CLEP, IB, SAT, ACT. 30 credit hours maximum toward bachelor's degree. Student must have passing scores (determined by state) for AP and CLEP exams. **Support services:** Learning center, pre-admission summer program, remedial instruction, study skills assistance, tutoring, writing center.

Majors. **Architecture:** Architecture. **Area/ethnic studies:** African-American. **Biology:** General. **Business:** Accounting, business admin. **Communications:** Journalism, public relations. **Computer sciences:** General, information technology. **Conservation:** Environmental science. **Education:** Early childhood, elementary, English, mathematics, music, physical, science, social science, trade/industrial. **Engineering:** Agricultural, chemical, civil, computer, electrical, industrial, mechanical. **English:** English lit. **Health services:** Health care admin, health information management, nursing (RN), pharmaceutical sciences, respiratory therapy technology. **History:** General. **Human services:** Social work. **Math:** General. **Philosophy/religion:** General. **Physical sciences:** Chemistry, physics. **Protective services:** Criminal justice. **Psychology:** General. **Social sciences:** Economics, political science, sociology. **Visual/performing arts:** Dramatic, graphic design, music, studio arts.

Most popular majors. Business/marketing 13%, health sciences 25%, security/protective services 12%, social sciences 7%.

Technology on campus. 4,000 workstations in dormitories, library, computer center, student center. Dormitories wired for high-speed internet access and linked to campus network. Commuter students can connect to campus network. Online course registration, online library, helpline, repair service, wireless network available.

Student life. **Freshman orientation:** Mandatory, $150 fee. Preregistration for classes offered. Two-and-a-half day session in fall. **Policies:** Student must have completed freshman year with 24 credit hours, 2.5 GPA and 30 hours of community service to be eligible for club or organization membership.

To maintain membership, student must maintain 2.0 GPA, be in good academic and judicial standing, and accrue 30 hours of community service annually. Freshmen not permitted cars on campus. **Housing:** Guaranteed on-campus for freshmen. Coed dorms, single-sex dorms, special housing for disabled, apartments, themed housing available. $350 partly refundable deposit, deadline 6/1. **Activities:** Bands, campus ministries, choral groups, dance, drama, film society, international student organizations, literary magazine, music ensembles, Model UN, musical theater, radio station, student government, student newspaper, symphony orchestra, TV station.

Athletics. NCAA. **Intercollegiate:** Baseball M, basketball, bowling W, cheerleading, cross-country, football (tackle) M, golf, softball W, swimming, tennis, track and field, volleyball W. **Intramural:** Badminton, basketball, bowling, cheerleading W, football (non-tackle), football (tackle) M, golf, gymnastics, racquetball, skiing, soccer, softball, swimming, table tennis, tennis, track and field, ultimate frisbee, volleyball, weight lifting, wrestling. **Team name:** Rattlers.

Student services. Adult student services, alcohol/substance abuse counseling, career counseling, services for economically disadvantaged, student employment services, financial aid counseling, health services, minority student services, on-campus daycare, personal counseling, placement for graduates, veterans' counselor, women's services. **Physically disabled:** Services for visually, speech, hearing impaired.

Contact. E-mail: ugrdadmissions@famu.edu
Phone: (850) 599-3796 Toll-free number: (866) 642-1198
Fax: (850) 599-3069
Barbara Cox, Director of Admissions, Florida Agricultural and Mechanical University, 444 Gamble Street Lucy Moten, Room 204, Tallahassee, FL 32307-3200

Florida Atlantic University

Boca Raton, Florida CB member
www.fau.edu CB code: 5229

- Public 4-year university
- Commuter campus in small city
- 24,230 degree-seeking undergraduates: 35% part-time, 57% women, 20% African American, 4% Asian American, 26% Hispanic/Latino, 4% Multi-racial, non-Hispanic, 2% international
- 4,655 degree-seeking graduate students
- 67% of applicants admitted
- SAT or ACT with writing required
- 48% graduate within 6 years

General. Founded in 1961. Regionally accredited. Courses and degree programs offered at additional sites in Palm Beach, Broward, and St. Lucie counties. **Degrees:** 5,665 bachelor's, 360 associate awarded; master's, professional, doctoral offered. **ROTC:** Army, Air Force. **Location:** 17 miles from Fort Lauderdale. **Calendar:** Semester, extensive summer session. **Full-time faculty:** 826 total; 78% have terminal degrees, 32% minority, 45% women. **Part-time faculty:** 490 total; 24% have terminal degrees, 23% minority, 56% women. **Class size:** 23% < 20, 50% 20-39, 8% 40-49, 10% 50-99, 9% >100. **Special facilities:** Environmental center, native fish research center, ocean engineering laboratory, marine research facility, robotics laboratory, harbor branch research, office of undergraduate research and inquiry.

Freshman class profile. 16,005 applied, 10,725 admitted, 3,479 enrolled.

Mid 50% test scores			
		Rank in top quarter:	35%
SAT critical reading:	480-570	Rank in top tenth:	11%
SAT math:	470-570	End year in good standing:	72%
SAT writing:	470-560	Return as sophomores:	77%
ACT composite:	20-24	Out-of-state:	10%
GPA 3.75 or higher:	47%	Live on campus:	59%
GPA 3.50-3.74:	19%	International:	4%
GPA 3.0-3.49:	31%	Fraternities:	4%
GPA 2.0-2.99:	3%	Sororities:	7%

Basis for selection. Secondary school record, standardized test scores most important. Recommendation, talent, ability also important. Top 20% of state high school graduates guaranteed admission. Audition recommended for theater majors. Portfolio recommended for art majors. **Home schooled:** Transcript of courses and grades required.

High school preparation. College-preparatory program required. 18 units required; 20 recommended. Required and recommended units include English 4, mathematics 4, social studies 3, science 3-4 (laboratory 2), foreign language 2 and academic electives 3.

2015-2016 Annual costs. Tuition/fees: $6,039; $21,595 out-of-state. Room/board: $11,748. Books/supplies: $1,240. Personal expenses: $2,462.

Financial aid. Non-need-based: Scholarships awarded for academics, athletics, leadership, music/drama, state residency.

Application procedures. Admission: Priority date 2/15; deadline 5/1 (receipt date). $30 fee, may be waived for applicants with need. Application must be submitted online. Admission notification on a rolling basis beginning on or about 10/1. Must reply by 5/1. Must reply by May 1 or within 2 week(s) if notified thereafter. **Financial aid:** Priority date 3/1, closing date 6/30. FAFSA required. Applicants notified on a rolling basis starting 3/15; must reply by 8/23.

Academics. Special study options: Accelerated study, combined bachelor's/graduate degree, cooperative education, cross-registration, distance learning, double major, dual enrollment of high school students, ESL, honors, independent study, internships, liberal arts/career combination, student-designed major, study abroad, teacher certification program, weekend college. **Credit/placement by examination:** AP, CLEP, IB. 45 credit hours maximum toward bachelor's degree. **Support services:** Learning center, pre-admission summer program, reduced course load, study skills assistance, tutoring, writing center.

Honors college/program. Most applicants have 3.5 GPA, 1280 SAT (exclusive of Writing) or 29 Enhanced ACT. Exceptional applicants who do not meet these criteria may be admitted on individual basis.

Majors. Architecture: Architecture, environmental design, urban/community planning. **Biology:** General. **Business:** Accounting, business admin, finance, hospitality admin, international, management information systems, marketing, real estate. **Communications:** Communications/speech/rhetoric, digital media. **Computer sciences:** General. **Education:** General, elementary, English, mathematics, music, science, social science, special ed. **Engineering:** Civil, computer, electrical, mechanical, ocean, surveying. **English:** English lit. **Foreign languages:** French, linguistics, Spanish. **Health services:** Health care admin, nursing (RN). **History:** General. **Human services:** General, social work. **Liberal arts:** Arts/sciences. **Math:** General. **Parks/recreation:** Exercise sciences. **Philosophy/religion:** Judaic, philosophy. **Physical sciences:** Chemistry, geology, physics. **Protective services:** Criminal justice. **Psychology:** General, psychobiology. **Social sciences:** General, anthropology, economics, geography, political science, sociology. **Visual/performing arts:** Art, dramatic, music, music management.

Most popular majors. Biology 7%, business/marketing 24%, education 7%, engineering/engineering technologies 6%, health sciences 8%, psychology 7%, security/protective services 8%, social sciences 9%.

Technology on campus. 1,000 workstations in dormitories, library, computer center, student center. Dormitories wired for high-speed internet access and linked to campus network. Commuter students can connect to campus network. Online course registration, online library, helpline, repair service, wireless network available.

Student life. Freshman orientation: Mandatory, $75 fee. Preregistration for classes offered. Held over a two day session. **Housing:** Guaranteed on-campus for freshmen. Coed dorms, single-sex dorms, apartments, themed housing available. $200 partly refundable deposit, deadline 8/1. **Activities:** Bands, campus ministries, choral groups, dance, drama, film society, international student organizations, literary magazine, music ensembles, Model UN, musical theater, opera, radio station, student government, student newspaper, symphony orchestra, TV station, Circle K, College Democrats, College Republicans, B'nai B'rith Hillel, Neumann Club, Christian College Fellowship, human rights organization, European student association, NAACP, Peace Finders.

Athletics. NCAA. **Intercollegiate:** Baseball M, basketball, cheerleading, cross-country, football (tackle) M, golf, soccer, softball W, swimming, tennis, track and field W, volleyball W. **Intramural:** Basketball, diving, football (non-tackle), rugby, soccer M, softball, table tennis, volleyball M. **Team name:** Owls.

Student services. Adult student services, alcohol/substance abuse counseling, chaplain/spiritual director, career counseling, student employment services, financial aid counseling, health services, minority student services, on-campus daycare, personal counseling, placement for graduates, veterans' counselor, women's services. **Physically disabled:** Services for visually, speech, hearing impaired.

Contact. E-mail: Admissions@fau.edu
Phone: (561) 297-3040 Toll-free number: (800) 299-4328
Fax: (561) 297-2758
Tracy Boulukos, Assistant Provost, Enrollment Management, Florida Atlantic University, 777 Glades Road, Boca Raton, FL 33431

Florida Career College: Boynton Beach
Boynton Beach, Florida
www.careercollege.edu

- For-profit 4-year technical and career college
- Small city

General. Regionally accredited. **Calendar:** Quarter.

Annual costs/financial aid. Total program costs including tuition, books and supplies: diploma, $14,475-$22,698; associate degree, $27,322-$44,003; Additional lab fees, supply fees, and technology fees vary by program.

Contact. Director of Admissions, 1749 North Congress Avenue, Boynton Beach, FL 33426

Florida Career College: Jacksonville
Jacksonville, Florida
www.careercollege.edu

- For-profit 4-year technical and career college
- Very large city

General. Regionally accredited. **Calendar:** Quarter.

Annual costs/financial aid. Total program costs including tuition, books and supplies: diploma, $14,475-$22,698; associate degree, $27,322-$44,003; Additional lab fees, supply fees, and technology fees vary by program.

Contact. Director of Admissions, 6600 Youngerman Circle, Jacksonville, FL 32244

Florida Career College: Lauderdale Lakes
Lauderdale Lakes, Florida
www.anthem.edu

- For-profit 4-year technical and career college
- Large town

General. Accredited by ACICS. **Calendar:** Quarter.

Annual costs/financial aid. Total program costs including tuition, books and supplies: diploma, $14,475-$22,698; associate degree, $27,322-$44,003; Additional lab fees, supply fees, and technology fees vary by program.

Contact. Phone: (954) 535-8700
Director of Admissions, 3383 North State Road 7, Lauderdale Lakes, FL 33319

Florida Career College: Riverview
Riverview, Florida
www.careercollege.edu

- For-profit 4-year technical and career college
- Large town

General. Regionally accredited. **Calendar:** Quarter.

Annual costs/financial aid. Total program costs including tuition, books and supplies: diploma, $14,475-$22,698; associate degree, $27,322-$44,003; Additional lab fees, supply fees, and technology fees vary by program.

Contact. Director of Admissions, 2662 South Falkenburg Road, Riverview, FL 33578

Florida College
Temple Terrace, Florida
www.floridacollege.edu   CB code: 5216

- Private 4-year liberal arts college
- Residential campus in large town

- 550 degree-seeking undergraduates: 2% part-time, 54% women, 6% African American, 6% Hispanic/Latino, 2% Native American, 5% Multiracial, non-Hispanic, 3% international
- 81% of applicants admitted
- SAT or ACT (ACT writing optional) required

General. Founded in 1944. Regionally accredited. **Degrees:** 79 bachelor's, 105 associate awarded. **ROTC:** Army, Air Force. **Location:** 2 miles from Tampa. **Calendar:** Semester, limited summer session. **Full-time faculty:** 35 total; 37% have terminal degrees, 9% minority, 29% women. **Part-time faculty:** 21 total; 48% have terminal degrees, 5% minority, 33% women. **Class size:** 68% < 20, 22% 20-39, 4% 40-49, 6% 50-99. **Special facilities:** Riverwalk.

Freshman class profile. 297 applied, 241 admitted, 181 enrolled.

Mid 50% test scores			
		GPA 3.50-3.74:	17%
SAT critical reading:	430-560	GPA 3.0-3.49:	23%
SAT math:	420-550	GPA 2.0-2.99:	14%
SAT writing:	410-570	Out-of-state:	65%
ACT composite:	19-25	Live on campus:	96%
GPA 3.75 or higher:	46%		

Basis for selection. 2 recommendations, 2.0 GPA required. Test scores, moral character important. **Home schooled:** Homeschool completion certification required. **Learning Disabled:** Provide voluntary declaration of disability form and documentation.

High school preparation. 16 units required. Required and recommended units include English 4, mathematics 3, social studies 2-3, science 2 (laboratory 2) and foreign language 2.

2015-2016 Annual costs. Tuition/fees: $16,074. Room/board: $8,090. Books/supplies: $1,300. Personal expenses: $1,500.

2014-2015 Financial aid. Need-based: 195 full-time freshmen applied for aid; 169 deemed to have need; 169 received aid. Average need met was 58%. Average scholarship/grant was $6,008; average loan $3,161. 55% of total undergraduate aid awarded as scholarships/grants, 45% as loans/jobs. **Non-need-based:** Awarded to 529 full-time undergraduates, including 212 freshmen. Scholarships awarded for academics, athletics, music/drama, state residency.

Application procedures. Admission: Priority date 5/1; deadline 8/1 (postmark date). $40 fee, may be waived for applicants with need. Admission notification on a rolling basis. **Financial aid:** Closing date 9/30. FAFSA required. Applicants notified on a rolling basis starting 3/30; must reply within 2 week(s) of notification.

Academics. Special study options: Cross-registration, distance learning, double major, independent study, teacher certification program. **Credit/placement by examination:** AP, CLEP, IB, SAT, ACT, institutional tests. 30 credit hours maximum toward associate degree, 30 toward bachelor's. **Support services:** Reduced course load, remedial instruction, study skills assistance, tutoring, writing center.

Majors. Business: Business admin. **Communications:** General, organizational. **Education:** Elementary. **History:** General, American. **Liberal arts:** Arts/sciences. **Theology:** Bible, religious ed. **Visual/performing arts:** Music.

Most popular majors. Business/marketing 37%, communications/journalism 8%, education 9%, history 6%, liberal arts 25%, visual/performing arts 9%.

Technology on campus. 85 workstations in library, computer center. Dormitories wired for high-speed internet access and linked to campus network. Online library, wireless network available.

Student life. Freshman orientation: Mandatory. Preregistration for classes offered. **Policies:** All campus residents expected to attend Sunday worship services. **Housing:** Guaranteed on-campus for all undergraduates. Single-sex dorms, special housing for disabled, wellness housing available. $150 partly refundable deposit, deadline 8/1. **Activities:** Bands, choral groups, drama, literary magazine, music ensembles, musical theater, student government, honor society, Circle K, Sowers club, LOVE.

Athletics. USCAA. **Intercollegiate:** Basketball, cheerleading W, cross-country, soccer, volleyball W. **Intramural:** Basketball, football (non-tackle), soccer, softball, ultimate frisbee, volleyball. **Team name:** Falcons.

Student services. Career counseling, financial aid counseling, health services, personal counseling, veterans' counselor.

Contact. E-mail: admission@floridacollege.edu
Phone: (813) 988-5131 ext. 152 Toll-free number: (800) 326-7655
Fax: (813) 899-1799
Paul Casebolt, Director of Admissions & Retention Services, Florida College, 119 North Glen Arven Avenue, Temple Terrace, FL 33617

Florida Gulf Coast University
Fort Myers, Florida   **CB member**
www.fgcu.edu   **CB code: 5221**

- Public 4-year university
- Residential campus in small city
- 13,430 degree-seeking undergraduates: 20% part-time, 55% women, 7% African American, 2% Asian American, 19% Hispanic/Latino, 3% Multiracial, non-Hispanic, 2% international
- 983 degree-seeking graduate students
- 61% of applicants admitted
- SAT or ACT with writing required
- 49% graduate within 6 years

General. Regionally accredited. **Degrees:** 2,061 bachelor's, 334 associate awarded; master's, professional, doctoral offered. **Location:** 100 miles from Tampa, 125 miles from Miami. **Calendar:** Semester, extensive summer session. **Full-time faculty:** 456 total; 75% have terminal degrees, 17% minority, 45% women. **Part-time faculty:** 246 total; 17% minority, 48% women. **Class size:** 19% < 20, 55% 20-39, 10% 40-49, 15% 50-99, less than 1% >100. **Special facilities:** Natural wetlands, observatory, campus beach.

Freshman class profile. 13,608 applied, 8,244 admitted, 2,704 enrolled.

Mid 50% test scores			
		GPA 2.0-2.99:	7%
SAT critical reading:	490-570	Rank in top quarter:	34%
SAT math:	480-570	Rank in top tenth:	13%
SAT writing:	480-560	Return as sophomores:	79%
ACT composite:	22-26	Out-of-state:	14%
GPA 3.75 or higher:	49%	Live on campus:	80%
GPA 3.50-3.74:	16%	International:	1%
GPA 3.0-3.49:	28%		

Basis for selection. Grades in academic units, test scores very important. **Home schooled:** Transcript of courses and grades required. 1010 SAT (exclusive of Writing) or 21 ACT required.

High school preparation. College-preparatory program required. 18 units required. Required units include English 4, mathematics 4, social studies 2, science 3 (laboratory 2), foreign language 2 and academic electives 2.

2015-2016 Annual costs. Tuition/fees: $6,118; $25,161 out-of-state. Room/board: $8,820. Books/supplies: $1,200. Personal expenses: $1,700.

2014-2015 Financial aid. Need-based: 1,944 full-time freshmen applied for aid; 1,271 deemed to have need; 1,271 received aid. Average need met was 51%. Average scholarship/grant was $5,070; average loan $6,799. 45% of total undergraduate aid awarded as scholarships/grants, 55% as loans/jobs. **Non-need-based:** Awarded to 2,492 full-time undergraduates, including 599 freshmen. Scholarships awarded for academics, alumni affiliation, athletics, leadership, minority status, music/drama, religious affiliation, state residency.

Application procedures. Admission: Closing date 2/15 (receipt date). $30 fee, may be waived for applicants with need. Admission notification on a rolling basis beginning on or about 9/1. Must reply by 5/1. **Financial aid:** Priority date 3/1, closing date 6/30. FAFSA, institutional form required. Applicants notified on a rolling basis starting 2/15.

Academics. Special study options: Accelerated study, combined bachelor's/graduate degree, cross-registration, distance learning, double major, dual enrollment of high school students, honors, independent study, internships, study abroad, teacher certification program, Washington semester. **Credit/placement by examination:** AP, CLEP, IB, SAT, ACT, institutional tests. 45 credit hours maximum toward bachelor's degree. Credit received from one exam program may not be duplicated by another, nor duplicated through dual enrollment credit. **Support services:** Learning center, reduced course load, remedial instruction, study skills assistance, tutoring, writing center.

Majors. Biology: General, biotechnology. **Business:** Accounting, business admin, finance, management information systems, marketing, resort management. **Communications:** Digital media, media studies. **Computer sciences:** General. **Conservation:** Environmental studies, water/wetlands/marine. **Education:** General, early childhood, elementary, music, secondary, special ed. **Engineering:** Biomedical, civil, environmental. **English:** English lit. **Foreign languages:** Spanish. **Health services:** Athletic training, clinical lab science, community health, nursing (RN). **History:** General. **Human services:** Social work. **Liberal arts:** Arts/sciences. **Math:** General. **Parks/recreation:** Exercise sciences. **Philosophy/religion:** Philosophy. **Physical sciences:** Chemistry. **Protective services:** Criminal justice, criminalistics. **Psychology:** General. **Social sciences:** Anthropology, economics, political science, sociology. **Visual/performing arts:** Art, dramatic, music performance.

Most popular majors. Business/marketing 24%, communications/journalism 10%, education 8%, health sciences 11%, psychology 7%, security/protective services 8%.

Technology on campus. 1,029 workstations in dormitories, library, computer center. Dormitories wired for high-speed internet access and linked to campus network. Commuter students can connect to campus network. Online course registration, online library, helpline, student web hosting, wireless network available.

Student life. Freshman orientation: Mandatory, $35 fee. Preregistration for classes offered. Two-day summer program prior to fall semester; families invited. **Policies:** Student code of conduct in effect. **Housing:** Coed dorms, special housing for disabled, apartments, wellness housing available. $50 partly refundable deposit, deadline 11/1. **Activities:** Campus ministries, international student organizations, literary magazine, Model UN, student government, student newspaper, College Republicans, College Democrats, Christian Campus Fellowship, Intervarsity Christian Fellowship, Navigators, Colleges Against Cancer, American Association of University Women Student Affiliates, human services student organization.

Athletics. NCAA. **Intercollegiate:** Baseball M, basketball, cross-country, golf, softball W, tennis, volleyball W. **Intramural:** Basketball, cross-country, football (non-tackle), soccer, softball, table tennis, tennis, volleyball, water polo. **Team name:** Eagles.

Student services. Adult student services, alcohol/substance abuse counseling, career counseling, student employment services, financial aid counseling, health services, minority student services, on-campus daycare, personal counseling, placement for graduates, veterans' counselor, women's services. **Physically disabled:** Services for visually, speech, hearing impaired.

Contact. E-mail: admissions@fgcu.edu
Phone: (239) 590-7878 Toll-free number: (888) 889-1095
Fax: (239) 590-7894
Marc Laviolette, Director of Admissions and Records, Florida Gulf Coast University, 10501 FGCU Boulevard South, Fort Myers, FL 33965-6565

Florida Institute of Technology

Melbourne, Florida

www.fit.edu

CB member
CB code: 5080

- Private 4-year university
- Residential campus in small city
- 3,320 degree-seeking undergraduates: 4% part-time, 29% women, 6% African American, 2% Asian American, 7% Hispanic/Latino, 2% Multiracial, non-Hispanic, 33% international
- 3,041 degree-seeking graduate students
- 57% of applicants admitted
- SAT or ACT (ACT writing optional), application essay required
- 57% graduate within 6 years

General. Founded in 1958. Regionally accredited. **Degrees:** 607 bachelor's awarded; master's, professional, doctoral offered. **ROTC:** Army. **Location:** 76 miles from Orlando. **Calendar:** Semester, limited summer session. **Full-time faculty:** 321 total; 89% have terminal degrees, 22% minority, 25% women. **Part-time faculty:** 241 total; 52% have terminal degrees, 14% minority, 31% women. **Class size:** 49% < 20, 41% 20-39, 6% 40-49, 4% 50-99, less than 1% >100. **Special facilities:** Botanical garden, center for sports and recreation, center for textile arts, art museum, 0.8-m telescope, center for aviation training and research, center for autism treatment, center for science and engineering.

Freshman class profile. 9,303 applied, 5,336 admitted, 645 enrolled.

Mid 50% test scores			
		Rank in top quarter:	59%
SAT critical reading:	520-620	Rank in top tenth:	31%
SAT math:	560-670	Return as sophomores:	79%
ACT composite:	24-29	Out-of-state:	53%
GPA 3.75 or higher:	49%	Live on campus:	84%
GPA 3.50-3.74:	18%	International:	27%
GPA 3.0-3.49:	27%	Fraternities:	10%
GPA 2.0-2.99:	6%	Sororities:	3%

Basis for selection. Applications reviewed with reference to specific degree programs or for admission to first-year programs in engineering, science and general studies. High school curriculum, GPA, class rank, SAT/ACT, teachers' recommendations, experiential essay, special classes, clubs or teams that involve research projects/opportunities, and advanced problem-solving techniques important. Interview recommended. **Home schooled:** Transcript of courses and grades required. Self-descriptive 1-page essay, proof of research project participation required. SAT Subject Test strongly recommended (English composition, Math Level II, any sciences related to desired area of study).

High school preparation. College-preparatory program recommended. 16 units required; 22 recommended. Required and recommended units include English 4, mathematics 3-4, social studies 2, history 2, science 3-4 (laboratory 3), foreign language 2, computer science 2 and academic electives 2.

2015-2016 Annual costs. Tuition/fees: $39,290. Room/board: $13,500. Books/supplies: $1,200. Personal expenses: $1,500.

2015-2016 Financial aid. Need-based: 439 full-time freshmen applied for aid; 383 deemed to have need; 383 received aid. Average need met was 87%. Average scholarship/grant was $27,045; average loan $3,436. 74% of total undergraduate aid awarded as scholarships/grants, 26% as loans/jobs. **Non-need-based:** Awarded to 2,725 full-time undergraduates, including 622 freshmen. Scholarships awarded for academics, alumni affiliation, athletics, music/drama, ROTC, state residency.

Application procedures. Admission: Priority date 2/1; no deadline. No application fee. Admission notification on a rolling basis beginning on or about 7/1. Must reply by May 1 or within 4 week(s) if notified thereafter. **Financial aid:** Priority date 3/1; no closing date. FAFSA, CSS PROFILE required. Applicants notified on a rolling basis starting 2/15; must reply by 5/1 or within 4 week(s) of notification.

Academics. Special study options: Accelerated study, combined bachelor's/graduate degree, cooperative education, cross-registration, distance learning, double major, dual enrollment of high school students, ESL, independent study, internships, student-designed major, study abroad, teacher certification program. Dual degrees in computer engineering/electrical engineering, chemical engineering/chemistry, molecular/marine biology. **Credit/placement by examination:** AP, CLEP, IB, institutional tests. **Support services:** Learning center, remedial instruction, study skills assistance, tutoring, writing center.

Majors. Biology: General, aquatic, biochemistry, biomedical sciences, conservation, marine, molecular. **Business:** Accounting, business admin, international, management information systems, marketing. **Communications:** General. **Computer sciences:** Computer science. **Conservation:** Environmental science. **Education:** Biology, chemistry, earth science, mathematics, middle, physics, science. **Engineering:** General, aerospace, biomedical, chemical, civil, computer, electrical, mechanical, ocean, software. **Liberal arts:** Humanities. **Math:** General, applied. **Parks/recreation:** Sports admin. **Physical sciences:** General, chemistry, meteorology, oceanography, physics, planetary. **Psychology:** General, forensic.

Most popular majors. Biology 9%, business/marketing 10%, engineering/engineering technologies 47%, psychology 7%, trade and industry 9%.

Technology on campus. 415 workstations in library, computer center, student center. Dormitories wired for high-speed internet access and linked to campus network. Commuter students can connect to campus network. Online course registration, online library, helpline, student web hosting, wireless network available.

Student life. Freshman orientation: Mandatory. Preregistration for classes offered. Held over three days in late August. **Policies:** Function in accordance with written constitution and bylaws approved by Dean of Students. **Housing:** Guaranteed on-campus for freshmen. Coed dorms, apartments, fraternity/sorority housing available. $200 fully refundable deposit, deadline 1/1. **Activities:** Bands, campus ministries, choral groups, dance, drama, film society, international student organizations, literary magazine, music ensembles, musical theater, radio station, student government, student newspaper, TV station, Newman Club, InterVarsity Christian Fellowship, Taiwanese student association, Saudi student union, National Society of Black Engineers, Society of Women Engineers, Korean student association, Caribbean students association, Chinese student and scholar association, Muslim student association.

Athletics. NCAA. **Intercollegiate:** Baseball M, basketball, cross-country, golf, lacrosse M, rowing (crew), soccer, softball W, swimming, tennis, track and field, volleyball W. **Intramural:** Badminton, bowling, football (non-tackle), soccer, softball, tennis, ultimate frisbee, volleyball, water polo. **Team name:** Panthers.

Student services. Alcohol/substance abuse counseling, chaplain/spiritual director, career counseling, student employment services, financial aid counseling, health services, personal counseling, veterans' counselor. **Physically disabled:** Services for visually, speech, hearing impaired.

Contact. E-mail: admission@fit.edu
Phone: (321) 674-8030 Toll-free number: (800) 888-4348
Fax: (321) 674-8004
Michael Perry, Director of Undergraduate Admission, Florida Institute of Technology, 150 West University Boulevard, Melbourne, FL 32901-6975

Florida International University
Miami, Florida   **CB member**
www.fiu.edu   **CB code: 5206**

- Public 4-year university
- Commuter campus in very large city
- 40,225 degree-seeking undergraduates: 37% part-time, 56% women, 12% African American, 3% Asian American, 67% Hispanic/Latino, 2% Multi-racial, non-Hispanic, 6% international
- 8,470 degree-seeking graduate students
- 50% of applicants admitted
- SAT or ACT with writing required
- 58% graduate within 6 years

General. Founded in 1965. Regionally accredited. **Degrees:** 9,051 bachelor's, 65 associate awarded; master's, professional, doctoral offered. **ROTC:** Army, Air Force. **Location:** 10 miles from downtown Miami. **Calendar:** Semester, extensive summer session. **Full-time faculty:** 1,232 total; 87% have terminal degrees, 46% minority, 42% women. **Part-time faculty:** 1,120 total; 44% have terminal degrees, 50% minority, 49% women. **Class size:** 21% < 20, 42% 20-39, 16% 40-49, 16% 50-99, 6% >100. **Special facilities:** Nature preserve, Biscayne Bay preserve, art museum, astroscience center, discovery lab, Wall of Wind and restaurant management lab.

Freshman class profile. 15,834 applied, 7,874 admitted, 2,835 enrolled.

Mid 50% test scores			
SAT critical reading:	520-600	**GPA 3.0-3.49:**	12%
SAT math:	510-600	**Rank in top quarter:**	46%
SAT writing:	510-590	**Rank in top tenth:**	18%
ACT composite:	23-26	**Out-of-state:**	4%
GPA 3.75 or higher:	65%	**Live on campus:**	22%
GPA 3.50-3.74:	23%	**International:**	5%

Basis for selection. Student's strong preparation; includes review of all academic credentials and complete file. Audition required for music performance and theater. Portfolio required for art and architecture. **Home schooled:** State high school equivalency certificate required. GED required if equivalency certificate is not available. **Learning Disabled:** Assistance provided to applicants with disabilities who do not meet standard admission criteria by seeking admission consideration based on disability when appropriate.

High school preparation. College-preparatory program required. 18 units required; 22 recommended. Required and recommended units include English 4, mathematics 4, social studies 3, science 3 (laboratory 2), foreign language 2 and academic electives 2-4.

2015-2016 Annual costs. Tuition/fees: $6,556; $18,955 out-of-state. Room/board: $10,870. Books/supplies: $1,462. Personal expenses: $2,456.

2014-2015 Financial aid. **Need-based:** 2,817 full-time freshmen applied for aid; 2,790 deemed to have need; 2,563 received aid. Average need met was 27%. Average scholarship/grant was $6,311; average loan $2,065. 61% of total undergraduate aid awarded as scholarships/grants, 39% as loans/jobs. **Non-need-based:** Awarded to 8,068 full-time undergraduates, including 1,960 freshmen. Scholarships awarded for academics, art, athletics, minority status, music/drama, state residency.

Application procedures. **Admission:** Priority date 5/1; deadline 11/1. $30 fee, may be waived for applicants with need. Application must be submitted online. Admission notification on a rolling basis. Must reply by May 1 or within 2 week(s) if notified thereafter. **Financial aid:** Priority date 3/1, closing date 5/15. FAFSA required. Applicants notified on a rolling basis; must reply by 5/1.

Academics. **Special study options:** Accelerated study, combined bachelor's/graduate degree, cooperative education, distance learning, double major, dual enrollment of high school students, exchange student, honors, independent study, internships, study abroad, teacher certification program, weekend college. **Credit/placement by examination:** AP, CLEP, IB, SAT, ACT, institutional tests. **Support services:** Learning center, pre-admission summer program, study skills assistance, tutoring, writing center.

Honors college/program. 3.5 weighted GPA, and 1850 SAT/28 ACT, 500 word essay required.

Majors. **Architecture:** Architecture, landscape. **Area/ethnic studies:** Asian, women's. **Biology:** General, marine. **Business:** Accounting, business admin, finance, hospitality admin, human resources, international, marketing, real estate. **Communications:** Communications/speech/rhetoric, media studies. **Computer sciences:** General, information technology. **Conservation:** Environmental studies. **Education:** Art, early childhood, elementary, physical, special ed. **Engineering:** Biomedical, civil, computer, electrical, environmental, mechanical. **English:** English lit. **Foreign languages:** French, Italian, Portuguese, Spanish. **Health services:** Dietetics, health care admin, nursing (RN). **History:** General. **Human services:** General, social work. **Liberal arts:** Arts/sciences. **Math:** General, statistics. **Parks/recreation:** Facilities management. **Philosophy/religion:** Philosophy, religion. **Physical sciences:** Chemistry, geology, physics. **Protective services:** Criminal justice. **Psychology:** General. **Social sciences:** Economics, geography, international relations, political science, sociology. **Visual/performing arts:** Art, art history/conservation, dramatic, music, studio arts.

Most popular majors. Biology 6%, business/marketing 29%, health sciences 7%, psychology 12%, security/protective services 6%, social sciences 9%.

Technology on campus. Dormitories wired for high-speed internet access and linked to campus network. Commuter students can connect to campus network. Online course registration, online library, helpline, repair service, wireless network available.

Student life. **Freshman orientation:** Mandatory, $100 fee. Preregistration for classes offered. Two-day overnight program. **Housing:** Coed dorms, apartments, fraternity/sorority housing available. $100 nonrefundable deposit. **Activities:** Bands, campus ministries, choral groups, drama, international student organizations, music ensembles, Model UN, opera, radio station, student government, student newspaper, symphony orchestra, over 150 student organizations available.

Athletics. NCAA. **Intercollegiate:** Baseball M, basketball, cross-country, diving W, football (tackle) M, golf W, soccer, softball, swimming W, tennis W, track and field, volleyball W. **Intramural:** Badminton, basketball, cross-country, football (non-tackle), golf W, racquetball, sailing, soccer, softball, swimming, table tennis, tennis, ultimate frisbee, volleyball, weight lifting. **Team name:** Golden Panthers.

Student services. Adult student services, alcohol/substance abuse counseling, career counseling, student employment services, financial aid counseling, health services, minority student services, on-campus daycare, personal counseling, placement for graduates, veterans' counselor, women's services. **Physically disabled:** Services for visually, speech, hearing impaired.

Contact. E-mail: admiss@fiu.edu
Phone: (305) 348-2363 Fax: (305) 348-3648
Luisa Havens, Director, Florida International University, Modesto Maidique Campus, PC 140, Miami, FL 33199

Florida Memorial University
Miami Gardens, Florida
www.fmuniv.edu   **CB code: 5217**

- Private 4-year liberal arts college affiliated with the American Baptist Churches in the USA
- Residential campus in very large city
- 1,399 degree-seeking undergraduates
- Application essay required

General. Founded in 1879. Regionally accredited. New sporting facilities. **Degrees:** 209 bachelor's awarded; master's offered. **ROTC:** Army. **Location:** 15 miles from downtown Miami. **Calendar:** Semester, limited summer session. **Full-time faculty:** 92 total. **Part-time faculty:** 51 total. **Class size:** 70% < 20, 28% 20-39, 1% 40-49, less than 1% 50-99. **Special facilities:** Black archives, airway science building with simulator and air traffic control tower.

Freshman class profile.

GPA 3.75 or higher:	1%	**GPA 2.0-2.99:**	71%
GPA 3.50-3.74:	5%	**Out-of-state:**	20%
GPA 3.0-3.49:	15%	**Live on campus:**	80%

Basis for selection. 2.0 GPA required. School achievement record, test scores, interview, recommendations, and alumni affiliation considered. SAT or ACT recommended. Interview recommended.

High school preparation. 15 units recommended. Recommended units include English 4, mathematics 4, social studies 2, science 3 and foreign language 2. College-preparatory program strongly recommended.

2015-2016 Annual costs. Tuition/fees: $15,280. Room/board: $5,040. Books/supplies: $1,500. Personal expenses: $3,500.

Financial aid. **Additional information:** Need-based financial aid available to part-time students taking 6 credits or more per semester.

Application procedures. **Admission:** No deadline. $50 fee, may be waived for applicants with need. Admission notification on a rolling basis. **Financial aid:** No deadline. Applicants notified on a rolling basis; must reply within 2 week(s) of notification.

Academics. **Special study options:** Combined bachelor's/graduate degree, cooperative education, double major, dual enrollment of high school students, honors, independent study, internships, liberal arts/career combination, study abroad, teacher certification program, weekend college. **Credit/placement by examination:** AP, CLEP, institutional tests. 30 credit hours maximum toward bachelor's degree. **Support services:** Learning center, pre-admission summer program, remedial instruction, study skills assistance, tutoring, writing center.

Majors. **Biology:** General. **Business:** Accounting, business admin, management information systems. **Computer sciences:** General, computer science. **Education:** Elementary, physical. **English:** English lit. **Health services:** Clinical lab science. **Human services:** General. **Math:** General. **Psychology:** General. **Social sciences:** Sociology. **Visual/performing arts:** Music.

Most popular majors. Biology 9%, business/marketing 17%, computer/information sciences 11%, education 21%, psychology 9%, social sciences 16%.

Technology on campus. 300 workstations in dormitories, library, computer center, student center. Dormitories wired for high-speed internet access and linked to campus network. Commuter students can connect to campus network. Online library, helpline, repair service, wireless network available.

Student life. **Freshman orientation:** Mandatory. Preregistration for classes offered. **Housing:** Guaranteed on-campus for freshmen. Single-sex dorms available. **Activities:** Jazz band, choral groups, international student organizations, music ensembles, musical theater, student government, student newspaper, TV station, Christian student union, broadcasting club, Junior NAACP, Toastmasters, Professional Women of Tomorrow.

Athletics. NAIA. **Intercollegiate:** Baseball M, basketball, track and field, volleyball W. **Intramural:** Baseball M, basketball, soccer M, softball W, swimming, tennis, volleyball. **Team name:** Figthing Lions.

Student services. Chaplain/spiritual director, career counseling, student employment services, health services, minority student services, personal counseling, placement for graduates.

Contact. E-mail: admit@fmuniv.edu
Phone: (305) 626-3750 Fax: (305) 623-1462
Peggy Martin, Director of Admissions, Florida Memorial University, 15800 NW 42nd Avenue, Miami Gardens, FL 33054

Florida Southern College
Lakeland, Florida
www.flsouthern.edu

CB member
CB code: 5218

- Private 4-year liberal arts college affiliated with the United Methodist Church
- Residential campus in small city
- 2,306 degree-seeking undergraduates: 2% part-time, 63% women, 5% African American, 2% Asian American, 11% Hispanic/Latino, 1% Native American, 2% Multi-racial, non-Hispanic, 5% international
- 310 degree-seeking graduate students
- 45% of applicants admitted
- SAT or ACT (ACT writing optional), application essay required
- 57% graduate within 6 years; 26% enter graduate study

General. Founded in 1885. Regionally accredited. Transitional school for gifted elementary-age students with dyslexia located on-campus. **Degrees:** 598 bachelor's awarded; master's, doctoral offered. **ROTC:** Army, Air Force. **Location:** 30 miles from Tampa, 40 miles from Orlando. **Calendar:** Semester, limited summer session. **Full-time faculty:** 132 total; 80% have terminal degrees, 17% minority, 48% women. **Part-time faculty:** 124 total; 30% have terminal degrees, 13% minority, 55% women. **Class size:** 59% < 20, 36% 20-39, 5% 40-49. **Special facilities:** Collection of Frank Lloyd Wright architecture, center for learning and literacy, tourism and education center, Melvin gallery, planetarium, greenhouse, three gardens.

Freshman class profile. 6,190 applied, 2,806 admitted, 698 enrolled.

Mid 50% test scores		Rank in top quarter:	59%
SAT critical reading:	520-620	Rank in top tenth:	24%
SAT math:	530-610	End year in good standing:	93%
SAT writing:	500-600	Return as sophomores:	80%
ACT composite:	24-29	Out-of-state:	41%
GPA 3.75 or higher:	49%	Live on campus:	95%
GPA 3.50-3.74:	19%	International:	4%
GPA 3.0-3.49:	26%	Fraternities:	35%
GPA 2.0-2.99:	6%	Sororities:	34%

Basis for selection. School achievement record most important, followed by test scores and recommendations. Character and motivation, demonstrated leadership and/or service, and extracurricular activities also important. Interview recommended. Audition required for music; audition recommended (required for scholarship consideration) for theater majors. Portfolio recommended (required for scholarship consideration) for art majors.

High school preparation. College-preparatory program required. 18 units required. Required and recommended units include English 4, mathematics 3, social studies 3, history 3, science 2 (laboratory 2), foreign language 2 and academic electives 1.

2015-2016 Annual costs. Tuition/fees: $31,460. Room/board: $10,210. Books/supplies: $1,222. Personal expenses: $1,608.

2015-2016 Financial aid. **Need-based:** 633 full-time freshmen applied for aid; 505 deemed to have need; 505 received aid. Average need met was 75%. Average scholarship/grant was $20,621; average loan $5,366. 68% of total undergraduate aid awarded as scholarships/grants, 32% as loans/jobs. **Non-need-based:** Awarded to 1,871 full-time undergraduates, including 530 freshmen. Scholarships awarded for academics, alumni affiliation, art, athletics, job skills, leadership, minority status, music/drama, religious affiliation, ROTC, state residency.

Application procedures. **Admission:** Priority date 3/1; no deadline. $30 fee, may be waived for applicants with need, free for online applicants. Admission notification on a rolling basis beginning on or about 1/15. Must reply by May 1 or within 2 week(s) if notified thereafter. Housing deposit refundable through 5/1 for regular decision students; not refundable for early decision students. **Financial aid:** Priority date 3/1, closing date 7/1. FAFSA, institutional form required. Applicants notified on a rolling basis starting 3/1; must reply within 3 week(s) of notification.

Academics. **Special study options:** Accelerated study, combined bachelor's/graduate degree, distance learning, double major, dual enrollment of high school students, external degree, honors, independent study, internships, liberal arts/career combination, New York semester, student-designed major, study abroad, teacher certification program, United Nations semester, Washington semester. BS Business Administration/MBA 3+2 (accelerated). BS Accounting/Master of Accountancy 3+2. FSC Pre-Med Honor's Program with USF. College of Medicine Medical Education Program. FSC-Duke University Cooperative 3+2 Master of Environmental Management or Forestry. Dual Degree Program with Washington University, St. Louis in Engineering. 3+/4+ Pharmacy, 3+4/4+4 DO, 4+4 Dental with Lake Erie College of Osteopathic Medicine. **Credit/placement by examination:** AP, CLEP, IB, SAT, ACT. 60 credit hours maximum toward bachelor's degree. **Support services:** Pre-admission summer program, reduced course load, study skills assistance, tutoring, writing center.

Majors. **Biology:** General, Biochemistry/molecular biology, biotechnology, exercise physiology, marine. **Business:** Accounting, business admin, small business admin. **Communications:** Media studies, organizational, persuasive communications, political, sports. **Computer sciences:** Computer science. **Conservation:** Environmental studies. **Education:** Art, elementary, music. **English:** Creative writing, general lit. **Foreign languages:** Spanish. **Health services:** Athletic training, health care admin, nursing (RN), predental, premedicine, preveterinary. **History:** General. **Liberal arts:** Humanities. **Math:** General. **Parks/recreation:** Sports admin. **Philosophy/religion:** Philosophy, religion. **Physical sciences:** Chemistry. **Psychology:** General. **Social sciences:** General, criminology, economics, political economy, political science. **Visual/performing arts:** Acting, art history/conservation, dance, digital arts, dramatic, music, music management, music performance, musical theater, studio arts, theater design.

Most popular majors. Biology 9%, business/marketing 25%, communications/journalism 9%, education 9%, health sciences 13%, psychology 6%, social sciences 12%, visual/performing arts 7%.

Technology on campus. 470 workstations in library, computer center. Dormitories wired for high-speed internet access and linked to campus network. Commuter students can connect to campus network. Online course registration, online library, helpline, wireless network available.

Student life. **Freshman orientation:** Mandatory, $100 fee. Preregistration for classes offered. Four-day program held prior to start of Fall classes.

Housing: Guaranteed on-campus for all undergraduates. Coed dorms, single-sex dorms, special housing for disabled, apartments, fraternity/sorority housing, themed housing, wellness housing available. $500 fully refundable deposit, deadline 5/1. **Activities:** Bands, campus ministries, choral groups, dance, drama, international student organizations, literary magazine, music ensembles, musical theater, opera, student government, student newspaper, symphony orchestra, TV station, Wesley Fellowship, Fellowship of Christian Athletes, Beyond Campus Ministries, Jewish student association, Sandwich Ministry to the homeless, multicultural student council, Catholic Student Ministries, student organization of Latinos.

Athletics. NCAA. **Intercollegiate:** Baseball M, basketball, cross-country, golf, lacrosse, soccer, softball W, swimming, tennis, track and field, volleyball W. **Intramural:** Basketball, bowling, football (non-tackle), golf, sand volleyball, soccer, softball, swimming, table tennis, tennis, ultimate frisbee, volleyball, water polo. **Team name:** Moccasins.

Student services. Adult student services, alcohol/substance abuse counseling, chaplain/spiritual director, career counseling, student employment services, financial aid counseling, health services, minority student services, personal counseling, placement for graduates.

Contact. E-mail: fscadm@flsouthern.edu
Phone: (863) 680-4131 Toll-free number: (800) 274-4131
Fax: (863) 680-4120
Arden Mitchell, Director of Admission, Florida Southern College, 111 Lake Hollingsworth Drive, Lakeland, FL 33801-5698

Florida State University

Tallahassee, Florida
www.fsu.edu

CB member
CB code: 5219

- Public 4-year university
- Residential campus in small city
- 32,290 degree-seeking undergraduates: 10% part-time, 55% women, 8% African American, 2% Asian American, 19% Hispanic/Latino, 3% Multiracial, non-Hispanic, 1% international
- 7,805 degree-seeking graduate students
- 56% of applicants admitted
- SAT or ACT with writing, application essay required
- 79% graduate within 6 years

General. Founded in 1851. Regionally accredited. **Degrees:** 8,421 bachelor's awarded; master's, professional, doctoral offered. **ROTC:** Army, Naval, Air Force. **Location:** 191 miles from Pensacola, 163 miles from Jacksonville. **Calendar:** Semester, extensive summer session. **Full-time faculty:** 1,382 total; 92% have terminal degrees, 20% minority, 39% women. **Part-time faculty:** 376 total; 92% have terminal degrees, 13% minority, 53% women. **Class size:** 33% < 20, 41% 20-39, 8% 40-49, 11% 50-99, 7% >100. **Special facilities:** Marine laboratory/aquarium, institute of molecular biophysics, national high magnetic field laboratory, music research center, accelerator, oceanographic institute, planetarium, reservation, golf course, Middle East center, institute of science and public affairs, center for the advancement of human rights.

Freshman class profile. 29,828 applied, 16,674 admitted, 6,100 enrolled.

Mid 50% test scores		Rank in top quarter:	75%
SAT critical reading:	560-640	Rank in top tenth:	38%
SAT math:	560-640	Return as sophomores:	93%
SAT writing:	560-640	Out-of-state:	11%
ACT composite:	25-29	Live on campus:	63%
GPA 3.75 or higher:	66%	International:	1%
GPA 3.50-3.74:	21%	Fraternities:	17%
GPA 3.0-3.49:	12%	Sororities:	25%
GPA 2.0-2.99:	1%		

Basis for selection. 3.8-4.3 academic GPA; 26-30 ACT composite; equivalent SAT total. In addition to the academic profile, a variety of other factors are also considered in the review process. These include the written essay, the rigor and quality of courses and curriculum, grade trends, class rank, strength of senior schedule in academic subjects, math level in the senior year, and number of years in a sequential world language. Audition required of music, dance, BFA theater majors. Portfolio required of BFA art, interior design majors. Departmental application required for motion picture, television, and recording art programs. **Home schooled:** Statement describing home school structure and mission, transcript of courses and grades required. Must provide detailed course syllabi with complete course description and names of textbooks used.

High school preparation. College-preparatory program required. 19 units required; 23 recommended. Required and recommended units include English 4, mathematics 4, social studies 1-2, history 2, science 3-4 (laboratory 2),

foreign language 2-4 and academic electives 3. Math courses must be algebra I and above; 2 units of same world language required; at least 4 units English with substantial writing requirements; social studies must include history. Additional consideration given for completion of higher level courses (AP, IB, honors, dual enrollment, calculus and/or foreign language IV or V) and for completion of 4 or more senior academic courses. The typical student accepted to Florida State has 4.5 units of English, 5.5 units of math, 4.5 units of natural science, 5 units of social science, and 3.5 units of world language.

2015-2016 Annual costs. Tuition/fees: $6,507; $21,673 out-of-state. Room/board: $10,264. Books/supplies: $1,000. Personal expenses: $2,728.

2014-2015 Financial aid. **Need-based:** 4,952 full-time freshmen applied for aid; 2,999 deemed to have need; 2,966 received aid. Average need met was 62%. Average scholarship/grant was $8,203; average loan $3,581. 56% of total undergraduate aid awarded as scholarships/grants, 44% as loans/jobs. **Non-need-based:** Awarded to 13,570 full-time undergraduates, including 2,933 freshmen. Scholarships awarded for academics, art, athletics, leadership, music/drama, ROTC, state residency.

Application procedures. **Admission:** Priority date 10/15; deadline 1/13 (receipt date). $30 fee. Application must be submitted online. Admission notification by 3/16. Must reply by May 1 or within 2 week(s) if notified thereafter. Those applying before 10/15 who are denied admission are given additional opportunities to improve application standing. **Financial aid:** No deadline. FAFSA required. Applicants notified on a rolling basis starting 4/5.

Academics. 2+2 distance learning available in cooperation with selected Florida community colleges includes programs in computer science, interdisciplinary social sciences, and nursing (RN to BSN). **Special study options:** Accelerated study, combined bachelor's/graduate degree, cooperative education, cross-registration, distance learning, double major, dual enrollment of high school students, ESL, honors, independent study, internships, study abroad, teacher certification program. Cooperative programs with Florida Agricultural and Mechanical University and Tallahassee Community College; degree in three years; International year abroad, year-round study abroad in England, Italy, Panama, Spain; summer study abroad in Australia, Brazil, China, Costa Rica, Croatia, Czech Republic, Ecuador, England, France, Ireland, Italy, Japan, Netherlands, Russia, Switzerland. **Credit/placement by examination:** AP, CLEP, IB, SAT, ACT, institutional tests. 30 credit hours maximum toward associate degree, 45 toward bachelor's. English AP credit not awarded for more than 1 exam. **Support services:** Learning center, reduced course load, study skills assistance, tutoring, writing center.

Majors. **Area/ethnic studies:** African-American, Asian, Near/Middle Eastern, Russian/Eastern European/Eurasian, Russian/Slavic. **Biology:** General, biochemistry, marine. **Business:** Accounting, actuarial science, business admin, finance, hospitality admin, human resources, insurance, international, management information systems, marketing, real estate, taxation. **Communications:** Advertising, public relations. **Computer sciences:** General, computer science. **Conservation:** Environmental science. **Education:** Early childhood, elementary, English, music, social science, special ed. **Engineering:** Chemical, civil, computer, electrical, environmental, industrial, mechanical, software. **English:** English lit. **Foreign languages:** Ancient Greek, Chinese, classics, French, German, Italian, Japanese, Latin, Russian, Spanish. **Health services:** Athletic training, audiology/speech pathology, dietetics, music therapy, nursing (RN), predental, premedicine, prepharmacy, preveterinary. **History:** General. **Human services:** Social work. **Liberal arts:** Humanities. **Math:** General, applied, computational, statistics. **Parks/recreation:** Sports admin. **Philosophy/religion:** Philosophy, religion. **Physical sciences:** Atmospheric science, chemistry, geology, physics. **Protective services:** Criminal justice. **Psychology:** General. **Social sciences:** General, applied economics, criminology, economics, geography, international relations, political science, sociology, U.S. government. **Visual/performing arts:** Acting, art history/conservation, cinematography, dance, dramatic, interior design, jazz, music, music theory/composition, musical theater, piano/keyboard, stringed instruments, studio arts, theater design, voice/opera. **Work/family studies:** Family studies.

Most popular majors. Biology 8%, business/marketing 18%, psychology 6%, security/protective services 7%, social sciences 17%.

Technology on campus. PC or laptop required. 2,958 workstations in dormitories, library, computer center, student center. Dormitories wired for high-speed internet access and linked to campus network. Commuter students can connect to campus network. Online course registration, online library, helpline, repair service, student web hosting, wireless network available.

Student life. **Freshman orientation:** Mandatory, $105 fee. Preregistration for classes offered. Held during summer. **Housing:** Coed dorms, special housing for disabled, apartments, fraternity/sorority housing, themed housing, wellness housing available. $225 partly refundable deposit. Honor residences and living and learning communities available. **Activities:** Bands, campus ministries, choral groups, dance, drama, film society, literary magazine, music ensembles, musical theater, opera, radio station, student government, student newspaper, symphony orchestra, TV station, Hillel, Christian student association, Catholic student union, Campus Crusade for Christ, College Democrats,

College Republicans, black student union, Hispanic student union, American civil liberties union.

Athletics. NCAA. **Intercollegiate:** Baseball M, basketball, cheerleading, cross-country, diving, football (tackle) M, golf, soccer W, softball W, swimming, tennis, track and field, volleyball W. **Intramural:** Basketball, bowling, field hockey, football (non-tackle), golf, racquetball, soccer, softball, swimming, table tennis, tennis, ultimate frisbee, volleyball, wrestling. **Team name:** Seminoles.

Student services. Adult student services, alcohol/substance abuse counseling, career counseling, student employment services, financial aid counseling, health services, legal services, minority student services, on-campus daycare, personal counseling, placement for graduates, veterans' counselor, women's services. **Physically disabled:** Services for visually, speech, hearing impaired.

Contact. E-mail: admissions@fsu.edu
Phone: (850) 644-6200 Fax: (850) 644-0197
Janice Finney, Director of Admissions, Florida State University, PO Box 3062400, Tallahassee, FL 32306-2400

Full Sail University
Winter Park, Florida
www.fullsail.edu
CB code: 3164

- For-profit 4-year visual arts and music college
- Commuter campus in very large city
- 17,318 undergraduates

General. Accredited by ACCSC. **Degrees:** 3,652 bachelor's, 137 associate awarded; master's offered. **Location:** 8 miles from Orlando. **Calendar:** Differs by program. **Full-time faculty:** 946 total. **Special facilities:** Recording studios, production suites, sound stages, green screen facility, motion capture production studio, game studio, live venue.

Basis for selection. Open admission, but selective for some programs. Applicants for game design and development bachelor's degree program must have an A average in Algebra II. Geometry, physics and programming experience also recommended. **Home schooled:** Diplomas recognized if applicant's state board of education recognizes them. **Learning Disabled:** Require documentation, not more than 3 years old, describing learning disabilities.

2015-2016 Annual costs. Tuition ranges from $31,000-$77,500 for the entire degree program, including books, lab fees, and other educational charges. Does not include Project LaunchBox - an Apple computer and software package.

Application procedures. Admission: No deadline. $75 fee. Admission notification on a rolling basis. **Financial aid:** No deadline. FAFSA required. Applicants notified on a rolling basis; must reply within 2 week(s) of notification.

Academics. Special study options: Accelerated study, combined bachelor's/graduate degree, cooperative education, internships. **Credit/placement by examination:** AP, CLEP, institutional tests. Students may take test-out exam in each course for which credit is being sought. If credit earned, tuition and program hours reduced accordingly. Minimum of 25% of degree program's semester hours or equivalent must be earned in residence to receive degree. **Support services:** Study skills assistance, tutoring, writing center. Cognitive development course offered at no charge. Tutoring available through Federal Work-Study program.

Majors. Communications technology: Animation/special effects. **Computer sciences:** Web page design. **Visual/performing arts:** Cinematography, game design.

Technology on campus. 56 workstations in library, computer center. Online library, helpline, repair service, wireless network available.

Student life. Freshman orientation: Mandatory. Preregistration for classes offered. **Policies:** Alcohol and drug-free facility. **Activities:** Student government.

Student services. Career counseling, financial aid counseling, placement for graduates.

Contact. E-mail: admissions@fullsail.com
Phone: (407) 679-6333 Toll-free number: (800) 226-7625
Mary Beth Plank-Mezo, Vice President of Admissions, Full Sail University, 3300 University Boulevard, Winter Park, FL 32792-7429

Hobe Sound Bible College
Hobe Sound, Florida
www.hsbc.edu
CB code: 5306

- Private 4-year Bible college affiliated with the interdenominational tradition
- Residential campus in small town
- 59 degree-seeking undergraduates
- SAT or ACT (ACT writing optional) required

General. Founded in 1960. Accredited by ABHE. **Degrees:** 29 bachelor's, 11 associate awarded. **Location:** 25 miles from West Palm Beach. **Calendar:** 4-1-4, limited summer session. **Full-time faculty:** 7 total. **Part-time faculty:** 6 total.

Basis for selection. Recommendations, essay, religious commitment important. **Home schooled:** Must submit official transcripts from reputable organizations documenting completion of all academic coursework required for high school diploma.

2015-2016 Annual costs. Tuition/fees: $6,090. Room/board: $5,840. Books/supplies: $450. Personal expenses: $2,000.

Financial aid. Non-need-based: Scholarships awarded for academics, leadership.

Application procedures. Admission: Closing date 8/25. $25 fee, may be waived for applicants with need. Admission notification on a rolling basis beginning on or about 3/1. **Financial aid:** Closing date 8/1. FAFSA required.

Academics. Double major required of all students in 4-year programs. All students complete major in Bible as well as major in Christian vocational field. **Special study options:** Distance learning, double major, dual enrollment of high school students, ESL, external degree, internships, teacher certification program. **Credit/placement by examination:** AP, CLEP, institutional tests. **Support services:** Reduced course load, remedial instruction.

Majors. Education: Elementary, English, mathematics, music. **Philosophy/religion:** Religion. **Theology:** Bible, missionary, sacred music, theology. **Visual/performing arts:** Music performance, piano/keyboard.

Technology on campus. 10 workstations in computer center.

Student life. Freshman orientation: Mandatory. Preregistration for classes offered. **Policies:** Religious observance required. **Housing:** Guaranteed on-campus for all undergraduates. Single-sex dorms, apartments available. Unmarried students under 25 required to live in campus dormitories or with parents. **Activities:** Concert band, choral groups, music ensembles, student government, Christian service organizations.

Athletics. Intramural: Basketball, football (tackle) M, racquetball, soccer, softball, tennis, volleyball.

Student services. Health services, personal counseling.

Contact. E-mail: admissions@hsbc.edu
Phone: (772) 546-5534 ext. 1015 Toll-free number: (800) 881-5534
Fax: (772) 545-1422
Joanna Wetherald, Director of Admissions, Hobe Sound Bible College, PO Box 1065, Hobe Sound, FL 33475

Hodges University
Naples, Florida
www.hodges.edu
CB code: 5307

- Private 4-year university
- Commuter campus in small city
- 1,476 degree-seeking undergraduates: 33% part-time, 62% women, 13% African American, 2% Asian American, 35% Hispanic/Latino, 1% Multiracial, non-Hispanic
- 236 degree-seeking graduate students

General. Founded in 1990. Regionally accredited. **Degrees:** 252 bachelor's, 166 associate awarded; master's offered. **Location:** 110 miles from Miami, 180 miles from Tampa. **Calendar:** Trimester, extensive summer session. **Full-time faculty:** 59 total; 56% have terminal degrees, 12% minority, 52% women. **Part-time faculty:** 60 total; 38% have terminal degrees, 18% minority, 42% women. **Class size:** 87% < 20, 13% 20-39.

Basis for selection. Essay and interview important; level of interest very important.

2015-2016 Annual costs. Tuition/fees: $16,400. Books/supplies: $1,200. Personal expenses: $2,144.

2015-2016 Financial aid. Need-based: 112 full-time freshmen applied for aid; 101 deemed to have need; 101 received aid. Average need met was 70%. Average scholarship/grant was $3,100; average loan $3,050. 62% of total undergraduate aid awarded as scholarships/grants, 38% as loans/jobs. **Non-need-based:** Awarded to 706 full-time undergraduates, including 73 freshmen. Scholarships awarded for academics.

Application procedures. Admission: No deadline. $20 fee. Admission notification on a rolling basis. **Financial aid:** Priority date 8/15; no closing date. FAFSA required. Applicants notified on a rolling basis starting 7/7.

Academics. Special study options: Accelerated study, cooperative education, distance learning, double major, ESL, independent study, internships, weekend college. **Credit/placement by examination:** AP, CLEP, IB, institutional tests. **Support services:** Remedial instruction, tutoring.

Majors. Business: Accounting, business admin. **Computer sciences:** Information technology. **Health services:** Health care admin. **Protective services:** Criminal justice.

Most popular majors. Business/marketing 38%, computer/information sciences 10%, health sciences 15%, interdisciplinary studies 19%, legal studies 8%, psychology 8%, security/protective services 7%.

Technology on campus. 500 workstations in library, computer center. Wireless network available.

Student life. Freshman orientation: Mandatory. Preregistration for classes offered. **Activities:** Literary magazine.

Student services. Career counseling, financial aid counseling, personal counseling, placement for graduates.

Contact. E-mail: admit@hodges.edu
Phone: (239) 513-1122 Toll-free number: (800) 466-8017
Fax: (239) 513-9071
Brent Passey, Cheif Admissions Officer, Hodges University, 2655 Northbrooke Drive, Naples, FL 34119

International Academy of Design and Technology: Orlando
Orlando, Florida
www.iadt.edu
CB code: 4366

- For-profit 4-year career college
- Very large city
- 460 undergraduates

General. Accredited by ACICS. **Degrees:** 61 bachelor's, 15 associate awarded. **Location:** Downtown. **Calendar:** Quarter, extensive summer session. **Full-time faculty:** 4 total. **Part-time faculty:** 49 total.

Basis for selection. Open admission.

2015-2016 Annual costs. Total program tuition: certificates, $22,400; associate degrees, $32,800; bachelor's degrees, $64,800.

Application procedures. Admission: No deadline. $50 fee. **Financial aid:** No deadline. FAFSA required.

Academics. Special study options: Accelerated study. **Credit/placement by examination:** AP, CLEP. **Support services:** Learning center, remedial instruction, tutoring.

Majors. Business: Fashion, marketing. **Computer sciences:** Computer graphics, webmaster. **Visual/performing arts:** Game design, interior design.

Technology on campus. Online course registration, online library available.

Student life. Freshman orientation: Mandatory. Preregistration for classes offered.

Contact. Phone: (407) 857-2300
Dawn Wolff, Director of Admissions, International Academy of Design and Technology: Orlando, 6039 S Rio Grande Avenue, Orlando, FL 32809

International Academy of Design and Technology: Tampa
Tampa, Florida
www.academy.edu
CB code: 7114

- For-profit 4-year visual arts and technical college
- Commuter campus in very large city
- 600 undergraduates
- Interview required

General. Accredited by ACICS. **Degrees:** 207 bachelor's, 74 associate awarded. **Calendar:** Quarter, extensive summer session. **Full-time faculty:** 9 total. **Part-time faculty:** 76 total.

Basis for selection. Open admission. Essay recommended. **Learning Disabled:** Auxiliary Aid Application available if disability is disclosed.

2015-2016 Annual costs. Associate programs: $32,800. Bachelor's programs: $64,800.

Financial aid. Non-need-based: Scholarships awarded for academics.

Application procedures. Admission: No deadline. $50 fee, may be waived for applicants with need. Admission notification on a rolling basis. **Financial aid:** No deadline. FAFSA required.

Academics. Special study options: Accelerated study, cooperative education, distance learning, independent study, internships, study abroad. **Credit/placement by examination:** AP, CLEP, IB, institutional tests. 67 credit hours maximum toward associate degree, 135 toward bachelor's. **Support services:** Learning center, study skills assistance, tutoring.

Majors. Business: Merchandising. **Communications technology:** Animation/special effects. **Computer sciences:** Web page design. **Visual/performing arts:** Digital arts, fashion design, film/cinema/video, game design, graphic design, interior design, photography.

Technology on campus. Wireless network available.

Student life. Freshman orientation: Available. Preregistration for classes offered.

Student services. Adult student services, student employment services, financial aid counseling, placement for graduates, veterans' counselor.

Contact. E-mail: admissions@academy.edu
Phone: (813) 881-0007 Toll-free number: (800) 222-3369
Fax: (813) 881-0008
Brent Passey, Vice President of Admissions and Marketing, International Academy of Design and Technology: Tampa, 5104 Eisenhower Boulevard, Tampa, FL 33634

ITT Technical Institute: Ft. Lauderdale
Ft. Lauderdale, Florida
www.itt-tech.edu
CB code: 2700

- For-profit 4-year technical college
- Commuter campus in small city
- 552 undergraduates
- Interview required

General. Accredited by ACICS. **Degrees:** 38 bachelor's, 142 associate awarded. **Calendar:** Quarter, extensive summer session. **Full-time faculty:** 13 total. **Part-time faculty:** 69 total.

Basis for selection. Satisfactory scores from on-site tests in English and mathematics required.

2015-2016 Annual costs. Per-credit-hour charge, $493; academic fee, $200. Certain programs require purchase of tools, which range from $150 to $655. All costs subject to change.

Application procedures. Admission: No deadline. $100 fee. Admission notification on a rolling basis. **Financial aid:** No deadline. FAFSA, institutional form required. Applicants notified on a rolling basis.

Academics. Credit/placement by examination: AP, CLEP. **Support services:** Learning center, tutoring.

Majors. Business: Business admin, construction management. **Computer sciences:** Security. **Protective services:** Law enforcement admin.

Technology on campus. Online library available.

Student life. Freshman orientation: Available. Preregistration for classes offered.

Student services. Career counseling, student employment services, placement for graduates.

Contact. Phone: (954) 476-9300 Toll-free number: (800) 488-7797 Britt Carpenter, Director of Recruitment, ITT Technical Institute: Ft. Lauderdale, 3401 South University Drive, Ft. Lauderdale, FL 33328

ITT Technical Institute: Jacksonville
Jacksonville, Florida
www.itt-tech.edu   **CB code: 2716**

- For-profit 4-year technical college
- Commuter campus in very large city
- 603 undergraduates
- Interview required

General. Accredited by ACICS. **Degrees:** 33 bachelor's, 145 associate awarded. **Calendar:** Quarter, extensive summer session. **Full-time faculty:** 14 total. **Part-time faculty:** 81 total.

Basis for selection. Satisfactory scores from on-site tests in English and mathematics required.

2015-2016 Annual costs. Per-credit-hour charge, $493; academic fee, $200. Certain programs require purchase of tools, which range from $150 to $655. All costs subject to change.

Application procedures. Admission: No deadline. No application fee. Admission notification on a rolling basis. **Financial aid:** No deadline. FAFSA, institutional form required. Applicants notified on a rolling basis.

Academics. Credit/placement by examination: AP, CLEP. **Support services:** Learning center, tutoring.

Majors. Business: Business admin. **Computer sciences:** Security. **Protective services:** Law enforcement admin.

Technology on campus. Online library available.

Student life. Freshman orientation: Available. Preregistration for classes offered.

Student services. Career counseling, student employment services, placement for graduates.

Contact. Phone: (904) 573-9100 Toll-free number: (800) 318-1264 Jorge Torres, Director of Recruitment, ITT Technical Institute: Jacksonville, 7011 A.C. Skinner Parkway, Suite 140, Jacksonville, FL 32256

ITT Technical Institute: Lake Mary
Lake Mary, Florida
www.itt-tech.edu

- For-profit 4-year technical college
- Commuter campus in large town
- 382 undergraduates

General. Accredited by ACICS. **Degrees:** 24 bachelor's, 75 associate awarded. **Calendar:** Quarter. **Full-time faculty:** 13 total. **Part-time faculty:** 51 total.

Basis for selection. Additional requirements for some programs.

2015-2016 Annual costs. Per-credit-hour charge, $493; academic fee, $200. Certain programs require purchase of tools, which range from $150 to $655. All costs subject to change.

Academics. Credit/placement by examination: AP, CLEP.

Majors. Business: Business admin, construction management. **Communications technology:** Animation/special effects. **Computer sciences:** Security. **Protective services:** Law enforcement admin.

Contact. Phone: (407) 660-2900 Toll-free number: (866) 489-8441 Fax: (407) 660-2566 Larry Johnson, Director of Recruitment, ITT Technical Institute: Lake Mary, 1400 International Parkway South, Lake Mary, FL 32746

ITT Technical Institute: Miami
Miami, Florida
www.itt-tech.edu   **CB code: 2733**

- For-profit 4-year technical college
- Commuter campus in large city
- 440 undergraduates
- Interview required

General. Accredited by ACICS. **Degrees:** 65 bachelor's, 153 associate awarded. **Calendar:** Quarter, extensive summer session. **Full-time faculty:** 12 total. **Part-time faculty:** 48 total.

Basis for selection. Satisfactory scores from on-site tests in English and mathematics required.

2015-2016 Annual costs. Per-credit-hour charge, $493; academic fee, $200. Certain programs require purchase of tools, which range from $150 to $655. All costs subject to change.

Application procedures. Admission: No deadline. No application fee. Admission notification on a rolling basis. **Financial aid:** No deadline. FAFSA, institutional form required. Applicants notified on a rolling basis.

Academics. Credit/placement by examination: AP, CLEP. **Support services:** Learning center, tutoring.

Majors. Business: Accounting technology, business admin, construction management. **Computer sciences:** Security. **Protective services:** Law enforcement admin.

Technology on campus. Online library available.

Student life. Freshman orientation: Available. Preregistration for classes offered.

Student services. Career counseling, student employment services, placement for graduates.

Contact. Phone: (305) 477-3080 Alan Arellano, Director of Recruitment, ITT Technical Institute: Miami, 7955 NW 12th Street, Suite 119, Miami, FL 33126

ITT Technical Institute: Tampa
Tampa, Florida
www.itt-tech.edu   **CB code: 2145**

- For-profit 4-year technical college
- Commuter campus in large city
- 471 undergraduates
- Interview required

General. Founded in 1981. Accredited by ACICS. **Degrees:** 21 bachelor's, 115 associate awarded. **Calendar:** Quarter, extensive summer session. **Full-time faculty:** 21 total. **Part-time faculty:** 53 total.

Basis for selection. Satisfactory scores from on-site English and mathematics tests required.

2015-2016 Annual costs. Per-credit-hour charge, $493; academic fee, $200. Certain programs require purchase of tools, which range from $150 to $655. All costs subject to change.

Application procedures. Admission: No deadline. No application fee. Admission notification on a rolling basis. **Financial aid:** No deadline. FAFSA, institutional form required. Applicants notified on a rolling basis.

Academics. Credit/placement by examination: AP, CLEP. **Support services:** Learning center, tutoring.

Majors. Business: Construction management. **Communications technology:** Animation/special effects. **Computer sciences:** Security. **Protective services:** Law enforcement admin.

Technology on campus. Online library available.

Student life. Freshman orientation: Available. Preregistration for classes offered.

Student services. Career counseling, student employment services, placement for graduates.

Contact. Phone: (813) 885-2244 Toll-free number: (800) 825-2831 Joe Rostkowski, Director of Recruitment, ITT Technical Institute: Tampa, 4809 Memorial Highway, Tampa, FL 33634

Jacksonville University
Jacksonville, Florida
www.ju.edu

CB member
CB code: 5331

- Private 4-year university and liberal arts college
- Residential campus in very large city
- 2,964 degree-seeking undergraduates: 31% part-time, 63% women, 15% African American, 2% Asian American, 8% Hispanic/Latino, 2% Multiracial, non-Hispanic, 4% international
- 993 degree-seeking graduate students
- 55% of applicants admitted
- Application essay required
- 41% graduate within 6 years

General. Founded in 1934. Regionally accredited. **Degrees:** 917 bachelor's awarded; master's, professional, doctoral offered. **ROTC:** Army, Naval. **Location:** 5 miles from downtown. **Calendar:** Semester, limited summer session. **Full-time faculty:** 203 total; 77% have terminal degrees, 9% minority, 50% women. **Part-time faculty:** 137 total; 33% have terminal degrees, 18% minority, 54% women. **Class size:** 74% < 20, 25% 20-39, less than 1% 40-49, less than 1% 50-99, less than 1% >100. **Special facilities:** Marine science research institute.

Freshman class profile. 3,718 applied, 2,035 admitted, 469 enrolled.

Mid 50% test scores			
SAT critical reading:	450-570	GPA 3.0-3.49:	31%
SAT math:	440-550	GPA 2.0-2.99:	16%
SAT writing:	430-530	Return as sophomores:	69%
ACT composite:	19-25	Out-of-state:	31%
GPA 3.75 or higher:	30%	Live on campus:	67%
GPA 3.50-3.74:	22%	International:	4%

Basis for selection. The most important factor in the admissions decision is the academic record; courses taken, grades attained, and class standing are considered. The GPA calculation is based on a weighted, recalculated core GPA. Submission of test scores is optional; submitted scores will be considered. Other factors which may be considered include personal statements, recommendations, leadership potential, extracurricular and service-related activities, special talents, and the ability to contribute positively to the campus community. SAT or ACT recommended. The submission of test scores is optional. Students are encouraged to submit SAT and/or ACT test scores if competitive. An audition is required of music dance, and theater majors. A portfolio is required for art, computer art, and design majors. An interview is required for students seeking placement in the Honors Program. **Home schooled:** Transcript of courses and grades, interview, letter of recommendation (nonparent) required. 2 letters of recommendation evaluating academic potential from qualified educator or evaluator outside of homeschool environment, portfolio that includes 2 writing samples of at least 100 words, bibliography of reading completed and texts used, and description of curriculum required. **Learning Disabled:** The Student Life Office coordinates services for students with disabilities and special needs. Applicants are encouraged to contact the Student Life Office to facilitate a complete understanding of all available resources and accommodations.

High school preparation. College-preparatory program required. 13 units required; 15 recommended. Required and recommended units include English 4, mathematics 3, social studies 3, science 3 (laboratory 2) and foreign language 2.

2015-2016 Annual costs. Tuition/fees: $32,620. Room/board: $11,540. Books/supplies: $1,500. Personal expenses: $1,212.

2015-2016 Financial aid. Need-based: 476 full-time freshmen applied for aid; 421 deemed to have need; 421 received aid. Average need met was 88%. Average scholarship/grant was $19,055; average loan $2,506. 65% of total undergraduate aid awarded as scholarships/grants, 35% as loans/jobs. **Non-need-based:** Awarded to 756 full-time undergraduates, including 171 freshmen. Scholarships awarded for academics, art, athletics, leadership, music/drama, ROTC.

Application procedures. Admission: Priority date 3/1; deadline 7/1 (postmark date). $30 fee, may be waived for applicants with need. Admission

notification on a rolling basis beginning on or about 11/1. Must reply by May 1 or within 2 week(s) if notified thereafter. Housing deposit of $300 is refundable if notice is given before May 1. Students are allowed up to one calendar year to enroll provided they do not attend another regional accredited college or university during that time. Students who do complete course work at another college or university must submit official transcripts of that work for review and approval before being allowed to enroll. **Financial aid:** Priority date 3/31; no closing date. FAFSA, institutional form required. Applicants notified on a rolling basis starting 2/20.

Academics. Special study options: Accelerated study, combined bachelor's/graduate degree, cooperative education, cross-registration, distance learning, double major, dual enrollment of high school students, ESL, exchange student, honors, independent study, internships, liberal arts/career combination, semester at sea, student-designed major, study abroad, teacher certification program, Washington semester. **Credit/placement by examination:** AP, CLEP, IB, SAT, ACT, institutional tests. 30 credit hours maximum toward associate degree, 30 toward bachelor's. **Support services:** Learning center, remedial instruction, study skills assistance, tutoring, writing center.

Majors. Architecture: Urban/community planning. **Biology:** General, marine. **Business:** General, accounting, business admin, entrepreneurial studies, finance, international, management science, managerial economics, marketing. **Communications:** Media studies. **Computer sciences:** General, information systems. **Conservation:** Environmental studies. **Education:** General, art, drama/dance, elementary, music, physical, special ed. **Engineering:** Applied physics, electrical, mechanical. **English:** English lit. **Foreign languages:** French, Germanic, Spanish. **Health services:** Clinical lab science, communication disorders, nursing (RN), predental, premedicine, prenursing, preveterinary. **History:** General. **Human services:** General. **Liberal arts:** Arts/sciences, humanities. **Math:** General. **Parks/recreation:** Exercise sciences, health/fitness, sports admin. **Philosophy/religion:** Philosophy. **Physical sciences:** Chemistry, physics. **Psychology:** General. **Social sciences:** Economics, geography, international relations, political science, sociology. **Theology:** Sacred music. **Visual/performing arts:** General, art, art history/conservation, commercial/advertising art, dance, dramatic, fashion design, film/cinema/video, jazz, multimedia, music, music history, music management, music performance, music theory/composition, piano/keyboard, studio arts, voice/opera.

Most popular majors. Business/marketing 9%, health sciences 57%.

Technology on campus. 400 workstations in dormitories, library, computer center, student center. Dormitories wired for high-speed internet access and linked to campus network. Commuter students can connect to campus network. Online course registration, online library, helpline, wireless network available.

Student life. Freshman orientation: Mandatory. Preregistration for classes offered. Occurs in the few days preceding first day of class. **Housing:** Guaranteed on-campus for freshmen. Coed dorms, single-sex dorms, special housing for disabled, apartments, fraternity/sorority housing, themed housing, wellness housing available. $300 partly refundable deposit, deadline 5/1. **Activities:** Bands, campus ministries, choral groups, dance, drama, international student organizations, literary magazine, music ensembles, Model UN, musical theater, opera, radio station, student government, student newspaper, symphony orchestra, TV station, Baptist Collegiate Ministries, Campus Outreach, Catholic Dolphins, College Republicans, Political Science Society, Black Student Union, International Students Association Club, The Cultural Diversity Appreciation Club, Career Development Center, Service Learning Center.

Athletics. NCAA. **Intercollegiate:** Baseball M, basketball, cross-country, football (tackle) M, golf, lacrosse, rowing (crew), sand volleyball W, soccer, softball W, track and field W, volleyball W. **Intramural:** Basketball, football (non-tackle), soccer, softball, ultimate frisbee, volleyball. **Team name:** Dolphins.

Student services. Adult student services, alcohol/substance abuse counseling, chaplain/spiritual director, career counseling, services for economically disadvantaged, student employment services, financial aid counseling, health services, minority student services, on-campus daycare, personal counseling, placement for graduates, veterans' counselor. **Physically disabled:** Services for visually, speech, hearing impaired.

Contact. E-mail: admissions@ju.edu
Phone: (904) 256-7000 Toll-free number: (800) 225-2027
Fax: (904) 256-7012
Thomas Taggart, Chief Admissions Officer, Jacksonville University, 2800 University Boulevard North, Jacksonville, FL 32211-3394

Johnson & Wales University: North Miami
North Miami, Florida
www.jwu.edu

CB code: 3441

- Private 4-year university
- Residential campus in large city

▶ 1,752 degree-seeking undergraduates: 10% part-time, 63% women, 31% African American, 23% Hispanic/Latino, 8% Multi-racial, non-Hispanic, 10% international

▶ 76% of applicants admitted

▶ 41% graduate within 6 years

General. Regionally accredited. **Degrees:** 357 bachelor's, 259 associate awarded. **Calendar:** Quarter, extensive summer session. **Full-time faculty:** 57 total. **Part-time faculty:** 22 total. **Class size:** 48% < 20, 41% 20-39, 11% 40-49.

Freshman class profile. 4,049 applied, 3,071 admitted, 425 enrolled.

GPA 3.75 or higher:	15%	Return as sophomores:	69%
GPA 3.50-3.74:	17%	Out-of-state:	51%
GPA 3.0-3.49:	37%	Live on campus:	82%
GPA 2.0-2.99:	29%	International:	5%

Basis for selection. Academic record, secondary school curriculum, GPA, class rank, and test scores important. Student motivation and interest given strong consideration. **Home schooled:** Transcript of courses and grades, state high school equivalency certificate required. SAT/ACT required.

High school preparation. College-preparatory program recommended. Required units include English 4, mathematics 3, social studies 2 and science 3.

2015-2016 Annual costs. Tuition/fees: $29,226. Room/board: $11,100. Books/supplies: $1,500. Personal expenses: $1,409.

2015-2016 Financial aid. Need-based: 298 full-time freshmen applied for aid; 263 deemed to have need; 263 received aid. Average need met was 69%. Average scholarship/grant was $10,213; average loan $3,371. 65% of total undergraduate aid awarded as scholarships/grants, 35% as loans/jobs. **Non-need-based:** Awarded to 1,377 full-time undergraduates, including 288 freshmen. Scholarships awarded for academics, alumni affiliation, leadership, state residency.

Application procedures. Admission: No deadline. No application fee. Admission notification on a rolling basis. Must reply by May 1 or within 2 week(s) if notified thereafter. **Financial aid:** No deadline. FAFSA required. Applicants notified on a rolling basis starting 3/1; must reply within 2 week(s) of notification.

Academics. Special study options: Accelerated study, cooperative education, dual enrollment of high school students, ESL, exchange student, honors, independent study, internships, study abroad. **Credit/placement by examination:** AP, CLEP, institutional tests. **Support services:** Learning center, reduced course load, remedial instruction, study skills assistance, tutoring, writing center.

Honors college/program. SAT/ACT required.

Majors. Business: General, apparel, business admin, entrepreneurial studies, event planning, fashion, hospitality admin, hospitality/recreation, hotel/motel admin, hotel/motel/restaurant management, international, managerial economics, marketing, merchandising, personal/financial services, resort management, restaurant/food services, retail management, retailing, selling, tourism promotion, tourism/travel, travel services. **Parks/recreation:** General, facilities management, golf management, sports admin. **Protective services:** Law enforcement admin. **Work/family studies:** Apparel marketing, clothing/textiles, food/nutrition, institutional food production.

Most popular majors. English 41%, family/consumer sciences 38%, legal studies 12%, security/protective services 9%.

Technology on campus. 60 workstations in library, computer center, student center. Dormitories wired for high-speed internet access and linked to campus network. Commuter students can connect to campus network. Online course registration, online library, helpline, repair service, wireless network available.

Student life. Freshman orientation: Mandatory, $300 fee. Preregistration for classes offered. **Housing:** Guaranteed on-campus for freshmen. Coed dorms, apartments, themed housing, wellness housing available. $300 nonrefundable deposit, deadline 5/1. All housing accessible for disabled students. **Activities:** Pep band, campus ministries, dance, international student organizations, music ensembles, student government, student newspaper.

Athletics. NAIA. **Intercollegiate:** Basketball, cross-country, golf, soccer, track and field. **Intramural:** Basketball M, football (non-tackle), soccer, softball, volleyball. **Team name:** Wildcats.

Student services. Adult student services, alcohol/substance abuse counseling, career counseling, student employment services, financial aid counseling, health services, personal counseling, placement for graduates, veterans'

counselor. **Physically disabled:** Services for visually, speech, hearing impaired.

Contact. E-mail: mia@admissions.jwu.edu
Phone: (866) 598-3567 Toll-free number: (800) 342-5598
Fax: (305) 892-7020
Heather Munns, Director of Admissions, Johnson & Wales University: North Miami, 1701 Northeast 127th Street, North Miami, FL 33181

Johnson University: Florida
Kissimmee, Florida
www.fcc.edu   CB code: 2167

▶ Private 4-year Bible and teachers college affiliated with the Christian Church

▶ Residential campus in small city

▶ 201 degree-seeking undergraduates

▶ SAT or ACT (ACT writing optional), application essay required

General. Founded in 1975. Regionally accredited; also accredited by ABHE. **Degrees:** 44 bachelor's, 6 associate awarded. **Location:** 20 miles from Orlando. **Calendar:** Semester, limited summer session. **Full-time faculty:** 11 total; 73% have terminal degrees, 9% minority, 27% women. **Part-time faculty:** 28 total; 21% have terminal degrees, 4% minority, 43% women. **Class size:** 73% < 20, 21% 20-39, 4% 40-49, 3% 50-99.

Basis for selection. Autobiographical essays, personal recommendation, and church references required. **Home schooled:** State high school equivalency certificate, letter of recommendation (nonparent) required.

2015-2016 Annual costs. Tuition/fees: $14,270. Room only: $3,200. Books/supplies: $850. Personal expenses: $3,960.

Financial aid. Non-need-based: Scholarships awarded for academics, alumni affiliation, leadership, music/drama, religious affiliation, state residency.

Application procedures. Admission: Priority date 3/1; deadline 5/1 (postmark date). $50 fee, may be waived for applicants with need. Admission notification on a rolling basis. **Financial aid:** Priority date 5/1, closing date 7/15. FAFSA, institutional form required. Applicants notified on a rolling basis starting 3/1.

Academics. Online degree completion students must be 23 years or older and transfer in 60 credits. **Special study options:** Accelerated study, distance learning, dual enrollment of high school students, independent study, internships, student-designed major, teacher certification program. **Credit/placement by examination:** AP, CLEP, IB. 15 credit hours maximum toward associate degree, 30 toward bachelor's. **Support services:** Reduced course load, study skills assistance, tutoring.

Majors. Education: Elementary. **Philosophy/religion:** Religion. **Theology:** Bible, missionary, pastoral counseling, sacred music, theology.

Most popular majors. Theological studies 92%.

Technology on campus. 8 workstations in library, student center. Dormitories wired for high-speed internet access and linked to campus network. Online course registration, online library, helpline, repair service, student web hosting, wireless network available.

Student life. Freshman orientation: Mandatory. Preregistration for classes offered. **Policies:** Spiritual development and community involvement expected; students must attend chapel and small groups (or equivalent) and perform community service projects. Religious observance required. **Housing:** Special housing for disabled, apartments, wellness housing available. $100 fully refundable deposit, deadline 7/15. **Activities:** Choral groups, music ensembles, student government, student newspaper, Christian service activities, mission group.

Athletics. NCCAA. **Intercollegiate:** Baseball M, basketball M, cross-country, soccer W, volleyball W. **Intramural:** Football (non-tackle), soccer, softball, table tennis, ultimate frisbee M. **Team name:** Suns.

Student services. Career counseling, financial aid counseling, personal counseling, veterans' counselor. **Physically disabled:** Services for visually impaired.

Contact. E-mail: JohnsonUFL@JohnsonU.edu
Phone: (407) 569-1172 Toll-free number: (877) 468-6322
Fax: (321) 206-2007
Kellie Spencer, Director of Admission, Johnson University: Florida, 1011 Bill Beck Boulevard, Kissimmee, FL 34744-4402

Jones College
Jacksonville, Florida
www.jones.edu   CB code: 5343

- Private 4-year business college
- Commuter campus in very large city
- 445 degree-seeking undergraduates
- Interview required

General. Founded in 1918. Accredited by ACICS. Online learning available. **Degrees:** 29 bachelor's, 35 associate awarded. **Calendar:** Trimester, extensive summer session. **Full-time faculty:** 6 total; 67% women. **Part-time faculty:** 59 total; 10% have terminal degrees, 51% women. **Class size:** 95% < 20, 5% 20-39.

Basis for selection. Open admission. **Home schooled:** State high school equivalency certificate required.

2015-2016 Annual costs. Tuition/fees: $9,240. Books/supplies: $1,600. Personal expenses: $1,435.

Financial aid. All financial aid based on need. **Additional information:** All new students offered Annie Harper Jones Scholarship during their first semester if enrolled in at least 6 hours.

Application procedures. Admission: No deadline. No application fee. Admission notification on a rolling basis. **Financial aid:** Priority date 8/1; no closing date. FAFSA required. Applicants notified on a rolling basis starting 7/1.

Academics. Special study options: Accelerated study, distance learning, double major, internships, weekend college. **Credit/placement by examination:** AP, CLEP, institutional tests. 15 credit hours maximum toward associate degree, 15 toward bachelor's. Life experience: 21 hours for bachelor's programs, 9 hours for associate programs. CLEP: 30 hours for bachelor's programs, 15 hours for associate programs. **Support services:** Reduced course load, remedial instruction, study skills assistance, tutoring.

Majors. Business: Business admin. **Computer sciences:** General. **Education:** Elementary. **Health services:** Medical assistant.

Most popular majors. Business/marketing 43%, computer/information sciences 6%, health sciences 18%, interdisciplinary studies 18%, legal studies 14%.

Technology on campus. 126 workstations in library, computer center. Commuter students can connect to campus network. Online library, wireless network available.

Student life. Freshman orientation: Mandatory. Preregistration for classes offered.

Student services. Career counseling, student employment services, financial aid counseling, placement for graduates, veterans' counselor.

Contact. E-mail: ghowze@jones.edu
Phone: (904) 743-1122 ext. 207
Toll-free number: (800) 331-0176 ext. 207 Fax: (904) 743-4446
Gregory Howze, Director of Admissions, Jones College, 5353 Arlington Expressway, Jacksonville, FL 32211

Jose Maria Vargas University
Pembroke Pines, Florida
www.jmvu.edu

- For-profit 4-year university
- Commuter campus in small city
- 154 degree-seeking undergraduates
- 5 graduate students

General. Regionally accredited; also accredited by ACICS. Bilingual education in English and Spanish. **Degrees:** 1 bachelor's, 8 associate awarded; master's offered. **Location:** 22 miles away from Miami. **Calendar:** Semester, extensive summer session. **Full-time faculty:** 3 total; 33% have terminal degrees, 33% minority, 67% women. **Part-time faculty:** 25 total; 52% have terminal degrees, 76% minority, 56% women. **Special facilities:** Art gallery, student center, graphic design lab, preschool education experimental lab.

Basis for selection. Open admission. Varies by program. **Learning Disabled:** Student may report disability to Student Development Department.

2015-2016 Annual costs. Books/supplies: $1,200.

Financial aid. Non-need-based: Scholarships awarded for academics.

Application procedures. Admission: No deadline. $50 fee. Admission notification on a rolling basis. **Financial aid:** No deadline. FAFSA, institutional form required. Applicants notified on a rolling basis; must reply within 2 week(s) of notification.

Academics. Special study options: Double major, dual enrollment of high school students, independent study, internships, weekend college. **Credit/placement by examination:** AP, CLEP, IB. **Support services:** Reduced course load, study skills assistance, tutoring.

Majors. Business: Business admin. **Education:** Early childhood. **Health services:** Mental health services. **Visual/performing arts:** Graphic design.

Technology on campus. 50 workstations in library, computer center, student center. Commuter students can connect to campus network. Online course registration, online library, repair service, wireless network available.

Student life. Freshman orientation: Mandatory, $640 fee. Preregistration for classes offered. Two-week program held before start of semester.

Student services. Career counseling, financial aid counseling, placement for graduates.

Contact. E-mail: admissions@jmvu.edu
Phone: (954) 322-4460 Toll-free number: (866) 650-5688
Fax: (954) 322-4131
Lelis Ortiz, University Registrar and Director of Admissions, Jose Maria Vargas University, 10131 Pines Boulevard, Pembroke Pines, FL 33026

Keiser University
West Palm Beach, Florida
www.keiseruniversity.edu   CB code: 7004

- Private 4-year health science and career college
- Commuter campus in large city
- 15,939 degree-seeking undergraduates: 46% part-time, 68% women
- 2,080 degree-seeking graduate students
- 66% of applicants admitted
- SAT or ACT, interview required

General. Founded in 1977. Regionally accredited. **Degrees:** 1,055 bachelor's, 3,593 associate awarded; master's, professional offered. **Location:** 35 miles from Miami. **Calendar:** Semester, extensive summer session. **Full-time faculty:** 882 total; 25% minority, 56% women. **Part-time faculty:** 615 total. **Class size:** 100% 20-39.

Freshman class profile. 8,680 applied, 5,687 admitted, 5,614 enrolled.

Basis for selection. 1430 SAT, 17 ACT, or 35-55 on Otis-Lennon evaluation test required.

2015-2016 Annual costs. Tuition/fees: $9,162. Books/supplies: $800.

Financial aid. Non-need-based: Scholarships awarded for academics, alumni affiliation, job skills, leadership.

Application procedures. Admission: No deadline. $55 fee. Admission notification on a rolling basis. **Financial aid:** No deadline. FAFSA required.

Academics. Special study options: Accelerated study, combined bachelor's/graduate degree, distance learning, dual enrollment of high school students, exchange student, independent study, internships, weekend college. **Credit/placement by examination:** AP, CLEP. **Support services:** Learning center, reduced course load, remedial instruction, study skills assistance, tutoring, writing center.

Majors. Biology: Biomedical sciences. **Business:** Accounting, business admin, management information systems. **Computer sciences:** Information technology. **Health services:** Health care admin, health information management, health services admin, nursing (RN). **Liberal arts:** Arts/sciences. **Protective services:** Computer forensics, forensics, homeland security, law enforcement admin. **Psychology:** General.

Technology on campus. Commuter students can connect to campus network. Online library, helpline, wireless network available.

Student life. Freshman orientation: Available. Preregistration for classes offered. **Activities:** Student government.

Athletics. NAIA. **Intercollegiate:** Baseball, basketball, golf M, volleyball M.

Student services. Career counseling, student employment services, financial aid counseling, placement for graduates.

Contact. E-mail: ResidentialAdmissions@keiseruniversity.edu
Phone: (954) 776-4456 Toll-free number: (800) 622-9000
Fax: (561) 640-3328
Jeffrey Greenip, Director of Enrollment Management and Admissions, Keiser University, 2600 North Military Trail, West Palm Beach, FL 33409

Lynn University
Boca Raton, Florida   **CB member**
www.lynn.edu   **CB code: 5437**

▶ Private 4-year university
▶ Residential campus in small city
▶ 1,957 degree-seeking undergraduates: 5% part-time, 48% women, 8% African American, 2% Asian American, 15% Hispanic/Latino, 1% Native American, 1% Multi-racial, non-Hispanic, 23% international
▶ 661 degree-seeking graduate students
▶ 76% of applicants admitted
▶ Application essay required
▶ 44% graduate within 6 years

General. Founded in 1962. Regionally accredited. **Degrees:** 439 bachelor's awarded; master's, doctoral offered. **ROTC:** Air Force. **Location:** 20 miles from Fort Lauderdale, 20 miles from West Palm Beach. **Calendar:** Semester, limited summer session. **Full-time faculty:** 114 total; 63% have terminal degrees, 4% minority, 40% women. **Part-time faculty:** 80 total; 45% have terminal degrees, 16% minority, 52% women. **Class size:** 49% < 20, 51% 20-39, less than 1% 40-49, less than 1% 50-99. **Special facilities:** Flight simulator, conservatory of music, performing arts center.

Freshman class profile. 3,770 applied, 2,864 admitted, 516 enrolled.

Mid 50% test scores		Rank in top quarter:	25%
SAT critical reading:	450-540	Rank in top tenth:	10%
SAT math:	450-550	End year in good standing:	77%
SAT writing:	430-540	Return as sophomores:	73%
ACT composite:	19-24	Out-of-state:	59%
GPA 3.75 or higher:	13%	Live on campus:	84%
GPA 3.50-3.74:	10%	International:	17%
GPA 3.0-3.49:	32%	Fraternities:	5%
GPA 2.0-2.99:	44%	Sororities:	8%

Basis for selection. School achievement record, high school counselor's recommendation, test scores important; class rank, school and community activities considered. Special consideration given to foreign and minority applicants. First-year students may apply without SAT or ACT scores. If student chooses to apply test optional, their application will be evaluated holistically with consideration given to various factors including high school grade point average, strength of curriculum, progression of courses taken, letters of recommendation, and through an interview process if deemed necessary. For first-year students interested in participating in an athletic program, or if the student is home-schooled, then they are required to submit standardized test scores. Interview recommended. Conservatory students must audition. **Learning Disabled:** Submit psychological testing in addition to other admission documents.

High school preparation. College-preparatory program recommended. 16 units recommended. Recommended units include English 4, mathematics 4, social studies 2, history 2 and science 4. Mathematics must include algebra I, algebra II, and either geometry, trigonometry, calculus, or analysis. Science must include biology and a physical science.

2016-2017 Annual costs. Tuition/fees: $36,150. Room/board: $11,640. Books/supplies: $800. Personal expenses: $3,866.

2015-2016 Financial aid. Need-based: 461 full-time freshmen applied for aid; 276 deemed to have need; 276 received aid. Average need met was 55%. Average scholarship/grant was $10,427; average loan $3,931. 66% of total undergraduate aid awarded as scholarships/grants, 34% as loans/jobs. **Non-need-based:** Awarded to 1,413 full-time undergraduates, including 528 freshmen. Scholarships awarded for academics, alumni affiliation, athletics, leadership, music/drama.

Application procedures. Admission: Priority date 12/1; deadline 8/1 (postmark date). $45 fee, may be waived for applicants with need. Application must be submitted online. Admission notification on a rolling basis beginning on or about 12/15. Must reply by May 1 or within 2 week(s) if notified thereafter. **Financial aid:** Priority date 3/1; no closing date. FAFSA required. Applicants notified on a rolling basis starting 2/1; must reply within 2 week(s) of notification.

Academics. Special study options: Accelerated study, combined bachelor's/graduate degree, distance learning, double major, dual enrollment of high school students, independent study, internships, study abroad, teacher certification program. **Credit/placement by examination:** AP, CLEP, IB, institutional tests. 30 credit hours maximum toward bachelor's degree. **Support services:** Learning center, reduced course load, remedial instruction, study skills assistance, tutoring, writing center. Academic coaching, assistive technology, diagnostic assessment, alternative testing environment.

Majors. Biology: General. **Business:** Business admin, entrepreneurial studies, event planning, fashion, hospitality admin, international, investments/securities, marketing. **Communications:** General, journalism, media studies, persuasive communications. **Conservation:** Environmental studies. **Education:** Elementary. **Parks/recreation:** Sports admin. **Protective services:** Forensics, law enforcement admin. **Psychology:** General. **Social sciences:** Political science. **Visual/performing arts:** Cinematography, dramatic, music performance, music theory/composition.

Most popular majors. Business/marketing 43%, communications/journalism 15%, parks/recreation 7%, psychology 9%, security/protective services 9%, visual/performing arts 7%.

Technology on campus. PC or laptop required. 250 workstations in library, computer center. Dormitories wired for high-speed internet access and linked to campus network. Online library, helpline, repair service, wireless network available.

Student life. Freshman orientation: Mandatory. Preregistration for classes offered. **Housing:** Guaranteed on-campus for all undergraduates. Coed dorms, special housing for disabled available. $200 partly refundable deposit, deadline 5/1. **Activities:** Campus ministries, dance, drama, film society, international student organizations, literary magazine, music ensembles, Model UN, musical theater, radio station, student government, student newspaper, symphony orchestra, TV station, Student activities board, Black Student Union, Chabad, Hillel, Gay-Straight Alliance, animal welfare club, criminal justice club, Knight of the Roundtable, Adults Supporting Kids, Blue Notez.

Athletics. NCAA. **Intercollegiate:** Baseball M, basketball, cross-country W, golf, lacrosse M, soccer, softball W, swimming W, tennis, volleyball W. **Intramural:** Basketball, football (non-tackle), golf, sand volleyball, soccer, tennis, ultimate frisbee, volleyball. **Team name:** Fighting Knights.

Student services. Adult student services, chaplain/spiritual director, career counseling, student employment services, financial aid counseling, health services, minority student services, personal counseling, placement for graduates, veterans' counselor.

Contact. E-mail: admission@lynn.edu
Phone: (561) 237-7900 Toll-free number: (800) 888-5966
Fax: (561) 237-7100
Stefano Papaleo, Director of Undergraduate Admission, Lynn University, 3601 North Military Trail, Boca Raton, FL 33431-5598

Miami International University of Art and Design
Miami, Florida
www.mymiu.edu   **CB code: 5327**

▶ For-profit 3-year university and visual arts college
▶ Commuter campus in very large city
▶ 3,167 degree-seeking undergraduates
▶ 41 graduate students
▶ Application essay, interview required

General. Founded in 1965. Regionally accredited. **Degrees:** 484 bachelor's, 166 associate awarded; master's offered. **Location:** 2 miles from downtown. **Calendar:** Quarter, extensive summer session. **Full-time faculty:** 102 total. **Part-time faculty:** 162 total.

Basis for selection. Academic record, essay, and how well the applicant's stated education and career goals relate to the chosen program of study. Admissions committee may request additional information or require the applicant to meet with Academic Director or Coordinator or other personnel prior to making final decision. ACCUPLACER, SAT/ACT required for placement and to determine the need for developmental course work in English and/or math. Portfolio of work may be required depending on program and campus chosen. **Home schooled:** Must submit official GED certificate or evidence of completion of state home schooling requirements. **Learning Disabled:** Students who require accommodations should advise the Student Affairs department during application process.

2015-2016 Annual costs. Tuition/fees: $22,105. Room only: $5,100. Books/supplies: $2,052. Personal expenses: $3,354.

Application procedures. Admission: No deadline. $50 fee. Admission notification on a rolling basis. Students encouraged to apply as early as possible prior to intended start date. **Financial aid:** Priority date 7/1; no closing date. FAFSA required. Applicants notified on a rolling basis starting 8/1.

Academics. Special study options: Distance learning, internships. **Credit/placement by examination:** AP, CLEP, IB, SAT, ACT, institutional tests. 22 credit hours maximum toward associate degree, 45 toward bachelor's. Official documents (CLEP or AP scores) related to transfer or proficiency credit must be received prior to class start. No more than 25% of program credits will be considered for any type of proficiency credit. **Support services:** Learning center, reduced course load, tutoring.

Majors. BACHELOR'S. Business: Apparel, fashion. **Communications:** Advertising. **Communications technology:** Animation/special effects, recording arts. **Computer sciences:** Computer graphics, web page design. **Visual/performing arts:** Cinematography, commercial photography, design, fashion design, game design, graphic design, interior design. **ASSOCIATE. Business:** Apparel, fashion. **Visual/performing arts:** Fashion design, graphic design.

Technology on campus. 87 workstations in library, computer center. Online library, student web hosting, wireless network available.

Student life. Freshman orientation: Mandatory. Preregistration for classes offered. Held the week before start of quarter for approximately 4 hours.

Student services. Career counseling, student employment services, financial aid counseling.

Contact. E-mail: kryan@aii.edu
Phone: (305) 428-5700 Toll-free number: (800) 225-9023
Fax: (305) 374-7946
Kevin Ryan, Senior Director of Admissions, Miami International University of Art and Design, 1501 Biscayne Boulevard, Suite 100, Miami, FL 33132-1418

New College of Florida
Sarasota, Florida   **CB member**
www.ncf.edu   **CB code: 5506**

- Public 4-year liberal arts college
- Residential campus in small city
- 852 degree-seeking undergraduates: 61% women, 3% African American, 3% Asian American, 16% Hispanic/Latino, 4% Multi-racial, non-Hispanic, 2% international
- 61% of applicants admitted
- SAT or ACT with writing, application essay required
- 71% graduate within 6 years; 32% enter graduate study

General. Founded in 1960. Regionally accredited. State legislatively-designated honors college for liberal arts and sciences. **Degrees:** 177 bachelor's awarded; master's offered. **Location:** 50 miles from Tampa, 2 miles from Sarasota. **Calendar:** 4-1-4. **Full-time faculty:** 78 total; 99% have terminal degrees, 12% minority, 50% women. **Part-time faculty:** 22 total; 82% have terminal degrees, 9% minority, 73% women. **Class size:** 73% < 20, 21% 20-39, 4% 40-49, 2% 50-99. **Special facilities:** High-field nuclear magnetic resonance spectrometer, hardware/software system for brain function analysis, scanning electron microscope, UV-visible and infrared spectrophotometer, inert atmosphere glove box, fine arts center, laboratories for environmental studies, anthropology, psychology, marine biology research facility and laboratories, academic resource center.

Freshman class profile. 1,655 applied, 1,009 admitted, 261 enrolled.

Mid 50% test scores			
SAT critical reading:	610-720	Rank in top quarter:	79%
SAT math:	560-660	Rank in top tenth:	43%
SAT writing:	570-670	End year in good standing:	81%
ACT composite:	27-31	Return as sophomores:	81%
GPA 3.75 or higher:	73%	Out-of-state:	18%
GPA 3.50-3.74:	15%	Live on campus:	97%
GPA 3.0-3.49:	12%	International:	2%

Basis for selection. Challenging course loads, strong grades, and writing ability are most important considerations. Class rank (if available), standardized test scores, recommendations, and extracurricular activities are also important. SAT/ACT requirement waived for students with Florida College

System AA degree. **Home schooled:** Transcript of courses and grades required. List of length and levels of study completed or planned for completion, textbook information and reading lists required. Additional information may be requested on a case by case basis. **Learning Disabled:** Students with any type of disability are invited to contact the admissions office to coordinate completion of the admissions requirements with high school graduation requirements. Additionally, students are encouraged to contact the college's disability services coordinator early to determine necessary documentation required.

High school preparation. College-preparatory program required. 18 units required; 20 recommended. Required and recommended units include English 4, mathematics 4, social studies 3-4, science 3-4 (laboratory 2), foreign language 2-4 and academic electives 2-4. History included in social studies.

2015-2016 Annual costs. Tuition/fees: $6,916; $29,944 out-of-state. Room/board: $8,932. Books/supplies: $1,200. Personal expenses: $2,170.

2015-2016 Financial aid. Need-based: 238 full-time freshmen applied for aid; 145 deemed to have need; 145 received aid. Average need met was 89%. Average scholarship/grant was $9,832; average loan $2,649. 68% of total undergraduate aid awarded as scholarships/grants, 32% as loans/jobs. **Non-need-based:** Awarded to 380 full-time undergraduates, including 116 freshmen. Scholarships awarded for academics, state residency.

Application procedures. Admission: Priority date 11/1; deadline 4/15 (postmark date). $30 fee, may be waived for applicants with need. Admission notification by 4/25. Admission notification on a rolling basis beginning on or about 4/1. Must reply by 5/1. **Financial aid:** Priority date 2/15; no closing date. FAFSA required. Applicants notified on a rolling basis starting 3/15; must reply by 5/1 or within 2 week(s) of notification.

Academics. All students required to complete three 4-week independent study projects, senior thesis, and oral baccalaureate exam before committee of faculty. **Special study options:** Cross-registration, double major, exchange student, honors, independent study, internships, semester at sea, student-designed major, study abroad, Washington semester. Academic contract, January Interterm (independent study), narrative evaluation/pass-fail, senior thesis, tutorials, undergraduate research. **Credit/placement by examination:** AP, CLEP, institutional tests. AP exam scores, IB higher-level exam scores, AICE A-level exam scores, and CLEP scores at certain levels may be used toward exemptions from Liberal Arts Curriculum requirements. **Support services:** Learning center, study skills assistance, tutoring, writing center.

Majors. Area/ethnic studies: European, French, German, Latin American, Spanish/Iberian. **Biology:** General, biochemistry, marine. **Conservation:** Environmental studies. **English:** English lit. **Foreign languages:** General, Chinese, classics, French, German, Russian, Spanish. **History:** General. **Human services:** Public policy. **Liberal arts:** Arts/sciences, humanities. **Math:** General, applied. **Philosophy/religion:** Philosophy, religion. **Physical sciences:** Chemistry, physics. **Psychology:** General. **Social sciences:** General, anthropology, economics, international relations, political science, sociology, urban studies. **Visual/performing arts:** Art history/conservation, music, studio arts.

Technology on campus. 123 workstations in library, computer center, student center. Dormitories wired for high-speed internet access and linked to campus network. Commuter students can connect to campus network. Online course registration, online library, helpline, student web hosting, wireless network available.

Student life. Freshman orientation: Mandatory, $145 fee. Preregistration for classes offered. Week-long program connecting new students with campus resources, academic info sessions, mini-classes and faculty advisors. **Policies:** All students required to live on campus unless granted waiver by office of residential life. **Housing:** Guaranteed on-campus for freshmen. Coed dorms, special housing for disabled, apartments, gender-neutral housing, themed housing, wellness housing available. Pets allowed in dorm rooms. Specialized housing options may be arranged in response to student interest. **Activities:** Jazz band, campus ministries, choral groups, dance, drama, film society, international student organizations, literary magazine, music ensembles, musical theater, radio station, student government, student newspaper, Inter-Faith Council, Hillel, Catholic Solidarity, Unitarian Universalists, Students Working for Equal Rights, Mental Health Alliance, China club, German club, Queery, Transwagger.

Athletics. Intercollegiate: Sailing. **Intramural:** Basketball, fencing, football (non-tackle), racquetball, swimming, table tennis, tennis, wrestling.

Student services. Alcohol/substance abuse counseling, chaplain/spiritual director, career counseling, student employment services, financial aid counseling, health services, on-campus daycare, personal counseling. **Physically disabled:** Services for visually, hearing impaired.

Contact. E-mail: admissions@ncf.edu
Phone: (941) 487-5000 Fax: (941) 487-5010
Kathleen Killion, Dean of Enrollment Services and Information Technology, New College of Florida, 5800 Bay Shore Road, Sarasota, FL 34243-2109

Nova Southeastern University
Fort Lauderdale, Florida
www.nova.edu
CB member
CB code: 5514

- Private 4-year university
- Commuter campus in small city
- 4,565 degree-seeking undergraduates: 30% part-time, 68% women, 18% African American, 9% Asian American, 32% Hispanic/Latino, 2% Multiracial, non-Hispanic, 5% international
- 18,558 degree-seeking graduate students
- 59% of applicants admitted
- SAT or ACT (ACT writing optional) required
- 44% graduate within 6 years

General. Founded in 1964. Regionally accredited. Field-based programs offered throughout the nation and at selected international sites. **Degrees:** 1,412 bachelor's, 2 associate awarded; master's, professional, doctoral offered. **Location:** 10 miles from Fort Lauderdale. **Calendar:** Trimester, limited summer session. **Full-time faculty:** 857 total; 79% have terminal degrees, 28% minority, 52% women. **Part-time faculty:** 842 total; 69% have terminal degrees, 27% minority, 60% women. **Class size:** 78% < 20, 19% 20-39, 2% 40-49, less than 1% 50-99, less than 1% >100. **Special facilities:** Center of Excellence for Coral Reef Ecosystems Science, dryland training, student educational center, nursing simulation labs, sales institute, neuro immune medicine clinical, health professions division museum, Hall of Fame, performing arts center, oceanographic center, law center, family village center, preschool.

Freshman class profile. 4,333 applied, 2,567 admitted, 657 enrolled.

Mid 50% test scores			
SAT critical reading:	490-610	Rank in top quarter:	60%
SAT math:	490-620	Rank in top tenth:	31%
ACT composite:	22-29	Return as sophomores:	80%
GPA 3.75 or higher:	67%	Out-of-state:	34%
GPA 3.50-3.74:	10%	Live on campus:	62%
GPA 3.0-3.49:	16%	International:	7%
GPA 2.0-2.99:	7%	Fraternities:	14%
		Sororities:	12%

Basis for selection. Test scores, GPA important. Career Development applicants (adult and evening/weekend) exempt from test score requirement; high school diploma or GED required. Interviews and essays are recommended. **Home schooled:** Information about home school program-of-study and GED score to demonstrate high school equivalence required.

High school preparation. College-preparatory program recommended. Recommended units include English 4, mathematics 3, social studies 3 and science 3.

2015-2016 Annual costs. Tuition/fees: $27,660. Room/board: $10,874. Books/supplies: $1,500. Personal expenses: $3,425.

2015-2016 Financial aid. All financial aid based on need. 566 full-time freshmen applied for aid; 473 deemed to have need; 458 received aid. Average need met was 81%. Average scholarship/grant was $18,946; average loan $2,344. 53% of total undergraduate aid awarded as scholarships/grants, 47% as loans/jobs.

Application procedures. Admission: Closing date 7/20 (receipt date). $50 fee, may be waived for applicants with need. Admission notification on a rolling basis. **Financial aid:** No deadline. FAFSA required. Applicants notified on a rolling basis.

Academics. Professional and liberal studies for traditional daytime students, career development for adult evening and weekend students. Core curriculum of liberal arts-based courses plus general education required. Supplemental Instruction available in a few courses. **Special study options:** Combined bachelor's/graduate degree, distance learning, double major, honors, independent study, internships, study abroad, teacher certification program. Dual admission with NSU graduate/professional programs. **Credit/placement by examination:** AP, CLEP, IB, SAT, ACT, institutional tests. 90 credit hours maximum toward bachelor's degree. **Support services:** Learning center, reduced course load, study skills assistance, tutoring, writing center. On-line tutoring.

Honors college/program. For admission, highly qualified students must complete an application, with their answers to two essay questions, which will be reviewed (with the applicants' academic record) by a faculty committee. Approximately, 10% of each year's entering student class-distributed across all majors-are accepted to participate. Honors courses are more interactive, discussion-based, and hands-on than other courses, but are not necessarily more challenging. Honors students get direct interaction with faculty. Honors seminars are unique courses offered only as Honors courses.

Majors. Area/ethnic studies: American. **Biology:** General, marine. **Business:** Accounting, business admin, finance, marketing. **Communications:** Communications/speech/rhetoric. **Computer sciences:** General, computer science. **Conservation:** Environmental science, environmental studies. **Education:** Early childhood, elementary, English, kindergarten/preschool, learning disabled, mathematics, physical, science, secondary, social studies, special ed. **Engineering:** Computer, software. **English:** English lit. **Health services:** Nursing (RN), recreational therapy, respiratory therapy technology, sonography, speech pathology. **History:** General. **Human services:** General. **Liberal arts:** Arts/sciences, humanities. **Parks/recreation:** Exercise sciences, sports admin. **Philosophy/religion:** Philosophy. **Physical sciences:** Chemistry. **Protective services:** Criminal justice. **Psychology:** General. **Social sciences:** Anthropology, international relations, sociology. **Visual/performing arts:** Dance, dramatic, music, studio arts. **Work/family studies:** Family studies.

Most popular majors. Biology 26%, business/marketing 15%, health sciences 29%, psychology 8%.

Technology on campus. 3,000 workstations in dormitories, library, computer center, student center. Dormitories wired for high-speed internet access and linked to campus network. Commuter students can connect to campus network. Online course registration, online library, helpline, student web hosting, wireless network available.

Student life. Freshman orientation: Mandatory. Preregistration for classes offered. **Housing:** Guaranteed on-campus for freshmen. Coed dorms, special housing for disabled, apartments, fraternity/sorority housing, themed housing available. $500 partly refundable deposit. Fraternity/sorority wing/floor available in one dormitory. **Activities:** Concert band, campus ministries, choral groups, dance, drama, international student organizations, music ensembles, musical theater, radio station, student government, student newspaper, TV station, black student association, psychology club, Hillel, pre-med society, Alpha Phi Omega, Salsa, Indian student association, international Muslim association.

Athletics. NCAA. **Intercollegiate:** Baseball M, basketball, cheerleading W, cross-country, diving, golf, rowing (crew) W, soccer, softball W, swimming, track and field, volleyball W. **Intramural:** Badminton, basketball, football (non-tackle), soccer, softball W, volleyball. **Team name:** Sharks.

Student services. Adult student services, alcohol/substance abuse counseling, career counseling, student employment services, financial aid counseling, health services, personal counseling. **Physically disabled:** Services for visually, speech, hearing impaired.

Contact. E-mail: admissions@nova.edu
Phone: (954) 262-8000 Toll-free number: (800) 338-4723 ext. 8000
Fax: (954) 262-3811
Mensima Biney, Director, Nova Southeastern University, 3301 College Avenue, Fort Lauderdale, FL 33314

Palm Beach Atlantic University
West Palm Beach, Florida
www.pba.edu
CB code: 5553

- Private 4-year university and liberal arts college affiliated with the interdenominational tradition
- Commuter campus in small city
- 2,587 degree-seeking undergraduates: 7% part-time, 65% women, 12% African American, 2% Asian American, 17% Hispanic/Latino, 3% Multiracial, non-Hispanic, 4% international
- 871 degree-seeking graduate students
- 93% of applicants admitted
- SAT or ACT (ACT writing optional), application essay required
- 44% graduate within 6 years; 21% enter graduate study

General. Founded in 1968. Regionally accredited. **Degrees:** 495 bachelor's awarded; master's, professional offered. **ROTC:** Army. **Location:** 46 miles from Fort Lauderdale, 70 miles from Miami, 170 miles from Orlando. **Calendar:** Semester, limited summer session. **Full-time faculty:** 174 total; 82% have terminal degrees, 13% minority, 47% women. **Part-time faculty:** 191 total; 47% have terminal degrees, 18% minority, 50% women. **Class size:** 61% < 20, 35% 20-39, 2% 40-49, 2% 50-99. **Special facilities:** Center for public policy, recital hall, chapel, center for experiential learning.

Freshman class profile. 1,504 applied, 1,397 admitted, 551 enrolled.

Mid 50% test scores			
		GPA 3.0-3.49:	27%
SAT critical reading:	480-590	GPA 2.0-2.99:	13%
SAT math:	460-590	End year in good standing:	82%
SAT writing:	460-580	Return as sophomores:	75%
ACT composite:	20-26	Out-of-state:	48%
GPA 3.75 or higher:	43%	Live on campus:	81%
GPA 3.50-3.74:	16%	International:	3%

Basis for selection. Secondary school record, recommendations, test scores, interview, application essay important. Audition required of music, theater and dance majors. **Learning Disabled:** Students requesting accommodations advised to meet with Assistant Director for Disability Services for an initial interview.

High school preparation. College-preparatory program recommended. Required and recommended units include English 4, mathematics 3, science 3 (laboratory 3), foreign language 2 and academic electives 5.

2015-2016 Annual costs. Tuition/fees: $27,050. Room/board: $8,932. Books/supplies: $1,000. Personal expenses: $1,905.

2015-2016 Financial aid. Need-based: 476 full-time freshmen applied for aid; 401 deemed to have need; 401 received aid. Average need met was 67%. Average scholarship/grant was $17,554; average loan $3,339. 73% of total undergraduate aid awarded as scholarships/grants, 27% as loans/jobs. **Non-need-based:** Awarded to 967 full-time undergraduates, including 257 freshmen. Scholarships awarded for academics, alumni affiliation, art, athletics, leadership, music/drama, ROTC, state residency.

Application procedures. Admission: No deadline. $50 fee, may be waived for applicants with need. Admission notification on a rolling basis beginning on or about 9/1. **Financial aid:** Priority date 5/1, closing date 5/1. FAFSA required. Applicants notified on a rolling basis starting 3/1; must reply by 5/1.

Academics. Reduced course load is available to learning disabled students without compromising financial aid benefits. Students need the appropriate medical documentation to be considered. **Special study options:** Accelerated study, combined bachelor's/graduate degree, distance learning, double major, dual enrollment of high school students, honors, independent study, internships, New York semester, student-designed major, study abroad, teacher certification program, Washington semester. **Credit/placement by examination:** AP, CLEP, IB, SAT, ACT, institutional tests. 32 credit hours maximum toward bachelor's degree. If enrolled in undergraduate evening adult program, the aggregate of credit by examination may not exceed 32 semester hours, excluding International Baccalaureate Credit. Maximum Professional Education Credit which may be awarded are as follows: 31 credit hours towards B.S. in Organizational Management; 37 credit hours towards B.S. in Psychology; or 39 credit hours towards B.A. in Ministry. **Support services:** Reduced course load, remedial instruction, study skills assistance, tutoring, writing center.

Honors college/program. 3.5 GPA and 26 ACT/1200 SAT required.

Majors. Biology: General. **Business:** Accounting, business admin, finance, international, marketing, organizational behavior. **Communications:** Communications/speech/rhetoric, journalism, public relations. **Computer sciences:** Computer science. **Education:** Art, biology, elementary, English, mathematics, music, physical. **English:** English lit. **Health services:** Athletic training, nursing (RN). **History:** General. **Math:** General. **Philosophy/religion:** Philosophy. **Physical sciences:** Forensic chemistry. **Psychology:** General. **Social sciences:** Political science. **Theology:** Bible, missionary, theology. **Visual/performing arts:** Cinematography, dance, dramatic, graphic design, music, music performance, music theory/composition, piano/keyboard, studio arts, voice/opera.

Most popular majors. Biology 6%, business/marketing 25%, education 6%, health sciences 10%, psychology 15%, theological studies 11%, visual/performing arts 10%.

Technology on campus. 350 workstations in dormitories, library, computer center, student center. Dormitories wired for high-speed internet access and linked to campus network. Commuter students can connect to campus network. Online course registration, online library, helpline, wireless network available.

Student life. Freshman orientation: Mandatory, $15 fee. Preregistration for classes offered. One-day program. **Policies:** Undergraduate students required to donate 45 hours of community service for each year of attendance. Religious observance required. **Housing:** Guaranteed on-campus for freshmen. Coed dorms, single-sex dorms, apartments, themed housing available. $300 fully refundable deposit, deadline 8/20. **Activities:** Bands, campus ministries, choral groups, dance, drama, international student organizations, literary magazine, music ensembles, musical theater, student government, student newspaper, symphony orchestra, College Republicans, Presidential Ambassadors, Black Student Union, Sigma Alpha Omega Fellowship Club, PBA Praise, Student Government, pre-pharmacy society, College Democrats, Fellowship of Christian Athletes, science club.

Athletics. NCAA. **Intercollegiate:** Baseball M, basketball, cross-country W, golf, soccer, softball W, tennis, volleyball W. **Intramural:** Basketball M, football (non-tackle), sand volleyball, softball. **Team name:** Sailfish.

Student services. Chaplain/spiritual director, career counseling, student employment services, financial aid counseling, health services, minority student services, personal counseling. **Physically disabled:** Services for visually, speech, hearing impaired.

Contact. E-mail: admit@pba.edu
Phone: (561) 803-2100 Toll-free number: (888) 468-6722
Fax: (561) 803-2115
Joe Sharp, Dean of Admissions, Palm Beach Atlantic University, 901 South Flagler Drive, West Palm Beach, FL 33416-4708

Rasmussen College: Fort Myers
Fort Myers, Florida
www.rasmussen.edu

- For-profit 4-year career college
- Small city
- 642 degree-seeking undergraduates

General. Regionally accredited. **Degrees:** 42 bachelor's, 151 associate awarded. **Calendar:** Quarter. **Full-time faculty:** 11 total. **Part-time faculty:** 49 total.

Freshman class profile. 229 applied, 158 admitted, 158 enrolled.

Basis for selection. Open admission, but selective for some programs.

2016-2017 Annual costs. Tuition/fees (projected): $13,455. **Additional information:** Full-time tuition varies according to program of study. Required course materials fee of $150 per course.

Application procedures. Admission: No deadline. No application fee. Admission notification on a rolling basis. **Financial aid:** No deadline. FAFSA, institutional form required. Applicants notified on a rolling basis.

Academics. Credit/placement by examination: AP, CLEP.

Majors. Business: Accounting, accounting/business management, business admin, finance, human resources, information resources management, marketing. **Computer sciences:** Computer science, security, system admin, web page design. **Health services:** Health care admin, health information management, nursing (RN). **Protective services:** Criminal justice, special ops. **Visual/performing arts:** Digital arts, game design.

Contact. Phone: (239) 477-2100
Susan Hammerstrom, Director of Admissions, Rasmussen College: Fort Myers, 9160 Forum Corporate Parkway, Suite 100, Fort Myers, FL 33905-7805

Rasmussen College: New Port Richey
New Port Richey, Florida
www.rasmussen.edu   **CB code: 3503**

- For-profit 4-year career college
- Commuter campus in small city
- 637 degree-seeking undergraduates

General. Regionally accredited. **Degrees:** 54 bachelor's, 200 associate awarded. **Location:** 30 miles from Tampa. **Calendar:** Quarter. **Full-time faculty:** 18 total. **Part-time faculty:** 16 total.

Freshman class profile. 222 applied, 172 admitted, 172 enrolled.

Basis for selection. Open admission, but selective for some programs. Some programs require entrance examinations and additional information.

2016-2017 Annual costs. Tuition/fees (projected): $13,455.

Application procedures. Admission: No deadline. No application fee. Admission notification on a rolling basis. **Financial aid:** No deadline. FAFSA, institutional form required. Applicants notified on a rolling basis.

Academics. Special study options: Distance learning, double major, honors, independent study, internships. **Credit/placement by examination:** AP, CLEP, IB, institutional tests. 45 credit hours maximum toward associate degree, 90 toward bachelor's. Limited to specific programs, and to courses. **Support services:** Learning center, remedial instruction, study skills assistance, tutoring, writing center.

Majors. Business: Accounting, accounting/business management, business admin, finance, human resources, information resources management, marketing. **Computer sciences:** Computer science, security, system admin, web page design. **Health services:** Health care admin, health information management, nursing (RN). **Protective services:** Criminal justice, special ops. **Visual/performing arts:** Digital arts, game design.

Technology on campus. 100 workstations in library, computer center, student center. Online course registration, online library, helpline, wireless network available.

Student life. Freshman orientation: Mandatory. Preregistration for classes offered.

Student services. Adult student services, career counseling, services for economically disadvantaged, student employment services, financial aid counseling, placement for graduates.

Contact. E-mail: susan.hammerstrom@rasmussen.edu
Phone: (727) 942-0069 Fax: (727) 938-5709
Susan Hammerstrom, Director of Admissions, Rasmussen College: New Port Richey, 8661 Citizens Drive, New Port Richey, FL 34654

Rasmussen College: Ocala
Ocala, Florida
www.rasmussen.edu   CB code: 3502

- For-profit 4-year career college
- Commuter campus in small city
- 1,305 degree-seeking undergraduates

General. Regionally accredited. **Degrees:** 72 bachelor's, 272 associate awarded. **Calendar:** Quarter. **Full-time faculty:** 28 total. **Part-time faculty:** 53 total.

Freshman class profile. 425 applied, 335 admitted, 335 enrolled.

Basis for selection. Open admission, but selective for some programs. Some programs require entrance examinations and additional information.

2016-2017 Annual costs. Tuition/fees (projected): $13,455.

Application procedures. Admission: No deadline. No application fee. Admission notification on a rolling basis. **Financial aid:** No deadline. FAFSA, institutional form required. Applicants notified on a rolling basis.

Academics. Special study options: Distance learning, double major, honors, independent study, internships. **Credit/placement by examination:** AP, CLEP, IB, institutional tests. 45 credit hours maximum toward associate degree, 90 toward bachelor's. Limited to specific programs, and to courses for which programs are available. **Support services:** Learning center, remedial instruction, study skills assistance, tutoring, writing center.

Majors. Business: Accounting, accounting/business management, business admin, finance, human resources, information resources management, marketing. **Computer sciences:** Computer science, security, system admin, web page design. **Health services:** Health care admin, health information management, nursing (RN). **Protective services:** Criminal justice, special ops. **Visual/performing arts:** Digital arts, game design.

Technology on campus. 100 workstations in library, computer center, student center. Online course registration, online library, helpline, wireless network available.

Student life. Freshman orientation: Mandatory. Preregistration for classes offered.

Student services. Adult student services, career counseling, services for economically disadvantaged, student employment services, financial aid counseling, placement for graduates.

Contact. E-mail: susan.hammerstrom@rasmussen.edu
Phone: (352) 629-1941 Fax: (352) 629-0926
Susan Hammerstrom, Director of Admissions, Rasmussen College: Ocala, 2221 Southwest 46th Court, Ocala, FL 34474

Rasmussen College: Tampa/Brandon
Tampa, Florida
www.rasmussen.edu

- For-profit 4-year branch campus and career college
- Large city
- 583 degree-seeking undergraduates

General. Regionally accredited. **Degrees:** 21 bachelor's, 111 associate awarded. **Calendar:** Quarter. **Full-time faculty:** 9 total. **Part-time faculty:** 43 total.

Freshman class profile. 258 applied, 192 admitted, 192 enrolled.

Basis for selection. Open admission, but selective for some programs.

2016-2017 Annual costs. Tuition/fees (projected): $13,455. **Additional information:** Full-time tuition varies according to program of study. Required course materials fee of $150 per course.

Application procedures. Admission: No deadline. No application fee. Admission notification on a rolling basis. **Financial aid:** No deadline. FAFSA, institutional form required. Applicants notified on a rolling basis.

Academics. Credit/placement by examination: AP, CLEP.

Majors. Business: Accounting, accounting/business management, business admin, finance, human resources, information resources management, marketing. **Computer sciences:** Computer science, security, system admin, web page design. **Health services:** Health care admin, health information management, nursing (RN). **Protective services:** Criminal justice, special ops. **Visual/performing arts:** Digital arts, game design.

Contact. Phone: (813) 246-7600
Susan Hammerstrom, Director of Admissions, Rasmussen College: Tampa/Brandon, 4042 Park Oak Boulevard, Tampa, FL 33610

Remington College of Nursing
Lake Mary, Florida
www.remingtoncollege.edu

- Private 4-year nursing college
- Large town
- 184 undergraduates

General. Regionally accredited; also accredited by ACCSC. **Degrees:** 86 bachelor's awarded. **Calendar:** Quarter. **Full-time faculty:** 2 total. **Part-time faculty:** 15 total.

Basis for selection. Open admission, but selective for some programs.

2015-2016 Annual costs. Total tuition for the accelerated BSN program is $42,000 plus a $50 application fee. Tuition includes books, supplies, uniforms (except shoes), malpractice insurance, lab fees, computer-assisted instruction and equipment.

Application procedures. Admission: Closing date 6/1. $50 fee. **Financial aid:** No deadline.

Academics. Credit/placement by examination: AP, CLEP.

Majors. Health services: Nursing (RN).

Contact. E-mail: admissions@remingtoncollege.edu
Remington College of Nursing, 660 Century Point, Lake Mary, FL 32746

Remington College: Tampa
Tampa, Florida
www.tampa.remingtoncollege.edu   CB code: 0123

- Private 4-year technical college
- Commuter campus in very large city
- 350 undergraduates
- Interview required

General. Founded in 1948. Accredited by ACCSC. **Degrees:** 4 bachelor's, 10 associate awarded. **Calendar:** Quarter, extensive summer session. **Full-time faculty:** 13 total. **Part-time faculty:** 7 total.

Basis for selection. Recommendations considered; Wonderlic test used.

2015-2016 Annual costs. Personal expenses: $1,200. **Additional information:** Diploma programs: $15,995-$19,990. Associate programs, $33,900. Bachelor's program: $24,700.

Financial aid. All financial aid based on need.

Application procedures. Admission: No deadline. $50 fee. Admission notification on a rolling basis. **Financial aid:** No deadline. FAFSA, institutional form required.

Academics. Special study options: Accelerated study, combined bachelor's/graduate degree, distance learning. **Credit/placement by examination:** AP, CLEP. **Support services:** Remedial instruction, tutoring.

Majors. Protective services: Law enforcement admin.

Technology on campus. 350 workstations in library, computer center. Online library, helpline, repair service, wireless network available.

Student life. Freshman orientation: Mandatory. Preregistration for classes offered.

Student services. Career counseling, student employment services, financial aid counseling, personal counseling, placement for graduates.

Contact. Phone: (813) 333-7939 Toll-free number: (800) 992-4850 Fax: (813) 935-7415
Gary Schwartz, Director of Recruiting, Remington College: Tampa, 6302 East Dr. Martin Luther King Jr. Boulevard, Tampa, FL 33619

Ringling College of Art and Design
Sarasota, Florida **CB member**
www.ringling.edu **CB code: 5573**

- Private 4-year visual arts college
- Residential campus in small city
- 1,258 degree-seeking undergraduates: 6% part-time, 63% women, 3% African American, 9% Asian American, 16% Hispanic/Latino, 1% Native American, 2% Multi-racial, non-Hispanic, 15% international
- 77% of applicants admitted
- Application essay required
- 70% graduate within 6 years

General. Founded in 1931. Regionally accredited. **Degrees:** 269 bachelor's awarded. **Location:** 50 miles from Tampa. **Calendar:** Semester, limited summer session. **Full-time faculty:** 96 total; 62% have terminal degrees, 5% minority, 30% women. **Part-time faculty:** 58 total; 38% have terminal degrees, 5% minority, 57% women. **Class size:** 81% < 20, 16% 20-39, 2% 40-49, 1% 50-99. **Special facilities:** Art library, art center, art galleries.

Freshman class profile. 1,492 applied, 1,142 admitted, 306 enrolled.

GPA 3.75 or higher:	22%	Return as sophomores:	83%
GPA 3.50-3.74:	17%	Out-of-state:	55%
GPA 3.0-3.49:	33%	Live on campus:	85%
GPA 2.0-2.99:	28%	International:	13%

Basis for selection. Portfolio, school achievement record, statement of purpose, and recommendations important. Interview recommended. Portfolio required. **Home schooled:** State high school equivalency certificate required. **Learning Disabled:** Students seeking special accommodations for learning disabilities must provide documentation of disability.

2015-2016 Annual costs. Tuition/fees: $41,480. Room/board: $13,850.

2015-2016 Financial aid. Need-based: Average need met was 50%. Average scholarship/grant was $17,652; average loan $6,969. 57% of total undergraduate aid awarded as scholarships/grants, 43% as loans/jobs. **Non-need-based:** Scholarships awarded for academics, art.

Application procedures. Admission: No deadline. $70 fee, may be waived for applicants with need. Admission notification on a rolling basis beginning on or about 9/1. **Financial aid:** Priority date 3/1; no closing date. FAFSA required. Applicants notified on a rolling basis starting 4/1.

Academics. Special study options: Dual enrollment of high school students, ESL, exchange student, independent study, internships, New York semester, study abroad. **Credit/placement by examination:** AP, CLEP, IB. 30 credit hours maximum toward bachelor's degree. **Support services:** Learning center, pre-admission summer program, remedial instruction, study skills assistance, tutoring, writing center.

Majors. Communications: Advertising. **Communications technology:** Animation/special effects. **Visual/performing arts:** Cinematography, commercial/advertising art, game design, graphic design, illustration, interior design, photography, studio arts, studio arts management.

Most popular majors. Communication technologies 23%, visual/performing arts 75%.

Technology on campus. PC or laptop required. 879 workstations in dormitories, library, computer center, student center. Dormitories wired for high-speed internet access and linked to campus network. Commuter students can connect to campus network. Online course registration, online library, helpline, repair service, student web hosting, wireless network available.

Student life. Freshman orientation: Mandatory. Preregistration for classes offered. Held the week prior to start of classes. **Housing:** Coed dorms, single-sex dorms, special housing for disabled, apartments, gender-neutral housing, themed housing, wellness housing available. $400 nonrefundable deposit. All housing accommodations are ADA compliant. **Activities:** Campus ministries, dance, drama, international student organizations, student government, TV station.

Athletics. Intramural: Basketball, football (non-tackle), soccer, table tennis, ultimate frisbee, volleyball, weight lifting. **Team name:** Fighting Armadillos.

Student services. Alcohol/substance abuse counseling, chaplain/spiritual director, career counseling, student employment services, financial aid counseling, health services, minority student services, personal counseling, placement for graduates, veterans' counselor, women's services. **Physically disabled:** Services for visually, hearing impaired.

Contact. E-mail: admissions@ringling.edu
Phone: (941) 351-5100 Toll-free number: (800) 255-7695
Fax: (941) 359-7517
James Dean, Dean of Admissions, Ringling College of Art and Design, 2700 North Tamiami Trail, Sarasota, FL 34234-5895

Rollins College
Winter Park, Florida **CB member**
www.rollins.edu **CB code: 5572**

- Private 4-year liberal arts college
- Residential campus in large town
- 1,948 degree-seeking undergraduates: 59% women, 3% African American, 3% Asian American, 14% Hispanic/Latino, 3% Multi-racial, non-Hispanic, 9% international
- 573 degree-seeking graduate students
- 60% of applicants admitted
- Application essay required
- 71% graduate within 6 years

General. Founded in 1885. Regionally accredited. **Degrees:** 623 bachelor's awarded; master's, doctoral offered. **Location:** 5 miles from Orlando. **Calendar:** Semester, limited summer session. **Full-time faculty:** 233 total; 92% have terminal degrees, 12% minority, 44% women. **Class size:** 71% < 20, 28% 20-39, less than 1% 50-99. **Special facilities:** 2 performing arts theaters, fine arts museum, boathouse, beach and nature walk at Lake Virginia, child development center, greenhouse, outdoor classroom.

Freshman class profile. 4,922 applied, 2,972 admitted, 493 enrolled.

Mid 50% test scores		GPA 2.0-2.99:	24%
SAT critical reading:	550-650	Rank in top quarter:	66%
SAT math:	560-660	Rank in top tenth:	34%
SAT writing:	550-650	End year in good standing:	99%
ACT composite:	24-29	Return as sophomores:	71%
GPA 3.75 or higher:	21%	Out-of-state:	50%
GPA 3.50-3.74:	18%	Live on campus:	88%
GPA 3.0-3.49:	37%	International:	7%

Basis for selection. School achievement record and GPA most important, followed by test scores, activities, essay, recommendations, and interview (required for merit scholarships and certain academic programs only). Students considered for merit scholarships, 3/2 Accelerated Management Program, or Honors Program required to submit SAT/ACT. All other students have option to apply under Test Score Waived Option and must submit personal representation of their strengths, interests, and/or passions as well as a teacher recommendation from junior or senior year core course. Auditions required for applicants seeking theater and/or music scholarships.

High school preparation. College-preparatory program recommended. 17 units required; 24 recommended. Required and recommended units include English 4, mathematics 3-4, social studies 2-3, history 2-3, science 2-4, foreign language 2-3 and academic electives 2-3. 3-4 units recommended for foreign language, social studies, history.

2015-2016 Annual costs. Tuition/fees: $44,760. Room/board: $13,910. Books/supplies: $1,244. Personal expenses: $3,620.

2015-2016 Financial aid. Need-based: 325 full-time freshmen applied for aid; 272 deemed to have need; 271 received aid. Average need met was 71%. Average scholarship/grant was $30,035; average loan $3,720. 84% of total undergraduate aid awarded as scholarships/grants, 16% as loans/jobs. **Non-need-based:** Awarded to 912 full-time undergraduates, including 219 freshmen. Scholarships awarded for academics, art, athletics, leadership, music/drama, state residency. **Additional information:** Audition required for theater arts and music scholarship applicants. Portfolio required for art scholarships.

Application procedures. Admission: Closing date 2/15 (postmark date). $50 fee, may be waived for applicants with need. Admission notification by 4/1. Must reply by 5/1. **Financial aid:** Priority date 3/1; no closing date. FAFSA required. Applicants notified on a rolling basis starting 3/1.

Academics. International business major featuring language training, internships, and study abroad available; pre-professional support services. **Special study options:** Accelerated study, combined bachelor's/graduate degree, cross-registration, double major, exchange student, honors, independent study, internships, student-designed major, study abroad, teacher certification program, Washington semester. **Credit/placement by examination:** AP, CLEP, IB, institutional tests. 76 credit hours maximum toward bachelor's degree. **Support services:** Learning center, reduced course load, study skills assistance, tutoring, writing center.

Honors college/program. Top 10% of entering freshman class admitted.

Majors. Area/ethnic studies: American, Asian, Latin American/Caribbean. **Biology:** General, biochemistry, Biochemistry/molecular biology, marine, molecular. **Business:** General, international, organizational behavior. **Communications:** General, organizational. **Computer sciences:** General. **Conservation:** Environmental studies. **Education:** Elementary. **English:** English lit. **Foreign languages:** Classics, French, Spanish. **History:** General. **Liberal arts:** Arts/sciences, humanities. **Math:** General. **Philosophy/religion:** Philosophy, religion. **Physical sciences:** Chemistry, physics. **Psychology:** General. **Social sciences:** Anthropology, economics, international relations, political science, sociology. **Visual/performing arts:** Art, art history/conservation, dramatic, music, studio arts.

Most popular majors. Biology 6%, business/marketing 14%, communications/journalism 14%, psychology 10%, social sciences 23%, visual/performing arts 10%.

Technology on campus. 187 workstations in library, computer center, student center. Dormitories wired for high-speed internet access and linked to campus network. Commuter students can connect to campus network. Online course registration, online library, helpline, repair service, student web hosting, wireless network available.

Student life. Freshman orientation: Mandatory. Preregistration for classes offered. Held just prior to fall semester. **Policies:** Freshmen not permitted cars on campus. **Housing:** Guaranteed on-campus for freshmen. Coed dorms, special housing for disabled, apartments, fraternity/sorority housing, gender-neutral housing, themed housing available. **Activities:** Bands, campus ministries, choral groups, dance, drama, film society, international student organizations, literary magazine, music ensembles, Model UN, musical theater, opera, radio station, student government, student newspaper, symphony orchestra, TV station, Hillel, Catholic Campus Ministry (Newman Club), Canterbury Club, Asian Student Association, Black Student Union, Caribbean Student Association, Latin American Student Association, Chinese Student Organization, Desi, Deutsch Student Society, College Democrats, Student Government Association, Join Us In Making Progress (JUMP), Eco-Rollins, Immersion: Citizens Take Action, Making Lives Better, Project Bridge, College Republicans, Rollins Relief, Rollins Awareness and Activism.

Athletics. NCAA. **Intercollegiate:** Baseball M, basketball, cross-country, golf, lacrosse, rowing (crew), sailing, skiing, soccer, softball W, swimming, tennis, volleyball W. **Intramural:** Baseball M, basketball, bowling, soccer, softball, table tennis, tennis, ultimate frisbee, volleyball W. **Team name:** Tars.

Student services. Alcohol/substance abuse counseling, chaplain/spiritual director, career counseling, financial aid counseling, health services, minority student services, personal counseling, veterans' counselor, women's services. **Physically disabled:** Services for visually, speech, hearing impaired.

Contact. E-mail: admission@rollins.edu
Phone: (407) 646-2161 Fax: (407) 646-1502
Holly Pohlig, Director of Admission, Rollins College, 1000 Holt Avenue, Campus Box 2720, Winter Park, FL 32789

Saint Leo University
Saint Leo, Florida   **CB member**
www.saintleo.edu   **CB code:** 5638

- Private 4-year university affiliated with the Roman Catholic Church
- Residential campus in rural community
- 2,367 degree-seeking undergraduates: 4% part-time, 54% women, 13% African American, 2% Asian American, 19% Hispanic/Latino, 3% Multiracial, non-Hispanic, 12% international
- 3,758 degree-seeking graduate students
- 73% of applicants admitted
- 42% graduate within 6 years

General. Founded in 1889. Regionally accredited. **Degrees:** 383 bachelor's, 22 associate awarded; master's, professional offered. **ROTC:** Army, Air Force. **Location:** 25 miles from Tampa. **Calendar:** Semester, limited summer session. **Full-time faculty:** 125 total; 82% have terminal degrees, 10% minority, 41% women. **Part-time faculty:** 87 total; 36% have terminal degrees, 13% minority, 63% women. **Class size:** 43% < 20, 57% 20-39. **Special facilities:** Center for Catholic and Jewish studies.

Freshman class profile. 3,865 applied, 2,803 admitted, 659 enrolled.

Mid 50% test scores			
SAT critical reading:	460-540	GPA 2.0-2.99:	19%
SAT math:	450-540	Rank in top quarter:	32%
SAT writing:	430-530	Rank in top tenth:	10%
ACT composite:	20-24	Return as sophomores:	71%
GPA 3.75 or higher:	32%	Out-of-state:	32%
GPA 3.50-3.74:	19%	Live on campus:	85%
GPA 3.0-3.49:	30%	International:	9%

Basis for selection. High school GPA, guidance counselor's recommendation, high school curriculum important. Interview recommended. **Home schooled:** Transcript of courses and grades, interview, letter of recommendation (nonparent) required. Bibliography of all high school reading material, 2 letters of recommendation, portfolio of sample work required.

High school preparation. College-preparatory program recommended. 16 units recommended. Recommended units include English 4, mathematics 3, social studies 3, science 2, foreign language 2 and academic electives 2. Algebra I and II, geometry strongly recommended. Those planning to study science should complete courses in biology and chemistry.

2015-2016 Annual costs. Tuition/fees: $20,830. Room/board: $9,870. Books/supplies: $1,720. Personal expenses: $1,372.

2015-2016 Financial aid. Need-based: 579 full-time freshmen applied for aid; 505 deemed to have need; 504 received aid. Average need met was 68%. Average scholarship/grant was $14,862; average loan $3,428. 64% of total undergraduate aid awarded as scholarships/grants, 36% as loans/jobs. **Non-need-based:** Awarded to 799 full-time undergraduates, including 206 freshmen. Scholarships awarded for academics, alumni affiliation, athletics, leadership, minority status, religious affiliation, state residency.

Application procedures. Admission: Priority date 1/15; no deadline. $40 fee, may be waived for applicants with need, free for online applicants. Admission notification on a rolling basis beginning on or about 7/1. Must reply by May 1 or within 2 week(s) if notified thereafter. **Financial aid:** Priority date 3/1; no closing date. FAFSA required. Applicants notified on a rolling basis starting 1/1.

Academics. Special study options: Combined bachelor's/graduate degree, distance learning, double major, dual enrollment of high school students, ESL, honors, independent study, internships, liberal arts/career combination, study abroad, teacher certification program, weekend college. Opportunity to study abroad in Italy, France, Ecuador, Spain, United Kingdom, Ireland, Australia, Germany, Scotland and Greece. Freshman English Composition classes for non-native speakers of English available. **Credit/placement by examination:** AP, CLEP, IB, institutional tests. 40 credit hours maximum toward associate degree, 40 toward bachelor's. **Support services:** Learning center, pre-admission summer program, reduced course load, remedial instruction, study skills assistance, tutoring, writing center.

Honors college/program. 3.5 GPA and 1150 SAT (exclusive of Writing) or 25 ACT required. Full honors curriculum consists of integrated sequence of 6 courses plus 2 research courses.

Majors. Biology: General. **Business:** Accounting, business admin, communications, hospitality admin, human resources, management science, marketing. **Computer sciences:** General. **Conservation:** Environmental studies. **Education:** Elementary, middle. **English:** Creative writing, English lit. **Health services:** Clinical lab science, health care admin. **History:** General. **Human services:** Community org/advocacy, social work. **Liberal arts:** Arts/

sciences. **Math:** General. **Parks/recreation:** Sports admin. **Philosophy/religion:** Religion. **Protective services:** Criminal justice, criminalistics, homeland security. **Psychology:** General. **Social sciences:** International relations, political science, sociology.

Most popular majors. Biology 7%, business/marketing 22%, computer/information sciences 10%, education 6%, parks/recreation 8%, psychology 8%, security/protective services 15%, social sciences 7%.

Technology on campus. 1,264 workstations in dormitories, library, student center. Dormitories wired for high-speed internet access and linked to campus network. Commuter students can connect to campus network. Online course registration, online library, helpline, repair service, student web hosting, wireless network available.

Student life. Freshman orientation: Mandatory, $300 fee. Preregistration for classes offered. Held over four days in August. **Policies:** Fish aquariums allowed. **Housing:** Guaranteed on-campus for all undergraduates. Coed dorms, single-sex dorms, apartments, themed housing available. $500 nonrefundable deposit, deadline 5/1. Freshmen-only Housing, Theme Housing, Wellness Housing. **Activities:** Campus ministries, choral groups, dance, drama, international student organizations, literary magazine, music ensembles, musical theater, student government, student newspaper, Samaritans, intercultural student association, Student Chaplain program, Pi Sigma Alpha, social work club, La Familia, students for environmental awareness, Fellowship of Christian Athletes, salsa club, Progressive Black Men.

Athletics. NCAA. **Intercollegiate:** Baseball M, basketball, cross-country, golf, lacrosse, soccer, softball W, swimming, tennis, volleyball W. **Intramural:** Basketball, field hockey, football (non-tackle), soccer, softball, tennis, ultimate frisbee, volleyball. **Team name:** Lions.

Student services. Adult student services, alcohol/substance abuse counseling, chaplain/spiritual director, career counseling, student employment services, financial aid counseling, health services, personal counseling, veterans' counselor. **Physically disabled:** Services for visually impaired.

Contact. E-mail: admissions@saintleo.edu
Phone: (352) 588-8283 Toll-free number: (800) 334-5532
Fax: (352) 588-8257
Reggie Hill, Assistant Vice President of Enrollment, Saint Leo University, Box 6665 MC2008, Saint Leo, FL 33574-6665

Saint Thomas University
Miami Gardens, Florida
www.stu.edu
CB code: 5076

▶ Private 4-year university affiliated with the Roman Catholic Church
▶ Commuter campus in very large city
▶ 882 degree-seeking undergraduates: 7% part-time, 51% women, 22% African American, 51% Hispanic/Latino, 1% Multi-racial, non-Hispanic, 11% international
▶ 1,736 degree-seeking graduate students
▶ 49% of applicants admitted
▶ SAT or ACT (ACT writing optional) required
▶ 44% graduate within 6 years

General. Founded in 1961. Regionally accredited. Multilocation institution. Affiliated with Archdiocese of Miami. **Degrees:** 233 bachelor's awarded; master's, professional, doctoral offered. **Location:** 10 miles from Miami. **Calendar:** Semester, extensive summer session. **Full-time faculty:** 104 total; 94% have terminal degrees, 35% minority, 42% women. **Part-time faculty:** 112 total; 21% have terminal degrees, 59% minority, 44% women. **Class size:** 68% < 20, 31% 20-39, less than 1% 40-49.

Freshman class profile. 1,570 applied, 768 admitted, 192 enrolled.

Mid 50% test scores		GPA 2.0-2.99:	33%
SAT math:	400-510	Rank in top quarter:	27%
SAT writing:	410-500	Rank in top tenth:	13%
ACT composite:	17-22	Return as sophomores:	55%
GPA 3.75 or higher:	16%	Out-of-state:	28%
GPA 3.50-3.74:	13%	Live on campus:	50%
GPA 3.0-3.49:	36%		

Basis for selection. High school grades, test scores primary factors. Class rank, interview, school, community activities, recommendations also considered. Interview recommended.

High school preparation. College-preparatory program recommended. 18 units required. Required units include English 4, mathematics 3, social studies 3, science 2 and academic electives 6.

2015-2016 Annual costs. Tuition/fees: $27,780. Room/board: $7,720. Books/supplies: $1,250. Personal expenses: $2,808.

2014-2015 Financial aid. Need-based: 46% of total undergraduate aid awarded as scholarships/grants, 54% as loans/jobs. **Non-need-based:** Scholarships awarded for academics, athletics, leadership.

Application procedures. Admission: No deadline. $40 fee, may be waived for applicants with need. Admission notification on a rolling basis. Must reply by May 1 or within 2 week(s) if notified thereafter. Applicants needing on-campus housing strongly encouraged to apply before 5/15. **Financial aid:** Priority date 4/1; no closing date. FAFSA required. Applicants notified on a rolling basis starting 3/1.

Academics. Special study options: Combined bachelor's/graduate degree, distance learning, double major, dual enrollment of high school students, ESL, honors, independent study, internships, liberal arts/career combination, teacher certification program. **Credit/placement by examination:** AP, CLEP, SAT, ACT, institutional tests. 45 credit hours maximum toward bachelor's degree. **Support services:** Learning center, pre-admission summer program, reduced course load, remedial instruction, study skills assistance, tutoring, writing center.

Majors. Biology: General. **Business:** Accounting, business admin, finance, hospitality admin, international, organizational behavior, tourism/travel. **Communications:** Communications/speech/rhetoric, media studies. **Computer sciences:** General, computer science. **Conservation:** Environmental studies. **Education:** Elementary, secondary, social studies. **English:** English lit. **Health services:** Health care admin, premedicine, preveterinary. **History:** General. **Liberal arts:** Arts/sciences. **Parks/recreation:** Sports admin. **Philosophy/religion:** Religion. **Physical sciences:** Chemistry. **Protective services:** Criminal justice. **Psychology:** General. **Social sciences:** Political science. **Theology:** Religious ed.

Most popular majors. Biology 10%, business/marketing 43%, psychology 6%, security/protective services 18%.

Technology on campus. 200 workstations in library, computer center. Dormitories linked to campus network. Online course registration, helpline, wireless network available.

Student life. Freshman orientation: Mandatory. Preregistration for classes offered. **Housing:** Single-sex dorms available. $225 fully refundable deposit. **Activities:** Campus ministries, international student organizations, student government, Global Leadership Pax Romana student society, Caribbean students association, Kreyol Nation, Students Working for Equal Rights.

Athletics. NAIA. **Intercollegiate:** Baseball M, cross-country, golf, soccer, softball W, tennis, volleyball W. **Intramural:** Golf, soccer M, softball, tennis, volleyball. **Team name:** Bobcats.

Student services. Adult student services, alcohol/substance abuse counseling, career counseling, student employment services, financial aid counseling, health services, personal counseling, placement for graduates. **Physically disabled:** Services for visually, hearing impaired.

Contact. E-mail: signup@stu.edu
Phone: (305) 628-6546 Toll-free number: (800) 367-9010
Fax: (305) 628-6591
Celso Alvarez, Dean of Enrollment, Saint Thomas University, 16401 Northwest 37th Avenue, Miami Gardens, FL 33054-6459

Schiller International University
Largo, Florida
www.schiller.edu
CB code: 0835

▶ For-profit 4-year university
▶ Commuter campus in small city
▶ 145 degree-seeking undergraduates

General. Founded in 1964. Accredited by ACICS. Campuses located in Largo, Florida; Heidelberg, Germany; Madrid, Spain; and Paris, France; as well as Schiller Online. Students may transfer between campuses without loss of time or credit. **Degrees:** 7 bachelor's, 1 associate awarded; master's offered. **Location:** 20 miles from Tampa. **Calendar:** Semester, extensive summer session. **Full-time faculty:** 2 total. **Part-time faculty:** 10 total.

Basis for selection. Open admission. Interviews recommended.

2015-2016 Annual costs. Books/supplies: $1,250. **Additional information:** Total program costs: associates $35,400-$47,190; bachelor's $35,400-$70,800.

Financial aid. Non-need-based: Scholarships awarded for academics, alumni affiliation, leadership, minority status, state residency. **Additional information:** Special scholarship program for US students studying abroad at European campuses of Schiller. Work-study available to students taking 2 or more courses.

Application procedures. Admission: No deadline. $20 fee. Application must be submitted on paper. Admission notification on a rolling basis. **Financial aid:** Closing date 4/1. FAFSA, institutional form required. Applicants notified on a rolling basis starting 5/1; must reply within 3 week(s) of notification.

Academics. Completion of intermediate level of at least one foreign language required for most undergraduate degree programs. **Special study options:** Accelerated study, cooperative education, distance learning, double major, ESL, internships, liberal arts/career combination, study abroad. **Credit/placement by examination:** AP, CLEP, IB, institutional tests. 16 credit hours maximum toward associate degree, 16 toward bachelor's. **Support services:** Study skills assistance, tutoring.

Majors. Business: General, banking/financial services, business admin, finance, hotel/motel admin, international, international marketing, marketing, tourism/travel. **Foreign languages:** French, German. **Social sciences:** International economics, international relations.

Most popular majors. Business/marketing 77%.

Technology on campus. Online library, wireless network available.

Student life. Freshman orientation: Mandatory. Preregistration for classes offered. **Activities:** Model UN, student government.

Student services. Adult student services, career counseling, services for economically disadvantaged, student employment services, financial aid counseling, personal counseling, placement for graduates.

Contact. E-mail: admissions@schiller.edu
Phone: (727) 736-5082 Toll-free number: (800) 261-9751
Fax: (727) 734-0359
Michele Geigle, President, Schiller International University, 8560 Ulmerton Road, Largo, FL 33771

Southeastern University
Lakeland, Florida
www.seu.edu   CB code: 5621

‣ Private 4-year liberal arts and teachers college affiliated with the Assemblies of God

‣ Residential campus in small city

‣ 3,412 degree-seeking undergraduates: 8% part-time, 55% women, 14% African American, 1% Asian American, 17% Hispanic/Latino, 1% Native Hawaiian/Pacific islander, 2% international

‣ 537 degree-seeking graduate students

‣ 46% of applicants admitted

‣ SAT or ACT (ACT writing optional), application essay required

‣ 39% graduate within 6 years

General. Founded in 1935. Regionally accredited. **Degrees:** 407 bachelor's, 21 associate awarded; master's offered. **ROTC:** Army. **Location:** 40 miles from Tampa, 50 miles from Orlando. **Calendar:** Semester, limited summer session. **Full-time faculty:** 128 total; 68% have terminal degrees, 16% minority, 62% women. **Class size:** 64% < 20, 34% 20-39, 1% 40-49, less than 1% 50-99.

Freshman class profile. 3,823 applied, 1,777 admitted, 979 enrolled.

Mid 50% test scores			
SAT critical reading:	430-550	GPA 3.0-3.49:	26%
SAT math:	410-530	GPA 2.0-2.99:	27%
SAT writing:	410-530	Return as sophomores:	67%
ACT composite:	17-23	Out-of-state:	36%
GPA 3.75 or higher:	30%	Live on campus:	61%
GPA 3.50-3.74:	15%	International:	1%

Basis for selection. Christian character essay required. Interview recommended for academically weak applicants. **Home schooled:** Transcript of courses and grades required.

High school preparation. College-preparatory program recommended. Recommended units include English 4, mathematics 4, social studies 4, science 4 (laboratory 1) and foreign language 2.

2015-2016 Annual costs. Tuition/fees: $22,840. Room/board: $9,148. Books/supplies: $1,600. Personal expenses: $1,200.

2014-2015 Financial aid. Need-based: 739 full-time freshmen applied for aid; 641 deemed to have need; 638 received aid. Average need met was 65%. Average scholarship/grant was $13,603; average loan $3,265. 57% of total undergraduate aid awarded as scholarships/grants, 43% as loans/jobs. **Non-need-based:** Awarded to 526 full-time undergraduates, including 173 freshmen. Scholarships awarded for academics, alumni affiliation, athletics, job skills, leadership, minority status, music/drama, religious affiliation, state residency.

Application procedures. Admission: Closing date 5/1 (postmark date). $40 fee, may be waived for applicants with need. Admission notification on a rolling basis. Must reply by 6/1. **Financial aid:** Priority date 2/15; no closing date. FAFSA required. Applicants notified on a rolling basis starting 3/15; must reply within 6 week(s) of notification.

Academics. Special study options: Distance learning, double major, dual enrollment of high school students, honors, independent study, internships, study abroad, teacher certification program. **Credit/placement by examination:** AP, CLEP, IB, SAT, ACT, institutional tests. 45 credit hours maximum toward bachelor's degree. **Support services:** Reduced course load, remedial instruction, study skills assistance, tutoring, writing center.

Majors. Biology: General. **Business:** General, accounting, finance, international, management information systems, marketing, organizational leadership. **Communications:** General, journalism, radio/TV. **Education:** Biology, elementary, English, mathematics, music, social science, special ed. **English:** English lit. **Health services:** Premedicine. **History:** General. **Human services:** Public policy, social work. **Math:** General. **Parks/recreation:** Sports admin. **Protective services:** Law enforcement admin. **Psychology:** General. **Theology:** Missionary, preministerial, sacred music. **Visual/performing arts:** Dramatic, film/cinema/video, music, music performance, piano/keyboard, voice/opera.

Most popular majors. Business/marketing 24%, communications/journalism 10%, education 10%, psychology 6%, public administration/social services 6%, theological studies 22%, visual/performing arts 7%.

Technology on campus. 158 workstations in library, computer center, student center. Dormitories wired for high-speed internet access and linked to campus network. Commuter students can connect to campus network. Online course registration, online library, helpline, wireless network available.

Student life. Freshman orientation: Mandatory. Preregistration for classes offered. **Policies:** Religious observance required. **Housing:** Guaranteed on-campus for freshmen. Single-sex dorms available. $200 fully refundable deposit, deadline 6/1. **Activities:** Bands, campus ministries, choral groups, dance, drama, international student organizations, music ensembles, musical theater, opera, radio station, student government, student newspaper, TV station, College Republicans, Habitat for Humanity, international justice mission, social work club, Christian Medical and Dental Association, student missions organization.

Athletics. NAIA, NCCAA. **Intercollegiate:** Baseball M, basketball, cheerleading, cross-country, football (tackle) M, golf M, soccer, softball W, tennis, volleyball W. **Intramural:** Basketball, football (non-tackle), soccer, softball, tennis, ultimate frisbee, volleyball. **Team name:** Fire.

Student services. Adult student services, chaplain/spiritual director, career counseling, student employment services, financial aid counseling, health services, personal counseling, placement for graduates.

Contact. E-mail: admission@seu.edu
Phone: (863) 667-5018 Toll-free number: (800) 500-8760
Fax: (863) 667-5200
Betania Torres, Director of Admission, Southeastern University, 1000 Longfellow Boulevard, Lakeland, FL 33801-6034

St. John Vianney College Seminary
Miami, Florida
www.sjvcs.edu   CB code: 5650

‣ Private 4-year liberal arts and seminary college for men affiliated with the Roman Catholic Church

‣ Residential campus in very large city

‣ 78 degree-seeking undergraduates: 3% women

‣ 31 degree-seeking graduate students

‣ Interview required

General. Founded in 1959. Regionally accredited. **Degrees:** 18 bachelor's awarded. **Location:** 12 miles from downtown. **Calendar:** Semester, limited summer session. **Full-time faculty:** 7 total. **Part-time faculty:** 11 total. **Class size:** 100% < 20.

Freshman class profile.

Out-of-state:	2%	Live on campus:	100%

Basis for selection. Interview, academic record, recommendations required. Those to be formed for priesthood should present evidence of vocation for priesthood and submit psychological and physical evaluations. Applicants referred by home (church) Diocesan Offices of Vocations.

High school preparation. 20 units required. Required units include English 4, mathematics 2, social studies 2, history 2, science 2, foreign language 2 and academic electives 6.

2015-2016 Annual costs. Tuition/fees: $14,760. Room/board: $11,000. Books/supplies: $800. Personal expenses: $2,000.

Application procedures. Admission: Priority date 6/30; deadline 7/15 (receipt date). No application fee. Admission notification on a rolling basis. **Financial aid:** No deadline. FAFSA required. Applicants notified on a rolling basis.

Academics. Fluency in both English and Spanish must be achieved. Students required to take at least 1 course in alternate language each semester. **Special study options:** Cross-registration, ESL, independent study. **Credit/placement by examination:** AP, CLEP, institutional tests. **Support services:** Pre-admission summer program, reduced course load, remedial instruction, study skills assistance, tutoring.

Majors. Philosophy/religion: Philosophy.

Technology on campus. 12 workstations in library, computer center. Online library, wireless network available.

Student life. Freshman orientation: Mandatory, $2,000 fee. Preregistration for classes offered. Three weeks during August. **Policies:** All sophomores and upperclassmen assigned weekly apostolic work at various locations. Religious observance required. **Housing:** Guaranteed on-campus for all undergraduates. **Activities:** Choral groups, drama, music ensembles, student government, student newspaper, apostolic works program.

Athletics. Intramural: Baseball M, basketball M, handball M, racquetball M, soccer M, softball M, swimming M, table tennis M, tennis M, volleyball M, weight lifting M.

Student services. Adult student services, career counseling, financial aid counseling, health services, personal counseling.

Contact. Phone: (305) 223-4561 ext. 115 Fax: (305) 223-0650
Ramon Santos, Academic Dean, St. John Vianney College Seminary, 2900 Southwest 87 Avenue, Miami, FL 33165-3244

Stetson University
DeLand, Florida
www.stetson.edu
CB member
CB code: 5630

- Private 4-year university
- Residential campus in large town
- 3,042 degree-seeking undergraduates: 2% part-time, 57% women, 8% African American, 2% Asian American, 15% Hispanic/Latino, 1% Native American, 3% Multi-racial, non-Hispanic, 5% international
- 1,222 degree-seeking graduate students
- 63% of applicants admitted
- Application essay required
- 64% graduate within 6 years; 27% enter graduate study

General. Founded in 1883. Regionally accredited. **Degrees:** 549 bachelor's awarded; master's, professional offered. **ROTC:** Army. **Location:** 20 miles from Daytona Beach, 40 miles from Orlando. **Calendar:** Semester, limited summer session. **Full-time faculty:** 265 total; 95% have terminal degrees, 17% minority, 45% women. **Part-time faculty:** 160 total; 64% have terminal degrees, 16% minority, 43% women. **Class size:** 54% < 20, 43% 20-39, 2% 40-49, less than 1% 50-99. **Special facilities:** Geological museum, greenhouse with growth chambers, digital arts laboratory, software development lab, aquatic research station, art center, environmental learning classroom, political archives, native plant landscape/garden, neuroscience research lab, DNA sequencing lab, courtroom classrooms, trading room and investment lab, 6 Beckerath organs, outdoor recreation and sport facilities including simplicity stables.

Freshman class profile.
11,216 applied, 7,119 admitted, 983 enrolled.

Mid 50% test scores			
SAT critical reading:	530-640	GPA 2.0-2.99:	5%
SAT math:	520-620	Rank in top quarter:	60%
SAT writing:	500-620	Rank in top tenth:	28%
ACT composite:	24-28	End year in good standing:	93%
GPA 3.75 or higher:	61%	Return as sophomores:	77%
GPA 3.50-3.74:	16%	Out-of-state:	31%
GPA 3.0-3.49:	18%	Live on campus:	88%
		International:	4%

Basis for selection. Applications reviewed individually and holistically, taking into consideration qualities of academic preparation (which includes both rigor of course work and grades), extracurricular activities, leadership potential, potential for adding a unique perspective, individual talents and character, recommendations, and, with the exception of test score optional candidates, ACT/SAT. Interview recommended. Audition required of music majors. Portfolio recommended for art majors.

High school preparation. College-preparatory program required. 14 units required. Required units include English 4, mathematics 3, social studies 2, science 3 and foreign language 2.

2015-2016 Annual costs. Tuition/fees: $41,590. Room/board: $11,944. Books/supplies: $1,200. Personal expenses: $1,000.

2015-2016 Financial aid. Need-based: 871 full-time freshmen applied for aid; 760 deemed to have need; 760 received aid. Average need met was 78%. Average scholarship/grant was $28,926; average loan $3,674. 79% of total undergraduate aid awarded as scholarships/grants, 21% as loans/jobs. **Non-need-based:** Awarded to 1,154 full-time undergraduates, including 375 freshmen. Scholarships awarded for academics, alumni affiliation, art, athletics, leadership, minority status, music/drama, religious affiliation, ROTC, state residency.

Application procedures. Admission: Priority date 12/1; no deadline. $50 fee, may be waived for applicants with need. Admission notification on a rolling basis beginning on or about 9/1. Must reply by May 1 or within 2 week(s) if notified thereafter. **Financial aid:** Priority date 3/15; no closing date. FAFSA required. Applicants notified on a rolling basis starting 3/1; must reply within 2 week(s) of notification.

Academics. Special study options: Accelerated study, combined bachelor's/graduate degree, distance learning, double major, honors, independent study, internships, liberal arts/career combination, student-designed major, study abroad, teacher certification program, Washington semester. **Credit/placement by examination:** AP, CLEP, IB, SAT, ACT, institutional tests. 32 credit hours maximum toward bachelor's degree. **Support services:** Learning center, reduced course load, study skills assistance, tutoring, writing center.

Majors. Area/ethnic studies: American, Russian/Slavic. **Biology:** General, aquatic, biochemistry, molecular. **Business:** Accounting, business admin, entrepreneurial studies, finance, international, management information systems, managerial economics, marketing. **Communications:** General. **Computer sciences:** General, computer science. **Conservation:** Environmental science. **Education:** Elementary, music. **English:** English lit. **Foreign languages:** French, German, Spanish. **History:** General. **Liberal arts:** Humanities. **Math:** General. **Parks/recreation:** Sports admin. **Philosophy/religion:** Philosophy, religion. **Physical sciences:** Chemistry, physics. **Psychology:** General. **Social sciences:** General, economics, geography, international relations, political science, sociology. **Visual/performing arts:** Art history/conservation, digital arts, dramatic, music, music performance, music technology, music theory/composition, piano/keyboard, stringed instruments, studio arts, voice/opera.

Most popular majors. Biology 9%, business/marketing 24%, health sciences 6%, psychology 11%, social sciences 11%, visual/performing arts 11%.

Technology on campus. 500 workstations in dormitories, library, computer center, student center. Dormitories wired for high-speed internet access and linked to campus network. Commuter students can connect to campus network. Online course registration, online library, helpline, repair service, student web hosting, wireless network available.

Student life. Freshman orientation: Mandatory, $100 fee. Preregistration for classes offered. Held the 4 days prior to start of classes. **Policies:** Students are required to live on campus until they have earned 90 credit hours. **Housing:** Guaranteed on-campus for freshmen. Coed dorms, single-sex dorms, apartments, fraternity/sorority housing, gender-neutral housing, themed housing, wellness housing available. $200 nonrefundable deposit. Pets allowed in dorm rooms. Family/partnered, pet-friendly, living-learning housing available. **Activities:** Bands, campus ministries, choral groups, dance, drama, film society, international student organizations, literary magazine, music ensembles, Model UN, musical theater, opera, student government, student newspaper, symphony orchestra, black student association, Caribbean student organization, Habitat for Humanity, Muslim student association, Hillel (JSO), Hatter Harvest, National Organization for Women, College Democrats, College Republicans.

Athletics. NCAA. **Intercollegiate:** Baseball M, basketball, cross-country, football (tackle) M, golf, lacrosse W, rowing (crew), sand volleyball W, soccer, softball W, tennis, volleyball W. **Intramural:** Basketball, sand volleyball, soccer, softball, ultimate frisbee, volleyball. **Team name:** Hatters.

Student services. Adult student services, alcohol/substance abuse counseling, chaplain/spiritual director, career counseling, student employment services, financial aid counseling, health services, minority student services, personal counseling, placement for graduates, veterans' counselor, women's services. **Physically disabled:** Services for visually, speech, hearing impaired.

Contact. E-mail: admissions@stetson.edu
Phone: (386) 822-7100 Toll-free number: (800) 688-0101
Fax: (386) 822-7112
Director of Admissions, Stetson University, Campus Box 8378, DeLand, FL 32723

Talmudic University
Miami Beach, Florida
www.talmudicu.edu   CB code: 0514

- Private 4-year rabbinical college for men affiliated with the Jewish faith
- Very large city
- 29 degree-seeking undergraduates
- Interview required

General. Founded in 1974. Accredited by AARTS. **Degrees:** 9 bachelor's awarded; master's offered. **Location:** 3 miles from downtown. **Calendar:** Semester, extensive summer session. **Full-time faculty:** 7 total. **Part-time faculty:** 4 total. **Class size:** 100% < 20. **Special facilities:** Rabbinical studies research library.

Freshman class profile.

Out-of-state:	60%	Live on campus:	100%

Basis for selection. Recommendations and personal interview most important. Essay recommended.

High school preparation. Recommended units include foreign language 2. Two Bible and Talmud, 1 Jewish thought recommended.

2015-2016 Annual costs. Tuition/fees: $13,000. Room/board: $8,000. Books/supplies: $900.

Financial aid. All financial aid based on need.

Application procedures. **Admission:** No deadline. $250 fee, may be waived for applicants with need. Admission notification on a rolling basis. **Financial aid:** No deadline. FAFSA, institutional form required. Applicants notified on a rolling basis.

Academics. **Special study options:** Cooperative education, distance learning, dual enrollment of high school students, honors, independent study, student-designed major, study abroad, weekend college. **Credit/placement by examination:** AP, CLEP. **Support services:** Remedial instruction, study skills assistance, tutoring.

Majors. **Philosophy/religion:** Judaic. **Theology:** Religious ed.

Technology on campus. 8 workstations in library, computer center. Online library available.

Student life. **Freshman orientation:** Available. Preregistration for classes offered. **Policies:** Students must be "Shomer Mitzvot". Religious observance required. **Housing:** Guaranteed on-campus for all undergraduates. Apartments available.

Student services. Adult student services, chaplain/spiritual director, career counseling, student employment services, financial aid counseling, health services, legal services, personal counseling.

Contact. Phone: (305) 534-0750 Toll-free number: (888) 825-6834
Fax: (305) 534-8444
Rabbi Yeshaya Greenberg, Dean of Students, Talmudic University, 4000 Alton Road, Miami Beach, FL 33140

Trinity Baptist College
Jacksonville, Florida
www.tbc.edu   CB code: 5780

- Private 4-year Bible and teachers college
- Very large city
- 280 degree-seeking undergraduates

General. Regionally accredited; also accredited by TRACS. **Degrees:** 40 bachelor's, 4 associate awarded; master's offered. **Calendar:** Semester. **Full-time faculty:** 12 total. **Part-time faculty:** 11 total.

Basis for selection. Applicant must meet school's high standard of Christian faith and academic rigor.

2015-2016 Annual costs. Tuition/fees: $11,040. Room/board: $6,270. Books/supplies: $1,500.

Application procedures. Admission: $30 fee.

Academics. **Credit/placement by examination:** AP, CLEP.

Majors. **Education:** Elementary, secondary, special ed. **Theology:** Missionary, pastoral counseling. **Visual/performing arts:** Music.

Contact. E-mail: admissions@tbc.edu
Phone: (800) 786-2206
Brandon Willis, Director of Enrollment Management, Trinity Baptist College, 800 Hammond Boulevard, Jacksonville, FL 32221

Trinity College of Florida
Trinity, Florida
www.trinitycollege.edu   CB code: 1979

- Private 4-year Bible college affiliated with the interdenominational tradition
- Commuter campus in small city
- 202 degree-seeking undergraduates: 18% part-time, 47% women, 25% African American, 1% Asian American, 14% Hispanic/Latino, 1% Multiracial, non-Hispanic, 1% international
- 75% of applicants admitted
- SAT or ACT (ACT writing optional), application essay required

General. Regionally accredited; also accredited by ABHE. **Degrees:** 30 bachelor's, 2 associate awarded. **Location:** 25 miles from Tampa. **Calendar:** Semester, limited summer session. **Full-time faculty:** 7 total; 57% have terminal degrees, 57% women. **Part-time faculty:** 21 total; 38% have terminal degrees, 5% minority, 24% women. **Class size:** 88% < 20, 12% 20-39.

Freshman class profile. 64 applied, 48 admitted, 32 enrolled.

Mid 50% test scores		GPA 3.50-3.74:	14%
SAT critical reading:	420-500	GPA 3.0-3.49:	38%
SAT math:	390-470	GPA 2.0-2.99:	34%
SAT writing:	370-470	Return as sophomores:	39%
ACT composite:	16-22	Out-of-state:	12%
GPA 3.75 or higher:	14%	Live on campus:	56%

Basis for selection. Applicants must provide evidence of Christian character and witness, GPA. Test scores are required for applicants with less than 24 college credits. Interviews are conducted when essay is unclear in any way. **Home schooled:** Transcript of courses and grades required. GED may be required if student is not registered with local superintendent or umbrella school. **Learning Disabled:** Need documentation of disability if requesting special accommodations.

High school preparation. 18 units required. Required units include English 4, mathematics 4, social studies 4, science 4 and foreign language 2.

2015-2016 Annual costs. Tuition/fees: $15,690. Room/board: $6,450. Books/supplies: $1,314. Personal expenses: $2,968.

2015-2016 Financial aid. **Need-based:** 28 full-time freshmen applied for aid; 25 deemed to have need; 25 received aid. Average need met was 48%. Average scholarship/grant was $7,445; average loan $6,567. 47% of total undergraduate aid awarded as scholarships/grants, 53% as loans/jobs. **Non-need-based:** Awarded to 13 full-time undergraduates, including 5 freshmen. Scholarships awarded for academics.

Application procedures. **Admission:** Closing date 7/31 (receipt date). $35 fee, may be waived for applicants with need. Admission notification on a rolling basis. Must reply by 7/31. **Financial aid:** Priority date 3/15, closing date 9/15. FAFSA, institutional form required. Applicants notified on a rolling basis starting 1/5; must reply within 2 week(s) of notification.

Academics. **Special study options:** Accelerated study, distance learning, double major, dual enrollment of high school students, honors, independent study, internships. **Credit/placement by examination:** AP, CLEP, SAT, ACT, institutional tests. 24 credit hours maximum toward associate degree, 24 toward bachelor's. **Support services:** Learning center, reduced course load, remedial instruction, tutoring, writing center.

Majors. **Business:** General. **Education:** Elementary. **Psychology:** Counseling. **Theology:** Missionary, pastoral counseling, preministerial, youth ministry.

Most popular majors. Business/marketing 19%, education 6%, psychology 6%, theological studies 63%.

Technology on campus. 16 workstations in library, computer center. Dormitories wired for high-speed internet access and linked to campus network. Online library, repair service, wireless network available.

Student life. Freshman orientation: Mandatory. Preregistration for classes offered. Held 4 days before classes begin. Includes assessment testing. **Policies:** Religious observance required. **Housing:** Guaranteed on-campus for all undergraduates. Single-sex dorms, special housing for disabled, apartments, wellness housing available. $150 fully refundable deposit, deadline 7/31. **Activities:** Campus ministries, choral groups, film society, student government.

Athletics. NCCAA. **Intercollegiate:** Basketball, soccer M, volleyball W. **Team name:** Tigers.

Student services. Alcohol/substance abuse counseling, chaplain/spiritual director, career counseling, financial aid counseling, personal counseling, placement for graduates.

Contact. E-mail: admissions@trinitycollege.edu
Phone: (727) 569-1411 ext. 306 Toll-free number: (800) 388-0869
Fax: (727) 569-1410
Rachel Noble, Director of Admissions, Trinity College of Florida, 2430 Welbilt Boulevard, Trinity, FL 34655-4401

University of Central Florida
Orlando, Florida
www.ucf.edu

CB member
CB code: 5233

- Public 4-year university
- Residential campus in very large city
- 54,120 degree-seeking undergraduates: 31% part-time, 55% women, 11% African American, 6% Asian American, 24% Hispanic/Latino, 4% Multi-racial, non-Hispanic, 1% international
- 8,140 degree-seeking graduate students
- 49% of applicants admitted
- SAT or ACT with writing required
- 71% graduate within 6 years; 15% enter graduate study

General. Founded in 1963. Regionally accredited. **Degrees:** 12,809 bachelor's, 471 associate awarded; master's, professional, doctoral offered. **ROTC:** Army, Air Force. **Location:** 13 miles from downtown. **Calendar:** Semester, extensive summer session. **Full-time faculty:** 1,434 total; 81% have terminal degrees, 26% minority, 43% women. **Part-time faculty:** 504 total; 36% have terminal degrees, 18% minority, 57% women. **Class size:** 27% < 20, 36% 20-39, 11% 40-49, 17% 50-99, 8% >100. **Special facilities:** Solar energy center, simulation and training institute, research/education in optics and lasers center, space education and research center, biomolecular sciences center, forensic science center, arboretum, observatory.

Freshman class profile. 35,572 applied, 17,279 admitted, 6,525 enrolled.

Mid 50% test scores		
SAT critical reading:	540-630	
SAT math:	540-640	
SAT writing:	510-610	
ACT composite:	24-28	
GPA 3.75 or higher:	66%	
GPA 3.50-3.74:	24%	
GPA 3.0-3.49:	10%	
Rank in top quarter:	74%	
Rank in top tenth:		33%
End year in good standing:		97%
Return as sophomores:		89%
Out-of-state:		8%
Live on campus:		66%
International:		1%
Fraternities:		8%
Sororities:		5%

Basis for selection. A thorough review of a student's high school GPA, rigor of coursework, standardized test scores, essays, letters of recommendation, and special talents. Essay recommended. Audition required of music

majors. Portfolio recommended for art majors. **Home schooled:** May be asked to provide details about the coursework and the teaching process.

High school preparation. College-preparatory program required. 18 units required. Required units include English 4, mathematics 4, social studies 3, science 3 (laboratory 2), foreign language 2 and academic electives 2.

2015-2016 Annual costs. Tuition/fees: $6,368; $22,467 out-of-state. Room/board: $9,554. Books/supplies: $1,146. Personal expenses: $2,772.

2014-2015 Financial aid. **Need-based:** 5,552 full-time freshmen applied for aid; 3,860 deemed to have need; 3,713 received aid. Average need met was 55%. Average scholarship/grant was $5,382; average loan $3,630. 55% of total undergraduate aid awarded as scholarships/grants, 45% as loans/jobs. **Non-need-based:** Awarded to 13,313 full-time undergraduates, including 3,062 freshmen. Scholarships awarded for academics, alumni affiliation, athletics, leadership, ROTC, state residency.

Application procedures. **Admission:** Closing date 5/1 (postmark date). $30 fee, may be waived for applicants with need. Application must be submitted online. Admission notification on a rolling basis beginning on or about 9/15. Must reply by May 1 or within 3 week(s) if notified thereafter. **Financial aid:** Priority date 3/1, closing date 6/30. FAFSA required. Applicants notified on a rolling basis starting 3/15; must reply within 3 week(s) of notification.

Academics. **Special study options:** Accelerated study, combined bachelor's/graduate degree, cooperative education, distance learning, double major, dual enrollment of high school students, ESL, honors, independent study, internships, study abroad, teacher certification program. **Credit/placement by examination:** AP, CLEP, IB, SAT, ACT, institutional tests. 45 credit hours maximum toward bachelor's degree. **Support services:** Learning center, pre-admission summer program, reduced course load, study skills assistance, tutoring, writing center.

Honors college/program. Requires separate application, admission based on GPA, test scores, and class rank. Small general and specialized honors courses, honors building, and residence hall available. Accepts approximately 500 freshmen in the fall.

Majors. **Architecture:** Architecture. **Area/ethnic studies:** Latin American. **Biology:** General, biomedical sciences, biotechnology. **Business:** General, accounting, business admin, event planning, finance, hospitality admin, managerial economics, marketing, real estate, restaurant/food services. **Communications:** Advertising, communications/speech/rhetoric, journalism, radio/TV. **Computer sciences:** General, information technology. **Education:** Art, early childhood, elementary, English, foreign languages, mathematics, music, physical, science, social science, trade/industrial. **Engineering:** Aerospace, civil, computer, electrical, environmental, industrial, laser/optical, mechanical, structural. **English:** English lit, rhetoric/composition. **Foreign languages:** French, Spanish. **Health services:** Athletic training, audiology/speech pathology, clinical lab science, health care admin, health information management, nursing (RN), predental, premedicine, prepharmacy, preveterinary. **History:** General. **Human services:** General, social work. **Liberal arts:** Humanities. **Math:** General, statistics. **Philosophy/religion:** Philosophy, religion. **Physical sciences:** Chemistry, physics. **Protective services:** Criminal justice, forensics. **Psychology:** General. **Social sciences:** General, anthropology, economics, political science, sociology. **Visual/performing arts:** Art, cinematography, digital arts, dramatic, music performance, photography, studio arts.

Most popular majors. Business/marketing 22%, education 7%, engineering/engineering technologies 7%, health sciences 16%, psychology 9%, social sciences 6%.

Technology on campus. 4,260 workstations in library, computer center, student center. Dormitories wired for high-speed internet access and linked to campus network. Commuter students can connect to campus network. Online course registration, online library, helpline, repair service, student web hosting, wireless network available.

Student life. Freshman orientation: Mandatory, $35 fee. Preregistration for classes offered. Ten sessions offered throughout spring and summer. 2-day event includes financial aid presentation, advising. **Housing:** Coed dorms, special housing for disabled, apartments, fraternity/sorority housing, themed housing, wellness housing available. $250 nonrefundable deposit. Living learning communities. **Activities:** Bands, campus ministries, choral groups, drama, film society, international student organizations, literary magazine, music ensembles, Model UN, musical theater, radio station, student government, student newspaper, symphony orchestra, TV station, campus activities board, African American student union, orientation team, Hispanic American student association, Korean student association, Indian student association, Christian student association, Jewish student union, Volunteer UCF, various political associations.

Athletics. NCAA. **Intercollegiate:** Baseball M, basketball, cross-country W, football (tackle) M, golf, rowing (crew) W, soccer, softball W, tennis, track and field W, volleyball W. **Intramural:** Badminton, baseball M, basketball, football (non-tackle), golf, racquetball, soccer, tennis, volleyball. **Team name:** Knights.

Student services. Adult student services, alcohol/substance abuse counseling, career counseling, student employment services, financial aid counseling, health services, legal services, minority student services, on-campus daycare, personal counseling, placement for graduates, veterans' counselor, women's services. **Physically disabled:** Services for visually, speech, hearing impaired.

Contact. E-mail: admission@ucf.edu
Phone: (407) 823-3000 Fax: (407) 823-5625
Gordon Chavis, Associate Vice President, University of Central Florida, Box 160111, Orlando, FL 32816-0111

University of Florida
Gainesville, Florida   CB member
www.ufl.edu   CB code: 5812

- Public 4-year university
- Residential campus in small city
- 33,972 degree-seeking undergraduates: 10% part-time, 55% women, 6% African American, 8% Asian American, 21% Hispanic/Latino, 1% Native Hawaiian/Pacific islander, 3% Multi-racial, non-Hispanic, 1% international
- 16,236 degree-seeking graduate students
- 48% of applicants admitted
- SAT or ACT (ACT writing optional), application essay required

General. Founded in 1853. Regionally accredited. **Degrees:** 8,603 bachelor's, 394 associate awarded; master's, professional, doctoral offered. **ROTC:** Army, Naval, Air Force. **Location:** 70 miles from Jacksonville. **Calendar:** Semester, limited summer session. **Special facilities:** Natural history museum, marine laboratory, wildlife sanctuary, citrus research center, bell carillon, pipe organ, center for performing arts, microkelvin laboratory, brain institute, nuclear reactor, art museum, cancer and genetics research center, emerging pathogens institute, nanoscale research facility, innovation district, arts and architecture fab lab.

Freshman class profile. 29,837 applied, 14,237 admitted, 7,204 enrolled.

Mid 50% test scores		GPA 3.50-3.74:	4%
SAT critical reading:	580-670	GPA 3.0-3.49:	1%
SAT math:	590-680	Rank in top quarter:	96%
SAT writing:	570-670	Rank in top tenth:	72%
ACT composite:	27-31	International:	1%
GPA 3.75 or higher:	95%		

Basis for selection. High school grades, academic course selection, SAT/ACT, extracurricular activities, awards, honors, recognitions, and special talents considered. SAT subject tests used strictly for placement purposes and not for admission, except for applicants from non-regionally accredited schools or home school applicants. College of Arts requires auditions for majors in the performing arts. **Home schooled:** Statement describing home school structure and mission, transcript of courses and grades, state high school equivalency certificate required. SAT Subject Test in math (level II-C), science, social science and foreign language required. Record of courses and grades through self-reported academic record, transcripts only required of enrolling students. **Learning Disabled:** Optional self disclosure; students receive extra review by disability resource center.

High school preparation. College-preparatory program required. 16 units required. Required units include English 4, mathematics 4, social studies 3, science 3 (laboratory 2) and foreign language 2. English units must include substantial writing; math units must include algebra I, formal geometry, algebra II; foreign language must be same language and must be sequential.

2015-2016 Annual costs. Tuition/fees: $6,381; $28,658 out-of-state. Room/board: $9,650.

2014-2015 Financial aid. Need-based: 5,467 full-time freshmen applied for aid; 3,344 deemed to have need; 3,296 received aid. Average need met was 99%. Average scholarship/grant was $7,874; average loan $3,990. 67% of total undergraduate aid awarded as scholarships/grants, 33% as loans/jobs. **Non-need-based:** Awarded to 15,333 full-time undergraduates, including 3,288 freshmen. Scholarships awarded for academics, alumni affiliation, art, athletics, leadership, minority status, music/drama, state residency.

Application procedures. Admission: Closing date 11/1 (postmark date). $30 fee, may be waived for applicants with need. Application must be submitted online. 2nd Friday of February. Must reply by 5/1. **Financial aid:** Priority date 3/15; no closing date. FAFSA required. Applicants notified on a rolling basis starting 4/15.

Academics. Special study options: Accelerated study, cooperative education, cross-registration, distance learning, double major, dual enrollment of high school students, ESL, exchange student, honors, independent study, internships, liberal arts/career combination, semester at sea, student-designed major, study abroad, teacher certification program, Washington semester. TV-delivered credit-bearing courses. **Credit/placement by examination:** AP, CLEP, IB, SAT, ACT, institutional tests. 45 credit hours maximum toward associate degree, 45 toward bachelor's. **Support services:** Learning center, reduced course load, study skills assistance, tutoring, writing center. Information technology training.

Majors. Architecture: Architecture, landscape. **Area/ethnic studies:** African-American, women's. **Biology:** General, bacteriology, botany, entomology, exercise physiology, zoology. **Business:** Accounting, business admin, finance, management science, marketing, real estate. **Communications:** Advertising, journalism, public relations, radio/TV. **Computer sciences:** General. **Conservation:** Environmental science, forestry, wildlife/wilderness. **Education:** Agricultural, art, elementary, music, special ed. **Engineering:** Aerospace, biological, biomedical, chemical, civil, computer, electrical, environmental, materials, mechanical, nuclear, systems. **English:** English lit. **Foreign languages:** Classics, French, German, linguistics, Portuguese, Russian, Spanish. **Health services:** Athletic training, audiology/speech pathology, community health, dietetics, nursing (RN). **History:** General. **Math:** General, statistics. **Parks/recreation:** Facilities management, sports admin. **Philosophy/religion:** Judaic, philosophy, religion. **Physical sciences:** Astronomy, chemistry, geology, physics. **Protective services:** Firefighting. **Psychology:** General. **Social sciences:** Anthropology, criminology, economics, geography, political science, sociology. **Visual/performing arts:** Art history/conservation, dance, digital arts, dramatic, graphic design, interior design, music, studio arts. **Work/family studies:** Family/community services.

Most popular majors. Agriculture 6%, biology 10%, business/marketing 12%, communications/journalism 8%, engineering/engineering technologies 14%, health sciences 7%, social sciences 12%.

Technology on campus. 1,512 workstations in library, student center. Dormitories wired for high-speed internet access and linked to campus network. Commuter students can connect to campus network. Online course registration, online library, helpline, student web hosting, wireless network available.

Student life. Freshman orientation: Mandatory, $180 fee. Preregistration for classes offered. Two-day program held various dates in May, June and July. **Policies:** Student code of conduct and honor code enforced; medical amnesty program; interpersonal violence prevention and alcohol education requirement. **Housing:** Coed dorms, special housing for disabled, apartments, fraternity/sorority housing, themed housing available. $200 nonrefundable deposit, deadline 5/1. Pets allowed in dorm rooms. Available living-learning communities: innovation academy, engineering, honors residential college, entrepreneurial, gatorWell, honors II, Returning Gators, pre-health, fine arts, ROTC, Leader Scholar Program, International House, Global, Infinity Hall. **Activities:** Bands, campus ministries, choral groups, dance, drama, film society, international student organizations, literary magazine, music ensembles, Model UN, musical theater, opera, radio station, student government, student newspaper, symphony orchestra, TV station, Over 1,000 student groups available.

Athletics. NCAA. **Intercollegiate:** Baseball M, basketball, cross-country, diving, football (tackle) M, golf, gymnastics W, lacrosse W, soccer W, softball W, swimming, tennis, track and field, volleyball W. **Intramural:** Basketball, bowling, football (non-tackle), golf, racquetball, sand volleyball, soccer, softball, swimming, table tennis, tennis, track and field, ultimate frisbee, volleyball. **Team name:** Gators.

Student services. Alcohol/substance abuse counseling, career counseling, services for economically disadvantaged, student employment services, financial aid counseling, health services, legal services, minority student services, on-campus daycare, personal counseling, placement for graduates, veterans' counselor. **Physically disabled:** Services for visually, speech, hearing impaired.

Contact. E-mail: webrequests@admissions.ufl.edu
Phone: (352) 392-1365
Zina Evans, Vice President Enrollment Management, University of Florida, 201 Criser Hall-PO Box 114000, Gainesville, FL 32611-4000

University of Miami
Coral Gables, Florida   CB member
www.miami.edu   CB code: 5815

- Private 4-year university
- Residential campus in small city

- 10,768 degree-seeking undergraduates: 4% part-time, 51% women, 8% African American, 6% Asian American, 22% Hispanic/Latino, 3% Multiracial, non-Hispanic, 14% international
- 5,626 degree-seeking graduate students
- 38% of applicants admitted
- SAT or ACT with writing, application essay required
- 82% graduate within 6 years; 33% enter graduate study

General. Founded in 1925. Regionally accredited. **Degrees:** 2,774 bachelor's awarded; master's, professional, doctoral offered. **ROTC:** Army, Air Force. **Location:** 9 miles from downtown. **Calendar:** Semester, extensive summer session. **Full-time faculty:** 1,131 total; 86% have terminal degrees, 32% minority, 40% women. **Part-time faculty:** 418 total; 56% have terminal degrees, 41% minority, 44% women. **Class size:** 54% < 20, 31% 20-39, 8% 40-49, 5% 50-99, 2% >100. **Special facilities:** Cinema, observatory, palmetum, marine science research vessels, broadcasting studios, concert hall, arboretum, performing arts theater, film studios, sound stage, museum, marine technology and life sciences seawater complex.

Freshman class profile. 33,415 applied, 12,624 admitted, 2,081 enrolled.

Mid 50% test scores			
SAT critical reading:	590-690	GPA 2.0-2.99:	5%
SAT math:	610-700	Rank in top quarter:	90%
SAT writing:	580-680	Rank in top tenth:	63%
ACT composite:	28-32	End year in good standing:	94%
GPA 3.75 or higher:	63%	Return as sophomores:	92%
GPA 3.50-3.74:	15%	Out-of-state:	65%
GPA 3.0-3.49:	17%	Live on campus:	83%
		International:	14%

Basis for selection. Transcript, standardized test scores, letters of recommendation, extra-curricular activities, and essay most important. SAT subject exams in math and one science required for dual-degree honors programs in medicine and in biochemistry and molecular biology. School of Architecture and Art BFA require portfolio. Theater Arts BFA requires audition/portfolio review. Audition required for all music majors. Dual Degree Honors Programs in Medicine and Biochemistry & Molecular Biology require interview. **Home schooled:** Statement describing home school structure and mission, transcript of courses and grades, letter of recommendation (nonparent) required.

High school preparation. College-preparatory program recommended. 20 units recommended. Recommended units include English 4, mathematics 4, social studies 3, history 2, science 3 (laboratory 2), foreign language 2, computer science 1 and visual/performing arts 1.

2015-2016 Annual costs. Tuition/fees: $45,724. Room/board: $13,066.

2015-2016 Financial aid. **Need-based:** 2,056 full-time freshmen applied for aid; 1,564 deemed to have need; 1,259 received aid. Average need met was 99%. Average scholarship/grant was $11,456; average loan $3,874. 90% of total undergraduate aid awarded as scholarships/grants, 10% as loans/jobs. **Non-need-based:** Awarded to 7,294 full-time undergraduates, including 1,728 freshmen. Scholarships awarded for academics, athletics, music/drama, ROTC, state residency.

Application procedures. **Admission:** Closing date 1/1 (postmark date). $70 fee, may be waived for applicants with need. Application must be submitted online. Admission notification by 4/15. Must reply by May 1 or within 2 week(s) if notified thereafter. **Financial aid:** Priority date 1/1, closing date 4/15. FAFSA, CSS PROFILE required. Applicants notified on a rolling basis starting 1/20; must reply by 5/1.

Academics. **Special study options:** Accelerated study, combined bachelor's/graduate degree, cooperative education, distance learning, double major, dual enrollment of high school students, ESL, exchange student, honors, independent study, internships, liberal arts/career combination, student-designed major, study abroad, teacher certification program, Washington semester, weekend college. **Credit/placement by examination:** AP, CLEP, IB, SAT, ACT, institutional tests. 60 credit hours maximum toward bachelor's degree. **Support services:** Learning center, reduced course load, remedial instruction, study skills assistance, tutoring, writing center.

Majors. **Architecture:** Architecture. **Area/ethnic studies:** African-American, American, Latin American, women's. **Biology:** General, biochemistry, exercise physiology, marine, microbiology/immunology, neuroscience. **Business:** Accounting, accounting technology, business admin, entrepreneurial studies, finance, human resources, international, managerial economics, marketing, real estate. **Communications:** Broadcast journalism, communications/speech/rhetoric, digital media, journalism, public relations. **Computer sciences:** Computer science, information systems. **Conservation:** Management/policy. **Education:** Elementary, music. **Engineering:** Aerospace, architectural, biomedical, civil, computer, electrical, engineering science, environmental, industrial, mechanical. **English:** English lit. **Foreign languages:** Classics, French, German, Spanish. **Health services:** Athletic training, health care admin, music therapy, nursing (RN), public health nursing. **History:**

General. **Math:** General. **Parks/recreation:** Sports admin. **Philosophy/religion:** Judaic, philosophy, religion. **Physical sciences:** Atmospheric science, chemistry, geology, meteorology, oceanography, physics. **Psychology:** General, community. **Social sciences:** Anthropology, criminology, economics, geography, international relations, political science, sociology. **Visual/performing arts:** Acting, art, art history/conservation, ceramics, cinematography, directing/producing, dramatic, graphic design, jazz, music, music performance, music theory/composition, painting, photography, piano/keyboard, printmaking, studio arts, theater arts management, voice/opera. **Work/family studies:** Family/community services.

Most popular majors. Biology 15%, business/marketing 19%, communications/journalism 10%, engineering/engineering technologies 10%, health sciences 9%, psychology 6%, social sciences 10%, visual/performing arts 6%.

Technology on campus. Dormitories wired for high-speed internet access and linked to campus network. Commuter students can connect to campus network. Online course registration, online library, helpline, repair service, student web hosting, wireless network available.

Student life. **Freshman orientation:** Mandatory. Preregistration for classes offered. Three-day event. **Policies:** The Honor Code protects the academic integrity of the University by encouraging consistent ethical behavior among its undergraduate students. Freshmen not permitted cars on campus. **Housing:** Guaranteed on-campus for freshmen. Coed dorms, special housing for disabled, apartments, fraternity/sorority housing, themed housing available. $500 nonrefundable deposit, deadline 5/1. Special interest housing available. **Activities:** Bands, campus ministries, choral groups, dance, drama, film society, international student organizations, literary magazine, music ensembles, Model UN, musical theater, opera, radio station, student government, student newspaper, symphony orchestra, TV station, Hillel, Canes Care for Canes, FunDay, SpectrUM, CERT (Canes Emergency Response Team), College Republicans, Planet Kreyol, Chinese Student Scholars Association, Association of Commuter Students, Federacion de Estudienates Cubanos.

Athletics. NCAA. **Intercollegiate:** Baseball M, basketball, cross-country, diving, football (tackle) M, golf W, rowing (crew) W, soccer W, swimming W, tennis, track and field, volleyball W. **Intramural:** Basketball, football (non-tackle), golf, sand volleyball, soccer, softball, table tennis, tennis, ultimate frisbee, volleyball, weight lifting. **Team name:** Hurricanes.

Student services. Adult student services, alcohol/substance abuse counseling, career counseling, services for economically disadvantaged, student employment services, financial aid counseling, health services, minority student services, on-campus daycare, personal counseling, placement for graduates, veterans' counselor, women's services. **Physically disabled:** Services for visually, hearing impaired.

Contact. E-mail: admission@miami.edu
Phone: (305) 284-4323 Fax: (305) 284-2507
Karen Long, Asst. VP of Undergraduate Admission & Marketing,
University of Miami, PO Box 248025, Coral Gables, FL 33124-4616

University of North Florida
Jacksonville, Florida   CB member
www.unf.edu   CB code: 5490

- Public 4-year university
- Residential campus in very large city
- 13,562 degree-seeking undergraduates: 30% part-time, 55% women, 9% African American, 4% Asian American, 10% Hispanic/Latino, 5% Multiracial, non-Hispanic, 1% international
- 1,735 degree-seeking graduate students
- 57% of applicants admitted
- SAT or ACT with writing required
- 55% graduate within 6 years

General. Founded in 1965. Regionally accredited. **Degrees:** 3,208 bachelor's, 261 associate awarded; master's, professional, doctoral offered. **ROTC:** Army, Naval. **Location:** 12 miles from downtown. **Calendar:** Semester, extensive summer session. **Full-time faculty:** 543 total; 81% have terminal degrees, 14% minority, 49% women. **Part-time faculty:** 357 total; 31% have terminal degrees, 12% minority, 58% women. **Class size:** 30% < 20, 49% 20-39, 12% 40-49, 6% 50-99, 4% >100. **Special facilities:** Nature trails, designated bird sanctuary, fine arts center, skate park, museum of contemporary art.

Freshman class profile. 10,901 applied, 6,171 admitted, 1,578 enrolled.

Mid 50% test scores			
SAT critical reading:	540-630	GPA 2.0-2.99:	3%
SAT math:	530-610	Rank in top quarter:	42%
SAT writing:	500-600	Rank in top tenth:	19%
ACT composite:	22-27	End year in good standing:	81%
GPA 3.75 or higher:	52%	Return as sophomores:	80%
GPA 3.50-3.74:	21%	Out-of-state:	4%
GPA 3.0-3.49:	24%	Live on campus:	94%
		International:	1%

Basis for selection. SAT/ACT and GPA based on 18 academic units very important. High school academic courses (not including electives) used for calculating GPA. Summer admission available for some students who do not meet fall admissions criteria. Audition required for music majors. **Home schooled:** Transcript of courses and grades required. Required to pass all sections of GED. **Learning Disabled:** Applicants should register with Disability Resource Center.

High school preparation. College-preparatory program required. 18 units required. Required units include English 4, mathematics 4, social studies 3, science 3 (laboratory 1), foreign language 2 and academic electives 2.

2015-2016 Annual costs. Tuition/fees: $6,394; $20,112 out-of-state. Room/board: $9,487. Books/supplies: $1,200. Personal expenses: $2,808.

2015-2016 Financial aid. Need-based: 1,282 full-time freshmen applied for aid; 857 deemed to have need; 807 received aid. Average need met was 90%. Average scholarship/grant was $7,680; average loan $3,220. 52% of total undergraduate aid awarded as scholarships/grants, 48% as loans/jobs. **Non-need-based:** Awarded to 3,379 full-time undergraduates, including 617 freshmen. Scholarships awarded for academics, athletics, leadership, minority status, music/drama, state residency.

Application procedures. Admission: No deadline. $30 fee, may be waived for applicants with need. Application must be submitted online. Admission notification on a rolling basis beginning on or about 1/6. **Financial aid:** Closing date 4/1. FAFSA required. Applicants notified on a rolling basis starting 3/15.

Academics. Special study options: Accelerated study, cooperative education, distance learning, double major, dual enrollment of high school students, ESL, honors, independent study, internships, student-designed major, study abroad, teacher certification program. **Credit/placement by examination:** AP, CLEP, IB, SAT, ACT, institutional tests. 30 credit hours maximum toward bachelor's degree. **Support services:** Learning center, pre-admission summer program, reduced course load, study skills assistance, tutoring, writing center.

Honors college/program. Two 250 word essays. In terms of GPA and test scores, students who are accepted into the Hicks Honors College usually have earned a weighted GPA of 4.0-4.9, and SAT of 1200-1510 or ACT of 26-36. Other material can be added to the Honors application such as a resume and/or a letter of recommendation.

Majors. Area/ethnic studies: French. **Biology:** General. **Business:** Accounting, banking/financial services, business admin, finance, international, managerial economics, marketing, transportation. **Communications:** Media studies. **Computer sciences:** General. **Education:** Art, Deaf/hearing impaired, early childhood, elementary, mathematics, middle, music, physical, secondary, special ed. **Engineering:** Civil, electrical, mechanical. **English:** English lit. **Foreign languages:** Sign language interpretation, Spanish. **Health services:** Athletic training, dietetics, health care admin, nursing (RN). **History:** General. **Human services:** Social work. **Math:** General, statistics. **Parks/recreation:** Sports admin. **Philosophy/religion:** Philosophy, religion. **Physical sciences:** Chemistry, physics. **Protective services:** Criminal justice. **Psychology:** General. **Social sciences:** Anthropology, economics, political science, sociology. **Visual/performing arts:** Art, art history/conservation, jazz, music performance, studio arts.

Most popular majors. Business/marketing 18%, communications/journalism 8%, education 6%, health sciences 17%, psychology 11%, security/protective services 6%, social sciences 7%.

Technology on campus. 850 workstations in library, computer center, student center. Dormitories wired for high-speed internet access and linked to campus network. Commuter students can connect to campus network. Online course registration, online library, helpline, student web hosting, wireless network available.

Student life. Freshman orientation: Mandatory, $35 fee. Preregistration for classes offered. One-and-one-half day program held several times during summer. **Policies:** Students must abide by drug/alcohol policy, student code of conduct, model bill of rights and responsibilities. Smoke-free campus. **Housing:** Guaranteed on-campus for freshmen. Coed dorms, special housing for disabled, apartments available. $300 partly refundable deposit. Living-learning communities available. **Activities:** Bands, campus ministries, choral groups, drama, international student organizations, literary magazine, music ensembles, radio station, student government, student newspaper, TV station, African American student union, Jewish student union, InterVarsity Christian Fellowship, College Republicans, Jeffersonian Society, The New Left, Muslim student association, Filipino student association, Golden Key international honor society.

Athletics. NCAA. **Intercollegiate:** Baseball M, basketball, cross-country, diving W, golf, soccer, softball W, swimming W, tennis, track and field, volleyball W. **Intramural:** Basketball, football (non-tackle), racquetball, soccer, softball, tennis, track and field, volleyball. **Team name:** Ospreys.

Student services. Adult student services, alcohol/substance abuse counseling, chaplain/spiritual director, career counseling, student employment services, financial aid counseling, health services, minority student services, on-campus daycare, personal counseling, placement for graduates, veterans' counselor, women's services. **Physically disabled:** Services for visually, speech, hearing impaired.

Contact. E-mail: admissions@unf.edu
Phone: (904) 620-2624 Toll-free number: (888) 808-0626
Fax: (904) 620-2414
Karen Lucas, Director of Admissions, University of North Florida, 1 UNF Drive, Jacksonville, FL 32224-7699

University of Phoenix: Central Florida
Orlando, Florida
www.phoenix.edu

- For-profit 4-year university and health science college
- Small city
- 1,100 degree-seeking undergraduates

General. Regionally accredited. **Degrees:** 865 bachelor's awarded; master's offered. **Calendar:** Differs by program. **Full-time faculty:** 15 total. **Part-time faculty:** 149 total.

Basis for selection. Open admission, but selective for some programs.

2015-2016 Annual costs. Per-credit-hour charge, $410 to $635, depending upon level and course of study. Books, material charges, and other fees vary by course and program. All fees are subject to change.

Application procedures. Admission: No deadline. No application fee. **Financial aid:** No deadline.

Academics. Credit/placement by examination: AP, CLEP.

Majors. Business: Accounting, accounting/business management, business admin, e-commerce, entrepreneurial studies, finance, human resources, marketing, operations. **Communications:** General. **Computer sciences:** Database management, networking, programming, security, support specialist, system admin, systems analysis, web page design, webmaster. **Education:** Elementary. **English:** English lit. **Health services:** Facilities admin, health information management, long term care admin, nursing (RN). **Human services:** General. **Protective services:** Disaster management, law enforcement admin, security management.

Student life. Freshman orientation: Mandatory. Preregistration for classes offered.

Contact. Toll-free number: (866) 766-0766
University of Phoenix: Central Florida, 8325 South Park Circle, Orlando, FL 32819

University of Phoenix: North Florida
Jacksonville, Florida
www.phoenix.edu

- For-profit 4-year university
- Very large city
- 1,100 degree-seeking undergraduates
- 180 graduate students

General. Regionally accredited. **Degrees:** 179 bachelor's awarded; master's offered. **Calendar:** Differs by program. **Full-time faculty:** 12 total. **Part-time faculty:** 125 total.

Basis for selection. Open admission, but selective for some programs.

2015-2016 Annual costs. Per-credit-hour charge, $410 to $635, depending upon level and course of study. Books, material charges, and other fees vary by course and program. All fees are subject to change.

Application procedures. Admission: No deadline. No application fee. **Financial aid:** No deadline.

Academics. Credit/placement by examination: AP, CLEP.

Majors. Business: Accounting, accounting/business management, business admin, e-commerce, entrepreneurial studies, finance, human resources, marketing, operations. **Communications:** General. **Computer sciences:** Database management, networking, programming, security, support specialist, system admin, systems analysis, web page design, webmaster. **Education:** Elementary. **English:** English lit. **Health services:** Facilities admin, health information management, long term care admin, nursing (RN). **Human services:** General. **Protective services:** Disaster management, law enforcement admin, security management.

Student life. Freshman orientation: Mandatory. Preregistration for classes offered.

Contact. Toll-free number: (866) 766-0766
University of Phoenix: North Florida, 4500 Salisbury Road, Jacksonville, FL 32216

University of Phoenix: South Florida
Miramar, Florida
www.phoenix.edu

- For-profit 4-year university
- Small city
- 1,400 degree-seeking undergraduates
- 366 graduate students

General. Regionally accredited. **Degrees:** 250 bachelor's awarded; master's offered. **Calendar:** Differs by program. **Full-time faculty:** 15 total. **Part-time faculty:** 241 total.

Basis for selection. Open admission, but selective for some programs.

2015-2016 Annual costs. Per-credit-hour charge, $410 to $635, depending upon level and course of study. Books, material charges, and other fees vary by course and program. All fees are subject to change.

Application procedures. Admission: No deadline. No application fee. **Financial aid:** No deadline.

Academics. Credit/placement by examination: AP, CLEP.

Majors. Business: Accounting, accounting/business management, business admin, e-commerce, entrepreneurial studies, finance, human resources, marketing, operations. **Communications:** General. **Computer sciences:** General, database management, networking, programming, security, support specialist, system admin, systems analysis, web page design, webmaster. **Education:** Elementary. **English:** English lit. **Health services:** Facilities admin, health information management, long term care admin, nursing (RN). **Human services:** General. **Protective services:** Disaster management, law enforcement admin, security management.

Student life. Freshman orientation: Mandatory. Preregistration for classes offered.

Contact. Toll-free number: (866) 766-0677
University of Phoenix: South Florida, 2400 SW 145th Street, Miramar, FL 33027-4145

University of Phoenix: West Florida
Temple Terrace, Florida
www.phoenix.edu

- For-profit 4-year university
- Large town
- 800 degree-seeking undergraduates

General. Regionally accredited. **Degrees:** 93 bachelor's awarded; master's offered. **Calendar:** Differs by program. **Full-time faculty:** 11 total. **Part-time faculty:** 103 total.

Basis for selection. Open admission, but selective for some programs.

2015-2016 Annual costs. Per-credit-hour charge, $410 to $635, depending upon level and course of study. Books, material charges, and other fees vary by course and program. All fees are subject to change.

Application procedures. Admission: No deadline. No application fee. **Financial aid:** No deadline.

Academics. Credit/placement by examination: AP, CLEP.

Majors. Business: Accounting, accounting/business management, business admin, e-commerce, entrepreneurial studies, finance, human resources, marketing, operations. **Communications:** General. **Computer sciences:** Database management, networking, programming, security, system admin, systems analysis, web page design, webmaster. **Education:** Elementary. **English:** English lit. **Health services:** Facilities admin, health information management, long term care admin, nursing (RN). **Human services:** General. **Protective services:** Disaster management, law enforcement admin, security management.

Student life. Freshman orientation: Mandatory. Preregistration for classes offered.

Contact. Toll-free number: (866) 766-0766
University of Phoenix: West Florida, 12802 Tampa Oaks Boulevard, Temple Terrace, FL 33637-1920

University of South Florida
Tampa, Florida   **CB member**
www.usf.edu   **CB code: 5828**

- Public 4-year university
- Commuter campus in very large city
- 30,314 degree-seeking undergraduates: 22% part-time, 55% women, 11% African American, 6% Asian American, 21% Hispanic/Latino, 4% Multi-racial, non-Hispanic, 5% international
- 9,930 degree-seeking graduate students
- 45% of applicants admitted
- SAT or ACT with writing required
- 67% graduate within 6 years

General. Founded in 1956. Regionally accredited. Regional institutional campuses in St. Petersburg and Sarasota/Manatee. **Degrees:** 8,171 bachelor's, 202 associate awarded; master's, professional, doctoral offered. **ROTC:** Army, Naval, Air Force. **Location:** 10 miles from downtown. **Calendar:** Semester, extensive summer session. **Full-time faculty:** 1,208 total; 84% have terminal degrees, 29% minority, 44% women. **Part-time faculty:** 526 total; 35% have terminal degrees, 28% minority, 55% women. **Class size:** 31% < 20, 44% 20-39, 10% 40-49, 11% 50-99, 4% >100. **Special facilities:** Art museums, weather station, botanical garden, anthropology museum.

Freshman class profile. 30,386 applied, 13,563 admitted, 2,642 enrolled.

Mid 50% test scores			
SAT critical reading:	530-630	GPA 2.0-2.99:	1%
SAT math:	540-640	Rank in top quarter:	59%
SAT writing:	510-600	Rank in top tenth:	34%
ACT composite:	24-28	Out-of-state:	10%
GPA 3.75 or higher:	63%	Live on campus:	78%
GPA 3.50-3.74:	17%	International:	7%
GPA 3.0-3.49:	19%	Fraternities:	10%
		Sororities:	15%

Basis for selection. GPA and test scores most important; higher grades compensate for lower test scores. Requirements higher for several degree programs. TOEFL OR IELTS required of non-native English speaking applicants. Audition required of music majors. Portfolio required of art majors. **Home schooled:** State high school equivalency certificate required.

High school preparation. College-preparatory program required. 19 units required; 22 recommended. Required and recommended units include English 4, mathematics 4, social studies 3, science 3-4 (laboratory 2-3), foreign language 2-4 and academic electives 3. Foreign language units must be in 1 language.

2015-2016 Annual costs. Tuition/fees: $6,410; $17,324 out-of-state. Room/board: $9,400. Books/supplies: $1,200. Personal expenses: $2,500.

2014-2015 Financial aid. Need-based: 3,537 full-time freshmen applied for aid; 2,680 deemed to have need; 2,568 received aid. Average need met was 62%. Average scholarship/grant was $9,173; average loan $4,949. 39% of total undergraduate aid awarded as scholarships/grants, 61% as loans/jobs. **Non-need-based:** Awarded to 3,009 full-time undergraduates, including

1,000 freshmen. Scholarships awarded for academics, art, athletics, leadership, music/drama, state residency. **Additional information:** Deferred tuition payment plan available for late financial aid recipients.

Application procedures. Admission: Closing date 3/1 (postmark date). $30 fee, may be waived for applicants with need. Admission notification by 4/15. Admission notification on a rolling basis beginning on or about 10/1. Must reply by May 1 or within 3 week(s) if notified thereafter. **Financial aid:** Priority date 3/1; no closing date. FAFSA required. Applicants notified on a rolling basis starting 3/15.

Academics. Special study options: Accelerated study, combined bachelor's/graduate degree, cooperative education, cross-registration, distance learning, double major, dual enrollment of high school students, exchange student, honors, internships, study abroad, teacher certification program, Washington semester, weekend college. **Credit/placement by examination:** AP, CLEP, IB, SAT, institutional tests. **Support services:** Learning center, pre-admission summer program, remedial instruction, tutoring, writing center.

Honors college/program. 3.8 GPA and 1300 SAT with 580 verbal/29 ACT with 29 English required.

Majors. Area/ethnic studies: African-American, American, women's. **Biology:** General, bacteriology, biomedical sciences. **Business:** General, accounting, business admin, finance, hospitality admin, international, management information systems, marketing. **Communications:** Communications/speech/rhetoric, media studies. **Computer sciences:** General, information technology. **Conservation:** Environmental science. **Education:** Early childhood, elementary, English, foreign languages, mathematics, music, physical, science, social science, special ed. **Engineering:** Chemical, civil, computer, electrical, industrial, mechanical. **English:** English lit. **Foreign languages:** Classics, French, German, Italian, Russian, Spanish. **Health services:** Athletic training, audiology/speech pathology, clinical lab science, health care admin, nursing (RN). **History:** General. **Human services:** Social work. **Liberal arts:** Humanities. **Math:** General, statistics. **Philosophy/religion:** Philosophy, religion. **Physical sciences:** Chemistry, geology, physics. **Psychology:** General. **Social sciences:** General, anthropology, criminology, economics, geography, international relations, political science, sociology. **Visual/performing arts:** Art, art history/conservation, dance, dramatic, music performance, studio arts.

Most popular majors. Biology 9%, business/marketing 17%, engineering/engineering technologies 6%, health sciences 18%, psychology 8%, social sciences 14%.

Technology on campus. PC or laptop required. 825 workstations in dormitories, library, computer center, student center. Dormitories wired for high-speed internet access and linked to campus network. Commuter students can connect to campus network. Online course registration, helpline, wireless network available.

Student life. Freshman orientation: Mandatory, $35 fee. Preregistration for classes offered. **Housing:** Coed dorms, single-sex dorms, special housing for disabled, apartments, gender-neutral housing, themed housing, wellness housing available. $225 partly refundable deposit, deadline 8/1. Grad student only and Medical student only housing available. **Activities:** Bands, campus ministries, choral groups, dance, drama, film society, international student organizations, literary magazine, music ensembles, musical theater, opera, radio station, student government, student newspaper, symphony orchestra, TV station, approximately 600 student organizations available.

Athletics. NCAA. **Intercollegiate:** Baseball M, basketball, cross-country, football (tackle) M, golf, soccer, softball W, tennis, track and field, volleyball W. **Intramural:** Badminton, basketball, bowling, cross-country, football (tackle) M, golf, racquetball, soccer, softball W, swimming, tennis, track and field, volleyball W, wrestling M. **Team name:** Bulls.

Student services. Adult student services, alcohol/substance abuse counseling, career counseling, student employment services, financial aid counseling, health services, legal services, minority student services, on-campus daycare, personal counseling, placement for graduates, veterans' counselor. **Physically disabled:** Services for visually, speech, hearing impaired.

Contact. E-mail: admissions@usf.edu
Phone: (813) 974-3350 Fax: (813) 974-9689
David Lee Henry, Director of Admissions, University of South Florida, 4202 East Fowler Avenue, SVC 1036, Tampa, FL 33620-9951

University of South Florida: Saint Petersburg
St. Petersburg, Florida   **CB member**
www.usfsp.edu

- Public 4-year university
- Small city

- 3,964 degree-seeking undergraduates: 33% part-time, 62% women, 8% African American, 4% Asian American, 16% Hispanic/Latino, 4% Multiracial, non-Hispanic
- 540 degree-seeking graduate students
- 47% of applicants admitted
- SAT or ACT with writing required
- 38% graduate within 6 years

General. Regionally accredited. **Degrees:** 842 bachelor's, 63 associate awarded; master's offered. **ROTC:** Army. **Calendar:** Semester. **Full-time faculty:** 133 total; 86% have terminal degrees, 23% minority, 50% women. **Part-time faculty:** 145 total; 54% have terminal degrees, 14% minority, 59% women. **Class size:** 34% < 20, 52% 20-39, 7% 40-49, 7% 50-99, less than 1% >100.

Freshman class profile. 5,119 applied, 2,399 admitted, 598 enrolled.

Mid 50% test scores			
SAT critical reading:	510-590	GPA 2.0-2.99:	10%
SAT math:	490-570	Rank in top quarter:	29%
ACT composite:	22-26	Rank in top tenth:	9%
GPA 3.75 or higher:	42%	Return as sophomores:	71%
GPA 3.50-3.74:	17%	Out-of-state:	5%
GPA 3.0-3.49:	31%	Live on campus:	69%

Basis for selection. Rigor of secondary school record, GPA, volunteer experience and standardized test scores considered. **Home schooled:** Transcript of courses and grades required. Students who are participating in an approved home schooling program are expected to provide acceptable transcripts for the equivalent of grades 9-12. A portfolio or additional documentation may be requested if deemed necessary to complete an appropriate evaluation for admission.

High school preparation. Required units include English 4, mathematics 4, social studies 3, science 3 (laboratory 2), foreign language 2 and academic electives 2.

2015-2016 Annual costs. Tuition/fees: $5,821; $16,736 out-of-state. Room/board: $9,645. Books/supplies: $1,000. Personal expenses: $1,250.

Application procedures. Admission: Priority date 1/2; deadline 4/15. $30 fee, may be waived for applicants with need. Admission notification on a rolling basis beginning on or about 10/1. Must reply by May 1 or within 2 week(s) if notified thereafter. **Financial aid:** Priority date 3/1; no closing date. FAFSA required.

Academics. Special study options: Distance learning, double major, dual enrollment of high school students, honors, independent study, internships, study abroad, teacher certification program. **Credit/placement by examination:** AP, SAT, ACT. **Support services:** Learning center, tutoring, writing center.

Majors. Biology: General. **Business:** Accounting, entrepreneurial studies, finance, international, management science, managerial economics, marketing. **Communications:** Journalism. **Conservation:** Environmental studies. **Education:** Special ed. **English:** English lit. **History:** General. **Liberal arts:** Arts/sciences. **Psychology:** General. **Social sciences:** Anthropology, criminology, economics, political science. **Visual/performing arts:** Art.

Most popular majors. Business/marketing 35%, education 10%, English 6%, psychology 13%, social sciences 18%.

Technology on campus. Dormitories wired for high-speed internet access and linked to campus network. Commuter students can connect to campus network. Online course registration, online library, student web hosting available.

Student life. Freshman orientation: Mandatory. Preregistration for classes offered. **Housing:** Coed dorms, special housing for disabled, themed housing available. $400 partly refundable deposit, deadline 4/15. **Activities:** Campus ministries, dance, international student organizations, literary magazine, radio station, student government, student newspaper.

Student services. Alcohol/substance abuse counseling, career counseling, financial aid counseling, health services, personal counseling, veterans' counselor. **Physically disabled:** Services for visually, speech, hearing impaired.

Contact. E-mail: admissions@usfsp.edu
Phone: (727) 873-4142
Holly Kickliter, Director of Admissions, University of South Florida: Saint Petersburg, 140 Seventh Avenue South, St. Petersburg, FL 33701

University of South Florida: Sarasota-Manatee
Sarasota, Florida
www.usfsm.edu

♦ Public 4-year university
♦ Commuter campus in small city
♦ 1,762 degree-seeking undergraduates: 45% part-time, 59% women, 6% African American, 2% Asian American, 15% Hispanic/Latino, 2% Multiracial, non-Hispanic, 1% international
♦ 175 degree-seeking graduate students
♦ 33% of applicants admitted
♦ SAT or ACT with writing required

General. Regionally accredited. The University of South Florida Sarasota-Manatee (USFSM), also known as USF Sarasota-Manatee, is a separately accredited, four-year institution in the University of South Florida System, which includes USF Tampa and USF St. Petersburg (USFSP). **Degrees:** 480 bachelor's, 2 associate awarded; master's offered. **Location:** 60 miles to Tampa. **Calendar:** Semester, extensive summer session. **Full-time faculty:** 80 total; 78% have terminal degrees, 18% minority, 56% women. **Part-time faculty:** 59 total; 39% have terminal degrees, 12% minority, 56% women. **Class size:** 55% < 20, 39% 20-39, 4% 40-49, 2% 50-99. **Special facilities:** Culinary Innovation Laboratory, Science Laboratories at Mote Marine Laboratory.

Freshman class profile. 487 applied, 159 admitted, 86 enrolled.

Mid 50% test scores			
		GPA 2.0-2.99:	4%
SAT critical reading:	520-600	Rank in top quarter:	53%
SAT math:	530-600	Rank in top tenth:	26%
SAT writing:	490-590	End year in good standing:	71%
ACT composite:	22-26	Return as sophomores:	78%
GPA 3.75 or higher:	49%	Out-of-state:	5%
GPA 3.50-3.74:	12%	International:	1%
GPA 3.0-3.49:	35%		

Basis for selection. 21 ACT/500 SAT on critical reading, math, and writing, and weighted high school GPA of 3.3 recommended. SAT Subject Tests recommended. Essay optional, but highly recommended. **Home schooled:** SAT subject tests in math, foreign language, science and social science required; requirement may be waived if the student provides official secondary or postsecondary transcript or official AP or CLEP exam results demonstrating college readiness in each of the four core subject areas above.

High school preparation. College-preparatory program required. 18 units required. Required units include English 4, mathematics 4, social studies 3, science 3 (laboratory 2), foreign language 2 and academic electives 2. 3 English units must include substantial writing. Math must be algebra 1 or above; 2 science units must include substantial work in lab. Foreign language units must be in same language.

2015-2016 Annual costs. Tuition/fees: $5,587; $16,502 out-of-state. Books/supplies: $1,200. Personal expenses: $2,500.

2014-2015 Financial aid. **Need-based:** 79 full-time freshmen applied for aid; 61 deemed to have need; 55 received aid. Average need met was 54%. Average scholarship/grant was $7,798; average loan $3,999. 45% of total undergraduate aid awarded as scholarships/grants, 55% as loans/jobs. **Non-need-based:** Awarded to 19 full-time undergraduates, including 7 freshmen. Scholarships awarded for academics, alumni affiliation, art, athletics, job skills, leadership, minority status, music/drama, religious affiliation, state residency.

Application procedures. **Admission:** Priority date 1/2; deadline 5/1 (postmark date). $30 fee, may be waived for applicants with need. Admission notification on a rolling basis. Must reply by May 1 or within 2 week(s) if notified thereafter. **Financial aid:** Priority date 3/1; no closing date. FAFSA required. Applicants notified on a rolling basis starting 3/15.

Academics. **Special study options:** Cross-registration, distance learning, double major, dual enrollment of high school students, honors, independent study, internships, study abroad, teacher certification program. **Credit/placement by examination:** AP, IB, institutional tests. 45 credit hours maximum toward bachelor's degree. **Support services:** Learning center, reduced course load, study skills assistance, tutoring, writing center.

Majors. **Biology:** General. **Business:** General, accounting, business admin, finance, hospitality admin, marketing. **Computer sciences:** Information technology. **Education:** Early childhood, elementary. **English:** English lit, technical writing. **Health services:** Communication disorders. **History:** General. **Psychology:** General. **Social sciences:** General, criminology.

Most popular majors. Business/marketing 41%, computer/information sciences 7%, education 6%, health sciences 12%, psychology 12%, social sciences 15%.

Technology on campus. PC or laptop required. 22 workstations in computer center. Commuter students can connect to campus network. Online course registration, online library, helpline, wireless network available.

Student life. **Freshman orientation:** Mandatory, $80 fee. Preregistration for classes offered. **Activities:** Campus ministries, film society, student government, student newspaper.

Athletics. **Team name:** Bulls.

Student services. Adult student services, alcohol/substance abuse counseling, chaplain/spiritual director, career counseling, student employment services, financial aid counseling, health services, personal counseling, placement for graduates, veterans' counselor. **Physically disabled:** Services for visually, speech, hearing impaired.

Contact. E-mail: admissions@sar.usf.edu
Phone: (941) 359-4330 Fax: (941) 359-4585
Andrew Telatovich, Director of Admissions, University of South Florida: Sarasota-Manatee, 8350 North Tamiami Trail, Sarasota, FL 34243

University of Tampa
Tampa, Florida **CB member**
www.ut.edu **CB code: 5819**

♦ Private 4-year university and liberal arts college
♦ Residential campus in large city
♦ 7,061 degree-seeking undergraduates: 3% part-time, 58% women, 5% African American, 11% international
♦ 876 degree-seeking graduate students
♦ 51% of applicants admitted
♦ SAT or ACT (ACT writing recommended) required
♦ 56% graduate within 6 years; 23% enter graduate study

General. Founded in 1931. Regionally accredited. **Degrees:** 1,412 bachelor's awarded; master's offered. **ROTC:** Army, Naval, Air Force. **Location:** 20 miles from St. Petersburg, 70 miles from Orlando. **Calendar:** Semester, extensive summer session. **Full-time faculty:** 295 total; 90% have terminal degrees, 14% minority, 43% women. **Part-time faculty:** 360 total; 37% have terminal degrees, 14% minority, 56% women. **Class size:** 41% < 20, 55% 20-39, less than 1% 40-49, 2% 50-99. **Special facilities:** Art and furniture museum, dance studio, art studio, marine science research vessel, marine science research laboratory.

Freshman class profile. 18,712 applied, 9,499 admitted, 1,801 enrolled.

Mid 50% test scores			
		Rank in top quarter:	45%
SAT critical reading:	490-580	Rank in top tenth:	18%
SAT math:	500-590	End year in good standing:	90%
SAT writing:	480-570	Return as sophomores:	75%
ACT composite:	22-26	Out-of-state:	82%
GPA 3.75 or higher:	17%	Live on campus:	93%
GPA 3.50-3.74:	22%	International:	9%
GPA 3.0-3.49:	44%	Fraternities:	11%
GPA 2.0-2.99:	17%	Sororities:	13%

Basis for selection. Secondary school record, test scores most important. Recommendations, talent/ability, character/personal qualities considered. Interview recommended. Auditions required of music and performing arts majors. Portfolio recommended for art majors. **Home schooled:** 11th year annual pupil's educational progress evaluation or annual assessment test results required, if available. **Learning Disabled:** Documentation required.

High school preparation. College-preparatory program required. 20 units required. Required units include English 4, mathematics 3, social studies 3, science 3 (laboratory 2), foreign language 2 and academic electives 3.

2015-2016 Annual costs. Tuition/fees: $27,044. Room/board: $9,900. Books/supplies: $1,200. Personal expenses: $1,965.

2014-2015 Financial aid. **Need-based:** 1,417 full-time freshmen applied for aid; 1,113 deemed to have need; 1,112 received aid. Average need met was 62%. Average scholarship/grant was $13,276; average loan $3,318. 61% of total undergraduate aid awarded as scholarships/grants, 39% as loans/jobs. **Non-need-based:** Awarded to 5,909 full-time undergraduates, including 1,645 freshmen. Scholarships awarded for academics, art, athletics, leadership, music/drama, ROTC.

Application procedures. **Admission:** Priority date 11/15; no deadline. $40 fee, may be waived for applicants with need. Admission notification on a rolling basis beginning on or about 10/1. Must reply by May 1 or within 4 week(s) if notified thereafter. **Financial aid:** Priority date 1/1; no closing date. FAFSA required. Applicants notified on a rolling basis starting 3/1; must reply by 5/1 or within 3 week(s) of notification.

Academics. **Special study options:** Combined bachelor's/graduate degree, double major, dual enrollment of high school students, ESL, honors, independent study, internships, liberal arts/career combination, semester at sea, study abroad, teacher certification program, Washington semester. Certificate of International Studies. **Credit/placement by examination:** AP, CLEP, IB, SAT, ACT, institutional tests. 30 credit hours maximum toward bachelor's degree. **Support services:** Learning center, reduced course load, study skills assistance, tutoring, writing center.

Majors. **Biology:** General, biochemistry, marine. **Business:** Accounting, business admin, entrepreneurial studies, finance, international, management information systems, management science, marketing. **Communications:** General, advertising, digital media, journalism, persuasive communications. **Computer sciences:** General, security. **Conservation:** Environmental studies. **Education:** Elementary, music, physical, secondary. **English:** English lit, writing. **Foreign languages:** Spanish. **Health services:** Athletic training, nursing (RN). **History:** General. **Liberal arts:** Arts/sciences. **Math:** General. **Parks/recreation:** Exercise sciences, health/fitness, sports admin. **Philosophy/religion:** Philosophy. **Physical sciences:** Chemistry. **Protective services:** Forensics. **Psychology:** General. **Social sciences:** Criminology, economics, political science, sociology. **Visual/performing arts:** Art, digital arts, dramatic, film/cinema/video, graphic design, music, music performance, musical theater.

Most popular majors. Biology 6%, business/marketing 29%, communications/journalism 12%, health sciences 9%, parks/recreation 8%, social sciences 11%, visual/performing arts 7%.

Technology on campus. 884 workstations in dormitories, library, computer center, student center. Dormitories wired for high-speed internet access and linked to campus network. Commuter students can connect to campus network. Online course registration, online library, helpline, student web hosting, wireless network available.

Student life. **Freshman orientation:** Mandatory, $75 fee. Preregistration for classes offered. **Housing:** Coed dorms, special housing for disabled, apartments, themed housing available. $500 fully refundable deposit, deadline 5/1. **Activities:** Bands, campus ministries, choral groups, dance, drama, film society, international student organizations, literary magazine, music ensembles, Model UN, musical theater, radio station, student government, student newspaper, symphony orchestra, TV station, over 140 student organizations.

Athletics. NCAA. **Intercollegiate:** Baseball M, basketball, cross-country, golf, lacrosse M, rowing (crew) W, soccer, softball W, swimming, tennis W, volleyball W. **Intramural:** Basketball, field hockey W, football (non-tackle) W, football (tackle) M, golf, soccer, softball, swimming, table tennis W, tennis, track and field, ultimate frisbee, volleyball. **Team name:** Spartans.

Student services. Adult student services, career counseling, student employment services, financial aid counseling, health services, minority student services, personal counseling, placement for graduates, veterans' counselor, women's services. **Physically disabled:** Services for visually, hearing impaired.

Contact. E-mail: admissions@ut.edu
Phone: (813) 253-6211 Toll-free number: (888) 646-2738
Fax: (813) 258-7398
Dennis Nostrand, Vice President for Enrollment, University of Tampa, 401 West Kennedy Boulevard, Tampa, FL 33606-1490

University of West Florida
Pensacola, Florida
www.uwf.edu   CB code: 5833

- Public 4-year university
- Commuter campus in small city
- 9,786 degree-seeking undergraduates: 28% part-time, 57% women, 13% African American, 3% Asian American, 9% Hispanic/Latino, 5% Multiracial, non-Hispanic, 2% international
- 2,278 degree-seeking graduate students
- 42% of applicants admitted
- SAT or ACT (ACT writing optional) required
- 47% graduate within 6 years

General. Founded in 1963. Regionally accredited. **Degrees:** 1,967 bachelor's, 112 associate awarded; master's, doctoral offered. **ROTC:** Army, Air Force. **Location:** 10 miles from downtown. **Calendar:** Semester, extensive summer session. **Full-time faculty:** 338 total; 18% minority, 44% women. **Part-time faculty:** 268 total; 10% minority, 52% women. **Class size:** 36%

< 20, 40% 20-39, 13% 40-49, 10% 50-99, 1% >100. **Special facilities:** Archaeology museum, nature preserve, science and engineering complex with holodeck.

Freshman class profile. 7,104 applied, 2,951 admitted, 1,293 enrolled.

Mid 50% test scores			
SAT critical reading:	470-570	GPA 2.0-2.99:	29%
SAT math:	460-550	Rank in top quarter:	38%
SAT writing:	450-540	Rank in top tenth:	14%
ACT composite:	20-26	Return as sophomores:	72%
GPA 3.75 or higher:	27%	Out-of-state:	8%
GPA 3.50-3.74:	15%	Live on campus:	54%
GPA 3.0-3.49:	28%	International:	2%

Basis for selection. School achievement record, test scores, and school curriculum most important. **Home schooled:** Transcript of courses and grades required. **Learning Disabled:** If requesting special consideration due to disability, student must provide documentation.

High school preparation. College-preparatory program recommended. 19 units required. Required units include English 4, mathematics 3, social studies 3, science 3 (laboratory 2), foreign language 2 and academic electives 4. Social studies includes history, economics, government, psychology, sociology and geography.

2015-2016 Annual costs. Tuition/fees: $6,569; $19,451 out-of-state. Room/board: $9,912. Books/supplies: $1,200. Personal expenses: $2,600.

2014-2015 Financial aid. **Need-based:** 1,032 full-time freshmen applied for aid; 809 deemed to have need; 785 received aid. Average need met was 53%. Average scholarship/grant was $6,752; average loan $3,438. 51% of total undergraduate aid awarded as scholarships/grants, 49% as loans/jobs. **Non-need-based:** Awarded to 705 full-time undergraduates, including 185 freshmen. Scholarships awarded for academics, alumni affiliation, art, athletics, minority status, music/drama, ROTC.

Application procedures. **Admission:** Closing date 6/30 (postmark date). $30 fee, may be waived for applicants with need. Admission notification on a rolling basis beginning on or about 10/1. Must apply by January 1 for scholarship consideration. **Financial aid:** Priority date 3/15; no closing date. FAFSA required. Applicants notified on a rolling basis starting 3/1.

Academics. Weekend program in nursing (BSN) available. **Special study options:** Cooperative education, distance learning, double major, dual enrollment of high school students, exchange student, honors, independent study, internships, study abroad, teacher certification program. **Credit/placement by examination:** AP, CLEP, IB, SAT, ACT, institutional tests. 30 credit hours maximum toward associate degree, 30 toward bachelor's. Up to 60 hours can be accepted, but academic department determines how credit counts toward degree. **Support services:** Learning center, remedial instruction, study skills assistance, tutoring, writing center.

Majors. **Biology:** General, marine. **Business:** General, accounting, business admin, finance, hospitality admin, management information systems, managerial economics, marketing. **Communications:** Media studies. **Computer sciences:** General, information technology. **Conservation:** Environmental science. **Education:** Art, early childhood, elementary, English, foreign languages, mathematics, mentally handicapped, middle, music, science, social science, special ed, trade/industrial. **Engineering:** Computer, electrical. **English:** English lit. **Foreign languages:** French, Spanish. **Health services:** Clinical lab science, community health services, nursing (RN). **History:** General. **Human services:** Social work. **Liberal arts:** Humanities. **Math:** General. **Parks/recreation:** Health/fitness. **Philosophy/religion:** Philosophy, religion. **Physical sciences:** Chemistry, oceanography, physics. **Protective services:** Criminal justice. **Psychology:** General. **Social sciences:** General, anthropology, economics, international relations, political science, sociology. **Visual/performing arts:** Art, art history/conservation, dramatic, music performance, studio arts.

Most popular majors. Business/marketing 13%, communications/journalism 6%, education 6%, health sciences 19%, parks/recreation 6%, psychology 6%, social sciences 8%.

Technology on campus. 300 workstations in dormitories, library, computer center, student center. Dormitories wired for high-speed internet access and linked to campus network. Commuter students can connect to campus network. Online course registration, online library, helpline, repair service, student web hosting, wireless network available.

Student life. **Freshman orientation:** Mandatory, $100 fee. Preregistration for classes offered. Two-day programs held throughout summer; includes parents. **Housing:** Coed dorms, apartments, fraternity/sorority housing, wellness housing available. $225 partly refundable deposit. **Activities:** Bands, campus ministries, choral groups, dance, drama, international student organizations, music ensembles, musical theater, radio station, student government, student newspaper, symphony orchestra, TV station, black student union, CLOVE, College Republicans.

Athletics. NCAA. **Intercollegiate:** Baseball M, basketball, cross-country, golf, soccer, softball W, tennis, track and field, volleyball W. **Intramural:** Badminton, basketball, bowling, fencing, football (non-tackle), handball, racquetball, soccer, swimming, table tennis, volleyball, water polo, weight lifting. **Team name:** Argonauts.

Student services. Alcohol/substance abuse counseling, career counseling, student employment services, financial aid counseling, health services, minority student services, on-campus daycare, personal counseling, placement for graduates, veterans' counselor. **Physically disabled:** Services for visually, speech, hearing impaired.

Contact. E-mail: admissions@uwf.edu
Phone: (850) 474-2230 Toll-free number: (800) 263-1074
Fax: (850) 474-3360
Katherine Condon, Director of Admissions, University of West Florida, 11000 University Parkway, Pensacola, FL 32514-5750

Warner University
Lake Wales, Florida
www.warner.edu
CB code: 5883

- Private 4-year liberal arts college affiliated with the Church of God
- Commuter campus in large town
- 1,027 degree-seeking undergraduates
- SAT or ACT (ACT writing optional), application essay required

General. Founded in 1968. Regionally accredited. Off-site locations including Lakeland Learning Center, Space Coast Learning Center in Melbourne, teaching site in Titusville. **Degrees:** 195 bachelor's, 72 associate awarded; master's offered. **Location:** 60 miles from Tampa, 55 miles from Orlando. **Calendar:** Semester, limited summer session. **Full-time faculty:** 41 total. **Part-time faculty:** 65 total. **Class size:** 72% < 20, 28% 20-39. **Special facilities:** Natural scrub brush preserve.

Freshman class profile.

GPA 3.75 or higher:	22%	Rank in top quarter:	27%
GPA 3.50-3.74:	13%	Rank in top tenth:	6%
GPA 3.0-3.49:	37%	Out-of-state:	18%
GPA 2.0-2.99:	28%	Live on campus:	79%

Basis for selection. Two of the following required: 2.25 GPA, top 50% of class, or 18 ACT/870 SAT (exclusive of Writing). ACT Residual test administered to those without scores or with scores too low. Interview recommended. Audition required of music majors. **Home schooled:** Statement describing home school structure and mission, transcript of courses and grades, interview, letter of recommendation (nonparent) required. GED or portfolio required of applicants without transcripts.

High school preparation. College-preparatory program recommended. Recommended units include English 4, mathematics 3, social studies 1, history 1, science 2, foreign language 2 and academic electives 2.

2015-2016 Annual costs. Tuition/fees: $19,754. Room/board: $7,924. Books/supplies: $1,400. Personal expenses: $1,800.

Financial aid. **Non-need-based:** Scholarships awarded for academics, alumni affiliation, art, athletics, leadership, music/drama, religious affiliation, state residency.

Application procedures. **Admission:** No deadline. $20 fee, may be waived for applicants with need. Admission notification on a rolling basis beginning on or about 9/15. **Financial aid:** Priority date 5/1; no closing date. FAFSA required. Applicants notified on a rolling basis starting 3/15; must reply within 2 week(s) of notification.

Academics. **Special study options:** Accelerated study, combined bachelor's/graduate degree, distance learning, double major, dual enrollment of high school students, ESL, independent study, internships, study abroad, teacher certification program, Washington semester. Online distance learning opportunities available for those interested in Organizational Management or Church Ministry. **Credit/placement by examination:** AP, CLEP, IB, SAT, ACT, institutional tests. **Support services:** Learning center, remedial instruction, study skills assistance, tutoring.

Majors. Biology: General. **Business:** Business admin. **Communications:** Communications/speech/rhetoric, journalism. **Education:** Elementary, English, music, physical, science, social science, special ed. **English:** English lit. **History:** General. **Human services:** Social work. **Parks/recreation:** Exercise sciences, sports admin. **Psychology:** General. **Social sciences:** General. **Theology:** Bible, sacred music, theology.

Most popular majors. Business/marketing 63%, education 18%.

Technology on campus. 69 workstations in library, computer center, student center. Dormitories wired for high-speed internet access. Commuter students can connect to campus network. Online library, helpline, repair service, wireless network available.

Student life. Freshman orientation: Mandatory. Preregistration for classes offered. Three-day program at start of fall semester. **Policies:** Student lifestyle agreement keeping with the moral and spiritual nature of the institution required. Religious observance required. **Housing:** Guaranteed on-campus for all undergraduates. Single-sex dorms, wellness housing available. $50 nonrefundable deposit, deadline 8/15. **Activities:** Campus ministries, choral groups, drama, music ensembles, student government, student newspaper, star throwers, missions, Young Americans.

Athletics. NAIA. **Intercollegiate:** Baseball M, basketball, cheerleading, cross-country, golf, soccer, softball W, tennis, track and field, volleyball. **Intramural:** Basketball, football (non-tackle), soccer, volleyball W. **Team name:** Royals.

Student services. Alcohol/substance abuse counseling, career counseling, student employment services, financial aid counseling, health services, personal counseling, placement for graduates.

Contact. E-mail: admissions@warner.edu
Phone: (863) 638-7212 Toll-free number: (800) 309-9563
Fax: (863) 638-7290
Jason Roe, Director of Admissions, Warner University, 13895 Highway 27, Lake Wales, FL 33859

Webber International University
Babson Park, Florida
www.webber.edu
CB member
CB code: 5893

- Private 4-year university and business college
- Residential campus in rural community
- 688 degree-seeking undergraduates
- SAT or ACT (ACT writing recommended) required

General. Founded in 1927. Regionally accredited. **Degrees:** 128 bachelor's, 2 associate awarded; master's offered. **Location:** 50 miles from Orlando, 60 miles from Tampa. **Calendar:** Semester, limited summer session. **Full-time faculty:** 21 total; 71% have terminal degrees, 10% minority, 33% women. **Part-time faculty:** 23 total; 30% have terminal degrees, 13% minority, 44% women. **Class size:** 43% < 20, 56% 20-39, less than 1% 40-49. **Special facilities:** Nature preserve.

Freshman class profile.

GPA 3.75 or higher:	17%	GPA 2.0-2.99:	39%
GPA 3.50-3.74:	15%	Out-of-state:	3%
GPA 3.0-3.49:	29%	Live on campus:	85%

Basis for selection. GPA and standardized test scores very important, followed by school record. Interview recommended. **Home schooled:** Transcript of courses and grades required. Proof of graduation with 2.0 GPA required. **Learning Disabled:** Documentation of disability required in order to adequately assist student in studies.

High school preparation. College-preparatory program recommended. 15 units recommended. Required and recommended units include English 4, mathematics 2-3, social studies 2, history 2, science 1-3, foreign language 1 and academic electives 4. 2 business courses recommended.

2015-2016 Annual costs. Tuition/fees: $22,326. Room/board: $8,712. Books/supplies: $1,148. Personal expenses: $3,454.

Financial aid. **Non-need-based:** Scholarships awarded for academics, athletics, leadership.

Application procedures. **Admission:** Priority date 5/1; deadline 8/1 (postmark date). $35 fee, may be waived for applicants with need. Admission notification on a rolling basis beginning on or about 12/1. Must reply by May 1 or within 4 week(s) if notified thereafter. **Financial aid:** Priority date 5/1, closing date 8/1. FAFSA, institutional form required. Applicants notified on a rolling basis starting 4/1; must reply within 4 week(s) of notification.

Academics. **Special study options:** Combined bachelor's/graduate degree, cooperative education, cross-registration, distance learning, double major, dual enrollment of high school students, ESL, exchange student, external degree, independent study, internships, weekend college. **Credit/placement by examination:** AP, CLEP, IB, institutional tests. 30 credit hours maximum toward associate degree, 30 toward bachelor's. No more than 6 semester hours credit awarded in each of 5 areas (English, humanities, science, social science, math). **Support services:** Reduced course load, remedial instruction, study skills assistance, tutoring.

Majors. Business: General, accounting, business admin, finance, hospitality admin, marketing. **Communications:** Communications/speech/rhetoric. **Computer sciences:** General. **Parks/recreation:** Facilities management. **Protective services:** Security management.

Most popular majors. Business/marketing 65%, computer/information sciences 8%, parks/recreation 20%.

Technology on campus. 92 workstations in library, computer center. Dormitories wired for high-speed internet access and linked to campus network. Commuter students can connect to campus network. Online library, helpline available.

Student life. Freshman orientation: Mandatory. Preregistration for classes offered. Five-day program immediately preceding semester opening. **Housing:** Guaranteed on-campus for freshmen. Single-sex dorms available. $205 fully refundable deposit, deadline 8/28. **Activities:** Marching band, international student organizations, student government, student newspaper, Fellowship of Christian Athletes, fishing club, marketing club, Phi Beta Lambda, photography club, Society of Hosteurs.

Athletics. NAIA. **Intercollegiate:** Baseball M, basketball, bowling, cross-country, football (tackle) M, golf, soccer, softball W, tennis, track and field, volleyball W. **Intramural:** Basketball, bowling, football (non-tackle), soccer, softball, table tennis, tennis. **Team name:** Warriors.

Student services. Adult student services, alcohol/substance abuse counseling, career counseling, student employment services, financial aid counseling, health services, personal counseling, placement for graduates, veterans' counselor, women's services.

Contact. E-mail: admissions@webber.edu
Phone: (863) 638-2910 Toll-free number: (800) 741-1844
Fax: (863) 638-1591
Mike Mattison, Director of Admission, Webber International University, 1201 North Scenic Highway, Babson Park, FL 33827-0096

Yeshiva Gedolah Rabbinical College
Miami Beach, Florida

▶ Private 4-year rabbinical college for men affiliated with the Jewish faith
▶ Very large city
▶ 46 degree-seeking undergraduates

General. Accredited by AARTS. **Degrees:** 5 bachelor's awarded; master's offered. **Calendar:** Semester. **Full-time faculty:** 4 total.

Basis for selection. Open admission.

2015-2016 Annual costs. Tuition/fees: $8,400. Room/board: $8,500.

Academics. Credit/placement by examination: AP, CLEP.

Majors. Philosophy/religion: Judaic. **Theology:** Religious ed, Talmudic.

Contact. Phone: (305) 673-5664
Yeshiva Gedolah Rabbinical College, 1140 Alton Road, Miami Beach, FL 33139

Georgia

Agnes Scott College

Decatur, Georgia — CB member
www.agnesscott.edu — CB code: 5002

- Private 4-year liberal arts college for women affiliated with the Presbyterian Church (USA)
- Residential campus in very large city
- 846 degree-seeking undergraduates: 1% part-time, 100% women, 34% African American, 6% Asian American, 10% Hispanic/Latino, 8% Multiracial, non-Hispanic, 8% international
- 62% of applicants admitted
- Application essay required
- 68% graduate within 6 years; 20% enter graduate study

General. Founded in 1889. Regionally accredited. **Degrees:** 184 bachelor's awarded. **ROTC:** Army, Air Force. **Location:** 6 miles from downtown Atlanta. **Calendar:** Semester, limited summer session. **Full-time faculty:** 73 total; 100% have terminal degrees, 16% minority, 64% women. **Part-time faculty:** 38 total; 60% have terminal degrees, 24% minority, 63% women. **Class size:** 73% < 20, 27% 20-39. **Special facilities:** Center for writing and speaking, sociology and anthropology research lab, language lab, electron microscope, observatory.

Freshman class profile. 1,461 applied, 902 admitted, 272 enrolled.

Mid 50% test scores			
SAT critical reading:	550-690	Rank in top quarter:	62%
SAT math:	510-640	Rank in top tenth:	29%
SAT writing:	550-670	Return as sophomores:	87%
ACT composite:	24-29	Out-of-state:	46%
GPA 3.75 or higher:	50%	Live on campus:	93%
GPA 3.50-3.74:	20%	International:	6%
GPA 3.0-3.49:	24%		
GPA 2.0-2.99:	6%		

Basis for selection. US Citizens must submit at least one of the following: SAT/ACT scores; an interview with an Agnes Scott College representative; a graded writing sample. Non-US citizens must submit SAT/ACT scores or complete a video interview. All home-schooled students must submit SAT I or ACT scores and SAT II Subject tests. Interview recommended. Audition required for music scholarship. **Home schooled:** Statement describing home school structure and mission, interview required. Applications must include at least one of the following: SAT/ACT, interview with College representative, graded writing sample, SAT Subject tests.

High school preparation. College-preparatory program recommended. 13 units recommended. Recommended units include English 4, mathematics 3, social studies 2, science 2 (laboratory 2) and foreign language 2.

2016-2017 Annual costs. Tuition/fees: $38,472. Room/board: $11,520. Books/supplies: $1,000. Personal expenses: $1,000.

2015-2016 Financial aid. Need-based: 249 full-time freshmen applied for aid; 220 deemed to have need; 220 received aid. Average need met was 84%. Average scholarship/grant was $27,535; average loan $3,391. 86% of total undergraduate aid awarded as scholarships/grants, 14% as loans/jobs. **Non-need-based:** Awarded to 348 full-time undergraduates, including 109 freshmen. Scholarships awarded for academics, leadership, minority status, music/drama, religious affiliation.

Application procedures. Admission: Priority date 1/15; deadline 3/15 (postmark date). No application fee. Application must be submitted online. Admission notification on a rolling basis beginning on or about 4/15. Must reply by May 1 or within 2 week(s) if notified thereafter. Scholarship applicants must apply for regular admission by 1/15. **Financial aid:** Priority date 2/15, closing date 5/1. FAFSA required. PROFILE required for early decision/early action applicants. Applicants notified on a rolling basis starting 3/1; must reply by 5/1 or within 3 week(s) of notification.

Academics. Special study options: Accelerated study, combined bachelor's/graduate degree, cross-registration, distance learning, double major, dual enrollment of high school students, exchange student, independent study, internships, liberal arts/career combination, student-designed major, study abroad, Washington semester. Internship opportunities guaranteed; over 250 internships and externships available in Atlanta and other cities. Language

Across the Curriculum links foreign languages to other disciplines. Opportunities to study at more than 123 universities in 33 countries. **Credit/placement by examination:** AP, CLEP, IB, SAT, ACT, institutional tests. 32 credit hours maximum toward bachelor's degree. **Support services:** Learning center, reduced course load, study skills assistance, tutoring, writing center.

Majors. Area/ethnic studies: African, women's. **Biology:** General, biochemistry, neuroscience. **Business:** Business admin. **English:** Creative writing, English lit. **Foreign languages:** Classics, French, German, Spanish. **History:** General. **Math:** General. **Philosophy/religion:** Philosophy, religion. **Physical sciences:** Astrophysics, chemistry, physics. **Psychology:** General. **Social sciences:** Economics, international relations, political science. **Visual/performing arts:** Art history/conservation, dance, dramatic, music, studio arts.

Most popular majors. Area/ethnic studies 6%, biology 14%, English 9%, foreign language 8%, health sciences 9%, physical sciences 6%, psychology 11%, social sciences 19%.

Technology on campus. 458 workstations in dormitories, library, computer center, student center. Dormitories wired for high-speed internet access and linked to campus network. Commuter students can connect to campus network. Online course registration, online library, helpline, repair service, wireless network available.

Student life. Freshman orientation: Mandatory. Preregistration for classes offered. Held 5 days prior to start of semester. **Housing:** Guaranteed on-campus for all undergraduates. Apartments, themed housing available. $350 nonrefundable deposit, deadline 5/1. **Activities:** Bands, campus ministries, choral groups, dance, drama, international student organizations, literary magazine, music ensembles, Model UN, musical theater, radio station, student government, student newspaper, symphony orchestra, Coalition of Student Multicultural Organizations, Affinity African West Indian Student Association, Religious Life Council, Baptist Collegiate Ministry, Daughters of Gaia, Fellowship of Christian Students, Campus Girl Scouts, Circle K, The Colonnade Club.

Athletics. NCAA. **Intercollegiate:** Basketball W, cross-country W, soccer W, softball W, tennis W, volleyball W. **Team name:** Scotties.

Student services. Adult student services, alcohol/substance abuse counseling, chaplain/spiritual director, career counseling, student employment services, financial aid counseling, health services, minority student services, personal counseling, placement for graduates, women's services. **Physically disabled:** Services for visually, speech, hearing impaired.

Contact. E-mail: admission@agnesscott.edu
Phone: (404) 471-6285 Toll-free number: (800) 868-8602
Fax: (404) 471-6414
Alexa Gaeta, Associate Vice President for Enrollment and Director of Admission, Agnes Scott College, 141 East College Avenue, Decatur, GA 30030-3797

Albany State University

Albany, Georgia — CB member
www.asurams.edu — CB code: 5004

- Public 4-year university
- Residential campus in small city
- 2,988 degree-seeking undergraduates: 15% part-time, 66% women, 90% African American, 2% Hispanic/Latino, 1% Multi-racial, non-Hispanic
- 492 degree-seeking graduate students
- 64% of applicants admitted
- SAT or ACT (ACT writing optional) required
- 31% graduate within 6 years

General. Founded in 1903. Regionally accredited. **Degrees:** 543 bachelor's awarded; master's offered. **ROTC:** Army. **Location:** 190 miles from Atlanta. **Calendar:** Semester, extensive summer session. **Full-time faculty:** 160 total; 73% have terminal degrees, 80% minority, 43% women. **Part-time faculty:** 18 total; 44% have terminal degrees, 100% minority, 44% women. **Class size:** 52% < 20, 43% 20-39, 3% 40-49, 2% 50-99. **Special facilities:** Natatorium, fitness center.

Freshman class profile. 2,196 applied, 1,399 admitted, 475 enrolled.

Mid 50% test scores			
SAT critical reading:	430-480	Rank in top quarter:	24%
SAT math:	410-470	Rank in top tenth:	10%
ACT composite:	17-19	Return as sophomores:	78%
GPA 3.75 or higher:	2%	Out-of-state:	7%
GPA 3.50-3.74:	11%	Live on campus:	72%
GPA 3.0-3.49:	30%		
GPA 2.0-2.99:	56%		

Basis for selection. 430 SAT Verbal, 400 SAT Math or 17 ACT English and Math, 2.22 high school GPA required. **Home schooled:** Transcript of courses and grades, state high school equivalency certificate required. SAT and satisfactory documentation of equivalent competence in each of the areas at the college-preparatory level. **Learning Disabled:** Register with Office of Counseling, Disability and Student Support Services.

High school preparation. College-preparatory program required. 17 units required. Required units include English 4, mathematics 4, social studies 3, history 3, science 4 and foreign language 2. 2 foreign language units must be same language emphasizing speaking, listening, reading and writing.

2015-2016 Annual costs. Tuition/fees: $6,460; $19,280 out-of-state. Room/board: $7,698. Books/supplies: $1,200. Personal expenses: $1,500.

Financial aid. Non-need-based: Scholarships awarded for academics, alumni affiliation, athletics, music/drama, ROTC, state residency.

Application procedures. Admission: Priority date 6/1; deadline 7/1. $25 fee, may be waived for applicants with need. Application must be submitted online. Admission notification on a rolling basis beginning on or about 9/30. Must reply within 24 hours. Early admission high school students must have permission from their high school to attend; must also meet certain GPA and SAT/ACT requirement. **Financial aid:** Priority date 4/15, closing date 6/30. FAFSA required. Applicants notified on a rolling basis starting 1/7; must reply within 2 week(s) of notification.

Academics. Special study options: Combined bachelor's/graduate degree, cooperative education, cross-registration, distance learning, double major, dual enrollment of high school students, honors, independent study, internships, liberal arts/career combination, study abroad, teacher certification program. 3+2 and 2+2 engineering program with Georgia Institute of Technology. **Credit/placement by examination:** AP, CLEP, SAT, ACT, institutional tests. 30 credit hours maximum toward bachelor's degree. Credit will be awarded based on the minimum scale score recommended for passing by the American Council on Education. **Support services:** Learning center, pre-admission summer program, remedial instruction, study skills assistance, tutoring, writing center. Advising via faculty, Academic Advising and Retention Center, University Testing Center, Veterans Assistance Program, Counseling and Disability Student Services, Honors Program.

Majors. Biology: General. **Business:** Accounting, business admin, logistics, management information systems, marketing. **Communications:** Media studies. **Computer sciences:** General, information systems. **Education:** Early childhood, mathematics, middle, music, physical, science, social science, special ed. **English:** English lit, rhetoric/composition. **Foreign languages:** Spanish. **Health services:** Nursing (RN). **History:** General. **Human services:** Social work. **Math:** General. **Parks/recreation:** Health/fitness. **Physical sciences:** Chemistry. **Protective services:** Criminal justice, fire services admin, forensics. **Psychology:** General. **Social sciences:** Political science, sociology. **Visual/performing arts:** Drawing, music.

Most popular majors. Business/marketing 18%, education 25%, public administration/social services 6%, security/protective services 14%, social sciences 7%.

Technology on campus. Dormitories wired for high-speed internet access and linked to campus network. Commuter students can connect to campus network. Online course registration, online library, helpline, wireless network available.

Student life. Freshman orientation: Mandatory, $50 fee. Preregistration for classes offered. **Housing:** Single-sex dorms, apartments available. **Activities:** Bands, choral groups, dance, drama, international student organizations, literary magazine, musical theater, radio station, TV station, Anointed Gospel Choir, NAACP, HIV Aids peer educators, Sigma Alpha Phi, peer educators, Campus Girl Scouts, Center for African American Male.

Athletics. NCAA. **Intercollegiate:** Baseball M, basketball, cheerleading, cross-country, football (tackle) M, softball W, tennis W, track and field, volleyball W. **Intramural:** Basketball M, football (tackle) M, track and field. **Team name:** Rams.

Student services. Adult student services, alcohol/substance abuse counseling, career counseling, services for economically disadvantaged, student employment services, financial aid counseling, health services, minority student services, personal counseling, veterans' counselor. **Physically disabled:** Services for visually, speech, hearing impaired.

Contact. E-mail: admissions@asurams.edu
Phone: (229) 430-4646 Toll-free number: (800) 822-7267
Fax: (229) 430-4105
Leslie Charles, Director of Admissions, Albany State University, 504 College Drive, Albany, GA 31705-2796

Argosy University: Atlanta
Atlanta, Georgia
www.argosy.edu/atlanta

- For-profit 4-year university
- Very large city
- 434 degree-seeking undergraduates

General. Regionally accredited. **Degrees:** 53 bachelor's, 5 associate awarded; master's, professional, doctoral offered. **Calendar:** Differs by program. **Full-time faculty:** 50 total. **Part-time faculty:** 36 total.

Basis for selection. Open admission.

2015-2016 Annual costs. Tuition/fees: $16,842. **Additional information:** Tuition indicated is for programs in the College of Arts and Sciences. College of Health Sciences programs are $575 per-credit-hour.

Application procedures. Admission: Closing date 9/13. $50 fee. Admission notification on a rolling basis. **Financial aid:** No deadline.

Academics. Credit/placement by examination: AP, CLEP.

Majors. Business: Business admin. **Liberal arts:** Arts/sciences. **Protective services:** Police science. **Psychology:** General.

Contact. E-mail: auaadmissions@argosy.edu
Phone: (770) 671-1200 Toll-free number: (888) 671-4777
Johanna Collins, Senior Director of Admissions, Argosy University: Atlanta, 980 Hammond Drive, Suite 100, Atlanta, GA 30328

Armstrong State University
Savannah, Georgia
www.armstrong.edu   CB code: 5012

- Public 4-year university
- Residential campus in small city
- 6,331 degree-seeking undergraduates: 27% part-time, 66% women, 25% African American, 3% Asian American, 7% Hispanic/Latino, 5% Multiracial, non-Hispanic, 2% international
- 772 degree-seeking graduate students
- 74% of applicants admitted
- SAT or ACT (ACT writing optional) required
- 33% graduate within 6 years

General. Founded in 1935. Regionally accredited. **Degrees:** 1,018 bachelor's, 69 associate awarded; master's, professional offered. **ROTC:** Army, Naval. **Location:** 250 miles from Atlanta; 150 miles from Jacksonville, FL. **Calendar:** Semester, extensive summer session. **Full-time faculty:** 265 total; 14% minority, 58% women. **Part-time faculty:** 179 total; 8% minority, 64% women. **Class size:** 41% < 20, 53% 20-39, 3% 40-49, 3% 50-99.

Freshman class profile. 2,328 applied, 1,721 admitted, 980 enrolled.

Mid 50% test scores			
		GPA 3.0-3.49:	38%
SAT critical reading:	460-550	GPA 2.0-2.99:	29%
SAT math:	450-530	Return as sophomores:	70%
SAT writing:	430-520	Out-of-state:	9%
ACT composite:	19-23	Live on campus:	48%
GPA 3.75 or higher:	17%	International:	1%
GPA 3.50-3.74:	16%	Sororities:	3%

Basis for selection. For regular admissions, 410 SAT math and 440 SAT verbal with combined scored of at least 900 and 2.5 GPA required. **Home schooled:** Transcript of courses and grades, letter of recommendation (non-parent) required. Applicants who do not complete accredited program must pass SAT Subject Tests to satisfy college prep requirements.

High school preparation. College-preparatory program required. Required units include English 4, mathematics 4, social studies 3, science 4 (laboratory 2) and foreign language 2.

2015-2016 Annual costs. Tuition/fees: $6,332; $19,152 out-of-state. Room/board: $10,498. Books/supplies: $3,000. Personal expenses: $7,899.

2014-2015 Financial aid. Need-based: 576 full-time freshmen applied for aid; 402 deemed to have need; 402 received aid. Average need met was 49%. Average scholarship/grant was $1,500; average loan $4,500. 50% of total undergraduate aid awarded as scholarships/grants, 50% as loans/jobs. **Non-need-based:** Awarded to 933 full-time undergraduates, including 318

freshmen. Scholarships awarded for academics, alumni affiliation, art, athletics, job skills, leadership, minority status, music/drama, ROTC, state residency. **Additional information:** Armstrong Commitment Fund provided to students in sophomore, junior or senior year. Students must demonstrate need, complete financial literacy training, and participate in community service activities.

Application procedures. Admission: $25 fee, may be waived for applicants with need. Admission notification on a rolling basis beginning on or about 10/1. **Financial aid:** Priority date 3/15, closing date 4/20. FAFSA required. Must reply within 2 week(s) of notification.

Academics. Special study options: Cooperative education, distance learning, double major, dual enrollment of high school students, honors, independent study, internships, study abroad, teacher certification program, weekend college. **Credit/placement by examination:** AP, CLEP, IB, SAT, ACT, institutional tests. 30 credit hours maximum toward associate degree, 30 toward bachelor's. **Support services:** Learning center, pre-admission summer program, reduced course load, remedial instruction, study skills assistance, tutoring, writing center.

Majors. Area/ethnic studies: Women's. **Biology:** General, biochemistry. **Business:** Managerial economics. **Computer sciences:** General, information systems. **Education:** Art, early childhood, English, mathematics, music, physical, special ed, speech impaired. **English:** English lit. **Foreign languages:** French, Spanish. **Health services:** Clinical lab science, medical radiologic technology/radiation therapy, nursing (RN), physical therapy, respiratory therapy technology, sonography. **History:** General. **Liberal arts:** Arts/sciences. **Math:** General. **Physical sciences:** Chemistry, physics. **Protective services:** Police science. **Psychology:** General. **Social sciences:** Economics, political science. **Visual/performing arts:** Art, dramatic, music.

Most popular majors. Biology 8%, education 11%, health sciences 44%, liberal arts 6%.

Technology on campus. 300 workstations in dormitories, library, computer center, student center. Dormitories wired for high-speed internet access and linked to campus network. Commuter students can connect to campus network. Online course registration, online library, helpline, wireless network available.

Student life. Freshman orientation: Mandatory, $75 fee. Preregistration for classes offered. One-day event prior to registration. **Housing:** Coed dorms, apartments available. **Activities:** Bands, campus ministries, choral groups, dance, drama, international student organizations, literary magazine, music ensembles, Model UN, musical theater, student government, student newspaper, NAACP, Baptist Collegiate Ministry, Hispanic outreach and leadership, Cercle Francais, Wesley Foundation, College Libertarians, Student Veterans of America, Gay-Straight Alliance, ASU Annointed Voices/Gospel Choir.

Athletics. NCAA. Intercollegiate: Baseball M, basketball, cross-country M, golf, soccer W, softball W, tennis, volleyball W. **Intramural:** Basketball, bowling, football (non-tackle), handball, sand volleyball, soccer, softball, table tennis, tennis, ultimate frisbee, volleyball. **Team name:** Pirates.

Student services. Adult student services, alcohol/substance abuse counseling, career counseling, student employment services, financial aid counseling, health services, minority student services, personal counseling, placement for graduates, veterans' counselor. **Physically disabled:** Services for visually, speech, hearing impaired.

Contact. E-mail: admissions.info@armstrong.edu
Phone: (912) 344-2503 Toll-free number: (800) 633-2349
Fax: (912) 344-3417
Joanne Landers, Director of Admissions, Armstrong State University, 11935 Abercorn Street, Savannah, GA 31419-1997

Art Institute of Atlanta
Atlanta, Georgia   **CB member**
www.artinstitutes.edu/atlanta   **CB code: 5429**

- For-profit 4-year culinary school and visual arts college
- Commuter campus in very large city
- 2,623 undergraduates
- Application essay, interview required

General. Founded in 1949. Regionally accredited. **Degrees:** 241 bachelor's, 135 associate awarded. **Location:** 12 miles from city center. **Calendar:** Quarter, extensive summer session. **Full-time faculty:** 131 total. **Part-time faculty:** 107 total. **Class size:** 58% < 20, 42% 20-39. **Special facilities:** Camera video studios, video editing suites, digital audio studio, professional photography studios, traditional darkroom, digital darkroom, digital image capture systems, motion capture lab, color-calibrated monitors, scanners, printers.

Basis for selection. GPA or GED transcript; ACT, SAT, ASSET or COMPASS; essay most important. Applicants for associate degree should have 2.0 GPA; 2.5 GPA for bachelor's degree. Test scores or life experience may be considered if GPA requirement not met. Students exempt from placement testing if one of the following apply: transfer credit in both English & math; 21 ACT; 500 SAT critical reading and math subscores. Portfolio required for national scholarship competition. **Home schooled:** Transcript of courses and grades, state high school equivalency certificate required. State or accreditation-issued credential for high school graduation is required along with transcript. If credential not available, students must have GED. **Learning Disabled:** Students should submit current documentation of disability to disability services coordinator at least 6 weeks before accommodations will be needed.

High school preparation. College-preparatory program required.

2015-2016 Annual costs. Books/supplies: $1,700. Personal expenses: $7,692. **Additional information:** Diploma programs: $20,381-$30,412, books and supplies $450-$600, room and board $15,024-$18,780. Associate programs: $44,354-$47,791, books and supplies $1,100-$1,450, room and board $30,048. Bachelor's programs: $88,047-$92,101, books and supplies $1,100-$2,250, room and board $56,340.

Financial aid. Non-need-based: Scholarships awarded for academics, art, state residency.

Application procedures. Admission: No deadline. $50 fee. Admission notification on a rolling basis. **Financial aid:** No deadline. FAFSA required. Applicants notified on a rolling basis starting 3/15.

Academics. Special study options: Accelerated study, distance learning, dual enrollment of high school students, honors, independent study, internships, study abroad, weekend college. **Credit/placement by examination:** AP, CLEP, IB, SAT, ACT, institutional tests. **Support services:** Learning center, pre-admission summer program, reduced course load, remedial instruction, study skills assistance, tutoring, writing center.

Majors. Communications: Advertising, digital media. **Communications technology:** Animation/special effects, graphic/printing, graphics, photo/film/video, recording arts. **Computer sciences:** Web page design, webmaster. **Visual/performing arts:** Cinematography, commercial photography, commercial/advertising art, fashion design, graphic design, illustration, interior design, multimedia, photography.

Most popular majors. Communication technologies 10%, computer/information sciences 24%, personal/culinary services 6%, visual/performing arts 56%.

Technology on campus. 385 workstations in dormitories, library, computer center. Dormitories wired for high-speed internet access. Online course registration, online library, helpline, student web hosting, wireless network available.

Student life. Freshman orientation: Available. Preregistration for classes offered. One day at beginning of each quarter. **Housing:** Guaranteed on-campus for all undergraduates. Coed dorms available. $250 fully refundable deposit. **Activities:** International student organizations, student government, Student Leadership Council.

Student services. Career counseling, student employment services, financial aid counseling, personal counseling, placement for graduates. **Physically disabled:** Services for visually, speech, hearing impaired.

Contact. E-mail: aia-admis@aii.edu
Phone: (770) 394-8300 Toll-free number: (800) 275-4242
Fax: (770) 394-0008
Joy McClure, Senior Director of Admissions, Art Institute of Atlanta, 6600 Peachtree Dunwoody Road, NE, Atlanta, GA 30328

Augusta University
Augusta, Georgia   **CB member**
www.augusta.edu   **CB code: 5406**

- Public 4-year university
- Commuter campus in small city
- 4,776 degree-seeking undergraduates: 25% African American, 2% Asian American, 6% Hispanic/Latino, 4% Multi-racial, non-Hispanic, 1% international
- 2,727 graduate students
- 74% of applicants admitted
- SAT or ACT (ACT writing optional) required
- 30% graduate within 6 years

General. Founded in 1828. Regionally accredited. **Degrees:** 1,013 bachelor's, 7 associate awarded; master's, professional, doctoral offered. **ROTC:** Army. **Location:** 157 miles from Atlanta. **Calendar:** Semester, extensive summer session. **Full-time faculty:** 962 total. **Part-time faculty:** 541 total.

Freshman class profile. 2,096 applied, 1,553 admitted, 775 enrolled.

Mid 50% test scores		Return as sophomores:	75%
SAT critical reading:	470-580	Out-of-state:	4%
SAT math:	460-560	International:	2%
ACT composite:	20-26		

Basis for selection. GED not accepted. High school GPA and standardized test scores most important. Freshman Index (FI) the FI is determined by the following formula(s): FI = SAT critical reading + SAT math + (High School GPA x 500) or FI = (ACT Composite x 42) + (High School GPA x 500) + 88.

High school preparation. College-preparatory program required. Required units include English 4, mathematics 4, social studies 3, science 4 (laboratory 4) and foreign language 2.

2015-2016 Annual costs. Tuition/fees: $10,418; $29,084 out-of-state. Room only: $4,600.

2015-2016 Financial aid. Need-based: 49% of total undergraduate aid awarded as scholarships/grants, 51% as loans/jobs. **Non-need-based:** Scholarships awarded for academics, alumni affiliation, art, athletics, job skills, leadership, minority status, music/drama, religious affiliation, ROTC, state residency.

Application procedures. Admission: Priority date 12/1; deadline 6/1. $50 fee, may be waived for applicants with need. Admission notification on a rolling basis. **Financial aid:** Closing date 3/1. FAFSA required. Applicants notified on a rolling basis starting 3/1; must reply within 2 week(s) of notification.

Academics. Special study options: Combined bachelor's/graduate degree, distance learning, double major, dual enrollment of high school students, honors, independent study, internships, study abroad, teacher certification program, United Nations semester. **Credit/placement by examination:** AP, CLEP, IB, institutional tests. **Support services:** Learning center, study skills assistance, tutoring, writing center.

Majors. Biology: General. **Business:** Accounting, business admin, finance, management information systems, marketing. **Communications:** Communications/speech/rhetoric. **Computer sciences:** General, information technology. **Education:** Early childhood, middle, music, physical, special ed. **English:** English lit. **Foreign languages:** General. **Health services:** Clinical lab science, dental hygiene, health information management, medical radiologic technology/radiation therapy, nuclear medical technology, nursing (RN), physician assistant, preop/surgical nursing, respiratory therapy technology. **History:** General. **Human services:** Social work. **Math:** General. **Parks/recreation:** Exercise sciences. **Physical sciences:** Chemistry, physics. **Protective services:** Criminal justice. **Psychology:** General. **Social sciences:** Anthropology, political science, sociology. **Visual/performing arts:** Multimedia, music, music performance.

Most popular majors. Business/marketing 14%, education 6%, health sciences 28%, parks/recreation 7%, psychology 7%, social sciences 6%.

Technology on campus. Dormitories wired for high-speed internet access and linked to campus network. Commuter students can connect to campus network. Online course registration, online library, helpline, wireless network available.

Student life. Freshman orientation: Mandatory, $60 fee. Preregistration for classes offered. **Housing:** Guaranteed on-campus for freshmen. Coed dorms, special housing for disabled, apartments, themed housing available. **Activities:** Bands, campus ministries, choral groups, dance, drama, international student organizations, literary magazine, music ensembles, Model UN, musical theater, opera, student government, student newspaper, symphony orchestra, Baptist Collegiate Ministries, Campus Crusade for Christ, Jewish Student Union, Muslim Student Association. The Lumin Society, Handy Helpers, Hispanic Health Clinic, Model UN, Black Student Union, College Republicans, Student Veterans Association, Indian Cultural Association, Lambda Alliance.

Athletics. NCAA. **Intercollegiate:** Baseball M, basketball, cross-country, golf M, softball W, tennis, track and field, volleyball W. **Intramural:** Badminton, basketball, football (non-tackle), golf, racquetball, soccer, softball, table tennis, ultimate frisbee, volleyball, weight lifting. **Team name:** Jaguars.

Student services. Adult student services, alcohol/substance abuse counseling, career counseling, student employment services, financial aid counseling, health services, minority student services, personal counseling, veterans' counselor.

Contact. E-mail: admissions@augusta.edu
Phone: (706) 737-1632 Fax: (706) 667-4355
Scott Argo, Director of Admissions, Augusta University, Benet House, 1120 15th Street, Augusta, GA 30912

Bauder College
Atlanta, Georgia
www.bauder.edu
CB code: 5070

- For-profit 4-year career college
- Commuter campus in very large city
- 751 undergraduates
- Application essay, interview required

General. Founded in 1964. Regionally accredited. Certified as a Pearson VUE Test Center. **Degrees:** 16 bachelor's, 141 associate awarded. **Location:** Downtown. **Calendar:** Quarter, extensive summer session. **Full-time faculty:** 40 total. **Part-time faculty:** 34 total.

Freshman class profile.

Out-of-state:	14%	Live on campus:	50%

Basis for selection. Open admission, but selective for some programs. Portfolio recommended for interior and fashion design majors. **Home schooled:** GED recommended.

2015-2016 Annual costs. Books/supplies: $900. Personal expenses: $1,100. **Additional information:** Bachelor's programs: Business Administration $70,125; Business Administration - Accounting $70,452; Business Administration - Fashion Merchandising $72,772; Criminal Justice $73,139. Associate programs: $34,275-$46,723. Certificate program: Medical Assisting $15,568. Diploma program: Practical Nursing $23,395.

Financial aid. All financial aid based on need.

Application procedures. Admission: No deadline. $10 fee. Application must be submitted on paper. Admission notification on a rolling basis. **Financial aid:** No deadline. FAFSA, institutional form required. Applicants notified on a rolling basis starting 7/15.

Academics. Special study options: Double major, internships. **Credit/placement by examination:** AP, CLEP. **Support services:** Reduced course load, remedial instruction, tutoring.

Majors. Business: Business admin. **Protective services:** Law enforcement admin.

Technology on campus. 38 workstations in library, computer center, student center. Online library, helpline, wireless network available.

Student life. Freshman orientation: Mandatory. Preregistration for classes offered. **Housing:** Cooperative housing available. **Activities:** Student government, student newspaper.

Student services. Alcohol/substance abuse counseling, career counseling, services for economically disadvantaged, student employment services, financial aid counseling, personal counseling, placement for graduates.

Contact. E-mail: admissions@bauder.edu
Phone: (404) 237-7573 Toll-free number: (800) 241-3797
Fax: (404) 237-1619
Director of Admissions, Bauder College, 384 Northyards Boulevard NW, Ste 190, Atlanta, GA 30313

Berry College
Mount Berry, Georgia
www.berry.edu
CB member
CB code: 5059

- Private 4-year liberal arts college
- Residential campus in large town
- 2,089 degree-seeking undergraduates: 1% part-time, 62% women, 5% African American, 1% Asian American, 7% Hispanic/Latino, 3% Multiracial, non-Hispanic, 1% international
- 119 degree-seeking graduate students
- 55% of applicants admitted
- SAT or ACT (ACT writing optional), application essay required
- 64% graduate within 6 years; 20% enter graduate study

General. Founded in 1902. Regionally accredited. **Degrees:** 419 bachelor's awarded; master's offered. **Location:** 72 miles from Atlanta; 75 miles from Chattanooga, TN. **Calendar:** Semester, limited summer session. **Full-time faculty:** 167 total; 89% have terminal degrees, 5% minority, 45% women. **Part-time faculty:** 60 total; 45% have terminal degrees, 5% minority, 37% women. **Class size:** 58% < 20, 40% 20-39, 2% 40-49. **Special facilities:** Museum, waterwheel, wildlife management area and refuge, equine center with boarding facilities, dairy and beef cattle research center, on-campus elementary and middle schools, child development center, science center with 60-foot Foucault pendulum, student campsites.

Freshman class profile. 4,347 applied, 2,407 admitted, 575 enrolled.

Mid 50% test scores		GPA 2.0-2.99:	4%
SAT critical reading:	530-630	Rank in top quarter:	62%
SAT math:	520-610	Rank in top tenth:	31%
SAT writing:	510-610	End year in good standing:	92%
ACT composite:	24-29	Return as sophomores:	83%
GPA 3.75 or higher:	60%	Out-of-state:	37%
GPA 3.50-3.74:	17%	Live on campus:	96%
GPA 3.0-3.49:	19%		

Basis for selection. School achievement record and test scores most important. Class rank, recommendations and essays considered. Interview recommended; auditions required of music and theater majors; portfolio recommended for art majors. **Home schooled:** Transcript of courses and grades, letter of recommendation (nonparent) required. Must meet or exceed academic profile of previous freshman class.

High school preparation. College-preparatory program required. 20 units required. Required units include English 4, mathematics 4, social studies 3, science 3, foreign language 2 and academic electives 4. Algebra I, geometry or trigonometry, algebra II and fourth year higher than algebra II required.

2015-2016 Annual costs. Tuition/fees: $31,996. Room/board: $11,190. Books/supplies: $1,000. Personal expenses: $1,198.

2015-2016 Financial aid. Need-based: 523 full-time freshmen applied for aid; 410 deemed to have need; 410 received aid. Average need met was 84%. Average scholarship/grant was $22,244; average loan $4,092. 78% of total undergraduate aid awarded as scholarships/grants, 22% as loans/jobs. **Non-need-based:** Awarded to 916 full-time undergraduates, including 262 freshmen. Scholarships awarded for academics, art, leadership, minority status, music/drama, religious affiliation. **Additional information:** All students encouraged to work on-campus up to 16 hours per week.

Application procedures. Admission: Priority date 2/1; deadline 7/22 (receipt date). $50 fee, may be waived for applicants with need, free for online applicants. Admission notification on a rolling basis beginning on or about 11/1. Must reply by May 1 or within 4 week(s) if notified thereafter. **Financial aid:** Priority date 3/1; no closing date. FAFSA required. Not require for domestic applicants. Applicants notified by 2/15; Applicants notified on a rolling basis starting 2/15; must reply by 5/1.

Academics. Special study options: Combined bachelor's/graduate degree, cross-registration, double major, dual enrollment of high school students, honors, independent study, internships, student-designed major, study abroad, teacher certification program. 3-2 nursing with Emory University; 3-2 engineering with Georgia Institute of Technology and Kennesaw State University. **Credit/placement by examination:** AP, CLEP, IB, SAT, ACT, institutional tests. **Support services:** Study skills assistance, tutoring, writing center.

Majors. Biology: General, biochemistry. **Business:** Accounting, business admin, finance, international, managerial economics, marketing. **Communications:** General. **Conservation:** Environmental science. **Education:** Art, early childhood, ESL, mathematics, middle, music, secondary. **English:** English lit. **Foreign languages:** French, German, Spanish. **Health services:** Nursing (RN), prenursing. **History:** General. **Math:** General. **Parks/recreation:** Exercise sciences. **Philosophy/religion:** General. **Physical sciences:** Chemistry, physics. **Psychology:** General. **Social sciences:** General, international relations, political science. **Visual/performing arts:** Art, music, music management, theater arts management.

Most popular majors. Agriculture 10%, biology 11%, business/marketing 23%, education 8%, parks/recreation 6%, psychology 7%.

Technology on campus. 200 workstations in library, computer center, student center. Dormitories wired for high-speed internet access and linked to campus network. Commuter students can connect to campus network. Online library, helpline, repair service, wireless network available.

Student life. Freshman orientation: Mandatory, $90 fee. Preregistration for classes offered. Sessions for students and parents in June based on date of prepayment. Additional orientation 4 days prior to start of classes. **Policies:** Limited visitation hours. Dry campus. Tobacco free campus. **Housing:** Guaranteed on-campus for all undergraduates. Coed dorms, single-sex dorms, apartments, wellness housing available. $100 fully refundable deposit, deadline 5/1. **Activities:** Bands, campus ministries, choral groups, dance, drama,

international student organizations, literary magazine, music ensembles, Model UN, musical theater, student government, student newspaper, symphony orchestra, Amnesty International, Wesley Foundation, Catholic Student Association, Habitat for Humanity, Canterbury Club, Campus Outreach, Fellowship of Christian Athletes, Young Democrats, College Republicans.

Athletics. NCAA. **Intercollegiate:** Baseball M, basketball, cross-country, diving, equestrian W, football (tackle) M, golf, lacrosse, soccer, softball W, swimming, tennis, track and field, volleyball W. **Intramural:** Basketball, bowling, cross-country, football (non-tackle), golf, racquetball, soccer, softball, swimming, tennis, ultimate frisbee, volleyball. **Team name:** Vikings.

Student services. Alcohol/substance abuse counseling, chaplain/spiritual director, career counseling, student employment services, financial aid counseling, health services, minority student services, on-campus daycare, personal counseling, placement for graduates, veterans' counselor, women's services. **Physically disabled:** Services for visually, hearing impaired.

Contact. E-mail: admissions@berry.edu
Phone: (706) 236-2215 Toll-free number: (800) 237-7942
Fax: (706) 290-2178
Brett Kennedy, Assistant Vice President of Admissions, Berry College, PO Box 490159, Mount Berry, GA 30149-0159

Beulah Heights University
Atlanta, Georgia
www.beulah.edu   CB code: 5082

▸ Private 5-year university, Bible, business and seminary college affiliated with the nondenominational tradition
▸ Commuter campus in very large city
▸ 400 degree-seeking undergraduates
▸ 212 graduate students
▸ Application essay required
▸ 32% graduate within 6 years

General. Accredited by ABHE. **Degrees:** 33 bachelor's, 17 associate awarded; master's, professional, doctoral offered. **Location:** Downtown. **Calendar:** Continuous, extensive summer session. **Full-time faculty:** 12 total; 67% have terminal degrees, 100% minority, 8% women. **Class size:** 70% < 20, 28% 20-39, 2% 40-49.

Freshman class profile.

End year in good standing:	71%	Out-of-state:	1%
Return as sophomores:	71%	Live on campus:	5%

Basis for selection. Open admission. Qualitative faith is important. Pastoral and personal references required. Applicants pursuing GED may be accepted prior to completion, but are not be eligible to receive degree until GED is received. **Home schooled:** State high school equivalency certificate required. Program must be approved by state; 16 ACT/900 SAT (exclusive of Writing) required.

High school preparation. College-preparatory program recommended.

2015-2016 Annual costs. Tuition/fees: $9,390. Room only: $5,000. Books/supplies: $400. Personal expenses: $600. **Additional information:** An additional fee of $100 is incurred for each on-line course in which a student is registered.

Application procedures. Admission: Closing date 8/1 (postmark date). $35 fee, may be waived for applicants with need. Application must be submitted on paper. Admission notification on a rolling basis. **Financial aid:** Priority date 2/1, closing date 6/30. FAFSA required. Applicants notified on a rolling basis.

Academics. Special study options: Accelerated study, cross-registration, distance learning, double major, ESL, independent study, internships, weekend college. **Credit/placement by examination:** AP, CLEP, IB, institutional tests. **Support services:** Learning center, reduced course load, remedial instruction, study skills assistance, tutoring, writing center.

Majors. Business: Business admin, organizational leadership. **Theology:** Bible.

Most popular majors. Business/marketing 30%, theological studies 70%.

Technology on campus. 30 workstations in dormitories, library, computer center, student center. Dormitories wired for high-speed internet access. Commuter students can connect to campus network. Online course registration, online library, student web hosting, wireless network available.

Student life. Freshman orientation: Mandatory. Preregistration for classes offered. **Policies:** Students are required to abide by the schools code of conduct and observe the schools rules and regulations. Religious observance required. **Housing:** Single-sex dorms, apartments, wellness housing available. $150 fully refundable deposit. **Activities:** Campus ministries, choral groups, international student organizations, student government, student newspaper, Club Give, international students association, Saturday Knight Live.

Student services. Adult student services, chaplain/spiritual director, career counseling, financial aid counseling, minority student services, personal counseling.

Contact. E-mail: admissions@beulah.edu
Phone: (404) 627-2681 ext. 104 Toll-free number: (888) 777-2422
Fax: (404) 627-0702
Arthur Breland, Director of Admissions, Beulah Heights University, 892 Berne Street SE, Atlanta, GA 30316

Brenau University
Gainesville, Georgia   **CB member**
www.brenau.edu   **CB code: 5066**

▶ Private 4-year university and liberal arts college for women
▶ Residential campus in large town
▶ 1,556 degree-seeking undergraduates: 37% part-time, 90% women, 32% African American, 2% Asian American, 8% Hispanic/Latino, 3% Multiracial, non-Hispanic, 2% international
▶ 1,310 degree-seeking graduate students
▶ 66% of applicants admitted
▶ SAT or ACT (ACT writing optional) required
▶ 51% graduate within 6 years

General. Founded in 1878. Regionally accredited. **Degrees:** 343 bachelor's, 2 associate awarded; master's, professional offered. **Location:** 45 miles from Atlanta, GA. **Calendar:** Semester, limited summer session. **Full-time faculty:** 123 total; 81% have terminal degrees, 16% minority, 76% women. **Part-time faculty:** 226 total; 46% have terminal degrees, 23% minority, 67% women. **Class size:** 88% < 20, 11% 20-39, less than 1% 40-49, less than 1% 50-99. **Special facilities:** Regional history museum, visual arts center, performing arts centers.

Freshman class profile. 2,324 applied, 1,525 admitted, 203 enrolled.

Mid 50% test scores			
SAT critical reading:	450-560	Out-of-state:	8%
SAT math:	440-530	Live on campus:	64%
SAT writing:	450-520	International:	2%
Return as sophomores:	58%	Sororities:	24%

Basis for selection. GPA and SAT/ACT weighted equally. Admission policies for evening/weekend college differ from day programs. SAT/ACT used for placement into math courses. Auditions required of performing arts majors. **Home schooled:** Transcript of courses and grades required. **Learning Disabled:** Learning disability must be professionally diagnosed.

High school preparation. College-preparatory program recommended. 16 units required. Required units include English 4, mathematics 4, social studies 3, science 3 and foreign language 2.

2015-2016 Annual costs. Tuition/fees: $25,878. Room/board: $11,998. Books/supplies: $1,300. Personal expenses: $1,600.

Financial aid. **Non-need-based:** Scholarships awarded for academics, art, athletics, leadership, music/drama.

Application procedures. Admission: Priority date 1/15; no deadline. $35 fee, may be waived for applicants with need. Admission notification on a rolling basis beginning on or about 8/1. **Financial aid:** Priority date 4/1; no closing date. FAFSA required. Applicants notified on a rolling basis starting 3/1.

Academics. Special study options: Accelerated study, combined bachelor's/graduate degree, cross-registration, distance learning, double major, honors, independent study, internships, liberal arts/career combination, study abroad, teacher certification program, weekend college. **Credit/placement by examination:** AP, CLEP, IB, institutional tests. 27 credit hours maximum toward bachelor's degree. Total of 27 hours for non-traditional students allowed. **Support services:** Learning center, reduced course load, remedial instruction, study skills assistance, tutoring, writing center.

Majors. Biology: General. **Business:** General, accounting, fashion, human resources, marketing, organizational leadership. **Communications:** Media

studies. **Education:** Art, drama/dance, early childhood, early childhood special, elementary, elementary special ed, junior high special ed, mentally handicapped, middle, music, secondary, secondary special ed, special ed. **English:** English lit. **Health services:** Nursing practice, physician assistant. **History:** General. **Liberal arts:** Arts/sciences. **Psychology:** General. **Social sciences:** Political science. **Visual/performing arts:** Arts management, dance, dramatic, fashion design, graphic design, interior design, music, music performance, musical theater, studio arts, studio arts management, theater design.

Most popular majors. Business/marketing 31%, education 10%, health sciences 33%, visual/performing arts 11%.

Technology on campus. PC or laptop required. 150 workstations in dormitories, library, computer center, student center. Dormitories wired for high-speed internet access and linked to campus network. Commuter students can connect to campus network. Online course registration, online library, helpline, repair service, student web hosting, wireless network available.

Student life. Freshman orientation: Mandatory. Preregistration for classes offered. **Policies:** Single students under 22 years of age required to live on campus unless living with family or legal guardian; alcohol-free campus; required convocation attendance. **Housing:** Guaranteed on-campus for all undergraduates. Special housing for disabled, apartments, fraternity/sorority housing available. **Activities:** Bands, campus ministries, choral groups, dance, drama, international student organizations, literary magazine, music ensembles, musical theater, radio station, student government, student newspaper, Brenau Fellowship Association, Eco-Friends, Fellowship of Christian Athletes, College Republicans, College Democrats, Silhouettes, Greek letter service organizations, student activities board.

Athletics. NAIA. **Intercollegiate:** Basketball W, cheerleading W, cross-country W, golf W, soccer W, softball W, swimming W, tennis W, track and field W, volleyball W. **Team name:** Golden Tigers.

Student services. Alcohol/substance abuse counseling, chaplain/spiritual director, career counseling, student employment services, financial aid counseling, health services, minority student services, personal counseling, placement for graduates, women's services. **Physically disabled:** Services for visually, speech, hearing impaired.

Contact. E-mail: admissions@brenau.edu
Phone: (770) 534-6100 Toll-free number: (800) 252-5119
Fax: (770) 538-4701
Ray Tatum, Senior Vice President for Enrollment Management & Student Services, Brenau University, 500 Washington Street SE, Gainesville, GA 30501

Brewton-Parker College
Mount Vernon, Georgia   **CB member**
www.bpc.edu   **CB code: 5068**

▶ Private 4-year liberal arts college affiliated with the Southern Baptist Convention
▶ Residential campus in small town
▶ 432 degree-seeking undergraduates
▶ SAT or ACT (ACT writing optional) required

General. Founded in 1904. Regionally accredited. **Degrees:** 62 bachelor's, 10 associate awarded. **Location:** 90 miles from Macon and Savannah. **Calendar:** Semester, limited summer session. **Full-time faculty:** 27 total. **Part-time faculty:** 36 total. **Class size:** 66% < 20, 33% 20-39, less than 1% 40-49. **Special facilities:** Living history museum, recital hall, greenhouse, nature trail.

Freshman class profile.

Out-of-state:	13%	Live on campus:	84%

Basis for selection. Students evaluated on SAT/ACT and high school performance. Audition and interview required of music majors.

High school preparation. College-preparatory program recommended. 13 units required. Required units include English 4, mathematics 3, social studies 3 and science 3.

2015-2016 Annual costs. Tuition/fees: $16,180. Room/board: $7,930. Books/supplies: $2,000. Personal expenses: $104.

Financial aid. **Non-need-based:** Scholarships awarded for academics, athletics, leadership, religious affiliation, state residency.

Application procedures. Admission: Closing date 8/1. $35 fee. Admission notification on a rolling basis beginning on or about 9/1. **Financial aid:**

Priority date 3/15, closing date 7/1. FAFSA required. Applicants notified on a rolling basis starting 3/15; must reply within 2 week(s) of notification.

Academics. Special study options: Distance learning, double major, dual enrollment of high school students, external degree, honors, independent study, internships, teacher certification program. **Credit/placement by examination:** AP, CLEP, SAT, ACT, institutional tests. 30 credit hours maximum toward associate degree, 30 toward bachelor's. **Support services:** Learning center, reduced course load, remedial instruction, study skills assistance, tutoring.

Majors. Biology: General. **Business:** General. **Communications:** Communications/speech/rhetoric. **Computer sciences:** General. **Education:** Early childhood, middle. **English:** English lit. **Foreign languages:** Spanish. **History:** General. **Math:** General. **Parks/recreation:** Sports admin. **Philosophy/religion:** Christian. **Psychology:** General. **Social sciences:** Criminology, political science, sociology. **Theology:** Bible, sacred music. **Visual/performing arts:** General.

Most popular majors. Biology 8%, business/marketing 32%, education 21%, English 7%, liberal arts 7%, parks/recreation 8%, public administration/social services 6%.

Technology on campus. 104 workstations in library, computer center. Dormitories wired for high-speed internet access. Online course registration, online library, wireless network available.

Student life. Freshman orientation: Mandatory, $100 fee. Preregistration for classes offered. Held the week and/or weekend before classes start. **Policies:** All day students required to live on campus except seniors, students residing with parents, students 22 or older. Religious observance required. **Housing:** Guaranteed on-campus for freshmen. Single-sex dorms available. $125 nonrefundable deposit. **Activities:** Campus ministries, choral groups, international student organizations, music ensembles, student government, ministerial association, Fellowship of Christian Athletes, Rotaract, Circle K, student activities council.

Athletics. NAIA. Intercollegiate: Baseball M, basketball, cheerleading, cross-country, golf M, soccer, softball W, volleyball W, wrestling M. **Intramural:** Basketball, football (non-tackle), softball, table tennis, tennis, volleyball. **Team name:** Barons.

Student services. Alcohol/substance abuse counseling, chaplain/spiritual director, financial aid counseling, health services, personal counseling, veterans' counselor. **Physically disabled:** Services for visually, speech, hearing impaired.

Contact. E-mail: admissions@bpc.edu
Phone: (912) 583-2241 ext. 265
Toll-free number: (800) 342-1087 ext. 265 Fax: (912) 583-3598
Kim Bell, Vice President for Enrollment Services, Brewton-Parker College, Brewton-Parker College # 2011, Mount Vernon, GA 30445

Carver College
Atlanta, Georgia
www.carver.edu

- Private 4-year Bible and liberal arts college
- Commuter campus in very large city
- 115 undergraduates
- Application essay required

General. Accredited by ABHE. **Degrees:** 17 bachelor's, 9 associate awarded. **Calendar:** Semester, limited summer session. **Full-time faculty:** 3 total. **Part-time faculty:** 12 total.

Basis for selection. Applicants assessed for admittance based on academic record, moral character and personal testimony of faith. Students who cannot meet the general entrance requirements may be given conditional admittance for probationary period.

2015-2016 Annual costs. Tuition/fees: $9,860. Room/board: $6,600. Books/supplies: $800.

Financial aid. All financial aid based on need.

Application procedures. Admission: No deadline. $35 fee, may be waived for applicants with need. Admission notification on a rolling basis. **Financial aid:** No deadline. FAFSA, institutional form required.

Academics. Remedial instruction offered, particularly for those whose first language is not English. **Special study options:** Independent study. **Credit/placement by examination:** AP, CLEP. Transfer credits offered for work done which may be same or similar to offered courses. **Support services:** Learning center, remedial instruction.

Majors. Theology: Bible.

Technology on campus. Commuter students can connect to campus network.

Student life. Freshman orientation: Mandatory. Preregistration for classes offered. Held Saturday before classes begin; includes opening ceremony for new students. Credit bearing 7-week freshman seminar class also required. **Policies:** Religious observance required. **Housing:** Single-sex dorms available. **Activities:** Choral groups, student government.

Athletics. NCCAA. Intercollegiate: Basketball M. **Team name:** Carver Cougars.

Student services. Financial aid counseling.

Contact. E-mail: admissions@carver.edu
Phone: (404) 527-4520 Fax: (404) 527-4524
Marj Patrick, Director of Enrollment Management, Carver College, 3870 Cascade Road, SW, Atlanta, GA 30331

Chamberlain College of Nursing: Atlanta
Atlanta, Georgia
www.chamberlain.edu   CB code: 6994

- For-profit 4-year nursing college
- Commuter campus in very large city
- 879 degree-seeking undergraduates
- SAT or ACT required

General. Degrees: 156 bachelor's awarded. **Calendar:** Semester. **Full-time faculty:** 9 total; 67% minority, 100% women. **Part-time faculty:** 6 total; 50% minority, 83% women.

Basis for selection. Admission decisions based on interview, proof of high school diploma/GED, and satisfactory test scores. For more information about such tests and scores, contact admissions office.

2015-2016 Annual costs. Tuition/fees: $18,160. Books/supplies: $1,400. Personal expenses: $2,452. **Additional information:** Tuition quoted is for Nursing courses at $590 per credit. Tuition and fees vary by program.

Application procedures. Admission: No deadline. $95 fee. Admission notification on a rolling basis.

Academics. Special study options: Accelerated study, distance learning. **Credit/placement by examination:** AP, CLEP.

Majors. Health services: Nursing (RN).

Contact. Phone: (404) 250-8500
Chamberlain College of Nursing: Atlanta, 5775 Peachtree Dunwoody Road Northeast, Atlanta, GA 30342

Clark Atlanta University
Atlanta, Georgia   CB member
www.cau.edu   CB code: 5110

- Private 4-year university affiliated with the United Methodist Church
- Residential campus in very large city
- 2,741 degree-seeking undergraduates: 4% part-time, 74% women, 84% African American, 2% international
- 920 degree-seeking graduate students
- 52% of applicants admitted
- SAT or ACT (ACT writing optional), application essay required
- 38% graduate within 6 years

General. Founded in 1869. Regionally accredited. Member of Atlanta University Center, a consortium of black private education institutions. **Degrees:** 448 bachelor's awarded; master's, doctoral offered. **ROTC:** Army, Naval. **Location:** 2 miles from downtown. **Calendar:** Semester, limited summer session. **Full-time faculty:** 173 total; 86% have terminal degrees, 88% minority, 42% women. **Part-time faculty:** 119 total; 53% have terminal degrees, 90% minority, 57% women. **Class size:** 46% < 20, 39% 20-39, 9% 40-49, 6% 50-99, less than 1% >100. **Special facilities:** Exhibition gallery, research center for science and technology.

Freshman class profile. 8,616 applied, 4,509 admitted, 844 enrolled.

Mid 50% test scores		Rank in top quarter:	20%
SAT critical reading:	380-470	Rank in top tenth:	3%
SAT math:	360-450	End year in good standing:	80%
ACT composite:	16-20	Return as sophomores:	67%
GPA 3.75 or higher:	6%	Out-of-state:	69%
GPA 3.50-3.74:	10%	Live on campus:	92%
GPA 3.0-3.49:	32%	International:	3%
GPA 2.0-2.99:	52%		

Basis for selection. Secondary school record most important. Test scores, recommendations, essay also important. Audition recommended for music and drama majors. **Home schooled:** Course work portfolio required.

High school preparation. College-preparatory program recommended. 18 units required. Required units include English 4, mathematics 3, social studies 3, science 3 (laboratory 1), foreign language 2 and academic electives 3.

2016-2017 Annual costs. Tuition/fees (projected): $21,945. Room/board: $10,478. Books/supplies: $1,500. Personal expenses: $1,603.

2015-2016 Financial aid. Need-based: 788 full-time freshmen applied for aid; 761 deemed to have need; 759 received aid. Average need met was 39%. Average scholarship/grant was $4,870; average loan $2,072. 53% of total undergraduate aid awarded as scholarships/grants, 47% as loans/jobs. **Non-need-based:** Awarded to 501 full-time undergraduates, including 155 freshmen. Scholarships awarded for academics, art, athletics, leadership, minority status, music/drama, religious affiliation, ROTC, state residency.

Application procedures. Admission: Priority date 3/1; deadline 6/1 (postmark date). $35 fee, may be waived for applicants with need. Admission notification on a rolling basis beginning on or about 1/1. **Financial aid:** Priority date 3/1; no closing date. FAFSA required. Applicants notified on a rolling basis starting 4/1.

Academics. Special study options: Accelerated study, combined bachelor's/graduate degree, cooperative education, cross-registration, double major, dual enrollment of high school students, exchange student, honors, independent study, internships, study abroad, teacher certification program, Washington semester, weekend college. **Credit/placement by examination:** AP, CLEP, IB, institutional tests. 45 credit hours maximum toward bachelor's degree. **Support services:** Learning center, reduced course load, study skills assistance, tutoring, writing center.

Majors. Biology: General. **Business:** Accounting, business admin, managerial economics. **Computer sciences:** General, computer science. **Education:** General, early childhood. **English:** English lit, rhetoric/composition. **Foreign languages:** French, Spanish. **History:** General. **Human services:** Social work. **Math:** General. **Philosophy/religion:** Philosophy, religion. **Physical sciences:** Chemistry, physics. **Protective services:** Criminal justice. **Psychology:** General. **Social sciences:** Political science, sociology. **Visual/performing arts:** Art, fashion design, music, theater history.

Most popular majors. Biology 11%, business/marketing 17%, communications/journalism 16%, psychology 14%, security/protective services 12%, visual/performing arts 8%.

Technology on campus. 650 workstations in dormitories, library, computer center, student center. Dormitories wired for high-speed internet access and linked to campus network. Commuter students can connect to campus network. Online course registration, online library, helpline, repair service, wireless network available.

Student life. Freshman orientation: Mandatory, $150 fee. Preregistration for classes offered. **Policies:** Drug/alcohol policy, sanctions for violations, policies governing Greek and other student organizations. **Housing:** Guaranteed on-campus for freshmen. Coed dorms, single-sex dorms, apartments available. $325 partly refundable deposit, deadline 6/1. **Activities:** Bands, campus ministries, choral groups, dance, drama, film society, international student organizations, literary magazine, music ensembles, musical theater, opera, radio station, student government, student newspaper, symphony orchestra, TV station, NAACP, pan-Hellenic council, Anointed Students in Fellowship, Campus Crusade for Christ, Christian Fellowship, National Council of Negro Women, Forensic Society, Gamma Sigma Sigma, Caribbean-oriented student organization.

Athletics. NCAA. **Intercollegiate:** Baseball M, basketball, cross-country, football (tackle) M, softball W, tennis W, track and field, volleyball W. **Intramural:** Basketball, football (non-tackle), tennis W, track and field. **Team name:** Panthers.

Student services. Alcohol/substance abuse counseling, chaplain/spiritual director, career counseling, student employment services, financial aid counseling, health services, personal counseling, placement for graduates, veterans' counselor, women's services. **Physically disabled:** Services for visually, speech, hearing impaired.

Contact. E-mail: cauadmissions@cau.edu
Phone: (404) 880-6605 Toll-free number: (800) 688-3228
Fax: (404) 880-6174
Lorri Rice, Director of Admissions, Clark Atlanta University, 223 James P. Brawley Drive, SW, Atlanta, GA 30314-4391

Clayton State University
Morrow, Georgia — CB member
www.clayton.edu — CB code: 5145

- Public 4-year university
- Commuter campus in small city
- 5,878 degree-seeking undergraduates: 41% part-time, 69% women, 66% African American, 5% Asian American, 3% Hispanic/Latino, 3% Multiracial, non-Hispanic, 1% international
- 425 degree-seeking graduate students
- 39% of applicants admitted
- SAT or ACT (ACT writing optional) required
- 32% graduate within 6 years

General. Founded in 1969. Regionally accredited. **Degrees:** 1,028 bachelor's, 48 associate awarded; master's offered. **ROTC:** Army, Naval, Air Force. **Location:** 12 miles from Atlanta. **Calendar:** Semester, extensive summer session. **Full-time faculty:** 249 total; 82% have terminal degrees, 40% minority, 53% women. **Part-time faculty:** 121 total. **Class size:** 45% < 20, 49% 20-39, 3% 40-49, 3% 50-99. **Special facilities:** Concert hall.

Freshman class profile. 2,774 applied, 1,070 admitted, 613 enrolled.

Mid 50% test scores		GPA 3.0-3.49:	31%
SAT critical reading:	440-520	GPA 2.0-2.99:	46%
SAT math:	420-500	Return as sophomores:	70%
ACT composite:	18-21	Out-of-state:	2%
GPA 3.75 or higher:	9%	Live on campus:	51%
GPA 3.50-3.74:	13%	International:	2%

Basis for selection. 17 ACT or 400 SAT math and 430 verbal required. Secondary school record also very important for health sciences, music, teacher education, and business programs. Auditions recommended for music majors. **Home schooled:** Must validate the completion of a college prep curriculum. SAT may be used to do so.

High school preparation. 16 units required; 22 recommended. Required and recommended units include English 4, mathematics 4, social studies 3, history 2, science 3-4 (laboratory 3), foreign language 2-3 and academic electives 2. Students not meeting college-preparatory requirements must take remedial classes before entering any program.

2015-2016 Annual costs. Tuition/fees: $6,312; $19,132 out-of-state. Room/board: $9,484. Books/supplies: $1,222. Personal expenses: $2,500.

2014-2015 Financial aid. Need-based: 412 full-time freshmen applied for aid; 375 deemed to have need; 375 received aid. Average need met was 52%. Average scholarship/grant was $6,535; average loan $3,402. **Non-need-based:** Awarded to 199 full-time undergraduates, including 66 freshmen. Scholarships awarded for academics, athletics, music/drama.

Application procedures. Admission: Priority date 2/1; no deadline. $40 fee, may be waived for applicants with need. Admission notification on a rolling basis beginning on or about 1/1. **Financial aid:** Priority date 7/15; no closing date. FAFSA required. Applicants notified on a rolling basis.

Academics. Special study options: Cooperative education, cross-registration, distance learning, double major, dual enrollment of high school students, exchange student, honors, independent study, internships, liberal arts/career combination, student-designed major, study abroad, teacher certification program. **Credit/placement by examination:** AP, CLEP, IB, institutional tests. **Support services:** Learning center, reduced course load, remedial instruction, study skills assistance, tutoring, writing center.

Majors. Biology: General. **Business:** General, accounting, business admin, logistics, marketing, office management. **Communications:** Communications/speech/rhetoric. **Computer sciences:** Computer science, information systems, information technology. **Education:** Middle. **English:** English lit. **Health services:** Dental hygiene, facilities admin, health care admin, nursing (RN). **History:** General. **Liberal arts:** Arts/sciences. **Math:** General. **Parks/recreation:** Sports admin. **Philosophy/religion:** Philosophy. **Physical sciences:** Chemistry. **Protective services:** Criminal justice. **Psychology:** Community. **Social sciences:** Political science, sociology. **Visual/performing arts:** Dramatic, music.

Most popular majors. Business/marketing 22%, health sciences 27%, liberal arts 11%, psychology 11%.

Technology on campus. PC or laptop required. Dormitories wired for high-speed internet access and linked to campus network. Online course registration, online library, helpline, repair service, student web hosting, wireless network available.

Student life. Freshman orientation: Mandatory, $40 fee. Preregistration for classes offered. **Housing:** Coed dorms available. **Activities:** Jazz band, choral groups, drama, film society, literary magazine, music ensembles, musical theater, opera, radio station, student government, student newspaper, approximately 20 student groups.

Athletics. NAIA, NCAA. **Intercollegiate:** Basketball, cross-country, golf M, soccer, tennis W, track and field. **Team name:** Lakers.

Student services. Adult student services, alcohol/substance abuse counseling, career counseling, student employment services, financial aid counseling, health services, minority student services, personal counseling, placement for graduates, veterans' counselor. **Physically disabled:** Services for visually, speech, hearing impaired.

Contact. E-mail: csu-info@clayton.edu
Phone: (678) 466-4115 Fax: (678) 466-4149
Stephen Jenkins, Director of Admissions, Clayton State University, 2000 Clayton State Boulevard, Morrow, GA 30260-0285

College of Coastal Georgia
Brunswick, Georgia   **CB member**
www.ccga.edu   **CB code: 5078**

- Public 4-year liberal arts college
- Commuter campus in large town
- 3,039 degree-seeking undergraduates: 36% part-time, 66% women, 18% African American, 2% Asian American, 5% Hispanic/Latino, 4% Multiracial, non-Hispanic, 1% international
- 72% of applicants admitted
- SAT or ACT (ACT writing optional) required

General. Founded in 1961. Regionally accredited. Students may take select courses at the Camden Center in Kingsland, Georgia. **Degrees:** 211 bachelor's, 220 associate awarded. **Location:** 70 miles from Savannah; 60 miles from Jacksonville, FL. **Calendar:** Semester, limited summer session. **Full-time faculty:** 88 total; 62% have terminal degrees, 11% minority, 53% women. **Part-time faculty:** 103 total; 31% have terminal degrees, 8% minority, 45% women. **Class size:** 43% < 20, 49% 20-39, 7% 40-49, less than 1% 50-99.

Freshman class profile. 1,600 applied, 1,147 admitted, 707 enrolled.

Mid 50% test scores			
		GPA 3.0-3.49:	33%
SAT critical reading:	430-530	GPA 2.0-2.99:	47%
SAT math:	410-510	Return as sophomores:	65%
ACT composite:	17-22	Out-of-state:	8%
GPA 3.75 or higher:	9%	Live on campus:	36%
GPA 3.50-3.74:	10%	International:	1%

Basis for selection. Additional requirements for career associate health science programs and all baccalaureate degree programs. SAT/ACT may be used to exempt students from placement testing. **Home schooled:** Statement describing home school structure and mission, transcript of courses and grades, letter of recommendation (nonparent) required. **Learning Disabled:** Students must go through accreditation process with system agency on learning disabilities to receive accommodations.

High school preparation. College-preparatory program recommended. 17 units recommended. Recommended units include English 4, mathematics 4, social studies 1, history 2, science 4 (laboratory 2) and foreign language 2.

2015-2016 Annual costs. Tuition/fees: $4,434; $12,692 out-of-state. Room/board: $9,416.

Financial aid. Non-need-based: Scholarships awarded for academics, alumni affiliation, athletics.

Application procedures. Admission: No deadline. $25 fee, may be waived for applicants with need. Application must be submitted online. Admission notification on a rolling basis beginning on or about 9/1. **Financial aid:** Priority date 6/1; no closing date. FAFSA required. Applicants notified on a rolling basis starting 4/1.

Academics. Special study options: Distance learning, double major, dual enrollment of high school students, honors, independent study, internships, liberal arts/career combination, study abroad, teacher certification program. **Credit/placement by examination:** AP, CLEP, IB, SAT, ACT, institutional tests. 24 credit hours maximum toward associate degree, 24 toward bachelor's.

Support services: Learning center, reduced course load, remedial instruction, study skills assistance, tutoring, writing center.

Majors. Area/ethnic studies: American. **Biology:** General. **Business:** Business admin. **Education:** Elementary, middle, special ed. **Foreign languages:** General. **Health services:** Health information management, nursing (RN). **Math:** General. **Protective services:** Law enforcement admin. **Psychology:** General.

Most popular majors. Business/marketing 23%, education 19%, health sciences 27%, psychology 16%, public administration/social services 8%.

Technology on campus. 350 workstations in library, computer center, student center. Dormitories linked to campus network. Commuter students can connect to campus network. Online course registration, online library, helpline, repair service, wireless network available.

Student life. Freshman orientation: Mandatory. Preregistration for classes offered. **Policies:** Exception to no-pets rule made for non-carnivorous fish in reasonable numbers kept in 10 gallon maximum aquarium. **Housing:** Guaranteed on-campus for freshmen. Coed dorms available. $250 partly refundable deposit, deadline 5/1. **Activities:** Pep band, campus ministries, dance, international student organizations, literary magazine, student government, student newspaper.

Athletics. NAIA. **Intercollegiate:** Basketball, golf, softball W, tennis, volleyball W. **Intramural:** Basketball, bowling M, cheerleading W, football (non-tackle), golf, sand volleyball, soccer, softball, ultimate frisbee. **Team name:** Mariners.

Student services. Adult student services, career counseling, services for economically disadvantaged, student employment services, financial aid counseling, health services, minority student services, personal counseling, placement for graduates, veterans' counselor. **Physically disabled:** Services for visually, speech, hearing impaired.

Contact. E-mail: admiss@ccga.edu
Phone: (912) 279-5730 Toll-free number: (800) 675-7235
Fax: (912) 262-3072
Clayton Daniels, Assistant Vice President for Enrollment Management, College of Coastal Georgia, One College Drive, Brunswick, GA 31520

Columbus State University
Columbus, Georgia   **CB member**
www.columbusstate.edu   **CB code: 5123**

- Public 4-year university and liberal arts college
- Commuter campus in small city
- 6,711 degree-seeking undergraduates: 27% part-time, 60% women, 37% African American, 2% Asian American, 6% Hispanic/Latino, 2% Multiracial, non-Hispanic, 1% international
- 1,489 degree-seeking graduate students
- 56% of applicants admitted
- SAT or ACT (ACT writing optional) required
- 31% graduate within 6 years

General. Founded in 1958. Regionally accredited. **Degrees:** 975 bachelor's, 22 associate awarded; master's, doctoral offered. **ROTC:** Army. **Location:** 100 miles from Atlanta. **Calendar:** Semester, extensive summer session. **Full-time faculty:** 287 total; 77% have terminal degrees, 26% minority, 42% women. **Part-time faculty:** 238 total; 28% have terminal degrees, 22% minority, 53% women. **Class size:** 46% < 20, 44% 20-39, 5% 40-49, 5% 50-99, less than 1% >100. **Special facilities:** Environmental learning center, space science center, fine and performing arts center.

Freshman class profile. 3,157 applied, 1,758 admitted, 1,021 enrolled.

Mid 50% test scores			
		GPA 2.0-2.99:	38%
SAT critical reading:	430-550	Rank in top quarter:	36%
SAT math:	420-540	Rank in top tenth:	15%
SAT writing:	410-530	Return as sophomores:	72%
ACT composite:	17-23	Out-of-state:	11%
GPA 3.75 or higher:	14%	Live on campus:	49%
GPA 3.50-3.74:	14%	Fraternities:	5%
GPA 3.0-3.49:	34%	Sororities:	5%

Basis for selection. GED not accepted. 2.3 GPA, 440 SAT Critical Reading/17 ACT English, and 410 SAT math/17 ACT math required. Students must be on track to graduate with college preparatory seal. Students with college prep deficiencies will be considered on individual basis. Interviews and auditions required of music majors. Portfolio recommended for art majors. **Home schooled:** Statement describing home school structure and mission, transcript of courses and grades required. 1000 SAT (exclusive of Writing),

Home School Credit Evaluation Table, letter from primary teacher certifying completion of high school and date of graduation and two letters of recommendation from non-family members required.

High school preparation. College-preparatory program required. 17 units required. Required units include English 4, mathematics 4, social studies 3, science 4 (laboratory 3) and foreign language 2. Social studies units required include U.S. history and world studies.

2015-2016 Annual costs. Tuition/fees: $7,056; $20,274 out-of-state. Room/board: $9,374. Books/supplies: $1,200. Personal expenses: $2,140.

2015-2016 Financial aid. Need-based: 861 full-time freshmen applied for aid; 691 deemed to have need; 687 received aid. Average need met was 70%. Average scholarship/grant was $4,994; average loan $3,483. 48% of total undergraduate aid awarded as scholarships/grants, 52% as loans/jobs. **Non-need-based:** Awarded to 2,030 full-time undergraduates, including 509 freshmen. Scholarships awarded for academics, alumni affiliation, art, athletics, job skills, leadership, minority status, music/drama, ROTC.

Application procedures. Admission: Priority date 5/15; deadline 6/30 (receipt date). $40 fee, may be waived for applicants with need. Admission notification on a rolling basis beginning on or about 9/1. **Financial aid:** Priority date 5/1; no closing date. FAFSA required. Applicants notified on a rolling basis starting 5/15; must reply within 4 week(s) of notification.

Academics. Special study options: Accelerated study, combined bachelor's/graduate degree, cooperative education, distance learning, double major, dual enrollment of high school students, ESL, honors, independent study, internships, liberal arts/career combination, study abroad, teacher certification program. **Credit/placement by examination:** AP, CLEP, IB, institutional tests. 30 credit hours maximum toward associate degree, 60 toward bachelor's. **Support services:** Learning center, reduced course load, remedial instruction, study skills assistance, tutoring, writing center.

Majors. Biology: General. **Business:** General, accounting, business admin, finance, management information systems, marketing. **Computer sciences:** General, information technology. **Education:** Art, biology, chemistry, drama/dance, early childhood, English, mathematics, middle, music, physical, science, secondary, social science, social studies, special ed. **English:** English lit, rhetoric/composition. **Foreign languages:** General. **Health services:** Nursing (RN). **History:** General. **Liberal arts:** Arts/sciences. **Math:** General. **Parks/recreation:** Exercise sciences. **Physical sciences:** Chemistry, geology. **Protective services:** Criminal justice. **Psychology:** General. **Social sciences:** Political science, sociology. **Visual/performing arts:** Art, dramatic, music, music performance.

Most popular majors. Business/marketing 15%, education 9%, English 7%, health sciences 25%, security/protective services 8%, visual/performing arts 7%.

Technology on campus. 1,150 workstations in dormitories, library, computer center, student center. Dormitories wired for high-speed internet access and linked to campus network. Commuter students can connect to campus network. Online course registration, online library, helpline, repair service, student web hosting, wireless network available.

Student life. Freshman orientation: Mandatory, $85 fee. Preregistration for classes offered. **Policies:** Entering freshmen from outside local area must live in student housing. **Housing:** Special housing for disabled, apartments, fraternity/sorority housing, themed housing, wellness housing available. $300 partly refundable deposit, deadline 5/15. Apartments take place of traditional dorms; weekday meals included in fee. **Activities:** Bands, campus ministries, choral groups, dance, drama, international student organizations, literary magazine, music ensembles, Model UN, musical theater, radio station, student government, student newspaper, symphony orchestra, TV station, College Republicans, Islamic association, Freethought Society, Cougars for Christ, CSU Democrats, minority student union, student political awareness, Westminster Fellowship, Baptist student union.

Athletics. NCAA. **Intercollegiate:** Baseball M, basketball, cross-country, golf, rifle, soccer W, softball W, tennis. **Intramural:** Badminton, basketball, football (tackle) M, skiing, soccer, softball, table tennis, tennis, volleyball. **Team name:** Cougars.

Student services. Adult student services, alcohol/substance abuse counseling, career counseling, student employment services, financial aid counseling, health services, minority student services, personal counseling, placement for graduates, veterans' counselor, women's services. **Physically disabled:** Services for visually, speech, hearing impaired.

Contact. E-mail: admissions@columbiastate.edu
Phone: (706) 568-2035 Toll-free number: (866) 264-2035
Fax: (706) 568-5091
Amy Clines, Director of Enrollment Services, Columbus State University, 4225 University Avenue, Columbus, GA 31907-5645

Covenant College
Lookout Mountain, Georgia
www.covenant.edu   CB code: 6124

- Private 4-year liberal arts college affiliated with the Presbyterian Church in America (PCA)
- Residential campus in small city
- 1,007 degree-seeking undergraduates: 1% part-time, 57% women, 2% African American, 2% Asian American, 3% Hispanic/Latino, 3% Multiracial, non-Hispanic, 3% international
- 58 degree-seeking graduate students
- 94% of applicants admitted
- SAT or ACT (ACT writing optional), application essay required
- 64% graduate within 6 years

General. Founded in 1955. Regionally accredited. **Degrees:** 239 bachelor's awarded; master's offered. **ROTC:** Army. **Location:** 120 miles from Atlanta, 5 miles from Chattanooga. **Calendar:** Semester, limited summer session. **Full-time faculty:** 65 total; 91% have terminal degrees, 9% minority, 22% women. **Part-time faculty:** 34 total; 24% have terminal degrees, 6% minority, 47% women. **Class size:** 56% < 20, 42% 20-39, less than 1% 40-49, less than 1% 50-99, less than 1% >100.

Freshman class profile. 615 applied, 578 admitted, 258 enrolled.

Mid 50% test scores			
SAT critical reading:	540-650	**GPA 2.0-2.99:**	5%
SAT math:	520-630	**Rank in top quarter:**	63%
SAT writing:	510-650	**Rank in top tenth:**	32%
ACT composite:	24-29	**Return as sophomores:**	85%
GPA 3.75 or higher:	47%	**Out-of-state:**	73%
GPA 3.50-3.74:	27%	**Live on campus:**	98%
GPA 3.0-3.49:	21%	**International:**	3%

Basis for selection. 1000 SAT (exclusive of Writing) or 21 ACT, 2.5 GPA, academic evaluation, church evaluation, and personal testimony of faith important. Students that do not meet minimum scores may be asked to provide additional information. Auditions required for music and voice majors. **Home schooled:** Transcript of courses and grades, letter of recommendation (nonparent) required.

High school preparation. College-preparatory program recommended. 14 units required; 16 recommended. Required and recommended units include English 4, mathematics 3, social studies 2, science 2, foreign language 2 and academic electives 3.

2015-2016 Annual costs. Tuition/fees: $31,320. Room/board: $9,170. Books/supplies: $1,100. Personal expenses: $800.

2014-2015 Financial aid. Need-based: 215 full-time freshmen applied for aid; 172 deemed to have need; 172 received aid. Average need met was 80%. Average scholarship/grant was $18,152; average loan $5,915. 72% of total undergraduate aid awarded as scholarships/grants, 28% as loans/jobs. **Non-need-based:** Awarded to 424 full-time undergraduates, including 111 freshmen. Scholarships awarded for academics, alumni affiliation, art, job skills, leadership, minority status, music/drama, religious affiliation, state residency.

Application procedures. Admission: Priority date 3/1; deadline 8/15. $35 fee, may be waived for applicants with need. Admission notification on a rolling basis beginning on or about 7/1. Must reply by May 1 or within 3 week(s) if notified thereafter. **Financial aid:** No deadline. FAFSA required. Applicants notified on a rolling basis starting 2/1; must reply within 3 week(s) of notification.

Academics. Special study options: Double major, dual enrollment of high school students, exchange student, independent study, internships, student-designed major, study abroad, teacher certification program, Washington semester. Dual engineering degree with Georgia Tech; cooperative nursing program with Emory University; bridge program for MSN with Vanderbilt University. **Credit/placement by examination:** AP, CLEP, IB, SAT, ACT, institutional tests. 30 credit hours maximum toward associate degree, 30 toward bachelor's. **Support services:** Reduced course load, remedial instruction, study skills assistance, tutoring, writing center.

Majors. Biology: General. **Business:** General. **Computer sciences:** General. **Education:** Elementary, English, history, mathematics, science. **English:** English lit. **Foreign languages:** French, Spanish. **History:** General. **Math:** General. **Philosophy/religion:** General, philosophy. **Physical sciences:** General, chemistry, physics. **Psychology:** General. **Social sciences:** General, economics, sociology. **Theology:** Bible. **Visual/performing arts:** Dramatic, music, music performance.

Most popular majors. Biology 9%, business/marketing 10%, education 14%, English 7%, interdisciplinary studies 9%, psychology 8%, social sciences 9%, visual/performing arts 10%.

Technology on campus. 130 workstations in dormitories, library, computer center. Dormitories linked to campus network. Commuter students can connect to campus network. Online library, helpline, repair service, wireless network available.

Student life. Freshman orientation: Mandatory, $355 fee. Preregistration for classes offered. Held the week prior to beginning of classes. **Policies:** Smoking, alcoholic beverages, and drugs prohibited. Students are to use wisdom and Christ-like discretion in applying Biblical principles to decisions regarding all areas of life. Religious observance required. **Housing:** Guaranteed on-campus for freshmen. Coed dorms, apartments available. **Activities:** Bands, campus ministries, choral groups, dance, drama, film society, international student organizations, literary magazine, music ensembles, musical theater, radio station, student government, student newspaper, Rotaract, Young Life, pre-law club, Psi Chi, Reformed University Fellowship, Evangelism Club.

Athletics. NCAA. **Intercollegiate:** Baseball M, basketball, cross-country, golf, soccer, softball W, tennis, volleyball W. **Intramural:** Basketball, football (non-tackle), football (tackle) M, soccer, volleyball. **Team name:** Scots.

Student services. Adult student services, chaplain/spiritual director, career counseling, student employment services, financial aid counseling, health services, personal counseling, placement for graduates.

Contact. E-mail: admissions@covenant.edu
Phone: (706) 820-2398 Toll-free number: (888) 451-2683
Fax: (706) 820-0893
Matthew Bryant, Director of Admissions, Covenant College, 14049 Scenic Highway, Lookout Mountain, GA 30750

Dalton State College
Dalton, Georgia
www.daltonstate.edu   CB code: 5167

▶ Public 4-year liberal arts and teachers college
▶ Commuter campus in large town
▶ 4,671 degree-seeking undergraduates
▶ SAT or ACT (ACT writing optional) required

General. Founded in 1963. Regionally accredited. **Degrees:** 367 bachelor's, 315 associate awarded. **Location:** 90 miles from Atlanta, 33 miles from Chattanooga. **Calendar:** Semester, limited summer session. **Full-time faculty:** 160 total. **Part-time faculty:** 56 total. **Class size:** 41% < 20, 53% 20-39, 5% 40-49, less than 1% 50-99.

Freshman class profile.

GPA 3.75 or higher:	14%	GPA 2.0-2.99:	36%
GPA 3.50-3.74:	13%	Out-of-state:	1%
GPA 3.0-3.49:	36%	Live on campus:	8%

Basis for selection. Mildly selective in admission requirements. All degree-seeking students whose COMPASS scores fall below the University System of Georgia minimums will not be admitted. SAT/ACT not required for certificate students. **Home schooled:** State high school equivalency certificate required.

High school preparation. College-preparatory program recommended. 16 units required. Required units include English 4, mathematics 4, social studies 1, history 2, science 3 and foreign language 2.

2015-2016 Annual costs. Tuition/fees: $4,056; $12,314 out-of-state. Room only: $4,500. Books/supplies: $1,000.

Financial aid. Non-need-based: Scholarships awarded for academics, leadership, minority status, state residency.

Application procedures. Admission: Priority date 12/1; deadline 7/1. $30 fee, may be waived for applicants with need. Admission notification on a rolling basis beginning on or about 12/1. **Financial aid:** No deadline. FAFSA required. Applicants notified on a rolling basis starting 4/1.

Academics. Special study options: Distance learning, double major, dual enrollment of high school students, ESL, internships, study abroad, teacher certification program, weekend college. **Credit/placement by examination:** AP, CLEP, SAT, ACT, institutional tests. Credit awarded only to admitted students and recorded only for those who enroll for credit courses. Credit awarded only for offered courses. **Support services:** Pre-admission summer program, remedial instruction, study skills assistance, tutoring, writing center.

Majors. Biology: General. **Business:** Accounting, business admin, management information systems, marketing, operations. **Education:** Early childhood. **English:** English lit. **Health services:** Nursing (RN). **History:** General. **Human services:** Social work. **Math:** General. **Physical sciences:** Chemistry. **Protective services:** Police science.

Most popular majors. Biology 11%, business/marketing 32%, education 29%, history 7%, legal studies 9%.

Technology on campus. 800 workstations in library, computer center, student center. Dormitories linked to campus network. Commuter students can connect to campus network. Online library, helpline, wireless network available.

Student life. Freshman orientation: Mandatory. Preregistration for classes offered. **Housing:** Coed dorms, special housing for disabled, apartments available. $200 fully refundable deposit. **Activities:** Campus ministries, drama, international student organizations, literary magazine, music ensembles, student government, student newspaper, social work club, LPN, Baptist student union, psychology club, Black Student Alliance, Phi Theta Kappa, Young Democrats, Progressive student union.

Athletics. Intercollegiate: Cheerleading. **Intramural:** Basketball, football (non-tackle), soccer, volleyball. **Team name:** Roadrunners.

Student services. Adult student services, career counseling, student employment services, financial aid counseling, personal counseling, placement for graduates, veterans' counselor. **Physically disabled:** Services for hearing impaired.

Contact. E-mail: admissions@daltonstate.edu
Phone: (706) 272-4436 Toll-free number: (800) 829-4436
Fax: (706) 272-2530
Jodi Johnson, Vice President for Enrollment Services, Dalton State College, 650 College Drive, Dalton, GA 30720

DeVry University: Decatur
Decatur, Georgia
www.devry.edu   CB code: 5715

▶ For-profit 4-year university
▶ Commuter campus in large town
▶ 1,684 degree-seeking undergraduates
▶ Interview required

General. Founded in 1969. Regionally accredited. Additional locations: Alpharetta, Atlanta Buckhead, Atlanta Cobb/Galleria, Atlanta Perimeter, Gwinnett, Henry County, Memphis, Nashville. **Degrees:** 357 bachelor's, 118 associate awarded; master's offered. **Location:** 15 miles from Atlanta. **Calendar:** Semester, extensive summer session. **Full-time faculty:** 41 total; 44% minority, 39% women. **Part-time faculty:** 111 total; 40% minority, 44% women.

Basis for selection. Applicants must have high school diploma or equivalent, or degree from accredited post-secondary institution, demonstrate proficiency in basic college-level skills through SAT/ACT or institution-administered placement exams, and be at least 17 years of age. New students may enter at beginning of any semester.

High school preparation. College-preparatory program recommended.

2015-2016 Annual costs. Tuition/fees: $17,132. Books/supplies: $1,320. Personal expenses: $2,376.

Financial aid. All financial aid based on need.

Application procedures. Admission: No deadline. $40 fee. Admission notification on a rolling basis. **Financial aid:** No deadline. FAFSA required. Applicants notified on a rolling basis.

Academics. Special study options: Accelerated study, distance learning, study abroad. **Credit/placement by examination:** AP, CLEP, institutional tests. **Support services:** Learning center, remedial instruction, tutoring.

Majors. Business: General, accounting, business admin, operations. **Communications:** General. **Computer sciences:** Information systems, networking, systems analysis, web page design. **Engineering:** Software. **Health services:** Health care admin.

Most popular majors. Business/marketing 70%, computer/information sciences 18%, engineering/engineering technologies 12%.

Technology on campus. 300 workstations in library, computer center. Online course registration, online library, helpline available.

Student life. Freshman orientation: Mandatory. Preregistration for classes offered. **Activities:** Toastmasters International, National Society of Black Engineers, Delta Pi Chi, Tau Alpha Pi, Sigma Beta Delta, Alpha Beta Kappa.

Athletics. Intramural: Basketball, football (non-tackle), softball, volleyball.

Student services. Career counseling, student employment services, financial aid counseling, placement for graduates, veterans' counselor. **Physically disabled:** Services for visually, hearing impaired.

Contact. E-mail: bsilva@admin.atl.devry.edu
Phone: (404) 292-2645 Toll-free number: (800) 221-4771
Fax: (404) 292-7011
DeVry University: Decatur, One West Court Square, Suite 100, Decatur, GA 30030-2556

Emmanuel College

Franklin Springs, Georgia   **CB member**
www.ec.edu   **CB code: 5184**

- Private 4-year liberal arts and teachers college affiliated with the Pentecostal Holiness Church
- Residential campus in rural community
- 762 degree-seeking undergraduates: 3% part-time, 44% women, 17% African American, 5% Hispanic/Latino, 1% Native Hawaiian/Pacific islander, 2% Multi-racial, non-Hispanic, 6% international
- 9% of applicants admitted
- SAT or ACT (ACT writing optional), application essay required
- 35% graduate within 6 years

General. Founded in 1919. Regionally accredited. **Degrees:** 136 bachelor's, 33 associate awarded. **Location:** 30 miles from Athens, 90 miles from Atlanta. **Calendar:** Semester, limited summer session. **Full-time faculty:** 68 total; 44% have terminal degrees, 6% minority, 29% women. **Part-time faculty:** 41 total; 7% have terminal degrees, 10% minority, 56% women. **Class size:** 68% < 20, 30% 20-39, 2% 40-49.

Freshman class profile. 5,692 applied, 539 admitted, 232 enrolled.

Mid 50% test scores		Return as sophomores:	63%
SAT critical reading:	390-540	Out-of-state:	25%
SAT math:	400-530	Live on campus:	59%
End year in good standing:	88%	International:	6%

Basis for selection. High school record and SAT/ACT important. Recommendations considered. Audition required and interview recommended for music majors. **Learning Disabled:** Must submit professional documentation of disability.

High school preparation. College-preparatory program recommended.

2015-2016 Annual costs. Tuition/fees: $18,870. Room/board: $7,200. Books/supplies: $1,200. Personal expenses: $1,500.

2015-2016 Financial aid. Need-based: 59% of total undergraduate aid awarded as scholarships/grants, 41% as loans/jobs. **Non-need-based:** Scholarships awarded for academics, art, athletics, job skills, leadership, music/drama, religious affiliation, state residency.

Application procedures. Admission: Closing date 8/1 (receipt date). $25 fee, may be waived for applicants with need. Admission notification on a rolling basis beginning on or about 1/1. **Financial aid:** Priority date 5/1, closing date 6/15. FAFSA, institutional form required. Applicants notified on a rolling basis starting 3/1; must reply within 2 week(s) of notification.

Academics. Special study options: Combined bachelor's/graduate degree, dual enrollment of high school students, honors, independent study, internships, teacher certification program. **Credit/placement by examination:** AP, CLEP, IB, SAT, ACT, institutional tests. 24 credit hours maximum toward associate degree, 24 toward bachelor's. **Support services:** Remedial instruction, study skills assistance, tutoring.

Majors. Biology: General. **Business:** Business admin. **Communications:** Communications/speech/rhetoric. **Computer sciences:** Computer graphics. **Education:** Business, elementary, English, history, mathematics, middle, music, physical. **English:** English lit. **Health services:** Premedicine, prepharmacy. **History:** General. **Math:** General. **Parks/recreation:** Exercise sciences, sports admin. **Protective services:** Law enforcement admin. **Psychology:** General. **Theology:** Pastoral counseling, sacred music. **Visual/performing arts:** Music.

Most popular majors. Biology 10%, business/marketing 18%, communications/journalism 9%, education 13%, parks/recreation 22%, psychology 12%, theological studies 10%.

Technology on campus. 70 workstations in library, computer center. Dormitories wired for high-speed internet access and linked to campus network. Commuter students can connect to campus network. Online course registration, online library, repair service, wireless network available.

Student life. Freshman orientation: Mandatory. Preregistration for classes offered. Held first 2 days of semester. **Policies:** Chapel attendance required for all full-time students. Students not living at home must reside in college housing through junior year. Religious observance required. **Housing:** Guaranteed on-campus for all undergraduates. Single-sex dorms, apartments, wellness housing available. $150 fully refundable deposit, deadline 8/1. **Activities:** Bands, campus ministries, choral groups, dance, drama, international student organizations, literary magazine, music ensembles, musical theater, student government, student newspaper, ministerial fellowship, missions fellowship, Students in Free Enterprise.

Athletics. NCAA, NCCAA. **Intercollegiate:** Archery, baseball M, basketball, bowling, cross-country, golf, lacrosse, rifle, soccer, softball W, swimming, tennis, track and field, volleyball, wrestling. **Intramural:** Basketball, soccer, softball, tennis, track and field, ultimate frisbee M, volleyball. **Team name:** Lions.

Student services. Adult student services, chaplain/spiritual director, career counseling, financial aid counseling, personal counseling, veterans' counselor.

Contact. E-mail: admission@ec.edu
Phone: (706) 245-7226 ext. 2874 Toll-free number: (800) 860-8800
Fax: (706) 245-2876
Wendy Vinson, Dean of Enrollment Management, Emmanuel College, 181 Spring Street, Franklin Springs, GA 30639-0129

Emory University

Atlanta, Georgia   **CB member**
www.emory.edu   **CB code: 5187**

- Private 4-year university affiliated with the United Methodist Church
- Residential campus in very large city
- 6,770 degree-seeking undergraduates: 1% part-time, 58% women, 9% African American, 19% Asian American, 8% Hispanic/Latino, 3% Multi-racial, non-Hispanic, 17% international
- 6,380 degree-seeking graduate students
- 24% of applicants admitted
- SAT or ACT with writing, application essay required
- 89% graduate within 6 years

General. Founded in 1836. Regionally accredited. **Degrees:** 1,901 bachelor's awarded; master's, professional, doctoral offered. **ROTC:** Army, Naval, Air Force. **Location:** 5 miles from downtown. **Calendar:** Semester, limited summer session. **Class size:** 61% < 20, 27% 20-39, 4% 40-49, 6% 50-99, 2% >100. **Special facilities:** Art, architecture and archaeology museum, biological field station, primate research center, 185 acre park, planetarium, healthcare facilities, access to the Center for Disease Control, manuscript, archives and rare book library, Carter Center.

Freshman class profile. 20,492 applied, 4,851 admitted, 1,357 enrolled.

Mid 50% test scores		GPA 2.0-2.99:	1%
SAT critical reading:	620-720	Rank in top quarter:	96%
SAT math:	650-770	Rank in top tenth:	83%
SAT writing:	640-730	Return as sophomores:	94%
ACT composite:	29-33	Out-of-state:	83%
GPA 3.75 or higher:	52%	Live on campus:	100%
GPA 3.50-3.74:	32%	International:	17%
GPA 3.0-3.49:	15%		

Basis for selection. GED not accepted. Challenging curriculum and community involvement important. SAT/ACT important, but not deciding factor. Diversity, character and maturity, and indications of interest considered. Alumni interviews available in limited number of cities. Students may audition for music programs or scholarships on-campus or via recorded performance. Art and other portfolios should be sent directly to department of interest. **Home schooled:** Letter of recommendation (nonparent) required. 3 SAT Subject Tests required (1 math and 2 of student's choice).

High school preparation. College-preparatory program recommended. 22 units recommended. Recommended units include English 4, mathematics 4, social studies 2, history 2, science 4 (laboratory 2), foreign language 4 and visual/performing arts 1. History should include country/region other than U.S.

2016-2017 Annual costs. Tuition/fees (projected): $47,954. Room/board: $13,486. Books/supplies: $1,224. Personal expenses: $1,486.

Financial aid. Non-need-based: Scholarships awarded for academics, art, leadership, music/drama, religious affiliation, state residency. **Additional information:** Loan replacement grant and loan cap program available to students from families with total annual incomes of $100,000 or less who demonstrate need for financial aid.

Application procedures. Admission: Closing date 1/1 (postmark date). $75 fee, may be waived for applicants with need. Admission notification by 4/1. Must reply by 5/1. **Financial aid:** Priority date 2/15, closing date 3/1. FAFSA, CSS PROFILE required. Applicants notified by 4/1; must reply by 5/1.

Academics. Special study options: Combined bachelor's/graduate degree, cooperative education, cross-registration, double major, dual enrollment of high school students, ESL, honors, independent study, internships, liberal arts/career combination, study abroad, Washington semester. 3-2 dual-degree program in engineering with Georgia Institute of Technology. **Credit/placement by examination:** AP, CLEP, IB, institutional tests. **Support services:** Learning center, pre-admission summer program, remedial instruction, study skills assistance, tutoring, writing center.

Majors. Area/ethnic studies: African, African-American, American, Asian, East Asian, French, German, Italian, Latin American, Near/Middle Eastern, Russian/Slavic, women's. **Biology:** General, biophysics, ecology, neuroscience. **Business:** Accounting, accounting/business management, business admin. **Communications:** Journalism. **Computer sciences:** Computer science. **Conservation:** Environmental studies. **Engineering:** Engineering science. **English:** Creative writing, English lit. **Foreign languages:** Ancient Greek, Arabic, Chinese, classics, comparative lit, Japanese, Latin, linguistics, Romance, Russian, Spanish. **Health services:** Medical radiologic technology/radiation therapy, nursing (RN). **History:** General. **Liberal arts:** Humanities. **Math:** General, applied, mathematics/statistics. **Parks/recreation:** Health/fitness. **Philosophy/religion:** Judaic, philosophy, religion. **Physical sciences:** Astronomy, chemistry, physics. **Psychology:** General, cognitive. **Social sciences:** Anthropology, economics, international relations, political science, research methodology, sociology. **Visual/performing arts:** General, art history/conservation, dance, dramatic, film/cinema/video, music, play/screenwriting, studio arts.

Most popular majors. Biology 17%, business/marketing 15%, health sciences 7%, psychology 6%, social sciences 23%.

Technology on campus. 1,000 workstations in dormitories, library, computer center, student center. Dormitories wired for high-speed internet access and linked to campus network. Commuter students can connect to campus network. Online course registration, online library, helpline, repair service, wireless network available.

Student life. Freshman orientation: Mandatory, $125 fee. Preregistration for classes offered. Five-day program held prior to start of classes. **Policies:** 2-year residency requirement. **Housing:** Guaranteed on-campus for freshmen. Coed dorms, apartments, fraternity/sorority housing, themed housing available. $200 nonrefundable deposit, deadline 5/1. Gender-neutral housing available. **Activities:** Bands, campus ministries, choral groups, dance, drama, film society, international student organizations, literary magazine, music ensembles, Model UN, musical theater, opera, radio station, student government, student newspaper, symphony orchestra, TV station, over 220 student clubs and organizations.

Athletics. NCAA. **Intercollegiate:** Baseball M, basketball, cross-country, diving, golf M, soccer, softball W, swimming, tennis, track and field, volleyball W. **Intramural:** Basketball, football (non-tackle), racquetball, soccer, softball, swimming, tennis, track and field, ultimate frisbee, volleyball. **Team name:** Eagles.

Student services. Alcohol/substance abuse counseling, chaplain/spiritual director, career counseling, student employment services, financial aid counseling, health services, legal services, minority student services, on-campus daycare, personal counseling, placement for graduates, women's services. **Physically disabled:** Services for visually, speech, hearing impaired.

Contact. E-mail: admiss@emory.edu
Phone: (404) 727-6036 Toll-free number: (800) 727-6036
Fax: (404) 727-4303
John Latting, Director of Admission, Emory University, 1390 Oxford Road NE, 3rd Floor, Atlanta, GA 30322

Fort Valley State University
Fort Valley, Georgia **CB member**
www.fvsu.edu **CB code: 5220**

- Public 4-year liberal arts and teachers college
- Residential campus in small town
- 3,250 undergraduates
- 320 graduate students
- SAT or ACT (ACT writing optional) required

General. Founded in 1895. Regionally accredited. 1890 land-grant institution. **Degrees:** 464 bachelor's awarded; master's offered. **ROTC:** Army. **Location:** 30 miles from Macon. **Calendar:** Semester, limited summer session. **Full-time faculty:** 143 total. **Part-time faculty:** 57 total. **Class size:** 49% < 20, 37% 20-39, 10% 40-49, 4% 50-99.

Freshman class profile.

GPA 3.75 or higher:	3%	**Rank in top quarter:**	24%
GPA 3.50-3.74:	4%	**Rank in top tenth:**	7%
GPA 3.0-3.49:	19%	**Out-of-state:**	3%
GPA 2.0-2.99:	61%	**Live on campus:**	93%

Basis for selection. High school transcript, test scores, physical examination important. Audition recommended for music education majors.

High school preparation. College-preparatory program required. 16 units required. Required units include English 4, mathematics 4, social studies 1, history 2, science 3 and foreign language 2.

2015-2016 Annual costs. Tuition/fees: $6,566; $19,386 out-of-state. Room/board: $7,778. Books/supplies: $1,320. Personal expenses: $500.

Financial aid. Non-need-based: Scholarships awarded for academics, athletics, music/drama. **Additional information:** Financial aid transcripts must be received from former institutions before application for aid will be considered complete and reviewed for awards.

Application procedures. Admission: Closing date 7/15. $20 fee. Admission notification on a rolling basis. **Financial aid:** Priority date 3/1; no closing date. FAFSA required. Applicants notified on a rolling basis starting 3/15; must reply within 1 week(s) of notification.

Academics. Special study options: Distance learning, double major, dual enrollment of high school students, ESL, internships, teacher certification program. **Credit/placement by examination:** AP, CLEP, SAT, ACT, institutional tests. 20 credit hours maximum toward associate degree, 45 toward bachelor's. **Support services:** Learning center, reduced course load, remedial instruction, tutoring, writing center.

Majors. Biology: General. **Business:** General, accounting, business admin, marketing, office management. **Communications:** Journalism, public relations. **Computer sciences:** General, information systems. **Education:** Agricultural, elementary, English, family/consumer sciences, foreign languages, French, mathematics, middle, music, physical, secondary. **Engineering:** Agricultural. **English:** English lit. **Health services:** Medical assistant, veterinary technology/assistant. **Human services:** Social work. **Liberal arts:** Arts/sciences. **Math:** General. **Physical sciences:** Chemistry. **Psychology:** General. **Social sciences:** Economics, political science, sociology. **Work/family studies:** General, child care management, child development, family studies, food/nutrition.

Most popular majors. Business/marketing 20%, education 8%, health sciences 8%, psychology 10%, public administration/social services 6%, security/protective services 11%.

Technology on campus. Dormitories linked to campus network. Commuter students can connect to campus network. Helpline available.

Student life. Freshman orientation: Mandatory. Preregistration for classes offered. **Housing:** Single-sex dorms available. $200 fully refundable deposit, deadline 8/5. **Activities:** Bands, campus ministries, choral groups, music ensembles, radio station, student government, student newspaper.

Athletics. NCAA. **Intercollegiate:** Basketball, cross-country, football (tackle) M, softball W, tennis, track and field, volleyball W. **Intramural:** Basketball, softball, swimming, tennis, track and field, volleyball. **Team name:** Wildcats.

Student services. Adult student services, career counseling, student employment services, health services, on-campus daycare, personal counseling, placement for graduates, veterans' counselor.

Contact. E-mail: admissap@fvsu.edu
Phone: (478) 825-6307 Toll-free number: (877) 462-3878
Fax: (478) 825-6394
Donovan Coley, Director of Admissions, Fort Valley State University,
1005 State University Drive, Fort Valley, GA 31030-4313

Georgia College and State University
Milledgeville, Georgia   CB member
www.gcsu.edu   CB code: 5252

- Public 4-year university and liberal arts college
- Residential campus in large town
- 5,935 degree-seeking undergraduates: 7% part-time, 60% women, 5% African American, 1% Asian American, 5% Hispanic/Latino, 3% Multiracial, non-Hispanic, 1% international
- 838 degree-seeking graduate students
- 76% of applicants admitted
- SAT or ACT (ACT writing optional), application essay required
- 60% graduate within 6 years

General. Founded in 1889. Regionally accredited. Branch campuses in Macon and Warner Robins offering junior, senior, and graduate level options. **Degrees:** 1,273 bachelor's awarded; master's, professional offered. **ROTC:** Army. **Location:** 95 miles from Atlanta, 30 miles from Macon. **Calendar:** Semester, limited summer session. **Full-time faculty:** 337 total; 73% have terminal degrees, 16% minority, 55% women. **Part-time faculty:** 99 total; 28% have terminal degrees, 6% minority, 61% women. **Class size:** 36% < 20, 53% 20-39, 5% 40-49, 5% 50-99. **Special facilities:** Art galleries, greenhouse, challenge/ropes course, former Governor's mansion, Flannery O'Connor collection, Georgia education museum and archives.

Freshman class profile. 3,968 applied, 3,002 admitted, 1,475 enrolled.

Mid 50% test scores		GPA 2.0-2.99:	7%
SAT critical reading:	530-620	End year in good standing:	93%
SAT math:	520-610	Return as sophomores:	86%
SAT writing:	510-600	Out-of-state:	1%
ACT composite:	23-27	Live on campus:	98%
GPA 3.75 or higher:	24%	Fraternities:	20%
GPA 3.50-3.74:	25%	Sororities:	46%
GPA 3.0-3.49:	44%		

Basis for selection. Total student portfolio and demonstrated potential for contribution to the university and probability for success. Test scores used in evaluating honors program candidates. Audition required of music and drama majors. **Home schooled:** Students from non-accredited home schools must have SAT/ACT equal to or above average of previous year's entering freshmen class; other documentation may be required. **Learning Disabled:** Students must identify themselves as disabled during admissions process.

High school preparation. College-preparatory program required. 17 units required. Required units include English 4, mathematics 4, social studies 3, science 4 (laboratory 2) and foreign language 2.

2015-2016 Annual costs. Tuition/fees: $9,170; $27,518 out-of-state. Room/board: $11,612. Books/supplies: $1,500. Personal expenses: $3,090.

2014-2015 Financial aid. Need-based: 1,266 full-time freshmen applied for aid; 767 deemed to have need; 761 received aid. Average need met was 25%. Average scholarship/grant was $4,544; average loan $3,302. 38% of total undergraduate aid awarded as scholarships/grants, 62% as loans/jobs. **Non-need-based:** Awarded to 2,391 full-time undergraduates, including 777 freshmen. Scholarships awarded for academics, alumni affiliation, art, athletics, leadership, music/drama, state residency.

Application procedures. Admission: Priority date 4/1; no deadline. $40 fee. Admission notification on a rolling basis. Must reply by May 1 or within 2 week(s) if notified thereafter. Options are available for dual enrollment of high school students who have completed at least the 10th grade. **Financial aid:** Priority date 3/1; no closing date. FAFSA, CSS PROFILE required. Applicants notified on a rolling basis starting 3/1.

Academics. Special study options: Accelerated study, combined bachelor's/graduate degree, distance learning, double major, ESL, external degree, honors, independent study, internships, student-designed major, study abroad, teacher certification program, Washington semester. 3-2 engineering program with Georgia Institute of Technology. **Credit/placement by examination:** AP, CLEP, IB, SAT, ACT, institutional tests. 30 credit hours maximum toward bachelor's degree. Students may earn a maximum of 24 hours credit through the IB program. **Support services:** Learning center, pre-admission summer program, reduced course load, study skills assistance, tutoring, writing center. Supplemental instruction.

Majors. Biology: General. **Business:** General, accounting, business admin, managerial economics, marketing. **Communications:** Journalism. **Computer sciences:** Computer science, webmaster. **Conservation:** Environmental science. **Education:** Early childhood, middle, music, special ed. **English:** English lit, rhetoric/composition. **Foreign languages:** French, Spanish. **Health services:** Athletic training, community health, music therapy, nursing (RN). **History:** General. **Liberal arts:** Arts/sciences. **Math:** General. **Parks/recreation:** General. **Philosophy/religion:** Philosophy. **Physical sciences:** Chemistry, physics. **Protective services:** Law enforcement admin. **Social sciences:** Geography, political science, sociology. **Visual/performing arts:** Art, dramatic, music.

Most popular majors. Biology 6%, business/marketing 22%, communications/journalism 7%, education 16%, health sciences 13%.

Technology on campus. 900 workstations in dormitories, library, computer center, student center. Dormitories wired for high-speed internet access and linked to campus network. Commuter students can connect to campus network. Online course registration, online library, helpline, wireless network available.

Student life. Freshman orientation: Available, $60 fee. Preregistration for classes offered. Several summer sessions available, with shorter programs held during the academic year. **Policies:** First-year students under the age of 21 required to live on campus for 2 consecutive semesters. Only pets allowed are fish in 10 gallon or smaller tanks. **Housing:** Guaranteed on-campus for freshmen. Coed dorms, special housing for disabled, apartments, themed housing available. $235 partly refundable deposit, deadline 5/1. **Activities:** Bands, campus ministries, choral groups, dance, drama, international student organizations, literary magazine, music ensembles, Model UN, musical theater, radio station, student government, student newspaper, TV station, Young Democrats, Hillel Society, Baptist Collegiate ministries, Campus Catholics, Young Americans for Liberty, Latino Student Alliance, international club.

Athletics. NCAA. **Intercollegiate:** Baseball M, basketball, cheerleading, cross-country, golf M, soccer W, softball W, tennis. **Intramural:** Basketball, football (non-tackle), sand volleyball, soccer, softball, ultimate frisbee, volleyball, water polo. **Team name:** Bobcats.

Student services. Adult student services, alcohol/substance abuse counseling, career counseling, student employment services, financial aid counseling, health services, minority student services, personal counseling, placement for graduates, veterans' counselor, women's services. **Physically disabled:** Services for visually, hearing impaired.

Contact. E-mail: admissions@gcsu.edu
Phone: (478) 445-1283 Toll-free number: (800) 342-0471
Fax: (478) 445-1914
Ramon Blakley, Director of Admissions, Georgia College and State University, Campus Box 23, Milledgeville, GA 31061-0490

Georgia Gwinnett College
Lawrenceville, Georgia
www.ggc.edu   CB code: 4796

- Public 4-year liberal arts college
- Commuter campus in large town
- 10,998 degree-seeking undergraduates: 30% part-time, 56% women, 33% African American, 9% Asian American, 16% Hispanic/Latino, 4% Multi-racial, non-Hispanic, 2% international
- 84% of applicants admitted
- SAT or ACT (ACT writing optional) required

General. Regionally accredited. **Degrees:** 814 bachelor's awarded. **ROTC:** Army. **Location:** 35 miles from Atlanta. **Calendar:** Semester, limited summer session. **Full-time faculty:** 419 total; 22% minority, 50% women. **Part-time faculty:** 231 total; 36% minority, 38% women. **Class size:** 48% < 20, 50% 20-39, 2% 40-49.

Freshman class profile. 3,612 applied, 3,041 admitted, 2,326 enrolled.

Mid 50% test scores		GPA 2.0-2.99:	62%
SAT critical reading:	410-430	Rank in top quarter:	9%
SAT math:	420-530	Rank in top tenth:	3%
SAT writing:	400-510	Return as sophomores:	67%
ACT composite:	17-22	Out-of-state:	3%
GPA 3.75 or higher:	4%	Live on campus:	18%
GPA 3.50-3.74:	6%	International:	2%
GPA 3.0-3.49:	25%		

Basis for selection. 2.0 GPA required for college prep students; 2.2 GPA required for tech prep students. **Home schooled:** Transcript of courses and grades required.

High school preparation. College-preparatory program recommended. 17 units required. Required units include English 4, mathematics 4, social studies 3, science 4 (laboratory 2) and foreign language 2.

2015-2016 Annual costs. Tuition/fees: $5,648; $16,152 out-of-state. Room/board: $12,300.

2015-2016 Financial aid. **Need-based:** 1,904 full-time freshmen applied for aid; 1,646 deemed to have need; 1,603 received aid. Average need met was 35%. Average scholarship/grant was $4,983; average loan $3,350. 58% of total undergraduate aid awarded as scholarships/grants, 42% as loans/jobs. **Non-need-based:** Awarded to 1,812 full-time undergraduates, including 473 freshmen. Scholarships awarded for academics, athletics.

Application procedures. **Admission:** Closing date 6/2 (receipt date). $20 fee, may be waived for applicants with need. Application must be submitted online. Admission notification on a rolling basis. **Financial aid:** Priority date 7/1; no closing date. FAFSA required. Applicants notified on a rolling basis starting 5/15.

Academics. **Special study options:** Double major, dual enrollment of high school students, ESL, independent study, internships, study abroad. **Credit/ placement by examination:** AP, CLEP, IB, SAT, ACT, institutional tests. 30 credit hours maximum toward bachelor's degree. **Support services:** Study skills assistance, tutoring, writing center.

Honors college/program. Applicants generally have 3.5 GPA and meet the following requirements: completed fewer than 24 college-level credit hours; submit essay that illustrates personal commitment to core values of scholarship, service, leadership and creativity; interview with selection committee; complete separate application, detailing co-curricular and extra-curricular activities. Rigor of high school program also considered.

Majors. **Biology:** General. **Business:** Business admin. **Computer sciences:** Information technology. **Conservation:** Environmental science. **Education:** Early childhood, special ed. **English:** English lit. **Health services:** Nursing (RN). **History:** General. **Math:** General. **Parks/recreation:** Exercise sciences. **Physical sciences:** Chemistry. **Protective services:** Criminal justice. **Psychology:** General. **Social sciences:** Political science.

Most popular majors. Biology 12%, business/marketing 34%, computer/ information sciences 7%, education 13%, psychology 10%, security/protective services 7%.

Technology on campus. 207 workstations in library, computer center, student center. Dormitories wired for high-speed internet access and linked to campus network. Commuter students can connect to campus network. Online course registration, online library, helpline, wireless network available.

Student life. **Freshman orientation:** Mandatory, $40 fee. Preregistration for classes offered. One-day sessions held prior to start of semester, with on-campus and online components. **Housing:** Guaranteed on-campus for freshmen. Coed dorms available. $250 nonrefundable deposit. **Activities:** Campus ministries, international student organizations, student government.

Athletics. NAIA. **Intercollegiate:** Baseball M, soccer, softball W, tennis. **Team name:** Grizzlies.

Student services. Adult student services, alcohol/substance abuse counseling, career counseling, services for economically disadvantaged, student employment services, financial aid counseling, health services, minority student services, personal counseling, veterans' counselor, women's services. **Physically disabled:** Services for visually, speech, hearing impaired.

Contact. E-mail: ggcadmissions@ggc.edu
Phone: (678) 407-5313 Toll-free number: (877) 704-4422
Fax: (678) 407-5747
Kristi McBride, Associate Director of Admissions, Georgia Gwinnett College, 1000 University Center Lane, Lawrenceville, GA 30043

Georgia Institute of Technology
Atlanta, Georgia   **CB member**
www.gatech.edu   **CB code: 5248**

- Public 4-year university
- Residential campus in large city
- 14,460 degree-seeking undergraduates: 6% part-time, 35% women, 7% African American, 19% Asian American, 7% Hispanic/Latino, 4% Multi-racial, non-Hispanic, 11% international
- 9,799 degree-seeking graduate students
- 32% of applicants admitted

- SAT or ACT with writing, application essay required
- 85% graduate within 6 years; 17% enter graduate study

General. Founded in 1885. Regionally accredited. **Degrees:** 3,274 bachelor's awarded; master's, doctoral offered. **ROTC:** Army, Naval, Air Force. **Location:** Downtown. **Calendar:** Semester, extensive summer session. **Full-time faculty:** 1,076 total; 84% have terminal degrees, 28% minority, 26% women. **Part-time faculty:** 99 total; 36% have terminal degrees, 26% minority, 41% women. **Class size:** 38% < 20, 27% 20-39, 9% 40-49, 19% 50-99, 7% >100. **Special facilities:** Advanced technology development center, carbon neutral lab, trading floor, fluid mechanics research laboratory with transonic open-return continuous wind tunnel, smart house, nanotechnology cleanroom with electron microscope, virtual factory laboratory, nanotechnology research center, mechanical properties research laboratory with scanning electron microscope, nuclear magnetic resonance spectroscopy center, ovarian cancer institute, paper museum, solar decathlon house, engineered biosystems building.

Freshman class profile. 27,277 applied, 8,775 admitted, 3,089 enrolled.

Mid 50% test scores		End year in good standing:	98%
SAT critical reading:	630-730	Return as sophomores:	97%
SAT math:	680-770	Out-of-state:	45%
SAT writing:	640-730	Live on campus:	98%
ACT composite:	30-33	International:	8%
GPA 3.75 or higher:	87%	Fraternities:	28%
GPA 3.50-3.74:	9%	Sororities:	36%
GPA 3.0-3.49:	4%		

Basis for selection. GED not accepted. Academic record, test scores, essay, honors, extracurricular activities, and work experience evaluated. **Home schooled:** For applicants from unaccredited home school programs, previous college coursework, SAT Subject Tests, AP/IB test scores, or a combination of these are recommended to assist in assessment of achievement and excellence in math, foreign language, social studies/social science and lab science.

High school preparation. College-preparatory program required. 17 units required. Required units include English 4, mathematics 4, social studies 3, science 4 (laboratory 2) and foreign language 2.

2015-2016 Annual costs. Tuition/fees: $12,204; $32,396 out-of-state. Room/board: $10,716.

2014-2015 Financial aid. **Need-based:** 1,634 full-time freshmen applied for aid; 806 deemed to have need; 783 received aid. Average need met was 84%. Average scholarship/grant was $7,953; average loan $3,788. 58% of total undergraduate aid awarded as scholarships/grants, 42% as loans/jobs. **Non-need-based:** Awarded to 6,666 full-time undergraduates, including 1,025 freshmen. Scholarships awarded for academics, athletics, leadership, music/drama, ROTC, state residency.

Application procedures. **Admission:** Priority date 10/15; deadline 1/10 (receipt date). $75 fee, may be waived for applicants with need. Application must be submitted online. Admission notification by 3/14. Must reply by 5/1. **Financial aid:** Priority date 2/15, closing date 2/15. FAFSA, institutional form required. CSS PROFILE required for domestic, first-time applicants. Applicants notified by 4/15; must reply by 5/1.

Academics. **Special study options:** Accelerated study, combined bachelor's/graduate degree, cooperative education, cross-registration, distance learning, dual enrollment of high school students, ESL, honors, independent study, internships, student-designed major, study abroad, teacher certification program, weekend college. Undergraduate research opportunities program, dual degree program (3-2); Regent's engineering transfer program with 16 colleges in the University System of Georgia. **Credit/placement by examination:** AP, CLEP, IB, institutional tests. 9 credit hours maximum toward bachelor's degree. **Support services:** Learning center, pre-admission summer program, reduced course load, remedial instruction, study skills assistance, tutoring, writing center.

Majors. **Architecture:** Architecture, building sciences. **Biology:** General, biochemistry. **Business:** Business admin, managerial economics. **Communications:** Digital media. **Computer sciences:** General. **Engineering:** Aerospace, biomedical, chemical, civil, computer, electrical, environmental, industrial, materials, mechanical, nuclear. **Foreign languages:** General. **History:** Science/technology. **Human services:** Public policy. **Math:** Applied. **Physical sciences:** Chemistry, physics. **Psychology:** Industrial. **Social sciences:** International relations. **Visual/performing arts:** Industrial design.

Most popular majors. Business/marketing 13%, computer/information sciences 9%, engineering/engineering technologies 61%.

Technology on campus. PC or laptop required. 1,000 workstations in library, computer center, student center. Dormitories wired for high-speed internet access and linked to campus network. Commuter students can connect to campus network. Online course registration, online library, helpline, repair service, student web hosting, wireless network available.

Student life. Freshman orientation: Available, $210 fee. Preregistration for classes offered. Each orientation session lasts two days, and several sessions are held in July and August. **Housing:** Coed dorms, single-sex dorms, special housing for disabled, apartments, fraternity/sorority housing, themed housing available. $600 partly refundable deposit, deadline 5/1. **Activities:** Bands, campus ministries, choral groups, dance, drama, film society, international student organizations, literary magazine, music ensembles, Model UN, musical theater, radio station, student government, student newspaper, symphony orchestra, TV station, Christian Campus Fellowship, Wesley Foundation, College Democrats, College Republicans, Association of Environmental Engineers and Scientists, National Society of Black Engineers, Society of Women Engineers, Society of Hispanic Professional Engineers.

Athletics. NCAA. **Intercollegiate:** Baseball M, basketball, cross-country, diving, football (tackle) M, golf M, softball W, swimming, tennis, track and field, volleyball W. **Intramural:** Basketball, soccer, volleyball. **Team name:** Yellow Jackets.

Student services. Career counseling, student employment services, financial aid counseling, health services, legal services, minority student services, on-campus daycare, personal counseling, placement for graduates, veterans' counselor, women's services. **Physically disabled:** Services for visually, speech, hearing impaired.

Contact. E-mail: admission@gatech.edu
Phone: (404) 894-4154 Fax: (404) 894-9511
Rick Clark, Director of Undergraduate Admissions, Georgia Institute of Technology, Office of Undergraduate Admissions, Atlanta, GA 30332-0320

Georgia Southern University
Statesboro, Georgia
www.georgiasouthern.edu

CB member
CB code: 5253

- Public 4-year university
- Residential campus in large town
- 17,173 degree-seeking undergraduates: 8% part-time, 50% women, 26% African American, 2% Asian American, 5% Hispanic/Latino, 2% Multiracial, non-Hispanic, 1% international
- 2,434 degree-seeking graduate students
- 60% of applicants admitted
- SAT or ACT with writing required
- 50% graduate within 6 years

General. Founded in 1906. Regionally accredited. Member of the University System of Georgia; Carnegie doctoral-research university. **Degrees:** 3,221 bachelor's awarded; master's, doctoral offered. **ROTC:** Army. **Location:** 50 miles from Savannah, 200 miles from Atlanta. **Calendar:** Semester, extensive summer session. **Full-time faculty:** 794 total; 84% have terminal degrees, 17% minority, 48% women. **Part-time faculty:** 90 total; 43% have terminal degrees, 4% minority, 56% women. **Class size:** 27% < 20, 52% 20-39, 10% 40-49, 6% 50-99, 4% >100. **Special facilities:** Bureau of business research and economic development, center for addiction recovery, center for Africana studies, center for bio-statistics and survey, center for education leadership, center for entrepreneurial learning and leadership, center for forensic studies in accounting, center for international schooling, center for international studies, center for Irish studies, center for retail studies, center for sustainability, center for wildlife education, center for gender studies, child development center, graduate academic services center (GASC), institute for coastal plain science, coastlands AHEC, national youth-at-risk center (NYAR), small business development center, black box theatre, performing arts center, garden of the coastal plain.

Freshman class profile. 10,098 applied, 6,082 admitted, 3,495 enrolled.

Mid 50% test scores		Rank in top quarter:	49%
SAT critical reading:	520-590	Rank in top tenth:	17%
SAT math:	510-590	End year in good standing:	84%
SAT writing:	480-570	Return as sophomores:	82%
ACT composite:	21-25	Out-of-state:	5%
GPA 3.75 or higher:	19%	Live on campus:	91%
GPA 3.50-3.74:	18%	International:	2%
GPA 3.0-3.49:	37%	Fraternities:	12%
GPA 2.0-2.99:	26%	Sororities:	20%

Basis for selection. GED not accepted. Test scores, high school GPA, and college preparatory curriculum considered. SAT and ACT not required for international or non-traditional applicants. TOEFL required for international applicants whose native language is not English. Students may be required to take placement exams. Audition required for music majors. **Home**

schooled: 1100 SAT (exclusive of Writing) or 24 ACT required. Per Board of Regents' policy, homeschooled students must take the SAT or ACT test and score at or above the average SAT score of the previous year's fall semester first-time freshman class. **Learning Disabled:** Admissions coordinated through student disability resource center.

High school preparation. College-preparatory program required. 17 units required. Required units include English 4, mathematics 4, social studies 3, science 4 (laboratory 2) and foreign language 2.

2015-2016 Annual costs. Tuition/fees: $7,318; $20,536 out-of-state. Room/board: $9,800. Books/supplies: $1,200. Personal expenses: $3,104.

2014-2015 Financial aid. Need-based: 3,270 full-time freshmen applied for aid; 2,306 deemed to have need; 2,255 received aid. Average need met was 55%. Average scholarship/grant was $7,098; average loan $4,183. 44% of total undergraduate aid awarded as scholarships/grants, 56% as loans/jobs. **Non-need-based:** Awarded to 515 full-time undergraduates, including 202 freshmen. Scholarships awarded for academics, alumni affiliation, art, athletics, leadership, minority status, music/drama, ROTC, state residency. **Additional information:** Majority of available scholarships are need-blind.

Application procedures. Admission: Priority date 4/1; deadline 5/1 (postmark date). $30 fee, may be waived for applicants with need. Admission notification on a rolling basis. **Financial aid:** Priority date 4/20; no closing date. FAFSA required. Applicants notified on a rolling basis starting 4/20.

Academics. Special study options: Accelerated study, combined bachelor's/graduate degree, cooperative education, distance learning, double major, dual enrollment of high school students, ESL, honors, independent study, internships, student-designed major, study abroad, teacher certification program, Washington semester. **Credit/placement by examination:** AP, CLEP, IB, institutional tests. 30 credit hours maximum toward bachelor's degree. For AP exams, more credit hours will be awarded for higher-than-minimum scores. **Support services:** Learning center, pre-admission summer program, reduced course load, remedial instruction, study skills assistance, tutoring, writing center.

Majors. Biology: General. **Business:** Accounting, business admin, finance, international, logistics, management information systems, managerial economics, marketing. **Communications:** Digital media, journalism, public relations. **Communications technology:** Graphic/printing. **Computer sciences:** General, information systems. **Education:** Elementary, middle, music, physical, special ed. **Engineering:** Civil, electrical, manufacturing, mechanical. **English:** English lit, rhetoric/composition, writing. **Health services:** Athletic training, nursing (RN), public health ed. **History:** General. **Math:** General. **Parks/recreation:** General, exercise sciences, sports admin. **Philosophy/religion:** Philosophy. **Physical sciences:** Chemistry, geology, physics. **Protective services:** Criminal justice. **Psychology:** General. **Social sciences:** Anthropology, economics, geography, international relations, political science, sociology. **Visual/performing arts:** Art, dramatic, graphic design, interior design, music performance. **Work/family studies:** Clothing/textiles, family studies, food/nutrition.

Most popular majors. Biology 6%, business/marketing 18%, communications/journalism 6%, education 6%, engineering/engineering technologies 8%, health sciences 6%, liberal arts 8%, parks/recreation 9%, psychology 6%.

Technology on campus. 3,872 workstations in dormitories, library, student center. Dormitories wired for high-speed internet access and linked to campus network. Commuter students can connect to campus network. Online course registration, online library, helpline, repair service, student web hosting, wireless network available.

Student life. Freshman orientation: Mandatory, $70 fee. Preregistration for classes offered. Freshman/parent program held for 2 days. **Policies:** Freshmen required to live on-campus. **Housing:** Guaranteed on-campus for freshmen. Coed dorms, special housing for disabled, apartments, themed housing available. $250 partly refundable deposit. **Activities:** Bands, campus ministries, choral groups, dance, drama, film society, international student organizations, literary magazine, music ensembles, musical theater, opera, radio station, student government, student newspaper, symphony orchestra.

Athletics. NCAA. **Intercollegiate:** Baseball M, basketball, cheerleading, cross-country W, diving W, football (tackle) M, golf M, rifle, soccer, softball W, swimming W, tennis, track and field W, volleyball W. **Intramural:** Archery, baseball M, basketball, bowling, cricket M, equestrian, fencing, football (non-tackle), golf, lacrosse, rifle, rugby, soccer, softball, swimming, tennis, ultimate frisbee, volleyball, weight lifting. **Team name:** Eagles.

Student services. Adult student services, career counseling, services for economically disadvantaged, student employment services, financial aid counseling, health services, legal services, minority student services, on-campus daycare, personal counseling, placement for graduates, veterans' counselor, women's services. **Physically disabled:** Services for visually, speech, hearing impaired.

Contact. E-mail: admissions@georgiasouthern.edu
Phone: (912) 478-5391 Fax: (912) 478-1156
Amy Smith, Director of Admission, Georgia Southern University, PO Box 8024, Statesboro, GA 30458

Georgia Southwestern State University

Americus, Georgia
www.gsw.edu
CB member
CB code: 5250

- Public 4-year university and liberal arts college
- Residential campus in large town
- 2,305 degree-seeking undergraduates: 29% part-time, 64% women, 29% African American, 1% Asian American, 3% Hispanic/Latino, 2% Multi-racial, non-Hispanic, 2% international
- 316 degree-seeking graduate students
- 72% of applicants admitted
- SAT or ACT (ACT writing optional) required
- 33% graduate within 6 years

General. Founded in 1906. Regionally accredited. **Degrees:** 527 bachelor's awarded; master's offered. **Location:** 135 miles of Atlanta. **Calendar:** Semester, limited summer session. **Full-time faculty:** 108 total; 75% have terminal degrees, 16% minority, 52% women. **Part-time faculty:** 45 total; 29% have terminal degrees, 4% minority, 73% women. **Class size:** 47% < 20, 44% 20-39, 8% 40-49, 1% 50-99, less than 1% >100. **Special facilities:** Observatory, glass blowing studio, golf course, indoor climbing wall.

Freshman class profile. 1,167 applied, 836 admitted, 381 enrolled.

Mid 50% test scores			
SAT critical reading:	440-530	Rank in top quarter:	40%
SAT math:	430-510	Rank in top tenth:	18%
SAT writing:	420-510	Return as sophomores:	74%
ACT composite:	18-24	Out-of-state:	4%
GPA 3.75 or higher:	20%	Live on campus:	69%
GPA 3.50-3.74:	16%	International:	2%
GPA 3.0-3.49:	34%	Fraternities:	6%
GPA 2.0-2.99:	30%	Sororities:	6%

Basis for selection. School achievement record, test scores most important. **Home schooled:** Statement describing home school structure and mission, transcript of courses and grades required. Copy of Declaration of Intent to Home School filed with the local Board of Education.

High school preparation. College-preparatory program required. 17 units required. Required and recommended units include English 4, mathematics 4, social studies 1, history 2, science 4 (laboratory 2), foreign language 2 and academic electives 2. The 3 units of social science must include 1 unit focusing on US studies and 1 focusing on world studies.

2015-2016 Annual costs. Tuition/fees: $6,234; $19,054 out-of-state. Room/board: $7,390. Books/supplies: $1,400. Personal expenses: $2,644.

2015-2016 Financial aid. Need-based: 350 full-time freshmen applied for aid; 272 deemed to have need; 270 received aid. Average need met was 58%. Average scholarship/grant was $4,941; average loan $3,435. 47% of total undergraduate aid awarded as scholarships/grants, 53% as loans/jobs. **Non-need-based:** Awarded to 712 full-time undergraduates, including 234 freshmen. Scholarships awarded for academics, alumni affiliation, art, athletics, leadership, music/drama, state residency.

Application procedures. Admission: Closing date 7/21 (postmark date). $25 fee, may be waived for applicants with need. Admission notification on a rolling basis. Must reply by May 1 or within 3 week(s) if notified thereafter. **Financial aid:** Priority date 4/15, closing date 6/15. FAFSA required. Applicants notified on a rolling basis starting 5/1; must reply within 8 week(s) of notification.

Academics. Special study options: Accelerated study, distance learning, double major, ESL, honors, internships, study abroad, teacher certification program. 3+2 program in engineering with Georgia Institute of Technology. **Credit/placement by examination:** AP, CLEP, IB, SAT, ACT, institutional tests. 30 credit hours maximum toward bachelor's degree. Credit by examination limited to 10 hours in the major discipline and 30 hours towards degree requirements. **Support services:** Learning center, reduced course load, remedial instruction, study skills assistance, tutoring, writing center.

Majors. Biology: General. **Business:** Accounting, business admin, human resources, marketing. **Computer sciences:** Computer science, information technology. **Education:** Elementary, middle, physical, special ed. **English:** English lit. **Health services:** Nursing (RN). **History:** General. **Math:** General.

Physical sciences: Chemistry, geology. **Protective services:** Law enforcement admin. **Psychology:** General. **Social sciences:** Political science, sociology. **Visual/performing arts:** Art, dramatic, music.

Most popular majors. Business/marketing 37%, education 23%, health sciences 15%, psychology 6%.

Technology on campus. 260 workstations in dormitories, library, computer center. Dormitories wired for high-speed internet access and linked to campus network. Commuter students can connect to campus network. Online course registration, online library, wireless network available.

Student life. Freshman orientation: Mandatory, $85 fee. Preregistration for classes offered. One-day session offered 3 times in summer, includes parents' program. **Housing:** Guaranteed on-campus for freshmen. Coed dorms, apartments, fraternity/sorority housing available. $250 nonrefundable deposit. **Activities:** Bands, campus ministries, choral groups, drama, international student organizations, literary magazine, student government, student newspaper, TV station, Habitat for Humanity, African student association, Student African American Brotherhood, ihelp peer educators, Christian student center, Presbyterian student center, Wesley Foundation, College Republicans, Young Democrats, Red Cross club.

Athletics. NCAA. **Intercollegiate:** Baseball M, basketball, cross-country W, golf M, soccer, softball W, tennis. **Intramural:** Basketball, football (non-tackle), racquetball, soccer, table tennis, tennis, ultimate frisbee, volleyball. **Team name:** Hurricanes.

Student services. Career counseling, student employment services, financial aid counseling, health services, personal counseling, veterans' counselor. **Physically disabled:** Services for visually, speech, hearing impaired.

Contact. E-mail: admissions@gsw.edu
Phone: (229) 928-1273 Toll-free number: (800) 338-0082
Fax: (229) 931-2983
Gaye Hayes, Vice President of Enrollment Management, Georgia Southwestern State University, 800 Georgia Southwestern State University Drive, Americus, GA 31709-9957

Georgia State University

Atlanta, Georgia
www.gsu.edu
CB member
CB code: 5251

- Public 4-year university
- Commuter campus in very large city
- 24,452 degree-seeking undergraduates: 23% part-time, 59% women, 42% African American, 12% Asian American, 10% Hispanic/Latino, 5% Multi-racial, non-Hispanic, 2% international
- 6,717 degree-seeking graduate students
- 58% of applicants admitted
- SAT or ACT (ACT writing optional), application essay required
- 54% graduate within 6 years

General. Founded in 1913. Regionally accredited. Courses offered at Alpharetta and Brookhaven Centers. Distance learning and web courses available in College of Health and Human Sciences and College of Education. **Degrees:** 4,780 bachelor's awarded; master's, professional, doctoral offered. **ROTC:** Army, Naval, Air Force. **Location:** Downtown. **Calendar:** Semester, extensive summer session. **Full-time faculty:** 1,219 total; 90% have terminal degrees, 26% minority, 46% women. **Part-time faculty:** 488 total; 55% have terminal degrees, 28% minority, 53% women. **Class size:** 18% < 20, 45% 20-39, 19% 40-49, 12% 50-99, 5% >100. **Special facilities:** Viral immunology center, writing studio, advanced biotechnology center, Asian studies center, multi-media instructional lab, child development center, performing arts center, language acquisition and research centers, military science leadership lab, music media center, learning disorders center, speech and language center, hearing center, art galleries, observatory, business and marketing research centers, women's studies institute, Confucius institute, digital arts and entertainment laboratory, digital aquarium, cinefest, lodge and recreation area.

Freshman class profile. 13,568 applied, 7,831 admitted, 3,682 enrolled.

Mid 50% test scores			
		GPA 2.0-2.99:	13%
SAT critical reading:	480-580	Rank in top quarter:	45%
SAT math:	470-580	Rank in top tenth:	16%
ACT composite:	20-25	Return as sophomores:	81%
GPA 3.75 or higher:	19%	Out-of-state:	4%
GPA 3.50-3.74:	24%	Live on campus:	57%
GPA 3.0-3.49:	44%	International:	2%

Basis for selection. GED not accepted. Grades achieved in 17 units of the required high school curriculum and SAT/ACT most important. Audition and interview required for music majors. Portfolio required for art majors.

Home schooled: Transcript of courses and grades required. Portfolio outlining subjects studied, titles of text books, assignment descriptions, and examples of coursework, tests, assignments.

High school preparation. College-preparatory program required. 17 units required. Required units include English 4, mathematics 4, social studies 3, science 4 (laboratory 2) and foreign language 2.

2015-2016 Annual costs. Tuition/fees: $10,686; $28,896 out-of-state. Room/board: $10,728. Books/supplies: $1,000. Personal expenses: $1,970.

2014-2015 Financial aid. Need-based: 3,494 full-time freshmen applied for aid; 2,985 deemed to have need; 2,937 received aid. Average need met was 62%. Average scholarship/grant was $5,089. 52% of total undergraduate aid awarded as scholarships/grants, 48% as loans/jobs. **Non-need-based:** Awarded to 13,826 full-time undergraduates, including 2,685 freshmen. Scholarships awarded for academics, alumni affiliation, art, athletics, job skills, leadership, minority status, music/drama, religious affiliation, ROTC, state residency.

Application procedures. Admission: Closing date 3/1 (receipt date). $60 fee, may be waived for applicants with need. Admission notification by 5/1. Must reply by 7/15. **Financial aid:** Closing date 4/1. FAFSA required. Applicants notified on a rolling basis starting 3/1.

Academics. Special study options: Combined bachelor's/graduate degree, cooperative education, cross-registration, distance learning, double major, dual enrollment of high school students, ESL, honors, independent study, internships, study abroad, teacher certification program. **Credit/placement by examination:** AP, CLEP, IB, institutional tests. 30 credit hours maximum toward bachelor's degree. **Support services:** Learning center, pre-admission summer program, reduced course load, study skills assistance, tutoring, writing center.

Honors college/program. Applicants should have 3.5 GPA and 1200 SAT with 500 verbal and math; around 200 students admitted each year.

Majors. Area/ethnic studies: African-American, women's. **Biology:** General, neuroscience. **Business:** Accounting, actuarial science, business admin, finance, hospitality admin, insurance, managerial economics, marketing, real estate. **Communications:** Communications/speech/rhetoric, journalism. **Computer sciences:** General, computer science. **Education:** Art, kindergarten/preschool, physical. **English:** English lit. **Foreign languages:** French, German, linguistics, Spanish. **Health services:** Dietetics, nursing (RN), respiratory therapy technology. **History:** General. **Human services:** Public policy, social work. **Math:** General. **Philosophy/religion:** Philosophy, religion. **Physical sciences:** Chemistry, geology, physics. **Protective services:** Criminal justice. **Psychology:** General. **Social sciences:** Anthropology, economics, geography, international economics, political science, sociology. **Visual/performing arts:** Drawing, film/cinema/video, music management, music performance.

Most popular majors. Biology 7%, business/marketing 27%, communications/journalism 6%, computer/information sciences 6%, education 6%, psychology 10%, social sciences 11%, visual/performing arts 7%.

Technology on campus. 982 workstations in library, computer center, student center. Dormitories wired for high-speed internet access and linked to campus network. Commuter students can connect to campus network. Online course registration, online library, helpline, student web hosting, wireless network available.

Student life. Freshman orientation: Mandatory, $56 fee. Preregistration for classes offered. Various types of meetings available. **Policies:** Student code of conduct in effect. **Housing:** Coed dorms, special housing for disabled, apartments, fraternity/sorority housing, themed housing available. $375 partly refundable deposit. **Activities:** Bands, campus ministries, choral groups, dance, drama, film society, international student organizations, literary magazine, music ensembles, Model UN, musical theater, opera, radio station, student government, student newspaper, symphony orchestra, TV station, Black Student Alliance, Women Computing in Atlanta, Bridge Builders, Global Peace Youth Corps, Hong Kong Student Association, International Student Association Council, Indian Student Association, African Students Association, Christian Students, Muslim Student Association.

Athletics. NCAA. **Intercollegiate:** Baseball M, basketball, cross-country, football (tackle) M, golf, sand volleyball W, soccer, softball W, tennis, track and field W, volleyball W. **Intramural:** Badminton, basketball, bowling, football (non-tackle), golf, racquetball, soccer, softball, table tennis, track and field M, ultimate frisbee, volleyball, water polo. **Team name:** Panthers.

Student services. Adult student services, alcohol/substance abuse counseling, career counseling, student employment services, financial aid counseling, health services, minority student services, on-campus daycare, personal counseling, veterans' counselor. **Physically disabled:** Services for visually, speech, hearing impaired.

Contact. E-mail: admissions@gsu.edu
Phone: (404) 413-2500 Fax: (404) 413-2002
Scott Burke, Director of Admissions, Georgia State University, Box 4009, Atlanta, GA 30302-4009

Herzing University: Atlanta
Atlanta, Georgia
www.herzing.edu   CB code: 2342

- For-profit 3-year business and technical college
- Commuter campus in very large city
- 393 undergraduates
- Interview required

General. Founded in 1949. Regionally accredited. **Degrees:** 76 bachelor's, 30 associate awarded; master's offered. **Location:** 120 miles from Birmingham, AL; 70 miles from Chattanooga, TN. **Calendar:** Semester, extensive summer session. **Full-time faculty:** 10 total. **Part-time faculty:** 25 total. **Class size:** 84% < 20, 16% 20-39.

Basis for selection. Entrance test and evaluation required. Competitive admission to some programs based on score. SAT/ACT may be used for academic advising.

2015-2016 Annual costs. Personal expenses: $2,700. **Additional information:** Tuition for diploma programs: $6,450-$8,555 per semester. Associate programs: $12,900 per year; Bachelor's programs: $12,900-$19,320 per year.

Financial aid. Non-need-based: Scholarships awarded for academics.

Application procedures. Admission: No deadline. No application fee. Admission notification on a rolling basis. **Financial aid:** No deadline. FAFSA, institutional form required. Applicants notified on a rolling basis.

Academics. Students train on types of equipment used in the field. **Special study options:** Distance learning, independent study, internships, liberal arts/career combination. **Credit/placement by examination:** AP, CLEP, IB, institutional tests. **Support services:** Learning center, study skills assistance, tutoring.

Majors. BACHELOR'S. Business: Accounting, accounting/business management, business admin, entrepreneurial studies, human resources, international. **Computer sciences:** Networking. **Health services:** Health care admin. **Protective services:** Criminal justice. **ASSOCIATE. Business:** Accounting, business admin. **Computer sciences:** Computer science. **Health services:** Massage therapy, medical assistant, surgical technology.

Most popular majors. Business/marketing 31%, computer/information sciences 41%.

Technology on campus. 157 workstations in library, computer center. Online library available.

Student life. Freshman orientation: Mandatory. Preregistration for classes offered. Held beginning of each term for 2 hours. **Activities:** Student government.

Student services. Career counseling, student employment services, financial aid counseling, personal counseling, placement for graduates, veterans' counselor.

Contact. E-mail: info@atl.herzing.edu
Phone: (404) 816-4533 Toll-free number: (800) 573-4533
Fax: (404) 816-5576
Annisa Elder, Director of Admissions, Herzing University: Atlanta, 3393 Peachtree Road NE, Suite 1003, Atlanta, GA 30326

ITT Technical Institute: Duluth
Duluth, Georgia
www.itt-tech.edu

- For-profit 4-year technical college
- Commuter campus in large town
- 591 undergraduates

General. Accredited by ACICS. **Degrees:** 38 bachelor's, 166 associate awarded. **Calendar:** Quarter. **Full-time faculty:** 10 total. **Part-time faculty:** 40 total.

Basis for selection. Admission requirements will vary by program.

2015-2016 Annual costs. Per-credit-hour charge, $493, will vary depending on program level and course of study. Academic fee, $300. Some programs require purchase of tools, ranging from $100 to $500.

Academics. Credit/placement by examination: AP, CLEP.

Majors. Business: Business admin, construction management, project management. **Communications technology:** Animation/special effects. **Computer sciences:** Security. **Protective services:** Law enforcement admin.

Contact. Phone: (866) 489-8818 Toll-free number: (866) 489-8818 Chip Hinton, Director of Recruitment, ITT Technical Institute: Duluth, 10700 Abbotts Bridge Road, Duluth, GA 30097

Kennesaw State University
Kennesaw, Georgia
www.kennesaw.edu

CB member
CB code: 5359

- Public 4-year university
- Commuter campus in large town
- 29,842 degree-seeking undergraduates: 24% part-time, 49% women, 20% African American, 4% Asian American, 9% Hispanic/Latino, 4% Multi-racial, non-Hispanic, 2% international
- 2,698 degree-seeking graduate students
- 59% of applicants admitted
- SAT or ACT (ACT writing optional) required
- 42% graduate within 6 years

General. Founded in 1963. Regionally accredited. **Degrees:** 4,377 bachelor's awarded; master's, doctoral offered. **ROTC:** Army, Air Force. **Location:** 27 miles from Atlanta. **Calendar:** Semester, limited summer session. **Full-time faculty:** 1,019 total; 78% have terminal degrees, 25% minority, 49% women. **Part-time faculty:** 736 total; 34% have terminal degrees, 24% minority, 59% women. **Class size:** 32% < 20, 49% 20-39, 7% 40-49, 10% 50-99, 2% >100. **Special facilities:** Museum of History and Holocaust Education; The Bentley Rare Book Gallery; Zuckerman Museum of Art; The 3D Center; Alternative Energy Innovation Center; Center for Advanced Materials Research and Education; Center for Student Leadership; The Civil War Center; The Entrepreneurship Center; The ESL Center; Mobile Application Development Center; Student Development Center; Visualization and Simulation Research Center.

Freshman class profile. 14,215 applied, 8,323 admitted, 5,032 enrolled.

Mid 50% test scores		Rank in top quarter:	45%
SAT critical reading:	510-590	Rank in top tenth:	35%
SAT math:	500-590	End year in good standing:	82%
SAT writing:	470-570	Return as sophomores:	78%
ACT composite:	21-25	Out-of-state:	12%
GPA 3.75 or higher:	13%	Live on campus:	57%
GPA 3.50-3.74:	17%	International:	1%
GPA 3.0-3.49:	43%	Fraternities:	2%
GPA 2.0-2.99:	27%	Sororities:	6%

Basis for selection. GED not accepted. Requirements include combined Critical Reading and Math total of 950 SAT (exclusive of Writing), (20 ACT), freshman index of at least 1940, with SAT-Critical Reading/Verbal of at least 490 (ACT 20) and SAT-Math of at least 460 (ACT 19), and GPA of at least 2.5 in the required H.S. curriculum as calculated by KSU. (The SAT essay portion must be submitted, but will not be used in the decision.). Audition required for dance and music programs. Portfolio required for art majors. **Home schooled:** Applicants are considered if they meet required high school curriculum preparedness on appropriate standardized subject matter tests (specific SAT II subject exams or through a portfolio review process) and meet or exceed required minimum freshmen SAT or ACT scores. **Learning Disabled:** Students must visit the Office for Student Disability Services and make an appointment to arrange an individual assistance plan. In most cases, certification of disability is required. Special services are based on medical and/or psychological certification of disability, eligibility for services by outside agencies, and ability to complete tasks required in courses.

High school preparation. College-preparatory program required. 17 units required. Required units include English 4, mathematics 4, social studies 3, science 4 (laboratory 2) and foreign language 2.

2015-2016 Annual costs. Tuition/fees: $7,326; $20,782 out-of-state. Room/board: $10,210.

Financial aid. Non-need-based: Scholarships awarded for academics, alumni affiliation, art, athletics, job skills, leadership, minority status, music/drama, ROTC, state residency.

Application procedures. Admission: Priority date 10/30; deadline 5/6 (receipt date). $40 fee, may be waived for applicants with need. Admission notification on a rolling basis beginning on or about 1/1. **Financial aid:** Priority date 4/1; no closing date. FAFSA required. Applicants notified on a rolling basis starting 4/1.

Academics. Special study options: Cooperative education, cross-registration, distance learning, double major, ESL, honors, internships, study abroad, teacher certification program, weekend college. **Credit/placement by examination:** AP, CLEP, IB, institutional tests. 30 credit hours maximum toward bachelor's degree. **Support services:** Learning center, reduced course load, remedial instruction, study skills assistance, tutoring, writing center.

Honors college/program. Honors opportunities available for students with 3.5 GPA and 1200 SAT (exclusive of Writing)/26 ACT.

Majors. Architecture: Architecture. **Area/ethnic studies:** African. **Biology:** General, biochemistry, biotechnology. **Business:** Accounting, business admin, construction management, finance, international, logistics, managerial economics, marketing, restaurant/food services, sales/distribution. **Communications:** Communications/speech/rhetoric, journalism, persuasive communications. **Computer sciences:** General, applications programming, computer science, information systems, information technology, security. **Conservation:** Environmental science. **Education:** Art, biology, early childhood, elementary, English, mathematics, middle, music, physical, physics, social studies. **Engineering:** Civil, construction, electrical, environmental, mechanical, software, systems. **English:** English lit. **Health services:** Public health ed. **History:** General. **Math:** General, applied. **Parks/recreation:** Exercise sciences, sports admin. **Philosophy/religion:** Philosophy. **Physical sciences:** Chemistry, physics. **Protective services:** Criminal justice. **Psychology:** General. **Social sciences:** Anthropology, geography, GIS/cartography, international relations, political science, sociology. **Visual/performing arts:** General, art, art history/conservation, dance, dramatic, music, music performance.

Most popular majors. Business/marketing 21%, communications/journalism 8%, computer/information sciences 8%, education 9%, engineering/engineering technologies 10%, psychology 6%, social sciences 7%.

Technology on campus. 4,649 workstations in library, computer center, student center. Dormitories wired for high-speed internet access and linked to campus network. Commuter students can connect to campus network. Online course registration, online library, helpline, repair service, student web hosting, wireless network available.

Student life. Freshman orientation: Mandatory, $65 fee. Preregistration for classes offered. **Housing:** Apartments available. $375 nonrefundable deposit. **Activities:** Bands, campus ministries, choral groups, dance, drama, international student organizations, literary magazine, music ensembles, Model UN, musical theater, opera, radio station, student government, student newspaper, symphony orchestra, Baptist Collegiate Ministries, Catholic Student Union, The Journey, College Libertarians of KSU, College Republicans, Young Americans for Liberty, African Students Association, International Student Association, Kiwanis Circle K, KSU Red Cross club.

Athletics. NCAA. **Intercollegiate:** Baseball M, basketball, cross-country, football (tackle) M, golf, lacrosse W, soccer W, softball W, tennis, track and field, volleyball W. **Intramural:** Basketball, bowling, football (non-tackle), golf, soccer, softball, tennis, ultimate frisbee, volleyball. **Team name:** Owls.

Student services. Adult student services, alcohol/substance abuse counseling, career counseling, services for economically disadvantaged, student employment services, financial aid counseling, health services, minority student services, personal counseling, placement for graduates, veterans' counselor. **Physically disabled:** Services for visually, speech, hearing impaired.

Contact. E-mail: ksuadmit@kennesaw.edu
Phone: (770) 423-6300 Fax: (470) 578-9169
Angela Evans, Director of Student Recruitment and Admissions, Kennesaw State University, 3391 Town Point Drive, Kennesaw, GA 30144

LaGrange College
LaGrange, Georgia
www.lagrange.edu

CB member
CB code: 5362

- Private 4-year liberal arts college affiliated with the United Methodist Church
- Residential campus in large town
- 905 degree-seeking undergraduates: 5% part-time, 50% women, 25% African American, 1% Asian American, 2% Hispanic/Latino, 3% Multi-racial, non-Hispanic
- 116 degree-seeking graduate students
- 57% of applicants admitted

▶ SAT or ACT (ACT writing optional), application essay required

▶ 46% graduate within 6 years

General. Founded in 1831. Regionally accredited. **Degrees:** 169 bachelor's awarded; master's offered. **Location:** 70 miles from Atlanta, 45 miles from Columbus. **Calendar:** 4-1-4, extensive summer session. **Full-time faculty:** 71 total; 1% have terminal degrees, 7% minority, 49% women. **Part-time faculty:** 36 total; 3% have terminal degrees, 14% minority, 44% women. **Class size:** 72% < 20, 24% 20-39, 3% 40-49, less than 1% 50-99. **Special facilities:** Performing arts auditorium, natatorium, art center.

Freshman class profile. 1,530 applied, 876 admitted, 269 enrolled.

Mid 50% test scores			
SAT critical reading:	450-550	GPA 3.0-3.49:	38%
SAT math:	440-550	GPA 2.0-2.99:	13%
SAT writing:	430-520	Rank in top quarter:	41%
ACT composite:	20-24	Rank in top tenth:	18%
GPA 3.75 or higher:	27%	Return as sophomores:	67%
GPA 3.50-3.74:	22%	Out-of-state:	23%
		Live on campus:	87%

Basis for selection. School achievement record and test scores most important. Interview and recommendations considered. Separate application typically during sophomore year for nursing applicants. **Home schooled:** Bibliography of high school readings, including textbooks, letter of recommendation from outside the home required.

High school preparation. College-preparatory program recommended. 14 units required; 16 recommended. Required and recommended units include English 4, mathematics 4, social studies 3, science 3 and foreign language 2.

2015-2016 Annual costs. Tuition/fees: $27,510. Room/board: $11,240. Books/supplies: $1,000. Personal expenses: $1,500.

2014-2015 Financial aid. **Need-based:** 225 full-time freshmen applied for aid; 213 deemed to have need; 213 received aid. Average need met was 75%. Average scholarship/grant was $15,282; average loan $3,274. 78% of total undergraduate aid awarded as scholarships/grants, 22% as loans/jobs. **Non-need-based:** Awarded to 142 full-time undergraduates, including 24 freshmen. Scholarships awarded for academics, art, leadership, music/drama, religious affiliation, state residency.

Application procedures. **Admission:** Priority date 5/15; deadline 8/31. No application fee. Admission notification on a rolling basis beginning on or about 10/1. Must reply by May 1 or within 2 week(s) if notified thereafter. **Financial aid:** Priority date 3/1; no closing date. FAFSA required. Applicants notified on a rolling basis starting 3/15; must reply within 4 week(s) of notification.

Academics. **Special study options:** Accelerated study, combined bachelor's/graduate degree, double major, dual enrollment of high school students, ESL, independent study, internships, student-designed major, study abroad, teacher certification program, Washington semester. Interim classes in January, Dual Engineering degree with Georgia Institute of Technology and Auburn University, Servant Scholars Program. **Credit/placement by examination:** AP, CLEP, IB, SAT, ACT, institutional tests. 6 credit hours maximum toward bachelor's degree. USAFI credit accepted. **Support services:** Reduced course load, remedial instruction, study skills assistance, tutoring, writing center.

Majors. Biology: General, biochemistry. **Business:** Accounting, business admin, nonprofit/public, organizational leadership. **Computer sciences:** General. **Education:** Elementary, mathematics, social studies. **Engineering:** General. **English:** English lit. **Foreign languages:** Spanish. **Health services:** Nursing (RN). **History:** General. **Liberal arts:** Arts/sciences. **Math:** General. **Parks/recreation:** Exercise sciences. **Philosophy/religion:** General, religion. **Physical sciences:** Chemistry. **Psychology:** General. **Social sciences:** Political science, sociology. **Visual/performing arts:** General, dramatic, music, music performance, music technology, musical theater.

Most popular majors. Biology 6%, business/marketing 14%, education 7%, health sciences 27%, parks/recreation 10%, psychology 7%, visual/performing arts 8%.

Technology on campus. 141 workstations in dormitories, library, computer center. Dormitories wired for high-speed internet access and linked to campus network. Commuter students can connect to campus network. Online library, helpline, student web hosting, wireless network available.

Student life. Freshman orientation: Mandatory. Preregistration for classes offered. Three 2-day summer orientation sessions available. **Policies:** Honor Code and Social Code. **Housing:** Guaranteed on-campus for all undergraduates. Coed dorms, single-sex dorms, special housing for disabled, apartments, fraternity/sorority housing, themed housing available. $100 partly refundable deposit. **Activities:** Pep band, campus ministries, choral groups, drama, international student organizations, literary magazine, music ensembles, musical theater, student government, student newspaper, symphony

orchestra, Wesley Fellowship, Baptist student union, Rotaract, interfaith council, black collegiate student union, Reformed Bible Study, Servant Fellows, Panther Toy Store, bus project.

Athletics. NCAA. **Intercollegiate:** Baseball M, basketball, cheerleading W, cross-country, football (tackle) M, golf M, lacrosse W, soccer, softball W, swimming, tennis, volleyball W. **Intramural:** Basketball, football (non-tackle), softball, table tennis, water polo. **Team name:** Panthers.

Student services. Adult student services, chaplain/spiritual director, career counseling, student employment services, financial aid counseling, health services, personal counseling, placement for graduates.

Contact. E-mail: admission@lagrange.edu
Phone: (706) 880-8005 Toll-free number: (800) 593-2885
Fax: (706) 880-8010
Michael Thomas, Director of Admission, LaGrange College, 601 Broad Street, LaGrange, GA 30240-2999

Life University
Marietta, Georgia
www.life.edu   CB code: 7006

▶ Private 4-year university

▶ Commuter campus in very large city

▶ 718 degree-seeking undergraduates: 27% part-time, 51% women

▶ 1,990 degree-seeking graduate students

▶ 59% of applicants admitted

General. Regionally accredited. **Degrees:** 93 bachelor's, 11 associate awarded; master's, professional offered. **Location:** 10 miles from downtown Atlanta. **Calendar:** Quarter, extensive summer session. **Full-time faculty:** 130 total; 86% have terminal degrees, 28% minority, 46% women. **Part-time faculty:** 54 total; 67% have terminal degrees, 22% minority, 44% women. **Class size:** 85% < 20, 12% 20-39, 3% 40-49. **Special facilities:** 19th Century Village, Fitness Trail.

Freshman class profile. 301 applied, 177 admitted, 93 enrolled.

End year in good standing:	86%	Out-of-state:	61%
Return as sophomores:	63%	Live on campus:	5%

Basis for selection. Standardized test scores and high school record most important. 2.0 GPA and 1430 SAT (including Writing) or 18 ACT important. SAT or ACT recommended. **Home schooled:** Transcript of courses and grades required. **Learning Disabled:** Letter from doctor required.

High school preparation. College-preparatory program recommended. Recommended units include English 4, mathematics 4, social studies 3, science 4, computer science 3 and academic electives 4.

2015-2016 Annual costs. Tuition/fees: $10,860. Books/supplies: $1,650. Personal expenses: $3,900.

2015-2016 Financial aid. **Need-based:** 82 full-time freshmen applied for aid; 74 deemed to have need; 74 received aid. Average need met was 24%. Average scholarship/grant was $5,000; average loan $3,500. 62% of total undergraduate aid awarded as scholarships/grants, 38% as loans/jobs. **Non-need-based:** Scholarships awarded for academics, alumni affiliation, athletics, leadership, minority status, state residency.

Application procedures. **Admission:** Closing date 9/7 (postmark date). $50 fee, may be waived for applicants with need. Admission notification on a rolling basis. **Financial aid:** Priority date 3/15; no closing date. FAFSA required. Applicants notified on a rolling basis starting 3/1.

Academics. **Special study options:** Accelerated study, combined bachelor's/graduate degree, dual enrollment of high school students, ESL, independent study, internships. **Credit/placement by examination:** AP, CLEP, SAT, ACT. **Support services:** Learning center, reduced course load, remedial instruction, study skills assistance, tutoring, writing center.

Majors. Biology: General, exercise physiology. **Business:** General, management information systems. **Computer sciences:** General. **Parks/recreation:** Exercise sciences. **Psychology:** General.

Most popular majors. Biology 35%, health sciences 13%, liberal arts 6%, parks/recreation 13%, psychology 13%.

Technology on campus. Dormitories wired for high-speed internet access and linked to campus network. Commuter students can connect to campus network. Online course registration, online library, helpline, wireless network available.

Student life. Freshman orientation: Mandatory. Preregistration for classes offered. Two-day program usually held on Thursday and Friday before quarter begins. **Housing:** Coed dorms, apartments, wellness housing available. $250 partly refundable deposit. Pets allowed in dorm rooms. **Activities:** International student organizations, student government, student newspaper.

Athletics. NAIA. **Intercollegiate:** Basketball M, bowling, cross-country, rugby, swimming, track and field M, weight lifting M, wrestling. **Intramural:** Basketball, bowling, cross-country, football (non-tackle), rugby, soccer, softball, swimming, volleyball, weight lifting W, wrestling. **Team name:** Eagles.

Student services. Alcohol/substance abuse counseling, career counseling, services for economically disadvantaged, student employment services, financial aid counseling, health services, minority student services, personal counseling. **Physically disabled:** Services for visually, speech, hearing impaired.

Contact. E-mail: admissions@life.edu
Phone: (770) 426-2884 Toll-free number: (800) 543-3202
Fax: (770) 426-2895
Stephanie Buchanan, Director of Admissions Operations, Life University, 1269 Barclay Circle, Marietta, GA 30060

Luther Rice University
Lithonia, Georgia
www.LutherRice.edu

- Private 4-year university, Bible and seminary college affiliated with the Baptist faith
- Commuter campus in very large city
- 408 degree-seeking undergraduates
- Application essay required

General. Regionally accredited; also accredited by TRACS. All degrees can be completed online. **Degrees:** 85 bachelor's awarded; master's, professional offered. **Location:** 19 miles from Atlanta. **Calendar:** Trimester, extensive summer session. **Full-time faculty:** 16 total; 81% have terminal degrees, 19% minority, 12% women. **Part-time faculty:** 18 total; 67% have terminal degrees, 6% minority, 11% women. **Class size:** 43% < 20, 50% 20-39, 7% 40-49.

Basis for selection. Open admission. **Home schooled:** Transcript of courses and grades, state high school equivalency certificate, letter of recommendation (nonparent) required. Bible knowledge test required.

2015-2016 Annual costs. Tuition/fees: $7,920. Books/supplies: $1,000.

2014-2015 Financial aid. Need-based: 3 full-time freshmen applied for aid; 1 deemed to have need; 1 received aid. 29% of total undergraduate aid awarded as scholarships/grants, 71% as loans/jobs. **Non-need-based:** Awarded to 27 full-time undergraduates, including 3 freshmen. Scholarships awarded for academics.

Application procedures. Admission: No deadline. $50 fee, may be waived for applicants with need. Admission notification on a rolling basis. **Financial aid:** No deadline. FAFSA required. Applicants notified on a rolling basis.

Academics. Special study options: Distance learning, external degree, independent study, internships, weekend college. **Credit/placement by examination:** AP, CLEP. **Support services:** Reduced course load, remedial instruction.

Technology on campus. Commuter students can connect to campus network. Online library, wireless network available.

Student life. Freshman orientation: Available. Preregistration for classes offered. **Activities:** Campus ministries, student government, student newspaper.

Student services. Alcohol/substance abuse counseling, chaplain/spiritual director, career counseling, student employment services, financial aid counseling, personal counseling, placement for graduates, veterans' counselor.

Contact. E-mail: admissions@LutherRice.edu
Phone: (770) 484-1204 Toll-free number: (800) 442-1577
Fax: (770) 484-1155
Gary Cook, Director of Admissions, Luther Rice University, 3038 Evans Mill Road, Lithonia, GA 30038

Mercer University
Macon, Georgia
www.mercer.edu
CB member
CB code: 5409

- Private 4-year university
- Residential campus in small city
- 2,851 degree-seeking undergraduates: 2% part-time, 50% women, 18% African American, 8% Asian American, 5% Hispanic/Latino, 4% Multiracial, non-Hispanic, 4% international
- 3,913 degree-seeking graduate students
- 67% of applicants admitted
- SAT or ACT (ACT writing optional), application essay required
- 61% graduate within 6 years; 37% enter graduate study

General. Founded in 1833. Regionally accredited. **Degrees:** 464 bachelor's awarded; master's, professional, doctoral offered. **ROTC:** Army. **Location:** 85 miles from Atlanta. **Calendar:** Semester, extensive summer session. **Full-time faculty:** 391 total; 92% have terminal degrees, 23% minority, 46% women. **Part-time faculty:** 324 total; 56% have terminal degrees, 24% minority, 57% women. **Class size:** 53% < 20, 40% 20-39, 3% 40-49, 4% 50-99, less than 1% >100. **Special facilities:** Opera house.

Freshman class profile. 4,559 applied, 3,049 admitted, 831 enrolled.

Mid 50% test scores			
SAT critical reading:	550-650	Rank in top quarter:	73%
SAT math:	560-660	Rank in top tenth:	45%
SAT writing:	530-630	Return as sophomores:	87%
ACT composite:	24-30	Out-of-state:	20%
GPA 3.75 or higher:	58%	Live on campus:	92%
GPA 3.50-3.74:	28%	International:	3%
GPA 3.0-3.49:	12%	Fraternities:	21%
GPA 2.0-2.99:	2%	Sororities:	21%

Basis for selection. Minimum admission requirements include GPA of 3.3 recalculated, ACT 23 or SAT 1060. Engineering applicants must have 500 or above on English portion of SAT and 560 or above on math portion. Recommendation letters optional. Interview recommended. Audition recommended for music majors. **Home schooled:** Transcript of courses and grades, interview required. 1100 SAT (exclusive of Writing) and certified transcript indicating college-preparatory curriculum, including titles of textbooks, required. SAT Subject Tests or AP exams may be substituted for certified transcript. **Learning Disabled:** Documentation from licensed professional required.

High school preparation. College-preparatory program required. 16 units required. Required units include English 4, mathematics 4, social studies 1, history 2, science 3 (laboratory 3) and foreign language 2.

2015-2016 Annual costs. Tuition/fees: $34,450. Room/board: $10,898. Books/supplies: $1,200. Personal expenses: $1,575.

2015-2016 Financial aid. Need-based: 827 full-time freshmen applied for aid; 609 deemed to have need; 609 received aid. Average need met was 89%. Average scholarship/grant was $25,648; average loan $8,776. 71% of total undergraduate aid awarded as scholarships/grants, 29% as loans/jobs. **Non-need-based:** Awarded to 1,426 full-time undergraduates, including 443 freshmen. Scholarships awarded for academics, art, athletics, job skills, leadership, music/drama, religious affiliation, ROTC, state residency.

Application procedures. Admission: Priority date 11/1; deadline 4/1 (postmark date). $50 fee, may be waived for applicants with need. Admission notification on a rolling basis beginning on or about 9/15. Must reply by May 1 or within 4 week(s) if notified thereafter. **Financial aid:** Priority date 4/1; no closing date. FAFSA, institutional form required. Applicants notified on a rolling basis starting 3/15; must reply within 2 week(s) of notification.

Academics. Special study options: Accelerated study, combined bachelor's/graduate degree, cooperative education, cross-registration, distance learning, double major, dual enrollment of high school students, ESL, honors, independent study, internships, liberal arts/career combination, student-designed major, study abroad, teacher certification program. **Credit/placement by examination:** AP, CLEP, IB, SAT, ACT, institutional tests. 32 credit hours maximum toward bachelor's degree. **Support services:** Learning center, pre-admission summer program, reduced course load, study skills assistance, tutoring.

Honors college/program. Applicants are required to have a 1280 SAT or 29 ACT with a minimum of a 3.7 GPA to be considered for the Honor's program. Mercer has five academic honors programs: Research, Service, International, Engineering, and Business. The requirements vary by program.

Majors. Area/ethnic studies: African, regional, women's. **Biology:** General, biochemistry, environmental. **Business:** General, accounting, finance, international, management information systems, marketing, training/development. **Communications:** Communications/speech/rhetoric, journalism, media studies. **Computer sciences:** Computer science, informatics, information systems. **Conservation:** Environmental science, environmental studies. **Education:** Early childhood, elementary, middle, music. **Engineering:** General, biomedical, computer, electrical, mechanical, software. **English:** Creative writing, English lit. **Foreign languages:** Classics, French, German, Latin, Spanish. **Health services:** Nursing (RN), predental, premedicine, prenursing, prepharmacy, prephysical therapy. **History:** General. **Human services:** Community org/advocacy. **Liberal arts:** Arts/sciences. **Math:** General. **Philosophy/religion:** Christian, philosophy. **Physical sciences:** Chemistry, physics. **Protective services:** Criminal justice. **Psychology:** General. **Social sciences:** Economics, international relations, political science, sociology. **Visual/performing arts:** Art, conducting, dramatic, music, music performance.

Most popular majors. Biology 16%, business/marketing 20%, communications/journalism 6%, engineering/engineering technologies 13%, foreign language 6%, psychology 6%, social sciences 7%.

Technology on campus. Dormitories wired for high-speed internet access and linked to campus network. Commuter students can connect to campus network. Online course registration, online library, helpline, repair service, wireless network available.

Student life. Freshman orientation: Mandatory. Preregistration for classes offered. 4-day program before semester begins. **Policies:** Alcohol not permitted on campus. **Housing:** Guaranteed on-campus for freshmen. Coed dorms, single-sex dorms, special housing for disabled, apartments, fraternity/sorority housing, themed housing available. **Activities:** Bands, campus ministries, choral groups, dance, drama, film society, international student organizations, literary magazine, music ensembles, musical theater, opera, radio station, student government, student newspaper, symphony orchestra, TV station, Cooperative Student Fellowship, Habitat for Humanity, Alpha Phi Omega National Service Fraternity, College Republicans, College Democrats, Engineers without Borders, housing center, Indian cultural exchange, organization of black students, Students for Environmental Action.

Athletics. NCAA. **Intercollegiate:** Baseball M, basketball, cross-country, football (tackle) M, golf, lacrosse, sand volleyball W, soccer, softball W, tennis, track and field W, volleyball W. **Intramural:** Basketball, football (non-tackle), golf, sand volleyball, soccer, softball, table tennis, tennis, ultimate frisbee. **Team name:** Bears.

Student services. Adult student services, alcohol/substance abuse counseling, chaplain/spiritual director, career counseling, services for economically disadvantaged, student employment services, financial aid counseling, health services, minority student services, personal counseling, placement for graduates. **Physically disabled:** Services for visually, speech, hearing impaired.

Contact. E-mail: admissions@mercer.edu
Phone: (478) 301-2650 Toll-free number: (800) 840-8577
Fax: (478) 301-2828
Kelly Holloway, Director of Freshman Admissions, Mercer University, 1501 Mercer University Drive, Macon, GA 31207-0001

Middle Georgia State College
Macon, Georgia
www.mga.edu   CB code: 5411

- Public 4-year liberal arts college
- Commuter campus in small city
- 7,164 degree-seeking undergraduates
- SAT or ACT (ACT writing optional) required

General. Founded in 1884. Regionally accredited. Eastman campus offers certificates and degrees for aviation careers. **Degrees:** 670 bachelor's, 470 associate awarded. **ROTC:** Army. **Location:** 85 miles from Atlanta. **Calendar:** Semester, limited summer session. **Full-time faculty:** 310 total. **Part-time faculty:** 103 total. **Special facilities:** Botanical garden.

Basis for selection. Applicants to bachelor's degree programs must have a minimum 430 SAT Critical Reading and 400 SAT Math, 17 ACT English and 17 ACT Math or COMPASS test scores of 70 English/ Writing, 78 Reading, and 37 Algebra, minimum freshman index of 1850, and complete required high school curriculum. Applicants to associate degree programs must have a minimum high school GPA of 2.0, submit SAT/ ACT or COMPASS scores, and have a maximum of 4 required high school deficiencies. Associate degree students may also use the COMPASS test for admission and placement purposes. **Home schooled:** Transcript of courses and grades required. Additional requirements for home schooled students.

High school preparation. College-preparatory program recommended. 13 units required; 17 recommended. Required and recommended units include

English 4, mathematics 3-4, social studies 1, history 2, science 3-4 (laboratory 1) and foreign language 2. 17 high school units required for admission to bachelor's programs.

2015-2016 Annual costs. Tuition/fees: $4,522; $13,308 out-of-state. Room/board: $8,210.

Financial aid. Non-need-based: Scholarships awarded for academics, alumni affiliation, art, athletics, job skills, leadership, minority status, music/drama, state residency.

Application procedures. Admission: Priority date 5/1; deadline 7/16 (receipt date). $25 fee, may be waived for applicants with need. Application must be submitted online. Admission notification on a rolling basis. Admissions application deadline: 30 days before first day of registration for term you wish to enroll. **Financial aid:** Closing date 7/16. FAFSA required. Applicants notified on a rolling basis starting 5/1.

Academics. Special study options: Accelerated study, distance learning, double major, dual enrollment of high school students, exchange student, honors, independent study, internships, study abroad, weekend college. Weekend college at Dublin campus only; Georgia Academy of Mathematics, Engineering and Science is 2-year residential joint enrollment program for gifted high school juniors and seniors to pursue associate degree utilizing dual credits. **Credit/placement by examination:** AP, CLEP, IB, SAT, ACT, institutional tests. 40 credit hours maximum toward associate degree, 40 toward bachelor's. **Support services:** Learning center, reduced course load, remedial instruction, study skills assistance, tutoring, writing center.

Majors. Biology: General. **Business:** Accounting, business admin, logistics, marketing, operations. **Communications:** Digital media. **Computer sciences:** Information technology. **Education:** Biology, early childhood, English, history, mathematics, middle. **English:** English lit. **Health services:** Health services admin, nursing (RN), respiratory therapy technology. **History:** General. **Math:** General. **Psychology:** General.

Technology on campus. Dormitories wired for high-speed internet access and linked to campus network. Commuter students can connect to campus network. Online course registration, online library, helpline, wireless network available.

Student life. Freshman orientation: Available, $25 fee. Preregistration for classes offered. One-day sessions held in fall, spring and summer. **Policies:** Alcohol not allowed on campus. Smoking in designated areas only. **Housing:** Guaranteed on-campus for all undergraduates. Coed dorms, wellness housing available. $150 nonrefundable deposit, deadline 7/1. **Activities:** Jazz band, campus ministries, choral groups, dance, drama, literary magazine, music ensembles, musical theater, student government, student newspaper, Baptist student union, Wesley Foundation, minority alliance club, Rotaract, cultural relations club, Young Republicans, Young Democrats, Fellowship of Christian Athletes.

Athletics. NJCAA. **Intercollegiate:** Baseball M, basketball, soccer, softball W. **Intramural:** Badminton, basketball, football (tackle), golf, handball M, softball, tennis, volleyball, weight lifting. **Team name:** Knights.

Student services. Adult student services, alcohol/substance abuse counseling, career counseling, services for economically disadvantaged, student employment services, financial aid counseling, health services, minority student services, personal counseling, veterans' counselor. **Physically disabled:** Services for visually, hearing impaired.

Contact. E-mail: admissions@mga.edu
Phone: (478) 471-2800 Toll-free number: (800) 272-7619
Fax: (478) 471-5343
Margaret Woodham, Director of Enrollment Services, Middle Georgia State College, 100 College Station Drive, Macon, GA 31206

Morehouse College
Atlanta, Georgia   CB member
www.morehouse.edu   CB code: 5415

- Private 4-year liberal arts college for men
- Residential campus in very large city
- 2,163 degree-seeking undergraduates: 4% part-time, 95% African American, 1% Hispanic/Latino, 2% international
- 76% of applicants admitted
- SAT or ACT (ACT writing recommended), application essay, interview required
- 53% graduate within 6 years

General. Founded in 1867. Regionally accredited. One of 4 members of Atlanta University Center sharing facilities including library. **Degrees:** 332

bachelor's awarded. **ROTC:** Army, Naval, Air Force. **Location:** 3 miles from downtown. **Calendar:** Semester, limited summer session. **Full-time faculty:** 160 total; 82% have terminal degrees, 76% minority, 36% women. **Part-time faculty:** 49 total; 29% have terminal degrees, 80% minority, 39% women. **Class size:** 50% < 20, 47% 20-39, 2% 40-49, 1% 50-99. **Special facilities:** Chapels, meditation room.

Freshman class profile. 2,288 applied, 1,738 admitted, 598 enrolled.

Mid 50% test scores		GPA 2.0-2.99:	40%
SAT critical reading:	440-550	Rank in top quarter:	30%
SAT math:	430-550	Rank in top tenth:	11%
SAT writing:	410-520	End year in good standing:	73%
ACT composite:	18-23	Return as sophomores:	83%
GPA 3.75 or higher:	15%	Out-of-state:	69%
GPA 3.50-3.74:	11%	Live on campus:	100%
GPA 3.0-3.49:	31%		

Basis for selection. Academic record most important, followed by test scores, counselor recommendation(s), school and community activities, and student leadership. SAT and SAT Subject Tests or ACT, SAT Subject Tests recommended.

High school preparation. College-preparatory program recommended. 11 units required; 16 recommended. Required and recommended units include English 4, mathematics 3, social studies 2, science 2, foreign language 2 and academic electives 3.

2016-2017 Annual costs. Tuition/fees: $26,742. Room/board: $13,322.

2015-2016 Financial aid. Need-based: 590 full-time freshmen applied for aid; 522 deemed to have need; 514 received aid. Average need met was 50%. Average scholarship/grant was $15,904; average loan $3,611. 80% of total undergraduate aid awarded as scholarships/grants, 20% as loans/jobs. **Non-need-based:** Awarded to 275 full-time undergraduates, including 63 freshmen. Scholarships awarded for academics, alumni affiliation, art, athletics, job skills, leadership, music/drama, ROTC, state residency.

Application procedures. Admission: Priority date 11/1; deadline 2/15 (postmark date). $50 fee, may be waived for applicants with need. Admission notification by 4/1. Admission notification on a rolling basis beginning on or about 3/15. Must reply by May 1 or within 2 week(s) if notified thereafter. **Financial aid:** Priority date 2/15, closing date 4/1. FAFSA required. Applicants notified on a rolling basis; must reply within 2 week(s) of notification.

Academics. Special study options: Combined bachelor's/graduate degree, cooperative education, cross-registration, double major, dual enrollment of high school students, exchange student, honors, independent study, internships, liberal arts/career combination, semester at sea, study abroad, teacher certification program. Dual degree program in engineering and architecture with other institutions. **Credit/placement by examination:** AP, CLEP, IB, SAT, ACT, institutional tests. 60 credit hours maximum toward bachelor's degree. **Support services:** Learning center, pre-admission summer program, reduced course load, remedial instruction, study skills assistance, tutoring, writing center.

Majors. Area/ethnic studies: African-American. **Biology:** General. **Business:** Business admin. **Computer sciences:** General. **Education:** Early childhood. **Engineering:** Applied physics, engineering science. **English:** English lit. **Foreign languages:** French, Spanish. **History:** General. **Math:** General. **Parks/recreation:** Health/fitness. **Philosophy/religion:** Philosophy, religion. **Physical sciences:** Chemistry, physics. **Psychology:** General. **Social sciences:** Economics, political science, sociology, urban studies. **Visual/performing arts:** Art, dramatic, film/cinema/video, music.

Most popular majors. Biology 9%, business/marketing 24%, English 6%, psychology 6%, social sciences 20%, visual/performing arts 8%.

Technology on campus. 1,158 workstations in library, computer center, student center. Dormitories wired for high-speed internet access and linked to campus network. Commuter students can connect to campus network. Online course registration, online library, helpline, repair service, wireless network available.

Student life. Freshman orientation: Mandatory, $588 fee. Preregistration for classes offered. Held several days before class begins each fall. **Housing:** Guaranteed on-campus for freshmen. Apartments, themed housing available. $588 nonrefundable deposit, deadline 5/1. **Activities:** Bands, campus ministries, choral groups, dance, drama, film society, international student organizations, literary magazine, music ensembles, Model UN, student government, student newspaper, symphony orchestra, Martin Luther King International Chapel Assistants, mentoring program, Frederick Douglass Tutorial Program, political science club, New Life Inspirational Gospel Choir, NAACP, Eagle Scout Association.

Athletics. NCAA. Intercollegiate: Baseball M, basketball M, cross-country M, football (tackle) M, golf M, tennis M, track and field M. **Intramural:** Basketball M, football (non-tackle) M, golf M, lacrosse M, rugby M, soccer M, swimming M, tennis M, volleyball M. **Team name:** Maroon Tigers.

Student services. Alcohol/substance abuse counseling, chaplain/spiritual director, career counseling, student employment services, financial aid counseling, health services, personal counseling, placement for graduates, veterans' counselor. **Physically disabled:** Services for visually, speech, hearing impaired.

Contact. E-mail: admissions@morehouse.edu
Phone: (404) 215-2632 Fax: (404) 572-3668
Darryl Isom, Director of Admissions and Recruitment, Morehouse College, 830 Westview Drive SW, Atlanta, GA 30314

Oglethorpe University
Atlanta, Georgia
www.oglethorpe.edu

CB member
CB code: 5521

▸ Private 4-year liberal arts college
▸ Residential campus in very large city
▸ 1,125 degree-seeking undergraduates: 6% part-time, 58% women, 18% African American, 3% Asian American, 10% Hispanic/Latino, 3% Multiracial, non-Hispanic, 7% international
▸ 78% of applicants admitted
▸ SAT or ACT (ACT writing recommended) required
▸ 53% graduate within 6 years

General. Founded in 1835. Regionally accredited. **Degrees:** 190 bachelor's awarded. **ROTC:** Army, Naval, Air Force. **Location:** 10 miles from downtown. **Calendar:** Semester, extensive summer session. **Full-time faculty:** 59 total; 92% have terminal degrees, 15% minority, 39% women. **Part-time faculty:** 39 total; 51% have terminal degrees, 13% minority, 51% women. **Class size:** 70% < 20, 30% 20-39. **Special facilities:** Art museum, performing arts center.

Freshman class profile. 2,768 applied, 2,172 admitted, 445 enrolled.

Mid 50% test scores		GPA 2.0-2.99:	9%
SAT critical reading:	530-630	Rank in top quarter:	58%
SAT math:	510-610	Rank in top tenth:	29%
SAT writing:	500-610	Return as sophomores:	73%
ACT composite:	22-28	Out-of-state:	26%
GPA 3.75 or higher:	40%	Live on campus:	84%
GPA 3.50-3.74:	24%	International:	5%
GPA 3.0-3.49:	27%		

Basis for selection. High school GPA and general academic record most important, followed by test scores. Recommendations required. Activities considered. Oglethorpe accepts the TOEFL for international students as well. Interview recommended.

High school preparation. College-preparatory program recommended. Required and recommended units include English 4, mathematics 3, social studies 3, science 2 and foreign language 2. Honors, AP, IB recommended where available.

2016-2017 Annual costs. Tuition/fees (projected): $35,425. Room/board: $12,710. Books/supplies: $1,100. Personal expenses: $2,000.

2015-2016 Financial aid. Need-based: 282 full-time freshmen applied for aid; 259 deemed to have need; 259 received aid. Average need met was 78%. Average scholarship/grant was $27,004; average loan $3,325. 78% of total undergraduate aid awarded as scholarships/grants, 22% as loans/jobs. **Non-need-based:** Awarded to 414 full-time undergraduates, including 102 freshmen. Scholarships awarded for academics, art, leadership, music/drama, religious affiliation, state residency.

Application procedures. Admission: $50 fee, may be waived for applicants with need. Admission notification on a rolling basis beginning on or about 12/5. Must reply by May 1 or within 3 week(s) if notified thereafter. **Financial aid:** Priority date 2/15; no closing date. FAFSA required. Applicants notified on a rolling basis starting 3/1; must reply by 5/1 or within 2 week(s) of notification.

Academics. Special study options: Accelerated study, cooperative education, cross-registration, double major, dual enrollment of high school students, ESL, exchange student, honors, independent study, internships, liberal arts/career combination, student-designed major, study abroad. Dual engineering degree program with Auburn University, Georgia Institute of Technology, University of Florida, Auburn University, Mercer University, University of Southern California; dual degree program in environmental studies with

Nicholas School of the Environment at Duke University; international partner degree program with Universite Catholique de Lille in France. **Credit/placement by examination:** AP, CLEP, IB, institutional tests. 32 credit hours maximum toward bachelor's degree. **Support services:** Learning center, study skills assistance, tutoring, writing center.

Majors. Area/ethnic studies: American. **Biology:** General. **Business:** Accounting, business admin, managerial economics, organizational behavior, training/development. **Communications:** Communications/speech/rhetoric. **English:** English lit, rhetoric/composition. **Foreign languages:** French, Japanese, Spanish. **Health services:** Predental, premedicine, prepharmacy, preveterinary. **History:** General. **Human services:** Social work. **Liberal arts:** Arts/sciences. **Math:** General. **Philosophy/religion:** Philosophy. **Physical sciences:** Chemistry, physics. **Psychology:** General. **Social sciences:** Economics, international relations, political science, sociology. **Visual/performing arts:** Art, art history/conservation, studio arts, theater history.

Most popular majors. English 22%, foreign language 39%, interdisciplinary studies 7%, psychology 10%, visual/performing arts 7%.

Technology on campus. 64 workstations in library, computer center. Dormitories wired for high-speed internet access and linked to campus network. Commuter students can connect to campus network. Helpline, wireless network available.

Student life. Freshman orientation: Mandatory, $125 fee. Preregistration for classes offered. Four day comprehensive program that utilizes the entire campus. **Housing:** Guaranteed on-campus for freshmen. Coed dorms, fraternity/sorority housing, themed housing available. $200 fully refundable deposit, deadline 5/1. **Activities:** Bands, campus ministries, choral groups, dance, drama, international student organizations, literary magazine, music ensembles, musical theater, radio station, student government, student newspaper, Catholic student association, black student caucus, Christian fellowship, environmentally concerned students, Jewish student union, Students Against Homophobia, APO service organization, Circle K.

Athletics. NCAA. **Intercollegiate:** Baseball M, basketball, cross-country, golf, lacrosse, soccer, tennis, track and field, volleyball W. **Intramural:** Badminton, basketball, lacrosse, softball, tennis, volleyball. **Team name:** Stormy Petrels.

Student services. Adult student services, alcohol/substance abuse counseling, career counseling, student employment services, financial aid counseling, health services, personal counseling. **Physically disabled:** Services for visually, speech, hearing impaired.

Contact. E-mail: admission@oglethorpe.edu
Phone: (404) 364-8307 Toll-free number: (800) 428-4484
Fax: (404) 364-8491
Lucy Leusch, Vice President for Enrollment and Financial Aid,
Oglethorpe University, 4484 Peachtree Road NE, Atlanta, GA 30319-2797

Paine College
Augusta, Georgia
www.paine.edu   CB code: 5530

♦ Private 4-year liberal arts college affiliated with the Christian Methodist Episcopal Church

♦ Residential campus in large city

♦ 551 degree-seeking undergraduates: 8% part-time, 59% women, 89% African American, 2% Hispanic/Latino, 2% Multi-racial, non-Hispanic, 3% international

♦ 31% of applicants admitted

♦ SAT or ACT (ACT writing optional), application essay required

General. Founded in 1882. Regionally accredited. **Degrees:** 101 bachelor's awarded. **ROTC:** Army. **Location:** 72 miles from Columbia, SC; 150 miles from Atlanta. **Calendar:** Semester, limited summer session. **Full-time faculty:** 52 total; 35% women. **Part-time faculty:** 14 total; 43% women. **Class size:** 80% < 20, 20% 20-39. **Special facilities:** Frank Yerby house replica.

Freshman class profile. 3,711 applied, 1,136 admitted, 131 enrolled.

GPA 3.75 or higher:	1%	Rank in top tenth:	5%
GPA 3.50-3.74:	5%	Return as sophomores:	33%
GPA 3.0-3.49:	19%	Out-of-state:	25%
GPA 2.0-2.99:	69%	Live on campus:	73%
Rank in top quarter:	15%	International:	1%

Basis for selection. School achievement record, test scores, and recommendations considered. 2.0 GPA required. Two letters of recommendation required. Short autobiographical essay-one page required. Georgia public secondary high school graduates must submit documentation demonstrating

a minimum of 500 on each of the Georgia High School Exit Exams. Essay must be typed. Interview recommended. **Learning Disabled:** Contact the Office of Disability Services to register with them and arrange an appointment.

High school preparation. College-preparatory program recommended. 16 units recommended. Recommended units include English 4, mathematics 3, social studies 2, history 1, science 3 and academic electives 3. Electives may include work in foreign languages, fine arts, health and physical education, and other courses that are consistent with the college curriculum.

2015-2016 Annual costs. Tuition/fees: $12,912. Room/board: $6,094. Books/supplies: $1,000. Personal expenses: $1,940.

Financial aid. Non-need-based: Scholarships awarded for academics, alumni affiliation, athletics, music/drama, religious affiliation, ROTC.

Application procedures. Admission: Closing date 7/1 (receipt date). $35 fee, may be waived for applicants with need. Admission notification on a rolling basis. **Financial aid:** Priority date 3/1; no closing date. FAFSA required. Applicants notified on a rolling basis starting 5/1; must reply within 2 week(s) of notification.

Academics. Special study options: Combined bachelor's/graduate degree, cooperative education, cross-registration, distance learning, dual enrollment of high school students, honors, independent study, internships, liberal arts/career combination, study abroad, teacher certification program. Dual degree in engineering and mathematics with Tuskegee University; cross-registration with Augusta University. **Credit/placement by examination:** AP, CLEP, SAT, ACT, institutional tests. **Support services:** Study skills assistance, tutoring. Individual and small-group tutoring in a variety of academic areas and includes an Internet-accessible computer lab.

Majors. Biology: General. **Business:** Accounting, business admin, international, management information systems, marketing. **Communications:** Broadcast journalism, journalism, persuasive communications. **Conservation:** Environmental science. **Education:** Elementary. **English:** English lit. **History:** General. **Math:** General. **Philosophy/religion:** Philosophy, religion. **Physical sciences:** Chemistry. **Psychology:** General, counseling, experimental, social. **Social sciences:** Criminology, sociology. **Visual/performing arts:** Dramatic.

Most popular majors. Business/marketing 25%, communications/journalism 17%, psychology 15%, social sciences 24%.

Technology on campus. 130 workstations in dormitories, library, computer center, student center. Dormitories wired for high-speed internet access and linked to campus network. Commuter students can connect to campus network. Online course registration, online library, helpline, repair service, wireless network available.

Student life. Freshman orientation: Mandatory, $117 fee. Preregistration for classes offered. Held at the beginning of each semester. **Housing:** Single-sex dorms, apartments, wellness housing available. $250 nonrefundable deposit, deadline 7/1. Honors housing available. **Activities:** Campus ministries, choral groups, dance, drama, international student organizations, literary magazine, music ensembles, student government, student newspaper, NAACP, pre-alumni club, National Pan Hellenic Council, Wesley Fellowship.

Athletics. NCAA. **Intercollegiate:** Baseball M, basketball, cross-country, golf M, softball W, track and field, volleyball W. **Intramural:** Badminton, baseball M, basketball, cross-country, softball, table tennis, track and field, volleyball, weight lifting. **Team name:** Lions.

Student services. Alcohol/substance abuse counseling, chaplain/spiritual director, career counseling, student employment services, financial aid counseling, health services, personal counseling, placement for graduates, veterans' counselor.

Contact. E-mail: PaineAdmissions@paine.edu
Phone: (706) 821-8320 Toll-free number: (800) 476-7703
Fax: (706) 821-8648
Charles Singley, Asst Dir of Admissions/Recruitment Coordinator, Paine College, 1235 15th Street, Augusta, GA 30901-3182

Piedmont College
Demorest, Georgia   CB member
www.piedmont.edu   CB code: 5537

♦ Private 4-year liberal arts and teachers college affiliated with the Christian Church

♦ Residential campus in rural community

♦ 1,259 degree-seeking undergraduates: 10% part-time, 67% women

♦ 980 graduate students

▶ 57% of applicants admitted

▶ SAT or ACT (ACT writing optional) required

▶ 46% graduate within 6 years

General. Founded in 1897. Regionally accredited. Independent, comprehensive, co-educational liberal arts college (with campuses in Demorest and Athens) affiliated with the National Association of Congregational Christian Churches and United Church of Christ. **Degrees:** 283 bachelor's awarded; master's, doctoral offered. **Location:** 30 miles from Gainesville, 75 miles from Atlanta. **Calendar:** Semester, limited summer session. **Full-time faculty:** 128 total; 74% have terminal degrees, 56% women. **Part-time faculty:** 110 total; 73% have terminal degrees, 50% women. **Class size:** 75% < 20, 24% 20-39, less than 1% 40-49. **Special facilities:** Athletic center, performing arts and communication center, pipe organ, residential village, commons, worship and music center.

Freshman class profile. 1,135 applied, 647 admitted, 281 enrolled.

Mid 50% test scores		ACT composite:	19-24
SAT critical reading:	430-550	Return as sophomores:	63%
SAT math:	440-550		

Basis for selection. GPA and standardized tests most important. Essay recommended. Interview recommended in some cases. **Home schooled:** Interview, letter of recommendation (nonparent) required. Transcript or portfolio detailing high school coursework completed, 2 letters of recommendation from sources outside home who have knowledge of student's academic/extracurricular achievements required. Interview with student and family may be required.

High school preparation. College-preparatory program recommended. 23 units recommended. Recommended units include English 4, mathematics 4, social studies 1, history 2, science 3 and foreign language 2.

2015-2016 Annual costs. Tuition/fees: $21,990. Room/board: $9,050. Books/supplies: $1,400. Personal expenses: $1,390.

2015-2016 Financial aid. Need-based: 252 full-time freshmen applied for aid; 227 deemed to have need; 227 received aid. Average need met was 75%. Average scholarship/grant was $17,050; average loan $3,337. 69% of total undergraduate aid awarded as scholarships/grants, 31% as loans/jobs. **Non-need-based:** Awarded to 296 full-time undergraduates, including 89 freshmen. Scholarships awarded for academics, alumni affiliation, art, leadership, music/drama, religious affiliation, state residency.

Application procedures. Admission: Closing date 7/1. No application fee. Admission notification on a rolling basis. **Financial aid:** Priority date 5/1; no closing date. FAFSA, institutional form required. Applicants notified on a rolling basis; must reply within 2 week(s) of notification.

Academics. Experiential learning credit allows students to document work experience for college credit as appropriate. **Special study options:** Accelerated study, combined bachelor's/graduate degree, distance learning, double major, dual enrollment of high school students, honors, independent study, internships, student-designed major, study abroad, teacher certification program, Washington semester. **Credit/placement by examination:** AP, CLEP. 30 credit hours maximum toward bachelor's degree. **Support services:** Learning center, study skills assistance, tutoring, writing center.

Majors. Biology: General. **Business:** Business admin. **Communications:** Media studies. **Conservation:** Environmental science. **Education:** Art, biology, chemistry, drama/dance, early childhood, English, history, mathematics, middle, science, secondary, Spanish. **English:** English lit. **Foreign languages:** Spanish. **Health services:** Athletic training, nursing (RN). **History:** General. **Math:** General. **Philosophy/religion:** Philosophy, religion. **Physical sciences:** Chemistry, physics. **Protective services:** Criminal justice. **Psychology:** General. **Social sciences:** General, political science, sociology. **Visual/performing arts:** Art, dramatic, music, musical theater, studio arts, theater design.

Most popular majors. Business/marketing 20%, education 17%, health sciences 25%, psychology 6%, social sciences 7%, visual/performing arts 8%.

Technology on campus. 240 workstations in dormitories, library, computer center, student center. Dormitories wired for high-speed internet access and linked to campus network. Commuter students can connect to campus network. Online course registration, online library, wireless network available.

Student life. Freshman orientation: Mandatory. Preregistration for classes offered. **Policies:** Unmarried students under 21 must live in dormitories or with relatives. **Housing:** Guaranteed on-campus for all undergraduates. Coed dorms, single-sex dorms, special housing for disabled, apartments, wellness housing available. $250 nonrefundable deposit. **Activities:** Pep band, campus ministries, choral groups, drama, film society, literary magazine, music ensembles, musical theater, radio station, student government, student newspaper, symphony orchestra, TV station, psychology club, Fellowship

of Christian Athletes, Student Association of Educators, literary society, science club, environmental club, Rotaract, history society, chemistry club.

Athletics. NCAA. **Intercollegiate:** Baseball M, basketball, cross-country, golf, lacrosse, soccer, softball W, tennis, volleyball W. **Intramural:** Basketball, football (non-tackle), rowing (crew), soccer, softball, table tennis, volleyball. **Team name:** Lions.

Student services. Chaplain/spiritual director, career counseling, financial aid counseling, health services, personal counseling, placement for graduates, veterans' counselor.

Contact. E-mail: ugrad@piedmont.edu
Phone: (706) 776-0103 Toll-free number: (800) 277-7020
Fax: (706) 776-6635
Brenda Boonstra, Director of Admissions, Piedmont College, 1021 Central Avenue, Demorest, GA 30535-0010

Point University
West Point, Georgia
www.point.edu   CB code: 5029

▶ Private 4-year Bible and liberal arts college affiliated with the Christian Church

▶ Residential campus in small town

▶ 1,337 degree-seeking undergraduates: 12% part-time, 48% women

▶ 49% of applicants admitted

▶ SAT or ACT (ACT writing optional) required

General. Founded in 1937. Regionally accredited. **Degrees:** 225 bachelor's, 155 associate awarded. **Location:** 80 miles from Atlanta, 80 miles from Montgomery, AL. **Calendar:** Semester, limited summer session. **Full-time faculty:** 35 total; 66% have terminal degrees, 23% minority, 54% women. **Part-time faculty:** 117 total; 21% have terminal degrees, 20% minority, 50% women. **Class size:** 72% < 20, 22% 20-39, 5% 40-49, less than 1% 50-99.

Freshman class profile. 862 applied, 423 admitted, 266 enrolled.

GPA 3.75 or higher:	16%	Rank in top quarter:	10%
GPA 3.50-3.74:	12%	Rank in top tenth:	5%
GPA 3.0-3.49:	44%	Out-of-state:	38%
GPA 2.0-2.99:	28%		

Basis for selection. Recommendations, scholastic ability, and test scores are most important. **Home schooled:** Transcript of courses and grades, letter of recommendation (nonparent) required.

High school preparation. College-preparatory program recommended. 23 units recommended. Recommended units include English 4, mathematics 4, social studies 3, science 4 (laboratory 2) and foreign language 2.

2015-2016 Annual costs. Tuition/fees: $18,500. Room/board: $6,600.

2014-2015 Financial aid. Need-based: 44% of total undergraduate aid awarded as scholarships/grants, 56% as loans/jobs. **Non-need-based:** Scholarships awarded for academics, athletics, leadership.

Application procedures. Admission: Priority date 7/1; deadline 8/1 (receipt date). $25 fee, may be waived for applicants with need. Admission notification on a rolling basis. **Financial aid:** Priority date 6/1, closing date 8/1. FAFSA required. Applicants notified on a rolling basis starting 3/1; must reply within 3 week(s) of notification.

Academics. Special study options: Accelerated study, distance learning, double major, dual enrollment of high school students, honors, independent study, teacher certification program. **Credit/placement by examination:** AP, CLEP, IB. 16 credit hours maximum toward associate degree, 32 toward bachelor's. **Support services:** Reduced course load, study skills assistance, tutoring, writing center.

Majors. Biology: General. **Business:** Accounting, business admin, marketing, organizational leadership. **Education:** Early childhood, middle. **English:** English lit. **History:** General. **Liberal arts:** Humanities. **Parks/recreation:** Exercise sciences. **Protective services:** Criminal justice. **Psychology:** General. **Social sciences:** Sociology. **Theology:** Bible. **Visual/performing arts:** Music. **Work/family studies:** Child development.

Most popular majors. Business/marketing 25%, education 8%, philosophy/religious studies 25%, psychology 27%.

Technology on campus. 72 workstations in library, computer center, student center. Dormitories wired for high-speed internet access. Commuter students can connect to campus network. Online course registration, online library, helpline, wireless network available.

Student life. Freshman orientation: Mandatory. Preregistration for classes offered. **Policies:** Religious observance required. **Housing:** Guaranteed on-campus for freshmen. Single-sex dorms, themed housing available. $100 nonrefundable deposit, deadline 8/1. **Activities:** Bands, campus ministries, choral groups, music ensembles, student government, religious organizations, Christian service clubs, service-oriented organizations.

Athletics. NAIA, NCCAA. **Intercollegiate:** Baseball M, basketball, cheerleading W, cross-country, football (tackle) M, golf, lacrosse, soccer, softball W, swimming, tennis, volleyball W. **Intramural:** Basketball, football (non-tackle), sand volleyball, soccer, softball, table tennis, ultimate frisbee, volleyball, weight lifting. **Team name:** Skyhawks.

Student services. Adult student services, alcohol/substance abuse counseling, chaplain/spiritual director, career counseling, student employment services, financial aid counseling, personal counseling, placement for graduates, veterans' counselor.

Contact. E-mail: admissions@point.edu
Phone: (706) 385-1202 Toll-free number: (855) 377-6168
Fax: (706) 645-9473
Rusty Hassell, Director of Admission, Point University, 507 West 10th Street, West Point, GA 31833

Reinhardt University
Waleska, Georgia — CB member
www.reinhardt.edu — CB code: 5568

- Private 4-year liberal arts and teachers college affiliated with the United Methodist Church
- Commuter campus in rural community
- 1,237 degree-seeking undergraduates: 9% part-time, 46% women
- 102 degree-seeking graduate students
- 91% of applicants admitted
- SAT or ACT (ACT writing optional) required

General. Founded in 1883. Regionally accredited. Off-campus center in Alpharetta. Additional sites for adult programs. **Degrees:** 215 bachelor's, 11 associate awarded; master's offered. **Location:** 50 miles from Atlanta. **Calendar:** Semester, extensive summer session. **Full-time faculty:** 77 total. **Class size:** 83% < 20, 16% 20-39, less than 1% 40-49. **Special facilities:** Indian history museum, visual arts center, performing arts center.

Freshman class profile. 1,158 applied, 1,051 admitted, 293 enrolled.

Out-of-state: 6% **Live on campus:** 68%

Basis for selection. School achievement record and standardized test scores most important. Interview recommended. Audition required of music majors. Portfolio required of art majors. **Home schooled:** Transcript of courses and grades, state high school equivalency certificate required. **Learning Disabled:** Recommend that students be counseled by Academic Support Office.

High school preparation. College-preparatory program recommended. 14 units required. Required and recommended units include English 4, mathematics 4, social studies 3, science 3 and foreign language 2.

2015-2016 Annual costs. Tuition/fees: $20,266. Room/board: $7,568. Books/supplies: $1,100. Personal expenses: $5,760.

2014-2015 Financial aid. Need-based: 298 full-time freshmen applied for aid; 252 deemed to have need; 250 received aid. Average need met was 57%. Average scholarship/grant was $11,105; average loan $3,191. 65% of total undergraduate aid awarded as scholarships/grants, 35% as loans/jobs. **Non-need-based:** Awarded to 431 full-time undergraduates, including 145 freshmen. Scholarships awarded for academics, art, athletics, music/drama, religious affiliation, state residency.

Application procedures. Admission: No deadline. $25 fee, may be waived for applicants with need. Admission notification on a rolling basis beginning on or about 9/1. **Financial aid:** Priority date 7/1, closing date 7/1. FAFSA required. Applicants notified on a rolling basis starting 3/1; must reply within 2 week(s) of notification.

Academics. Special study options: Accelerated study, cooperative education, distance learning, double major, dual enrollment of high school students, external degree, honors, independent study, internships, liberal arts/career combination, study abroad, teacher certification program, weekend college. **Credit/placement by examination:** AP, CLEP, SAT, ACT, institutional

tests. 15 credit hours maximum toward associate degree, 30 toward bachelor's. **Support services:** Learning center, pre-admission summer program, reduced course load, remedial instruction, study skills assistance, tutoring, writing center.

Majors. Biology: General. **Business:** General, accounting, business admin. **Communications:** Communications/speech/rhetoric. **Education:** General, biology, early childhood, elementary, English, mathematics, middle, music, physical. **English:** English lit. **Foreign languages:** General. **History:** General. **Liberal arts:** Arts/sciences. **Math:** General. **Parks/recreation:** Sports admin. **Philosophy/religion:** Religion. **Protective services:** Police science. **Psychology:** General. **Social sciences:** Political science, sociology. **Visual/performing arts:** Art, music, studio arts.

Most popular majors. Business/marketing 15%, education 29%, liberal arts 23%, visual/performing arts 11%.

Technology on campus. 170 workstations in dormitories, library, computer center, student center. Dormitories wired for high-speed internet access and linked to campus network. Commuter students can connect to campus network. Online course registration, online library, helpline, student web hosting, wireless network available.

Student life. Freshman orientation: Mandatory, $100 fee. Preregistration for classes offered. One- or 2-day program. **Housing:** Guaranteed on-campus for freshmen. Coed dorms, single-sex dorms, special housing for disabled, apartments available. $200 fully refundable deposit, deadline 8/15. Honors house available. **Activities:** Bands, campus ministries, choral groups, drama, film society, international student organizations, literary magazine, music ensembles, musical theater, student government, student newspaper, symphony orchestra, TV station, Baptist collegiate ministry, Wesley Fellowship, Athletes for Christ Everyday, Phi Theta Kappa, Circle-K International, Habitat for Humanity, breast cancer awareness committee.

Athletics. NAIA. **Intercollegiate:** Baseball M, basketball, cheerleading, cross-country, golf M, lacrosse, soccer, softball W, tennis. **Intramural:** Basketball, football (non-tackle), soccer, softball, volleyball. **Team name:** Eagles.

Student services. Adult student services, alcohol/substance abuse counseling, chaplain/spiritual director, career counseling, student employment services, financial aid counseling, health services, personal counseling, placement for graduates, veterans' counselor. **Physically disabled:** Services for visually, speech, hearing impaired.

Contact. E-mail: admissions@mail.reinhardt.edu
Phone: (770) 720-5526 Toll-free number: (877) 343-4273
Fax: (770) 720-5602
Julie Fleming, Director of Admissions, Reinhardt University, 7300 Reinhardt Circle, Waleska, GA 30183-2981

Savannah College of Art and Design
Savannah, Georgia — CB member
www.scad.edu — CB code: 5631

- Private 4-year visual arts and performing arts college
- Residential campus in small city
- 9,939 degree-seeking undergraduates: 17% part-time, 66% women, 11% African American, 8% Asian American, 8% Hispanic/Latino, 1% Native American, 16% international
- 2,267 degree-seeking graduate students
- 69% of applicants admitted
- SAT or ACT (ACT writing optional) required
- 67% graduate within 6 years

General. Founded in 1978. Regionally accredited. Degrees offered in Savannah and Atlanta, Georgia; Hong Kong; Lacoste, France; and online through SCAD eLearning. **Degrees:** 1,857 bachelor's awarded; master's offered. **Location:** 250 miles from Atlanta, 150 miles from Jacksonville, FL. **Calendar:** Quarter, limited summer session. **Full-time faculty:** 526 total; 81% have terminal degrees, 10% minority, 41% women. **Part-time faculty:** 169 total; 72% have terminal degrees, 7% minority, 54% women. **Class size:** 71% < 20, 29% 20-39. **Special facilities:** Art museums, 2 vintage diners, amphitheater, restored 1921 theater, restored 1946 theater, equestrian center.

Freshman class profile. 10,303 applied, 7,117 admitted, 2,156 enrolled.

Mid 50% test scores		GPA 3.0-3.49:	30%
SAT critical reading:	480-600	GPA 2.0-2.99:	16%
SAT math:	460-580	Return as sophomores:	85%
SAT writing:	460-590	Out-of-state:	81%
ACT composite:	20-26	Live on campus:	86%
GPA 3.75 or higher:	37%	International:	15%
GPA 3.50-3.74:	17%		

Basis for selection. In general, SAT score of 1000, ACT score of 21 and/or a 3.0 GPA are required. Exceptions may be made for applicants of unusual motivation and ability. Additional materials may be requested if an applicant does not meet or exceed regular admission standards. All applicants may submit supporting materials such as portfolio, recommendations, statement of purpose and/or may interview. SAT or ACT scores are not required of non-U.S. applicants. Domestic applicants who have been graduated from high school two or more years at the time their file is reviewed for admission are not required to submit test scores. Interview and/or portfolio recommended. Essay recommended for historic preservation, art history, and architectural history programs. Portfolio or audition required for scholarship consideration. **Home schooled:** Statement describing home school structure and mission, transcript of courses and grades, state high school equivalency certificate required. **Learning Disabled:** Documentation of specific nature of disability required.

High school preparation. College-preparatory program recommended.

2015-2016 Annual costs. Tuition/fees: $34,470. Room/board: $13,677.

2015-2016 Financial aid. **Need-based:** 1,437 full-time freshmen applied for aid; 1,172 deemed to have need; 1,172 received aid. Average need met was 16%. Average scholarship/grant was $5,363; average loan $3,005. 24% of total undergraduate aid awarded as scholarships/grants, 76% as loans/jobs. **Non-need-based:** Awarded to 7,247 full-time undergraduates, including 1,950 freshmen. Scholarships awarded for academics, alumni affiliation, art, athletics, job skills, leadership, minority status, music/drama, ROTC. **Additional information:** Degree-seeking students can be awarded maximum of one scholarship from the college, but may receive additional scholarships from other sources, as well as additional forms of financial aid. Scholarships based on academic achievement are awarded through the admission office.

Application procedures. **Admission:** No deadline. $70 fee. Admission notification on a rolling basis beginning on or about 9/1. The recommended deadline for reply is 5/1. **Financial aid:** No deadline. FAFSA required. Applicants notified on a rolling basis starting 3/1; must reply within 4 week(s) of notification.

Academics. **Special study options:** Combined bachelor's/graduate degree, distance learning, double major, dual enrollment of high school students, ESL, independent study, internships, study abroad. Off-campus programs in Europe and other art centers. Cross registration available at SCAD-Atlanta through membership in ARCHE. **Credit/placement by examination:** AP, CLEP, IB, SAT, ACT. 15 credit hours maximum toward bachelor's degree. A maximum of 90 quarter hours of undergraduate credit for a bachelor's degree may be given for appropriate courses. A maximum of 45 quarter hours of CLEP credit may be awarded. Transfer credit from all sources may not exceed 90 quarter hours. **Support services:** Learning center, pre-admission summer program, reduced course load, study skills assistance, tutoring, writing center.

Majors. **Architecture:** Architecture, history/criticism. **Communications:** Digital media, radio/TV. **Communications technology:** Animation/special effects, recording arts. **English:** Technical writing. **Visual/performing arts:** Art history/conservation, cinematography, commercial/advertising art, dramatic, fashion design, fiber arts, game design, graphic design, illustration, industrial design, interior design, metal/jewelry, painting, photography, play/screenwriting, printmaking, sculpture, theater design. **Work/family studies:** Apparel marketing, merchandising.

Most popular majors. Communications/journalism 16%, communication technologies 14%, family/consumer sciences 7%, visual/performing arts 56%.

Technology on campus. 3,450 workstations in dormitories, library, computer center, student center. Dormitories wired for high-speed internet access and linked to campus network. Commuter students can connect to campus network. Online course registration, online library, helpline, repair service, student web hosting, wireless network available.

Student life. **Freshman orientation:** Mandatory. Preregistration for classes offered. Held before the start of classes. An optional 2-day summer program is offered during summer for a nominal fee. **Housing:** Coed dorms, single-sex dorms, special housing for disabled, apartments available. $250 nonrefundable deposit, deadline 6/1. Freshmen-only halls. Accommodations for disabled students are available on a case-by-case basis. **Activities:** Campus ministries, choral groups, dance, drama, film society, international student organizations, literary magazine, music ensembles, musical theater, radio station, student newspaper, TV station, American Institute of Architecture Students, Industrial Design Student Association, United Student Forum, student activities council, Serve, Intercultural Student Association, art history society, Society for Collegiate Journalists, Engage.

Athletics. NAIA. **Intercollegiate:** Bowling, cross-country, equestrian, golf, lacrosse, soccer, swimming, table tennis, tennis, track and field. **Intramural:** Badminton, basketball, sand volleyball, soccer, table tennis, volleyball. **Team name:** Bees.

Student services. Adult student services, alcohol/substance abuse counseling, career counseling, student employment services, financial aid counseling, health services, personal counseling, placement for graduates, veterans' counselor. **Physically disabled:** Services for visually, speech, hearing impaired.

Contact. E-mail: admission@scad.edu
Phone: (912) 525-5100 Toll-free number: (800) 869-7223
Fax: (912) 525-5986
Jenny Jaquillard, Executive Director of Admissions, Recruitment & Events, Savannah College of Art and Design, PO Box 2072, Savannah, GA 31402-2072

Savannah State University
Savannah, Georgia   **CB member**
www.savannahstate.edu   **CB code: 5609**

- Public 4-year business, liberal arts and teachers college
- Residential campus in small city
- 4,635 degree-seeking undergraduates: 12% part-time, 58% women, 83% African American, 8% Hispanic/Latino, 3% Multi-racial, non-Hispanic, 1% international
- 155 degree-seeking graduate students
- 33% of applicants admitted
- SAT or ACT (ACT writing optional) required

General. Founded in 1890. Regionally accredited. **Degrees:** 492 bachelor's, 6 associate awarded; master's offered. **ROTC:** Army, Naval. **Location:** 250 miles from Atlanta; 120 miles from Jacksonville, FL. **Calendar:** Semester, extensive summer session. **Full-time faculty:** 191 total; 71% minority, 47% women. **Part-time faculty:** 29 total; 66% minority, 76% women. **Class size:** 41% < 20, 30% 20-39, 5% 40-49, 12% 50-99, 12% >100. **Special facilities:** Marine biology dock, college archives, natural estuary.

Freshman class profile. 6,977 applied, 2,318 admitted, 1,186 enrolled.

Basis for selection. Test score and high school GPA are very important. Students lacking complete college-preparatory requirements admitted on provisional basis. **Home schooled:** Transcript of courses and grades, state high school equivalency certificate required. Declaration of Intent to Home School; Iowa TAP, SAT Subject Tests, California Achievement Test, Stanford Achievement Test or other national standardized high school summation exam; completion of collegiate-preparatory curriculum; student and primary teacher certification of completion of high school and date of graduation required.

High school preparation. College-preparatory program required. 17 units required. Required units include English 4, mathematics 4, social studies 3, science 4 (laboratory 2) and foreign language 2. For students that graduated high school prior to 2012: 16 Required High School Curriculum (CPC) units (4 math courses; 3 sciences; 3 social sciences; 2 years of same foreign language).

2015-2016 Annual costs. Tuition/fees: $6,616; $19,436 out-of-state. Room/board: $8,040. Books/supplies: $1,500. Personal expenses: $800.

Financial aid. **Non-need-based:** Scholarships awarded for academics, alumni affiliation, music/drama.

Application procedures. **Admission:** Closing date 7/15. No application fee. Application must be submitted online. Admission notification on a rolling basis. **Financial aid:** Closing date 4/1. FAFSA required. Applicants notified on a rolling basis starting 4/15; must reply within 2 week(s) of notification.

Academics. **Special study options:** Combined bachelor's/graduate degree, cooperative education, cross-registration, double major, dual enrollment of high school students, ESL, exchange student, honors, independent study, internships, study abroad. **Credit/placement by examination:** AP, CLEP, institutional tests. 45 credit hours maximum toward bachelor's degree. **Support services:** Learning center, pre-admission summer program, remedial instruction, study skills assistance, tutoring, writing center.

Majors. **Area/ethnic studies:** African. **Biology:** General, marine. **Business:** Accounting, business admin, marketing. **Communications:** Media studies. **Computer sciences:** Information systems. **Education:** Middle. **English:** English lit. **History:** General. **Human services:** Social work. **Math:** General. **Physical sciences:** Chemistry. **Protective services:** Forensics, homeland security, law enforcement admin. **Psychology:** Developmental. **Social sciences:** Political science, sociology. **Visual/performing arts:** General.

Most popular majors. Biology 10%, business/marketing 19%, communications/journalism 8%, engineering/engineering technologies 8%, psychology 8%, public administration/social services 7%, security/protective services 16%, social sciences 8%.

Technology on campus. 420 workstations in dormitories, library, computer center, student center. Dormitories wired for high-speed internet access and linked to campus network. Commuter students can connect to campus network. Online course registration, helpline, repair service, wireless network available.

Student life. Freshman orientation: Available, $60 fee. Preregistration for classes offered. Available various times leading up to fall semester. Private appointments upon request. **Housing:** Single-sex dorms, apartments available. **Activities:** Bands, campus ministries, choral groups, dance, drama, international student organizations, literary magazine, music ensembles, radio station, student government, student newspaper, Achievers of Today & Tomorrow, Caribbean student association, College Democrats, DC & Beyond, National Council of Negro Women, non-traditional student organization, Sisters Striving for Excellence, Way of Real Discovery.

Athletics. NCAA. **Intercollegiate:** Baseball M, basketball, bowling W, cross-country, football (tackle) M, golf, softball W, tennis W, track and field, volleyball W. **Intramural:** Baseball M, bowling, softball W, table tennis. **Team name:** Tigers.

Student services. Alcohol/substance abuse counseling, career counseling, student employment services, financial aid counseling, health services, personal counseling, placement for graduates, veterans' counselor. **Physically disabled:** Services for visually, speech, hearing impaired.

Contact. E-mail: admissions@savannahstate.edu
Phone: (912) 358-4338 Toll-free number: (800) 788-0478
Fax: (912) 358-3171
Descatur Potier, Asst VP Enrollment Services, Savannah State University, Office of Admissions and Recruitment, Savannah, GA 31404

Shorter University
Rome, Georgia   **CB member**
www.shorter.edu   **CB code: 5616**

◗ Private 4-year liberal arts college affiliated with the Southern Baptist Convention
◗ Residential campus in large town
◗ 1,300 full-time, degree-seeking undergraduates
◗ SAT or ACT (ACT writing recommended), application essay required

General. Founded in 1873. Regionally accredited. **Degrees:** 348 bachelor's, 23 associate awarded; master's offered. **Location:** 70 miles from Atlanta; 65 miles from Chattanooga, TN. **Calendar:** Semester, limited summer session. **Full-time faculty:** 85 total. **Part-time faculty:** 71 total. **Class size:** 50% < 20, 48% 20-39, 2% 40-49, less than 1% >100.

Freshman class profile.

GPA 3.75 or higher:	31%	Rank in top tenth:	21%
GPA 3.50-3.74:	10%	Out-of-state:	14%
GPA 3.0-3.49:	28%	Live on campus:	74%
GPA 2.0-2.99:	30%	Fraternities:	7%
Rank in top quarter:	47%	Sororities:	33%

Basis for selection. School rank, completion of college prep program, letters of recommendation, formal demonstrations of competencies recommended. Auditions required of music and drama majors. Portfolios required of art majors. **Home schooled:** Interview may be required.

High school preparation. College-preparatory program required. 16 units required. Required units include English 4, mathematics 4, history 3, science 3 and foreign language 2. Math units should include 2 algebra, 1 geometry.

2015-2016 Annual costs. Tuition/fees: $20,976. Room/board: $9,500. Books/supplies: $1,200. Personal expenses: $3,958.

Financial aid. Non-need-based: Scholarships awarded for academics, art, athletics, music/drama, religious affiliation, state residency. **Additional information:** Cost is reduced for all in-state students by state tuition equalization grant program. College matches for out-of-state full-time students.

Application procedures. Admission: No deadline. $25 fee, may be waived for applicants with need. Admission notification on a rolling basis beginning on or about 1/1. Must reply by May 1 or within 2 week(s) if notified thereafter. **Financial aid:** Priority date 4/1; no closing date. FAFSA, institutional form required. Applicants notified on a rolling basis starting 3/1; must reply within 2 week(s) of notification.

Academics. Special study options: Combined bachelor's/graduate degree, cross-registration, distance learning, double major, dual enrollment of high school students, honors, independent study, internships, student-designed major, study abroad, teacher certification program, weekend college. **Credit/**

placement by examination: AP, CLEP, IB, SAT, institutional tests. 30 credit hours maximum toward bachelor's degree. **Support services:** Learning center, pre-admission summer program, remedial instruction, study skills assistance, tutoring, writing center.

Majors. Biology: General. **Business:** Accounting, business admin, managerial economics. **Communications:** Communications/speech/rhetoric, public relations. **Computer sciences:** General. **Conservation:** General, environmental studies. **Education:** Art, elementary, mathematics, middle, music. **English:** English lit. **Foreign languages:** French, Spanish. **History:** General. **Liberal arts:** Arts/sciences. **Math:** General. **Parks/recreation:** Sports admin. **Philosophy/religion:** Religion. **Physical sciences:** Chemistry. **Psychology:** General. **Social sciences:** General, sociology. **Theology:** Sacred music, theology. **Visual/performing arts:** Dramatic, piano/keyboard, studio arts, voice/opera.

Most popular majors. Biology 7%, business/marketing 26%, education 17%, history 6%, liberal arts 8%, parks/recreation 6%, visual/performing arts 12%.

Technology on campus. 50 workstations in library, computer center. Dormitories wired for high-speed internet access and linked to campus network. Online course registration, online library, helpline, wireless network available.

Student life. Freshman orientation: Mandatory, $150 fee. Preregistration for classes offered. Several summer overnight sessions from June to August during which freshmen take placement exams. **Policies:** All housing is alcohol-, drug- and smoke-free. **Housing:** Guaranteed on-campus for freshmen. Single-sex dorms, apartments, wellness housing available. $200 fully refundable deposit, deadline 7/18. **Activities:** Bands, campus ministries, choral groups, dance, drama, film society, international student organizations, literary magazine, music ensembles, Model UN, musical theater, opera, radio station, student government, student newspaper, TV station, Baptist student union, relations society, Fellowship of Christian Athletes, optimist club.

Athletics. NAIA. **Intercollegiate:** Baseball M, basketball, cheerleading, cross-country, football (tackle) M, golf, lacrosse, soccer, softball W, tennis, track and field, volleyball W, wrestling M. **Intramural:** Basketball, bowling, football (non-tackle), soccer, softball, table tennis, tennis, track and field, volleyball. **Team name:** Hawks.

Student services. Adult student services, alcohol/substance abuse counseling, chaplain/spiritual director, career counseling, student employment services, financial aid counseling, health services, personal counseling, placement for graduates. **Physically disabled:** Services for visually, hearing impaired.

Contact. E-mail: admissions@shorter.edu
Phone: (706) 233-7319 Toll-free number: (800) 868-6980
Fax: (706) 233-7224
Patrick McElhaney, Director of Admissions, Shorter University, 315 Shorter Avenue, Rome, GA 30165

South Georgia State College
Douglas, Georgia
www.sgsc.edu   **CB code: 5619**

◗ Public 4-year liberal arts college
◗ Commuter campus in large town
◗ 2,635 degree-seeking undergraduates: 31% part-time, 63% women, 31% African American, 1% Asian American, 6% Hispanic/Latino, 1% Multiracial, non-Hispanic
◗ 60% of applicants admitted

General. Founded in 1906. Regionally accredited. **Degrees:** 33 bachelor's, 309 associate awarded. **Location:** 212 miles from Atlanta, 140 miles from Jacksonville, Florida. **Calendar:** Semester, extensive summer session. **Full-time faculty:** 62 total. **Part-time faculty:** 49 total. **Special facilities:** Mobile nursing clinic, endangered pine/wiregrass plot.

Freshman class profile. 1,986 applied, 1,195 admitted, 1,011 enrolled.

Basis for selection. SAT/ACT required of nursing students. COMPASS placement test required of applicants without SAT/ACT. Applicants who score below 400 SAT math (17 ACT math) or 430 SAT verbal (17 ACT English) also required to take placement tests. **Home schooled:** Statement describing home school structure and mission, transcript of courses and grades required. **Learning Disabled:** Documentation required so appropriate services can be provided.

High school preparation. College-preparatory program recommended. 17 units recommended. Recommended units include English 4, mathematics 4, social studies 3, science 4 (laboratory 3) and foreign language 2.

2015-2016 Annual costs. Tuition/fees: $3,756; $11,350 out-of-state. Room/board: $8,250. Books/supplies: $660.

Financial aid. Non-need-based: Scholarships awarded for academics.

Application procedures. Admission: No deadline. $20 fee, may be waived for applicants with need. Admission notification on a rolling basis. **Financial aid:** Priority date 6/1; no closing date. FAFSA, institutional form required. Applicants notified on a rolling basis starting 7/6; must reply within 2 week(s) of notification.

Academics. Special study options: Combined bachelor's/graduate degree, distance learning, dual enrollment of high school students, independent study. **Credit/placement by examination:** AP, CLEP, IB, institutional tests. 30 credit hours maximum toward associate degree. **Support services:** Learning center, remedial instruction, study skills assistance, tutoring.

Majors. Biology: General. **Health services:** Nursing (RN).

Technology on campus. 235 workstations in dormitories, library, computer center, student center. Dormitories wired for high-speed internet access. Online course registration, online library, wireless network available.

Student life. Freshman orientation: Mandatory. Preregistration for classes offered. **Housing:** Single-sex dorms, special housing for disabled available. $250 fully refundable deposit, deadline 6/30. **Activities:** Campus ministries, choral groups, drama, international student organizations, student government, cultural exchange club, debate society, Association of Nursing Students, College Democrats, College Republicans, students for social awareness, student organization for multicultural unity, Phi Beta Lambda.

Athletics. NJCAA. **Intercollegiate:** Baseball M, basketball M, cross-country, soccer W, softball W, swimming. **Intramural:** Basketball, softball, swimming, tennis. **Team name:** Hawks.

Student services. Alcohol/substance abuse counseling, career counseling, student employment services, financial aid counseling, personal counseling, veterans' counselor. **Physically disabled:** Services for speech impaired.

Contact. E-mail: admissions@sgsc.edu
Phone: (912) 260-4206 Toll-free number: (800) 342-6364
Fax: (912) 260-4441
Angela Wasdin, Director of Admissions, South Georgia State College, 100 West College Park Drive, Douglas, GA 31533-5098

South University: Savannah
Savannah, Georgia
www.southuniversity.edu   CB code: 5157

▸ For-profit 4-year university
▸ Commuter campus in small city
▸ 777 undergraduates
▸ Interview required

General. Founded in 1899. Regionally accredited. **Degrees:** 81 bachelor's, 97 associate awarded; master's, professional offered. **Location:** 225 miles from Atlanta; 165 miles from Jacksonville, FL. **Calendar:** Quarter, extensive summer session. **Full-time faculty:** 45 total. **Part-time faculty:** 63 total.

Basis for selection. Test scores and school achievement record considered. SAT or ACT recommended. Computerized placement test may be submitted in place of test scores for admission. **Home schooled:** Students must provide evidence that homeschooling was conducted in accordance with state laws (certificate of attendance or completion is not sufficient).

2015-2016 Annual costs. Associate programs: $44,615-$50,250, books and supplies $3,200-$3,600. Bachelor's programs: $44,665-$83,500, books and supplies $3,200-$6,000.

Application procedures. Admission: No deadline. $50 fee. Admission notification on a rolling basis. **Financial aid:** No deadline. FAFSA required. Applicants notified on a rolling basis starting 9/1.

Academics. Special study options: Combined bachelor's/graduate degree, distance learning, internships. **Credit/placement by examination:** AP, CLEP, IB, SAT, ACT, institutional tests. **Support services:** Learning center, remedial instruction, study skills assistance, tutoring.

Majors. Business: Business admin. **Computer sciences:** Information technology. **Health services:** Health care admin, nursing (RN). **Protective services:** Law enforcement admin. **Psychology:** General.

Most popular majors. Business/marketing 17%, health sciences 69%, security/protective services 6%.

Technology on campus. Commuter students can connect to campus network. Online library, helpline, repair service, wireless network available.

Student life. Freshman orientation: Mandatory. Preregistration for classes offered. **Housing:** Apartments available.

Student services. Career counseling, student employment services, financial aid counseling, placement for graduates, veterans' counselor.

Contact. Phone: (912) 201-8100 Toll-free number: (866) 629-2901
Fax: (912) 201-8070
Danielle Maddox, Director of Admissions, South University: Savannah, 709 Mall Boulevard, Savannah, GA 31406

Spelman College
Atlanta, Georgia   CB member
www.spelman.edu   CB code: 5628

▸ Private 4-year liberal arts college for women
▸ Residential campus in very large city
▸ 2,142 degree-seeking undergraduates: 2% part-time, 100% women, 96% African American, 2% Multi-racial, non-Hispanic, 1% international
▸ 48% of applicants admitted
▸ SAT or ACT (ACT writing optional), application essay required
▸ 74% graduate within 6 years; 32% enter graduate study

General. Founded in 1881. Regionally accredited. One of 5 members of Atlanta University Center sharing facilities, resources, and activities. Students may take courses at other undergraduate schools in Atlanta University Consortium. **Degrees:** 462 bachelor's awarded. **ROTC:** Army, Naval, Air Force. **Location:** 2 miles from downtown. **Calendar:** Semester. **Full-time faculty:** 180 total; 87% have terminal degrees, 86% minority, 71% women. **Part-time faculty:** 70 total; 81% minority, 67% women. **Class size:** 58% < 20, 38% 20-39, 2% 40-49, 2% 50-99, less than 1% >100. **Special facilities:** Women's research and resource center, fine arts museum, digital moving image salon, comprehensive writing center, center for health disparities research and education, center for global education, center for leadership and civic engagement, women in spiritual discernment of ministry center.

Freshman class profile. 5,051 applied, 2,441 admitted, 566 enrolled.

Mid 50% test scores			
SAT critical reading:	470-570	GPA 3.0-3.49:	33%
SAT math:	450-550	GPA 2.0-2.99:	5%
SAT writing:	450-550	Rank in top quarter:	62%
ACT composite:	20-23	Rank in top tenth:	23%
GPA 3.75 or higher:	38%	Return as sophomores:	90%
GPA 3.50-3.74:	24%	Out-of-state:	75%
		Live on campus:	99%

Basis for selection. GED not accepted. School achievement record, letters of recommendation, test scores, leadership, activities, and essay are used for admission decisions. Portfolio required of art majors.

High school preparation. College-preparatory program required. 16 units required; 20 recommended. Required and recommended units include English 4, mathematics 2-4, social studies 2, history 1, science 2-3 (laboratory 1-2), foreign language 2-3 and academic electives 6. Math must include algebra and geometry. 2 years of same foreign language required. Social studies should include 2 years of history.

2015-2016 Annual costs. Tuition/fees: $26,388. Room/board: $12,363. Books/supplies: $2,000. Personal expenses: $2,500.

2015-2016 Financial aid. Need-based: 544 full-time freshmen applied for aid; 495 deemed to have need; 494 received aid. Average need met was 35%. Average scholarship/grant was $11,056; average loan $3,722. 75% of total undergraduate aid awarded as scholarships/grants, 25% as loans/jobs. **Non-need-based:** Awarded to 57 full-time undergraduates, including 11 freshmen. Scholarships awarded for academics, alumni affiliation, music/drama, state residency.

Application procedures. Admission: Closing date 2/1 (postmark date). $35 fee, may be waived for applicants with need. Admission notification by 4/1. Must reply by 5/1. **Financial aid:** Priority date 2/1; no closing date. FAFSA, institutional form required. Applicants notified on a rolling basis starting 2/15; must reply within 2 week(s) of notification.

Academics. Special study options: Combined bachelor's/graduate degree, cooperative education, cross-registration, double major, dual enrollment of high school students, exchange student, honors, independent study, internships, semester at sea, student-designed major, study abroad, teacher certification program, Washington semester. **Credit/placement by examination:** AP, CLEP, IB, institutional tests. 16 credit hours maximum toward bachelor's degree. **Support services:** Learning center, pre-admission summer program, study skills assistance, tutoring, writing center.

Majors. Area/ethnic studies: Women's. **Biology:** General, biochemistry. **Computer sciences:** General. **Conservation:** Environmental science, environmental studies. **Education:** Early childhood. **Engineering:** General. **English:** English lit. **Foreign languages:** French, Spanish. **History:** General. **Math:** General. **Philosophy/religion:** Philosophy, religion. **Physical sciences:** Chemistry, physics. **Psychology:** General. **Social sciences:** Economics, international relations, political science, sociology, sociology/anthropology. **Visual/performing arts:** Dramatic, music, studio arts.

Most popular majors. Biology 12%, English 9%, psychology 22%, social sciences 30%.

Technology on campus. 102 workstations in dormitories, library, computer center, student center. Dormitories wired for high-speed internet access and linked to campus network. Commuter students can connect to campus network. Online course registration, online library, helpline, repair service, wireless network available.

Student life. Freshman orientation: Mandatory. Preregistration for classes offered. One-week program prior to registration. **Policies:** Freshmen not permitted cars on campus. **Housing:** Guaranteed on-campus for freshmen. Themed housing available. $100 nonrefundable deposit, deadline 5/1. **Activities:** Bands, campus ministries, choral groups, dance, drama, film society, international student organizations, literary magazine, music ensembles, Model UN, musical theater, opera, student government, student newspaper, symphony orchestra, Women in Spiritual Discernment of Ministry, Atlanta University Center, Muslim student association, National Catholic Student Coalition-Auc Chapter, Caribbean American student association, Asian culture club, Social Justice Fellows, Student Health Associates & Peer Educators, Pauline E. Drake Scholars.

Athletics. Team name: Jaguars.

Student services. Adult student services, chaplain/spiritual director, career counseling, student employment services, financial aid counseling, health services, personal counseling, placement for graduates, women's services. **Physically disabled:** Services for visually, speech, hearing impaired.

Contact. E-mail: admiss@spelman.edu
Phone: (404) 681-3643 ext. 5193 Toll-free number: (800) 982-2411
Fax: (404) 270-5201
Tiffany Nelson, Director of Admissions, Spelman College, 350 Spelman Lane SW, Campus Box 277, Atlanta, GA 30314-4399

Thomas University
Thomasville, Georgia
www.thomasu.edu   CB code: 5072

- Private 4-year university and liberal arts college
- Commuter campus in large town
- 745 degree-seeking undergraduates

General. Founded in 1950. Regionally accredited. **Degrees:** 162 bachelor's, 54 associate awarded; master's offered. **Location:** 60 miles from Albany, GA; 35 miles from Tallahassee, FL. **Calendar:** Semester, extensive summer session. **Full-time faculty:** 58 total; 45% have terminal degrees, 7% minority. **Part-time faculty:** 76 total; 26% have terminal degrees, 13% minority. **Class size:** 85% < 20, 14% 20-39, less than 1% 40-49.

Basis for selection. Open admission, but selective for some programs. Special requirements for nursing program. All students must take the Multiple Assessment Programs & Services examination and successfully complete remedial courses before enrolling in academic courses. **Home schooled:** Transcript of courses and grades, state high school equivalency certificate required.

2015-2016 Annual costs. Tuition/fees: $16,400. Room only: $4,650. Books/supplies: $1,500. Personal expenses: $3,120.

Financial aid. Non-need-based: Scholarships awarded for academics, athletics, leadership, state residency.

Application procedures. Admission: No deadline. $35 fee. Admission notification on a rolling basis. **Financial aid:** Priority date 5/1; no closing date. FAFSA required. Applicants notified on a rolling basis.

Academics. Special study options: Accelerated study, combined bachelor's/graduate degree, distance learning, dual enrollment of high school students, internships, liberal arts/career combination, teacher certification program. **Credit/placement by examination:** AP, CLEP, institutional tests. 40 credit hours maximum toward associate degree, 40 toward bachelor's. Total of 40 hours applies to credit by examination and prior work/life experience credit combined. **Support services:** Learning center, reduced course load, remedial instruction, study skills assistance, tutoring, writing center.

Majors. Biology: General. **Business:** General, accounting, management information systems, marketing. **Education:** Early childhood, elementary, middle, music, secondary. **English:** English lit. **Health services:** Nursing (RN), staff services technology. **History:** General. **Human services:** Social work. **Liberal arts:** Arts/sciences. **Protective services:** Criminal justice. **Psychology:** General. **Social sciences:** General, anthropology.

Most popular majors. Biology 6%, business/marketing 8%, education 21%, interdisciplinary studies 7%, science technologies 9%, security/protective services 14%.

Technology on campus. 50 workstations in library, computer center. Dormitories wired for high-speed internet access and linked to campus network. Commuter students can connect to campus network. Online course registration, online library, helpline, wireless network available.

Student life. Freshman orientation: Available. Preregistration for classes offered. Half-day program held every semester. **Housing:** Guaranteed on-campus for freshmen. Coed dorms, apartments available. $300 deposit. **Activities:** Jazz band, choral groups, drama, literary magazine, music ensembles, student government, student newspaper.

Athletics. NAIA. **Intercollegiate:** Baseball M, golf, soccer, softball W. **Team name:** Night Hawks.

Student services. Adult student services, alcohol/substance abuse counseling, career counseling, student employment services, financial aid counseling, personal counseling, placement for graduates, veterans' counselor. **Physically disabled:** Services for visually, hearing impaired.

Contact. E-mail: admissions@thomasu.edu
Phone: (229) 226-1621 ext. 124
Toll-free number: (800) 538-9784 ext. 124 Fax: (229) 226-1679
Rita Gigliano, Director of Admissions, Thomas University, 1501 Millpond Road, Thomasville, GA 31792-7499

Toccoa Falls College
Toccoa Falls, Georgia   CB member
www.tfc.edu   CB code: 5799

- Private 4-year Bible and liberal arts college affiliated with the Christian and Missionary Alliance
- Residential campus in large town
- 773 degree-seeking undergraduates: 9% part-time, 53% women, 8% African American, 8% Asian American, 4% Hispanic/Latino, 2% Multiracial, non-Hispanic, 1% international
- 45% of applicants admitted
- SAT or ACT (ACT writing recommended), application essay required
- 47% graduate within 6 years

General. Founded in 1907. Regionally accredited; also accredited by ABHE. **Degrees:** 140 bachelor's, 10 associate awarded. **Location:** 90 miles from Atlanta; 60 miles from Greenville, SC. **Calendar:** 4-1-4, limited summer session. **Full-time faculty:** 40 total; 60% have terminal degrees, 8% minority, 28% women. **Part-time faculty:** 59 total; 19% have terminal degrees, 2% minority, 42% women. **Class size:** 68% < 20, 30% 20-39, 1% 40-49, less than 1% 50-99. **Special facilities:** 186-foot waterfall, 1898 hydroelectric generator, nature trails, nature museum.

Freshman class profile. 759 applied, 345 admitted, 150 enrolled.

Mid 50% test scores		GPA 2.0-2.99:	18%
SAT critical reading:	450-580	Rank in top quarter:	43%
SAT math:	430-520	Rank in top tenth:	25%
ACT composite:	18-26	Return as sophomores:	66%
GPA 3.75 or higher:	29%	Out-of-state:	34%
GPA 3.50-3.74:	19%	Live on campus:	88%
GPA 3.0-3.49:	34%		

Basis for selection. Evidence of Christian commitment, character, capacity and desire to learn considered. Index score calculated by multiplying unweighted GPA by best total standardized test score. Personal statement of Christian faith required.

High school preparation. College-preparatory program recommended. 19 units recommended. Recommended units include English 4, mathematics 3, social studies 3, science 3 and academic electives 6.

2016-2017 Annual costs. Tuition/fees (projected): $22,910. Room/board: $7,635. Books/supplies: $1,000. Personal expenses: $2,580.

2014-2015 Financial aid. Need-based: 135 full-time freshmen applied for aid; 119 deemed to have need; 119 received aid. Average need met was 64%. Average scholarship/grant was $13,981; average loan $3,271. 68% of total undergraduate aid awarded as scholarships/grants, 32% as loans/jobs. **Non-need-based:** Awarded to 135 full-time undergraduates, including 38 freshmen. Scholarships awarded for academics.

Application procedures. Admission: Priority date 5/1; deadline 8/1 (postmark date). $25 fee, may be waived for applicants with need. Admission notification on a rolling basis beginning on or about 3/1. Must reply by May 1 or within 2 week(s) if notified thereafter. **Financial aid:** Priority date 5/1, closing date 8/1. FAFSA, institutional form required. Applicants notified on a rolling basis starting 3/1; must reply within 2 week(s) of notification.

Academics. All students complete at least 30 credit hours of Bible/Theology courses (15 credit hours for associate degrees and for Teacher Education bachelor degrees). **Special study options:** Distance learning, double major, dual enrollment of high school students, independent study, internships, study abroad, teacher certification program. **Credit/placement by examination:** AP, CLEP, SAT, ACT, institutional tests. 30 credit hours maximum toward associate degree, 45 toward bachelor's. **Support services:** Learning center, reduced course load, study skills assistance, tutoring.

Majors. Biology: General. **Business:** Business admin, nonprofit/public, organizational leadership. **Communications:** General. **Education:** Elementary, English, history, middle, music, science. **English:** English lit. **Foreign languages:** Biblical. **History:** General. **Parks/recreation:** Outdoor education, sports admin. **Philosophy/religion:** Christian, philosophy. **Psychology:** Counseling. **Theology:** Bible, missionary, pastoral counseling, religious ed, youth ministry. **Visual/performing arts:** Music, music performance. **Work/family studies:** Family/community services.

Most popular majors. Business/marketing 8%, education 14%, parks/recreation 6%, psychology 16%, theological studies 38%.

Technology on campus. 60 workstations in library, computer center. Dormitories wired for high-speed internet access and linked to campus network. Commuter students can connect to campus network. Online course registration, online library, helpline, student web hosting, wireless network available.

Student life. Freshman orientation: Mandatory. Preregistration for classes offered. Held 1 week in fall and throughout spring semester. **Policies:** Students attend weekly church services and participate in student ministry field assignments. Religious observance required. **Housing:** Guaranteed on-campus for freshmen. Single-sex dorms, apartments, wellness housing available. $200 fully refundable deposit. **Activities:** Bands, campus ministries, choral groups, drama, international student organizations, music ensembles, radio station, student government, student newspaper, over 50 different ministry opportunities.

Athletics. NCCAA. **Intercollegiate:** Baseball M, basketball, cross-country, soccer, volleyball W. **Intramural:** Basketball, football (non-tackle), soccer, softball, ultimate frisbee. **Team name:** Screaming Eagles.

Student services. Chaplain/spiritual director, career counseling, student employment services, financial aid counseling, health services, personal counseling. **Physically disabled:** Services for visually impaired.

Contact. E-mail: admissions@tfc.edu
Phone: (706) 886-7299 ext. 5380 Toll-free number: (888) 785-5624
Fax: (706) 282-6012
Zack Whitt, Director of Admission, Toccoa Falls College, PO Box 800899, Toccoa Falls, GA 30598

Truett-McConnell College
Cleveland, Georgia
www.truett.edu

CB member
CB code: 5798

- Private 4-year liberal arts college affiliated with the Southern Baptist Convention
- Residential campus in small town
- 752 degree-seeking undergraduates: 9% part-time, 56% women, 8% African American, 1% Asian American, 4% Hispanic/Latino, 2% international
- 20 degree-seeking graduate students

- 91% of applicants admitted
- SAT or ACT (ACT writing optional), application essay required
- 34% graduate within 6 years

General. Founded in 1946. Regionally accredited. Associated with Baptist Convention of the State of Georgia. **Degrees:** 91 bachelor's awarded. **Location:** 75 miles from Atlanta, 25 miles from Gainesville. **Calendar:** Semester, limited summer session. **Full-time faculty:** 50 total; 46% have terminal degrees. **Part-time faculty:** 65 total. **Class size:** 63% < 20, 24% 20-39, 2% 40-49, 10% 50-99. **Special facilities:** World Missions Center, Creation Research Center.

Freshman class profile. 485 applied, 442 admitted, 210 enrolled.

Mid 50% test scores			
SAT critical reading:	430-510	Rank in top quarter:	33%
SAT math:	410-510	Rank in top tenth:	13%
SAT writing:	410-500	Return as sophomores:	62%
ACT composite:	18-22	Out-of-state:	9%
GPA 3.75 or higher:	27%	Live on campus:	79%
GPA 3.50-3.74:	24%	International:	2%
GPA 3.0-3.49:	30%		
GPA 2.0-2.99:	18%		

Basis for selection. 2.0 GPA and 710 SAT or 15 ACT required. Students with lower scores may apply and are reviewed by an appeal committee. Audition required of music majors. **Home schooled:** Transcript of courses and grades required. Letter from local school board stating that student has completed homeschool program requirements and placement exams required. **Learning Disabled:** Students may request accommodations upon presentation of appropriate documentation of disability. Determination of reasonable accommodations made on individual basis.

High school preparation. College-preparatory program recommended. Recommended units include English 4, mathematics 3, social studies 3, science 3 and foreign language 2.

2015-2016 Annual costs. Tuition/fees: $17,900. Room/board: $7,220. Books/supplies: $1,600. Personal expenses: $1,500.

2015-2016 Financial aid. Need-based: 199 full-time freshmen applied for aid; 178 deemed to have need; 178 received aid. Average need met was 64%. Average scholarship/grant was $11,579; average loan $3,697. 65% of total undergraduate aid awarded as scholarships/grants, 35% as loans/jobs. **Non-need-based:** Awarded to 228 full-time undergraduates, including 72 freshmen. Scholarships awarded for academics, alumni affiliation, athletics, leadership, minority status, music/drama, religious affiliation, state residency.

Application procedures. Admission: Closing date 8/1 (receipt date). $25 fee, may be waived for applicants with need, free for online applicants. Admission notification on a rolling basis. Must reply by May 1 or within 1 week(s) if notified thereafter. **Financial aid:** Priority date 4/1; no closing date. FAFSA, institutional form required. Applicants notified on a rolling basis starting 3/15; must reply within 2 week(s) of notification.

Academics. Special study options: Distance learning, double major, dual enrollment of high school students, independent study. **Credit/placement by examination:** AP, CLEP, SAT, ACT, institutional tests. 30 credit hours maximum toward associate degree, 30 toward bachelor's. **Support services:** Remedial instruction, tutoring.

Majors. Biology: General. **Business:** General. **Education:** Early childhood, middle, music. **English:** English lit. **Health services:** Nursing (RN). **History:** General. **Parks/recreation:** Exercise sciences. **Protective services:** Criminal justice. **Psychology:** General. **Theology:** Bible, missionary, sacred music, youth ministry. **Visual/performing arts:** Music.

Most popular majors. Business/marketing 22%, education 11%, health sciences 9%, psychology 18%, theological studies 23%, visual/performing arts 8%.

Technology on campus. 45 workstations in library, student center. Dormitories wired for high-speed internet access and linked to campus network. Online course registration, helpline, wireless network available.

Student life. Freshman orientation: Mandatory. Preregistration for classes offered. Three days prior to start of fall classes and Monday before start of spring classes. **Policies:** Tobacco-free campus. Religious observance required. **Housing:** Single-sex dorms, apartments, wellness housing available. $100 fully refundable deposit. **Activities:** Bands, campus ministries, choral groups, music ensembles, student government.

Athletics. NAIA. **Intercollegiate:** Baseball M, basketball, cross-country, golf, lacrosse W, soccer, softball W, volleyball W, wrestling M. **Intramural:** Basketball, football (non-tackle), volleyball. **Team name:** Bears.

Student services. Career counseling, student employment services, financial aid counseling, veterans' counselor.

Contact. E-mail: admissions@truett.edu
Phone: (706) 865-2134 Toll-free number: (800) 226-8621
Fax: (706) 865-3110
Andrew Gailey, Director of Admissions, Truett-McConnell College, 100
Alumni Drive, Cleveland, GA 30528

University of Georgia
Athens, Georgia
CB member
www.uga.edu
CB code: 5813

◗ Public 4-year university

◗ Residential campus in small city

◗ 27,328 degree-seeking undergraduates: 6% part-time, 57% women, 7%
African American, 10% Asian American, 5% Hispanic/Latino, 4% Multi-
racial, non-Hispanic, 2% international

◗ 8,417 degree-seeking graduate students

◗ 53% of applicants admitted

◗ SAT or ACT (ACT writing optional), application essay required

◗ 84% graduate within 6 years

General. Founded in 1785. Regionally accredited. **Degrees:** 6,935 bachelor's awarded; master's, professional, doctoral offered. **ROTC:** Army, Air
Force. **Location:** 70 miles from Atlanta. **Calendar:** Semester, extensive
summer session. **Full-time faculty:** 1,918 total; 93% have terminal degrees,
20% minority, 38% women. **Special facilities:** Regional botanical garden,
golf course, performing arts center, regional art museum.

Freshman class profile. 21,945 applied, 11,604 admitted, 5,274 enrolled.

Mid 50% test scores		Rank in top quarter:	88%
SAT critical reading:	570-660	Rank in top tenth:	53%
SAT math:	580-670	Return as sophomores:	95%
SAT writing:	560-660	Out-of-state:	11%
ACT composite:	26-30	Live on campus:	98%
GPA 3.75 or higher:	74%	International:	2%
GPA 3.50-3.74:	20%	Fraternities:	21%
GPA 3.0-3.49:	6%	Sororities:	11%

Basis for selection. GPA in core academic courses, rigor of course selection, and best combination of SAT/ACT important. Applications reviewed for
conduct issues, recommendations, and satisfactory completion of all courses
including required college preparatory courses. Provided the student applied
by our deadline of January 15th. Audition required of music majors.

High school preparation. College-preparatory program required. 17 units
required; 19 recommended. Required and recommended units include English
4, mathematics 4, social studies 3, history 2, science 4 (laboratory 2), foreign
language 2-3 and academic electives 1.

2015-2016 Annual costs. Tuition/fees: $11,622; $29,832 out-of-state.
Room/board: $9,436. Personal expenses: $2,780.

2015-2016 Financial aid. Need-based: 4,429 full-time freshmen applied
for aid; 2,328 deemed to have need; 2,304 received aid. Average need met
was 78%. Average scholarship/grant was $10,210; average loan $3,260. 68%
of total undergraduate aid awarded as scholarships/grants, 32% as loans/jobs.
Non-need-based: Awarded to 3,661 full-time undergraduates, including 828
freshmen. Scholarships awarded for academics, athletics, ROTC, state residency.

Application procedures. Admission: Priority date 10/15; deadline 1/15
(postmark date). $60 fee, may be waived for applicants with need. Admission
notification by 4/1. Must reply by 5/1. **Financial aid:** Priority date 3/1; no
closing date. FAFSA required. Applicants notified on a rolling basis starting
5/1; must reply within 2 week(s) of notification.

Academics. Special study options: Accelerated study, combined bachelor's/graduate degree, cooperative education, cross-registration, distance
learning, double major, dual enrollment of high school students, exchange
student, external degree, honors, independent study, internships, liberal arts/
career combination, student-designed major, study abroad, teacher certification program, Washington semester. **Credit/placement by examination:**
AP, CLEP, IB, institutional tests. Unlimited number of hours of credit by
examination may be counted toward bachelor's degree. **Support services:**
Learning center, pre-admission summer program, reduced course load, remedial instruction, study skills assistance, tutoring, writing center.

Majors. Architecture: Landscape. **Area/ethnic studies:** African-
American, Latin American/Caribbean, women's. **Biology:** General, Biochem-
istry/molecular biology, biotechnology, botany, cell/histology, ecology, entomology, genetics, microbiology. **Business:** General, accounting, business
admin, fashion, finance, insurance, international, management information
systems, managerial economics, marketing, real estate. **Communications:**

Advertising, broadcast journalism, communications/speech/rhetoric, digital
media, journalism, public relations. **Computer sciences:** Computer science.
Conservation: Environmental science, forestry, nature tourism, wildlife/wil-
derness. **Education:** Agricultural, early childhood, English, family/consumer
sciences, foreign languages, mathematics, middle, music, science, social studies, special ed. **Engineering:** Agricultural, biochemical, biological, civil,
computer, electrical, environmental, mechanical. **English:** English lit.
Foreign languages: Ancient Greek, Arabic, Chinese, classics, comparative
lit, French, German, Italian, Japanese, linguistics, Romance, Russian, Spanish.
Health services: Athletic training, communication disorders, dietetics, environmental health, music therapy, pharmaceutical sciences, public health ed.
History: General. **Human services:** Social work. **Liberal arts:** Arts/sciences.
Math: General, statistics. **Parks/recreation:** Exercise sciences, health/fit-
ness, sports admin. **Philosophy/religion:** Philosophy, religion. **Physical sciences:** Astronomy, chemistry, environmental chemistry, geology, physics.
Protective services: Law enforcement admin. **Psychology:** General. **Social
sciences:** Anthropology, geography, international relations, political science,
sociology. **Visual/performing arts:** Art, art history/conservation, dance, dramatic, film/cinema/video, music, music performance, music theory/composi-
tion, studio arts. **Work/family studies:** Communication, consumer economics, family resources, family studies, food/nutrition, housing.

Most popular majors. Biology 9%, business/marketing 23%, communica-
tions/journalism 11%, education 6%, psychology 6%, social sciences 9%.

Technology on campus. Dormitories wired for high-speed internet
access and linked to campus network. Commuter students can connect to
campus network. Online course registration, online library, helpline, repair
service, student web hosting, wireless network available.

Student life. Freshman orientation: Mandatory. Preregistration for
classes offered. Two-day sessions offered during summer. **Housing:** Guaranteed on-campus for freshmen. Coed dorms, single-sex dorms, special housing
for disabled, apartments, fraternity/sorority housing, themed housing available. Honors and language focused housing available. **Activities:** Bands,
campus ministries, choral groups, dance, drama, film society, international
student organizations, literary magazine, music ensembles, Model UN,
musical theater, opera, radio station, student government, student newspaper,
symphony orchestra.

Athletics. NCAA. **Intercollegiate:** Baseball M, basketball, cross-country,
diving, equestrian W, football (tackle) M, golf, gymnastics W, soccer W,
softball W, swimming, tennis, track and field, volleyball W. **Intramural:**
Badminton, basketball, football (non-tackle), football (tackle), golf, racquetball, soccer, softball, tennis, ultimate frisbee, volleyball, water polo.
Team name: Bulldogs.

Student services. Adult student services, alcohol/substance abuse counseling, career counseling, student employment services, financial aid counseling, health services, legal services, minority student services, on-campus
daycare, personal counseling, placement for graduates, veterans' counselor,
women's services. **Physically disabled:** Services for visually, speech, hearing impaired.

Contact. E-mail: adm-info@uga.edu
Phone: (706) 542-8776 Fax: (706) 542-1466
Patrick Winter, Associate Vice President, University of Georgia, Terrell
Hall, Athens, GA 30602-1633

University of North Georgia
Dahlonega, Georgia
CB member
www.ung.edu
CB code: 5497

◗ Public 4-year university and liberal arts college

◗ Commuter campus in large town

◗ 16,048 degree-seeking undergraduates: 28% part-time, 55% women, 4%
African American, 3% Asian American, 11% Hispanic/Latino, 3% Multi-
racial, non-Hispanic, 2% international

◗ 454 degree-seeking graduate students

◗ 64% of applicants admitted

◗ SAT or ACT (ACT writing optional) required

◗ 54% graduate within 6 years

General. Founded in 1873. Regionally accredited. On January 8, 2013, the
consolidation of North Georgia College & State University and Gainesville
State College officially became the University of North Georgia. **Degrees:**
1,312 bachelor's, 820 associate awarded; master's, professional offered.
ROTC: Army. **Location:** 70 miles from Atlanta. **Calendar:** Semester, extensive summer session. **Class size:** 30% < 20, 64% 20-39, 3% 40-49, 3% 50-
99, less than 1% >100. **Special facilities:** Observatory, rappelling tower,
planetarium, nature preserve.

Freshman class profile. 5,623 applied, 3,622 admitted, 1,711 enrolled.

Mid 50% test scores			
SAT critical reading:	510-600	GPA 3.0-3.49:	36%
SAT math:	500-590	GPA 2.0-2.99:	4%
SAT writing:	480-570	Return as sophomores:	80%
ACT composite:	22-26	Out-of-state:	2%
GPA 3.75 or higher:	32%	Live on campus:	27%
GPA 3.50-3.74:	28%	International:	1%

Basis for selection. High school academic GPA and SAT/ACT scores. Freshmen applying to associate degree programs must take COMPASS exam if SAT/ACT requirements are not met. Baccalaureate admissions are more selective. Students must provide certification of immunization against communicable diseases. Commuting students must apply for permission to commute. Audition recommended for music majors. Portfolio recommended for art majors. **Home schooled:** Must provide a portfolio of documents, per University instructions.

High school preparation. College-preparatory program recommended. 17 units required. Required units include English 4, mathematics 4, social studies 3, science 4 (laboratory 2) and foreign language 2.

2015-2016 Annual costs. Tuition/fees: $7,178; $20,720 out-of-state. Room/board: $7,642.

2014-2015 Financial aid. Need-based: 2,672 full-time freshmen applied for aid; 1,790 deemed to have need; 1,701 received aid. Average need met was 68%. Average scholarship/grant was $5,945; average loan $3,775. 56% of total undergraduate aid awarded as scholarships/grants, 44% as loans/jobs. **Non-need-based:** Awarded to 721 full-time undergraduates, including 322 freshmen. Scholarships awarded for academics, alumni affiliation, art, athletics, leadership, minority status, music/drama, ROTC, state residency.

Application procedures. Admission: Priority date 11/15; deadline 2/15. $30 fee, may be waived for applicants with need. Admission notification on a rolling basis. Must reply by May 1 or within 2 week(s) if notified thereafter. **Financial aid:** No deadline. FAFSA required. Applicants notified on a rolling basis starting 4/1; must reply within 2 week(s) of notification.

Academics. Special study options: Accelerated study, combined bachelor's/graduate degree, cooperative education, distance learning, double major, dual enrollment of high school students, ESL, honors, internships, liberal arts/career combination, study abroad, teacher certification program. Dual degree program in engineering with Georgia Institute of Technology and Clemson University. **Credit/placement by examination:** AP, CLEP, SAT, ACT, institutional tests. 30 credit hours maximum toward associate degree, 30 toward bachelor's. **Support services:** Learning center, pre-admission summer program, reduced course load, remedial instruction, study skills assistance, tutoring, writing center.

Honors college/program. Admission by application to program coordinator. 2 letters of recommendation and 1150 SAT or 3.5 GPA required.

Majors. Biology: General. **Business:** Accounting, business admin, finance, marketing. **Communications:** Digital media. **Computer sciences:** General, information systems. **Conservation:** Environmental studies. **Education:** Art, early childhood, elementary, middle, music, physical, secondary, special ed. **English:** English lit. **Foreign languages:** General. **Health services:** Athletic training, nursing (RN). **History:** General. **Math:** General. **Physical sciences:** Chemistry, physics. **Protective services:** Criminal justice. **Social sciences:** International relations, political science, sociology. **Visual/performing arts:** Commercial/advertising art, music performance, studio arts, theater design.

Most popular majors. Biology 7%, business/marketing 23%, education 25%, psychology 6%, security/protective services 6%, social sciences 7%.

Technology on campus. Dormitories linked to campus network. Commuter students can connect to campus network. Online course registration, online library, helpline, repair service, student web hosting, wireless network available.

Student life. Freshman orientation: Available, $105 fee. Preregistration for classes offered. Two-day overnight program held 4 times during summer; students stay in residence halls. **Policies:** Cadets who have earned 90 semester hours may elect to leave Corps to become civilian students. Those leaving the Corps prior to earning 90 hours will be ineligible to enroll in courses for one year. **Housing:** Single-sex dorms, apartments, themed housing available. $250 fully refundable deposit, deadline 5/1. Military housing available. **Activities:** Bands, campus ministries, choral groups, dance, drama, film society, international student organizations, literary magazine, music ensembles, Model UN, musical theater, radio station, student government, student newspaper, symphony orchestra, Commuter Council, Students of Caribbean Ancestry, Voices for Women, Habitat for Humanity, Wesley Foundation, Gay Straight Alliance, Graduate Student Senate.

Athletics. NCAA. **Intercollegiate:** Baseball M, basketball, cheerleading W, cross-country W, golf, rifle, soccer, softball W, tennis. **Intramural:** Basketball, football (non-tackle), softball, table tennis, ultimate frisbee, volleyball, water polo. **Team name:** Nighthawks.

Student services. Alcohol/substance abuse counseling, career counseling, student employment services, financial aid counseling, health services, minority student services, personal counseling, placement for graduates, veterans' counselor, women's services. **Physically disabled:** Services for visually, speech, hearing impaired.

Contact. E-mail: bacheloradmissions@ung.edu
Phone: (706) 864-1800 Toll-free number: (800) 498-9581
Fax: (706) 864-1478
Molly Potts, Executive Director, Undergraduate Admissions, University of North Georgia, 82 College Circle, Dahlonega, GA 30597

University of Phoenix: Atlanta
Sandy Springs, Georgia
www.phoenix.edu

- For-profit 4-year university
- Small city
- 1,700 degree-seeking undergraduates

General. Regionally accredited. **Degrees:** 764 bachelor's awarded; master's offered. **Calendar:** Differs by program. **Full-time faculty:** 13 total. **Part-time faculty:** 169 total.

Basis for selection. Open admission.

2015-2016 Annual costs. Per-credit-hour charge $395 to $610, depending upon level and course of study; electronic course materials fee range between $95 and $200 if applicable. Book and material charges may vary by course and program. All fees are subject to change.

Application procedures. Admission: No deadline. No application fee. **Financial aid:** No deadline.

Academics. Credit/placement by examination: AP, CLEP.

Majors. Business: Accounting, accounting/business management, business admin, e-commerce, entrepreneurial studies, finance, human resources, marketing, operations. **Communications:** General. **Computer sciences:** Database management, networking, programming, security, system admin, systems analysis, web page design, webmaster. **Health services:** Facilities admin, health information management, long term care admin, nursing (RN). **Human services:** General. **Protective services:** Disaster management, law enforcement admin, security management.

Student life. Freshman orientation: Mandatory. Preregistration for classes offered.

Contact. Toll-free number: (866) 766-0766
University of Phoenix: Atlanta, 1625 W. Fountainhead Pkwy, Tempe, AZ 85282

University of Phoenix: Augusta
Augusta, Georgia
www.phoenix.edu

- For-profit 4-year university
- Commuter campus in small city
- 930 degree-seeking undergraduates

General. Regionally accredited. **Degrees:** 166 bachelor's awarded; master's offered. **Calendar:** Differs by program. **Full-time faculty:** 14 total. **Part-time faculty:** 123 total.

Basis for selection. Open admission.

2015-2016 Annual costs. Per-credit-hour charge $410 to $635, depending upon level and course of study; electronic course materials fee $95-$200 if applicable. Book and material charges may vary by course and program. All fees are subject to change.

Application procedures. Admission: No deadline. No application fee.

Academics. Credit/placement by examination: AP, CLEP.

Majors. Business: Accounting, accounting/business management, business admin, e-commerce, entrepreneurial studies, finance, human resources, marketing, operations. **Communications:** General. **Computer sciences:** Database management, networking, programming, security, system admin, systems analysis, web page design, webmaster. **Health services:** Facilities admin, health information management, long term care admin. **Human services:** General. **Protective services:** Disaster management, law enforcement admin, security management.

Student life. Freshman orientation: Mandatory. Preregistration for classes offered.

Contact. Toll-free number: (866) 766-0766
University of Phoenix: Augusta, 1625 W. Fountainhead Pkwy, Tempe, AZ 85282

University of Phoenix: Columbus
Columbus, Georgia
www.phoenix.edu

‣ For-profit 4-year university
‣ Small city
‣ 1,000 degree-seeking undergraduates

General. Regionally accredited. **Degrees:** 99 bachelor's awarded; master's offered. **Calendar:** Differs by program. Other Academic Calendar. **Full-time faculty:** 10 total. **Part-time faculty:** 86 total.

Basis for selection. Open admission.

2015-2016 Annual costs. Per-credit-hour charge $395 to $630, depending upon level and course of study; electronic course materials fee $95-$200, if applicable. Book and material charges may vary by course and program. All fees are subject to change.

Application procedures. Admission: No deadline. No application fee. **Financial aid:** No deadline.

Academics. Credit/placement by examination: AP, CLEP.

Majors. Business: Accounting, accounting/business management, business admin, e-commerce, entrepreneurial studies, finance, human resources, marketing, operations. **Communications:** General. **Computer sciences:** Database management, networking, programming, security, system admin, systems analysis, web page design, webmaster. **Health services:** Facilities admin, health information management, long term care admin, nursing (RN). **Human services:** General. **Protective services:** Disaster management, law enforcement admin, security management.

Student life. Freshman orientation: Mandatory. Preregistration for classes offered.

Contact. Toll-free number: (866) 766-0766
University of Phoenix: Columbus, 7200 N. Lake Drive, Columbus, GA 31909

University of Phoenix: Savannah
Savannah, Georgia
www.phoenix.edu

‣ For-profit 4-year university
‣ Commuter campus in small city
‣ 490 degree-seeking undergraduates

General. Regionally accredited. **Degrees:** 65 bachelor's awarded; master's offered. **Calendar:** Differs by program. Other Academic Calendar. **Full-time faculty:** 9 total. **Part-time faculty:** 80 total.

Basis for selection. Open admission.

2015-2016 Annual costs. Per-credit-hour charge $395 to $635, depending upon level and course of study; electronic course materials fee $95-$200, if applicable. Book and material charges may vary by course and program. All fees are subject to change.

Application procedures. Admission: No deadline. No application fee. **Financial aid:** No deadline.

Academics. Credit/placement by examination: AP, CLEP.

Majors. Business: Accounting, accounting/business management, business admin, e-commerce, entrepreneurial studies, finance, human resources, marketing, operations. **Communications:** General. **Computer sciences:** Database management, networking, programming, security, system admin, systems analysis, web page design, webmaster. **Health services:** Facilities admin, health information management, long term care admin, nursing (RN). **Human services:** General. **Protective services:** Disaster management, law enforcement admin, security management.

Student life. Freshman orientation: Mandatory. Preregistration for classes offered.

Contact. Toll-free number: (866) 766-0766
University of Phoenix: Savannah, 1625 W. Fountainhead Pkwy, Tempe, AZ 85282

University of West Georgia
Carrollton, Georgia
www.westga.edu
CB member
CB code: 5900

‣ Public 4-year university
‣ Commuter campus in large town
‣ 10,753 degree-seeking undergraduates: 18% part-time, 63% women, 37% African American, 1% Asian American, 5% Hispanic/Latino, 3% Multi-racial, non-Hispanic, 1% international
‣ 2,081 degree-seeking graduate students
‣ 57% of applicants admitted
‣ SAT or ACT (ACT writing optional) required
‣ 39% graduate within 6 years

General. Founded in 1906. Regionally accredited. Additional instructional site locations in Douglasville and Newnan. **Degrees:** 1,587 bachelor's awarded; master's, doctoral offered. **ROTC:** Air Force. **Location:** 50 miles from Atlanta. **Calendar:** Semester, limited summer session. **Full-time faculty:** 423 total; 77% have terminal degrees, 20% minority, 57% women. **Part-time faculty:** 271 total; 38% have terminal degrees, 20% minority, 60% women. **Class size:** 34% < 20, 47% 20-39, 8% 40-49, 7% 50-99, 3% >100. **Special facilities:** Observatory, performing arts center, archaeological laboratory, technology enhanced learning center, coliseum, football stadium, campus center.

Freshman class profile. 7,679 applied, 4,381 admitted, 2,410 enrolled.

Mid 50% test scores			
SAT critical reading:	440-520	**GPA 2.0-2.99:**	37%
SAT math:	420-500	**Return as sophomores:**	73%
SAT writing:	420-510	**Out-of-state:**	3%
ACT composite:	18-22	**Live on campus:**	73%
GPA 3.75 or higher:	13%	**International:**	1%
GPA 3.50-3.74:	14%	**Fraternities:**	8%
GPA 3.0-3.49:	36%	**Sororities:**	11%

Basis for selection. SAT/ACT, GPA in college preparatory subjects, and system-mandated college preparatory curriculum. **Home schooled:** 430 SAT verbal and 410 SAT math or 17 ACT English and math required. Must submit academic portfolio booklets detailing all 16 high school college prep courses.

High school preparation. College-preparatory program recommended. 17 units required. Required units include English 4, mathematics 4, social studies 1, history 2, science 4 (laboratory 2) and foreign language 2.

2015-2016 Annual costs. Tuition/fees: $7,188; $20,406 out-of-state. Room/board: $9,698. Books/supplies: $1,500. Personal expenses: $1,800.

2015-2016 Financial aid. Need-based: 2,253 full-time freshmen applied for aid; 1,879 deemed to have need; 1,851 received aid. Average need met was 46%. Average scholarship/grant was $4,961; average loan $3,400. 52% of total undergraduate aid awarded as scholarships/grants, 48% as loans/jobs. **Non-need-based:** Awarded to 1,501 full-time undergraduates, including 498 freshmen. Scholarships awarded for academics, alumni affiliation, art, athletics, job skills, leadership, minority status, music/drama, religious affiliation.

Application procedures. Admission: Priority date 2/1; deadline 6/1 (receipt date). $40 fee, may be waived for applicants with need. Admission notification on a rolling basis beginning on or about 9/1. **Financial aid:** Priority date 4/1, closing date 7/1. FAFSA required. Applicants notified on a rolling basis starting 5/1.

Academics. Special study options: Accelerated study, cooperative education, cross-registration, distance learning, double major, dual enrollment of high school students, external degree, honors, independent study, internships, study abroad, teacher certification program. **Credit/placement by examination:** AP, CLEP, IB, SAT, ACT, institutional tests. 30 credit hours maximum toward bachelor's degree. **Support services:** Learning center, reduced course load, study skills assistance, tutoring, writing center.

Majors. Biology: General. **Business:** Accounting, business admin, finance, management information systems, managerial economics, marketing, real estate. **Communications:** Journalism. **Computer sciences:** General. **Education:** Elementary, music, physical, special ed. **English:** English lit. **Health services:** Nursing (RN), speech pathology. **History:** General. **Math:** General. **Parks/recreation:** Facilities management. **Philosophy/religion:** Philosophy. **Physical sciences:** Chemistry, geology, physics. **Psychology:** General. **Social sciences:** Anthropology, criminology, economics, geography, international economics, international relations, political science, sociology. **Visual/performing arts:** Art, dramatic, music performance, music theory/composition.

Most popular majors. Biology 6%, business/marketing 22%, communications/journalism 6%, education 13%, health sciences 14%, psychology 9%, social sciences 15%.

Technology on campus. 1,200 workstations in dormitories, library, computer center, student center. Dormitories wired for high-speed internet access and linked to campus network. Online course registration, online library, helpline, repair service, student web hosting, wireless network available.

Student life. Freshman orientation: Mandatory. Preregistration for classes offered. Held beginning of semester; includes registration assistance and presentation of available services. **Policies:** Freshmen required to reside on-campus unless married or living with parents, relatives, or legal guardians. **Housing:** Guaranteed on-campus for freshmen. Coed dorms, special housing for disabled, apartments, fraternity/sorority housing, themed housing, wellness housing available. $150 nonrefundable deposit. **Activities:** Bands, campus ministries, choral groups, dance, drama, international student organizations, literary magazine, music ensembles, musical theater, opera, radio station, student government, student newspaper, TV station.

Athletics. NCAA. **Intercollegiate:** Baseball M, basketball, cross-country, football (tackle) M, golf, soccer W, softball W, tennis W, track and field W, volleyball W. **Intramural:** Basketball, football (non-tackle), sand volleyball, soccer, softball, ultimate frisbee, volleyball. **Team name:** Wolves.

Student services. Adult student services, career counseling, student employment services, financial aid counseling, health services, minority student services, on-campus daycare, personal counseling, placement for graduates, veterans' counselor. **Physically disabled:** Services for visually, speech, hearing impaired.

Contact. E-mail: admiss@westga.edu
Phone: (678) 839-4000 Fax: (678) 839-4747
Justin Barlow, Director of Admissions, University of West Georgia, 1601 Maple Street, Carrollton, GA 30118

Valdosta State University
Valdosta, Georgia
www.valdosta.edu

CB member
CB code: 5855

- Public 4-year university
- Commuter campus in small city
- 8,744 degree-seeking undergraduates: 17% part-time, 59% women, 36% African American, 1% Asian American, 5% Hispanic/Latino, 3% Multiracial, non-Hispanic, 3% international
- 2,398 degree-seeking graduate students
- 50% of applicants admitted
- SAT or ACT (ACT writing optional) required
- 36% graduate within 6 years

General. Founded in 1906. Regionally accredited. **Degrees:** 1,682 bachelor's, 39 associate awarded; master's, professional, doctoral offered. **ROTC:** Air Force. **Location:** 124 miles from Jacksonville, FL, 226 miles from Atlanta. **Calendar:** Semester, extensive summer session. **Full-time faculty:** 467 total; 80% have terminal degrees, 18% minority, 49% women. **Part-time faculty:** 139 total; 31% have terminal degrees, 17% minority, 58% women. **Class size:** 51% < 20, 41% 20-39, 4% 40-49, 3% 50-99, 1% >100. **Special facilities:** Planetarium, herbarium, observatory, archives museum, pedestrian mall, camellia garden, amphitheatre.

Freshman class profile. 5,564 applied, 2,806 admitted, 1,387 enrolled.

Mid 50% test scores			
SAT critical reading:	460-550	GPA 2.0-2.99:	33%
SAT math:	450-530	Return as sophomores:	69%
SAT writing:	440-530	Out-of-state:	8%
ACT composite:	19-23	Live on campus:	77%
GPA 3.75 or higher:	16%	International:	2%
GPA 3.50-3.74:	16%	Fraternities:	14%
GPA 3.0-3.49:	35%	Sororities:	20%

Basis for selection. Georgia State Board of Regents minimum requirements for each section, 430 Critical Reading (SAT subscore) and 400 Math (SAT subscore), with minimum total score of 900 SAT (Math and Critical Reading only) or 17 English (ACT subscore) and 17 Math (ACT subscore) with an ACT Composite score of 19. A Freshman Index (FI) of 2040 calculated using total SAT Score, exclusive of Writing + (500 x high school academic GPA) or (ACT composite x 42) + 88 + (500 x high school GPA). Specific degree programs may require an interview, audition, essay, or personal statement for acceptance into the program. **Home schooled:** Letter of recommendation (nonparent) required. 1050 SAT with 430 critical reading/400 math or 19 ACT with 17 English/17 math, official transcripts from any high school and colleges attended, and copy of Declaration of Intent to Home School as filed with your local Board of Education required. Portfolio must include information about each course used to satisfy CPC requirements and list of educational resources used, course outline or syllabus, and outcomes assessment. Also include any extracurricular activities and/or academic achievements, letter from primary teacher certifying completion of high school and a date of graduation, and two letters of recommendation from non-family members such as employer, clergy, civic leader, or tutor. **Learning Disabled:** Untimed SAT/ACT accepted.

High school preparation. College-preparatory program required. 17 units required. Required units include English 4, mathematics 4, social studies 3, history 2, science 4 (laboratory 2) and foreign language 2.

2015-2016 Annual costs. Tuition/fees: $7,342; $20,560 out-of-state. Room/board: $7,912. Books/supplies: $1,200. Personal expenses: $1,660.

2014-2015 Financial aid. Need-based: 1,427 full-time freshmen applied for aid; 1,168 deemed to have need; 1,168 received aid. Average need met was 98%. Average scholarship/grant was $6,943; average loan $3,389. 34% of total undergraduate aid awarded as scholarships/grants, 66% as loans/jobs. **Non-need-based:** Awarded to 339 full-time undergraduates, including 96 freshmen. Scholarships awarded for academics, art, athletics, minority status, music/drama, ROTC, state residency.

Application procedures. Admission: Closing date 6/15 (receipt date). $40 fee, may be waived for applicants with need. Admission notification by 9/1. Admission notification on a rolling basis beginning on or about 8/1. **Financial aid:** Priority date 4/1, closing date 3/1. FAFSA required. Applicants notified on a rolling basis starting 3/15.

Academics. Special study options: Accelerated study, cooperative education, distance learning, double major, dual enrollment of high school students, ESL, external degree, honors, independent study, internships, study abroad, teacher certification program, weekend college. **Credit/placement by examination:** AP, CLEP, IB, SAT, ACT, institutional tests. 30 credit hours maximum toward associate degree, 30 toward bachelor's. **Support services:** Study skills assistance, tutoring, writing center.

Honors college/program. Entering freshmen with a combined quantitative and verbal SAT score of 1170 or higher (ACT composite score of 26 or higher) and a high school grade point average of B+ (3.2) or higher are eligible to apply. Currently enrolled students at VSU with cumulative grade point average of 3.2 or higher after completing 15 hours are also eligible to apply.

Majors. Biology: General. **Business:** Accounting, administrative services, business admin, finance, international, managerial economics, marketing, organizational leadership. **Communications:** Communications/speech/rhetoric, media studies. **Computer sciences:** General, information systems. **Education:** Art, early childhood, middle, physical, special ed, trade/industrial. **English:** English lit. **Foreign languages:** French, sign language interpretation, Spanish. **Health services:** Athletic training, health care admin, nursing (RN), speech pathology. **History:** General. **Math:** General, applied. **Philosophy/religion:** General. **Physical sciences:** Astronomy, chemistry, geology, physics. **Protective services:** Criminal justice. **Psychology:** General. **Social sciences:** Political science, sociology/anthropology. **Visual/performing arts:** Art, dance, dramatic, interior design, music, music performance.

Most popular majors. Business/marketing 21%, communications/journalism 9%, education 11%, health sciences 11%, psychology 9%, security/protective services 6%.

Technology on campus. 1,733 workstations in library, computer center, student center. Dormitories wired for high-speed internet access and linked to campus network. Commuter students can connect to campus network. Online course registration, online library, helpline, repair service, student web hosting, wireless network available.

Student life. Freshman orientation: Available, $55 fee. Preregistration for classes offered. One-day programs offered to all first-year and transfer students entering their first semester. **Policies:** Student organizations must be registered with the Office of Student Life. **Housing:** Coed dorms, special housing for disabled, apartments, fraternity/sorority housing, themed housing available. $300 partly refundable deposit, deadline 4/15. Honors housing available. **Activities:** Bands, campus ministries, choral groups, dance, drama, film society, international student organizations, literary magazine, music ensembles, Model UN, musical theater, opera, radio station, student government, student newspaper, symphony orchestra, TV station, Baptist Collegiate Ministries, Catholic Newman Center, Black Student League, Fellowship of Christian Athletes, Hillel, Latin American Students Association, Students Against Violating the Environment, Wesley Foundation, College Republicans, College Democrats.

Athletics. NCAA. **Intercollegiate:** Baseball M, basketball, cheerleading, cross-country, football (tackle) M, golf M, soccer W, softball W, tennis, volleyball W. **Intramural:** Basketball, bowling, football (non-tackle), golf, racquetball, soccer, softball, table tennis, tennis, ultimate frisbee, volleyball. **Team name:** Blazers.

Student services. Adult student services, alcohol/substance abuse counseling, career counseling, student employment services, financial aid counseling, health services, minority student services, personal counseling, placement for graduates, veterans' counselor. **Physically disabled:** Services for visually, speech, hearing impaired.

Contact. E-mail: admissions@valdosta.edu
Phone: (229) 333-5791 Toll-free number: (800) 618-1878
Fax: (229) 333-5482
Ryan Hogan, Director of Admissions, Valdosta State University, 1500 North Patterson Street, Valdosta, GA 31698-0170

Wesleyan College
Macon, Georgia
www.wesleyancollege.edu
CB member
CB code: 5895

▶ Private 4-year nursing and liberal arts college for women affiliated with the United Methodist Church
▶ Residential campus in small city
▶ 660 degree-seeking undergraduates: 22% part-time, 100% women, 27% African American, 2% Asian American, 4% Hispanic/Latino, 3% Multiracial, non-Hispanic, 24% international
▶ 48 degree-seeking graduate students
▶ 42% of applicants admitted
▶ SAT or ACT (ACT writing optional), application essay required
▶ 59% graduate within 6 years; 56% enter graduate study

General. Founded in 1836. Regionally accredited. **Degrees:** 135 bachelor's awarded; master's offered. **ROTC:** Army. **Location:** 75 miles of Atlanta. **Calendar:** Semester, limited summer session. **Full-time faculty:** 54 total; 93% have terminal degrees, 9% minority, 68% women. **Part-time faculty:** 1 total; 100% minority. **Class size:** 78% < 20, 21% 20-39, less than 1% 40-49, less than 1% 50-99. **Special facilities:** Equestrian facilities, arboretum, lake, Confucius Institute.

Freshman class profile. 848 applied, 353 admitted, 119 enrolled.

Mid 50% test scores		End year in good standing:	88%
SAT critical reading:	480-580	Return as sophomores:	79%
SAT math:	440-560	Out-of-state:	8%
SAT writing:	450-580	Live on campus:	96%
ACT composite:	19-25	International:	15%

Basis for selection. Academic performance in college preparatory courses, standardized test scores, extra-curricular activities and recommendations most important. Interview recommended; required for scholarship competitions. Audition required of music or theater students interested in performance arts scholarship. Portfolio required of art majors. **Home schooled:** Statement describing home school structure and mission, transcript of courses and grades, letter of recommendation (nonparent) required. Diplomas issued by parents are recognized. Student may provide bibliography of high school literature and essay to evaluate exposure and thinking skills. Extra-curricular activities, counselor interviews considered. **Learning Disabled:** Student support team available through student services.

High school preparation. College-preparatory program required. 15 units required; 22 recommended. Required and recommended units include English 4, mathematics 3-4, social studies 3-4, science 3-4 (laboratory 2-3), foreign language 2-4 and academic electives 2.

2015-2016 Annual costs. Tuition/fees: $20,290. Room/board: $9,020. Books/supplies: $2,000. Personal expenses: $2,000.

2014-2015 Financial aid. **Need-based:** 83 full-time freshmen applied for aid; 81 deemed to have need; 81 received aid. Average need met was 77%. Average scholarship/grant was $16,450; average loan $4,895. 63% of total

undergraduate aid awarded as scholarships/grants, 37% as loans/jobs. **Non-need-based:** Awarded to 177 full-time undergraduates, including 37 freshmen. Scholarships awarded for academics, alumni affiliation, art, job skills, leadership, minority status, music/drama, religious affiliation, state residency.

Application procedures. Admission: Priority date 3/1; deadline 6/1 (postmark date). $30 fee, may be waived for applicants with need, free for online applicants. Admission notification on a rolling basis beginning on or about 10/1. Must reply by May 1 or within 3 week(s) if notified thereafter. **Financial aid:** Closing date 4/15. FAFSA, institutional form required. Applicants notified on a rolling basis starting 3/1; must reply by 5/1 or within 3 week(s) of notification.

Academics. Special study options: Accelerated study, cross-registration, double major, dual enrollment of high school students, exchange student, honors, independent study, internships, liberal arts/career combination, student-designed major, study abroad, teacher certification program. **Credit/placement by examination:** AP, CLEP, IB, institutional tests. 30 credit hours maximum toward bachelor's degree. **Support services:** Learning center, pre-admission summer program, reduced course load, study skills assistance, tutoring, writing center.

Majors. Area/ethnic studies: Women's. **Biology:** General, neuroscience. **Business:** Accounting, business admin, international. **Communications:** Advertising, communications/speech/rhetoric. **Conservation:** Environmental studies. **Education:** Early childhood. **English:** English lit. **Foreign languages:** French, Spanish. **Health services:** Nursing (RN). **History:** General. **Liberal arts:** Arts/sciences. **Math:** General, applied. **Philosophy/religion:** Philosophy, religion. **Physical sciences:** Chemistry. **Psychology:** General. **Social sciences:** Economics, international relations, political science. **Visual/performing arts:** Art history/conservation, dramatic, music, studio arts. **Work/family studies:** Family studies.

Most popular majors. Biology 9%, business/marketing 22%, education 7%, health sciences 19%, psychology 10%, social sciences 8%, visual/performing arts 10%.

Technology on campus. 63 workstations in library, student center. Dormitories wired for high-speed internet access and linked to campus network. Commuter students can connect to campus network. Online course registration, online library, helpline, repair service, wireless network available.

Student life. Freshman orientation: Mandatory. Preregistration for classes offered. Held in August prior to start of classes. **Policies:** Students required to live on campus unless married or living with immediate family in the local area. Honor Code used. **Housing:** Guaranteed on-campus for all undergraduates. Special housing for disabled, apartments available. $150 deposit, deadline 7/1. **Activities:** Campus ministries, choral groups, dance, drama, international student organizations, literary magazine, Model UN, musical theater, student government, student newspaper, honor council, Mortar board, Young Democrats, Circle K, College Republicans, Council on Religions Concerns, American Chemical Society, Wesleyan Disciples.

Athletics. NCAA. **Intercollegiate:** Basketball W, equestrian W, soccer W, softball W, tennis W. **Team name:** Wolves.

Student services. Adult student services, alcohol/substance abuse counseling, chaplain/spiritual director, career counseling, student employment services, financial aid counseling, health services, minority student services, personal counseling, placement for graduates, women's services. **Physically disabled:** Services for visually impaired.

Contact. E-mail: admission@wesleyancollege.edu
Phone: (478) 757-5206 Toll-free number: (800) 447-6610
Fax: (478) 757-4030
C. Stephen Farr, Vice President for Enrollment Services, Wesleyan College, 4760 Forsyth Road, Macon, GA 31210-4462

Westwood College: Atlanta Midtown
Atlanta, Georgia
www.westwood.edu/locations/georgia/atlanta-midtown-campus

▶ For-profit 3-year career college
▶ Commuter campus in very large city
▶ 969 degree-seeking undergraduates
▶ Interview required

General. Regionally accredited; also accredited by ACICS. This Westwood College campus offers a unique hands-on, career-focused curriculum providing associate degrees that can be earned in as little as three months and bachelor's degrees that can be earned in as little as three years. Degree programs are available in the fields of technology, healthcare, business, design and justice. **Degrees:** 38 bachelor's, 103 associate awarded. **Calendar:** Differs by program. **Full-time faculty:** 10 total. **Part-time faculty:** 35 total.

Basis for selection. Rigor of secondary school, interview, student's ability and character, residency considered. **Home schooled:** Transcript of courses and grades, state high school equivalency certificate required.

2015-2016 Annual costs. Books/supplies: $1,106. **Additional information:** Computer-Aided Design/Architectural Drafting: AAS $39,067. Graphic Design: AAS $40,978; BS $78,120. Electronics Technology: AOS $35,525. Information Technology: AOS $35,525. Information and Network Technologies: BS $71,050. Business Administration: AAS $37,128; BS $74,256. Construction Management: AAS $37,128; BS $74,256. Criminal Justice: AAS $39,417; BS $78,834. Health Information Technology: AAS $41,096. Healthcare Office Administration: AAS $35,959. Medical Assisting: Diploma $25,685; AAS $35,959. Additional costs and fees such as books, tool kits, lab fee and online fees may apply.

Application procedures. Admission: No deadline. No application fee. Admission notification on a rolling basis.

Academics. Credit/placement by examination: AP, CLEP, IB, institutional tests. 75 credit hours maximum toward associate degree, 75 toward bachelor's.

Majors. BACHELOR'S. Business: Accounting/business management, business admin, construction management, marketing. **Computer sciences:** LAN/WAN management. **Health services:** Health care admin. **Protective services:** Law enforcement admin. **Visual/performing arts:** Graphic design. **ASSOCIATE. Business:** Business admin, construction management. **Computer sciences:** Networking. **Health services:** Health information technology, medical assistant, office admin. **Protective services:** Law enforcement admin. **Visual/performing arts:** Graphic design.

Technology on campus. 160 workstations in computer center, student center.

Student life. Freshman orientation: Mandatory. Preregistration for classes offered. **Activities:** Student government, student newspaper.

Student services. Adult student services, student employment services.

Contact. E-mail: admissionsrepresentativesww-campus@westwood.edu
Phone: (404) 745-9862
Sanjay Ketty, Field Admissions Director, Westwood College: Atlanta Midtown, 231 Peachtree St. NE, Suite 100, Atlanta, GA 30303

Westwood College: Northlake
Atlanta, Georgia
www.westwood.edu/locations/georgia/atlanta-northlake-campus

▸ For-profit 4-year career college
▸ Very large city
▸ 855 degree-seeking undergraduates

General. Regionally accredited; also accredited by ACICS. This Westwood College campus offers a unique hands-on, career-focused curriculum providing associate degrees that can be earned in as little as three months and bachelor's degrees that can be earned in as little as three years. Degree programs are available in the fields of technology, healthcare, business, design and justice. **Degrees:** 27 bachelor's, 108 associate awarded. **Calendar:** Differs by program. **Full-time faculty:** 10 total. **Part-time faculty:** 44 total.

Basis for selection. Rigor of secondary school, interview, student's ability and character, residency considered. SAT or ACT recommended.

2015-2016 Annual costs. Books/supplies: $1,106. **Additional information:** Computer-Aided Design/Architectural Drafting: AAS $39,067. Graphic Design: AAS $40,978; BS $78,120. Electronics Technology: AOS $35,525. Information Technology: AOS $35,525. Information and Network Technologies: BS $71,050. Business Administration: AAS $37,128; BS $74,256. Construction Management: AAS $37,128; BS $74,256. Criminal Justice: AAS $39,417; BS $78,834. Health Information Technology: AAS $41,096. Healthcare Office Administration: AAS $35,959. Medical Assisting: Diploma $25,685; AAS $35,959. Additional costs and fees such as books, tool kits, lab fee and online fees may apply.

Application procedures. Admission: No deadline. No application fee. Admission notification on a rolling basis.

Academics. Credit/placement by examination: AP, CLEP, institutional tests.

Majors. Business: Accounting/business management, business admin, construction management, marketing. **Computer sciences:** LAN/WAN management. **Health services:** Health care admin. **Protective services:** Law enforcement admin. **Visual/performing arts:** Design.

Contact. E-mail: AdmissionsRepresentativesWW-Campus@westwood.edu
Phone: (770) 743-3000 Toll-free number: (866) 821-6145
Brian LaCourse, Director of Admissions, Westwood College: Northlake, 2220 Parklake Drive NE, Atlanta, GA 30345

Young Harris College
Young Harris, Georgia
www.yhc.edu   **CB code: 5990**

▸ Private 4-year liberal arts college affiliated with the United Methodist Church
▸ Residential campus in rural community
▸ 1,166 degree-seeking undergraduates
▸ SAT or ACT (ACT writing recommended) required

General. Founded in 1886. Regionally accredited. Affiliated with the United Methodist Church and welcomes students from all backgrounds. **Degrees:** 147 bachelor's, 6 associate awarded. **Location:** 90 miles from Atlanta. **Calendar:** Semester, limited summer session. **Full-time faculty:** 77 total; 73% have terminal degrees, 43% women. **Part-time faculty:** 28 total; 18% have terminal degrees, 39% women. **Special facilities:** Planetarium, black box theater, observatory, climbing wall, cross country trail, 18-hole disc golf course, LEED Silver Certified residence hall, predatory beetle lab, bee keeping institute, national forest.

Freshman class profile.

GPA 3.75 or higher:	15%	**GPA 3.0-3.49:**	39%
GPA 3.50-3.74:	21%	**GPA 2.0-2.99:**	25%

Basis for selection. Heavy emphasis on academic GPA and SAT/ACT scores. High school record, interview considered. **Home schooled:** Transcript of courses and grades required. Possible GED requirement dependent upon SAT/ACT scores. **Learning Disabled:** Psycho-educational analysis required.

High school preparation. College-preparatory program recommended. Recommended units include English 4, mathematics 4, social studies 3, science 3 and foreign language 2.

2015-2016 Annual costs. Tuition/fees: $28,197. Room/board: $9,876. Books/supplies: $1,390. Personal expenses: $1,100.

2014-2015 Financial aid. Need-based: 929 full-time freshmen applied for aid; 836 deemed to have need; 836 received aid. Average need met was 78%. Average scholarship/grant was $19,671; average loan $3,679. 79% of total undergraduate aid awarded as scholarships/grants, 21% as loans/jobs. **Non-need-based:** Awarded to 473 full-time undergraduates, including 473 freshmen. Scholarships awarded for academics, art, athletics, job skills, leadership, music/drama, state residency.

Application procedures. Admission: Priority date 1/1; no deadline. $30 fee. Admission notification on a rolling basis beginning on or about 9/15. **Financial aid:** Priority date 5/1; no closing date. FAFSA required. Applicants notified on a rolling basis starting 2/15; must reply within 2 week(s) of notification.

Academics. Special study options: Dual enrollment of high school students, honors, internships, study abroad, teacher certification program. **Credit/placement by examination:** AP, CLEP, IB, institutional tests. Student may exempt computer science 101 but will not receive credit. **Support services:** Pre-admission summer program, reduced course load, remedial instruction, study skills assistance, tutoring, writing center.

Majors. Biology: General. **Education:** General, elementary, middle, music. **English:** Creative writing, English lit. **Health services:** Predental, premedicine, prenursing, prepharmacy, preveterinary. **History:** General. **Math:** General. **Philosophy/religion:** Religion. **Physical sciences:** Chemistry. **Psychology:** General. **Visual/performing arts:** Art, music, musical theater, theater arts management.

Most popular majors. Biology 26%, business/marketing 27%, communications/journalism 8%, English 13%, history 11%, visual/performing arts 15%.

Technology on campus. 99 workstations in dormitories, library, computer center. Commuter students can connect to campus network. Online course registration, online library, helpline, wireless network available.

Student life. Freshman orientation: Mandatory. Preregistration for classes offered. **Housing:** Guaranteed on-campus for all undergraduates. Coed dorms, single-sex dorms, apartments available. $300 fully refundable deposit. **Activities:** Bands, campus ministries, choral groups, dance, drama, international student organizations, literary magazine, music ensembles, musical theater, student government, student newspaper, Wesley Fellowship, Baptist campus ministries, Catholic student association, College Republicans, Bonner Leaders, Fellowship of Christian Athletes, Buddhist Meditation & Mindfulness Gathering, Multicultural student club, Third World 1st, College Democrats.

Athletics. NCAA. **Intercollegiate:** Baseball M, basketball, cheerleading, cross-country, golf, lacrosse, soccer, softball W, tennis, ultimate frisbee. **Intramural:** Basketball, football (non-tackle), soccer, softball, ultimate frisbee, volleyball. **Team name:** Mountain Lions.

Student services. Alcohol/substance abuse counseling, chaplain/spiritual director, career counseling, student employment services, financial aid counseling, health services, personal counseling, women's services. **Physically disabled:** Services for visually, speech, hearing impaired.

Contact. E-mail: admissions@yhc.edu
Phone: (706) 379-3111 Toll-free number: (800) 241-3754
Fax: (706) 379-3108
Clinton Hobbs, Vice President for Enrollment Management, Young Harris College, PO Box 116, Young Harris, GA 30582-0116

Hawaii

Argosy University: Hawaii
Honolulu, Hawaii
www.argosy.edu/hawaii

- For-profit 4-year university
- Large city
- 431 degree-seeking undergraduates: 39% part-time, 61% women
- 502 graduate students

General. Regionally accredited. **Degrees:** 69 bachelor's, 4 associate awarded; master's, professional, doctoral offered. **Calendar:** Differs by program. **Full-time faculty:** 14 total. **Part-time faculty:** 58 total.

Basis for selection. Open admission.

2015-2016 Annual costs. Tuition/fees: $16,842. **Additional information:** Tuition indicated is for programs in the College of Arts and Sciences. College of Health Sciences programs are $575 per credit-hour.

Application procedures. Admission: Closing date 9/13. $50 fee. **Financial aid:** No deadline.

Academics. Credit/placement by examination: AP, CLEP.

Majors. Business: Business admin. **Liberal arts:** Arts/sciences. **Protective services:** Police science. **Psychology:** General.

Contact. E-mail: auhonadmissions@argosy.edu
Phone: (808) 791-5214 Toll-free number: (888) 323-2777
Paul Billington, Senior Director of Admissions, Argosy University: Hawaii, 400 ASB Tower, 1001 Bishop Street, Honolulu, HI 96813

Brigham Young University-Hawaii
Laie, Hawaii
www.byuh.edu   CB code: 4106

- Private 4-year university and liberal arts college affiliated with the Church of Jesus Christ of Latter-day Saints
- Residential campus in small town
- 2,681 degree-seeking undergraduates
- Application essay, interview required

General. Founded in 1955. Regionally accredited. **Degrees:** 714 bachelor's, 133 associate awarded. **ROTC:** Army, Naval, Air Force. **Location:** 38 miles from Honolulu. **Calendar:** Semester, limited summer session. **Full-time faculty:** 118 total. **Part-time faculty:** 129 total. **Class size:** 54% < 20, 40% 20-39, 4% 40-49, 2% 50-99, less than 1% >100. **Special facilities:** Center for Hawaiian language and cultural studies, museum of natural history, Polynesian cultural center, Pacific Islands collection housed in university archives, Pacific Islands research room.

Freshman class profile.

GPA 3.75 or higher:	21%	GPA 2.0-2.99:	15%
GPA 3.50-3.74:	20%	Out-of-state:	76%
GPA 3.0-3.49:	44%	Live on campus:	90%

Basis for selection. GED not accepted. Interview, essay, recommendations very important. Test scores also important. 3.0 GPA required for domestic students. ACT recommended. Audition required for music majors. Portfolio required for art majors. Ecclesiastical interviews required for all students. Essays may make difference in admission.

High school preparation. Recommended units include English 4, mathematics 2, social studies 3, history 2 and science 2.

2015-2016 Annual costs. Tuition/fees: $5,100. Room/board: $5,802. Books/supplies: $1,300. Personal expenses: $3,088. **Additional information:** 100% higher tuition and per credit hour charges for students who are not members of The Church of Jesus Christ of Latter-day Saints.

Financial aid. Non-need-based: Scholarships awarded for academics, art, athletics, leadership, music/drama, state residency.

Application procedures. Admission: Closing date 2/15 (receipt date). $30 fee. Admission notification on a rolling basis beginning on or about 4/1. Must reply by 8/25. **Financial aid:** Closing date 3/15. FAFSA required. Applicants notified by 5/1; must reply by 8/31.

Academics. Special study options: Cooperative education, double major, ESL, honors, independent study, internships, student-designed major, teacher certification program. **Credit/placement by examination:** AP, CLEP, IB, institutional tests. **Support services:** Learning center, remedial instruction, study skills assistance, tutoring, writing center.

Majors. Area/ethnic studies: Pacific. **Biology:** General, biochemistry. **Business:** Accounting, business admin. **Computer sciences:** Computer science, information systems, information technology. **Education:** Art, biology, business, chemistry, elementary, English, ESL, mathematics, music, physical, physics, science, secondary, social science, special ed. **English:** English lit. **History:** General. **Human services:** Social work. **Liberal arts:** Arts/sciences. **Math:** General. **Parks/recreation:** Exercise sciences, health/fitness. **Psychology:** General. **Social sciences:** Political science. **Visual/performing arts:** Art, piano/keyboard, studio arts, voice/opera.

Most popular majors. Business/marketing 25%, computer/information sciences 7%, education 19%, interdisciplinary studies 13%, parks/recreation 6%, psychology 8%, public administration/social services 6%.

Technology on campus. 465 workstations in dormitories, library, computer center, student center. Dormitories wired for high-speed internet access and linked to campus network. Online course registration, online library, helpline, repair service, wireless network available.

Student life. Freshman orientation: Mandatory. Preregistration for classes offered. Two-week program at beginning of semester, includes luau, campus and island tour. **Policies:** All first-time, non-local freshmen required to live on campus until sophomore standing achieved. Religious observance required. **Housing:** Guaranteed on-campus for freshmen. Single-sex dorms, apartments, wellness housing available. $50 deposit, deadline 4/30. **Activities:** Bands, choral groups, dance, drama, film society, literary magazine, music ensembles, student government, student newspaper.

Athletics. NCAA. **Intercollegiate:** Basketball, cross-country, golf M, soccer, softball W, tennis, volleyball W. **Intramural:** Basketball, bowling, cross-country, golf, racquetball, rugby, soccer, softball, swimming, table tennis, tennis, volleyball, water polo M, weight lifting. **Team name:** Seasiders.

Student services. Chaplain/spiritual director, career counseling, student employment services, financial aid counseling, health services, personal counseling, placement for graduates, veterans' counselor, women's services. **Physically disabled:** Services for visually, speech, hearing impaired.

Contact. E-mail: admissions@byuh.edu
Phone: (808) 675-3738 Fax: (808) 675-3741
Arapata Meha, Dean of Admissions and Records, Brigham Young University-Hawaii, 55-220 Kulanui Street, #1973, Laie, HI 96762-1294

Chaminade University of Honolulu
Honolulu, Hawaii   CB member
www.chaminade.edu   CB code: 4105

- Private 4-year university affiliated with the Roman Catholic Church
- Commuter campus in large city
- 1,217 degree-seeking undergraduates: 2% part-time, 71% women, 3% African American, 38% Asian American, 4% Hispanic/Latino, 1% Native American, 20% Native Hawaiian/Pacific islander, 15% Multiracial, non-Hispanic, 2% international
- 639 degree-seeking graduate students
- 82% of applicants admitted
- SAT or ACT (ACT writing optional), application essay required
- 46% graduate within 6 years

General. Founded in 1955. Regionally accredited. Campus shared with St. Louis School. **Degrees:** 420 bachelor's, 87 associate awarded; master's offered. **ROTC:** Army, Air Force. **Location:** 2 miles from Waikiki. **Calendar:** Semester, limited summer session. **Full-time faculty:** 88 total; 30% minority, 43% women. **Part-time faculty:** 60 total; 28% minority, 43% women. **Class size:** 57% < 20, 42% 20-39, less than 1% 40-49, less than 1% 50-99. **Special facilities:** Montessori laboratory preschool, observatory, theater.

Freshman class profile. 895 applied, 734 admitted, 215 enrolled.

Mid 50% test scores			
SAT critical reading:	430-520	GPA 2.0-2.99:	24%
SAT math:	440-540	Rank in top quarter:	5%
ACT composite:	19-22	Rank in top tenth:	3%
GPA 3.75 or higher:	27%	Return as sophomores:	74%
GPA 3.50-3.74:	20%	Out-of-state:	33%
GPA 3.0-3.49:	29%	Live on campus:	48%

Basis for selection. School achievement record, test scores, statement of purpose important. Interview recommended for marginal students.

High school preparation. College-preparatory program required. Required and recommended units include English 4, mathematics 3-4, social studies 3 and science 2-4. 4 units of college prep required.

2015-2016 Annual costs. Tuition/fees: $21,924. Room/board: $12,290. Books/supplies: $1,600. Personal expenses: $1,334. **Additional information:** Nursing tuition $26,930.

2014-2015 Financial aid. Need-based: 215 full-time freshmen applied for aid; 180 deemed to have need; 180 received aid. Average need met was 74%. Average scholarship/grant was $4,858; average loan $3,264. **Non-need-based:** Awarded to 1,239 full-time undergraduates, including 242 freshmen. Scholarships awarded for academics, athletics, minority status, religious affiliation, ROTC, state residency.

Application procedures. Admission: No deadline. $50 fee, may be waived for applicants with need. Admission notification on a rolling basis. **Financial aid:** Priority date 2/15; no closing date. FAFSA required. Must reply within 4 week(s) of notification.

Academics. Special study options: Accelerated study, distance learning, double major, dual enrollment of high school students, exchange student, independent study, internships, semester at sea, study abroad, teacher certification program. **Credit/placement by examination:** AP, CLEP, IB, SAT, ACT, institutional tests. 30 credit hours maximum toward associate degree, 30 toward bachelor's. **Support services:** Learning center, pre-admission summer program, remedial instruction, study skills assistance, tutoring.

Majors. Biology: General. **Business:** Accounting, business admin, marketing. **Communications:** Broadcast journalism, communications/speech/rhetoric, media studies, public relations. **Computer sciences:** General, computer science. **Conservation:** Environmental studies. **Education:** Early childhood, elementary, secondary. **English:** English lit. **Health services:** Nursing (RN). **History:** General. **Liberal arts:** Arts/sciences. **Philosophy/religion:** Religion. **Protective services:** Criminalistics, forensics. **Psychology:** General. **Social sciences:** General, international relations, political science. **Visual/performing arts:** Interior design.

Most popular majors. Biology 9%, business/marketing 11%, communications/journalism 6%, health sciences 21%, psychology 9%, security/protective services 25%.

Technology on campus. 100 workstations in dormitories, library, computer center, student center. Dormitories wired for high-speed internet access and linked to campus network. Online library, helpline, repair service, wireless network available.

Student life. Freshman orientation: Mandatory, $140 fee. Preregistration for classes offered. **Housing:** Guaranteed on-campus for freshmen. Coed dorms, single-sex dorms, special housing for disabled, apartments available. $300 nonrefundable deposit, deadline 5/1. **Activities:** Campus ministries, choral groups, dance, drama, literary magazine, musical theater, radio station, student government, student newspaper, Lumana'i O Samoa, Hawaiian club, Rotaract club, Black Cultures United, Environmental club, La Familia, Marianas club, Temana Tahitian club, Micronesian club, civic engagement club.

Athletics. NCAA. **Intercollegiate:** Basketball, cross-country, golf M, soccer, softball W, tennis W, volleyball W. **Intramural:** Basketball, cheerleading. **Team name:** Silverswords.

Student services. Adult student services, chaplain/spiritual director, career counseling, services for economically disadvantaged, student employment services, financial aid counseling, health services, personal counseling, placement for graduates. **Physically disabled:** Services for visually, speech, hearing impaired.

Contact. E-mail: admissions@chaminade.edu
Phone: (808) 735-4735 Toll-free number: (800) 735-3733
Fax: (808) 739-4647
Shauna Pimentel-Motooka, Director of Admissions, Chaminade University of Honolulu, 3140 Waialae Avenue, Honolulu, HI 96816

Hawaii Pacific University
Honolulu, Hawaii
www.hpu.edu

CB member
CB code: 4352

- Private 4-year university and liberal arts college
- Commuter campus in large city
- 3,940 degree-seeking undergraduates: 28% part-time, 58% women, 5% African American, 17% Asian American, 15% Hispanic/Latino, 2% Native Hawaiian/Pacific islander, 16% Multi-racial, non-Hispanic, 11% international
- 784 degree-seeking graduate students
- 91% of applicants admitted
- SAT or ACT (ACT writing optional) required
- 49% graduate within 6 years

General. Founded in 1965. Regionally accredited. Two main campuses and marine research facility (The Oceanic Institute) connected by free shuttle service. Programs offered for military personnel and their dependents and for older students. Satellite campus on 6 military installations on Oahu. **Degrees:** 842 bachelor's, 117 associate awarded; master's offered. **ROTC:** Army, Air Force. **Calendar:** Semester, extensive summer session. **Full-time faculty:** 240 total; 43% women. **Part-time faculty:** 267 total; 48% women. **Class size:** 57% < 20, 39% 20-39, 3% 40-49, 1% 50-99. **Special facilities:** Research boat, theater, oceanic institute.

Freshman class profile. 3,449 applied, 3,149 admitted, 504 enrolled.

Mid 50% test scores			
SAT critical reading:	440-550	GPA 3.0-3.49:	27%
SAT math:	440-560	GPA 2.0-2.99:	18%
SAT writing:	420-530	Return as sophomores:	70%
ACT composite:	19-24	Out-of-state:	60%
GPA 3.75 or higher:	34%	Live on campus:	31%
GPA 3.50-3.74:	21%	International:	7%

Basis for selection. Academic record, test scores most important. Interview also important, recommendations considered. Essay recommended. **Home schooled:** Transcript of courses and grades, interview, letter of recommendation (nonparent) required.

High school preparation. College-preparatory program recommended. 15 units recommended. Recommended units include English 4, mathematics 3, social studies 2, history 2, science 3 (laboratory 1) and foreign language 2. Additional science and math required for nursing and marine science.

2016-2017 Annual costs. Tuition/fees (projected): $23,460. Room/board: $13,899. Books/supplies: $1,200. Personal expenses: $1,546.

Financial aid. Non-need-based: Scholarships awarded for academics, alumni affiliation, athletics, leadership, music/drama, ROTC.

Application procedures. Admission: $50 fee, may be waived for applicants with need. Admission notification on a rolling basis. Must reply by May 1 or within 4 week(s) if notified thereafter. **Financial aid:** Priority date 3/1; no closing date. FAFSA required. Applicants notified on a rolling basis starting 4/1; must reply within 3 week(s) of notification.

Academics. All students complete core requirements based on following themes: global systems, world cultures, communication skills, research/epistemology, values and choices. **Special study options:** Accelerated study, combined bachelor's/graduate degree, cooperative education, distance learning, double major, dual enrollment of high school students, ESL, honors, independent study, internships, liberal arts/career combination, student-designed major, study abroad, teacher certification program. 3-2 engineering program with University of Southern California, Washington University (St. Louis). **Credit/placement by examination:** AP, CLEP, IB, SAT, ACT, institutional tests. 36 credit hours maximum toward associate degree, 36 toward bachelor's. **Support services:** Learning center, reduced course load, remedial instruction, study skills assistance, tutoring.

Majors. Biology: General, marine. **Business:** General, accounting, banking/financial services, business admin, communications, entrepreneurial studies, finance, human resources, international, international finance, management information systems, managerial economics, marketing, tourism/travel. **Communications:** Advertising, communications/speech/rhetoric, digital media, journalism, media studies, public relations. **Computer sciences:** General, computer science. **Conservation:** Environmental science, environmental studies. **Education:** Elementary, ESL. **English:** English lit. **Foreign languages:** Comparative lit. **Health services:** Nursing (RN), premedicine. **History:** General, military. **Human services:** General, social work. **Liberal arts:** Arts/sciences, humanities. **Math:** General, applied. **Physical sciences:** Oceanography. **Protective services:** Law enforcement admin. **Psychology:** General. **Social sciences:** General, anthropology, economics, international relations, political science, sociology. **Work/family studies:** Family studies.

Most popular majors. Biology 6%, business/marketing 25%, communications/journalism 7%, health sciences 26%, psychology 6%.

Technology on campus. Dormitories wired for high-speed internet access and linked to campus network. Commuter students can connect to campus network. Online course registration, online library, helpline, student web hosting, wireless network available.

Student life. Freshman orientation: Available, $120 fee. Preregistration for classes offered. Week of activities including on-campus sessions and off-campus activities. **Housing:** Coed dorms, apartments, wellness housing available. $200 partly refundable deposit, deadline 5/1. **Activities:** Bands, campus ministries, choral groups, dance, drama, film society, international student organizations, literary magazine, music ensembles, Model UN, musical theater, student government, student newspaper, symphony orchestra, Rotaract, President's Hosts, Christian Fellowship, American marketing association, hiking club, honors societies, computing club, Students In Free Enterprise.

Athletics. NCAA. **Intercollegiate:** Baseball M, basketball, cheerleading, cross-country, golf M, soccer, softball W, tennis, volleyball W. **Team name:** Sharks.

Student services. Adult student services, alcohol/substance abuse counseling, chaplain/spiritual director, career counseling, student employment services, financial aid counseling, personal counseling, placement for graduates, veterans' counselor.

Contact. E-mail: admissions@hpu.edu
Phone: (808) 544-0238 Toll-free number: (866) 225-5478
Fax: (808) 544-1136
Marissa Bratton, Director of Admissions, Hawaii Pacific University, 1 Aloha Tower Drive, Honolulu, HI 96813

University of Hawaii at Hilo

Hilo, Hawaii	**CB member**
www.hilo.hawaii.edu	**CB code: 4869**

▸ Public 4-year university and liberal arts college

▸ Commuter campus in large town

▸ 3,124 degree-seeking undergraduates: 19% part-time, 61% women, 1% African American, 17% Asian American, 13% Hispanic/Latino, 1% Native American, 11% Native Hawaiian/Pacific islander, 31% Multiracial, non-Hispanic, 4% international

▸ 552 degree-seeking graduate students

▸ 71% of applicants admitted

▸ SAT or ACT with writing required

▸ 39% graduate within 6 years

General. Founded in 1970. Regionally accredited. **Degrees:** 749 bachelor's awarded; master's, professional, doctoral offered. **ROTC:** Army. **Location:** 200 miles from Honolulu. **Calendar:** Semester, limited summer session. **Full-time faculty:** 267 total; 75% have terminal degrees, 52% minority, 50% women. **Part-time faculty:** 93 total; 31% have terminal degrees, 39% minority, 61% women. **Class size:** 47% < 20, 44% 20-39, 6% 40-49, 3% 50-99. **Special facilities:** Active volcanoes study center, space science center, small business development center, marine education center, 110-acre farm laboratory.

Freshman class profile. 1,534 applied, 1,091 admitted, 382 enrolled.

Mid 50% test scores		GPA 3.0-3.49:	37%
SAT critical reading:	410-520	GPA 2.0-2.99:	21%
SAT math:	420-530	Rank in top quarter:	50%
SAT writing:	400-510	Rank in top tenth:	23%
ACT composite:	16-22	Return as sophomores:	63%
GPA 3.75 or higher:	24%	Out-of-state:	30%
GPA 3.50-3.74:	18%	International:	2%

Basis for selection. High school GPA in academic subjects, SAT/ACT, class rank, and school recommendation considered. **Home schooled:** Transcript of courses and grades required.

High school preparation. College-preparatory program required. 17 units required; 23 recommended. Required and recommended units include English 4, mathematics 3-4, science 3-4 (laboratory 1), foreign language 2 and academic electives 7-8. 3 math beyond pre-algebra, 7 academic electives not including physical education or ROTC required. 4 math and 4 science recommended for science and business majors.

2015-2016 Annual costs. Tuition/fees: $7,332; $19,788 out-of-state. Room/board: $8,414.

Financial aid. Non-need-based: Scholarships awarded for academics, art, leadership, music/drama, state residency. **Additional information:** Hawaii student incentive grants and tuition waivers (merit and need-based) available to Hawaii residents at participating institutions.

Application procedures. Admission: Priority date 3/1; deadline 7/1 (postmark date). $50 fee, may be waived for applicants with need. Admission notification on a rolling basis beginning on or about 10/1. Must reply by May 1 or within 2 week(s) if notified thereafter. **Financial aid:** Priority date 3/1; no closing date. FAFSA required. Applicants notified on a rolling basis starting 3/1; must reply within 3 week(s) of notification.

Academics. Special study options: Combined bachelor's/graduate degree, cross-registration, distance learning, double major, dual enrollment of high school students, ESL, exchange student, honors, independent study, internships, semester at sea, student-designed major, study abroad, teacher certification program. Marine sciences and astronomy summer programs. **Credit/placement by examination:** AP, CLEP, IB, SAT, ACT, institutional tests. 30 credit hours maximum toward bachelor's degree. **Support services:** Learning center, tutoring, writing center.

Majors. Area/ethnic studies: Japanese, Native American. **Biology:** General, marine. **Business:** Accounting, business admin. **Communications:** Communications/speech/rhetoric. **Computer sciences:** Computer science. **Conservation:** Environmental science, environmental studies. **Engineering:** General. **English:** English lit. **Foreign languages:** Linguistics. **Health services:** Nursing (RN). **History:** General. **Human services:** General. **Liberal arts:** Arts/sciences. **Math:** General. **Parks/recreation:** Exercise sciences. **Philosophy/religion:** Philosophy. **Physical sciences:** Astronomy, chemistry, geology, physics. **Protective services:** Criminal justice. **Psychology:** General. **Social sciences:** Anthropology, economics, geography, political science, sociology. **Visual/performing arts:** Art, music.

Most popular majors. Biology 10%, business/marketing 9%, communications/journalism 8%, health sciences 11%, parks/recreation 6%, psychology 12%, social sciences 15%.

Technology on campus. 600 workstations in dormitories, library, computer center, student center. Commuter students can connect to campus network. Online course registration, online library, helpline, repair service, wireless network available.

Student life. Freshman orientation: Available, $75 fee. Preregistration for classes offered. Held for one week before the start of classes. **Housing:** Coed dorms, special housing for disabled, apartments available. $100 deposit. Student housing units available for mobility-impaired students. **Activities:** Bands, choral groups, dance, drama, international student organizations, literary magazine, music ensembles, musical theater, radio station, student government, student newspaper, Samoan club, Delta Sigma Pi business fraternity, World Hope, Rotoract, Bayanihan club, Bahai Club, Chuukese student association, Earth Action, Nihon no kai.

Athletics. NCAA. **Intercollegiate:** Baseball M, basketball, cross-country W, golf, soccer, softball W, tennis, volleyball W. **Intramural:** Archery, badminton, basketball, bowling, cross-country, golf, softball, table tennis, tennis, volleyball. **Team name:** Vulcans.

Student services. Career counseling, services for economically disadvantaged, student employment services, financial aid counseling, health services, minority student services, personal counseling, placement for graduates, women's services. **Physically disabled:** Services for visually, speech, hearing impaired.

Contact. E-mail: uhhadm@hawaii.edu
Phone: (808) 932-7446 Toll-free number: (800) 897-4456
Fax: (808) 932-7459
Zach Street, Director of Admissions, University of Hawaii at Hilo, 200 West Kawili Street, Hilo, HI 96720-4091

University of Hawaii at Manoa

Honolulu, Hawaii	**CB member**
www.manoa.hawaii.edu	**CB code: 4867**

▸ Public 4-year university

▸ Commuter campus in very large city

▸ 13,320 degree-seeking undergraduates: 16% part-time, 55% women, 2% African American, 41% Asian American, 2% Hispanic/Latino, 17% Native Hawaiian/Pacific islander, 15% Multi-racial, non-Hispanic, 3% international

▸ 4,754 degree-seeking graduate students

▸ 81% of applicants admitted

♦ SAT or ACT with writing required
♦ 57% graduate within 6 years

General. Founded in 1907. Regionally accredited. **Degrees:** 3,404 bachelor's awarded; master's, professional, doctoral offered. **ROTC:** Army, Air Force. **Location:** 3 miles from downtown. **Calendar:** Semester, extensive summer session. **Full-time faculty:** 1,201 total; 90% have terminal degrees, 45% minority, 46% women. **Part-time faculty:** 258 total; 93% have terminal degrees, 64% minority, 45% women. **Class size:** 50% < 20, 31% 20-39, 6% 40-49, 8% 50-99, 5% >100. **Special facilities:** Institute for astronomy, observatories, arboretum, East-West center, Japanese tea house and garden, Hawaiian studies center, Korean studies center.

Freshman class profile. 7,658 applied, 6,234 admitted, 1,903 enrolled.

Mid 50% test scores			
SAT critical reading:	480-580	Rank in top quarter:	56%
SAT math:	500-610	Rank in top tenth:	25%
SAT writing:	470-570	Return as sophomores:	78%
ACT composite:	21-26	Out-of-state:	39%
GPA 3.75 or higher:	33%	Live on campus:	57%
GPA 3.50-3.74:	20%	International:	2%
GPA 3.0-3.49:	35%	Fraternities:	1%
GPA 2.0-2.99:	12%	Sororities:	1%

Basis for selection. School achievement record, test scores, and class rank important. **Home schooled:** State high school equivalency certificate required. In absence of official transcript from accredited school, students must submit GED results in addition to other requirements.

High school preparation. College-preparatory program required. 22 units required. Required units include English 4, mathematics 3, social studies 3, science 3 and academic electives 5. 4 other college preparatory courses required.

2015-2016 Annual costs. Tuition/fees: $11,164; $31,516 out-of-state. Room/board: $10,980.

2014-2015 Financial aid. Need-based: 1,412 full-time freshmen applied for aid; 940 deemed to have need; 934 received aid. Average need met was 76%. Average scholarship/grant was $9,904; average loan $3,907. 64% of total undergraduate aid awarded as scholarships/grants, 36% as loans/jobs. **Non-need-based:** Awarded to 3,978 full-time undergraduates, including 623 freshmen. Scholarships awarded for academics, alumni affiliation, art, athletics, leadership, music/drama, ROTC, state residency. **Additional information:** Hawaii student incentive grants and tuition waivers (merit and need-based) available to Hawaii residents at participating institutions.

Application procedures. Admission: Priority date 1/5; deadline 3/1 (receipt date). $70 fee, may be waived for applicants with need. Admission notification on a rolling basis beginning on or about 9/1. Must reply by May 1 or within 2 week(s) if notified thereafter. **Financial aid:** Priority date 3/1; no closing date. FAFSA required. Applicants notified on a rolling basis starting 4/1; must reply by 5/1 or within 4 week(s) of notification.

Academics. Special study options: Cooperative education, distance learning, double major, ESL, exchange student, honors, independent study, internships, semester at sea, student-designed major, study abroad, teacher certification program. **Credit/placement by examination:** AP, CLEP, IB, SAT, ACT, institutional tests. 30 credit hours maximum toward bachelor's degree. **Support services:** Learning center, pre-admission summer program, remedial instruction, study skills assistance, tutoring, writing center.

Majors. Architecture: Environmental design. **Area/ethnic studies:** American, Asian, Native American. **Biology:** General, botany, cellular/molecular, marine, microbiology, zoology. **Business:** General, accounting, business admin, finance, human resources, international, management information systems, marketing, tourism/travel. **Communications:** Communications/speech/rhetoric, journalism. **Computer sciences:** General, computer science. **Conservation:** Environmental science, management/policy. **Education:** Elementary, ESL, secondary, special ed. **Engineering:** Agricultural, civil, electrical, mechanical. **English:** English lit. **Foreign languages:** Chinese, classics, Filipino/Tagalog, French, German, Japanese, Korean, Russian, Spanish. **Health services:** Audiology/speech pathology, clinical lab science, dental hygiene, nursing (RN). **History:** General. **Human services:** Social work. **Liberal arts:** Arts/sciences. **Math:** General. **Parks/recreation:** Exercise sciences. **Philosophy/religion:** Philosophy, religion. **Physical sciences:** Astrophysics, chemistry, geology, meteorology, physics. **Psychology:** General. **Social sciences:** Anthropology, economics, geography, political science, sociology. **Visual/performing arts:** Art, dance, dramatic, music. **Work/family studies:** General, clothing/textiles.

Most popular majors. Biology 7%, business/marketing 20%, education 6%, engineering/engineering technologies 7%, health sciences 7%, psychology 6%, social sciences 9%.

Technology on campus. 1,500 workstations in dormitories, library, computer center, student center. Dormitories wired for high-speed internet access and linked to campus network. Commuter students can connect to campus network. Online course registration, online library, helpline, repair service, student web hosting, wireless network available.

Student life. Freshman orientation: Available, $80 fee. Preregistration for classes offered. Two-day program. **Housing:** Guaranteed on-campus for freshmen. Coed dorms, special housing for disabled, apartments, themed housing available. $400 nonrefundable deposit. **Activities:** Bands, campus ministries, choral groups, dance, drama, film society, international student organizations, literary magazine, music ensembles, musical theater, radio station, student government, student newspaper, symphony orchestra, over 150 registered organizations.

Athletics. NCAA. **Intercollegiate:** Baseball M, basketball, cheerleading, cross-country W, diving, football (tackle) M, golf, sailing, soccer W, softball W, swimming, tennis, track and field W, volleyball, water polo W. **Intramural:** Badminton, basketball, cross-country, golf, soccer, softball, table tennis, tennis, track and field W, volleyball, weight lifting. **Team name:** Warriors, Rainbow Warriors, Rainbows, Rainbow Wahine.

Student services. Adult student services, alcohol/substance abuse counseling, career counseling, services for economically disadvantaged, student employment services, financial aid counseling, health services, minority student services, on-campus daycare, personal counseling, placement for graduates, veterans' counselor, women's services. **Physically disabled:** Services for visually, speech, hearing impaired.

Contact. E-mail: uhmanoa.admissions@hawaii.edu
Phone: (808) 956-8975 Toll-free number: (800) 823-9771
Fax: (808) 956-4148
Roxie Shabazz, Assistant Vice Chancellor for Enrollment Management & Director of Admissions, University of Hawaii at Manoa, 2600 Campus Road, QLCSS 001, Honolulu, HI 96822

University of Hawaii: West Oahu
Kapolei, Hawaii   **CB member**
www.uhwo.hawaii.edu   **CB code: 1042**

♦ Public 4-year liberal arts and teachers college
♦ Commuter campus in large town
♦ 2,517 degree-seeking undergraduates: 43% part-time, 65% women, 2% African American, 38% Asian American, 1% Hispanic/Latino, 30% Native Hawaiian/Pacific islander, 15% Multi-racial, non-Hispanic
♦ 70% of applicants admitted

General. Founded in 1976. Regionally accredited. **Degrees:** 439 bachelor's awarded. **ROTC:** Army, Air Force. **Location:** 10 miles from Honolulu. **Calendar:** Semester, limited summer session. **Full-time faculty:** 77 total; 83% have terminal degrees, 49% minority, 44% women. **Class size:** 39% < 20, 52% 20-39, 9% 40-49.

Freshman class profile. 892 applied, 626 admitted, 254 enrolled.

Mid 50% test scores			
		GPA 3.0-3.49:	36%
SAT critical reading:	390-490	GPA 2.0-2.99:	37%
SAT math:	400-520	Rank in top quarter:	40%
SAT writing:	400-490	Rank in top tenth:	13%
ACT composite:	16-21	Return as sophomores:	67%
GPA 3.75 or higher:	12%	Out-of-state:	4%
GPA 3.50-3.74:	15%		

Basis for selection. Students with 2.7 GPA and 22 credits of required high school coursework will be automatically accepted. **Home schooled:** State high school equivalency certificate required.

High school preparation. College-preparatory program required. 22 units required. Required units include English 4, mathematics 3, social studies 3, science 3 and academic electives 5. Math credits must include Algebra II and Geometry. 4 credits of college prep coursework (language, fine arts, etc.) also required.

2015-2016 Annual costs. Tuition/fees: $7,152; $19,608 out-of-state. Books/supplies: $1,246. Personal expenses: $1,422.

2014-2015 Financial aid. Need-based: 126 full-time freshmen applied for aid; 126 deemed to have need; 126 received aid. Average need met was 50%. Average scholarship/grant was $727; average loan $592. 40% of total undergraduate aid awarded as scholarships/grants, 60% as loans/jobs. **Non-need-based:** Awarded to 191 full-time undergraduates, including 11 freshmen. Scholarships awarded for academics.

Application procedures. Admission: Priority date 3/1; deadline 8/1 (postmark date). $50 fee, may be waived for applicants with need. Application must be submitted on paper. Admission notification on a rolling basis beginning on or about 12/15. Must reply by May 1 or within 3 week(s) if notified thereafter. **Financial aid:** Priority date 4/1; no closing date. FAFSA required. Applicants notified on a rolling basis starting 4/1; must reply within 2 week(s) of notification.

Academics. Special study options: Distance learning, double major, dual enrollment of high school students, internships, teacher certification program. **Credit/placement by examination:** AP, CLEP, IB, SAT, ACT, institutional tests. 42 credit hours maximum toward bachelor's degree. 21 lower division and 21 upper division credits may be earned through examination. **Support services:** Study skills assistance, tutoring, writing center.

Majors. Area/ethnic studies: Pacific. **Business:** Accounting, business admin. **Computer sciences:** LAN/WAN management. **Education:** Early childhood, elementary. **English:** English lit. **History:** General. **Human services:** General. **Philosophy/religion:** Philosophy. **Protective services:** Law enforcement admin. **Psychology:** General. **Social sciences:** General, anthropology, economics, political science, sociology.

Most popular majors. Business/marketing 32%, education 7%, interdisciplinary studies 8%, public administration/social services 25%, social sciences 24%.

Technology on campus. 18 workstations in computer center. Commuter students can connect to campus network. Online course registration, online library, helpline, student web hosting, wireless network available.

Student life. Freshman orientation: Available. Preregistration for classes offered. **Activities:** Concert band, student government, accounting club, anthropology/sociology club, business club, economics club, Hawaiian-Pacific Club, humanities club, political science club, psychology association, students in free enterprise.

Athletics. Team name: Pueo.

Student services. Career counseling, student employment services, financial aid counseling, veterans' counselor. **Physically disabled:** Services for visually, hearing impaired.

Contact. E-mail: admissions@uhwo.hawaii.edu
Phone: (808) 454-4700 Fax: (808) 453-6075
Robyn Oshiro, Admissions Specialist, University of Hawaii: West Oahu, 91-1001 Farrington Highway, Kapolei, HI 96707

University of Phoenix: Hawaii
Honolulu, Hawaii
www.phoenix.edu

- For-profit 4-year university
- Large city
- 1,300 degree-seeking undergraduates

General. Regionally accredited. **Degrees:** 285 bachelor's awarded; master's offered. **Calendar:** Differs by program. Other academic calendar. **Full-time faculty:** 22 total. **Part-time faculty:** 193 total.

Basis for selection. Open admission, but selective for some programs.

2015-2016 Annual costs. Per-credit-hour charge, $410 to $635, depending upon level and course of study. Books, material charges, and other fees vary by course and program. All fees are subject to change.

Application procedures. Admission: No deadline. No application fee. **Financial aid:** No deadline.

Academics. Credit/placement by examination: AP, CLEP.

Majors. Business: Accounting/business management, business admin, e-commerce, entrepreneurial studies, finance, human resources, marketing, operations. **Computer sciences:** Database management, networking, programming, security, system admin, systems analysis, web page design, webmaster. **Education:** Elementary. **Health services:** Facilities admin, health information management, long term care admin, nursing (RN). **Human services:** General. **Protective services:** Disaster management, law enforcement admin, security management.

Student life. Freshman orientation: Mandatory. Preregistration for classes offered.

Contact. Toll-free number: (866) 766-0766
University of Phoenix: Hawaii, 745 Fort Street, Honolulu, HI 96813

Idaho

Boise Bible College
Boise, Idaho
www.boisebible.edu   CB code: 0891

- Private 4-year Bible college affiliated with the nondenominational tradition
- Residential campus in small city
- 144 degree-seeking undergraduates
- SAT or ACT (ACT writing optional), application essay required

General. Founded in 1945. Accredited by ABHE. **Degrees:** 36 bachelor's, 12 associate awarded. **Location:** 4 miles from downtown. **Calendar:** Semester. **Full-time faculty:** 10 total. **Part-time faculty:** 5 total.

Basis for selection. Christian conduct or ethical code standards based on signed student statement, recommendation of home church minister, 1 employment/school reference, and 1 personal reference required. School achievement important. **Home schooled:** Transcript of courses and grades required. GED or transcripts from homeschooling agency recommended. Applicants submitting home-prepared transcripts advised to consult admissions office.

High school preparation. Recommended units include English 4, mathematics 2, history 2 and foreign language 1.

2015-2016 Annual costs. Tuition/fees: $11,670. Room/board: $3,150. Books/supplies: $605. Personal expenses: $1,210.

Financial aid. Non-need-based: Scholarships awarded for academics, leadership, music/drama, religious affiliation.

Application procedures. Admission: Priority date 5/1; deadline 8/1 (receipt date). $25 fee. Application must be submitted on paper. Admission notification on a rolling basis. Must reply by 6/1 or 3 weeks after acceptance date if accepted after 6/1. **Financial aid:** Priority date 5/1; no closing date. FAFSA, institutional form required. Applicants notified on a rolling basis starting 5/2; must reply by 8/1 or within 2 week(s) of notification.

Academics. Special study options: Distance learning, double major, independent study, internships. **Credit/placement by examination:** AP, CLEP, IB, SAT, ACT, institutional tests. ABHE Bible Knowledge Test. **Support services:** Reduced course load, remedial instruction.

Majors. Theology: Bible, missionary, pastoral counseling, religious ed, sacred music, theology, youth ministry.

Technology on campus. 7 workstations in library, computer center.

Student life. Freshman orientation: Mandatory, $50 fee. Preregistration for classes offered. Two days of training and testing, followed by whitewater boat trip. **Policies:** Religious observance required. **Housing:** Guaranteed on-campus for freshmen. Single-sex dorms available. $150 deposit, deadline 7/1. Trailer hookups for married students available. **Activities:** Choral groups, music ensembles, student government, student newspaper, Christian service missions club.

Athletics. Intramural: Basketball, football (non-tackle) M, soccer, volleyball. **Team name:** Lions.

Student services. Adult student services, career counseling, student employment services, financial aid counseling, health services, personal counseling, placement for graduates, veterans' counselor.

Contact. E-mail: boisebible@boisebible.edu
Phone: (208) 376-7731 Toll-free number: (800) 893-7755
Fax: (208) 376-7743
Michael Maglish, Admissions Director, Boise Bible College, 8695 West Marigold Street, Boise, ID 83714-1220

Boise State University
Boise, Idaho   CB member
www.boisestate.edu   CB code: 4018

- Public 4-year university
- Commuter campus in small city
- 15,964 degree-seeking undergraduates: 25% part-time, 53% women, 2% African American, 2% Asian American, 11% Hispanic/Latino, 1% Native American, 4% Multi-racial, non-Hispanic, 5% international
- 2,426 degree-seeking graduate students
- 80% of applicants admitted
- 38% graduate within 6 years

General. Founded in 1932. Regionally accredited. **Degrees:** 3,154 bachelor's, 168 associate awarded; master's, doctoral offered. **ROTC:** Army. **Location:** Downtown. **Calendar:** Semester, extensive summer session. **Full-time faculty:** 713 total; 69% have terminal degrees, 10% minority, 48% women. **Part-time faculty:** 19 total; 5% minority, 79% women. **Class size:** 35% < 20, 46% 20-39, 8% 40-49, 8% 50-99, 3% >100. **Special facilities:** Performing arts center, technology center, natural area, world center for birds of prey research.

Freshman class profile. 8,155 applied, 6,489 admitted, 2,192 enrolled.

Mid 50% test scores		Rank in top quarter:	40%
SAT critical reading:	460-570	Rank in top tenth:	15%
SAT math:	460-570	Return as sophomores:	76%
SAT writing:	440-550	Out-of-state:	39%
ACT composite:	20-26	Live on campus:	57%
GPA 3.75 or higher:	24%	International:	5%
GPA 3.50-3.74:	23%	Fraternities:	3%
GPA 3.0-3.49:	38%	Sororities:	8%
GPA 2.0-2.99:	15%		

Basis for selection. Admission based on GPA and SAT/ACT. Applicants without high school diploma or GED may petition for admission. Interview required for nursing majors. **Home schooled:** State high school equivalency certificate required.

High school preparation. College-preparatory program recommended. Recommended units include English 8, mathematics 6, social studies 5, science 6 (laboratory 2), foreign language 2 and academic electives 3. Recommended history credits are counted with social studies credits. Academic elective credits are a total of 3 credits that are a combination of electives (e.g., humanities, fine arts, and 1.5 units other college preparatory).

2015-2016 Annual costs. Tuition/fees: $6,876; $20,926 out-of-state. Room/board: $6,938.

2014-2015 Financial aid. Need-based: 1,421 full-time freshmen applied for aid; 1,348 deemed to have need; 1,312 received aid. Average need met was 62%. Average scholarship/grant was $5,245; average loan $3,191. 38% of total undergraduate aid awarded as scholarships/grants, 62% as loans/jobs. **Non-need-based:** Awarded to 935 full-time undergraduates, including 377 freshmen. Scholarships awarded for academics, alumni affiliation, art, athletics, music/drama.

Application procedures. Admission: $50 fee, may be waived for applicants with need. Admission notification on a rolling basis beginning on or about 4/1. Strongly recommended that students apply January-March. **Financial aid:** Priority date 2/15; no closing date. FAFSA required. Applicants notified on a rolling basis starting 3/15; must reply by 4/12 or within 4 week(s) of notification.

Academics. Basque studies program abroad. **Special study options:** Distance learning, double major, dual enrollment of high school students, exchange student, honors, independent study, internships, student-designed major, study abroad, teacher certification program, weekend college. **Credit/placement by examination:** AP, CLEP, SAT, ACT, institutional tests. 21 credit hours maximum toward associate degree, 42 toward bachelor's. **Support services:** Learning center, pre-admission summer program, reduced course load, remedial instruction, study skills assistance, tutoring, writing center.

Honors college/program. 3.5 GPA, 27 ACT or 1200 SAT required.

Majors. Area/ethnic studies: General. **Biology:** General. **Business:** General, accounting, accounting/finance, business admin, construction management, finance, international, logistics, managerial economics, marketing. **Communications:** Communications/speech/rhetoric, media studies. **Computer sciences:** Computer science, information systems. **Conservation:** Environmental studies. **Education:** Art, bilingual, biology, chemistry, early childhood special, elementary, elementary special ed, English, French, German, history, mathematics, music, physical, physics, science, social science,

Spanish, special ed, speech. **Engineering:** Civil, electrical, mechanical, pre-engineering. **English:** English lit, technical writing. **Foreign languages:** French, German, Spanish. **Health services:** Athletic training, environmental health, health information management, nursing (RN), nursing practice, pre-chiropractic, predental, premedicine, prenursing, preoccupational therapy, preoptometry, prepharmacy, prephysical therapy, preveterinary, radiologic technology/medical imaging, respiratory therapy technology. **History:** General. **Human services:** Social work. **Liberal arts:** Arts/sciences. **Math:** General, applied. **Parks/recreation:** Exercise sciences, health/fitness. **Philosophy/religion:** Philosophy. **Physical sciences:** Chemistry, geology, geophysics, physics. **Protective services:** Criminal justice, law enforcement admin. **Psychology:** General. **Social sciences:** General, anthropology, economics, political science, sociology. **Visual/performing arts:** Art history/conservation, commercial/advertising art, design, dramatic, game design, music, music management, music performance, music theory/composition.

Most popular majors. Business/marketing 19%, communications/journalism 7%, health sciences 21%, social sciences 7%.

Technology on campus. 900 workstations in dormitories, library, computer center, student center. Dormitories wired for high-speed internet access and linked to campus network. Commuter students can connect to campus network. Online course registration, online library, helpline, wireless network available.

Student life. Freshman orientation: Mandatory, $75 fee. Preregistration for classes offered. **Housing:** Coed dorms, apartments available. $250 partly refundable deposit, deadline 5/31. **Activities:** Bands, choral groups, dance, drama, film society, international student organizations, literary magazine, music ensembles, musical theater, radio station, student government, student newspaper, symphony orchestra, Afro-Black Student Alliance, Native American Association, Organization de Estudiantes Latino-Americanos, Saudi Women Inspiration, Latter-day Saints Student Association, Young Life College, Alternative Mobility Adventure Seekers, Net Impact.

Athletics. NCAA. **Intercollegiate:** Basketball, cheerleading, cross-country, football (tackle) M, golf, gymnastics W, soccer W, softball W, swimming W, tennis, track and field, volleyball W, wrestling M. **Intramural:** Baseball M, basketball, bowling, handball, racquetball, rodeo, soccer M, softball W, swimming, tennis, volleyball W. **Team name:** Broncos.

Student services. Adult student services, alcohol/substance abuse counseling, career counseling, student employment services, financial aid counseling, health services, legal services, minority student services, on-campus daycare, personal counseling, placement for graduates, veterans' counselor, women's services. **Physically disabled:** Services for visually, speech, hearing impaired.

Contact. E-mail: bsuinfo@boisestate.edu
Phone: (208) 426-1000 ext. 1 Toll-free number: (800) 824-7017
Fax: (208) 426-3765
Kelly Talbert, Director of Admissions, Boise State University, 1910 University Drive, Boise, ID 83725-1320

Brigham Young University-Idaho
Rexburg, Idaho
www.byui.edu   CB code: 4657

- Private 4-year university affiliated with the Church of Jesus Christ of Latter-day Saints
- Residential campus in large town
- 20,390 degree-seeking undergraduates
- SAT or ACT (ACT writing optional), application essay required

General. Founded in 1888. Regionally accredited. **Degrees:** 3,650 bachelor's, 1,484 associate awarded. **ROTC:** Army. **Location:** 30 miles from Idaho Falls, 240 miles from Salt Lake City. **Calendar:** Semester, extensive summer session. **Full-time faculty:** 481 total. **Part-time faculty:** 283 total. **Special facilities:** Observatory, planetarium, livestock center, off-campus outdoor educational facility, leadership and service institute, arboretum, horticultural gardens.

Freshman class profile.

GPA 3.75 or higher:	23%	GPA 3.0-3.49:	40%
GPA 3.50-3.74:	30%	GPA 2.0-2.99:	7%

Basis for selection. Religious affiliation, recommendations most important. High school record, test scores, personal essay, extracurricular activities also important. Interview with student's ecclesiastical leader required. Auditions required for music, dance, theater majors. **Home schooled:** GED or Compass test required.

2015-2016 Annual costs. Tuition/fees: $3,830. Room/board: $4,000. Books/supplies: $818. Personal expenses: $1,630.

Financial aid. Non-need-based: Scholarships awarded for academics, alumni affiliation, art, leadership, music/drama. **Additional information:** Application deadline for merit scholarships 3/1.

Application procedures. Admission: Priority date 12/1; deadline 2/1 (postmark date). $35 fee. Application must be submitted online. Admission notification by 4/1. Admission notification on a rolling basis beginning on or about 10/15. **Financial aid:** Priority date 5/1; no closing date. FAFSA required. Applicants notified on a rolling basis starting 2/1.

Academics. Special study options: Accelerated study, distance learning, double major, independent study, internships, student-designed major, study abroad, teacher certification program, urban semester. **Credit/placement by examination:** AP, CLEP, IB, institutional tests. **Support services:** Learning center, reduced course load, remedial instruction, study skills assistance, tutoring, writing center.

Majors. Architecture: Interior. **Biology:** General, zoology. **Business:** Accounting, business admin. **Communications:** Advertising, broadcast journalism, communications/speech/rhetoric, journalism, public relations. **Computer sciences:** General, computer science. **Conservation:** Environmental science, wildlife/wilderness. **Education:** Art, biology, chemistry, drama/dance, elementary, English, family/consumer sciences, history, mathematics, music, physics, science, social studies, Spanish. **Engineering:** Computer, mechanical. **English:** English lit, writing. **Health services:** Nursing (RN), predental, premedicine, prepharmacy, preveterinary. **History:** General. **Liberal arts:** Arts/sciences. **Math:** General. **Parks/recreation:** General. **Physical sciences:** Chemistry, geology, physics. **Psychology:** General. **Social sciences:** Economics, international relations, political science, sociology. **Visual/performing arts:** Art, interior design, music, photography. **Work/family studies:** Food/nutrition.

Most popular majors. Agriculture 7%, biology 7%, education 20%, health sciences 7%, liberal arts 6%, social sciences 6%, visual/performing arts 10%.

Technology on campus. PC or laptop required. 2,500 workstations in dormitories, library, computer center, student center. Dormitories wired for high-speed internet access and linked to campus network. Commuter students can connect to campus network. Online course registration, online library, helpline, student web hosting, wireless network available.

Student life. Freshman orientation: Available. Preregistration for classes offered. **Policies:** Students encouraged to attend weekly devotional at which noted church leaders speak. Religious observance required. **Housing:** Single-sex dorms, apartments, wellness housing available. $175 deposit. **Activities:** Bands, choral groups, dance, drama, international student organizations, literary magazine, music ensembles, musical theater, radio station, student government, student newspaper, symphony orchestra, TV station, Lambda Delta Sigma, Sigma Gamma Chi, business club, married student association, outdoor club.

Athletics. Intramural: Archery, badminton, baseball, basketball, bowling, cheerleading, cross-country, diving, fencing, field hockey, football (non-tackle), football (tackle), golf, ice hockey, lacrosse, racquetball, rodeo, skiing, skin diving, soccer, softball, swimming, table tennis, tennis, track and field, ultimate frisbee, volleyball, water polo, wrestling M. **Team name:** Vikings.

Student services. Career counseling, student employment services, financial aid counseling, health services, personal counseling, placement for graduates, veterans' counselor. **Physically disabled:** Services for visually, hearing impaired.

Contact. E-mail: admissions@byui.edu
Phone: (208) 496-1300 Fax: (208) 496-1303
Tyler Williams, Director of Admissions, Brigham Young University-Idaho, 120 Kimball Building, Rexburg, ID 83460-1615

College of Idaho
Caldwell, Idaho   CB member
www.collegeofidaho.edu   CB code: 4060

- Private 4-year liberal arts college
- Residential campus in large town
- 1,034 degree-seeking undergraduates: 3% part-time, 51% women, 2% African American, 2% Asian American, 14% Hispanic/Latino, 1% Native American, 1% Native Hawaiian/Pacific islander, 3% Multi-racial, non-Hispanic, 7% international
- 31 degree-seeking graduate students
- 90% of applicants admitted

‣ Application essay required
‣ 68% graduate within 6 years

General. Founded in 1891. Regionally accredited. **Degrees:** 222 bachelor's awarded; master's offered. **ROTC:** Army. **Location:** 30 miles from Boise. **Calendar:** Semester. **Full-time faculty:** 84 total; 83% have terminal degrees, 6% minority, 43% women. **Part-time faculty:** 56 total; 25% have terminal degrees, 9% minority, 54% women. **Class size:** 58% < 20, 37% 20-39, 4% 40-49, 1% 50-99. **Special facilities:** Planetarium, herbarium, center for the performing and fine arts, art gallery, natural history museum.

Freshman class profile. 955 applied, 863 admitted, 201 enrolled.

Mid 50% test scores		GPA 2.0-2.99:	16%
SAT critical reading:	460-590	Return as sophomores:	82%
SAT math:	470-600	Out-of-state:	37%
SAT writing:	450-570	Live on campus:	94%
ACT composite:	20-26	International:	6%
GPA 3.75 or higher:	37%	Fraternities:	12%
GPA 3.50-3.74:	14%	Sororities:	8%
GPA 3.0-3.49:	27%		

Basis for selection. Academic record, test scores, extracurricular activities, essay, teacher recommendation important. Interview, campus visit recommended. Audition required of music, theater major; portfolio required of art majors. **Home schooled:** Transcript of courses and grades, letter of recommendation (nonparent) required. Course descriptions required. **Learning Disabled:** Student must submit a request for accommodations, submit appropriate documentation of the diagnosed disability from a qualified treatment provider completed within the last 3 years; provide a signed release of information form with contact information to the Student Disability Services Office; and schedule an appointment with the Disability Services Coordinator.

High school preparation. College-preparatory program recommended. Recommended units include English 4, mathematics 3, social studies 2, history 2, science 2, foreign language 2 and academic electives 4.

2016-2017 Annual costs. Tuition/fees (projected): $27,425. Room/board: $8,990. Books/supplies: $1,200. Personal expenses: $1,500.

2015-2016 Financial aid. Need-based: 177 full-time freshmen applied for aid; 156 deemed to have need; 156 received aid. Average need met was 87%. Average scholarship/grant was $3,831; average loan $3,391. 59% of total undergraduate aid awarded as scholarships/grants, 41% as loans/jobs. **Non-need-based:** Awarded to 1,095 full-time undergraduates, including 114 freshmen. Scholarships awarded for academics, alumni affiliation, athletics, job skills, ROTC.

Application procedures. Admission: Priority date 11/15; deadline 2/16 (postmark date). No application fee. Admission notification on a rolling basis beginning on or about 10/15. Must reply by May 1 or within 2 week(s) if notified thereafter. **Financial aid:** Priority date 2/1; no closing date. FAFSA, institutional form required. Applicants notified on a rolling basis starting 3/15; must reply within 3 week(s) of notification.

Academics. Special study options: Combined bachelor's/graduate degree, cross-registration, double major, dual enrollment of high school students, ESL, honors, independent study, internships, study abroad, teacher certification program, Washington semester. BS/Pharm.D, Pharmacy; BS/BS, Medical Laboratory Science; BS/BS, Nursing; and BS/BS, Speech Language Pathology & Audiology with Idaho State University. BS/BS, BA or BS/JD, Law with University of Idaho. **Credit/placement by examination:** AP, CLEP, IB, SAT, ACT. **Support services:** Learning center, reduced course load, study skills assistance, tutoring, writing center.

Majors. Biology: General. **Business:** Accounting, business admin. **Computer sciences:** General. **Conservation:** Environmental studies. **Education:** Bilingual, elementary, multi-level teacher, music, physical. **English:** Creative writing, English lit. **Foreign languages:** Spanish. **Health services:** Audiology/speech pathology, clinical lab science, prenursing, prepharmacy. **History:** General. **Math:** General, applied. **Parks/recreation:** Exercise sciences. **Philosophy/religion:** Philosophy, religion. **Physical sciences:** General, chemistry. **Psychology:** General. **Social sciences:** International relations, political science, sociology/anthropology. **Visual/performing arts:** Dramatic, music, music theory/composition, studio arts.

Most popular majors. Biology 7%, business/marketing 15%, education 6%, health sciences 8%, mathematics 8%, psychology 13%, social sciences 10%, visual/performing arts 7%.

Technology on campus. 250 workstations in dormitories, library, computer center, student center. Dormitories wired for high-speed internet access and linked to campus network. Commuter students can connect to campus network. Online course registration, online library, helpline, repair service, student web hosting, wireless network available.

Student life. Freshman orientation: Mandatory. Preregistration for classes offered. One-day sessions to assist students and parents. **Policies:** Freshmen, sophomores and juniors under age 21 must live on campus unless living with parents or relatives. All buildings smoke-free. Honor Code has been implemented for all students. **Housing:** Guaranteed on-campus for freshmen. Coed dorms, special housing for disabled, apartments, fraternity/sorority housing, themed housing, wellness housing available. $300 nonrefundable deposit, deadline 8/1. Academic communities (minimum GPA) available. **Activities:** Bands, campus ministries, choral groups, dance, drama, film society, international student organizations, literary magazine, music ensembles, Model UN, musical theater, opera, student government, student newspaper, symphony orchestra, over 30 activities or organizations.

Athletics. NAIA. **Intercollegiate:** Baseball M, basketball, cross-country, golf, skiing, soccer, softball W, swimming, tennis W, track and field, volleyball W. **Intramural:** Badminton, basketball, football (non-tackle), soccer, softball, ultimate frisbee, volleyball. **Team name:** Coyotes.

Student services. Alcohol/substance abuse counseling, chaplain/spiritual director, career counseling, student employment services, financial aid counseling, health services, minority student services, personal counseling, placement for graduates, women's services. **Physically disabled:** Services for hearing impaired.

Contact. E-mail: admissions@collegeofidaho.edu
Phone: (208) 459-5305 Toll-free number: (800) 224-3246
Fax: (208) 459-5757
Lorna Hunter, Vice President for Enrollment Management, College of Idaho, 2112 Cleveland Boulevard, Caldwell, ID 83605-4432

Idaho State University
Pocatello, Idaho
www.isu.edu

CB code: 4355

‣ Public 4-year university
‣ Commuter campus in small city
‣ 8,977 degree-seeking undergraduates: 23% part-time, 50% women, 1% African American, 1% Asian American, 10% Hispanic/Latino, 1% Native American, 3% Multi-racial, non-Hispanic, 14% international
‣ 1,822 degree-seeking graduate students
‣ 99% of applicants admitted
‣ SAT or ACT (ACT writing optional) required
‣ 31% graduate within 6 years

General. Founded in 1901. Regionally accredited. Designated by State Board of Education as institution specializing in health-related programs. **Degrees:** 1,155 bachelor's, 374 associate awarded; master's, professional, doctoral offered. **ROTC:** Army. **Location:** 150 miles from Salt Lake City, 230 miles from Boise. **Calendar:** Semester, limited summer session. **Full-time faculty:** 585 total; 51% have terminal degrees, 9% minority, 45% women. **Part-time faculty:** 149 total; 5% minority, 53% women. **Class size:** 66% < 20, 27% 20-39, 3% 40-49, 3% 50-99, less than 1% >100. **Special facilities:** Natural history museum, accelerator center, geographical information systems center, performing arts center.

Freshman class profile. 3,057 applied, 3,020 admitted, 1,466 enrolled.

Mid 50% test scores		GPA 2.0-2.99:	31%
SAT critical reading:	420-540	Rank in top quarter:	31%
SAT math:	420-530	Rank in top tenth:	11%
SAT writing:	400-510	End year in good standing:	74%
ACT composite:	19-25	Return as sophomores:	71%
GPA 3.75 or higher:	24%	Out-of-state:	9%
GPA 3.50-3.74:	17%	Live on campus:	30%
GPA 3.0-3.49:	27%		

Basis for selection. For general admissions, predicted GPA of 1.5 (based on core GPA and test scores) required. Students not meeting those standards can be admitted conditionally or by petition or admission will be deferred. ACT preferred. Interview recommended. Audition recommended for music majors. Portfolio recommended for experiential credit-seeking applicants. **Home schooled:** GED required.

High school preparation. College-preparatory program required. 16 units required. Required and recommended units include English 4, mathematics 3-4, social studies 2.5, science 3 (laboratory 1) and foreign language 1. 1.5 units in humanities, speech, studio/performing arts required.

2015-2016 Annual costs. Tuition/fees: $6,784; $20,182 out-of-state. Room/board: $6,338. Books/supplies: $1,000. Personal expenses: $4,013.

2014-2015 Financial aid. Need-based: 1,100 full-time freshmen applied for aid; 910 deemed to have need; 894 received aid. Average need met was

48%. Average scholarship/grant was $4,992; average loan $3,051. 37% of total undergraduate aid awarded as scholarships/grants, 63% as loans/jobs. **Non-need-based:** Awarded to 2,107 full-time undergraduates, including 699 freshmen. Scholarships awarded for academics, alumni affiliation, art, athletics, leadership, minority status, music/drama, ROTC, state residency.

Application procedures. Admission: Priority date 8/1; no deadline. $50 fee, may be waived for applicants with need. Admission notification on a rolling basis beginning on or about 3/1. High school students who graduate early may petition admissions committee to enroll full time. **Financial aid:** Priority date 3/1; no closing date. FAFSA required. Applicants notified on a rolling basis starting 4/1.

Academics. Special study options: Accelerated study, combined bachelor's/graduate degree, cooperative education, cross-registration, distance learning, double major, dual enrollment of high school students, ESL, exchange student, honors, independent study, internships, liberal arts/career combination, student-designed major, study abroad, teacher certification program, weekend college. **Credit/placement by examination:** AP, CLEP, IB, SAT, ACT, institutional tests. 32 credit hours maximum toward associate degree, 64 toward bachelor's. Credit by challenge exam not permitted for courses already taken, or for courses that are prerequisites to courses already completed. **Support services:** Learning center, remedial instruction, study skills assistance, tutoring, writing center.

Majors. Biology: General, biochemistry, botany, ecology, microbiology, zoology. **Business:** General, accounting, administrative services, business admin, finance, human resources, insurance, marketing. **Communications:** Communications/speech/rhetoric, media studies. **Communications technology:** Desktop publishing. **Computer sciences:** General, applications programming, information systems, networking, web page design. **Conservation:** Environmental science. **Education:** Early childhood, elementary, health, music, physical, secondary, special ed. **Engineering:** Civil, electrical, mechanical, nuclear. **English:** English lit. **Foreign languages:** French, German, sign language interpretation, Spanish. **General:** Carpentry. **Health services:** Audiology/speech pathology, clinical lab science, dental hygiene, dietetics, health care admin, health information technology, massage therapy, medical assistant, medical radiologic technology/radiation therapy, nursing (RN), physical therapy assistant. **History:** General. **Human services:** Social work. **Math:** General, statistics. **Philosophy/religion:** Philosophy. **Physical sciences:** Chemistry, geology, physics. **Protective services:** Disaster management, firefighting, police science. **Psychology:** General. **Social sciences:** Anthropology, economics, international relations, political science, sociology. **Visual/performing arts:** Art, dramatic, music, music performance. **Work/family studies:** General, child care service.

Most popular majors. Biology 6%, business/marketing 12%, education 13%, engineering/engineering technologies 7%, health sciences 23%, social sciences 6%.

Technology on campus. 200 workstations in dormitories, library, computer center, student center. Dormitories wired for high-speed internet access and linked to campus network. Commuter students can connect to campus network. Online course registration, online library, helpline, student web hosting, wireless network available.

Student life. Freshman orientation: Available. Preregistration for classes offered. Held several times before classes begin in both fall and spring semesters. **Policies:** In order to be eligible for housing, student must be taking 6 credits per semester and be working towards a degree. **Housing:** Coed dorms, single-sex dorms, special housing for disabled, apartments, wellness housing available. $150 partly refundable deposit, deadline 8/23. Housing modified for disabled available on request, subject to waiting list. Graduate housing is also available. **Activities:** Bands, campus ministries, choral groups, dance, drama, international student organizations, literary magazine, music ensembles, musical theater, opera, radio station, student government, student newspaper, symphony orchestra, TV station, Newman Center, Latter-day Saints Institute, student ambassadors, Young Democrats, Young Republicans, Campus Crusade for Christ, Associated Black Students, Native Americans United, Cooperative Wilderness Handicapped Outdoor Group.

Athletics. NCAA. **Intercollegiate:** Basketball, cheerleading, cross-country, football (tackle) M, golf W, soccer W, softball W, tennis, track and field, volleyball W. **Intramural:** Badminton, basketball, bowling, fencing, football (non-tackle) M, golf, judo, racquetball, soccer, softball, table tennis, tennis, ultimate frisbee, volleyball. **Team name:** Bengals.

Student services. Adult student services, alcohol/substance abuse counseling, career counseling, student employment services, financial aid counseling, health services, legal services, minority student services, on-campus daycare, personal counseling, placement for graduates, veterans' counselor, women's services. **Physically disabled:** Services for visually, speech, hearing impaired.

Contact. E-mail: admiss@isu.edu
Phone: (208) 282-2475 Fax: (208) 282-4511
Nicole Roseberg, Director, Idaho State University, 921 South 8th Stop 8270, Pocatello, ID 83209-8270

ITT Technical Institute: Boise
Boise, Idaho
www.itt-tech.edu   **CB code: 3596**

- For-profit 4-year technical college
- Commuter campus in small city
- 274 undergraduates
- Interview required

General. Founded in 1906. Accredited by ACICS. **Degrees:** 25 bachelor's, 72 associate awarded. **Calendar:** Quarter, extensive summer session. **Full-time faculty:** 16 total. **Part-time faculty:** 37 total.

Basis for selection. Satisfactory scores from on-site English and mathematics tests required.

2015-2016 Annual costs. Per-credit-hour charge, $493; academic fee, $200. Certain programs require purchase of tools, which range from $500 to $655. All costs subject to change.

Application procedures. Admission: No deadline. $100 fee. Admission notification on a rolling basis. **Financial aid:** No deadline. FAFSA, institutional form required. Applicants notified on a rolling basis.

Academics. Credit/placement by examination: AP, CLEP. **Support services:** Tutoring.

Majors. Business: Business admin, construction management. **Communications technology:** Animation/special effects. **Computer sciences:** Programming, security. **Protective services:** Law enforcement admin.

Technology on campus. Online library available.

Student life. Freshman orientation: Available. Preregistration for classes offered.

Student services. Career counseling, student employment services, placement for graduates.

Contact. Phone: (208) 322-8844 Toll-free number: (800) 666-4888
Fax: (208) 322-0173
Terry Lowder, Director of Recruitment, ITT Technical Institute: Boise, 12302 West Explorer Drive, Boise, ID 83713-1529

Lewis-Clark State College
Lewiston, Idaho
www.lcsc.edu   **CB code: 4385**

- Public 4-year liberal arts and technical college
- Commuter campus in large town
- 3,035 degree-seeking undergraduates: 26% part-time, 62% women, 1% African American, 1% Asian American, 6% Hispanic/Latino, 3% Native American, 2% Multi-racial, non-Hispanic, 3% international
- 99% of applicants admitted

General. Founded in 1893. Regionally accredited. Courses offered at outreach centers (Orofino, Grangeville, Coeur d'Alene, and Lapwai). **Degrees:** 544 bachelor's, 204 associate awarded. **ROTC:** Army, Naval, Air Force. **Location:** 300 miles from Boise, 100 miles from Spokane, WA. **Calendar:** Semester, limited summer session. **Full-time faculty:** 173 total; 59% women. **Part-time faculty:** 80 total; 64% women. **Class size:** 64% < 20, 31% 20-39, 4% 40-49, 1% 50-99, less than 1% >100. **Special facilities:** Biodiversity museum and collection, geographical information systems center.

Freshman class profile. 1,117 applied, 1,104 admitted, 553 enrolled.

Mid 50% test scores			
		GPA 2.0-2.99:	37%
SAT critical reading:	410-520	Rank in top quarter:	23%
SAT math:	410-510	Rank in top tenth:	6%
ACT composite:	18-23	Out-of-state:	21%
GPA 3.75 or higher:	15%	Live on campus:	40%
GPA 3.50-3.74:	15%	International:	4%
GPA 3.0-3.49:	30%		

Basis for selection. High school courses, GPA, test scores considered. Students may be asked to take COMPASS test under certain circumstances. **Home schooled:** Must have predicted college GPA of 2.0 based on ACT/SAT. Must have acceptable performance on 2 testing indicators: GED score of 500 (50 if tested before 2002) or higher, or other standardized diagnostic test such as ACT, SAT, COMPASS, ASSET, or CPT.

High school preparation. College-preparatory program required. 15 units required. Required units include English 4, mathematics 3, social studies 2.5, science 3 (laboratory 1), academic electives 1.5.

2015-2016 Annual costs. Tuition/fees: $6,000; $17,000 out-of-state. Room/board: $6,360. Books/supplies: $1,520. Personal expenses: $1,960.

2014-2015 Financial aid. Need-based: 463 full-time freshmen applied for aid; 378 deemed to have need; 378 received aid. Average need met was 57%. Average scholarship/grant was $5,185; average loan $2,906. 51% of total undergraduate aid awarded as scholarships/grants, 49% as loans/jobs. **Non-need-based:** Awarded to 930 full-time undergraduates, including 349 freshmen. Scholarships awarded for academics, alumni affiliation, art, athletics, job skills, leadership, minority status, music/drama, religious affiliation.

Application procedures. Admission: Closing date 8/8 (receipt date). No application fee. Admission notification on a rolling basis. **Financial aid:** Closing date 3/1. FAFSA, institutional form required. Applicants notified on a rolling basis starting 4/15; must reply within 2 week(s) of notification.

Academics. Communications/speech lab to help students prepare for speeches and presentations. **Special study options:** Accelerated study, combined bachelor's/graduate degree, cooperative education, distance learning, double major, dual enrollment of high school students, independent study, internships, liberal arts/career combination, student-designed major, study abroad, teacher certification program. **Credit/placement by examination:** AP, CLEP, IB, SAT, ACT, institutional tests. 16 credit hours maximum toward associate degree, 32 toward bachelor's. **Support services:** Learning center, reduced course load, remedial instruction, study skills assistance, tutoring, writing center.

Majors. Biology: General. **Business:** Accounting technology, administrative services, business admin, hospitality admin, small business admin. **Communications:** Communications/speech/rhetoric. **Communications technology:** Graphic/printing. **Computer sciences:** General, computer science, webmaster. **Education:** Elementary, English, mathematics, physical, science, social science. **English:** Creative writing, English lit. **Health services:** Management/clinical assistant, nursing (RN), office assistant. **Human services:** Social work. **Math:** General. **Parks/recreation:** Exercise sciences. **Physical sciences:** Chemistry. **Protective services:** Corrections, criminal justice, firefighting. **Psychology:** General. **Social sciences:** General. **Work/family studies:** Child development.

Most popular majors. Business/marketing 23%, education 9%, health sciences 24%, liberal arts 6%, public administration/social services 10%.

Technology on campus. 455 workstations in dormitories, library, computer center, student center. Dormitories wired for high-speed internet access and linked to campus network. Commuter students can connect to campus network. Online course registration, online library, helpline, student web hosting, wireless network available.

Student life. Freshman orientation: Mandatory, $35 fee. Preregistration for classes offered. One-day session held in August. **Housing:** Coed dorms, apartments, themed housing available. $200 partly refundable deposit. **Activities:** Jazz band, campus ministries, drama, international student organizations, literary magazine, radio station, student government, student newspaper, Native American Indian Student Organization, Ambassadors' Club, Criminal Justice Society, Idaho Student Lobby, Business Student Organization, Latter-Day Saints Student Association, College Democrats, College Republicans.

Athletics. NAIA. **Intercollegiate:** Baseball M, basketball, cross-country, golf, tennis, track and field, volleyball W. **Intramural:** Badminton, baseball, basketball, bowling, football (non-tackle), golf, soccer, softball, volleyball. **Team name:** Warriors.

Student services. Adult student services, alcohol/substance abuse counseling, career counseling, services for economically disadvantaged, student employment services, financial aid counseling, health services, minority student services, on-campus daycare, personal counseling, placement for graduates, veterans' counselor, women's services. **Physically disabled:** Services for visually, speech, hearing impaired.

Contact. E-mail: admissions@lcsc.edu
Phone: (208) 792-2210 Toll-free number: (800) 933-5272
Fax: (208) 792-2876
Nikol Luther, Registrar/Director of Admissions, Lewis-Clark State College, 500 Eighth Avenue, Lewiston, ID 83501-2698

New Saint Andrews College
Moscow, Idaho
www.nsa.edu   CB code: 3855

- Private 4-year liberal arts college affiliated with the Christian Church
- Residential campus in large town

- 139 degree-seeking undergraduates: 6% part-time, 55% women, 1% Asian American, 4% Hispanic/Latino, 1% Native American, 1% Multiracial, non-Hispanic, 11% international
- 20 degree-seeking graduate students
- 100% of applicants admitted
- SAT or ACT (ACT writing optional), application essay required
- 63% graduate within 6 years; 18% enter graduate study

General. Regionally accredited; also accredited by TRACS. **Degrees:** 26 bachelor's, 6 associate awarded; master's offered. **Location:** 80 miles from Spokane, Washington. **Calendar:** Semester. **Full-time faculty:** 6 total; 83% have terminal degrees, 17% minority. **Part-time faculty:** 9 total; 44% have terminal degrees, 11% women. **Class size:** 57% < 20, 36% 20-39, 4% 40-49, 4% 50-99.

Freshman class profile. 63 applied, 63 admitted, 49 enrolled.

Mid 50% test scores		End year in good standing:	95%
SAT critical reading:	570-720	Return as sophomores:	93%
SAT math:	510-630	Out-of-state:	81%
SAT writing:	550-660	International:	16%
ACT composite:	21-28		

Basis for selection. Academic achievement and test scores very important. **Home schooled:** Letter of recommendation (nonparent) required.

2016-2017 Annual costs. Tuition/fees: $12,100. Books/supplies: $1,200.

Financial aid. Non-need-based: Scholarships awarded for academics.

Application procedures. Admission: Priority date 2/15; deadline 8/1 (postmark date). $40 fee. Admission notification by 2/15. Admission notification on a rolling basis beginning on or about 12/1. **Financial aid:** Priority date 2/15, closing date 5/15. Institutional form required. Must reply within 2 week(s) of notification.

Academics. Special study options: Dual enrollment of high school students. **Credit/placement by examination:** AP, CLEP. **Support services:** Pre-admission summer program, reduced course load, remedial instruction, study skills assistance, tutoring.

Majors. Liberal arts: Arts/sciences.

Technology on campus. 5 workstations in library. Commuter students can connect to campus network. Online course registration, wireless network available.

Student life. Freshman orientation: Mandatory. Preregistration for classes offered. **Policies:** Religious observance required. **Activities:** Campus ministries, choral groups, drama, music ensembles, musical theater, Students for the Relief of the Oppressed.

Athletics. Intramural: Rugby M, volleyball W.

Student services. Chaplain/spiritual director, career counseling, financial aid counseling, personal counseling.

Contact. E-mail: admissions@nsa.edu
Phone: (208) 882-1566 ext. 113 Fax: (208) 882-4293
Brenda Schlect, Director of Admissions, New Saint Andrews College, PO Box 9025, Moscow, ID 83843

Northwest Nazarene University
Nampa, Idaho
www.nnu.edu   CB code: 4544

- Private 4-year university affiliated with the Church of the Nazarene
- Residential campus in small city
- 1,290 degree-seeking undergraduates: 10% part-time, 60% women, 2% African American, 2% Asian American, 7% Hispanic/Latino, 1% Native American, 4% Multi-racial, non-Hispanic, 3% international
- 712 degree-seeking graduate students
- 55% of applicants admitted
- SAT or ACT (ACT writing optional), application essay required
- 49% graduate within 6 years

General. Founded in 1913. Regionally accredited. **Degrees:** 260 bachelor's, 1 associate awarded; master's, professional, doctoral offered. **ROTC:** Army. **Location:** 18 miles from Boise. **Calendar:** Semester, limited summer session. **Full-time faculty:** 128 total; 66% have terminal degrees; 8% minority, 57% women. **Part-time faculty:** 1 total; 100% have terminal degrees, 100%

women. **Class size:** 66% < 20, 27% 20-39, 3% 40-49, 4% 50-99. **Special facilities:** Depository for federal government publications.

Freshman class profile. 1,589 applied, 870 admitted, 258 enrolled.

Mid 50% test scores			
		GPA 2.0-2.99:	17%
SAT critical reading:	460-580	Rank in top quarter:	52%
SAT math:	460-570	Rank in top tenth:	26%
SAT writing:	440-560	Return as sophomores:	74%
ACT composite:	21-25	Out-of-state:	11%
GPA 3.75 or higher:	39%	Live on campus:	76%
GPA 3.50-3.74:	20%	International:	1%
GPA 3.0-3.49:	23%		

Basis for selection. For unconditional admission 2 of following criteria must be met: 2.5 GPA, class rank in top 50%, 18 ACT. Provisional admission available. Interview recommended for students with provisional admission.

High school preparation. College-preparatory program recommended. 15 units recommended. Recommended units include English 4, mathematics 3, social studies 1.5, history 1.5, science 3 and foreign language 2.

2016-2017 Annual costs. Tuition/fees (projected): $28,150. Room/board: $7,000. Books/supplies: $1,200. Personal expenses: $1,280.

2015-2016 Financial aid. **Need-based:** Average need met was 77%. Average scholarship/grant was $16,946; average loan $7,511. 65% of total undergraduate aid awarded as scholarships/grants, 35% as loans/jobs. **Non-need-based:** Scholarships awarded for academics, athletics, leadership, music/drama, religious affiliation, ROTC.

Application procedures. **Admission:** Priority date 3/1; deadline 8/15. $40 fee, may be waived for applicants with need. Admission notification on a rolling basis beginning on or about 9/15. **Financial aid:** Priority date 3/1; no closing date. FAFSA required. Applicants notified on a rolling basis starting 2/15; must reply within 3 week(s) of notification.

Academics. **Special study options:** Accelerated study, combined bachelor's/graduate degree, cooperative education, cross-registration, distance learning, double major, dual enrollment of high school students, ESL, exchange student, honors, independent study, internships, liberal arts/career combination, student-designed major, study abroad, teacher certification program. **Credit/placement by examination:** AP, CLEP, IB, SAT, ACT, institutional tests. 31 credit hours maximum toward bachelor's degree. **Support services:** Learning center, reduced course load, remedial instruction, study skills assistance, tutoring, writing center.

Majors. **Biology:** General, biochemistry, ecology. **Business:** Accounting, business admin, international, marketing, office management. **Communications:** Communications/speech/rhetoric, media studies. **Computer sciences:** Computer science. **Education:** General, art, biology, chemistry, elementary, English, health, history, mathematics, music, physical, physics, psychology, secondary, social science, Spanish. **Engineering:** Aerospace, applied physics, chemical, civil, electrical. **English:** English lit. **Foreign languages:** Spanish. **Health services:** Nursing (RN), physician assistant, predental, premedicine, prepharmacy, preveterinary. **History:** General. **Human services:** Social work. **Liberal arts:** Arts/sciences. **Math:** General. **Parks/recreation:** General, exercise sciences, health/fitness, sports admin. **Philosophy/religion:** Philosophy, religion. **Physical sciences:** Chemistry, physics. **Psychology:** General, industrial. **Social sciences:** General, international relations, political science. **Theology:** Bible, missionary, pastoral counseling, religious ed, sacred music, youth ministry. **Visual/performing arts:** Ceramics, graphic design, music, music performance, music theory/composition, piano/keyboard, voice/opera.

Most popular majors. Biology 6%, business/marketing 18%, education 8%, health sciences 15%, liberal arts 7%, philosophy/religious studies 8%, public administration/social services 6%.

Technology on campus. 275 workstations in dormitories, library, computer center, student center. Dormitories wired for high-speed internet access and linked to campus network. Commuter students can connect to campus network. Online library, helpline, repair service, student web hosting, wireless network available.

Student life. **Freshman orientation:** Mandatory. Preregistration for classes offered. **Policies:** All students required to live on campus until senior year or age 21. Religious observance required. **Housing:** Guaranteed on-campus for all undergraduates. Single-sex dorms, special housing for disabled, apartments available. $250 fully refundable deposit. Some rental units available. **Activities:** Bands, campus ministries, choral groups, drama, film society, international student organizations, music ensembles, musical theater, opera, student government, student newspaper, symphony orchestra, summer ministries, Circle-K, urban ministries club, social work clubs, Angels Ministry, PALS ministry, AIDS ministry, Fellowship of Christian Athletes, multicultural affairs club.

Athletics. NCAA. **Intercollegiate:** Baseball M, basketball, cross-country, golf M, soccer W, softball W, track and field, volleyball W. **Intramural:** Basketball, cross-country, football (non-tackle), softball, volleyball. **Team name:** Crusaders.

Student services. Adult student services, alcohol/substance abuse counseling, chaplain/spiritual director, career counseling, student employment services, financial aid counseling, health services, minority student services, personal counseling, placement for graduates. **Physically disabled:** Services for visually, hearing impaired.

Contact. E-mail: admissions@nnu.edu
Phone: (208) 467-8000 Toll-free number: (877) 668-4968
Fax: (208) 467-8645
Mike Marston, Director of Admissions, Northwest Nazarene University, 623 South University Boulevard, Nampa, ID 83686-5897

University of Idaho
Moscow, Idaho
www.uidaho.edu   CB code: 4843

- Public 4-year university
- Residential campus in large town
- 7,826 degree-seeking undergraduates: 7% part-time, 47% women
- 2,097 degree-seeking graduate students
- 72% of applicants admitted
- SAT or ACT (ACT writing optional) required
- 57% graduate within 6 years

General. Founded in 1889. Regionally accredited. Residential land-grant high-research university. **Degrees:** 2,015 bachelor's awarded; master's, professional, doctoral offered. **ROTC:** Army, Naval, Air Force. **Location:** 90 miles from Spokane, Washington. **Calendar:** Semester, extensive summer session. **Full-time faculty:** 558 total; 78% have terminal degrees, 13% minority, 36% women. **Part-time faculty:** 145 total; 17% have terminal degrees, 5% minority, 47% women. **Class size:** 53% < 20, 34% 20-39, 4% 40-49, 6% 50-99, 3% >100. **Special facilities:** Arboretum and botanical garden, CAVE IQ 3-D visualization image station, 18-hole golf course, art gallery, international jazz collection, indoor climbing facility, herbarium, farm-scale biodiesel production facility.

Freshman class profile. 6,248 applied, 4,476 admitted, 1,588 enrolled.

Mid 50% test scores			
		Rank in top quarter:	42%
SAT critical reading:	470-590	Rank in top tenth:	17%
SAT math:	470-580	Return as sophomores:	80%
SAT writing:	440-560	Out-of-state:	24%
ACT composite:	20-26	Live on campus:	84%
GPA 3.75 or higher:	28%	International:	3%
GPA 3.50-3.74:	20%	Fraternities:	13%
GPA 3.0-3.49:	33%	Sororities:	11%
GPA 2.0-2.99:	19%		

Basis for selection. Applicants must have 3.0 GPA, or 2.2 to 3.0 GPA with high SAT/ACT scores. Recommendations, essay required of applicants with nonstandard high school diploma and adults long out of high school. **Home schooled:** Letter of recommendation (nonparent) required. Copy of GED test results; 3 signed letters of recommendation from individuals who know of and can attest to applicant's academic ability; written statement from applicant including goals, education and/or professional objective; explanation of past academic performance required.

High school preparation. College-preparatory program recommended. 15 units required. Required units include English 4, mathematics 3, social studies 2.5, science 3 (laboratory 1), academic electives 1.5. 1 unit humanities recommended; course should emphasize history, appreciation, theory, analysis, and/or critique. Foreign language strongly recommended.

2015-2016 Annual costs. Tuition/fees: $7,020; $21,024 out-of-state. Room/board: $8,328. Books/supplies: $1,448. Personal expenses: $2,454.

2014-2015 Financial aid. **Need-based:** 1,446 full-time freshmen applied for aid; 1,099 deemed to have need; 1,079 received aid. Average need met was 80%. Average scholarship/grant was $4,660; average loan $5,474. 51% of total undergraduate aid awarded as scholarships/grants, 49% as loans/jobs. **Non-need-based:** Awarded to 4,539 full-time undergraduates, including 1,222 freshmen. Scholarships awarded for academics, alumni affiliation, art, athletics, leadership, minority status, music/drama, ROTC, state residency.

Application procedures. **Admission:** Priority date 2/15; deadline 8/1 (receipt date). $60 fee. Admission notification on a rolling basis. **Financial aid:** Priority date 2/15; no closing date. FAFSA required. Applicants notified on a rolling basis starting 3/30; must reply within 4 week(s) of notification.

Academics. Special study options: Accelerated study, combined bachelor's/graduate degree, cooperative education, cross-registration, distance learning, double major, dual enrollment of high school students, ESL, exchange student, honors, independent study, internships, study abroad, teacher certification program. **Credit/placement by examination:** AP, CLEP, IB, SAT, ACT, institutional tests. 48 credit hours maximum toward bachelor's degree. **Support services:** Learning center, pre-admission summer program, reduced course load, remedial instruction, study skills assistance, tutoring, writing center.

Majors. Architecture: Architecture, landscape. **Area/ethnic studies:** Latin American. **Biology:** General, biochemistry, conservation, microbiology, molecular. **Business:** Accounting, business admin, finance, human resources, management information systems, managerial economics, marketing. **Communications:** Advertising, digital media, journalism, organizational, public relations. **Computer sciences:** Computer science, modeling/simulation. **Conservation:** General, environmental science, fisheries, forest management, forest sciences, nature tourism, wildlife/wilderness, wood science. **Education:** Elementary, physical, secondary, voc/tech. **Engineering:** Biological, chemical, civil, computer, electrical, materials, mechanical. **English:** Creative writing, English lit, technical writing. **Foreign languages:** General, French, Spanish. **Health services:** Athletic training. **History:** General. **Math:** General, applied, biological. **Parks/recreation:** Facilities management. **Philosophy/religion:** Philosophy. **Physical sciences:** Chemistry, geology, physics. **Psychology:** General. **Social sciences:** Anthropology, economics, geography, international relations, political science, sociology. **Visual/performing arts:** Art, dance, dramatic, interior design, music history, music management, music performance, music theory/composition, studio arts. **Work/family studies:** Clothing/textiles, family resources, family studies, food/nutrition.

Most popular majors. Agriculture 6%, business/marketing 17%, communications/journalism 6%, education 6%, engineering/engineering technologies 9%, psychology 8%, social sciences 7%.

Technology on campus. 530 workstations in dormitories, library, computer center, student center. Dormitories wired for high-speed internet access and linked to campus network. Commuter students can connect to campus network. Online course registration, online library, helpline, repair service, student web hosting, wireless network available.

Student life. Freshman orientation: Available, $50 fee. Preregistration for classes offered. Three- to four-day event held the week before classes start. **Policies:** First-year, first-time freshmen required to live on campus. **Housing:** Guaranteed on-campus for freshmen. Coed dorms, single-sex dorms, special housing for disabled, apartments, cooperative housing, fraternity/sorority housing, themed housing available. $250 partly refundable deposit, deadline 9/6. **Activities:** Bands, campus ministries, choral groups, dance, drama, film society, international student organizations, literary magazine, music ensembles, Model UN, musical theater, opera, radio station, student government, student newspaper, symphony orchestra, TV station, Circle K International, environmental club, Engineers Without Borders, Native American student association, Campus Christian Fellowship, Soil Stewards, Lutheran Campus Ministries, Movimiento Activista Social, Brotherhood Empowerment Against Rape, international affairs club.

Athletics. NCAA. **Intercollegiate:** Basketball, cross-country, diving W, football (tackle) M, golf, soccer W, swimming W, tennis, track and field, volleyball W. **Intramural:** Badminton, basketball, football (non-tackle), golf, racquetball, soccer, softball, swimming, track and field, ultimate frisbee, volleyball, weight lifting. **Team name:** Vandals.

Student services. Adult student services, career counseling, services for economically disadvantaged, student employment services, financial aid counseling, health services, legal services, minority student services, on-campus daycare, personal counseling, veterans' counselor, women's services. **Physically disabled:** Services for visually, speech, hearing impaired.

Contact. E-mail: admissions@uidaho.edu
Phone: (208) 885-6326 Toll-free number: (888) 884-3246
Fax: (208) 885-9119
Cezar Mesquita, Director of Admissions, University of Idaho, 875 Perimeter Drive MS 4264, Moscow, ID 83844-4264

University of Phoenix: Idaho
Meridian, Idaho
www.phoenix.edu

- For-profit 4-year university
- Small city
- 410 degree-seeking undergraduates

General. Regionally accredited. **Degrees:** 103 bachelor's awarded; master's offered. **Calendar:** Differs by program. Other academic calendar. **Full-time faculty:** 7 total. **Part-time faculty:** 80 total.

Basis for selection. Open admission, but selective for some programs.

2015-2016 Annual costs. Per-credit-hour charge, $410 to $635, depending upon level and course of study. Books, material charges, and other fees vary by course and program. All fees are subject to change.

Application procedures. Admission: No deadline. No application fee. **Financial aid:** No deadline.

Academics. Credit/placement by examination: AP, CLEP.

Majors. Business: Accounting, accounting/business management, business admin, e-commerce, entrepreneurial studies, finance, human resources, marketing, operations. **Communications:** Communications/speech/rhetoric. **Computer sciences:** Database management, networking, programming, security, system admin, systems analysis, web page design, webmaster. **Conservation:** Environmental studies. **English:** English lit. **Health services:** Facilities admin, health information management, long term care admin. **Human services:** General. **Protective services:** Law enforcement admin.

Student life. Freshman orientation: Mandatory. Preregistration for classes offered.

Contact. Toll-free number: (866) 766-0766
University of Phoenix: Idaho, 1422 South Tech Lane, Meridian, ID 83642-5114

Illinois

American Academy of Art

Chicago, Illinois

www.aaart.edu   CB code: 1013

- Private 4-year visual arts college
- Commuter campus in very large city
- 317 degree-seeking undergraduates: 29% part-time, 60% women, 11% African American, 5% Asian American, 26% Hispanic/Latino, 3% Multiracial, non-Hispanic
- Interview required
- 51% graduate within 6 years

General. Founded in 1923. Accredited by ACCSC. The Academy hosts the Bill L. Parks Gallery which arranges showings of student, faculty and visiting artist work, as well as exhibitions of past and new works from the Academy's permanent collection. **Degrees:** 78 bachelor's awarded. **Location:** The Academy is located in the City of Chicago. **Calendar:** Semester, extensive summer session. **Full-time faculty:** 26 total; 4% have terminal degrees, 8% minority, 50% women. **Class size:** 76% < 20, 24% 20-39.

Freshman class profile.

Return as sophomores: 72% **Out-of-state:**   24%

Basis for selection. Open admission.

2015-2016 Annual costs. Tuition/fees: $31,050. Books/supplies: $800.

Financial aid. **Non-need-based:** Scholarships awarded for art.

Application procedures. **Admission:** No deadline. $25 fee, may be waived for applicants with need. Admission notification on a rolling basis. Essay explaining desire to enter art school used for counseling purposes. **Financial aid:** No deadline. FAFSA, institutional form required. Applicants notified on a rolling basis.

Academics. **Special study options:** Accelerated study, independent study, internships, study abroad. **Credit/placement by examination:** AP, CLEP, institutional tests. **Support services:** Pre-admission summer program.

Majors. **Communications:** Advertising. **Computer sciences:** Computer graphics. **Visual/performing arts:** General, commercial/advertising art, design, drawing, multimedia, painting, studio arts.

Technology on campus. 70 workstations in library, computer center.

Student life. **Freshman orientation:** Mandatory. Preregistration for classes offered. 2-day program held in weeks before classes start. **Housing:** Coed dorms available.

Student services. Career counseling, student employment services, financial aid counseling, placement for graduates, veterans' counselor.

Contact. E-mail: info@aaart.edu
Phone: (312) 461-0600 Toll-free number: (888) 461-0600
Fax: (312) 294-9570
Stuart Rosenbloom, Director of Admissions, American Academy of Art, 332 South Michigan Avenue, Suite 300, Chicago, IL 60604-4302

American InterContinental University

Schaumburg, Illinois

www.aiuniv.edu   CB code: 2486

- For-profit 4-year virtual college
- Small city
- 10,876 degree-seeking undergraduates
- Interview required

General. Founded in 1977. Regionally accredited. Additional campuses in Houston and Atlanta. **Degrees:** 1,938 bachelor's, 787 associate awarded; master's offered. **Calendar:** Quarter. **Full-time faculty:** 87 total. **Part-time faculty:** 532 total.

Basis for selection. Open admission. **Home schooled:** Transcript of courses and grades required. The University Registrar Department will work with students to discuss what additional documentation may be required.

2015-2016 Annual costs. Associate programs: $27,180. Bachelor's programs: $54,360.

Application procedures. **Admission:** No deadline. No application fee. Admission notification on a rolling basis. **Financial aid:** No deadline.

Academics. **Credit/placement by examination:** AP, CLEP, IB, institutional tests. **Support services:** Learning center, reduced course load, tutoring.

Majors. **Business:** Business admin. **Computer sciences:** Information technology. **Protective services:** Law enforcement admin.

Technology on campus. Online library, helpline available.

Student life. **Freshman orientation:** Mandatory. Preregistration for classes offered.

Contact. Toll-free number: (855) 377-1888
American InterContinental University, 231 N. Martingale Rd 6th Floor, Schaumburg, IL 60173

Argosy University: Chicago

Chicago, Illinois

www.argosy.edu/chicago   CB code: 3922

- For-profit 4-year university
- Very large city
- 247 degree-seeking undergraduates: 66% part-time, 72% women
- 611 graduate students

General. Regionally accredited. **Degrees:** 23 bachelor's awarded; master's, professional, doctoral offered. **Calendar:** Differs by program, extensive summer session. **Full-time faculty:** 31 total. **Part-time faculty:** 135 total.

Basis for selection. 18 ACT, 850 SAT (exclusive of Writing) or passing score on institution's entrance exam required. Other requirements vary by program. SAT or ACT recommended.

2015-2016 Annual costs. Tuition/fees: $16,842. **Additional information:** Tuition indicated is for programs in the College of Arts and Sciences. College of Health Sciences programs are $575 per-credit-hour.

Application procedures. **Admission:** Closing date 9/13. $50 fee. Admission notification on a rolling basis. **Financial aid:** No deadline.

Academics. **Special study options:** Distance learning. **Credit/placement by examination:** AP, CLEP.

Majors. **Business:** Business admin. **Psychology:** General.

Most popular majors. Psychology 96%.

Technology on campus. Online library available.

Contact. Phone: (312) 201-0200 Toll-free number: (800) 626-4123
Christa Holton, Senior Director of Admissions, Argosy University: Chicago, 225 North Michigan Avenue, Suite 1300, Chicago, IL 60601

Argosy University: Schaumburg

Schaumburg, Illinois

www.argosy.edu/schaumburg   CB code: 6227

- For-profit 4-year university
- Small city
- 90 degree-seeking undergraduates: 56% part-time, 57% women
- 259 graduate students

General. Regionally accredited. **Degrees:** 36 bachelor's awarded; master's, professional, doctoral offered. **Calendar:** Differs by program. **Full-time faculty:** 21 total. **Part-time faculty:** 69 total.

Basis for selection. Open admission.

2015-2016 Annual costs. Tuition/fees: $16,842. **Additional information:** Tuition indicated is for programs in the College of Arts and Sciences. College of Health Sciences programs are $575 per-credit-hour.

Application procedures. Admission: No deadline. $50 fee.

Academics. Credit/placement by examination: AP, CLEP.

Majors. Business: Business admin. **Liberal arts:** Arts/sciences. **Protective services:** Police science. **Psychology:** General.

Contact. Phone: (847) 969-4910 Toll-free number: (866) 290-2777 Catherine Curran, Senior Director of Admissions, Argosy University: Schaumburg, 999 North Plaza Drive, Suite 111, Schaumburg, IL 60173-5403

Augustana College
Rock Island, Illinois
www.augustana.edu

CB member
CB code: 1025

- Private 4-year liberal arts college affiliated with the Evangelical Lutheran Church in America
- Residential campus in large city
- 2,454 degree-seeking undergraduates: 58% women, 4% African American, 2% Asian American, 10% Hispanic/Latino, 4% Multi-racial, non-Hispanic, 4% international
- 49% of applicants admitted
- 76% graduate within 6 years; 37% enter graduate study

General. Founded in 1860. Regionally accredited. **Degrees:** 573 bachelor's awarded. **Location:** 165 miles from Chicago. **Calendar:** Quarter, limited summer session. **Full-time faculty:** 191 total; 93% have terminal degrees, 15% minority, 45% women. **Part-time faculty:** 63 total; 32% have terminal degrees, 11% minority, 62% women. **Class size:** 64% < 20, 34% 20-39, 2% 40-49. **Special facilities:** Planetarium, observatory, map library, geology museum, Swedish immigration research center, research foundation, 500 acres of environmental laboratories, educational technology center, scanning electron microscope, 3D printer, high-field NMR, x-ray diffractometer, scanning tunneling microscope, HeliFlux station magnetometer.

Freshman class profile. 6,712 applied, 3,312 admitted, 678 enrolled.

Mid 50% test scores			
SAT critical reading:	530-640	Rank in top quarter:	62%
SAT math:	510-690	Rank in top tenth:	27%
SAT writing:	510-640	End year in good standing:	90%
ACT composite:	22-29	Return as sophomores:	86%
GPA 3.75 or higher:	19%	Out-of-state:	16%
GPA 3.50-3.74:	18%	Live on campus:	94%
GPA 3.0-3.49:	38%	International:	4%
GPA 2.0-2.99:	25%	Fraternities:	39%
		Sororities:	47%

Basis for selection. GED not accepted. GPA, class rank, test scores, high school curriculum most important. Extracurricular activities and essay important. Academic honors and special qualifications also considered. Test optional for those who interview and submit a photocopy of a graded high school paper. Interview and essay required of freshman honors program applicants, recommended for all applicants. Essay required of academically marginal applicants and for certain departmental programs. Portfolio required of applicants to some art programs. Audition recommended for music and theater majors.

High school preparation. College-preparatory program recommended. 16 units recommended. Required and recommended units include English 3-4, mathematics 3-4, social studies 1-2, history 1, science 3-4 (laboratory 2), foreign language 1-2 and academic electives 4.

2015-2016 Annual costs. Tuition/fees: $38,466. Room/board: $9,746. Books/supplies: $1,000. Personal expenses: $800.

2014-2015 Financial aid. Need-based: 663 full-time freshmen applied for aid; 578 deemed to have need; 576 received aid. Average need met was 87%. Average scholarship/grant was $24,025; average loan $3,721. 74% of total undergraduate aid awarded as scholarships/grants, 26% as loans/jobs. **Non-need-based:** Awarded to 835 full-time undergraduates, including 256 freshmen. Scholarships awarded for academics, alumni affiliation, art, music/drama, religious affiliation.

Application procedures. Admission: Priority date 2/1; no deadline. No application fee. Admission notification on a rolling basis beginning on or about 11/1. Must reply by 5/1. **Financial aid:** Priority date 2/1; no closing date. FAFSA, institutional form required. Applicants notified on a rolling basis starting 3/1; must reply by 5/1.

Academics. Term-abroad programs in Asia, Europe, and South America. Internship programs in cities throughout United States and in South America, Europe, Asia, Africa, and Australia. Exchange programs with universities in People's Republic of China, Peru, and Sweden. Summer language study programs in Sweden, France, Ecuador and Israel. Team-taught, interdisciplinary honors sequence available. June registration for classes. **Special study options:** Accelerated study, combined bachelor's/graduate degree, double major, honors, independent study, internships, liberal arts/career combination, student-designed major, study abroad, teacher certification program. 3-2 forestry and environmental management program with Duke University, 3-2 landscape architecture program with University of Illinois at Urbana-Champaign, 3-2 engineering program with Northern Illinois University, Washington University, and other ABET accredited institutions, 3-2 occupational therapy program with Washington University, early selection programs in dentistry with University of Iowa. **Credit/placement by examination:** AP, CLEP, IB, SAT, ACT, institutional tests. More than 18 hours of credit by examination must be approved by the Dean of the College. **Support services:** Learning center, pre-admission summer program, reduced course load, remedial instruction, study skills assistance, tutoring, writing center.

Majors. Area/ethnic studies: African, Asian, women's. **Biology:** General, biochemistry, neuroscience. **Business:** Accounting, business admin, finance, international, management information systems, marketing. **Communications:** Communications/speech/rhetoric. **Computer sciences:** Computer science. **Conservation:** Environmental studies. **Education:** General, art, biology, chemistry, earth science, elementary, English, foreign languages, French, geography, German, history, Latin, mathematics, music, physical, physics, science, secondary, social science, Spanish, speech. **Engineering:** Applied physics. **English:** Creative writing, English lit, writing. **Foreign languages:** Ancient Greek, classics, French, German, Latin, Scandinavian, Spanish. **Health services:** Communication disorders, premedicine. **History:** General. **Math:** General, applied. **Philosophy/religion:** Philosophy, religion. **Physical sciences:** Chemistry, geology, physics. **Psychology:** General. **Social sciences:** Anthropology, economics, geography, political science, sociology, sociology/anthropology. **Visual/performing arts:** Art, art history/conservation, dramatic, graphic design, jazz, music, music performance, music theory/composition, piano/keyboard, voice/opera.

Most popular majors. Biology 21%, business/marketing 18%, health sciences 8%, psychology 7%, social sciences 10%.

Technology on campus. 500 workstations in dormitories, library, computer center, student center. Dormitories wired for high-speed internet access and linked to campus network. Commuter students can connect to campus network. Online course registration, online library, helpline, repair service, student web hosting, wireless network available.

Student life. Freshman orientation: Mandatory. Preregistration for classes offered. Three-day program held before start of fall classes. **Policies:** Students represented on all major faculty/administrative committees and act as observers at Board of Trustees meetings. Student life governed by Bill of Student Rights and code of social conduct. Campus judiciary process includes student participation. Lower-division students not living with parents required to live on campus unless released to live off-campus by student services office. **Housing:** Guaranteed on-campus for freshmen. Coed dorms, special housing for disabled, apartments, wellness housing available. $150 nonrefundable deposit, deadline 6/1. **Activities:** Bands, campus ministries, choral groups, dance, drama, international student organizations, literary magazine, music ensembles, Model UN, musical theater, opera, radio station, student government, student newspaper, symphony orchestra, black student union, Asian student organization, Latinos Unidos, multicultural programming board, feminist forum, Intervarsity Christian Fellowship, Muslim student association, Viking Volunteers, College Republicans/Democrats, Habitat for Humanity.

Athletics. NCAA. **Intercollegiate:** Baseball M, basketball, cross-country, diving, football (tackle) M, golf, lacrosse, soccer, softball W, swimming, tennis, track and field, volleyball W, wrestling M. **Intramural:** Badminton, basketball, bowling, cross-country, fencing, football (non-tackle), golf, handball, racquetball, rowing (crew), skiing, soccer, softball, swimming M, table tennis, tennis, track and field, volleyball, water polo, wrestling M. **Team name:** Vikings.

Student services. Alcohol/substance abuse counseling, chaplain/spiritual director, career counseling, student employment services, financial aid counseling, health services, minority student services, personal counseling, placement for graduates, women's services. **Physically disabled:** Services for visually, speech, hearing impaired.

Contact. E-mail: admissions@augustana.edu
Phone: (309) 794-7341 Toll-free number: (800) 798-8100
Fax: (309) 794-8797
W. Kent Barnds, Vice President of Enrollment, Augustana College, 639 38th Street, Rock Island, IL 61201-2296

Aurora University
Aurora, Illinois
www.aurora.edu   CB code: 1027

- Private 4-year university
- Commuter campus in large city
- 3,567 degree-seeking undergraduates: 12% part-time, 64% women, 8% African American, 2% Asian American, 25% Hispanic/Latino, 3% Multiracial, non-Hispanic
- 1,686 degree-seeking graduate students
- 77% of applicants admitted
- SAT or ACT (ACT writing optional) required
- 56% graduate within 6 years

General. Founded in 1893. Regionally accredited. George Williams College of Aurora University is branch campus in Williams Bay, Wisconsin, offering bachelor degrees in applied psychology, criminal justice (emphasis in conservation), environmental science (sustainability), nursing, parks and recreation leadership, and social work. **Degrees:** 803 bachelor's awarded; master's, doctoral offered. **ROTC:** Army. **Location:** 40 miles from Chicago. **Calendar:** Semester, extensive summer session. **Full-time faculty:** 159 total; 10% minority, 56% women. **Part-time faculty:** 342 total; 43% minority, 67% women. **Class size:** 53% < 20, 47% 20-39. **Special facilities:** Native American cultures center, collection of Jenks Memorial Collection of Adventual Materials.

Freshman class profile. 2,843 applied, 2,196 admitted, 630 enrolled.

Mid 50% test scores		GPA 3.0-3.49:	35%
SAT critical reading:	450-550	GPA 2.0-2.99:	34%
SAT math:	460-530	Return as sophomores:	70%
ACT composite:	19-23	Out-of-state:	21%
GPA 3.75 or higher:	17%	Live on campus:	54%
GPA 3.50-3.74:	14%	International:	1%

Basis for selection. High school achievement record most important, followed by test scores. Recommendations considered. Interview and essay recommended. **Home schooled:** State high school equivalency certificate, interview required. Writing sample (graded paper or personal statement) required.

High school preparation. College-preparatory program required. 16 units required. Required units include English 4, mathematics 3, social studies 3, science 3 and academic electives 3.

2016-2017 Annual costs. Tuition/fees: $22,830. Room/board: $10,000. Books/supplies: $1,000. Personal expenses: $1,584.

2015-2016 Financial aid. Need-based: 586 full-time freshmen applied for aid; 534 deemed to have need; 534 received aid. Average need met was 78%. Average scholarship/grant was $15,972; average loan $3,234. 65% of total undergraduate aid awarded as scholarships/grants, 35% as loans/jobs. **Non-need-based:** Awarded to 926 full-time undergraduates, including 186 freshmen. Scholarships awarded for academics, alumni affiliation, art, music/drama, religious affiliation, ROTC, state residency. **Additional information:** Undocumented students may be considered for limited institutional financial aid based on an internal financial aid document.

Application procedures. Admission: No deadline. No application fee. Admission notification on a rolling basis beginning on or about 9/1. Candidates may apply early and have until May 1 to have tuition and housing deposits refunded. **Financial aid:** Priority date 1/1; no closing date. FAFSA required. Applicants notified on a rolling basis starting 3/1.

Academics. Special study options: Accelerated study, cross-registration, distance learning, double major, independent study, internships, liberal arts/career combination, student-designed major, study abroad, teacher certification program. **Credit/placement by examination:** AP, CLEP, SAT, ACT, institutional tests. 30 credit hours maximum toward bachelor's degree. **Support services:** Learning center, pre-admission summer program, reduced course load, remedial instruction, study skills assistance, tutoring, writing center.

Majors. Area/ethnic studies: Disability. **Biology:** General. **Business:** General, accounting, actuarial science, business admin, finance, management information systems, management science, marketing. **Communications:** Communications/speech/rhetoric. **Computer sciences:** Computer science. **Education:** Bilingual, elementary, physical, secondary, special ed. **English:** English lit, writing. **Foreign languages:** Spanish. **Health services:** General, athletic training, nursing (RN). **History:** General. **Human services:** Social work, youth services. **Liberal arts:** Arts/sciences. **Math:** General. **Parks/recreation:** General, sports admin. **Philosophy/religion:** Philosophy, religion. **Protective services:** Criminal justice. **Psychology:** General. **Social

sciences:** Political science, sociology. **Visual/performing arts:** Art, dramatic, music.

Most popular majors. Business/marketing 20%, communications/journalism 7%, education 8%, health sciences 23%, psychology 7%, public administration/social services 13%, security/protective services 9%.

Technology on campus. 90 workstations in library, computer center, student center. Dormitories wired for high-speed internet access and linked to campus network. Commuter students can connect to campus network. Online library, helpline, wireless network available.

Student life. Freshman orientation: Mandatory. Preregistration for classes offered. Day-long sessions held each May and June for admitted first-year students and their parents. **Policies:** Alcohol and smoke-free campus. **Housing:** Coed dorms available. $100 fully refundable deposit, deadline 5/1. **Activities:** Pep band, campus ministries, choral groups, drama, literary magazine, music ensembles, Model UN, musical theater, radio station, student government, student newspaper, Black Student Association, Latin American Student Organization, Students for Wellness, Fellowship of Christian Athletes, Circle K International, Intervarsity Christian Fellowship, political science club, Future Leaders of the Work, Aurora University Human Rights Organization, A.R.I.S.E (Awareness, Responsibility, Integrity Sisterhood Empowerment.

Athletics. NCAA. **Intercollegiate:** Baseball M, basketball, bowling W, cross-country, football (tackle) M, golf, ice hockey, lacrosse, soccer, softball W, tennis, track and field, volleyball W. **Intramural:** Badminton, basketball, football (tackle), racquetball, soccer, table tennis, volleyball. **Team name:** Spartans.

Student services. Adult student services, alcohol/substance abuse counseling, chaplain/spiritual director, career counseling, services for economically disadvantaged, student employment services, financial aid counseling, health services, minority student services, personal counseling, placement for graduates. **Physically disabled:** Services for visually, speech, hearing impaired.

Contact. E-mail: admission@aurora.edu
Phone: (630) 844-5533 Toll-free number: (800) 742-5281
Fax: (630) 844-6191
James Lancaster, Dean of Freshman Admission, Aurora University, 347 South Gladstone Avenue, Aurora, IL 60506-4892

Benedictine University
Lisle, Illinois
www.ben.edu   CB code: 1707

- Private 4-year university and liberal arts college affiliated with the Roman Catholic Church
- Commuter campus in large town
- 3,749 degree-seeking undergraduates
- 2,489 graduate students
- SAT or ACT with writing, application essay required

General. Founded in 1887. Regionally accredited. **Degrees:** 916 bachelor's, 20 associate awarded; master's, doctoral offered. **ROTC:** Army. **Location:** 25 miles from Chicago. **Calendar:** Semester, extensive summer session. **Full-time faculty:** 166 total; 82% have terminal degrees, 14% minority, 53% women. **Part-time faculty:** 553 total; 19% have terminal degrees, 20% minority, 53% women. **Class size:** 71% < 20, 28% 20-39, less than 1% 40-49, less than 1% 50-99, less than 1% >100. **Special facilities:** Nature museum, Benedictine abbey, arboretum, Fermi nuclear accelerator laboratories, Argonne national laboratories.

Freshman class profile.

GPA 3.75 or higher:	28%	Rank in top quarter:	35%
GPA 3.50-3.74:	12%	Rank in top tenth:	12%
GPA 3.0-3.49:	28%	Out-of-state:	26%
GPA 2.0-2.99:	31%	Live on campus:	42%

Basis for selection. Require rank in top half of class and 21 ACT. Candidates falling below these criteria reviewed by admissions committee. Audition required of musical instrument and voice majors.

High school preparation. College-preparatory program required. Required units include mathematics 4, history 3, science 3 (laboratory 3) and foreign language 2.

2015-2016 Annual costs. Tuition/fees: $29,620. Room/board: $8,630. Books/supplies: $1,480. Personal expenses: $2,500.

Financial aid. Non-need-based: Scholarships awarded for academics, alumni affiliation, athletics, leadership, music/drama, ROTC, state residency.

Application procedures. Admission: Priority date 8/30; no deadline. $40 fee, may be waived for applicants with need. Admission notification on a rolling basis beginning on or about 9/1. **Financial aid:** Priority date 3/1; no closing date. FAFSA required. Applicants notified on a rolling basis starting 2/1; must reply within 2 week(s) of notification.

Academics. Special study options: Accelerated study, combined bachelor's/graduate degree, cooperative education, cross-registration, distance learning, double major, dual enrollment of high school students, ESL, exchange student, honors, independent study, internships, study abroad, teacher certification program, weekend college. Engineering degree program with Illinois Institute of Technology. **Credit/placement by examination:** AP, CLEP, ACT, institutional tests. 30 credit hours maximum toward bachelor's degree. **Support services:** Learning center, reduced course load, remedial instruction, study skills assistance, tutoring, writing center.

Majors. Biology: General, biochemistry, molecular. **Business:** Accounting, finance, international, managerial economics, marketing, organizational behavior. **Communications:** Communications/speech/rhetoric, publishing. **Computer sciences:** Computer science, information systems. **Conservation:** Environmental science. **Education:** Elementary, special ed. **Engineering:** Engineering science. **English:** English lit. **Foreign languages:** Spanish. **Health services:** Clinical lab science, health care admin, nuclear medical technology, nursing (RN), sonography. **History:** General. **Math:** General. **Parks/recreation:** Exercise sciences. **Philosophy/religion:** Philosophy. **Physical sciences:** Chemistry, physics. **Psychology:** General. **Social sciences:** General, economics, international relations, political science, sociology. **Theology:** Theology. **Visual/performing arts:** Graphic design, music, studio arts, studio arts management. **Work/family studies:** Food/nutrition.

Most popular majors. Biology 6%, business/marketing 35%, health sciences 22%, psychology 8%, social sciences 8%.

Technology on campus. 200 workstations in dormitories, library, computer center, student center. Dormitories wired for high-speed internet access and linked to campus network. Commuter students can connect to campus network. Online course registration, online library, helpline, wireless network available.

Student life. Freshman orientation: Mandatory, $75 fee. Preregistration for classes offered. Summer parent and student program. Student program 3 days prior to first day of classes. **Housing:** Coed dorms, single-sex dorms, apartments, themed housing available. $150 nonrefundable deposit, deadline 8/1. **Activities:** Bands, campus ministries, choral groups, dance, international student organizations, music ensembles, Model UN, student government, student newspaper, TV station, Muslim student association, African-American student union, Knights of Columbus, Daughters of Isabella, Students for Life, Relay for Life, Best Buddies, South Asian student association, Democracy Matters, Hindu student association.

Athletics. NCAA. **Intercollegiate:** Baseball M, basketball, cross-country, football (tackle) M, golf, lacrosse, soccer, softball W, tennis W, track and field, volleyball W. **Intramural:** Basketball, bowling, football (non-tackle), softball, table tennis, volleyball. **Team name:** Eagles.

Student services. Adult student services, chaplain/spiritual director, career counseling, student employment services, financial aid counseling, health services, personal counseling, placement for graduates. **Physically disabled:** Services for visually, speech, hearing impaired.

Contact. E-mail: admissions@ben.edu
Phone: (630) 829-6300 Toll-free number: (888) 829-6363
Fax: (630) 829-6301
Kari Gibbons, Dean of Enrollment, Benedictine University, 5700 College Road, Lisle, IL 60532

Blackburn College
Carlinville, Illinois
www.blackburn.edu

CB member
CB code: 1065

- Private 4-year liberal arts college affiliated with the Presbyterian Church (USA)
- Residential campus in small town
- 579 degree-seeking undergraduates: 3% part-time, 54% women, 13% African American, 1% Asian American, 2% Hispanic/Latino, 3% Multiracial, non-Hispanic
- 55% of applicants admitted
- SAT or ACT (ACT writing optional) required
- 42% graduate within 6 years

General. Founded in 1837. Regionally accredited. **Degrees:** 108 bachelor's awarded. **Location:** 40 miles from Springfield, 60 miles from St. Louis. **Calendar:** Semester, limited summer session. **Full-time faculty:** 37 total; 95% have terminal degrees, 3% minority, 43% women. **Part-time faculty:** 21 total; 14% have terminal degrees, 10% minority, 52% women. **Class size:** 71% < 20, 25% 20-39, 3% 40-49.

Freshman class profile. 1,078 applied, 598 admitted, 160 enrolled.

Mid 50% test scores			
SAT critical reading:	370-520	Rank in top quarter:	36%
SAT math:	420-510	Rank in top tenth:	14%
ACT composite:	19-24	Return as sophomores:	65%
GPA 3.75 or higher:	28%	Out-of-state:	10%
GPA 3.50-3.74:	10%	Live on campus:	79%
GPA 3.0-3.49:	33%		
GPA 2.0-2.99:	28%		

Basis for selection. High school academic record, substantiated by test scores, most important. Interview recommended. Audition recommended for music majors. Portfolio recommended for art majors. **Home schooled:** Statement describing home school structure and mission, transcript of courses and grades, state high school equivalency certificate required.

High school preparation. College-preparatory program recommended. 16 units recommended. Recommended units include English 4, mathematics 3, social studies 2, history 2, science 3 and foreign language 2.

2016-2017 Annual costs. Tuition/fees (projected): $21,162. Room/board: $7,364. Books/supplies: $700. Personal expenses: $800.

2014-2015 Financial aid. Need-based: 156 full-time freshmen applied for aid; 136 deemed to have need; 136 received aid. Average need met was 76%. Average scholarship/grant was $13,988; average loan $2,948. 70% of total undergraduate aid awarded as scholarships/grants, 30% as loans/jobs. **Non-need-based:** Awarded to 140 full-time undergraduates, including 49 freshmen. Scholarships awarded for academics, state residency. **Additional information:** Each resident student works 160 hours per semester.

Application procedures. Admission: No deadline. $20 fee, may be waived for applicants with need. Admission notification on a rolling basis beginning on or about 10/15. **Financial aid:** Priority date 3/1; no closing date. FAFSA required. Applicants notified on a rolling basis starting 3/1; must reply within 4 week(s) of notification.

Academics. Special study options: Accelerated study, combined bachelor's/graduate degree, cooperative education, double major, dual enrollment of high school students, independent study, internships, student-designed major, study abroad, teacher certification program, Washington semester. British studies semester, Mexico studies semester. **Credit/placement by examination:** AP, CLEP, SAT, ACT, institutional tests. 30 credit hours maximum toward bachelor's degree. **Support services:** Learning center, reduced course load, remedial instruction, study skills assistance, tutoring, writing center.

Majors. Area/ethnic studies: Latin American. **Biology:** General, biochemistry, environmental, molecular. **Business:** Accounting, business admin, marketing, organizational leadership, training/development. **Communications:** Communications/speech/rhetoric. **Computer sciences:** Computer science. **Conservation:** Environmental studies. **Education:** Art, biology, elementary, English, evaluation, mathematics, physical, social science, teacher assistance. **English:** English lit. **Foreign languages:** Spanish. **Health services:** Clinical lab science. **History:** General. **Human services:** General. **Math:** General, financial. **Parks/recreation:** Health/fitness. **Physical sciences:** Chemistry. **Protective services:** Criminal justice. **Psychology:** General. **Social sciences:** Political science. **Visual/performing arts:** Art, music, musical theater, theater arts management.

Most popular majors. Biology 14%, business/marketing 26%, education 6%, English 6%, parks/recreation 8%, psychology 9%, security/protective services 10%, visual/performing arts 7%.

Technology on campus. 75 workstations in library, computer center. Dormitories linked to campus network. Helpline, wireless network available.

Student life. Freshman orientation: Mandatory. Preregistration for classes offered. One-day summer orientation and two-day fall orientation prior to beginning of semester. **Policies:** Participation in student-managed work program required for all resident students. Resident students work 160 hours per semester to reduce costs and gain valuable career skills. Alcohol allowed for students 21 and older. All residence halls are smoke-free. **Housing:** Guaranteed on-campus for all undergraduates. Coed dorms, single-sex dorms, gender-neutral housing, themed housing, wellness housing available. Quiet study housing available. **Activities:** Concert band, campus ministries, choral groups, dance, drama, literary magazine, music ensembles, Model UN, musical theater, radio station, student government, student newspaper, Cultural Expressions, Habitat for Humanity chapter, Catacombs, Newman Club, Common Ground, Republican club, health and wellness club, fishing club, Beavers Against Destructive Decisions, psychology club.

Athletics. NCAA. **Intercollegiate:** Baseball M, basketball, cross-country, golf M, soccer, softball W, tennis W, volleyball W. **Intramural:** Badminton, basketball, racquetball, softball, swimming, table tennis, tennis, volleyball, water polo. **Team name:** Beavers.

Student services. Adult student services, alcohol/substance abuse counseling, chaplain/spiritual director, career counseling, student employment services, financial aid counseling, minority student services, personal counseling, placement for graduates. **Physically disabled:** Services for visually, hearing impaired.

Contact. E-mail: alisha.kapp@blackburn.edu
Phone: (217) 854-3231 Toll-free number: (800) 233-3550
Fax: (217) 854-3713
Alisha Kapp, Director of Admissions, Blackburn College, 700 College Avenue, Carlinville, IL 62626

Blessing-Rieman College of Nursing
Quincy, Illinois
www.brcn.edu   **CB code: 0139**

◗ Private 4-year health science and nursing college
◗ Commuter campus in large town
◗ 233 degree-seeking undergraduates: 18% part-time, 87% women, 5% African American, 2% Asian American, 1% Hispanic/Latino
◗ 17 degree-seeking graduate students
◗ 58% of applicants admitted
◗ SAT or ACT (ACT writing optional) required

General. Founded in 1891. Regionally accredited. Joint degree programs with Culver-Stockton College and Quincy University leading to BS in Nursing. General education classes held at partner campus, with nursing classes at BRC campus and clinical experiences at Blessing Hospital, a regional medical facility and magnet hospital. BRC also offer an Associate of Science in Respiratory Care Degree program. **Degrees:** 61 bachelor's awarded; master's offered. **Location:** 120 miles from St. Louis, 100 miles from Springfield. **Calendar:** Semester, limited summer session. **Full-time faculty:** 29 total; 21% have terminal degrees, 97% women. **Part-time faculty:** 7 total; 86% women. **Class size:** 71% < 20, 29% 20-39. **Special facilities:** Simulation center, community health simulation apartment.

Freshman class profile. 630 applied, 368 admitted, 88 enrolled.

GPA 3.75 or higher:	15%	GPA 2.0-2.99:	26%
GPA 3.50-3.74:	21%	Return as sophomores:	80%
GPA 3.0-3.49:	36%	Out-of-state:	50%

Basis for selection. 3.0 GPA and 22 ACT required. **Home schooled:** Transcript of courses and grades required.

High school preparation. Required units include English 4, mathematics 2, social studies 3, science 4 (laboratory 2). Biology, chemistry, algebra suggested.

2016-2017 Annual costs. Tuition/fees: $22,900. Books/supplies: $2,000. Personal expenses: $1,400.

2014-2015 Financial aid. **Need-based:** 39% of total undergraduate aid awarded as scholarships/grants, 61% as loans/jobs. **Non-need-based:** Scholarships awarded for academics, alumni affiliation, leadership, state residency. **Additional information:** Financial aid for freshmen and sophomores administered by Culver-Stockton College and Quincy University. Institution does not have first time, full-time students, only junior and senior students.

Application procedures. **Admission:** No deadline. No application fee. Admission notification on a rolling basis. **Financial aid:** Priority date 3/1, closing date 4/1. FAFSA required.

Academics. **Special study options:** Accelerated study, combined bachelor's/graduate degree, internships. **Credit/placement by examination:** AP, CLEP, SAT, ACT, institutional tests. **Support services:** Learning center, study skills assistance, tutoring.

Majors. **Health services:** Nursing (RN).

Technology on campus. 60 workstations in dormitories, library, computer center. Dormitories wired for high-speed internet access and linked to campus network. Online library, helpline, wireless network available.

Student life. **Policies:** Immunization and background check required for sophomore level and up. **Housing:** Men's and women's dormitories available at Culver-Stockton College and Quincy University. **Activities:** Student government, student nurses organization.

Student services. Alcohol/substance abuse counseling, career counseling, student employment services, financial aid counseling, health services, on-campus daycare, personal counseling, placement for graduates.

Contact. E-mail: admissions@brcn.edu
Phone: (217) 228-5520 ext. 6949
Toll-free number: (800) 877-9140 ext. 6949 Fax: (217) 223-4661
Jenna Crabtree, Admissions Coordinator, Blessing-Rieman College of Nursing, PO Box 7005, Quincy, IL 62305

Bradley University
Peoria, Illinois   **CB member**
www.bradley.edu   **CB code: 1070**

◗ Private 4-year university
◗ Residential campus in large city
◗ 4,436 degree-seeking undergraduates: 5% part-time, 51% women
◗ 899 degree-seeking graduate students
◗ 66% of applicants admitted
◗ SAT or ACT (ACT writing optional), application essay required
◗ 74% graduate within 6 years; 17% enter graduate study

General. Founded in 1897. Regionally accredited. **Degrees:** 1,142 bachelor's awarded; master's, doctoral offered. **ROTC:** Army. **Location:** 162 miles from Chicago, 169 miles from St. Louis. **Calendar:** Semester, limited summer session. **Full-time faculty:** 343 total; 83% have terminal degrees, 18% minority, 41% women. **Part-time faculty:** 210 total; 6% minority, 47% women. **Class size:** 62% < 20, 35% 20-39, 2% 40-49, less than 1% 50-99, less than 1% >100. **Special facilities:** Two art galleries.

Freshman class profile. 9,186 applied, 6,033 admitted, 929 enrolled.

Mid 50% test scores		Rank in top quarter:	58%
SAT critical reading:	500-620	Rank in top tenth:	22%
SAT math:	520-650	End year in good standing:	96%
SAT writing:	470-610	Return as sophomores:	86%
ACT composite:	23-28	Out-of-state:	21%
GPA 3.75 or higher:	43%	Live on campus:	92%
GPA 3.50-3.74:	22%	International:	1%
GPA 3.0-3.49:	27%	Fraternities:	32%
GPA 2.0-2.99:	8%	Sororities:	41%

Basis for selection. High school curriculum, GPA, test scores, special talents, co-curricular activities, letters of recommendation, personal statement and educational goals important. Student's academic interest, motivation level and quality of secondary school education also considered. SAT or ACT is required of traditional freshman. Interview recommended. Audition required of music majors and recommended for theater majors. Portfolio recommended for art majors. **Home schooled:** Statement describing home school structure and mission required. Record of courses taken, grades earned, personal statement, letter of recommendation and record of activities or club memberships required. Interview may be required, otherwise highly recommended.

High school preparation. College-preparatory program required. 16 units required; 22 recommended. Required and recommended units include English 4-5, mathematics 3-4, social studies 2-3, history 2, science 2-3 (laboratory 2-3) and foreign language 2. Additional requirements for business, science, engineering, music, nursing and health science majors.

2015-2016 Annual costs. Tuition/fees: $31,480. Room/board: $9,700.

2014-2015 Financial aid. **Need-based:** 837 full-time freshmen applied for aid; 647 deemed to have need; 646 received aid. Average need met was 72%. Average scholarship/grant was $15,901; average loan $4,704. 72% of total undergraduate aid awarded as scholarships/grants, 28% as loans/jobs. **Non-need-based:** Awarded to 1,250 full-time undergraduates, including 252 freshmen. Scholarships awarded for academics, alumni affiliation, art, athletics, leadership, minority status, music/drama.

Application procedures. **Admission:** Priority date 2/1; no deadline. $35 fee, may be waived for applicants with need, free for online applicants. Admission notification on a rolling basis beginning on or about 10/1. Must reply by May 1 or within 2 week(s) if notified thereafter. **Financial aid:** Priority date 3/1; no closing date. FAFSA required. Applicants notified on a rolling basis starting 3/1; must reply by 5/1 or within 2 week(s) of notification.

Academics. **Special study options:** Accelerated study, combined bachelor's/graduate degree, cooperative education, distance learning, double major, honors, independent study, internships, liberal arts/career combination, student-designed major, study abroad, teacher certification program, Washington semester. **Credit/placement by examination:** AP, CLEP, IB, institutional tests. 60 credit hours maximum toward bachelor's degree. **Support**

services: Learning center, reduced course load, study skills assistance, tutoring, writing center.

Majors. Biology: General, biochemistry, biomedical sciences, cellular/molecular, ecology/evolutionary. **Business:** Accounting, actuarial science, auditing, business admin, construction management, entrepreneurial studies, finance, hospitality admin, human resources, insurance, international, logistics, management information systems, managerial economics, marketing, selling, small business admin. **Communications:** General, advertising, digital media, journalism, organizational, persuasive communications, photojournalism, public relations, radio/TV, sports. **Communications technology:** Animation/special effects, graphics. **Computer sciences:** General, computer science, information systems, information technology. **Conservation:** Environmental science. **Education:** General, art, biology, chemistry, drama/dance, early childhood, elementary, English, family/consumer sciences, French, history, learning disabled, mathematics, mentally handicapped, music, physics, psychology, science, social science, social studies, Spanish, speech. **Engineering:** Applied physics, civil, computer, construction, electrical, industrial, manufacturing, mechanical. **English:** English lit. **Foreign languages:** French, Spanish. **Health services:** Clinical lab science, dietetics, nursing (RN), predental, premedicine, preoccupational therapy, prephysical therapy, preveterinary. **History:** General. **Human services:** Social work. **Liberal arts:** Arts/sciences, humanities. **Math:** General. **Philosophy/religion:** Philosophy, religion. **Physical sciences:** Chemistry, physics. **Protective services:** Law enforcement admin. **Psychology:** General. **Social sciences:** Economics, international relations, political science, sociology. **Visual/performing arts:** Acting, art, art history/conservation, ceramics, directing/producing, dramatic, drawing, game design, graphic design, music, music management, music performance, music theory/composition, painting, photography, printmaking, sculpture, studio arts, voice/opera. **Work/family studies:** General, food/nutrition, merchandising.

Most popular majors. Business/marketing 16%, communications/journalism 11%, education 8%, engineering/engineering technologies 15%, health sciences 11%.

Technology on campus. 103 workstations in dormitories, library, computer center. Dormitories wired for high-speed internet access and linked to campus network. Commuter students can connect to campus network. Online course registration, helpline, student web hosting, wireless network available.

Student life. Freshman orientation: Mandatory. Preregistration for classes offered. 12 2-1/2 day sessions throughout summer. **Housing:** Guaranteed on-campus for all undergraduates. Coed dorms, apartments, fraternity/sorority housing available. $100 partly refundable deposit, deadline 6/1. Service and leadership floor for women and honors program floor available. **Activities:** Bands, campus ministries, choral groups, dance, drama, film society, international student organizations, literary magazine, music ensembles, musical theater, radio station, student government, student newspaper, symphony orchestra, TV station, Alpha Phi Omega, Hillel, InterVarsity Christian Fellowship, Cru, Newman Center, Amnesty International, Habitat for Humanity, Beyond Prejudice, Association of Latin American Students, NAACP student chapter.

Athletics. NCAA. **Intercollegiate:** Baseball M, basketball, cheerleading, cross-country, golf, soccer M, softball W, tennis W, track and field, volleyball W. **Intramural:** Badminton, basketball, bowling, football (tackle) M, golf, handball, racquetball, softball W, swimming, table tennis, tennis, volleyball, wrestling M. **Team name:** Braves.

Student services. Alcohol/substance abuse counseling, career counseling, student employment services, financial aid counseling, health services, minority student services, personal counseling, placement for graduates.

Contact. E-mail: admissions@bradley.edu
Phone: (309) 677-1000 Toll-free number: (800) 447-6460
Fax: (309) 677-2797
Justin Ball, Associate Vice President for Undergraduate Admissions, Bradley University, 1501 W. Bradley Avenue, Peoria, IL 61625

Chamberlain College of Nursing: Addison
Addison, Illinois
www.chamberlain.edu   **CB code: 5759**

- For-profit 4-year nursing college
- Commuter campus in large town
- 11,988 degree-seeking undergraduates
- SAT or ACT required

General. Regionally accredited. **Degrees:** 5,164 bachelor's awarded; master's offered. **Location:** 30 miles from Chicago. **Calendar:** Semester. **Full-time faculty:** 60 total; 7% minority, 97% women. **Part-time faculty:** 293 total; 16% minority, 92% women.

Basis for selection. ACT composite of 21 or SAT critical reading/mathematics score of 990, or admissions assessment score of 175; high school cumulative GPA of 2.75.

2015-2016 Annual costs. Tuition/fees: $18,160. Books/supplies: $1,400. Personal expenses: $2,452.

Application procedures. Admission: No deadline. $95 fee. Admission notification on a rolling basis.

Academics. Special study options: Accelerated study, distance learning. **Credit/placement by examination:** AP, CLEP.

Majors. Health services: Nursing (RN).

Contact. Chamberlain College of Nursing: Addison, 1221 North Swift Road, Addison, IL 60101-6106

Chamberlain College of Nursing: Chicago
Chicago, Illinois
www.chamberlain.edu/nursing-schools/campuses/Chicago-Illinois   **CB code: 6504**

- For-profit 4-year nursing college
- Very large city
- 892 degree-seeking undergraduates
- SAT or ACT, interview required

General. Regionally accredited. **Degrees:** 5,164 bachelor's awarded; master's, doctoral offered. **Calendar:** Semester. **Full-time faculty:** 19 total; 37% minority, 84% women. **Part-time faculty:** 38 total; 40% minority, 90% women.

Basis for selection. Secondary school record, class rank, GPA most important; interview also important.

2015-2016 Annual costs. Tuition/fees: $18,160. Books/supplies: $1,400. Personal expenses: $2,452. **Additional information:** Tuition quoted is for Nursing courses at $590 per credit. Tuition and fees vary by program.

Application procedures. Admission: No deadline. $95 fee. Admission notification on a rolling basis.

Academics. Special study options: Accelerated study, distance learning. **Credit/placement by examination:** AP, CLEP.

Majors. Health services: Nursing (RN).

Contact. Chamberlain College of Nursing: Chicago, 3300 North Campbell Avenue, Chicago, IL 60618

Chicago State University
Chicago, Illinois
www.csu.edu   **CB code: 1118**

- Public 4-year university
- Commuter campus in very large city
- 3,437 degree-seeking undergraduates
- SAT or ACT (ACT writing optional), application essay, interview required

General. Founded in 1867. Regionally accredited. **Degrees:** 661 bachelor's awarded; master's, doctoral offered. **ROTC:** Army. **Location:** 12 miles from downtown. **Calendar:** Semester, limited summer session. **Full-time faculty:** 269 total; 39% have terminal degrees, 53% minority, 52% women. **Part-time faculty:** 97 total; 2% have terminal degrees, 52% women. **Class size:** 60% < 20, 40% 20-39, less than 1% 40-49, less than 1% 50-99. **Special facilities:** Electron microscopy laboratory, video conference room, center of African heritage and culture, Gwendolyn Brooks writing center, aquaponics laboratory, and small business development center.

Freshman class profile.

GPA 3.75 or higher:	5%	GPA 2.0-2.99:	41%
GPA 3.50-3.74:	7%	Out-of-state:	4%
GPA 3.0-3.49:	21%	Live on campus:	28%

Basis for selection. GPA, standardized test scores, and subject/units completed important. Based on GPA and test score, student may need to complete on-campus interview. Letters of recommendation are also required. Student test scores must be received before admission can be granted.

High school preparation. 15 units required. Required units include English 4, mathematics 3, social studies 3, science 3 and academic electives 2. 2 units foreign language, music, vocational education or art.

2015-2016 Annual costs. Tuition/fees: $11,758; $20,458 out-of-state. Room/board: $8,723. Books/supplies: $1,800. Personal expenses: $3,000.

Financial aid. Non-need-based: Scholarships awarded for academics, athletics, ROTC, state residency. **Additional information:** Freshmen of outstanding academic ability and talent eligible for Scholars Program full-tuition scholarship.

Application procedures. Admission: No deadline. $25 fee, may be waived for applicants with need. Admission notification on a rolling basis. **Financial aid:** Priority date 3/1; no closing date. FAFSA, institutional form required.

Academics. Special study options: Combined bachelor's/graduate degree, cooperative education, distance learning, double major, dual enrollment of high school students, ESL, honors, independent study, internships, liberal arts/career combination, student-designed major, study abroad, teacher certification program. **Credit/placement by examination:** AP, CLEP, SAT, ACT, institutional tests. 60 credit hours maximum toward bachelor's degree. **Support services:** Learning center, remedial instruction, study skills assistance, tutoring, writing center.

Honors college/program. Students must have a minimum ACT composite of 23; high school G.P.A. of 3.5; or top 10% of their high school class. Second semester freshmen and first semester sophomores with a 3.25 cumulative GPA at Chicago State University or another accredited institution are also eligible.

Majors. Area/ethnic studies: African-American. **Biology:** General, bacteriology, biochemistry, environmental, molecular. **Business:** Accounting, business admin, fashion, finance, management information systems. **Communications:** Broadcast journalism. **Computer sciences:** General, data processing, information systems. **Education:** General, art, biology, business, chemistry, early childhood, elementary, English, health, history, mathematics, mentally handicapped, multi-level teacher, music, physical, secondary, technology/industrial arts. **English:** English lit, rhetoric/composition, technical writing. **Foreign languages:** Spanish. **Health services:** Health information management, nursing (RN). **History:** General. **Math:** General. **Parks/recreation:** Health/fitness. **Physical sciences:** Chemistry, physics. **Psychology:** General. **Social sciences:** Anthropology, economics, geography, political science, sociology. **Visual/performing arts:** Art, commercial/advertising art, music.

Most popular majors. Business/marketing 12%, health sciences 9%, liberal arts 30%, psychology 13%, security/protective services 8%, social sciences 8%.

Technology on campus. 156 workstations in dormitories, library, computer center, student center. Dormitories wired for high-speed internet access. Commuter students can connect to campus network. Online course registration, online library, helpline, wireless network available.

Student life. Freshman orientation: Mandatory. Preregistration for classes offered. One-day programs in July and August. **Housing:** Coed dorms available. $125 deposit, deadline 8/1. **Activities:** Bands, choral groups, dance, drama, literary magazine, music ensembles, radio station, student government, student newspaper, TV station, 71 clubs and organizations.

Athletics. NCAA. **Intercollegiate:** Baseball M, basketball, cross-country, golf, soccer W, tennis, track and field, volleyball W. **Intramural:** Basketball, football (non-tackle), swimming, volleyball. **Team name:** Cougars.

Student services. Adult student services, alcohol/substance abuse counseling, chaplain/spiritual director, career counseling, services for economically disadvantaged, student employment services, financial aid counseling, health services, minority student services, personal counseling, placement for graduates, veterans' counselor, women's services. **Physically disabled:** Services for visually, speech, hearing impaired.

Contact. E-mail: ug-admissions@csu.edu
Phone: (773) 995-2513 Fax: (773) 995-3820
John Martinez, Associate Director of Admissions, Chicago State University, 9501 South King Drive, Chicago, IL 60628

Columbia College Chicago
Chicago, Illinois
www.colum.edu

CB member
CB code: 1135

⬩ Private 4-year visual arts and liberal arts college
⬩ Residential campus in very large city

⬩ 8,519 degree-seeking undergraduates
⬩ Application essay required

General. Founded in 1890. Regionally accredited. **Degrees:** 1,919 bachelor's awarded; master's offered. **Location:** Downtown. **Calendar:** Semester, limited summer session. **Full-time faculty:** 374 total; 50% have terminal degrees, 17% minority, 47% women. **Part-time faculty:** 1,086 total. **Class size:** 76% < 20, 23% 20-39, less than 1% 40-49, less than 1% 50-99, less than 1% >100. **Special facilities:** Media production center, film/video sound stage, contemporary photography museum, photography studios, dance performance space, theater, audio technology center, psychoacoustic classroom, animation facilities, reverb chamber, book and paper arts center, black music research center, community media workshop, international Latino cultural center, community arts partnership center, concert hall, student boutique, art galleries.

Freshman class profile.

GPA 3.75 or higher:	21%	Rank in top quarter:	29%
GPA 3.50-3.74:	15%	Rank in top tenth:	8%
GPA 3.0-3.49:	32%	Out-of-state:	53%
GPA 2.0-2.99:	31%	Live on campus:	73%

Basis for selection. Proof of high school graduation (or earned GED), letter of recommendation, and essay required. All freshmen take COMPASS placement test on campus. SAT and SAT Subject Tests or ACT recommended. Interview recommended. **Home schooled:** Transcript of courses and grades required. **Learning Disabled:** Student must have regular earned GED or high school diploma.

High school preparation. College-preparatory program recommended.

2015-2016 Annual costs. Tuition/fees: $24,344. Room/board: $13,482. Books/supplies: $1,600. Personal expenses: $2,090.

Financial aid. Non-need-based: Scholarships awarded for academics, art, leadership, music/drama, state residency.

Application procedures. Admission: Priority date 5/1; no deadline. $35 fee, may be waived for applicants with need. Application must be submitted online. Admission notification on a rolling basis beginning on or about 11/1. **Financial aid:** Priority date 5/1; no closing date. FAFSA, institutional form required. Accepted but not required for domestic applicants. Applicants notified on a rolling basis.

Academics. Special study options: Cooperative education, distance learning, double major, ESL, exchange student, honors, independent study, internships, liberal arts/career combination, student-designed major, study abroad, teacher certification program. Semester in Los Angeles. **Credit/placement by examination:** AP, CLEP, IB, SAT, ACT, institutional tests. 62 credit hours maximum toward bachelor's degree. **Support services:** Learning center, reduced course load, remedial instruction, study skills assistance, tutoring, writing center.

Majors. Architecture: Interior. **Business:** Business admin, fashion, marketing. **Communications:** Advertising, broadcast journalism, journalism, public relations, radio/TV. **Communications technology:** Animation/special effects, recording arts. **Computer sciences:** Web page design. **Education:** Art, early childhood, kindergarten/preschool. **English:** Creative writing. **Foreign languages:** Sign language interpretation. **Liberal arts:** Arts/sciences. **Visual/performing arts:** General, acting, art, art history/conservation, cinematography, commercial/advertising art, dance, design, directing/producing, dramatic, fashion design, film/cinema/video, game design, graphic design, illustration, industrial design, interior design, jazz, multimedia, music, music management, music performance, photography, play/screenwriting, studio arts, studio arts management, theater design, voice/opera.

Most popular majors. Business/marketing 17%, communications/journalism 9%, communication technologies 7%, visual/performing arts 60%.

Technology on campus. 851 workstations in dormitories, library, computer center, student center. Dormitories wired for high-speed internet access and linked to campus network. Commuter students can connect to campus network. Online course registration, helpline, wireless network available.

Student life. Freshman orientation: Mandatory. Preregistration for classes offered. Parent orientation and parent weekend program available. **Housing:** Coed dorms, apartments available. $500 nonrefundable deposit. **Activities:** Bands, campus ministries, choral groups, dance, drama, film society, international student organizations, literary magazine, music ensembles, musical theater, radio station, student government, student newspaper, TV station, Association of Black Journalists, Black Actor's Guild, Black Ink, Latino Alliance, environmental campus organization, Hillel, Common Ground, Asian-American Cultural Affairs.

Athletics. Intramural: Baseball, basketball, soccer. **Team name:** Renegades.

Student services. Adult student services, alcohol/substance abuse counseling, career counseling, services for economically disadvantaged, student employment services, financial aid counseling, health services, minority student services, personal counseling, placement for graduates, veterans' counselor, women's services. **Physically disabled:** Services for visually, speech, hearing impaired.

Contact. E-mail: admissions@colum.edu
Phone: (312) 369-7130 Fax: (312) 369-8024
Murphy Monroe, Assistant Vice President Admission/Enrollment Management, Columbia College Chicago, 600 South Michigan Avenue, Chicago, IL 60605-1996

Concordia University Chicago
River Forest, Illinois — CB member
www.cuchicago.edu — CB code: 1140

- Private 4-year university and liberal arts college affiliated with the Lutheran Church - Missouri Synod
- Residential campus in large town
- 1,441 degree-seeking undergraduates
- SAT or ACT (ACT writing optional) required

General. Founded in 1864. Regionally accredited. **Degrees:** 318 bachelor's awarded; master's, doctoral offered. **Location:** 10 miles from Chicago. **Calendar:** Semester, limited summer session. **Full-time faculty:** 256 total; 59% have terminal degrees, 15% minority, 60% women. **Part-time faculty:** 170 total; 7% have terminal degrees, 11% minority, 49% women. **Class size:** 65% < 20, 34% 20-39, less than 1% 50-99. **Special facilities:** Early childhood education laboratory school, curriculum center (teacher's resource), human performance laboratory.

Freshman class profile.

GPA 3.75 or higher:	12%	Rank in top quarter:	9%
GPA 3.50-3.74:	8%	Rank in top tenth:	9%
GPA 3.0-3.49:	29%	Out-of-state:	30%
GPA 2.0-2.99:	49%	Live on campus:	72%

Basis for selection. School achievement record most important, particularly in college preparatory courses. SAT/ACT considered, personal statement is optional. SAT Subject Test scores must be received before orientation for fall-term admission. Interview recommended. Essay and interview required for students who do not meet academic admission requirements. **Home schooled:** Statement describing home school structure and mission, transcript of courses and grades required. Syllabus for each course, personal statement or essay describing an important event or individual, certificate of completion from home school (if available), official transcripts of any college work completed required.

High school preparation. College-preparatory program recommended. Required and recommended units include English 4, mathematics 3, social studies 2, history 1, science 2-4 (laboratory 2) and foreign language 2.

2015-2016 Annual costs. Tuition/fees: $29,520. Room/board: $8,992. Books/supplies: $1,200. Personal expenses: $800.

2014-2015 Financial aid. Need-based: 290 full-time freshmen applied for aid; 271 deemed to have need; 271 received aid. Average need met was 76%. Average scholarship/grant was $19,060; average loan $3,206. 78% of total undergraduate aid awarded as scholarships/grants, 22% as loans/jobs. **Non-need-based:** Awarded to 311 full-time undergraduates, including 59 freshmen. Scholarships awarded for academics, alumni affiliation, music/drama, religious affiliation.

Application procedures. Admission: No application fee. Admission notification on a rolling basis beginning on or about 10/1. Admissions application deadline is August. Date varies. Must reply by May 1 or within specified timeframe if notified thereafter. Housing deposit fully refundable prior to May 1. **Financial aid:** Priority date 2/1, closing date 6/1. FAFSA required. Applicants notified on a rolling basis starting 1/24.

Academics. Special study options: Accelerated study, combined bachelor's/graduate degree, cross-registration, distance learning, double major, dual enrollment of high school students, exchange student, honors, independent study, internships, study abroad, teacher certification program. **Credit/placement by examination:** AP, CLEP, IB, SAT, ACT, institutional tests. 12 credit hours maximum toward bachelor's degree. **Support services:** Learning center, reduced course load, study skills assistance, tutoring, writing center.

Majors. Area/ethnic studies: Women's. **Biology:** General. **Business:** Accounting, business admin, communications, marketing, nonprofit/public. **Communications:** Communications/speech/rhetoric, journalism. **Computer**

sciences: General. **Conservation:** Environmental science. **Education:** General, art, biology, chemistry, computer, early childhood, elementary, English, history, mathematics, multi-level teacher, music, physical, science, secondary, social science, special ed. **English:** English lit. **Foreign languages:** Biblical, Spanish. **Health services:** EMT paramedic. **History:** General. **Human services:** Social work. **Math:** General. **Parks/recreation:** Exercise sciences, sports admin. **Philosophy/religion:** Philosophy, religion. **Physical sciences:** General, chemistry, geology. **Psychology:** General. **Social sciences:** Criminology, geography, political science, sociology. **Theology:** Religious ed, sacred music, theology. **Visual/performing arts:** General, art, commercial/advertising art, dramatic, music.

Most popular majors. Business/marketing 22%, education 31%, parks/recreation 9%, psychology 7%, social sciences 8%.

Technology on campus. 85 workstations in library, computer center, student center. Dormitories wired for high-speed internet access and linked to campus network. Commuter students can connect to campus network. Online course registration, helpline, repair service, student web hosting, wireless network available.

Student life. Freshman orientation: Mandatory. Preregistration for classes offered. Overnight sessions held over the summer that allow students to meet each other, finalize academic schedules, and learn about university resources. **Housing:** Guaranteed on-campus for freshmen. Coed dorms, special housing for disabled, apartments, themed housing available. $200 nonrefundable deposit, deadline 7/15. **Activities:** Bands, campus ministries, choral groups, drama, literary magazine, music ensembles, musical theater, radio station, student government, student newspaper, TV station, Habitat for Humanity, Fellowship of Christian Athletes, Latin student union, Black student union, College Republicans, Human Rights Club, Green FCC Committee, history club.

Athletics. NCAA. **Intercollegiate:** Baseball M, basketball, cheerleading, cross-country, football (tackle) M, soccer, softball W, tennis, track and field, volleyball W. **Intramural:** Basketball, bowling, football (non-tackle), softball, tennis, ultimate frisbee, volleyball. **Team name:** Cougars.

Student services. Adult student services, alcohol/substance abuse counseling, chaplain/spiritual director, career counseling, student employment services, financial aid counseling, health services, on-campus daycare, personal counseling, placement for graduates. **Physically disabled:** Services for visually, speech, hearing impaired.

Contact. E-mail: admission@cuchicago.edu
Phone: (877) 282-4422 Toll-free number: (800) 285-2668
Fax: (708) 209-3473
Gwen Kanelos, Assistant Vice President for Enrollment, Concordia University Chicago, 7400 Augusta Street, River Forest, IL 60305-1499

DePaul University
Chicago, Illinois — CB member
www.depaul.edu — CB code: 1165

- Private 4-year university affiliated with the Roman Catholic Church
- Commuter campus in very large city
- 15,683 degree-seeking undergraduates: 13% part-time, 53% women, 8% African American, 8% Asian American, 18% Hispanic/Latino, 4% Multiracial, non-Hispanic, 3% international
- 7,405 degree-seeking graduate students
- 72% of applicants admitted
- Application essay required
- 73% graduate within 6 years

General. Founded in 1898. Regionally accredited. Campuses in Chicago's Loop and Lincoln Park neighborhoods and two suburban locations. **Degrees:** 3,776 bachelor's awarded; master's, professional, doctoral offered. **ROTC:** Army. **Calendar:** Continuous, extensive summer session. **Full-time faculty:** 914 total; 86% have terminal degrees, 20% minority, 46% women. **Part-time faculty:** 971 total; 5% have terminal degrees, 15% minority, 45% women. **Class size:** 35% < 20, 54% 20-39, 9% 40-49, 1% 50-99, less than 1% >100. **Special facilities:** LEED-Certified environmental science and chemistry building with greenhouse and green roof, digital cinema laboratory with motion-capture system, green-screen studio, converged newsroom, 10 specialized computer research labs including artificial intelligence, biomedics informatics, mobile e-commerce.

Freshman class profile. 19,628 applied, 14,129 admitted, 2,519 enrolled.

Mid 50% test scores		GPA 2.0-2.99:	14%
SAT critical reading:	520-620	Rank in top quarter:	54%
SAT math:	490-610	Rank in top tenth:	20%
ACT composite:	22-28	Return as sophomores:	84%
GPA 3.75 or higher:	37%	Out-of-state:	41%
GPA 3.50-3.74:	20%	Live on campus:	70%
GPA 3.0-3.49:	29%	International:	3%

Basis for selection. Rigor of secondary school record, academic GPA, standardized test score very important. Class rank, recommendation(s), extracurricular activities, talent/ability, character, volunteer and work experience, level of applicant's interest important. Interview, first generation, alumni/ae relation, geographical location, state residency, religious affiliation, application essay, racial or ethnic status considered. SAT or ACT recommended. ACT/SAT are optional. Students who do not submit test scores will be required to send responses to several short essay questions. Audition required for music and acting. Interview or portfolio review required for design, technical, or theater studies. **Home schooled:** Transcript of courses and grades required. Home schooled applicants must submit test scores for consideration. Official community college transcripts for any courses taken required. Listing of textbooks used, especially in math and sciences, recommended. **Learning Disabled:** Students are required to complete an Enrollment Request form and submit documentation from a licensed professional in order to register with the CSD. All documentation must be current. The CSD will advise the student of any additional documentation needed to support their request.

High school preparation. College-preparatory program required. 12 units required; 14 recommended. Required and recommended units include English 4, mathematics 3, science 3 (laboratory 2) and foreign language 2. 2 units social science/humanities required.

2015-2016 Annual costs. Tuition/fees: $36,361. Room/board: $12,873. Books/supplies: $1,104. Personal expenses: $1,500.

2014-2015 Financial aid. Need-based: 2,180 full-time freshmen applied for aid; 1,806 deemed to have need; 1,803 received aid. Average need met was 65%. Average scholarship/grant was $1,969; average loan $3,601. 72% of total undergraduate aid awarded as scholarships/grants, 28% as loans/ jobs. Non-need-based: Awarded to 9,009 full-time undergraduates, including 2,243 freshmen. Scholarships awarded for academics, art, athletics, leadership, music/drama, ROTC, state residency.

Application procedures. Admission: Priority date 11/15; deadline 2/1. No application fee. Application must be submitted online. Admission notification by 3/15. Must reply by May 1 or within 2 week(s) if notified thereafter. Applications are considered on a space-available basis after February 1. Early Action applicants will be notified of a decision by January 15. Regular notification applicants will receive a decision by March 15. Music and Theatre applicants will be notified of a decision by April 1. **Financial aid:** Priority date 3/1; no closing date. FAFSA required. Applicants notified on a rolling basis starting 3/15.

Academics. Special study options: Accelerated study, combined bachelor's/graduate degree, distance learning, double major, ESL, honors, independent study, internships, liberal arts/career combination, study abroad, teacher certification program, weekend college. **Credit/placement by examination:** AP, CLEP, IB, SAT, ACT, institutional tests. Senior year residency requirement excludes CLEP, AP or IB credits. For transfer students, CLEP, IB or AP credits combined with transfer credits from 2-year institutions may total no more than 99 hours, and combined with transfer credits from 4-year institutions may total no more than 132 hours. **Support services:** Learning center, pre-admission summer program, reduced course load, remedial instruction, study skills assistance, tutoring, writing center. Experiential Service Learning, Senior Year Capstone, Religious Dimensions.

Honors college/program. Each Honors application is individually reviewed, taking into consideration all components of a student's academic profile, particularly content and quality of essay responses.

Majors. Architecture: History/criticism. **Area/ethnic studies:** African-American, American, Chinese, Japanese, Latin American, women's. **Biology:** General. **Business:** Accounting, business admin, e-commerce, finance, hospitality admin, human resources, management information systems, management science, managerial economics, marketing, organizational behavior, real estate. **Communications:** General, communications/speech/rhetoric, journalism, media studies. **Communications technology:** Animation/special effects. **Computer sciences:** Applications programming, computer graphics, computer science, information systems, information technology, networking, programming, security, web page design. **Conservation:** Environmental science, environmental studies. **Education:** Art, early childhood, elementary, health, multi-level teacher, music, physical, secondary, special ed. **English:** Creative writing, English lit, rhetoric/composition. **Foreign languages:** Arabic, French, German, Italian, Spanish. **Health services:** Clinical lab science, nursing (RN). **History:** General. **Human services:** Community org/advocacy, public policy. **Liberal arts:** Arts/sciences. **Math:** General. **Parks/recreation:**

Exercise sciences, health/fitness. **Philosophy/religion:** Islamic, Judaic, philosophy, religion. **Physical sciences:** Chemistry, physics. **Psychology:** General, educational. **Social sciences:** General, anthropology, economics, geography, international relations, political science, sociology, urban studies. **Visual/performing arts:** Acting, art, art history/conservation, cinematography, commercial/advertising art, digital arts, dramatic, jazz, music, music management, music performance, music theory/composition, play/screenwriting, studio arts management, theater design, theater history.

Most popular majors. Business/marketing 28%, communications/journalism 15%, computer/information sciences 6%, liberal arts 10%, psychology 7%, social sciences 7%, visual/performing arts 6%.

Technology on campus. Dormitories wired for high-speed internet access and linked to campus network. Commuter students can connect to campus network. Online course registration, online library, helpline, repair service, student web hosting, wireless network available.

Student life. Freshman orientation: Mandatory, $170 fee. Preregistration for classes offered. Two-day, overnight program. **Housing:** Coed dorms, special housing for disabled, apartments, themed housing available. $400 fully refundable deposit. **Activities:** Bands, campus ministries, choral groups, dance, drama, film society, international student organizations, literary magazine, music ensembles, Model UN, musical theater, opera, radio station, student government, student newspaper, symphony orchestra.

Athletics. NCAA. **Intercollegiate:** Basketball, cross-country, golf M, soccer, softball W, tennis, track and field, volleyball W. **Intramural:** Badminton, basketball, football (non-tackle), racquetball, soccer, softball, table tennis, tennis, volleyball, water polo. **Team name:** Blue Demons.

Student services. Adult student services, alcohol/substance abuse counseling, chaplain/spiritual director, career counseling, services for economically disadvantaged, student employment services, financial aid counseling, health services, legal services, minority student services, personal counseling, veterans' counselor, women's services. **Physically disabled:** Services for visually, speech, hearing impaired.

Contact. E-mail: admission@depaul.edu
Phone: (312) 362-8300 Toll-free number: (800) 433-7285
Fax: (312) 362-5749
Carlene Klaas, Dean of Undergraduate Admission, DePaul University, 1 East Jackson Boulevard Suite 9000, Chicago, IL 60604-2287

DeVry University: Chicago
Chicago, Illinois
www.devry.edu   **CB code: 1171**

- For-profit 4-year university
- Commuter campus in very large city
- 1,149 degree-seeking undergraduates
- Interview required

General. Founded in 1931. Regionally accredited. Additional locations: Addison, Chicago Loop, Chicago O'Hare, Downers Grove, Elgin, Gurnee, Lincolnshire, Naperville, Schaumburg, Tinley Park; Merrillville (IN); Edina, St. Louis Park (MN); Milwaukee, Waukesha (WI). **Degrees:** 2,439 bachelor's, 889 associate awarded; master's offered. **Location:** 6 miles from downtown. **Calendar:** Semester, extensive summer session. **Full-time faculty:** 37 total; 22% minority, 32% women. **Part-time faculty:** 93 total; 13% minority, 33% women.

Basis for selection. Applicants must have high school diploma or equivalent, or degree from an accredited postsecondary institution, demonstrate proficiency in basic college-level skills through ACT scores or institution-administered placement examinations, and be at least 17 years of age. New students may enter at beginning of any semester. SAT/ACT or DeVry-administered admissions test required for all.

High school preparation. College-preparatory program recommended.

2015-2016 Annual costs. Tuition/fees: $17,132. Books/supplies: $1,320. Personal expenses: $2,376. **Additional information:** Annual tuition: $10,810-$21,163; fees $50-$90.

Financial aid. All financial aid based on need.

Application procedures. Admission: No deadline. $44 fee. Admission notification on a rolling basis. **Financial aid:** No deadline. FAFSA required. Applicants notified on a rolling basis.

Academics. Special study options: Accelerated study, distance learning, study abroad. **Credit/placement by examination:** AP, CLEP, institutional tests. **Support services:** Learning center, remedial instruction, tutoring.

Majors. Business: General, business admin. **Communications:** General. **Computer sciences:** Networking, systems analysis, web page design. **Engineering:** Biomedical, electrical. **Health services:** Clinical lab science.

Most popular majors. Business/marketing 57%, computer/information sciences 32%, engineering/engineering technologies 11%.

Technology on campus. 600 workstations in library, computer center. Online course registration, online library, helpline available.

Student life. Freshman orientation: Mandatory. Preregistration for classes offered. **Housing:** Private apartments, student-plan housing, private rooms available. **Activities:** Student government, student newspaper, Muslim student association, Alpha Beta Gamma, Alpha Chi, Bible club, National Society of Black Engineers, Tau Alpha Pi.

Student services. Career counseling, student employment services, financial aid counseling, placement for graduates, veterans' counselor. **Physically disabled:** Services for visually, hearing impaired.

Contact. E-mail: admissions2@devry.edu
Phone: (773) 929-6550 Toll-free number: (800) 383-3879
Fax: (773) 697-2710
DeVry University: Chicago, 3300 North Campbell Avenue, Chicago, IL 60618-5994

DeVry University: Online
Addison, Illinois
www.devry.edu   CB code: 3816

- For-profit 4-year virtual college
- Small city
- 14,794 degree-seeking undergraduates

General. Regionally accredited. **Degrees:** 2,439 bachelor's, 889 associate awarded; master's offered. **Calendar:** Semester. **Full-time faculty:** 28 total; 18% minority, 32% women. **Part-time faculty:** 2,781 total; 20% minority, 50% women.

Basis for selection. Applicants must have high school diploma or equivalent, or degree from accredited post-secondary institution, demonstrate proficiency in basic college-level skills through SAT or ACT scores or institution-administered placement examinations, and be at least 17 years of age.

High school preparation. College-preparatory program recommended.

2015-2016 Annual costs. Tuition/fees: $17,132. Books/supplies: $1,320. Personal expenses: $2,376.

Financial aid. Non-need-based: Scholarships awarded for academics.

Application procedures. Admission: No deadline. $40 fee. Admission notification on a rolling basis. **Financial aid:** No deadline. FAFSA required. Applicants notified on a rolling basis.

Academics. Special study options: Accelerated study, distance learning. **Credit/placement by examination:** AP, CLEP.

Majors. Business: General, business admin, e-commerce. **Communications:** General. **Computer sciences:** Networking, systems analysis, web page design. **Engineering:** Software. **Health services:** Health care admin. **Visual/performing arts:** Game design.

Most popular majors. Business/marketing 78%, computer/information sciences 18%.

Contact. DeVry University: Online, One Tower Lane, Oakbrook Terrace, IL 60181

Dominican University
River Forest, Illinois
www.dom.edu   CB member   CB code: 1667

- Private 4-year university and liberal arts college affiliated with the Roman Catholic Church
- Commuter campus in large town
- 2,241 degree-seeking undergraduates: 8% part-time, 66% women, 7% African American, 3% Asian American, 48% Hispanic/Latino, 1% Multiracial, non-Hispanic, 3% international
- 1,144 degree-seeking graduate students

- 63% of applicants admitted
- SAT or ACT (ACT writing optional), application essay required
- 59% graduate within 6 years; 32% enter graduate study

General. Founded in 1901. Regionally accredited. **Degrees:** 429 bachelor's awarded; master's, doctoral offered. **Location:** 10 miles from downtown Chicago. **Calendar:** Semester, limited summer session. **Full-time faculty:** 167 total; 87% have terminal degrees, 17% minority, 56% women. **Part-time faculty:** 295 total; 42% have terminal degrees, 22% minority, 67% women. **Class size:** 64% < 20, 35% 20-39, less than 1% 40-49, less than 1% 50-99. **Special facilities:** Food science laboratory, cadaver lab, hospital simulation lab, children's literature center.

Freshman class profile. 4,161 applied, 2,611 admitted, 484 enrolled.

Mid 50% test scores			
SAT critical reading:	440-580	GPA 3.0-3.49:	29%
SAT math:	420-550	GPA 2.0-2.99:	19%
SAT writing:	400-480	Rank in top quarter:	51%
ACT composite:	19-24	Rank in top tenth:	23%
GPA 3.75 or higher:	36%	Return as sophomores:	79%
GPA 3.50-3.74:	16%	Out-of-state:	6%
		Live on campus:	38%

Basis for selection. Rank in upper half of class, 2.75 GPA, ACT/SAT at or above national average, and 16 units college prep work. Interview recommended. **Home schooled:** Transcript of courses and grades required.

High school preparation. College-preparatory program recommended. 16 units required. Required and recommended units include English 4, mathematics 3, social studies 1, history 2, science 3 (laboratory 2), foreign language 2 and academic electives 1.

2015-2016 Annual costs. Tuition/fees: $30,670. Room/board: $9,380. Books/supplies: $1,200. Personal expenses: $1,340.

2015-2016 Financial aid. Need-based: 458 full-time freshmen applied for aid; 435 deemed to have need; 435 received aid. Average need met was 76%. Average scholarship/grant was $21,975; average loan $3,333. 67% of total undergraduate aid awarded as scholarships/grants, 33% as loans/jobs. **Non-need-based:** Awarded to 310 full-time undergraduates, including 65 freshmen. Scholarships awarded for academics, alumni affiliation, art, minority status, religious affiliation.

Application procedures. Admission: No deadline. $25 fee, may be waived for applicants with need. Admission notification on a rolling basis beginning on or about 10/15. Must reply by 5/1. Maximum period of postponement is one semester. **Financial aid:** Priority date 2/15; no closing date. FAFSA required. Applicants notified on a rolling basis starting 3/15; must reply within 2 week(s) of notification.

Academics. Special study options: Accelerated study, combined bachelor's/graduate degree, cross-registration, distance learning, double major, dual enrollment of high school students, ESL, honors, independent study, internships, liberal arts/career combination, study abroad, teacher certification program, Washington semester. **Credit/placement by examination:** AP, CLEP, IB, institutional tests. 28 credit hours maximum toward bachelor's degree. **Support services:** Learning center, pre-admission summer program, reduced course load, remedial instruction, study skills assistance, tutoring, writing center.

Majors. Area/ethnic studies: African-American, American, women's. **Biology:** General, neuroscience. **Business:** Accounting, business admin, fashion, finance, international, marketing. **Communications:** Communications/speech/rhetoric, journalism, public relations. **Computer sciences:** Computer science, informatics. **Conservation:** Environmental science. **Education:** Early childhood, elementary, history, multi-level teacher. **Engineering:** General. **English:** English lit. **Foreign languages:** French, Italian, Spanish. **Health services:** Dietetics, nursing (RN), occupational therapy, physical therapy, premedicine, prepharmacy. **History:** General. **Liberal arts:** Arts/sciences. **Math:** General. **Philosophy/religion:** Philosophy. **Physical sciences:** Chemistry. **Psychology:** General, clinical. **Social sciences:** Criminology, economics, international relations, political science, sociology. **Theology:** Theology. **Visual/performing arts:** Art, art history/conservation, commercial/advertising art, dramatic, fashion design, film/cinema/video, music, photography, sculpture, studio arts. **Work/family studies:** Food/nutrition.

Most popular majors. Business/marketing 23%, health sciences 14%, interdisciplinary studies 8%, psychology 10%, social sciences 13%.

Technology on campus. 550 workstations in dormitories, library, computer center, student center. Dormitories wired for high-speed internet access and linked to campus network. Commuter students can connect to campus network. Online course registration, online library, helpline, wireless network available.

Student life. Freshman orientation: Mandatory. Preregistration for classes offered. Two-day program with overnight on campus. **Housing:** Guaranteed on-campus for freshmen. Coed dorms, single-sex dorms, special housing for disabled, apartments, wellness housing available. $300 partly refundable deposit, deadline 5/1. Pets allowed in dorm rooms. **Activities:** Concert band, campus ministries, choral groups, dance, drama, international student organizations, literary magazine, Model UN, musical theater, student government, student newspaper, Students for Peace and Justice, Organization of Latino Americans, eco club, black student union, Polish club, gospel choir, Team KIVA, Domestic Abuse Stops Here, Campus Crusade for Christ.

Athletics. NCAA. **Intercollegiate:** Baseball M, basketball, cross-country, golf M, soccer, softball W, tennis, volleyball. **Intramural:** Basketball, bowling, football (non-tackle). **Team name:** Stars.

Student services. Chaplain/spiritual director, career counseling, student employment services, financial aid counseling, health services, on-campus daycare, personal counseling, placement for graduates, veterans' counselor. **Physically disabled:** Services for visually, speech, hearing impaired.

Contact. E-mail: domadmis@dom.edu
Phone: (708) 524-6800 Toll-free number: (800) 828-8475
Fax: (708) 524-6864
Glenn Hamilton, Assistant Vice President for Enrollment Management, Dominican University, 7900 West Division Street, River Forest, IL 60305-1099

East-West University
Chicago, Illinois
www.eastwest.edu   **CB member**
    CB code: 0798

- Private 4-year university
- Commuter campus in very large city
- 512 degree-seeking undergraduates
- Interview required

General. Founded in 1978. Regionally accredited. **Degrees:** 77 bachelor's, 12 associate awarded. **Calendar:** Quarter, limited summer session. **Full-time faculty:** 17 total. **Part-time faculty:** 59 total.

Basis for selection. Open admission, but selective for some programs. SAT or ACT recommended.

High school preparation. College-preparatory program recommended.

2015-2016 Annual costs. Tuition/fees: $20,145. Room/board: $8,811. Books/supplies: $1,800.

Financial aid. Non-need-based: Scholarships awarded for academics. **Additional information:** Foreign students eligible for institutional scholarship.

Application procedures. Admission: Priority date 5/1; no deadline. $50 fee, may be waived for applicants with need. Admission notification on a rolling basis. **Financial aid:** Closing date 3/31. FAFSA required. Applicants notified on a rolling basis starting 1/4; must reply within 4 week(s) of notification.

Academics. Special study options: Cooperative education, double major, ESL, honors, independent study, internships. **Credit/placement by examination:** AP, CLEP, institutional tests. Interview recommended for placement. **Support services:** Tutoring.

Majors. Business: Business admin. **Communications:** Communications/ speech/rhetoric. **Computer sciences:** General. **Liberal arts:** Arts/sciences. **Math:** General.

Most popular majors. Business/marketing 32%, computer/information sciences 11%, engineering/engineering technologies 16%, liberal arts 40%.

Technology on campus. 10 workstations in computer center. Online library available.

Student life. Freshman orientation: Available. Preregistration for classes offered. **Activities:** Drama, literary magazine, student government, student newspaper.

Athletics. Team name: Phantom.

Student services. Adult student services, alcohol/substance abuse counseling, career counseling, student employment services, financial aid counseling, health services, minority student services.

Contact. E-mail: seeyou@eastwest.edu
Phone: (312) 939-0111 Toll-free number: (877) 398-9376
Fax: (312) 939-0083
Bryan Lambert, Director of Admissions, East-West University, 816 South Michigan Avenue, Chicago, IL 60605-2185

Eastern Illinois University
Charleston, Illinois
www.eiu.edu   **CB code: 1199**

- Public 4-year university
- Residential campus in large town
- 7,063 degree-seeking undergraduates: 12% part-time, 59% women, 19% African American, 1% Asian American, 6% Hispanic/Latino, 2% Multiracial, non-Hispanic, 1% international
- 1,257 degree-seeking graduate students
- 50% of applicants admitted
- SAT or ACT (ACT writing recommended) required
- 58% graduate within 6 years

General. Founded in 1895. Regionally accredited. On-line courses and off-campus sites in Carterville, Champaign-Urbana, Chicago-American Indian Association of Illinois, Danville, Decatur, Effingham, Grayslake-University Center at College of Lake County, Mattoon, Mount Vernon, Olney, River Grove, Schaumburg, and Vandalia. **Degrees:** 1,875 bachelor's awarded; master's offered. **ROTC:** Army. **Location:** 57 miles from Champaign, IL;110 miles from Indianapolis, IN; 147 miles from St. Louis, MO. **Calendar:** Semester, limited summer session. **Full-time faculty:** 468 total; 79% have terminal degrees, 14% minority, 46% women. **Part-time faculty:** 129 total; 15% have terminal degrees, 6% minority, 57% women. **Class size:** 43% < 20, 49% 20-39, 5% 40-49, 3% 50-99, less than 1% >100. **Special facilities:** Arts center, greenhouse, observatory, renewable energy center, scanning electron microscope, laboratory school exhibit.

Freshman class profile. 9,103 applied, 4,571 admitted, 1,143 enrolled.

Mid 50% test scores		End year in good standing:	81%
ACT composite:	19-24	Return as sophomores:	75%
GPA 3.75 or higher:	13%	Out-of-state:	5%
GPA 3.50-3.74:	11%	Live on campus:	95%
GPA 3.0-3.49:	31%	International:	3%
GPA 2.0-2.99:	45%	Fraternities:	22%
Rank in top quarter:	31%	Sororities:	23%
Rank in top tenth:	9%		

Basis for selection. Applicants must meet one of following: rank in top quarter of class based on 6 or more semesters or 3.0 GPA and 18 ACT/860 SAT; rank in top one-half based on 6 or more semesters or have 2.5 GPA and 19 ACT/910 SAT; rank in the top three-quarters of class based on 6 or more semesters or have 2.25 GPA and 22 ACT/1020 SAT. Gateway admissions program for students with at least 16 ACT and 2.0 GPA. Audition required of music majors. **Home schooled:** GED requirement may be waived with acceptable ACT score. Students must present a transcript of all courses completed with grades listed for each class.

High school preparation. College-preparatory program recommended. 15 units required. Required and recommended units include English 4, mathematics 3, social studies 3, science 3 (laboratory 3), foreign language 2 and academic electives 2. Significant science lab experience required.

2015-2016 Annual costs. Tuition/fees: $11,312; $13,442 out-of-state. Room/board: $9,546. Books/supplies: $150. Personal expenses: $1,152.

2015-2016 Financial aid. Need-based: 1,053 full-time freshmen applied for aid; 794 deemed to have need; 786 received aid. Average need met was 64%. Average scholarship/grant was $3,629; average loan $3,165. 51% of total undergraduate aid awarded as scholarships/grants, 49% as loans/jobs. **Non-need-based:** Awarded to 3,026 full-time undergraduates, including 618 freshmen. Scholarships awarded for academics, art, athletics, leadership, music/drama, ROTC.

Application procedures. Admission: Closing date 8/15 (receipt date). $30 fee, may be waived for applicants with need. Admission notification on a rolling basis beginning on or about 8/1. Must reply by May 1 or within 2 week(s) if notified thereafter. Consult university for possible cut-off date. **Financial aid:** Priority date 3/1; no closing date. FAFSA required. Applicants notified on a rolling basis starting 3/1; must reply within 2 week(s) of notification.

Academics. Many workshops available on-line in podcasts. **Special study options:** Accelerated study, combined bachelor's/graduate degree, distance learning, double major, ESL, exchange student, honors, independent study, internships, semester at sea, study abroad, teacher certification program.

Credit/placement by examination: AP, CLEP, IB, SAT, ACT, institutional tests. Credit will count toward graduation and may be used to fullfill graduation requirements but does not carry a grade. Credit by exam will only be applied toward degree if not used toward high school graduation. All residency and degree requirements must still be met. **Support services:** Learning center, pre-admission summer program, reduced course load, remedial instruction, study skills assistance, tutoring, writing center.

Honors college/program. 26 ACT or equivalent SAT or higher; upper 10% of high school class, or 3.5 GPA; permission of the Dean of the Honors College.

Majors. Area/ethnic studies: African-American. **Biology:** General. **Business:** Accounting, business admin, finance, management science, marketing. **Communications:** General, journalism. **Computer sciences:** General. **Education:** Adult/continuing, elementary, health, kindergarten/preschool, middle, science, social science, special ed, voc/tech. **Engineering:** General. **English:** English lit. **Foreign languages:** General. **Health services:** Athletic training, clinical lab science, communication disorders, nursing (RN). **History:** General. **Liberal arts:** Arts/sciences. **Math:** General. **Parks/recreation:** Exercise sciences, facilities management. **Philosophy/religion:** Philosophy. **Physical sciences:** Chemistry, geology, physics. **Psychology:** General. **Social sciences:** Economics, geography, political science, sociology. **Visual/performing arts:** Art, dramatic, music. **Work/family studies:** General.

Most popular majors. Business/marketing 11%, communications/journalism 10%, education 11%, family/consumer sciences 9%, liberal arts 10%, parks/recreation 11%, psychology 7%, social sciences 7%.

Technology on campus. 706 workstations in dormitories, library, computer center, student center. Dormitories wired for high-speed internet access and linked to campus network. Commuter students can connect to campus network. Online course registration, online library, helpline, repair service, student web hosting, wireless network available.

Student life. Freshman orientation: Mandatory, $100 fee. Preregistration for classes offered. One-day session held in June and July; includes advisement and registration. Students also participate in a transition program that starts 3 days before the semester and runs for the first 40 days. **Housing:** Guaranteed on-campus for freshmen. Coed dorms, single-sex dorms, apartments, fraternity/sorority housing available. $50 nonrefundable deposit. **Activities:** Bands, campus ministries, choral groups, dance, drama, film society, international student organizations, literary magazine, music ensembles, musical theater, radio station, student government, student newspaper, symphony orchestra, TV station, Association of International Students, Black Student Union, Minority Student Health, College Democrats, College Republicans, Christian Campus Fellowship, Newman Catholic Center, Korean Student Association, Study Abroad Society, University Board.

Athletics. NCAA. **Intercollegiate:** Baseball M, basketball, cross-country, football (tackle) M, golf, soccer, softball W, swimming, tennis, track and field, volleyball W. **Intramural:** Badminton, basketball, bowling, football (non-tackle), racquetball, soccer, softball, table tennis, tennis, volleyball. **Team name:** Panthers.

Student services. Adult student services, alcohol/substance abuse counseling, career counseling, services for economically disadvantaged, student employment services, financial aid counseling, health services, legal services, minority student services, personal counseling, placement for graduates, veterans' counselor, women's services. **Physically disabled:** Services for visually, speech, hearing impaired.

Contact. E-mail: admissions@eiu.edu
Phone: (217) 581-2223 Toll-free number: (877) 581-2348
Fax: (217) 581-7060
Chris Dearth, Director of Admissions, Eastern Illinois University, 600 Lincoln Avenue, Charleston, IL 61920

Elmhurst College

| Elmhurst, Illinois | CB member |
| www.elmhurst.edu | CB code: 1204 |

- Private 4-year liberal arts college affiliated with the United Church of Christ
- Residential campus in large town
- 2,752 degree-seeking undergraduates: 4% part-time, 60% women, 5% African American, 6% Asian American, 17% Hispanic/Latino, 3% Multiracial, non-Hispanic
- 458 degree-seeking graduate students
- 55% of applicants admitted
- SAT or ACT (ACT writing optional) required
- 67% graduate within 6 years

General. Founded in 1871. Regionally accredited. **Degrees:** 706 bachelor's awarded; master's offered. **ROTC:** Army, Air Force. **Location:** 16 miles from Chicago. **Calendar:** 4-1-4, limited summer session. **Full-time faculty:** 141 total; 80% have terminal degrees, 9% minority, 61% women. **Part-time faculty:** 210 total; 22% have terminal degrees, 9% minority, 56% women. **Class size:** 59% < 20, 40% 20-39, less than 1% 40-49, less than 1% 50-99. **Special facilities:** 2 nuclear accelerators, 4 electron microscopes, Impressionist art collection, computer science and technology center, media center, sound studio, greenhouse.

Freshman class profile. 3,620 applied, 1,983 admitted, 478 enrolled.

Mid 50% test scores		GPA 3.50-3.74:	17%
SAT critical reading:	490-600	GPA 3.0-3.49:	35%
SAT math:	490-610	GPA 2.0-2.99:	23%
SAT writing:	460-590	Rank in top quarter:	54%
ACT composite:	21-26	Rank in top tenth:	23%
GPA 3.75 or higher:	25%	Return as sophomores:	79%

Basis for selection. School achievement record, including grades and course levels, most important, followed by test scores. Applicants should rank in top half of class. Activities and counselor recommendations also important. Interview and essay recommended for all applicants, required of academically marginal applicants. Audition required of music majors. Portfolio recommended for art majors. **Home schooled:** Interview strongly recommended.

High school preparation. College-preparatory program recommended. 16 units required; 21 recommended. Required and recommended units include English 4, mathematics 2-3, social studies 2-3, history 1-2, science 2-3 (laboratory 2-3), foreign language 1-2 and academic electives 4. Chemistry required for nursing applicants. 3 mathematics required for most business administration and computer-related specialties applicants.

2015-2016 Annual costs. Tuition/fees: $34,450. Room/board: $9,816. Books/supplies: $1,000. Personal expenses: $1,334.

2015-2016 Financial aid. Need-based: 468 full-time freshmen applied for aid; 408 deemed to have need; 408 received aid. Average need met was 80%. Average scholarship/grant was $24,766; average loan $3,467. 83% of total undergraduate aid awarded as scholarships/grants, 17% as loans/jobs. **Non-need-based:** Awarded to 1,203 full-time undergraduates, including 192 freshmen. Scholarships awarded for academics, alumni affiliation, art, minority status, music/drama, religious affiliation, ROTC, state residency.

Application procedures. Admission: Priority date 4/15; no deadline. No application fee. Admission notification on a rolling basis beginning on or about 10/1. Must reply by May 1 or within 2 week(s) if notified thereafter. **Financial aid:** Priority date 2/1; no closing date. FAFSA required. Applicants notified on a rolling basis starting 2/16; must reply within 3 week(s) of notification.

Academics. Special study options: Accelerated study, combined bachelor's/graduate degree, cooperative education, double major, dual enrollment of high school students, honors, independent study, internships, liberal arts/career combination, study abroad, teacher certification program, Washington semester. 3+2 engineering with Illinois Institute of Technology, University of Illinois at Urbana-Champaign, and Washington University (MO). **Credit/placement by examination:** AP, CLEP, IB, institutional tests. 48 credit hours maximum toward bachelor's degree. **Support services:** Learning center, pre-admission summer program, reduced course load, study skills assistance, tutoring, writing center.

Majors. Area/ethnic studies: American. **Biology:** General. **Business:** Accounting, business admin, finance, international, logistics, marketing. **Communications:** Communications/speech/rhetoric. **Computer sciences:** Computer science, information systems. **Conservation:** Management/policy. **Education:** General, agricultural, biology, chemistry, early childhood, elementary, English, French, German, history, kindergarten/preschool, mathematics, music, physical, physics, secondary, Spanish, special ed. **English:** English lit. **Foreign languages:** French, German, Spanish. **Health services:** Nursing (RN), predental, premedicine, prepharmacy, preveterinary, speech pathology. **History:** General. **Liberal arts:** Arts/sciences. **Math:** General. **Parks/recreation:** Exercise sciences, health/fitness, sports admin. **Philosophy/religion:** Philosophy. **Physical sciences:** Chemistry, physics. **Protective services:** Criminal justice, law enforcement admin. **Psychology:** General. **Social sciences:** Criminology, economics, geography, political science, sociology, urban studies. **Theology:** Preministerial, theology. **Visual/performing arts:** Art, dramatic, music, music management.

Most popular majors. Biology 6%, business/marketing 21%, education 8%, English 7%, health sciences 14%, psychology 11%.

Technology on campus. 800 workstations in library, computer center, student center. Dormitories wired for high-speed internet access and linked to campus network. Commuter students can connect to campus network. Online library, helpline, repair service, wireless network available.

Student life. Freshman orientation: Mandatory, $225 fee. Preregistration for classes offered. Three-day program held immediately prior to term. **Policies:** Each residence hall is self-governing. **Housing:** Coed dorms, apartments available. $300 nonrefundable deposit. **Activities:** Bands, campus ministries, choral groups, drama, international student organizations, literary magazine, music ensembles, musical theater, radio station, student government, student newspaper, over 90 organizations.

Athletics. NCAA. **Intercollegiate:** Baseball M, basketball, bowling W, cross-country, football (tackle) M, golf, lacrosse, soccer, softball W, tennis, track and field, volleyball W, wrestling M. **Intramural:** Basketball, football (tackle) M, golf, racquetball, softball, volleyball. **Team name:** Blue Jays.

Student services. Adult student services, chaplain/spiritual director, career counseling, student employment services, financial aid counseling, health services, minority student services, personal counseling, placement for graduates, veterans' counselor.

Contact. E-mail: admit@elmhurst.edu
Phone: (630) 617-3400 Toll-free number: (800) 697-1871
Fax: (630) 617-5501
Stephanie Levenson, Executive Director of Admission, Elmhurst College, 190 South Prospect Avenue, Elmhurst, IL 60126-3296

Eureka College
Eureka, Illinois
www.eureka.edu
CB member
CB code: 1206

▶ Private 4-year liberal arts college affiliated with the Christian Church (Disciples of Christ)
▶ Residential campus in small town
▶ 654 degree-seeking undergraduates
▶ SAT or ACT (ACT writing optional) required

General. Founded in 1855. Regionally accredited. **Degrees:** 163 bachelor's awarded. **Location:** 140 miles from Chicago. **Calendar:** Semester, limited summer session. **Full-time faculty:** 40 total; 80% have terminal degrees, 42% women. **Part-time faculty:** 35 total; 37% have terminal degrees, 51% women. **Class size:** 78% < 20, 22% 20-39, less than 1% 40-49. **Special facilities:** Ronald Reagan Museum, peace garden, lilac arboretum, labyrinth, fitness center.

Freshman class profile.

GPA 3.75 or higher:	27%	Rank in top quarter:	35%
GPA 3.50-3.74:	13%	Rank in top tenth:	19%
GPA 3.0-3.49:	26%	Out-of-state:	8%
GPA 2.0-2.99:	34%	Live on campus:	86%

Basis for selection. Class rank, high school GPA, ACT scores, and high school curriculum most important. Recommendations and interviews also important. Must have minimum ACT composite of 17 and high school GPA of 2.3. **Home schooled:** Interview required.

High school preparation. College-preparatory program recommended. 14 units recommended. Recommended units include English 4, mathematics 3, social studies 2, history 2, science 2 (laboratory 2) and foreign language 2.

2015-2016 Annual costs. Tuition/fees: $20,510. Room/board: $8,635. Books/supplies: $1,000. Personal expenses: $510.

Financial aid. Non-need-based: Scholarships awarded for academics, alumni affiliation, art, leadership, music/drama, religious affiliation.

Application procedures. Admission: Closing date 8/15 (postmark date). No application fee. Admission notification by 8/20. Admission notification on a rolling basis beginning on or about 9/1. Must reply by May 1 or within 3 week(s) if notified thereafter. **Financial aid:** Priority date 4/15; no closing date. FAFSA required. Applicants notified on a rolling basis starting 2/1; must reply by 5/1 or within 3 week(s) of notification.

Academics. Special study options: Double major, honors, independent study, internships, student-designed major, study abroad, teacher certification program, Washington semester, weekend college. Students who began as freshmen, have a record of leadership and service, and hold a 3.5 GPA at the end of their sophomore year qualify for a mentorship paid for by the college. **Credit/placement by examination:** AP, CLEP, ACT, institutional tests. **Support services:** Learning center, reduced course load, remedial instruction, study skills assistance, tutoring, writing center.

Honors college/program. Admitted by invitation, includes advanced and special classes, advanced general education requirements along with thesis preparation and presentation, honors seminars on special topics.

Majors. Biology: General, environmental. **Business:** General, accounting, business admin, finance, management information systems, marketing. **Communications:** Communications/speech/rhetoric, media studies, public relations. **Computer sciences:** General, computer science. **Education:** General, elementary, middle, multi-level teacher, secondary, special ed. **Engineering:** General. **English:** Creative writing, English lit, writing. **Health services:** Predental, premedicine, prenursing, preveterinary. **History:** General. **Liberal arts:** Arts/sciences. **Math:** General. **Philosophy/religion:** Philosophy, religion. **Physical sciences:** Chemistry. **Protective services:** Law enforcement admin. **Psychology:** General. **Social sciences:** Political science. **Visual/performing arts:** Art, dramatic, music performance, studio arts management.

Most popular majors. Biology 6%, business/marketing 21%, communications/journalism 7%, education 14%, history 8%, parks/recreation 8%, security/protective services 9%.

Technology on campus. 50 workstations in dormitories, library, computer center, student center. Dormitories wired for high-speed internet access and linked to campus network. Commuter students can connect to campus network. Online library, helpline, repair service available.

Student life. Freshman orientation: Mandatory. Preregistration for classes offered. Held at start of school year. **Policies:** All single students under 24 not living with parents required to live on campus. **Housing:** Guaranteed on-campus for all undergraduates. Coed dorms, single-sex dorms, fraternity/sorority housing available. $150 fully refundable deposit, deadline 8/14. **Activities:** Pep band, campus ministries, choral groups, dance, drama, international student organizations, literary magazine, music ensembles, musical theater, student government, student newspaper, Disciples on Campus, PRIDE, Young Republicans, Campus Democrats, Catholic Salve Regina Newman Center, Campus Crusade for Christ, Black student union, Habitat for Humanity, Student Foundation, International Healthcare Development Program.

Athletics. NCAA. **Intercollegiate:** Baseball M, basketball, cross-country, diving, football (tackle) M, golf, soccer, softball W, swimming, tennis, track and field, volleyball W. **Intramural:** Badminton, basketball, bowling, football (non-tackle), golf, softball, swimming, table tennis, tennis, volleyball. **Team name:** Red Devils.

Student services. Adult student services, alcohol/substance abuse counseling, chaplain/spiritual director, career counseling, student employment services, financial aid counseling, health services, personal counseling, placement for graduates.

Contact. E-mail: admissions@eureka.edu
Phone: (309) 467-6350 Toll-free number: (888) 438-7352
Fax: (309) 467-6576
Kurt Krile, Dean of Admissions and Financial Aid, Eureka College, 300 East College Avenue, Eureka, IL 61530-1500

Governors State University
University Park, Illinois
www.govst.edu
CB code: 0807

▶ Public 4-year university
▶ Commuter campus in large town
▶ 3,526 degree-seeking undergraduates: 47% part-time, 66% women, 38% African American, 1% Asian American, 11% Hispanic/Latino, 2% Multiracial, non-Hispanic, 1% international
▶ 2,194 degree-seeking graduate students
▶ SAT or ACT (ACT writing optional) required

General. Founded in 1969. Regionally accredited. **Degrees:** 899 bachelor's awarded; master's, professional, doctoral offered. **Location:** 30 miles from Chicago. **Calendar:** Semester, extensive summer session. **Full-time faculty:** 222 total; 72% have terminal degrees, 33% minority, 61% women. **Part-time faculty:** 265 total; 20% have terminal degrees, 25% minority, 55% women. **Class size:** 60% < 20, 37% 20-39, 2% 40-49, less than 1% 50-99. **Special facilities:** 750-acre campus, nature trails, 6 small lakes, sculpture park, prairie restoration.

Freshman class profile. 1,114 applied, 433 admitted, 203 enrolled.

Mid 50% test scores		GPA 3.0-3.49:	24%
SAT critical reading:	460-570	GPA 2.0-2.99:	54%
SAT math:	400-500	Rank in top quarter:	33%
SAT writing:	430-450	Rank in top tenth:	14%
ACT composite:	17-21	Live on campus:	74%
GPA 3.75 or higher:	11%	International:	1%
GPA 3.50-3.74:	8%		

Basis for selection. Open admission, but selective for some programs. 60 semester hours or associate degree required. Additional special criteria for selected undergraduate majors. Special admissions for applicants not meeting stated requirements available by petition. Institutional examinations required of nursing applicants. ACT/PEP required of nursing applicants from diploma program.

High school preparation. 4 units required. Required units include English 3, mathematics 2, social studies 2, science 2 (laboratory 2) and foreign language 2.

2015-2016 Annual costs. Tuition/fees: $10,246; $18,406 out-of-state. Room only: $5,238. Books/supplies: $900. Personal expenses: $4,000. **Additional information:** Board plans are declining balance, so lower and higher balances are available and can be changed at any time.

2014-2015 Financial aid. Need-based: 41% of total undergraduate aid awarded as scholarships/grants, 59% as loans/jobs. **Non-need-based:** Scholarships awarded for academics.

Application procedures. Admission: Priority date 11/15; deadline 4/1. $25 fee, may be waived for applicants with need. Admission notification on a rolling basis beginning on or about 11/1. Must reply by May 1 or within 2 week(s) if notified thereafter. **Financial aid:** Priority date 5/1, closing date 10/1. FAFSA required. Applicants notified on a rolling basis starting 3/1; must reply within 2 week(s) of notification.

Academics. Special study options: Distance learning, double major, dual enrollment of high school students, ESL, honors, independent study, internships, student-designed major, study abroad, teacher certification program. Dual admission with several community colleges. **Credit/placement by examination:** AP, CLEP, IB, SAT, ACT, institutional tests. 60 credit hours maximum toward bachelor's degree.

Majors. Biology: General. **Business:** Accounting, business admin, management information systems. **Communications:** Broadcast journalism, communications/speech/rhetoric, journalism. **Computer sciences:** General, computer science. **Education:** Biology, chemistry, early childhood, elementary, English, mathematics. **English:** English lit. **Health services:** Health care admin, nursing (RN), speech pathology. **Human services:** General, social work. **Liberal arts:** Arts/sciences. **Math:** General. **Physical sciences:** Chemistry. **Protective services:** Criminal justice. **Psychology:** General. **Social sciences:** General. **Visual/performing arts:** Art.

Most popular majors. Business/marketing 16%, health sciences 19%, liberal arts 18%, psychology 12%, security/protective services 10%.

Technology on campus. 300 workstations in dormitories, library, computer center, student center. Dormitories wired for high-speed internet access and linked to campus network. Commuter students can connect to campus network. Online course registration, online library, helpline, wireless network available.

Student life. Policies: A minimum of seven students can seek chartering as a student club or organization through the Office of Student Life. All organizations must renew their charters each academic year. **Housing:** Coed dorms, apartments available. $200 fully refundable deposit. **Activities:** Choral groups, drama, international student organizations, literary magazine, musical theater, student government, student newspaper, Art Forum, Association of Latin American Students, Black Student Union, Chinese students association, Japanese philosophy, art and culture club, Spanish reading club, table tennis club, wellness club, over 30 co-curricular professional service organizations.

Athletics. Intercollegiate: Basketball, cross-country, golf. **Intramural:** Table tennis. **Team name:** Jaguars.

Student services. Adult student services, alcohol/substance abuse counseling, career counseling, services for economically disadvantaged, student employment services, financial aid counseling, minority student services, on-campus daycare, personal counseling, veterans' counselor. **Physically disabled:** Services for visually, speech, hearing impaired.

Contact. E-mail: admission@govst.edu
Phone: (708) 534-4490 Fax: (708) 534-1640
Yakeea Daniels, Director of Admissions, Governors State University, One University Parkway, University Park, IL 60484

Greenville College
Greenville, Illinois
www.greenville.edu   CB code: 1256

♦ Private 4-year liberal arts college affiliated with the Free Methodist Church of North America
♦ Residential campus in small town

♦ 1,042 degree-seeking undergraduates: 2% part-time, 51% women, 10% African American, 1% Asian American, 6% Hispanic/Latino, 1% Native American, 2% international
♦ 145 degree-seeking graduate students
♦ 72% of applicants admitted
♦ SAT or ACT (ACT writing recommended), application essay required
♦ 57% graduate within 6 years

General. Founded in 1892. Regionally accredited. Academic and Christian values emphasized. **Degrees:** 229 bachelor's awarded; master's offered. **Location:** 50 miles from St. Louis, 190 miles from Indianapolis. **Calendar:** 4-1-4, limited summer session. **Full-time faculty:** 60 total; 80% have terminal degrees, 12% minority, 33% women. **Part-time faculty:** 120 total; 17% have terminal degrees, 6% minority, 54% women. **Class size:** 59% < 20, 31% 20-39, 5% 40-49, 5% 50-99, less than 1% >100. **Special facilities:** Sculpture collection, Frank Lloyd Wright architectural drawings, 140 acre field station and nature preserve, observatory, environmental education center.

Freshman class profile. 568 applied, 410 admitted, 260 enrolled.

Mid 50% test scores			
SAT critical reading:	440-550	GPA 3.0-3.49:	27%
SAT math:	430-540	GPA 2.0-2.99:	27%
SAT writing:	410-520	Return as sophomores:	65%
ACT composite:	19-25	Out-of-state:	40%
GPA 3.75 or higher:	29%	Live on campus:	94%
GPA 3.50-3.74:	17%	International:	1%

Basis for selection. Secondary school record, standardized test scores, application essay, and religious affiliation or commitment very important. Extracurricular activities, talent/ability and character considered. SAT, ACT, SAT Subject Test scores must be received by institution's drop/add date. Interview required of academically weak applicants. Audition recommended for music majors. **Home schooled:** Transcript of courses and grades required.

High school preparation. College-preparatory program recommended. 11 units recommended. Recommended units include English 4, mathematics 2, science 2 (laboratory 1) and foreign language 2. Math recommendation includes algebra and geometry.

2015-2016 Annual costs. Tuition/fees: $25,088. Room/board: $8,288. Books/supplies: $250. Personal expenses: $1,564.

2014-2015 Financial aid. Need-based: 245 full-time freshmen applied for aid; 225 deemed to have need; 225 received aid. Average need met was 77%. Average scholarship/grant was $16,806; average loan $3,518. 68% of total undergraduate aid awarded as scholarships/grants, 32% as loans/jobs. **Non-need-based:** Awarded to 196 full-time undergraduates, including 56 freshmen. Scholarships awarded for academics, alumni affiliation, art, minority status, religious affiliation.

Application procedures. Admission: No deadline. $30 fee, may be waived for applicants with need, free for online applicants. Admission notification on a rolling basis beginning on or about 7/10. Housing deposit refundable prior to 5/1. **Financial aid:** Priority date 2/1; no closing date. FAFSA required. Applicants notified on a rolling basis starting 3/1.

Academics. Special study options: Accelerated study, combined bachelor's/graduate degree, cooperative education, cross-registration, distance learning, double major, dual enrollment of high school students, ESL, external degree, honors, independent study, internships, liberal arts/career combination, semester at sea, student-designed major, study abroad, teacher certification program, urban semester, Washington semester. **Credit/placement by examination:** AP, CLEP, IB, SAT, ACT, institutional tests. 32 credit hours maximum toward bachelor's degree. **Support services:** Learning center, reduced course load, remedial instruction, study skills assistance, tutoring.

Honors college/program. McAllester Scholars must have an ACT of 28.

Majors. Biology: General, environmental. **Business:** Accounting, business admin, management information systems, marketing, organizational behavior. **Communications:** Media studies, public relations. **Computer sciences:** General. **Education:** Biology, chemistry, elementary, English, history, mathematics, music, physical, physics, Spanish, special ed. **English:** English lit, rhetoric/composition. **Foreign languages:** Spanish. **Health services:** Predental, premedicine, prenursing, preveterinary. **History:** General. **Human services:** Social work. **Liberal arts:** Arts/sciences. **Math:** General. **Parks/recreation:** General, exercise sciences, sports admin. **Philosophy/religion:** Philosophy, religion. **Physical sciences:** Chemistry, physics. **Protective services:** Law enforcement admin. **Psychology:** General. **Social sciences:** Sociology. **Theology:** Pastoral counseling, youth ministry. **Visual/performing arts:** Art, music, music management.

Most popular majors. Biology 11%, business/marketing 24%, education 15%, visual/performing arts 7%.

Technology on campus. 75 workstations in library, computer center. Dormitories wired for high-speed internet access and linked to campus network. Commuter students can connect to campus network. Online library, helpline, repair service, wireless network available.

Student life. Freshman orientation: Mandatory. Preregistration for classes offered. **Policies:** Signed statements of Christian values and academic honesty requested. Required chapel. All single students not living at home must live in college housing. Religious observance required. **Housing:** Guaranteed on-campus for all undergraduates. Single-sex dorms, apartments, wellness housing available. $200 partly refundable deposit. Upper division students may live in college-owned houses. **Activities:** Bands, campus ministries, choral groups, drama, music ensembles, musical theater, radio station, student government, student newspaper, Habitat for Humanity, campus activities board, student outreach, Circle K, e-cafe, Mosaic, prison initiative, music and entertainment industry student association.

Athletics. NCAA, NCCAA. **Intercollegiate:** Baseball M, basketball, cross-country, football (tackle) M, soccer, softball W, tennis, track and field, volleyball. **Intramural:** Basketball, football (non tackle), soccer, volleyball. **Team name:** Panthers.

Student services. Adult student services, career counseling, student employment services, financial aid counseling, personal counseling, placement for graduates.

Contact. E-mail: admissions@greenville.edu
Phone: (618) 664-7100 Toll-free number: (800) 345-4440
Fax: (618) 664-9841
Karl Hatton, Dean of Admissions, Greenville College, 315 East College Avenue, Greenville, IL 62246

Hebrew Theological College
Skokie, Illinois
www.htc.edu   **CB code: 0817**

- Private 4-year liberal arts and rabbinical college affiliated with the Jewish faith
- Residential campus in small city
- 475 degree-seeking undergraduates
- 97% of applicants admitted
- SAT or ACT (ACT writing optional), application essay, interview required

General. Regionally accredited. Co-ed on separate campuses. Program designated as master's level is Rabbinic Ordination. **Degrees:** 46 bachelor's awarded; master's offered. **Location:** 15 miles from downtown. **Calendar:** Semester, limited summer session. **Full-time faculty:** 12 total. **Part-time faculty:** 42 total. **Class size:** 92% < 20, 8% 20-39.

Freshman class profile. 403 applied, 390 admitted, 351 enrolled.

Mid 50% test scores			
SAT critical reading:	490-600	SAT writing:	460-570
SAT math:	450-570	ACT composite:	19-25

Basis for selection. Admissions decisions are reached by reviewing academic records, assessment data, and application materials in conjunction with input from personal interviews and recommendations.

2015-2016 Annual costs. Tuition/fees: $11,430. Room/board: $10,390. Books/supplies: $1,400. Personal expenses: $2,685.

Application procedures. Admission: No deadline. $100 fee, may be waived for applicants with need. Application must be submitted on paper. Admission notification on a rolling basis.

Academics. Special study options: Combined bachelor's/graduate degree, distance learning, double major, dual enrollment of high school students, independent study, teacher certification program. **Credit/placement by examination:** AP, CLEP, institutional tests. 15 credit hours maximum toward bachelor's degree. **Support services:** Remedial instruction, tutoring, writing center.

Majors. Business: General, accounting. **Education:** Elementary, special ed. **English:** English lit. **Liberal arts:** Arts/sciences. **Philosophy/religion:** Judaic. **Psychology:** General.

Technology on campus. 30 workstations in library, computer center. Dormitories wired for high-speed internet access.

Student life. Freshman orientation: Mandatory. Preregistration for classes offered. **Policies:** Religious observance required. **Housing:** Guaranteed on-campus for all undergraduates. Single-sex dorms, apartments available.

Student services. Chaplain/spiritual director, career counseling, student employment services, financial aid counseling, personal counseling.

Contact. E-mail: admissions@htc.edu
Phone: (847) 982-2500 Fax: (847) 674-6381
Rabbi Joshua Zisook, Director of Admissions, Hebrew Theological College, 7135 North Carpenter Road, Skokie, IL 60077

Illinois College
Jacksonville, Illinois   **CB member**
www.ic.edu   **CB code: 1315**

- Private 4-year liberal arts college affiliated with the Presbyterian Church (USA)
- Residential campus in large town
- 942 degree-seeking undergraduates: 52% women, 12% African American, 1% Asian American, 10% Hispanic/Latino, 4% Multi-racial, non-Hispanic, 4% international
- 3 degree-seeking graduate students
- 61% of applicants admitted
- 70% graduate within 6 years

General. Founded in 1829. Regionally accredited. New England style quad and architecture. **Degrees:** 213 bachelor's awarded; master's offered. **Location:** 30 miles from Springfield, 90 miles from St. Louis. **Calendar:** Semester, limited summer session. **Full-time faculty:** 84 total; 83% have terminal degrees, 10% minority, 43% women. **Part-time faculty:** 20 total; 30% have terminal degrees, 5% minority, 50% women. **Class size:** 75% < 20, 23% 20-39, 2% 40-49. **Special facilities:** Biology station, observatory.

Freshman class profile. 2,431 applied, 1,471 admitted, 240 enrolled.

Mid 50% test scores			
SAT critical reading:	430-530	GPA 2.0-2.99:	16%
SAT math:	430-630	Rank in top quarter:	51%
SAT writing:	400-550	Rank in top tenth:	23%
ACT composite:	18-25	Return as sophomores:	79%
GPA 3.75 or higher:	35%	Out-of-state:	23%
GPA 3.50-3.74:	19%	Live on campus:	96%
GPA 3.0-3.49:	30%	International:	5%

Basis for selection. Core course GPA, rank in top half of class, test scores, 1 letter of recommendation from teacher, 1 letter of recommendation from guidance counselor important. Interview recommended, essay considered. **Home schooled:** Transcript of courses and grades, letter of recommendation (nonparent) required.

High school preparation. College-preparatory program recommended. 16 units required; 20 recommended. Required and recommended units include English 4, mathematics 3, social studies 1, history 1, science 2-3 (laboratory 2-3), foreign language 2 and academic electives 3.

2015-2016 Annual costs. Tuition/fees: $31,660. Room/board: $9,190. Personal expenses: $900.

2014-2015 Financial aid. Need-based: 240 full-time freshmen applied for aid; 222 deemed to have need; 222 received aid. Average need met was 87%. Average scholarship/grant was $22,274; average loan $4,416. 73% of total undergraduate aid awarded as scholarships/grants, 27% as loans/jobs. **Non-need-based:** Awarded to 256 full-time undergraduates, including 63 freshmen. Scholarships awarded for academics, art, music/drama.

Application procedures. Admission: Priority date 12/1; no deadline. No application fee. Admission notification on a rolling basis beginning on or about 9/1. Must reply by May 1 or within 2 week(s) if notified thereafter. **Financial aid:** Priority date 1/31; no closing date. FAFSA required. Applicants notified on a rolling basis starting 2/15; must reply within 2 week(s) of notification.

Academics. Special study options: Combined bachelor's/graduate degree, cross-registration, double major, dual enrollment of high school students, honors, independent study, internships, liberal arts/career combination, student-designed major, study abroad, teacher certification program, Washington semester. **Credit/placement by examination:** AP, CLEP, IB, SAT, ACT, institutional tests. 84 credit hours maximum toward bachelor's degree. **Support services:** Reduced course load, study skills assistance, tutoring, writing center.

Majors. Area/ethnic studies: American. **Biology:** General, environmental. **Business:** Accounting, finance, management information systems, managerial economics. **Computer sciences:** Computer science. **Education:** Early childhood, elementary, physical. **English:** English lit, rhetoric/composition. **Foreign languages:** French, German, Spanish. **History:** General. **Math:** General. **Philosophy/religion:** Philosophy, religion. **Physical sciences:** Chemistry, physics. **Psychology:** General. **Social sciences:** Economics, political science, sociology. **Visual/performing arts:** Art, dramatic, music, studio arts.

Most popular majors. Biology 21%, business/marketing 10%, English 8%, history 6%, interdisciplinary studies 15%, psychology 13%, social sciences 9%.

Technology on campus. 125 workstations in library, computer center. Dormitories wired for high-speed internet access and linked to campus network. Commuter students can connect to campus network. Online course registration, online library, helpline, repair service, student web hosting, wireless network available.

Student life. Freshman orientation: Mandatory. Preregistration for classes offered. Overnight program and several summer sessions are available. **Policies:** Student representation on faculty committees. **Housing:** Guaranteed on-campus for all undergraduates. Coed dorms, single-sex dorms, apartments, themed housing available. Honors housing available. **Activities:** Bands, campus ministries, choral groups, dance, drama, international student organizations, literary magazine, music ensembles, Model UN, radio station, student government, student newspaper, symphony orchestra, Young Republicans, Young Democrats, Alpha Phi Omega, men's and women's literary societies, debate club, Action Jacksonville.

Athletics. NCAA. **Intercollegiate:** Baseball M, basketball, cheerleading, cross-country, football (tackle) M, golf, soccer, softball W, tennis, track and field, volleyball W. **Intramural:** Basketball, cricket, football (non-tackle) M, handball, racquetball, softball, volleyball. **Team name:** Blueboys, Lady Blues.

Student services. Alcohol/substance abuse counseling, chaplain/spiritual director, career counseling, student employment services, financial aid counseling, health services, personal counseling, placement for graduates. **Physically disabled:** Services for visually, hearing impaired.

Contact. E-mail: admissions@mail.ic.edu
Phone: (217) 245-3030 Toll-free number: (866) 464-5265
Fax: (217) 245-3034
Barb Lundberg, Vice President for Enrollment, Illinois College, 1101 West College Avenue, Jacksonville, IL 62650

Illinois Institute of Art: Chicago
Chicago, Illinois
www.ilic.artinstitutes.edu   **CB code: 2908**

- For-profit 4-year visual arts college
- Commuter campus in very large city
- 1,807 undergraduates
- Application essay required

General. Founded in 1916. Regionally accredited; also accredited by ACCSC. Branch campus at Woodfield in Schaumburg. **Degrees:** 264 bachelor's, 92 associate awarded. **Calendar:** Semester. **Full-time faculty:** 76 total. **Part-time faculty:** 145 total. **Special facilities:** Computer graphics laboratories, exhibit galleries, incentive studio.

Basis for selection. Secondary school record, interview, and personal statement most important. SAT or ACT recommended for placement and evaluation. Portfolio required for advertising design, illustration, photography, fashion design, fashion illustration majors.

High school preparation. Recommended units include English 4, mathematics 3, social studies 2, science 3 and foreign language 1. Recommend art, interior design, drafting, fashion.

2015-2016 Annual costs. Books/supplies: $1,000. **Additional information:** Diploma programs: $23,334-$27,665, books and supplies $800-$950. Associate programs: $44,019-$46,802, books and supplies $1,500. Bachelor's programs: $87,489-$92,372, books and supplies $3,000.

Application procedures. Admission: No deadline. $150 fee. Admission notification on a rolling basis. **Financial aid:** Priority date 5/1; no closing date. FAFSA required. Applicants notified on a rolling basis.

Academics. Credit/placement by examination: AP, CLEP. **Support services:** Reduced course load.

Majors. Business: Fashion. **Communications:** Advertising. **Visual/performing arts:** Commercial/advertising art, fashion design, interior design.

Technology on campus. 25 workstations in computer center.

Student life. Activities: Student Positive Action Committee.

Contact. E-mail: antonj@aii.edu
Phone: (312) 280-3500 Toll-free number: (800) 351-3450
Janice Anton, Senior Director of Admissions, Illinois Institute of Art: Chicago, 350 North Orleans Street, Chicago, IL 60654

Illinois Institute of Art: Schaumburg
Schaumburg, Illinois
www.artinstitutes.edu/schaumburg   **CB code: 3043**

- For-profit 3-year visual arts and career college
- Commuter campus in small city
- 902 undergraduates
- Application essay, interview required

General. Regionally accredited; also accredited by ACCSC. **Degrees:** 196 bachelor's, 9 associate awarded. **Location:** 26 miles from Chicago. **Calendar:** Quarter, extensive summer session. **Full-time faculty:** 37 total. **Part-time faculty:** 48 total. **Special facilities:** Gallery, motion capture studio, lighting lab, sound lab, green room.

Basis for selection. Open admission. SAT or ACT recommended. Portfolios required for some majors. **Home schooled:** Transcript of courses and grades required.

2015-2016 Annual costs. Books/supplies: $987. Personal expenses: $2,628. **Additional information:** Associate programs: $43,620-$44,019, books and supplies $1,500. Bachelor's programs: $87,090-$88,584, books and supplies $3,000.

Financial aid. Non-need-based: Scholarships awarded for academics, art.

Application procedures. Admission: No deadline. $50 fee. Admission notification on a rolling basis. **Financial aid:** Priority date 3/1; no closing date. FAFSA required.

Academics. Special study options: Accelerated study, internships, liberal arts/career combination, study abroad. **Credit/placement by examination:** AP, CLEP. **Support services:** Learning center, pre-admission summer program, reduced course load, remedial instruction, study skills assistance, tutoring.

Majors. BACHELOR'S. Business: Fashion, hospitality admin, special products marketing. **Communications:** Advertising. **Communications technology:** Graphics, photo/film/video. **Computer sciences:** Webmaster. **Visual/performing arts:** General, art, commercial/advertising art, design, game design, interior design, multimedia. **ASSOCIATE. Communications technology:** Graphics. **Computer sciences:** Webmaster. **Visual/performing arts:** Design.

Student life. Freshman orientation: Mandatory. Preregistration for classes offered. Held the week before school begins. **Housing:** Single-sex dorms available. $200 deposit. Dormitory-style living in college-leased apartments available. **Activities:** Literary magazine, student government, student newspaper.

Student services. Adult student services, career counseling, student employment services, financial aid counseling, personal counseling, placement for graduates, veterans' counselor.

Contact. E-mail: ILISadmissions@aii.edu
Phone: (847) 619-3450 Toll-free number: (800) 314-3450
Fax: (847) 619-3064
Jamie Carson, Senior Director of Admissions, Illinois Institute of Art: Schaumburg, 1000 North Plaza Drive, Schaumburg, IL 60173

Illinois Institute of Technology
Chicago, Illinois   **CB member**
www.iit.edu   **CB code: 1318**

- Private 4-year university and engineering college
- Residential campus in very large city

- 2,923 degree-seeking undergraduates: 5% part-time, 30% women, 6% African American, 13% Asian American, 16% Hispanic/Latino, 2% Multi-racial, non-Hispanic, 26% international
- 4,685 degree-seeking graduate students
- 53% of applicants admitted
- SAT or ACT (ACT writing optional), application essay required
- 73% graduate within 6 years

General. Founded in 1890. Regionally accredited. **Degrees:** 587 bachelor's awarded; master's, professional, doctoral offered. **ROTC:** Army, Naval, Air Force. **Location:** 3 miles from downtown. **Calendar:** Semester, extensive summer session. **Full-time faculty:** 423 total; 95% have terminal degrees, 19% minority. **Part-time faculty:** 377 total; 22% minority. **Class size:** 54% < 20, 29% 20-39, 8% 40-49, 8% 50-99, 1% >100. **Special facilities:** Prototyping shop.

Freshman class profile. 4,403 applied, 2,321 admitted, 479 enrolled.

Mid 50% test scores		GPA 2.0-2.99:	2%
SAT critical reading:	520-640	Rank in top quarter:	77%
SAT math:	640-740	Rank in top tenth:	45%
SAT writing:	520-640	Return as sophomores:	92%
ACT composite:	25-31	Out-of-state:	25%
GPA 3.75 or higher:	40%	Live on campus:	73%
GPA 3.50-3.74:	30%	International:	20%
GPA 3.0-3.49:	28%		

Basis for selection. Admission decisions based on academic performance, strength of curriculum, test scores, counselor recommendations, and application essay. Class rank, interview, extracurricular activities, alumni relationship, volunteer and work experience also considered. Interview recommended. Portfolio optional for first-year freshmen entering College of Architecture. **Home schooled:** Statement describing home school structure and mission, letter of recommendation (nonparent) required.

High school preparation. College-preparatory program recommended. 15 units required; 19 recommended. Required and recommended units include English 4, mathematics 4, social studies 2, history 2, science 3 (laboratory 2), foreign language 2, computer science 1 and visual/performing arts 1. Technology and other courses recommended but not required.

2015-2016 Annual costs. Tuition/fees: $43,680. Room/board: $11,300. Books/supplies: $1,200. Personal expenses: $3,028.

2014-2015 Financial aid. Need-based: 309 full-time freshmen applied for aid; 283 deemed to have need; 283 received aid. Average need met was 83%. Average scholarship/grant was $32,136; average loan $3,657. 80% of total undergraduate aid awarded as scholarships/grants, 20% as loans/jobs. **Non-need-based:** Awarded to 1,214 full-time undergraduates, including 206 freshmen. Scholarships awarded for academics, alumni affiliation, leadership, ROTC.

Application procedures. Admission: Priority date 12/1; deadline 8/1. No application fee. Application must be submitted online. Admission notification on a rolling basis beginning on or about 10/1. 2 weeks if communicated with admission. **Financial aid:** Priority date 2/1; no closing date. FAFSA required. Applicants notified on a rolling basis starting 3/1.

Academics. Interprofessional Projects Program provides team-based learning environment in which students from various concentrations and disciplines work together to solve real-world problems. Research opportunities for undergraduates in science, engineering, technology and mathematics. **Special study options:** Combined bachelor's/graduate degree, cooperative education, cross-registration, distance learning, double major, ESL, independent study, internships, liberal arts/career combination, study abroad, teacher certification program. Joint enrollment at 2 institutions. **Credit/placement by examination:** AP, CLEP, IB, SAT, ACT, institutional tests. 18 credit hours maximum toward bachelor's degree. No limit for advanced placement credit. **Support services:** Learning center, study skills assistance, tutoring, writing center.

Majors. Architecture: Architecture. **Biology:** General, biochemistry, biophysics. **Business:** Business admin, operations. **Communications:** Journalism, technical/scientific. **Computer sciences:** General, computer science, information technology, web page design. **Education:** Physics. **Engineering:** Aerospace, applied physics, architectural, biomedical, chemical, civil, computer, electrical, materials, mechanical. **Health services:** Prepharmacy. **Liberal arts:** Arts/sciences. **Math:** Applied. **Physical sciences:** Chemistry, physics. **Psychology:** General. **Social sciences:** General, political science, sociology.

Most popular majors. Architecture 17%, computer/information sciences 13%, engineering/engineering technologies 51%.

Technology on campus. 500 workstations in dormitories, library, computer center, student center. Dormitories wired for high-speed internet access and linked to campus network. Online course registration, online library, helpline, student web hosting, wireless network available.

Student life. Freshman orientation: Mandatory, $150 fee. Preregistration for classes offered. Five summer sessions. Welcome Week held prior to start of classes. **Policies:** Student organizations register each semester, are nondiscriminatory and prohibit hazing. **Housing:** Guaranteed on-campus for all undergraduates. Coed dorms, apartments, fraternity/sorority housing available. Men's/women's floors in residence halls available. **Activities:** Concert band, campus ministries, choral groups, dance, drama, film society, international student organizations, literary magazine, music ensembles, musical theater, radio station, student government, student newspaper, TV station, Red Cross club, Engineers Without Borders, Greek Council, Haiti Outreach, InterVarsity Christian Fellowship, Latinos Involved in Further Education, National Society of Black Engineers, Society of Women Engineers, Union Board.

Athletics. NAIA. **Intercollegiate:** Baseball M, cross-country, diving, soccer, swimming, volleyball W. **Intramural:** Badminton, basketball, bowling, field hockey, football (non-tackle), racquetball, soccer, softball, squash, table tennis, ultimate frisbee, volleyball, wrestling. **Team name:** Scarlet Hawks.

Student services. Alcohol/substance abuse counseling, career counseling, student employment services, financial aid counseling, health services, legal services, minority student services, personal counseling, placement for graduates, women's services. **Physically disabled:** Services for visually, hearing impaired.

Contact. E-mail: admission@iit.edu
Phone: (312) 567-3025 Toll-free number: (800) 448-2329
Fax: (312) 567-6939
Alfred Nunez, Director of Undergraduate Admission, Illinois Institute of Technology, 10 West 33rd Street, Chicago, IL 60616-3793

Illinois State University
Normal, Illinois **CB member**
www.ilstu.edu **CB code: 1319**

- Public 4-year university
- Residential campus in small city
- 18,343 degree-seeking undergraduates: 7% part-time, 55% women, 8% African American, 2% Asian American, 9% Hispanic/Latino, 3% Multi-racial, non-Hispanic
- 2,182 degree-seeking graduate students
- 80% of applicants admitted
- SAT or ACT (ACT writing optional) required
- 73% graduate within 6 years; 18% enter graduate study

General. Founded in 1857. Regionally accredited. **Degrees:** 4,322 bachelor's awarded; master's, professional, doctoral offered. **ROTC:** Army. **Location:** 132 miles from Chicago, 168 miles from St. Louis. **Calendar:** Semester, limited summer session. **Full-time faculty:** 877 total; 82% have terminal degrees, 15% minority, 51% women. **Part-time faculty:** 387 total; 28% have terminal degrees, 7% minority, 64% women. **Class size:** 35% < 20, 51% 20-39, 4% 40-49, 6% 50-99, 4% >100. **Special facilities:** 610-acre farm, horticulture center, planetarium, museum of nations, laboratory school, university galleries.

Freshman class profile. 13,323 applied, 10,642 admitted, 3,630 enrolled.

Mid 50% test scores		Return as sophomores:	82%
ACT composite:	21-26	Out-of-state:	3%
GPA 3.75 or higher:	25%	Live on campus:	97%
GPA 3.50-3.74:	16%	Fraternities:	9%
GPA 3.0-3.49:	35%	Sororities:	22%
GPA 2.0-2.99:	24%		

Basis for selection. School achievement record and test scores most important. Auditions and portfolio review may be required for some majors in the College of Fine Arts.

High school preparation. College-preparatory program recommended. 15 units required. Required units include English 4, mathematics 3, social studies 2, science 2 (laboratory 2), foreign language 2 and academic electives 2. 2 units required in foreign language and/or fine arts.

2016-2017 Annual costs. Tuition/fees (projected): $13,666; $21,482 out-of-state. Room/board: $9,850. Books/supplies: $991. Personal expenses: $3,010.

Financial aid. Non-need-based: Scholarships awarded for academics, alumni affiliation, art, athletics, leadership, music/drama, ROTC.

Application procedures. Admission: Priority date 11/15; deadline 4/1 (receipt date). $50 fee, may be waived for applicants with need. Admission notification on a rolling basis beginning on or about 9/1. Must reply by 5/1. **Financial aid:** Priority date 3/1; no closing date. FAFSA required. Applicants notified on a rolling basis starting 4/1; must reply within 2 week(s) of notification.

Academics. Special study options: Accelerated study, combined bachelor's/graduate degree, cooperative education, distance learning, double major, dual enrollment of high school students, ESL, exchange student, honors, independent study, internships, student-designed major, study abroad, teacher certification program. **Credit/placement by examination:** AP, CLEP, SAT, ACT, institutional tests. 39 credit hours maximum toward associate degree, 18 toward bachelor's. Credit earned through CLEP shall count toward general education and graduation requirements only. A student may not use CLEP to raise grades or remove failures in courses already taken. All credit for CLEP shall be considered credit at the 100-level. **Support services:** Learning center, remedial instruction, study skills assistance, tutoring, writing center.

Majors. Biology: General, biochemistry, cellular/molecular. **Business:** Accounting, business admin, construction management, finance, insurance, international, management information systems, management science, marketing. **Communications:** Communications/speech/rhetoric, journalism, media studies, public relations. **Communications technology:** Graphics. **Computer sciences:** Computer science, information technology, networking. **Education:** Business, elementary, health, kindergarten/preschool, middle, music, physical, social studies, special ed, technology/industrial arts. **English:** English lit. **Foreign languages:** French, German, Spanish. **Health services:** Athletic training, audiology/speech pathology, clinical lab science, environmental health, health information management, nursing (RN), occupational health. **History:** General. **Human services:** Social work. **Liberal arts:** Arts/sciences. **Math:** General. **Parks/recreation:** Exercise sciences, facilities management. **Philosophy/religion:** Philosophy. **Physical sciences:** Chemistry, geology, physics. **Protective services:** Criminal justice. **Psychology:** General. **Social sciences:** Anthropology, economics, geography, political science, sociology. **Visual/performing arts:** Art, dramatic, music, music performance, studio arts. **Work/family studies:** General.

Most popular majors. Business/marketing 19%, communications/journalism 6%, education 15%, health sciences 9%, social sciences 6%.

Technology on campus. PC or laptop required. 2,445 workstations in dormitories, library, computer center, student center. Dormitories wired for high-speed internet access and linked to campus network. Commuter students can connect to campus network. Online course registration, online library, helpline, repair service, student web hosting, wireless network available.

Student life. Freshman orientation: Mandatory, $50 fee. Preregistration for classes offered. Two-day sessions held each week from mid-June to end of July. **Housing:** Guaranteed on-campus for freshmen. Coed dorms, special housing for disabled, apartments, fraternity/sorority housing, themed housing, wellness housing available. $300 nonrefundable deposit. **Activities:** Bands, campus ministries, choral groups, dance, drama, film society, international student organizations, literary magazine, music ensembles, Model UN, musical theater, opera, radio station, student government, student newspaper, symphony orchestra, TV station, more than 300 student organizations.

Athletics. NCAA. **Intercollegiate:** Baseball M, basketball, cross-country, diving W, football (tackle) M, golf, gymnastics W, soccer W, softball W, swimming W, tennis, track and field, volleyball W. **Intramural:** Badminton, basketball, football (non-tackle), golf, handball, soccer, softball, tennis, ultimate frisbee, volleyball. **Team name:** Redbirds.

Student services. Adult student services, alcohol/substance abuse counseling, career counseling, services for economically disadvantaged, student employment services, financial aid counseling, health services, legal services, minority student services, on-campus daycare, personal counseling, placement for graduates, veterans' counselor, women's services. **Physically disabled:** Services for visually, speech, hearing impaired.

Contact. E-mail: admissions@ilstu.edu
Phone: (309) 438-2181 Toll-free number: (800) 366-2478
Fax: (309) 438-3932
Jeff Mavros, Director of Admissions, Illinois State University, Campus Box 2200, Normal, IL 61790-2200

Illinois Wesleyan University

Bloomington, Illinois   **CB member**
www.iwu.edu   **CB code: 1320**

◗ Private 4-year university and liberal arts college
◗ Residential campus in small city

◗ 1,834 degree-seeking undergraduates: 1% part-time, 56% women, 4% African American, 4% Asian American, 7% Hispanic/Latino, 3% Multiracial, non-Hispanic, 9% international
◗ 62% of applicants admitted
◗ SAT or ACT (ACT writing optional), application essay required

General. Founded in 1850. Regionally accredited. The nearly $16 million 48,700-square-foot classroom facility State Farm Hall opened for classes in the fall of 2013. **Degrees:** 425 bachelor's awarded. **ROTC:** Army. **Location:** 125 miles from Chicago, 165 miles from St. Louis. **Calendar:** Semester. **Full-time faculty:** 150 total; 95% have terminal degrees, 9% minority, 43% women. **Part-time faculty:** 63 total; 51% have terminal degrees, 10% minority, 64% women. **Class size:** 65% < 20, 31% 20-39, 3% 40-49, less than 1% 50-99, less than 1% >100. **Special facilities:** Observatory, natural sciences research labs, computerized music lab, social science research lab, visual anthropology lab, student-managed real-dollar investment portfolio program, nursing lab, lab theatre producing original works by undergraduates, Action Research Center (supporting community-based student research for academic credit).

Freshman class profile. 3,744 applied, 2,318 admitted, 450 enrolled.

Mid 50% test scores		
SAT critical reading:	490-620	
SAT math:	660-760	
ACT composite:	25-32	
Rank in top quarter:	69%	
Rank in top tenth:	34%	
End year in good standing:	93%	

Return as sophomores:	93%
Out-of-state:	16%
Live on campus:	100%
International:	9%
Fraternities:	25%
Sororities:	32%

Basis for selection. Test scores, class rank, high school record, and essay or personal statement most important. Interview strongly recommended. Audition required for bachelor of music or BFA in theater or music theater. Portfolio review required for BFA in art. **Home schooled:** Transcript of courses and grades required. **Learning Disabled:** Students welcome to submit information on learning disabilities as part of application review process.

High school preparation. College-preparatory program recommended. 15 units recommended. Recommended units include English 4, mathematics 3, social studies 2, science 3 (laboratory 2) and foreign language 3. Biology and chemistry are required for admission to nursing and biology.

2015-2016 Annual costs. Tuition/fees: $42,490. Room/board: $9,796. Books/supplies: $800. Personal expenses: $1,600.

2015-2016 Financial aid. Need-based: 389 full-time freshmen applied for aid; 300 deemed to have need; 300 received aid. Average need met was 87%. Average scholarship/grant was $26,251; average loan $4,318. 80% of total undergraduate aid awarded as scholarships/grants, 20% as loans/jobs. **Non-need-based:** Awarded to 736 full-time undergraduates, including 191 freshmen. Scholarships awarded for academics, art, music/drama.

Application procedures. Admission: No deadline. No application fee. Admission notification on a rolling basis beginning on or about 1/15. Must reply by May 1 or within 2 week(s) if notified thereafter. **Financial aid:** Priority date 3/1; no closing date. FAFSA, institutional form required. Applicants notified on a rolling basis starting 3/1; must reply by 5/1.

Academics. Optional 3-week May Term provides opportunities for students to pursue experimental courses, travel courses, internships, or independent research projects. Fall Term in London and Spring Term in Madrid led by Illinois Wesleyan faculty members where students may earn General Education credit during these terms. **Special study options:** Combined bachelor's/graduate degree, double major, exchange student, honors, independent study, internships, New York semester, student-designed major, study abroad, teacher certification program, United Nations semester, urban semester, Washington semester. 3-2 cooperative program in engineering with Washington University, Case Western Reserve University, and Northwestern University; 3-2 program in forestry and environmental management with Duke University; 3-2 program in occupational therapy with Washington University, 2-2 program in engineering with the University of Illinois, and a nonguaranteed cooperative program in engineering with Dartmouth College. **Credit/placement by examination:** AP, CLEP, IB, institutional tests. 32 credit hours maximum toward bachelor's degree. Limit of 16 hours (equivalent to four courses) may count toward general education credit. Up to 16 additional hours (equivalent to four courses) can be awarded as elective credit. **Support services:** Reduced course load, study skills assistance, tutoring, writing center.

Majors. Area/ethnic studies: African, American, Asian, Latin American, Russian/Eastern European/Eurasian, Western European, women's. **Biology:** General. **Business:** Accounting, business admin, insurance, international. **Computer sciences:** General. **Conservation:** Environmental studies. **Education:** General, biology, chemistry, elementary, English, French, history, mathematics, music, physics, Spanish. **English:** English lit. **Foreign languages:** Classics, French, German, Spanish. **Health services:** Nursing (RN). **History:** General. **Math:** General. **Philosophy/religion:** Philosophy, religion. **Physical**

sciences: Chemistry, physics. **Psychology:** General. **Social sciences:** Anthropology, economics, political science, sociology. **Visual/performing arts:** Acting, art, dramatic, music, music performance, music theory/composition, musical theater, piano/keyboard, stringed instruments, theater design, voice/opera.

Most popular majors. Biology 8%, business/marketing 23%, health sciences 7%, psychology 11%, social sciences 10%, visual/performing arts 9%.

Technology on campus. 400 workstations in dormitories, library, computer center, student center. Dormitories wired for high-speed internet access and linked to campus network. Commuter students can connect to campus network. Online course registration, online library, helpline, repair service, student web hosting, wireless network available.

Student life. Freshman orientation: Mandatory. Preregistration for classes offered. Held 5-6 days prior to start of classes. **Policies:** No smoking permitted in residence halls. Beer and wine permitted in designated areas for students of legal age. **Housing:** Guaranteed on-campus for freshmen. Coed dorms, special housing for disabled, apartments, fraternity/sorority housing available. Groups of students with common curricular or co-curricular interests are able to propose and implement theme housing communities. **Activities:** Bands, campus ministries, choral groups, dance, drama, film society, international student organizations, literary magazine, music ensembles, Model UN, musical theater, opera, radio station, student government, student newspaper, symphony orchestra, TV station, black student union, InterVarsity Christian Fellowship, Alpha Phi Omega, Council of Latin American Student Enrichment, Habitat for Humanity, several environmental concerns organizations, Amnesty International, Pan-Asian student association, College Democrats, College Republicans.

Athletics. NCAA. **Intercollegiate:** Baseball M, basketball, cross-country, diving, football (tackle) M, golf, lacrosse, soccer, softball W, swimming, tennis, track and field, volleyball W. **Intramural:** Badminton, basketball, football (non-tackle), golf, soccer, softball, tennis, volleyball. **Team name:** Titans.

Student services. Alcohol/substance abuse counseling, chaplain/spiritual director, career counseling, student employment services, financial aid counseling, health services, minority student services, personal counseling, placement for graduates. **Physically disabled:** Services for visually, speech, hearing impaired.

Contact. E-mail: iwuadmit@iwu.edu
Phone: (309) 556-3031 Toll-free number: (800) 332-2498
Fax: (309) 556-3820
Bob Geraty, Dean of Admissions, Illinois Wesleyan University, PO Box 2900, Bloomington, IL 61702-2900

International Academy of Design and Technology: Chicago
Chicago, Illinois
www.iadtchicago.edu   **CB code: 3363**

- For-profit 4-year visual arts and technical college
- Commuter campus in very large city
- 229 undergraduates
- Interview required

General. Founded in 1977. Accredited by ACICS. **Degrees:** 67 bachelor's, 8 associate awarded. **Location:** Downtown. **Calendar:** Quarter, extensive summer session. **Full-time faculty:** 14 total. **Part-time faculty:** 99 total. **Class size:** 53% < 20, 44% 20-39, 3% 40-49.

Basis for selection. Open admission. **Home schooled:** Transcript of courses and grades required. Should be registered with state or accrediting agency.

2015-2016 Annual costs. Associate degree program tuition $38,400. Bachelor's degree program tuition $72,000. Books included in tuition. Application fee $50.

Financial aid. All financial aid based on need. **Additional information:** College work study programs available to day and evening students.

Application procedures. Admission: No deadline. $20 fee. Admission notification on a rolling basis. **Financial aid:** No deadline. FAFSA required. Applicants notified on a rolling basis.

Academics. Special study options: Distance learning, independent study, internships, study abroad, weekend college. **Credit/placement by examination:** AP, CLEP, IB, institutional tests. 40 credit hours maximum toward

associate degree, 100 toward bachelor's. **Support services:** Learning center, reduced course load, remedial instruction, study skills assistance, tutoring.

Majors. Business: Fashion. **Communications technology:** Animation/special effects. **Computer sciences:** Information technology. **Protective services:** Computer forensics. **Visual/performing arts:** Commercial/advertising art, fashion design, game design, graphic design, interior design.

Most popular majors. Business/marketing 31%, communication technologies 14%, visual/performing arts 53%.

Technology on campus. 386 workstations in library, computer center, student center. Online course registration, online library, wireless network available.

Student life. Freshman orientation: Mandatory. Preregistration for classes offered. **Activities:** Student newspaper, Fashion Council, merchandising management club, information technology club, video and animation club, Omega Pi Delta, International Interior Design Association, graphic design club, international club, chess club, movie club.

Student services. Adult student services, career counseling, student employment services, financial aid counseling, personal counseling, placement for graduates, veterans' counselor. **Physically disabled:** Services for visually impaired.

Contact. Phone: (312) 980-9200 Toll-free number: (877) 222-3369
Fax: (312) 541-3929
Ernest Cochran, Vice President of Admissions, International Academy of Design and Technology: Chicago, One North State Street, Suite 500, Chicago, IL 60602

ITT Technical Institute: Arlington Heights
Arlington Heights, Illinois
www.itt-tech.edu   **CB code: 4271**

- For-profit 4-year technical college
- Commuter campus in small city
- 248 undergraduates
- Interview required

General. Founded in 1986. Accredited by ACICS. **Degrees:** 11 bachelor's, 67 associate awarded. **Location:** 20 miles from Chicago. **Calendar:** Quarter, extensive summer session. **Full-time faculty:** 10 total. **Part-time faculty:** 45 total.

Basis for selection. Satisfactory scores required on English and math tests.

2015-2016 Annual costs. Per-credit-hour charge, $493, will vary depending on program level and course of study. Academic fee, $200. Some programs require purchase of tools, which could cost an additional $500. All costs subject to change.

Application procedures. Admission: No deadline. No application fee. Admission notification on a rolling basis. **Financial aid:** No deadline. FAFSA, institutional form required. Applicants notified on a rolling basis.

Academics. Credit/placement by examination: AP, CLEP, institutional tests. **Support services:** Learning center, tutoring.

Majors. Business: Construction management, e-commerce, retail management. **Computer sciences:** Security. **Protective services:** Law enforcement admin. **Visual/performing arts:** Game design.

Technology on campus. Online library available.

Student life. Freshman orientation: Available. Preregistration for classes offered.

Student services. Career counseling, student employment services.

Contact. Phone: (847) 454-1800
Cesar Rodriguez, Director of Recruitment, ITT Technical Institute: Arlington Heights, 3800 North Wilke Road, Arlington Heights, IL 60004

Judson University
Elgin, Illinois
www.judsonu.edu   **CB code: 1351**

- Private 4-year university and liberal arts college affiliated with the American Baptist Churches in the USA
- Residential campus in small city

- 1,077 degree-seeking undergraduates: 32% part-time, 59% women, 8% African American, 2% Asian American, 16% Hispanic/Latino, 1% Multiracial, non-Hispanic, 3% international
- 161 degree-seeking graduate students
- 52% graduate within 6 years

General. Founded in 1963. Regionally accredited. **Degrees:** 239 bachelor's awarded; master's, doctoral offered. **ROTC:** Army. **Location:** 40 miles from Chicago. **Calendar:** Continuous, limited summer session. **Full-time faculty:** 64 total; 88% have terminal degrees, 16% minority, 47% women. **Part-time faculty:** 117 total; 25% minority, 46% women. **Class size:** 74% < 20, 23% 20-39, 2% 40-49, less than 1% 50-99. **Special facilities:** Gold LEED certified academic center.

Freshman class profile. 653 applied, 461 admitted, 156 enrolled.

Mid 50% test scores			
		GPA 2.0-2.99:	16%
SAT critical reading:	520-570	Rank in top quarter:	44%
SAT math:	450-590	Rank in top tenth:	22%
ACT composite:	21-26	End year in good standing:	80%
GPA 3.75 or higher:	33%	Return as sophomores:	73%
GPA 3.50-3.74:	19%	Out-of-state:	29%
GPA 3.0-3.49:	32%	Live on campus:	79%

Basis for selection. Open admission, but selective for some programs. School achievement record, class rank, and test scores are important. Audition recommended for performing arts majors. Portfolio recommended for art majors. Essay required for architecture majors. **Home schooled:** Transcript of courses and grades required. **Learning Disabled:** Students need documentation, including medical, when requesting services.

High school preparation. College-preparatory program recommended. Recommended units include English 4, mathematics 3, social studies 2, science 2 (laboratory 2).

2016-2017 Annual costs. Tuition/fees (projected): $28,700. Room/board: $9,650. Books/supplies: $1,300. Personal expenses: $1,500.

2015-2016 Financial aid. Need-based: 171 full-time freshmen applied for aid; 160 deemed to have need; 160 received aid. Average need met was 68%. Average scholarship/grant was $10,414; average loan $4,317. 68% of total undergraduate aid awarded as scholarships/grants, 32% as loans/jobs. **Non-need-based:** Awarded to 910 full-time undergraduates, including 108 freshmen. Scholarships awarded for academics, alumni affiliation, art, athletics, leadership, music/drama, religious affiliation.

Application procedures. Admission: No deadline. $50 fee, may be waived for applicants with need. Admission notification on a rolling basis beginning on or about 10/1. **Financial aid:** Priority date 2/15, closing date 5/1. FAFSA required. Applicants notified on a rolling basis starting 3/1; must reply by 5/1 or within 4 week(s) of notification.

Academics. Special study options: Accelerated study, distance learning, double major, honors, independent study, internships, student-designed major, study abroad, teacher certification program, urban semester, Washington semester. **Credit/placement by examination:** AP, CLEP, IB, institutional tests. 30 credit hours maximum toward bachelor's degree. **Support services:** Learning center, reduced course load, remedial instruction, study skills assistance, tutoring, writing center.

Majors. Architecture: Architecture. **Biology:** General, biochemistry. **Business:** Accounting, business admin, human resources, marketing. **Communications:** Communications/speech/rhetoric, organizational. **Conservation:** Environmental studies. **Education:** Early childhood, early childhood special, elementary, learning disabled, physical, secondary. **English:** English lit. **History:** General. **Math:** General. **Parks/recreation:** Sports admin. **Physical sciences:** Chemistry. **Protective services:** Criminal justice. **Psychology:** General, applied. **Social sciences:** Sociology. **Theology:** Bible, lay ministry, sacred music, theology, youth ministry. **Visual/performing arts:** Art, arts management, film/cinema/video, graphic design, interior design, music management, music performance, photography, play/screenwriting, studio arts.

Most popular majors. Architecture 9%, business/marketing 33%, communications/journalism 9%, psychology 7%, public administration/social services 9%, theological studies 7%, visual/performing arts 6%.

Technology on campus. 150 workstations in dormitories, library, computer center, student center. Dormitories wired for high-speed internet access and linked to campus network. Commuter students can connect to campus network. Online course registration, online library, helpline, wireless network available.

Student life. Freshman orientation: Mandatory. Preregistration for classes offered. **Policies:** Chapel services held 3 mornings a week. Religious observance required. **Housing:** Guaranteed on-campus for all undergraduates. Coed dorms, single-sex dorms, special housing for disabled, apartments,

wellness housing available. $150 fully refundable deposit. **Activities:** Concert band, campus ministries, choral groups, drama, international student organizations, music ensembles, musical theater, student government, symphony orchestra, Judson Student Organization, University Ministries, B.A.S.I.C. (Brothers and Sisters in Christ), Fellowship of Christian Athletes, International Justice Mission-Judson Chapter, Student Sustainability Committee.

Athletics. NAIA, NCCAA. **Intercollegiate:** Baseball M, basketball, bowling, cheerleading, cross-country, golf, lacrosse M, soccer, softball W, tennis, track and field, volleyball W. **Intramural:** Basketball, football (tackle), soccer, volleyball. **Team name:** Eagles.

Student services. Adult student services, chaplain/spiritual director, career counseling, student employment services, financial aid counseling, health services, personal counseling, placement for graduates. **Physically disabled:** Services for visually, speech, hearing impaired.

Contact. E-mail: admissions@judsonu.edu
Phone: (847) 628-2510 Toll-free number: (800) 879-5376
Fax: (847) 628-2526
Nathan McNeely, Director of Admissions, Judson University, 1151 North State Street, Elgin, IL 60123-1404

Kendall College
Chicago, Illinois
www.kendall.edu   CB code: 1366

- For-profit 4-year culinary school and teachers college
- Commuter campus in very large city
- 1,516 undergraduates
- Application essay, interview required

General. Founded in 1934. Regionally accredited. Internships required in every major. **Degrees:** 289 bachelor's, 120 associate awarded. **Location:** Downtown. **Calendar:** Quarter, extensive summer session. **Full-time faculty:** 42 total. **Part-time faculty:** 125 total. **Class size:** 60% < 20, 40% 20-39.

Basis for selection. High school record most important, followed by test scores, class rank, recommendations and interview. Placement test required of all incoming students. SAT or ACT recommended.

High school preparation. Recommended units include English 4, mathematics 2, social studies 2, science 2 and foreign language 2. Specific academic units required for certain majors.

2015-2016 Annual costs. Tuition/fees: $25,248. Room only: $10,350. Books/supplies: $1,800. **Additional information:** Tuition and fees quoted are for School of Culinary Arts.

Financial aid. Non-need-based: Scholarships awarded for academics, alumni affiliation, job skills.

Application procedures. Admission: No deadline. $50 fee, may be waived for applicants with need. Admission notification on a rolling basis. Must reply by May 1 or within 4 week(s) if notified thereafter. **Financial aid:** Priority date 4/15; no closing date. FAFSA required. Applicants notified on a rolling basis starting 1/1; must reply within 2 week(s) of notification.

Academics. Special study options: Accelerated study, combined bachelor's/graduate degree, distance learning, internships, study abroad, teacher certification program. Hybrid coursework. **Credit/placement by examination:** AP, CLEP, IB, institutional tests. 24 credit hours maximum toward associate degree, 48 toward bachelor's. **Support services:** Learning center, reduced course load, remedial instruction, study skills assistance, tutoring, writing center.

Majors. Business: Business admin, hospitality admin. **Education:** Early childhood.

Most popular majors. Business/marketing 41%, education 50%, personal/culinary services 9%.

Technology on campus. 45 workstations in library, computer center, student center. Dormitories wired for high-speed internet access and linked to campus network. Commuter students can connect to campus network. Online course registration, online library, helpline, wireless network available.

Student life. Freshman orientation: Mandatory. Preregistration for classes offered. One-day event held 1 week before start of quarter. **Policies:** Visible photo IDs required on campus at all times. **Housing:** Coed dorms, wellness housing available. $350 nonrefundable deposit. **Activities:** International student organizations, student government, National Society for Minorities in Hospitality, black student union, Latinos Juntos, Kendall HOPE, Kendall Pride.

Athletics. Team name: The Viking.

Student services. Adult student services, career counseling, student employment services, financial aid counseling, personal counseling, placement for graduates.

Contact. E-mail: kendalladmissions@kendall.edu
Phone: (312) 752-2020 Toll-free number: (866) 667-3344
Fax: (312) 752-2021
Jeanette Konieczka, Admissions Manager, Kendall College, 900 N. North Branch Street, Chicago, IL 60642-4278

Knox College
Galesburg, Illinois
www.knox.edu

CB member
CB code: 1372

- Private 4-year liberal arts college
- Residential campus in large town
- 1,374 degree-seeking undergraduates: 1% part-time, 59% women, 8% African American, 6% Asian American, 14% Hispanic/Latino, 3% Multiracial, non-Hispanic, 12% international
- 64% of applicants admitted
- Application essay required
- 77% graduate within 6 years; 23% enter graduate study

General. Founded in 1837. Regionally accredited. **Degrees:** 316 bachelor's awarded. **Location:** 200 miles from Chicago, 200 miles from St. Louis. **Calendar:** Trimester. **Full-time faculty:** 115 total; 95% have terminal degrees, 16% minority, 43% women. **Part-time faculty:** 27 total; 33% have terminal degrees, 15% minority, 41% women. **Class size:** 71% < 20, 28% 20-39, less than 1% 40-49, less than 1% 50-99. **Special facilities:** Biological field station, farm with two high tunnels, historic landmark site of the 1858 Lincoln-Douglas Debates.

Freshman class profile. 3,445 applied, 2,198 admitted, 387 enrolled.

Mid 50% test scores			
SAT critical reading:	580-630	**Rank in top tenth:**	34%
SAT math:	590-660	**End year in good standing:**	83%
SAT writing:	580-630	**Return as sophomores:**	83%
ACT composite:	23-29	**Out-of-state:**	48%
Rank in top quarter:	67%	**Live on campus:**	98%
		International:	14%

Basis for selection. Primary emphasis placed on rigor of high school courses, grades, writing abilities, and personal qualities. Preparation of the application, recommendations, and interviews are particularly helpful in identifying personal qualities. Class rank, extracurricular activities, special skills, and talents also considered. Preference given to students who have taken advantage of academic opportunities offered by high school, including honors, Advanced Placement, International Baccalaureate and/or college level courses. SAT or ACT recommended. Interviews are strongly recommended; auditions or portfolios required for scholarships in arts and writing. **Home schooled:** Statement describing home school structure and mission, transcript of courses and grades, interview required. Applicants should provide detailed documentation of coursework completed, including course syllabi as appropriate. SAT/ACT required. Interviews strongly recommended. **Learning Disabled:** Students with learning disabilities who require accommodations may submit documentation for evaluation by the Center for Teaching and Learning. This evaluation is for informational purposes only and not used in conjunction with admission.

High school preparation. College-preparatory program required. 20 units recommended. Recommended units include English 4, mathematics 4, social studies 2, history 2, science 4 (laboratory 2), foreign language 3 and academic electives 1.

2015-2016 Annual costs. Tuition/fees: $41,847. Room/board: $9,012. Books/supplies: $900.

2015-2016 Financial aid. Need-based: 347 full-time freshmen applied for aid; 316 deemed to have need; 316 received aid. Average need met was 91%. Average scholarship/grant was $32,565; average loan $4,892. 82% of total undergraduate aid awarded as scholarships/grants, 18% as loans/jobs. **Non-need-based:** Awarded to 385 full-time undergraduates, including 100 freshmen. Scholarships awarded for academics, art, leadership, music/drama.

Application procedures. Admission: Closing date 1/15 (postmark date). $50 fee, may be waived for applicants with need. Application must be submitted online. Admission notification by 3/30. Must reply by May 1 or within 2 week(s) if notified thereafter. **Financial aid:** Priority date 2/1; no closing date. FAFSA, institutional form required. Applicants notified on a rolling basis starting 2/15; must reply by 5/1.

Academics. Clinical Psychology Term, Green Oaks Term, Japan Term, Open Studio, Repertory Theatre Term, and StartUp Term are offered to provide students with a focused, hands-on exploration of a single field of study over the course of an entire term. Peace Corps Preparatory Program, prepares students for the Peace Corps or other international service programs. The Law Scholars Program with Indiana University Maurer School of Law. Kemper Scholars Program provides students with scholarships, practical experience, and opportunities to explore careers. **Special study options:** Combined bachelor's/graduate degree, double major, ESL, independent study, internships, student-designed major, study abroad, teacher certification program, urban semester, Washington semester. **Credit/placement by examination:** AP, CLEP, IB, SAT, ACT, institutional tests. 9 credit hours maximum toward bachelor's degree. **Support services:** Learning center, tutoring. TRIO Achievement Program.

Majors. Area/ethnic studies: African-American, American, Asian, Latin American, women's. **Biology:** General, biochemistry, neuroscience. **Computer sciences:** Computer science. **Conservation:** Environmental studies. **Education:** Elementary, secondary, social science. **English:** Creative writing, English lit. **Foreign languages:** General, ancient Greek, classics, French, German, Latin, Spanish. **History:** General. **Math:** General, financial. **Philosophy/religion:** Philosophy. **Physical sciences:** Chemistry, physics. **Psychology:** General. **Social sciences:** Anthropology, economics, international relations, political science, sociology. **Visual/performing arts:** Art history/conservation, dramatic, music, studio arts.

Most popular majors. Biology 10%, computer/information sciences 6%, education 9%, English 11%, foreign language 6%, psychology 6%, social sciences 27%, visual/performing arts 9%.

Technology on campus. 250 workstations in library, computer center, student center. Dormitories wired for high-speed internet access and linked to campus network. Commuter students can connect to campus network. Online library, helpline, student web hosting, wireless network available.

Student life. Freshman orientation: Mandatory. Preregistration for classes offered. Five-day program held immediately prior to the beginning of fall term. **Policies:** Students required to be on-board when living on campus. Exceptions made for health and/or religious concerns. Academic work conducted under an Honor Code. **Housing:** Guaranteed on-campus for freshmen. Coed dorms, single-sex dorms, special housing for disabled, apartments, fraternity/sorority housing, themed housing available. $300 non-refundable deposit, deadline 5/1. Pets allowed in dorm rooms. **Activities:** Jazz band, choral groups, dance, drama, film society, international student organizations, literary magazine, music ensembles, Model UN, radio station, student government, student newspaper, symphony orchestra, TV station, Intervarsity Christian Fellowship, Islamic Club, Newman Club, Blessings in A Backpack, Best Buddies, Knox Conservatives, Knox Democrats, Harambee, Habitat for Humanity, Common Ground.

Athletics. NCAA. **Intercollegiate:** Baseball M, basketball, cross-country, diving, football (tackle) M, golf, soccer, softball W, swimming, tennis, track and field, volleyball W. **Intramural:** Basketball, soccer, softball. **Team name:** Prairie Fire.

Student services. Career counseling, services for economically disadvantaged, financial aid counseling, health services, minority student services, personal counseling, women's services. **Physically disabled:** Services for hearing impaired.

Contact. E-mail: admission@knox.edu
Phone: (309) 341-7100 Toll-free number: (800) 678-5669
Fax: (309) 341-7070
Paul Steenis, Dean of Admission, Knox College, 2 East South Street, Galesburg, IL 61401

Lake Forest College
Lake Forest, Illinois
www.lakeforest.edu

CB member
CB code: 1392

- Private 4-year liberal arts college
- Residential campus in large town
- 1,559 degree-seeking undergraduates: 1% part-time, 56% women, 7% African American, 5% Asian American, 17% Hispanic/Latino, 3% Multiracial, non-Hispanic, 8% international
- 28 degree-seeking graduate students
- 55% of applicants admitted
- Application essay required

General. Founded in 1857. Regionally accredited. **Degrees:** 370 bachelor's awarded; master's offered. **Location:** 30 miles from Chicago. **Calendar:** Semester, limited summer session. **Full-time faculty:** 98 total; 98% have terminal degrees, 14% minority, 42% women. **Part-time faculty:** 98 total;

51% have terminal degrees, 6% minority, 53% women. **Class size:** 62% < 20, 38% 20-39, less than 1% 40-49. **Special facilities:** Rhetoric and production room, electronic music studio, technology resource center, Center for Chicago Programs, vegetable garden, three art galleries.

Freshman class profile. 3,373 applied, 1,855 admitted, 358 enrolled.

Mid 50% test scores			
SAT critical reading:	480-610	GPA 3.0-3.49:	27%
SAT math:	500-600	GPA 2.0-2.99:	14%
SAT writing:	460-580	Rank in top quarter:	64%
ACT composite:	22-28	Rank in top tenth:	39%
GPA 3.75 or higher:	38%	Out-of-state:	43%
GPA 3.50-3.74:	21%	Live on campus:	89%
		International:	9%

Basis for selection. Holistic approach to candidate review with emphasis on academic preparedness and character. SAT or ACT recommended. ACT/SAT optional except for applicants for highest academic scholarships and for international students. Interviews highly recommended, required for certain scholarships and for students who do not submit standardized test scores. Audition required for theater and music scholarships. Portfolio required for art, foreign language, and writing scholarships. **Home schooled:** Statement describing home school structure and mission, transcript of courses and grades, interview, letter of recommendation (nonparent) required. SAT/ACT scores.

High school preparation. College-preparatory program required. Required and recommended units include English 4, mathematics 3-4, social studies 3, science 3-4 (laboratory 2) and foreign language 2. 1 honors or AP course recommended.

2015-2016 Annual costs. Tuition/fees: $42,644. Room/board: $9,570. Books/supplies: $1,000. Personal expenses: $600.

Financial aid. Non-need-based: Scholarships awarded for academics, alumni affiliation, art, leadership, music/drama.

Application procedures. Admission: Priority date 2/15; no deadline. No application fee. Application must be submitted online. Must reply by May 1 or within 3 week(s) if notified thereafter. **Financial aid:** Priority date 2/15, closing date 5/1. FAFSA required. Applicants notified on a rolling basis starting 3/1; must reply by 5/1 or within 2 week(s) of notification.

Academics. Special study options: Accelerated study, combined bachelor's/graduate degree, double major, honors, independent study, internships, liberal arts/career combination, student-designed major, study abroad, teacher certification program, urban semester, Washington semester. 3-year BA programs in communication and philosophy. Accelerated dual degree programs with select schools in law, international relations, and pharmacy (3-4). **Credit/placement by examination:** AP, CLEP, IB, SAT, ACT, institutional tests. **Support services:** Learning center, study skills assistance, tutoring, writing center.

Majors. Area/ethnic studies: American, Asian, Latin American. **Biology:** General, neuroscience. **Business:** General, accounting, finance, marketing. **Communications:** Communications/speech/rhetoric. **Computer sciences:** Computer science. **Conservation:** Environmental studies. **Education:** General. **English:** English lit. **Foreign languages:** French, Spanish. **History:** General. **Math:** General. **Philosophy/religion:** Philosophy, religion. **Physical sciences:** Chemistry, physics. **Psychology:** General. **Social sciences:** Economics, international relations, political science, sociology/anthropology. **Visual/performing arts:** Art, art history/conservation, music, theater arts management.

Most popular majors. Biology 10%, business/marketing 10%, communications/journalism 11%, English 6%, psychology 7%, social sciences 20%, visual/performing arts 6%.

Technology on campus. 135 workstations in library, computer center, student center. Dormitories wired for high-speed internet access and linked to campus network. Commuter students can connect to campus network. Online course registration, online library, helpline, repair service, student web hosting, wireless network available.

Student life. Freshman orientation: Mandatory, $200 fee. Preregistration for classes offered. Six-day program held on-campus in August. Additional five-day pre-orientation program held for traditionally underrepresented, minority, international, first-generation, and GLBT students, but open to all students. **Policies:** Freshmen not permitted cars on campus. **Housing:** Guaranteed on-campus for freshmen. Coed dorms, special housing for disabled, apartments available. $500 nonrefundable deposit, deadline 5/1. **Activities:** Bands, campus ministries, choral groups, dance, drama, international student organizations, literary magazine, music ensembles, Model UN, musical theater, radio station, student government, student newspaper, symphony orchestra, Amnesty International, Habitat for Humanity, Circle K, League for Environmental Awareness and Protection, United Black Association, Latinos Unidos, United Asia, PRIDE, Hillel, Intervarsity.

Athletics. NCAA. **Intercollegiate:** Basketball, cross-country, diving, football (tackle) M, golf, handball, ice hockey, soccer, softball W, swimming, tennis, volleyball W. **Intramural:** Badminton, basketball, football (nontackle), ice hockey, racquetball, soccer, softball, table tennis, tennis, volleyball. **Team name:** Foresters.

Student services. Alcohol/substance abuse counseling, career counseling, student employment services, financial aid counseling, health services, minority student services, personal counseling, placement for graduates, women's services. **Physically disabled:** Services for visually, hearing impaired.

Contact. E-mail: admissions@lakeforest.edu
Phone: (847) 735-5000 Toll-free number: (800) 828-4751
Fax: (847) 735-6271
Chris Ellertson, Vice President for Enrollment, Lake Forest College, 555 North Sheridan Road, Lake Forest, IL 60045-2338

Lakeview College of Nursing
Danville, Illinois
www.lakeviewcol.edu   **CB code: 0149**

- Private two-year upper-division nursing college
- Commuter campus in large town
- Application essay required

General. Founded in 1894. Regionally accredited. **Degrees:** 141 bachelor's awarded. **Articulation:** Agreements with Danville Area Community College, Eastern Illinois University. **Location:** 35 miles from Urbana-Champaign, 130 miles from Chicago. **Calendar:** Semester, limited summer session. **Full-time faculty:** 20 total. **Part-time faculty:** 8 total.

Student profile. 324 degree-seeking undergraduates.

Women:	86%	Out-of-state:	2%
Part-time:	18%	25 or older:	83%

Basis for selection. High school transcript, college transcript, application essay required. Based on interview, references, and transcripts. Applicant must have completed 33 credit hours of general course work with 2.5 GPA prior to admission. Transfer accepted as juniors.

2015-2016 Annual costs. Tuition/fees: $14,400. Books/supplies: $700.

Application procedures. Admission: Rolling admission. $100 fee. Application must be submitted on paper. National League for Nursing examinations used to determine advanced placement for entering students who already have RN degree. **Financial aid:** Priority date 4/15, no deadline. FAFSA, institutional form required.

Academics. BS in nursing requires total of 125 credit hours. 95% of entering students complete degree in 5 years or less. **Special study options:** Distance learning, honors, independent study. **Credit/placement by examination:** AP, CLEP. **Support services:** Reduced course load, study skills assistance, tutoring.

Majors. Health services: Nursing (RN).

Technology on campus. 12 workstations in library, computer center.

Student life. Activities: Student government, student newspaper, Illinois Student Nurses Association, National Student Nurses Association.

Student services. Adult student services, career counseling, financial aid counseling, health services, personal counseling, veterans' counselor.

Contact. E-mail: admissions@lakeviewcol.edu
Phone: (217) 443-5238
Connie Young, Director of Enrollment/Registrar, Lakeview College of Nursing, 903 North Logan Avenue, Danville, IL 61832

Lewis University
Romeoville, Illinois   **CB member**
www.lewisu.edu   **CB code: 1404**

- Private 4-year university affiliated with the Roman Catholic Church
- Commuter campus in large town
- 4,529 degree-seeking undergraduates: 16% part-time, 57% women, 6% African American, 4% Asian American, 19% Hispanic/Latino, 3% Multiracial, non-Hispanic, 1% international
- 1,934 degree-seeking graduate students

- 62% of applicants admitted
- SAT or ACT (ACT writing optional) required
- 66% graduate within 6 years

General. Founded in 1932. Regionally accredited. Comprehensive Catholic university sponsored by De La Salle Christian Brothers. **Degrees:** 1,160 bachelor's, 2 associate awarded; master's, doctoral offered. **ROTC:** Army, Air Force. **Location:** 30 miles from Chicago. **Calendar:** Semester, extensive summer session. **Full-time faculty:** 232 total; 78% have terminal degrees, 14% minority, 51% women. **Part-time faculty:** 443 total; 18% have terminal degrees, 15% minority, 48% women. **Class size:** 69% < 20, 30% 20-39, less than 1% 40-49, less than 1% 50-99. **Special facilities:** Science center, aviation center with airport and Boeing 737 jet, nursing simulation labs, all digital radio station and broadcast TV studio with digital robotics, fine arts center, art gallery, music studios.

Freshman class profile. 5,728 applied, 3,542 admitted, 702 enrolled.

Mid 50% test scores		Rank in top quarter:	41%
SAT critical reading:	500-560	Rank in top tenth:	16%
SAT math:	500-600	Return as sophomores:	84%
SAT writing:	430-530	Out-of-state:	8%
ACT composite:	21-25	Live on campus:	50%
GPA 3.75 or higher:	26%	International:	1%
GPA 3.50-3.74:	16%	Fraternities:	2%
GPA 3.0-3.49:	36%	Sororities:	2%
GPA 2.0-2.99:	22%		

Basis for selection. Applicants must have graduated from an approved high school with a combination of GPA, class rank, and ACT/SAT which indicates a strong likelihood of success in university studies. Admission to biology or chemistry department programs requires 21 ACT; nursing requires 20 ACT. Interview recommended. **Home schooled:** Statement describing home school structure and mission, transcript of courses and grades required.

High school preparation. College-preparatory program required. 18 units required; 22 recommended. Required and recommended units include English 3-4, mathematics 2-3, social studies 2, history 1, science 2 (laboratory 1), foreign language 2 and academic electives 8. 1 year chemistry and 2 years math at 2.0 level or above strongly recommended for nursing applicants.

2015-2016 Annual costs. Tuition/fees: $29,040. Room/board: $9,930. Books/supplies: $1,000. Personal expenses: $1,830.

2015-2016 Financial aid. Need-based: 668 full-time freshmen applied for aid; 604 deemed to have need; 604 received aid. Average need met was 81%. Average scholarship/grant was $16,992; average loan $3,366. 55% of total undergraduate aid awarded as scholarships/grants, 45% as loans/jobs. **Non-need-based:** Awarded to 1,114 full-time undergraduates, including 201 freshmen. Scholarships awarded for academics, alumni affiliation, art, athletics, music/drama, religious affiliation, ROTC.

Application procedures. Admission: Priority date 4/15; no deadline. $40 fee, may be waived for applicants with need. Admission notification on a rolling basis beginning on or about 10/1. Must reply by May 1 or within 2 week(s) if notified thereafter. **Financial aid:** Priority date 2/1, closing date 5/1. FAFSA required. Applicants notified on a rolling basis starting 2/1; must reply by 5/1 or within 2 week(s) of notification.

Academics. Accelerated degree completion program available to students 24 years and older. **Special study options:** Accelerated study, distance learning, double major, dual enrollment of high school students, ESL, honors, independent study, internships, liberal arts/career combination, student-designed major, study abroad, teacher certification program, weekend college. **Credit/placement by examination:** AP, CLEP, IB, ACT, institutional tests. 60 credit hours maximum toward bachelor's degree. **Support services:** Learning center, pre-admission summer program, reduced course load, remedial instruction, study skills assistance, tutoring, writing center. Academic resource center provides academic, career and tutorial services; center for academic technology solutions offers IMPACT Lab for assistance with development of multimedia projects, receiving individual instruction or attending technology workshops/seminars; library services, academic computing facilities, instructional technology support services, and academic support workshops for adult students.

Majors. Biology: General, biochemistry, biomedical sciences. **Business:** General, accounting, business admin, e-commerce, finance, human resources, information resources management, international, management information systems, managerial economics, marketing, organizational leadership. **Communications:** Communications/speech/rhetoric, digital media, journalism, media studies, organizational, public relations, radio/TV. **Computer sciences:** Computer science, information systems, security. **Conservation:** Environmental science. **Education:** Early childhood special, elementary, middle, secondary, Spanish, special ed. **Engineering:** Computer. **English:** English lit. **Foreign languages:** Spanish. **Health services:** Athletic training, dental hygiene, health care admin, nuclear medical technology, nursing (RN), radiation protection, radiologic technology/medical imaging, sonography.

History: General. **Human services:** General, community org/advocacy, social work. **Liberal arts:** Arts/sciences. **Math:** General. **Parks/recreation:** Exercise sciences, sports admin. **Philosophy/religion:** Philosophy, religion. **Physical sciences:** Chemical physics, chemistry, physics. **Protective services:** Criminal justice, fire services admin, forensics, security services. **Psychology:** General. **Social sciences:** International relations, political science, sociology. **Visual/performing arts:** Art, commercial/advertising art, design, dramatic, drawing, music, music management, painting.

Most popular majors. Business/marketing 21%, health sciences 18%, psychology 6%, security/protective services 14%, trade and industry 11%.

Technology on campus. 350 workstations in library, computer center. Dormitories wired for high-speed internet access and linked to campus network. Commuter students can connect to campus network. Online course registration, online library, helpline, wireless network available.

Student life. Freshman orientation: Mandatory, $130 fee. Preregistration for classes offered. Two-day summer program includes parent program. Welcome Weekend for new students held before first day of fall classes. **Housing:** Coed dorms, special housing for disabled, themed housing available. $100 fully refundable deposit, deadline 5/1. Pets allowed in dorm rooms. Handicapped accessibility available in most residence halls. **Activities:** Bands, campus ministries, choral groups, dance, drama, international student organizations, literary magazine, music ensembles, musical theater, radio station, student government, student newspaper, symphony orchestra, TV station, peer ministry, Latin American student organization, black student union, South Asian student association, Best Buddies, InterVarsity Christian Fellowship, P.E.A.C.E., STAND, Students for Life.

Athletics. NCAA. **Intercollegiate:** Baseball M, basketball, cheerleading W, cross-country, golf, soccer, softball W, swimming, tennis, track and field, volleyball. **Intramural:** Badminton, basketball, bowling, football (non-tackle), rugby, sand volleyball, softball, table tennis, volleyball. **Team name:** Flyers.

Student services. Adult student services, alcohol/substance abuse counseling, chaplain/spiritual director, career counseling, student employment services, financial aid counseling, health services, minority student services, personal counseling, placement for graduates, veterans' counselor. **Physically disabled:** Services for visually, hearing impaired.

Contact. E-mail: admissions@lewisu.edu
Phone: (815) 836-5250 Toll-free number: (800) 897-9000
Fax: (815) 836-5002
Ryan Cockerill, Director of Admission, Lewis University, Unit #297, Romeoville, IL 60446-2200

Lincoln Christian University
Lincoln, Illinois
www.lincolnchristian.edu **CB code:** 1405

- Private 4-year university and Bible college affiliated with the Church of Christ
- Residential campus in large town
- 514 degree-seeking undergraduates: 21% part-time, 45% women, 9% African American, 1% Asian American, 4% Hispanic/Latino, 1% Native American, 2% Multi-racial, non-Hispanic, 3% international
- 350 degree-seeking graduate students
- 60% of applicants admitted
- SAT or ACT (ACT writing recommended), application essay required
- 54% graduate within 6 years

General. Founded in 1944. Regionally accredited; also accredited by ABHE, ATS. **Degrees:** 134 bachelor's, 24 associate awarded; master's, professional, doctoral offered. **Location:** 30 miles from Springfield. **Calendar:** Semester, limited summer session. **Full-time faculty:** 50 total; 40% have terminal degrees, 4% minority, 24% women. **Part-time faculty:** 20 total; 90% have terminal degrees, 70% women. **Class size:** 88% < 20, 10% 20-39, 1% 40-49, less than 1% 50-99.

Freshman class profile. 247 applied, 149 admitted, 90 enrolled.

Mid 50% test scores		GPA 3.0-3.49:	32%
SAT critical reading:	420-460	GPA 2.0-2.99:	28%
SAT math:	410-510	Return as sophomores:	65%
SAT writing:	370-440	Out-of-state:	38%
ACT composite:	19-25	Live on campus:	99%
GPA 3.75 or higher:	25%	International:	7%
GPA 3.50-3.74:	15%		

Basis for selection. Recommendation of applicant's church leaders as to suitability for church-related vocations very important. High school record (core courses) and ACT scores also considered. Subscores of writing and English, application essay also important. Interview recommended. Audition required of music majors. **Home schooled:** List of involvement outside of education/academics required. **Learning Disabled:** Students with self-reported learning disabilities are referred to Academic Resource Center.

High school preparation. College-preparatory program recommended. 14 units recommended. Recommended units include English 4, mathematics 3, history 3, science 2 and foreign language 2.

2015-2016 Annual costs. Tuition/fees: $17,400. Room/board: $7,430. Books/supplies: $1,000. Personal expenses: $3,382.

2014-2015 Financial aid. Need-based: 66 full-time freshmen applied for aid; 56 deemed to have need; 56 received aid. Average need met was 51%. Average scholarship/grant was $8,297; average loan $3,188. 55% of total undergraduate aid awarded as scholarships/grants, 45% as loans/jobs. **Non-need-based:** Awarded to 50 full-time undergraduates, including 15 freshmen. Scholarships awarded for academics.

Application procedures. Admission: No deadline. $25 fee, may be waived for applicants with need. Admission notification on a rolling basis. **Financial aid:** Priority date 3/1; no closing date. FAFSA required. Applicants notified on a rolling basis starting 3/1; must reply within 4 week(s) of notification.

Academics. Special study options: Distance learning, double major, dual enrollment of high school students, honors, independent study, internships, study abroad, weekend college. Study abroad through the CCCU-BestSemester program. **Credit/placement by examination:** AP, CLEP, ACT, institutional tests. **Support services:** Learning center, reduced course load, remedial instruction, study skills assistance, tutoring, writing center.

Majors. Business: Organizational leadership. **Philosophy/religion:** Philosophy. **Psychology:** General. **Theology:** Bible, missionary, pastoral counseling, youth ministry.

Most popular majors. Business/marketing 23%, liberal arts 10%, psychology 8%, public administration/social services 9%, theological studies 49%.

Technology on campus. 51 workstations in library, computer center, student center. Dormitories wired for high-speed internet access and linked to campus network. Commuter students can connect to campus network. Online course registration, online library, helpline, repair service, wireless network available.

Student life. Freshman orientation: Mandatory, $300 fee. Preregistration for classes offered. **Policies:** Religious observance required. **Housing:** Guaranteed on-campus for all undergraduates. Single-sex dorms, apartments, wellness housing available. $150 fully refundable deposit, deadline 8/10. **Activities:** Campus ministries, choral groups, drama, international student organizations, music ensembles, musical theater, student government, volunteer groups in local health care institutions, missions interest groups, Christian service and outreach groups.

Athletics. NAIA, NCCAA. **Intercollegiate:** Baseball M, basketball, soccer, volleyball W. **Intramural:** Badminton, basketball, soccer, ultimate frisbee, volleyball. **Team name:** Red Lions.

Student services. Student employment services, financial aid counseling, health services, personal counseling. **Physically disabled:** Services for visually, hearing impaired.

Contact. E-mail: enroll@lincolnchristian.edu
Phone: (217) 732-3168 ext. 2251 Toll-free number: (888) 522-5228
Fax: (217) 732-4199
Jessica Hanson, Senior Director of Enrollment, Lincoln Christian University, 100 Campus View Drive, Lincoln, IL 62656-2111

Loyola University Chicago
Chicago, Illinois
www.luc.edu

CB member
CB code: 1412

- Private 4-year university affiliated with the Roman Catholic Church
- Residential campus in very large city
- 10,276 degree-seeking undergraduates: 7% part-time, 65% women, 4% African American, 12% Asian American, 14% Hispanic/Latino, 5% Multi-racial, non-Hispanic, 5% international
- 5,307 degree-seeking graduate students
- 71% of applicants admitted
- SAT or ACT (ACT writing optional), application essay required
- 74% graduate within 6 years

General. Founded in 1870. Regionally accredited. Three main campuses: the Lake Shore Campus, Water Tower Campus and Health Sciences Campus. Additional campuses in Woodstock, Vernon Hills, and Italy. **Degrees:** 2,212 bachelor's awarded; master's, professional, doctoral offered. **ROTC:** Army, Naval, Air Force. **Calendar:** Semester, extensive summer session. **Full-time faculty:** 767 total; 96% have terminal degrees, 15% minority, 48% women. **Part-time faculty:** 865 total; 14% minority, 53% women. **Class size:** 45% < 20, 39% 20-39, 10% 40-49, 5% 50-99, 1% >100. **Special facilities:** Theaters, art museums, digital media labs, convergence media studio, language learning resource center, neuroscience labs, clean energy lab, mock trial room, performance and specialized fine arts rooms, clinical simulation nursing laboratory, histology lab, geothermal system, ecodome greenhouse, aquaponics system showcase, artificial stream research facility, retreat and ecology.

Freshman class profile. 21,553 applied, 15,360 admitted, 2,194 enrolled.

Mid 50% test scores			
SAT critical reading:	520-630	Rank in top quarter:	70%
SAT math:	520-630	Rank in top tenth:	33%
SAT writing:	520-630	End year in good standing:	98.7%
ACT composite:	24-29	Return as sophomores:	86%
GPA 3.75 or higher:	51%	Out-of-state:	40%
GPA 3.50-3.74:	19%	Live on campus:	85%
GPA 3.0-3.49:	22%	International:	5%
GPA 2.0-2.99:	8%	Fraternities:	10%
		Sororities:	19%

Basis for selection. High school GPA, rigor of high school curriculum, ACT/SAT, recommendation letter and essay important. Personal interviews recommended but not required.

High school preparation. College-preparatory program required. 15 units required; 20 recommended. Required and recommended units include English 4, mathematics 3-4, social studies 2, history 1-2, science 3, foreign language 2 and academic electives 3. Additional requirements for certain majors.

2016-2017 Annual costs. Tuition/fees (projected): $42,032. Room/board: $13,770. Books/supplies: $1,200. Personal expenses: $1,600.

2015-2016 Financial aid. Need-based: 1,823 full-time freshmen applied for aid; 1,504 deemed to have need; 1,499 received aid. Average need met was 80%. Average scholarship/grant was $20,960; average loan $3,947. 66% of total undergraduate aid awarded as scholarships/grants, 34% as loans/jobs. **Non-need-based:** Awarded to 3,065 full-time undergraduates, including 780 freshmen. Scholarships awarded for academics, art, athletics, leadership, music/drama, religious affiliation, ROTC.

Application procedures. Admission: Priority date 12/1; no deadline. No application fee. Admission notification on a rolling basis beginning on or about 10/15. Separate application, recommendation and essay required for admission to Interdisciplinary Honors Program. Must apply by 3/1. **Financial aid:** Priority date 3/1; no closing date. FAFSA required. Applicants notified on a rolling basis starting 2/15; must reply within 3 week(s) of notification.

Academics. Special study options: Accelerated study, combined bachelor's/graduate degree, distance learning, double major, dual enrollment of high school students, ESL, external degree, honors, independent study, internships, study abroad, teacher certification program, Washington semester. School of professional studies offers part-time evening programs leading to bachelor's degrees; cooperative programs with Erikson Institute for Early Education and St. Joseph's Seminary; study abroad in 55 countries. **Credit/placement by examination:** AP, CLEP, IB, SAT, ACT, institutional tests. 24 credit hours maximum toward bachelor's degree. **Support services:** Learning center, pre-admission summer program, reduced course load, study skills assistance, tutoring, writing center.

Majors. Area/ethnic studies: African-American, women's. **Biology:** General, biochemistry, bioinformatics, biophysics. **Business:** Accounting, communications, entrepreneurial studies, finance, human resources, international, management information systems, managerial economics, marketing, office management, operations. **Communications:** Advertising, communications/speech/rhetoric, digital media, journalism. **Computer sciences:** General, information technology, security. **Conservation:** General, environmental science, environmental studies. **Education:** Bilingual, early childhood, elementary, mathematics, science, secondary, special ed. **English:** English lit. **Foreign languages:** Ancient Greek, classics, French, Italian, Latin, Spanish. **Health services:** Clinical lab science, clinical nutrition, health care admin, nursing (RN), physical therapy. **History:** General. **Human services:** Social work. **Math:** General, statistics. **Philosophy/religion:** Philosophy. **Physical sciences:** Chemistry, physics. **Protective services:** Criminal justice, forensics. **Psychology:** General, applied. **Social sciences:** Anthropology, international relations, political science, sociology. **Theology:** Pastoral counseling, religious ed, theology. **Visual/performing arts:** Art history/conservation, dance, design, dramatic, music, studio arts.

Most popular majors. Biology 15%, business/marketing 20%, communications/journalism 7%, health sciences 12%, psychology 11%, social sciences 10%.

Technology on campus. 1,300 workstations in library, computer center, student center. Dormitories wired for high-speed internet access and linked to campus network. Commuter students can connect to campus network. Online course registration, online library, helpline, wireless network available.

Student life. Freshman orientation: Mandatory, $350 fee. Preregistration for classes offered. Two-day program at Lake Shore campus. **Housing:** Guaranteed on-campus for freshmen. Coed dorms, special housing for disabled, apartments available. Living learning community floors available. **Activities:** Bands, campus ministries, choral groups, dance, drama, film society, international student organizations, literary magazine, music ensembles, Model UN, musical theater, radio station, student government, student newspaper, TV station, Agape Christian Fellowship, College Republicans, College Democrats, student environmental alliance, Bible Fellowship, African Student Alliance, American Red Cross, Latin American student organization, Habitat for Humanity, South Asian Student Alliance.

Athletics. NCAA. **Intercollegiate:** Basketball, cross-country, golf, soccer, softball W, track and field, volleyball. **Intramural:** Badminton, basketball, football (non-tackle), racquetball, soccer, table tennis, tennis, volleyball. **Team name:** Ramblers.

Student services. Adult student services, alcohol/substance abuse counseling, chaplain/spiritual director, career counseling, services for economically disadvantaged, student employment services, financial aid counseling, health services, minority student services, on-campus daycare, personal counseling, placement for graduates, veterans' counselor, women's services. **Physically disabled:** Services for visually, speech, hearing impaired.

Contact. E-mail: admission@luc.edu
Phone: (773) 508-3075 Toll-free number: (800) 262-2373
Fax: (773) 508-8926
Erin Moriarty, Director of Admissions, Loyola University Chicago, 1032 West Sheridan Road., Chicago, IL 60660

MacMurray College

Jacksonville, Illinois
www.mac.edu

CB member
CB code: 1435

- Private 4-year liberal arts college affiliated with the United Methodist Church
- Residential campus in large town
- 571 degree-seeking undergraduates
- 63% of applicants admitted
- SAT or ACT (ACT writing recommended) required

General. Founded in 1846. Regionally accredited. **Degrees:** 111 bachelor's awarded. **Location:** 30 miles from Springfield. **Calendar:** Semester, limited summer session. **Full-time faculty:** 34 total. **Part-time faculty:** 28 total. **Class size:** 59% < 20, 39% 20-39, 2% 40-49, 1% 50-99.

Freshman class profile. 959 applied, 601 admitted, 130 enrolled.

Mid 50% test scores		
	SAT math:	420-460
SAT critical reading:	390-430 ACT composite:	17-22

Basis for selection. Holistic view using core courses, ACT/SAT scores, and rigor of academic curriculum. Nursing students must have 20 ACT/ 950 SAT, 2.5 core GPA, and high school chemistry with grade of "C" or better for direct entry. Interview recommended for academically deficient applicants. Portfolio recommended for art scholarship.

2015-2016 Annual costs. Tuition/fees: $24,172. Room/board: $8,112. Books/supplies: $1,100. Personal expenses: $800. **Additional information:** Two year frozen tuition plan in place. Students receive one tuition increase across 4 years. Students residing on campus all 4 years receive 8th semester of room and board free.

Financial aid. Non-need-based: Scholarships awarded for academics, alumni affiliation, leadership, religious affiliation, state residency. **Additional information:** Merit scholarships for accepted, enrolled freshman and transfer students based on academic record and notified upon admission. Frozen tuition offered for full-time degree seeking new students for their first two years. Students residing on campus for four years will get the 8th semester of room and board waived.

Application procedures. Admission: Priority date 4/9; no deadline. No application fee. Admission notification on a rolling basis beginning on or about 9/1. **Financial aid:** Priority date 2/1; no closing date. FAFSA required. Applicants notified on a rolling basis starting 3/1; must reply within 2 week(s) of notification.

Academics. Special study options: Combined bachelor's/graduate degree, cooperative education, distance learning, double major, dual enrollment of

high school students, independent study, internships, liberal arts/career combination, student-designed major, study abroad, teacher certification program, weekend college. **Credit/placement by examination:** AP, CLEP, IB, institutional tests. 32 credit hours maximum toward bachelor's degree. **Support services:** Learning center, reduced course load, study skills assistance, tutoring, writing center.

Majors. Biology: General. **Business:** Accounting, business admin, finance, management information systems. **Communications:** Journalism. **Computer sciences:** General, computer science. **Education:** Biology, Deaf/hearing impaired, elementary, emotionally handicapped, English, history, learning disabled, mathematics, music, physical, secondary, Spanish, special ed. **Engineering:** General. **English:** English lit. **Foreign languages:** French, sign language interpretation, Spanish. **Health services:** Nursing (RN), predental, premedicine, preveterinary. **History:** General. **Human services:** Social work. **Math:** General. **Parks/recreation:** Sports admin. **Philosophy/religion:** Philosophy, religion. **Physical sciences:** Chemistry, physics. **Protective services:** Homeland security. **Psychology:** General. **Social sciences:** International relations, political science. **Visual/performing arts:** Art, dramatic, music.

Most popular majors. Security/protective services 9%.

Technology on campus. 75 workstations in dormitories, library, computer center. Dormitories wired for high-speed internet access and linked to campus network. Online library, helpline, wireless network available.

Student life. Freshman orientation: Mandatory. Preregistration for classes offered. Two-day acclimation to campus life held prior to start of classes. **Housing:** Guaranteed on-campus for all undergraduates. Coed dorms, single-sex dorms, special housing for disabled available. $150 fully refundable deposit. **Activities:** Campus ministries, choral groups, drama, international student organizations, literary magazine, student government.

Athletics. NCAA. **Intercollegiate:** Baseball M, basketball, football (tackle) M, golf, soccer, softball W, volleyball W. **Intramural:** Basketball, soccer, softball, volleyball. **Team name:** Highlanders.

Student services. Alcohol/substance abuse counseling, chaplain/spiritual director, career counseling, student employment services, financial aid counseling, health services, personal counseling, placement for graduates, veterans' counselor. **Physically disabled:** Services for visually, hearing impaired.

Contact. E-mail: admissions@mac.edu
Phone: (217) 479-7056 Toll-free number: (800) 252-7485
Fax: (217) 291-0702
Tressman Goode, Director of Admissions, MacMurray College, 447 East College Avenue, Jacksonville, IL 62650-2590

McKendree University

Lebanon, Illinois
www.mckendree.edu

CB code: 1456

- Private 4-year university and liberal arts college affiliated with the United Methodist Church
- Residential campus in small town
- 2,292 degree-seeking undergraduates: 21% part-time, 54% women, 14% African American, 1% Asian American, 5% Hispanic/Latino, 1% Native American, 2% Multi-racial, non-Hispanic, 2% international
- 630 degree-seeking graduate students
- 63% of applicants admitted
- SAT or ACT (ACT writing optional), application essay required
- 56% graduate within 6 years; 18% enter graduate study

General. Founded in 1828. Regionally accredited. **Degrees:** 508 bachelor's, 9 associate awarded; master's, doctoral offered. **ROTC:** Army, Air Force. **Location:** 12 miles from Belleville, 23 miles from St. Louis. **Calendar:** Semester, limited summer session. **Full-time faculty:** 104 total; 80% have terminal degrees, 11% minority, 59% women. **Part-time faculty:** 168 total; 21% have terminal degrees, 8% minority, 51% women. **Class size:** 77% < 20, 23% 20-39. **Special facilities:** Center for the arts, golf course.

Freshman class profile. 1,904 applied, 1,209 admitted, 362 enrolled.

Mid 50% test scores			
		Rank in top quarter:	34%
SAT critical reading:	450-550	Rank in top tenth:	12%
SAT math:	420-530	End year in good standing:	99%
SAT writing:	400-490	Return as sophomores:	71%
ACT composite:	19-24	Out-of-state:	23%
GPA 3.75 or higher:	23%	Live on campus:	91%
GPA 3.50-3.74:	18%	Fraternities:	5%
GPA 3.0-3.49:	31%	Sororities:	16%
GPA 2.0-2.99:	28%		

Basis for selection. High school records, including rigor of curriculum, test scores, recommendations, evidence of student leadership and desire to succeed in rigorous academic environment. Each application is reviewed holistically, and while not required for admission, college prep curriculum recommended. Interviews recommended. Audition required of music majors and minors. Portfolio recommended for art majors. **Home schooled:** Statement describing home school structure and mission, transcript of courses and grades, letter of recommendation (nonparent) required. Applicants must submit description of courses studied and 3 letters of recommendation from other than parents.

High school preparation. College-preparatory program recommended. 16 units recommended. Recommended units include English 4, mathematics 2, social studies 2, history 1, science 2 (laboratory 1), foreign language 1 and academic electives 4.

2016-2017 Annual costs. Tuition/fees (projected): $28,740. Room/board: $9,200. Books/supplies: $1,000. Personal expenses: $1,200.

2015-2016 Financial aid. Need-based: Average need met was 75%. Average scholarship/grant was $20,705; average loan $3,887. 69% of total undergraduate aid awarded as scholarships/grants, 31% as loans/jobs. **Non-need-based:** Scholarships awarded for academics, alumni affiliation, art, athletics, leadership, music/drama, religious affiliation.

Application procedures. Admission: No deadline. No application fee. Admission notification on a rolling basis beginning on or about 9/15. Must reply by May 1 or within 4 week(s) if notified thereafter. **Financial aid:** No deadline. FAFSA required. Applicants notified by 3/1.

Academics. Special study options: Accelerated study, combined bachelor's/graduate degree, distance learning, double major, dual enrollment of high school students, external degree, honors, independent study, internships, liberal arts/career combination, student-designed major, study abroad, teacher certification program. 3-2 and 3-3 occupational therapy program with Washington University; 3-2 engineering transfer option with several institutions. **Credit/placement by examination:** AP, CLEP, IB, SAT, ACT, institutional tests. 36 credit hours maximum toward associate degree, 64 toward bachelor's. **Support services:** Learning center, reduced course load, remedial instruction, study skills assistance, tutoring, writing center. In addition to face to face assistance, some academic tutoring and writing assistance is provided online. Academic recovery program for students on academic probation. First-generation student success program.

Honors college/program. Admission requirements: 3.6 GPA and 27 ACT; about 120 freshman admitted.

Majors. Biology: General. **Business:** Accounting, business admin, human resources, management science, marketing. **Communications:** Communications/speech/rhetoric, organizational, persuasive communications. **Computer sciences:** Computer science, information systems, information technology. **Conservation:** Environmental studies. **Education:** General, art, biology, chemistry, elementary, health, history, middle, music, physical, science, secondary, social science, special ed. **English:** English lit, rhetoric/composition. **Foreign languages:** Spanish. **Health services:** Athletic training, nursing (RN), occupational therapy, prechiropractic, predental, premedicine, preoccupational therapy, preoptometry, prepharmacy, prephysical therapy, preveterinary. **History:** General. **Human services:** Social work. **Liberal arts:** Arts/sciences. **Math:** General, computational. **Parks/recreation:** Exercise sciences, sports admin. **Philosophy/religion:** Philosophy, religion. **Physical sciences:** Chemistry. **Protective services:** Law enforcement admin. **Psychology:** General. **Social sciences:** General, economics, international relations, political science, sociology. **Visual/performing arts:** Dramatic, music, studio arts.

Most popular majors. Business/marketing 34%, education 7%, health sciences 22%, psychology 7%, social sciences 7%.

Technology on campus. 205 workstations in dormitories, library, computer center. Dormitories wired for high-speed internet access and linked to campus network. Commuter students can connect to campus network. Online course registration, online library, helpline, repair service, student web hosting, wireless network available.

Student life. Freshman orientation: Mandatory, $50 fee. Preregistration for classes offered. Three day program held weekend before start of classes. **Policies:** Students required to live on campus unless 21 years of age, of senior class standing, married, commuting from the home of a parent or legal guardian, or a veteran with at least two years active military duty. **Housing:** Guaranteed on-campus for all undergraduates. Coed dorms, special housing for disabled, apartments, themed housing, wellness housing available. $200 fully refundable deposit. Living learning communities based on interests; faculty in residence program available. **Activities:** Bands, campus ministries, choral groups, dance, drama, film society, international student organizations, literary magazine, music ensembles, Model UN, musical theater, radio station,

student government, student newspaper, Campus Christian Fellowship, Students Against Social Injustice, Black Student Organization, Service Organizations, Resident Hall Association, Inter-Greek Council, Community Service Fellows, Young Feminists.

Athletics. NCAA. **Intercollegiate:** Baseball M, basketball, bowling, cheerleading, cross-country, diving, fencing, football (tackle) M, golf, ice hockey, lacrosse W, soccer, softball W, swimming, tennis, track and field, volleyball, water polo, weight lifting, wrestling. **Intramural:** Basketball, football (non-tackle), softball, ultimate frisbee, volleyball. **Team name:** Bearcats.

Student services. Adult student services, alcohol/substance abuse counseling, chaplain/spiritual director, career counseling, student employment services, financial aid counseling, health services, minority student services, personal counseling, placement for graduates, veterans' counselor. **Physically disabled:** Services for visually, speech, hearing impaired.

Contact. E-mail: inquiry@mckendree.edu
Phone: (618) 537-6400 Toll-free number: (800) 232-7228 ext. 6400
Fax: (618) 537-6496
Chris Hall, Vice President for Admission and Financial Aid, McKendree University, 701 College Road, Lebanon, IL 62254-1299

Methodist College
Peoria, Illinois   **CB member**
www.methodistcol.edu   **CB code: 1503**

- Private 4-year health science college
- Small city
- 603 degree-seeking undergraduates
- 3 graduate students
- ACT (writing optional) required

General. Regionally accredited. **Degrees:** 111 bachelor's awarded. **Calendar:** Semester. **Full-time faculty:** 34 total. **Part-time faculty:** 25 total.

Freshman class profile. 12 enrolled.

Mid 50% test scores	ACT composite:	20-24

Basis for selection. Admission is based on GPA (2.5+) and ACT Composite score (19+). ACT's collected from all, used only for applicants with less than 30 college credits.

2015-2016 Annual costs. Tuition/fees: $30,726. Room only: $9,682. Books/supplies: $1,500. Personal expenses: $1,000.

Application procedures. Admission: Priority date 2/15; deadline 4/15. $50 fee.

Academics. Credit/placement by examination: AP, CLEP.

Majors. Health services: Nursing education.

Contact. E-mail: admissions@methodistcol.edu
Phone: (309) 671-5143
Keith Branham, Dean of Enrollment Management, Methodist College, 415 St. Mark Court, Peoria, IL 61603

Midstate College
Peoria, Illinois
www.midstate.edu   **CB code: 3329**

- For-profit 4-year business college
- Commuter campus in small city
- 521 degree-seeking undergraduates: 70% part-time, 77% women
- Application essay, interview required

General. Founded in 1888. Regionally accredited. **Degrees:** 49 bachelor's, 68 associate awarded. **Location:** 165 miles from Chicago. **Calendar:** Quarter, extensive summer session. **Full-time faculty:** 24 total; 58% women. **Part-time faculty:** 64 total; 61% women. **Class size:** 99% < 20, 1% 20-39.

Basis for selection. Open admission, but selective for some programs and for out-of-state students. Academic record, personal ability, and desire to succeed. Some programs have additional requirements. Entrance examination required of all applicants. To ensure compliance with state regulations, students from out-of-state must be approved to enroll.

2015-2016 Annual costs. Tuition/fees: $16,230. Books/supplies: $1,050.

Financial aid. Non-need-based: Scholarships awarded for academics.

Application procedures. Admission: No deadline. $25 fee. Admission notification on a rolling basis. **Financial aid:** No deadline. FAFSA, institutional form required. Applicants notified on a rolling basis; must reply within 4 week(s) of notification.

Academics. Special study options: Distance learning, internships. **Credit/placement by examination:** AP, CLEP, IB, institutional tests. 23 credit hours maximum toward associate degree, 47 toward bachelor's. **Support services:** Learning center, reduced course load, remedial instruction, study skills assistance, tutoring.

Majors. Business: Accounting, business admin. **Computer sciences:** Information systems. **Health services:** Health care admin.

Most popular majors. Business/marketing 73%, health sciences 18%.

Technology on campus. 109 workstations in library, computer center, student center. Commuter students can connect to campus network. Online library, helpline, repair service, wireless network available.

Student life. Freshman orientation: Mandatory. Preregistration for classes offered. Held first day of each quarter.

Student services. Career counseling, student employment services, financial aid counseling, personal counseling, placement for graduates, veterans' counselor.

Contact. E-mail: admissions@midstate.edu
Phone: (309) 692-4092 Toll-free number: (800) 251-4299
Fax: (309) 692-3893
Ashley Spain, Director of Marketing & Enrollment, Midstate College, 411 West Northmoor Road, Peoria, IL 61614-3558

Millikin University
Decatur, Illinois
www.millikin.edu

CB member
CB code: 1470

▸ Private 4-year university affiliated with the Presbyterian Church (USA)
▸ Residential campus in small city
▸ 2,013 degree-seeking undergraduates: 2% part-time, 58% women, 14% African American, 1% Asian American, 6% Hispanic/Latino, 4% Multi-racial, non-Hispanic, 2% international
▸ 87 degree-seeking graduate students
▸ 60% of applicants admitted
▸ SAT or ACT (ACT writing optional) required
▸ 60% graduate within 6 years; 17% enter graduate study

General. Founded in 1901. Regionally accredited. **Degrees:** 453 bachelor's awarded; master's, professional offered. **Location:** 180 miles from Chicago, 120 miles from St. Louis. **Calendar:** Semester, limited summer session. **Full-time faculty:** 141 total; 80% have terminal degrees, 6% minority, 48% women. **Part-time faculty:** 131 total; 16% have terminal degrees, 8% minority, 64% women. **Class size:** 62% < 20, 36% 20-39, less than 1% 40-49, less than 1% 50-99, less than 1% >100. **Special facilities:** Art museums, 32-track recording studio, computer imaging center, greenhouse, observatory, performance center, 24-hour computer labs, video-conferencing classroom, proscenium theater, science center, 3-D arts building, student-owned and operated publishing company, record label, business incubator, fine art press.

Freshman class profile. 3,540 applied, 2,124 admitted, 420 enrolled.

Mid 50% test scores			
SAT critical reading:	480-590	Rank in top quarter:	38%
SAT math:	460-590	Rank in top tenth:	17%
SAT writing:	450-590	End year in good standing:	86%
ACT composite:	20-26	Return as sophomores:	73%
GPA 3.75 or higher:	27%	Out-of-state:	20%
GPA 3.50-3.74:	17%	Live on campus:	86%
GPA 3.0-3.49:	30%	International:	1%
GPA 2.0-2.99:	25%	Fraternities:	17%
		Sororities:	20%

Basis for selection. School achievement record is most important. Class rank, GPA, recommendations, test scores important. Applicant should rank in top half of class. Character references considered. Interview recommended. Audition required of music, music/theater majors. Portfolio required of art majors.

High school preparation. College-preparatory program recommended. 15 units required; 16 recommended. Required and recommended units include English 4, mathematics 3, social studies 2, history 2, science 3 and foreign language 2.

2015-2016 Annual costs. Tuition/fees: $30,630. Room/board: $9,916.

2014-2015 Financial aid. Need-based: 461 full-time freshmen applied for aid; 418 deemed to have need; 418 received aid. Average need met was 85%. Average scholarship/grant was $9,192; average loan $4,348. 67% of total undergraduate aid awarded as scholarships/grants, 33% as loans/jobs. **Non-need-based:** Awarded to 1,749 full-time undergraduates, including 460 freshmen. Scholarships awarded for academics, alumni affiliation, art, leadership, minority status, music/drama.

Application procedures. Admission: Priority date 5/1; no deadline. No application fee. Application must be submitted online. Admission notification on a rolling basis beginning on or about 9/15. **Financial aid:** Priority date 1/31; no closing date. FAFSA required. Applicants notified on a rolling basis starting 3/1; must reply by 5/1 or within 4 week(s) of notification.

Academics. Small business consulting and accelerated adult education available. **Special study options:** Accelerated study, combined bachelor's/graduate degree, double major, ESL, exchange student, honors, independent study, internships, student-designed major, study abroad, teacher certification program, United Nations semester, urban semester, Washington semester. **Credit/placement by examination:** AP, CLEP, IB, ACT, institutional tests. 30 credit hours maximum toward bachelor's degree. To receive CLEP credit student must not have attended secondary school in the past 3 years; CLEP credit cannot count in the major and may not be used if the equivalent course has been attempted. **Support services:** Learning center, reduced course load, study skills assistance, tutoring, writing center.

Majors. Biology: General, molecular. **Business:** Accounting, business admin, entrepreneurial studies, international, management information systems, marketing, organizational leadership. **Communications:** Communications/speech/rhetoric. **Education:** Art, biology, chemistry, early childhood, elementary, English, mathematics, music, physical, social science. **English:** Creative writing, English lit. **Foreign languages:** Spanish. **Health services:** Art therapy, athletic training, nursing (RN), prechiropractic, predental, premedicine, preoccupational therapy, preoptometry, prepharmacy, prephysical therapy, preveterinary. **History:** General. **Math:** General, applied. **Parks/recreation:** Sports admin. **Philosophy/religion:** Philosophy. **Physical sciences:** Chemistry, physics. **Psychology:** General. **Social sciences:** Political science, sociology. **Visual/performing arts:** Commercial/advertising art, dramatic, music, music performance, musical theater, piano/keyboard, studio arts, theater design, voice/opera.

Most popular majors. Business/marketing 22%, communications/journalism 6%, education 11%, health sciences 13%, visual/performing arts 20%.

Technology on campus. 200 workstations in dormitories, library, computer center, student center. Dormitories wired for high-speed internet access and linked to campus network. Commuter students can connect to campus network. Online course registration, online library, helpline, student web hosting, wireless network available.

Student life. Freshman orientation: Mandatory, $100 fee. Preregistration for classes offered. Held the 5 days before beginning of classes. **Policies:** Three-year residential requirement for full-time, undergraduate students (freshmen, sophomores, juniors); there are exceptions to this policy. Freshmen not permitted cars on campus. **Housing:** Guaranteed on-campus for freshmen. Coed dorms, special housing for disabled, apartments, fraternity/sorority housing available. $150 fully refundable deposit, deadline 5/1. Single-gender floors; living-learning communities. **Activities:** Bands, choral groups, dance, drama, film society, international student organizations, literary magazine, music ensembles, Model UN, musical theater, opera, radio station, student government, student newspaper, symphony orchestra, student senate, Latin American student organization, Inter-Fraternity Council, Multicultural Voices of Praise, multicultural student council, Inter-Varsity Christian Fellowship, Up 'Til Dawn, environmental affairs council, university center board.

Athletics. NCAA. **Intercollegiate:** Baseball M, basketball, cross-country, football (tackle) M, golf, soccer, softball W, swimming, tennis W, track and field, volleyball W, wrestling M. **Intramural:** Basketball, bowling, football (non-tackle), soccer, softball, ultimate frisbee, volleyball. **Team name:** Big Blue.

Student services. Adult student services, alcohol/substance abuse counseling, career counseling, services for economically disadvantaged, student employment services, financial aid counseling, health services, minority student services, personal counseling, placement for graduates, women's services. **Physically disabled:** Services for visually, speech impaired.

Contact. E-mail: admis@millikin.edu
Phone: (217) 424-6210 Toll-free number: (800) 373-7733
Fax: (217) 425-4669
Kevin McIntyre, Dean of Admission, Millikin University, 1184 West Main Street, Decatur, IL 62522-2084

Monmouth College

Monmouth, Illinois
www.monmouthcollege.edu

CB member
CB code: 1484

- Private 4-year liberal arts college affiliated with the Presbyterian Church (USA)
- Residential campus in small town
- 1,174 degree-seeking undergraduates: 1% part-time, 52% women, 10% African American, 2% Asian American, 12% Hispanic/Latino, 1% Native American, 2% Multi-racial, non-Hispanic, 6% international
- 62% of applicants admitted
- SAT or ACT (ACT writing optional) required
- 58% graduate within 6 years; 18% enter graduate study

General. Founded in 1853. Regionally accredited. **Degrees:** 269 bachelor's awarded. **ROTC:** Army. **Location:** 180 miles from Chicago, 60 miles from Peoria. **Calendar:** Semester. **Full-time faculty:** 92 total; 88% have terminal degrees, 5% minority, 42% women. **Part-time faculty:** 41 total; 49% have terminal degrees, 5% minority, 49% women. **Class size:** 70% < 20, 30% 20-39, less than 1% 40-49. **Special facilities:** Prairie-habitat biology field station, educational garden and farm, nature preserve, virgin prairie plots, freshwater pond for field research on amphibians and reptiles, art and antiquities collection, U.S. First Ladies letter collection, Native American artifacts collection and lab, federal government documents repository.

Freshman class profile. 2,657 applied, 1,658 admitted, 272 enrolled.

Mid 50% test scores		End year in good standing:	82%
ACT composite:	20-26	Return as sophomores:	74%
GPA 3.75 or higher:	28%	Out-of-state:	11%
GPA 3.50-3.74:	11%	Live on campus:	97%
GPA 3.0-3.49:	33%	International:	4%
GPA 2.0-2.99:	28%	Fraternities:	9%
Rank in top quarter:	36%	Sororities:	24%
Rank in top tenth:	13%		

Basis for selection. Record of academic achievement is most important, followed by test scores, class rank, recommendations of counselor and teachers, and record of leadership and initiative. Interview highly recommended. Well-written essay adds to application, but is not required.

High school preparation. College-preparatory program recommended. 10 units required; 22 recommended. Required and recommended units include English 4, mathematics 2-4, social studies 1, history 1-2, science 2-3 (laboratory 1-2), foreign language 2, visual/performing arts 2 and academic electives 2.

2015-2016 Annual costs. Tuition/fees: $34,200. Room/board: $8,060. Books/supplies: $1,200. Personal expenses: $1,150.

2015-2016 Financial aid. Need-based: 257 full-time freshmen applied for aid; 237 deemed to have need; 237 received aid. Average need met was 88%. Average scholarship/grant was $26,884; average loan $3,573. 85% of total undergraduate aid awarded as scholarships/grants, 15% as loans/jobs. **Non-need-based:** Awarded to 311 full-time undergraduates, including 69 freshmen. Scholarships awarded for academics, art, leadership, music/drama, religious affiliation.

Application procedures. Admission: No deadline. No application fee. Admission notification on a rolling basis beginning on or about 9/15. Must reply by May 1 or within 2 week(s) if notified thereafter. **Financial aid:** Priority date 1/1; no closing date. FAFSA required. Applicants notified on a rolling basis starting 2/15; must reply by 5/1 or within 2 week(s) of notification.

Academics. Special study options: Combined bachelor's/graduate degree, double major, ESL, exchange student, honors, independent study, internships, semester at sea, student-designed major, study abroad, teacher certification program, urban semester, Washington semester. Off-campus (domestic and study abroad) programs available in cooperation with Associated Colleges of the Midwest and other study-abroad organizations, plus institutional off-campus programs and student-exchange agreements with universities in Ireland, France, Greece, Mexico, Morocco, Senegal, Scotland and Sweden. Monmouth College belongs to the International Student Exchange Program (ISEP). **Credit/placement by examination:** AP, CLEP, IB, SAT, ACT, institutional tests. 16 credit hours maximum toward bachelor's degree. IB diploma and A level examinations may result in transfer credits. **Support services:** Learning center, pre-admission summer program, remedial instruction, study skills assistance, tutoring, writing center.

Majors. Biology: General, biochemistry. **Business:** Accounting, business admin, international, managerial economics. **Communications:** Communications/speech/rhetoric, public relations. **Computer sciences:** Computer science. **Conservation:** Environmental science. **Education:** General, elementary, physical. **English:** English lit, rhetoric/composition. **Foreign languages:** Ancient Greek, classics, French, Latin, Spanish. **Health services:** Health care admin. **History:** General. **Human services:** Social work. **Liberal arts:** Arts/sciences. **Math:** General. **Philosophy/religion:** Philosophy, religion. **Physical sciences:** Chemistry, physics. **Psychology:** General. **Social sciences:** Anthropology, economics, international relations, political science, sociology. **Visual/performing arts:** Art, dramatic, music, studio arts, studio arts management.

Most popular majors. Business/marketing 20%, communications/journalism 14%, education 8%, history 7%, parks/recreation 6%, psychology 8%, social sciences 10%.

Technology on campus. 140 workstations in dormitories, library, computer center, student center. Dormitories wired for high-speed internet access and linked to campus network. Commuter students can connect to campus network. Online course registration, online library, helpline, student web hosting, wireless network available.

Student life. Freshman orientation: Mandatory, $190 fee. Preregistration for classes offered. Held before start of fall semester. **Policies:** All students required to live on campus unless they are married or live with family. **Housing:** Guaranteed on-campus for all undergraduates. Coed dorms, single-sex dorms, special housing for disabled, apartments, cooperative housing, fraternity/sorority housing, gender-neutral housing, themed housing, wellness housing available. $200 partly refundable deposit. **Activities:** Bands, campus ministries, choral groups, dance, drama, film society, international student organizations, literary magazine, music ensembles, musical theater, radio station, student government, student newspaper, symphony orchestra, TV station, Circle K, international club, Rotaract, LGBTQIA-Spectrum, UMOJA (Swahili for Unity), Raices, Colleges Against Cancer, Newman Club, Muslim Community at Monmouth, campus outreach, Colorful Voices of Praise.

Athletics. NCAA. **Intercollegiate:** Baseball M, basketball, cross-country, diving, football (tackle) M, golf, lacrosse, soccer, softball W, swimming, tennis, track and field, volleyball W, water polo. **Intramural:** Archery, badminton, football (non-tackle), sand volleyball, soccer, swimming, table tennis, tennis, ultimate frisbee, volleyball. **Team name:** Fighting Scots.

Student services. Alcohol/substance abuse counseling, chaplain/spiritual director, career counseling, services for economically disadvantaged, student employment services, financial aid counseling, health services, minority student services, personal counseling, placement for graduates, women's services. **Physically disabled:** Services for visually, speech, hearing impaired.

Contact. E-mail: admissions@monmouthcollege.edu
Phone: (309) 457-2131 Toll-free number: (800) 747-2687
Fax: (309) 457-2141
Nicholas Spaeth, Assoc. VP for Admission, Monmouth College, 700 East Broadway, Monmouth, IL 61462-1998

Moody Bible Institute

Chicago, Illinois
www.moody.edu

CB code: 1486

- Private 4-year Bible and seminary college affiliated with the interdenominational tradition
- Residential campus in very large city
- 2,976 degree-seeking undergraduates
- SAT or ACT with writing, application essay required

General. Founded in 1886. Regionally accredited; also accredited by ABHE. **Degrees:** 546 bachelor's, 34 associate awarded; master's offered. **Location:** Downtown. **Calendar:** Semester, limited summer session. **Full-time faculty:** 98 total. **Part-time faculty:** 178 total. **Class size:** 33% < 20, 55% 20-39, 4% 40-49, 4% 50-99, 4% >100.

Freshman class profile.

Out-of-state:	81%	Live on campus:	98%

Basis for selection. Rank in top half of graduating class and/or high school GPA above 2.0. Applicants must have been Christians for at least 1 year. Membership in Evangelical Protestant Church and recommendation from church leadership required. Interview recommended. Audition required of music majors. **Home schooled:** ACT plus GED or SAT required.

High school preparation. College-preparatory program recommended.

2015-2016 Annual costs. Tuition/fees: $12,290. Room/board: $11,870. Books/supplies: $918. Personal expenses: $2,692.

Financial aid. All financial aid based on need. **Additional information:** Aid available to upperclassmen is based on private and not federal/state sources.

Application procedures. Admission: Priority date 12/1; deadline 3/1 (postmark date). $50 fee, may be waived for applicants with need. Admission notification by 4/1. Must reply by May 1 or within 6 week(s) if notified thereafter. **Financial aid:** No deadline. Institutional form required. Applicants notified on a rolling basis; must reply by 7/1.

Academics. Special study options: Distance learning, honors, independent study, internships, study abroad. **Credit/placement by examination:** AP, CLEP, IB, institutional tests. 15 credit hours maximum toward associate degree, 30 toward bachelor's. **Support services:** Learning center, reduced course load, study skills assistance, tutoring, writing center.

Majors. Communications: Communications/speech/rhetoric. **Education:** ESL. **Theology:** Bible, missionary, pastoral counseling, religious ed, sacred music, theology, youth ministry.

Most popular majors. Theological studies 88%.

Technology on campus. 50 workstations in dormitories, library, computer center. Dormitories wired for high-speed internet access and linked to campus network. Commuter students can connect to campus network. Online course registration, online library, helpline, repair service, wireless network available.

Student life. Freshman orientation: Mandatory. Preregistration for classes offered. Held for main and regional campus students at the beginning of fall term. **Policies:** Students are required to subscribe to and follow community life standards published in the student handbook. Religious observance required. **Housing:** Guaranteed on-campus for all undergraduates. Single-sex dorms, special housing for disabled, apartments available. $350 nonrefundable deposit, deadline 5/1. **Activities:** Bands, campus ministries, choral groups, drama, international student organizations, music ensembles, radio station, student government, student newspaper, Student Missionary Fellowship, Gospel teams, Embrace, international student fellowship, Big Brother/Big Sister Program, married students fellowship, residence activities council, Hispanic student fellowship, student wives fellowship.

Athletics. NCCAA. **Intercollegiate:** Basketball, soccer M, volleyball. **Intramural:** Badminton, basketball, cross-country, football (non-tackle), racquetball, soccer, swimming, table tennis, tennis, ultimate frisbee, volleyball, water polo. **Team name:** Archers.

Student services. Career counseling, student employment services, financial aid counseling, health services, minority student services, on-campus daycare, personal counseling, placement for graduates, veterans' counselor. **Physically disabled:** Services for visually impaired.

Contact. E-mail: admissions@moody.edu
Phone: (312) 329-4400 Toll-free number: (800) 967-4624
Fax: (312) 329-8955
Charles Dresser, Dean of Admissions, Moody Bible Institute, 820 N LaSalle Boulevard, Chicago, IL 60610

National University of Health Sciences
Lombard, Illinois
www.nuhs.edu
CB code: 1567

- Private 4-year university and health science college
- Commuter campus in large town
- 130 undergraduates

General. Regionally accredited. **Degrees:** 33 bachelor's, 2 associate awarded; master's, professional offered. **Location:** 20 miles from Chicago. **Calendar:** Trimester, extensive summer session. **Full-time faculty:** 69 total. **Part-time faculty:** 57 total. **Special facilities:** Learning resource center, medical library, onsite clinic.

Basis for selection. Associate degree and certificate programs require 2.0 GPA or GED; bachelor's completion program in biomedical science requires minimum of 60 semester hours of prerequisite courses. Must be 18 years of age and of good moral character.

2015-2016 Annual costs. Tuition/fees: $11,368. Books/supplies: $800. **Additional information:** Tuition and fees quoted are for Bachelor's program: Biomedical Science. Associate program: Massage Therapy $12,702, books and supplies $400.

Application procedures. Admission: $55 fee, may be waived for applicants with need. **Financial aid:** No deadline.

Academics. College of Professional Studies offers doctor of chiropractic, doctor of naturopathy, and master's degrees in acupuncture and Oriental Medicine. Primary undergraduate enrollment is in bachelor of biomedical science completion program and certificate programs in massage therapy

and chiropractic assistance. Accelerated prerequisite program available for students needing to complete science entrance requirements. **Special study options:** Internships. **Credit/placement by examination:** AP, CLEP. **Support services:** Learning center, reduced course load, study skills assistance, tutoring.

Majors. Biology: Biomedical sciences.

Technology on campus. 75 workstations in library. Dormitories wired for high-speed internet access and linked to campus network. Online course registration, helpline, student web hosting, wireless network available.

Student life. Freshman orientation: Mandatory. Preregistration for classes offered. Half day program designed to familiarize new students with the campus, key people and where to go for help. **Policies:** Must be 21 to live on campus. **Housing:** Apartments available. Pets allowed in dorm rooms. **Activities:** Student government, student newspaper, student chiropractic organizations, professional sororities and fraternities, christian chiropractic association.

Athletics. Intramural: Basketball, golf, soccer, softball, tennis, volleyball.

Student services. Financial aid counseling, health services.

Contact. E-mail: admissions@nuhs.edu
Phone: (630) 889-6566 Toll-free number: (800) 826-6285
Fax: (630) 889-6554
Victoria Sweeney, Director of Communications and Enrollment Services, National University of Health Sciences, 200 East Roosevelt Road, Lombard, IL 60148-4583

National-Louis University
Chicago, Illinois
www.nl.edu
CB member
CB code: 1551

- Private 4-year university and teachers college
- Commuter campus in very large city
- 1,213 degree-seeking undergraduates: 49% part-time, 78% women, 36% African American, 3% Asian American, 31% Hispanic/Latino, 2% Multiracial, non-Hispanic, 1% international
- 2,747 degree-seeking graduate students
- SAT or ACT required

General. Founded in 1886. Regionally accredited. Additional in-state locations in Skokie, Wheeling, Lisle and Elgin. Field programs available on and off campus. Out-of-state campuses located in Milwaukee/Beloit, and Tampa. **Degrees:** 449 bachelor's awarded; master's, doctoral offered. **Location:** Downtown. **Calendar:** Quarter, limited summer session. **Full-time faculty:** 213 total; 75% have terminal degrees, 11% minority, 66% women. **Part-time faculty:** 308 total; 15% minority, 69% women. **Special facilities:** Elementary demonstration school for practice teaching and observation.

Basis for selection. Rank in top half of high school class, score 19 ACT, 1150 SAT (exclusive of Writing) and 2 letters of recommendation from counselors or teachers. Interview and essay recommended.

High school preparation. Recommended units include English 4, mathematics 3, social studies 3, science 2 (laboratory 1) and foreign language 2. 1 unit U.S. government or U.S. history recommended.

2015-2016 Annual costs. Tuition/fees: $15,915. Books/supplies: $1,350.

Financial aid. Non-need-based: Scholarships awarded for academics.

Application procedures. Admission: No deadline. $40 fee, may be waived for applicants with need. Admission notification on a rolling basis. **Financial aid:** Priority date 4/15; no closing date. FAFSA, institutional form required. Applicants notified on a rolling basis starting 5/1; must reply within 2 week(s) of notification.

Academics. Degree-completion programs available in allied health leadership, management, and applied behavioral science. Field classes offered evenings/weekends. **Special study options:** Accelerated study, combined bachelor's/graduate degree, distance learning, double major, dual enrollment of high school students, ESL, honors, independent study, internships, liberal arts/career combination, teacher certification program. **Credit/placement by examination:** AP, CLEP. 132 credit hours maximum toward bachelor's degree. **Support services:** Learning center, pre-admission summer program, reduced course load, remedial instruction, study skills assistance, tutoring, writing center.

Majors. Biology: General. **Business:** Accounting, business admin. **Computer sciences:** Information systems. **Education:** Early childhood, elementary. **English:** English lit. **Health services:** Clinical lab science, health care admin, medical radiologic technology/radiation therapy, respiratory therapy technology, substance abuse counseling. **Liberal arts:** Arts/sciences. **Math:** General, applied. **Psychology:** General. **Social sciences:** General, anthropology, economics.

Most popular majors. Business/marketing 30%, education 12%, health sciences 6%, interdisciplinary studies 36%, public administration/social services 6%.

Technology on campus. Commuter students can connect to campus network. Online course registration, online library, helpline, repair service, wireless network available.

Student life. Freshman orientation: Available. Preregistration for classes offered. **Activities:** Association of Latino Scholars, debate club, Sigma Beta Theta Multicultural Co-Ed Fraternity, Student Veterans Association, National Society of Leadership and Success.

Student services. Adult student services, alcohol/substance abuse counseling, career counseling, student employment services, financial aid counseling, health services, personal counseling, placement for graduates, veterans' counselor. **Physically disabled:** Services for visually, speech, hearing impaired.

Contact. E-mail: admissions@nl.edu
Phone: (847) 947-5718 Toll-free number: (800) 443-5522 ext. 5718
Fax: (847) 465-5730
Ken Kasprzak, Admissions Director, National-Louis University, 122 South Michigan Avenue, Chicago, IL 60603

North Central College
Naperville, Illinois   **CB member**
www.northcentralcollege.edu   **CB code: 1555**

- Private 4-year liberal arts college affiliated with the United Methodist Church
- Residential campus in small city
- 2,633 degree-seeking undergraduates: 2% part-time, 54% women, 4% African American, 2% Asian American, 11% Hispanic/Latino, 3% Multiracial, non-Hispanic, 2% international
- 226 degree-seeking graduate students
- 57% of applicants admitted
- SAT or ACT (ACT writing optional) required
- 67% graduate within 6 years; 18% enter graduate study

General. Founded in 1861. Regionally accredited. **Degrees:** 735 bachelor's awarded; master's offered. **ROTC:** Army, Air Force. **Location:** 25 miles from Chicago. **Calendar:** Quarter, limited summer session. **Full-time faculty:** 142 total; 91% have terminal degrees, 16% minority, 54% women. **Part-time faculty:** 132 total; 36% have terminal degrees, 5% minority, 51% women. **Class size:** 39% < 20, 60% 20-39, less than 1% 40-49. **Special facilities:** Fermi accelerator laboratory, Argonne laboratory, arboretum, aquarium, anthropology museum.

Freshman class profile. 7,307 applied, 4,177 admitted, 599 enrolled.

Mid 50% test scores			
		Rank in top tenth:	22%
ACT composite:	22-27	End year in good standing:	86%
GPA 3.75 or higher:	38%	Return as sophomores:	80%
GPA 3.50-3.74:	19%	Out-of-state:	10%
GPA 3.0-3.49:	31%	Live on campus:	77%
GPA 2.0-2.99:	12%	International:	1%
Rank in top quarter:	54%		

Basis for selection. Academic record, SAT or ACT scores, and personal character all considered important. Interview and essay recommended for marginal students. **Home schooled:** Interview required. Review of the student's portfolio and curriculum, writing sample, interview with the Director of Freshman Admission, interview with a faculty member may be required. **Learning Disabled:** Students who self-identify are referred to the academic support center.

High school preparation. College-preparatory program required. 16 units required; 19 recommended. Required and recommended units include English 4, mathematics 3, social studies 2, history 1, science 3 (laboratory 2-3), foreign language 3 and academic electives 3.

2015-2016 Annual costs. Tuition/fees: $35,421. Room/board: $10,545. Books/supplies: $1,200. Personal expenses: $1,182.

2015-2016 Financial aid. Need-based: 558 full-time freshmen applied for aid; 484 deemed to have need; 484 received aid. Average need met was 81%. Average scholarship/grant was $23,861; average loan $3,429. 70% of total undergraduate aid awarded as scholarships/grants, 30% as loans/jobs. **Non-need-based:** Awarded to 767 full-time undergraduates, including 172 freshmen. Scholarships awarded for academics, art, leadership, minority status, music/drama, religious affiliation, ROTC, state residency.

Application procedures. Admission: Priority date 4/15; no deadline. $25 fee, may be waived for applicants with need, free for online applicants. Admission notification on a rolling basis beginning on or about 10/1. Must reply by May 1 or within 4 week(s) if notified thereafter. **Financial aid:** No deadline. FAFSA required. Applicants notified on a rolling basis starting 3/1; must reply within 4 week(s) of notification.

Academics. Special study options: Accelerated study, combined bachelor's/graduate degree, cross-registration, double major, dual enrollment of high school students, ESL, exchange student, honors, independent study, internships, liberal arts/career combination, New York semester, student-designed major, study abroad, teacher certification program, United Nations semester, urban semester, Washington semester. Independent study project grants; 3-2 engineering program with Universities of Illinois at Urbana-Champaign and Minnesota; 5-year bachelor's/master's degree programs. **Credit/placement by examination:** AP, CLEP, IB, SAT, ACT, institutional tests. 28 credit hours maximum toward bachelor's degree. Students must be tested or otherwise assessed in order for experiential credit to be awarded. **Support services:** Pre-admission summer program, reduced course load, remedial instruction, study skills assistance, tutoring, writing center.

Majors. Area/ethnic studies: East Asian. **Biology:** General, biochemistry. **Business:** Accounting, actuarial science, business admin, finance, human resources, international, marketing, small business admin. **Communications:** Communications/speech/rhetoric, journalism, organizational, radio/TV. **Communications technology:** Animation/special effects. **Computer sciences:** Computer science. **Education:** General, art, elementary, music, physical. **English:** Creative writing, English lit. **Foreign languages:** Chinese, classics, French, German, Japanese, Spanish. **Health services:** Athletic training, medical radiologic technology/radiation therapy, nuclear medical technology. **History:** General. **Liberal arts:** Arts/sciences. **Math:** General, applied. **Parks/recreation:** Exercise sciences, health/fitness, sports admin. **Philosophy/religion:** Philosophy, religion. **Physical sciences:** Analytical chemistry, chemistry, physics. **Psychology:** General. **Social sciences:** General, anthropology, economics, political science, sociology, sociology/anthropology. **Visual/performing arts:** Art, art history/conservation, dramatic, graphic design, jazz, music, musical theater, theater design.

Most popular majors. Business/marketing 24%, parks/recreation 9%, psychology 13%, social sciences 11%, visual/performing arts 9%.

Technology on campus. 360 workstations in dormitories, library, computer center, student center. Dormitories wired for high-speed internet access and linked to campus network. Commuter students can connect to campus network. Online course registration, online library, helpline, repair service, student web hosting, wireless network available.

Student life. Freshman orientation: Available, $125 fee. Preregistration for classes offered. Four one-day orientations held in June, two in August. **Policies:** Freshmen not permitted cars on campus. **Housing:** Guaranteed on-campus for all undergraduates. Coed dorms, single-sex dorms, special housing for disabled, wellness housing available. $100 nonrefundable deposit, deadline 5/1. **Activities:** Bands, campus ministries, choral groups, dance, drama, international student organizations, literary magazine, music ensembles, Model UN, musical theater, opera, radio station, student government, student newspaper, United Methodist student organization, Black Student Association, Fellowship of Christian Athletes, Raza Unida, Cardinals in Action, Green Scene, commuter student organization, ENACTUS (Students in Free Enterprise), Japan club, Chinese club.

Athletics. NCAA. **Intercollegiate:** Baseball M, basketball, cross-country, football (tackle) M, golf, lacrosse, soccer, softball W, swimming, tennis, track and field, triathlon W, volleyball, wrestling M. **Intramural:** Basketball, bowling, cheerleading, football (tackle) M, golf, softball, table tennis, volleyball. **Team name:** Cardinals.

Student services. Adult student services, alcohol/substance abuse counseling, chaplain/spiritual director, career counseling, student employment services, financial aid counseling, health services, minority student services, personal counseling, placement for graduates, veterans' counselor. **Physically disabled:** Services for visually, hearing impaired.

Contact. E-mail: admissions@noctrl.edu
Phone: (630) 637-5800 Toll-free number: (800) 411-1861
Fax: (630) 637-5819
Martha Stolze, Dean of Admission, North Central College, 30 North Brainard Street, Naperville, IL 60566-7063

North Park University

Chicago, Illinois   **CB member**
www.northpark.edu   **CB code: 1556**

- Private 4-year university and liberal arts college affiliated with the Evangelical Covenant Church of America
- Residential campus in very large city
- 2,140 degree-seeking undergraduates
- 49% of applicants admitted
- SAT or ACT (ACT writing recommended), application essay required

General. Founded in 1891. Regionally accredited. Offers Christian, urban, and intercultural education. **Degrees:** 535 bachelor's awarded; master's, professional offered. **ROTC:** Army, Air Force. **Location:** 8 miles from downtown. **Calendar:** Semester, limited summer session. **Full-time faculty:** 116 total; 56% women. **Part-time faculty:** 225 total. **Class size:** 58% < 20, 36% 20-39, 3% 40-49, 3% 50-99. **Special facilities:** Nursing simulation lab.

Freshman class profile. 3,927 applied, 1,920 admitted, 358 enrolled.

Mid 50% test scores			
SAT critical reading:	450-580	GPA 3.0-3.49:	35%
SAT math:	460-590	GPA 2.0-2.99:	35%
SAT writing:	450-570	Rank in top quarter:	37%
ACT composite:	24-19	Rank in top tenth:	16%
GPA 3.75 or higher:	16%	Out-of-state:	33%
GPA 3.50-3.74:	14%	Live on campus:	66%

Basis for selection. Full review of student's record, including courses taken, GPA, class rank, test scores, recommendations, essay or writing sample, co-curricular involvements, and community service. Nursing has an early admission option available to high achieving students. Interview may be required for some applicants. All students who visit campus may schedule an appointment with an admission counselor. **Home schooled:** Transcript of courses and grades, letter of recommendation (nonparent) required. **Learning Disabled:** Provides and coordinates support services and reasonable accommodations to aid students with disabilities through Center for Academic Services.

High school preparation. College-preparatory program recommended. Recommended units include English 4, mathematics 3, social studies 1, history 1, science 3 and foreign language 2.

2015-2016 Annual costs. Tuition/fees: $25,740. Room/board: $8,580. Books/supplies: $1,000. Personal expenses: $2,100.

Financial aid. **Non-need-based:** Scholarships awarded for academics, art, music/drama, religious affiliation.

Application procedures. **Admission:** Priority date 12/1; deadline 4/1 (receipt date). $40 fee, may be waived for applicants with need. Admission notification on a rolling basis beginning on or about 9/15. Must reply by May 1 or within 4 week(s) if notified thereafter. **Financial aid:** Priority date 5/1, closing date 8/1. FAFSA required. Applicants notified on a rolling basis starting 10/1; must reply by 5/1 or within 3 week(s) of notification.

Academics. **Special study options:** Accelerated study, combined bachelor's/graduate degree, distance learning, double major, ESL, exchange student, honors, independent study, internships, liberal arts/career combination, student-designed major, study abroad, teacher certification program, Washington semester. **Credit/placement by examination:** AP, CLEP, IB, SAT, ACT, institutional tests. 30 credit hours maximum toward bachelor's degree. **Support services:** Pre-admission summer program, reduced course load, remedial instruction, study skills assistance, tutoring, writing center.

Majors. **Area/ethnic studies:** African-American, Scandinavian. **Biology:** General. **Business:** General, business admin, nonprofit/public, organizational behavior. **Communications:** Advertising, communications/speech/rhetoric. **Conservation:** Environmental studies. **Education:** Early childhood, elementary, middle, multi-level teacher, secondary. **Engineering:** General. **English:** English lit. **Foreign languages:** French, Scandinavian, Spanish. **Health services:** Athletic training, nursing (RN). **History:** General. **Math:** General. **Parks/recreation:** Exercise sciences. **Philosophy/religion:** Philosophy. **Physical sciences:** Chemistry, physics. **Protective services:** Law enforcement admin. **Psychology:** General, counseling. **Social sciences:** Political science, sociology. **Theology:** Bible, theology, youth ministry. **Visual/performing arts:** Art, music, music performance.

Most popular majors. Biology 6%, business/marketing 23%, communications/journalism 6%, health sciences 26%.

Technology on campus. 100 workstations in dormitories, library, computer center, student center. Dormitories wired for high-speed internet access and linked to campus network. Commuter students can connect to campus network. Online course registration, online library, helpline, wireless network available.

Student life. **Freshman orientation:** Mandatory. Preregistration for classes offered. Begins 3 days before start of classes. **Policies:** Alcohol-free campus and smoke-free buildings. Visiting hours in residence halls for persons of opposite sex. Freshmen not permitted cars on campus. **Housing:** Guaranteed on-campus for all undergraduates. Coed dorms, single-sex dorms, apartments, themed housing available. $250 nonrefundable deposit, deadline 5/1. **Activities:** Bands, campus ministries, choral groups, drama, literary magazine, music ensembles, musical theater, opera, student government, student newspaper, symphony orchestra, African student club, black student association, Latino American student organization, Middle Eastern student association, East Asian student association, South Asian student association, Scandinavian student association, Urban Outreach.

Athletics. NCAA. **Intercollegiate:** Baseball M, basketball, cross-country, football (tackle) M, golf, rowing (crew) W, soccer, softball W, tennis W, track and field, volleyball W. **Intramural:** Basketball, football (non-tackle), soccer, volleyball. **Team name:** Vikings.

Student services. Adult student services, alcohol/substance abuse counseling, chaplain/spiritual director, career counseling, services for economically disadvantaged, student employment services, financial aid counseling, health services, minority student services, personal counseling, placement for graduates.

Contact. E-mail: admissions@northpark.edu
Phone: (773) 244-5500 Toll-free number: (800) 888-6728
Fax: (773) 244-5243
Jared Christensen, Senior Director of Undergraduate Enrollment, North Park University, 3225 West Foster Avenue Box 19, Chicago, IL 60625-4895

Northeastern Illinois University

Chicago, Illinois   **CB member**
www.neiu.edu   **CB code: 1090**

- Public 4-year university
- Commuter campus in very large city
- 7,979 degree-seeking undergraduates: 44% part-time, 56% women, 10% African American, 9% Asian American, 37% Hispanic/Latino, 2% Multiracial, non-Hispanic, 4% international
- 1,355 degree-seeking graduate students
- 66% of applicants admitted
- ACT (writing optional) required

General. Founded in 1961. Regionally accredited. Two extension centers serve Hispanic and African-American communities. To support our diverse student body at the main campus, we feature the Angelina Pedroso Center for Diversity and Intercultural Affairs, the Veterans Center, the Women's Center, the LGBTQA Resource Center, and the Office of Student Disability Services. **Degrees:** 1,578 bachelor's awarded; master's offered. **ROTC:** Army, Air Force. **Calendar:** Semester, limited summer session. **Full-time faculty:** 374 total; 82% have terminal degrees, 30% minority, 54% women. **Part-time faculty:** 251 total; 38% have terminal degrees, 27% minority, 47% women. **Class size:** 43% < 20, 52% 20-39, 4% 40-49, less than 1% 50-99, less than 1% >100. **Special facilities:** Ensemble Espanol, The Jewel Box Series, recital hall, art gallery, white oak preserve.

Freshman class profile. 4,539 applied, 3,009 admitted, 749 enrolled.

Mid 50% test scores			
ACT composite:	16-20	Rank in top quarter:	13%
GPA 3.75 or higher:	7%	Rank in top tenth:	3%
GPA 3.50-3.74:	7%	Return as sophomores:	61%
GPA 3.0-3.49:	20%	Out-of-state:	3%
GPA 2.0-2.99:	62%	International:	3%
		Sororities:	1%

Basis for selection. Rank in top half of graduating class or 19 ACT/equivalent SAT required. Audition recommended for dance and music majors. Portfolio recommended for art majors.

High school preparation. 15 units required. Required units include English 4, mathematics 3, social studies 3, science 3 and visual/performing arts 2. 2 additional units in fine arts, music, art, foreign languages, or vocational education. (Only 1 vocational education course accepted.).

2016-2017 Annual costs. Tuition/fees (projected): $11,698; $20,098 out-of-state. Books/supplies: $2,400. Personal expenses: $2,988.

2015-2016 Financial aid. **Need-based:** 622 full-time freshmen applied for aid; 498 deemed to have need; 419 received aid. Average need met was

18%. Average scholarship/grant was $7,550; average loan $3,057. 75% of total undergraduate aid awarded as scholarships/grants, 25% as loans/jobs. **Non-need-based:** Awarded to 568 full-time undergraduates, including 47 freshmen. Scholarships awarded for academics, art, leadership, music/drama, ROTC.

Application procedures. Admission: Closing date 7/1 (receipt date). $30 fee, may be waived for applicants with need. Admission notification on a rolling basis beginning on or about 9/1. Must reply by 7/1. **Financial aid:** Priority date 2/28; no closing date. FAFSA required. Applicants notified on a rolling basis starting 3/15; must reply within 2 week(s) of notification.

Academics. Special study options: Distance learning, double major, dual enrollment of high school students, ESL, honors, independent study, internships, liberal arts/career combination, student-designed major, study abroad, teacher certification program, weekend college. **Credit/placement by examination:** AP, CLEP, IB, ACT, institutional tests. 30 credit hours maximum toward bachelor's degree. **Support services:** Learning center, pre-admission summer program, remedial instruction, study skills assistance, tutoring, writing center. TRIO program.

Majors. Area/ethnic studies: Women's. **Biology:** General. **Business:** General, accounting, business admin, finance, marketing. **Computer sciences:** Computer science. **Conservation:** Environmental studies. **Education:** Bilingual, early childhood, elementary, physical, special ed. **English:** English lit. **Foreign languages:** French, Spanish. **Health services:** Community health services. **History:** General. **Human services:** Social work. **Liberal arts:** Arts/sciences. **Math:** General. **Philosophy/religion:** Philosophy. **Physical sciences:** Chemistry, geology, physics. **Protective services:** Criminal justice. **Psychology:** General. **Social sciences:** Anthropology, economics, geography, political science, sociology. **Visual/performing arts:** Art, music.

Most popular majors. Biology 6%, business/marketing 17%, communications/journalism 6%, education 8%, mathematics 7%, psychology 8%, public administration/social services 9%, security/protective services 6%, social sciences 7%.

Technology on campus. PC or laptop required. 560 workstations in library, computer center, student center. Commuter students can connect to campus network. Online course registration, online library, helpline, student web hosting, wireless network available.

Student life. Freshman orientation: Mandatory, $65 fee. Preregistration for classes offered. Full day program held during summer for fall term and in December for spring term. **Policies:** Smoking is not allowed anywhere on campus. **Activities:** Bands, campus ministries, choral groups, dance, drama, film society, international student organizations, literary magazine, music ensembles, Model UN, musical theater, opera, radio station, student government, student newspaper, symphony orchestra, Catholic student association, Muslim student association, Bible fellowship, Gay/Lesbian/Bisexual/Transgender and Queer Alliance, justice studies club, Latinos in Power, Model Illinois Government, Students for Justice in Palestine, Undocumented Resilient & Organized Club, UTATU Collective.

Athletics. Intramural: Basketball, football (non-tackle), soccer, volleyball. **Team name:** Eagles.

Student services. Adult student services, alcohol/substance abuse counseling, career counseling, student employment services, financial aid counseling, health services, minority student services, on-campus daycare, personal counseling, placement for graduates, veterans' counselor, women's services. **Physically disabled:** Services for visually, speech, hearing impaired.

Contact. E-mail: admrec@neiu.edu
Phone: (773) 442-4000 Fax: (773) 442-4020
Catherine Curran, Director of Admissions, Northeastern Illinois University, 5500 North St. Louis Avenue, Chicago, IL 60625

Northern Illinois University
DeKalb, Illinois **CB member**
www.niu.edu **CB code: 1559**

- Public 4-year university
- Residential campus in large town
- 14,952 degree-seeking undergraduates: 12% part-time, 49% women, 16% African American, 5% Asian American, 15% Hispanic/Latino, 3% Multi-racial, non-Hispanic, 2% international
- 4,472 degree-seeking graduate students
- 50% of applicants admitted
- SAT or ACT required
- 50% graduate within 6 years

General. Founded in 1895. Regionally accredited. Field campus in Oregon. **Degrees:** 3,507 bachelor's awarded; master's, professional, doctoral offered. **ROTC:** Army. **Location:** 65 miles from Chicago. **Calendar:** Semester, extensive summer session. **Full-time faculty:** 847 total; 82% have terminal degrees, 25% minority, 46% women. **Part-time faculty:** 252 total; 48% have terminal degrees, 16% minority, 55% women. **Class size:** 46% < 20, 38% 20-39, 5% 40-49, 9% 50-99, 2% >100. **Special facilities:** Observatory, Burma art collection, anthropology museum, historic scenic collection, history of education museum and research collection.

Freshman class profile. 17,081 applied, 8,598 admitted, 2,259 enrolled.

Mid 50% test scores		Rank in top tenth:	13%
ACT composite:	19-25	End year in good standing:	93%
GPA 3.75 or higher:	21%	Return as sophomores:	72%
GPA 3.50-3.74:	14%	Out-of-state:	5%
GPA 3.0-3.49:	33%	Live on campus:	91%
GPA 2.0-2.99:	32%	International:	1%
Rank in top quarter:	36%		

Basis for selection. 19 ACT required of applicants who rank in top half of class, 23 ACT required of applicants in top two-thirds of class or with high school equivalency certificate. Interview required of CHANCE program applicants. Audition required of music majors. Portfolio recommended for art majors.

High school preparation. College-preparatory program required. 15 units required. Required and recommended units include English 4, mathematics 2-4, social studies 2-3, history 1, science 2-4 (laboratory 1-2) and foreign language 1-2. One unit of art, film, music, theater, or foreign language required. Mathematics must include algebra and/or geometry. Social sciences must include US history or a combination of US history and government.

2015-2016 Annual costs. Tuition/fees: $12,202; $15,988 out-of-district; $21,242 out-of-state. Room/board: $9,670. Books/supplies: $1,400. Personal expenses: $1,800.

2014-2015 Financial aid. Need-based: 2,361 full-time freshmen applied for aid; 2,025 deemed to have need; 2,020 received aid. Average need met was 63%. Average scholarship/grant was $9,083; average loan $3,443. 44% of total undergraduate aid awarded as scholarships/grants, 56% as loans/jobs. **Non-need-based:** Awarded to 1,523 full-time undergraduates, including 490 freshmen. Scholarships awarded for academics, alumni affiliation, art, athletics, leadership, music/drama, ROTC.

Application procedures. Admission: Priority date 3/1; deadline 8/1. $40 fee, may be waived for applicants with need. Admission notification on a rolling basis. **Financial aid:** Priority date 3/1; no closing date. FAFSA required. Applicants notified on a rolling basis starting 3/15.

Academics. Special study options: Cooperative education, distance learning, double major, dual enrollment of high school students, honors, independent study, internships, student-designed major, study abroad, teacher certification program. **Credit/placement by examination:** AP, CLEP, institutional tests. Credit by examination not awarded for courses that are prerequisites for courses for which the student already has credit or is currently enrolled. **Support services:** Learning center, tutoring, writing center.

Majors. Biology: General. **Business:** General, accounting, business admin, finance, management science, marketing, operations. **Communications:** Communications/speech/rhetoric, journalism. **Computer sciences:** Computer science. **Conservation:** Environmental studies. **Education:** General, art, early childhood, elementary, health, physical, special ed. **Engineering:** Electrical, industrial, mechanical. **English:** English lit. **Foreign languages:** French, German, Russian, Spanish. **Health services:** Athletic training, clinical lab science, communication disorders, community health services, dietetics, nursing (RN), physical therapy, public health nursing. **History:** General. **Liberal arts:** Arts/sciences. **Math:** General. **Parks/recreation:** Health/fitness. **Philosophy/religion:** Philosophy. **Physical sciences:** Atmospheric science, chemistry, geology, physics. **Psychology:** General. **Social sciences:** Anthropology, economics, geography, political science, sociology. **Visual/performing arts:** Art, art history/conservation, dramatic, music, music performance, studio arts. **Work/family studies:** Clothing/textiles, family studies, food/nutrition.

Most popular majors. Business/marketing 15%, communications/journalism 8%, education 6%, engineering/engineering technologies 6%, health sciences 18%, psychology 6%, social sciences 9%.

Technology on campus. 1,500 workstations in dormitories, library, computer center, student center. Dormitories wired for high-speed internet access. Commuter students can connect to campus network. Online course registration, online library, helpline, wireless network available.

Student life. Freshman orientation: Mandatory, $60 fee. Preregistration for classes offered. **Housing:** Guaranteed on-campus for freshmen. Coed dorms, special housing for disabled, apartments, fraternity/sorority housing available. $150 deposit. Quiet and alcohol-free lifestyle floors, 21 and over student floors, honors floors available. **Activities:** Bands, campus ministries, choral groups, dance, drama, film society, international student organizations, music ensembles, Model UN, musical theater, opera, radio station, student government, student newspaper, symphony orchestra, TV station, numerous organizations available.

Athletics. NCAA. **Intercollegiate:** Baseball M, basketball, cross-country W, football (tackle) M, golf, gymnastics W, soccer, softball W, tennis, track and field W, volleyball W, wrestling M. **Intramural:** Badminton, basketball, football (non-tackle), football (tackle) M, golf, racquetball, sailing, soccer, softball, table tennis, tennis, ultimate frisbee, volleyball. **Team name:** Huskies.

Student services. Career counseling, student employment services, health services, legal services, minority student services, on-campus daycare, personal counseling, placement for graduates, veterans' counselor, women's services. **Physically disabled:** Services for visually, speech, hearing impaired.

Contact. E-mail: admissions@niu.edu
Phone: (815) 753-0446 Toll-free number: (800) 892-3050
Fax: (815) 753-8312
Dani Rollins, Director of Admissions, Northern Illinois University, 1425 West Lincoln Highway, DeKalb, IL 60115-2854

Northwestern University
Evanston, Illinois
www.northwestern.edu

CB member
CB code: 1565

- Private 4-year university
- Residential campus in small city
- 8,819 degree-seeking undergraduates: 6% part-time, 50% women
- 12,538 degree-seeking graduate students
- 13% of applicants admitted
- SAT or ACT with writing, application essay required
- 93% graduate within 6 years

General. Founded in 1851. Regionally accredited. **Degrees:** 2,275 bachelor's awarded; master's, professional, doctoral offered. **ROTC:** Army, Naval, Air Force. **Location:** 12 miles from downtown Chicago. **Calendar:** Quarter, limited summer session. **Special facilities:** Nanotechnology center, fine-arts complex, dance center, observatory, engineering design center, tennis center.

Freshman class profile. 32,122 applied, 4,248 admitted, 2,018 enrolled.

Mid 50% test scores			
SAT critical reading:	690-760	Return as sophomores:	97%
SAT math:	710-800	Out-of-state:	71%
ACT composite:	31-34	Live on campus:	99%
Rank in top quarter:	100%	Fraternities:	71%
Rank in top tenth:	91%	Sororities:	32%

Basis for selection. Academic record, essays, test scores, activity record, school recommendations most important. Audition required for music majors. **Home schooled:** 3 SAT Subject Tests required. Math Level 1 or 2 for students who plan to study sciences or engineering, Math Level 2 preferable, plus 2 other SAT Subject Tests of applicant's choice from different subject areas required.

High school preparation. College-preparatory program required. 16 units recommended. Recommended units include English 4, mathematics 3, social studies 2, history 2, science 2 (laboratory 2), foreign language 2 and academic electives 1.

2015-2016 Annual costs. Tuition/fees: $49,047. Room/board: $14,936.

2015-2016 Financial aid. Need-based: 1,188 full-time freshmen applied for aid; 982 deemed to have need; 982 received aid. Average need met was 100%. Average scholarship/grant was $42,088; average loan $3,961. 90% of total undergraduate aid awarded as scholarships/grants, 10% as loans/jobs. **Non-need-based:** Awarded to 768 full-time undergraduates, including 193 freshmen. Scholarships awarded for athletics, music/drama.

Application procedures. Admission: Closing date 1/1 (postmark date). $75 fee, may be waived for applicants with need. Admission notification by 4/1. Must reply by May 1 or within 2 week(s) if notified thereafter. **Financial aid:** Priority date 3/5, closing date 3/5. FAFSA, CSS PROFILE required. Applicants notified by 4/15; must reply by 5/1 or within 2 week(s) of notification.

Academics. One unit of credit awarded for each course; 45-48 units required for graduation. **Special study options:** Accelerated study, combined bachelor's/graduate degree, cooperative education, double major, honors,

independent study, internships, liberal arts/career combination, student-designed major, study abroad, teacher certification program. **Credit/placement by examination:** AP, CLEP, IB, institutional tests. **Support services:** Learning center, study skills assistance, tutoring, writing center.

Majors. Area/ethnic studies: African-American, American, Asian, European, women's. **Biology:** General, ecology, neuroscience. **Business:** Organizational behavior. **Communications:** Broadcast journalism, communications/speech/rhetoric, journalism, radio/TV. **Computer sciences:** General, computer science, information systems. **Conservation:** Environmental science, environmental studies. **Education:** General, learning disabled, mathematics, music, secondary. **Engineering:** General, biomedical, chemical, civil, computer, electrical, engineering science, environmental, industrial, manufacturing, materials, mechanical. **English:** Creative writing, English lit. **Foreign languages:** Classics, comparative lit, East Asian, French, German, Italian, linguistics, Slavic, Spanish. **Health services:** Communication disorders, pre-medicine. **History:** General. **Human services:** Community org/advocacy, public policy. **Liberal arts:** Arts/sciences. **Math:** General, applied, statistics. **Philosophy/religion:** Philosophy, religion. **Physical sciences:** Chemistry, geology, materials science, physics. **Psychology:** General, cognitive, community. **Social sciences:** Anthropology, economics, geography, international relations, political science, sociology, urban studies. **Visual/performing arts:** General, art, art history/conservation, dance, dramatic, jazz, music, music performance, music theory/composition, musicology, piano/keyboard, stringed instruments, theater history, voice/opera.

Most popular majors. Communications/journalism 15%, engineering/engineering technologies 13%, psychology 8%, social sciences 25%, visual/performing arts 7%.

Technology on campus. PC or laptop required. Dormitories wired for high-speed internet access and linked to campus network. Commuter students can connect to campus network. Online course registration, online library, helpline, repair service, student web hosting, wireless network available.

Student life. Freshman orientation: Mandatory. Preregistration for classes offered. **Housing:** Guaranteed on-campus for freshmen. Coed dorms, single-sex dorms, fraternity/sorority housing, themed housing, wellness housing available. $200 nonrefundable deposit, deadline 5/1. **Activities:** Bands, campus ministries, choral groups, dance, drama, film society, international student organizations, literary magazine, music ensembles, Model UN, musical theater, opera, radio station, student government, student newspaper, symphony orchestra, TV station.

Athletics. NCAA. **Intercollegiate:** Baseball M, basketball, cheerleading, cross-country W, diving, fencing W, field hockey W, football (tackle) M, golf, lacrosse W, soccer, softball W, swimming, tennis, volleyball W, wrestling M. **Intramural:** Basketball, football (non-tackle), ice hockey, soccer, softball, volleyball. **Team name:** Wildcats.

Student services. Adult student services, alcohol/substance abuse counseling, chaplain/spiritual director, career counseling, student employment services, financial aid counseling, health services, minority student services, personal counseling, placement for graduates, women's services. **Physically disabled:** Services for visually, speech, hearing impaired.

Contact. E-mail: ug-admission@northwestern.edu
Phone: (847) 491-7271
Christopher Watson, Dean of Undergraduate Admission, Northwestern University, 1801 Hinman Avenue, Evanston, IL 60208-3060

Olivet Nazarene University
Bourbonnais, Illinois
www.olivet.edu

CB member
CB code: 1596

- Private 4-year university and liberal arts college affiliated with the Church of the Nazarene
- Residential campus in small city
- 3,389 degree-seeking undergraduates: 10% part-time, 61% women, 8% African American, 2% Asian American, 7% Hispanic/Latino, 2% Multiracial, non-Hispanic, 1% international
- 1,132 degree-seeking graduate students
- 77% of applicants admitted
- SAT or ACT (ACT writing optional) required
- 61% graduate within 6 years

General. Founded in 1907. Regionally accredited. **Degrees:** 887 bachelor's, 7 associate awarded; master's, doctoral offered. **ROTC:** Army. **Location:** 60 miles from Chicago. **Calendar:** Semester, limited summer session. **Full-time faculty:** 136 total; 41% women. **Part-time faculty:** 306 total; 59% women. **Special facilities:** Planetarium, observatory, science museum, distance learning classroom.

Freshman class profile. 4,133 applied, 3,165 admitted, 734 enrolled.

Mid 50% test scores		Out-of-state:	43%
ACT composite:	20-27	Live on campus:	92%
Return as sophomores:	77%	International:	1%

Basis for selection. 2.0 GPA in college-preparatory subjects, ranking in top three-quarters of class, 18 ACT, 2 recommendations required. Writing portion of the ACT highly encouraged. Interview recommended. Audition required of music majors. Portfolios required for art scholarship applicants. **Home schooled:** Statement describing home school structure and mission, transcript of courses and grades, state high school equivalency certificate, interview, letter of recommendation (nonparent) required. ACT scores required.

High school preparation. College-preparatory program recommended. 15 units required. Required and recommended units include English 4, mathematics 3, social studies 4, history 2, science 3 and foreign language 2.

2015-2016 Annual costs. Tuition/fees: $32,790. Room/board: $7,900. Books/supplies: $1,000. Personal expenses: $400.

2015-2016 Financial aid. Need-based: 700 full-time freshmen applied for aid; 631 deemed to have need; 631 received aid. Average need met was 80%. Average scholarship/grant was $21,424; average loan $2,465. 77% of total undergraduate aid awarded as scholarships/grants, 23% as loans/jobs. **Non-need-based:** Awarded to 1,125 full-time undergraduates, including 256 freshmen. Scholarships awarded for academics, alumni affiliation, art, athletics, leadership, music/drama, religious affiliation, ROTC, state residency.

Application procedures. Admission: Closing date 5/15 (postmark date). $25 fee, may be waived for applicants with need, free for online applicants. Admission notification on a rolling basis. **Financial aid:** Priority date 3/1; no closing date. Applicants notified on a rolling basis starting 1/15; must reply within 2 week(s) of notification.

Academics. Special study options: Accelerated study, distance learning, double major, honors, independent study, internships, liberal arts/career combination, student-designed major, study abroad, teacher certification program, Washington semester. Council of Christian Colleges and Universities study programs (international and domestic). **Credit/placement by examination:** AP, CLEP, IB, ACT, institutional tests. **Support services:** Learning center, pre-admission summer program, reduced course load, remedial instruction, study skills assistance, tutoring. Academic coaching center.

Majors. Biology: General, zoology. **Business:** General, accounting, business admin, fashion, finance, international, marketing. **Communications:** Communications/speech/rhetoric, media studies. **Computer sciences:** General, computer science, information systems, programming. **Conservation:** Environmental studies. **Education:** Art, biology, chemistry, early childhood, elementary, English, family/consumer sciences, foreign languages, health, history, mathematics, music, physical, science, secondary, social science, social studies, Spanish. **Engineering:** General. **English:** English lit. **Foreign languages:** General, Spanish. **Health services:** Athletic training, dietetics, nursing (RN). **History:** General. **Human services:** Public policy, social work. **Liberal arts:** Arts/sciences. **Math:** General. **Parks/recreation:** Exercise sciences, sports admin. **Philosophy/religion:** Religion. **Physical sciences:** Chemistry, geology. **Protective services:** Criminal justice. **Psychology:** General. **Social sciences:** General, economics, political science, sociology. **Theology:** Bible, missionary, pastoral counseling, religious ed, sacred music, theology, youth ministry. **Visual/performing arts:** Art, music, music performance, piano/keyboard, voice/opera. **Work/family studies:** General, family/community services, housing.

Technology on campus. 125 workstations in library, computer center, student center. Dormitories wired for high-speed internet access and linked to campus network. Commuter students can connect to campus network. Online library, helpline, repair service, student web hosting, wireless network available.

Student life. Freshman orientation: Mandatory. Preregistration for classes offered. Three-day program held on second and third weekends in June. Comprehensive for students and parents. **Policies:** Chapel convocations held twice weekly. Religious observance required. **Housing:** Guaranteed on-campus for all undergraduates. Single-sex dorms, special housing for disabled, apartments available. **Activities:** Bands, campus ministries, choral groups, drama, international student organizations, literary magazine, music ensembles, musical theater, radio station, student government, student newspaper, symphony orchestra, social service clubs, spiritual life groups.

Athletics. NAIA, NCCAA. **Intercollegiate:** Baseball M, basketball, cheerleading, cross-country, football (tackle) M, golf M, soccer, softball W, swimming, tennis, track and field, volleyball W. **Intramural:** Badminton, basketball, bowling, cross-country, football (non-tackle) W, golf, handball, racquetball, soccer, softball, table tennis, tennis, track and field, volleyball. **Team name:** Tigers.

Student services. Adult student services, alcohol/substance abuse counseling, chaplain/spiritual director, career counseling, services for economically disadvantaged, student employment services, financial aid counseling, health services, personal counseling, placement for graduates, veterans' counselor. **Physically disabled:** Services for visually, hearing impaired.

Contact. E-mail: admissions@olivet.edu
Phone: (815) 939-5203 Toll-free number: (800) 648-1463
Fax: (815) 939-5069
Susan Wolff, Dean of Undergraduate Enrollment, Olivet Nazarene University, One University Avenue, Bourbonnais, IL 60914

Principia College
Elsah, Illinois   **CB member**
www.principiacollege.edu   **CB code: 1630**

- Private 4-year liberal arts college affiliated with the First Church of Christ, Scientist (Christian Science)
- Residential campus in rural community
- 449 degree-seeking undergraduates: 2% part-time, 50% women, 2% African American, 1% Asian American, 4% Hispanic/Latino, 2% Multiracial, non-Hispanic, 16% international
- 75% of applicants admitted
- SAT or ACT with writing, application essay required
- 80% graduate within 6 years

General. Founded in 1910. Regionally accredited. All faculty, staff, and students are Christian Scientists. **Degrees:** 110 bachelor's awarded. **Location:** 35 miles from St. Louis. **Calendar:** Semester, limited summer session. **Full-time faculty:** 62 total; 63% have terminal degrees, 6% minority, 48% women. **Special facilities:** Museum, astronomical observatory telescope, media center, tropical aviary, science center with mammoth excavation, Christian Science practitioner's office, natatorium, dance studios, 3,069-pipe organ, 39 bronze bell carillon.

Freshman class profile. 159 applied, 120 admitted, 79 enrolled.

Mid 50% test scores		GPA 2.0-2.99:	24%
SAT critical reading:	460-590	Rank in top quarter:	32%
SAT math:	470-610	Rank in top tenth:	21%
SAT writing:	460-570	End year in good standing:	98%
ACT composite:	21-27	Return as sophomores:	88%
GPA 3.75 or higher:	31%	Out-of-state:	93%
GPA 3.50-3.74:	22%	Live on campus:	100%
GPA 3.0-3.49:	23%	International:	9%

Basis for selection. High school transcript, admissions application and essay or personal statement most important. Test scores important as well. Applicant must be practicing Christian Scientist. Foreign language SAT Subject Test required for placement purposes. Interview recommended. **Home schooled:** Must submit curricula program from accredited high school or accepted agency, plus GED.

High school preparation. 16 units required; 20 recommended. Required and recommended units include English 4, mathematics 3-4, social studies 2, history 1-2, science 3-4 (laboratory 1-2), foreign language 2-3 and academic electives 2.

2016-2017 Annual costs. Tuition/fees (projected): $27,980. Room/board: $11,030. Books/supplies: $1,000. Personal expenses: $1,000.

2015-2016 Financial aid. Need-based: 59 full-time freshmen applied for aid; 51 deemed to have need; 51 received aid. Average need met was 99%. Average scholarship/grant was $26,094; average loan $5,727. 86% of total undergraduate aid awarded as scholarships/grants, 14% as loans/jobs. **Non-need-based:** Awarded to 285 full-time undergraduates, including 72 freshmen. Scholarships awarded for academics, alumni affiliation, leadership.

Application procedures. Admission: No deadline. No application fee. Application must be submitted online. Admission notification on a rolling basis beginning on or about 10/15. Must reply by May 1 or within 2 week(s) if notified thereafter. **Financial aid:** Closing date 3/1. Institutional form, CSS PROFILE required. Applicants notified by 4/1.

Academics. Special study options: Combined bachelor's/graduate degree, distance learning, double major, dual enrollment of high school students, honors, independent study, internships, liberal arts/career combination, student-designed major, study abroad. 3-2 engineering with University of Minnesota. UND arrangement is students take classes here via distance learning. **Credit/placement by examination:** AP, CLEP, IB, institutional tests. **Support services:** Learning center, reduced course load, study skills assistance, tutoring, writing center.

Majors. Biology: General. **Business:** Business admin. **Communications:** Media studies. **Computer sciences:** General, computer science. **Conservation:** General. **Education:** Elementary. **Engineering:** Engineering science. **English:** English lit. **Foreign languages:** General, French, Spanish. **History:** General. **Liberal arts:** Arts/sciences, humanities. **Math:** General. **Philosophy/religion:** Philosophy, religion. **Physical sciences:** Chemistry, physics. **Social sciences:** General, anthropology, economics, political science, sociology. **Visual/performing arts:** Art history/conservation, dramatic, music, studio arts.

Most popular majors. Biology 7%, business/marketing 17%, communications/journalism 8%, education 7%, English 7%, philosophy/religious studies 6%, social sciences 10%, visual/performing arts 19%.

Technology on campus. 250 workstations in dormitories, library, computer center, student center. Dormitories wired for high-speed internet access and linked to campus network. Online course registration, online library, helpline, student web hosting, wireless network available.

Student life. Freshman orientation: Mandatory. Preregistration for classes offered. One week orientation program offered each semester prior to start of classes in August and January. **Policies:** Students required to comply with standards of Christian Science. No alcoholic beverages, smoking, drugs. High moral standards and behavior expected. Standards maintained regarding abstinence from premarital sex or homosexual activity. Religious observance required. **Housing:** Guaranteed on-campus for all undergraduates. Coed dorms, single-sex dorms, apartments, wellness housing available. $100 nonrefundable deposit, deadline 5/1. Single-sex wings, 8 person cottages for non-traditional students available. **Activities:** Bands, choral groups, dance, drama, international student organizations, music ensembles, musical theater, radio station, student government, student newspaper, symphony orchestra, TV station, Christian Science organization, black student union, Latin American student organization, student volunteer program, public affairs conference.

Athletics. NCAA. **Intercollegiate:** Baseball M, basketball, cross-country, diving, soccer, swimming, tennis, track and field, volleyball W. **Intramural:** Basketball, soccer, softball, volleyball W. **Team name:** Panthers.

Student services. Adult student services, career counseling, student employment services, financial aid counseling, health services, on-campus daycare, personal counseling.

Contact. E-mail: collegeadmissions@principia.edu
Phone: (618) 374-5181 Toll-free number: (800) 277-4648 ext. 2802
Fax: (618) 374-4000
Tami Gavaletz, Director of Admissions and Financial Aid, Principia College, One Maybeck Place, Elsah, IL 62028-9799

Quincy University
Quincy, Illinois
www.quincy.edu

CB code: 1645

▶ Private 4-year university and liberal arts college affiliated with the Roman Catholic Church

▶ Residential campus in large town

▶ 1,065 degree-seeking undergraduates: 4% part-time, 54% women, 12% African American, 1% Asian American, 5% Hispanic/Latino, 2% Multiracial, non-Hispanic

▶ 96 degree-seeking graduate students

▶ 63% of applicants admitted

▶ SAT or ACT (ACT writing optional), application essay required

▶ 52% graduate within 6 years

General. Founded in 1860. Regionally accredited. **Degrees:** 262 bachelor's awarded; master's offered. **Location:** 300 miles from Chicago, 275 miles from Indianapolis, 120 miles from St. Louis, 100 miles from Springfield, IL. **Calendar:** Semester, limited summer session. **Full-time faculty:** 52 total; 10% minority, 44% women. **Part-time faculty:** 62 total; 48% have terminal degrees, 3% minority, 60% women. **Class size:** 71% < 20, 28% 20-39, less than 1% 40-49. **Special facilities:** Theater, multi-media and graphic design labs, environmental studies institute, TV production studio, rare books archive, hospital simulation lab, aviation facility with simulator, university chapel and non-denominational praise/worship chapel, art gallery, mock trial courtroom, center for music.

Freshman class profile. 1,553 applied, 984 admitted, 278 enrolled.

Mid 50% test scores			
SAT critical reading:	480-590	Rank in top quarter:	32%
SAT math:	430-520	Rank in top tenth:	8%
ACT composite:	19-24	Return as sophomores:	69%
GPA 3.75 or higher:	22%	Out-of-state:	36%
GPA 3.50-3.74:	21%	Live on campus:	72%
GPA 3.0-3.49:	29%	Fraternities:	4%
GPA 2.0-2.99:	28%	Sororities:	9%

Basis for selection. School achievement record is most important. Applicants for BS in nursing must have the minimum of a 22 ACT composite and 3.0 high school GPA and meet other requirements. May also require references and/or writing sample. Audition required of music majors. Portfolio recommended for art majors. **Home schooled:** Letter of recommendation (nonparent) required. Required documentation may vary. **Learning Disabled:** Must submit documentation of disability.

High school preparation. College-preparatory program recommended. 16 units recommended. Recommended units include English 4, mathematics 3, social studies 3, science 3, foreign language 2, computer science .5, visual/performing arts .5. Courses in computers and the arts recommended.

2015-2016 Annual costs. Tuition/fees: $26,998. Room/board: $10,000. Books/supplies: $1,250.

2015-2016 Financial aid. Need-based: 266 full-time freshmen applied for aid; 240 deemed to have need; 239 received aid. Average need met was 87%. Average scholarship/grant was $19,246; average loan $5,131. 73% of total undergraduate aid awarded as scholarships/grants, 27% as loans/jobs. **Non-need-based:** Awarded to 177 full-time undergraduates, including 61 freshmen. Scholarships awarded for academics, alumni affiliation, art, athletics, leadership, music/drama.

Application procedures. Admission: Priority date 5/1; no deadline. $25 fee. Admission notification on a rolling basis beginning on or about 9/1. **Financial aid:** Priority date 3/21; no closing date. FAFSA required. Applicants notified on a rolling basis starting 3/1; must reply by 5/1 or within 2 week(s) of notification.

Academics. Study abroad program offers 94 programs in 30 countries. A variety of service projects are available. **Special study options:** Accelerated study, distance learning, double major, dual enrollment of high school students, honors, independent study, internships, student-designed major, study abroad, teacher certification program, Washington semester. 3-1 program in medical technology with various hospitals; learning communities, service learning, evening courses, Washington Semester Program, credit for life experiences (CARE). **Credit/placement by examination:** AP, CLEP, IB, SAT, ACT, institutional tests. 40 credit hours maximum toward bachelor's degree. Combined total of 40 semester hours of credit from nontraditional sources accepted toward a bachelor's degree, including a maximum of 30 semester hours of credit through CLEP. **Support services:** Learning center, pre-admission summer program, reduced course load, remedial instruction, study skills assistance, tutoring, writing center.

Majors. Biology: General. **Business:** Accounting, business admin, finance, management science, marketing. **Communications:** General. **Computer sciences:** Computer science, information systems, webmaster. **Education:** Elementary, multi-level teacher, music, physical, special ed. **English:** English lit. **Foreign languages:** Sign language interpretation. **Health services:** Clinical lab science, nursing (RN). **History:** General. **Liberal arts:** Arts/sciences, humanities. **Math:** General. **Parks/recreation:** Health/fitness, sports admin. **Physical sciences:** Chemistry. **Protective services:** Criminal justice, forensics. **Psychology:** General, forensic. **Social sciences:** Political science. **Theology:** Sacred music. **Visual/performing arts:** Graphic design, music.

Most popular majors. Biology 10%, business/marketing 21%, communications/journalism 6%, education 14%, health sciences 9%, parks/recreation 7%, psychology 7%, security/protective services 7%.

Technology on campus. 139 workstations in library, computer center. Dormitories wired for high-speed internet access and linked to campus network. Commuter students can connect to campus network. Online course registration, online library, helpline, wireless network available.

Student life. Freshman orientation: Mandatory, $150 fee. Preregistration for classes offered. Held 4 days prior to the beginning of fall semester and first day of spring semester for first-time/transfer students. **Policies:** Full-time, first-time, regular undergraduate students required to live on campus until they have attained senior standing unless living locally with immediate family who are permanent residents, or given permission from the Vice President for Student Affairs to live off campus. **Housing:** Guaranteed on-campus for all undergraduates. Coed dorms, special housing for disabled, apartments, fraternity/sorority housing, themed housing available. Honors housing and on campus houses available; student living center. **Activities:** Bands, campus ministries, choral groups, dance, drama, film society, literary magazine, music ensembles, musical theater, student government, student newspaper, symphony orchestra, Circle K International, environmental club, minority student association, Peers 2 Peers, student programming board, Haiti Connection, Koinonia Retreat, Voices of Praise, Brothers of Unity.

Athletics. NCAA. **Intercollegiate:** Baseball M, basketball, cross-country, football (tackle) M, golf, soccer, softball W, swimming W, tennis, volleyball. **Intramural:** Basketball, bowling, football (non-tackle), racquetball, soccer, softball, table tennis, volleyball. **Team name:** Hawks.

Student services. Alcohol/substance abuse counseling, chaplain/spiritual director, career counseling, student employment services, financial aid counseling, health services, minority student services, personal counseling, placement for graduates, women's services. **Physically disabled:** Services for visually, hearing impaired.

Contact. E-mail: admissions@quincy.edu
Phone: (217) 228-5210 Toll-free number: (800) 688-4295
Fax: (217) 228-5479
Abby Wayman, Director of Admissions, Quincy University, 1800 College Avenue, Quincy, IL 62301-2699

Rasmussen College: Mokena/Tinley Park
Mokena, Illinois
www.rasmussen.edu

- For-profit 4-year career college
- Large town
- 234 degree-seeking undergraduates
- 75% of applicants admitted

General. Regionally accredited. **Degrees:** 33 bachelor's, 48 associate awarded. **Calendar:** Quarter. **Full-time faculty:** 1 total. **Part-time faculty:** 23 total.

Freshman class profile. 153 applied, 115 admitted, 115 enrolled.

Basis for selection. Admission requirements vary by program.

2016-2017 Annual costs. Tuition/fees (projected): $13,455.

Application procedures. Admission: No deadline. No application fee. Admission notification on a rolling basis. **Financial aid:** No deadline. FAFSA, institutional form required. Applicants notified on a rolling basis.

Academics. Credit/placement by examination: AP, CLEP.

Majors. Business: Accounting, accounting/business management, business admin, finance, human resources, information resources management, marketing. **Computer sciences:** Computer science, security, system admin. **Health services:** Health care admin, health information management. **Protective services:** Criminal justice, special ops. **Visual/performing arts:** Digital arts, game design.

Contact. Phone: (815) 534-3300
Susan Hammerstrom, Director of Admissions, Rasmussen College: Mokena/Tinley Park, 8650 West Spring Lake Road, Mokena, IL 60448

Resurrection University
Chicago, Illinois
www.resu.edu   CB code: 1927

- Private two-year upper-division health science and nursing college affiliated with the Roman Catholic Church
- Commuter campus in very large city
- 96% of applicants admitted
- Test scores, application essay required

General. Founded in 1982. Regionally accredited. Facilities located in St.Elizabeth's Hospital. **Degrees:** 197 bachelor's awarded; master's, professional offered. **Location:** 7 miles from downtown Chicago. **Calendar:** Semester, limited summer session. **Full-time faculty:** 30 total. **Part-time faculty:** 32 total. **Class size:** 20% < 20, 23% 20-39, 26% 40-49, 31% 50-99. **Special facilities:** In-hospital location, health sciences library, nursing clinical skills laboratory.

Student profile. 391 degree-seeking undergraduates, 65 graduate students. 190 applied as first time-transfer students, 182 admitted, 119 enrolled.

Basis for selection. College transcript, application essay, standardized test scores required. Natural and behavioral science grades more heavily

weighted. Recommendation and essay required. Must have 2.75 science GPA. Satisfactory score on TEAS required. Transfer accepted as juniors.

2015-2016 Annual costs. Tuition/fees: $25,142. Books/supplies: $1,400.

Financial aid. Non-need-based: Scholarships awarded for academics, alumni affiliation.

Application procedures. Admission: $50 fee. Application must be submitted online. **Financial aid:** Priority date 4/1, no deadline. Applicants notified on a rolling basis starting 4/1; must reply within 3 weeks of notification. FAFSA required.

Academics. Special study options: Accelerated study, combined bachelor's/graduate degree, independent study. Evening and weekend BS completion program for registered nurses. **Credit/placement by examination:** AP, CLEP.

Majors. Health services: Nursing (RN).

Technology on campus. PC or laptop required. 10 workstations in library, computer center. Online library, wireless network available.

Student life. Activities: Student government.

Student services. Career counseling, student employment services, health services, personal counseling.

Contact. E-mail: admissions@resu.edu
Phone: (773) 252-6464 Fax: (773) 227-3838
Ron de los Santos, Director of Enrollment Management, Resurrection University, 1431 North Claremont Avenue, Chicago, IL 60622

Robert Morris University: Chicago
Chicago, Illinois   CB member
www.robertmorris.edu   CB code: 1670

- Private 4-year university
- Commuter campus in very large city
- 2,681 degree-seeking undergraduates: 5% part-time, 50% women, 27% African American, 3% Asian American, 29% Hispanic/Latino, 2% Multiracial, non-Hispanic, 1% international
- 349 degree-seeking graduate students
- 24% of applicants admitted
- 73% graduate within 6 years; 20% enter graduate study

General. Founded in 1913. Regionally accredited. Additional locations in Arlington Heights, Bensenville, DuPage, Elgin, Lake County, Orland Park, Peoria, Schaumburg, and Springfield. **Degrees:** 542 bachelor's, 423 associate awarded; master's offered. **ROTC:** Army. **Location:** Downtown. **Calendar:** Five, 10-week sessions. Extensive summer session. **Full-time faculty:** 71 total; 31% have terminal degrees, 28% minority, 42% women. **Part-time faculty:** 151 total; 17% have terminal degrees, 27% minority, 54% women. **Class size:** 51% < 20, 45% 20-39, 3% 40-49, less than 1% 50-99. **Special facilities:** Student-run restaurant, art gallery.

Freshman class profile. 2,945 applied, 704 admitted, 608 enrolled.

Mid 50% test scores		Rank in top quarter:	17%
ACT composite:	16-21	Rank in top tenth:	4%
GPA 3.75 or higher:	6%	End year in good standing:	83%
GPA 3.50-3.74:	7%	Return as sophomores:	50%
GPA 3.0-3.49:	18%	Out-of-state:	12%
GPA 2.0-2.99:	63%	Live on campus:	20%

Basis for selection. Must submit high school transcript or GED for review. Secondary school record, class rank, GPA, and interview most important. Extra curricular activities and level of interest considered. Meeting with admissions counselor and campus visit strongly recommended. **Home schooled:** Transcript of courses and grades, state high school equivalency certificate required. Curriculum documentation, state certification, and standardized exam with acceptable achievement level required.

High school preparation. College-preparatory program recommended. 16 units recommended. Recommended units include English 4, mathematics 3, social studies 2, history 3, science 2 (laboratory 1) and foreign language 2.

2016-2017 Annual costs. Tuition/fees (projected): $25,950. Room/board: $12,600. Books/supplies: $1,500. Personal expenses: $2,592.

2014-2015 Financial aid. Need-based: 835 full-time freshmen applied for aid; 809 deemed to have need; 780 received aid. Average need met was 51%. Average scholarship/grant was $12,301; average loan $3,855. 50% of

total undergraduate aid awarded as scholarships/grants, 50% as loans/jobs. **Non-need-based:** Awarded to 4,314 full-time undergraduates, including 1,129 freshmen. Scholarships awarded for academics, art, athletics, leadership, music/drama, ROTC, state residency.

Application procedures. Admission: No deadline. $20 fee, may be waived for applicants with need. Admission notification on a rolling basis. **Financial aid:** No deadline. FAFSA required. Applicants notified on a rolling basis.

Academics. Special study options: Accelerated study, combined bachelor's/graduate degree, double major, honors, internships, study abroad. Master's Advantage and dual degree. **Credit/placement by examination:** AP, CLEP. **Support services:** Learning center, reduced course load, study skills assistance, tutoring, writing center.

Majors. Business: Accounting, business admin. **Computer sciences:** Information technology. **Visual/performing arts:** Graphic design.

Most popular majors. Business/marketing 64%, computer/information sciences 7%, interdisciplinary studies 23%, visual/performing arts 6%.

Technology on campus. 1,360 workstations in library, computer center, student center. Online library, helpline, repair service, student web hosting, wireless network available.

Student life. Freshman orientation: Mandatory. Preregistration for classes offered. Held 1-4 weeks prior to commencement of classes. Students required to attend one 2 1/2-hour session. **Policies:** Students required to abide by student code of conduct and housing policies. **Housing:** Coed dorms, apartments available. $300 fully refundable deposit, deadline 5/1. **Activities:** Bands, choral groups, dance, drama, international student organizations, literary magazine, music ensembles, student newspaper, Interior arts and design club, mobile applications and game idea club, UNA-USA, Warriors to Scholars, Culinary Society.

Athletics. NAIA, USCAA. **Intercollegiate:** Baseball M, basketball, bowling, cheerleading, cross-country, football (tackle) M, golf, ice hockey, lacrosse, soccer, softball W, tennis W, track and field, volleyball. **Intramural:** Bowling, cross-country, football (non-tackle), golf, softball, volleyball. **Team name:** Eagles.

Student services. Adult student services, alcohol/substance abuse counseling, career counseling, services for economically disadvantaged, student employment services, financial aid counseling, personal counseling, placement for graduates, veterans' counselor. **Physically disabled:** Services for visually, speech, hearing impaired.

Contact. E-mail: ais@robertmorris.edu
Phone: (312) 935-4400 Toll-free number: (800) 762-5960
Fax: (312) 935-4182
Nicole Cafillio, Senior Vice President for Enrollment Management, Robert Morris University: Chicago, 401South State Street, Chicago, IL 60605

Rockford University
Rockford, Illinois
www.rockford.edu

CB member
CB code: 1665

+ Private 4-year liberal arts college
+ Residential campus in small city
+ 1,033 degree-seeking undergraduates: 11% part-time, 60% women, 9% African American, 2% Asian American, 14% Hispanic/Latino, 3% Multiracial, non-Hispanic, 1% international
+ 153 degree-seeking graduate students
+ SAT or ACT (ACT writing optional) required
+ 42% graduate within 6 years

General. Founded in 1847. Regionally accredited. **Degrees:** 277 bachelor's awarded; master's offered. **Location:** 90 miles from Chicago. **Calendar:** Semester, limited summer session. **Full-time faculty:** 76 total; 70% have terminal degrees, 3% minority, 49% women. **Part-time faculty:** 89 total; 16% have terminal degrees, 7% minority, 61% women. **Class size:** 82% < 20, 17% 20-39, less than 1% 40-49, less than 1% 50-99. **Special facilities:** Theater, nursing lab, center for civic engagement.

Freshman class profile. 168 enrolled.

Mid 50% test scores			
SAT critical reading:	400-560	GPA 3.0-3.49:	31%
SAT math:	430-520	GPA 2.0-2.99:	38%
SAT writing:	430-550	Return as sophomores:	66%
ACT composite:	19-24	Out-of-state:	20%
GPA 3.75 or higher:	17%	Live on campus:	71%
GPA 3.50-3.74:	14%	International:	2%

Basis for selection. School achievement record and test scores are most important. Recommendations and activities also are considered. Auditions required of theater arts and musical theater performance majors. Personal statements required of students who fall below standard admission criteria.

High school preparation. College-preparatory program recommended. 15 units recommended. Recommended units include English 4, mathematics 3, social studies 3, science 3 (laboratory 3) and academic electives 2.

2015-2016 Annual costs. Tuition/fees: $28,330. Room/board: $7,940. Books/supplies: $1,200. Personal expenses: $2,250.

2014-2015 Financial aid. Need-based: 142 full-time freshmen applied for aid; 134 deemed to have need; 134 received aid. Average need met was 71%. Average scholarship/grant was $16,491; average loan $3,907. 61% of total undergraduate aid awarded as scholarships/grants, 39% as loans/jobs. **Non-need-based:** Awarded to 152 full-time undergraduates, including 30 freshmen. Scholarships awarded for academics, alumni affiliation, leadership, minority status, music/drama, state residency.

Application procedures. Admission: Closing date 8/15. No application fee. Admission notification on a rolling basis beginning on or about 6/15. **Financial aid:** Priority date 3/1; no closing date. FAFSA required. Applicants notified on a rolling basis starting 3/1; must reply within 4 week(s) of notification.

Academics. Community-based learning opportunities available. **Special study options:** Accelerated study, double major, dual enrollment of high school students, ESL, exchange student, honors, independent study, internships, semester at sea, study abroad, teacher certification program, United Nations semester, Washington semester, weekend college. **Credit/placement by examination:** AP, CLEP, SAT, ACT, institutional tests. **Support services:** Learning center, reduced course load, remedial instruction, study skills assistance, tutoring, writing center.

Majors. Biology: General, biochemistry. **Business:** Accounting, business admin. **Computer sciences:** General. **Education:** General, early childhood, elementary, physical, special ed. **English:** English lit. **Foreign languages:** Classics, French, Latin, Romance, Spanish. **Health services:** Nursing (RN). **History:** General. **Liberal arts:** Humanities. **Math:** General. **Philosophy/religion:** Philosophy. **Physical sciences:** Chemistry. **Psychology:** General. **Social sciences:** General, economics, international relations, political science. **Visual/performing arts:** Art, art history/conservation, dramatic, music, music history, musical theater.

Most popular majors. Biology 6%, business/marketing 22%, education 16%, family/consumer sciences 6%, health sciences 23%, social sciences 8%.

Technology on campus. Dormitories wired for high-speed internet access and linked to campus network. Commuter students can connect to campus network. Helpline, repair service, wireless network available.

Student life. Freshman orientation: Mandatory. Preregistration for classes offered. Four-day program held the week prior to beginning of fall classes. **Policies:** Alcohol and guest policies, Academic Honor Code in place. **Housing:** Coed dorms, special housing for disabled, themed housing, wellness housing available. Special housing available for first-year students. **Activities:** Campus ministries, choral groups, dance, drama, international student organizations, literary magazine, music ensembles, musical theater, radio station, student government, student newspaper, multicultural club, ELITE Leadership Program.

Athletics. NCAA. **Intercollegiate:** Baseball M, basketball, cross-country, football (tackle) M, soccer M, softball W, track and field, volleyball W. **Team name:** Regents.

Student services. Alcohol/substance abuse counseling, chaplain/spiritual director, career counseling, student employment services, financial aid counseling, health services, personal counseling. **Physically disabled:** Services for visually, hearing impaired.

Contact. E-mail: admissions@rockford.edu
Phone: (815) 226-4050 Toll-free number: (800) 892-2984
Fax: (815) 226-2822
Jennifer Nordstrom, Associate Vice President for Undergraduate Admission, Rockford University, 5050 East State Street, Rockford, IL 61108-2311

Roosevelt University
Chicago, Illinois
www.roosevelt.edu

CB member
CB code: 1666

+ Private 4-year university
+ Commuter campus in very large city

- 3,727 degree-seeking undergraduates
- 2,320 graduate students
- SAT or ACT (ACT writing optional) required

General. Founded in 1945. Regionally accredited. Additional campus in Schaumburg. **Degrees:** 896 bachelor's awarded; master's, professional, doctoral offered. **Location:** Downtown. **Calendar:** Semester, extensive summer session. **Full-time faculty:** 247 total; 90% have terminal degrees, 26% minority, 45% women. **Part-time faculty:** 486 total; 89% have terminal degrees, 17% minority, 45% women. **Class size:** 60% < 20, 36% 20-39, 3% 40-49, less than 1% 50-99, less than 1% >100.

Freshman class profile.

GPA 3.75 or higher:	26%	Rank in top tenth:	2%
GPA 3.50-3.74:	14%	Out-of-state:	21%
GPA 3.0-3.49:	28%	Live on campus:	60%
GPA 2.0-2.99:	32%	Sororities:	5%
Rank in top quarter:	6%		

Basis for selection. Recent secondary school performance most crucial. Personal statement and recommended interview can be used to communicate special circumstances. Placement evaluation required for all admitted, degree-seeking undergraduate students. Test results must be submitted by first year or transfer applicants with scores less than 2 years old. Interview recommended for early admission and borderline applicants. Audition required of music and theater majors. Portfolio recommended for music and theater majors. **Home schooled:** Statement describing home school structure and mission, letter of recommendation (nonparent) required. **Learning Disabled:** Students are encouraged to visit with director of disability services.

High school preparation. College-preparatory program required. 11 units required; 23 recommended. Required and recommended units include English 4, mathematics 3-4, social studies 2-3, history 2, science 2-3 (laboratory 2-3), foreign language 2 and computer science 2. Extensive work in English, history, mathematics, foreign language, and science recommended.

2015-2016 Annual costs. Tuition/fees: $27,300. Room/board: $12,980. Books/supplies: $1,200. Personal expenses: $4,400.

Financial aid. Non-need-based: Scholarships awarded for academics, alumni affiliation, art, job skills, minority status.

Application procedures. Admission: Priority date 8/15; no deadline. $25 fee, may be waived for applicants with need. Admission notification on a rolling basis beginning on or about 10/15. Admission deposit requested within two weeks of admission decision. Housing deposit fully refundable before 6/1. **Financial aid:** Priority date 3/1; no closing date. FAFSA, institutional form required. Applicants notified on a rolling basis starting 2/1; must reply within 2 week(s) of notification.

Academics. Special study options: Accelerated study, combined bachelor's/graduate degree, distance learning, double major, dual enrollment of high school students, ESL, exchange student, honors, independent study, internships, student-designed major, study abroad, teacher certification program. **Credit/placement by examination:** AP, CLEP, SAT, ACT, institutional tests. 30 credit hours maximum toward bachelor's degree. **Support services:** Learning center, pre-admission summer program, reduced course load, remedial instruction, study skills assistance, tutoring, writing center.

Majors. Area/ethnic studies: African-American, women's. **Biology:** General, biochemistry. **Business:** General, accounting, actuarial science, casino management, event planning, finance, hospitality admin, hotel/motel admin, hotel/motel/restaurant management, human resources, management science, marketing, organizational behavior, organizational leadership, restaurant/food services, tourism/travel. **Communications:** General, journalism, media studies, organizational. **Computer sciences:** Computer science. **Education:** Early childhood, elementary, music, secondary, special ed. **English:** English lit. **Health services:** Clinical lab science, medical radiologic technology/radiation therapy, nuclear medical technology. **History:** General. **Liberal arts:** Arts/sciences. **Math:** General. **Philosophy/religion:** Philosophy. **Physical sciences:** Chemistry. **Protective services:** Criminal justice. **Psychology:** General. **Social sciences:** Economics, international relations, political science, sociology. **Visual/performing arts:** Acting, art history/conservation, dramatic, jazz, music, music performance, music theory/composition, musical theater, piano/keyboard, stringed instruments, voice/opera.

Most popular majors. Biology 6%, business/marketing 36%, psychology 15%, security/protective services 6%, social sciences 7%, visual/performing arts 8%.

Technology on campus. 250 workstations in dormitories, library, computer center, student center. Dormitories wired for high-speed internet access and linked to campus network. Commuter students can connect to campus network. Online course registration, online library, helpline available.

Student life. Freshman orientation: Mandatory, $60 fee. Preregistration for classes offered. Held in spring and summer. New Student Orientation program for students: 4 day program prior to start of fall classes. **Policies:** University housing is only available at the Chicago campus. **Housing:** Guaranteed on-campus for freshmen. Coed dorms, apartments, gender-neutral housing available. $500 fully refundable deposit, deadline 5/1. **Activities:** Bands, choral groups, dance, drama, international student organizations, literary magazine, music ensembles, musical theater, opera, radio station, student government, student newspaper, symphony orchestra, Black student union, association of Latin American students, RU Proud (LGBTQIA organization), Muslim student association, Colleges Against Cancer, Alpha Phi Omega service fraternity, Vietnamese student association.

Athletics. NAIA. **Intercollegiate:** Baseball M, basketball, cross-country, golf M, soccer, softball W, tennis, track and field, volleyball W. **Intramural:** Basketball, football (non-tackle). **Team name:** Lakers.

Student services. Adult student services, alcohol/substance abuse counseling, career counseling, student employment services, financial aid counseling, personal counseling, placement for graduates, veterans' counselor. **Physically disabled:** Services for visually, hearing impaired.

Contact. E-mail: admission@roosevelt.edu
Phone: (312) 341-2101 Toll-free number: (877) 277-5978
Fax: (847) 619-8636
Eric Weems, Associate Provost, Enrollment, Roosevelt University, 430 S Michigan Ave, Chicago, IL 60605-1394

Rush University
Chicago, Illinois
www.rushu.rush.edu   **CB code: 3262**

- Private two-year upper-division health science and nursing college
- Commuter campus in very large city

General. Founded in 1971. Regionally accredited. **Degrees:** 58 bachelor's awarded; master's, professional, doctoral offered. **Location:** 2 miles from downtown. **Calendar:** Quarter, limited summer session. **Full-time faculty:** 917 total; 30% minority, 54% women. **Special facilities:** Clinical and laboratory facilities.

Student profile. 134 degree-seeking undergraduates, 935 degree-seeking graduate students. 100% entered as juniors.

Women:	66%	Multi-racial, non-Hispanic:	1%
African American:	8%	Part-time:	26%
Asian American:	10%	Out-of-state:	2%
Hispanic/Latino:	25%	Live on campus:	7%
Native American:	1%	25 or older:	62%
Native Hawaiian/Pacific islander:	1%		

2015-2016 Annual costs. Tuition/fees: $33,857. Books/supplies: $857. Personal expenses: $680.

Financial aid. Non-need-based: Scholarships awarded for academics, minority status.

Application procedures. Admission: No application fee. Application must be submitted online. Application deadlines vary by program. **Financial aid:** Priority date 3/1.

Academics. Provides education based on the teacher-practitioner model. **Special study options:** Distance learning, internships. **Credit/placement by examination:** AP, CLEP.

Majors. Health services: Clinical lab science, perfusion technology, respiratory therapy technology.

Technology on campus. 140 workstations in library, computer center, student center. Commuter students can connect to campus network. Online library, helpline, wireless network available.

Student life. Policies: Funds available for official student groups. **Housing:** Apartments available. **Activities:** Student government, Christian Fellowship, National Student Nurses' Association chapter, Lesbian/Gay/Bisexual/Allies, Medical/Nursing students for choice.

Student services. Career counseling, student employment services, financial aid counseling, minority student services, on-campus daycare, personal counseling.

Contact. E-mail: rush_admissions@rush.edu
Phone: (312) 942-7100 Fax: (312) 942-2219
Rush University, College Admissions, Chicago, IL 60612

Saint Anthony College of Nursing
Rockford, Illinois
www.sacn.edu CB code: 3923

- Private two-year upper-division nursing college affiliated with the Roman Catholic Church
- Commuter campus in small city
- Test scores, application essay required

General. Regionally accredited. The RN to BSN program is 22 months in length and is offered in a hybrid format (each class is 50% in-class time, 50% online). **Degrees:** 81 bachelor's awarded; master's, doctoral offered. **Articulation:** Rock Valley College, McHenry County College, Highland Community College, Sauk Valley Community College, Kishwaukee College, Blackhawk Technical College, Black Hawk College, College of DuPage, College of Lake County, Elgin Community College, Harper College, Heartland Community College, Illinois Central College, Illinois Valley Community College, Judson College, Northern Illinois University, Rasmussen College, Rockford University, University of Wisconsin, Waubonsee Community College. **Location:** 80 miles from Chicago. **Calendar:** Semester, limited summer session. **Full-time faculty:** 19 total; 16% have terminal degrees, 10% minority, 95% women. **Part-time faculty:** 24 total; 29% have terminal degrees, 88% women. **Class size:** 33% < 20, 29% 20-39, 12% 40-49, 25% 50-99. **Special facilities:** Nursing simulation labs.

Student profile. 233 degree-seeking undergraduates. 100% entered as juniors. 75% transferred from two-year, 25% transferred from four-year institutions.

Out-of-state: 8% 25 or older: 62%

Basis for selection. College transcript, application essay, standardized test scores required. 64 credits required in specific pre-nursing and general education courses. Transfer accepted as juniors.

2015-2016 Annual costs. Tuition/fees: $23,566. Books/supplies: $3,400. Personal expenses: $2,500.

Financial aid. Non-need-based: Scholarships awarded for academics, leadership.

Application procedures. Admission: Priority date 9/15; deadline 2/15. $50 fee. Application must be submitted on paper. **Financial aid:** Closing date 6/30. Applicants notified on a rolling basis starting 4/15.

Academics. Special study options: Independent study. **Credit/placement by examination:** AP, CLEP.

Majors. Health services: Nursing (RN).

Technology on campus. 104 workstations in library, computer center. Commuter students can connect to campus network. Online course registration, online library, helpline, wireless network available.

Student life. Activities: Student government.

Student services. Alcohol/substance abuse counseling, chaplain/spiritual director, career counseling, financial aid counseling, health services, legal services, personal counseling, women's services.

Contact. E-mail: admissions@sacn.edu
Phone: (815) 227-2141 Fax: (815) 227-2730
April Lipnitzky, Supervisor of Enrollment Management, Saint Anthony College of Nursing, 5658 East State Street, Rockford, IL 61108-2468

Saint Xavier University
Chicago, Illinois CB member
www.sxu.edu CB code: 1708

- Private 4-year university affiliated with the Roman Catholic Church
- Commuter campus in very large city
- 2,940 degree-seeking undergraduates
- SAT or ACT (ACT writing optional), application essay required

General. Founded in 1847. Regionally accredited. Affiliated with Sisters of Mercy. **Degrees:** 693 bachelor's awarded; master's offered. **ROTC:** Air Force. **Location:** 20 miles from downtown. **Calendar:** Semester, limited summer session. **Full-time faculty:** 168 total. **Part-time faculty:** 230 total. **Class size:** 40% < 20, 56% 20-39, 2% 40-49, 1% 50-99. **Special facilities:** Music performance studio, reading clinic, speech clinic, learning disabilities clinic, mathematics laboratory.

Freshman class profile.

GPA 3.75 or higher:	30%	Rank in top quarter:	50%
GPA 3.50-3.74:	14%	Rank in top tenth:	22%
GPA 3.0-3.49:	32%	Out-of-state:	7%
GPA 2.0-2.99:	24%	Live on campus:	46%

Basis for selection. GPA, test scores most important. Counselor recommendation, class rank considered. Interview recommended for borderline applicants. Audition required of music majors.

High school preparation. College-preparatory program recommended. 16 units recommended. Recommended units include English 4, mathematics 3, foreign language 2 and academic electives 3. 4 units of science and social studies combined.

2015-2016 Annual costs. Tuition/fees: $30,920. Room/board: $10,620. Books/supplies: $1,200. Personal expenses: $1,150.

Financial aid. Non-need-based: Scholarships awarded for academics, athletics, music/drama.

Application procedures. Admission: No deadline. $25 fee, may be waived for applicants with need, free for online applicants. Admission notification on a rolling basis. Must reply by May 1 or within 4 week(s) if notified thereafter. **Financial aid:** Priority date 2/15; no closing date. FAFSA required. Applicants notified on a rolling basis starting 2/1; must reply by 5/1 or within 2 week(s) of notification.

Academics. Special study options: Accelerated study, cooperative education, distance learning, double major, dual enrollment of high school students, ESL, external degree, honors, independent study, internships, liberal arts/career combination, semester at sea, student-designed major, study abroad, teacher certification program. **Credit/placement by examination:** AP, CLEP, institutional tests. 27 credit hours maximum toward bachelor's degree. **Support services:** Learning center, pre-admission summer program, reduced course load, remedial instruction, study skills assistance, tutoring, writing center.

Majors. Biology: General. **Business:** General, accounting, international. **Communications:** Communications/speech/rhetoric, organizational. **Computer sciences:** General, computer science. **Education:** General, art, biology, history, mathematics, music, secondary, social science, Spanish. **English:** English lit. **Foreign languages:** Spanish. **Health services:** Nursing (RN), premedicine, prepharmacy, speech pathology. **History:** General. **Liberal arts:** Arts/sciences. **Math:** General. **Philosophy/religion:** Philosophy, religion. **Physical sciences:** Chemistry. **Protective services:** Criminal justice. **Psychology:** General, industrial. **Social sciences:** General, international relations, political science, sociology. **Theology:** Pastoral counseling. **Visual/performing arts:** Music, studio arts, voice/opera.

Most popular majors. Business/marketing 25%, education 38%, health sciences 15%.

Technology on campus. 700 workstations in dormitories, library, computer center, student center. Dormitories wired for high-speed internet access and linked to campus network. Commuter students can connect to campus network. Online course registration, online library, helpline, student web hosting, wireless network available.

Student life. Freshman orientation: Mandatory, $100 fee. Preregistration for classes offered. Two-day overnight orientation held in summer. **Housing:** Guaranteed on-campus for freshmen. Coed dorms, special housing for disabled, apartments available. $100 nonrefundable deposit, deadline 5/1. **Activities:** Bands, campus ministries, choral groups, film society, international student organizations, literary magazine, music ensembles, radio station, student government, student newspaper, symphony orchestra, Black student organization, Hispanic student organization, student activities board, student nurses association, Muslim student association, Celtic Connection, Fellowship of Christian Athletes, Xi Delta.

Athletics. NAIA. **Intercollegiate:** Baseball M, basketball, cross-country, football (tackle) M, soccer, softball W, volleyball W. **Intramural:** Basketball M, bowling, volleyball. **Team name:** Cougars.

Student services. Adult student services, alcohol/substance abuse counseling, chaplain/spiritual director, career counseling, services for economically disadvantaged, student employment services, financial aid counseling, health services, on-campus daycare, personal counseling, placement for graduates, veterans' counselor. **Physically disabled:** Services for speech impaired.

Contact. E-mail: admissions@sxu.edu
Phone: (773) 298-3050 Toll-free number: (800) 462-9288
Fax: (773) 298-3076
Brian Hotzfield, Director of Admission, Saint Xavier University, 3700 West 103rd Street, Chicago, IL 60655

School of the Art Institute of Chicago
Chicago, Illinois
www.saic.edu

CB member
CB code: 1713

- Private 4-year visual arts college
- Commuter campus in very large city
- 2,843 degree-seeking undergraduates: 8% part-time, 72% women, 3% African American, 12% Asian American, 9% Hispanic/Latino, 3% Multiracial, non-Hispanic, 32% international
- 748 degree-seeking graduate students
- 67% of applicants admitted
- SAT or ACT (ACT writing optional), application essay required
- 60% graduate within 6 years

General. Founded in 1866. Regionally accredited. **Degrees:** 533 bachelor's awarded; master's offered. **Location:** Downtown Chicago. **Calendar:** Semester, extensive summer session. **Full-time faculty:** 168 total; 87% have terminal degrees, 18% minority, 46% women. **Part-time faculty:** 596 total; 81% have terminal degrees, 16% minority, 52% women. **Class size:** 83% < 20, 15% 20-39, less than 1% 40-49, less than 1% 50-99, less than 1% >100. **Special facilities:** Art collection, film center, video data bank, poetry center, art galleries, fashion resource center, artists' book collection, Roger Brown house museum and study collection.

Freshman class profile. 4,219 applied, 2,814 admitted, 815 enrolled.

Return as sophomores:	81%	Live on campus:	89%
Out-of-state:	80%	International:	30%

Basis for selection. Portfolio very important, statement of purpose, 500 SAT Critical Reading or 20 ACT English, academic credentials, and recommendations also considered. Interview recommended. Portfolio required.

High school preparation. Advanced-level study of art recommended.

2015-2016 Annual costs. Tuition/fees: $43,960. Room/board: $12,850. Books/supplies: $1,770. Personal expenses: $1,370.

2014-2015 Financial aid. Non-need-based: Scholarships awarded for academics, art.

Application procedures. Admission: Priority date 12/1; deadline 5/1 (receipt date). $65 fee, may be waived for applicants with need. Application must be submitted online. Admission notification on a rolling basis beginning on or about 10/1. **Financial aid:** Priority date 3/15; no closing date. FAFSA required. Applicants notified on a rolling basis starting 3/1.

Academics. Interdisciplinary curriculum allows students to personalize education or concentrate on single discipline. **Special study options:** Cooperative education, cross-registration, double major, ESL, exchange student, independent study, internships, New York semester, student-designed major, study abroad, teacher certification program. Interdisciplinary curriculum with 6 credit off-campus study requirement, "credit/no-credit" grading system. **Credit/placement by examination:** AP, CLEP, IB. 18 credit hours maximum toward bachelor's degree. DANTES scores accepted. **Support services:** Learning center, pre-admission summer program, reduced course load, remedial instruction, study skills assistance, tutoring.

Majors. Architecture: Interior. **Communications:** Digital media. **Communications technology:** Animation/special effects, desktop publishing, graphics, photo/film/video, recording arts. **Education:** Art. **English:** Creative writing. **Visual/performing arts:** General, art, art history/conservation, ceramics, cinematography, design, digital arts, drawing, fashion design, fiber arts, graphic design, industrial design, interior design, multimedia, painting, photography, printmaking, sculpture, studio arts.

Most popular majors. Visual/performing arts 98%.

Technology on campus. PC or laptop required. 350 workstations in dormitories, library, computer center. Dormitories wired for high-speed internet access and linked to campus network. Commuter students can connect to campus network. Online library, helpline, repair service, student web hosting, wireless network available.

Student life. Freshman orientation: Mandatory, $100 fee. Preregistration for classes offered. Four days prior to beginning of class. First day open to parents, family and friends. **Housing:** Coed dorms, special housing for disabled, wellness housing available. $550 nonrefundable deposit. **Activities:** Campus ministries, dance, drama, film society, international student organizations, literary magazine, radio station, student government, student newspaper, TV station, Black at SAIC, Hillel, InterVarsity, Korean student association, Latin American student organization, Oxfam, Taiwanese student organization.

Student services. Alcohol/substance abuse counseling, career counseling, student employment services, financial aid counseling, health services, minority student services, personal counseling, placement for graduates, veterans' counselor. **Physically disabled:** Services for visually, speech, hearing impaired.

Contact. E-mail: admiss@saic.edu
Phone: (312) 629-6100 Toll-free number: (800) 232-7242
Fax: (312) 629-6101
Asia Mitchell, Director of Undergraduate Admissions, School of the Art Institute of Chicago, 36 South Wabash Avenue, Chicago, IL 60603

Shimer College
Chicago, Illinois
www.shimer.edu

CB code: 1717

- Private 4-year liberal arts college
- Residential campus in very large city
- 76 degree-seeking undergraduates: 21% part-time, 54% women, 13% African American, 8% Asian American, 9% Hispanic/Latino, 1% Multiracial, non-Hispanic
- Application essay, interview required
- 68% graduate within 6 years

General. Founded in 1853. Regionally accredited. Located on campus of Illinois Institute of Technology. **Degrees:** 19 bachelor's awarded. **ROTC:** Army, Naval, Air Force. **Location:** 3 miles from downtown. **Calendar:** Semester, limited summer session. **Full-time faculty:** 9 total; 100% have terminal degrees, 22% minority, 33% women. **Part-time faculty:** 3 total; 67% have terminal degrees, 33% women. **Class size:** 100% < 20.

Freshman class profile.

GPA 3.75 or higher:	25%	Return as sophomores:	73%
GPA 3.50-3.74:	14%	Out-of-state:	55%
GPA 3.0-3.49:	14%	Live on campus:	42%
GPA 2.0-2.99:	47%		

Basis for selection. Essays and interviews most important. Test scores, GPA, recommendations, motivation, maturity considered. Demonstrated writing skills and interest in and enthusiasm about Great Books curriculum and discussion method important. Early entrants and other applicants who do not have high school diplomas may be required to submit GED; applicants without high school diplomas who are too young to take GED may be required to complete additional approved testing in order to comply with financial aid regulations.

High school preparation. College-preparatory program recommended. 15 units recommended. Recommended units include English 4, mathematics 3, history 2, science 3, foreign language 2 and visual/performing arts 1.

2015-2016 Annual costs. Tuition/fees: $34,004. Room/board: $11,516. Books/supplies: $750. Personal expenses: $3,000.

Financial aid. Non-need-based: Scholarships awarded for academics, alumni affiliation.

Application procedures. Admission: Priority date 5/1; no deadline. $25 fee, may be waived for applicants with need. Admission notification on a rolling basis beginning on or about 9/15. Must reply by May 1 or within 2 week(s) if notified thereafter. **Financial aid:** No deadline. FAFSA required. Applicants notified on a rolling basis starting 3/15; must reply by 5/1.

Academics. Curriculum is based on The Great Books of Western Culture. **Special study options:** Accelerated study, combined bachelor's/graduate degree, cross-registration, double major, dual enrollment of high school students, independent study, liberal arts/career combination. **Credit/placement by examination:** AP, CLEP, institutional tests. Shimer Institutional placement examinations may result in credit; no outside testing is accepted. **Support services:** Reduced course load, study skills assistance, tutoring, writing center.

Majors. Liberal arts: Arts/sciences, humanities. **Social sciences:** General.

Most popular majors. Liberal arts 78%, social sciences 22%.

Technology on campus. 25 workstations in dormitories, library, computer center, student center. Dormitories wired for high-speed internet access and linked to campus network. Commuter students can connect to campus network. Helpline, wireless network available.

Student life. Freshman orientation: Mandatory, $100 fee. Preregistration for classes offered. Held 3-4 days prior to start of classes. **Housing:** Guaranteed on-campus for freshmen. Coed dorms, special housing for disabled, apartments, themed housing available. $600 fully refundable deposit, deadline 5/1. **Activities:** Bands, campus ministries, choral groups, dance, drama, film society, international student organizations, literary magazine, music ensembles, radio station, student government, student newspaper, symphony orchestra, American Red Cross, Catholic campus ministry, gays/lesbians/allies and more, Hillel, Hindu student council, gospel choir, Muslim students association, chess club.

Athletics. Intramural: Basketball, football (non-tackle), soccer, softball, track and field, volleyball. **Team name:** Flaming Smelts.

Student services. Adult student services, alcohol/substance abuse counseling, career counseling, student employment services, financial aid counseling, health services, personal counseling, placement for graduates.

Contact. E-mail: admission@shimer.edu
Phone: (312) 235-3555 Toll-free number: (800) 215-7173
Fax: (888) 808-3133
Director of Enrollment Services, Shimer College, 3424 South State Street, Chicago, IL 60616

Southern Illinois University Carbondale
Carbondale, Illinois   **CB member**
www.siu.edu   **CB code: 1726**

- Public 4-year university
- Residential campus in large town
- 12,858 degree-seeking undergraduates: 12% part-time, 46% women, 19% African American, 2% Asian American, 8% Hispanic/Latino, 3% Multi-racial, non-Hispanic, 4% international
- 4,220 degree-seeking graduate students
- 81% of applicants admitted
- SAT or ACT (ACT writing optional) required
- 45% graduate within 6 years

General. Founded in 1869. Regionally accredited. **Degrees:** 3,259 bachelor's, 102 associate awarded; master's, professional, doctoral offered. **ROTC:** Army, Air Force. **Location:** 100 miles from St. Louis. **Calendar:** Semester, extensive summer session. **Full-time faculty:** 812 total; 79% have terminal degrees, 23% minority, 37% women. **Part-time faculty:** 88 total; 72% have terminal degrees, 7% minority, 44% women. **Class size:** 55% < 20, 35% 20-39, 3% 40-49, 5% 50-99, 3% >100. **Special facilities:** University press, coal research center, technology center, outdoor education laboratory, university farms, center for study of crime, electron microscopy center, cooperative wildlife research laboratory, cooperative fisheries research laboratory, vivarium, airport training facility, laboratory theater, center for archaeological investigations, small business incubator, public policy institute, dental and medical clinics, environmental center, media center,.

Freshman class profile. 10,648 applied, 8,605 admitted, 2,177 enrolled.

Mid 50% test scores			
SAT critical reading:	460-610	Rank in top tenth:	10%
SAT math:	470-600	End year in good standing:	80%
ACT composite:	19-25	Return as sophomores:	68%
GPA 3.75 or higher:	17%	Out-of-state:	15%
GPA 3.50-3.74:	15%	Live on campus:	94%
GPA 3.0-3.49:	24%	International:	1%
GPA 2.0-2.99:	41%	Fraternities:	5%
Rank in top quarter:	32%	Sororities:	4%

Basis for selection. Core GPA and ACT most important. Holistic approach using these two items along with core unit courses and other available academic information. Interviews required for major scholarships only, not for admission. **Learning Disabled:** Special requirements only apply for certain programs.

High school preparation. College-preparatory program required. 15 units required; 16 recommended. Required and recommended units include English 4, mathematics 3-4, social studies 3, science 3 (laboratory 3) and academic electives 2.

2015-2016 Annual costs. Tuition/fees: $13,137; $26,390 out-of-state. Room/board: $9,996. Books/supplies: $1,100. Personal expenses: $1,218.

2015-2016 Financial aid. **Need-based:** 2,027 full-time freshmen applied for aid; 1,719 deemed to have need; 1,703 received aid. Average need met was 62%. Average scholarship/grant was $8,675; average loan $3,403. 47% of total undergraduate aid awarded as scholarships/grants, 53% as loans/jobs. **Non-need-based:** Awarded to 3,043 full-time undergraduates, including 786

freshmen. Scholarships awarded for academics, alumni affiliation, art, athletics, leadership, minority status, music/drama, ROTC, state residency. **Additional information:** Need-based financial aid available to part-time students enrolled in minimum of 6 semester hours.

Application procedures. Admission: Priority date 12/1; deadline 5/1 (postmark date). $40 fee, may be waived for applicants with need. Admission notification on a rolling basis beginning on or about 9/1. Must reply by May 1 or within 2 week(s) if notified thereafter. **Financial aid:** Priority date 3/1; no closing date. FAFSA required. Applicants notified on a rolling basis starting 3/15.

Academics. Special study options: Accelerated study, combined bachelor's/graduate degree, cooperative education, distance learning, double major, dual enrollment of high school students, ESL, exchange student, honors, independent study, internships, student-designed major, study abroad, teacher certification program. Workforce education and development weekend program. **Credit/placement by examination:** AP, CLEP, IB, SAT, ACT, institutional tests. 15 credit hours maximum toward associate degree, 30 toward bachelor's. **Support services:** Learning center, pre-admission summer program, reduced course load, remedial instruction, study skills assistance, tutoring, writing center.

Majors. Architecture: Architecture. **Area/ethnic studies:** African-American. **Biology:** General, botany, microbiology, physiology, zoology. **Business:** Accounting, business admin, finance, management science, managerial economics, marketing. **Communications:** Journalism, radio/TV. **Computer sciences:** Computer science, information systems. **Conservation:** Forestry. **Education:** Early childhood, elementary, health, physical, special ed, trade/industrial. **Engineering:** Civil, computer, electrical, mechanical, mining. **English:** English lit. **Foreign languages:** General, linguistics. **Health services:** Communication disorders, dental hygiene, health care admin, medical radiologic technology/radiation therapy. **History:** General. **Human services:** Social work. **Liberal arts:** Arts/sciences. **Math:** General. **Parks/recreation:** General, exercise sciences, sports admin. **Philosophy/religion:** Philosophy. **Physical sciences:** Chemistry, geology, physics. **Protective services:** Fire services admin. **Psychology:** General. **Social sciences:** General, anthropology, criminology, economics, geography, political science, sociology. **Visual/performing arts:** Art, cinematography, design, dramatic, interior design, music, studio arts. **Work/family studies:** Clothing/textiles, food/nutrition.

Most popular majors. Business/marketing 8%, education 14%, engineering/engineering technologies 12%, health sciences 8%, social sciences 6%.

Technology on campus. 1,900 workstations in dormitories, library, computer center. Dormitories wired for high-speed internet access and linked to campus network. Commuter students can connect to campus network. Online course registration, online library, helpline, repair service, wireless network available.

Student life. Freshman orientation: Mandatory, $150 fee. Preregistration for classes offered. **Housing:** Guaranteed on-campus for freshmen. Coed dorms, single-sex dorms, special housing for disabled, apartments, fraternity/sorority housing, themed housing available. $150 nonrefundable deposit. Living learning communities available. **Activities:** Bands, campus ministries, choral groups, dance, drama, film society, international student organizations, literary magazine, music ensembles, Model UN, musical theater, opera, radio station, student government, student newspaper, symphony orchestra, TV station, More than 400 student organizations.

Athletics. NCAA. Intercollegiate: Baseball M, basketball, cheerleading, cross-country, diving, football (tackle) M, golf, softball W, swimming, tennis, track and field, volleyball W. **Intramural:** Badminton, basketball, football (non-tackle), racquetball, soccer, softball, swimming, table tennis, tennis, track and field, volleyball. **Team name:** Salukis.

Student services. Adult student services, alcohol/substance abuse counseling, career counseling, services for economically disadvantaged, student employment services, financial aid counseling, health services, legal services, minority student services, on-campus daycare, personal counseling, placement for graduates, veterans' counselor, women's services. **Physically disabled:** Services for visually, speech, hearing impaired.

Contact. E-mail: admissions@siu.edu
Phone: (618) 536-4405 Fax: (618) 453-3250
Josephine Koonce Evans, Director of Undergraduate Admissions, Southern Illinois University Carbondale, Undergraduate Admissions, Mailcode 4710, Carbondale, IL 62901

Southern Illinois University Edwardsville
Edwardsville, Illinois   **CB member**
www.siue.edu   **CB code: 1759**

- Public 4-year university
- Residential campus in large town

- 11,717 degree-seeking undergraduates: 15% part-time, 53% women, 15% African American, 2% Asian American, 4% Hispanic/Latino, 3% Multi-racial, non-Hispanic, 1% international
- 2,484 degree-seeking graduate students
- 88% of applicants admitted
- SAT or ACT (ACT writing optional) required
- 49% graduate within 6 years

General. Founded in 1957. Regionally accredited. **Degrees:** 2,415 bachelor's awarded; master's, professional, doctoral offered. **ROTC:** Army, Air Force. **Location:** 18 miles from St. Louis. **Calendar:** Semester, extensive summer session. **Full-time faculty:** 605 total; 80% have terminal degrees, 22% minority, 49% women. **Part-time faculty:** 240 total; 42% have terminal degrees, 11% minority, 44% women. **Class size:** 42% < 20, 47% 20-39, 8% 40-49, 2% 50-99, 2% >100. **Special facilities:** Museum, arboretum, greenhouse, engineering labs, clinical nursing facility, observatory, applied research and technology park, corn-to-ethanol research center, biotechnology laboratory incubator, pharmaceutical care lab.

Freshman class profile. 7,764 applied, 6,869 admitted, 2,096 enrolled.

Rank in top quarter:	45%	Live on campus:	68%
Rank in top tenth:	19%	International:	1%
Return as sophomores:	84%	Fraternities:	8%
Out-of-state:	15%	Sororities:	9%

Basis for selection. GPA, ACT/SAT, high school course work most important. Audition recommended for music majors; portfolio recommended for art majors.

High school preparation. College-preparatory program required. 15 units required. Required and recommended units include English 4, mathematics 3, social studies 3, science 3 (laboratory 3), foreign language 2 and academic electives 2. At least 2 years of history or government required; 2 years foreign language, music, dance, theater, art, or vocational education (1 year maximum) electives recommended; 1 year chemistry and 1 year biology required.

2015-2016 Annual costs. Tuition/fees: $10,247; $21,740 out-of-state. Room/board: $9,570. Books/supplies: $840. Personal expenses: $1,399.

2015-2016 Financial aid. All financial aid based on need. 1,870 full-time freshmen applied for aid; 1,373 deemed to have need; 1,340 received aid. Average need met was 66%. Average scholarship/grant was $8,069; average loan $3,533. 42% of total undergraduate aid awarded as scholarships/grants, 58% as loans/jobs.

Application procedures. **Admission:** Priority date 12/1; deadline 5/1 (postmark date). $30 fee, may be waived for applicants with need. Admission notification on a rolling basis beginning on or about 9/15. Must reply by May 1 or within 2 week(s) if notified thereafter. **Financial aid:** Priority date 3/1, closing date 6/1. FAFSA required. Applicants notified on a rolling basis starting 3/15; must reply within 4 week(s) of notification.

Academics. Senior project required. **Special study options:** Accelerated study, combined bachelor's/graduate degree, cooperative education, cross-registration, distance learning, double major, ESL, honors, independent study, internships, student-designed major, study abroad, teacher certification program. Independent study; elementary and secondary teacher certificate programs in art, music, social studies, English, kinesiology, biology, chemistry, foreign languages, history, math, physics, speech communication. **Credit/placement by examination:** AP, CLEP, SAT, ACT, institutional tests. 32 credit hours maximum toward bachelor's degree. Placement tests required for some students in reading, writing and/or math; determination based on test scores and GPA. **Support services:** Learning center, pre-admission summer program, reduced course load, remedial instruction, study skills assistance, tutoring, writing center.

Majors. **Biology:** General. **Business:** Accounting, business admin, management information systems, managerial economics. **Communications:** Communications/speech/rhetoric, media studies. **Computer sciences:** Computer science. **Education:** Early childhood, elementary, health, middle, science, special ed. **Engineering:** Civil, computer, electrical, industrial, mechanical. **English:** English lit. **Foreign languages:** General. **Health services:** Audiology/speech pathology, clinical nutrition, nursing (RN). **History:** General. **Human services:** Social work. **Liberal arts:** Arts/sciences. **Math:** General. **Parks/recreation:** Exercise sciences. **Philosophy/religion:** Philosophy. **Physical sciences:** Chemistry, physics. **Protective services:** Criminal justice. **Psychology:** General. **Social sciences:** Anthropology, economics, geography, political science, sociology. **Visual/performing arts:** Art, dramatic, music, studio arts.

Most popular majors. Biology 6%, business/marketing 19%, education 8%, engineering/engineering technologies 8%, health sciences 15%, psychology 7%, social sciences 6%.

Technology on campus. 600 workstations in dormitories, library, computer center, student center. Dormitories wired for high-speed internet access and linked to campus network. Commuter students can connect to campus network. Online course registration, online library, helpline, student web hosting, wireless network available.

Student life. **Freshman orientation:** Mandatory, $150 fee. Preregistration for classes offered. Two-day overnight summer program. **Housing:** Coed dorms, special housing for disabled, apartments, wellness housing available. $300 nonrefundable deposit, deadline 5/1. Focused-interest communities available. **Activities:** Bands, campus ministries, choral groups, dance, drama, international student organizations, literary magazine, music ensembles, musical theater, opera, radio station, student government, student newspaper, symphony orchestra, more than 200 organizations and honor societies available.

Athletics. NCAA. **Intercollegiate:** Baseball M, basketball, cheerleading, cross-country, golf, soccer, softball W, tennis, track and field, volleyball W, wrestling M. **Intramural:** Badminton, basketball, bowling, cheerleading, cross-country, fencing, football (non-tackle), golf, racquetball, soccer, softball, table tennis, tennis, volleyball, water polo, weight lifting. **Team name:** Cougars.

Student services. Alcohol/substance abuse counseling, career counseling, services for economically disadvantaged, student employment services, financial aid counseling, health services, legal services, on-campus daycare, personal counseling, placement for graduates, veterans' counselor. **Physically disabled:** Services for visually, speech, hearing impaired.

Contact. E-mail: admissions@siue.edu
Phone: (618) 650-3705 Toll-free number: (800) 447-7483
Fax: (618) 650-5013
Todd Burrell, Director of Admissions, Southern Illinois University Edwardsville, Rendleman Hall, Rm 2120, Edwardsville, IL 62026-1600

St. Augustine College
Chicago, Illinois
www.staugustine.edu   CB code: 0697

- Private 4-year liberal arts college affiliated with the Episcopal Church
- Commuter campus in very large city
- 1,754 degree-seeking undergraduates

General. Founded in 1980. Regionally accredited. St. Augustine College was founded as a bilingual institution of higher education supporting the Hispanic community. **Degrees:** 18 bachelor's, 285 associate awarded. **Location:** Chicago's North Metro Area. **Calendar:** Semester, limited summer session. **Full-time faculty:** 28 total. **Part-time faculty:** 151 total.

Basis for selection. Open admission, but selective for some programs. Admission to the Bachelor of Social Work (upper level) requires 2.75 GPA and completion of certain prerequisite courses; admission to the A.A.S. in Respiratory Therapy requires 2.67 GPA in specific prerequisite courses. **Home schooled:** Placement test in English, math, and Spanish required.

2015-2016 Annual costs. Tuition/fees: $12,300. Books/supplies: $600. Personal expenses: $150.

Application procedures. **Admission:** No deadline. No application fee. Application must be submitted on paper. Admission notification on a rolling basis. **Financial aid:** No deadline. FAFSA, institutional form required. Applicants notified on a rolling basis.

Academics. **Special study options:** Cooperative education, double major, ESL, independent study, internships, liberal arts/career combination. **Credit/placement by examination:** AP, CLEP, IB, institutional tests. **Support services:** Learning center, pre-admission summer program, remedial instruction, tutoring.

Majors. **Human services:** Social work.

Most popular majors. Public administration/social services 11%.

Technology on campus. 100 workstations in library, computer center. Online library, wireless network available.

Student life. **Freshman orientation:** Mandatory. Preregistration for classes offered.

Student services. Adult student services, alcohol/substance abuse counseling, career counseling, services for economically disadvantaged, financial aid counseling, minority student services, on-campus daycare, personal counseling, placement for graduates.

Contact. Phone: (773) 878-8756 Fax: (773) 878-0937
Honorio Morales, Director of Admission, St. Augustine College, 1345
West Argyle, Chicago, IL 60640-3501

St. Francis Medical Center College of Nursing
Peoria, Illinois
www.sfmccon.edu   CB code: 1756

◆ Private two-year upper-division nursing college affiliated with the
 Roman Catholic Church
◆ Commuter campus in small city
◆ 63% of applicants admitted
◆ Application essay required

General. Founded in 1905. Regionally accredited. Located at large medical center. National League of Nursing accredited. NCA accredited. Offers experience at Tazewell County, Fulton County, Peoria City/County Health Departments, Human Service Center and other community agencies. **Degrees:** 186 bachelor's awarded; master's, doctoral offered. **Location:** 180 miles from Chicago, 160 miles from St. Louis. **Calendar:** Semester, limited summer session. **Full-time faculty:** 36 total; 33% have terminal degrees, 97% women. **Part-time faculty:** 19 total; 5% have terminal degrees, 95% women. **Class size:** 42% < 20, 28% 20-39, 25% 40-49, 5% 50-99.

Student profile. 402 degree-seeking undergraduates, 270 degree-seeking graduate students. 224 applied as first time-transfer students, 141 admitted, 101 enrolled. 100% entered as juniors. 95% transferred from two-year, 5% transferred from four-year institutions.

Women:	90%	Part-time:	29%
African American:	1%	Out-of-state:	1%
Asian American:	4%	Live on campus:	23%
Hispanic/Latino:	2%	25 or older:	57%

Basis for selection. High school transcript, college transcript, application essay required. Enrollment depends on satisfactory completion of 62 semester hours of a specified prenursing curriculum. Applications may be submitted after satisfactory completion of 30 semester hours of required prenursing courses. Must include 8 semester hours of physical/life sciences. 2.5 GPA required. Transfer accepted as juniors, seniors.

2016-2017 Annual costs. Tuition/fees: $19,980. Room only: $3,500. Books/supplies: $1,218. Personal expenses: $1,944.

Financial aid. **Need-based:** 265 applied for aid; 201 deemed to have need; 201 received aid. Average need met was 40%. 36% of total undergraduate aid awarded as scholarships/grants, 64% as loans/jobs. **Non-need-based:** Awarded to 20 undergraduates. Scholarships awarded for academics, alumni affiliation. **Additional information:** OSF Saint Francis Medical Center Education student loan available to full-time students on a limited basis. Tuition waiver program for hospital employees available.

Application procedures. **Admission:** Deadline 9/1. $50 fee. Application must be submitted on paper. Admission notification 10/1. **Financial aid:** No deadline. Applicants notified on a rolling basis starting 5/15; must reply within 4 weeks of notification. FAFSA, institutional form required.

Academics. **Special study options:** Accelerated study, combined bachelor's/graduate degree, distance learning. **Credit/placement by examination:** AP, CLEP.

Majors. Health services: Nursing (RN).

Technology on campus. 60 workstations in library, computer center. Dormitories linked to campus network. Commuter students can connect to campus network. Online library, helpline, repair service, wireless network available.

Student life. **Housing:** Coed dorms, wellness housing available. **Activities:** Student government, Christian fellowship, student nurses' association, minority association.

Student services. Adult student services, alcohol/substance abuse counseling, services for economically disadvantaged, financial aid counseling, health services, personal counseling.

Contact. E-mail: janice.farquharson@osfhealthcare.org
Phone: (309) 655-2245 Fax: (309) 624-8973
Janice Farquharson, Director of Admissions and Recruitment, St. Francis Medical Center College of Nursing, 511 NE Greenleaf Street, Peoria, IL 61603-3783

St. John's College
Springfield, Illinois
www.stjohnscollegespringfield.edu

◆ Private two-year upper-division nursing college affiliated with the
 Roman Catholic Church
◆ Commuter campus in small city
◆ 53% of applicants admitted
◆ Test scores required

General. **Degrees:** 61 bachelor's awarded. **Articulation:** Lincoln Land Community College. **Location:** 220 miles from Chicago, 100 miles from St. Louis. **Calendar:** Semester, limited summer session. **Full-time faculty:** 11 total; 27% have terminal degrees, 100% women. **Part-time faculty:** 10 total; 10% have terminal degrees, 10% minority, 100% women. **Special facilities:** Simulation lab.

Student profile. 121 degree-seeking undergraduates. 118 applied as first time-transfer students, 62 admitted, 62 enrolled. 66% transferred from two-year, 34% transferred from four-year institutions.

Women:	84%	Multi-racial, non-Hispanic:	1%
African American:	2%	Part-time:	12%
Asian American:	2%	25 or older:	41%

Basis for selection. High school transcript, college transcript, standardized test scores required. Transfer accepted as juniors.

2015-2016 Annual costs. Tuition/fees: $19,237. Books/supplies: $1,500. Personal expenses: $2,000.

Financial aid. **Need-based:** 108 applied for aid; 108 deemed to have need; 108 received aid. Average need met was 30%. 35% of total undergraduate aid awarded as scholarships/grants, 65% as loans/jobs. **Non-need-based:** Awarded to 2 undergraduates. Scholarships awarded for alumni affiliation, minority status.

Application procedures. **Admission:** Priority date 10/15. $60 fee. **Financial aid:** Priority date 2/15, no deadline. Applicants notified on a rolling basis starting 4/1; must reply within 12 weeks of notification.

Academics. **Special study options:** Accelerated study, combined bachelor's/graduate degree, distance learning. **Credit/placement by examination:** AP, CLEP.

Majors. Health services: Nursing (RN).

Technology on campus. PC or laptop required. 23 workstations in library, computer center. Commuter students can connect to campus network. Online library, helpline, wireless network available.

Student life. **Activities:** Student government.

Student services. Alcohol/substance abuse counseling, chaplain/spiritual director, financial aid counseling, health services, personal counseling.

Contact. E-mail: admissions@stjohnscollegespringfield.edu
Phone: (217) 525-5628 Fax: (217) 757-6870
Britni Caruso, Admissions Officer, St. John's College, 729 East Carpenter Street, Springfield, IL 62702-5321

Telshe Yeshiva-Chicago
Chicago, Illinois
                                                      CB code: 7009

◆ Private 4-year rabbinical college for men affiliated with the Jewish faith
◆ Very large city
◆ 67 degree-seeking undergraduates

General. Accredited by AARTS. **Degrees:** 2 bachelor's awarded; master's offered. **Calendar:** Differs by program. **Full-time faculty:** 5 total. **Part-time faculty:** 5 total.

Basis for selection. Open admission. GPA important, test scores and recommendations required.

2015-2016 Annual costs. Tuition/fees: $13,500.

Application procedures. **Admission:** No deadline. No application fee.

Academics. **Credit/placement by examination:** AP, CLEP.

Majors. Theology: Talmudic.

Contact. Phone: (773) 463-7738 Fax: (773) 463-2894
Director of Admissions, Telshe Yeshiva-Chicago, 3535 West Foster
Avenue, Chicago, IL 60625

Trinity Christian College
Palos Heights, Illinois
www.trnty.edu   **CB code: 1820**

- Private 4-year liberal arts college
- Residential campus in very large city
- 1,152 degree-seeking undergraduates: 15% part-time, 68% women, 10% African American, 1% Asian American, 13% Hispanic/Latino, 2% Multiracial, non-Hispanic, 5% international
- 79 degree-seeking graduate students
- SAT or ACT (ACT writing optional), application essay, interview required
- 62% graduate within 6 years

General. Founded in 1959. Regionally accredited. **Degrees:** 321 bachelor's awarded; master's offered. **Location:** 20 miles from downtown Chicago. **Calendar:** Semester, limited summer session. **Full-time faculty:** 85 total; 65% have terminal degrees, 13% minority, 52% women. **Part-time faculty:** 69 total; 14% have terminal degrees, 10% minority, 55% women. **Class size:** 57% < 20, 41% 20-39, 1% 40-49, less than 1% 50-99. **Special facilities:** Dutch heritage center archives.

Freshman class profile.

GPA 3.75 or higher:	36%	Rank in top tenth:	20%
GPA 3.50-3.74:	21%	Return as sophomores:	82%
GPA 3.0-3.49:	26%	Out-of-state:	52%
GPA 2.0-2.99:	16%	Live on campus:	85%
Rank in top quarter:	42%	International:	9%

Basis for selection. Secondary school record, high school GPA, and standardized test scores most important. ACT recommended. Statement of religious faith required. **Home schooled:** Transcript of courses and grades required. Applicants may substitute an academic portfolio plus verification that the home-school program has been completed. If the student has been part of an association that issues transcripts, a transcript should be provided. **Learning Disabled:** Documented diagnosis of disability is requested.

High school preparation. College-preparatory program recommended. 16 units required; 18 recommended. Required and recommended units include English 3-4, mathematics 3-4, social studies 2-3, history 2, science 2-3 and foreign language 2. One 3-year major in mathematics, science, or social studies, and 2 2-year minors in mathematics, science, social studies, or foreign language recommended.

2015-2016 Annual costs. Tuition/fees: $26,440. Room/board: $9,390. Books/supplies: $650. Personal expenses: $1,910.

2015-2016 Financial aid. Need-based: 175 full-time freshmen applied for aid; 151 deemed to have need; 151 received aid. Average scholarship/grant was $4,109; average loan $3,671. 72% of total undergraduate aid awarded as scholarships/grants, 28% as loans/jobs. **Non-need-based:** Awarded to 244 full-time undergraduates, including 56 freshmen. Scholarships awarded for academics, alumni affiliation, art, athletics, leadership, minority status, music/drama, religious affiliation. **Additional information:** High school transcripts and ACT/SAT required for merit scholarships.

Application procedures. Admission: No deadline. $30 fee, may be waived for applicants with need. Admission notification on a rolling basis beginning on or about 9/1. Must reply by May 1 or within 2 week(s) if notified thereafter. **Financial aid:** Priority date 2/15; no closing date. FAFSA required. Applicants notified on a rolling basis starting 3/1; must reply by 5/1 or within 2 week(s) of notification.

Academics. Special study options: Accelerated study, distance learning, double major, dual enrollment of high school students, ESL, honors, independent study, internships, liberal arts/career combination, study abroad, teacher certification program, urban semester. **Credit/placement by examination:** AP, CLEP, IB, SAT, ACT, institutional tests. 30 credit hours maximum toward bachelor's degree. **Support services:** Learning center, reduced course load, remedial instruction, study skills assistance, tutoring, writing center.

Honors college/program. Must have 28 ACT, be in top 10% of high school class, and have 3.5 high school GPA. 13-19 semester hours of unique courses. Approximately 15 freshmen admitted each year.

Majors. Biology: General, biochemistry, bioinformatics. **Business:** General, accounting, communications, entrepreneurial studies, finance, marketing. **Communications:** Communications/speech/rhetoric. **Computer sciences:** General, computer science. **Conservation:** Environmental science. **Education:** Art, biology, business, chemistry, elementary, English, history, mathematics, middle, music, physical, Spanish, special ed. **English:** English lit. **Foreign languages:** Spanish. **Health services:** Nursing (RN), speech pathology. **History:** General. **Human services:** Social work. **Math:** General. **Parks/recreation:** Exercise sciences. **Philosophy/religion:** Philosophy. **Physical sciences:** Chemistry. **Protective services:** Criminal justice. **Psychology:** General. **Theology:** Theology. **Visual/performing arts:** Digital arts, graphic design, music, studio arts.

Most popular majors. Business/marketing 19%, education 31%, health sciences 13%, psychology 7%.

Technology on campus. 140 workstations in dormitories, library, computer center. Dormitories wired for high-speed internet access and linked to campus network. Commuter students can connect to campus network. Helpline, wireless network available.

Student life. Freshman orientation: Mandatory, $225 fee. Preregistration for classes offered. Two-day program in early July and two-week program in late August. **Housing:** Guaranteed on-campus for all undergraduates. Coed dorms available. $150 fully refundable deposit, deadline 9/1. **Activities:** Bands, campus ministries, choral groups, drama, literary magazine, music ensembles, student government, student newspaper, religious drama club, theology club, pro-life, Bread for the World, Inter-Varsity Fellowship, Big Brother/Big Sister, Association for Public Justice, PACE literacy program in Cook County jail.

Athletics. NAIA, NCCAA. **Intercollegiate:** Baseball M, basketball, cross-country, golf, soccer, softball W, track and field, volleyball. **Intramural:** Basketball, racquetball, soccer, volleyball. **Team name:** Trolls.

Student services. Adult student services, alcohol/substance abuse counseling, chaplain/spiritual director, career counseling, student employment services, financial aid counseling, minority student services, personal counseling, placement for graduates, veterans' counselor. **Physically disabled:** Services for visually, speech, hearing impaired.

Contact. E-mail: admissions@trnty.edu
Phone: (708) 239-4708 Toll-free number: (866) 874-6463 ext. 4708
Fax: (708) 239-4826
Jeremy Klyn, Director of Admissions, Trinity Christian College, 6601 West College Drive, Palos Heights, IL 60463

Trinity College of Nursing & Health Sciences
Rock Island, Illinois
www.trinitycollegeqc.edu   **CB code: 2555**

- Private 4-year health science and nursing college
- Commuter campus in large city
- 219 degree-seeking undergraduates: 37% part-time, 96% women
- 7 degree-seeking graduate students
- 60% of applicants admitted
- 75% graduate within 6 years

General. Affiliated with UnityPoint Health. **Degrees:** 37 bachelor's, 37 associate awarded; master's offered. **Location:** 180 miles from Chicago. **Calendar:** Semester, limited summer session. **Full-time faculty:** 16 total; 12% have terminal degrees, 94% women. **Part-time faculty:** 3 total; 100% women. **Class size:** 64% < 20, 28% 20-39, 8% 50-99. **Special facilities:** Learning labs with hospital simulation rooms, health sciences library, founders library, anatomage table.

Freshman class profile. 5 applied, 3 admitted, 1 enrolled.

GPA 3.50-3.74:	100%	Rank in top quarter:	100%

Basis for selection. Requirements and placement standards vary by program. GPA, ACT, previous college credit, and quality of work in general education courses considered for admission to health care programs. Students applying to the accelerated BSN program are required to write a personal essay in a letter form addressing professional attributes, ability to manage an accelerated curriculum and career goals. **Home schooled:** Transcript of courses and grades required.

High school preparation. College-preparatory program recommended. Required units include English 4, mathematics 3, social studies 3, science 3 (laboratory 1).

2016-2017 Annual costs. Tuition/fees (projected): $23,404. Books/supplies: $2,082. Personal expenses: $4,241.

2015-2016 Financial aid. All financial aid based on need. 47% of total undergraduate aid awarded as scholarships/grants, 53% as loans/jobs.

Application procedures. Admission: Priority date 11/1; no deadline. $50 fee, may be waived for applicants with need. Admission notification on a rolling basis beginning on or about 12/20. Accepted students have 2 weeks from receipt of acceptance letter to reply and pay $100 tuition deposit to hold their seat in the program. **Financial aid:** No deadline. FAFSA, institutional form required. Applicants notified on a rolling basis starting 1/1.

Academics. Special study options: Accelerated study, distance learning, dual enrollment of high school students, internships. 15 month accelerated BSN program for students with bachelors degree. **Credit/placement by examination:** AP, CLEP, institutional tests. 18 credit hours maximum toward associate degree, 18 toward bachelor's. **Support services:** Study skills assistance.

Majors. Health services: Nursing (RN).

Technology on campus. 20 workstations in library, computer center. Commuter students can connect to campus network. Online library, helpline, wireless network available.

Student life. Freshman orientation: Mandatory. Preregistration for classes offered. **Activities:** Student government.

Student services. Alcohol/substance abuse counseling, chaplain/spiritual director, career counseling, financial aid counseling, health services, minority student services, personal counseling.

Contact. E-mail: lori.perez@trinitycollegeqc.edu
Phone: (309) 779-7812 Fax: (309) 779-7748
Lenore Knock, Director of Student Services and External Relations, Trinity College of Nursing & Health Sciences, 2122 25th Avenue, Rock Island, IL 61201-5317

Trinity International University
Deerfield, Illinois
www.tiu.edu   **CB code: 1810**

- Private 4-year university and liberal arts college affiliated with the Evangelical Free Church of America
- Residential campus in large town
- 1,010 degree-seeking undergraduates
- SAT or ACT (ACT writing optional), application essay required

General. Founded in 1897. Regionally accredited. Off-campus programs available through Christian College Consortium. **Degrees:** 193 bachelor's awarded; master's, professional offered. **Location:** 25 miles from Chicago. **Calendar:** Semester, limited summer session. **Full-time faculty:** 79 total. **Part-time faculty:** 223 total. **Class size:** 41% < 20, 39% 20-39, 16% 40-49, 5% 50-99. **Special facilities:** Seminary facilities.

Freshman class profile.

GPA 3.75 or higher:	29%	Rank in top quarter:	43%
GPA 3.50-3.74:	14%	Rank in top tenth:	37%
GPA 3.0-3.49:	27%	Out-of-state:	51%
GPA 2.0-2.99:	30%	Live on campus:	93%

Basis for selection. School achievement record, test scores, recommendations, evidence of Christian commitment, essays most important. Interview recommended for borderline applicants. **Home schooled:** Transcript of courses and grades required.

High school preparation. College-preparatory program required. Required units include English 4, mathematics 2, social studies 2, history 2, science 2 (laboratory 1), foreign language 2 and visual/performing arts 2.

2015-2016 Annual costs. Tuition/fees: $28,700. Room/board: $8,830. Books/supplies: $1,200. Personal expenses: $1,480.

2014-2015 Financial aid. Need-based: 149 full-time freshmen applied for aid; 133 deemed to have need; 133 received aid. Average need met was 71%. Average scholarship/grant was $6,990; average loan $4,001. **Non-need-based:** Awarded to 539 full-time undergraduates, including 147 freshmen. Scholarships awarded for academics, alumni affiliation, athletics, minority status, music/drama, religious affiliation.

Application procedures. Admission: No deadline. $25 fee, may be waived for applicants with need. Admission notification on a rolling basis beginning on or about 7/1. **Financial aid:** Priority date 4/1; no closing date. FAFSA required. Applicants notified on a rolling basis starting 2/15; must reply within 4 week(s) of notification.

Academics. Special study options: Accelerated study, combined bachelor's/graduate degree, cooperative education, cross-registration, distance learning, double major, dual enrollment of high school students, exchange student, honors, independent study, internships, liberal arts/career combination, student-designed major, study abroad, teacher certification program, urban semester, Washington semester. REACH (for nontraditional students with previous college credit), graduate courses available to undergraduates with junior or senior standing. **Credit/placement by examination:** AP, CLEP, IB, SAT, ACT, institutional tests. Permission and approval by department chair required. May not be used to satisfy senior residency requirement. **Support services:** Learning center, remedial instruction, study skills assistance, tutoring, writing center.

Majors. Biology: General. **Business:** General, accounting, human resources, management science, marketing, nonprofit/public, organizational behavior, training/development. **Communications:** Communications/speech/rhetoric. **Education:** Biology, elementary, English, history, mathematics, music, physical, secondary. **English:** English lit. **Health services:** Athletic training, physical therapy, physician assistant, premedicine, prephysical therapy. **History:** General. **Liberal arts:** Humanities. **Math:** General. **Parks/recreation:** Health/fitness. **Philosophy/religion:** Philosophy. **Protective services:** Computer forensics, criminal justice, law enforcement admin. **Psychology:** General. **Social sciences:** General. **Theology:** Bible, pastoral counseling, preministerial, religious ed, sacred music, theology, youth ministry. **Visual/performing arts:** Music, music pedagogy, music performance, music theory/composition, piano/keyboard, voice/opera.

Most popular majors. Business/marketing 22%, education 26%, health sciences 7%, liberal arts 6%, psychology 10%, theological studies 17%.

Technology on campus. 100 workstations in library, computer center, student center. Dormitories wired for high-speed internet access and linked to campus network. Commuter students can connect to campus network. Online course registration, online library, helpline, repair service, student web hosting, wireless network available.

Student life. Freshman orientation: Mandatory. Preregistration for classes offered. Orientation held the week before classes each fall and spring. Generally lasts entire week. **Policies:** Community expectations, general patterns of Christian lifestyle, policy on drug and alcohol abuse. Religious observance required. **Housing:** Guaranteed on-campus for freshmen. Single-sex dorms, special housing for disabled, apartments, wellness housing available. $50 partly refundable deposit, deadline 5/1. Pets allowed in dorm rooms. **Activities:** Bands, campus ministries, choral groups, dance, drama, international student organizations, music ensembles, musical theater, student government, student newspaper, symphony orchestra, Association of Believers for Black America, Global Christian Movement, Kappa Tau, Discipleship Cabinet, FAT Thursdays, Chapel Cabinet, Kids on Kampus, Wives Fellowship, Men's Ministry.

Athletics. NAIA, NCCAA. **Intercollegiate:** Baseball M, basketball, cross-country, football (tackle) M, soccer, softball W, volleyball W. **Intramural:** Baseball M, basketball, bowling, football (non-tackle) M, racquetball, rugby M, soccer, softball, table tennis, volleyball. **Team name:** Trojans.

Student services. Alcohol/substance abuse counseling, chaplain/spiritual director, career counseling, student employment services, financial aid counseling, health services, minority student services, on-campus daycare, personal counseling, placement for graduates. **Physically disabled:** Services for visually impaired.

Contact. E-mail: admissions@tiu.edu
Phone: (847) 317-7000 Toll-free number: (800) 822-3225
Fax: (847) 317-8097
Jordan Bryant, Director of Undergraduate Admissions, Trinity International University, 2065 Half Day Road, Deerfield, IL 60015

University of Chicago
Chicago, Illinois   **CB member**
www.uchicago.edu   **CB code: 1832**

- Private 4-year university and liberal arts college
- Residential campus in very large city
- 5,830 degree-seeking undergraduates: 1% part-time, 47% women, 5% African American, 17% Asian American, 9% Hispanic/Latino, 3% Multiracial, non-Hispanic, 11% international
- 6,946 degree-seeking graduate students
- 8% of applicants admitted
- SAT or ACT (ACT writing optional), application essay required
- 92% graduate within 6 years

General. Founded in 1891. Regionally accredited. **Degrees:** 1,326 bachelor's awarded; master's, professional, doctoral offered. **ROTC:** Army, Air

Force. **Location:** 7 miles from downtown Chicago. **Calendar:** Quarter, extensive summer session. **Full-time faculty:** 1,305 total; 100% have terminal degrees, 20% minority, 31% women. **Part-time faculty:** 445 total; 58% have terminal degrees, 19% minority, 33% women. **Class size:** 78% < 20, 14% 20-39, 3% 40-49, 5% 50-99, less than 1% >100. **Special facilities:** Institute for research in economics, brain research imaging center, institute for clinical excellence, center for the art of East Asia, comprehensive cancer center, computation institute, crime lab, cultural policy center, economic research center, energy policy institute, center for computational science, institute for the humanities, clinical research center, institute for molecular engineering, institute of politics, center for the study of American Culture, Oriental Institute and more.

Freshman class profile. 30,069 applied, 2,521 admitted, 1,537 enrolled.

Mid 50% test scores			
SAT critical reading:	720-800	GPA 3.0-3.49:	4%
SAT math:	720-800	Rank in top quarter:	99%
SAT writing:	700-780	Rank in top tenth:	98%
ACT composite:	32-35	Return as sophomores:	99%
GPA 3.75 or higher:	84%	Out-of-state:	84%
GPA 3.50-3.74:	12%	Live on campus:	100%
		International:	13%

Basis for selection. Secondary school record, recommendations, essay, talent/ability and character/personal qualities very important. Interview optional -- Alumni in area or on campus interviews. **Home schooled:** Interview required.

High school preparation. 19 units recommended. Recommended units include English 4, mathematics 4, social studies 2, history 2, science 4 and foreign language 3.

2015-2016 Annual costs. Tuition/fees: $50,193. Room/board: $14,772.

2015-2016 Financial aid. Need-based: 937 full-time freshmen applied for aid; 724 deemed to have need; 724 received aid. Average need met was 100%. Average scholarship/grant was $46,854. 96% of total undergraduate aid awarded as scholarships/grants, 4% as loans/jobs. **Non-need-based:** Scholarships awarded for academics, leadership. **Additional information:** No Barriers program replaces student loans with grants in all need-based financial aid packages. Grants offered instead of loans in all need based financial aid packages. Families who apply for financial aid do not have to pay a college application fee. Funding available for summer and school-year internships, research positions, study abroad, and career exploration treks for all majors and interests.

Application procedures. Admission: Closing date 1/1 (postmark date). $75 fee, may be waived for applicants with need. Admission notification by 4/1. Must reply by 5/1. Must be submitted by November 1st. **Financial aid:** Closing date 2/15. FAFSA, institutional form required. Applicants notified by 4/1; must reply by 5/1.

Academics. Special study options: Accelerated study, combined bachelor's/graduate degree, cross-registration, double major, dual enrollment of high school students, exchange student, independent study, internships, student-designed major, study abroad, teacher certification program. **Credit/placement by examination:** AP, CLEP, IB, institutional tests. 30 credit hours maximum toward bachelor's degree. **Support services:** Learning center, pre-admission summer program, study skills assistance, tutoring, writing center.

Majors. Area/ethnic studies: General, African, African-American, German, Latin American, Russian/Slavic, Slavic, South Asian, women's. **Biology:** General. **Computer sciences:** General. **Conservation:** Environmental science, environmental studies. **English:** English lit. **Foreign languages:** Classics, comparative lit, linguistics, Slavic, South Asian. **History:** General, science/technology. **Human services:** Public policy. **Liberal arts:** Arts/sciences, humanities. **Math:** General, applied, statistics. **Philosophy/religion:** Judaic, philosophy, religion. **Physical sciences:** Chemistry, geophysics, physics. **Psychology:** General. **Social sciences:** Anthropology, economics, geography, international relations, political science, sociology. **Theology:** Theology. **Visual/performing arts:** General, art history/conservation, directing/producing, film/cinema/video, music.

Most popular majors. Biology 9%, foreign language 6%, mathematics 9%, physical sciences 8%, psychology 6%, public administration/social services 6%, social sciences 35%.

Technology on campus. 400 workstations in dormitories, library, computer center, student center. Dormitories wired for high-speed internet access and linked to campus network. Commuter students can connect to campus network. Online course registration, online library, helpline, repair service, student web hosting, wireless network available.

Student life. Freshman orientation: Mandatory. Preregistration for classes offered. Held week before classes begin. **Housing:** Guaranteed on-campus for all undergraduates. Coed dorms, special housing for disabled, apartments available. $500 nonrefundable deposit, deadline 5/1. Single sex

floors available in some buildings. **Activities:** Bands, campus ministries, choral groups, dance, drama, film society, international student organizations, literary magazine, music ensembles, Model UN, musical theater, radio station, student government, student newspaper, symphony orchestra, TV station, UChicago Democrats, College Republicans, Health Leads, Peer Health Advocates, Multicultural Students Association, ACLUChicago, Organization of Black Students, Queers & Associates.

Athletics. NCAA. Intercollegiate: Baseball M, basketball, cross-country, diving, football (tackle) M, soccer, softball W, swimming, tennis, track and field, volleyball W, wrestling M. **Intramural:** Badminton, basketball, bowling, football (non-tackle), racquetball, soccer, softball, swimming, table tennis, tennis, track and field, ultimate frisbee, volleyball. **Team name:** Maroons.

Student services. Adult student services, chaplain/spiritual director, career counseling, services for economically disadvantaged, student employment services, financial aid counseling, health services, minority student services, personal counseling, placement for graduates, veterans' counselor, women's services. **Physically disabled:** Services for visually, speech, hearing impaired.

Contact. E-mail: collegeadmissions@uchicago.edu
Phone: (773) 702-8650 Fax: (773) 702-4199
James Nondorf, Vice President for Enrollment and Student Advancement
Dean of College Admissions and Financial Aid, University of Chicago, 1101 East 58th Street, Chicago, IL 60637

University of Illinois at Chicago
Chicago, Illinois — CB member
www.uic.edu — CB code: 1851

- Public 4-year university
- Commuter campus in very large city
- 17,368 degree-seeking undergraduates: 8% part-time, 50% women, 8% African American, 22% Asian American, 28% Hispanic/Latino, 3% Multi-racial, non-Hispanic, 2% international
- 10,877 degree-seeking graduate students
- 77% of applicants admitted
- SAT or ACT (ACT writing optional), application essay required
- 60% graduate within 6 years

General. Founded in 1946. Regionally accredited. Medical, dental, nursing and pharmacy colleges, and medical center within university complex. **Degrees:** 3,687 bachelor's awarded; master's, professional, doctoral offered. **ROTC:** Army, Naval, Air Force. **Location:** One mile from downtown. **Calendar:** Semester, limited summer session. **Full-time faculty:** 1,141 total; 85% have terminal degrees, 25% minority, 49% women. **Part-time faculty:** 431 total; 64% have terminal degrees, 18% minority, 54% women. **Class size:** 35% < 20, 38% 20-39, 7% 40-49, 10% 50-99, 10% >100. **Special facilities:** Jane Addams' Hull House museum, prairie preserve, health sciences center, software technologies research facility.

Freshman class profile. 15,664 applied, 12,007 admitted, 3,508 enrolled.

Mid 50% test scores			
SAT critical reading:	460-580	Rank in top quarter:	63%
SAT math:	520-660	Rank in top tenth:	23%
SAT writing:	470-580	Return as sophomores:	81%
ACT composite:	21-26	Out-of-state:	4%
GPA 3.75 or higher:	13%	Live on campus:	36%
GPA 3.50-3.74:	16%	International:	3%
GPA 3.0-3.49:	44%	Fraternities:	4%
GPA 2.0-2.99:	27%	Sororities:	4%

Basis for selection. Class rank, GPA, and test scores most important. High school course selection and personal statement strongly considered. Auditions required of music and theater majors. Portfolio required of art majors. **Home schooled:** Transcript of courses and grades required. **Learning Disabled:** Students may add learning disability information to personal essay.

High school preparation. College-preparatory program required. 15 units required. Required and recommended units include English 4, mathematics 3-4, social studies 3, science 3 and foreign language 2. Additional course requirements vary with college and program.

2015-2016 Annual costs. Tuition/fees: $13,762; $26,618 out-of-state. Room/board: $10,728. Books/supplies: $1,400. Personal expenses: $2,176.

2014-2015 Financial aid. Need-based: 2,737 full-time freshmen applied for aid; 2,377 deemed to have need; 2,258 received aid. Average need met was 62%. Average scholarship/grant was $13,834; average loan $3,608. 63% of total undergraduate aid awarded as scholarships/grants, 37% as loans/jobs.

Non-need-based: Awarded to 888 full-time undergraduates, including 239 freshmen. Scholarships awarded for academics, art, athletics, ROTC.

Application procedures. Admission: Closing date 1/15 (postmark date). $50 fee, may be waived for applicants with need. Admission notification on a rolling basis beginning on or about 11/30. Must reply by 5/2. **Financial aid:** Priority date 2/1; no closing date. FAFSA required. Applicants notified on a rolling basis starting 3/15; must reply by 5/1.

Academics. Special study options: Accelerated study, combined bachelor's/graduate degree, cooperative education, cross-registration, distance learning, double major, dual enrollment of high school students, honors, independent study, internships, student-designed major, study abroad, teacher certification program. **Credit/placement by examination:** AP, CLEP, IB, institutional tests. 30 credit hours maximum toward bachelor's degree. **Support services:** Learning center, pre-admission summer program, remedial instruction, study skills assistance, tutoring, writing center.

Majors. Architecture: Architecture. **Area/ethnic studies:** African-American, German, Latin American. **Biology:** General, biochemistry, neuroscience. **Business:** Accounting, business admin, entrepreneurial studies, finance, management science, marketing. **Communications:** Communications/speech/rhetoric. **Computer sciences:** Computer science, information systems. **Education:** Art, biology, chemistry, elementary, English, French, German, history, mathematics, physics, Spanish. **Engineering:** Applied physics, biomedical, chemical, civil, computer, electrical, industrial, mechanical. **English:** English lit. **Foreign languages:** Classics, French, Italian, Polish, Russian, Spanish. **Health services:** Dietetics, health information management, nursing (RN), predental. **History:** General. **Liberal arts:** Arts/sciences. **Math:** General, statistics. **Parks/recreation:** Exercise sciences. **Philosophy/religion:** Philosophy. **Physical sciences:** Chemistry, geology, physics. **Protective services:** Criminal justice. **Psychology:** General. **Social sciences:** Anthropology, economics, political science, sociology, urban studies. **Visual/performing arts:** Art history/conservation, cinematography, dramatic, graphic design, industrial design, music, photography, studio arts.

Most popular majors. Biology 13%, business/marketing 15%, engineering/engineering technologies 13%, health sciences 8%, psychology 13%, social sciences 8%.

Technology on campus. 1,333 workstations in dormitories, library, computer center, student center. Dormitories wired for high-speed internet access and linked to campus network. Commuter students can connect to campus network. Online course registration, online library, helpline, student web hosting, wireless network available.

Student life. Freshman orientation: Mandatory, $149 fee. Preregistration for classes offered. Two-day, overnight offered from early June to mid-August. **Housing:** Coed dorms, special housing for disabled, apartments, themed housing available. $100 fully refundable deposit, deadline 3/1. Presidential Award House, honors, entrepreneur, women in science and engineering floors available. **Activities:** Bands, campus ministries, choral groups, dance, drama, international student organizations, music ensembles, musical theater, radio station, student government, symphony orchestra, over 200 student groups available.

Athletics. NCAA. **Intercollegiate:** Baseball M, basketball, cheerleading, cross-country, diving, gymnastics, soccer M, softball W, swimming, tennis, track and field, volleyball W. **Intramural:** Badminton, basketball, bowling, cross-country, football (non-tackle), racquetball, soccer, softball, table tennis, tennis, volleyball. **Team name:** Flames.

Student services. Adult student services, alcohol/substance abuse counseling, career counseling, services for economically disadvantaged, student employment services, financial aid counseling, health services, legal services, minority student services, on-campus daycare, personal counseling, placement for graduates, veterans' counselor, women's services. **Physically disabled:** Services for visually, speech, hearing impaired.

Contact. E-mail: admit@uic.edu
Phone: (312) 996-4350 Fax: (312) 413-7628
Thomas Glenn, Executive Director Admissions and Records, University of Illinois at Chicago, Office of Admissions and Records, UIC, PO Box 5220, Chicago, IL 60607-5220

University of Illinois at Urbana-Champaign
Champaign, Illinois — CB member
http://illinois.edu — CB code: 1836

- Public 4-year university
- Residential campus in small city
- 32,170 degree-seeking undergraduates: 2% part-time, 44% women, 6% African American, 17% Asian American, 10% Hispanic/Latino, 3% Multi-racial, non-Hispanic, 16% international

- 12,020 degree-seeking graduate students
- 66% of applicants admitted
- SAT or ACT (ACT writing optional), application essay required
- 85% graduate within 6 years

General. Founded in 1867. Regionally accredited. **Degrees:** 8,024 bachelor's awarded; master's, professional, doctoral offered. **ROTC:** Army, Naval; Air Force. **Location:** 130 miles from Chicago, 125 miles from Indianapolis. **Calendar:** Semester, extensive summer session. **Full-time faculty:** 1,970 total; 94% have terminal degrees, 27% minority, 35% women. **Part-time faculty:** 3 total; 100% have terminal degrees. **Class size:** 41% < 20, 33% 20-39, 6% 40-49, 11% 50-99, 9% >100. **Special facilities:** Natural history museum, museum of world history and culture, performing and visual arts centers, 37 public libraries, institute of genomic biology, institute for advanced science and technology, computer science center, national center for supercomputing applications, arboretum, observatory, hiking trails, Japanese house and gardens, ice arena.

Freshman class profile. 34,277 applied, 22,471 admitted, 7,565 enrolled.

Mid 50% test scores			
SAT critical reading:	570-680	Return as sophomores:	93%
SAT math:	700-790	Out-of-state:	14%
SAT writing:	590-690	Live on campus:	99%
ACT composite:	26-31	International:	15%
Rank in top quarter:	86%	Fraternities:	23%
Rank in top tenth:	53%	Sororities:	23%

Basis for selection. High school course work, personal essay, class rank, SAT/ACT most important. Audition required of dance, music, theater (performance) majors. Professional interest statement required of all applicants. **Home schooled:** Provide detailed information about home school environment/coursework; applicants should contact admissions office early in high school career with questions or concerns. **Learning Disabled:** Recommended that students address disability and any accommodations they receive in required personal statement section.

High school preparation. College-preparatory program required. 15.5 units required; 24 recommended. Required and recommended units include English 4, mathematics 3.5-4, social studies 2-4, science 2-4 (laboratory 2-4), foreign language 2-4 and academic electives 2-4. Specific subject requirements vary with college and program.

2015-2016 Annual costs. Tuition/fees: $15,626; $30,786 out-of-state. Room/board: $11,010. Books/supplies: $1,200. Personal expenses: $2,500.

2014-2015 Financial aid. Need-based: 5,882 full-time freshmen applied for aid; 3,346 deemed to have need; 3,133 received aid. Average need met was 68%. Average scholarship/grant was $14,644; average loan $4,455. 61% of total undergraduate aid awarded as scholarships/grants, 39% as loans/jobs. **Non-need-based:** Awarded to 5,436 full-time undergraduates, including 1,496 freshmen. Scholarships awarded for academics, alumni affiliation, art, athletics, leadership, minority status, music/drama, ROTC, state residency.

Application procedures. Admission: Priority date 11/1; deadline 12/1 (postmark date). $50 fee, may be waived for applicants with need. Admission notification by 2/5. Admission notification on a rolling basis beginning on or about 2/5. Must reply by May 1 or within 2 week(s) if notified thereafter. **Financial aid:** Priority date 3/15; no closing date. FAFSA required. Applicants notified on a rolling basis starting 3/1; must reply by 5/1 or within 3 week(s) of notification.

Academics. Students generally declare a major upon enrollment. Students without a declared major may apply for the general curriculum option in the Division of General Studies. **Special study options:** Accelerated study, combined bachelor's/graduate degree, cooperative education, cross-registration, distance learning, double major, dual enrollment of high school students, ESL, exchange student, honors, independent study, internships, liberal arts/career combination, semester at sea, student-designed major, study abroad, teacher certification program, Washington semester. Honors programs, campus honors, Illinois Leadership & Entrepreneurial programs. **Credit/placement by examination:** AP, CLEP, IB, SAT, ACT, institutional tests. Unlimited credit hours may be counted toward a degree. **Support services:** Learning center, reduced course load, study skills assistance, tutoring, writing center.

Majors. Architecture: Architecture, landscape, urban/community planning. **Area/ethnic studies:** East Asian, Latin American, Russian/Slavic, women's. **Biology:** General, biochemistry, biophysics, biotechnology, botany, cell/histology, cellular/molecular, entomology, microbiology, physiology, plant molecular. **Business:** General, accounting, accounting/business management, actuarial science, auditing, banking/financial services, business admin, entrepreneurial studies, finance, financial planning, hospitality admin, human resources, insurance, logistics, management information systems, management science, market research, marketing, operations, organizational behavior, purchasing, real estate, sales/distribution. **Communications:** Advertising, broadcast journalism, communications/speech/rhetoric, journalism, media studies, organizational. **Computer sciences:** General, computer science, programming, security. **Conservation:** General, environmental science, forest sciences, urban forestry, wildlife/wilderness. **Education:** Agricultural, art, biology, chemistry, early childhood, early childhood special, elementary, English, foreign languages, French, German, history, kindergarten/preschool, Latin, mathematics, multi-level teacher, multiple handicapped, music, physical, physics, science, secondary, social science, social studies, Spanish, special ed. **Engineering:** General, aerospace, agricultural, applied physics, biomedical, ceramic, chemical, civil, computer, computer hardware, construction, electrical, engineering mechanics, environmental, geotechnical, industrial, manufacturing, materials, mechanical, metallurgical, nuclear, operations research, polymer, software, structural, transportation, water resource. **English:** English lit, rhetoric/composition, writing. **Foreign languages:** Classics, comparative lit, East Asian, French, German, Hebrew, Italian, linguistics, Portuguese, Russian, Spanish. **Health services:** Athletic training, audiology/hearing, audiology/speech pathology, community health, dietetics, environmental health, health services admin, preveterinary, vocational rehab counseling. **History:** General. **Liberal arts:** Arts/sciences, humanities. **Math:** General, computational, statistics. **Parks/recreation:** General, exercise sciences, sports admin. **Philosophy/religion:** Philosophy, religion. **Physical sciences:** Astronomy, atmospheric science, chemistry, geology, materials science, physics. **Psychology:** General. **Social sciences:** Anthropology, economics, geography, political science, sociology. **Visual/performing arts:** Acting, art history/conservation, crafts, dance, directing/producing, dramatic, film/cinema/video, graphic design, jazz, music, music history, music performance, music theory/composition, painting, photography, sculpture, studio arts, theater history, voice/opera. **Work/family studies:** Child development, consumer economics, family studies, human nutrition.

Most popular majors. Agriculture 6%, biology 7%, business/marketing 12%, communications/journalism 8%, engineering/engineering technologies 20%, social sciences 8%.

Technology on campus. Dormitories wired for high-speed internet access and linked to campus network. Commuter students can connect to campus network. Online course registration, online library, helpline, repair service, student web hosting, wireless network available.

Student life. Freshman orientation: Mandatory. Preregistration for classes offered. One-day program, held end of May through July. **Policies:** Freshmen required to live on campus (or campus-approved housing) unless over 21 years, married, or living with parents. **Housing:** Guaranteed on-campus for freshmen. Coed dorms, single-sex dorms, special housing for disabled, apartments, cooperative housing, fraternity/sorority housing, themed housing, wellness housing available. $150 fully refundable deposit, deadline 5/15. Living/learning communities available. **Activities:** Bands, campus ministries, choral groups, dance, drama, film society, international student organizations, literary magazine, music ensembles, Model UN, musical theater, opera, radio station, student government, student newspaper, symphony orchestra, TV station, more than 1,000 registered student organizations.

Athletics. NCAA. **Intercollegiate:** Baseball M, basketball, cheerleading, cross-country, diving W, football (tackle) M, golf, gymnastics, soccer W, softball W, swimming W, tennis, track and field, volleyball W, wrestling M. **Intramural:** Badminton, basketball, cross-country, diving, football (non-tackle), football (tackle) M, golf, racquetball, soccer, softball W, tennis, volleyball, wrestling M. **Team name:** Fighting Illini.

Student services. Alcohol/substance abuse counseling, career counseling, services for economically disadvantaged, student employment services, financial aid counseling, health services, legal services, minority student services, on-campus daycare, personal counseling, placement for graduates, veterans' counselor, women's services. **Physically disabled:** Services for visually, speech, hearing impaired.

Contact. E-mail: admissions@illinois.edu
Phone: (217) 333-0302 Fax: (217) 244-4614
Keith Marshall, Assistant Provost for Enrollment Management, University of Illinois at Urbana-Champaign, 901 West Illinois, Urbana, IL 61801-3028

University of Illinois: Springfield

Springfield, Illinois — **CB member**
www.uis.edu — **CB code: 0834**

- Public 4-year university and liberal arts college
- Commuter campus in small city
- 2,857 degree-seeking undergraduates: 35% part-time, 51% women, 16% African American, 4% Asian American, 7% Hispanic/Latino, 3% Multiracial, non-Hispanic, 5% international
- 2,311 degree-seeking graduate students
- 63% of applicants admitted
- SAT or ACT (ACT writing optional) required
- 48% graduate within 6 years

General. Founded in 1969. Regionally accredited. Smallest campus of University of Illinois system. **Degrees:** 693 bachelor's awarded; master's, doctoral offered. **Location:** 95 miles from St. Louis, 200 miles from Chicago. **Calendar:** Semester, extensive summer session. **Full-time faculty:** 223 total; 84% have terminal degrees, 15% minority, 47% women. **Part-time faculty:** 157 total; 30% have terminal degrees, 17% minority, 46% women. **Class size:** 51% < 20, 42% 20-39, 5% 40-49, 2% 50-99. **Special facilities:** Observatory, studio theater.

Freshman class profile. 1,524 applied, 962 admitted, 268 enrolled.

Mid 50% test scores			
SAT critical reading:	430-530	Rank in top quarter:	46%
SAT math:	510-600	Rank in top tenth:	19%
SAT writing:	430-600	Return as sophomores:	77%
ACT composite:	20-26	Out-of-state:	12%
GPA 3.75 or higher:	36%	Live on campus:	83%
GPA 3.50-3.74:	13%	International:	3%
GPA 3.0-3.49:	25%		
GPA 2.0-2.99:	26%		

Basis for selection. GPA, rank, record, completion of college-preparatory program, recommendations, admission test scores, and formal demonstration of competencies all fully considered. ACT/SAT required if applicant has fewer than 30 semester hours of college transfer coursework. Personal or telephone interview may be required.

High school preparation. College-preparatory program required. 15 units required. Required units include English 4, mathematics 3, social studies 3, science 3 (laboratory 2) and visual/performing arts 2. Visual arts can be substituted with foreign language.

2015-2016 Annual costs. Tuition/fees: $11,413; $20,938 out-of-state. Room/board: $11,550.

2014-2015 Financial aid. Need-based: 281 full-time freshmen applied for aid; 233 deemed to have need; 229 received aid. Average need met was 80%. Average scholarship/grant was $13,210; average loan $3,237. 50% of total undergraduate aid awarded as scholarships/grants, 50% as loans/jobs. **Non-need-based:** Awarded to 436 full-time undergraduates, including 113 freshmen. Scholarships awarded for academics, alumni affiliation, art, athletics, job skills, leadership, minority status, music/drama, state residency.

Application procedures. Admission: Priority date 5/1; no deadline. $50 fee, may be waived for applicants with need. Admission notification on a rolling basis beginning on or about 10/1. Recommend May 1 but will accept as space permits. **Financial aid:** Priority date 3/1, closing date 11/15. FAFSA required. Applicants notified on a rolling basis starting 1/1; must reply within 3 week(s) of notification.

Academics. Special study options: Combined bachelor's/graduate degree, distance learning, ESL, honors, independent study, internships, study abroad, teacher certification program. **Credit/placement by examination:** AP, CLEP, IB, ACT, institutional tests. 30 credit hours maximum toward bachelor's degree. **Support services:** Learning center, reduced course load, remedial instruction, study skills assistance, tutoring, writing center.

Majors. Biology: General. **Business:** Accounting, business admin. **Communications:** General. **Computer sciences:** Computer science, security, systems analysis. **Conservation:** Environmental studies. **English:** English lit. **Health services:** Clinical lab science. **History:** General. **Human services:** Social work. **Liberal arts:** Arts/sciences. **Math:** General. **Philosophy/religion:** Philosophy. **Physical sciences:** Chemistry. **Protective services:** Criminal justice. **Psychology:** General. **Social sciences:** Economics, political science, sociology/anthropology. **Visual/performing arts:** Studio arts.

Most popular majors. Business/marketing 26%, communications/journalism 7%, computer/information sciences 15%, liberal arts 6%, psychology 8%, security/protective services 6%.

Technology on campus. 550 workstations in dormitories, library, computer center, student center. Dormitories wired for high-speed internet access and linked to campus network. Commuter students can connect to campus network. Online course registration, online library, helpline, student web hosting, wireless network available.

Student life. Freshman orientation: Mandatory. Preregistration for classes offered. **Housing:** Guaranteed on-campus for freshmen. Coed dorms, special housing for disabled, apartments, gender-neutral housing, themed housing, wellness housing available. $250 partly refundable deposit. Family housing available. **Activities:** Bands, campus ministries, choral groups, dance, drama, film society, international student organizations, music ensembles, Model UN, radio station, student government, student newspaper, Catholic Student Organization, Chinese Bible Christian Student Association, Christian Student Fellowship, Church of the Living God International Campus Ministry at UIS, Epic Praise for Christ, Springfield University Bible Fellowship, Voices in Praise, American Red Cross at UIS, College Republicans, Young Americans for Liberty.

Athletics. NCAA. **Intercollegiate:** Baseball M, basketball, cross-country, golf, soccer, softball W, tennis, track and field W, volleyball W. **Intramural:** Badminton, basketball, cricket, football (non-tackle), handball, racquetball, soccer, softball, squash, table tennis, track and field, ultimate frisbee, volleyball. **Team name:** Prairie Stars.

Student services. Alcohol/substance abuse counseling, career counseling, student employment services, financial aid counseling, health services, minority student services, on-campus daycare, personal counseling, veterans' counselor, women's services. **Physically disabled:** Services for visually, speech, hearing impaired.

Contact. E-mail: admissions@uis.edu
Phone: (217) 206-4847 Toll-free number: (800) 977-4847
Fax: (217) 206-6620
Fernando Planas, Director of Admissions, University of Illinois: Springfield, One University Plaza, MS UHB 1080, Springfield, IL 62703

University of Phoenix: Chicago
Schaumburg, Illinois
www.phoenix.edu

- For-profit 4-year university
- Small city
- 781 undergraduates

General. Regionally accredited. **Degrees:** 199 bachelor's awarded; master's offered. **Calendar:** Differs by program. **Full-time faculty:** 19 total. **Part-time faculty:** 213 total.

Basis for selection. Open admission.

2015-2016 Annual costs. Per-credit-hour charge $410 to $635, depending upon level and course of study; electronic course materials fee $95, if applicable. Book and material charges may vary by course and program. All fees are subject to change.

Application procedures. Admission: No deadline. No application fee. **Financial aid:** No deadline.

Academics. Credit/placement by examination: AP, CLEP.

Majors. Business: Accounting/business management, business admin, e-commerce, entrepreneurial studies, finance, human resources, marketing, operations. **Computer sciences:** Programming, security, system admin, systems analysis, web page design, webmaster. **Health services:** Facilities admin, long term care admin. **Human services:** General. **Protective services:** Law enforcement admin.

Student life. Freshman orientation: Mandatory. Preregistration for classes offered.

Contact. Toll-free number: (866) 766-0766
University of Phoenix: Chicago, 1625 W. Fountainhead Pkwy, Tempe, AZ 85282

University of St. Francis
Joliet, Illinois
www.stfrancis.edu
CB code: 1130

- Private 4-year university and liberal arts college affiliated with the Roman Catholic Church
- Commuter campus in small city
- 1,325 degree-seeking undergraduates: 4% part-time, 64% women, 7% African American, 2% Asian American, 18% Hispanic/Latino, 3% Multiracial, non-Hispanic, 2% international
- 1,188 degree-seeking graduate students
- 51% of applicants admitted
- SAT or ACT (ACT writing optional) required
- 65% graduate within 6 years; 19% enter graduate study

General. Founded in 1920. Regionally accredited. **Degrees:** 300 bachelor's awarded; master's, doctoral offered. **ROTC:** Army. **Location:** 35 miles from Chicago. **Calendar:** Semester, extensive summer session. **Full-time faculty:**

100 total; 69% have terminal degrees, 16% minority, 65% women. **Part-time faculty:** 204 total; 26% have terminal degrees, 13% minority, 58% women. **Class size:** 71% < 20, 29% 20-39. **Special facilities:** Cadaver lab, Mac labs, SimLabs for nursing students, mock trial courtroom, business incubator, art and design complex with studio spaces for senior students, greenhouse, on-campus beehives, outdoor challenge course.

Freshman class profile. 1,423 applied, 719 admitted, 181 enrolled.

Mid 50% test scores			
SAT critical reading:	470-530	GPA 2.0-2.99:	17%
SAT math:	470-630	Rank in top quarter:	43%
SAT writing:	450-490	Rank in top tenth:	16%
ACT composite:	21-25	End year in good standing:	95%
GPA 3.75 or higher:	31%	Return as sophomores:	81%
GPA 3.50-3.74:	16%	Out-of-state:	7%
GPA 3.0-3.49:	36%	Live on campus:	51%
		International:	2%

Basis for selection. High school GPA and rank, test scores important. Essay and letters of recommendation required and interview recommended for students who do not meet admissions requirements. **Home schooled:** Transcript of courses and grades, state high school equivalency certificate required.

High school preparation. College-preparatory program required. 17 units required. Required units include English 4, mathematics 3, social studies 2, science 2 (laboratory 1) and academic electives 3. 3 units required from 2 areas: foreign language, music/art, or computer science.

2015-2016 Annual costs. Tuition/fees: $29,950. Room/board: $9,084. Books/supplies: $800. Personal expenses: $2,000.

2015-2016 Financial aid. Need-based: 173 full-time freshmen applied for aid; 158 deemed to have need; 158 received aid. Average need met was 79%. Average scholarship/grant was $8,815; average loan $3,637. 69% of total undergraduate aid awarded as scholarships/grants, 31% as loans/jobs. **Non-need-based:** Awarded to 1,322 full-time undergraduates, including 195 freshmen. Scholarships awarded for academics, alumni affiliation, art, athletics, leadership, minority status, music/drama, religious affiliation, state residency.

Application procedures. Admission: Priority date 5/1; deadline 8/1 (receipt date). No application fee. Admission notification on a rolling basis beginning on or about 9/1. Must reply by 5/1. **Financial aid:** Priority date 2/15; no closing date. FAFSA, institutional form required. Applicants notified on a rolling basis starting 2/15.

Academics. Special study options: Combined bachelor's/graduate degree, distance learning, double major, dual enrollment of high school students, ESL, honors, independent study, internships, semester at sea, student-designed major, study abroad, teacher certification program, Washington semester. **Credit/placement by examination:** AP, CLEP, IB, SAT, ACT, institutional tests. 33 credit hours maximum toward bachelor's degree. **Support services:** Learning center, pre-admission summer program, reduced course load, remedial instruction, study skills assistance, tutoring, writing center.

Majors. Biology: General. **Business:** Accounting, actuarial science, business admin, entrepreneurial studies, finance, human resources, international, logistics, management science, marketing, organizational behavior. **Communications:** Advertising, broadcast journalism, media studies, public relations, radio/TV. **Computer sciences:** Computer science, information technology, webmaster. **Conservation:** Environmental science. **Education:** Art, elementary, English, mathematics, music, science, social studies, special ed. **English:** English lit. **Health services:** Clinical lab science, facilities admin, health care admin, medical radiologic technology/radiation therapy, nuclear medical technology, nursing (RN), predental, premedicine, prepharmacy, prephysical therapy, preveterinary, radiologic technology/medical imaging, recreational therapy, substance abuse counseling. **History:** General. **Human services:** Social work. **Liberal arts:** Arts/sciences. **Math:** General. **Parks/recreation:** Facilities management. **Protective services:** Law enforcement admin. **Psychology:** General. **Social sciences:** Political science. **Theology:** Theology. **Visual/performing arts:** General, music, music performance.

Most popular majors. Biology 8%, business/marketing 8%, education 11%, health sciences 30%, parks/recreation 6%, public administration/social services 6%, security/protective services 6%.

Technology on campus. 417 workstations in dormitories, library, computer center, student center. Dormitories wired for high-speed internet access and linked to campus network. Commuter students can connect to campus network. Online course registration, online library, helpline, wireless network available.

Student life. Freshman orientation: Mandatory, $120 fee. Preregistration for classes offered. **Policies:** Visitation between 9am and 2am. Overnight guests must sign in at Marian desk. Marian Hall is alcohol-free. All halls close during major breaks (fall break, winter break, spring break) unless special permission received to remain in hall. **Housing:** Guaranteed on-campus for freshmen. Coed dorms, special housing for disabled, apartments, themed housing, wellness housing available. $50 fully refundable deposit, deadline 5/1. **Activities:** Campus ministries, choral groups, dance, drama, international student organizations, music ensembles, musical theater, opera, radio station, student government, student newspaper, symphony orchestra, TV station, Brother 2 Brother, Black Student Association, Council for Environmental Awareness, Fellowship of Christian Athletes, HOUSE, international club, Criminal Justice & Pre-Law Society, Mock Trial, Pro-Life Group, Sister 2 Sister, social work club, Unidos Vamos a Alcanzar, History Club.

Athletics. NAIA. **Intercollegiate:** Baseball M, basketball, bowling, cheerleading, cross-country, football (tackle) M, golf, soccer, softball W, tennis, track and field, volleyball W. **Intramural:** Basketball, bowling, table tennis, volleyball. **Team name:** Saints.

Student services. Adult student services, alcohol/substance abuse counseling, chaplain/spiritual director, career counseling, student employment services, financial aid counseling, health services, minority student services, personal counseling, placement for graduates. **Physically disabled:** Services for visually, speech, hearing impaired.

Contact. E-mail: admissions@stfrancis.edu
Phone: (815) 740-2270 Toll-free number: (800) 735-7500
Fax: (815) 740-5078
Cynthia Lambert, Director Undergraduate Admissions, University of St. Francis, 500 Wilcox Street, Joliet, IL 60435

VanderCook College of Music
Chicago, Illinois
www.vandercook.edu CB code: 1872

- Private 4-year music and teachers college
- Residential campus in very large city
- 104 degree-seeking undergraduates: 8% part-time, 43% women, 8% African American, 2% Asian American, 21% Hispanic/Latino, 4% Multiracial, non-Hispanic, 2% international
- 42 degree-seeking graduate students
- 96% of applicants admitted
- Application essay, interview required
- 65% graduate within 6 years

General. Founded in 1909. Regionally accredited. Full access to all student services at Illinois Institute of Technology. **Degrees:** 27 bachelor's awarded; master's offered. **Location:** 3 miles from downtown. **Calendar:** Semester. **Full-time faculty:** 9 total; 67% have terminal degrees, 33% minority, 78% women. **Part-time faculty:** 24 total; 8% have terminal degrees, 29% women. **Class size:** 74% < 20, 23% 20-39, 3% 50-99. **Special facilities:** MIDI/electronic music laboratory, archival collection of recordings, photographs, sheet music and materials from early 20th century to the present.

Freshman class profile. 47 applied, 45 admitted, 21 enrolled.

Mid 50% test scores		
SAT critical reading:	400-470	GPA 3.0-3.49: 25%
SAT math:	480-610	GPA 2.0-2.99: 20%
SAT writing:	480-510	Return as sophomores: 80%
ACT composite:	22-28	Out-of-state: 30%
GPA 3.75 or higher:	45%	Live on campus: 60%
GPA 3.50-3.74:	10%	International: 5%

Basis for selection. Academic credentials, SAT or ACT scores and recommendations are weighed along with student's musical audition and interview. Audition required. **Home schooled:** Applicants should obtain experience performing with a concert band or chorus. A minimum of three credits of music is recommended.

High school preparation. College-preparatory program recommended. 15 units recommended. Recommended units include English 3, mathematics 2, social studies 3, science 2, foreign language 2 and academic electives 3. Art may be substituted for foreign language.

2015-2016 Annual costs. Tuition/fees: $26,300. Room/board: $11,516. Books/supplies: $1,900. Personal expenses: $2,310.

2014-2015 Financial aid. Need-based: 27 full-time freshmen applied for aid; 19 deemed to have need; 19 received aid. Average scholarship/grant was $6,591; average loan $3,362. 52% of total undergraduate aid awarded as scholarships/grants, 48% as loans/jobs. **Non-need-based:** Awarded to 106 full-time undergraduates, including 25 freshmen. Scholarships awarded for academics, music/drama. **Additional information:** Musical talent considered for partial tuition waiver.

Application procedures. Admission: Priority date 4/1; no deadline. $35 fee. Application must be submitted on paper. Admission notification on a rolling basis. Must reply by 5/1. Accepted candidates should submit non-refundable tuition deposit of $100 by May 1 as indication of intent to enroll. **Financial aid:** Priority date 3/1; no closing date. FAFSA required. Applicants notified on a rolling basis starting 5/1; must reply within 2 week(s) of notification.

Academics. Special study options: Teacher certification program. **Credit/placement by examination:** AP, CLEP, IB, SAT, ACT, institutional tests. 18 credit hours maximum toward bachelor's degree. **Support services:** Remedial instruction, tutoring.

Majors. Education: Music.

Technology on campus. 21 workstations in dormitories, library, computer center, student center. Dormitories wired for high-speed internet access and linked to campus network. Commuter students can connect to campus network. Wireless network available.

Student life. Freshman orientation: Mandatory. Preregistration for classes offered. **Housing:** Guaranteed on-campus for all undergraduates. Coed dorms, apartments, fraternity/sorority housing available. Apartments for single students over 23 available. **Activities:** Bands, choral groups, music ensembles, musical theater, radio station.

Student services. Career counseling, student employment services, health services, personal counseling, placement for graduates.

Contact. E-mail: admissions@vandercook.edu
Phone: (312) 225-6288 ext. 230 Fax: (312) 225-5211
LeeAnn Meyer, Director of Admissions and Retention, VanderCook College of Music, 3140 South Federal Street, Chicago, IL 60616-3731

Western Illinois University
Macomb, Illinois
www.wiu.edu CB code: 1900

- Public 4-year university
- Residential campus in large town
- 9,141 degree-seeking undergraduates: 11% part-time, 50% women, 19% African American, 1% Asian American, 11% Hispanic/Latino, 2% Multiracial, non-Hispanic, 2% international
- 1,953 degree-seeking graduate students
- 60% of applicants admitted
- SAT or ACT (ACT writing optional) required
- 53% graduate within 6 years

General. Founded in 1899. Regionally accredited. **Degrees:** 2,218 bachelor's awarded; master's, doctoral offered. **ROTC:** Army. **Location:** 83 miles from Rock Island, 78 miles from Peoria. **Calendar:** Semester, limited summer session. **Full-time faculty:** 632 total; 72% have terminal degrees, 17% minority, 45% women. **Part-time faculty:** 47 total; 28% have terminal degrees, 2% minority, 57% women. **Class size:** 51% < 20, 42% 20-39, 5% 40-49, 3% 50-99, less than 1% >100. **Special facilities:** Geology museum, life sciences station, 92-acre nature retreat, university farm, multicultural center.

Freshman class profile. 10,877 applied, 6,534 admitted, 1,535 enrolled.

Mid 50% test scores		
ACT composite:	18-23	Rank in top quarter: 31%
GPA 3.75 or higher:	17%	Rank in top tenth: 10%
GPA 3.50-3.74:	11%	Return as sophomores: 68%
GPA 3.0-3.49:	35%	Out-of-state: 6%
GPA 2.0-2.99:	37%	Live on campus: 92%
		International: 1%

Basis for selection. Standardized test scores and GPA very important. Audition required for music majors. **Home schooled:** Transcript of courses and grades required.

High school preparation. College-preparatory program recommended. 15 units recommended. Recommended units include English 4, mathematics 3, social studies 3, science 3 and academic electives 2. 2 units of art, film, foreign language, music, speech, theater, journalism, religion, philosophy or vocational education also recommended.

2015-2016 Annual costs. Tuition/fees: $11,508; $15,910 out-of-state. Room/board: $9,580. **Additional information:** Student Insurance $690/semester or $1380 for full academic year.

2015-2016 Financial aid. Need-based: 1,387 full-time freshmen applied for aid; 1,210 deemed to have need; 1,178 received aid. Average need met was 61%. Average scholarship/grant was $9,935; average loan $3,481. 63%

of total undergraduate aid awarded as scholarships/grants, 37% as loans/jobs. **Non-need-based:** Awarded to 3,381 full-time undergraduates, including 927 freshmen. Scholarships awarded for academics, alumni affiliation, art, athletics, leadership, minority status, music/drama, ROTC. **Additional information:** University funded need-based grant and work program continued for student's undergraduate career with emphasis on graduating in 4 years and maintaining an average of 15 hours/semester and satisfactory academic performance.

Application procedures. Admission: Priority date 5/15; no deadline. $30 fee, may be waived for applicants with need. Admission notification on a rolling basis beginning on or about 9/15. **Financial aid:** No deadline. FAFSA required. Applicants notified on a rolling basis starting 1/15.

Academics. Some academic support services available on weekends (Sundays). **Special study options:** Combined bachelor's/graduate degree, distance learning, double major, dual enrollment of high school students, ESL, honors, independent study, internships, student-designed major, study abroad, teacher certification program, weekend college. **Credit/placement by examination:** AP, CLEP, IB, SAT, ACT, institutional tests. 30 credit hours maximum toward bachelor's degree. **Support services:** Remedial instruction, study skills assistance, tutoring, writing center. Math help centers, mentoring program.

Honors college/program. 28 ACT or upper 10% of class and 24 ACT required.

Majors. Area/ethnic studies: African-American, women's. **Biology:** General. **Business:** Accounting, business admin, construction management, finance, human resources, logistics, management information systems, managerial economics, marketing. **Communications:** Communications/speech/rhetoric, journalism, radio/TV. **Communications technology:** Graphic/printing. **Computer sciences:** General, networking. **Education:** Bilingual, educational technology, elementary, health, special ed. **Engineering:** Electrical. **English:** English lit. **Foreign languages:** French, Spanish. **Health services:** Athletic training, clinical lab science, communication disorders, health care admin, nursing (RN). **History:** General. **Human services:** Social work. **Liberal arts:** Arts/sciences. **Math:** General. **Parks/recreation:** Exercise sciences, facilities management. **Philosophy/religion:** Philosophy, religion. **Physical sciences:** Chemistry, forensic chemistry, geology, meteorology, physics. **Protective services:** Homeland security, law enforcement admin. **Psychology:** General. **Social sciences:** Economics, geography, political science, sociology. **Visual/performing arts:** Art, dramatic, music, music performance, musical theater, studio arts. **Work/family studies:** General.

Most popular majors. Business/marketing 14%, communications/journalism 6%, liberal arts 12%, parks/recreation 7%, security/protective services 18%.

Technology on campus. 1,036 workstations in dormitories, library, computer center. Dormitories wired for high-speed internet access and linked to campus network. Commuter students can connect to campus network. Online course registration, online library, helpline, wireless network available.

Student life. Freshman orientation: Mandatory. Preregistration for classes offered. Two-day orientation session held prior to beginning of classes. **Housing:** Guaranteed on-campus for all undergraduates. Coed dorms, special housing for disabled, apartments, fraternity/sorority housing, themed housing, wellness housing available. $50 nonrefundable deposit, deadline 7/20. **Activities:** Bands, campus ministries, choral groups, dance, drama, film society, international student organizations, literary magazine, music ensembles, Model UN, musical theater, opera, radio station, student government, student newspaper, symphony orchestra, TV station, 67 special-interest organizations, 5 service organizations, 14 religious organizations, 32 national honorary and professional fraternities.

Athletics. NCAA. **Intercollegiate:** Baseball M, basketball, cheerleading, cross-country, diving, football (tackle) M, golf, soccer, softball W, swimming, tennis, track and field, volleyball W. **Intramural:** Badminton, basketball, bowling, cross-country, football (non-tackle), football (tackle) M, golf, handball, lacrosse M, racquetball, rugby, skin diving, soccer, softball, swimming, table tennis, tennis, volleyball, water polo. **Team name:** Leathernecks.

Student services. Adult student services, alcohol/substance abuse counseling, career counseling, student employment services, financial aid counseling, health services, legal services, minority student services, on-campus daycare, personal counseling, placement for graduates, veterans' counselor, women's services. **Physically disabled:** Services for visually, speech, hearing impaired.

Contact. E-mail: admissions@wiu.edu
Phone: (309) 298-3157 Toll-free number: (877) 742-5948
Fax: (309) 298-3111
Andrew Borst, Director of Admissions, Western Illinois University, 1 University Circle, Macomb, IL 61455-1390

Westwood College: Chicago Loop
Chicago, Illinois
www.westwood.edu/locations/illinois/chicago-loop-campus

◗ For-profit 4-year technical and career college
◗ Commuter campus in very large city
◗ 417 degree-seeking undergraduates

General. Regionally accredited; also accredited by ACICS. This Westwood College campus offers a unique hands-on, career-focused curriculum providing associate degrees that can be earned in as little as three months and bachelor's degrees that can be earned in as little as three years. Degree programs are available in the fields of technology, healthcare, business, design and justice. **Degrees:** 72 bachelor's, 27 associate awarded. **Calendar:** Differs by program. **Full-time faculty:** 4 total. **Part-time faculty:** 54 total.

Basis for selection. Admission based on interview, applicant's level of interest and test scores. SAT or ACT recommended.

High school preparation. 4 units required.

2015-2016 Annual costs. Books/supplies: $1,106. **Additional information:** Computer-Aided Design/Architectural Drafting: AAS $39,067. Graphic Design: AAS $40,978; BAS $78,120. Information and Network Technologies: AAS $35,525; BAS $71,050. Software Development: BAS $71,050. Business Administration: BAS $74,256. Construction Management: AAS $37,128; BAS $74,256. Criminal Justice: BAS $78,834. Medical Assisting: Diploma $25,685. Additional costs and fees such as books, tool kits, lab fee and online fees may apply.

Application procedures. Admission: Closing date 8/1. No application fee. **Financial aid:** No deadline.

Academics. Special study options: Independent study, internships. **Credit/placement by examination:** AP, CLEP, SAT, ACT, institutional tests.

Majors. Business: Accounting/business management, construction management, marketing. **Communications technology:** Animation/special effects. **Computer sciences:** LAN/WAN management. **Health services:** Health care admin. **Protective services:** Law enforcement admin. **Visual/performing arts:** Design.

Contact. E-mail: AdmissionsRepresentativesWW-Campus@westwood.edu
Phone: (312) 739-0850 Toll-free number: (800) 693-5411
Fax: (312) 739-1004
Gus Pyroulis, Director of Admissions, Westwood College: Chicago Loop, One North State Street, Suite 1000, Chicago, IL 60602

Westwood College: DuPage
Woodridge, Illinois
www.westwood.edu/locations/illinois/dupage-campus
CB code: 5096

◗ For-profit 4-year career college
◗ Commuter campus in large city
◗ 499 degree-seeking undergraduates
◗ Interview required

General. Regionally accredited; also accredited by ACICS. This Westwood College campus offers a unique hands-on, career-focused curriculum providing associate degrees that can be earned in as little as three months and bachelor's degrees that can be earned in as little as three years. Degree programs are available in the fields of technology, healthcare, business, design and justice. **Degrees:** 71 bachelor's, 5 associate awarded. **Location:** 20 miles from downtown Chicago. **Calendar:** Quarter. **Full-time faculty:** 1 total. **Part-time faculty:** 28 total.

Basis for selection. Successful completion of ACCUPLACER test and interview required prior to admission; SAT/ACT scores may be used in lieu of ACCUPLACER. SAT or ACT recommended.

2015-2016 Annual costs. Computer-Aided Design/Architectural Drafting: AAS $39,067. Graphic Design: AAS $40,978; BAS $78,120. Information and Network Technologies: AAS $35,525; BAS $71,050. Software Development: BAS $71,050. Business Administration: BAS $74,256. Construction Management: AAS $37,128; BAS $74,256. Criminal Justice: BAS $78,834. Medical Assisting: Diploma $25,685. Additional costs and fees such as books, tool kits, lab fee and online fees may apply.

Application procedures. Admission: No deadline. No application fee. Admission notification on a rolling basis.

Academics. Special study options: Accelerated study, independent study. **Credit/placement by examination:** AP, CLEP, institutional tests.

Majors. Business: Construction management. **Computer sciences:** LAN/WAN management. **Visual/performing arts:** Design.

Student life. Activities: Student government.

Contact. E-mail: AdmissionsRepresentativesWW-Campus@westwood.edu
Phone: (630) 434-7655 Toll-free number: (866) 721-7647
Fax: (630) 743-0667
Jim Galas, Assistant Director of Admissions, Westwood College: DuPage, 7155 Janes Avenue, Woodridge, IL 60517

Westwood College: O'Hare Airport
Chicago, Illinois
www.westwood.edu/locations/illinois/ohare-airport-campus

- For-profit 4-year career college
- Commuter campus in very large city
- 784 degree-seeking undergraduates
- Application essay, interview required

General. Regionally accredited; also accredited by ACICS. This Westwood College campus offers a unique hands-on, career-focused curriculum providing associate degrees that can be earned in as little as three months and bachelor's degrees that can be earned in as little as three years. Degree programs are available in the fields of technology, healthcare, business, design and justice. **Degrees:** 108 bachelor's, 11 associate awarded. **Location:** Downtown. **Calendar:** Differs by program. **Full-time faculty:** 8 total. **Part-time faculty:** 34 total.

Basis for selection. Institutional test (ACCUPLACER) and interview most important. Developmental courses may be required for those who do not pass entrance examination. Assessment given to all students; passing score required for admission to college programs.

2015-2016 Annual costs. Books/supplies: $1,106. Personal expenses: $400. **Additional information:** Computer-Aided Design/Architectural Drafting: AAS $39,067. Graphic Design: AAS $40,978; BAS $78,120. Information and Network Technologies: AAS $35,525; BAS $71,050. Software Development: BAS $71,050. Business Administration: BAS $74,256. Construction Management: AAS $37,128; BAS $74,256. Criminal Justice: BAS $78,834. Medical Assisting: Diploma $25,685. Additional costs and fees such as books, tool kits, lab fee and online fees may apply.

Application procedures. Admission: No deadline. No application fee. Application must be submitted on paper. Admission notification on a rolling basis. **Financial aid:** Priority date 3/1, closing date 6/30. FAFSA, institutional form required.

Academics. Special study options: Accelerated study, cooperative education, distance learning, double major, independent study, internships, liberal arts/career combination, study abroad. **Credit/placement by examination:** AP, CLEP, institutional tests. **Support services:** Learning center, reduced course load, remedial instruction, study skills assistance, tutoring, writing center.

Majors. Business: Accounting/business management, construction management, marketing. **Health services:** Health care admin. **Protective services:** Law enforcement admin. **Visual/performing arts:** Design.

Technology on campus. Commuter students can connect to campus network. Online library, wireless network available.

Student life. Freshman orientation: Mandatory. Preregistration for classes offered. **Housing:** Wellness housing available. **Activities:** Student government, student newspaper.

Student services. Adult student services, alcohol/substance abuse counseling, career counseling, student employment services, financial aid counseling, minority student services, personal counseling, placement for graduates, veterans' counselor, women's services. **Physically disabled:** Services for visually, hearing impaired.

Contact. E-mail: AdmissionsRepresentativesWW-Campus@westwood.edu
Phone: (773) 380-6800 Toll-free number: (877) 235-2457
Michael Favia, Director of Admissions, Westwood College: O'Hare Airport, 8501 West Higgins Road, Chicago, IL 60631

Westwood College: River Oaks
Calumet City, Illinois
www.westwood.edu/locations/illinois/river-oaks-campus

- For-profit 4-year career college
- Commuter campus in very large city
- 548 degree-seeking undergraduates
- Interview required

General. Regionally accredited; also accredited by ACICS. This Westwood College campus offers a unique hands-on, career-focused curriculum providing associate degrees that can be earned in as little as three months and bachelor's degrees that can be earned in as little as three years. Degree programs are available in the fields of technology, healthcare, business, design and justice. **Degrees:** 53 bachelor's, 32 associate awarded. **Calendar:** Differs by program. **Full-time faculty:** 9 total. **Part-time faculty:** 32 total.

Basis for selection. Institutional test (ACCUPLACER) and interview most important. Developmental courses may be required for those who do not pass entrance examination. SAT or ACT recommended. **Home schooled:** Interview required.

2015-2016 Annual costs. Books/supplies: $1,106. **Additional information:** Computer-Aided Design/Architectural Drafting: AAS $39,067. Graphic Design: AAS $40,978; BAS $78,120. Information and Network Technologies: AAS $35,525; BAS $71,050. Software Development: BAS $71,050. Business Administration: BAS $74,256. Construction Management: AAS $37,128; BAS $74,256. Criminal Justice: BAS $78,834. Medical Assisting: Diploma $25,685. Additional costs and fees such as books, tool kits, lab fee and online fees may apply.

Application procedures. Admission: No deadline. No application fee. Admission notification on a rolling basis. **Financial aid:** FAFSA, institutional form required.

Academics. Credit/placement by examination: AP, CLEP, institutional tests.

Majors. Business: Accounting/business management, construction management, marketing. **Computer sciences:** LAN/WAN management. **Health services:** Health care admin. **Protective services:** Law enforcement admin. **Visual/performing arts:** Design.

Contact. E-mail: AdmissionsRepresentativesWW-Campus@westwood.edu
Phone: (708) 832-1988 Toll-free number: (888) 549-4960
James Galas, Director of Admissions, Westwood College: River Oaks, 80 River Oaks Center Drive, Suite 111, Calumet City, IL 60409-5802

Wheaton College
Wheaton, Illinois
www.wheaton.edu

CB member
CB code: 1905

- Private 4-year liberal arts college affiliated with the nondenominational tradition
- Residential campus in small city
- 2,447 degree-seeking undergraduates: 2% part-time, 53% women, 3% African American, 9% Asian American, 6% Hispanic/Latino, 5% Multiracial, non-Hispanic, 3% international
- 401 degree-seeking graduate students
- 71% of applicants admitted
- SAT or ACT (ACT writing optional), application essay required
- 89% graduate within 6 years; 27% enter graduate study

General. Founded in 1860. Regionally accredited. **Degrees:** 588 bachelor's awarded; master's, professional, doctoral offered. **ROTC:** Army, Air Force. **Location:** 25 miles from Chicago. **Calendar:** Semester, limited summer session. **Full-time faculty:** 204 total; 96% have terminal degrees, 13% minority, 35% women. **Part-time faculty:** 101 total; 39% have terminal degrees, 11% minority, 46% women. **Class size:** 57% < 20, 35% 20-39, 3% 40-49, 3% 50-99, 2% >100.

Freshman class profile. 1,971 applied, 1,390 admitted, 605 enrolled.

Mid 50% test scores			
SAT critical reading:	600-710	Rank in top quarter:	81%
SAT math:	600-700	Rank in top tenth:	54%
SAT writing:	590-700	End year in good standing:	97%
ACT composite:	27-32	Return as sophomores:	95%
GPA 3.75 or higher:	54%	Out-of-state:	74%
GPA 3.50-3.74:	25%	Live on campus:	100%
GPA 3.0-3.49:	18%	International:	3%
		GPA 2.0-2.99:	3%

Basis for selection. Evidence of a vital Christian experience, moral character, personal integrity, social concern, academic ability, and desire for a liberal arts education as defined by the college are most important. Interview recommended. Audition required of music majors. **Home schooled:** Statement describing home school structure and mission required. Applicants advised to take the ACT to satisfy the "Ability to Benefit" requirements. **Learning Disabled:** Personal interview required at enrollment. Must contact Academic Support Coordinator to request services or equipment and provide documentation/diagnosis of disability.

High school preparation. College-preparatory program required. 15 units required; 19 recommended. Required and recommended units include English 4, mathematics 3-4, social studies 3-4, science 3-4 and foreign language 2-3.

2015-2016 Annual costs. Tuition/fees: $32,950. Room/board: $9,200. Books/supplies: $1,120. Personal expenses: $1,300.

2015-2016 Financial aid. Need-based: 455 full-time freshmen applied for aid; 353 deemed to have need; 352 received aid. Average need met was 88%. Average scholarship/grant was $22,035; average loan $4,923. 78% of total undergraduate aid awarded as scholarships/grants, 22% as loans/jobs. **Non-need-based:** Awarded to 903 full-time undergraduates, including 259 freshmen. Scholarships awarded for academics, alumni affiliation, art, minority status, music/drama.

Application procedures. Admission: Closing date 1/10 (receipt date). $50 fee, may be waived for applicants with need. Admission notification by 4/1. Must reply by May 1 or within 2 week(s) if notified thereafter. **Financial aid:** Priority date 2/15; no closing date. FAFSA, institutional form required. Applicants notified on a rolling basis starting 3/1.

Academics. Special study options: Combined bachelor's/graduate degree, cross-registration, double major, exchange student, independent study, internships, liberal arts/career combination, student-designed major, study abroad, teacher certification program, urban semester, Washington semester. **Credit/placement by examination:** AP, CLEP, IB, SAT, ACT, institutional tests. 76 credit hours maximum toward bachelor's degree. **Support services:** Study skills assistance, tutoring, writing center.

Majors. Biology: General. **Business:** Managerial economics. **Communications:** Communications/speech/rhetoric. **Computer sciences:** Computer science. **Conservation:** Environmental science. **Education:** Elementary, music, secondary, social studies. **Engineering:** General. **English:** English lit. **Foreign languages:** Classics, French, German, Spanish. **Health services:** Nursing (RN). **History:** General. **Math:** General, applied. **Philosophy/religion:** Philosophy. **Physical sciences:** Chemistry, geology, physics. **Psychology:** General. **Social sciences:** Anthropology, archaeology, economics, international relations, political science, sociology, urban studies. **Theology:** Bible, religious ed. **Visual/performing arts:** Art, music, music history, music pedagogy, music performance, music theory/composition.

Most popular majors. Business/marketing 10%, communications/journalism 8%, English 8%, health sciences 7%, social sciences 12%, theological studies 8%, visual/performing arts 10%.

Technology on campus. 325 workstations in dormitories, library, computer center, student center. Dormitories wired for high-speed internet access and linked to campus network. Commuter students can connect to campus network. Online course registration, online library, helpline, wireless network available.

Student life. Freshman orientation: Mandatory. Preregistration for classes offered. Five-day program during week before classes begin. Optional pre-orientation offered during the 2-weeks before orientation begins. **Policies:** All college and college-related functions are alcohol and tobacco free. Religious observance required. Freshmen not permitted cars on campus. **Housing:** Guaranteed on-campus for freshmen. Coed dorms, single-sex dorms, apartments, cooperative housing available. Housing for disabled provided as needed. **Activities:** Bands, campus ministries, choral groups, dance, drama, film society, international student organizations, literary magazine, music ensembles, Model UN, musical theater, opera, radio station, student government, student newspaper, symphony orchestra, TV station, Christian Service Council, gospel choir, Honduras Project, International Justice Mission, Koinonia, Solidarity Cabinet, World Christian Fellowship, William Osborne Society, Unidad Cristiana.

Athletics. NCAA. **Intercollegiate:** Baseball M, basketball, cross-country, football (tackle) M, golf, soccer, softball W, swimming, tennis, track and field, volleyball W, wrestling M. **Intramural:** Basketball, golf, sand volleyball, soccer, softball M, ultimate frisbee, volleyball. **Team name:** Thunder.

Student services. Chaplain/spiritual director, career counseling, student employment services, financial aid counseling, health services, minority student services, personal counseling, placement for graduates, veterans' counselor. **Physically disabled:** Services for visually, speech, hearing impaired.

Contact. E-mail: admissions@wheaton.edu
Phone: (630) 752-5011 Toll-free number: (800) 222-2419
Fax: (630) 752-5285
Shawn Leftwich, Director of Undergraduate Admissions, Wheaton College, 501 College Avenue, Wheaton, IL 60187-5593

Indiana

Anderson University
Anderson, Indiana
www.anderson.edu

CB member
CB code: 1016

▸ Private 4-year liberal arts college affiliated with the Church of God
▸ Residential campus in small city
▸ 1,760 degree-seeking undergraduates: 9% part-time, 61% women, 6% African American, 1% Asian American, 2% Hispanic/Latino, 3% Multiracial, non-Hispanic, 3% international
▸ 415 degree-seeking graduate students
▸ 60% of applicants admitted
▸ SAT or ACT with writing required
▸ 54% graduate within 6 years

General. Founded in 1917. Regionally accredited. **Degrees:** 386 bachelor's, 1 associate awarded; master's, doctoral offered. **Location:** 45 miles from Indianapolis. **Calendar:** Semester, limited summer session. **Full-time faculty:** 129 total; 74% have terminal degrees, 11% minority, 40% women. **Part-time faculty:** 148 total; 7% have terminal degrees, 10% minority, 48% women. **Class size:** 68% < 20, 28% 20-39, 2% 40-49, 2% 50-99, less than 1% >100. **Special facilities:** Religious art collection, museum of Bible and Near Eastern studies, glass studio, wellness center.

Freshman class profile. 2,620 applied, 1,562 admitted, 422 enrolled.

Mid 50% test scores			
SAT critical reading:	470-560	Rank in top quarter:	53%
SAT math:	470-570	Rank in top tenth:	24%
ACT composite:	21-25	End year in good standing:	86%
GPA 3.75 or higher:	36%	Return as sophomores:	75%
GPA 3.50-3.74:	19%	Out-of-state:	25%
GPA 3.0-3.49:	30%	Live on campus:	90%
GPA 2.0-2.99:	15%	International:	2%

Basis for selection. Rank in top half of class, test scores, reference important. School, church, and community activities also considered. Additional requirements for nursing, athletic training, and educational programs. Essay recommended. Interview required of academically weak applicants. Audition required of music majors. Portfolio recommended for art majors. **Home schooled:** Interview may be required.

High school preparation. College-preparatory program required. 17 units required; 30 recommended. Required and recommended units include English 4, mathematics 3-4, social studies 1-2, history 1-2, science 3-4 (laboratory 3-4), foreign language 2-3, computer science 1, visual/performing arts 1 and academic electives 5.

2015-2016 Annual costs. Tuition/fees: $27,600. Room/board: $9,380. Books/supplies: $1,200. Personal expenses: $1,800.

Financial aid. Non-need-based: Scholarships awarded for academics, alumni affiliation, art, leadership, minority status, music/drama, religious affiliation.

Application procedures. Admission: Priority date 1/15; deadline 7/1. $25 fee, may be waived for applicants with need, free for online applicants. Admission notification on a rolling basis beginning on or about 9/1. Must reply by May 1 or within 2 week(s) if notified thereafter. **Financial aid:** Priority date 3/1; no closing date. FAFSA required. Applicants notified on a rolling basis starting 3/1.

Academics. Special study options: Accelerated study, combined bachelor's/graduate degree, cross-registration, distance learning, double major, dual enrollment of high school students, honors, independent study, internships, student-designed major, study abroad, teacher certification program, urban semester. **Credit/placement by examination:** AP, CLEP, IB, SAT, ACT, institutional tests. 30 credit hours maximum toward bachelor's degree. **Support services:** Learning center, pre-admission summer program, reduced course load, tutoring.

Majors. Biology: General, biochemistry. **Business:** Accounting, business admin, entrepreneurial studies, finance, international, managerial economics, marketing, organizational leadership. **Communications:** Persuasive communications. **Computer sciences:** Computer science, information systems. **Education:** General, elementary, English, mathematics, music, physical, social

studies, Spanish. **Engineering:** Electrical, mechanical. **English:** English lit. **Foreign languages:** Spanish. **Health services:** Athletic training, nursing (RN). **History:** General. **Human services:** Social work. **Math:** General, financial. **Parks/recreation:** Exercise sciences, sports admin. **Philosophy/religion:** Religion. **Physical sciences:** General, chemistry, physics. **Protective services:** Criminal justice. **Psychology:** General. **Social sciences:** Political science, sociology. **Theology:** Bible, sacred music, theology, youth ministry. **Visual/performing arts:** Arts management, cinematography, dance, design, music, music management, music performance, music theory/composition, musical theater, voice/opera. **Work/family studies:** Family systems.

Most popular majors. Business/marketing 17%, education 11%, health sciences 17%, psychology 7%, visual/performing arts 9%.

Technology on campus. 300 workstations in dormitories, library, computer center, student center. Dormitories linked to campus network. Commuter students can connect to campus network. Online course registration, wireless network available.

Student life. Freshman orientation: Mandatory. Preregistration for classes offered. **Policies:** Religious observance required. **Housing:** Coed dorms, single-sex dorms, apartments, wellness housing available. $100 nonrefundable deposit, deadline 5/1. **Activities:** Bands, campus ministries, choral groups, dance, drama, international student organizations, literary magazine, music ensembles, Model UN, musical theater, opera, radio station, student government, student newspaper, symphony orchestra, multicultural student union, Religious Life Council, business club, women's clubs, men's clubs.

Athletics. NCAA. **Intercollegiate:** Baseball M, basketball, cross-country, football (tackle) M, golf, soccer, softball W, tennis, track and field, volleyball W. **Intramural:** Badminton, basketball, bowling, soccer, softball, tennis, volleyball. **Team name:** Ravens.

Student services. Adult student services, chaplain/spiritual director, career counseling, student employment services, financial aid counseling, health services, minority student services, personal counseling, placement for graduates, veterans' counselor. **Physically disabled:** Services for visually, speech impaired.

Contact. E-mail: info@anderson.edu
Phone: (765) 641-4080 Toll-free number: (800) 428-6414
Fax: (765) 641-4091
Julie Short, Associate Director of Admissions, Anderson University, 1100 East Fifth Street, Anderson, IN 46012-3495

Ball State University
Muncie, Indiana
www.bsu.edu

CB member
CB code: 1051

▸ Public 4-year university
▸ Residential campus in small city
▸ 15,689 degree-seeking undergraduates: 7% part-time, 59% women
▸ 4,389 degree-seeking graduate students
▸ 61% of applicants admitted
▸ 61% graduate within 6 years

General. Founded in 1918. Regionally accredited. **Degrees:** 3,682 bachelor's, 57 associate awarded; master's, professional, doctoral offered. **ROTC:** Army. **Location:** 56 miles from Indianapolis. **Calendar:** Semester, extensive summer session. **Full-time faculty:** 1,017 total; 74% have terminal degrees, 7% minority, 47% women. **Part-time faculty:** 228 total; 38% have terminal degrees, 7% minority, 64% women. **Class size:** 42% < 20, 46% 20-39, 6% 40-49, 4% 50-99, 2% >100. **Special facilities:** Planetarium, nature preserves, institute for wellness and gerontology, art museum, media design center, glass center, communication and media building, institute for digital fabrication, virtual studios, School of Nursing's simulation and information technology center.

Freshman class profile. 22,147 applied, 13,399 admitted, 3,503 enrolled.

Mid 50% test scores			
		GPA 2.0-2.99:	14%
SAT critical reading:	510-600	Rank in top quarter:	50%
SAT math:	500-590	Rank in top tenth:	19%
SAT writing:	490-580	Return as sophomores:	82%
ACT composite:	20-24	Out-of-state:	16%
GPA 3.75 or higher:	28%	Live on campus:	90%
GPA 3.50-3.74:	20%	Fraternities:	13%
GPA 3.0-3.49:	38%	Sororities:	17%

Basis for selection. High school curriculum, HS GPA, academic GPA, standardized test scores; College of Fine Arts and College of Architecture and Planning programs have supplemental applications. Non-traditional applicants typically do not have to submit standardized test scores. Audition required of music, dance and theater majors; portfolio recommended for art and architecture majors. **Home schooled:** Statement describing home school structure and mission, transcript of courses and grades required. **Learning Disabled:** Students may self-disclose if they choose.

High school preparation. College-preparatory program required. Required and recommended units include English 4, mathematics 3-4, social studies 2, history 1, science 3 (laboratory 2) and foreign language 3. Social studies includes history.

2015-2016 Annual costs. Tuition/fees: $9,498; $25,016 out-of-state. Room/board: $9,656. Books/supplies: $1,320. Personal expenses: $1,860.

2015-2016 Financial aid. **Need-based:** 3,287 full-time freshmen applied for aid; 2,506 deemed to have need; 2,506 received aid. Average need met was 67%. Average scholarship/grant was $5,490; average loan $3,534. 44% of total undergraduate aid awarded as scholarships/grants, 56% as loans/jobs. **Non-need-based:** Awarded to 7,290 full-time undergraduates, including 2,343 freshmen. Scholarships awarded for academics, athletics, leadership, minority status, music/drama, ROTC, state residency.

Application procedures. **Admission:** Priority date 3/1; deadline 8/10 (postmark date). $55 fee, may be waived for applicants with need. Application must be submitted online. Admission notification on a rolling basis. Must reply by May 1 or within 2 week(s) if notified thereafter. **Financial aid:** Priority date 3/15; no closing date. FAFSA required. Applicants notified on a rolling basis starting 4/1.

Academics. All undergraduates must meet writing proficiency requirement. **Special study options:** Accelerated study, combined bachelor's/graduate degree, cooperative education, distance learning, double major, dual enrollment of high school students, ESL, external degree, honors, independent study, internships, liberal arts/career combination, student-designed major, study abroad, teacher certification program. **Credit/placement by examination:** AP, CLEP, IB, SAT, ACT, institutional tests. 15 credit hours maximum toward associate degree, 63 toward bachelor's. **Support services:** Learning center, pre-admission summer program, reduced course load, study skills assistance, tutoring, writing center.

Majors. **Architecture:** Architecture, environmental design, landscape, urban/community planning. **Area/ethnic studies:** Women's. **Biology:** General. **Business:** General, accounting, actuarial science, construction management, entrepreneurial studies, finance, human resources, insurance, international, management information systems, management science, managerial economics, marketing, selling. **Communications:** Advertising, communications/speech/rhetoric, journalism, persuasive communications, radio/TV. **Computer sciences:** General. **Conservation:** General. **Education:** Biology, business, chemistry, early childhood, earth science, elementary, elementary special ed, multiple handicapped, music, physical, physics, science, social studies, technology/industrial arts. **Engineering:** General. **English:** English lit. **Foreign languages:** Classics, French, German, Japanese, Spanish. **Health services:** Athletic training, audiology/speech pathology, clinical lab science, community health, dental hygiene, dietetics, nursing (RN), physical therapy, predental, premedicine, preveterinary, respiratory therapy technology. **History:** General. **Human services:** Social work. **Liberal arts:** Arts/sciences. **Math:** General. **Parks/recreation:** Exercise sciences, sports admin. **Philosophy/religion:** Philosophy, religion. **Physical sciences:** Astronomy, chemistry, geology, physics. **Protective services:** Criminal justice. **Psychology:** General. **Social sciences:** General, anthropology, geography, political science, sociology. **Visual/performing arts:** Art, dance, dramatic, music. **Work/family studies:** General.

Most popular majors. Business/marketing 16%, communications/journalism 13%, education 12%, health sciences 8%, liberal arts 8%, visual/performing arts 6%.

Technology on campus. 888 workstations in dormitories, library, computer center, student center. Dormitories wired for high-speed internet access and linked to campus network. Commuter students can connect to campus network. Online course registration, online library, helpline, repair service, student web hosting, wireless network available.

Student life. **Freshman orientation:** Mandatory, $100 fee. Preregistration for classes offered. 2-day program held in June and July. **Policies:** All students required to live in university housing unless they will be 21 years of age prior to beginning of term for which they are enrolling, have 24 or more semester hours, are married or are custodial parent of a dependent child, or are living with their parents within 60-mile radius of campus. **Housing:** Guaranteed on-campus for freshmen. Coed dorms, single-sex dorms, special housing for disabled, apartments, fraternity/sorority housing, themed housing available. $125 nonrefundable deposit. Living/learning communities available. **Activities:** Bands, campus ministries, choral groups, dance, drama, film society, international student organizations, literary magazine, music ensembles, opera, radio station, student government, student newspaper, symphony orchestra, TV station, more than 380 student organizations.

Athletics. NCAA. **Intercollegiate:** Baseball M, basketball, cheerleading, cross-country W, diving, field hockey W, football (tackle) M, golf, gymnastics

W, soccer W, softball W, swimming, tennis, track and field W, volleyball. **Intramural:** Badminton, basketball, bowling, football (non-tackle), golf, racquetball, soccer, softball, swimming, table tennis, tennis, track and field, ultimate frisbee, volleyball. **Team name:** Cardinals.

Student services. Adult student services, alcohol/substance abuse counseling, career counseling, services for economically disadvantaged, student employment services, financial aid counseling, health services, legal services, minority student services, on-campus daycare, personal counseling, placement for graduates, veterans' counselor, women's services. **Physically disabled:** Services for visually, speech, hearing impaired.

Contact. E-mail: askus@bsu.edu
Phone: (765) 285-8300 Toll-free number: (800) 482-4278
Fax: (765) 285-1632
Chris Munchel, Director of Undergraduate Admisisons, Ball State University, Office of Admissions, Ball State University, Muncie, IN 47306-0855

Bethel College
Mishawaka, Indiana
www.bethelcollege.edu — CB code: 1079

- Private 4-year liberal arts college affiliated with the Missionary Church
- Residential campus in small city
- 1,432 degree-seeking undergraduates: 18% part-time, 65% women, 11% African American, 1% Asian American, 6% Hispanic/Latino, 3% Multiracial, non-Hispanic, 1% international
- 230 graduate students
- 66% of applicants admitted
- SAT or ACT (ACT writing optional) required
- 64% graduate within 6 years; 13% enter graduate study

General. Founded in 1947. Regionally accredited. **Degrees:** 400 bachelor's, 56 associate awarded; master's offered. **ROTC:** Army, Air Force. **Location:** 90 miles from Chicago. 140 miles from Indianapolis. **Calendar:** Semester, limited summer session. **Full-time faculty:** 75 total; 59% have terminal degrees, 11% minority, 48% women. **Part-time faculty:** 130 total; 22% have terminal degrees, 4% minority, 54% women. **Class size:** 66% < 20, 29% 20-39, 3% 40-49, 2% 50-99, less than 1% >100. **Special facilities:** Otis Bowen museum and archives, missionary church archives.

Freshman class profile. 1,938 applied, 1,288 admitted, 281 enrolled.

Mid 50% test scores			
SAT critical reading:	440-560	GPA 2.0-2.99:	23%
SAT math:	440-560	Rank in top quarter:	47%
SAT writing:	420-540	Rank in top tenth:	20%
ACT composite:	19-26	Return as sophomores:	78%
GPA 3.75 or higher:	33%	Out-of-state:	36%
GPA 3.50-3.74:	21%	Live on campus:	89%
GPA 3.0-3.49:	22%	International:	2%

Basis for selection. School achievement record, test scores, character recommendations, personal statement important. Interview recommended for all applicants, required for some scholarship awards. Audition/portfolio required of art, music and theater majors for scholarship consideration. **Learning Disabled:** Provide documentation of assessment and accommodations suggested (IEP).

High school preparation. College-preparatory program recommended. 17 units recommended. Recommended units include English 4, mathematics 3, social studies 1, history 2, science 1 (laboratory 1), foreign language 2 and academic electives 3.

2016-2017 Annual costs. Tuition/fees (projected): $27,380. Room/board: $8,470. Books/supplies: $1,200. Personal expenses: $1,600.

2015-2016 Financial aid. **Non-need-based:** Awarded to 132 full-time undergraduates, including 33 freshmen. Scholarships awarded for academics, alumni affiliation, art, athletics, job skills, leadership, minority status, music/drama, religious affiliation, ROTC.

Application procedures. **Admission:** Priority date 12/1; deadline 8/15 (postmark date). No application fee. Admission notification on a rolling basis beginning on or about 10/1. Priority date of May 1 to guarantee place in class. Students may enroll after May 1 on a rolling basis. **Financial aid:** Priority date 3/1, closing date 3/10. FAFSA, institutional form required. Applicants notified on a rolling basis starting 3/1.

Academics. **Special study options:** Accelerated study, cross-registration, distance learning, double major, dual enrollment of high school students, exchange student, honors, independent study, internships, liberal arts/career combination, student-designed major, study abroad, teacher certification program, urban semester, Washington semester. Off-campus study options available through consortium programs in Nashville, Los Angeles, Washington DC, Australia, China, Costa Rica, England, Jordan, Uganda. **Credit/placement by examination:** AP, CLEP, IB, SAT, ACT, institutional tests. **Support services:** Learning center, reduced course load, remedial instruction, study skills assistance, tutoring, writing center.

Majors. Biology: General, cellular/molecular. **Business:** Accounting, business admin, financial planning. **Communications:** Communications/speech/rhetoric. **Education:** Biology, chemistry, early childhood, elementary, English, ESL, mathematics, middle, music, physical, physics, science, secondary, social studies. **Engineering:** General, engineering science. **English:** English lit. **Foreign languages:** Sign language interpretation, Spanish. **Health services:** International public health, nursing (RN). **History:** General. **Liberal arts:** Arts/sciences, humanities. **Math:** General, applied. **Parks/recreation:** Exercise sciences, sports admin, sports studies. **Philosophy/religion:** General, Christian, philosophy, religion. **Physical sciences:** Chemistry. **Protective services:** Criminal justice. **Psychology:** General. **Social sciences:** General, sociology. **Theology:** Bible, missionary, theology, youth ministry. **Visual/performing arts:** Design, dramatic, music performance, studio arts, theater arts management.

Most popular majors. Business/marketing 26%, education 9%, health sciences 14%, liberal arts 9%, public administration/social services 7%, theological studies 8%.

Technology on campus. 160 workstations in dormitories, library, computer center, student center. Dormitories wired for high-speed internet access and linked to campus network. Commuter students can connect to campus network. Online library, helpline, repair service, wireless network available.

Student life. Freshman orientation: Mandatory. Preregistration for classes offered. Saturday through Wednesday before classes begin. Includes trip to Chicago and small group activities. **Policies:** Chapel service 3 times per week; full-time traditional students required to attend specified number each semester; students agree to the community life covenant. Religious observance required. Freshmen not permitted cars on campus. **Housing:** Guaranteed on-campus for freshmen. Single-sex dorms, special housing for disabled, apartments, themed housing available. $100 nonrefundable deposit. **Activities:** Bands, campus ministries, choral groups, drama, international student organizations, literary magazine, music ensembles, musical theater, opera, radio station, student government, student newspaper, symphony orchestra, Black Student Fellowship, International Student Fellowship, Students for Life, service learning/community service, cross-cultural ministries, Rotoract, Young Republicans, Residential Hall/Non-Profit Dorm Match, special interest clubs.

Athletics. NAIA, NCCAA. **Intercollegiate:** Baseball M, basketball, cheerleading, cross-country, golf, lacrosse W, rugby M, soccer, softball W, tennis, track and field, volleyball W. **Intramural:** Baseball M, basketball, football (non-tackle) M, soccer, softball, tennis, volleyball. **Team name:** Pilots.

Student services. Adult student services, alcohol/substance abuse counseling, chaplain/spiritual director, career counseling, student employment services, financial aid counseling, health services, minority student services, personal counseling, placement for graduates. **Physically disabled:** Services for visually, hearing impaired.

Contact. E-mail: admissions@bethelcollege.edu
Phone: (574) 807-7600 Toll-free number: (800) 422-4101
Fax: (574) 807-7650
Andrea Helmuth, Director of Admission, Bethel College, 1001 Bethel Circle, Mishawaka, IN 46545-5591

Butler University
Indianapolis, Indiana — CB member
www.butler.edu — CB code: 1073

▶ Private 4-year university
▶ Residential campus in very large city
▶ 4,001 degree-seeking undergraduates: 1% part-time, 60% women, 4% African American, 3% Asian American, 4% Hispanic/Latino, 2% Multiracial, non-Hispanic
▶ 754 degree-seeking graduate students
▶ 70% of applicants admitted
▶ SAT or ACT (ACT writing optional), application essay required
▶ 75% graduate within 6 years; 22% enter graduate study

General. Founded in 1855. Regionally accredited. **Degrees:** 792 bachelor's awarded; master's, professional offered. **ROTC:** Army, Air Force. **Location:**

5 miles from downtown. **Calendar:** Semester, limited summer session. **Full-time faculty:** 363 total; 79% have terminal degrees, 9% minority, 47% women. **Part-time faculty:** 199 total. **Class size:** 64% < 20, 33% 20-39, 1% 40-49, less than 1% 50-99, 1% >100. **Special facilities:** Observatory, planetarium, herbarium, performing arts auditorium, canal, nature preserve.

Freshman class profile. 9,943 applied, 7,003 admitted, 1,025 enrolled.

Mid 50% test scores			
SAT critical reading:	520-620	GPA 2.0-2.99:	4%
SAT math:	530-630	Rank in top quarter:	77%
SAT writing:	510-610	Rank in top tenth:	49%
ACT composite:	25-30	End year in good standing:	97%
GPA 3.75 or higher:	57%	Return as sophomores:	92%
GPA 3.50-3.74:	20%	Out-of-state:	53%
GPA 3.0-3.49:	19%	Live on campus:	95%

Basis for selection. Overall academic preparation as well as other considerations including personal statement and extracurricular activities. A minimum 3.3 cumulative GPA and 1200 SAT (CR+M) or 26 ACT is required for applicants to the Pharmacy or Health Sciences-Physician's Assistant programs for consideration. Additionally, four years of math and science courses are strongly recommended for applicants applying to any STEM related program; standard requirement for consideration is 3 years. Separate application and audition/interview is required for all applicants to the Jordan College of the Arts. **Home schooled:** Statement describing home school structure and mission, transcript of courses and grades, letter of recommendation (nonparent) required.

High school preparation. College-preparatory program required. 17 units required; 20 recommended. Required and recommended units include English 4, mathematics 3-4, social studies 2, history 2, science 3-4 (laboratory 3) and foreign language 2.

2015-2016 Annual costs. Tuition/fees: $37,010. Room/board: $12,055. Books/supplies: $1,000. Personal expenses: $1,650.

2015-2016 Financial aid. Need-based: 985 full-time freshmen applied for aid; 641 deemed to have need; 641 received aid. Average need met was 73%. Average scholarship/grant was $22,533; average loan $3,982. 71% of total undergraduate aid awarded as scholarships/grants, 29% as loans/jobs. **Non-need-based:** Scholarships awarded for academics, alumni affiliation, athletics, leadership, music/drama.

Application procedures. Admission: Priority date 11/1; deadline 2/1 (postmark date). No application fee. Admission notification by 2/20. Admission notification on a rolling basis beginning on or about 12/20. Must reply by May 1 or within 2 week(s) if notified thereafter. **Financial aid:** Priority date 3/1; no closing date. FAFSA required. Applicants notified by 3/15; Applicants notified on a rolling basis starting 3/15; must reply within 3 week(s) of notification.

Academics. Special study options: Accelerated study, combined bachelor's/graduate degree, cross-registration, distance learning, double major, dual enrollment of high school students, exchange student, honors, independent study, internships, liberal arts/career combination, student-designed major, study abroad, teacher certification program, Washington semester. Dual-degree engineering program with Indiana University-Purdue University Indianapolis, cooperative program in business. **Credit/placement by examination:** AP, CLEP, IB, SAT, ACT, institutional tests. **Support services:** Learning center, reduced course load, study skills assistance, tutoring, writing center.

Majors. Area/ethnic studies: Women's. **Biology:** General. **Business:** Accounting, actuarial science, entrepreneurial studies, finance, insurance, international, management information systems, marketing. **Communications:** Digital media, journalism, organizational, public relations, radio/TV, sports. **Communications technology:** Recording arts. **Computer sciences:** General. **Conservation:** Environmental studies. **Education:** General, early childhood, elementary, kindergarten/preschool, middle, music, secondary. **Engineering:** Software. **English:** Creative writing, English lit. **Foreign languages:** French, German, Latin, modern Greek, Spanish. **Health services:** Communication disorders, health care admin, pharmaceutical sciences, physician assistant. **History:** General. **Liberal arts:** Arts/sciences. **Math:** General. **Philosophy/religion:** Philosophy, religion. **Physical sciences:** Chemistry, physics. **Protective services:** Criminal justice. **Psychology:** General. **Social sciences:** Anthropology, criminology, economics, international relations, political science, sociology, urban studies. **Visual/performing arts:** Arts management, dance, dramatic, jazz, music, music management, music pedagogy, music performance, music theory/composition, piano/keyboard, stringed instruments, studio arts management, voice/opera.

Most popular majors. Biology 6%, business/marketing 27%, communications/journalism 8%, education 11%, health sciences 11%, social sciences 8%, visual/performing arts 11%.

Technology on campus. 450 workstations in dormitories, library, computer center, student center. Dormitories wired for high-speed internet access

and linked to campus network. Commuter students can connect to campus network. Online course registration, online library, helpline, repair service, wireless network available.

Student life. Freshman orientation: Mandatory, $150 fee. Preregistration for classes offered. Four-day program held in August. **Housing:** Guaranteed on-campus for all undergraduates. Coed dorms, single-sex dorms, apartments, fraternity/sorority housing, themed housing available. $300 fully refundable deposit, deadline 5/1. **Activities:** Bands, campus ministries, choral groups, dance, drama, film society, international student organizations, literary magazine, music ensembles, Model UN, musical theater, opera, radio station, student government, student newspaper, symphony orchestra, TV station, Campus Crusade for Christ, Muslim Student Association, Hillel, LCMS-U, Young Americans for Liberty, Butler University College Republicans, Black Student Union, Asian Culture Enthusiasts, Latino Unidos, Best Buddies.

Athletics. NCAA. Intercollegiate: Baseball M, basketball, cross-country, football (tackle) M, golf, soccer, softball W, swimming W, tennis, track and field, volleyball W. **Intramural:** Badminton, baseball M, basketball, bowling, football (non-tackle), golf, soccer, softball, swimming, table tennis, tennis, track and field, ultimate frisbee, volleyball, weight lifting. **Team name:** Bulldogs.

Student services. Alcohol/substance abuse counseling, career counseling, student employment services, financial aid counseling, health services, minority student services, personal counseling, placement for graduates. **Physically disabled:** Services for visually, speech, hearing impaired.

Contact. E-mail: admission@butler.edu
Phone: (317) 940-8100 Toll-free number: (888) 940-8100
Fax: (317) 940-8150
Aimee Rust-Scheuermann, Director of Admission, Butler University, 4600 Sunset Avenue, Indianapolis, IN 46208

Calumet College of St. Joseph
Whiting, Indiana
www.ccsj.edu
CB code: 1776

- Private 4-year liberal arts college affiliated with the Roman Catholic Church
- Commuter campus in small city
- 881 degree-seeking undergraduates
- 218 graduate students
- 33% of applicants admitted
- Application essay required

General. Founded in 1951. Regionally accredited. **Degrees:** 196 bachelor's, 16 associate awarded; master's offered. **Location:** 20 miles from Chicago. **Calendar:** Semester, limited summer session. **Full-time faculty:** 30 total; 67% have terminal degrees, 20% minority, 37% women. **Part-time faculty:** 106 total; 32% have terminal degrees, 18% minority, 39% women. **Class size:** 75% < 20, 24% 20-39, less than 1% 50-99, less than 1% >100.

Freshman class profile. 496 applied, 164 admitted, 132 enrolled.

Mid 50% test scores			
SAT critical reading:	390-520	GPA 3.50-3.74:	9%
SAT math:	390-490	GPA 3.0-3.49:	17%
SAT writing:	370-500	GPA 2.0-2.99:	52%
ACT composite:	16-22	Rank in top quarter:	14%
GPA 3.75 or higher:	4%	Rank in top tenth:	6%

Basis for selection. High school record most important. ACT/COMPASS Assessment Test, rank top half of class, 2.0 GPA required. Acuplace testing used for placement. Essay used to place students in English courses as part of placement exam. SAT or ACT recommended. Interview recommended. **Home schooled:** State high school equivalency certificate required.

High school preparation. College-preparatory program recommended. 15 units recommended. Recommended units include English 4, mathematics 3, social studies 3, science 2 (laboratory 1) and foreign language 1.

2015-2016 Annual costs. Tuition/fees: $17,000. Books/supplies: $1,500. Personal expenses: $1,140.

2014-2015 Financial aid. Need-based: 100 full-time freshmen applied for aid; 92 deemed to have need; 87 received aid. Average need met was 66%. Average scholarship/grant was $6,429; average loan $3,073. 50% of total undergraduate aid awarded as scholarships/grants, 50% as loans/jobs. **Non-need-based:** Awarded to 480 full-time undergraduates, including 106 freshmen. Scholarships awarded for academics, alumni affiliation, art, athletics, leadership, music/drama. **Additional information:** Immediate computerized estimate of financial aid eligibility available to students applying in

person. Students with a zero EFC who are state aid and Pell Grant recipients receive institutional aid to cover tuition.

Application procedures. Admission: No deadline. No application fee. Admission notification on a rolling basis. **Financial aid:** Priority date 3/10; no closing date. FAFSA required. Applicants notified on a rolling basis starting 4/30; must reply within 2 week(s) of notification.

Academics. Special study options: Accelerated study, cooperative education, double major, dual enrollment of high school students, ESL, honors, independent study, internships, liberal arts/career combination, student-designed major, teacher certification program. **Credit/placement by examination:** AP, CLEP, institutional tests. 12 credit hours maximum toward associate degree, 15 toward bachelor's. **Support services:** Learning center, reduced course load, remedial instruction, study skills assistance, tutoring, writing center.

Majors. Business: General, accounting, business admin, organizational behavior. **Computer sciences:** General. **Education:** General, elementary. **English:** English lit. **Liberal arts:** Arts/sciences. **Philosophy/religion:** Religion. **Protective services:** Police science. **Psychology:** General. **Social sciences:** General. **Visual/performing arts:** Studio arts.

Most popular majors. Biology 6%, business/marketing 28%, security/protective services 42%.

Technology on campus. 72 workstations in library, computer center, student center. Online library, wireless network available.

Student life. Freshman orientation: Mandatory, $85 fee. Preregistration for classes offered. Held 1 week before classes begin, followed up by mentoring program. **Activities:** Pep band, campus ministries, dance, drama, literary magazine, student government, student newspaper, Los Amigos, EON club, Veterans Unit Organization, criminal justice club, media and fine arts club, creative writing club, paralegal studies club, booster club, human services club, educators club, G.I.V.E.

Athletics. NAIA. Intercollegiate: Baseball M, basketball, bowling, cross-country, golf, soccer, softball W, tennis, track and field, volleyball, wrestling M. **Team name:** Crimson Wave.

Student services. Adult student services, chaplain/spiritual director, career counseling, student employment services, financial aid counseling, on-campus daycare, personal counseling, placement for graduates, veterans' counselor.

Contact. E-mail: admissions@ccsj.edu
Phone: (219) 473-4215 Toll-free number: (877) 700-9100
Fax: (219) 473-4336
Carl Cuttone, Director of Enrollment Management, Calumet College of St. Joseph, 2400 New York Avenue, Whiting, IN 46394-2195

Chamberlain College of Nursing: Indianapolis
Indianapolis, Indiana
www.chamberlain.edu
CB code: 7906

- For-profit 4-year nursing college
- Commuter campus in very large city
- 219 degree-seeking undergraduates

General. Degrees: 23 bachelor's awarded. **Calendar:** Semester. **Full-time faculty:** 3 total; 100% women.

Basis for selection. Admission decisions based on interview, proof of high school diploma/GED, and satisfactory test scores. For more information about such tests and scores, contact admissions office.

2015-2016 Annual costs. Tuition/fees: $18,160.

Application procedures. Admission: No deadline. $95 fee. Admission notification on a rolling basis.

Academics. Credit/placement by examination: AP, CLEP.

Majors. Health services: Nursing (RN).

Contact. Toll-free number: (877) 751-5783
Chamberlain College of Nursing: Indianapolis, 9100 Keystone Crossing, Suite 600, Indianapolis, IN 46240

Crossroads Bible College
Indianapolis, Indiana
www.crossroads.edu   CB code: 3811

- Private 4-year Bible college
- Commuter campus in very large city
- 249 undergraduates
- Application essay required

General. Regionally accredited; also accredited by ABHE. **Degrees:** 25 bachelor's, 14 associate awarded. **Calendar:** Semester, limited summer session. **Full-time faculty:** 7 total; 29% have terminal degrees, 71% minority, 29% women.

Basis for selection. Applicants evaluated on basis of test scores, academic performance, references, essays. SAT or ACT recommended. **Home schooled:** Transcript of courses and grades required.

High school preparation. College-preparatory program recommended. Recommended units include English 4.

2015-2016 Annual costs. Tuition/fees: $12,400. Books/supplies: $950.

2014-2015 Financial aid. All financial aid based on need. 9 full-time freshmen applied for aid; 9 deemed to have need; 9 received aid. Average need met was 100%. Average scholarship/grant was $5,500; average loan $4,500. 43% of total undergraduate aid awarded as scholarships/grants, 57% as loans/jobs.

Application procedures. Admission: No deadline. $35 fee, may be waived for applicants with need. Admission notification on a rolling basis. **Financial aid:** Priority date 3/1, closing date 3/10. FAFSA, institutional form required. Applicants notified on a rolling basis; must reply within 2 week(s) of notification.

Academics. Special study options: Accelerated study, distance learning, dual enrollment of high school students, independent study, internships. **Credit/placement by examination:** AP, CLEP, SAT, ACT, institutional tests. 15 credit hours maximum toward associate degree, 15 toward bachelor's. **Support services:** Reduced course load, tutoring, writing center.

Majors. Business: Business admin. **Theology:** Pastoral counseling, religious ed, urban ministry.

Most popular majors. Business/marketing 8%, interdisciplinary studies 8%, philosophy/religious studies 80%.

Technology on campus. PC or laptop required. Commuter students can connect to campus network. Wireless network available.

Student life. Freshman orientation: Mandatory. Preregistration for classes offered. **Policies:** Religious observance required. **Activities:** Campus ministries.

Student services. Financial aid counseling.

Contact. E-mail: admissions@crossroads.edu
Phone: (317) 789-8271 Fax: (317) 789-8253
John Crowder, Dean of Enrollment Management, Crossroads Bible College, 601 North Shortridge Road, Indianapolis, IN 46219

DePauw University
Greencastle, Indiana   CB member
www.depauw.edu   CB code: 1166

- Private 4-year music and liberal arts college affiliated with the United Methodist Church
- Residential campus in small town
- 2,223 degree-seeking undergraduates: 54% women, 5% African American, 4% Asian American, 4% Hispanic/Latino, 7% Multi-racial, non-Hispanic, 8% international
- 65% of applicants admitted
- SAT or ACT (ACT writing optional), application essay required
- 82% graduate within 6 years

General. Founded in 1837. Regionally accredited. **Degrees:** 501 bachelor's awarded. **ROTC:** Army, Air Force. **Location:** 45 miles from Indianapolis. **Calendar:** 4-1-4. **Full-time faculty:** 210 total; 20% minority, 42% women. **Part-time faculty:** 39 total; 28% have terminal degrees, 8% minority, 54% women. **Class size:** 72% < 20, 28% 20-39, less than 1% 40-49. **Special**

facilities: Nature park and arboretum, ethnographic museums, closed circuit tv studio facilities, music instructional technology studio, digital media laboratory, visual resources library with digital image collection, digital video studio, observatory, 2 theaters, 2 music concert halls, concert pipe organ.

Freshman class profile. 5,182 applied, 3,356 admitted, 596 enrolled.

Mid 50% test scores			
SAT critical reading:	510-620	Rank in top quarter:	76%
SAT math:	550-670	Rank in top tenth:	41%
SAT writing:	520-620	Return as sophomores:	94%
ACT composite:	25-29	Out-of-state:	61%
GPA 3.75 or higher:	55%	Live on campus:	100%
GPA 3.50-3.74:	23%	International:	7%
GPA 3.0-3.49:	20%	Fraternities:	68%
GPA 2.0-2.99:	2%	Sororities:	63%

Basis for selection. Academic achievement and preparation, demonstrated verbal and quantitative skills, evidence of continuing commitment to learning most important. Interview strongly recommended. Audition required for School of Music candidates. **Home schooled:** Transcript of courses and grades, interview required.

High school preparation. College-preparatory program recommended. 22 units recommended. Recommended units include English 4, mathematics 4, social studies 4, science 4 (laboratory 2) and foreign language 4.

2015-2016 Annual costs. Tuition/fees: $44,678. Room/board: $11,700. Books/supplies: $900. Personal expenses: $1,000.

Financial aid. Non-need-based: Scholarships awarded for academics, alumni affiliation, leadership, music/drama.

Application procedures. Admission: Closing date 2/1 (postmark date). No application fee. Admission notification on a rolling basis beginning on or about 12/15. Must reply by May 1 or within 2 week(s) if notified thereafter. **Financial aid:** Priority date 2/15, closing date 3/1. FAFSA, CSS PROFILE required. Applicants notified on a rolling basis starting 3/15; must reply by 5/1.

Academics. Demonstrated competence in writing, quantitative reasoning, and oral communication required of all students. Seminar, thesis, project, or comprehensive examination in major also required. More than 700 students participate in off-campus winter term programs; 40% study off-campus. **Special study options:** Combined bachelor's/graduate degree, double major, dual enrollment of high school students, exchange student, honors, independent study, internships, student-designed major, study abroad, teacher certification program. Science research fellows, media fellows, management fellows, Bonner Scholars, Posse Scholars, Instructional Technology Associate's Program (ITAP) Interns. **Credit/placement by examination:** AP, CLEP, IB, SAT, ACT, institutional tests. 32 credit hours maximum toward bachelor's degree. **Support services:** Learning center, study skills assistance, tutoring, writing center.

Majors. Area/ethnic studies: African-American, East Asian, women's. **Biology:** General, biochemistry. **Communications:** Media studies. **Computer sciences:** Computer science. **Conservation:** Environmental science. **Education:** Music. **English:** English lit, writing. **Foreign languages:** Ancient Greek, classics, French, German, Latin, Romance, Spanish. **Health services:** Athletic training. **History:** General. **Math:** General. **Parks/recreation:** Exercise sciences. **Philosophy/religion:** Philosophy, religion. **Physical sciences:** Chemistry, geology, physics. **Psychology:** General. **Social sciences:** Anthropology, economics, political science, sociology. **Visual/performing arts:** Art history/conservation, dramatic, film/cinema/video, music, music management, music performance, music theory/composition, studio arts.

Most popular majors. Biology 11%, communications/journalism 10%, computer/information sciences 8%, English 9%, social sciences 20%, visual/performing arts 7%.

Technology on campus. PC or laptop required. 413 workstations in dormitories, library, computer center, student center. Dormitories wired for high-speed internet access and linked to campus network. Commuter students can connect to campus network. Online course registration, online library, helpline, repair service, student web hosting, wireless network available.

Student life. Freshman orientation: Mandatory. Preregistration for classes offered. Four-day program in August. **Housing:** Guaranteed on-campus for all undergraduates. Coed dorms, special housing for disabled, apartments, fraternity/sorority housing available. $400 nonrefundable deposit, deadline 5/1. **Activities:** Bands, campus ministries, dance, drama, film society, international student organizations, literary magazine, music ensembles, Model UN, musical theater, opera, radio station, student government, student newspaper, symphony orchestra, TV station, African American students association, union board, coalition for women's concerns, College Republicans, College Democrats, Habitat for Humanity, Christian fellowship, United DePauw, Latino concerns committee.

Athletics. NCAA. **Intercollegiate:** Baseball M, basketball, cheerleading, cross-country, diving, field hockey W, football (tackle) M, golf, soccer, softball W, swimming, tennis, track and field, volleyball W. **Intramural:** Badminton, basketball, bowling, football (non-tackle), golf, racquetball, soccer, softball, table tennis, tennis, volleyball. **Team name:** Tigers.

Student services. Alcohol/substance abuse counseling, chaplain/spiritual director, career counseling, student employment services, financial aid counseling, health services, minority student services, on-campus daycare, personal counseling, placement for graduates, women's services. **Physically disabled:** Services for visually, hearing impaired.

Contact. E-mail: admission@depauw.edu
Phone: (765) 658-4006 Toll-free number: (800) 447-2495
Fax: (765) 658-4007
Earl Macam, Director of Admission, DePauw University, 101 East Seminary Street, Greencastle, IN 46135-1611

Earlham College
Richmond, Indiana
www.earlham.edu

CB member
CB code: 1195

- Private 4-year liberal arts and seminary college affiliated with the Society of Friends (Quaker)
- Residential campus in large town
- 935 degree-seeking undergraduates: 1% part-time, 57% women, 12% African American, 5% Asian American, 6% Hispanic/Latino, 1% Native American, 21% international
- 79 degree-seeking graduate students
- 62% of applicants admitted
- Application essay required
- 66% graduate within 6 years

General. Founded in 1847. Regionally accredited; also accredited by ATS. **Degrees:** 177 bachelor's awarded; master's offered. **Location:** 70 miles from Indianapolis; 45 miles from Dayton, Ohio. **Calendar:** Semester. **Full-time faculty:** 111 total; 95% have terminal degrees, 10% minority, 58% women. **Part-time faculty:** 11 total; 64% have terminal degrees, 54% women. **Class size:** 79% < 20, 18% 20-39, 2% 40-49, less than 1% 50-99. **Special facilities:** Center for science and technology, center for the visual and performing arts, center for integrated learning and international programs office, observatory, greenhouse.

Freshman class profile. 2,549 applied, 1,571 admitted, 255 enrolled.

Mid 50% test scores			
SAT critical reading:	550-700	GPA 2.0-2.99:	6%
SAT math:	560-690	Rank in top quarter:	71%
SAT writing:	590-680	Rank in top tenth:	43%
ACT composite:	25-31	End year in good standing:	90%
GPA 3.75 or higher:	40%	Return as sophomores:	82%
GPA 3.50-3.74:	27%	Out-of-state:	82%
GPA 3.0-3.49:	27%	Live on campus:	98%
		International:	27%

Basis for selection. Combination of GPA, quality of high school program, application essay, recommendations, and extracurricular activities are important. Test scores are optional. If students submit their scores, they will be considered along with many other factors in admissions decisions. Interview preferred. **Home schooled:** Statement describing home school structure and mission, interview, letter of recommendation (nonparent) required. Portfolio or other evidence of learning, test scores, and essay.

High school preparation. College-preparatory program recommended. Required and recommended units include English 4, mathematics 3-4, social studies 4, history 2, science 3-4 (laboratory 2), foreign language 2-4 and visual/performing arts 1.

2015-2016 Annual costs. Tuition/fees: $44,390. Room/board: $9,120. Books/supplies: $1,000. Personal expenses: $1,030.

2014-2015 Financial aid. **Need-based:** 254 full-time freshmen applied for aid; 240 deemed to have need; 240 received aid. Average need met was 93%. Average scholarship/grant was $31,777; average loan $4,318. 83% of total undergraduate aid awarded as scholarships/grants, 17% as loans/jobs. **Non-need-based:** Awarded to 297 full-time undergraduates, including 96 freshmen. Scholarships awarded for academics, leadership, minority status, religious affiliation.

Application procedures. **Admission:** Priority date 12/1; deadline 2/15 (postmark date). No application fee. Admission notification by 4/1. Must reply by 5/1. **Financial aid:** Priority date 3/1, closing date 3/1. FAFSA required. Applicants notified on a rolling basis starting 3/15; must reply by 5/1.

Academics. **Special study options:** Accelerated study, combined bachelor's/graduate degree, cross-registration, double major, dual enrollment of high school students, ESL, independent study, internships, New York semester, student-designed major, study abroad, urban semester. Teacher certification at Master's level only. **Credit/placement by examination:** AP, CLEP, IB, institutional tests. 18 credit hours maximum toward bachelor's degree. **Support services:** Learning center, pre-admission summer program, reduced course load, study skills assistance, tutoring, writing center.

Majors. **Area/ethnic studies:** African-American, Japanese, Latin American, women's. **Biology:** General, biochemistry, neuroscience. **Business:** Nonprofit/public. **Computer sciences:** General. **Conservation:** Environmental science, environmental studies. **English:** English lit. **Foreign languages:** Classics, comparative lit, French, German, Spanish. **Health services:** Premedicine. **History:** General. **Math:** General. **Philosophy/religion:** Philosophy, religion. **Physical sciences:** Chemistry, geology, physics. **Psychology:** General. **Social sciences:** Economics, political science, sociology. **Visual/performing arts:** Art, dramatic, music.

Most popular majors. Biology 21%, business/marketing 6%, foreign language 6%, interdisciplinary studies 19%, psychology 9%, social sciences 10%, visual/performing arts 7%.

Technology on campus. 150 workstations in library, computer center. Dormitories wired for high-speed internet access and linked to campus network. Commuter students can connect to campus network. Online course registration, online library, helpline, repair service, student web hosting, wireless network available.

Student life. **Freshman orientation:** Mandatory. Preregistration for classes offered. Five-day program held just prior to beginning of fall semester. **Policies:** Community and academic honor codes. **Housing:** Guaranteed on-campus for all undergraduates. Coed dorms, single-sex dorms, special housing for disabled, cooperative housing, themed housing, wellness housing available. Friendship houses available. **Activities:** Jazz band, campus ministries, choral groups, dance, drama, film society, international student organizations, literary magazine, music ensembles, Model UN, radio station, student government, student newspaper, symphony orchestra, Young Friends, Questing Catholics, Christian Fellowship, Jewish student union, Muslim student union, Bahai club, Amnesty International, Model UN, Coalition for Racial Justice, Fellowship of Christian Athletes.

Athletics. NCAA. **Intercollegiate:** Baseball M, basketball, cross-country, field hockey W, football (tackle) M, golf, soccer, tennis, track and field, volleyball W. **Intramural:** Basketball, bowling, football (non-tackle) M, racquetball, soccer, triathlon. **Team name:** Quakers.

Student services. Chaplain/spiritual director, career counseling, student employment services, financial aid counseling, health services, minority student services, on-campus daycare, personal counseling, placement for graduates, women's services. **Physically disabled:** Services for visually, speech, hearing impaired.

Contact. E-mail: admission@earlham.edu
Phone: (765) 983-1600 Toll-free number: (800) 327-5426
Fax: (765) 983-1560
Jonathan Stroud, VP for Enrollment and Communications, Earlham College, 801 National Road West, Richmond, IN 47374-4095

Franklin College
Franklin, Indiana
www.franklincollege.edu

CB member
CB code: 1228

- Private 4-year liberal arts college affiliated with the American Baptist Churches in the USA
- Residential campus in large town
- 1,012 degree-seeking undergraduates: 52% women, 4% African American, 1% Asian American, 2% Hispanic/Latino, 4% Multi-racial, non-Hispanic, 2% international
- 70% of applicants admitted
- SAT or ACT (ACT writing optional), application essay required
- 60% graduate within 6 years

General. Founded in 1834. Regionally accredited. **Degrees:** 191 bachelor's awarded. **ROTC:** Army. **Location:** 20 miles from Indianapolis. **Calendar:** 4-1-4, limited summer session. **Full-time faculty:** 75 total; 85% have terminal degrees, 8% minority, 48% women. **Part-time faculty:** 36 total; 28% have terminal degrees, 3% minority, 39% women. **Class size:** 66% < 20, 34% 20-39, less than 1% 40-49.

Freshman class profile. 2,023 applied, 1,412 admitted, 290 enrolled.

Mid 50% test scores			
SAT critical reading:	440-540	Rank in top quarter:	43%
SAT math:	450-540	Rank in top tenth:	16%
SAT writing:	430-520	Return as sophomores:	80%
ACT composite:	19-24	Out-of-state:	6%
GPA 3.75 or higher:	27%	Live on campus:	90%
GPA 3.50-3.74:	18%	International:	1%
GPA 3.0-3.49:	39%	Fraternities:	24%
GPA 2.0-2.99:	16%	Sororities:	48%

Basis for selection. Class rank, test scores, essay and counselor recommendations important. Extracurricular activities considered. Interview recommended for all. **Home schooled:** Transcript of courses and grades, interview, letter of recommendation (nonparent) required. Submit research paper(s), art work, community service projects, educational trip or programs, writing samples, other pertinent documents. Formal interview on campus required. **Learning Disabled:** Students with learning disabilities asked to schedule meeting with Director of Academic Support Services.

High school preparation. Required and recommended units include English 4, mathematics 4, social studies 3, science 2 and foreign language 2.

2015-2016 Annual costs. Tuition/fees: $29,025. Room/board: $9,040. Books/supplies: $1,200. Personal expenses: $2,000.

2014-2015 Financial aid. **Need-based:** 320 full-time freshmen applied for aid; 281 deemed to have need; 281 received aid. Average need met was 71%. Average scholarship/grant was $17,782; average loan $3,454. 70% of total undergraduate aid awarded as scholarships/grants, 30% as loans/jobs. **Non-need-based:** Awarded to 254 full-time undergraduates, including 81 freshmen. Scholarships awarded for academics, alumni affiliation, art, minority status, music/drama, religious affiliation, state residency.

Application procedures. **Admission:** Priority date 12/1; no deadline. $40 fee, may be waived for applicants with need, free for online applicants. Admission notification on a rolling basis beginning on or about 9/1. **Financial aid:** Priority date 3/1, closing date 3/10. FAFSA, institutional form required. Applicants notified on a rolling basis starting 3/1; must reply by 5/1 or within 4 week(s) of notification.

Academics. **Special study options:** Combined bachelor's/graduate degree, cross-registration, double major, exchange student, independent study, internships, liberal arts/career combination, semester at sea, student-designed major, study abroad, teacher certification program, Washington semester. **Credit/placement by examination:** AP, CLEP, IB, SAT, ACT, institutional tests. 30 credit hours maximum toward bachelor's degree. **Support services:** Learning center, remedial instruction, study skills assistance, tutoring, writing center.

Majors. **Biology:** General. **Business:** General, accounting, finance, marketing. **Communications:** Broadcast journalism, digital media, journalism, persuasive communications. **Computer sciences:** Computer science, programming. **Education:** Biology, chemistry, elementary, English, French, history, mathematics, physical, social studies, Spanish. **English:** Creative writing, English lit. **Foreign languages:** French, Spanish. **Health services:** Athletic training. **History:** General. **Math:** General, applied. **Parks/recreation:** Exercise sciences. **Philosophy/religion:** Philosophy, religion. **Physical sciences:** Chemistry. **Psychology:** General. **Social sciences:** Criminology, economics, political science, sociology. **Visual/performing arts:** Art history/conservation, dramatic, music, studio arts.

Most popular majors. Biology 10%, business/marketing 10%, communications/journalism 15%, education 9%, English 6%, health sciences 8%, mathematics 6%, social sciences 10%, visual/performing arts 7%.

Technology on campus. 250 workstations in dormitories, library, student center. Dormitories wired for high-speed internet access and linked to campus network. Commuter students can connect to campus network. Online course registration, online library, helpline, repair service, wireless network available.

Student life. **Freshman orientation:** Mandatory. Preregistration for classes offered. Session held 4 days prior to start of classes. **Policies:** All students must live on campus until senior year unless living with family. **Housing:** Guaranteed on-campus for all undergraduates. Coed dorms, single-sex dorms, special housing for disabled, fraternity/sorority housing, themed housing, wellness housing available. $100 deposit, deadline 5/1. **Activities:** Bands, campus ministries, choral groups, dance, drama, literary magazine, music ensembles, Model UN, musical theater, radio station, student government, student newspaper, student association for the support of multiculturalism, Habitat for Humanity, college mentors for kids, Fellowship of Christian Athletes, ODK Leadership, international club.

Athletics. NCAA. **Intercollegiate:** Baseball M, basketball, cheerleading, cross-country, diving, football (tackle) M, golf, lacrosse W, soccer, softball W, swimming, tennis, track and field, volleyball W. **Intramural:** Basketball, bowling, football (non-tackle), racquetball, softball, volleyball. **Team name:** Grizzlies.

Student services. Alcohol/substance abuse counseling, chaplain/spiritual director, career counseling, student employment services, financial aid counseling, health services, minority student services, personal counseling, placement for graduates, veterans' counselor, women's services.

Contact. E-mail: admissions@franklincollege.edu
Phone: (317) 738-8062 Toll-free number: (800) 852-0232
Fax: (317) 738-8274
Jennifer Bostrom, Director of Admissions, Franklin College, 101 Branigin Boulevard, Franklin, IN 46131-2623

Goshen College
Goshen, Indiana
www.goshen.edu   **CB code: 1251**

- Private 4-year liberal arts college affiliated with the Mennonite Church
- Residential campus in large town
- 756 degree-seeking undergraduates: 6% part-time, 58% women, 4% African American, 2% Asian American, 17% Hispanic/Latino, 2% Multiracial, non-Hispanic, 9% international
- 63 degree-seeking graduate students
- 63% of applicants admitted
- SAT or ACT (ACT writing optional), application essay required
- 66% graduate within 6 years; 16% enter graduate study

General. Founded in 1894. Regionally accredited. 1,150 acre environmental study facilities located 30 miles from campus. **Degrees:** 234 bachelor's awarded; master's offered. **Location:** 25 miles from South Bend, 120 miles from Chicago. **Calendar:** Semester, limited summer session. **Full-time faculty:** 67 total; 66% have terminal degrees, 9% minority, 51% women. **Part-time faculty:** 39 total; 20% have terminal degrees, 3% minority, 67% women. **Class size:** 72% < 20, 27% 20-39, less than 1% 40-49, less than 1% 50-99. **Special facilities:** Concert and recital halls, x-ray precision laboratory, electron microscope, marine biology laboratory in Florida Keys, Mennonite historical library and archives, laboratory kindergarten and child care center, media production studio, environmental education center, student-run coffee shop.

Freshman class profile. 797 applied, 505 admitted, 177 enrolled.

Mid 50% test scores			
SAT critical reading:	440-580	GPA 2.0-2.99:	16%
SAT math:	500-640	Rank in top quarter:	46%
SAT writing:	410-540	Rank in top tenth:	22%
ACT composite:	21-27	End year in good standing:	87%
GPA 3.75 or higher:	39%	Return as sophomores:	78%
GPA 3.50-3.74:	14%	Out-of-state:	32%
GPA 3.0-3.49:	29%	Live on campus:	68%
		International:	7%

Basis for selection. GPA, ACT/SAT, class rank, and high school curriculum important. Nursing and education programs require 2.7 and 2.8 college GPAs respectively for entrance and continuation. **Home schooled:** Statement describing home school structure and mission, transcript of courses and grades required. **Learning Disabled:** Documentation of disability and special requirements dated within last 3 years required. Exit interview with high school special needs counselor, if working with one, required.

High school preparation. College-preparatory program recommended. 16 units recommended. Recommended units include English 4, mathematics 3, history 3, science 3 and foreign language 3.

2016-2017 Annual costs. Tuition/fees (projected): $32,200. Room/board: $10,300. Books/supplies: $900. Personal expenses: $1,200.

2015-2016 Financial aid. **Need-based:** 152 full-time freshmen applied for aid; 134 deemed to have need; 134 received aid. Average need met was 88%. Average scholarship/grant was $25,103; average loan $3,933. 73% of total undergraduate aid awarded as scholarships/grants, 27% as loans/jobs. **Non-need-based:** Awarded to 317 full-time undergraduates, including 183 freshmen. Scholarships awarded for academics, art, athletics, job skills, leadership, minority status, music/drama.

Application procedures. **Admission:** Priority date 12/15; deadline 8/15 (postmark date). $25 fee, may be waived for applicants with need. Admission notification on a rolling basis beginning on or about 10/1. Must reply by May 1 or within 4 week(s) if notified thereafter. **Financial aid:** Priority date 3/1; no closing date. FAFSA required. Applicants notified on a rolling basis starting 2/1; must reply by 5/1 or within 2 week(s) of notification.

Academics. Practicum/internship and senior seminar required in all majors. International/Intercultural education through domestic or international study service term. Study abroad incorporates language study, academic and cultural learning and community service. Students live in homes of host families. **Special study options:** Combined bachelor's/graduate degree, cross-registration, double major, dual enrollment of high school students, independent study, internships, liberal arts/career combination, student-designed major, study abroad, teacher certification program, urban semester, Washington semester. **Credit/placement by examination:** AP, CLEP, IB, SAT, ACT, institutional tests. No limit on credit by examination. **Support services:** Learning center, pre-admission summer program, reduced course load, remedial instruction, study skills assistance, tutoring, writing center.

Majors. Biology: General, molecular. **Business:** General, accounting, business admin, marketing. **Communications:** General, broadcast journalism, journalism, public relations. **Computer sciences:** Computer science, informatics, information systems. **Conservation:** Environmental science. **Education:** General, art, biology, business, chemistry, elementary, English, ESL, mathematics, music, physical, physics, science, secondary, social studies, Spanish, special ed. **English:** English lit, writing. **Foreign languages:** American Sign Language, sign language interpretation, Spanish. **Health services:** Nursing (RN). **History:** General, applied. **Human services:** Social work. **Math:** General. **Physical sciences:** Chemistry, physics. **Psychology:** General. **Social sciences:** Sociology. **Theology:** Bible, youth ministry. **Visual/performing arts:** Art, cinematography, dramatic, music.

Most popular majors. Biology 8%, business/marketing 11%, education 6%, health sciences 21%, interdisciplinary studies 8%, visual/performing arts 11%.

Technology on campus. 130 workstations in dormitories, library, computer center, student center. Dormitories wired for high-speed internet access and linked to campus network. Commuter students can connect to campus network. Online course registration, online library, helpline, student web hosting, wireless network available.

Student life. Freshman orientation: Mandatory. Preregistration for classes offered. One-day sessions in June, plus 3 days prior to beginning of fall semester. **Policies:** No smoking, drinking alcoholic beverages, firearms or fireworks on-campus. **Housing:** Guaranteed on-campus for all undergraduates. Coed dorms, single-sex dorms, special housing for disabled, apartments, wellness housing available. $200 nonrefundable deposit, deadline 5/1. **Activities:** Bands, campus ministries, choral groups, drama, film society, international student organizations, music ensembles, musical theater, opera, radio station, student government, student newspaper, symphony orchestra, TV station, black student union, Latino student union, women's association, Catholic student association, eco-pax club, peace club, Fellowship of Christian Athletes, social work action association, nursing students association, business club.

Athletics. NAIA. **Intercollegiate:** Baseball M, basketball, cross-country, soccer, softball W, tennis, track and field, volleyball W. **Intramural:** Badminton, basketball, soccer, table tennis, volleyball. **Team name:** Maple Leafs.

Student services. Adult student services, alcohol/substance abuse counseling, chaplain/spiritual director, career counseling, student employment services, financial aid counseling, health services, minority student services, on-campus daycare, personal counseling, placement for graduates, veterans' counselor, women's services. **Physically disabled:** Services for visually, speech, hearing impaired.

Contact. E-mail: admission@goshen.edu
Phone: (574) 535-7535 Toll-free number: (800) 348-7422
Fax: (574) 535-7609
Adela Hufford, Director of Admissions, Goshen College, 1700 South Main Street, Goshen, IN 46526-4724

Grace College
Winona Lake, Indiana
www.grace.edu
CB code: 1252

- Private 4-year liberal arts college affiliated with the Brethren Church
- Residential campus in small town
- 1,604 degree-seeking undergraduates: 8% part-time, 56% women, 6% African American, 1% Asian American, 4% Hispanic/Latino, 2% Multiracial, non-Hispanic
- 374 degree-seeking graduate students
- 78% of applicants admitted
- SAT or ACT (ACT writing recommended), application essay required
- 67% graduate within 6 years

General. Founded in 1948. Regionally accredited. Students may be able to graduate with a bachelor's degree in either three or four years, or may take advantage of a combined bachelor's and master's degree in four years. **Degrees:** 271 bachelor's, 33 associate awarded; master's, doctoral offered. **Location:** 40 miles from Fort Wayne, 50 miles from South Bend. **Calendar:** Semester, extensive summer session. **Full-time faculty:** 49 total; 63% have terminal degrees, 8% minority, 35% women. **Part-time faculty:** 150 total; 27% have terminal degrees, 12% minority, 45% women. **Class size:** 57% < 20, 35% 20-39, 4% 40-49, 4% 50-99. **Special facilities:** Creation science center, Winona history museum.

Freshman class profile. 3,850 applied, 2,999 admitted, 412 enrolled.

Mid 50% test scores			
SAT critical reading:	460-580	GPA 2.0-2.99:	13%
SAT math:	450-580	Rank in top quarter:	53%
ACT composite:	21-27	Rank in top tenth:	22%
GPA 3.75 or higher:	47%	Return as sophomores:	80%
GPA 3.50-3.74:	13%	Out-of-state:	33%
GPA 3.0-3.49:	26%	Live on campus:	92%

Basis for selection. References, religious affiliation/commitment, high school class rank, test scores most important. Interview recommended for music and art majors. Audition recommended for music majors. Portfolio recommended for art majors. **Home schooled:** Transcript of courses and grades required.

High school preparation. College-preparatory program recommended. Required and recommended units include English 3-4, mathematics 2-4, social studies 2-3, history 2-3, science 2-3 (laboratory 2-3) and foreign language 2-4.

2015-2016 Annual costs. Tuition/fees: $22,450. Room/board: $8,160. Books/supplies: $1,300. Personal expenses: $1,000.

Financial aid. Non-need-based: Scholarships awarded for academics, art, athletics, leadership, minority status, music/drama, religious affiliation, state residency.

Application procedures. Admission: Priority date 12/1; deadline 8/1 (postmark date). $30 fee, may be waived for applicants with need, free for online applicants. Admission notification on a rolling basis beginning on or about 9/15. Must reply by May 1 or within 2 week(s) if notified thereafter. **Financial aid:** Closing date 3/1. FAFSA required. Applicants notified on a rolling basis starting 3/1; must reply by 5/1.

Academics. Special study options: Accelerated study, combined bachelor's/graduate degree, cooperative education, cross-registration, distance learning, double major, dual enrollment of high school students, exchange student, honors, independent study, internships, liberal arts/career combination, study abroad, teacher certification program. **Credit/placement by examination:** AP, CLEP, IB, SAT, ACT, institutional tests. 30 credit hours maximum toward associate degree, 30 toward bachelor's. **Support services:** Learning center, reduced course load, remedial instruction, study skills assistance, tutoring, writing center.

Majors. Biology: General, environmental. **Business:** General, accounting, business admin, finance, financial planning, hospitality/recreation, international, management information systems, marketing, nonprofit/public. **Communications:** Communications/speech/rhetoric, journalism, sports. **Computer sciences:** Web page design. **Conservation:** Environmental science, environmental studies. **Education:** Art, biology, business, elementary, English, French, mathematics, social studies, Spanish, special ed. **Engineering:** Biomedical, civil, mechanical. **English:** English lit. **Foreign languages:** General, French, Spanish. **History:** General. **Math:** General. **Parks/recreation:** Exercise sciences, sports admin, sports studies. **Physical sciences:** General. **Protective services:** Criminal justice. **Psychology:** General. **Social sciences:** Political science, sociology. **Theology:** Bible, lay ministry, missionary, youth ministry. **Visual/performing arts:** General, dramatic, drawing, film/cinema/video, graphic design, illustration, photography.

Most popular majors. Business/marketing 30%, education 13%, psychology 20%, theological studies 10%.

Technology on campus. 160 workstations in dormitories, library, computer center, student center. Dormitories wired for high-speed internet access and linked to campus network. Commuter students can connect to campus network. Online course registration, online library, helpline, repair service, wireless network available.

Student life. Freshman orientation: Mandatory. Preregistration for classes offered. Weekend program held at beginning of fall semester. **Policies:** Students are to refrain from use of alcoholic beverages, illegal drugs, tobacco, sexual misconduct, morally degrading media and literature, coarse or obscene language or any other conduct inconsistent with the goals and traditions of the college. Religious observance required. **Housing:** Guaranteed on-campus for all undergraduates. Single-sex dorms, apartments available. $200 nonrefundable deposit, deadline 5/1. **Activities:** Bands, campus ministries, choral groups, drama, international student organizations, literary magazine, music ensembles, musical theater, student government, student newspaper, symphony orchestra.

Athletics. NAIA, NCCAA. **Intercollegiate:** Baseball M, basketball, cross-country, golf, soccer, softball W, tennis, track and field, volleyball W. **Intramural:** Badminton, basketball, football (non-tackle) M, soccer, table tennis, volleyball. **Team name:** Lancers.

Student services. Chaplain/spiritual director, career counseling, student employment services, financial aid counseling, health services, personal counseling, placement for graduates, veterans' counselor. **Physically disabled:** Services for visually impaired.

Contact. E-mail: admissions@grace.edu
Phone: (574) 372-5100 ext. 6008
Toll-free number: (800) 544-7223 ext. 6008 Fax: (574) 372-5120
Cynthia Sisson, Vice President of Enrollment Management, Grace College, 200 Seminary Drive, Winona Lake, IN 46590

Hanover College
Hanover, Indiana   **CB member**
www.hanover.edu   **CB code: 1290**

- Private 4-year liberal arts college affiliated with the Presbyterian Church (USA)
- Residential campus in rural community
- 1,127 degree-seeking undergraduates: 59% women, 4% African American, 2% Asian American, 2% Hispanic/Latino, 1% Native American, 1% Multi-racial, non-Hispanic, 4% international
- 61% of applicants admitted
- SAT or ACT (ACT writing recommended), application essay required
- 67% graduate within 6 years; 22% enter graduate study

General. Founded in 1827. Regionally accredited. **Degrees:** 243 bachelor's awarded. **Location:** 45 miles from Louisville, KY; 70 miles from Cincinnati, OH; 90 miles from Indianapolis. **Calendar:** 4-1-4. 4-4-1. **Full-time faculty:** 97 total; 97% have terminal degrees, 8% minority, 44% women. **Part-time faculty:** 4 total; 50% have terminal degrees, 50% women. **Class size:** 73% < 20, 26% 20-39, less than 1% 40-49, less than 1% 50-99. **Special facilities:** Human cadaver lab, geology museum, observatory, national wildlife refuge.

Freshman class profile. 3,355 applied, 2,056 admitted, 304 enrolled.

Mid 50% test scores			
SAT critical reading:	480-610	GPA 2.0-2.99:	5%
SAT math:	470-600	Rank in top quarter:	54%
SAT writing:	460-570	Rank in top tenth:	20%
ACT composite:	22-27	End year in good standing:	95%
GPA 3.75 or higher:	40%	Return as sophomores:	82%
GPA 3.50-3.74:	18%	Out-of-state:	26%
GPA 3.0-3.49:	37%	Live on campus:	97%
		International:	2%

Basis for selection. GED not accepted. Selection of and performance in academic courses most important. Interview recommended. **Home schooled:** Transcript of courses and grades required.

High school preparation. College-preparatory program required. 18 units required; 26 recommended. Required and recommended units include English 4, mathematics 3-4, social studies 2-3, history 2-3, science 3-4 (laboratory 2-3), foreign language 2-4, visual/performing arts 1 and academic electives 2-3.

2015-2016 Annual costs. Tuition/fees: $34,514. Room/board: $10,452. Books/supplies: $1,200. Personal expenses: $900.

2014-2015 Financial aid. Need-based: 79% of total undergraduate aid awarded as scholarships/grants, 21% as loans/jobs. **Non-need-based:** Scholarships awarded for academics, alumni affiliation, art, leadership, minority status, music/drama, religious affiliation, state residency.

Application procedures. Admission: No deadline. No application fee. Admission notification on a rolling basis beginning on or about 9/1. Must reply by May 1 or within 2 week(s) if notified thereafter. **Financial aid:** Priority date 3/1; no closing date. FAFSA required. Applicants notified by 3/1.

Academics. Students take only one course in the 4-week May term. **Special study options:** Double major, dual enrollment of high school students, independent study, internships, student-designed major, study abroad, teacher certification program, Washington semester. Business Scholars Program, City Semesters (internships or student teaching): Philadelphia Center, Washington Center, Associated Colleges of the Midwest. **Credit/placement by examination:** AP, CLEP, IB, institutional tests. **Support services:** Learning center,

reduced course load, study skills assistance, tutoring, writing center. Help securing electronic textbooks.

Majors. Biology: General, biochemistry. **Communications:** Communications/speech/rhetoric. **Computer sciences:** General. **Conservation:** Environmental science. **Education:** Elementary. **English:** English lit. **Foreign languages:** Classics, French, German, Spanish. **History:** General. **Math:** General. **Parks/recreation:** Exercise sciences, health/fitness. **Philosophy/religion:** Philosophy. **Physical sciences:** Chemistry, geology, physics. **Psychology:** General. **Social sciences:** Anthropology, economics, political science, sociology. **Theology:** Theology. **Visual/performing arts:** Art history/conservation, dramatic, music, studio arts.

Most popular majors. Biology 11%, communications/journalism 12%, history 6%, parks/recreation 11%, physical sciences 12%, psychology 7%, social sciences 16%.

Technology on campus. 205 workstations in library, computer center, student center. Dormitories wired for high-speed internet access and linked to campus network. Commuter students can connect to campus network. Online course registration, online library, helpline, student web hosting, wireless network available.

Student life. Freshman orientation: Available. Preregistration for classes offered. Five 1-day orientation and fall class registration sessions in April, May, June, and August. Additional orientation starts 1 week before classes begin. **Housing:** Guaranteed on-campus for all undergraduates. Coed dorms, single-sex dorms, apartments, fraternity/sorority housing, themed housing, wellness housing available. $300 fully refundable deposit, deadline 5/1. **Activities:** Bands, campus ministries, choral groups, dance, drama, film society, international student organizations, literary magazine, music ensembles, musical theater, radio station, student government, student newspaper, symphony orchestra, TV station, Campus Fellowship, political and social service organizations, academic clubs, Christian Life, Love Out Loud (LGBT group), Kaleidoscope.

Athletics. NCAA. **Intercollegiate:** Baseball M, basketball, cross-country, football (tackle) M, golf, lacrosse, soccer, softball W, tennis, track and field, volleyball W. **Intramural:** Basketball, football (non-tackle) W, football (tackle) M, racquetball, soccer, softball, ultimate frisbee, volleyball. **Team name:** Panthers.

Student services. Alcohol/substance abuse counseling, chaplain/spiritual director, career counseling, student employment services, financial aid counseling, health services, minority student services, personal counseling, placement for graduates. **Physically disabled:** Services for visually, hearing impaired.

Contact. E-mail: admission@hanover.edu
Phone: (812) 866-7021 Toll-free number: (800) 213-2178
Fax: (812) 866-7098
Chris Gage, Dean of Admission, Hanover College, PO Box 108, Hanover, IN 47243-0108

Holy Cross College
Notre Dame, Indiana   **CB member**
www.hcc-nd.edu   **CB code: 1309**

- Private 4-year liberal arts college affiliated with the Roman Catholic Church
- Residential campus in small city
- 546 degree-seeking undergraduates: 1% part-time, 39% women
- 91% of applicants admitted
- SAT or ACT (ACT writing recommended) required

General. Founded in 1966. Regionally accredited. **Degrees:** 72 bachelor's, 2 associate awarded. **ROTC:** Army, Air Force. **Location:** 140 miles from Indianapolis, 90 miles from Chicago. **Calendar:** Semester, limited summer session. **Full-time faculty:** 26 total; 54% have terminal degrees, 23% minority, 42% women. **Part-time faculty:** 40 total; 38% have terminal degrees, 8% minority, 55% women.

Freshman class profile. 623 applied, 564 admitted, 139 enrolled.

Mid 50% test scores			
SAT critical reading:	430-540	GPA 3.0-3.49:	33%
SAT math:	410-540	GPA 2.0-2.99:	39%
ACT composite:	18-24	End year in good standing:	65%
GPA 3.75 or higher:	18%	Out-of-state:	50%
GPA 3.50-3.74:	10%	Live on campus:	90%

Basis for selection. Application, high school transcripts, ACT/SAT scores. Students may also submit an essay and/or letters of recommendation, but these items are optional. Admission decisions are reached based on material submitted. Student who are transferring to Holy Cross with 24 or more transferrable credits (those with a grade of C or higher) are not required to submit test scores. Essay or personal statement strongly encouraged. Interview recommended. **Home schooled:** Statement describing home school structure and mission, transcript of courses and grades required.

High school preparation. College-preparatory program recommended. Required and recommended units include English 4, mathematics 3-4, social studies 2-4, science 2-4 and foreign language 2.

2015-2016 Annual costs. Tuition/fees: $27,950. Room/board: $9,975. Books/supplies: $1,200. Personal expenses: $1,100.

2014-2015 Financial aid. Need-based: 93 full-time freshmen applied for aid; 72 deemed to have need; 72 received aid. Average need met was 61%. Average scholarship/grant was $15,400; average loan $3,700. 85% of total undergraduate aid awarded as scholarships/grants, 15% as loans/jobs. **Non-need-based:** Awarded to 477 full-time undergraduates, including 113 freshmen. Scholarships awarded for academics, athletics, state residency.

Application procedures. Admission: Priority date 3/1; deadline 8/15. No application fee. Admission notification on a rolling basis beginning on or about 10/1. Must reply by May 1 or within 3 week(s) if notified thereafter. **Financial aid:** Priority date 3/1; no closing date. FAFSA required. Applicants notified on a rolling basis starting 5/1; must reply within 2 week(s) of notification.

Academics. Special study options: Cross-registration, double major, dual enrollment of high school students, ESL, honors, internships, liberal arts/career combination, study abroad, teacher certification program. Service learning. **Credit/placement by examination:** AP, CLEP, IB, SAT, ACT, institutional tests. 30 credit hours maximum toward associate degree, 30 toward bachelor's. **Support services:** Learning center, reduced course load, remedial instruction, study skills assistance, tutoring, writing center.

Majors. Business: General. **Communications:** General. **Education:** Elementary. **English:** English lit. **History:** General. **Liberal arts:** Arts/sciences. **Psychology:** General. **Theology:** Theology. **Visual/performing arts:** Art.

Technology on campus. 95 workstations in library, computer center, student center. Dormitories wired for high-speed internet access and linked to campus network. Commuter students can connect to campus network. Online course registration, online library, helpline, repair service, student web hosting, wireless network available.

Student life. Freshman orientation: Mandatory. Preregistration for classes offered. Held 3 days prior to start of fall classes. **Housing:** Single-sex dorms, special housing for disabled, apartments available. $200 partly refundable deposit, deadline 5/3. **Activities:** Bands, campus ministries, choral groups, drama, literary magazine, music ensembles, student government, student newspaper, mission team, Right to Life, multicultural organization.

Athletics. NAIA. **Intercollegiate:** Baseball M, basketball, cross-country, golf, soccer. **Intramural:** Basketball, football (non-tackle), table tennis, volleyball. **Team name:** Saints.

Student services. Alcohol/substance abuse counseling, chaplain/spiritual director, career counseling, student employment services, financial aid counseling, health services, personal counseling, placement for graduates.

Contact. E-mail: admissions@hcc-nd.edu
Phone: (574) 239-8400 Fax: (574) 239-8323
Brian Studebaker, Director of Enrollment Management, Holy Cross College, 54515 State Road 933 North, Notre Dame, IN 46556-0308

Huntington University
Huntington, Indiana
www.huntington.edu

CB code: 1304

- Private 4-year liberal arts college affiliated with the United Brethren in Christ
- Residential campus in large town
- 947 degree-seeking undergraduates: 6% part-time, 57% women
- 231 degree-seeking graduate students
- 84% of applicants admitted
- SAT or ACT (ACT writing recommended), application essay required
- 66% graduate within 6 years; 10% enter graduate study

General. Founded in 1897. Regionally accredited. Branch campuses in Fort Wayne and Columbia City. **Degrees:** 241 bachelor's, 4 associate awarded; master's, professional offered. **Location:** 20 miles from Fort Wayne. **Calendar:** 4-1-4, limited summer session. **Full-time faculty:** 55 total; 87% have terminal degrees, 2% minority, 38% women. **Part-time faculty:** 51 total; 24% have terminal degrees, 6% minority, 45% women. **Class size:** 71% < 20, 24% 20-39, 4% 40-49, 1% 50-99. **Special facilities:** Life Sciences Education Consortium, simulated nursing lab, radio telescope, disc golf course, herbarium, greenhouse, Thornhill Nature Preserve, film studio with green screen, animation (film) lab, tv studio, radio studio, theater auditorium, studio theater, Enterprise Resource Center (for internships), career services center, Office of Student Success, student-run marketing firm, portable ice rink.

Freshman class profile. 942 applied, 790 admitted, 209 enrolled.

Mid 50% test scores			
SAT critical reading:	440-560	GPA 3.0-3.49:	24%
SAT math:	440-580	GPA 2.0-2.99:	20%
SAT writing:	430-540	Rank in top quarter:	49%
ACT composite:	20-26	Rank in top tenth:	17%
GPA 3.75 or higher:	35%	Return as sophomores:	79%
GPA 3.50-3.74:	20%	Out-of-state:	27%
		Live on campus:	91%

Basis for selection. Class rank in top half, satisfactory test scores, 2.3 GPA most important. Selected students with 860 SAT (exclusive of Writing), 2.0 GPA, or rank in top 50% of class may be admitted on a minimum load. Interview recommended. Audition required of music majors. Portfolio required for art scholarships. Essay required for presidential scholarships. Test required for journalism scholarships. **Home schooled:** Transcript of courses and grades required. **Learning Disabled:** Documentation of learning disability required in some cases where both GPA and standardized test results are below minimum requirement for admission.

High school preparation. College-preparatory program recommended. 20 units required. Required and recommended units include English 4, mathematics 3, social studies 3, science 3, foreign language 2, visual/performing arts 1 and academic electives 7.

2016-2017 Annual costs. Tuition/fees: $25,400. Room/board: $8,456. Books/supplies: $1,000. Personal expenses: $1,350.

2015-2016 Financial aid. Need-based: 207 full-time freshmen applied for aid; 188 deemed to have need; 159 received aid. Average need met was 82%. Average scholarship/grant was $15,542; average loan $2,770. 59% of total undergraduate aid awarded as scholarships/grants, 41% as loans/jobs. **Non-need-based:** Awarded to 366 full-time undergraduates, including 107 freshmen. Scholarships awarded for academics, alumni affiliation, art, athletics, leadership, minority status, music/drama, religious affiliation. **Additional information:** Loan repayment program offered to qualifying students. This program helps students payback their loans after graduation based on their income.

Application procedures. Admission: Priority date 3/1; deadline 8/1 (receipt date). $25 fee, may be waived for applicants with need. Application must be submitted online. Admission notification on a rolling basis beginning on or about 10/1. Education majors must apply separately to the Education Department before entering those major classes. Performance grants also require a separate application process for those majoring in music, theatre, art, and communication. **Financial aid:** Priority date 3/10; no closing date. FAFSA required. Applicants notified on a rolling basis starting 2/15; must reply by 5/1.

Academics. Special study options: Accelerated study, combined bachelor's/graduate degree, distance learning, double major, dual enrollment of high school students, ESL, honors, independent study, internships, semester at sea, study abroad, teacher certification program, urban semester, Washington semester. TESOL certificate. **Credit/placement by examination:** AP, CLEP, institutional tests. 38 credit hours maximum toward bachelor's degree. **Support services:** Learning center, pre-admission summer program, reduced course load, remedial instruction, study skills assistance, tutoring, writing center. Resume building, internships, job training skills available.

Majors. Biology: General, biochemistry. **Business:** General, accounting, accounting/finance, business admin, entrepreneurial studies, human resources, managerial economics, marketing, nonprofit/public, small business admin. **Communications:** Broadcast journalism, communications/speech/rhetoric, digital media, journalism, public relations, radio/TV. **Computer sciences:** General, computer science. **Education:** General, art, biology, business, chemistry, elementary, English, mathematics, music, physical, science, secondary, social studies, special ed. **English:** General lit, writing. **Health services:** Nursing practice, pharmaceutical sciences, premedicine. **History:** General. **Human services:** Social work. **Math:** General. **Parks/recreation:** General, exercise sciences, health/fitness, outdoor education, sports admin, sports studies. **Philosophy/religion:** Philosophy, religion. **Physical sciences:** Chemistry. **Psychology:** General. **Social sciences:** Political science, sociology. **Theology:** Bible, missionary, religious ed, youth ministry. **Visual/performing arts:** Art, cinematography, dramatic, film/cinema/video, graphic design, music, music management, music performance, piano/keyboard, studio arts, theater design, voice/opera.

Most popular majors. Business/marketing 19%, communication technologies 6%, education 15%, health sciences 9%, parks/recreation 6%, theological studies 13%, visual/performing arts 9%.

Technology on campus. 209 workstations in dormitories, library, computer center, student center. Dormitories wired for high-speed internet access and linked to campus network. Online course registration, online library, helpline, student web hosting, wireless network available.

Student life. Freshman orientation: Mandatory. Preregistration for classes offered. Three-day orientation held immediately before first semester. **Policies:** Chapel/convocation attendance required 2 out of 4 weekly programs. Use of alcohol, drugs, and tobacco prohibited. Religious observance required. **Housing:** Guaranteed on-campus for all undergraduates. Coed dorms, single-sex dorms, special housing for disabled, apartments, themed housing available. $150 fully refundable deposit, deadline 8/30. **Activities:** Bands, campus ministries, choral groups, dance, drama, film society, international student organizations, literary magazine, music ensembles, musical theater, radio station, student government, student newspaper, TV station, Acting on AIDS, Amnesty International, Global Vision, Habitat for Humanity, Mu Kappa, volunteer service center, psychology, social work student council, nursing student council.

Athletics. NAIA, NCCAA. **Intercollegiate:** Baseball M, basketball, bowling, cross-country, golf, soccer, softball W, tennis, track and field, volleyball W. **Intramural:** Basketball, football (non-tackle), racquetball, soccer, softball, ultimate frisbee, volleyball. **Team name:** Foresters.

Student services. Adult student services, alcohol/substance abuse counseling, chaplain/spiritual director, career counseling, student employment services, financial aid counseling, health services, minority student services, on-campus daycare, personal counseling, placement for graduates, women's services. **Physically disabled:** Services for visually, speech, hearing impaired.

Contact. E-mail: admissions@huntington.edu
Phone: (260) 359-4000 Toll-free number: (800) 642-6493
Fax: (260) 358-3699
Nate Perry, Director of Undergraduate Admissions, Huntington University, 2303 College Avenue, Huntington, IN 46750-1237

Indiana Institute of Technology

Fort Wayne, Indiana
www.indianatech.edu

CB member
CB code: 1323

- Private 4-year business and engineering college
- Residential campus in large city
- 6,873 degree-seeking undergraduates
- 70% of applicants admitted
- SAT or ACT (ACT writing optional) required

General. Founded in 1930. Regionally accredited. **Degrees:** 563 bachelor's, 244 associate awarded; master's, professional, doctoral offered. **ROTC:** Army. **Location:** 125 miles from Indianapolis, 165 miles from Chicago, 165 miles from Detroit. **Calendar:** Semester, limited summer session. **Full-time faculty:** 45 total. **Part-time faculty:** 230 total. **Class size:** 81% < 20, 19% 20-39. **Special facilities:** Computer-aided design center, outdoor amphitheater, 200 seat on-campus movie theater, bowling alley, Leadership in Energy and Environmental Design (LEED,) geothermal certified building, wind turbine.

Freshman class profile. 3,016 applied, 2,099 admitted, 406 enrolled.

Mid 50% test scores			
SAT critical reading:	400-520	GPA 3.50-3.74:	10%
SAT math:	410-550	GPA 3.0-3.49:	30%
SAT writing:	380-490	GPA 2.0-2.99:	48%
ACT composite:	18-24	Rank in top quarter:	28%
GPA 3.75 or higher:	9%	Rank in top tenth:	8%
		Out-of-state:	28%

Basis for selection. High school or transfer organization GPA and ACT/SAT are the most important, however applicants are individually evaluated and, when necessary, given consideration based on other criteria. Minimum admissions requirements vary based upon program. Interviews, essays, or personal statements may be used to enhance an acceptance decision. Letters of recommendation may be requested for admission. **Home schooled:** Transcript of courses and grades required. For out-of-state students, require certification that homeschool organization is registered with that state.

High school preparation. College-preparatory program recommended.

2015-2016 Annual costs. Tuition/fees: $25,600. Room/board: $9,470. Personal expenses: $3,044.

Application procedures. Admission: No deadline. $50 fee, may be waived for applicants with need, free for online applicants. Admission notification on a rolling basis beginning on or about 9/15.

Academics. Special study options: Accelerated study, combined bachelor's/graduate degree, cross-registration, distance learning, double major, dual enrollment of high school students, ESL, exchange student, external degree, honors, independent study, internships, student-designed major. **Credit/placement by examination:** AP, CLEP, IB, SAT, ACT, institutional tests. **Support services:** Remedial instruction, study skills assistance, tutoring.

Majors. Business: Accounting, business admin, organizational leadership. **Communications:** Communications/speech/rhetoric. **Computer sciences:** Computer science, networking, security, webmaster. **Education:** Elementary, physical. **Engineering:** Biomedical, computer, electrical, environmental, industrial, mechanical, software. **Health services:** Recreational therapy. **Parks/recreation:** Facilities management, sports admin. **Protective services:** Criminalistics, law enforcement admin. **Psychology:** General. **Work/family studies:** Apparel marketing.

Most popular majors. Business/marketing 68%, computer/information sciences 7%, engineering/engineering technologies 6%, security/protective services 7%.

Technology on campus. 430 workstations in library, computer center. Dormitories wired for high-speed internet access and linked to campus network. Commuter students can connect to campus network. Online course registration, online library, helpline, repair service, student web hosting, wireless network available.

Student life. Freshman orientation: Mandatory. Preregistration for classes offered. One-day program held on campus that emphasizes new students familiarizing themselves with individuals and resources on campus, as well as promoting leadership building and opportunities. **Housing:** Guaranteed on-campus for freshmen. Coed dorms, special housing for disabled, apartments, fraternity/sorority housing, wellness housing available. $350 fully refundable deposit. **Activities:** Bands, campus ministries, choral groups, dance, international student organizations, student government, student newspaper, student board, black student association, Indiana Tech Gaming Society, Society for Women Engineers, American Society of Mechanical Engineers, Society for Human Resource Management, Society of Automotive Engineering, Collegiate Cyber Defense Team, Sport Recreation and Leisure Society.

Athletics. NAIA. **Intercollegiate:** Baseball M, basketball, bowling, cheerleading, cross-country, golf, lacrosse, soccer, softball W, tennis, track and field, volleyball W, wrestling M. **Intramural:** Badminton, basketball, bowling, soccer, volleyball. **Team name:** Warriors.

Student services. Adult student services, chaplain/spiritual director, career counseling, services for economically disadvantaged, student employment services, financial aid counseling, health services, legal services, placement for graduates. **Physically disabled:** Services for visually, speech, hearing impaired.

Contact. E-mail: admissions@indianatech.edu
Phone: (260) 422-5561 ext. 3103
Toll-free number: (800) 937-2448 ext. 3103 Fax: (260) 422-7696
Robert Confer, Director of Admissions, Indiana Institute of Technology, 1600 E Washington Blvd, Fort Wayne, IN 46803

Indiana State University

Terre Haute, Indiana
www.indstate.edu

CB member
CB code: 1322

- Public 4-year university
- Residential campus in small city
- 10,737 degree-seeking undergraduates: 10% part-time, 53% women, 19% African American, 1% Asian American, 4% Hispanic/Latino, 4% Multi-racial, non-Hispanic, 6% international
- 2,280 degree-seeking graduate students
- 71% of applicants admitted
- SAT or ACT (ACT writing optional) required
- 35% graduate within 6 years

General. Founded in 1865. Regionally accredited. **Degrees:** 1,784 bachelor's awarded; master's, professional, doctoral offered. **ROTC:** Army, Air Force. **Location:** 70 miles from Indianapolis. **Calendar:** Semester, extensive summer session. **Full-time faculty:** 505 total; 76% have terminal degrees, 16% minority, 46% women. **Part-time faculty:** 188 total; 25% have terminal degrees, 6% minority, 58% women. **Class size:** 28% < 20, 49% 20-39, 12% 40-49, 10% 50-99, 2% >100. **Special facilities:** Observatory, museum, flight simulator.

Freshman class profile. 14,312 applied, 10,104 admitted, 2,784 enrolled.

Mid 50% test scores			
SAT critical reading:	400-510	Rank in top quarter:	24%
SAT math:	400-510	Rank in top tenth:	8%
SAT writing:	390-490	Return as sophomores:	64%
ACT composite:	16-22	Out-of-state:	11%
GPA 3.75 or higher:	12%	Live on campus:	82%
GPA 3.50-3.74:	10%	International:	2%
GPA 3.0-3.49:	30%	Fraternities:	21%
GPA 2.0-2.99:	48%	Sororities:	18%

Basis for selection. Students who rank in top 50% of high school class usually admitted. High school curriculum, GPA, test scores, class rank, type of high school, and interview all considered. Interview required of some scholarship applicants, recommended for applicants below 50th percentile of high school graduating class. Essay recommended. Audition required of music majors. Portfolio recommended for art majors.

High school preparation. College-preparatory program required. 20 units recommended. Recommended units include English 4, mathematics 4, social studies 2, history 1, science 3 (laboratory 3), foreign language 1 and academic electives 2. 3 or more units in career area recommended. 1 unit health & safety/physical education recommended.

2015-2016 Annual costs. Tuition/fees: $8,580; $18,708 out-of-state. Room/board: $9,000. Books/supplies: $1,140. Personal expenses: $1,744.

2014-2015 Financial aid. All financial aid based on need. 2,581 full-time freshmen applied for aid; 2,158 deemed to have need; 2,083 received aid. Average need met was 81%. Average scholarship/grant was $5,589; average loan $3,079. 52% of total undergraduate aid awarded as scholarships/grants, 48% as loans/jobs. **Additional information:** Financial aid application deadline March 1 for Indiana residents applying for state grant.

Application procedures. Admission: Priority date 7/1; deadline 8/15 (postmark date). $25 fee, may be waived for applicants with need. Admission notification on a rolling basis. **Financial aid:** Priority date 3/1, closing date 7/1. FAFSA required. Applicants notified on a rolling basis starting 3/15.

Academics. Special study options: Accelerated study, cooperative education, distance learning, double major, dual enrollment of high school students, ESL, honors, independent study, internships, study abroad, teacher certification program. **Credit/placement by examination:** AP, CLEP, SAT, ACT, institutional tests. 31 credit hours maximum toward bachelor's degree. **Support services:** Learning center, pre-admission summer program, remedial instruction, study skills assistance, tutoring, writing center.

Majors. Architecture: Interior. **Area/ethnic studies:** African-American. **Biology:** General. **Business:** Accounting, business admin, construction management, finance, human resources, insurance, management information systems, marketing, office management. **Communications:** Communications/speech/rhetoric. **Computer sciences:** General, information technology. **Education:** Art, business, elementary, physical, science, social studies, special ed, trade/industrial. **English:** English lit. **Health services:** Athletic training, audiology/speech pathology, clinical lab science, community health services, nursing (RN). **History:** General. **Human services:** Social work. **Liberal arts:** Arts/sciences. **Math:** General. **Parks/recreation:** Exercise sciences, facilities management. **Philosophy/religion:** Philosophy. **Physical sciences:** Chemistry, geology, physics. **Psychology:** General. **Social sciences:** Anthropology, criminology, economics, geography, political science. **Visual/performing arts:** Art, dramatic, music, music performance, studio arts. **Work/family studies:** General, clothing/textiles, family studies, food/nutrition.

Most popular majors. Business/marketing 16%, education 9%, engineering/engineering technologies 9%, health sciences 20%, parks/recreation 7%, social sciences 11%.

Technology on campus. PC or laptop required. 846 workstations in library, computer center, student center. Dormitories wired for high-speed internet access and linked to campus network. Commuter students can connect to campus network. Online course registration, online library, helpline, repair service, student web hosting, wireless network available.

Student life. Freshman orientation: Mandatory. Preregistration for classes offered. One-day program includes registering for their first semester coursework. **Housing:** Guaranteed on-campus for freshmen. Coed dorms, single-sex dorms, special housing for disabled, apartments, fraternity/sorority housing, themed housing available. Apartments for students with dependent children and special housing for freshmen available. Special housing for freshmen. **Activities:** Bands, campus ministries, choral groups, dance, drama, film society, international student organizations, literary magazine, music ensembles, musical theater, radio station, student government, student newspaper, symphony orchestra, 290 student organizations available.

Athletics. NCAA. **Intercollegiate:** Baseball M, basketball, cross-country, diving W, football (tackle) M, golf W, soccer W, softball W, swimming W, track and field, volleyball W. **Intramural:** Badminton, basketball, football (non-tackle), handball, racquetball, soccer, softball, swimming, tennis, ultimate frisbee, volleyball. **Team name:** Sycamores.

Student services. Adult student services, alcohol/substance abuse counseling, career counseling, student employment services, financial aid counseling, health services, minority student services, on-campus daycare, personal counseling, placement for graduates, veterans' counselor, women's services. **Physically disabled:** Services for visually, speech, hearing impaired.

Contact. E-mail: admissions@indstate.edu
Phone: (812) 237-2121 Toll-free number: (800) 468-6478
Fax: (812) 237-8023
Richard Toomey, Director, Indiana State University, Office of Admissions, John W. Moore Welcome Center, Terre Haute, IN 47809-9989

Indiana University Bloomington
Bloomington, Indiana
www.iub.edu

CB member
CB code: 1324

- Public 4-year university
- Residential campus in small city
- 32,694 degree-seeking undergraduates: 3% part-time, 50% women, 4% African American, 4% Asian American, 5% Hispanic/Latino, 4% Multiracial, non-Hispanic, 11% international
- 9,894 degree-seeking graduate students
- 78% of applicants admitted
- SAT or ACT with writing, application essay required
- 77% graduate within 6 years

General. Founded in 1820. Regionally accredited. **Degrees:** 7,339 bachelor's, 14 associate awarded; master's, professional, doctoral offered. **ROTC:** Army, Air Force. **Location:** 50 miles from Indianapolis. **Calendar:** Semester, extensive summer session. **Full-time faculty:** 2,059 total; 78% have terminal degrees, 20% minority, 40% women. **Part-time faculty:** 320 total; 31% have terminal degrees, 11% minority, 48% women. **Class size:** 35% < 20, 38% 20-39, 8% 40-49, 12% 50-99, 6% >100. **Special facilities:** Cyclotron, 2 observatories, museum of anthropology/history/folklore, rare book library, outdoor educational center, center for excellence in education, garden and nature center, arboretum, automated virtual environment.

Freshman class profile. 34,483 applied, 26,892 admitted, 7,875 enrolled.

Mid 50% test scores			
SAT critical reading:	520-630	GPA 3.0-3.49:	27%
SAT math:	540-660	GPA 2.0-2.99:	4%
SAT writing:	510-620	Rank in top quarter:	68%
ACT composite:	24-30	Rank in top tenth:	34%
GPA 3.75 or higher:	48%	Return as sophomores:	89%
GPA 3.50-3.74:	21%	Out-of-state:	39%
		Live on campus:	95%

Basis for selection. Strength of student's college preparatory program, senior year program, grade trends, class rank (if provided), and SAT or ACT test scores important. SAT Subject Tests recommended. Campus visit encouraged. Audition required for majority of music majors. **Learning Disabled:** Current and comprehensive documentation of disability required to receive services.

High school preparation. College-preparatory program required. 17 units required. Required units include English 4, mathematics 3.5, social studies 3, science 3 (laboratory 2), foreign language 2, academic electives 1.5. Indiana residents must be on track to complete a Core 40 curriculum, a Core 40 Academic Honors curriculum, or the equivalent as a condition of being offered admission. Additional math credits recommended for students intending to pursue science degree. Additional world language credits recommended for all.

2015-2016 Annual costs. Tuition/fees: $10,388; $33,741 out-of-state. Room/board: $9,795. Books/supplies: $1,230. Personal expenses: $2,096.

2014-2015 Financial aid. Need-based: 5,442 full-time freshmen applied for aid; 3,479 deemed to have need; 3,277 received aid. Average need met was 66%. Average scholarship/grant was $11,891; average loan $3,077. 63% of total undergraduate aid awarded as scholarships/grants, 37% as loans/jobs. **Non-need-based:** Awarded to 11,166 full-time undergraduates, including 2,162 freshmen. Scholarships awarded for academics, art, athletics, leadership, minority status, music/drama, religious affiliation, ROTC. **Additional information:** Majority of institutional gift aid merit-based. Some need-based grants go to merit winners with financial need.

Application procedures. Admission: Priority date 2/1; no deadline. $60 fee, may be waived for applicants with need. Admission notification on a rolling basis. Must reply by May 1 or within 3 week(s) if notified thereafter.

Financial aid: Priority date 3/10; no closing date. FAFSA required. Applicants notified on a rolling basis starting 4/1.

Academics. Special study options: Accelerated study, combined bachelor's/graduate degree, cooperative education, distance learning, double major, dual enrollment of high school students, ESL, external degree, honors, independent study, internships, liberal arts/career combination, semester at sea, student-designed major, study abroad, teacher certification program, United Nations semester, Washington semester. **Credit/placement by examination:** AP, CLEP, IB, SAT, ACT, institutional tests. **Support services:** Learning center, pre-admission summer program, reduced course load, remedial instruction, study skills assistance, tutoring, writing center.

Honors college/program. Admissions based on 31 ACT/1360-1380 SAT and 3.95 GPA or top 5% class rank; 32-33 ACT/1390-1460 SAT and 3.90 GPA or top 7.5% class rank; 34-36 ACT/1470 SAT and 3.85 GPA or top 10% class rank.

Majors. Area/ethnic studies: African-American, American, Central Asian, East Asian, folklore, South Asian. **Biology:** General, animal behavior, biochemistry, biotechnology, microbiology, neuroscience, vision science. **Business:** General, labor studies. **Communications:** Communications/speech/rhetoric, digital media, journalism, media studies. **Communications technology:** Recording arts. **Computer sciences:** Computer science, informatics. **Conservation:** Environmental science, environmental studies. **Education:** Art, biology, chemistry, early childhood, elementary, English, foreign languages, French, German, health, Latin, mathematics, music, physics, secondary, social studies, Spanish, special ed. **Engineering:** General. **English:** English lit. **Foreign languages:** Ancient Greek, classics, comparative lit, East Asian, French, Germanic, Italian, linguistics, Portuguese, Semitic, Slavic, Spanish. **Health services:** Athletic training, audiology/speech pathology, community health, nursing (RN). **History:** General. **Human services:** General, social work. **Liberal arts:** Arts/sciences. **Math:** General, statistics. **Parks/recreation:** General, exercise sciences. **Philosophy/religion:** Judaic, philosophy, religion. **Physical sciences:** Astronomy, chemistry, geology, physics. **Protective services:** Criminal justice. **Psychology:** General. **Social sciences:** Anthropology, economics, geography, international relations, political science, sociology. **Visual/performing arts:** Art, art history/conservation, ballet, dance, dramatic, fashion design, game design, interior design, music performance, musical theater, studio arts, studio arts management. **Work/family studies:** Clothing/textiles.

Most popular majors. Biology 8%, business/marketing 18%, communications/journalism 8%, education 7%, parks/recreation 8%, public administration/social services 7%, social sciences 9%.

Technology on campus. 2,218 workstations in dormitories, library, computer center, student center. Dormitories wired for high-speed internet access and linked to campus network. Commuter students can connect to campus network. Online course registration, online library, helpline, repair service, student web hosting, wireless network available.

Student life. Freshman orientation: Mandatory, $149 fee. Preregistration for classes offered. Held for two days during the summer for students and their parents. **Housing:** Guaranteed on-campus for freshmen. Coed dorms, single-sex dorms, special housing for disabled, apartments, cooperative housing, fraternity/sorority housing, themed housing available. $300 partly refundable deposit, deadline 7/1. Residential language houses, living/learning centers, wellness center, African-American living/learning center, honors college floors, first-year academic interest group housing available. **Activities:** Bands, campus ministries, choral groups, dance, drama, international student organizations, literary magazine, music ensembles, musical theater, opera, radio station, student government, student newspaper, symphony orchestra, TV station, Amnesty International, bass fishing club, Buddhist Study Association, caving club, Chabad House, Chinese calligraphy club, Hoosier Happiness, investment banking club, Latinos Unidos, Muslim Student Union.

Athletics. NCAA. **Intercollegiate:** Baseball M, basketball, cross-country, diving, field hockey W, football (tackle) M, golf, rowing (crew) W, soccer, softball W, swimming, tennis, track and field, volleyball W, water polo W, wrestling M. **Intramural:** Badminton, basketball, football (non-tackle), handball, racquetball, soccer, softball, table tennis, tennis, ultimate frisbee, volleyball. **Team name:** Hoosiers.

Student services. Adult student services, alcohol/substance abuse counseling, chaplain/spiritual director, career counseling, services for economically disadvantaged, student employment services, financial aid counseling, health services, legal services, minority student services, on-campus daycare, personal counseling, placement for graduates, veterans' counselor, women's services. **Physically disabled:** Services for visually, speech, hearing impaired.

Contact. E-mail: iuadmit@indiana.edu
Phone: (812) 855-0661 Fax: (812) 855-5102
Sacha Thieme, Executive Director of Admissions, Indiana University Bloomington, 300 North Jordan Avenue, Bloomington, IN 47405-1106

Indiana University East
Richmond, Indiana
www.iue.edu   CB code: 1194

♦ Public 4-year university
♦ Commuter campus in large town
♦ 3,173 degree-seeking undergraduates: 39% part-time, 65% women, 4% African American, 1% Asian American, 3% Hispanic/Latino, 3% Multiracial, non-Hispanic, 1% international
♦ 132 degree-seeking graduate students
♦ 62% of applicants admitted
♦ SAT or ACT with writing required

General. Founded in 1971. Regionally accredited. **Degrees:** 665 bachelor's awarded; master's offered. **Location:** 70 miles from Indianapolis. **Calendar:** Semester, extensive summer session. **Full-time faculty:** 107 total; 62% have terminal degrees, 20% minority, 64% women. **Part-time faculty:** 189 total; 17% have terminal degrees, 6% minority, 58% women. **Class size:** 64% < 20, 32% 20-39, 2% 40-49, 2% 50-99.

Freshman class profile. 1,311 applied, 816 admitted, 354 enrolled.

Mid 50% test scores			
SAT critical reading:	430-520	GPA 3.0-3.49:	35%
SAT math:	430-530	GPA 2.0-2.99:	38%
SAT writing:	410-510	Rank in top quarter:	30%
ACT composite:	18-23	Rank in top tenth:	9%
GPA 3.75 or higher:	15%	Return as sophomores:	64%
GPA 3.50-3.74:	12%	Out-of-state:	17%

Basis for selection. High school graduates from Indiana expected to earn Indiana Core 40, Core 40 with Academic Honors or Core 40 with Technical Honors Diploma. Out-of-state students expected to complete minimum of 28 semesters of college prep courses. Applicants should rank in upper half of graduating class. SAT/ACT should meet or exceed the Indiana median scores; students with GED should have above average score. Interview recommended. **Home schooled:** Must graduate from national accredited home school program or take GED.

High school preparation. College-preparatory program required. 17 units required. Required units include English 4, mathematics 3, social studies 3, science 3 (laboratory 3) and academic electives 4. Recent high school graduates from Indiana are expected to complete the Core 40 curriculum. Out-of-state students are expected to complete a minimum of 28 semester hours of college prep courses listed. The four units of academic electives include additional Math, Lab Science, Social Science, Computer Science, Foreign Language, or other college-prep courses.

2015-2016 Annual costs. Tuition/fees: $6,930; $18,379 out-of-state. Books/supplies: $1,148. Personal expenses: $2,096.

2014-2015 Financial aid. Need-based: 385 full-time freshmen applied for aid; 319 deemed to have need; 314 received aid. Average need met was 66%. Average scholarship/grant was $7,210; average loan $2,761. 50% of total undergraduate aid awarded as scholarships/grants, 50% as loans/jobs. **Non-need-based:** Awarded to 266 full-time undergraduates, including 87 freshmen. Scholarships awarded for academics, alumni affiliation, leadership.

Application procedures. Admission: No deadline. $35 fee, may be waived for applicants with need. Admission notification on a rolling basis. **Financial aid:** Priority date 3/10; no closing date. FAFSA, institutional form required. Applicants notified on a rolling basis starting 5/1; must reply within 2 week(s) of notification.

Academics. Special study options: Accelerated study, cooperative education, cross-registration, distance learning, double major, dual enrollment of high school students, external degree, honors, independent study, internships, study abroad, teacher certification program, weekend college. State-wide technology program with Purdue University. **Credit/placement by examination:** AP, CLEP, IB, SAT, ACT, institutional tests. **Support services:** Remedial instruction, study skills assistance, tutoring, writing center.

Majors. Biology: General, biochemistry, biotechnology. **Business:** General. **Communications:** Communications/speech/rhetoric. **Computer sciences:** Informatics. **Education:** Elementary, secondary. **English:** English lit. **Health services:** Nursing (RN). **History:** General. **Human services:** Social work. **Liberal arts:** Humanities. **Math:** General. **Protective services:** Law enforcement admin. **Psychology:** General. **Social sciences:** Political science, sociology. **Visual/performing arts:** Art.

Most popular majors. Business/marketing 27%, education 7%, health sciences 22%, liberal arts 11%, psychology 6%.

Technology on campus. 187 workstations in library, computer center, student center. Commuter students can connect to campus network. Online course registration, online library, helpline, student web hosting, wireless network available.

Student life. Freshman orientation: Mandatory, $50 fee. Preregistration for classes offered. Day long event conducted prior to the start of each semester. **Activities:** Pep band, choral groups, dance, drama, literary magazine, music ensembles, student government, student newspaper, TV station, Aspiring Artists Redefining Tradition, Campus Christian Fellowship, Environmental Club, The Foam Dart Society, LGBTQS Alliance, National Alliance for Mental Illness, Stocks and Investment Club, Student Veteran's Organization, Whovians, World Languages and Cultures Club.

Athletics. NAIA. Intercollegiate: Basketball, cross-country, golf, tennis, track and field, volleyball W. **Intramural:** Basketball, cross-country, golf, softball, tennis, track and field, volleyball W. **Team name:** Red Wolves.

Student services. Adult student services, career counseling, student employment services, financial aid counseling, health services, personal counseling, placement for graduates. **Physically disabled:** Services for visually, speech, hearing impaired.

Contact. E-mail: applynow@iue.edu
Phone: (765) 973-8208 Toll-free number: (800) 959-3278
Fax: (765) 973-8209
Molly Vanderpool, Director of Admissions, Indiana University East, 2325 Chester Boulevard, Richmond, IN 47374-1289

Indiana University Kokomo
Kokomo, Indiana
www.iuk.edu   CB code: 1337

- Public 4-year university
- Commuter campus in large town
- 2,778 degree-seeking undergraduates: 23% part-time, 67% women, 4% African American, 1% Asian American, 5% Hispanic/Latino, 1% Native American, 2% Multi-racial, non-Hispanic, 1% international
- 116 degree-seeking graduate students
- 71% of applicants admitted
- SAT or ACT (ACT writing recommended) required

General. Founded in 1945. Regionally accredited. **Degrees:** 555 bachelor's, 13 associate awarded; master's offered. **ROTC:** Army. **Location:** 50 miles from Indianapolis. **Calendar:** Semester, limited summer session. **Full-time faculty:** 117 total; 59% have terminal degrees, 13% minority, 61% women. **Part-time faculty:** 116 total; 9% have terminal degrees, 9% minority, 60% women. **Class size:** 49% < 20, 44% 20-39, 5% 40-49, 2% 50-99. **Special facilities:** Observatory.

Freshman class profile. 1,534 applied, 1,094 admitted, 594 enrolled.

Mid 50% test scores		GPA 3.0-3.49:	33%
SAT critical reading:	420-520	GPA 2.0-2.99:	39%
SAT math:	420-520	Rank in top quarter:	29%
SAT writing:	410-500	Rank in top tenth:	6%
ACT composite:	18-23	Return as sophomores:	65%
GPA 3.75 or higher:	15%	Out-of-state:	1%
GPA 3.50-3.74:	12%	International:	1%

Basis for selection. Test scores, class rank, course work important. In-state applicants should be in top half of graduating class (top third for out-of-state applicants). SAT score of 950 or higher (critical reading plus mathematical reasoning) or ACT composite score of 20 or higher required. Students who have been out of high school for three or more years are not required to submit SAT or ACT scores.

High school preparation. College-preparatory program required. 20 units required. Required and recommended units include English 4, mathematics 3, social studies 3, science 3, foreign language 2 and academic electives 7. If a student has not earned an Academic Honors or Core 40 high school diploma, your high school preparation should include a minimum of at least the 40 college preparatory courses listed. The academic electives include foreign language, additional mathematics, laboratory science, social science, computer science or other college preparatory courses.

2015-2016 Annual costs. Tuition/fees: $6,941; $18,379 out-of-state. Books/supplies: $1,148. Personal expenses: $2,096.

2014-2015 Financial aid. Need-based: 469 full-time freshmen applied for aid; 365 deemed to have need; 342 received aid. Average need met was 65%. Average scholarship/grant was $7,641; average loan $2,774. 55% of total undergraduate aid awarded as scholarships/grants, 45% as loans/jobs. **Non-need-based:** Awarded to 202 full-time undergraduates, including 77 freshmen. Scholarships awarded for academics, athletics, leadership.

Application procedures. Admission: Priority date 3/1; no deadline. $35 fee, may be waived for applicants with need. Admission notification on a rolling basis. **Financial aid:** Priority date 3/10; no closing date. FAFSA required. Applicants notified on a rolling basis starting 3/25; must reply within 4 week(s) of notification.

Academics. Special study options: Accelerated study, cross-registration, distance learning, double major, dual enrollment of high school students, ESL, external degree, honors, independent study, internships, liberal arts/career combination, study abroad, teacher certification program. **Credit/placement by examination:** AP, CLEP, IB, SAT, ACT, institutional tests. **Support services:** Learning center, reduced course load, remedial instruction, tutoring, writing center.

Majors. Biology: General, biochemistry. **Business:** General, hospitality admin. **Communications:** Communications/speech/rhetoric, digital media. **Computer sciences:** Informatics. **Education:** Early childhood, elementary, secondary. **English:** English lit. **Health services:** General, medical radiologic technology/radiation therapy, nursing (RN). **Human services:** General. **Liberal arts:** Humanities. **Math:** General. **Physical sciences:** Chemistry. **Protective services:** Criminal justice. **Psychology:** General. **Social sciences:** Sociology. **Visual/performing arts:** Art, studio arts.

Most popular majors. Business/marketing 9%, health sciences 49%, liberal arts 9%, psychology 6%.

Technology on campus. 325 workstations in library, computer center. Commuter students can connect to campus network. Online course registration, helpline, student web hosting, wireless network available.

Student life. Freshman orientation: Available, $50 fee. Preregistration for classes offered. One day event designed to provide new students with information on activities and services on the campus and to promote and enhance student success. Orientation date is based on admit date. **Activities:** Concert band, choral groups, dance, drama, international student organizations, literary magazine, music ensembles, Model UN, radio station, student government, student newspaper, Actions for Animals, Cougar Advocates for Diversity, drama club, Enactus, Nurses Christian Fellowship, Saudi students club, Secular Student Alliance, Student Veterans Organization, SumAntics, Young Americans for Liberty.

Athletics. NAIA. Intercollegiate: Basketball, cross-country, golf, volleyball W. **Intramural:** Basketball, soccer, softball. **Team name:** Cougars.

Student services. Adult student services, career counseling, student employment services, financial aid counseling, minority student services, personal counseling, placement for graduates, veterans' counselor. **Physically disabled:** Services for visually, hearing impaired.

Contact. E-mail: iuadmis@iuk.edu
Phone: (765) 455-9217 Toll-free number: (888) 875-4485
Fax: (765) 455-9537
Angie Siders, Director of Admissions, Indiana University Kokomo, Kelley Student Center, Room 230, Kokomo, IN 46902-9003

Indiana University Northwest
Gary, Indiana
www.iun.edu   CB code: 1338

- Public 4-year university
- Commuter campus in small city
- 4,117 degree-seeking undergraduates: 29% part-time, 69% women, 18% African American, 2% Asian American, 20% Hispanic/Latino, 3% Multi-racial, non-Hispanic
- 354 degree-seeking graduate students
- 79% of applicants admitted
- SAT or ACT with writing required

General. Founded in 1948. Regionally accredited. **Degrees:** 532 bachelor's, 75 associate awarded; master's offered. **ROTC:** Army. **Location:** 35 miles from Chicago. **Calendar:** Semester, limited summer session. **Full-time faculty:** 167 total; 71% have terminal degrees, 28% minority, 53% women. **Part-time faculty:** 197 total; 19% have terminal degrees, 19% minority, 64% women. **Class size:** 37% < 20, 52% 20-39, 4% 40-49, 6% 50-99, less than 1% >100.

Freshman class profile. 1,573 applied, 1,247 admitted, 652 enrolled.

Mid 50% test scores		GPA 3.0-3.49:	24%
SAT critical reading:	410-520	GPA 2.0-2.99:	51%
SAT math:	400-510	Rank in top quarter:	32%
SAT writing:	400-500	Rank in top tenth:	11%
ACT composite:	17-23	Return as sophomores:	66%
GPA 3.75 or higher:	12%	Out-of-state:	3%
GPA 3.50-3.74:	10%	International:	1%

Basis for selection. Indiana Core 40 (college prep) diploma, or an equivalent diploma now state mandated for entering freshmen. School achievement record and test scores most important. Applicants should be in top half of class and have 2.0 high school GPA or better.

High school preparation. College-preparatory program required. 20 units required. Required and recommended units include English 4, mathematics 3, social studies 2, history 1, science 3 (laboratory 3), foreign language 2 and academic electives 7. The seven academic electives include a required one credit of physical education, and a half credit in health & wellness. Two and a half credits more must be directed electives in world languages, fine arts, or career-technical courses.

2015-2016 Annual costs. Tuition/fees: $6,963; $18,379 out-of-state. Books/supplies: $1,066. Personal expenses: $2,096.

2014-2015 Financial aid. Need-based: 590 full-time freshmen applied for aid; 431 deemed to have need; 398 received aid. Average need met was 68%. Average scholarship/grant was $7,243; average loan $2,776. 54% of total undergraduate aid awarded as scholarships/grants, 46% as loans/jobs. **Non-need-based:** Awarded to 291 full-time undergraduates, including 67 freshmen. Scholarships awarded for academics, athletics.

Application procedures. Admission: Priority date 7/1; no deadline. $35 fee, may be waived for applicants with need. Admission notification on a rolling basis. **Financial aid:** Priority date 3/10; no closing date. FAFSA required. Applicants notified on a rolling basis starting 4/15; must reply by 6/30.

Academics. Special study options: Accelerated study, cooperative education, distance learning, double major, dual enrollment of high school students, external degree, honors, independent study, internships, liberal arts/career combination, student-designed major, study abroad, teacher certification program, Washington semester, weekend college. **Credit/placement by examination:** AP, CLEP, IB, SAT, ACT, institutional tests. **Support services:** Learning center, pre-admission summer program, reduced course load, remedial instruction, tutoring, writing center.

Majors. Area/ethnic studies: African-American. **Biology:** General. **Business:** General, actuarial science, labor studies. **Communications:** Communications/speech/rhetoric. **Computer sciences:** Computer science, informatics. **Education:** Biology, chemistry, elementary, English, mathematics, secondary, social studies. **English:** English lit. **Foreign languages:** French, Spanish. **Health services:** Dental hygiene, health services admin, nursing (RN), radiologic technology/medical imaging. **History:** General. **Human services:** General, social work. **Math:** General. **Philosophy/religion:** Philosophy. **Physical sciences:** Chemistry, geology. **Protective services:** Criminal justice. **Psychology:** General. **Social sciences:** Anthropology, economics, political science, sociology. **Visual/performing arts:** Dramatic, studio arts.

Most popular majors. Business/marketing 11%, education 7%, health sciences 30%, liberal arts 13%, psychology 8%, public administration/social services 7%, security/protective services 8%.

Technology on campus. 605 workstations in library, computer center, student center. Commuter students can connect to campus network. Online course registration, helpline, student web hosting, wireless network available.

Student life. Freshman orientation: Mandatory, $50 fee. Preregistration for classes offered. One-day event. **Activities:** Campus ministries, choral groups, dance, drama, film society, international student organizations, literary magazine, music ensembles, musical theater, radio station, student government, student newspaper, art club, Asian American Association, Bible study club, Connectionz, Habitat for Humanity, Love Your Melon Campus Crew, modern languages club, Muslim Student Association, Public Relations Student Society of America, Student Ambassadors.

Athletics. NAIA. **Intercollegiate:** Basketball, cross-country, volleyball W. **Intramural:** Basketball, volleyball. **Team name:** Red Hawks.

Student services. Adult student services, career counseling, student employment services, financial aid counseling, health services, personal counseling, placement for graduates, veterans' counselor, women's services. **Physically disabled:** Services for visually impaired.

Contact. E-mail: admit@iun.edu
Phone: (219) 980-6991 Toll-free number: (888) 968-7486
Fax: (219) 981-4219
Dorothy Frink, Director of Admissions and Strategic Recruitment, Indiana University Northwest, 3400 Broadway, Gary, IN 46408

Indiana University South Bend
South Bend, Indiana
www.iusb.edu   CB code: 1339

- Public 4-year university
- Commuter campus in small city
- 5,165 degree-seeking undergraduates: 26% part-time, 61% women, 8% African American, 1% Asian American, 9% Hispanic/Latino, 3% Multiracial, non-Hispanic, 3% international
- 507 degree-seeking graduate students
- 76% of applicants admitted
- SAT or ACT with writing required

General. Founded in 1922. Regionally accredited. Off-campus course offerings in Elkhart and Plymouth. **Degrees:** 789 bachelor's, 11 associate awarded; master's offered. **ROTC:** Army, Naval, Air Force. **Location:** 95 miles from Chicago. **Calendar:** Semester, limited summer session. **Full-time faculty:** 268 total; 70% have terminal degrees, 22% minority, 48% women. **Part-time faculty:** 208 total; 18% have terminal degrees, 11% minority, 54% women. **Class size:** 49% < 20, 44% 20-39, 5% 40-49, 2% 50-99, less than 1% >100.

Freshman class profile. 2,299 applied, 1,752 admitted, 906 enrolled.

Mid 50% test scores			
SAT critical reading:	420-530	Rank in top quarter:	25%
SAT math:	420-530	Rank in top tenth:	7%
SAT writing:	400-510	Return as sophomores:	66%
ACT composite:	18-23	Out-of-state:	2%
GPA 3.75 or higher:	10%	Live on campus:	25%
GPA 3.50-3.74:	11%	International:	3%
GPA 3.0-3.49:	36%		

GPA 2.0-2.99: 43%

Basis for selection. Indiana high school graduates are expected to complete the Core 40 curriculum and are strongly encouraged to earn the Academic Honors Diploma. Out-of-state students are expected to complete a comparable college-prep curriculum. Interview recommended for academically weak applicants or those with unusual circumstances. Audition required of music majors. Portfolios required for some art majors. **Home schooled:** Applicants to degree-seeking programs must meet institution's requirement for college-prep courses.

High school preparation. College-preparatory program required. 20 units required. Required and recommended units include English 4, mathematics 3, social studies 3, science 3 (laboratory 3), foreign language 2 and academic electives 7. Indiana high school graduates are expected to complete the Core 40 curriculum and are strongly encouraged to earn the Academic Honors Diploma. Out-of-state students are expected to complete a comparable college-prep curriculum.

2015-2016 Annual costs. Tuition/fees: $6,986; $18,379 out-of-state. Room only: $7,150. Books/supplies: $1,148. Personal expenses: $2,096.

2014-2015 Financial aid. Need-based: 804 full-time freshmen applied for aid; 680 deemed to have need; 658 received aid. Average need met was 63%. Average scholarship/grant was $7,169; average loan $2,882. 54% of total undergraduate aid awarded as scholarships/grants, 46% as loans/jobs. **Non-need-based:** Awarded to 442 full-time undergraduates, including 146 freshmen. Scholarships awarded for academics, athletics.

Application procedures. Admission: Priority date 7/31; no deadline. $35 fee, may be waived for applicants with need. Admission notification on a rolling basis. **Financial aid:** Priority date 3/10; no closing date. FAFSA, institutional form required. Applicants notified on a rolling basis starting 5/1.

Academics. Most allied health programs must be completed at Indianapolis campus. **Special study options:** Accelerated study, cross-registration, distance learning, double major, dual enrollment of high school students, ESL, external degree, honors, independent study, internships, liberal arts/career combination, study abroad, teacher certification program, weekend college. Electrical, mechanical engineering, computer technology with Purdue University on Indiana University South Bend campus; Northern Indiana Consortium for Education (part of 6 member institutions sharing library resources, faculty expertise, and academic strengths). **Credit/placement by examination:** AP, CLEP, IB, institutional tests. 90 credit hours maximum toward bachelor's degree. **Support services:** Learning center, pre-admission summer program, reduced course load, remedial instruction, tutoring, writing center.

Majors. Biology: General, biochemistry. **Business:** General, actuarial science, labor studies. **Communications:** Communications/speech/rhetoric, digital media. **Computer sciences:** Computer science, informatics. **Conservation:** Environmental studies. **Education:** Art, biology, chemistry, elementary, English, French, German, mathematics, music, physics, science, secondary, social studies, Spanish, special ed. **English:** English lit. **Foreign languages:**

French, German, Spanish. **Health services:** General, dental hygiene, medical radiologic technology/radiation therapy, nursing (RN). **History:** General. **Human services:** Social work. **Math:** General, applied. **Philosophy/religion:** Philosophy. **Physical sciences:** Chemistry, physics. **Protective services:** Criminal justice. **Psychology:** General. **Social sciences:** Anthropology, economics, political science, sociology. **Visual/performing arts:** Art, dramatic, music, music performance, studio arts.

Most popular majors. Business/marketing 19%, communications/journalism 8%, education 10%, health sciences 17%, liberal arts 13%.

Technology on campus. 775 workstations in dormitories, library, computer center, student center. Dormitories wired for high-speed internet access and linked to campus network. Commuter students can connect to campus network. Online course registration, online library, helpline, student web hosting, wireless network available.

Student life. Freshman orientation: Mandatory, $35 fee. Preregistration for classes offered. Two and a half hour sessions held in May, June, July and August. **Housing:** Coed dorms, apartments available. $200 nonrefundable deposit. **Activities:** Bands, choral groups, dance, drama, film society, literary magazine, music ensembles, musical theater, opera, student government, student newspaper, symphony orchestra, Affordable travel club, Black Student Union, Campus Bible Fellowship, Feminist Student Union, film studies club, Japanese club, Latino Student Union, sustainability club, Theatre Guild, Titan Productions.

Athletics. NAIA. **Intercollegiate:** Baseball M, basketball, cross-country, golf M, volleyball W. **Intramural:** Badminton, basketball, bowling, football (non-tackle), racquetball, soccer, softball, table tennis, tennis, volleyball. **Team name:** Titans.

Student services. Adult student services, chaplain/spiritual director, career counseling, student employment services, on-campus daycare, personal counseling, placement for graduates, veterans' counselor. **Physically disabled:** Services for visually, speech, hearing impaired.

Contact. E-mail: admissions@iusb.edu
Phone: (574) 520-4839 Fax: (574) 520-4834
Connie Peterson-Miller, Director of Admissions, Indiana University South Bend, 1700 Mishawaka Avenue, South Bend, IN 46634-7111

Indiana University Southeast
New Albany, Indiana
www.ius.edu

CB member
CB code: 1314

- Public 4-year university
- Commuter campus in large town
- 5,228 degree-seeking undergraduates: 34% part-time, 59% women, 6% African American, 1% Asian American, 4% Hispanic/Latino, 3% Multiracial, non-Hispanic
- 349 degree-seeking graduate students
- 85% of applicants admitted
- SAT or ACT with writing required
- 32% graduate within 6 years

General. Founded in 1941. Regionally accredited. **Degrees:** 864 bachelor's, 59 associate awarded; master's offered. **ROTC:** Army, Air Force. **Location:** 10 miles from Louisville. **Calendar:** Semester, limited summer session. **Full-time faculty:** 211 total; 73% have terminal degrees, 17% minority, 52% women. **Part-time faculty:** 272 total; 20% have terminal degrees, 9% minority, 60% women. **Class size:** 50% < 20, 45% 20-39, 4% 40-49, less than 1% 50-99. **Special facilities:** Cultural and community center.

Freshman class profile. 1,930 applied, 1,632 admitted, 926 enrolled.

Mid 50% test scores			
SAT critical reading:	420-530	GPA 3.0-3.49:	32%
SAT math:	410-520	GPA 2.0-2.99:	40%
SAT writing:	410-510	Rank in top quarter:	31%
ACT composite:	18-23	Rank in top tenth:	9%
GPA 3.75 or higher:	14%	Return as sophomores:	62%
GPA 3.50-3.74:	13%	Out-of-state:	22%
		Live on campus:	21%

Basis for selection. Core 40 with Academic Honors diploma or Core 40 with Technical Honors; 3.0 GPA and Core 40 diploma (or 28 college preparatory high school courses for non-Indiana residents and those graduating prior to 2011); 2.5 GPA and 950 SAT or 20 ACT and Core 40 diploma (or 28 college preparatory high school courses for non-Indiana residents) required. Conditional admission may be offered to students who are not eligible for full admission. Interview recommended.

High school preparation. College-preparatory program required. 20 units required. Required and recommended units include English 4, mathematics 3, social studies 3, science 3 (laboratory 3), foreign language 2 and academic electives 7. High school graduates from Indiana are expected to complete the Core 40 curriculum. Out-of-state students are expected to complete a minimum of 28 semester hours of college preparatory courses.

2015-2016 Annual costs. Tuition/fees: $6,949; $18,379 out-of-state. Room only: $6,410. Books/supplies: $1,148. Personal expenses: $2,096.

2014-2015 Financial aid. Need-based: 822 full-time freshmen applied for aid; 646 deemed to have need; 622 received aid. Average need met was 60%. Average scholarship/grant was $6,628; average loan $3,077. 53% of total undergraduate aid awarded as scholarships/grants, 47% as loans/jobs. **Non-need-based:** Awarded to 372 full-time undergraduates, including 124 freshmen. Scholarships awarded for academics, art, athletics, leadership, minority status, music/drama.

Application procedures. Admission: Priority date 8/17; no deadline. $35 fee, may be waived for applicants with need. Admission notification on a rolling basis. **Financial aid:** Closing date 3/10. FAFSA required. Applicants notified on a rolling basis starting 5/1; must reply within 3 week(s) of notification.

Academics. Special study options: Accelerated study, cross-registration, distance learning, double major, dual enrollment of high school students, ESL, external degree, honors, independent study, internships, student-designed major, study abroad, teacher certification program, weekend college. Member of Metroversity consortium of institutions of higher education in Louisville area. **Credit/placement by examination:** AP, CLEP, IB, institutional tests. **Support services:** Reduced course load, remedial instruction, study skills assistance, tutoring, writing center.

Majors. Biology: General. **Business:** General. **Communications:** Communications/speech/rhetoric, journalism. **Computer sciences:** Computer science, informatics. **Education:** Biology, elementary, English, mathematics, secondary, social studies, special ed. **English:** English lit. **Foreign languages:** French, German, Spanish. **Health services:** Clinical lab science, health information management, nursing (RN). **History:** General. **Math:** General. **Philosophy/religion:** Philosophy. **Physical sciences:** Chemistry, physics. **Protective services:** Criminal justice. **Psychology:** General. **Social sciences:** Economics, geography, international relations, political science, sociology. **Visual/performing arts:** Art, music, studio arts.

Most popular majors. Business/marketing 18%, education 11%, health sciences 12%, liberal arts 11%, psychology 10%, security/protective services 6%, social sciences 6%.

Technology on campus. 924 workstations in dormitories, library, computer center, student center. Dormitories wired for high-speed internet access and linked to campus network. Commuter students can connect to campus network. Online course registration, online library, helpline, student web hosting, wireless network available.

Student life. Freshman orientation: Mandatory, $50 fee. Preregistration for classes offered. Day-long event held April-August. **Housing:** Apartments available. $175 partly refundable deposit. **Activities:** Bands, choral groups, dance, drama, international student organizations, literary magazine, music ensembles, Model UN, student government, student newspaper, symphony orchestra, Asian Pop Culture, Christian Student Fellowship, Civil Liberties Union, College Democrats, College Republicans, Gamer's Society, Gay Straight Alliance, Model United Nations, Student Veterans Organization, Young Americans for Liberty.

Athletics. NAIA. **Intercollegiate:** Baseball M, basketball, softball W, tennis, volleyball W. **Intramural:** Basketball, football (non-tackle), golf, sand volleyball, soccer, softball, ultimate frisbee, volleyball, weight lifting M. **Team name:** Grenadiers.

Student services. Adult student services, alcohol/substance abuse counseling, chaplain/spiritual director, career counseling, student employment services, financial aid counseling, minority student services, on-campus daycare, personal counseling, placement for graduates, veterans' counselor. **Physically disabled:** Services for visually, speech, hearing impaired.

Contact. E-mail: admissions@ius.edu
Phone: (812) 941-2212 Toll-free number: (800) 852-8835
Fax: (812) 941-2595
Chris Crews, Director of Admission, Indiana University Southeast, 4201 Grant Line Road, New Albany, IN 47150-6405

Indiana University-Purdue University Fort Wayne

Fort Wayne, Indiana
www.ipfw.edu

CB member
CB code: 1336

- Public 4-year university and branch campus college
- Commuter campus in large city
- 8,746 degree-seeking undergraduates
- SAT or ACT (ACT writing optional) required

General. Founded in 1964. Regionally accredited. Degrees awarded through Indiana University or Purdue University, depending on course of study. **Degrees:** 1,374 bachelor's, 231 associate awarded; master's offered. **ROTC:** Army. **Location:** 110 miles from Indianapolis. **Calendar:** Semester, limited summer session. **Full-time faculty:** 403 total; 85% have terminal degrees, 22% minority, 44% women. **Part-time faculty:** 411 total; 11% have terminal degrees, 53% women. **Class size:** 49% < 20, 44% 20-39, 3% 40-49, 3% 50-99, less than 1% >100. **Special facilities:** Lake biological research station.

Freshman class profile.

GPA 3.75 or higher:	18%	Rank in top quarter:	38%
GPA 3.50-3.74:	15%	Rank in top tenth:	14%
GPA 3.0-3.49:	31%	Out-of-state:	5%
GPA 2.0-2.99:	36%	Live on campus:	23%

Basis for selection. Class rank should be in top half of high school class and a greater than 2.8 cumulative GPA. TOEFL or Michigan Test may be used to assess English proficiency. Audition required of music majors. Portfolio required of visual arts majors. **Home schooled:** Transcript of courses and grades required.

High school preparation. College-preparatory program required. 20 units required. Required units include English 4, mathematics 3, social studies 3, science 3, foreign language 2 and academic electives 5. Additional requirements vary by program.

2015-2016 Annual costs. Tuition/fees: $8,080; $19,408 out-of-state. Room only: $5,980. Books/supplies: $1,400. Personal expenses: $1,000.

2014-2015 Financial aid. **Need-based:** 1,354 full-time freshmen applied for aid; 1,099 deemed to have need; 1,003 received aid. Average need met was 47%. Average scholarship/grant was $4,566; average loan $2,936. 45% of total undergraduate aid awarded as scholarships/grants, 55% as loans/jobs. **Non-need-based:** Awarded to 1,613 full-time undergraduates, including 522 freshmen. Scholarships awarded for academics, alumni affiliation, art, athletics, leadership, minority status, music/drama, ROTC, state residency.

Application procedures. **Admission:** Closing date 8/1. $50 fee, may be waived for applicants with need. Admission notification on a rolling basis beginning on or about 11/1. **Financial aid:** Priority date 3/10; no closing date. FAFSA required. Applicants notified on a rolling basis starting 4/1; must reply within 3 week(s) of notification.

Academics. **Special study options:** Accelerated study, cooperative education, distance learning, double major, dual enrollment of high school students, ESL, exchange student, honors, independent study, internships, liberal arts/career combination, student-designed major, study abroad, teacher certification program, Washington semester, weekend college. **Credit/placement by examination:** AP, CLEP, IB, institutional tests. Hours of credit awarded by examination varies by program. **Support services:** Learning center, preadmission summer program, remedial instruction, study skills assistance, tutoring, writing center.

Majors. **Area/ethnic studies:** Women's. **Biology:** General. **Business:** General, accounting, business admin, finance, hospitality admin, hotel/motel admin, labor relations, managerial economics, marketing, operations. **Communications:** Communications/speech/rhetoric. **Computer sciences:** General, information technology. **Education:** Art, biology, chemistry, elementary, English, French, German, history, mathematics, music, physics, science, secondary, social studies, Spanish, speech. **Engineering:** Civil, computer, electrical, mechanical. **English:** British lit, English lit, technical writing, writing. **Foreign languages:** French, German, Spanish. **Health services:** Audiology/speech pathology, clinical lab science, clinical lab technology, community health services, health care admin, health services admin, mental health services, music therapy, nursing (RN), predental, premedicine, preveterinary, substance abuse counseling. **History:** General. **Human services:** General, public policy. **Math:** General, computational, statistics. **Philosophy/religion:** Philosophy. **Physical sciences:** Chemistry, geology, physics. **Psychology:** General. **Social sciences:** Anthropology, economics, political science, sociology. **Visual/performing arts:** Art, commercial/advertising art, crafts, dramatic, drawing, graphic design, interior design, music, music performance, painting, photography, piano/keyboard, printmaking, sculpture, studio arts, voice/opera.

Most popular majors. Business/marketing 16%, engineering/engineering technologies 11%, health sciences 13%, liberal arts 15%, psychology 6%, public administration/social services 7%, visual/performing arts 6%.

Technology on campus. 642 workstations in dormitories, library, computer center, student center. Dormitories wired for high-speed internet access and linked to campus network. Commuter students can connect to campus network. Online course registration, online library, helpline, repair service, student web hosting, wireless network available.

Student life. **Freshman orientation:** Mandatory, $30 fee. Preregistration for classes offered. Eight-hour program; 15 dates available between June and August; Freshmen Fest held 2 days in late August. **Housing:** Apartments available. $150 fully refundable deposit. **Activities:** Bands, campus ministries, choral groups, dance, drama, film society, international student organizations, literary magazine, music ensembles, musical theater, opera, student government, student newspaper, symphony orchestra, TV station, Hispanos Unidos, InterVarsity Christian Fellowship, Bangladesh student association, College Republicans, University Democrats, Global Christian Fellowship, Free Bible Now, Campus Ministry, Vietnamese Student Association, Campus Atheists and Agnostics.

Athletics. NCAA. **Intercollegiate:** Baseball M, basketball, cross-country, golf, soccer, softball W, tennis, track and field W, volleyball. **Intramural:** Basketball, football (non-tackle), golf, racquetball, sand volleyball, soccer, softball W, tennis, ultimate frisbee, volleyball. **Team name:** Mastodons.

Student services. Adult student services, alcohol/substance abuse counseling, chaplain/spiritual director, career counseling, student employment services, financial aid counseling, health services, minority student services, personal counseling, placement for graduates, veterans' counselor, women's services. **Physically disabled:** Services for visually, speech, hearing impaired.

Contact. E-mail: ask@ipfw.edu
Phone: (260) 481-6812 Toll-free number: (800) 324-4739
Fax: (260) 481-5450
Tonishea Jackson, Director of Admissions, Indiana University-Purdue University Fort Wayne, 2101 East Coliseum Boulevard, Fort Wayne, IN 46805-1499

Indiana University-Purdue University Indianapolis

Indianapolis, Indiana
www.iupui.edu

CB member
CB code: 1325

- Public 4-year university
- Commuter campus in very large city
- 21,217 degree-seeking undergraduates: 20% part-time, 56% women, 10% African American, 4% Asian American, 6% Hispanic/Latino, 4% Multi-racial, non-Hispanic, 4% international
- 7,827 degree-seeking graduate students
- 70% of applicants admitted
- SAT or ACT with writing required
- 45% graduate within 6 years

General. Founded in 1969. Regionally accredited. **Degrees:** 3,922 bachelor's, 126 associate awarded; master's, professional, doctoral offered. **ROTC:** Army, Air Force. **Calendar:** Semester, extensive summer session. **Full-time faculty:** 2,269 total; 84% have terminal degrees, 23% minority, 41% women. **Part-time faculty:** 1,058 total; 29% have terminal degrees, 14% minority, 52% women. **Class size:** 37% < 20, 44% 20-39, 8% 40-49, 9% 50-99, 2% >100.

Freshman class profile. 13,529 applied, 9,425 admitted, 3,929 enrolled.

Mid 50% test scores		GPA 3.0-3.49:	43%
SAT critical reading:	440-560	GPA 2.0-2.99:	17%
SAT math:	450-560	Rank in top quarter:	43%
SAT writing:	430-540	Rank in top tenth:	15%
ACT composite:	19-25	Return as sophomores:	74%
GPA 3.75 or higher:	22%	Out-of-state:	3%
GPA 3.50-3.74:	18%	Live on campus:	36%

Basis for selection. Admissions committee looks for students who have excelled in the completion of a rigorous high school curriculum and has achieved outstanding performance on the SAT/ACT. Portfolio recommended for some art applicants. **Home schooled:** Transcript of courses and grades required.

High school preparation. College-preparatory program required. 20 units required. Required and recommended units include English 4, mathematics 3, social studies 3, science 3 (laboratory 3), foreign language 3 and academic electives 7. The units of academic electives can be a combination of additional mathematics, laboratory science, social science, computer science, foreign language, or other courses of college preparatory nature.

2015-2016 Annual costs. Tuition/fees: $9,056; $29,774 out-of-state. Room/board: $8,154. Books/supplies: $1,148. Personal expenses: $2,096.

2014-2015 Financial aid. Need-based: 3,431 full-time freshmen applied for aid; 2,644 deemed to have need; 2,552 received aid. Average need met was 68%. Average scholarship/grant was $9,403; average loan $3,306. 55% of total undergraduate aid awarded as scholarships/grants, 45% as loans/jobs. **Non-need-based:** Awarded to 2,561 full-time undergraduates, including 680 freshmen. Scholarships awarded for academics, ROTC.

Application procedures. Admission: Closing date 5/1. $55 fee, may be waived for applicants with need. Admission notification on a rolling basis. Must reply by May 1 or within 3 week(s) if notified thereafter. Application deadlines for nursing and allied health programs range from October 15 to February 1. **Financial aid:** Priority date 3/10; no closing date. FAFSA required. Applicants notified on a rolling basis starting 4/1.

Academics. Special study options: Accelerated study, cooperative education, cross-registration, distance learning, double major, dual enrollment of high school students, ESL, exchange student, external degree, honors, independent study, internships, liberal arts/career combination, student-designed major, study abroad, teacher certification program. **Credit/placement by examination:** AP, CLEP, IB, SAT, ACT, institutional tests. Policy varies by school. **Support services:** Learning center, reduced course load, remedial instruction, tutoring, writing center.

Majors. Area/ethnic studies: African-American. **Biology:** General, biotechnology, neuroscience. **Business:** General, labor studies, operations, tourism/travel. **Communications:** Communications/speech/rhetoric, digital media, journalism, technical/scientific. **Computer sciences:** Computer science, informatics. **Conservation:** Environmental science. **Education:** Art, elementary, English, social studies, Spanish. **Engineering:** General, biomedical, computer, electrical, mechanical. **English:** English lit. **Foreign languages:** French, German, sign language interpretation, Spanish. **Health services:** Clinical lab science, cytotechnology, health care admin, health information management, health services admin, medical radiologic technology/radiation therapy, nuclear medical technology, nursing (RN), premedicine, prepharmacy, preveterinary, radiation protection, respiratory therapy technology. **History:** General. **Human services:** General, social work. **Math:** General. **Parks/recreation:** Exercise sciences. **Philosophy/religion:** Philosophy, religion. **Physical sciences:** Chemistry, geology, physics. **Protective services:** Criminal justice, forensics. **Psychology:** General. **Social sciences:** Anthropology, economics, geography, international relations, political science, sociology. **Visual/performing arts:** Art history/conservation, interior design, music technology, studio arts.

Most popular majors. Business/marketing 15%, engineering/engineering technologies 8%, health sciences 19%, liberal arts 9%.

Technology on campus. 1,158 workstations in dormitories, library, computer center, student center. Dormitories wired for high-speed internet access and linked to campus network. Commuter students can connect to campus network. Online course registration, online library, helpline, repair service, student web hosting, wireless network available.

Student life. Freshman orientation: Mandatory, $110 fee. Preregistration for classes offered. **Policies:** Smoking policy, code of conduct. **Housing:** Coed dorms, special housing for disabled, apartments, themed housing, wellness housing available. $50 nonrefundable deposit, deadline 5/1. **Activities:** Bands, campus ministries, dance, drama, film society, international student organizations, literary magazine, music ensembles, Model UN, student government, student newspaper, Amateur Radio Association, Campus Coalition Against Trafficking, Cosplay club, forensic science club, Global Medical and Dental Brigades, International club, mock trial club, robotics club, Swing Cats, Timmy Global Health.

Athletics. NCAA. **Intercollegiate:** Basketball, cheerleading, cross-country, diving, golf, soccer, softball W, swimming, tennis, track and field, volleyball W. **Intramural:** Basketball, football (non-tackle), golf, racquetball, soccer, softball, ultimate frisbee, volleyball, water polo. **Team name:** Jaguars.

Student services. Adult student services, chaplain/spiritual director, career counseling, student employment services, financial aid counseling, health services, minority student services, on-campus daycare, personal counseling, placement for graduates, veterans' counselor, women's services. **Physically disabled:** Services for visually, speech, hearing impaired.

Contact. E-mail: apply@iupui.edu
Phone: (317) 274-4591 Fax: (317) 278-1862
Yohlunda Mosley, Director of Undergraduate Admissions, Indiana University-Purdue University Indianapolis, 420 University Boulevard, CE 255, Indianapolis, IN 46202-5143

Indiana Wesleyan University
Marion, Indiana
www.indwes.edu   **CB code: 1446**

- Private 4-year university and liberal arts college affiliated with the Wesleyan Church
- Residential campus in large town
- 2,752 degree-seeking undergraduates: 2% part-time, 66% women, 3% African American, 1% Asian American, 4% Hispanic/Latino, 3% Multiracial, non-Hispanic, 1% international
- 230 degree-seeking graduate students
- 96% of applicants admitted
- SAT or ACT (ACT writing recommended), application essay required
- 65% graduate within 6 years

General. Founded in 1920. Regionally accredited. **Degrees:** 663 bachelor's, 2 associate awarded; master's, doctoral offered. **ROTC:** Army. **Location:** 65 miles from Indianapolis, 57 miles from Fort Wayne. **Calendar:** Semester, extensive summer session. **Full-time faculty:** 160 total; 77% have terminal degrees, 10% minority, 43% women. **Part-time faculty:** 106 total; 21% have terminal degrees, 4% minority, 49% women. **Class size:** 66% < 20, 27% 20-39, 5% 40-49, 2% 50-99, less than 1% >100.

Freshman class profile. 2,444 applied, 2,340 admitted, 656 enrolled.

Mid 50% test scores			
SAT critical reading:	470-590	GPA 3.0-3.49:	28%
SAT math:	460-590	GPA 2.0-2.99:	11%
SAT writing:	450-570	Rank in top quarter:	58%
ACT composite:	21-27	Rank in top tenth:	30%
GPA 3.75 or higher:	44%	Return as sophomores:	82%
GPA 3.50-3.74:	17%	Out-of-state:	54%
		Live on campus:	97%

Basis for selection. 2.6 GPA and 880 SAT (Math and Critical Reading) or 18 ACT required to qualify for regular admission. Applicants who do not meet the requirements for regular admission may request special consideration. Interested students are encouraged to apply for admission at the close of their junior year in high school. Audition recommended for music majors. Portfolio required for art majors. **Home schooled:** Transcript of courses and grades, letter of recommendation (nonparent) required. Transcript must have GPA on 4.0 scale. Recommendation from pastor required.

High school preparation. College-preparatory program recommended. 21 units recommended. Recommended units include English 4, mathematics 3, social studies 3, science 3, foreign language 2 and academic electives 5. 1 unit of Health/PE.

2015-2016 Annual costs. Tuition/fees: $24,728. Room/board: $7,988. Books/supplies: $1,392. Personal expenses: $1,558.

2014-2015 Financial aid. Need-based: 626 full-time freshmen applied for aid; 538 deemed to have need; 538 received aid. Average need met was 93%. Average scholarship/grant was $8,673; average loan $3,772. 62% of total undergraduate aid awarded as scholarships/grants, 38% as loans/jobs. **Non-need-based:** Awarded to 1,783 full-time undergraduates, including 600 freshmen. Scholarships awarded for academics, alumni affiliation, art, athletics, music/drama, ROTC.

Application procedures. Admission: Priority date 3/1; no deadline. No application fee. Admission notification on a rolling basis beginning on or about 9/1. **Financial aid:** Closing date 3/10. FAFSA, institutional form required. Applicants notified on a rolling basis starting 3/10.

Academics. Special study options: Accelerated study, cross-registration, distance learning, double major, honors, independent study, internships, New York semester, semester at sea, study abroad, teacher certification program, United Nations semester, urban semester, Washington semester. **Credit/placement by examination:** AP, CLEP, SAT, ACT, institutional tests. 18 credit hours maximum toward associate degree, 40 toward bachelor's. Credit through examination (CLEP/DANTES/Advance Placement) may only be awarded with official test scores from an official testing center and an Indiana Wesleyan University individual assessment. The maximum number of credits awarded shall be limited to a total of 40 semester hours for the baccalaureate degrees and 18 semester hours for the associate degrees, and ordinarily will not be applied to upper-division requirements in the major (junior and senior levels). It is the responsibility of the student to obtain approval from the appropriate division for the application of credits to the majors. The College of Arts and Sciences does not accept the College Composition CLEP test. **Support services:** Learning center, reduced course load, remedial instruction, study skills assistance, tutoring, writing center.

Honors college/program. Combined SAT score of 1320 or higher (Math/Critical Reading), combined SAT score of 1980 or higher (Math/Critical Reading/Writing), composite ACT score of 30 or higher, rank in the top 10

Four-Year Colleges

percent of graduating class, GPA of 3.7 or higher (on a 4.0 scale); 30 selected. Honors College students must have a willingness to engage in a learning community and a transformative education that goes well beyond knowledge accumulation and career preparation.

Majors. Biology: General, Biochemistry/molecular biology, exercise physiology. **Business:** Accounting, business admin, entrepreneurial studies, finance, managerial economics, marketing, organizational behavior. **Communications:** General, communications/speech/rhetoric, journalism, media studies, persuasive communications, public relations. **Computer sciences:** Computer graphics, computer science, information technology, programming, web page design. **Education:** Art, business, elementary, English, mathematics, middle, music, physical, science, secondary, social studies. **Engineering:** Pre-engineering, software. **English:** English lit, writing. **Foreign languages:** Spanish. **Health services:** Athletic training, nursing (RN), predental, premedicine, prepharmacy, preveterinary, substance abuse counseling. **History:** General. **Human services:** Public policy, social work. **Math:** General. **Parks/recreation:** Facilities management, sports admin. **Philosophy/religion:** General. **Physical sciences:** Chemistry. **Protective services:** Criminal justice. **Psychology:** General. **Social sciences:** General, economics, international relations, political science, sociology. **Theology:** Bible, pastoral counseling, religious ed, sacred music, theology, youth ministry. **Visual/performing arts:** Ceramics, drawing, game design, interior design, music, music theory/composition, painting, photography, printmaking, studio arts, theater arts management.

Most popular majors. Business/marketing 12%, education 11%, health sciences 26%, psychology 7%, theological studies 8%, visual/performing arts 7%.

Technology on campus. 823 workstations in dormitories, library, computer center, student center. Dormitories wired for high-speed internet access and linked to campus network. Commuter students can connect to campus network. Online course registration, online library, helpline, repair service, wireless network available.

Student life. Freshman orientation: Mandatory. Preregistration for classes offered. Held the weekend before the semester begins. **Policies:** Weekly chapel attendance required. Religious observance required. **Housing:** Guaranteed on-campus for all undergraduates. Single-sex dorms, special housing for disabled, apartments, themed housing, wellness housing available. $100 fully refundable deposit, deadline 8/15. **Activities:** Bands, campus ministries, choral groups, dance, drama, film society, international student organizations, literary magazine, music ensembles, Model UN, musical theater, opera, radio station, student government, student newspaper, symphony orchestra, TV station, Creation Care Alliance, Divine Purpose Gospel Choir, Doulos (Acting on AIDS), student activities council, World Christian Fellowship, La Amistad Hispanica, College Republicans.

Athletics. NAIA, NCCAA. **Intercollegiate:** Baseball M, basketball, cross-country, golf, soccer, softball W, swimming W, tennis, track and field, volleyball W. **Intramural:** Badminton, basketball, bowling, football (non-tackle), golf, racquetball, soccer, softball, swimming, table tennis, tennis, volleyball, weight lifting. **Team name:** Wildcats.

Student services. Adult student services, alcohol/substance abuse counseling, chaplain/spiritual director, career counseling, services for economically disadvantaged, student employment services, financial aid counseling, health services, minority student services, personal counseling, placement for graduates, veterans' counselor. **Physically disabled:** Services for visually, speech, hearing impaired.

Contact. E-mail: admissions@indwes.edu
Phone: (765) 677-2138 Toll-free number: (866) 468-6498
Fax: (765) 677-2333
Adam Farmer, Director of Admissions, Indiana Wesleyan University, 4201 South Washington Street, Marion, IN 46953-4999

International Business College
Fort Wayne, Indiana
www.ibcfortwayne.edu   CB code: 1330

▶ For-profit 4-year business and community college
▶ Small city
▶ 406 undergraduates
▶ Interview required

General. Founded in 1889. Accredited by ACICS. Branch campus located in Indianapolis. **Degrees:** 64 bachelor's, 160 associate awarded. **Location:** 4 miles from downtown. **Calendar:** Semester, extensive summer session. **Full-time faculty:** 15 total. **Part-time faculty:** 9 total.

Freshman class profile.

Out-of-state: 30% **Live on campus:**   45%

Basis for selection. Open admission, but selective for some programs. Each applicant's academic record is reviewed.

2015-2016 Annual costs. Tuition/fees: $13,920. Books/supplies: $900. **Additional information:** Estimated costs of books and supplies vary depending upon degree program and can range from $700 to $4,400. All costs, including tuition, are subject to change.

Application procedures. Admission: No deadline. $50 fee. Admission notification on a rolling basis. **Financial aid:** Closing date 5/1. Applicants notified by 9/15.

Academics. Special study options: Internships. **Credit/placement by examination:** AP, CLEP. **Support services:** Tutoring.

Majors. Business: General, business admin.

Technology on campus. 146 workstations in library, computer center. Wireless network available.

Student life. Freshman orientation: Available. Preregistration for classes offered. **Housing:** College maintains non-campus housing accommodations. **Activities:** Student government, accounting club, secretarial club, medical assistants club, veterinary technicians club.

Student services. Career counseling, student employment services, personal counseling, placement for graduates.

Contact. E-mail: admission@ibcfortwayne.edu
Phone: (260) 459-4500 Toll-free number: (800) 589-6363
Fax: (260) 436-1896
Gena Hopkins, Director of Admissions, International Business College, 5699 Coventry Lane, Fort Wayne, IN 46804

ITT Technical Institute: Fort Wayne
Fort Wayne, Indiana
www.itt-tech.edu   CB code: 0650

▶ For-profit 4-year technical college
▶ Commuter campus in large city
▶ 220 undergraduates
▶ Interview required

General. Founded in 1967. Accredited by ACICS. **Degrees:** 28 bachelor's, 76 associate awarded. **Location:** 122 miles from Indianapolis. **Calendar:** Quarter, extensive summer session. **Full-time faculty:** 10 total. **Part-time faculty:** 33 total.

Basis for selection. Satisfactory scores from on-site tests in English and mathematics required.

2015-2016 Annual costs. Per-credit-hour charge, $493. Required fees: $200. Some programs require purchase of tools, which could cost an additional $100 to $655, depending on program. All costs subject to change.

Application procedures. Admission: No deadline. No application fee. Admission notification on a rolling basis. **Financial aid:** No deadline. FAFSA, institutional form required. Applicants notified on a rolling basis.

Academics. Credit/placement by examination: AP, CLEP. **Support services:** Learning center, tutoring.

Majors. Business: Accounting technology, business admin, construction management, e-commerce. **Communications technology:** Animation/special effects. **Computer sciences:** Programming, security, system admin. **Protective services:** Law enforcement admin.

Technology on campus. Online library available.

Student life. Freshman orientation: Available. Preregistration for classes offered.

Student services. Career counseling, student employment services, placement for graduates.

Contact. Phone: (260) 484-4107 Toll-free number: (800) 866-4488
Fax: (260) 484-0860
Mike Frantom, Director of Recruitment, ITT Technical Institute: Fort Wayne, 2810 Dupont Commerce Court, Fort Wayne, IN 46825

ITT Technical Institute: Indianapolis
Indianapolis, Indiana
www.itt-tech.edu   **CB code: 0640**

- For-profit 4-year technical college
- Commuter campus in very large city
- 3,407 undergraduates
- 140 graduate students
- Interview required

General. Founded in 1956. Accredited by ACICS. **Degrees:** 372 bachelor's, 813 associate awarded; master's offered. **Location:** 10 miles from downtown. **Calendar:** Quarter, extensive summer session. **Full-time faculty:** 19 total. **Part-time faculty:** 376 total.

Basis for selection. Satisfactory score from on-site tests in English and mathematics required.

2015-2016 Annual costs. Per-credit-hour charge ranges $426-$493 depending on program level and course of study; academic fee, $200. Some programs require purchase of tools, which could cost an additional $100 to $675. All costs subject to change.

Application procedures. Admission: No deadline. No application fee. Admission notification on a rolling basis. **Financial aid:** No deadline. FAFSA, institutional form required. Applicants notified on a rolling basis.

Academics. Special study options: Distance learning. **Credit/placement by examination:** AP, CLEP. **Support services:** Learning center, tutoring.

Majors. Business: Accounting technology, business admin, construction management, e-commerce. **Communications technology:** Animation/special effects. **Computer sciences:** Programming, security. **Protective services:** Law enforcement admin.

Technology on campus. Online library available.

Student life. Freshman orientation: Available. Preregistration for classes offered.

Student services. Career counseling, student employment services, placement for graduates. **Physically disabled:** Services for speech impaired.

Contact. Phone: (317) 875-8640 Toll-free number: (800) 937-4488 Fax: (317) 875-8641
Greg Goralski, Director of Recruitment, ITT Technical Institute: Indianapolis, 9511 Angola Court, Indianapolis, IN 46268-1119

Manchester University
North Manchester, Indiana   **CB member**
www.manchester.edu   **CB code: 1440**

- Private 4-year pharmacy and liberal arts college affiliated with the Church of the Brethren
- Residential campus in small town
- 1,239 degree-seeking undergraduates: 1% part-time, 52% women, 6% African American, 1% Asian American, 6% Hispanic/Latino, 3% Multi-racial, non-Hispanic, 3% international
- 290 degree-seeking graduate students
- 74% of applicants admitted
- 55% graduate within 6 years

General. Founded in 1889. Regionally accredited. **Degrees:** 249 bachelor's awarded; master's, professional offered. **Location:** 35 miles from Fort Wayne, 100 miles from Indianapolis. **Calendar:** 4-1-4, limited summer session. **Full-time faculty:** 82 total; 87% have terminal degrees, 10% minority, 43% women. **Part-time faculty:** 17 total; 24% have terminal degrees, 41% women. **Class size:** 56% < 20, 42% 20-39, 1% 40-49, less than 1% 50-99. **Special facilities:** Observatory, 100-acre environmental studies and retreat center.

Freshman class profile. 2,822 applied, 2,079 admitted, 396 enrolled.

Mid 50% test scores			
		GPA 3.0-3.49:	30%
SAT critical reading:	430-550	**GPA 2.0-2.99:**	27%
SAT math:	440-550	**Rank in top quarter:**	44%
SAT writing:	410-530	**Rank in top tenth:**	15%
ACT composite:	19-26	**Return as sophomores:**	69%
GPA 3.75 or higher:	26%	**Out-of-state:**	13%
GPA 3.50-3.74:	17%	**Live on campus:**	94%

Basis for selection. School achievement record most important, with emphasis on college-preparatory courses, followed by SAT or ACT scores, class rank, recommendations. SAT or ACT recommended. Essay recommended for academically borderline applicants. Audition recommended for music majors. **Home schooled:** Provide full information in detailed cover letter with application. **Learning Disabled:** School reviews ability to meet student needs.

High school preparation. College-preparatory program required. 14 units required; 22 recommended. Required and recommended units include English 4, mathematics 2-3, social studies 1-2, history 1-2, science 2-3 (laboratory 2), foreign language 2, computer science 1, visual/performing arts 1 and academic electives 2.

2016-2017 Annual costs. Tuition/fees: $30,802. Room/board: $9,620. Books/supplies: $1,000. Personal expenses: $776.

2015-2016 Financial aid. Need-based: Average need met was 85%. Average scholarship/grant was $22,106; average loan $3,337. 75% of total undergraduate aid awarded as scholarships/grants, 25% as loans/jobs. **Non-need-based:** Scholarships awarded for academics, alumni affiliation, leadership, minority status, music/drama, religious affiliation. **Additional information:** Students automatically considered for all scholarship programs.

Application procedures. Admission: Priority date 12/31; no deadline. $25 fee, may be waived for applicants with need, free for online applicants. Admission notification on a rolling basis beginning on or about 9/1. Must reply by May 1 or within 3 week(s) if notified thereafter. For deferred admission, maximum period of postponement is 1 year. **Financial aid:** Priority date 3/1; no closing date. FAFSA required. Applicants notified on a rolling basis starting 3/20.

Academics. Students required to earn 2 credits in Values, Ideas and the Arts. **Special study options:** Accelerated study, combined bachelor's/graduate degree, distance learning, double major, dual enrollment of high school students, exchange student, honors, independent study, internships, liberal arts/career combination, student-designed major, study abroad, teacher certification program, urban semester. 3-1 medical technology programs with area hospitals, 3-2 engineering dual-degree program with Washington University (MO) and others. **Credit/placement by examination:** AP, CLEP, IB, SAT, ACT, institutional tests. First year students take college proficiency tests to place out of the first year of modern language. Unlimited credit hours by examination may be counted toward associate or bachelor's degree. **Support services:** Learning center, reduced course load, study skills assistance, tutoring, writing center.

Majors. Area/ethnic studies: Women's. **Biology:** General, biochemistry, environmental. **Business:** General, accounting, business admin, finance, marketing. **Communications:** Broadcast journalism, communications/speech/rhetoric, journalism, media studies. **Computer sciences:** General, computer science. **Conservation:** General, environmental studies. **Education:** General, art, biology, chemistry, elementary, English, foreign languages, French, health, history, mathematics, mentally handicapped, middle, multi-level teacher, music, physical, physics, science, secondary, social science, social studies, Spanish, special ed. **Engineering:** General. **English:** English lit. **Foreign languages:** General, French, Spanish. **Health services:** Athletic training, clinical lab science, predental, premedicine, prepharmacy, preveterinary. **History:** General. **Human services:** Social work. **Liberal arts:** Arts/sciences. **Math:** General. **Parks/recreation:** Exercise sciences, sports admin. **Philosophy/religion:** Philosophy, religion. **Physical sciences:** Chemistry, physics. **Protective services:** Criminal justice. **Psychology:** General. **Social sciences:** General, economics, political science, sociology. **Theology:** Preministerial. **Visual/performing arts:** Art, music, music performance, music theory/composition.

Most popular majors. Business/marketing 23%, education 9%, parks/recreation 13%, psychology 7%, public administration/social services 6%.

Technology on campus. 222 workstations in dormitories, library. Dormitories wired for high-speed internet access and linked to campus network. Commuter students can connect to campus network. Online library, helpline, student web hosting, wireless network available.

Student life. Freshman orientation: Mandatory. Preregistration for classes offered. Held the 4 days prior to start of fall classes. **Policies:** Students under 21 required to live on-campus unless living with family. **Housing:** Guaranteed on-campus for freshmen. Coed dorms, single-sex dorms, special housing for disabled, apartments available. $250 fully refundable deposit, deadline 5/1. **Activities:** Bands, campus ministries, choral groups, dance, drama, film society, international student organizations, literary magazine, music ensembles, Model UN, musical theater, opera, radio station, student government, student newspaper, symphony orchestra, Political science club, Black Student Union, Hispanos Unidos, Habitat for Humanity, volunteer corps, Intercollegiate Ministries, environmental group, Circle K.

Athletics. NCAA. **Intercollegiate:** Baseball M, basketball, cross-country, equestrian W, football (tackle) M, golf, soccer, softball W, swimming, tennis, track and field, volleyball W, wrestling M. **Intramural:** Basketball, football (non-tackle), soccer, softball, volleyball. **Team name:** Spartans.

Student services. Chaplain/spiritual director, career counseling, student employment services, financial aid counseling, health services, minority student services, personal counseling, placement for graduates, veterans' counselor. **Physically disabled:** Services for visually, hearing impaired.

Contact. E-mail: admitinfo@manchester.edu
Phone: (260) 982-5055 Toll-free number: (800) 852-3648
Fax: (260) 982-5239
Adam Hohman, Director of Admissions, Manchester University, 604 East College Avenue, North Manchester, IN 46962-0365

Marian University
Indianapolis, Indiana   CB member
www.marian.edu   CB code: 1442

- Private 4-year university and liberal arts college affiliated with the Roman Catholic Church
- Residential campus in very large city
- 1,969 degree-seeking undergraduates: 14% part-time, 61% women, 12% African American, 2% Asian American, 5% Hispanic/Latino, 2% Multi-racial, non-Hispanic, 1% international
- 775 degree-seeking graduate students
- 55% of applicants admitted
- SAT or ACT with writing required
- 54% graduate within 6 years; 10% enter graduate study

General. Founded in 1851. Regionally accredited. **Degrees:** 501 bachelor's, 29 associate awarded; master's, professional offered. **ROTC:** Army. **Location:** 4 miles from downtown. **Calendar:** Semester, limited summer session. **Full-time faculty:** 148 total; 68% have terminal degrees, 14% minority, 51% women. **Part-time faculty:** 135 total; 13% have terminal degrees, 8% minority, 64% women. **Class size:** 68% < 20, 31% 20-39, less than 1% 40-49, 1% 50-99. **Special facilities:** Archives (materials on development of education in Archdiocese), 35 acre wetlands biology/ecology laboratory, Allison and Wheeler-Stokely mansions, Japanese tea house and garden, undergraduate seminary.

Freshman class profile. 2,072 applied, 1,148 admitted, 293 enrolled.

Mid 50% test scores		GPA 2.0-2.99:	23%
SAT critical reading:	460-560	Rank in top quarter:	43%
SAT math:	470-560	Rank in top tenth:	18%
SAT writing:	430-540	End year in good standing:	92%
ACT composite:	20-26	Return as sophomores:	79%
GPA 3.75 or higher:	32%	Out-of-state:	18%
GPA 3.50-3.74:	16%	Live on campus:	85%
GPA 3.0-3.49:	29%	International:	1%

Basis for selection. School achievement record, test scores, recommendations important. Interview recommended. Essay recommended for academically weak applicants.

High school preparation. College-preparatory program required. 20 units required; 22 recommended. Required and recommended units include English 4, mathematics 2-3, social studies 1, history 1, science 2-3 (laboratory 2), foreign language 1 and academic electives 9.

2015-2016 Annual costs. Tuition/fees: $30,500. Room/board: $9,436. Books/supplies: $1,200. Personal expenses: $3,748.

Financial aid. Non-need-based: Scholarships awarded for academics, alumni affiliation, art, athletics, leadership, music/drama, religious affiliation.

Application procedures. Admission: Priority date 3/1; deadline 8/1 (receipt date). $35 fee, may be waived for applicants with need, free for online applicants. Admission notification on a rolling basis beginning on or about 9/1. Must reply by May 1 or within 2 week(s) if notified thereafter. **Financial aid:** Closing date 3/15. FAFSA, institutional form required. Applicants notified on a rolling basis starting 3/15; must reply within 2 week(s) of notification.

Academics. Special study options: Accelerated study, cooperative education, cross-registration, distance learning, double major, dual enrollment of high school students, honors, independent study, internships, liberal arts/career combination, study abroad, teacher certification program. **Credit/placement by examination:** AP, CLEP, IB, SAT, ACT, institutional tests. 30 credit hours maximum toward associate degree, 60 toward bachelor's. **Support services:** Learning center, reduced course load, remedial instruction, study skills assistance, tutoring, writing center.

Majors. Biology: General. **Business:** Accounting, business admin, finance, human resources, marketing. **Communications:** Communications/speech/rhetoric. **Education:** General, elementary, leadership, music, physical, secondary, special ed. **English:** English lit. **Foreign languages:** Spanish. **Health services:** Clinical lab science, nursing (RN). **History:** General. **Math:** General. **Parks/recreation:** Exercise sciences, health/fitness, sports admin, **Philosophy/religion:** Christian, philosophy. **Physical sciences:** Chemistry. **Psychology:** General. **Social sciences:** Political science, sociology. **Theology:** Pastoral counseling, religious ed, sacred music, theology. **Visual/performing arts:** Commercial/advertising art, graphic design, music, music performance, studio arts.

Most popular majors. Business/marketing 22%, education 7%, health sciences 49%.

Technology on campus. 118 workstations in dormitories, library, computer center, student center. Dormitories wired for high-speed internet access and linked to campus network. Online course registration, online library, helpline, wireless network available.

Student life. Freshman orientation: Mandatory. Preregistration for classes offered. Held weekend prior to start of school. Community service project required. **Policies:** Drinking under the age of 21 on campus prohibited. **Housing:** Guaranteed on-campus for freshmen. Coed dorms, special housing for disabled, apartments, cooperative housing, themed housing, wellness housing available. $125 fully refundable deposit, deadline 5/1. College-owned apartments for students 21 or older, voluntary spiritual living community, nonsmoking areas, houses, suite-style rooms, singles available. **Activities:** Bands, campus ministries, choral groups, dance, drama, international student organizations, literary magazine, music ensembles, Model UN, musical theater, student government, student newspaper, service organization, community ministries, Union for Black Identity, Fellowship of Christian Athletes, Catholic Relief Services, College Mentors for Kids, international club, Japan and anime culture club, Justice League, Model UN.

Athletics. NAIA. **Intercollegiate:** Baseball M, basketball, bowling, cheerleading, cross-country, football (tackle) M, golf, lacrosse W, soccer, softball W, tennis, track and field, volleyball W. **Intramural:** Basketball, football (non-tackle), racquetball, softball W, ultimate frisbee, volleyball W. **Team name:** Knights.

Student services. Adult student services, alcohol/substance abuse counseling, chaplain/spiritual director, career counseling, student employment services, financial aid counseling, health services, personal counseling, placement for graduates. **Physically disabled:** Services for visually, hearing impaired.

Contact. E-mail: admissions@marian.edu
Phone: (317) 955-6300 Toll-free number: (800) 772-7264
Fax: (317) 955-6401
Luann Brames, Director of Freshmen Admission, Marian University, 3200 Cold Spring Road, Indianapolis, IN 46222-1997

Martin University
Indianapolis, Indiana
www.martin.edu   CB code: 1379

- Private 4-year university and liberal arts college
- Commuter campus in very large city
- 286 degree-seeking undergraduates

General. Founded in 1977. Regionally accredited. **Degrees:** 58 bachelor's awarded; master's offered. **Calendar:** Semester, extensive summer session. **Full-time faculty:** 26 total. **Part-time faculty:** 1 total.

Basis for selection. Open admission.

2015-2016 Annual costs. Tuition/fees: $15,590. Books/supplies: $1,400. Personal expenses: $1,000.

Application procedures. Admission: Priority date 3/1; no deadline. $25 fee, may be waived for applicants with need. Application must be submitted on paper. Admission notification on a rolling basis. **Financial aid:** Priority date 5/1, closing date 6/30. FAFSA required. Applicants notified on a rolling basis starting 6/1; must reply within 2 week(s) of notification.

Academics. Special study options: Accelerated study, cross-registration, double major, internships, liberal arts/career combination, student-designed major. **Credit/placement by examination:** AP, CLEP. **Support services:** Learning center, remedial instruction, study skills assistance, tutoring.

Majors. Biology: General. **Business:** General, accounting, business admin, human resources, insurance. **Conservation:** Environmental science. **Education:** General, early childhood, kindergarten/preschool. **Health services:**

Genetic counseling, substance abuse counseling. **Liberal arts:** Arts/sciences, humanities. **Math:** General. **Philosophy/religion:** Religion. **Physical sciences:** Chemistry. **Protective services:** Criminal justice. **Psychology:** General, counseling. **Social sciences:** General, sociology.

Technology on campus. 14 workstations in computer center.

Student life. Freshman orientation: Available. Preregistration for classes offered. **Activities:** Choral groups, dance, drama, music ensembles, student government.

Student services. Adult student services, career counseling, student employment services, veterans' counselor.

Contact. E-mail: hglinsey@martin.edu
Phone: (317) 917-3308 Fax: (317) 543-4790
Ron Goodwin, Director of Admissions, Martin University, 2171 Avondale Place, Indianapolis, IN 46218

Oakland City University
Oakland City, Indiana
www.oak.edu   CB code: 1585

- Private 4-year university and liberal arts college affiliated with the Baptist General Conference
- Commuter campus in small town
- 539 degree-seeking undergraduates: 42% part-time, 51% women, 9% African American, 2% Hispanic/Latino, 1% Multi-racial, non-Hispanic, 4% international
- 133 degree-seeking graduate students
- 55% of applicants admitted
- 55% graduate within 6 years

General. Founded in 1885. Regionally accredited. Branches in Rockport, Evansville, Bedford, and Plainfield. Accelerated degrees offered at several off-campus sites (National Guard bases and civilian locations). **Degrees:** 155 bachelor's, 49 associate awarded; master's, professional, doctoral offered. **Location:** 30 miles from Evansville. **Calendar:** Semester, limited summer session. **Full-time faculty:** 38 total; 76% have terminal degrees, 10% minority, 50% women. **Part-time faculty:** 165 total; 62% have terminal degrees, 8% minority, 48% women. **Class size:** 91% < 20, 9% 20-39.

Freshman class profile. 832 applied, 460 admitted, 84 enrolled.

Mid 50% test scores			
SAT critical reading:	420-500	GPA 3.0-3.49:	38%
		GPA 2.0-2.99:	39%
SAT math:	410-510	Return as sophomores:	72%
ACT composite:	17-22	Out-of-state:	13%
GPA 3.75 or higher:	7%	Live on campus:	55%
GPA 3.50-3.74:	10%	International:	8%

Basis for selection. 2.5 GPA or average mean score of 450 on GED required. SAT/ACT test scores most important; 1250 on SAT or 18 ACT required. Recommendations considered. Interview and essay recommended. **Home schooled:** Transcript of courses and grades required.

High school preparation. College-preparatory program recommended. 15 units recommended. Recommended units include English 4, mathematics 3, social studies 1, history 2, science 3 (laboratory 1) and foreign language 1.

2015-2016 Annual costs. Tuition/fees: $22,800. Room/board: $9,030. Books/supplies: $1,400. Personal expenses: $5,569.

2014-2015 Financial aid. Need-based: 74 full-time freshmen applied for aid; 74 deemed to have need; 74 received aid. Average need met was 70%. Average scholarship/grant was $4,726; average loan $10,907. 57% of total undergraduate aid awarded as scholarships/grants, 43% as loans/jobs. **Non-need-based:** Scholarships awarded for academics, athletics, minority status, religious affiliation.

Application procedures. Admission: No deadline. No application fee. Admission notification on a rolling basis beginning on or about 8/24. Must reply by May 1 or within 4 week(s) if notified thereafter. **Financial aid:** Priority date 3/10; no closing date. FAFSA required. Applicants notified on a rolling basis starting 5/1.

Academics. Special study options: Accelerated study, combined bachelor's/graduate degree, cross-registration, distance learning, double major, dual enrollment of high school students, independent study, internships, liberal arts/career combination, teacher certification program, weekend college. **Credit/placement by examination:** AP, CLEP, IB, institutional tests. 16 credit hours maximum toward associate degree, 32 toward bachelor's. **Support services:** Learning center, pre-admission summer program, reduced

course load, remedial instruction, study skills assistance, tutoring, writing center.

Majors. Biology: General. **Business:** Business admin, operations. **Communications:** General. **Education:** Art, biology, business, early childhood, elementary, English, mathematics, physical, science, social studies, special ed. **English:** English lit. **History:** General. **Liberal arts:** Humanities. **Math:** General. **Parks/recreation:** Health/fitness. **Philosophy/religion:** Religion. **Protective services:** Criminal justice. **Psychology:** General, counseling. **Theology:** Sacred music. **Visual/performing arts:** Art, music.

Most popular majors. Biology 6%, business/marketing 42%, education 13%, security/protective services 19%.

Technology on campus. 200 workstations in library, computer center, student center. Dormitories wired for high-speed internet access and linked to campus network. Commuter students can connect to campus network. Online course registration, online library, helpline, wireless network available.

Student life. Freshman orientation: Mandatory, $75 fee. Preregistration for classes offered. One day immediately before each semester. **Housing:** Guaranteed on-campus for all undergraduates. Single-sex dorms, apartments, wellness housing available. $100 fully refundable deposit, deadline 7/22. **Activities:** Pep band, campus ministries, choral groups, drama, literary magazine, music ensembles, musical theater, student government, student newspaper, Student Government Association, Student Christian Association, FOCUS Missions Club, Psychology Club.

Athletics. NCAA, NCCAA. **Intercollegiate:** Baseball M, basketball, cheerleading W, cross-country, golf, soccer, softball W, tennis, volleyball W. **Intramural:** Basketball, bowling, football (non-tackle), softball, table tennis, tennis, volleyball. **Team name:** Mighty Oaks.

Student services. Adult student services, alcohol/substance abuse counseling, chaplain/spiritual director, career counseling, services for economically disadvantaged, student employment services, financial aid counseling, health services, personal counseling, placement for graduates, veterans' counselor.

Contact. E-mail: ocuadmit@oak.edu
Phone: (812) 749-4781 ext. 222 Toll-free number: (800) 737-5125
Fax: (812) 749-1433
Mariah McDaniel, Director of Admissions, Oakland City University, 138 North Lucretia Street, Oakland City, IN 47660

Purdue University
West Lafayette, Indiana
www.purdue.edu   CB member / CB code: 1631

- Public 4-year university
- Residential campus in small city
- 29,325 degree-seeking undergraduates: 4% part-time, 43% women, 3% African American, 6% Asian American, 4% Hispanic/Latino, 2% Multi-racial, non-Hispanic, 18% international
- 9,635 degree-seeking graduate students
- 59% of applicants admitted
- SAT or ACT with writing, application essay required

General. Founded in 1869. Regionally accredited. **Degrees:** 6,972 bachelor's, 37 associate awarded; master's, professional, doctoral offered. **ROTC:** Army, Naval, Air Force. **Location:** 65 miles from Indianapolis. **Calendar:** Semester, extensive summer session. **Full-time faculty:** 2,256 total; 98% have terminal degrees, 24% minority, 33% women. **Part-time faculty:** 337 total; 87% have terminal degrees, 13% minority, 50% women. **Class size:** 39% < 20, 36% 20-39, 8% 40-49, 12% 50-99, 6% >100. **Special facilities:** Linear accelerator, horticultural park, concert hall, 3 theaters, outdoor concert facility, 2 professional golf courses, on-campus airport, center for data perceptualization.

Freshman class profile. 45,023 applied, 26,524 admitted, 6,812 enrolled.

Mid 50% test scores			
SAT critical reading:	520-630	GPA 3.0-3.49:	18%
SAT math:	560-700	GPA 2.0-2.99:	2%
SAT writing:	520-640	Rank in top quarter:	79%
ACT composite:	25-31	Rank in top tenth:	43%
GPA 3.75 or higher:	55%	Out-of-state:	39%
GPA 3.50-3.74:	25%	Live on campus:	94%
		International:	16%

Basis for selection. Rigor of high school curriculum, standardized test scores, GPA and information provided by both applicant and high school counselor considered. Interview required for veterinary medicine, veterinary technology and pharmacy applicants.

413

High school preparation. College-preparatory program required. 4 units required. Required units include English 4, mathematics 3, science 3 (laboratory 2) and foreign language 3.

2015-2016 Annual costs. Tuition/fees: $10,002; $28,804 out-of-state. Room/board: $10,030. Books/supplies: $1,220. Personal expenses: $1,570. **Additional information:** Differential general service fees: Engineering and new beginning Computer Science undergraduate students pay an additional $2,050 per academic year. Management undergraduate students pay an additional $1,436 per academic year. School of Technology undergraduate students pay an additional $572 per academic year.

2015-2016 Financial aid. **Need-based:** 4,898 full-time freshmen applied for aid; 3,318 deemed to have need; 3,318 received aid. Average need met was 83%. Average scholarship/grant was $13,865; average loan $3,759. 54% of total undergraduate aid awarded as scholarships/grants, 46% as loans/jobs. **Non-need-based:** Awarded to 8,199 full-time undergraduates, including 2,310 freshmen. Scholarships awarded for academics, athletics, leadership, music/drama, ROTC, state residency. **Additional information:** Cooperative work for credit available in many programs. Purdue Promise replaces need based loans with institutional funds after and in conjunction with federal and state eligibility for high-need students; maximum allowable family income is $50,000.

Application procedures. **Admission:** Priority date 2/1; no deadline. $60 fee, may be waived for applicants with need. Application must be submitted online. Admission notification on a rolling basis. Notified by 12/12. Must reply by 5/1. **Financial aid:** Priority date 3/1; no closing date. FAFSA required. Applicants notified by 4/15.

Academics. Minimal number of courses outside major allowed on pass/fail basis, not to exceed 20% of total credit hours required. **Special study options:** Accelerated study, combined bachelor's/graduate degree, cooperative education, cross-registration, distance learning, double major, dual enrollment of high school students, ESL, honors, independent study, internships, liberal arts/career combination, New York semester, study abroad, teacher certification program, weekend college. **Credit/placement by examination:** AP, CLEP, IB, SAT, ACT, institutional tests. **Support services:** Learning center, pre-admission summer program, reduced course load, remedial instruction, study skills assistance, tutoring, writing center.

Majors. **Architecture:** Landscape. **Area/ethnic studies:** African-American, Asian, French, German, Japanese, women's. **Biology:** General, biochemistry, Biochemistry/molecular biology, botany, cellular/molecular, entomology, microbiology, molecular, plant genetics, zoology. **Business:** Accounting, accounting/business management, accounting/finance, actuarial science, business admin, construction management, fashion, financial planning, hospitality admin, hospitality/recreation, hotel/motel admin, human resources, labor studies, management information systems, marketing, operations, organizational behavior, retailing, selling, telecom management, tourism/travel, training/development. **Communications:** Advertising, broadcast journalism, communications/speech/rhetoric, journalism, organizational, persuasive communications, public relations. **Computer sciences:** General, computer graphics, computer science, information systems, LAN/WAN management, networking, programming, systems analysis. **Conservation:** General, environmental science, fisheries, forestry, wildlife/wilderness. **Education:** General, agricultural, art, biology, chemistry, developmentally delayed, early childhood, early childhood special, elementary, elementary special ed, family/consumer sciences, foreign languages, French, German, health, kindergarten/preschool, mathematics, multi-level teacher, physical, physics, secondary, social studies, Spanish, technology/industrial arts. **Engineering:** Aerospace, agricultural, biomedical, chemical, civil, computer, construction, electrical, industrial, materials, mechanical, nuclear, surveying. **English:** Creative writing, English lit, technical writing. **Foreign languages:** General, classics, comparative lit, East Asian, French, German, Italian, Japanese, linguistics, Russian, Spanish. **Health services:** Athletic training, audiology/hearing, audiology/speech pathology, clinical lab science, dietetic technician, dietetics, nursing (RN), occupational health, occupational therapy, predental, premedicine, speech pathology, veterinary technology/assistant. **History:** General. **Human services:** Social work. **Liberal arts:** Arts/sciences, humanities. **Math:** General, applied, statistics. **Parks/recreation:** Exercise sciences, facilities management, health/fitness, sports studies. **Philosophy/religion:** Philosophy, religion. **Physical sciences:** Atmospheric science, chemistry, geology, meteorology, physics. **Protective services:** Law enforcement admin. **Psychology:** General. **Social sciences:** General, anthropology, political science, sociology. **Visual/performing arts:** General, acting, art, art history/conservation, design, dramatic, fashion design, film/cinema/video, interior design, music, photography, studio arts, theater arts management. **Work/family studies:** General, apparel marketing, clothing/textiles, family studies, family/community services, food/nutrition.

Most popular majors. Agriculture 7%, business/marketing 18%, engineering/engineering technologies 28%, health sciences 7%, social sciences 6%.

Technology on campus. 1,137 workstations in dormitories, library, computer center, student center. Dormitories wired for high-speed internet access and linked to campus network. Commuter students can connect to campus network. Online course registration, helpline, student web hosting, wireless network available.

Student life. **Freshman orientation:** Available, $320 fee. Preregistration for classes offered. Held the week before classes. **Policies:** Nondiscrimination, anti-harassment, anti-hazing policies; bill of students' rights. Freshmen not permitted cars on campus. **Housing:** Coed dorms, single-sex dorms, special housing for disabled, apartments, cooperative housing, fraternity/sorority housing available. $100 nonrefundable deposit, deadline 5/5. Honors College, Living Learning Communities. **Activities:** Bands, campus ministries, choral groups, dance, drama, international student organizations, literary magazine, music ensembles, Model UN, musical theater, radio station, student government, student newspaper, TV station, over 850 organizations.

Athletics. NCAA. **Intercollegiate:** Baseball M, basketball, cross-country, diving, football (tackle) M, golf, soccer W, softball W, swimming, tennis, track and field, volleyball W, wrestling M. **Intramural:** Badminton, basketball, bowling, cross-country, football (non-tackle), golf, handball, racquetball, sand volleyball, soccer, softball, swimming, table tennis, tennis, ultimate frisbee, volleyball, water polo. **Team name:** Boilermakers.

Student services. Adult student services, alcohol/substance abuse counseling, career counseling, services for economically disadvantaged, student employment services, financial aid counseling, health services, legal services, minority student services, on-campus daycare, personal counseling, placement for graduates, veterans' counselor, women's services. **Physically disabled:** Services for visually, speech, hearing impaired.

Contact. E-mail: admissions@purdue.edu
Phone: (765) 494-1776 Fax: (765) 494-0544
Pamela Horne, Dean of Admissions, Purdue University, 475 Stadium Mall Drive, West Lafayette, IN 47907-2050

Purdue University Calumet
Hammond, Indiana   CB member
www.purduecal.edu   CB code: 1638

- Public 4-year university and branch campus college
- Commuter campus in small city
- 8,408 degree-seeking undergraduates: 42% part-time, 57% women, 11% African American, 2% Asian American, 17% Hispanic/Latino, 2% Multiracial, non-Hispanic, 7% international
- 879 degree-seeking graduate students
- 65% of applicants admitted
- SAT or ACT (ACT writing optional) required
- 30% graduate within 6 years

General. Founded in 1943. Regionally accredited. Experiential learning curricular components required by all undergraduate students. **Degrees:** 1,497 bachelor's, 1 associate awarded; master's, professional offered. **ROTC:** Army. **Location:** 20 miles from Chicago. **Calendar:** Semester, extensive summer session. **Full-time faculty:** 270 total; 67% have terminal degrees, 30% minority, 49% women. **Part-time faculty:** 236 total; 16% have terminal degrees, 16% minority, 54% women. **Class size:** 30% < 20, 56% 20-39, 6% 40-49, 7% 50-99, 1% >100.

Freshman class profile. 2,669 applied, 1,725 admitted, 1,035 enrolled.

Mid 50% test scores			
		GPA 2.0-2.99:	42%
SAT critical reading:	430-530	Rank in top quarter:	40%
SAT math:	420-540	Rank in top tenth:	16%
SAT writing:	420-510	Return as sophomores:	70%
GPA 3.75 or higher:	15%	Out-of-state:	11%
GPA 3.50-3.74:	10%	Live on campus:	16%
GPA 3.0-3.49:	32%	International:	7%

Basis for selection. Class rank, grade average in subjects related to degree objectives, trends in achievement throughout high school, satisfactory high school subject matter requirements, strength of college preparatory program, and standardized test results most important. Graduation from high school with minimum of 15 units of credit required. **Home schooled:** Transcript of courses and grades required.

High school preparation. College-preparatory program required. 15 units required; 19 recommended. Required and recommended units include English 4, mathematics 3-4, social studies 1, history 1-2, science 3-4 (laboratory 1), foreign language 2 and academic electives 1. Course requirements vary according to program.

2015-2016 Annual costs. Tuition/fees: $7,360; $16,625 out-of-state. Room/board: $7,368. Books/supplies: $1,500. Personal expenses: $2,221.

2014-2015 Financial aid. Need-based: 836 full-time freshmen applied for aid; 657 deemed to have need; 616 received aid. Average need met was 12%. Average scholarship/grant was $5,060; average loan $2,303. 39% of total undergraduate aid awarded as scholarships/grants, 61% as loans/jobs. **Non-need-based:** Awarded to 1,242 full-time undergraduates, including 320 freshmen. Scholarships awarded for academics, athletics, state residency.

Application procedures. Admission: Closing date 8/1. $25 fee, may be waived for applicants with need. Admission notification on a rolling basis. **Financial aid:** Priority date 3/10, closing date 6/30. FAFSA required. Applicants notified on a rolling basis starting 4/15; must reply within 2 week(s) of notification.

Academics. Special study options: Accelerated study, combined bachelor's/graduate degree, cooperative education, distance learning, double major, dual enrollment of high school students, ESL, honors, independent study, internships, study abroad, teacher certification program, weekend college. **Credit/placement by examination:** AP, CLEP, SAT, ACT, institutional tests. **Support services:** Learning center, study skills assistance, tutoring, writing center.

Honors college/program. While there are no firm minimal scores for admission, students with 3.5 GPA and 1100 SAT (exclusive of Writing)/25 ACT will enhance their chances of admission significantly. Strong record of extracurricular engagement also expected. Admission to the Honors College is on a rolling basis.

Majors. Biology: General. **Business:** General, accounting, business admin, hotel/motel admin, operations. **Communications:** Communications/speech/rhetoric. **Computer sciences:** Computer science. **Education:** General, elementary. **Engineering:** General, civil, computer, electrical, mechanical. **English:** English lit. **Foreign languages:** General. **Health services:** Clinical lab science, nursing (RN). **History:** General. **Math:** General. **Philosophy/religion:** Philosophy. **Physical sciences:** General, chemistry, physics. **Psychology:** General. **Social sciences:** Political science, sociology. **Work/family studies:** Family studies.

Most popular majors. Business/marketing 15%, communications/journalism 6%, engineering/engineering technologies 12%, health sciences 43%.

Technology on campus. 1,500 workstations in library, computer center, student center. Dormitories wired for high-speed internet access and linked to campus network. Commuter students can connect to campus network. Online course registration, online library, helpline, wireless network available.

Student life. Freshman orientation: Mandatory, $30 fee. Preregistration for classes offered. Orientation runs approximately 5-6 hours and includes applying for financial aid, academic support services, counseling, and overview of academic areas. **Housing:** Apartments available. $200 deposit. **Activities:** Pep band, campus ministries, choral groups, dance, drama, international student organizations, student government, student newspaper, American Association of University Women; Black Student Union; Chinese Student Association; InterVarsity Christian Fellowship; LGBTQIA; Los Latinos, National Society of Black Engineers; Social Justice Club; Society of Hispanic Professional Engineers; Veterans Enlisted Students Association.

Athletics. NAIA. **Intercollegiate:** Baseball M, basketball, cheerleading, cross-country, golf M, soccer, softball W, tennis, volleyball W. **Intramural:** Badminton, basketball, bowling, football (non-tackle), golf, racquetball, sailing, soccer, softball, table tennis, volleyball. **Team name:** Peregrines.

Student services. Adult student services, alcohol/substance abuse counseling, career counseling, student employment services, financial aid counseling, health services, on-campus daycare, personal counseling, placement for graduates, veterans' counselor. **Physically disabled:** Services for visually, speech, hearing impaired.

Contact. E-mail: adms@purduecal.edu
Phone: (219) 989-2213 Fax: (219) 989-2775
Eric Felver, Director of Admissions, Admissions and Recruitment, Purdue University Calumet, 2200 169th Street, Hammond, IN 46323-2094

Purdue University North Central

Westville, Indiana
www.pnc.edu

CB member
CB code: 1640

- Public 4-year university
- Commuter campus in rural community
- 3,514 degree-seeking undergraduates
- 48 graduate students

General. Founded in 1943. Regionally accredited. **Degrees:** 486 bachelor's, 55 associate awarded; master's offered. **Location:** 10 miles from Michigan City, 13 miles from Laporte. **Calendar:** Semester, limited summer session.

Full-time faculty: 125 total; 61% have terminal degrees, 18% minority, 47% women. **Part-time faculty:** 156 total; 13% have terminal degrees, 2% minority, 62% women. **Class size:** 52% < 20, 43% 20-39, 2% 40-49, 2% 50-99, less than 1% >100.

Freshman class profile.

GPA 3.75 or higher:	9%	Rank in top quarter:	25%
GPA 3.50-3.74:	10%	Rank in top tenth:	7%
GPA 3.0-3.49:	29%	Out-of-state:	2%
GPA 2.0-2.99:	50%		

Basis for selection. Academic record and test scores important. SAT or ACT recommended. Interview recommended for academically weak applicants.

High school preparation. College-preparatory program recommended. 15 units recommended. Recommended units include English 4, mathematics 3, social studies 1, history 1, science 3 (laboratory 3) and foreign language 2.

2015-2016 Annual costs. Tuition/fees: $7,358; $17,516 out-of-state.

Financial aid. Non-need-based: Scholarships awarded for academics, athletics, leadership.

Application procedures. Admission: Priority date 8/1; no deadline. No application fee. Admission notification on a rolling basis. **Financial aid:** Priority date 3/10, closing date 6/30. FAFSA required. Applicants notified on a rolling basis starting 4/1; must reply by 8/1 or within 2 week(s) of notification.

Academics. Special study options: Distance learning, double major, dual enrollment of high school students, honors, independent study, internships, study abroad, teacher certification program, weekend college. **Credit/placement by examination:** AP, CLEP, SAT, ACT, institutional tests. **Support services:** Learning center, reduced course load, remedial instruction, tutoring, writing center.

Majors. Biology: General. **Business:** Human resources, operations. **Communications:** Communications/speech/rhetoric. **Computer sciences:** Networking. **Education:** Early childhood, elementary. **Engineering:** Electrical, mechanical. **English:** English lit. **Health services:** Nursing (RN). **History:** General. **Human services:** Social work. **Liberal arts:** Arts/sciences. **Psychology:** General.

Most popular majors. Biology 7%, business/marketing 23%, education 11%, engineering/engineering technologies 14%, health sciences 13%, interdisciplinary studies 6%, liberal arts 14%.

Technology on campus. 330 workstations in library, computer center. Commuter students can connect to campus network. Online course registration, online library, helpline, wireless network available.

Student life. Freshman orientation: Available. Preregistration for classes offered. **Activities:** Campus ministries, choral groups, drama, literary magazine, student government, student newspaper, Active Voices, Alpha Phi Alpha, Christian bible study, Rotaract club, TRIO service club.

Athletics. NAIA. **Intercollegiate:** Baseball M, basketball M, golf M, softball W, volleyball W. **Team name:** Panthers.

Student services. Career counseling, student employment services, financial aid counseling, on-campus daycare, personal counseling, placement for graduates, veterans' counselor. **Physically disabled:** Services for visually, hearing impaired.

Contact. E-mail: admissions@pnc.edu
Phone: (219) 785-5505 Toll-free number: (800) 782-1231
Fax: (219) 785-5653
Janice Whisler, Director Enrollment Outreach Recruitment, Purdue University North Central, 1401 South US Highway 421, Westville, IN 46391-9542

Rose-Hulman Institute of Technology

Terre Haute, Indiana
www.rose-hulman.edu

CB member
CB code: 1668

- Private 4-year engineering college
- Residential campus in small city
- 2,233 degree-seeking undergraduates: 1% part-time, 22% women, 2% African American, 4% Asian American, 3% Hispanic/Latino, 4% Multiracial, non-Hispanic, 12% international
- 85 degree-seeking graduate students

- 58% of applicants admitted
- SAT or ACT (ACT writing optional) required
- 77% graduate within 6 years; 16% enter graduate study

General. Founded in 1874. Regionally accredited. **Degrees:** 446 bachelor's awarded; master's offered. **ROTC:** Army, Air Force. **Location:** 73 miles from Indianapolis. **Calendar:** Quarter, limited summer session. **Full-time faculty:** 181 total; 99% have terminal degrees, 13% minority, 21% women. **Part-time faculty:** 12 total; 100% have terminal degrees, 8% minority, 50% women. **Class size:** 38% < 20, 61% 20-39, less than 1% 40-49, less than 1% 50-99. **Special facilities:** Advanced learning center, observatory, center for technological research with industry.

Freshman class profile. 4,331 applied, 2,503 admitted, 545 enrolled.

Mid 50% test scores		Rank in top tenth:	69%
SAT critical reading:	550-670	End year in good standing:	85%
SAT math:	630-750	Return as sophomores:	93%
SAT writing:	550-660	Out-of-state:	64%
ACT composite:	28-32	Live on campus:	99%
GPA 3.75 or higher:	81%	International:	12%
GPA 3.50-3.74:	13%	Fraternities:	33%
GPA 3.0-3.49:	6%	Sororities:	39%
Rank in top quarter:	90%		

Basis for selection. GED not accepted. Primary consideration given to school achievement record and subjects taken. Applicants must rank in top quarter of graduating class. Test scores also very important. Recommendations important. Extracurricular and leadership activities, alumni ties considered. Interviews, although not required, can be determining factor. **Home schooled:** Statement describing home school structure and mission, transcript of courses and grades, letter of recommendation (nonparent) required. Lab courses must have been taken at high school or community college.

High school preparation. College-preparatory program required. 16 units required. Required and recommended units include English 4, mathematics 4-5, social studies 2, science 2-3 (laboratory 2) and academic electives 4.

2015-2016 Annual costs. Tuition/fees: $45,141. Room/board: $12,660. Books/supplies: $1,500. Personal expenses: $1,500. **Additional information:** Required fees for incoming freshman students include mandatory purchase of laptop computer, which is a $2,400 expense, activity fees, health services fee, technology fee, and Residence Hall Association fee.

2015-2016 Financial aid. **Need-based:** 429 full-time freshmen applied for aid; 340 deemed to have need; 340 received aid. Average need met was 77%. Average scholarship/grant was $25,954; average loan $3,367. 72% of total undergraduate aid awarded as scholarships/grants, 28% as loans/jobs. **Non-need-based:** Awarded to 2,174 full-time undergraduates, including 541 freshmen. Scholarships awarded for academics, minority status, ROTC.

Application procedures. Admission: Priority date 11/1; deadline 2/1 (postmark date). $40 fee, may be waived for applicants with need. Application must be submitted online. 3/15. Must reply by 5/1. **Financial aid:** Priority date 3/1; no closing date. FAFSA required. Applicants notified on a rolling basis starting 3/10; must reply by 5/1.

Academics. Area minor programs in science, engineering, humanities and social sciences. Additional certificate and interdisciplinary programs available in imaging systems, German technical translation, semiconductor materials and devices, management studies, and consulting engineering. **Special study options:** Accelerated study, cooperative education, cross-registration, double major, independent study, internships, study abroad. **Credit/placement by examination:** AP, CLEP, IB, institutional tests. **Support services:** Learning center, reduced course load, study skills assistance, tutoring, writing center.

Majors. **Biology:** General, biochemistry. **Computer sciences:** Computer science. **Engineering:** Applied physics, biomedical, chemical, civil, computer, electrical, mechanical, software. **Math:** General. **Physical sciences:** Chemistry, physics. **Social sciences:** Economics.

Most popular majors. Computer/information sciences 9%, engineering/engineering technologies 80%.

Technology on campus. PC or laptop required. 14 workstations in library. Dormitories wired for high-speed internet access and linked to campus network. Commuter students can connect to campus network. Online course registration, online library, helpline, repair service, student web hosting, wireless network available.

Student life. Freshman orientation: Mandatory. Preregistration for classes offered. **Housing:** Guaranteed on-campus for freshmen. Coed dorms, single-sex dorms, apartments, fraternity/sorority housing, themed housing available. Pets allowed in dorm rooms. **Activities:** Bands, choral groups, dance, drama, international student organizations, literary magazine, music ensembles, musical theater, radio station, student government, student newspaper, Inter-Varsity Christian Fellowship, Circle K, National Society of Black

Engineers, student activities board, Society of Woman Engineers, Alpha Phi Omega service fraternity.

Athletics. NCAA. **Intercollegiate:** Baseball M, basketball, cross-country, diving, football (tackle) M, golf, rifle, soccer, softball W, swimming, tennis, track and field, volleyball W. **Intramural:** Badminton, basketball, bowling, cross-country, football (non-tackle), golf, racquetball, soccer, softball, swimming, table tennis, tennis, track and field, ultimate frisbee, volleyball. **Team name:** Fightin' Engineers.

Student services. Alcohol/substance abuse counseling, career counseling, student employment services, financial aid counseling, health services, personal counseling, placement for graduates.

Contact. E-mail: admissions@rose-hulman.edu
Phone: (812) 877-8213 Toll-free number: (800) 248-7448
Fax: (812) 877-8941
Lisa Norton, Dean of Admissions, Rose-Hulman Institute of Technology, Office of Admissions, Terre Haute, IN 47803-3999

Saint Joseph's College
Rensselaer, Indiana   CB member
www.saintjoe.edu   CB code: 1697

- Private 4-year liberal arts college affiliated with the Roman Catholic Church
- Residential campus in small town
- 1,009 degree-seeking undergraduates: 6% part-time, 56% women, 10% African American, 5% Hispanic/Latino, 3% Multi-racial, non-Hispanic, 2% international
- 15 degree-seeking graduate students
- 71% of applicants admitted
- SAT or ACT (ACT writing optional) required
- 54% graduate within 6 years

General. Founded in 1889. Regionally accredited. **Degrees:** 225 bachelor's, 2 associate awarded; master's offered. **Location:** 80 miles from Chicago, 90 miles from Indianapolis. **Calendar:** Semester, limited summer session. **Full-time faculty:** 79 total; 76% have terminal degrees, 5% minority, 53% women. **Part-time faculty:** 48 total; 42% have terminal degrees, 4% minority, 52% women. **Class size:** 78% < 20, 21% 20-39, 1% 40-49, less than 1% 50-99. **Special facilities:** Two nature preserves for biological research, instructional facility for sustainable food production.

Freshman class profile. 1,596 applied, 1,136 admitted, 249 enrolled.

Mid 50% test scores		GPA 2.0-2.99:	42%
SAT critical reading:	420-530	Rank in top quarter:	25%
SAT math:	420-540	Rank in top tenth:	13%
ACT composite:	19-24	Return as sophomores:	66%
GPA 3.75 or higher:	16%	Out-of-state:	34%
GPA 3.50-3.74:	11%	Live on campus:	91%
GPA 3.0-3.49:	31%	International:	5%

Basis for selection. For applicants with requirement deficiencies, admissions decision may be deferred until additional requirements (which may include an interview, recommendations, further course work, or an essay) are evaluated. Limited number of these applicants will be admitted under the Freshman Academic Support Program. Interview, college visit recommended. **Home schooled:** Statement describing home school structure and mission, transcript of courses and grades required. **Learning Disabled:** After admission, documentation of learning disability must be submitted to Director of Counseling Services in order to receive academic accommodations.

High school preparation. College-preparatory program recommended. 15 units recommended. Recommended units include English 4, mathematics 3, social studies 3, science 3 (laboratory 2) and foreign language 2. 10 recommended units must be from English, foreign language, social studies, math, and natural science. 3 units distributed among social studies, history, and academic electives.

2015-2016 Annual costs. Tuition/fees: $28,690. Room/board: $8,900. Books/supplies: $900. Personal expenses: $800.

2014-2015 Financial aid. **Need-based:** 221 full-time freshmen applied for aid; 200 deemed to have need; 200 received aid. Average need met was 80%. Average scholarship/grant was $19,894; average loan $4,101. 70% of total undergraduate aid awarded as scholarships/grants, 30% as loans/jobs. **Non-need-based:** Awarded to 371 full-time undergraduates, including 78 freshmen. Scholarships awarded for academics, alumni affiliation, athletics, music/drama, religious affiliation.

Application procedures. Admission: No deadline. $25 fee, may be waived for applicants with need, free for online applicants. Admission notification on a rolling basis beginning on or about 9/1. Must reply by May 1 or within 2 week(s) if notified thereafter. **Financial aid:** Priority date 3/1; no closing date. FAFSA required. Applicants notified on a rolling basis starting 3/1; must reply by 5/1 or within 2 week(s) of notification.

Academics. Core program is a sequence of 10 interdisciplinary courses and seeks to integrate Christian humanism with critical appraisal of human condition. **Special study options:** Accelerated study, cross-registration, double major, dual enrollment of high school students, honors, independent study, internships, liberal arts/career combination, student-designed major, study abroad, teacher certification program, Washington semester. **Credit/placement by examination:** AP, CLEP, IB, SAT, ACT, institutional tests. **Support services:** Learning center, reduced course load, study skills assistance, tutoring, writing center.

Majors. Biology: General, biochemistry. **Business:** Accounting, business admin. **Communications:** Communications/speech/rhetoric, media studies. **Computer sciences:** General. **Education:** Elementary. **English:** Creative writing, English lit. **Health services:** Athletic training, clinical lab science, nursing (RN), predental, premedicine, preveterinary. **History:** General. **Math:** General. **Parks/recreation:** Health/fitness, sports admin. **Philosophy/religion:** Philosophy. **Physical sciences:** Chemistry. **Protective services:** Criminal justice. **Psychology:** General. **Social sciences:** Economics, international relations, political science, sociology. **Theology:** Pastoral counseling. **Visual/performing arts:** Directing/producing, music history, music management, studio arts.

Most popular majors. Biology 11%, business/marketing 16%, health sciences 27%, parks/recreation 13%, psychology 6%.

Technology on campus. 69 workstations in library, computer center, student center. Dormitories wired for high-speed internet access and linked to campus network. Online course registration, helpline, student web hosting, wireless network available.

Student life. Freshman orientation: Mandatory. Preregistration for classes offered. One-day optional early registrations in April, June and July; 4-day required orientation in August. **Policies:** All buildings are smoke-free. **Housing:** Guaranteed on-campus for all undergraduates. Coed dorms, single-sex dorms, special housing for disabled, apartments available. $200 nonrefundable deposit, deadline 8/15. Graduate housing available. **Activities:** Bands, campus ministries, choral groups, dance, drama, literary magazine, music ensembles, Model UN, musical theater, radio station, student government, student newspaper, TV station, charitable society, Habitat for Humanity, Kairos Team, College Republicans, College Democrats, peer ministry, Right to Life, volunteer corps, diversity coalition, St. Thomas Aquinas Catholic Society, Knights of Columbus.

Athletics. NCAA. **Intercollegiate:** Baseball M, basketball, cross-country, football (tackle) M, golf, soccer, softball W, tennis, track and field, volleyball W. **Intramural:** Basketball, football (non-tackle), softball, ultimate frisbee, volleyball. **Team name:** Pumas.

Student services. Career counseling, financial aid counseling, health services, personal counseling, placement for graduates. **Physically disabled:** Services for visually impaired.

Contact. E-mail: admissions@saintjoe.edu
Phone: (219) 866-6170 Toll-free number: (800) 447-8781
Fax: (219) 866-6122
Saint Joseph's College, Box 890, Rensselaer, IN 47978-0890

Saint Mary's College

Notre Dame, Indiana	
www.saintmarys.edu	**CB member**
	CB code: 1702

- Private 4-year liberal arts college for women affiliated with the Roman Catholic Church
- Residential campus in small city
- 1,559 degree-seeking undergraduates: 1% part-time, 100% women, 2% African American, 2% Asian American, 11% Hispanic/Latino, 3% Multi-racial, non-Hispanic, 1% international
- 38 degree-seeking graduate students
- 80% of applicants admitted
- SAT or ACT (ACT writing optional), application essay required
- 79% graduate within 6 years; 29% enter graduate study

General. Founded in 1844. Regionally accredited. **Degrees:** 332 bachelor's awarded; master's, professional offered. **ROTC:** Army, Naval, Air Force. **Location:** 3 miles from South Bend, 90 miles from Chicago. **Calendar:**

Semester, limited summer session. **Full-time faculty:** 133 total; 86% have terminal degrees, 14% minority, 69% women. **Part-time faculty:** 73 total; 41% have terminal degrees, 8% minority, 66% women. **Class size:** 53% < 20, 46% 20-39, less than 1% 40-49, 1% 50-99. **Special facilities:** Performing arts center, greenhouse, galleries.

Freshman class profile. 1,722 applied, 1,384 admitted, 419 enrolled.

Mid 50% test scores			
		GPA 2.0-2.99:	2%
SAT critical reading:	500-620	Rank in top quarter:	62%
SAT math:	480-590	Rank in top tenth:	28%
SAT writing:	500-620	End year in good standing:	98%
ACT composite:	22-28	Return as sophomores:	90%
GPA 3.75 or higher:	51%	Out-of-state:	72%
GPA 3.50-3.74:	20%	Live on campus:	98%
GPA 3.0-3.49:	27%	International:	1%

Basis for selection. School achievement record, high school transcript, GPA, test scores, activities important. Essay, class rank, school recommendations considered. ACT Writing is not required. Interview recommended. Audition recommended for music majors. Portfolio recommended for art majors. **Home schooled:** Statement describing home school structure and mission, transcript of courses and grades required.

High school preparation. College-preparatory program recommended. 16 units required; 20 recommended. Required and recommended units include English 4, mathematics 3-4, social studies 2, history 3, science 2-4 (laboratory 2) and foreign language 2-4. 3 additional units distributed among English, math, science, foreign language, and social studies required. 2 years of same foreign language required.

2015-2016 Annual costs. Tuition/fees: $37,400. Room/board: $11,320. Books/supplies: $1,000. Personal expenses: $950.

2015-2016 Financial aid. Need-based: 363 full-time freshmen applied for aid; 299 deemed to have need; 299 received aid. Average need met was 88%. Average scholarship/grant was $16,542; average loan $3,348. 76% of total undergraduate aid awarded as scholarships/grants, 24% as loans/jobs. **Non-need-based:** Awarded to 1,403 full-time undergraduates, including 374 freshmen. Scholarships awarded for academics, art, music/drama. **Additional information:** Saint Mary's also accepts veteran benefits and participates in the Yellow Ribbon Program, through which 100% of a student's tuition and fees can be paid.

Application procedures. Admission: Priority date 2/15; no deadline. No application fee. Admission notification on a rolling basis beginning on or about 12/15. Must reply by May 1 or within 3 week(s) if notified thereafter. **Financial aid:** Closing date 3/1. FAFSA required. Applicants notified on a rolling basis starting 12/15.

Academics. Special study options: Combined bachelor's/graduate degree, cross-registration, distance learning, double major, ESL, exchange student, independent study, internships, liberal arts/career combination, student-designed major, study abroad, teacher certification program, Washington semester. Distance learning offered during summer terms. Campus in Rome, Italy and study abroad programs in Ireland, Spain, France, Argentina, Austria, Australia, England, South Africa, Uganda, Morocco, Puerto Rico, South Korea, Greece, Honduras, Ecuador, China, and Nicaragua. Women's Studies in Europe. Summer European study tour. Academic and extra-curricular co-exchange with University of Notre Dame. Volunteer service opportunities in the U.S. and abroad. **Credit/placement by examination:** AP, CLEP, IB, institutional tests. 30 credit hours maximum toward bachelor's degree. **Support services:** Reduced course load, study skills assistance, tutoring, writing center.

Majors. Biology: General. **Business:** Accounting, business admin, management information systems. **Communications:** Communications/speech/rhetoric. **Education:** Elementary. **English:** British lit, creative writing. **Foreign languages:** Spanish. **Health services:** Communication disorders, nursing (RN). **History:** General. **Human services:** Social work. **Liberal arts:** Humanities. **Math:** General, applied, statistics. **Philosophy/religion:** Philosophy, religion. **Physical sciences:** Chemistry. **Psychology:** General. **Social sciences:** Economics, political science, sociology. **Visual/performing arts:** Art, dramatic, music, studio arts.

Most popular majors. Biology 6%, business/marketing 10%, communications/journalism 9%, education 7%, English 7%, health sciences 19%, psychology 6%, social sciences 8%.

Technology on campus. 291 workstations in dormitories, library, computer center, student center. Dormitories wired for high-speed internet access and linked to campus network. Commuter students can connect to campus network. Online course registration, online library, helpline, student web hosting, wireless network available.

Student life. Freshman orientation: Mandatory. Preregistration for classes offered. Held weekend prior to beginning of fall semester. **Policies:** Educational judicial system guaranteeing certain due process rights to all students involved in discipline situation; student judicial board provides opportunity for peer review system. **Housing:** Guaranteed on-campus for freshmen. Special housing for disabled, apartments available. $400 fully refundable deposit, deadline 5/1. Pets allowed in dorm rooms. **Activities:** Bands, campus ministries, choral groups, dance, drama, international student organizations, literary magazine, music ensembles, musical theater, opera, radio station, student government, student newspaper, TV station, neighborhood study help program, Community of International Lay Apostolate, Urban Plunge community program, Circle-K, World Hunger Coalition, Student Alliance for Women's Colleges, Right to Life, Women for the Environment, Sisters of Nefertiti, La Fuerza.

Athletics. NCAA. **Intercollegiate:** Basketball W, cross-country W, golf W, lacrosse W, soccer W, softball W, tennis W, volleyball W. **Intramural:** Basketball W, soccer W, tennis W, volleyball W. **Team name:** Belles.

Student services. Chaplain/spiritual director, career counseling, student employment services, financial aid counseling, health services, minority student services, on-campus daycare, personal counseling, women's services. **Physically disabled:** Services for visually, speech, hearing impaired.

Contact. E-mail: admission@saintmarys.edu
Phone: (574) 284-4587 Toll-free number: (800) 551-7621
Fax: (574) 284-4841
Sarah Dvorak, Director of Admissions, Saint Mary's College, 122 Le Mans Hall, Notre Dame, IN 46556-5001

St. Mary-of-the-Woods College
Saint Mary of the Woods, Indiana   CB member
www.smwc.edu   CB code: 1704

- Private 4-year liberal arts college affiliated with the Roman Catholic Church
- Residential campus in rural community
- 592 degree-seeking undergraduates: 34% part-time, 96% women
- 202 degree-seeking graduate students
- 59% of applicants admitted
- SAT or ACT (ACT writing optional), application essay required
- 53% graduate within 6 years

General. Founded in 1840. Regionally accredited. Traditional campus program open to women only. Distance education undergraduate programs and graduate programs open to men and women. **Degrees:** 150 bachelor's, 1 associate awarded; master's offered. **ROTC:** Army, Air Force. **Location:** 5 miles from Terre Haute, 82 miles from Indianapolis. **Calendar:** Semester, limited summer session. **Full-time faculty:** 48 total. **Part-time faculty:** 94 total. **Class size:** 97% < 20, 3% 20-39. **Special facilities:** Equine indoor and outdoor arenas, wildlife habitat restoration areas.

Freshman class profile. 283 applied, 168 admitted, 73 enrolled.

Mid 50% test scores			
		GPA 3.0-3.49:	41%
SAT critical reading:	420-530	GPA 2.0-2.99:	27%
SAT math:	410-500	Rank in top quarter:	31%
SAT writing:	400-500	Rank in top tenth:	2%
ACT composite:	19-23	Return as sophomores:	77%
GPA 3.75 or higher:	18%	Out-of-state:	81%
GPA 3.50-3.74:	13%	International:	8%

Basis for selection. School achievement record, test scores most important. Recommendations considered. Interview recommended. Audition required of music majors. Portfolio required of art and journalism majors. **Home schooled:** Descriptions of courses taken while in high school requested. **Learning Disabled:** Meeting with Learning Resource Coordinator strongly recommended, IEP report required.

High school preparation. Recommended units include English 4, mathematics 3, social studies 3, science 3 (laboratory 3) and foreign language 2.

2015-2016 Annual costs. Tuition/fees: $28,932. Room/board: $10,500. Books/supplies: $1,600. Personal expenses: $3,040.

Financial aid. Non-need-based: Scholarships awarded for academics, alumni affiliation, art, athletics, leadership, minority status, music/drama, state residency. **Additional information:** Portfolio or audition required of applicants who wish to be considered for Creative Arts Scholarship.

Application procedures. Admission: No deadline. No application fee. Admission notification on a rolling basis beginning on or about 8/1. **Financial aid:** Priority date 3/1; no closing date. FAFSA required. Applicants notified on a rolling basis starting 12/1; must reply within 6 week(s) of notification.

Academics. Special study options: Cross-registration, distance learning, double major, ESL, external degree, honors, independent study, internships, student-designed major, study abroad, teacher certification program. Students throughout the country and abroad do course work on-line from home. Exchange program with Providence University in Taiwan. International Agreements with Regent's College, London, and others. **Credit/placement by examination:** AP, CLEP, IB, SAT, ACT, institutional tests. 30 credit hours maximum toward associate degree, 30 toward bachelor's. **Support services:** Learning center, reduced course load, study skills assistance, tutoring, writing center.

Honors college/program. SAT/ACT, GPA, teacher recommendations, and written essays considered; average of 12 first-year students selected each year. Students complete specially-designed Honors Program courses to fulfill general studies requirements.

Majors. Biology: General. **Business:** Accounting, business admin, human resources, marketing, nonprofit/public. **Education:** Art, biology, developmentally delayed, early childhood, elementary, kindergarten/preschool, multi-level teacher, social studies, special ed. **English:** English lit, technical writing. **Health services:** Clinical lab science, health care admin, music therapy, nursing (RN). **Liberal arts:** Arts/sciences, humanities. **Math:** General. **Psychology:** General. **Social sciences:** General, criminology. **Visual/performing arts:** Art, graphic design, music, theater arts management.

Most popular majors. Business/marketing 15%, education 26%, psychology 14%, public administration/social services 9%.

Technology on campus. 85 workstations in dormitories, library, computer center, student center. Dormitories wired for high-speed internet access and linked to campus network. Commuter students can connect to campus network. Online library, helpline, wireless network available.

Student life. Freshman orientation: Mandatory, $125 fee. Preregistration for classes offered. Three-day program before classes start for traditional undergraduate; requires service component. **Policies:** All students in traditional on-campus program whose families do not live in a contiguous county must live on-campus all 4 years. **Housing:** Guaranteed on-campus for all undergraduates. Single-sex dorms, special housing for disabled available. **Activities:** Campus ministries, choral groups, dance, drama, international student organizations, literary magazine, music ensembles, musical theater, student government, student newspaper, Habitat for Humanity, literacy volunteers, environmentalist activities, peace and justice committee, arts and issues committee, United Way, sustainability club.

Athletics. USCAA. **Intercollegiate:** Basketball W, cross-country W, equestrian W, golf W, soccer W, softball W. **Team name:** Pomeroys.

Student services. Adult student services, alcohol/substance abuse counseling, chaplain/spiritual director, career counseling, student employment services, financial aid counseling, health services, on-campus daycare, personal counseling, placement for graduates. **Physically disabled:** Services for visually, hearing impaired.

Contact. E-mail: smwcadms@smwc.edu
Phone: (812) 535-5106 Toll-free number: (800) 926-7692
Fax: (812) 535-5010
Karen Dyer, Vice President of Enrollment Management, St. Mary-of-the-Woods College, 1 St Mary of Woods Coll, Saint Mary of the Woods, IN 47876-1099

Taylor University
Upland, Indiana   CB member
www.taylor.edu   CB code: 1802

- Private 4-year university and liberal arts college affiliated with the inter-denominational tradition
- Residential campus in small town
- 1,888 degree-seeking undergraduates: 3% part-time, 55% women, 3% African American, 3% Asian American, 3% Hispanic/Latino, 1% Native American, 5% international
- 41 degree-seeking graduate students
- 85% of applicants admitted
- SAT or ACT (ACT writing recommended), application essay required
- 77% graduate within 6 years; 24% enter graduate study

General. Founded in 1846. Regionally accredited. Christ-centered, covenant community committed to service. **Degrees:** 476 bachelor's, 6 associate awarded; master's offered. **Location:** 20 miles from Muncie, 70 miles from Indianapolis. **Calendar:** 4-1-4, limited summer session. **Full-time faculty:** 128 total; 88% have terminal degrees, 6% minority, 27% women. **Part-time faculty:** 86 total; 42% have terminal degrees, 2% minority, 46% women.

Class size: 59% < 20, 32% 20-39, 4% 40-49, 4% 50-99, 1% >100. **Special facilities:** Photo-voltaic solar array, wind turbines, arboretum, environmental studies laboratory, NASA-approved clean room, particle accelerator, NASA project space research equipment, C.S. Lewis collection of original manuscripts.

Freshman class profile. 1,716 applied, 1,460 admitted, 522 enrolled.

Mid 50% test scores			
SAT critical reading:	490-640	GPA 2.0-2.99:	5%
SAT math:	490-640	Rank in top quarter:	65%
SAT writing:	490-600	Rank in top tenth:	36%
ACT composite:	24-30	End year in good standing:	93%
GPA 3.75 or higher:	60%	Return as sophomores:	87%
GPA 3.50-3.74:	15%	Out-of-state:	61%
GPA 3.0-3.49:	20%	Live on campus:	97%
		International:	3%

Basis for selection. High school transcript, test scores important. Recommend rank in top 25% of graduating class with 3.3 GPA and 1000 SAT (exclusive of Writing). Recommendations from applicant's pastor and counselor required. Cocurricular activities considered. Audition required for music majors. Portfolio recommended for art majors. Interviews required for some financial and academic programs. **Home schooled:** Letter of recommendation (nonparent) required.

High school preparation. College-preparatory program recommended. 15 units required. Required and recommended units include English 4, mathematics 3-4, social studies 2-3, science 3-4 (laboratory 3-4), foreign language 2, computer science 1, visual/performing arts 1 and academic electives 3.

2015-2016 Annual costs. Tuition/fees: $30,270. Room/board: $8,497. Books/supplies: $1,200. Personal expenses: $2,200. **Additional information:** Per-credit hour charge for 1 to 6 hours: $841; for 7 to 11 hours: $1,058.

2015-2016 Financial aid. **Need-based:** 445 full-time freshmen applied for aid; 345 deemed to have need; 345 received aid. Average need met was 76%. Average scholarship/grant was $17,653; average loan $4,429. 68% of total undergraduate aid awarded as scholarships/grants, 32% as loans/jobs. **Non-need-based:** Awarded to 831 full-time undergraduates, including 237 freshmen. Scholarships awarded for academics, alumni affiliation, art, athletics, leadership, minority status, music/drama, religious affiliation, state residency.

Application procedures. Admission: No deadline. $25 fee, may be waived for applicants with need, free for online applicants. Admission notification on a rolling basis beginning on or about 10/1. Must reply by May 1 or within 2 week(s) if notified thereafter. **Financial aid:** Closing date 3/10. FAFSA required. Applicants notified on a rolling basis starting 3/1; must reply by 5/1.

Academics. Special study options: Combined bachelor's/graduate degree, cooperative education, distance learning, double major, dual enrollment of high school students, ESL, exchange student, honors, independent study, internships, semester at sea, student-designed major, study abroad, teacher certification program, urban semester, Washington semester. **Credit/placement by examination:** AP, CLEP, IB, institutional tests. 30 credit hours maximum toward associate degree, 30 toward bachelor's. **Support services:** Learning center, remedial instruction, study skills assistance, tutoring, writing center.

Majors. Biology: General, biochemistry. **Business:** Accounting, business admin, finance, international, managerial economics, marketing. **Communications:** Communications/speech/rhetoric, digital media, journalism, persuasive communications, public relations. **Computer sciences:** Computer science. **Conservation:** Environmental science. **Education:** General, art, elementary, English, mathematics, music, physical, science, social studies, Spanish. **Engineering:** Applied physics, computer, environmental, systems. **English:** English lit, technical writing. **Foreign languages:** Spanish. **Health services:** Health behavior. **History:** General. **Human services:** Social work. **Math:** General, applied. **Parks/recreation:** Exercise sciences, sports admin. **Philosophy/religion:** Philosophy. **Physical sciences:** Chemistry, physics. **Psychology:** General. **Social sciences:** Geography, international economic development, international relations, political science, sociology. **Theology:** Bible, religious ed. **Visual/performing arts:** Art, cinematography, dramatic, music, music performance, music theory/composition.

Most popular majors. Biology 6%, business/marketing 18%, communications/journalism 7%, education 14%, parks/recreation 8%, psychology 7%, visual/performing arts 8%.

Technology on campus. 500 workstations in library, computer center. Dormitories wired for high-speed internet access and linked to campus network. Commuter students can connect to campus network. Online course registration, online library, helpline, repair service, student web hosting, wireless network available.

Student life. Freshman orientation: Available, $15 fee. Preregistration for classes offered. One-day session held twice in June. **Policies:** Students

and faculty sign Life Together Covenant explaining expectations and responsibilities of living in Christian community where faith is integrated with academic progress. Religious observance required. **Housing:** Guaranteed on-campus for freshmen. Single-sex dorms, apartments, wellness housing available. $50 nonrefundable deposit, deadline 5/1. Some off-campus apartments available to upperclassmen with special permission. **Activities:** Bands, choral groups, drama, film society, international student organizations, literary magazine, music ensembles, musical theater, opera, radio station, student government, student newspaper, symphony orchestra, TV station, Missions Service program, Multicultural Society, Missionary kids organizations, community service programs, Global Outreach, Fellow Christian Athletes, Carpenter's Hands Ministry, High School Youth Conference, Acting on AIDS.

Athletics. NAIA, NCCAA. **Intercollegiate:** Baseball M, basketball, cross-country, football (tackle) M, golf, soccer, softball W, tennis, track and field, volleyball W. **Intramural:** Badminton, basketball, football (non-tackle), golf, racquetball, soccer, softball, table tennis, tennis, volleyball. **Team name:** Trojans.

Student services. Chaplain/spiritual director, career counseling, student employment services, financial aid counseling, health services, minority student services, personal counseling, placement for graduates. **Physically disabled:** Services for visually, speech, hearing impaired.

Contact. E-mail: admissions@taylor.edu
Phone: (765) 998-5134 Toll-free number: (800) 882-3456
Fax: (765) 998-4925
Amy Barnett, Director of Admissions, Taylor University, 236 West Reade Avenue, Upland, IN 46989-1001

Trine University
Angola, Indiana
www.trine.edu
CB member
CB code: 1811

- Private 4-year university and engineering college
- Residential campus in small town
- 1,738 degree-seeking undergraduates: 2% part-time, 28% women, 3% African American, 1% Asian American, 4% Hispanic/Latino, 2% Multiracial, non-Hispanic, 9% international
- 265 degree-seeking graduate students
- 78% of applicants admitted
- SAT or ACT (ACT writing optional) required
- 56% graduate within 6 years

General. Founded in 1884. Regionally accredited. **Degrees:** 264 bachelor's, 6 associate awarded; master's, professional offered. **ROTC:** Air Force. **Location:** 40 miles from Fort Wayne; 80 miles from Toledo, Ohio. **Calendar:** Semester, limited summer session. **Full-time faculty:** 89 total; 9% minority, 36% women. **Part-time faculty:** 123 total; 3% minority, 46% women. **Class size:** 48% < 20, 51% 20-39, less than 1% 40-49, less than 1% 50-99. **Special facilities:** Educational media resource center, 18 hole championship golf course, student-operated radio station.

Freshman class profile. 3,217 applied, 2,498 admitted, 457 enrolled.

Mid 50% test scores			
SAT critical reading:	450-570	Rank in top quarter:	54%
SAT math:	500-620	Rank in top tenth:	21%
ACT composite:	21-27	Return as sophomores:	73%
GPA 3.75 or higher:	39%	Out-of-state:	46%
GPA 3.50-3.74:	19%	Live on campus:	91%
GPA 3.0-3.49:	27%	International:	1%
GPA 2.0-2.99:	15%	Fraternities:	5%
		Sororities:	1%

Basis for selection. School achievement, class rank, test scores, school and community activities, and recommendations important. Interview and essay recommended. **Home schooled:** Statement describing home school structure and mission, transcript of courses and grades required. **Learning Disabled:** Must submit clinical evaluation of learning disability completed within 5 years prior to enrollment.

High school preparation. College-preparatory program required. 18 units required. Required units include English 4, mathematics 3, social studies 3, science 3 (laboratory 2) and academic electives 3. 3 1/2 years of math, physics, and chemistry required for engineering, math and computer science majors.

2015-2016 Annual costs. Tuition/fees: $30,350. Room/board: $10,200. Books/supplies: $1,200. Personal expenses: $2,000. **Additional information:** Tuition for engineering students: $32,300.

2014-2015 Financial aid. **Need-based:** 485 full-time freshmen applied for aid; 442 deemed to have need; 442 received aid. Average need met was 80%. Average scholarship/grant was $5,796; average loan $4,533. 64% of total undergraduate aid awarded as scholarships/grants, 36% as loans/jobs. **Non-need-based:** Awarded to 1,478 full-time undergraduates, including 515 freshmen. Scholarships awarded for academics, alumni affiliation, minority status, music/drama.

Application procedures. Admission: Priority date 6/1; deadline 8/1. No application fee. Application must be submitted online. Admission notification by 8/1. Admission notification on a rolling basis. **Financial aid:** Priority date 3/1; no closing date. FAFSA required. Applicants notified on a rolling basis starting 3/10; must reply by 5/1 or within 2 week(s) of notification.

Academics. Special study options: Accelerated study, combined bachelor's/graduate degree, cooperative education, distance learning, double major, dual enrollment of high school students, ESL, honors, independent study, internships, student-designed major, study abroad, teacher certification program. **Credit/placement by examination:** AP, CLEP, IB, institutional tests. **Support services:** Learning center, reduced course load, remedial instruction, study skills assistance, tutoring, writing center.

Majors. Biology: General. **Business:** Accounting, business admin, entrepreneurial studies, finance, operations. **Communications:** Communications/speech/rhetoric. **Computer sciences:** Computer science, informatics. **Education:** Elementary, English, health, mathematics, middle, physical, science, social studies. **Engineering:** Chemical, civil, computer, electrical, mechanical. **Health services:** Premedicine. **Math:** General. **Parks/recreation:** Golf management, health/fitness, sports admin. **Physical sciences:** Chemistry. **Protective services:** Criminal justice, forensics. **Psychology:** General. **Social sciences:** General.

Most popular majors. Business/marketing 13%, education 7%, engineering/engineering technologies 47%, parks/recreation 9%, psychology 6%, security/protective services 9%.

Technology on campus. 600 workstations in dormitories, library, computer center, student center. Dormitories wired for high-speed internet access and linked to campus network. Commuter students can connect to campus network. Online library, helpline, wireless network available.

Student life. Freshman orientation: Mandatory. Preregistration for classes offered. Held 3 days at start of fall semester. **Housing:** Guaranteed on-campus for all undergraduates. Coed dorms, single-sex dorms, apartments, fraternity/sorority housing available. $150 nonrefundable deposit, deadline 5/1. Honors housing; independent fraternity/sorority housing available. **Activities:** Bands, campus ministries, choral groups, dance, drama, international student organizations, music ensembles, radio station, student government, student newspaper, Circle K, Newman Fellowship, InterVarsity Christian Fellowship, Christian campus house, multicultural student association, Students Against Destructive Decisions, Habitat for Humanity, SPEAK (environmental/ecological concerns).

Athletics. NCAA. **Intercollegiate:** Baseball M, basketball, cross-country, football (tackle) M, golf, lacrosse, soccer, softball W, tennis, track and field, volleyball W, wrestling M. **Intramural:** Basketball, cheerleading, football (non-tackle) M, soccer, volleyball. **Team name:** Thunder.

Student services. Alcohol/substance abuse counseling, chaplain/spiritual director, career counseling, student employment services, financial aid counseling, health services, personal counseling, placement for graduates, veterans' counselor.

Contact. E-mail: admit@trine.edu
Phone: (260) 665-4100 Toll-free number: (800) 347-4878
Fax: (260) 665-4578
Stuart Jones, Dean of Admission, Trine University, One University Avenue, Angola, IN 46703

University of Evansville
Evansville, Indiana
www.evansville.edu   CB code: 1208

- Private 4-year university and liberal arts college affiliated with the United Methodist Church
- Residential campus in small city
- 2,161 degree-seeking undergraduates: 4% part-time, 54% women, 3% African American, 1% Asian American, 3% Hispanic/Latino, 2% Multiracial, non-Hispanic, 14% international
- 164 degree-seeking graduate students
- 71% of applicants admitted
- 69% graduate within 6 years; 23% enter graduate study

General. Founded in 1854. Regionally accredited. **Degrees:** 562 bachelor's, 7 associate awarded; master's, professional offered. **ROTC:** Army. **Location:**

170 miles from Indianapolis and St. Louis. **Calendar:** Semester, limited summer session. **Full-time faculty:** 169 total; 85% have terminal degrees, 13% minority, 43% women. **Part-time faculty:** 65 total; 2% minority, 60% women. **Class size:** 66% < 20, 29% 20-39, 4% 40-49, 1% 50-99.

Freshman class profile. 3,916 applied, 2,765 admitted, 515 enrolled.

Mid 50% test scores			
SAT critical reading:	500-610	Rank in top quarter:	66%
SAT math:	510-630	Rank in top tenth:	33%
SAT writing:	480-600	End year in good standing:	91%
ACT composite:	23-29	Return as sophomores:	81%
		Out-of-state:	40%
GPA 3.75 or higher:	47%	Live on campus:	80%
GPA 3.50-3.74:	21%	International:	12%
GPA 3.0-3.49:	24%	Fraternities:	33%
GPA 2.0-2.99:	8%	Sororities:	26%

Basis for selection. Weighted GPA utilized. Extracurricular activities important. Subjective review of all submitted materials with emphasis on transcript and test score. Earned grades, curriculum, and performance are looked at in relation to peers. SAT or ACT recommended. Interview recommended. Audition required of music and theater majors. **Home schooled:** Transcript of courses and grades required. Test score must come from testing agency. **Learning Disabled:** Students requesting accommodations must provide documentation of the disability and the significant impact of the disability on academic functioning.

High school preparation. College-preparatory program required. 15 units required; 20 recommended. Required and recommended units include English 4, mathematics 3-4, social studies 1, history 3-4, science 3-4 (laboratory 3-4), foreign language 2 and academic electives 1. 1 or more physics, additional chemistry and math recommended for engineering programs. 1 chemistry required for nursing program.

2015-2016 Annual costs. Tuition/fees: $32,946. Room/board: $11,240.

2015-2016 Financial aid. Need-based: Average need met was 86%. Average scholarship/grant was $24,275; average loan $3,459. 80% of total undergraduate aid awarded as scholarships/grants, 20% as loans/jobs. **Non-need-based:** Awarded to 960 full-time undergraduates, including 154 freshmen. Scholarships awarded for academics, alumni affiliation, art, athletics, music/drama, religious affiliation.

Application procedures. Admission: No deadline. No application fee. Admission notification on a rolling basis beginning on or about 8/15. Must reply by May 1 or within 2 week(s) if notified thereafter. **Financial aid:** Priority date 3/1; no closing date. FAFSA required. Applicants notified on a rolling basis starting 3/1; must reply by 8/1.

Academics. Special study options: Accelerated study, cooperative education, distance learning, double major, dual enrollment of high school students, ESL, honors, independent study, internships, student-designed major, study abroad, teacher certification program. British Campus at Harlaxton College and undergraduate research. **Credit/placement by examination:** AP, CLEP, IB, SAT, ACT, institutional tests. 6 credit hours maximum toward associate degree, 6 toward bachelor's. **Support services:** Study skills assistance, tutoring, writing center. Supplemental instruction available in several traditionally challenging courses.

Majors. Biology: General, biochemistry, neuroscience. **Business:** Accounting, business admin, finance, international, marketing, organizational leadership. **Communications:** General, health, sports. **Computer sciences:** Computer science. **Conservation:** Environmental science, environmental studies. **Education:** General, art, biology, chemistry, drama/dance, elementary, English, French, German, mathematics, music, physics, social studies, Spanish, special ed. **Engineering:** Civil, computer, electrical, mechanical. **English:** Creative writing, English lit, writing. **Foreign languages:** Classics, French, German, Spanish. **Health services:** Athletic training, clinical lab science, health care admin, music therapy, nursing (RN), predental, premedicine, preoptometry, prepharmacy, preveterinary. **History:** General. **Liberal arts:** Arts/sciences. **Math:** General. **Parks/recreation:** Exercise sciences, sports admin. **Philosophy/religion:** Philosophy. **Physical sciences:** Chemistry, physics. **Protective services:** Criminal justice. **Psychology:** General. **Social sciences:** Archaeology, economics, international relations, political science, sociology. **Theology:** Bible, theology. **Visual/performing arts:** Art, art history/conservation, design, dramatic, music, music management, music performance, theater arts management.

Most popular majors. Business/marketing 13%, education 7%, engineering/engineering technologies 9%, English 7%, health sciences 14%, parks/recreation 10%, social sciences 8%, visual/performing arts 8%.

Technology on campus. 385 workstations in dormitories, library, student center. Dormitories wired for high-speed internet access and linked to campus network. Commuter students can connect to campus network. Online course registration, online library, helpline, repair service, student web hosting, wireless network available.

Student life. Freshman orientation: Mandatory. Preregistration for classes offered. 3 1/2 day program held prior to beginning of semester. One session includes testing, advising, and registration. **Housing:** Guaranteed on-campus for freshmen. Coed dorms, single-sex dorms, apartments, fraternity/sorority housing, themed housing available. $300 nonrefundable deposit. **Activities:** Bands, campus ministries, choral groups, dance, drama, film society, international student organizations, literary magazine, music ensembles, Model UN, musical theater, opera, radio station, student government, student newspaper, symphony orchestra, Black Student Union, Hillel, Kappa Chi (service), Habitat for Humanity, Circle K, College Democrats, College Republicans, Student Christian Fellowship, Asian culture club.

Athletics. NCAA. **Intercollegiate:** Baseball M, basketball, cross-country, diving, golf, soccer, softball W, swimming, tennis W, volleyball W. **Intramural:** Badminton, basketball, football (non-tackle), golf, racquetball, sand volleyball, soccer, softball, tennis, ultimate frisbee, volleyball. **Team name:** Purple Aces.

Student services. Adult student services, alcohol/substance abuse counseling, chaplain/spiritual director, career counseling, student employment services, financial aid counseling, health services, minority student services, personal counseling, placement for graduates, veterans' counselor. **Physically disabled:** Services for visually, speech, hearing impaired.

Contact. E-mail: admission@evansville.edu
Phone: (812) 488-2468 Toll-free number: (800) 423-8633 ext. 2468
Fax: (812) 488-4076
Scott Henne, Dean of Admission, University of Evansville, 1800 Lincoln Avenue, Evansville, IN 47722

University of Indianapolis
Indianapolis, Indiana
www.uindy.edu

CB member
CB code: 1321

- Private 4-year university and liberal arts college affiliated with the United Methodist Church
- Residential campus in very large city
- 4,139 degree-seeking undergraduates: 16% part-time, 64% women, 9% African American, 1% Asian American, 4% Hispanic/Latino, 3% Multiracial, non-Hispanic, 9% international
- 1,263 degree-seeking graduate students
- 73% of applicants admitted
- SAT or ACT (ACT writing optional) required
- 56% graduate within 6 years

General. Founded in 1902. Regionally accredited. **Degrees:** 822 bachelor's, 72 associate awarded; master's, professional, doctoral offered. **ROTC:** Army. **Location:** 5 miles from downtown. **Calendar:** Semester, limited summer session. **Full-time faculty:** 234 total; 73% have terminal degrees, 7% minority, 56% women. **Part-time faculty:** 301 total; 16% have terminal degrees, 9% minority, 56% women. **Class size:** 62% < 20, 37% 20-39, 1% 40-49, less than 1% 50-99. **Special facilities:** Observatory, fine arts center.

Freshman class profile. 7,216 applied, 5,297 admitted, 960 enrolled.

Mid 50% test scores			
SAT critical reading:	450-560	Rank in top quarter:	55%
SAT math:	460-560	Rank in top tenth:	21%
SAT writing:	450-540	Return as sophomores:	75%
ACT composite:	20-25	Out-of-state:	10%
GPA 3.75 or higher:	36%	Live on campus:	81%
GPA 3.50-3.74:	18%	International:	5%
GPA 3.0-3.49:	31%	GPA 2.0-2.99:	15%

Basis for selection. Recommendations, GPA, SAT/ACT, class rank important. Involvement in extracurricular activities considered. Essay recommended. Interview recommended for borderline applicants. Audition required of music majors. Portfolio recommended for art majors. **Home schooled:** Transcript of courses and grades required. **Learning Disabled:** Students with learning disabilities may apply to the BUILD program through separate application process.

High school preparation. College-preparatory program recommended. 20 units recommended. Recommended units include English 4, mathematics 3, social studies 2, history 2, science 3 (laboratory 3), foreign language 2, computer science 1 and visual/performing arts 2.

2015-2016 Annual costs. Tuition/fees: $26,150. Room/board: $9,930. Books/supplies: $1,250. Personal expenses: $2,030.

2014-2015 Financial aid. Need-based: 878 full-time freshmen applied for aid; 775 deemed to have need; 775 received aid. Average need met was 67%. Average scholarship/grant was $8,338; average loan $3,728. 89% of total undergraduate aid awarded as scholarships/grants, 11% as loans/jobs. **Non-need-based:** Awarded to 3,173 full-time undergraduates, including 971 freshmen. Scholarships awarded for academics, alumni affiliation, art, athletics, music/drama, religious affiliation, state residency.

Application procedures. Admission: No deadline. No application fee. Admission notification on a rolling basis beginning on or about 9/1. **Financial aid:** Closing date 3/10. FAFSA, institutional form required. Applicants notified on a rolling basis starting 3/1; must reply within 3 week(s) of notification.

Academics. Special study options: Accelerated study, combined bachelor's/graduate degree, cross-registration, double major, dual enrollment of high school students, ESL, honors, independent study, internships, liberal arts/career combination, student-designed major, study abroad, teacher certification program, Washington semester. Baccalaureate for University of Indianapolis Learning Disabled (BUILD), Wellness, Judaic-Christian Traditions, New Student Experience. **Credit/placement by examination:** AP, CLEP, IB, SAT, ACT, institutional tests. 3-8 hours awarded for International Baccalaureate based on scores. **Support services:** Learning center, pre-admission summer program, reduced course load, remedial instruction, study skills assistance, tutoring, writing center.

Honors college/program. Presidential Scholars, Dean's Scholars, or Lugar Scholars with Distinguished Admission invited to participate. Students make formal application to Honors College in second semester for full admission to the College.

Majors. Biology: General, cell/histology. **Business:** Accounting, business admin, entrepreneurial studies, international, management information systems, managerial economics, marketing, tourism/travel. **Communications:** Communications/speech/rhetoric, journalism. **Computer sciences:** General, computer science, information systems. **Conservation:** Environmental science. **Education:** General, art, biology, business, chemistry, elementary, English, foreign languages, French, history, mathematics, music, physical, physics, science, secondary, social studies, Spanish, speech. **English:** Creative writing, English lit. **Foreign languages:** French, German, Spanish. **Health services:** Art therapy, athletic training, clinical lab science, clinical lab technology, nursing (RN), public health ed, respiratory therapy technology. **History:** General. **Human services:** Social work. **Math:** General. **Parks/recreation:** Exercise sciences, sports admin. **Philosophy/religion:** Philosophy, religion. **Physical sciences:** Chemistry, geology, physics. **Protective services:** Law enforcement admin. **Psychology:** General. **Social sciences:** Anthropology, archaeology, economics, international relations, political science, sociology. **Visual/performing arts:** Art, commercial/advertising art, design, dramatic, music, music performance.

Most popular majors. Business/marketing 23%, education 6%, health sciences 18%, liberal arts 7%, parks/recreation 7%, psychology 6%.

Technology on campus. 222 workstations in dormitories, library, computer center, student center. Dormitories wired for high-speed internet access and linked to campus network. Commuter students can connect to campus network. Online course registration, online library, helpline, wireless network available.

Student life. Freshman orientation: Mandatory, $40 fee. Preregistration for classes offered. Student attends one of 6 summer registration programs. **Housing:** Coed dorms, single-sex dorms, apartments available. $50 partly refundable deposit, deadline 5/1. **Activities:** Bands, campus ministries, choral groups, dance, drama, international student organizations, literary magazine, music ensembles, musical theater, opera, radio station, student government, student newspaper, TV station, Young Democrats, Young Republicans, Fellowship of Christian Athletes, Circle-K, social service, honorary societies, Catholic student association.

Athletics. NCAA. **Intercollegiate:** Baseball M, basketball, cross-country, diving, football (tackle) M, golf, soccer, softball W, swimming, tennis, track and field, volleyball W, wrestling M. **Intramural:** Basketball, football (non-tackle) M, soccer, softball, volleyball. **Team name:** Greyhounds.

Student services. Adult student services, chaplain/spiritual director, career counseling, student employment services, financial aid counseling, health services, personal counseling, placement for graduates, veterans' counselor. **Physically disabled:** Services for visually, speech, hearing impaired.

Contact. E-mail: admissions@uindy.edu
Phone: (317) 788-3216 Toll-free number: (800) 232-8634
Fax: (317) 788-3300
Ron Wilks, Director of Admissions, University of Indianapolis, 1400 East Hanna Avenue, Indianapolis, IN 46227-3697

University of Notre Dame
Notre Dame, Indiana

CB member
CB code: 1841

www.nd.edu

- Private 4-year university affiliated with the Roman Catholic Church
- Residential campus in small city
- 8,425 degree-seeking undergraduates: 48% women, 4% African American, 6% Asian American, 11% Hispanic/Latino, 4% Multi-racial, non-Hispanic, 6% international
- 3,645 degree-seeking graduate students
- 20% of applicants admitted
- SAT or ACT (ACT writing optional), application essay required
- 97% graduate within 6 years; 28% enter graduate study

General. Founded in 1842. Regionally accredited. Notre Dame Study Centers in Washington, DC; Dublin, Ireland; London, England; Rome, Italy; several other countries. **Degrees:** 2,128 bachelor's awarded; master's, professional, doctoral offered. **ROTC:** Army, Naval, Air Force. **Location:** 90 miles from Chicago. **Calendar:** Semester, extensive summer session. **Full-time faculty:** 1,119 total; 91% have terminal degrees, 17% minority, 30% women. **Part-time faculty:** 190 total; 60% have terminal degrees, 7% minority, 42% women. **Special facilities:** Germ-free research facility, radiation laboratory, nature preserve for biological research, wind-tunnel research facility, art museum, performing arts center.

Freshman class profile. 18,157 applied, 3,595 admitted, 2,007 enrolled.

Mid 50% test scores			
SAT critical reading:	670-760	Rank in top tenth:	91%
SAT math:	680-770	Return as sophomores:	98%
SAT writing:	650-750	Out-of-state:	92%
ACT composite:	32-34	Live on campus:	100%
Rank in top quarter:	98%	International:	7%

Basis for selection. GED not accepted. Essay and writing skills, teacher recommendation, extracurricular activities, and short answer responses on application important. 3 SAT Subject Tests recommended for home schooled students. Music sample recommended for music majors. Portfolio for art and architecture majors. **Home schooled:** SAT Subject Tests recommended in foreign language, science and history.

High school preparation. College-preparatory program recommended. 16 units required; 20 recommended. Required and recommended units include English 4, mathematics 3-4, history 2-4, science 2-4 (laboratory 2), foreign language 2-4 and academic electives 3.

2015-2016 Annual costs. Tuition/fees: $47,929. Room/board: $13,846. Books/supplies: $1,050. Personal expenses: $1,200.

2014-2015 Financial aid. Need-based: 1,346 full-time freshmen applied for aid; 886 deemed to have need; 886 received aid. Average need met was 100%. Average scholarship/grant was $35,998; average loan $3,622. 85% of total undergraduate aid awarded as scholarships/grants, 15% as loans/jobs. **Non-need-based:** Awarded to 2,836 full-time undergraduates, including 654 freshmen. Scholarships awarded for academics, athletics, ROTC.

Application procedures. Admission: Closing date 1/1 (postmark date). $75 fee, may be waived for applicants with need. Application must be submitted online. Admission notification by 4/10. Must reply by May 1 or within 2 week(s) if notified thereafter. **Financial aid:** Priority date 2/15; no closing date. FAFSA, CSS PROFILE required. Applicants notified on a rolling basis starting 3/28; must reply by 5/1.

Academics. Special study options: Cross-registration, double major, dual enrollment of high school students, exchange student, honors, independent study, internships, liberal arts/career combination, student-designed major, study abroad, teacher certification program, Washington semester. Teacher certification available only through cross-registration with St. Mary's College; triple majors, quadruple majors, triple degrees, double majors within dual degrees. **Credit/placement by examination:** AP, CLEP, IB, institutional tests. Students with HL score of 6 or 7 eligible to receive credit in anthropology, biology, chemistry, English, French, German, Greek, Latin, math, music, physics, psychology, Spanish, economics, Arabic, Chinese, Italian, Japanese, Russian. **Support services:** Learning center, study skills assistance, tutoring, writing center.

Majors. Architecture: Architecture. **Area/ethnic studies:** African-American, American. **Biology:** General, biochemistry. **Business:** General, accounting, finance, management information systems, marketing. **Computer sciences:** General. **Conservation:** Environmental science. **Education:** Science. **Engineering:** Aerospace, chemical, civil, computer, electrical, environmental, mechanical. **English:** English lit. **Foreign languages:** Ancient Greek, Arabic, Chinese, classics, French, German, Italian, Japanese, Romance, Russian, Spanish. **Health services:** Premedicine. **History:** General. **Liberal arts:** Arts/sciences. **Math:** General. **Philosophy/religion:** Philosophy. **Physical sciences:** Chemistry, physics. **Psychology:** General. **Social sciences:** Anthropology, economics, political science, sociology. **Theology:** Theology. **Visual/performing arts:** Art history/conservation, design, dramatic, music, studio arts.

Most popular majors. Business/marketing 24%, engineering/engineering technologies 11%, foreign language 6%, health sciences 7%, social sciences 14%.

Technology on campus. 232 workstations in dormitories, library, computer center, student center. Dormitories wired for high-speed internet access and linked to campus network. Commuter students can connect to campus network. Online course registration, online library, helpline, repair service, wireless network available.

Student life. Freshman orientation: Mandatory. Preregistration for classes offered. **Policies:** Freshmen not permitted cars on campus. **Housing:** Guaranteed on-campus for freshmen. Single-sex dorms available. Requests for ground level housing or housing suitable for a disabled student will be honored. **Activities:** Bands, campus ministries, choral groups, dance, drama, film society, international student organizations, literary magazine, music ensembles, musical theater, opera, radio station, student government, student newspaper, symphony orchestra, more than 400 clubs and organizations available.

Athletics. NCAA. **Intercollegiate:** Baseball M, basketball, cross-country, diving, fencing, football (tackle) M, golf, ice hockey M, lacrosse, rowing (crew) W, soccer, softball W, swimming, tennis, track and field, volleyball W. **Intramural:** Badminton, baseball M, basketball, bowling, cross-country, football (non-tackle), football (tackle) M, golf, ice hockey M, lacrosse, racquetball, sand volleyball, soccer, softball, table tennis, tennis, ultimate frisbee, volleyball. **Team name:** Fighting Irish.

Student services. Alcohol/substance abuse counseling, chaplain/spiritual director, career counseling, student employment services, health services, minority student services, personal counseling, placement for graduates, veterans' counselor. **Physically disabled:** Services for visually, hearing impaired.

Contact. E-mail: admissions@nd.edu
Phone: (574) 631-7505 Fax: (574) 631-8865
Donald Bishop, Assistant Vice President Undergraduate Enrollment, University of Notre Dame, 220 Main Building, Notre Dame, IN 46556

University of Phoenix: Indianapolis
Indianapolis, Indiana

www.phoenix.edu

- For-profit 4-year university
- Very large city
- 275 undergraduates
- 40 graduate students

General. Regionally accredited. **Degrees:** 61 bachelor's awarded; master's offered. **Calendar:** Differs by program. **Full-time faculty:** 9 total. **Part-time faculty:** 146 total.

Basis for selection. Open admission, but selective for some programs.

2015-2016 Annual costs. Per-credit-hour charge, $395 to $635, depending upon level and course of study. Books, material charges, and other fees vary by course and program. All fees are subject to change.

Application procedures. Admission: No deadline. No application fee. **Financial aid:** No deadline.

Academics. Credit/placement by examination: AP, CLEP.

Majors. Business: Accounting/business management, business admin, e-commerce, entrepreneurial studies, finance, human resources, marketing, operations. **Communications:** General. **Computer sciences:** Database management, networking, programming, security, system admin, systems analysis, web page design, webmaster. **Education:** Elementary. **Health services:** Facilities admin, health information management, long term care admin, nursing (RN). **Human services:** General. **Protective services:** Disaster management, law enforcement admin, security management.

Student life. Freshman orientation: Mandatory. Preregistration for classes offered.

Contact. Toll-free number: (866) 766-0766
University of Phoenix: Indianapolis, 1625 West Fountainhead Parkway, Tempe, AZ 85282

University of Saint Francis
Fort Wayne, Indiana
www.sf.edu   **CB code: 1693**

- Private 4-year university and liberal arts college affiliated with the Roman Catholic Church
- Commuter campus in large city
- 1,745 degree-seeking undergraduates: 14% part-time, 71% women, 7% African American, 1% Asian American, 6% Hispanic/Latino, 2% Multiracial, non-Hispanic, 1% international
- 425 degree-seeking graduate students
- 95% of applicants admitted
- SAT or ACT (ACT writing optional) required
- 56% graduate within 6 years; 15% enter graduate study

General. Founded in 1890. Regionally accredited. **Degrees:** 315 bachelor's, 148 associate awarded; master's offered. **Location:** 125 miles from Indianapolis,150 miles from Chicago. **Calendar:** Semester, limited summer session. **Full-time faculty:** 125 total; 47% have terminal degrees, 2% minority, 64% women. **Part-time faculty:** 145 total; 12% have terminal degrees, 6% minority, 70% women. **Class size:** 63% < 20, 35% 20-39, 1% 40-49, less than 1% 50-99. **Special facilities:** Art galleries, planetarium, nature preserve, cadaver lab, health sciences simulation lab, performing arts center.

Freshman class profile. 991 applied, 944 admitted, 372 enrolled.

Mid 50% test scores			
SAT critical reading:	430-530	GPA 2.0-2.99:	28%
SAT math:	430-540	Rank in top quarter:	47%
SAT writing:	420-530	Rank in top tenth:	17%
ACT composite:	18-24	Return as sophomores:	68%
GPA 3.75 or higher:	30%	Out-of-state:	11%
GPA 3.50-3.74:	14%	Live on campus:	53%
GPA 3.0-3.49:	27%	International:	1%

Basis for selection. High school achievement record, rank, and test scores are important. Additional requirements for admissions to dual-accept, healthcare, or business majors may be needed. Applicants for these programs are encouraged to contact the Office of Admissions. SAT and SAT Subject Tests or ACT recommended. Interview and/or essay/personal statement may be required for certain majors or programs. Additional testing may be required for students entering into certain programs. **Home schooled:** Letter of recommendation (nonparent) required. Bibliography of books read, list of extracurricular activities, and the letter of recommendation from person other than parent must be submitted. **Learning Disabled:** Students with learning disabilities are encouraged to contact our disability services coordinator to discuss classroom accommodations. No special admissions procedures are required.

High school preparation. College-preparatory program recommended. 21 units required; 28 recommended. Required and recommended units include English 4, mathematics 3-4, social studies 2-3, history 1, science 2-3 and academic electives 1-4.

2015-2016 Annual costs. Tuition/fees: $27,220. Room/board: $8,830.

2014-2015 Financial aid. Need-based: 274 full-time freshmen applied for aid; 254 deemed to have need; 254 received aid. Average need met was 73%. Average scholarship/grant was $16,670; average loan $2,890. 60% of total undergraduate aid awarded as scholarships/grants, 40% as loans/jobs. **Non-need-based:** Awarded to 298 full-time undergraduates, including 85 freshmen. Scholarships awarded for academics, art, athletics, music/drama, state residency.

Application procedures. Admission: No deadline. No application fee. Admission notification on a rolling basis beginning on or about 8/1. **Financial aid:** Priority date 3/10; no closing date. FAFSA required. Applicants notified on a rolling basis starting 3/1; must reply by 8/1.

Academics. Special study options: Cross-registration, distance learning, double major, dual enrollment of high school students, honors, independent study, internships, student-designed major, teacher certification program. **Credit/placement by examination:** AP, CLEP, IB, SAT, ACT, institutional tests. 15 credit hours maximum toward associate degree, 30 toward bachelor's. **Support services:** Learning center, reduced course load, remedial instruction, study skills assistance, tutoring, writing center. Available on a case by case basis.

Majors. Biology: General. **Business:** General, accounting, business admin, finance, insurance, marketing. **Communications:** General. **Conservation:** Environmental science. **Education:** General, art, biology, business, chemistry, elementary, English, health, mathematics, secondary, social studies, special ed. **English:** English lit. **Health services:** General, art therapy, clinical lab science, health care admin, nursing (RN). **History:** General. **Human**

services: Social work. **Liberal arts:** Arts/sciences. **Math:** General. **Philosophy/religion:** Philosophy. **Physical sciences:** Chemistry, forensic chemistry. **Protective services:** Criminal justice. **Psychology:** Developmental. **Social sciences:** Political science, sociology. **Theology:** Lay ministry, theology. **Visual/performing arts:** Art history/conservation, dance, design, digital arts, music technology, studio arts.

Most popular majors. Business/marketing 13%, health sciences 50%, visual/performing arts 9%.

Technology on campus. 498 workstations in dormitories, library, computer center, student center. Dormitories wired for high-speed internet access and linked to campus network. Commuter students can connect to campus network. Online course registration, online library, helpline, repair service, wireless network available.

Student life. Freshman orientation: Mandatory, $100 fee. Preregistration for classes offered. Held on several pre-scheduled dates throughout the spring and early summer for fall admits; normally takes up to four hours. **Policies:** No alcohol allowed in residence halls; no smoking on campus property; full-time students under 21 not living at home or with a guardian must live in residence halls. **Housing:** Guaranteed on-campus for all undergraduates. Coed dorms, special housing for disabled, apartments available. $200 fully refundable deposit, deadline 6/30. **Activities:** Bands, campus ministries, choral groups, drama, film society, literary magazine, music ensembles, musical theater, student government, student newspaper, Student Government Organization, Peer Ministers, Legacy, Culturas Unidas, Brotherhood, Cougars Care service club, Logos, Cougars for Faith, Family and Life.

Athletics. NAIA. **Intercollegiate:** Baseball M, basketball, cross-country, football (tackle) M, golf, soccer, softball W, tennis, track and field, volleyball W. **Intramural:** Basketball, soccer, softball, ultimate frisbee, volleyball. **Team name:** Cougars.

Student services. Chaplain/spiritual director, career counseling, student employment services, financial aid counseling, health services, personal counseling, placement for graduates. **Physically disabled:** Services for visually, hearing impaired.

Contact. E-mail: admis@sf.edu
Phone: (260) 399-8000 Toll-free number: (800) 729-4732
Fax: (260) 399-8152
Maria Gerber, Director of Undergraduate Admissions, University of Saint Francis, 2701 Spring Street, Fort Wayne, IN 46808

University of Southern Indiana
Evansville, Indiana
www.usi.edu   **CB code: 1335**

- Public 4-year university and liberal arts college
- Commuter campus in small city
- 8,058 degree-seeking undergraduates: 15% part-time, 61% women, 4% African American, 1% Asian American, 3% Hispanic/Latino, 2% Multiracial, non-Hispanic, 2% international
- 876 degree-seeking graduate students
- 69% of applicants admitted
- SAT or ACT (ACT writing recommended) required
- 41% graduate within 6 years

General. Founded in 1965. Regionally accredited. Credit courses offered at various off-campus sites in Evansville and surrounding areas. **Degrees:** 1,566 bachelor's, 79 associate awarded; master's, professional offered. **ROTC:** Army. **Location:** 150 miles from Indianapolis. **Calendar:** Semester, limited summer session. **Full-time faculty:** 347 total; 69% have terminal degrees, 7% minority, 54% women. **Part-time faculty:** 330 total; 23% have terminal degrees, 4% minority, 62% women. **Class size:** 40% < 20, 53% 20-39, 3% 40-49, 2% 50-99, 1% >100.

Freshman class profile. 6,216 applied, 4,310 admitted, 1,690 enrolled.

Mid 50% test scores			
SAT critical reading:	440-550	Rank in top quarter:	33%
SAT math:	450-550	Rank in top tenth:	12%
SAT writing:	420-530	Return as sophomores:	71%
ACT composite:	19-24	Out-of-state:	7%
GPA 3.75 or higher:	18%	Live on campus:	66%
GPA 3.50-3.74:	18%	International:	1%
GPA 3.0-3.49:	33%	Fraternities:	5%
GPA 2.0-2.99:	31%	Sororities:	2%

Basis for selection. 2.0 GPA required for out-of-state applicants. 900 SAT (exclusive of Writing) required for applicants to health programs. Students accepted at 1 of 3 levels based on academic record and test scores. Placement test administered prior to registration. SAT/ACT used to place students at 1 of 3 levels within institution. **Home schooled:** Transcript of courses and grades required.

High school preparation. College-preparatory program recommended. 18 units recommended. Recommended units include English 4, mathematics 4, social studies 2, history 2, science 2, foreign language 2 and academic electives 2. 2 units computer and/or art recommended.

2015-2016 Annual costs. Tuition/fees: $7,397; $17,179 out-of-state. Room/board: $8,276. Books/supplies: $1,140. Personal expenses: $1,582.

2015-2016 Financial aid. Need-based: 1,539 full-time freshmen applied for aid; 1,081 deemed to have need; 1,081 received aid. Average need met was 80%. Average scholarship/grant was $8,137; average loan $3,288. 42% of total undergraduate aid awarded as scholarships/grants, 58% as loans/jobs. **Non-need-based:** Awarded to 3,043 full-time undergraduates, including 837 freshmen. Scholarships awarded for academics, art, athletics, leadership, music/drama, state residency.

Application procedures. Admission: Closing date 8/15 (receipt date). $40 fee, may be waived for applicants with need. Admission notification on a rolling basis beginning on or about 7/1. Applicants accepted through first week of classes, but encouraged to apply by August 15 for fall and January 1 for spring. **Financial aid:** Priority date 3/1; no closing date. FAFSA required. Applicants notified on a rolling basis starting 4/1; must reply by 4/1.

Academics. Special study options: Combined bachelor's/graduate degree, cooperative education, distance learning, double major, dual enrollment of high school students, ESL, honors, independent study, internships, study abroad, teacher certification program. **Credit/placement by examination:** AP, CLEP, SAT, ACT, institutional tests. 42 credit hours maximum toward associate degree, 90 toward bachelor's. **Support services:** Learning center, reduced course load, remedial instruction, study skills assistance, tutoring, writing center.

Majors. Biology: General, biochemistry, biophysics. **Business:** General, accounting, business admin, entrepreneurial studies, finance, marketing, office management, operations. **Communications:** Advertising, journalism, media studies, radio/TV. **Computer sciences:** General, computer science. **Conservation:** Environmental science. **Education:** Business, early childhood, elementary, physical. **Engineering:** General. **English:** English lit. **Foreign languages:** French, German, Spanish. **Health services:** Dental hygiene, health care admin, medical radiologic technology/radiation therapy, nursing (RN). **History:** General. **Human services:** Social work. **Liberal arts/sciences:** Arts/sciences. **Math:** General. **Parks/recreation:** Exercise sciences, sports admin. **Philosophy/religion:** Philosophy. **Physical sciences:** Chemistry, geology. **Protective services:** Criminal justice. **Psychology:** General. **Social sciences:** General, anthropology, economics, international relations, political science, sociology. **Visual/performing arts:** Art, dramatic.

Most popular majors. Business/marketing 16%, communications/journalism 6%, education 6%, health sciences 25%, parks/recreation 6%.

Technology on campus. 306 workstations in dormitories, library, computer center, student center. Dormitories wired for high-speed internet access and linked to campus network. Commuter students can connect to campus network. Online course registration, online library, helpline, repair service, wireless network available.

Student life. Freshman orientation: Mandatory, $65 fee. Preregistration for classes offered. Two-day program, includes parent participation. **Housing:** Coed dorms, special housing for disabled, apartments, fraternity/sorority housing, themed housing available. $200 partly refundable deposit. **Activities:** Bands, campus ministries, choral groups, dance, drama, film society, international student organizations, literary magazine, radio station, student government, student newspaper, TV station, Chi Alpha Campus Ministry, Student Christian Fellowship, Young Life, College Democrats, College Republicans, Black Student Union, International Club, Latinos Unidos/Hispanic Student Union, Riley Dance Marathon, Colleges Against Cancer.

Athletics. NCAA. **Intercollegiate:** Baseball M, basketball, cheerleading, cross-country, golf, soccer, softball W, tennis, track and field, volleyball W. **Intramural:** Badminton, basketball, bowling, cross-country, football (non-tackle), golf, soccer, softball, swimming, table tennis, tennis, volleyball. **Team name:** Screaming Eagles.

Student services. Adult student services, alcohol/substance abuse counseling, chaplain/spiritual director, career counseling, services for economically disadvantaged, student employment services, financial aid counseling, health services, minority student services, on-campus daycare, personal counseling, placement for graduates, veterans' counselor. **Physically disabled:** Services for visually, speech, hearing impaired.

Contact. E-mail: enroll@usi.edu
Phone: (812) 464-1765 Toll-free number: (800) 467-1965
Fax: (812) 465-7154
Mark Rusk, Director of Admission, University of Southern Indiana, 8600 University Boulevard, Evansville, IN 47712

Valparaiso University
Valparaiso, Indiana
www.valpo.edu

CB member
CB code: 1874

- Private 4-year university affiliated with the Lutheran Church
- Residential campus in large town
- 3,141 degree-seeking undergraduates: 2% part-time, 52% women, 6% African American, 2% Asian American, 8% Hispanic/Latino, 3% Multi-racial, non-Hispanic, 7% international
- 1,338 degree-seeking graduate students
- 82% of applicants admitted
- SAT or ACT (ACT writing recommended), application essay required
- 67% graduate within 6 years; 21% enter graduate study

General. Founded in 1859. Regionally accredited. **Degrees:** 710 bachelor's, 1 associate awarded; master's, professional offered. **ROTC:** Army, Air Force. **Location:** 55 miles from Chicago. **Calendar:** Semester, limited summer session. **Full-time faculty:** 312 total; 83% have terminal degrees, 12% minority, 43% women. **Part-time faculty:** 102 total; 53% have terminal degrees, 9% minority, 49% women. **Class size:** 47% < 20, 45% 20-39, 3% 40-49, 4% 50-99, less than 1% >100. **Special facilities:** Electron microscope, observatory, storm chasing equipment, weather station, Doppler Radar facility, planetarium, center for learning and information resources, virtual nursing learning center, scientific visualization laboratory, solar research facility, engineering innovation center.

Freshman class profile. 6,657 applied, 5,452 admitted, 742 enrolled.

Mid 50% test scores		Rank in top quarter:	64%
SAT critical reading:	490-600	Rank in top tenth:	35%
SAT math:	510-630	End year in good standing:	84%
SAT writing:	480-590	Return as sophomores:	82%
ACT composite:	23-29	Out-of-state:	59%
GPA 3.75 or higher:	51%	Live on campus:	86%
GPA 3.50-3.74:	19%	International:	2%
GPA 3.0-3.49:	26%	Fraternities:	29%
GPA 2.0-2.99:	4%	Sororities:	21%

Basis for selection. High school record most important. Test scores next in importance, followed by recommendations and activities. Nature of high school program considered. Interview recommended. Audition required of music majors. Portfolio recommended for art majors. **Home schooled:** Transcript of courses and grades required. Must specify primary educator and provide course description list or reading list. **Learning Disabled:** Student should submit suitable documentation to the Disability Support Services Office following admission into the University in order to determine eligibility of services.

High school preparation. College-preparatory program recommended. 16 units required; 19 recommended. Required and recommended units include English 4, mathematics 3-4, social studies 1, history 2, science 2-3 (laboratory 2-3), foreign language 2 and academic electives 3.

2015-2016 Annual costs. Tuition/fees: $36,160. Room/board: $10,520. Books/supplies: $1,200. Personal expenses: $870. **Additional information:** Engineering students pay an additional $740 fee.

2014-2015 Financial aid. Need-based: 650 full-time freshmen applied for aid; 570 deemed to have need; 568 received aid. Average need met was 94%. Average scholarship/grant was $24,489; average loan $4,852. 70% of total undergraduate aid awarded as scholarships/grants, 30% as loans/jobs. **Non-need-based:** Awarded to 1,129 full-time undergraduates, including 223 freshmen. Scholarships awarded for academics, alumni affiliation, art, athletics, leadership, music/drama, religious affiliation, ROTC, state residency. **Additional information:** Financial assistance based on need, academic record, talent available through university.

Application procedures. Admission: Priority date 12/1; no deadline. No application fee. Admission notification on a rolling basis beginning on or about 10/1. Must reply by May 1 or within 4 week(s) if notified thereafter. **Financial aid:** Priority date 3/1; no closing date. FAFSA required. Applicants notified on a rolling basis starting 3/1.

Academics. Special study options: Accelerated study, combined bachelor's/graduate degree, cooperative education, cross-registration, distance learning, double major, ESL, exchange student, honors, independent study, internships, liberal arts/career combination, student-designed major, study abroad, teacher certification program, urban semester, Washington semester. **Credit/placement by examination:** AP, CLEP, IB, institutional tests. **Support services:** Learning center, reduced course load, study skills assistance, tutoring, writing center.

Honors college/program. Approximately 80-90 students enroll per year in Christ College, the Honors College. Must demonstrate academic excellence in high school, intellectual curiosity, and leadership skills. Program integrates history, literature, philosophy, religion, and art.

Majors. Area/ethnic studies: American, East Asian. **Biology:** General, biochemistry. **Business:** Accounting, actuarial science, finance, international, management science, marketing. **Communications:** General, digital media. **Computer sciences:** Computer science. **Conservation:** Environmental science. **Education:** Art, biology, chemistry, drama/dance, elementary, English, foreign languages, French, geography, German, history, mathematics, middle, music, physical, physics, psychology, science, secondary, social science, Spanish. **Engineering:** Civil, computer, electrical, mechanical. **English:** Creative writing, English lit, technical writing. **Foreign languages:** Classics, French, German, Spanish. **Health services:** Health care admin, nursing (RN). **History:** General. **Human services:** Social work. **Liberal arts:** Humanities. **Math:** General. **Parks/recreation:** Exercise sciences, health/fitness, sports admin. **Philosophy/religion:** Philosophy. **Physical sciences:** Astronomy, atmospheric science, chemistry, geology, physics. **Psychology:** General. **Social sciences:** General, criminology, economics, geography, international economics, international relations, political science, sociology. **Theology:** Theology. **Visual/performing arts:** Art, dramatic, music, music performance, music theory/composition, piano/keyboard, voice/opera.

Most popular majors. Biology 6%, business/marketing 12%, engineering/engineering technologies 9%, health sciences 18%, physical sciences 6%, social sciences 9%.

Technology on campus. 500 workstations in dormitories, library, computer center, student center. Dormitories wired for high-speed internet access and linked to campus network. Commuter students can connect to campus network. Online course registration, online library, helpline, student web hosting, wireless network available.

Student life. Freshman orientation: Mandatory, $145 fee. Preregistration for classes offered. Overnight program held in June. **Policies:** Freshmen not permitted cars on campus. **Housing:** Guaranteed on-campus for all undergraduates. Coed dorms, single-sex dorms, apartments, fraternity/sorority housing, themed housing, wellness housing available. $100 fully refundable deposit, deadline 5/1. **Activities:** Bands, campus ministries, choral groups, dance, drama, international student organizations, literary magazine, music ensembles, musical theater, radio station, student government, student newspaper, symphony orchestra, Alpha Phi Omega, Earthtones, InterVarsity Christian Fellowship, St. Teresa of Avila, Black Student Organization, Asian American Association, Latinos in Valparaiso for Excellence, College Democrats, College Republicans.

Athletics. NCAA. **Intercollegiate:** Baseball M, basketball, bowling W, cross-country, diving, football (tackle) M, golf, soccer, softball W, swimming, tennis, track and field, volleyball W. **Intramural:** Badminton, basketball, bowling, football (non-tackle), golf, racquetball, sand volleyball, soccer, softball, table tennis, tennis, triathlon, ultimate frisbee, volleyball. **Team name:** Crusaders.

Student services. Adult student services, alcohol/substance abuse counseling, chaplain/spiritual director, career counseling, services for economically disadvantaged, student employment services, financial aid counseling, health services, legal services, minority student services, personal counseling, placement for graduates. **Physically disabled:** Services for visually impaired.

Contact. E-mail: undergrad.admission@valpo.edu
Phone: (219) 464-5011 Toll-free number: (888) 468-2576
Fax: (219) 464-6898
Bart Harvey, Director of Freshman Admission and Operations, Valparaiso University, Kretzmann Hall, 1700 Chapel Drive, Valparaiso, IN 46383-6493

Wabash College
Crawfordsville, Indiana
www.wabash.edu

CB member
CB code: 1895

- Private 4-year liberal arts college for men
- Residential campus in large town
- 867 degree-seeking undergraduates: 6% African American, 1% Asian American, 7% Hispanic/Latino, 3% Multi-racial, non-Hispanic, 7% international
- 61% of applicants admitted
- SAT or ACT (ACT writing recommended), application essay required
- 73% graduate within 6 years; 9% enter graduate study

General. Founded in 1832. Regionally accredited. **Degrees:** 229 bachelor's awarded. **Location:** 45 miles from Indianapolis, 125 miles from Chicago. **Calendar:** Semester. **Full-time faculty:** 80 total; 99% have terminal degrees, 10% minority, 35% women. **Part-time faculty:** 25 total; 88% have terminal degrees, 24% minority, 44% women. **Class size:** 72% < 20, 23% 20-39, 3%

40-49, 2% 50-99. **Special facilities:** Two biology field stations, qualitative and quantitative skills center, electron microscope, parallel computer, nature preserve, archival center, Center of Inquiry in the Liberal Arts, Wabash Center for Teaching and Learning in Theology and Religion.

Freshman class profile. 1,247 applied, 766 admitted, 238 enrolled.

Mid 50% test scores			
SAT critical reading:	510-610	Rank in top quarter:	71%
SAT math:	530-640	Rank in top tenth:	35%
SAT writing:	470-600	End year in good standing:	90%
ACT composite:	22-28	Return as sophomores:	85%
GPA 3.75 or higher:	44%	Out-of-state:	22%
GPA 3.50-3.74:	24%	Live on campus:	100%
GPA 3.0-3.49:	27%	International:	6%
GPA 2.0-2.99:	5%	Fraternities:	50%

Basis for selection. Class rank, school achievement, recommendation, essay and test scores important. Interview recommended. Character and personal qualities considered. **Learning Disabled:** All students considered on an individual basis.

High school preparation. College-preparatory program required. Recommended units include English 4, mathematics 4, social studies 2, history 2, science 2 (laboratory 2), foreign language 2 and academic electives 2.

2015-2016 Annual costs. Tuition/fees: $39,980. Room/board: $9,360.

2015-2016 Financial aid. Need-based: 228 full-time freshmen applied for aid; 184 deemed to have need; 183 received aid. Average need met was 93%. Average scholarship/grant was $28,590; average loan $3,326. 80% of total undergraduate aid awarded as scholarships/grants, 20% as loans/jobs. **Non-need-based:** Awarded to 154 full-time undergraduates, including 52 freshmen. Scholarships awarded for academics, art, leadership, music/drama.

Application procedures. Admission: Priority date 12/1; no deadline. $40 fee, may be waived for applicants with need. Admission notification on a rolling basis beginning on or about 12/1. Must reply by May 1 or within 2 week(s) if notified thereafter. **Financial aid:** Closing date 2/15. FAFSA required. Applicants notified by 3/31; must reply by 5/1 or within 2 week(s) of notification.

Academics. Special study options: Combined bachelor's/graduate degree, double major, independent study, internships, New York semester, semester at sea, student-designed major, study abroad, teacher certification program, United Nations semester, urban semester, Washington semester. Internships with off-campus organizations; study abroad in approximately 40 countries; 3-2 engineering programs with Purdue University/Columbia University/Washington University in St. Louis; 4-1 program with Indiana University Kelley School of Business leading to a BA-MS in accounting; new Financial Economics major; interdisciplinary minors in Hispanic Studies, Asian Studies, Multicultural American Studies, International Studies, and Gender Studies. **Credit/placement by examination:** AP, CLEP, IB, SAT, ACT, institutional tests. AP credit based on AP exam scores and subsequent coursework. **Support services:** Learning center, study skills assistance, tutoring, writing center.

Majors. Area/ethnic studies: Spanish/Iberian. **Biology:** General, biochemistry. **English:** English lit, rhetoric/composition. **Foreign languages:** Ancient Greek, classics, French, German, Latin, Spanish. **History:** General. **Liberal arts:** Humanities. **Math:** General. **Philosophy/religion:** Philosophy, religion. **Physical sciences:** Chemistry, physics. **Psychology:** General. **Social sciences:** Applied economics, economics, political science. **Visual/performing arts:** Art, dramatic, music.

Most popular majors. Biology 9%, English 11%, foreign language 10%, history 15%, mathematics 8%, philosophy/religious studies 7%, physical sciences 6%, psychology 8%, social sciences 21%.

Technology on campus. 335 workstations in dormitories, library, computer center, student center. Dormitories wired for high-speed internet access and linked to campus network. Commuter students can connect to campus network. Online course registration, online library, helpline, repair service, student web hosting, wireless network available.

Student life. Freshman orientation: Mandatory. Preregistration for classes offered. Held 5 days leading up to start of classes. **Policies:** Gentleman's Rule. **Housing:** Guaranteed on-campus for freshmen. Special housing for disabled, apartments, fraternity/sorority housing available. $100 nonrefundable deposit, deadline 6/1. **Activities:** Bands, campus ministries, choral groups, dance, drama, film society, international student organizations, literary magazine, music ensembles, musical theater, radio station, student government, student newspaper, symphony orchestra, Alpha Phi Omega, Fellowship of Christian Athletes, Muslim Student Association, Malcolm X Institute of Black Studies, Unidos Por Sangre, International Student Association, College Republicans, College Democrats, College Mentors for Kids.

Athletics. NCAA. **Intercollegiate:** Baseball M, basketball M, cross-country M, diving M, football (tackle) M, golf M, lacrosse M, soccer M, swimming M, tennis M, track and field M, wrestling M. **Intramural:** Badminton M, basketball M, bowling M, cross-country M, football (non-tackle) M, golf M, racquetball M, soccer M, softball M, swimming M, table tennis M, tennis M, track and field M, ultimate frisbee M, volleyball M, weight lifting M, wrestling M. **Team name:** Little Giants.

Student services. Adult student services, alcohol/substance abuse counseling, career counseling, student employment services, financial aid counseling, health services, minority student services, personal counseling, placement for graduates. **Physically disabled:** Services for visually, speech, hearing impaired.

Contact. E-mail: admissions@wabash.edu
Phone: (765) 361-6225 Toll-free number: (800) 345-5385
Fax: (765) 361-6437
Michael Thorp, Dean for Enrollment Management, Wabash College, PO Box 352, Crawfordsville, IN 47933

Iowa

Allen College
Waterloo, Iowa
www.allencollege.edu

CB code: 3610

- Private 4-year health science and nursing college
- Commuter campus in small city
- 370 degree-seeking undergraduates
- 241 graduate students
- SAT or ACT (ACT writing optional), application essay required

General. Regionally accredited. **Degrees:** 181 bachelor's, 14 associate awarded; master's, professional offered. **ROTC:** Army. **Calendar:** Semester, limited summer session. **Full-time faculty:** 38 total; 37% have terminal degrees, 3% minority, 95% women. **Part-time faculty:** 16 total; 19% have terminal degrees, 12% minority, 94% women. **Class size:** 75% < 20, 16% 20-39, 4% 40-49, 6% 50-99.

Basis for selection. Academic achievement, extra-curricular involvement, leadership, community service, diversity, and other applicable life experiences considered.

High school preparation. 4 units required. Required units include English 4, mathematics 3, social studies 3, science 3 (laboratory 2).

2015-2016 Annual costs. Tuition/fees: $19,530. Room/board: $7,281. Books/supplies: $1,200. Personal expenses: $2,727.

2014-2015 Financial aid. Need-based: 1 full-time freshmen applied for aid; 1 deemed to have need; 1 received aid. Average need met was 58%. Average scholarship/grant was $18,130; average loan $4,500. 42% of total undergraduate aid awarded as scholarships/grants, 58% as loans/jobs. **Non-need-based:** Scholarships awarded for academics, leadership, minority status, ROTC.

Application procedures. Admission: Priority date 3/1; deadline 8/1 (receipt date). $50 fee, may be waived for applicants with need. Admission notification on a rolling basis. Must reply by May 1 or within 4 week(s) if notified thereafter. **Financial aid:** Priority date 5/1; no closing date. FAFSA, institutional form required. Applicants notified on a rolling basis starting 5/1; must reply within 2 week(s) of notification.

Academics. Special study options: Accelerated study, combined bachelor's/graduate degree, cooperative education, distance learning, external degree, honors, independent study, internships, liberal arts/career combination. **Credit/placement by examination:** AP, CLEP, IB. **Support services:** Learning center, study skills assistance, tutoring, writing center.

Majors. Health services: Clinical lab science, dental hygiene, nuclear medical technology, nursing (RN), sonography.

Technology on campus. 32 workstations in dormitories, library, computer center. Dormitories wired for high-speed internet access. Online library, helpline, wireless network available.

Student life. Freshman orientation: Mandatory. Preregistration for classes offered. Includes registration, assessment testing, and completion of mandatory health career training. **Housing:** Coed dorms, single-sex dorms, special housing for disabled, apartments, cooperative housing, wellness housing available. Additional housing available at local cooperating campus. **Activities:** Choral groups, student government.

Student services. Alcohol/substance abuse counseling, chaplain/spiritual director, career counseling, financial aid counseling, health services, minority student services, personal counseling, placement for graduates, women's services. **Physically disabled:** Services for visually, speech, hearing impaired.

Contact. E-mail: admissions@allencollege.edu
Phone: (319) 226-2014 Fax: (319) 226-2010
Molly Quinn, Director of Admissions, Allen College, 1825 Logan Avenue, Waterloo, IA 50703

Briar Cliff University
Sioux City, Iowa
www.briarcliff.edu

CB member
CB code: 6046

- Private 4-year university and liberal arts college affiliated with the Roman Catholic Church
- Residential campus in small city
- 942 degree-seeking undergraduates: 17% part-time, 56% women, 7% African American, 1% Asian American, 11% Hispanic/Latino, 1% Native American, 1% Native Hawaiian/Pacific islander, 2% Multi-racial, non-Hispanic, 4% international
- 126 degree-seeking graduate students
- 53% of applicants admitted
- SAT or ACT (ACT writing optional) required
- 48% graduate within 6 years

General. Founded in 1930. Regionally accredited. **Degrees:** 231 bachelor's awarded; master's, professional offered. **ROTC:** Army. **Location:** 90 miles from Omaha, Nebraska, 80 miles from Sioux Falls, South Dakota. **Calendar:** Semester, limited summer session. **Full-time faculty:** 61 total; 79% have terminal degrees, 3% minority, 44% women. **Part-time faculty:** 33 total; 21% have terminal degrees, 46% women. **Class size:** 64% < 20, 32% 20-39, 2% 40-49, 2% 50-99. **Special facilities:** Prairie nature preserve, human anatomy/cadaver laboratory, integrated media lab, nursing simulation lab, entrepreneurship lab, music lab.

Freshman class profile. 1,741 applied, 919 admitted, 185 enrolled.

Mid 50% test scores			
SAT critical reading:	410-500	GPA 2.0-2.99:	34%
SAT math:	430-520	Rank in top quarter:	39%
ACT composite:	19-23	Rank in top tenth:	14%
GPA 3.75 or higher:	25%	Return as sophomores:	70%
GPA 3.50-3.74:	13%	Out-of-state:	49%
GPA 3.0-3.49:	28%	Live on campus:	85%
		International:	8%

Basis for selection. 2.0 GPA and 18 ACT required for full acceptance. Students not meeting requirement may be accepted conditionally or may appeal admission decision if not accepted. Interview and essay recommended. **Home schooled:** Transcript of high school work should be obtained from the school district where the student resides full time. **Learning Disabled:** Students should submit official documentation directly to Student Support Services office.

High school preparation. College-preparatory program recommended. 16 units required. Required units include English 4, mathematics 4, history 3, science 3 and foreign language 2.

2015-2016 Annual costs. Tuition/fees: $27,910. Room/board: $8,124. Books/supplies: $1,188. Personal expenses: $1,886.

2014-2015 Financial aid. Need-based: 206 full-time freshmen applied for aid; 173 deemed to have need; 173 received aid. Average need met was 34%. Average scholarship/grant was $15,058; average loan $3,865. 74% of total undergraduate aid awarded as scholarships/grants, 26% as loans/jobs. **Non-need-based:** Awarded to 808 full-time undergraduates, including 266 freshmen. Scholarships awarded for academics, alumni affiliation, art, athletics, music/drama, religious affiliation.

Application procedures. Admission: No deadline. $20 fee, may be waived for applicants with need, free for online applicants. Admission notification on a rolling basis beginning on or about 6/1. **Financial aid:** Priority date 3/15; no closing date. FAFSA required. Applicants notified on a rolling basis starting 3/15; must reply by 5/1 or within 4 week(s) of notification.

Academics. Special study options: Accelerated study, cross-registration, distance learning, double major, dual enrollment of high school students, honors, independent study, internships, liberal arts/career combination, student-designed major, study abroad, teacher certification program, urban semester. Radiologic technology 1-2-1 program, medical technology 3-1 program. **Credit/placement by examination:** AP, CLEP, IB, SAT, ACT, institutional tests. 45 credit hours maximum toward bachelor's degree. Examinations must be taken before student enters last 30 hours of study. **Support services:** Learning center, pre-admission summer program, reduced course load, remedial instruction, study skills assistance, tutoring, writing center.

Majors. Biology: General. **Business:** Accounting, business admin, human resources, management information systems. **Communications:** Digital media, media studies. **Communications technology:** Graphics. **Computer sciences:** General, computer science. **Conservation:** Environmental science. **Education:** General, art, biology, chemistry, elementary, English, history, mathematics, music, physical, reading, science, secondary, social science. **English:** Creative writing, English lit, writing. **Foreign languages:** Spanish.

Health services: Clinical lab science, medical radiologic technology/radiation therapy, nursing (RN). **History:** General. **Human services:** Social work. **Math:** General. **Parks/recreation:** Exercise sciences, health/fitness, sports admin. **Physical sciences:** Chemistry. **Protective services:** Law enforcement admin. **Psychology:** General. **Social sciences:** Political science, sociology. **Theology:** Theology. **Visual/performing arts:** Art, dramatic, film/cinema/video, graphic design, music.

Most popular majors. Biology 6%, business/marketing 23%, education 12%, parks/recreation 10%, physical sciences 7%, social sciences 6%, visual/performing arts 6%.

Technology on campus. 100 workstations in dormitories, library, computer center, student center. Dormitories wired for high-speed internet access and linked to campus network. Commuter students can connect to campus network. Online library, helpline, repair service, wireless network available.

Student life. Freshman orientation: Mandatory, $125 fee. Preregistration for classes offered. Offered on three separate occasions the summer prior to fall semester. **Housing:** Guaranteed on-campus for freshmen. Coed dorms, themed housing available. $100 fully refundable deposit, deadline 5/1. Pets allowed in dorm rooms. Quad suites available. **Activities:** Jazz band, campus ministries, choral groups, dance, international student organizations, literary magazine, radio station, student government, student newspaper, Best Buddies, BCCares, Champions of Characters Council of Athletes, College Democrats, College Republicans, criminal justice club, departmental clubs, ethnic relations club, mentors in violence prevention.

Athletics. NAIA. **Intercollegiate:** Baseball M, basketball, cheerleading W, cross-country, football (tackle) M, golf, soccer, softball W, tennis, track and field, volleyball W, wrestling M. **Intramural:** Basketball, bowling, football (non-tackle) M, golf, soccer, softball, table tennis, tennis, volleyball. **Team name:** Chargers.

Student services. Alcohol/substance abuse counseling, chaplain/spiritual director, career counseling, services for economically disadvantaged, student employment services, financial aid counseling, health services, minority student services, personal counseling, placement for graduates. **Physically disabled:** Services for visually impaired.

Contact. E-mail: admissions@briarcliff.edu
Phone: (712) 279-5200 Toll-free number: (800) 662-3303 ext. 5200
Fax: (712) 279-1632
Brian Eben, Assistant Vice President for Enrollment Management, Briar Cliff University, 3303 Rebecca Street, Sioux City, IA 51104-2324

Buena Vista University
Storm Lake, Iowa
www.bvu.edu   CB code: 6047

◗ Private 4-year liberal arts college affiliated with the Presbyterian Church (USA)
◗ Residential campus in large town
◗ 864 degree-seeking undergraduates: 1% part-time, 52% women, 2% African American, 2% Asian American, 7% Hispanic/Latino, 3% Multiracial, non-Hispanic, 8% international
◗ 109 degree-seeking graduate students
◗ 68% of applicants admitted
◗ SAT or ACT (ACT writing optional) required
◗ 51% graduate within 6 years; 17% enter graduate study

General. Founded in 1891. Regionally accredited. 15 branch sites throughout Iowa and online programs provide educational opportunities for nontraditional students. **Degrees:** 611 bachelor's awarded; master's offered. **ROTC:** Army. **Location:** 150 miles from Des Moines, 80 miles from Sioux City. **Calendar:** 4-1-4, limited summer session. **Full-time faculty:** 76 total; 76% have terminal degrees, 10% minority, 49% women. **Part-time faculty:** 30 total; 3% have terminal degrees, 3% minority, 67% women. **Class size:** 69% < 20, 30% 20-39, less than 1% 40-49, less than 1% 50-99. **Special facilities:** Multimedia production facilities, underground buildings, information technology center, digitally-controlled acoustic music practice rooms, recording studio, greenhouse with three environmental growth chambers, 3200-acre natural glacier lake and surrounding wetlands serve as an outdoor laboratory.

Freshman class profile. 1,372 applied, 934 admitted, 223 enrolled.

Mid 50% test scores		Rank in top quarter:	41%
ACT composite:	19-24	Rank in top tenth:	15%
GPA 3.75 or higher:	33%	Return as sophomores:	78%
GPA 3.50-3.74:	17%	Out-of-state:	28%
GPA 3.0-3.49:	29%	Live on campus:	99%
GPA 2.0-2.99:	21%	International:	7%

Basis for selection. High school GPA and curriculum, rank in class, standardized test scores, interview, school and community activities important. ACT recommended. Essay recommended.

High school preparation. College-preparatory program recommended. 15 units recommended. Recommended units include English 4, mathematics 4, social studies 3, science 3 (laboratory 1).

2015-2016 Annual costs. Tuition/fees: $31,318. Room/board: $9,046. Books/supplies: $885. Personal expenses: $817.

2015-2016 Financial aid. Need-based: 201 full-time freshmen applied for aid; 178 deemed to have need; 177 received aid. Average need met was 86%. Average scholarship/grant was $24,691; average loan $5,002. 81% of total undergraduate aid awarded as scholarships/grants, 19% as loans/jobs. **Non-need-based:** Awarded to 278 full-time undergraduates, including 69 freshmen. Scholarships awarded for academics, art, minority status, music/drama. **Additional information:** Portfolio required of art scholarship applicants, audition required of music and drama scholarship applicants.

Application procedures. Admission: No deadline. No application fee. Admission notification on a rolling basis. **Financial aid:** Priority date 6/1; no closing date. FAFSA required. Applicants notified on a rolling basis starting 2/15.

Academics. Special study options: Combined bachelor's/graduate degree, distance learning, double major, dual enrollment of high school students, ESL, external degree, honors, independent study, internships, student-designed major, study abroad, teacher certification program, Washington semester. Rollins Fellows (competitive international internships). **Credit/placement by examination:** AP, CLEP, IB, ACT, institutional tests. 21 credit hours maximum toward bachelor's degree. **Support services:** Learning center, reduced course load, remedial instruction, study skills assistance, tutoring, writing center.

Majors. Biology: General, biochemistry. **Business:** General, accounting, banking/financial services, business admin, entrepreneurial studies, human resources, managerial economics, marketing, organizational leadership. **Communications:** Communications/speech/rhetoric, digital media, media studies, organizational. **Computer sciences:** Computer science, information technology, systems analysis. **Conservation:** Environmental science. **Education:** General, art, biology, business, chemistry, computer, elementary, English, history, mathematics, music, physical, physics, psychology, reading, science, social science, Spanish, special ed, speech. **English:** English lit. **Foreign languages:** Spanish. **Health services:** Athletic training. **History:** General. **Human services:** General, social work. **Math:** General. **Parks/recreation:** Exercise sciences, sports admin. **Philosophy/religion:** Philosophy. **Physical sciences:** Chemistry, physics. **Protective services:** Criminal justice. **Psychology:** General. **Social sciences:** General, political science, sociology. **Visual/performing arts:** Art, commercial/advertising art, music management, music performance, music technology, studio arts management, theater arts management, theater history.

Most popular majors. Business/marketing 31%, education 21%, interdisciplinary studies 18%, psychology 11%, security/protective services 7%.

Technology on campus. PC or laptop required. 400 workstations in dormitories, library, computer center, student center. Dormitories wired for high-speed internet access and linked to campus network. Commuter students can connect to campus network. Online course registration, online library, helpline, repair service, wireless network available.

Student life. Freshman orientation: Mandatory. Preregistration for classes offered. Two-day orientation offered during summer. **Housing:** Guaranteed on-campus for all undergraduates. Coed dorms, single-sex dorms, special housing for disabled, wellness housing available. $200 nonrefundable deposit. **Activities:** Bands, campus ministries, choral groups, drama, international student organizations, music ensembles, musical theater, radio station, student government, student newspaper, TV station, BV Buddies, Esprit de Corps, IMPACT, RAICES, Student Activities Board, Student Mobilizing Outreach & Volunteer Efforts, Students Concerned About Tomorrow's Environment, Student Senate.

Athletics. NCAA. **Intercollegiate:** Baseball M, basketball, cross-country, football (tackle) M, golf, soccer, softball W, tennis, track and field, volleyball W, wrestling M. **Intramural:** Basketball, football (non-tackle) M, racquetball, softball, table tennis, tennis, volleyball. **Team name:** Beavers.

Student services. Adult student services, alcohol/substance abuse counseling, chaplain/spiritual director, career counseling, student employment services, financial aid counseling, health services, minority student services, personal counseling, placement for graduates, veterans' counselor. **Physically disabled:** Services for visually, speech, hearing impaired.

Contact. E-mail: admissions@bvu.edu
Phone: (712) 749-2235 Toll-free number: (800) 383-9600
Fax: (712) 749-2035
Michael Fox, Director of Admissions, Buena Vista University, 610 West Fourth Street, Storm Lake, IA 50588

Central College

Pella, Iowa
www.central.edu

CB member
CB code: 6087

- Private 4-year liberal arts college affiliated with the Reformed Church in America
- Residential campus in large town
- 1,225 degree-seeking undergraduates: 1% part-time, 52% women, 2% African American, 1% Asian American, 4% Hispanic/Latino, 1% Multiracial, non-Hispanic
- 64% of applicants admitted
- SAT or ACT (ACT writing optional) required
- 67% graduate within 6 years

General. Founded in 1853. Regionally accredited. International study centers in England, Yucatan, Wales, Spain, and Austria **Degrees:** 331 bachelor's awarded. **Location:** 40 miles from Des Moines. **Calendar:** Semester, limited summer session. **Full-time faculty:** 100 total; 88% have terminal degrees, 12% minority, 45% women. **Part-time faculty:** 5 total; 20% have terminal degrees, 20% minority, 80% women. **Class size:** 69% < 20, 29% 20-39, 1% 40-49, less than 1% 50-99. **Special facilities:** 79-acre field station, glassblowing studio, classrooms with lecture-capture technology, three LEED-rated facilities.

Freshman class profile. 3,071 applied, 1,974 admitted, 317 enrolled.

Mid 50% test scores			
SAT critical reading:	410-560	GPA 2.0-2.99:	10%
SAT math:	470-600	Rank in top quarter:	54%
ACT composite:	20-26	Rank in top tenth:	23%
GPA 3.75 or higher:	41%	Return as sophomores:	78%
GPA 3.50-3.74:	19%	Out-of-state:	27%
GPA 3.0-3.49:	30%	Live on campus:	100%

Basis for selection. High school curriculum, GPA, class rank, test scores important. Recommendations, school and community activities, alumni affiliation also considered. Interview and essay recommended. Audition recommended for music and theater majors; required for scholarships. Portfolio recommended for art majors; required for scholarships. **Home schooled:** Transcript of courses and grades, state high school equivalency certificate required.

High school preparation. College-preparatory program required. 13 units recommended. Recommended units include English 4, mathematics 2, social studies 3, science 2 (laboratory 2) and foreign language 2.

2015-2016 Annual costs. Tuition/fees: $33,345. Room/board: $9,980. Books/supplies: $1,114. Personal expenses: $1,947.

2015-2016 Financial aid. Need-based: 307 full-time freshmen applied for aid; 270 deemed to have need; 270 received aid. Average need met was 83%. Average scholarship/grant was $25,326; average loan $2,811. 78% of total undergraduate aid awarded as scholarships/grants, 22% as loans/jobs. **Non-need-based:** Awarded to 330 full-time undergraduates, including 309 freshmen. Scholarships awarded for academics, alumni affiliation, art, minority status, music/drama, religious affiliation, state residency. **Additional information:** Funds are awarded to students who qualify as National Merit Finalists.

Application procedures. Admission: Closing date 8/15 (receipt date). $25 fee, may be waived for applicants with need, free for online applicants. Admission notification on a rolling basis beginning on or about 6/15. Must reply by 5/1. **Financial aid:** Priority date 3/1; no closing date. FAFSA required. Applicants notified on a rolling basis starting 3/1; must reply by 5/1 or within 2 week(s) of notification.

Academics. All students take first-year seminar in which faculty members from all academic divisions provide interdisciplinary introduction to the liberal arts. **Special study options:** Combined bachelor's/graduate degree, cooperative education, distance learning, double major, dual enrollment of high school students, honors, independent study, internships, student-designed major, study abroad, teacher certification program, urban semester, Washington semester. Study abroad in 5 locations and programs in Chicago and Washington, DC. Dual degree programs in physical therapy, chiropractic and nursing. **Credit/placement by examination:** AP, CLEP, IB, SAT, ACT, institutional tests. Maximum of 24 semester hours for Advanced Placement (AP), International Baccalaureate (IB), Post-Secondary Enrollment Option (PSEO), and dual-enrollment programs will be awarded. Central does not award any credit for College Level Examination Program (CLEP) tests. **Support services:** Learning center, reduced course load, study skills assistance, tutoring, writing center. Each student assigned a class dean to serve as academic mentor and resource for seeking out support services.

Majors. Biology: General, biochemistry, exercise physiology. **Business:** Accounting, actuarial science, business admin, international. **Communications:** Communications/speech/rhetoric. **Computer sciences:** General, information systems. **Conservation:** Environmental studies. **Education:** Elementary, music. **Engineering:** General, electrical, mechanical. **English:** English lit. **Foreign languages:** French, German, linguistics, Spanish. **Health services:** Athletic training. **History:** General. **Math:** General. **Philosophy/religion:** Philosophy, religion. **Physical sciences:** Chemistry, physics. **Psychology:** General. **Social sciences:** General, anthropology, economics, political science, sociology. **Visual/performing arts:** Art, dramatic, music.

Most popular majors. Biology 24%, business/marketing 17%, education 10%, psychology 6%, social sciences 12%.

Technology on campus. 200 workstations in dormitories, library, computer center, student center. Dormitories wired for high-speed internet access and linked to campus network. Commuter students can connect to campus network. Online course registration, online library, helpline, repair service, student web hosting, wireless network available.

Student life. Freshman orientation: Mandatory. Preregistration for classes offered. Choice of 1 of 4 days in late June to meet with academic advisor and register for classes. In-depth Welcome Week activities begin immediately prior to start of fall classes. **Policies:** To be recognized, new student organizations must share the mission and values of the college. **Housing:** Guaranteed on-campus for all undergraduates. Coed dorms, single-sex dorms, special housing for disabled, fraternity/sorority housing, themed housing available. $200 fully refundable deposit, deadline 5/1. Sustainability (GREEN) housing available. **Activities:** Bands, campus ministries, choral groups, dance, drama, literary magazine, music ensembles, student government, symphony orchestra, Central volunteer center, Students Concerned About the Environment, Coalition for a Multicultural Campus, Common Ground, Habitat for Humanity, Amnesty International, Dance Marathon, Fellowship of Christian Athletes, College Democrats, College Republicans.

Athletics. NCAA. **Intercollegiate:** Baseball M, basketball, cross-country, football (tackle) M, golf, soccer, softball W, tennis, track and field, volleyball W, wrestling M. **Intramural:** Basketball, football (non-tackle), racquetball, softball, volleyball. **Team name:** Dutch.

Student services. Alcohol/substance abuse counseling, chaplain/spiritual director, career counseling, services for economically disadvantaged, student employment services, financial aid counseling, health services, minority student services, personal counseling, placement for graduates, veterans' counselor. **Physically disabled:** Services for visually, speech, hearing impaired.

Contact. E-mail: admission@central.edu
Phone: (641) 628-5286 Toll-free number: (877) 462-3687
Fax: (641) 628-5983
Chevy Freiburger, Director of Admission, Central College, 812 University Street, Pella, IA 50219-1999

Clarke University

Dubuque, Iowa
www.clarke.edu

CB code: 6099

- Private 4-year university and liberal arts college affiliated with the Roman Catholic Church
- Residential campus in small city
- 861 degree-seeking undergraduates: 8% part-time, 66% women, 4% African American, 1% Asian American, 7% Hispanic/Latino, 2% Multiracial, non-Hispanic, 1% international
- 207 graduate students
- 72% of applicants admitted
- SAT or ACT (ACT writing optional) required
- 57% graduate within 6 years

General. Founded in 1843. Regionally accredited. **Degrees:** 222 bachelor's, 1 associate awarded; master's, professional offered. **ROTC:** Army. **Location:** 150 miles from Chicago. **Calendar:** Semester, limited summer session. **Full-time faculty:** 89 total; 84% have terminal degrees, 3% minority, 67% women. **Part-time faculty:** 2 total; 50% women. **Class size:** 69% < 20, 29% 20-39, 1% 40-49, less than 1% 50-99. **Special facilities:** Planetarium, art and communications laboratory, writing center, art slide library, computerized mathematics laboratory, nursing laboratory, human gross anatomy laboratory with A.D.A.M. software.

Freshman class profile. 1,257 applied, 904 admitted, 180 enrolled.

Mid 50% test scores			
		Rank in top quarter:	42%
ACT composite:	20-25	Rank in top tenth:	13%
GPA 3.75 or higher:	28%	Return as sophomores:	76%
GPA 3.50-3.74:	16%	Out-of-state:	66%
GPA 3.0-3.49:	36%	Live on campus:	84%
GPA 2.0-2.99:	20%	International:	1%

Basis for selection. High school record of primary importance. Particular attention paid to grades on college preparatory course work and test scores. Interview required of the academically weak. Auditions required of music and drama majors. Portfolio required of art majors. **Home schooled:** Transcript of courses and grades required.

High school preparation. College-preparatory program recommended. 20 units recommended. Recommended units include English 4, mathematics 3, social studies 3, science 3 (laboratory 2), foreign language 2 and academic electives 3. 4 college preparatory science, recommended for physical therapy program.

2015-2016 Annual costs. Tuition/fees: $29,940. Room/board: $9,000. Books/supplies: $1,180. Personal expenses: $1,844.

2015-2016 Financial aid. Need-based: 168 full-time freshmen applied for aid; 151 deemed to have need; 151 received aid. Average need met was 84%. Average scholarship/grant was $22,043; average loan $3,299. 74% of total undergraduate aid awarded as scholarships/grants, 26% as loans/jobs. **Non-need-based:** Awarded to 1,030 full-time undergraduates, including 280 freshmen. Scholarships awarded for academics, alumni affiliation, art, athletics, leadership, music/drama. **Additional information:** Reduced tuition for family members of BVMs.

Application procedures. Admission: No deadline. $25 fee; may be waived for applicants with need, free for online applicants. Admission notification on a rolling basis beginning on or about 6/16. **Financial aid:** Priority date 4/15; no closing date. FAFSA required. Applicants notified on a rolling basis starting 3/15; must reply by 5/1 or within 2 week(s) of notification.

Academics. Special study options: Accelerated study, cross-registration, distance learning, double major, honors, independent study, internships, student-designed major, study abroad, teacher certification program. **Credit/placement by examination:** AP, CLEP, IB, SAT, ACT, institutional tests. 15 credit hours maximum toward associate degree, 30 toward bachelor's. Students applying for prior learning assessment (PLA) credit must be 24 years of age or older. Maximum of 30 credits granted for PLA, CLEP or DANTES within 5-year period. If more than 15 PLA credits are awarded based on portfolio evaluation, additional credit up to 30 hours must be matched by regular college credit. PLA does not count toward the 30 hour residency requirement and is awarded only after 5 hours in degree program are completed. Guidelines may vary by department. **Support services:** Learning center, reduced course load, remedial instruction, study skills assistance, tutoring, writing center.

Majors. Biology: General, biochemistry. **Business:** Accounting, business admin. **Communications:** General. **Computer sciences:** General. **Conservation:** Environmental studies. **Education:** Elementary, music, secondary. **English:** English lit. **Foreign languages:** Spanish. **Health services:** Athletic training, nursing (RN), predental, premedicine, prepharmacy, preveterinary. **History:** General. **Human services:** Social work. **Liberal arts:** Arts/sciences. **Math:** General. **Parks/recreation:** Sports admin. **Philosophy/religion:** Philosophy, religion. **Physical sciences:** Chemistry. **Psychology:** General. **Visual/performing arts:** Art history/conservation, dramatic, graphic design, music performance, musical theater, studio arts.

Most popular majors. Business/marketing 15%, education 10%, health sciences 28%, psychology 13%.

Technology on campus. 237 workstations in dormitories, library, computer center, student center. Dormitories wired for high-speed internet access and linked to campus network. Commuter students can connect to campus network. Online course registration, online library, helpline, wireless network available.

Student life. Freshman orientation: Mandatory. Preregistration for classes offered. **Housing:** Guaranteed on-campus for freshmen. Coed dorms, single-sex dorms, apartments available. **Activities:** Bands, campus ministries, choral groups, dance, drama, literary magazine, music ensembles, musical theater, student government, Life & Justice, Prayer, Black Student Union, Spanish club, Alliance, social work club.

Athletics. NAIA. **Intercollegiate:** Baseball M, basketball, bowling, cheerleading W, cross-country, golf, lacrosse, soccer, softball W, track and field, volleyball. **Intramural:** Basketball, bowling, football (non-tackle), softball, table tennis, tennis, volleyball. **Team name:** Crusaders.

Student services. Adult student services, alcohol/substance abuse counseling, chaplain/spiritual director, career counseling, student employment services, financial aid counseling, health services, minority student services, personal counseling. **Physically disabled:** Services for visually, hearing impaired.

Contact. E-mail: admissions@clarke.edu
Phone: (563) 588-6316 Toll-free number: (800) 383-2345
Fax: (563) 588-6789
Beth Triplett, Vice President for Enrollment Management, Clarke University, 1550 Clarke Drive, Dubuque, IA 52001-3198

Coe College

Cedar Rapids, Iowa
www.coe.edu

CB member
CB code: 6101

- Private 4-year nursing and liberal arts college affiliated with the Presbyterian Church (USA)
- Residential campus in small city
- 1,338 degree-seeking undergraduates: 1% part-time, 58% women, 6% African American, 3% Asian American, 9% Hispanic/Latino, 3% Multiracial, non-Hispanic, 1% international
- 63% of applicants admitted
- SAT or ACT (ACT writing optional), application essay required
- 67% graduate within 6 years

General. Founded in 1851. Regionally accredited. **Degrees:** 279 bachelor's awarded; master's offered. **ROTC:** Army, Air Force. **Location:** 230 miles from Chicago, 300 miles from Minneapolis-St. Paul. **Calendar:** Semester, limited summer session. **Full-time faculty:** 96 total; 6% minority, 44% women. **Part-time faculty:** 81 total; 1% have terminal degrees, 5% minority, 60% women. **Class size:** 72% < 20, 26% 20-39, less than 1% 40-49, less than 1% 50-99. **Special facilities:** Infrared spectrometer, analytical physiology units, music library, wilderness field station.

Freshman class profile. 3,457 applied, 2,190 admitted, 368 enrolled.

Mid 50% test scores			
SAT critical reading:	520-630	GPA 2.0-2.99:	8%
SAT math:	500-640	Rank in top quarter:	55%
SAT writing:	520-610	Rank in top tenth:	27%
ACT composite:	22-27	Return as sophomores:	77%
GPA 3.75 or higher:	44%	Out-of-state:	55%
GPA 3.50-3.74:	19%	Live on campus:	90%
GPA 3.0-3.49:	29%	Fraternities:	23%
		Sororities:	24%

Basis for selection. School achievement record and test scores most important. Recommendations and school activities also important. Interview and community activities considered. **Home schooled:** GED and portfolio required. **Learning Disabled:** Submission of disability assessment required.

High school preparation. College-preparatory program recommended. 18 units recommended. Recommended units include English 4, mathematics 3, social studies 3, science 3 (laboratory 1), foreign language 2 and academic electives 2.

2015-2016 Annual costs. Tuition/fees: $39,080. Room/board: $8,510. Books/supplies: $1,000. Personal expenses: $1,670.

2015-2016 Financial aid. Need-based: 353 full-time freshmen applied for aid; 317 deemed to have need; 317 received aid. Average need met was 85%. Average scholarship/grant was $29,510; average loan $4,487. 79% of total undergraduate aid awarded as scholarships/grants, 21% as loans/jobs. **Non-need-based:** Awarded to 373 full-time undergraduates, including 102 freshmen. Scholarships awarded for academics, alumni affiliation, art, music/drama, ROTC, state residency.

Application procedures. Admission: Priority date 12/10; deadline 3/1 (postmark date). $30 fee, may be waived for applicants with need, free for online applicants. Admission notification on a rolling basis beginning on or about 10/1. Must reply by 5/1. **Financial aid:** Priority date 3/1; no closing date. FAFSA required. Applicants notified on a rolling basis starting 3/15; must reply by 5/1 or within 2 week(s) of notification.

Academics. Writing emphasis courses required. Semester practicum required for all students. **Special study options:** Cross-registration, double major, dual enrollment of high school students, ESL, exchange student, honors, independent study, internships, New York semester, student-designed major, study abroad, teacher certification program, urban semester, Washington semester. Oak Ridge science semester; research program at wilderness field station- Minnesota Superior National Forest; tropical field research in Costa Rica; travel abroad to England, Hong Kong, India, Italy, Japan, Russia, Latin America, Czech Republic, Tanzania, Germany, Sweden, Spain, France, Korea, Thailand, Ireland. **Credit/placement by examination:** AP, CLEP, IB, SAT, ACT, institutional tests. **Support services:** Pre-admission summer program, reduced course load, study skills assistance, tutoring, writing center.

Majors. Area/ethnic studies: African-American, American, Asian, French, German, Spanish/Iberian. **Biology:** General, biochemistry, molecular. **Business:** Accounting, business admin, international. **Communications:** Communications/speech/rhetoric, organizational, public relations. **Computer sciences:** Computer science. **Conservation:** Environmental science, environmental studies. **Education:** General, art, elementary, middle, music, physical, science, secondary. **Engineering:** Pre-engineering. **English:** Creative writing, English lit, rhetoric/composition. **Foreign languages:** Classics, French, German, Spanish. **Health services:** Athletic training, nursing (RN), predental, premedicine, prephysical therapy, preveterinary. **History:** General. **Math:** General. **Parks/recreation:** Health/fitness. **Philosophy/religion:** Philosophy, religion. **Physical sciences:** General, chemistry, physics. **Psychology:** General, industrial. **Social sciences:** Economics, political science, sociology. **Visual/performing arts:** Acting, art, art history/conservation, ceramics, directing/producing, dramatic, film/cinema/video, music, music performance, music theory/composition, painting, photography, studio arts, theater design.

Most popular majors. Biology 11%, business/marketing 18%, communications/journalism 7%, health sciences 7%, psychology 10%, social sciences 6%, visual/performing arts 7%.

Technology on campus. Dormitories wired for high-speed internet access and linked to campus network. Commuter students can connect to campus network. Online course registration, online library, helpline, student web hosting, wireless network available.

Student life. Freshman orientation: Mandatory, $150 fee. Preregistration for classes offered. Four or five-day program. **Policies:** Students must live on campus unless residing with relatives or granted off-campus permission by Department of Residence Life. **Housing:** Guaranteed on-campus for all undergraduates. Coed dorms, single-sex dorms, special housing for disabled, apartments, fraternity/sorority housing, themed housing available. $250 nonrefundable deposit, deadline 5/1. Living-learning communities available. **Activities:** Bands, campus ministries, choral groups, dance, drama, film society, international student organizations, literary magazine, music ensembles, Model UN, musical theater, radio station, student government, student newspaper, symphony orchestra, black self-education organization, Friends club, Egalitarians Supporting the Advancement of Women, Christian Fellowship, College Republicans, Habitat for Humanity, green club, College Democrats, Fellowship of Christian Athletes.

Athletics. NCAA. **Intercollegiate:** Baseball M, basketball, cheerleading W, cross-country, diving, football (tackle) M, golf, soccer, softball W, swimming, tennis, track and field, volleyball W, wrestling M. **Intramural:** Badminton, basketball, football (non-tackle) M, racquetball, soccer, softball, squash, table tennis, tennis, volleyball, wrestling M. **Team name:** Kohawks.

Student services. Adult student services, alcohol/substance abuse counseling, chaplain/spiritual director, career counseling, student employment services, financial aid counseling, health services, minority student services, personal counseling, placement for graduates.

Contact. E-mail: admission@coe.edu
Phone: (319) 399-8500 Toll-free number: (877) 225-5263
Fax: (319) 399-8816
Julie Staker, Dean of Admission, Coe College, 1220 First Avenue NE, Cedar Rapids, IA 52402

Cornell College
Mount Vernon, Iowa
www.cornellcollege.edu

CB member
CB code: 6119

- Private 4-year liberal arts college affiliated with the United Methodist Church
- Residential campus in small town
- 1,031 degree-seeking undergraduates: 51% women
- 70% of applicants admitted
- SAT or ACT (ACT writing optional), application essay required
- 68% graduate within 6 years

General. Founded in 1853. Regionally accredited. **Degrees:** 262 bachelor's awarded. **Location:** 15 miles from Cedar Rapids, 20 miles from Iowa City. **Calendar:** Eight terms of 3 and 1/2 weeks; one course per term. Limited summer session. **Full-time faculty:** 89 total; 96% have terminal degrees, 8% minority, 52% women. **Part-time faculty:** 35 total; 66% have terminal degrees, 14% minority, 60% women. **Class size:** 71% < 20, 29% 20-39. **Special facilities:** Geology museum, observatory, Chicago center, creative writing house.

Freshman class profile. 1,936 applied, 1,364 admitted, 552 enrolled.

Mid 50% test scores			
SAT critical reading:	510-660	GPA 3.0-3.49:	33%
SAT math:	500-640	GPA 2.0-2.99:	17%
SAT writing:	490-630	Rank in top quarter:	45%
ACT composite:	23-29	Rank in top tenth:	25%
GPA 3.75 or higher:	33%	Return as sophomores:	82%
GPA 3.50-3.74:	17%	Out-of-state:	85%
		Live on campus:	100%

Basis for selection. Academic record, essay, co-curricular involvement, evidence of character, standardized test score, letters of reference, and recommended optional interview important. Primary consideration given to academic performance in college preparatory courses. Portfolio required for art

scholarship applicants. Audition required for music and theater scholarship applicants. **Home schooled:** Transcript of courses and grades, interview, letter of recommendation (nonparent) required. Applicants asked to provide as many documents pertaining to their education as possible.

High school preparation. College-preparatory program recommended. 15 units recommended. Recommended units include English 4, mathematics 3, social studies 3, science 3, foreign language 2 and academic electives 1. As many advanced, honors, and/or AP courses as possible recommended.

2016-2017 Annual costs. Tuition/fees (projected): $38,925. Room/board: $8,700. Books/supplies: $1,118. Personal expenses: $1,845.

2015-2016 Financial aid. Need-based: 239 full-time freshmen applied for aid; 210 deemed to have need; 210 received aid. Average need met was 80%. Average scholarship/grant was $25,076; average loan $3,450. 78% of total undergraduate aid awarded as scholarships/grants, 22% as loans/jobs. **Non-need-based:** Awarded to 324 full-time undergraduates, including 134 freshmen. Scholarships awarded for academics, alumni affiliation, art, leadership, minority status, music/drama, religious affiliation.

Application procedures. Admission: Priority date 12/1; no deadline. $30 fee, may be waived for applicants with need, free for online applicants. Admission notification on a rolling basis beginning on or about 12/1. Must reply by May 1 or within 2 week(s) if notified thereafter. **Financial aid:** Priority date 3/1; no closing date. FAFSA required. Applicants notified on a rolling basis starting 3/1; must reply by 5/1 or within 2 week(s) of notification.

Academics. Special study options: Accelerated study, combined bachelor's/graduate degree, double major, ESL, exchange student, independent study, internships, liberal arts/career combination, semester at sea, student-designed major, study abroad, teacher certification program, urban semester, Washington semester. **Credit/placement by examination:** AP, CLEP, IB, institutional tests. 32 credit hours maximum toward bachelor's degree. **Support services:** Learning center, study skills assistance, tutoring, writing center.

Majors. Area/ethnic studies: German, Latin American, Russian/Slavic, women's. **Biology:** General, biochemistry, Biochemistry/molecular biology, ecology, molecular, molecular biochemistry. **Computer sciences:** Computer science. **Conservation:** Environmental studies. **Education:** General, art, biology, chemistry, elementary, English, foreign languages, French, German, history, mathematics, middle, multi-level teacher, music, physical, physics, science, secondary, social science, social studies, Spanish. **English:** Creative writing, English lit. **Foreign languages:** General, classics, French, German, Russian, Spanish. **Health services:** Prechiropractic, predental, premedicine, prenursing, preoptometry, prepharmacy, prephysical therapy, preveterinary. **History:** General. **Math:** General, mathematics/statistics, statistics. **Parks/recreation:** Exercise sciences, health/fitness. **Philosophy/religion:** Philosophy, religion. **Physical sciences:** Chemistry, geology, physics. **Psychology:** General. **Social sciences:** Anthropology, archaeology, economics, international relations, political science, sociology. **Visual/performing arts:** Art, art history/conservation, dramatic, music, music history, music performance, music theory/composition, stringed instruments, studio arts, theater design, voice/opera.

Most popular majors. Biology 14%, education 8%, English 6%, psychology 10%, social sciences 15%, visual/performing arts 9%.

Technology on campus. 190 workstations in library, computer center, student center. Dormitories wired for high-speed internet access and linked to campus network. Commuter students can connect to campus network. Online course registration, online library, helpline, repair service, student web hosting, wireless network available.

Student life. Freshman orientation: Mandatory. Preregistration for classes offered. Five-day orientation held before fall classes begin. **Housing:** Guaranteed on-campus for freshmen. Coed dorms, single-sex dorms, apartments, gender-neutral housing, themed housing, wellness housing available. $300 nonrefundable deposit, deadline 5/1. First-year halls/floors available. **Activities:** Bands, campus ministries, choral groups, dance, drama, film society, international student organizations, literary magazine, music ensembles, musical theater, opera, radio station, student government, student newspaper, symphony orchestra, Alpha Phi Omega, alumni student association, Fellowship of Christian Athletes, black awareness cultural organization, women's action group, Young Democrats, College Republicans, Habitat for Humanity, Organization for Latino Awareness, lunch buddies/youth mentoring.

Athletics. NCAA. **Intercollegiate:** Baseball M, basketball, cross-country, football (tackle) M, soccer, softball W, tennis, track and field, volleyball W, wrestling M. **Intramural:** Badminton, basketball, bowling, football (non-tackle), racquetball, soccer, softball, table tennis, track and field, ultimate frisbee, volleyball. **Team name:** Rams.

Student services. Alcohol/substance abuse counseling, chaplain/spiritual director, career counseling, student employment services, financial aid counseling, health services, minority student services, personal counseling, women's services. **Physically disabled:** Services for visually, speech, hearing impaired.

Contact. E-mail: admissions@cornellcollege.edu
Phone: (319) 895-4215 Toll-free number: (800) 747-1112
Fax: (319) 895-4451
Marie Schofer, Director of Admission, Cornell College, 600 First Street SW, Mount Vernon, IA 52314-1098

Divine Word College
Epworth, Iowa
www.dwci.edu   **CB code: 6174**

▶ Private 4-year liberal arts and seminary college affiliated with the Roman Catholic Church
▶ Residential campus in rural community
▶ 47 degree-seeking undergraduates
▶ Application essay, interview required

General. Founded in 1912. Regionally accredited. **Degrees:** 25 bachelor's, 3 associate awarded. **Location:** 15 miles from Dubuque. **Calendar:** Semester. **Full-time faculty:** 18 total. **Part-time faculty:** 7 total.

Basis for selection. Desire to pursue vocation to missionary priesthood or Brotherhood most important. SAT or ACT recommended. Minnesota Multiphasic Personality Inventory used for admission and counseling. **Home schooled:** Transcript of courses and grades, state high school equivalency certificate, interview, letter of recommendation (nonparent) required.

High school preparation. College-preparatory program recommended.

2015-2016 Annual costs. Tuition/fees: $12,600. Room/board: $3,500. Books/supplies: $500.

Application procedures. Admission: Closing date 7/15. $25 fee, may be waived for applicants with need. Admission notification on a rolling basis beginning on or about 1/1. **Financial aid:** Priority date 8/31; no closing date. Applicants notified on a rolling basis starting 8/1.

Academics. Special study options: Double major, dual enrollment of high school students, ESL, independent study. **Credit/placement by examination:** AP, CLEP, institutional tests. **Support services:** Reduced course load, remedial instruction, tutoring.

Majors. Philosophy/religion: Philosophy, religion.

Technology on campus. 26 workstations in computer center.

Student life. Freshman orientation: Mandatory. Preregistration for classes offered. **Policies:** All students live in dormitories on campus. Religious observance required. **Housing:** Single-sex dorms available. **Activities:** Campus ministries, choral groups, student government, Vietnamese student organization, Sudanese student organization, social justice committee, Right to Life committee.

Athletics. Intramural: Basketball M, soccer M, swimming M, table tennis M, tennis M, volleyball M.

Student services. Career counseling, health services, personal counseling.

Contact. E-mail: svdvocations@dwci.edu
Phone: (563) 876-3332 Toll-free number: (800) 553-3321
Fax: (563) 876-5515
Len Uhal, Vice President for Admissions, Divine Word College, 102 Jacoby Drive SW, Epworth, IA 52045

Dordt College
Sioux Center, Iowa
www.dordt.edu   **CB code: 6171**

▶ Private 4-year liberal arts college affiliated with the Christian Reformed Church
▶ Residential campus in small town
▶ 1,351 degree-seeking undergraduates
▶ 71% of applicants admitted
▶ SAT or ACT (ACT writing optional) required

General. Founded in 1955. Regionally accredited. **Degrees:** 277 bachelor's, 21 associate awarded; master's offered. **Location:** 45 miles from Sioux City; 55 miles from Sioux Falls, SD. **Calendar:** Semester. **Full-time faculty:** 80 total; 75% have terminal degrees, 4% minority, 38% women. **Part-time faculty:** 25 total; 40% have terminal degrees, 60% women. **Class size:** 59% < 20, 31% 20-39, 5% 40-49, 4% 50-99, less than 1% >100. **Special facilities:** Farm, biotechnology research facility, natural prairie plot, digital media lab, radio station, education program learning resource center, pre-school.

Freshman class profile. 1,238 applied, 880 admitted, 351 enrolled.

Mid 50% test scores			
SAT critical reading:	460-640	GPA 3.0-3.49:	24%
SAT math:	490-640	GPA 2.0-2.99:	14%
SAT writing:	450-610	Rank in top quarter:	35%
ACT composite:	21-28	Rank in top tenth:	17%
GPA 3.75 or higher:	41%	Out-of-state:	61%
GPA 3.50-3.74:	21%	Live on campus:	90%

Basis for selection. School achievement record, high school GPA, test scores, religious affiliation or commitment important. Applicants with less than 2.25 GPA considered on individual basis, may be admitted provisionally. Interview recommended for academically borderline applicants. **Home schooled:** Transcript of courses and grades required. Must submit certified GPA. **Learning Disabled:** Copies of prior testing and interview with learning disabilities advisor required.

High school preparation. College-preparatory program required. 19 units required; 25 recommended. Required and recommended units include English 3-4, mathematics 2-3, social studies 1, history 2, science 2-4, foreign language 2-3 and academic electives 6. 10 units must be in social science, English, foreign language, natural science, or math. Math must include algebra, geometry.

2015-2016 Annual costs. Tuition/fees: $28,280. Room/board: $8,350. Books/supplies: $900. Personal expenses: $2,000.

2015-2016 Financial aid. Need-based: 62% of total undergraduate aid awarded as scholarships/grants, 38% as loans/jobs. **Non-need-based:** Scholarships awarded for academics, alumni affiliation, art, athletics, leadership, music/drama, religious affiliation.

Application procedures. Admission: Closing date 7/31. $25 fee, may be waived for applicants with need, free for online applicants. Admission notification on a rolling basis beginning on or about 10/1. Must reply by May 1 or within 1 week(s) if notified thereafter. **Financial aid:** Priority date 4/1; no closing date. FAFSA, institutional form required. Applicants notified on a rolling basis starting 3/1; must reply within 3 week(s) of notification.

Academics. Special study options: Combined bachelor's/graduate degree, double major, ESL, exchange student, honors, independent study, internships, liberal arts/career combination, student-designed major, study abroad, teacher certification program, urban semester, Washington semester. Iowa Legislative Intern program; China, England, Costa Rica, Russia, Latin America, Netherlands, and Germany semesters; Los Angeles-Film Institute semester, Chicago Metro semester, American Studies semester. **Credit/placement by examination:** AP, CLEP, IB, SAT, ACT, institutional tests. Registrar makes determination on case-by-case basis. Some credit may be given for work experience. **Support services:** Learning center, reduced course load, remedial instruction, study skills assistance, tutoring.

Majors. Biology: General. **Business:** General, accounting, accounting/business management, actuarial science, information resources management, marketing. **Communications:** Broadcast journalism, communications/speech/rhetoric, digital media, journalism, media studies, public relations. **Communications technology:** General, graphics. **Computer sciences:** General, computer science, information systems, LAN/WAN management, system admin. **Conservation:** General, environmental studies. **Education:** General, art, biology, business, chemistry, drama/dance, elementary, English, foreign languages, health, history, mathematics, middle, music, physical, physics, reading, science, secondary, social science, social studies, Spanish, special ed, speech. **Engineering:** General, agricultural, biomedical, chemical, civil, computer, construction, electrical, mechanical. **English:** English lit, rhetoric/composition, writing. **Foreign languages:** Dutch/Flemish, Spanish. **Health services:** Athletic training, clinical lab science, clinical lab technology, nursing (RN), predental, premedicine, prepharmacy, preveterinary. **History:** General. **Human services:** General, social work. **Liberal arts:** Arts/sciences. **Math:** General, mathematics/statistics. **Parks/recreation:** General, exercise sciences, health/fitness, sports admin. **Philosophy/religion:** Philosophy, religion. **Physical sciences:** General, chemistry, physics. **Protective services:** Police science. **Psychology:** General. **Social sciences:** General, political science. **Theology:** Missionary, sacred music, theology, youth ministry. **Visual/performing arts:** Art, commercial/advertising art, design, dramatic, music, piano/keyboard, stringed instruments, voice/opera.

Most popular majors. Business/marketing 8%, education 22%, health sciences 8%, parks/recreation 7%.

Technology on campus. 200 workstations in dormitories, library, computer center, student center. Dormitories wired for high-speed internet access and linked to campus network. Commuter students can connect to campus network. Online course registration, online library, helpline, wireless network available.

Student life. Freshman orientation: Mandatory. Preregistration for classes offered. Two-day program prior to beginning of classes. **Policies:** No smoking or alcohol allowed on-campus. Religious observance required. **Housing:** Guaranteed on-campus for all undergraduates. Single-sex dorms, special housing for disabled, apartments available. $200 fully refundable deposit, deadline 6/1. **Activities:** Bands, campus ministries, choral groups, dance, drama, film society, international student organizations, literary magazine, music ensembles, musical theater, opera, radio station, student government, student newspaper, symphony orchestra, 50 clubs and student organizations available.

Athletics. NAIA. **Intercollegiate:** Baseball M, basketball, cross-country, football (tackle) M, golf, ice hockey M, soccer, softball W, track and field, volleyball W. **Intramural:** Badminton, basketball, bowling, cross-country, field hockey, golf, racquetball, soccer, softball, swimming, tennis, volleyball, weight lifting. **Team name:** Defenders.

Student services. Adult student services, alcohol/substance abuse counseling, chaplain/spiritual director, career counseling, student employment services, financial aid counseling, health services, minority student services, personal counseling, placement for graduates, veterans' counselor, women's services. **Physically disabled:** Services for visually, speech, hearing impaired.

Contact. E-mail: admission@dordt.edu
Phone: (712) 722-6080 Toll-free number: (800) 343-6738
Fax: (712) 722-6035
Quentin Van Essen, Executive Director of Admissions, Dordt College, 498 Fourth Avenue, NE, Sioux Center, IA 51250

Drake University
Des Moines, Iowa
www.drake.edu

CB member
CB code: 6168

- Private 4-year university
- Residential campus in large city
- 3,269 degree-seeking undergraduates: 3% part-time, 57% women, 4% African American, 3% Asian American, 4% Hispanic/Latino, 2% Multiracial, non-Hispanic, 7% international
- 1,608 degree-seeking graduate students
- 67% of applicants admitted
- SAT or ACT (ACT writing optional), application essay required
- 75% graduate within 6 years

General. Founded in 1881. Regionally accredited. **Degrees:** 788 bachelor's awarded; master's, professional, doctoral offered. **ROTC:** Army, Air Force. **Location:** 150 miles from Omaha, NE; 194 miles from Kansas City, MO. **Calendar:** Semester, extensive summer session. **Full-time faculty:** 289 total; 92% have terminal degrees, 14% minority, 46% women. **Part-time faculty:** 167 total; 20% have terminal degrees, 8% minority, 54% women. **Class size:** 31% < 20, 50% 20-39, 12% 40-49, 4% 50-99, 2% >100. **Special facilities:** Observatory, greenhouse.

Freshman class profile. 6,514 applied, 4,356 admitted, 803 enrolled.

Mid 50% test scores		Rank in top quarter:	69%
SAT critical reading:	520-670	Rank in top tenth:	37%
SAT math:	550-690	Return as sophomores:	88%
ACT composite:	24-30	Out-of-state:	72%
GPA 3.75 or higher:	57%	Live on campus:	97%
GPA 3.50-3.74:	19%	International:	3%
GPA 3.0-3.49:	20%	Fraternities:	37%
GPA 2.0-2.99:	4%	Sororities:	27%

Basis for selection. High school academic record, test scores, extracurricular activities, counselor recommendation, and essay important. Comprehensive review completed and each item in student's file considered. Interview recommended for all, required for some. Audition required of music and theater majors. Portfolio recommended for art majors.

High school preparation. College-preparatory program recommended. 16 units recommended. Recommended units include English 4, mathematics 3, social studies 4, science 2 (laboratory 1) and foreign language 2.

2015-2016 Annual costs. Tuition/fees: $33,696. Room/board: $9,596. Books/supplies: $1,100. Personal expenses: $2,000.

2015-2016 Financial aid. Need-based: 687 full-time freshmen applied for aid; 546 deemed to have need; 546 received aid. Average need met was 76%. Average scholarship/grant was $19,158; average loan $3,109. 65% of total undergraduate aid awarded as scholarships/grants, 35% as loans/jobs. **Non-need-based:** Awarded to 1,524 full-time undergraduates, including 363 freshmen. Scholarships awarded for academics, alumni affiliation, art, athletics, minority status, music/drama, ROTC, state residency.

Application procedures. Admission: Priority date 3/1; no deadline. $25 fee, may be waived for applicants with need, free for online applicants. Admission notification on a rolling basis beginning on or about 10/15. Must reply by 5/1. **Financial aid:** No deadline. FAFSA required. Applicants notified on a rolling basis starting 3/1; must reply by 5/1 or within 3 week(s) of notification.

Academics. Peer support through academic departments and residence halls offered. **Special study options:** Accelerated study, combined bachelor's/graduate degree, cooperative education, distance learning, double major, dual enrollment of high school students, ESL, honors, independent study, internships, liberal arts/career combination, semester at sea, student-designed major, study abroad, teacher certification program, Washington semester. **Credit/placement by examination:** AP, CLEP, IB, institutional tests. 66 credit hours maximum toward bachelor's degree. **Support services:** Study skills assistance, tutoring, writing center.

Majors. Biology: General, biochemistry, cellular/molecular, neuroscience, pharmacology. **Business:** General, accounting, actuarial science, finance, international, management information systems, management science, managerial economics, marketing. **Communications:** Advertising, broadcast journalism, communications/speech/rhetoric, journalism, media studies, public relations, radio/TV. **Computer sciences:** General, computer science, information technology. **Conservation:** Environmental science, management/policy. **Education:** Curriculum, elementary, mathematics, music, secondary. **English:** English lit, rhetoric/composition, writing. **Health services:** Pharmaceutical sciences. **History:** General. **Math:** General. **Philosophy/religion:** Ethics, philosophy, religion. **Physical sciences:** Astronomy, chemistry, physics. **Psychology:** General. **Social sciences:** General, anthropology, economics, international relations, political science, sociology. **Visual/performing arts:** Acting, art history/conservation, commercial/advertising art, directing/producing, dramatic, drawing, music, music management, music performance, painting, printmaking, sculpture, theater design.

Most popular majors. Biology 8%, business/marketing 34%, communications/journalism 9%, education 7%, English 6%, psychology 6%, social sciences 8%, visual/performing arts 7%.

Technology on campus. 4,900 workstations in dormitories, library, computer center, student center. Dormitories wired for high-speed internet access and linked to campus network. Commuter students can connect to campus network. Online course registration, online library, helpline, repair service, student web hosting, wireless network available.

Student life. Freshman orientation: Available, $90 fee. Preregistration for classes offered. Four 1-1/2 day sessions held in June; includes parents. **Policies:** Student leaders must maintain 2.0 GPA. Students must live on-campus first 2 years following high school. **Housing:** Guaranteed on-campus for freshmen. Coed dorms, apartments, fraternity/sorority housing, themed housing available. $250 nonrefundable deposit, deadline 5/1. **Activities:** Bands, choral groups, dance, drama, international student organizations, literary magazine, music ensembles, Model UN, musical theater, radio station, student government, student newspaper, symphony orchestra, coalition of black students, Best Buddies, College Republicans, College Democrats, La Fuerza Latina, Alpha Phi Omega, South Asian student association, Rainbow Union, Drake Hillel.

Athletics. NCAA. **Intercollegiate:** Basketball, cheerleading, cross-country, football (tackle) M, golf, rowing (crew) W, soccer, softball W, tennis, track and field, volleyball W. **Intramural:** Badminton, basketball, football (non-tackle), football (tackle) M, golf, racquetball, soccer, swimming, tennis, volleyball. **Team name:** Bulldogs.

Student services. Career counseling, student employment services, financial aid counseling, health services, legal services, personal counseling, placement for graduates. **Physically disabled:** Services for visually, speech, hearing impaired.

Contact. E-mail: admission@drake.edu
Phone: (515) 271-3181 Toll-free number: (800) 443-7253
Fax: (515) 271-2831
Laura Linn, Director of Admission, Drake University, 2507 University Avenue, Des Moines, IA 50311-4505

Emmaus Bible College
Dubuque, Iowa
www.emmaus.edu   CB code: 1215

- Private 4-year Bible college affiliated with the Brethren Church
- Residential campus in small city
- 232 degree-seeking undergraduates: 4% part-time, 56% women, 6% African American, 2% Asian American, 6% Hispanic/Latino, 1% Native American, 1% Native Hawaiian/Pacific islander, 3% Multi-racial, non-Hispanic
- 34% of applicants admitted
- SAT or ACT (ACT writing optional), application essay required
- 75% graduate within 6 years

General. Founded in 1942. Accredited by ABHE. **Degrees:** 31 bachelor's, 9 associate awarded. **Location:** 90 miles from Waterloo, 150 miles from Chicago. **Calendar:** Semester, limited summer session. **Full-time faculty:** 23 total; 30% have terminal degrees, 17% minority, 22% women. **Part-time faculty:** 15 total; 7% have terminal degrees, 7% minority, 60% women. **Class size:** 82% < 20, 11% 20-39, 2% 40-49, 5% 50-99.

Freshman class profile. 432 applied, 147 admitted, 59 enrolled.

Mid 50% test scores			
SAT critical reading:	450-650	GPA 2.0-2.99:	12%
SAT math:	400-630	Rank in top quarter:	28%
ACT composite:	20-26	Rank in top tenth:	6%
GPA 3.75 or higher:	37%	Return as sophomores:	83%
GPA 3.50-3.74:	22%	Out-of-state:	51%
GPA 3.0-3.49:	26%	Live on campus:	91%

Basis for selection. Recommendations and essay most important. GPA also important. Tests not required of students who have earned 24 college credits or are at least 25 years of age. **Home schooled:** Transcript of courses and grades, letter of recommendation (nonparent) required.

2016-2017 Annual costs. Tuition/fees (projected): $16,580. Room/board: $7,100. Books/supplies: $600. Personal expenses: $1,125.

Financial aid. Non-need-based: Scholarships awarded for academics, leadership, minority status, music/drama, religious affiliation.

Application procedures. Admission: Priority date 8/1; no deadline. $25 fee, may be waived for applicants with need. Admission notification on a rolling basis. Must reply by May 1 or within 2 week(s) if notified thereafter. **Financial aid:** No deadline. FAFSA required. Applicants notified on a rolling basis starting 3/1; must reply within 2 week(s) of notification.

Academics. Special study options: Cooperative education, distance learning, double major, dual enrollment of high school students, ESL, independent study, internships, teacher certification program. **Credit/placement by examination:** AP, CLEP, IB, institutional tests. 9 credit hours maximum toward associate degree, 18 toward bachelor's. **Support services:** Reduced course load, remedial instruction, study skills assistance, tutoring.

Majors. Business: Business admin. **Computer sciences:** General. **Education:** Business, elementary, English, ESL, history, music, psychology, secondary. **Psychology:** Counseling. **Theology:** Bible, missionary, theology, youth ministry.

Most popular majors. Business/marketing 6%, education 23%, psychology 10%, theological studies 35%.

Technology on campus. 60 workstations in library, computer center, student center. Dormitories wired for high-speed internet access and linked to campus network. Online course registration, online library, wireless network available.

Student life. Freshman orientation: Mandatory. Preregistration for classes offered. Held 4 days immediately preceding first day of class. **Policies:** No smoking, alcohol consumption, dancing. Religious observance required. **Housing:** Guaranteed on-campus for all undergraduates. Single-sex dorms available. $170 nonrefundable deposit, deadline 7/9. **Activities:** Campus ministries, choral groups, drama, international student organizations, music ensembles, student government, symphony orchestra.

Athletics. NCCAA. **Intercollegiate:** Basketball, soccer M, volleyball W. **Intramural:** Badminton, basketball, cross-country, football (non-tackle), golf, racquetball, soccer, softball, table tennis, tennis, ultimate frisbee, volleyball. **Team name:** Eagles.

Student services. Chaplain/spiritual director, career counseling, student employment services, financial aid counseling, health services, personal counseling, veterans' counselor.

Contact. E-mail: admissions@emmaus.edu
Phone: (563) 588-8000 ext. 1310 Fax: (563) 588-1216
Laurel Rasmussen, Director of Enrollment, Emmaus Bible College, 2570 Asbury Road, Dubuque, IA 52001

Faith Baptist Bible College and Theological Seminary
Ankeny, Iowa
www.faith.edu   CB code: 6214

- Private 4-year Bible and seminary college affiliated with the General Association of Regular Baptist Churches
- Residential campus in large town
- 227 degree-seeking undergraduates
- 39 graduate students
- 64% of applicants admitted
- SAT or ACT (ACT writing optional), application essay required
- 47% graduate within 6 years

General. Founded in 1921. Regionally accredited; also accredited by ABHE. **Degrees:** 37 bachelor's, 30 associate awarded; master's offered. **Location:** 6 miles from Des Moines. **Calendar:** Semester, limited summer session. **Full-time faculty:** 16 total; 62% have terminal degrees, 6% minority, 19% women. **Part-time faculty:** 14 total; 36% have terminal degrees, 7% minority, 29% women. **Class size:** 74% < 20, 14% 20-39, 4% 40-49, 8% 50-99.

Freshman class profile. 137 applied, 88 admitted, 69 enrolled.

Mid 50% test scores			
SAT critical reading:	480-640	GPA 3.0-3.49:	28%
SAT math:	340-660	GPA 2.0-2.99:	11%
SAT writing:	400-600	Rank in top quarter:	44%
ACT composite:	20-25	Rank in top tenth:	20%
GPA 3.75 or higher:	39%	Return as sophomores:	86%
GPA 3.50-3.74:	20%	Out-of-state:	43%
		Live on campus:	99%

Basis for selection. Recommendations, church affiliation, character qualities important. Interview recommended for borderline applicants. **Home schooled:** Transcript of courses and grades required. **Learning Disabled:** Request for accommodation must be submitted.

High school preparation. College-preparatory program required. Recommended units include English 4, mathematics 4, social studies 3, history 4, science 3 (laboratory 3), foreign language 2 and computer science 4.

2015-2016 Annual costs. Tuition/fees: $16,600. Room/board: $6,732. Books/supplies: $1,164.

Financial aid. Non-need-based: Scholarships awarded for academics, leadership, music/drama.

Application procedures. Admission: Priority date 6/1; deadline 8/1 (postmark date). $45 fee. Application must be submitted online. Admission notification on a rolling basis. **Financial aid:** Priority date 4/1; no closing date. FAFSA required. Applicants notified on a rolling basis starting 3/15.

Academics. Special study options: Distance learning, double major, dual enrollment of high school students, independent study, internships, study abroad, teacher certification program. **Credit/placement by examination:** AP, CLEP, SAT, ACT, institutional tests. 6 credit hours maximum toward associate degree, 12 toward bachelor's. **Support services:** Learning center, pre-admission summer program, reduced course load, remedial instruction, study skills assistance, tutoring, writing center.

Majors. Business: Administrative services. **Education:** Elementary, English, middle, music, secondary. **Theology:** Bible, missionary, religious ed, sacred music, theology. **Visual/performing arts:** Music.

Most popular majors. Education 40%, theological studies 54%.

Technology on campus. 46 workstations in dormitories, library, computer center, student center. Dormitories wired for high-speed internet access and linked to campus network. Commuter students can connect to campus network. Online library, repair service, wireless network available.

Student life. Freshman orientation: Mandatory. Preregistration for classes offered. Held weekend before classes start in fall. **Policies:** All single students under the age of 23 and not living at home must live in the residence halls. Religious observance required. **Housing:** Guaranteed on-campus for all undergraduates. Single-sex dorms, special housing for disabled, apartments available. $200 nonrefundable deposit, deadline 6/1. **Activities:** Bands, campus ministries, choral groups, drama, music ensembles, student government, student missionary fellowship, missionary kids fellowship, student association, Future Christian Teachers Association, Future Preacher's Association.

Athletics. NCCAA. **Intercollegiate:** Basketball, cross-country, soccer, track and field, volleyball W. **Intramural:** Basketball, soccer. **Team name:** Eagles.

Student services. Chaplain/spiritual director, career counseling, student employment services, financial aid counseling, health services, personal counseling, placement for graduates, veterans' counselor, women's services.

Contact. E-mail: admissions@faith.edu
Phone: (515) 964-0601 ext. 241 Toll-free number: (888) 324-8448
Fax: (515) 964-1638
Mark Davis, Director of Admissions, Faith Baptist Bible College and Theological Seminary, 1900 NW Fourth Street, Ankeny, IA 50023

Graceland University
Lamoni, Iowa
www.graceland.edu   **CB code: 6249**

- Private 4-year university and liberal arts college affiliated with the Community of Christ
- Residential campus in rural community
- 1,375 degree-seeking undergraduates: 10% part-time, 56% women, 10% African American, 1% Asian American, 11% Hispanic/Latino, 1% Native Hawaiian/Pacific islander, 4% Multi-racial, non-Hispanic, 3% international
- 655 degree-seeking graduate students
- 48% of applicants admitted
- SAT or ACT (ACT writing optional) required
- 51% graduate within 6 years

General. Founded in 1895. Regionally accredited. Additional campus in Independence, Missouri. Evening and weekend programs offered at Indian Hills Community College and North Central Missouri College. **Degrees:** 396 bachelor's awarded; master's, doctoral offered. **Location:** 75 miles from Des Moines, 110 miles from Kansas City. **Calendar:** Trimester, limited summer session. **Full-time faculty:** 88 total; 74% have terminal degrees, 10% minority, 56% women. **Part-time faculty:** 77 total; 18% have terminal degrees, 4% minority, 60% women. **Class size:** 66% < 20, 26% 20-39, 5% 40-49, 3% 50-99. **Special facilities:** International health center, nuclear magnetic resonance spectrometer, ultra-centrifuge, -80 degrees freezer, free enterprise study center, Shaw Center for the Performing Arts.

Freshman class profile. 2,153 applied, 1,031 admitted, 290 enrolled.

Mid 50% test scores		GPA 2.0-2.99:	35%
SAT critical reading:	370-450	Rank in top quarter:	18%
SAT math:	410-490	Rank in top tenth:	12%
ACT composite:	18-24	Return as sophomores:	60%
GPA 3.75 or higher:	20%	Out-of-state:	20%
GPA 3.50-3.74:	13%	Live on campus:	95%
GPA 3.0-3.49:	32%	International:	3%

Basis for selection. Rank in upper 50% of class, 2.5 GPA, 21 ACT or 960 SAT important. Applicants who do not meet admissions criteria may be considered and will be required to take developmental courses if accepted. Some applicants must test for Chance Program prior to being considered. Interview required of applicants who do not meet admissions requirements, recommended for others. Portfolio recommended of art majors. Theater and music majors submit performance application and audition. **Home schooled:** Transcript of courses and grades required. 2.5 GPA plus two of the following required: 21 ACT/960 SAT; portfolio demonstrating the breadth and depth of learning by the applicant and sufficient preparation for college success; home school transcript prepared by the teachers/parents, an independent or supervising teacher, or an organization with whom the student is registered or affiliated.

High school preparation. College-preparatory program recommended. 13 units recommended. Recommended units include English 4, mathematics 3, social studies 3, science 2 and foreign language 1.

2016-2017 Annual costs. Tuition/fees: $27,010. Room/board: $8,280. Books/supplies: $1,190. Personal expenses: $1,886.

2015-2016 Financial aid. **Need-based:** 266 full-time freshmen applied for aid; 249 deemed to have need; 248 received aid. Average need met was 80%. Average scholarship/grant was $21,114; average loan $3,694. 67% of total undergraduate aid awarded as scholarships/grants, 33% as loans/jobs. **Non-need-based:** Awarded to 655 full-time undergraduates, including 154

freshmen. Scholarships awarded for academics, alumni affiliation, art, athletics, job skills, leadership, music/drama, religious affiliation. **Additional information:** Founders Scholarship will supplement other gift aid until percentage of calculated need has been met.

Application procedures. **Admission:** No deadline. No application fee. Admission notification on a rolling basis. **Financial aid:** No deadline. FAFSA required. Applicants notified on a rolling basis starting 2/1; must reply within 2 week(s) of notification.

Academics. Distance Learning programs delivered to online cohorts and at multiple off-campus locations. Nursing program delivered through online study and on-campus residency sessions. **Special study options:** Accelerated study, combined bachelor's/graduate degree, distance learning, double major, dual enrollment of high school students, honors, independent study, internships, liberal arts/career combination, student-designed major, study abroad, teacher certification program. **Credit/placement by examination:** AP, CLEP, IB, SAT, ACT, institutional tests. 30 credit hours maximum toward bachelor's degree. Credit by standardized examinations is awarded based on American Council on Education recommendations. **Support services:** Learning center, reduced course load, remedial instruction, study skills assistance, tutoring, writing center.

Majors. Biology: General. **Business:** Accounting, business admin, organizational leadership. **Communications:** Communications/speech/rhetoric, organizational. **Communications technology:** Desktop publishing. **Computer sciences:** General, web page design. **Education:** Elementary, physical. **English:** English lit. **Foreign languages:** Spanish. **Health services:** Nursing (RN). **History:** General. **Human services:** Social work. **Liberal arts:** Arts/sciences. **Math:** General. **Parks/recreation:** Health/fitness, sports admin. **Philosophy/religion:** Religion. **Physical sciences:** Chemistry. **Protective services:** Criminal justice, law enforcement admin. **Psychology:** General. **Social sciences:** Economics. **Visual/performing arts:** Art, commercial/advertising art, design, dramatic, music performance, theater arts management. **Work/family studies:** Food/nutrition.

Most popular majors. Business/marketing 16%, education 21%, health sciences 23%, parks/recreation 7%.

Technology on campus. 106 workstations in library, student center. Dormitories wired for high-speed internet access and linked to campus network. Commuter students can connect to campus network. Online library, helpline, student web hosting, wireless network available.

Student life. Freshman orientation: Mandatory. Preregistration for classes offered. Early 1-day orientation sessions in spring and summer. Additional 2-3 day orientation at beginning of semester. **Policies:** No tobacco, alcohol, or drug use on campus. Students required to live on campus through sophomore year unless married, living with relatives or over age 24. **Housing:** Guaranteed on-campus for freshmen. Coed dorms, single-sex dorms, apartments available. $200 fully refundable deposit, deadline 5/1. Accommodations exist in residence halls for disabled students. **Activities:** Bands, campus ministries, choral groups, dance, drama, international student organizations, literary magazine, music ensembles, radio station, student government, student newspaper, symphony orchestra, religious clubs, environmental sustainability club, Outreach International, Students for Free Enterprise, Habitat for Humanity, Young Republicans, Young Democrats, black student union, New Latino Generation club, gay/straight alliance.

Athletics. NAIA. **Intercollegiate:** Baseball M, basketball, bowling, cheerleading, cross-country, football (tackle) M, golf, soccer, softball W, tennis, track and field, volleyball, wrestling M. **Intramural:** Badminton, baseball M, basketball, cross-country, football (non-tackle), golf, handball, sand volleyball, soccer, softball, table tennis, tennis, track and field, volleyball. **Team name:** Yellowjackets.

Student services. Adult student services, alcohol/substance abuse counseling, chaplain/spiritual director, career counseling, services for economically disadvantaged, student employment services, financial aid counseling, health services, minority student services, personal counseling, placement for graduates, veterans' counselor. **Physically disabled:** Services for visually impaired.

Contact. E-mail: admissions@graceland.edu
Phone: (641) 784-5196 Toll-free number: (866) 472-0053
Fax: (641) 784-5480
Kevin Brown, Director of Admissions, Graceland University, 1 University Place, Lamoni, IA 50140

Grand View University
Des Moines, Iowa
www.admissions.grandview.edu   **CB member**   **CB code: 6251**

- Private 4-year university and liberal arts college affiliated with the Evangelical Lutheran Church in America
- Residential campus in large city

- 1,889 degree-seeking undergraduates: 14% part-time, 55% women, 8% African American, 3% Asian American, 4% Hispanic/Latino, 3% Multi-racial, non-Hispanic, 2% international
- 67 degree-seeking graduate students
- 98% of applicants admitted
- SAT or ACT (ACT writing recommended) required
- 47% graduate within 6 years

General. Founded in 1896. Regionally accredited. **Degrees:** 636 bachelor's awarded; master's offered. **ROTC:** Army, Air Force. **Location:** 200 miles from Kansas City, 250 miles from Minneapolis-St. Paul. **Calendar:** Semester, extensive summer session. **Full-time faculty:** 95 total; 66% have terminal degrees, 5% minority, 54% women. **Part-time faculty:** 119 total; 24% have terminal degrees, 7% minority, 56% women. **Class size:** 70% < 20, 30% 20-39, less than 1% 50-99.

Freshman class profile. 784 applied, 770 admitted, 267 enrolled.

Mid 50% test scores			
SAT critical reading:	380-580	Rank in top quarter:	33%
SAT math:	400-540	Rank in top tenth:	14%
SAT writing:	340-570	Return as sophomores:	74%
ACT composite:	18-23	Out-of-state:	17%
GPA 3.75 or higher:	17%	Live on campus:	86%
GPA 3.50-3.74:	16%	International:	2%
GPA 3.0-3.49:	35%		
GPA 2.0-2.99:	31%		

Basis for selection. Individualized evaluation of applicant's secondary school record and SAT/ACT. **Home schooled:** Transcript of courses and grades required.

High school preparation. College-preparatory program recommended. 15 units recommended. Recommended units include English 4, mathematics 3, social studies 3, science 3 and foreign language 2.

2016-2017 Annual costs. Tuition/fees (projected): $25,474. Room/board: $8,172. Books/supplies: $812. Personal expenses: $2,204.

2015-2016 Financial aid. Need-based: 253 full-time freshmen applied for aid; 220 deemed to have need; 220 received aid. Average need met was 84%. Average scholarship/grant was $19,812; average loan $3,955. 62% of total undergraduate aid awarded as scholarships/grants, 38% as loans/jobs. **Non-need-based:** Awarded to 607 full-time undergraduates, including 257 freshmen. Scholarships awarded for academics, alumni affiliation, art, athletics, music/drama, religious affiliation, ROTC.

Application procedures. Admission: Closing date 8/15 (receipt date). No application fee. Admission notification on a rolling basis beginning on or about 9/15. **Financial aid:** Priority date 3/1; no closing date. Applicants notified on a rolling basis starting 3/1; must reply by 5/1 or within 3 week(s) of notification.

Academics. University emphasizes integration of liberal arts core with career-related majors. Internships are primary focus in many majors. **Special study options:** Accelerated study, cooperative education, cross-registration, distance learning, double major, dual enrollment of high school students, ESL, exchange student, honors, independent study, internships, liberal arts/career combination, student-designed major, study abroad, teacher certification program, Washington semester, weekend college. **Credit/placement by examination:** AP, CLEP, SAT, ACT, institutional tests. 32 credit hours maximum toward bachelor's degree. ACT PEP credit accepted, DANTES accepted. **Support services:** Learning center, reduced course load, remedial instruction, study skills assistance, tutoring, writing center.

Majors. Biology: General, biochemistry, biotechnology. **Business:** General, accounting, entrepreneurial studies, finance, hospitality admin, human resources, marketing, real estate. **Communications:** Broadcast journalism, journalism, media studies, public relations, radio/TV. **Computer sciences:** General, information technology, programming. **Education:** Art, elementary, English, music, physical, secondary. **English:** English lit. **Foreign languages:** Spanish. **Health services:** Nursing (RN), premedicine, prepharmacy. **History:** General. **Liberal arts:** Arts/sciences. **Math:** Applied. **Parks/recreation:** Exercise sciences, health/fitness, sports admin. **Philosophy/religion:** Religion. **Protective services:** Criminal justice. **Psychology:** General. **Social sciences:** General, political science. **Visual/performing arts:** Dramatic, graphic design, music, studio arts.

Most popular majors. Business/marketing 21%, education 10%, health sciences 13%, liberal arts 6%, parks/recreation 7%, visual/performing arts 7%.

Technology on campus. 336 workstations in dormitories, library, computer center, student center. Dormitories wired for high-speed internet access and linked to campus network. Commuter students can connect to campus network. Online course registration, online library, helpline, student web hosting, wireless network available.

Student life. Freshman orientation: Mandatory. Preregistration for classes offered. **Housing:** Coed dorms, apartments available. $200 fully refundable deposit. **Activities:** Bands, campus ministries, choral groups, dance, drama, international student organizations, literary magazine, music ensembles, radio station, student government, student newspaper, TV station, Education club, Nursing Student Association, campus fellowship, diversity alliance, art club, photography club, Viking Brigade, Viking Volunteers, Fellowship of Christian Athletes.

Athletics. NAIA. **Intercollegiate:** Baseball M, basketball, bowling, cheerleading W, cross-country, football (tackle) M, golf, soccer, softball W, tennis, track and field, volleyball, wrestling M. **Intramural:** Badminton, basketball, football (non-tackle), soccer, softball, swimming, table tennis, track and field, volleyball. **Team name:** Vikings.

Student services. Adult student services, alcohol/substance abuse counseling, chaplain/spiritual director, career counseling, student employment services, financial aid counseling, health services, minority student services, personal counseling, placement for graduates, veterans' counselor. **Physically disabled:** Services for visually, speech, hearing impaired.

Contact. E-mail: admissions@GrandView.edu
Phone: (515) 263-2810 Toll-free number: (800) 444-6083
Fax: (515) 263-2974
Ryan Thompson, Director of Admissions, Grand View University, 1200 Grandview Avenue, Des Moines, IA 50316-1599

Grinnell College
Grinnell, Iowa
www.grinnell.edu

CB member
CB code: 6252

- Private 4-year liberal arts college
- Residential campus in small town
- 1,667 degree-seeking undergraduates: 55% women, 6% African American, 7% Asian American, 7% Hispanic/Latino, 5% Multi-racial, non-Hispanic, 16% international
- 25% of applicants admitted
- SAT or ACT (ACT writing optional), application essay required
- 86% graduate within 6 years; 15% enter graduate study

General. Founded in 1846. Regionally accredited. **Degrees:** 402 bachelor's awarded. **Location:** 55 miles from Des Moines, 70 miles from Iowa City. **Calendar:** Semester, limited summer session. **Full-time faculty:** 171 total; 98% have terminal degrees, 20% minority, 45% women. **Part-time faculty:** 38 total; 42% have terminal degrees, 8% minority, 45% women. **Class size:** 69% < 20, 31% 20-39. **Special facilities:** 365-acre environmental research area, observatory.

Freshman class profile. 6,414 applied, 1,598 admitted, 442 enrolled.

Mid 50% test scores			
SAT critical reading:	640-740	End year in good standing:	93%
SAT math:	660-770	Return as sophomores:	94%
ACT composite:	30-33	Out-of-state:	88%
Rank in top quarter:	96%	Live on campus:	100%
Rank in top tenth:	81%	International:	17%

Basis for selection. Scholastic ability plus extracurricular pursuits, accomplishments most important. Curiosity, motivation, persistence, social and emotional maturity stressed. Interview recommended. **Home schooled:** Statement describing home school structure and mission, transcript of courses and grades, interview, letter of recommendation (nonparent) required. Copy of curriculum, writing sample required. SAT Subject Tests strongly recommended.

High school preparation. College-preparatory program recommended. 20 units recommended. Recommended units include English 4, mathematics 4, social studies 3, history 3, science 3 (laboratory 3) and foreign language 3.

2016-2017 Annual costs. Tuition/fees (projected): $48,758. Room/board: $11,980. Books/supplies: $900. Personal expenses: $1,100.

2015-2016 Financial aid. Need-based: 362 full-time freshmen applied for aid; 306 deemed to have need; 306 received aid. Average need met was 100%. Average scholarship/grant was $37,426; average loan $3,979. 86% of total undergraduate aid awarded as scholarships/grants, 14% as loans/jobs. **Non-need-based:** Awarded to 429 full-time undergraduates, including 129 freshmen. Scholarships awarded for academics, state residency. **Additional information:** Need-blind admission policy, 100% of demonstrated institutional need met for all domestic students, with loan cap programs. Students may apply financial aid to off-campus study programs.

Application procedures. Admission: Closing date 1/15 (postmark date). No application fee. Admission notification by 4/1. Must reply by May 1 or within 2 week(s) if notified thereafter. **Financial aid:** Closing date 2/1. FAFSA, CSS PROFILE required. Applicants notified by 4/1; must reply by 5/1.

Academics. Internships available in public agencies, private organizations, and corporations. Advanced research opportunities available for students in all majors. **Special study options:** Accelerated study, double major, dual enrollment of high school students, independent study, internships, liberal arts/career combination, student-designed major, study abroad, teacher certification program, urban semester, Washington semester. Study abroad available in more than 30 countries. Other programs include study in Washington, 3-2 engineering, architecture, and law. **Credit/placement by examination:** AP, CLEP, IB, institutional tests. **Support services:** Learning center, reduced course load, study skills assistance, tutoring, writing center.

Majors. Area/ethnic studies: Women's. **Biology:** General, biochemistry. **Computer sciences:** Computer science. **English:** English lit. **Foreign languages:** Chinese, classics, French, German, Russian, Spanish. **History:** General. **Math:** General. **Philosophy/religion:** Philosophy, religion. **Physical sciences:** Chemistry, physics. **Psychology:** General. **Social sciences:** Anthropology, economics, political science, sociology. **Visual/performing arts:** Art history/conservation, dramatic, music, studio arts.

Most popular majors. Biology 15%, English 7%, foreign language 11%, history 6%, physical sciences 7%, psychology 8%, social sciences 25%, visual/performing arts 6%.

Technology on campus. 400 workstations in dormitories, library, computer center, student center. Dormitories wired for high-speed internet access and linked to campus network. Commuter students can connect to campus network. Online library, helpline, student web hosting, wireless network available.

Student life. Freshman orientation: Mandatory. Preregistration for classes offered. Four day session held the weekend before start of classes. **Policies:** All residence halls and college-owned off-campus houses are self-governing: residents decide how their individual hall will operate and share responsibility for budget, quiet hours, social policy, regulations. **Housing:** Guaranteed on-campus for all undergraduates. Coed dorms, special housing for disabled, cooperative housing, themed housing, wellness housing available. $200 nonrefundable deposit, deadline 5/1. Pets allowed in dorm rooms. **Activities:** Bands, campus ministries, choral groups, dance, drama, film society, international student organizations, literary magazine, music ensembles, Model UN, musical theater, radio station, student government, student newspaper, symphony orchestra, Young Muslims Sisters, Chalutzim, Concerned Black Students, Asian and Asian American Association, Coalition of Environmental Activists, Campus Democrats, Feminist Action Coalition, Alternative Break, Student Organization of Latinas/os, social justice action groups.

Athletics. NCAA. **Intercollegiate:** Baseball M, basketball, cross-country, diving, football (tackle) M, golf, soccer, softball W, swimming, tennis, track and field, volleyball W. **Intramural:** Badminton, basketball, football (non-tackle), racquetball, rowing (crew), soccer, softball, table tennis, tennis, volleyball. **Team name:** Pioneers.

Student services. Alcohol/substance abuse counseling, chaplain/spiritual director, career counseling, student employment services, financial aid counseling, health services, minority student services, personal counseling, placement for graduates, veterans' counselor. **Physically disabled:** Services for visually, speech, hearing impaired.

Contact. E-mail: admission@grinnell.edu
Phone: (641) 269-3600 Toll-free number: (800) 247-0113
Fax: (641) 269-4800
Gregory Sneed, Director of Admission, Grinnell College, 1103 Park Street, 2nd Floor, Grinnell, IA 50112-1690

Hamilton Technical College
Davenport, Iowa
www.hamiltontechcollege.edu   **CB code: 1588**

- For-profit 3-year technical college
- Commuter campus in large city
- 90 degree-seeking undergraduates: 7% women
- Interview required

General. Founded in 1969. Accredited by ACCSC. **Degrees:** 25 bachelor's, 34 associate awarded. **Location:** 190 miles from Des Moines, 175 miles from Chicago. **Calendar:** Semester, extensive summer session. **Full-time faculty:** 9 total; 22% minority, 33% women. **Part-time faculty:** 2 total.

Basis for selection. Open admission. Pseudoisochromatic Color Plates vision test required of all applicants. **Home schooled:** Transcript of courses and grades, state high school equivalency certificate required.

2015-2016 Annual costs. Diploma programs: Medical Assisting Technology, $12,390; Medical/Insurance Coding Specialist Program, $12,390. Associate degree program: Electronics Engineering Technology, $35,820. Bachelor's program: Electronics Engineering Technology, $47,760. Books and lab fee included.

Application procedures. Admission: No deadline. No application fee. Admission notification on a rolling basis. Applicant must be 17 or older and if 17, he/she must provide a co-signer (parent/legal guardian). **Financial aid:** No deadline. FAFSA, institutional form required. Applicants notified on a rolling basis.

Academics. Credit/placement by examination: AP, CLEP. 35 credit hours maximum toward associate degree, 60 toward bachelor's. **Support services:** Learning center, tutoring.

Technology on campus. 125 workstations in library, computer center. Wireless network available.

Student life. Freshman orientation: Mandatory. Preregistration for classes offered.

Student services. Career counseling, student employment services, financial aid counseling, placement for graduates.

Contact. E-mail: admissions@hamiltontechcollege.com
Phone: (563) 386-3570 Toll-free number: (866) 966-4825
Fax: (563) 386-6756
Brian Beert, Dean of Students and Enrollment, Hamilton Technical College, 1011 East 53rd Street, Davenport, IA 52807

Iowa State University
Ames, Iowa
www.iastate.edu   **CB member**   **CB code: 6306**

- Public 4-year university
- Residential campus in small city
- 29,520 degree-seeking undergraduates: 5% part-time, 43% women, 3% African American, 3% Asian American, 5% Hispanic/Latino, 2% Multiracial, non-Hispanic, 7% international
- 5,680 degree-seeking graduate students
- 87% of applicants admitted
- SAT or ACT (ACT writing optional) required
- 71% graduate within 6 years

General. Founded in 1858. Regionally accredited. **Degrees:** 5,687 bachelor's awarded; master's, professional, doctoral offered. **ROTC:** Army, Naval, Air Force. **Location:** 30 miles from Des Moines. **Calendar:** Semester, extensive summer session. **Full-time faculty:** 1,603 total; 93% have terminal degrees, 22% minority, 37% women. **Part-time faculty:** 281 total; 54% have terminal degrees, 8% minority, 56% women. **Class size:** 32% < 20, 36% 20-39, 8% 40-49, 15% 50-99, 9% >100. **Special facilities:** Observatory, nature preserve, research park, molecular biology building, computation center, center for designing foods, Department of Energy laboratory, virtual reality applications center, crop utilization center, transportation research and education center, sustainable environmental technologies center, gardens, field-oriented lakeside research facility.

Freshman class profile. 19,164 applied, 16,702 admitted, 6,230 enrolled.

Mid 50% test scores			
SAT critical reading:	460-620	Rank in top quarter:	54%
SAT math:	500-640	Rank in top tenth:	22%
ACT composite:	22-28	Return as sophomores:	87%
GPA 3.75 or higher:	31%	Out-of-state:	40%
GPA 3.50-3.74:	24%	Live on campus:	94%
GPA 3.0-3.49:	35%	International:	4%
GPA 2.0-2.99:	10%	Fraternities:	17%
		Sororities:	28%

Basis for selection. Students admitted if they achieve 245 Regent Admission Index (RAI) and meet course requirements. RAI is calculated using ACT, class rank, GPA, and number of years of course requirement. **Home schooled:** Emphasis placed on standardized examinations.

High school preparation. College-preparatory program required. 12 units required; 19 recommended. Required and recommended units include English 4, mathematics 3-4, social studies 2-4, science 3-4 (laboratory 2 3) and foreign language 2-3. 2 years of foreign language required for Colleges of

Liberal Arts & Sciences, and Engineering; 3 years of social studies required for College of Liberal Arts & Sciences.

2015-2016 Annual costs. Tuition/fees: $7,736; $20,856 out-of-state. Room/board: $8,070. Books/supplies: $1,035. Personal expenses: $2,030.

2014-2015 Financial aid. Need-based: 5,091 full-time freshmen applied for aid; 3,103 deemed to have need; 3,062 received aid. Average need met was 82%. Average scholarship/grant was $8,389; average loan $3,308. 55% of total undergraduate aid awarded as scholarships/grants, 45% as loans/jobs. **Non-need-based:** Awarded to 15,457 full-time undergraduates, including 3,729 freshmen. Scholarships awarded for academics, alumni affiliation, art, athletics, leadership, minority status, music/drama, ROTC, state residency. **Additional information:** Short-term loan program available to meet unplanned needs. Financial counseling clinic provides budget and credit education assistance.

Application procedures. Admission: Priority date 7/1; no deadline. $40 fee, may be waived for applicants with need. Admission notification on a rolling basis beginning on or about 7/1. Must reply by May 1 or within 2 week(s) if notified thereafter. **Financial aid:** Priority date 3/1; no closing date. FAFSA required. Applicants notified on a rolling basis starting 4/1; must reply by 5/1.

Academics. Classes offered over the Internet, by videotape, at distant locations through the state's fiber-optic communication network, and at off-campus locations taught face-to-face by the university's professors. **Special study options:** Accelerated study, combined bachelor's/graduate degree, cooperative education, cross-registration, distance learning, double major, dual enrollment of high school students, ESL, exchange student, external degree, honors, independent study, internships, liberal arts/career combination, student-designed major, study abroad, teacher certification program, Washington semester. National Collegiate Honors Council Honors Semester. Combined bachelor's/graduate programs include: landscape architecture, agriculture and biosystems engineering, biochemistry and biophysics, electrical and computer engineering, civil and construction engineering, chemical engineering, food science and human nutrition, material science engineering, zoology and genetics. **Credit/placement by examination:** AP, CLEP, IB, SAT, ACT, institutional tests. No limit on number of hours of credit by examination that may be counted toward degree. **Support services:** Learning center, pre-admission summer program, reduced course load, remedial instruction, study skills assistance, tutoring, writing center.

Majors. Architecture: Architecture, landscape, urban/community planning. **Area/ethnic studies:** Women's. **Biology:** General, biochemistry, bioinformatics, biophysics, entomology, genetics, microbiology. **Business:** General, accounting, finance, hospitality admin, logistics, management information systems, managerial economics, marketing, operations, statistics. **Communications:** Advertising, communications/speech/rhetoric, journalism. **Computer sciences:** General. **Conservation:** Environmental science, environmental studies, forestry. **Education:** General, agricultural, early childhood, elementary, family/consumer sciences, health, kindergarten/preschool, music, technology/industrial arts, trade/industrial. **Engineering:** General, aerospace, agricultural, chemical, civil, computer, construction, electrical, industrial, materials, mechanical, software. **English:** English lit, rhetoric/composition, technical writing. **Foreign languages:** General, linguistics. **Health services:** Dietetics, medical illustrating, premedicine, preveterinary. **History:** General. **Liberal arts:** Arts/sciences. **Math:** General, statistics. **Parks/recreation:** Exercise sciences. **Philosophy/religion:** Philosophy, religion. **Physical sciences:** Chemistry, geology, materials science, physics, planetary. **Psychology:** General. **Social sciences:** Anthropology, economics, international relations, political science, sociology. **Visual/performing arts:** General, art, commercial/advertising art, design, fashion design, graphic design, industrial design, interior design, music. **Work/family studies:** General, apparel marketing, clothing/textiles, family resources, family/community services, food/nutrition, housing, human nutrition, institutional food production, textile manufacture.

Most popular majors. Agriculture 12%, biology 6%, business/marketing 19%, engineering/engineering technologies 20%.

Technology on campus. 2,400 workstations in dormitories, library, computer center, student center. Dormitories wired for high-speed internet access and linked to campus network. Commuter students can connect to campus network. Online course registration, online library, helpline, repair service, student web hosting, wireless network available.

Student life. Freshman orientation: Available. Preregistration for classes offered. Two-day, overnight program. **Housing:** Guaranteed on-campus for all undergraduates. Coed dorms, single-sex dorms, special housing for disabled, apartments, cooperative housing, fraternity/sorority housing, themed housing, wellness housing available. $135 partly refundable deposit, deadline 9/1. Learning communities, non-smoking, non-alcohol, graduate/adult undergrad housing available. **Activities:** Bands, campus ministries, choral groups, dance, drama, film society, international student organizations, literary magazine, music ensembles, Model UN, musical theater, opera, radio station, student government, student newspaper, symphony orchestra, TV station, more than 500 clubs and organizations.

Athletics. NCAA. **Intercollegiate:** Basketball, cross-country, football (tackle) M, golf, gymnastics W, soccer W, softball W, swimming W, tennis W, track and field, volleyball W, wrestling M. **Intramural:** Badminton, basketball, bowling, boxing M, cross-country, diving, golf, handball, ice hockey, racquetball, skiing, soccer, softball, squash, swimming, table tennis, tennis, volleyball, water polo, weight lifting, wrestling. **Team name:** Cyclones.

Student services. Adult student services, alcohol/substance abuse counseling, career counseling, student employment services, financial aid counseling, health services, legal services, minority student services, on-campus daycare, personal counseling, placement for graduates, veterans' counselor, women's services. **Physically disabled:** Services for visually, speech, hearing impaired.

Contact. E-mail: admissions@iastate.edu
Phone: (515) 294-5836 Toll-free number: (800) 262-3810
Fax: (515) 294-2592
Katherine Johnson Suski, Director of Admissions, Iowa State University, 100 Enrollment Services Center, Ames, IA 50011-2011

Iowa Wesleyan College
Mount Pleasant, Iowa CB member
www.iwc.edu CB code: 6308

▸ Private 4-year liberal arts college affiliated with the United Methodist Church
▸ Residential campus in small town
▸ 578 degree-seeking undergraduates
▸ SAT or ACT (ACT writing optional) required

General. Founded in 1842. Regionally accredited. **Degrees:** 122 bachelor's awarded. **Location:** 47 miles from Iowa City, 25 miles from Burlington. **Calendar:** Semester, limited summer session. **Full-time faculty:** 51 total; 59% have terminal degrees, 10% minority, 55% women. **Part-time faculty:** 48 total; 17% have terminal degrees, 67% women. **Class size:** 88% < 20, 12% 20-39. **Special facilities:** Public interest institute, Harlan-Lincoln house and museum.

Freshman class profile.

GPA 3.75 or higher:	19%	Rank in top tenth:	8%
GPA 3.50-3.74:	14%	Out-of-state:	60%
GPA 3.0-3.49:	31%	Live on campus:	91%
GPA 2.0-2.99:	33%	Sororities:	8%
Rank in top quarter:	34%		

Basis for selection. Upper 50% class rank preferred. Automatic acceptance with 2.5 GPA and 19 ACT. Transfer students who have 24 or more credits are not required to submit ACT. Audition recommended for music majors. Portfolio recommended for art, creative programs majors. Essay recommended for applicants who do not meet regular admission requirements. **Home schooled:** Transcript of courses and grades required. GED or portfolio may be substituted for high school transcript requirement.

High school preparation. College-preparatory program recommended. 16 units recommended. Recommended units include English 4, mathematics 3, social studies 3, science 2 (laboratory 2) and academic electives 4.

2015-2016 Annual costs. Tuition/fees: $27,286. Room/board: $9,576. Books/supplies: $1,114. Personal expenses: $1,600.

Financial aid. Non-need-based: Scholarships awarded for academics, alumni affiliation, art, music/drama.

Application procedures. Admission: No deadline. $20 fee, may be waived for applicants with need, free for online applicants. Admission notification on a rolling basis beginning on or about 9/15. Must reply by May 1 or within 2 week(s) if notified thereafter. **Financial aid:** Priority date 4/1; no closing date. FAFSA required. Applicants notified on a rolling basis starting 1/1; must reply within 2 week(s) of notification.

Academics. Special study options: Combined bachelor's/graduate degree, cross-registration, distance learning, double major, dual enrollment of high school students, exchange student, independent study, internships, liberal arts/career combination, student-designed major, study abroad, teacher certification program, Washington semester. **Credit/placement by examination:** AP, CLEP, IB, institutional tests. 30 credit hours maximum toward bachelor's degree. **Support services:** Learning center, reduced course load, study skills assistance, tutoring, writing center.

Majors. Biology: General. **Business:** General, accounting, business admin. **Communications:** General, communications/speech/rhetoric. **Education:** General, art, biology, chemistry, early childhood, elementary, English, foundations, health, history, mathematics, middle, music, physical, physics, secondary, social studies, technology/industrial arts. **English:** English lit. **Health services:** Nursing (RN), nursing practice, predental, premedicine, prepharmacy, prephysical therapy, preveterinary. **History:** General. **Parks/recreation:** Exercise sciences, health/fitness. **Philosophy/religion:** General, Christian, philosophy, religion. **Physical sciences:** Chemistry. **Protective services:** Forensics, law enforcement admin. **Psychology:** General. **Social sciences:** Sociology. **Visual/performing arts:** Design, music, studio arts.

Most popular majors. Biology 7%, business/marketing 28%, education 17%, health sciences 11%, parks/recreation 17%, psychology 6%.

Technology on campus. 110 workstations in library, computer center. Dormitories wired for high-speed internet access and linked to campus network. Commuter students can connect to campus network. Online library, repair service, wireless network available.

Student life. Freshman orientation: Mandatory. Preregistration for classes offered. Five-day program held week before classes begin. **Policies:** All full-time, unmarried students under the age of 23 who do not live with parents within a 30 mile radius of campus are required to live in college residential facilities. Exemptions may be made for students with dependent children and veterans. **Housing:** Guaranteed on-campus for all undergraduates. Coed dorms, single-sex dorms, wellness housing available. $100 nonrefundable deposit, deadline 8/20. **Activities:** Bands, campus ministries, choral groups, international student organizations, literary magazine, music ensembles, radio station, student government, symphony orchestra, Black Awareness Organization, Fellowship of Christian Athletics, Bacchus, Unidad.

Athletics. NCAA. **Intercollegiate:** Baseball M, basketball, cross-country, football (tackle) M, golf, soccer, softball W, track and field, volleyball W. **Intramural:** Badminton, basketball, bowling, football (non-tackle), softball, table tennis, volleyball. **Team name:** Tigers.

Student services. Adult student services, alcohol/substance abuse counseling, chaplain/spiritual director, career counseling, student employment services, financial aid counseling, health services, personal counseling.

Contact. E-mail: admit@iwc.edu
Phone: (319) 385-6231 Toll-free number: (800) 582-2383 ext. 6231
Fax: (319) 385-6240
Iowa Wesleyan College, 601 North Main Street, Mount Pleasant, IA 52641-1398

Kaplan University: Cedar Falls
Cedar Falls, Iowa
www.kaplanuniversity.edu/cedar-falls-iowa.aspx

- For-profit 4-year university and branch campus college
- Commuter campus in small city
- 386 undergraduates
- Application essay, interview required

General. Degrees: 24 bachelor's, 87 associate awarded; master's offered. **Location:** 120 miles from Des Moines. **Calendar:** Differs by program, extensive summer session. **Full-time faculty:** 12 total. **Part-time faculty:** 32 total. **Class size:** 64% < 20, 33% 20-39, 3% 40-49.

Basis for selection. Open admission, but selective for some programs. Entrance test required for most programs.

2015-2016 Annual costs. Diploma programs: $11,501-$23,410. Associate programs: $30,654-$35,763. Bachelor's programs: $35,763-$66,417.

Financial aid. All financial aid based on need.

Application procedures. Admission: No deadline. $20 fee. Application must be submitted on paper. Admission notification on a rolling basis. **Financial aid:** No deadline. FAFSA, institutional form required. Applicants notified on a rolling basis.

Academics. Special study options: Cooperative education, distance learning. **Credit/placement by examination:** AP, CLEP, institutional tests. 32 credit hours maximum toward associate degree. **Support services:** Learning center, tutoring.

Majors. Business: Business admin.

Student life. Freshman orientation: Available, $20 fee. Preregistration for classes offered. **Activities:** Student government, student newspaper.

Student services. Student employment services, financial aid counseling, personal counseling, placement for graduates.

Contact. Phone: (319) 277-0220 Toll-free number: (800) 728-1220
Fax: (319) 243-2961
Jill Hansen, Director of Admissions, Kaplan University: Cedar Falls, 7009 Nordic Drive, Cedar Falls, IA 50613

Kaplan University: Davenport
Davenport, Iowa
www.kaplanuniversity.edu/davenport-iowa.aspx
CB code: 5848

- For-profit 4-year university
- Residential campus in large city
- 40,349 undergraduates
- Interview required

General. Founded in 1937. Regionally accredited. **Degrees:** 4,285 bachelor's, 3,362 associate awarded; master's, professional offered. **Location:** 165 miles from Des Moines, 180 miles from Chicago. **Calendar:** Quarter, extensive summer session. **Full-time faculty:** 6 total. **Part-time faculty:** 33 total.

Basis for selection. Open admission, but selective for some programs.

2015-2016 Annual costs. Diploma programs: $11,501-$23,410. Associate programs: $30,654-$35,763. Bachelor's programs: $35,763-$66,417.

Financial aid. Non-need-based: Scholarships awarded for academics.

Application procedures. Admission: No deadline. $25 fee, may be waived for applicants with need. Admission notification on a rolling basis. **Financial aid:** No deadline. FAFSA, institutional form required. Applicants notified on a rolling basis starting 3/4; must reply by 6/15 or within 2 week(s) of notification.

Academics. Special study options: Distance learning, double major, honors, internships, teacher certification program. **Credit/placement by examination:** AP, CLEP, institutional tests. 22 credit hours maximum toward associate degree, 45 toward bachelor's. Up to 25% of all credit in a particular program can be earned through examination. **Support services:** Learning center, reduced course load, remedial instruction, study skills assistance, tutoring, writing center.

Majors. Business: Business admin. **Communications:** Communications/speech/rhetoric. **Computer sciences:** Information technology, networking. **Health services:** Nursing (RN). **Protective services:** Criminal justice. **Psychology:** General.

Most popular majors. Business/marketing 35%, computer/information sciences 12%, health sciences 7%, legal studies 19%, security/protective services 28%.

Technology on campus. 121 workstations in library, student center. Online course registration, online library, helpline, student web hosting, wireless network available.

Student life. Freshman orientation: Mandatory, $20 fee. Preregistration for classes offered. **Activities:** Student government, student newspaper.

Student services. Career counseling, student employment services, financial aid counseling, personal counseling, placement for graduates.

Contact. Phone: (563) 355-3500 Toll-free number: (800) 747-1035
Fax: (563) 355-1320
Jason Wilebski, Director of Admissions, Kaplan University: Davenport, 1801 East Kimberly Road, Suite 1, Davenport, IA 52807-2095

Kaplan University: Des Moines
Urbandale, Iowa
www.kaplanuniversity.edu/des-moines-iowa.aspx
CB code: 3388

- For-profit 4-year university
- Commuter campus in large city
- 780 undergraduates
- Interview required

General. Regionally accredited. **Degrees:** 98 bachelor's, 201 associate awarded; master's offered. **Location:** 4 miles from Des Moines. **Calendar:**

Differs by program, extensive summer session. **Full-time faculty:** 11 total. **Part-time faculty:** 51 total.

Basis for selection. Open admission, but selective for some programs.

2015-2016 Annual costs. Personal expenses: $1,500. **Additional information:** Diploma programs: $11,501-$23,410. Associate programs: $30,654-$35,763. Bachelor's programs: $35,763-$66,417.

Financial aid. All financial aid based on need.

Application procedures. Admission: No deadline. $20 fee. Application must be submitted on paper. Admission notification on a rolling basis. **Financial aid:** Priority date 6/30; no closing date. FAFSA, institutional form required.

Academics. Special study options: Accelerated study, distance learning, independent study, internships, liberal arts/career combination. **Credit/placement by examination:** AP, CLEP, institutional tests. 32 credit hours maximum toward associate degree, 32 toward bachelor's. **Support services:** Learning center, remedial instruction, study skills assistance, tutoring.

Majors. Business: Accounting, business admin. **Computer sciences:** Information technology. **Protective services:** Law enforcement admin.

Technology on campus. 195 workstations in library, computer center. Commuter students can connect to campus network. Online library, repair service available.

Student life. Freshman orientation: Mandatory, $20 fee. Preregistration for classes offered. **Activities:** Student government, student newspaper.

Student services. Adult student services, career counseling, student employment services, financial aid counseling, placement for graduates.

Contact. Phone: (515) 727-2100 Toll-free number: (800) 383-0253 Fax: (515) 727-2115
Mark Bandy, Director of Admissions, Kaplan University: Des Moines, 4655 121st Street, Urbandale, IA 50323

Kaplan University: Mason City
Mason City, Iowa
www.kaplanuniversity.edu/mason-city-iowa.aspx
CB code: 6289

- For-profit 4-year branch campus college
- Commuter campus in large town
- 213 undergraduates
- 23 graduate students
- Interview required

General. Regionally accredited. **Degrees:** 38 bachelor's, 41 associate awarded; master's offered. **Location:** 127 miles from Des Moines. **Calendar:** Differs by program, extensive summer session. **Full-time faculty:** 2 total. **Part-time faculty:** 5 total. **Class size:** 92% < 20, 8% 20-39.

Basis for selection. Open admission. **Home schooled:** Transcript of courses and grades, state high school equivalency certificate required. GED required.

2015-2016 Annual costs. Personal expenses: $5,408. **Additional information:** Diploma programs: $11,501-$23,410. Associate programs: $30,654-$35,763. Bachelor's programs: $35,763-$66,417.

Financial aid. Non-need-based: Scholarships awarded for academics.

Application procedures. Admission: No deadline. $20 fee. Application must be submitted on paper. Admission notification on a rolling basis. **Financial aid:** No deadline. FAFSA required. Applicants notified on a rolling basis.

Academics. Special study options: Accelerated study, combined bachelor's/graduate degree, distance learning, dual enrollment of high school students, independent study, internships, student-designed major, study abroad, teacher certification program. **Credit/placement by examination:** AP, CLEP. **Support services:** Learning center, study skills assistance, tutoring.

Majors. Business: Accounting, business admin. **Computer sciences:** Information technology.

Technology on campus. 140 workstations in library, computer center. Commuter students can connect to campus network. Online library, helpline, repair service, wireless network available.

Student life. Freshman orientation: Mandatory, $20 fee. Preregistration for classes offered. **Activities:** Student government.

Student services. Adult student services, student employment services, financial aid counseling, placement for graduates. **Physically disabled:** Services for hearing impaired.

Contact. E-mail: jvalencia@kaplan.edu
Phone: (641) 423-2530 Toll-free number: (800) 274-2530
Fax: (641) 423-7512
Julie Valencia, Campus President, Kaplan University: Mason City, Plaza West 2570 Fourth Street, SW, Mason City, IA 50401

Loras College
Dubuque, Iowa
www.loras.edu
CB code: 6370

- Private 4-year liberal arts college affiliated with the Roman Catholic Church
- Residential campus in small city
- 1,444 degree-seeking undergraduates: 2% part-time, 48% women, 2% African American, 1% Asian American, 6% Hispanic/Latino, 2% Multiracial, non-Hispanic, 1% international
- 66 degree-seeking graduate students
- 95% of applicants admitted
- SAT or ACT (ACT writing optional) required
- 70% graduate within 6 years; 16% enter graduate study

General. Founded in 1839. Regionally accredited. **Degrees:** 312 bachelor's awarded; master's offered. **ROTC:** Army. **Location:** 180 miles from Chicago. **Calendar:** Semester, extensive summer session. **Full-time faculty:** 103 total; 97% have terminal degrees, 3% minority, 37% women. **Part-time faculty:** 52 total; 31% have terminal degrees, 4% minority, 62% women. **Class size:** 45% < 20, 55% 20-39, less than 1% 40-49. **Special facilities:** Planetarium, observatory, residential arts complex, regional history archive.

Freshman class profile. 1,250 applied, 1,187 admitted, 389 enrolled.

Mid 50% test scores		Rank in top tenth:	22%
SAT critical reading:	460-540	End year in good standing:	86%
SAT math:	460-570	Return as sophomores:	81%
ACT composite:	21-26	Out-of-state:	62%
GPA 3.75 or higher:	34%	Live on campus:	95%
GPA 3.50-3.74:	19%	International:	1%
GPA 3.0-3.49:	27%	Fraternities:	2%
GPA 2.0-2.99:	20%	Sororities:	4%
Rank in top quarter:	46%		

Basis for selection. High school academic record, college prep course work, and test scores are most important. Interview and personal statement recommended. **Learning Disabled:** Students must be admitted to the college before being eligible for acceptance into the enhanced learning disabilities program. All students applying for the enhanced learning disabilities program must have materials submitted by the required date. All files reviewed by the learning disabilities program.

High school preparation. College-preparatory program recommended. 16 units recommended. Recommended units include English 4, mathematics 4, social studies 3, science 3 (laboratory 2) and academic electives 2.

2016-2017 Annual costs. Tuition/fees (projected): $31,525. Room/board: $7,697. Books/supplies: $1,100. Personal expenses: $659.

2015-2016 Financial aid. Need-based: 363 full-time freshmen applied for aid; 313 deemed to have need; 313 received aid. Average need met was 85%. Average scholarship/grant was $17,682; average loan $3,855. 86% of total undergraduate aid awarded as scholarships/grants, 14% as loans/jobs. **Non-need-based:** Awarded to 976 full-time undergraduates, including 223 freshmen. Scholarships awarded for academics, art. **Additional information:** Audition or portfolio recommended for music and art financial aid applicants.

Application procedures. Admission: No deadline. $25 fee, may be waived for applicants with need, free for online applicants. Admission notification on a rolling basis. **Financial aid:** Priority date 4/15; no closing date. FAFSA required. Applicants notified on a rolling basis starting 3/1; must reply within 3 week(s) of notification.

Academics. Athletic Training 3+2 dual degree program awards a bachelor's degree in kinesiology and a master's degree in athletic training. **Special study options:** Combined bachelor's/graduate degree, cross-registration, distance learning, double major, dual enrollment of high school students, exchange student, honors, independent study, internships, student-designed major, study abroad, teacher certification program, urban semester, Washington semester.

Undergraduate neuroscience, undergraduate and graduate Business Analytics. Graduate courses open to undergraduates if certain requirements are met. **Credit/placement by examination:** AP, CLEP, IB, SAT, ACT. 30 credit hours maximum toward bachelor's degree. **Support services:** Learning center, pre-admission summer program, reduced course load, remedial instruction, study skills assistance, tutoring, writing center.

Majors. Biology: General, biochemistry, neuroscience. **Business:** General, accounting, business admin, finance, management information systems, management science, marketing. **Communications:** Media studies, public relations. **Computer sciences:** Computer science. **Education:** Elementary. **Engineering:** Applied physics. **English:** Creative writing, English lit. **Foreign languages:** Spanish. **Health services:** Athletic training. **History:** General. **Human services:** Social work. **Liberal arts:** Arts/sciences. **Math:** General. **Parks/recreation:** Exercise sciences, sports admin. **Philosophy/religion:** Philosophy, religion. **Physical sciences:** Chemistry. **Protective services:** Criminal justice. **Psychology:** General. **Social sciences:** Economics, international relations, political science, sociology. **Visual/performing arts:** Music.

Most popular majors. Biology 7%, business/marketing 17%, communications/journalism 8%, education 7%, parks/recreation 9%, psychology 6%, social sciences 9%.

Technology on campus. PC or laptop required. 5 workstations in library, computer center. Dormitories wired for high-speed internet access and linked to campus network. Commuter students can connect to campus network. Online course registration, online library, helpline, repair service, student web hosting, wireless network available.

Student life. Freshman orientation: Mandatory. Preregistration for classes offered. Four sessions offered May-June. **Policies:** To qualify to live off campus, students must be 21, have 80 hours of credit, or live with their parents. **Housing:** Guaranteed on-campus for freshmen. Coed dorms, apartments, themed housing available. $100 fully refundable deposit. **Activities:** Bands, campus ministries, choral groups, drama, international student organizations, literary magazine, music ensembles, radio station, student government, student newspaper, TV station, Dance Marathon, Habitat for Humanity, Black Student Union, Daughters of Isabella, DuHealth Committee, Knights of Columbus, Social Work Club, Peace and Justice Club, Environmental Action Forum.

Athletics. NCAA. **Intercollegiate:** Baseball M, basketball, cross-country, diving, football (tackle) M, golf, lacrosse W, soccer, softball W, swimming, tennis, track and field, volleyball, wrestling M. **Intramural:** Basketball, cheerleading, racquetball, soccer, softball, volleyball. **Team name:** Duhawks.

Student services. Adult student services, alcohol/substance abuse counseling, chaplain/spiritual director, career counseling, financial aid counseling, health services, minority student services, personal counseling, placement for graduates. **Physically disabled:** Services for visually, speech, hearing impaired.

Contact. E-mail: admission@loras.edu
Phone: (563) 588-7236 Toll-free number: (800) 245-6727
Fax: (563) 588-7119
Mary Ellen Carroll, Vice President for Enrollment Management, Loras College, 1450 Alta Vista Street, Dubuque, IA 52001-0178

Luther College
Decorah, Iowa
www.luther.edu
CB code: 6375

- Private 4-year liberal arts college affiliated with the Evangelical Lutheran Church in America
- Residential campus in small town
- 2,286 degree-seeking undergraduates: 55% women, 2% African American, 2% Asian American, 4% Hispanic/Latino, 2% Multi-racial, non-Hispanic, 6% international
- 67% of applicants admitted
- SAT or ACT (ACT writing optional) required
- 78% graduate within 6 years; 16% enter graduate study

General. Founded in 1861. Regionally accredited. **Degrees:** 553 bachelor's awarded. **Location:** 70 miles from Rochester, MN; 50 miles from LaCrosse, WI. **Calendar:** 4-1-4, limited summer session. **Full-time faculty:** 177 total; 93% have terminal degrees, 11% minority, 48% women. **Part-time faculty:** 57 total; 40% have terminal degrees, 5% minority, 58% women. **Class size:** 60% < 20, 37% 20-39, 1% 40-49, less than 1% 50-99, less than 1% >100. **Special facilities:** Planetarium, Norwegian-American museum, biology field study areas, cadaver laboratory, wind turbine, solar field, aquatic center.

Freshman class profile. 3,896 applied, 2,606 admitted, 624 enrolled.

Mid 50% test scores			
SAT critical reading:	500-630	GPA 2.0-2.99:	4%
SAT math:	480-640	Rank in top quarter:	62%
SAT writing:	480-610	Rank in top tenth:	31%
ACT composite:	23-29	End year in good standing:	93%
GPA 3.75 or higher:	56%	Return as sophomores:	85%
GPA 3.50-3.74:	19%	Out-of-state:	69%
GPA 3.0-3.49:	21%	Live on campus:	100%
		International:	6%

Basis for selection. Rigor of high school curriculum most important, followed by test scores and teacher recommendation(s). Applicants should rank in top half of high school class. Audition recommended for music scholarships. Portfolio recommended for art majors. Interview recommended for some students. **Home schooled:** If graduate of non-diploma-granting organization, evidence of preparation for college required. Must provide at least 2 of the following: home school transcript listing all courses; detailed portfolio of high school work completed; bibliography of major books read, with brief essay on one of the selected works; additional reference letter completed by an educator assessing the applicant's academic preparation; scores from any AP exams and/or GED test results.

High school preparation. College-preparatory program recommended. 14 units recommended. Recommended units include English 4, mathematics 3, social studies 3, science 2 (laboratory 1) and foreign language 2.

2015-2016 Annual costs. Tuition/fees: $39,190. Room/board: $7,920. Books/supplies: $1,040. Personal expenses: $1,725.

2015-2016 Financial aid. Need-based: 534 full-time freshmen applied for aid; 456 deemed to have need; 456 received aid. Average need met was 89%. Average scholarship/grant was $24,313; average loan $4,796. 79% of total undergraduate aid awarded as scholarships/grants, 21% as loans/jobs. **Non-need-based:** Awarded to 521 full-time undergraduates, including 177 freshmen. Scholarships awarded for academics, alumni affiliation, art, minority status, music/drama.

Application procedures. Admission: No deadline. No application fee. Admission notification on a rolling basis beginning on or about 9/1. Must reply by May 1 or within 4 week(s) if notified thereafter. **Financial aid:** Priority date 3/1; no closing date. FAFSA, institutional form required. Applicants notified on a rolling basis starting 3/15; must reply by 5/1 or within 4 week(s) of notification.

Academics. Special study options: Combined bachelor's/graduate degree, double major, dual enrollment of high school students, honors, independent study, internships, student-designed major, study abroad, teacher certification program, Washington semester. **Credit/placement by examination:** AP, CLEP, IB, institutional tests. No limit, but student must satisfy residency requirement. **Support services:** Learning center, pre-admission summer program, remedial instruction, study skills assistance, tutoring, writing center.

Majors. Area/ethnic studies: African-American, Russian/Slavic, women's. **Biology:** General. **Business:** Accounting, business admin, management information systems. **Communications:** Communications/speech/rhetoric. **Computer sciences:** Computer science. **Conservation:** Environmental studies. **Education:** Elementary. **English:** English lit. **Foreign languages:** Biblical, classics, French, German, Scandinavian, Spanish. **Health services:** Athletic training, nursing (RN). **History:** General. **Human services:** Social work. **Math:** General, mathematics/statistics. **Parks/recreation:** Health/fitness. **Philosophy/religion:** Philosophy, religion. **Physical sciences:** Chemistry, physics. **Psychology:** General. **Social sciences:** Anthropology, economics, political science, sociology. **Visual/performing arts:** Art, dance, dramatic, multimedia, music.

Most popular majors. Biology 12%, business/marketing 10%, health sciences 6%, psychology 8%, social sciences 10%, visual/performing arts 13%.

Technology on campus. 600 workstations in dormitories, library, computer center, student center. Dormitories wired for high-speed internet access and linked to campus network. Commuter students can connect to campus network. Online course registration, online library, helpline, repair service, student web hosting, wireless network available.

Student life. Freshman orientation: Mandatory. Preregistration for classes offered. Held prior to start of classes. **Housing:** Guaranteed on-campus for all undergraduates. Coed dorms, special housing for disabled, apartments, wellness housing available. Sustainability house, clusters, quiet floors, honors floor available, house for women. **Activities:** Bands, campus ministries, choral groups, dance, drama, international student organizations, literary magazine, music ensembles, Model UN, musical theater, opera, radio station, student government, student newspaper, symphony orchestra, various religious and political clubs, black student union, Asian student association, Phi Beta Kappa, Amnesty International, Alpha Phi Omega, Habitat for Humanity, PALS/Big Brothers Big Sisters.

Athletics. NCAA. Intercollegiate: Baseball M, basketball, cross-country, diving, football (tackle) M, golf, soccer, softball W, swimming, tennis, track and field, volleyball W, wrestling M. **Intramural:** Archery, badminton, basketball, football (non-tackle), handball, racquetball, soccer, softball, table tennis, tennis, track and field, ultimate frisbee, volleyball. **Team name:** Norse.

Student services. Alcohol/substance abuse counseling, chaplain/spiritual director, career counseling, student employment services, financial aid counseling, health services, minority student services, personal counseling, placement for graduates. **Physically disabled:** Services for visually, hearing impaired.

Contact. E-mail: admissions@luther.edu
Phone: (563) 387-1287 Toll-free number: (800) 458-8437
Fax: (563) 387-2159
Scot Schaeffer, Vice President for Enrollment Management, Luther College, 700 College Drive, Decorah, IA 52101-1042

Maharishi University of Management
Fairfield, Iowa
www.mum.edu   **CB code: 4497**

▶ Private 4-year university and liberal arts college

▶ Residential campus in small town

▶ 344 degree-seeking undergraduates: 35% part-time, 51% women, 7% African American, 3% Asian American, 8% Hispanic/Latino, 1% Native American, 1% Native Hawaiian/Pacific islander, 3% Multi-racial, non-Hispanic, 38% international

▶ 1,138 degree-seeking graduate students

▶ 37% of applicants admitted

▶ Application essay required

▶ 39% graduate within 6 years

General. Founded in 1971. Regionally accredited. **Degrees:** 125 bachelor's awarded; master's, doctoral offered. **Location:** 60 miles from Iowa City, 110 miles from Des Moines. **Calendar:** Semester, limited summer session. **Full-time faculty:** 118 total; 34% have terminal degrees, 19% minority, 28% women. **Part-time faculty:** 49 total; 49% have terminal degrees, 14% minority, 24% women. **Class size:** 80% < 20, 9% 20-39, 5% 40-49, 5% 50-99. **Special facilities:** Buildings for practice of transcendental meditation, organic greenhouses, college prep-school, indoor rock-climbing wall, basketball and tennis courts, weight training room, sustainable student center.

Freshman class profile. 84 applied, 31 admitted, 21 enrolled.

GPA 3.75 or higher:	23%	Rank in top tenth:	15%
GPA 3.50-3.74:	17%	Return as sophomores:	91%
GPA 3.0-3.49:	23%	Out-of-state:	84%
GPA 2.0-2.99:	32%	Live on campus:	77%
Rank in top quarter:	25%	International:	10%

Basis for selection. Academics, grades, academic test scores, recommendations, high school and college transcripts, advanced placement tests, extracurricular activities, work experience, interview with admissions officer, and essay important. Test recommended for applicants who have a low GPA. Students encouraged to visit campus for 4-day weekend. **Home schooled:** Must supply detailed record of courses and objectives. Home school certification required.

High school preparation. College-preparatory program recommended. 15 units recommended. Recommended units include English 4, mathematics 3, social studies 1, science 2 (laboratory 1) and computer science 1.

2015-2016 Annual costs. Tuition/fees: $26,530. Room/board: $7,400. Books/supplies: $1,200. Personal expenses: $2,000.

Financial aid. Additional information: Students may earn scholarships through volunteer staff program.

Application procedures. Admission: No deadline. $25 fee, may be waived for applicants with need. Application must be submitted online. Notified by six weeks after application. **Financial aid:** Priority date 7/15, closing date 7/30. FAFSA required. Applicants notified on a rolling basis starting 3/1; must reply within 4 week(s) of notification.

Academics. Offers consciousness-based education through Transcendental Meditation technique. **Special study options:** Distance learning, double major, ESL, independent study, internships, student-designed major, study abroad, teacher certification program. **Credit/placement by examination:** AP, CLEP, IB, institutional tests. 12 credit hours maximum toward bachelor's degree. **Support services:** Study skills assistance.

Majors. Business: Business admin. **Communications:** Media studies. **Computer sciences:** Computer science. **Education:** Elementary, secondary. **English:** English lit. **Health services:** Premedicine. **Math:** General. **Visual/performing arts:** Studio arts.

Most popular majors. Business/marketing 50%, communications/journalism 10%, natural resources/environmental science 10%, visual/performing arts 6%.

Technology on campus. 400 workstations in library, computer center, student center. Dormitories wired for high-speed internet access and linked to campus network. Commuter students can connect to campus network. Online library, helpline available.

Student life. Freshman orientation: Mandatory. Preregistration for classes offered. One-day program held the first day of class. **Policies:** Daily practice of Transcendental Meditation program by all students, faculty, and staff. Smoking, alcohol and drugs not permitted on campus. Organic, vegetarian food served in dining halls. **Housing:** Guaranteed on-campus for all undergraduates. Single-sex dorms, apartments available. $100 fully refundable deposit, deadline 7/15. **Activities:** Concert band, choral groups, international student organizations, music ensembles, radio station, student government, student newspaper, many clubs and activities available.

Athletics. Team name: Flyers.

Student services. Career counseling, financial aid counseling, health services, on-campus daycare, personal counseling, placement for graduates.

Contact. E-mail: admissions@mum.edu
Phone: (641) 472-1110 Toll-free number: (800) 369-6480
Fax: (641) 472-1179
Michelle Paton, U.S. Director of Admissions, Maharishi University of Management, Office of Admissions, Fairfield, IA 52557

Mercy College of Health Sciences
Des Moines, Iowa
www.mchs.edu   **CB code: 2803**

▶ Private 4-year health science college affiliated with the Roman Catholic Church

▶ Commuter campus in large city

▶ 789 degree-seeking undergraduates: 44% part-time, 88% women

General. Regionally accredited. **Degrees:** 87 bachelor's, 174 associate awarded. **Location:** Downtown. **Calendar:** Semester, extensive summer session. **Full-time faculty:** 47 total; 23% have terminal degrees, 2% minority, 83% women. **Part-time faculty:** 56 total; 11% have terminal degrees, 7% minority, 64% women. **Class size:** 74% < 20, 22% 20-39, 1% 40-49, 3% 50-99. **Special facilities:** Science and health care laboratory facilities.

Basis for selection. GPA, test scores very important. **Home schooled:** Transcript signed by student's academic evaluator documenting courses taken, credit earned in each course, and letter grade achieved; 2.25 GPA and 18 ACT required.

2015-2016 Annual costs. Tuition/fees: $16,268. Books/supplies: $1,540. Personal expenses: $5,004.

Financial aid. Non-need-based: Scholarships awarded for academics, minority status.

Application procedures. Admission: Closing date 6/15 (receipt date). No application fee. Admission notification on a rolling basis. **Financial aid:** Priority date 4/15, closing date 7/1. FAFSA required. Applicants notified on a rolling basis starting 3/1; must reply within 3 week(s) of notification.

Academics. Special study options: Accelerated study, distance learning, dual enrollment of high school students. Practicum experience in clinical settings. **Credit/placement by examination:** AP, CLEP. 24 credit hours maximum toward associate degree, 24 toward bachelor's. **Support services:** Learning center, study skills assistance, tutoring, writing center.

Majors. Health services: Health care admin, nursing (RN), premedicine. **Liberal arts:** Arts/sciences.

Technology on campus. 61 workstations in library, computer center. Commuter students can connect to campus network. Online course registration, online library, wireless network available.

Student life. Freshman orientation: Mandatory. Preregistration for classes offered. Held prior to beginning classes. **Activities:** Campus ministries, student government, science club, professional organizations.

Student services. Chaplain/spiritual director, career counseling, student employment services, financial aid counseling, health services, personal counseling, veterans' counselor.

Contact. E-mail: admissions@mchs.edu
Phone: (515) 643-6715 Toll-free number: (800) 637-2994 ext. 6715
Fax: (515) 643-6702
Melinda Tingle-Williams, Director of Admissions, Mercy College of Health Sciences, 921 Sixth Avenue, Des Moines, IA 50309-1200

Morningside College
Sioux City, Iowa
www.morningside.edu   **CB code: 6415**

- Private 4-year liberal arts college affiliated with the United Methodist Church
- Residential campus in small city
- 1,268 degree-seeking undergraduates: 2% part-time, 53% women
- 886 degree-seeking graduate students
- 56% of applicants admitted
- SAT or ACT (ACT writing optional) required
- 55% graduate within 6 years

General. Founded in 1894. Regionally accredited. All full-time students receive notebook computers. **Degrees:** 295 bachelor's awarded; master's offered. **ROTC:** Army. **Location:** 90 miles from Omaha, NE; 90 miles from Sioux Falls, SD. **Calendar:** Semester, limited summer session. **Full-time faculty:** 85 total; 74% have terminal degrees, 2% minority, 52% women. **Part-time faculty:** 162 total; 28% have terminal degrees, 74% women. **Class size:** 64% < 20, 36% 20-39. **Special facilities:** Biology research station.

Freshman class profile. 4,556 applied, 2,551 admitted, 372 enrolled.

Mid 50% test scores		Rank in top quarter:	43%
ACT composite:	20-26	Rank in top tenth:	16%
GPA 3.75 or higher:	29%	Return as sophomores:	74%
GPA 3.50-3.74:	19%	Out-of-state:	47%
GPA 3.0-3.49:	34%	Live on campus:	92%
GPA 2.0-2.99:	18%		

Basis for selection. 20 ACT/1410 SAT and either rank in top half of class or 2.5 GPA required. Interview recommended. Audition or audition tape recommended for music majors and theater applicants. Portfolio recommended for art majors. **Home schooled:** Transcript of courses and grades required. Home School Credit Evaluation form may be submitted in place of transcript.

High school preparation. College-preparatory program recommended. 10 units recommended. Recommended units include English 3, mathematics 2, social studies 3 and science 2. 4 units math and science required of math or science majors.

2015-2016 Annual costs. Tuition/fees: $28,155. Room/board: $8,710.

Financial aid. Non-need-based: Scholarships awarded for academics, alumni affiliation, art, athletics, music/drama, religious affiliation.

Application procedures. Admission: Priority date 8/15; no deadline. No application fee. Admission notification on a rolling basis. Must reply by 5/1. **Financial aid:** Priority date 3/1; no closing date. FAFSA required. Applicants notified on a rolling basis starting 3/15.

Academics. Special study options: Distance learning, double major, dual enrollment of high school students, honors, independent study, internships, liberal arts/career combination, student-designed major, study abroad, teacher certification program, United Nations semester, Washington semester. **Credit/placement by examination:** AP, CLEP, IB, SAT, ACT, institutional tests. 32 credit hours maximum toward bachelor's degree. Maximum 12 hours may be used for general studies core requirements. **Support services:** Learning center, reduced course load, remedial instruction, study skills assistance, tutoring, writing center.

Majors. Biology: General. **Business:** Business admin, communications. **Communications:** Advertising, media studies. **Computer sciences:** Programming. **Education:** Art, biology, chemistry, elementary, English, history, mathematics, music, physics, science, Spanish, special ed. **Engineering:** Applied physics. **English:** English lit. **Foreign languages:** Spanish. **Health services:** Clinical lab science, nursing (RN). **History:** General, American. **Math:** General. **Philosophy/religion:** Philosophy, religion. **Physical sciences:** Chemistry, physics. **Psychology:** General, counseling, industrial. **Social sciences:** International relations, political science. **Visual/performing arts:** Dramatic, graphic design, music, music performance, photography, studio arts.

Most popular majors. Biology 14%, business/marketing 20%, communications/journalism 6%, education 19%, health sciences 9%, psychology 7%, visual/performing arts 6%.

Technology on campus. PC or laptop required. Dormitories wired for high-speed internet access and linked to campus network. Commuter students can connect to campus network. Online library, helpline, repair service, student web hosting, wireless network available.

Student life. Freshman orientation: Mandatory. Preregistration for classes offered. Held 4 days before school begins. **Housing:** Guaranteed on-campus for freshmen. Coed dorms, apartments, fraternity/sorority housing, wellness housing available. Apartments for adult non-traditional students available. **Activities:** Bands, campus ministries, choral groups, dance, drama, international student organizations, literary magazine, music ensembles, musical theater, radio station, student government, student newspaper, TV station, Civic Union, Campus Ministries, Project Hope, Alpha Psi Omega, Delta Sigma Phi Fraternity, Morningside College Republicans, Morningside College Democrats, Gay Straight Alliance, Crossed by Colors, SERVE (Serving Everyone Respectfully through Volunteer Efforts).

Athletics. NAIA. **Intercollegiate:** Baseball M, basketball, cross-country, football (tackle) M, golf, soccer, softball W, swimming, tennis, track and field, volleyball W. **Intramural:** Basketball, bowling, football (non-tackle), golf, soccer, softball, swimming, tennis, track and field, volleyball. **Team name:** Mustangs.

Student services. Alcohol/substance abuse counseling, chaplain/spiritual director, career counseling, student employment services, financial aid counseling, health services, minority student services, personal counseling, placement for graduates, veterans' counselor. **Physically disabled:** Services for visually, speech, hearing impaired.

Contact. E-mail: mscadm@morningside.edu
Phone: (712) 274-5000 ext. 5111 Toll-free number: (800) 831-0806
Fax: (712) 274-5101
Stephanie Peters, Director of Admissions, Morningside College, 1501 Morningside Avenue, Sioux City, IA 51106

Mount Mercy University
Cedar Rapids, Iowa
www.mtmercy.edu   **CB code: 6417**

- Private 4-year liberal arts college affiliated with the Roman Catholic Church
- Residential campus in small city
- 1,535 degree-seeking undergraduates: 38% part-time, 71% women, 7% African American, 2% Asian American, 2% Hispanic/Latino, 1% Native American, 2% Multi-racial, non-Hispanic, 3% international
- 328 degree-seeking graduate students
- 61% of applicants admitted
- SAT or ACT (ACT writing optional) required
- 65% graduate within 6 years; 12% enter graduate study

General. Founded in 1928. Regionally accredited. Available adult accelerated program with evening classes. **Degrees:** 421 bachelor's awarded; master's offered. **Location:** 220 miles from Chicago. **Calendar:** 4-1-4, limited summer session. **Full-time faculty:** 81 total; 64% have terminal degrees, 10% minority, 64% women. **Part-time faculty:** 68 total; 24% have terminal degrees, 9% minority, 46% women. **Class size:** 57% < 20, 39% 20-39, 3% 40-49, 2% 50-99. **Special facilities:** Campus buildings connected by tunnel system.

Freshman class profile. 1,108 applied, 672 admitted, 235 enrolled.

Mid 50% test scores		Rank in top quarter:	38%
ACT composite:	19-23	Rank in top tenth:	12%
GPA 3.75 or higher:	27%	Return as sophomores:	78%
GPA 3.50-3.74:	20%	Out-of-state:	19%
GPA 3.0-3.49:	31%	Live on campus:	93%
GPA 2.0-2.99:	21%	International:	6%

Basis for selection. 2.5 GPA, rank in top half of class, 20 ACT required. **Home schooled:** Transcript of courses and grades, letter of recommendation (nonparent) required. Submit records of studies or detailed account of subjects and materials.

High school preparation. College-preparatory program recommended. Recommended units include English 4, mathematics 3, social studies 3, history 3, science 3 (laboratory 1) and foreign language 2.

2015-2016 Annual costs. Tuition/fees: $28,226. Room/board: $8,600. Books/supplies: $1,200. Personal expenses: $2,090.

2015-2016 Financial aid. Need-based: 221 full-time freshmen applied for aid; 192 deemed to have need; 191 received aid. Average need met was 85%. Average scholarship/grant was $22,373; average loan $3,460. 69% of total undergraduate aid awarded as scholarships/grants, 31% as loans/jobs. **Non-need-based:** Scholarships awarded for academics, alumni affiliation, art, athletics, leadership, music/drama, religious affiliation.

Application procedures. Admission: Closing date 8/15 (receipt date). No application fee. Admission notification on a rolling basis. Must reply by May 1 or within 2 week(s) if notified thereafter. **Financial aid:** Priority date 3/1; no closing date. FAFSA required. Applicants notified on a rolling basis starting 3/15; must reply by 5/1 or within 3 week(s) of notification.

Academics. Special study options: Accelerated study, cross-registration, double major, dual enrollment of high school students, honors, independent study, internships, liberal arts/career combination, study abroad, teacher certification program. **Credit/placement by examination:** AP, CLEP, IB, ACT, institutional tests. 60 credit hours maximum toward bachelor's degree. **Support services:** Learning center, remedial instruction, study skills assistance, tutoring, writing center.

Majors. Biology: General. **Business:** General, accounting, actuarial science, business admin, finance, management information systems, marketing. **Communications:** Communications/speech/rhetoric, digital media, journalism, public relations. **Computer sciences:** General, computer science. **Conservation:** General. **Education:** Elementary, secondary. **English:** English lit, rhetoric/composition. **Health services:** Clinical lab science, health care admin, nursing (RN). **History:** General. **Human services:** Social work. **Math:** General. **Philosophy/religion:** Philosophy, religion. **Protective services:** Law enforcement admin. **Psychology:** General. **Social sciences:** International relations, political science, sociology. **Visual/performing arts:** Art, graphic design, music.

Most popular majors. Business/marketing 37%, education 8%, health sciences 30%, security/protective services 6%.

Technology on campus. 165 workstations in dormitories, library, computer center. Dormitories wired for high-speed internet access and linked to campus network. Commuter students can connect to campus network. Online course registration, online library, helpline, wireless network available.

Student life. Freshman orientation: Available. Preregistration for classes offered. Three-day orientation held prior to start of fall term; 3 one-day orientation/registration sessions in spring and summer. **Housing:** Guaranteed on-campus for freshmen. Coed dorms, apartments, themed housing, wellness housing available. $200 nonrefundable deposit, deadline 8/15. Living learning communities. **Activities:** Pep band, campus ministries, choral groups, dance, drama, international student organizations, literary magazine, music ensembles, musical theater, student government, student newspaper, M2AP-Activites Board, math and computer science club, association of nursing students, LGBTQ, Honors Students Assc, Veterans Association, Black Student Union, Peer Ministry Team, international club, criminal justice association.

Athletics. NAIA. **Intercollegiate:** Baseball M, basketball, bowling, cheerleading W, cross-country, golf, soccer, softball W, track and field, volleyball W. **Intramural:** Basketball, football (non-tackle) M, racquetball, soccer, softball, table tennis, tennis, volleyball. **Team name:** Mustangs.

Student services. Adult student services, alcohol/substance abuse counseling, chaplain/spiritual director, career counseling, student employment services, financial aid counseling, health services, minority student services, personal counseling, placement for graduates, veterans' counselor. **Physically disabled:** Services for visually, speech, hearing impaired.

Contact. E-mail: admission@mtmercy.edu
Phone: (319) 368-6460 Toll-free number: (800) 248-4504
Fax: (319) 363-5270
Terri Crumley, Dean of Admissions, Mount Mercy University, 1330 Elmhurst Drive NE, Cedar Rapids, IA 52402-4797

Northwestern College
Orange City, Iowa
www.nwciowa.edu
CB code: 6490

▶ Private 4-year liberal arts college affiliated with the Reformed Church in America
▶ Residential campus in small town
▶ 1,084 degree-seeking undergraduates: 3% part-time, 57% women, 2% African American, 1% Asian American, 5% Hispanic/Latino, 2% Multiracial, non-Hispanic, 3% international
▶ 90 degree-seeking graduate students
▶ 72% of applicants admitted

▶ SAT or ACT (ACT writing optional) required
▶ 67% graduate within 6 years; 15% enter graduate study

General. Founded in 1882. Regionally accredited. **Degrees:** 241 bachelor's awarded; master's offered. **Location:** 45 miles from Sioux City, 70 miles from Sioux Falls, South Dakota. **Calendar:** Semester, limited summer session. **Full-time faculty:** 82 total; 87% have terminal degrees, 5% minority, 38% women. **Part-time faculty:** 63 total; 8% minority, 68% women. **Class size:** 68% < 20, 30% 20-39, 2% 40-49, less than 1% 50-99. **Special facilities:** Natural prairie restoration project.

Freshman class profile. 1,234 applied, 890 admitted, 260 enrolled.

Mid 50% test scores			
		GPA 2.0-2.99:	8%
SAT critical reading:	490-630	Rank in top quarter:	57%
SAT math:	450-660	Rank in top tenth:	25%
SAT writing:	450-610	End year in good standing:	91%
ACT composite:	22-28	Return as sophomores:	82%
GPA 3.75 or higher:	54%	Out-of-state:	47%
GPA 3.50-3.74:	17%	Live on campus:	99%
GPA 3.0-3.49:	20%	International:	4%

Basis for selection. 2.0 High School GPA required. Rank in top half of class and test scores above 50th percentile most important. Recommendations also important. Interview and essay recommended. Audition recommended for theater and music majors. Portfolio recommended for art majors. **Learning Disabled:** Students provide documentation to Director of Academic Support upon admittance.

High school preparation. College-preparatory program recommended. 16 units recommended. Recommended units include English 4, mathematics 3, social studies 3, science 3 and foreign language 3.

2015-2016 Annual costs. Tuition/fees: $28,950. Room/board: $8,750. Books/supplies: $1,200.

2015-2016 Financial aid. Need-based: 231 full-time freshmen applied for aid; 181 deemed to have need; 181 received aid. Average need met was 94%. Average scholarship/grant was $6,370; average loan $4,322. 68% of total undergraduate aid awarded as scholarships/grants, 32% as loans/jobs. **Non-need-based:** Awarded to 1,184 full-time undergraduates, including 306 freshmen. Scholarships awarded for academics, alumni affiliation, art, athletics, music/drama, religious affiliation, state residency.

Application procedures. Admission: Priority date 6/1; no deadline. No application fee. Admission notification on a rolling basis beginning on or about 10/1. **Financial aid:** Priority date 4/1, closing date 6/30. FAFSA required. Applicants notified on a rolling basis starting 3/15; must reply within 3 week(s) of notification.

Academics. Special study options: Distance learning, double major, dual enrollment of high school students, ESL, honors, independent study, internships, liberal arts/career combination, student-designed major, study abroad, teacher certification program, urban semester, Washington semester. American Studies Program (Washington, D.C.), AuSable Institute of Environmental Studies Program (Michigan), Los Angeles Film Studies Semester, Chicago Metropolitan Studies Program, China Studies Program (Xiaman), Middle East Studies Program (Cairo), Oxford Summer Program (Oxford), Russian Studies Program, Contemporary Music Center (Martha's Vineyard, MA), Latin American Studies Program (Costa Rica), Oxford Honours Programme (England), Trinity Christian College: Semester in Spain, Creation Care Study Program, Summer Institute of Journalism (Washington, D.C.), Semester in Romania, Semester in Oman. **Credit/placement by examination:** AP, CLEP, IB, SAT, ACT, institutional tests. 24 credit hours maximum toward bachelor's degree. **Support services:** Learning center, reduced course load, remedial instruction, study skills assistance, tutoring, writing center.

Majors. Biology: General, biochemistry, environmental, genomics. **Business:** Accounting, actuarial science, business admin, finance, human resources, managerial economics, marketing. **Communications:** Journalism, public relations. **Computer sciences:** General, computer science. **Education:** General, biology, business, elementary, English, music, physical. **English:** English lit, rhetoric/composition. **Foreign languages:** Spanish, translation. **Health services:** Athletic training, clinical lab science, nursing (RN). **History:** General. **Human services:** Social work. **Liberal arts:** Arts/sciences, humanities. **Math:** General. **Parks/recreation:** Exercise sciences, sports admin. **Philosophy/religion:** Philosophy, religion. **Physical sciences:** Chemistry. **Protective services:** Law enforcement admin. **Psychology:** General. **Social sciences:** Economics, political science, sociology. **Theology:** Religious ed, sacred music. **Visual/performing arts:** Art, dramatic, music.

Most popular majors. Biology 7%, business/marketing 15%, education 15%, health sciences 12%, parks/recreation 7%, social sciences 6%, visual/performing arts 6%.

Technology on campus. 250 workstations in dormitories, library, computer center, student center. Dormitories wired for high-speed internet access

and linked to campus network. Commuter students can connect to campus network. Online course registration, online library, helpline, repair service, wireless network available.

Student life. Freshman orientation: Available. Preregistration for classes offered. Five orientation days for the upcoming fall are held on Mondays throughout the spring semester. **Policies:** Use of alcohol prohibited on campus. Resident living required for all students unless granted commuting status, married, or living with parents. Religious observance required. **Housing:** Guaranteed on-campus for all undergraduates. Single-sex dorms, special housing for disabled, apartments, wellness housing available. $100 fully refundable deposit, deadline 8/1. **Activities:** Bands, campus ministries, choral groups, dance, drama, international student organizations, literary magazine, music ensembles, student government, student newspaper, symphony orchestra, TV station, student activities council, Fellowship of Christian Athletes, College Republicans, Campus Democrats, Sigma Tau, Spanish club, education club, business club, future physician's club, justice and service team.

Athletics. NAIA. **Intercollegiate:** Baseball M, basketball, cheerleading, cross-country, football (tackle) M, golf, soccer, softball W, tennis W, track and field, volleyball W, wrestling M. **Intramural:** Badminton, basketball, bowling, football (non-tackle), golf, racquetball, sand volleyball, soccer, softball, table tennis, tennis, ultimate frisbee, volleyball. **Team name:** Red Raiders.

Student services. Alcohol/substance abuse counseling, chaplain/spiritual director, career counseling, student employment services, financial aid counseling, health services, minority student services, personal counseling, placement for graduates, veterans' counselor. **Physically disabled:** Services for visually, speech, hearing impaired.

Contact. E-mail: admissions@nwciowa.edu
Phone: (712) 707-7130 Toll-free number: (800) 747-4757
Fax: (712) 707-7164
Jackie Davis, Director of Admissions, Northwestern College, 101 Seventh Street SW, Orange City, IA 51041

Shiloh University
Kalona, Iowa
www.shilohuniversity.edu   **CB code: 7362**

▶ Private 4-year virtual Bible college affiliated with the Christian Church
▶ Small town
▶ 13 degree-seeking undergraduates: 100% part-time, 62% women
▶ 17 degree-seeking graduate students
▶ 100% of applicants admitted
▶ Application essay required

General. Regionally accredited; also accredited by DETC. **Degrees:** 1 associate awarded; master's, professional offered. **Location:** 25 miles from Iowa City. **Calendar:** Trimester, extensive summer session. **Full-time faculty:** 2 total. **Part-time faculty:** 25 total.

Freshman class profile. 2 applied, 2 admitted, 2 enrolled.

Basis for selection. Required admissions essay; test scores recommended. SAT and SAT Subject Tests or ACT recommended. **Home schooled:** Transcript of courses and grades required.

2016-2017 Annual costs. Tuition/fees (projected): $4,520. Books/supplies: $1,000.

Application procedures. Admission: Closing date 6/6. No application fee.

Academics. Special study options: Distance learning. **Credit/placement by examination:** AP, CLEP, IB, SAT, ACT, institutional tests. 15 credit hours maximum toward associate degree, 30 toward bachelor's. **Support services:** Reduced course load, study skills assistance, writing center.

Majors. Theology: Bible.

Technology on campus. PC or laptop required.

Contact. E-mail: admissions@shilohuniversity.edu
Phone: (319) 656-2447 Fax: (319) 656-2448
Andrew Thompson, Director of Admissions, Shiloh University, 100 Shiloh Drive, Kalona, IA 52247

Simpson College
Indianola, Iowa   **CB member**
www.simpson.edu   **CB code: 6650**

▶ Private 4-year liberal arts college affiliated with the United Methodist Church
▶ Residential campus in large town
▶ 1,602 degree-seeking undergraduates: 11% part-time, 54% women
▶ 50 degree-seeking graduate students
▶ 89% of applicants admitted
▶ SAT or ACT (ACT writing optional) required
▶ 68% graduate within 6 years; 17% enter graduate study

General. Founded in 1860. Regionally accredited. **Degrees:** 365 bachelor's awarded; master's offered. **Location:** 12 miles from Des Moines. **Calendar:** 4-4-1. Extensive summer session. **Full-time faculty:** 95 total; 86% have terminal degrees, 2% minority, 46% women. **Part-time faculty:** 103 total; 23% have terminal degrees, 2% minority, 47% women. **Class size:** 70% < 20, 27% 20-39, 2% 40-49, 1% 50-99. **Special facilities:** Antebellum-era literature collection, cadaver laboratory, art galleries, education lab, Iowa history center, urban studies institute, vocational and integrative learning center, public policy center.

Freshman class profile. 1,271 applied, 1,137 admitted, 322 enrolled.

Mid 50% test scores		Return as sophomores:	81%
ACT composite:	21-27	Out-of-state:	21%
Rank in top quarter:	52%	Live on campus:	97%
Rank in top tenth:	24%	Fraternities:	24%
End year in good standing:	98%	Sororities:	30%

Basis for selection. High school record, class rank, GPA, and ACT/SAT most important, Recommendations also considered. Campus visit/interview recommended. Audition strongly recommended for music, drama majors. Portfolio strongly recommended for art majors. **Home schooled:** Letter of recommendation (nonparent) required. Must submit transcript(s) with course content descriptions. **Learning Disabled:** Should submit documentation of disability to ensure adequate facilities and programming can be provided.

High school preparation. College-preparatory program recommended. 16 units recommended. Recommended units include English 4, mathematics 3, social studies 3, science 3 (laboratory 3) and foreign language 3. English units should include composition, literature; math units should include 2 algebra, 1 geometry; 4 units math strongly recommended of math or science majors. Foreign language units should be one language.

2015-2016 Annual costs. Tuition/fees: $34,175. Room/board: $7,963. Books/supplies: $1,188. Personal expenses: $1,922.

2015-2016 Financial aid. Need-based: 322 full-time freshmen applied for aid; 267 deemed to have need; 267 received aid. Average need met was 83%. Average scholarship/grant was $23,831; average loan $4,842. 75% of total undergraduate aid awarded as scholarships/grants, 25% as loans/jobs. **Non-need-based:** Awarded to 384 full-time undergraduates, including 95 freshmen. Scholarships awarded for academics, alumni affiliation, art, leadership, minority status, music/drama, religious affiliation. **Additional information:** Music and theater scholarships based on audition. Art scholarships based on portfolio.

Application procedures. Admission: Priority date 5/1; no deadline. No application fee. Admission notification on a rolling basis beginning on or about 9/1. $200 enrollment deposit required; nonrefundable after May 1. **Financial aid:** Priority date 4/1; no closing date. FAFSA required. Applicants notified on a rolling basis starting 3/15; must reply by 5/1 or within 3 week(s) of notification.

Academics. Special study options: Combined bachelor's/graduate degree, cooperative education, double major, independent study, internships, liberal arts/career combination, student-designed major, study abroad, teacher certification program, Washington semester. 3-2 and 4-2 engineering program with Washington University in St. Louis, Iowa State University, and Institute of Technology, University of Minnesota, Minneapolis. 3 year-15 months nursing program with Allen College, and 3 + 3 program with Drake University, Des Moines, IA. **Credit/placement by examination:** AP, CLEP, IB, SAT, ACT, institutional tests. 24 credit hours maximum toward bachelor's degree. **Support services:** Learning center, pre-admission summer program, reduced course load, study skills assistance, tutoring, writing center. Tutoring services offered free of charge.

Majors. Biology: General, biochemistry. **Business:** Accounting, actuarial science, business admin, international, management information systems, marketing. **Communications:** Persuasive communications. **Computer sciences:** Computer science, information systems. **Conservation:** Environmental science. **Education:** General, elementary, music, physical. **Engineering:**

Pre-engineering. **English:** English lit. **Foreign languages:** French, German, Spanish. **Health services:** Athletic training, health care admin, predental, premedicine, prenursing, preoptometry, prepharmacy, prephysical therapy, preveterinary. **History:** General. **Liberal arts:** Arts/sciences. **Math:** General. **Parks/recreation:** Exercise sciences, sports admin. **Philosophy/religion:** Philosophy, religion. **Physical sciences:** Chemistry, physics. **Protective services:** Criminal justice, forensics. **Psychology:** General. **Social sciences:** Economics, international relations, political science, sociology. **Theology:** Preministerial. **Visual/performing arts:** Art, dramatic, graphic design, music, music performance, studio arts.

Most popular majors. Business/marketing 13%, social sciences 45%.

Technology on campus. 374 workstations in dormitories, library, computer center, student center. Dormitories wired for high-speed internet access and linked to campus network. Commuter students can connect to campus network. Online course registration, online library, helpline, wireless network available.

Student life. Freshman orientation: Mandatory. Preregistration for classes offered. Four 1-day summer registration programs in June. Fall orientation held first week students are on campus. **Housing:** Guaranteed on-campus for all undergraduates. Coed dorms, apartments, fraternity/sorority housing, gender-neutral housing, themed housing, wellness housing available. $200 fully refundable deposit, deadline 5/1. Single sex rooms and floors in co-ed dorms; medical single rooms available. **Activities:** Bands, campus ministries, choral groups, dance, drama, international student organizations, literary magazine, music ensembles, Model UN, musical theater, opera, radio station, student government, student newspaper, symphony orchestra, Religious Life Community, interfaith fellowship, Alpha Phi Omega service fraternity, College Democrats, College Republicans, Fellowship of Christian Athletes, Habitat for Humanity, Catholic Worker House, Center for Vocation and Integrative Learning.

Athletics. NCAA. **Intercollegiate:** Baseball M, basketball, cheerleading, cross-country, diving, football (tackle) M, golf, soccer, softball W, swimming, tennis, track and field, volleyball W, wrestling M. **Intramural:** Badminton, basketball, football (non-tackle), golf, racquetball, soccer, softball, swimming, table tennis, tennis, volleyball, weight lifting. **Team name:** Storm.

Student services. Adult student services, alcohol/substance abuse counseling, chaplain/spiritual director, career counseling, services for economically disadvantaged, student employment services, financial aid counseling, health services, minority student services, personal counseling, veterans' counselor, women's services. **Physically disabled:** Services for visually, speech, hearing impaired.

Contact. E-mail: admiss@simpson.edu
Phone: (515) 961-1624 Toll-free number: (800) 362-2454 ext. 1624
Fax: (515) 961-1870
Deborah Tierney, Vice President for Enrollment, Simpson College, 701 North C Street, Indianola, IA 50125

St. Ambrose University
Davenport, Iowa
www.sau.edu   CB code: 6617

- Private 4-year university and business college affiliated with the Roman Catholic Church
- Residential campus in small city
- 2,499 degree-seeking undergraduates: 10% part-time, 57% women, 3% African American, 1% Asian American, 6% Hispanic/Latino, 2% Multiracial, non-Hispanic, 3% international
- 776 degree-seeking graduate students
- 73% of applicants admitted
- SAT or ACT (ACT writing optional) required
- 63% graduate within 6 years; 31% enter graduate study

General. Founded in 1882. Regionally accredited. **Degrees:** 611 bachelor's awarded; master's, professional, doctoral offered. **Location:** Located on Iowa-Illinois border at Mississippi River. 180 miles from Des Moines, 175 miles from Chicago, 266 miles from St. Louis, and 162 miles from Madison. **Calendar:** Semester, extensive summer session. **Full-time faculty:** 219 total; 78% have terminal degrees, 10% minority, 52% women. **Part-time faculty:** 75 total; 1% have terminal degrees, 16% minority, 67% women. **Class size:** 71% < 20, 29% 20-39, less than 1% 40-49, less than 1% >100. **Special facilities:** Transmission electron microscope, cable television channel, observatory, national prairie garden, radio station.

Freshman class profile. 2,546 applied, 1,858 admitted, 448 enrolled.

Mid 50% test scores		Rank in top tenth:	15%
ACT composite:	20-25	End year in good standing:	92%
GPA 3.75 or higher:	23%	Return as sophomores:	78%
GPA 3.50-3.74:	17%	Out-of-state:	31%
GPA 3.0-3.49:	31%	Live on campus:	94%
GPA 2.0-2.99:	29%	International:	2%
Rank in top quarter:	40%		

Basis for selection. 2.5 GPA and 20 ACT/950 SAT or 18-19 ACT/870-950 SAT and rank in top half of class required. Students who graduated from high school 5+ years ago do not have to supply ACT or SAT scores. Interview recommended. Portfolio required for art majors. **Home schooled:** Students without high school diploma required to obtain passing score on GED with 18 ACT or 870 SAT.

High school preparation. College-preparatory program recommended. 18 units recommended. Recommended units include English 4, mathematics 3, social studies 1, history 1, science 2 (laboratory 2), foreign language 1 and academic electives 4.

2015-2016 Annual costs. Tuition/fees: $28,380. Room/board: $9,582. Books/supplies: $1,200. Personal expenses: $1,814.

Financial aid. Non-need-based: Scholarships awarded for academics, alumni affiliation, art, athletics, minority status, music/drama. **Additional information:** Iowa applicants must apply for financial aid by July 1. Audition required for music, drama scholarship applicants.

Application procedures. Admission: No deadline. No application fee. Admission notification on a rolling basis beginning on or about 10/1. Must reply by May 1 or within 2 week(s) if notified thereafter. **Financial aid:** Priority date 3/15; no closing date. FAFSA required. Applicants notified on a rolling basis starting 2/1; must reply within 2 week(s) of notification.

Academics. Special study options: Accelerated study, combined bachelor's/graduate degree, cooperative education, distance learning, double major, honors, independent study, internships, liberal arts/career combination, student-designed major, study abroad, teacher certification program. Service learning program in which students work as volunteers for community and earn 1-3 semester hours credit, license preparation for occupational therapy on campus, accounting majors volunteer to work on income tax forms for low income families on campus. **Credit/placement by examination:** AP, CLEP, IB, SAT, ACT, institutional tests. 64 credit hours maximum toward bachelor's degree. **Support services:** Learning center, pre-admission summer program, reduced course load, remedial instruction, study skills assistance, tutoring, writing center.

Majors. Area/ethnic studies: Women's. **Biology:** General, neuroscience. **Business:** General, accounting, business admin, finance, international, management science, marketing, organizational behavior. **Communications:** Communications/speech/rhetoric, journalism, media studies, public relations, radio/TV. **Computer sciences:** General, computer science, information systems, LAN/WAN management, security, systems analysis. **Education:** General, art, biology, business, chemistry, early childhood, elementary, English, foreign languages, French, German, health, history, mathematics, music, physical, physics, psychology, science, secondary, social science, Spanish, speech. **Engineering:** General, applied physics, industrial, mechanical. **English:** English lit, writing. **Foreign languages:** French, German, Spanish. **Health services:** Nursing (RN). **History:** General. **Human services:** General. **Math:** General, applied. **Parks/recreation:** Exercise sciences, health/fitness, sports admin. **Philosophy/religion:** Philosophy. **Physical sciences:** Chemistry, physics. **Protective services:** Criminal justice, criminalistics. **Psychology:** General, forensic. **Social sciences:** Economics, political science, sociology. **Visual/performing arts:** Art history/conservation, commercial/advertising art, design, dramatic, graphic design, multimedia, music, painting, printmaking, studio arts, theater arts management.

Most popular majors. Business/marketing 25%, education 12%, health sciences 20%, psychology 13%.

Technology on campus. 190 workstations in library, computer center, student center. Dormitories wired for high-speed internet access and linked to campus network. Commuter students can connect to campus network. Online course registration, online library, helpline, wireless network available.

Student life. Freshman orientation: Mandatory, $75 fee. Preregistration for classes offered. Held 2 days per month in April, June, August. **Policies:** All campus buildings smoke-free. **Housing:** Guaranteed on-campus for freshmen. Coed dorms, single-sex dorms, special housing for disabled, apartments, themed housing, wellness housing available. $250 partly refundable deposit, deadline 5/1. Townhouses for seniors, houses for juniors and seniors available. **Activities:** Bands, campus ministries, choral groups, dance, drama, international student organizations, literary magazine, music ensembles, Model UN, musical theater, radio station, student government, student newspaper, symphony orchestra, TV station, Multicultural Affairs Community Action Club,

Military and Veterans Organization (MAVO), Model UN Society, Ambrosians for Peace and Justice, Dance Marathon, Habitat for Humanity, Sexual Assault Awareness Team, Student Government Association, Green Life, Fellowship of Christian Athletes.

Athletics. NAIA. **Intercollegiate:** Baseball M, basketball, bowling, cheerleading, cross-country, football (tackle) M, golf, lacrosse M, soccer, softball W, tennis, track and field, volleyball. **Intramural:** Badminton, basketball, bowling, football (non-tackle), sand volleyball, softball, volleyball. **Team name:** Fighting Bees.

Student services. Adult student services, alcohol/substance abuse counseling, chaplain/spiritual director, career counseling, student employment services, financial aid counseling, health services, minority student services, on-campus daycare, personal counseling, placement for graduates, veterans' counselor. **Physically disabled:** Services for visually, speech, hearing impaired.

Contact. E-mail: admit@sau.edu
Phone: (563) 333-6300 Toll-free number: (800) 383-2627
Fax: (563) 333-6243
Allison Conklin, Associate Director of First Year Admissions, St. Ambrose University, 518 West Locust Street, Davenport, IA 52803-2898

University of Dubuque
Dubuque, Iowa   CB member
www.dbq.edu   CB code: 6869

- Private 4-year university and seminary college affiliated with the Presbyterian Church (USA)
- Residential campus in small city
- 1,834 degree-seeking undergraduates: 11% part-time, 41% women, 14% African American, 2% Asian American, 9% Hispanic/Latino, 3% Multiracial, non-Hispanic, 3% international
- 338 degree-seeking graduate students
- 77% of applicants admitted
- SAT or ACT (ACT writing optional), application essay required
- 44% graduate within 6 years

General. Founded in 1852. Regionally accredited. **Degrees:** 366 bachelor's awarded; master's, professional offered. **ROTC:** Army. **Location:** 94 miles from Madison, WI; 180 miles from Chicago, IL. **Calendar:** 4-1-4, limited summer session. **Full-time faculty:** 75 total; 69% have terminal degrees, 16% minority, 43% women. **Part-time faculty:** 109 total. **Class size:** 75% < 20, 24% 20-39, less than 1% 40-49, less than 1% 50-99. **Special facilities:** Floating laboratory on Mississippi River, curriculum laboratory for teachers, aviation operations center, studio laboratory for animation program, wetland area management, science center.

Freshman class profile. 1,457 applied, 1,128 admitted, 447 enrolled.

Mid 50% test scores		Rank in top quarter:	22%
SAT critical reading:	420-490	Rank in top tenth:	7%
SAT math:	390-500	Out-of-state:	68%
ACT composite:	17-23	Live on campus:	89%
GPA 3.75 or higher:	10%	International:	6%
GPA 3.50-3.74:	16%	Fraternities:	5%
GPA 3.0-3.49:	25%	Sororities:	10%
GPA 2.0-2.99:	44%		

Basis for selection. High school graduate or equivalent (GED) is required. Rolling admission; must receive test scores before final enrollment. Recommendations required. **Learning Disabled:** Students must request assistance.

High school preparation. College-preparatory program recommended. 16 units required. Required and recommended units include English 4, mathematics 3, social studies 3, science 3, foreign language 2 and academic electives 3.

2015-2016 Annual costs. Tuition/fees: $27,895. Room/board: $9,070. Books/supplies: $950.

Financial aid. Non-need-based: Scholarships awarded for academics, alumni affiliation, leadership, music/drama, religious affiliation, ROTC.

Application procedures. Admission: No deadline. $25 fee, may be waived for applicants with need. Admission notification on a rolling basis beginning on or about 9/1. Must reply by May 1 or within 4 week(s) if notified thereafter. **Financial aid:** Priority date 4/1; no closing date. FAFSA required. Applicants notified on a rolling basis starting 3/1; must reply within 3 week(s) of notification.

Academics. In addition to traditional courses, an accelerated adult degree program called LIFE: Learning Institute for Fulfillment and Engagement offered. **Special study options:** Accelerated study, combined bachelor's/graduate degree, cooperative education, distance learning, double major, honors, independent study, internships, liberal arts/career combination, student-designed major, study abroad, teacher certification program. Undergraduate students may take graduate courses. Off-campus study: semester-away programs. **Credit/placement by examination:** AP, CLEP, IB, SAT, ACT, institutional tests. 24 credit hours maximum toward associate degree, 24 toward bachelor's. **Support services:** Learning center, reduced course load, remedial instruction, study skills assistance, tutoring, writing center.

Majors. Biology: General. **Business:** Accounting, business admin, human resources, marketing. **Communications:** General. **Computer sciences:** General, computer graphics, data processing. **Conservation:** Environmental science. **Education:** Biology, chemistry, elementary, English, environmental, health, mathematics, physical, science. **English:** English lit. **Health services:** Health care admin, nursing (RN). **Liberal arts:** Arts/sciences. **Math:** General. **Parks/recreation:** Exercise sciences, health/fitness, sports admin, sports studies. **Philosophy/religion:** Christian, philosophy, religion. **Physical sciences:** Chemistry. **Protective services:** Criminal justice, forensics. **Psychology:** General. **Social sciences:** Sociology.

Most popular majors. Business/marketing 26%, education 10%, health sciences 6%, parks/recreation 6%, psychology 6%, security/protective services 13%, trade and industry 12%.

Technology on campus. 200 workstations in dormitories, library, computer center, student center. Dormitories wired for high-speed internet access and linked to campus network. Commuter students can connect to campus network. Online course registration, online library, helpline, wireless network available.

Student life. Freshman orientation: Mandatory, $100 fee. Preregistration for classes offered. Held 4 days prior to beginning of class. **Policies:** Students required to live on-campus through junior year or until they reach 21 years of age unless living with parents within 50 miles of campus. **Housing:** Guaranteed on-campus for freshmen. Coed dorms, special housing for disabled, apartments, wellness housing available. $200 fully refundable deposit, deadline 6/1. Houses and townhouses available. **Activities:** Bands, campus ministries, choral groups, dance, drama, film society, international student organizations, literary magazine, music ensembles, musical theater, student government, student newspaper, social service organizations, service fraternity, environmental group, student activities board, College Republicans, College Democrats.

Athletics. NCAA. **Intercollegiate:** Baseball M, basketball, cross-country, football (tackle) M, golf, lacrosse, soccer, softball W, tennis, track and field, volleyball W, wrestling M. **Intramural:** Badminton, basketball, football (non-tackle), golf, handball, lacrosse, racquetball, rugby, soccer, softball, table tennis, tennis, ultimate frisbee, volleyball. **Team name:** Spartans.

Student services. Alcohol/substance abuse counseling, chaplain/spiritual director, career counseling, student employment services, financial aid counseling, health services, minority student services, on-campus daycare, personal counseling, placement for graduates, veterans' counselor.

Contact. E-mail: admssns@dbq.edu
Phone: (563) 589-3200 Toll-free number: (800) 722-5583
Fax: (563) 589-3690
Robert Broshous, Dean of Admission, University of Dubuque, 2000 University Avenue, Dubuque, IA 52001-5099

University of Iowa
Iowa City, Iowa   CB member
www.uiowa.edu   CB code: 6681

- Public 4-year university
- Residential campus in small city
- 21,927 degree-seeking undergraduates: 10% part-time, 52% women, 3% African American, 4% Asian American, 7% Hispanic/Latino, 3% Multiracial, non-Hispanic, 12% international
- 7,003 degree-seeking graduate students
- 81% of applicants admitted
- SAT or ACT (ACT writing recommended) required
- 72% graduate within 6 years

General. Founded in 1847. Regionally accredited. **Degrees:** 5,419 bachelor's awarded; master's, professional, doctoral offered. **ROTC:** Army, Air Force. **Location:** 20 miles from Cedar Rapids, 110 miles from Des Moines. **Calendar:** Semester, extensive summer session. **Full-time faculty:** 1,433 total; 97% have terminal degrees, 19% minority, 32% women. **Part-time**

faculty: 130 total; 97% have terminal degrees, 8% minority, 37% women. **Class size:** 52% <20, 31% 20-39, 4% 40-49, 8% 50-99, 5% >100. **Special facilities:** Hydraulics laboratory, riverside environmental research station, field campus, nature preserve, accelerator, observatory, natural history museum, driving simulator, TILE classrooms, learning commons, native birds-of-prey rehabilitation and research project.

Freshman class profile. 26,222 applied, 21,171 admitted, 5,241 enrolled.

Mid 50% test scores		End year in good standing:	87%
SAT critical reading:	460-630	Return as sophomores:	85%
SAT math:	540-690	Out-of-state:	41%
ACT composite:	23-28	Live on campus:	96%
GPA 3.75 or higher:	46%	International:	12%
GPA 3.50-3.74:	21%	Fraternities:	13%
GPA 3.0-3.49:	28%	Sororities:	22%
GPA 2.0-2.99:	6%		

Basis for selection. Regent Admission Index (RAI) computed based on ACT/SAT, class rank, GPA and number of high school core courses. Iowa residents must have 245 RAI; nonresidents must have 255 RAI. College of Engineering applicants must also demonstrate As or Bs in math and science courses; have 25 ACT with 25 ACT math or 1130 SAT (exclusive of Writing) with 620 SAT math. Admission to BSN program requires satisfactory completion of pre-nursing courses. Audition required of music, dance majors. **Home schooled:** Transcript of courses and grades required. Personal essay describing home school experience strongly recommended and required in certain circumstances.

High school preparation. College-preparatory program required. 15 units required. Required and recommended units include English 4, mathematics 3-4, social studies 3, science 3 and foreign language 2. Math units must include 2 algebra, 1 geometry. Science units must include 2 of the following: biology, chemistry, and physics. Engineering majors require fourth unit of higher math, 1 chemistry and 1 physics, and 2 units social studies.

2015-2016 Annual costs. Tuition/fees: $8,104; $27,890 out-of-state. Room/board: $9,728.

2014-2015 Financial aid. Need-based: 3,333 full-time freshmen applied for aid; 2,214 deemed to have need; 2,214 received aid. Average need met was 70%. Average scholarship/grant was $8,695; average loan $4,310. 55% of total undergraduate aid awarded as scholarships/grants, 45% as loans/jobs. **Non-need-based:** Awarded to 6,414 full-time undergraduates, including 2,489 freshmen. Scholarships awarded for academics, alumni affiliation, art, athletics, leadership, music/drama, ROTC, state residency.

Application procedures. Admission: Closing date 4/1 (postmark date). $40 fee, may be waived for applicants with need. Application must be submitted online. Admission notification on a rolling basis beginning on or about 8/1. Must reply by May 1 or within 2 week(s) if notified thereafter. **Financial aid:** Priority date 3/1; no closing date. FAFSA, institutional form required. Applicants notified on a rolling basis starting 3/1; must reply by 5/1 or within 2 week(s) of notification.

Academics. Bachelor of liberal studies, bachelor of applied studies, bachelor in business administration may be earned with distance education course work. **Special study options:** Accelerated study, combined bachelor's/graduate degree, cooperative education, distance learning, double major, dual enrollment of high school students, ESL, exchange student, external degree, honors, independent study, internships, liberal arts/career combination, New York semester, semester at sea, student-designed major, study abroad, teacher certification program, Washington semester. **Credit/placement by examination:** AP, CLEP, IB, SAT, ACT, institutional tests. 30 credit hours maximum toward bachelor's degree. **Support services:** Learning center, pre-admission summer program, reduced course load, remedial instruction, study skills assistance, tutoring, writing center.

Majors. Area/ethnic studies: African-American, American, Asian, women's. **Biology:** General, biochemistry, microbiology. **Business:** Accounting, actuarial science, business admin, finance, human resources, labor relations, management information systems, management science, managerial economics, marketing. **Communications:** Communications/speech/rhetoric, journalism, media studies. **Computer sciences:** General, computer science. **Conservation:** Environmental science, environmental studies. **Education:** Elementary, science. **Engineering:** General, biomedical, chemical, civil, electrical, industrial, mechanical. **English:** English lit. **Foreign languages:** Chinese, classics, comparative lit, French, German, Italian, Japanese, linguistics, Portuguese, Russian, Spanish. **Health services:** Athletic training, audiology/speech pathology, clinical lab science, nuclear medical technology, nursing (RN), radiologic technology/medical imaging. **History:** General. **Human services:** Social work. **Liberal arts:** Arts/sciences. **Math:** General, statistics. **Parks/recreation:** General, exercise sciences, sports admin, sports studies. **Philosophy/religion:** Philosophy, religion. **Physical sciences:** Astronomy, chemistry, geology, physics. **Psychology:** General. **Social sciences:** Anthropology, economics, geography, international relations, political science, sociology. **Visual/performing arts:** Art, art history/conservation, dance, dramatic, film/cinema/video, music.

Most popular majors. Business/marketing 19%, communications/journalism 8%, engineering/engineering technologies 8%, parks/recreation 12%, social sciences 10%.

Technology on campus. 1,386 workstations in dormitories, library, computer center, student center. Dormitories wired for high-speed internet access and linked to campus network. Commuter students can connect to campus network. Online course registration, online library, helpline, repair service, student web hosting, wireless network available.

Student life. Freshman orientation: Mandatory, $250 fee. Preregistration for classes offered. Several one-and-a-half-day programs throughout the summer, with concurrent parent/guardian program offered. **Policies:** Non-smoking campus. **Housing:** Coed dorms, special housing for disabled, apartments, fraternity/sorority housing, gender-neutral housing, themed housing, wellness housing available. $75 nonrefundable deposit, deadline 6/15. Living-learning communities, leased apartments for upperclass students available. **Activities:** Bands, campus ministries, choral groups, dance, drama, film society, international student organizations, literary magazine, music ensembles, Model UN, musical theater, opera, radio station, student government, student newspaper, symphony orchestra, TV station, College Republicans, University Democrats, Hispanic Society, black student union, Christian Fellowship, environmental coalition, Gay/Lesbian/Bisexual/Transgendered and Allied Union, honor societies, Habitat for Humanity, global health club.

Athletics. NCAA. **Intercollegiate:** Baseball M, basketball, cheerleading, cross-country, diving, field hockey W, football (tackle) M, golf, gymnastics, rowing (crew) W, soccer W, softball W, swimming, tennis, track and field, volleyball W, wrestling M. **Intramural:** Badminton, basketball, bowling, football (non-tackle), golf, racquetball, soccer, softball, swimming, table tennis, tennis, volleyball, wrestling. **Team name:** Hawkeyes.

Student services. Adult student services, alcohol/substance abuse counseling, career counseling, services for economically disadvantaged, student employment services, financial aid counseling, health services, legal services, minority student services, on-campus daycare, personal counseling, placement for graduates, veterans' counselor, women's services. **Physically disabled:** Services for visually, speech, hearing impaired.

Contact. E-mail: admissions@uiowa.edu
Phone: (319) 335-3847 Fax: (319) 335-1535
Brent Gage, Associate Vice President for Enrollment Management, University of Iowa, 107 Calvin Hall, Iowa City, IA 52242-1396

University of Northern Iowa
Cedar Falls, Iowa — CB member
www.uni.edu — CB code: 6307

- Public 4-year university
- Residential campus in small city
- 9,934 degree-seeking undergraduates: 9% part-time, 57% women, 3% African American, 1% Asian American, 3% Hispanic/Latino, 2% Multiracial, non-Hispanic, 4% international
- 1,812 degree-seeking graduate students
- 80% of applicants admitted
- SAT or ACT (ACT writing optional) required
- 68% graduate within 6 years

General. Founded in 1876. Regionally accredited. **Degrees:** 2,303 bachelor's awarded; master's, doctoral offered. **ROTC:** Army. **Location:** 63 miles from Cedar Rapids. **Calendar:** Semester, limited summer session. **Full-time faculty:** 556 total; 78% have terminal degrees, 15% minority, 48% women. **Part-time faculty:** 184 total; 35% have terminal degrees, 12% minority, 60% women. **Class size:** 36% <20, 50% 20-39, 8% 40-49, 5% 50-99, 2% >100. **Special facilities:** Performing arts center, center for energy and environmental education, NASA teacher resource center, observatory, natural preserve, museum.

Freshman class profile. 5,364 applied, 4,271 admitted, 1,916 enrolled.

Mid 50% test scores		Rank in top tenth:	18%
ACT composite:	25-20	Return as sophomores:	80%
GPA 3.75 or higher:	34%	Out-of-state:	7%
GPA 3.50-3.74:	21%	Live on campus:	91%
GPA 3.0-3.49:	32%	International:	2%
GPA 2.0-2.99:	13%	Fraternities:	6%
Rank in top quarter:	48%	Sororities:	8%

Basis for selection. High school GPA, rank in top half of class, completion of high school curriculum requirements most important. In the absence of class rank, standardized test scores may carry greater weight. Audition required of music majors. Interview may be recommended for borderline applicants who do not meet admission requirements. **Home schooled:** Statement describing home school structure and mission, transcript of courses and grades required.

High school preparation. College-preparatory program required. 15 units required. Required and recommended units include English 4, mathematics 3, social studies 3, science 3 (laboratory 1), foreign language 2 and academic electives 2. English units must include 1 composition. Math units must include algebra, geometry and advanced algebra. 2 electives required in subjects listed above and/or fine arts.

2015-2016 Annual costs. Tuition/fees: $7,817; $18,005 out-of-state. Room/board: $8,320. Books/supplies: $900. Personal expenses: $2,146.

2014-2015 Financial aid. **Need-based:** 1,520 full-time freshmen applied for aid; 1,036 deemed to have need; 1,010 received aid. Average need met was 68%. Average scholarship/grant was $4,866; average loan $3,225. 57% of total undergraduate aid awarded as scholarships/grants, 43% as loans/jobs. **Non-need-based:** Awarded to 3,594 full-time undergraduates, including 1,160 freshmen. Scholarships awarded for academics, alumni affiliation, art, athletics, leadership, minority status, music/drama, ROTC, state residency.

Application procedures. **Admission:** Closing date 8/16 (postmark date). $40 fee. Admission notification on a rolling basis beginning on or about 9/1. **Financial aid:** No deadline. FAFSA required. Applicants notified on a rolling basis starting 3/15.

Academics. Bachelor of liberal studies external undergraduate degree completion program available to both Iowa and non-resident students. **Special study options:** Accelerated study, combined bachelor's/graduate degree, cooperative education, distance learning, double major, dual enrollment of high school students, ESL, exchange student, external degree, honors, independent study, internships, liberal arts/career combination, student-designed major, study abroad, teacher certification program, Washington semester, weekend college. Combined bachelors/masters degree programs (BA/MA, BS/MS, BA/MS); undergraduate dual degree majors; undergraduate and graduate certificates. **Credit/placement by examination:** AP, CLEP, IB, ACT, institutional tests. 32 credit hours maximum toward bachelor's degree. **Support services:** Learning center, pre-admission summer program, reduced course load, remedial instruction, study skills assistance, tutoring, writing center.

Majors. **Area/ethnic studies:** American, Latin American. **Biology:** General, biochemistry, biomedical sciences, ecology, microbiology. **Business:** Accounting, business admin, construction management, finance, management information systems, marketing, real estate. **Communications:** Communications/speech/rhetoric, digital media, organizational, public relations. **Communications technology:** Graphics. **Computer sciences:** General, computer science, networking. **Conservation:** Environmental science. **Education:** Business, elementary, ESL, foreign languages, health, kindergarten/preschool, middle, music, physical, reading, science, social science, speech, technology/industrial arts. **Engineering:** Applied physics. **English:** English lit, rhetoric/composition. **Foreign languages:** Spanish. **Health services:** Athletic training, speech pathology. **History:** General. **Human services:** General, social work. **Liberal arts:** Arts/sciences, humanities. **Math:** General, applied. **Parks/recreation:** General, health/fitness. **Philosophy/religion:** Philosophy, religion. **Physical sciences:** Chemistry, geology, physics. **Psychology:** General. **Social sciences:** Anthropology, applied economics, criminology, econometrics, economics, geography, political science, sociology. **Visual/performing arts:** Acting, art, art history/conservation, dramatic, interior design, music, music performance, music theory/composition, studio arts, theater design. **Work/family studies:** Clothing/textiles, family/community services.

Most popular majors. Biology 6%, business/marketing 18%, communications/journalism 8%, education 16%, parks/recreation 6%, social sciences 7%, visual/performing arts 6%.

Technology on campus. 2,500 workstations in dormitories, library, computer center, student center. Dormitories wired for high-speed internet access and linked to campus network. Online course registration, online library, helpline, student web hosting, wireless network available.

Student life. **Freshman orientation:** Mandatory, $125 fee. Preregistration for classes offered. Nine 2-day sessions in summer and immediately preceding beginning of semesters. **Housing:** Guaranteed on-campus for all undergraduates. Coed dorms, single-sex dorms, apartments, fraternity/sorority housing, themed housing, wellness housing available. $200 partly refundable deposit. **Activities:** Bands, campus ministries, choral groups, dance, drama, international student organizations, literary magazine, music ensembles, Model UN, musical theater, opera, radio station, student government, student newspaper, symphony orchestra, Amnesty International, Asian American student union, black student union, Campus Crusade for Christ, Catholic student association, College Republicans, conservation club, Fellowship of Christian Athletes, Habitat for Humanity, Democrat club.

Athletics. NCAA. **Intercollegiate:** Basketball, cross-country, diving W, football (tackle) M, golf, soccer W, softball W, swimming W, tennis W, track

and field, volleyball W, wrestling M. **Intramural:** Badminton, basketball, bowling, cheerleading, cross-country, football (non-tackle), football (tackle) M, golf, racquetball, soccer, softball, swimming, table tennis, tennis, track and field, volleyball, weight lifting, wrestling M. **Team name:** Panthers.

Student services. Adult student services, alcohol/substance abuse counseling, career counseling, services for economically disadvantaged, student employment services, financial aid counseling, health services, minority student services, on-campus daycare, personal counseling, placement for graduates, veterans' counselor. **Physically disabled:** Services for visually, speech, hearing impaired.

Contact. E-mail: admissions@uni.edu
Phone: (319) 273-2281 Fax: (319) 273-2885
Matthew Kroeger, Director of Admissions, University of Northern Iowa, 1227 West 27th Street, Cedar Falls, IA 50614-0018

University of Phoenix: Des Moines
Des Moines, Iowa
www.phoenix.edu

- For-profit 4-year university
- Small city
- 30 undergraduates

General. Regionally accredited. **Degrees:** 5 bachelor's awarded; master's offered. **Calendar:** Differs by program. **Full-time faculty:** 2 total. **Part-time faculty:** 3 total.

Basis for selection. Open admission.

2015-2016 Annual costs. Per-credit-hour charge $410 to $635, depending upon level and course of study; electronic course materials fee $95 and more than $200, if applicable. Book and material charges may vary by course and program. All fees are subject to change.

Application procedures. **Admission:** No deadline. No application fee. **Financial aid:** No deadline.

Academics. **Credit/placement by examination:** AP, CLEP.

Majors. **Business:** Accounting/business management, business admin, finance, human resources, marketing. **Human services:** General.

Student life. **Freshman orientation:** Mandatory. Preregistration for classes offered.

Contact. Toll-free number: (866) 766-0766
University of Phoenix: Des Moines, 1625 W. Fountainhead Pkwy, Tempe, AZ 85282

Upper Iowa University
Fayette, Iowa
www.uiu.edu   **CB code: 6885**

- Private 4-year university and liberal arts college
- Residential campus in rural community
- 4,022 degree-seeking undergraduates: 39% part-time, 62% women
- 686 degree-seeking graduate students
- 68% of applicants admitted
- SAT or ACT (ACT writing optional) required
- 41% graduate within 6 years

General. Founded in 1857. Regionally accredited. 20 US education centers, online and independent study programs, education centers in Hong Kong and Malaysia. **Degrees:** 1,799 bachelor's, 140 associate awarded; master's offered. **Location:** 50 miles from Waterloo, 70 miles from Cedar Rapids. **Calendar:** Semester, limited summer session. **Full-time faculty:** 78 total; 72% have terminal degrees, 3% minority, 54% women. **Part-time faculty:** 533 total; 39% have terminal degrees, 12% minority, 50% women. **Class size:** 82% < 20, 17% 20-39, less than 1% 40-49, less than 1% 50-99. **Special facilities:** Electron microscope lab, greenhouse, television and media lab with computer animation suite, Apple computer lab.

Freshman class profile. 1,637 applied, 1,112 admitted, 223 enrolled.

Mid 50% test scores		Out-of-state:	39%
ACT composite:	17-22	Live on campus:	99%
Return as sophomores:	42%	Fraternities:	64%

Basis for selection. 2.0 GPA, 17 ACT/810 SAT important. Interview recommended for academically weak applicants. Portfolio recommended for art majors. **Home schooled:** Transcript of courses and grades required. Letters of recommendation strongly encouraged. GED or proof of completed coursework required.

High school preparation. 14 units recommended. Recommended units include English 4, mathematics 3, social studies 2, history 1, science 3 (laboratory 1).

2015-2016 Annual costs. Tuition/fees: $28,138. Room/board: $8,058. Books/supplies: $1,400. Personal expenses: $2,600.

2014-2015 Financial aid. Need-based: 232 full-time freshmen applied for aid; 222 deemed to have need; 221 received aid. Average need met was 65%. Average scholarship/grant was $16,563; average loan $2,610. 46% of total undergraduate aid awarded as scholarships/grants, 54% as loans/jobs. **Non-need-based:** Awarded to 424 full-time undergraduates, including 243 freshmen. Scholarships awarded for academics, alumni affiliation, athletics.

Application procedures. Admission: No deadline. No application fee. Admission notification on a rolling basis. Enrollment deposit is refundable until May 1st. **Financial aid:** Priority date 3/1; no closing date. FAFSA required. Applicants notified on a rolling basis starting 3/1; must reply within 9 week(s) of notification.

Academics. 2 consecutive 8-week terms equal one semester. **Special study options:** Accelerated study, combined bachelor's/graduate degree, distance learning, double major, dual enrollment of high school students, ESL, external degree, honors, independent study, internships, liberal arts/career combination, student-designed major, study abroad, teacher certification program. **Credit/placement by examination:** AP, CLEP, IB, SAT, ACT, institutional tests. 30 credit hours maximum toward associate degree, 30 toward bachelor's. **Support services:** Learning center, remedial instruction, study skills assistance, tutoring, writing center.

Majors. Area/ethnic studies: American. **Biology:** General. **Business:** General, accounting, business admin, finance, human resources, international, management information systems. **Communications:** Communications/speech/rhetoric. **Computer sciences:** Information technology. **Conservation:** General, environmental science, forestry. **Education:** General, biology, chemistry, early childhood, elementary, health, history, kindergarten/preschool, middle, physical, reading, science, secondary, social science, social studies, special ed. **English:** English lit. **Health services:** Athletic training, facilities admin, health care admin, physical therapy assistant, predental, premedicine, prepharmacy, preveterinary. **Liberal arts:** Arts/sciences. **Math:** General. **Parks/recreation:** Facilities management, health/fitness. **Physical sciences:** Chemistry. **Protective services:** Criminal justice. **Psychology:** General. **Social sciences:** General, criminology, sociology. **Visual/performing arts:** Art, commercial/advertising art, studio arts, studio arts management.

Most popular majors. Business/marketing 43%, health sciences 7%, psychology 11%, public administration/social services 20%, social sciences 15%.

Technology on campus. 600 workstations in dormitories, library, computer center, student center. Dormitories wired for high-speed internet access and linked to campus network. Commuter students can connect to campus network. Online course registration, online library, helpline, repair service, wireless network available.

Student life. Freshman orientation: Mandatory. Preregistration for classes offered. Small group sessions held during the early spring and summer. Include financial aid counseling for parents and students. **Housing:** Guaranteed on-campus for all undergraduates. Coed dorms, single-sex dorms available. $250 fully refundable deposit. Suite-style housing available. **Activities:** Pep band, campus ministries, choral groups, dance, drama, international student organizations, student government, student newspaper, Peacocks for Progress, diversity club, Fellowship of Christian Athletes, Chi Alpha.

Athletics. NCAA. **Intercollegiate:** Baseball M, basketball, cross-country W, football (tackle) M, golf, soccer, softball W, tennis W, volleyball W, wrestling M. **Intramural:** Badminton, basketball, bowling, football (tackle), soccer M, softball, table tennis, volleyball. **Team name:** Peacocks.

Student services. Alcohol/substance abuse counseling, career counseling, student employment services, financial aid counseling, health services, personal counseling, placement for graduates.

Contact. E-mail: admission@uiu.edu
Phone: (563) 425-5281 Toll-free number: (800) 553-4150 ext. 2
Fax: (563) 425-5323
Anthony DiJohn, Executive Director of Admissions, Upper Iowa University, Parker Fox Hall, Fayette, IA 52142

Waldorf University

Forest City, Iowa
www.waldorf.edu

CB member
CB code: 6925

- Private 4-year liberal arts college affiliated with the Evangelical Lutheran Church in America
- Residential campus in small town
- 1,764 degree-seeking undergraduates: 21% part-time, 38% women, 16% African American, 2% Asian American, 9% Hispanic/Latino, 1% Native American, 2% Multi-racial, non-Hispanic, 2% international
- 208 degree-seeking graduate students
- 66% of applicants admitted
- SAT or ACT (ACT writing optional) required

General. Founded in 1903. Regionally accredited. **Degrees:** 334 bachelor's, 42 associate awarded; master's offered. **Location:** 125 miles from Des Moines. **Calendar:** Semester, limited summer session. **Full-time faculty:** 43 total; 60% have terminal degrees, 5% minority, 54% women. **Part-time faculty:** 100 total; 35% have terminal degrees, 11% minority, 48% women. **Class size:** 68% < 20, 32% 20-39. **Special facilities:** Digital multimedia lab, exercise physiology laboratory with hydrostatic metabolic chamber, GeoWall, FM radio station, cable access TV station.

Freshman class profile. 873 applied, 577 admitted, 187 enrolled.

GPA 3.75 or higher:	7%	End year in good standing:	94%
GPA 3.50-3.74:	1%	Return as sophomores:	53%
GPA 3.0-3.49:	32%	Out-of-state:	85%
GPA 2.0-2.99:	57%	Live on campus:	96%
Rank in top quarter:	10%	International:	2%
Rank in top tenth:	4%		

Basis for selection. School record and test scores most important, recommendations important, class rank considered. Interview recommended. Audition and portfolio recommended for music, theater majors. **Home schooled:** Transcript of courses and grades required. **Learning Disabled:** Interview during campus visit required.

High school preparation. College-preparatory program recommended. 16 units recommended. Recommended units include English 4, mathematics 3, social studies 4, science 3 and foreign language 2.

2015-2016 Annual costs. Tuition/fees: $20,884. Room/board: $6,994. Books/supplies: $1,188. Personal expenses: $1,845.

2015-2016 Financial aid. Need-based: Average need met was 70%. Average scholarship/grant was $15,383; average loan $4,218. 50% of total undergraduate aid awarded as scholarships/grants, 50% as loans/jobs. **Non-need-based:** Scholarships awarded for academics, alumni affiliation, athletics, job skills, leadership, music/drama, religious affiliation, state residency.

Application procedures. Admission: No deadline. No application fee. Admission notification on a rolling basis beginning on or about 9/10. **Financial aid:** Priority date 3/1; no closing date. FAFSA, institutional form required. Applicants notified on a rolling basis starting 3/1; must reply within 2 week(s) of notification.

Academics. Special study options: Accelerated study, combined bachelor's/graduate degree, distance learning, double major, dual enrollment of high school students, honors, independent study, internships, study abroad, teacher certification program. **Credit/placement by examination:** AP, CLEP, SAT, ACT, institutional tests. 8 credit hours maximum toward associate degree, 8 toward bachelor's. **Support services:** Learning center, reduced course load, remedial instruction, study skills assistance, tutoring, writing center.

Majors. Biology: General. **Business:** General, international, organizational behavior. **Education:** Elementary, music, physical, secondary. **English:** Creative writing, English lit. **History:** General. **Parks/recreation:** Sports admin. **Protective services:** Fire services admin, law enforcement admin. **Psychology:** General. **Visual/performing arts:** Dramatic, music. **Work/family studies:** Food/nutrition.

Most popular majors. Business/marketing 28%, psychology 10%, security/protective services 43%.

Technology on campus. 18 workstations in library. Dormitories wired for high-speed internet access and linked to campus network. Commuter students can connect to campus network. Online library, repair service, wireless network available.

Student life. Freshman orientation: Mandatory. Preregistration for classes offered. Held 2 days prior to start of school. Summer orientation for families in July. Program part of First Year Seminar Course focused on social transition, social decision making, campus resources, academic services and community. **Policies:** No alcohol or smoking allowed in residence halls. Three year residency requirement. Campus housing/meal plan. **Housing:** Guaranteed on-campus for all undergraduates. Coed dorms, single-sex dorms, special housing for disabled, apartments, themed housing, wellness housing available. $125 fully refundable deposit, deadline 9/10. Single rooms, community service-based housing available. **Activities:** Concert band, campus ministries, choral groups, drama, international student organizations, literary magazine, music ensembles, musical theater, radio station, student government, student newspaper, TV station, Student Warrior Activities Team, Active Catholics to Serve, Global Culture Club, Amnesty International, awareness ambassadors, praise and worship groups, history club, Gay Straight Alliance, Campus Democrats/Republicans, Black Student Union.

Athletics. NAIA. **Intercollegiate:** Baseball M, basketball, bowling, cheerleading, cross-country, football (tackle) M, golf, soccer, softball W, track and field, volleyball W, wrestling. **Intramural:** Badminton, basketball, bowling, football (non-tackle), racquetball, skiing, soccer, softball, table tennis, tennis, ultimate frisbee, volleyball, weight lifting. **Team name:** Warriors.

Student services. Alcohol/substance abuse counseling, chaplain/spiritual director, career counseling, student employment services, financial aid counseling, health services, personal counseling, placement for graduates. **Physically disabled:** Services for visually, hearing impaired.

Contact. E-mail: admissions@waldorf.edu
Phone: (641) 585-8112 Toll-free number: (800) 292-1903
Fax: (641) 585-8125
Scott Pitcher, Director of Admissions, Waldorf University, 106 South Sixth Street, Forest City, IA 50436-1713

Wartburg College
Waverly, Iowa
www.wartburg.edu
CB code: 6926

‣ Private 4-year liberal arts college affiliated with the Evangelical Lutheran Church in America

‣ Residential campus in small town

‣ 1,537 degree-seeking undergraduates: 4% part-time, 52% women, 5% African American, 1% Asian American, 3% Hispanic/Latino, 2% Multiracial, non-Hispanic, 8% international

‣ 74% of applicants admitted

‣ SAT or ACT (ACT writing optional) required

‣ 69% graduate within 6 years; 24% enter graduate study

General. Founded in 1852. Regionally accredited. **Degrees:** 350 bachelor's awarded. **Location:** 15 miles from Waterloo-Cedar Falls. **Calendar:** 4-4-1. Limited summer session. **Full-time faculty:** 105 total; 90% have terminal degrees, 5% minority, 44% women. **Part-time faculty:** 71 total; 7% have terminal degrees, 1% minority, 51% women. **Class size:** 60% < 20, 36% 20-39, 2% 40-49, 2% 50-99. **Special facilities:** Planetarium/observatory, prairie preserve, math simulation laboratory, institute for leadership education, music laboratory, science center, center for community engagement.

Freshman class profile. 2,147 applied, 1,585 admitted, 366 enrolled.

Mid 50% test scores			
SAT critical reading:	430-620	GPA 2.0-2.99:	13%
SAT math:	510-650	Rank in top quarter:	58%
SAT writing:	440-590	Rank in top tenth:	26%
ACT composite:	21-27	End year in good standing:	91%
GPA 3.75 or higher:	42%	Return as sophomores:	80%
GPA 3.50-3.74:	21%	Out-of-state:	30%
GPA 3.0-3.49:	23%	Live on campus:	98%
		International:	7%

Basis for selection. Class rank, GPA, courses taken, test scores, recommendations important. Students with 18 ACT or below or who rank in lower half of high school class are reviewed by admission and scholarship committee for final decision. Interview recommended. Audition recommended for music majors. Portfolio recommended for art majors. **Learning Disabled:** Documentation of disability required.

High school preparation. College-preparatory program required. 15 units recommended. Recommended units include English 4, mathematics 3, social studies 2, science 3, foreign language 2 and computer science 1.

2015-2016 Annual costs. Tuition/fees: $37,190. Room/board: $9,010.

2014-2015 Financial aid. **Need-based:** 409 full-time freshmen applied for aid; 357 deemed to have need; 357 received aid. Average need met was 84%. Average scholarship/grant was $23,885; average loan $4,658. 76% of total undergraduate aid awarded as scholarships/grants, 24% as loans/jobs. **Non-need-based:** Awarded to 610 full-time undergraduates, including 169

---

freshmen. Scholarships awarded for academics, alumni affiliation, leadership, music/drama, religious affiliation.

Application procedures. **Admission:** Priority date 5/1; no deadline. No application fee. Admission notification on a rolling basis beginning on or about 9/1. **Financial aid:** Priority date 3/1; no closing date. FAFSA required. Applicants notified on a rolling basis starting 3/1; must reply within 2 week(s) of notification.

Academics. **Special study options:** Accelerated study, combined bachelor's/graduate degree, double major, dual enrollment of high school students, honors, independent study, internships, student-designed major, study abroad, teacher certification program, urban semester, Washington semester. Urban academic internship experience in Denver, CO; Washington Center Academic Internship Program; cultural immersions in U.S. and around the world; Leadership Minor; deferred admission program with the University of Iowa College of Dentistry, community-based learning courses and first-year seminars. **Credit/placement by examination:** AP, CLEP, SAT, ACT, institutional tests. **Support services:** Learning center, reduced course load, remedial instruction, study skills assistance, tutoring, writing center.

Majors. **Biology:** General, biochemistry, neuroscience. **Business:** Accounting, business admin, finance, international, marketing. **Communications:** Broadcast journalism, communications/speech/rhetoric, journalism, public relations. **Computer sciences:** General, information systems. **Conservation:** Environmental science, environmental studies. **Education:** Art, elementary, history, music, physical. **Engineering:** Engineering science. **English:** English lit, rhetoric/composition. **Foreign languages:** French, German, Spanish. **Health services:** Clinical lab science, music therapy. **History:** General. **Human services:** Social work. **Math:** General. **Parks/recreation:** Sports admin. **Philosophy/religion:** Philosophy, religion. **Physical sciences:** Chemistry, physics. **Psychology:** General. **Social sciences:** Economics, international relations, political science, sociology. **Theology:** Pastoral counseling, religious ed, sacred music. **Visual/performing arts:** Art, commercial/advertising art, dramatic, music, music performance, music theory/composition.

Most popular majors. Biology 16%, business/marketing 21%, communications/journalism 9%, education 9%, social sciences 8%.

Technology on campus. 275 workstations in dormitories, library, computer center, student center. Dormitories wired for high-speed internet access and linked to campus network. Commuter students can connect to campus network. Online course registration, online library, helpline, wireless network available.

Student life. **Freshman orientation:** Mandatory. Preregistration for classes offered. Two-day program in summer; continues in fall for 1 week. **Housing:** Guaranteed on-campus for freshmen. Coed dorms, single-sex dorms, apartments, themed housing available. $250 nonrefundable deposit, deadline 5/1. Suite-style housing available. **Activities:** Bands, campus ministries, choral groups, dance, drama, film society, international student organizations, literary magazine, music ensembles, Model UN, musical theater, opera, radio station, student government, student newspaper, symphony orchestra, TV station, Adopt a Grandparent, Catholic Knights, Fellowship of Christian Athletes, Habitat for Humanity, Manna Student Senate, Wartburg Republicans La Mesa Espanola, German Club Best Buddies, EARTH, Students for Peace and Justice, Volunteer Action Center.

Athletics. NCAA. **Intercollegiate:** Baseball M, basketball, cross-country, football (tackle) M, golf, lacrosse W, soccer, softball W, tennis, track and field, volleyball W, wrestling M. **Intramural:** Basketball, bowling, football (non-tackle), racquetball, softball, tennis, volleyball. **Team name:** Knights.

Student services. Alcohol/substance abuse counseling, chaplain/spiritual director, career counseling, student employment services, financial aid counseling, health services, minority student services, personal counseling.

Contact. E-mail: admissions@wartburg.edu
Phone: (319) 352-8264 Toll-free number: (800) 772-2085
Fax: (319) 352-8579
Todd Coleman, Assistant Vice President for Admissions, Wartburg College, 100 Wartburg Boulevard, PO Box 1003, Waverly, IA 50677-0903

William Penn University
Oskaloosa, Iowa
www.wmpenn.edu
CB code: 6943

‣ Private 4-year university and liberal arts college affiliated with the Society of Friends (Quaker)

‣ Residential campus in large town

- 1,464 degree-seeking undergraduates: 7% part-time, 46% women, 19% African American, 1% Asian American, 8% Hispanic/Latino, 1% Native American, 1% Native Hawaiian/Pacific islander, 2% Multi-racial, non-Hispanic, 5% international
- 84 degree-seeking graduate students
- 57% of applicants admitted
- SAT or ACT (ACT writing optional) required
- 32% graduate within 6 years

General. Founded in 1873. Regionally accredited. Strong emphasis on leadership development. **Degrees:** 303 bachelor's, 67 associate awarded; master's offered. **Location:** 60 miles from Des Moines. **Calendar:** Semester, limited summer session. **Full-time faculty:** 40 total; 45% have terminal degrees, 2% minority, 35% women. **Part-time faculty:** 60 total; 3% have terminal degrees, 5% minority, 40% women. **Class size:** 59% < 20, 38% 20-39, less than 1% 40-49, 1% 50-99. **Special facilities:** Applied technology laboratories, theater, Middle Eastern art collection, prairie wildlife preserve.

Freshman class profile. 1,151 applied, 661 admitted, 309 enrolled.

Rank in top quarter:	16%	International:	7%
End year in good standing:	77%	Fraternities:	1%
Return as sophomores:	54%	Sororities:	1%
Live on campus:	80%		

Basis for selection. Class rank, test scores, high school GPA important. Extracurricular activities, alumni relationship, recommendation, personal essay considered. Essay required if student does not have ACT/SAT. Interview and essay recommended for academically marginal applicants. **Home schooled:** Transcript of courses and grades, state high school equivalency certificate required.

High school preparation. College-preparatory program recommended. 15 units required. Required and recommended units include English 4, mathematics 3, social studies 2, history 2, science 3 and academic electives 3.

2015-2016 Annual costs. Tuition/fees: $23,930. Room/board: $6,544. Books/supplies: $1,198. Personal expenses: $2,418.

2014-2015 Financial aid. Need-based: 197 full-time freshmen applied for aid; 164 deemed to have need; 164 received aid. Average scholarship/grant was $6,304. **Non-need-based:** Scholarships awarded for academics, alumni affiliation, athletics, leadership, music/drama, religious affiliation.

Application procedures. Admission: No deadline. No application fee. Admission notification on a rolling basis. **Financial aid:** Priority date 7/1; no closing date. FAFSA required. Applicants notified on a rolling basis starting 1/1; must reply within 3 week(s) of notification.

Academics. College for Working Adults (CWA) degree program. Leadership core curriculum replaces general education requirements. **Special study options:** Accelerated study, combined bachelor's/graduate degree, distance learning, double major, dual enrollment of high school students, independent study, internships, liberal arts/career combination, study abroad, teacher certification program. 3+2 engineering program with Iowa State University. **Credit/placement by examination:** AP, CLEP, IB, SAT, ACT, institutional tests. 16 credit hours maximum toward associate degree, 32 toward bachelor's. **Support services:** Learning center, reduced course load, remedial instruction, study skills assistance, tutoring, writing center.

Majors. Biology: General. **Business:** Accounting, business admin. **Communications:** General, broadcast journalism, digital media, public relations. **Computer sciences:** General, information technology. **Conservation:** Environmental studies. **Education:** Elementary, secondary. **Engineering:** Mechanical, software. **English:** English lit. **History:** General, American. **Math:** General, applied. **Parks/recreation:** Exercise sciences, health/fitness, sports admin. **Psychology:** General. **Social sciences:** Criminology, sociology, U.S. government. **Visual/performing arts:** Studio arts.

Most popular majors. Business/marketing 33%, education 19%, health sciences 7%, parks/recreation 12%, social sciences 6%.

Technology on campus. 125 workstations in dormitories, library, computer center, student center. Dormitories wired for high-speed internet access and linked to campus network. Commuter students can connect to campus network. Online library, helpline, repair service, wireless network available.

Student life. Freshman orientation: Mandatory. Preregistration for classes offered. Student services orientation held weekend before classes start; Penn Pride Experience held for first year students the day prior to classes starting. **Policies:** Student Code of Conduct identifies academic conduct, conduct toward society, general conduct, and conduct toward others. **Housing:** Guaranteed on-campus for freshmen. Coed dorms, single-sex dorms, special housing for disabled, apartments, wellness housing available. $100 partly refundable deposit, deadline 8/1. **Activities:** Bands, campus ministries, choral groups, dance, drama, international student organizations, literary magazine, music ensembles, musical theater, radio station, student government, student newspaper, literary magazine, Students for Minority Interests, Presidents Diplomats, education club, Greek Council, honor societies, computer club.

Athletics. NAIA. **Intercollegiate:** Baseball M, basketball, bowling, cheerleading, cross-country, football (tackle) M, golf, soccer, softball W, track and field, volleyball W, wrestling M. **Intramural:** Basketball, football (non-tackle) M, softball, table tennis, tennis, ultimate frisbee, volleyball. **Team name:** Lady Statesmen, Statesmen.

Student services. Adult student services, alcohol/substance abuse counseling, chaplain/spiritual director, career counseling, services for economically disadvantaged, student employment services, financial aid counseling, health services, minority student services, personal counseling, placement for graduates, veterans' counselor. **Physically disabled:** Services for visually, hearing impaired.

Contact. E-mail: admissions@wmpenn.edu
Phone: (641) 673-1012 Toll-free number: (800) 779-7366
Fax: (641) 673-2113
Kerra Strong, Vice President for Enrollment Management, William Penn University, 201 Trueblood Avenue, Oskaloosa, IA 52577

Kansas

Baker University

Baldwin City, Kansas
www.bakeru.edu

CB member
CB code: 6031

- Private 4-year liberal arts and teachers college affiliated with the United Methodist Church
- Residential campus in small town
- 793 degree-seeking undergraduates: 1% part-time, 47% women, 10% African American, 1% Asian American, 7% Hispanic/Latino, 3% Native American, 1% Native Hawaiian/Pacific islander, 2% Multi-racial, non-Hispanic, 3% international
- 82% of applicants admitted
- SAT or ACT (ACT writing optional) required
- 67% graduate within 6 years; 21% enter graduate study

General. Founded in 1858. Regionally accredited. College of Arts and Sciences in Baldwin City, KS. Also available (Overland Park, Topeka), School of Professional and Graduate Studies, School of Education and School of Nursing. **Degrees:** 150 bachelor's awarded. **ROTC:** Army, Air Force. **Location:** 15 miles from Lawrence, KS. 35 miles from Kansas City, Missouri. **Calendar:** 4-1-4; limited summer session. **Full-time faculty:** 60 total; 80% have terminal degrees, 5% minority, 52% women. **Part-time faculty:** 23 total; 35% have terminal degrees, 52% women. **Class size:** 67% < 20, 29% 20-39, 3% 40-49, less than 1% 50-99. **Special facilities:** Wetlands discover center, telescope, bible collections.

Freshman class profile. 889 applied, 729 admitted, 182 enrolled.

Mid 50% test scores		End year in good standing:	86.2%
ACT composite:	20-25	Return as sophomores:	77%
GPA 3.75 or higher:	30%	Out-of-state:	31%
GPA 3.50-3.74:	22%	Live on campus:	97%
GPA 3.0-3.49:	33%	International:	3%
GPA 2.0-2.99:	15%	Fraternities:	51%
Rank in top quarter:	43%	Sororities:	50%
Rank in top tenth:	17%		

Basis for selection. Strong core curriculum during high school very important. GPA, class rank, course selection, ACT or SAT, and recommendation from high school core teacher or guidance counselor important. Involvement in school, community and church activities considered. Interview and essay recommended. Audition recommended for music and theater majors. Portfolio recommended for art majors. **Home schooled:** Interview, letter of recommendation (nonparent) required.

High school preparation. College-preparatory program recommended. 17 units recommended. Recommended units include English 4, mathematics 3, social studies 3, science 3 (laboratory 1) and foreign language 2. One fine arts and one computing course recommended.

2015-2016 Annual costs. Tuition/fees: $30,080. Room/board: $8,270. Books/supplies: $1,200. Personal expenses: $1,350.

2015-2016 Financial aid. Need-based: Average scholarship/grant was $4,837; average loan $3,269. 56% of total undergraduate aid awarded as scholarships/grants, 44% as loans/jobs. **Non-need-based:** Scholarships awarded for academics, alumni affiliation, art, athletics, music/drama, religious affiliation.

Application procedures. Admission: Priority date 3/1; no deadline. No application fee. Admission notification on a rolling basis beginning on or about 9/15. **Financial aid:** Priority date 3/1; no closing date. FAFSA required. Applicants notified on a rolling basis starting 3/1; must reply within 6 week(s) of notification.

Academics. Liberal arts core required; stresses critical thinking skills, strong writing and oral communication ability, and application of these skills to various academic disciplines. **Special study options:** Accelerated study, combined bachelor's/graduate degree, double major, honors, independent study, internships, liberal arts/career combination, student-designed major, study abroad, teacher certification program. **Credit/placement by examination:** AP, CLEP, IB, SAT, ACT, institutional tests. **Support services:** Learning center, reduced course load, study skills assistance, tutoring, writing center.

Majors. Biology: General. **Business:** General, accounting, international. **Communications:** Media studies. **Computer sciences:** Computer science. **Education:** Art, elementary, middle, music, secondary. **English:** English lit. **Foreign languages:** French, German, Spanish. **History:** General. **Math:** General. **Parks/recreation:** Exercise sciences, health/fitness, sports admin. **Philosophy/religion:** Philosophy, religion. **Physical sciences:** Chemistry, physics. **Psychology:** General. **Social sciences:** Economics, sociology. **Visual/performing arts:** Art history/conservation, dramatic, music, studio arts.

Most popular majors. Business/marketing 23%, communications/journalism 6%, education 10%, parks/recreation 21%, psychology 6%, social sciences 8%.

Technology on campus. 140 workstations in dormitories, library, computer center. Dormitories wired for high-speed internet access. Online library, helpline, wireless network available.

Student life. Freshman orientation: Mandatory. Preregistration for classes offered. Five one-day programs held in June and July. **Policies:** Students required to live in campus or Greek housing unless granted permission to live off-campus. **Housing:** Guaranteed on-campus for freshmen. Coed dorms, single-sex dorms, special housing for disabled, apartments, fraternity/sorority housing available. $100 nonrefundable deposit. **Activities:** Bands, campus ministries, choral groups, dance, drama, international student organizations, literary magazine, music ensembles, radio station, student government, student newspaper, TV station, Student Senate, Student Activities Council, Baker Serves, Mungano, Panhellic Council, Interfraternity Council, Baker Ambassadors, Speech Choir, BRaV, ParMentors.

Athletics. NAIA. **Intercollegiate:** Baseball M, basketball, bowling W, cheerleading, cross-country, football (tackle) M, golf, soccer, softball W, tennis, track and field, volleyball W, wrestling M. **Intramural:** Basketball, football (non-tackle), softball, table tennis, volleyball. **Team name:** Wildcats.

Student services. Alcohol/substance abuse counseling, chaplain/spiritual director, career counseling, student employment services, financial aid counseling, health services, minority student services, personal counseling, placement for graduates, veterans' counselor, women's services. **Physically disabled:** Services for visually, hearing impaired.

Contact. E-mail: admission@bakeru.edu
Phone: (785) 594-8325 Fax: (785) 594-8353
Kevin Kropf, Director of Enrollment Management, Baker University, 618 Eighth Street, Baldwin City, KS 66006-0065

Barclay College

Haviland, Kansas
www.barclaycollege.edu

CB code: 6228

- Private 4-year Bible college affiliated with the Society of Friends (Quaker)
- Residential campus in rural community
- 233 degree-seeking undergraduates: 19% part-time, 50% women, 12% African American, 4% Hispanic/Latino, 1% Native American, 3% Multi-racial, non-Hispanic, 2% international
- 37 degree-seeking graduate students
- 75% of applicants admitted
- ACT (writing optional), application essay, interview required
- 41% graduate within 6 years

General. Founded in 1917. Accredited by ABHE. **Degrees:** 34 bachelor's, 7 associate awarded; master's offered. **Location:** 100 miles from Wichita, 65 miles from Dodge City. **Calendar:** Semester, limited summer session. **Full-time faculty:** 17 total; 47% have terminal degrees, 6% minority, 24% women. **Part-time faculty:** 24 total; 42% have terminal degrees, 33% women. **Class size:** 87% < 20, 8% 20-39, less than 1% 40-49, 4% 50-99.

Freshman class profile. 95 applied, 71 admitted, 50 enrolled.

Mid 50% test scores		Return as sophomores:	53%
SAT critical reading:	380-670	Out-of-state:	68%
SAT math:	330-530	Live on campus:	90%
SAT writing:	390-550	International:	4%
ACT composite:	18-23		

Basis for selection. Personal references and commitment to Christian vocation important. Committee reviews file and conducts phone interview. Audition recommended for music majors.

2015-2016 Annual costs. Tuition/fees: $14,990. Room/board: $8,000. Books/supplies: $1,600. Personal expenses: $1,200.

Financial aid. Non-need-based: Scholarships awarded for academics, alumni affiliation, leadership, music/drama, state residency.

Application procedures. Admission: Closing date 9/1. $25 fee, may be waived for applicants with need, free for online applicants. Admission notification on a rolling basis. **Financial aid:** Priority date 5/31, closing date 7/15. FAFSA, institutional form required. Applicants notified on a rolling basis starting 1/1; must reply within 4 week(s) of notification.

Academics. Each student has Bible major in addition to individually chosen major. Emphasis on practicums and internships. **Special study options:** Combined bachelor's/graduate degree, cooperative education, distance learning, double major, dual enrollment of high school students, independent study, internships, liberal arts/career combination, study abroad, teacher certification program. Cooperative classes with Pratt Community College cooperative programs with Fort Hays State University. **Credit/placement by examination:** AP, CLEP, IB, SAT, ACT, institutional tests. 15 credit hours maximum toward associate degree, 30 toward bachelor's. **Support services:** Learning center, remedial instruction, study skills assistance, tutoring, writing center.

Majors. Business: General, business admin. **Education:** Elementary. **Philosophy/religion:** Religion. **Psychology:** General. **Theology:** Bible, missionary, pastoral counseling, sacred music, theology, youth ministry.

Most popular majors. Business/marketing 27%, education 6%, psychology 6%, theological studies 61%.

Technology on campus. 25 workstations in dormitories, library, computer center. Dormitories wired for high-speed internet access and linked to campus network. Commuter students can connect to campus network. Online course registration, online library, helpline, repair service, wireless network available.

Student life. Freshman orientation: Mandatory. Preregistration for classes offered. **Policies:** Christian and social work required. Religious observance required. **Housing:** Guaranteed on-campus for freshmen. Single-sex dorms, wellness housing available. $50 deposit. **Activities:** Jazz band, choral groups, drama, music ensembles, student government.

Athletics. Intercollegiate: Basketball, cheerleading W, golf, soccer M, tennis, volleyball W. **Intramural:** Baseball, basketball, bowling, softball, volleyball. **Team name:** Bears.

Student services. Chaplain/spiritual director, career counseling, student employment services, financial aid counseling, health services, personal counseling, placement for graduates.

Contact. E-mail: admissions@barclaycollege.edu
Phone: (620) 862-5252 ext. 21 Toll-free number: (800) 862-0226
Fax: (620) 862-5242
Justin Kendall, Director of Admissions, Barclay College, 607 North Kingman, Haviland, KS 67059

Benedictine College
Atchison, Kansas
www.benedictine.edu

CB member
CB code: 6056

- Private 4-year liberal arts college affiliated with the Roman Catholic Church
- Residential campus in large town
- 1,868 degree-seeking undergraduates: 1% part-time, 54% women, 3% African American, 1% Asian American, 5% Hispanic/Latino, 5% Multiracial, non-Hispanic, 3% international
- 46 degree-seeking graduate students
- 99% of applicants admitted
- SAT or ACT (ACT writing optional) required
- 68% graduate within 6 years; 10% enter graduate study

General. Founded in 1858. Regionally accredited. **Degrees:** 349 bachelor's awarded; master's offered. **ROTC:** Army. **Location:** 45 miles from Kansas City, Missouri. **Calendar:** Semester, limited summer session. **Full-time faculty:** 105 total; 72% have terminal degrees, 7% minority, 34% women. **Part-time faculty:** 60 total; 22% have terminal degrees, 8% minority, 57% women. **Class size:** 52% < 20, 44% 20-39, 3% 40-49, 1% 50-99.

Freshman class profile. 2,355 applied, 2,325 admitted, 508 enrolled.

Mid 50% test scores		Rank in top quarter:	44%
SAT critical reading:	510-660	Rank in top tenth:	22%
SAT math:	490-630	End year in good standing:	94%
ACT composite:	21-28	Return as sophomores:	77%
GPA 3.75 or higher:	45%	Out-of-state:	74%
GPA 3.50-3.74:	19%	Live on campus:	99%
GPA 3.0-3.49:	24%	International:	1%
GPA 2.0-2.99:	12%		

Basis for selection. Applicant must satisfy 2 of following requirements: GPA above 2.0, rank in top half of class, requisite ACT or SAT scores. Recommendations and interview considered. Interview recommended for academically weak applicants.

High school preparation. College-preparatory program recommended. Recommended units include English 4, mathematics 3, social studies 2, history 1, science 2 and foreign language 2.

2015-2016 Annual costs. Tuition/fees: $26,250. Room/board: $9,165.

2015-2016 Financial aid. Need-based: 439 full-time freshmen applied for aid; 369 deemed to have need; 369 received aid. Average need met was 76%. Average scholarship/grant was $17,135; average loan $3,940. 64% of total undergraduate aid awarded as scholarships/grants, 36% as loans/jobs. **Non-need-based:** Awarded to 839 full-time undergraduates, including 215 freshmen. Scholarships awarded for academics, alumni affiliation, art, athletics, job skills, leadership, minority status, music/drama, religious affiliation, state residency.

Application procedures. Admission: No deadline. $50 fee, may be waived for applicants with need, free for online applicants. Admission notification on a rolling basis. **Financial aid:** Priority date 4/1; no closing date. FAFSA required. Applicants notified on a rolling basis starting 2/1; must reply within 2 week(s) of notification.

Academics. Special study options: Distance learning, double major, dual enrollment of high school students, ESL, honors, independent study, internships, student-designed major, study abroad, teacher certification program. **Credit/placement by examination:** AP, CLEP, IB, SAT, ACT, institutional tests. **Support services:** Learning center, reduced course load, study skills assistance, tutoring, writing center.

Honors college/program. Admit 25 total students. Minimum 3.75 high school GPA and 29 ACT. Some courses are distinct, but most are shared with the rest of the student body.

Majors. Biology: General, biochemistry. **Business:** Accounting, business admin, finance, international, marketing. **Communications:** Journalism, media studies. **Computer sciences:** Computer science. **Education:** General, art, elementary, music, physical, secondary, special ed. **Engineering:** General, mechanical. **English:** English lit. **Foreign languages:** General, French, Spanish. **Health services:** Athletic training, nursing practice. **History:** General. **Liberal arts:** Arts/sciences. **Math:** General. **Philosophy/religion:** Philosophy. **Physical sciences:** Astronomy, chemistry, physics. **Psychology:** General. **Social sciences:** General, criminology, economics, political science, sociology. **Theology:** Religious ed, theology. **Visual/performing arts:** Art, dramatic, music, theater arts management.

Most popular majors. Business/marketing 21%, education 20%, social sciences 8%, theological studies 8%.

Technology on campus. 89 workstations in library, computer center. Dormitories wired for high-speed internet access and linked to campus network. Commuter students can connect to campus network. Online course registration, online library, helpline, wireless network available.

Student life. Freshman orientation: Mandatory. Preregistration for classes offered. Weekend program before classes commence. **Housing:** Guaranteed on-campus for freshmen. Single-sex dorms, apartments available. $100 fully refundable deposit. Off-campus college-owned housing available. **Activities:** Bands, campus ministries, choral groups, dance, drama, international student organizations, literary magazine, music ensembles, musical theater, opera, student government, student newspaper, symphony orchestra, Ravens Respect Life, Knights of Columbus, Hunger Coalition, Fellowship of Catholic University Students, Enactus, Black Student Union, Communion & Liberation, swing & social dance club, Oblates of St. Benedict.

Athletics. NAIA. Intercollegiate: Baseball M, basketball, cheerleading, cross-country, football (tackle) M, lacrosse, soccer, softball W, track and field, volleyball W, wrestling M. **Intramural:** Baseball M, basketball, football (non-tackle), soccer, softball, volleyball. **Team name:** Ravens.

Student services. Alcohol/substance abuse counseling, chaplain/spiritual director, career counseling, student employment services, financial aid counseling, health services, personal counseling, placement for graduates. **Physically disabled:** Services for visually, speech, hearing impaired.

Contact. E-mail: bcadmiss@benedictine.edu
Phone: (913) 367-5340 Toll-free number: (800) 467-5340
Fax: (913) 367-5462
Pete Helgesen, Dean of Enrollment Management, Benedictine College, 1020 North Second Street, Atchison, KS 66002-1499

Bethany College
Lindsborg, Kansas
www.bethanylb.edu

CB code: 6034

- Private 4-year liberal arts college affiliated with the Evangelical Lutheran Church in America
- Residential campus in small town
- 629 degree-seeking undergraduates: 2% part-time, 39% women, 16% African American, 1% Asian American, 19% Hispanic/Latino, 1% Native American, 3% Multi-racial, non-Hispanic
- 99% of applicants admitted
- SAT or ACT (ACT writing optional) required
- 43% graduate within 6 years

General. Founded in 1881. Regionally accredited. **Degrees:** 119 bachelor's awarded. **Location:** 20 miles from Salina, 72 miles from Wichita. **Calendar:** 4-1-4, limited summer session.

Freshman class profile. 1,650 applied, 1,638 admitted, 188 enrolled.

Mid 50% test scores			
SAT critical reading:	410-510	GPA 2.0-2.99:	37%
SAT math:	410-520	Rank in top quarter:	20%
SAT writing:	380-490	Rank in top tenth:	8%
ACT composite:	18-23	Out-of-state:	54%
GPA 3.75 or higher:	20%	Live on campus:	98%
GPA 3.50-3.74:	11%	Fraternities:	16%
GPA 3.0-3.49:	31%	Sororities:	18%

Basis for selection. High school GPA, course selection, trends in grades, and standardized test scores are weighed with an interview, letters of recommendation and exhibited leadership qualities. A student's future curriculum participation and involvement are also considered. Interview and essay recommended for some. Audition required of music and theater majors. Portfolio required of art majors.

High school preparation. College-preparatory program recommended. Recommended units include English 4, mathematics 3, social studies 3, science 3 (laboratory 2) and foreign language 2.

2015-2016 Annual costs. Tuition/fees: $26,550. Room/board: $8,100. Books/supplies: $1,000. Personal expenses: $2,600.

Financial aid. Non-need-based: Scholarships awarded for academics, alumni affiliation, art, athletics, job skills, leadership, minority status, music/drama, religious affiliation, ROTC, state residency. **Additional information:** State financial aid deadline March 15.

Application procedures. Admission: Priority date 2/1; no deadline. No application fee. Admission notification on a rolling basis beginning on or about 9/1. **Financial aid:** Priority date 3/1; no closing date. FAFSA required. Applicants notified on a rolling basis; must reply by 8/22.

Academics. Special study options: Combined bachelor's/graduate degree, cross-registration, distance learning, double major, dual enrollment of high school students, honors, independent study, internships, student-designed major, study abroad, teacher certification program, urban semester, Washington semester. Special education program with Associated Colleges of Central Kansas. **Credit/placement by examination:** AP, CLEP, IB, SAT, ACT. 32 credit hours maximum toward bachelor's degree. **Support services:** Learning center, reduced course load, remedial instruction, study skills assistance, tutoring, writing center.

Majors. Biology: General. **Business:** Accounting, business admin, finance, managerial economics, marketing, sales/distribution. **Communications:** Communications/speech/rhetoric. **Education:** General, art, biology, business, chemistry, elementary, English, health, history, mathematics, music, physical, secondary, social science. **English:** English lit, rhetoric/composition. **Health services:** Art therapy, athletic training. **History:** General. **Liberal arts:** Arts/sciences. **Math:** General. **Parks/recreation:** Facilities management, sports admin. **Philosophy/religion:** Christian. **Physical sciences:** Chemistry, physics. **Protective services:** Criminal justice, police science. **Psychology:** General. **Social sciences:** General, economics, sociology. **Visual/performing arts:** Art, graphic design, music, music performance.

Technology on campus. 50 workstations in library, computer center. Dormitories wired for high-speed internet access and linked to campus network. Commuter students can connect to campus network. Online library available.

Student life. Freshman orientation: Mandatory. Preregistration for classes offered. One week of activities prior to first day of classes; planned and organized by returning students. **Policies:** No alcohol allowed on campus.

Full-time students required to live on campus until age 22 or special consideration given. **Housing:** Guaranteed on-campus for freshmen. Coed dorms, single-sex dorms, special housing for disabled, apartments available. $100 deposit, deadline 8/1. **Activities:** Bands, campus ministries, choral groups, dance, drama, international student organizations, music ensembles, musical theater, student government, student newspaper, symphony orchestra, Blue Key, Gold Key, Alpha Omega, Chi Alpha, Beta Tau Sigma, International Student's Organization, departmental organizations, honorary societies, Green Team, Student Government Association.

Athletics. NAIA. **Intercollegiate:** Baseball M, basketball, cross-country, football (tackle) M, golf, soccer, softball W, tennis, track and field, volleyball W, wrestling M. **Intramural:** Basketball, football (non-tackle), racquetball, soccer, softball, table tennis, volleyball, weight lifting. **Team name:** Swedes.

Student services. Alcohol/substance abuse counseling, chaplain/spiritual director, career counseling, student employment services, financial aid counseling, health services, minority student services, personal counseling, placement for graduates, veterans' counselor.

Contact. E-mail: admissions@bethanylb.edu
Phone: (785) 227-3380 ext. 8113
Toll-free number: (800) 826-2281 ext. 8113 Fax: (785) 227-8993
Matt Pfannenstiel, Dean of Admissions & Financial Aid, Bethany College, 335 East Swensson, Lindsborg, KS 67456-1897

Bethel College
North Newton, Kansas
www.bethelks.edu

CB code: 6037

- Private 4-year liberal arts college affiliated with the Mennonite Church
- Residential campus in large town
- 525 degree-seeking undergraduates: 3% part-time, 52% women, 14% African American, 1% Asian American, 6% Hispanic/Latino, 1% Native American, 4% Multi-racial, non-Hispanic, 2% international
- 53% of applicants admitted
- SAT or ACT (ACT writing optional) required
- 60% graduate within 6 years

General. Founded in 1887. Regionally accredited. **Degrees:** 83 bachelor's awarded. **Location:** 25 miles from Wichita. **Calendar:** 4-1-4, limited summer session. **Full-time faculty:** 44 total; 66% have terminal degrees, 7% minority, 59% women. **Part-time faculty:** 28 total; 14% have terminal degrees, 4% minority, 61% women. **Class size:** 71% < 20, 26% 20-39, 2% 40-49, less than 1% 50-99, less than 1% >100. **Special facilities:** Natural history museum, 80-acre natural history field laboratory, institute for peace and conflict resolution, Mennonite library and archives, observatory, conservatory.

Freshman class profile. 862 applied, 459 admitted, 130 enrolled.

Mid 50% test scores			
		Rank in top quarter:	41%
ACT composite:	21-24	Rank in top tenth:	22%
GPA 3.75 or higher:	39%	Return as sophomores:	65%
GPA 3.50-3.74:	12%	Out-of-state:	49%
GPA 3.0-3.49:	26%	Live on campus:	96%
GPA 2.0-2.99:	23%	International:	2%

Basis for selection. Automatic admission generally given to students with high school GPA of 2.5 and ACT score of at least 19 or SAT of at least 890 (exclusive of Writing). Essay recommended for academically weak applicants. Audition recommended for drama and music majors. Portfolio recommended for art majors. **Home schooled:** Evaluative transcript or GED score. ACT or SAT score is also required.

High school preparation. College-preparatory program recommended. 16 units recommended. Recommended units include English 4, mathematics 4, social studies 3, science 3 and foreign language 2.

2015-2016 Annual costs. Tuition/fees: $25,410. Room/board: $8,110. Books/supplies: $900. Personal expenses: $2,400.

2015-2016 Financial aid. Need-based: Average need met was 80%. Average scholarship/grant was $5,489; average loan $5,639. 74% of total undergraduate aid awarded as scholarships/grants, 26% as loans/jobs. **Non-need-based:** Scholarships awarded for academics, alumni affiliation, art, athletics, minority status, music/drama, religious affiliation, state residency.

Application procedures. Admission: Closing date 8/1. $20 fee, may be waived for applicants with need. Admission notification on a rolling basis beginning on or about 9/1. **Financial aid:** Priority date 4/1; no closing date. FAFSA, institutional form required. Applicants notified on a rolling basis starting 2/1; must reply within 2 week(s) of notification.

Academics. Curriculum founded on general education program in liberal arts and sciences. Distinctive elements include peace, justice and conflict studies, convocation, and cross-cultural learning requirements and senior capstone course focusing on basic issues of faith and life. **Special study options:** Cross-registration, double major, dual enrollment of high school students, independent study, internships, liberal arts/career combination, student-designed major, study abroad, teacher certification program, urban semester, Washington semester. **Credit/placement by examination:** AP, CLEP, IB, SAT, ACT, institutional tests. **Support services:** Learning center, study skills assistance, tutoring.

Majors. Biology: General. **Business:** General. **Communications:** Media studies. **Education:** Elementary. **English:** English lit. **Health services:** Athletic training, nursing (RN). **History:** General. **Human services:** Social work. **Math:** General. **Parks/recreation:** Health/fitness. **Philosophy/religion:** Religion. **Physical sciences:** Chemistry. **Psychology:** General. **Visual/performing arts:** Music, studio arts.

Most popular majors. Biology 10%, education 13%, health sciences 37%, physical sciences 6%, public administration/social services 14%.

Technology on campus. 56 workstations in library, computer center. Dormitories wired for high-speed internet access and linked to campus network. Commuter students can connect to campus network. Helpline, repair service, student web hosting, wireless network available.

Student life. Freshman orientation: Mandatory. Preregistration for classes offered. Held the Wednesday through Monday before classes begin. **Policies:** Chapel services voluntary. Two weekly convocations required and credited as part of general education. **Housing:** Guaranteed on-campus for all undergraduates. Coed dorms, special housing for disabled available. **Activities:** Bands, campus ministries, choral groups, drama, international student organizations, literary magazine, music ensembles, musical theater, opera, radio station, student government, student newspaper, symphony orchestra, Student Community Action Network for voluntary services, peace club, Bethel Christian Fellowship, service corps-disaster response, Fellowship of Christian Athletes, environmental action club, Catholic student organization.

Athletics. NAIA. **Intercollegiate:** Basketball, cross-country, football (tackle) M, golf, soccer, softball W, tennis, track and field, volleyball W. **Intramural:** Badminton, basketball, football (non-tackle), golf, racquetball, softball, table tennis, tennis, ultimate frisbee, volleyball. **Team name:** Threshers.

Student services. Alcohol/substance abuse counseling, chaplain/spiritual director, career counseling, student employment services, financial aid counseling, health services, minority student services, personal counseling. **Physically disabled:** Services for visually, hearing impaired.

Contact. E-mail: admissions@bethelks.edu
Phone: (316) 284-5230 Toll-free number: (800) 522-1887 ext. 230
Fax: (316) 284-5870
Todd Moore, Vice President for Admissions, Bethel College, 300 E 27th Street, North Newton, KS 67117-8061

Central Christian College of Kansas
McPherson, Kansas
www.centralchristian.edu   **CB code: 6088**

- Private 4-year liberal arts college affiliated with the Free Methodist Church of North America
- Residential campus in large town
- 1,043 degree-seeking undergraduates: 2% part-time, 53% women, 27% African American, 1% Asian American, 6% Hispanic/Latino, 2% Native American, 2% Multi-racial, non-Hispanic, 1% international
- 61% of applicants admitted
- SAT or ACT (ACT writing recommended) required
- 32% graduate within 6 years

General. Founded in 1884. Regionally accredited. **Degrees:** 107 bachelor's, 10 associate awarded. **Location:** 55 miles from Wichita. **Calendar:** 4-1-4, limited summer session. **Full-time faculty:** 22 total. **Part-time faculty:** 102 total. **Class size:** 92% < 20, 7% 20-39, less than 1% 50-99.

Freshman class profile. 700 applied, 424 admitted, 338 enrolled.

Mid 50% test scores			
		GPA 3.0-3.49:	37%
SAT critical reading:	360-500	**GPA 2.0-2.99:**	21%
SAT math:	380-560	**Rank in top quarter:**	25%
SAT writing:	360-470	**Rank in top tenth:**	10%
ACT composite:	18-23	**Return as sophomores:**	61%
GPA 3.75 or higher:	24%	**Out-of-state:**	74%
GPA 3.50-3.74:	18%	**Live on campus:**	96%

Basis for selection. Admissions decisions are based on a composite score drawn from ACT/SAT and prior GPA, along with a recommendation from the admissions counselor. TOEFL scores are required for international students from non-English speaking countries. Interview and essay recommended. **Home schooled:** Transcript of courses and grades required. **Learning Disabled:** Provide Individualized Education Program (IEP).

High school preparation. College-preparatory program recommended. 22 units required. Required units include English 4, mathematics 2, social studies 2, history 1, science 2 (laboratory 1). One computer technology course recommended.

2016-2017 Annual costs. Tuition/fees (projected): $24,690. Room/board: $7,950. Books/supplies: $1,200. Personal expenses: $1,000.

Financial aid. Non-need-based: Scholarships awarded for academics, alumni affiliation, athletics, leadership, music/drama, religious affiliation.

Application procedures. Admission: No deadline. No application fee. Admission notification on a rolling basis. **Financial aid:** Priority date 3/1; no closing date. FAFSA required. Applicants notified on a rolling basis starting 3/1; must reply within 4 week(s) of notification.

Academics. Special study options: Accelerated study, cooperative education, cross-registration, distance learning, double major, dual enrollment of high school students, independent study, internships, liberal arts/career combination, student-designed major, teacher certification program, urban semester, Washington semester. **Credit/placement by examination:** AP, CLEP, IB, SAT, ACT, institutional tests. 30 credit hours maximum toward associate degree, 30 toward bachelor's. CLEP Score of 50 or higher required to accept credit. **Support services:** Learning center, reduced course load, remedial instruction, study skills assistance, tutoring, writing center.

Majors. Biology: General, exercise physiology. **Business:** Accounting, business admin, organizational behavior, small business admin. **Communications:** Communications/speech/rhetoric, media studies, organizational, persuasive communications. **Education:** Elementary, English, history, multi-level teacher, physical, secondary, social studies. **English:** English lit, rhetoric/composition. **History:** General. **Liberal arts:** Arts/sciences. **Math:** General. **Parks/recreation:** Exercise sciences, sports admin. **Philosophy/religion:** General. **Physical sciences:** Chemistry. **Psychology:** General. **Social sciences:** General. **Theology:** Pastoral counseling, sacred music. **Visual/performing arts:** Music, music performance, piano/keyboard.

Most popular majors. Business/marketing 13%, history 9%, security/protective services 44%, theological studies 10%.

Technology on campus. 40 workstations in dormitories, library, computer center, student center. Dormitories wired for high-speed internet access. Commuter students can connect to campus network. Online course registration, online library, helpline, repair service, wireless network available.

Student life. Freshman orientation: Mandatory, $30 fee. Preregistration for classes offered. Fall semester first seven weeks. Interterm and Spring 1-2 days. **Policies:** Students must sign a life-style covenant. Alcohol, smoking, drugs not allowed on campus. Students 23 years of age or older can request to live off campus. **Housing:** Guaranteed on-campus for all undergraduates. Single-sex dorms, apartments, wellness housing available. $200 fully refundable deposit, deadline 8/1. **Activities:** Bands, campus ministries, choral groups, dance, drama, music ensembles, musical theater, radio station, student government, student newspaper, Christian service organization, Flying Tigers, performing arts club, PBL, student activities council.

Athletics. NAIA, NCCAA. **Intercollegiate:** Baseball M, basketball, cheerleading, cross-country, golf, soccer, softball W, tennis, volleyball W. **Intramural:** Badminton, basketball, football (non-tackle), soccer, softball, table tennis, tennis, ultimate frisbee, volleyball. **Team name:** Tigers.

Student services. Adult student services, chaplain/spiritual director, career counseling, student employment services, financial aid counseling, health services, personal counseling, placement for graduates. **Physically disabled:** Services for visually, speech impaired.

Contact. E-mail: admissions@centralchristian.edu
Phone: (620) 241-0723 ext. 337
Toll-free number: (800) 835-0078 ext. 337 Fax: (620) 241-6032
Tina Golden, Deputy Director of Admissions, Central Christian College of Kansas, 1200 South Main, McPherson, KS 67460-5740

Emporia State University
Emporia, Kansas
www.emporia.edu   **CB code: 6335**

- Public 4-year university
- Residential campus in large town

- 3,730 degree-seeking undergraduates: 6% part-time, 60% women, 5% African American, 1% Asian American, 7% Hispanic/Latino, 1% Native American, 7% Multi-racial, non-Hispanic, 8% international
- 1,974 degree-seeking graduate students
- 87% of applicants admitted
- SAT or ACT (ACT writing optional) required
- 42% graduate within 6 years

General. Founded in 1863. Regionally accredited. **Degrees:** 709 bachelor's awarded; master's, doctoral offered. **Location:** 50 miles from Topeka, 77 miles from Wichita. **Calendar:** Semester, extensive summer session. **Full-time faculty:** 254 total; 79% have terminal degrees, 13% minority, 46% women. **Part-time faculty:** 22 total; 41% have terminal degrees, 77% women. **Class size:** 47% < 20, 41% 20-39, 6% 40-49, 6% 50-99, less than 1% >100. **Special facilities:** Planetarium, natural history reserve, natural history museum, National Teachers Hall of Fame, Great Plains study center, center for early childhood education, memorial to fallen educators.

Freshman class profile. 1,736 applied, 1,510 admitted, 735 enrolled.

Mid 50% test scores		End year in good standing:	76%
ACT composite:	19-25	Return as sophomores:	72%
GPA 3.75 or higher:	26%	Out-of-state:	8%
GPA 3.50-3.74:	19%	Live on campus:	81%
GPA 3.0-3.49:	29%	International:	5%
GPA 2.0-2.99:	24%	Fraternities:	19%
Rank in top quarter:	36%	Sororities:	15%
Rank in top tenth:	13%		

Basis for selection. Applicants must have one of following: minimum ACT score of 21, rank in top third of high school class, minimum 2.0 GPA in Kansas Core Curriculum for in-state students, or 2.5 GPA for out-of-state students. Limited number of students who do not meet qualifications may be admitted through 10% exceptions window. ACT scores must be received by end of first semester of study. **Home schooled:** State high school equivalency certificate required. GED must be submitted.

High school preparation. College-preparatory program recommended. Required units include English 4, mathematics 3, social studies 3, science 3 and academic electives 1. 1 computer technology recommended. These units required for students who do not have minimum ACT score of 21, or in top 1/3 of high school class.

2015-2016 Annual costs. Tuition/fees: $5,936; $18,524 out-of-state. Room/board: $7,967. Books/supplies: $800. Personal expenses: $2,200.

2015-2016 Financial aid. Need-based: 662 full-time freshmen applied for aid; 529 deemed to have need; 527 received aid. Average need met was 64%. Average scholarship/grant was $5,937; average loan $5,106. 46% of total undergraduate aid awarded as scholarships/grants, 54% as loans/jobs. **Non-need-based:** Awarded to 762 full-time undergraduates, including 210 freshmen. Scholarships awarded for academics, alumni affiliation, art, athletics, job skills, leadership, minority status, music/drama, religious affiliation, state residency. **Additional information:** Institution's own payment plan is available.

Application procedures. Admission: No deadline. $30 fee, may be waived for applicants with need. Admission notification on a rolling basis. Must reply by May 1 or within 2 week(s) if notified thereafter. **Financial aid:** Priority date 3/15; no closing date. FAFSA required. Applicants notified on a rolling basis starting 2/2; must reply within 2 week(s) of notification.

Academics. Special study options: Distance learning, double major, dual enrollment of high school students, honors, independent study, internships, student-designed major, study abroad, teacher certification program. Career development center and programs, continuing education courses, evening program, interdisciplinary or interdepartmental courses of study, learning assistance programs, pass-fail grading option, service members' opportunity college, summer sessions, tutorial program, trio programs. **Credit/placement by examination:** AP, CLEP, IB, ACT, institutional tests. 30 credit hours maximum toward bachelor's degree. **Support services:** Learning center, remedial instruction, tutoring, writing center.

Honors college/program. To participate in the program, entering freshmen must have an ACT composite score of 26 or higher OR a high school GPA of 3.5 or better. Students transferring from other colleges or ESU students who have completed at least one semester of college must have a GPA of 3.5 or better. Students in the Honors College will be prepared to be agents of change for the common good in their respective communities, and will experience specific training in Civic Leadership and Community Engagement.

Majors. Biology: General, Biochemistry/molecular biology. **Business:** Accounting, business admin, human resources, marketing. **Communications:** Communications/speech/rhetoric. **Computer sciences:** General, information systems, security. **Education:** Elementary, health, music, secondary, speech.

English: English lit. **Foreign languages:** General. **Health services:** Athletic training, nursing (RN), public health ed, vocational rehab counseling. **History:** General. **Liberal arts:** Arts/sciences. **Math:** General. **Parks/recreation:** General. **Physical sciences:** General, chemistry, geology, physics. **Psychology:** General. **Social sciences:** General, economics, political science, sociology. **Visual/performing arts:** Art, dramatic, music.

Most popular majors. Business/marketing 13%, education 23%, health sciences 11%, liberal arts 6%, social sciences 10%.

Technology on campus. 410 workstations in dormitories, library, computer center, student center. Dormitories wired for high-speed internet access and linked to campus network. Commuter students can connect to campus network. Online course registration, online library, helpline, repair service, student web hosting, wireless network available.

Student life. Freshman orientation: Available, $35 fee. Preregistration for classes offered. One-day program for students and parents; held during summer and prior to start of classes. **Housing:** Guaranteed on-campus for freshmen. Coed dorms, single-sex dorms, special housing for disabled, cooperative housing, fraternity/sorority housing, themed housing, wellness housing available. $145 partly refundable deposit, deadline 7/1. **Activities:** Bands, campus ministries, choral groups, dance, drama, film society, international student organizations, literary magazine, music ensembles, musical theater, opera, student government, student newspaper, symphony orchestra, Black Student Union, Hispanic American leadership organization, Catholic Campus Community, Christian student center, Black women's network, Muslim student association, Fellowship of Christian Athletes, Arabic language club, East Asian club, Campus Crusade for Christ.

Athletics. NCAA. **Intercollegiate:** Baseball M, basketball, cheerleading, cross-country, football (tackle) M, soccer W, softball W, tennis, track and field, volleyball W. **Intramural:** Badminton, basketball, football (non-tackle), soccer, softball, table tennis, volleyball. **Team name:** Hornets.

Student services. Adult student services, alcohol/substance abuse counseling, career counseling, services for economically disadvantaged, student employment services, financial aid counseling, health services, legal services, minority student services, on-campus daycare, personal counseling, placement for graduates, veterans' counselor, women's services. **Physically disabled:** Services for visually, speech, hearing impaired.

Contact. E-mail: go2esu@emporia.edu
Phone: (620) 341-5465 Toll-free number: (877) 468-6378
Fax: (620) 341-5599
Laura Eddy, Director of Admissions, Emporia State University, One Kellogg Circle, Campus Box 4034, Emporia, KS 66801-5415

Fort Hays State University

Hays, Kansas
www.fhsu.edu

CB member
CB code: 6218

- Public 4-year university
- Commuter campus in large town
- 11,503 degree-seeking undergraduates: 51% part-time, 61% women, 4% African American, 1% Asian American, 7% Hispanic/Latino, 2% Multi-racial, non-Hispanic, 29% international
- 2,096 degree-seeking graduate students
- 86% of applicants admitted
- 42% graduate within 6 years

General. Founded in 1902. Regionally accredited. **Degrees:** 2,494 bachelor's, 106 associate awarded; master's offered. **Location:** 170 miles from Wichita, 270 miles from Kansas City. **Calendar:** Semester, extensive summer session. **Full-time faculty:** 315 total; 61% have terminal degrees, 10% minority, 45% women. **Part-time faculty:** 229 total; 2% have terminal degrees, 4% minority, 53% women. **Class size:** 43% < 20, 50% 20-39, 3% 40-49, 4% 50-99, less than 1% >100.

Freshman class profile. 2,337 applied, 2,007 admitted, 962 enrolled.

Mid 50% test scores		Rank in top tenth:	13%
ACT composite:	18-24	Return as sophomores:	69%
GPA 3.75 or higher:	30%	Out-of-state:	23%
GPA 3.50-3.74:	19%	Live on campus:	74%
GPA 3.0-3.49:	28%	International:	2%
GPA 2.0-2.99:	22%	Fraternities:	5%
Rank in top quarter:	32%	Sororities:	7%

Basis for selection. One of the following required: 21 ACT, rank in top third of high school class, or 2.0 GPA on Kansas pre-college curriculum (2.5 GPA for out-of-state students). Audition recommended for music majors.

Four-Year Colleges

High school preparation. College-preparatory program recommended. 14 units recommended. Recommended units include English 4, mathematics 3, social studies 2, history 1, science 3 and computer science 1.

2015-2016 Annual costs. Tuition/fees: $4,654; $13,657 out-of-state. Room/board: $7,477. Books/supplies: $900. Personal expenses: $2,082.

2014-2015 Financial aid. Need-based: 516 full-time freshmen applied for aid; 429 deemed to have need; 414 received aid. Average need met was 47%. Average scholarship/grant was $4,879; average loan $2,847. 37% of total undergraduate aid awarded as scholarships/grants, 63% as loans/jobs. **Non-need-based:** Awarded to 779 full-time undergraduates, including 168 freshmen. Scholarships awarded for academics, alumni affiliation, art, job skills, leadership, minority status, music/drama, state residency.

Application procedures. Admission: No deadline. $30 fee. Admission notification on a rolling basis. **Financial aid:** Priority date 3/1; no closing date. FAFSA, institutional form required. Applicants notified on a rolling basis starting 3/15; must reply within 2 week(s) of notification.

Academics. Special study options: Combined bachelor's/graduate degree, distance learning, double major, dual enrollment of high school students, ESL, exchange student, external degree, honors, independent study, internships, liberal arts/career combination, student-designed major, study abroad, teacher certification program, United Nations semester, weekend college. **Credit/placement by examination:** AP, CLEP, ACT, institutional tests. **Support services:** Learning center, pre-admission summer program, reduced course load, remedial instruction, study skills assistance, tutoring, writing center.

Majors. Biology: General. **Business:** General, accounting, business admin, market research, marketing, office management. **Communications:** Communications/speech/rhetoric. **Computer sciences:** General. **Education:** Business, elementary, music, physical, technology/industrial arts, trade/industrial. **English:** English lit. **Foreign languages:** General. **Health services:** Physical therapy assistant, sonography. **History:** General. **Human services:** Social work. **Math:** General. **Philosophy/religion:** Philosophy. **Physical sciences:** Chemistry, geology, physics. **Protective services:** Criminal justice. **Psychology:** General. **Social sciences:** Economics, political science, sociology. **Visual/performing arts:** Art, music.

Most popular majors. Business/marketing 46%, education 12%, health sciences 7%, liberal arts 10%.

Technology on campus. 1,400 workstations in dormitories, library, computer center, student center. Dormitories linked to campus network. Commuter students can connect to campus network. Online course registration, helpline, repair service, wireless network available.

Student life. Freshman orientation: Mandatory, $25 fee. Preregistration for classes offered. Three-day program before start of classes; includes skills training. **Housing:** Guaranteed on-campus for freshmen. Coed dorms, single-sex dorms, apartments, fraternity/sorority housing available. $35 nonrefundable deposit. **Activities:** Bands, campus ministries, choral groups, dance, drama, international student organizations, literary magazine, music ensembles, Model UN, musical theater, opera, radio station, student government, student newspaper, symphony orchestra, TV station, Campus Crusade for Christ, Disciples of the Catholic Campus Center, black student union, Hispanic American leadership organization, Young Republicans, Young Democrats.

Athletics. NCAA. **Intercollegiate:** Baseball M, basketball, cross-country, football (tackle) M, golf, gymnastics W, rodeo, soccer M, softball W, tennis, track and field, volleyball W, wrestling M. **Intramural:** Archery, badminton, baseball M, basketball, bowling, cross-country, diving, fencing, field hockey W, gymnastics W, racquetball, soccer, softball, swimming, table tennis, tennis, track and field, volleyball, water polo, wrestling M. **Team name:** Tigers.

Student services. Adult student services, career counseling, student employment services, financial aid counseling, health services, on-campus daycare, personal counseling, placement for graduates, veterans' counselor. **Physically disabled:** Services for visually, speech, hearing impaired.

Contact. E-mail: tigers@fhsu.edu
Phone: (785) 628-3478 Toll-free number: (888) 628-3478
Fax: (800) 432-0428
Tricia Cline, Director of Admissions, Fort Hays State University, 600 Park Street, Hays, KS 67601

Friends University
Wichita, Kansas
www.friends.edu — CB code: 6224

- Private 4-year university and liberal arts college affiliated with the non-denominational tradition
- Commuter campus in large city

- 1,417 degree-seeking undergraduates
- 538 graduate students

General. Founded in 1898. Regionally accredited. **Degrees:** 404 bachelor's, 11 associate awarded; master's offered. **Location:** 1 mile from downtown. **Calendar:** Semester, limited summer session. **Full-time faculty:** 74 total; 78% have terminal degrees, 5% minority, 42% women. **Part-time faculty:** 157 total; 8% minority, 51% women. **Class size:** 62% < 20, 35% 20-39, 3% 50-99, less than 1% >100. **Special facilities:** Art center, observatory, Quaker collection.

Freshman class profile.

GPA 3.75 or higher:	23%	Rank in top quarter:	33%
GPA 3.50-3.74:	17%	Rank in top tenth:	12%
GPA 3.0-3.49:	33%	Out-of-state:	22%
GPA 2.0-2.99:	26%	Live on campus:	65%

Basis for selection. ACT score multiplied by GPA must equal 45 or above for admission. Those with a score of less than 45 but equal to 20 or above are admitted provisionally. SAT and SAT Subject Tests or ACT recommended. Audition required for music, dance, and theater programs. Portfolio required for art program. **Home schooled:** Transcript of courses and grades, interview, letter of recommendation (nonparent) required. Interview and letter of recommendation is required for early admit home schooled applicants.

High school preparation. College-preparatory program recommended. 19 units recommended. Recommended units include English 3, mathematics 3, social studies 2, history 2, science 1 (laboratory 1), foreign language 2 and computer science 1.

2015-2016 Annual costs. Tuition/fees: $25,830. Room/board: $7,320. Books/supplies: $1,500. Personal expenses: $1,800.

2014-2015 Financial aid. Need-based: 167 full-time freshmen applied for aid; 149 deemed to have need; 149 received aid. Average need met was 81%. Average scholarship/grant was $7,423; average loan $3,188. 67% of total undergraduate aid awarded as scholarships/grants, 33% as loans/jobs. **Non-need-based:** Awarded to 1,386 full-time undergraduates, including 254 freshmen. Scholarships awarded for academics, alumni affiliation, art, athletics, leadership, music/drama, religious affiliation.

Application procedures. Admission: No deadline. $35 fee. Admission notification on a rolling basis. **Financial aid:** Priority date 3/15; no closing date. FAFSA required. Applicants notified on a rolling basis starting 3/1; must reply within 3 week(s) of notification.

Academics. Special study options: Accelerated study, cross-registration, distance learning, double major, dual enrollment of high school students, exchange student, honors, internships, student-designed major, study abroad, teacher certification program. Degree completion programs for working adults. **Credit/placement by examination:** AP, CLEP, IB, SAT, ACT, institutional tests. 15 credit hours maximum toward associate degree, 60 toward bachelor's. **Support services:** Reduced course load, remedial instruction, study skills assistance, tutoring, writing center.

Majors. Biology: General, environmental, wildlife. **Business:** Accounting, business admin, e-commerce, human resources, international, management information systems, management science, marketing, nonprofit/public. **Communications:** General. **Computer sciences:** General, information systems, programming. **Education:** Art, business, early childhood, elementary, English, history, mathematics, middle, music, physical, science, secondary, social science, Spanish, speech. **English:** English lit. **Foreign languages:** Spanish. **Health services:** Health care admin, radiologic technology/medical imaging. **History:** General. **Liberal arts:** Arts/sciences. **Math:** General. **Parks/recreation:** Health/fitness, sports admin. **Philosophy/religion:** General, Christian, religion. **Physical sciences:** Chemistry. **Protective services:** Criminal justice. **Psychology:** General. **Social sciences:** Political science, sociology. **Theology:** Youth ministry. **Visual/performing arts:** Art, ballet, dance, dramatic, music, music performance.

Technology on campus. 360 workstations in dormitories, library, computer center. Dormitories wired for high-speed internet access and linked to campus network. Commuter students can connect to campus network. Online course registration, online library, helpline, wireless network available.

Student life. Freshman orientation: Mandatory. Preregistration for classes offered. Held in early August and early January. **Policies:** Students are expected to follow Community Life Standards set forth by the University. **Housing:** Coed dorms, apartments available. $100 nonrefundable deposit. Married students should contact housing director for options. **Activities:** Bands, campus ministries, choral groups, dance, drama, international student organizations, literary magazine, music ensembles, Model UN, musical theater, opera, student government, student newspaper, symphony orchestra, Acts of Faith, History/Political Science Club, The Group, Young Democrats, Student Government Association, Friends Enterprise Club.

Athletics. NAIA. **Intercollegiate:** Baseball M, basketball, cheerleading, cross-country, football (tackle) M, golf M, soccer, softball W, tennis, track and field, volleyball W. **Intramural:** Basketball, football (non-tackle), soccer, softball, table tennis, ultimate frisbee, volleyball. **Team name:** Falcons.

Student services. Adult student services, alcohol/substance abuse counseling, chaplain/spiritual director, career counseling, student employment services, financial aid counseling, health services, personal counseling, placement for graduates, veterans' counselor. **Physically disabled:** Services for visually, speech, hearing impaired.

Contact. E-mail: admissions@friends.edu
Phone: (316) 295-5100 Toll-free number: (800) 794-6945
Fax: (316) 295-5020
Jim Allen, Director of CBASE Admissions, Friends University, 2100 West University Avenue, Wichita, KS 67213

Grantham University
Lenexa, Kansas
www.grantham.edu   **CB code: 2244**

- For-profit 4-year virtual university
- Large city
- 11,092 degree-seeking undergraduates: 35% African American, 1% Asian American, 6% Hispanic/Latino, 1% Native American, 2% Multiracial, non-Hispanic
- 1,992 graduate students
- Interview required

General. Founded in 1951. Accredited by DETC. **Degrees:** 1,065 bachelor's, 925 associate awarded; master's offered. **Location:** 20 miles from Kansas City. **Calendar:** Differs by program, extensive summer session. **Full-time faculty:** 44 total; 20% have terminal degrees. **Part-time faculty:** 319 total; 34% have terminal degrees. **Class size:** 73% < 20, 27% 20-39.

Freshman class profile. 4,528 applied, 3,149 admitted, 1,959 enrolled.

Basis for selection. Open admission, but selective for some programs. **Home schooled:** Transcript of courses and grades, interview, letter of recommendation (nonparent) required. Application essay, evidence of the coursework completed and level of performance, and telephone interview required of all home school applicants. **Learning Disabled:** Reasonable accommodations or services provided to qualified students with disabilities.

2015-2016 Annual costs. Tuition/fees: $16,108. Room/board: $13,568. Books/supplies: $664.

Application procedures. Admission: No deadline. No application fee. Application must be submitted online. Admission notification on a rolling basis. **Financial aid:** No deadline. FAFSA required.

Academics. Special study options: Accelerated study, combined bachelor's/graduate degree, distance learning, independent study, internships, weekend college. **Credit/placement by examination:** AP, CLEP, IB. 45 credit hours maximum toward associate degree, 90 toward bachelor's. **Support services:** Learning center, reduced course load, remedial instruction, study skills assistance, tutoring, writing center.

Majors. Business: Accounting, business admin, human resources, information resources management. **Computer sciences:** Computer science, networking. **Protective services:** Law enforcement admin.

Most popular majors. Business/marketing 32%, computer/information sciences 12%, engineering/engineering technologies 12%, interdisciplinary studies 27%, security/protective services 13%.

Technology on campus. PC or laptop required. Online course registration, online library, helpline available.

Student life. Freshman orientation: Mandatory. Preregistration for classes offered. Student Success course familiarizes students with procedures to navigate within Grantham University's online learning environment.

Athletics. Team name: Fighting Eagles.

Student services. Adult student services, career counseling, financial aid counseling, veterans' counselor.

Contact. E-mail: admissions@grantham.edu
Toll-free number: (888) 947-2684
Jared Parlette, Vice President of Student Enrollment, Grantham University, 16025 W 113th Street, Lenexa, KS 66219

Haskell Indian Nations University
Lawrence, Kansas
www.haskell.edu   **CB code: 0919**

- Public 4-year university
- Residential campus in small city
- 803 degree-seeking undergraduates: 4% part-time, 52% women, 100% Native American
- 55% of applicants admitted
- SAT or ACT (ACT writing optional), application essay required

General. Founded in 1884. Regionally accredited. Federally owned and operated college provides educational benefits to Federally recognized North American Indians who are under jurisdiction of Bureau of Indian Affairs. **Degrees:** 94 bachelor's, 100 associate awarded. **ROTC:** Army. **Location:** Lawrence, KS. **Calendar:** Semester, limited summer session. **Full-time faculty:** 36 total; 31% have terminal degrees, 78% minority, 50% women. **Part-time faculty:** 45 total; 24% have terminal degrees, 40% minority, 60% women. **Class size:** 59% < 20, 38% 20-39, 4% 40-49. **Special facilities:** Cultural center, wetlands.

Freshman class profile. 327 applied, 179 admitted, 177 enrolled.

Mid 50% test scores			
		GPA 3.50-3.74:	9%
SAT math:	390-470	GPA 3.0-3.49:	30%
SAT writing:	350-430	GPA 2.0-2.99:	50%
ACT composite:	16-19	Out-of-state:	77%
GPA 3.75 or higher:	4%	Live on campus:	89%

Basis for selection. ACT/SAT scores, secondary school Grade Point Average (GPA) or GED scores and secondary school class ranking. Applicant must be a member of a federally-recognized tribe or quarter degree descendant of tribal member recognized by the Bureau of Indian Affairs. ACT/SAT scores are not required for student over 21 years of age. **Learning Disabled:** Must provide IEP from high school and test scores not more than 2 years old.

High school preparation. College-preparatory program recommended. Recommended units include English 4, mathematics 4, history 2, science 2 (laboratory 1) and foreign language 1.

2015-2016 Annual costs. Tuition/fees: $1,610. Room/board: $248. Books/supplies: $210. Personal expenses: $1,400.

Financial aid. Additional information: Some personal expenses may be offset by Bureau of Indian Affairs grants. Most students qualify for only minimum Pell grant.

Application procedures. Admission: Closing date 6/1 (receipt date). $10 fee. Application must be submitted on paper. Admission notification on a rolling basis beginning on or about 6/1. **Financial aid:** Priority date 5/15; no closing date. FAFSA required. Applicants notified on a rolling basis starting 3/15; must reply within 9 week(s) of notification.

Academics. Special study options: Internships, student-designed major, teacher certification program. **Credit/placement by examination:** AP, CLEP, institutional tests. 10 credit hours maximum toward associate degree. **Support services:** Learning center, reduced course load, remedial instruction, tutoring, writing center.

Majors. Area/ethnic studies: Native American. **Business:** Business admin. **Conservation:** General. **Education:** General, elementary.

Most popular majors. Area/ethnic studies 30%, business/marketing 48%, education 11%, natural resources/environmental science 11%.

Technology on campus. 200 workstations in dormitories, library, computer center, student center. Dormitories wired for high-speed internet access and linked to campus network. Online library, helpline, repair service, wireless network available.

Student life. Freshman orientation: Mandatory. Preregistration for classes offered. Three days preceding start of classes. **Housing:** Coed dorms, single-sex dorms, special housing for disabled, apartments available. **Activities:** Pep band, campus ministries, film society, literary magazine, student government, student newspaper, TV station, Native American clubs, Phi Beta Lambda (service organization), Baptist Student Union, LIGHT House (Lutheran organization), Catholic Center.

Athletics. NAIA. **Intercollegiate:** Basketball, cross-country, football (tackle) M, golf M, softball, track and field, volleyball. **Intramural:** Basketball, softball, volleyball. **Team name:** Indians.

Student services. Adult student services, alcohol/substance abuse counseling, career counseling, student employment services, financial aid counseling, health services, on-campus daycare, personal counseling, placement for graduates, veterans' counselor, women's services.

Contact. E-mail: admissions@haskell.edu
Phone: (785) 749-8454 Fax: (785) 749-8429
Dorothy Stites, Director of Admissions, Haskell Indian Nations University, 155 Indian Avenue #5031, Lawrence, KS 66046-4800

Kansas State University
Manhattan, Kansas   **CB member**
www.k-state.edu   **CB code: 6334**

- Public 4-year university
- Residential campus in small city
- 19,443 degree-seeking undergraduates: 9% part-time, 48% women, 4% African American, 1% Asian American, 7% Hispanic/Latino, 3% Multiracial, non-Hispanic, 6% international
- 3,995 degree-seeking graduate students
- 95% of applicants admitted
- 62% graduate within 6 years

General. Founded in 1863. Regionally accredited. Additional campuses at Salina, Kansas and Olathe, Kansas. Off-campus sites include Fort Riley and Fort Leavenworth army bases. **Degrees:** 3,887 bachelor's, 43 associate awarded; master's, professional, doctoral offered. **ROTC:** Army, Air Force. **Location:** 120 miles from Kansas City, Missouri. **Calendar:** Semester, extensive summer session. **Full-time faculty:** 1,085 total; 84% have terminal degrees, 16% minority, 42% women. **Part-time faculty:** 192 total; 54% have terminal degrees, 5% minority, 52% women. **Class size:** 41% < 20, 38% 20-39, 8% 40-49, 8% 50-99, 6% >100. **Special facilities:** Native prairie for biological research, laser laboratory, cancer research center, nuclear reactor, insect zoo, biosecurity research institute.

Freshman class profile. 9,178 applied, 8,712 admitted, 3,624 enrolled.

Mid 50% test scores		Rank in top quarter:	47%
ACT composite:	22-28	Rank in top tenth:	22%
GPA 3.75 or higher:	38%	Return as sophomores:	87%
GPA 3.50-3.74:	20%	Out-of-state:	18%
GPA 3.0-3.49:	28%	Live on campus:	74%
GPA 2.0-2.99:	14%	International:	3%

Basis for selection. Minimum 2.0 GPA on Kansas pre-college curriculum (2.5 GPA for out-of-state students) plus one of following required: minimum ACT score of 21 or rank in top third of high school class. ACT tests may be used to meet State of Kansas admissions requirements, but are not required. SAT or ACT recommended. ACT tests may be used to meet State of Kansas admissions requirements, but are not required. Audition recommended for music and theater majors. Portfolio recommended for art and architecture majors. **Home schooled:** Admission based on ACT or SAT scores or GED scores. Achieve a 21 or higher composite score on the ACT or a 980 or higher on the SAT.

High school preparation. College-preparatory program required. 16 units required. Required units include English 4, mathematics 3, social studies 3, science 3 and academic electives 3.

2015-2016 Annual costs. Tuition/fees: $9,350; $23,429 out-of-state. Room/board: $8,380. Books/supplies: $856. Personal expenses: $3,860.

2014-2015 Financial aid. **Need-based:** 2,853 full-time freshmen applied for aid; 1,955 deemed to have need; 1,916 received aid. Average need met was 78%. Average scholarship/grant was $4,578; average loan $3,669. 43% of total undergraduate aid awarded as scholarships/grants, 57% as loans/jobs. **Non-need-based:** Awarded to 6,486 full-time undergraduates, including 2,173 freshmen. Scholarships awarded for academics, alumni affiliation, art, athletics, leadership, music/drama, ROTC, state residency.

Application procedures. **Admission:** No deadline. $30 fee, may be waived for applicants with need. Admission notification on a rolling basis. **Financial aid:** Priority date 3/1; no closing date. FAFSA required. Applicants notified on a rolling basis starting 4/1; must reply within 2 week(s) of notification.

Academics. **Special study options:** Accelerated study, combined bachelor's/graduate degree, cooperative education, distance learning, double major, ESL, exchange student, honors, independent study, internships, study abroad, teacher certification program. **Credit/placement by examination:** AP, CLEP, IB, SAT, ACT. 10 credit hours maximum toward associate degree, 20 toward bachelor's. PEP, DANTES exams accepted for credit. **Support**

services: Learning center, pre-admission summer program, reduced course load, remedial instruction, study skills assistance, tutoring, writing center.

Majors. **Architecture:** Architecture. **Area/ethnic studies:** General, women's. **Biology:** General, biochemistry, microbiology, wildlife. **Business:** General, accounting, business admin, entrepreneurial studies, finance, financial planning, hospitality admin, marketing. **Communications:** Communications/speech/rhetoric, journalism. **Computer sciences:** General, information systems. **Conservation:** Environmental studies, management/policy. **Education:** Agricultural, art, elementary, family/consumer sciences, music, secondary. **Engineering:** Agricultural, architectural, chemical, civil, computer, electrical, industrial, mechanical. **English:** English lit. **Foreign languages:** General. **Health services:** Athletic training, communication disorders, dietetics, preveterinary. **History:** General. **Human services:** Social work. **Liberal arts:** Humanities. **Math:** General, statistics. **Parks/recreation:** Exercise sciences, facilities management. **Philosophy/religion:** Philosophy. **Physical sciences:** General, chemistry, geology, physics. **Psychology:** General. **Social sciences:** General, anthropology, economics, geography, political science, sociology. **Visual/performing arts:** Dramatic, interior design, music, music performance, studio arts. **Work/family studies:** General, child development, clothing/textiles, family studies, human nutrition.

Most popular majors. Agriculture 13%, business/marketing 18%, education 7%, engineering/engineering technologies 13%, family/consumer sciences 7%, social sciences 10%.

Technology on campus. 547 workstations in dormitories, library, computer center, student center. Dormitories wired for high-speed internet access and linked to campus network. Commuter students can connect to campus network. Online course registration, online library, helpline, repair service, wireless network available.

Student life. **Freshman orientation:** Available, $25 fee. Preregistration for classes offered. **Housing:** Coed dorms, single-sex dorms, apartments, cooperative housing, fraternity/sorority housing available. $400 fully refundable deposit. Honors housing available. **Activities:** Bands, campus ministries, choral groups, dance, drama, international student organizations, music ensembles, musical theater, radio station, student government, student newspaper, symphony orchestra, TV station, 340 religious, political, ethnic, and social service clubs and organizations available.

Athletics. NCAA. **Intercollegiate:** Baseball M, basketball, cross-country, football (tackle) M, golf, rowing (crew) W, soccer W, tennis W, track and field, volleyball W. **Intramural:** Badminton, basketball, bowling, cross-country, golf, handball, soccer, softball, squash, swimming, table tennis, tennis, track and field, volleyball, water polo, wrestling M. **Team name:** Wildcats.

Student services. Adult student services, alcohol/substance abuse counseling, career counseling, student employment services, financial aid counseling, health services, legal services, minority student services, on-campus daycare, personal counseling, placement for graduates, veterans' counselor, women's services. **Physically disabled:** Services for visually, speech, hearing impaired.

Contact. E-mail: k-state@k-state.edu
Phone: (785) 532-6250 Toll-free number: (800) 432-8270
Fax: (785) 532-6393
Larry Moeder, Assistant Vice President for Student Financial Assistance and Admissions, Kansas State University, 119 Anderson Hall, Manhattan, KS 66506

Kansas Wesleyan University
Salina, Kansas
www.kwu.edu   **CB code: 6337**

- Private 4-year university and liberal arts college affiliated with the United Methodist Church
- Residential campus in large town
- 665 degree-seeking undergraduates: 7% part-time, 48% women, 9% African American, 15% Hispanic/Latino, 1% Native American, 2% Multi-racial, non-Hispanic, 2% international
- 58 degree-seeking graduate students
- 62% of applicants admitted
- SAT or ACT (ACT writing optional) required
- 41% graduate within 6 years; 23% enter graduate study

General. Founded in 1886. Regionally accredited. **Degrees:** 145 bachelor's, 2 associate awarded; master's offered. **Location:** 90 miles from Wichita, 180 miles from Kansas City. **Calendar:** Semester, limited summer session. **Full-time faculty:** 41 total; 58% have terminal degrees, 7% minority, 51% women.

Part-time faculty: 79 total; 15% have terminal degrees, 6% minority, 57% women. **Class size:** 69% < 20, 27% 20-39, 3% 40-49, less than 1% 50-99.

Freshman class profile. 818 applied, 504 admitted, 160 enrolled.

Mid 50% test scores			
SAT critical reading:	430-520	Rank in top quarter:	29%
SAT math:	480-550	Rank in top tenth:	14%
ACT composite:	20-24	End year in good standing:	89%
GPA 3.75 or higher:	23%	Return as sophomores:	63%
GPA 3.50-3.74:	25%	Out-of-state:	63%
GPA 3.0-3.49:	36%	Live on campus:	96%
GPA 2.0-2.99:	16%	International:	1%

Basis for selection. Applicant must have ACT composite score of 18 or SAT combined score of 860 (exclusive of Writing) and high school GPA of 2.5 or rank in top half of class. ACT or SAT Scores are required of all degree seeking freshman & transfer students who have earned less than 24 transferable college credit hours. International Students from non-English speaking countries are not required to submit and ACT/SAT, however they must submit a TOEFL. Interview recommended for academically weak applicants. Audition recommended for music majors. Portfolio recommended for art majors. **Home schooled:** Transcript of courses and grades required.

High school preparation. Recommended units include English 4, mathematics 3, social studies 3, science 3 (laboratory 1), foreign language 2, computer science 1, visual/performing arts 1 and academic electives 8.

2016-2017 Annual costs. Tuition/fees: $28,000. Room/board: $8,600. Books/supplies: $800. Personal expenses: $1,924.

2014-2015 Financial aid. Need-based: 141 full-time freshmen applied for aid; 127 deemed to have need; 127 received aid. Average need met was 74%. Average scholarship/grant was $9,003; average loan $3,851. 62% of total undergraduate aid awarded as scholarships/grants, 38% as loans/jobs. **Non-need-based:** Awarded to 694 full-time undergraduates, including 172 freshmen. Scholarships awarded for academics, alumni affiliation, art, athletics, job skills, music/drama, religious affiliation. **Additional information:** Awards available for residence hall students: minimum $7,000 for 3.0 GPA plus ACT score of 22 or SAT of 950 (exclusive of Writing); minimum $8,000 for 3.5 GPA plus ACT score of 22 or SAT score of 1030 (exclusive of Writing); minimum $9,000 for 3.75 GPA plus ACT score of 25 or SAT score of 1140 (exclusive of Writing). Application deadline March 15.

Application procedures. Admission: No deadline. $20 fee, may be waived for applicants with need. Admission notification on a rolling basis. **Financial aid:** Closing date 3/15. FAFSA required. Applicants notified on a rolling basis starting 2/1; must reply by 8/1 or within 3 week(s) of notification.

Academics. Special study options: Combined bachelor's/graduate degree, cross-registration, distance learning, double major, dual enrollment of high school students, honors, independent study, internships, liberal arts/career combination, student-designed major, study abroad, teacher certification program, Washington semester. **Credit/placement by examination:** AP, CLEP, IB, SAT, ACT, institutional tests. 30 credit hours maximum toward bachelor's degree. Students scoring 50 or above on the CLEP exam will receive credit according to the corresponding course. Credit by Examination: To receive credit by examination, a student must arrange with the instructor of the course to take the examination and have the examination graded before the date listed in the academic calendar. Credit is granted to students who earn "A" or "B" on the examination. Credit by examination is not used in determining students' course loads since the courses are considered completed when the examinations are taken. Application for credit by examination is made to the Registrar and approved by the department offering the course. **Support services:** Learning center, reduced course load, remedial instruction, study skills assistance, tutoring, writing center.

Majors. Biology: General. **Business:** Accounting, business admin, human resources, marketing, organizational leadership. **Communications:** Communications/speech/rhetoric, public relations. **Computer sciences:** General, computer science. **Conservation:** Environmental science, environmental studies. **Education:** Art, elementary, English, secondary. **Engineering:** Preengineering. **English:** English lit, writing. **Health services:** Nursing (RN). **History:** General. **Liberal arts:** Arts/sciences. **Math:** General. **Parks/recreation:** Exercise sciences, health/fitness, sports admin. **Philosophy/religion:** Philosophy, religion. **Physical sciences:** Chemistry, forensic chemistry, physics. **Protective services:** Disaster management, law enforcement admin. **Psychology:** General, applied, counseling, family, medical. **Social sciences:** Sociology. **Visual/performing arts:** General, dramatic, drawing, graphic design, music, music performance, painting, photography.

Most popular majors. Business/marketing 19%, education 8%, health sciences 22%, parks/recreation 11%, visual/performing arts 6%.

Technology on campus. 50 workstations in library, computer center, student center. Dormitories wired for high-speed internet access and linked to campus network. Commuter students can connect to campus network.

Online course registration, online library, helpline, repair service, wireless network available.

Student life. Freshman orientation: Available. Preregistration for classes offered. Held during the summer. **Housing:** Guaranteed on-campus for freshmen. Coed dorms, single-sex dorms, apartments available. $200 nonrefundable deposit, deadline 8/15. **Activities:** Bands, campus ministries, choral groups, dance, drama, international student organizations, literary magazine, music ensembles, musical theater, radio station, student government, student newspaper, symphony orchestra, TV station, Art club, Alpha Chi, Phi Alpha Alpha Theta, SNO, SPES, Coyote Sports Gaming Network, drama club, KKWU NewsDesk, Multicultural Student Union.

Athletics. NAIA. **Intercollegiate:** Baseball M, basketball, bowling, cheerleading, cross-country, football (tackle) M, golf, soccer, softball W, tennis, track and field, volleyball W, wrestling M. **Intramural:** Basketball, soccer, softball, volleyball, weight lifting. **Team name:** Coyotes.

Student services. Adult student services, chaplain/spiritual director, career counseling, student employment services, financial aid counseling, minority student services, personal counseling, placement for graduates, veterans' counselor. **Physically disabled:** Services for visually, speech, hearing impaired.

Contact. E-mail: admissions@kwu.edu
Phone: (785) 833-2285 Fax: (785) 404-1485
Esteban Paredes, Director of Admissions, Kansas Wesleyan University, 100 East Claflin Avenue, Salina, KS 67401-6196

Manhattan Christian College
Manhattan, Kansas
www.mccks.edu   **CB code: 6392**

- Private 4-year Bible college affiliated with the Christian Church
- Residential campus in small city
- 294 degree-seeking undergraduates: 22% part-time, 44% women
- SAT or ACT (ACT writing optional), application essay required

General. Founded in 1927. Regionally accredited; also accredited by ABHE. Students have access to Kansas State University library and facilities at student rates. **Degrees:** 48 bachelor's, 10 associate awarded. **ROTC:** Army, Air Force. **Location:** 130 miles from Kansas City. **Calendar:** Semester, limited summer session. **Full-time faculty:** 10 total. **Part-time faculty:** 27 total.

Freshman class profile.

Out-of-state:	38%	Live on campus:	98%

Basis for selection. High school record, test scores, recommendations important. Character recommendations required. Interview recommended. Audition required for music majors. **Home schooled:** Transcript of courses and grades required.

High school preparation. College-preparatory program recommended. Recommended units include English 4, mathematics 2 and science 2.

2015-2016 Annual costs. Tuition/fees: $14,290. Room/board: $8,254. Books/supplies: $2,000. Personal expenses: $1,982.

Financial aid. Non-need-based: Scholarships awarded for academics, leadership, music/drama.

Application procedures. Admission: Priority date 4/1; no deadline. $25 fee, may be waived for applicants with need. Admission notification on a rolling basis beginning on or about 10/15. **Financial aid:** Priority date 4/1; no closing date. FAFSA required. Applicants notified on a rolling basis starting 4/1; must reply within 2 week(s) of notification.

Academics. Special study options: Combined bachelor's/graduate degree, distance learning, double major, dual enrollment of high school students, internships, liberal arts/career combination. Dual degree program with Kansas State University and Manhattan Area Technical College. **Credit/placement by examination:** AP, CLEP, IB, SAT, ACT, institutional tests. 18 credit hours maximum toward associate degree, 36 toward bachelor's. **Support services:** Reduced course load, study skills assistance, tutoring.

Majors. Business: Business admin. **Philosophy/religion:** Religion. **Theology:** Bible, missionary, pastoral counseling, preministerial, religious ed, sacred music, theology, youth ministry.

Most popular majors. Business/marketing 26%, philosophy/religious studies 74%.

Technology on campus. 12 workstations in library. Commuter students can connect to campus network. Online course registration, repair service, wireless network available.

Student life. Freshman orientation: Mandatory. Preregistration for classes offered. Three-day program held prior to start of classes. **Policies:** Religious observance required. **Housing:** Guaranteed on-campus for freshmen. Single-sex dorms, apartments available. $125 fully refundable deposit, deadline 6/1. **Activities:** Campus ministries, choral groups, drama, music ensembles, student government.

Athletics. NCCAA. **Intercollegiate:** Baseball M, basketball, cross-country, soccer, volleyball W. **Team name:** Thunder.

Student services. Career counseling, student employment services, financial aid counseling, health services, personal counseling, placement for graduates. **Physically disabled:** Services for speech impaired.

Contact. E-mail: admit@mccks.edu
Phone: (785) 539-3571 Toll-free number: (877) 246-4622
Fax: (785) 776-9251
Nick Brown, Director of Admissions, Manhattan Christian College, 1415 Anderson Avenue, Manhattan, KS 66502

McPherson College
McPherson, Kansas
www.mcpherson.edu CB code: 6404

- Private 4-year liberal arts college affiliated with the Church of the Brethren
- Residential campus in large town
- 643 degree-seeking undergraduates: 4% part-time, 38% women, 10% African American, 1% Asian American, 12% Hispanic/Latino, 1% Native American, 2% Multi-racial, non-Hispanic, 4% international
- 34 degree-seeking graduate students
- 45% of applicants admitted
- SAT or ACT (ACT writing optional) required
- 50% graduate within 6 years

General. Founded in 1887. Regionally accredited. **Degrees:** 114 bachelor's awarded; master's offered. **Location:** 60 miles from Wichita. **Calendar:** 4-1-4. **Full-time faculty:** 34 total; 15% have terminal degrees, 15% minority, 32% women. **Part-time faculty:** 41 total; 7% have terminal degrees, 10% minority, 46% women. **Class size:** 77% < 20, 23% 20-39.

Freshman class profile. 1,070 applied, 479 admitted, 388 enrolled.

Mid 50% test scores		GPA 2.0-2.99:	23%
SAT critical reading:	460-580	Rank in top quarter:	40%
SAT math:	440-550	Rank in top tenth:	12%
ACT composite:	15-24	Return as sophomores:	56%
GPA 3.75 or higher:	19%	Out-of-state:	56%
GPA 3.50-3.74:	19%	Live on campus:	97%
GPA 3.0-3.49:	39%	International:	3%

Basis for selection. Satisfactory high school performance or completion of GED, corresponding standardized test scores, and appropriate personal qualities. Portfolio required for auto restoration program. **Home schooled:** Transcript of courses and grades required.

High school preparation. College-preparatory program recommended.

2015-2016 Annual costs. Tuition/fees: $25,977. Room/board: $8,450. Books/supplies: $1,300. Personal expenses: $2,580.

2014-2015 Financial aid. Need-based: 167 full-time freshmen applied for aid; 152 deemed to have need; 152 received aid. Average need met was 100%. Average scholarship/grant was $5,653; average loan $10,879. 27% of total undergraduate aid awarded as scholarships/grants, 73% as loans/jobs. **Non-need-based:** Awarded to 921 full-time undergraduates, including 306 freshmen. Scholarships awarded for academics, alumni affiliation, art, athletics, music/drama, religious affiliation, state residency.

Application procedures. Admission: Priority date 3/1; no deadline. $25 fee, may be waived for applicants with need, free for online applicants. Admission notification on a rolling basis beginning on or about 6/1. Must reply by May 1 or within 4 week(s) if notified thereafter. **Financial aid:** Priority date 3/1; no closing date. FAFSA required. Applicants notified on a rolling basis starting 3/1; must reply within 3 week(s) of notification.

Academics. Special study options: Cross-registration, double major, dual enrollment of high school students, ESL, exchange student, independent study, internships, liberal arts/career combination, student-designed major,

---

study abroad, teacher certification program, urban semester. **Credit/placement by examination:** AP, CLEP, IB, institutional tests. No more than 6 credit hours will be accepted in the area of college composition. **Support services:** Learning center, reduced course load, remedial instruction, study skills assistance, tutoring, writing center.

Majors. Biology: General. **Business:** Accounting, business admin, finance, international. **Communications:** Communications/speech/rhetoric. **Education:** General, art, biology, business, chemistry, computer, early childhood, elementary, English, foreign languages, history, mathematics, middle, music, physical, science, social studies, Spanish, special ed, speech, technology/industrial arts. **English:** English lit. **Foreign languages:** General, Spanish. **Health services:** Predental, premedicine, prepharmacy, preveterinary. **History:** General. **Liberal arts:** Arts/sciences. **Math:** General. **Parks/recreation:** Health/fitness. **Physical sciences:** Chemistry. **Psychology:** General. **Social sciences:** Sociology. **Visual/performing arts:** Art, dramatic, music, music performance.

Most popular majors. Biology 6%, business/marketing 19%, education 7%, engineering/engineering technologies 18%, parks/recreation 14%, public administration/social services 6%, social sciences 9%.

Technology on campus. 72 workstations in dormitories, library, computer center, student center. Dormitories wired for high-speed internet access and linked to campus network. Commuter students can connect to campus network. Online course registration, online library, helpline, repair service, wireless network available.

Student life. Freshman orientation: Mandatory. Preregistration for classes offered. Held in August for 2-3 days. **Policies:** No alcohol permitted on campus. Unmarried students under 23 years old are required to live in residence halls. **Housing:** Guaranteed on-campus for freshmen. Coed dorms, single-sex dorms, apartments available. $150 fully refundable deposit, deadline 5/1. **Activities:** Bands, campus ministries, choral groups, dance, drama, music ensembles, musical theater, student government, student newspaper, 28 clubs and organizations available.

Athletics. NAIA. **Intercollegiate:** Baseball M, basketball, cheerleading, cross-country, football (tackle) M, softball W, tennis, track and field, volleyball W. **Intramural:** Badminton, basketball, football (non-tackle), football (tackle) M, handball, racquetball, soccer, softball, table tennis, ultimate frisbee, volleyball. **Team name:** Bulldogs.

Student services. Adult student services, chaplain/spiritual director, career counseling, student employment services, financial aid counseling, health services, personal counseling, placement for graduates. **Physically disabled:** Services for visually, hearing impaired.

Contact. E-mail: admiss@mcpherson.edu
Phone: (620) 242-0400 Toll-free number: (800) 695-7402
Fax: (620) 241-8443
Christi Hopkins, Vice President for Enrollment, McPherson College, 1600 East Euclid Street, McPherson, KS 67460-1402

MidAmerica Nazarene University
Olathe, Kansas
www.mnu.edu CB code: 6437

- Private 4-year university and liberal arts college affiliated with the Church of the Nazarene
- Residential campus in small city
- 1,329 degree-seeking undergraduates: 20% part-time, 58% women, 13% African American, 1% Asian American, 4% Hispanic/Latino, 1% Native American, 1% Native Hawaiian/Pacific islander, 5% Multi-racial, non-Hispanic
- 438 degree-seeking graduate students
- SAT or ACT (ACT writing optional) required
- 50% graduate within 6 years

General. Founded in 1966. Regionally accredited. **Degrees:** 504 bachelor's, 22 associate awarded; master's offered. **ROTC:** Army, Air Force. **Location:** 19 miles from Kansas City. **Calendar:** Semester, limited summer session. **Full-time faculty:** 81 total; 64% have terminal degrees, 48% women. **Part-time faculty:** 140 total. **Class size:** 75% < 20, 19% 20-39, 4% 40-49, 2% 50-99. **Special facilities:** Cultural events center.

Freshman class profile. 191 enrolled.

Mid 50% test scores		Return as sophomores:	74%
ACT composite:	19-25	Live on campus:	72%

Basis for selection. Secondary school record, class rank, test scores, and moral principles important. Nursing, elementary education, and secondary education programs have higher standards for admission. Interview recommended for music, nursing, elementary and secondary education programs. Audition recommended for music majors. **Home schooled:** Transcript of courses and grades, letter of recommendation (nonparent) required.

High school preparation. College-preparatory program recommended. 15 units recommended. Recommended units include English 4, mathematics 3, social studies 3, science 3 and foreign language 1.

2016-2017 Annual costs. Tuition/fees (projected): $27,650. Room/board: $7,900. Books/supplies: $1,200. Personal expenses: $1,454.

Financial aid. Non-need-based: Scholarships awarded for academics, athletics, music/drama, religious affiliation, ROTC.

Application procedures. Admission: Priority date 3/1; deadline 8/1 (postmark date). $25 fee. Admission notification on a rolling basis. **Financial aid:** Priority date 3/1; no closing date. FAFSA required. Applicants notified on a rolling basis starting 1/30; must reply within 2 week(s) of notification.

Academics. Students may earn bachelor's degree through professional program division. **Special study options:** Accelerated study, combined bachelor's/graduate degree, distance learning, double major, dual enrollment of high school students, honors, independent study, internships, student-designed major, study abroad, teacher certification program, Washington semester. **Credit/placement by examination:** AP, CLEP, IB, SAT, ACT, institutional tests. 34 credit hours maximum toward associate degree, 34 toward bachelor's. **Support services:** Learning center, reduced course load, remedial instruction, study skills assistance, tutoring.

Majors. Biology: General. **Business:** General, accounting, business admin, communications, human resources, marketing, organizational leadership. **Communications:** Communications/speech/rhetoric, media studies. **Computer sciences:** Computer science. **Education:** General, biology, elementary, English, history, mathematics, middle, music, physical, secondary, social studies, Spanish, special ed, speech. **English:** English lit. **Foreign languages:** Spanish. **Health services:** Athletic training, nursing (RN). **History:** General. **Human services:** General. **Math:** General. **Parks/recreation:** Exercise sciences, health/fitness, sports admin. **Philosophy/religion:** Religion. **Physical sciences:** Chemistry, forensic chemistry, physics. **Protective services:** Law enforcement admin. **Psychology:** General, industrial. **Social sciences:** General, sociology, urban studies. **Theology:** Bible, missionary, pastoral counseling, religious ed, sacred music, youth ministry. **Visual/performing arts:** General, graphic design, music, music pedagogy, music performance, theater arts management, voice/opera.

Most popular majors. Business/marketing 30%, health sciences 40%.

Technology on campus. 90 workstations in library, computer center. Dormitories wired for high-speed internet access and linked to campus network. Commuter students can connect to campus network. Online course registration, online library, helpline, wireless network available.

Student life. Freshman orientation: Mandatory, $700 fee. Preregistration for classes offered. **Policies:** Religious observance required. **Housing:** Guaranteed on-campus for freshmen. Single-sex dorms, special housing for disabled, apartments, wellness housing available. $100 fully refundable deposit, deadline 8/21. **Activities:** Bands, campus ministries, choral groups, drama, international student organizations, literary magazine, music ensembles, musical theater, radio station, student government, symphony orchestra, TV station, Associated Student Government, Brothers and Sisters United, Covenant Groups, International club, medical careers club, ministry groups, Pi Lambda Theta (education), Psi Chi (psychology honors), SIFE, Sigma Chi.

Athletics. NAIA. **Intercollegiate:** Baseball M, basketball, cheerleading, football (tackle) M, soccer, softball W, volleyball W. **Intramural:** Basketball, bowling, football (non-tackle), golf, soccer, softball, table tennis, tennis, volleyball. **Team name:** Pioneers.

Student services. Adult student services, alcohol/substance abuse counseling, chaplain/spiritual director, financial aid counseling, health services, minority student services, personal counseling, veterans' counselor. **Physically disabled:** Services for visually, speech, hearing impaired.

Contact. E-mail: admissions@mnu.edu
Phone: (913) 971-3380 Toll-free number: (800) 800-8887
Fax: (913) 971-3481
Derrry Ebert, Assoc VP and Dean for Traditional Enrollment, MidAmerica Nazarene University, 2030 East College Way, Olathe, KS 66062-1899

Newman University
Wichita, Kansas　　　　　　　　　　　　**CB member**
www.newmanu.edu　　　　　　　　　　　　**CB code: 6615**

- Private 4-year university and liberal arts college affiliated with the Roman Catholic Church
- Commuter campus in large city
- 1,126 degree-seeking undergraduates: 12% part-time, 66% women, 5% African American, 5% Asian American, 13% Hispanic/Latino, 1% Native American, 3% Multi-racial, non-Hispanic, 6% international
- 426 degree-seeking graduate students
- 56% of applicants admitted
- 46% graduate within 6 years

General. Founded in 1933. Regionally accredited. The university is a sponsored ministry of the Adorers of the Blood of Christ and is named after Blessed John Henry Cardinal Newman. **Degrees:** 266 bachelor's, 55 associate awarded; master's offered. **Location:** 160 miles from Oklahoma City, 180 miles from Kansas City. **Calendar:** Semester, limited summer session. **Full-time faculty:** 87 total; 48% have terminal degrees, 6% minority, 63% women. **Part-time faculty:** 150 total. **Class size:** 69% < 20, 28% 20-39, 2% 40-49, less than 1% 50-99. **Special facilities:** Photography laboratory, cadaver laboratory.

Freshman class profile. 1,284 applied, 715 admitted, 163 enrolled.

Mid 50% test scores			
ACT composite:	20-27.5	Rank in top quarter:	53%
		Rank in top tenth:	26%
GPA 3.75 or higher:	39%	Return as sophomores:	71%
GPA 3.50-3.74:	25%	Out-of-state:	15%
GPA 3.0-3.49:	25%	Live on campus:	53%
GPA 2.0-2.99:	11%	International:	10%

Basis for selection. Minimum GPA 2.0, minimum ACT composite score of 18, or SAT score of 1290 (including Writing). Caliber of high school curriculum important. Portfolio recommended for art majors. **Learning Disabled:** Applicants should submit medical evaluation and recommendation.

High school preparation. College-preparatory program recommended. Recommended units include English 4, mathematics 3, social studies 3 and science 3.

2015-2016 Annual costs. Tuition/fees: $25,720. Room/board: $7,340. Books/supplies: $956. Personal expenses: $1,450.

Financial aid. Non-need-based: Scholarships awarded for academics, art, athletics, leadership, music/drama.

Application procedures. Admission: No deadline. No application fee. Admission notification on a rolling basis beginning on or about 10/1. Must reply by 5/1. **Financial aid:** Closing date 3/1. FAFSA required. Applicants notified on a rolling basis starting 2/1.

Academics. Special study options: Accelerated study, combined bachelor's/graduate degree, cooperative education, cross-registration, distance learning, double major, dual enrollment of high school students, honors, independent study, internships, liberal arts/career combination, student-designed major, study abroad, teacher certification program. **Credit/placement by examination:** AP, CLEP, IB, ACT, institutional tests. 12 credit hours maximum toward bachelor's degree. **Support services:** Learning center, remedial instruction, study skills assistance, tutoring, writing center.

Majors. Biology: General, biochemistry. **Business:** Accounting, business admin, management information systems. **Communications:** Media studies, sports. **Computer sciences:** Information systems. **Education:** General, early childhood special, elementary, middle, secondary. **English:** English lit. **Health services:** Nursing (RN), sonography. **History:** General. **Liberal arts:** Arts/sciences. **Math:** General. **Philosophy/religion:** Philosophy. **Physical sciences:** Chemistry, forensic chemistry. **Protective services:** Forensics, law enforcement admin. **Psychology:** General, counseling. **Social sciences:** Sociology. **Theology:** Pastoral counseling, theology. **Visual/performing arts:** Art.

Most popular majors. Biology 16%, business/marketing 11%, education 14%, health sciences 26%, psychology 8%.

Technology on campus. 90 workstations in dormitories, library, computer center, student center. Dormitories wired for high-speed internet access and linked to campus network. Commuter students can connect to campus network. Online library, helpline, repair service, student web hosting, wireless network available.

Student life. Freshman orientation: Mandatory, $160 fee. Preregistration for classes offered. Weekend prior to first day of class. **Policies:** Freshmen required to live in college housing for first 2 years if not living with parents. **Housing:** Guaranteed on-campus for freshmen. Coed, dorms, apartments, wellness housing available. $75 nonrefundable deposit. **Activities:** Bands, campus ministries, choral groups, dance, drama, international student organizations, literary magazine, music ensembles, musical theater, student government, student newspaper, Koinonia, Service Scholars, Newman Club, Peer Educators, Kansas Catholic College Student Convention, Peer Ministers.

Athletics. NCAA. **Intercollegiate:** Baseball M, basketball, cross-country, golf, soccer, softball W, tennis, volleyball W, wrestling M. **Intramural:** Basketball, football (tackle), table tennis, volleyball. **Team name:** Jets.

Student services. Adult student services, chaplain/spiritual director, career counseling, student employment services, financial aid counseling, personal counseling, placement for graduates. **Physically disabled:** Services for visually, speech, hearing impaired.

Contact. E-mail: admissions@newmanu.edu
Phone: (316) 942-4291 ext. 2144 Toll-free number: (877) 639-6268
Fax: (316) 942-4483
Norm Jones, Vice President for Enrollment Management, Newman University, 3100 McCormick, Wichita, KS 67213-2097

Ottawa University
Ottawa, Kansas — **CB member**
www.ottawa.edu — **CB code: 6547**

▶ Private 4-year university and liberal arts college affiliated with the American Baptist Churches in the USA
▶ Residential campus in large town
▶ 533 degree-seeking undergraduates
▶ Application essay required

General. Founded in 1865. Regionally accredited. Degree programs offered at additional campuses in Overland Park, KS; Phoenix, AZ; Milwaukee, WI; Jeffersonville, IN; and through Ottawa Online. **Degrees:** 104 bachelor's awarded; master's offered. **Location:** 45 miles from Kansas City. **Calendar:** Semester, limited summer session. **Full-time faculty:** 27 total. **Part-time faculty:** 17 total. **Class size:** 76% < 20, 24% 20-39, less than 1% 40-49.

Freshman class profile.

GPA 3.75 or higher:	19%	Rank in top quarter:	36%
GPA 3.50-3.74:	17%	Rank in top tenth:	12%
GPA 3.0-3.49:	37%	Out-of-state:	42%
GPA 2.0-2.99:	25%	Live on campus:	99%

Basis for selection. Class ranking, cumulative GPA, standardized test scores, and personal essay are considered in the admissions decision. SAT or ACT recommended. Auditions recommended for music and drama majors. Portfolio recommended for art majors. **Home schooled:** Transcript of courses and grades required. Must take ACT or SAT. Require a sample of most recent written work/portfolio.

High school preparation. College-preparatory program recommended. Recommended units include English 4, mathematics 3, social studies 1, history 2, science 3 (laboratory 2) and foreign language 1.

2015-2016 Annual costs. Tuition/fees: $26,204. Room/board: $9,194. Books/supplies: $1,100. Personal expenses: $2,000.

Financial aid. Non-need-based: Scholarships awarded for academics, alumni affiliation, athletics, music/drama, religious affiliation.

Application procedures. Admission: Priority date 6/1; no deadline. $25 fee, may be waived for applicants with need. Admission notification on a rolling basis. **Financial aid:** Priority date 3/15; no closing date. FAFSA required. Applicants notified on a rolling basis starting 2/1; must reply within 4 week(s) of notification.

Academics. Special study options: Distance learning, double major, dual enrollment of high school students, independent study, internships, liberal arts/career combination, student-designed major, study abroad, teacher certification program. **Credit/placement by examination:** AP, CLEP, IB. **Support services:** Learning center, reduced course load, study skills assistance, tutoring.

Majors. Biology: General. **Business:** Accounting/business management, business admin. **Communications:** Communications/speech/rhetoric. **Computer sciences:** Information technology. **Education:** Elementary. **English:** English lit. **History:** General. **Math:** General. **Parks/recreation:** General, exercise sciences, health/fitness. **Philosophy/religion:** Religion. **Psychology:** General. **Social sciences:** Sociology. **Visual/performing arts:** Art, dramatic, music.

Most popular majors. Biology 6%, business/marketing 27%, communications/journalism 10%, education 11%, parks/recreation 22%.

Technology on campus. 59 workstations in library, computer center. Dormitories wired for high-speed internet access and linked to campus network. Commuter students can connect to campus network. Online course registration, online library, helpline, wireless network available.

Student life. Freshman orientation: Mandatory. Preregistration for classes offered. **Housing:** Guaranteed on-campus for freshmen. Coed dorms, single-sex dorms available. $150 fully refundable deposit. Pets allowed in dorm rooms. **Activities:** Jazz band, campus ministries, choral groups, dance, drama, music ensembles, radio station, student government, student newspaper, symphony orchestra, Christian Faith in Action, voluntary service organization, Whole Earth club, Fellowship of Christian Athletes, student activities force, Cognoscenti (literary group), Amnesty International.

Athletics. NAIA. **Intercollegiate:** Baseball M, basketball, cross-country, football (tackle) M, golf M, soccer, softball W, track and field, volleyball W. **Intramural:** Basketball, handball, racquetball, soccer, softball, track and field, volleyball. **Team name:** Braves.

Student services. Alcohol/substance abuse counseling, chaplain/spiritual director, career counseling, student employment services, financial aid counseling, health services, personal counseling, placement for graduates.

Contact. E-mail: admiss@ottawa.edu
Phone: (785) 242-5200 ext. 5421
Toll-free number: (800) 755-5200 ext. 5421 Fax: (785) 229-1008
Steed Bell, Manager of New Student Enrollment, Ottawa University, 1001 South Cedar Street, #17, Ottawa, KS 66067-3399

Pittsburg State University
Pittsburg, Kansas
www.pittstate.edu — **CB code: 6336**

▶ Public 4-year university
▶ Residential campus in large town
▶ 5,700 degree-seeking undergraduates: 6% part-time, 47% women, 4% African American, 1% Asian American, 5% Hispanic/Latino, 1% Native American, 6% Multi-racial, non-Hispanic, 3% international
▶ 1,033 degree-seeking graduate students
▶ 82% of applicants admitted
▶ SAT or ACT (ACT writing optional) required
▶ 48% graduate within 6 years

General. Founded in 1903. Regionally accredited. **Degrees:** 1,187 bachelor's, 20 associate awarded; master's offered. **ROTC:** Army. **Location:** 120 miles from Kansas City. **Calendar:** Semester, limited summer session. **Full-time faculty:** 316 total; 81% have terminal degrees, 11% minority, 40% women. **Part-time faculty:** 92 total; 42% have terminal degrees, 3% minority, 59% women. **Class size:** 45% < 20, 43% 20-39, 6% 40-49, 6% 50-99. **Special facilities:** Planetarium, observatory, field biology reserve, nature reach, herbarium, gorilla village, mammal collection, natural history reserve, Timmons Chapel, hiking/biking trail, art gallery, Performing Arts Center.

Freshman class profile. 2,631 applied, 2,169 admitted, 1,059 enrolled.

Mid 50% test scores		GPA 2.0-2.99:	22%
ACT composite:	18-23	Return as sophomores:	74%
GPA 3.75 or higher:	23%	Out-of-state:	35%
GPA 3.50-3.74:	14%	International:	2%
GPA 3.0-3.49:	30%		

Basis for selection. Academics, school record, class rank and test scores most important. **Home schooled:** GED, record of course content and completion required.

High school preparation. College-preparatory program required. 17 units recommended. Recommended units include English 4, mathematics 4, social studies 3, science 3 and computer science 3.

2015-2016 Annual costs. Tuition/fees: $6,508; $16,978 out-of-state. Room/board: $7,372. Books/supplies: $1,000. Personal expenses: $2,436.

2014-2015 Financial aid. Need-based: Average scholarship/grant was $5,990; average loan $3,293. 48% of total undergraduate aid awarded as scholarships/grants, 52% as loans/jobs. **Non-need-based:** Scholarships awarded for academics, alumni affiliation, art, athletics, leadership, minority status, music/drama, ROTC.

Application procedures. Admission: No deadline. $30 fee, may be waived for applicants with need. Admission notification on a rolling basis.

Financial aid: Priority date 3/1; no closing date. FAFSA required. Applicants notified on a rolling basis starting 3/1; must reply within 2 week(s) of notification.

Academics. **Special study options:** Accelerated study, distance learning, double major, dual enrollment of high school students, honors, independent study, internships, student-designed major, study abroad, teacher certification program. **Credit/placement by examination:** AP, CLEP, IB, ACT, institutional tests. **Support services:** Learning center, tutoring, writing center.

Honors college/program. Separate application required. Criteria for selection include minimum 28 ACT score, pre-college curriculum with minimum 3.5 GPA, references, record of participation in academic and other extracurricular activities. 36 incoming freshmen are accepted each year.

Majors. **Biology:** General. **Business:** General, accounting, construction management, finance, international, marketing. **Communications:** Communications/speech/rhetoric. **Communications technology:** Printing management. **Computer sciences:** General, systems analysis. **Education:** Art, biology, chemistry, elementary, English, family/consumer sciences, French, history, mathematics, music, physical, physics, psychology, science, Spanish, technology/industrial arts. **English:** English lit. **Foreign languages:** French, Spanish. **Health services:** Clinical lab science, nursing (RN). **History:** General. **Human services:** Social work. **Liberal arts:** Arts/sciences. **Math:** General. **Parks/recreation:** General, exercise sciences. **Physical sciences:** Chemistry, physics. **Protective services:** Criminal justice. **Psychology:** General. **Social sciences:** Economics, geography, political science, sociology. **Visual/performing arts:** Art, graphic design, music performance. **Work/family studies:** General.

Most popular majors. Business/marketing 18%, education 13%, engineering/engineering technologies 14%, health sciences 8%, psychology 6%.

Technology on campus. 1,250 workstations in dormitories, library, computer center, student center. Dormitories wired for high-speed internet access and linked to campus network. Commuter students can connect to campus network. Online course registration, online library, repair service, student web hosting, wireless network available.

Student life. **Freshman orientation:** Mandatory, $30 fee. Preregistration for classes offered. Eight individual sessions are offered and last approximately eight hours each. **Policies:** Guns, smoking, hazing prohibited. **Housing:** Guaranteed on-campus for freshmen. Coed dorms, apartments, themed housing, wellness housing available. $100 partly refundable deposit. **Activities:** Bands, campus ministries, choral groups, drama, international student organizations, literary magazine, music ensembles, Model UN, opera, radio station, student government, student newspaper, TV station, Over 150 clubs and organizations available.

Athletics. NCAA. **Intercollegiate:** Baseball M, basketball, cheerleading, cross-country, football (tackle) M, golf M, softball W, track and field, volleyball W. **Intramural:** Badminton, basketball, football (non-tackle), golf, handball, racquetball, sand volleyball W, soccer, softball, table tennis, volleyball, water polo M. **Team name:** Gorillas.

Student services. Alcohol/substance abuse counseling, career counseling, student employment services, financial aid counseling, health services, legal services, minority student services, personal counseling, placement for graduates, veterans' counselor. **Physically disabled:** Services for visually, speech, hearing impaired.

Contact. E-mail: psuadmit@pittstate.edu
Phone: (620) 235-4251 Toll-free number: (800) 854-7488
Fax: (620) 235-6003
Melinda Roelfs, Director of Admission, Pittsburg State University, 1701 South Broadway, Pittsburg, KS 66762

Southwestern College
Winfield, Kansas
www.sckans.edu   **CB code: 6670**

- Private 4-year liberal arts college affiliated with the United Methodist Church
- Residential campus in large town
- 1,147 degree-seeking undergraduates: 59% part-time, 41% women, 12% African American, 1% Asian American, 8% Hispanic/Latino, 2% Native American, 3% Multi-racial, non-Hispanic, 5% international
- 279 degree-seeking graduate students
- 91% of applicants admitted
- SAT or ACT (ACT writing optional), application essay required
- 44% graduate within 6 years

General. Founded in 1885. Regionally accredited. Laptop computers issued to all full-time students enrolled at main campus. **Degrees:** 477 bachelor's, 2 associate awarded; master's, doctoral offered. **Location:** 40 miles from Wichita. **Calendar:** Semester, limited summer session. **Full-time faculty:** 49 total; 67% have terminal degrees, 8% minority, 47% women. **Part-time faculty:** 125 total; 18% have terminal degrees, 13% minority, 56% women. **Class size:** 83% < 20, 16% 20-39, less than 1% 40-49. **Special facilities:** Biological field station.

Freshman class profile. 362 applied, 330 admitted, 90 enrolled.

Mid 50% test scores			
SAT critical reading:	440-480	Rank in top quarter:	34%
SAT math:	450-570	Rank in top tenth:	8%
ACT composite:	19-24	End year in good standing:	81%
GPA 3.75 or higher:	19%	Return as sophomores:	65%
GPA 3.50-3.74:	15%	Out-of-state:	51%
GPA 3.0-3.49:	44%	Live on campus:	84%
GPA 2.0-2.99:	22%	International:	10%

Basis for selection. School achievement record, test scores, and personal essay statement most important. Portfolio required. Interview recommended for nursing majors. Audition required for music and drama majors.

High school preparation. College-preparatory program recommended. 14 units recommended. Recommended units include English 4, mathematics 3, social studies 1, history 2, science 2 (laboratory 1). Two units of foreign language, oral communications, computer science, or any combination of the three required.

2015-2016 Annual costs. Tuition/fees: $25,946. Room/board: $7,080. Books/supplies: $1,000. Personal expenses: $3,381.

2014-2015 Financial aid. **Need-based:** 94 full-time freshmen applied for aid; 88 deemed to have need; 88 received aid. Average need met was 68%. Average scholarship/grant was $15,738; average loan $4,724. 51% of total undergraduate aid awarded as scholarships/grants, 49% as loans/jobs. **Non-need-based:** Awarded to 198 full-time undergraduates, including 49 freshmen. Scholarships awarded for academics, athletics, leadership, music/drama.

Application procedures. **Admission:** Closing date 8/25 (receipt date). $25 fee, may be waived for applicants with need. Admission notification on a rolling basis beginning on or about 9/15. Must reply by May 1 or within 3 week(s) if notified thereafter. **Financial aid:** Priority date 4/1; no closing date. FAFSA, institutional form required. Applicants notified on a rolling basis starting 2/1; must reply within 2 week(s) of notification.

Academics. **Special study options:** Accelerated study, distance learning, double major, honors, independent study, internships, student-designed major, study abroad, teacher certification program, urban semester, Washington semester. **Credit/placement by examination:** AP, CLEP, ACT. 30 credit hours maximum toward bachelor's degree. **Support services:** Learning center, reduced course load, remedial instruction, study skills assistance, tutoring, writing center.

Majors. **Biology:** General, biochemistry, marine. **Business:** Accounting, business admin, finance, management information systems, marketing, operations, organizational leadership, training/development. **Communications:** General, communications/speech/rhetoric, digital media, journalism, radio/TV. **Computer sciences:** Computer science, programming. **Education:** Early childhood, elementary, English, mathematics, music, physical, speech. **English:** Creative writing, general lit. **Health services:** Athletic training, health care admin, nursing (RN). **History:** General. **Liberal arts:** Arts/sciences. **Math:** General. **Parks/recreation:** Sports admin, sports studies. **Philosophy/religion:** General, Christian. **Physical sciences:** Chemistry. **Protective services:** Criminal justice, security management. **Psychology:** General. **Visual/performing arts:** Digital arts, dramatic, film/cinema/video, game design, music, music performance, musical theater, theater design.

Most popular majors. Business/marketing 42%, computer/information sciences 9%, education 11%, health sciences 7%, security/protective services 12%.

Technology on campus. PC or laptop required. 15 workstations in library, computer center, student center. Dormitories wired for high-speed internet access and linked to campus network. Commuter students can connect to campus network. Online library, helpline, repair service, student web hosting, wireless network available.

Student life. **Freshman orientation:** Mandatory. Preregistration for classes offered. Three-day orientation held before upperclassmen arrive on campus. **Policies:** Drug and alcohol-free campus. **Housing:** Guaranteed on-campus for freshmen. Coed dorms, single-sex dorms, apartments available. $150 partly refundable deposit. **Activities:** Bands, campus ministries, choral groups, dance, drama, international student organizations, music ensembles, musical theater, radio station, student government, student newspaper, symphony orchestra, TV station, Discipleship Southwestern, Student Foundation, international club, Leadership Southwestern, outreach teams, Student African American Brotherhood, Black Student Union.

Athletics. NAIA. **Intercollegiate:** Basketball, cross-country, football (tackle) M, golf, soccer, softball W, tennis, track and field, volleyball W. **Intramural:** Basketball, softball, tennis, volleyball. **Team name:** Moundbuilders.

Student services. Adult student services, alcohol/substance abuse counseling, chaplain/spiritual director, career counseling, student employment services, financial aid counseling, health services, minority student services, personal counseling, placement for graduates, veterans' counselor. **Physically disabled:** Services for visually, hearing impaired.

Contact. E-mail: scadmit@sckans.edu
Phone: (620) 229-6236 Toll-free number: (800) 846-1543 ext. 6236
Fax: (620) 229-6344
Dean Clark, Vice President for Enrollment Management, Southwestern College, 100 College Street, Winfield, KS 67156

Sterling College
Sterling, Kansas
www.sterling.edu　　　　　　　　　**CB code: 6684**

▶ Private 4-year liberal arts college
▶ Residential campus in small town
▶ 659 degree-seeking undergraduates: 6% part-time, 47% women
▶ 41% of applicants admitted
▶ SAT or ACT (ACT writing optional), application essay required
▶ 38% graduate within 6 years

General. Founded in 1887. Regionally accredited. **Degrees:** 119 bachelor's awarded. **Location:** 20 miles from Hutchinson, 70 miles from Wichita. **Calendar:** 4-1-4, limited summer session. **Full-time faculty:** 40 total; 52% have terminal degrees, 15% minority, 35% women. **Part-time faculty:** 34 total; 6% have terminal degrees, 3% minority, 47% women. **Class size:** 70% < 20, 29% 20-39, 1% 40-49, less than 1% 50-99.

Freshman class profile. 1,118 applied, 463 admitted, 140 enrolled.

Mid 50% test scores		GPA 3.0-3.49:	27%
SAT critical reading:	380-460	GPA 2.0-2.99:	31%
SAT math:	410-520	Rank in top quarter:	18%
SAT writing:	400-500	Rank in top tenth:	16%
ACT composite:	19-24	Return as sophomores:	61%
GPA 3.75 or higher:	22%	Out-of-state:	50%
GPA 3.50-3.74:	20%	Live on campus:	100%

Basis for selection. High school record, test scores, recommendations from school counselor and pastor important; commitment to Christian values and service also important. Interview recommended. Audition required of performing arts majors. Portfolio recommended for art majors. **Home schooled:** Transcript of courses and grades required. State certification of the home school or GED strongly recommended for athletic eligibility. **Learning Disabled:** Must provide official documentation with recommended accommodations.

High school preparation. College-preparatory program recommended. 18 units recommended. Recommended units include English 4, mathematics 3, social studies 1, history 2, science 3 (laboratory 2), foreign language 2, computer science 1 and academic electives 1. Physical education recommended.

2015-2016 Annual costs. Tuition/fees: $23,350. Room/board: $8,110. Books/supplies: $1,200. Personal expenses: $1,082.

2015-2016 Financial aid. **Need-based:** Average need met was 88%. Average scholarship/grant was $12,180; average loan $5,008. 67% of total undergraduate aid awarded as scholarships/grants, 33% as loans/jobs. **Non-need-based:** Scholarships awarded for academics, alumni affiliation, art, athletics, leadership, music/drama.

Application procedures. **Admission:** Priority date 3/1; no deadline. $25 fee, may be waived for applicants with need, free for online applicants. Admission notification on a rolling basis beginning on or about 9/15. **Financial aid:** Priority date 3/15; no closing date. FAFSA required. Applicants notified on a rolling basis starting 2/1; must reply within 2 week(s) of notification.

Academics. **Special study options:** Distance learning, double major, dual enrollment of high school students, honors, independent study, internships, liberal arts/career combination, student-designed major, study abroad, teacher certification program, urban semester, Washington semester. **Credit/placement by examination:** AP, CLEP, IB, SAT, ACT, institutional tests. **Support**

services: Learning center, reduced course load, remedial instruction, study skills assistance, tutoring, writing center.

Majors. **Biology:** General. **Business:** Business admin. **Communications:** Communications/speech/rhetoric. **Education:** Elementary, mathematics, music. **English:** English lit. **Health services:** Athletic training. **History:** General. **Math:** General. **Parks/recreation:** Health/fitness, sports admin. **Philosophy/religion:** General. **Physical sciences:** Chemistry. **Psychology:** General. **Theology:** Bible, missionary, religious ed, theology, urban ministry, youth ministry. **Visual/performing arts:** Art, dramatic, music.

Most popular majors. Business/marketing 15%, communications/journalism 8%, education 15%, health sciences 6%, parks/recreation 18%, psychology 6%, theological studies 6%, visual/performing arts 6%.

Technology on campus. 120 workstations in dormitories, library, computer center, student center. Dormitories wired for high-speed internet access and linked to campus network. Commuter students can connect to campus network. Online library, helpline, wireless network available.

Student life. **Freshman orientation:** Mandatory. Preregistration for classes offered. Three-day program prior to start of fall classes; includes service project. **Policies:** Prohibition of alcohol and tobacco products. All students under age 23 required to live in campus dormitories unless married or with dependents, living at home with parents, 5th-year senior, or by special circumstances. Religious observance required. **Housing:** Guaranteed on-campus for all undergraduates. Single-sex dorms, wellness housing available. $100 partly refundable deposit, deadline 8/1. **Activities:** Bands, campus ministries, choral groups, dance, drama, literary magazine, music ensembles, musical theater, radio station, student government, student newspaper, Future Science Professionals Association, Alpha Phi Omega, Fellowship of Christian Athletes, behavioral science club, Habitat for Humanity, Chi Beta Sigma, Pi Kappa Delta, Catholic student association.

Athletics. NAIA. **Intercollegiate:** Baseball M, basketball, cross-country, football (tackle) M, golf, soccer, softball W, track and field, volleyball W. **Intramural:** Basketball, football (non-tackle), sand volleyball, soccer, softball, table tennis, volleyball. **Team name:** Warriors.

Student services. Chaplain/spiritual director, career counseling, student employment services, financial aid counseling, health services, personal counseling, veterans' counselor.

Contact. E-mail: admissions@sterling.edu
Phone: (620) 278-4275 Toll-free number: (800) 346-1017
Fax: (620) 278-4416
Dennis Dutton, Director of Admissions, Sterling College, 125 West Cooper, Sterling, KS 67579

Tabor College
Hillsboro, Kansas
www.tabor.edu　　　　　　　　　**CB code: 6815**

▶ Private 4-year liberal arts college affiliated with the Mennonite Brethren Church
▶ Residential campus in small town
▶ 669 degree-seeking undergraduates: 18% part-time, 48% women, 10% African American, 1% Asian American, 13% Hispanic/Latino, 1% Native American, 4% Multi-racial, non-Hispanic, 2% international
▶ 40 degree-seeking graduate students
▶ 55% of applicants admitted
▶ SAT or ACT (ACT writing optional), application essay required
▶ 41% graduate within 6 years; 7% enter graduate study

General. Founded in 1908. Regionally accredited. School of Adult and Graduate Studies in Wichita offers degree completion, R.N. to B.S.N., as well as several bachelor and masters level programs. Degrees are offered in a variety of formats, dependent on the degree choice, including online-only. Honors Program available to select undergraduates. **Degrees:** 180 bachelor's, 1 associate awarded; master's offered. **Location:** 50 miles from Wichita. **Calendar:** Continuous, limited summer session. **Full-time faculty:** 38 total; 63% have terminal degrees, 8% minority, 53% women. **Part-time faculty:** 41 total; 17% have terminal degrees, 7% minority, 63% women. **Class size:** 70% < 20, 25% 20-39, 4% 40-49, 1% 50-99. **Special facilities:** Center for Mennonite Brethren Studies.

Freshman class profile. 592 applied, 328 admitted, 150 enrolled.

Mid 50% test scores		Rank in top tenth:	13%
ACT composite:	19-25	End year in good standing:	80%
GPA 3.75 or higher:	27%	Return as sophomores:	60%
GPA 3.50-3.74:	19%	Out-of-state:	43%
GPA 3.0-3.49:	25%	Live on campus:	99%
GPA 2.0-2.99:	29%	International:	5%
Rank in top quarter:	36%		

Basis for selection. Life values and objectives, desire for Christian growth, and personal interviews are important factors. Students must have a minimum ACT score of 18 as well as an ACT/GPA (4.0 scale) product of 45 or above to be considered for admission. Tabor College is interested in men and women who are academically prepared and qualified to do college work, and in those who are willing to become involved in the type of community life offered at Tabor College. Admission is granted to students who meet requirements set in each of these areas. Prospective students are able to set up an audition in music or drama during one of their visits to campus prior to their arrival on campus in the fall. Such an audition is recommended for anyone interested in music or drama. **Learning Disabled:** Prospective students must provide an IEP if special accommodations are requested.

High school preparation. 17 units recommended. Recommended units include English 4, mathematics 3, social studies 2, history 2, science 3 and foreign language 1.

2015-2016 Annual costs. Tuition/fees: $25,320. Room/board: $8,880. Books/supplies: $1,200. Personal expenses: $2,500.

2014-2015 Financial aid. Need-based: 147 full-time freshmen applied for aid; 119 deemed to have need; 119 received aid. Average need met was 73%. Average scholarship/grant was $5,535; average loan $4,209. 38% of total undergraduate aid awarded as scholarships/grants, 62% as loans/jobs. **Non-need-based:** Awarded to 906 full-time undergraduates, including 291 freshmen. Scholarships awarded for academics, alumni affiliation, art, athletics, leadership, music/drama, religious affiliation.

Application procedures. Admission: No deadline. $50 fee, may be waived for applicants with need. Admission notification on a rolling basis beginning on or about 9/1. Must reply by May 1 or within 4 week(s) if notified thereafter. **Financial aid:** Priority date 3/1; no closing date. FAFSA required. Applicants notified on a rolling basis starting 3/1; must reply within 5 week(s) of notification.

Academics. The overall commitment is to develop holistic collegiate-level competence, and a distinctly Christian lifestyle and world view. These attributes are developed through the curriculum as well as through student life activities. **Special study options:** Accelerated study, combined bachelor's/graduate degree, cross-registration, distance learning, double major, dual enrollment of high school students, exchange student, honors, independent study, internships, student-designed major, study abroad, teacher certification program, Washington semester. **Credit/placement by examination:** AP, CLEP, IB, SAT, ACT. 30 credit hours maximum toward bachelor's degree. **Support services:** Learning center, reduced course load, remedial instruction, study skills assistance, tutoring, writing center. Career counseling is also offered.

Majors. Biology: General, biochemistry. **Business:** Accounting/finance, business admin, marketing. **Communications:** Communications/speech/rhetoric. **Conservation:** Management/policy. **Education:** General, elementary, music, physical, secondary. **English:** English lit. **Health services:** Athletic training. **History:** General. **Human services:** Social work. **Math:** General. **Parks/recreation:** Health/fitness, sports admin. **Philosophy/religion:** Christian. **Physical sciences:** Chemistry. **Psychology:** General. **Social sciences:** Criminology. **Theology:** Missionary, preministerial, youth ministry. **Visual/performing arts:** Dramatic, graphic design, music performance, painting, studio arts.

Most popular majors. Business/marketing 16%, education 9%, health sciences 27%, parks/recreation 13%, philosophy/religious studies 7%, visual/performing arts 6%.

Technology on campus. 58 workstations in dormitories, library, computer center. Dormitories wired for high-speed internet access. Online course registration, online library, wireless network available.

Student life. Freshman orientation: Mandatory. Preregistration for classes offered. Three-day program prior to fall semester; includes a service day. **Policies:** Religious observance required. **Housing:** Guaranteed on-campus for freshmen. Single-sex dorms, themed housing available. $175 fully refundable deposit, deadline 8/1. Students required to live on campus until age 23. **Activities:** Bands, campus ministries, choral groups, drama, music ensembles, student government, student newspaper, Campus Ministries Council, Multicultural Student Union, Fellowship of Christian Athletes, CHUMS, Science, Math, business and social work clubs, music-related organizations.

Athletics. NAIA. **Intercollegiate:** Baseball M, basketball, cheerleading, cross-country, football (tackle) M, soccer, softball W, swimming, tennis, track and field, volleyball W. **Intramural:** Basketball, football (non-tackle), soccer, volleyball. **Team name:** Bluejays.

Student services. Chaplain/spiritual director, career counseling, student employment services, financial aid counseling, minority student services, personal counseling, placement for graduates. **Physically disabled:** Services for visually, hearing impaired.

Contact. E-mail: admissions@tabor.edu
Phone: (620) 947-3121 ext. 1723 Toll-free number: (800) 822-6799
Fax: (620) 947-6276
Lee Waldron, Director of Admissions, Tabor College, 400 South Jefferson, Hillsboro, KS 67063-7135

University of Kansas
Lawrence, Kansas — CB member
www.ku.edu — CB code: 6871

- Public 4-year university
- Residential campus in small city
- 18,278 degree-seeking undergraduates: 9% part-time, 49% women, 4% African American, 4% Asian American, 7% Hispanic/Latino, 5% Multiracial, non-Hispanic, 6% international
- 5,972 graduate students
- 93% of applicants admitted
- SAT or ACT (ACT writing optional) required
- 61% graduate within 6 years; 29% enter graduate study

General. Founded in 1866. Regionally accredited. **Degrees:** 3,682 bachelor's awarded; master's, professional, doctoral offered. **ROTC:** Army, Naval, Air Force. **Location:** 40 miles from Kansas City, 30 miles from Topeka. **Calendar:** Semester, extensive summer session. **Full-time faculty:** 1,174 total; 91% have terminal degrees, 20% minority, 38% women. **Part-time faculty:** 367 total; 34% have terminal degrees, 12% minority, 52% women. **Class size:** 48% < 20, 37% 20-39, 4% 40-49, 6% 50-99, 5% >100. **Special facilities:** 12 libraries: art and architecture, engineering, music and dance, maps, research, rare books and special collections; art and natural history museums; art and design gallery; space technology center; institute for life span studies; performing arts center and organ recital hall; Kansas ecological reserves; design lab; flight research lab; radar systems and remote sensing lab; film studio; center for the humanities; multicultural resource center; institute of politics; engineering research and development center.

Freshman class profile. 15,155 applied, 14,165 admitted, 4,187 enrolled.

Mid 50% test scores		Rank in top quarter:	56%
ACT composite:	22-28	Rank in top tenth:	26%
GPA 3.75 or higher:	44%	Return as sophomores:	80%
GPA 3.50-3.74:	18%	Out-of-state:	33%
GPA 3.0-3.49:	25%	Live on campus:	63%
GPA 2.0-2.99:	13%	International:	7%

Basis for selection. Admission to College of Liberal Arts and Sciences requires one of following for in-state students: completion of required college preparatory curriculum with 2.0 GPA, AND 3.0+ overall GPA and 24+ ACT (1090+ SAT) OR 3.25+ overall GPA and 21+ ACT (980+ SAT). For out-of-state students: completion of required college preparatory curriculum with 2.5+ GPA, AND 3.0+ overall GPA and 24+ ACT (1090+ SAT) OR 3.25+ overall GPA and 21+ ACT (980+ SAT). An admissions review committee will review, on a case-by-case basis, the applications that do not meet the above criteria. Home school. Audition required for music performance, music education, music therapy, and dance. Essay and portfolio required for admission to Visual Art majors. **Home schooled:** Students graduating from a non-accredited school must meet the overall GPA and test score requirements listed.

High school preparation. College-preparatory program required. 16 units required; 17 recommended. Required and recommended units include English 4, mathematics 3-4, social studies 3, science 3 and academic electives 3. 1 science unit must be chemistry or physics. 4 units mathematics recommended for mathematics, engineering and architecture majors. Social studies units include history.

2015-2016 Annual costs. Tuition/fees: $10,802; $26,640 out-of-state. Room/board: $10,076. Books/supplies: $1,040. Personal expenses: $1,170.

2014-2015 Financial aid. Need-based: 3,127 full-time freshmen applied for aid; 2,067 deemed to have need; 2,008 received aid. Average need met was 73%. Average scholarship/grant was $7,001; average loan $3,409. 43% of total undergraduate aid awarded as scholarships/grants, 57% as loans/jobs. **Non-need-based:** Awarded to 3,646 full-time undergraduates, including 1,238 freshmen. Scholarships awarded for academics, alumni affiliation, art, athletics, leadership, minority status, music/drama, ROTC, state residency.

Application procedures. Admission: Priority date 11/1; no deadline. $30 fee. Admission notification on a rolling basis beginning on or about 9/1. Must reply by May 1 or within 2 week(s) if notified thereafter. **Financial**

aid: Priority date 3/1; no closing date. FAFSA required. Applicants notified on a rolling basis starting 4/1; must reply within 4 week(s) of notification.

Academics. Special study options: Accelerated study, combined bachelor's/graduate degree, cooperative education, distance learning, double major, dual enrollment of high school students, ESL, honors, independent study, internships, liberal arts/career combination, study abroad, teacher certification program, Washington semester. **Credit/placement by examination:** AP, CLEP, IB, SAT, ACT, institutional tests. **Support services:** Learning center, remedial instruction, study skills assistance, tutoring, writing center. Advising Center, Office of First Year Experience, International Student Services, Nontraditional Students, Veterans Upward Bound.

Honors college/program. Admission to the University Honors Program is highly competitive. While no ACT/SAT or GPA scores guarantee acceptance or denial, last year accepted students averaged a 32 ACT composite score and a 3.95 unweighted high school GPA. Because each applicant's curriculum, resume, co-curricular summary, and essay are also reviewed, students with test scores and grades lower than these averages may be accepted.

Majors. Architecture: History/criticism. **Area/ethnic studies:** African, American, European, Latin American, Russian/Slavic, women's. **Biology:** General, biochemistry, biotechnology, microbiology, molecular. **Business:** General, accounting, business admin, finance, logistics, management information systems, marketing. **Communications:** Communications/speech/rhetoric, journalism. **Computer sciences:** General, information technology. **Conservation:** Environmental studies. **Education:** Art, early childhood, elementary, English, foreign languages, history, mathematics, middle, music, physical, science, secondary, social studies. **Engineering:** Aerospace, applied physics, architectural, chemical, civil, computer, electrical, mechanical, petroleum. **English:** English lit. **Foreign languages:** Classics, East Asian, French, Germanic, linguistics, Slavic, Spanish. **Health services:** Athletic training, communication disorders, community health services, music therapy. **History:** General. **Human services:** General, social work. **Liberal arts:** Arts/sciences, humanities. **Math:** General. **Parks/recreation:** Exercise sciences, health/fitness, sports admin. **Philosophy/religion:** Judaic, philosophy, religion. **Physical sciences:** Astronomy, atmospheric science, chemistry, geology, physics. **Psychology:** General, developmental. **Social sciences:** Anthropology, economics, geography, political science, sociology. **Visual/performing arts:** Art history/conservation, brass instruments, ceramics, dance, design, dramatic, fiber arts, film/cinema/video, graphic design, illustration, industrial design, metal/jewelry, music, music performance, music theory/composition, musicology, painting, percussion instruments, piano/keyboard, printmaking, sculpture, stringed instruments, studio arts, theater design, voice/opera, woodwind instruments.

Most popular majors. Business/marketing 16%, communications/journalism 10%, engineering/engineering technologies 9%, health sciences 12%, social sciences 8%, visual/performing arts 6%.

Technology on campus. 1,500 workstations in dormitories, library, computer center, student center. Dormitories wired for high-speed internet access and linked to campus network. Commuter students can connect to campus network. Online course registration, online library, helpline, student web hosting, wireless network available.

Student life. Freshman orientation: Available. Preregistration for classes offered. One-day program throughout summer; several 2 day program dates available. **Policies:** No alcohol or guns permitted on campus, no smoking in any buildings. Parking by permit only. **Housing:** Coed dorms, single-sex dorms, apartments, cooperative housing, fraternity/sorority housing, themed housing, wellness housing available. Scholarship halls available to students with high scholastic achievement and financial need. **Activities:** Bands, choral groups, dance, drama, international student organizations, literary magazine, music ensembles, Model UN, musical theater, opera, radio station, student government, student newspaper, symphony orchestra, TV station, over 511 student organizations and activities available.

Athletics. NCAA. **Intercollegiate:** Baseball M, basketball, cross-country, football (tackle) M, golf, rowing (crew) W, soccer W, softball W, swimming W, tennis W, track and field, volleyball W. **Intramural:** Basketball, football (non-tackle), golf, racquetball, soccer, softball, table tennis, tennis, ultimate frisbee, volleyball. **Team name:** Jayhawks.

Student services. Adult student services, alcohol/substance abuse counseling, career counseling, services for economically disadvantaged, student employment services, financial aid counseling, health services, legal services, minority student services, on-campus daycare, personal counseling, placement for graduates, veterans' counselor, women's services. **Physically disabled:** Services for visually, speech, hearing impaired.

Contact. E-mail: adm@ku.edu
Phone: (785) 864-3911 Fax: (785) 864-5017
Lisa Pinamonti Kress, Director of Admissions, University of Kansas, 1502 Iowa Street, Lawrence, KS 66045-7576

468

University of Kansas Medical Center
Kansas City, Kansas
www.kumc.edu   CB code: 0414

▶ Public two-year upper-division university and health science college
▶ Commuter campus in very large city

General. Founded in 1905. Regionally accredited. **Degrees:** 217 bachelor's awarded; master's, professional, doctoral offered. **Location:** Downtown. **Calendar:** Semester, limited summer session.

Student profile. 504 degree-seeking undergraduates, 1,932 degree-seeking graduate students. 102 applied as first time-transfer students.

Women:	86%	International:	3%
African American:	3%	Part-time:	28%
Asian American:	5%	Out-of-state:	15%
Hispanic/Latino:	6%	25 or older:	37%
Multi-racial, non-Hispanic:	3%		

Basis for selection. College transcript required. Admissions regulations, policies, and application closing dates vary by degree program. Transfer accepted as juniors, seniors.

2015-2016 Annual costs. Tuition/fees: $9,903; $24,549 out-of-state. Books/supplies: $1,300.

Financial aid. Need-based: 268 applied for aid; 244 deemed to have need; 232 received aid. Average need met was 64%. 32% of total undergraduate aid awarded as scholarships/grants, 68% as loans/jobs. **Non-need-based:** Awarded to 25 undergraduates. Scholarships awarded for academics, leadership, state residency.

Application procedures. Admission: $60 fee. Application must be submitted online. Admissions deadlines vary by academic school and program.

Academics. Assessment and reading skills screened. Assistance offered in reviewing APA-style papers. **Special study options:** Combined bachelor's/graduate degree, distance learning, ESL, honors, independent study, internships, study abroad. **Credit/placement by examination:** AP, CLEP.

Majors. Health services: Clinical lab science, cytotechnology, health information management, nursing (RN), respiratory therapy technology.

Technology on campus. 120 workstations in library, computer center, student center. Commuter students can connect to campus network. Online library, helpline, student web hosting, wireless network available.

Student life. Activities: Campus ministries, choral groups, international student organizations, student government, American Indian Health Student Association, Care 4 Kids, Christian Medical Fellowship, Chinese Student and Scholar's Association, community outreach program, Healthcare Professionals for Human Rights, Latino Medical Student Association, student governing council, Student Recycling Program, KUMC Kids.

Athletics. Intramural: Basketball, racquetball, soccer, softball, ultimate frisbee, volleyball.

Student services. Chaplain/spiritual director, career counseling, financial aid counseling, health services, legal services, personal counseling. **Physically disabled:** Services for visually, speech, hearing impaired.

Contact. E-mail: kumcadmissions@kumc.edu
Phone: (913) 588-6211
University of Kansas Medical Center, KUMC Office of Admissions, Mail Stop 4005, Kansas City, KS 66160

University of St. Mary
Leavenworth, Kansas
www.stmary.edu   CB code: 6630

▶ Private 4-year university affiliated with the Roman Catholic Church
▶ Residential campus in large town
▶ 793 degree-seeking undergraduates: 22% part-time, 60% women, 12% African American, 1% Asian American, 16% Hispanic/Latino, 1% Native Hawaiian/Pacific islander, 3% Multi-racial, non-Hispanic, 1% international
▶ 527 degree-seeking graduate students
▶ 49% of applicants admitted
▶ SAT or ACT (ACT writing optional) required
▶ 41% graduate within 6 years

General. Founded in 1923. Regionally accredited. **Degrees:** 202 bachelor's, 2 associate awarded; master's, professional offered. **ROTC:** Army, Air Force. **Location:** 26 miles from Kansas City. **Calendar:** Semester, limited summer session. **Full-time faculty:** 65 total; 71% have terminal degrees, 15% minority, 60% women. **Part-time faculty:** 228 total; 10% have terminal degrees, 13% minority, 64% women. **Class size:** 68% < 20, 30% 20-39, 1% 40-49, less than 1% 50-99. **Special facilities:** Sacred Scripture and History of the Catholic Church in Kansas collections in library.

Freshman class profile. 933 applied, 458 admitted, 135 enrolled.

Mid 50% test scores			
SAT critical reading:	410-490	GPA 3.0-3.49:	37%
SAT math:	450-520	GPA 2.0-2.99:	25%
ACT composite:	19-23	Rank in top quarter:	10%
GPA 3.75 or higher:	19%	Return as sophomores:	75%
GPA 3.50-3.74:	19%	Out-of-state:	48%
		Live on campus:	76%

Basis for selection. 2.5 GPA, 18 ACT, 870 SAT (exclusive of Writing) required. Applicants below required GPA or ACT/SAT may be considered for admission. Portfolio recommended for fine and applied arts majors.

High school preparation. College-preparatory program recommended. 12 units required; 24 recommended. Required and recommended units include English 4, mathematics 2-4, social studies 2, history 2-4, science 2-4 (laboratory 2), foreign language 2 and academic electives 2. 1-2 computer programming recommended.

2015-2016 Annual costs. Tuition/fees: $25,620. Room/board: $7,750. Books/supplies: $2,426. Personal expenses: $590.

2014-2015 Financial aid. **Need-based:** 91 full-time freshmen applied for aid; 81 deemed to have need; 81 received aid. Average need met was 88%. Average scholarship/grant was $6,658; average loan $3,476. 57% of total undergraduate aid awarded as scholarships/grants, 43% as loans/jobs. **Non-need-based:** Awarded to 679 full-time undergraduates, including 181 freshmen. Scholarships awarded for academics, art, athletics, leadership, music/drama, religious affiliation.

Application procedures. **Admission:** No deadline. $25 fee, may be waived for applicants with need. Admission notification on a rolling basis. Must reply by May 1 or within 4 week(s) if notified thereafter. **Financial aid:** Priority date 4/1; no closing date. FAFSA required. Applicants notified on a rolling basis starting 2/15; must reply within 2 week(s) of notification.

Academics. **Special study options:** Accelerated study, distance learning, double major, dual enrollment of high school students, exchange student, honors, independent study, internships, student-designed major, study abroad, teacher certification program. Degree completion programs. **Credit/placement by examination:** AP, CLEP, IB, SAT, ACT, institutional tests. 30 credit hours maximum toward bachelor's degree. **Support services:** Learning center, remedial instruction, study skills assistance, tutoring.

Majors. **Biology:** General. **Business:** General, accounting, business admin. **Computer sciences:** Information technology. **Education:** Elementary. **English:** English lit. **Health services:** Health care admin, health information technology, medical informatics, nursing (RN). **History:** General. **Liberal arts:** Arts/sciences. **Math:** General. **Parks/recreation:** Sports admin. **Physical sciences:** Chemistry. **Psychology:** General, applied, community. **Social sciences:** Criminology, political science. **Theology:** Pastoral counseling, theology. **Visual/performing arts:** Art, dramatic, music. **Work/family studies:** Child development.

Most popular majors. Business/marketing 8%, health sciences 53%.

Technology on campus. 45 workstations in library, student center. Dormitories wired for high-speed internet access and linked to campus network. Commuter students can connect to campus network. Online course registration, online library, helpline, repair service, wireless network available.

Student life. **Freshman orientation:** Mandatory. Preregistration for classes offered. Three-day program at beginning of fall semester. **Housing:** Guaranteed on-campus for freshmen. Coed dorms available. $100 nonrefundable deposit. **Activities:** Concert band, campus ministries, choral groups, dance, drama, international student organizations, literary magazine, music ensembles, musical theater, opera, student government, Bacchus, Aristotle Club, Amnesty International, Students in Free Enterprise, Young Democrats, Campus Republicans.

Athletics. NAIA. **Intercollegiate:** Baseball M, basketball, cheerleading, cross-country, football (tackle) M, soccer, softball W, track and field, volleyball W. **Intramural:** Basketball, bowling, racquetball, softball, table tennis, volleyball. **Team name:** Spires.

Student services. Adult student services, alcohol/substance abuse counseling, chaplain/spiritual director, career counseling, student employment services, financial aid counseling, health services, personal counseling, placement for graduates, veterans' counselor.

Contact. E-mail: admissions@stmary.edu
Phone: (913) 758-6118 Toll-free number: (800) 752-7043
Fax: (913) 758-6140
Kitti O'Donnell, Director of Admissions Operations, University of St. Mary, 4100 South Fourth Street Trafficway, Leavenworth, KS 66048

Washburn University
Topeka, Kansas
www.washburn.edu
CB code: 6928

- Public 4-year university
- Commuter campus in small city
- 4,900 degree-seeking undergraduates: 25% part-time, 59% women, 6% African American, 1% Asian American, 8% Hispanic/Latino, 1% Native American, 4% Multi-racial, non-Hispanic, 3% international
- 822 degree-seeking graduate students
- 36% graduate within 6 years

General. Founded in 1865. Regionally accredited. **Degrees:** 773 bachelor's, 195 associate awarded; master's, professional offered. **ROTC:** Army, Naval, Air Force. **Location:** 60 miles from Kansas City. **Calendar:** Semester, extensive summer session. **Full-time faculty:** 286 total; 84% have terminal degrees, 14% minority, 55% women. **Part-time faculty:** 268 total; 37% have terminal degrees, 11% minority, 64% women. **Class size:** 49% < 20, 43% 20-39, 6% 40-49, 2% 50-99, less than 1% >100. **Special facilities:** Concert hall, observatory, planetarium, 30-acre natural study and research area.

Freshman class profile. 1,458 applied, 1,440 admitted, 813 enrolled.

Mid 50% test scores		End year in good standing:	81%
ACT composite:	19-25	Return as sophomores:	68%
GPA 3.75 or higher:	36%	Out-of-state:	10%
GPA 3.50-3.74:	16%	Live on campus:	46%
GPA 3.0-3.49:	27%	International:	2%
GPA 2.0-2.99:	19%	Fraternities:	9%
Rank in top quarter:	34%	Sororities:	15%
Rank in top tenth:	13%		

Basis for selection. Open admission, but selective for some programs. Special requirements for health science programs, nursing, school of business, and education. ACT or ASSET required of all students for placement purposes. **Home schooled:** Students with an ACT composite score less than 23 are required to submit a General Educational Development (GED) test score.

High school preparation. College-preparatory program recommended. Recommended units include English 4, mathematics 3, social studies 3, history 1, science 3, foreign language 2 and computer science 1.

2015-2016 Annual costs. Tuition/fees: $7,910; $17,750 out-of-state. Room/board: $6,830. Books/supplies: $1,000. Personal expenses: $2,538.

2015-2016 Financial aid. **Need-based:** 699 full-time freshmen applied for aid; 456 deemed to have need; 456 received aid. Average need met was 39%. Average scholarship/grant was $4,850; average loan $3,438. 45% of total undergraduate aid awarded as scholarships/grants, 55% as loans/jobs. **Non-need-based:** Awarded to 1,819 full-time undergraduates, including 498 freshmen. Scholarships awarded for academics, alumni affiliation, art, athletics, job skills, leadership, minority status, music/drama, religious affiliation, ROTC, state residency.

Application procedures. **Admission:** Closing date 8/1. $20 fee, may be waived for applicants with need. Admission notification on a rolling basis beginning on or about 9/1. **Financial aid:** Priority date 2/15; no closing date. FAFSA required. Applicants notified on a rolling basis starting 4/1; must reply within 4 week(s) of notification.

Academics. **Special study options:** Combined bachelor's/graduate degree, cooperative education, cross-registration, distance learning, double major, dual enrollment of high school students, ESL, honors, independent study, internships, liberal arts/career combination, student-designed major, study abroad, teacher certification program. Transformational Experience. **Credit/placement by examination:** AP, CLEP, institutional tests. **Support services:** Learning center, remedial instruction, study skills assistance, tutoring, writing center.

Majors. **Biology:** General, biochemistry. **Business:** General, accounting, business admin, entrepreneurial studies, finance, international, managerial economics, marketing. **Communications:** Communications/speech/rhetoric, media studies. **Computer sciences:** General. **Education:** General, art, biology, chemistry, early childhood, elementary, English, French, German, history, mathematics, music, physical, secondary, Spanish. **English:** English lit. **Foreign languages:** French, German, Spanish. **Health services:** Athletic training, clinical lab science, nursing (RN), predental, premedicine, prepharmacy, preveterinary, sonography. **History:** General. **Human services:** General, social work. **Liberal arts:** Arts/sciences. **Math:** General. **Parks/recreation:** Exercise sciences, health/fitness, sports admin. **Philosophy/religion:** Philosophy, religion. **Physical sciences:** Chemistry, physics, theoretical physics. **Protective services:** Corrections, criminal justice, forensics, law enforcement admin, police science, security services. **Psychology:** General. **Social sciences:** Anthropology, economics, political science, sociology. **Visual/performing arts:** General, art, art history/conservation, dramatic, music, music performance, studio arts.

Most popular majors. Business/marketing 13%, communications/journalism 8%, education 8%, health sciences 28%, security/protective services 7%.

Technology on campus. 542 workstations in dormitories, library, computer center, student center. Dormitories wired for high-speed internet access and linked to campus network. Commuter students can connect to campus network. Online course registration, online library, helpline, student web hosting, wireless network available.

Student life. Freshman orientation: Available. Preregistration for classes offered. Full day session in summer; 3-day session prior to start of classes. **Housing:** Coed dorms, apartments, fraternity/sorority housing, wellness housing available. $300 partly refundable deposit. **Activities:** Bands, campus ministries, choral groups, dance, drama, film society, international student organizations, literary magazine, music ensembles, Model UN, musical theater, student government, student newspaper, symphony orchestra, TV station, Hispanic American Leadership Organization, Black Student Union, Learning in the Community, Literacy Education Action Project, Oxfam America Club, Christian Challenge, Alternative Spring Break, Ichabod Civitan Club, Bods Feeding Bods.

Athletics. NCAA. **Intercollegiate:** Baseball M, basketball, cheerleading, football (tackle) M, golf M, soccer W, softball W, tennis, volleyball W. **Intramural:** Badminton, basketball, football (non-tackle), handball, soccer, softball, table tennis, tennis, triathlon, volleyball. **Team name:** Ichabods.

Student services. Adult student services, alcohol/substance abuse counseling, career counseling, services for economically disadvantaged, student employment services, financial aid counseling, health services, minority student services, personal counseling, placement for graduates, veterans' counselor. **Physically disabled:** Services for visually, hearing impaired.

Contact. E-mail: admissions@washburn.edu
Phone: (785) 670-1030 Toll-free number: (877) 281-2637
Fax: (785) 670-1113
Kris Klima, Director, Admissions, Washburn University, 1700 SW College Avenue, Morgan 100, Topeka, KS 66621

Wichita State University
Wichita, Kansas — CB member
www.wichita.edu — CB code: 6884

- Public 4-year university
- Commuter campus in large city
- 11,060 degree-seeking undergraduates: 23% part-time, 53% women, 6% African American, 7% Asian American, 11% Hispanic/Latino, 1% Native American, 4% Multi-racial, non-Hispanic, 6% international
- 2,804 degree-seeking graduate students
- 95% of applicants admitted
- 43% graduate within 6 years

General. Founded in 1895. Regionally accredited. **Degrees:** 1,976 bachelor's, 72 associate awarded; master's, professional, doctoral offered. **Calendar:** Semester, extensive summer session. **Full-time faculty:** 534 total; 73% have terminal degrees, 17% minority, 45% women. **Part-time faculty:** 294 total; 25% have terminal degrees, 12% minority, 62% women. **Class size:** 47% < 20, 35% 20-39, 7% 40-49, 9% 50-99, 2% >100. **Special facilities:** Outdoor sculpture garden, wind tunnels, Marcusson pipe organ, flow-visualization water tunnel, National Aviation Research Institute, observatory, anthropology museum, bowling alley.

Freshman class profile. 5,431 applied, 5,145 admitted, 1,429 enrolled.

Mid 50% test scores			
SAT critical reading:	450-580	Rank in top tenth:	20%
SAT math:	470-600	End year in good standing:	73%
ACT composite:	21-26	Return as sophomores:	72%
GPA 3.75 or higher:	29%	Out-of-state:	13%
GPA 3.50-3.74:	22%	Live on campus:	42%
GPA 3.0-3.49:	28%	International:	3%
GPA 2.0-2.99:	19%	Fraternities:	8%
Rank in top quarter:	45%	Sororities:	9%

Basis for selection. In-state criteria: 21 ACT or greater or SAT score of 980 or greater, rank in top 1/3 of high school graduating class, or minimum 2.00 GPA in pre-college curriculum. Out-of-state criteria: 21 ACT or greater or SAT score of 980 or greater, rank in top 1/3 of high school graduating class, or minimum 2.5 GPA in pre-college curriculum. SAT or ACT recommended. **Home schooled:** State high school equivalency certificate required. ACT required.

High school preparation. College-preparatory program recommended. 17 units required. Required units include English 4, mathematics 3, social studies 3, science 3 (laboratory 1) and academic electives 3.

2015-2016 Annual costs. Tuition/fees: $7,528; $15,852 out-of-state.

2014-2015 Financial aid. Need-based: 1,346 full-time freshmen applied for aid; 745 deemed to have need; 736 received aid. Average need met was 72%. Average scholarship/grant was $4,486; average loan $3,728. 45% of total undergraduate aid awarded as scholarships/grants, 55% as loans/jobs. **Non-need-based:** Awarded to 3,456 full-time undergraduates, including 982 freshmen. Scholarships awarded for academics, alumni affiliation, art, athletics.

Application procedures. Admission: No deadline. $30 fee. Admission notification on a rolling basis. **Financial aid:** Priority date 3/1; no closing date. FAFSA required. Applicants notified on a rolling basis starting 10/15; must reply by 5/1 or within 2 week(s) of notification.

Academics. 24-hour study room with Internet access. All library databases and other software maintained for student use. **Special study options:** Accelerated study, cooperative education, cross-registration, distance learning, double major, dual enrollment of high school students, ESL, exchange student, honors, independent study, internships, liberal arts/career combination, study abroad, teacher certification program, Washington semester. **Credit/placement by examination:** AP, CLEP, IB, SAT, ACT, institutional tests. 15 credit hours maximum toward associate degree, 30 toward bachelor's. **Support services:** Learning center, pre-admission summer program, reduced course load, remedial instruction, study skills assistance, tutoring, writing center. TRIO Student Support Services, Disability Services.

Honors college/program. Students with less than 24 credit hours must have a high school GPA of 3.7 or higher or an ACT composite score of 27. Students with 24 or more credit hours must have a college GPA of 3.5 or higher.

Majors. Area/ethnic studies: General, women's. **Biology:** General, biochemistry. **Business:** Accounting, business admin, entrepreneurial studies, finance, human resources, international, management information systems, marketing. **Communications:** Communications/speech/rhetoric. **Education:** General, art, early childhood, elementary, ESL, music, physical, secondary. **Engineering:** General, aerospace, biomedical, computer, electrical, industrial, manufacturing, mechanical, software. **English:** English lit. **Foreign languages:** General, French, Latin, Spanish. **Health services:** Athletic training, clinical lab science, communication disorders, dental hygiene, health care admin. **History:** General. **Human services:** Social work. **Liberal arts:** Arts/sciences. **Math:** General. **Parks/recreation:** Exercise sciences, sports admin. **Philosophy/religion:** Philosophy. **Physical sciences:** Chemistry, geology, physics. **Protective services:** Criminal justice, forensics. **Psychology:** General. **Social sciences:** Anthropology, economics, political science, sociology. **Visual/performing arts:** General, art, art history/conservation, dramatic, graphic design, music, music performance, music theory/composition, musical theater, studio arts, voice/opera.

Most popular majors. Business/marketing 20%, education 9%, engineering/engineering technologies 14%, health sciences 17%.

Technology on campus. 1,500 workstations in dormitories, library, computer center, student center. Dormitories wired for high-speed internet access and linked to campus network. Commuter students can connect to campus network. Online course registration, online library, helpline, wireless network available.

Student life. Freshman orientation: Mandatory. Preregistration for classes offered. Held prior to fall semester and spring semester. **Policies:** Freshmen are required to live on campus, however, exceptions are made for freshmen who are 21 or older, married, living with a parent, legal guardian, grandparent, aunt or uncle in the greater Sedgwick County area, are taking fewer than 9 credit hours, or living in official Greek housing. **Housing:** Guaranteed on-campus for freshmen. Coed dorms, fraternity/sorority housing available. $200 nonrefundable deposit. **Activities:** Bands, campus ministries, choral groups, dance, drama, film society, international student organizations, literary magazine, music ensembles, Model UN, musical theater, opera, radio station, student government, student newspaper, symphony orchestra, TV station, Campus Ministry International, Muslim Student Association, Christian Challenge, WSU College Republicans, WSU College Democrats, Black Student Union, Cultural Ambassador Program, Saudi Student Association, Community Service Board, Global Awareness Student Project.

Athletics. NCAA. **Intercollegiate:** Baseball M, basketball, bowling, cheerleading, cross-country, golf, softball W, tennis, track and field, volleyball W. **Intramural:** Badminton, basketball, football (non-tackle), golf, racquetball, rowing (crew), soccer, softball, swimming, table tennis, tennis, volleyball. **Team name:** Shockers.

Student services. Adult student services, alcohol/substance abuse counseling, chaplain/spiritual director, career counseling, services for economically disadvantaged, student employment services, financial aid counseling, health services, minority student services, on-campus daycare, personal counseling, placement for graduates, veterans' counselor, women's services. **Physically disabled:** Services for visually, speech, hearing impaired.

Contact. E-mail: admissions@wichita.edu
Phone: (316) 978-3085 Toll-free number: (800) 362-2594
Bobby Gandu, Director of Admissions, Wichita State University, 1845 Fairmount, Box 124, Wichita, KS 67260-0124

Kentucky

Alice Lloyd College
Pippa Passes, Kentucky
www.alc.edu   CB code: 1098

◆ Private 4-year liberal arts college
◆ Residential campus in rural community
◆ 214 degree-seeking undergraduates: 55% women
◆ 33% of applicants admitted
◆ SAT or ACT (ACT writing optional), interview required

General. Founded in 1923. Regionally accredited. **Degrees:** 74 bachelor's awarded. **Location:** 150 miles from Lexington; 100 miles from Huntington, West Virginia. **Calendar:** Semester. **Full-time faculty:** 29 total; 59% have terminal degrees, 3% minority, 52% women. **Part-time faculty:** 20 total; 25% have terminal degrees, 50% women. **Class size:** 56% < 20, 39% 20-39, 4% 40-49, 1% 50-99. **Special facilities:** Appalachian history collection, photographic archives.

Freshman class profile. 4,810 applied, 1,611 admitted, 182 enrolled.

GPA 3.75 or higher:	30%	Rank in top quarter:	28%
GPA 3.50-3.74:	23%	Rank in top tenth:	19%
GPA 3.0-3.49:	34%	Out-of-state:	8%
GPA 2.0-2.99:	13%	Live on campus:	90%

Basis for selection. High school record and test scores important. Interview recommended. **Home schooled:** Transcript of courses and grades, interview required.

High school preparation. 12 units required. Required units include English 4, mathematics 3, social studies 2 and science 3.

2015-2016 Annual costs. Tuition/fees: $11,460. Room/board: $5,940. Books/supplies: $1,400. Personal expenses: $2,600.

Financial aid. Non-need-based: Scholarships awarded for academics, athletics, minority status, state residency. **Additional information:** All students receive financial aid through student work program. No student denied admission because of inability to pay. All full-time students required to work minimum of 10 hours per week.

Application procedures. Admission: Priority date 5/1; no deadline. No application fee. Admission notification on a rolling basis beginning on or about 9/1. **Financial aid:** Closing date 2/1. FAFSA required. Applicants notified on a rolling basis starting 5/1; must reply by 8/1 or within 4 week(s) of notification.

Academics. Scholarships for graduate work following graduation. **Special study options:** Double major, independent study, internships, liberal arts/career combination, student-designed major, study abroad, teacher certification program, Washington semester. **Credit/placement by examination:** AP, CLEP, IB, SAT, ACT, institutional tests. 30 credit hours maximum toward bachelor's degree. Limited number of hours of credit by examination may be counted toward degree, decided on individual basis. **Support services:** Reduced course load, remedial instruction, study skills assistance, tutoring, writing center.

Majors. Biology: General. **Business:** Business admin. **Education:** Biology, elementary, English, mathematics, middle, physical, social studies. **English:** English lit. **History:** General. **Parks/recreation:** Exercise sciences, sports admin. **Social sciences:** Sociology.

Most popular majors. Biology 30%, business/marketing 14%, education 20%, English 7%, history 8%, social sciences 13%.

Technology on campus. 80 workstations in library, computer center. Dormitories wired for high-speed internet access and linked to campus network. Online library, helpline, repair service, wireless network available.

Student life. Freshman orientation: Mandatory. Preregistration for classes offered. Held 3 days before start of first semester. **Policies:** Zero tolerance of on-campus alcohol and/or drug usage or possession. **Housing:** Guaranteed on-campus for all undergraduates. Single-sex dorms available. $50 deposit, deadline 5/15. **Activities:** Choral groups, drama, radio station, student government, student newspaper, Students for Christ, Baptist student union, cultural diversity club, children's outreach club, community service volunteers, Circle K.

Athletics. NAIA. **Intercollegiate:** Baseball M, basketball, cheerleading W, cross-country, golf, softball W, tennis, volleyball. **Intramural:** Basketball, bowling, football (non-tackle), racquetball, soccer, softball, swimming, table tennis, tennis, volleyball, weight lifting. **Team name:** Eagles.

Student services. Alcohol/substance abuse counseling, career counseling, student employment services, financial aid counseling, health services, on-campus daycare, personal counseling, placement for graduates, veterans' counselor.

Contact. E-mail: admissions@alc.edu
Phone: (606) 368-6036 Toll-free number: (888) 280-4252
Fax: (606) 368-6215
Angela Phipps, Director of Admissions, Alice Lloyd College, 100 Purpose Road, Pippa Passes, KY 41844

Asbury University
Wilmore, Kentucky   CB member
www.asbury.edu   CB code: 1019

◆ Private 4-year university and liberal arts college affiliated with the inter-denominational tradition
◆ Residential campus in small town
◆ 1,526 degree-seeking undergraduates: 12% part-time, 60% women, 4% African American, 1% Asian American, 3% Hispanic/Latino, 6% Multi-racial, non-Hispanic, 2% international
◆ 230 degree-seeking graduate students
◆ 57% of applicants admitted
◆ SAT or ACT (ACT writing optional), application essay required
◆ 63% graduate within 6 years

General. Founded in 1890. Regionally accredited. **Degrees:** 292 bachelor's, 1 associate awarded; master's offered. **ROTC:** Army, Air Force. **Location:** 20 miles from Lexington. **Calendar:** Semester, limited summer session. **Full-time faculty:** 94 total; 78% have terminal degrees, 4% minority, 36% women. **Part-time faculty:** 146 total; 45% women. **Class size:** 59% < 20, 30% 20-39, 7% 40-49, 4% 50-99. **Special facilities:** TV and recording studios, film sets, television news bureau, film sound stage, black box theater, indoor horseback riding arena, farm and horse stables, ropes challenge course.

Freshman class profile. 1,620 applied, 921 admitted, 309 enrolled.

Mid 50% test scores			
		GPA 2.0-2.99:	6%
SAT critical reading:	490-620	Rank in top quarter:	51%
SAT math:	470-610	Rank in top tenth:	25%
ACT composite:	21-27	Return as sophomores:	81%
GPA 3.75 or higher:	46%	Out-of-state:	52%
GPA 3.50-3.74:	17%	Live on campus:	96%
GPA 3.0-3.49:	30%	International:	3%

Basis for selection. Careful consideration given to academic records, test scores, application essays, references, and ability to benefit. Probationary acceptance possible if GPA below 2.5. ACT may be required prior to admission to teacher education program; both ACT and SAT required for presidential level scholarships. Interview may be recommended for academically weak applicants. Audition required for music majors. Portfolio recommended for art majors. Scholarship competition for academic scholars. **Home schooled:** Transcript of courses and grades, state high school equivalency certificate required.

High school preparation. College-preparatory program recommended. 15 units recommended. Recommended units include English 4, mathematics 3, social studies 1, history 1, science 2 (laboratory 2) and foreign language 2.

2016-2017 Annual costs. Tuition/fees: $28,829. Room/board: $6,748. Books/supplies: $1,240. Personal expenses: $1,395.

Financial aid. Non-need-based: Scholarships awarded for academics, alumni affiliation, art, athletics, leadership, minority status, music/drama, religious affiliation, ROTC, state residency.

Application procedures. Admission: Priority date 5/1; no deadline. No application fee. Admission notification on a rolling basis. $200 pre-tuition deposit required of all full-time students. Refundable until 5/1. **Financial aid:** Priority date 3/1; no closing date. FAFSA required. Applicants notified on a rolling basis starting 1/31; must reply within 4 week(s) of notification.

Academics. Special study options: Double major, dual enrollment of high school students, exchange student, internships, study abroad, teacher certification program, urban semester, Washington semester. Limited exchange program with colleges in Christian College Consortium, 3-2 program in engineering with the University of Kentucky. **Credit/placement by examination:** AP, CLEP, IB, SAT, ACT, institutional tests. Military, life experience and non-accredited college credit is limited to a combined 24.0 credit maximum. Bachelor's degree allows a combined 75-credit maximum from AP tests, CLEP tests, life experience credit, military service credit, and institution transfer credit. **Support services:** Study skills assistance, tutoring, writing center.

Majors. **Biology:** General, biochemistry. **Business:** General, accounting, business admin, marketing. **Communications:** General, journalism. **Education:** Art, educational technology, elementary, middle, music, physical. **Engineering:** Pre-engineering. **English:** Creative writing, English lit. **Foreign languages:** Classics, French, Spanish. **History:** General. **Human services:** Social work. **Math:** General, computational, financial. **Parks/recreation:** Facilities management, health/fitness, sports admin. **Philosophy/religion:** Philosophy. **Physical sciences:** Chemistry. **Psychology:** General. **Social sciences:** General, political science, sociology. **Theology:** Bible, missionary, religious ed, sacred music, youth ministry. **Visual/performing arts:** Dramatic, music, studio arts.

Most popular majors. Agriculture 6%, business/marketing 8%, communications/journalism 22%, education 12%, parks/recreation 6%, psychology 7%, theological studies 12%, visual/performing arts 6%.

Technology on campus. 225 workstations in dormitories, library, computer center, student center. Dormitories wired for high-speed internet access and linked to campus network. Commuter students can connect to campus network. Online course registration, online library, helpline, repair service, wireless network available.

Student life. **Freshman orientation:** Mandatory. Preregistration for classes offered. Held the week before classes start. **Policies:** Christian values stressed. Religious observance required. Freshmen not permitted cars on campus. **Housing:** Guaranteed on-campus for freshmen. Single-sex dorms, apartments available. **Activities:** Bands, campus ministries, choral groups, drama, literary magazine, music ensembles, musical theater, opera, radio station, student government, student newspaper, symphony orchestra, TV station, Christian Service Association, One Mission Society Student Fellowship, Salvation Army Student Fellowship, Sacred Life ministry, Tumbling Team outreach ministry, Asbury Outdoors, World Gospel Mission Student Involvement, Lead On leadership development, Allelon Student Leadership Council for intercultural programs.

Athletics. NAIA, NCCAA. **Intercollegiate:** Baseball M, basketball, cross-country, diving, golf, lacrosse, soccer, softball W, swimming, tennis, volleyball W. **Intramural:** Basketball, football (non-tackle), golf, racquetball, soccer, softball, volleyball. **Team name:** Eagles.

Student services. Adult student services, chaplain/spiritual director, career counseling, student employment services, financial aid counseling, health services, minority student services, personal counseling.

Contact. E-mail: admissions@asbury.edu
Phone: (859) 858-3511 ext. 2142 Toll-free number: (800) 888-1818
Fax: (859) 858-3921
Brandon Combs, Director of Admissions, Asbury University, One Macklem Drive, Wilmore, KY 40390-1198

Beckfield College
Florence, Kentucky
www.beckfield.edu
CB code: 3404

- For-profit 4-year nursing and career college
- Commuter campus in large town
- 808 degree-seeking undergraduates
- Interview required

General. Accredited by ACICS. **Degrees:** 27 bachelor's, 193 associate awarded. **Location:** 10 miles from Cincinnati. **Calendar:** Quarter, extensive summer session. **Full-time faculty:** 33 total; 3% have terminal degrees, 6% minority, 70% women. **Part-time faculty:** 91 total; 10% have terminal degrees, 1% minority, 59% women. **Class size:** 100% < 20. **Special facilities:** Fire arms training simulator.

Basis for selection. Open admission, but selective for some programs. Nursing program requires qualifying ACT/SAT scores. Certificate programs require an earned degree for admission. Personal training and medical massage therapy programs require qualifying ACT Compass scores. **Home schooled:** Transcript of courses and grades required. Accredited home study course will be considered for admission.

2015-2016 Annual costs. Tuition/fees: $18,350. Books/supplies: $2,000. Personal expenses: $2,484.

Financial aid. All financial aid based on need. **Additional information:** Deadline for filing of financial aid forms is end of first week of classes.

Application procedures. **Admission:** No deadline. No application fee. **Financial aid:** FAFSA required. Applicants notified on a rolling basis.

Academics. **Special study options:** Combined bachelor's/graduate degree, independent study, internships. **Credit/placement by examination:** AP, CLEP, IB, institutional tests. **Support services:** Reduced course load, remedial instruction, study skills assistance, tutoring.

Majors. **Business:** Business admin. **Health services:** Nursing (RN). **Protective services:** Law enforcement admin.

Technology on campus. PC or laptop required. 90 workstations in library, computer center. Online course registration, online library, wireless network available.

Student life. **Freshman orientation:** Mandatory. Preregistration for classes offered. Held for half-day 3 days before beginning of quarter.

Athletics. **Team name:** Bulldogs.

Student services. Alcohol/substance abuse counseling, career counseling, student employment services, financial aid counseling, personal counseling, placement for graduates, veterans' counselor.

Contact. Phone: (859) 371-9393 Fax: (859) 371-5096
Michele Mumma, Director of Admissions, Beckfield College, 16 Spiral Drive, Florence, KY 41042

Bellarmine University
Louisville, Kentucky
www.bellarmine.edu
CB member
CB code: 1056

- Private 4-year university and liberal arts college affiliated with the Roman Catholic Church
- Residential campus in very large city
- 2,584 degree-seeking undergraduates: 5% part-time, 65% women, 4% African American, 2% Asian American, 3% Hispanic/Latino, 3% Multiracial, non-Hispanic, 1% international
- 725 degree-seeking graduate students
- 84% of applicants admitted
- SAT or ACT (ACT writing optional), application essay required
- 67% graduate within 6 years

General. Founded in 1950. Regionally accredited. **Degrees:** 504 bachelor's awarded; master's, professional, doctoral offered. **ROTC:** Army, Air Force. **Location:** 7 miles from downtown, 100 miles from Cincinnati. **Calendar:** Semester, extensive summer session. **Full-time faculty:** 167 total; 83% have terminal degrees, 10% minority, 54% women. **Part-time faculty:** 281 total; 40% have terminal degrees, 8% minority, 57% women. **Class size:** 54% < 20, 45% 20-39, 1% 40-49, less than 1% 50-99.

Freshman class profile. 5,885 applied, 4,940 admitted, 709 enrolled.

Mid 50% test scores			
SAT critical reading:	500-590	Rank in top quarter:	59%
SAT math:	500-610	Rank in top tenth:	25%
ACT composite:	22-27	Return as sophomores:	81%
GPA 3.75 or higher:	35%	Out-of-state:	34%
GPA 3.50-3.74:	22%	Live on campus:	71%
GPA 3.0-3.49:	32%	International:	1%
GPA 2.0-2.99:	11%	Fraternities:	1%
		Sororities:	1%

Basis for selection. Admissions based on 2.5 GPA, college preparatory curriculum, 21 ACT or 1000 SAT (exclusive of Writing), strong high school recommendation, submission of acceptable essay (if requested). Applicants not meeting requirements may be admitted on strength of each criterion. School activities also considered. Interview recommended. Audition required of music majors. Portfolio recommended for art majors. **Home schooled:** Transcript of courses and grades, letter of recommendation (nonparent) required.

High school preparation. College-preparatory program required. 22 units required; 26 recommended. Required and recommended units include English 4, mathematics 3-4, social studies 2-3, history 1-2, science 3-4 (laboratory 2), foreign language 2 and academic electives 5-7.

2015-2016 Annual costs. Tuition/fees: $37,650. Room/board: $11,360. Books/supplies: $788. Personal expenses: $3,382.

2015-2016 Financial aid. Need-based: 678 full-time freshmen applied for aid; 584 deemed to have need; 584 received aid. Average need met was 77%. Average scholarship/grant was $23,542; average loan $3,316. 81% of total undergraduate aid awarded as scholarships/grants, 19% as loans/jobs. **Non-need-based:** Awarded to 1,269 full-time undergraduates, including 358 freshmen. Scholarships awarded for academics, alumni affiliation, art, athletics, leadership, minority status, music/drama, religious affiliation, ROTC, state residency.

Application procedures. Admission: Priority date 2/1; deadline 8/15 (postmark date). $25 fee, may be waived for applicants with need, free for online applicants. Admission notification on a rolling basis beginning on or about 9/1. Must reply by May 1 or within 3 week(s) if notified thereafter. **Financial aid:** Priority date 2/1; no closing date. FAFSA required. Applicants notified by 3/15; Applicants notified on a rolling basis starting 3/15; must reply by 5/1.

Academics. Special study options: Accelerated study, combined bachelor's/graduate degree, cross-registration, double major, dual enrollment of high school students, honors, independent study, internships, liberal arts/career combination, semester at sea, student-designed major, study abroad, teacher certification program, Washington semester. **Credit/placement by examination:** AP, CLEP, IB, institutional tests. **Support services:** Learning center, reduced course load, study skills assistance, tutoring, writing center.

Honors college/program. Admission is by invitation; prospective students encouraged to contact the director with a letter describing interest in program. Accepted students usually have 28 ACT and rank in top 10% of graduating class. Love of learning, intellectual curiosity, and desire to pursue advanced education important.

Majors. Biology: General, Biochemistry/molecular biology. **Business:** Accounting, actuarial science, business admin, finance. **Communications:** Communications/speech/rhetoric. **Computer sciences:** General. **Conservation:** Environmental science, environmental studies. **Education:** Elementary, middle, secondary, special ed. **Engineering:** Computer. **English:** English lit. **Foreign languages:** Spanish. **Health services:** Clinical lab science, nursing (RN), physical therapy, respiratory therapy technology. **History:** General. **Liberal arts:** Arts/sciences. **Math:** General. **Parks/recreation:** Exercise sciences, sports admin. **Philosophy/religion:** Philosophy. **Physical sciences:** Chemistry, physics. **Protective services:** Criminal justice. **Psychology:** General. **Social sciences:** Economics, political science, sociology. **Theology:** Theology. **Visual/performing arts:** Design, dramatic, music, studio arts, studio arts management.

Most popular majors. Biology 6%, business/marketing 17%, health sciences 36%, parks/recreation 6%, psychology 9%.

Technology on campus. 430 workstations in dormitories, library, computer center, student center. Dormitories wired for high-speed internet access and linked to campus network. Commuter students can connect to campus network. Online course registration, online library, helpline, repair service, wireless network available.

Student life. Freshman orientation: Mandatory, $400 fee. Preregistration for classes offered. Off-campus and on-campus 3-day session held in August before classes begin. **Housing:** Guaranteed on-campus for freshmen. Coed dorms, single-sex dorms, special housing for disabled, apartments, fraternity/sorority housing, themed housing available. $200 partly refundable deposit, deadline 5/1. Pets allowed in dorm rooms. Suites available to upperclassmen. Apartments for single students are available for students 21 and over. When possible, international students are housed with U.S. students in designated buildings. Fraternity/sorority designated housing areas are available by request. They are not offered yearly if there is no interest. **Activities:** Bands, campus ministries, choral groups, dance, drama, film society, international student organizations, literary magazine, music ensembles, musical theater, radio station, student government, student newspaper, Catholic Student Association, Fellowship of Christian Athletes, Hillel, Highland Community Ministries, Habitat for Humanity, InterVarsity Christian Fellowship, Black Student Union, Best Buddies, Youth in Government, Colleges Against Cancer.

Athletics. NCAA. **Intercollegiate:** Baseball M, basketball, cheerleading, cross-country, field hockey W, golf, lacrosse M, soccer, softball W, swimming, tennis, track and field, volleyball W. **Intramural:** Basketball, football (non-tackle), golf, handball, soccer, softball, swimming, table tennis, tennis, ultimate frisbee, volleyball. **Team name:** Knights.

Student services. Adult student services, chaplain/spiritual director, career counseling, student employment services, financial aid counseling, health services, personal counseling, placement for graduates. **Physically disabled:** Services for visually, hearing impaired.

Contact. E-mail: admissions@bellarmine.edu
Phone: (502) 272-8131 Toll-free number: (800) 274-4723 ext. 8131
Fax: (502) 272-8002
Timothy Sturgeon, Dean of Admissions, Bellarmine University, 2001 Newburg Road, Louisville, KY 40205

Berea College
Berea, Kentucky
www.berea.edu

CB member
CB code: 1060

- Private 4-year liberal arts college
- Residential campus in small town
- 1,593 degree-seeking undergraduates: 58% women, 16% African American, 2% Asian American, 8% Hispanic/Latino, 5% Multi-racial, non-Hispanic, 8% international
- 37% of applicants admitted
- SAT or ACT (ACT writing optional), application essay, interview required
- 63% graduate within 6 years

General. Founded in 1855. Regionally accredited. Each student is provided with a laptop computer. Departmental computer labs offer access to specialized functions such as video editing and graphical production. **Degrees:** 338 bachelor's awarded. **Location:** 40 miles from Lexington, 100 miles from Louisville. **Calendar:** Semester, limited summer session. **Full-time faculty:** 133 total; 92% have terminal degrees, 13% minority, 47% women. **Part-time faculty:** 47 total; 60% have terminal degrees, 11% minority, 60% women. **Class size:** 79% < 20, 20% 20-39, less than 1% 40-49, less than 1% 50-99. **Special facilities:** Appalachian gallery, planetarium and observatory, geology museum, Ecovillage, child development laboratory, early technology lab, crafts program.

Freshman class profile. 1,635 applied, 597 admitted, 432 enrolled.

Mid 50% test scores			
SAT critical reading:	550-640	Rank in top quarter:	67%
SAT math:	520-620	Rank in top tenth:	24%
SAT writing:	500-610	Return as sophomores:	86%
ACT composite:	22-26	Out-of-state:	52%
GPA 3.75 or higher:	26%	Live on campus:	97%
GPA 3.50-3.74:	20%	International:	7%
GPA 3.0-3.49:	41%		
GPA 2.0-2.99:	13%		

Basis for selection. Admissions based on comprehensive review of application including academic credentials, recommendations, essay, financial eligibility, and interview. **Home schooled:** List of courses and titles of textbooks required if transcript is not available.

High school preparation. College-preparatory program recommended. 13 units recommended. Recommended units include English 4, mathematics 3, social studies 2, science 2 (laboratory 2) and foreign language 2.

2015-2016 Annual costs. Tuition/fees: $24,870. Room/board: $6,410. Books/supplies: $700. Personal expenses: $1,600. **Additional information:** Only those with financial need admitted. All students awarded 4-year tuition scholarship. Amount of scholarship varies depending on financial need and presence of any additional outside scholarships. Resources cover entire cost of tuition, which totals $24,300. Financial aid and scholarships available for meeting additional costs of room/board ($6,410) and fees ($570), depending on financial need. Every student is provided a personal notebook computer by the college.

2015-2016 Financial aid. All financial aid based on need. 432 full-time freshmen applied for aid; 432 deemed to have need; 432 received aid. Average need met was 96%. Average scholarship/grant was $32,957; average loan $908. 92% of total undergraduate aid awarded as scholarships/grants, 8% as loans/jobs.

Application procedures. Admission: Closing date 4/30. No application fee. Admission notification on a rolling basis beginning on or about 11/1. Must reply by 5/1. $50 deposit required. **Financial aid:** Priority date 2/1; no closing date. FAFSA required. Applicants notified on a rolling basis starting 11/1; must reply by 5/1.

Academics. Special study options: Combined bachelor's/graduate degree, double major, ESL, exchange student, honors, independent study, internships, student-designed major, study abroad, teacher certification program. 3-2 engineering program with the University of Kentucky. **Credit/placement by examination:** AP, CLEP, SAT, ACT, institutional tests. Unlimited number of credit hours may be counted toward degree. **Support services:** Learning center, remedial instruction, study skills assistance, tutoring, writing center.

Majors. Area/ethnic studies: African-American, Asian, women's. **Biology:** General, neuroanatomy. **Business:** General, accounting, finance, marketing. **Communications:** Media studies. **Computer sciences:** General. **Education:** General, art, elementary, family/consumer sciences, kindergarten/preschool, middle, music, secondary, technology/industrial arts. **English:** British lit, creative writing, English lit. **Foreign languages:** French, German, Latin, Spanish. **Health services:** Nursing (RN). **History:** General. **Math:** General, applied. **Parks/recreation:** Exercise sciences, health/fitness. **Philosophy/**

religion: Philosophy, religion. **Physical sciences:** Chemistry, physics. **Psychology:** General. **Social sciences:** Economics, political science, sociology. **Visual/performing arts:** Art, art history/conservation, dramatic, music, music performance, studio arts, voice/opera. **Work/family studies:** General.

Most popular majors. Area/ethnic studies 6%, biology 8%, business/marketing 7%, education 6%, engineering/engineering technologies 6%, English 6%, psychology 6%, social sciences 7%, visual/performing arts 8%.

Technology on campus. Dormitories wired for high-speed internet access and linked to campus network. Online course registration, online library, helpline, repair service, wireless network available.

Student life. Freshman orientation: Mandatory. Preregistration for classes offered. **Policies:** Freshmen not permitted cars on campus. **Housing:** Guaranteed on-campus for all undergraduates. Single-sex dorms, apartments available. Apartments for single parent students, ecovillage, Deep Green residence hall available. **Activities:** Bands, campus ministries, choral groups, dance, drama, international student organizations, literary magazine, music ensembles, student government, student newspaper, religious organizations, People Who Care, Students for Appalachia, Habitat for Humanity, Cosmopolitan Club.

Athletics. NCAA. **Intercollegiate:** Baseball M, basketball, cross-country, golf M, soccer, softball W, tennis, track and field, volleyball W. **Intramural:** Basketball, football (non-tackle), soccer, ultimate frisbee, volleyball. **Team name:** Mountaineers.

Student services. Adult student services, alcohol/substance abuse counseling, chaplain/spiritual director, career counseling, services for economically disadvantaged, student employment services, financial aid counseling, health services, minority student services, on-campus daycare, personal counseling, placement for graduates, veterans' counselor, women's services. **Physically disabled:** Services for visually, speech, hearing impaired.

Contact. E-mail: askadmissions@berea.edu
Phone: (859) 985-3500 Toll-free number: (800) 326-5948
Fax: (859) 985-3512
Luke Hodson, Director of Admissions, Berea College, CPO 2220, Berea, KY 40404

Brescia University
Owensboro, Kentucky
www.brescia.edu   **CB code: 1071**

▸ Private 4-year university and liberal arts college affiliated with the Roman Catholic Church

▸ Commuter campus in small city

▸ 1,024 degree-seeking undergraduates: 25% part-time, 77% women, 13% African American, 6% Hispanic/Latino, 1% Native American, 1% Multiracial, non-Hispanic, 1% international

▸ 18 degree-seeking graduate students

▸ 48% of applicants admitted

▸ SAT or ACT (ACT writing optional), application essay required

▸ 30% graduate within 6 years

General. Founded in 1950. Regionally accredited. Social Work program accredited by the Council on Social Work Education. Online associate and bachelor's degree completion programs. **Degrees:** 138 bachelor's, 24 associate awarded; master's offered. **Location:** 120 miles from Louisville; 120 miles from Nashville, TN. **Calendar:** Semester, limited summer session. **Full-time faculty:** 44 total; 61% have terminal degrees, 54% women. **Part-time faculty:** 60 total; 27% have terminal degrees, 68% women. **Class size:** 88% < 20, 12% 20-39. **Special facilities:** Observatory, greenhouse, clay studio.

Freshman class profile. 4,153 applied, 1,991 admitted, 151 enrolled.

GPA 3.75 or higher:	19%	**Return as sophomores:**	61%
GPA 3.50-3.74:	18%	**Out-of-state:**	20%
GPA 3.0-3.49:	36%	**Live on campus:**	83%
GPA 2.0-2.99:	27%	**International:**	1%

Basis for selection. Students admitted based on GPA and ACT/SAT. **Home schooled:** Transcript of courses and grades required. **Learning Disabled:** Applicants should inform admission counselor of learning disability and arrange appointment with Student Support Services staff member if requesting assistance.

High school preparation. College-preparatory program required. 17 units recommended. Recommended units include English 4, mathematics 3, social studies 2, history 2, science 2, foreign language 2 and academic electives 2. 2 units in fine arts, 2 units in computer science also recommended.

2015-2016 Annual costs. Tuition/fees: $20,840. Room/board: $8,750. Books/supplies: $1,000. Personal expenses: $1,800.

2014-2015 Financial aid. Need-based: 51% of total undergraduate aid awarded as scholarships/grants, 49% as loans/jobs. **Non-need-based:** Scholarships awarded for academics, alumni affiliation, art, athletics, minority status, music/drama, religious affiliation, state residency.

Application procedures. Admission: No deadline. $25 fee, may be waived for applicants with need. Admission notification on a rolling basis beginning on or about 9/1. **Financial aid:** Priority date 8/1, closing date 8/23. FAFSA required. Applicants notified on a rolling basis starting 3/1; must reply within 3 week(s) of notification.

Academics. Special study options: Accelerated study, combined bachelor's/graduate degree, cross-registration, distance learning, double major, dual enrollment of high school students, exchange student, honors, independent study, internships, liberal arts/career combination, student-designed major, study abroad, teacher certification program, weekend college. **Credit/placement by examination:** AP, CLEP, IB, SAT, ACT, institutional tests. 18 credit hours maximum toward associate degree, 36 toward bachelor's. **Support services:** Learning center, pre-admission summer program, reduced course load, remedial instruction, study skills assistance, tutoring, writing center.

Honors college/program. Students with a 3.5 GPA and a 25+ on the ACT may apply to the Honors College. In addition to alternative housing options, opportunities to hear guest lectures, off-campus activities, and other club-type activities, students in the Honors College enroll in four exclusive and unique general education courses, a research methods course, and an Honors capstone course.

Majors. Biology: General. **Business:** General, accounting, business admin. **Computer sciences:** General. **Education:** Art, elementary, middle, secondary, social studies, Spanish, special ed. **English:** English lit. **Foreign languages:** Spanish. **Health services:** Audiology/speech pathology, clinical lab science. **History:** General. **Human services:** Social work. **Math:** Applied. **Philosophy/religion:** Religion. **Physical sciences:** Chemistry. **Psychology:** General. **Social sciences:** Political science. **Theology:** Pastoral counseling, theology. **Visual/performing arts:** Art, graphic design.

Most popular majors. Business/marketing 20%, health sciences 16%, psychology 8%, public administration/social services 40%.

Technology on campus. 77 workstations in library, computer center. Dormitories wired for high-speed internet access and linked to campus network. Commuter students can connect to campus network. Online library, helpline, repair service, wireless network available.

Student life. Freshman orientation: Mandatory, $200 fee. Preregistration for classes offered. Saturday-Tuesday program held prior to start of classes. **Housing:** Guaranteed on-campus for freshmen. Coed dorms, single-sex dorms, special housing for disabled, apartments, themed housing available. $100 fully refundable deposit, deadline 8/23. Shared apartment houses available. **Activities:** Bands, campus ministries, choral groups, drama, international student organizations, music ensembles, student government, student newspaper, Fellowship of Christian Athletes, social work club, Council for Exceptional Children, Grave Robbers, St. Angela's Messengers, Alternative Spring Break, Right to Life, psychology club.

Athletics. NAIA. **Intercollegiate:** Baseball M, basketball, cross-country, golf, soccer, softball W, tennis, track and field, volleyball W. **Intramural:** Basketball, racquetball, table tennis, volleyball. **Team name:** Bearcats.

Student services. Adult student services, alcohol/substance abuse counseling, chaplain/spiritual director, career counseling, services for economically disadvantaged, student employment services, financial aid counseling, personal counseling, placement for graduates, veterans' counselor, women's services. **Physically disabled:** Services for visually, speech, hearing impaired.

Contact. E-mail: admissions@brescia.edu
Phone: (270) 686-4241 Toll-free number: (877) 273-7242
Fax: (270) 686-4314
Chris Houk, Vice President for Enrollment Management, Brescia University, 717 Frederica Street, Owensboro, KY 42301-3023

Campbellsville University
Campbellsville, Kentucky   **CB member**
www.campbellsville.edu   **CB code: 1097**

▸ Private 4-year university affiliated with the Baptist faith
▸ Residential campus in large town
▸ 2,098 degree-seeking undergraduates: 11% part-time, 55% women, 12% African American, 2% Hispanic/Latino, 1% Multi-racial, non-Hispanic, 10% international

▶ 431 degree-seeking graduate students
▶ 76% of applicants admitted
▶ SAT or ACT (ACT writing optional) required
▶ 37% graduate within 6 years

General. Founded in 1906. Regionally accredited. **Degrees:** 328 bachelor's, 84 associate awarded; master's offered. **ROTC:** Army. **Location:** 80 miles from Louisville; 140 miles from Nashville, Tennessee. **Calendar:** Semester, extensive summer session. **Full-time faculty:** 157 total; 60% have terminal degrees, 12% minority, 51% women. **Part-time faculty:** 122 total; 26% minority, 70% women. **Class size:** 57% < 20, 41% 20-39, 1% 40-49, less than 1% 50-99. **Special facilities:** Educational and research woodland, American Civil War institute, fine arts center with computer-enhanced practice room with acoustical adjustment system.

Freshman class profile. 2,579 applied, 1,949 admitted, 514 enrolled.

GPA 3.75 or higher:	24%	Rank in top tenth:	12%
GPA 3.50-3.74:	15%	Return as sophomores:	58%
GPA 3.0-3.49:	25%	Out-of-state:	15%
GPA 2.0-2.99:	33%	Live on campus:	75%
Rank in top quarter:	37%		

Basis for selection. Achievement in strong high school program and satisfactory SAT/ACT most important. Special consideration for entry to basic skills program may be given to other highly motivated and potentially successful applicants. Interview and essay recommended. **Home schooled:** State high school equivalency certificate required.

High school preparation. College-preparatory program recommended. 21 units recommended. Recommended units include English 4, mathematics 3, social studies 2, history 2, science 3 (laboratory 1), foreign language 1 and academic electives 6. At least 2 units in the arts recommended for academic elective.

2016-2017 Annual costs. Tuition/fees: $24,596. Room/board: $7,896. Books/supplies: $1,100. Personal expenses: $1,800.

2014-2015 Financial aid. Need-based: 685 full-time freshmen applied for aid; 644 deemed to have need; 637 received aid. Average need met was 73%. Average scholarship/grant was $15,817; average loan $3,052. 75% of total undergraduate aid awarded as scholarships/grants, 25% as loans/jobs. **Non-need-based:** Awarded to 465 full-time undergraduates, including 153 freshmen. Scholarships awarded for academics, art, athletics, leadership, minority status, music/drama, religious affiliation, state residency. **Additional information:** Matching scholarships available for students whose church contributes $200 annually. Performance grants available to members of marching band.

Application procedures. Admission: Priority date 4/15; no deadline. $20 fee, may be waived for applicants with need. Admission notification on a rolling basis beginning on or about 1/2. **Financial aid:** Priority date 1/31; no closing date. FAFSA required. Applicants notified on a rolling basis starting 3/15; must reply by 5/1 or within 2 week(s) of notification.

Academics. Special study options: Accelerated study, cooperative education, distance learning, double major, dual enrollment of high school students, ESL, exchange student, honors, independent study, internships, study abroad, teacher certification program, Washington semester. **Credit/placement by examination:** AP, CLEP, institutional tests. 32 credit hours maximum toward bachelor's degree. Institutional/departmental examinations given in some areas. **Support services:** Learning center, pre-admission summer program, reduced course load, remedial instruction, study skills assistance, tutoring, writing center.

Majors. Biology: General. **Business:** General, accounting, business admin, marketing, office management. **Communications:** Broadcast journalism, communications/speech/rhetoric, journalism, public relations. **Computer sciences:** General. **Education:** General, art, biology, chemistry, early childhood, elementary, English, ESL, health, history, mathematics, middle, music, physical, physics, reading, science, secondary, social science, social studies, special ed. **English:** English lit. **Foreign languages:** Spanish. **Health services:** Athletic training, nursing (RN), predental, premedicine, prepharmacy, preveterinary. **History:** General. **Human services:** Social work. **Math:** General. **Parks/recreation:** General, exercise sciences, health/fitness. **Physical sciences:** Chemistry, physics. **Protective services:** Law enforcement admin. **Psychology:** General. **Social sciences:** General, economics, political science, sociology. **Theology:** Bible, religious ed, sacred music. **Visual/performing arts:** Art, conducting, dramatic, music, music performance, music theory/composition, piano/keyboard, studio arts, voice/opera.

Most popular majors. Biology 6%, business/marketing 24%, education 11%, public administration/social services 11%, security/protective services 9%, theological studies 8%.

Technology on campus. 250 workstations in dormitories, library, computer center, student center. Dormitories wired for high-speed internet access and linked to campus network. Commuter students can connect to campus network. Online course registration, online library, repair service, wireless network available.

Student life. Freshman orientation: Mandatory. Preregistration for classes offered. Held in May, June, July, and early August. **Policies:** Religious observance required. **Housing:** Guaranteed on-campus for all undergraduates. Single-sex dorms, apartments, wellness housing available. $100 deposit, deadline 7/1. **Activities:** Bands, campus ministries, choral groups, dance, drama, international student organizations, literary magazine, music ensembles, musical theater, opera, radio station, student government, student newspaper, symphony orchestra, TV station, Baptist Campus Ministries, Young Republicans, Young Democrats, Student Government Association, Fellowship of Christian Athletes, student ambassadors, Green Minds.

Athletics. NAIA, NCCAA. **Intercollegiate:** Archery, baseball M, basketball, bowling, cheerleading, cross-country, football (tackle) M, golf, soccer, softball W, swimming, tennis, track and field, volleyball W, wrestling. **Intramural:** Basketball, football (non-tackle), sand volleyball, soccer, softball, swimming, table tennis, tennis. **Team name:** Tigers.

Student services. Adult student services, alcohol/substance abuse counseling, chaplain/spiritual director, career counseling, student employment services, financial aid counseling, health services, personal counseling, placement for graduates, veterans' counselor.

Contact. E-mail: admissions@campbellsville.edu
Phone: (270) 789-5220 Toll-free number: (800) 264-6014
Fax: (270) 789-5071
David Walters, Vice President for Admissions, Campbellsville University, 1 University Drive, Campbellsville, KY 42718-2799

Centre College
Danville, Kentucky   **CB member**
www.centre.edu   **CB code: 1109**

▶ Private 4-year liberal arts college affiliated with the Presbyterian Church (USA)
▶ Residential campus in large town
▶ 1,355 degree-seeking undergraduates: 50% women, 5% African American, 4% Asian American, 3% Hispanic/Latino, 3% Multi-racial, non-Hispanic, 7% international
▶ 71% of applicants admitted
▶ SAT or ACT (ACT writing recommended), application essay required
▶ 86% graduate within 6 years; 27% enter graduate study

General. Founded in 1819. Regionally accredited. **Degrees:** 329 bachelor's awarded. **ROTC:** Army, Air Force. **Location:** 35 miles from Lexington, 85 miles from Louisville. **Calendar:** 4-1-4. **Full-time faculty:** 124 total; 98% have terminal degrees, 3% minority, 42% women. **Part-time faculty:** 20 total; 40% have terminal degrees, 15% minority, 55% women. **Class size:** 60% < 20, 40% 20-39. **Special facilities:** Regional performing arts center, hot glass studio.

Freshman class profile. 2,716 applied, 1,933 admitted, 374 enrolled.

Mid 50% test scores			
SAT critical reading:	540-660	Rank in top quarter:	84%
SAT math:	570-740	Rank in top tenth:	54%
ACT composite:	26-31	End year in good standing:	96%
GPA 3.75 or higher:	46%	Return as sophomores:	89%
GPA 3.50-3.74:	18%	Out-of-state:	45%
GPA 3.0-3.49:	26%	Live on campus:	99%
GPA 2.0-2.99:	10%	International:	8%

Basis for selection. Achievement and quality of high school program most important. Recommendations, test scores, academic and nonacademic interests, experiences considered. Interview recommended.

High school preparation. College-preparatory program required. 13 units required; 20 recommended. Required and recommended units include English 4, mathematics 3-4, social studies 2, history 2, science 2-4 (laboratory 2), foreign language 2-4 and visual/performing arts 1.

2015-2016 Annual costs. Tuition/fees: $38,200. Room/board: $9,620. Books/supplies: $1,500. Personal expenses: $1,000.

2015-2016 Financial aid. Need-based: 299 full-time freshmen applied for aid; 226 deemed to have need; 226 received aid. Average need met was 87%. Average scholarship/grant was $29,311; average loan $3,718. 87% of total undergraduate aid awarded as scholarships/grants, 13% as loans/jobs. **Non-need-based:** Awarded to 546 full-time undergraduates, including 141

freshmen. Scholarships awarded for academics, alumni affiliation, art, leadership, music/drama, ROTC.

Application procedures. Admission: Closing date 1/15 (postmark date). No application fee. Admission notification by 3/15. Must reply by May 1 or within 2 week(s) if notified thereafter. **Financial aid:** Priority date 1/31, closing date 1/31. FAFSA, institutional form required. Applicants notified by 3/19; Applicants notified on a rolling basis starting 3/19; must reply by 5/1.

Academics. Unusual courses and off-campus study options offered during 3-week winter term. Long-term study abroad sites in England, France, Mexico, Japan, and Ireland. Winter-term international locations vary. **Special study options:** Combined bachelor's/graduate degree, cross-registration, double major, honors, independent study, internships, student-designed major, study abroad, Washington semester. Science semester at Oak Ridge National Laboratories, Tennessee, and 5 other national science laboratories, 3-2 engineering program with Columbia University (NY), Washington University (MO), Vanderbilt University (TN), and University of Kentucky. **Credit/placement by examination:** AP, CLEP, IB, SAT, ACT, institutional tests. **Support services:** Study skills assistance, tutoring, writing center.

Majors. Biology: General, biochemistry, molecular. **Computer sciences:** Computer science. **Conservation:** Environmental studies. **English:** English lit. **Foreign languages:** Classics, French, German, Spanish. **History:** General. **Math:** General. **Philosophy/religion:** Philosophy, religion. **Physical sciences:** Chemical physics, chemistry, physics. **Psychology:** General. **Social sciences:** Anthropology, economics, international relations, political science, sociology. **Visual/performing arts:** Art, dramatic, music.

Most popular majors. Biology 10%, English 6%, foreign language 7%, history 7%, interdisciplinary studies 8%, psychology 11%, social sciences 31%.

Technology on campus. 425 workstations in dormitories, library, computer center, student center. Dormitories wired for high-speed internet access and linked to campus network. Commuter students can connect to campus network. Online course registration, helpline, repair service, student web hosting, wireless network available.

Student life. Freshman orientation: Mandatory. Preregistration for classes offered. Held at beginning of fall term. **Housing:** Guaranteed on-campus for all undergraduates. Coed dorms, single-sex dorms, special housing for disabled, apartments, fraternity/sorority housing, themed housing available. **Activities:** Bands, campus ministries, choral groups, dance, drama, film society, international student organizations, literary magazine, music ensembles, musical theater, opera, student government, student newspaper, symphony orchestra, student activities council, volunteer services, diversity student union, Christian Fellowship, Campus Democrats and Republicans, ecumenical organization, peace organization, student environmental organization, Muslim student association.

Athletics. NCAA. **Intercollegiate:** Baseball M, basketball, cross-country, diving, field hockey W, football (tackle) M, golf, lacrosse, soccer, softball W, swimming, tennis, track and field, volleyball W. **Intramural:** Badminton, basketball, bowling, football (non-tackle), racquetball, rugby M, soccer, softball, tennis, volleyball. **Team name:** Colonels.

Student services. Alcohol/substance abuse counseling, chaplain/spiritual director, career counseling, student employment services, financial aid counseling, health services, minority student services, personal counseling, placement for graduates. **Physically disabled:** Services for visually, hearing impaired.

Contact. E-mail: admission@centre.edu
Phone: (859) 238-5350 Toll-free number: (800) 423-6236
Fax: (859) 238-5373
Bob Nesmith, Director of Admission, Centre College, 600 West Walnut Street, Danville, KY 40422-1394

Clear Creek Baptist Bible College
Pineville, Kentucky
www.ccbbc.edu   **CB code: 5975**

- Private 4-year Bible college affiliated with the Southern Baptist Convention
- Residential campus in small town
- 135 degree-seeking undergraduates
- Application essay, interview required

General. Founded in 1926. Regionally accredited; also accredited by ABHE. Bible college affiliated with Kentucky Baptist Convention that trains individuals for local church ministry, missions, or seminary preparation. **Degrees:** 21 bachelor's, 5 associate awarded. **Location:** 110 miles from

Lexington, 76 miles from Knoxville, TN. **Calendar:** Semester, limited summer session. **Full-time faculty:** 6 total; 83% have terminal degrees. **Part-time faculty:** 18 total; 50% have terminal degrees, 17% women. **Class size:** 92% < 20, 8% 20-39. **Special facilities:** Family life center, hiking/walking trails, campus thrift store.

Freshman class profile.

Out-of-state: 54% Live on campus: 70%

Basis for selection. Open admission, but selective for some programs. Recommendations by church required. **Home schooled:** Transcript of courses and grades required.

High school preparation. Recommended units include English 4, mathematics 3, social studies 2, history 2, science 2, foreign language 2 and computer science 1.

2015-2016 Annual costs. Tuition/fees: $8,310. Room/board: $3,570. Books/supplies: $1,200. Personal expenses: $1,000.

2015-2016 Financial aid. Need-based: 10 full-time freshmen applied for aid; 10 deemed to have need; 10 received aid. Average need met was 50%. Average scholarship/grant was $6,365. 88% of total undergraduate aid awarded as scholarships/grants, 12% as loans/jobs. **Non-need-based:** Awarded to 52 full-time undergraduates, including 3 freshmen. Scholarships awarded for academics, alumni affiliation, religious affiliation.

Application procedures. Admission: Priority date 7/15; no deadline. $40 fee, may be waived for applicants with need. Admission notification on a rolling basis. **Financial aid:** Priority date 6/30; no closing date. FAFSA, institutional form required. Applicants notified on a rolling basis starting 6/1; must reply by 8/1.

Academics. Special study options: Distance learning, double major, dual enrollment of high school students, independent study, internships. **Credit/placement by examination:** AP, CLEP, institutional tests. **Support services:** Reduced course load, remedial instruction, study skills assistance, tutoring.

Majors. Theology: Bible.

Technology on campus. 12 workstations in library, computer center. Dormitories wired for high-speed internet access and linked to campus network. Online course registration, online library, wireless network available.

Student life. Freshman orientation: Available. Preregistration for classes offered. Four-day program held week of registration. **Policies:** Dress code; no tobacco, alcohol, or drugs on campus. Religious observance required. **Housing:** Single-sex dorms, apartments available. $50 nonrefundable deposit. Cottages, family housing available. **Activities:** Campus ministries, choral groups, drama, music ensembles, student government, Women's Missionary Union, Brotherhood, Young Disciples, Acteens, Royal Ambassadors, Girls in Action, Mission Friends.

Athletics. Intramural: Basketball, football (non-tackle), softball, swimming, table tennis, tennis, volleyball.

Student services. Chaplain/spiritual director, career counseling, student employment services, financial aid counseling, health services, on-campus daycare, personal counseling, placement for graduates, veterans' counselor.

Contact. E-mail: admissions@ccbbc.edu
Phone: (606) 337-1072 Toll-free number: (866) 340-3196
Fax: (606) 337-2372
Ed Goodman, Director of Admissions, Clear Creek Baptist Bible College, 300 Clear Creek Road, Pineville, KY 40977-9754

Eastern Kentucky University
Richmond, Kentucky   **CB member**
www.eku.edu   **CB code: 1200**

- Public 4-year university
- Residential campus in large town
- 13,493 degree-seeking undergraduates: 16% part-time, 57% women
- 2,443 degree-seeking graduate students
- 71% of applicants admitted
- SAT or ACT (ACT writing optional) required

General. Founded in 1906. Regionally accredited. Courses offered at additional sites in Corbin, Danville, Manchester, Lancaster, London, Somerset, and Barbourville. **Degrees:** 2,532 bachelor's, 195 associate awarded; master's, professional offered. **ROTC:** Army. **Location:** 28 miles from Lexington, 110 miles from Cincinnati. **Calendar:** Semester, extensive summer session. **Full-time faculty:** 637 total; 82% have terminal degrees, 12% minority,

49% women. **Part-time faculty:** 507 total; 52% have terminal degrees, 9% minority, 57% women. **Class size:** 48% < 20, 44% 20-39, 4% 40-49, 3% 50-99, 1% >100. **Special facilities:** Planetarium, nature preserves, law enforcement facilities, music library.

Freshman class profile. 10,215 applied, 7,213 admitted, 2,821 enrolled.

Out-of-state:	17%	**Fraternities:**	13%
Live on campus:	69%	**Sororities:**	8%

Basis for selection. Applicants must have a minimum cumulative high school grade point average of 2.5 on a 4.0 scale or a minimum ACT composite score of 20 or SAT combined score of 950 or higher and meet the Kentucky Pre-college curriculum and have submitted an official six-semester high school transcript, or a General Equivalency Diploma, or documentation indicating completion of an EKU approved home-school or distance learning high school program. Adult Learners may use Residual ACT, Compass Test, or University Placement Exam results in place of test scores. Applicants without college preparatory courses subject to remediation. ACT only required for placement for in-state applicants. Interview recommended. Audition recommended for music majors. Portfolio recommended for art and graphic art majors. **Home schooled:** Transcript of courses and grades required.

High school preparation. 25 units required. Required units include English 4, mathematics 3, social studies 3, science 3 (laboratory 1), foreign language 2 and academic electives 7. Art, drama, music, and computer science also recommended.

2015-2016 Annual costs. Tuition/fees: $8,600; $18,090 out-of-state. Room/board: $8,360. Books/supplies: $1,000. Personal expenses: $1,500.

Financial aid. Non-need-based: Scholarships awarded for academics, alumni affiliation, art, athletics, job skills, leadership, minority status, music/drama, ROTC, state residency.

Application procedures. Admission: Closing date 8/1. $30 fee, may be waived for applicants with need. Admission notification on a rolling basis beginning on or about 8/1. **Financial aid:** No deadline. FAFSA required. Applicants notified on a rolling basis starting 4/1.

Academics. Special study options: Cooperative education, distance learning, double major, ESL, honors, independent study, internships, liberal arts/career combination, student-designed major, study abroad, teacher certification program. **Credit/placement by examination:** AP, CLEP, SAT, ACT, institutional tests. 30 credit hours maximum toward associate degree, 65 toward bachelor's. **Support services:** Learning center, pre-admission summer program, reduced course load, remedial instruction, study skills assistance, tutoring, writing center.

Majors. Area/ethnic studies: Canadian. **Biology:** General, bacteriology, ecology. **Business:** General, accounting, business admin, fashion, finance, insurance, management information systems, managerial economics, marketing, office management. **Communications:** Broadcast journalism, communications/speech/rhetoric, journalism, public relations. **Computer sciences:** General, computer science. **Conservation:** Management/policy, wildlife/wilderness. **Education:** Art, biology, business, Deaf/hearing impaired, elementary, family/consumer sciences, geography, mathematics, middle, music, physical, science, Spanish, special ed, speech impaired, technology/industrial arts, trade/industrial. **Engineering:** Engineering science. **English:** English lit, rhetoric/composition. **Foreign languages:** General, French, German, sign language interpretation, Spanish. **Health services:** Clinical lab assistant, clinical lab science, clinical lab technology, EMT paramedic, health care admin, health information management, health information technology, medical assistant, nursing (RN), predental, premedicine, preop/surgical nursing, prepharmacy. **History:** General. **Human services:** Social work. **Liberal arts:** Arts/sciences. **Math:** General, statistics. **Parks/recreation:** General, facilities management. **Philosophy/religion:** Philosophy. **Physical sciences:** Chemistry, geology, physics. **Protective services:** Corrections, fire safety technology, forensics, police science, security services. **Psychology:** General. **Social sciences:** Anthropology, economics, geography, political science, sociology. **Visual/performing arts:** Art, ceramics, dramatic, drawing, interior design, music, painting, printmaking, sculpture, studio arts. **Work/family studies:** Family studies, food/nutrition, housing.

Most popular majors. Business/marketing 12%, education 14%, health sciences 16%, security/protective services 13%.

Technology on campus. 250 workstations in dormitories, library, computer center, student center. Dormitories wired for high-speed internet access and linked to campus network. Commuter students can connect to campus network. Online course registration, online library, helpline, wireless network available.

Student life. Freshman orientation: Mandatory. Preregistration for classes offered. **Policies:** Students required to live on-campus until age 21 unless living with parent or guardian. **Housing:** Guaranteed on-campus for freshmen. Coed dorms, single-sex dorms, apartments, fraternity/sorority housing available. $100 fully refundable deposit. **Activities:** Bands, choral groups, dance, drama, literary magazine, music ensembles, musical theater, radio station, student government, student newspaper, symphony orchestra, 160 organizations available.

Athletics. NCAA. **Intercollegiate:** Baseball M, basketball, cheerleading, cross-country, football (tackle) M, golf, soccer W, softball W, swimming, tennis, track and field, volleyball W. **Intramural:** Basketball, football (tackle) M, golf, racquetball, softball, tennis, volleyball. **Team name:** Colonels.

Student services. Alcohol/substance abuse counseling, chaplain/spiritual director, career counseling, student employment services, financial aid counseling, health services, personal counseling, placement for graduates, veterans' counselor. **Physically disabled:** Services for visually, speech, hearing impaired.

Contact. E-mail: admissions@eku.edu
Phone: (859) 622-2106 Toll-free number: (800) 465-9191
Fax: (859) 622-8024
Brett Morris, Director of Admissions, Eastern Kentucky University, SSB CPO 54, 521 Lancaster Avenue, Richmond, KY 40475-3102

Georgetown College
Georgetown, Kentucky
www.georgetowncollege.edu   CB code: 1249

▸ Private 4-year liberal arts college affiliated with the Baptist faith
▸ Residential campus in large town
▸ 978 degree-seeking undergraduates: 7% part-time, 53% women, 7% African American, 1% Asian American, 4% Hispanic/Latino, 4% Multiracial, non-Hispanic, 1% international
▸ 380 degree-seeking graduate students
▸ 68% of applicants admitted
▸ SAT or ACT (ACT writing optional) required
▸ 57% graduate within 6 years

General. Founded in 1829. Regionally accredited. **Degrees:** 226 bachelor's awarded; master's offered. **ROTC:** Army, Air Force. **Location:** 12 miles from Lexington, 60 miles from Louisville, 70 miles from Cincinnati, OH. **Calendar:** Semester, limited summer session. **Full-time faculty:** 84 total; 94% have terminal degrees, 6% minority, 46% women. **Part-time faculty:** 65 total; 29% have terminal degrees, 12% minority, 49% women. **Class size:** 77% < 20, 23% 20-39. **Special facilities:** Planetarium, Foucault pendulum, arboretum, fine arts building and gallery, center for solids analysis, center for Christian discernment and academic leadership.

Freshman class profile. 2,145 applied, 1,452 admitted, 282 enrolled.

Mid 50% test scores		GPA 2.0-2.99:	25%
SAT critical reading:	440-530	Rank in top quarter:	44%
SAT math:	460-560	Rank in top tenth:	17%
ACT composite:	20-25	Return as sophomores:	89%
GPA 3.75 or higher:	26%	Out-of-state:	23%
GPA 3.50-3.74:	20%	Live on campus:	96%
GPA 3.0-3.49:	29%	International:	1%

Basis for selection. School achievement record, test scores, and rank in top half of class most important. Interview recommended for academically weak or special needs applicants. Audition recommended for music and communication arts majors. Portfolio recommended for art majors. **Home schooled:** Transcript of courses and grades required. Essay required.

High school preparation. College-preparatory program recommended. 20 units recommended. Recommended units include English 4, mathematics 3, social studies 2, science 3 and foreign language 2.

2015-2016 Annual costs. Tuition/fees: $34,280. Room/board: $8,710. Books/supplies: $1,250. Personal expenses: $1,620. **Additional information:** A new, all-day dining plan will begin in the fall of 2015. Students will have flexible meal times with a continuous dining program called the 'Carte Blanche Meal Plan' offering unlimited meal swipes.

2014-2015 Financial aid. Need-based: 263 full-time freshmen applied for aid; 244 deemed to have need; 244 received aid. Average need met was 88%. Average scholarship/grant was $15,317; average loan $2,575. 72% of total undergraduate aid awarded as scholarships/grants, 28% as loans/jobs. **Non-need-based:** Awarded to 779 full-time undergraduates, including 245 freshmen. Scholarships awarded for academics, alumni affiliation, art, athletics, leadership, music/drama, religious affiliation, ROTC, state residency.

Application procedures. Admission: Priority date 5/1; deadline 8/15 (postmark date). $30 fee, may be waived for applicants with need, free for online applicants. Admission notification on a rolling basis beginning on or about 10/1. Must reply by May 1 or within 4 week(s) if notified thereafter. **Financial aid:** Priority date 2/1; no closing date. FAFSA required. Applicants notified by 3/1; Applicants notified on a rolling basis starting 3/1; must reply by 5/1.

Academics. **Special study options:** Accelerated study, cooperative education, distance learning, double major, dual enrollment of high school students, ESL, honors, independent study, internships, liberal arts/career combination, student-designed major, study abroad, teacher certification program. Spanish Immersion program; 3-2 programs in Nursing and in Engineering with the University of Kentucky; joint degree programs with Regents Park College at Oxford University; programs in public policy and in diplomacy with the Patterson School of Diplomacy and International Commerce; Consortium for Global Education. **Credit/placement by examination:** AP, CLEP, IB, SAT, ACT, institutional tests. **Support services:** Study skills assistance, tutoring, writing center.

Majors. **Area/ethnic studies:** American, European, German. **Biology:** General. **Business:** General, accounting. **Communications:** Media studies. **Computer sciences:** General. **Education:** Elementary, middle, music, secondary. **English:** English lit. **Foreign languages:** French, German, Spanish. **Health services:** Athletic training, predental, prenursing, prepharmacy, preveterinary. **History:** General. **Math:** General. **Philosophy/religion:** Philosophy, religion. **Physical sciences:** Chemistry, physics. **Psychology:** General. **Social sciences:** Economics, political science, sociology. **Visual/performing arts:** Dramatic, music, studio arts.

Most popular majors. Biology 12%, business/marketing 13%, communications/journalism 12%, health sciences 6%, parks/recreation 10%, psychology 10%, social sciences 8%.

Technology on campus. 115 workstations in library, computer center, student center. Dormitories wired for high-speed internet access and linked to campus network. Commuter students can connect to campus network. Online course registration, online library, helpline, repair service, wireless network available.

Student life. **Freshman orientation:** Mandatory. Preregistration for classes offered. Four-day session held prior to beginning of fall semester. Orientation/registration weekends offered. **Policies:** An academic honor code enforced. The NEXUS Program offers a wide variety of events designed to create engagement and connections among the cultural, intellectual, and spiritual aspects of life in the campus community. Students choose at least six such events each semester. **Housing:** Guaranteed on-campus for freshmen. Single-sex dorms, apartments, fraternity/sorority housing available. $200 nonrefundable deposit, deadline 5/1. Minidorms of fewer than 80 students, some apartments for upperclassmen, newly constructed townhouses on campus including a limited number of units accessible for students with mobility limitations available. **Activities:** Bands, campus ministries, choral groups, dance, drama, literary magazine, music ensembles, Model UN, radio station, student government, student newspaper, Baptist Campus Ministry, Chapel Leadership Team, Catholic Student Association, Fellowship of Christian Athletes, Union of Black Leaders, Habitat for Humanity, Conflict-Free Campus Initiative, Community-based Experiential Learning Program, Harper Gatton Leadership Medallion Program.

Athletics. NAIA. **Intercollegiate:** Baseball M, basketball, cheerleading W, cross-country, football (tackle) M, golf, lacrosse W, soccer, softball W, tennis, track and field, volleyball W. **Intramural:** Basketball, equestrian, football (non-tackle), golf, racquetball, soccer, softball, table tennis, tennis, volleyball. **Team name:** Tigers.

Student services. Alcohol/substance abuse counseling, chaplain/spiritual director, career counseling, student employment services, financial aid counseling, health services, minority student services, personal counseling, placement for graduates, veterans' counselor.

Contact. E-mail: admissions@georgetowncollege.edu
Phone: (502) 863-8009 Toll-free number: (800) 788-9985
Fax: (502) 868-7733
Michelle Lynch, Vice President Enrollment Management, Georgetown College, 400 East College Street, Georgetown, KY 40324-1696

ITT Technical Institute: Louisville
Louisville, Kentucky
www.itt-tech.edu   **CB code: 2728**

- For-profit 4-year technical college
- Large city
- 547 undergraduates
- Interview required

General. Accredited by ACICS. **Degrees:** 22 bachelor's, 179 associate awarded. **Calendar:** Quarter, extensive summer session. **Full-time faculty:** 18 total. **Part-time faculty:** 66 total.

Basis for selection. Satisfactory scores from on-site tests in English and mathematics required.

2015-2016 Annual costs. Per-credit-hour charge, $493, will vary depending on program level and course of study. Academic fee, $200. Some programs require purchase of tools, which could cost an additional $150 to $655. All costs subject to change.

Application procedures. **Admission:** No deadline. No application fee. Admission notification on a rolling basis. **Financial aid:** No deadline. FAFSA, institutional form required. Applicants notified on a rolling basis.

Academics. **Credit/placement by examination:** AP, CLEP. **Support services:** Learning center, tutoring.

Majors. **Business:** Business admin, construction management, e-commerce. **Communications technology:** Animation/special effects. **Computer sciences:** Security. **Protective services:** Law enforcement admin.

Technology on campus. Online library available.

Student services. Career counseling, student employment services, placement for graduates.

Contact. Phone: (502) 327-7424
Steve Allen, Director of Recruitment, ITT Technical Institute: Louisville, 9500 Ormsby Station Road, Louisville, KY 40223

Kentucky Christian University
Grayson, Kentucky
www.kcu.edu   **CB code: 1377**

- Private 4-year university and Bible college
- Residential campus in small town
- 564 degree-seeking undergraduates: 12% part-time, 47% women
- 35 degree-seeking graduate students
- SAT or ACT (ACT writing optional), application essay required

General. Founded in 1919. Regionally accredited. **Degrees:** 108 bachelor's awarded; master's offered. **Location:** 25 miles from Ashland, 100 miles from Lexington. **Calendar:** Semester, limited summer session. **Full-time faculty:** 34 total; 56% have terminal degrees, 3% minority, 41% women. **Part-time faculty:** 30 total; 20% have terminal degrees, 40% women. **Class size:** 72% < 20, 25% 20-39, 3% 40-49.

Freshman class profile.

GPA 3.75 or higher:	20%	Rank in top quarter:	33%
GPA 3.50-3.74:	14%	Rank in top tenth:	15%
GPA 3.0-3.49:	26%	Out-of-state:	54%
GPA 2.0-2.99:	38%	Live on campus:	86%

Basis for selection. High school grades and rank in class, ACT or SAT test scores, personal references, and religious commitment considered. Interview recommended for academically weak. **Home schooled:** Transcript of courses and grades, letter of recommendation (nonparent) required. **Learning Disabled:** Students with special needs should contact the Vice President of Student Services or the Director of Campus Counseling to make arrangements for special accommodations.

High school preparation. College-preparatory program recommended. 12 units required; 25 recommended. Required and recommended units include English 4, mathematics 4, social studies 4, history 4, science 4 (laboratory 1), foreign language 2 and academic electives 2.

2015-2016 Annual costs. Tuition/fees: $17,810. Room/board: $7,800.

Financial aid. Non-need-based: Scholarships awarded for academics, alumni affiliation, leadership, minority status, music/drama, religious affiliation.

Application procedures. **Admission:** Closing date 8/1 (receipt date). $30 fee, may be waived for applicants with need, free for online applicants. Admission notification on a rolling basis. **Financial aid:** Priority date 3/1; no closing date. FAFSA required. Applicants notified on a rolling basis starting 3/15; must reply within 2 week(s) of notification.

Academics. All students required to major in Bible as a second degree. **Special study options:** Combined bachelor's/graduate degree, distance learning, double major, dual enrollment of high school students, independent study, internships, liberal arts/career combination, study abroad, teacher certification program. **Credit/placement by examination:** AP, CLEP, SAT, ACT, institutional tests. 59 credit hours maximum toward bachelor's degree. **Support services:** Learning center, reduced course load, remedial instruction, study skills assistance, tutoring, writing center.

Majors. Biology: General. **Business:** Business admin. **Education:** Elementary, English, mathematics, middle, social studies. **Health services:** Nursing (RN). **History:** General. **Human services:** Social work. **Liberal arts:** Humanities. **Psychology:** Counseling. **Theology:** Bible, sacred music. **Visual/performing arts:** Music management, music performance.

Most popular majors. Business/marketing 6%, education 10%, health sciences 21%, history 6%, interdisciplinary studies 18%, psychology 7%, public administration/social services 21%, theological studies 9%.

Technology on campus. 52 workstations in library, computer center, student center. Dormitories wired for high-speed internet access and linked to campus network. Commuter students can connect to campus network. Online library, helpline, repair service, wireless network available.

Student life. Freshman orientation: Mandatory. Preregistration for classes offered. **Policies:** All students under 26 not living with parents must live in on-campus housing. Religious observance required. **Housing:** Guaranteed on-campus for all undergraduates. Single-sex dorms, special housing for disabled, apartments available. $100 nonrefundable deposit, deadline 8/1. **Activities:** Bands, campus ministries, choral groups, drama, music ensembles, student government, Global Mission Awareness, Pi Chi Delta, Collegiate Music Educators National Conference, Herodotus Society, Laos Protos, American Association of Christian Counselors, Students in Free Enterprise.

Athletics. NAIA, NCCAA. **Intercollegiate:** Archery, basketball, cheerleading, cross-country, football (tackle) M, soccer, softball W, volleyball W. **Intramural:** Basketball, football (non-tackle) M, soccer, softball, table tennis, volleyball. **Team name:** Knights.

Student services. Chaplain/spiritual director, career counseling, financial aid counseling, health services, minority student services, personal counseling, women's services. **Physically disabled:** Services for visually, hearing impaired.

Contact. E-mail: knights@kcu.edu
Phone: (606) 474-3266 Toll-free number: (800) 522-3181
Fax: (606) 474-3155
Heather Stacy, Director of Admissions, Kentucky Christian University, 100 Academic Parkway, Grayson, KY 41143-2205

Kentucky Mountain Bible College
Jackson, Kentucky
www.kmbc.edu   CB code: 1384

▶ Private 4-year Bible college affiliated with the Kentucky Mountain Holiness Association
▶ Residential campus in rural community
▶ 67 degree-seeking undergraduates: 18% part-time, 43% women
▶ 54% of applicants admitted
▶ ACT (writing optional), application essay required
▶ 47% graduate within 6 years; 25% enter graduate study

General. Founded in 1931. Accredited by ABHE. **Degrees:** 12 bachelor's, 3 associate awarded. **Location:** 75 miles from Lexington. **Calendar:** 4-1-4. **Part-time faculty:** 17 total; 6% have terminal degrees, 29% women. **Class size:** 95% < 20, 5% 20-39. **Special facilities:** Radio station, hiking tails in several hundred acres of woodland.

Freshman class profile. 69 applied, 37 admitted, 25 enrolled.

Mid 50% test scores		Rank in top tenth:	11%
ACT composite:	18-24	End year in good standing:	92%
GPA 3.75 or higher:	15%	Return as sophomores:	85%
GPA 3.50-3.74:	40%	Out-of-state:	19%
GPA 3.0-3.49:	30%	Live on campus:	94%
Rank in top quarter:	44%		

Basis for selection. All students must have C average or above and provide 2 recommendations. 15 ACT required. Provisional admission granted. Interview recommended.

High school preparation. 18 units required. Required and recommended units include English 4, mathematics 2, history 2 and science 2. A total of 10 units in English, math, science or language required out of 18 units.

2015-2016 Annual costs. Tuition/fees: $7,460. Room/board: $4,750. Books/supplies: $500. Personal expenses: $2,205.

2015-2016 Financial aid. Need-based: 14 full-time freshmen applied for aid; 14 deemed to have need; 14 received aid. Average need met was 65%. Average scholarship/grant was $5,393; average loan $6,625. 66% of total undergraduate aid awarded as scholarships/grants, 34% as loans/jobs. **Non-need-based:** Scholarships awarded for academics, job skills, leadership, music/drama.

Application procedures. Admission: Priority date 6/1; no deadline. $25 fee, may be waived for applicants with need. Admission notification on a rolling basis. **Financial aid:** Priority date 5/1; no closing date. FAFSA, institutional form required. Applicants notified on a rolling basis starting 3/15.

Academics. Special study options: Distance learning, dual enrollment of high school students, independent study, internships, teacher certification program. **Credit/placement by examination:** AP, CLEP, ACT, institutional tests. 20 credit hours maximum toward associate degree, 20 toward bachelor's. **Support services:** Reduced course load, remedial instruction, study skills assistance, tutoring.

Majors. Communications: Communications/speech/rhetoric. **Education:** Elementary. **Theology:** Missionary, religious ed, sacred music, theology.

Technology on campus. 4 workstations in library, computer center. Dormitories wired for high-speed internet access and linked to campus network. Commuter students can connect to campus network. Online library, repair service, wireless network available.

Student life. Freshman orientation: Mandatory. Preregistration for classes offered. Two-day program held immediately before semester; includes Bible-knowledge testing. **Policies:** No pets, except fish and turtles, allowed in dorms. Religious observance required. **Housing:** Guaranteed on-campus for all undergraduates. Single-sex dorms, apartments, wellness housing available. Pets allowed in dorm rooms. **Activities:** Campus ministries, choral groups, drama, radio station, student government, student newspaper, missionary student involvement group, student council, class organizations.

Student services. Chaplain/spiritual director, financial aid counseling, health services, personal counseling.

Contact. E-mail: kmbc@kmbc.edu
Phone: (606) 693-5000 ext. 130
Toll-free number: (800) 879-5622 ext. 130 Fax: (888) 742-1124
David Lorimer, Director of Admissions, Kentucky Mountain Bible College, 855 Highway 541, Jackson, KY 41339

Kentucky State University
Frankfort, Kentucky   **CB member**
www.kysu.edu   **CB code: 1368**

▶ Public 4-year university and liberal arts college
▶ Residential campus in large town
▶ 1,286 degree-seeking undergraduates: 15% part-time, 59% women, 57% African American, 1% Asian American, 3% Hispanic/Latino, 2% Multiracial, non-Hispanic
▶ 150 degree-seeking graduate students
▶ 38% of applicants admitted
▶ SAT or ACT (ACT writing optional) required

General. Founded in 1886. Regionally accredited. 1890 Land Grant institution, Historically Black College/University. **Degrees:** 270 bachelor's, 62 associate awarded; master's, professional offered. **ROTC:** Army, Air Force. **Location:** 50 miles from Louisville, 25 miles from Lexington. **Calendar:** Semester, limited summer session. **Full-time faculty:** 121 total; 78% have terminal degrees, 42% minority, 35% women. **Part-time faculty:** 8 total; 62% have terminal degrees, 12% minority, 50% women. **Class size:** 77% < 20, 23% 20-39, less than 1% 50-99. **Special facilities:** Center of excellence for the study of Kentucky African Americans, center for families and children, aquaculture production technologies laboratory, floating science lab (Kentucky River Thoroughbred), research and demonstration farm.

Freshman class profile. 4,666 applied, 1,787 admitted, 210 enrolled.

Mid 50% test scores		GPA 2.0-2.99:	49%
SAT critical reading:	380-480	Rank in top quarter:	26%
SAT math:	450-570	Rank in top tenth:	3.9%
SAT writing:	380-480	End year in good standing:	93%
ACT composite:	17-22	Return as sophomores:	60%
GPA 3.75 or higher:	12%	Out-of-state:	33%
GPA 3.50-3.74:	12%	Live on campus:	82%
GPA 3.0-3.49:	25%		

Basis for selection. Regular admission: 2.5 high school GPA or 18 ACT. **Home schooled:** Statement describing home school structure and mission, transcript of courses and grades required. **Learning Disabled:** Provide proof of individualized education plan (IEP).

High school preparation. College-preparatory program required. 19 units required. Required units include English 4, mathematics 3, social studies 3, history 3, science 3 and foreign language 2. Physical education .5, health education .5.

2015-2016 Annual costs. Tuition/fees: $7,754; $18,056 out-of-state. Room/board: $6,690. Books/supplies: $1,300. Personal expenses: $1,890.

2015-2016 Financial aid. Need-based: 192 full-time freshmen applied for aid; 182 deemed to have need; 182 received aid. Average need met was 87%. Average scholarship/grant was $9,987; average loan $3,733. 49% of total undergraduate aid awarded as scholarships/grants, 51% as loans/jobs. **Non-need-based:** Awarded to 162 full-time undergraduates, including 44 freshmen. Scholarships awarded for academics, alumni affiliation, art, athletics, leadership, music/drama.

Application procedures. Admission: Priority date 11/1; deadline 7/1. $30 fee, may be waived for applicants with need. Admission notification on a rolling basis beginning on or about 9/15. **Financial aid:** Priority date 4/15; no closing date. FAFSA required. Applicants notified on a rolling basis starting 3/15; must reply within 4 week(s) of notification.

Academics. Special study options: Combined bachelor's/graduate degree, cooperative education, distance learning, double major, dual enrollment of high school students, honors, independent study, internships, liberal arts/career combination, semester at sea, student-designed major, teacher certification program. **Credit/placement by examination:** AP, CLEP, IB, SAT, ACT. 15 credit hours maximum toward associate degree, 30 toward bachelor's. Up to one-fourth the minimum number of semester credit hours required for completion of a baccalaureate degree or an associate degree at KSU may be earned through any combination of credit by examination and credit for life experience. **Support services:** Learning center, pre-admission summer program, reduced course load, remedial instruction, study skills assistance, tutoring, writing center.

Honors college/program. High school GPA 3.0 and 21 ACT.

Majors. Area/ethnic studies: African. **Biology:** General. **Business:** General. **Computer sciences:** General, information technology. **Education:** Elementary, physical. **English:** English lit. **Foreign languages:** Spanish. **Health services:** Nursing (RN). **Human services:** General, social work. **Liberal arts:** Arts/sciences. **Math:** General. **Physical sciences:** Chemistry. **Protective services:** Criminal justice. **Psychology:** General. **Social sciences:** General, political science. **Visual/performing arts:** Music, studio arts. **Work/family studies:** Family studies.

Most popular majors. Biology 6%, business/marketing 9%, computer/information sciences 7%, education 7%, health sciences 7%, liberal arts 13%, psychology 9%, public administration/social services 10%, security/protective services 10%.

Technology on campus. 127 workstations in dormitories, library, computer center, student center. Dormitories wired for high-speed internet access and linked to campus network. Online library, helpline, wireless network available.

Student life. Freshman orientation: Mandatory. Preregistration for classes offered. **Policies:** Maintaining the required GPA and in good financial standing to become Greek. **Housing:** Coed dorms, single-sex dorms available. $310 nonrefundable deposit. Special dorm rooms for disabled students available. **Activities:** Bands, campus ministries, choral groups, dance, international student organizations, music ensembles, student government, student newspaper, symphony orchestra, Royal Phaze, Alpha Phi Omega, NAACP, KSU Girls Rock, spring dance team, Apostolic Lighthouse, creative writing club, Wesley Foundation, Student Ambassadors, Whitney Young Student Council.

Athletics. NCAA. **Intercollegiate:** Baseball M, basketball, cheerleading W, cross-country, football (tackle) M, golf M, softball W, track and field, volleyball W. **Intramural:** Badminton, basketball, football (non-tackle), gymnastics, racquetball, volleyball. **Team name:** Thorobreds.

Student services. Adult student services, alcohol/substance abuse counseling, chaplain/spiritual director, career counseling, student employment services, financial aid counseling, health services, on-campus daycare, personal counseling, placement for graduates, veterans' counselor. **Physically disabled:** Services for visually, speech, hearing impaired.

Contact. E-mail: admissions@kysu.edu
Phone: (502) 597-6813 Toll-free number: (877) 367-5978
Fax: (502) 597-5814
Andrea Houston, Special Projects Coordinator, Kentucky State University, 400 East Main Street, ASB 312, Frankfort, KY 40601

Kentucky Wesleyan College
Owensboro, Kentucky
www.kwc.edu   CB code: 1369

◗ Private 4-year liberal arts college affiliated with the United Methodist Church
◗ Residential campus in small city
◗ 691 degree-seeking undergraduates: 4% part-time, 47% women, 15% African American, 1% Hispanic/Latino
◗ SAT or ACT (ACT writing optional) required
◗ 42% graduate within 6 years

General. Founded in 1858. Regionally accredited. **Degrees:** 99 bachelor's awarded. **ROTC:** Army. **Location:** 116 miles from Louisville; 120 miles from Nashville, TN. **Calendar:** Semester, extensive summer session. **Full-time faculty:** 45 total; 69% have terminal degrees, 7% minority, 56% women. **Part-time faculty:** 37 total; 16% have terminal degrees, 8% minority, 46% women. **Class size:** 84% < 20, 14% 20-39, 1% 40-49, less than 1% 50-99. **Special facilities:** Center for the sciences, center for the arts, fully computerized writing workshop, center for business studies.

Freshman class profile.

GPA 3.75 or higher:	22%	**Return as sophomores:**	61%
GPA 3.50-3.74:	18%	**Out-of-state:**	33%
GPA 3.0-3.49:	30%	**Live on campus:**	66%
GPA 2.0-2.99:	29%	**Fraternities:**	17%
Rank in top quarter:	39%	**Sororities:**	32%
Rank in top tenth:	13%		

Basis for selection. Secondary school record very important. Test scores, GPA, class rank, and school activities important. **Home schooled:** Transcript of courses and grades required.

High school preparation. College-preparatory program recommended. 13 units required. Required and recommended units include English 4, mathematics 3, social studies 3, science 3 and foreign language 2.

2015-2016 Annual costs. Tuition/fees: $23,250. Room/board: $8,150. Books/supplies: $1,400. Personal expenses: $2,090.

2014-2015 Financial aid. Need-based: 222 full-time freshmen applied for aid; 207 deemed to have need; 206 received aid. Average need met was 74%. Average scholarship/grant was $15,663; average loan $3,153. 75% of total undergraduate aid awarded as scholarships/grants, 25% as loans/jobs. **Non-need-based:** Awarded to 150 full-time undergraduates, including 49 freshmen. Scholarships awarded for academics, alumni affiliation, art, athletics, leadership, music/drama, religious affiliation, state residency.

Application procedures. Admission: No deadline. No application fee. Admission notification on a rolling basis beginning on or about 9/1. **Financial aid:** Priority date 1/1; no closing date. FAFSA required. Applicants notified on a rolling basis starting 2/15; must reply within 2 week(s) of notification.

Academics. Special study options: Combined bachelor's/graduate degree, distance learning, double major, dual enrollment of high school students, independent study, internships, liberal arts/career combination, student-designed major, study abroad, teacher certification program, Washington semester. **Credit/placement by examination:** AP, CLEP, IB, SAT, ACT, institutional tests. 42 credit hours maximum toward bachelor's degree. International Baccalaureate Diploma credit will be awarded for advanced course scores of 6 or 7, with up to 10 hours of credit awarded. **Support services:** Learning center, reduced course load, remedial instruction, study skills assistance, tutoring, writing center.

Majors. Biology: General, zoology. **Business:** General, accounting, business admin. **Communications:** Communications/speech/rhetoric. **Computer sciences:** General. **Education:** Art, biology, chemistry, elementary, English, mathematics, middle, physical, social studies, Spanish. **English:** English lit. **Foreign languages:** Spanish. **History:** General. **Math:** General. **Parks/recreation:** Sports admin. **Philosophy/religion:** Religion. **Physical sciences:** Chemistry, physics. **Protective services:** Criminal justice. **Psychology:** General. **Social sciences:** Political science. **Visual/performing arts:** Art, music management, music performance, studio arts.

Most popular majors. Biology 11%, business/marketing 12%, communications/journalism 7%, education 11%, parks/recreation 6%, psychology 8%, security/protective services 11%, visual/performing arts 11%.

Technology on campus. 125 workstations in dormitories, library, computer center, student center. Dormitories wired for high-speed internet access and linked to campus network. Commuter students can connect to campus network. Online course registration, online library, helpline, repair service, wireless network available.

Student life. Freshman orientation: Mandatory, $125 fee. Preregistration for classes offered. **Housing:** Guaranteed on-campus for freshmen. Coed dorms, single-sex dorms, apartments, fraternity/sorority housing available. $100 fully refundable deposit, deadline 8/28. **Activities:** Bands, campus ministries, choral groups, dance, drama, international student organizations, literary magazine, music ensembles, musical theater, radio station, student government, student newspaper, student activities programming board, Baptist Student Union, United Methodist Student Fellowship, Brothers and Sisters in Christ, Criminal Justice Association, College Republicans, Young Democrats, Fellowship of Christian Athletes, psychology club.

Athletics. NCAA. **Intercollegiate:** Baseball M, basketball, cross-country, football (tackle) M, golf, soccer, softball W, tennis W, track and field, volleyball W. **Intramural:** Basketball, bowling, football (non-tackle), soccer, softball, table tennis, tennis, volleyball. **Team name:** Panthers.

Student services. Alcohol/substance abuse counseling, chaplain/spiritual director, career counseling, student employment services, financial aid counseling, health services, personal counseling, placement for graduates. **Physically disabled:** Services for visually impaired.

Contact. E-mail: rsmith@kwc.edu
Phone: (270) 852-3120 Toll-free number: (800) 999-0592
Fax: (270) 852-3133
Rashad Smith, Director of Admissions, Kentucky Wesleyan College, 3000 Frederica Street, Owensboro, KY 42301

Lindsey Wilson College
Columbia, Kentucky
www.lindsey.edu
CB code: 1409

▶ Private 4-year liberal arts college affiliated with the United Methodist Church

▶ Residential campus in small town

▶ 2,100 degree-seeking undergraduates: 2% part-time, 59% women, 9% African American, 1% Hispanic/Latino, 2% Multi-racial, non-Hispanic

▶ 436 degree-seeking graduate students

▶ 34% graduate within 6 years

General. Founded in 1903. Regionally accredited. **Degrees:** 439 bachelor's, 15 associate awarded; master's, doctoral offered. **Location:** 100 miles from Louisville. **Calendar:** Semester, limited summer session. **Full-time faculty:** 111 total. **Part-time faculty:** 137 total. **Class size:** 63% < 20, 37% 20-39, less than 1% 40-49.

Freshman class profile. 2,870 applied, 2,010 admitted, 514 enrolled.

Mid 50% test scores		Rank in top quarter:	33%
ACT composite:	19-24	Rank in top tenth:	13%
GPA 3.75 or higher:	23%	Return as sophomores:	61%
GPA 3.50-3.74:	12%	Out-of-state:	17%
GPA 3.0-3.49:	36%	Live on campus:	72%
GPA 2.0-2.99:	28%		

Basis for selection. Open admission, but selective for some programs. Special requirements for education, human services and nursing programs. Interview recommended. **Home schooled:** Transcript of courses and grades required.

High school preparation. College-preparatory program recommended.

2015-2016 Annual costs. Tuition/fees: $23,162. Room/board: $8,900. Books/supplies: $1,000. Personal expenses: $2,963.

2015-2016 Financial aid. All financial aid based on need. 514 full-time freshmen applied for aid; 484 deemed to have need; 484 received aid. Average scholarship/grant was $11,170; average loan $8,112. 74% of total undergraduate aid awarded as scholarships/grants, 26% as loans/jobs.

Application procedures. Admission: Priority date 6/1; no deadline. No application fee. Admission notification on a rolling basis beginning on or about 9/1. **Financial aid:** Priority date 3/1; no closing date. FAFSA, institutional form required. Applicants notified on a rolling basis starting 5/1; must reply within 2 week(s) of notification.

Academics. Special study options: Double major, dual enrollment of high school students, honors, independent study, internships, student-designed major, study abroad, teacher certification program, Washington semester, weekend college. On-campus and extension evening program for associate degree in business management and computer science, weekend extension program in human services. **Credit/placement by examination:** AP, CLEP. 16 credit hours maximum toward associate degree, 32 toward bachelor's.

Support services: Learning center, reduced course load, remedial instruction, study skills assistance, tutoring, writing center.

Majors. Area/ethnic studies: American. **Biology:** General. **Business:** Business admin. **Communications:** Communications/speech/rhetoric, journalism. **Education:** Art, biology, elementary, English, mathematics, middle, music, physical, secondary, social science. **English:** English lit. **History:** General. **Liberal arts:** Humanities. **Math:** General. **Parks/recreation:** Health/fitness. **Philosophy/religion:** Christian. **Protective services:** Criminal justice. **Psychology:** General. **Social sciences:** General. **Visual/performing arts:** Studio arts, theater arts management.

Most popular majors. Business/marketing 9%, education 7%, public administration/social services 51%, security/protective services 6%.

Technology on campus. 100 workstations in library, computer center, student center. Dormitories wired for high-speed internet access and linked to campus network. Commuter students can connect to campus network. Online course registration, online library, helpline, repair service, wireless network available.

Student life. Freshman orientation: Mandatory. Preregistration for classes offered. **Policies:** All students not living with family must live in campus housing. **Housing:** Single-sex dorms, apartments, wellness housing available. $45 nonrefundable deposit. **Activities:** Bands, campus ministries, choral groups, dance, drama, international student organizations, literary magazine, music ensembles, student government, student newspaper, symphony orchestra, Bonner Scholars, Humanity Hands, student activities board, student ambassadors.

Athletics. NAIA. **Intercollegiate:** Baseball M, basketball, bowling, cross-country, football (tackle) M, golf, soccer, softball W, swimming, tennis, track and field, volleyball W, wrestling M. **Intramural:** Basketball, football (non-tackle), racquetball, soccer, softball, swimming, table tennis, tennis, ultimate frisbee, volleyball. **Team name:** Blue Raiders.

Student services. Alcohol/substance abuse counseling, chaplain/spiritual director, career counseling, student employment services, financial aid counseling, health services, minority student services, personal counseling, placement for graduates, veterans' counselor, women's services. **Physically disabled:** Services for visually impaired.

Contact. E-mail: admissions@lindsey.edu
Phone: (270) 384-8100 Toll-free number: (800) 264-0138
Fax: (270) 384-8591
Charity Ferguson, Director of Admissions, Lindsey Wilson College, 210 Lindsey Wilson Street, Columbia, KY 42728

Midway College
Midway, Kentucky
www.midway.edu
CB member
CB code: 1467

▶ Private 4-year liberal arts college for women affiliated with the Christian Church (Disciples of Christ)

▶ Residential campus in small town

▶ 916 degree-seeking undergraduates

▶ 111 graduate students

▶ SAT or ACT (ACT writing optional) required

▶ 56% graduate within 6 years

General. Founded in 1847. Regionally accredited. Men admitted to evening, weekend and online programs. **Degrees:** 212 bachelor's, 99 associate awarded; master's offered. **ROTC:** Army, Air Force. **Location:** 12 miles from Lexington, 60 miles from Louisville. **Calendar:** Semester, limited summer session. **Full-time faculty:** 44 total. **Part-time faculty:** 96 total. **Class size:** 80% < 20, 19% 20-39, 1% 40-49. **Special facilities:** Equine science center, riding arena, campus farm.

Freshman class profile.

GPA 3.75 or higher:	15%	Rank in top quarter:	42%
GPA 3.50-3.74:	23%	Rank in top tenth:	16%
GPA 3.0-3.49:	36%	Out-of-state:	9%
GPA 2.0-2.99:	24%	Live on campus:	45%

Basis for selection. High school record and test scores important. Essay and letters of recommendation encouraged. More competitive requirements established for certain programs such as biology, education, nursing. Interview required for majors in nursing; also required of academically weak. Essay recommended for students who are conditionally admitted.

High school preparation. 15 units required. Required and recommended units include English 4, mathematics 2, social studies 1, history 1 and science 2. Specific college-preparatory program required for some majors.

2016-2017 Annual costs. Tuition/fees: $23,250. Room/board: $8,400. Books/supplies: $1,500. Personal expenses: $1,000.

Financial aid. Non-need-based: Scholarships awarded for academics, alumni affiliation, art, athletics, leadership, minority status, religious affiliation. **Additional information:** Audition required of applicants for music scholarships.

Application procedures. Admission: Priority date 4/1; no deadline. $25 fee, may be waived for applicants with need. Admission notification on a rolling basis. Must reply by May 1 or within 4 week(s) if notified thereafter. **Financial aid:** No deadline. FAFSA, institutional form required. Applicants notified on a rolling basis; must reply within 4 week(s) of notification.

Academics. Special study options: Accelerated study, cooperative education, distance learning, double major, dual enrollment of high school students, independent study, internships, liberal arts/career combination, study abroad, teacher certification program. Evening programs in business, nursing, and teacher certification. **Credit/placement by examination:** AP, CLEP, IB, ACT, institutional tests. 12 credit hours maximum toward associate degree, 12 toward bachelor's. **Support services:** Learning center, reduced course load, remedial instruction, study skills assistance, tutoring, writing center.

Majors. Biology: General, ecology. **Business:** General, human resources, organizational behavior. **Computer sciences:** General. **Conservation:** Environmental science. **Education:** Elementary, middle, multi-level teacher, secondary, special ed. **English:** English lit. **Health services:** Health care admin, nursing (RN), pharmaceutical sciences, predental, premedicine, preoptometry, prepharmacy. **Liberal arts:** Arts/sciences. **Math:** General. **Parks/recreation:** Sports admin. **Protective services:** Disaster management, homeland security, security services. **Psychology:** General.

Technology on campus. 60 workstations in dormitories, library, computer center, student center. Dormitories wired for high-speed internet access and linked to campus network. Commuter students can connect to campus network. Online course registration, online library, helpline, wireless network available.

Student life. Freshman orientation: Mandatory. Preregistration for classes offered. Two-three day orientation prior to start of term. **Policies:** All students under 21, unmarried, and not living at home required to live in campus housing. **Housing:** Guaranteed on-campus for all undergraduates. Special housing for disabled, wellness housing available. $100 nonrefundable deposit, deadline 5/1. **Activities:** Campus ministries, choral groups, international student organizations, student government, commuters committee, Fellowship of Christian Athletes, Disciples on Campus, Ruth Slack Roach Scholars.

Athletics. NAIA. **Intercollegiate:** Archery W, basketball W, cross-country W, equestrian W, golf W, soccer W, softball W, tennis W, track and field W, volleyball W. **Team name:** Eagles.

Student services. Adult student services, chaplain/spiritual director, career counseling, student employment services, financial aid counseling, health services, minority student services, personal counseling, placement for graduates, veterans' counselor, women's services.

Contact. E-mail: admissions@midway.edu
Phone: (859) 846-5347 Toll-free number: (800) 755-0031
Fax: (859) 846-5787
Stephanie Whaley, Dean of Enrollment Services, Midway College, 512 East Stephens Street, Midway, KY 40347-1120

Morehead State University
Morehead, Kentucky **CB member**
www.moreheadstate.edu **CB code: 1487**

- Public 4-year university
- Residential campus in large town
- 7,038 degree-seeking undergraduates: 13% part-time, 60% women, 4% African American, 1% Hispanic/Latino, 2% Multi-racial, non-Hispanic, 2% international
- 978 degree-seeking graduate students
- 85% of applicants admitted
- SAT or ACT (ACT writing optional) required
- 46% graduate within 6 years

General. Founded in 1922. Regionally accredited. **Degrees:** 1,166 bachelor's, 164 associate awarded; master's, doctoral offered. **ROTC:** Army. **Location:** 65 miles from Lexington, 70 miles from Huntington, WV. **Calendar:** Semester, extensive summer session. **Full-time faculty:** 349 total; 72% have terminal degrees, 7% minority, 47% women. **Part-time faculty:** 89 total;

3% minority, 58% women. **Class size:** 55% < 20, 37% 20-39, 6% 40-49, 2% 50-99, less than 1% >100. **Special facilities:** Planetarium, agriculture complex, outdoor learning center at Cave Run, Kentucky folk art center, space science center, space tracking radio telescope, Center for Traditional Music.

Freshman class profile. 4,888 applied, 4,174 admitted, 1,461 enrolled.

Mid 50% test scores		
SAT critical reading:	430-550	Rank in top quarter: 44%
SAT math:	420-550	Rank in top tenth: 18%
SAT writing:	388-520	Return as sophomores: 66%
ACT composite:	20-25	Out-of-state: 13%
GPA 3.75 or higher:	29%	Live on campus: 77%
GPA 3.50-3.74:	19%	International: 3%
GPA 3.0-3.49:	30%	Fraternities: 4%
GPA 2.0-2.99:	21%	Sororities: 8%

Basis for selection. Test scores and GPA used to calculate index to determine admission. Status and review of pre-college curriculum important. Some professional programs such as teaching, nursing, and music have additional criteria. Interview recommended for applicants to specialized allied health programs. Audition recommended for music majors. Students not meeting academic requirements may request an interview and submit additional documentation in order to be admitted with conditions. **Home schooled:** Statement describing home school structure and mission, transcript of courses and grades required.

High school preparation. College-preparatory program required. 24 units required. Required and recommended units include English 4, mathematics 3, social studies 3, science 3, foreign language 2, computer science 1, visual/performing arts 1 and academic electives 7. 1 unit health and PE.

2015-2016 Annual costs. Tuition/fees: $7,966; $20,114 out-of-state. Room/board: $8,300. Books/supplies: $1,200. Personal expenses: $1,651.

Financial aid. Non-need-based: Scholarships awarded for academics, alumni affiliation, art, athletics, leadership, minority status, music/drama, ROTC, state residency.

Application procedures. Admission: No deadline. $30 fee, may be waived for applicants with need. Admission notification on a rolling basis. **Financial aid:** Priority date 3/15; no closing date. FAFSA required. Applicants notified on a rolling basis.

Academics. 2-year transfer programs in pre-chiropractic, pre-dentistry, pre-engineering, pre-forestry, pre-law, pre-medicine, pre-optometry, pre-pharmacy, pre-physical therapy, pre-veterinary medicine, and others offered. **Special study options:** Accelerated study, cooperative education, cross-registration, distance learning, double major, dual enrollment of high school students, ESL, honors, independent study, internships, student-designed major, study abroad, teacher certification program, Washington semester, weekend college. **Credit/placement by examination:** AP, CLEP, IB, SAT, ACT, institutional tests. 16 credit hours maximum toward associate degree, 32 toward bachelor's. **Support services:** Learning center, pre-admission summer program, remedial instruction, study skills assistance, tutoring, writing center.

Majors. Biology: General. **Business:** Accounting, business admin, finance, management information systems, managerial economics, marketing, real estate. **Communications:** Communications/speech/rhetoric. **Computer sciences:** General. **Education:** Business, early childhood, elementary, health, middle, physical, special ed. **English:** Creative writing, English lit. **Foreign languages:** French, Spanish. **Health services:** Medical radiologic technology/radiation therapy, nursing (RN). **History:** General. **Human services:** Social work. **Math:** General. **Parks/recreation:** Exercise sciences. **Philosophy/religion:** Philosophy. **Physical sciences:** Chemistry, geology, physics. **Psychology:** General. **Social sciences:** General, geography, political science, sociology. **Visual/performing arts:** Dramatic, music, studio arts.

Most popular majors. Business/marketing 13%, education 10%, health sciences 12%, liberal arts 12%, public administration/social services 7%.

Technology on campus. 2,100 workstations in library, computer center, student center. Dormitories wired for high-speed internet access and linked to campus network. Commuter students can connect to campus network. Online course registration, online library, helpline, repair service, student web hosting, wireless network available.

Student life. Freshman orientation: Mandatory. Preregistration for classes offered. Held several times in June and July. **Housing:** Coed dorms, special housing for disabled, fraternity/sorority housing available. $100 fully refundable deposit. Limited housing for agricultural students at the University Farm; housing for handicapped students; some private rooms available. **Activities:** Bands, campus ministries, choral groups, dance, drama, international student organizations, literary magazine, music ensembles, musical theater, opera, radio station, student government, student newspaper, symphony orchestra, TV station, six religious organizations, Young Democrats, Young Republicans, several service organizations.

Athletics. NCAA. **Intercollegiate:** Baseball M, basketball, cheerleading, cross-country, football (tackle) M, golf M, rifle, soccer W, softball W, tennis, track and field, volleyball W. **Intramural:** Archery, badminton, basketball, bowling, football (non-tackle) M, golf, racquetball, soccer, softball, swimming, table tennis, tennis, track and field, volleyball. **Team name:** Eagles.

Student services. Adult student services, alcohol/substance abuse counseling, career counseling, services for economically disadvantaged, student employment services, financial aid counseling, health services, minority student services, personal counseling, veterans' counselor. **Physically disabled:** Services for visually, speech, hearing impaired.

Contact. E-mail: admissions@moreheadstate.edu
Phone: (606) 783-2000 Toll-free number: (800) 585-6781
Fax: (606) 783-5038
Holly Pollock, Assistant Vice President of Enrollment Services, Morehead State University, 100 Admissions Center, Morehead, KY 40351

Murray State University
Murray, Kentucky   **CB member**
www.murraystate.edu   **CB code: 1494**

- Public 4-year university
- Residential campus in large town
- 7,891 degree-seeking undergraduates: 11% part-time, 58% women, 8% African American, 1% Asian American, 2% Hispanic/Latino, 2% Multi-racial, non-Hispanic, 4% international
- 1,667 degree-seeking graduate students
- 91% of applicants admitted
- SAT or ACT (ACT writing optional) required
- 48% graduate within 6 years; 41% enter graduate study

General. Founded in 1922. Regionally accredited. **Degrees:** 1,512 bachelor's, 18 associate awarded; master's, professional, doctoral offered. **ROTC:** Army. **Location:** 115 miles from Nashville, TN. **Calendar:** Semester, limited summer session. **Full-time faculty:** 455 total; 77% have terminal degrees, 17% minority, 42% women. **Part-time faculty:** 253 total; 30% have terminal degrees, 9% minority, 62% women. **Class size:** 58% < 20, 34% 20-39, 5% 40-49, 3% 50-99, less than 1% >100. **Special facilities:** Arboretum, biological research station, watershed studies institute, mid-America remote sensing center, chemical services laboratory, museum and cultural events center, fine arts center, financial services center, agricultural research farms, veterinary research center, agricultural exposition center.

Freshman class profile. 4,874 applied, 4,416 admitted, 1,468 enrolled.

GPA 3.75 or higher:	36%	Return as sophomores:	72%
GPA 3.50-3.74:	20%	Out-of-state:	39%
GPA 3.0-3.49:	26%	Live on campus:	79%
GPA 2.0-2.99:	17%	International:	4%
Rank in top quarter:	45%	Fraternities:	19%
Rank in top tenth:	18%	Sororities:	22%
End year in good standing:	94%		

Basis for selection. Rigor of secondary school record, class rank, academic GPA, recommendations, and standardized test scores very important. For unconditional admission to a baccalaureate program, students must meet the following criteria: scored at least 18 on the ACT or at least 870 on the SAT; completed pre-college high school curriculum requirements; ranked in top half of high school class or earned a GPA of 3.0 or greater; and requires no developmental courses. Students who need to take one developmental course, but meet all other admission criteria, may be admitted conditionally to a baccalaureate program. Interview recommended for art, music, nursing majors. Auditions recommended for music majors. Portfolio recommended for art majors. **Home schooled:** Transcript of courses and grades required. Students may be asked to verify lab experience and provide GED if ACT score is less than average. **Learning Disabled:** Students should contact Office of Student Disability Services.

High school preparation. College-preparatory program required. 22 units required. Required and recommended units include English 4, mathematics 3-4, social studies 3, history 3, science 3-4 (laboratory 1), foreign language 2, computer science 1, visual/performing arts 1 and academic electives 5. 1 art appreciation required. Social sciences must include U.S. history and world civilization. 1 arts and 1 computer science recommended. Math must include 3 units at the algebra 1 level or higher. Sciences must include biology and chemistry or physics.

2015-2016 Annual costs. Tuition/fees: $7,608; $20,712 out-of-state. Room/board: $8,206. Books/supplies: $1,345. Personal expenses: $2,665. **Additional information:** Murray State has multiple regional tuition rates for residents of states in our region. Regional rates are substantially lower than the out-of-state tuition rate.

2014-2015 Financial aid. **Need-based:** 1,302 full-time freshmen applied for aid; 1,028 deemed to have need; 1,027 received aid. Average need met was 34%. Average scholarship/grant was $6,496; average loan $5,071. 47% of total undergraduate aid awarded as scholarships/grants, 53% as loans/jobs. **Non-need-based:** Awarded to 947 full-time undergraduates, including 314 freshmen. Scholarships awarded for academics, alumni affiliation, art, athletics, job skills, leadership, minority status, music/drama, ROTC, state residency. **Additional information:** Racer Promise grant, for first-time freshman from our 18-county service region who demonstrate financial need, covers up to 8 semesters of mandatory tuition and fees.

Application procedures. **Admission:** Closing date 8/10. $40 fee, may be waived for applicants with need. Admission notification on a rolling basis. **Financial aid:** Priority date 2/1; no closing date. FAFSA, institutional form required. Applicants notified on a rolling basis starting 3/15; must reply by 5/1.

Academics. **Special study options:** Combined bachelor's/graduate degree, cooperative education, cross-registration, distance learning, double major, dual enrollment of high school students, ESL, exchange student, external degree, honors, independent study, internships, student-designed major, study abroad, teacher certification program, weekend college. Cooperative center for study in Britain, Kentucky Institute for International Studies, national and international student exchange. **Credit/placement by examination:** AP, CLEP, IB, SAT, ACT, institutional tests. **Support services:** Learning center, pre-admission summer program, reduced course load, remedial instruction, study skills assistance, tutoring, writing center. Oral communications center, mathematical studies and career center. Student Support Services provides retention services to first-generation students. Office of Multicultural Affairs provides services to underrepresented minority students.

Honors college/program. Admission based on standardized test scores, GPA, evidence of creative and leadership abilities as displayed in extracurricular interests and activities, and faculty recommendation. An average of 120 freshman are accepted each year. Required components of the academic program includes honors seminars, study abroad, foreign language, the honors sequence, and a minimum 3.2 grade point average.

Majors. **Biology:** General. **Business:** General, accounting, business admin, finance, international, logistics, marketing. **Communications:** Advertising, journalism, organizational, public relations, radio/TV. **Communications technology:** Graphics. **Computer sciences:** Computer science, information systems, information technology. **Conservation:** Wildlife/wilderness. **Education:** Early childhood, elementary, ESL, health, middle, special ed, trade/industrial. **Engineering:** Applied physics. **English:** Creative writing, English lit. **Foreign languages:** French, German, Japanese, Spanish. **Health services:** Athletic training, audiology/speech pathology, community health, nursing (RN), veterinary technology/assistant. **History:** General. **Human services:** General, social work, youth services. **Liberal arts:** Arts/sciences. **Math:** General. **Parks/recreation:** Exercise sciences, outdoor education. **Philosophy/religion:** Philosophy. **Physical sciences:** Chemistry, geology, physics. **Protective services:** Criminal justice. **Psychology:** General. **Social sciences:** Economics, international relations, political science, sociology. **Visual/performing arts:** Dramatic, music, music management, studio arts. **Work/family studies:** Food/nutrition.

Most popular majors. Business/marketing 13%, communications/journalism 7%, education 10%, engineering/engineering technologies 8%, health sciences 16%, liberal arts 8%, public administration/social services 6%.

Technology on campus. Dormitories wired for high-speed internet access and linked to campus network. Commuter students can connect to campus network. Online course registration, online library, helpline, repair service, student web hosting, wireless network available.

Student life. **Freshman orientation:** Available, $130 fee. Preregistration for classes offered. **Policies:** Only documented comfort or service animals are allowed in dorms. **Housing:** Guaranteed on-campus for freshmen. Coed dorms, single-sex dorms, special housing for disabled, apartments, fraternity/sorority housing, wellness housing available. $150 fully refundable deposit, deadline 7/31. Pets allowed in dorm rooms. **Activities:** Bands, campus ministries, choral groups, dance, drama, film society, international student organizations, literary magazine, music ensembles, Model UN, musical theater, opera, radio station, student government, student newspaper, symphony orchestra, TV station, Murray Christian Fellowship; Muslim Student Organization; College Republicans; College Democrats; Black Student Council; International Student Organization; Rotaract Club; Murray Environmental Student Society; MSU Student Ambassadors; Campus Outreach.

Athletics. NCAA. **Intercollegiate:** Baseball M, basketball, cross-country, football (tackle) M, golf, rifle, soccer W, softball W, tennis, track and field W, volleyball W. **Intramural:** Basketball, bowling, football (non-tackle), golf, racquetball, soccer, softball, swimming, table tennis, tennis, ultimate frisbee, volleyball, water polo. **Team name:** Racers.

Student services. Adult student services, alcohol/substance abuse counseling, career counseling, services for economically disadvantaged, student

employment services, financial aid counseling, health services, minority student services, personal counseling, placement for graduates, veterans' counselor, women's services. **Physically disabled:** Services for visually, speech, hearing impaired.

Contact. E-mail: msu.admissions@murraystate.edu
Phone: (270) 809-3741 Toll-free number: (800) 272-4678
Fax: (270) 809-3780
Lesa Harris, Director of Undergraduate Admissions, Murray State University, 102 Curris Center, Murray, KY 42071

Northern Kentucky University
Highland Heights, Kentucky
CB member
www.nku.edu
CB code: 1574

- Public 4-year university
- Commuter campus in small town
- 11,302 degree-seeking undergraduates: 18% part-time, 55% women, 7% African American, 1% Asian American, 3% Hispanic/Latino, 2% Multiracial, non-Hispanic, 3% international
- 2,082 degree-seeking graduate students
- 92% of applicants admitted
- SAT or ACT (ACT writing optional) required
- 40% graduate within 6 years

General. Founded in 1968. Regionally accredited. **Degrees:** 2,214 bachelor's, 84 associate awarded; master's, professional, doctoral offered. **ROTC:** Army, Air Force. **Location:** 7 miles from Cincinnati, Ohio. **Calendar:** Semester, extensive summer session. **Full-time faculty:** 583 total; 69% have terminal degrees, 12% minority, 53% women. **Part-time faculty:** 423 total; 25% have terminal degrees, 6% minority, 53% women. **Class size:** 38% < 20, 54% 20-39, 5% 40-49, 2% 50-99, less than 1% >100. **Special facilities:** Planetarium, anthropology museum, biology museum, cadaver lab, informatics building, recreation center.

Freshman class profile. 7,397 applied, 6,797 admitted, 2,266 enrolled.

Mid 50% test scores		Rank in top quarter:	32%
SAT critical reading:	460-590	Rank in top tenth:	11%
SAT math:	460-570	End year in good standing:	81%
SAT writing:	440-550	Return as sophomores:	69%
ACT composite:	20-26	Out-of-state:	35%
GPA 3.75 or higher:	27%	Live on campus:	47%
GPA 3.50-3.74:	15%	International:	1%
GPA 3.0-3.49:	28%	Fraternities:	11%
GPA 2.0-2.99:	27%	Sororities:	19%

Basis for selection. GPA, pre-college curriculum and ACT/SAT/COMPASS scores. ACT and/or SAT scores are used to determine whether a placement test is required based on CPE standards. Tests required of all students ACT/SAT for students under 21; students over 21 years of age may use ACT/SAT/COMPASS scores. Auditions/interviews/essays can be required for specific programs. **Home schooled:** Transcript of courses and grades required. Homeschool transcripts must be notarized.

High school preparation. College-preparatory program required. Required and recommended units include English 4, mathematics 3-4, social studies 3, history 3, science 3, foreign language 2 and computer science 1.

2015-2016 Annual costs. Tuition/fees: $9,120; $13,584 out-of-district; $17,856 out-of-state. Room/board: $9,078.

2014-2015 Financial aid. **Need-based:** 1,858 full-time freshmen applied for aid; 1,468 deemed to have need; 1,465 received aid. Average need met was 68%. Average scholarship/grant was $5,994; average loan $3,476. 42% of total undergraduate aid awarded as scholarships/grants, 58% as loans/jobs. **Non-need-based:** Awarded to 4,737 full-time undergraduates, including 1,468 freshmen. Scholarships awarded for academics, alumni affiliation, art, athletics, leadership, music/drama, ROTC, state residency.

Application procedures. **Admission:** Priority date 5/1; deadline 8/15 (postmark date). $40 fee, may be waived for applicants with need. Admission notification on a rolling basis. Must reply by May 1 or within 2 week(s) if notified thereafter. **Financial aid:** Priority date 2/1; no closing date. FAFSA required. Applicants notified on a rolling basis starting 3/15.

Academics. **Special study options:** Accelerated study, combined bachelor's/graduate degree, cooperative education, cross-registration, distance learning, double major, dual enrollment of high school students, ESL, exchange student, honors, independent study, internships, liberal arts/career combination, semester at sea, student-designed major, study abroad, teacher certification program, weekend college. **Credit/placement by examination:** AP, CLEP, IB, SAT, ACT, institutional tests. 37 credit hours maximum

toward bachelor's degree. Credit awarded for CLEP, military, vocational, and National Occupational Competency Testing Institute exams. **Support services:** Learning center, reduced course load, remedial instruction, study skills assistance, tutoring, writing center.

Majors. **Area/ethnic studies:** Women's. **Biology:** General. **Business:** General, accounting, business admin, construction management, entrepreneurial studies, finance, management information systems, managerial economics, marketing, organizational behavior, training/development. **Communications:** Broadcast journalism, communications/speech/rhetoric, journalism, public relations, radio/TV. **Computer sciences:** General, information systems, information technology. **Conservation:** Environmental science. **Education:** Business, elementary, foreign languages, kindergarten/preschool, middle, music, physical, science, secondary, special ed, trade/industrial, voc/tech. **English:** English lit, rhetoric/composition. **Foreign languages:** French, German, Spanish. **Health services:** Athletic training, nursing (RN), radiologic technology/medical imaging, respiratory therapy technology. **History:** General. **Human services:** Social work. **Liberal arts:** Arts/sciences. **Math:** General, statistics. **Parks/recreation:** Sports admin. **Philosophy/religion:** Philosophy. **Physical sciences:** Chemistry, geology, physics. **Protective services:** Criminal justice. **Psychology:** General. **Social sciences:** General, anthropology, geography, international relations, political science, sociology. **Visual/performing arts:** Commercial/advertising art, dramatic, music, studio arts.

Most popular majors. Business/marketing 25%, communications/journalism 9%, computer/information sciences 7%, education 6%, health sciences 11%, visual/performing arts 7%.

Technology on campus. 250 workstations in library, computer center, student center. Dormitories wired for high-speed internet access and linked to campus network. Commuter students can connect to campus network. Online course registration, online library, helpline, repair service, student web hosting, wireless network available.

Student life. **Freshman orientation:** Mandatory, $100 fee. Preregistration for classes offered. 3-day program before classes begin in August. **Policies:** Student organizations required to register annually and attend student organization sessions annually. **Housing:** Coed dorms, special housing for disabled, apartments, fraternity/sorority housing, themed housing available. $200 nonrefundable deposit, deadline 5/1. **Activities:** Bands, campus ministries, choral groups, dance, drama, film society, international student organizations, literary magazine, music ensembles, Model UN, musical theater, radio station, student government, student newspaper, TV station, Baptist student union, Newman Center, Schools for Schools, Up Till Dawn, Black united students, Common Ground, College Republicans, Campus Democrats, Latino student union.

Athletics. NCAA. **Intercollegiate:** Baseball M, basketball, cheerleading, cross-country, golf, soccer, softball W, tennis, track and field, volleyball W. **Intramural:** Basketball, field hockey, football (non-tackle), soccer, softball, tennis, ultimate frisbee, volleyball. **Team name:** Norse.

Student services. Adult student services, alcohol/substance abuse counseling, career counseling, services for economically disadvantaged, student employment services, financial aid counseling, health services, minority student services, on-campus daycare, personal counseling, placement for graduates, veterans' counselor. **Physically disabled:** Services for visually, speech, hearing impaired.

Contact. E-mail: admitnku@nku.edu
Phone: (859) 572-5220 Toll-free number: (800) 637-9948
Fax: (859) 572-6665
Melissa Gorbandt, Director of Admissions - Outreach, Northern Kentucky University, Administrative Center 400, Northern Kentucky University, Highland Heights, KY 41099

Southern Baptist Theological Seminary
Louisville, Kentucky
www.sbts.edu

- Private 5-year Bible and seminary college affiliated with the Southern Baptist Convention
- Very large city
- 799 undergraduates
- 2,627 graduate students

General. Founded in 1859. Regionally accredited. **Degrees:** 58 bachelor's, 8 associate awarded; master's, doctoral offered. **Calendar:** Semester, limited summer session. **Full-time faculty:** 74 total. **Part-time faculty:** 22 total.

Basis for selection. The Southern Baptist Theological Seminary/Boyce College reviews applications and admits based on a combination of academic standards, test scores, church membership & activity, along with personal understanding and commitment to the gospel of Jesus Christ. ACT or SAT exam is required for admission for all students applying with less than 15 college credit hours or less than 24 years of age. **Home schooled:** Transcript of courses and grades, letter of recommendation (nonparent) required.

2015-2016 Annual costs. Tuition/fees: $10,870. Books/supplies: $1,000.

Application procedures. Admission: Priority date 7/15; no deadline. $35 fee. **Financial aid:** Closing date 8/1.

Academics. Credit/placement by examination: AP, CLEP.

Majors. Theology: Bible, missionary, pastoral counseling, youth ministry.

Student life. Housing: Coed dorms available.

Athletics. Team name: Bulldogs.

Contact. E-mail: admissions@sbts.edu
Phone: (502) 897-4200
Kody Gibson, Director of Admissions, Southern Baptist Theological Seminary, 2825 Lexington Road, Louisville, KY 40280

Spalding University
Louisville, Kentucky   **CB member**
www.spalding.edu   **CB code: 1552**

▶ Private 4-year university affiliated with the Roman Catholic Church
▶ Commuter campus in very large city
▶ 1,122 degree-seeking undergraduates: 18% part-time, 70% women, 20% African American, 2% Asian American, 3% Hispanic/Latino, 3% Multi-racial, non-Hispanic
▶ 936 degree-seeking graduate students
▶ 52% of applicants admitted
▶ SAT or ACT (ACT writing optional) required
▶ 43% graduate within 6 years

General. Founded in 1814. Regionally accredited. **Degrees:** 269 bachelor's, 1 associate awarded; master's, professional, doctoral offered. **ROTC:** Army, Air Force. **Location:** One mile from downtown. **Calendar:** Differs by program, extensive summer session. **Class size:** 75% < 20, 25% 20-39, less than 1% 40-49. **Special facilities:** Historical collection of Edith Stein works, Huff Art Gallery.

Freshman class profile. 1,406 applied, 727 admitted, 196 enrolled.

Mid 50% test scores		GPA 3.0-3.49:	29%
SAT math:	480-600	GPA 2.0-2.99:	26%
ACT composite:	18-23	Return as sophomores:	77%
GPA 3.75 or higher:	27%	Out-of-state:	16%
GPA 3.50-3.74:	18%		

Basis for selection. Adult Accelerated Program cumulative high school GPA of 2.5 or higher or GED of 50 or higher required. Applicants who do not meet the stated automatic admission criteria must submit personal statement. **Home schooled:** Transcript of courses and grades, state high school equivalency certificate required.

High school preparation. College-preparatory program recommended. 13 units recommended. Recommended units include English 4, mathematics 3, social studies 2, science 2 and foreign language 2.

2015-2016 Annual costs. Tuition/fees: $23,887. Room/board: $8,400. Books/supplies: $1,260. Personal expenses: $3,564.

Financial aid. Non-need-based: Scholarships awarded for academics, alumni affiliation, art, leadership.

Application procedures. Admission: No deadline. $20 fee, may be waived for applicants with need. Admission notification on a rolling basis. **Financial aid:** Priority date 1/1; no closing date. FAFSA required. Applicants notified on a rolling basis starting 3/31.

Academics. Special study options: Accelerated study, combined bachelor's/graduate degree, cross-registration, distance learning, double major, dual enrollment of high school students, independent study, internships, study abroad, teacher certification program, weekend college. **Credit/placement by examination:** AP, CLEP, SAT, ACT, institutional tests. 30 credit hours maximum toward associate degree, 30 toward bachelor's. **Support services:** Learning center, reduced course load, remedial instruction, study skills assistance, tutoring, writing center.

Majors. Business: General, accounting, accounting/business management. **Communications:** Communications/speech/rhetoric, media studies. **Education:** General, elementary, middle, secondary, special ed. **English:** Creative writing. **Health services:** Nursing (RN). **Human services:** Social work. **Liberal arts:** Arts/sciences, humanities. **Psychology:** General. **Social sciences:** General. **Visual/performing arts:** Studio arts.

Most popular majors. Business/marketing 15%, health sciences 49%, psychology 14%.

Technology on campus. 250 workstations in dormitories, library. Dormitories wired for high-speed internet access and linked to campus network. Commuter students can connect to campus network. Online course registration, online library, helpline, wireless network available.

Student life. Freshman orientation: Mandatory. Preregistration for classes offered. Three-day overnight program including a full-day off campus trip to the Nazareth campus. AAP and online orientations held about one week prior to the beginning of each session. **Housing:** Coed dorms, single-sex dorms, wellness housing available. $100 nonrefundable deposit. **Activities:** Campus ministries, dance, international student organizations, radio station, student government, Best Buddies. Multicultural student association, The Undergraduate Artist Movement, campus activities board, Egan Service Living, residence hall activities council, Student Government Association, SU Gay Straight Alliance, Joyful Praise Liturgical Dance Team.

Athletics. NCAA, USCAA. **Intercollegiate:** Baseball M, basketball, bowling W, cross-country, golf, soccer, softball W, track and field, volleyball W. **Team name:** Golden Eagles.

Student services. Adult student services, alcohol/substance abuse counseling, chaplain/spiritual director, career counseling, services for economically disadvantaged, student employment services, financial aid counseling, minority student services, personal counseling, veterans' counselor. **Physically disabled:** Services for visually, speech, hearing impaired.

Contact. E-mail: admissions@spalding.edu
Phone: (502) 585-7111 Toll-free number: (800) 896-8941 ext. 2111
Fax: (502) 992-2418
Matthew Elder, Director, Undergraduate Admissions, Spalding University, 845 S Third Street, Louisville, KY 40203

St. Catharine College
St. Catharine, Kentucky
www.sccky.edu   **CB code: 1690**

▶ Private 4-year health science and liberal arts college affiliated with the Roman Catholic Church
▶ Commuter campus in small town
▶ 539 degree-seeking undergraduates: 5% part-time, 57% women
▶ 13 degree-seeking graduate students

General. Founded in 1931. Regionally accredited. **Degrees:** 101 bachelor's, 49 associate awarded; master's offered. **Location:** 50 miles from Louisville and Lexington. **Calendar:** Semester, limited summer session. **Full-time faculty:** 63 total; 13% minority, 65% women. **Class size:** 86% < 20, 14% 20-39, less than 1% 40-49.

Freshman class profile. 633 applied, 366 admitted, 137 enrolled.

Out-of-state:	19%	Live on campus:	71%

Basis for selection. Open admission, but selective for some programs. Students must submit their application, transcripts, test scores and have received a minimum ACT score of 15 (SAT equivalent) in English, Mathematics, and Reading as a traditional/nontraditional student. Scores from other tests such as Compass and Kyote are accepted as well. Transfers must have a 2.0 minimum cumulative GPA and a 2.0 or higher during the last semester attended. **Learning Disabled:** The paperwork for any students who have an IEP is submitted to Sr. Mary Angela Shaughnessy, the ADA Services Coordinator for Saint Catharine College.

High school preparation. Recommended units include English 4, mathematics 4, social studies 2, history 1, science 2 (laboratory 2) and foreign language 2. Aligns with Kentucky high school graduate general education requirements.

2015-2016 Annual costs. Tuition/fees: $19,832. Room/board: $9,412. Books/supplies: $700. Personal expenses: $1,200.

Financial aid. All financial aid based on need.

Application procedures. Admission: No deadline. No application fee. Admission notification on a rolling basis. **Financial aid:** Priority date 3/15;

no closing date. FAFSA, institutional form required. Applicants notified on a rolling basis.

Academics. Special study options: Combined bachelor's/graduate degree, distance learning, double major, dual enrollment of high school students, honors, independent study, internships, liberal arts/career combination, student-designed major, study abroad, teacher certification program, weekend college. **Credit/placement by examination:** AP, CLEP, IB, institutional tests. 35 credit hours maximum toward associate degree, 35 toward bachelor's. **Support services:** Learning center, pre-admission summer program, reduced course load, remedial instruction, study skills assistance, tutoring.

Majors. Biology: General. **Business:** Business admin. **Education:** Elementary, middle. **English:** English lit. **Health services:** Athletic training, medical radiologic technology/radiation therapy, nursing (RN), radiologic technology/medical imaging. **Liberal arts:** Arts/sciences. **Parks/recreation:** Sports admin. **Protective services:** Law enforcement admin. **Psychology:** General. **Visual/performing arts:** General.

Most popular majors. Business/marketing 22%, health sciences 34%, liberal arts 8%, parks/recreation 6%, psychology 12%, security/protective services 9%.

Technology on campus. 60 workstations in library, computer center. Dormitories wired for high-speed internet access. Commuter students can connect to campus network. Online course registration, online library, wireless network available.

Student life. Freshman orientation: Mandatory, $40 fee. Preregistration for classes offered. Two-day program held before start of classes. **Housing:** Single-sex dorms, special housing for disabled, wellness housing available. $25 deposit, deadline 8/15. **Activities:** Campus ministries, choral groups, drama, literary magazine, student government, student newspaper, Phi Theta Kappa, Student Ambassadors, Health Occupations Student Association, Alpha Chi Omega, Student Government Association.

Athletics. NAIA. **Intercollegiate:** Baseball M, basketball, bowling, cross-country, golf, soccer, softball W, swimming M, tennis M, track and field, volleyball W, wrestling M. **Team name:** Patriots.

Student services. Chaplain/spiritual director, career counseling, student employment services, financial aid counseling, legal services, on-campus daycare, personal counseling, veterans' counselor.

Contact. E-mail: admissions@sccky.edu
Phone: (859) 336-5082 ext. 1227 Fax: (859) 336-5031
Ashley Dudgeon, Director of Admissions, St. Catharine College, 2735 Bardstown Road, St. Catharine, KY 40061

Sullivan University
Louisville, Kentucky
www.sullivan.edu   CB code: 0811

- For-profit 4-year university
- Commuter campus in large city
- 2,498 degree-seeking undergraduates: 38% part-time, 60% women, 18% African American, 1% Asian American, 9% Multi-racial, non-Hispanic
- 1,175 degree-seeking graduate students
- Interview required

General. Founded in 1962. Regionally accredited. **Degrees:** 355 bachelor's, 451 associate awarded; master's, professional, doctoral offered. **Location:** 110 miles from Indianapolis, 110 miles from Cincinnati. **Calendar:** Quarter, extensive summer session. **Full-time faculty:** 152 total. **Part-time faculty:** 156 total. **Special facilities:** University-operated fine dining restaurant.

Basis for selection. Test scores, interview, high school record important. SAT or ACT recommended. Institutional exam required for placement if no ACT or SAT scores are available.

2015-2016 Annual costs. Program and housing costs vary by program. For more information, you may visit http://pages.sullivan.edu/pdf/SULO_supplementA.pdf.

Financial aid. All financial aid based on need.

Application procedures. Admission: No deadline. $50 fee. Application must be submitted online. Admission notification on a rolling basis. **Financial aid:** No deadline. FAFSA required. Applicants notified on a rolling basis starting 1/2.

Academics. Day classes meet Monday-Thursday; special program on Friday for additional help. Night/weekend classes meet Monday-Sunday. **Special**

study options: Accelerated study, combined bachelor's/graduate degree, distance learning, double major, independent study, internships, weekend college. **Credit/placement by examination:** AP, CLEP, SAT, ACT, institutional tests. **Support services:** Reduced course load, remedial instruction, study skills assistance, tutoring.

Majors. Business: Accounting, business admin, hospitality admin, human resources. **Computer sciences:** Information technology. **Health services:** Health information management, nursing (RN). **Protective services:** Criminal justice.

Technology on campus. 102 workstations in dormitories, library, computer center. Dormitories wired for high-speed internet access. Commuter students can connect to campus network. Online library, helpline, wireless network available.

Student life. Freshman orientation: Mandatory. Preregistration for classes offered. One-day sessions held at beginning of quarter. **Housing:** Coed dorms, special housing for disabled, wellness housing available. $95 nonrefundable deposit, deadline 9/30. Housing available for students under 21. **Activities:** Choral groups, drama, film society, musical theater, Student activities committee, culinary competition team, student paralegal association, Sullivan Christian Fellowship, Celebrate Kids!, and Student Veterans of America.

Athletics. Intramural: Basketball, bowling, football (non-tackle), softball, table tennis, ultimate frisbee, volleyball.

Student services. Chaplain/spiritual director, career counseling, financial aid counseling, placement for graduates.

Contact. E-mail: admissions@sullivan.edu
Phone: (502) 456-6505 Toll-free number: (800) 844-1354
Fax: (502) 456-0040
Nina Martinez, Vice President of Admissions, Sullivan University, 3101 Bardstown Road, Louisville, KY 40205

Thomas More College
Crestview Hills, Kentucky   CB member
www.thomasmore.edu   CB code: 1876

- Private 4-year liberal arts college affiliated with the Roman Catholic Church
- Residential campus in small town
- 1,308 degree-seeking undergraduates: 3% part-time, 52% women, 7% African American, 2% Hispanic/Latino, 3% Multi-racial, non-Hispanic, 1% international
- 178 degree-seeking graduate students
- 88% of applicants admitted
- SAT or ACT (ACT writing optional) required
- 47% graduate within 6 years; 29% enter graduate study

General. Founded in 1921. Regionally accredited. **Degrees:** 232 bachelor's, 66 associate awarded; master's offered. **ROTC:** Army, Air Force. **Location:** 8 miles from Cincinnati. **Calendar:** Semester, limited summer session. **Full-time faculty:** 75 total; 79% have terminal degrees, 5% minority, 47% women. **Part-time faculty:** 53 total; 15% have terminal degrees, 4% minority, 49% women. **Class size:** 74% < 20, 26% 20-39, less than 1% 50-99. **Special facilities:** Biology field station, observatory.

Freshman class profile. 1,518 applied, 1,341 admitted, 276 enrolled.

Mid 50% test scores		Rank in top quarter:	31%
SAT critical reading:	400-490	Rank in top tenth:	11%
SAT math:	420-510	End year in good standing:	65%
ACT composite:	20-24	Return as sophomores:	66%
GPA 3.75 or higher:	23%	Out-of-state:	49%
GPA 3.50-3.74:	12%	Live on campus:	59%
GPA 3.0-3.49:	32%	International:	1%
GPA 2.0-2.99:	32%		

Basis for selection. Students must have C+ average or 2.5 GPA, 20 ACT English/480 SAT verbal, and 20 ACT/1010 SAT. Students not meeting these requirements may be conditionally admitted.

High school preparation. College-preparatory program required. 17 units required. Required units include English 4, mathematics 3, social studies 3, science 3, foreign language 2, computer science 1 and visual/performing arts 1.

2016-2017 Annual costs. Tuition/fees: $29,450. Room/board: $7,304. Personal expenses: $1,654.

2014-2015 Financial aid. Need-based: 267 full-time freshmen applied for aid; 248 deemed to have need; 248 received aid. Average need met was 74%. Average scholarship/grant was $17,415; average loan $3,637. 68% of total undergraduate aid awarded as scholarships/grants, 32% as loans/jobs. **Non-need-based:** Awarded to 298 full-time undergraduates, including 62 freshmen. Scholarships awarded for academics, alumni affiliation, art, leadership, minority status, music/drama, religious affiliation, ROTC, state residency.

Application procedures. Admission: Closing date 8/15 (postmark date). $25 fee, may be waived for applicants with need, free for online applicants. Admission notification on a rolling basis beginning on or about 10/1. **Financial aid:** Closing date 3/15. FAFSA required. Applicants notified on a rolling basis starting 3/1; must reply by 5/1.

Academics. Special study options: Accelerated study, cooperative education, cross-registration, distance learning, double major, dual enrollment of high school students, honors, independent study, internships, student-designed major, study abroad, teacher certification program. **Credit/placement by examination:** AP, CLEP, IB, SAT, ACT, institutional tests. 30 credit hours maximum toward associate degree, 60 toward bachelor's. **Support services:** Learning center, reduced course load, remedial instruction, study skills assistance, tutoring, writing center.

Majors. Biology: General, biochemistry. **Business:** Accounting, business admin. **Communications:** Communications/speech/rhetoric. **Computer sciences:** General. **Conservation:** Environmental science. **Education:** Art, business, elementary, middle, secondary, Spanish. **English:** English lit. **Foreign languages:** Spanish. **Health services:** Athletic training, clinical lab science, health care admin, nursing (RN). **History:** General. **Liberal arts:** Arts/sciences, humanities. **Math:** General. **Parks/recreation:** Sports admin. **Philosophy/religion:** Philosophy, religion. **Physical sciences:** Chemistry, physics. **Protective services:** Criminal justice, forensics. **Psychology:** General. **Social sciences:** Economics, political science, sociology. **Visual/performing arts:** Art history/conservation, dramatic, studio arts.

Most popular majors. Biology 8%, business/marketing 40%, health sciences 8%.

Technology on campus. 96 workstations in dormitories, library, computer center. Dormitories wired for high-speed internet access and linked to campus network. Commuter students can connect to campus network. Online library, helpline, wireless network available.

Student life. Freshman orientation: Mandatory, $125 fee. Preregistration for classes offered. One day registration/orientation program held once per month from April through August. **Housing:** Coed dorms, single-sex dorms, special housing for disabled available. $100 nonrefundable deposit, deadline 5/15. **Activities:** Bands, campus ministries, choral groups, dance, drama, international student organizations, literary magazine, music ensembles, student government, student activities board, residence hall government association, African American Society, Habitat for Humanity, business society, social issues commune, student government association, campus ministry, international student organization.

Athletics. NCAA. Intercollegiate: Baseball M, basketball, bowling, cross-country, football (tackle) M, golf, lacrosse W, soccer, softball W, tennis, track and field, volleyball W, wrestling M. **Intramural:** Basketball, football (non-tackle), sand volleyball, soccer, softball, volleyball. **Team name:** Saints.

Student services. Adult student services, alcohol/substance abuse counseling, chaplain/spiritual director, career counseling, student employment services, financial aid counseling, health services, minority student services, personal counseling, placement for graduates, veterans' counselor. **Physically disabled:** Services for visually, speech, hearing impaired.

Contact. E-mail: admissions@thomasmore.edu
Phone: (859) 344-3332 Toll-free number: (800) 825-4557
Fax: (859) 344-3444
Chris Powers, Vice President of Enrollment Management, Thomas More College, 333 Thomas More Parkway, Crestview Hills, KY 41017-3495

Transylvania University
Lexington, Kentucky
www.transy.edu

CB member
CB code: 1808

▸ Private 4-year liberal arts college affiliated with the Christian Church (Disciples of Christ)
▸ Residential campus in large city
▸ 1,055 degree-seeking undergraduates: 1% part-time, 58% women, 3% African American, 2% Asian American, 6% Hispanic/Latino, 3% Multiracial, non-Hispanic, 4% international
▸ 93% of applicants admitted

▸ Application essay required
▸ 73% graduate within 6 years; 38% enter graduate study

General. Founded in 1780. Regionally accredited. **Degrees:** 195 bachelor's awarded. **ROTC:** Army, Air Force. **Location:** 80 miles from Louisville; 80 miles from Cincinnati, Ohio. **Calendar:** 4-1-4, limited summer session. **Full-time faculty:** 85 total; 95% have terminal degrees, 7% minority, 45% women. **Part-time faculty:** 28 total; 32% have terminal degrees, 4% minority, 57% women. **Class size:** 71% < 20, 29% 20-39. **Special facilities:** Museum of early scientific apparatus, special library collections of early medical and scientific works and Kentucky books.

Freshman class profile. 1,538 applied, 1,425 admitted, 311 enrolled.

Mid 50% test scores		Rank in top tenth:	39%
SAT critical reading:	520-640	End year in good standing:	95%
SAT math:	500-660	Return as sophomores:	85%
ACT composite:	24-30	Out-of-state:	24%
GPA 3.75 or higher:	66%	Live on campus:	91%
GPA 3.50-3.74:	12%	International:	3%
GPA 3.0-3.49:	16%	Fraternities:	46%
GPA 2.0-2.99:	6%	Sororities:	56%
Rank in top quarter:	76%		

Basis for selection. Rigor of curriculum, GPA, and test scores most important. Recommendations, essay, extracurricular activities, excellence of character and high personal goals important. Interview recommended. Audition required for music scholarship applicants. Portfolio required for art scholarship applicants. **Learning Disabled:** Students should meet with coordinator of disability services.

High school preparation. College-preparatory program required. 20 units required; 22 recommended. Required and recommended units include English 4, mathematics 3-4, social studies 2, history 1, science 3-4 (laboratory 2-3), foreign language 2 and academic electives 2. Broad high school curriculum important to allow full participation in required liberal arts course work. Solid background in English highly recommended.

2015-2016 Annual costs. Tuition/fees: $34,370. Room/board: $9,560. Books/supplies: $1,000. Personal expenses: $1,350.

2015-2016 Financial aid. Need-based: 281 full-time freshmen applied for aid; 228 deemed to have need; 228 received aid. Average need met was 84%. Average scholarship/grant was $23,656; average loan $3,135. 81% of total undergraduate aid awarded as scholarships/grants, 19% as loans/jobs. **Non-need-based:** Awarded to 443 full-time undergraduates, including 130 freshmen. Scholarships awarded for academics, art, leadership, minority status, music/drama, religious affiliation, state residency. **Additional information:** Auditions and portfolios required for music and art scholarships respectively. Essays required for other scholarship programs. Applications for William T. Young scholarships must be received by December 1.

Application procedures. Admission: Priority date 2/1; no deadline. No application fee. Admission notification on a rolling basis beginning on or about 11/1. Must reply by May 1 or within 4 week(s) if notified thereafter. **Financial aid:** Priority date 1/1; no closing date. FAFSA required. Applicants notified by 3/15; Applicants notified on a rolling basis starting 3/15; must reply by 5/1 or within 2 week(s) of notification.

Academics. Special study options: Combined bachelor's/graduate degree, double major, independent study, internships, liberal arts/career combination, student-designed major, study abroad, teacher certification program, Washington semester. **Credit/placement by examination:** AP, CLEP, IB, SAT, ACT, institutional tests. No limit to credit for AP or IB. **Support services:** Learning center, study skills assistance, tutoring, writing center.

Majors. Biology: General, neuroscience. **Business:** General, accounting. **Communications:** Communications/speech/rhetoric. **Computer sciences:** General. **Education:** Elementary, foundations, middle, music, physical. **English:** English lit. **Foreign languages:** Classics, French, German, Spanish. **History:** General. **Liberal arts:** Arts/sciences. **Math:** General. **Parks/recreation:** Exercise sciences. **Philosophy/religion:** Philosophy, religion. **Physical sciences:** Chemistry, physics. **Psychology:** General. **Social sciences:** Anthropology, economics, political science, sociology, sociology/anthropology. **Visual/performing arts:** Art history/conservation, dramatic, music performance, music technology, studio arts.

Most popular majors. Biology 9%, business/marketing 15%, foreign language 9%, psychology 9%, social sciences 12%, visual/performing arts 6%.

Technology on campus. 200 workstations in dormitories, library, computer center, student center. Dormitories wired for high-speed internet access and linked to campus network. Commuter students can connect to campus network. Online course registration, online library, helpline, repair service, student web hosting, wireless network available.

Student life. Freshman orientation: Mandatory. Preregistration for classes offered. Orientation begins the weekend prior to August term (three-week term for new students only). **Housing:** Guaranteed on-campus for freshmen. Coed dorms, single-sex dorms, special housing for disabled, apartments, themed housing available. Efficiency apartment option for upperclassmen; two units with facilities for disabled students available. **Activities:** Bands, campus ministries, choral groups, dance, drama, literary magazine, music ensembles, musical theater, opera, radio station, student government, student newspaper, Diversity Action Council, College Democrats, College Republicans, Alternative Spring Break, Campus Crusade, student government association, student activities board, student alumni association, Environmental Rights and Responsibilities Alliance.

Athletics. NCAA. **Intercollegiate:** Baseball M, basketball, cross-country, diving, equestrian, field hockey W, golf, lacrosse, soccer, softball W, swimming, tennis, track and field, volleyball W. **Intramural:** Badminton, basketball, bowling, cross-country, football (non-tackle), golf, racquetball, soccer, softball, swimming, table tennis, tennis, volleyball. **Team name:** Pioneers.

Student services. Alcohol/substance abuse counseling, chaplain/spiritual director, career counseling, student employment services, financial aid counseling, health services, minority student services, personal counseling, veterans' counselor. **Physically disabled:** Services for visually, hearing impaired.

Contact. E-mail: admissions@transy.edu
Phone: (859) 233-8242 Toll-free number: (800) 872-6798
Fax: (859) 281-3649
Rhyan Conyers, Vice President for Enrollment and Dean of Admissions, Transylvania University, 300 North Broadway, Lexington, KY 40508-1797

Union College
Barbourville, Kentucky
www.unionky.edu
CB code: 1825

- Private 4-year liberal arts and teachers college affiliated with the United Methodist Church
- Residential campus in small town
- 794 degree-seeking undergraduates: 6% part-time, 47% women, 12% African American, 1% Asian American, 2% Hispanic/Latino, 5% Multiracial, non-Hispanic, 8% international
- 197 degree-seeking graduate students
- 69% of applicants admitted
- SAT or ACT (ACT writing optional) required
- 32% graduate within 6 years

General. Founded in 1879. Regionally accredited. **Degrees:** 120 bachelor's awarded; master's offered. **Location:** 107 miles from Lexington; 107 miles from Knoxville, TN. **Calendar:** Semester, limited summer session. **Full-time faculty:** 54 total; 50% have terminal degrees, 11% minority, 46% women. **Part-time faculty:** 53 total; 47% have terminal degrees, 8% minority, 49% women. **Class size:** 77% < 20, 23% 20-39.

Freshman class profile. 1,332 applied, 920 admitted, 213 enrolled.

Mid 50% test scores		GPA 2.0-2.99:	37%
ACT composite:	18-23	Return as sophomores:	56%
GPA 3.75 or higher:	21%	Out-of-state:	33%
GPA 3.50-3.74:	12%	Live on campus:	86%
GPA 3.0-3.49:	29%	International:	8%

Basis for selection. School achievement record, course work, class rank, SAT/ACT important. ACT preferred for all, required for teacher education program. Interview recommended. **Home schooled:** Statement describing home school structure and mission, transcript of courses and grades, state high school equivalency certificate, letter of recommendation (nonparent) required. Academic calendar with attendance required. Submission of writing sample, summary of travel-related experience or work history may be requested. **Learning Disabled:** Students must provide documentation to coordinator of special program to receive necessary accommodations.

High school preparation. College-preparatory program recommended. Recommended units include English 4, mathematics 3, social studies 2, science 2 (laboratory 2) and foreign language 1.

2015-2016 Annual costs. Tuition/fees: $24,075. Room/board: $7,000. Books/supplies: $1,470. Personal expenses: $1,680.

2015-2016 Financial aid. **Need-based:** Average need met was 68%. Average scholarship/grant was $18,504; average loan $3,667. 71% of total undergraduate aid awarded as scholarships/grants, 29% as loans/jobs. **Non-need-based:** Scholarships awarded for academics, alumni affiliation, athletics, leadership, music/drama, religious affiliation.

Application procedures. Admission: No deadline. $10 fee, may be waived for applicants with need. Admission notification on a rolling basis. **Financial aid:** Priority date 2/1; no closing date. FAFSA required. Applicants notified on a rolling basis starting 2/15; must reply within 2 week(s) of notification.

Academics. Special study options: Combined bachelor's/graduate degree, cross-registration, distance learning, honors, independent study, internships, student-designed major, study abroad, teacher certification program. **Credit/placement by examination:** AP, CLEP, SAT, ACT, institutional tests. 30 credit hours maximum toward bachelor's degree. **Support services:** Learning center, remedial instruction, study skills assistance, tutoring, writing center.

Majors. Area/ethnic studies: Latin American. **Biology:** General. **Business:** Accounting, business admin, marketing. **Communications:** Media studies. **Computer sciences:** Information technology. **Education:** Elementary, health, middle, physical, science, social studies, special ed. **English:** English lit. **Health services:** General, athletic training, nursing (RN), nursing practice. **History:** General. **Human services:** Social work. **Math:** General. **Parks/recreation:** Exercise sciences, facilities management, sports admin. **Philosophy/religion:** Religion. **Physical sciences:** Chemistry. **Protective services:** Law enforcement admin. **Psychology:** General. **Social sciences:** Sociology. **Visual/performing arts:** General.

Most popular majors. Biology 6%, business/marketing 30%, education 17%, health sciences 11%, parks/recreation 7%, psychology 6%, security/protective services 7%.

Technology on campus. 230 workstations in dormitories, library, computer center, student center. Dormitories wired for high-speed internet access and linked to campus network. Commuter students can connect to campus network. Online course registration, online library, wireless network available.

Student life. Freshman orientation: Mandatory, $100 fee. Preregistration for classes offered. One-day sessions offered in May, June, and July. **Housing:** Guaranteed on-campus for freshmen. Single-sex dorms, apartments available. $100 fully refundable deposit, deadline 4/9. Private rooms occasionally available to upperclassmen. **Activities:** Pep band, campus ministries, choral groups, drama, international student organizations, student government, Fellowship of Christian Athletes, Appalachian wilderness club, Baptist student union, Methodist student organizations, Newman club, student ambassadors, science society, philosophy society.

Athletics. NAIA. **Intercollegiate:** Baseball M, basketball, bowling, cross-country, football (tackle) M, golf, soccer, softball W, swimming, tennis, track and field, volleyball W. **Intramural:** Basketball, football (non-tackle), soccer, softball, table tennis, tennis, volleyball. **Team name:** Bulldogs.

Student services. Alcohol/substance abuse counseling, chaplain/spiritual director, career counseling, services for economically disadvantaged, student employment services, financial aid counseling, health services, personal counseling, placement for graduates. **Physically disabled:** Services for visually, hearing impaired.

Contact. E-mail: enrollme@unionky.edu
Phone: (606) 546-1617 Toll-free number: (800) 489-8646
Fax: (606) 546-1667
Craig Grooms, Director of Undergraduate Enrollment, Union College, 310 College Street, Box 005, Barbourville, KY 40906

University of Kentucky
Lexington, Kentucky
www.uky.edu
CB member
CB code: 1837

- Public 4-year university
- Commuter campus in large city
- 22,247 degree-seeking undergraduates
- SAT or ACT (ACT writing optional) required

General. Founded in 1865. Regionally accredited. **Degrees:** 4,238 bachelor's awarded; master's, professional, doctoral offered. **ROTC:** Army, Air Force. **Location:** 80 miles from Louisville, 90 miles from Cincinnati. **Calendar:** Semester, limited summer session. **Special facilities:** Center for the arts, Van de Graaff accelerator, equine research center, center for the humanities.

Freshman class profile.

Mid 50% test scores		GPA 3.50-3.74:	17%
SAT critical reading:	500-620	GPA 3.0-3.49:	24%
SAT math:	510-630	GPA 2.0-2.99:	14%
SAT writing:	490-610	Rank in top quarter:	57%
ACT composite:	22-28	Rank in top tenth:	30%
GPA 3.75 or higher:	45%	Out-of-state:	37%

489

Basis for selection. Test scores and GPA should indicate potential for academic success. Required course work and extracurricular activities also considered. Students out of high school 2 years or more with no college credit admitted on probationary basis. Audition required of music majors. **Home schooled:** List of textbooks, attendance record and 2 letters of recommendation from persons outside family required.

High school preparation. College-preparatory program required. 24 units required. Required units include English 4, mathematics 3, social studies 3, science 3 (laboratory 1), foreign language 2, visual/performing arts 1 and academic electives 7. Health .5, physical education .5.

2015-2016 Annual costs. Tuition/fees: $10,936; $24,268 out-of-state. Room/board: $9,086. Books/supplies: $1,000. Personal expenses: $2,406.

Financial aid. Non-need-based: Scholarships awarded for academics, alumni affiliation, art, athletics, job skills, leadership, minority status, music/drama, ROTC, state residency.

Application procedures. Admission: No deadline. $50 fee, may be waived for applicants with need. Admission notification on a rolling basis. Reply by 5/1 preferred. **Financial aid:** Closing date 2/15. FAFSA required. Applicants notified on a rolling basis starting 4/1; must reply within 3 week(s) of notification.

Academics. Special study options: Accelerated study, combined bachelor's/graduate degree, cooperative education, distance learning, double major, ESL, exchange student, honors, independent study, internships, study abroad, teacher certification program, weekend college. **Credit/placement by examination:** AP, CLEP, IB, SAT, ACT, institutional tests. Students who receive Advanced Placement credit for a course may apply this credit the same way credit earned by passing a course is applied. **Support services:** Learning center, reduced course load, remedial instruction, tutoring, writing center.

Majors. Architecture: Architecture, landscape. **Area/ethnic studies:** Latin American. **Biology:** General, bacteriology, biotechnology. **Business:** General, accounting, finance, hospitality admin, management science, managerial economics, marketing. **Communications:** Communications/speech/rhetoric, journalism, persuasive communications, radio/TV. **Computer sciences:** General, information systems. **Conservation:** General, environmental studies, forest sciences. **Education:** Art, early childhood, elementary, health, middle, music, physical, science, social studies, special ed, voc/tech. **Engineering:** Agricultural, chemical, civil, computer, electrical, materials, mechanical, mining. **English:** English lit, rhetoric/composition. **Foreign languages:** Chinese, classics, French, German, Japanese, linguistics, Russian, Spanish. **Health services:** Audiology/speech pathology, clinical lab science, health care admin, nursing (RN), physician assistant, prephysical therapy. **History:** General. **Human services:** Social work. **Math:** General, financial. **Philosophy/religion:** Philosophy. **Physical sciences:** Chemistry, geology, physics. **Psychology:** General. **Social sciences:** Anthropology, economics, geography, political science, sociology. **Visual/performing arts:** Art history/conservation, arts management, dramatic, interior design, music history, music performance, studio arts. **Work/family studies:** General, clothing/textiles, consumer economics, family studies, food/nutrition, human nutrition.

Most popular majors. Agriculture 7%, business/marketing 17%, communications/journalism 9%, education 10%, engineering/engineering technologies 9%, health sciences 6%, psychology 6%, social sciences 6%.

Technology on campus. 1,000 workstations in dormitories, library, computer center, student center. Dormitories wired for high-speed internet access and linked to campus network. Commuter students can connect to campus network. Online course registration, online library, helpline, repair service, student web hosting, wireless network available.

Student life. Freshman orientation: Mandatory, $40 fee. Preregistration for classes offered. $20 additional charge per guest. **Housing:** Coed dorms, single-sex dorms, special housing for disabled, apartments, cooperative housing, fraternity/sorority housing, themed housing, wellness housing available. $50 deposit, deadline 6/1. **Activities:** Bands, campus ministries, choral groups, dance, drama, international student organizations, literary magazine, music ensembles, musical theater, opera, radio station, student government, student newspaper, symphony orchestra, more than 300 organizations available.

Athletics. NCAA. **Intercollegiate:** Baseball M, basketball, cross-country, diving, football (tackle) M, golf, gymnastics W, rifle, soccer, softball W, swimming, tennis, track and field, volleyball W. **Intramural:** Archery, badminton, basketball, bowling, cross-country, fencing, field hockey W, football (non-tackle), golf, handball, ice hockey M, lacrosse, racquetball, rugby M, skiing, soccer, softball, squash, swimming, table tennis, tennis, track and field, volleyball, wrestling M. **Team name:** Wildcats.

Student services. Adult student services, alcohol/substance abuse counseling, career counseling, student employment services, financial aid counseling, health services, minority student services, on-campus daycare, personal counseling, placement for graduates, veterans' counselor, women's services. **Physically disabled:** Services for visually, speech, hearing impaired.

Contact. E-mail: admissions@uky.edu
Phone: (859) 257-2000 Toll-free number: (866) 900-4685
Fax: (859) 257-3823
Don Witt, Assistant Provost for Enrollment Management, University of Kentucky, 100 Funkhouser Building, Lexington, KY 40506-0054

University of Louisville
Louisville, Kentucky   **CB member**
www.louisville.edu   **CB code: 1838**

- Public 4-year university
- Commuter campus in very large city
- 14,844 degree-seeking undergraduates: 18% part-time, 50% women, 11% African American, 3% Asian American, 4% Hispanic/Latino, 4% Multi-racial, non-Hispanic, 1% international
- 5,230 degree-seeking graduate students
- 72% of applicants admitted
- SAT or ACT (ACT writing optional) required
- 53% graduate within 6 years

General. Founded in 1798. Regionally accredited. **Degrees:** 2,832 bachelor's, 25 associate awarded; master's, professional, doctoral offered. **ROTC:** Army, Air Force. **Location:** 3 miles from downtown, 92 miles from Cincinnati. **Calendar:** Semester, extensive summer session. **Full-time faculty:** 824 total; 87% have terminal degrees, 20% minority, 45% women. **Part-time faculty:** 439 total; 40% have terminal degrees, 11% minority, 59% women. **Class size:** 34% < 20, 51% 20-39, 6% 40-49, 7% 50-99, 2% >100. **Special facilities:** Planetarium, computer-aided engineering building with robotics laboratory, rapid prototype facility with Sinterstation 2000 system, photographic archives.

Freshman class profile. 9,430 applied, 6,758 admitted, 2,797 enrolled.

Mid 50% test scores			
SAT critical reading:	490-620	GPA 2.0-2.99:	10%
SAT math:	510-620	Return as sophomores:	79%
ACT composite:	22-29	Out-of-state:	18%
GPA 3.75 or higher:	47%	Live on campus:	72%
GPA 3.50-3.74:	18%	International:	1%
GPA 3.0-3.49:	24%	Fraternities:	16%
		Sororities:	20%

Basis for selection. High school grades, curriculum, and test scores very important. Diagnostic testing/interview option for students lacking requirements. Partnership with local community college for those lacking required academic units. SAT/ACT score reports must be received by registration before first day of class. **Home schooled:** Transcript of courses and grades required.

High school preparation. College-preparatory program required. 22 units required. Required and recommended units include English 4; mathematics 3-4, social studies 3, science 3-4 (laboratory 1), foreign language 2-3, visual/performing arts 1 and academic electives 5. 1 physical education and health (.5 each). History requirement included in social studies, 5 electives must be rigorous.

2015-2016 Annual costs. Tuition/fees: $10,744; $24,632 out-of-state. Room/board: $8,120. Books/supplies: $1,000. Personal expenses: $3,382.

Financial aid. Non-need-based: Scholarships awarded for academics, art, athletics, leadership, minority status, music/drama, ROTC, state residency.

Application procedures. Admission: Priority date 2/15; deadline 8/24 (receipt date). $50 fee, may be waived for applicants with need. Admission notification on a rolling basis. Must reply by 2/15. **Financial aid:** Priority date 2/15; no closing date. FAFSA required. Applicants notified on a rolling basis starting 4/1.

Academics. Special study options: Accelerated study, combined bachelor's/graduate degree, cooperative education, cross-registration, distance learning, double major, dual enrollment of high school students, ESL, exchange student, honors, independent study, internships, semester at sea, student-designed major, study abroad, teacher certification program. **Credit/placement by examination:** AP, CLEP, IB, SAT, ACT, institutional tests. 24 credit hours maximum toward bachelor's degree. **Support services:** Learning center, pre-admission summer program, reduced course load, remedial instruction, study skills assistance, tutoring, writing center.

Majors. Area/ethnic studies: African-American, women's. **Biology:** General. **Business:** Accounting, finance, management information systems, managerial economics, marketing. **Communications:** Communications/speech/

rhetoric. **Education:** Elementary, multi-level teacher, trade/industrial. **Engineering:** Biomedical, chemical, civil, computer, electrical, industrial, mechanical. **English:** English lit. **Foreign languages:** French, sign language interpretation, Spanish. **Health services:** Dental hygiene, music therapy, nursing (RN). **History:** General. **Human services:** Social work. **Liberal arts:** Arts/sciences, humanities. **Math:** General. **Parks/recreation:** Health/fitness, sports admin. **Philosophy/religion:** Philosophy. **Physical sciences:** Atmospheric science, chemistry, physics. **Protective services:** Law enforcement admin. **Psychology:** General. **Social sciences:** Anthropology, economics, geography, political science, sociology. **Visual/performing arts:** Art history/conservation, dramatic, music, studio arts.

Most popular majors. Business/marketing 13%, communications/journalism 9%, education 8%, engineering/engineering technologies 10%, health sciences 9%, parks/recreation 10%, psychology 8%, social sciences 7%.

Technology on campus. 400 workstations in dormitories, library, computer center, student center. Dormitories wired for high-speed internet access and linked to campus network. Commuter students can connect to campus network. Online course registration, online library, helpline, repair service, student web hosting, wireless network available.

Student life. Freshman orientation: Mandatory, $125 fee. Preregistration for classes offered. **Housing:** Guaranteed on-campus for freshmen. Coed dorms, single-sex dorms, special housing for disabled, apartments, fraternity/sorority housing, themed housing available. $200 fully refundable deposit, deadline 7/18. Special residence hall floors with in-house computer facilities for honors students, coed suites available. **Activities:** Bands, campus ministries, choral groups, dance, drama, international student organizations, literary magazine, music ensembles, musical theater, opera, radio station, student government, student newspaper, symphony orchestra, Association of Black Students, Authentic, Baptist campus ministry, College Democrats, College Republicans, Commonground, debate society, L-Raisers, Rho Lambda Honor Society, Society of Hispanic Professional Engineers.

Athletics. NCAA. **Intercollegiate:** Baseball M, basketball, cross-country, diving, field hockey W, football (tackle) M, golf, soccer, softball W, swimming, tennis, track and field, volleyball W. **Intramural:** Badminton, basketball, bowling, cheerleading, football (non-tackle) M, golf, racquetball, soccer, swimming, table tennis, tennis, track and field, volleyball. **Team name:** Cardinals.

Student services. Alcohol/substance abuse counseling, chaplain/spiritual director, career counseling, student employment services, financial aid counseling, health services, legal services, minority student services, on-campus daycare, personal counseling, placement for graduates, women's services. **Physically disabled:** Services for visually, speech, hearing impaired.

Contact. E-mail: admitme@louisville.edu
Phone: (502) 852-6531 Toll-free number: (800) 334-8635 ext. 6531
Fax: (502) 852-4776
Jenny Sawyer, Director of Admissions, University of Louisville, 2211 South Brook Street, Louisville, KY 40292

University of Phoenix: Louisville
Louisville, Kentucky
www.phoenix.edu

- For-profit 4-year career college
- Very large city
- 184 undergraduates

General. Regionally accredited. **Degrees:** 21 bachelor's awarded; master's offered. **Calendar:** Differs by program.

Basis for selection. Open admission.

2015-2016 Annual costs. Per-credit-hour charge, depending upon level and course of study. Books, material charges, and other fees vary by course and program. All fees are subject to change.

Application procedures. Admission: No deadline. No application fee. **Financial aid:** No deadline.

Academics. Credit/placement by examination: AP, CLEP.

Majors. Business: Accounting/business management, business admin, e-commerce, entrepreneurial studies, finance, human resources, marketing, operations. **Communications:** General. **Computer sciences:** Programming, security, system admin, systems analysis, web page design, webmaster. **Health services:** Facilities admin, health information management, long term care admin. **Human services:** General. **Protective services:** Disaster management, law enforcement admin.

Student life. Freshman orientation: Mandatory. Preregistration for classes offered.

Contact. University of Phoenix: Louisville, 10400 Linn Station Road, Louisville, KY 40223-3839

University of Pikeville
Pikeville, Kentucky   **CB member**
www.upike.edu   **CB code: 1625**

- Private 4-year university and liberal arts college affiliated with the Presbyterian Church (USA)
- Residential campus in small town
- 1,244 degree-seeking undergraduates: 2% part-time, 51% women, 12% African American, 1% Asian American, 2% Hispanic/Latino, 4% international
- 627 degree-seeking graduate students
- 36% graduate within 6 years; 16% enter graduate study

General. Founded in 1889. Regionally accredited. **Degrees:** 241 bachelor's, 23 associate awarded; master's, professional offered. **Location:** 150 miles from Lexington; 140 miles from Charleston, WV. **Calendar:** Semester, limited summer session. **Full-time faculty:** 69 total; 59% have terminal degrees, 3% minority, 56% women. **Part-time faculty:** 82 total; 8% have terminal degrees, 1% minority, 48% women. **Class size:** 57% < 20, 39% 20-39, 1% 40-49, 3% 50-99.

Freshman class profile. 2,408 applied, 2,408 admitted, 314 enrolled.

Mid 50% test scores			
SAT critical reading:	410-460	GPA 2.0-2.99:	38%
SAT math:	400-470	Rank in top quarter:	27%
ACT composite:	18-23	Rank in top tenth:	14%
GPA 3.75 or higher:	17%	End year in good standing:	74%
GPA 3.50-3.74:	13%	Return as sophomores:	58%
GPA 3.0-3.49:	27%	Out-of-state:	22%
		Live on campus:	81%

Basis for selection. Open admission, but selective for some programs. 19 ACT required for nursing, 21 ACT required for education majors.

High school preparation. College-preparatory program recommended. 13 units recommended. Recommended units include English 4, mathematics 3, social studies 1.5, history 1.5 and science 3.

2016-2017 Annual costs. Tuition/fees: $19,600. Room/board: $8,376. Books/supplies: $2,500. Personal expenses: $3,000.

2015-2016 Financial aid. All financial aid based on need. Average need met was 82%. Average scholarship/grant was $18,100; average loan $3,442. 67% of total undergraduate aid awarded as scholarships/grants, 33% as loans/jobs.

Application procedures. Admission: Priority date 3/15; deadline 8/15 (receipt date). No application fee. Admission notification on a rolling basis beginning on or about 9/15. **Financial aid:** Priority date 2/15; no closing date. FAFSA required. Applicants notified on a rolling basis starting 2/1; must reply by 5/1.

Academics. Special study options: Combined bachelor's/graduate degree, double major, dual enrollment of high school students, ESL, internships, liberal arts/career combination, student-designed major, study abroad, teacher certification program, Washington semester. **Credit/placement by examination:** AP, CLEP, institutional tests. 15 credit hours maximum toward associate degree, 15 toward bachelor's. **Support services:** Reduced course load, remedial instruction, study skills assistance, tutoring.

Majors. Biology: General. **Business:** Business admin. **Communications:** Communications/speech/rhetoric. **Computer sciences:** General. **Education:** Elementary, middle. **English:** English lit. **Foreign languages:** Spanish. **Health services:** Nursing (RN). **History:** General. **Human services:** Social work. **Math:** General. **Philosophy/religion:** Religion. **Physical sciences:** Chemistry. **Protective services:** Criminal justice. **Psychology:** General. **Social sciences:** Sociology. **Visual/performing arts:** Art, film/cinema/video.

Most popular majors. Biology 17%, business/marketing 20%, communications/journalism 10%, education 6%, psychology 10%, security/protective services 9%.

Technology on campus. 308 workstations in library, computer center. Dormitories wired for high-speed internet access and linked to campus network. Commuter students can connect to campus network. Online library, wireless network available.

Student life. Freshman orientation: Mandatory. Preregistration for classes offered. Held first 3 days before start of classes. **Policies:** No alcohol allowed on campus. **Housing:** Coed dorms, single-sex dorms, themed housing available. $100 nonrefundable deposit, deadline 5/1. **Activities:** Pep band, campus ministries, choral groups, dance, student government, student newspaper, TV station, academic team, Appalachian Association for Justice, Baptist student union, Blessed Unity of God, Fellowship of Christian Athletes, Lambda Sigma society, Phi Beta Lambda, Psi Chi, Sigma Tau Delta, Young Republicans.

Athletics. NAIA. **Intercollegiate:** Baseball M, basketball, bowling, cheerleading, cross-country, football (tackle) M, golf, lacrosse W, soccer, softball W, tennis, track and field, volleyball W. **Intramural:** Basketball, softball. **Team name:** Bears.

Student services. Alcohol/substance abuse counseling, chaplain/spiritual director, career counseling, student employment services, financial aid counseling, health services, personal counseling, veterans' counselor.

Contact. E-mail: wewantyou@Upike.edu
Phone: (606) 218-5251 Toll-free number: (866) 232-7700
Fax: (606) 218-5255
Teresa Lockhart, Vice President, Enrollment Management, University of Pikeville, 147 Sycamore Street, Pikeville, KY 41501-1194

University of the Cumberlands
Williamsburg, Kentucky
www.ucumberlands.edu

CB member
CB code: 1145

▶ Private 4-year university and liberal arts college affiliated with the Baptist faith
▶ Residential campus in small town
▶ 1,817 degree-seeking undergraduates: 9% part-time, 54% women, 6% African American, 2% Hispanic/Latino, 1% Multi-racial, non-Hispanic, 5% international
▶ 3,282 degree-seeking graduate students
▶ 68% of applicants admitted
▶ SAT or ACT (ACT writing optional) required
▶ 37% graduate within 6 years

General. Founded in 1889. Regionally accredited. **Degrees:** 386 bachelor's, 3 associate awarded; master's, professional, doctoral offered. **Location:** 100 miles from Lexington; 65 miles from Knoxville, TN. **Calendar:** Continuous, limited summer session. **Full-time faculty:** 154 total; 6% minority, 44% women. **Part-time faculty:** 263 total; 11% minority, 59% women. **Class size:** 67% < 20, 31% 20-39, less than 1% 40-49, less than 1% 50-99, less than 1% >100. **Special facilities:** Life science museum, conference center and inn.

Freshman class profile. 2,440 applied, 1,667 admitted, 436 enrolled.

Mid 50% test scores		Rank in top quarter:	40%
SAT critical reading:	430-540	Rank in top tenth:	17%
SAT math:	460-550	End year in good standing:	95%
ACT composite:	19-25	Return as sophomores:	65%
GPA 3.75 or higher:	36%	Out-of-state:	34%
GPA 3.50-3.74:	15%	Live on campus:	90%
GPA 3.0-3.49:	25%	International:	4%
GPA 2.0-2.99:	24%		

Basis for selection. Test scores and GPA paramount. School achievement and activities also considered. **Home schooled:** Transcript of courses and grades required. Must have GED or high school transcript.

High school preparation. College-preparatory program recommended. Required and recommended units include English 4, mathematics 3, social studies 1-2 and science 2-3.

2015-2016 Annual costs. Tuition/fees: $22,000. Room/board: $8,500. Books/supplies: $1,200. Personal expenses: $3,000.

2015-2016 Financial aid. Need-based: 414 full-time freshmen applied for aid; 388 deemed to have need; 388 received aid. Average need met was 80%. Average scholarship/grant was $18,932; average loan $3,438. 73% of total undergraduate aid awarded as scholarships/grants, 27% as loans/jobs. **Non-need-based:** Awarded to 523 full-time undergraduates, including 146 freshmen. Scholarships awarded for academics, athletics, job skills, leadership, music/drama, religious affiliation, state residency.

Application procedures. Admission: Priority date 3/1; deadline 8/15 (receipt date). No application fee. Admission notification on a rolling basis beginning on or about 9/1. **Financial aid:** Priority date 2/1; no closing date.

FAFSA required. Applicants notified on a rolling basis starting 3/1; must reply within 2 week(s) of notification.

Academics. Individualized or computerized tutoring assistance. **Special study options:** Accelerated study, combined bachelor's/graduate degree, cooperative education, distance learning, double major, dual enrollment of high school students, honors, independent study, internships, liberal arts/career combination, student-designed major, study abroad, teacher certification program. **Credit/placement by examination:** AP, CLEP, IB, SAT, ACT, institutional tests. 30 credit hours maximum toward bachelor's degree. **Support services:** Learning center, reduced course load, remedial instruction, study skills assistance, tutoring, writing center.

Majors. Biology: General. **Business:** Accounting, business admin, management information systems. **Communications:** Communications/speech/rhetoric, journalism. **Education:** Art, elementary, health, middle, music, physical, secondary, social studies, Spanish, special ed. **Engineering:** Pre-engineering. **English:** English lit. **Foreign languages:** Spanish. **History:** General. **Math:** General. **Parks/recreation:** Health/fitness, sports admin. **Philosophy/religion:** Christian. **Physical sciences:** Chemistry, physics. **Protective services:** Criminal justice. **Psychology:** General. **Social sciences:** Political science. **Theology:** Missionary, religious ed, sacred music. **Visual/performing arts:** Dramatic, music, studio arts.

Most popular majors. Biology 8%, business/marketing 34%, parks/recreation 9%, psychology 16%, public administration/social services 7%, security/protective services 6%.

Technology on campus. 207 workstations in dormitories, library, computer center, student center. Dormitories wired for high-speed internet access and linked to campus network. Commuter students can connect to campus network. Online course registration, online library, helpline, wireless network available.

Student life. Freshman orientation: Mandatory. Preregistration for classes offered. One-day session in summer. **Policies:** All students required to complete 40-hour community service project. Religious observance required. **Housing:** Guaranteed on-campus for all undergraduates. Single-sex dorms available. $125 fully refundable deposit, deadline 8/15. **Activities:** Bands, campus ministries, choral groups, dance, drama, international student organizations, literary magazine, music ensembles, musical theater, radio station, student government, student newspaper, TV station, Baptist Campus Ministries, Fellowship of Christian Athletes, Appalachian Ministries, Mountain Outreach, Student Government Association, College Democrats, College Republicans.

Athletics. NAIA. **Intercollegiate:** Archery, baseball M, basketball, bowling, cheerleading, cross-country, football (tackle) M, golf, lacrosse, soccer, softball W, swimming, tennis, track and field, volleyball W, wrestling. **Intramural:** Badminton, basketball, football (non-tackle), golf, sand volleyball, softball, table tennis, ultimate frisbee, volleyball. **Team name:** Patriots.

Student services. Alcohol/substance abuse counseling, chaplain/spiritual director, career counseling, services for economically disadvantaged, student employment services, financial aid counseling, health services, personal counseling, placement for graduates, veterans' counselor, women's services. **Physically disabled:** Services for visually, speech, hearing impaired.

Contact. E-mail: admiss@ucumberlands.edu
Phone: (606) 539-4241 Toll-free number: (800) 343-1609
Fax: (606) 539-4303
Erica Harris, Director of Admissions, University of the Cumberlands, 6178 College Station Drive, Williamsburg, KY 40769

Western Kentucky University
Bowling Green, Kentucky
www.wku.edu

CB member
CB code: 1901

▶ Public 4-year university
▶ Residential campus in small city
▶ 15,119 degree-seeking undergraduates: 14% part-time, 56% women, 10% African American, 1% Asian American, 3% Hispanic/Latino, 3% Multi-racial, non-Hispanic, 6% international
▶ 2,474 degree-seeking graduate students
▶ 93% of applicants admitted
▶ SAT or ACT (ACT writing optional) required
▶ 50% graduate within 6 years

General. Founded in 1906. Regionally accredited. **Degrees:** 2,704 bachelor's, 244 associate awarded; master's, professional offered. **ROTC:** Army, Air Force. **Location:** 110 miles from Louisville; 65 miles from Nashville, TN. **Calendar:** Semester, extensive summer session. **Full-time faculty:** 776

total; 74% have terminal degrees, 18% minority, 52% women. **Part-time faculty:** 409 total; 22% have terminal degrees, 7% minority, 54% women. **Class size:** 49% < 20, 38% 20-39, 8% 40-49, 4% 50-99, 1% >100. **Special facilities:** University farm, planetarium, observatory, Kentucky museum.

Freshman class profile. 8,957 applied, 8,303 admitted, 3,121 enrolled.

Mid 50% test scores		Rank in top tenth:	22%
SAT critical reading:	430-580	End year in good standing:	75%
SAT math:	440-570	Return as sophomores:	72%
ACT composite:	19-26	Out-of-state:	20%
GPA 3.75 or higher:	27%	Live on campus:	80%
GPA 3.50-3.74:	15%	International:	3%
GPA 3.0-3.49:	27%	Fraternities:	13%
GPA 2.0-2.99:	30%	Sororities:	23%
Rank in top quarter:	44%		

Basis for selection. Students must meet one of the following requirements for admission: ACT composite of 20 or greater, or SAT (math + critical reading) of 940 or higher, or Unweighted high school GPA of 2.50 or higher, or Achieve the required Composite Admission Index (CAI) score.

High school preparation. College-preparatory program recommended. 22 units required. Required units include English 4, mathematics 3, social studies 3, history 1, science 3 (laboratory 1), foreign language 2 and academic electives 5. 0.5 credit required in each health and physical education.

2015-2016 Annual costs. Tuition/fees: $9,482; $24,132 out-of-state. Room/board: $7,368. Books/supplies: $1,000. Personal expenses: $1,834.

2014-2015 Financial aid. Need-based: 2,697 full-time freshmen applied for aid; 2,053 deemed to have need; 2,028 received aid. Average need met was 40%. Average scholarship/grant was $5,222; average loan $3,000. 53% of total undergraduate aid awarded as scholarships/grants, 47% as loans/jobs. **Non-need-based:** Awarded to 7,650 full-time undergraduates, including 2,311 freshmen. Scholarships awarded for academics, alumni affiliation, art, athletics, job skills, leadership, minority status, music/drama, religious affiliation, ROTC, state residency.

Application procedures. Admission: Closing date 8/1 (postmark date). $45 fee, may be waived for applicants with need. Admission notification on a rolling basis. **Financial aid:** Priority date 2/15; no closing date. FAFSA required. Applicants notified on a rolling basis starting 3/1.

Academics. Special study options: Accelerated study, combined bachelor's/graduate degree, cooperative education, distance learning, double major, dual enrollment of high school students, ESL, honors, independent study, internships, semester at sea, student-designed major, study abroad, teacher certification program, weekend college. **Credit/placement by examination:** AP, CLEP, IB, SAT, ACT, institutional tests. Unlimited number of hours of credit by examination may be counted toward degree. **Support services:** Learning center, pre-admission summer program, reduced course load, remedial instruction, study skills assistance, tutoring, writing center.

Honors college/program. 27 ACT/1210 SAT, 3.8 unweighted GPA, or top 15% of graduating high school class required.

Majors. Architecture: Technology. **Area/ethnic studies:** Asian. **Biology:** General, biochemistry. **Business:** Accounting, business admin, entrepreneurial studies, finance, hospitality admin, international, management information systems, management science, managerial economics, marketing, organizational leadership. **Communications:** Advertising, broadcast journalism, communications/speech/rhetoric, journalism, organizational, photojournalism, public relations, radio/TV. **Computer sciences:** General, information technology. **Education:** Business, early childhood, elementary, family/consumer sciences, middle, multi-level teacher, physical, special ed, trade/industrial. **Engineering:** Civil, electrical, mechanical. **English:** English lit. **Foreign languages:** Arabic, Chinese, French, German, Spanish. **Health services:** Clinical lab science, communication disorders, community health, dental hygiene, environmental health, health care admin, health information management, nursing (RN). **History:** General. **Human services:** Social work. **Math:** General. **Parks/recreation:** Exercise sciences, facilities management, sports studies. **Philosophy/religion:** Religion. **Physical sciences:** General, chemistry, geology, meteorology, physics. **Psychology:** General. **Social sciences:** General, anthropology, criminology, econometrics, economics, geography, GIS/cartography, international relations, political science, sociology. **Visual/performing arts:** Art history/conservation, dance, dramatic, music performance, studio arts. **Work/family studies:** Clothing/textiles.

Most popular majors. Business/marketing 15%, communications/journalism 7%, education 9%, health sciences 11%, liberal arts 10%, parks/recreation 6%, social sciences 8%.

Technology on campus. 354 workstations in dormitories, library, computer center. Dormitories wired for high-speed internet access and linked to campus network. Commuter students can connect to campus network. Online course registration, online library, helpline, repair service, student web hosting, wireless network available.

Student life. Freshman orientation: Mandatory, $75 fee. Preregistration for classes offered. One-day program; several dates available. **Housing:** Coed dorms, single-sex dorms, apartments, fraternity/sorority housing, themed housing, wellness housing available. $150 partly refundable deposit. Special housing available for Honors College students and Gatton Academy students. On-campus apartments available to juniors and seniors. **Activities:** Bands, campus ministries, choral groups, dance, drama, film society, international student organizations, literary magazine, music ensembles, Model UN, musical theater, opera, radio station, student government, student newspaper, symphony orchestra, TV station, American Democracy Project, Amnesty International, Black Student Alliance, College Republicans, College Democrats, Campus Crusade, Green Party, Habitat for Humanity, NAACP, Women in Transition.

Athletics. NCAA. **Intercollegiate:** Baseball M, basketball, cross-country, football (tackle) M, golf, soccer W, softball W, tennis, track and field, volleyball W. **Intramural:** Badminton, basketball, football (non-tackle), handball, racquetball, sand volleyball, soccer, softball, swimming, table tennis, ultimate frisbee, volleyball. **Team name:** Hilltoppers.

Student services. Adult student services, alcohol/substance abuse counseling, career counseling, services for economically disadvantaged, student employment services, financial aid counseling, health services, legal services, minority student services, personal counseling, placement for graduates, veterans' counselor, women's services. **Physically disabled:** Services for visually, speech, hearing impaired.

Contact. E-mail: admission@wku.edu
Phone: (270) 745-2551 Toll-free number: (800) 495-8463
Fax: (270) 745-6133
Jace Lux, Director of Recruitment and Admissions, Western Kentucky University, 1906 College Heights Boulevard #11020, Bowling Green, KY 42101

Louisiana

Centenary College of Louisiana
Shreveport, Louisiana   **CB member**
www.centenary.edu   **CB code: 6082**

▶ Private 4-year liberal arts college affiliated with the United Methodist Church

▶ Residential campus in large city

▶ 518 degree-seeking undergraduates: 2% part-time, 56% women, 35% African American, 3% Asian American, 6% Hispanic/Latino, 1% Native American, 5% Multi-racial, non-Hispanic, 2% international

▶ 65 graduate students

▶ 67% of applicants admitted

▶ SAT or ACT (ACT writing optional), application essay required

▶ 55% graduate within 6 years

General. Founded in 1825. Regionally accredited. **Degrees:** 133 bachelor's awarded; master's offered. **Location:** 325 miles from New Orleans, 189 miles from Dallas. **Calendar:** Semester. Hybrid. Extensive summer session. **Full-time faculty:** 57 total; 96% have terminal degrees, 9% minority, 37% women. **Part-time faculty:** 32 total; 28% have terminal degrees, 3% minority, 59% women. **Class size:** 86% < 20, 14% 20-39, less than 1% 40-49. **Special facilities:** Amphitheater, playhouse, music library, archives, Jack London collection, arboretum.

Freshman class profile. 747 applied, 501 admitted, 157 enrolled.

Mid 50% test scores		GPA 3.0-3.49:	34%
SAT critical reading:	490-590	GPA 2.0-2.99:	9%
SAT math:	490-610	Return as sophomores:	74%
ACT composite:	21-28	Out-of-state:	49%
GPA 3.75 or higher:	37%	International:	3%
GPA 3.50-3.74:	20%		

Basis for selection. Academic achievement record, high school GPA, test scores, essay, letters of recommendation. Extracurricular activities and leadership ability considered. Audition required of music, theater, dance majors. Portfolio recommended for art majors. **Home schooled:** Transcript of courses and grades, letter of recommendation (nonparent) required.

High school preparation. College-preparatory program recommended. 15 units recommended. Recommended units include English 4, mathematics 3, social studies 3, science 3 and foreign language 2.

2015-2016 Annual costs. Tuition/fees: $33,900. Room/board: $12,350. Books/supplies: $1,200. Personal expenses: $1,500.

2015-2016 Financial aid. Need-based: 146 full-time freshmen applied for aid; 131 deemed to have need; 131 received aid. Average need met was 68%. Average scholarship/grant was $22,356; average loan $3,297. 85% of total undergraduate aid awarded as scholarships/grants, 15% as loans/jobs. **Non-need-based:** Awarded to 401 full-time undergraduates, including 116 freshmen. Scholarships awarded for academics, alumni affiliation, art, music/drama, religious affiliation, state residency.

Application procedures. Admission: Priority date 2/15; deadline 8/1 (postmark date). No application fee. Admission notification by 4/1. Admission notification on a rolling basis. **Financial aid:** Priority date 2/15; no closing date. FAFSA required. Applicants notified on a rolling basis starting 3/15; must reply by 5/1.

Academics. Special study options: Combined bachelor's/graduate degree, double major, exchange student, honors, independent study, internships, student-designed major, study abroad, Washington semester. 3-2 engineering program, 3-2 communication disorders program. **Credit/placement by examination:** AP, CLEP, IB, SAT, ACT, institutional tests. 40 credit hours maximum toward bachelor's degree. Credit awarded only when the student has not already attempted to earn credit in a college classroom at or below the level of the subject covered by the exam. **Support services:** Learning center, reduced course load, study skills assistance, tutoring, writing center.

Majors. Biology: General, biochemistry, biophysics, neuroscience. **Business:** Business admin. **Communications:** Media studies. **English:** English lit. **Foreign languages:** French. **History:** General. **Math:** General. **Philosophy/**

religion: Philosophy, religion. **Physical sciences:** Chemistry, geology, physics. **Psychology:** General. **Social sciences:** Economics, political science, sociology. **Visual/performing arts:** General, art, dramatic, music, studio arts.

Most popular majors. Biology 29%, business/marketing 13%, communications/journalism 6%, physical sciences 6%, psychology 6%, social sciences 12%, visual/performing arts 10%.

Technology on campus. 250 workstations in dormitories, library, computer center. Dormitories linked to campus network. Commuter students can connect to campus network. Online course registration, online library, student web hosting, wireless network available.

Student life. Freshman orientation: Mandatory, $100 fee. Preregistration for classes offered. Held in the summer before fall courses begin. **Policies:** Students participate on enrollment management committee, academic affairs committee, student/faculty discipline and other college-wide committees. All students 21 years of age or younger are required to live in college housing. **Housing:** Guaranteed on-campus for all undergraduates. Coed dorms, fraternity/sorority housing available. $250 nonrefundable deposit, deadline 5/1. Living-learning communities available. **Activities:** Campus ministries, choral groups, drama, film society, international student organizations, literary magazine, music ensembles, Model UN, musical theater, opera, radio station, student government, student newspaper, symphony orchestra, church careers institute, United Methodist Student Movement, Baptist Collegiate Ministry, Canterbury House, Fellowship of Christian Athletes, Student Government Association, Young Democrats, Young Republicans, Students for Diversity, Office of Global Engagement.

Athletics. NCAA. **Intercollegiate:** Baseball M, basketball, cross-country, golf, gymnastics W, lacrosse M, soccer, softball W, swimming, tennis, volleyball W. **Intramural:** Badminton, basketball, football (non-tackle), golf, lacrosse, racquetball, sand volleyball, soccer, softball, table tennis, tennis, ultimate frisbee, volleyball. **Team name:** Gents/Ladies.

Student services. Alcohol/substance abuse counseling, chaplain/spiritual director, career counseling, student employment services, financial aid counseling, health services, personal counseling, veterans' counselor. **Physically disabled:** Services for visually impaired.

Contact. E-mail: admission@centenary.edu
Phone: (318) 869-5131 Toll-free number: (800) 234-4448
Fax: (318) 869-5005
Peter Colbert, Director of Admission, Centenary College of Louisiana, Office of Admission, Shreveport, LA 71104

Dillard University
New Orleans, Louisiana   **CB member**
www.dillard.edu   **CB code: 6164**

▶ Private 4-year university and liberal arts college affiliated with the United Church of Christ

▶ Residential campus in large city

▶ 1,200 degree-seeking undergraduates

▶ SAT or ACT (ACT writing optional), application essay required

General. Founded in 1869. Regionally accredited. **Degrees:** 192 bachelor's awarded. **ROTC:** Army, Naval, Air Force. **Calendar:** Semester, limited summer session. **Full-time faculty:** 65 total; 82% minority, 51% women. **Part-time faculty:** 59 total; 83% minority, 71% women. **Class size:** 60% < 20, 35% 20-39, 4% 40-49, 1% 50-99, less than 1% >100.

Freshman class profile.

GPA 3.75 or higher:	8%	Rank in top quarter:	23%
GPA 3.50-3.74:	9%	Rank in top tenth:	9%
GPA 3.0-3.49:	30%	Out-of-state:	35%
GPA 2.0-2.99:	52%	Live on campus:	61%

Basis for selection. Preference to applicants in top 25% of class with 2.5 GPA. Test scores, class rank, participation in extracurricular activities and community projects considered. Interview recommended. **Home schooled:** Recommended that student apply for state diploma.

High school preparation. 19 units required. Required and recommended units include English 4, mathematics 3, social studies 3, science 3, foreign language 2 and academic electives 6.

2015-2016 Annual costs. Tuition/fees: $16,252. Room/board: $9,766. Books/supplies: $1,200. Personal expenses: $1,970.

Financial aid. All financial aid based on need.

Application procedures. Admission: Priority date 12/1; deadline 7/1 (postmark date). $35 fee, may be waived for applicants with need. Admission notification on a rolling basis. Must reply by May 1 or within 2 week(s) if notified thereafter. **Financial aid:** Priority date 12/1, closing date 3/1. FAFSA, institutional form required. Applicants notified on a rolling basis starting 3/1; must reply by 5/1 or within 2 week(s) of notification.

Academics. Special study options: Combined bachelor's/graduate degree, double major, dual enrollment of high school students, exchange student, honors, independent study, internships, liberal arts/career combination, study abroad, teacher certification program. **Credit/placement by examination:** AP, CLEP, IB, SAT, ACT, institutional tests. 20 credit hours maximum toward bachelor's degree. **Support services:** Learning center, pre-admission summer program, reduced course load, remedial instruction, tutoring, writing center.

Majors. Area/ethnic studies: African. **Biology:** General. **Business:** Accounting, business admin, finance. **Communications:** Communications/speech/rhetoric. **Computer sciences:** Computer science. **Education:** Early childhood, early childhood special, elementary, secondary, special ed. **English:** English lit. **Foreign languages:** General. **Health services:** Nursing (RN), public health ed. **History:** General. **Math:** General. **Philosophy/religion:** Philosophy, religion. **Physical sciences:** Chemistry, physics. **Psychology:** General. **Social sciences:** Economics, political science, sociology, urban studies. **Visual/performing arts:** Art, dramatic, music, studio arts management.

Most popular majors. Biology 7%, business/marketing 14%, communications/journalism 12%, health sciences 23%, psychology 13%, social sciences 17%.

Technology on campus. 400 workstations in dormitories, library, computer center. Dormitories wired for high-speed internet access and linked to campus network. Commuter students can connect to campus network. Online library, helpline, repair service available.

Student life. Freshman orientation: Mandatory, $350 fee. Preregistration for classes offered. One-week program held the week before classes begin; includes advising and registration. **Housing:** Guaranteed on-campus for freshmen. Coed dorms, single-sex dorms, special housing for disabled, apartments, wellness housing available. $300 nonrefundable deposit, deadline 5/1. **Activities:** Jazz band, choral groups, dance, drama, music ensembles, musical theater, radio station, student government, student newspaper, service sororities and fraternities, honor societies, religious groups, NAACP, Santa Filomena, Young Republicans, Baptist student union.

Athletics. NAIA. **Intercollegiate:** Basketball, cross-country, track and field, volleyball W. **Intramural:** Basketball, football (non-tackle), football (tackle) M, softball, tennis, volleyball. **Team name:** Bleu Devils.

Student services. Chaplain/spiritual director, career counseling, student employment services, financial aid counseling, health services, personal counseling, placement for graduates.

Contact. E-mail: admission@dillard.edu
Phone: (504) 816-4670 Toll-free number: (800) 216-6637
Fax: (504) 816-4895
Thomas Steffen, Director of Admissions, Dillard University, 2601 Gentilly Boulevard, New Orleans, LA 70122-3097

Grambling State University
Grambling, Louisiana
www.gram.edu
CB code: 6250

- Public 4-year university
- Residential campus in small town
- 4,153 degree-seeking undergraduates
- 916 graduate students
- SAT or ACT (ACT writing optional) required

General. Founded in 1901. Regionally accredited. **Degrees:** 592 bachelor's, 8 associate awarded; master's, doctoral offered. **ROTC:** Army, Air Force. **Location:** 35 miles from Monroe, 65 miles from Shreveport. **Calendar:** Semester, limited summer session. **Full-time faculty:** 194 total; 66% have terminal degrees, 11% minority, 48% women. **Part-time faculty:** 24 total; 75% minority, 50% women. **Class size:** 43% < 20, 41% 20-39, 9% 40-49, 7% 50-99.

Freshman class profile.

GPA 3.75 or higher:	4%	Rank in top quarter:	22%
GPA 3.50-3.74:	6%	Rank in top tenth:	8%
GPA 3.0-3.49:	25%	Out-of-state:	46%
GPA 2.0-2.99:	64%		

Basis for selection. 2.0 GPA or 20 ACT and completion of 17.5 high school core units required for in-state applicants. Graduates of non-Louisiana high schools must complete the required units plus have either a 2.0 GPA and 20 ACT or have a 23 ACT. Neither group can require more than 1 developmental course. **Home schooled:** State high school equivalency certificate required.

High school preparation. College-preparatory program required. 19 units required. Required units include English 4, mathematics 3, history 3, science 3, foreign language 2, computer science .5 and visual/performing arts 1. One additional unit of advanced math (geometry or above) or advanced science required (biology II, chemistry II, physics, or above). Foreign language units must be of the same language.

2015-2016 Annual costs. Tuition/fees: $7,063; $16,086 out-of-state. Room/board: $6,478. Books/supplies: $1,749. Personal expenses: $4,428.

Financial aid. Non-need-based: Scholarships awarded for academics, alumni affiliation, art, athletics, job skills, leadership, minority status, music/drama, religious affiliation, ROTC, state residency.

Application procedures. Admission: Priority date 4/1; deadline 8/15 (receipt date). $20 fee, may be waived for applicants with need. Admission notification on a rolling basis. **Financial aid:** Priority date 4/1, closing date 6/1. FAFSA required. Applicants notified on a rolling basis starting 3/1; must reply within 2 week(s) of notification.

Academics. Special study options: Cooperative education, cross-registration, distance learning, double major, exchange student, honors, independent study, internships, study abroad, teacher certification program. **Credit/placement by examination:** AP, CLEP, SAT, ACT, institutional tests. 30 credit hours maximum toward associate degree, 30 toward bachelor's. **Support services:** Learning center, reduced course load, remedial instruction, study skills assistance, tutoring, writing center.

Honors college/program. 25 ACT/SAT equivalent and 3.5 GPA required.

Majors. Biology: General. **Business:** Accounting, business admin, hotel/motel admin, managerial economics, marketing. **Communications:** Media studies. **Computer sciences:** Computer science, information systems. **Education:** Art, biology, early childhood, elementary, English, French, mathematics, middle, music, physical, physics, social studies, special ed. **English:** English lit. **Foreign languages:** French, Spanish. **Health services:** Nursing (RN). **History:** General. **Human services:** Social work. **Math:** General. **Parks/recreation:** General. **Physical sciences:** Chemistry, physics. **Protective services:** Criminal justice. **Psychology:** General. **Social sciences:** Political science, sociology. **Visual/performing arts:** Art, dramatic, music performance. **Work/family studies:** Child development.

Most popular majors. Biology 7%, business/marketing 19%, communications/journalism 7%, health sciences 11%, public administration/social services 6%, security/protective services 21%.

Technology on campus. 300 workstations in dormitories, library, computer center, student center. Dormitories wired for high-speed internet access and linked to campus network. Commuter students can connect to campus network. Online course registration, online library, helpline, wireless network available.

Student life. Freshman orientation: Mandatory. Preregistration for classes offered. **Housing:** Single-sex dorms, special housing for disabled, apartments, wellness housing available. $50 fully refundable deposit, deadline 7/15. **Activities:** Bands, campus ministries, choral groups, dance, drama, international student organizations, music ensembles, Model UN, opera, radio station, student government, student newspaper, symphony orchestra, TV station, Bayou Boyz social organization, Favrot student union, College Democrats, Ladies of Essence, NAACP, Bayou Girlz.

Athletics. NCAA. **Intercollegiate:** Baseball M, basketball, bowling W, cross-country, football (tackle) M, golf W, soccer W, softball W, tennis, track and field, volleyball W. **Intramural:** Badminton, baseball M, basketball, bowling, cross-country, golf, gymnastics M, softball W, swimming, tennis, track and field, volleyball. **Team name:** Tigers.

Student services. Career counseling, student employment services, financial aid counseling, health services, personal counseling, placement for graduates, veterans' counselor. **Physically disabled:** Services for visually, speech, hearing impaired.

Contact. E-mail: admissions@gram.edu
Phone: (318) 274-6183 Toll-free number: (888) 863-3655
Fax: (318) 274-3292
Cherlyn Hatter, Director of Admissions and Recruitment, Grambling State University, 403 Main Street, GSU Box 4200, Grambling, LA 71245

Herzing University: Kenner
Kenner, Louisiana
www.herzing.edu   CB code: 3430

▶ For-profit 4-year branch campus and technical college
▶ Commuter campus in very large city
▶ 305 degree-seeking undergraduates
▶ Interview required

General. Regionally accredited. **Degrees:** 26 bachelor's, 63 associate awarded; master's offered. **Location:** 10 miles from downtown New Orleans. **Calendar:** Semester, extensive summer session. **Full-time faculty:** 15 total. **Part-time faculty:** 13 total. **Class size:** 16% < 20, 84% 20-39.

Basis for selection. Wonderlic entrance test required.

2015-2016 Annual costs. Personal expenses: $1,566. **Additional information:** Certificate programs: $13,670 to $26,820. Associate programs: $26,180 to $53,640. Bachelor's programs: $61,515 to $88,065.

Application procedures. Admission: No deadline. No application fee. **Financial aid:** No deadline.

Academics. Special study options: Combined bachelor's/graduate degree, distance learning, liberal arts/career combination, weekend college. **Credit/placement by examination:** AP, CLEP, IB, institutional tests. **Support services:** Learning center, reduced course load, study skills assistance, tutoring.

Majors. Business: Accounting, accounting/business management, business admin, entrepreneurial studies, human resources, international, marketing. **Computer sciences:** Networking. **Health services:** Health care admin. **Protective services:** Criminal justice, homeland security. **Visual/performing arts:** Graphic design.

Technology on campus. 115 workstations in library, computer center, student center. Online library, helpline, repair service available.

Student life. Freshman orientation: Mandatory. Preregistration for classes offered. **Activities:** Student government.

Student services. Career counseling, student employment services, financial aid counseling, placement for graduates. **Physically disabled:** Services for visually, hearing impaired.

Contact. E-mail: info@nor.herzing.edu
Phone: (504) 733-0074 Fax: (504) 733-0020
Chrissy Kalivitis, Director of Admissions, Herzing University: Kenner, 2500 Williams Boulevard, Kenner, LA 70062

ITT Technical Institute: St. Rose
St. Rose, Louisiana
www.itt-tech.edu   CB code: 2766

▶ For-profit 4-year technical college
▶ Commuter campus in small town
▶ 414 undergraduates
▶ Interview required

General. Accredited by ACICS. **Degrees:** 55 bachelor's, 114 associate awarded. **Calendar:** Quarter, extensive summer session. **Full-time faculty:** 12 total. **Part-time faculty:** 35 total.

Basis for selection. Satisfactory scores from on-site tests in English and math required.

2015-2016 Annual costs. Per-credit-hour charge, $493, will vary depending on program level and course of study. Academic fee, $200. Some programs require purchase of tools, which could cost an additional $100 to $500. All costs subject to change.

Application procedures. Admission: No deadline. No application fee. Admission notification on a rolling basis. **Financial aid:** No deadline. FAFSA, institutional form required. Applicants notified on a rolling basis.

Academics. Credit/placement by examination: AP, CLEP. **Support services:** Learning center, tutoring.

Majors. Business: Business admin, construction management. **Communications technology:** Animation/special effects. **Computer sciences:** Programming, security. **Protective services:** Law enforcement admin.

Technology on campus. Online library available.

Student life. Freshman orientation: Available. Preregistration for classes offered.

Student services. Career counseling, student employment services, placement for graduates.

Contact. Phone: (504) 463-0338 Toll-free number: (866) 463-0338 Heidi Munoz, Director of Recruitment, ITT Technical Institute: St. Rose, 140 James Drive East, St. Rose, LA 70087

Louisiana College
Pineville, Louisiana
www.lacollege.edu   CB code: 6371

▶ Private 4-year liberal arts college affiliated with the Southern Baptist Convention
▶ Residential campus in small city
▶ 881 degree-seeking undergraduates: 3% part-time, 47% women, 28% African American, 1% Asian American, 3% Hispanic/Latino, 1% Native American, 1% Multi-racial, non-Hispanic, 3% international
▶ 90 degree-seeking graduate students
▶ 69% of applicants admitted
▶ SAT or ACT (ACT writing optional) required
▶ 32% graduate within 6 years

General. Founded in 1906. Regionally accredited. **Degrees:** 176 bachelor's, 24 associate awarded; master's offered. **ROTC:** Army. **Location:** 110 miles from Shreveport, 140 miles from Baton Rouge. **Calendar:** Semester, limited summer session. **Full-time faculty:** 72 total; 62% have terminal degrees, 57% women. **Class size:** 71% < 20, 25% 20-39, 4% 40-49.

Freshman class profile. 756 applied, 525 admitted, 212 enrolled.

Mid 50% test scores			
SAT math:	380-470	GPA 3.0-3.49:	22%
SAT writing:	440-470	GPA 2.0-2.99:	31%
ACT composite:	18-23	Return as sophomores:	59%
GPA 3.75 or higher:	29%	Out-of-state:	9%
GPA 3.50-3.74:	13%	International:	2%

Basis for selection. 20 ACT (930 SAT) and 2.0 GPA OR 17 ACT (810 SAT), 2.0 GPA and rank in upper 50% of graduating class required. Interview required of nursing, respiratory care majors. Portfolio recommended for art majors.

High school preparation. 17 units required. Required units include English 4, mathematics 3, social studies 3, science 3 (laboratory 2) and academic electives 4.

2015-2016 Annual costs. Tuition/fees: $15,070. Room/board: $5,186. Books/supplies: $1,200. Personal expenses: $1,970.

Financial aid. Non-need-based: Scholarships awarded for academics, art, leadership, music/drama, ROTC.

Application procedures. Admission: Closing date 8/15. $25 fee, may be waived for applicants with need. Admission notification on a rolling basis. Must reply by May 1 or within 2 week(s) if notified thereafter. **Financial aid:** Priority date 3/31; no closing date. FAFSA, institutional form required. Applicants notified on a rolling basis starting 3/1; must reply by 5/1 or within 2 week(s) of notification.

Academics. Special study options: Distance learning, double major, dual enrollment of high school students, independent study, internships, liberal arts/career combination, student-designed major, study abroad, teacher certification program. **Credit/placement by examination:** AP, CLEP, SAT, ACT, institutional tests. 30 credit hours maximum toward bachelor's degree. **Support services:** Pre-admission summer program, reduced course load, remedial instruction, tutoring, writing center.

Majors. Biology: General. **Business:** General, accounting, business admin, finance, marketing. **Communications:** Communications/speech/rhetoric, journalism, media studies. **Computer sciences:** Webmaster. **Education:** General, art, business, elementary, English, foreign languages, French, health, mathematics, middle, music, physical, physically handicapped, science, secondary, social studies, Spanish. **English:** English lit. **Foreign languages:** General, French. **Health services:** Athletic training, clinical lab technology, nursing (RN), physical therapy assistant, predental, premedicine, prepharmacy, preveterinary. **History:** General. **Human services:** General, social work. **Math:** General. **Parks/recreation:** Health/fitness. **Philosophy/religion:** Religion. **Physical sciences:** Chemistry. **Protective services:** Law enforcement admin. **Psychology:** General. **Social sciences:** General, economics, political science. **Theology:** Religious ed, sacred music. **Visual/performing arts:** Commercial/advertising art, dramatic, music, music pedagogy, music performance, piano/keyboard, studio arts, voice/opera.

Most popular majors. Biology 8%, business/marketing 12%, education 10%, health sciences 21%, parks/recreation 8%, philosophy/religious studies 7%, visual/performing arts 7%.

Technology on campus. 323 workstations in library, computer center, student center. Dormitories wired for high-speed internet access and linked to campus network. Commuter students can connect to campus network. Online course registration, online library, helpline, repair service, wireless network available.

Student life. Freshman orientation: Mandatory. Preregistration for classes offered. **Policies:** Religious observance required. **Housing:** Guaranteed on-campus for all undergraduates. Single-sex dorms, apartments, wellness housing available. $75 nonrefundable deposit, deadline 8/1. **Activities:** Bands, campus ministries, choral groups, drama, international student organizations, literary magazine, music ensembles, musical theater, opera, radio station, student government, student newspaper, Lamda Chi Beta, Delta Xi Omega, Sigma Theta, Kappa Tau Beta, Union Board, church vocation fellowship, Fellowship of Christian Athletes, Jacob's Society.

Athletics. NCAA, NCCAA. **Intercollegiate:** Baseball M, basketball, cheerleading, cross-country, football (tackle) M, golf, soccer, softball W, tennis. **Intramural:** Badminton, basketball, bowling, golf, softball, swimming, table tennis, tennis, volleyball. **Team name:** Wildcats.

Student services. Chaplain/spiritual director, career counseling, student employment services, financial aid counseling, health services, personal counseling, placement for graduates. **Physically disabled:** Services for visually impaired.

Contact. E-mail: admissions@lacollege.edu
Phone: (318) 487-7259 Toll-free number: (800) 487-1906
Fax: (318) 487-7550
Brandon Bannon, Director of Enrollment Management and Admissions, Louisiana College, LC Box 566, Pineville, LA 71359

Louisiana State University and Agricultural and Mechanical College

Baton Rouge, Louisiana
www.lsu.edu

CB member
CB code: 6373

- Public 4-year university and agricultural college
- Commuter campus in small city
- 24,904 degree-seeking undergraduates: 6% part-time, 52% women, 12% African American, 4% Asian American, 6% Hispanic/Latino, 2% Multiracial, non-Hispanic, 2% international
- 5,175 degree-seeking graduate students
- 77% of applicants admitted
- SAT or ACT (ACT writing optional) required
- 67% graduate within 6 years; 27% enter graduate study

General. Founded in 1860. Regionally accredited. **Degrees:** 4,649 bachelor's awarded; master's, professional, doctoral offered. **ROTC:** Army, Naval, Air Force. **Location:** 80 miles from New Orleans. **Calendar:** Semester, extensive summer session. **Full-time faculty:** 1,278 total; 88% have terminal degrees, 18% minority, 35% women. **Part-time faculty:** 172 total; 63% have terminal degrees, 11% minority, 40% women. **Class size:** 36% < 20, 35% 20-39, 7% 40-49, 13% 50-99, 9% >100. **Special facilities:** Herbarium, natural science museum, rural life museum, museum of art, Civil War center, biomedical research center, coastal ecology center, center for advanced microstructures and devices.

Freshman class profile. 17,429 applied, 13,480 admitted, 5,624 enrolled.

Mid 50% test scores		Rank in top quarter:	52%
SAT critical reading:	510-620	Rank in top tenth:	26%
SAT math:	510-640	End year in good standing:	88%
ACT composite:	23-28	Return as sophomores:	85%
GPA 3.75 or higher:	29%	Out-of-state:	18%
GPA 3.50-3.74:	24%	Live on campus:	66%
GPA 3.0-3.49:	39%	International:	1%
GPA 2.0-2.99:	8%		

Basis for selection. Criteria include number of academic units earned, GPA, ACT or SAT scores. Students must also meet minimum Board of Regents Master Plan requirements. Applicants not meeting course units, grades and/or test score requirements may be considered by faculty admissions

committee. Audition required for MDA majors. Portfolio requirements for some majors in Art & Design. **Home schooled:** Statement describing home school structure and mission, transcript of courses and grades, state high school equivalency certificate required. Students with ACT score below 26 will be reviewed by admission committee. **Learning Disabled:** Students with learning disabilities who do not meet regular admission requirements may appeal to the faculty admissions committee and must submit documentation of disability diagnosis.

High school preparation. College-preparatory program required. 19 units required. Required units include English 4, mathematics 4, social studies 3, history 1, science 4, foreign language 2 and visual/performing arts 1. Specific courses required in some subject areas.

2015-2016 Annual costs. Tuition/fees: $8,827; $26,236 out-of-state. Room/board: $11,200. Books/supplies: $1,500. Personal expenses: $2,004.

Financial aid. Non-need-based: Scholarships awarded for academics, athletics, music/drama, ROTC.

Application procedures. Admission: Priority date 11/15; deadline 4/15 (receipt date). $40 fee. Application must be submitted online. Admission notification on a rolling basis. Recommend responding by May 1. **Financial aid:** Priority date 4/1; no closing date. FAFSA, institutional form required. Applicants notified on a rolling basis starting 12/15; must reply by 5/1.

Academics. Special study options: Accelerated study, cooperative education, cross-registration, distance learning, double major, dual enrollment of high school students, ESL, exchange student, honors, independent study, internships, student-designed major, study abroad, teacher certification program. **Credit/placement by examination:** AP, CLEP, IB, SAT, ACT, institutional tests. 30 credit hours maximum toward bachelor's degree. **Support services:** Learning center, study skills assistance, tutoring, writing center.

Honors college/program. 30 ACT with 30 English, or 29 ACT with 31 English, or 1330 SAT (exclusive of Writing) with 660 Verbal. 3.5 GPA and essay required. ACT/SAT writing component required.

Majors. Architecture: Architecture, interior, landscape. **Biology:** General, biochemistry, microbiology. **Business:** Accounting, business admin, construction management, fashion, finance, international, management science, managerial economics, marketing. **Communications:** Communications/speech/rhetoric, media studies. **Computer sciences:** Computer science. **Conservation:** Environmental science, management/policy. **Education:** Adult/continuing, agricultural, early childhood, elementary, music, physical. **Engineering:** Biomedical, chemical, civil, computer, electrical, environmental, industrial, mechanical, petroleum. **English:** English lit. **Foreign languages:** French, Spanish. **Health services:** Athletic training, audiology/speech pathology. **History:** General. **Liberal arts:** Arts/sciences. **Math:** General. **Parks/recreation:** Sports admin. **Philosophy/religion:** Philosophy. **Physical sciences:** Chemistry, geology, oceanography, physics. **Psychology:** General. **Social sciences:** Anthropology, economics, geography, political science, sociology. **Visual/performing arts:** Dramatic, music, music performance, studio arts. **Work/family studies:** General.

Most popular majors. Biology 8%, business/marketing 21%, communications/journalism 7%, education 10%, engineering/engineering technologies 13%, social sciences 7%.

Technology on campus. 1,180 workstations in dormitories, library, student center. Dormitories wired for high-speed internet access and linked to campus network. Commuter students can connect to campus network. Online course registration, online library, helpline, student web hosting, wireless network available.

Student life. Freshman orientation: Mandatory, $140 fee. Preregistration for classes offered. Held in June, July, and August. **Housing:** Coed dorms, single-sex dorms, special housing for disabled, apartments, fraternity/sorority housing, themed housing available. $250 nonrefundable deposit. **Activities:** Bands, campus ministries, choral groups, dance, drama, film society, international student organizations, literary magazine, music ensembles, musical theater, opera, radio station, student government, student newspaper, symphony orchestra, TV station, various organizations available.

Athletics. NCAA. **Intercollegiate:** Baseball M, basketball, cross-country, diving, football (tackle) M, golf, gymnastics W, sand volleyball, soccer W, softball W, swimming, tennis, track and field, volleyball W. **Intramural:** Badminton, basketball, football (non-tackle), golf, racquetball, sand volleyball, soccer, softball, table tennis, tennis, ultimate frisbee, volleyball. **Team name:** Tigers.

Student services. Adult student services, alcohol/substance abuse counseling, career counseling, student employment services, financial aid counseling, health services, minority student services, on-campus daycare, personal counseling, placement for graduates, veterans' counselor, women's services. **Physically disabled:** Services for visually, speech, hearing impaired.

Contact. E-mail: admissions@lsu.edu
Phone: (225) 578-1175 Fax: (225) 578-4433
Charlotte Tullos, Associate Vice Chancellor, Enrollment Management,
Louisiana State University and Agricultural and Mechanical College, 1146
Pleasant Hall, Baton Rouge, LA 70803-2750

Louisiana State University at Alexandria
Alexandria, Louisiana
www.lsua.edu   CB code: 1632

▶ Public 4-year university
▶ Commuter campus in small city
▶ 3,104 undergraduates: 18% African American, 1% Asian American, 3%
  Hispanic/Latino, 4% Native American, 3% Multi-racial, non-Hispanic,
  3% international
▶ SAT or ACT (ACT writing optional) required

General. Founded in 1959. Regionally accredited. **Degrees:** 314 bachelor's,
149 associate awarded. **ROTC:** Army. **Location:** 10 miles from downtown.
Calendar: Semester, extensive summer session. **Full-time faculty:** 81 total;
60% have terminal degrees, 17% minority, 59% women. **Part-time faculty:**
89 total; 21% have terminal degrees, 15% minority, 61% women. **Class size:**
48% < 20, 42% 20-39, 5% 40-49, 5% 50-99, less than 1% >100.

Freshman class profile. 1,017 enrolled.

Mid 50% test scores		Rank in top quarter:	29%
ACT composite:	18-22	Rank in top tenth:	9%
GPA 3.75 or higher:	10%	Return as sophomores:	66%
GPA 3.50-3.74:	12%	Out-of-state:	5%
GPA 3.0-3.49:	34%	Live on campus:	28%
GPA 2.0-2.99:	42%	International:	6%

Basis for selection. GED not accepted. High school curriculum, GPA,
ACT or SAT, and no need for developmental course work (determined by
having an ACT score of 18 English and 19 Math). Completion of Regents
high school core curriculum and a HS GPA of 2.0 required, along with either
a 20 ACT Composite or 2.0 GPA in core courses. COMPASS Scores are
also accepted to determine if developmental coursework is needed. **Home
schooled:** Applicants must submit transcript of high school level work with
graduation date.

High school preparation. College-preparatory program required. 19 units
required. Required units include English 4, mathematics 4, social studies 4,
science 4, foreign language 2 and visual/performing arts 2. 2 Health & PE.

2015-2016 Annual costs. Tuition/fees: $6,158; $13,150 out-of-state.
Books/supplies: $1,200. Personal expenses: $1,726.

2014-2015 Financial aid. Need-based: 238 full-time freshmen applied
for aid; 238 deemed to have need; 238 received aid. Average need met was
98%. Average scholarship/grant was $4,517; average loan $2,601. 58% of
total undergraduate aid awarded as scholarships/grants, 42% as loans/jobs.
Non-need-based: Awarded to 686 full-time undergraduates, including 228
freshmen. Scholarships awarded for academics, athletics, ROTC.

Application procedures. Admission: Priority date 8/1; no deadline. $20
fee. Admission notification on a rolling basis. **Financial aid:** No deadline.
FAFSA required. Applicants notified on a rolling basis starting 3/1; must
reply within 3 week(s) of notification.

Academics. Special study options: Accelerated study, cross-registration,
distance learning, dual enrollment of high school students, honors, independent study, internships, teacher certification program. **Credit/placement by
examination:** AP, CLEP, SAT, ACT, institutional tests. Credit by examination limited to one-fourth number of hours required for degree. **Support
services:** Learning center, pre-admission summer program, remedial instruction, study skills assistance, tutoring, writing center.

Majors. Biology: General. **Business:** Business admin. **Education:** General,
elementary. **Health services:** Nursing (RN). **History:** General. **Liberal arts:**
Arts/sciences. **Math:** General. **Psychology:** General.

Most popular majors. Biology 7%, business/marketing 20%, education
8%, English 7%, health sciences 7%, liberal arts 20%, psychology 14%,
security/protective services 7%.

Technology on campus. 163 workstations in library, computer center,
student center. Commuter students can connect to campus network.

Student life. Freshman orientation: Mandatory, $35 fee. Preregistration
for classes offered. **Housing:** Coed dorms, special housing for disabled,
apartments available. **Activities:** Campus ministries, choral groups, dance,

drama, international student organizations, musical theater, student government, Baptist ministry, Catholic student organization, Apostolic student fellowship, Canterbury club, College Republicans, College Democrats, international student organization, nontraditional student organization, Identity, Circle K.

Athletics. Intramural: Basketball, cross-country, football (non-tackle) M,
soccer, softball, tennis, volleyball. **Team name:** Generals.

Student services. Adult student services, chaplain/spiritual director,
career counseling, student employment services, financial aid counseling,
minority student services, on-campus daycare, personal counseling, placement for graduates, veterans' counselor.

Contact. Phone: (318) 473-6508 Toll-free number: (888) 473-6416
Shelly Kieffer, Director of Admissions and Recruiting, Louisiana State
University at Alexandria, 8100 Highway 71 South, Alexandria, LA
71302-9121

Louisiana State University Health Sciences Center
New Orleans, Louisiana
www.lsuhsc.edu   CB code: 1192

▶ Public two-year upper-division health science and nursing college
▶ Commuter campus in large city
▶ Test scores, application essay, interview required

General. Founded in 1931. Regionally accredited. **Degrees:** 330 bachelor's,
9 associate awarded; master's, professional, doctoral offered. **Articulation:**
Agreement with University of New Orleans. **Location:** Downtown. **Calendar:** Continuous, limited summer session. **Full-time faculty:** 713 total. **Part-
time faculty:** 134 total.

Student profile. 877 degree-seeking undergraduates, 837 degree-seeking
graduate students.

Women:	86%	Part-time:	33%
African American:	10%	Out-of-state:	1%
Asian American:	7%	Live on campus:	20%
Hispanic/Latino:	6%	25 or older:	28%

Basis for selection. College transcript, application essay, interview, standardized test scores required. Application closing, notification, and response
dates vary by program. Transfer accepted as sophomores, juniors, seniors.

2015-2016 Annual costs. Tuition/fees: $6,093; $11,717 out-of-state.
Room only: $4,797. Books/supplies: $2,500.

Financial aid. Non-need-based: Scholarships awarded for academics.

Application procedures. Admission: $50 fee. **Financial aid:** FAFSA,
institutional form required.

Academics. Special study options: Double major, honors, independent
study, internships. **Credit/placement by examination:** AP, CLEP.

Majors. Health services: Cardiovascular technology, clinical lab science,
dental hygiene, nursing (RN).

Technology on campus. 227 workstations in dormitories, library, computer center, student center. Dormitories wired for high-speed internet access
and linked to campus network. Commuter students can connect to campus
network. Online library, helpline, repair service, wireless network available.

Student life. Housing: Coed dorms, apartments available. **Activities:** Student government.

Student services. Alcohol/substance abuse counseling, career counseling,
financial aid counseling, health services, personal counseling. **Physically
disabled:** Services for visually, speech, hearing impaired.

Contact. Phone: (504) 568-4808
Louisiana State University Health Sciences Center, 433 Bolivar Street,
New Orleans, LA 70112-2223

Louisiana State University in Shreveport
Shreveport, Louisiana
www.lsus.edu   CB code: 6355

▶ Public 4-year university and teachers college
▶ Commuter campus in large city

- 2,444 degree-seeking undergraduates: 25% part-time, 60% women, 23% African American, 2% Asian American, 5% Hispanic/Latino, 1% Native American, 4% Multi-racial, non-Hispanic, 2% international
- 1,625 degree-seeking graduate students
- 81% of applicants admitted
- SAT or ACT (ACT writing optional) required
- 37% graduate within 6 years

General. Founded in 1965. Regionally accredited. **Degrees:** 455 bachelor's awarded; master's, professional offered. **ROTC:** Army. **Location:** 180 miles from Dallas. **Calendar:** Semester, extensive summer session. **Full-time faculty:** 117 total; 87% have terminal degrees, 20% minority, 43% women. **Part-time faculty:** 61 total; 12% minority, 61% women. **Class size:** 57% < 20, 29% 20-39, 7% 40-49, 5% 50-99, 3% >100. **Special facilities:** Life science museum, pioneer heritage center.

Freshman class profile. 602 applied, 489 admitted, 357 enrolled.

Mid 50% test scores		GPA 2.0-2.99:	20%
SAT critical reading:	460-520	Return as sophomores:	65%
SAT math:	470-500	Out-of-state:	6%
ACT composite:	20-24	International:	2%
GPA 3.75 or higher:	19%	Fraternities:	1%
GPA 3.50-3.74:	23%	Sororities:	1%
GPA 3.0-3.49:	38%		

Basis for selection. Completion of Regents high school core curriculum of 19 course units and one of the following required: 2.0 GPA, high school rank in top 50% of class, or 20 ACT. For early admission, principal's recommendation, 29 ACT, 15 specific high school units, 3.0 GPA required. Regardless of age, students who have accumulated at least 18 term hours of non-developmental college credit may transfer if all transfer requirements met. **Home schooled:** GED required.

High school preparation. College-preparatory program required. 19 units required. Required units include English 4, mathematics 4, social studies 4, science 4, foreign language 2 and visual/performing arts 1.

2015-2016 Annual costs. Tuition/fees: $6,903; $20,057 out-of-state. Books/supplies: $1,200. Personal expenses: $1,941.

Financial aid. Non-need-based: Scholarships awarded for academics, athletics.

Application procedures. Admission: No deadline. $20 fee. Admission notification on a rolling basis. **Financial aid:** No deadline. Applicants notified on a rolling basis.

Academics. Special study options: Accelerated study, combined bachelor's/graduate degree, distance learning, double major, dual enrollment of high school students, honors, independent study, internships, teacher certification program, Washington semester. Cooperative education program with Southern University at Shreveport. **Credit/placement by examination:** AP, CLEP, SAT, ACT, institutional tests. 60 credit hours maximum toward bachelor's degree. **Support services:** Learning center, remedial instruction, study skills assistance, tutoring, writing center.

Honors college/program. 3.0 unweighted high school GPA; ACT score of 24 or higher required.

Majors. Biology: General. **Business:** Accounting, banking/financial services, business admin, financial planning, managerial economics, marketing. **Communications:** Media studies. **Computer sciences:** Computer science. **Education:** Art, biology, chemistry, early childhood, elementary, English, mathematics, physics, science, social studies. **English:** English lit, rhetoric/composition. **History:** General. **Liberal arts:** Arts/sciences. **Math:** General. **Parks/recreation:** Health/fitness. **Physical sciences:** Chemistry, physics. **Protective services:** Criminal justice. **Psychology:** General. **Social sciences:** Sociology. **Visual/performing arts:** General, digital arts, dramatic, graphic design.

Most popular majors. Biology 11%, business/marketing 22%, education 9%, health sciences 10%, liberal arts 14%, psychology 8%.

Technology on campus. 250 workstations in library, computer center, student center. Commuter students can connect to campus network. Online course registration, online library, helpline, student web hosting, wireless network available.

Student life. Freshman orientation: Mandatory. Preregistration for classes offered. **Housing:** Pets allowed in dorm rooms. **Activities:** Campus ministries, dance, drama, literary magazine, radio station, student government, student newspaper, Baptist student union, College Republicans, government and law society, Catholic student union, Rotaract, foreign language club, psychology club, black student association.

Athletics. NAIA. **Intercollegiate:** Baseball M, basketball, cross-country, tennis W. **Intramural:** Badminton, basketball, cross-country, football (non-tackle), golf, racquetball, soccer, softball, swimming, table tennis, tennis, track and field, triathlon, volleyball. **Team name:** Pilots.

Student services. Career counseling, student employment services, financial aid counseling, minority student services, personal counseling, placement for graduates, veterans' counselor. **Physically disabled:** Services for visually, speech, hearing impaired.

Contact. E-mail: admissions@lsus.edu
Phone: (318) 797-5061 Toll-free number: (800) 229-5957
Fax: (318) 797-5286
Kimberly Thornton, Director of Admissions, Louisiana State University in Shreveport, One University Place, Shreveport, LA 71115-2399

Louisiana Tech University	
Ruston, Louisiana	**CB member**
www.latech.edu	**CB code: 6372**

- Public 4-year university
- Commuter campus in large town
- 7,629 degree-seeking undergraduates
- SAT or ACT (ACT writing optional) required

General. Founded in 1894. Regionally accredited. **Degrees:** 1,235 bachelor's, 55 associate awarded; master's, doctoral offered. **ROTC:** Army, Air Force. **Location:** 70 miles from Shreveport, 30 miles from Monroe. **Calendar:** Quarter, extensive summer session. **Full-time faculty:** 352 total; 76% have terminal degrees. **Part-time faculty:** 81 total; 22% have terminal degrees. **Class size:** 54% < 20, 33% 20-39, 6% 40-49, 7% 50-99, 1% >100. **Special facilities:** Natural history museum, on-campus lab school, arboretum, planetarium, rehabilitation science and biomedical engineering center, micro-manufacturing institute, water resource center.

Freshman class profile.

GPA 3.75 or higher:	29%	Rank in top quarter:	45%
GPA 3.50-3.74:	21%	Rank in top tenth:	18%
GPA 3.0-3.49:	32%	Out-of-state:	14%
GPA 2.0-2.99:	18%	Live on campus:	35%

Basis for selection. GED not accepted. High school record, test scores most important. Special talents, school and community activities, recommendations considered. To be admitted, applicant must need no more than one remedial course. Admission deadline for scholarship consideration is January 2 for the following fall term. ACT recommended. **Home schooled:** Applicants must have 2.5 GPA, 23 ACT/1060 SAT (exclusive of Writing).

High school preparation. College-preparatory program required. 19 units required. Required units include English 4, mathematics 4, social studies 4, science 4, foreign language 2 and visual/performing arts 1. 2 algebra required. Social studies must include 1 U.S. history. 4.5 units of electives from foreign language, sciences, math, social studies, speech, advanced fine arts, or computer literacy required. Prefer English courses that emphasize grammar, composition, and literature.

2015-2016 Annual costs. Tuition/fees: $8,463; $25,980 out-of-state. Room/board: $5,670. Books/supplies: $1,800. Personal expenses: $1,500.

Financial aid. Non-need-based: Scholarships awarded for academics, alumni affiliation, art, athletics, job skills, leadership, music/drama, ROTC, state residency.

Application procedures. Admission: Closing date 7/31 (receipt date). $20 fee. Admission notification on a rolling basis beginning on or about 6/1. **Financial aid:** Priority date 4/15; no closing date. FAFSA, institutional form required. Applicants notified on a rolling basis starting 4/1; must reply within 3 week(s) of notification.

Academics. Special study options: Combined bachelor's/graduate degree, distance learning, double major, dual enrollment of high school students, honors, independent study, internships, study abroad, teacher certification program. Cooperative programs with Grambling State University. **Credit/placement by examination:** AP, CLEP, SAT, ACT, institutional tests. 30 credit hours maximum toward associate degree, 30 toward bachelor's. **Support services:** Remedial instruction, study skills assistance, tutoring.

Majors. Architecture: Architecture, interior. **Biology:** General. **Business:** Accounting, business admin, finance, human resources, management information systems, management science, managerial economics, marketing. **Communications:** Journalism. **Computer sciences:** Computer science. **Conservation:** General, forest resources, forestry. **Education:** Art, early childhood, elementary, French, music, physical, secondary, special ed, speech impaired.

Engineering: Biomedical, chemical, civil, electrical, mechanical. **English:** English lit, rhetoric/composition. **Foreign languages:** French, Spanish. **Health services:** Audiology/speech pathology, clinical lab science, health information management. **History:** General. **Liberal arts:** Arts/sciences. **Math:** General. **Parks/recreation:** Health/fitness. **Physical sciences:** Chemistry, geology, physics. **Psychology:** General. **Social sciences:** Geography, political science, sociology. **Visual/performing arts:** Art, commercial/advertising art, music, music performance, photography. **Work/family studies:** Family studies.

Most popular majors. Business/marketing 16%, engineering/engineering technologies 17%, health sciences 6%, liberal arts 10%, social sciences 7%.

Technology on campus. 1,800 workstations in dormitories, library, computer center. Dormitories linked to campus network.

Student life. Freshman orientation: Available, $100 fee. Preregistration for classes offered. Four sessions offered during summer. **Housing:** Guaranteed on-campus for freshmen. Single-sex dorms, special housing for disabled, apartments, themed housing available. $50 partly refundable deposit, deadline 7/15. **Activities:** Bands, campus ministries, choral groups, dance, drama, film society, international student organizations, music ensembles, musical theater, radio station, student government, student newspaper, TV station, Wesley Foundation, Baptist student union, Union Board, College Republicans, Campus Crusade for Christ, international student association, NAACP, Circle K, Angel Flight.

Athletics. NCAA. **Intercollegiate:** Baseball M, basketball, bowling W, cross-country, football (tackle) M, golf M, soccer W, softball W, tennis W, track and field, volleyball W. **Intramural:** Badminton, basketball, bowling, golf M, racquetball, soccer, softball, tennis, volleyball. **Team name:** Bulldogs (M), Lady Techsters (W).

Student services. Chaplain/spiritual director, career counseling, student employment services, financial aid counseling, health services, legal services, minority student services, personal counseling, placement for graduates, veterans' counselor, women's services. **Physically disabled:** Services for speech impaired.

Contact. E-mail: bulldog@latech.edu
Phone: (318) 257-3036 Toll-free number: (800) 528-3241
Fax: (318) 257-2499
Joan Edinger, Director of Admissions, College of Basic and Career Studies, Louisiana Tech University, Box 3178, Ruston, LA 71272

Loyola University New Orleans

New Orleans, Louisiana   **CB member**
www.loyno.edu   **CB code: 6374**

- Private 4-year university and liberal arts college affiliated with the Roman Catholic Church
- Residential campus in large city
- 2,583 degree-seeking undergraduates: 6% part-time, 60% women, 17% African American, 4% Asian American, 16% Hispanic/Latino, 1% Native American, 4% Multi-racial, non-Hispanic, 3% international
- 1,367 degree-seeking graduate students
- 90% of applicants admitted
- SAT or ACT (ACT writing optional), application essay required
- 66% graduate within 6 years; 55% enter graduate study

General. Founded in 1912. Regionally accredited. **Degrees:** 645 bachelor's awarded; master's, professional, doctoral offered. **ROTC:** Army, Naval, Air Force. **Location:** Uptown. **Calendar:** Semester, limited summer session. **Full-time faculty:** 257 total; 91% have terminal degrees, 18% minority, 45% women. **Part-time faculty:** 173 total; 51% have terminal degrees, 10% minority, 39% women. **Class size:** 54% < 20, 42% 20-39, 2% 40-49, 2% 50-99, less than 1% >100. **Special facilities:** Humanities lab, multimedia classrooms, information technology computer labs, computer science lab, graphics lab, visual arts lab, ad club/communications lab, RATHE business computer lab, multi-media training center, audio recording studio, editing studio, library learning commons, multimedia exhibit room, career development center, writing across the curriculum writing service.

Freshman class profile. 3,591 applied, 3,243 admitted, 667 enrolled.

Mid 50% test scores			
		Rank in top tenth:	8%
SAT critical reading:	520-620	End year in good standing:	84%
SAT math:	480-610	Return as sophomores:	77%
ACT composite:	22-28	Out-of-state:	60%
GPA 3.75 or higher:	35%	Live on campus:	84%
GPA 3.50-3.74:	18%	International:	1%
GPA 3.0-3.49:	29%	Fraternities:	9%
GPA 2.0-2.99:	18%	Sororities:	16%
Rank in top quarter:	20%		

Basis for selection. High school performance, test scores, counselor/teacher evaluation, personal essay, extracurricular activity, community involvement and work experience all considered. SAT/ACT can be waived for students for whom English is not their native language. TOEFL/ELTS can be submitted in place of ACT/SAT. Interview recommended. Audition required for music, theater arts and dance majors. Portfolio required for visual arts program applicants. **Home schooled:** Require proof of high school graduation or its equivalent.

High school preparation. College-preparatory program recommended. 17 units required; 22 recommended. Required and recommended units include English 4, mathematics 2-3, social studies 2, science 2-3 (laboratory 1) and foreign language 2.

2016-2017 Annual costs. Tuition/fees: $38,504. Room/board: $12,808. Books/supplies: $1,224. Personal expenses: $1,968.

2015-2016 Financial aid. Need-based: 591 full-time freshmen applied for aid; 514 deemed to have need; 513 received aid. Average need met was 80%. Average scholarship/grant was $29,994; average loan $3,672. 80% of total undergraduate aid awarded as scholarships/grants, 20% as loans/jobs. **Non-need-based:** Awarded to 812 full-time undergraduates, including 194 freshmen. Scholarships awarded for academics, alumni affiliation, art, athletics, music/drama, ROTC.

Application procedures. Admission: Priority date 12/1; no deadline. No application fee. Admission notification on a rolling basis beginning on or about 12/12. Must reply by May 1 or within 2 week(s) if notified thereafter. Must reply by May 1 or within 2 weeks if notified thereafter. Students recommended by high school principals and considered ready for college work by the Committee on Admissions may be admitted immediately following completion of junior year of high school. Program intended to serve applicants of unusual promise who will benefit from beginning college careers a year early. **Financial aid:** Priority date 3/1; no closing date. FAFSA required. Applicants notified by 3/30; must reply within 2 week(s) of notification.

Academics. Jesuit tradition of contributing to the liberal education of the whole person emphasized. **Special study options:** Accelerated study, combined bachelor's/graduate degree, cross-registration, distance learning, double major, dual enrollment of high school students, ESL, exchange student, honors, independent study, internships, liberal arts/career combination, student-designed major, study abroad, teacher certification program, Washington semester. Interdisciplinary majors and minors, student-designed minors available. **Credit/placement by examination:** AP, CLEP, IB, SAT, ACT, institutional tests. 30 credit hours maximum toward bachelor's degree. At least 25 percent of the semester credit hours required for the degree must be earned through instruction offered by Loyola. Unless special permission is granted by the dean for the student to pursue coursework elsewhere, the last 30 credit hours must be completed at Loyola. **Support services:** Learning center, reduced course load, remedial instruction, study skills assistance, tutoring, writing center. Peer tutoring is available in all introductory common curriculum courses and in major courses across the curriculum. When warranted, reader and transcriber services are provided for all exams, and if recorded course materials (books and other texts) are not available Loyola provides text to voice alternatives.

Majors. Biology: General. **Business:** Accounting, business admin, finance, international, managerial economics, marketing. **Communications:** Communications/speech/rhetoric. **Conservation:** Environmental science. **Education:** Music. **English:** Creative writing, English lit. **Foreign languages:** General, ancient Greek, French, Latin, Spanish. **Health services:** Music therapy, predental, premedicine, preveterinary. **History:** General. **Math:** General, computational. **Philosophy/religion:** Christian, philosophy, religion. **Physical sciences:** Chemistry, physics. **Protective services:** Criminal justice, forensics. **Psychology:** General. **Social sciences:** General, criminology, economics, political science, sociology. **Visual/performing arts:** General, art, arts management, commercial/advertising art, dramatic, graphic design, jazz, music, music management, music performance, music theory/composition, studio arts.

Most popular majors. Business/marketing 22%, communications/journalism 8%, English 8%, psychology 13%, social sciences 14%, visual/performing arts 16%.

Technology on campus. 525 workstations in dormitories, library, computer center, student center. Dormitories wired for high-speed internet access and linked to campus network. Commuter students can connect to campus network. Online course registration, online library, helpline, repair service, student web hosting, wireless network available.

Student life. Freshman orientation: Mandatory, $250 fee. Preregistration for classes offered. **Housing:** Guaranteed on-campus for freshmen. Coed dorms, special housing for disabled, apartments, themed housing, wellness housing available. $200 nonrefundable deposit, deadline 5/1. Honors Community, SPARK Service and Ministry Community, Leadership Community available. **Activities:** Bands, campus ministries, choral groups, dance, drama, film society, international student organizations, literary magazine, music ensembles, musical theater, opera, radio station, student government, student newspaper, symphony orchestra, TV station, Black Student Union, Loyola University Community Action Program (LUCAP), Muslim student association, Loyola Asian Student Organization, Wolfpack Diversity Team, Women's Resource Center, Loyola Society for Civic Engagement, Active Minds at Loyola University (organization to destigmatize mental health disorders).

Athletics. NAIA. **Intercollegiate:** Baseball M, basketball, cheerleading, cross-country, golf, swimming, tennis, track and field, volleyball W. **Intramural:** Basketball, football (non-tackle), soccer, softball, table tennis, volleyball, weight lifting. **Team name:** Wolfpack.

Student services. Adult student services, alcohol/substance abuse counseling, chaplain/spiritual director, career counseling, student employment services, financial aid counseling, health services, minority student services, on-campus daycare, personal counseling, placement for graduates, women's services. **Physically disabled:** Services for visually, speech, hearing impaired.

Contact. E-mail: admit@loyno.edu
Phone: (504) 865-3240 Toll-free number: (800) 456-9652
Fax: (504) 865-3383
Susan Oaks, Director of Admissions, Loyola University New Orleans, 6363 St. Charles Avenue, New Orleans, LA 70118-6195

McNeese State University
Lake Charles, Louisiana
www.mcneese.edu   **CB code: 6403**

- Public 4-year university
- Commuter campus in small city
- 6,598 degree-seeking undergraduates: 14% part-time, 60% women, 18% African American, 2% Asian American, 3% Hispanic/Latino, 1% Native American, 2% Multi-racial, non-Hispanic, 7% international
- 660 degree-seeking graduate students
- 82% of applicants admitted
- SAT or ACT (ACT writing optional) required
- 41% graduate within 6 years

General. Founded in 1939. Regionally accredited. **Degrees:** 1,081 bachelor's, 101 associate awarded; master's offered. **Location:** 193 miles from New Orleans, 124 miles from Houston. **Calendar:** Semester, extensive summer session. **Full-time faculty:** 260 total. **Part-time faculty:** 170 total. **Special facilities:** Environmental research center, vertebrate museum, farm, community health care clinic, meat processing plant, Southwest Louisiana Entrepreneurial and Economic Development Center.

Freshman class profile. 3,002 applied, 2,463 admitted, 1,439 enrolled.

Mid 50% test scores			
SAT critical reading:	440-530	**GPA 2.0-2.99:**	22%
SAT math:	470-580	**Rank in top quarter:**	41%
ACT composite:	20-24	**Rank in top tenth:**	18%
GPA 3.75 or higher:	27%	**Return as sophomores:**	67%
GPA 3.50-3.74:	20%	**Out-of-state:**	9%
GPA 3.0-3.49:	31%	**International:**	10%

Basis for selection. Completion of the Regents' High School Core 4 Curriculum; need no developmental courses; 2.35 GPA; and ONE of the following: 2.0 core GPA as reported by Department of Education OR 20 ACT/ 940 SAT. Audition required of music majors. **Home schooled:** Transcript of courses and grades required. Letter from State Board of Education approving the home school program required. **Learning Disabled:** Applicants should register with Office of Services for Students with Disabilities.

High school preparation. College-preparatory program required. 19 units required. Required units include English 4, mathematics 4, social studies 4, science 4, foreign language 2 and visual/performing arts 1.

2015-2016 Annual costs. Tuition/fees: $6,658; $12,000 out-of-state. Room/board: $5,664. Books/supplies: $1,220. Personal expenses: $2,002.

Financial aid. Non-need-based: Scholarships awarded for academics, alumni affiliation, art, athletics, leadership, minority status, music/drama, state residency. **Additional information:** Books may be charged and paid in 2 installments during semester.

Application procedures. Admission: $20 fee. Admission notification on a rolling basis. **Financial aid:** Priority date 5/1; no closing date. FAFSA, institutional form required. Applicants notified on a rolling basis.

Academics. Special study options: Accelerated study, cooperative education, distance learning, double major, dual enrollment of high school students,

ESL, honors, independent study, internships, study abroad, teacher certification program. **Credit/placement by examination:** AP, CLEP, SAT, ACT, institutional tests. 24 credit hours maximum toward associate degree, 45 toward bachelor's. **Support services:** Learning center, tutoring, writing center.

Honors college/program. Excellent high school record including a college-preparatory background, 3.4 GPA, 27 ACT/1210 SAT, written essay, interview, 3 recommendations from teachers, principals or guidance counselors, and acceptance by the University for enrollment.

Majors. Biology: General. **Business:** Accounting, business admin, finance, marketing. **Communications:** Media studies. **Computer sciences:** Computer science. **Conservation:** Wildlife/wilderness. **Education:** Early childhood, elementary, physical. **Engineering:** General. **English:** English lit. **Health services:** Clinical lab science, health services admin, nursing (RN), radiologic technology/medical imaging. **History:** General. **Liberal arts:** Arts/sciences. **Math:** General. **Parks/recreation:** Exercise sciences. **Physical sciences:** Chemistry. **Protective services:** Criminal justice. **Psychology:** General. **Social sciences:** Political science, sociology. **Visual/performing arts:** Art, music performance.

Most popular majors. Business/marketing 14%, education 6%, engineering/engineering technologies 7%, health sciences 17%, liberal arts 14%, social sciences 6%.

Technology on campus. 450 workstations in dormitories, library, computer center, student center, student center. Dormitories wired for high-speed internet access and linked to campus network. Commuter students can connect to campus network. Online course registration, online library, helpline, student web hosting, wireless network available.

Student life. Freshman orientation: Mandatory, $100 fee. Preregistration for classes offered. Five conferences offered in summer. **Housing:** Coed dorms, apartments, fraternity/sorority housing available. $345 partly refundable deposit. **Activities:** Bands, campus ministries, choral groups, dance, drama, international student organizations, literary magazine, music ensembles, musical theater, opera, student government, student newspaper, symphony orchestra, 108 organizations available.

Athletics. NCAA. **Intercollegiate:** Baseball M, basketball, cheerleading, cross-country, football (tackle) M, golf, rodeo, soccer W, softball W, tennis W, track and field, volleyball W. **Intramural:** Football (non-tackle), racquetball, soccer, table tennis, tennis, volleyball, water polo. **Team name:** Cowboys.

Student services. Adult student services, alcohol/substance abuse counseling, chaplain/spiritual director, career counseling, student employment services, financial aid counseling, health services, minority student services, personal counseling, placement for graduates, veterans' counselor. **Physically disabled:** Services for visually, speech, hearing impaired.

Contact. E-mail: admissions@mcneese.edu
Phone: (337) 475-5504 Toll-free number: (800) 622-3352 ext. 5504
Fax: (337) 475-5151
Kara Smith, Director of Admissions and Recruiting, McNeese State University, MSU Box 91740, Lake Charles, LA 70609-1740

New Orleans Baptist Theological Seminary
New Orleans, Louisiana
www.nobts.edu   **CB code: 5034**

- Private 4-year Bible and seminary college affiliated with the Southern Baptist Convention
- Very large city
- 1,230 degree-seeking undergraduates
- Application essay, interview required

General. Regionally accredited; also accredited by ATS. **Degrees:** 90 bachelor's, 5 associate awarded; master's, professional, doctoral offered. **Calendar:** Semester, limited summer session. **Full-time faculty:** 50 total. **Part-time faculty:** 156 total. **Special facilities:** Learning extension centers in Baton Rouge, Lake Charles, and Shreveport. Other centers in Mississippi, Alabama, Florida, and Georgia.

Basis for selection. Must be at least 18 years old and a Christian for at least one year.

2015-2016 Annual costs. Tuition/fees: $6,605. Room only: $2,350. Books/supplies: $600.

Application procedures. Admission: No deadline. $25 fee, may be waived for applicants with need. Admission notification on a rolling basis. **Financial aid:** Closing date 4/30.

Academics. Credit/placement by examination: AP, CLEP. 30 credit hours maximum toward bachelor's degree.

Majors. Philosophy/religion: Christian. **Theology:** Bible, religious ed, sacred music.

Student life. Freshman orientation: Mandatory. Preregistration for classes offered. **Housing:** Single-sex dorms, apartments available.

Contact. E-mail: leavelladmission@nobts.edu
Phone: (504) 282-4455
Paul Gregoire, Registrar and Dean of Admissions, New Orleans Baptist Theological Seminary, 3939 Gentilly Boulevard, New Orleans, LA 70126-4858

Nicholls State University
Thibodaux, Louisiana
www.nicholls.edu   **CB code: 6221**

- Public 4-year university
- Commuter campus in large town
- 5,256 degree-seeking undergraduates: 13% part-time, 63% women, 20% African American, 1% Asian American, 3% Hispanic/Latino, 2% Native American, 3% Multi-racial, non-Hispanic, 2% international
- 604 degree-seeking graduate students
- 90% of applicants admitted
- SAT or ACT (ACT writing optional) required
- 41% graduate within 6 years

General. Founded in 1948. Regionally accredited. **Degrees:** 958 bachelor's, 209 associate awarded; master's offered. **Location:** 60 miles from New Orleans, 75 miles from Baton Rouge. **Calendar:** Semester, extensive summer session. **Full-time faculty:** 257 total; 59% have terminal degrees, 13% minority, 52% women. **Part-time faculty:** 54 total; 28% have terminal degrees, 17% minority, 46% women. **Class size:** 39% < 20, 46% 20-39, 5% 40-49, 9% 50-99, 1% >100. **Special facilities:** Marine research facility, culinary institute, center for women and government, marine biology laboratory, center for study of dyslexia, center for economic education, small business development center, center for traditional boat building, economic council.

Freshman class profile. 2,399 applied, 2,164 admitted, 1,212 enrolled.

Mid 50% test scores		GPA 2.0-2.99:	29%
SAT critical reading:	440-540	Rank in top quarter:	42%
SAT math:	470-610	Rank in top tenth:	17%
SAT writing:	430-510	Out-of-state:	4%
ACT composite:	20-24	Live on campus:	47%
GPA 3.75 or higher:	18%	International:	2%
GPA 3.50-3.74:	18%	Fraternities:	13%
GPA 3.0-3.49:	35%	Sororities:	16%

Basis for selection. Louisiana residents must meet Board of Regents Core (TOPS Core) requirement, have no need for developmental coursework, and meet at least one of the following: 21 ACT or 2.0 GPA. Students who are not Louisiana residents will meet different admissions requirements.

High school preparation. College-preparatory program recommended. 19 units required. Required units include English 4, mathematics 4, social studies 2, history 2, science 4, foreign language 2 and visual/performing arts 1.

2015-2016 Annual costs. Tuition/fees: $7,378; $18,310 out-of-state. Room/board: $9,290. Books/supplies: $1,200. Personal expenses: $2,042.

2014-2015 Financial aid. Need-based: 1,113 full-time freshmen applied for aid; 768 deemed to have need; 760 received aid. Average need met was 64%. Average scholarship/grant was $8,207; average loan $2,551. 63% of total undergraduate aid awarded as scholarships/grants, 37% as loans/jobs. **Non-need-based:** Awarded to 818 full-time undergraduates, including 263 freshmen. Scholarships awarded for academics, athletics, leadership, minority status, music/drama, state residency.

Application procedures. Admission: Priority date 8/15; no deadline. $20 fee ($30 out-of-state). Admission notification on a rolling basis. **Financial aid:** Priority date 4/15, closing date 6/30. FAFSA, institutional form required. Applicants notified on a rolling basis.

Academics. Special study options: Cooperative education, cross-registration, distance learning, double major, dual enrollment of high school students, honors, independent study, internships, study abroad, teacher certification program. **Credit/placement by examination:** AP, CLEP, SAT, ACT, institutional tests. 15 credit hours maximum toward associate degree, 30 toward bachelor's. **Support services:** Learning center, pre-admission summer program, reduced course load, remedial instruction, study skills assistance, tutoring, writing center.

Majors. Biology: General. **Business:** Accounting, business admin, finance, management information systems, marketing. **Communications:** Media studies. **Education:** Art, business, early childhood, early childhood special, elementary, English, mathematics, middle, music, physical, science, social studies. **English:** English lit. **Health services:** Athletic training, audiology/speech pathology, dietetics, nursing (RN). **History:** General. **Math:** General. **Physical sciences:** Chemistry. **Psychology:** General. **Social sciences:** Political science, sociology. **Visual/performing arts:** Music, studio arts. **Work/family studies:** General.

Most popular majors. Business/marketing 24%, education 11%, health sciences 17%, liberal arts 14%.

Technology on campus. 304 workstations in dormitories, library, computer center. Dormitories wired for high-speed internet access and linked to campus network. Commuter students can connect to campus network. Online course registration, online library, wireless network available.

Student life. Freshman orientation: Mandatory, $50 fee. Preregistration for classes offered. **Housing:** Guaranteed on-campus for all undergraduates. Coed dorms, apartments available. $250 partly refundable deposit, deadline 8/15. **Activities:** Bands, campus ministries, choral groups, dance, drama, film society, international student organizations, literary magazine, music ensembles, Model UN, musical theater, radio station, student government, student newspaper, TV station, Baptist student union, Circle K, Young Democrats, Support for Older and Returning Students, Order of Athena, Young Republicans, UNITE, Newman club, Muslim student association.

Athletics. NCAA. **Intercollegiate:** Baseball M, basketball, cross-country, football (tackle) M, golf M, soccer W, softball W, tennis, track and field W, volleyball W. **Intramural:** Basketball, football (non-tackle), soccer, softball, tennis, volleyball. **Team name:** Colonels.

Student services. Adult student services, alcohol/substance abuse counseling, chaplain/spiritual director, career counseling, services for economically disadvantaged, student employment services, financial aid counseling, health services, legal services, minority student services, personal counseling, placement for graduates, veterans' counselor, women's services. **Physically disabled:** Services for visually, speech, hearing impaired.

Contact. E-mail: nicholls@nicholls.edu
Phone: (985) 448-4507 Toll-free number: (877) 642-4655
Fax: (985) 448-4929
Becky Durocher, Director of Admissions, Nicholls State University, PO Box 2004-NSU, Thibodaux, LA 70310

Northwestern State University
Natchitoches, Louisiana
www.nsula.edu   **CB code: 6492**

- Public 4-year university
- Commuter campus in large town
- 6,836 degree-seeking undergraduates: 27% part-time, 68% women, 31% African American, 1% Asian American, 5% Hispanic/Latino, 2% Native American, 4% Multi-racial, non-Hispanic, 1% international
- 1,099 degree-seeking graduate students
- 65% of applicants admitted
- SAT or ACT (ACT writing optional) required

General. Founded in 1884. Regionally accredited. Additional campuses in Shreveport, Leesville, Alexandria, and off-campus sites. **Degrees:** 1,069 bachelor's, 264 associate awarded; master's, professional offered. **ROTC:** Army. **Location:** 75 miles from Shreveport, 57 miles from Alexandria. **Calendar:** Semester, extensive summer session. **Full-time faculty:** 286 total; 57% have terminal degrees, 13% minority, 59% women. **Part-time faculty:** 241 total; 26% have terminal degrees, 19% minority, 67% women. **Class size:** 47% < 20, 43% 20-39, 5% 40-49, 5% 50-99, less than 1% >100. **Special facilities:** Regional folklife center, Creole heritage center, southern studies institute, heritage resources laboratory, preservation technology and training center, aquaculture center.

Freshman class profile. 4,100 applied, 2,665 admitted, 1,216 enrolled.

Mid 50% test scores		GPA 2.0-2.99:	29%
SAT critical reading:	420-550	Rank in top quarter:	73%
SAT math:	450-550	Rank in top tenth:	15%
SAT writing:	410-470	Return as sophomores:	69%
ACT composite:	19-24	Out-of-state:	12%
GPA 3.75 or higher:	17%	Live on campus:	55%
GPA 3.50-3.74:	18%	International:	1%
GPA 3.0-3.49:	35%		

Basis for selection. In-state applicants must have required 19 unit college preparatory program, 2.35 GPA, need no more than one developmental class, and have one of the following: 20 ACT/940 SAT or 2.0 core GPA. Out-of-state and homeschooled students must have between 17-19 units of college preparatory program and meet the rest of the qualifications above or have 23 ACT/1050 SAT and need no more than one developmental course. All EFRs are required to have an ACT/SAT score. The COMPASS test is also used in some cases.

High school preparation. College-preparatory program required. 19 units required. Required units include English 4, mathematics 4, science 4 (laboratory 2), foreign language 4 and visual/performing arts 1.

2015-2016 Annual costs. Tuition/fees: $7,006; $17,794 out-of-state. Room/board: $8,584. Books/supplies: $1,220. Personal expenses: $2,004.

2014-2015 Financial aid. Need-based: 1,082 full-time freshmen applied for aid; 857 deemed to have need; 850 received aid. Average scholarship/grant was $8,160; average loan $5,854. 46% of total undergraduate aid awarded as scholarships/grants, 54% as loans/jobs. **Non-need-based:** Awarded to 713 full-time undergraduates, including 279 freshmen. Scholarships awarded for academics, alumni affiliation, art, athletics, job skills, leadership, minority status, music/drama, religious affiliation, ROTC, state residency.

Application procedures. Admission: No deadline. $20 fee, may be waived for applicants with need. Admission notification on a rolling basis. Applications may be submitted after fall deadline but consideration is not guaranteed. **Financial aid:** Priority date 5/1; no closing date. FAFSA, institutional form required. Applicants notified on a rolling basis starting 5/1; must reply within 4 week(s) of notification.

Academics. Special study options: Cooperative education, distance learning, double major, dual enrollment of high school students, exchange student, honors, independent study, internships, study abroad, teacher certification program. **Credit/placement by examination:** AP, CLEP, IB, SAT, ACT, institutional tests. 30 credit hours maximum toward associate degree, 60 toward bachelor's. Maximum semester hours of credit by examination may not exceed half the number of credits required for degree. **Support services:** Learning center, pre-admission summer program, reduced course load, remedial instruction, study skills assistance, tutoring, writing center.

Honors college/program. 19 units of Louisiana Regents' high school core curriculum or comparable curriculum, 27 ACT with no subscore below 20 or 1220 SAT with no subscore below 480, and 3.3 unweighted GPA in Regents' curriculum or comparable curriculum recommended.

Majors. Biology: General. **Business:** Accounting, business admin, hospitality admin, organizational leadership. **Communications:** Communications/speech/rhetoric. **Computer sciences:** Information systems. **Education:** Early childhood, elementary, English, family/consumer sciences, mathematics, middle, music, physical. **English:** English lit. **Health services:** Nursing (RN), radiologic technology/medical imaging, substance abuse counseling. **History:** General. **Human services:** Social work. **Liberal arts:** Arts/sciences. **Math:** General. **Parks/recreation:** Health/fitness. **Physical sciences:** General. **Protective services:** Criminal justice. **Psychology:** General. **Visual/performing arts:** Dramatic, music performance, studio arts. **Work/family studies:** General.

Most popular majors. Biology 6%, business/marketing 12%, health sciences 26%, liberal arts 13%, psychology 10%, security/protective services 6%.

Technology on campus. Dormitories linked to campus network. Commuter students can connect to campus network. Online course registration, online library, helpline, student web hosting, wireless network available.

Student life. Freshman orientation: Available, $80 fee. Preregistration for classes offered. One to two-day program held 3 times during the summer; includes program for parents. **Housing:** Coed dorms, special housing for disabled, apartments, fraternity/sorority housing, themed housing available. $175 partly refundable deposit, deadline 3/5. **Activities:** Bands, campus ministries, choral groups, dance, drama, international student organizations, literary magazine, music ensembles, musical theater, opera, radio station, student government, student newspaper, symphony orchestra, TV station, Baptist collegiate ministry, Catholic student organization, Fellowship of Christian Athletes, Wesley campus ministries, Purple Jackets, College Republicans, College Democrats, African-American Caucus, Native American culture association, student government association.

Athletics. NCAA. **Intercollegiate:** Baseball M, basketball, cross-country, football (tackle) M, soccer W, softball W, tennis W, track and field, volleyball W. **Intramural:** Badminton, basketball, bowling, football (non-tackle), golf, racquetball, soccer, softball, swimming, table tennis, tennis, volleyball, water polo. **Team name:** Demons.

Student services. Adult student services, alcohol/substance abuse counseling, chaplain/spiritual director, career counseling, services for economically disadvantaged, student employment services, financial aid counseling, health services, minority student services, personal counseling, placement for graduates, veterans' counselor. **Physically disabled:** Services for visually, speech, hearing impaired.

Contact. E-mail: applications@nsula.edu
Phone: (318) 357-4078 Toll-free number: (800) 767-8115
Fax: (318) 357-4660
Andrea Maley, Director of Admissions, Northwestern State University, 175 Sam Sibley Drive, Student Services Center, Suite 235, Natchitoches, LA 71497

Our Lady of the Lake College
Baton Rouge, Louisiana
www.ololcollege.edu   CB code: 3928

- Private 4-year health science and nursing college affiliated with the Roman Catholic Church
- Commuter campus in large city
- 1,485 degree-seeking undergraduates
- 156 graduate students
- SAT or ACT (ACT writing optional) required

General. Regionally accredited. **Degrees:** 259 bachelor's, 64 associate awarded; master's, professional offered. **ROTC:** Army, Air Force. **Calendar:** Semester, extensive summer session. **Full-time faculty:** 85 total. **Part-time faculty:** 89 total. **Class size:** 50% < 20, 41% 20-39, 4% 40-49, 4% 50-99.

Basis for selection. High school record and test scores are important. **Home schooled:** State high school equivalency certificate required.

High school preparation. College-preparatory program recommended. Required units include English 4, mathematics 3, social studies 3, science 3, foreign language 2, computer science .5 and academic electives 2.

2015-2016 Annual costs. Tuition/fees: $14,816.

Application procedures. Admission: Closing date 7/1 (receipt date). $35 fee. Admission notification on a rolling basis. **Financial aid:** Priority date 3/1; no closing date. FAFSA, institutional form required.

Academics. Special study options: Combined bachelor's/graduate degree, distance learning. **Credit/placement by examination:** AP, CLEP, ACT, institutional tests. 15 credit hours maximum toward associate degree, 30 toward bachelor's. **Support services:** Learning center, reduced course load, study skills assistance, tutoring, writing center.

Majors. Biology: General, biomedical sciences. **Health services:** Clinical lab science, facilities admin, health care admin, health services admin, nursing (RN), premedicine. **Liberal arts:** Humanities. **Psychology:** General.

Most popular majors. Health sciences 98%.

Technology on campus. 150 workstations in library. Commuter students can connect to campus network. Online library, helpline, wireless network available.

Student life. Freshman orientation: Mandatory. Preregistration for classes offered. One-day program held before classes begin. **Policies:** Smoke-free campus. **Activities:** Campus ministries, student government, American College of Healthcare Executives, Beta Epsilon Fraternity of Radiologic Technology Students, Beta Sigma Mu, Christian student fellowship, clinical laboratory scientist association, cultural arts association, Epsilon Mu Theta, math and science association, Phi Theta Alpha.

Student services. Adult student services, chaplain/spiritual director, career counseling, financial aid counseling, personal counseling.

Contact. E-mail: admission@ololcollege.edu
Phone: (225) 768-1700 Toll-free number: (877) 242-3509
Fax: (225) 768-1726
Rebecca Cannon, Director of Enrollment Management, Our Lady of the Lake College, 5414 Brittany Drive, Baton Rouge, LA 70808

Southeastern Louisiana University
Hammond, Louisiana
www.southeastern.edu   CB code: 6656

- Public 4-year university
- Commuter campus in large town

◆ 11,028 degree-seeking undergraduates: 13% part-time, 62% women, 18% African American, 1% Asian American, 8% Hispanic/Latino, 7% Multi-racial, non-Hispanic, 2% international

◆ 910 degree-seeking graduate students

◆ 87% of applicants admitted

◆ SAT or ACT (ACT writing optional) required

◆ 37% graduate within 6 years

General. Founded in 1925. Regionally accredited. **Degrees:** 1,933 bachelor's, 13 associate awarded; master's, professional, doctoral offered. **ROTC:** Army. **Location:** 50 miles from New Orleans, 40 miles from Baton Rouge. **Calendar:** Semester, extensive summer session. **Full-time faculty:** 482 total; 67% have terminal degrees, 13% minority, 56% women. **Part-time faculty:** 113 total; 48% have terminal degrees, 7% minority, 59% women. **Class size:** 35% < 20, 53% 20-39, 6% 40-49, 6% 50-99, less than 1% >100. **Special facilities:** Environmental research station, maritime museum, contemporary art gallery, performing arts theater.

Freshman class profile. 3,738 applied, 3,242 admitted, 2,420 enrolled.

Mid 50% test scores		Rank in top tenth:	10%
ACT composite:	20-24	End year in good standing:	56%
GPA 3.75 or higher:	15%	Return as sophomores:	64%
GPA 3.50-3.74:	15%	Out-of-state:	3%
GPA 3.0-3.49:	35%	Live on campus:	42%
GPA 2.0-2.99:	35%	International:	1%
Rank in top quarter:	31%		

Basis for selection. In-state applicants must have a 21 ACT with ACT Math score of 19 or higher and an ACT English score of 18 or higher (or a high school core GPA of 2.0 or higher on a 4.0 scale), and a 2.0 high school GPA on a 4 point scale, and satisfy Board of Regents High School Core Curriculum (4 units of English, Math, Science, Social Studies, 2 units of Foreign Language & 1 unit of Art) with no developmental course requirement. Audition recommended for music majors. **Home schooled:** Program must be state-approved; applicant must have 23 ACT with no more than 1 developmental course requirement. **Learning Disabled:** No special requirements or procedures.

High school preparation. College-preparatory program required. 19 units required. Required units include English 4, mathematics 4, social studies 4, science 4, foreign language 2 and visual/performing arts 1.

2015-2016 Annual costs. Tuition/fees: $7,280; $19,758 out-of-state. Room/board: $7,370. Books/supplies: $1,220. Personal expenses: $2,000.

2014-2015 Financial aid. **Need-based:** 2,235 full-time freshmen applied for aid; 1,654 deemed to have need; 1,629 received aid. Average scholarship/grant was $4,967; average loan $2,996. 59% of total undergraduate aid awarded as scholarships/grants, 41% as loans/jobs. **Non-need-based:** Awarded to 4,492 full-time undergraduates, including 1,440 freshmen. Scholarships awarded for academics, athletics, job skills, leadership, music/drama, state residency.

Application procedures. Admission: Closing date 8/1 (postmark date). $20 fee. Admission notification on a rolling basis beginning on or about 10/1. **Financial aid:** Priority date 5/1; no closing date. FAFSA, institutional form required. Applicants notified on a rolling basis starting 4/1; must reply within 2 week(s) of notification.

Academics. Special study options: Accelerated study, cross-registration, distance learning, double major, dual enrollment of high school students, ESL, honors, independent study, internships, study abroad, teacher certification program. **Credit/placement by examination:** AP, CLEP, SAT, ACT, institutional tests. 30 credit hours maximum toward bachelor's degree. Credit will not be given through CLEP in last 30 hours. **Support services:** Learning center, remedial instruction, study skills assistance, tutoring, writing center.

Majors. Biology: General. **Business:** Accounting, business admin, finance, logistics, marketing. **Communications:** Communications/speech/rhetoric. **Computer sciences:** Computer science, information technology. **Education:** Early childhood, elementary, English, middle, physical, social studies. **English:** English lit. **Foreign languages:** Spanish. **Health services:** Athletic training, audiology/speech pathology, health services admin, nursing (RN), public health ed. **History:** General. **Human services:** Social work. **Math:** General. **Parks/recreation:** Sports admin. **Physical sciences:** Chemistry, physics. **Protective services:** Criminal justice. **Psychology:** General. **Social sciences:** Political science, sociology. **Visual/performing arts:** Art, music performance. **Work/family studies:** General.

Most popular majors. Business/marketing 23%, education 12%, health sciences 13%, liberal arts 12%.

Technology on campus. 1,300 workstations in library, computer center, student center. Dormitories wired for high-speed internet access and linked to campus network. Commuter students can connect to campus network.

Online course registration, online library, helpline, repair service, student web hosting, wireless network available.

Student life. Freshman orientation: Mandatory, $100 fee. Preregistration for classes offered. Sessions held during summer or at beginning of first semester; students pay room and board for summer session. **Housing:** Coed dorms, single-sex dorms, apartments, fraternity/sorority housing available. $150 fully refundable deposit, deadline 6/15. Honors housing. **Activities:** Bands, dance, drama, international student organizations, literary magazine, music ensembles, radio station, student government, student newspaper, TV station, Baptist collegiate ministries, student government association, Wesley Foundation, campus activities board, black student union, Circle K International, Best Buddies, Campus Crusade for Christ, College republicans, Nepalese Student Association.

Athletics. NCAA. **Intercollegiate:** Baseball M, basketball, cross-country, football (tackle) M, golf M, soccer W, softball W, tennis W, track and field, volleyball W. **Intramural:** Badminton, basketball, football (non-tackle), racquetball, soccer, softball, volleyball, weight lifting. **Team name:** Lions, Lady Lions.

Student services. Adult student services, alcohol/substance abuse counseling, career counseling, services for economically disadvantaged, student employment services, financial aid counseling, health services, minority student services, personal counseling, placement for graduates, veterans' counselor. **Physically disabled:** Services for visually, speech, hearing impaired.

Contact. E-mail: admissions@selu.edu
Phone: (985) 549-2066 Toll-free number: (800) 222-7358
Fax: (985) 549-5882
Lori Fairburn, Director of Enrollment Services, Southeastern Louisiana University, SLU 10752, Hammond, LA 70402

Southern University and Agricultural and Mechanical College

Baton Rouge, Louisiana
www.subr.edu CB code: 6663

◆ Public 4-year university

◆ Commuter campus in large city

◆ 5,285 degree-seeking undergraduates: 13% part-time, 65% women

◆ 440 degree-seeking graduate students

◆ SAT or ACT (ACT writing optional) required

◆ 35% graduate within 6 years

General. Founded in 1880. Regionally accredited. **Degrees:** 652 bachelor's awarded; master's, professional, doctoral offered. **ROTC:** Army, Naval, Air Force. **Location:** 80 miles from New Orleans. **Calendar:** Semester, extensive summer session. **Full-time faculty:** 271 total; 92% minority, 44% women. **Part-time faculty:** 116 total; 94% minority, 63% women. **Special facilities:** Experimental (laboratory) farm, human simulation laboratory, outdoor learning resource center, intramural sports center, Center for Teaching and Learning Excellence (CTLE), center for international education, career services, black heritage museum.

Freshman class profile.

Mid 50% test scores		GPA 3.50-3.74:	8%
ACT composite:	17-21	GPA 3.0-3.49:	30%
GPA 3.75 or higher:	7%	GPA 2.0-2.99:	54%

Basis for selection. Minimum overall high school GPA of 2.0; and require only one developmental course by having a minimum ACT English score of 18 or Math score of 19 (SAT verbal score of 450 or SAT Math score of 460); and one of the following: core GPA of 2.0 or ACT composite score of 20 (SAT composite score of 940). **Home schooled:** Transcript of courses and grades required. Completion of Board of Regents' high school core curriculum; Minimum ACT English score of 18 or math score of 19 (SAT verbal score of 450 or SAT math score of 460; one of the following: minimum high school GPA of 2.0 on a 4.0 scale or core GPA of 2.0 or ACT composite score of 20 (SAT composite score of 940).

High school preparation. College-preparatory program required. 19 units required. Required units include English 4, mathematics 4, social studies 4, science 4, foreign language 2 and visual/performing arts 1.

2015-2016 Annual costs. Tuition/fees: $6,766; $16,116 out-of-state. Room/board: $6,232. Books/supplies: $1,220. Personal expenses: $2,003.

2015-2016 Financial aid. Need-based: 1,147 full-time freshmen applied for aid; 1,073 deemed to have need; 1,054 received aid. 60% of total undergraduate aid awarded as scholarships/grants, 40% as loans/jobs. **Non-need-based:** Scholarships awarded for academics, athletics, ROTC, state residency.

Application procedures. Admission: Closing date 7/1 (postmark date). $20 fee. Admission notification on a rolling basis. Admission can be deferred for 2 semesters. High school students admitted early must be in good academic standing and have approval from their high school. **Financial aid:** Priority date 1/31, closing date 3/30. FAFSA required. Applicants notified on a rolling basis starting 5/1; must reply within 3 week(s) of notification.

Academics. Special study options: Combined bachelor's/graduate degree, cooperative education, cross-registration, distance learning, double major, dual enrollment of high school students, exchange student, honors, independent study, internships, study abroad, teacher certification program, weekend college. **Credit/placement by examination:** AP, CLEP, SAT, ACT, institutional tests. 30 credit hours maximum toward bachelor's degree. **Support services:** Learning center, pre-admission summer program, reduced course load, remedial instruction, study skills assistance, tutoring, writing center.

Honors college/program. Students must have an ACT score of 23 (1070 SAT) and 3.0 GPA.

Majors. Biology: General. **Business:** Accounting, business admin, finance, marketing. **Communications:** Media studies. **Computer sciences:** Computer science. **Conservation:** Urban forestry. **Education:** Elementary, middle. **Engineering:** Civil, electrical, mechanical. **English:** English lit. **Health services:** Audiology/speech pathology, nursing (RN), recreational therapy, vocational rehab counseling. **History:** General. **Human services:** Social work. **Physical sciences:** Chemistry. **Protective services:** Criminal justice. **Psychology:** General. **Social sciences:** Political science, sociology. **Visual/performing arts:** Music performance. **Work/family studies:** General.

Most popular majors. Business/marketing 12%, engineering/engineering technologies 9%, health sciences 22%, psychology 6%, security/protective services 10%, social sciences 6%.

Technology on campus. 344 workstations in dormitories, library, computer center, student center. Dormitories wired for high-speed internet access and linked to campus network. Commuter students can connect to campus network. Online course registration, online library, helpline, wireless network available.

Student life. Freshman orientation: Mandatory. Preregistration for classes offered. Two-day program held during registration. **Policies:** First-time, first-year students must obtain special permission to have a car on campus. All first-time freshmen are required to live on campus. **Housing:** Guaranteed on-campus for freshmen. Single-sex dorms, special housing for disabled, apartments, wellness housing available. $150 partly refundable deposit, deadline 12/20. **Activities:** Bands, campus ministries, choral groups, dance, drama, international student organizations, literary magazine, music ensembles, musical theater, student government, student newspaper, TV station, Catholic student club, Way of Holiness Ministries, Nation of Islam student association, Alpha Sigma Omega Delta, social service organizations, Student Government Association, African student organization, National Society of Black Engineers, criminal justice club, Student Nurses Association, Student Rehabilitation Association.

Athletics. NCAA. **Intercollegiate:** Baseball M, basketball, bowling W, cross-country, football (tackle) M, soccer W, softball W, tennis W, track and field, volleyball W. **Intramural:** Football (non-tackle). **Team name:** Jaguars.

Student services. Career counseling, student employment services, financial aid counseling, health services, personal counseling, placement for graduates, veterans' counselor. **Physically disabled:** Services for visually, speech, hearing impaired.

Contact. E-mail: admit@subr.edu
Phone: (225) 771-2430 Toll-free number: (800) 256-1531
Fax: (225) 771-2500
Anthony Jackson, Assistant Vice Chancellor of Student Affairs and Enrollment Mgmt/ Director of Admission, Southern University and Agricultural and Mechanical College, T.H. Harris Hall, Baton Rouge, LA 70813

Southern University at New Orleans
New Orleans, Louisiana
www.suno.edu   **CB code: 1647**

▶ Public 4-year university
▶ Commuter campus in large city
▶ 2,390 degree-seeking undergraduates
▶ ACT (writing optional) required

General. Founded in 1959. Regionally accredited. Part of Southern University System. **Degrees:** 306 bachelor's, 30 associate awarded; master's offered. **ROTC:** Army, Naval, Air Force. **Location:** Downtown. **Calendar:** Semester, limited summer session. **Full-time faculty:** 113 total. **Part-time faculty:** 34

total. **Class size:** 49% < 20, 47% 20-39, 3% 40-49, less than 1% 50-99, less than 1% >100.

Basis for selection. Applicants must complete Louisiana Board of Regents high school core curriculum (also TOPS core curriculum); require no more than 1 remedial course for immediate admission; and satisfy one of the following: 2.0 GPA or 20 ACT (950 SAT) or rank to top 50% of class. ACT required by state law for placement.

High school preparation. 16 units recommended. Recommended units include English 4, mathematics 3, social studies 3, science 3 (laboratory 2) and foreign language 1.

2015-2016 Annual costs. Tuition/fees: $5,781; $14,682 out-of-state. Room/board: $8,620. Books/supplies: $1,000.

Financial aid. All financial aid based on need.

Application procedures. Admission: No deadline. $20 fee ($15 out-of-state). Admission notification on a rolling basis. **Financial aid:** Closing date 4/15. FAFSA required. Applicants notified by 5/15; must reply within 1 week(s) of notification.

Academics. Special study options: Combined bachelor's/graduate degree, cooperative education, cross-registration, distance learning, double major, dual enrollment of high school students, internships, teacher certification program, weekend college. **Credit/placement by examination:** AP, CLEP. 30 credit hours maximum toward bachelor's degree. **Support services:** Reduced course load, remedial instruction, study skills assistance, tutoring, writing center.

Majors. Biology: General. **Business:** Entrepreneurial studies, management information systems. **Education:** Early childhood, elementary. **English:** English lit. **Health services:** Health information management, substance abuse counseling. **Human services:** General, social work. **Physical sciences:** Physics. **Protective services:** Criminal justice. **Psychology:** General. **Social sciences:** Sociology. **Work/family studies:** Family studies.

Most popular majors. Biology 6%, business/marketing 21%, computer/information sciences 10%, liberal arts 17%, psychology 15%, public administration/social services 10%, security/protective services 13%.

Technology on campus. 60 workstations in library, computer center. Online library, helpline, wireless network available.

Student life. Freshman orientation: Available. Preregistration for classes offered. **Housing:** Wellness housing available. **Activities:** Student government.

Athletics. NAIA. **Intercollegiate:** Basketball, cross-country. **Team name:** Knights.

Student services. Chaplain/spiritual director, career counseling, student employment services, financial aid counseling, health services, personal counseling, placement for graduates. **Physically disabled:** Services for visually, speech, hearing impaired.

Contact. Phone: (504) 286-5000 ext. 5314 Fax: (504) 284-5481
Shawn Vinnett, Director of Recruitment, Admissions, & Retention, Southern University at New Orleans, 6801 Press Drive, New Orleans, LA 70126

Southwest University
Kenner, Louisiana
www.southwest.edu

▶ For-profit 4-year virtual university
▶ Very large city
▶ 601 degree-seeking undergraduates

General. Accredited by DETC. **Degrees:** 52 bachelor's awarded; master's offered. **Calendar:** Differs by program. **Full-time faculty:** 6 total. **Part-time faculty:** 41 total.

Basis for selection. Open admission.

2015-2016 Annual costs. Tuition/fees: $8,550.

Application procedures. Admission: No deadline. $75 fee. Admission notification on a rolling basis.

Academics. Special study options: Accelerated study, distance learning, double major, independent study. **Credit/placement by examination:** AP, CLEP.

Majors. Business: Business admin, management science. **Protective services:** Law enforcement admin.

Technology on campus. Online library available.

Student services. Adult student services, veterans' counselor.

Contact. E-mail: admissions@southwest.edu
Phone: (504) 468-2900 Toll-free number: (800) 433-5923
Fax: (504) 468-3213
Lydia Ocmand, Director of Admissions, Southwest University, 2200
Veterans Memorial Boulevard, Kenner, LA 70062-4005

St. Joseph Seminary College
St. Benedict, Louisiana
www.sjasc.edu   CB code: 6689

- Private 4-year liberal arts and seminary college for men affiliated with the Roman Catholic Church
- Residential campus in rural community
- 137 degree-seeking undergraduates
- SAT or ACT (ACT writing optional), application essay required

General. Founded in 1891. Regionally accredited. Non-seminarian students may attend. **Degrees:** 23 bachelor's awarded. **Location:** 40 miles from New Orleans. **Calendar:** Semester. **Full-time faculty:** 13 total; 31% have terminal degrees, 31% women. **Part-time faculty:** 12 total; 25% have terminal degrees, 8% minority, 17% women. **Class size:** 69% < 20, 31% 20-39. **Special facilities:** 1,200 acres of forest, Romanesque abbey church.

Freshman class profile.

Out-of-state: 20% Live on campus: 100%

Basis for selection. Recommendation by diocesan bishop, academic standing, and test scores required. Interview, essay required by dioceses prior to application to college. **Home schooled:** State high school equivalency certificate required.

High school preparation. 10 units recommended. Recommended units include English 3, mathematics 2, history 1, science 2 and foreign language 2. Additional units in English, second foreign language, social science and math recommended.

2015-2016 Annual costs. Tuition/fees: $16,410. Room/board: $14,120. Books/supplies: $1,220. Personal expenses: $2,003.

Financial aid. Non-need-based: Scholarships awarded for academics, leadership.

Application procedures. Admission: No deadline. No application fee. Application must be submitted on paper. **Financial aid:** Priority date 3/15; no closing date. FAFSA required. Applicants notified on a rolling basis starting 7/1; must reply within 4 week(s) of notification.

Academics. Writing Center has extended hours to include evenings and weekends if needed by students. **Special study options:** ESL. **Credit/placement by examination:** AP, CLEP, IB, institutional tests. 24 credit hours maximum toward bachelor's degree. **Support services:** Remedial instruction, tutoring, writing center.

Majors. Liberal arts: Arts/sciences.

Technology on campus. 14 workstations in dormitories, library, computer center. Dormitories wired for high-speed internet access. Online library, repair service, wireless network available.

Student life. Freshman orientation: Mandatory. Preregistration for classes offered. **Policies:** Closed formation weekends. Religious observance required. **Housing:** Guaranteed on-campus for all undergraduates. **Activities:** Campus ministries, choral groups, student government.

Athletics. Intramural: Basketball M, football (non-tackle) M, softball M, tennis M, volleyball M. **Team name:** Ravens.

Student services. Chaplain/spiritual director, financial aid counseling, health services, personal counseling, veterans' counselor. **Physically disabled:** Services for visually, speech, hearing impaired.

Contact. E-mail: registrar@sjasc.edu
Phone: (985) 867-2273 Fax: (985) 327-1085
Casey Edler, Registrar, St. Joseph Seminary College, 75376 River Road, St. Benedict, LA 70457-9990

Tulane University
New Orleans, Louisiana   CB member
www.tulane.edu   CB code: 6832

- Private 4-year university
- Residential campus in very large city
- 8,262 degree-seeking undergraduates: 18% part-time, 59% women, 8% African American, 3% Asian American, 6% Hispanic/Latino, 3% Multiracial, non-Hispanic, 3% international
- 5,110 degree-seeking graduate students
- 30% of applicants admitted
- SAT or ACT (ACT writing recommended), application essay required
- 83% graduate within 6 years; 45% enter graduate study

General. Founded in 1834. Regionally accredited. **Degrees:** 1,740 bachelor's, 82 associate awarded; master's, professional, doctoral offered. **ROTC:** Army, Naval, Air Force. **Location:** 4 miles from downtown. **Calendar:** Semester, limited summer session. **Full-time faculty:** 704 total; 96% have terminal degrees, 18% minority, 41% women. **Part-time faculty:** 500 total; 48% have terminal degrees, 18% minority, 44% women. **Class size:** 65% < 20, 25% 20-39, 6% 40-49, 3% 50-99, 1% >100. **Special facilities:** Jazz archive, Louisiana collection of historical materials, Southeastern architecture archive, center for research on women, political economy institute, center for Latin American studies, middle American research institute, center for bio-environmental research, performing arts center, Amistad research center, art center.

Freshman class profile. 26,257 applied, 8,008 admitted, 1,719 enrolled.

Mid 50% test scores		Rank in top quarter:	85%
SAT critical reading:	620-710	Rank in top tenth:	55%
SAT math:	620-700	Return as sophomores:	92%
SAT writing:	640-720	Out-of-state:	87%
ACT composite:	29-32	Live on campus:	99%
GPA 3.75 or higher:	31%	International:	3%
GPA 3.50-3.74:	23%	Fraternities:	35%
GPA 3.0-3.49:	37%	Sororities:	56%
GPA 2.0-2.99:	8%		

Basis for selection. High school achievement record most important, followed by test scores, recommendation, personal qualities; special consideration for children of alumni and minority applicants. Candidates should be in top third of graduating class with 3.5 GPA. Audition recommended for music majors. Portfolio recommended for architecture, art majors. **Home schooled:** Statement describing home school structure and mission, state high school equivalency certificate, letter of recommendation (nonparent) required. Completed application for admission, 2 SAT subject tests in subject of choice in addition to a SAT or ACT Test Score.

High school preparation. College-preparatory program required. Recommended units include English 4, mathematics 4, social studies 3, science 4 (laboratory 4), foreign language 3 and academic electives 3.

2015-2016 Annual costs. Tuition/fees: $49,638. Room/board: $13,758. Books/supplies: $1,200. Personal expenses: $1,058.

2014-2015 Financial aid. Need-based: 1,017 full-time freshmen applied for aid; 645 deemed to have need; 645 received aid. Average need met was 96%. Average scholarship/grant was $30,318; average loan $6,224. 72% of total undergraduate aid awarded as scholarships/grants, 28% as loans/jobs. **Non-need-based:** Awarded to 3,013 full-time undergraduates, including 797 freshmen. Scholarships awarded for academics, athletics, leadership, music/drama, ROTC, state residency.

Application procedures. Admission: Closing date 1/15 (postmark date). No application fee. Admission notification by 4/1. Admission notification on a rolling basis. Must reply by May 1 or within 2 week(s) if notified thereafter. **Financial aid:** Priority date 2/15; no closing date. FAFSA, CSS PROFILE required. Applicants notified on a rolling basis starting 3/15.

Academics. Special study options: Accelerated study, combined bachelor's/graduate degree, cooperative education, cross-registration, distance learning, double major, dual enrollment of high school students, ESL, exchange student, honors, independent study, internships, liberal arts/career combination, student-designed major, study abroad, teacher certification program, Washington semester. **Credit/placement by examination:** AP, CLEP, IB, institutional tests. **Support services:** Learning center, study skills assistance, tutoring, writing center.

Majors. Architecture: Architecture. **Area/ethnic studies:** African, American, Asian, German, Latin American, Russian/Slavic, women's. **Biology:** General, biochemistry, cell/histology, ecology, evolutionary, molecular, neuroscience. **Business:** General, accounting, business admin, finance, management information systems, marketing. **Communications:** Media studies.

Conservation: Environmental science, environmental studies. **Engineering:** Applied physics, biomedical, chemical. **English:** English lit. **Foreign languages:** Classics, French, German, Italian, linguistics, modern Greek, Portuguese, Russian, Spanish. **History:** General. **Math:** General. **Philosophy/religion:** Judaic, philosophy. **Physical sciences:** Chemistry, geology, physics. **Protective services:** Homeland security. **Psychology:** General. **Social sciences:** Anthropology, economics, international economics, political science, sociology, urban studies. **Visual/performing arts:** Art, art history/conservation, dance, dramatic, multimedia, music, music performance, music theory/composition, musical theater, studio arts, theater history.

Most popular majors. Biology 9%, business/marketing 23%, communications/journalism 6%, health sciences 8%, psychology 6%, social sciences 15%.

Technology on campus. 556 workstations in dormitories, library, computer center, student center. Dormitories wired for high-speed internet access and linked to campus network. Commuter students can connect to campus network. Online course registration, online library, helpline, repair service, student web hosting, wireless network available.

Student life. Freshman orientation: Mandatory, $400 fee. Preregistration for classes offered. **Policies:** Alcohol, substance abuse and sexual harassment policies in place. Freshmen not permitted cars on campus. **Housing:** Guaranteed on-campus for freshmen. Coed dorms, single-sex dorms, special housing for disabled, apartments, fraternity/sorority housing, themed housing, wellness housing available. $250 fully refundable deposit, deadline 5/1. Honors program residence hall, language floors, women in science, healthy lifestyle, engineering and technology, performing and creative arts, pre-med and pre-law special living floors, quiet-study floors, and international living floors available. **Activities:** Bands, campus ministries, choral groups, dance, drama, film society, international student organizations, literary magazine, music ensembles, musical theater, radio station, student government, student newspaper, symphony orchestra, TV station, Hillel, Episcopal center, Inter-Varsity Christian Fellowship, Catholic center, Baptist student union, African-American Congress, Latin American students association, Amnesty International.

Athletics. NCAA. **Intercollegiate:** Baseball M, basketball, cross-country, diving W, football (tackle) M, golf W, swimming W, tennis, track and field, volleyball W. **Intramural:** Badminton, basketball, racquetball, soccer, softball, tennis, triathlon, volleyball. **Team name:** Green Wave.

Student services. Alcohol/substance abuse counseling, chaplain/spiritual director, career counseling, services for economically disadvantaged, student employment services, financial aid counseling, health services, legal services, minority student services, on-campus daycare, personal counseling, placement for graduates, veterans' counselor, women's services. **Physically disabled:** Services for visually, speech, hearing impaired.

Contact. E-mail: undergrad.admission@tulane.edu
Phone: (504) 865-5731 Toll-free number: (800) 873-9283
Fax: (504) 862-8715
Earl Retif, Vice President for Enrollment Management and University Registrar, Tulane University, 6823 St. Charles Avenue, New Orleans, LA 70118-5680

University of Holy Cross
New Orleans, Louisiana
www.olhcc.edu   **CB code: 6002**

▸ Private 4-year liberal arts college affiliated with the Roman Catholic Church
▸ Commuter campus in very large city
▸ 940 degree-seeking undergraduates
▸ ACT required

General. Founded in 1916. Regionally accredited. Campus offerings available for senior citizens. **Degrees:** 134 bachelor's, 5 associate awarded; master's, professional offered. **ROTC:** Army, Naval, Air Force. **Location:** 3 miles from downtown. **Calendar:** Semester, limited summer session. **Full-time faculty:** 47 total. **Part-time faculty:** 85 total. **Class size:** 100% 50-99. **Special facilities:** Training and counseling center.

Basis for selection. 2.5 GPA and 20 ACT required. Applicants with less than 2.5 GPA and 17 ACT will be denied, and can appeal to be accepted conditionally. Students entering directly from high school required to submit ACT. English and math proficiency tests required.

High school preparation. 17.5 units recommended. Recommended units include English 4, mathematics 2, social studies 3, science 4 and foreign language 2. Computer literacy .5.

2015-2016 Annual costs. Tuition/fees: $13,360. Books/supplies: $1,200. Personal expenses: $1,970.

Financial aid. Non-need-based: Scholarships awarded for academics, state residency.

Application procedures. Admission: Priority date 12/14; no deadline. $25 fee. Admission notification on a rolling basis. **Financial aid:** Priority date 7/1; no closing date. FAFSA required. Applicants notified on a rolling basis starting 5/15; must reply within 4 week(s) of notification.

Academics. Special study options: Cross-registration, distance learning, dual enrollment of high school students, exchange student, honors, independent study, internships, study abroad, teacher certification program. **Credit/placement by examination:** AP, CLEP, institutional tests. 60 credit hours maximum toward bachelor's degree. **Support services:** Learning center, pre-admission summer program, reduced course load, remedial instruction, study skills assistance, tutoring.

Majors. Biology: General. **Business:** Accounting, business admin. **Education:** Business, elementary, English, mathematics, school counseling, secondary, social studies, special ed. **English:** English lit. **Health services:** Medical radiologie technology/radiation therapy. **History:** General. **Liberal arts:** Arts/sciences. **Social sciences:** General.

Technology on campus. 68 workstations in library, computer center. Commuter students can connect to campus network. Online library, wireless network available.

Student life. Freshman orientation: Mandatory. Preregistration for classes offered. **Activities:** Campus ministries, choral groups, international student organizations, literary magazine, student government, student newspaper, Rotaract Club, various honor societies.

Athletics. Intramural: Soccer M, softball, volleyball. **Team name:** Hurricanes.

Student services. Adult student services, chaplain/spiritual director, career counseling, student employment services, financial aid counseling, health services, personal counseling, placement for graduates, veterans' counselor.

Contact. E-mail: admissions@olhcc.edu
Phone: (504) 394-7744 ext. 175 Toll-free number: (800) 259-7744
Fax: (504) 394-1182
Kobi Sloane, Registrar, University of Holy Cross, 4123 Woodland Drive, New Orleans, LA 70131-7399

University of Louisiana at Lafayette
Lafayette, Louisiana   **CB member**
www.louisiana.edu   **CB code: 6672**

▸ Public 4-year university
▸ Commuter campus in small city
▸ 15,091 degree-seeking undergraduates: 15% part-time, 56% women, 22% African American, 2% Asian American, 4% Hispanic/Latino, 2% Multi-racial, non-Hispanic, 2% international
▸ 1,619 degree-seeking graduate students
▸ 55% of applicants admitted
▸ SAT or ACT (ACT writing optional) required
▸ 45% graduate within 6 years

General. Founded in 1898. Regionally accredited. **Degrees:** 2,542 bachelor's awarded; master's, doctoral offered. **ROTC:** Army. **Location:** 130 miles from New Orleans, 200 miles from Houston. **Calendar:** Semester, extensive summer session. **Full-time faculty:** 601 total; 62% have terminal degrees, 17% minority, 45% women. **Part-time faculty:** 192 total; 18% have terminal degrees, 8% minority, 60% women. **Class size:** 34% < 20, 44% 20-39, 13% 40-49, 6% 50-99, 2% >100. **Special facilities:** 2 nuclear accelerators, 2 electron microscopes, CAD/CAM laboratory, Acadian folklore archives, confocal microscope, atomic force microscope, immersive technology center, on-campus restaurant and hotel, nursery school laboratory, television production studio, marine research facility.

Freshman class profile. 10,899 applied, 6,023 admitted, 3,179 enrolled.

Mid 50% test scores		Rank in top quarter:	46%
SAT critical reading:	460-590	Rank in top tenth:	21%
SAT math:	470-590	Return as sophomores:	76%
ACT composite:	21-25	Out-of-state:	5%
GPA 3.75 or higher:	20%	Live on campus:	58%
GPA 3.50-3.74:	17%	International:	1%
GPA 3.0-3.49:	39%	Fraternities:	11%
GPA 2.0-2.99:	24%	Sororities:	14%

Basis for selection. In-state applicants must meet one of the following: 2.5 GPA or 23 ACT/1050 SAT. Out-of-state or home schooled applicants must meet one of the following: 1) successfully complete 17 out of 19 credits from Core 4 curriculum with 2.5 GPA and have 23 ACT/1050 SAT; 2) 26 ACT/1170 SAT; 3) meet in-state student requirements and complete all 19 units of Louisiana Board of Regents high school Core 4 curriculum. Audition required of music majors. Portfolio required of art, architecture majors. Essays required for some applicants.

High school preparation. College-preparatory program required. Required units include English 4, mathematics 4, social studies 1, history 2, science 3, foreign language 2 and visual/performing arts 1. Suggested electives: .5 unit computer science, 1 unit fine arts, 1 unit speech.

2015-2016 Annual costs. Tuition/fees: $8,552; $22,280 out-of-state. Room/board: $8,566. Books/supplies: $1,220. Personal expenses: $2,003.

2014-2015 Financial aid. All financial aid based on need. 2,740 full-time freshmen applied for aid; 1,843 deemed to have need; 1,825 received aid. Average need met was 61%. Average scholarship/grant was $7,695; average loan $3,133. 56% of total undergraduate aid awarded as scholarships/grants, 44% as loans/jobs.

Application procedures. Admission: Priority date 7/20; no deadline. $25 fee. Admission notification on a rolling basis. **Financial aid:** Priority date 5/1; no closing date. FAFSA required. Applicants notified on a rolling basis starting 4/1; must reply within 2 week(s) of notification.

Academics. Special study options: Accelerated study, cooperative education, cross-registration, distance learning, double major, dual enrollment of high school students, exchange student, honors, independent study, internships, student-designed major, study abroad, teacher certification program. **Credit/placement by examination:** AP, CLEP, SAT, ACT, institutional tests. 30 credit hours maximum toward bachelor's degree. **Support services:** Learning center, reduced course load, remedial instruction, study skills assistance, tutoring, writing center.

Majors. Architecture: Architecture, interior. **Biology:** General, conservation, microbiology. **Business:** Accounting, business admin, fashion, finance, hospitality admin, insurance, management information systems, managerial economics, marketing. **Communications:** Communications/speech/rhetoric, media studies, public relations. **Computer sciences:** Computer science. **Conservation:** Land use planning, management/policy. **Education:** Agricultural, art, biology, business, chemistry, early childhood, early childhood special, elementary, English, family/consumer sciences, French, German, mathematics, middle, music, physical, physics, science, secondary, social studies, Spanish, special ed, speech, technology/industrial arts. **Engineering:** Chemical, civil, computer, electrical, mechanical, petroleum. **Foreign languages:** General. **Health services:** Athletic training, audiology/speech pathology, dental hygiene, dietetics, health information management, nursing (RN). **History:** General. **Math:** General. **Physical sciences:** Chemistry, geology, physics. **Protective services:** Criminal justice. **Psychology:** General. **Social sciences:** Anthropology, political science, sociology. **Visual/performing arts:** General, art, film/cinema/video, industrial design, music performance. **Work/family studies:** Family studies.

Most popular majors. Business/marketing 16%, education 12%, engineering/engineering technologies 12%, health sciences 19%, liberal arts 10%.

Technology on campus. 2,000 workstations in dormitories, library, computer center, student center. Commuter students can connect to campus network. Online course registration, online library, helpline, wireless network available.

Student life. Freshman orientation: Mandatory, $75 fee. Preregistration for classes offered. **Housing:** Single-sex dorms, apartments, fraternity/sorority housing available. $50 deposit, deadline 6/15. **Activities:** Bands, campus ministries, choral groups, dance, drama, international student organizations, literary magazine, music ensembles, musical theater, opera, radio station, student government, student newspaper, symphony orchestra, Young Republicans, Young Democrats, Omega Phi Alpha, Afro-American student groups.

Athletics. NCAA. **Intercollegiate:** Baseball M, basketball, cheerleading, cross-country, football (tackle) M, golf M, soccer W, softball W, tennis, track and field, volleyball W. **Intramural:** Basketball, football (non-tackle), racquetball, soccer, softball, tennis, volleyball, water polo. **Team name:** Ragin' Cajuns.

Student services. Adult student services, career counseling, student employment services, financial aid counseling, health services, minority student services, on-campus daycare, personal counseling, placement for graduates, veterans' counselor. **Physically disabled:** Services for visually, speech, hearing impaired.

Contact. E-mail: enroll@louisiana.edu
Phone: (337) 482-6553 Toll-free number: (800) 752-6553
Fax: (337) 482-1112
Andy Benoit, Director of Undergraduate Admission and Recruitment, University of Louisiana at Lafayette, Box 41210, Lafayette, LA 70504-1210

University of Louisiana at Monroe
Monroe, Louisiana   CB member
www.ulm.edu   CB code: 6482

- Public 4-year university
- Commuter campus in small city
- 5,981 degree-seeking undergraduates: 17% part-time, 65% women, 25% African American, 2% Asian American, 2% Hispanic/Latino, 3% Multiracial, non-Hispanic, 3% international
- 1,214 degree-seeking graduate students
- 94% of applicants admitted
- SAT or ACT (ACT writing optional) required
- 41% graduate within 6 years

General. Founded in 1931. Regionally accredited. **Degrees:** 1,005 bachelor's, 51 associate awarded; master's, professional, doctoral offered. **ROTC:** Army. **Location:** 90 miles from Shreveport, 120 miles from Jackson, Mississippi. **Calendar:** Semester, limited summer session. **Full-time faculty:** 288 total; 12% minority, 55% women. **Part-time faculty:** 127 total; 16% minority, 71% women. **Class size:** 34% < 20, 41% 20-39, 9% 40-49, 13% 50-99, 3% >100. **Special facilities:** National Public Radio station, Louisiana state cancer tumor registry archives, regional small business development center, weather research center, museum of natural history, flight simulator.

Freshman class profile. 3,187 applied, 2,997 admitted, 1,300 enrolled.

Mid 50% test scores		Rank in top quarter:	52%
SAT math:	500-660	Rank in top tenth:	22%
SAT writing:	440-550	End year in good standing:	85%
ACT composite:	20-25	Return as sophomores:	74%
GPA 3.75 or higher:	31%	Out-of-state:	7%
GPA 3.50-3.74:	23%	Live on campus:	56%
GPA 3.0-3.49:	29%	International:	6%
GPA 2.0-2.99:	17%		

Basis for selection. Students who do not meet defined admissions criteria are evaluated on other evidence of academic promise for potential admission by exception. Only limited number of students will be granted admission by exception. **Home schooled:** Transcript of courses and grades required. Must submit official transcript of grades and official proof of graduation or original diploma to admissions office.

High school preparation. College-preparatory program required. 19 units required. Required units include English 4, mathematics 4, social studies 4, science 4, foreign language 2 and visual/performing arts 1.

2015-2016 Annual costs. Tuition/fees: $7,658; $19,758 out-of-state. Room/board: $7,048.

2015-2016 Financial aid. Need-based: 92% of total undergraduate aid awarded as scholarships/grants, 8% as loans/jobs. **Non-need-based:** Scholarships awarded for academics, alumni affiliation, art, athletics, job skills, leadership, minority status, music/drama, religious affiliation, ROTC, state residency.

Application procedures. Admission: Priority date 4/1; no deadline. $20 fee, may be waived for applicants with need. Admission notification on a rolling basis. **Financial aid:** Closing date 6/30. FAFSA required. Applicants notified on a rolling basis starting 6/1; must reply within 2 week(s) of notification.

Academics. Credit hours toward graduation may be earned through examination, military service, correspondence and extension courses taken through accredited extension divisions of other colleges and universities. **Special study options:** Accelerated study, combined bachelor's/graduate degree, cooperative education, distance learning, double major, dual enrollment of high school students, ESL, honors, independent study, internships, study abroad, teacher certification program. Evening college. **Credit/placement by examination:** AP, CLEP, SAT, ACT, institutional tests. 22 credit hours maximum toward associate degree, 43 toward bachelor's. Maximum of one-third of credits required for degree may be earned through examination, military experience, and correspondence courses. **Support services:** Learning center, reduced course load, remedial instruction, study skills assistance, tutoring, writing center.

Majors. Biology: General, toxicology. **Business:** Accounting, business admin, construction management, finance, insurance, management information systems, marketing. **Communications:** Communications/speech/rhetoric, media studies. **Computer sciences:** Computer science. **Education:** Biology, chemistry, elementary, English, mathematics, secondary, social studies. **English:** English lit. **Foreign languages:** General. **Health services:** Audiology/speech pathology, clinical lab science, dental hygiene, health care admin, nursing (RN), radiologic technology/medical imaging. **History:** General. **Human services:** Social work. **Math:** General. **Parks/recreation:** Exercise sciences. **Physical sciences:** Atmospheric science. **Protective services:** Criminal justice. **Psychology:** General. **Social sciences:** Political science, sociology. **Visual/performing arts:** Music performance, studio arts.

Most popular majors. Biology 6%, business/marketing 13%, education 6%, health sciences 30%, liberal arts 9%, parks/recreation 6%, psychology 8%.

Technology on campus. Dormitories wired for high-speed internet access and linked to campus network. Commuter students can connect to campus network. Online course registration, online library, helpline, repair service, student web hosting, wireless network available.

Student life. Freshman orientation: Mandatory. Preregistration for classes offered. Five regular sessions plus one computer PREP session available. **Housing:** Coed dorms, single-sex dorms, apartments, fraternity/sorority housing, wellness housing available. $500 partly refundable deposit, deadline 5/1. **Activities:** Bands, campus ministries, choral groups, dance, drama, international student organizations, literary magazine, music ensembles, musical theater, opera, radio station, student government, student newspaper, symphony orchestra.

Athletics. NCAA. **Intercollegiate:** Baseball M, basketball, cheerleading, cross-country, football (tackle) M, golf, sand volleyball W, soccer W, softball W, swimming, track and field, volleyball W. **Intramural:** Basketball, cross-country, football (non-tackle), golf, racquetball, sand volleyball, soccer, softball, swimming, tennis, track and field, volleyball, weight lifting. **Team name:** Warhawks.

Student services. Adult student services, alcohol/substance abuse counseling, chaplain/spiritual director, career counseling, student employment services, financial aid counseling, health services, on-campus daycare, personal counseling, placement for graduates, veterans' counselor. **Physically disabled:** Services for visually, speech, hearing impaired.

Contact. E-mail: admit@ulm.edu
Phone: (318) 342-5430 Toll-free number: (800) 372-5127
Fax: (318) 342-1915
Mary Schmeer, Director of Enrollment & Scholarships, University of Louisiana at Monroe, 700 University Avenue, Monroe, LA 71209-1160

University of New Orleans
New Orleans, Louisiana   **CB member**
www.uno.edu   **CB code: 6379**

- Public 4-year university
- Commuter campus in very large city
- 6,185 degree-seeking undergraduates: 23% part-time, 50% women, 16% African American, 8% Asian American, 12% Hispanic/Latino, 4% Multiracial, non-Hispanic, 4% international
- 1,700 degree-seeking graduate students
- 58% of applicants admitted
- SAT or ACT (ACT writing optional) required
- 35% graduate within 6 years

General. Founded in 1956. Regionally accredited. **Degrees:** 1,248 bachelor's awarded; master's, doctoral offered. **ROTC:** Army, Naval, Air Force. **Calendar:** Semester, extensive summer session. **Full-time faculty:** 270 total; 66% have terminal degrees, 21% minority, 36% women. **Part-time faculty:** 132 total; 33% have terminal degrees, 17% minority, 44% women. **Class size:** 37% < 20, 45% 20-39, 7% 40-49, 8% 50-99, 2% >100. **Special facilities:** Museum of southern art, gallery, motion picture and television production facility, marine engineering tow tank, fine arts gallery, coastal education and research facility, student dining and entertainment center.

Freshman class profile. 3,932 applied, 2,267 admitted, 922 enrolled.

Mid 50% test scores		GPA 2.0-2.99:	39%
SAT critical reading:	460-600	Rank in top quarter:	32%
SAT math:	480-630	Rank in top tenth:	14%
ACT composite:	20-24	Return as sophomores:	62%
GPA 3.75 or higher:	11%	Out-of-state:	7%
GPA 3.50-3.74:	12%	Live on campus:	29%
GPA 3.0-3.49:	37%	International:	4%

Basis for selection. Students who graduate from state-approved high schools must complete academic core curriculum and require no remedial coursework. Test score and GPA requirements: 19 ACT Math/460 SAT Math, 18 ACT English/450 SAT English, 23 ACT/1060 SAT composite or 2.5 GPA. Students with less than 2.0 GPA will not be admitted. Out-of-state and home school applicants who do not meet academic core curriculum must satisfy the minimum ACT scores listed above or have 26 ACT/1170 SAT and require no remediation. Audition or interview required of music majors; fine arts studio majors may apply for bypass credit for 1000 level studio courses by submitting portfolio. **Home schooled:** In-state students must complete academic core curriculum and require no remedial coursework. Test score and GPA requirements: 19 ACT Math/460 SAT Math, 18 ACT English/450 SAT English, 23 ACT/1060 SAT composite or 2.5 GPA. Out-of-state and home school applicants who do not meet academic core curriculum must satisfy the minimum ACT scores listed above or have 26 ACT/1170 SAT and require no remediation. **Learning Disabled:** Learning Disability Documentation Packet must be completed by an appropriate professional, along with a copy of the evaluation, including test scores. New students must meet with ODS staff member to complete registration with the office and have accommodations determined.

High school preparation. College-preparatory program required. 19 units required. Required units include English 4, mathematics 4, social studies 4, science 4, foreign language 2 and visual/performing arts 1.

2015-2016 Annual costs. Tuition/fees: $8,094; $21,911 out-of-state. Room/board: $9,515. Books/supplies: $1,220. Personal expenses: $2,003.

2015-2016 Financial aid. Need-based: 856 full-time freshmen applied for aid; 728 deemed to have need; 691 received aid. Average need met was 66%. Average scholarship/grant was $5,873; average loan $3,286. 63% of total undergraduate aid awarded as scholarships/grants, 37% as loans/jobs. **Non-need-based:** Awarded to 1,761 full-time undergraduates, including 556 freshmen. Scholarships awarded for academics, athletics, music/drama. **Additional information:** Students in good academic and financial standing eligible to participate in Extended Payment Plan option.

Application procedures. Admission: Priority date 1/15; deadline 7/25 (receipt date). $20 fee. Application must be submitted online. Admission notification on a rolling basis. **Financial aid:** Priority date 1/15; no closing date. FAFSA required. Applicants notified on a rolling basis starting 3/15.

Academics. Special study options: Cooperative education, cross-registration, distance learning, double major, dual enrollment of high school students, ESL, exchange student, honors, independent study, internships, study abroad, teacher certification program, Washington semester, weekend college. **Credit/placement by examination:** AP, CLEP, IB, SAT, ACT, institutional tests. 30 credit hours maximum toward bachelor's degree. **Support services:** Learning center, study skills assistance, tutoring, writing center. Math tutor center, first generation mentoring program.

Majors. Biology: General. **Business:** Accounting, business admin, finance, hospitality admin, marketing. **Computer sciences:** Computer science. **Education:** Elementary, secondary. **Engineering:** Civil, electrical, marine, mechanical. **English:** English lit. **Foreign languages:** General. **Health services:** Health services admin. **History:** General. **Math:** General. **Parks/recreation:** Health/fitness. **Philosophy/religion:** Philosophy. **Physical sciences:** Chemistry, geology, physics. **Psychology:** General. **Social sciences:** Anthropology, political science, sociology, urban studies. **Visual/performing arts:** Art history/conservation, dramatic, music, studio arts.

Most popular majors. Biology 10%, business/marketing 31%, engineering/engineering technologies 9%, interdisciplinary studies 10%, psychology 7%, visual/performing arts 12%.

Technology on campus. 1,300 workstations in library, computer center, student center. Dormitories wired for high-speed internet access and linked to campus network. Commuter students can connect to campus network. Online course registration, online library, helpline, wireless network available.

Student life. Freshman orientation: Mandatory, $100 fee. Preregistration for classes offered. One and a half-day program; fee includes housing and meals. **Housing:** Coed dorms, special housing for disabled, apartments, themed housing available. $300 partly refundable deposit. **Activities:** Bands, campus ministries, choral groups, dance, drama, film society, international student organizations, literary magazine, music ensembles, Model UN, student government, student newspaper, over 120 registered clubs and organizations available.

Athletics. NCAA. **Intercollegiate:** Baseball M, basketball, cross-country, golf M, sand volleyball W, tennis, track and field, volleyball W. **Intramural:** Basketball, football (non-tackle), soccer, softball, volleyball. **Team name:** Privateers.

Student services. Adult student services, alcohol/substance abuse counseling, career counseling, student employment services, financial aid counseling, health services, minority student services, personal counseling, placement for graduates, veterans' counselor, women's services. **Physically disabled:** Services for visually, speech, hearing impaired.

Contact. E-mail: pec@uno.edu
Phone: (504) 280-6595 Toll-free number: (800) 256-5866
Fax: (504) 280-3973
Susan Dandridge, Director of Admissions, University of New Orleans, University of New Orleans, 105 Earl K. Long Library, New Orleans, LA 70148

University of Phoenix: Baton Rouge
Baton Rouge, Louisiana
www.phoenix.edu

- For-profit 4-year career college
- Small city
- 865 undergraduates

General. Regionally accredited. **Degrees:** 87 bachelor's awarded; master's offered. **Calendar:** Differs by program. **Part-time faculty:** 4 total.

Basis for selection. Open admission, but selective for some programs.

2015-2016 Annual costs. Per-credit-hour charge, $410 to $635, depending upon level and course of study. Books, material charges, and other fees vary by course and program. All fees are subject to change. .

Application procedures. Admission: No deadline. No application fee.

Academics. Credit/placement by examination: AP, CLEP.

Majors. Business: Accounting, accounting/business management, business admin, e-commerce, entrepreneurial studies, finance, human resources, marketing, operations. **Communications:** General. **Computer sciences:** Database management, networking, programming, security, system admin, systems analysis, web page design, webmaster. **English:** English lit. **Health services:** Facilities admin, health information management, nursing (RN). **Human services:** General. **Protective services:** Disaster management, law enforcement admin, security management.

Student life. Freshman orientation: Mandatory. Preregistration for classes offered.

Contact. Toll-free number: (866) 766-0766
University of Phoenix: Baton Rouge, 2431 South Acadian Thruway, Baton Rouge, LA 70808-2300

University of Phoenix: Louisiana
Metairie, Louisiana
www.phoenix.edu

- For-profit 4-year career college
- Small city
- 530 undergraduates

General. Regionally accredited. **Degrees:** 57 bachelor's awarded; master's offered. **Calendar:** Differs by program. **Full-time faculty:** 26 total. **Part-time faculty:** 218 total.

Basis for selection. Open admission, but selective for some programs.

2015-2016 Annual costs. Per-credit-hour charge, $395 to $635, depending upon level and course of study. Books, material charges, and other fees vary by course and program. All fees are subject to change.

Application procedures. Admission: No deadline. No application fee. **Financial aid:** No deadline.

Academics. Credit/placement by examination: AP, CLEP.

Majors. Business: Accounting, accounting/business management, business admin, e-commerce, entrepreneurial studies, finance, human resources, marketing, operations. **Communications:** General. **Computer sciences:** Database management, networking, programming, security, system admin, systems analysis, web page design, webmaster. **English:** English lit. **Health services:** Facilities admin, health information management, long term care admin, nursing (RN). **Human services:** General. **Protective services:** Disaster management, law enforcement admin, security management.

Student life. Freshman orientation: Mandatory. Preregistration for classes offered.

Contact. Toll-free number: (866) 766-0766
University of Phoenix: Louisiana, One Galleria Boulevard, Suite 725, Metairie, LA 70001-2082

University of Phoenix: Shreveport
Bossier City, Louisiana
www.phoenix.edu

- For-profit 4-year career college
- Small city
- 310 undergraduates

General. Regionally accredited. **Degrees:** 25 bachelor's awarded; master's offered. **Calendar:** Differs by program. **Part-time faculty:** 3 total.

Basis for selection. Open admission, but selective for some programs.

2015-2016 Annual costs. Per-credit-hour charge, $410 to $635, depending upon level and course of study. Books, material charges, and other fees vary by course and program. All fees are subject to change.

Application procedures. Admission: No deadline. No application fee.

Academics. Credit/placement by examination: AP, CLEP.

Majors. Business: Accounting, accounting/business management, business admin, e-commerce, entrepreneurial studies, finance, human resources, marketing, operations. **Communications:** General. **Computer sciences:** Database management, networking, programming, security, system admin, systems analysis, web page design, webmaster. **English:** English lit. **Health services:** Facilities admin, health information management, long term care admin. **Human services:** General. **Protective services:** Disaster management, law enforcement admin, security management.

Student life. Freshman orientation: Mandatory. Preregistration for classes offered.

Contact. Toll-free number: (866) 766-0766
University of Phoenix: Shreveport, 350 Plaza Loop Drive, Bossier City, LA 71111-4390

Xavier University of Louisiana
New Orleans, Louisiana   **CB member**
www.xula.edu   **CB code: 6975**

- Private 4-year university affiliated with the Roman Catholic Church
- Commuter campus in very large city
- 2,344 degree-seeking undergraduates: 4% part-time, 73% women, 76% African American, 10% Asian American, 4% Hispanic/Latino, 3% Multiracial, non-Hispanic, 2% international
- 602 degree-seeking graduate students
- 66% of applicants admitted
- SAT or ACT (ACT writing recommended) required
- 38% graduate within 6 years

General. Founded in 1915. Regionally accredited. **Degrees:** 358 bachelor's awarded; master's, professional offered. **ROTC:** Army, Naval, Air Force. **Location:** One mile from downtown. **Calendar:** Semester, limited summer session. **Full-time faculty:** 220 total; 97% have terminal degrees, 44% minority, 47% women. **Part-time faculty:** 28 total; 61% have terminal degrees, 54% minority, 32% women. **Class size:** 41% < 20, 44% 20-39, 13% 40-49, 3% 50-99, less than 1% >100.

Freshman class profile. 4,847 applied, 3,187 admitted, 684 enrolled.

Mid 50% test scores			
SAT critical reading:	450-550	GPA 3.0-3.49:	25%
SAT math:	420-560	GPA 2.0-2.99:	22%
SAT writing:	420-540	Rank in top quarter:	57%
ACT composite:	20-26	Rank in top tenth:	31%
GPA 3.75 or higher:	37%	Out-of-state:	50%
GPA 3.50-3.74:	15%	Live on campus:	55%

Basis for selection. High school record or GED scores, standardized test results, and recommendation from counselor important. Interview recommended for academically weak. Audition required for music majors. Portfolio required for art majors.

High school preparation. College-preparatory program recommended. 16 units required. Required and recommended units include English 4, mathematics 2-4, social studies 1, history 1, science 2-3, foreign language 1 and academic electives 7. Math must include 1 algebra.

2015-2016 Annual costs. Tuition/fees: $22,349. Room/board: $8,200. Books/supplies: $1,220. Personal expenses: $2,003.

Financial aid. Non-need-based: Scholarships awarded for academics, art, athletics, music/drama.

Application procedures. Admission: Priority date 3/1; deadline 7/1 (postmark date). No application fee. Admission notification on a rolling basis beginning on or about 10/15. Must reply by May 1 or within 2 week(s) if notified thereafter. **Financial aid:** Priority date 1/1; no closing date. FAFSA required. Applicants notified on a rolling basis starting 4/1; must reply within 2 week(s) of notification.

Academics. Special study options: Accelerated study, combined bachelor's/graduate degree, cooperative education, cross-registration, distance learning, double major, dual enrollment of high school students, exchange student, honors, independent study, internships, study abroad, teacher certification program. AFAM Studies, Women's Studies, Confucius Institute. **Credit/placement by examination:** AP, CLEP, SAT, ACT, institutional tests. 30 credit hours maximum toward bachelor's degree. **Support services:** Learning center, pre-admission summer program, reduced course load, remedial instruction, study skills assistance, tutoring, writing center.

Majors. Biology: General, biochemistry, microbiology. **Business:** Accounting, business admin, finance, management science, marketing. **Communications:** Media studies. **Computer sciences:** General, computer science. **Education:** General, art, biology, chemistry, early childhood, elementary, English, foreign languages, French, history, mathematics, multi-level teacher, music, physical, science, social studies, Spanish, special ed. **Engineering:** Computer. **English:** English lit. **Foreign languages:** French, Spanish. **Health services:** Premedicine, prepharmacy, speech pathology. **History:** General. **Math:** General, statistics. **Philosophy/religion:** Philosophy. **Physical sciences:** Chemistry, physics. **Psychology:** General. **Social sciences:** Political science, sociology. **Theology:** Theology. **Visual/performing arts:** Art, music, music performance, piano/keyboard, stringed instruments, voice/opera.

Most popular majors. Biology 37%, business/marketing 9%, health sciences 6%, physical sciences 14%, psychology 13%.

Technology on campus. 350 workstations in dormitories, library, computer center. Dormitories wired for high-speed internet access and linked to campus network. Commuter students can connect to campus network. Online course registration, online library, helpline available.

Student life. Freshman orientation: Mandatory, $150 fee. Preregistration for classes offered. One-week program. **Policies:** All recognized student organizations must perform 2 community service activities per semester. **Housing:** Coed dorms, single-sex dorms, special housing for disabled, wellness housing available. $100 nonrefundable deposit. **Activities:** Bands, campus ministries, choral groups, dance, drama, international student organizations, literary magazine, music ensembles, opera, radio station, student government, student newspaper, symphony orchestra, TV station, over 30 organizations.

Athletics. NAIA. **Intercollegiate:** Basketball, cross-country, tennis, volleyball W. **Intramural:** Basketball, cheerleading, football (non-tackle), softball, swimming, table tennis, tennis, track and field, volleyball. **Team name:** Gold Rush.

Student services. Adult student services, alcohol/substance abuse counseling, chaplain/spiritual director, career counseling, student employment services, financial aid counseling, health services, personal counseling, placement for graduates, veterans' counselor, women's services. **Physically disabled:** Services for visually, speech, hearing impaired.

Contact. E-mail: apply@xula.edu
Phone: (504) 520-7388 Toll-free number: (877) 928-4378
Fax: (504) 520-7941
Winston Brown, Dean of Admissions, Xavier University of Louisiana, One Drexel Drive, New Orleans, LA 70125-1098

Maine

Bates College

Lewiston, Maine
www.bates.edu

CB member
CB code: 3076

- Private 4-year liberal arts college
- Residential campus in small city
- 1,792 degree-seeking undergraduates: 51% women
- 22% of applicants admitted
- Application essay required
- 88% graduate within 6 years

General. Founded in 1855. Regionally accredited. **Degrees:** 484 bachelor's awarded. **Location:** 35 miles from Portland. **Calendar:** 4-4-1 semester system. **Full-time faculty:** 170 total; 92% have terminal degrees, 16% minority, 51% women. **Part-time faculty:** 13 total; 69% have terminal degrees, 8% minority, 69% women. **Class size:** 68% < 20, 23% 20-39, 6% 40-49, 3% 50-99. **Special facilities:** Mountain conservation area, Edmund S. Muskie Archives, art museum, art center, observatory.

Freshman class profile. 5,651 applied, 1,231 admitted, 516 enrolled.

Mid 50% test scores			
SAT critical reading:	590-710	Rank in top tenth:	69%
SAT math:	600-700	Return as sophomores:	95%
SAT writing:	610-710	Out-of-state:	90%
ACT composite:	28-32	Live on campus:	100%
Rank in top quarter:	95%	International:	8%

Basis for selection. GED not accepted. School achievement record with an emphasis on rigor of curriculum, recommendations, special talents, leadership, essays are all of equal importance. Submission of standardized test scores is optional for admission. Interviews are recommended. **Home schooled:** Statement describing home school structure and mission, letter of recommendation (nonparent) required. Interview encouraged but not required for all applicants, including home school students.

High school preparation. College-preparatory program required. 17 units required; 23 recommended. Required and recommended units include English 4, mathematics 3-4, social studies 3-4, history 3-4, science 3-4 (laboratory 2-3) and foreign language 2-4. History included in social studies requirement.

2015-2016 Annual costs. Tuition/fees: $48,735. Room/board: $14,105. Books/supplies: $800. Personal expenses: $950.

2015-2016 Financial aid. All financial aid based on need. 254 full-time freshmen applied for aid; 215 deemed to have need; 215 received aid. Average need met was 100%. Average scholarship/grant was $41,230; average loan $2,197. 92% of total undergraduate aid awarded as scholarships/grants, 8% as loans/jobs. **Additional information:** Priority date for filing required financial aid forms for early decision students is 11/15.

Application procedures. Admission: Closing date 1/1 (postmark date). $60 fee, may be waived for applicants with need. Admission notification by 4/1. Must reply by 5/1. **Financial aid:** Closing date 2/15. FAFSA, CSS PROFILE required. Applicants notified by 4/1; must reply by 5/1.

Academics. One major plus a combination of two general education concentrations are required, (each of which faculty designed around a coherent theme and is comprised of four courses). Also required are three writing attentive courses; one course focused on scientific reasoning, one course on laboratory experience, and one course on quantitative literacy. All majors require a senior thesis or capstone project. **Special study options:** Accelerated study, combined bachelor's/graduate degree, cross-registration, double major, exchange student, honors, independent study, internships, liberal arts/career combination, student-designed major, study abroad, teacher certification program. Marine studies program at Mystic Seaport, liberal arts-engineering dual degree program with 5 universities. **Credit/placement by examination:** AP, CLEP, IB, institutional tests. **Support services:** Learning center, reduced course load, study skills assistance, tutoring, writing center.

Majors. Area/ethnic studies: African-American, American, East Asian, women's. **Biology:** General, biochemistry, neuroscience. **Conservation:** Environmental studies. **Engineering:** General. **English:** English lit, rhetoric/composition. **Foreign languages:** Chinese, French, German, Japanese, Spanish. **History:** General. **Math:** General. **Philosophy/religion:** Philosophy, religion. **Physical sciences:** Chemistry, geology, physics. **Psychology:** General. **Social sciences:** Anthropology, economics, political science, sociology. **Visual/performing arts:** Art, dance, dramatic, music.

Most popular majors. Biology 11%, English 8%, foreign language 7%, history 7%, natural resources/environmental science 6%, physical sciences 7%, psychology 8%, social sciences 28%, visual/performing arts 7%.

Technology on campus. 400 workstations in library, computer center. Dormitories wired for high-speed internet access and linked to campus network. Commuter students can connect to campus network. Online course registration, online library, helpline, repair service, student web hosting, wireless network available.

Student life. Freshman orientation: Mandatory. Preregistration for classes offered. Held 5 days prior to start of classes. **Housing:** Guaranteed on-campus for all undergraduates. Coed dorms, single-sex dorms, themed housing, wellness housing available. $300 nonrefundable deposit, deadline 5/1. Quiet/Study. **Activities:** Bands, campus ministries, choral groups, dance, drama, film society, international student organizations, literary magazine, music ensembles, Model UN, radio station, student government, student newspaper, symphony orchestra, Amandla!, Bates Christian Fellowship, Bates Democrats, Hindu Awareness Group, College Republicans, Women's Advocacy Group, Hillel, Latinos Unidos, Mushahada Association, OUTFront, Queer Peers.

Athletics. NCAA. **Intercollegiate:** Baseball M, basketball, cross-country, diving, field hockey W, football (tackle) M, golf, lacrosse, rowing (crew), skiing, soccer, softball W, squash, swimming, tennis, track and field, volleyball W. **Intramural:** Basketball, bowling, football (non-tackle), handball, ice hockey, lacrosse W, racquetball, soccer, softball, squash, table tennis, tennis, volleyball. **Team name:** Bobcats.

Student services. Alcohol/substance abuse counseling, chaplain/spiritual director, career counseling, student employment services, financial aid counseling, health services, minority student services, personal counseling, placement for graduates, women's services. **Physically disabled:** Services for visually, hearing impaired.

Contact. E-mail: admission@bates.edu
Phone: (207) 786-6000 Toll-free number: (855) 228-3755
Fax: (207) 786-6025
Leigh Weisenburger, Dean of Admission and Financial Aid, Bates College, 23 Campus Avenue, Lindholm House, Lewiston, ME 04240

Bowdoin College

Brunswick, Maine
www.bowdoin.edu

CB member
CB code: 3089

- Private 4-year liberal arts college
- Residential campus in large town
- 1,794 degree-seeking undergraduates: 50% women, 5% African American, 7% Asian American, 12% Hispanic/Latino, 6% Multi-racial, non-Hispanic, 5% international
- 15% of applicants admitted
- Application essay required
- 93% graduate within 6 years; 20% enter graduate study

General. Founded in 1794. Regionally accredited. **Degrees:** 474 bachelor's awarded. **Location:** 25 miles from Portland, 120 miles from Boston. **Calendar:** Semester. **Full-time faculty:** 190 total; 100% have terminal degrees, 15% minority, 50% women. **Part-time faculty:** 50 total; 84% have terminal degrees, 10% minority, 52% women. **Class size:** 68% < 20, 27% 20-39, 2% 40-49, 2% 50-99. **Special facilities:** Museum of art, arctic museum, language media center, women's resource center, electronic classroom, coastal studies center and marine laboratory, screening rooms, production studios, multimedia lab, African American center, crafts center, ceramics studio, photography darkroom, printmaking studio, woodworking studio, sculpture studio, dance studio, scientific station located in the Bay of Fundy, educational research and development program, theaters, music halls, recording studio, community service resource center, environmental studies center, and visual arts center.

Freshman class profile. 6,790 applied, 1,010 admitted, 500 enrolled.

Mid 50% test scores			
SAT critical reading:	690-770	Rank in top tenth:	84%
SAT math:	690-770	Return as sophomores:	97%
SAT writing:	690-770	Out-of-state:	90%
ACT composite:	31-34	Live on campus:	100%
Rank in top quarter:	98%	International:	5%

Basis for selection. GED not accepted. Academic record, level of challenge represented in the candidate's course work, counselor/teacher recommendations, interview, quality of application and essay, character and personal qualities, extracurricular activities, talents and abilities, and overall academic potential most important. Test scores considered, but not required. Motivation of candidate also considered. SAT or ACT scores are not required for admission to Bowdoin. However, applicants who wish to submit their scores as part of their application should do so no later than January 1st. SAT I scores are required for home school applicants. Interview recommended. Candidates with unusual talent in music, theater or visual arts encouraged to complete Arts Supplement when applying for admission. Audition recommended for music majors. Portfolio recommended for art majors. **Home schooled:** Applicants applying from systems providing written evaluations rather than grades are required to submit either SAT or ACT plus SAT Subject Test results. SAT Subject Tests should include Math Level 1 or Math Level 2 and one science. Personal interview strongly recommended. Must submit the Home School Supplement.

High school preparation. College-preparatory program required. 20 units recommended. Recommended units include English 4, mathematics 4, social studies 4, science 4 (laboratory 3) and foreign language 4. Arts, music and computer science or computer literacy recommended.

2015-2016 Annual costs. Tuition/fees: $48,212. Room/board: $13,142. Books/supplies: $836. Personal expenses: $1,250.

2015-2016 Financial aid. Need-based: 280 full-time freshmen applied for aid; 225 deemed to have need; 225 received aid. Average need met was 100%. Average scholarship/grant was $42,165. 96% of total undergraduate aid awarded as scholarships/grants, 4% as loans/jobs. **Non-need-based:** Awarded to 51 full-time undergraduates, including 20 freshmen. Scholarships awarded for academics, leadership. **Additional information:** Regardless of financial circumstances, students admitted will receive the money they need to attend. International students for regular admission must submit their financial aid applications by January 1st.

Application procedures. Admission: Closing date 1/1 (receipt date). $60 fee, may be waived for applicants with need. 04/05. Must reply by May 1 or within 1 week(s) if notified thereafter. **Financial aid:** Closing date 2/15. FAFSA, CSS PROFILE required. Applicants notified by 4/5; must reply by 5/1 or within 1 week(s) of notification.

Academics. Most students pursue independent scholarly research, working closely with a faculty advisor, through an independent study or honors project. About half of the student body studies abroad for one or 2 semesters, usually during the junior year. First-year seminars are limited to 16 first-year students and emphasize college-level reading and writing. Interdisciplinary and self-designed majors are available. **Special study options:** Accelerated study, combined bachelor's/graduate degree, double major, exchange student, independent study, liberal arts/career combination, student-designed major, study abroad, teacher certification program, Washington semester. 3-2 or 4-2 Engineering Degree Programs with Dartmouth College, California Institute of Technology, Columbia University and University of Maine, Orono; and 3-3 Legal Studies Degree Program with Columbia University Law School, first-year seminars, summer research fellowships, service-learning courses, The Writing Project, Quantitative Reasoning Program, Legal Studies Advisory Group, Health Professions Advising, EMS Writing Tutor. Pass/Fail grading options are available. **Credit/placement by examination:** AP, CLEP, IB, institutional tests. **Support services:** Learning center, reduced course load, study skills assistance, tutoring, writing center.

Majors. Area/ethnic studies: African, Asian, Latin American, Russian/Eastern European/Eurasian, women's. **Biology:** General, biochemistry, neuroscience. **Computer sciences:** Computer science. **Conservation:** Environmental studies. **Education:** Mathematics. **English:** English lit. **Foreign languages:** Classics, French, German, Romance, Russian, Spanish. **History:** General. **Math:** General. **Philosophy/religion:** Philosophy, religion. **Physical sciences:** Chemical physics, chemistry, geology, physics. **Psychology:** General. **Social sciences:** Anthropology, archaeology, econometrics, economics, political science, sociology. **Visual/performing arts:** Art history/conservation, music, studio arts, theater history.

Most popular majors. Biology 12%, foreign language 9%, mathematics 7%, natural resources/environmental science 6%, physical sciences 9%, social sciences 28%, visual/performing arts 6%.

Technology on campus. 450 workstations in dormitories, library, computer center, student center. Dormitories wired for high-speed internet access and linked to campus network. Commuter students can connect to campus network. Online course registration, online library, helpline, repair service, student web hosting, wireless network available.

Student life. Freshman orientation: Mandatory. Preregistration for classes offered. Nine-day event at the end of August, which includes outdoor and community service trips for the first four days. The orientation fee is waived for all students who receive financial aid. **Policies:** Honor code, social code, judicial authority, drug and alcohol policies, policies on sexual misconduct, smoking, illegal drugs, discrimination, information technology use, residential life. Freshmen not permitted cars on campus. **Housing:** Guaranteed on-campus for freshmen. Coed dorms, special housing for disabled, apartments, wellness housing available. Four small college houses and 8 college system houses available. **Activities:** Bands, choral groups, dance, drama, film society, international student organizations, literary magazine, music ensembles, Model UN, musical theater, radio station, student government, student newspaper, African American Society, Green Bowdoin, Muslim Student Association, Asian Students Association, Latin American Students' Organization, Hillel, Catholic Students Union, College Democrats, College Republicans, Africa Alliance.

Athletics. NCAA. **Intercollegiate:** Baseball M, basketball, cross-country, diving, field hockey W, football (tackle) M, golf, ice hockey, lacrosse, rugby W, sailing, skiing, soccer, softball W, squash, swimming, tennis, track and field, volleyball W. **Intramural:** Badminton, basketball, ice hockey, soccer, softball. **Team name:** Polar Bears.

Student services. Alcohol/substance abuse counseling, chaplain/spiritual director, career counseling, student employment services, health services, minority student services, on-campus daycare, personal counseling, placement for graduates, women's services. **Physically disabled:** Services for visually, speech, hearing impaired.

Contact. E-mail: admissions@bowdoin.edu
Phone: (207) 725-3100 Fax: (207) 725-3101
Scott Meiklejohn, Dean of Admissions and Student Aid, Bowdoin College, 5000 College Station, Brunswick, ME 04011-8441

Colby College
Waterville, Maine
www.colby.edu

CB member
CB code: 3280

- Private 4-year liberal arts college
- Residential campus in large town
- 1,857 degree-seeking undergraduates: 52% women
- 23% of applicants admitted
- Application essay required
- 94% graduate within 6 years

General. Founded in 1813. Regionally accredited. **Degrees:** 491 bachelor's awarded. **ROTC:** Army. **Location:** 180 miles from Boston, 75 miles from Portland. **Calendar:** 4-1-4. **Full-time faculty:** 180 total; 95% have terminal degrees, 16% minority, 45% women. **Part-time faculty:** 32 total; 81% have terminal degrees, 62% women. **Class size:** 76% < 20, 20% 20-39, 4% 40-49, 1% 50-99. **Special facilities:** Museum of art, art and music library, electronic music center, multicultural center, astronomical observatory, 35-cm (14-inch) telescope on research-grade computer-controlled mount with liquid-nitrogen cooled CCD camera, organic garden, arboretum and bird sanctuary, research greenhouses, kettle-hole research bog, professional blacksmith's forge, woodworking shop, Nordic ski trails, boathouse, 450-feet waterfront, community radio station, scanning and transmission electron microscopes, four-capillary DNA sequencer, flow cytometer, laser flash photolysis, 400-MHz NMR, x-ray diffractometer, spectrophotometers, chromatographs, GIS lab, microcalorimeters, piezometers (groundwater monitoring wells), research vessel and remote-sensing buoy for biogeochemical lake research, biomass facility.

Freshman class profile. 7,593 applied, 1,710 admitted, 508 enrolled.

Mid 50% test scores			
SAT critical reading:	630-720	Rank in top tenth:	63%
SAT math:	640-740	End year in good standing:	98%
SAT writing:	630-730	Return as sophomores:	93%
ACT composite:	29-32	Out-of-state:	87%
Rank in top quarter:	94%	Live on campus:	100%
		International:	12%

Basis for selection. School record and personal qualities very important. Test scores, recommendations, potential contribution to college life, and essay important. Interview, social, economic, racial, and geographic diversity considered. Interview recommended (on-campus, or alumni available). Portfolios submitted via SlideRoom. **Home schooled:** Letter of recommendation (nonparent) required.

High school preparation. College-preparatory program recommended. 16 units recommended. Recommended units include English 4, mathematics 3, social studies 2, science 2 (laboratory 2), foreign language 3 and academic electives 2. Social studies units recommended could include history courses.

2015-2016 Annual costs. Tuition/fees: $49,120. Room/board: $12,610. Books/supplies: $700. Personal expenses: $1,032.

2015-2016 Financial aid. Need-based: 253 full-time freshmen applied for aid; 211 deemed to have need; 211 received aid. Average need met was

100%. Average scholarship/grant was $43,762; average loan $2,925. 95% of total undergraduate aid awarded as scholarships/grants, 5% as loans/jobs. **Non-need-based:** Awarded to 26 full-time undergraduates, including 4 freshmen. **Additional information:** Packaged loans have been replaced with institutional grants.

Application procedures. **Admission:** Closing date 1/1 (postmark date). No application fee. Admission notification by 4/1. Must reply by 5/1. All entering students responsible for $300 admissions deposit, which is credited at time of registration. **Financial aid:** Closing date 2/1. FAFSA required. Required if they want to be eligible for any aid beyond federal aid. Applicants notified by 4/1; must reply by 5/1.

Academics. **Special study options:** Combined bachelor's/graduate degree, cross-registration, double major, dual enrollment of high school students, exchange student, honors, independent study, internships, semester at sea, student-designed major, study abroad, teacher certification program, Washington semester. Numerous research, service learning, and internship opportunities; paid summer research assistantships; coordinated 3-2 engineering program with Dartmouth and 4-2 engineering program with Columbia; Idea Network of Biomedical Research Excellence (partnerships with Jackson Labs, Mt. Desert Island Biological Labs, and other colleges), exchange programs with Howard University, Claremont Colleges, Clark Atlanta University; January Program term for focused studies; extensive study-abroad opportunities; study and internship opportunities in Washington, D.C.; Colby Achievement Program in the Sciences (CAPS) program for incoming students from diverse backgrounds. **Credit/placement by examination:** AP, CLEP, IB, institutional tests. 12 credit hours maximum toward bachelor's degree. When appropriate, distribution requirements, as well as certain requirements for the major, may be absolved by examination without course enrollment at the discretion of the department concerned. Matriculated students may earn credit by examination in 100- or 200-level courses to a maximum of 12 hours. Departmental examinations or external examinations approved by the department may be used, with credit given for the equivalent of at least C-level work. The cost of each examination is paid by the student. The college will exempt students from the language requirement for attaining before entrance a score of 64 in a SAT Subject Test in a foreign language or for attaining a score of 64 in Colby's placement test during first-year orientation; in either case, no academic credit will be granted. **Support services:** Pre-admission summer program, reduced course load, study skills assistance, tutoring, writing center.

Majors. **Area/ethnic studies:** African-American, American, East Asian, Latin American, women's. **Biology:** General, biochemistry, cell/histology, computational, ecology/evolutionary, environmental, molecular, neuroscience. **Computer sciences:** Computer science. **Conservation:** Environmental science, environmental studies. **Education:** General. **English:** Creative writing, English lit. **Foreign languages:** Classics, French, German, Russian, Spanish. **History:** General. **Math:** General, mathematics/statistics. **Philosophy/religion:** Philosophy, religion. **Physical sciences:** Chemistry, environmental chemistry, geology, physics. **Psychology:** General. **Social sciences:** Anthropology, economics, international relations, political science, sociology. **Visual/performing arts:** Art, art history/conservation, dramatic, music, studio arts.

Most popular majors. Area/ethnic studies 7%, biology 10%, English 7%, interdisciplinary studies 11%, natural resources/environmental science 6%, physical sciences 7%, psychology 6%, social sciences 25%.

Technology on campus. 400 workstations in library, computer center, student center. Dormitories wired for high-speed internet access and linked to campus network. Commuter students can connect to campus network. Online course registration, online library, helpline, repair service, student web hosting, wireless network available.

Student life. **Freshman orientation:** Mandatory, $275 fee. Preregistration for classes offered. A weeklong orientation program including a one-day community involvement project and a three-day outdoor orientation trip, plus a variety of on-campus programs, all held the week before classes begin. **Policies:** Students participate in forming policies and governing social and community activities through student government and serving on official college committees up to and including the Board of Trustees. **Housing:** Guaranteed on-campus for all undergraduates. Coed dorms, apartments, themed housing, wellness housing available. $300 nonrefundable deposit, deadline 5/1. Quiet, chem-free, green houses available. **Activities:** Bands, choral groups, dance, drama, film society, international student organizations, literary magazine, music ensembles, Model UN, musical theater, radio station, student government, student newspaper, symphony orchestra, Approximately 110 student clubs and organizations.

Athletics. NCAA. **Intercollegiate:** Baseball M, basketball, cross-country, diving, field hockey W, football (tackle) M, golf, ice hockey, lacrosse, rowing (crew), skiing, soccer, softball W, squash, swimming, tennis, track and field, volleyball W. **Intramural:** Basketball, field hockey, football (non-tackle), soccer, softball. **Team name:** Mules.

Student services. Alcohol/substance abuse counseling, chaplain/spiritual director, career counseling, student employment services, financial aid counseling, health services, minority student services, personal counseling, placement for graduates, women's services. **Physically disabled:** Services for visually, hearing impaired.

Contact. E-mail: admissions@colby.edu
Phone: (207) 859-4800 Toll-free number: (800) 723-3032
Fax: (207) 859-4828
Matthew Proto, Vice President and Dean of Admissions, Colby College, 4800 Mayflower Hill, Waterville, ME 04901-8848

College of the Atlantic
Bar Harbor, Maine
www.coa.edu   CB code: 3305

- Private 4-year liberal arts college
- Residential campus in small town
- 333 degree-seeking undergraduates: 2% part-time, 70% women, 1% African American, 3% Asian American, 5% Hispanic/Latino, 2% Multiracial, non-Hispanic, 17% international
- 10 degree-seeking graduate students
- 76% of applicants admitted
- Application essay required
- 70% graduate within 6 years

General. Founded in 1969. Regionally accredited. **Degrees:** 80 bachelor's awarded; master's offered. **Location:** 300 miles from Boston, 50 miles from Bangor. **Calendar:** Trimester, limited summer session. **Full-time faculty:** 27 total; 93% have terminal degrees, 7% minority, 41% women. **Part-time faculty:** 19 total; 58% have terminal degrees, 5% minority, 42% women. **Class size:** 94% < 20, 6% 20-39. **Special facilities:** Natural history museum, marine mammal research center, two offshore island research centers, sustainable business incubator, two college-owned organic farms, herbarium, greenhouses, ocean-going vessels, ceramics studio, taxidermy lab, community garden.

Freshman class profile. 400 applied, 302 admitted, 81 enrolled.

Mid 50% test scores			
		GPA 2.0-2.99:	6%
SAT critical reading:	590-680	Rank in top quarter:	47%
SAT math:	540-630	Rank in top tenth:	26%
SAT writing:	580-670	End year in good standing:	92%
ACT composite:	28-32	Return as sophomores:	80%
GPA 3.75 or higher:	37%	Out-of-state:	74%
GPA 3.50-3.74:	31%	Live on campus:	100%
GPA 3.0-3.49:	26%	International:	19%

Basis for selection. Academic record and ability, motivation, intellectual enthusiasm, independence, creativity, commitment to ecological concerns and to the college's mission very important. High school record, recommendations, and an (optional) interview are all considered important. Interviews are recommended. For those unable to come to campus, COA can conduct interviews via phone or Skype. **Home schooled:** Thorough outline of topics covered, books read, homework completed, a description of the evaluation process used in assessing work, and the progress made over the years. Standardized test scores recommended. **Learning Disabled:** Meeting with academic dean recommended.

High school preparation. 15 units required; 19 recommended. Required and recommended units include English 4, mathematics 3-4, social studies 2, history 2, science 2-3 (laboratory 2), foreign language 2 and academic electives 1.

2015-2016 Annual costs. Tuition/fees: $42,084. Room/board: $9,432. Books/supplies: $600. Personal expenses: $555.

Financial aid. **Non-need-based:** Scholarships awarded for academics, leadership. **Additional information:** Low-cost classes available for local residents; some business courses covered by grant to the college.

Application procedures. **Admission:** Closing date 2/15 (postmark date). $50 fee, may be waived for applicants with need. Admission notification by 4/1. Must reply by May 1 or within 2 week(s) if notified thereafter. **Financial aid:** Closing date 2/15. FAFSA, institutional form required. Applicants notified by 4/1; must reply by 5/1.

Academics. Interdisciplinary, hands-on curriculum consists of problem-solving course work, strong mentorships, seminars, independent study, tutorials, specialized skill courses, and supervised internships away from college. Each student designs his or her own major; no two students follow same path. **Special study options:** Independent study, internships, semester at sea, student-designed major, study abroad, teacher certification program. Winter term program in Yucatan, Mexico and (less frequently) Guatemala. Study abroad in Vichy, France. Consortium agreement (Eco-League) with five other colleges for student exchanges: Alaska Pacific University, Dickinson College, Green Mountain College, Northland College, Prescott College; academic partnership with National Outdoor Leadership School; exchange agreement with The New School. Residencies (one term of self-directed study) under direction of faculty members. **Credit/placement by examination:** AP, CLEP, IB. 30 credit hours maximum toward bachelor's degree. **Support services:** Reduced course load, remedial instruction, study skills assistance, tutoring, writing center.

Majors. Architecture: Landscape. **Area/ethnic studies:** General, gay/lesbian, Latin American/Caribbean, women's. **Biology:** General, animal behavior, animal physiology, aquatic, botany, conservation, ecology, ecology/evolutionary, embryology, entomology, environmental, evolutionary, genetics, marine, microbiology/immunology, mycology, plant physiology, wildlife, zoology. **Business:** Entrepreneurial studies, nonprofit/public. **Communications:** General. **Conservation:** General, environmental science, environmental studies. **Education:** Biology, elementary, social studies. **English:** Child lit, creative writing, English lit, general lit, writing. **Health services:** Holistic, massage therapy. **History:** General, applied. **Human services:** Community org/advocacy, education policy, international policy, public policy. **Liberal arts:** Arts/sciences, humanities. **Math:** General. **Parks/recreation:** Outdoor education. **Philosophy/religion:** General, philosophy. **Physical sciences:** Chemistry, geology. **Psychology:** General, environmental. **Social sciences:** General, anthropology, applied economics, cultural anthropology, economics, GIS/cartography, international economic development, international economics, international relations, political economy, political science, research methodology, U.S. government. **Visual/performing arts:** General, art, art history/conservation, ceramics, cinematography, commercial/advertising art, crafts, design, digital arts, documentaries, dramatic, drawing, film/cinema/video, graphic design, illustration, multimedia, music, music history, painting, photography, play/screenwriting, printmaking, sculpture, studio arts.

Technology on campus. 32 workstations in library, computer center, student center. Dormitories wired for high-speed internet access and linked to campus network. Online course registration, online library, helpline, student web hosting, wireless network available.

Student life. Freshman orientation: Mandatory, $120 fee. Preregistration for classes offered. Four days on campus, plus an optional 6-day outdoor adventure trip. **Housing:** Guaranteed on-campus for freshmen. Coed dorms, special housing for disabled, themed housing, wellness housing available. $150 nonrefundable deposit, deadline 5/1. **Activities:** Bands, choral groups, dance, drama, international student organizations, literary magazine, music ensembles, student government, student newspaper, outing club, poetry group, spectrum (LGBT), sustainability committee, meditation group, earth in brackets (international environmental issues), chess club, futbol club, foreign policy club.

Athletics. Intramural: Badminton, basketball, cricket, ice hockey, sailing, soccer, softball, table tennis, ultimate frisbee, volleyball, water polo. **Team name:** Black Flies.

Student services. Alcohol/substance abuse counseling, career counseling, student employment services, financial aid counseling, health services, minority student services, personal counseling, placement for graduates. **Physically disabled:** Services for visually, hearing impaired.

Contact. E-mail: inquiry@coa.edu
Phone: (207) 801-5641 Toll-free number: (800) 528-0025
Fax: (207) 288-4126
Heather Albert-Knopp, Dean of Admission, College of the Atlantic, 105 Eden Street, Bar Harbor, ME 04609

Husson University
Bangor, Maine
www.husson.edu

CB member
CB code: 3440

- Private 4-year business and health science college
- Commuter campus in large town
- 2,595 degree-seeking undergraduates: 15% part-time, 53% women, 4% African American, 1% Asian American, 2% Hispanic/Latino, 1% Native American, 1% Multi-racial, non-Hispanic, 2% international
- 704 degree-seeking graduate students
- 78% of applicants admitted
- SAT or ACT with writing, application essay required
- 44% graduate within 6 years; 30% enter graduate study

General. Founded in 1898. Regionally accredited. **Degrees:** 523 bachelor's, 32 associate awarded; master's, professional offered. **ROTC:** Army, Naval. **Location:** 125 miles from Portland. **Calendar:** Semester, extensive summer session. **Full-time faculty:** 151 total; 59% have terminal degrees, 5% minority, 48% women. **Part-time faculty:** 197 total; 26% have terminal degrees, 2% minority, 52% women. **Class size:** 59% < 20, 40% 20-39, 1% 40-49. **Special facilities:** Center for Family Business, nature trails.

Freshman class profile. 2,066 applied, 1,610 admitted, 538 enrolled.

Mid 50% test scores			
SAT critical reading:	430-530	Rank in top quarter:	39%
SAT math:	430-540	Rank in top tenth:	11%
SAT writing:	420-520	End year in good standing:	85%
ACT composite:	18-23	Return as sophomores:	73%
GPA 3.75 or higher:	12%	Out-of-state:	27%
GPA 3.50-3.74:	29%	Live on campus:	80%
GPA 3.0-3.49:	35%	International:	1%
GPA 2.0-2.99:	23%	Fraternities:	3%
		Sororities:	5%

Basis for selection. Class rank and school achievement record most important. Counselor recommendations and SAT scores considered. Test scores most important for nursing applicants and occupational and physical therapy applicants, as well as students interested in Pharmacy. Test scores are used only for placement purposes for business and humanities school applicants. SAT recommended but not required for 2-year program. Interview recommended. **Home schooled:** Transcript of courses and grades, state high school equivalency certificate, letter of recommendation (nonparent) required. GED required for financial aid to be awarded. **Learning Disabled:** School must be apprised of special accommodation needs at time of payment of tuition deposit.

High school preparation. College-preparatory program recommended. Recommended units include English 4, mathematics 3, social studies 1, history 1, science 3 (laboratory 2).

2015-2016 Annual costs. Tuition/fees: $16,582. Room/board: $8,922. Books/supplies: $1,150. Personal expenses: $2,000. **Additional information:** Some programs have additional lab fees, $800 per year for programs within the New England School of Communications.

2015-2016 Financial aid. Need-based: 492 full-time freshmen applied for aid; 437 deemed to have need; 437 received aid. Average need met was 78%. Average scholarship/grant was $9,205; average loan $3,278. 51% of total undergraduate aid awarded as scholarships/grants, 49% as loans/jobs. **Non-need-based:** Awarded to 1,324 full-time undergraduates, including 311 freshmen. Scholarships awarded for academics, leadership.

Application procedures. Admission: Priority date 3/1; deadline 8/15 (postmark date). $40 fee, may be waived for applicants with need. Admission notification on a rolling basis beginning on or about 12/1. Must reply by May 1 or within 2 week(s) if notified thereafter. **Financial aid:** Priority date 4/15; no closing date. FAFSA required. Applicants notified on a rolling basis starting 4/1; must reply by 5/1 or within 2 week(s) of notification.

Academics. Strong liberal arts core within business and health programs. **Special study options:** Combined bachelor's/graduate degree, cooperative education, distance learning, double major, dual enrollment of high school students, ESL, independent study, internships, liberal arts/career combination, student-designed major, study abroad, teacher certification program, weekend college. **Credit/placement by examination:** AP, CLEP, IB, SAT, institutional tests. 15 credit hours maximum toward associate degree, 30 toward bachelor's. **Support services:** Learning center, pre-admission summer program, reduced course load, remedial instruction, study skills assistance, tutoring, writing center.

Majors. Biology: General. **Business:** General, accounting, accounting/business management, banking/financial services, business admin, entrepreneurial studies, finance, hospitality admin, hospitality/recreation, hotel/motel admin, international, international marketing, management information systems, managerial economics, market research, marketing, public finance, sales/distribution, small business admin. **Communications:** Digital media, journalism, persuasive communications, radio/TV, sports. **Communications technology:** Photo/film/video, recording arts. **Computer sciences:** General. **Education:** Biology, elementary, English, physical, secondary. **English:** English lit. **Health services:** Nursing (RN), prepharmacy. **Liberal arts:** Arts/sciences. **Parks/recreation:** Facilities management, health/fitness, sports admin. **Physical sciences:** Chemistry. **Protective services:** Criminal justice, law enforcement admin. **Psychology:** General. **Social sciences:** Criminology. **Visual/performing arts:** Theater design.

Most popular majors. Business/marketing 29%, communication technologies 11%, health sciences 20%, psychology 12%, security/protective services 11%.

Technology on campus. 131 workstations in library, computer center, student center. Dormitories wired for high-speed internet access and linked to campus network. Commuter students can connect to campus network. Online course registration, online library, helpline, student web hosting, wireless network available.

Student life. Freshman orientation: Mandatory, $100 fee. Preregistration for classes offered. Held during the summer and the weekend before classes start. **Housing:** Guaranteed on-campus for all undergraduates. Coed dorms, wellness housing available. Suite living for sophomores and up available. **Activities:** Pep band, campus ministries, choral groups, drama, international student organizations, literary magazine, music ensembles, musical theater, radio station, student government, Campus Crusade for Christ, Chi Alpha, political clubs.

Athletics. NCAA. **Intercollegiate:** Baseball M, basketball, cross-country, diving, field hockey W, football (tackle) M, golf, lacrosse, soccer, softball W, swimming, tennis W, track and field, volleyball W. **Intramural:** Basketball, football (non-tackle), lacrosse, soccer, softball, swimming, tennis, ultimate frisbee, volleyball. **Team name:** Eagles.

Student services. Adult student services, alcohol/substance abuse counseling, chaplain/spiritual director, career counseling, student employment services, financial aid counseling, health services, personal counseling, placement for graduates, veterans' counselor.

Contact. E-mail: admit@husson.edu
Phone: (207) 941-7100 Toll-free number: (800) 448-7766
Fax: (207) 941-7935
John Champoli, Director of Admissions, Husson University, 1 College Circle, Bangor, ME 04401-2999

Maine College of Art
Portland, Maine
www.meca.edu

CB member
CB code: 3701

- Private 4-year visual arts college
- Commuter campus in small city
- 430 degree-seeking undergraduates: 4% part-time, 70% women
- 33 degree-seeking graduate students
- 98% of applicants admitted
- Application essay required

General. Founded in 1882. Regionally accredited. Personal studio space for all juniors and seniors. **Degrees:** 80 bachelor's awarded; master's offered. **Location:** 100 miles from Boston. **Calendar:** Semester. **Full-time faculty:** 16 total; 100% have terminal degrees, 12% minority. **Part-time faculty:** 60 total; 58% have terminal degrees, 3% minority. **Class size:** 68% < 20, 28% 20-39, 3% 40-49. **Special facilities:** 3 art galleries, visual arts library.

Freshman class profile. 411 applied, 403 admitted, 118 enrolled.

GPA 3.75 or higher:	10%	Rank in top quarter:	31%
GPA 3.50-3.74:	12%	Rank in top tenth:	10%
GPA 3.0-3.49:	37%	Out-of-state:	68%
GPA 2.0-2.99:	41%	Live on campus:	98%

Basis for selection. Decision based on interview and portfolio in conjunction with high school achievement record; essay, recommendations important, test scores considered. Interview recommended. Portfolio required. **Home schooled:** Transcript of courses and grades, letter of recommendation (nonparent) required. Show evidence through state's certification of completion of high school program or GED. **Learning Disabled:** Once admitted, submit proper documentation to student affairs director and request specific accommodations.

High school preparation. 27 units recommended. Recommended units include English 4, mathematics 3, social studies 4, history 4, science 3, visual/performing arts 4 and academic electives 3. 4 units of art strongly recommended.

2015-2016 Annual costs. Tuition/fees: $32,290. Room/board: $10,872. Books/supplies: $1,250. Personal expenses: $1,000.

Financial aid. Non-need-based: Scholarships awarded for academics, art.

Application procedures. Admission: Priority date 3/1; no deadline. $40 fee, may be waived for applicants with need. Admission notification on a rolling basis beginning on or about 1/2. Students strongly encouraged to reply by May 1 or within 3 weeks if notified thereafter. **Financial aid:** Priority date 3/1; no closing date. FAFSA required. Applicants notified on a rolling basis starting 2/15; must reply within 2 week(s) of notification.

Academics. 1 to 2 year foundation program in drawing, color, digital imaging, and 2 and 3 dimensional design, followed by transitional year, and final 2 years in major. **Special study options:** Accelerated study, combined bachelor's/graduate degree, cross-registration, exchange student, independent study, internships, liberal arts/career combination, New York semester, study abroad, teacher certification program. Mobility program with 36 AICAD (Associated Independent Colleges of Art and Design) across the country and

in Canada, cross-registration program with 4 other colleges and universities in the greater Portland area; special exchange program with Hanoi Fine Arts College, Vietnam; BFA credit available through Provincetown (MA) Fine Arts Work Center. **Credit/placement by examination:** AP, CLEP. **Support services:** Learning center, study skills assistance, tutoring, writing center.

Majors. Visual/performing arts: Art, ceramics, graphic design, illustration, metal/jewelry, painting, photography, printmaking, sculpture, studio arts.

Technology on campus. 106 workstations in library, computer center, student center. Dormitories wired for high-speed internet access and linked to campus network. Commuter students can connect to campus network. Online library, helpline, student web hosting, wireless network available.

Student life. Freshman orientation: Mandatory. Preregistration for classes offered. Held the week before the start of classes. **Housing:** Coed dorms, wellness housing available. $200 partly refundable deposit. **Activities:** Film society, student government, student senate, community action group, green (ecology) group, movie club, peer mentor scholarships.

Student services. Adult student services, alcohol/substance abuse counseling, career counseling, student employment services, financial aid counseling, minority student services, personal counseling.

Contact. E-mail: admissions@meca.edu
Phone: (207) 699-5026 Toll-free number: (800) 699-1509
Fax: (207) 699-5080
Megan Lloyd, Director of Admissions, Maine College of Art, 522 Congress Street, Portland, ME 04101

Maine Maritime Academy
Castine, Maine
www.mainemaritime.edu

CB code: 3505

- Public 4-year maritime college
- Residential campus in rural community
- 1,037 degree-seeking undergraduates: 1% part-time, 13% women
- 29 degree-seeking graduate students
- SAT or ACT (ACT writing optional) required

General. Founded in 1941. Regionally accredited. **Degrees:** 213 bachelor's, 3 associate awarded; master's offered. **ROTC:** Army, Naval. **Location:** 38 miles from Bangor. **Calendar:** Semester. **Full-time faculty:** 65 total; 35% have terminal degrees, 5% minority, 18% women. **Part-time faculty:** 28 total; 54% women. **Special facilities:** 500-foot training ship, 40-foot marine research vessel, 80-foot oceangoing tugboat and 230-foot barge, two-masted arctic schooner, steam and diesel engine laboratories, power plant simulators, bridge simulator, tanker labs, planetarium, ocean classrooms.

Freshman class profile.

Out-of-state:	41%	Live on campus:	95%

Basis for selection. High school academic record followed by SAT/ACT test scores the most important. Interview, school and community activities, work ethic, and recommendations also considered. Interview and personal statement are highly recommended. **Home schooled:** Transcript of courses and grades, letter of recommendation (nonparent) required. ACT/SAT scores and possible evaluation of transcripts/course records by Maine Department of Education.

High school preparation. College-preparatory program required. Required and recommended units include English 4, mathematics 4, social studies 2, history 2, science 2-3 (laboratory 2-3) and foreign language 2. 1 unit computer literacy recommended.

2015-2016 Annual costs. Tuition/fees: $12,788; $17,668 out-of-district; $25,372 out-of-state. Room/board: $9,830. Books/supplies: $1,000. Personal expenses: $800. **Additional information:** USCG mandated Training Cruise/Co-ops have additional fees.

Financial aid. Non-need-based: Scholarships awarded for academics, leadership, religious affiliation, state residency.

Application procedures. Admission: Priority date 11/30; deadline 3/1 (receipt date). No application fee. Application must be submitted online. Admission notification by 4/1. Admission notification on a rolling basis beginning on or about 12/30. Must reply by 5/1. **Financial aid:** Closing date 4/15. FAFSA required. Applicants notified on a rolling basis starting 4/1; must reply within 4 week(s) of notification.

Academics. Special study options: Cooperative education, double major, honors, internships, student-designed major, study abroad, teacher certification program. Training cruise for USCG unlimited license majors; 90 days after freshman year and 45 days after junior year. Internships/Co-ops required for other majors. **Credit/placement by examination:** AP, CLEP. **Support services:** Study skills assistance, tutoring, writing center.

Majors. Biology: Marine. **Business:** General, business admin, entrepreneurial studies, international, logistics. **Engineering:** Marine, systems. **Physical sciences:** Oceanography.

Most popular majors. Biology 8%, business/marketing 7%, engineering/engineering technologies 55%, trade and industry 29%.

Technology on campus. PC or laptop required. 40 workstations in dormitories, library, student center. Dormitories wired for high-speed internet access and linked to campus network. Commuter students can connect to campus network. Online course registration, online library, helpline, repair service, wireless network available.

Student life. Freshman orientation: Mandatory. Preregistration for classes offered. Two days available through 4 different sessions in July, August. **Policies:** Regimental lifestyle optional for the 2-year program and those majoring in power engineering, ocean studies, international business, and small vessel operations. Regiment is mandatory for United States Coast Guard unlimited license programs (marine transportation and marine engineering). No military obligation. Students required to live on-campus unless married, over age 23, or have completed 2 or more years of active military service or 6 semesters of study. Freshmen not permitted cars on campus. **Housing:** Guaranteed on-campus for all undergraduates. Coed dorms, apartments, wellness housing available. **Activities:** Bands, choral groups, drama, international student organizations, music ensembles, student government, Alpha Phi Omega, other service organizations.

Athletics. NCAA. **Intercollegiate:** Basketball, cross-country, football (tackle) M, golf M, lacrosse, sailing, soccer, volleyball W. **Intramural:** Basketball, football (tackle), golf M, handball, racquetball, rifle, sailing, skiing, soccer, softball, squash, tennis, volleyball, water polo, wrestling. **Team name:** Mariners.

Student services. Alcohol/substance abuse counseling, career counseling, student employment services, financial aid counseling, health services, personal counseling, placement for graduates, veterans' counselor, women's services.

Contact. E-mail: admissions@mma.edu
Phone: (207) 326-2207 Toll-free number: (800) 227-8465
Fax: (207) 326-2515
Jeffrey Wright, Director of Admissions, Maine Maritime Academy, Pleasant Street, Castine, ME 04420

Saint Joseph's College of Maine
Standish, Maine   **CB member**
www.sjcme.edu   **CB code: 3755**

- Private 4-year liberal arts college affiliated with the Roman Catholic Church
- Residential campus in small town
- 960 degree-seeking undergraduates
- 1,725 graduate students
- SAT or ACT (ACT writing optional), application essay required

General. Founded in 1912. Regionally accredited. The campus is a short drive from the culture and entertainment city of Portland, Maine. Associate's, bachelor's, and master's degrees are also offered to nontraditional students through online education. **Degrees:** 288 bachelor's, 5 associate awarded; master's offered. **ROTC:** Army. **Location:** 18 miles from Portland, 120 miles from Boston. **Calendar:** Semester, limited summer session. **Full-time faculty:** 68 total. **Part-time faculty:** 65 total. **Class size:** 60% < 20, 36% 20-39, 2% 40-49, 1% 50-99.

Freshman class profile.

Rank in top quarter:	35%	Out-of-state:	35%
Rank in top tenth:	11%		

Basis for selection. School record, class rank, national test scores, recommendations, essays, extracurricular activities are all considered. Interview optional, but recommended.

High school preparation. College-preparatory program recommended. 20 units recommended. Recommended units include English 4, mathematics 3, social studies 3, science 3, foreign language 1, visual/performing arts 1 and academic electives 5. Laboratory biology and laboratory chemistry required of nursing and science applicants. For any intended major, transcripts from candidates for admission should include 16 or more college-preparatory courses.

2015-2016 Annual costs. Tuition/fees: $33,820. Room/board: $12,510. Books/supplies: $1,200. Personal expenses: $1,200.

Financial aid. Non-need-based: Scholarships awarded for academics, alumni affiliation, leadership.

Application procedures. Admission: Priority date 3/1; no deadline. No application fee. Admission notification on a rolling basis beginning on or about 12/17. Must reply by May 1 or within 2 week(s) if notified thereafter. **Financial aid:** Priority date 3/1; no closing date. FAFSA, institutional form required. Applicants notified on a rolling basis starting 3/1; must reply within 3 week(s) of notification.

Academics. College belongs to Greater Portland Alliance, a 5-college consortium with cross registration. **Special study options:** Combined bachelor's/graduate degree, cooperative education, cross-registration, distance learning, double major, honors, independent study, internships, liberal arts/career combination, semester at sea, student-designed major, study abroad, teacher certification program, Washington semester. **Credit/placement by examination:** AP, CLEP, SAT, ACT, institutional tests. 30 credit hours maximum toward bachelor's degree. **Support services:** Study skills assistance, tutoring, writing center.

Majors. Biology: General. **Business:** Accounting, business admin, finance, human resources, international, marketing. **Communications:** Digital media, journalism, public relations. **Conservation:** Environmental science, environmental studies. **Education:** Biology, elementary, English, history, mathematics, physical. **English:** English lit. **Health services:** Medical radiologic technology/radiation therapy, nursing (RN). **History:** General. **Math:** General. **Parks/recreation:** Exercise sciences, sports admin. **Philosophy/religion:** Philosophy. **Physical sciences:** Chemistry. **Protective services:** Criminal justice. **Psychology:** General. **Social sciences:** General, political science, sociology. **Theology:** Theology.

Most popular majors. Biology 6%, business/marketing 20%, communications/journalism 8%, education 13%, health sciences 21%, parks/recreation 6%, social sciences 6%.

Technology on campus. 102 workstations in library, computer center, student center. Dormitories wired for high-speed internet access and linked to campus network. Commuter students can connect to campus network. Helpline, repair service, wireless network available.

Student life. Freshman orientation: Available, $50 fee. Preregistration for classes offered. Two-day session in June or July. **Policies:** Mass available daily on campus. **Housing:** Guaranteed on-campus for all undergraduates. Coed dorms, single-sex dorms, wellness housing available. $100 deposit, deadline 5/1. **Activities:** Campus ministries, choral groups, dance, drama, literary magazine, student government, student newspaper, Habitat for Humanity, High Adventure, Superkids, business club, campus ministry, culture and heritage club, interhall council, student nurses association.

Athletics. NCAA. **Intercollegiate:** Baseball M, basketball, cross-country, field hockey W, golf M, lacrosse, soccer, softball W, swimming, track and field M, volleyball W. **Intramural:** Basketball, football (non-tackle), soccer, softball, swimming, volleyball. **Team name:** Monks.

Student services. Alcohol/substance abuse counseling, chaplain/spiritual director, career counseling, student employment services, financial aid counseling, health services, personal counseling, placement for graduates, veterans' counselor. **Physically disabled:** Services for visually, speech, hearing impaired.

Contact. E-mail: admission@sjcme.edu
Phone: (207) 893-7746 Toll-free number: (800) 338-7057
Fax: (207) 893-7862
Nikolas Ray, Dean of Admission, Saint Joseph's College of Maine, 278 Whites Bridge Road, Standish, ME 04084-5236

Thomas College
Waterville, Maine   **CB member**
www.thomas.edu   **CB code: 3903**

- Private 4-year business, liberal arts and teachers college
- Residential campus in large town
- 855 degree-seeking undergraduates: 6% part-time, 49% women, 4% African American, 1% Asian American, 2% Hispanic/Latino, 9% Multiracial, non-Hispanic, 2% international
- 155 degree-seeking graduate students
- 88% of applicants admitted
- Application essay required
- 44% graduate within 6 years

517

General. Founded in 1894. Regionally accredited. Evening division (undergraduate and graduate) on trimester system. **Degrees:** 154 bachelor's, 6 associate awarded; master's offered. **Location:** 75 miles from Portland. **Calendar:** Semester, limited summer session. **Full-time faculty:** 34 total; 65% have terminal degrees, 6% minority, 29% women. **Part-time faculty:** 34 total; 12% have terminal degrees, 6% minority, 38% women. **Class size:** 54% < 20, 46% 20-39.

Freshman class profile. 1,079 applied, 949 admitted, 250 enrolled.

GPA 3.75 or higher:	7%	Rank in top tenth:	21%
GPA 3.50-3.74:	9%	End year in good standing:	88%
GPA 3.0-3.49:	37%	Return as sophomores:	70%
GPA 2.0-2.99:	43%	Out-of-state:	20%
Rank in top quarter:	34%	Live on campus:	80%

Basis for selection. Academic transcripts most important. Letters of recommendation, college essay, SAT, ACT and/or TOEFL Exam scores also important. Recommend minimum 2.0 overall GPA, rank in top half of class. Thomas is a test-optional college. Interview recommended. **Home schooled:** Statement describing home school structure and mission, transcript of courses and grades, state high school equivalency certificate, letter of recommendation (nonparent) required.

High school preparation. College-preparatory program recommended. 16 units recommended. Recommended units include English 4, mathematics 3, social studies 2, history 2, science 3 and foreign language 2.

2015-2016 Annual costs. Tuition/fees: $24,300. Room/board: $10,430. Books/supplies: $800. Personal expenses: $1,000.

2015-2016 Financial aid. **Need-based:** Average need met was 85%. Average scholarship/grant was $16,101; average loan $4,026. 78% of total undergraduate aid awarded as scholarships/grants, 22% as loans/jobs. **Non-need-based:** Scholarships awarded for academics, alumni affiliation, leadership, state residency.

Application procedures. Admission: Closing date 8/15 (postmark date). $40 fee, may be waived for applicants with need. Admission notification on a rolling basis beginning on or about 11/1. Must reply by May 1 or within 4 week(s) if notified thereafter. **Financial aid:** Priority date 2/15; no closing date. FAFSA required. Applicants notified on a rolling basis starting 3/15; must reply within 2 week(s) of notification.

Academics. Special study options: Accelerated study, combined bachelor's/graduate degree, cross-registration, double major, dual enrollment of high school students, exchange student, independent study, internships, study abroad, teacher certification program, Washington semester. **Credit/placement by examination:** AP, CLEP. 15 credit hours maximum toward associate degree, 15 toward bachelor's. **Support services:** Learning center, reduced course load, study skills assistance, tutoring.

Majors. Business: Accounting, business admin, entrepreneurial studies, finance, hospitality admin, hotel/motel admin, human resources, international, marketing. **Communications:** Persuasive communications. **Computer sciences:** General, computer science. **Education:** Early childhood, elementary, secondary. **English:** English lit. **Military:** Cyber ops. **Parks/recreation:** Sports admin. **Protective services:** Criminal justice, law enforcement admin. **Psychology:** General, forensic. **Social sciences:** U.S. government.

Most popular majors. Business/marketing 41%, education 8%, parks/recreation 8%, psychology 14%, security/protective services 18%.

Technology on campus. 275 workstations in dormitories, library, computer center, student center. Dormitories wired for high-speed internet access and linked to campus network. Commuter students can connect to campus network. Online course registration, online library, helpline, repair service, student web hosting, wireless network available.

Student life. Freshman orientation: Mandatory. Preregistration for classes offered. Three-day program held at the end of August; extended programs during fall semester. One day program in January for new students entering for spring semester. **Housing:** Coed dorms, themed housing, wellness housing available. $100 nonrefundable deposit, deadline 5/1. **Activities:** Dance, drama, international student organizations, student government, Service Society, international club, Campus Crusades for Christ (CRU), Sacred Circle.

Athletics. NCAA. **Intercollegiate:** Baseball M, basketball, cross-country, field hockey W, lacrosse, soccer, softball W, tennis. **Intramural:** Badminton, basketball, football (non-tackle), soccer, softball, table tennis, tennis, ultimate frisbee, volleyball. **Team name:** Terriers.

Student services. Alcohol/substance abuse counseling, chaplain/spiritual director, career counseling, student employment services, financial aid counseling, health services, personal counseling, placement for graduates, veterans' counselor. **Physically disabled:** Services for hearing impaired.

Contact. E-mail: admiss@thomas.edu
Phone: (207) 859-1101 Toll-free number: (800) 339-7001
Fax: (207) 859-1114
Jonathan Kent, VP for Enrollment Management, Thomas College, 180 West River Road, Waterville, ME 04901

Unity College
Unity, Maine
www.unity.edu
CB code: 3925

- Private 4-year liberal arts college
- Residential campus in rural community
- 643 degree-seeking undergraduates: 1% part-time, 51% women, 1% African American, 2% Asian American, 2% Hispanic/Latino, 1% Native American, 4% Multi-racial, non-Hispanic
- 91% of applicants admitted
- Application essay required
- 54% graduate within 6 years; 25% enter graduate study

General. Founded in 1965. Regionally accredited. **Degrees:** 113 bachelor's, 2 associate awarded. **Location:** 16 miles from Waterville; 23 miles from Belfast. **Calendar:** Semester, limited summer session. **Full-time faculty:** 42 total; 83% have terminal degrees, 57% women. **Part-time faculty:** 31 total; 52% have terminal degrees, 45% women. **Class size:** 58% < 20, 39% 20-39, 3% 40-49, less than 1% 50-99. **Special facilities:** Wetlands research areas, outdoor pottery kiln, outdoor classroom.

Freshman class profile. 831 applied, 756 admitted, 198 enrolled.

Mid 50% test scores			
SAT critical reading:	440-580	GPA 2.0-2.99:	32%
SAT math:	440-560	Rank in top quarter:	32%
SAT writing:	450-540	Rank in top tenth:	18%
ACT composite:	20-25	End year in good standing:	85%
GPA 3.75 or higher:	16%	Return as sophomores:	66%
GPA 3.50-3.74:	21%	Out-of-state:	71%
GPA 3.0-3.49:	31%	Live on campus:	97%
		International:	1%

Basis for selection. High school transcripts, interviews, recommendations and essay are most important for acceptance decisions. Test scores are not required but are highly recommended. SAT or ACT recommended. Interview is optional but recommended. **Home schooled:** State high school equivalency certificate, interview required. Informative portfolio required.

High school preparation. College-preparatory program recommended. 18 units recommended. Required and recommended units include English 4, mathematics 4, social studies 3, history 3, science 3 (laboratory 3) and foreign language 2.

2015-2016 Annual costs. Tuition/fees: $26,800. Room/board: $9,800. Books/supplies: $500. Personal expenses: $600.

2015-2016 Financial aid. Need-based: 157 full-time freshmen applied for aid; 140 deemed to have need; 140 received aid. Average need met was 72%. Average scholarship/grant was $13,825; average loan $6,432. 61% of total undergraduate aid awarded as scholarships/grants, 39% as loans/jobs. **Non-need-based:** Awarded to 122 full-time undergraduates, including 38 freshmen. Scholarships awarded for academics, leadership, minority status.

Application procedures. Admission: Priority date 12/15; deadline 2/15 (postmark date). No application fee. Admission notification by 6/15. Admission notification on a rolling basis beginning on or about 9/15. Must reply by 5/1. **Financial aid:** Priority date 3/1; no closing date. FAFSA required. Applicants notified on a rolling basis starting 3/10; must reply within 2 week(s) of notification.

Academics. Special study options: Accelerated study, double major, honors, independent study, internships, liberal arts/career combination, semester at sea, study abroad, teacher certification program, Washington semester. **Credit/placement by examination:** AP, CLEP, IB, SAT, ACT, institutional tests. 15 credit hours maximum toward associate degree, 15 toward bachelor's. **Support services:** Learning center, reduced course load, study skills assistance, tutoring, writing center.

Majors. Biology: Environmental, marine, wildlife. **Conservation:** Enforcement, environmental science, nature tourism, wildlife/wilderness. **Education:** Secondary. **Health services:** Recreational therapy. **Parks/recreation:** Outdoor education. **Visual/performing arts:** Studio arts.

Most popular majors. Biology 31%, natural resources/environmental science 57%.

Technology on campus. 140 workstations in dormitories, library, computer center, student center. Dormitories wired for high-speed internet access and linked to campus network. Commuter students can connect to campus network. Online course registration, online library, helpline, student web hosting, wireless network available.

Student life. Freshman orientation: Mandatory, $100 fee. Preregistration for classes offered. Five-day outdoor wilderness-based program in summer and 2-day on-campus orientation before classes begin. **Policies:** Students are required to live on campus unless they are 21 years of age, married, live with their parents (within 50 miles of the campus), or have earned a minimum of 60 credits. **Housing:** Guaranteed on-campus for freshmen. Coed dorms, single-sex dorms, special housing for disabled, cooperative housing, themed housing, wellness housing available. $100 nonrefundable deposit, deadline 4/1. **Activities:** Choral groups, drama, literary magazine, student government, Constructive Activists, search and rescue crew, trail crew; groups devoted to environmental awareness, recycling, community service, and sustainability.

Athletics. USCAA. **Intercollegiate:** Basketball, cross-country, soccer, volleyball W. **Intramural:** Basketball, football (non-tackle), soccer, softball, volleyball. **Team name:** Rams.

Student services. Alcohol/substance abuse counseling, chaplain/spiritual director, career counseling, student employment services, financial aid counseling, health services, personal counseling, placement for graduates, veterans' counselor, women's services. **Physically disabled:** Services for visually, hearing impaired.

Contact. E-mail: admissions@unity.edu
Phone: (207) 509-7100 Toll-free number: (800) 624-1024
Fax: (207) 512-1212
Joe Saltalamachia, Director of Admissions, Unity College, P.O. 532, Unity, ME 04988-0532

University of Maine
Orono, Maine — CB member
www.umaine.edu — CB code: 3916

- Public 4-year university
- Residential campus in large town
- 8,677 degree-seeking undergraduates: 8% part-time, 47% women, 2% African American, 2% Asian American, 3% Hispanic/Latino, 1% Native American, 3% Multi-racial, non-Hispanic, 2% international
- 1,464 degree-seeking graduate students
- 91% of applicants admitted
- SAT or ACT (ACT writing optional), application essay required
- 55% graduate within 6 years

General. Founded in 1865. Regionally accredited. **Degrees:** 1,554 bachelor's awarded; master's, doctoral offered. **ROTC:** Army, Naval. **Location:** 5 miles from Bangor. **Calendar:** Semester, extensive summer session. **Full-time faculty:** 493 total; 85% have terminal degrees, 8% minority, 35% women. **Part-time faculty:** 352 total; 25% have terminal degrees, 7% minority, 56% women. **Class size:** 41% < 20, 36% 20-39, 7% 40-49, 12% 50-99, 5% >100. **Special facilities:** Astronomy center, art museum, innovative media, research and commercialization center, studio art center, center for the arts, recital hall, arboretum, ornamental trial garden, farm and home museum, marine center, arena and stadium, advance manufacturing center, Franco-American center, foster center for student innovation, laboratory for surface science and technology, advanced structures and composites center.

Freshman class profile. 11,044 applied, 10,073 admitted, 2,047 enrolled.

Mid 50% test scores			
SAT critical reading:	480-600	GPA 2.0-2.99:	20%
SAT math:	480-610	Rank in top quarter:	46%
SAT writing:	460-580	Rank in top tenth:	19%
ACT composite:	21-28	Return as sophomores:	76%
GPA 3.75 or higher:	27%	Out-of-state:	35%
GPA 3.50-3.74:	9%	Live on campus:	92%
GPA 3.0-3.49:	44%	International:	1%

Basis for selection. Strong emphasis on grades earned, GPA, class rank (if available) and standardized test scores. Academic requirements for admission may vary by program. SAT or ACT scores are waived for transfers with more than 12 completed credits or applicants age 20 and older. Interviews available. Audition required of music majors. Portfolio recommended for art majors. **Home schooled:** Statement describing home school structure and mission, transcript of courses and grades, state high school equivalency certificate, letter of recommendation (nonparent) required. GED requirement may be waived if thorough records submitted.

High school preparation. College-preparatory program required. 17 units required; 21 recommended. Required and recommended units include English 4, mathematics 3-4, social studies 2, history 1, science 2-4 (laboratory 2-3), foreign language 2 and academic electives 4. 1 unit physical education required of all College of Education candidates.

2015-2016 Annual costs. Tuition/fees: $10,610; $28,880 out-of-state. Room/board: $9,576. Books/supplies: $1,000. **Additional information:** New England Regional Student Program tuition is $12,570.

2015-2016 Financial aid. Need-based: 1,873 full-time freshmen applied for aid; 1,489 deemed to have need; 1,469 received aid. Average need met was 82%. Average scholarship/grant was $10,561; average loan $3,762. 52% of total undergraduate aid awarded as scholarships/grants, 48% as loans/jobs. **Non-need-based:** Awarded to 1,070 full-time undergraduates, including 457 freshmen. Scholarships awarded for academics, alumni affiliation, art, athletics, job skills, leadership, minority status, music/drama, religious affiliation, ROTC, state residency. **Additional information:** Financial aid is available for students entering in the spring.

Application procedures. Admission: Priority date 2/1; no deadline. $40 fee, may be waived for applicants with need. Admission notification on a rolling basis beginning on or about 2/1. Must reply by May 1 or within 2 week(s) if notified thereafter. **Financial aid:** Priority date 3/1, closing date 5/15. FAFSA required. Applicants notified on a rolling basis starting 3/15.

Academics. Special study options: Accelerated study, combined bachelor's/graduate degree, cooperative education, distance learning, double major, dual enrollment of high school students, ESL, exchange student, honors, independent study, internships, liberal arts/career combination, semester at sea, study abroad, teacher certification program. **Credit/placement by examination:** AP, CLEP, IB, institutional tests. 15 credit hours maximum toward bachelor's degree. Duplicate credit may not be granted. Each department may develop or adopt examinations other than CLEP examinations for the purpose of granting credit for specific courses. **Support services:** Reduced course load, remedial instruction, study skills assistance, tutoring, writing center.

Honors college/program. Admission for first-time and transfer students based on test scores and high school record.

Majors. Area/ethnic studies: Women's. **Biology:** General, bacteriology, biochemistry, botany, ecology, microbiology, molecular, pathology, zoology. **Business:** Accounting, business admin, finance, marketing. **Communications:** General, journalism, media studies. **Computer sciences:** Computer science. **Conservation:** General, environmental science, forest sciences, forestry, water/wetlands/marine, wildlife/wilderness, wood science. **Education:** General, art, biology, chemistry, elementary, English, foreign languages, French, history, mathematics, music, physical, science, secondary, social studies, Spanish. **Engineering:** General, agricultural, applied physics, biomedical, chemical, civil, computer, electrical, mechanical, surveying. **English:** English lit, rhetoric/composition. **Foreign languages:** General, French, German, Spanish. **Health services:** Athletic training, clinical lab science, communication disorders, nursing (RN). **History:** General. **Human services:** Social work. **Liberal arts:** Arts/sciences. **Math:** General. **Parks/recreation:** Facilities management. **Philosophy/religion:** Philosophy. **Physical sciences:** Chemistry, geology, physics. **Psychology:** General. **Social sciences:** Anthropology, economics, international relations, political science, sociology. **Visual/performing arts:** Art history/conservation, dramatic, music, music performance, studio arts. **Work/family studies:** Family studies.

Most popular majors. Biology 6%, business/marketing 13%, communications/journalism 6%, education 9%, engineering/engineering technologies 18%, health sciences 7%, psychology 6%, social sciences 9%.

Technology on campus. 500 workstations in library, computer center, student center. Dormitories wired for high-speed internet access and linked to campus network. Commuter students can connect to campus network. Online course registration, online library, helpline, repair service, student web hosting, wireless network available.

Student life. Freshman orientation: Available. Preregistration for classes offered. Two-day events in June, parents invited to special sessions. Four-day welcome program in fall prior to the beginning of school. **Housing:** Guaranteed on-campus for freshmen. Coed dorms, special housing for disabled, apartments, fraternity/sorority housing, themed housing, wellness housing available. Academic grouping wings, men-only sections, women-only sections available. **Activities:** Bands, campus ministries, choral groups, dance, drama, film society, international student organizations, literary magazine, music ensembles, musical theater, opera, radio station, student government, student newspaper, symphony orchestra, Hillel, Campus Crusade for Christ, Muslim Student Association, Black Student Union, Asian Student Association, International Students Association, Alternative Breaks, Engineers Without Borders, Green Team.

Athletics. NCAA. **Intercollegiate:** Baseball M, basketball, cross-country, diving, field hockey W, football (tackle) M, ice hockey, soccer W, softball W, swimming, track and field, volleyball W. **Intramural:** Badminton, basketball, field hockey, football (non-tackle), ice hockey, racquetball, skiing, soccer, softball, swimming, table tennis, tennis, track and field, triathlon, ultimate frisbee, volleyball, water polo. **Team name:** Black Bears.

Student services. Adult student services, alcohol/substance abuse counseling, chaplain/spiritual director, career counseling, services for economically disadvantaged, student employment services, financial aid counseling, health services, legal services, minority student services, on-campus daycare, personal counseling, placement for graduates, veterans' counselor, women's services. **Physically disabled:** Services for visually, speech, hearing impaired.

Contact. E-mail: umaineadmissions@maine.edu
Phone: (207) 581-1561 Toll-free number: (877) 486-2364
Fax: (207) 581-1213
Sharon Oliver, Senior Director of Admissions, University of Maine, 5713 Chadbourne Hall, Orono, ME 04469-5713

University of Maine at Augusta	
Augusta, Maine	**CB member**
www.uma.edu	**CB code: 3929**

▶ Public 4-year university
▶ Commuter campus in large town
▶ 3,964 degree-seeking undergraduates: 61% part-time, 74% women

General. Founded in 1965. Regionally accredited. Additional centers in Rockland, Brunswick, Rumford, Saco, Ellsworth, South Paris, East Millinocket, Houlton; additional campus in Bangor. **Degrees:** 444 bachelor's, 221 associate awarded. **ROTC:** Army, Naval, Air Force. **Location:** 2 miles from downtown, 65 miles from Portland. **Calendar:** Semester, extensive summer session. **Full-time faculty:** 97 total; 55% have terminal degrees, 59% women. **Part-time faculty:** 182 total; 10% have terminal degrees, 2% minority, 56% women. **Class size:** 72% < 20, 26% 20-39, 2% 40-49, less than 1% 50-99. **Special facilities:** Holocaust and human rights center.

Freshman class profile. 747 applied, 728 admitted, 419 enrolled.

Basis for selection. Open admission, but selective for some programs. High school achievement record and test scores considered for admission to allied health and bachelor's degree programs. Talent/ability assessed for admission to music programs. TOEFL is requested of non-native English speakers. Interviews required of dental hygiene and medical laboratory technology majors. Audition required of music majors. **Home schooled:** Transcript of courses and grades required. Documentation of high school completion required.

High school preparation. College-preparatory program recommended. 17.5 units required. Required and recommended units include English 4, mathematics 2-3, social studies 2, history 2, science 2-3 (laboratory 2-3). Applicants to health science programs must have biology, chemistry, and Algebra II. Business administration and public administration applicants must have Algebra II and geometry.

2015-2016 Annual costs. Tuition/fees: $7,448; $16,688 out-of-state. Books/supplies: $1,200. Personal expenses: $1,800. **Additional information:** New England Regional Student Program tuition is $9,750.

2015-2016 Financial aid. Need-based: 42% of total undergraduate aid awarded as scholarships/grants, 58% as loans/jobs. **Non-need-based:** Scholarships awarded for academics, athletics, leadership, music/drama, state residency.

Application procedures. Admission: Priority date 6/15; deadline 8/1 (receipt date). $40 fee, may be waived for applicants with need. Admission notification on a rolling basis beginning on or about 10/1. Must reply by May 1 or within 2 week(s) if notified thereafter. **Financial aid:** Priority date 3/1; no closing date. FAFSA required. Applicants notified on a rolling basis starting 3/15; must reply within 2 week(s) of notification.

Academics. Special study options: Combined bachelor's/graduate degree, cross-registration, distance learning, double major, dual enrollment of high school students, honors, independent study, internships, liberal arts/career combination, student-designed major, study abroad, teacher certification program. **Credit/placement by examination:** AP, CLEP, institutional tests. 45 credit hours maximum toward associate degree, 90 toward bachelor's. **Support services:** Reduced course load, remedial instruction, study skills assistance, tutoring.

Majors. Architecture: Technology. **Biology:** General. **Business:** Accounting, business admin, financial planning. **Computer sciences:** Information technology, security. **English:** English lit. **Health services:** Clinical nurse leader, dental hygiene, mental health services, veterinary technology/assistant.

Human services: General. **Liberal arts:** Arts/sciences, library science. **Protective services:** Law enforcement admin. **Social sciences:** General. **Visual/performing arts:** Music, studio arts.

Most popular majors. Business/marketing 14%, health sciences 30%, liberal arts 24%, library sciences 6%, security/protective services 8%.

Technology on campus. 415 workstations in library, computer center, student center. Commuter students can connect to campus network. Online course registration, online library, student web hosting, wireless network available.

Student life. Freshman orientation: Available. Preregistration for classes offered. One-day program held 1 week prior to start of each semester and mid-summer. **Activities:** Jazz band, drama, international student organizations, literary magazine, music ensembles, student government, student newspaper, Art and Architectural Student Association, Gay Lesbian Bisexual Transgender Friends and Associates, Honors English Program, English Society, Student Nursing Association, Pi Alpha Alpha, College Republicans, Mental Health and Human Services Club, Campus Crusade for Christ.

Athletics. USCAA. **Intercollegiate:** Basketball, bowling, cross-country, golf, soccer. **Intramural:** Basketball, racquetball, soccer. **Team name:** Moose.

Student services. Adult student services, alcohol/substance abuse counseling, career counseling, services for economically disadvantaged, financial aid counseling, personal counseling, veterans' counselor. **Physically disabled:** Services for visually, hearing impaired.

Contact. E-mail: umaadm@maine.edu
Phone: (207) 621-3465 Toll-free number: (877) 862-1234
Fax: (207) 621-3333
Pamela Proulx-Curry, Dean of Enrollment Services, University of Maine at Augusta, 46 University Drive, Augusta, ME 04330

University of Maine at Farmington	
Farmington, Maine	**CB member**
www.umf.maine.edu	**CB code: 3506**

▶ Public 4-year liberal arts and teachers college
▶ Residential campus in small town
▶ 1,766 degree-seeking undergraduates: 5% part-time, 66% women, 2% African American, 1% Asian American, 2% Hispanic/Latino, 1% Native American, 2% Multi-racial, non-Hispanic
▶ 131 degree-seeking graduate students
▶ 83% of applicants admitted
▶ Application essay required
▶ 59% graduate within 6 years

General. Founded in 1863. Regionally accredited. **Degrees:** 348 bachelor's awarded; master's offered. **Location:** 38 miles from Augusta, 80 miles from Portland. **Calendar:** Semester, extensive summer session. **Full-time faculty:** 113 total; 88% have terminal degrees, 7% minority, 58% women. **Part-time faculty:** 60 total; 38% have terminal degrees, 2% minority, 67% women. **Class size:** 63% < 20, 34% 20-39, 1% 40-49, 1% 50-99. **Special facilities:** Observatory, learning center, on-site nursery school and day care as a teaching environment, art gallery, radio station.

Freshman class profile. 1,614 applied, 1,346 admitted, 448 enrolled.

Mid 50% test scores		GPA 2.0-2.99:	46%
SAT critical reading:	440-570	Rank in top quarter:	40%
SAT math:	430-550	Rank in top tenth:	13%
SAT writing:	430-550	End year in good standing:	89%
GPA 3.75 or higher:	11%	Return as sophomores:	75%
GPA 3.50-3.74:	8%	Out-of-state:	20%
GPA 3.0-3.49:	31%	Live on campus:	94%

Basis for selection. Rigor of high school academic program and GPA most important. Class rank, essay, and recommendations also important. SAT scores not required for admission, but considered if submitted. SAT scores also used for placement in first-year courses. Accuplacer placement tests required for students with SAT scores below 500 Writing or 490 Math. Interview recommended. 12-14 page writing sample required for Creative Writing BFA. **Home schooled:** Statement describing home school structure and mission, letter of recommendation (nonparent) required. Additional information may be requested upon review of application. **Learning Disabled:** Students may submit disclosure of learning disability to Learning Assistance Center after admission.

High school preparation. College-preparatory program required. Required and recommended units include English 4, mathematics 3, social studies 3, science 3 (laboratory 2) and foreign language 2. Algebra I and II and geometry required. Two years of same foreign language recommended. General college preparatory program required for all except those admitted to the Johnson Scholars program.

2015-2016 Annual costs. Tuition/fees: $9,217; $18,305 out-of-state. Room/board: $8,970. Books/supplies: $840. Personal expenses: $2,054. **Additional information:** New England Regional Student Program tuition is $12,544.

2014-2015 Financial aid. Need-based: 405 full-time freshmen applied for aid; 351 deemed to have need; 351 received aid. Average need met was 86%. Average scholarship/grant was $8,538; average loan $5,304. 49% of total undergraduate aid awarded as scholarships/grants, 51% as loans/jobs. **Non-need-based:** Awarded to 88 full-time undergraduates, including 47 freshmen. Scholarships awarded for academics, leadership, minority status, music/drama, state residency. **Additional information:** Freshman students from Franklin County, Maine, offered free on-campus housing for their first year at UMF. Federal processor must receive FAFSA by 3/1 in order for applicant to receive priority consideration from campus.

Application procedures. Admission: No deadline. No application fee. Admission notification on a rolling basis beginning on or about 11/15. Must reply by May 1 or within 3 week(s) if notified thereafter. **Financial aid:** Priority date 3/1; no closing date. FAFSA required. Applicants notified on a rolling basis starting 3/15.

Academics. Interdisciplinary first-year seminar and Co-Labs (a group of courses organized around a theme with emphasis on student projects) available. **Special study options:** Accelerated study, cross-registration, distance learning, double major, dual enrollment of high school students, exchange student, honors, independent study, internships, liberal arts/career combination, student-designed major, study abroad, teacher certification program. **Credit/placement by examination:** AP, CLEP, IB, SAT, institutional tests. 16 credit hours maximum toward bachelor's degree. CLEP tests must have been taken prior to matriculation. **Support services:** Learning center, pre-admission summer program, reduced course load, remedial instruction, study skills assistance, tutoring, writing center. Supplemental Instruction program available for certain courses; walk-in tutoring available in math and writing, and tutoring in other subjects available upon request.

Majors. Biology: General. **Business:** Actuarial science, managerial economics, organizational leadership. **Computer sciences:** Computer science. **Conservation:** Environmental science, environmental studies. **Education:** Biology, chemistry, early childhood, early childhood special, earth science, elementary, English, health, kindergarten/preschool, mathematics, physics, secondary, social science, special ed. **English:** Creative writing, English lit. **Health services:** Community health services, health information management, rehabilitation science. **History:** General. **Liberal arts:** Arts/sciences. **Math:** General. **Philosophy/religion:** General. **Physical sciences:** Geology. **Psychology:** General. **Social sciences:** Geography, political science, sociology/anthropology. **Visual/performing arts:** General, art, multimedia, music.

Most popular majors. Business/marketing 6%, education 34%, English 8%, health sciences 16%, psychology 13%.

Technology on campus. 220 workstations in library, computer center, student center. Dormitories wired for high-speed internet access and linked to campus network. Commuter students can connect to campus network. Online course registration, online library, helpline, student web hosting, wireless network available.

Student life. Freshman orientation: Available, $230 fee. Preregistration for classes offered. Four-day program held immediately prior to the start of classes. **Policies:** Good Samaritan policy that shields residents from a judicial process for drugs and alcohol if they come forward to seek help for a friend or themselves and if they are in crisis because of drug or alcohol use. **Housing:** Guaranteed on-campus for all undergraduates. Coed dorms, single-sex dorms, special housing for disabled, cooperative housing, gender-neutral housing, themed housing, wellness housing available. Honors and scholars housing, medical single rooms, independent living environment, educational themed, artist infinity, outdoors pursuits and suite style living available. **Activities:** Campus ministries, choral groups, dance, drama, international student organizations, literary magazine, music ensembles, musical theater, radio station, student government, student newspaper, symphony orchestra, TV station, Justice Uniting Students Together, student environmental and political awareness club, Amnesty International, Inter-Varsity Christian Fellowship, Campus Residence Council, student admissions club, Alpha Phi Omega, Writers Guild, Newman Club, student-run entertainment board.

Athletics. NCAA. **Intercollegiate:** Baseball M, basketball, cross-country, field hockey W, golf M, lacrosse, skiing, soccer, softball W, track and field. **Intramural:** Basketball, football (non-tackle), soccer, softball, swimming, tennis, volleyball. **Team name:** Beavers.

Student services. Adult student services, alcohol/substance abuse counseling, career counseling, services for economically disadvantaged, student employment services, financial aid counseling, health services, on-campus daycare, personal counseling, placement for graduates, veterans' counselor, women's services. **Physically disabled:** Services for visually, speech, hearing impaired.

Contact. E-mail: umfadmit@maine.edu
Phone: (207) 778-7050 Fax: (207) 778-8182
Jared Cash, Vice President for Enrollment, University of Maine at Farmington, 246 Main Street, Farmington, ME 04938

University of Maine at Fort Kent
Fort Kent, Maine   **CB member**
www.umfk.maine.edu   **CB code: 3393**

◗ Public 4-year university and branch campus college
◗ Commuter campus in small town
◗ 990 degree-seeking undergraduates: 41% part-time, 72% women, 4% African American, 1% Asian American, 2% Hispanic/Latino, 1% Native American, 2% Multi-racial, non-Hispanic, 11% international
◗ 89% of applicants admitted
◗ Application essay required
◗ 39% graduate within 6 years

General. Founded in 1878. Regionally accredited. Bilingual Franco-American region. **Degrees:** 157 bachelor's, 41 associate awarded. **Location:** 200 miles from Bangor, 21 miles from Edmundston, Canada. **Calendar:** Semester, extensive summer session. **Full-time faculty:** 33 total; 58% have terminal degrees, 9% minority, 39% women. **Part-time faculty:** 54 total; 6% have terminal degrees, 4% minority, 67% women. **Class size:** 79% < 20, 19% 20-39, less than 1% 40-49, 2% 50-99. **Special facilities:** 16-acre biological park, Acadian Archives, interactive television site, Northern Maine Center for Rural Health Science, Center for Sustainable Rural Development.

Freshman class profile. 215 applied, 192 admitted, 124 enrolled.

Mid 50% test scores			
SAT critical reading:	400-480	**GPA 2.0-2.99:**	31%
SAT math:	400-500	**Rank in top quarter:**	7%
SAT writing:	380-480	**Rank in top tenth:**	1%
ACT composite:	15-19	**Return as sophomores:**	70%
GPA 3.75 or higher:	16%	**Out-of-state:**	15%
GPA 3.50-3.74:	11%	**Live on campus:**	62%
GPA 3.0-3.49:	34%	**Fraternities:**	1%
		Sororities:	1%

Basis for selection. High school courses and achievement record most important. Recommendations considered. SAT, ACT scores, or on-campus placement exams required. SAT and SAT Subject Tests or ACT recommended. Interview recommended.

High school preparation. College-preparatory program recommended. 16 units required. Required and recommended units include English 4, mathematics 2, science 2 (laboratory 2) and foreign language 2. Biology and chemistry required for nursing and environmental studies.

2015-2016 Annual costs. Tuition/fees: $7,575; $10,875 out-of-state. Room/board: $7,910. Books/supplies: $1,000. Personal expenses: $1,000.

2014-2015 Financial aid. Need-based: 109 full-time freshmen applied for aid; 93 deemed to have need; 93 received aid. Average need met was 85%. Average scholarship/grant was $6,133; average loan $5,436. 52% of total undergraduate aid awarded as scholarships/grants, 48% as loans/jobs. **Non-need-based:** Awarded to 43 full-time undergraduates, including 10 freshmen. Scholarships awarded for academics, leadership.

Application procedures. Admission: Priority date 6/1; deadline 8/15. $40 fee, may be waived for applicants with need. Admission notification on a rolling basis. **Financial aid:** Priority date 3/1; no closing date. FAFSA, institutional form, CSS PROFILE required. Applicants notified on a rolling basis starting 3/15.

Academics. Special study options: Cross-registration, distance learning, double major, dual enrollment of high school students, honors, independent study, internships, student-designed major, teacher certification program. **Credit/placement by examination:** AP, CLEP, IB, SAT, institutional tests. 30 credit hours maximum toward associate degree, 90 toward bachelor's. **Support services:** Learning center, pre-admission summer program, reduced course load, remedial instruction, tutoring, writing center.

Majors. Biology: General. **Business:** General, business admin, e-commerce, management information systems. **Computer sciences:** General, information technology. **Conservation:** Environmental science, management/policy. **Education:** General, business, elementary, English, multi-level teacher, music, science, secondary, social studies. **English:** American lit, British lit,

English lit. **Foreign languages:** General, comparative lit, French. **Health services:** Nursing (RN). **Human services:** Social work. **Liberal arts:** Arts/sciences. **Psychology:** General. **Social sciences:** General.

Most popular majors. Business/marketing 14%, education 8%, health sciences 52%, liberal arts 7%, social sciences 7%.

Technology on campus. 100 workstations in dormitories, library, computer center, student center. Dormitories wired for high-speed internet access and linked to campus network. Commuter students can connect to campus network. Online course registration, helpline, repair service, student web hosting, wireless network available.

Student life. Freshman orientation: Mandatory. Preregistration for classes offered. Three-day social and educational orientation; includes workshops. **Housing:** Coed dorms, single-sex dorms, special housing for disabled available. $100 fully refundable deposit, deadline 8/15. **Activities:** Campus ministries, drama, international student organizations, student government, student newspaper, Christian Fellowship, Newman Club.

Athletics. NAIA. **Intercollegiate:** Basketball, skiing, soccer, volleyball W. **Intramural:** Baseball, basketball, golf, ice hockey M, racquetball, skiing, soccer, softball, table tennis, tennis, volleyball, weight lifting. **Team name:** Bengals.

Student services. Adult student services, alcohol/substance abuse counseling, career counseling, services for economically disadvantaged, financial aid counseling, health services, personal counseling, placement for graduates, veterans' counselor. **Physically disabled:** Services for visually, speech, hearing impaired.

Contact. E-mail: umfkadm@maine.edu
Toll-free number: (888) 879-8635 Fax: (207) 834-7609
Jill Cairns, Director of Admissions, University of Maine at Fort Kent, 23 University Drive, Fort Kent, ME 04743

University of Maine at Machias
Machias, Maine
www.umm.maine.edu

CB member
CB code: 3956

- Public 4-year university and liberal arts college
- Commuter campus in rural community
- 574 degree-seeking undergraduates: 25% part-time, 65% women
- SAT or ACT (ACT writing optional), application essay required

General. Founded in 1909. Regionally accredited. **Degrees:** 86 bachelor's, 9 associate awarded. **Location:** 85 miles from Bangor, 65 miles from Bar Harbor. **Calendar:** Semester, limited summer session. **Special facilities:** Institute for applied marine research and education, mariculture student research facility, greenhouse, GIS lab, early childhood center, field station, international park, sail loft.

Freshman class profile.

Out-of-state:	15%	Live on campus:	64%

Basis for selection. Applicants should rank in top half of class and have a B average. Recommendations and test scores important. Essay and outstanding nonacademic achievement (extracurricular, community, military, life, or work) considered. SAT/ACT not required of applicants for associate of science degree. Test score for fall-term admission must be received before first day of classes. Interview recommended. **Home schooled:** Statement describing home school structure and mission, transcript of courses and grades required. Records of all completed coursework plus documentation verifying proficiency in coursework (such as examples of writing, math skills). Portfolio beneficial for some coursework. Standardized test scores required; campus visit with interview important. **Learning Disabled:** Students evaluated on results of required college preparatory work. Documentation of disability important if seeking assistance from Student Resource Center.

High school preparation. College-preparatory program required. 11 units required. Required and recommended units include English 4, mathematics 3, social studies 2, science 2 (laboratory 2), foreign language 2, computer science 1 and academic electives 3. Social studies may include history. Computer applications, fine arts also recommended.

2015-2016 Annual costs. Tuition/fees: $7,480; $19,300 out-of-state. Room/board: $8,486. Books/supplies: $800. Personal expenses: $1,600. **Additional information:** New England Regional Student Program tuition is $9,990.

Financial aid. Non-need-based: Scholarships awarded for academics, athletics.

Application procedures. Admission: Closing date 8/15 (receipt date). $40 fee, may be waived for applicants with need. Admission notification on a rolling basis. Must reply by May 1 or within 2 week(s) if notified thereafter. **Financial aid:** Priority date 3/1; no closing date. FAFSA required. Applicants notified on a rolling basis starting 3/1.

Academics. Internships and/or cooperative education program available in business studies, recreation management, biology, environmental studies, and behavioral science. **Special study options:** Cooperative education, distance learning, double major, dual enrollment of high school students, independent study, internships, student-designed major, study abroad, teacher certification program. **Credit/placement by examination:** AP, CLEP, SAT, ACT, institutional tests. **Support services:** Learning center, reduced course load, remedial instruction, study skills assistance, tutoring, writing center.

Majors. Biology: General, ecology, marine. **Business:** General, accounting, business admin, hospitality admin, hospitality/recreation, marketing, office management, office/clerical, tourism promotion, tourism/travel. **Conservation:** General, environmental studies. **Education:** Elementary, secondary. **English:** English lit. **Health services:** Mental health services. **History:** General. **Liberal arts:** Arts/sciences. **Parks/recreation:** General, facilities management. **Psychology:** General. **Visual/performing arts:** General.

Most popular majors. Biology 16%, business/marketing 16%, education 7%, English 7%, liberal arts 12%, parks/recreation 11%, psychology 25%.

Technology on campus. 117 workstations in dormitories, library, computer center. Dormitories wired for high-speed internet access and linked to campus network. Commuter students can connect to campus network. Online course registration, online library, helpline, repair service, wireless network available.

Student life. Freshman orientation: Available. Preregistration for classes offered. Orientation in June, August, and January. **Policies:** Students over 21 may drink in their rooms. Firearms must be stored in safe in Resident Director's office. **Housing:** Guaranteed on-campus for all undergraduates. Coed dorms, special housing for disabled, themed housing available. $100 nonrefundable deposit. Pets allowed in dorm rooms. **Activities:** Bands, choral groups, dance, drama, literary magazine, music ensembles, radio station, student government, Newman Club, Students of Service.

Athletics. NAIA. **Intercollegiate:** Basketball, cross-country, soccer, volleyball W. **Intramural:** Basketball, cheerleading W, fencing, football (nontackle), soccer, softball W, water polo. **Team name:** Clippers.

Student services. Career counseling, student employment services, financial aid counseling, health services, on-campus daycare, personal counseling, placement for graduates, veterans' counselor.

Contact. E-mail: ummadmissions@maine.edu
Phone: (207) 255-1318 Toll-free number: (888) 468-6866
Fax: (207) 255-1363
David Dollins, Director of Admissions, University of Maine at Machias, 116 O'Brien Avenue, Machias, ME 04654-1397

University of Maine at Presque Isle
Presque Isle, Maine
www.umpi.edu

CB code: 3008

- Public 4-year university
- Commuter campus in small town
- 833 degree-seeking undergraduates: 21% part-time, 62% women, 3% African American, 2% Hispanic/Latino, 3% Native American, 3% Multiracial, non-Hispanic, 8% international
- 77% of applicants admitted
- Application essay required
- 45% graduate within 6 years

General. Founded in 1903. Regionally accredited. **Degrees:** 147 bachelor's, 31 associate awarded. **Location:** 165 miles from Bangor. **Calendar:** Semester, limited summer session. **Full-time faculty:** 42 total; 57% have terminal degrees, 5% minority, 48% women. **Part-time faculty:** 60 total; 23% have terminal degrees, 60% women. **Class size:** 71% < 20, 29% 20-39.

Freshman class profile. 1,442 applied, 1,112 admitted, 202 enrolled.

Mid 50% test scores		GPA 2.0-2.99:	34%
SAT critical reading:	390-530	Rank in top quarter:	15%
SAT math:	400-530	Rank in top tenth:	3%
SAT writing:	380-510	Return as sophomores:	65%
ACT composite:	18-23	Out-of-state:	1%
GPA 3.75 or higher:	23%	Live on campus:	36%
GPA 3.50-3.74:	5%	International:	8%
GPA 3.0-3.49:	35%		

Basis for selection. Admissions based on secondary school record, class rank, recommendations, and essay. Standardized tests are used to determine some merit awards and as one of several factors for placement. Interview recommended for academically borderline. Portfolio required of bachelor of fine arts applicants. **Home schooled:** Transcript of courses and grades, state high school equivalency certificate, letter of recommendation (nonparent) required.

High school preparation. College-preparatory program recommended. 16 units recommended. Recommended units include English 4, mathematics 3, social studies 3, science 2 (laboratory 2), foreign language 2 and academic electives 2. Medical laboratory technology and nursing programs: 4 English, 1 biology w/lab, 1 chemistry w/lab, 2 math, 1 social studies, 6 electives, totaling 15.

2015-2016 Annual costs. Tuition/fees: $7,436; $10,736 out-of-state. Room/board: $8,044. Books/supplies: $900. Personal expenses: $1,100. **Additional information:** New England Regional Student Program tuition is $9,900.

2015-2016 Financial aid. Need-based: 166 full-time freshmen applied for aid; 141 deemed to have need; 141 received aid. Average need met was 87%. Average scholarship/grant was $8,150; average loan $4,223. 60% of total undergraduate aid awarded as scholarships/grants, 40% as loans/jobs. **Non-need-based:** Awarded to 54 full-time undergraduates, including 23 freshmen. Scholarships awarded for academics.

Application procedures. Admission: No deadline. $40 fee, may be waived for applicants with need. Admission notification on a rolling basis beginning on or about 10/1. **Financial aid:** Priority date 4/1; no closing date. FAFSA required. Applicants notified on a rolling basis starting 3/1; must reply within 2 week(s) of notification.

Academics. Special study options: Accelerated study, combined bachelor's/graduate degree, distance learning, double major, dual enrollment of high school students, exchange student, honors, independent study, internships, study abroad, teacher certification program. **Credit/placement by examination:** AP, CLEP, IB, SAT, ACT, institutional tests. 15 credit hours maximum toward associate degree, 30 toward bachelor's. Scores of 3, 4, and 5 acceptable on AP tests; hours awarded decided on case-by-case basis. **Support services:** Learning center, reduced course load, remedial instruction, study skills assistance, tutoring, writing center.

Majors. Biology: General. **Business:** Business admin. **Conservation:** Environmental studies. **Education:** General, art, elementary, physical, secondary. **English:** English lit. **Health services:** Athletic training. **History:** General. **Human services:** Social work. **Liberal arts:** Arts/sciences. **Math:** General. **Physical sciences:** Geology. **Protective services:** Criminal justice. **Psychology:** General. **Social sciences:** Political science. **Visual/performing arts:** Art, studio arts.

Most popular majors. Biology 6%, business/marketing 16%, education 18%, liberal arts 20%, psychology 9%, public administration/social services 6%.

Technology on campus. 120 workstations in library, computer center, student center. Dormitories wired for high-speed internet access and linked to campus network. Commuter students can connect to campus network. Online course registration, helpline, wireless network available.

Student life. Freshman orientation: Available. Preregistration for classes offered. Held the Friday prior to opening. **Policies:** Smoking-free campus. **Housing:** Guaranteed on-campus for all undergraduates. Coed dorms, special housing for disabled, apartments available. **Activities:** Campus ministries, choral groups, dance, international student organizations, radio station, student government, student newspaper, Campus Crusade for Christ, Fellowship of Christian Athletes, Presque Isle Student Ministries, College Republicans, College Democrats, Kappa Delta Phi, Kappa Delta Phi NAS, Phi Eta Sigma National Honors Society, international students club.

Athletics. NCAA. **Intercollegiate:** Baseball M, basketball, cross-country, golf M, skiing, soccer, softball W, volleyball W. **Intramural:** Baseball, basketball, soccer, softball, tennis, volleyball. **Team name:** Owls.

Student services. Alcohol/substance abuse counseling, chaplain/spiritual director, career counseling, student employment services, financial aid counseling, health services, on-campus daycare, personal counseling. **Physically disabled:** Services for visually, speech, hearing impaired.

Contact. E-mail: admissions@umpi.edu
Phone: (207) 768-9532 Fax: (207) 768-9777
Erin Benson, Director of Admissions, University of Maine at Presque Isle, 181 Main Street, Presque Isle, ME 04769

University of New England
Biddeford, Maine
www.une.edu

CB member
CB code: 3751

- Private 4-year university
- Residential campus in small city
- 2,271 degree-seeking undergraduates: 1% part-time, 71% women, 1% African American, 3% Asian American, 1% Multi-racial, non-Hispanic
- 3,947 degree-seeking graduate students
- 85% of applicants admitted
- SAT or ACT (ACT writing recommended) required
- 65% graduate within 6 years; 40% enter graduate study

General. Founded in 1831. Regionally accredited. **Degrees:** 439 bachelor's awarded; master's, professional, doctoral offered. **ROTC:** Army. **Location:** Biddeford campus is 15 miles from Portland. **Calendar:** Semester, limited summer session. **Full-time faculty:** 265 total; 76% have terminal degrees, 8% minority, 53% women. **Part-time faculty:** 270 total; 55% have terminal degrees, 5% minority, 57% women. **Class size:** 48% < 20, 40% 20-39, 7% 40-49, 5% 50-99. **Special facilities:** Center for the Health Sciences.

Freshman class profile. 4,416 applied, 3,760 admitted, 626 enrolled.

Mid 50% test scores			
SAT critical reading:	480-580	GPA 3.0-3.49:	37%
SAT math:	480-590	GPA 2.0-2.99:	19%
SAT writing:	470-560	End year in good standing:	95%
ACT composite:	20-29	Return as sophomores:	75%
GPA 3.75 or higher:	22%	Out-of-state:	72%
GPA 3.50-3.74:	21%	Live on campus:	96%

Basis for selection. School achievement is most important, Standardized test scores important. School, community activities considered. Exposure to healthcare careers recommended if seeking admission to health science majors. Rigor of curriculum considered. Essay recommended. Interview required for nursing program, recommended for all, strongly recommended for academically weaker students. **Home schooled:** Statement describing home school structure and mission, transcript of courses and grades required.

High school preparation. College-preparatory program recommended. 16 units required; 20 recommended. Required and recommended units include English 4, mathematics 3-4, social studies 1-2, history 1-2, science 2-3 (laboratory 2-3), foreign language 2 and academic electives 2-4.

2015-2016 Annual costs. Tuition/fees: $34,660. Room/board: $12,920. Books/supplies: $1,400. Personal expenses: $1,400.

Financial aid. Non-need-based: Scholarships awarded for academics.

Application procedures. Admission: Priority date 12/1; deadline 2/15 (postmark date). $40 fee, may be waived for applicants with need. Admission notification on a rolling basis beginning on or about 12/15. Must reply by May 1 or within 4 week(s) if notified thereafter. **Financial aid:** Priority date 5/1; no closing date. FAFSA required. Applicants notified on a rolling basis starting 2/1.

Academics. Special study options: Accelerated study, combined bachelor's/graduate degree, cooperative education, cross-registration, distance learning, double major, dual enrollment of high school students, honors, independent study, internships, liberal arts/career combination, student-designed major, study abroad, teacher certification program. Accelerated program available for certain majors such as Nursing, where incoming students already hold an Associate level degree/work as Registered Nurse. **Credit/placement by examination:** AP, CLEP, IB, SAT, ACT, institutional tests. **Support services:** Learning center, reduced course load, remedial instruction, study skills assistance, tutoring, writing center.

Majors. Biology: General, animal behavior, biochemistry, marine, neuroscience. **Business:** Business admin, communications. **Conservation:** Environmental science, environmental studies. **Education:** General, art, elementary. **English:** English lit. **Health services:** General, athletic training, dental hygiene, nursing (RN). **History:** General. **Human services:** Social work. **Liberal arts:** Arts/sciences. **Math:** General, applied. **Parks/recreation:** Exercise sciences, sports admin. **Physical sciences:** Chemistry. **Psychology:** General, psychobiology, social. **Social sciences:** Demography, political science, sociology. **Visual/performing arts:** Design.

Most popular majors. Biology 29%, health sciences 45%, parks/recreation 8%.

Technology on campus. 170 workstations in dormitories, library, computer center, student center. Dormitories wired for high-speed internet access and linked to campus network. Commuter students can connect to campus

network. Online course registration, online library, helpline, student web hosting, wireless network available.

Student life. Freshman orientation: Mandatory. Preregistration for classes offered. Varying sessions held over the summer for Fall starts. **Housing:** Guaranteed on-campus for freshmen. Coed dorms, single-sex dorms, special housing for disabled, gender-neutral housing, themed housing, wellness housing available. $200 partly refundable deposit, deadline 5/1. **Activities:** Bands, campus ministries, dance, drama, international student organizations, literary magazine, music ensembles, musical theater, student government, student newspaper, United Cross-Cultural club, Habitat for Humanity, college community mentoring, Gay/Straight (and In Between) Alliance.

Athletics. NCAA. Intercollegiate: Basketball, cross-country, field hockey W, golf M, ice hockey, lacrosse, soccer, softball W, swimming W, volleyball W. **Intramural:** Handball, racquetball, soccer, volleyball. **Team name:** Nor-easters.

Student services. Adult student services, alcohol/substance abuse counseling, chaplain/spiritual director, career counseling, student employment services, financial aid counseling, health services, minority student services, personal counseling, placement for graduates, veterans' counselor.

Contact. E-mail: admissions@une.edu
Phone: (207) 283-0170 ext. 2297 Toll-free number: (800) 477-4863
Fax: (207) 602-5900
Scott Steinberg, Dean of University Admission, University of New England, 11 Hills Beach Road, Biddeford, ME 04005

University of Southern Maine
Portland, Maine — CB member
www.usm.maine.edu — CB code: 3691

▶ Public 4-year university
▶ Commuter campus in small city
▶ 5,359 degree-seeking undergraduates: 31% part-time, 57% women, 4% African American, 2% Asian American, 2% Hispanic/Latino, 1% Native American, 3% Multi-racial, non-Hispanic, 1% international
▶ 1,417 degree-seeking graduate students
▶ 88% of applicants admitted
▶ SAT or ACT with writing, application essay required
▶ 33% graduate within 6 years

General. Founded in 1878. Regionally accredited. **Degrees:** 1,257 bachelor's awarded; master's, professional, doctoral offered. **ROTC:** Army, Air Force. **Location:** 110 miles from Boston. **Calendar:** Semester, extensive summer session. **Full-time faculty:** 248 total; 84% have terminal degrees, 7% minority, 48% women. **Part-time faculty:** 293 total; 20% have terminal degrees, 4% minority, 60% women. **Class size:** 50% <20, 42% 20-39, 4% 40-49, 3% 50-99, less than 1% >100. **Special facilities:** Planetarium, cartographic collection, Olympic-sized ice arena.

Freshman class profile. 3,402 applied, 2,986 admitted, 705 enrolled.

Mid 50% test scores		GPA 3.0-3.49:	37%
SAT critical reading:	420-550	GPA 2.0-2.99:	40%
SAT math:	440-550	Rank in top quarter:	26%
SAT writing:	430-540	Rank in top tenth:	5%
ACT composite:	19-25	Out-of-state:	23%
GPA 3.75 or higher:	11%	Live on campus:	63%
GPA 3.50-3.74:	9%	International:	1%

Basis for selection. Level and content of academic program with performance or achievement record, class rank, and standardized test scores most important. Counselor recommendation, essay, and experience outside classroom also important. Interview recommended for all. Audition required of music majors. **Home schooled:** Transcript of courses and grades, letter of recommendation (nonparent) required. SAT or ACT, annual assessment of courses, and GED required for financial aid purposes. **Learning Disabled:** Must be otherwise qualified for admission; may be asked to provide documentation.

High school preparation. 16 units required. Required and recommended units include English 4, mathematics 3, social studies 2-3, history 1, science 2-3 (laboratory 2-3).

2015-2016 Annual costs. Tuition/fees: $8,540; $20,900 out-of-state. Room/board: $9,400. Books/supplies: $1,346. **Additional information:** New England Regional Student Program tuition is $11,400.

2014-2015 Financial aid. Need-based: 654 full-time freshmen applied for aid; 523 deemed to have need; 522 received aid. Average need met was 73%. Average scholarship/grant was $7,212; average loan $5,845. 43% of total undergraduate aid awarded as scholarships/grants, 57% as loans/jobs. **Non-need-based:** Awarded to 235 full-time undergraduates, including 87 freshmen. Scholarships awarded for academics, music/drama, state residency.

Application procedures. Admission: Priority date 2/15; no deadline. $40 fee, may be waived for applicants with need. Admission notification on a rolling basis beginning on or about 1/1. **Financial aid:** Priority date 2/15; no closing date. FAFSA required. Applicants notified on a rolling basis starting 3/15; must reply by 5/1 or within 2 week(s) of notification.

Academics. Special study options: Combined bachelor's/graduate degree, cooperative education, cross-registration, distance learning, double major, dual enrollment of high school students, ESL, exchange student, honors, independent study, internships, liberal arts/career combination, student-designed major, study abroad, teacher certification program, weekend college. Preengineering program with University of Maine at Orono, living/learning scholars program, Greater Portland Alliance; cross registration with University of New England, St. Joseph's (Maine), Southern Maine Technical College, and Maine College of Art. **Credit/placement by examination:** AP, CLEP, IB, SAT, ACT, institutional tests. No numerical limit. Students must meet all course requirements and 30 credit residency for BA/BS and 15 credit residency for AA/AS degrees. **Support services:** Learning center, reduced course load, remedial instruction, study skills assistance, tutoring, writing center.

Honors college/program. Honors application required. Several course options available. Interdisciplinary curriculum with small seminar classes.

Majors. Area/ethnic studies: Women's. **Biology:** General, biochemistry, exercise physiology. **Business:** Accounting, accounting/finance, business admin, finance, marketing, tourism/travel. **Communications:** Communications/speech/rhetoric, media studies. **Computer sciences:** Computer science. **Conservation:** Environmental science, environmental studies. **Education:** Adult/continuing, art, elementary, music, technology/industrial arts, trade/industrial, voc/tech. **Engineering:** General, electrical, mechanical. **English:** English lit. **Foreign languages:** Linguistics. **Health services:** Athletic training, environmental health, nursing (RN), psychiatric nursing, recreational therapy. **History:** General. **Human services:** Social work. **Liberal arts:** Arts/sciences, humanities. **Math:** General. **Parks/recreation:** Exercise sciences, health/fitness. **Philosophy/religion:** Philosophy. **Physical sciences:** General, chemistry, physics. **Psychology:** General. **Social sciences:** Criminology, economics, political science, sociology. **Visual/performing arts:** Art, dramatic, music, music performance, studio arts.

Most popular majors. Business/marketing 19%, communications/journalism 6%, engineering/engineering technologies 6%, health sciences 19%, social sciences 13%.

Technology on campus. 219 workstations in dormitories, library, computer center, student center. Dormitories wired for high-speed internet access and linked to campus network. Commuter students can connect to campus network. Online course registration, online library, helpline, repair service, wireless network available.

Student life. Freshman orientation: Mandatory. Preregistration for classes offered. Sessions in summer and fall. **Policies:** Smoking is not allowed within 50 feet of any dormitory. **Housing:** Coed dorms, special housing for disabled, apartments, themed housing, wellness housing available. **Activities:** Bands, campus ministries, choral groups, dance, drama, international student organizations, literary magazine, music ensembles, Model UN, musical theater, opera, radio station, student government, student newspaper, symphony orchestra, American Indian student association, Environmental Coalition, College Republicans, Alliance of Sexual Diversity, Women's Forum, Bahai Association, ethnic student association.

Athletics. NCAA. Intercollegiate: Baseball M, basketball, cheerleading, cross-country, field hockey W, golf, ice hockey, lacrosse, soccer, softball W, tennis, track and field, volleyball W, wrestling M. **Intramural:** Basketball, cheerleading W, football (non-tackle), football (tackle) M, ice hockey, lacrosse, racquetball, rugby, sailing, skiing, soccer, softball, squash, table tennis, tennis, volleyball, weight lifting. **Team name:** Huskies.

Student services. Adult student services, alcohol/substance abuse counseling, chaplain/spiritual director, career counseling, services for economically disadvantaged, student employment services, financial aid counseling, health services, legal services, minority student services, personal counseling, placement for graduates, veterans' counselor, women's services. **Physically disabled:** Services for visually impaired, speech, hearing impaired.

Contact. E-mail: usmadm@usm.maine.edu
Phone: (207) 780-5670 Toll-free number: (800) 800-4876 ext. 5670
Fax: (207) 780-5640
Jonathan Barker, Director of Technology for Undergraduate Admission, University of Southern Maine, PO Box 9300, Portland, ME 04104

Maryland

Bowie State University

Bowie, Maryland — CB member
www.bowiestate.edu — CB code: 5401

- Public 4-year university
- Commuter campus in small city
- 4,298 degree-seeking undergraduates: 18% part-time, 62% women, 86% African American, 1% Asian American, 3% Hispanic/Latino, 4% Multiracial, non-Hispanic, 1% international
- 1,054 degree-seeking graduate students
- 53% of applicants admitted
- SAT or ACT (ACT writing optional) required
- 36% graduate within 6 years

General. Founded in 1865. Regionally accredited. Limited courses offered at off-site locations. **Degrees:** 801 bachelor's awarded; master's, doctoral offered. **ROTC:** Army, Air Force. **Location:** 25 miles from Baltimore, 20 miles from Washington, DC. **Calendar:** Semester, extensive summer session. **Full-time faculty:** 216 total; 95% have terminal degrees, 84% minority, 50% women. **Part-time faculty:** 192 total; 80% have terminal degrees, 90% minority, 54% women. **Class size:** 45% < 20, 50% 20-39, 5% 40-49, less than 1% 50-99. **Special facilities:** NASA operations and control center, art gallery, green house, super computer center (limited access).

Freshman class profile. 3,180 applied, 1,680 admitted, 591 enrolled.

Mid 50% test scores		GPA 3.0-3.49:	22%
SAT critical reading:	410-490	GPA 2.0-2.99:	63%
SAT math:	400-470	Out-of-state:	13%
SAT writing:	390-470	Live on campus:	95%
ACT composite:	15-20	International:	1%
GPA 3.75 or higher:	3%	Fraternities:	3%
GPA 3.50-3.74:	6%	Sororities:	2%

Basis for selection. School achievement record in college-prep curriculum, test scores, minimum GPA of 2.0, counselor/school recommendation important. Audition required for music program. Portfolio required for art program. Praxis I required for education program. **Home schooled:** Statement describing home school structure and mission required.

High school preparation. Required units include English 4, mathematics 3, social studies 1, history 2, science 3 and foreign language 2.

2015-2016 Annual costs. Tuition/fees: $7,657; $18,140 out-of-state. Room/board: $10,850. Books/supplies: $1,338. Personal expenses: $1,804.

2014-2015 Financial aid. Need-based: 461 full-time freshmen applied for aid; 460 deemed to have need; 460 received aid. Average need met was 48%. Average scholarship/grant was $7,856; average loan $3,368. 50% of total undergraduate aid awarded as scholarships/grants, 50% as loans/jobs. **Non-need-based:** Awarded to 2,349 full-time undergraduates, including 434 freshmen. Scholarships awarded for academics, alumni affiliation, art, athletics, music/drama, state residency.

Application procedures. Admission: No deadline. $40 fee, may be waived for applicants with need. Admission notification on a rolling basis. **Financial aid:** Closing date 3/1. FAFSA required. Applicants notified on a rolling basis starting 4/1; must reply within 2 week(s) of notification.

Academics. Special study options: Combined bachelor's/graduate degree, cooperative education, cross-registration, distance learning, double major, dual enrollment of high school students, exchange student, honors, independent study, internships, liberal arts/career combination, study abroad, teacher certification program. Dual degree programs in engineering and dentistry with cooperating universities. **Credit/placement by examination:** AP, CLEP, institutional tests. 60 credit hours maximum toward bachelor's degree. **Support services:** Learning center, pre-admission summer program, reduced course load, remedial instruction, tutoring, writing center.

Majors. Biology: General. **Business:** Business admin. **Communications technology:** Radio/TV. **Computer sciences:** Computer science. **Education:** Elementary, kindergarten/preschool, science. **English:** English lit. **Health services:** Nursing (RN). **History:** General. **Human services:** Social work. **Math:** General. **Psychology:** General. **Social sciences:** Sociology. **Visual/performing arts:** Art, dramatic. **Work/family studies:** Child development.

Most popular majors. Business/marketing 24%, communication technologies 15%, English 16%, health sciences 6%, psychology 9%, social sciences 8%.

Technology on campus. 150 workstations in dormitories, library, computer center. Dormitories wired for high-speed internet access and linked to campus network. Commuter students can connect to campus network. Online course registration, online library, helpline, repair service, wireless network available.

Student life. Freshman orientation: Mandatory, $75 fee. Preregistration for classes offered. One-day session in the 2nd or 3rd week of August. **Policies:** Zero tolerance policy for illegal substance use and violence. Freshmen not permitted cars on campus. **Housing:** Coed dorms, single-sex dorms, apartments, wellness housing available. $150 fully refundable deposit, deadline 5/29. **Activities:** Bands, campus ministries, choral groups, dance, drama, international student organizations, music ensembles, musical theater, radio station, student government, student newspaper, TV station, NAACP, Greater Washington Urban League chapter, commuter senate.

Athletics. NCAA. **Intercollegiate:** Basketball, bowling W, cross-country, football (tackle) M, softball W, tennis W, track and field, volleyball W. **Intramural:** Basketball, football (non-tackle), golf, gymnastics, racquetball, soccer, softball, swimming, table tennis, tennis, volleyball, weight lifting. **Team name:** Bulldogs.

Student services. Adult student services, alcohol/substance abuse counseling, chaplain/spiritual director, career counseling, student employment services, financial aid counseling, health services, personal counseling, placement for graduates, veterans' counselor. **Physically disabled:** Services for visually, hearing impaired.

Contact. Phone: (301) 860-3415 Fax: (301) 860-3438
Angela, Acting-Director of Admission, Bowie State University, 14000 Jericho Park Road, Bowie, MD 20715

Capitol Technology University

Laurel, Maryland
www.capitol-college.edu — CB code: 5101

- Private 4-year business and engineering college
- Commuter campus in large town
- 441 degree-seeking undergraduates
- SAT or ACT (ACT writing optional), application essay required

General. Founded in 1964. Regionally accredited. **Degrees:** 85 bachelor's, 3 associate awarded; master's, doctoral offered. **ROTC:** Army. **Location:** 19 miles from Washington, DC, 22 miles from Baltimore. **Calendar:** Semester, limited summer session. **Full-time faculty:** 14 total. **Part-time faculty:** 62 total. **Special facilities:** Video lab, interactive computer classrooms, two engineering labs, telecommunications lab.

Basis for selection. Academic preparation, school record and test scores most important. Mathematics foundation necessary for successful completion of programs. Interview and essay recommended.

High school preparation. 20 units required. Required and recommended units include English 4, mathematics 3-4, social studies 2, history 2, science 1-3 (laboratory 1-2) and academic electives 2-3. Math units include algebra I, geometry, algebra II/trigonometry. Calculus recommended for advanced standing.

2015-2016 Annual costs. Tuition/fees: $23,508. Room only: $5,180. Books/supplies: $1,200. Personal expenses: $1,900. **Additional information:** On-campus room charge is for triple occupancy room.

Financial aid. Non-need-based: Scholarships awarded for academics, alumni affiliation, leadership, minority status.

Application procedures. Admission: Priority date 5/1; no deadline. $25 fee, may be waived for applicants with need, free for online applicants. Admission notification on a rolling basis beginning on or about 3/1. Must reply by May 1 or within 3 week(s) if notified thereafter. **Financial aid:** Priority date 3/1; no closing date. FAFSA, institutional form required. Applicants notified on a rolling basis starting 4/1; must reply by 5/1 or within 3 week(s) of notification.

Academics. Special study options: Combined bachelor's/graduate degree, cooperative education, distance learning, double major, independent study, liberal arts/career combination, weekend college. **Credit/placement by examination:** AP, CLEP, institutional tests. **Support services:** Learning center, pre-admission summer program, reduced course load, remedial instruction, tutoring.

Majors. Business: Business admin. **Computer sciences:** Computer science. **Engineering:** Computer, electrical, software.

Most popular majors. Business/marketing 12%, computer/information sciences 29%, engineering/engineering technologies 59%.

Technology on campus. 60 workstations in library, computer center. Dormitories wired for high-speed internet access and linked to campus network. Helpline, wireless network available.

Student life. Freshman orientation: Mandatory. Preregistration for classes offered. **Housing:** Coed dorms available. $200 deposit, deadline 5/1. **Activities:** Drama, literary magazine, radio station, student government, student newspaper, computer club, chess club, robotics club, music club, Society of Black Engineers, Society of Women Engineers.

Athletics. Intramural: Basketball M, boxing M, fencing M, golf M, soccer M, softball M, table tennis, tennis, track and field, volleyball, water polo.

Student services. Adult student services, career counseling, student employment services, personal counseling, placement for graduates, veterans' counselor.

Contact. E-mail: admissions@capitol-college.edu
Phone: (301) 369-2800 Toll-free number: (800) 950-1992
Fax: (301) 953-1442
George Walls, Director of Admissions, Capitol Technology University, 11301 Springfield Road, Laurel, MD 20708

Coppin State University
Baltimore, Maryland   **CB member**
www.coppin.edu   **CB code: 5122**

- Public 4-year liberal arts college
- Commuter campus in very large city
- 2,885 degree-seeking undergraduates
- 463 graduate students
- SAT or ACT (ACT writing optional) required

General. Founded in 1900. Regionally accredited. Manages Rosemont Elementary School; educational corridor between Coppin and selected elementary, middle, and high schools; mentorship program with elementary students. **Degrees:** 416 bachelor's awarded; master's offered. **ROTC:** Army. **Location:** 50 miles from Washington, DC. **Calendar:** Semester, extensive summer session. **Full-time faculty:** 127 total. **Part-time faculty:** 144 total.

Freshman class profile.

GPA 3.75 or higher:	3%	GPA 2.0-2.99:	61%
GPA 3.50-3.74:	5%	Out-of-state:	16%
GPA 3.0-3.49:	20%		

Basis for selection. 2.5 GPA and predictive index based on test scores and school achievement record. Essay recommended. Interview recommended for nursing majors. Portfolio recommended for art majors. **Home schooled:** Program must be certified by Maryland Department of Education.

High school preparation. 16 units required. Required units include English 4, mathematics 3, social studies 3, science 2 (laboratory 2) and foreign language 2. 2 years of advanced tech program courses can be substituted for foreign language requirement.

2015-2016 Annual costs. Tuition/fees: $6,362; $11,886 out-of-state. Room/board: $9,359. Books/supplies: $700. Personal expenses: $3,085.

Financial aid. Non-need-based: Scholarships awarded for academics, alumni affiliation, athletics, ROTC, state residency. **Additional information:** Funds allocated by State of Maryland for minority students enrolled for at least 6 credits who are Maryland residents and US citizens (Minority Grant).

Application procedures. Admission: Closing date 7/15. $35 fee, may be waived for applicants with need. Admission notification on a rolling basis beginning on or about 3/15. **Financial aid:** Priority date 3/1; no closing date. FAFSA required. Applicants notified on a rolling basis starting 4/15; must reply within 2 week(s) of notification.

Academics. Special study options: Accelerated study, combined bachelor's/graduate degree, cooperative education, distance learning, double major, dual enrollment of high school students, external degree, honors, independent study, internships, liberal arts/career combination, study abroad, teacher certification program, weekend college. 3-2 programs in engineering, pharmacy, dentistry, physical therapy. **Credit/placement by examination:** AP, CLEP, IB, SAT, institutional tests. 30 credit hours maximum toward bachelor's

degree. **Support services:** Learning center, pre-admission summer program, remedial instruction, study skills assistance, tutoring, writing center.

Majors. Biology: General. **Business:** Management science. **Computer sciences:** Computer science. **Education:** Biology, chemistry, early childhood, elementary, mathematics, secondary, special ed. **English:** English lit. **Health services:** Health information management, nursing (RN). **History:** General. **Human services:** Social work. **Liberal arts:** Arts/sciences. **Math:** General. **Parks/recreation:** Sports admin. **Physical sciences:** Chemistry. **Protective services:** Criminal justice. **Psychology:** General. **Social sciences:** General, political science, sociology. **Visual/performing arts:** Art.

Technology on campus. 371 workstations in dormitories, library, computer center, student center. Dormitories wired for high-speed internet access and linked to campus network. Commuter students can connect to campus network. Online course registration, online library, helpline, repair service, student web hosting, wireless network available.

Student life. Freshman orientation: Mandatory. Preregistration for classes offered. **Housing:** Coed dorms, special housing for disabled, wellness housing available. $150 deposit. **Activities:** Campus ministries, choral groups, dance, drama, film society, international student organizations, music ensembles, radio station, student government, student newspaper, TV station, criminal justice club, gospel choir, history club, psychology club, Thurgood Marshall Club, social work association.

Athletics. NCAA. Intercollegiate: Baseball M, basketball, bowling W, cheerleading W, cross-country, golf W, softball W, tennis, track and field, volleyball W. **Intramural:** Basketball, football (non-tackle), softball, tennis, volleyball. **Team name:** Eagles.

Student services. Adult student services, alcohol/substance abuse counseling, career counseling, services for economically disadvantaged, student employment services, financial aid counseling, health services, minority student services, personal counseling, placement for graduates, veterans' counselor, women's services. **Physically disabled:** Services for visually, hearing impaired.

Contact. E-mail: admissions@coppin.edu
Phone: (410) 951-3600 Toll-free number: (800) 635-3674
Fax: (410) 523-7351
Michelle Gross, Director of Admissions, Coppin State University, 2500 West North Avenue, Baltimore, MD 21216

Frostburg State University
Frostburg, Maryland   **CB member**
www.frostburg.edu   **CB code: 5402**

- Public 4-year university and teachers college
- Residential campus in small town
- 4,850 degree-seeking undergraduates: 15% part-time, 51% women, 31% African American, 2% Asian American, 5% Hispanic/Latino, 4% Multiracial, non-Hispanic, 1% international
- 768 degree-seeking graduate students
- 63% of applicants admitted
- SAT or ACT (ACT writing optional) required
- 53% graduate within 6 years

General. Founded in 1898. Regionally accredited. Center in Hagerstown offers upper-division undergraduate and graduate courses. **Degrees:** 1,028 bachelor's awarded; master's, doctoral offered. **Location:** 150 miles from Baltimore,150 miles from Washington DC. **Calendar:** Semester, limited summer session. **Full-time faculty:** 248 total; 91% have terminal degrees, 13% minority, 41% women. **Part-time faculty:** 133 total; 16% have terminal degrees, 4% minority, 54% women. **Class size:** 47% < 20, 47% 20-39, 3% 40-49, 3% 50-99, less than 1% >100. **Special facilities:** Planetarium, arboretum, electron microscope, exploratorium.

Freshman class profile. 3,911 applied, 2,481 admitted, 933 enrolled.

Mid 50% test scores			
SAT critical reading:	430-530	GPA 2.0-2.99:	46%
SAT math:	430-530	Rank in top quarter:	27%
SAT writing:	410-510	Rank in top tenth:	9%
ACT composite:	17-22	Return as sophomores:	77%
GPA 3.75 or higher:	14%	Out-of-state:	5%
GPA 3.50-3.74:	10%	Live on campus:	76%
GPA 3.0-3.49:	30%	International:	2%

Basis for selection. High school record and SAT/ACT most important. Interview recommended. Audition required of music majors. Portfolio required of art majors.

High school preparation. 18 units required. Required units include English 4, mathematics 4, social studies 3, science 3 (laboratory 2) and foreign language 2.

2015-2016 Annual costs. Tuition/fees: $8,488; $20,588 out-of-state. Room/board: $8,672. Books/supplies: $750. Personal expenses: $900.

2014-2015 Financial aid. Need-based: 854 full-time freshmen applied for aid; 631 deemed to have need; 630 received aid. Average need met was 60%. Average scholarship/grant was $7,515; average loan $3,217. 63% of total undergraduate aid awarded as scholarships/grants, 37% as loans/jobs. **Non-need-based:** Awarded to 1,606 full-time undergraduates, including 340 freshmen. Scholarships awarded for academics, leadership, minority status.

Application procedures. Admission: No deadline. $30 fee, may be waived for applicants with need. Admission notification on a rolling basis beginning on or about 11/1. Must reply by May 1 or within 4 week(s) if notified thereafter. **Financial aid:** Priority date 3/1; no closing date. FAFSA required. Applicants notified on a rolling basis starting 3/15; must reply within 3 week(s) of notification.

Academics. Special study options: Combined bachelor's/graduate degree, distance learning, double major, dual enrollment of high school students, honors, independent study, internships, study abroad, teacher certification program. International student exchange program, dual degree program, combined bachelor's program. **Credit/placement by examination:** AP, CLEP, IB, institutional tests. 30 credit hours maximum toward bachelor's degree. **Support services:** Learning center, reduced course load, remedial instruction, tutoring, writing center.

Majors. Architecture: Urban/community planning. **Biology:** General. **Business:** Accounting, business admin. **Communications:** Communications/speech/rhetoric. **Computer sciences:** General, information systems, information technology, security. **Conservation:** General, environmental studies, fisheries, wildlife/wilderness. **Education:** Early childhood, elementary, English, mathematics, multi-level teacher, music, physical, social science. **Engineering:** General. **English:** English lit, rhetoric/composition. **Foreign languages:** General. **Health services:** Nursing (RN), predental, premedicine, prenursing, prepharmacy, preveterinary. **History:** General. **Human services:** Social work. **Liberal arts:** Arts/sciences. **Math:** General. **Parks/recreation:** General, exercise sciences, health/fitness, sports admin. **Philosophy/religion:** Philosophy. **Physical sciences:** Chemistry, physics. **Protective services:** Police science. **Psychology:** General. **Social sciences:** General, economics, geography, international relations, political science, sociology. **Visual/performing arts:** General, commercial/advertising art, dramatic, music, studio arts.

Most popular majors. Biology 7%, business/marketing 13%, education 9%, health sciences 10%, liberal arts 7%, parks/recreation 6%, psychology 9%, social sciences 7%.

Technology on campus. 668 workstations in dormitories, library, computer center, student center. Dormitories wired for high-speed internet access and linked to campus network. Commuter students can connect to campus network. Online course registration, online library, helpline, wireless network available.

Student life. Freshman orientation: Mandatory. Preregistration for classes offered. **Housing:** Coed dorms, single-sex dorms, special housing for disabled, wellness housing available. $100 deposit. **Activities:** Bands, campus ministries, choral groups, dance, drama, literary magazine, music ensembles, Model UN, radio station, student government, student newspaper, TV station, social, religious, political, and ethnic organizations.

Athletics. NCAA. **Intercollegiate:** Baseball M, basketball, cross-country, diving, field hockey W, football (tackle) M, lacrosse, soccer, softball W, swimming, tennis, track and field, volleyball W. **Intramural:** Basketball, field hockey, football (tackle), golf, lacrosse, racquetball, rugby M, soccer, softball, table tennis, tennis, volleyball, weight lifting, wrestling M. **Team name:** Bobcats.

Student services. Chaplain/spiritual director, career counseling, student employment services, health services, minority student services, personal counseling, placement for graduates, veterans' counselor. **Physically disabled:** Services for visually, speech, hearing impaired.

Contact. E-mail: fsuadmissions@frostburg.edu
Phone: (301) 687-4201 Fax: (301) 687-7074
Patricia Gregory, Director of Admissions, Frostburg State University, 101 Braddock Road, Frostburg, MD 21532-1099

Goucher College
Baltimore, Maryland
www.goucher.edu

CB member
CB code: 5257

- Private 4-year liberal arts college
- Residential campus in small city
- 1,466 degree-seeking undergraduates: 1% part-time, 68% women, 12% African American, 4% Asian American, 9% Hispanic/Latino, 4% Multiracial, non-Hispanic, 3% international
- 445 degree-seeking graduate students
- 78% of applicants admitted
- Application essay required
- 69% graduate within 6 years; 32% enter graduate study

General. Founded in 1885. Regionally accredited. **Degrees:** 327 bachelor's awarded; master's offered. **ROTC:** Army, Air Force. **Location:** 8 miles from downtown Baltimore. **Calendar:** Semester, limited summer session. **Full-time faculty:** 138 total; 88% have terminal degrees, 15% minority, 61% women. **Part-time faculty:** 47 total; 26% have terminal degrees, 6% minority, 64% women. **Class size:** 72% < 20, 27% 20-39, less than 1% 40-49, less than 1% 50-99. **Special facilities:** Equestrian stables and riding areas, community garden, wooded trails, center for community service programming, research and teaching labs, international commons to facilitate cultural exchange, three multi-purpose performance spaces, robotics lab, observatory, advanced teaching labs for physics and computer science, research labs for math, physics, and psychology, technology/learning center, international technology and media center, centers for writing, math, and politics.

Freshman class profile. 3,577 applied, 2,777 admitted, 390 enrolled.

Mid 50% test scores			
SAT critical reading:	500-630	GPA 2.0-2.99:	37%
SAT math:	480-590	Rank in top quarter:	47%
SAT writing:	500-610	Rank in top tenth:	22%
ACT composite:	23-28	End year in good standing:	96%
GPA 3.75 or higher:	14%	Return as sophomores:	82%
GPA 3.50-3.74:	16%	Out-of-state:	73%
GPA 3.0-3.49:	33%	Live on campus:	98%
		International:	4%

Basis for selection. All credentials are carefully reviewed, with particular attention paid to personal qualities and intellectual promise. Offers Common Application option. Institution has an application option requesting student-submitted videos as the decisive factor for admission. Students may choose not to submit transcripts, test scores, and other traditional application materials. Instead, applicants may send institution a straightforward, two-minute video about how they see themselves flourishing at the college. Interview recommended. **Home schooled:** Statement describing home school structure and mission, transcript of courses and grades, state high school equivalency certificate, letter of recommendation (nonparent) required.

High school preparation. College-preparatory program recommended. 16 units required; 20 recommended. Required and recommended units include English 4, mathematics 3-4, social studies 3, science 2-3 (laboratory 2-3), foreign language 2-4 and academic electives 2.

2015-2016 Annual costs. Tuition/fees: $42,180. Room/board: $12,460. Books/supplies: $1,000. Personal expenses: $868.

2015-2016 Financial aid. Need-based: 312 full-time freshmen applied for aid; 265 deemed to have need; 265 received aid. Average need met was 80%. Average scholarship/grant was $29,973; average loan $2,995. 82% of total undergraduate aid awarded as scholarships/grants, 18% as loans/jobs. **Non-need-based:** Awarded to 554 full-time undergraduates, including 169 freshmen. Scholarships awarded for academics, art, music/drama.

Application procedures. Admission: Priority date 2/1; deadline 8/1 (postmark date). $55 fee, may be waived for applicants with need. Application must be submitted online. Admission notification by 4/1. Admission notification on a rolling basis. Must reply by May 1 or within 2 week(s) if notified thereafter. **Financial aid:** Priority date 2/1, closing date 4/1. FAFSA, CSS PROFILE required. Applicants notified on a rolling basis starting 3/1; must reply by 5/1 or within 2 week(s) of notification.

Academics. Special study options: Combined bachelor's/graduate degree, cross-registration, distance learning, double major, dual enrollment of high school students, independent study, internships, student-designed major, study abroad, teacher certification program. Community-based service, service learning. **Credit/placement by examination:** AP, CLEP, institutional tests. 30 credit hours maximum toward bachelor's degree. **Support services:** Learning center, reduced course load, study skills assistance, tutoring, writing center.

Majors. Area/ethnic studies: American, women's. **Biology:** General, Biochemistry/molecular biology. **Business:** Business admin. **Communications:**

Communications/speech/rhetoric. **Computer sciences:** General. **Conservation:** Environmental studies. **Education:** Elementary, special ed. **English:** English lit. **Foreign languages:** French, Russian, Spanish. **History:** General. **Math:** General. **Philosophy/religion:** Philosophy, religion. **Physical sciences:** Chemistry, physics. **Psychology:** General. **Social sciences:** Anthropology, economics, international relations, political science, sociology, sociology/anthropology. **Visual/performing arts:** Art history/conservation, dance, dramatic, music, studio arts.

Most popular majors. Business/marketing 6%, communications/journalism 6%, English 6%, foreign language 8%, psychology 12%, social sciences 15%, visual/performing arts 11%.

Technology on campus. 246 workstations in library. Dormitories wired for high-speed internet access and linked to campus network. Commuter students can connect to campus network. Online course registration, online library, helpline, student web hosting, wireless network available.

Student life. Freshman orientation: Mandatory. Preregistration for classes offered. Five-day program held in August, just prior to start of classes. **Housing:** Guaranteed on-campus for freshmen. Coed dorms, single-sex dorms, special housing for disabled, apartments, gender-neutral housing, themed housing, wellness housing available. $100 nonrefundable deposit, deadline 5/1. Quiet, art, and language houses available. **Activities:** Bands, campus ministries, choral groups, dance, drama, film society, international student organizations, literary magazine, music ensembles, Model UN, musical theater, opera, radio station, student government, student newspaper, symphony orchestra, TV station, Umoja Black Student Alliance, Hispanic Organization for Learning and Awareness, Asian Student Union, Goucher Christian Fellowship, Hillel, Goucher International Student Association, Model Senate, Roosevelt Institute, Rotaract Club.

Athletics. NCAA. **Intercollegiate:** Basketball, cross-country, equestrian, field hockey W, lacrosse, soccer, swimming, tennis, track and field, volleyball W. **Intramural:** Basketball, soccer, softball, ultimate frisbee. **Team name:** Gophers.

Student services. Adult student services, alcohol/substance abuse counseling, chaplain/spiritual director, career counseling, services for economically disadvantaged, student employment services, financial aid counseling, health services, minority student services, personal counseling, placement for graduates, veterans' counselor, women's services. **Physically disabled:** Services for visually, hearing impaired.

Contact. E-mail: admissions@goucher.edu
Phone: (410) 337-6100 Toll-free number: (800) 468-2437
Fax: (410) 337-6354
Carlton Surbeck, Director of Admissions, Goucher College, 1021 Dulaney Valley Road, Baltimore, MD 21204-2753

Hood College
Frederick, Maryland **CB member**
www.hood.edu **CB code: 5296**

⭢ Private 4-year liberal arts college
⭢ Residential campus in small city
⭢ 1,246 degree-seeking undergraduates: 6% part-time, 63% women, 12% African American, 3% Asian American, 9% Hispanic/Latino, 5% Multiracial, non-Hispanic, 2% international
⭢ 852 degree-seeking graduate students
⭢ 79% of applicants admitted
⭢ Application essay required
⭢ 63% graduate within 6 years; 31% enter graduate study

General. Founded in 1893. Regionally accredited. **Degrees:** 352 bachelor's awarded; master's, professional offered. **ROTC:** Army. **Location:** 52 miles from Baltimore; 52 miles from Washington, DC. **Calendar:** Semester, limited summer session. **Full-time faculty:** 100 total; 95% have terminal degrees, 18% minority, 58% women. **Part-time faculty:** 164 total; 35% have terminal degrees, 6% minority, 57% women. **Class size:** 75% < 20, 24% 20-39, less than 1% 40-49. **Special facilities:** Psychology and preschool laboratories, observatory, trading room, mock trial courtroom.

Freshman class profile. 1,636 applied, 1,286 admitted, 258 enrolled.

Mid 50% test scores			
SAT critical reading:	470-600	**GPA 2.0-2.99:**	13%
SAT math:	470-600	**Rank in top quarter:**	42%
SAT writing:	460-570	**Rank in top tenth:**	21%
ACT composite:	19-27	**End year in good standing:**	80%
GPA 3.75 or higher:	25%	**Return as sophomores:**	75%
GPA 3.50-3.74:	27%	**Out-of-state:**	29%
GPA 3.0-3.49:	35%	**Live on campus:**	83%
		International:	2%

Basis for selection. High school record, class rank, test scores important. Recommendations, contributions to school, family and community, essay considered. SAT/ACT optional. Interview recommended. **Home schooled:** Interview, letter of recommendation (nonparent) required. Must interview and present bibliography of all reading materials used; two recommendations; partial portfolio of work.

High school preparation. College-preparatory program required. 16 units required; 21 recommended. Required and recommended units include English 4, mathematics 3-4, social studies 3, history 2, science 3-4 (laboratory 2), foreign language 2-3, computer science 1, visual/performing arts 1 and academic electives 1.

2015-2016 Annual costs. Tuition/fees: $35,150. Room/board: $11,840. Books/supplies: $1,200. Personal expenses: $1,550.

2015-2016 Financial aid. Need-based: 233 full-time freshmen applied for aid; 197 deemed to have need; 197 received aid. Average need met was 78%. Average scholarship/grant was $25,594; average loan $3,728. 77% of total undergraduate aid awarded as scholarships/grants, 23% as loans/jobs. **Non-need-based:** Awarded to 375 full-time undergraduates, including 92 freshmen. Scholarships awarded for academics, alumni affiliation, leadership, minority status, music/drama, ROTC, state residency.

Application procedures. Admission: Priority date 2/15; no deadline. $35 fee, may be waived for applicants with need, free for online applicants. Admission notification on a rolling basis beginning on or about 10/1. Must reply by May 1 or within 2 week(s) if notified thereafter. Rolling admission offered. Admission decisions will be mailed within two weeks of receipt of completed application file. First round of admission decisions will be mailed on October 1. Students are recommended to apply prior to March 1; however, decisions will continue to be made after March 1 based on availability of space in the first-year class. **Financial aid:** Priority date 2/15; no closing date. FAFSA, institutional form required. Applicants notified on a rolling basis starting 3/1; must reply by 5/1 or within 4 week(s) of notification.

Academics. Students in all fields may earn academic credits for internships. Opportunities available for students to earn degree in 3 years, 2 degrees in 4 years, or bachelor's and master's in 5 years. **Special study options:** Combined bachelor's/graduate degree, double major, dual enrollment of high school students, honors, independent study, internships, liberal arts/career combination, semester at sea, student-designed major, study abroad, teacher certification program, Washington semester. **Credit/placement by examination:** AP, CLEP, IB, SAT, ACT, institutional tests. 30 credit hours maximum toward bachelor's degree. **Support services:** Learning center, pre-admission summer program, reduced course load, remedial instruction, study skills assistance, tutoring, writing center.

Honors college/program. We have a highly selective Honors Program that admits a limited number of outstanding students each year. Students take two honors seminars their freshman year augmented by field trips.

Majors. Area/ethnic studies: Latin American, Near/Middle Eastern. **Biology:** General, biochemistry. **Business:** Accounting, business admin. **Communications:** General, public relations. **Computer sciences:** Computer science. **Conservation:** Environmental studies. **Education:** Early childhood, special ed. **English:** English lit. **Foreign languages:** French, German, Spanish. **History:** General. **Human services:** Social work. **Math:** General. **Philosophy/religion:** Philosophy, religion. **Physical sciences:** Chemistry. **Protective services:** Criminal justice. **Psychology:** General. **Social sciences:** Economics, political science, sociology. **Visual/performing arts:** Art, music.

Most popular majors. Biology 8%, business/marketing 7%, communications/journalism 6%, education 11%, English 8%, history 6%, psychology 9%, social sciences 7%, visual/performing arts 6%.

Technology on campus. 500 workstations in dormitories, library, computer center, student center. Dormitories wired for high-speed internet access and linked to campus network. Commuter students can connect to campus network. Online course registration, online library, helpline, wireless network available.

Student life. Freshman orientation: Mandatory. Preregistration for classes offered. Weekend program in May or June for preregistration with final program 4 days prior to start of classes. **Policies:** Students responsible for governing themselves through honor code. **Housing:** Guaranteed on-campus for all undergraduates. Coed dorms, special housing for disabled, apartments available. French, German, Spanish language houses available. **Activities:** Jazz band, campus ministries, choral groups, dance, drama, international student organizations, literary magazine, music ensembles, Model UN, musical theater, radio station, student government, student newspaper, black student union, Circle K, La Union Latina, Best Buddies, Intervarsity Christian Fellowship, College Democrats, Jewish student union, College Republicans.

Athletics. NCAA. **Intercollegiate:** Basketball, cross-country, field hockey W, golf, lacrosse, soccer, softball W, swimming, tennis, track and field, volleyball W. **Intramural:** Basketball, football (non-tackle) M, football (tackle) M, soccer, table tennis, volleyball W. **Team name:** Blazers.

Student services. Adult student services, alcohol/substance abuse counseling, chaplain/spiritual director, career counseling, student employment services, financial aid counseling, health services, minority student services, personal counseling, placement for graduates, veterans' counselor, women's services. **Physically disabled:** Services for speech, hearing impaired.

Contact. E-mail: admission@hood.edu
Phone: (301) 696-3400 Toll-free number: (800) 922-1599
Fax: (301) 696-3819
Jennifer Decker, Director of Admissions, Hood College, 401 Rosemont Avenue, Frederick, MD 21701-8575

ITT Technical Institute: Owings Mills
Owings Mills, Maryland
www.itt-tech.edu

- For-profit 4-year business and technical college
- Large town
- 555 undergraduates

General. Accredited by ACICS. **Degrees:** 108 bachelor's, 168 associate awarded. **Calendar:** Quarter. **Full-time faculty:** 19 total. **Part-time faculty:** 58 total.

Basis for selection. Additional requirements for some programs.

2015-2016 Annual costs. Per-credit-hour charge, $493; academic fee, $200. Certain programs require purchase of tools, which range from $100 to $500. All costs subject to change.

Academics. Credit/placement by examination: AP, CLEP.

Majors. Business: Construction management, e-commerce. **Communications technology:** Animation/special effects. **Computer sciences:** Security, system admin.

Most popular majors. Business/marketing 14%, computer/information sciences 62%, engineering/engineering technologies 23%.

Contact. ITT Technical Institute: Owings Mills, 11301 Red Run Boulevard, Owings Mills, MD 21117

Johns Hopkins University
Baltimore, Maryland   **CB member**
www.jhu.edu   **CB code: 5332**

- Private 4-year university
- Residential campus in very large city
- 5,334 degree-seeking undergraduates: 49% women, 6% African American, 23% Asian American, 13% Hispanic/Latino, 5% Multi-racial, non-Hispanic, 10% international
- 1,968 degree-seeking graduate students
- 13% of applicants admitted
- SAT or ACT (ACT writing optional), application essay required
- 94% graduate within 6 years; 37% enter graduate study

General. Founded in 1876. Regionally accredited. Centers in Bologna and Florence, Italy and in Nanjing, China. **Degrees:** 1,714 bachelor's awarded; master's, professional, doctoral offered. **ROTC:** Army, Air Force. **Location:** 4 miles from downtown Baltimore, 40 miles from Washington, D.C. **Calendar:** 4-1-4, limited summer session. **Full-time faculty:** 576 total; 93% have terminal degrees, 14% minority, 31% women. **Part-time faculty:** 64 total; 84% have terminal degrees, 14% minority, 39% women. **Class size:** 73% <20, 14% 20-39, 3% 40-49, 5% 50-99, 4% >100. **Special facilities:** Archaeological museum, museum of art, learning commons, DaVinci Robot, undergraduate teaching labs, space telescope science institute, special collections library, Brody Learning Commons (high-tech collaborative learning and meeting spaces), extreme materials lab, film center.

Freshman class profile. 24,716 applied, 3,251 admitted, 1,299 enrolled.

Mid 50% test scores		
SAT critical reading:	690-760	
SAT math:	710-790	
SAT writing:	690-770	
ACT composite:	32-34	
GPA 3.75 or higher:	86%	
GPA 3.50-3.74:	12%	
GPA 3.0-3.49:	2%	

Rank in top quarter:	99%
Rank in top tenth:	92%
Return as sophomores:	97%
Out-of-state:	91%
Live on campus:	99%
International:	9%
Fraternities:	20%
Sororities:	20%

Basis for selection. Applicant's accomplishments, goals, and fit with our community. Admitted applicants are well-rounded students with strong academic achievement, intellectual curiosity, and passion for learning. Students interested in pursuing the biomedical engineering major must indicate BME as their first choice major and are admitted based on evaluation of credentials and space availability. SAT and SAT Subject Tests or ACT recommended. Early Decision applicants should have test scores in by 11/1. Recommend two SAT Subject Tests. SAT Math Level 2 recommended for students applying to school of engineering. Interview optional. Audition required of applicants to dual-degree program with Peabody Institute. **Home schooled:** Statement describing home school structure and mission, transcript of courses and grades, letter of recommendation (nonparent) required. Secondary school report must include summary of program, complete transcript with course descriptions, bibliography of textbooks, description of evaluation methods, and actual grades or evaluations.

High school preparation. College-preparatory program recommended. Recommended units include English 4, mathematics 4, social studies 2, history 2, science 4 and foreign language 4. 4 units of all academic core subjects strongly recommended.

2015-2016 Annual costs. Tuition/fees: $49,210. Room/board: $14,540. Books/supplies: $1,210. Personal expenses: $1,036.

2014-2015 Financial aid. Need-based: 914 full-time freshmen applied for aid; 717 deemed to have need; 717 received aid. Average need met was 99%. Average scholarship/grant was $35,792; average loan $3,301. 86% of total undergraduate aid awarded as scholarships/grants, 14% as loans/jobs. **Non-need-based:** Awarded to 679 full-time undergraduates, including 250 freshmen. Scholarships awarded for academics, athletics, leadership, ROTC, state residency. **Additional information:** Selected students receive aid packages without loan expectation, including grants to full need. Private merit aid does not reduce Hopkins grant.

Application procedures. Admission: Closing date 1/1 (postmark date). $70 fee, may be waived for applicants with need. Admission notification by 4/1. Must reply by May 1 or within 1 week(s) if notified thereafter. **Financial aid:** Closing date 3/1. FAFSA, CSS PROFILE required. Applicants notified by 4/1; must reply by 5/1.

Academics. Learning is multidimensional and occurs both inside and outside the classroom. Undergraduates have access to graduate professors and researchers at affiliated campuses, including the schools of Medicine, Nursing, Public Health, Advanced International Studies, plus the Peabody Institute. **Special study options:** Combined bachelor's/graduate degree, cross-registration, double major, independent study, internships, student-designed major, study abroad, Washington semester. Combined Bachelor's/Master's programs; Double Degree-Bachelor of Arts and Bachelor of Music. **Credit/placement by examination:** AP, CLEP, IB, institutional tests. **Support services:** Pre-admission summer program, reduced course load, study skills assistance, tutoring, writing center. Peer-led team learning, departmental help rooms (math, chemistry, physics), undergraduate teaching labs, learning den, research librarians. Student Support Services (SSS) program promotes the success of students from underrepresented populations by providing mentoring, academic support, advising, career development, and community service services.

Majors. Area/ethnic studies: African-American, East Asian, Near/Middle Eastern. **Biology:** General, biophysics, cellular/molecular, neuroscience. **Computer sciences:** General, security. **Conservation:** Environmental studies. **Engineering:** General, biomedical, chemical, civil, computer, electrical, engineering mechanics, environmental, materials, mechanical. **English:** Creative writing, English lit. **Foreign languages:** Classics, French, German, Italian, Latin, Romance, Spanish. **History:** General, science/technology. **Human services:** Public policy. **Math:** General, applied, statistics. **Philosophy/religion:** Philosophy. **Physical sciences:** Chemistry, geology, physics. **Psychology:** General. **Social sciences:** General, anthropology, archaeology, economics, geography, GIS/cartography, international relations, political science, sociology. **Visual/performing arts:** Art history/conservation.

Most popular majors. Biology 11%, engineering/engineering technologies 19%, health sciences 25%, social sciences 12%.

Technology on campus. 140 workstations in dormitories, library, computer center. Dormitories wired for high-speed internet access and linked to campus network. Commuter students can connect to campus network. Online course registration, online library, helpline, repair service, student web hosting, wireless network available.

Student life. Freshman orientation: Mandatory. Preregistration for classes offered. Five-day intensive program held the week prior to the start of fall classes. **Policies:** Freshmen and sophomores required to live on campus unless living with a parent or legal guardian within commuting distance. Students joining fraternities and sororities must have completed one semester and be in good academic standing. Freshmen not permitted cars on campus. **Housing:** Guaranteed on-campus for freshmen. Coed dorms, special housing for disabled, apartments, wellness housing available. $200 nonrefundable deposit, deadline 5/29. Vacation housing floors available. Specific spaces accessible or modified for disabled students. **Activities:** Bands, campus ministries, choral groups, dance, drama, film society, international student organizations, literary magazine, music ensembles, Model UN, musical theater, radio station, student government, student newspaper, symphony orchestra, Interfaith Center (26 groups), Multicultural Affairs (25 groups), Center for Social Concern (60 groups), 27 political/advocacy groups.

Athletics. NCAA. **Intercollegiate:** Baseball M, basketball, cross-country, fencing, field hockey W, football (tackle) M, lacrosse, soccer, swimming, tennis, track and field, volleyball W, water polo M, wrestling M. **Intramural:** Basketball, football (non-tackle), soccer, volleyball, water polo. **Team name:** Blue Jays.

Student services. Alcohol/substance abuse counseling, chaplain/spiritual director, career counseling, student employment services, financial aid counseling, health services, minority student services, personal counseling, placement for graduates, women's services. **Physically disabled:** Services for visually, speech, hearing impaired.

Contact. E-mail: gotojhu@jhu.edu
Phone: (410) 516-8171 Fax: (410) 516-6025
Ellen Kim, Director of Undergraduate Admissions, Johns Hopkins University, 3400 North Charles Street, Mason Hall, Baltimore, MD 21218-2683

Johns Hopkins University: Peabody Conservatory of Music
Baltimore, Maryland
www.peabody.jhu.edu   **CB code: 5532**

- Private 4-year music college
- Residential campus in very large city
- 265 degree-seeking undergraduates
- 45% of applicants admitted
- SAT or ACT, application essay required

General. Founded in 1857. Regionally accredited. **Degrees:** 78 bachelor's awarded; master's, doctoral offered. **Location:** 36 miles from Washington, DC. **Calendar:** Semester. **Full-time faculty:** 82 total; 30% women. **Part-time faculty:** 87 total; 38% women. **Class size:** 89% < 20, 8% 20-39, 1% 40-49, 2% 50-99. **Special facilities:** Concert halls.

Freshman class profile. 760 applied, 345 admitted, 86 enrolled.

Out-of-state:	74%	Live on campus:	100%

Basis for selection. Audition most important; secondary school record, test scores also important. Interview recommended. Audition required. **Home schooled:** Statement describing home school structure and mission, state high school equivalency certificate required.

High school preparation. College-preparatory program recommended.

2015-2016 Annual costs. Tuition/fees: $44,050. Room/board: $14,200. Books/supplies: $1,000. Personal expenses: $1,600.

Financial aid. Non-need-based: Scholarships awarded for academics, music/drama.

Application procedures. Admission: Priority date 12/1; deadline 4/1 (postmark date). $120 fee, may be waived for applicants with need. Admission notification by 4/1. Must reply by 5/1. Must apply by December 15 for guarantee of scholarship consideration. **Financial aid:** Closing date 2/1. FAFSA, institutional form required. Applicants notified by 4/1; must reply by 5/1.

Academics. Special study options: Cross-registration, double major, ESL, independent study, internships, study abroad, teacher certification program. **Credit/placement by examination:** AP, CLEP, IB, institutional tests. 8 credit hours maximum toward bachelor's degree. **Support services:** Remedial instruction, tutoring.

Majors. Communications technology: Recording arts. **Education:** Music. **Visual/performing arts:** Music performance, music theory/composition, piano/keyboard, voice/opera.

Most popular majors. Education 10%, visual/performing arts 90%.

Technology on campus. 28 workstations in dormitories, library, computer center. Dormitories wired for high-speed internet access and linked to campus network. Commuter students can connect to campus network. Online course registration, online library, helpline, repair service, wireless network available.

Student life. Freshman orientation: Available. Preregistration for classes offered. **Housing:** Guaranteed on-campus for freshmen. Coed dorms, single-sex dorms available. $250 partly refundable deposit, deadline 1/7. **Activities:** Bands, choral groups, music ensembles, opera, student government, symphony orchestra.

Student services. Alcohol/substance abuse counseling, career counseling, student employment services, financial aid counseling, health services, personal counseling, placement for graduates. **Physically disabled:** Services for visually, speech, hearing impaired.

Contact. E-mail: admissions@peabody.jhu.edu
Phone: (410) 234-4848 Toll-free number: (800) 368-2521
Fax: (410) 659-8102
David Lane, Director of Admissions, Johns Hopkins University: Peabody Conservatory of Music, One East Mount Vernon Place, Baltimore, MD 21202

Loyola University Maryland
Baltimore, Maryland   **CB member**
www.loyola.edu   **CB code: 5370**

- Private 4-year university affiliated with the Roman Catholic Church
- Residential campus in very large city
- 4,031 degree-seeking undergraduates: 1% part-time, 58% women, 6% African American, 4% Asian American, 9% Hispanic/Latino, 2% Multiracial, non-Hispanic
- 1,872 degree-seeking graduate students
- 61% of applicants admitted
- Application essay required
- 81% graduate within 6 years

General. Founded in 1852. Regionally accredited. **Degrees:** 908 bachelor's awarded; master's, professional, doctoral offered. **ROTC:** Army, Air Force. **Location:** 42 miles from Washington, DC; 101 miles from Philadelphia. **Calendar:** Semester, extensive summer session. **Full-time faculty:** 364 total; 85% have terminal degrees, 17% minority, 48% women. **Part-time faculty:** 196 total; 5% have terminal degrees, 19% minority, 50% women. **Class size:** 40% < 20, 59% 20-39, less than 1% 40-49, less than 1% 50-99, less than 1% >100. **Special facilities:** Fitness and aquatic center.

Freshman class profile. 13,867 applied, 8,449 admitted, 1,033 enrolled.

Mid 50% test scores			
		GPA 2.0-2.99:	8%
SAT critical reading:	550-650	Rank in top quarter:	62%
SAT math:	560-640	Rank in top tenth:	26%
ACT composite:	25-29	Return as sophomores:	87%
GPA 3.75 or higher:	22%	Out-of-state:	83%
GPA 3.50-3.74:	32%	Live on campus:	98%
GPA 3.0-3.49:	38%	International:	1%

Basis for selection. All applicants are admitted on the condition that they satisfactorily complete their secondary school courses. **Home schooled:** Letter of recommendation (nonparent) required. SAT/ACT required.

High school preparation. College-preparatory program required. 15 units required; 19 recommended. Required and recommended units include English 4, mathematics 3-4, social studies 2-3, history 2-3, science 3-4, foreign language 3-4, computer science 1 and visual/performing arts 1.

2015-2016 Annual costs. Tuition/fees: $45,200. Room/board: $13,310. Books/supplies: $1,240. Personal expenses: $1,000.

2014-2015 Financial aid. Need-based: 858 full-time freshmen applied for aid; 662 deemed to have need; 662 received aid. Average need met was 93%. Average scholarship/grant was $21,995; average loan $4,190. 73% of total undergraduate aid awarded as scholarships/grants, 27% as loans/jobs. **Non-need-based:** Awarded to 1,381 full-time undergraduates, including 464 freshmen. Scholarships awarded for academics, athletics, ROTC.

Application procedures. Admission: Priority date 11/1; deadline 1/15 (postmark date). $60 fee, may be waived for applicants with need. Admission notification by 3/15. Must reply by May 1 or within 3 week(s) if notified thereafter. **Financial aid:** Closing date 2/15. FAFSA, CSS PROFILE required. Applicants notified by 3/15; must reply by 5/1.

Academics. Service learning courses available. **Special study options:** Combined bachelor's/graduate degree, cross-registration, double major, exchange student, honors, independent study, internships, liberal arts/career combination, study abroad, teacher certification program. **Credit/placement**

by examination: AP, CLEP, IB, institutional tests. **Support services:** Learning center, reduced course load, remedial instruction, study skills assistance, tutoring, writing center.

Majors. Biology: General. **Business:** General, accounting. **Communications:** Communications/speech/rhetoric. **Computer sciences:** General. **Education:** Elementary. **Engineering:** General, electrical. **English:** Creative writing, English lit. **Foreign languages:** Classics, French, German, Latin, Spanish. **Health services:** Speech pathology. **History:** General. **Math:** Applied. **Philosophy/religion:** Philosophy, religion. **Physical sciences:** Chemistry, physics. **Psychology:** General. **Social sciences:** Economics, political science, sociology. **Visual/performing arts:** Art.

Most popular majors. Biology 6%, business/marketing 33%, communications/journalism 11%, health sciences 6%, psychology 9%, social sciences 9%.

Technology on campus. 775 workstations in dormitories, library, computer center, student center. Dormitories wired for high-speed internet access and linked to campus network. Commuter students can connect to campus network. Online course registration, online library, helpline, student web hosting, wireless network available.

Student life. Freshman orientation: Mandatory, $165 fee. Preregistration for classes offered. Held 5 times in summer; parents invited to attend. **Policies:** Freshmen not permitted cars on campus. **Housing:** Guaranteed on-campus for freshmen. Coed dorms, themed housing, wellness housing available. $300 nonrefundable deposit, deadline 5/1. **Activities:** Jazz band, campus ministries, choral groups, dance, drama, film society, international student organizations, literary magazine, music ensembles, musical theater, radio station, student government, student newspaper, TV station.

Athletics. NCAA. **Intercollegiate:** Basketball, cross-country, diving, golf M, lacrosse, rowing (crew), soccer, swimming, tennis, track and field W, volleyball W. **Intramural:** Basketball, football (non-tackle) M, racquetball, soccer, softball, tennis, volleyball. **Team name:** Greyhounds.

Student services. Alcohol/substance abuse counseling, chaplain/spiritual director, career counseling, student employment services, financial aid counseling, health services, minority student services, personal counseling, placement for graduates, women's services. **Physically disabled:** Services for visually, speech, hearing impaired.

Contact. E-mail: admissions@loyola.edu
Phone: (410) 617-5012 Toll-free number: (800) 221-9107
Fax: (410) 617-2176
Elena Hicks, Director of Undergraduate Admission, Loyola University Maryland, 4501 North Charles Street, Baltimore, MD 21210-2699

Maryland Institute College of Art
Baltimore, Maryland
www.mica.edu

CB member
CB code: 5399

- Private 4-year visual arts college
- Residential campus in very large city
- 1,761 degree-seeking undergraduates: 1% part-time, 74% women, 6% African American, 13% Asian American, 3% Hispanic/Latino, 10% Multi-racial, non-Hispanic, 16% international
- 401 degree-seeking graduate students
- 47% of applicants admitted
- SAT or ACT (ACT writing optional), application essay required
- 73% graduate within 6 years; 11% enter graduate study

General. Founded in 1826. Regionally accredited. **Degrees:** 427 bachelor's awarded; master's offered. **ROTC:** Army. **Location:** 180 miles from New York City, 50 miles from Washington, DC. **Calendar:** Semester, extensive summer session. **Full-time faculty:** 159 total; 76% have terminal degrees, 11% minority, 53% women. **Part-time faculty:** 211 total; 75% have terminal degrees, 11% minority, 53% women. **Class size:** 85% < 20, 14% 20-39, less than 1% 40-49, less than 1% 50-99. **Special facilities:** Nature library, graphics laboratory, independent studios, digital print studio, smart textile classroom, 3D fabrication studio, ABOX and BBOX performance spaces.

Freshman class profile. 3,818 applied, 1,808 admitted, 411 enrolled.

Mid 50% test scores		Return as sophomores:	88%
SAT critical reading:	520-650	Out-of-state:	82%
SAT math:	480-630	Live on campus:	88%
SAT writing:	500-630	International:	23%
End year in good standing:	98%		

Basis for selection. Emphasis placed on artistic ability as demonstrated in portfolio, academic achievement, test scores, GPA, and level of coursework.

Essays, recommendations, interview, and extra-curricular activities also considered. An interview is recommended, a portfolio of 12-20 pieces of artwork is required, and a list of activities, interests, and honors needs to be submitted. **Learning Disabled:** Students with documented learning disabilities not required to submit SAT or ACT test scores.

High school preparation. College-preparatory program required. 24 units required. Required and recommended units include English 4, mathematics 2-3, social studies 4, history 3-4, science 2-3 (laboratory 1) and academic electives 6. 2 studio art required, 4 studio art recommended, 1 art history recommended.

2015-2016 Annual costs. Tuition/fees: $43,870. Room/board: $12,030. Books/supplies: $1,450. Personal expenses: $725.

Financial aid. Non-need-based: Scholarships awarded for academics, art.

Application procedures. Admission: Closing date 2/1 (receipt date). $70 fee, may be waived for applicants with need. Admission notification by 3/4. Admission notification on a rolling basis beginning on or about 2/28. Must reply by 5/1. **Financial aid:** Closing date 2/15. FAFSA, institutional form required. Applicants notified by 4/6; must reply by 5/1.

Academics. One-third of course work in liberal arts and two-thirds in studio art required for graduation. Minors available in academic subjects. Independent studio and study requirement sometimes met by job internships. Foundation program required in the first year. **Special study options:** Accelerated study, combined bachelor's/graduate degree, cross-registration, distance learning, double major, dual enrollment of high school students, exchange student, independent study, internships, liberal arts/career combination, New York semester, student-designed major, study abroad, teacher certification program. AICAD Mobility Program; cooperative exchange programs with Johns Hopkins University, Goucher College, Peabody Conservatory of Music, University of Baltimore, Loyola College, Notre Dame College, University of Maryland Baltimore County, Morgan State University, Baltimore Hebrew Institute and Towson University; and 5-year BFA/MAT. **Credit/placement by examination:** AP, CLEP, IB, institutional tests. 24 credit hours maximum toward bachelor's degree. **Support services:** Learning center, pre-admission summer program, reduced course load, remedial instruction, study skills assistance, tutoring, writing center.

Majors. Education: Art. **Visual/performing arts:** Art history/conservation, ceramics, drawing, fiber arts, film/cinema/video, game design, graphic design, illustration, interior design, multimedia, painting, photography, printmaking, sculpture.

Most popular majors. Education 6%, visual/performing arts 94%.

Technology on campus. 600 workstations in dormitories, library, computer center, student center. Dormitories wired for high-speed internet access and linked to campus network. Commuter students can connect to campus network. Online library, helpline, student web hosting, wireless network available.

Student life. Freshman orientation: Mandatory, $175 fee. Preregistration for classes offered. **Housing:** Guaranteed on-campus for freshmen. Coed dorms, special housing for disabled, apartments, themed housing, wellness housing available. $550 partly refundable deposit, deadline 5/1. **Activities:** Campus ministries, choral groups, dance, drama, film society, international student organizations, literary magazine, music ensembles, musical theater, radio station, student government, Koinonia Christian Fellowship, Hispanic Latino Student Union, Students of Sustainability, Asian Student Alliance, Black Student Union, MICatholic, Chinese Student Association, Mission in Christian Artists, Student Voice Association, and Agape Christian Fellowship.

Student services. Adult student services, alcohol/substance abuse counseling, career counseling, student employment services, financial aid counseling, health services, minority student services, personal counseling.

Contact. E-mail: admissions@mica.edu
Phone: (410) 225-2222 Fax: (410) 225-2337
Theresa Bedoya, Vice President and Dean of Admission and Financial Aid, Maryland Institute College of Art, 1300 Mount Royal Avenue, Baltimore, MD 21217-4134

McDaniel College
Westminster, Maryland
www.mcdaniel.edu

CB member
CB code: 5898

- Private 4-year liberal arts college
- Residential campus in large town
- 1,621 degree-seeking undergraduates: 1% part-time, 53% women, 14% African American, 4% Asian American, 6% Hispanic/Latino, 1% international

- 1,023 degree-seeking graduate students
- 80% of applicants admitted
- SAT or ACT (ACT writing optional), application essay required
- 70% graduate within 6 years

General. Founded in 1867. Regionally accredited. **Degrees:** 358 bachelor's awarded; master's offered. **ROTC:** Army. **Location:** 30 miles from Baltimore, 60 miles from Washington, DC. **Calendar:** 4-1-4, limited summer session. **Full-time faculty:** 110 total; 97% have terminal degrees, 12% minority, 54% women. **Part-time faculty:** 268 total; 31% have terminal degrees, 8% minority, 53% women. **Special facilities:** 9-hole golf course, video production laboratory, photography studio, human performance laboratory, graphics laboratory, observatory, student research science labs.

Freshman class profile. 2,864 applied, 2,286 admitted, 432 enrolled.

Mid 50% test scores		Rank in top quarter:	51%
SAT critical reading:	480-590	Rank in top tenth:	26%
SAT math:	480-590	Return as sophomores:	75%
ACT composite:	20-27	Out-of-state:	58%
GPA 3.75 or higher:	33%	Live on campus:	98%
GPA 3.50-3.74:	16%	Fraternities:	15%
GPA 3.0-3.49:	32%	Sororities:	31%
GPA 2.0-2.99:	19%		

Basis for selection. Rigor of course work completed and academic performance, test scores, writing skills, personal and academic accomplishments, recommendations by counselors and teachers, leadership and participation in non-academic activities. SAT Optional policy for students who rank in the top ten percent of their graduating classes, or in the absence of school rank, have a cumulative academic GPA above 3.5. Academic recommendations required. Interview recommended. **Home schooled:** Statement describing home school structure and mission, transcript of courses and grades, letter of recommendation (nonparent) required. Must submit documentation used to satisfy your state graduation requirement.

High school preparation. College-preparatory program required. 16 units required; 19 recommended. Required and recommended units include English 4, mathematics 3-4, social studies 3, science 3-4 (laboratory 3) and foreign language 3-4.

2015-2016 Annual costs. Tuition/fees: $39,500. Room/board: $10,300. Books/supplies: $1,200. Personal expenses: $970.

2015-2016 Financial aid. Need-based: 398 full-time freshmen applied for aid; 352 deemed to have need; 352 received aid. Average need met was 84%. Average scholarship/grant was $31,233; average loan $3,365. 87% of total undergraduate aid awarded as scholarships/grants, 13% as loans/jobs. **Non-need-based:** Awarded to 542 full-time undergraduates, including 151 freshmen. Scholarships awarded for academics, ROTC, state residency.

Application procedures. Admission: Priority date 2/16; no deadline. $50 fee, may be waived for applicants with need. Admission notification by 3/7. Admission notification on a rolling basis beginning on or about 11/24. Must reply by May 1 or within 2 week(s) if notified thereafter. **Financial aid:** Priority date 3/1; no closing date. FAFSA required. Applicants notified on a rolling basis starting 3/1; must reply by 5/1 or within 2 week(s) of notification.

Academics. January term offered as 2-credit period of concentrated study. May include travel, classroom study or independent study (including internships). **Special study options:** Accelerated study, distance learning, double major, dual enrollment of high school students, exchange student, honors, independent study, internships, New York semester, semester at sea, student-designed major, study abroad, teacher certification program, United Nations semester, Washington semester. **Credit/placement by examination:** AP, CLEP, IB, SAT, ACT, institutional tests. 32 credit hours maximum toward bachelor's degree. **Support services:** Learning center, reduced course load, remedial instruction, study skills assistance, tutoring, writing center.

Majors. Area/ethnic studies: Asian, Near/Middle Eastern. **Biology:** General, biochemistry, environmental. **Business:** Business admin. **Communications:** Communications/speech/rhetoric. **Computer sciences:** General. **Conservation:** Environmental science. **English:** English lit. **Foreign languages:** French, German, Spanish. **History:** General. **Human services:** Social work. **Math:** General. **Parks/recreation:** Exercise sciences. **Philosophy/religion:** Philosophy, religion. **Physical sciences:** Chemistry, physics. **Psychology:** General. **Social sciences:** Economics, political science, sociology. **Visual/performing arts:** Art, art history/conservation, dramatic, film/cinema/video, music.

Most popular majors. Biology 8%, business/marketing 8%, English 6%, history 6%, parks/recreation 11%, psychology 9%, public administration/social services 6%, social sciences 11%, visual/performing arts 9%.

Technology on campus. 175 workstations in library, computer center. Dormitories wired for high-speed internet access and linked to campus network. Commuter students can connect to campus network. Online course registration, online library, helpline, repair service, wireless network available.

Student life. Freshman orientation: Mandatory. Preregistration for classes offered. Five-day program. **Policies:** Freshmen not permitted cars on campus. **Housing:** Guaranteed on-campus for freshmen. Coed dorms, special housing for disabled, apartments, fraternity/sorority housing, themed housing, wellness housing available. **Activities:** Bands, campus ministries, choral groups, dance, drama, film society, international student organizations, literary magazine, music ensembles, Model UN, musical theater, opera, radio station, student government, student newspaper, symphony orchestra, TV station, Africa's Legacy club, Asian community coalition, Best Buddies, Catholic Campus ministries, Heroes Helping Hopkins, Intervarsity Christian Fellowship, Jewish student union, Spanish club, German club, French club.

Athletics. NCAA. **Intercollegiate:** Baseball M, basketball, cross-country, field hockey W, football (tackle) M, golf, lacrosse, soccer, softball W, swimming, tennis, track and field, volleyball W, wrestling M. **Intramural:** Badminton, basketball, football (non-tackle) M, golf, soccer, softball, volleyball. **Team name:** Green Terror.

Student services. Career counseling, student employment services, financial aid counseling, health services, minority student services, personal counseling. **Physically disabled:** Services for visually, hearing impaired.

Contact. E-mail: admissions@mcdaniel.edu
Phone: (410) 857-2230 Toll-free number: (800) 638-5005
Fax: (410) 857-2757
Florence Hines, Vice President for Enrollment Management and Dean of Admissions, McDaniel College, 2 College Hill, Westminster, MD 21157-4390

Morgan State University
Baltimore, Maryland — CB member
www.morgan.edu — CB code: 5416

- Public 4-year university
- Commuter campus in large city
- 6,294 degree-seeking undergraduates: 11% part-time, 54% women, 83% African American, 1% Asian American, 4% Hispanic/Latino, 3% Multiracial, non-Hispanic, 7% international
- 1,383 degree-seeking graduate students
- 67% of applicants admitted
- SAT and SAT Subject Tests or ACT (ACT writing optional) required
- 31% graduate within 6 years

General. Founded in 1867. Regionally accredited. **Degrees:** 933 bachelor's awarded; master's, doctoral offered. **ROTC:** Army. **Location:** 45 miles from Washington, DC, 100 miles from Philadelphia. **Calendar:** Semester, limited summer session. **Full-time faculty:** 416 total; 69% have terminal degrees, 52% minority, 42% women. **Part-time faculty:** 232 total; 18% have terminal degrees, 62% minority, 51% women. **Class size:** 44% < 20, 53% 20-39, 2% 40-49, less than 1% 50-99, less than 1% >100. **Special facilities:** Historical and government documents collections, special collections of African American history, super computer, engineering complex.

Freshman class profile. 5,090 applied, 3,396 admitted, 1,168 enrolled.

Mid 50% test scores		GPA 3.0-3.49:	22%
SAT critical reading:	400-480	GPA 2.0-2.99:	62%
SAT math:	400-490	Return as sophomores:	76%
SAT writing:	390-470	Out-of-state:	29%
GPA 3.75 or higher:	6%	International:	8%
GPA 3.50-3.74:	9%		

Basis for selection. School achievement record and test scores most important. 820 SAT (exclusive of Writing) with 2.5 high school GPA or 900 SAT (exclusive of Writing) with 2.0 high school GPA, principal's recommendation, and parents' consent form (for minors) required. Interview and essay recommended. Audition recommended for music majors. **Home schooled:** State high school equivalency certificate required. State-recognized diploma required. **Learning Disabled:** Students with learning disability must provide documentation and take untimed SAT with assistance from counseling center.

High school preparation. College-preparatory program recommended. 21 units required. Required units include English 4, mathematics 3, social studies 3, history 3, science 3, foreign language 2 and academic electives 3. History can be substituted for social studies; computer science can be used in place of foreign language.

2015-2016 Annual costs. Tuition/fees: $7,508; $17,182 out-of-state. Room/board: $10,246. Books/supplies: $2,000. Personal expenses: $2,395.

Application procedures. Admission: Priority date 11/15; deadline 2/15. $45 fee, may be waived for applicants with need. Admission notification by 4/15. Admission notification on a rolling basis beginning on or about 2/15. Must reply by May 1 or within 2 week(s) if notified thereafter. **Financial aid:** Priority date 4/1; no closing date. FAFSA required. Applicants notified on a rolling basis starting 6/1; must reply within 2 week(s) of notification.

Academics. Special study options: Accelerated study, combined bachelor's/graduate degree, cooperative education, distance learning, double major, ESL, honors, independent study, internships, student-designed major, study abroad, teacher certification program, weekend college. **Credit/placement by examination:** AP, CLEP, SAT, ACT, institutional tests. 46 credit hours maximum toward bachelor's degree. Proficiency tests in general education requirements. **Support services:** Learning center, pre-admission summer program, reduced course load, remedial instruction, study skills assistance, tutoring, writing center.

Majors. Architecture: Architecture, environmental design. **Area/ethnic studies:** African-American. **Biology:** General. **Business:** Accounting, business admin, finance, hospitality admin, marketing. **Computer sciences:** Computer science, information systems, networking. **Education:** Elementary, health, physical, science. **Engineering:** General, applied physics, civil, electrical, industrial. **English:** English lit, rhetoric/composition. **Health services:** Staff services technology. **History:** General. **Math:** General. **Physical sciences:** Chemistry, physics. **Psychology:** General. **Social sciences:** Economics, political science, sociology. **Visual/performing arts:** Dramatic, music, studio arts. **Work/family studies:** Food/nutrition.

Most popular majors. Business/marketing 24%, communications/journalism 10%, education 8%, engineering/engineering technologies 12%, social sciences 8%.

Technology on campus. Dormitories wired for high-speed internet access and linked to campus network. Commuter students can connect to campus network. Online course registration, online library, helpline, repair service, student web hosting, wireless network available.

Student life. Freshman orientation: Mandatory. Preregistration for classes offered. Held twice during summer for 5 days. **Housing:** Coed dorms, single-sex dorms, special housing for disabled, apartments, fraternity/sorority housing, wellness housing available. $200 nonrefundable deposit, deadline 7/1. **Activities:** Bands, campus ministries, choral groups, dance, drama, international student organizations, musical theater, radio station, student government, Council on Religious Life.

Athletics. NCAA. **Intercollegiate:** Basketball, bowling W, cheerleading W, cross-country, football (tackle) M, softball W, tennis, track and field, volleyball W. **Intramural:** Basketball, cross-country, handball, racquetball, rifle, soccer, softball, swimming, table tennis, tennis, track and field, volleyball. **Team name:** Bears.

Student services. Alcohol/substance abuse counseling, career counseling, student employment services, health services, on-campus daycare, personal counseling, placement for graduates, veterans' counselor. **Physically disabled:** Services for visually, speech, hearing impaired.

Contact. E-mail: admissions@morgan.edu
Phone: (443) 885-3000 Toll-free number: (800) 332-6674
Fax: (443) 885-8260
Shonda Gray, Director of Admissions/Recruitment, Morgan State University, 1700 East Cold Spring Lane, Baltimore, MD 21251

Mount St. Mary's University
Emmitsburg, Maryland   CB member
www.msmary.edu   CB code: 5421

- Private 4-year university and liberal arts college affiliated with the Roman Catholic Church
- Residential campus in rural community
- 1,786 degree-seeking undergraduates: 5% part-time, 54% women, 12% African American, 3% Asian American, 9% Hispanic/Latino, 5% Multiracial, non-Hispanic, 1% international
- 460 degree-seeking graduate students
- 67% of applicants admitted
- SAT or ACT (ACT writing optional) required
- 69% graduate within 6 years; 26% enter graduate study

General. Founded in 1808. Regionally accredited. **Degrees:** 442 bachelor's awarded; master's offered. **ROTC:** Army. **Location:** 65 miles from Washington, DC, 50 miles from Baltimore. **Calendar:** Semester, limited summer session. **Full-time faculty:** 126 total; 91% have terminal degrees, 7% minority, 41% women. **Part-time faculty:** 94 total; 14% have terminal degrees, 11% minority, 36% women. **Class size:** 46% < 20, 54% 20-39. **Special facilities:** 300 acre recreation area.

Freshman class profile. 6,113 applied, 4,105 admitted, 506 enrolled.

Mid 50% test scores		GPA 2.0-2.99:	26%
SAT critical reading:	460-570	Rank in top quarter:	31%
SAT math:	450-560	Rank in top tenth:	14%
SAT writing:	450-560	End year in good standing:	85%
ACT composite:	18-24	Return as sophomores:	75%
GPA 3.75 or higher:	28%	Out-of-state:	42%
GPA 3.50-3.74:	14%	Live on campus:	94%
GPA 3.0-3.49:	30%		

Basis for selection. High school record most important followed by character, extracurricular activities, level of applicant's interest. Interview and essay welcomed but not required. **Home schooled:** Letter of recommendation (nonparent) required. **Learning Disabled:** Current and valid documentation of disability, including functional limitations and the impact of disability on academic performance, is required.

High school preparation. 16 units required. Required units include English 4, mathematics 3, social studies 3, science 3 (laboratory 2), foreign language 2 and academic electives 1.

2015-2016 Annual costs. Tuition/fees: $37,500. Room/board: $12,400. Books/supplies: $1,300. Personal expenses: $800.

2015-2016 Financial aid. Need-based: 455 full-time freshmen applied for aid; 379 deemed to have need; 379 received aid. Average need met was 72%. Average scholarship/grant was $22,784; average loan $4,269. 74% of total undergraduate aid awarded as scholarships/grants, 26% as loans/jobs. **Non-need-based:** Awarded to 767 full-time undergraduates, including 232 freshmen. Scholarships awarded for academics, art, athletics, leadership, ROTC.

Application procedures. Admission: Priority date 12/1; deadline 3/1 (postmark date). $45 fee, may be waived for applicants with need. Admission notification by 5/1. Admission notification on a rolling basis beginning on or about 11/1. Must reply by 5/1. **Financial aid:** Closing date 3/1. FAFSA required. Applicants notified on a rolling basis starting 2/14; must reply by 5/1.

Academics. Veritas program is integrated with every academic major and includes leadership development and cultural components. Undergraduate professional studies in business, criminal justice and human services are offered in an accelerated format offered off-campus; open to adult students only. **Special study options:** Accelerated study, combined bachelor's/graduate degree, cross-registration, double major, dual enrollment of high school students, honors, independent study, internships, liberal arts/career combination, student-designed major, study abroad, teacher certification program, Washington semester, weekend college. 3-2 with University of Maryland (BS Biology, BS Nursing); 3-2 with Shenandoah University in Nursing (BS Biology, BS Nursing); 4-4 with Lake Erie College of Osteopathic Medicine (BS in Biology, DO in Osteopathic Medicine). **Credit/placement by examination:** AP, CLEP, IB, institutional tests. 30 credit hours maximum toward bachelor's degree. **Support services:** Learning center, reduced course load, remedial instruction, study skills assistance, tutoring, writing center.

Majors. Biology: General, biochemistry. **Business:** General, accounting, information resources management. **Communications:** Communications/speech/rhetoric. **Computer sciences:** General. **Conservation:** Environmental studies. **Education:** Elementary, social science. **English:** English lit. **Foreign languages:** French, German, Spanish. **History:** General. **Math:** General. **Parks/recreation:** Sports admin. **Philosophy/religion:** Philosophy. **Physical sciences:** Chemistry. **Psychology:** General. **Social sciences:** Criminology, economics, international relations, political science, sociology. **Theology:** Theology. **Visual/performing arts:** General. **Work/family studies:** Family/community services.

Most popular majors. Biology 8%, business/marketing 27%, communications/journalism 6%, education 7%, psychology 6%, social sciences 23%.

Technology on campus. 80 workstations in library, computer center, student center. Dormitories wired for high-speed internet access and linked to campus network. Commuter students can connect to campus network. Online course registration, online library, helpline, repair service, student web hosting, wireless network available.

Student life. Freshman orientation: Mandatory, $250 fee. Preregistration for classes offered. Choice of 1 of 2 weekends in June for pre-registration and 3-day weekend in August. **Housing:** Guaranteed on-campus for all undergraduates. Coed dorms, special housing for disabled, apartments, themed housing, wellness housing available. **Activities:** Bands, campus ministries, choral groups, dance, drama, international student organizations, literary magazine, music ensembles, musical theater, radio station, student government, student newspaper, TV station, Maryland Student Legislature, European Union Simulation, Amnesty International, Campaign to End the Death Penalty, Students for Life, Community Outreach Realizing Equality, Women's Empowerment, Fellowship of Catholic University Students, Black Student Union, Hispanic Cultural Association.

Athletics. NCAA. **Intercollegiate:** Baseball M, basketball, cross-country, lacrosse, soccer W, softball W, swimming W, tennis, track and field. **Intramural:** Basketball, field hockey W, football (non-tackle) M, racquetball, skiing, soccer, softball, swimming, tennis, volleyball. **Team name:** Mountaineers.

Student services. Adult student services, alcohol/substance abuse counseling, chaplain/spiritual director, career counseling, student employment services, financial aid counseling, health services, minority student services, personal counseling, placement for graduates. **Physically disabled:** Services for visually, hearing impaired.

Contact. E-mail: admissions@msmary.edu
Phone: (301) 447-5214 Toll-free number: (800) 448-4347
Fax: (301) 447-5860
Michael Post, Dean of Admissions and Enrollment Management, Mount St. Mary's University, 16300 Old Emmitsburg Road, Emmitsburg, MD 21727

Ner Israel Rabbinical College
Baltimore, Maryland
CB code: 0839

▶ Private 4-year rabbinical college for men affiliated with the Jewish faith
▶ Very large city
▶ 287 degree-seeking undergraduates: 7% international
▶ 200 degree-seeking graduate students
▶ Interview required

General. Accredited by AARTS. **Degrees:** 55 bachelor's awarded; master's, professional, doctoral offered. **Location:** 5 miles from Baltimore city. **Calendar:** Semester, limited summer session. **Full-time faculty:** 20 total.

Basis for selection. Interview, character, religious affiliation most important. High school record and recommendations also important. **Home schooled:** Transcript of courses and grades, state high school equivalency certificate, interview, letter of recommendation (nonparent) required.

2015-2016 Annual costs. Tuition/fees: $10,900. Room/board: $6,600.

Application procedures. Admission: No deadline. $100 fee, may be waived for applicants with need. Admission notification on a rolling basis. **Financial aid:** Closing date 3/1.

Academics. Special study options: Teacher certification program. **Credit/ placement by examination:** AP, CLEP, institutional tests. 21 credit hours maximum toward bachelor's degree.

Majors. Theology: Talmudic.

Student life. Policies: Religious observance required. **Housing:** Guaranteed on-campus for all undergraduates.

Student services. Physically disabled: Services for visually, speech, hearing impaired.

Contact. Phone: (410) 484-7200
Rabbi Beryl Weisbord, Admissions Director, Ner Israel Rabbinical College, 400 Mount Wilson Lane, Baltimore, MD 21208

Notre Dame of Maryland University
Baltimore, Maryland
www.ndm.edu
CB member
CB code: 5114

▶ Private 4-year liberal arts college for women affiliated with the Roman Catholic Church
▶ Residential campus in very large city
▶ 1,009 degree-seeking undergraduates: 49% part-time, 95% women
▶ 1,599 graduate students
▶ SAT or ACT (ACT writing recommended), application essay required

General. Founded in 1873. Regionally accredited. **Degrees:** 299 bachelor's awarded; master's, professional, doctoral offered. **ROTC:** Army. **Location:** 5 miles from Baltimore, 37 miles from Washington, DC. **Calendar:** Semester, limited summer session. **Full-time faculty:** 125 total. **Part-time faculty:** 9 total. **Class size:** 78% < 20, 22% 20-39. **Special facilities:** Planetarium, photography laboratories, art gallery, chapel.

Freshman class profile.

GPA 3.75 or higher:	15%	Rank in top quarter:	49%
GPA 3.50-3.74:	48%	Rank in top tenth:	25%
GPA 3.0-3.49:	15%	Out-of-state:	15%
GPA 2.0-2.99:	22%	Live on campus:	77%

Basis for selection. Careful evaluation of academic record, high school curriculum, test scores, recommendations, personal abilities/talents and goals, intellectual potential and eagerness to learn and be challenged. Students should take SAT by December of senior year. Interview and campus visit highly recommended. Portfolio recommended for art majors. **Home schooled:** Transcript or GED required. **Learning Disabled:** Students with learning disabilities should self-report during admissions process.

High school preparation. College-preparatory program required. 18 units required. Required units include English 4, mathematics 3, social studies 2, science 2 (laboratory 2), foreign language 3 and academic electives 4.

2015-2016 Annual costs. Tuition/fees: $33,670. Room/board: $10,930. Books/supplies: $1,200. Personal expenses: $1,000.

Financial aid. Non-need-based: Scholarships awarded for academics, alumni affiliation, art, leadership, music/drama, ROTC. **Additional information:** Maximum consideration for financial aid if application received by February 15. Auditions and portfolios in areas of art, music and writing considered for scholarships.

Application procedures. Admission: Priority date 2/1; no deadline. $45 fee, may be waived for applicants with need. Admission notification on a rolling basis beginning on or about 12/1. Must reply by May 1 or within 2 week(s) if notified thereafter. **Financial aid:** Priority date 2/15; no closing date. FAFSA required. Applicants notified on a rolling basis starting 3/15; must reply by 5/1 or within 2 week(s) of notification.

Academics. Special study options: Accelerated study, combined bachelor's/graduate degree, cross-registration, distance learning, double major, dual enrollment of high school students, ESL, honors, independent study, internships, liberal arts/career combination, study abroad, teacher certification program, weekend college. 3-2 programs in engineering and nursing with Johns Hopkins University; academic consortium with seven local colleges and universities. **Credit/placement by examination:** AP, CLEP, IB, SAT, ACT, institutional tests. 30 credit hours maximum toward bachelor's degree. AP, CLEP and IB credits are posted upon admissions to college. Students should send testing information with their admissions application or prior to start of their first semester. **Support services:** Learning center, pre-admission summer program, reduced course load, remedial instruction, study skills assistance, tutoring, writing center.

Majors. Biology: General, neuroscience. **Business:** General, finance, international, nonprofit/public. **Communications:** General, digital media, media studies. **Computer sciences:** General, computer science. **Education:** Early childhood, elementary, secondary, special ed. **Engineering:** General. **English:** English lit. **Foreign languages:** General, classics, French, Spanish. **Health services:** Medical radiologic technology/radiation therapy. **History:** General. **Human services:** Community org/advocacy. **Liberal arts:** Arts/ sciences. **Math:** General. **Philosophy/religion:** Philosophy, religion. **Physical sciences:** Chemistry, physics. **Psychology:** General, industrial. **Social sciences:** Criminology, economics, international relations, political science. **Visual/performing arts:** Art, art history/conservation, photography, studio arts.

Technology on campus. 80 workstations in dormitories, library, computer center, student center. Dormitories wired for high-speed internet access and linked to campus network. Commuter students can connect to campus network. Online course registration, online library, helpline, repair service, wireless network available.

Student life. Freshman orientation: Mandatory. Preregistration for classes offered. Two-day program in June; 4-day program prior to start of school in late August/early September. **Policies:** Must abide by honor code. **Housing:** Guaranteed on-campus for all undergraduates. Wellness housing available. $500 nonrefundable deposit, deadline 5/1. **Activities:** Campus ministries, choral groups, dance, drama, international student organizations, literary magazine, music ensembles, musical theater, radio station, student government, student newspaper, TV station, community service organization, Hispanic society, Black student organization, inter-organizational council, student environmental organization, international student organization, campus ministry student organization, student health educators.

Athletics. NCAA. **Intercollegiate:** Basketball W, field hockey W, lacrosse W, soccer W, softball W, swimming W, tennis W, volleyball W. **Team name:** Gators.

Student services. Adult student services, alcohol/substance abuse counseling, chaplain/spiritual director, career counseling, services for economically disadvantaged, student employment services, financial aid counseling, health services, personal counseling, placement for graduates, veterans' counselor, women's services. **Physically disabled:** Services for visually, speech, hearing impaired.

Contact. E-mail: admiss@ndm.edu
Phone: (410) 532-5330 Toll-free number: (800) 435-0200
Fax: (410) 532-6287
Angela Baumler, Assistant Director of Admissions, Notre Dame of Maryland University, 4701 North Charles Street, Baltimore, MD 21210

Salisbury University
Salisbury, Maryland   **CB member**
www.salisbury.edu   **CB code: 5403**

▸ Public 4-year university and liberal arts college
▸ Residential campus in large town
▸ 7,612 degree-seeking undergraduates: 6% part-time, 57% women, 13% African American, 3% Asian American, 4% Hispanic/Latino, 1% Native American, 4% Multi-racial, non-Hispanic, 1% international
▸ 754 degree-seeking graduate students
▸ 61% of applicants admitted
▸ Application essay required
▸ 67% graduate within 6 years; 20% enter graduate study

General. Founded in 1925. Regionally accredited. **Degrees:** 1,935 bachelor's awarded; master's, professional, doctoral offered. **ROTC:** Army, Air Force. **Location:** 30 miles from Ocean City, 120 miles from Baltimore, 120 miles from Washington DC. **Calendar:** 4-1-4, limited summer session. **Full-time faculty:** 415 total; 85% have terminal degrees, 16% minority, 49% women. **Part-time faculty:** 241 total; 21% have terminal degrees, 8% minority, 67% women. **Class size:** 32% < 20, 61% 20-39, 4% 40-49, 2% 50-99, less than 1% >100. **Special facilities:** Research center, museum of business and entrepreneurship, museum of wildfowl art, literacy center, theater, medical simulation center.

Freshman class profile. 8,360 applied, 5,069 admitted, 1,189 enrolled.

Mid 50% test scores			
SAT critical reading:	540-620	Rank in top quarter:	54%
SAT math:	540-620	Rank in top tenth:	20%
SAT writing:	530-610	End year in good standing:	85%
ACT composite:	21-26	Return as sophomores:	82%
GPA 3.75 or higher:	45%	Out-of-state:	19%
GPA 3.50-3.74:	31%	Live on campus:	99%
GPA 3.0-3.49:	19%	International:	1%
GPA 2.0-2.99:	5%	Fraternities:	10%
		Sororities:	10%

Basis for selection. Rigor of secondary school record, including level of courses, depth of subjects and academic GPA most important. Activities, leadership roles, artistic or athletic talents and ability to contribute to a culturally diverse community also considered. The admissions review process considers the qualifications of all applicants in a holistic manner. The students' high school curriculum, performance in academic coursework and on standardized tests like the SAT and/or ACT (where applicable), essay, recommendations, leadership experience, community service, talents, extracurricular activities and the ability to contribute to the diverse academic community at SU are many of the qualifications considered for admission. SAT/ACT optional for students with 3.5 GPA or higher (on 4.0 scale). Auditions required for music and BFA art programs, once admission to university is granted.

High school preparation. College-preparatory program recommended. 15 units required; 21 recommended. Required and recommended units include English 4, mathematics 4, social studies 3, science 3-4 (laboratory 2-3), foreign language 2-3 and academic electives 3.

2015-2016 Annual costs. Tuition/fees: $9,086; $17,432 out-of-state. Room/board: $11,010. Books/supplies: $1,300. Personal expenses: $1,500.

2014-2015 Financial aid. Need-based: 985 full-time freshmen applied for aid; 593 deemed to have need; 572 received aid. Average need met was 51%. Average scholarship/grant was $6,323; average loan $3,128. 41% of total undergraduate aid awarded as scholarships/grants, 59% as loans/jobs. **Non-need-based:** Awarded to 911 full-time undergraduates, including 281 freshmen. Scholarships awarded for academics, alumni affiliation, art, leadership, music/drama, ROTC, state residency.

Application procedures. Admission: Closing date 1/15 (postmark date). $50 fee, may be waived for applicants with need. Application must be submitted online. Admission notification by 3/15. Must reply by 5/1. **Financial aid:** Priority date 3/1, closing date 12/31. FAFSA required. Applicants notified by 3/15; must reply by 5/1.

Academics. Special study options: Accelerated study, combined bachelor's/graduate degree, cooperative education, cross-registration, distance learning, double major, dual enrollment of high school students, ESL, exchange student, honors, independent study, internships, student-designed major, study abroad, teacher certification program, Washington semester. Learning disabilities services, off-campus study, summer sessions for credit, pass/fail grading option, certificate programs. **Credit/placement by examination:** AP, CLEP, IB, institutional tests. 60 credit hours maximum toward bachelor's degree. Institution will apply a maximum of 60 semester hours of course work toward the completion of a Baccalaureate degree for acceptable credit by examination scores. **Support services:** Learning center, study skills assistance, tutoring, writing center. Academic counseling, math tutoring.

Honors college/program. GPA, SAT/ACT and separate admissions essay most important; must be admitted into Honors program with supplemental application.

Majors. Biology: General, ecology. **Business:** Accounting, business admin, finance, international, managerial economics, marketing. **Communications:** Communications/speech/rhetoric. **Computer sciences:** General, information systems. **Conservation:** Environmental science. **Education:** Early childhood, elementary, ESL, health, physical. **English:** English lit. **Foreign languages:** French, Spanish. **Health services:** Athletic training, clinical lab science, nursing (RN), respiratory therapy technology. **History:** General. **Human services:** Social work. **Liberal arts:** Arts/sciences. **Math:** General. **Parks/recreation:** Exercise sciences. **Philosophy/religion:** Philosophy. **Physical sciences:** Chemistry, physics. **Psychology:** General. **Social sciences:** Economics, geography, political science, sociology. **Visual/performing arts:** Art, dramatic, music, studio arts.

Most popular majors. Biology 6%, business/marketing 15%, communications/journalism 8%, education 10%, health sciences 8%, parks/recreation 7%, psychology 7%, social sciences 6%.

Technology on campus. 500 workstations in dormitories, library, computer center, student center. Dormitories wired for high-speed internet access and linked to campus network. Commuter students can connect to campus network. Online course registration, online library, helpline, repair service, student web hosting, wireless network available.

Student life. Freshman orientation: Mandatory, $150 fee. Preregistration for classes offered. Held for a full-day; parents and family members are welcome to attend. **Policies:** Class attendance policies set by individual instructor. Hazing prohibited. **Housing:** Guaranteed on-campus for freshmen. Coed dorms, special housing for disabled, apartments, themed housing, wellness housing available. $300 nonrefundable deposit, deadline 5/1. Living/learning communities. **Activities:** Bands, campus ministries, choral groups, dance, drama, film society, international student organizations, literary magazine, music ensembles, Model UN, musical theater, opera, radio station, student government, student newspaper, symphony orchestra, TV station, All Nations for Christ, Muslim Student Association, Young Life; College Democrats, College Republicans, African Student Association, Asian and Pacific Islanders club, Student United Way, Habitat for Humanity, Active Minds.

Athletics. NCAA. **Intercollegiate:** Baseball M, basketball, cross-country, field hockey W, football (tackle) M, lacrosse, soccer, softball W, swimming, tennis, track and field, volleyball W. **Intramural:** Basketball, football (non-tackle), racquetball, sand volleyball, soccer, softball, volleyball. **Team name:** Sea Gulls.

Student services. Adult student services, alcohol/substance abuse counseling, career counseling, student employment services, financial aid counseling, health services, minority student services, personal counseling, veterans' counselor, women's services. **Physically disabled:** Services for visually, speech, hearing impaired.

Contact. E-mail: admissions@salisbury.edu
Phone: (410) 543-6161 Toll-free number: (888) 543-0148
Fax: (410) 546-6016
Elizabeth Skoglund, Director of Admissions, Salisbury University, 1101 Camden Avenue, Salisbury, MD 21801

St. John's College
Annapolis, Maryland   **CB member**
www.sjc.edu   **CB code: 5598**

▸ Private 4-year liberal arts college
▸ Residential campus in large town

- 406 degree-seeking undergraduates: 45% women
- 45 degree-seeking graduate students
- 78% of applicants admitted
- Application essay required
- 71% graduate within 6 years

General. Founded in 1784. Regionally accredited. Two campuses: Annapolis, Maryland and Santa Fe, New Mexico. Students can alternate studies between the two without sacrificing any time toward graduation, quality of instruction, or benefit of the curriculum. Students select a "home" campus but may elect to spend a year (or more) at the sister location across the country. **Degrees:** 97 bachelor's awarded; master's offered. **Location:** 35 miles from Washington, DC; 30 miles from Baltimore. **Calendar:** Semester. **Full-time faculty:** 75 total; 80% have terminal degrees, 11% minority, 32% women. **Part-time faculty:** 6 total; 33% have terminal degrees, 17% women. **Class size:** 99% < 20, less than 1% >100. **Special facilities:** Planetarium, observatory, boathouse, art gallery, music library.

Freshman class profile. 332 applied, 260 admitted, 105 enrolled.

Mid 50% test scores		Rank in top quarter:	49%
SAT critical reading:	620-740	Rank in top tenth:	33%
SAT math:	590-700	Return as sophomores:	81%
SAT writing:	600-700	Out-of-state:	49%
ACT composite:	24-30	Live on campus:	92%

Basis for selection. Holistic approach, where the applicant's essays, academic record and recommendations are considered. Standardized test scores are required from home-schooled and international applicants, as well as those who have not and will not graduate from high school. Two required essays and one optional. Interviews are recommended, but not required. **Home schooled:** Statement describing home school structure and mission, letter of recommendation (nonparent) required. A GED or a GED equivalent must be accompanied by an SAT/ACT test score.

High school preparation. College-preparatory program recommended. Recommended units include English 4, mathematics 3, social studies 3, science 3, foreign language 2, academic electives 2.5. Additional 2.5 electives spread among academic or arts offerings recommended.

2016-2017 Annual costs. Tuition/fees: $50,228. Room/board: $11,888. Books/supplies: $630. Personal expenses: $400.

2015-2016 Financial aid. Need-based: 85 full-time freshmen applied for aid; 72 deemed to have need; 72 received aid. Average need met was 85%. Average scholarship/grant was $31,235; average loan $3,715. 82% of total undergraduate aid awarded as scholarships/grants, 18% as loans/jobs. **Non-need-based:** Awarded to 155 full-time undergraduates, including 52 freshmen. Scholarships awarded for academics. **Additional information:** All applicants automatically considered for merit scholarships, and all students completing the FAFSA are considered for need-based financial aid.

Application procedures. Admission: Priority date 1/15; no deadline. No application fee. Admission notification on a rolling basis beginning on or about 12/15. Must reply by May 1 or within 3 week(s) if notified thereafter. **Financial aid:** Priority date 2/15; no closing date. FAFSA required. International students must complete CSS PROFILE. Applicants notified on a rolling basis starting 12/15; must reply by 5/1 or within 2 week(s) of notification.

Academics. Special study options: Cross-registration, internships. **Credit/placement by examination:** AP, CLEP. **Support services:** Tutoring, writing center.

Majors. Liberal arts: Arts/sciences.

Technology on campus. 26 workstations in library, computer center. Dormitories wired for high-speed internet access and linked to campus network. Commuter students can connect to campus network. Online library, helpline, wireless network available.

Student life. Freshman orientation: Mandatory. Preregistration for classes offered. Two-day program held after registration and prior to start of classes. **Policies:** Freshmen are required to live on campus. Freshmen not permitted cars on campus. **Housing:** Guaranteed on-campus for freshmen. Coed dorms, single-sex dorms, wellness housing available. $300 nonrefundable deposit, deadline 5/1. **Activities:** Campus ministries, choral groups, dance, drama, film society, international student organizations, literary magazine, music ensembles, musical theater, student government, student newspaper, symphony orchestra, environmental issues club, LGBTQ alliance, community service club, vegan/vegetarian club, Orthodox Christian Fellowship, Jewish student group, Chinese teahouse, committee on student life, delegate council, student committee on instruction.

Athletics. Intercollegiate: Fencing, rowing (crew), sailing. **Intramural:** Basketball, football (non-tackle), handball, soccer, volleyball.

Student services. Alcohol/substance abuse counseling, career counseling, student employment services, financial aid counseling, health services, personal counseling, placement for graduates, women's services.

Contact. E-mail: annapolis.admissions@sjc.edu
Phone: (410) 626-2522 Toll-free number: (800) 727-9238
Fax: (410) 269-7916
Benjamin Baum, Director of Admissions, St. John's College, 60 College Avenue, Annapolis, MD 21401

St. Mary's College of Maryland
St. Mary's City, Maryland
www.smcm.edu
CB member
CB code: 5601

- Public 4-year liberal arts college
- Residential campus in small town
- 1,725 degree-seeking undergraduates: 3% part-time, 57% women, 8% African American, 3% Asian American, 8% Hispanic/Latino, 4% Multiracial, non-Hispanic, 1% international
- 27 degree-seeking graduate students
- 79% of applicants admitted
- SAT or ACT (ACT writing optional), application essay required
- 78% graduate within 6 years; 48% enter graduate study

General. Founded in 1840. Regionally accredited. **Degrees:** 501 bachelor's awarded; master's offered. **Location:** 70 miles from Washington, DC. **Calendar:** Semester, limited summer session. **Full-time faculty:** 141 total; 97% have terminal degrees, 18% minority, 48% women. **Part-time faculty:** 49 total; 24% have terminal degrees, 12% minority, 53% women. **Class size:** 72% < 20, 26% 20-39, 2% 40-49. **Special facilities:** Archaeological site of Historic St. Mary's City, electron microscope, marine research vessel, fresh and salt water research facilities, comprehensive neuroscience laboratory facilities.

Freshman class profile. 1,675 applied, 1,320 admitted, 394 enrolled.

Mid 50% test scores		GPA 3.0-3.49:	38%
SAT critical reading:	530-640	GPA 2.0-2.99:	18%
SAT math:	500-620	Return as sophomores:	85%
SAT writing:	510-620	Out-of-state:	8%
ACT composite:	22-28	Live on campus:	96%
GPA 3.75 or higher:	19%	International:	1%
GPA 3.50-3.74:	25%		

Basis for selection. High school record most important, with careful attention paid to co-curricular activities (including work and family responsibilities), essays, letters of recommendation, and standardized test scores. Interviews optional. Supplemental essay required via Common Application. **Home schooled:** Statement describing home school structure and mission, transcript of courses and grades, letter of recommendation (nonparent) required. Personal statement.

High school preparation. College-preparatory program recommended. 20 units required; 24 recommended. Required and recommended units include English 4, mathematics 3-4, social studies 2-3, history 1, science 3 (laboratory 2) and foreign language 4.

2015-2016 Annual costs. Tuition/fees: $13,895; $28,745 out-of-state. Room/board: $12,290. Books/supplies: $1,200. Personal expenses: $1,025.

2015-2016 Financial aid. Need-based: 320 full-time freshmen applied for aid; 210 deemed to have need; 207 received aid. Average need met was 73%. Average scholarship/grant was $10,337; average loan $3,327. 63% of total undergraduate aid awarded as scholarships/grants, 37% as loans/jobs. **Non-need-based:** Awarded to 867 full-time undergraduates, including 236 freshmen. Scholarships awarded for academics, alumni affiliation.

Application procedures. Admission: Priority date 11/1; deadline 2/15 (postmark date). $50 fee, may be waived for applicants with need. Admission notification by 3/1. Must reply by 5/1. **Financial aid:** Priority date 2/28; no closing date. FAFSA required. Applicants notified by 4/1; must reply by 5/1.

Academics. Special study options: Cross-registration, double major, dual enrollment of high school students, exchange student, honors, independent study, internships, liberal arts/career combination, semester at sea, student-designed major, study abroad, Washington semester. International study programs in Argentina, Australia, China, Costa Rica, England, France, the Gambia, Germany, Japan, India, Ireland, Thailand, and many other short-term study tours around the world. Opportunities for participating in colonial and archaeological research. **Credit/placement by examination:** AP, CLEP, IB, institutional tests. 45 credit hours maximum toward bachelor's degree. **Support services:** Pre-admission summer program, reduced course load, study skills assistance, tutoring, writing center.

Majors. **Area/ethnic studies:** Asian. **Biology:** General, biochemistry. **Computer sciences:** General. **Conservation:** Environmental studies. **English:** English lit. **Foreign languages:** General. **History:** General. **Human services:** Public policy. **Liberal arts:** Humanities. **Math:** General. **Philosophy/religion:** Philosophy, religion. **Physical sciences:** Chemistry, physics. **Psychology:** General. **Social sciences:** Anthropology, economics, political science, sociology. **Visual/performing arts:** Art, dramatic, music.

Most popular majors. Biology 15%, English 9%, psychology 14%, social sciences 26%, visual/performing arts 8%.

Technology on campus. 400 workstations in library, computer center, student center. Dormitories wired for high-speed internet access and linked to campus network. Commuter students can connect to campus network. Online course registration, online library, helpline, student web hosting, wireless network available.

Student life. **Freshman orientation:** Mandatory, $100 fee. Preregistration for classes offered. Four-day program held Thursday-Sunday prior to start of fall semester. **Policies:** Membership in student organizations is available to all full-time, degree-seeking students. Elected student leaders must be in good standing with the institution in order to serve. **Housing:** Guaranteed on-campus for all undergraduates. Coed dorms, single-sex dorms, special housing for disabled, apartments, gender-neutral housing, themed housing, wellness housing available. $500 nonrefundable deposit, deadline 5/1: Pets allowed in dorm rooms. Townhouses and suites available for upper-class students. **Activities:** Bands, campus ministries, choral groups, dance, drama, international student organizations, literary magazine, music ensembles, Model UN, musical theater, radio station, student government, student newspaper, symphony orchestra, black student union, College Republicans, College Democrats, Amnesty International, For Goodness Sake, Hillel, Habitat for Humanity, student environmental action coalition, Intervarsity Christian Fellowship, St. Mary's Triangle and Rainbow Society, Students for a Democratic Society.

Athletics. NCAA. **Intercollegiate:** Baseball M, basketball, cross-country, field hockey W, lacrosse, sailing, soccer, swimming, tennis, volleyball W. **Intramural:** Badminton, basketball, cross-country, field hockey, football (non-tackle), soccer, volleyball. **Team name:** Seahawks.

Student services. Adult student services, alcohol/substance abuse counseling, career counseling, services for economically disadvantaged, student employment services, financial aid counseling, health services, minority student services, personal counseling, placement for graduates, veterans' counselor, women's services. **Physically disabled:** Services for visually, hearing impaired.

Contact. E-mail: admissions@smcm.edu
Phone: (240) 895-5000 Toll-free number: (800) 492-7181
Fax: (240) 895-5001
Gary Sherman, Vice President of Enrollment Managment and Dean of Admissions, St. Mary's College of Maryland, 18952 East Fisher Road, St. Mary's City, MD 20686-3001

Stevenson University
Stevenson, Maryland **CB member**
www.stevenson.edu **CB code: 5856**

- Private 4-year university
- Residential campus in very large city
- 3,665 degree-seeking undergraduates: 15% part-time, 67% women, 27% African American, 3% Asian American, 5% Hispanic/Latino, 4% Multiracial, non-Hispanic
- 483 degree-seeking graduate students
- 60% of applicants admitted
- SAT or ACT (ACT writing optional), application essay required
- 56% graduate within 6 years

General. Founded in 1947. Regionally accredited. **Degrees:** 841 bachelor's awarded; master's offered. **ROTC:** Army, Air Force. **Location:** 8 miles from Baltimore. **Calendar:** Semester, extensive summer session. **Full-time faculty:** 144 total; 73% have terminal degrees, 16% minority, 55% women. **Part-time faculty:** 327 total; 35% have terminal degrees, 13% minority, 50% women. **Class size:** 68% < 20, 32% 20-39. **Special facilities:** Nursing skills lab, moot courtroom.

Freshman class profile. 5,747 applied, 3,433 admitted, 1,417 enrolled.

Mid 50% test scores			
SAT critical reading:	450-550	GPA 3.0-3.49:	36%
SAT math:	450-560	GPA 2.0-2.99:	17%
SAT writing:	450-550	Rank in top quarter:	48%
ACT composite:	19-24	Rank in top tenth:	18%
GPA 3.75 or higher:	25%	Out-of-state:	32%
GPA 3.50-3.74:	22%	Live on campus:	86%

Basis for selection. High school record and test scores most important. Optional interview, recommendations, essay, extracurricular activities also important. Interviews recommended.

High school preparation. College-preparatory program recommended. 17 units required. Required units include English 4, mathematics 3, social studies 2, history 1, science 3 (laboratory 2).

2015-2016 Annual costs. Tuition/fees: $30,998. Room/board: $12,720. Books/supplies: $1,250. Personal expenses: $1,080.

2014-2015 Financial aid. **Need-based:** 655 full-time freshmen applied for aid; 579 deemed to have need; 579 received aid. Average need met was 61%. Average scholarship/grant was $17,771; average loan $3,298. 66% of total undergraduate aid awarded as scholarships/grants, 34% as loans/jobs. **Non-need-based:** Awarded to 733 full-time undergraduates, including 166 freshmen. Scholarships awarded for academics, art. **Additional information:** Cooperative Education Program allows students to work in their field of study with area corporations.

Application procedures. **Admission:** Priority date 3/1; no deadline. $40 fee, may be waived for applicants with need, free for online applicants. Admission notification on a rolling basis beginning on or about 12/1. Must reply by May 1 or within 2 week(s) if notified thereafter. **Financial aid:** Priority date 2/15; no closing date. FAFSA required. Applicants notified on a rolling basis starting 3/15; must reply by 5/1 or within 2 week(s) of notification.

Academics. Advanced technology programs, forensic science program and forensic studies programs offered. Cooperative education program available to third- and fourth-year students. Career Architecture, a program for personal and professional development, is integrated into all programs. **Special study options:** Accelerated study, cooperative education, cross-registration, distance learning, dual enrollment of high school students, independent study, internships, liberal arts/career combination, student-designed major, study abroad, teacher certification program, Washington semester. **Credit/placement by examination:** AP, CLEP, IB, SAT, ACT, institutional tests. 15 credit hours maximum toward associate degree, 30 toward bachelor's. **Support services:** Learning center, pre-admission summer program, reduced course load, remedial instruction, study skills assistance, tutoring, writing center.

Majors. **Biology:** General, biochemistry, biotechnology. **Business:** Accounting, business admin, communications, fashion, management information systems. **Communications:** Digital media. **Computer sciences:** Information systems, networking. **Conservation:** Environmental science. **Education:** Elementary, kindergarten/preschool, middle. **English:** English lit. **Health services:** Clinical lab science, nursing (RN). **History:** Applied. **Math:** Applied. **Physical sciences:** Chemistry. **Protective services:** Law enforcement admin. **Psychology:** General. **Visual/performing arts:** Acting, design, fashion design, film/cinema/video. **Work/family studies:** Family/community services.

Most popular majors. Business/marketing 23%, computer/information sciences 8%, education 7%, health sciences 21%, security/protective services 9%, visual/performing arts 7%.

Technology on campus. 89 workstations in library, computer center, student center. Dormitories wired for high-speed internet access and linked to campus network. Commuter students can connect to campus network. Online course registration, online library, helpline, repair service, wireless network available.

Student life. **Freshman orientation:** Mandatory. Preregistration for classes offered. Full-day program, conducted by major, held during June. Freshmen also attend second orientation in August, prior to start of fall semester. **Housing:** Coed dorms, apartments, themed housing available. Suite style housing (2 bedrooms, share bath); accommodations made for students with disabilities. **Activities:** Bands, campus ministries, choral groups, dance, drama, international student organizations, literary magazine, music ensembles, musical theater, radio station, student government, student newspaper, TV station, black student union, Service Corps, Campus Crusade for Christ, Extreme Acts, activities and program board, accounting association, Students Helping Students.

Athletics. NCAA. **Intercollegiate:** Baseball M, basketball, cheerleading W, cross-country, field hockey W, football (tackle) M, golf, ice hockey W, lacrosse, soccer, softball W, tennis, track and field, volleyball. **Intramural:** Basketball M, football (non-tackle) M, soccer, table tennis, tennis, track and field, volleyball. **Team name:** Mustangs.

Student services. Adult student services, alcohol/substance abuse counseling, career counseling, student employment services, financial aid counseling, health services, minority student services, personal counseling, placement for graduates, veterans' counselor. **Physically disabled:** Services for visually, speech, hearing impaired.

Contact. E-mail: admissions@stevenson.edu
Phone: (410) 486-7001 Toll-free number: (877) 468-6852
Fax: (443) 352-4440
Mark Hergan, Vice President for Enrollment Management, Stevenson University, 1525 Greenspring Valley Road, Stevenson, MD 21153-0641

Towson University
Towson, Maryland
www.towson.edu

CB member
CB code: 5404

- Public 4-year university
- Commuter campus in small city
- 18,806 degree-seeking undergraduates: 11% part-time, 60% women, 18% African American, 5% Asian American, 6% Hispanic/Latino, 4% Multi-racial, non-Hispanic, 2% international
- 3,161 degree-seeking graduate students
- 73% of applicants admitted
- SAT or ACT (ACT writing optional), application essay required
- 70% graduate within 6 years

General. Founded in 1866. Regionally accredited. **Degrees:** 4,422 bachelor's awarded; master's, professional, doctoral offered. **ROTC:** Army, Air Force. **Location:** 8 miles from downtown Baltimore. **Calendar:** Semester, extensive summer session. **Full-time faculty:** 899 total; 79% have terminal degrees, 19% minority, 56% women. **Part-time faculty:** 779 total; 28% have terminal degrees, 16% minority, 57% women. **Class size:** 30% < 20, 63% 20-39, 5% 40-49, 3% 50-99, less than 1% >100. **Special facilities:** 3D printing lab, art galleries, Asian arts and culture center, media center, speech and language center, planetarium/observatory, herbarium, nursing simulation center, regional medical centers, field station, biodiversity center.

Freshman class profile. 10,947 applied, 8,033 admitted, 2,714 enrolled.

Mid 50% test scores			
SAT critical reading:	500-580	Rank in top quarter:	45%
SAT math:	500-590	Rank in top tenth:	18%
SAT writing:	490-580	Return as sophomores:	86%
ACT composite:	21-25	Out-of-state:	25%
GPA 3.75 or higher:	37%	Live on campus:	85%
GPA 3.50-3.74:	23%	International:	2%
GPA 3.0-3.49:	37%	Fraternities:	10%
GPA 2.0-2.99:	3%	Sororities:	15%

Basis for selection. Official high school transcript (GPA), standardized test scores (SAT or ACT), college essay, letters of recommendation (optional), and extracurricular activities list (optional). Interview recommended. Audition required of music, dance, acting majors. Portfolio required of certain art majors. **Home schooled:** Coursework/transcripts verified by either a homeschool agency or the school district where the student lives showing they have met all requirements to graduate high school.

High school preparation. 22 units required. Required units include English 4, mathematics 4, social studies 3, science 3 (laboratory 2), foreign language 2 and academic electives 6.

2015-2016 Annual costs. Tuition/fees: $9,182; $20,788 out-of-state. Room/board: $11,638. Books/supplies: $1,080. Personal expenses: $1,500.

2015-2016 Financial aid. Need-based: 2,353 full-time freshmen applied for aid; 1,599 deemed to have need; 1,491 received aid. Average need met was 57%. Average scholarship/grant was $8,290; average loan $3,194. 60% of total undergraduate aid awarded as scholarships/grants, 40% as loans/jobs. **Non-need-based:** Awarded to 3,627 full-time undergraduates, including 1,101 freshmen. Scholarships awarded for academics, alumni affiliation, art, athletics, leadership, music/drama, ROTC, state residency.

Application procedures. Admission: Priority date 12/1; deadline 1/15 (receipt date). $45 fee, may be waived for applicants with need. Application must be submitted online. Admission notification on a rolling basis beginning on or about 11/6. Must reply by 5/1. **Financial aid:** Priority date 2/15; no closing date. FAFSA required. Applicants notified on a rolling basis starting 3/21; must reply within 2 week(s) of notification.

Academics. Special study options: Combined bachelor's/graduate degree, cooperative education, cross-registration, distance learning, double major, dual enrollment of high school students, ESL, exchange student, honors, independent study, internships, liberal arts/career combination, student-designed major, study abroad, teacher certification program. **Credit/placement by examination:** AP, CLEP, IB, SAT, ACT, institutional tests. 45 credit hours maximum toward bachelor's degree. Portfolio reviews, oral exams, demonstrations or written reports/papers considered for credit. **Support services:** Learning center, remedial instruction, study skills assistance, tutoring, writing center.

Honors college/program. No minimum score requirements, but average is GPA of 4.11 and SAT of 1900 or ACT of 28. The middle 50% ranges for those scores are GPA 3.94-4.34, SAT 1810-1990, and ACT 27-30. Applicants must submit a separate essay and resume, and have the option for a letter of recommendation from a classroom instructor. The approximate number of freshmen admitted: 160. Academic program: four-year program of 24 units, composed of 3 units of Honors English, 15 units of Honors course equivalents and seminars, and 6 units of electives or experiential learning.

Majors. Area/ethnic studies: American, deaf, women's. **Biology:** General. **Business:** Accounting, business admin, e-commerce. **Communications:** General, media studies. **Computer sciences:** Computer science, information systems, information technology. **Conservation:** General. **Education:** Art, early childhood, elementary, elementary special ed, middle, music, physical, special ed. **English:** English lit. **Foreign languages:** General. **Health services:** General, athletic training, audiology/speech pathology, health care admin, nursing (RN), occupational therapy. **History:** General. **Math:** General. **Parks/recreation:** Exercise sciences, sports admin. **Philosophy/religion:** Philosophy, religion. **Physical sciences:** Chemistry, geology, physics. **Protective services:** Forensics. **Psychology:** General. **Social sciences:** General, economics, geography, international relations, political science, sociology/anthropology, urban studies. **Visual/performing arts:** Acting, art, art history/conservation, dance, dramatic, music, studio arts. **Work/family studies:** Family systems.

Most popular majors. Business/marketing 14%, communications/journalism 8%, education 10%, health sciences 12%, parks/recreation 7%, psychology 8%, social sciences 10%, visual/performing arts 6%.

Technology on campus. 2,500 workstations in dormitories, library, computer center, student center. Dormitories wired for high-speed internet access and linked to campus network. Commuter students can connect to campus network. Online course registration, online library, helpline, repair service, student web hosting, wireless network available.

Student life. Freshman orientation: Mandatory. Preregistration for classes offered. **Policies:** Students play active role in university governance. **Housing:** Guaranteed on-campus for freshmen. Coed dorms, special housing for disabled, apartments, gender-neutral housing available. $350 nonrefundable deposit, deadline 5/1. Alcohol free floors, Honors housing, STEM housing, Service floor: Tigers Serving, American Sign Language Floor, SAGE Community. **Activities:** Bands, campus ministries, choral groups, dance, drama, film society, international student organizations, literary magazine, music ensembles, Model UN, musical theater, opera, radio station, student government, student newspaper, symphony orchestra, TV station, Black Student Union, Hillel, Alternative Break Connections, Students Helping Honduras, Queer Student Union, Bethel Campus Fellowship, Chabad, Chinese American Student Union, College Democrats, College Republicans.

Athletics. NCAA. **Intercollegiate:** Baseball M, basketball, cross-country W, diving, field hockey W, football (tackle) M, golf, gymnastics W, lacrosse, soccer W, softball W, swimming, tennis W, track and field W, volleyball W. **Intramural:** Basketball, football (non-tackle), soccer, ultimate frisbee, volleyball. **Team name:** Tigers.

Student services. Adult student services, alcohol/substance abuse counseling, career counseling, student employment services, financial aid counseling, health services, minority student services, on-campus daycare, personal counseling, placement for graduates, veterans' counselor, women's services. **Physically disabled:** Services for visually, speech, hearing impaired.

Contact. E-mail: admissions@towson.edu
Phone: (410) 704-2113 Fax: (410) 704-3030
David Fedorchak, Director of Admissions, Towson University, 8000 York Road, Towson, MD 21252-0001

United States Naval Academy
Annapolis, Maryland
www.usna.edu

CB member
CB code: 5809

- Public 4-year military college
- Residential campus in large town
- 4,525 degree-seeking undergraduates: 25% women, 7% African American, 7% Asian American, 11% Hispanic/Latino, 1% Native Hawaiian/Pacific islander, 8% Multi-racial, non-Hispanic, 1% international
- 9% of applicants admitted
- SAT or ACT (ACT writing optional), application essay, interview required
- 86% graduate within 6 years; 6% enter graduate study

General. Founded in 1845. Regionally accredited. **Degrees:** 1,081 bachelor's awarded. **Location:** 30 miles from Baltimore, 32 miles from Washington,

DC. **Calendar:** Semester, limited summer session. **Full-time faculty:** 554 total; 66% have terminal degrees, 12% minority, 29% women. **Part-time faculty:** 38 total; 10% have terminal degrees, 34% minority, 45% women. **Class size:** 70% < 20, 30% 20-39, less than 1% 40-49, less than 1% 50-99. **Special facilities:** Observatory, planetarium, satellite earth station, oceanographic research vessel, weather station, tow tanks, propulsion laboratory, transonic and hypersonic wind tunnels, Naval museum, sailing center, yard patrol squadron, golf course.

Freshman class profile. 16,101 applied, 1,373 admitted, 1,195 enrolled.

Mid 50% test scores			
SAT critical reading:	570-680	Rank in top quarter:	81%
SAT math:	610-700	Rank in top tenth:	58%
GPA 3.75 or higher:	75%	End year in good standing:	98%
GPA 3.50-3.74:	13%	Return as sophomores:	98%
GPA 3.0-3.49:	10%	Out-of-state:	94%
GPA 2.0-2.99:	2%	Live on campus:	100%
		International:	1%

Basis for selection. Test scores, school achievement record, interview, recommendations of school officials, participation in sports, school, and community activities important. Rank in top 40% of class usually required. Successful candidate must be qualified medically, pass a candidate physical fitness assessment, and be nominated by an official source.

High school preparation. College-preparatory program recommended. Recommended units include English 4, mathematics 4, history 2, science 2 (laboratory 2) and foreign language 2. Familiarity with the use of personal computers, including the Windows operating system, word processing, spreadsheets, and the Internet required.

2016-2017 Annual costs. The Naval Academy does not charge tuition, room, board, or any other fees. Medical and dental care is provided by the United States Government. Each midshipman receives a monthly salary to cover costs of books, supplies, uniform, laundry, and equipment including a computer and a printer.

Application procedures. Admission: Closing date 1/31 (receipt date). No application fee. Application must be submitted online. Admission notification on a rolling basis beginning on or about 9/1. Must reply by May 1 or within 2 week(s) if notified thereafter. Nomination essential prior to consideration for appointment. Nominating authorities include President, Vice President, Secretary of Navy, members of Congress, delegates to Congress, governors of United States Territories, and resident commissioner of Puerto Rico. Applicants for presidential appointments limited by law to sons and daughters of career military personnel, active or retired. Applicants encouraged to apply to the Academy and nominating authority by May one year prior to desired admission. **Financial aid:** No deadline.

Academics. Military environment and organization under student leadership with military officer supervision. Professional training at US bases and with units of the United States Navy and United States Marine Corps during summer months. Graduates receive B.S. degree with a major in one of 25 disciplines, plus commission as Ensign in US Navy or Second Lieutenant in US Marine Corps. **Special study options:** Double major, exchange student, honors, independent study, study abroad. Qualified students have opportunities to begin work in second semester of senior year towards a Master's degree at local graduate schools. Selected midshipmen can also engage in research with thesis, or work towards honors in their majors. **Credit/placement by examination:** AP, CLEP, IB, SAT, ACT, institutional tests. Midshipmen take local examinations after admission for placement. AP Exam scores also used for validation of some courses. **Support services:** Learning center, remedial instruction, study skills assistance, tutoring, writing center.

Majors. Computer sciences: General, information technology. **Engineering:** General, aerospace, computer hardware, electrical, marine, mechanical, nuclear, ocean, operations research, systems. **English:** English lit. **Foreign languages:** Arabic, Chinese. **History:** General. **Math:** General. **Military:** Cyber ops. **Physical sciences:** General, chemistry, oceanography, physics. **Social sciences:** Econometrics, economics, political science.

Most popular majors. Engineering/engineering technologies 41%, physical sciences 16%, social sciences 24%.

Technology on campus. PC or laptop required. 400 workstations in dormitories, library, computer center. Dormitories wired for high-speed internet access and linked to campus network. Online course registration, online library, helpline, repair service, wireless network available.

Student life. Freshman orientation: Mandatory. Preregistration for classes offered. All freshmen (plebes) report in late June/early July for approximately 6 weeks of military indoctrination. **Policies:** The Naval Academy has an Honor Concept administered by the Brigade of Midshipmen. Freshmen not permitted cars on campus. **Housing:** Guaranteed on-campus for all undergraduates. Coed dorms, wellness housing available. Midshipmen must live in the dormitory on campus all four years. **Activities:** Bands, campus ministries, choral groups, dance, drama, film society, international student organizations, literary magazine, music ensembles, Model UN, musical theater, radio station,

student government, student newspaper, symphony orchestra, Fellowship of Christian Athletes, Black Studies Club, Midshipmen Action Group, Officers' Christian Fellowship, Foreign Affairs Conference, Joy Bright Hancock Organization, Navy Spectrum, ALLIES/Civil Military Relations, Korean American Midshipmen Club, Japanese American Midshipmen Club, Muslim Midshipmen Club, Chinese Culture Club.

Athletics. NCAA. **Intercollegiate:** Baseball M, basketball, cross-country, diving, football (tackle) M, golf, gymnastics M, lacrosse, rifle, rowing (crew), sailing, soccer, squash M, swimming, tennis, track and field, volleyball W, water polo M, weight lifting, wrestling M. **Intramural:** Basketball, football (non-tackle), lacrosse, racquetball, soccer, softball, volleyball. **Team name:** Midshipmen.

Student services. Alcohol/substance abuse counseling, chaplain/spiritual director, career counseling, health services, legal services, minority student services, personal counseling, placement for graduates, women's services.

Contact. E-mail: webmail@usna.edu
Phone: (410) 293-4361 Toll-free number: (888) 249-7707
Fax: (410) 293-1815
Dean of Admissions, United States Naval Academy, 52 King George Street, Annapolis, MD 21402-1318

University of Baltimore
Baltimore, Maryland   **CB member**
www.ubalt.edu   **CB code: 5810**

▶ Public 4-year university and liberal arts college
▶ Commuter campus in very large city
▶ 3,307 degree-seeking undergraduates: 38% part-time, 58% women, 47% African American, 5% Asian American, 5% Hispanic/Latino, 4% Multiracial, non-Hispanic, 2% international
▶ 2,685 degree-seeking graduate students
▶ 53% of applicants admitted
▶ SAT or ACT (ACT writing optional), application essay required
▶ 32% graduate within 6 years

General. Founded in 1925. Regionally accredited. **Degrees:** 694 bachelor's awarded; master's, professional, doctoral offered. **ROTC:** Army. **Location:** Midtown Baltimore. **Calendar:** Semester, extensive summer session. **Full-time faculty:** 197 total. **Part-time faculty:** 233 total. **Class size:** 30% < 20, 64% 20-39, 7% 40-49. **Special facilities:** Center for excellence in learning and teaching, veterans center, center for digital communication, commerce and culture, center for entrepreneurship and innovation, career and professional development center, forensic lab.

Freshman class profile. 674 applied, 355 admitted, 141 enrolled.

Mid 50% test scores			
SAT critical reading:	450-550	GPA 3.0-3.49:	27%
SAT math:	420-530	GPA 2.0-2.99:	46%
SAT writing:	430-530	End year in good standing:	87%
ACT composite:	18-23	Return as sophomores:	71%
GPA 3.75 or higher:	16%	Out-of-state:	9%
GPA 3.50-3.74:	10%	International:	1%

Basis for selection. Application, high school transcript, standardized test scores (ACT/SAT) and personal essay. **Home schooled:** Transcript of courses and grades, state high school equivalency certificate, interview required.

High school preparation. 22 units required; 24 recommended. Required and recommended units include English 4, mathematics 3, social studies 3, history 3, science 3, foreign language 1-2, computer science 1-2 and academic electives 4.

2015-2016 Annual costs. Tuition/fees: $8,326; $19,744 out-of-state. Books/supplies: $730.

Application procedures. Admission: Closing date 4/1 (postmark date). $30 fee, may be waived for applicants with need. Admission notification on a rolling basis beginning on or about 10/1. Must reply by May 1 or within 2 week(s) if notified thereafter. **Financial aid:** No deadline. FAFSA, institutional form required. Applicants notified on a rolling basis.

Academics. All undergraduate students take 9 hours in an upper-level core curriculum in a general humanities-based general education. **Special study options:** Accelerated study, combined bachelor's/graduate degree, cooperative education, cross-registration, distance learning, dual enrollment of high school students, exchange student, honors, independent study, internships, student-designed major, study abroad, weekend college. **Credit/placement by examination:** AP, CLEP, IB, SAT, ACT, institutional tests. 30 credit hours maximum toward bachelor's degree. **Support services:** Learning center, pre-admission summer program, reduced course load, remedial instruction, study skills assistance, tutoring, writing center.

Majors. Business: General, accounting, business admin, communications, entrepreneurial studies, finance, human resources, international, management information systems, managerial economics, marketing, real estate. **Communications:** Public relations. **Computer sciences:** General, modeling/simulation. **Conservation:** Environmental studies. **English:** English lit. **Health services:** Health care admin. **History:** General. **Liberal arts:** Arts/sciences. **Protective services:** Criminal justice, forensics. **Psychology:** General. **Social sciences:** Political science. **Visual/performing arts:** Game design.

Most popular majors. Business/marketing 40%, computer/information sciences 10%, health sciences 7%, security/protective services 11%.

Technology on campus. 155 workstations in dormitories, library, computer center, student center. Dormitories wired for high-speed internet access and linked to campus network. Commuter students can connect to campus network. Online library, helpline, wireless network available.

Student life. Freshman orientation: Mandatory, $100 fee. Preregistration for classes offered. **Housing:** Guaranteed on-campus for freshmen. Coed dorms available. **Activities:** International student organizations, literary magazine, student government, student newspaper, 60 student organizations.

Athletics. Intramural: Badminton, basketball, golf, judo, racquetball, rowing (crew), skiing, soccer W, table tennis, tennis, volleyball.

Student services. Career counseling, student employment services, financial aid counseling, health services, personal counseling, placement for graduates, veterans' counselor. **Physically disabled:** Services for visually, speech, hearing impaired.

Contact. E-mail: admission@ubalt.edu
Phone: (410) 837-4777 Toll-free number: (877) 277-5982
Fax: (410) 837-4793
Heeseung Lee, AVP Admission, University of Baltimore, 1420 North Charles Street, Baltimore, MD 21201-5779

University of Maryland: Baltimore
Baltimore, Maryland
www.umaryland.edu   CB code: 0527

- Public two-year upper-division university and health science college
- Commuter campus in very large city
- 44% of applicants admitted

General. Founded in 1807. Regionally accredited. **Degrees:** 333 bachelor's awarded; master's, professional, doctoral offered. **Articulation:** Agreements with all Maryland community colleges. **Location:** Downtown. **Calendar:** 4-1-4, limited summer session. **Full-time faculty:** 441 total; 63% have terminal degrees, 25% minority, 66% women. **Part-time faculty:** 591 total; 43% have terminal degrees, 18% minority, 62% women. **Special facilities:** Dental, medical, pharmacy and nursing museums; law library, health sciences library, center for health policy and health services research, center for research on aging, center for vaccine development, biotechnology institute, center for health and homeland security.

Student profile. 860 degree-seeking undergraduates, 5,370 degree-seeking graduate students. 806 applied as first time-transfer students, 357 admitted, 267 enrolled.

Women:	86%	International:	2%
African American:	19%	Part-time:	28%
Asian American:	13%	Out-of-state:	6%
Hispanic/Latino:	5%	25 or older:	56%
Multi-racial, non-Hispanic:	3%		

Basis for selection. College transcript required. Undergraduate deadlines range from February 1 to August 15 (nursing, dental hygiene, medical technology). Transfer accepted as juniors, seniors.

2015-2016 Annual costs. Tuition/fees: $10,143; $32,779 out-of-state. Books/supplies: $1,955. Personal expenses: $1,000. **Additional information:** Tuition and fees vary by program.

Financial aid. Additional information: Maryland state deadline 3/1.

Application procedures. Admission: $50 fee. Admission process, fees, and dates differ among undergraduate programs (nursing, dental hygiene, medical technology). **Financial aid:** FAFSA required.

Academics. Special study options: Combined bachelor's/graduate degree, distance learning, double major. **Credit/placement by examination:** AP, CLEP, institutional tests. 30 credit hours maximum toward bachelor's degree.

Majors. Health services: Clinical lab science, dental hygiene, nursing (RN).

Technology on campus. 100 workstations in library, computer center, student center. Dormitories wired for high-speed internet access and linked to campus network. Commuter students can connect to campus network. Online library, helpline, wireless network available.

Student life. Housing: Apartments available. **Activities:** International student organizations, student government, Jewish student association, Muslim student and scholars association, United Students of African Descent, Project Jump Start.

Athletics. Intramural: Badminton, basketball, football (non-tackle), golf, racquetball, soccer, softball, squash, table tennis, volleyball.

Student services. Alcohol/substance abuse counseling, career counseling, services for economically disadvantaged, student employment services, financial aid counseling, health services, minority student services, on-campus daycare, personal counseling, placement for graduates, women's services. **Physically disabled:** Services for visually, speech, hearing impaired.

Contact. E-mail: gradinfo@umaryland.edu
Phone: (410) 706-7480 Fax: (410) 706-4053
Ryan Holtz, University Registrar, University of Maryland: Baltimore, 220 Arch Street, Baltimore, MD 21201

University of Maryland: Baltimore County
Baltimore, Maryland   CB member
www.umbc.edu   CB code: 5835

- Public 4-year university
- Residential campus in large city
- 11,144 degree-seeking undergraduates: 14% part-time, 45% women, 17% African American, 20% Asian American, 6% Hispanic/Latino, 4% Multi-racial, non-Hispanic, 4% international
- 2,501 degree-seeking graduate students
- 59% of applicants admitted
- SAT or ACT (ACT writing optional), application essay required
- 61% graduate within 6 years

General. Founded in 1963. Regionally accredited. **Degrees:** 2,432 bachelor's awarded; master's, doctoral offered. **ROTC:** Army, Naval, Air Force. **Location:** 35 miles from Washington, DC. **Calendar:** 4-1-4, extensive summer session. **Full-time faculty:** 527 total; 86% have terminal degrees, 24% minority, 47% women. **Part-time faculty:** 298 total; 36% have terminal degrees, 19% minority, 44% women. **Class size:** 39% < 20, 39% 20-39, 10% 40-49, 8% 50-99, 4% >100. **Special facilities:** Research telescope, greenhouse, research spectrometers, nuclear magnetic resonance machines, electron microscope facility, imaging/digital art laboratory, healthcare informatics laboratory, two galleries - contemporary art and photography, conservation and environmental research area.

Freshman class profile. 10,629 applied, 6,316 admitted, 1,559 enrolled.

Mid 50% test scores			
SAT critical reading:	540-640	GPA 2.0-2.99:	7%
SAT math:	570-670	Rank in top quarter:	56%
SAT writing:	530-630	Rank in top tenth:	27%
ACT composite:	24-29	Return as sophomores:	86%
GPA 3.75 or higher:	53%	Out-of-state:	8%
GPA 3.50-3.74:	18%	Live on campus:	72%
GPA 3.0-3.49:	21%	International:	5%

Basis for selection. High school record, test scores important. SAT or ACT scores must be received prior to completed application. Audition required for music, dance, theater majors. Portfolio required for visual arts majors.

High school preparation. College-preparatory program required. Required units include English 4, mathematics 4, science 3 and foreign language 2. 3 credits required in social studies or history.

2015-2016 Annual costs. Tuition/fees: $11,006; $23,770 out-of-state. Room/board: $10,868. Books/supplies: $1,200. Personal expenses: $1,524.

2014-2015 Financial aid. Need-based: 1,252 full-time freshmen applied for aid; 820 deemed to have need; 748 received aid. Average need met was 61%. Average scholarship/grant was $8,994; average loan $3,389. 67% of total undergraduate aid awarded as scholarships/grants, 33% as loans/jobs. **Non-need-based:** Awarded to 2,149 full-time undergraduates, including 603 freshmen. Scholarships awarded for academics, alumni affiliation, art, athletics, music/drama.

Application procedures. Admission: Priority date 11/1; deadline 2/1 (postmark date). $50 fee, may be waived for applicants with need. Admission notification on a rolling basis beginning on or about 2/1. Must reply by May 1 or within 2 week(s) if notified thereafter. **Financial aid:** Priority date 2/14; no closing date. FAFSA required. Applicants notified on a rolling basis starting 3/25; must reply within 2 week(s) of notification.

Academics. Special study options: Accelerated study, combined bachelor's/graduate degree, cooperative education, cross-registration, double major, dual enrollment of high school students, ESL, honors, independent study, internships, liberal arts/career combination, semester at sea, student-designed major, study abroad, teacher certification program. **Credit/placement by examination:** AP, CLEP, IB, institutional tests. 60 credit hours maximum toward bachelor's degree. **Support services:** Learning center, study skills assistance, tutoring, writing center.

Honors college/program. Minimum 1300 SAT (exclusive of Writing) and 3.5 GPA required. Approximately 140 students accepted each year, with average SAT of 1300 (exclusive of Writing) and 3.81 GPA. Each semester 40-50 courses offered along with non-curricular activities.

Majors. Area/ethnic studies: African-American, American. **Biology:** General, Biochemistry/molecular biology, bioinformatics. **Communications:** Media studies. **Computer sciences:** General, computer science, information systems. **Conservation:** Environmental science, environmental studies. **Education:** Physics. **Engineering:** General, chemical, computer, mechanical. **English:** English lit. **Foreign languages:** General, linguistics. **Health services:** EMT paramedic. **History:** General. **Human services:** Social work. **Math:** General, statistics. **Philosophy/religion:** Philosophy. **Physical sciences:** Chemistry, physics. **Psychology:** General. **Social sciences:** Anthropology, economics, geography, political science, sociology. **Visual/performing arts:** General, acting, art, dance, dramatic, music, studio arts.

Most popular majors. Biology 16%, computer/information sciences 15%, engineering/engineering technologies 7%, psychology 13%, social sciences 13%, visual/performing arts 6%.

Technology on campus. 1,100 workstations in dormitories, library, computer center, student center. Dormitories wired for high-speed internet access and linked to campus network. Commuter students can connect to campus network. Online course registration, online library, helpline, repair service, student web hosting, wireless network available.

Student life. Freshman orientation: Mandatory, $125 fee. Preregistration for classes offered. Held June and July. Separate program for honors college students. **Housing:** Guaranteed on-campus for freshmen. Coed dorms, special housing for disabled, apartments, gender-neutral housing, themed housing available. $200 nonrefundable deposit, deadline 5/1. **Activities:** Bands, campus ministries, choral groups, dance, drama, film society, international student organizations, literary magazine, music ensembles, Model UN, musical theater, radio station, student government, student newspaper, symphony orchestra, Black student union, Chinese student association, Jewish student association, Korean club, gay and lesbian organization, progressive action committee, Christian Fellowship, women's union.

Athletics. NCAA. **Intercollegiate:** Baseball M, basketball, cross-country, lacrosse, soccer, softball W, swimming, tennis, track and field, volleyball W. **Intramural:** Lacrosse, soccer, softball W, swimming, tennis, track and field, volleyball W. **Team name:** Retrievers.

Student services. Adult student services, alcohol/substance abuse counseling, chaplain/spiritual director, career counseling, services for economically disadvantaged, student employment services, financial aid counseling, health services, minority student services, on-campus daycare, personal counseling, placement for graduates, veterans' counselor, women's services. **Physically disabled:** Services for visually, hearing impaired.

Contact. E-mail: admissions@umbc.edu
Phone: (410) 455-2291 Toll-free number: (800) 862-2482
Fax: (410) 455-1094
Dale Bittinger, Director of Admissions, University of Maryland: Baltimore County, 1000 Hilltop Circle, Baltimore, MD 21250

University of Maryland: College Park

College Park, Maryland — **CB member**
www.maryland.edu — **CB code: 5814**

- Public 4-year university
- Commuter campus in large town
- 26,889 degree-seeking undergraduates: 6% part-time, 46% women, 13% African American, 16% Asian American, 9% Hispanic/Latino, 4% Multiracial, non-Hispanic, 4% international
- 10,260 degree-seeking graduate students

- 45% of applicants admitted
- SAT or ACT with writing, application essay required
- 86% graduate within 6 years; 21% enter graduate study

General. Founded in 1856. Regionally accredited. Research and internship opportunities at Smithsonian Institution, National Institutes for Health, NASA, US Capitol, White House, FBI, Department of Agriculture, other federal agencies. **Degrees:** 7,166 bachelor's awarded; master's, professional, doctoral offered. **ROTC:** Army, Naval, Air Force. **Location:** 30 miles from Baltimore, 3 miles from Washington, DC. **Calendar:** Semester, extensive summer session. **Full-time faculty:** 1,813 total; 92% have terminal degrees, 22% minority, 37% women. **Part-time faculty:** 675 total; 55% have terminal degrees, 15% minority, 41% women. **Class size:** 46% < 20, 32% 20-39, 6% 40-49, 11% 50-99, 6% >100. **Special facilities:** National Archives II, astronomy observatory, engineering wind tunnel, space systems lab, nuclear reactor, performing arts center, center for young children, agricultural biotechnology, superconductivity research, institute for systems research, fire and rescue institute.

Freshman class profile. 28,301 applied, 12,637 admitted, 3,937 enrolled.

Mid 50% test scores			
SAT critical reading:	590-690	Rank in top tenth:	70%
SAT math:	620-730	Return as sophomores:	95%
		Out-of-state:	30%
GPA 3.75 or higher:	87%	Live on campus:	93%
GPA 3.50-3.74:	7%	International:	2%
GPA 3.0-3.49:	5%	Fraternities:	15%
GPA 2.0-2.99:	1%	Sororities:	22%
Rank in top quarter:	88%		

Basis for selection. Academic record, rigor of the high school academic program, standardized test scores, class rank (if available), essay, extracurricular activities, counselor recommendation, and other letters of recommendation reviewed. The date provided for latest date by which SAT or ACT scores must be received for fall-term admission is for early action admissions. For regular decision applications, the deadline is January 20. Audition required of music majors. Drawing required of applicants to architecture program. **Home schooled:** Statement describing home school structure and mission, transcript of courses and grades, letter of recommendation (nonparent) required. Transcript should include description of course work, books used, method of evaluation and actual grades or evaluation. Letter of recommendation required and must be from academic professional.

High school preparation. College-preparatory program recommended. 16 units required. Required units include English 4, mathematics 4, social studies 3, science 3 (laboratory 2) and foreign language 2. Social studies units must include history.

2015-2016 Annual costs. Tuition/fees: $9,996; $31,144 out-of-state. Room/board: $10,972. Books/supplies: $1,130. Personal expenses: $1,868. **Additional information:** For the upcoming academic year, the tuition figure for junior and senior undergraduate students in business, engineering, and computer science majors is $700 higher, regardless of residency.

2014-2015 Financial aid. Need-based: 3,174 full-time freshmen applied for aid; 1,695 deemed to have need; 1,681 received aid. Average need met was 78%. Average scholarship/grant was $11,040; average loan $4,663. 53% of total undergraduate aid awarded as scholarships/grants, 47% as loans/jobs. **Non-need-based:** Awarded to 4,096 full-time undergraduates, including 1,094 freshmen. Scholarships awarded for academics, art, athletics, leadership, music/drama, ROTC, state residency. **Additional information:** Prepaid tuition plans available through state.

Application procedures. Admission: Priority date 11/1; deadline 1/20 (receipt date). $65 fee, may be waived for applicants with need. Application must be submitted online. Admission notification by 4/1. Admission notification on a rolling basis. Must reply by May 1 or within 4 week(s) if notified thereafter. Housing deposit refundable in full if requested before 5/1. After 5/1, no refund will be given. Housing deposit is part of the $400 confirmation fee. **Financial aid:** Priority date 2/15; no closing date. FAFSA required. Applicants notified on a rolling basis starting 4/1; must reply by 5/1.

Academics. Special study options: Accelerated study, combined bachelor's/graduate degree, cooperative education, cross-registration, distance learning, double major, dual enrollment of high school students, ESL, exchange student, external degree, honors, independent study, internships, liberal arts/career combination, semester at sea, student-designed major, study abroad, teacher certification program. Living/learning programs. **Credit/placement by examination:** AP, CLEP, IB, SAT, ACT, institutional tests. 60 credit hours maximum toward bachelor's degree. Information on specific credit by examination policies may be found on the college website. **Support services:** Learning center, pre-admission summer program, reduced course load, remedial instruction, study skills assistance, tutoring, writing center.

Majors. Architecture: Architecture, landscape. **Area/ethnic studies:** African-American, American, Russian/Slavic, women's. **Biology:** General, biochemistry, ecology, microbiology. **Business:** General, accounting, finance, international, logistics, management science, marketing. **Communications:** Communications/speech/rhetoric, journalism. **Computer sciences:** General, information systems. **Conservation:** General, environmental science. **Education:** Art, elementary, health, kindergarten/preschool, middle, music, physical, secondary, special ed. **Engineering:** Aerospace, agricultural, chemical, civil, computer, electrical, materials, mechanical. **English:** English lit. **Foreign languages:** Arabic, Chinese, classics, French, German, Iranian, Italian, Japanese, linguistics, Romance, Russian, Spanish. **Health services:** Communication disorders, predental, preveterinary. **History:** General. **Math:** General. **Parks/recreation:** Exercise sciences. **Philosophy/religion:** Judaic, philosophy. **Physical sciences:** General, astronomy, atmospheric science, chemistry, geology, physics. **Psychology:** General. **Social sciences:** Anthropology, criminology, economics, geography, political science, sociology. **Visual/performing arts:** Art history/conservation, dance, dramatic, film/cinema/video, music, music performance, studio arts. **Work/family studies:** Family/community services.

Most popular majors. Biology 10%, business/marketing 14%, communications/journalism 6%, engineering/engineering technologies 12%, social sciences 17%.

Technology on campus. 3,890 workstations in dormitories, library, computer center, student center. Dormitories wired for high-speed internet access and linked to campus network. Commuter students can connect to campus network. Online course registration, online library, helpline, repair service, student web hosting, wireless network available.

Student life. Freshman orientation: Mandatory, $176 fee. Preregistration for classes offered. Two-day program. **Housing:** Guaranteed on-campus for freshmen. Coed dorms, single-sex dorms, special housing for disabled, apartments, cooperative housing, fraternity/sorority housing, themed housing, wellness housing available. $400 fully refundable deposit, deadline 5/1. Living/learning housing available. **Activities:** Bands, campus ministries, choral groups, dance, drama, film society, international student organizations, literary magazine, music ensembles, Model UN, musical theater, opera, radio station, student government, student newspaper, symphony orchestra, TV station, Black student union, Asian American student union, Latino student union, Native American student union, Alpha Phi Omega, Habitat for Humanity.

Athletics. NCAA. **Intercollegiate:** Baseball M, basketball, cross-country W, field hockey W, football (tackle) M, golf, gymnastics W, lacrosse, soccer, softball W, tennis W, track and field, volleyball W, wrestling M. **Intramural:** Basketball, football (non-tackle), racquetball, sand volleyball, soccer, softball, table tennis, tennis, volleyball. **Team name:** Terrapins.

Student services. Adult student services, alcohol/substance abuse counseling, chaplain/spiritual director, career counseling, services for economically disadvantaged, student employment services, financial aid counseling, health services, legal services, minority student services, on-campus daycare, personal counseling, placement for graduates, veterans' counselor, women's services. **Physically disabled:** Services for visually, speech, hearing impaired.

Contact. E-mail: ApplyMaryland@umd.edu
Phone: (301) 314-8385 Toll-free number: (800) 422-5867
Fax: (301) 314-9693
Barbara Gill, Director of Undergraduate Admissions, University of Maryland: College Park, Mitchell Building, College Park, MD 20742-5235

University of Maryland: Eastern Shore
Princess Anne, Maryland   **CB member**
www.umes.edu   **CB code: 5400**

- Public 4-year university
- Residential campus in rural community
- 3,573 degree-seeking undergraduates: 8% part-time, 54% women, 75% African American, 1% Asian American, 3% Hispanic/Latino, 8% Multiracial, non-Hispanic, 3% international
- 710 degree-seeking graduate students
- 49% of applicants admitted
- SAT or ACT (ACT writing optional) required
- 33% graduate within 6 years

General. Founded in 1886. Regionally accredited. **Degrees:** 577 bachelor's awarded; master's, professional, doctoral offered. **Location:** 12 miles from Salisbury. **Calendar:** Semester, extensive summer session. **Full-time faculty:** 230 total; 81% have terminal degrees, 63% minority, 44% women. **Part-time faculty:** 125 total; 20% have terminal degrees, 42% minority, 56% women. **Class size:** 55% < 20, 40% 20-39, 2% 40-49, 3% 50-99, less than 1% >100. **Special facilities:** Arts and technology center, performing arts center, foreign language instructional center, education center.

Freshman class profile. 7,249 applied, 3,556 admitted, 1,020 enrolled.

Mid 50% test scores		GPA 3.0-3.49:	24%
SAT critical reading:	380-470	GPA 2.0-2.99:	66%
SAT math:	370-460	End year in good standing:	71%
SAT writing:	360-450	Return as sophomores:	68%
ACT composite:	15-18	Out-of-state:	20%
GPA 3.75 or higher:	5%	Live on campus:	93%
GPA 3.50-3.74:	4%	International:	3%

Basis for selection. School record, class rank, and test scores are important. Interview recommended for honors program and physical therapy applicants. Audition required for music majors. **Home schooled:** Transcript of courses and grades, letter of recommendation (nonparent) required. Must demonstrate compliance with state and local education regulations.

High school preparation. College-preparatory program recommended. 20 units required. Required units include English 4, mathematics 4, social studies 3, science 2, foreign language 2 and academic electives 6.

2015-2016 Annual costs. Tuition/fees: $7,625; $16,687 out-of-state. Room/board: $9,114. Books/supplies: $1,500. Personal expenses: $1,800.

2014-2015 Financial aid. Need-based: 739 full-time freshmen applied for aid; 661 deemed to have need; 637 received aid. Average need met was 24%. 68% of total undergraduate aid awarded as scholarships/grants, 32% as loans/jobs. **Non-need-based:** Awarded to 834 full-time undergraduates, including 212 freshmen. Scholarships awarded for academics, alumni affiliation, art, athletics, leadership, music/drama, ROTC, state residency.

Application procedures. Admission: Priority date 4/15; deadline 6/30. $25 fee, may be waived for applicants with need. Admission notification on a rolling basis. **Financial aid:** Priority date 3/1, closing date 4/1. FAFSA required. Applicants notified on a rolling basis starting 4/15.

Academics. Special study options: Accelerated study, cooperative education, cross-registration, distance learning, double major, dual enrollment of high school students, exchange student, honors, independent study, internships, liberal arts/career combination, New York semester, study abroad, teacher certification program. **Credit/placement by examination:** AP, CLEP, IB, institutional tests. 60 credit hours maximum toward bachelor's degree. **Support services:** Learning center, pre-admission summer program, reduced course load, remedial instruction, study skills assistance, tutoring, writing center.

Majors. Area/ethnic studies: African-American. **Biology:** General, biochemistry, ecology. **Business:** Accounting, business admin, finance, hospitality admin, marketing. **Computer sciences:** General. **Conservation:** Urban forestry. **Education:** Art, business, music, special ed, technology/industrial arts. **Engineering:** General. **English:** English lit. **History:** General. **Math:** General. **Parks/recreation:** Exercise sciences, golf management. **Physical sciences:** Chemistry. **Protective services:** Police science. **Psychology:** General. **Social sciences:** Sociology. **Visual/performing arts:** Jazz, music. **Work/family studies:** General.

Most popular majors. Biology 11%, business/marketing 11%, family/consumer sciences 7%, health sciences 13%, parks/recreation 8%, security/protective services 19%, social sciences 8%.

Technology on campus. 450 workstations in dormitories, library, computer center, student center. Dormitories wired for high-speed internet access and linked to campus network. Commuter students can connect to campus network. Online course registration, online library, helpline, wireless network available.

Student life. Freshman orientation: Mandatory. Preregistration for classes offered. Five-day program held in late August. **Housing:** Coed dorms, single-sex dorms, apartments, wellness housing available. $300 partly refundable deposit, deadline 5/1. **Activities:** Bands, campus ministries, choral groups, dance, drama, international student organizations, music ensembles, radio station, student government, Women of Respect Tact and Honor, Men of Distinction, Praise Fellowship, Stars Status, Gospel choir, Caribbean International Association, African Student Association, NAACP.

Athletics. NCAA. **Intercollegiate:** Baseball M, basketball, bowling W, cross-country, golf M, softball W, tennis, track and field, volleyball W. **Team name:** Hawks.

Student services. Adult student services, alcohol/substance abuse counseling, chaplain/spiritual director, career counseling, services for economically disadvantaged, student employment services, financial aid counseling, health services, legal services, minority student services, on-campus daycare, personal counseling, placement for graduates, veterans' counselor, women's services. **Physically disabled:** Services for visually, speech, hearing impaired.

Contact. E-mail: umesadmissions@umes.edu
Phone: (410) 651-6410 Fax: (410) 651-7922
Jinawa McNeil, Director of Admissions and Recruitment, University of
Maryland: Eastern Shore, Student Development Center, Suite 1140,
Princess Anne, MD 21853

University of Maryland: University College
Adelphi, Maryland
www.umuc.edu   CB code: 0551

- Public 4-year virtual university
- Commuter campus in large town
- 36,118 degree-seeking undergraduates: 76% part-time, 46% women, 27% African American, 4% Asian American, 12% Hispanic/Latino, 1% Native American, 1% Native Hawaiian/Pacific islander, 4% Multi-racial, non-Hispanic, 1% international
- 12,702 degree-seeking graduate students

General. Founded in 1947. Regionally accredited. Courses held at over 20 locations throughout Maryland, Virginia and Washington, DC; held at more than locations throughout Europe and Asia. Associate degree programs available only to active military personnel. More than 80% of courses are offered online; no degree program can be completed without online courses. **Degrees:** 5,102 bachelor's awarded; master's, professional offered. **Location:** 9 miles from Washington, DC. **Calendar:** Semester, extensive summer session. **Full-time faculty:** 145 total; 89% have terminal degrees, 18% minority, 47% women. **Part-time faculty:** 2,666 total; 59% have terminal degrees, 28% minority, 44% women. **Class size:** 65% < 20, 35% 20-39.

Freshman class profile. 1,453 applied, 1,453 admitted, 783 enrolled.

Out-of-state: 52% **International:**   1%

Basis for selection. Open admission.

2015-2016 Annual costs. Tuition/fees: $7,146; $12,426 out-of-state. Personal expenses: $3,350.

2014-2015 Financial aid. Need-based: 162 full-time freshmen applied for aid; 156 deemed to have need; 79 received aid. Average need met was 23%. Average scholarship/grant was $3,012; average loan $2,480. 48% of total undergraduate aid awarded as scholarships/grants, 52% as loans/jobs. **Non-need-based:** Awarded to 556 full-time undergraduates, including 2 freshmen. Scholarships awarded for academics, leadership.

Application procedures. Admission: No deadline. $50 fee. Admission notification on a rolling basis. **Financial aid:** Priority date 6/1; no closing date. FAFSA required. Applicants notified on a rolling basis starting 5/1; must reply within 2 week(s) of notification.

Academics. Degree programs offered primarily for adults attending part-time. No traditional freshman class. **Special study options:** Accelerated study, cooperative education, cross-registration, distance learning, double major, dual enrollment of high school students, external degree, independent study, internships, teacher certification program, weekend college. **Credit/placement by examination:** AP, CLEP, IB, institutional tests. 30 credit hours maximum toward associate degree, 60 toward bachelor's. **Support services:** Tutoring, writing center.

Majors. Area/ethnic studies: Asian. **Biology:** Biotechnology. **Business:** Accounting, business admin, finance, human resources, marketing. **Communications:** Communications/speech/rhetoric. **Communications technology:** Graphics. **Computer sciences:** General, information systems, security. **Conservation:** General. **English:** English lit. **Health services:** Nursing (RN). **History:** General. **Human services:** General. **Liberal arts:** Arts/sciences. **Protective services:** Criminal justice, forensics. **Psychology:** General. **Social sciences:** General, political science.

Most popular majors. Business/marketing 23%, computer/information sciences 43%, psychology 8%, security/protective services 7%.

Technology on campus. 404 workstations in computer center. Commuter students can connect to campus network. Online course registration, online library, helpline, wireless network available.

Student life. Freshman orientation: Available. Preregistration for classes offered.

Student services. Adult student services, alcohol/substance abuse counseling, career counseling, student employment services, financial aid counseling, personal counseling, veterans' counselor **Physically disabled:** Services for visually, speech, hearing impaired.

Contact. E-mail: admissions@umuc.edu
Phone: (800) 888-8682 Toll-free number: (800) 888-8682
Fax: (240) 684-2153
Insiya Bream, Director of Admissions, University of Maryland: University
College, 1616 McCormick Drive, Largo, MD 20774

University of Phoenix: Maryland
Columbia, Maryland
www.phoenix.edu

- For-profit 4-year university
- Small city
- 395 undergraduates

General. Regionally accredited. **Degrees:** 124 bachelor's awarded; master's offered. **Calendar:** Differs by program. Other academic calendar. **Full-time faculty:** 18 total. **Part-time faculty:** 83 total.

Basis for selection. Open admission, but selective for some programs.

2015-2016 Annual costs. Per-credit-hour charge, $410 to $745, depending upon level and course of study. Books, material charges, and other fees vary by course and program. All fees are subject to change.

Application procedures. Admission: No deadline. No application fee. **Financial aid:** No deadline.

Academics. Credit/placement by examination: AP, CLEP.

Majors. Business: Accounting/business management, business admin, e-commerce. **Computer sciences:** General, database management, networking, programming, security, system admin, systems analysis, web page design, webmaster.

Student life. Freshman orientation: Mandatory. Preregistration for classes offered.

Contact. Toll-free number: (866) 766-0766
University of Phoenix: Maryland, 8830 Stanford Boulevard, Columbia,
MD 21045

Washington Adventist University
Takoma Park, Maryland
www.wau.edu   CB code: 5890

- Private 4-year liberal arts college affiliated with the Seventh-day Adventists
- Residential campus in large town
- 765 degree-seeking undergraduates
- 167 graduate students
- SAT or ACT (ACT writing optional) required

General. Founded in 1904. Regionally accredited. **Degrees:** 205 bachelor's, 11 associate awarded; master's offered. **Location:** One mile from Washington, DC. **Calendar:** Semester, limited summer session.

Basis for selection. For regular admission, a freshman must have a high school GPA of 2.75 and have an ACT verbal score of 17 or SAT verbal score of 470. School achievement record is considered, test scores are very important, and recommendations are considered. Freshmen with a high school GPA of 2.50 to 2.74 and a minimum ACT verbal score of 16 or SAT verbal score of 400 will be admitted conditionally through the Enrichment Program. Other stipulations apply. Audition required of music majors. **Home schooled:** Transcript of courses and grades required. Recognized high school diploma or GED required. **Learning Disabled:** Students must provide written documentation of disabilities and submit written request for all needed services for review by the Disabilities Coordinator three months before registration.

High school preparation. 18 units required; 29 recommended. Required and recommended units include English 4, mathematics 2-4, social studies 2, history 4, science 2-4 (laboratory 2), foreign language 2, computer science 1 and academic electives 4. One unit of computer science also recommended.

2015-2016 Annual costs. Tuition/fees: $22,790. Room/board: $8,650. Books/supplies: $1,200.

Financial aid. Non-need-based: Scholarships awarded for academics, alumni affiliation, athletics, religious affiliation.

Application procedures. Admission: Closing date 8/1 (postmark date). $25 fee, may be waived for applicants with need, free for online applicants. Admission notification on a rolling basis. **Financial aid:** Priority date 3/1, closing date 3/31. FAFSA required. Applicants notified on a rolling basis starting 5/31; must reply within 4 week(s) of notification.

Academics. Special study options: Accelerated study, combined bachelor's/graduate degree, cooperative education, cross-registration, distance learning, double major, dual enrollment of high school students, ESL, external degree, honors, independent study, internships, liberal arts/career combination, student-designed major, study abroad, teacher certification program, Washington semester. Co-Op Programs: Business, Biochemistry, Communications/Journalism, Computer Science, English. **Credit/placement by examination:** AP, CLEP, SAT, ACT, institutional tests. 12 credit hours maximum toward associate degree, 24 toward bachelor's. CLEP business exams not accepted for traditional business majors. **Support services:** Learning center, reduced course load, remedial instruction, study skills assistance, tutoring, writing center.

Majors. Biology: General, biochemistry. **Business:** Accounting, business admin, marketing, organizational behavior. **Communications:** Broadcast journalism, communications/speech/rhetoric, journalism. **Computer sciences:** General, computer science, information systems. **Education:** General, elementary, English, mathematics, music, physical, science, secondary. **English:** English lit. **Health services:** Health care admin, nursing (RN), predental, premedicine, prepharmacy, preveterinary. **History:** General. **Liberal arts:** Arts/sciences. **Math:** General. **Parks/recreation:** Health/fitness, sports admin. **Philosophy/religion:** Religion. **Physical sciences:** Chemistry. **Psychology:** General, counseling. **Social sciences:** Political science. **Theology:** Religious ed, theology. **Visual/performing arts:** Music, music performance.

Technology on campus. Dormitories wired for high-speed internet access and linked to campus network. Commuter students can connect to campus network. Online library, wireless network available.

Student life. Freshman orientation: Mandatory, $150 fee. Preregistration for classes offered. **Policies:** Attendance required at weekly chapel service. Resident students required to attend dormitory worships. Religious observance required. **Housing:** Guaranteed on-campus for freshmen. Single-sex dorms, apartments available. $200 fully refundable deposit, deadline 8/15. **Activities:** Bands, campus ministries, choral groups, international student organizations, literary magazine, music ensembles, musical theater, radio station, student government, student newspaper, symphony orchestra, Humanitas, Loaves and Fishes, Shepherd's Hands, Teach-a-Kid, Youth-to-Youth, student mission club.

Athletics. NCAA. **Intercollegiate:** Basketball, cross-country, soccer, track and field. **Intramural:** Basketball M, soccer M. **Team name:** Shock.

Student services. Adult student services, chaplain/spiritual director, career counseling, student employment services, financial aid counseling, health services, personal counseling, placement for graduates, veterans' counselor.

Contact. E-mail: enroll@wau.edu
Phone: (301) 891-4080 Toll-free number: (800) 835-4212
Fax: (301) 891-4563
Wanda Colon-Canales, Director of Admissions, Washington Adventist University, 7600 Flower Avenue, Takoma Park, MD 20912

Washington College

Chestertown, Maryland
www.washcoll.edu

CB member
CB code: 5888

- Private 4-year liberal arts college
- Residential campus in small town
- 1,386 degree-seeking undergraduates: 56% women, 5% African American, 2% Asian American, 3% Hispanic/Latino, 1% Native American, 2% Multi-racial, non-Hispanic, 10% international
- 4 degree-seeking graduate students
- 54% of applicants admitted
- SAT or ACT (ACT writing optional), application essay required
- 75% graduate within 6 years

General. Founded in 1782. Regionally accredited. **Degrees:** 347 bachelor's awarded; master's offered. **Location:** 70 miles from Baltimore; 75 miles from Washington, DC. **Calendar:** Semester, limited summer session. **Full-time faculty:** 113 total; 86% have terminal degrees, 17% minority, 45% women. **Part-time faculty:** 51 total; 41% have terminal degrees, 16% minority, 45% women. **Class size:** 70% < 20, 28% 20-39, 1% 40-49, 1% 50-99. **Special facilities:** Literary House, CV Starr Center for the Study of the American Experience, Center for Environment and Society, Center for the Arts.

Freshman class profile. 6,847 applied, 3,702 admitted, 391 enrolled.

Mid 50% test scores			
SAT critical reading:	530-650	Rank in top quarter:	62%
SAT math:	540-640	Rank in top tenth:	34%
SAT writing:	540-650	Return as sophomores:	83%
ACT composite:	25-30	Out-of-state:	56%
GPA 3.75 or higher:	39%	Live on campus:	98%
GPA 3.50-3.74:	19%	International:	9%
GPA 3.0-3.49:	27%	Fraternities:	9%
GPA 2.0-2.99:	15%	Sororities:	14%

Basis for selection. High school program rigor and grades are very important; class rank, test scores, and essay are important. Interview recommended. **Home schooled:** Interview required.

High school preparation. College-preparatory program required. 16 units required; 20 recommended. Required and recommended units include English 4, mathematics 3-4, social studies 2, history 2, science 3-4 (laboratory 2-3) and foreign language 2-4.

2015-2016 Annual costs. Tuition/fees: $43,850. Room/board: $10,612. Books/supplies: $1,250. Personal expenses: $1,500.

2015-2016 Financial aid. Need-based: 308 full-time freshmen applied for aid; 266 deemed to have need; 266 received aid. Average need met was 91%. Average scholarship/grant was $29,630; average loan $3,429. 86% of total undergraduate aid awarded as scholarships/grants, 14% as loans/jobs. **Non-need-based:** Awarded to 613 full-time undergraduates, including 164 freshmen. Scholarships awarded for academics, art, music/drama.

Application procedures. Admission: Closing date 2/15 (postmark date). $50 fee, may be waived for applicants with need, free for online applicants. Admission notification on a rolling basis beginning on or about 10/1. Must reply by May 1 or within 2 week(s) if notified thereafter. Applicants applying after 2/15 may be wait-listed. **Financial aid:** Priority date 3/1; no closing date. FAFSA required. Applicants notified on a rolling basis starting 1/5; must reply by 5/1 or within 2 week(s) of notification.

Academics. Special study options: Combined bachelor's/graduate degree, cross-registration, double major, dual enrollment of high school students, exchange student, honors, independent study, internships, liberal arts/career combination, student-designed major, study abroad, teacher certification program, Washington semester. **Credit/placement by examination:** AP, CLEP, IB, SAT, ACT, institutional tests. **Support services:** Learning center, reduced course load, study skills assistance, tutoring, writing center.

Majors. Area/ethnic studies: American. **Biology:** General. **Business:** General. **Computer sciences:** Computer science. **Conservation:** Environmental science, environmental studies. **Education:** General. **English:** English lit. **Foreign languages:** French, German, Spanish. **History:** General. **Liberal arts:** Arts/sciences, humanities. **Math:** General. **Philosophy/religion:** Philosophy. **Physical sciences:** Chemistry, physics. **Psychology:** General. **Social sciences:** Anthropology, economics, international relations, political science, sociology. **Visual/performing arts:** Art, dramatic, music.

Most popular majors. Biology 10%, business/marketing 18%, English 7%, history 6%, natural resources/environmental science 6%, psychology 9%, social sciences 20%, visual/performing arts 6%.

Technology on campus. 150 workstations in dormitories, library, computer center, student center. Dormitories wired for high-speed internet access and linked to campus network. Commuter students can connect to campus network. Online course registration, online library, helpline, repair service, student web hosting, wireless network available.

Student life. Freshman orientation: Mandatory. Preregistration for classes offered. Held Thursday-Sunday before fall classes begin. **Housing:** Guaranteed on-campus for freshmen. Coed dorms, single-sex dorms, apartments, fraternity/sorority housing, themed housing, wellness housing available. $200 nonrefundable deposit, deadline 6/1. **Activities:** Bands, campus ministries, choral groups, dance, drama, international student organizations, literary magazine, music ensembles, Model UN, musical theater, student government, student newspaper, College Republicans, Christian Fellowship, Amnesty International, Hillel, Black Student Alliance, Cleopatra's Daughters, College Democrats, Best Buddies, Newman Club.

Athletics. NCAA. **Intercollegiate:** Baseball M, basketball, field hockey W, lacrosse, rowing (crew), sailing, soccer, softball W, swimming, tennis, volleyball W. **Intramural:** Basketball, fencing, golf M, ice hockey M, racquetball, rugby, sailing, soccer, softball, squash, tennis, volleyball. **Team name:** Shoremen/Shorewomen.

Student services. Adult student services, alcohol/substance abuse counseling, career counseling, student employment services, financial aid counseling, health services, minority student services, personal counseling, placement for graduates, veterans' counselor. **Physically disabled:** Services for hearing impaired.

Contact. E-mail: wc_admissions@washcoll.edu
Phone: (410) 778-7700 Toll-free number: (800) 422-1782
Fax: (410) 778-7287
Bradly Booke, Director of Admissions, Washington College, 300 Washington Avenue, Chestertown, MD 21620-1197

Yeshiva College of the Nations Capital
Silver Spring, Maryland

- Private 4-year rabbinical college for men affiliated with the Jewish faith
- Residential campus in small city
- 23 degree-seeking undergraduates

General. Accredited by AARTS. **Calendar:** Differs by program. **Full-time faculty:** 3 total. **Part-time faculty:** 3 total.

Basis for selection. Open admission.

2015-2016 Annual costs. Tuition/fees: $9,700. Room/board: $9,200.

Academics. Credit/placement by examination: AP, CLEP.

Majors. Philosophy/religion: Judaic. Theology: Talmudic.

Contact. Phone: (301) 593-2534
David Hyatt, Academic Dean, Yeshiva College of the Nations Capital, 1216 Arcola Avenue, Silver Spring, MD 20902

Massachusetts

American International College
Springfield, Massachusetts
www.aic.edu

CB member
CB code: 3002

- Private 4-year health science and liberal arts college
- Residential campus in small city
- 1,478 degree-seeking undergraduates: 6% part-time, 60% women, 25% African American, 1% Asian American, 14% Hispanic/Latino, 3% Multi-racial, non-Hispanic, 3% international
- 2,022 degree-seeking graduate students
- 64% of applicants admitted
- SAT or ACT (ACT writing optional) required
- 38% graduate within 6 years

General. Founded in 1885. Regionally accredited. **Degrees:** 270 bachelor's, 3 associate awarded; master's, professional, doctoral offered. **ROTC:** Army, Air Force. **Location:** 90 miles from Boston; 27 miles from Hartford, Connecticut. **Calendar:** Semester, extensive summer session. **Full-time faculty:** 74 total; 64% have terminal degrees, 16% minority, 58% women. **Part-time faculty:** 366 total; 13% have terminal degrees, 7% minority, 63% women. **Class size:** 50% < 20, 44% 20-39, less than 1% 40-49, 4% 50-99, less than 1% >100. **Special facilities:** Cultural arts center, performing arts center, anatomical laboratory, communications media laboratory.

Freshman class profile. 2,053 applied, 1,315 admitted, 343 enrolled.

Mid 50% test scores			
SAT critical reading:	390-480	GPA 3.0-3.49:	26%
SAT math:	400-500	GPA 2.0-2.99:	57%
SAT writing:	380-480	Return as sophomores:	72%
ACT composite:	16-23	Out-of-state:	54%
GPA 3.75 or higher:	5%	Live on campus:	80%
GPA 3.50-3.74:	6%	International:	5%

Basis for selection. Must have satisfied school's graduation requirements except for one course in English and one course in Social Studies. Must have unqualified approval of school counselor or principal and must possess strong academic skills and maturity necessary for success in college. Essay or personal statement recommended. **Home schooled:** Statement describing home school structure and mission, transcript of courses and grades, interview, letter of recommendation (nonparent) required. **Learning Disabled:** Wechsler Adult Intelligence Scale, interview, diagnostic documentation recommended.

High school preparation. College-preparatory program required. 16 units recommended. Recommended units include English 4, mathematics 3, social studies 2, science 2 (laboratory 2), foreign language 1 and academic electives 4.

2015-2016 Annual costs. Tuition/fees: $31,870. Room/board: $12,900. Books/supplies: $1,200. Personal expenses: $1,000.

2014-2015 Financial aid. Need-based: 297 full-time freshmen applied for aid; 288 deemed to have need; 288 received aid. Average need met was 67%. Average scholarship/grant was $22,092; average loan $3,293. 68% of total undergraduate aid awarded as scholarships/grants, 32% as loans/jobs. **Non-need-based:** Awarded to 373 full-time undergraduates, including 77 freshmen. Scholarships awarded for academics, athletics.

Application procedures. Admission: Priority date 12/1; no deadline. No application fee. Admission notification on a rolling basis beginning on or about 10/1. **Financial aid:** Priority date 5/1; no closing date. FAFSA required. Applicants notified on a rolling basis starting 2/15; must reply within 2 week(s) of notification.

Academics. Special study options: Accelerated study, combined bachelor's/graduate degree, cross-registration, distance learning, double major, dual enrollment of high school students, honors, independent study, internships, study abroad, teacher certification program, Washington semester. **Credit/placement by examination:** AP, CLEP, IB, institutional tests. 30 credit hours maximum toward bachelor's degree. **Support services:** Learning center, reduced course load, remedial instruction, study skills assistance, tutoring, writing center.

Majors. Area/ethnic studies: American. **Biology:** General, biochemistry. **Business:** General, accounting, business admin, finance, international, management science, managerial economics, marketing. **Communications:** General, media studies. **English:** English lit. **Health services:** Health care admin, nursing (RN), preoccupational therapy, prephysical therapy. **History:** General. **Liberal arts:** Arts/sciences. **Parks/recreation:** Sports admin. **Physical sciences:** Chemistry. **Protective services:** Criminal justice, law enforcement admin. **Psychology:** General. **Social sciences:** Criminology, economics, international relations, political science, sociology. **Visual/performing arts:** General, dramatic.

Most popular majors. Business/marketing 16%, health sciences 39%, psychology 7%, security/protective services 11%, social sciences 9%.

Technology on campus. 100 workstations in dormitories, library, computer center, student center. Dormitories wired for high-speed internet access and linked to campus network. Commuter students can connect to campus network. Online course registration, online library, helpline, wireless network available.

Student life. Freshman orientation: Mandatory. Preregistration for classes offered. Several two-day programs in June and July and just prior to start of fall term. **Policies:** Freshmen not permitted cars on campus. **Housing:** Guaranteed on-campus for all undergraduates. Coed dorms, single-sex dorms, apartments available. $200 nonrefundable deposit, deadline 5/1. **Activities:** Pep band, campus ministries, dance, drama, international student organizations, literary magazine, Model UN, student government, student newspaper, Model Congress, minority student organizations, Partners, Best Buddies, Intervarsity Christian Fellowship, Young Professionals for International Cooperation, Students in Free Enterprise, student entrepreneur group.

Athletics. NCAA. **Intercollegiate:** Baseball M, basketball, cheerleading, cross-country, field hockey W, football (tackle) M, golf, ice hockey M, lacrosse, rugby, soccer, softball W, tennis, track and field, volleyball W, wrestling M. **Intramural:** Basketball, football (non-tackle) M, softball, volleyball. **Team name:** Yellow Jackets.

Student services. Adult student services, alcohol/substance abuse counseling, chaplain/spiritual director, career counseling, services for economically disadvantaged, student employment services, financial aid counseling, health services, minority student services, personal counseling, placement for graduates, veterans' counselor, women's services. **Physically disabled:** Services for visually, hearing impaired.

Contact. E-mail: inquiry@aic.edu
Phone: (413) 205-3201 Toll-free number: (800) 242-3142
Fax: (413) 205-3051
Janelle Holmboe, Dean of Admissions, American International College, 1000 State Street, Springfield, MA 01109

Amherst College
Amherst, Massachusetts
www.amherst.edu

CB member
CB code: 3003

- Private 4-year liberal arts college
- Residential campus in large town
- 1,795 degree-seeking undergraduates: 50% women, 12% African American, 14% Asian American, 13% Hispanic/Latino, 5% Multi-racial, non-Hispanic, 10% international
- 14% of applicants admitted
- SAT and SAT Subject Tests or ACT (ACT writing recommended), application essay required
- 95% graduate within 6 years; 17% enter graduate study

General. Founded in 1821. Regionally accredited. **Degrees:** 471 bachelor's awarded. **ROTC:** Army, Air Force. **Location:** 90 miles from Boston, 150 miles from New York City. **Calendar:** Semester. **Full-time faculty:** 211 total; 98% have terminal degrees, 21% minority, 49% women. **Part-time faculty:** 74 total; 84% have terminal degrees, 8% minority, 46% women. **Class size:** 70% < 20, 24% 20-39, 4% 40-49, 2% 50-99, less than 1% >100. **Special facilities:** Observatory, planetarium, Center for Russian Culture, Emily Dickinson Homestead, Center for Community Engagement, Book and Plow Farm, Mead Art Museum, Beneski Museum of Natural History.

Freshman class profile. 8,568 applied, 1,210 admitted, 477 enrolled.

Mid 50% test scores			
SAT critical reading:	680-780	Rank in top tenth:	86%
SAT math:	680-780	Return as sophomores:	98%
SAT writing:	680-770	Out-of-state:	89%
ACT composite:	31-34	Live on campus:	100%
Rank in top quarter:	96%	International:	9%

Basis for selection. Grades, test scores, essays, recommendations, independent work, quality of individual's secondary school program, and achievements outside of classroom are important.

High school preparation. College-preparatory program recommended. Recommended units include English 4, mathematics 4, social studies 2, history 2, science 3 (laboratory 1) and foreign language 3.

2015-2016 Annual costs. Tuition/fees: $50,562. Room/board: $13,210. Books/supplies: $1,000. Personal expenses: $1,800.

2015-2016 Financial aid. All financial aid based on need. 322 full-time freshmen applied for aid; 259 deemed to have need; 259 received aid. Average need met was 100%. Average scholarship/grant was $49,514; average loan $404. 95% of total undergraduate aid awarded as scholarships/grants, 5% as loans/jobs.

Application procedures. Admission: Closing date 1/1 (postmark date). $60 fee, may be waived for applicants with need. Application must be submitted online. Admission notification by 4/1. Must reply by 5/1. **Financial aid:** Priority date 2/15; no closing date. FAFSA, CSS PROFILE required. Applicants notified by 4/1; must reply by 5/1.

Academics. First-year students must choose 1 first-year seminar from a range of 29 special topics, often interdisciplinary. No core curriculum and no distribution requirements. Students select major at end of sophomore year. **Special study options:** Cross-registration, double major, exchange student, independent study, internships, student-designed major, study abroad, teacher certification program. Member of 5-college consortium. **Credit/placement by examination:** AP, CLEP, IB, institutional tests. **Support services:** Study skills assistance, tutoring, writing center.

Majors. Architecture: History/criticism. **Area/ethnic studies:** African, African-American, American, Asian, European, Russian/Eastern European/Eurasian, Western European, women's. **Biology:** General, neuroscience. **Computer sciences:** Computer science. **Conservation:** Environmental studies. **English:** English lit. **Foreign languages:** Ancient Greek, classics, French, German, Latin, Russian, Spanish. **History:** General. **Math:** General. **Philosophy/religion:** Philosophy, religion. **Physical sciences:** Astronomy, chemistry, geology, physics. **Psychology:** General. **Social sciences:** Anthropology, economics, political science, sociology. **Visual/performing arts:** Dance, dramatic, music, studio arts.

Most popular majors. Biology 11%, English 8%, foreign language 7%, history 7%, legal studies 9%, mathematics 9%, physical sciences 6%, psychology 7%, social sciences 20%, visual/performing arts 7%.

Technology on campus. 254 workstations in library, computer center, student center. Dormitories wired for high-speed internet access and linked to campus network. Commuter students can connect to campus network. Online library, helpline, repair service, wireless network available.

Student life. Freshman orientation: Mandatory. Preregistration for classes offered. Eight-day orientation with events planned by student groups and cultural organizations. **Policies:** Freshmen not permitted cars on campus. **Housing:** Guaranteed on-campus for all undergraduates. Coed dorms, cooperative housing, themed housing, wellness housing available. Language and other theme houses available including French/Spanish, Russian/German, Chinese/Japanese, Latino, African American, health and wellness house, cooperative house, and arts house. Men's and women's floors available to all students. **Activities:** Bands, campus ministries, choral groups, dance, drama, film society, international student organizations, literary magazine, music ensembles, Model UN, musical theater, opera, radio station, student government, student newspaper, symphony orchestra, Amherst Christian Fellowship, Christian Worship Series, Hillel, Muslim Student Association, multifaith council, Newman Catholic club, Adventist Christians Together to Serve, Big Brothers Big Sisters, Political Union, Reader to Reader, Inc, GlobeMEd.

Athletics. NCAA. **Intercollegiate:** Baseball M, basketball, cross-country, diving, field hockey W, football (tackle) M, golf, ice hockey, lacrosse, soccer, softball W, squash, swimming, tennis, track and field, volleyball W. **Intramural:** Badminton, basketball, football (non-tackle), golf, ice hockey, soccer, softball, squash, table tennis, tennis, volleyball.

Student services. Alcohol/substance abuse counseling, chaplain/spiritual director, career counseling, services for economically disadvantaged, student employment services, financial aid counseling, health services, minority student services, personal counseling, placement for graduates, women's services. **Physically disabled:** Services for visually, speech, hearing impaired.

Contact. E-mail: admission@amherst.edu
Phone: (413) 542-2328 Fax: (413) 542-2040
Cate Zolkos, Dean of Admission, Amherst College, PO Box 5000, Amherst, MA 01002-5000

Anna Maria College
Paxton, Massachusetts
www.annamaria.edu

CB member
CB code: 3005

- Private 4-year liberal arts college affiliated with the Roman Catholic Church
- Residential campus in small town
- 1,123 degree-seeking undergraduates: 28% part-time, 61% women, 11% African American, 2% Asian American, 8% Hispanic/Latino, 2% Multiracial, non-Hispanic
- 323 degree-seeking graduate students
- 80% of applicants admitted
- Application essay required

General. Founded in 1946. Regionally accredited. **Degrees:** 252 bachelor's awarded; master's offered. **ROTC:** Air Force. **Location:** 8 miles from Worcester, 40 miles from Boston. **Calendar:** Semester, limited summer session. **Full-time faculty:** 38 total; 55% have terminal degrees, 10% minority, 50% women. **Class size:** 78% < 20, 21% 20-39, less than 1% 40-49. **Special facilities:** Nature trails, arts building.

Freshman class profile. 1,785 applied, 1,429 admitted, 235 enrolled.

GPA 3.75 or higher:	6%	Return as sophomores:	65%
GPA 3.50-3.74:	8%	Out-of-state:	31%
GPA 3.0-3.49:	31%	Live on campus:	77%
GPA 2.0-2.99:	50%		

Basis for selection. High school record most important, followed by recommendations, and school and community activities. Test scores optional for all students except for those majoring in paramedic science. Interviews recommended. Auditions required for music majors, portfolios required for art majors. **Learning Disabled:** Students with a diagnosed learning disability should submit any diagnostic tests completed along with copy of an individualized educational plan, if available.

High school preparation. College-preparatory program recommended. 21 units required. Required units include English 4, mathematics 3, social studies 2, history 2, science 3 (laboratory 1), foreign language 2 and academic electives 4.

2015-2016 Annual costs. Tuition/fees: $35,074. Room/board: $13,112. Books/supplies: $2,000.

2014-2015 Financial aid. Non-need-based: Scholarships awarded for academics, music/drama.

Application procedures. Admission: Priority date 3/1; no deadline. $25 fee, may be waived for applicants with need. Admission notification on a rolling basis. **Financial aid:** Priority date 3/1; no closing date. FAFSA required. Applicants notified on a rolling basis starting 4/1.

Academics. Special study options: Accelerated study, combined bachelor's/graduate degree, cooperative education, cross-registration, distance learning, double major, honors, independent study, internships, liberal arts/career combination, student-designed major, study abroad, teacher certification program, Washington semester. Member of Higher Education Consortium of Central Massachusetts. **Credit/placement by examination:** AP, CLEP, institutional tests. 30 credit hours maximum toward bachelor's degree. **Support services:** Learning center, reduced course load, remedial instruction, study skills assistance, tutoring, writing center.

Majors. Biology: General. **Business:** Business admin, management information systems. **Communications:** Media studies. **Conservation:** Environmental science, environmental studies. **Education:** General, art, early childhood, elementary, English, history, kindergarten/preschool, middle, music, secondary. **English:** English lit. **Health services:** Art therapy, music therapy, nursing (RN), prenursing. **History:** General. **Human services:** Public policy, social work. **Liberal arts:** Arts/sciences, humanities. **Philosophy/religion:** Philosophy. **Protective services:** Firefighting, forensics, law enforcement admin. **Psychology:** General. **Social sciences:** Political science, sociology. **Theology:** Theology. **Visual/performing arts:** Art, graphic design, music, music performance, piano/keyboard, studio arts management, voice/opera.

Most popular majors. Health sciences 41%, public administration/social services 6%, security/protective services 33%.

Technology on campus. 86 workstations in dormitories, library, computer center, student center. Dormitories wired for high-speed internet access and linked to campus network. Commuter students can connect to campus network. Online course registration, online library, helpline, wireless network available.

Student life. Freshman orientation: Mandatory. Preregistration for classes offered. **Housing:** Guaranteed on-campus for freshmen. Coed dorms, special housing for disabled, wellness housing available. $300 nonrefundable deposit, deadline 5/1. **Activities:** Bands, campus ministries, choral groups, dance, drama, music ensembles, musical theater, student government, student newspaper.

Athletics. NCAA. **Intercollegiate:** Baseball M, basketball, cross-country, field hockey W, football (tackle) M, golf, lacrosse, soccer, softball W, tennis W, volleyball W. **Intramural:** Baseball, basketball, football (non-tackle), volleyball. **Team name:** AMCATS.

Student services. Alcohol/substance abuse counseling, chaplain/spiritual director, career counseling, student employment services, financial aid counseling, health services, minority student services, personal counseling, placement for graduates. **Physically disabled:** Services for visually, speech, hearing impaired.

Contact. E-mail: admission@annamaria.edu
Phone: (508) 849-3360 Toll-free number: (800) 344-4586 ext. 360
Fax: (508) 849-3362
Peter Miller, Dean of Admissions and Financial Aid, Anna Maria College, 50 Sunset Lane, Box O, Paxton, MA 01612-1198

Assumption College
Worcester, Massachusetts
www.assumption.edu
CB member
CB code: 3009

- Private 4-year liberal arts college affiliated with the Roman Catholic Church
- Residential campus in small city
- 1,979 degree-seeking undergraduates: 59% women, 6% African American, 2% Asian American, 7% Hispanic/Latino, 2% Multi-racial, non-Hispanic, 2% international
- 408 degree-seeking graduate students
- 76% of applicants admitted
- Application essay required
- 73% graduate within 6 years; 24% enter graduate study

General. Founded in 1904. Regionally accredited. **Degrees:** 482 bachelor's awarded; master's offered. **ROTC:** Army, Air Force. **Location:** 45 miles from Boston. **Calendar:** Semester, limited summer session. **Full-time faculty:** 144 total; 92% have terminal degrees, 6% minority, 43% women. **Part-time faculty:** 80 total; 56% have terminal degrees, 6% minority, 48% women. **Class size:** 41% < 20, 58% 20-39, 2% 40-49, less than 1% 50-99. **Special facilities:** French institute (academic research center for study of Francophone questions), Assumption College Rome study abroad campus.

Freshman class profile. 4,769 applied, 3,614 admitted, 570 enrolled.

Mid 50% test scores			
SAT critical reading:	510-600	Rank in top quarter:	43%
SAT math:	510-610	Rank in top tenth:	12%
ACT composite:	23-26	End year in good standing:	87%
GPA 3.75 or higher:	22%	Return as sophomores:	83%
GPA 3.50-3.74:	22%	Out-of-state:	38%
GPA 3.0-3.49:	34%	Live on campus:	92%
GPA 2.0-2.99:	21%	International:	3%

Basis for selection. School achievement most important, followed by class rank in top 40%, extracurricular activities, interview, recommendations. **Home schooled:** Statement describing home school structure and mission, letter of recommendation (nonparent) required. Submit Official Educational Records if associated with a home school program.

High school preparation. College-preparatory program required. 18 units required. Required units include English 4, mathematics 3, history 2, science 2, foreign language 2 and academic electives 5.

2015-2016 Annual costs. Tuition/fees: $36,160. Room/board: $11,264. Books/supplies: $1,000. Personal expenses: $1,000.

2015-2016 Financial aid. Need-based: 506 full-time freshmen applied for aid; 430 deemed to have need; 430 received aid. Average need met was 72%. Average scholarship/grant was $20,067; average loan $3,687. 74% of total undergraduate aid awarded as scholarships/grants, 26% as loans/jobs. **Non-need-based:** Awarded to 722 full-time undergraduates, including 243 freshmen. Scholarships awarded for academics, athletics, music/drama.

Application procedures. Admission: Closing date 2/15 (postmark date). $50 fee, may be waived for applicants with need. Admission notification on a rolling basis beginning on or about 3/15. Must reply by May 1 or within 2 week(s) if notified thereafter. **Financial aid:** Closing date 2/15. FAFSA required. Applicants notified on a rolling basis starting 2/16; must reply by 5/1.

Academics. Special study options: Combined bachelor's/graduate degree, cross-registration, double major, honors, independent study, internships, New York semester, semester at sea, student-designed major, study abroad, teacher certification program, Washington semester. Worcester Consortium gerontology studies program; 3-2 engineering program (BA/BS) with Worcester Polytechnic Institute. Students may register for courses at 11 area colleges. Volunteer programs available: comprehensive 2-week programs in Mexico and Puerto Rico, 1-week spring break programs in various locations. Study abroad available in Rome. **Credit/placement by examination:** AP, CLEP, IB, institutional tests. **Support services:** Learning center, study skills assistance, tutoring, writing center.

Majors. Area/ethnic studies: Latin American. **Biology:** General, biotechnology, molecular. **Business:** Accounting, actuarial science, business admin, international, marketing. **Communications:** Organizational. **Computer sciences:** General. **Conservation:** Environmental science. **Education:** Multi-level teacher. **English:** English lit. **Foreign languages:** General, classics, French, Italian, Spanish. **History:** General. **Math:** General. **Philosophy/religion:** Philosophy. **Physical sciences:** Chemistry. **Psychology:** General. **Social sciences:** Criminology, economics, political science, sociology. **Theology:** Theology. **Visual/performing arts:** Art history/conservation, graphic design, music, studio arts.

Most popular majors. Biology 12%, business/marketing 21%, communications/journalism 6%, English 10%, health sciences 10%, history 6%, psychology 9%, social sciences 11%.

Technology on campus. 361 workstations in dormitories, library, computer center, student center. Dormitories wired for high-speed internet access and linked to campus network. Commuter students can connect to campus network. Online course registration, online library, helpline, repair service, student web hosting, wireless network available.

Student life. Freshman orientation: Mandatory, $400 fee. Preregistration for classes offered. Two-day program held in June. **Policies:** Freshmen not permitted cars on campus. **Housing:** Guaranteed on-campus for all undergraduates. Coed dorms, single-sex dorms, special housing for disabled, themed housing, wellness housing available. Freshman dorms, substance-free dorms, living/learning center available. **Activities:** Bands, campus ministries, choral groups, dance, drama, film society, literary magazine, music ensembles, musical theater, student government, student newspaper, TV station, ALANA network, College Democrats, College Republicans, student volunteer organization, students advocating change, student health network, service program, Omicron Delta Kappa leadership circle, retreat programs.

Athletics. NCAA. **Intercollegiate:** Baseball M, basketball, cross-country, field hockey W, football (tackle) M, golf M, ice hockey M, lacrosse, rowing (crew) W, soccer, softball W, swimming W, tennis, track and field, volleyball W. **Intramural:** Basketball, football (non-tackle), golf, ice hockey, racquetball, soccer, softball, volleyball. **Team name:** Greyhounds.

Student services. Alcohol/substance abuse counseling, chaplain/spiritual director, career counseling, student employment services, financial aid counseling, health services, minority student services, personal counseling, placement for graduates. **Physically disabled:** Services for visually, speech, hearing impaired.

Contact. E-mail: admiss@assumption.edu
Phone: (508) 767-7285 Toll-free number: (866) 477-7776
Fax: (508) 799-4412
Evan Lipp, Vice President for Enrollment Management, Assumption College, 500 Salisbury Street, Worcester, MA 01609-1296

Babson College
Babson Park, Massachusetts
www.babson.edu
CB member
CB code: 3075

- Private 4-year business college
- Residential campus in large town
- 2,141 degree-seeking undergraduates: 48% women, 5% African American, 12% Asian American, 10% Hispanic/Latino, 2% Multi-racial, non-Hispanic, 26% international
- 904 degree-seeking graduate students
- 26% of applicants admitted
- SAT or ACT (ACT writing optional), application essay required
- 89% graduate within 6 years

General. Founded in 1919. Regionally accredited. **Degrees:** 536 bachelor's awarded; master's offered. **ROTC:** Army. **Location:** 14 miles from Boston.

Calendar: Semester, extensive summer session. **Full-time faculty:** 194 total; 85% have terminal degrees, 17% minority, 38% women. **Part-time faculty:** 66 total; 44% have terminal degrees, 8% minority, 46% women. **Class size:** 21% < 20, 61% 20-39, 17% 40-49. **Special facilities:** Entrepreneurship center, woman's leadership center, social entrepreneurship institute, investment center, first year entrepreneurship program.

Freshman class profile. 7,516 applied, 1,977 admitted, 528 enrolled.

Mid 50% test scores		Out-of-state:	75%
SAT critical reading:	580-720	Live on campus:	100%
SAT math:	620-720	International:	25%
SAT writing:	590-660	Fraternities:	16%
ACT composite:	27-30	Sororities:	31%
Return as sophomores:	96%		

Basis for selection. Academic performance and level of course work (college preparatory, honors, Advanced Placement) most important; followed by academic motivation, including interest in learning and willingness to challenge oneself; test scores; writing ability; involvement in cocurricular activities and/or work experience; leadership, creativity, enthusiasm. **Home schooled:** Statement describing home school structure and mission, transcript of courses and grades, state high school equivalency certificate, letter of recommendation (nonparent) required. Applicants must provide information about completed courses, schooling, testing, and diploma requirements.

High school preparation. College-preparatory program required. 20 units required. Required and recommended units include English 4, mathematics 4, social studies 4, science 3 and foreign language 4. Pre-calculus strongly recommended.

2016-2017 Annual costs. Tuition/fees (projected): $48,288. Room/board: $15,376. Books/supplies: $1,050.

2015-2016 Financial aid. All financial aid based on need. Average need met was 98%. Average scholarship/grant was $38,761; average loan $3,840. 87% of total undergraduate aid awarded as scholarships/grants, 13% as loans/jobs.

Application procedures. Admission: Priority date 11/1; deadline 1/1 (postmark date). $75 fee, may be waived for applicants with need. Admission notification by 4/1. Must reply by 5/1. **Financial aid:** Priority date 2/15, closing date 2/15. FAFSA, CSS PROFILE required. Applicants notified by 4/1; must reply by 5/1.

Academics. Special study options: Accelerated study, combined bachelor's/graduate degree, cross-registration, exchange student, honors, independent study, internships, liberal arts/career combination, student-designed major, study abroad. Study abroad program to Russia, China and India over one semester Semester in San Francisco. **Credit/placement by examination:** AP, CLEP, IB, institutional tests. **Support services:** Reduced course load, study skills assistance, tutoring, writing center.

Majors. Business: General, accounting, accounting/business management, accounting/finance, auditing, business admin, communications, entrepreneurial studies, finance, international, international finance, international marketing, investments/securities, management information systems, management science, managerial economics, marketing, office management, operations, sales/distribution, small business admin, statistics. **Communications:** Advertising. **Computer sciences:** General, information systems.

Technology on campus. PC or laptop required. Dormitories wired for high-speed internet access and linked to campus network. Commuter students can connect to campus network. Online course registration, online library, helpline, repair service, wireless network available.

Student life. Freshman orientation: Mandatory. Preregistration for classes offered. Three-day program preceding start of classes. **Policies:** First-year students required to live on-campus. **Housing:** Guaranteed on-campus for all undergraduates. Coed dorms, apartments, fraternity/sorority housing, themed housing, wellness housing available. $500 nonrefundable deposit, deadline 5/1. **Activities:** Jazz band, campus ministries, choral groups, dance, drama, international student organizations, literary magazine, music ensembles, musical theater, radio station, student government, student newspaper, TV station, 100 organizations available.

Athletics. NCAA. **Intercollegiate:** Baseball M, basketball, cross-country, diving, field hockey W, golf M, ice hockey M, lacrosse, skiing; soccer, softball W, swimming, tennis, track and field, volleyball W. **Intramural:** Basketball, football (non-tackle), ice hockey, racquetball, soccer, softball, squash, tennis, volleyball, water polo. **Team name:** Beavers.

Student services. Alcohol/substance abuse counseling, chaplain/spiritual director, career counseling, student employment services, financial aid counseling, health services, minority student services, personal counseling, placement for graduates, women's services. **Physically disabled:** Services for visually, speech, hearing impaired.

Contact. E-mail: ugradadmission@babson.edu
Phone: (781) 239-5522 Toll-free number: (800) 488-3696
Fax: (781) 239-4135
Courtney Minden, Director of Undergraduate Admission, Babson College, 231 Forest Street, Babson Park, MA 02457-0310

Bard College at Simon's Rock
Great Barrington, Massachusetts
www.simons-rock.edu   CB code: 3795

- Private 4-year liberal arts college
- Residential campus in small town
- 325 degree-seeking undergraduates: 1% part-time, 61% women, 4% African American, 10% Asian American, 3% Hispanic/Latino, 6% Multiracial, non-Hispanic, 14% international
- 89% of applicants admitted
- Application essay, interview required
- 49% graduate within 6 years

General. Founded in 1964. Regionally accredited. Provides students with the opportunity to begin college in a residential environment after completing the 10th or 11th grade. **Degrees:** 36 bachelor's, 99 associate awarded. **Location:** 135 miles from Boston, 132 miles from New York. **Calendar:** Semester. **Full-time faculty:** 46 total; 94% have terminal degrees, 11% minority, 56% women. **Part-time faculty:** 24 total; 38% have terminal degrees, 8% minority, 54% women. **Class size:** 97% < 20, 3% 20-39. **Special facilities:** Theaters, dance studio, 3-D design studio, wood/metal studio, sculpture terrace, wood-fired kiln.

Freshman class profile. 199 applied, 178 admitted, 117 enrolled.

Mid 50% test scores		GPA 3.0-3.49:	31%
SAT critical reading:	640-750	GPA 2.0-2.99:	11%
SAT math:	610-650	Return as sophomores:	78%
SAT writing:	610-700	Out-of-state:	75%
ACT composite:	28-30	Live on campus:	93%
GPA 3.75 or higher:	43%	International:	10%
GPA 3.50-3.74:	15%		

Basis for selection. School achievement record, essays, recommendations (counselor and teacher), interview most important. Institutional testing used for math and foreign language placement. Students in home schooled or ungraded schooling should submit test scores if available. **Home schooled:** Statement describing home school structure and mission, transcript of courses and grades, interview required.

High school preparation. 10 units recommended. Recommended units include English 2, mathematics 2, social studies 2, history 2, science 2 and foreign language 2. Applicants who have completed 10th or 11th grade should have 2 or 3 years college-preparatory curriculum respectively.

2015-2016 Annual costs. Tuition/fees: $50,859. Room/board: $13,660. Books/supplies: $1,000. Personal expenses: $840.

Financial aid. Non-need-based: Scholarships awarded for academics, alumni affiliation, minority status, state residency.

Application procedures. Admission: Priority date 2/1; deadline 5/1 (postmark date). $50 fee, may be waived for applicants with need. Admission notification on a rolling basis beginning on or about 11/15. Must reply by May 1 or within 2 week(s) if notified thereafter. **Financial aid:** Priority date 2/15; no closing date. FAFSA, CSS PROFILE required. Applicants notified on a rolling basis starting 3/15; must reply within 2 week(s) of notification.

Academics. Upper-class students may take tutorials, independent projects, and extended campus projects (internships or courses). Seniors must complete 8-credit, year-long senior thesis project. **Special study options:** Combined bachelor's/graduate degree, double major, external degree, independent study, internships, semester at sea, student-designed major, study abroad, Washington semester. Bard Globalization and International Affairs, 3/2 engineering program with Columbia University, articulation agreements with Lincoln College at Oxford University and the Centre for New Writing at the University of Manchester, articulation agreement with the International Center for Photography/Bard. **Credit/placement by examination:** AP, CLEP, institutional tests. **Support services:** Learning center, reduced course load, remedial instruction, study skills assistance, tutoring, writing center.

Majors. Area/ethnic studies: African-American, Asian, East Asian, French, German, Spanish/Iberian. **Biology:** General. **Computer sciences:** Computer science. **Conservation:** Environmental studies. **Engineering:** Pre-engineering. **English:** Creative writing, English lit, general lit. **Foreign languages:** Classics, French, German, linguistics, Spanish. **Health services:** Premedicine. **History:** General. **Liberal arts:** Arts/sciences. **Math:** General, applied. **Philosophy/religion:** Philosophy. **Physical sciences:** Chemistry, physics. **Psychology:** General. **Social sciences:** Geography, political science. **Visual/performing arts:** General, acting, art history/conservation, ceramics, cinematography, dance, dramatic, film/cinema/video, multimedia, music, photography, play/screenwriting, studio arts, theater design.

Most popular majors. Computer/information sciences 6%, English 13%, interdisciplinary studies 14%, liberal arts 14%, social sciences 10%, visual/performing arts 21%.

Technology on campus. 62 workstations in dormitories, library, student center. Dormitories wired for high-speed internet access and linked to campus network. Commuter students can connect to campus network. Online library, helpline, student web hosting, wireless network available.

Student life. Freshman orientation: Mandatory, $600 fee. Preregistration for classes offered. One-week writing and thinking workshop held prior to start of semester in August. **Policies:** Dry campus. No smoking on campus. Freshmen not permitted cars on campus. **Housing:** Guaranteed on-campus for freshmen. Coed dorms, single-sex dorms, apartments available. Pets allowed in dorm rooms. Senior only houses. **Activities:** Bands, campus ministries, choral groups, dance, drama, film society, international student organizations, literary magazine, music ensembles, Model UN, student government, symphony orchestra, black student union, community conservation and clean up, chemistry club, international students club, Latino/a students alliance, QueerSA, women's center.

Athletics. Intercollegiate: Basketball, soccer, swimming. **Intramural:** Archery, basketball, cross-country, racquetball, soccer, squash, swimming, tennis, ultimate frisbee, volleyball, weight lifting. **Team name:** Llamas.

Student services. Alcohol/substance abuse counseling, chaplain/spiritual director, career counseling, student employment services, financial aid counseling, health services, minority student services, personal counseling, placement for graduates, women's services. **Physically disabled:** Services for visually, speech, hearing impaired.

Contact. E-mail: admit@simons-rock.edu
Phone: (413) 528-7312 Toll-free number: (800) 235-7186
Fax: (413) 541-0081
Mary Davidson, Dean of the College, Bard College at Simon's Rock, Office of Admission, Great Barrington, MA 01230-1990

Bay Path University
Longmeadow, Massachusetts
www.baypath.edu
CB code: 3078

- Private 4-year liberal arts college for women
- Residential campus in large town
- 1,849 degree-seeking undergraduates: 20% part-time, 100% women, 14% African American, 2% Asian American, 19% Hispanic/Latino, 2% Multi-racial, non-Hispanic
- 1,251 degree-seeking graduate students
- 77% of applicants admitted
- 57% graduate within 6 years

General. Founded in 1897. Regionally accredited. Member of 8-college consortium. Women as Empowered Learners and Leaders Program (WELL) is the foundation of the Bay Path education. The program offers courses that hone in on academic and professional skills, including a senior capstone course that requires students to implement their learning into a community-based project. **Degrees:** 370 bachelor's, 30 associate awarded; master's offered. **ROTC:** Army, Air Force. **Location:** 5 miles from Springfield; 23 miles from Hartford, Connecticut. **Calendar:** Semester, limited summer session. **Full-time faculty:** 56 total. **Part-time faculty:** 255 total. **Class size:** 83% < 20, 16% 20-39, less than 1% 40-49. **Special facilities:** Academic development center, occupational therapy laboratory, physicians assistant laboratory, career development center.

Freshman class profile. 1,148 applied, 887 admitted, 178 enrolled.

GPA 3.75 or higher:	15%	Rank in top tenth:	18%
GPA 3.50-3.74:	17%	End year in good standing:	88%
GPA 3.0-3.49:	33%	Return as sophomores:	79%
GPA 2.0-2.99:	35%	Out-of-state:	54%
Rank in top quarter:	42%	Live on campus:	63%

Basis for selection. High school transcript and performance, class rank, GPA, SAT or ACT, letters of recommendation, and essay. Interview and essay or personal statement recommended. **Home schooled:** Statement describing home school structure and mission, transcript of courses and grades, state high school equivalency certificate, letter of recommendation (nonparent) required.

High school preparation. College-preparatory program recommended. Required and recommended units include English 4, mathematics 3, social studies 2, history 1, science 2-3 (laboratory 2-3) and foreign language 2.

2015-2016 Annual costs. Tuition/fees: $31,785. Room/board: $13,045. Books/supplies: $1,100. Personal expenses: $1,100.

2015-2016 Financial aid. Need-based: 166 full-time freshmen applied for aid; 160 deemed to have need; 160 received aid. Average need met was 76%. Average scholarship/grant was $24,193; average loan $4,051. 69% of total undergraduate aid awarded as scholarships/grants, 31% as loans/jobs. **Non-need-based:** Scholarships awarded for academics.

Application procedures. Admission: Priority date 12/15; deadline 8/1. $25 fee, may be waived for applicants with need, free for online applicants. Admission notification on a rolling basis beginning on or about 9/15. Must reply by May 1 or within 2 week(s) if notified thereafter. **Financial aid:** Priority date 3/1; no closing date. FAFSA required. Applicants notified on a rolling basis starting 3/1; must reply within 2 week(s) of notification.

Academics. Summer school offerings available online at substantial discount; open to rising high school juniors and seniors. **Special study options:** Accelerated study, combined bachelor's/graduate degree, cooperative education, cross-registration, distance learning, double major, ESL, exchange student, honors, independent study, internships, liberal arts/career combination, student-designed major, study abroad, teacher certification program, Washington semester, weekend college. **Credit/placement by examination:** AP, CLEP, IB, institutional tests. 30 credit hours maximum toward associate degree, 60 toward bachelor's. **Support services:** Learning center, pre-admission summer program, study skills assistance, tutoring, writing center.

Honors college/program. Admissions based on 1500 SAT/equivalent ACT, 3.50 GPA, demonstrated evidence of past academic achievement and commitment to extra-curricular activities and community service; 20-30 admitted each year.

Majors. Biology: General, biochemistry, biomedical sciences, biotechnology, neurobiology/behavior, neuroscience. **Business:** Accounting, business admin, human resources, marketing. **Computer sciences:** Security. **Education:** Biology, early childhood, elementary. **Health services:** Preoccupational therapy. **Liberal arts:** Arts/sciences. **Protective services:** Criminalistics, forensics. **Psychology:** General, developmental, forensic. **Visual/performing arts:** Interior design.

Most popular majors. Business/marketing 28%, education 10%, health sciences 9%, liberal arts 14%, psychology 19%, security/protective services 9%.

Technology on campus. 235 workstations in dormitories, library, computer center, student center. Dormitories wired for high-speed internet access and linked to campus network. Commuter students can connect to campus network. Online course registration, online library, helpline, wireless network available.

Student life. Freshman orientation: Mandatory. Preregistration for classes offered. Two-part program: Advising Days in June and July covers placement testing, academic advising, and course registration. Welcome Week held the end of August. **Policies:** No smoking or alcohol in dormitories. **Housing:** Guaranteed on-campus for all undergraduates. Wellness housing available. $300 nonrefundable deposit, deadline 5/1. **Activities:** Choral groups, dance, drama, international student organizations, music ensembles, Model UN, musical theater, student government, Interfaith council, Habitat for Humanity, Women of Culture, Alliance, Phi Beta Lambda, Bay Path Christian Fellowship, native cultures club.

Athletics. NCAA. **Intercollegiate:** Basketball W, cross-country W, field hockey W, lacrosse W, soccer W, softball W, tennis W, volleyball W. **Team name:** Wildcats.

Student services. Adult student services, career counseling, student employment services, financial aid counseling, health services, minority student services, personal counseling, placement for graduates, women's services.

Contact. E-mail: admiss@baypath.edu
Phone: (413) 565-1000 ext. 1331
Toll-free number: (800) 782-7284 ext. 1331 Fax: (413) 565-1105
Dawn Bryden, Dean of Admissions, Bay Path University, 588 Longmeadow Street, Longmeadow, MA 01106

Becker College
Worcester, Massachusetts
www.becker.edu
CB member
CB code: 3079

- Private 4-year liberal arts college
- Residential campus in small city

- 2,036 degree-seeking undergraduates: 22% part-time, 60% women, 7% African American, 2% Asian American, 9% Hispanic/Latino, 3% Multiracial, non-Hispanic, 1% international
- 5 degree-seeking graduate students
- 67% of applicants admitted
- SAT or ACT (ACT writing optional) required

General. Founded in 1887. Regionally accredited. Campuses in Worcester and Leicester. **Degrees:** 300 bachelor's, 115 associate awarded; master's offered. **ROTC:** Army, Air Force. **Location:** 49 miles from Boston; 39 miles from Providence, Rhode Island. **Calendar:** Semester, limited summer session. **Full-time faculty:** 43 total; 72% have terminal degrees, 9% minority, 63% women. **Part-time faculty:** 187 total; 15% have terminal degrees, 9% minority, 60% women. **Class size:** 51% < 20, 44% 20-39, 4% 40-49, 1% 50-99. **Special facilities:** Veterinary clinic, 55-acre off-campus stable for equine programs and equestrian athletic team, digital games institute, working crime scene lab, on-campus mental health clinic for graduate program, center for global citizenship, nursing SIM lab.

Freshman class profile. 3,258 applied, 2,176 admitted, 407 enrolled.

Mid 50% test scores			
SAT critical reading:	450-550	GPA 2.0-2.99:	43%
SAT math:	450-560	Rank in top quarter:	27%
SAT writing:	430-540	Rank in top tenth:	4%
ACT composite:	19-25	Return as sophomores:	74%
GPA 3.75 or higher:	11%	Out-of-state:	46%
GPA 3.50-3.74:	11%	Live on campus:	79%
GPA 3.0-3.49:	33%	International:	2%

Basis for selection. High school record, GPA, test scores very important. Recommendations, class rank important. Interview, level of applicants interest, essay, extracurricular activities considered. Additional prerequisites for nursing, veterinary technology, veterinary science programs. Essay recommended. **Home schooled:** Statement describing home school structure and mission, transcript of courses and grades, state high school equivalency certificate, letter of recommendation (nonparent) required. Official transcript/documentation required from high school with which student is affiliated.

High school preparation. College-preparatory program required. 18 units recommended. Recommended units include English 4, mathematics 3, social studies 2, history 2, science 3 (laboratory 2) and foreign language 2. 1 chemistry with lab, 1 biology with lab required for nursing, veterinary technician, veterinary science, pre-vet programs. Specific math requirements for health science programs including nursing and veterinary-related majors. For more detail please visit the links below.

2015-2016 Annual costs. Tuition/fees: $34,080. Room/board: $12,400.

2015-2016 Financial aid. **Need-based:** 380 full-time freshmen applied for aid; 353 deemed to have need; 353 received aid. Average need met was 64%. Average scholarship/grant was $9,038; average loan $3,449. 92% of total undergraduate aid awarded as scholarships/grants, 8% as loans/jobs. **Non-need-based:** Awarded to 1,472 full-time undergraduates, including 399 freshmen. Scholarships awarded for academics, state residency.

Application procedures. Admission: Priority date 2/15; no deadline. No application fee. Admission notification on a rolling basis beginning on or about 11/1. Must reply by May 1 or within 2 week(s) if notified thereafter. **Financial aid:** Priority date 3/15; no closing date. FAFSA required. Applicants notified on a rolling basis starting 3/15.

Academics. Special study options: Accelerated study, combined bachelor's/graduate degree, cooperative education, cross-registration, distance learning, double major, dual enrollment of high school students, independent study, internships, liberal arts/career combination, semester at sea, study abroad, teacher certification program. **Credit/placement by examination:** AP, CLEP, IB, SAT, ACT, institutional tests. 30 credit hours maximum toward associate degree, 60 toward bachelor's. **Support services:** Learning center, reduced course load, remedial instruction, study skills assistance, tutoring, writing center.

Majors. Biology: General. **Business:** Business admin, management science, marketing. **Communications:** Intercultural. **Computer sciences:** General. **Education:** Early childhood, elementary. **Health services:** Community health services, nursing (RN), prephysical therapy, preveterinary, veterinary technology/assistant. **Liberal arts:** Arts/sciences. **Parks/recreation:** Exercise sciences, sports admin. **Protective services:** Forensics, law enforcement admin. **Psychology:** General. **Visual/performing arts:** Game design, graphic design.

Most popular majors. Business/marketing 19%, health sciences 13%, parks/recreation 9%, psychology 14%, visual/performing arts 34%.

Technology on campus. 325 workstations in dormitories, library, computer center, student center. Dormitories wired for high-speed internet access. Online course registration, online library, helpline, wireless network available.

Student life. Freshman orientation: Mandatory. Preregistration for classes offered. Three, day and a half overnight sessions in early- mid June, on both campuses. **Housing:** Guaranteed on-campus for freshmen. Coed dorms, apartments, gender-neutral housing, themed housing, wellness housing available. $100 nonrefundable deposit, deadline 6/1. **Activities:** Campus ministries, choral groups, dance, drama, international student organizations, music ensembles, musical theater, student government, Gay-Straight Alliance, Lambing Club, Muzunte Turtle Club, National Student Nurses Association, Japanese society, ALANA, Active Minds, International Student Organization, Global Citizenship, Habitat for Humanity.

Athletics. NCAA. **Intercollegiate:** Baseball M, basketball, equestrian, field hockey W, football (tackle) M, golf M, ice hockey, lacrosse, soccer, softball W, tennis, volleyball W. **Intramural:** Basketball. **Team name:** Hawks.

Student services. Adult student services, alcohol/substance abuse counseling, chaplain/spiritual director, career counseling, student employment services, financial aid counseling, health services, personal counseling. **Physically disabled:** Services for visually, speech, hearing impaired.

Contact. E-mail: admissions@becker.edu
Phone: (508) 373-9400 Toll-free number: (877) 523-2537
Fax: (508) 890-1500
Michael Perron, Director of Admissions, Becker College, Office of Admissions, Worcester, MA 01609

Bentley University
Waltham, Massachusetts
www.bentley.edu

CB member
CB code: 3096

- Private 4-year university and business college
- Residential campus in small city
- 4,137 degree-seeking undergraduates: 1% part-time, 40% women, 3% African American, 8% Asian American, 7% Hispanic/Latino, 2% Multiracial, non-Hispanic, 14% international
- 1,347 degree-seeking graduate students
- 42% of applicants admitted
- SAT or ACT (ACT writing optional), application essay required
- 89% graduate within 6 years; 14% enter graduate study

General. Founded in 1917. Regionally accredited. **Degrees:** 1,063 bachelor's awarded; master's, doctoral offered. **ROTC:** Army, Air Force. **Location:** 10 miles from Boston. **Calendar:** Semester, limited summer session. **Full-time faculty:** 289 total; 78% have terminal degrees, 16% minority, 40% women. **Part-time faculty:** 195 total; 42% have terminal degrees, 10% minority, 40% women. **Class size:** 26% < 20, 74% 20-39, less than 1% 40-49. **Special facilities:** Accounting center, academic technology center, center for arts and sciences, center for business ethics, center for languages and international collaboration, center for marketing technology, center for quantitative analysis, design and usability center, center for financial services, enterprise risk management program, media and culture labs and studio, trading room, Women's Leadership Institute, service-learning center, center for international students and scholars, multicultural center, writing center, spiritual life center, center for women in business, center for integration of science and industry.

Freshman class profile. 8,346 applied, 3,532 admitted, 915 enrolled.

Mid 50% test scores			
SAT critical reading:	540-640	End year in good standing:	99%
SAT math:	600-690	Return as sophomores:	95%
SAT writing:	550-650	Out-of-state:	61%
ACT composite:	26-30	Live on campus:	98%
Rank in top quarter:	72%	International:	13%
Rank in top tenth:	38%	Fraternities:	10%
		Sororities:	17%

Basis for selection. We holistically review all components of a student's admission file to assess academic preparedness as well as personal contributions to his/her school and community. While we will thoroughly review a student's secondary school transcript and standardized test scores, we will also consider their school activities, community involvement and/or work experiences along with recommendation letters. SAT or ACT is required of all students. If English is not your first spoken language, you'll also need to submit official results of the test of English as a Foreign language (TOEFL) or the International English Testing Systems (IELTS) exams. Interviews strongly recommended. **Home schooled:** Statement describing home school structure and mission, transcript of courses and grades, state high school equivalency certificate, letter of recommendation (nonparent) required.

High school preparation. College-preparatory program required. 19 units required. Required and recommended units include English 4, mathematics 4, social studies 3-4, science 3-4 (laboratory 2-3) and foreign language 3-4.

History is combined with social studies. Two additional units in English, math, social or lab science, or foreign language are recommended.

2015-2016 Annual costs. Tuition/fees: $44,085. Room/board: $14,520. Books/supplies: $1,200. Personal expenses: $1,200.

2014-2015 Financial aid. Need-based: 707 full-time freshmen applied for aid; 492 deemed to have need; 491 received aid. Average need met was 94%. Average scholarship/grant was $30,356; average loan $3,882. 82% of total undergraduate aid awarded as scholarships/grants, 18% as loans/jobs. **Non-need-based:** Awarded to 1,162 full-time undergraduates, including 344 freshmen. Scholarships awarded for academics, athletics, leadership, minority status.

Application procedures. Admission: Closing date 1/7 (postmark date). $50 fee, may be waived for applicants with need. Must reply by 5/1. **Financial aid:** Closing date 2/1. FAFSA required. CSS PROFILE is required of students who want to be considered for institutional need-based grants. Deadlines for receipt of CSS Profile: Early Decision 12/1; Regular Decision, 2/1. Applicants notified by 3/31.

Academics. Special study options: Accelerated study, combined bachelor's/graduate degree, cross-registration, distance learning, double major, exchange student, honors, independent study, internships, liberal arts/career combination, New York semester, semester at sea, student-designed major, study abroad, Washington semester. 5-year Bachelor's/Master's programs in Business Administration, Accountancy, Finance, Marketing Analytics, Information Technology, Financial Planning, and Taxation. **Credit/placement by examination:** AP, CLEP, IB, SAT, institutional tests. 30 credit hours maximum toward bachelor's degree. **Support services:** Learning center, reduced course load, study skills assistance, tutoring, writing center. Disability services, CIS sandbox (IT course assistance), ESOL Center for Foreign Language Tutoring lab, Economics-Finance-Stat tutoring lab.

Majors. Business: General, accounting, accounting/finance, actuarial science, business admin, communications, finance, managerial economics, marketing, sales/distribution. **Communications:** Media studies. **Computer sciences:** General, information systems. **Foreign languages:** Spanish. **Health services:** Health services admin. **History:** General. **Human services:** Public policy. **Liberal arts:** Arts/sciences. **Math:** General. **Philosophy/religion:** Philosophy.

Most popular majors. Business/marketing 93%.

Technology on campus. PC or laptop required. 4,472 workstations in dormitories, library, computer center, student center. Dormitories wired for high-speed internet access and linked to campus network. Commuter students can connect to campus network. Online course registration, online library, helpline, repair service, student web hosting, wireless network available.

Student life. Policies: Academic honesty system, minimum GPA for student leaders, travel and liability waivers for off-campus events. Freshmen not permitted cars on campus. **Housing:** Guaranteed on-campus for all undergraduates. Coed dorms, special housing for disabled, apartments, themed housing, wellness housing available. $500 nonrefundable deposit, deadline 5/1. Global living floors, women's leadership floor available. **Activities:** Jazz band, campus ministries, choral groups, dance, drama, film society, international student organizations, literary magazine, music ensembles, Model UN, musical theater, radio station, student government, student newspaper, TV station, Black United Body, South Asian student association, La Cultura Latina, PRIDE, Green Society, Islamic Community, Circle K, Habitat For Humanity, Hillel, Christian Fellowship.

Athletics. NCAA. **Intercollegiate:** Baseball M, basketball, cross-country, diving, field hockey W, football (tackle) M, golf M, ice hockey M, lacrosse, soccer, softball W, swimming, tennis, track and field, volleyball W. **Intramural:** Basketball, football (non-tackle) M, soccer, softball, ultimate frisbee, volleyball. **Team name:** Falcons.

Student services. Adult student services, alcohol/substance abuse counseling, chaplain/spiritual director, career counseling, services for economically disadvantaged, student employment services, financial aid counseling, health services, minority student services, personal counseling, placement for graduates, veterans' counselor, women's services. **Physically disabled:** Services for visually, speech, hearing impaired.

Contact. E-mail: ugadmission@bentley.edu
Phone: (781) 891-2244 Toll-free number: (800) 523-2354
Fax: (781) 891-3414
Bentley University, 175 Forest Street, Waltham, MA 02452-4705

Berklee College of Music
Boston, Massachusetts
www.berklee.edu

CB member
CB code: 3107

- Private 4-year music college
- Commuter campus in very large city
- 5,112 degree-seeking undergraduates: 16% part-time, 33% women, 5% African American, 4% Asian American, 8% Hispanic/Latino, 5% Multiracial, non-Hispanic, 33% international
- 160 degree-seeking graduate students
- 26% of applicants admitted
- Application essay, interview required
- 49% graduate within 6 years

General. Founded in 1945. Regionally accredited. **Degrees:** 841 bachelor's awarded; master's offered. **Calendar:** Semester, extensive summer session. **Full-time faculty:** 255 total; less than 1% have terminal degrees, 20% minority, 26% women. **Part-time faculty:** 433 total; less than 1% have terminal degrees, 14% minority, 31% women. **Class size:** 90% < 20, 10% 20-39, less than 1% 40-49, less than 1% 50-99. **Special facilities:** Performance center, student-run music venue and coffee house, music technology facilities and practice spaces, synthesizer laboratories, recording studios, film scoring laboratories, technology labs, media center.

Freshman class profile. 7,682 applied, 2,012 admitted, 945 enrolled.

GPA 3.75 or higher:	14%	Return as sophomores:	85%
GPA 3.50-3.74:	26%	Out-of-state:	54%
GPA 3.0-3.49:	35%	Live on campus:	76%
GPA 2.0-2.99:	25%	International:	30%

Basis for selection. Musical training and experience, recommendations, academic record, test scores, extracurricular music activities, interview important. Auditions required. **Home schooled:** Statement describing home school structure and mission, state high school equivalency certificate required. **Learning Disabled:** Students with disabilities should contact Special Services Coordinator.

High school preparation. Recommended units include English 4, mathematics 1, history 1, science 1 (laboratory 1) and academic electives 6. Minimum 2 years recent formal musical study on principal instrument covering standard methods/materials and/or significant practical performance experience plus knowledge of written-music fundamentals normally required of all applicants.

2015-2016 Annual costs. Tuition/fees: $40,082. Room/board: $17,546. Books/supplies: $474. Personal expenses: $1,203.

2015-2016 Financial aid. Need-based: 412 full-time freshmen applied for aid; 352 deemed to have need; 338 received aid. Average need met was 33%. Average scholarship/grant was $12,674; average loan $3,694. 52% of total undergraduate aid awarded as scholarships/grants, 48% as loans/jobs. **Non-need-based:** Awarded to 1,771 full-time undergraduates, including 365 freshmen. Scholarships awarded for academics, music/drama.

Application procedures. Admission: Priority date 11/1; deadline 1/15 (postmark date). $150 fee, may be waived for applicants with need. Application must be submitted online. Admission notification by 3/31. Must reply by 5/1. Applicants should submit completed application materials well in advance of deadline to ensure placement in desired entry class. **Financial aid:** Priority date 3/1, closing date 4/15. FAFSA, CSS PROFILE required. Applicants notified on a rolling basis starting 1/31; must reply within 2 week(s) of notification.

Academics. Bachelor's degree program includes 30 credits general education courses. Four-year professional diploma available (not including general education). **Special study options:** Cooperative education, cross-registration, distance learning, double major, dual enrollment of high school students, ESL, independent study, internships, student-designed major, study abroad, teacher certification program. ProArts Consortium with Boston Architectural Center, Boston Conservatory, Emerson College, Massachusetts College of Art, School of the Museum of Fine Arts. **Credit/placement by examination:** AP, CLEP, institutional tests. 60 credit hours maximum toward bachelor's degree. **Support services:** Learning center, pre-admission summer program, tutoring, writing center.

Majors. Education: Music. **Health services:** Music therapy. **Visual/performing arts:** Jazz, music, music management, music performance, music technology, music theory/composition.

Most popular majors. Visual/performing arts 96%.

Technology on campus. PC or laptop required. 50 workstations in dormitories, library, computer center. Dormitories wired for high-speed internet access and linked to campus network. Online library, helpline, repair service, student web hosting, wireless network available.

Student life. Freshman orientation: Available. Preregistration for classes offered. Series of events before and during registration week. **Housing:** Coed dorms, special housing for disabled available. $300 nonrefundable deposit, deadline 5/1. Residence space limited. **Activities:** Bands, campus ministries, choral groups, dance, drama, film society, international student organizations, literary magazine, music ensembles, musical theater, opera, radio station, student government, student newspaper, symphony orchestra, black student union, Christian Fellowship, Berklee Cares, women musicians' network, Latinos association, GLBT Allies at Berklee, Korean student association, Amnesty International.

Athletics. Intramural: Basketball, football (non-tackle), ice hockey, soccer. **Team name:** IceCats.

Student services. Career counseling, student employment services, minority student services, personal counseling, veterans' counselor. **Physically disabled:** Services for visually impaired.

Contact. E-mail: admissions@berklee.edu
Phone: (617) 747-2221 Toll-free number: (800) 237-5533
Fax: (617) 747-2047
Damien Bracken, Director of Admissions/OSSE, Berklee College of Music, 1140 Boylston Street, Boston, MA 02215

Boston Architectural College
Boston, Massachusetts
www.the-bac.edu

CB member
CB code: 1168

- Private 6-year architecture and design college
- Commuter campus in very large city
- 329 degree-seeking undergraduates: 2% part-time, 34% women, 8% African American, 8% Asian American, 14% Hispanic/Latino, 4% Multiracial, non-Hispanic, 12% international
- 366 degree-seeking graduate students

General. Founded in 1889. Regionally accredited. Practice-based learning with simultaneous employment in field and academic study. **Degrees:** 53 bachelor's awarded; master's offered. **Location:** Downtown. **Calendar:** Semester, limited summer session. **Part-time faculty:** 264 total; 59% have terminal degrees, 14% minority, 43% women. **Class size:** 95% < 20, 4% 20-39, 1% 40-49. **Special facilities:** On-campus gallery of architectural and interior design, CAD lab, photography studio, 3-D printer, wood shop, laser cutter, laser printer.

Freshman class profile. 181 applied, 106 admitted, 36 enrolled.

Basis for selection. Open admission, but selective for some programs. Creative exercise required. **Learning Disabled:** Students with learning disabilities are strongly encouraged to notify the Learning Resource Center of any special accommodations prior to matriculation.

High school preparation. College-preparatory program recommended.

2015-2016 Annual costs. Tuition/fees: $20,666. Books/supplies: $2,600. Personal expenses: $5,122.

Financial aid. Non-need-based: Scholarships awarded for academics, art, leadership.

Application procedures. Admission: No deadline. $50 fee, may be waived for applicants with need. Admission notification on a rolling basis beginning on or about 3/1. **Financial aid:** Priority date 4/15; no closing date. FAFSA required. Applicants notified on a rolling basis starting 3/30; must reply within 2 week(s) of notification.

Academics. Students are required to earn work hours while attending school. The BAC Practice Department assists students in tracking the hours they earn and have additional supports in place to assist students as they search for applicable jobs. **Special study options:** Combined bachelor's/graduate degree, cross-registration, distance learning, independent study, internships, liberal arts/career combination, study abroad. **Credit/placement by examination:** AP, CLEP, institutional tests. **Support services:** Learning center, study skills assistance, tutoring, writing center.

Majors. Architecture: Architecture, interior, landscape.

Technology on campus. 84 workstations in computer center. Online course registration, online library, helpline, student web hosting, wireless network available.

Student life. Freshman orientation: Mandatory. Preregistration for classes offered. **Policies:** Campus compact, sexual harassment policy, studio culture statement, alcohol and substance abuse policy, anti-hazing policy. Freshmen not permitted cars on campus. **Housing:** Housing at Fisher College for enrolled degree students available. **Activities:** International student organizations, student government, Atelier, American Institute of Architectural Students, Interior Design Society, National Organization of Minority Architecture Students, American Society of Landscape Architect Student Chapter, The Green Team, Studio Q (LGBT community), Veterans Community Collective, mentorship program.

Student services. Adult student services, alcohol/substance abuse counseling, career counseling, services for economically disadvantaged, student employment services, financial aid counseling, health services, legal services, minority student services, personal counseling, veterans' counselor. **Physically disabled:** Services for visually, speech, hearing impaired.

Contact. E-mail: admissions@the-bac.edu
Phone: (617) 585-0123 Fax: (617) 585-0121
Meredith Spinnato, Director of Admissions, Boston Architectural College, 320 Newbury Street, Boston, MA 02115-2795

Boston Baptist College
Boston, Massachusetts
www.boston.edu

CB code: 4323

- Private 4-year Bible college affiliated with the Baptist faith
- Very large city
- 89 degree-seeking undergraduates
- SAT or ACT required

General. Regionally accredited; also accredited by TRACS. **Degrees:** 13 bachelor's awarded. **Calendar:** Semester. **Full-time faculty:** 17 total. **Part-time faculty:** 2 total.

Basis for selection. Test scores, recommendation very important. **Home schooled:** Letter of recommendation (nonparent) required.

High school preparation. College-preparatory program recommended.

2015-2016 Annual costs. Tuition/fees: $15,040. Room/board: $8,102. Books/supplies: $100.

Financial aid. Non-need-based: Scholarships awarded for academics, alumni affiliation, job skills, leadership, religious affiliation.

Application procedures. Admission: Priority date 11/2; deadline 3/15. $50 fee, may be waived for applicants with need. **Financial aid:** No deadline. FAFSA, institutional form required.

Academics. Special study options: Dual enrollment of high school students. **Credit/placement by examination:** AP, CLEP.

Majors. Theology: Bible.

Student life. Freshman orientation: Available. Preregistration for classes offered. Session held in mid-August before start of classes. **Activities:** Campus ministries, drama, music ensembles.

Contact. E-mail: admissions@boston.edu
Phone: (617) 364-3510 ext. 230
Karen Fox, Director of Admissions, Boston Baptist College, 950 Metropolitan Avenue, Boston, MA 02136

Boston College
Chestnut Hill, Massachusetts
www.bc.edu

CB member
CB code: 3083

- Private 4-year university affiliated with the Roman Catholic Church
- Residential campus in small city
- 9,192 degree-seeking undergraduates: 53% women, 4% African American, 10% Asian American, 10% Hispanic/Latino, 3% Multi-racial, non-Hispanic, 6% international
- 4,513 graduate students
- 29% of applicants admitted
- SAT or ACT (ACT writing optional), application essay required
- 91% graduate within 6 years; 34% enter graduate study

General. Founded in 1863. Regionally accredited. **Degrees:** 2,315 bachelor's awarded; master's, professional, doctoral offered. **ROTC:** Army, Naval, Air Force. **Location:** 6 miles from downtown Boston. **Calendar:** Semester, extensive summer session. **Full-time faculty:** 786 total; 94% have terminal degrees, 16% minority, 40% women. **Part-time faculty:** 744 total; 95% have terminal degrees, 15% minority, 54% women. **Class size:** 52% < 20, 33% 20-39, 8% 40-49, 5% 50-99, 2% >100. **Special facilities:** Observatory, theater, arts center, chemistry center, art museum, rare books and special collections library.

Freshman class profile. 29,486 applied, 8,405 admitted, 2,162 enrolled.

Mid 50% test scores			
SAT critical reading:	620-720	**Rank in top tenth:**	81%
SAT math:	640-750	**Return as sophomores:**	95%
SAT writing:	640-730	**Out-of-state:**	76%
ACT composite:	30-33	**Live on campus:**	100%
Rank in top quarter:	95%	**International:**	7%

Basis for selection. Evidence of academic ability, intellectual curiosity, strength of character, motivation, creativity, energy, and promise for personal growth and development very important. Recommendations by counselors and teachers, required personal statement and extracurricular activities important. SAT Subject Tests are optional. If an applicant would like to highlight an academic strength in a specific area, they are welcome to submit SAT Subject Tests for consideration. Portfolio recommended for studio art majors. Students interested in music, theater, or dance encouraged to send examples of work via DVD or CD. **Learning Disabled:** May provide documentation of disability at option of applicant.

High school preparation. College-preparatory program required. 20 units recommended. Recommended units include English 4, mathematics 4, social studies 4, science 4 (laboratory 4) and foreign language 4. 4 combined social studies and history recommended. 2 laboratory science (including 1 chemistry) required of nursing applicants.

2015-2016 Annual costs. Tuition/fees: $49,324. Room/board: $13,496. Books/supplies: $1,250. Personal expenses: $1,250.

2014-2015 Financial aid. **Need-based:** 1,171 full-time freshmen applied for aid; 926 deemed to have need; 926 received aid. Average need met was 100%. Average scholarship/grant was $34,324; average loan $3,502. 83% of total undergraduate aid awarded as scholarships/grants, 17% as loans/jobs. **Non-need-based:** Awarded to 562 full-time undergraduates, including 124 freshmen. Scholarships awarded for academics, athletics, leadership, ROTC.

Application procedures. **Admission:** Closing date 1/1 (postmark date). $75 fee, may be waived for applicants with need. Admission notification by 4/15. Must reply by 5/1. BC's has an enrollment confirmation fee of $500 which is due by 5/1. There is no longer a separate housing deposit. **Financial aid:** Priority date 2/1; no closing date. FAFSA, CSS PROFILE required. Applicants notified on a rolling basis starting 4/1.

Academics. **Special study options:** Accelerated study, combined bachelor's/graduate degree, cross-registration, distance learning, double major, ESL, exchange student, honors, independent study, internships, liberal arts/career combination, student-designed major, study abroad, teacher certification program, Washington semester. Tufts Medical School early acceptance, 5th year master's program can be combined with bachelor's degree attainment in certain fields. **Credit/placement by examination:** AP, CLEP, IB. 24 credit hours maximum toward bachelor's degree. **Support services:** Learning center, pre-admission summer program, reduced course load, study skills assistance, tutoring, writing center.

Majors. **Area/ethnic studies:** Chicano/Hispanic-American/Latino. **Biology:** General, biochemistry. **Business:** Accounting, business admin, finance, human resources, management information systems, managerial economics, operations. **Communications:** Communications/speech/rhetoric. **Computer sciences:** General, computer science, information systems. **Education:** Elementary, secondary. **English:** English lit. **Foreign languages:** Ancient Greek, classics, French, German, Italian, Latin, linguistics, Russian, Spanish. **Health services:** Nursing (RN). **History:** General. **Math:** General. **Philosophy/religion:** Philosophy. **Physical sciences:** Chemistry, geology, geophysics, physics. **Psychology:** General. **Social sciences:** Economics, international relations, political science, sociology. **Visual/performing arts:** Art history/conservation, dramatic, film/cinema/video, music, studio arts.

Most popular majors. Biology 8%, business/marketing 21%, communications/journalism 8%, English 6%, psychology 10%, social sciences 20%.

Technology on campus. 1,000 workstations in library, computer center, student center. Dormitories wired for high-speed internet access and linked to campus network. Commuter students can connect to campus network. Online course registration, online library, helpline, repair service, student web hosting, wireless network available.

Student life. **Freshman orientation:** Mandatory, $444 fee. Preregistration for classes offered. Three-day, 2-night program; 4-6 scheduled options offered during summer. **Policies:** Alcohol prohibited for students under 21, smoking prohibited in all residence halls. Halogen lights, space heaters, egg crate style foam mattress pads, and candles prohibited in dorm rooms. Freshmen not permitted cars on campus. **Housing:** Guaranteed on-campus for freshmen. Coed dorms, single-sex dorms, special housing for disabled, apartments, themed housing, wellness housing available. Honors house, multicultural floor, 24-hour quiet living floor, social justice floor available. Apartment-style housing and townhouse-style housing available for upperclassmen. **Activities:** Bands, campus ministries, choral groups, dance, drama, film society, international student organizations, literary magazine, music ensembles, musical theater, radio station, student government, student newspaper, symphony orchestra, TV station, 4Boston, Amnesty International, Appalachia volunteers, Asian caucus, black student forum, Buddhist club, Hillel, Ignatian Society, Puerto Rican association, Muslim students association.

Athletics. NCAA. **Intercollegiate:** Baseball M, basketball, cross-country, diving, fencing, field hockey W, football (tackle) M, golf, ice hockey, lacrosse W, rowing (crew) W, sailing, skiing, soccer, softball W, swimming, tennis, track and field, volleyball W. **Intramural:** Basketball, football (non-tackle), golf, ice hockey, racquetball, soccer, softball, squash, tennis, ultimate frisbee, volleyball. **Team name:** Eagles.

Student services. Alcohol/substance abuse counseling, chaplain/spiritual director, career counseling, services for economically disadvantaged, student employment services, financial aid counseling, health services, minority student services, on-campus daycare, personal counseling, placement for graduates, veterans' counselor, women's services. **Physically disabled:** Services for visually, speech, hearing impaired.

Contact. Phone: (617) 552-3100 Toll-free number: (800) 360-2522 Fax: (617) 552-0798
John Mahoney, Director of Undergraduate Admission, Boston College, 140 Commonwealth Avenue, Devlin Hall 208, Chestnut Hill, MA 02467-3809

Boston Conservatory
Boston, Massachusetts
www.bostonconservatory.edu

CB member
CB code: 3084

- Private 4-year music and performing arts college
- Commuter campus in very large city
- 565 degree-seeking undergraduates: 1% part-time, 63% women, 4% African American, 2% Asian American, 9% Hispanic/Latino, 2% Multiracial, non-Hispanic, 9% international
- 235 degree-seeking graduate students
- 46% of applicants admitted
- Application essay required
- 77% graduate within 6 years

General. Founded in 1867. Regionally accredited. **Degrees:** 117 bachelor's awarded; master's offered. **Location:** Downtown. **Calendar:** Semester, limited summer session. **Full-time faculty:** 87 total; 18% have terminal degrees, 6% minority, 39% women. **Part-time faculty:** 105 total; 9% have terminal degrees, 11% minority, 52% women. **Class size:** 90% < 20, 7% 20-39, less than 1% 40-49, less than 1% 50-99, less than 1% >100.

Freshman class profile. 1,216 applied, 558 admitted, 182 enrolled.

End year in good standing:	100%	**Live on campus:**	98%
Return as sophomores:	91%	**International:**	4%
Out-of-state:	94%		

Basis for selection. Audition carries most weight. Academic record and artistic background strongly considered. Test scores, recommendations, personal essay important. SAT or ACT tests are not required. Audition required. Interview required of music education, composition and multidisciplinary stage management majors. **Home schooled:** Statement describing home school structure and mission, transcript of courses and grades, state high school equivalency certificate required.

High school preparation. College-preparatory program recommended. Recommended units include English 4, mathematics 3, social studies 2, history 2, science 2 and foreign language 2.

2015-2016 Annual costs. Tuition/fees: $43,800. Room/board: $17,242. Books/supplies: $780. Personal expenses: $1,294.

2014-2015 Financial aid. **Need-based:** 102 full-time freshmen applied for aid; 84 deemed to have need; 84 received aid. Average need met was 42%. Average scholarship/grant was $19,012; average loan $3,215. 63% of total undergraduate aid awarded as scholarships/grants, 37% as loans/jobs. **Non-need-based:** Scholarships awarded for music/drama.

Application procedures. Admission: Closing date 12/15 (receipt date). $110 fee, may be waived for applicants with need. Application must be submitted online. Admission notification by 4/1. Must reply by May 1 or within 2 week(s) if notified thereafter. **Financial aid:** Priority date 3/1; no closing date. FAFSA required. Applicants notified by 4/1; must reply by 5/1.

Academics. Special study options: Cross-registration, ESL, independent study, teacher certification program. **Credit/placement by examination:** AP, CLEP, institutional tests. 75 credit hours maximum toward bachelor's degree. **Support services:** Pre-admission summer program, study skills assistance, tutoring, writing center.

Majors. Visual/performing arts: Acting, brass instruments, dance, music performance, music theory/composition, musical theater, percussion instruments, piano/keyboard, stringed instruments, theater design, voice/opera, woodwind instruments.

Technology on campus. 20 workstations in library, computer center. Dormitories linked to campus network. Online library, helpline, wireless network available.

Student life. Freshman orientation: Mandatory. Preregistration for classes offered. Held the week prior to the first day of classes in the fall. **Housing:** Guaranteed on-campus for freshmen. Coed dorms available. $250 nonrefundable deposit, deadline 5/1. Graduate housing available. **Activities:** International student organizations, literary magazine, student government, student newspaper.

Student services. Career counseling, student employment services, financial aid counseling, health services, personal counseling.

Contact. E-mail: admissions@bostonconservatory.edu
Phone: (617) 912-9153 Fax: (617) 536-3176
Brian Calhoon, Director of Admissions, Boston Conservatory, 8 The Fenway, Boston, MA 02215

Boston University
Boston, Massachusetts
www.bu.edu

CB member
CB code: 3087

- Private 4-year university
- Residential campus in very large city
- 16,456 degree-seeking undergraduates: 2% part-time, 61% women, 4% African American, 14% Asian American, 11% Hispanic/Latino, 4% Multi-racial, non-Hispanic, 20% international
- 13,653 degree-seeking graduate students
- 33% of applicants admitted
- SAT or ACT (ACT writing optional), application essay required
- 85% graduate within 6 years; 12% enter graduate study

General. Founded in 1839. Regionally accredited. **Degrees:** 4,406 bachelor's awarded; master's, professional, doctoral offered. **ROTC:** Army, Naval, Air Force. **Location:** Downtown. **Calendar:** Semester, extensive summer session. **Full-time faculty:** 1,699 total; 88% have terminal degrees, 14% minority, 41% women. **Part-time faculty:** 957 total; 9% minority, 40% women. **Class size:** 58% < 20, 22% 20-39, 6% 40-49, 10% 50-99, 4% >100. **Special facilities:** Biodiversity station in Ecuador, dedicated management library, planetarium, National Public Radio station, 20th century archives, theater company, center for remote sensing, speech, language and hearing clinic, culinary center, communication multimedia lab, EPIC (engineering product innovation center).

Freshman class profile. 54,781 applied, 17,871 admitted, 3,629 enrolled.

Mid 50% test scores			
SAT critical reading:	570-680	Rank in top quarter:	89%
SAT math:	620-730	Rank in top tenth:	58%
SAT writing:	600-690	Return as sophomores:	93%
ACT composite:	27-31	Out-of-state:	84%
GPA 3.75 or higher:	33%	Live on campus:	99%
GPA 3.50-3.74:	41%	International:	24%
GPA 3.0-3.49:	26%	Fraternities:	5%
		Sororities:	15%

Basis for selection. Evidence of strong academic performance in challenging college-prep curriculum most important. SAT Subject Tests in Chemistry and Math (level 2) required for accelerated medical and dental programs. SAT Subject test in foreign language is recommended for accelerated medical and dental programs. Interview required for accelerated medical/dental programs, all non-performance theater arts majors. Audition required for music, theater performance programs. Portfolio required of visual arts, stage management, theatrical design majors. **Home schooled:** Statement describing home school structure and mission required. Students should contact Office of Admissions prior to application.

High school preparation. College-preparatory program required. 15 units required; 20 recommended. Required and recommended units include English 4, mathematics 3-4, social studies 3-4, science 3-4 (laboratory 3-4) and foreign language 2-4. Pre-calculus required, calculus recommended. Social studies includes history.

2015-2016 Annual costs. Tuition/fees: $48,436. Room/board: $14,520. Books/supplies: $1,000. Personal expenses: $1,320.

2015-2016 Financial aid. Need-based: 1,401 full-time freshmen applied for aid; 1,320 deemed to have need; 1,320 received aid. Average need met was 93%. Average scholarship/grant was $35,715; average loan $5,640. 81% of total undergraduate aid awarded as scholarships/grants, 19% as loans/jobs. **Non-need-based:** Awarded to 1,903 full-time undergraduates, including 382 freshmen. Scholarships awarded for academics, alumni affiliation, art, athletics, leadership, music/drama, religious affiliation, ROTC, state residency. **Additional information:** Financial aid deadline for early decision applicants: 11/1; Financial Aid deadline for early decision 2 applicants: 1/3. Graduates of Boston's public high schools who complete financial aid application and demonstrate need will be awarded financial aid packages that contain no loans and meet full demonstrated need.

Application procedures. Admission: Closing date 1/3 (receipt date). $80 fee, may be waived for applicants with need. Application must be submitted online. Admission notification by 4/1. Must reply by 5/1. **Financial aid:** Closing date 2/1. FAFSA, CSS PROFILE required. Applicants notified on a rolling basis starting 4/1; must reply by 5/1 or within 2 week(s) of notification.

Academics. Howard Thurman Center (HTC) hosts receptions for African American, Latino, LGBTQ and Veteran students at the start of each school year and introduces new minority students to upperclassmen leaders from the various cultural groups on campus. The Thurman Center offers a variety of programs to support students of diverse ethnic, racial, and national backgrounds. **Special study options:** Accelerated study, combined bachelor's/graduate degree, cooperative education, cross-registration, distance learning, double major, dual enrollment of high school students, ESL, exchange student, honors, independent study, internships, liberal arts/career combination, semester at sea, student-designed major, study abroad, teacher certification program, Washington semester, weekend college. Study abroad and internships available in South and Central America, Europe, Africa, China, Pacific Rim, Russia. Field study in marine science at Woods Hole Institute, in environmental/ecological science in Ecuador, and at Photonics Center, combined bachelor's/master's degrees, 6-year physical therapy (BS/DPT) program, 7-year accelerated MD, DMD programs. **Credit/placement by examination:** AP, CLEP, IB, SAT, ACT, institutional tests. 32 credit hours maximum toward bachelor's degree. Credits assigned vary by school and college. Scores higher than minimums may result in additional credit depending on department. **Support services:** Learning center, study skills assistance, tutoring, writing center.

Majors. Architecture: History/criticism. **Area/ethnic studies:** American, deaf, East Asian, European, French, Italian, Latin American, Near/Middle Eastern, Russian/Slavic. **Biology:** General, conservation, ecology, environmental, marine, molecular, neuroscience. **Business:** Accounting, business admin, entrepreneurial studies, finance, hospitality admin, international, international finance, management information systems, market research, marketing, operations, organizational behavior. **Communications:** General, communications/speech/rhetoric, journalism. **Computer sciences:** Computer science. **Education:** General, art, bilingual, chemistry, Deaf/hearing impaired, early childhood, elementary, English, Latin, mathematics, music, science, social studies, special ed. **Engineering:** General, biomedical, computer, electrical, manufacturing, mechanical. **English:** English lit. **Foreign languages:** Ancient Greek, Chinese, classics, French, German, Hispanic and Latin American, Italian, Japanese, Korean, Latin, linguistics, Russian, Spanish. **Health services:** Athletic training, clinical lab technology, communication disorders, dental lab technology, kinesiotherapy, predental, premedicine, rehabilitation science. **History:** General. **Math:** General. **Philosophy/religion:** Philosophy, religion. **Physical sciences:** Astronomy, astrophysics, chemistry, geology, geophysics, physics, planetary. **Protective services:** Criminal justice. **Psychology:** General. **Social sciences:** Anthropology, archaeology, economics, geography, international relations, political science, sociology, urban studies. **Visual/performing arts:** General, acting, art history/conservation, directing/producing, film/cinema/video, graphic design, music performance, music theory/composition, musicology, painting, piano/keyboard, printmaking, sculpture, stringed instruments, theater design.

Most popular majors. Biology 8%, business/marketing 20%, communications/journalism 15%, engineering/engineering technologies 7%, health sciences 9%, psychology 6%, social sciences 15%.

Technology on campus. 2,000 workstations in dormitories, library, computer center, student center. Dormitories wired for high-speed internet access and linked to campus network. Commuter students can connect to campus network. Online course registration, online library, helpline, repair service, student web hosting, wireless network available.

Student life. Freshman orientation: Mandatory, $250 fee. Preregistration for classes offered. Two-day program throughout summer includes optional half-day Common Ground program. **Policies:** Campus residents must abide by guest/visitor policy. **Housing:** Guaranteed on-campus for all undergraduates. Coed dorms, single-sex dorms, special housing for disabled, apartments, cooperative housing, gender-neutral housing, themed housing, wellness housing available. $650 nonrefundable deposit, deadline 5/1. Specialty halls/floors for groups of students with common interest or academic major, special housing for Kilachand Honors College, gender neutral housing available. **Activities:** Bands, campus ministries, choral groups, dance, drama, film society, international student organizations, literary magazine, music ensembles, Model UN, musical theater, opera, radio station, student government, student newspaper, symphony orchestra, TV station, over 450 student organizations available.

Athletics. NCAA. **Intercollegiate:** Basketball, cross-country, diving, field hockey W, golf W, ice hockey, lacrosse, rowing (crew), soccer, softball W, swimming, tennis, track and field. **Intramural:** Basketball, football (non-tackle), ice hockey W, soccer, softball, volleyball, water polo. **Team name:** Terriers.

Student services. Adult student services, alcohol/substance abuse counseling, chaplain/spiritual director, career counseling, student employment services, financial aid counseling, health services, minority student services, personal counseling, placement for graduates, veterans' counselor, women's services. **Physically disabled:** Services for visually, speech, hearing impaired.

Contact. E-mail: admissions@bu.edu
Phone: (617) 353-2300 Fax: (617) 353-9695
Kelly Walter, Associate Vice President and Executive Director of Admissions, Boston University, 233 Bay State Road, Boston, MA 02215

Brandeis University
Waltham, Massachusetts
www.brandeis.edu

CB member
CB code: 3092

- Private 4-year university
- Residential campus in small city
- 3,610 degree-seeking undergraduates: 57% women, 5% African American, 13% Asian American, 7% Hispanic/Latino, 3% Multi-racial, non-Hispanic, 20% international
- 1,984 degree-seeking graduate students
- 34% of applicants admitted
- SAT or ACT with writing, application essay required
- 87% graduate within 6 years

General. Founded in 1948. Regionally accredited. **Degrees:** 957 bachelor's awarded; master's, doctoral offered. **ROTC:** Army, Air Force. **Location:** 10 miles from Boston. **Calendar:** Semester, limited summer session. **Full-time faculty:** 358 total; 95% have terminal degrees, 12% minority, 42% women. **Part-time faculty:** 162 total; 54% have terminal degrees, 4% minority, 40% women. **Class size:** 61% < 20, 23% 20-39, 5% 40-49, 7% 50-99, 4% >100. **Special facilities:** Medical sciences research center, spatial orientation laboratory, center for complex systems, art museum, materials research science and engineering center.

Freshman class profile. 10,528 applied, 3,582 admitted, 802 enrolled.

Mid 50% test scores		GPA 2.0-2.99:	2%
SAT critical reading:	600-700	Rank in top quarter:	91%
SAT math:	650-770	Rank in top tenth:	71%
SAT writing:	640-710	Return as sophomores:	92%
ACT composite:	29-32	Out-of-state:	76%
GPA 3.75 or higher:	60%	Live on campus:	99%
GPA 3.50-3.74:	27%	International:	20%
GPA 3.0-3.49:	11%		

Basis for selection. Academic record, extracurricular activities, essay, recommendations and standardized tests considered. Brandeis has a test-flexible policy and no longer requires that domestic applicants submit SAT or ACT scores for the purpose of admission. Interview recommended. **Home schooled:** Statement describing home school structure and mission, letter of recommendation (nonparent) required. Detailed description of curriculum; information regarding any affiliation with state or national homeschooling organization; secondary letter of recommendation from outside teacher if course work was taken beyond the home school or, when not available, from employer, coach, art instructor or other community leader; supplemental essay describing why student chose to be home-schooled; and graded paper required.

High school preparation. College-preparatory program required. 20 units recommended. Recommended units include English 4, mathematics 4, social studies 4, science 4 (laboratory 2) and foreign language 4.

2015-2016 Annual costs. Tuition/fees: $49,598. Room/board: $13,706. Books/supplies: $1,000. Personal expenses: $1,500.

2014-2015 Financial aid. Need-based: 501 full-time freshmen applied for aid; 413 deemed to have need; 411 received aid. Average need met was 97%. Average scholarship/grant was $38,299; average loan $3,256. 81% of total undergraduate aid awarded as scholarships/grants, 19% as loans/jobs. **Non-need-based:** Awarded to 290 full-time undergraduates, including 137 freshmen. Scholarships awarded for academics.

Application procedures. Admission: Closing date 1/1 (receipt date). $75 fee, may be waived for applicants with need. Admission notification by 4/1. Must reply by May 1 or within 2 week(s) if notified thereafter. **Financial aid:** Priority date 2/1; no closing date. FAFSA, CSS PROFILE required. Applicants notified by 4/1; must reply by 5/1.

Academics. Special study options: Accelerated study, combined bachelor's/graduate degree, cross-registration, distance learning, double major, exchange student, independent study, internships, semester at sea, student-designed major, study abroad, teacher certification program, Washington semester. 5-year BA/MA programs in international economics and finance, computer science, computational linguistics, and Near Eastern and Judaic studies; early admission to Mt. Sinai Medical School and Tufts Medical School. **Credit/placement by examination:** AP, CLEP, IB, institutional tests. **Support services:** Reduced course load, remedial instruction, study skills assistance, tutoring, writing center.

Majors. Area/ethnic studies: African-American, American, East Asian, European, French, German, Latin American, Near/Middle Eastern, Russian/Slavic, Spanish/Iberian, women's. **Biology:** General, biochemistry, biophysics, neuroscience. **Business:** General. **Computer sciences:** Computer science. **Conservation:** Environmental studies. **Education:** General. **English:** Creative writing, English lit. **Foreign languages:** Classics, comparative lit, linguistics. **Health services:** Health care admin. **History:** General. **Math:** General. **Philosophy/religion:** Philosophy. **Physical sciences:** Chemistry, physics. **Psychology:** General. **Social sciences:** Anthropology, economics, political science, sociology, U.S. government. **Visual/performing arts:** Art history/conservation, dramatic, film/cinema/video, music, studio arts.

Most popular majors. Area/ethnic studies 7%, biology 15%, business/marketing 8%, interdisciplinary studies 7%, psychology 9%, public administration/social services 7%, social sciences 20%.

Technology on campus. 104 workstations in library, computer center, student center. Dormitories wired for high-speed internet access and linked to campus network. Commuter students can connect to campus network. Online course registration, online library, helpline, repair service, student web hosting, wireless network available.

Student life. Freshman orientation: Mandatory, $200 fee. Preregistration for classes offered. Five-day program begins weekend before Labor Day weekend. **Policies:** Freshmen not permitted cars on campus. **Housing:** Guaranteed on-campus for freshmen. Coed dorms, single-sex dorms, apartments, themed housing available. Thematic learning communities available. **Activities:** Bands, campus ministries, choral groups, dance, drama, film society, international student organizations, literary magazine, music ensembles, musical theater, radio station, student government, student newspaper, symphony orchestra, TV station, more than 250 student-run recognized clubs and organizations.

Athletics. NCAA. **Intercollegiate:** Baseball M, basketball, cross-country, diving, fencing, soccer, softball W, swimming, tennis, track and field, volleyball W. **Intramural:** Badminton, basketball, cross-country, football (non-tackle), golf, soccer, softball, squash, swimming, tennis, volleyball, water polo. **Team name:** Judges.

Student services. Alcohol/substance abuse counseling, chaplain/spiritual director, career counseling, services for economically disadvantaged, student employment services, financial aid counseling, health services, minority student services, personal counseling, placement for graduates, veterans' counselor, women's services. **Physically disabled:** Services for visually, speech, hearing impaired.

Contact. E-mail: admissions@brandeis.edu
Phone: (781) 736-3500 Toll-free number: (800) 622-0622
Fax: (781) 736-3536
Jennifer Walker, Dean of Admissions, Brandeis University, 415 South Street, MS003, Waltham, MA 02453

Bridgewater State University
Bridgewater, Massachusetts
www.bridgew.edu

CB member
CB code: 3517

- Public 4-year university
- Commuter campus in large town

♦ 9,497 degree-seeking undergraduates: 17% part-time, 59% women, 9% African American, 2% Asian American, 6% Hispanic/Latino, 3% Multiracial, non-Hispanic

♦ 1,238 degree-seeking graduate students

♦ 81% of applicants admitted

♦ SAT or ACT (ACT writing recommended) required

♦ 58% graduate within 6 years; 21% enter graduate study

General. Founded in 1840. Regionally accredited. **Degrees:** 1,942 bachelor's awarded; master's offered. **ROTC:** Army, Air Force. **Location:** 28 miles from Boston; 35 miles from Providence, RI. **Calendar:** Semester, extensive summer session. **Full-time faculty:** 335 total; 94% have terminal degrees, 17% minority, 52% women. **Part-time faculty:** 475 total; 36% have terminal degrees, 7% minority, 54% women. **Class size:** 42% < 20, 56% 20-39, 1% 40-49, less than 1% 50-99. **Special facilities:** Observatory, greenhouse, art gallery.

Freshman class profile. 5,867 applied, 4,735 admitted, 1,528 enrolled.

Mid 50% test scores		GPA 2.0-2.99:	40%
SAT critical reading:	440-550	End year in good standing:	79%
SAT math:	450-550	Return as sophomores:	79%
GPA 3.75 or higher:	11%	Out-of-state:	5%
GPA 3.50-3.74:	11%	Live on campus:	73%
GPA 3.0-3.49:	38%		

Basis for selection. High school achievement and completion of college preparatory courses are most important. Test scores, essay, extracurricular activities are also important. Class rank, recommendations considered. Essay recommended. Interviews are required for some performing arts majors. **Learning Disabled:** Exemption from admissions standardized testing upon documentation of diagnostic test results. Must complete 17 required academic courses with 3.0 GPA or present evidence of potential for academic success.

High school preparation. College-preparatory program required. 17 units required. Required units include English 4, mathematics 4, social studies 2, science 3 (laboratory 2), foreign language 2 and academic electives 2.

2015-2016 Annual costs. Tuition/fees: $8,474; $14,614 out-of-state. Room/board: $11,700. Books/supplies: $800. Personal expenses: $1,700.

2014-2015 Financial aid. Need-based: 1,448 full-time freshmen applied for aid; 1,117 deemed to have need; 1,093 received aid. Average scholarship/grant was $3,045; average loan $1,852. 49% of total undergraduate aid awarded as scholarships/grants, 51% as loans/jobs. **Non-need-based:** Awarded to 827 full-time undergraduates, including 268 freshmen. Scholarships awarded for academics, alumni affiliation, minority status, ROTC, state residency. **Additional information:** Tuition and/or fee waivers for Native Americans. Work-study programs available to half-time and full-time students.

Application procedures. Admission: Priority date 2/15; no deadline. $50 fee, may be waived for applicants with need. Admission notification on a rolling basis beginning on or about 12/15. Must reply by 5/1. **Financial aid:** Priority date 3/1; no closing date. FAFSA required. Applicants notified by 4/1; Applicants notified on a rolling basis starting 4/1.

Academics. Special study options: Accelerated study, combined bachelor's/graduate degree, cross-registration, distance learning, double major, dual enrollment of high school students, ESL, exchange student, honors, independent study, internships, study abroad, teacher certification program, Washington semester, weekend college. **Credit/placement by examination:** AP, CLEP, IB, institutional tests. Hours of credit are evaluated on a case by case basis. **Support services:** Learning center, pre-admission summer program, reduced course load, remedial instruction, study skills assistance, tutoring, writing center.

Majors. Biology: General. **Business:** Accounting, accounting/finance, management science. **Communications:** Communications/speech/rhetoric. **Computer sciences:** Computer science. **Education:** Art, biology, drama/dance, early childhood, elementary, English, health, music, physical, special ed. **English:** English lit. **Foreign languages:** Spanish. **Health services:** Athletic training, communication disorders, kinesiotherapy. **History:** General. **Human services:** Social work. **Math:** General. **Philosophy/religion:** Philosophy. **Physical sciences:** Chemistry, geochemistry, geology, physics. **Protective services:** Criminal justice. **Psychology:** General. **Social sciences:** Anthropology, economics, geography, political science, sociology. **Visual/performing arts:** Music, studio arts.

Most popular majors. Business/marketing 16%, communications/journalism 7%, education 20%, psychology 12%, security/protective services 11%, social sciences 7%.

Technology on campus. PC or laptop required. 780 workstations in library, computer center, student center. Dormitories wired for high-speed internet access and linked to campus network. Commuter students can connect

to campus network. Online course registration, online library, helpline, repair service, student web hosting, wireless network available.

Student life. Freshman orientation: Mandatory, $160 fee. Preregistration for classes offered. **Policies:** Tobacco-free policy. Freshmen not permitted cars on campus. **Housing:** Coed dorms, special housing for disabled, apartments, themed housing available. $300 nonrefundable deposit, deadline 5/1. Break housing for athletes, student teachers, and international students. **Activities:** Bands, campus ministries, choral groups, dance, drama, film society, international student organizations, literary magazine, music ensembles, musical theater, radio station, student government, student newspaper, TV station, Christian Fellowship, College Democrats, Afro-American society, international club, La Sociedad Latina, Amnesty International, Big Brothers/Big Sisters, Habitat for Humanity.

Athletics. NCAA. **Intercollegiate:** Baseball M, basketball, cross-country, diving, field hockey W, football (tackle) M, lacrosse W, soccer, softball W, swimming, tennis, track and field, volleyball W, wrestling M. **Intramural:** Badminton, basketball, field hockey W, football (tackle), lacrosse M, soccer, softball, tennis, volleyball. **Team name:** Bears.

Student services. Adult student services, alcohol/substance abuse counseling, chaplain/spiritual director, career counseling, student employment services, financial aid counseling, health services, minority student services, on-campus daycare, personal counseling, placement for graduates, veterans' counselor, women's services. **Physically disabled:** Services for visually, speech, hearing impaired.

Contact. E-mail: admission@bridgew.edu
Phone: (508) 531-1237 Fax: (508) 531-1746
Gregg Meyer, Dean of University Admissions, Bridgewater State University, Office of Admission-Welcome Center, Bridgewater, MA 02325

Cambridge College
Cambridge, Massachusetts   CB member
www.cambridgecollege.edu   CB code: 3612

♦ Private 4-year liberal arts and teachers college

♦ Commuter campus in small city

♦ 1,048 degree-seeking undergraduates

♦ 2,064 graduate students

♦ Application essay required

General. Regionally accredited. **Degrees:** 208 bachelor's awarded; master's, doctoral offered. **Calendar:** Trimester, extensive summer session. **Full-time faculty:** 24 total; 75% have terminal degrees, 38% minority, 54% women. **Part-time faculty:** 410 total; 59% have terminal degrees, 34% minority, 59% women. **Class size:** 87% < 20, 13% 20-39.

Basis for selection. Open admission.

2015-2016 Annual costs. Tuition/fees: $13,400. Books/supplies: $750. Personal expenses: $900.

Financial aid. All financial aid based on need.

Application procedures. Admission: No deadline. $50 fee, may be waived for applicants with need. Admission notification on a rolling basis beginning on or about 9/1. **Financial aid:** Priority date 7/15; no closing date. Institutional form required. Applicants notified on a rolling basis starting 6/1.

Academics. Special study options: Accelerated study, distance learning, double major, honors, independent study, internships, liberal arts/career combination, student-designed major, weekend college. **Credit/placement by examination:** AP, CLEP. **Support services:** Learning center, reduced course load, remedial instruction, study skills assistance, tutoring, writing center.

Majors. Business: General. **Liberal arts:** Arts/sciences. **Psychology:** General, community.

Most popular majors. Business/marketing 29%, interdisciplinary studies 43%, psychology 17%.

Technology on campus. Commuter students can connect to campus network. Online course registration, online library, wireless network available.

Student life. Freshman orientation: Mandatory. Preregistration for classes offered. **Activities:** Student government.

Student services. Adult student services, career counseling, services for economically disadvantaged, financial aid counseling. **Physically disabled:** Services for visually, speech, hearing impaired.

Contact. E-mail: admit@cambridgecollege.edu
Phone: (617) 868-1000 Toll-free number: (800) 877-4723
Fax: (617) 349-3561
Denise Haile, Director of Admissions, Cambridge College, 1000
Massachusetts Avenue, Cambridge, MA 02138-5304

Clark University
Worcester, Massachusetts
www.clarku.edu
CB member
CB code: 3279

- Private 4-year university and liberal arts college
- Residential campus in small city
- 2,331 degree-seeking undergraduates: 1% part-time, 61% women, 4% African American, 7% Asian American, 7% Hispanic/Latino, 2% Multi-racial, non-Hispanic, 15% international
- 1,064 degree-seeking graduate students
- 55% of applicants admitted
- Application essay required
- 83% graduate within 6 years; 42% enter graduate study

General. Founded in 1887. Regionally accredited. **Degrees:** 519 bachelor's awarded; master's, doctoral offered. **ROTC:** Army, Air Force. **Location:** 50 miles from Boston. **Calendar:** Semester, limited summer session. **Full-time faculty:** 203 total; 96% have terminal degrees, 21% minority, 45% women. **Part-time faculty:** 109 total; 6% minority, 41% women. **Class size:** 55% < 20, 36% 20-39, 3% 40-49, 5% 50-99, less than 1% >100. **Special facilities:** Robert Goddard exhibition, map library, rare book room, NMR research facility, observatory, electronic music facility, arboretum, crafts studio, 2 theaters, environmental education laboratory, student-run recycling center, pulsed magnetic field laboratory, Holocaust studies center.

Freshman class profile. 8,045 applied, 4,430 admitted, 671 enrolled.

Mid 50% test scores			
		GPA 2.0-2.99:	5%
SAT critical reading:	560-670	Rank in top quarter:	77%
SAT math:	560-670	Rank in top tenth:	44%
SAT writing:	560-670	End year in good standing:	89%
ACT composite:	26-30	Return as sophomores:	87%
GPA 3.75 or higher:	48%	Out-of-state:	64%
GPA 3.50-3.74:	25%	Live on campus:	97%
GPA 3.0-3.49:	22%	International:	16%

Basis for selection. School achievement record and courses, recommendations, test scores are optional. Special talents, accomplishments, motivation, and individual circumstances, including outside activities and jobs, also important. Interview recommended. Portfolio recommended for art majors. **Learning Disabled:** Students should self-identify as soon as possible.

High school preparation. College-preparatory program required. 16 units recommended. Recommended units include English 4, mathematics 3, social studies 2, history 2, science 3 (laboratory 2) and foreign language 2.

2015-2016 Annual costs. Tuition/fees: $41,940. Room/board: $8,200. Books/supplies: $800. Personal expenses: $700.

2015-2016 Financial aid. Need-based: 476 full-time freshmen applied for aid; 379 deemed to have need; 374 received aid. Average need met was 93%. Average scholarship/grant was $27,747; average loan $4,671. 80% of total undergraduate aid awarded as scholarships/grants, 20% as loans/jobs. **Non-need-based:** Awarded to 1,261 full-time undergraduates, including 371 freshmen. Scholarships awarded for academics, leadership.

Application procedures. Admission: Closing date 1/15 (receipt date). $60 fee, may be waived for applicants with need. Admission notification by 4/1. Must reply by May 1 or within 2 week(s) if notified thereafter. **Financial aid:** Closing date 2/1. FAFSA, CSS PROFILE required. Applicants notified by 3/31; must reply by 5/1 or within 2 week(s) of notification.

Academics. Interdisciplinary majors, special programs, and accelerated bachelor's/master's program with fifth-year tuition-free available. **Special study options:** Combined bachelor's/graduate degree, cross-registration, double major, ESL, independent study, internships, liberal arts/career combination, student-designed major, study abroad, teacher certification program, Washington semester. Courses at Bermuda Biological Station, May term at Clark European Center in Luxembourg, semester-long environmental science program at marine biological laboratory at Woods Hole Oceanographic Institute. 3-2 engineering program with Columbia University. **Credit/placement by examination:** AP, CLEP, IB, institutional tests. 16 credit hours maximum toward bachelor's degree. **Support services:** Learning center, pre-admission summer program, reduced course load, study skills assistance, tutoring, writing center.

Majors. Area/ethnic studies: Women's. **Biology:** General, biochemistry, bioinformatics, molecular. **Business:** General, business admin. **Communications:** Communications/speech/rhetoric. **Computer sciences:** General, computer science. **Conservation:** Environmental science, environmental studies. **English:** English lit. **Foreign languages:** General, classics, comparative lit, French, Spanish. **History:** General. **Human services:** General. **Liberal arts:** Arts/sciences. **Math:** General. **Philosophy/religion:** Philosophy. **Physical sciences:** Chemistry, physics. **Psychology:** General. **Social sciences:** Economics, geography, international relations, political science, sociology. **Visual/performing arts:** General, art, art history/conservation, dramatic, film/cinema/video, music, studio arts.

Most popular majors. Biology 10%, business/marketing 6%, communications/journalism 6%, psychology 17%, social sciences 28%, visual/performing arts 6%.

Technology on campus. 322 workstations in dormitories, library, computer center, student center. Dormitories wired for high-speed internet access and linked to campus network. Commuter students can connect to campus network. Online course registration, online library, helpline, student web hosting, wireless network available.

Student life. Freshman orientation: Mandatory, $200 fee. Preregistration for classes offered. Program held during week prior to fall semester. **Housing:** Guaranteed on-campus for freshmen. Coed dorms, single-sex dorms, special housing for disabled, apartments, themed housing, wellness housing available. $100 nonrefundable deposit, deadline 5/1. Some university-owned off-campus housing available. Quiet house and other special interest houses available. **Activities:** Bands, campus ministries, choral groups, dance, drama, film society, international student organizations, literary magazine, music ensembles, Model UN, musical theater, radio station, student government, student newspaper, symphony orchestra, TV station, 130 student clubs and organizations.

Athletics. NCAA. **Intercollegiate:** Baseball M, basketball, cross-country, diving, field hockey W, lacrosse M, rowing (crew), soccer, softball W, swimming, tennis, volleyball W. **Intramural:** Basketball, racquetball, soccer, softball, water polo. **Team name:** Cougars.

Student services. Adult student services, alcohol/substance abuse counseling, chaplain/spiritual director, career counseling, services for economically disadvantaged, student employment services, financial aid counseling, health services, minority student services, personal counseling, placement for graduates, women's services. **Physically disabled:** Services for visually, speech, hearing impaired.

Contact. E-mail: admissions@clarku.edu
Phone: (508) 793-7431 Toll-free number: (800) 462-5275
Fax: (508) 793-8821
Donald Honeman, Dean of Admissions, Clark University, 950 Main Street, Worcester, MA 01610-1477

College of the Holy Cross
Worcester, Massachusetts
www.holycross.edu
CB member
CB code: 3282

- Private 4-year liberal arts college affiliated with the Roman Catholic Church
- Residential campus in small city
- 2,885 degree-seeking undergraduates: 50% women, 3% African American, 5% Asian American, 10% Hispanic/Latino, 3% Multi-racial, non-Hispanic, 2% international
- 37% of applicants admitted
- Application essay required
- 92% graduate within 6 years; 14% enter graduate study

General. Founded in 1843. Regionally accredited. Campus is a registered arboretum. **Degrees:** 725 bachelor's awarded. **ROTC:** Army, Naval, Air Force. **Location:** 45 miles from Boston. **Calendar:** Semester. **Full-time faculty:** 296 total; 94% have terminal degrees, 14% minority, 44% women. **Part-time faculty:** 38 total; 58% have terminal degrees, 16% minority, 58% women. **Class size:** 66% < 20, 32% 20-39, 1% 40-49, less than 1% 50-99. **Special facilities:** Research-level scientific equipment, Nuclear Magnetic Resonance equipment, scanning electron and confocal microscopes, greenhouse, chamber music hall.

Freshman class profile. 6,595 applied, 2,442 admitted, 738 enrolled.

Mid 50% test scores			
		Rank in top tenth:	61%
SAT critical reading:	600-690	Return as sophomores:	96%
SAT math:	620-690	Out-of-state:	57%
SAT writing:	610-700	Live on campus:	99%
ACT composite:	28-31	International:	4%
Rank in top quarter:	89%		

Basis for selection. Candidates urged to complete the most challenging college-preparatory program available at their school. Evidence of superior achievement in analytical reading and writing are of particular importance. Advanced placement and honors courses recommended. Standardized test scores are optional. Students may submit scores if they believe the results present a fuller picture of their achievements and potential. Students who do not submit scores will not be at any disadvantage in admissions decisions. Personal interview optional but highly recommended. **Home schooled:** On-campus interview highly encouraged. Applicants should submit course work samples, personal statement, and college transcripts if applicable. If homeschooling associated with particular organization or program, submit description. **Learning Disabled:** Students with disabilities encouraged to contact Office of Disability Services any time prior to application or after acceptance to the College.

High school preparation. College-preparatory program recommended. 20 units recommended. Recommended units include English 4, mathematics 4, social studies 2, history 2, science 4 (laboratory 2) and foreign language 4.

2015-2016 Annual costs. Tuition/fees: $47,176. Room/board: $12,748. Books/supplies: $700. Personal expenses: $900.

2015-2016 Financial aid. Need-based: 469 full-time freshmen applied for aid; 404 deemed to have need; 404 received aid. Average need met was 100%. Average scholarship/grant was $34,015; average loan $4,937. 76% of total undergraduate aid awarded as scholarships/grants, 24% as loans/jobs. **Non-need-based:** Awarded to 190 full-time undergraduates, including 58 freshmen. Scholarships awarded for academics, athletics, music/drama, state residency. **Additional information:** Cost of tuition above amount of Pell Grant waived for Worcester residents whose families earn less than $50,000.

Application procedures. Admission: Closing date 1/15 (receipt date). $60 fee, may be waived for applicants with need. Application must be submitted online. Admission notification by 4/1. Must reply by 5/1. **Financial aid:** Closing date 2/1. FAFSA required. CSS PROFILE required of all students applying for institutional aid. Applicants notified by 4/1; must reply by 5/1.

Academics. Students encouraged to participate in Oxford-style tutorials. 32 courses of 1 or more units required for graduation; 10-14 courses of 1 or more units required in major. **Special study options:** Accelerated study, cross-registration, double major, dual enrollment of high school students, exchange student, honors, independent study, internships, liberal arts/career combination, semester at sea, student-designed major, study abroad, teacher certification program, Washington semester. First-year living and learning academic enrichment program. **Credit/placement by examination:** AP, CLEP, IB, institutional tests. Language placement determined by departmental testing. **Support services:** Learning center, study skills assistance, tutoring, writing center.

Majors. Architecture: History/criticism. **Area/ethnic studies:** Asian, deaf, Latin American. **Biology:** General. **Business:** Accounting. **Computer sciences:** General. **Conservation:** Environmental studies. **English:** English lit. **Foreign languages:** Chinese, classics, comparative lit, French, German, Italian, Russian, Spanish. **History:** General. **Math:** General. **Philosophy/religion:** Philosophy, religion. **Physical sciences:** Chemistry, physics. **Psychology:** General. **Social sciences:** Anthropology, economics, political science, sociology. **Visual/performing arts:** Art history/conservation, dramatic, music, studio arts.

Most popular majors. Biology 7%, English 9%, foreign language 8%, history 7%, mathematics 6%, physical sciences 7%, psychology 13%, social sciences 34%.

Technology on campus. 485 workstations in dormitories, library, computer center, student center. Dormitories wired for high-speed internet access and linked to campus network. Commuter students can connect to campus network. Online course registration, online library, helpline, repair service, student web hosting, wireless network available.

Student life. Freshman orientation: Available, $230 fee. Preregistration for classes offered. Two-day programs available in mid-June; 3-day orientation prior to fall registration. **Policies:** Responsible drinking policy for students 21 and older. Initiation hazing prohibited. Freshmen not permitted cars on campus. **Housing:** Guaranteed on-campus for all undergraduates. Coed dorms, special housing for disabled, apartments, wellness housing available. $500 nonrefundable deposit, deadline 5/1. **Activities:** Bands, campus ministries, choral groups, dance, drama, international student organizations, literary magazine, music ensembles, Model UN, musical theater, radio station, student government, student newspaper, black student union, Purple Key society, student program for urban development, women's forum, Latin American student organization, Asian student society, Muslim student association, Appalachia service project, Habitat for Humanity, Association of bisexuals/gays/lesbians.

Athletics. NCAA. **Intercollegiate:** Baseball M, basketball, cross-country, diving, field hockey W, football (tackle) M, golf, ice hockey, lacrosse, rowing (crew), soccer, softball W, swimming, tennis, track and field, volleyball

W. **Intramural:** Basketball, football (non-tackle), handball, soccer, softball, volleyball, water polo. **Team name:** Crusaders.

Student services. Alcohol/substance abuse counseling, chaplain/spiritual director, career counseling, student employment services, financial aid counseling, health services, minority student services, personal counseling, placement for graduates, veterans' counselor, women's services. **Physically disabled:** Services for visually, hearing impaired.

Contact. E-mail: admissions@holycross.edu
Phone: (508) 793-2443 Toll-free number: (800) 442-2421
Fax: (508) 793-3888
Ann McDermott, Director of Admissions, College of the Holy Cross, One College Street, Worcester, MA 01610-2395

Curry College
Milton, Massachusetts
www.curry.edu

CB member
CB code: 3285

- Private 4-year liberal arts college
- Residential campus in large town
- 2,691 degree-seeking undergraduates: 25% part-time, 62% women, 9% African American, 2% Asian American, 6% Hispanic/Latino, 2% Multiracial, non-Hispanic, 2% international
- 221 degree-seeking graduate students
- 88% of applicants admitted
- Application essay required
- 47% graduate within 6 years

General. Founded in 1879. Regionally accredited. **Degrees:** 676 bachelor's awarded; master's offered. **ROTC:** Army. **Location:** 7 miles from downtown Boston. **Calendar:** Semester, limited summer session. **Full-time faculty:** 125 total; 82% have terminal degrees, 6% minority, 65% women. **Part-time faculty:** 365 total; 26% have terminal degrees, 7% minority, 68% women. **Class size:** 62% < 20, 38% 20-39. **Special facilities:** HD television studio with virtual stet technology, including 3D video production, 4K RED Camera production, sports remote production unit.

Freshman class profile. 5,554 applied, 4,871 admitted, 602 enrolled.

Mid 50% test scores			
SAT critical reading:	420-510	GPA 2.0-2.99:	64%
SAT math:	420-520	Rank in top quarter:	21%
SAT writing:	410-510	Rank in top tenth:	4%
ACT composite:	18-22	End year in good standing:	82%
GPA 3.75 or higher:	3%	Return as sophomores:	69%
GPA 3.50-3.74:	6%	Out-of-state:	35%
GPA 3.0-3.49:	27%	Live on campus:	88%
		International:	2%

Basis for selection. High school record, recommendations, and extracurricular activities most important. Test scores are also important. Interviews strongly recommended. **Home schooled:** Statement describing home school structure and mission, transcript of courses and grades, state high school equivalency certificate required. **Learning Disabled:** SAT/ACT not required or considered for applicants to Program for the Advancement of Learning. Wechsler Adult Intelligence Scale required.

High school preparation. College-preparatory program recommended. 16 units required. Required and recommended units include English 4, mathematics 3, social studies 2, history 2, science 2 (laboratory 1) and foreign language 2. 3 math through algebra II, 1 chemistry, and 1 biology required for nursing applicants.

2015-2016 Annual costs. Tuition/fees: $36,445. Room/board: $13,900.

2015-2016 Financial aid. Need-based: 487 full-time freshmen applied for aid; 487 deemed to have need; 487 received aid. Average need met was 69%. Average scholarship/grant was $24,802; average loan $3,595. 79% of total undergraduate aid awarded as scholarships/grants, 21% as loans/jobs. **Non-need-based:** Awarded to 489 full-time undergraduates, including 144 freshmen. Scholarships awarded for academics, alumni affiliation, leadership.

Application procedures. Admission: Priority date 4/1; no deadline. $50 fee, may be waived for applicants with need. Admission notification on a rolling basis beginning on or about 11/1. Must reply by May 1 or within 2 week(s) if notified thereafter. **Financial aid:** Priority date 3/1; no closing date. FAFSA required. Applicants notified on a rolling basis starting 3/1; must reply by 5/1 or within 2 week(s) of notification.

Academics. Special study options: Accelerated study, cross-registration, double major, ESL, honors, independent study, internships, liberal arts/career combination, New York semester, semester at sea, student-designed major, study abroad, teacher certification program. **Credit/placement by examination:** AP, CLEP, IB, SAT, institutional tests. 60 credit hours maximum toward bachelor's degree. **Support services:** Learning center, reduced course load, remedial instruction, study skills assistance, tutoring, writing center. Speaking center, Academic Enrichment Center, Program for Advancement of Learning.

Majors. Biology: General, biochemistry. **Business:** Business admin. **Computer sciences:** General. **Education:** General, early childhood, elementary, special ed. **English:** English lit. **Health services:** Nursing (RN). **Liberal arts:** Arts/sciences. **Philosophy/religion:** Philosophy. **Protective services:** Criminal justice. **Psychology:** General. **Social sciences:** Sociology. **Visual/performing arts:** Graphic design, studio arts.

Most popular majors. Business/marketing 12%, communications/journalism 10%, health sciences 45%, psychology 8%, security/protective services 12%.

Technology on campus. 245 workstations in dormitories, library, computer center, student center. Dormitories wired for high-speed internet access and linked to campus network. Commuter students can connect to campus network. Online course registration, online library, helpline, student web hosting, wireless network available.

Student life. Freshman orientation: Available, $150 fee. Preregistration for classes offered. Four summer 2-day programs and 2-day August program available. **Policies:** Freshmen not permitted cars on campus. **Housing:** Coed dorms, single-sex dorms, special housing for disabled, themed housing available. $300 partly refundable deposit, deadline 5/1. **Activities:** Campus ministries, choral groups, dance, drama, film society, international student organizations, literary magazine, music ensembles, musical theater, radio station, student government, student newspaper, TV station, student government association, campus activities board, community service organization, Hillel, One Curry, Newman club, multicultural student union, gay straight alliance, politics & history club, Amnesty International.

Athletics. NCAA. Intercollegiate: Baseball M, basketball, cross-country W, football (tackle) M, ice hockey M, lacrosse, soccer, softball W, tennis, volleyball W. **Intramural:** Badminton, basketball, field hockey W, football (non-tackle), golf, skiing, soccer, softball, tennis, ultimate frisbee, volleyball. **Team name:** Colonels.

Student services. Adult student services, alcohol/substance abuse counseling, chaplain/spiritual director, career counseling, student employment services, financial aid counseling, health services, minority student services, on-campus daycare, personal counseling, placement for graduates, veterans' counselor, women's services. **Physically disabled:** Services for visually, hearing impaired.

Contact. E-mail: curryadm@curry.edu
Phone: (617) 333-2210 Toll-free number: (800) 669-0686
Fax: (617) 333-2114
Jane Fidler, Dean of Admission, Curry College, 1071 Blue Hill Avenue, Milton, MA 02186-9984

Eastern Nazarene College
Quincy, Massachusetts
www.enc.edu

CB member
CB code: 3365

▶ Private 4-year liberal arts college affiliated with the Church of the Nazarene

▶ Residential campus in small city

▶ 911 degree-seeking undergraduates: 1% part-time, 63% women, 24% African American, 2% Asian American, 12% Hispanic/Latino, 4% Multiracial, non-Hispanic, 3% international

▶ 188 degree-seeking graduate students

▶ 62% of applicants admitted

▶ SAT or ACT (ACT writing recommended) required

▶ 65% graduate within 6 years

General. Founded in 1900. Regionally accredited. **Degrees:** 234 bachelor's, 22 associate awarded; master's offered. **ROTC:** Army, Air Force. **Location:** 2 miles from Boston. **Calendar:** Semester, limited summer session. **Full-time faculty:** 37 total. **Part-time faculty:** 90 total. **Class size:** 80% < 20, 16% 20-39, 1% 40-49, 3% 50-99, less than 1% >100. **Special facilities:** Arboretum; early childhood education center; center for history, law, and government; business center.

Freshman class profile. 1,129 applied, 695 admitted, 187 enrolled.

GPA 3.75 or higher:	10%	Rank in top tenth:	13%
GPA 3.50-3.74:	13%	Out-of-state:	45%
GPA 3.0-3.49:	37%	Live on campus:	77%
GPA 2.0-2.99:	34%	International:	1%
Rank in top quarter:	32%		

Basis for selection. Applicants should demonstrate academic achievement, extracurricular involvement, and community engagement. ACCUPLACER test may also be required. Audition required of students intending to major in music. **Home schooled:** Statement describing home school structure and mission, transcript of courses and grades, interview, letter of recommendation (nonparent) required.

High school preparation. College-preparatory program required. 15 units required. Required and recommended units include English 4, mathematics 2-4, social studies 1-2, history 1-2, science 2-4 (laboratory 2-4), foreign language 2-4, visual/performing arts 1-2 and academic electives 5.

2016-2017 Annual costs. Tuition/fees (projected): $30,815. Room/board: $9,140. Books/supplies: $1,200. Personal expenses: $1,160.

Financial aid. Non-need-based: Scholarships awarded for academics, alumni affiliation, leadership, religious affiliation, ROTC. **Additional information:** Participant in Massachusetts University pre-payment plan.

Application procedures. Admission: Priority date 1/1; no deadline. No application fee. Application must be submitted online. Admission notification on a rolling basis. **Financial aid:** Priority date 3/1, closing date 8/1. FAFSA, institutional form required. Applicants notified on a rolling basis starting 3/14; must reply by 8/1 or within 2 week(s) of notification.

Academics. Special study options: Accelerated study, combined bachelor's/graduate degree, cross-registration, double major, dual enrollment of high school students, exchange student, honors, independent study, internships, liberal arts/career combination, semester at sea, study abroad, teacher certification program, urban semester, Washington semester. **Credit/placement by examination:** AP, CLEP, IB, SAT, ACT, institutional tests. **Support services:** Learning center, pre-admission summer program, remedial instruction, study skills assistance, tutoring, writing center.

Majors. Biology: General, biochemistry. **Business:** General, accounting, accounting/business management, accounting/finance, business admin, marketing. **Communications:** Journalism. **Conservation:** Environmental science, environmental studies. **Education:** General, biology, business, chemistry, early childhood, elementary, English, history, kindergarten/preschool, mathematics, middle, music, physical, physics, science, social studies, special ed. **Engineering:** General, applied physics, computer, electrical. **English:** Creative writing, English lit. **Health services:** Movement therapy, predental, premedicine, prenursing, prepharmacy, preveterinary. **History:** General. **Human services:** Social work. **Liberal arts:** Arts/sciences. **Math:** General. **Parks/recreation:** Health/fitness, sports admin. **Philosophy/religion:** Religion. **Physical sciences:** Chemistry, physics. **Protective services:** Criminal justice, forensics, law enforcement admin, police science. **Psychology:** General, clinical, counseling, developmental, social. **Theology:** Pastoral counseling, preministerial, sacred music, theology, youth ministry. **Visual/performing arts:** Dramatic, music, music history, music management, music pedagogy, music performance, music theory/composition, piano/keyboard, stringed instruments, theater arts management, voice/opera.

Most popular majors. Business/marketing 14%, communications/journalism 6%, education 9%, English 6%, liberal arts 11%, philosophy/religious studies 6%, psychology 16%, social sciences 6%.

Technology on campus. 98 workstations in library, computer center, student center. Dormitories wired for high-speed internet access and linked to campus network. Commuter students can connect to campus network. Online library, helpline, repair service, wireless network available.

Student life. Freshman orientation: Mandatory. Preregistration for classes offered. **Policies:** Students must abstain from use of illegal drugs, alcohol and tobacco, and are to avoid attendance at bars, clubs, or other activities or places of entertainment that promote themes of inappropriate sexuality, violence, profanity, pornography or activities demeaning to human life. Religious observance required. **Housing:** Guaranteed on-campus for all undergraduates. Coed dorms, single-sex dorms, special housing for disabled, apartments available. $300 nonrefundable deposit, deadline 8/25. **Activities:** Bands, campus ministries, choral groups, dance, drama, film society, literary magazine, music ensembles, musical theater, student government, student newspaper, symphony orchestra, ACTS/JUMP, Barnabas, Big Brother Big Sister, Causeway, Fellowship of Christian Athletes, Germantown Tutoring, Open Hand Open Heart, Refiner's Fire, Students for Social Justice, Women of Grace.

Athletics. NCAA. Intercollegiate: Baseball M, basketball, cross-country, soccer, softball W, tennis, track and field, volleyball. **Intramural:** Basketball, field hockey W, football (non-tackle), lacrosse, skiing, soccer, ultimate frisbee M, volleyball. **Team name:** Lions.

Student services. Adult student services, alcohol/substance abuse counseling, chaplain/spiritual director, career counseling, services for economically disadvantaged, student employment services, financial aid counseling, health services, minority student services, personal counseling, placement for graduates, veterans' counselor, women's services. **Physically disabled:** Services for visually impaired.

Contact. E-mail: admissions@enc.edu
Phone: (617) 745-3711 Toll-free number: (800) 883-6288
Fax: (617) 745-3992
Brian Parker, Director of Admissions, Eastern Nazarene College, 23 East Elm Avenue, Quincy, MA 02170

Elms College
Chicopee, Massachusetts
www.elms.edu

CB member
CB code: 3283

- Private 4-year liberal arts college affiliated with the Roman Catholic Church
- Residential campus in small city
- 1,268 degree-seeking undergraduates: 24% part-time, 77% women, 7% African American, 2% Asian American, 10% Hispanic/Latino
- 380 degree-seeking graduate students
- 75% of applicants admitted
- SAT or ACT (ACT writing optional), application essay required
- 67% graduate within 6 years

General. Founded in 1928. Regionally accredited. **Degrees:** 415 bachelor's, 22 associate awarded; master's, professional offered. **ROTC:** Army, Air Force. **Location:** 2 miles from Springfield; 30 miles from Hartford, Connecticut. **Calendar:** Semester, limited summer session. **Full-time faculty:** 60 total; 2% minority, 65% women. **Part-time faculty:** 117 total; 12% minority, 73% women. **Class size:** 70% < 20, 29% 20-39, less than 1% 40-49, less than 1% 50-99. **Special facilities:** Rare book collection, Federal Depository, Irish cultural center, Polish center for discovery and learning.

Freshman class profile. 832 applied, 623 admitted, 186 enrolled.

Mid 50% test scores		GPA 3.50-3.74:	16%
SAT critical reading:	440-530	GPA 3.0-3.49:	30%
SAT math:	430-540	GPA 2.0-2.99:	28%
SAT writing:	430-530	Return as sophomores:	82%
ACT composite:	19-24	Out-of-state:	42%
GPA 3.75 or higher:	26%	Live on campus:	69%

Basis for selection. Students should rank in top half of high school class; 2.8 GPA, 1000 SAT (exclusive of Writing) recommended. Interview recommended. **Home schooled:** Transcript of courses and grades, letter of recommendation (nonparent) required.

High school preparation. College-preparatory program recommended. 15 units required; 22 recommended. Required and recommended units include English 4, mathematics 2-4, social studies 1-2, history 2, science 2-4 (laboratory 2) and foreign language 2-4. Algebra II, biology, chemistry required for nursing applicants.

2015-2016 Annual costs. Tuition/fees: $32,335. Room/board: $11,708. Books/supplies: $1,150. Personal expenses: $1,650.

2015-2016 Financial aid. Need-based: 176 full-time freshmen applied for aid; 169 deemed to have need; 169 received aid. Average need met was 72%. Average scholarship/grant was $22,523; average loan $3,416. 61% of total undergraduate aid awarded as scholarships/grants, 39% as loans/jobs. **Non-need-based:** Awarded to 127 full-time undergraduates, including 31 freshmen. Scholarships awarded for academics, alumni affiliation, leadership, religious affiliation, state residency.

Application procedures. Admission: No deadline. $30 fee, may be waived for applicants with need. Admission notification by 12/10. Admission notification on a rolling basis. Must reply by May 1 or within 2 week(s) if notified thereafter. **Financial aid:** Priority date 3/1; no closing date. FAFSA required. Applicants notified on a rolling basis starting 3/15; must reply by 5/1 or within 2 week(s) of notification.

Academics. Tutor training certified by College Reading and Learning Association. **Special study options:** Combined bachelor's/graduate degree, cross-registration, distance learning, double major, dual enrollment of high school students, ESL, exchange student, honors, independent study, internships, liberal arts/career combination, study abroad, teacher certification program, Washington semester, weekend college. **Credit/placement by examination:** AP, CLEP, IB, SAT, ACT, institutional tests. 12 credit hours maximum toward bachelor's degree. **Support services:** Learning center, reduced course load, study skills assistance, tutoring, writing center.

Majors. Area/ethnic studies: American, Spanish/Iberian. **Biology:** General. **Business:** Accounting, accounting/business management, business admin, international, marketing. **Communications:** Communications/speech/rhetoric. **Computer sciences:** General. **Education:** General, bilingual, Deaf/hearing impaired, early childhood, elementary, English, ESL, secondary, special ed. **English:** English lit. **Foreign languages:** Spanish. **Health services:** Audiology/hearing, audiology/speech pathology, communication disorders, facilities admin, health care admin, health services admin, nursing (RN), pediatric nursing, predental, premedicine, preop/surgical nursing, preveterinary, public health nursing, speech pathology, speech-language pathology assistant. **History:** General, American, European. **Human services:** Social work. **Liberal arts:** Arts/sciences. **Math:** General. **Parks/recreation:** Sports admin. **Philosophy/religion:** Religion. **Physical sciences:** Chemistry. **Protective services:** Law enforcement admin. **Psychology:** General. **Social sciences:** International relations, sociology. **Visual/performing arts:** Studio arts.

Most popular majors. Business/marketing 11%, education 10%, health sciences 44%, psychology 7%, public administration/social services 11%.

Technology on campus. 70 workstations in dormitories, library, computer center, student center. Dormitories wired for high-speed internet access and linked to campus network. Commuter students can connect to campus network. Helpline, wireless network available.

Student life. Freshman orientation: Mandatory. Preregistration for classes offered. One-day programs held in June and August. **Housing:** Guaranteed on-campus for all undergraduates. Coed dorms, special housing for disabled, wellness housing available. **Activities:** Concert band, campus ministries, choral groups, dance, drama, international student organizations, literary magazine, music ensembles, student government, student newspaper, student government association, social work club, international club, speech pathology and audiology club, Student Ambassadors organization, student nurse association, drama club.

Athletics. NCAA. **Intercollegiate:** Baseball M, basketball, cross-country, field hockey W, golf M, lacrosse W, soccer, softball W, swimming, volleyball. **Intramural:** Baseball M, basketball, cross-country, field hockey W, football (non-tackle), golf M, lacrosse W, soccer, softball W, swimming, ultimate frisbee, volleyball. **Team name:** Blazers.

Student services. Adult student services, alcohol/substance abuse counseling, chaplain/spiritual director, career counseling, student employment services, financial aid counseling, health services, minority student services, personal counseling, placement for graduates. **Physically disabled:** Services for visually, speech, hearing impaired.

Contact. E-mail: admissions@elms.edu
Phone: (413) 592-3189 Toll-free number: (800) 255-3567
Fax: (413) 594-2781
Joseph Wagner, Director of Admission, Elms College, 291 Springfield Street, Chicopee, MA 01013-2839

Emerson College
Boston, Massachusetts
www.emerson.edu

CB member
CB code: 3367

- Private 4-year college of communication and the arts
- Residential campus in very large city
- 3,784 degree-seeking undergraduates: 1% part-time, 60% women, 3% African American, 4% Asian American, 11% Hispanic/Latino, 4% Multiracial, non-Hispanic, 7% international
- 671 degree-seeking graduate students
- 49% of applicants admitted
- SAT or ACT (ACT writing optional), application essay required
- 80% graduate within 6 years

General. Founded in 1880. Regionally accredited. **Degrees:** 969 bachelor's awarded; master's offered. **Calendar:** Semester, limited summer session. **Full-time faculty:** 202 total; 73% have terminal degrees, 19% minority, 45% women. **Part-time faculty:** 277 total; 43% have terminal degrees, 11% minority, 50% women. **Class size:** 67% < 20, 30% 20-39, 2% 40-49, 1% 50-99, less than 1% >100. **Special facilities:** Two historic theaters, performance and production center, sound treated television studios, integrated digital newsroom, film production facilities and film screening room, clinics/programs to observe speech and hearing therapy, marketing research suite.

Freshman class profile. 8,618 applied, 4,225 admitted, 915 enrolled.

Mid 50% test scores		Rank in top quarter:	67%
SAT critical reading:	560-670	Rank in top tenth:	27%
SAT math:	540-640	Return as sophomores:	87%
SAT writing:	560-660	Out-of-state:	76%
ACT composite:	25-29	Live on campus:	97%
GPA 3.75 or higher:	44%	International:	9%
GPA 3.50-3.74:	22%	Fraternities:	1%
GPA 3.0-3.49:	30%	Sororities:	2%
GPA 2.0-2.99:	4%		

Basis for selection. Secondary school record, recommendations, writing competency, and personal qualities as seen in extracurricular activities, community involvement, demonstrated leadership important. Performing arts applicants must submit theatrical resume and, depending upon the major, either audition/interview or submit portfolio/essay. Candidates for film program must submit either a 5-8 minute video (20MB) accompanied by statement describing their role in its production or 5-10 page script. **Home schooled:** State high school equivalency certificate required. Common Application Home School Supplement required.

High school preparation. College-preparatory program required. 16 units required; 20 recommended. Required and recommended units include English 4, mathematics 3, social studies 3, (laboratory 3), foreign language 3 and academic electives 4.

2015-2016 Annual costs. Tuition/fees: $41,052. Room/board: $15,700. Books/supplies: $1,000. Personal expenses: $2,478.

2015-2016 Financial aid. Need-based: 692 full-time freshmen applied for aid; 472 deemed to have need; 472 received aid. Average need met was 62%. Average scholarship/grant was $20,145; average loan $3,989. 60% of total undergraduate aid awarded as scholarships/grants, 40% as loans/jobs. **Non-need-based:** Awarded to 1,025 full-time undergraduates, including 170 freshmen. Scholarships awarded for academics, leadership, music/drama, state residency. **Additional information:** Massachusetts Loan Plan available for parents of dependent undergraduates.

Application procedures. Admission: Closing date 1/15 (postmark date). $65 fee, may be waived for applicants with need. Admission notification by 4/1. Must reply by May 1 or within 2 week(s) if notified thereafter. **Financial aid:** Closing date 3/1. FAFSA, CSS PROFILE required. Applicants notified by 4/1; must reply by 5/1 or within 3 week(s) of notification.

Academics. Special study options: Cross-registration, double major, honors, independent study, internships, liberal arts/career combination, student-designed major, study abroad, teacher certification program, Washington semester. Study and internship programs in Los Angeles and Washington, DC. Course cross-registration through the six-member Boston ProArts Consortium (Berklee College of Music, Boston Architectural Center, Boston Conservatory, Emerson, Massachusetts College of Art, School of the Museum of Fine Arts). **Credit/placement by examination:** AP, CLEP, IB, SAT, ACT, institutional tests. 32 credit hours maximum toward bachelor's degree. Math requirement waived with 550 SAT math or 24 ACT math. **Support services:** Learning center, reduced course load, study skills assistance, tutoring, writing center.

Majors. Business: Communications, marketing. **Communications:** Advertising, broadcast journalism, communications/speech/rhetoric, journalism, media studies, political, public relations, publishing. **Education:** Autistic, Deaf/hearing impaired, drama/dance, speech, speech impaired. **English:** Creative writing, rhetoric/composition. **Health services:** Audiology/hearing, audiology/speech pathology, communication disorders, speech pathology. **Visual/performing arts:** General, acting, cinematography, directing/producing, dramatic, film/cinema/video, play/screenwriting, theater arts management, theater design.

Most popular majors. Business/marketing 15%, communications/journalism 36%, English 13%, visual/performing arts 30%.

Technology on campus. 480 workstations in dormitories, library, computer center, student center. Dormitories wired for high-speed internet access and linked to campus network. Commuter students can connect to campus network. Online course registration, online library, helpline, repair service, wireless network available.

Student life. Freshman orientation: Mandatory, $150 fee. Preregistration for classes offered. Multi-day event preceding first day of classes that includes computer workshops, library tours, advising, social activities, and field trips around Boston. **Housing:** Coed dorms, themed housing, wellness housing available. $500 nonrefundable deposit, deadline 5/1. **Activities:** Campus ministries, choral groups, dance, drama, film society, international student organizations, literary magazine, music ensembles, Model UN, musical theater, radio station, student government, student newspaper, TV station, Hillel,

Newman club, Goodnews Fellowship, Islamic community, Alliance of Gays and Lesbians and Everyone, Latino student organization, international club, Earth Emerson, Asian Students for Intercultural Awareness, Amnesty International.

Athletics. NCAA. **Intercollegiate:** Baseball M, basketball, cross-country, golf, lacrosse, soccer, softball W, tennis, track and field, volleyball W. **Team name:** Lions.

Student services. Adult student services, chaplain/spiritual director, career counseling, student employment services, financial aid counseling, health services, minority student services, personal counseling, placement for graduates. **Physically disabled:** Services for visually, speech, hearing impaired.

Contact. E-mail: admission@emerson.edu
Phone: (617) 824-8600 Fax: (617) 824-8609
Michael Lynch, Director of Undergraduate Admission, Emerson College, 120 Boylston Street, Boston, MA 02116-4624

Emmanuel College
Boston, Massachusetts
www.emmanuel.edu

CB member
CB code: 3368

- Private 4-year liberal arts college affiliated with the Roman Catholic Church
- Residential campus in very large city
- 1,865 degree-seeking undergraduates: 5% part-time, 74% women, 5% African American, 4% Asian American, 9% Hispanic/Latino, 2% Multiracial, non-Hispanic, 2% international
- 190 degree-seeking graduate students
- 68% of applicants admitted
- Application essay required
- 64% graduate within 6 years

General. Founded in 1919. Regionally accredited. Students can cross-register at Simmons College, Wentworth Institute of Technology, Wheelock College, Massachusetts College of Art, and Massachusetts College of Pharmacy and Health Sciences. **Degrees:** 487 bachelor's awarded; master's offered. **ROTC:** Army, Air Force. **Calendar:** Semester, limited summer session. **Full-time faculty:** 94 total; 78% have terminal degrees, 16% minority, 62% women. **Part-time faculty:** 107 total; 32% have terminal degrees, 12% minority, 67% women. **Class size:** 40% < 20, 59% 20-39, less than 1% 40-49.

Freshman class profile. 6,516 applied, 4,463 admitted, 555 enrolled.

Mid 50% test scores		GPA 3.0-3.49:	27%
SAT critical reading:	520-610	GPA 2.0-2.99:	12%
SAT math:	510-600	Return as sophomores:	75%
SAT writing:	510-600	Out-of-state:	46%
ACT composite:	23-27	Live on campus:	92%
GPA 3.75 or higher:	40%	International:	2%
GPA 3.50-3.74:	21%		

Basis for selection. High school curriculum and record, eassy, GPA very important. Extracurricular activites, volunteer work, level of interest important. Class rank, test scores, interview considered. **Home schooled:** Transcript of courses and grades, state high school equivalency certificate, letter of recommendation (nonparent) required.

High school preparation. College-preparatory program required. 16 units required. Required units include English 4, mathematics 3, social studies 3, science 3 (laboratory 2) and foreign language 3.

2015-2016 Annual costs. Tuition/fees: $36,504. Room/board: $13,920. Books/supplies: $880. Personal expenses: $1,701.

2015-2016 Financial aid. Need-based: 500 full-time freshmen applied for aid; 454 deemed to have need; 454 received aid. Average need met was 76%. Average scholarship/grant was $23,170; average loan $3,660. 68% of total undergraduate aid awarded as scholarships/grants, 32% as loans/jobs. **Non-need-based:** Awarded to 1,754 full-time undergraduates, including 552 freshmen. Scholarships awarded for academics, alumni affiliation, leadership.

Application procedures. Admission: Priority date 11/1; deadline 2/15. $60 fee, may be waived for applicants with need, free for online applicants. Admission notification on a rolling basis beginning on or about 12/15. Must reply by May 1 or within 2 week(s) if notified thereafter. **Financial aid:** Priority date 2/15; no closing date. FAFSA required. Applicants notified on a rolling basis starting 3/1.

Academics. One-semester Capstone Experience required, may take the form of a seminar, internship, research project or creative project. **Special**

study options: Accelerated study, combined bachelor's/graduate degree, cross-registration, distance learning, double major, exchange student, honors, independent study, internships, liberal arts/career combination, New York semester, semester at sea, student-designed major, study abroad, teacher certification program, Washington semester. **Credit/placement by examination:** AP, CLEP, IB, institutional tests. A student achieving an AP score of 4 or 5 will receive credit for one course and advanced placement in that subject area. A student achieving higher level IB exam results of four, five, six or seven will be reviewed by the appropriate department at Emmanuel and entitle students to credits equivalent to at least one course. **Support services:** Learning center, reduced course load, remedial instruction, study skills assistance, tutoring, writing center.

Majors. Area/ethnic studies: American. **Biology:** General, biochemistry, biostatistics, neuroscience, physiology. **Business:** Accounting, business admin. **Communications:** Communications/speech/rhetoric. **Education:** Elementary, secondary. **English:** English lit. **Foreign languages:** Spanish. **Health services:** Art therapy. **History:** General. **Liberal arts:** Arts/sciences. **Math:** General. **Parks/recreation:** Sports admin. **Philosophy/religion:** Philosophy, religion. **Physical sciences:** Chemistry, forensic chemistry. **Psychology:** General, counseling, developmental. **Social sciences:** Criminology, international relations, political science, sociology, U.S. government. **Visual/performing arts:** Graphic design, studio arts.

Most popular majors. Biology 14%, business/marketing 16%, communications/journalism 8%, education 9%, health sciences 10%, liberal arts 6%, psychology 10%, social sciences 7%.

Technology on campus. 284 workstations in dormitories, library, computer center, student center. Online course registration, online library, helpline, student web hosting, wireless network available.

Student life. Freshman orientation: Mandatory, $280 fee. Preregistration for classes offered. Four 2-day sessions held during the summer, one 2-day in August, and one 2-day in January. **Policies:** Alcohol and tobacco free campus. Freshmen not permitted cars on campus. **Housing:** Guaranteed on-campus for all undergraduates. Coed dorms, special housing for disabled, themed housing available. $200 nonrefundable deposit, deadline 5/1. **Activities:** Campus ministries, choral groups, dance, drama, international student organizations, literary magazine, music ensembles, Model UN, musical theater, radio station, student government, student newspaper, symphony orchestra, 1804 Society, Political Forum, Model UN, Asian Student Association, Black Student Union, Armenian Club, International Student Association, HUELLAS, community outreach, OUTspoken.

Athletics. NCAA. **Intercollegiate:** Basketball, cross-country, golf M, lacrosse, soccer, softball W, track and field, volleyball. **Team name:** Saints.

Student services. Adult student services, alcohol/substance abuse counseling, chaplain/spiritual director, career counseling, student employment services, financial aid counseling, health services, minority student services, personal counseling, placement for graduates, veterans' counselor. **Physically disabled:** Services for visually, speech, hearing impaired.

Contact. E-mail: enroll@emmanuel.edu
Phone: (617) 735-9715 Fax: (617) 735-9801
Sandra Robbins, Dean of Enrollment, Emmanuel College, 400 The Fenway, Boston, MA 02115

Endicott College
Beverly, Massachusetts
www.endicott.edu

CB member
CB code: 3369

- Private 4-year liberal arts college
- Residential campus in large town
- 2,979 degree-seeking undergraduates: 10% part-time, 62% women, 2% African American, 1% Asian American, 5% Hispanic/Latino, 1% Multiracial, non-Hispanic, 2% international
- 948 degree-seeking graduate students
- 73% of applicants admitted
- Application essay required
- 71% graduate within 6 years; 14% enter graduate study

General. Founded in 1939. Regionally accredited. **Degrees:** 616 bachelor's, 27 associate awarded; master's, professional, doctoral offered. **ROTC:** Army. **Location:** 24 miles from Boston. **Calendar:** Semester, limited summer session. **Full-time faculty:** 98 total; 68% have terminal degrees, 7% minority, 57% women. **Part-time faculty:** 371 total; 36% have terminal degrees, 7% minority, 57% women. **Class size:** 55% < 20, 45% 20-39. **Special facilities:** Science labs, nursing labs, fine arts studios, recital hall, black box theater, nature trails, private beaches and marshland, student-run restaurant/classroom for hospitality, archives museum.

Freshman class profile. 4,009 applied, 2,918 admitted, 815 enrolled.

Mid 50% test scores			
SAT critical reading:	490-580	GPA 2.0-2.99:	28%
SAT math:	490-590	Rank in top quarter:	44%
SAT writing:	480-540	Rank in top tenth:	14%
ACT composite:	21-26	End year in good standing:	85%
GPA 3.75 or higher:	19%	Return as sophomores:	86%
GPA 3.50-3.74:	14%	Out-of-state:	56%
GPA 3.0-3.49:	38%	Live on campus:	96%
		International:	2%

Basis for selection. School achievement record most important. Class rank, essay, volunteer work, extracurricular activities, leadership also important. Teacher, counselor recommendations considered. Interview recommended. **Home schooled:** Verification that curriculum has been certified by local school system or state, or GED.

High school preparation. College-preparatory program recommended. 16 units recommended. Recommended units include English 4, mathematics 3, social studies 2, history 1, science 2 and academic electives 4. 1 chemistry with laboratory, 2 algebra and 1 geometry or equivalent higher level math required for nursing programs.

2015-2016 Annual costs. Tuition/fees: $30,292. Room/board: $14,112. Books/supplies: $1,210. Personal expenses: $1,072.

2015-2016 Financial aid. Need-based: 757 full-time freshmen applied for aid; 557 deemed to have need; 556 received aid. Average need met was 60%. Average scholarship/grant was $9,714; average loan $3,585. 75% of total undergraduate aid awarded as scholarships/grants, 25% as loans/jobs. **Non-need-based:** Awarded to 1,777 full-time undergraduates, including 623 freshmen. Scholarships awarded for academics, alumni affiliation, art, job skills, leadership, music/drama, religious affiliation, ROTC, state residency.

Application procedures. Admission: Closing date 2/15 (postmark date). $50 fee, may be waived for applicants with need. Admission notification on a rolling basis beginning on or about 11/1. Must reply by May 1 or within 1 week(s) if notified thereafter. **Financial aid:** Priority date 3/15; no closing date. FAFSA, institutional form required. Applicants notified on a rolling basis starting 3/15; must reply within 2 week(s) of notification.

Academics. Three internships required of most traditional undergraduates. Adult undergraduate programs available on the main campus, at offsite centers in Boston, MA, Gloucester, MA, several instructional locations across the state and online. **Special study options:** Accelerated study, combined bachelor's/graduate degree, cross-registration, distance learning, double major, dual enrollment of high school students, ESL, exchange student, honors, independent study, internships, liberal arts/career combination, semester at sea, student-designed major, study abroad, teacher certification program, weekend college. Single parent program, 5-year bachelor/master programs, ROTC Army. Adult undergraduate programs available on the main campus, at offsite centers in Boston, MA, Gloucester, MA, several instructional locations across the state and online. **Credit/placement by examination:** AP, CLEP, IB, SAT, institutional tests. 32 credit hours maximum toward associate degree, 85 toward bachelor's. **Support services:** Learning center, study skills assistance, tutoring, writing center.

Majors. Biology: Biotechnology. **Business:** Accounting, business admin, entrepreneurial studies, finance, hospitality admin, hotel/motel/restaurant management, international, marketing. **Communications:** Digital media, media studies, persuasive communications. **Computer sciences:** Computer science. **Conservation:** Environmental science. **Education:** Early childhood, elementary, physical, secondary. **Engineering:** Biomedical. **English:** English lit. **Health services:** Athletic training, nursing (RN). **History:** General. **Liberal arts:** Arts/sciences. **Math:** General, applied. **Parks/recreation:** Exercise sciences, sports admin. **Protective services:** Criminal justice. **Psychology:** General. **Social sciences:** Political science. **Visual/performing arts:** Graphic design, interior design, photography, studio arts.

Most popular majors. Business/marketing 28%, communications/journalism 8%, education 7%, health sciences 11%, parks/recreation 10%, psychology 9%, visual/performing arts 7%.

Technology on campus. 285 workstations in library, computer center. Dormitories wired for high-speed internet access and linked to campus network. Commuter students can connect to campus network. Online course registration, online library, helpline, repair service, wireless network available.

Student life. Freshman orientation: Available. Preregistration for classes offered. Held in July and September; includes preparation for fall course assignment. **Policies:** Freshmen not permitted cars on campus. **Housing:** Guaranteed on-campus for freshmen. Coed dorms, single-sex dorms, special housing for disabled, apartments, themed housing, wellness housing available. $500 deposit, deadline 5/1. Single-Parent housing, Ocean-Front, Academic, Healthy Living, Suites, Apartments, Converted Mansions, Modular Housing available. **Activities:** Bands, campus ministries, choral groups, dance, drama, film society, international student organizations, literary magazine, music ensembles, Model UN, musical theater, student government, student newspaper, TV station, Coast-2-Coast (intercultural), ALANA, EC Alliance, Random Cards of Kindness, Rotaract service club.

Athletics. NCAA. **Intercollegiate:** Baseball M, basketball, cross-country, equestrian, field hockey W, football (tackle) M, golf M, ice hockey, lacrosse, soccer, softball W, tennis, volleyball. **Intramural:** Basketball, football (non-tackle), lacrosse, racquetball, soccer, softball. **Team name:** Gulls.

Student services. Adult student services, alcohol/substance abuse counseling, chaplain/spiritual director, career counseling, financial aid counseling, health services, minority student services, personal counseling, veterans' counselor, women's services. **Physically disabled:** Services for visually, speech, hearing impaired.

Contact. E-mail: admission@endicott.edu
Phone: (978) 921-1000 Toll-free number: (800) 325-1114
Fax: (978) 232-2520
Thomas Redman, Vice President for Admissions and Financial Aid, Endicott College, 376 Hale Street, Beverly, MA 01915-9985

Fisher College
Boston, Massachusetts
www.fisher.edu
CB member
CB code: 3391

- Private 4-year business and liberal arts college
- Residential campus in very large city
- 1,608 degree-seeking undergraduates: 28% part-time, 67% women, 11% African American, 1% Asian American, 10% Hispanic/Latino, 2% Multiracial, non-Hispanic, 9% international
- 21 degree-seeking graduate students
- 70% of applicants admitted
- 46% graduate within 6 years

General. Founded in 1903. Regionally accredited. Branch campuses in Boston, North Attleboro and New Bedford. **Degrees:** 186 bachelor's, 166 associate awarded. **ROTC:** Army. **Location:** Downtown Boston. **Calendar:** Semester, limited summer session. **Full-time faculty:** 34 total; 62% have terminal degrees, 9% minority, 56% women. **Part-time faculty:** 147 total; 12% minority, 50% women. **Class size:** 74% < 20, 26% 20-39, less than 1% 40-49. **Special facilities:** Fashion laboratory.

Freshman class profile. 2,674 applied, 1,875 admitted, 278 enrolled.

Mid 50% test scores		GPA 3.0-3.49:	6%
SAT critical reading:	350-460	GPA 2.0-2.99:	56%
SAT math:	350-460	Return as sophomores:	58%
ACT composite:	16-21	Out-of-state:	26%
GPA 3.75 or higher:	2%	Live on campus:	49%
GPA 3.50-3.74:	3%	International:	7%

Basis for selection. High school GPA, test scores, personal essays and recommendation letters reviewed. Essay recommended. **Home schooled:** Statement describing home school structure and mission required. **Learning Disabled:** Accommodation review available upon request. Students requesting review should submit latest IEP as well as current psychoeducational testing.

High school preparation. College-preparatory program recommended. 12 units required. Required units include English 4, mathematics 3, social studies 3 and science 2.

2015-2016 Annual costs. Tuition/fees: $28,942. Room/board: $15,082. Books/supplies: $1,800. Personal expenses: $1,750.

2014-2015 Financial aid. Need-based: 246 full-time freshmen applied for aid; 207 deemed to have need; 205 received aid. Average scholarship/grant was $19,263; average loan $4,752. 71% of total undergraduate aid awarded as scholarships/grants, 29% as loans/jobs. **Non-need-based:** Awarded to 119 full-time undergraduates, including 57 freshmen. Scholarships awarded for academics.

Application procedures. Admission: No deadline. $50 fee, may be waived for applicants with need, free for online applicants. Admission notification on a rolling basis. **Financial aid:** Priority date 3/15; no closing date. FAFSA required. Applicants notified on a rolling basis starting 3/1.

Academics. Special study options: Accelerated study, distance learning, honors, independent study, liberal arts/career combination, study abroad, weekend college. **Credit/placement by examination:** AP, CLEP, IB, institutional tests. 30 credit hours maximum toward associate degree, 75 toward bachelor's. Institution follows ACE guide for credit by examination. **Support

services: Learning center, reduced course load, remedial instruction, study skills assistance, tutoring, writing center.

Majors. Biology: General. **Business:** Accounting, business admin, fashion, finance, hospitality admin, human resources, management information systems, management science, marketing, organizational leadership. **Communications:** Advertising, journalism, media studies, public relations. **Computer sciences:** General. **Education:** Early childhood. **Health services:** Health information management, nursing (RN). **Human services:** General. **Liberal arts:** Arts/sciences. **Protective services:** Law enforcement admin. **Psychology:** General. **Visual/performing arts:** Cinematography.

Most popular majors. Business/marketing 56%, communications/journalism 8%, education 8%.

Technology on campus. 60 workstations in dormitories, library, computer center, student center. Dormitories wired for high-speed internet access and linked to campus network. Online course registration, helpline, repair service available.

Student life. Freshman orientation: Mandatory. Preregistration for classes offered. Several 1-day preregistration days scheduled throughout summer with full 2-day orientation program prior to start of classes. **Housing:** Coed dorms, single-sex dorms available. $500 fully refundable deposit, deadline 5/14. **Activities:** Dance, drama, international student organizations, literary magazine, musical theater, student government.

Athletics. NAIA. **Intercollegiate:** Baseball M, basketball, soccer, softball W. **Team name:** Falcons.

Student services. Adult student services, alcohol/substance abuse counseling, career counseling, student employment services, financial aid counseling, health services, personal counseling, placement for graduates, veterans' counselor.

Contact. E-mail: admissions@fisher.edu
Phone: (617) 236-8818
Robert Melaragni, Dean of Admissions, Fisher College, Office of Admissions, Boston, MA 02116

Fitchburg State University
Fitchburg, Massachusetts
www.fitchburgstate.edu
CB member
CB code: 3518

- Public 4-year liberal arts and teachers college
- Residential campus in small city
- 4,048 degree-seeking undergraduates: 15% part-time, 54% women
- 884 degree-seeking graduate students
- 75% of applicants admitted
- SAT or ACT (ACT writing optional), application essay required
- 53% graduate within 6 years

General. Founded in 1894. Regionally accredited. **Degrees:** 759 bachelor's awarded; master's offered. **ROTC:** Army. **Location:** 50 miles from Boston, 25 miles from Worcester. **Calendar:** Semester, limited summer session. **Full-time faculty:** 203 total; 96% have terminal degrees, 12% minority, 52% women. **Part-time faculty:** 98 total; 28% have terminal degrees, 5% minority, 51% women. **Class size:** 42% < 20, 57% 20-39, less than 1% 40-49, 1% 50-99. **Special facilities:** 120-acre conservation area, teacher education laboratory school.

Freshman class profile. 3,998 applied, 2,989 admitted, 789 enrolled.

Mid 50% test scores		GPA 2.0-2.99:	38%
SAT critical reading:	440-540	End year in good standing:	84%
SAT math:	450-550	Return as sophomores:	75%
SAT writing:	420-530	Out-of-state:	9%
ACT composite:	19-23	Live on campus:	64%
GPA 3.75 or higher:	14%	Fraternities:	2%
GPA 3.50-3.74:	11%	Sororities:	3%
GPA 3.0-3.49:	37%		

Basis for selection. Secondary school record, test scores, essay important. Recommendations considered. Interview recommended for nursing, undeclared major, computer science, business administration, communications/media majors. **Learning Disabled:** Students with professionally diagnosed learning disabilities exempt from standardized test requirements.

High school preparation. 16 units required. Required units include English 4, mathematics 3, social studies 1, history 1, science 3 (laboratory 2), foreign language 2 and academic electives 2. Additional units of math and science preferred for nursing, computer science, and business applicants.

2015-2016 Annual costs. Tuition/fees: $9,935; $16,015 out-of-state. Room/board: $9,210. Books/supplies: $800. Personal expenses: $1,500.

2014-2015 Financial aid. Need-based: 707 full-time freshmen applied for aid; 510 deemed to have need; 494 received aid. Average need met was 76%. Average scholarship/grant was $6,068; average loan $3,239. 54% of total undergraduate aid awarded as scholarships/grants, 46% as loans/jobs. **Non-need-based:** Awarded to 853 full-time undergraduates, including 280 freshmen. Scholarships awarded for academics, alumni affiliation, leadership, ROTC, state residency.

Application procedures. Admission: Priority date 1/1; no deadline. $40 fee, may be waived for applicants with need. Admission notification on a rolling basis beginning on or about 12/1. Must reply by May 1 or within 2 week(s) if notified thereafter. **Financial aid:** Priority date 3/1; no closing date. FAFSA required. Applicants notified on a rolling basis starting 3/15; must reply within 2 week(s) of notification.

Academics. Many major programs include internship, practicum, or clinical experience. All degree programs require completion of 48 credits in liberal arts and sciences. **Special study options:** Cross-registration, distance learning, double major, dual enrollment of high school students, honors, independent study, internships, liberal arts/career combination, student-designed major, study abroad, teacher certification program. **Credit/placement by examination:** AP, CLEP, institutional tests. 60 credit hours maximum toward bachelor's degree. **Support services:** Learning center, pre-admission summer program, reduced course load, remedial instruction, study skills assistance, tutoring, writing center.

Honors college/program. Admissions based on high school preparation, test scores, and leadership potential. Students complete integrated sequence of courses over 4-year period and are expected to demonstrate leadership through extracurricular activities, volunteer positions, and service learning placements. 3.3 GPA required to continue in the program.

Majors. Architecture: Technology. **Biology:** General, biomedical sciences, biotechnology, environmental, exercise physiology, neurobiology/behavior. **Business:** Accounting, business admin, finance, international, management science, marketing. **Communications:** Communications/speech/rhetoric, digital media. **Computer sciences:** General, computer science. **Education:** General, biology, early childhood, elementary, English, geography, history, mathematics, middle, secondary, special ed, technology/industrial arts, trade/industrial. **English:** English lit, technical writing. **Health services:** Nursing (RN). **History:** General. **Liberal arts:** Arts/sciences. **Math:** General, applied. **Parks/recreation:** Exercise sciences, sports admin. **Physical sciences:** Chemistry. **Protective services:** Criminal justice. **Psychology:** General, cognitive, developmental, industrial. **Social sciences:** Economics, geography, international economics, international relations, political science, sociology, U.S. government. **Visual/performing arts:** Cinematography, dramatic, graphic design, photography, theater design.

Most popular majors. Biology 9%, business/marketing 13%, education 7%, health sciences 11%, interdisciplinary studies 10%, psychology 6%, security/protective services 6%, visual/performing arts 15%.

Technology on campus. PC or laptop required. 150 workstations in dormitories, library, computer center, student center. Dormitories wired for high-speed internet access and linked to campus network. Commuter students can connect to campus network. Online course registration, online library, helpline, repair service, wireless network available.

Student life. Freshman orientation: Mandatory. Preregistration for classes offered. Testing, academic advising, registration for classes are key components of the program. **Housing:** Coed dorms, special housing for disabled, apartments, wellness housing available. $150 nonrefundable deposit, deadline 5/1. Quiet halls available. **Activities:** Bands, choral groups, dance, drama, film society, literary magazine, Model UN, radio station, student government, student newspaper, Student government association, Christian Fellowship, Black Student Union, Habitat for Humanity, Latin American student organization, MASSPIRG, Asian cultural society, First Responders, Rotoracy club.

Athletics. NCAA. **Intercollegiate:** Baseball M, basketball, cross-country, field hockey W, football (tackle) M, ice hockey M, lacrosse W, soccer, softball W, track and field. **Intramural:** Basketball, bowling, football (non-tackle), handball, racquetball, soccer, softball, swimming, table tennis, ultimate frisbee, volleyball, water polo. **Team name:** Falcons.

Student services. Alcohol/substance abuse counseling, career counseling, services for economically disadvantaged, student employment services, financial aid counseling, health services, minority student services, personal counseling. **Physically disabled:** Services for visually, speech, hearing impaired.

Contact. E-mail: admissions@fitchburgstate.edu
Phone: (978) 665-3144 Toll-free number: (800) 705-9692
Fax: (978) 665-4540
Sean Ganas, Director of Admissions, Fitchburg State University, 160 Pearl Street, Fitchburg, MA 01420-2697

Framingham State University

Framingham, Massachusetts   CB member
www.framingham.edu   CB code: 3519

- Public 4-year university
- Residential campus in small city
- 4,288 degree-seeking undergraduates: 11% part-time, 64% women, 8% African American, 3% Asian American, 11% Hispanic/Latino, 4% Multiracial, non-Hispanic
- 987 degree-seeking graduate students
- 71% of applicants admitted
- SAT or ACT (ACT writing optional) required
- 56% graduate within 6 years; 14% enter graduate study

General. Founded in 1839. Regionally accredited. **Degrees:** 908 bachelor's awarded; master's offered. **Location:** 20 miles from Boston. **Calendar:** Semester, extensive summer session. **Full-time faculty:** 194 total; 16% minority, 57% women. **Part-time faculty:** 143 total; 13% minority, 59% women. **Class size:** 41% < 20, 57% 20-39, 1% 40-49, less than 1% 50-99. **Special facilities:** Center for global education, center for social research, economic research center, challenger learning center, NASA educator resource center, STEM education network, child development laboratory, education curriculum library, entrepreneur innovation center, institute for food and nutrition, children's hospital food study, greenhouse, planetarium.

Freshman class profile. 4,803 applied, 3,401 admitted, 855 enrolled.

Mid 50% test scores			
SAT critical reading:	430-540	GPA 3.50-3.74:	11%
SAT math:	440-540	GPA 3.0-3.49:	31%
SAT writing:	430-530	GPA 2.0-2.99:	47%
ACT composite:	19-24	Return as sophomores:	74%
GPA 3.75 or higher:	11%	Out-of-state:	4%
		Live on campus:	83%

Basis for selection. Strength of high school curriculum, weighted GPA, class rank, test scores most important. Some attention given to organized and volunteer activities, special talents, and recommendations (when requested). Consideration given to students whose educational opportunities have been limited due to economic disadvantage. Admission standards policy of Massachusetts Department of Higher Education requires 17 college-preparatory courses with 3.0 recalculated GPA. Students with lower GPA may qualify based on sliding scale combining SAT/ACT scores with GPA. Portfolio required of studio art majors. Essay may be required for selected applicants. Interviews welcomed but not required. **Home schooled:** Transcript of courses and grades required. Students may be required to submit results of additional nationally tests, such as SAT Subject Tests. **Learning Disabled:** Students with diagnosed learning disability must submit psychoeducational testing current within last 3 years.

High school preparation. College-preparatory program required. 17 units required; 21 recommended. Required and recommended units include English 4, mathematics 4, social studies 1-2, history 1-2, science 3-4 (laboratory 2-3), foreign language 2-4 and academic electives 2. Math must include algebra I, algebra II, geometry, and an additional math course senior year. Additional unit of math strongly recommended for computer science, math, pre-engineering, and science majors. Additional units of biology, chemistry, physics recommended for science majors. Foreign language must be 2 units of same language. All units must be college-preparatory level.

2015-2016 Annual costs. Tuition/fees: $8,700; $14,780 out-of-state. Room/board: $10,834. Books/supplies: $1,000. Personal expenses: $1,640.

2014-2015 Financial aid. Need-based: 754 full-time freshmen applied for aid; 576 deemed to have need; 576 received aid. Average need met was 60%. Average scholarship/grant was $5,200; average loan $4,550. 37% of total undergraduate aid awarded as scholarships/grants, 63% as loans/jobs. **Non-need-based:** Awarded to 572 full-time undergraduates, including 221 freshmen. Scholarships awarded for academics.

Application procedures. Admission: Priority date 2/15; no deadline. $50 fee, may be waived for applicants with need. Admission notification on a rolling basis beginning on or about 2/15. Must reply by May 1 or within 2 week(s) if notified thereafter. Students should contact admissions office after priority date of 2/15 to determine if applications are still being accepted. Some majors and on-campus housing may be filled by priority date. Application fee waiver available to students who submit College Board fee waiver. **Financial aid:** Priority date 3/1; no closing date. FAFSA required. Applicants notified on a rolling basis starting 3/15; must reply by 5/1 or within 2 week(s) of notification.

Academics. E-tutoring available on-line. **Special study options:** Cooperative education, cross-registration, distance learning, double major, ESL, honors, independent study, internships, liberal arts/career combination, student-designed major, study abroad, teacher certification program, Washington semester. Cooperative education program for Computer Science majors. **Credit/placement by examination:** AP, CLEP, IB, SAT, institutional tests. 64 credit hours maximum toward bachelor's degree. **Support services:** Learning center, reduced course load, remedial instruction, study skills assistance, tutoring, writing center. Supplemental instruction.

Majors. Biology: General. **Business:** General, accounting, finance, knowledge management, marketing. **Computer sciences:** General. **Conservation:** Environmental science. **Education:** Art, early childhood, elementary. **Engineering:** General. **English:** English lit. **Foreign languages:** Sign language interpretation, Spanish. **Health services:** Nursing (RN). **History:** General. **Liberal arts:** Arts/sciences. **Math:** General. **Physical sciences:** Chemistry, geology. **Psychology:** General. **Social sciences:** Criminology, economics, geography, political science, sociology. **Visual/performing arts:** Art. **Work/family studies:** Clothing/textiles, food/nutrition.

Most popular majors. Business/marketing 16%, communication technologies 8%, family/consumer sciences 12%, liberal arts 6%, psychology 10%, social sciences 19%.

Technology on campus. PC or laptop required. 216 workstations in library, computer center, student center. Dormitories wired for high-speed internet access and linked to campus network. Online course registration, online library, helpline, repair service, wireless network available.

Student life. Freshman orientation: Mandatory. Preregistration for classes offered. 7 one-day sessions in June. **Policies:** All clubs are required to re-register with the university on an annual basis. **Housing:** Coed dorms, single-sex dorms, special housing for disabled, gender-neutral housing, themed housing available. $150 nonrefundable deposit, deadline 5/1. **Activities:** Concert band, campus ministries, choral groups, dance, drama, film society, literary magazine, musical theater, radio station, student government, student newspaper, Black student union, Christian fellowship, Pride Alliance, wildlife club, Alternate Spring Break, community service club, Student Leaders in Diversity.

Athletics. NCAA. **Intercollegiate:** Baseball M, basketball, cross-country, field hockey W, football (tackle) M, ice hockey M, lacrosse W, soccer, softball W, volleyball W. **Intramural:** Basketball, football (non-tackle), golf, soccer, volleyball. **Team name:** Rams.

Student services. Alcohol/substance abuse counseling, chaplain/spiritual director, career counseling, services for economically disadvantaged, student employment services, financial aid counseling, health services, legal services, minority student services, on-campus daycare, personal counseling, placement for graduates, veterans' counselor, women's services. **Physically disabled:** Services for visually, speech, hearing impaired.

Contact. E-mail: admissions@framingham.edu
Phone: (508) 626-4500 Fax: (508) 626-4017
Shayna Eddy, Associate Dean/Director of Undergraduate Admissions, Framingham State University, PO Box 9101, Framingham, MA 01701-9101

Franklin W. Olin College of Engineering
Needham, Massachusetts   **CB member**
www.olin.edu   **CB code: 2824**

- Private 4-year engineering college
- Residential campus in large town
- 333 degree-seeking undergraduates: 48% women, 16% Asian American, 5% Hispanic/Latino, 7% Multi-racial, non-Hispanic, 8% international
- 11% of applicants admitted
- SAT or ACT with writing, application essay, interview required
- 93% graduate within 6 years; 14% enter graduate study

General. Regionally accredited. **Degrees:** 81 bachelor's awarded. **Location:** 14 miles from Boston. **Calendar:** Semester. **Full-time faculty:** 37 total; 97% have terminal degrees, 22% minority, 46% women. **Part-time faculty:** 18 total; 44% have terminal degrees, 6% minority, 17% women. **Class size:** 56% < 20, 43% 20-39, 1% 50-99.

Freshman class profile. 1,075 applied, 118 admitted, 76 enrolled.

Mid 50% test scores			
		GPA 3.0-3.49:	4%
SAT critical reading:	710-800	**End year in good standing:**	98%
SAT math:	730-800	**Return as sophomores:**	91%
SAT writing:	680-770	**Out-of-state:**	90%
ACT composite:	32-35	**Live on campus:**	100%
GPA 3.75 or higher:	74%	**International:**	8%
GPA 3.50-3.74:	22%		

Basis for selection. Secondary school achievement, course rigor, test scores, personal character most important; creativity and entrepreneurial spirit also very important. Cultural, economic, geographic diversity encouraged. Candidates required to attend 1 of 3 weekends on campus to participate in a design project, individual interviews, and team exercises. Incoming class is selected from this group. Financial support provided if needed. **Home schooled:** Statement describing home school structure and mission, transcript of courses and grades, letter of recommendation (nonparent) required.

High school preparation. College-preparatory program required. Recommended units include English 4, mathematics 4, social studies 2, history 2, science 4 (laboratory 3) and foreign language 2. 1 calculus unit and 1 physics unit required.

2015-2016 Annual costs. Tuition/fees: $48,181. Room/board: $15,600. Books/supplies: $300. Personal expenses: $460. **Additional information:** Required fees include a laptop fee charged to all first year students. Health insurance is also available for those who do not have it for an additional fee.

2015-2016 Financial aid. Need-based: 50 full-time freshmen applied for aid; 36 deemed to have need; 36 received aid. Average need met was 100%. Average scholarship/grant was $42,883; average loan $2,949. 95% of total undergraduate aid awarded as scholarships/grants, 5% as loans/jobs. **Non-need-based:** Awarded to 340 full-time undergraduates, including 76 freshmen. Scholarships awarded for academics, leadership. **Additional information:** Financial aid forms not needed for the Olin Tuition Scholarship, which all students receive. FAFSA is required to apply for need-based aid.

Application procedures. Admission: Closing date 1/1 (postmark date). $80 fee, may be waived for applicants with need. Application must be submitted online. Admission notification by 3/21. Must reply by May 1 or within 2 week(s) if notified thereafter. **Financial aid:** Closing date 2/15. FAFSA required. Applicants notified by 3/21; must reply by 5/1 or within 2 week(s) of notification.

Academics. Special study options: Cross-registration, exchange student, independent study, internships, student-designed major, study abroad. **Credit/placement by examination:** AP, CLEP. **Support services:** Study skills assistance, tutoring, writing center.

Majors. Engineering: General, electrical, mechanical.

Technology on campus. PC or laptop required. Dormitories wired for high-speed internet access and linked to campus network. Commuter students can connect to campus network. Online course registration, online library, helpline, repair service, student web hosting, wireless network available.

Student life. Freshman orientation: Mandatory. Preregistration for classes offered. Held the 3 days before classes begin in late August. **Policies:** All students sign an honor code that addresses personal and academic integrity. **Housing:** Guaranteed on-campus for all undergraduates. Coed dorms, special housing for disabled available. **Activities:** Campus ministries, choral groups, drama, international student organizations, music ensembles, student government, student newspaper, Christian fellowship, volunteerism club, Korean club, martial arts club, Chinese club, Catholic association, art club, environmental club, women engineers, a cappella clubs.

Student services. Alcohol/substance abuse counseling, chaplain/spiritual director, career counseling, student employment services, financial aid counseling, health services, minority student services, personal counseling, placement for graduates, women's services. **Physically disabled:** Services for hearing impaired.

Contact. E-mail: info@olin.edu
Phone: (781) 292-2222 Fax: (781) 292-2210
Emily Roper-Doten, Dean of Admission and Financial Aid, Franklin W. Olin College of Engineering, 1000 Olin Way, Needham, MA 02492

Gordon College
Wenham, Massachusetts   **CB member**
www.gordon.edu   **CB code: 3417**

- Private 4-year liberal arts college affiliated with the nondenominational tradition
- Residential campus in small town
- 1,664 degree-seeking undergraduates: 2% part-time, 62% women, 4% African American, 4% Asian American, 7% Hispanic/Latino, 4% Multi-racial, non-Hispanic, 8% international
- 254 degree-seeking graduate students
- 93% of applicants admitted
- SAT or ACT with writing, application essay, interview required
- 69% graduate within 6 years; 22% enter graduate study

General. Founded in 1889. Regionally accredited. **Degrees:** 382 bachelor's awarded; master's offered. **ROTC:** Army. **Location:** 25 miles from Boston. **Calendar:** Semester, limited summer session. **Full-time faculty:** 101 total; 87% have terminal degrees, 15% minority, 39% women. **Part-time faculty:** 93 total; 4% minority, 66% women. **Class size:** 60% < 20, 33% 20-39, 5% 40-49, 2% 50-99, less than 1% >100. **Special facilities:** Science center, electron microscope, gene sequencing machine, gross anatomy and physiology cadaver lab, indoor rock gym, ropes course, center for balance, mobility and wellness, prayer chapel.

Freshman class profile. 1,832 applied, 1,708 admitted, 441 enrolled.

Mid 50% test scores		GPA 2.0-2.99:	9%
SAT critical reading:	480-620	Rank in top quarter:	61%
SAT math:	470-610	Rank in top tenth:	26%
SAT writing:	460-620	End year in good standing:	89%
ACT composite:	23-29	Return as sophomores:	85%
GPA 3.75 or higher:	43%	Out-of-state:	67%
GPA 3.50-3.74:	20%	Live on campus:	97%
GPA 3.0-3.49:	28%	International:	6%

Basis for selection. High school course selection and grades, class rank, essay of Christian commitment, test scores, references, interview, school and community activities considered. Gordon College participates in the International Bachelorette Diploma Program. TOEFL iBT exam accepted for non-U.S. citizens. Audition required of music majors, portfolio required of visual art majors, additional materials required of Social Work program, personal statement of faith required of all. **Home schooled:** Statement describing home school structure and mission, letter of recommendation (nonparent) required. Information regarding course of study, including description of curriculum and reading list required. **Learning Disabled:** Students with diagnosed learning disability may submit documentation with application, as well as any learning plans used through high school. Some requirements may be substituted with appropriate documentation.

High school preparation. College-preparatory program required. 18 units required; 22 recommended. Required and recommended units include English 4, mathematics 2-3, social studies 2, science 2-3 (laboratory 1), foreign language 2-4 and academic electives 5. Academic profile should include AP, honors, or accelerated courses.

2015-2016 Annual costs. Tuition/fees: $35,386. Room/board: $10,218. Books/supplies: $800. Personal expenses: $1,000.

2015-2016 Financial aid. Need-based: 378 full-time freshmen applied for aid; 314 deemed to have need; 314 received aid. Average need met was 76%. Average scholarship/grant was $22,519; average loan $3,752. 70% of total undergraduate aid awarded as scholarships/grants, 30% as loans/jobs. **Non-need-based:** Awarded to 643 full-time undergraduates, including 166 freshmen. Scholarships awarded for academics, alumni affiliation, art, leadership, minority status, music/drama, ROTC, state residency.

Application procedures. Admission: Priority date 2/1; deadline 8/1 (receipt date). $50 fee, may be waived for applicants with need. Admission notification on a rolling basis beginning on or about 9/15. Must reply by May 1 or within 2 week(s) if notified thereafter. **Financial aid:** Priority date 3/1; no closing date. FAFSA required. Applicants notified on a rolling basis starting 2/15; must reply by 5/1.

Academics. Special study options: Combined bachelor's/graduate degree, cooperative education, cross-registration, double major, exchange student, honors, independent study, internships, liberal arts/career combination, student-designed major, study abroad, teacher certification program, urban semester, Washington semester. Oregon Extension; Outdoor Education Immersion Semester; LaVida Wilderness Expedition; co-op programs. **Credit/placement by examination:** AP, CLEP, IB, institutional tests. 32 credit hours maximum toward bachelor's degree. AP exams allow maximum of 32 credits. **Support services:** Learning center, reduced course load, study skills assistance, tutoring, writing center.

Majors. Biology: General, exercise physiology. **Business:** Accounting, business admin, finance. **Communications:** Communications/speech/rhetoric. **Computer sciences:** Computer science. **Education:** Early childhood, elementary, middle, music, secondary, special ed. **Engineering:** Applied physics. **English:** English lit. **Foreign languages:** General, French, German, linguistics, Spanish. **History:** General. **Human services:** Social work. **Math:** General. **Parks/recreation:** General. **Philosophy/religion:** Christian, philosophy. **Physical sciences:** Chemistry, physics. **Psychology:** General. **Social sciences:** Economics, international relations, political science, sociology. **Theology:** Youth ministry. **Visual/performing arts:** Art, dramatic, music, music performance.

Most popular majors. Biology 10%, business/marketing 12%, communications/journalism 7%, education 9%, English 6%, foreign language 7%, psychology 6%, social sciences 10%, visual/performing arts 7%.

Technology on campus. 100 workstations in dormitories, library, computer center, student center. Dormitories wired for high-speed internet access and linked to campus network. Commuter students can connect to campus network. Online course registration, online library, helpline, repair service, wireless network available.

Student life. Freshman orientation: Mandatory, $100 fee. Preregistration for classes offered. Five-day program held in the days prior to start of semester; includes program for parents during first two days. **Policies:** No alcohol or smoking allowed on campus or at college-sponsored events. Religious observance required. **Housing:** Guaranteed on-campus for all undergraduates. Coed dorms, single-sex dorms, special housing for disabled, apartments, themed housing available. $250 nonrefundable deposit, deadline 5/1. **Activities:** Bands, campus ministries, choral groups, dance, drama, film society, international student organizations, literary magazine, music ensembles, Model UN, musical theater, radio station, student government, student newspaper, symphony orchestra, Office of Community Engagement, Advocates for Cultural Diversity, Advocates for Sustainable Futures, Social Justice Initiatives, fellowship group for children of missionaries, ministry to deaf persons, outreach service, short-term mission trips, Amnesty International, ALANA.

Athletics. NCAA. **Intercollegiate:** Baseball M, basketball, cross-country, field hockey W, lacrosse, soccer, softball W, swimming, tennis, track and field, volleyball W. **Intramural:** Badminton, basketball, football (non-tackle), racquetball, sand volleyball, soccer, water polo. **Team name:** Fighting Scots.

Student services. Alcohol/substance abuse counseling, chaplain/spiritual director, career counseling, student employment services, financial aid counseling, health services, minority student services, personal counseling, placement for graduates. **Physically disabled:** Services for visually, speech, hearing impaired.

Contact. E-mail: admissions@gordon.edu
Phone: (978) 867-4218 Toll-free number: (866) 464-6736
Fax: (978) 867-4682
Amy France, Director of Admissions, Gordon College, 255 Grapevine Road, Wenham, MA 01984-1899

Hampshire College
Amherst, Massachusetts
www.hampshire.edu

CB member
CB code: 3447

▶ Private 4-year liberal arts college
▶ Residential campus in large town
▶ 1,396 degree-seeking undergraduates: 61% women
▶ 70% of applicants admitted
▶ Application essay required

General. Founded in 1965. Regionally accredited. **Degrees:** 291 bachelor's awarded. **ROTC:** Army. **Location:** 90 miles from Boston, 20 miles from Springfield. **Calendar:** 4-1-4. **Full-time faculty:** 119 total; 26% minority, 51% women. **Part-time faculty:** 46 total; 20% minority, 67% women. **Class size:** 68% < 20, 32% 20-39. **Special facilities:** Bioshelter (integrated greenhouse/aquaculture facility), farm center, electronic music production studio, extensive film and photography facilities, fabrication center, national Yiddish book center, picturebook art museum, creativity center.

Freshman class profile. 2,071 applied, 1,450 admitted, 374 enrolled.

GPA 3.75 or higher:	29%	Rank in top quarter:	52%
GPA 3.50-3.74:	22%	Rank in top tenth:	19%
GPA 3.0-3.49:	32%	Out-of-state:	81%
GPA 2.0-2.99:	17%	Live on campus:	97%

Basis for selection. Criteria include desire to do rigorous independent work, school record, academic writing samples, recommendations, school and community activities. Test blind admission policy; SAT and ACT scores are not considered as part of admissions and financial aid decisions. Interview recommended. **Home schooled:** Common Application's Home School Supplement required.

High school preparation. College-preparatory program required. 16 units required; 20 recommended. Required and recommended units include English 4, mathematics 3-4, history 3-4, science 3-4 (laboratory 2) and foreign language 3-4.

2016-2017 Annual costs. Tuition/fees (projected): $50,550. Room/board: $13,274. Books/supplies: $850. Personal expenses: $900.

2015-2016 Financial aid. Need-based: 81% of total undergraduate aid awarded as scholarships/grants, 19% as loans/jobs. **Non-need-based:** Scholarships awarded for academics, art, leadership, music/drama.

Application procedures. Admission: Priority date 11/15; deadline 1/15 (receipt date). No application fee. Admission notification by 4/1. Must reply by 5/1. **Financial aid:** Closing date 2/1. FAFSA, CSS PROFILE required. Applicants notified by 4/1; must reply by 5/1 or within 2 week(s) of notification.

Academics. All students pursue individualized program of study. Requirements for graduation not based on credit, but on completion of division one courses in all 5 schools, an independent concentration consisting of combination of courses, independent project work, year-long thesis. **Special study options:** Cross-registration, exchange student, independent study, internships, liberal arts/career combination, student-designed major, study abroad, teacher certification program. Member 5-college consortium; may take classes at other member institutions. **Credit/placement by examination:** AP, CLEP. **Support services:** Study skills assistance, writing center.

Majors. Architecture: Architecture. **Area/ethnic studies:** General, African, African-American, American, East Asian, European, gay/lesbian, Latin American, Native American, Near/Middle Eastern, South Asian, women's. **Biology:** General, animal behavior, neuroscience. **Business:** Entrepreneurial studies. **Communications:** Communications/speech/rhetoric. **Computer sciences:** Computer graphics, computer science. **Conservation:** Environmental studies. **Education:** General. **English:** Creative writing, English lit, general lit. **Foreign languages:** Linguistics. **Health services:** Public health ed. **History:** General. **Human services:** Public policy. **Math:** General. **Philosophy/religion:** Philosophy, religion. **Physical sciences:** Astronomy, chemistry, geology, physics. **Psychology:** General. **Social sciences:** Anthropology, economics, international economics, international relations, political science, sociology, urban studies. **Visual/performing arts:** Art history/conservation, dance, design, dramatic, film/cinema/video, music, studio arts.

Most popular majors. Area/ethnic studies 8%, biology 9%, English 12%, social sciences 9%, visual/performing arts 34%.

Technology on campus. 215 workstations in library, computer center, student center. Dormitories wired for high-speed internet access and linked to campus network. Commuter students can connect to campus network. Online course registration, online library, helpline, repair service, student web hosting, wireless network available.

Student life. Freshman orientation: Mandatory, $200 fee. Preregistration for classes offered. Program held during week immediately before matriculation. **Housing:** Guaranteed on-campus for freshmen. Coed dorms, single-sex dorms, special housing for disabled, apartments, cooperative housing, themed housing, wellness housing available. $400 nonrefundable deposit, deadline 5/1. **Activities:** Jazz band, choral groups, dance, drama, film society, international student organizations, literary magazine, music ensembles, musical theater, opera, radio station, student government, student newspaper, Re-Radicalization of Hampshire College, Students for Justice in Palestine, Pan Asian student association, RAICES, Christian Fellowship, College Quakers, College Democrats, SISTERS, Union of Activists, Building Awareness Across Bars.

Athletics. USCAA. **Intercollegiate:** Basketball, cross-country, fencing, soccer. **Intramural:** Basketball.

Student services. Alcohol/substance abuse counseling, chaplain/spiritual director, career counseling, financial aid counseling, health services, minority student services, on-campus daycare, personal counseling, women's services. **Physically disabled:** Services for visually, speech, hearing impaired.

Contact. E-mail: admissions@hampshire.edu
Phone: (413) 559-5471 Toll-free number: (877) 937-4267
Fax: (413) 559-5631
Meredith Twombly, Dean of Admissions & Financial Aid, Hampshire College, 893 West Street, Amherst, MA 01002-9988

Harvard College
Cambridge, Massachusetts   CB member
www.college.harvard.edu   CB code: 3434

- Private 4-year university and liberal arts college
- Residential campus in small city
- 6,638 degree-seeking undergraduates: 47% women, 7% African American, 20% Asian American, 10% Hispanic/Latino, 6% Multi-racial, non-Hispanic, 12% international
- 4,032 degree-seeking graduate students
- 6% of applicants admitted
- SAT or ACT with writing, SAT Subject Tests, application essay, interview required
- 98% graduate within 6 years

General. Founded in 1636. Regionally accredited. Harvard College is the undergraduate program within Harvard University, part of the faculty of arts and sciences, and offers programs in liberal arts. **Degrees:** 1,610 bachelor's awarded; master's, doctoral offered. **ROTC:** Army, Naval, Air Force. **Location:** 3 miles from Boston. **Calendar:** Semester, extensive summer session. **Full-time faculty:** 965 total; 85% have terminal degrees, 20% minority, 34% women. **Part-time faculty:** 187 total; 75% have terminal degrees, 14% minority, 43% women. **Class size:** 73% < 20, 12% 20-39, 3% 40-49, 7% 50-99, 4% >100. **Special facilities:** Museum of Scandinavian and Germanic art, experimental forest in New York state, center for study of Italian Renaissance in Florence, center for Byzantine studies (Washington, DC), Smithsonian astrophysical observatory.

Freshman class profile. 37,307 applied, 2,080 admitted, 1,660 enrolled.

Mid 50% test scores			
SAT critical reading:	700-800	GPA 3.0-3.49:	3%
SAT math:	700-800	Rank in top quarter:	99%
SAT writing:	710-790	Rank in top tenth:	95%
ACT composite:	32-35	Return as sophomores:	97%
GPA 3.75 or higher:	90%	Out-of-state:	83%
GPA 3.50-3.74:	7%	Live on campus:	100%
		International:	13%

Basis for selection. Secondary school record most important; character, creative ability in some discipline or activity, leadership, liveliness of mind, demonstrated stamina and ability to carry out demanding college program, and strong sense of social responsibility important. Normally two SAT Subject Tests required, but students may apply without them if the cost of the tests represents a financial hardship or if they prefer to have their application considered without them. Application will be evaluated on the basis of all submitted information. Interview with alumnus/alumna required of all applicants if possible; documentation of special talents encouraged.

High school preparation. College-preparatory program recommended. Recommended units include English 4, mathematics 4, social studies 3, history 2, science 4 and foreign language 4. Applicants encouraged to take rigorous courses and make the most of any opportunities for enrichment.

2015-2016 Annual costs. Tuition/fees: $45,278. Room/board: $15,381. Books/supplies: $1,000. Personal expenses: $2,741.

2014-2015 Financial aid. All financial aid based on need. 1,030 full-time freshmen applied for aid; 868 deemed to have need; 868 received aid. Average need met was 100%. Average scholarship/grant was $48,671; average loan $3,544. 94% of total undergraduate aid awarded as scholarships/grants, 6% as loans/jobs.

Application procedures. Admission: Closing date 1/1 (postmark date). $75 fee, may be waived for applicants with need. Admission notification by 4/1. Must reply by 5/1. **Financial aid:** Closing date 2/1. FAFSA, CSS PROFILE required. Applicants notified by 4/1; must reply by 5/1 or within 2 week(s) of notification.

Academics. Require 12 one-term courses for completion of major and 32 one-term courses for graduation. **Special study options:** Accelerated study, cross-registration, double major, exchange student, honors, independent study, student-designed major, study abroad, teacher certification program. **Credit/placement by examination:** AP, CLEP, IB, institutional tests. SAT Subject Test policy varies depending on subject matter and score. Sophomore standing available on basis of 4 AP exams with qualifying scores, or on basis of IB scores. Students with fewer than 4 AP qualifying scores eligible for placement in more challenging courses. **Support services:** Learning center, study skills assistance, tutoring, writing center.

Majors. Area/ethnic studies: African-American, East Asian, Near/Middle Eastern, women's. **Biology:** General, biochemistry, evolutionary, neurobiology/anatomy. **Computer sciences:** Computer science. **Conservation:** Environmental studies. **Engineering:** Engineering science. **English:** English lit. **Foreign languages:** Ancient Greek, classics, comparative lit, German, Latin, linguistics, Romance, Sanskrit, Slavic. **History:** General, science/technology. **Liberal arts:** Arts/sciences. **Math:** General, applied, statistics. **Philosophy/religion:** Philosophy, religion. **Physical sciences:** Chemistry, geology, molecular physics, physics. **Psychology:** General. **Social sciences:** General, anthropology, economics, political science, sociology. **Visual/performing arts:** General, art history/conservation, music.

Most popular majors. Biology 14%, computer/information sciences 6%, history 9%, mathematics 9%, physical sciences 7%, psychology 6%, social sciences 29%.

Technology on campus. 605 workstations in dormitories, library, computer center. Dormitories wired for high-speed internet access and linked to campus network. Commuter students can connect to campus network. Online course registration, online library, helpline, repair service, student web hosting, wireless network available.

Student life. Freshman orientation: Mandatory. Preregistration for classes offered. Week-long program in early September. **Policies:** All freshmen live together. Other students and some faculty members reside in 13 on-campus houses, self-contained communities offering seminars and tutorials. **Housing:** Guaranteed on-campus for all undergraduates. Coed dorms, special housing for disabled, apartments, cooperative housing available. **Activities:** Bands, campus ministries, choral groups, dance, drama, film society, international student organizations, literary magazine, music ensembles, Model UN, musical theater, opera, radio station, student government, student newspaper, symphony orchestra, TV station, over 400 official clubs available.

Athletics. NCAA. **Intercollegiate:** Baseball M, basketball, cross-country, diving, fencing, field hockey W, football (tackle) M, golf, ice hockey, lacrosse, rowing (crew), rugby W, sailing, skiing, soccer, softball W, squash, swimming, tennis, track and field, volleyball, water polo, wrestling M. **Intramural:** Badminton, basketball, cross-country, fencing, football (non-tackle), ice hockey, rowing (crew), soccer, squash, swimming, table tennis, tennis, ultimate frisbee, volleyball. **Team name:** Crimson.

Student services. Alcohol/substance abuse counseling, chaplain/spiritual director, career counseling, services for economically disadvantaged, student employment services, financial aid counseling, health services, on-campus daycare, personal counseling, placement for graduates, women's services. **Physically disabled:** Services for visually, speech, hearing impaired.

Contact. E-mail: college@fas.harvard.edu
Phone: (617) 495-1551 Fax: (617) 495-8821
William Fitzsimmons, Dean of Admissions, Harvard College, 86 Brattle Street, Cambridge, MA 02138

Hellenic College/Holy Cross
Brookline, Massachusetts   **CB member**
www.hchc.edu   **CB code: 3449**

- Private 4-year liberal arts and seminary college affiliated with the Eastern Orthodox Church
- Residential campus in large town
- 91 degree-seeking undergraduates
- SAT or ACT (ACT writing optional), application essay, interview required

General. Founded in 1937. Regionally accredited. **Degrees:** 20 bachelor's awarded; master's offered. **Location:** 5 miles from downtown Boston. **Calendar:** Semester, limited summer session. **Full-time faculty:** 13 total; 85% have terminal degrees, 54% women. **Part-time faculty:** 23 total; 35% have terminal degrees, 35% women. **Class size:** 49% < 20, 51% 20-39.

Freshman class profile.

GPA 3.75 or higher:	16%	GPA 2.0-2.99:	20%
GPA 3.50-3.74:	24%	Out-of-state:	90%
GPA 3.0-3.49:	40%	Live on campus:	95%

Basis for selection. High school achievement, GPA, 2 recommendations from instructors, test scores very important, school and community activities also important. For religious studies majors, 2 letters from clergy important if members of Orthodox Christian Church. **Home schooled:** Transcript of courses and grades, state high school equivalency certificate required.

High school preparation. 15 units required. Required units include English 4, mathematics 2, social studies 2, history 2, science 3 and foreign language 2.

2015-2016 Annual costs. Tuition/fees: $22,490. Room/board: $16,192. Books/supplies: $600. Personal expenses: $1,000. **Additional information:** Parking 425 Health Insurance 2007.

Financial aid. All financial aid based on need.

Application procedures. Admission: Priority date 5/1; deadline 8/1 (receipt date). $50 fee, may be waived for applicants with need. Admission notification on a rolling basis. Students who apply by December 1 eligible to have application fee waived and receive priority consideration for scholarships; early applications encouraged. **Financial aid:** Closing date 4/1. FAFSA, institutional form required. Applicants notified by 4/1; must reply within 2 week(s) of notification.

Academics. Special study options: Cross-registration, exchange student, honors, independent study, internships, liberal arts/career combination, study abroad. **Credit/placement by examination:** AP, CLEP, IB, institutional tests. Credit granted varies by degree program. **Support services:** Reduced course load, remedial instruction, tutoring, writing center.

Majors. Education: Elementary. **Liberal arts:** Arts/sciences. **Psychology:** General. **Theology:** Theology.

Technology on campus. Dormitories linked to campus network. Online library, helpline, repair service, wireless network available.

Student life. Freshman orientation: Mandatory. Preregistration for classes offered. **Policies:** Religious observance required for some students. **Housing:** Guaranteed on-campus for freshmen. Single-sex dorms, apartments available. $400 nonrefundable deposit. **Activities:** Campus ministries, choral groups, dance, music ensembles, student government, several Orthodox groups, prison ministry, missions group.

Athletics. Intramural: Basketball, soccer M, table tennis, tennis, volleyball.

Student services. Chaplain/spiritual director, career counseling, student employment services, financial aid counseling, personal counseling, placement for graduates.

Contact. E-mail: admissions@hchc.edu
Phone: (617) 850-1260 Toll-free number: (866) 424-2338
Fax: (617) 850-1460
Gregory Floor, Director of Admissions, Hellenic College/Holy Cross, 50 Goddard Avenue, Brookline, MA 02445

Lasell College
Newton, Massachusetts   **CB member**
www.lasell.edu   **CB code: 3481**

- Private 4-year business and liberal arts college
- Residential campus in small city
- 1,810 degree-seeking undergraduates: 1% part-time, 66% women, 5% African American, 2% Asian American, 8% Hispanic/Latino, 3% Multiracial, non-Hispanic, 6% international
- 384 degree-seeking graduate students
- 78% of applicants admitted
- SAT or ACT (ACT writing optional), application essay required
- 52% graduate within 6 years; 9% enter graduate study

General. Founded in 1851. Regionally accredited. **Degrees:** 295 bachelor's awarded; master's offered. **Location:** 8 miles from Boston. **Calendar:** Semester, limited summer session. **Full-time faculty:** 87 total; 74% have terminal degrees, 23% minority, 63% women. **Part-time faculty:** 176 total; 30% have terminal degrees, 7% minority, 58% women. **Class size:** 66% < 20, 34% 20-39. **Special facilities:** Academic achievement center, center for community-based learning, center for teaching and learning, child study centers, institute for ethics, diversity and inclusion, center for research on aging and intergenerational studies, technology for learning center, cultural center, small business institute.

Freshman class profile. 3,171 applied, 2,478 admitted, 490 enrolled.

Mid 50% test scores			
		GPA 3.0-3.49:	27%
SAT critical reading:	440-530	GPA 2.0-2.99:	48%
SAT math:	430-530	Return as sophomores:	75%
SAT writing:	430-530	Out-of-state:	47%
ACT composite:	18-23	Live on campus:	87%
GPA 3.75 or higher:	10%	International:	5%
GPA 3.50-3.74:	12%		

Basis for selection. GPA, curriculum, class rank, interview, recommendations, extracurricular activities, personal essay, and standardized test scores considered. Interview recommended and campus visit is strongly recommended. **Home schooled:** Transcript of courses and grades, letter of recommendation (nonparent) required.

High school preparation. College-preparatory program required. 11 units required; 17 recommended. Required and recommended units include English 4, mathematics 3-4, social studies 1-2, history 1-2, science 2-3 (laboratory 2-3) and foreign language 2.

2016-2017 Annual costs. Tuition/fees: $33,600. Room/board: $13,900. Books/supplies: $1,000. Personal expenses: $2,000.

2014-2015 Financial aid. Need-based: 450 full-time freshmen applied for aid; 401 deemed to have need; 400 received aid. Average need met was 73%. Average scholarship/grant was $22,400; average loan $2,500. 73% of total undergraduate aid awarded as scholarships/grants, 27% as loans/jobs. **Non-need-based:** Awarded to 402 full-time undergraduates, including 102 freshmen. Scholarships awarded for academics, alumni affiliation, leadership.

Application procedures. Admission: Priority date 11/15; no deadline. $40 fee, may be waived for applicants with need, free for online applicants. Admission notification on a rolling basis beginning on or about 12/15. Length of deferment after admission is limited to 1 year. **Financial aid:** Priority date 2/15; no closing date. FAFSA required. Applicants notified on a rolling basis starting 2/15; must reply by 5/1 or within 2 week(s) of notification.

Academics. Special study options: Accelerated study, combined bachelor's/graduate degree, cross-registration, distance learning, double major, ESL, exchange student, honors, independent study, internships, liberal arts/ career combination, student-designed major, study abroad, teacher certification program, Washington semester. **Credit/placement by examination:** AP, CLEP, IB, SAT, ACT, institutional tests. **Support services:** Learning center, reduced course load, remedial instruction, study skills assistance, tutoring.

Honors college/program. Honors Program admission is determined at the time of College admission. Approximately 12% of admits are honors.

Majors. Business: Accounting, accounting/business management, accounting/finance, apparel, business admin, entrepreneurial studies, event planning, fashion, finance, hospitality admin, international, management science, marketing. **Communications:** Advertising, digital media, journalism, media studies, public relations, radio/TV, sports. **Conservation:** Environmental studies. **Education:** Early childhood, elementary, English, history, mathematics, secondary. **English:** English lit. **Health services:** Athletic training. **History:** General. **Liberal arts:** Humanities. **Math:** Applied. **Parks/recreation:** Exercise sciences, sports admin. **Protective services:** Law enforcement admin. **Psychology:** General. **Social sciences:** General, sociology. **Visual/performing arts:** Fashion design, graphic design, studio arts management. **Work/ family studies:** Apparel marketing, clothing/textiles, fashion consultant, merchandising.

Most popular majors. Business/marketing 32%, communications/journalism 20%, parks/recreation 13%, visual/performing arts 8%.

Technology on campus. 200 workstations in dormitories, library, computer center, student center. Dormitories wired for high-speed internet access and linked to campus network. Commuter students can connect to campus network. Online course registration, online library, helpline, wireless network available.

Student life. Freshman orientation: Mandatory, $60 fee. Preregistration for classes offered. Two-day sessions held in June prior to fall enrollment; additional three-day program held before classes begin. **Policies:** Freshmen not permitted cars on campus. **Housing:** Guaranteed on-campus for all undergraduates. Coed dorms, single-sex dorms, gender-neutral housing, themed housing, wellness housing available. $200 nonrefundable deposit, deadline 5/1. **Activities:** Jazz band, campus ministries, choral groups, dance, drama, international student organizations, literary magazine, music ensembles, musical theater, radio station, student government, student newspaper, Ninos de Veracruz, Multicultural Student Union, Students Advocating for Equality, Fashion and Service Society, Hope for Humanity, Environmental Action Task Force, mentoring club, Nica Sister City club, Habitat for Humanity, Newman Society.

Athletics. NCAA. **Intercollegiate:** Baseball M, basketball, cross-country, field hockey W, lacrosse, soccer, softball W, track and field, volleyball. **Intramural:** Football (non-tackle). **Team name:** Lasers.

Student services. Alcohol/substance abuse counseling, chaplain/spiritual director, career counseling, student employment services, financial aid counseling, health services, personal counseling, placement for graduates. **Physically disabled:** Services for visually, speech, hearing impaired.

Contact. E-mail: info@lasell.edu
Phone: (617) 243-2225 Toll-free number: (888) 527-3554
Fax: (617) 243-2380
James Tweed, Assistant Vice President for Enrollment Management,
Lasell College, 1844 Commonwealth Avenue, Newton, MA 02466-2709

Lesley University
Cambridge, Massachusetts
www.lesley.edu

CB member
CB code: 3483

- Private 4-year liberal arts and teachers college
- Residential campus in very large city
- 1,418 degree-seeking undergraduates
- SAT or ACT with writing, application essay required

General. Founded in 1909. Regionally accredited. Lesley University includes 2 undergraduate colleges, Lesley College and The Art Institute of Boston. Main campus in Cambridge. **Degrees:** 453 bachelor's awarded; master's, doctoral offered. **Calendar:** Semester, limited summer session. **Full-time faculty:** 84 total; 92% have terminal degrees, 11% minority, 57%

women. **Part-time faculty:** 165 total; 28% have terminal degrees, 57% women. **Class size:** 78% < 20, 22% 20-39. **Special facilities:** Teaching resources center, media production facility, fine arts studios.

Freshman class profile.

GPA 3.75 or higher:	9%	Rank in top quarter:	43%
GPA 3.50-3.74:	16%	Rank in top tenth:	11%
GPA 3.0-3.49:	39%	Out-of-state:	42%
GPA 2.0-2.99:	35%	Live on campus:	86%

Basis for selection. Primary focus given to academic record, both grades and challenging courses. Test scores, recommendations, interview, community service, leadership experience also considered.

High school preparation. College-preparatory program required. 16 units required; 20 recommended. Required and recommended units include English 4, mathematics 3-4, social studies 1-2, history 1-2, science 3-4 (laboratory 2), foreign language 2 and academic electives 4. 2 units visual/performing arts recommended for some programs in art or expressive therapies.

2015-2016 Annual costs. Tuition/fees: $25,200. Room/board: $14,830. Books/supplies: $700. Personal expenses: $1,580.

2015-2016 Financial aid. Need-based: Average need met was 80%. Average scholarship/grant was $8,614; average loan $3,805. 56% of total undergraduate aid awarded as scholarships/grants, 44% as loans/jobs. **Non-need-based:** Scholarships awarded for academics, art, leadership, minority status, state residency.

Application procedures. Admission: Priority date 2/15; no deadline. No application fee. Admission notification on a rolling basis beginning on or about 1/15. Must reply by May 1 or within 2 week(s) if notified thereafter. **Financial aid:** Priority date 2/15; no closing date. FAFSA required. Applicants notified on a rolling basis starting 2/1.

Academics. Students complete between 450 and 650 hours of significant internship experience that begins freshman year. **Special study options:** Accelerated study, combined bachelor's/graduate degree, cross-registration, distance learning, double major, dual enrollment of high school students, exchange student, honors, independent study, internships, liberal arts/career combination, New York semester, student-designed major, study abroad, teacher certification program, Washington semester. Studio courses. **Credit/ placement by examination:** AP, CLEP, IB, SAT, ACT, institutional tests. 16 credit hours maximum toward bachelor's degree. **Support services:** Learning center, pre-admission summer program, reduced course load, study skills assistance, tutoring, writing center.

Majors. Area/ethnic studies: American. **Biology:** General. **Business:** Business admin. **Communications technology:** General. **Conservation:** Environmental studies. **Education:** General, art, early childhood, early childhood special, elementary, English, kindergarten/preschool, mathematics, middle, science, secondary, social studies, special ed. **English:** English lit. **Health services:** Art therapy. **Liberal arts:** Arts/sciences. **Math:** General. **Social sciences:** General. **Visual/performing arts:** Art, studio arts. **Work/family studies:** Child development, family studies.

Most popular majors. Business/marketing 7%, English 8%, health sciences 10%, liberal arts 13%, psychology 22%, visual/performing arts 22%.

Technology on campus. 195 workstations in dormitories, library, computer center, student center. Dormitories wired for high-speed internet access and linked to campus network. Commuter students can connect to campus network. Online course registration, online library, helpline, wireless network available.

Student life. Freshman orientation: Mandatory. Preregistration for classes offered. Begins 1 week prior to start of classes. **Housing:** Coed dorms, single-sex dorms, themed housing, wellness housing available. $300 nonrefundable deposit, deadline 5/1. Victorian houses and suite-style residences available. **Activities:** Campus ministries, choral groups, dance, drama, international student organizations, literary magazine, musical theater, student government, student newspaper, women for social justice, Hillel, Third Wave women's group, Prism, Students for a Free Tibet, ALANA, Christian Fellowship.

Athletics. NCAA. **Intercollegiate:** Baseball M, basketball, cross-country, soccer, softball W, tennis, track and field M, volleyball. **Team name:** Lynx.

Student services. Adult student services, alcohol/substance abuse counseling, chaplain/spiritual director, career counseling, student employment services, financial aid counseling, health services, minority student services, personal counseling, placement for graduates. **Physically disabled:** Services for visually, speech, hearing impaired.

Contact. E-mail: admissions@lesley.edu
Phone: (617) 349-8800 Toll-free number: (800) 999-1959 ext. 8800
Fax: (617) 349-8810
Deb Kocar, Director of Admissions, Lesley University, 29 Everett Street, Cambridge, MA 02140-2790

Massachusetts College of Art and Design
Boston, Massachusetts CB member
www.massart.edu CB code: 3516

- Public 4-year visual arts college
- Residential campus in very large city
- 1,736 degree-seeking undergraduates: 11% part-time, 71% women, 3% African American, 8% Asian American, 10% Hispanic/Latino, 1% Multiracial, non-Hispanic, 4% international
- 104 degree-seeking graduate students
- 71% of applicants admitted
- SAT or ACT with writing, application essay required
- 72% graduate within 6 years

General. Founded in 1873. Regionally accredited. **Degrees:** 364 bachelor's awarded; master's offered. **Calendar:** Semester, extensive summer session. **Full-time faculty:** 115 total. **Part-time faculty:** 152 total. **Class size:** 83% < 20, 17% 20-39. **Special facilities:** 7 art galleries, sculpture shop, glass furnaces, ceramic kilns, video and film studios, performance and studio spaces, Polaroid 20X24 camera.

Freshman class profile. 1,273 applied, 908 admitted, 293 enrolled.

Mid 50% test scores		GPA 3.0-3.49:	45%
SAT critical reading:	470-600	GPA 2.0-2.99:	13%
SAT math:	460-590	Return as sophomores:	92%
SAT writing:	460-590	Out-of-state:	33%
ACT composite:	21-27	Live on campus:	89%
GPA 3.75 or higher:	21%	International:	4%
GPA 3.50-3.74:	21%		

Basis for selection. Emphasis on portfolio, academic record, essay, test scores, recommendations. 3.0 GPA recommended. For GPA between 2.3 and 2.9, SAT/ACT considered in combination with GPA on sliding scale. Applicants must meet Massachusetts public college admission standards. Portfolio of 15-20 pieces of artwork completed in the past two years required. Work may also be submitted in digital or time-based formats. **Home schooled:** Transcript of courses and grades required. Students who earn high school diploma must provide course curriculum that includes evaluations/grades as well as SAT or ACT scores. Students who do not earn high school diploma must submit official GED exam scores. **Learning Disabled:** Testing may be waived for applicants with professionally certified learning disabilities.

High school preparation. College-preparatory program required. 17 units required. Required units include English 4, mathematics 2, social studies 2, science 2 (laboratory 2), foreign language 2, visual/performing arts 2 and academic electives 2. 1 additional math or science required. Electives include at least 2 academic units of computer science, humanities, or visual and performing arts. Social Studies requirement must include 1 U.S. history course. Foreign language units must be in same language.

2015-2016 Annual costs. Tuition/fees: $11,725; $31,225 out-of-state. Room/board: $13,175. Books/supplies: $2,100. Personal expenses: $1,400.

2014-2015 Financial aid. Need-based: 254 full-time freshmen applied for aid; 198 deemed to have need; 198 received aid. Average scholarship/grant was $9,005; average loan $3,425. 65% of total undergraduate aid awarded as scholarships/grants, 35% as loans/jobs. **Non-need-based:** Awarded to 212 full-time undergraduates, including 44 freshmen. Scholarships awarded for academics, art, leadership, state residency. **Additional information:** Tuition waiver available to Vietnam veterans.

Application procedures. Admission: Priority date 2/1; no deadline. $50 fee, may be waived for applicants with need. Admission notification on a rolling basis. Must reply by May 1 or within 3 week(s) if notified thereafter. **Financial aid:** Priority date 3/1; no closing date. FAFSA required. Applicants notified on a rolling basis starting 3/15; must reply within 3 week(s) of notification.

Academics. Three-year certificates available. **Special study options:** Cross-registration, distance learning, double major, exchange student, independent study, internships, liberal arts/career combination, student-designed major, study abroad. Member of American Independent Colleges of Art and Design (AICAD), College Academic Program Sharing (CAPS), Colleges of the Fenway, and Pro Arts Consortium. Exchange programs available in Holland, England, Germany, Ireland, Italy, France. Study abroad available in Spain, Greece, China, Mexico. **Credit/placement by examination:** AP,

CLEP, IB, institutional tests. **Support services:** Pre-admission summer program, reduced course load, remedial instruction, study skills assistance, tutoring, writing center.

Majors. Architecture: Environmental design. **Education:** Art. **Visual/performing arts:** Art history/conservation, ceramics, cinematography, design, fashion design, fiber arts, film/cinema/video, graphic design, industrial design, metal/jewelry, multimedia, painting, photography, printmaking, sculpture, studio arts.

Most popular majors. Visual/performing arts 95%.

Technology on campus. 370 workstations in library, computer center. Dormitories wired for high-speed internet access and linked to campus network. Commuter students can connect to campus network. Online course registration, online library, helpline, wireless network available.

Student life. Freshman orientation: Mandatory. Preregistration for classes offered. **Housing:** Guaranteed on-campus for freshmen. Coed dorms available. $240 nonrefundable deposit, deadline 5/1. **Activities:** Dance, drama, film society, music ensembles, radio station, student government, student newspaper, TV station, minority student organization, gay/lesbian organization, student-run design firm, international student organization, non-traditional student organization.

Athletics. Intramural: Basketball, cross-country, field hockey, football (non-tackle), ice hockey, soccer, softball W, table tennis, tennis, volleyball.

Student services. Adult student services, career counseling, student employment services, financial aid counseling, health services, personal counseling, placement for graduates, veterans' counselor. **Physically disabled:** Services for visually, hearing impaired.

Contact. E-mail: admissions@massart.edu
Phone: (617) 879-7222 Fax: (617) 879-7250
Lauren Wilshusen, Director of Admissions, Massachusetts College of Art and Design, 621 Huntington Avenue, Boston, MA 02115-5882

Massachusetts College of Liberal Arts
North Adams, Massachusetts CB member
www.mcla.edu CB code: 3521

- Public 4-year liberal arts college
- Residential campus in large town
- 1,423 degree-seeking undergraduates: 11% part-time, 63% women, 9% African American, 2% Asian American, 8% Hispanic/Latino, 1% Native American, 3% Multi-racial, non-Hispanic
- 98 degree-seeking graduate students
- 73% of applicants admitted
- SAT or ACT (ACT writing optional), application essay required
- 52% graduate within 6 years

General. Founded in 1894. Regionally accredited. **Degrees:** 386 bachelor's awarded; master's offered. **Location:** 45 miles from Albany, NY; 65 miles from Springfield. **Calendar:** Semester, limited summer session. **Full-time faculty:** 90 total; 77% have terminal degrees, 11% minority, 50% women. **Part-time faculty:** 78 total; 1% minority, 56% women. **Class size:** 64% < 20, 36% 20-39, less than 1% 40-49.

Freshman class profile. 2,091 applied, 1,535 admitted, 260 enrolled.

Mid 50% test scores		GPA 2.0-2.99:	43%
SAT critical reading:	440-580	Rank in top quarter:	43%
SAT math:	450-550	Rank in top tenth:	16%
ACT composite:	21-25	Return as sophomores:	74%
GPA 3.75 or higher:	15%	Out-of-state:	30%
GPA 3.50-3.74:	10%	Live on campus:	85%
GPA 3.0-3.49:	32%		

Basis for selection. Secondary school record most important; test scores, essay also important; recommendations, extracurricular activities considered. Interview recommended. **Home schooled:** State high school equivalency certificate required. **Learning Disabled:** Massachusetts law prohibits requiring standardized test scores from students with documented learning disabilities.

High school preparation. College-preparatory program required. 17 units required. Required units include English 4, mathematics 4, science 3 (laboratory 2), foreign language 2 and academic electives 2.

2015-2016 Annual costs. Tuition/fees: $9,650; $18,595 out-of-state. Room/board: $9,828.

2015-2016 Financial aid. Need-based: 264 full-time freshmen applied for aid; 203 deemed to have need; 203 received aid. Average need met was 81%. Average scholarship/grant was $7,614; average loan $3,273. 45% of total undergraduate aid awarded as scholarships/grants, 55% as loans/jobs. **Non-need-based:** Awarded to 343 full-time undergraduates, including 118 freshmen. Scholarships awarded for academics, art, leadership, minority status, music/drama.

Application procedures. Admission: Priority date 3/1; no deadline. $40 fee, may be waived for applicants with need. Admission notification on a rolling basis beginning on or about 12/1. Must reply by May 1 or within 2 week(s) if notified thereafter. **Financial aid:** Priority date 3/1; no closing date. FAFSA required. Applicants notified on a rolling basis starting 3/1; must reply by 5/1 or within 2 week(s) of notification.

Academics. Special study options: Accelerated study, combined bachelor's/graduate degree, cross-registration, distance learning, double major, dual enrollment of high school students, exchange student, honors, independent study, internships, liberal arts/career combination, semester at sea, student-designed major, study abroad, teacher certification program, Washington semester, weekend college. **Credit/placement by examination:** AP, CLEP, IB, SAT, institutional tests. **Support services:** Learning center, pre-admission summer program, reduced course load, remedial instruction, study skills assistance, tutoring, writing center.

Majors. Biology: General, biotechnology. **Business:** Accounting, business admin, entrepreneurial studies, international, management information systems, marketing. **Communications:** General, broadcast journalism, journalism, persuasive communications. **Computer sciences:** General. **Conservation:** Environmental studies. **Education:** General. **English:** Creative writing, English lit, general lit, technical writing, writing. **Health services:** Athletic training, premedicine, prephysical therapy. **History:** General. **Human services:** Public policy. **Liberal arts:** Arts/sciences. **Math:** General. **Philosophy/religion:** Philosophy. **Physical sciences:** Chemistry, physics. **Psychology:** General. **Social sciences:** Political science, sociology. **Visual/performing arts:** General, art, music, studio arts management, theater arts management.

Most popular majors. Biology 6%, business/marketing 14%, English 15%, interdisciplinary studies 13%, psychology 10%, social sciences 11%, visual/performing arts 8%.

Technology on campus. PC or laptop required. 140 workstations in dormitories, library, computer center, student center. Dormitories wired for high-speed internet access and linked to campus network. Commuter students can connect to campus network. Online course registration, online library, helpline, wireless network available.

Student life. Freshman orientation: Mandatory, $75 fee. Preregistration for classes offered. **Housing:** Guaranteed on-campus for all undergraduates. Coed dorms, special housing for disabled, themed housing, wellness housing available. $100 nonrefundable deposit. **Activities:** Bands, choral groups, dance, drama, international student organizations, literary magazine, music ensembles, musical theater, radio station, student government, student newspaper, TV station, Interfaith association, Campus Christian Fellowship, Jewish student organization, Newman club, gay and lesbian student society, multicultural society.

Athletics. NCAA. Intercollegiate: Baseball M, basketball, cross-country, golf M, lacrosse W, soccer, softball W, tennis, volleyball W. **Intramural:** Basketball, bowling, equestrian, football (non-tackle), skiing, soccer, softball, swimming, table tennis, tennis, ultimate frisbee, volleyball, water polo M. **Team name:** Trailblazers.

Student services. Adult student services, alcohol/substance abuse counseling, career counseling, services for economically disadvantaged, student employment services, financial aid counseling, health services, minority student services, personal counseling, placement for graduates, veterans' counselor, women's services. **Physically disabled:** Services for visually, hearing impaired.

Contact. E-mail: admissions@mcla.edu
Phone: (413) 662-5410 Toll-free number: (800) 969-6252
Fax: (413) 662-5179
Gina Puc, Director of Admissions, Massachusetts College of Liberal Arts, 375 Church Street, North Adams, MA 01247

Massachusetts Institute of Technology

Cambridge, Massachusetts — **CB member**
web.mit.edu — **CB code: 3514**

- Private 4-year university
- Residential campus in small city

- 4,474 degree-seeking undergraduates: 1% part-time, 46% women, 6% African American, 25% Asian American, 15% Hispanic/Latino, 6% Multi-racial, non-Hispanic, 10% international
- 6,631 degree-seeking graduate students
- 8% of applicants admitted
- SAT or ACT (ACT writing optional), SAT Subject Tests, application essay required
- 92% graduate within 6 years; 31% enter graduate study

General. Founded in 1861. Regionally accredited. **Degrees:** 1,099 bachelor's awarded; master's, doctoral offered. **ROTC:** Army, Naval, Air Force. **Location:** One mile from Boston. **Calendar:** 4-1-4, limited summer session. **Full-time faculty:** 1,246 total; 92% have terminal degrees, 18% minority, 25% women. **Part-time faculty:** 298 total; 72% have terminal degrees, 8% minority, 34% women. **Class size:** 64% < 20, 18% 20-39, 5% 40-49, 9% 50-99, 4% >100. **Special facilities:** Museum, visual arts center, numerous laboratories and centers.

Freshman class profile. 18,306 applied, 1,519 admitted, 1,106 enrolled.

Mid 50% test scores		End year in good standing:	98%
SAT critical reading:	680-780	Return as sophomores:	98%
SAT math:	750-800	Out-of-state:	90%
SAT writing:	690-780	Live on campus:	100%
ACT composite:	33-35	International:	9%
Rank in top quarter:	100%	Fraternities:	54%
Rank in top tenth:	98%	Sororities:	41%

Basis for selection. Important factors include character, creativity, grades, leadership, love of learning, personal accomplishments, HS curriculum, recommendations, resiliency, test scores. An applicant's context is considered. Non-native English speakers have the option of taking TOEFL in place of SAT or ACT. Others must take SAT or ACT. All students must take two SAT Subject Tests, one each in math and science. Interviews very strongly recommended.

High school preparation. College-preparatory program recommended. Recommended units include English 4, mathematics 4, social studies 2, science 4 and foreign language 2.

2015-2016 Annual costs. Tuition/fees: $46,704. Room/board: $13,730. Books/supplies: $1,000. Personal expenses: $1,816.

2014-2015 Financial aid. All financial aid based on need. 832 full-time freshmen applied for aid; 641 deemed to have need; 641 received aid. Average need met was 100%. Average scholarship/grant was $39,882; average loan $2,869. 91% of total undergraduate aid awarded as scholarships/grants, 9% as loans/jobs. **Additional information:** Filing deadline 2/15 for CSS PROFILE.

Application procedures. Admission: Closing date 1/1 (postmark date). $75 fee, may be waived for applicants with need. Admission notification by 3/20. Must reply by May 1 or within 2 week(s) if notified thereafter. **Financial aid:** Priority date 2/15, closing date 2/15. FAFSA, CSS PROFILE required. Applicants notified by 3/14; must reply by 5/1.

Academics. Special study options: Combined bachelor's/graduate degree, cooperative education, cross-registration, double major, internships, semester at sea, study abroad, teacher certification program. Undergraduate research opportunities program, independent activities period, freshman learning communities. **Credit/placement by examination:** AP, CLEP, IB, institutional tests. **Support services:** Learning center, pre-admission summer program, study skills assistance, tutoring, writing center.

Majors. Architecture: Architecture, urban/community planning. **Biology:** General, computational, neuroscience. **Business:** General. **Communications:** Media studies. **Computer sciences:** Computer science. **Engineering:** Aerospace, biomedical, biomolecular, chemical, civil, electrical, environmental, materials, mechanical, nuclear. **English:** Creative writing, English lit. **Foreign languages:** General, linguistics. **History:** General. **Liberal arts:** Arts/sciences. **Math:** General. **Philosophy/religion:** Philosophy. **Physical sciences:** Chemistry, geology, physics. **Social sciences:** Anthropology, economics, political science. **Visual/performing arts:** Dramatic, music.

Most popular majors. Biology 8%, computer/information sciences 23%, engineering/engineering technologies 39%, mathematics 9%, physical sciences 8%.

Technology on campus. 1,100 workstations in dormitories, library, computer center, student center. Dormitories wired for high-speed internet access and linked to campus network. Commuter students can connect to campus network. Online course registration, online library, helpline, repair service, student web hosting, wireless network available.

Student life. Freshman orientation: Mandatory. Preregistration for classes offered. Held last 2 weeks of August. Includes programs for parents and international students. Additional 25 optional pre-orientation programs held week prior to orientation. **Policies:** Many undergraduate buildings designated smoke-free. Freshmen not permitted cars on campus. **Housing:** Guaranteed on-campus for freshmen. Coed dorms, single-sex dorms, special housing for disabled, apartments, cooperative housing, fraternity/sorority housing, gender-neutral housing, themed housing available. Independent living group housing, housing for students with children, cultural theme housing, and living learning communities available. **Activities:** Bands, campus ministries, choral groups, dance, drama, film society, international student organizations, literary magazine, music ensembles, Model UN, musical theater, radio station, student government, student newspaper, symphony orchestra, TV station, over 450 recognized organizations available.

Athletics. NCAA. **Intercollegiate:** Baseball M, basketball, cross-country, diving, fencing, field hockey W, football (tackle) M, lacrosse, rifle, rowing (crew), sailing, soccer, softball W, squash M, swimming, tennis, track and field, volleyball, water polo M. **Intramural:** Badminton, basketball, football (non-tackle), ice hockey, soccer, softball, table tennis, tennis, ultimate frisbee, volleyball, water polo. **Team name:** Engineers.

Student services. Alcohol/substance abuse counseling, chaplain/spiritual director, career counseling, student employment services, financial aid counseling, health services, on-campus daycare, personal counseling, placement for graduates. **Physically disabled:** Services for visually, speech, hearing impaired.

Contact. E-mail: admissions@mit.edu
Phone: (617) 253-3400 Fax: (617) 258-8304
Stuart Schmill, Dean of Admissions, Massachusetts Institute of Technology, 77 Massachusetts Avenue, Room 3-108, Cambridge, MA 02139-4307

Massachusetts Maritime Academy
Buzzards Bay, Massachusetts   CB member
www.maritime.edu   CB code: 3515

- Public 4-year engineering and maritime college
- Residential campus in small town
- 1,537 degree-seeking undergraduates: 2% part-time, 12% women, 1% African American, 1% Asian American, 4% Hispanic/Latino, 3% Multiracial, non-Hispanic, 1% international
- 103 degree-seeking graduate students
- 74% of applicants admitted
- SAT or ACT (ACT writing recommended), application essay required
- 72% graduate within 6 years

General. Founded in 1891. Regionally accredited. **Degrees:** 285 bachelor's awarded; master's offered. **ROTC:** Army, Naval. **Location:** Located in Buzzards Bay, MA (55 miles from Boston; 50 miles from Providence, Rhode Island). **Calendar:** 4-1-4, limited summer session. **Full-time faculty:** 80 total; 64% have terminal degrees, 15% minority, 31% women. **Part-time faculty:** 39 total; 15% have terminal degrees, 5% minority, 26% women. **Class size:** 35% < 20, 61% 20-39, 2% 40-49, 2% 50-99. **Special facilities:** 540-foot training ship with classrooms, labs, and library; 360 degree state-of-the art navigation and shiphandling full mission simulator; tugboat simulator; diesel liquid cargo simulator; electronic and navigation lab; global maritime distress and safety system lab; integrated navigational lab; hands-on aquaculture center; 248-foot tall 660-kilowatt wind turbine; biodiesel regenerator.

Freshman class profile. 824 applied, 610 admitted, 385 enrolled.

Mid 50% test scores			
SAT critical reading:	480-570	GPA 3.50-3.74:	9%
SAT math:	500-590	GPA 3.0-3.49:	41%
SAT writing:	460-550	GPA 2.0-2.99:	38%
ACT composite:	20-23	Return as sophomores:	93%
GPA 3.75 or higher:	12%	Out-of-state:	21%
		Live on campus:	100%

Basis for selection. School achievement record, test scores, extracurricular accomplishments most important. Character and personality emphasized; leadership potential desirable. SAT Subject Tests recommended. Interview recommended.

High school preparation. College-preparatory program required. 17 units required; 18 recommended. Required and recommended units include English 4, mathematics 4, social studies 1, history 1, science 3-4 (laboratory 2-3), foreign language 2 and academic electives 2.

2015-2016 Annual costs. Tuition/fees: $7,256; $22,310 out-of-state. Room/board: $11,120. Books/supplies: $1,000. Personal expenses: $1,000.

2015-2016 Financial aid. **Need-based:** 361 full-time freshmen applied for aid; 257 deemed to have need; 257 received aid. Average need met was 77%. Average scholarship/grant was $9,304; average loan $3,245. 65% of total undergraduate aid awarded as scholarships/grants, 35% as loans/jobs. **Non-need-based:** Awarded to 92 full-time undergraduates, including 41 freshmen. Scholarships awarded for academics, alumni affiliation, leadership.

Application procedures. Admission: Priority date 2/15; no deadline. $50 fee, may be waived for applicants with need. Admission notification on a rolling basis. Must reply by May 1 or within 2 week(s) if notified thereafter. **Financial aid:** Priority date 5/1; no closing date. FAFSA, institutional form required. Applicants notified on a rolling basis starting 3/20.

Academics. Technical and practical training for third assistant engineer and third mate licenses. Graduates may apply for commissions in U.S. Navy, Coast Guard, Marine Reserve, Army, or Air Force. **Special study options:** Cooperative education, double major, dual enrollment of high school students, internships, semester at sea, study abroad. **Credit/placement by examination:** AP, CLEP, IB, institutional tests. **Support services:** Learning center, pre-admission summer program, reduced course load, study skills assistance, tutoring, writing center.

Majors. Business: International. **Conservation:** Environmental science. **Engineering:** General, marine, systems.

Most popular majors. Business/marketing 14%, engineering/engineering technologies 44%, natural resources/environmental science 12%, security/protective services 12%, trade and industry 19%.

Technology on campus. PC or laptop required. 130 workstations in dormitories, library. Dormitories wired for high-speed internet access and linked to campus network. Commuter students can connect to campus network. Online course registration, online library, helpline, repair service, student web hosting, wireless network available.

Student life. Freshman orientation: Mandatory, $1,164 fee. Preregistration for classes offered. Held last 2 weeks of August, paramilitary style orientation. **Policies:** No mandatory military obligation. **Housing:** Guaranteed on-campus for all undergraduates. Coed dorms, wellness housing available. $400 nonrefundable deposit, deadline 5/1. **Activities:** Bands, drama, literary magazine, music ensembles, student government, student newspaper, Newman Club, marine careers group, Association of Industrial Plant Engineers.

Athletics. NCAA. **Intercollegiate:** Baseball M, cross-country, football (tackle) M, lacrosse, rowing (crew), sailing, soccer, softball W, track and field, volleyball W. **Intramural:** Basketball, football (non-tackle), soccer, water polo. **Team name:** Buccaneers.

Student services. Adult student services, alcohol/substance abuse counseling, chaplain/spiritual director, career counseling, student employment services, financial aid counseling, health services, minority student services, personal counseling, placement for graduates, veterans' counselor, women's services.

Contact. E-mail: admissions@maritime.edu
Toll-free number: (800) 544-3411
CDR. Liz Daly, Director of Admissions, Massachusetts Maritime Academy, 101 Academy Drive, Buzzards Bay, MA 02532

MCPHS University
Boston, Massachusetts   CB member
www.mcphs.edu   CB code: 3512

- Private 4-year health science and pharmacy college
- Commuter campus in very large city
- 3,877 degree-seeking undergraduates: 5% part-time, 70% women, 7% African American, 24% Asian American, 5% Hispanic/Latino, 1% Multiracial, non-Hispanic, 13% international
- 3,122 degree-seeking graduate students
- 87% of applicants admitted
- SAT or ACT (ACT writing optional), application essay required
- 72% graduate within 6 years

General. Founded in 1823. Regionally accredited. Member of Fenway College Consortium, 14-college library consortium, Worcester Consortium, and Manchester Area College Consortium. Students have access to Harvard Medical School library. Accelerated PharmD program available at Worcester campus and Manchester campus; Physician Assistant program and Nursing also offered at Boston, Manchester, and Worcester campuses. **Degrees:** 898 bachelor's awarded; master's, professional, doctoral offered. **ROTC:** Army, Naval, Air Force. **Calendar:** Semester, limited summer session. **Full-time faculty:** 297 total; 91% have terminal degrees. **Part-time faculty:** 389 total. **Class size:** 24% < 20, 47% 20-39, 9% 40-49, 9% 50-99, 11% >100. **Special facilities:** Pharmacy practice lab, dental hygiene clinic, patient assessment lab, nursing skills and technology lab.

Freshman class profile. 4,867 applied, 4,213 admitted, 783 enrolled.

Mid 50% test scores			
SAT critical reading:	460-570	GPA 3.50-3.74:	22%
SAT math:	490-610	GPA 3.0-3.49:	36%
SAT writing:	470-580	GPA 2.0-2.99:	14%
ACT composite:	20-26	Return as sophomores:	84%
GPA 3.75 or higher:	28%	International:	16%

Basis for selection. School academic record most important, with emphasis on math and science courses. Student's interest, aptitude for pharmacy and allied health fields considered. **Home schooled:** Require documentation of curriculum and program of study; equivalency exam. **Learning Disabled:** Must submit documents to Academic Support Services.

High school preparation. College-preparatory program required. 16 units required. Required units include English 4, mathematics 3, social studies 1, history 1, science 2 (laboratory 2) and academic electives 5.

2015-2016 Annual costs. Tuition/fees: $30,530. Room/board: $15,174. Books/supplies: $988.

2015-2016 Financial aid. Need-based: 617 full-time freshmen applied for aid; 545 deemed to have need; 545 received aid. Average need met was 40%. Average scholarship/grant was $11,523; average loan $4,664. 45% of total undergraduate aid awarded as scholarships/grants, 55% as loans/jobs. **Non-need-based:** Scholarships awarded for academics.

Application procedures. Admission: No deadline. No application fee. Admission notification on a rolling basis beginning on or about 12/17. Must reply by May 1 or within 2 week(s) if notified thereafter. **Financial aid:** Priority date 3/15; no closing date. FAFSA required. Applicants notified on a rolling basis starting 3/15.

Academics. Special study options: Accelerated study, combined bachelor's/graduate degree, cross-registration, distance learning, double major, independent study, internships, study abroad. **Credit/placement by examination:** AP, CLEP, IB, SAT, ACT, institutional tests. 6 credit hours maximum toward bachelor's degree. CLEP exams must be taken before student's first semester of enrollment in order for credit to be granted. **Support services:** Learning center, reduced course load, study skills assistance, tutoring, writing center.

Majors. Biology: Pharmacology/toxicology. **Health services:** Dental hygiene, medical radiologic technology/radiation therapy, MRI technology, nuclear medical technology, nursing (RN), pharmaceutical sciences, prechiropractic, predental, premedicine, preoccupational therapy, preoptometry, prephysical therapy, preveterinary, radiologic technology/medical imaging, sonography. **Physical sciences:** Chemistry. **Psychology:** Medical.

Most popular majors. Health sciences 97%.

Technology on campus. 752 workstations in dormitories, library, computer center, student center. Dormitories wired for high-speed internet access and linked to campus network. Commuter students can connect to campus network. Online library, helpline, wireless network available.

Student life. Freshman orientation: Mandatory, $100 fee. Preregistration for classes offered. Two-day overnight program in summer; 1-day freshman parent orientation. **Policies:** Identification must be worn and displayed while on campus. Academic honesty policy, alcohol and drug abuse policies; electronic communications policy; good neighbor policy; hazing policy; smoke-free policy; sexual harassment policy. **Housing:** Guaranteed on-campus for freshmen. Coed dorms available. $250 fully refundable deposit, deadline 9/1. **Activities:** Concert band, choral groups, dance, drama, international student organizations, literary magazine, music ensembles, musical theater, student government, student newspaper, symphony orchestra, Academy of Student Pharmacists, Kappa Psi fraternity, Vietnamese student association, Black student union, physician assistant student society, campus activities board, student government association, Indian student organization, Asian student association.

Athletics. Intramural: Badminton, basketball, bowling, field hockey, football (non-tackle), racquetball, soccer, softball, table tennis, tennis, volleyball. **Team name:** Cardinals.

Student services. Adult student services, alcohol/substance abuse counseling, career counseling, student employment services, financial aid counseling, health services, minority student services, personal counseling, placement for graduates, veterans' counselor, women's services. **Physically disabled:** Services for visually, speech, hearing impaired.

Contact. E-mail: admissions@mcphs.edu
Phone: (617) 879-5964 Toll-free number: (800) 225-5506
Fax: (617) 732-2118
Kathleen Ryan, Executive Director of Admission, MCPHS University, 179 Longwood Avenue, Boston, MA 02115-5896

Merrimack College
North Andover, Massachusetts — **CB member**
www.merrimack.edu — **CB code: 3525**

- Private 4-year business and liberal arts college affiliated with the Roman Catholic Church
- Residential campus in large town
- 3,161 degree-seeking undergraduates: 3% part-time, 52% women, 3% African American, 1% Asian American, 5% Hispanic/Latino, 1% Multiracial, non-Hispanic, 5% international
- 433 degree-seeking graduate students
- 79% of applicants admitted
- Application essay required
- 71% graduate within 6 years

General. Founded in 1947. Regionally accredited. Associated with Augustinian Friars. **Degrees:** 562 bachelor's awarded; master's offered. **ROTC:** Air Force. **Location:** 25 miles from Boston. **Calendar:** Semester, limited summer session. **Full-time faculty:** 165 total; 87% have terminal degrees, 10% minority, 46% women. **Part-time faculty:** 209 total; 12% minority, 55% women. **Class size:** 40% < 20, 59% 20-39, less than 1% 40-49, less than 1% 50-99. **Special facilities:** Writers house, markets lab, astronomy dome and telescope, center for the arts, diversity education center, center for Augustinian study, center for biotechnology and biomedical sciences, center for engaged democracy, center for the study of Jewish-Christian-Muslim relations, radio frequency identification technology lab.

Freshman class profile. 7,751 applied, 6,121 admitted, 828 enrolled.

GPA 3.75 or higher:	12%	Return as sophomores:	83%
GPA 3.50-3.74:	11%	Out-of-state:	35%
GPA 3.0-3.49:	37%	Live on campus:	88%
GPA 2.0-2.99:	39%	International:	3%

Basis for selection. Academic achievement, strength of curriculum, community involvement, extracurricular activities, essay, application, references important. Interview recommended. **Home schooled:** State high school equivalency certificate required. Submit state certificate of completion, list of coursework, essay, two letters of recommendation from people outside the home. Interview highly recommended.

High school preparation. College-preparatory program required. 13 units required. Required units include English 4, mathematics 3, history 2, science 2 and foreign language 2. Math subject matter must be sequential through Algebra II. Advanced math course required of all science and engineering applicants. Prospective engineering students must have 3 units in science including 1 physics. Health science, biology, chemistry, computer science, engineering, mathematics, physics, or sports medicine applicants must have 1 additional unit in both math and science.

2015-2016 Annual costs. Tuition/fees: $37,270. Room/board: $13,875. Books/supplies: $1,000. Personal expenses: $450.

2015-2016 Financial aid. Need-based: 696 full-time freshmen applied for aid; 604 deemed to have need; 603 received aid. Average need met was 62%. Average scholarship/grant was $19,404; average loan $3,378. 66% of total undergraduate aid awarded as scholarships/grants, 34% as loans/jobs. **Non-need-based:** Awarded to 1,086 full-time undergraduates, including 322 freshmen. Scholarships awarded for academics, alumni affiliation, athletics, leadership, music/drama, religious affiliation.

Application procedures. Admission: Closing date 2/15 (postmark date). No application fee. Admission notification by 4/15. Admission notification on a rolling basis beginning on or about 3/15. Must reply by 5/1. Incoming students pay freshmen/transfer deposit of $500 due by 5/1. **Financial aid:** Priority date 2/15; no closing date. FAFSA required. Applicants notified by 3/15; Applicants notified on a rolling basis.

Academics. Math center offers free, drop-in tutoring. Writing intensive courses available in all areas. **Special study options:** Accelerated study, combined bachelor's/graduate degree, cooperative education, cross-registration, double major, dual enrollment of high school students, honors, independent study, internships, liberal arts/career combination, student-designed major, study abroad, teacher certification program, Washington semester. 5-year combined BA/BS program, continuing ed program, Bachelor's Completion program. Cross-registration available through college's membership in 10-college consortium. **Credit/placement by examination:** AP, CLEP, IB, institutional tests. **Support services:** Learning center, reduced course load, remedial instruction, study skills assistance, tutoring, writing center. Math Center.

Majors. Area/ethnic studies: Italian, women's. **Biology:** General, biochemistry. **Business:** Accounting, business admin, finance, international, marketing. **Computer sciences:** Computer science, information technology. **Conservation:** Environmental science. **Education:** General, biology, chemistry, early childhood, elementary, elementary special ed, English, French, history, junior high special ed, mathematics, middle, multi-level teacher, physics, secondary, secondary special ed, Spanish, special ed. **Engineering:** Civil, electrical, mechanical. **English:** English lit. **Foreign languages:** French, Romance, Spanish. **Health services:** Athletic training, prephysical therapy. **History:** General. **Liberal arts:** Arts/sciences. **Math:** General. **Parks/recreation:** Sports admin. **Philosophy/religion:** Philosophy, religion. **Physical sciences:** Chemistry, physics. **Protective services:** Law enforcement admin. **Psychology:** General. **Social sciences:** Economics, political science, sociology. **Visual/performing arts:** Art history/conservation, dramatic. **Work/family studies:** Family studies, family/community services.

Most popular majors. Business/marketing 30%, communications/journalism 6%, family/consumer sciences 14%, health sciences 9%, security/protective services 6%.

Technology on campus. Dormitories wired for high-speed internet access and linked to campus network. Online course registration, online library, helpline, repair service, wireless network available.

Student life. Freshman orientation: Mandatory. Preregistration for classes offered. Two-day June sessions and August pre-class orientation. **Policies:** All residence halls are drug-free. Freshmen not permitted cars on campus. **Housing:** Guaranteed on-campus for freshmen. Coed dorms, special housing for disabled, apartments, themed housing, wellness housing available. Townhouses, theme housing available for upperclassmen. Austin Scholars and Honors residential programs available to selected students. **Activities:** Bands, campus ministries, choral groups, dance, drama, film society, international student organizations, music ensembles, Model UN, musical theater, radio station, student government, student newspaper, TV station, ALANA, Best Buddies, CRU, Gay/Straight Alliance, Green Team, Interfaith Alliance.

Athletics. NCAA. **Intercollegiate:** Baseball M, basketball, cross-country, field hockey W, football (tackle) M, golf W, ice hockey, lacrosse, rowing (crew) W, soccer, softball W, swimming W, tennis, track and field, volleyball W. **Intramural:** Badminton, basketball, ice hockey, soccer. **Team name:** Warriors.

Student services. Adult student services, alcohol/substance abuse counseling, chaplain/spiritual director, career counseling, student employment services, financial aid counseling, health services, minority student services, personal counseling, placement for graduates. **Physically disabled:** Services for visually, speech impaired.

Contact. E-mail: admission@merrimack.edu
Phone: (978) 837-5000 ext. 5100 Fax: (978) 837-5133
Darren Conine, Director of Undergraduate Admissions, Merrimack College, 510 Turnpike Street, Suite 201, North Andover, MA 01845

Montserrat College of Art
Beverly, Massachusetts
www.montserrat.edu

CB member
CB code: 9101

- Private 4-year visual arts college
- Residential campus in large town
- 378 degree-seeking undergraduates
- Application essay required

General. Founded in 1970. Regionally accredited. **Degrees:** 73 bachelor's awarded. **Location:** 20 miles from Boston. **Calendar:** Semester, limited summer session. **Full-time faculty:** 61 total; 3% have terminal degrees, 2% minority, 49% women. **Part-time faculty:** 20 total; 15% have terminal degrees, 10% minority, 45% women. **Class size:** 89% < 20, 11% 20-39. **Special facilities:** Computer design laboratories, college-operated galleries, student-operated galleries, YMCA and MFA memberships.

Freshman class profile.

GPA 3.75 or higher:	9%	GPA 2.0-2.99:	44%
GPA 3.50-3.74:	13%	Out-of-state:	55%
GPA 3.0-3.49:	32%	Live on campus:	95%

Basis for selection. Visual art portfolio most important. High school record, interview, artist statement, and letters of recommendation required of BFA applicants. If personal visit is impractical, portfolio in digital or slide form may be sent; follow-up telephone interview will be conducted. SAT or ACT required for applicants with GED. Interview recommended; portfolio required. **Home schooled:** Transcript of courses and grades, state high school equivalency certificate, letter of recommendation (nonparent) required. Must take SAT/ACT and successfully pass GED. **Learning Disabled:** Official documentation of disability and any previous accommodation plans required if accommodation requested.

High school preparation. College-preparatory program recommended. Recommended units include English 4, social studies 2, history 2 and visual/performing arts 2. Visual arts courses including drawing recommended.

2015-2016 Annual costs. Tuition/fees: $29,550. Room only: $8,600. Books/supplies: $1,200. Personal expenses: $1,300.

Financial aid. Non-need-based: Scholarships awarded for academics, art.

Application procedures. Admission: Priority date 2/15; no deadline. $50 fee, may be waived for applicants with need. Admission notification on a rolling basis beginning on or about 12/15. Must reply by May 1 or within 3 week(s) if notified thereafter. **Financial aid:** Priority date 3/1; no closing date. FAFSA, institutional form required. Applicants notified on a rolling basis starting 3/1; must reply by 5/1 or within 2 week(s) of notification.

Academics. In addition to frequent class critiques, students' work is reviewed by faculty panel in semester-end evaluations. **Special study options:** Cross-registration, double major, dual enrollment of high school students, exchange student, independent study, internships, New York semester, student-designed major, study abroad, teacher certification program. Summer study abroad opportunities in Italy and Japan; winter study abroad opportunities in Africa and Spain; on-campus winter session classes available. **Credit/placement by examination:** AP, CLEP, IB. **Support services:** Learning center, pre-admission summer program, reduced course load, remedial instruction, study skills assistance, tutoring, writing center.

Majors. Visual/performing arts: Crafts, digital arts, graphic design, illustration, painting, photography, printmaking, sculpture, studio arts.

Technology on campus. 158 workstations in dormitories, library, computer center, student center. Dormitories wired for high-speed internet access. Online library, helpline, wireless network available.

Student life. Freshman orientation: Mandatory, $100 fee. Preregistration for classes offered. **Policies:** Student Handbook policies enforced. Freshmen not permitted cars on campus. **Housing:** Coed dorms, single-sex dorms, wellness housing available. $275 nonrefundable deposit, deadline 5/1. **Activities:** Dance, drama, music ensembles, student government, student newspaper, Food Not Bombs, community service corp, Student Voice, Intervarsity, Big Table Talks.

Athletics. Intramural: Basketball, football (tackle), ultimate frisbee.

Student services. Alcohol/substance abuse counseling, career counseling, student employment services, financial aid counseling, health services, personal counseling, placement for graduates. **Physically disabled:** Services for visually, speech, hearing impaired.

Contact. E-mail: admissions@montserrat.edu
Phone: (978) 921-4242 ext. 1153
Toll-free number: (800) 836-0487 ext. 1153 Fax: (978) 921-4241
Jeffrey Newell, Director of Admissions, Montserrat College of Art, 23 Essex Street, Beverly, MA 01915

Mount Holyoke College
South Hadley, Massachusetts
www.mtholyoke.edu

CB member
CB code: 3529

- Private 4-year liberal arts college for women
- Residential campus in large town
- 2,099 degree-seeking undergraduates: 1% part-time, 100% women
- 63 degree-seeking graduate students
- 50% of applicants admitted
- Application essay required
- 85% graduate within 6 years; 22% enter graduate study

General. Founded in 1837. Regionally accredited. Member of 5-college consortium with Amherst College, Hampshire College, Smith College, and University of Massachusetts at Amherst. Member of 12 College Exchange with Amherst College, Bowdoin, Connecticut College, Dartmouth College, O'Neill National Theatre Institute, Smith College, Trinity College, Vassar, Wellesley College, Wesleyan University, Wheaton College, Williams/Mystic Seaport Program in Maritime Studies. Member of Women's College Exchange Program with Mills College and Spelman College. **Degrees:** 628 bachelor's awarded; master's offered. **ROTC:** Army, Air Force. **Location:** 10 miles from Springfield; 40 miles from Hartford, CT. **Calendar:** Semester, limited summer session. **Full-time faculty:** 186 total; 98% have terminal degrees, 25% minority, 58% women. **Part-time faculty:** 48 total; 92% have terminal degrees, 4% minority, 58% women. **Class size:** 70% < 20, 25% 20-39, 4% 40-49, less than 1% 50-99, 1% >100. **Special facilities:** Nuclear accelerator, nuclear magnetic resonance equipment, electron microscope, bronze-casting foundry, solar greenhouse, Japanese meditation garden and tea house, equestrian center, language learning center with satellite communication and interactive video, child study center, global initiatives center, greenhouse and botanical garden, leadership and liberal arts center, art museum, center for the environment, observatory, spiritual places.

Freshman class profile. 3,858 applied, 1,932 admitted, 523 enrolled.

Mid 50% test scores		GPA 3.0-3.49:	14%
SAT critical reading:	620-730	GPA 2.0-2.99:	2%
SAT math:	610-740	Rank in top quarter:	90%
SAT writing:	630-720	Rank in top tenth:	58%
ACT composite:	29-32	Return as sophomores:	90%
GPA 3.75 or higher:	56%	Out-of-state:	77%
GPA 3.50-3.74:	28%	Live on campus:	100%

Basis for selection. School record, writing, and evaluations most important; special talents, particular goals, and character considered. Personal interview on campus recommended if candidate lives within 200 miles of college, or with alumna admissions representative if applicant resides outside of area. **Home schooled:** Detailed outline of study and SAT Subject Tests or ACT required.

High school preparation. College-preparatory program recommended. Recommended units include English 4, mathematics 4, history 3, science 4 (laboratory 3), foreign language 4 and academic electives 1.

2015-2016 Annual costs. Tuition/fees: $43,886. Room/board: $12,860. Books/supplies: $950. Personal expenses: $950.

2015-2016 Financial aid. Need-based: 400 full-time freshmen applied for aid; 336 deemed to have need; 336 received aid. Average need met was 100%. Average scholarship/grant was $32,332; average loan $3,468. 83% of total undergraduate aid awarded as scholarships/grants, 17% as loans/jobs. **Non-need-based:** Awarded to 573 full-time undergraduates, including 160 freshmen. Scholarships awarded for academics, leadership.

Application procedures. Admission: Closing date 1/15 (postmark date). $60 fee, may be waived for applicants with need, free for online applicants. Admission notification by 4/1. Must reply by 5/1. **Financial aid:** Priority date 2/15, closing date 3/1. FAFSA, CSS PROFILE required. Applicants notified by 4/1; must reply by 5/1.

Academics. Honor system and self-scheduled examinations practiced. **Special study options:** Combined bachelor's/graduate degree, cross-registration, distance learning, double major, exchange student, independent study, internships, liberal arts/career combination, student-designed major, study abroad, teacher certification program, Washington semester. Community-based learning courses and first-year seminars. **Credit/placement by examination:** AP, CLEP, IB, institutional tests. 32 credit hours maximum toward bachelor's degree. Credit will not satisfy any distribution or language requirement, but may satisfy some prerequisites. **Support services:** Reduced course load, study skills assistance, tutoring, writing center.

Majors. Architecture: Architecture. **Area/ethnic studies:** African-American, Asian, East Asian, German, Latin American/Caribbean, Near/Middle Eastern, Russian/Slavic, South Asian. **Biology:** General, biochemistry, neuroscience. **Computer sciences:** Computer science. **Conservation:** Environmental studies. **Education:** General. **English:** English lit. **Foreign languages:** Ancient Greek, classics, French, Italian, Latin, Romance, Spanish. **History:** General. **Math:** General, statistics. **Philosophy/religion:** Philosophy, religion. **Physical sciences:** Astronomy, chemistry, geology, physics. **Psychology:** General. **Social sciences:** Anthropology, economics, geography, international relations, political science, sociology. **Visual/performing arts:** Art history/conservation, dance, dramatic, film/cinema/video, music, studio arts.

Most popular majors. Biology 9%, English 7%, psychology 8%, social sciences 27%, visual/performing arts 8%.

Technology on campus. 456 workstations in dormitories, library, computer center, student center. Dormitories wired for high-speed internet access and linked to campus network. Commuter students can connect to campus network. Online course registration, online library, helpline, repair service, student web hosting, wireless network available.

Student life. Freshman orientation: Available. Preregistration for classes offered. Program held week before start of classes. **Policies:** Smoke-free campus. **Housing:** Guaranteed on-campus for all undergraduates. Special housing for disabled, apartments available. Kosher/halal kitchen available; special accommodations by need. **Activities:** Jazz band, campus ministries, choral groups, dance, drama, film society, international student organizations, literary magazine, music ensembles, Model UN, radio station, student government, student newspaper, symphony orchestra, Amnesty International, Animal Welfare Association, multi-faith council, Jewish student union, Asian students association, Best Buddies, Creating Awareness and Unity for Social Equality, Kuch Karo: Pakistani Students for Change, Chinese Christian Fellowship.

Athletics. NCAA. **Intercollegiate:** Basketball W, cross-country W, diving W, equestrian W, field hockey W, golf W, lacrosse W, rowing (crew) W, soccer W, squash W, swimming W, tennis W, track and field W, volleyball W. **Team name:** Lyons.

Student services. Adult student services, alcohol/substance abuse counseling, chaplain/spiritual director, career counseling, student employment services, financial aid counseling, health services, minority student services, personal counseling, placement for graduates, veterans' counselor, women's services. **Physically disabled:** Services for visually, speech, hearing impaired.

Contact. E-mail: admission@mtholyoke.edu
Phone: (413) 538-2023 Fax: (413) 538-2409
Gail Berson, Vice President for Enrollment and Dean of Admissions, Mount Holyoke College, Newhall Center, South Hadley, MA 01075-1488

Mount Ida College
Newton, Massachusetts
www.mountida.edu

CB member
CB code: 3530

- Private 4-year business and liberal arts college
- Residential campus in small city
- 1,290 degree-seeking undergraduates
- SAT or ACT (ACT writing recommended) required

General. Founded in 1899. Regionally accredited. **Degrees:** 225 bachelor's, 130 associate awarded; master's offered. **Location:** 8 miles from downtown Boston. **Calendar:** Semester, limited summer session. **Full-time faculty:** 64 total; 66% have terminal degrees, 8% minority, 62% women. **Part-time faculty:** 117 total; 32% have terminal degrees, 15% minority, 49% women. **Special facilities:** Darkroom, blueprint making facility, veterinary kennel and operating facility, dental laboratory, design labs.

Freshman class profile.

Out-of-state:	43%	Live on campus:	86%

Basis for selection. School record, GPA, recommendations, test scores, and essay most important. Essay or personal statement, campus visit strongly recommended. Interviews may be required.

High school preparation. College-preparatory program recommended. 14 units recommended. Recommended units include English 4, mathematics 3, social studies 2, science 3 (laboratory 3) and foreign language 2. 4 math and 2 physical science strongly recommended for science majors.

2015-2016 Annual costs. Tuition/fees: $32,300. Room/board: $13,000. Books/supplies: $1,000. Personal expenses: $1,272.

Application procedures. Admission: No deadline. $45 fee, may be waived for applicants with need, free for online applicants. Admission notification on a rolling basis beginning on or about 10/1. **Financial aid:** Priority date 4/15; no closing date. FAFSA, institutional form required. Applicants notified on a rolling basis starting 3/1; must reply within 3 week(s) of notification.

Academics. Professionally intensive courses of study coupled with liberal arts requirements. **Special study options:** Distance learning, double major, ESL, honors, independent study, internships, semester at sea, study abroad, teacher certification program. **Credit/placement by examination:** AP, CLEP, IB, institutional tests. **Support services:** Learning center, reduced course load, remedial instruction, study skills assistance, tutoring, writing center.

Majors. Area/ethnic studies: American. **Biology:** General. **Business:** Business admin, fashion, hospitality admin. **Communications technology:** Animation/special effects. **Education:** Early childhood. **English:** English lit. **Health services:** Veterinary technology/assistant. **Liberal arts:** Arts/sciences. **Parks/recreation:** Sports admin. **Protective services:** Criminal justice, forensics. **Psychology:** General. **Visual/performing arts:** Fashion design, graphic design, interior design.

Most popular majors. Business/marketing 31%, communication technologies 10%, education 6%, health sciences 13%, security/protective services 9%, visual/performing arts 16%.

Technology on campus. 122 workstations in library, computer center. Dormitories wired for high-speed internet access and linked to campus network. Commuter students can connect to campus network. Online library, wireless network available.

Student life. Freshman orientation: Mandatory. Preregistration for classes offered. Held in July. Activities also held prior to first day of class in late August. **Policies:** Freshmen not permitted cars on campus. **Housing:**

Guaranteed on-campus for freshmen. Coed dorms, single-sex dorms, special housing for disabled, themed housing, wellness housing available. $300 partly refundable deposit. **Activities:** Choral groups, dance, drama, international student organizations, literary magazine, student government, student newspaper, black student achievement coalition, gay/lesbian and everyone else, student association for Latino and Spanish Americans, volunteers in action.

Athletics. NCAA. **Intercollegiate:** Basketball, cheerleading, cross-country, equestrian W, football (tackle) M, lacrosse, soccer, softball W, tennis W, volleyball. **Intramural:** Basketball, football (non-tackle), rugby, soccer, ultimate frisbee. **Team name:** Mustangs.

Student services. Adult student services, alcohol/substance abuse counseling, chaplain/spiritual director, career counseling, services for economically disadvantaged, student employment services, financial aid counseling, health services, minority student services, personal counseling, placement for graduates.

Contact. E-mail: admissions@mountida.edu
Phone: (617) 928-4553 Fax: (617) 928-4507
Justeane Odams, Admissions Director, Mount Ida College, 777 Dedham Street, Newton, MA 02459

New England Conservatory of Music
Boston, Massachusetts
www.necmusic.edu

CB member
CB code: 3659

- Private 4-year music college
- Commuter campus in very large city
- 381 degree-seeking undergraduates: 4% part-time, 44% women, 3% African American, 11% Asian American, 3% Hispanic/Latino, 6% Multiracial, non-Hispanic, 35% international
- 312 degree-seeking graduate students
- 32% of applicants admitted
- Application essay required
- 84% graduate within 6 years

General. Founded in 1867. Regionally accredited. In close proximity to Symphony Hall. Faculty includes members of Boston Symphony Orchestra. **Degrees:** 84 bachelor's awarded; master's, doctoral offered. **Location:** 2 miles from downtown. **Calendar:** Semester, limited summer session. **Full-time faculty:** 102 total; 39% have terminal degrees, 7% minority, 34% women. **Part-time faculty:** 133 total; 10% have terminal degrees, 38% minority, 32% women. **Class size:** 81% < 20, 18% 20-39, less than 1% 40-49. **Special facilities:** Listening library.

Freshman class profile. 1,170 applied, 379 admitted, 98 enrolled.

End year in good standing:	95%	Live on campus:	95%
Return as sophomores:	86%	International:	37%
Out-of-state:	85%		

Basis for selection. Audition most important, followed by recommendations, high school record, essay. Live or recorded auditions required. **Home schooled:** Transcript of courses and grades required. Must provide curriculum overview.

2015-2016 Annual costs. Tuition/fees: $43,055. Room/board: $13,240. Books/supplies: $700. Personal expenses: $2,200.

2014-2015 Financial aid. **Need-based:** 55 full-time freshmen applied for aid; 40 deemed to have need; 40 received aid. Average need met was 56%. Average scholarship/grant was $19,742; average loan $4,366. 71% of total undergraduate aid awarded as scholarships/grants, 29% as loans/jobs. **Non-need-based:** Scholarships awarded for academics, music/drama.

Application procedures. **Admission:** Priority date 11/1; deadline 12/1. $115 fee. Application must be submitted online. Admission notification by 4/1. Must reply by May 1 or within 2 week(s) if notified thereafter. **Financial aid:** Closing date 12/1. FAFSA, institutional form required. Applicants notified by 4/1; must reply by 5/1 or within 2 week(s) of notification.

Academics. Undergraduate diploma available in lieu of bachelor's degree (performance-oriented, with fewer academic requirements). Artist's diploma (professional degree) available for particularly gifted performers. Graduate diploma also available. **Special study options:** Cross-registration, dual enrollment of high school students, ESL, independent study, internships, study abroad. 5-year double degree program with Tufts University; 5-year AB/MM program with Harvard University. **Credit/placement by examination:** AP, CLEP, IB, institutional tests. 12 credit hours maximum toward bachelor's degree. **Support services:** Remedial instruction, tutoring, writing center.

Majors. Visual/performing arts: Brass instruments, jazz, music, music history, music performance, music theory/composition, musicology, percussion instruments, piano/keyboard, stringed instruments, voice/opera, woodwind instruments.

Technology on campus. 83 workstations in library, computer center, student center. Commuter students can connect to campus network. Online course registration, online library, helpline, wireless network available.

Student life. Freshman orientation: Mandatory. Preregistration for classes offered. Held 1 week before start of classes; includes significant testing in Music Theory as well as re-hearings by major department. **Policies:** Freshmen not permitted cars on campus. **Housing:** Guaranteed on-campus for freshmen. Coed dorms available. $525 fully refundable deposit, deadline 6/1. **Activities:** Bands, choral groups, music ensembles, opera, student government, student newspaper, symphony orchestra, Fellowship with Christ, African-American student union, Early Society, The Penguin.

Athletics. Team name: Penguins.

Student services. Career counseling, student employment services, financial aid counseling, health services, personal counseling, placement for graduates. **Physically disabled:** Services for visually impaired.

Contact. E-mail: ADMStaff@necmusic.edu
Phone: (617) 585-1101 Fax: (617) 585-1115
Alex Powell, Assistant Dean for Admissions, New England Conservatory of Music, 290 Huntington Avenue, Boston, MA 02115-5018

Newbury College
Brookline, Massachusetts
www.newbury.edu

CB member
CB code: 3639

- Private 4-year business and liberal arts college
- Residential campus in large city
- 867 degree-seeking undergraduates
- 78% of applicants admitted
- Application essay required

General. Founded in 1962. Regionally accredited. **Degrees:** 152 bachelor's, 16 associate awarded. **Location:** 3 miles from downtown Boston. **Calendar:** Semester, limited summer session. **Full-time faculty:** 35 total; 34% have terminal degrees, 11% minority, 43% women. **Part-time faculty:** 72 total; 28% have terminal degrees, 25% minority, 40% women. **Class size:** 57% < 20, 43% 20-39. **Special facilities:** Seven culinary arts production kitchens, on-campus restaurant open to the public.

Freshman class profile. 2,758 applied, 2,155 admitted, 317 enrolled.

Mid 50% test scores		SAT writing:	360-460
SAT critical reading:	380-470	Out-of-state:	31%
SAT math:	380-480	Live on campus:	55%

Basis for selection. Holistic approach includes application, essay, high school transcript, extra-curricular activities and 2 letters of recommendation. Standardized test scores are optional. Students may submit scores if they believe the results present a fuller picture of their achievements and potential. Students who do not submit scores will not be at any disadvantage in admissions decisions. Interviews recommended. **Home schooled:** Statement describing home school structure and mission, transcript of courses and grades, interview required.

High school preparation. College-preparatory program recommended. Recommended units include English 4, mathematics 3, social studies 3, history 3, science 3, foreign language 2 and computer science 1.

2015-2016 Annual costs. Tuition/fees: $31,408. Room/board: $13,740. Books/supplies: $1,500. Personal expenses: $1,000.

Financial aid. All financial aid based on need.

Application procedures. Admission: Priority date 12/1; no deadline. No application fee. Admission notification on a rolling basis beginning on or about 11/1. Must reply by May 1 or within 4 week(s) if notified thereafter. **Financial aid:** Priority date 3/1, closing date 5/1. FAFSA required. Applicants notified on a rolling basis starting 3/1; must reply by 5/1 or within 2 week(s) of notification.

Academics. Academic Enrichment Program available for students entering who demonstrate need for academic support. **Special study options:** Accelerated study, distance learning, double major, honors, independent study, internships, liberal arts/career combination, student-designed major, study abroad, weekend college. **Credit/placement by examination:** AP, CLEP, IB, institutional tests. 30 credit hours maximum toward associate degree, 60 toward bachelor's. **Support services:** Learning center, reduced course load, remedial instruction, study skills assistance, tutoring.

Majors. Business: Accounting, business admin, fashion, hospitality admin, hotel/motel admin, international, marketing, restaurant/food services. **Communications:** Communications/speech/rhetoric, journalism, media studies. **Computer sciences:** General, computer graphics, computer science. **Health services:** Health care admin. **Protective services:** Law enforcement admin. **Psychology:** General. **Visual/performing arts:** Graphic design, interior design.

Most popular majors. Business/marketing 36%, communications/journalism 6%, parks/recreation 8%, personal/culinary services 10%, psychology 18%, security/protective services 6%, visual/performing arts 10%.

Technology on campus. 125 workstations in dormitories, library, computer center, student center. Dormitories wired for high-speed internet access and linked to campus network. Commuter students can connect to campus network. Online library, helpline, repair service, wireless network available.

Student life. Freshman orientation: Mandatory, $175 fee. Preregistration for classes offered. Information sessions and activities held a few days before each semester. **Policies:** Freshmen not permitted cars on campus. **Housing:** Guaranteed on-campus for freshmen. Coed dorms available. $250 fully refundable deposit, deadline 5/1. Summer housing available. **Activities:** Choral groups, dance, drama, international student organizations, radio station, student government, TV station, international student organization, Habitat for Humanity, innkeepers club, business club, radio club, student programming board, games club, quidditch club, Newbury Players: Improv Troupe, step team.

Athletics. NCAA. **Intercollegiate:** Baseball M, basketball, cross-country, lacrosse W, soccer, softball W, track and field, volleyball. **Team name:** Nighthawks.

Student services. Alcohol/substance abuse counseling, career counseling, student employment services, financial aid counseling, personal counseling, placement for graduates.

Contact. E-mail: admissions@newbury.edu
Phone: (617) 730-7007 Toll-free number: (800) 639-2879
Fax: (617) 731-9618
Ken Sawada, Director of Admissions, Newbury College, 129 Fisher Avenue, Brookline, MA 02445

Nichols College
Dudley, Massachusetts **CB member**
www.nichols.edu **CB code: 3666**

- Private 4-year business and liberal arts college
- Residential campus in rural community
- 1,256 degree-seeking undergraduates: 8% part-time, 38% women
- 187 degree-seeking graduate students
- 76% of applicants admitted
- Application essay required
- 44% graduate within 6 years; 18% enter graduate study

General. Founded in 1815. Regionally accredited. **Degrees:** 304 bachelor's awarded; master's offered. **ROTC:** Army, Air Force. **Location:** 20 miles from Worcester, 50 miles from Boston. **Calendar:** Semester, limited summer session. **Full-time faculty:** 47 total; 47% have terminal degrees, 4% minority. **Part-time faculty:** 44 total; 20% have terminal degrees, 2% minority, 39% women. **Class size:** 41% < 20, 58% 20-39, less than 1% 40-49. **Special facilities:** Policy and cultural institute, financial classroom.

Freshman class profile. 2,487 applied, 1,881 admitted, 324 enrolled.

Mid 50% test scores			
		GPA 3.50-3.74:	8%
SAT critical reading:	420-510	GPA 3.0-3.49:	27%
SAT math:	440-530	GPA 2.0-2.99:	56%
SAT writing:	410-500	Return as sophomores:	71%
ACT composite:	17-22	Out-of-state:	37%
GPA 3.75 or higher:	4%	Live on campus:	91%

Basis for selection. Secondary school record most important followed by recommendations, essay, interview, and activity sheet or resume; test scores important for most. Students with 3.0 GPA can choose to waive standardized test scores. Tests not required for students with 3.0 unweighted GPA. Interview recommended. **Home schooled:** Statement describing home school structure and mission, transcript of courses and grades, state high school equivalency certificate, interview, letter of recommendation (nonparent) required.

High school preparation. College-preparatory program recommended. 16 units required. Required and recommended units include English 4, mathematics 3-4, social studies 2-3, science 2-3 (laboratory 2-3), foreign language 2 and academic electives 5. 2 foreign language recommended for liberal arts majors.

2015-2016 Annual costs. Tuition/fees: $33,300. Room/board: $12,600. Books/supplies: $1,050. Personal expenses: $1,200.

2014-2015 Financial aid. Need-based: 383 full-time freshmen applied for aid; 337 deemed to have need; 337 received aid. Average need met was 73%. Average scholarship/grant was $17,842; average loan $2,529. 66% of total undergraduate aid awarded as scholarships/grants, 34% as loans/jobs. **Non-need-based:** Awarded to 244 full-time undergraduates, including 68 freshmen. Scholarships awarded for academics, alumni affiliation, leadership, ROTC.

Application procedures. Admission: Priority date 3/1; no deadline. $25 fee, may be waived for applicants with need, free for online applicants. Admission notification on a rolling basis beginning on or about 10/1. Must reply by May 1 or within 2 week(s) if notified thereafter. **Financial aid:** Priority date 3/1, closing date 6/1. FAFSA required. Applicants notified on a rolling basis starting 2/26; must reply within 4 week(s) of notification.

Academics. One-credit Professional Development Seminar program required each year; coursework helps with resume writing, building a work portfolio, and successful interviewing skills. **Special study options:** Accelerated study, combined bachelor's/graduate degree, cooperative education, cross-registration, distance learning, double major, exchange student, honors, independent study, internships, New York semester, semester at sea, study abroad, urban semester, Washington semester. **Credit/placement by examination:** AP, CLEP, IB, SAT, ACT. 30 credit hours maximum toward bachelor's degree. **Support services:** Learning center, reduced course load, remedial instruction, study skills assistance, tutoring, writing center.

Majors. Business: Accounting, business admin, communications, finance, hospitality/recreation, human resources, international, management information systems, managerial economics, marketing, training/development. **English:** English lit. **History:** General. **Math:** General. **Parks/recreation:** Sports admin. **Protective services:** Criminal justice. **Psychology:** General. **Social sciences:** Economics.

Most popular majors. Business/marketing 70%, parks/recreation 16%, security/protective services 12%.

Technology on campus. 150 workstations in dormitories, library, computer center, student center. Dormitories wired for high-speed internet access and linked to campus network. Commuter students can connect to campus network. Online course registration, online library, helpline, repair service, wireless network available.

Student life. Freshman orientation: Mandatory. Preregistration for classes offered. Overnight pre-college summer programs for students and parents. **Housing:** Guaranteed on-campus for all undergraduates. Coed dorms, single-sex dorms, special housing for disabled, apartments, themed housing, wellness housing available. $250 deposit, deadline 5/1. **Activities:** Campus ministries, dance, drama, international student organizations, literary magazine, radio station, student government, Institute for American Values, Republican club, Young Democrats, Umoja.

Athletics. NCAA. **Intercollegiate:** Baseball M, basketball, cross-country, field hockey W, football (tackle) M, golf M, ice hockey, lacrosse, soccer, softball W, tennis, track and field. **Intramural:** Basketball, football (non-tackle), racquetball, soccer, softball M, volleyball. **Team name:** Bison.

Student services. Alcohol/substance abuse counseling, chaplain/spiritual director, career counseling, student employment services, financial aid counseling, health services, minority student services, personal counseling, placement for graduates, women's services.

Contact. E-mail: admissions@nichols.edu
Phone: (800) 470-3379 Toll-free number: (800) 470-3379
Fax: (508) 943-9885
Emily Reardon, Associate Director of Admissions, Nichols College, PO Box 5000, Dudley, MA 01571-5000

Northeastern University
Boston, Massachusetts **CB member**
www.northeastern.edu **CB code: 3667**

- Private 4-year university
- Residential campus in very large city

- 17,913 degree-seeking undergraduates: 50% women, 4% African American, 12% Asian American, 7% Hispanic/Latino, 4% Multi-racial, non-Hispanic, 19% international
- 6,954 graduate students
- 28% of applicants admitted
- SAT or ACT (ACT writing optional), application essay required
- 84% graduate within 6 years

General. Founded in 1898. Regionally accredited. **Degrees:** 3,621 bachelor's awarded; master's, professional, doctoral offered. **ROTC:** Army, Naval, Air Force. **Calendar:** Semester, extensive summer session. **Full-time faculty:** 1,257 total; 94% have terminal degrees, 16% minority, 40% women. **Part-time faculty:** 403 total; 11% minority, 45% women. **Class size:** 65% < 20, 18% 20-39, 10% 40-49, 5% 50-99, 2% >100. **Special facilities:** Complex network research center, drug discovery center, chemical and biological analysis institute, high rate nanomanufacturing center, subsurface sensing and imaging systems center, information assurance institute, urban health research institute, urban and regional policy center, African-American institute, race and justice institute, global innovation management institute, homeland security research facility.

Freshman class profile. 50,523 applied, 14,388 admitted, 2,797 enrolled.

Mid 50% test scores			
SAT critical reading:	660-740	Return as sophomores:	97%
SAT math:	680-770	Out-of-state:	76%
SAT writing:	640-730	Live on campus:	99%
ACT composite:	31-34	International:	17%
Rank in top quarter:	94%	Fraternities:	5%
Rank in top tenth:	70%	Sororities:	7%

Basis for selection. Academic assessment which includes applicant's curriculum in context of course work available in secondary school, performance as measured by grades and grade trends, preparation for undergraduate major, and standardized testing. Recommendations, personal statement, activities, interests, and applicant's fit and readiness considered. For students whose native language is not English, a proof of English language proficiency is required. To satisfy this requirement, students should submit results of a TOEFL, IELTS or Pearson Test of English (PTE) exam. Students who are applying for science-based majors should take a SAT subject test in science as their second exam. Applicants to College of Engineering must submit a physics Subject Test. For students applying from secondary schools located outside the US, standardized tests (SAT/ACT) are not required and are not considered for admission. Portfolios/auditions required for studio art, music technology programs. Interviews offered to select candidates for whom the Admission Committee would like additional information. **Home schooled:** Statement describing home school structure and mission, transcript of courses and grades, letter of recommendation (nonparent) required. Applicants must submit a Common Application and Secondary School Report, academic portfolio/transcript consistent with home state guidelines, and list of all textbooks used. Proof that all requirements for official high school diploma have been met, GED, or certificate of completion from local school district or state board of education also required. ACT with Writing or SAT with Writing, plus two SAT Subject Tests, including math and additional test of choice, are required.

High school preparation. College-preparatory program required. 17 units required. Required and recommended units include English 4, mathematics 3-4, social studies 3, history 2, science 3-4 (laboratory 2) and foreign language 2-3. Each department and college of university may have more specific recommendations for additional preparation.

2015-2016 Annual costs. Tuition/fees: $45,530. Room/board: $15,000. Books/supplies: $1,000. Personal expenses: $900.

2015-2016 Financial aid. Need-based: 1,888 full-time freshmen applied for aid; 1,243 deemed to have need; 1,243 received aid. Average need met was 100%. Average scholarship/grant was $32,339; average loan $4,608. 77% of total undergraduate aid awarded as scholarships/grants, 23% as loans/jobs. **Non-need-based:** Awarded to 6,930 full-time undergraduates, including 1,303 freshmen. Scholarships awarded for academics, athletics, leadership, ROTC.

Application procedures. Admission: Closing date 1/1 (receipt date). $75 fee, may be waived for applicants with need. Admission notification by 4/1. Must reply by 5/1. **Financial aid:** Priority date 2/15; no closing date. FAFSA, CSS PROFILE required. Applicants notified by 4/1; must reply by 5/1.

Academics. Special study options: Accelerated study, combined bachelor's/graduate degree, cooperative education, cross-registration, distance learning, double major, ESL, exchange student, honors, independent study, internships, liberal arts/career combination, semester at sea, student-designed major, study abroad, teacher certification program, Washington semester. **Credit/placement by examination:** AP, CLEP, IB, institutional tests. **Support services:** Learning center, pre-admission summer program, reduced course load, remedial instruction, study skills assistance, tutoring, writing center.

Honors college/program. Top 20% of incoming freshmen class automatically reviewed for admission. Admissions based on high school academic record/GPA and SAT/ACT.

Majors. Architecture: Architecture, history/criticism, landscape. **Area/ethnic studies:** African-American, Asian. **Biology:** General, biochemistry, biophysics, neuroscience. **Business:** General, accounting, business admin, entrepreneurial studies, finance, human resources, international, logistics, management information systems, marketing. **Communications:** General, communications/speech/rhetoric, journalism, media studies. **Communications technology:** Animation/special effects. **Computer sciences:** General, information systems. **Conservation:** Environmental science, environmental studies. **Engineering:** General, chemical, civil, computer, electrical, industrial, mechanical. **English:** English lit. **Foreign languages:** American Sign Language, linguistics, Spanish. **Health services:** Audiology/speech pathology, nursing (RN), pharmaceutical sciences, rehabilitation science. **History:** General. **Math:** General. **Philosophy/religion:** Judaic, philosophy, religion. **Physical sciences:** Chemistry, geology, physics. **Protective services:** Criminal justice. **Psychology:** General. **Social sciences:** Cultural anthropology, economics, international relations, political science, sociology. **Visual/performing arts:** Art, digital arts, dramatic, film/cinema/video, graphic design, multimedia, music, studio arts.

Most popular majors. Biology 8%, business/marketing 23%, communications/journalism 6%, engineering/engineering technologies 14%, health sciences 15%, social sciences 10%.

Technology on campus. 1,993 workstations in dormitories, library, computer center, student center, student center. Dormitories wired for high-speed internet access and linked to campus network. Commuter students can connect to campus network. Online course registration, online library, helpline, repair service, student web hosting, wireless network available.

Student life. Freshman orientation: Mandatory, $350 fee. Preregistration for classes offered. **Policies:** Freshmen not permitted cars on campus. **Housing:** Guaranteed on-campus for freshmen. Coed dorms, special housing for disabled, apartments, gender-neutral housing, themed housing, wellness housing available. $400 nonrefundable deposit, deadline 5/1. **Activities:** Bands, campus ministries, choral groups, dance, drama, film society, international student organizations, literary magazine, music ensembles, Model UN, musical theater, radio station, student government, student newspaper, symphony orchestra, TV station, 400 student organizations available.

Athletics. NCAA. **Intercollegiate:** Baseball M, basketball, cross-country, diving W, field hockey W, ice hockey, rowing (crew), soccer, swimming W, track and field, volleyball W. **Intramural:** Basketball, football (non-tackle) M, ice hockey, lacrosse, racquetball, soccer, softball, tennis, volleyball, water polo. **Team name:** Huskies.

Student services. Alcohol/substance abuse counseling, chaplain/spiritual director, career counseling, services for economically disadvantaged, student employment services, financial aid counseling, health services, legal services, minority student services, on-campus daycare, personal counseling, placement for graduates, veterans' counselor, women's services. **Physically disabled:** Services for visually, speech, hearing impaired.

Contact. E-mail: admissions@neu.edu
Phone: (617) 373-2200 Fax: (617) 373-8780
Ronne Turner, Associate Vice President for Enrollment and Dean of Admissions, Northeastern University, 200 Kerr Hall, Boston, MA 02115

Northpoint Bible College
Haverhill, Massachusetts
www.northpoint.edu   **CB code: 3942**

- Private 4-year Bible college affiliated with the Assemblies of God
- Residential campus in small city
- 234 degree-seeking undergraduates: 15% part-time, 42% women
- 9 degree-seeking graduate students
- SAT or ACT (ACT writing optional), application essay required

General. Accredited by ABHE. **Degrees:** 42 bachelor's, 11 associate awarded; master's offered. **Location:** 40 miles from Boston. **Calendar:** Semester, limited summer session.

Freshman class profile.

Mid 50% test scores			
SAT critical reading:	480-560	GPA 3.50-3.74:	13%
SAT math:	460-570	GPA 3.0-3.49:	30%
SAT writing:	440-570	GPA 2.0-2.99:	43%
ACT composite:	15-19	Out-of-state:	79%
GPA 3.75 or higher:	7%	Live on campus:	61%

Basis for selection. References are weighed heavily in correlation with student's application material and personal statements. SAT/ACT for class placement only. **Home schooled:** Transcript of courses and grades required. Applicants must produce diploma and transcript that verify graduation by the state department of education, local school district or accrediting association. Curriculum used and a copy of the student's state home school requirements must also be submitted. Students who cannot produce this must submit GED.

2015-2016 Annual costs. Tuition/fees: $11,150. Room/board: $8,350.

2015-2016 Financial aid. Need-based: 37% of total undergraduate aid awarded as scholarships/grants, 63% as loans/jobs. **Non-need-based:** Scholarships awarded for academics, leadership, minority status, music/drama, state residency.

Application procedures. Admission: No deadline. $35 fee, may be waived for applicants with need. Admission notification on a rolling basis. Letter of Intent with deposit (tuition and board) required one month after notification. High school transcript, immunization record, health certificate, 2 references (including pastoral recommendation) required. **Financial aid:** Priority date 6/1; no closing date. FAFSA required. Applicants notified on a rolling basis; must reply within 4 week(s) of notification.

Academics. Special study options: Double major, independent study, internships, weekend college. **Credit/placement by examination:** AP, CLEP, SAT, ACT. **Support services:** Learning center, reduced course load, study skills assistance.

Majors. Theology: Bible.

Technology on campus. 12 workstations in computer center. Dormitories wired for high-speed internet access. Commuter students can connect to campus network. Online course registration, online library, wireless network available.

Student life. Freshman orientation: Mandatory. Preregistration for classes offered. **Policies:** Nightly curfew of 11:00, except for Fridays (11:30 or midnight for seniors). Chapel attendance required Monday through Thursday. No alcohol, drugs, or smoking permitted on-campus or off-campus. Full-time students assigned to assist in area church. Religious observance required. **Housing:** Guaranteed on-campus for all undergraduates. Single-sex dorms available. $100 fully refundable deposit. **Activities:** Campus ministries, choral groups, music ensembles, student government.

Student services. Chaplain/spiritual director, financial aid counseling.

Contact. E-mail: admissions@northpoint.edu
Phone: (978) 478-3400 Toll-free number: (800) 356-4014
Fax: (978) 478-3406
Amy Maranville, Registrar, Northpoint Bible College, 320 South Main Street, Haverhill, MA 01835

Pine Manor College
Chestnut Hill, Massachusetts   CB member
www.pmc.edu   CB code: 3689

- Private 4-year liberal arts college
- Residential campus in very large city
- 354 degree-seeking undergraduates: 3% part-time, 63% women
- 39 degree-seeking graduate students
- 71% of applicants admitted
- Application essay required
- 35% graduate within 6 years

General. Founded in 1911. Regionally accredited. **Degrees:** 26 bachelor's, 5 associate awarded; master's offered. **ROTC:** Army, Air Force. **Location:** 5 miles from Boston. **Calendar:** Semester, limited summer session. **Full-time faculty:** 13 total. **Part-time faculty:** 48 total. **Class size:** 78% < 20, 22% 20-39. **Special facilities:** Child study center.

Freshman class profile. 764 applied, 542 admitted, 97 enrolled.

GPA 3.75 or higher:	3%	Return as sophomores:	46%
GPA 3.50-3.74:	8%	Out-of-state:	52%
GPA 3.0-3.49:	13%	Live on campus:	73%
GPA 2.0-2.99:	59%		

Basis for selection. School achievement record, test scores, GPA, and recommendations important. Rolling deadline for SAT/ACT score submission. Interview recommended. **Home schooled:** Statement describing home school structure and mission, transcript of courses and grades required. **Learning Disabled:** Students may be required to submit learning disability documentation.

High school preparation. College-preparatory program recommended. 14 units recommended. Required and recommended units include English 4, mathematics 2, social studies 1, science 2 (laboratory 1), foreign language 2 and academic electives 1.

2015-2016 Annual costs. Tuition/fees: $27,105. Room/board: $12,890. Books/supplies: $800. Personal expenses: $1,000.

Financial aid. Non-need-based: Scholarships awarded for academics, alumni affiliation, leadership.

Application procedures. Admission: Priority date 7/15; deadline 8/15. $25 fee, may be waived for applicants with need. Admission notification on a rolling basis beginning on or about 9/1. Must reply by May 1 or within 2 week(s) if notified thereafter. **Financial aid:** Priority date 5/1; no closing date. FAFSA required. Applicants notified on a rolling basis starting 4/1; must reply by 5/1 or within 2 week(s) of notification.

Academics. All students required to participate in internship program. **Special study options:** Cross-registration, double major, honors, independent study, internships, liberal arts/career combination, student-designed major, study abroad, teacher certification program. Students with sophomore status or higher eligible to take courses offered by Marine Studies Consortium. **Credit/placement by examination:** AP, CLEP, IB, institutional tests. 24 credit hours maximum toward bachelor's degree. **Support services:** Learning center, reduced course load, study skills assistance, tutoring, writing center.

Majors. Biology: General. **Business:** Business admin. **Communications:** Media studies. **Education:** Early childhood. **English:** English lit. **Health services:** General. **Psychology:** General. **Social sciences:** Political science. **Visual/performing arts:** General.

Most popular majors. Biology 13%, business/marketing 21%, communications/journalism 9%, education 13%, health sciences 9%, psychology 13%, social sciences 13%, visual/performing arts 9%.

Technology on campus. 108 workstations in dormitories, library, computer center, student center. Dormitories wired for high-speed internet access and linked to campus network. Commuter students can connect to campus network. Online course registration, helpline, repair service available.

Student life. Freshman orientation: Mandatory, $150 fee. Preregistration for classes offered. Held in June and September. **Housing:** Guaranteed on-campus for freshmen. Coed dorms, single-sex dorms, wellness housing available. $250 nonrefundable deposit, deadline 8/15. Quiet residence halls available. **Activities:** Choral groups, dance, drama, literary magazine, Model UN, radio station, student government, student newspaper, Ladies of Various Ebony Shades, African American/Latina/Asian/Native American and All club, Alianza Latina, bisexuals/gays/lesbians and allies in diversity club, Cape Verdean student alliance, dance ensemble, student government association, student health advisory board, Imani Christian club, Camerata singers.

Athletics. NCAA. **Intercollegiate:** Basketball, cross-country, soccer, softball W, volleyball W. **Team name:** Gators.

Student services. Alcohol/substance abuse counseling, career counseling, services for economically disadvantaged, student employment services, financial aid counseling, health services, minority student services, personal counseling, placement for graduates, women's services.

Contact. E-mail: admission@pmc.edu
Phone: (617) 731-7011 Toll-free number: (800) 762-1357
Fax: (617) 731-7102
Stephen Secora, Director of Admissions, Pine Manor College, 400 Heath Street, Chestnut Hill, MA 02467

Regis College
Weston, Massachusetts   CB member
www.regiscollege.edu   CB code: 3723

- Private 4-year health science and liberal arts college affiliated with the Roman Catholic Church
- Residential campus in large town
- 1,235 degree-seeking undergraduates: 22% part-time, 79% women, 19% African American, 4% Asian American, 11% Hispanic/Latino, 1% Multiracial, non-Hispanic, 2% international
- 719 degree-seeking graduate students
- 84% of applicants admitted
- Application essay required
- 47% graduate within 6 years

General. Founded in 1927. Regionally accredited. College founded by Sisters of St. Joseph of Boston. **Degrees:** 319 bachelor's, 109 associate awarded; master's, professional offered. **ROTC:** Army. **Location:** 12 miles from Boston. **Calendar:** Semester, limited summer session. **Full-time faculty:** 96 total; 70% have terminal degrees, 9% minority, 76% women. **Part-time faculty:** 114 total; 36% have terminal degrees, 9% minority, 75% women. **Class size:** 65% < 20, 34% 20-39, 1% 40-49, less than 1% 50-99. **Special facilities:** Philatelic museum, fine arts center, 2 digital imaging studios, music laboratory with electronic keyboards and computers.

Freshman class profile. 2,023 applied, 1,704 admitted, 269 enrolled.

Mid 50% test scores			
SAT critical reading:	440-520	GPA 2.0-2.99:	44%
SAT math:	430-540	Rank in top quarter:	35%
SAT writing:	420-520	Rank in top tenth:	10%
ACT composite:	19-26	End year in good standing:	92%
GPA 3.75 or higher:	8%	Return as sophomores:	82%
GPA 3.50-3.74:	13%	Out-of-state:	24%
GPA 3.0-3.49:	35%	Live on campus:	88%
		International:	2%

Basis for selection. All credentials within student's file reviewed. At times, interview or additional grades requested or guidance counselors called. Scores are required for the Nursing program only. Interview highly recommended. **Home schooled:** Statement describing home school structure and mission, transcript of courses and grades, letter of recommendation (nonparent) required. **Learning Disabled:** Should apprise Director of Student Disabilities of disability status and document condition to receive appropriate accommodations.

High school preparation. College-preparatory program recommended. 16 units required. Required and recommended units include English 4, mathematics 3, social studies 2-4, science 2 (laboratory 1), foreign language 2-3 and academic electives 3. 4 math and 4 science recommended for nursing.

2015-2016 Annual costs. Tuition/fees: $37,540. Room/board: $14,380. Books/supplies: $1,000. Personal expenses: $1,520.

2015-2016 Financial aid. Need-based: 257 full-time freshmen applied for aid; 240 deemed to have need; 240 received aid. Average need met was 60%. Average scholarship/grant was $21,525; average loan $3,361. 68% of total undergraduate aid awarded as scholarships/grants, 32% as loans/jobs. **Non-need-based:** Awarded to 486 full-time undergraduates, including 144 freshmen. Scholarships awarded for academics, alumni affiliation. **Additional information:** Family tuition discount scholarship offered during any semester in which 2 or more unmarried, dependent siblings attend as full-time undergraduates.

Application procedures. Admission: Priority date 2/15; deadline 6/1 (postmark date). $50 fee, may be waived for applicants with need. Admission notification on a rolling basis beginning on or about 12/20. Must reply by May 1 or within 2 week(s) if notified thereafter. Students encouraged to apply by January 1. **Financial aid:** Priority date 2/15; no closing date. FAFSA required. Applicants notified on a rolling basis starting 3/15.

Academics. Online tutoring assistance, professional math and writing tutor, and academic skills workshops available. Academic Center for Excellence offers academic coaching. **Special study options:** Accelerated study, combined bachelor's/graduate degree, cross-registration, double major, dual enrollment of high school students, ESL, exchange student, honors, independent study, internships, student-designed major, study abroad, teacher certification program, Washington semester. **Credit/placement by examination:** AP, CLEP, IB, SAT, ACT, institutional tests. 24 credit hours maximum toward bachelor's degree. **Support services:** Learning center, reduced course load, remedial instruction, study skills assistance, tutoring, writing center.

Majors. Biology: General, biochemistry. **Business:** General. **Communications:** General. **Education:** Mathematics. **English:** English lit. **Foreign languages:** Spanish. **Health services:** Medical assistant, nursing (RN), radiologic technology/medical imaging. **History:** General. **Human services:** Social work. **Liberal arts:** Arts/sciences. **Parks/recreation:** Health/fitness. **Physical sciences:** Chemistry. **Psychology:** General. **Social sciences:** International relations, political science, sociology.

Most popular majors. Health sciences 71%.

Technology on campus. 196 workstations in library, computer center. Dormitories wired for high-speed internet access and linked to campus network. Commuter students can connect to campus network. Online course registration, online library, helpline, wireless network available.

Student life. Freshman orientation: Mandatory, $195 fee. Preregistration for classes offered. Two-day summer session and 2-day fall session during opening weekend. **Policies:** Must complete series of effective decision-making courses in order to obtain guest privileges. All residences smoke-free. Freshmen not permitted cars on campus. **Housing:** Guaranteed on-campus for all undergraduates. Coed dorms, single-sex dorms, special housing

for disabled, wellness housing available. $450 nonrefundable deposit, deadline 5/1. Quiet floors available. **Activities:** Campus ministries, choral groups, dance, drama, international student organizations, literary magazine, music ensembles, Model UN, musical theater, radio station, student government, Asian-American Association, Black Student Organization, Campus Ministry, Cape Verdean Student Association, Dance Company, Dynasty Step Squad, education club, Gay Straight Alliance, glee club, international club.

Athletics. NCAA. **Intercollegiate:** Basketball, cross-country, diving, field hockey W, lacrosse, soccer, softball W, swimming, tennis, track and field, volleyball. **Intramural:** Basketball, soccer, volleyball. **Team name:** Regis Pride.

Student services. Adult student services, alcohol/substance abuse counseling, chaplain/spiritual director, career counseling, services for economically disadvantaged, student employment services, financial aid counseling, health services, minority student services, on-campus daycare, personal counseling, placement for graduates, veterans' counselor. **Physically disabled:** Services for visually, hearing impaired.

Contact. E-mail: admission@regiscollege.edu
Phone: (781) 768-7100 Toll-free number: (866) 438-7344
Fax: (781) 768-7071
Zakaree Harris, Director of Admission, Regis College, 235 Wellesley Street, Weston, MA 02493-1571

Salem State University	
Salem, Massachusetts	**CB member**
www.salemstate.edu	**CB code: 3522**

- Public 4-year university
- Commuter campus in large town
- 7,134 degree-seeking undergraduates
- 1,637 graduate students
- SAT or ACT (ACT writing optional) required

General. Founded in 1854. Regionally accredited. **Degrees:** 1,594 bachelor's awarded; master's offered. **ROTC:** Army, Air Force. **Location:** 15 miles from Boston. **Calendar:** Semester, extensive summer session. **Class size:** 55% < 20, 43% 20-39, 1% 40-49, less than 1% 50-99. **Special facilities:** Media facility, center for creative and performing arts, observatories, glass blowing studio.

Freshman class profile.

GPA 3.75 or higher:	13%	GPA 2.0-2.99:	41%
GPA 3.50-3.74:	13%	Out-of-state:	5%
GPA 3.0-3.49:	33%	Live on campus:	65%

Basis for selection. Students with 3.0 GPA and college prep curriculum admitted. Students with less than 3.0 GPA admitted with balancing SAT/ACT scores. Special consideration possible. Some majors require higher GPA. Recommendations considered. Portfolio required for art applicants. Audition required for music applicants. **Home schooled:** State high school equivalency certificate required.

High school preparation. College-preparatory program required. 16 units required; 18 recommended. Required and recommended units include English 4, mathematics 3-4, social studies 2, history 1-3, science 3 (laboratory 3), foreign language 2, computer science 1 and visual/performing arts 1. Additional requirements for some programs.

2015-2016 Annual costs. Tuition/fees: $9,246; $15,386 out-of-state. Room/board: $12,464. Books/supplies: $1,000.

Financial aid. Non-need-based: Scholarships awarded for academics.

Application procedures. Admission: Closing date 4/15. $40 fee, may be waived for applicants with need. Admission notification on a rolling basis beginning on or about 12/1. Must reply by May 1 or within 2 week(s) if notified thereafter. **Financial aid:** Priority date 3/1, closing date 9/1. FAFSA required. Applicants notified on a rolling basis starting 3/15; must reply within 2 week(s) of notification.

Academics. Reading lab available. **Special study options:** Accelerated study, combined bachelor's/graduate degree, cross-registration, distance learning, double major, dual enrollment of high school students, ESL, honors, independent study, internships, semester at sea, student-designed major, study abroad, teacher certification program, Washington semester. **Credit/placement by examination:** AP, CLEP, SAT, institutional tests. **Support services:** Learning center, pre-admission summer program, reduced course load, remedial instruction, tutoring, writing center.

Majors. Biology: General, biochemistry, ecology, marine. **Business:** Accounting, accounting/finance, business admin, entrepreneurial studies, finance, hospitality admin, human resources, international, management information systems, managerial economics, marketing, tourism/travel. **Communications:** Advertising, communications/speech/rhetoric, journalism, media studies, public relations. **Computer sciences:** General. **Education:** General, early childhood, elementary, middle, physical, secondary, Spanish. **English:** Creative writing, English lit, technical writing, writing. **Foreign languages:** Comparative lit, Spanish, translation. **Health services:** Athletic training, clinical lab science, nuclear medical technology, nursing (RN). **History:** General, American, applied, European. **Human services:** Social work. **Liberal arts:** Arts/sciences. **Math:** General. **Parks/recreation:** General, exercise sciences, health/fitness, sports admin. **Physical sciences:** Chemistry, geology. **Protective services:** Fire services admin, law enforcement admin. **Psychology:** General. **Social sciences:** Economics, geography, GIS/cartography, political science, sociology. **Visual/performing arts:** Acting, art, art history/conservation, commercial/advertising art, dramatic, drawing, music, painting, photography, printmaking, sculpture, theater design, theater history.

Most popular majors. Business/marketing 22%, communications/journalism 6%, education 9%, health sciences 13%, psychology 8%, security/protective services 9%.

Technology on campus. PC or laptop required. 255 workstations in library, computer center, student center. Dormitories wired for high-speed internet access and linked to campus network. Commuter students can connect to campus network. Online course registration, online library, helpline, repair service, student web hosting, wireless network available.

Student life. Freshman orientation: Mandatory, $175 fee. Preregistration for classes offered. Sessions held prior to start of semester. **Housing:** Coed dorms, apartments, themed housing, wellness housing available. $225 nonrefundable deposit, deadline 5/1. **Activities:** Bands, campus ministries, choral groups, dance, drama, international student organizations, literary magazine, music ensembles, musical theater, radio station, student government, student newspaper, Hispanic-American society, multicultural student association, Asian student association, community service group, campus educators on sexual assault, political science academy, student action resource team.

Athletics. NCAA. **Intercollegiate:** Baseball M, basketball, cross-country, field hockey W, golf M, ice hockey M, lacrosse, soccer, softball W, tennis. **Intramural:** Cheerleading W, football (non-tackle), rugby, ultimate frisbee, volleyball. **Team name:** Vikings.

Student services. Adult student services, alcohol/substance abuse counseling, chaplain/spiritual director, career counseling, services for economically disadvantaged, student employment services, financial aid counseling, health services, legal services, minority student services, on-campus daycare, personal counseling, placement for graduates, veterans' counselor, women's services. **Physically disabled:** Services for visually, speech, hearing impaired.

Contact. E-mail: admissions@salemstate.edu
Phone: (978) 542-6200 Fax: (978) 542-6893
Mary Dunn, Assistant Dean of Undergraduate Admissions, Salem State University, 352 Lafayette Street, Salem, MA 01970-5353

School of the Museum of Fine Arts
Boston, Massachusetts
www.smfa.edu   CB code: 3794

- Private 4-year visual arts college
- Commuter campus in very large city
- 278 degree-seeking undergraduates: 11% part-time, 73% women, 2% African American, 3% Asian American, 12% Hispanic/Latino, 4% Multiracial, non-Hispanic, 12% international
- 149 degree-seeking graduate students
- 83% of applicants admitted
- Application essay required
- 54% graduate within 6 years

General. Founded in 1876. The SMFA is a division of the Museum of Fine Arts, Boston, and maintains partnerships with Tufts University, Northeastern University, and the ProArts Consortium, which offers studio courses at five other Boston visual and performing arts schools for no additional cost. **Degrees:** 93 bachelor's awarded; master's offered. **Location:** One mile from downtown. **Calendar:** Semester, limited summer session. **Full-time faculty:** 40 total; 85% have terminal degrees, 12% minority, 68% women. **Part-time faculty:** 49 total; 82% have terminal degrees, 12% minority, 71% women. **Class size:** 92% < 20, 8% 20-39.

Freshman class profile. 371 applied, 307 admitted, 37 enrolled.

GPA 3.75 or higher:	29%	Return as sophomores:	78%
GPA 3.50-3.74:	18%	Out-of-state:	61%
GPA 3.0-3.49:	21%	Live on campus:	62%
GPA 2.0-2.99:	26%	International:	3%
End year in good standing:	94%		

Basis for selection. Portfolio, level of applicant's interest, GPA, quality and content of essays are very important. Previous schooling, recommendation, and personal qualities are also considered. Volunteer work and work experience are considered if submitted. Portfolio required; interviews available. **Home schooled:** Transcript of courses and grades, state high school equivalency certificate, letter of recommendation (nonparent) required. Must submit both an official home-schooled transcript and GED/state equivalency scores in order to be considered for admission. Official transcripts must be submitted from any high school attended. Interviews are strongly recommended.

High school preparation. College-preparatory program recommended. 23 units recommended. Recommended units include English 4, mathematics 3, social studies 2, history 2, science 3 (laboratory 2), foreign language 2, computer science 1 and visual/performing arts 2.

2015-2016 Annual costs. Tuition/fees: $41,228. Room only: $10,950. Books/supplies: $1,600. Personal expenses: $2,000.

2015-2016 Financial aid. Need-based: Average need met was 46%. Average scholarship/grant was $5,591; average loan $4,452. 46% of total undergraduate aid awarded as scholarships/grants, 54% as loans/jobs. **Non-need-based:** Scholarships awarded for academics, art.

Application procedures. Admission: Priority date 2/15; no deadline. $65 fee, may be waived for applicants with need. Admission notification on a rolling basis beginning on or about 1/15. Must reply by May 1 or within 2 week(s) if notified thereafter. Students may apply early and request early notification of admission. **Financial aid:** Closing date 3/15. FAFSA required. Applicants notified by 4/1; Applicants notified on a rolling basis starting 4/1; must reply by 5/1 or within 2 week(s) of notification.

Academics. Special study options: Cross-registration, double major, exchange student, independent study, internships, liberal arts/career combination, student-designed major, study abroad, teacher certification program. 5-year Dual Degree BFA/BA with Tufts University, studio art elective diploma program, extensive exchange and cross-registration opportunities within Boston and around the world. All programs are interdisciplinary with no studio requirements or foundation programs. **Credit/placement by examination:** AP, CLEP. **Support services:** Reduced course load, study skills assistance, writing center.

Majors. Communications technology: Animation/special effects. **Visual/performing arts:** Art, ceramics, cinematography, design, digital arts, drawing, graphic design, illustration, metal/jewelry, multimedia, painting, photography, printmaking, sculpture, studio arts.

Technology on campus. 182 workstations in library, computer center, student center. Dormitories wired for high-speed internet access. Online course registration, helpline, wireless network available.

Student life. Freshman orientation: Mandatory, $125 fee. Preregistration for classes offered. Held during last week in August. **Housing:** Guaranteed on-campus for freshmen. Coed dorms available. $300 nonrefundable deposit, deadline 5/1. Professional off-campus housing assistance available. **Activities:** Film society, international student organizations, student government, student newspaper, Food bank club; diversity committee; Otakus Lounge.

Student services. Alcohol/substance abuse counseling, career counseling, student employment services, financial aid counseling, personal counseling. **Physically disabled:** Services for hearing impaired.

Contact. E-mail: admissions@smfa.edu
Phone: (617) 369-3626 Toll-free number: (800) 643-6078
Fax: (617) 369-4264
Angela Jones, Director of Admissions, School of the Museum of Fine Arts, 230 The Fenway, Boston, MA 02115

Simmons College
Boston, Massachusetts   CB member
www.simmons.edu   CB code: 3761

- Private 4-year health science and liberal arts college for women
- Residential campus in very large city

- 1,706 degree-seeking undergraduates: 6% part-time, 100% women, 7% African American, 9% Asian American, 6% Hispanic/Latino, 4% Multiracial, non-Hispanic, 3% international
- 3,726 degree-seeking graduate students
- 58% of applicants admitted
- SAT or ACT (ACT writing recommended), application essay required
- 74% graduate within 6 years; 23% enter graduate study

General. Founded in 1899. Regionally accredited. **Degrees:** 430 bachelor's awarded; master's, professional, doctoral offered. **ROTC:** Army. **Location:** 2 miles from downtown Boston. **Calendar:** Semester, extensive summer session. **Full-time faculty:** 218 total; 18% minority, 74% women. **Part-time faculty:** 626 total; 12% minority, 85% women. **Class size:** 66% < 20, 26% 20-39, 4% 40-49, 3% 50-99. **Special facilities:** Art gallery, technology resource center.

Freshman class profile. 4,575 applied, 2,634 admitted, 476 enrolled.

Mid 50% test scores		GPA 2.0-2.99:	18%
SAT critical reading:	540-630	Rank in top quarter:	72%
SAT math:	520-610	Rank in top tenth:	35%
SAT writing:	530-630	End year in good standing:	98%
ACT composite:	24-29	Return as sophomores:	85%
GPA 3.75 or higher:	20%	Out-of-state:	53%
GPA 3.50-3.74:	19%	Live on campus:	93%
GPA 3.0-3.49:	43%	International:	4%

Basis for selection. School achievement record most important. Test scores, 2 recommendations, essay, interview (if available), personal qualities also important. Interests, accomplishments considered. **Home schooled:** Statement describing home school structure and mission, transcript of courses and grades, letter of recommendation (nonparent) required.

High school preparation. College-preparatory program required. 4 units required. Required and recommended units include English 4, mathematics 3-4, social studies 3, history 2-3, science 4 (laboratory 3), foreign language 3-4 and academic electives 3-4.

2015-2016 Annual costs. Tuition/fees: $37,380. Room/board: $14,040. Books/supplies: $1,280. Personal expenses: $1,700.

2015-2016 Financial aid. Need-based: 411 full-time freshmen applied for aid; 368 deemed to have need; 368 received aid. Average need met was 77%. Average scholarship/grant was $27,573; average loan $3,105. 82% of total undergraduate aid awarded as scholarships/grants, 18% as loans/jobs. **Non-need-based:** Awarded to 377 full-time undergraduates, including 135 freshmen. Scholarships awarded for academics, alumni affiliation.

Application procedures. Admission: Priority date 11/1; deadline 2/1 (postmark date). $55 fee, may be waived for applicants with need, free for online applicants. Admission notification by 3/15. Must reply by 5/1. **Financial aid:** Priority date 3/1; no closing date. FAFSA, institutional form required. Applicants notified on a rolling basis starting 3/15.

Academics. Special study options: Accelerated study, combined bachelor's/graduate degree, cross-registration, distance learning, double major, exchange student, honors, independent study, internships, liberal arts/career combination, semester at sea, student-designed major, study abroad, teacher certification program, Washington semester. Exchange program with Mills College, Spelman College, Colleges of the Fenway, double degree programs with Massachusetts College of Pharmacy. **Credit/placement by examination:** AP, CLEP, IB, SAT, ACT, institutional tests. **Support services:** Learning center, reduced course load, study skills assistance, tutoring, writing center.

Majors. Area/ethnic studies: African, American, East Asian, women's. **Biology:** General, biochemistry, biostatistics. **Business:** Accounting, accounting/finance, business admin, finance, international, management information systems, marketing, sales/distribution. **Communications:** Advertising, communications/speech/rhetoric, public relations. **Computer sciences:** General, information technology, system admin. **Conservation:** Environmental science. **Education:** General, early childhood, elementary, ESL, secondary, special ed. **English:** American lit, British lit, English lit. **Foreign languages:** French, Spanish. **Health services:** Dietetics, medical informatics, nursing (RN), physical therapy, public health ed. **History:** General. **Human services:** Public policy, social work. **Liberal arts:** Arts/sciences. **Math:** General. **Parks/recreation:** Exercise sciences. **Philosophy/religion:** Philosophy. **Physical sciences:** Chemistry, physics. **Psychology:** General, psychobiology. **Social sciences:** Economics, international relations, political science, sociology. **Visual/performing arts:** Art, commercial/advertising art, music, studio arts management. **Work/family studies:** Institutional food production, merchandising.

Most popular majors. Business/marketing 8%, health sciences 41%, parks/recreation 6%, social sciences 9%.

Technology on campus. 570 workstations in dormitories, library, computer center, student center. Dormitories wired for high-speed internet access and linked to campus network. Commuter students can connect to campus network. Online course registration, online library, helpline, student web hosting, wireless network available.

Student life. Freshman orientation: Mandatory, $99 fee. Preregistration for classes offered. Optional program held in June; mandatory program held the day before classes begin. **Policies:** Residency requirement for first-year students, service animals allowed in dorm rooms. Freshmen not permitted cars on campus. **Housing:** Guaranteed on-campus for freshmen. Special housing for disabled, themed housing, wellness housing available. $250 nonrefundable deposit, deadline 5/1. **Activities:** Bands, campus ministries, choral groups, dance, drama, international student organizations, literary magazine, music ensembles, Model UN, musical theater, radio station, student government, student newspaper, student government association, black student organization, organizacion Latino Americana, Hillel, Amnesty International, women's center, The Alliance, chemistry-physics liaison, dance company.

Athletics. NCAA. **Intercollegiate:** Basketball W, cross-country W, diving W, field hockey W, lacrosse W, rowing (crew) W, soccer W, softball W, swimming W, tennis W, track and field W, volleyball W. **Intramural:** Basketball, soccer, volleyball. **Team name:** Sharks.

Student services. Adult student services, alcohol/substance abuse counseling, chaplain/spiritual director, career counseling, student employment services, financial aid counseling, health services, personal counseling, placement for graduates, women's services. **Physically disabled:** Services for visually, speech, hearing impaired.

Contact. E-mail: ugadm@simmons.edu
Phone: (617) 521-2051 Toll-free number: (800) 345-8468
Fax: (617) 521-3190
Ellen Johnson, Director of Undergraduate Admission, Simmons College, 300 The Fenway, Boston, MA 02115-5898

Smith College
Northampton, Massachusetts   CB member
www.smith.edu   CB code: 3762

- Private 4-year liberal arts college for women
- Residential campus in large town
- 2,473 degree-seeking undergraduates: 1% part-time, 100% women, 5% African American, 12% Asian American, 10% Hispanic/Latino, 5% Multi-racial, non-Hispanic, 14% international
- 396 degree-seeking graduate students
- 38% of applicants admitted
- Application essay required
- 87% graduate within 6 years

General. Founded in 1871. Regionally accredited. **Degrees:** 665 bachelor's awarded; master's, doctoral offered. **ROTC:** Army, Air Force. **Location:** 35 miles from Hartford, Connecticut; 90 miles from Boston. **Calendar:** Semester. **Full-time faculty:** 273 total; 99% have terminal degrees, 18% minority, 55% women. **Part-time faculty:** 25 total; 92% have terminal degrees, 12% minority, 52% women. **Class size:** 68% < 20, 24% 20-39, 2% 40-49, 5% 50-99, less than 1% >100. **Special facilities:** Physiology and horticultural laboratories, printmaking studio, darkroom and sculpture (including bronze casting studio) facilities, dance, theater and television studios, electronic music studio, recital hall, digital design studio, animal care facilities, electron microscopes, on-campus elementary school, multimedia language lab, greenhouses, astronomy observatories.

Freshman class profile. 5,006 applied, 1,897 admitted, 609 enrolled.

Mid 50% test scores		GPA 3.0-3.49:	8%
SAT critical reading:	620-740	Rank in top quarter:	90%
SAT math:	620-720	Rank in top tenth:	64%
SAT writing:	630-720	Return as sophomores:	90%
ACT composite:	28-32	Out-of-state:	83%
GPA 3.75 or higher:	65%	Live on campus:	100%
GPA 3.50-3.74:	27%	International:	16%

Basis for selection. Secondary school record, including GPA and difficulty of courses, recommendations most important. Class rank, essay, school and community activities and test scores also important. Interview strongly recommended, may be conducted off-campus by alumna. **Home schooled:** Statement describing home school structure and mission, transcript of courses and grades, letter of recommendation (nonparent) required. Submit portfolio and evaluation of coursework and sample of short research or analytical paper with evaluator's remarks.

High school preparation. College-preparatory program required. 16 units recommended. Recommended units include English 4, mathematics 3, history 2, science 3 (laboratory 3), foreign language 3 and academic electives 1. 3 units of 1 foreign language or 2 each of 2 languages recommended.

2015-2016 Annual costs. Tuition/fees: $46,288. Room/board: $15,470. Books/supplies: $800. Personal expenses: $1,376.

2015-2016 Financial aid. Need-based: Average need met was 100%. Average scholarship/grant was $41,802; average loan $3,289. 88% of total undergraduate aid awarded as scholarships/grants, 12% as loans/jobs. **Non-need-based:** Scholarships awarded for academics, state residency. **Additional information:** Financial aid policy guarantees to meet full financial need, as calculated by college, of all admitted students who have met application deadlines.

Application procedures. Admission: Closing date 1/15 (postmark date). No application fee. Notification by early April. Must reply by May 1 or within 1 week(s) if notified thereafter. **Financial aid:** Closing date 2/15. FAFSA, institutional form, CSS PROFILE required. Applicants notified by 4/1; must reply by 5/1.

Academics. Academic honor code; writing course required in first year. **Special study options:** Accelerated study, cross-registration, double major, exchange student, honors, independent study, internships, semester at sea, student-designed major, study abroad, teacher certification program, Washington semester. Member of Five College Consortium, program in engineering and technology, engineering science program within liberal arts curriculum leading to BS degree, post-baccalaureate certificate in American studies (available to international students). **Credit/placement by examination:** AP, CLEP, IB, institutional tests. 32 credit hours maximum toward bachelor's degree. **Support services:** Learning center, study skills assistance, tutoring, writing center.

Majors. Area/ethnic studies: African-American, American, Asian, Latin American, women's. **Biology:** General, biochemistry, neuroscience. **Computer sciences:** Computer science. **Education:** General. **Engineering:** General, biomedical, chemical, civil, computer, electrical, engineering mechanics, engineering science, environmental, mechanical. **English:** English lit. **Foreign languages:** Ancient Greek, classics, comparative lit, East Asian, French, German, Italian, Latin, Portuguese, Russian, Spanish. **History:** General. **Math:** General. **Philosophy/religion:** Philosophy, religion. **Physical sciences:** Astronomy, astrophysics, chemistry, geology, physics. **Psychology:** General. **Social sciences:** Anthropology, economics, political science, sociology. **Visual/performing arts:** Art, art history/conservation, dance, dramatic, film/cinema/video, studio arts.

Most popular majors. Area/ethnic studies 7%, biology 12%, foreign language 10%, psychology 9%, social sciences 24%, visual/performing arts 9%.

Technology on campus. 532 workstations in dormitories, library, computer center, student center. Dormitories wired for high-speed internet access and linked to campus network. Commuter students can connect to campus network. Online course registration, online library, helpline, repair service, student web hosting, wireless network available.

Student life. Freshman orientation: Mandatory. Preregistration for classes offered. Program held 4-5 days prior to beginning of classes; includes parent day. **Policies:** Each residence self-governed within framework of college regulations. Residents determine house responsibilities. **Housing:** Guaranteed on-campus for all undergraduates. Cooperative housing, wellness housing available. $500 nonrefundable deposit, deadline 5/1. French-speaking house, senior house, nontraditional age house, apartment complexes for juniors and seniors, housing for students with children available. **Activities:** Bands, campus ministries, choral groups, dance, drama, international student organizations, literary magazine, music ensembles, Model UN, musical theater, radio station, student government, student newspaper, TV station, service organizations, women's resource center, black student alliance, Asian student association, Hillel, Newman Club, Christian council, international relations club, Latina organization, Native American organization.

Athletics. NCAA. **Intercollegiate:** Basketball W, cross-country W, diving W, equestrian W, field hockey W, lacrosse W, rowing (crew) W, skiing W, soccer W, softball W, squash W, swimming W, tennis W, track and field W, volleyball W. **Intramural:** Basketball W, soccer W. **Team name:** Pioneers.

Student services. Adult student services, alcohol/substance abuse counseling, chaplain/spiritual director, career counseling, services for economically disadvantaged, student employment services, financial aid counseling, health services, minority student services, on-campus daycare, personal counseling, placement for graduates, women's services. **Physically disabled:** Services for visually, speech, hearing impaired.

Contact. E-mail: admission@smith.edu
Phone: (413) 585-2500 Toll-free number: (800) 383-3232
Fax: (413) 585-2527
Debra Shaver, Director of Admission, Smith College, 7 College Lane, Northampton, MA 01063

Springfield College

Springfield, Massachusetts   **CB member**
www.springfieldcollege.edu   **CB code: 3763**

- Private 4-year health science and liberal arts college
- Residential campus in small city
- 2,138 degree-seeking undergraduates
- 1,082 graduate students
- SAT or ACT with writing, application essay required

General. Founded in 1885. Regionally accredited. Adult weekend programs at 11 sites across the country. **Degrees:** 525 bachelor's awarded; master's, professional, doctoral offered. **ROTC:** Army, Air Force. **Location:** 90 miles from Boston; 26 miles from Hartford, Connecticut. **Calendar:** Semester, limited summer session. **Full-time faculty:** 181 total; 83% have terminal degrees, 9% minority, 50% women. **Part-time faculty:** 172 total; 62% women. **Class size:** 46% < 20, 52% 20-39, less than 1% 40-49, less than 1% 50-99, less than 1% >100. **Special facilities:** 57-acre campground and outdoor adventure area.

Freshman class profile.

GPA 3.75 or higher:	19%	Rank in top quarter:	38%
GPA 3.50-3.74:	10%	Rank in top tenth:	13%
GPA 3.0-3.49:	22%	Out-of-state:	60%
GPA 2.0-2.99:	42%	Live on campus:	96%

Basis for selection. School achievement record, essay, extracurricular activities, personal references, and test scores important. Portfolio required of art majors. **Home schooled:** Statement describing home school structure and mission, transcript of courses and grades, letter of recommendation (nonparent) required.

High school preparation. College-preparatory program required. 16 units required. Required and recommended units include English 4, mathematics 3, social studies 2, history 1, science 3 (laboratory 2) and foreign language 3. Emphasis on science for majors in allied health fields.

2015-2016 Annual costs. Tuition/fees: $34,455. Room/board: $13,410. Books/supplies: $1,000. Personal expenses: $1,200.

2015-2016 Financial aid. Need-based: 512 full-time freshmen applied for aid; 450 deemed to have need; 450 received aid. Average need met was 78%. Average scholarship/grant was $22,834; average loan $3,166. 68% of total undergraduate aid awarded as scholarships/grants, 32% as loans/jobs. **Non-need-based:** Awarded to 355 full-time undergraduates, including 113 freshmen. Scholarships awarded for academics, alumni affiliation, art, leadership, minority status, music/drama, state residency.

Application procedures. Admission: Priority date 3/1; deadline 4/1 (postmark date). $50 fee, may be waived for applicants with need. Admission notification on a rolling basis beginning on or about 12/1. Must reply by May 1 or within 2 week(s) if notified thereafter. Application closing date for athletic training, physical therapy majors 12/1; closing date for physician assistant and occupational therapy majors 1/15. **Financial aid:** Priority date 3/15; no closing date. FAFSA, institutional form required. Applicants notified on a rolling basis starting 2/7; must reply within 2 week(s) of notification.

Academics. Emphasis on practical fieldwork experiences to supplement classroom learning. **Special study options:** Combined bachelor's/graduate degree, cross-registration, double major, ESL, independent study, internships, liberal arts/career combination, study abroad, teacher certification program, weekend college. **Credit/placement by examination:** AP, CLEP, IB, SAT, ACT, institutional tests. 30 credit hours maximum toward bachelor's degree. **Support services:** Learning center, reduced course load, remedial instruction, study skills assistance, tutoring, writing center.

Majors. Biology: General. **Business:** Business admin. **Communications:** General, broadcast journalism, journalism, media studies, radio/TV, sports. **Computer sciences:** General, computer graphics, information systems. **Conservation:** General, environmental studies. **Education:** Art, early childhood, elementary, health, physical, secondary, special ed. **English:** English lit. **Health services:** Art therapy, athletic training, EMT paramedic, health care admin, predental, public health ed, recreational therapy. **History:** General. **Human services:** Community org/advocacy. **Liberal arts:** Arts/sciences. **Math:** General. **Parks/recreation:** Exercise sciences, facilities management, health/fitness, sports admin. **Protective services:** Law enforcement admin. **Psychology:** General. **Social sciences:** Sociology. **Visual/performing arts:** Art, dance.

Technology on campus. 235 workstations in dormitories, library, computer center, student center. Dormitories wired for high-speed internet access and linked to campus network. Commuter students can connect to campus network. Online course registration, helpline, wireless network available.

Student life. Freshman orientation: Mandatory, $125 fee. Preregistration for classes offered. Four-day program immediately preceding fall semester. **Policies:** Freshmen not permitted cars on campus. **Housing:** Guaranteed on-campus for all undergraduates. Coed dorms, single-sex dorms, special housing for disabled, apartments, wellness housing available. **Activities:** Campus ministries, choral groups, dance, drama, international student organizations, literary magazine, music ensembles, musical theater, radio station, student government, student newspaper, environmental club, Fellowship of Christian Athletes, Habitat for Humanity, Hillel, Newman community, outreach committee, student society for cultural diversity, Students Against Violence Everywhere.

Athletics. NCAA. **Intercollegiate:** Baseball M, basketball, cross-country, diving, field hockey W, football (tackle) M, golf, gymnastics, lacrosse, soccer, softball W, swimming, tennis, track and field, volleyball, wrestling M. **Intramural:** Basketball, bowling, field hockey, football (non-tackle), golf, handball, lacrosse, racquetball, soccer, softball, swimming, tennis, track and field, ultimate frisbee, volleyball, wrestling M. **Team name:** Pride.

Student services. Adult student services, alcohol/substance abuse counseling, chaplain/spiritual director, career counseling, student employment services, financial aid counseling, health services, minority student services, on-campus daycare, personal counseling, placement for graduates, veterans' counselor, women's services. **Physically disabled:** Services for visually, speech, hearing impaired.

Contact. E-mail: admissions@springfieldcollege.edu
Phone: (413) 748-3136 Toll-free number: (800) 343-1257
Fax: (413) 748-3694
Richard Veres, Director of Admissions, Springfield College, 263 Alden Street, Springfield, MA 01109

Stonehill College
Easton, Massachusetts   **CB member**
www.stonehill.edu   **CB code: 3770**

◗ Private 4-year liberal arts college affiliated with the Roman Catholic Church

◗ Residential campus in large town

◗ 2,481 degree-seeking undergraduates: 60% women, 5% African American, 2% Asian American, 4% Hispanic/Latino, 2% Multi-racial, non-Hispanic, 1% international

◗ 75% of applicants admitted

◗ Application essay required

◗ 87% graduate within 6 years; 25% enter graduate study

General. Founded in 1948. Regionally accredited. **Degrees:** 515 bachelor's awarded. **ROTC:** Army. **Location:** 19 miles from Boston, 25 miles from Providence, Rhode Island. **Calendar:** Semester, limited summer session. **Full-time faculty:** 157 total; 91% have terminal degrees, 10% minority, 41% women. **Part-time faculty:** 125 total; 44% have terminal degrees, 7% minority, 50% women. **Class size:** 49% < 20, 50% 20-39, 1% 40-49, less than 1% 50-99. **Special facilities:** Institute for law and society, observatory, science center, industrial history collection (shovel museum), center for non-profit management, theater, ice rink.

Freshman class profile. 5,892 applied, 4,429 admitted, 656 enrolled.

Mid 50% test scores			
SAT critical reading:	510-600	**GPA 2.0-2.99:**	20%
SAT math:	510-620	**Rank in top quarter:**	59%
SAT writing:	500-610	**Rank in top tenth:**	27%
ACT composite:	22-27	**End year in good standing:**	91%
GPA 3.75 or higher:	15%	**Return as sophomores:**	89%
GPA 3.50-3.74:	20%	**Out-of-state:**	39%
GPA 3.0-3.49:	45%	**Live on campus:**	94%
		International:	1%

Basis for selection. The admission review focuses on the depth and strength of the high school curriculum and the grades achieved in college preparatory classes, as well as class rank if provided, and teacher and counselor recommendations. In and out of school involvement and essays are also considered. Stonehill College is SAT optional. Interview recommended. **Home schooled:** Statement describing home school structure and mission, transcript of courses and grades required. Common Application Home Schooled Supplement form required.

High school preparation. College-preparatory program required. 16 units required; 20 recommended. Required and recommended units include English 4, mathematics 3-4, history 3-4, science 3-4 (laboratory 3) and foreign language 3-4. Foreign language units should be in same language. 3 combined units in history, political science, social science required. Math units should consist of algebra I, algebra II, and geometry. Additional units in science and math recommended for science applicants. Additional math units recommended for business applicants.

2015-2016 Annual costs. Tuition/fees: $38,550. Room/board: $14,720. Books/supplies: $893. Personal expenses: $835.

2015-2016 Financial aid. Need-based: 556 full-time freshmen applied for aid; 429 deemed to have need; 429 received aid. Average need met was 92%. Average scholarship/grant was $25,498; average loan $3,679. 79% of total undergraduate aid awarded as scholarships/grants, 21% as loans/jobs. **Non-need-based:** Awarded to 980 full-time undergraduates, including 328 freshmen. Scholarships awarded for academics, athletics, leadership, ROTC.

Application procedures. Admission: Closing date 1/15 (postmark date). $60 fee, may be waived for applicants with need. Application must be submitted online. Admission notification by 3/15. Must reply by 5/1. **Financial aid:** Priority date 12/1, closing date 2/1. FAFSA, CSS PROFILE required. Applicants notified by 4/1; must reply by 5/1.

Academics. Special study options: Combined bachelor's/graduate degree, cross-registration, double major, dual enrollment of high school students, exchange student, honors, independent study, internships, liberal arts/career combination, New York semester, student-designed major, study abroad, teacher certification program, Washington semester, Full-semester international internship sites in Belgrade, Dublin, London, Madrid, Paris, and Yerevan; 3-2 BA/BS chemical engineering, BA/BS computer engineering, BA/BS aeronautical engineering, BA/BS civil engineering, BA/BS electrical engineering, BA/BS mechanical engineering, and BS/BS environmental engineering programs with The University of Notre Dame, Indiana; Los Angeles semester, and Sea Education Association (SEA) semester; Stonehill Undergraduate Research Experience (SURE) program. **Credit/placement by examination:** AP, CLEP, IB, SAT, ACT, institutional tests. **Support services:** Learning center, pre-admission summer program, reduced course load, study skills assistance, tutoring, writing center.

Majors. Area/ethnic studies: American. **Biology:** General, biochemistry, neuroscience. **Business:** Accounting, business admin, finance, international, marketing. **Communications:** Communications/speech/rhetoric. **Computer sciences:** Computer science. **Conservation:** Environmental science, environmental studies. **Education:** General. **English:** English lit. **Foreign languages:** General, French, Spanish. **Health services:** Health care admin. **History:** General. **Math:** General. **Philosophy/religion:** Philosophy, religion. **Physical sciences:** Chemistry, physics. **Psychology:** General. **Social sciences:** Criminology, economics, sociology. **Visual/performing arts:** General, art history/conservation, arts management, graphic design, studio arts.

Most popular majors. Biology 11%, business/marketing 20%, communications/journalism 7%, psychology 11%, social sciences 14%.

Technology on campus. 404 workstations in library, computer center, student center. Dormitories wired for high-speed internet access and linked to campus network. Commuter students can connect to campus network. Online course registration, online library, helpline, wireless network available.

Student life. Freshman orientation: Mandatory. Preregistration for classes offered. Two-day program in June and four-day fall program. **Policies:** Freshmen not permitted cars on campus. **Housing:** Coed dorms, single-sex dorms, special housing for disabled, wellness housing available. $750 nonrefundable deposit, deadline 5/1. Special interest housing proposals considered for groups. **Activities:** Concert band, campus ministries, choral groups, dance, drama, film society, international student organizations, literary magazine, music ensembles, Model UN, musical theater, radio station, student government, student newspaper, Asian American Society, Diversity on Campus, PRIDE, Activism club, Desi, Habitat for Humanity, College Democrats, Good News club, Enactus, Disability Enlightenment Project.

Athletics. NCAA. **Intercollegiate:** Baseball M, basketball, cross-country, equestrian W, field hockey W, football (tackle) M, ice hockey M, lacrosse W, soccer, softball W, tennis, track and field, volleyball W. **Intramural:** Basketball, field hockey, football (non-tackle), sand volleyball, soccer, softball, tennis, ultimate frisbee, volleyball. **Team name:** Skyhawks.

Student services. Adult student services, alcohol/substance abuse counseling, chaplain/spiritual director, career counseling, services for economically disadvantaged, student employment services, financial aid counseling, health services, minority student services, personal counseling, placement for graduates, women's services. **Physically disabled:** Services for visually, speech, hearing impaired.

Contact. E-mail: admission@stonehill.edu
Phone: (508) 565-1373 Toll-free number: (888) 694-4554
Fax: (508) 565-1545
Joseph Dacey, Dean of Admission, Stonehill College, 320 Washington Street, Easton, MA 02357-0100

Suffolk University
Boston, Massachusetts
CB member
www.suffolk.edu
CB code: 3771

- Private 4-year university
- Commuter campus in very large city
- 5,454 degree-seeking undergraduates: 5% part-time, 54% women, 6% African American, 8% Asian American, 12% Hispanic/Latino, 2% Multiracial, non-Hispanic, 23% international
- 2,449 degree-seeking graduate students
- 82% of applicants admitted
- SAT or ACT with writing required
- 52% graduate within 6 years; 12% enter graduate study

General. Founded in 1906. Regionally accredited. Campus in Spain, branch campus in North Andover. **Degrees:** 1,323 bachelor's, 2 associate awarded; master's, professional, doctoral offered. **ROTC:** Army. **Location:** Downtown. **Calendar:** Semester, extensive summer session. **Full-time faculty:** 328 total; 92% have terminal degrees, 17% minority, 43% women. **Part-time faculty:** 374 total; 33% have terminal degrees, 8% minority, 43% women. **Class size:** 42% < 20, 54% 20-39, 4% 40-49, less than 1% 50-99. **Special facilities:** Poetry center, energy research lab, political research center, television studio, field station, river station.

Freshman class profile. 8,662 applied, 7,139 admitted, 1,380 enrolled.

Mid 50% test scores			
SAT critical reading:	460-560	**GPA 2.0-2.99:**	34%
SAT math:	450-560	**Rank in top quarter:**	40%
SAT writing:	450-560	**Rank in top tenth:**	11%
ACT composite:	20-25	**End year in good standing:**	96%
GPA 3.75 or higher:	15%	**Return as sophomores:**	74%
GPA 3.50-3.74:	13%	**Out-of-state:**	36%
GPA 3.0-3.49:	38%	**Live on campus:**	66%
		International:	18%

Basis for selection. High school record including courses taken, level of study, class rank, test scores, essay important. Counselor recommendation considered. Interview recommended. Portfolio required for BFA program applicants. **Home schooled:** Transcript of courses and grades, state high school equivalency certificate, letter of recommendation (nonparent) required. Admission interview highly recommended. Transcript/Record of courses and grades or written evaluation of work required.

High school preparation. College-preparatory program recommended. 17 units required; 27 recommended. Required and recommended units include English 4, mathematics 3-4, social studies 1-2, history 1-3, science 2-4 (laboratory 1-3), foreign language 2-4 and computer science 3.

2015-2016 Annual costs. Tuition/fees: $33,934. Room/board: $14,648. Books/supplies: $1,200. Personal expenses: $2,276.

2015-2016 Financial aid. Need-based: 971 full-time freshmen applied for aid; 876 deemed to have need; 876 received aid. Average need met was 69%. Average scholarship/grant was $9,604; average loan $3,463. 66% of total undergraduate aid awarded as scholarships/grants, 34% as loans/jobs. **Non-need-based:** Awarded to 3,277 full-time undergraduates, including 1,254 freshmen. Scholarships awarded for academics, alumni affiliation. **Additional information:** Foreign students may apply for institutional employment awards.

Application procedures. Admission: Priority date 2/15; deadline 7/30 (postmark date). $50 fee, may be waived for applicants with need. Admission notification on a rolling basis beginning on or about 3/20. Must reply by May 1 or within 2 week(s) if notified thereafter. Strongly suggest housing deposit before March 15. Housing awarded on first-come first-served basis by date of the admission deposit. **Financial aid:** Closing date 3/1. FAFSA required. Applicants notified on a rolling basis starting 2/5; must reply by 5/1 or within 2 week(s) of notification.

Academics. Special study options: Accelerated study, combined bachelor's/graduate degree, cooperative education, cross-registration, distance learning, double major, ESL, honors, independent study, internships, liberal arts/career combination, study abroad, Washington semester. **Credit/placement by examination:** AP, CLEP, IB, SAT, ACT, institutional tests. 30 credit hours maximum toward associate degree, 30 toward bachelor's. **Support services:** Learning center, pre-admission summer program, reduced course load, remedial instruction, study skills assistance, tutoring, writing center.

Majors. Area/ethnic studies: Asian, French, Latin American. **Biology:** General, radiobiology. **Business:** Accounting, business admin, entrepreneurial studies, finance, international, marketing. **Communications:** Advertising, broadcast journalism, communications/speech/rhetoric, journalism, media studies, organizational, political, public relations. **Communications technology:** Radio/TV. **Computer sciences:** General, computer science, information systems. **Conservation:** Environmental science. **Engineering:** Computer, electrical, environmental. **English:** English lit. **Foreign languages:** General, French, Spanish. **History:** General. **Liberal arts:** Humanities. **Math:** General. **Philosophy/religion:** Philosophy. **Physical sciences:** Chemistry, physics. **Psychology:** General. **Social sciences:** Economics, political science, sociology. **Visual/performing arts:** General, dramatic, interior design, theater history.

Most popular majors. Business/marketing 38%, communications/journalism 16%, psychology 7%, social sciences 16%.

Technology on campus. 539 workstations in dormitories, library, computer center, student center, student center. Dormitories wired for high-speed internet access and linked to campus network. Commuter students can connect to campus network. Online course registration, online library, helpline, wireless network available.

Student life. Freshman orientation: Mandatory, $85 fee. Preregistration for classes offered. Three-day orientation held in June and August. **Housing:** Coed dorms, apartments available. $600 nonrefundable deposit, deadline 5/1. **Activities:** Campus ministries, choral groups, dance, drama, international student organizations, literary magazine, music ensembles, Model UN, musical theater, radio station, student government, student newspaper, TV station, Islamic cultural society, Newman club, Jewish society, finance committee, student government association, student judiciary review board, Jumpstart Inc., S.O.U.L.S., Best Buddies, Up 'Til Dawn.

Athletics. NCAA. **Intercollegiate:** Baseball M, basketball, cross-country, golf M, ice hockey M, soccer, softball W, tennis, volleyball W. **Intramural:** Basketball, football (non-tackle), soccer W, table tennis, volleyball. **Team name:** Rams.

Student services. Adult student services, alcohol/substance abuse counseling, chaplain/spiritual director, career counseling, student employment services, financial aid counseling, health services, minority student services, personal counseling, placement for graduates, veterans' counselor, women's services. **Physically disabled:** Services for visually, speech, hearing impaired.

Contact. E-mail: admission@suffolk.edu
Phone: (617) 573-8460 Toll-free number: (800) 678-3365
Fax: (617) 557-1574
Jeanne Aversa, Director of Admissions, Suffolk University, 8 Ashburton Place, Boston, MA 02108

Tufts University
Medford, Massachusetts
CB member
www.tufts.edu
CB code: 3901

- Private 4-year university
- Residential campus in small city
- 5,236 degree-seeking undergraduates: 1% part-time, 50% women, 4% African American, 11% Asian American, 6% Hispanic/Latino, 4% Multiracial, non-Hispanic, 9% international
- 5,650 degree-seeking graduate students
- 16% of applicants admitted
- SAT and SAT Subject Tests or ACT with writing, application essay required
- 93% graduate within 6 years

General. Founded in 1852. Regionally accredited. **Degrees:** 1,385 bachelor's awarded; master's, professional, doctoral offered. **ROTC:** Army, Naval, Air Force. **Location:** 5 miles from Boston. **Calendar:** Semester, limited summer session. **Full-time faculty:** 682 total; 7% have terminal degrees, 21% minority, 42% women. **Part-time faculty:** 313 total; 3% have terminal degrees, 13% minority, 50% women. **Class size:** 67% < 20, 22% 20-39, 3% 40-49, 5% 50-99, 3% >100. **Special facilities:** Computer-aided design laboratory, arts center, theater in the round, center for scientific visualization, engineering product development center, center for the humanities, art gallery.

Freshman class profile. 19,063 applied, 3,069 admitted, 1,360 enrolled.

Mid 50% test scores			
SAT critical reading:	680-750	**Rank in top tenth:**	90%
SAT math:	690-770	**Return as sophomores:**	97%
SAT writing:	680-750	**Out-of-state:**	79%
ACT composite:	30-33	**Live on campus:**	100%
Rank in top quarter:	99%	**International:**	11%

Basis for selection. School achievement most important. School recommendations, test scores, character, personal qualities, extracurricular participation, and special talents are also important. Geographic distribution, alumni relationship, minority status, socioeconomic status are all considered. For applicants who submit SAT: 2 SAT Subject Tests required of applicants to the School of Arts and Sciences. Math 1 or 2 and either physics or chemistry recommended for applicants to the School of Engineering. Interview optional but recommended. **Home schooled:** Statement describing home school structure and mission, transcript of courses and grades, letter of recommendation (nonparent) required.

High school preparation. College-preparatory program required. Required and recommended units include English 4, mathematics 4, social studies 4, science 4 and foreign language 3-4.

2015-2016 Annual costs. Tuition/fees: $50,604. Room/board: $13,094. Books/supplies: $800. Personal expenses: $1,402.

2015-2016 Financial aid. All financial aid based on need. 665 full-time freshmen applied for aid; 513 deemed to have need; 496 received aid. Average need met was 100%. Average scholarship/grant was $40,048; average loan $2,459. 89% of total undergraduate aid awarded as scholarships/grants, 11% as loans/jobs. **Additional information:** Students from families with incomes less than $60,000 receive aid awards in which student loans are replaced by grants.

Application procedures. Admission: Closing date 1/1 (postmark date). $70 fee, may be waived for applicants with need. Application must be submitted online. Admission notification by 4/1. Must reply by 5/1. **Financial aid:** Closing date 2/15. FAFSA, CSS PROFILE required. Applicants notified by 4/1; must reply by 5/1.

Academics. Special study options: Combined bachelor's/graduate degree, cross-registration, double major, dual enrollment of high school students, exchange student, independent study, internships, semester at sea, student-designed major, study abroad, teacher certification program, Washington semester. Experimental College, semester exchange with Lincoln University and Swarthmore College, combined degree programs with New England Conservatory of Music (BA/BM), School of the Museum of Fine Arts (BA/BFA), European Center in Talloires, France. **Credit/placement by examination:** AP, CLEP, IB, SAT, institutional tests. Limit 1 year of credit by acceleration. **Support services:** Learning center, study skills assistance, tutoring, writing center.

Majors. Area/ethnic studies: African, African-American, American, Asian, East Asian, European, Latin American, Near/Middle Eastern, Russian/Eastern European/Eurasian, Russian/Slavic, Western European, women's. **Biology:** General, biochemistry, ecology. **Communications:** Media studies. **Computer sciences:** General, computer science, information systems, programming. **Conservation:** Environmental studies. **Education:** General, early childhood. **Engineering:** General, applied physics, architectural, biomedical, chemical, civil, computer, electrical, engineering science, environmental, mechanical. **English:** English lit. **Foreign languages:** General, ancient Greek, Chinese, classics, comparative lit, French, German, Italian, Japanese, Latin, Russian, Spanish. **History:** General. **Liberal arts:** Arts/sciences. **Math:** General, applied. **Philosophy/religion:** Philosophy, religion. **Physical sciences:** Astronomy, astrophysics, chemistry, geology, physics. **Psychology:** General, clinical, cognitive. **Social sciences:** Anthropology, archaeology, economics, international relations, political science, sociology. **Visual/performing arts:** Art history/conservation, film/cinema/video, music, music history, music theory/composition, musicology, studio arts, theater history.

Most popular majors. Biology 9%, computer/information sciences 6%, engineering/engineering technologies 9%, interdisciplinary studies 7%, psychology 6%, social sciences 29%, visual/performing arts 7%.

Technology on campus. 500 workstations in library, computer center. Dormitories wired for high-speed internet access and linked to campus network. Commuter students can connect to campus network. Online course registration, online library, helpline, repair service, student web hosting, wireless network available.

Student life. Freshman orientation: Mandatory. Preregistration for classes offered. Three-day on-campus program prior to beginning of fall semester. **Policies:** Freshmen not permitted cars on campus. **Housing:** Guaranteed on-campus for freshmen. Coed dorms, single-sex dorms, special housing for disabled, apartments, fraternity/sorority housing, gender-neutral housing, themed housing, wellness housing available. Culture, special interest, language houses available. **Activities:** Bands, campus ministries, choral groups, dance, drama, film society, international student organizations, literary magazine, music ensembles, Model UN, musical theater, opera, radio station, student government, student newspaper, symphony orchestra, TV station, 300 student organizations available.

Athletics. NCAA. **Intercollegiate:** Baseball M, basketball, cross-country, diving, fencing W, field hockey W, football (tackle) M, golf, ice hockey M, lacrosse, rowing (crew), sailing, soccer, softball W, squash, swimming, tennis, track and field, volleyball W. **Intramural:** Badminton, basketball, football (non-tackle), handball, lacrosse, soccer, softball, volleyball. **Team name:** Jumbos.

Student services. Adult student services, alcohol/substance abuse counseling, chaplain/spiritual director, career counseling, services for economically disadvantaged, student employment services, financial aid counseling, health services, legal services, minority student services, on-campus daycare, personal counseling, placement for graduates, women's services. **Physically disabled:** Services for visually, speech, hearing impaired.

Contact. E-mail: undergraduate.admissions@tufts.edu
Phone: (617) 627-3170 Fax: (617) 627-3860
Lee Coffin, Dean of Admissions and Enrollment Management, Tufts University, Bendetson Hall, Medford, MA 02155

University of Massachusetts Amherst

Amherst, Massachusetts   CB member
www.umass.edu   CB code: 3917

- Public 4-year university
- Residential campus in large town
- 22,405 degree-seeking undergraduates: 6% part-time, 49% women, 4% African American, 9% Asian American, 5% Hispanic/Latino, 3% Multiracial, non-Hispanic, 4% international
- 5,908 degree-seeking graduate students
- 58% of applicants admitted
- SAT or ACT (ACT writing recommended), application essay required
- 78% graduate within 6 years; 18% enter graduate study

General. Founded in 1863. Regionally accredited. **Degrees:** 5,683 bachelor's, 54 associate awarded; master's, professional, doctoral offered. **ROTC:** Army, Air Force. **Location:** 90 miles from Boston, 30 miles from Springfield. **Calendar:** Semester, limited summer session. **Full-time faculty:** 1,295 total; 95% have terminal degrees, 23% minority, 44% women. **Part-time faculty:** 178 total; 74% have terminal degrees, 7% minority, 53% women. **Class size:** 50% < 20, 28% 20-39, 4% 40-49, 9% 50-99, 9% >100. **Special facilities:** Observatory, botanical gardens, sports arena with ice rink, contemporary art museum, recreation center.

Freshman class profile. 40,010 applied, 23,308 admitted, 4,661 enrolled.

Mid 50% test scores			
		GPA 2.0-2.99:	1%
SAT critical reading:	550-640	Rank in top quarter:	73%
SAT math:	580-670	Rank in top tenth:	32%
ACT composite:	25-30	Return as sophomores:	91%
GPA 3.75 or higher:	58%	Out-of-state:	23%
GPA 3.50-3.74:	29%	Live on campus:	99%
GPA 3.0-3.49:	12%	International:	7%

Basis for selection. High school grades and test scores most important, followed by extracurricular activities, essay, and recommendations. Audition required of music and dance majors. Portfolio required of art and architecture majors. **Home schooled:** Transcript of courses and grades required. Detailed transcript required. **Learning Disabled:** Applicants must submit diagnostic data and/or individualized educational plan. Massachusetts residents with documented learning disabilities not required to submit standardized test scores for admissions consideration.

High school preparation. College-preparatory program required. 17 units required. Required units include English 4, mathematics 4, social studies 2, science 3 (laboratory 2), foreign language 2 and computer science 2.

2015-2016 Annual costs. Tuition/fees: $14,356; $30,689 out-of-state. Room/board: $12,028. Books/supplies: $1,000. Personal expenses: $1,000.

2014-2015 Financial aid. Need-based: 4,143 full-time freshmen applied for aid; 2,718 deemed to have need; 2,661 received aid. Average need met was 81%. Average scholarship/grant was $10,480; average loan $3,685. 54% of total undergraduate aid awarded as scholarships/grants, 46% as loans/jobs. **Non-need-based:** Awarded to 3,276 full-time undergraduates, including 985 freshmen. Scholarships awarded for academics, art, athletics, music/drama, state residency.

Application procedures. Admission: Closing date 1/15 (postmark date). $75 fee, may be waived for applicants with need. Notified early March through April. Must reply by May 1 or within 2 week(s) if notified thereafter. **Financial aid:** Priority date 3/1; no closing date. FAFSA required. Applicants notified on a rolling basis starting 4/1; must reply by 5/1 or within 2 week(s) of notification.

Academics. Students may take courses at Amherst, Hampshire, Mt. Holyoke and Smith Colleges at no extra charge. **Special study options:** Accelerated study, combined bachelor's/graduate degree, cooperative education, cross-registration, distance learning, double major, dual enrollment of high school students, ESL, exchange student, honors, independent study, internships, liberal arts/career combination, student-designed major, study abroad, teacher certification program. **Credit/placement by examination:** AP, CLEP, IB, institutional tests. 30 credit hours maximum toward bachelor's degree. Credit awarded for International Baccalaureate scores of 4-7. **Support services:** Learning center, reduced course load, study skills assistance, tutoring, writing center.

Honors college/program. First-year students admitted by invitation, approximately 600 freshmen admitted. Interdisciplinary seminars, enriched honors courses, colloquia, independent study, service learning offered; honors thesis, project, or activity required.

Majors. Architecture: Architecture, environmental design, landscape. **Area/ethnic studies:** African-American, German, Near/Middle Eastern, Russian/Slavic, women's. **Biology:** General, Biochemistry/molecular biology, exercise physiology, microbiology. **Business:** Accounting, business admin, finance, hospitality admin, marketing, operations. **Communications:** Communications/speech/rhetoric, journalism. **Computer sciences:** Computer science. **Conservation:** General, environmental science. **Education:** General. **Engineering:** Chemical, civil, computer, electrical, industrial, mechanical. **English:** English lit. **Foreign languages:** Chinese, classics, comparative lit, French, Italian, Japanese, linguistics, Portuguese, Spanish. **General:** Building construction. **Health services:** Communication disorders, nursing (RN), predental, premedicine, preveterinary. **History:** General. **Liberal arts:** Humanities. **Math:** General. **Parks/recreation:** Sports admin. **Philosophy/religion:** Judaic, philosophy. **Physical sciences:** Astronomy, chemistry, geology, physics. **Psychology:** General. **Social sciences:** Anthropology, economics, geography, political science, sociology. **Visual/performing arts:** Art history/ conservation, dance, dramatic, music, music performance, studio arts.

Most popular majors. Biology 10%, business/marketing 15%, communications/journalism 6%, engineering/engineering technologies 7%, health sciences 8%, interdisciplinary studies 6%, psychology 8%, social sciences 10%.

Technology on campus. 400 workstations in library, computer center. Dormitories linked to campus network. Commuter students can connect to campus network. Online course registration, online library, helpline, repair service, student web hosting, wireless network available.

Student life. Freshman orientation: Mandatory. Preregistration for classes offered. Two-and-a-half-day sessions in June or July, make-up orientation at end of August, and 3-day session in September at beginning of school year. **Policies:** Students required to live on-campus through freshman year unless eligible for housing exemption (parents of dependent children, veterans, commuting students). **Housing:** Guaranteed on-campus for freshmen. Coed dorms, single-sex dorms, special housing for disabled, apartments, fraternity/sorority housing, themed housing, wellness housing available. Special interest housing; residential academic programs for first-year students. Gradual penalty for cancellation of housing up to $300. **Activities:** Bands, campus ministries, choral groups, dance, drama, film society, international student organizations, literary magazine, music ensembles, Model UN, musical theater, opera, radio station, student government, student newspaper, symphony orchestra, TV station, over 300 student organizations.

Athletics. NCAA. **Intercollegiate:** Baseball M, basketball, cross-country, diving, field hockey W, football (tackle) M, ice hockey M, lacrosse, rowing (crew) W, soccer, softball W, swimming, tennis W, track and field. **Intramural:** Badminton, basketball, field hockey W, football (non-tackle), ice hockey M, racquetball, sand volleyball, soccer, softball, table tennis, tennis, ultimate frisbee, volleyball. **Team name:** Minutemen, Minutewomen.

Student services. Adult student services, alcohol/substance abuse counseling, chaplain/spiritual director, career counseling, student employment services, financial aid counseling, health services, legal services, minority student services, on-campus daycare, personal counseling, placement for graduates, veterans' counselor, women's services. **Physically disabled:** Services for visually, speech, hearing impaired.

Contact. E-mail: mail@admissions.umass.edu
Phone: (413) 545-0222 Fax: (413) 545-4312
Jon Westover, Sr. Associate Director of Freshmen Admissions, University of Massachusetts Amherst, University Admissions Center, Amherst, MA 01003-9291

University of Massachusetts Boston

Boston, Massachusetts
www.umb.edu

CB member
CB code: 3924

- Public 4-year university
- Commuter campus in very large city
- 12,397 degree-seeking undergraduates: 25% part-time, 55% women
- 3,582 degree-seeking graduate students
- 69% of applicants admitted
- SAT or ACT (ACT writing recommended), application essay required
- 42% graduate within 6 years

General. Founded in 1964. Regionally accredited. One of 5 campuses of the University of Massachusetts. **Degrees:** 2,442 bachelor's awarded; master's, professional, doctoral offered. **ROTC:** Army, Naval, Air Force. **Location:** 3 miles from downtown. **Calendar:** Semester, extensive summer session. **Full-time faculty:** 699 total; 6% have terminal degrees, 22% minority, 51% women. **Part-time faculty:** 572 total; 2% have terminal degrees, 11% minority, 58% women. **Class size:** 41% < 20, 49% 20-39, 4% 40-49, 4% 50-99, 1% >100. **Special facilities:** Tropical greenhouse, observatory, adaptive computer laboratory.

Freshman class profile. 9,365 applied, 6,467 admitted, 1,680 enrolled.

Mid 50% test scores			
SAT critical reading:	470-570	GPA 3.0-3.49:	34%
SAT math:	480-590	GPA 2.0-2.99:	33%
GPA 3.75 or higher:	18%	Return as sophomores:	78%
GPA 3.50-3.74:	15%	Out-of-state:	8%

Basis for selection. School achievement record, range of test scores, GPA most important. Recommendations, essay also important. Extracurricular activities considered. Grades for college preparatory background should be B- or better. Interview recommended for nontraditional students.

High school preparation. College-preparatory program required. 17 units required. Required units include English 4, mathematics 4, social studies 1, history 1, science 3 (laboratory 2), foreign language 2 and academic electives 2.

2015-2016 Annual costs. Tuition/fees: $12,682; $29,920 out-of-state. Books/supplies: $800. Personal expenses: $1,240.

2014-2015 Financial aid. Need-based: 1,060 full-time freshmen applied for aid; 929 deemed to have need; 929 received aid. Average need met was 90%. Average scholarship/grant was $9,909; average loan $3,077. 58% of total undergraduate aid awarded as scholarships/grants, 42% as loans/jobs. **Non-need-based:** Awarded to 424 full-time undergraduates, including 143 freshmen. Scholarships awarded for academics, leadership, state residency. **Additional information:** Some Massachusetts state employees and Massachusetts Vietnam veterans eligible for tuition waiver. Some waivers available based on talent and academic excellence.

Application procedures. Admission: Priority date 3/1; deadline 4/1. $60 fee ($60 out-of-state), may be waived for applicants with need. Admission notification on a rolling basis beginning on or about 4/30. Must reply by May 1 or within 3 week(s) if notified thereafter. **Financial aid:** Priority date 3/1; no closing date. FAFSA required. Applicants notified on a rolling basis starting 3/6.

Academics. Special study options: Combined bachelor's/graduate degree, cooperative education, cross-registration, distance learning, double major, dual enrollment of high school students, ESL, exchange student, honors, independent study, internships, liberal arts/career combination, student-designed major, study abroad, teacher certification program. 2-2 programs in engineering with area institutions. **Credit/placement by examination:** AP, CLEP, SAT, ACT, institutional tests. 90 credit hours maximum toward bachelor's degree. **Support services:** Learning center, pre-admission summer program, reduced course load, remedial instruction, study skills assistance, tutoring, writing center.

Majors. Area/ethnic studies: African-American, American, Asian, women's. **Biology:** General, biochemistry. **Business:** Business admin. **Communications:** General. **Computer sciences:** General, information technology. **Education:** Early childhood. **Engineering:** Applied physics, computer, electrical. **English:** English lit. **Foreign languages:** Classics, French, Italian, Spanish. **Health services:** Nursing (RN). **History:** General. **Human services:** General, community org/advocacy. **Math:** General. **Parks/recreation:** Health/fitness. **Philosophy/religion:** Philosophy. **Physical sciences:** Chemistry, geology, physics. **Protective services:** Criminal justice. **Psychology:** General. **Social sciences:** General, anthropology, economics, political science, sociology. **Visual/performing arts:** Art, dramatic, music.

Most popular majors. Biology 7%, business/marketing 18%, health sciences 17%, parks/recreation 6%, psychology 13%, social sciences 11%.

Technology on campus. 350 workstations in library, computer center, student center. Commuter students can connect to campus network. Online course registration, online library, helpline, repair service, wireless network available.

Student life. Freshman orientation: Mandatory. Preregistration for classes offered. **Housing:** Housing referral services available. **Activities:** Bands, campus ministries, choral groups, dance, drama, film society, international student organizations, literary magazine, music ensembles, Model UN, radio station, student government, student newspaper, symphony orchestra.

Athletics. NCAA. **Intercollegiate:** Baseball M, basketball, cross-country, ice hockey M, lacrosse M, soccer, softball W, tennis, track and field, volleyball W. **Intramural:** Basketball, ice hockey M, racquetball, sailing, soccer, softball, squash, tennis, volleyball. **Team name:** Beacons.

Student services. Adult student services, alcohol/substance abuse counseling, chaplain/spiritual director, career counseling, services for economically disadvantaged, student employment services, health services, legal services, minority student services, on-campus daycare, personal counseling, placement for graduates, veterans' counselor, women's services. **Physically disabled:** Services for visually, speech, hearing impaired.

Contact. E-mail: enrollment.info@umb.edu
Phone: (617) 287-6000 Fax: (617) 287-5999
John Drew, Director of Admissions, University of Massachusetts Boston, 100 Morrissey Boulevard, Boston, MA 02125-3393

University of Massachusetts Dartmouth

Dartmouth, Massachusetts — **CB member**
www.umassd.edu — **CB code: 3786**

- Public 4-year university
- Residential campus in large town
- 7,054 degree-seeking undergraduates: 12% part-time, 48% women, 14% African American, 4% Asian American, 8% Hispanic/Latino, 3% Multiracial, non-Hispanic, 1% international
- 1,455 degree-seeking graduate students
- 76% of applicants admitted
- SAT or ACT (ACT writing optional), application essay required
- 46% graduate within 6 years; 26% enter graduate study

General. Founded in 1895. Regionally accredited. **Degrees:** 1,328 bachelor's awarded; master's, professional, doctoral offered. **ROTC:** Army. **Location:** 60 miles from Boston; 30 miles from Providence, Rhode Island. **Calendar:** Semester, extensive summer session. **Full-time faculty:** 392 total; 88% have terminal degrees, 21% minority, 45% women. **Part-time faculty:** 207 total; 37% have terminal degrees, 12% minority, 58% women. **Class size:** 37% < 20, 41% 20-39, 11% 40-49, 9% 50-99, 2% >100. **Special facilities:** Observatory, marine research vessel, coastal marine laboratory, full art studios, Jewish culture and Portuguese studies centers, Robert F. Kennedy assassination archive.

Freshman class profile. 7,591 applied, 5,789 admitted, 1,430 enrolled.

Mid 50% test scores			
SAT critical reading:	450-560	**Rank in top quarter:**	38%
SAT math:	470-570	**Rank in top tenth:**	13%
SAT writing:	430-550	**End year in good standing:**	86%
ACT composite:	19-25	**Return as sophomores:**	75%
GPA 3.75 or higher:	16%	**Out-of-state:**	5%
GPA 3.50-3.74:	13%	**Live on campus:**	78%
GPA 3.0-3.49:	36%		
GPA 2.0-2.99:	35%		

Basis for selection. High school record, test scores most important; class rank, essay, recommendations considered. 2.0 GPA required; 3.0 GPA recommended. Except if out of high school for more than 3 years, MA learning disable can receive waiver with documentation. Audition required for music majors; portfolio required for design majors. **Home schooled:** State high school equivalency certificate required. Must get certification or equivalency from local high school. **Learning Disabled:** SAT scores may be waived for Massachusetts students with documented disability.

High school preparation. College-preparatory program required. 16 units required. Required units include English 4, mathematics 4, social studies 1, history 1, science 3 (laboratory 2), foreign language 2 and academic electives 1. 1 U.S. history required. Programs in science, engineering and business require additional math. Science and engineering require physical science. 2 foreign language must be same language. Academic electives should be college prep courses.

2015-2016 Annual costs. Tuition/fees: $12,588; $26,173 out-of-state. Room/board: $11,622. Books/supplies: $1,200. Personal expenses: $1,072.

2015-2016 Financial aid. Need-based: 1,278 full-time freshmen applied for aid; 1,071 deemed to have need; 1,071 received aid. Average met met was 87%. Average scholarship/grant was $9,351; average loan $3,264. 54% of total undergraduate aid awarded as scholarships/grants, 46% as loans/jobs. **Non-need-based:** Awarded to 601 full-time undergraduates, including 188 freshmen. Scholarships awarded for academics, minority status, ROTC, state residency.

Application procedures. Admission: Priority date 3/1; no deadline. $60 fee, may be waived for applicants with need. Admission notification on a rolling basis beginning on or about 1/1. Must reply by May 1 or within 3 week(s) if notified thereafter. Competitive programs may be filled by March 1. Nursing closes by late January. Freshman applicants advised to apply before end of December and not later than March. **Financial aid:** Priority date 3/1; no closing date. FAFSA required.

Academics. Alternative admissions program for academically disadvantaged Massachusetts residents; program offers special freshman curriculum and counseling support. **Special study options:** Combined bachelor's/graduate degree, cooperative education, cross-registration, distance learning, double major, dual enrollment of high school students, ESL, exchange student, honors, independent study, internships, semester at sea, student-designed major, study abroad, teacher certification program, Washington semester. **Credit/placement by examination:** AP, CLEP, IB, SAT, ACT, institutional tests. 30 credit hours maximum toward bachelor's degree. **Support services:** Learning center, reduced course load, remedial instruction, study skills assistance, tutoring, writing center.

Majors. Area/ethnic studies: Women's. **Biology:** General. **Business:** General, accounting, business admin, finance, management information systems, marketing, operations. **Computer sciences:** General. **Education:** Art. **Engineering:** Biomedical, civil, computer, electrical, mechanical, software. **English:** English lit. **Foreign languages:** French, Portuguese, Spanish. **Health services:** Clinical lab science, cytotechnology, health care admin, nursing (RN). **History:** General. **Liberal arts:** Arts/sciences. **Math:** General. **Philosophy/religion:** Philosophy. **Physical sciences:** Chemistry, physics. **Psychology:** General. **Social sciences:** Criminology, economics, political science, sociology, sociology/anthropology. **Visual/performing arts:** General, art history/conservation, ceramics, design, digital arts, fiber arts, illustration, metal/jewelry, music, painting, photography, sculpture, studio arts.

Most popular majors. Biology 6%, business/marketing 27%, engineering/engineering technologies 13%, health sciences 12%, psychology 8%, social sciences 9%, visual/performing arts 9%.

Technology on campus. 650 workstations in dormitories, library, computer center, student center. Dormitories wired for high-speed internet access and linked to campus network. Commuter students can connect to campus network. Helpline, repair service, wireless network available.

Student life. Freshman orientation: Mandatory, $250 fee. Preregistration for classes offered. Three-day, 2-night program in June and July. **Housing:** Coed dorms, special housing for disabled, apartments, themed housing, wellness housing available. $200 partly refundable deposit. Quiet, substance-free, smoke-free, program-dedicated suites, first year living learning communities available. **Activities:** Bands, choral groups, dance, drama, international student organizations, literary magazine, music ensembles, Model UN, radio station, student government, student newspaper, symphony orchestra, Portuguese Center, Frederick Douglas Unity House, Kekeli West African Drum and Dance Club, Student Veteran Association, Asian Student Association, MASSPIRG, Habitat for Humanity, Student Government Association.

Athletics. NCAA. **Intercollegiate:** Baseball M, basketball, cross-country, diving, equestrian W, field hockey W, football (tackle) M, golf M, ice hockey M, lacrosse, sailing W, soccer, softball W, swimming, tennis, track and field, volleyball W. **Intramural:** Badminton, basketball, football (non-tackle), soccer, table tennis, tennis, volleyball, water polo M. **Team name:** Corsairs.

Student services. Adult student services, alcohol/substance abuse counseling, chaplain/spiritual director, career counseling, student employment services, financial aid counseling, health services, minority student services, personal counseling, placement for graduates, women's services. **Physically disabled:** Services for visually, speech, hearing impaired.

Contact. E-mail: admissions@umassd.edu
Phone: (508) 999-8605 Fax: (508) 999-8755
Kathleen Magnusson, Director of Undergraduate Admissions, University of Massachusetts Dartmouth, 285 Old Westport Road, Dartmouth, MA 02747-2300

University of Massachusetts Lowell

Lowell, Massachusetts — **CB member**
www.uml.edu — **CB code: 3911**

- Public 4-year university
- Residential campus in small city
- 12,494 degree-seeking undergraduates: 23% part-time, 38% women, 6% African American, 9% Asian American, 10% Hispanic/Latino, 3% Multiracial, non-Hispanic, 3% international
- 3,706 degree-seeking graduate students
- 57% of applicants admitted
- SAT or ACT (ACT writing optional), application essay required
- 56% graduate within 6 years

General. Founded in 1894. Regionally accredited. **Degrees:** 2,388 bachelor's, 49 associate awarded; master's, professional, doctoral offered. **ROTC:** Army, Air Force. **Location:** 40 miles from Boston, 45 miles from Worcester. **Calendar:** Semester, extensive summer session. **Full-time faculty:** 565 total; 91% have terminal degrees, 24% minority, 43% women. **Part-time faculty:** 547 total; 36% have terminal degrees, 9% minority, 45% women. **Class size:** 59% <20, 21% 20-39, 15% 40-49, 3% 50-99, less than 1% >100. **Special facilities:** Tsongas industrial history center, teaching and research laboratories in sound recording technology, digital imaging, wellness resource room, boathouse.

Freshman class profile. 10,638 applied, 6,020 admitted, 1,600 enrolled.

Mid 50% test scores			
SAT critical reading:	520-620	GPA 2.0-2.99:	12%
SAT math:	550-650	Rank in top quarter:	49%
SAT writing:	500-600	Rank in top tenth:	20%
ACT composite:	23-29	Return as sophomores:	86%
GPA 3.75 or higher:	33%	Out-of-state:	11%
GPA 3.50-3.74:	18%	Live on campus:	82%
GPA 3.0-3.49:	37%	International:	3%

Basis for selection. Academic assessment, including curriculum, performance as measured by grades and grade trends, preparation for undergraduate major, and standardized testing. Recommendations, essay, and extracurricular activities considered. Audition required of music majors. Art portfolio required of art majors. **Home schooled:** Statement describing home school structure and mission, transcript of courses and grades, state high school equivalency certificate, letter of recommendation (nonparent) required. **Learning Disabled:** Students with a documented learning difference can have standardized testing requirement waived with appropriate testing documentation.

High school preparation. College-preparatory program required. 17 units required. Required and recommended units include English 4, mathematics 4, social studies 2, science 3-4 (laboratory 3), foreign language 2 and academic electives 2. 1 social studies unit must be U.S. History.

2015-2016 Annual costs. Tuition/fees: $13,427; $20,540 out-of-state. Room/board: $11,670. Books/supplies: $1,200. Personal expenses: $926. **Additional information:** The required fees above or In-State students are $11973. The required fees for Out of State students are $20,558.

2014-2015 Financial aid. **Need-based:** 1,412 full-time freshmen applied for aid; 1,019 deemed to have need; 1,019 received aid. Average need met was 90%. Average scholarship/grant was $9,343; average loan $3,438. 46% of total undergraduate aid awarded as scholarships/grants, 54% as loans/jobs. **Non-need-based:** Awarded to 1,269 full-time undergraduates, including 425 freshmen. Scholarships awarded for academics, alumni affiliation, art, athletics, leadership, minority status, music/drama, ROTC, state residency.

Application procedures. **Admission:** Priority date 11/1; deadline 2/1 (postmark date). $60 fee, may be waived for applicants with need. Admission notification by 12/15. Notified by 3/15. Must reply by May 1 or within 2 week(s) if notified thereafter. Must reply within 2 weeks of notification of acceptance. **Financial aid:** Priority date 3/1; no closing date. FAFSA required. Applicants notified on a rolling basis starting 3/21.

Academics. Special focus on applied science and technology; coursework emphasizes context and implications of each discipline. Funded research initiatives available in nanotechnology, bioinformatics, advanced materials, photonics. **Special study options:** Accelerated study, combined bachelor's/graduate degree, cooperative education, cross-registration, distance learning, double major, dual enrollment of high school students, honors, independent study, internships, study abroad, teacher certification program, Washington semester. **Credit/placement by examination:** AP, CLEP, IB, SAT, ACT, institutional tests. 30 credit hours maximum toward associate degree, 30 toward bachelor's. **Support services:** Learning center, pre-admission summer program, reduced course load, study skills assistance, tutoring, writing center.

Honors college/program. U Mass Lowell's Honors College admitted 1710 first-year students for the Fall 2015 semester. Enrollment in the Honors College is open to all majors and has more rigorous admissions standards.

Majors. **Area/ethnic studies:** American. **Biology:** General. **Business:** Business admin. **Computer sciences:** Computer science, information systems. **Engineering:** Chemical, civil, computer, electrical, mechanical, polymer. **English:** English lit. **Foreign languages:** General. **Health services:** Community health services, environmental health, nursing (RN). **History:** General. **Liberal arts:** Arts/sciences. **Math:** General, applied. **Philosophy/religion:** Philosophy. **Physical sciences:** Chemistry, physics. **Protective services:** Law enforcement admin. **Psychology:** General. **Social sciences:** Economics, political science, sociology. **Visual/performing arts:** Music, music management, music performance.

Most popular majors. Business/marketing 18%, computer/information sciences 11%, engineering/engineering technologies 16%, health sciences 11%, psychology 9%, security/protective services 11%.

Technology on campus. 2,145 workstations in dormitories, library, computer center, student center. Dormitories wired for high-speed internet access and linked to campus network. Commuter students can connect to campus network. Online course registration, online library, helpline, wireless network available.

Student life. **Freshman orientation:** Mandatory. Preregistration for classes offered. Overnight, two-day sessions are available 10 times throughout the summer. They are organized by major. There are 4 one-day sessions, two happening right before "opening" to accommodate out-of-state and international students. A family program is also available. **Housing:** Coed dorms, apartments, themed housing, wellness housing available. $200 fully refundable deposit, deadline 5/1. Living learning communities. **Activities:** Bands, campus ministries, choral groups, dance, drama, international student organizations, literary magazine, music ensembles, Model UN, radio station, student government, student newspaper, Abundant Life Christian Fellowship, Chi Alpha, Latter-day Saints Student Association, Association of Students of African Origin, Cambodian Student Association, Latin American Student Association, Community Service Organization, College Democrats, College Republicans.

Athletics. NCAA. **Intercollegiate:** Baseball M, basketball, cross-country, field hockey W, golf M, ice hockey M, lacrosse, soccer, softball W, track and field, volleyball W. **Intramural:** Baseball, basketball, football (non-tackle), ice hockey, racquetball, skiing, soccer, softball, squash, swimming, table tennis, tennis, ultimate frisbee, volleyball, weight lifting. **Team name:** River Hawks.

Student services. Alcohol/substance abuse counseling, chaplain/spiritual director, career counseling, student employment services, financial aid counseling, health services, minority student services, personal counseling, placement for graduates, veterans' counselor. **Physically disabled:** Services for visually, speech, hearing impaired.

Contact. E-mail: admissions@uml.edu
Phone: (978) 934-3931 Toll-free number: (800) 410-4607
Fax: (978) 934-3086
Kerri Johnston, Associate Dean of Enrollment and Director of Undergraduate Admissions, University of Massachusetts Lowell, University Crossing, Suite 420, 220 Pawtucket Street, Lowell, MA 01854-2874

University of Phoenix: Boston
Braintree, Massachusetts
www.phoenix.edu

- For-profit 4-year university
- Commuter campus in large town
- 179 undergraduates
- 40 graduate students

General. Regionally accredited. **Degrees:** 48 bachelor's awarded; master's offered. **Calendar:** Differs by program. **Full-time faculty:** 6 total. **Part-time faculty:** 46 total.

Basis for selection. Open admission, but selective for some programs.

2015-2016 Annual costs. Per-credit-hour charge, $410 to $635, depending upon level and course of study. Books, material charges, and other fees vary by course and program. All fees are subject to change.

Application procedures. **Admission:** No deadline. No application fee. **Financial aid:** No deadline.

Academics. **Credit/placement by examination:** AP, CLEP.

Majors. **Business:** Accounting/business management, business admin, e-commerce, entrepreneurial studies, finance, human resources, marketing, operations. **Computer sciences:** Database management, networking, programming, security, system admin, systems analysis, web page design, webmaster. **Human services:** General.

Student life. **Freshman orientation:** Mandatory. Preregistration for classes offered.

Contact. Toll-free number: (866) 766-0766
University of Phoenix: Boston, 19 Granite Street, Braintree, MA 02184-1744

Wellesley College
Wellesley, Massachusetts
www.wellesley.edu

CB member
CB code: 3957

- Private 4-year liberal arts college for women
- Residential campus in large town
- 2,188 degree-seeking undergraduates: 100% women, 5% African American, 23% Asian American, 11% Hispanic/Latino, 6% Multi-racial, non-Hispanic, 12% international
- 30% of applicants admitted
- SAT and SAT Subject Tests or ACT with writing, application essay required
- 93% graduate within 6 years

General. Founded in 1870. Regionally accredited. **Degrees:** 545 bachelor's awarded. **ROTC:** Army, Air Force. **Location:** 12 miles from Boston. **Calendar:** Semester, limited summer session. **Full-time faculty:** 298 total; 96% have terminal degrees, 22% minority, 56% women. **Part-time faculty:** 58 total; 86% have terminal degrees, 21% minority, 62% women. **Class size:** 73% < 20, 27% 20-39, less than 1% 40-49. **Special facilities:** Science center with X-ray diffractometer, nuclear magnetic resonance, spectrometers (NMR and microMRI), electron microscopes, argon and dye lasers, observatory with three telescopes (6-, 12-, and 24-inch), cultural center, greenhouses, botanic gardens, arboretum, media and technology center with linear editing room for video, digital-based video editing suite, plotter, film recorder, slide scanner.

Freshman class profile. 4,555 applied, 1,380 admitted, 595 enrolled.

Mid 50% test scores			
SAT critical reading:	640-740	Rank in top tenth:	80%
SAT math:	650-750	Return as sophomores:	95%
SAT writing:	650-750	Out-of-state:	87%
ACT composite:	29-33	Live on campus:	100%
Rank in top quarter:	95%	International:	14%

Basis for selection. Evidence in student's record, both in and out of the classroom, of ability to meet rigorous academic standards and willingness to engage in the community is important. Candidates should have taken full advantage of the opportunities available to them in high school. 2 SAT Subject Tests required if SAT is submitted; at least one quantitative Subject Test recommended. Interviews recommended; on- and off-campus interviews available. **Home schooled:** Statement describing home school structure and mission, transcript of courses and grades, letter of recommendation (nonparent) required. Applicants must meet homeschooling requirements of their state.

High school preparation. College-preparatory program recommended. Recommended units include English 4, mathematics 4, social studies 4, history 4, science 3 (laboratory 2) and foreign language 4.

2015-2016 Annual costs. Tuition/fees: $46,836. Room/board: $14,504. Books/supplies: $800. Personal expenses: $1,250.

2015-2016 Financial aid. All financial aid based on need. Average need met was 100%. Average scholarship/grant was $46,277; average loan $2,678. 92% of total undergraduate aid awarded as scholarships/grants, 8% as loans/jobs. **Additional information:** No student will graduate with more than $12,825 in packaged student loans. Students from families with a calculated income between $60,000 and $100,000 will graduate with no more than $8,600 in packaged student loans. Students from families with the greatest need ($60,000 income or less) will graduate with $0 in packaged student loans; their packages will consist of scholarship and work-study money.

Application procedures. Admission: Closing date 1/15 (postmark date). $50 fee, may be waived for applicants with need, free for online applicants. Admission notification by 4/1. Must reply by 5/1. **Financial aid:** Priority date 2/15; no closing date. FAFSA, CSS PROFILE required. Applicants notified by 4/1; must reply by 5/1.

Academics. Special study options: Cross-registration, double major, exchange student, honors, independent study, internships, semester at sea, student-designed major, study abroad, teacher certification program, Washington semester. **Credit/placement by examination:** AP, CLEP, IB, institutional tests. 16 credit hours maximum toward bachelor's degree. Students may receive credit for score of 5 on most AP exams or a 5, 6, or 7 on most IB exams. **Support services:** Learning center, reduced course load, study skills assistance, tutoring, writing center.

Majors. Architecture: Architecture. **Area/ethnic studies:** African, African-American, American, Asian, East Asian, European, French, German, Latin American, Near/Middle Eastern, Russian/Eastern European/Eurasian, Russian/Slavic, South Asian, women's. **Biology:** General, biochemistry, neuroscience. **Computer sciences:** General, computer science. **Conservation:**

Environmental studies. **Engineering:** General. **English:** English lit. **Foreign languages:** General, African, ancient Greek, Arabic, Chinese, classics, comparative lit, French, German, Italian, Japanese, Latin, linguistics, Russian, Spanish. **History:** General. **Math:** General. **Philosophy/religion:** Judaic, philosophy, religion. **Physical sciences:** Astronomy, astrophysics, chemistry, geology, physics. **Psychology:** General. **Social sciences:** Anthropology, archaeology, economics, international relations, political science, sociology. **Visual/performing arts:** Art history/conservation, dramatic, music, music history, studio arts.

Most popular majors. Area/ethnic studies 9%, biology 11%, computer/information sciences 6%, foreign language 8%, psychology 9%, social sciences 27%, visual/performing arts 7%.

Technology on campus. 481 workstations in dormitories, library, computer center, student center. Dormitories wired for high-speed internet access and linked to campus network. Commuter students can connect to campus network. Online course registration, online library, helpline, repair service, student web hosting, wireless network available.

Student life. Freshman orientation: Mandatory. Preregistration for classes offered. Held the week before classes begin. **Policies:** Honor Code in effect. **Housing:** Guaranteed on-campus for all undergraduates. Special housing for disabled, apartments, cooperative housing, themed housing available. Pets allowed in dorm rooms. French, Spanish and other language houses available. **Activities:** Jazz band, campus ministries, choral groups, dance, drama, film society, international student organizations, literary magazine, music ensembles, Model UN, radio station, student government, student newspaper, symphony orchestra, TV station, black student club, Latina student club, Asian student union, Hillel, Al-Muslimat, Intervarsity Christian Fellowship, political and legislative action organization, Best Buddies, Habitat for Humanity.

Athletics. NCAA. **Intercollegiate:** Basketball W, cross-country W, diving W, fencing W, field hockey W, golf W, lacrosse W, rowing (crew) W, soccer W, softball W, squash W, swimming W, tennis W, track and field W, volleyball W. **Intramural:** Basketball W, ice hockey W, racquetball W, rowing (crew) W, rugby W, sailing W, soccer W, table tennis W. **Team name:** Wellesley Blue.

Student services. Adult student services, alcohol/substance abuse counseling, chaplain/spiritual director, career counseling, services for economically disadvantaged, student employment services, financial aid counseling, health services, minority student services, on-campus daycare, personal counseling, placement for graduates, women's services. **Physically disabled:** Services for visually, hearing impaired.

Contact. E-mail: admission@wellesley.edu
Phone: (781) 283-2270 Fax: (781) 283-3678
Jennifer Desjarlais, Dean of Admission and Financial Aid, Wellesley College, 106 Central Street, Wellesley, MA 02481-8203

Wentworth Institute of Technology
Boston, Massachusetts
www.wit.edu

CB member
CB code: 3958

- Private 4-year engineering and technical college
- Residential campus in very large city
- 4,288 degree-seeking undergraduates: 9% part-time, 19% women, 4% African American, 7% Asian American, 3% Hispanic/Latino, 6% Multi-racial, non-Hispanic, 7% international
- 252 degree-seeking graduate students
- 67% of applicants admitted
- SAT or ACT (ACT writing optional), application essay required
- 66% graduate within 6 years; 20% enter graduate study

General. Founded in 1904. Regionally accredited. Mandatory cooperative education program. Member of Colleges of the Fenway. **Degrees:** 706 bachelor's, 25 associate awarded; master's offered. **ROTC:** Army, Air Force. **Location:** 2 miles from downtown. **Calendar:** Semester, limited summer session. **Full-time faculty:** 151 total; 70% have terminal degrees, 15% minority, 33% women. **Part-time faculty:** 220 total; 14% minority, 40% women. **Class size:** 41% < 20, 56% 20-39, less than 1% 40-49, 2% 50-99. **Special facilities:** Internet radio station.

Freshman class profile. 6,975 applied, 4,650 admitted, 965 enrolled.

Mid 50% test scores			
SAT critical reading:	470-580	GPA 3.0-3.49:	40%
SAT math:	520-630	GPA 2.0-2.99:	40%
SAT writing:	450-560	End year in good standing:	83%
ACT composite:	20-27	Return as sophomores:	84%
GPA 3.75 or higher:	8%	Out-of-state:	37%
GPA 3.50-3.74:	12%	Live on campus:	77%
		International:	9%

Basis for selection. School achievement record most important, followed by test scores. Teacher recommendations, personal statement, extracurricular activities also considered. **Home schooled:** Transcript of courses and grades, letter of recommendation (nonparent) required. Course content description may be requested.

High school preparation. College-preparatory program recommended. 10 units required; 11 recommended. Required and recommended units include English 4, mathematics 3-4, science 2 (laboratory 1). 3 college-preparatory math, 1 physics recommended for many programs. Additional math required for some.

2015-2016 Annual costs. Tuition/fees: $30,760. Room/board: $13,390. Books/supplies: $1,500.

2015-2016 Financial aid. Need-based: 875 full-time freshmen applied for aid; 776 deemed to have need; 776 received aid. Average scholarship/grant was $5,651; average loan $3,686. 26% of total undergraduate aid awarded as scholarships/grants, 74% as loans/jobs. **Non-need-based:** Awarded to 3,567 full-time undergraduates, including 1,016 freshmen. Scholarships awarded for academics, leadership, ROTC, state residency.

Application procedures. Admission: Priority date 2/15; no deadline. $50 fee, may be waived for applicants with need. Admission notification on a rolling basis beginning on or about 10/30. Must reply by 5/1. **Financial aid:** Priority date 3/1; no closing date. FAFSA required. Applicants notified on a rolling basis starting 3/15; must reply within 2 week(s) of notification.

Academics. Electromechanical Engineering requires 5 years. All bachelor's candidates required to complete 2 semesters full-time co-op. **Special study options:** Combined bachelor's/graduate degree, cooperative education, cross-registration, distance learning, study abroad. Cross-registration with Simmons College, Emmanuel College, Wheelock College, Massachusetts College of Pharmacy and Health Sciences, Massachusetts College of Art (Colleges of the Fenway). **Credit/placement by examination:** AP, CLEP, IB, institutional tests. 32 credit hours maximum toward associate degree, 64 toward bachelor's. Students may only receive maximum of one half of total credit requirement from credit by examination. **Support services:** Learning center, reduced course load, study skills assistance, tutoring, writing center.

Majors. Architecture: Architecture. **Business:** Business admin, construction management, operations, project management. **Computer sciences:** Computer science, information systems, networking. **Engineering:** General, biomedical, civil, computer, electrical, electromechanical, mechanical. **Math:** Applied. **Visual/performing arts:** Industrial design, interior design.

Most popular majors. Architecture 17%, business/marketing 25%, computer/information sciences 13%, engineering/engineering technologies 37%, visual/performing arts 8%.

Technology on campus. PC or laptop required. 191 workstations in library, computer center. Dormitories wired for high-speed internet access and linked to campus network. Commuter students can connect to campus network. Online course registration, online library, helpline, repair service, student web hosting, wireless network available.

Student life. Freshman orientation: Mandatory. Preregistration for classes offered. Week-long session held week before classes begin. **Policies:** Alcohol permitted in certain residential halls if every resident of the room is 21 or older. Smoke-free campus. Freshmen not permitted cars on campus. **Housing:** Coed dorms available. $500 nonrefundable deposit, deadline 5/1. Apartments available for upperclassmen. **Activities:** Choral groups, international student organizations, radio station, student government, Honor society, Society of Women Engineers, Student Association of Interior Design, National Society of Black Engineers, Society of Hispanic Professional Engineers, Architecture club, American Society of Civil Engineers, Society of Manufacturing Engineers, Institute of Electrical & Electronic Engineers, Industrial Design Society of America.

Athletics. NCAA. **Intercollegiate:** Baseball M, basketball, cross-country M, golf M, ice hockey M, lacrosse, rowing (crew) M, soccer, softball W, tennis, track and field M, volleyball. **Team name:** Leopards.

Student services. Alcohol/substance abuse counseling, career counseling, student employment services, financial aid counseling, health services, minority student services, personal counseling, placement for graduates, veterans' counselor, women's services. **Physically disabled:** Services for hearing impaired.

Contact. E-mail: admissions@wit.edu
Phone: (617) 989-4000 Toll-free number: (800) 556-0610
Fax: (617) 989-4010
Maureen Dischino, Executive Director, Wentworth Institute of Technology, 550 Huntington Avenue, Boston, MA 02115

Western New England University
Springfield, Massachusetts   **CB member**
www.wne.edu   **CB code: 3962**

- Private 4-year university
- Residential campus in small city
- 2,726 degree-seeking undergraduates: 5% part-time, 39% women, 6% African American, 3% Asian American, 8% Hispanic/Latino, 1% Multiracial, non-Hispanic, 3% international
- 1,179 degree-seeking graduate students
- 80% of applicants admitted
- SAT or ACT (ACT writing optional), application essay required
- 57% graduate within 6 years

General. Founded in 1919. Regionally accredited. **Degrees:** 582 bachelor's awarded; master's, professional, doctoral offered. **ROTC:** Army, Air Force. **Location:** 85 miles from Boston, 25 miles from Hartford, Ct. **Calendar:** Semester, limited summer session. **Full-time faculty:** 229 total; 88% have terminal degrees, 12% minority, 42% women. **Part-time faculty:** 148 total; 40% have terminal degrees, 3% minority, 40% women. **Class size:** 53% < 20, 47% 20-39, less than 1% 40-49.

Freshman class profile. 6,207 applied, 4,988 admitted, 719 enrolled.

Mid 50% test scores			
SAT critical reading:	470-570	Rank in top quarter:	47%
SAT math:	490-610	Rank in top tenth:	22%
ACT composite:	22-27	Return as sophomores:	77%
GPA 3.75 or higher:	32%	Out-of-state:	50%
GPA 3.50-3.74:	11%	Live on campus:	84%
GPA 3.0-3.49:	26%	International:	2%
GPA 2.0-2.99:	31%		

Basis for selection. School achievement record, test scores, recommendation most important. Interview, class rank, application essay, extracurricular activities also considered.

High school preparation. College-preparatory program required. 10 units required; 18 recommended. Required and recommended units include English 4, mathematics 2-4, social studies 1-2, history 1-2, science 1-2 (laboratory 1-2) and foreign language 2. 1 American history required. Additional science and math required for certain programs.

2015-2016 Annual costs. Tuition/fees: $34,030. Room/board: $12,896. Books/supplies: $1,240. Personal expenses: $1,520.

2015-2016 Financial aid. Need-based: 662 full-time freshmen applied for aid; 600 deemed to have need; 600 received aid. Average need met was 74%. Average scholarship/grant was $20,850; average loan $3,778. 67% of total undergraduate aid awarded as scholarships/grants, 33% as loans/jobs. **Non-need-based:** Awarded to 564 full-time undergraduates, including 139 freshmen. Scholarships awarded for academics, music/drama, ROTC.

Application procedures. Admission: Priority date 2/15; no deadline. $40 fee, may be waived for applicants with need. Admission notification on a rolling basis beginning on or about 10/1. Must reply by May 1 or within 2 week(s) if notified thereafter. **Financial aid:** Priority date 4/15; no closing date. FAFSA required. Applicants notified on a rolling basis starting 3/1; must reply by 5/1 or within 2 week(s) of notification.

Academics. Special study options: Accelerated study, combined bachelor's/graduate degree, cross-registration, distance learning, double major, dual enrollment of high school students, ESL, exchange student, honors, independent study, internships, student-designed major, study abroad, teacher certification program, Washington semester. 3+3 law program. Accelerated part-time degree completion. 3+2 programs for completion of MBA or MSA for a variety of majors. **Credit/placement by examination:** AP, CLEP, IB, SAT, ACT, institutional tests. **Support services:** Pre-admission summer program, reduced course load, study skills assistance, tutoring, writing center. Math and science centers.

Majors. Area/ethnic studies: American. **Biology:** General, neuroscience. **Business:** General, accounting, actuarial science, business admin, entrepreneurial studies, finance, information resources management, international, management information systems, marketing. **Communications:** General, communications/speech/rhetoric, digital media, journalism, media studies, public relations. **Computer sciences:** Computer science, information systems. **Education:** Biology, business, chemistry, elementary, English, history, mathematics, psychology, secondary. **Engineering:** Biomedical, civil, computer, electrical, industrial, mechanical. **English:** Creative writing, English lit. **History:** General. **Human services:** Social work. **Liberal arts:** Arts/sciences. **Math:** General. **Parks/recreation:** Sports admin. **Philosophy/religion:** Philosophy. **Physical sciences:** Chemistry, forensic chemistry. **Protective services:** Criminal justice, forensics. **Psychology:** General. **Social sciences:** Economics, political science, sociology. **Visual/performing arts:** Arts management.

Most popular majors. Business/marketing 27%, engineering/engineering technologies 20%, psychology 9%, security/protective services 9%.

Technology on campus. 530 workstations in dormitories, library, computer center, student center. Dormitories wired for high-speed internet access and linked to campus network. Commuter students can connect to campus network. Online library, helpline, repair service, wireless network available.

Student life. Freshman orientation: Available. Preregistration for classes offered. Two-day program held over summer for students and parents. Parents assessed meals and materials fee. **Housing:** Guaranteed on-campus for freshmen. Coed dorms, special housing for disabled, apartments, themed housing available. $400 nonrefundable deposit, deadline 5/1. **Activities:** Bands, campus ministries, choral groups, dance, drama, film society, international student organizations, literary magazine, music ensembles, Model UN, musical theater, radio station, student government, student newspaper, TV station, United and Mutually Equal, Community Action Rewards Everyone, Global Sustainability Club, Social Workers Advocating Together, Gay/Straight Alliance, Sexual Misconduct Advocate Response Team, Feminists Unite, Hillel, Muslim Student Association, Cornerstone Christian Fellowship.

Athletics. NCAA. **Intercollegiate:** Baseball M, basketball, cross-country, field hockey W, football (tackle) M, golf M, ice hockey M, lacrosse, soccer, softball W, swimming W, tennis, volleyball W, wrestling M. **Intramural:** Badminton, basketball, football (non-tackle), handball, soccer, softball, table tennis, ultimate frisbee, volleyball, water polo. **Team name:** Golden Bears.

Student services. Adult student services, alcohol/substance abuse counseling, chaplain/spiritual director, career counseling, student employment services, financial aid counseling, health services, minority student services, personal counseling, veterans' counselor. **Physically disabled:** Services for visually, speech, hearing impaired.

Contact. E-mail: learn@wne.edu
Phone: (413) 782-1321 Toll-free number: (800) 325-1122 ext. 1321
Fax: (413) 782-1777
Bryan Gross, Vice President for Enrollment Management, Western New England University, 1215 Wilbraham Road, Springfield, MA 01119-2684

Westfield State University
Westfield, Massachusetts
www.westfield.ma.edu

CB member
CB code: 3523

- Public 4-year university
- Residential campus in large town
- 5,459 degree-seeking undergraduates: 10% part-time, 54% women, 4% African American, 2% Asian American, 9% Hispanic/Latino, 4% Multiracial, non-Hispanic
- 563 degree-seeking graduate students
- 80% of applicants admitted
- SAT or ACT (ACT writing optional) required
- 63% graduate within 6 years

General. Founded in 1838. Regionally accredited. **Degrees:** 1,515 bachelor's awarded; master's offered. **ROTC:** Army, Air Force. **Location:** 10 miles from Springfield, 100 miles from Boston. **Calendar:** Semester, limited summer session. **Full-time faculty:** 238 total; 87% have terminal degrees, 16% minority, 50% women. **Part-time faculty:** 281 total; 22% have terminal degrees, 10% minority, 58% women. **Class size:** 38% < 20, 60% 20-39, 1% 40-49, 1% 50-99, less than 1% >100. **Special facilities:** Television production studio, radio station, natural history museum/collections, GIS lab, 2 art galleries.

Freshman class profile. 5,140 applied, 4,092 admitted, 1,292 enrolled.

Mid 50% test scores		GPA 3.50-3.74:	11%
SAT critical reading:	450-540	GPA 3.0-3.49:	34%
SAT math:	460-550	GPA 2.0-2.99:	44%
SAT writing:	430-530	Return as sophomores:	79%
ACT composite:	20-24	Out-of-state:	6%
GPA 3.75 or higher:	11%	Live on campus:	84%

Basis for selection. Rigor of secondary school record, academic grade point average, and standardized testing are the most important factors. Personal essay and recommendations may be considered if submitted. Extracurricular activities, community involvement, and family educational background may also be considered. Audition required of music majors. Portfolio required of art majors. Essay and interview may be required of nursing majors. **Home schooled:** Requirements based on AACROA standards. **Learning Disabled:** SAT/ACT requirement waived for students with documented learning disability. Interview required for some at request of Director of Disability Services.

High school preparation. College-preparatory program required. 17 units required. Required units include English 4, mathematics 4, social studies 1, history 1, science 3 (laboratory 2), foreign language 2 and academic electives 2.

2015-2016 Annual costs. Tuition/fees: $8,815; $14,895 out-of-state. Room/board: $10,691. Books/supplies: $1,100. Personal expenses: $1,534. **Additional information:** Tuition for New England Regional Program: $1,455.

2014-2015 Financial aid. Need-based: 1,157 full-time freshmen applied for aid; 819 deemed to have need; 805 received aid. Average need met was 60%. Average scholarship/grant was $5,770; average loan $3,162. 39% of total undergraduate aid awarded as scholarships/grants, 61% as loans/jobs. **Non-need-based:** Awarded to 629 full-time undergraduates, including 261 freshmen. Scholarships awarded for academics.

Application procedures. Admission: Closing date 3/1 (postmark date). $50 fee, may be waived for applicants with need. Admission notification by 3/15. Admission notification on a rolling basis beginning on or about 1/15. Must reply by May 1 or within 2 week(s) if notified thereafter. Maximum period of deferred admission: 1 semester. **Financial aid:** Priority date 3/1; no closing date. FAFSA required. Applicants notified on a rolling basis starting 4/1; must reply within 2 week(s) of notification.

Academics. Special study options: Cross-registration, distance learning, double major, dual enrollment of high school students, exchange student, honors, independent study, internships, semester at sea, student-designed major, study abroad, teacher certification program, Washington semester. **Credit/placement by examination:** AP, CLEP, institutional tests. 60 credit hours maximum toward bachelor's degree. Maximum of 3 credits awarded for AP tests in English. Students taking CLEP tests in English Composition with Essay or Freshman Composition must also submit writing portfolio; portfolio evaluated before credit can be awarded. Maximum of 3 credits awarded for composition. **Support services:** Learning center, pre-admission summer program, reduced course load, study skills assistance, tutoring, writing center.

Majors. Architecture: Urban/community planning. **Area/ethnic studies:** General. **Biology:** General. **Business:** General. **Communications:** Communications/speech/rhetoric. **Computer sciences:** Computer science, information systems. **Conservation:** Environmental science. **Education:** Elementary, kindergarten/preschool, special ed, technology/industrial arts. **English:** English lit. **Foreign languages:** Spanish. **Health services:** Athletic training, nursing (RN). **History:** General. **Human services:** Social work. **Liberal arts:** Arts/sciences. **Math:** General. **Parks/recreation:** Health/fitness. **Physical sciences:** General, chemistry. **Protective services:** Criminal justice. **Psychology:** General. **Social sciences:** Economics, political science, sociology. **Visual/performing arts:** Art, dramatic, music.

Most popular majors. Business/marketing 13%, communications/journalism 7%, education 9%, liberal arts 16%, psychology 8%, security/protective services 12%, social sciences 6%.

Technology on campus. 642 workstations in dormitories, library, computer center, student center. Dormitories wired for high-speed internet access and linked to campus network. Commuter students can connect to campus network. Online course registration, online library, helpline, student web hosting, wireless network available.

Student life. Freshman orientation: Available. Preregistration for classes offered. Several 2-day sessions held in June and August; includes mandatory testing, course selection. **Policies:** Non-smoking campus. Freshmen not permitted cars on campus. **Housing:** Coed dorms, special housing for disabled, apartments, themed housing available. $150 nonrefundable deposit, deadline 5/1. Living/learning (academic intensive), quiet living, honors housing available. **Activities:** Bands, campus ministries, choral groups, dance, drama, international student organizations, literary magazine, music ensembles, Model UN, musical theater, radio station, student government, student newspaper, TV station, 31 academic clubs, Christian Fellowship, Circle K, Intervarsity Christian Group, Latino Association, Queer-Straight Alliance, Students Advocating for Gender Equality, Wounded Warriors, Jewish and Muslim student organizations.

Athletics. NCAA. **Intercollegiate:** Baseball M, basketball, cheerleading W, cross-country, field hockey W, football (tackle) M, golf, ice hockey M, lacrosse W, soccer, softball W, swimming W, track and field, volleyball W. **Intramural:** Basketball M, football (non-tackle), soccer, softball M, ultimate frisbee, volleyball. **Team name:** Owls.

Student services. Adult student services, alcohol/substance abuse counseling, career counseling, services for economically disadvantaged, student employment services, financial aid counseling, health services, minority student services, personal counseling, placement for graduates, veterans' counselor. **Physically disabled:** Services for visually, speech, hearing impaired.

Contact. E-mail: admissions@westfield.ma.edu
Phone: (413) 572-5218 Fax: (413) 572-0520
Kelly Hart, Director of Admissions, Westfield State University, 577
Western Avenue, Westfield, MA 01086-1630

Wheaton College
Norton, Massachusetts
www.wheatoncollege.edu

CB member
CB code: 3963

- Private 4-year liberal arts college
- Residential campus in large town
- 1,565 degree-seeking undergraduates: 64% women, 6% African American, 5% Asian American, 7% Hispanic/Latino, 3% Multi-racial, non-Hispanic, 10% international
- 65% of applicants admitted
- Application essay required
- 79% graduate within 6 years; 21% enter graduate study

General. Founded in 1834. Regionally accredited. **Degrees:** 435 bachelor's awarded. **ROTC:** Army. **Location:** 35 miles from Boston; 20 miles from Providence, Rhode Island. **Calendar:** Semester, limited summer session. **Full-time faculty:** 129 total; 88% have terminal degrees, 18% minority, 53% women. **Part-time faculty:** 60 total; 45% have terminal degrees, 8% minority, 58% women. **Class size:** 68% < 20, 26% 20-39, 4% 40-49, 2% 50-99. **Special facilities:** Nursery school and early childhood lab, geographic information system lab, imaging center for undergraduate collaboration, language lab, WHALE lab, observatory.

Freshman class profile. 4,322 applied, 2,790 admitted, 417 enrolled.

Mid 50% test scores			
		GPA 2.0-2.99:	24%
SAT critical reading:	550-660	Rank in top quarter:	60%
SAT math:	550-670	Rank in top tenth:	26%
SAT writing:	540-650	End year in good standing:	95%
ACT composite:	25-30	Return as sophomores:	86%
GPA 3.75 or higher:	26%	Out-of-state:	65%
GPA 3.50-3.74:	17%	Live on campus:	99%
GPA 3.0-3.49:	33%	International:	14%

Basis for selection. Academic achievement, writing ability, difficulty of high school curriculum and co-curricular achievement considered. Test are optional. Interviews strongly recommended. **Home schooled:** Statement describing home school structure and mission, transcript of courses and grades required. **Learning Disabled:** Students who have diagnosed learning difference encouraged to submit supporting testing for review.

High school preparation. College-preparatory program required. Required and recommended units include English 4, mathematics 3, social studies 3, history 3, science 3 and foreign language 3. English should emphasize composition skills. History and social studies are considered to be one category.

2015-2016 Annual costs. Tuition/fees: $47,700. Room/board: $12,165. Books/supplies: $940. Personal expenses: $760.

2015-2016 Financial aid. Need-based: 332 full-time freshmen applied for aid; 282 deemed to have need; 282 received aid. Average need met was 93%. Average scholarship/grant was $33,905; average loan $3,953. 76% of total undergraduate aid awarded as scholarships/grants, 24% as loans/jobs. **Non-need-based:** Awarded to 443 full-time undergraduates, including 116 freshmen. Scholarships awarded for academics.

Application procedures. Admission: Priority date 11/15; deadline 1/15 (postmark date). $60 fee, may be waived for applicants with need. Admission notification by 4/1. Admission notification on a rolling basis beginning on or about 12/15. Must reply by May 1 or within 2 week(s) if notified thereafter. **Financial aid:** Closing date 2/1. FAFSA, CSS PROFILE required. Applicants notified by 4/1; must reply by 5/1.

Academics. Special study options: Accelerated study, combined bachelor's/graduate degree, cooperative education, cross-registration, double major, dual enrollment of high school students, ESL, exchange student, external degree, honors, independent study, internships, liberal arts/career combination, semester at sea, student-designed major, study abroad, teacher certification program, Washington semester, weekend college. Junior year abroad; Bhutan-Faculty led study abroad program, Brown/Wheaton Program; Salt, Marine Biological Lab, Williams-Mystic, National Theater, Twelve College Exchange. **Credit/placement by examination:** AP, CLEP, IB, institutional tests. 8 credit hours maximum toward bachelor's degree. **Support services:** Learning center, pre-admission summer program, reduced course load, study skills assistance, tutoring, writing center.

Majors. Area/ethnic studies: American, Asian, French, Italian, Russian/Slavic, women's. **Biology:** General, biochemistry, bioinformatics, neuroscience. **Business:** General. **Computer sciences:** Computer science. **Conservation:** Environmental science. **English:** Creative writing, English lit. **Foreign languages:** Classics, German, Latin, modern Greek, Russian. **History:** General. **Liberal arts:** Arts/sciences. **Math:** General. **Philosophy/religion:** Philosophy, religion. **Physical sciences:** Chemistry, physics. **Psychology:** General, psychobiology. **Social sciences:** Anthropology, economics, international relations, political science, sociology. **Visual/performing arts:** Art history/conservation, film/cinema/video, music, studio arts.

Most popular majors. Area/ethnic studies 9%, biology 13%, English 9%, psychology 12%, social sciences 22%, visual/performing arts 12%.

Technology on campus. 282 workstations in library, computer center, student center. Dormitories wired for high-speed internet access and linked to campus network. Commuter students can connect to campus network. Online course registration, online library, helpline, repair service, student web hosting, wireless network available.

Student life. Freshman orientation: Available. Preregistration for classes offered. Three 2-day programs offered in June and August. Core Orientation Program includes class registration. Parents are encouraged to attend. **Housing:** Guaranteed on-campus for all undergraduates. Coed dorms, single-sex dorms, special housing for disabled, themed housing, wellness housing available. Suite-style group housing, quiet housing available. **Activities:** Bands, campus ministries, choral groups, dance, drama, film society, international student organizations, literary magazine, music ensembles, Model UN, musical theater, radio station, student government, student newspaper, symphony orchestra, Hillel, Christian Fellowship, Interfaith Alliance, student government association, Amnesty International, Habitat for Humanity, black student association, Latino student association, Asian American coalition.

Athletics. NCAA. **Intercollegiate:** Baseball M, basketball, cross-country, diving, field hockey W, lacrosse, soccer, softball W, swimming, synchronized swimming W, tennis, track and field, volleyball W. **Intramural:** Badminton, basketball, football (non-tackle), soccer, softball, tennis, volleyball. **Team name:** Lyons.

Student services. Alcohol/substance abuse counseling, career counseling, student employment services, financial aid counseling, health services, minority student services, personal counseling, placement for graduates, women's services. **Physically disabled:** Services for visually, hearing impaired.

Contact. E-mail: admission@wheatoncollege.edu
Phone: (508) 286-8251 Toll-free number: (800) 394-6003
Fax: (508) 286-8271
Grant Gosselin, Vice President of Enrollment and Dean of Admission and Student Aid, Wheaton College, 26 East Main Street, Norton, MA 02766

Wheelock College
Boston, Massachusetts
www.wheelock.edu

CB member
CB code: 3964

- Private 4-year liberal arts and teachers college
- Residential campus in very large city
- 809 degree-seeking undergraduates: 1% part-time, 84% women, 13% African American, 4% Asian American, 11% Hispanic/Latino, 3% Multi-racial, non-Hispanic, 2% international
- 339 degree-seeking graduate students
- 95% of applicants admitted
- SAT or ACT (ACT writing optional), application essay required
- 64% graduate within 6 years

General. Founded in 1888. Regionally accredited. Member of the Colleges of the Fenway. **Degrees:** 189 bachelor's awarded; master's offered. **Calendar:** Semester, limited summer session. **Full-time faculty:** 69 total; 26% minority, 74% women. **Part-time faculty:** 111 total; 15% minority, 79% women. **Class size:** 57% < 20, 42% 20-39, less than 1% 50-99.

Freshman class profile. 1,331 applied, 1,270 admitted, 217 enrolled.

Mid 50% test scores			
		GPA 2.0-2.99:	50%
SAT critical reading:	410-540	Rank in top quarter:	33%
SAT math:	400-520	Rank in top tenth:	11%
SAT writing:	410-530	Return as sophomores:	68%
ACT composite:	18-24	Out-of-state:	43%
GPA 3.75 or higher:	8%	Live on campus:	82%
GPA 3.50-3.74:	10%	International:	2%
GPA 3.0-3.49:	28%		

Basis for selection. School achievement and record most important. Test scores, school and community activities considered. Interview recommended.

High school preparation. College-preparatory program required. 16 units required. Required units include English 4, mathematics 3, social studies 1, history 2, science 2 (laboratory 1) and academic electives 3. Child development courses considered.

2015-2016 Annual costs. Tuition/fees: $33,835. Room/board: $14,000. Books/supplies: $880. Personal expenses: $1,400.

2015-2016 Financial aid. Need-based: 197 full-time freshmen applied for aid; 185 deemed to have need; 185 received aid. Average need met was 67%. Average scholarship/grant was $23,325; average loan $3,373. 68% of total undergraduate aid awarded as scholarships/grants, 32% as loans/jobs. **Non-need-based:** Awarded to 175 full-time undergraduates, including 45 freshmen. Scholarships awarded for academics, leadership, state residency.

Application procedures. Admission: Priority date 3/1; deadline 5/1 (postmark date). No application fee. Admission notification on a rolling basis beginning on or about 1/20. Must reply by May 1 or within 2 week(s) if notified thereafter. **Financial aid:** Priority date 2/15; no closing date. FAFSA required. Applicants notified on a rolling basis starting 3/1; must reply by 5/1.

Academics. Special study options: Combined bachelor's/graduate degree, cross-registration, distance learning, double major, dual enrollment of high school students, honors, independent study, internships, liberal arts/career combination, study abroad, teacher certification program. **Credit/placement by examination:** AP, CLEP, institutional tests. 32 credit hours maximum toward bachelor's degree. **Support services:** Learning center, pre-admission summer program, reduced course load, study skills assistance, tutoring, writing center.

Majors. Area/ethnic studies: American. **Communications:** Media studies. **Education:** Early childhood, elementary, special ed. **Human services:** Social work, youth services. **Liberal arts:** Arts/sciences, humanities. **Math:** General. **Visual/performing arts:** General. **Work/family studies:** Child care management, child development, family studies.

Most popular majors. Education 20%, family/consumer sciences 13%, psychology 32%, public administration/social services 14%, visual/performing arts 6%.

Technology on campus. 120 workstations in dormitories, library, computer center, student center. Dormitories wired for high-speed internet access and linked to campus network. Commuter students can connect to campus network. Online course registration, online library, helpline, repair service, wireless network available.

Student life. Freshman orientation: Mandatory, $200 fee. Preregistration for classes offered. Two-day program held in summer; students have choice of 2 sessions. **Housing:** Guaranteed on-campus for freshmen. Coed dorms, single-sex dorms available. $100 nonrefundable deposit, deadline 5/1. **Activities:** Dance, drama, international student organizations, literary magazine, musical theater, student government, social work club, women's center, Boston Association for the Education of Young Children, child life council, sign language club, Bible study, juvenile justice and youth advocacy council.

Athletics. NCAA. **Intercollegiate:** Basketball, cross-country, field hockey W, lacrosse, soccer, softball W, tennis M. **Intramural:** Basketball, racquetball, soccer, softball, squash, volleyball. **Team name:** Wildcats.

Student services. Alcohol/substance abuse counseling, career counseling, student employment services, financial aid counseling, health services, minority student services, personal counseling, placement for graduates, women's services. **Physically disabled:** Services for visually, speech, hearing impaired.

Contact. E-mail: undergrad@wheelock.edu
Phone: (617) 879-2206 Toll-free number: (800) 734-5212
Fax: (617) 879-2449
Lisa Slavin, Director of Undergraduate Admissions, Wheelock College, 200 The Riverway, Boston, MA 02215-4104

Williams College
Williamstown, Massachusetts
www.williams.edu

CB member
CB code: 3965

- Private 4-year liberal arts college
- Residential campus in small town
- 2,065 degree-seeking undergraduates: 51% women, 8% African American, 12% Asian American, 13% Hispanic/Latino, 6% Multi-racial, non-Hispanic, 8% international
- 52 degree-seeking graduate students
- 18% of applicants admitted

- SAT or ACT (ACT writing optional), SAT Subject Tests, application essay required
- 96% graduate within 6 years

General. Founded in 1793. Regionally accredited. **Degrees:** 522 bachelor's awarded; master's offered. **ROTC:** Air Force. **Location:** 35 miles from Albany, NY; 150 miles from Boston. **Calendar:** 4-1-4. **Full-time faculty:** 266 total; 97% have terminal degrees, 20% minority, 44% women. **Part-time faculty:** 84 total; 75% have terminal degrees, 18% minority, 45% women. **Class size:** 78% < 20, 15% 20-39, 4% 40-49, 3% 50-99, less than 1% >100. **Special facilities:** Performing arts center, experimental forest, environmental studies center, observatory, electron-scanning microscope, transmission microscopes, studio art center, nuclear magnetic resonance imager, college museum, center for educational technology.

Freshman class profile. 6,883 applied, 1,212 admitted, 551 enrolled.

Mid 50% test scores			
SAT critical reading:	670-780	Rank in top tenth:	93%
SAT math:	660-770	Return as sophomores:	97%
SAT writing:	670-780	Out-of-state:	87%
ACT composite:	31-34	Live on campus:	100%
Rank in top quarter:	98%	International:	8%

Basis for selection. School achievement record, character and personal promise, test scores, essay important. College seeks diversity of social, economic, and geographic backgrounds. Leadership and accomplishment in extracurricular activities also considered.

High school preparation. College-preparatory program required. Recommended units include English 4, mathematics 4, social studies 4, science 4 (laboratory 3) and foreign language 4.

2015-2016 Annual costs. Tuition/fees: $50,070. Room/board: $13,220. Books/supplies: $800. Personal expenses: $1,500.

2015-2016 Financial aid. Need-based: 348 full-time freshmen applied for aid; 276 deemed to have need; 276 received aid. Average need met was 100%. Average scholarship/grant was $48,376; average loan $2,728. 93% of total undergraduate aid awarded as scholarships/grants, 7% as loans/jobs.

Application procedures. Admission: Closing date 1/1 (postmark date). $65 fee, may be waived for applicants with need. Notified by first week of April. Must reply by May 1 or within 1 week(s) if notified thereafter. **Financial aid:** Priority date 2/1; no closing date. FAFSA, CSS PROFILE required. Applicants notified by 4/1; must reply by 5/1.

Academics. Special study options: Combined bachelor's/graduate degree, cross-registration, double major, independent study, student-designed major, study abroad. Summer science research program, Williams in Oxford, Mystic maritime studies program, tutorials, 3-2 engineering program with Columbia University. **Credit/placement by examination:** AP, CLEP, IB, institutional tests. **Support services:** Pre-admission summer program, study skills assistance, tutoring, writing center.

Majors. Area/ethnic studies: American, Asian, women's. **Biology:** General. **Computer sciences:** Computer science. **Conservation:** Environmental science. **English:** English lit. **Foreign languages:** Chinese, classics, comparative lit, French, German, Japanese, Russian, Spanish. **History:** General. **Math:** General, statistics. **Philosophy/religion:** Philosophy, religion. **Physical sciences:** Astronomy, astrophysics, chemistry, geology, physics. **Psychology:** General. **Social sciences:** Anthropology, economics, political economy, political science, sociology. **Visual/performing arts:** Art history/conservation, dramatic, music, studio arts.

Most popular majors. Biology 8%, English 9%, foreign language 7%, history 9%, mathematics 8%, physical sciences 10%, psychology 8%, social sciences 23%, visual/performing arts 6%.

Technology on campus. 247 workstations in library, computer center, student center. Dormitories wired for high-speed internet access and linked to campus network. Commuter students can connect to campus network. Online course registration, online library, helpline, repair service, student web hosting, wireless network available.

Student life. Freshman orientation: Mandatory. Preregistration for classes offered. **Policies:** Freshmen not permitted cars on campus. **Housing:** Guaranteed on-campus for all undergraduates. Coed dorms, cooperative housing available. $200 nonrefundable deposit, deadline 5/1. **Activities:** Bands, campus ministries, choral groups, dance, drama, film society, international student organizations, literary magazine, music ensembles, musical theater, opera, radio station, student government, student newspaper, symphony orchestra, black student union, Purple Key, Asian Link, Hispanic students club, Korean club, minority coalition, nonviolent alternatives committee, women's club, Hillel, LGBTQ student organization.

Athletics. NCAA. **Intercollegiate:** Baseball M, basketball, cross-country, diving, field hockey W, football (tackle) M, golf, ice hockey, lacrosse, rowing (crew), skiing, soccer, softball W, squash, swimming, tennis, track and field, volleyball W, wrestling M. **Intramural:** Badminton, basketball, ice hockey M, soccer, softball, volleyball. **Team name:** Ephs.

Student services. Alcohol/substance abuse counseling, chaplain/spiritual director, career counseling, services for economically disadvantaged, student employment services, financial aid counseling, health services, minority student services, on-campus daycare, personal counseling, placement for graduates. **Physically disabled:** Services for visually, hearing impaired.

Contact. E-mail: admission@williams.edu
Phone: (413) 597-2211 Fax: (413) 597-4052
Richard Nesbitt, Director of Admission, Williams College, PO BOX 487, Williamstown, MA 01267

Worcester Polytechnic Institute
Worcester, Massachusetts
www.wpi.edu
CB member
CB code: 3969

- Private 4-year university
- Residential campus in small city
- 4,177 degree-seeking undergraduates: 2% part-time, 33% women, 2% African American, 5% Asian American, 8% Hispanic/Latino, 3% Multiracial, non-Hispanic, 12% international
- 1,962 degree-seeking graduate students
- 49% of applicants admitted
- Application essay required
- 85% graduate within 6 years; 33% enter graduate study

General. Founded in 1865. Regionally accredited. Participation by most students in overseas or off-campus projects; over 38 project centers located throughout North America, Central America, Africa, Australia, Asia and Europe. **Degrees:** 958 bachelor's awarded; master's, doctoral offered. **ROTC:** Army, Naval, Air Force. **Location:** 35 miles from Boston. **Calendar:** Quarter, limited summer session. **Full-time faculty:** 359 total; 94% have terminal degrees, 18% minority, 28% women. **Part-time faculty:** 155 total; 46% have terminal degrees, 6% minority, 23% women. **Class size:** 66% < 20, 21% 20-39, 4% 40-49, 7% 50-99, 3% >100. **Special facilities:** Centers for life sciences and bioengineering, biomaterials, bioprocessing, comparative neuroimaging, molecular sensors, nanoscience and technology, untethered healthcare, water research, computer-controlled machining, holographic studies and laser technology, wireless information network studies, fuel cell, industrial math and statistics, fire science laboratory, pavement research laboratory, atomic force microscopy laboratory.

Freshman class profile. 10,172 applied, 4,938 admitted, 1,093 enrolled.

Mid 50% test scores			
SAT critical reading:	570-680	Rank in top quarter:	91%
SAT math:	640-740	Rank in top tenth:	65%
SAT writing:	560-670	Return as sophomores:	96%
ACT composite:	27-32	Out-of-state:	58%
GPA 3.75 or higher:	73%	Live on campus:	96%
GPA 3.50-3.74:	17%	International:	11%
GPA 3.0-3.49:	10%	Fraternities:	23%
		Sororities:	43%

Basis for selection. High school record including academic rigor most important. Extracurricular activities, recommendations, motivation, creativity, initiative important. In lieu of test scores, students may submit alternative documentation of potential for academic success. SAT/ACT or alternative materials that will better reflect the applicant's potential for success (Flex Path) required. Students who choose the Flex Path encouraged to submit examples of academic work or extracurricular projects that reflect a high level of organization, motivation, creativity and problem-solving ability. Interviews offered, but not required. **Home schooled:** Statement describing home school structure and mission, transcript of courses and grades, letter of recommendation (nonparent) required. Submit as much relevant support material as possible and outside recommendations. Detailed course descriptions recommended.

High school preparation. College-preparatory program required. 10 units required. Required and recommended units include English 4, mathematics 4, social studies 2, history 1, science 2-4 (laboratory 2), foreign language 2 and computer science 1. Math requirement includes algebra, geometry, trigonometry and pre-calculus. Science should include physics, chemistry, or biology.

2015-2016 Annual costs. Tuition/fees: $45,590. Room/board: $13,410. Books/supplies: $1,000. Personal expenses: $1,200.

2014-2015 Financial aid. Need-based: 875 full-time freshmen applied for aid; 709 deemed to have need; 708 received aid. Average need met was 79%. Average scholarship/grant was $23,869; average loan $2,838. 82% of total undergraduate aid awarded as scholarships/grants, 18% as loans/jobs. **Non-need-based:** Awarded to 2,183 full-time undergraduates, including 530 freshmen. Scholarships awarded for academics, leadership, minority status, ROTC.

Application procedures. Admission: Closing date 2/1 (postmark date). $65 fee, may be waived for applicants with need. Admission notification by 4/1. Must reply by May 1 or within 2 week(s) if notified thereafter. **Financial aid:** Priority date 2/1; no closing date. FAFSA, CSS PROFILE required. Applicants notified on a rolling basis starting 4/1; must reply by 5/1 or within 2 week(s) of notification.

Academics. Special study options: Accelerated study, combined bachelor's/graduate degree, cooperative education, cross-registration, distance learning, double major, ESL, independent study, internships, liberal arts/career combination, student-designed major, study abroad, teacher certification program. Completion of degree-required projects at off-campus locations (international and domestic) supervised by institution's faculty; students resides at site for 2 months after having prepared for the experience for 2 months while on campus. **Credit/placement by examination:** AP, CLEP, IB, institutional tests. **Support services:** Pre-admission summer program, reduced course load, study skills assistance, tutoring, writing center.

Majors. Biology: General, biochemistry, bioinformatics, biotechnology. **Business:** Actuarial science, business admin, management information systems, management science, operations. **Computer sciences:** Artificial intelligence, computer science, web page design. **Conservation:** Environmental studies. **Engineering:** Aerospace, applied physics, architectural, biomedical, chemical, civil, electrical, environmental, industrial, mechanical, systems. **English:** Technical writing. **Health services:** Predental, premedicine, preveterinary. **Liberal arts:** Humanities. **Math:** General, applied. **Physical sciences:** Chemistry, physics. **Psychology:** General. **Social sciences:** General, economics. **Visual/performing arts:** Game design.

Most popular majors. Computer/information sciences 11%, engineering/engineering technologies 68%.

Technology on campus. 300 workstations in dormitories, library, computer center, student center. Dormitories wired for high-speed internet access and linked to campus network. Commuter students can connect to campus network. Online course registration, online library, helpline, repair service, student web hosting, wireless network available.

Student life. Freshman orientation: Available, $200 fee. Preregistration for classes offered. Program held in late August. **Policies:** Freshmen not permitted cars on campus. **Housing:** Guaranteed on-campus for freshmen. Coed dorms, special housing for disabled, apartments, fraternity/sorority housing, wellness housing available. **Activities:** Bands, campus ministries, choral groups, dance, drama, international student organizations, literary magazine, music ensembles, musical theater, radio station, student government, student newspaper, symphony orchestra, African American cultural society, volunteer tutoring group, Big Brother/Big Sister, World House, European student association, Asian society, Hispanic student association, women's awareness group, students for social awareness, Amnesty International.

Athletics. NCAA. **Intercollegiate:** Baseball M, basketball, cross-country, field hockey W, football (tackle) M, rowing (crew), soccer, softball W, swimming, track and field, volleyball W, wrestling M. **Intramural:** Basketball, cross-country, fencing, football (non-tackle) M, racquetball, soccer, softball, swimming, table tennis, volleyball, water polo M, wrestling M. **Team name:** Engineers.

Student services. Adult student services, alcohol/substance abuse counseling, chaplain/spiritual director, career counseling, student employment services, financial aid counseling, health services, minority student services, personal counseling, placement for graduates, veterans' counselor, women's services. **Physically disabled:** Services for visually, speech, hearing impaired.

Contact. E-mail: admissions@wpi.edu
Phone: (508) 831-5286 Fax: (508) 831-5875
Andrew Palumbo, Dean of Admissions and Financial Aid, Worcester Polytechnic Institute, 100 Institute Road, Worcester, MA 01609-2280

Worcester State University
Worcester, Massachusetts
www.worcester.edu
CB member
CB code: 3524

- Public 4-year liberal arts and teachers college
- Commuter campus in small city

- 5,049 degree-seeking undergraduates: 19% part-time, 59% women, 8% African American, 4% Asian American, 9% Hispanic/Latino, 3% Multi-racial, non-Hispanic, 1% international
- 559 degree-seeking graduate students
- 69% of applicants admitted
- SAT or ACT with writing, application essay required
- 51% graduate within 6 years

General. Founded in 1874. Regionally accredited. **Degrees:** 1,008 bachelor's awarded; master's offered. **ROTC:** Army, Naval, Air Force. **Location:** 45 miles from Boston; 65 miles from Hartford, Connecticut. **Calendar:** Semester, extensive summer session. **Full-time faculty:** 203 total; 81% have terminal degrees, 18% minority, 58% women. **Part-time faculty:** 214 total; 22% have terminal degrees, 11% minority, 62% women. **Class size:** 71% < 20, 28% 20-39, less than 1% 50-99. **Special facilities:** Photographic labs, multimedia classrooms with satellite connectivity, speech/language/hearing clinic.

Freshman class profile. 3,703 applied, 2,539 admitted, 814 enrolled.

Mid 50% test scores			
SAT critical reading:	460-550	GPA 3.0-3.49:	33%
SAT math:	470-560	GPA 2.0-2.99:	34%
SAT writing:	440-540	Return as sophomores:	77%
ACT composite:	20-25	Out-of-state:	6%
GPA 3.75 or higher:	19%	Live on campus:	64%
GPA 3.50-3.74:	14%	International:	1%

Basis for selection. Secondary school record most important; test scores important; extracurricular activities considered. **Home schooled:** Student must submit documentation that home school plan meets district curriculum standards. **Learning Disabled:** SAT waiver available for students with learning disabilities with Individualized Education Plan.

High school preparation. College-preparatory program required. 17 units required. Required units include English 4, mathematics 4, social studies 1, history 1, science 3 (laboratory 2), foreign language 2 and academic electives 2. History unit must be US history.

2015-2016 Annual costs. Tuition/fees: $8,857; $14,937 out-of-state. Room/board: $11,560. Books/supplies: $984. Personal expenses: $2,200.

2014-2015 Financial aid. Need-based: 743 full-time freshmen applied for aid; 561 deemed to have need; 548 received aid. Average need met was 77%. Average scholarship/grant was $4,811; average loan $2,756. 54% of total undergraduate aid awarded as scholarships/grants, 46% as loans/jobs. **Non-need-based:** Awarded to 966 full-time undergraduates, including 284 freshmen. Scholarships awarded for academics, ROTC. **Additional information:** Veterans, Native Americans and those certified by Massachusetts Rehabilitation Commission and Massachusetts Commission for the Blind considered for tuition waivers while funds available. Tuition also waived for needy Massachusetts residents and in-state National Guard members.

Application procedures. Admission: Priority date 3/1; deadline 5/1 (receipt date). $50 fee, may be waived for applicants with need. Admission notification on a rolling basis beginning on or about 1/2. Must reply by May 1 or within 2 week(s) if notified thereafter. **Financial aid:** Priority date 3/1, closing date 5/1. FAFSA, institutional form required. Applicants notified on a rolling basis starting 3/1; must reply within 3 week(s) of notification.

Academics. Special study options: Accelerated study, combined bachelor's/graduate degree, cross-registration, distance learning, double major, dual enrollment of high school students, ESL, exchange student, honors, independent study, internships, liberal arts/career combination, study abroad, teacher certification program. Foreign exchange student program. **Credit/placement by examination:** AP, CLEP, IB, institutional tests. 30 credit hours maximum toward bachelor's degree. **Support services:** Learning center, pre-admission summer program, reduced course load, remedial instruction, study skills assistance, tutoring, writing center.

Majors. Biology: General, biotechnology. **Business:** Business admin. **Communications:** Communications/speech/rhetoric, media studies. **Communications technology:** Radio/TV. **Computer sciences:** General. **Education:** Early childhood, elementary, health. **English:** English lit. **Foreign languages:** Spanish. **Health services:** Adult health nursing, communication disorders, community health services, nursing (RN). **History:** General. **Math:** General. **Physical sciences:** General, chemistry. **Protective services:** Criminal justice. **Psychology:** General. **Social sciences:** Economics, geography, sociology, urban studies. **Visual/performing arts:** General.

Most popular majors. Biology 8%, business/marketing 17%, communications/journalism 6%, education 6%, health sciences 21%, psychology 12%, security/protective services 8%, social sciences 6%.

Technology on campus. PC or laptop required. 500 workstations in dormitories, library, computer center, student center. Dormitories wired for high-speed internet access and linked to campus network. Commuter students can connect to campus network. Online course registration, online library, helpline, repair service, student web hosting, wireless network available.

Student life. Freshman orientation: Mandatory, $75 fee. Preregistration for classes offered. Four-hour parent orientation in Spring; 4-1/2 day session for students last week in August. **Housing:** Coed dorms, single-sex dorms, special housing for disabled available. $150 nonrefundable deposit, deadline 2/15. **Activities:** Bands, campus ministries, choral groups, dance, drama, literary magazine, music ensembles, radio station, student government, student newspaper, TV station, student events committee, Third World alliance, campus ambassadors, gay-straight alliance, surreal games and sci-fi, ski/snow board club.

Athletics. NCAA. **Intercollegiate:** Baseball M, basketball, cross-country, field hockey W, football (tackle) M, golf M, ice hockey M, lacrosse W, soccer, softball W, tennis W, track and field, volleyball. **Intramural:** Basketball, soccer, softball W, volleyball. **Team name:** Lancers.

Student services. Adult student services, alcohol/substance abuse counseling, chaplain/spiritual director, career counseling, services for economically disadvantaged, student employment services, financial aid counseling, health services, minority student services, personal counseling, placement for graduates, veterans' counselor, women's services. **Physically disabled:** Services for visually, speech, hearing impaired.

Contact. E-mail: admissions@worcester.edu
Phone: (508) 929-8040 Fax: (508) 929-8183
Joseph DiCarlo, Director of Admissions, Worcester State University, Office of Undergraduate Admission, Worcester, MA 01602-2597

Michigan

Adrian College
Adrian, Michigan
www.adrian.edu

CB member
CB code: 1001

- Private 4-year liberal arts college affiliated with the United Methodist Church
- Residential campus in large town
- 1,655 full-time, degree-seeking undergraduates: 9% African American, 5% Hispanic/Latino, 3% Multi-racial, non-Hispanic
- 28 graduate students
- 61% of applicants admitted
- SAT or ACT (ACT writing optional) required
- 54% graduate within 6 years

General. Founded in 1859. Regionally accredited. **Degrees:** 314 bachelor's, 1 associate awarded; master's offered. **ROTC:** Army. **Location:** 75 miles from Detroit, 30 miles from Toledo, OH. **Calendar:** Semester, limited summer session. **Full-time faculty:** 91 total; 87% have terminal degrees, 50% women. **Part-time faculty:** 93 total. **Special facilities:** Arboretum, observatory and planetarium, solar greenhouse, Sojourner Truth Underground Railroad Center, WVAC radio and television studios, education curriculum center, human anatomy laboratory, writing center.

Freshman class profile. 5,284 applied, 3,231 admitted, 515 enrolled.

Mid 50% test scores			
SAT critical reading:	410-540	Live on campus:	95%
SAT math:	440-570	Fraternities:	9%
ACT composite:	19-24	Sororities:	5%

Out-of-state: 20%

Basis for selection. School achievement most important, followed by test scores. Applicants should rank in top half of high school class. School recommendations and extracurricular activities considered. ACT preferred.

High school preparation. College-preparatory program recommended. 15 units recommended. Recommended units include English 4, mathematics 3, social studies 1, history 1, science 2 (laboratory 1), foreign language 2 and academic electives 2.

2016-2017 Annual costs. Tuition/fees (projected): $34,500. Room/board: $11,000. Books/supplies: $1,800.

2014-2015 Financial aid. Need-based: 452 full-time freshmen applied for aid; 423 deemed to have need; 423 received aid. Average need met was 75%. Average scholarship/grant was $22,052; average loan $3,581. 71% of total undergraduate aid awarded as scholarships/grants, 29% as loans/jobs. **Non-need-based:** Awarded to 277 full-time undergraduates, including 88 freshmen. Scholarships awarded for academics, alumni affiliation, art, leadership, music/drama, religious affiliation, ROTC, state residency.

Application procedures. Admission: Closing date 3/15 (receipt date). No application fee. Admission notification on a rolling basis beginning on or about 9/1. **Financial aid:** Priority date 3/1; no closing date. FAFSA required. Applicants notified on a rolling basis starting 3/15; must reply by 5/1 or within 2 week(s) of notification.

Academics. Special study options: Combined bachelor's/graduate degree, double major, dual enrollment of high school students, honors, independent study, internships, semester at sea, student-designed major, study abroad, teacher certification program, Washington semester. **Credit/placement by examination:** AP, CLEP, IB, institutional tests. 15 credit hours maximum toward associate degree, 30 toward bachelor's. **Support services:** Learning center, pre-admission summer program, reduced course load, remedial instruction, study skills assistance, tutoring, writing center.

Majors. Biology: General. **Business:** Accounting, business admin, international, marketing. **Communications:** Communications/speech/rhetoric. **Conservation:** Environmental science, environmental studies. **Education:** Art, biology, English, French, German, health, history, mathematics, music, physical, science, social studies, Spanish. **English:** English lit. **Foreign languages:** French, German, Japanese, Spanish. **Health services:** Athletic training, predental, premedicine, prepharmacy, preveterinary. **History:** General. **Human services:** Social work. **Math:** General. **Parks/recreation:** Exercise sciences. **Philosophy/religion:** Philosophy, religion. **Physical sciences:** Chemistry, geology, physics. **Protective services:** Law enforcement admin. **Psychology:**

General. **Social sciences:** Economics, political science, sociology. **Theology:** Preministerial. **Visual/performing arts:** Art, arts management, dramatic, interior design, music, music performance, musical theater, studio arts, studio arts management.

Most popular majors. Biology 11%, business/marketing 21%, communications/journalism 6%, education 9%, parks/recreation 11%, security/protective services 6%, visual/performing arts 9%.

Technology on campus. 180 workstations in library, computer center, student center. Dormitories wired for high-speed internet access and linked to campus network. Commuter students can connect to campus network. Online course registration, online library, helpline, student web hosting, wireless network available.

Student life. Freshman orientation: Mandatory, $350 fee. Preregistration for classes offered. Week-long program in August. **Policies:** All full-time students required to live on campus for 4 years. Exemptions based on local residence, marital status, 5th year senior or part-time student may be made by application to the Housing Office. Health insurance mandatory for all students registered for 12 hours or more. All motor vehicles possessed or used on campus must be registered every academic year. **Housing:** Guaranteed on-campus for all undergraduates. Coed dorms, single-sex dorms, apartments, fraternity/sorority housing, themed housing available. $100 deposit, deadline 7/1. **Activities:** Bands, campus ministries, choral groups, dance, drama, international student organizations, literary magazine, music ensembles, Model UN, musical theater, opera, radio station, student government, student newspaper, symphony orchestra, Adrian Latinos Moviendose Adelente, African-American Leaders Promoting Higher Achievement, Safe Place, Feminist Empowerment Movement, Green Action Club, Campus Crusade for Christ, Catholic Student Association, Circle K.

Athletics. NCAA. **Intercollegiate:** Baseball M, basketball, bowling W, cross-country, football (tackle) M, golf, ice hockey, lacrosse, soccer, softball W, tennis, track and field, volleyball, wrestling. **Intramural:** Basketball, football (non-tackle), lacrosse, racquetball, soccer, softball, tennis, volleyball. **Team name:** Bulldogs.

Student services. Adult student services, alcohol/substance abuse counseling, chaplain/spiritual director, career counseling, student employment services, financial aid counseling, health services, minority student services, personal counseling, placement for graduates. **Physically disabled:** Services for visually, speech, hearing impaired.

Contact. E-mail: admissions@adrian.edu
Phone: (517) 265-5161 ext. 4326 Toll-free number: (800) 877-2246
Fax: (517) 264-3878
Erin DeSmet, Director for Admissions, Adrian College, 110 South Madison Street, Adrian, MI 49221-2575

Albion College
Albion, Michigan
www.albion.edu

CB member
CB code: 1007

- Private 4-year liberal arts college affiliated with the United Methodist Church
- Residential campus in small town
- 1,360 degree-seeking undergraduates: 50% women, 6% African American, 2% Asian American, 5% Hispanic/Latino, 2% Multi-racial, non-Hispanic, 3% international
- 79% of applicants admitted
- SAT or ACT (ACT writing optional), application essay required
- 64% graduate within 6 years; 39% enter graduate study

General. Founded in 1835. Regionally accredited. **Degrees:** 264 bachelor's awarded. **Location:** 55 miles from Lansing, 55 miles from Ann Arbor. **Calendar:** Semester, limited summer session. **Full-time faculty:** 97 total; 94% have terminal degrees, 7% minority, 45% women. **Part-time faculty:** 47 total; 40% have terminal degrees, 2% minority, 38% women. **Class size:** 63% < 20, 35% 20-39, 2% 40-49. **Special facilities:** Science complex, 144-acre nature center, observatory, equestrian center.

Freshman class profile. 2,803 applied, 2,227 admitted, 455 enrolled.

Mid 50% test scores			
SAT critical reading:	500-590	Rank in top quarter:	52%
SAT math:	420-570	Rank in top tenth:	21%
ACT composite:	22-27	Return as sophomores:	80%
GPA 3.75 or higher:	27%	Out-of-state:	22%
GPA 3.50-3.74:	23%	Live on campus:	99%
GPA 3.0-3.49:	35%	International:	3%

GPA 2.0-2.99: 15%

Basis for selection. School achievement record, ACT/SAT test scores, recommendations from counselor or other contacts, extracurricular activities, and essay. Interview recommended. Programs of Distinction require interviews and/or a separate application. **Home schooled:** Letter of recommendation (nonparent) required.

High school preparation. College-preparatory program recommended. 17 units recommended. Recommended units include English 4, mathematics 4, social studies 2, science 3 (laboratory 2) and foreign language 2.

2015-2016 Annual costs. Tuition/fees: $39,088. Room/board: $11,060. Books/supplies: $800. Personal expenses: $600.

2015-2016 Financial aid. Need-based: 411 full-time freshmen applied for aid; 362 deemed to have need; 362 received aid. Average need met was 91%. Average scholarship/grant was $32,079; average loan $4,268. 85% of total undergraduate aid awarded as scholarships/grants, 15% as loans/jobs. **Non-need-based:** Awarded to 1,311 full-time undergraduates, including 447 freshmen. Scholarships awarded for academics, alumni affiliation, art, leadership, music/drama.

Application procedures. Admission: Priority date 12/1; no deadline. No application fee. Application must be submitted online. Admission notification on a rolling basis beginning on or about 10/15. Must reply by May 1 or within 2 week(s) if notified thereafter. **Financial aid:** Priority date 2/15; no closing date. FAFSA required. Applicants notified on a rolling basis starting 3/15.

Academics. Special study options: Combined bachelor's/graduate degree, distance learning, double major, dual enrollment of high school students, honors, independent study, internships, liberal arts/career combination, New York semester, semester at sea, student-designed major, study abroad, teacher certification program, urban semester, Washington semester. First Year Experience, Honors Program, Center for Sustainability & the Environment, Institute for Leadership in Public Policy & Service, Institute for Business & Management, Institute for Healthcare Professions, Center for Teacher Development, FURSCA (Foundation for Undergraduate Research, Scholarship, and Creative Activity). **Credit/placement by examination:** AP, CLEP, IB, institutional tests. 12 credit hours maximum toward bachelor's degree. No more than eight units of credit can be obtained through any combination of locally designed departmental examinations and CLEP. No more than 12 units of credit can be obtained through any combination of the AP exams, locally designed departmental examinations, and CLEP exams. **Support services:** Learning center, reduced course load, study skills assistance, tutoring, writing center. Academic coaching, organization and college level study skills sessions. Student mentoring program.

Majors. Area/ethnic studies: General, Latin American, women's. **Biology:** General, biochemistry. **Business:** Accounting, business admin, finance. **Communications:** General, media studies. **Conservation:** General, environmental science, environmental studies. **Engineering:** General. **English:** Creative writing, English lit, technical writing. **Foreign languages:** French, German, Spanish. **Health services:** Athletic training. **History:** General. **Human services:** Public policy. **Liberal arts:** Arts/sciences. **Math:** General. **Parks/recreation:** Exercise sciences. **Philosophy/religion:** Philosophy, religion. **Physical sciences:** Chemistry, geology, physics. **Psychology:** General. **Social sciences:** Anthropology, economics, international economics, political science, sociology, sociology/anthropology. **Visual/performing arts:** Art, art history/conservation, dramatic, music, music performance, studio arts.

Most popular majors. Biology 14%, business/marketing 10%, communications/journalism 8%, psychology 10%, social sciences 19%, visual/performing arts 7%.

Technology on campus. 185 workstations in dormitories, library, computer center, student center. Dormitories wired for high-speed internet access and linked to campus network. Commuter students can connect to campus network. Online course registration, online library, helpline, repair service, student web hosting, wireless network available.

Student life. Freshman orientation: Mandatory. Preregistration for classes offered. Several two day sessions held over the summer. **Policies:** All students required to reside and board on campus. Exemptions granted to students commuting from home (reside with parents or legal guardians within 25 miles of campus), married students, students with legal dependents, students age 23 or older (housing can be provided if desired), and United States veterans. **Housing:** Guaranteed on-campus for all undergraduates. Coed dorms, single-sex dorms, special housing for disabled, apartments, cooperative housing, fraternity/sorority housing, themed housing available. Special interest and male/female annexes available. **Activities:** Bands, campus ministries, choral groups, dance, drama, international student organizations, literary magazine, music ensembles, musical theater, opera, radio station, student government, student newspaper, symphony orchestra, Over 100 campus organizations available.

Athletics. NCAA. **Intercollegiate:** Baseball M, basketball, cross-country, diving, equestrian, football (tackle) M, golf, lacrosse, soccer, softball W,

swimming, tennis, track and field, volleyball W. **Intramural:** Basketball, football (non-tackle), racquetball, rugby, soccer, softball, swimming, tennis, ultimate frisbee, volleyball. **Team name:** Britons.

Student services. Alcohol/substance abuse counseling, chaplain/spiritual director, career counseling, services for economically disadvantaged, student employment services, financial aid counseling, health services, minority student services, personal counseling, placement for graduates, veterans' counselor, women's services. **Physically disabled:** Services for visually, speech, hearing impaired.

Contact. E-mail: admission@albion.edu
Phone: (517) 629-0321 Toll-free number: (800) 858-6770
Fax: (517) 629-0569
Amanda Dubiel, Director of Admissions, Albion College, 611 East Porter Street, Albion, MI 49224-1831

Alma College

Alma, Michigan
www.alma.edu

CB member
CB code: 1010

- Private 4-year liberal arts college affiliated with the Presbyterian Church (USA)
- Residential campus in large town
- 1,345 degree-seeking undergraduates: 1% part-time, 57% women, 4% African American, 1% Asian American, 4% Hispanic/Latino, 2% Multiracial, non-Hispanic, 1% international
- 68% of applicants admitted
- SAT or ACT (ACT writing optional), application essay required
- 59% graduate within 6 years

General. Founded in 1886. Regionally accredited. **Degrees:** 299 bachelor's awarded. **ROTC:** Army. **Location:** 50 miles from Lansing, 45 miles from Saginaw. **Calendar:** 4-4-1 semester system. Limited summer session. **Full-time faculty:** 96 total; 82% have terminal degrees, 12% minority, 43% women. **Part-time faculty:** 71 total; 38% have terminal degrees, 7% minority, 56% women. **Class size:** 68% < 20, 29% 20-39, 2% 40-49, 1% 50-99. **Special facilities:** Planetarium, performing arts center, climbing wall, ecological station, bike trail.

Freshman class profile. 2,479 applied, 1,675 admitted, 336 enrolled.

Mid 50% test scores			
SAT critical reading:	520-650	GPA 2.0-2.99:	19%
SAT math:	510-670	Rank in top quarter:	50%
SAT writing:	500-650	Rank in top tenth:	22%
ACT composite:	21-27	Return as sophomores:	84%
GPA 3.75 or higher:	36%	Out-of-state:	8%
GPA 3.50-3.74:	21%	Live on campus:	95%
GPA 3.0-3.49:	24%	International:	2%

Basis for selection. Applicant should be in top half of class, have 3.0 high school GPA or 22 ACT or 1030 SAT (exclusive of Writing). Co-curricular activities considered. Portfolio recommended for art majors. Interview recommended for all, strongly recommended for academically weak and those whose grades and test scores show discrepancies.

High school preparation. College-preparatory program recommended. 16 units required. Required and recommended units include English 4, mathematics 3, social studies 3, science 3 and foreign language 2.

2015-2016 Annual costs. Tuition/fees: $35,806. Room/board: $9,822. Books/supplies: $800. Personal expenses: $1,216.

2015-2016 Financial aid. Need-based: 318 full-time freshmen applied for aid; 289 deemed to have need; 289 received aid. Average need met was 81%. Average scholarship/grant was $27,491; average loan $3,825. 78% of total undergraduate aid awarded as scholarships/grants, 22% as loans/jobs. **Non-need-based:** Awarded to 345 full-time undergraduates, including 88 freshmen. Scholarships awarded for academics, alumni affiliation, art, minority status, music/drama, religious affiliation. **Additional information:** Auditions required for music, drama, dance scholarship candidates. Portfolios required for art scholarship candidates.

Application procedures. Admission: No deadline. $25 fee, may be waived for applicants with need, free for online applicants. Admission notification on a rolling basis beginning on or about 9/1. The May 1 deadline is encouraged. **Financial aid:** Priority date 3/1; no closing date. FAFSA required. Applicants notified on a rolling basis starting 3/1; must reply within 3 week(s) of notification.

Academics. One-month spring term provides special opportunities for study in United States or overseas. Students required to complete 2 spring terms. **Special study options:** Combined bachelor's/graduate degree, double major, dual enrollment of high school students, honors, independent study, internships, New York semester, student-designed major, study abroad, teacher certification program, urban semester, Washington semester. Pre-engineering 3-2 programs with Kettering University, University of Michigan, Michigan Technological University; pre-occupational therapy 3-2 program with Washington University (MO). **Credit/placement by examination:** AP, CLEP, IB, SAT, ACT, institutional tests. 32 credit hours maximum toward bachelor's degree. **Support services:** Pre-admission summer program, reduced course load, remedial instruction, study skills assistance, tutoring, writing center.

Majors. **Biology:** General, biochemistry. **Business:** Accounting, business admin, finance, international, marketing. **Communications:** Media studies. **Conservation:** Environmental studies. **Education:** General, early childhood special, elementary, secondary, special ed. **English:** English lit. **Foreign languages:** French, German, Spanish. **Health services:** Health care admin. **History:** General. **Math:** General. **Parks/recreation:** Exercise sciences, health/fitness. **Philosophy/religion:** Philosophy, religion. **Physical sciences:** Chemistry, physics. **Psychology:** General. **Social sciences:** Anthropology, economics, political science, sociology. **Visual/performing arts:** Dance, design, dramatic, music.

Most popular majors. Biology 10%, business/marketing 15%, communications/journalism 7%, education 6%, English 6%, health sciences 16%, psychology 9%, social sciences 7%, visual/performing arts 8%.

Technology on campus. 318 workstations in dormitories, library, computer center, student center. Dormitories wired for high-speed internet access and linked to campus network. Commuter students can connect to campus network. Online course registration, online library, helpline, student web hosting, wireless network available.

Student life. Freshman orientation: Mandatory, $350 fee. Preregistration for classes offered. Held last week of August prior to start of the fall term. **Housing:** Guaranteed on-campus for all undergraduates. Coed dorms, special housing for disabled, apartments, fraternity/sorority housing, themed housing available. $200 nonrefundable deposit, deadline 5/1. **Activities:** Bands, campus ministries, choral groups, dance, drama, international student organizations, literary magazine, music ensembles, Model UN, radio station, student government, student newspaper, symphony orchestra, College Republicans, College Democrats, Amnesty International, Big Brothers/Big Sisters, Catholic Student Organization, International Club, Multicultural Student Union.

Athletics. NCAA. **Intercollegiate:** Baseball M, basketball, bowling W, cheerleading, cross-country, diving, football (tackle) M, golf, lacrosse, soccer, softball W, swimming, tennis, track and field, volleyball W, wrestling M. **Intramural:** Basketball, soccer W, softball, volleyball. **Team name:** Scots.

Student services. Alcohol/substance abuse counseling, chaplain/spiritual director, career counseling, services for economically disadvantaged, student employment services, financial aid counseling, health services, minority student services, personal counseling. **Physically disabled:** Services for visually, hearing impaired.

Contact. E-mail: admissions@alma.edu
Phone: (989) 463-7139 Toll-free number: (800) 321-2562
Fax: (989) 463-7057
Craig Aimar, Director of Admissions, Alma College, 614 West Superior Street, Alma, MI 48801-1599

Andrews University
Berrien Springs, Michigan
www.andrews.edu   **CB code: 1030**

- Private 4-year university affiliated with the Seventh-day Adventists
- Residential campus in small town
- 1,504 degree-seeking undergraduates: 8% part-time, 56% women, 19% African American, 15% Asian American, 14% Hispanic/Latino, 2% Multi-racial, non-Hispanic, 18% international
- 1,585 degree-seeking graduate students
- 39% of applicants admitted
- SAT or ACT (ACT writing optional), application essay required
- 54% graduate within 6 years

General. Founded in 1874. Regionally accredited. **Degrees:** 416 bachelor's, 8 associate awarded; master's, doctoral offered. **Location:** 10 miles from St. Joseph-Benton Harbor; 25 miles from South Bend, IN. **Calendar:** Semester, limited summer session. **Full-time faculty:** 233 total; 72% have terminal degrees, 29% minority, 42% women. **Part-time faculty:** 67 total; 36% have terminal degrees, 27% minority, 48% women. **Class size:** 70% < 20, 22%

20-39, 5% 40-49, 3% 50-99. **Special facilities:** Natural history museum, archaeology museum, performing arts center, arboretum.

Freshman class profile. 2,201 applied, 863 admitted, 274 enrolled.

Mid 50% test scores			
SAT critical reading:	480-620	GPA 2.0-2.99:	12%
SAT math:	480-620	Rank in top quarter:	41%
SAT writing:	480-600	Rank in top tenth:	18%
ACT composite:	20-27	Return as sophomores:	80%
GPA 3.75 or higher:	41%	Out-of-state:	73%
GPA 3.50-3.74:	18%	Live on campus:	86%
GPA 3.0-3.49:	29%	International:	12%

Basis for selection. School achievement record, test scores, recommendations important. Interview recommended. Audition recommended for music majors. Portfolios recommended for architecture, art majors. **Home schooled:** Portfolio required. **Learning Disabled:** Must advise student services of learning disability prior to admission interview and testing.

High school preparation. College-preparatory program recommended. 13 units required; 15 recommended. Required and recommended units include English 3-4, mathematics 2-3, social studies 1, history 2, science 2 and academic electives 3. Additional 1 unit chemistry, 1 unit physics, 1 unit computer recommended.

2015-2016 Annual costs. Tuition/fees: $27,000. Room/board: $8,532. Books/supplies: $1,100. Personal expenses: $1,100.

2015-2016 Financial aid. Need-based: 209 full-time freshmen applied for aid; 182 deemed to have need; 182 received aid. Average need met was 86%. Average scholarship/grant was $6,386; average loan $3,437. 97% of total undergraduate aid awarded as scholarships/grants, 3% as loans/jobs. **Non-need-based:** Awarded to 1,395 full-time undergraduates, including 269 freshmen. Scholarships awarded for academics, job skills, leadership, music/drama.

Application procedures. Admission: No deadline. $30 fee. Admission notification on a rolling basis beginning on or about 1/1. **Financial aid:** Priority date 3/31; no closing date. FAFSA, institutional form, CSS PROFILE required. Applicants notified on a rolling basis starting 3/15.

Academics. Special study options: Accelerated study, combined bachelor's/graduate degree, cooperative education, distance learning, double major, dual enrollment of high school students, ESL, honors, internships, student-designed major, study abroad, teacher certification program. **Credit/placement by examination:** AP, CLEP, IB, institutional tests. 32 credit hours maximum toward associate degree, 32 toward bachelor's. DANTES (for nontraditional students). **Support services:** Learning center, pre-admission summer program, reduced course load, remedial instruction, study skills assistance, tutoring, writing center.

Majors. Architecture: Architecture. **Biology:** General, biochemistry, biophysics, botany, molecular, neuroscience, zoology. **Business:** Accounting, business admin, entrepreneurial studies, finance, managerial economics, nonprofit/public, training/development. **Communications:** Communications/speech/rhetoric, journalism, public relations. **Communications technology:** General. **Computer sciences:** General, information systems. **Education:** Elementary, mathematics, secondary, social science, social studies. **Engineering:** General, electrical, industrial, mechanical. **English:** English lit. **Foreign languages:** French, Spanish. **Health services:** Audiology/speech pathology, clinical lab science, dietetics, nursing (RN). **History:** General. **Human services:** Social work. **Liberal arts:** Arts/sciences. **Math:** General. **Philosophy/religion:** Religion. **Physical sciences:** Chemistry, physics. **Psychology:** General. **Social sciences:** General, anthropology, economics, international economic development, political science, sociology. **Theology:** Religious ed, sacred music, theology, youth ministry. **Visual/performing arts:** General, art, art history/conservation, ceramics, commercial/advertising art, design, graphic design, multimedia, music, music performance, painting, photography, printmaking, studio arts. **Work/family studies:** Family studies, food/nutrition.

Most popular majors. Biology 10%, business/marketing 10%, health sciences 21%, visual/performing arts 6%.

Technology on campus. 130 workstations in dormitories, library, computer center. Dormitories wired for high-speed internet access and linked to campus network. Commuter students can connect to campus network. Online course registration, online library, helpline, repair service, student web hosting, wireless network available.

Student life. Freshman orientation: Mandatory. Preregistration for classes offered. Held week before fall registration. **Policies:** Students expected to abide by mission-driven ethical and moral standards of the university. Resident students required to live in dorm until age 22. Religious observance required. **Housing:** Guaranteed on-campus for all undergraduates. Single-sex dorms, apartments, wellness housing available. $250 deposit. **Activities:** Concert band, choral groups, drama, international student organizations, music ensembles, musical theater, radio station, student government, student newspaper, symphony orchestra, Christian Youth Action.

Athletics. Intramural: Badminton, basketball, field hockey, football (non-tackle), soccer, softball, triathlon, volleyball.

Student services. Chaplain/spiritual director, career counseling, student employment services, financial aid counseling, health services, on-campus daycare, personal counseling, placement for graduates, veterans' counselor. **Physically disabled:** Services for visually, speech, hearing impaired.

Contact. E-mail: enroll@andrews.edu
Toll-free number: (800) 253-2874 Fax: (269) 471-3228
Randy Graves, Vice President for Enrollment Management, Andrews University, 100 US Highway 31, Berrien Springs, MI 49104

Aquinas College
Grand Rapids, Michigan
www.aquinas.edu   **CB code: 1018**

▸ Private 4-year liberal arts college affiliated with the Roman Catholic Church
▸ Residential campus in small city
▸ 1,692 degree-seeking undergraduates: 9% part-time, 60% women, 3% African American, 1% Asian American, 6% Hispanic/Latino, 3% Multiracial, non-Hispanic, 1% international
▸ 110 graduate students
▸ 72% of applicants admitted
▸ SAT or ACT (ACT writing optional) required
▸ 58% graduate within 6 years

General. Founded in 1886. Regionally accredited. **Degrees:** 348 bachelor's, 4 associate awarded; master's offered. **ROTC:** Army. **Location:** 140 miles from Detroit, 180 miles from Chicago. **Calendar:** Semester, extensive summer session. **Full-time faculty:** 86 total; 81% have terminal degrees, 9% minority, 40% women. **Part-time faculty:** 137 total; 18% have terminal degrees, 8% minority, 50% women. **Class size:** 63% < 20, 34% 20-39, 2% 40-49, less than 1% 50-99. **Special facilities:** Nature trails, community theater, center for sustainability, greenhouse, astronomy tower.

Freshman class profile. 2,635 applied, 1,908 admitted, 605 enrolled.

Mid 50% test scores		GPA 2.0-2.99:	17%
ACT composite:	21-26	Out-of-state:	8%
GPA 3.75 or higher:	35%	Live on campus:	84%
GPA 3.50-3.74:	22%	International:	1%
GPA 3.0-3.49:	26%		

Basis for selection. GED not accepted. 2.5 GPA in academic subjects, test scores important. Interview required for applicants with above average test scores but less than 2.5 GPA in academic subjects and recommended for others. Audition recommended for music majors. Portfolio recommended for art majors. **Home schooled:** Transcript of courses and grades required. Greater emphasis placed on ACT/SAT. Students may be required to complete Ability to Benefit test. **Learning Disabled:** Students must meet with Academic Achievement Center to express needed accommodations prior to enrollment.

High school preparation. College-preparatory program recommended. 16 units required. Required and recommended units include English 4, mathematics 4, social studies 3, science 3 and foreign language 2.

2016-2017 Annual costs. Tuition/fees: $30,062. Room/board: $8,814. Books/supplies: $872. Personal expenses: $850.

2015-2016 Financial aid. Need-based: 337 full-time freshmen applied for aid; 309 deemed to have need; 309 received aid. Average need met was 81%. Average scholarship/grant was $21,588; average loan $1,984. 76% of total undergraduate aid awarded as scholarships/grants, 24% as loans/jobs. **Non-need-based:** Scholarships awarded for academics, alumni affiliation, art, athletics, leadership, minority status, music/drama.

Application procedures. Admission: Priority date 5/1; no deadline. No application fee. Admission notification on a rolling basis beginning on or about 8/1. **Financial aid:** Priority date 3/1; no closing date. FAFSA required. Applicants notified on a rolling basis starting 3/1; must reply within 2 week(s) of notification.

Academics. Special study options: Cooperative education, cross-registration, distance learning, double major, dual enrollment of high school students, exchange student, honors, independent study, internships, liberal arts/career combination, student-designed major, study abroad, teacher certification program, urban semester. **Credit/placement by examination:** AP,

CLEP, institutional tests. 30 credit hours maximum toward bachelor's degree. **Support services:** Learning center, remedial instruction, study skills assistance, tutoring, writing center.

Majors. Biology: General. **Business:** Accounting, accounting/finance, business admin, communications, human resources, international, management information systems. **Communications:** General, journalism. **Computer sciences:** General. **Conservation:** Environmental science, environmental studies. **Education:** General, art, bilingual, biology, chemistry, elementary, English, ESL, French, geography, history, learning disabled, multi-level teacher, music, physical, physically handicapped, reading, science, secondary, social studies, Spanish, special ed. **English:** Creative writing, English lit. **Foreign languages:** French, German, Spanish. **Health services:** Athletic training. **History:** General. **Human services:** Community org/advocacy. **Liberal arts:** Arts/sciences, humanities. **Math:** General. **Parks/recreation:** General, health/fitness, sports admin. **Philosophy/religion:** Philosophy, religion. **Physical sciences:** Chemistry. **Psychology:** General. **Social sciences:** General, economics, geography, international relations, political science, sociology. **Theology:** Sacred music, theology. **Visual/performing arts:** Acting, art, art history/conservation, ceramics, directing/producing, dramatic, drawing, jazz, music, music management, music performance, painting, photography, printmaking, sculpture, studio arts, studio arts management, theater arts management, theater design.

Most popular majors. Biology 7%, business/marketing 17%, education 9%, English 6%, foreign language 7%, parks/recreation 7%, psychology 8%, social sciences 8%, visual/performing arts 6%.

Technology on campus. 173 workstations in dormitories, library, computer center, student center. Dormitories wired for high-speed internet access and linked to campus network. Commuter students can connect to campus network. Online library, helpline, wireless network available.

Student life. Freshman orientation: Mandatory, $100 fee. Preregistration for classes offered. Three-day program held week before classes begin. **Policies:** Students serve on administrative and faculty committees. **Housing:** Guaranteed on-campus for freshmen. Coed dorms, apartments, themed housing available. $200 deposit, deadline 8/15. **Activities:** Bands, campus ministries, choral groups, dance, drama, international student organizations, literary magazine, music ensembles, Model UN, radio station, student government, student newspaper, community action volunteers, social action commission, community senate, Bible study, College Democrats, College Republicans, Catholic studies club, Habitat for Humanity.

Athletics. NAIA. **Intercollegiate:** Baseball M, basketball, bowling M, cross-country, golf, ice hockey M, lacrosse, soccer, softball W, tennis, track and field, volleyball W. **Intramural:** Basketball, fencing M, golf, ice hockey M, lacrosse, skiing, soccer, softball, tennis, volleyball. **Team name:** Saints.

Student services. Adult student services, alcohol/substance abuse counseling, chaplain/spiritual director, career counseling, services for economically disadvantaged, student employment services, financial aid counseling, health services, minority student services, personal counseling, placement for graduates, veterans' counselor, women's services. **Physically disabled:** Services for visually, speech, hearing impaired.

Contact. E-mail: admissions@aquinas.edu
Phone: (616) 632-2900 Toll-free number: (800) 678-9593
Fax: (616) 732-4469
Angela Schlosser-Bacon, Director of Admissions, Aquinas College, 1607 Robinson Road Southeast, Grand Rapids, MI 49506-1799

Art Institute of Michigan
Novi, Michigan
www.artinstitutes.edu/detroit   **CB code: 5750**

▸ For-profit 4-year branch campus and visual arts college
▸ Commuter campus in large city
▸ 986 undergraduates
▸ Application essay, interview required

General. Regionally accredited; also accredited by ACCSC. **Degrees:** 79 bachelor's, 111 associate awarded. **Calendar:** Quarter. **Full-time faculty:** 8 total. **Part-time faculty:** 89 total.

Basis for selection. Academic record and interview very important. SAT or ACT recommended. **Home schooled:** Transcript of courses and grades, state high school equivalency certificate required.

2015-2016 Annual costs. Tuition/fees: $19,125. Room only: $6,000.

Application procedures. Admission: Closing date 10/13 (receipt date). $50 fee, may be waived for applicants with need. Admission notification on a rolling basis. **Financial aid:** Closing date 10/12.

Academics. Credit/placement by examination: AP, CLEP, SAT, ACT.

Majors. Business: Apparel. **Communications technology:** Recording arts. **Computer sciences:** Computer graphics, web page design. **Visual/performing arts:** Commercial photography, graphic design, interior design.

Contact. Phone: (248) 675-3800 Toll-free number: (800) 479-0087 Fax: (248) 675-3830
Lynne Mills, Director of Admissions, Art Institute of Michigan, 28175 Cabot Drive, Novi, MI 48377

Baker College of Allen Park
Allen Park, Michigan
www.baker.edu   CB code: 6588

- Private 4-year business and health science college
- Commuter campus in large city
- 4,000 undergraduates

General. Regionally accredited. **Degrees:** 164 bachelor's, 361 associate awarded. **Location:** 10 miles from Detroit. **Calendar:** Quarter, limited summer session. **Full-time faculty:** 2 total; 50% women. **Part-time faculty:** 86 total; 13% have terminal degrees, 60% women.

Basis for selection. Open admission, but selective for some programs. **Home schooled:** Transcript of courses and grades required.

2015-2016 Annual costs. Tuition/fees: $10,800. Books/supplies: $1,800.

Application procedures. Admission: No deadline. $20 fee, may be waived for applicants with need. Admission notification on a rolling basis.

Academics. Special study options: Combined bachelor's/graduate degree, cooperative education, distance learning, double major, dual enrollment of high school students, independent study, internships, teacher certification program. **Credit/placement by examination:** AP, CLEP. **Support services:** Learning center, remedial instruction, study skills assistance, tutoring.

Majors. Business: Human resources. **Computer sciences:** Information technology. **Education:** Elementary, middle, secondary.

Technology on campus. 208 workstations in library, computer center, student center. Online library, helpline, wireless network available.

Student life. Freshman orientation: Mandatory. Preregistration for classes offered.

Contact. Phone: (313) 425-3700 Toll-free number: (800) 767-4120 Fax: (313) 425-3776
Steve Peterson, Vice President for Admissions, Baker College of Allen Park, 4500 Enterprise Drive, Allen Park, MI 48101

Baker College of Auburn Hills
Auburn Hills, Michigan
www.baker.edu   CB code: 1457

- Private 4-year business and technical college
- Commuter campus in small city
- 3,400 undergraduates

General. Founded in 1990. Regionally accredited. Part of multi-campus system specializing in career education. **Degrees:** 208 bachelor's, 290 associate awarded. **Location:** 30 miles from Detroit. **Calendar:** Quarter, limited summer session. **Full-time faculty:** 11 total; 18% have terminal degrees, 46% women. **Part-time faculty:** 144 total; 15% have terminal degrees, 55% women. **Class size:** 45% < 20, 55% 20-39.

Basis for selection. Open admission, but selective for some programs. Specific entrance requirements for allied health programs and bachelor of business leadership degree program. Interview recommended.

2015-2016 Annual costs. Tuition/fees: $10,800. Books/supplies: $1,000.

Financial aid. Non-need-based: Scholarships awarded for academics, alumni affiliation.

Application procedures. Admission: No deadline. $20 fee, may be waived for applicants with need. Admission notification on a rolling basis. **Financial aid:** Priority date 2/21, closing date 9/1. FAFSA, institutional form required. Applicants notified on a rolling basis starting 4/1.

Academics. 2+2 system allows students to begin required courses in major while completing associate degree. **Special study options:** Accelerated study, combined bachelor's/graduate degree, distance learning, double major, dual enrollment of high school students, independent study, liberal arts/career combination, teacher certification program. **Credit/placement by examination:** AP, CLEP, IB, institutional tests. 48 credit hours maximum toward associate degree, 96 toward bachelor's. **Support services:** Learning center, reduced course load, remedial instruction, study skills assistance, tutoring, writing center.

Majors. Business: General, accounting, business admin, management science. **Education:** General, elementary, middle, multi-level teacher, secondary.

Technology on campus. 131 workstations in library, computer center, student center. Commuter students can connect to campus network. Helpline available.

Student life. Freshman orientation: Mandatory. Preregistration for classes offered. **Activities:** Accounting club, management club, interior design society, society of automotive engineers, marketing club.

Student services. Career counseling, student employment services, financial aid counseling, personal counseling, placement for graduates, veterans' counselor. **Physically disabled:** Services for visually, hearing impaired.

Contact. Phone: (248) 340-0600 Toll-free number: (888) 429-0410
Nicole Chirco, Director of Admissions, Baker College of Auburn Hills, 1500 University Drive, Auburn Hills, MI 48326

Baker College of Cadillac
Cadillac, Michigan
www.baker.edu   CB code: 1381

- Private 4-year business and health science college
- Commuter campus in large town
- 1,800 undergraduates

General. Founded in 1911. Regionally accredited. Part of multicampus system specializing in career education. **Degrees:** 46 bachelor's, 216 associate awarded. **Location:** 90 miles from Grand Rapids, 45 miles from Traverse City. **Calendar:** Quarter, limited summer session. **Full-time faculty:** 4 total; 25% women. **Part-time faculty:** 101 total; 5% have terminal degrees, 52% women. **Class size:** 68% < 20, 31% 20-39, 1% 40-49. **Special facilities:** Mock operating room, massage therapy room.

Basis for selection. Open admission. Some allied health programs require health appraisal. Interview recommended.

2015-2016 Annual costs. Tuition/fees: $10,800. Room only: $3,000. Books/supplies: $1,800.

Financial aid. Non-need-based: Scholarships awarded for academics.

Application procedures. Admission: No deadline. $20 fee, may be waived for applicants with need. Admission notification on a rolling basis beginning on or about 10/1. **Financial aid:** Priority date 2/21; no closing date. FAFSA, institutional form required. Applicants notified on a rolling basis starting 5/1.

Academics. Special study options: Accelerated study, combined bachelor's/graduate degree, cooperative education, distance learning, double major, dual enrollment of high school students, external degree, independent study, internships, liberal arts/career combination, weekend college. 2+2 bachelor's degree and bachelor of business leadership degree. **Credit/placement by examination:** AP, CLEP, IB, institutional tests. 48 credit hours maximum toward associate degree, 96 toward bachelor's. **Support services:** Learning center, reduced course load, remedial instruction, study skills assistance, tutoring, writing center.

Majors. Business: Accounting, business admin, human resources, office management. **Computer sciences:** Computer science.

Technology on campus. 154 workstations in library, computer center. Commuter students can connect to campus network. Online library, helpline, repair service available.

Student life. Freshman orientation: Mandatory. Preregistration for classes offered. **Activities:** Student activities group, professional student organizations.

Student services. Career counseling, student employment services, financial aid counseling, personal counseling, placement for graduates, veterans' counselor. **Physically disabled:** Services for visually, hearing impaired.

Contact. E-mail: mike.tisdale@baker.edu
Phone: (231) 876-3100 Toll-free number: (888) 313-3463
Fax: (231) 775-8505
Audrey Charmoli, Director of Admissions, Baker College of Cadillac,
9600 East 13th Street, Cadillac, MI 49601

Baker College of Clinton Township
Clinton Township, Michigan
www.baker.edu
CB code: 1386

- Private 4-year business and technical college
- Commuter campus in very large city
- 3,618 degree-seeking undergraduates

General. Founded in 1911. Regionally accredited. Part of multicampus
system specializing in career education. **Degrees:** 229 bachelor's, 436 associate awarded. **Location:** 15 miles from Detroit. **Calendar:** Quarter, limited
summer session. **Full-time faculty:** 17 total; 18% have terminal degrees,
76% women. **Part-time faculty:** 191 total; 11% have terminal degrees, 61%
women. **Class size:** 25% < 20, 74% 20-39, less than 1% 40-49.

Basis for selection. Open admission, but selective for some programs.
Physical exam may be required for some programs. Interview recommended.
Learning Disabled: Students must complete special needs intake form signed
by professional.

High school preparation. College-preparatory program recommended.
Recommended units include English 4, mathematics 4, social studies 2,
science 3 and foreign language 4.

2015-2016 Annual costs. Tuition/fees: $10,800. Books/supplies: $1,800.
Personal expenses: $2,000.

Financial aid. Non-need-based: Scholarships awarded for academics,
minority status.

Application procedures. Admission: Priority date 9/1; no deadline. $20
fee, may be waived for applicants with need. Admission notification on a
rolling basis. **Financial aid:** Priority date 2/21, closing date 9/1. FAFSA,
institutional form required. Applicants notified on a rolling basis starting 4/1.

Academics. 2+2 system allows students to begin required courses in major
while completing associate degree. **Special study options:** Accelerated study,
combined bachelor's/graduate degree, cooperative education, distance learning, double major, dual enrollment of high school students, external degree,
independent study, internships, teacher certification program. **Credit/place-
ment by examination:** AP, CLEP, IB, institutional tests. 48 credit hours
maximum toward associate degree, 96 toward bachelor's. **Support services:**
Learning center, reduced course load, remedial instruction, study skills assistance, tutoring, writing center.

Majors. Business: Accounting, administrative services, business admin,
human resources, management science, office management. **Computer sciences:** General, computer science. **Education:** Elementary, middle, multi-
level teacher, secondary. **Health services:** Health care admin, nursing (RN),
office admin.

Technology on campus. 120 workstations in library, computer center.
Commuter students can connect to campus network. Helpline available.

Student life. Freshman orientation: Mandatory. Preregistration for
classes offered.

Student services. Adult student services, career counseling, student
employment services, financial aid counseling, personal counseling, placement for graduates, veterans' counselor. **Physically disabled:** Services for
visually, hearing impaired.

Contact. E-mail: adm_mc@baker.edu
Phone: (586) 791-3000 Toll-free number: (888) 272-2842
Fax: (586) 791-6610
Annette Looser, Vice President for Admissions, Baker College of Clinton
Township, 34950 Little Mack Avenue, Clinton Township, MI 48035

Baker College of Flint
Flint, Michigan
www.baker.edu
CB code: 0806

- Private 4-year business and technical college
- Commuter campus in large city
- 5,500 undergraduates

General. Founded in 1911. Regionally accredited. Corporate services division offers degree-granting programs on campus and/or at work site, coordinated with corporate training and professional development programs. Part
of multicampus system specializing in career education. **Degrees:** 164 bachelor's, 464 associate awarded. **Location:** 10 miles from downtown, 60 miles
from Detroit. **Calendar:** Quarter, limited summer session. **Full-time faculty:**
40 total; 15% have terminal degrees, 58% women. **Part-time faculty:** 275
total; 12% have terminal degrees, 59% women. **Special facilities:** Polysomnography sleep lab, orthotic/prosthetic lab.

Freshman class profile.

Out-of-state: 2% Live on campus: 5%

Basis for selection. Open admission, but selective for some programs.
Health applicants must have health appraisal. Occupational therapy applicants
must present minimum of 1 year biology, 1 year chemistry/physics, 2 years
math including algebra or equivalent. All health programs require 2.0 GPA
for entrance to professional classes. Class size may be limited. Trucking
programs require drug screening prior to enrollment acceptance. Interview
recommended.

2015-2016 Annual costs. Tuition/fees: $10,800. Room only: $3,000.
Books/supplies: $1,800.

Financial aid. Non-need-based: Scholarships awarded for academics,
minority status.

Application procedures. Admission: Priority date 9/1; no deadline. $20
fee, may be waived for applicants with need. Admission notification on a
rolling basis. **Financial aid:** Priority date 2/21, closing date 9/1. FAFSA,
institutional form required. Applicants notified on a rolling basis starting 4/1.

Academics. 2+2 system allows students to begin required courses in major
while completing associate degree. Calendar based on 10-week quarters.
Special study options: Accelerated study, combined bachelor's/graduate
degree, cooperative education, distance learning, double major, dual enrollment of high school students, external degree, independent study, internships.
Credit/placement by examination: AP, CLEP, IB, institutional tests. 48
credit hours maximum toward associate degree, 96 toward bachelor's. **Support services:** Learning center, reduced course load, remedial instruction,
study skills assistance, tutoring, writing center.

Majors. Business: Accounting, business admin, management information
systems, office management, operations. **Computer sciences:** General. **Education:** Elementary, middle, multi-level teacher, secondary. **Engineering:**
Mechanical. **Health services:** Health care admin, health information management, nursing (RN). **Visual/performing arts:** Commercial/advertising art,
interior design.

Most popular majors. Business/marketing 65%, health sciences 25%.

Technology on campus. 300 workstations in library, computer center.
Commuter students can connect to campus network. Helpline available.

Student life. Freshman orientation: Mandatory. Preregistration for
classes offered. **Housing:** Guaranteed on-campus for freshmen. Coed dorms,
wellness housing available. $50 deposit, deadline 9/20. **Activities:** Literary
magazine, National Association of Accountants, American Marketing Association, Interior Design Society, travel club, environmental club, physical therapy assistant club, medical assistants student organization, Health Information
Management Association, graphic communications club, Society of Manufacturing Engineers student chapter.

Athletics. Intramural: Basketball, volleyball.

Student services. Career counseling, student employment services, on-
campus daycare, personal counseling, placement for graduates, veterans'
counselor. **Physically disabled:** Services for visually, hearing impaired.

Contact. E-mail: adm-fl@baker.edu
Phone: (810) 766-4000 Toll-free number: (800) 964-4299
Fax: (810) 766-4293
Jodi Cunez, Director of Admissions, Baker College of Flint, 1050 West
Bristol Road, Flint, MI 48507

Baker College of Jackson
Jackson, Michigan
www.baker.edu
CB code: 1887

- Private 4-year career college
- Commuter campus in small city
- 2,009 undergraduates

General. Founded in 1994. Regionally accredited. Part of multicampus system specializing in career education. **Degrees:** 160 bachelor's, 260 associate awarded. **ROTC:** Army. **Location:** 40 miles from Lansing, 40 miles from Ann Arbor. **Calendar:** Quarter, limited summer session.

Basis for selection. Open admission, but selective for some programs. Physical exam may be required for allied health programs. All health programs require specific GPA. Interview recommended. **Home schooled:** Transcript of courses and grades required.

2015-2016 Annual costs. Tuition/fees: $10,800. Books/supplies: $975.

Financial aid. Non-need-based: Scholarships awarded for academics, minority status.

Application procedures. Admission: No deadline. $20 fee, may be waived for applicants with need. Admission notification on a rolling basis. **Financial aid:** Priority date 2/21, closing date 9/1. FAFSA, institutional form required. Applicants notified on a rolling basis starting 4/1.

Academics. 2+2 system allows students to begin required courses in major while completing associate degree. **Special study options:** Accelerated study, combined bachelor's/graduate degree, cooperative education, distance learning, double major, dual enrollment of high school students, external degree, independent study, internships, teacher certification program. **Credit/placement by examination:** AP, CLEP, IB, institutional tests. 48 credit hours maximum toward associate degree, 96 toward bachelor's. **Support services:** Learning center, reduced course load, remedial instruction, study skills assistance, tutoring, writing center.

Majors. Business: General, accounting. **Education:** Elementary, middle, multi-level teacher, secondary.

Technology on campus. 114 workstations in library, computer center. Commuter students can connect to campus network. Helpline, wireless network available.

Student life. Freshman orientation: Mandatory. Preregistration for classes offered. **Activities:** Student government.

Student services. Adult student services, career counseling, student employment services, financial aid counseling, personal counseling, placement for graduates, veterans' counselor. **Physically disabled:** Services for visually, hearing impaired.

Contact. E-mail: adm-jk@baker.edu
Phone: (517) 788-7800 Toll-free number: (888) 343-3683
Fax: (517) 789-7331
Kevin Pnacek, Vice President for Admissions, Baker College of Jackson, 2800 Springport Road, Jackson, MI 49202

Baker College of Muskegon
Muskegon, Michigan
www.baker.edu   CB code: 1527

- Private 4-year business and technical college
- Commuter campus in small city
- 4,500 undergraduates

General. Founded in 1888. Regionally accredited. Part of multicampus system specializing in career education. All associate degree programs include internship, co-op or clinical affiliation experience. **Degrees:** 155 bachelor's, 494 associate awarded. **Location:** 40 miles from Grand Rapids. **Calendar:** Quarter, limited summer session. **Full-time faculty:** 37 total. **Part-time faculty:** 232 total. **Class size:** 38% < 20, 57% 20-39, 3% 40-49, 2% 50-99. **Special facilities:** Restaurant run by culinary and food and beverage management students.

Basis for selection. Open admission, but selective for some programs. 2.75 GPA required for admission to occupational therapy assisting, physical therapist assisting, veterinary technician, surgical technology, teacher preparation. Class size may be limited in some programs. Physical examination, background check required for some programs. Interview recommended. **Home schooled:** Basic skills placement assessments in math, language arts, and reading part of orientation/registration process. **Learning Disabled:** Learning disability must be documented and presented to counseling staff before registering for classes.

2015-2016 Annual costs. Tuition/fees: $10,800. Room only: $3,000. Books/supplies: $1,800. Personal expenses: $2,000.

Financial aid. Non-need-based: Scholarships awarded for academics, minority status.

Application procedures. Admission: Priority date 9/1; no deadline. $20 fee, may be waived for applicants with need. Admission notification on a rolling basis. **Financial aid:** Priority date 2/21; no closing date. FAFSA, institutional form required. Applicants notified on a rolling basis starting 4/1.

Academics. 2+2 system allows students to begin required courses in major while completing associate degree. Maximum number of credits awarded for prior work and/or life experiences, 48 for associate and 144 for bachelor. **Special study options:** Accelerated study, combined bachelor's/graduate degree, cooperative education, distance learning, double major, dual enrollment of high school students, external degree, independent study, internships, liberal arts/career combination, teacher certification program. Accelerated bachelor of business administration offered in weekend delivery format. **Credit/placement by examination:** AP, CLEP, IB, institutional tests. 48 credit hours maximum toward associate degree, 144 toward bachelor's. **Support services:** Learning center, reduced course load, remedial instruction, study skills assistance, tutoring.

Majors. Business: Accounting, accounting/business management, administrative services, business admin, human resources, management science, marketing, office management, restaurant/food services. **Computer sciences:** General, computer science, information systems, systems analysis. **Education:** Elementary, kindergarten/preschool, middle, multi-level teacher, secondary. **Health services:** Health care admin.

Technology on campus. 180 workstations in dormitories, library, computer center. Dormitories wired for high-speed internet access and linked to campus network. Commuter students can connect to campus network. Online course registration, online library, helpline, wireless network available.

Student life. Freshman orientation: Mandatory. Preregistration for classes offered. 3-4 hour session prior to start of quarter; includes COMPASS testing, registration, academic advising. **Policies:** No drug or alcohol use permitted anywhere on campus or in residence halls. **Housing:** Coed dorms, special housing for disabled, apartments, wellness housing available. $50 deposit, deadline 9/1. **Activities:** Student government, travel club, rehab club, residence hall association, culinary arts club, human resource management club.

Athletics. Intramural: Bowling.

Student services. Adult student services, career counseling, student employment services, financial aid counseling, personal counseling, placement for graduates, veterans' counselor. **Physically disabled:** Services for visually, hearing impaired.

Contact. E-mail: kathy.jacobson@baker.edu
Phone: (231) 777-5200 Toll-free number: (800) 937-0337
Fax: (231) 777-5201
Kathy Jacobson, Vice President and Director of Admissions, Baker College of Muskegon, 1903 Marquette Avenue, Muskegon, MI 49442

Baker College of Owosso
Owosso, Michigan
www.baker.edu   CB code: 5270

- Private 4-year business and technical college
- Commuter campus in large town
- 3,000 undergraduates

General. Founded in 1911. Regionally accredited. Part of multicampus system, with affiliated graduate school, specializing in career education. Master's degree available at Flint campus. **Degrees:** 89 bachelor's, 339 associate awarded. **Location:** 30 miles from Lansing, 300 miles from Flint. **Calendar:** Quarter, limited summer session. **Full-time faculty:** 8 total; 25% have terminal degrees, 50% women. **Part-time faculty:** 136 total; 14% have terminal degrees, 57% women. **Special facilities:** Diesel technology center.

Freshman class profile.

Out-of-state: 3% **Live on campus:**   30%

Basis for selection. Open admission, but selective for some programs. Limited enrollment for medical programs.

2015-2016 Annual costs. Tuition/fees: $10,800. Room only: $3,000. Books/supplies: $1,800.

Financial aid. Non-need-based: Scholarships awarded for academics, minority status.

Application procedures. Admission: Priority date 9/1; no deadline. $20 fee, may be waived for applicants with need. Admission notification on a rolling basis. **Financial aid:** Priority date 2/21, closing date 9/1. FAFSA, institutional form required. Applicants notified on a rolling basis starting 4/1.

Academics. 2+2 system allows students to begin required courses in major while completing associate degree. **Special study options:** Accelerated study, combined bachelor's/graduate degree, cooperative education, distance learning, double major, dual enrollment of high school students, external degree, independent study, internships. **Credit/placement by examination:** AP, CLEP, IB, institutional tests. 48 credit hours maximum toward associate degree, 96 toward bachelor's. **Support services:** Learning center, reduced course load, remedial instruction, study skills assistance, tutoring, writing center.

Majors. Business: Accounting, administrative services, business admin, human resources, management information systems, marketing, office management. **Communications technology:** Graphics. **Computer sciences:** General, computer graphics, computer science. **Education:** Elementary, middle, multi-level teacher, secondary. **Health services:** Health care admin.

Technology on campus. 226 workstations in dormitories, library, computer center. Dormitories wired for high-speed internet access. Commuter students can connect to campus network. Online library, helpline available.

Student life. Freshman orientation: Mandatory. Preregistration for classes offered. **Housing:** Guaranteed on-campus for freshmen. Coed dorms, wellness housing available. $50 deposit. **Activities:** Student newspaper, accounting club, MLT club, interior design club, radiology club, graphics club.

Athletics. Intramural: Basketball, volleyball.

Student services. Adult student services, career counseling, services for economically disadvantaged, student employment services, financial aid counseling, on-campus daycare, personal counseling, placement for graduates, veterans' counselor. **Physically disabled:** Services for visually, speech, hearing impaired.

Contact. E-mail: michael.konopacke@baker.edu
Phone: (989) 729-3350 Toll-free number: (800) 879-3797
Fax: (989) 729-3359
Michael Konopacke, Vice President of Admissions, Baker College of Owosso, 1020 South Washington Street, Owosso, MI 48867

Baker College of Port Huron
Port Huron, Michigan
www.baker.edu
CB code: 1413

▶ Private 4-year business and technical college
▶ Commuter campus in large town
▶ 1,200 undergraduates

General. Founded in 1911. Regionally accredited. Part of multicampus system specializing in career education. **Degrees:** 64 bachelor's, 150 associate awarded; master's offered. **Location:** 60 miles from Detroit. **Calendar:** Quarter, limited summer session. **Full-time faculty:** 12 total; 17% have terminal degrees, 67% women. **Part-time faculty:** 114 total; 6% have terminal degrees, 56% women. **Class size:** 58% < 20, 37% 20-39, 1% 40-49, 4% 50-99. **Special facilities:** Dental hygiene clinic.

Basis for selection. Open admission, but selective for some programs. Specific entrance requirements for health and human services programs. Waiting list for Dental Hygiene. Interview recommended.

2015-2016 Annual costs. Tuition/fees: $10,800. Room only: $3,000. Books/supplies: $1,800.

Financial aid. All financial aid based on need.

Application procedures. Admission: Priority date 9/1; no deadline. $20 fee, may be waived for applicants with need. Admission notification on a rolling basis. **Financial aid:** Priority date 2/21; no closing date. FAFSA, institutional form required. Applicants notified on a rolling basis starting 4/1.

Academics. 2+2 system allows students to begin required courses in major while completing associate degree. Accelerated BBA available. **Special study options:** Accelerated study, combined bachelor's/graduate degree, cooperative education, distance learning, double major, dual enrollment of high school students, external degree, independent study, internships, liberal arts/career combination. **Credit/placement by examination:** AP, CLEP, IB, institutional tests. 48 credit hours maximum toward associate degree, 96 toward bachelor's. **Support services:** Learning center, reduced course load, remedial instruction, study skills assistance, tutoring, writing center.

Majors. Business: General, accounting, administrative services, business admin, human resources, international, management information systems, marketing, office management. **Computer sciences:** General, computer science, information systems. **Health services:** Health care admin.

Technology on campus. 229 workstations in library, computer center. Commuter students can connect to campus network. Online course registration, helpline available.

Student life. Freshman orientation: Mandatory. Preregistration for classes offered. **Activities:** Dental hygiene society.

Student services. Adult student services, career counseling, student employment services, personal counseling, placement for graduates, veterans' counselor. **Physically disabled:** Services for visually, hearing impaired.

Contact. E-mail: daniel.kenny@baker.edu
Phone: (810) 985-7000 Toll-free number: (888) 262-2442
Fax: (810) 985-7066
Daniel Kenny, Vice President of Admissions, Baker College of Port Huron, 3403 Lapeer Road, Port Huron, MI 48060-2597

Calvin College
Grand Rapids, Michigan
www.calvin.edu
CB member
CB code: 1095

▶ Private 4-year liberal arts college affiliated with the Christian Reformed Church
▶ Residential campus in large city
▶ 3,788 degree-seeking undergraduates: 2% part-time, 55% women, 3% African American, 4% Asian American, 4% Hispanic/Latino, 4% Multiracial, non-Hispanic, 10% international
▶ 88 degree-seeking graduate students
▶ 74% of applicants admitted
▶ Application essay required
▶ 73% graduate within 6 years; 16% enter graduate study

General. Founded in 1876. Regionally accredited. **Degrees:** 801 bachelor's awarded; master's offered. **ROTC:** Army. **Location:** 150 miles from Detroit and Chicago. **Calendar:** 4-1-4, limited summer session. **Full-time faculty:** 262 total; 89% have terminal degrees, 10% minority, 36% women. **Part-time faculty:** 96 total; 29% have terminal degrees, 9% minority, 60% women. **Class size:** 36% < 20, 60% 20-39, 4% 40-49, less than 1% 50-99. **Special facilities:** Ecosystem preserve and interpretive center, TV studio, integrated scientific research experimental laboratory, observatory, greenhouse, human performance lab, community garden, speech pathology clinic.

Freshman class profile. 3,824 applied, 2,840 admitted, 944 enrolled.

Mid 50% test scores			
SAT critical reading:	520-670	Rank in top quarter:	56%
SAT math:	530-670	Rank in top tenth:	28%
ACT composite:	23-30	End year in good standing:	96%
GPA 3.75 or higher:	53%	Return as sophomores:	86%
GPA 3.50-3.74:	20%	Out-of-state:	45%
GPA 3.0-3.49:	19%	Live on campus:	95%
GPA 2.0-2.99:	8%	International:	9%

Basis for selection. Genuine interest in Christian goals of college and 2.5 GPA required. Recommendation, personal statement important. Minimum 20 ACT or 470 SAT Verbal and 470 SAT Math recommended. GED accepted only for those age 19 years or over. **Home schooled:** Letter of recommendation (nonparent) required. Must provide some form of transcript with grades.

High school preparation. College-preparatory program required. 12 units required; 17 recommended. Required and recommended units include English 3-4, mathematics 3-3, social studies 2-3, science 2-2 (laboratory 1), foreign language 2 and academic electives 3-3. Math must include algebra and geometry.

2015-2016 Annual costs. Tuition/fees: $30,660. Room/board: $9,690. Books/supplies: $1,000. Personal expenses: $1,300.

2015-2016 Financial aid. Need-based: 853 full-time freshmen applied for aid; 652 deemed to have need; 652 received aid. Average need met was 78%. Average scholarship/grant was $19,240; average loan $4,059. 68% of total undergraduate aid awarded as scholarships/grants, 32% as loans/jobs. **Non-need-based:** Awarded to 1,411 full-time undergraduates, including 361 freshmen. Scholarships awarded for academics, alumni affiliation, art, leadership, minority status, music/drama, religious affiliation, state residency.

Application procedures. Admission: Priority date 12/15; deadline 8/15 (postmark date). $35 fee, may be waived for applicants with need. Admission notification on a rolling basis beginning on or about 11/1. Must reply by May 1 or within 4 week(s) if notified thereafter. **Financial aid:** Priority date 2/15; no closing date. FAFSA required. Applicants notified on a rolling basis starting 3/15.

Academics. Special study options: Combined bachelor's/graduate degree, distance learning, double major, dual enrollment of high school students, honors, independent study, internships, student-designed major, study abroad, teacher certification program, urban semester, Washington semester. Overseas programs with Central College, January interim exchange with other colleges, academically-based service-learning. **Credit/placement by examination:** AP, CLEP, IB, institutional tests. **Support services:** Learning center, reduced course load, remedial instruction, study skills assistance, tutoring, writing center. Peer academic coaching, proactive academic advising for academically at-risk students.

Majors. Area/ethnic studies: Asian. **Biology:** General, biochemistry. **Business:** Accounting, business admin, communications, management information systems. **Communications:** Communications/speech/rhetoric, digital media, media studies, organizational. **Computer sciences:** Computer science. **Conservation:** Environmental science, environmental studies. **Education:** Art, bilingual, biology, chemistry, early childhood, earth science, elementary, English, foreign languages, French, German, history, mathematics, middle, music, physical, physics, reading, science, secondary, social science, social studies, Spanish, special ed. **Engineering:** General, chemical, civil, electrical, mechanical. **English:** English lit, general lit, rhetoric/composition, writing. **Foreign languages:** Chinese, Dutch/Flemish, French, German, Japanese, linguistics, Spanish. **Health services:** Nursing (RN), occupational therapy, predental, premedicine, preoccupational therapy, preoptometry, prepharmacy, prephysical therapy, preveterinary, recreational therapy, speech pathology. **History:** General. **Human services:** General, social work. **Math:** General. **Parks/recreation:** General, exercise sciences, health/fitness, sports admin. **Philosophy/religion:** Philosophy, religion. **Physical sciences:** Chemistry, geology, physics. **Psychology:** General. **Social sciences:** General, economics, geography, international economic development, international relations, political science, sociology. **Theology:** Bible, sacred music. **Visual/performing arts:** General, art, cinematography, film/cinema/video, graphic design, music, music history, music performance, music theory/composition, studio arts.

Most popular majors. Biology 8%, business/marketing 12%, education 13%, engineering/engineering technologies 6%, foreign language 6%, health sciences 11%, social sciences 7%.

Technology on campus. 900 workstations in dormitories, library, computer center. Dormitories wired for high-speed internet access and linked to campus network. Commuter students can connect to campus network. Online course registration, online library, helpline, student web hosting, wireless network available.

Student life. Freshman orientation: Mandatory, $250 fee. Preregistration for classes offered. Two-day program on-campus held in summer. Numerous options for week-long wilderness orientation also available. **Policies:** Strong emphasis on student leadership and service. Religious observance strongly expected and encouraged. First- and second-year students (under 21) not living at home required to live in residence halls. **Housing:** Guaranteed on-campus for freshmen. Single-sex dorms, apartments, themed housing, wellness housing available. Project Neighborhood houses available. **Activities:** Bands, campus ministries, choral groups, dance, drama, film society, international student organizations, literary magazine, music ensembles, Model UN, musical theater, student government, student newspaper, symphony orchestra, Amnesty International, Asia Club, Calvin College Democrats, Calvin College Conservatives, Democracy Matters, Engineers Without Borders, Environmental Stewardship, Global Business Brigades, International Health and Development.

Athletics. NCAA. **Intercollegiate:** Baseball M, basketball, cross-country, diving, golf, lacrosse, soccer, softball W, swimming, tennis, track and field, volleyball W. **Intramural:** Badminton, basketball, football (non-tackle), golf, racquetball, soccer, softball, swimming, table tennis, tennis, track and field, volleyball, water polo. **Team name:** Knights.

Student services. Adult student services, alcohol/substance abuse counseling, chaplain/spiritual director, career counseling, student employment services, financial aid counseling, health services, minority student services, personal counseling, placement for graduates. **Physically disabled:** Services for visually, speech, hearing impaired.

Contact. E-mail: admissions@calvin.edu
Phone: (616) 526-6106 Toll-free number: (800) 688-0122
Fax: (616) 526-6777
Ben Arendt, Director of Admissions, Calvin College, 3201 Burton Street Southeast, Grand Rapids, MI 49546

Central Michigan University
Mount Pleasant, Michigan

www.cmich.edu

CB member

CB code: 1106

- ◗ Public 4-year university
- ◗ Residential campus in large town
- ◗ 19,954 degree-seeking undergraduates: 12% part-time, 56% women, 8% African American, 1% Asian American, 4% Hispanic/Latino, 1% Native American, 3% Multi-racial, non-Hispanic, 2% international
- ◗ 6,183 degree-seeking graduate students
- ◗ 69% of applicants admitted
- ◗ SAT or ACT (ACT writing recommended) required
- ◗ 59% graduate within 6 years

General. Founded in 1892. Regionally accredited. 60 off-campus locations in the United States and surrounding countries. **Degrees:** 4,118 bachelor's awarded; master's, professional, doctoral offered. **ROTC:** Army, Air Force. **Location:** 70 miles from Lansing. **Calendar:** Semester, limited summer session. **Full-time faculty:** 798 total; 82% have terminal degrees, 19% minority, 42% women. **Part-time faculty:** 338 total; 34% have terminal degrees, 11% minority, 49% women. **Class size:** 32% < 20, 50% 20-39, 10% 40-49, 5% 50-99, 3% >100. **Special facilities:** Center for clinical care and education, English language institute, center for applied research and rural studies, Michigan services for children and young adults who are deaf-blind, psychological training and consultation center, language learning center, biological station, conservation genetics lab, water research center, museum of cultural and natural history, historical library, 255-acre natural woodland.

Freshman class profile. 18,269 applied, 12,674 admitted, 3,443 enrolled.

Mid 50% test scores			
SAT critical reading:	470-560	GPA 2.0-2.99:	17%
SAT math:	430-580	Rank in top quarter:	40%
SAT writing:	460-560	Rank in top tenth:	17%
ACT composite:	20-25	Return as sophomores:	78%
GPA 3.75 or higher:	25%	Out-of-state:	7%
GPA 3.50-3.74:	18%	Live on campus:	97%
GPA 3.0-3.49:	40%	Fraternities:	7%
		Sororities:	6%

Basis for selection. School achievement record, test scores, and recommendations are important. ACT recommended. Interview and essay are recommended of some. Auditions may be required for music majors. **Learning Disabled:** Students are prompted to register with Student Disability Services following admission.

High school preparation. College-preparatory program recommended. 21 units recommended. Recommended units include English 4, mathematics 4, social studies 2, history 2, science 4 (laboratory 1), foreign language 2, computer science 1 and visual/performing arts 2.

2015-2016 Annual costs. Tuition/fees: $11,850; $23,670 out-of-state. Room/board: $9,088. Books/supplies: $1,000. Personal expenses: $484.

2014-2015 Financial aid. Need-based: 3,402 full-time freshmen applied for aid; 2,478 deemed to have need; 2,402 received aid. Average need met was 83%. Average scholarship/grant was $8,017; average loan $6,075. 39% of total undergraduate aid awarded as scholarships/grants, 61% as loans/jobs. **Non-need-based:** Awarded to 2,681 full-time undergraduates, including 1,099 freshmen. Scholarships awarded for academics, alumni affiliation, art, athletics, leadership, minority status, music/drama, ROTC, state residency. **Additional information:** Tuition waiver for Native American students qualifying under state program criteria.

Application procedures. Admission: Priority date 10/1; deadline 7/1 (receipt date). $35 fee, may be waived for applicants with need. Admission notification on a rolling basis. Must reply by 5/1. **Financial aid:** Priority date 3/1; no closing date. FAFSA required. Applicants notified on a rolling basis starting 4/1.

Academics. Special study options: Combined bachelor's/graduate degree, distance learning, double major, dual enrollment of high school students, ESL, honors, independent study, internships, semester at sea, student-designed major, study abroad, teacher certification program, Washington semester. Leadership Institute, Pre-professional studies, Recognition of Cultural Competency, First Year Experience, NcNair Scholars Program. **Credit/placement by examination:** AP, CLEP, IB, SAT, ACT, institutional tests. 40 credit hours maximum toward bachelor's degree. Credit by examination may not be used to repeat any course previously taken. **Support services:** Learning center, pre-admission summer program, reduced course load, remedial instruction, study skills assistance, tutoring, writing center.

Honors college/program. Applicants must have 3.75 GPA or 3.6 GPA and 25 ACT.

Majors. Architecture: Interior. **Area/ethnic studies:** European, women's. **Biology:** General, biochemistry, biomedical sciences, neuroscience. **Business:** Accounting, actuarial science, business admin, entrepreneurial studies, fashion, finance, financial planning, hospitality admin, hotel/motel admin, human resources, international, logistics, management information systems, marketing, operations, purchasing, real estate, retail management. **Communications:** Advertising, communications/speech/rhetoric, journalism, organizational, photojournalism, public relations. **Computer sciences:** Computer science, information technology. **Conservation:** General, environmental science, environmental studies, land use planning. **Education:** Art, biology, business, chemistry, early childhood, earth science, elementary, emotionally handicapped, English, family/consumer sciences, French, geography, German, health, history, mathematics, mentally handicapped, music, physical, physics, science, social studies, Spanish, speech, technology/industrial arts. **Engineering:** Electrical, manufacturing, mechanical. **English:** Creative writing, English lit. **Foreign languages:** French, German, Spanish. **Health services:** Athletic training, clinical lab science, communication disorders, dietetics, health care admin, public health ed, recreational therapy. **History:** General. **Human services:** Community org/advocacy, social work. **Liberal arts:** Arts/sciences. **Math:** General, statistics. **Parks/recreation:** General, exercise sciences, facilities management, health/fitness, sports admin, sports studies. **Philosophy/religion:** Philosophy, religion. **Physical sciences:** Astronomy, chemistry, geology, meteorology, oceanography, physics. **Psychology:** General. **Social sciences:** General, anthropology, economics, geography, GIS/cartography, international relations, political science, sociology. **Visual/performing arts:** Acting, art, dramatic, graphic design, music, music theory/composition, musical theater, studio arts, theater design. **Work/family studies:** Child development, family systems, institutional food production.

Most popular majors. Business/marketing 24%, communications/journalism 8%, education 11%, health sciences 7%, parks/recreation 8%, psychology 8%, social sciences 7%.

Technology on campus. 3,000 workstations in dormitories, library, computer center, student center. Dormitories wired for high-speed internet access and linked to campus network. Commuter students can connect to campus network. Online course registration, online library, helpline, repair service, student web hosting, wireless network available.

Student life. Freshman orientation: Mandatory, $175 fee. Preregistration for classes offered. One-day sessions; morning refreshments and lunch provided. **Housing:** Guaranteed on-campus for freshmen. Coed dorms, special housing for disabled, apartments, cooperative housing, fraternity/sorority housing, themed housing, wellness housing available. $800 partly refundable deposit, deadline 5/1. Residential Colleges (Business Administration, Education & Human Services, Health Professions, Science & Technology, School of Music) available. **Activities:** Bands, campus ministries, choral groups, dance, drama, film society, international student organizations, literary magazine, music ensembles, Model UN, musical theater, opera, radio station, student government, student newspaper, symphony orchestra, TV station, Asian cultural organization, Hispanic student organization, North American Indian student organization, organization for Black unity, gay/lesbian/bisexual club, College Republicans, University Democrats, Baha'i club, Campus Crusade for Christ, Fellowship of Christian Athletes.

Athletics. NCAA. **Intercollegiate:** Baseball M, basketball, cross-country, field hockey W, football (tackle) M, gymnastics W, soccer W, softball W, track and field, volleyball W, wrestling M. **Intramural:** Basketball, football (non-tackle), golf, racquetball, soccer, softball, table tennis, tennis, volleyball, wrestling M. **Team name:** Chippewas.

Student services. Alcohol/substance abuse counseling, career counseling, services for economically disadvantaged, student employment services, financial aid counseling, health services, minority student services, personal counseling, placement for graduates, veterans' counselor. **Physically disabled:** Services for visually, speech, hearing impaired.

Contact. E-mail: cmuadmit@cmich.edu
Phone: (989) 774-3076 Toll-free number: (888) 292-5366
Fax: (989) 774-7267
Thomas Speakman, Director of Admissions, Central Michigan University, Admissions Office, Mount Pleasant, MI 48859

Cleary University
Howell, Michigan
www.cleary.edu
CB code: 1123

- Private 4-year university and business college
- Commuter campus in small city
- 206 full-time, degree-seeking undergraduates

General. Founded in 1883. Regionally accredited. Classroom facility in Washtenaw County; extension sites in Genesee and Montcalm Counties. **Degrees:** 85 bachelor's awarded; master's offered. **Location:** 55 miles from Detroit, 27 miles from Ann Arbor, 35 miles from Lansing, 30 miles from Flint. **Calendar:** Semester, limited summer session. **Full-time faculty:** 6 total. **Part-time faculty:** 101 total. **Class size:** 89% < 20, 11% 20-39. **Special facilities:** Disc-golf course, center for innovation and entrepreneurship, micro-business incubator.

Freshman class profile.

Out-of-state:	9%	Live on campus:	6%

Basis for selection. Open admission, but selective for some programs. Traditional students must have graduated high school with 2.5 GPA and have 19 ACT. Additional admissions requirements for Executive BBA program. Regular, special, guest, dual, provisional, transfer, and international admissions available. Applicants with below 2.5 GPA may be accepted if probable success in chosen program indicated.

High school preparation. 24 units recommended. Recommended units include English 4, mathematics 2, social studies 2, history 2, science 2 and academic electives 12.

2015-2016 Annual costs. Tuition/fees: $18,750. Personal expenses: $1,692.

Financial aid. All financial aid based on need. **Additional information:** Filing electronically preferred; paper applications available. Tuition guarantee based on continuous enrollment. Essay and recommendations required for scholarship consideration.

Application procedures. Admission: Closing date 8/15. $25 fee, may be waived for applicants with need. Admission notification on a rolling basis. **Financial aid:** Priority date 3/1; no closing date. FAFSA required. Applicants notified on a rolling basis starting 3/1; must reply within 2 week(s) of notification.

Academics. Compressed academic calendar reduces time to degree completion. First-time college students can complete bachelor's degree in 3.5 years. **Special study options:** Accelerated study, combined bachelor's/graduate degree, cooperative education, distance learning, double major, dual enrollment of high school students, honors, independent study, internships. **Credit/placement by examination:** AP, CLEP, institutional tests. 45 credit hours maximum toward bachelor's degree. **Support services:** Pre-admission summer program, reduced course load, remedial instruction, study skills assistance, tutoring.

Majors. Business: Accounting, business admin, communications, entrepreneurial studies, event planning, finance, financial planning, human resources, marketing, organizational leadership, sales/distribution.

Technology on campus. PC or laptop required. 26 workstations in computer center, student center. Commuter students can connect to campus network. Online library, helpline, wireless network available.

Student life. Freshman orientation: Mandatory. Preregistration for classes offered. Held two weeks prior to the start of classes, with on-campus and on-line components. Students instructed in the use of learning management software, electronic research tools, library resources, and academic support services. **Housing:** Guaranteed on-campus for freshmen.

Athletics. USCAA. **Intercollegiate:** Baseball M, bowling, cross-country, golf, lacrosse, soccer, softball W, tennis. **Team name:** Cougars.

Student services. Adult student services, career counseling, student employment services, financial aid counseling, personal counseling, placement for graduates, veterans' counselor.

Contact. E-mail: admissions@cleary.edu
Phone: (517) 338-3330 Toll-free number: (888) 525-3279
Fax: (517) 338-3336
Carrie Bonofiglio, Director of Admissions, Cleary University, 3750 Cleary Drive, Howell, MI 48843

College for Creative Studies
Detroit, Michigan
www.collegeforcreativestudies.edu
CB member
CB code: 1035

- Private 4-year visual arts college
- Commuter campus in very large city
- 1,376 degree-seeking undergraduates
- 58 graduate students
- SAT or ACT with writing required

General. Founded in 1926. Regionally accredited. **Degrees:** 247 bachelor's awarded; master's offered. **Calendar:** Semester, limited summer session.

Full-time faculty: 48 total; 52% have terminal degrees, 10% minority, 23% women. **Part-time faculty:** 241 total; 41% women. **Special facilities:** Foundry, computer studios, wood shop, metal shop, glassblowing studio, ceramic studio, fiber studio, large capacity spray booth, rapid prototype equipment.

Freshman class profile.

Out-of-state: 15%   **Live on campus:** 68%

Basis for selection. Art portfolio, test scores, and high school record important. 2.5 GPA required. Art portfolio required for all applicants. **Home schooled:** Transcript of courses and grades required. May be required to submit GED.

High school preparation. College-preparatory program recommended. 13 units recommended. Recommended units include English 4, mathematics 3, social studies 2, science 2 and foreign language 2. College-preparatory program recommended, art courses highly recommended.

2015-2016 Annual costs. Tuition/fees: $38,950. Room/board: $8,450. Books/supplies: $2,600. Personal expenses: $1,700.

Financial aid. Non-need-based: Scholarships awarded for academics, art.

Application procedures. Admission: Priority date 2/1; deadline 7/1 (postmark date). $35 fee, may be waived for applicants with need, free for online applicants. Admission notification on a rolling basis beginning on or about 9/1. Must reply by May 1 or within 3 week(s) if notified thereafter. **Financial aid:** Priority date 7/1; no closing date. FAFSA required. Applicants notified on a rolling basis starting 2/15; must reply within 3 week(s) of notification.

Academics. Special study options: Combined bachelor's/graduate degree, cooperative education, double major, dual enrollment of high school students, ESL, exchange student, independent study, internships, New York semester, study abroad, teacher certification program. Advanced students may petition for 1 semester in New York studio space. **Credit/placement by examination:** AP, CLEP, IB, SAT, ACT. 6 credit hours maximum toward bachelor's degree. **Support services:** Learning center, pre-admission summer program, reduced course load, remedial instruction, study skills assistance, tutoring, writing center.

Majors. Business: Transportation. **Communications:** Advertising, digital media. **Communications technology:** Animation/special effects. **Visual/performing arts:** Ceramics, cinematography, commercial photography, commercial/advertising art, crafts, design, drawing, fiber arts, film/cinema/video, game design, graphic design, illustration, industrial design, interior design, metal/jewelry, multimedia, painting, photography, printmaking, sculpture, studio arts.

Technology on campus. 400 workstations in dormitories, library, computer center, student center. Dormitories wired for high-speed internet access and linked to campus network. Commuter students can connect to campus network. Online course registration, online library, helpline, student web hosting, wireless network available.

Student life. Freshman orientation: Mandatory. Preregistration for classes offered. **Housing:** Coed dorms available. $200 fully refundable deposit, deadline 5/1. **Activities:** Student government, student newspaper, black artists researching trends, industrial design club, graphic design club.

Student services. Alcohol/substance abuse counseling, career counseling, student employment services, financial aid counseling, health services, minority student services, personal counseling, placement for graduates. **Physically disabled:** Services for hearing impaired.

Contact. E-mail: admissions@collegeforcreativestudies.edu
Phone: (313) 664-7425 Toll-free number: (800) 952-2787
Fax: (313) 872-2739
Lori Watson, Director of Admissions, College for Creative Studies, 201 East Kirby, Detroit, MI 48202-4034

Concordia University
Ann Arbor, Michigan
www.cuaa.edu   CB code: 1094

- Private 4-year liberal arts and teachers college affiliated with the Lutheran Church - Missouri Synod
- Residential campus in small city
- 562 full-time, degree-seeking undergraduates
- SAT or ACT (ACT writing optional) required

General. Founded in 1962. Regionally accredited. **Degrees:** 77 bachelor's, 1 associate awarded; master's offered. **ROTC:** Army, Air Force. **Location:** 40 miles from Detroit. **Calendar:** Semester, limited summer session. **Full-time faculty:** 37 total. **Part-time faculty:** 52 total. **Class size:** 85% < 20, 14% 20-39, less than 1% 40-49. **Special facilities:** Earhart Manor (certified Michigan Historical Landmark).

Basis for selection. School achievement record most important. Test scores and rank in top half of class also important. Interview and essay recommended. Audition recommended for music majors. Portfolio recommended for art majors. **Home schooled:** Letter of recommendation (nonparent) required. 300-500 word personal statement and resume or extracurricular activities sheet required. **Learning Disabled:** Require an explanation of the disability and written recommended accommodations from an appropriate professional.

High school preparation. 20 units recommended. Recommended units include English 4, mathematics 3, social studies 2, science 2 (laboratory 2), foreign language 2 and academic electives 5. Math should include two units of algebra and one unit of geometry.

2015-2016 Annual costs. Tuition/fees: $26,895. Room/board: $9,300. Books/supplies: $1,500. Personal expenses: $2,450.

2015-2016 Financial aid. Need-based: 167 full-time freshmen applied for aid; 156 deemed to have need; 156 received aid. Average need met was 70%. Average scholarship/grant was $16,876; average loan $4,899. 68% of total undergraduate aid awarded as scholarships/grants, 32% as loans/jobs. **Non-need-based:** Awarded to 172 full-time undergraduates, including 49 freshmen. Scholarships awarded for academics, alumni affiliation, art, athletics, leadership, music/drama, religious affiliation.

Application procedures. Admission: No deadline. $25 fee, may be waived for applicants with need, free for online applicants. Admission notification on a rolling basis. **Financial aid:** Closing date 3/1. FAFSA required. Applicants notified on a rolling basis starting 3/1; must reply within 3 week(s) of notification.

Academics. Special study options: Accelerated study, cross-registration, distance learning, double major, dual enrollment of high school students, ESL, exchange student, independent study, internships, liberal arts/career combination, student-designed major, study abroad, teacher certification program, weekend college. Accelerated degree program for mature students. **Credit/placement by examination:** AP, CLEP, IB, institutional tests. 32 credit hours maximum toward associate degree, 32 toward bachelor's. **Support services:** Learning center, pre-admission summer program, reduced course load, remedial instruction, study skills assistance, tutoring, writing center.

Majors. Biology: General. **Business:** Business admin. **Communications:** General. **Education:** Art, biology, elementary, English, mathematics, multilevel teacher, music, physical, science, secondary, social studies. **English:** English lit. **Foreign languages:** Biblical. **Health services:** Premedicine, prepharmacy, prephysical therapy. **Math:** General. **Parks/recreation:** Exercise sciences, health/fitness. **Philosophy/religion:** Religion. **Protective services:** Law enforcement admin. **Psychology:** General. **Social sciences:** General. **Theology:** Preministerial. **Visual/performing arts:** Art, music. **Work/family studies:** Family studies.

Most popular majors. Business/marketing 26%, education 33%, family/consumer sciences 13%, psychology 6%, security/protective services 10%.

Technology on campus. 60 workstations in library, computer center, student center. Dormitories wired for high-speed internet access and linked to campus network. Commuter students can connect to campus network. Online library, helpline, repair service, student web hosting, wireless network available.

Student life. Freshman orientation: Mandatory, $125 fee. Preregistration for classes offered. Three-day program includes academic, social, and orientation events. **Policies:** Students must live on campus (or with parents/guardian) until attaining junior status or 21 years of age. **Housing:** Guaranteed on-campus for all undergraduates. Single-sex dorms, apartments, wellness housing available. $100 nonrefundable deposit, deadline 8/15. **Activities:** Bands, campus ministries, choral groups, dance, drama, literary magazine, music ensembles, musical theater, student government, student newspaper, several religious and community service groups.

Athletics. NAIA. **Intercollegiate:** Baseball M, basketball, bowling, cheerleading, cross-country, football (tackle) M, golf, soccer, softball W, track and field, volleyball W. **Intramural:** Badminton, basketball, football (non-tackle), soccer, softball, table tennis, ultimate frisbee, volleyball. **Team name:** Cardinals.

Student services. Adult student services, alcohol/substance abuse counseling, chaplain/spiritual director, career counseling, student employment services, financial aid counseling, health services, personal counseling, placement for graduates, women's services. **Physically disabled:** Services for visually, speech, hearing impaired.

Contact. E-mail: admissions@cuaa.edu
Phone: (734) 995-7322 Toll-free number: (800) 253-0680
Fax: (734) 995-4610
Jon Bahr, Director of Undergraduate Admissions, Concordia University, 4090 Geddes Road, Ann Arbor, MI 48105

Cornerstone University
Grand Rapids, Michigan
www.cornerstone.edu

CB code: 1253

◗ Private 4-year university and liberal arts college affiliated with the interdenominational tradition

◗ Residential campus in small city

◗ 1,912 degree-seeking undergraduates: 22% part-time, 61% women, 14% African American, 1% Asian American, 4% Hispanic/Latino, 1% Native American, 1% Multi-racial, non-Hispanic, 2% international

◗ 547 graduate students

◗ SAT or ACT (ACT writing recommended), application essay required

◗ 61% graduate within 6 years

General. Founded in 1941. Regionally accredited. Listed in the top 100 online universities by US News & World Report. **Degrees:** 444 bachelor's, 36 associate awarded; master's offered. **ROTC:** Army. **Location:** 4 miles from downtown. **Calendar:** Semester, limited summer session. **Full-time faculty:** 56 total; 61% have terminal degrees, 9% minority, 34% women. **Part-time faculty:** 70 total; 16% have terminal degrees, 4% minority, 41% women. **Class size:** 56% < 20, 40% 20-39, 2% 40-49, 2% 50-99.

Freshman class profile.

Mid 50% test scores			
SAT critical reading:	480-590	**GPA 2.0-2.99:**	18%
SAT math:	470-590	**Rank in top quarter:**	37%
SAT writing:	450-580	**Rank in top tenth:**	13%
ACT composite:	20-25	**Return as sophomores:**	76%
GPA 3.75 or higher:	37%	**Out-of-state:**	24%
GPA 3.50-3.74:	18%	**Live on campus:**	88%
GPA 3.0-3.49:	27%	**International:**	4%

Basis for selection. Statement of Christian commitment, pastoral reference, 2.5 high school GPA, and ACT score of 19. Students with lower scores and GPA may be admitted conditionally. Audition required for music majors.

High school preparation. Required units include English 4, mathematics 3, social studies 3, history 3, science 2, foreign language 2 and academic electives 4.

2015-2016 Annual costs. Tuition/fees: $26,100. Room/board: $8,560. Books/supplies: $800. Personal expenses: $1,482.

2015-2016 Financial aid. Need-based: 298 full-time freshmen applied for aid; 261 deemed to have need; 261 received aid. Average need met was 70%. Average scholarship/grant was $17,747; average loan $3,606. 79% of total undergraduate aid awarded as scholarships/grants, 21% as loans/jobs. **Non-need-based:** Scholarships awarded for academics, athletics, music/drama. **Additional information:** Audition required for music scholarship applicants.

Application procedures. Admission: Closing date 8/15 (receipt date). No application fee. Admission notification on a rolling basis beginning on or about 8/1. **Financial aid:** Priority date 3/1; no closing date. FAFSA required. Applicants notified on a rolling basis starting 3/1.

Academics. All students complete an internship in major field. Core curriculum required of all students across all majors. **Special study options:** Accelerated study, combined bachelor's/graduate degree, cross-registration, distance learning, double major, dual enrollment of high school students, ESL, honors, independent study, internships, student-designed major, study abroad, teacher certification program, urban semester, Washington semester. **Credit/placement by examination:** AP, CLEP, IB, SAT, ACT, institutional tests. 15 credit hours maximum toward associate degree, 30 toward bachelor's. CLEP, DANTES. **Support services:** Learning center, reduced course load, remedial instruction, study skills assistance, tutoring, writing center.

Honors college/program. Requires 28 ACT; 12-15 admitted annually.

Majors. Biology: General, environmental. **Business:** Accounting, business admin, financial planning, international, management information systems, management science, marketing. **Communications:** Broadcast journalism,

communications/speech/rhetoric, digital media, health, journalism, media studies, sports. **Communications technology:** Graphics, photo/film/video. **Computer sciences:** General. **Conservation:** Environmental science, environmental studies. **Education:** Biology, early childhood, elementary, English, history, mathematics, music, physical, science, secondary, social science, social studies, voc/tech. **English:** American lit, English lit, rhetoric/composition, technical writing. **Foreign languages:** Spanish. **Health services:** Community health services, predental, premedicine, preoccupational therapy, preveterinary. **History:** General. **Human services:** Social work. **Math:** General. **Parks/recreation:** Exercise sciences, sports admin. **Psychology:** General, counseling, developmental, family. **Social sciences:** General, economics. **Theology:** Bible, youth ministry. **Visual/performing arts:** Music, music performance, music theory/composition. **Work/family studies:** Family systems.

Most popular majors. Business/marketing 44%, education 9%, psychology 13%, theological studies 8%.

Technology on campus. PC or laptop required. 62 workstations in dormitories, library, computer center, student center. Dormitories wired for high-speed internet access and linked to campus network. Commuter students can connect to campus network. Online course registration, online library, helpline, repair service, wireless network available.

Student life. Freshman orientation: Mandatory. Preregistration for classes offered. Four-day program held prior to start of Fall classes. **Policies:** Dry campus; chapel attendance required. Students under 21 with fewer than 63 credit hours must live on campus unless living with immediate family. Religious observance required. **Housing:** Guaranteed on-campus for all undergraduates. Single-sex dorms, special housing for disabled, apartments available. $150 fully refundable deposit, deadline 9/1. All housing is alcohol, drug, and smoke-free. **Activities:** Bands, campus ministries, choral groups, drama, international student organizations, literary magazine, music ensembles, musical theater, student government, student newspaper, ACTS poverty and justice organization, Night of Nets malaria project team, multi-cultural organization, MU Kappa, Sigma Beta Delta Honors Business Society, Cultural Diversity Committee, Social Work Student Group, YES Student Education Group.

Athletics. NAIA. **Intercollegiate:** Baseball M, basketball, bowling, cheerleading, cross-country, golf, soccer, softball W, track and field, volleyball W. **Intramural:** Basketball, football (non-tackle), ice hockey M, racquetball, sand volleyball, soccer, softball, volleyball. **Team name:** Golden Eagles.

Student services. Adult student services, alcohol/substance abuse counseling, chaplain/spiritual director, career counseling, student employment services, financial aid counseling, health services, personal counseling, placement for graduates, veterans' counselor. **Physically disabled:** Services for visually, speech, hearing impaired.

Contact. E-mail: admissions@cornerstone.edu
Phone: (616) 222-1426 Toll-free number: (800) 787-9778
Fax: (616) 222-1418
Lisa Link, Executive Director of Enrollment, Cornerstone University, 1001 East Beltline NE, Grand Rapids, MI 49525-5897

Davenport University
Grand Rapids, Michigan
www.davenport.edu

CB code: 1183

◗ Private 4-year university and business college

◗ Commuter campus in small city

◗ 5,864 degree-seeking undergraduates

◗ 2,092 graduate students

◗ 93% of applicants admitted

◗ 39% graduate within 6 years

General. Founded in 1866. Regionally accredited. Locations in Battle Creek, Flint, Holland, downtown Grand Rapids, Kalamazoo, Lansing, Livonia, Midland, Saginaw, Traverse City, and Warren. **Degrees:** 4,719 bachelor's, 1,039 associate awarded; master's offered. **ROTC:** Army. **Location:** 10 miles from Grand Rapids. **Calendar:** Semester, extensive summer session. **Full-time faculty:** 156 total; 26% have terminal degrees, 9% minority, 61% women. **Part-time faculty:** 737 total; 22% have terminal degrees, 16% minority, 55% women. **Class size:** 74% < 20, 26% 20-39.

Freshman class profile. 2,129 applied, 1,983 admitted, 677 enrolled.

Out-of-state:	1%	**Live on campus:**	31%

Basis for selection. GPA and test scores important; prospective students without ACT or SAT scores may take standard COMPASS assessment as arranged by a Davenport representative. SAT or ACT recommended. Interview recommended.

High school preparation. College-preparatory program recommended. Recommended units include English 4 and mathematics 3.

2015-2016 Annual costs. Tuition/fees: $19,750. Room/board: $10,078. Books/supplies: $1,200. Personal expenses: $1,752.

Financial aid. Non-need-based: Scholarships awarded for academics, alumni affiliation, athletics, leadership.

Application procedures. Admission: No deadline. $25 fee. Admission notification on a rolling basis beginning on or about 9/1. **Financial aid:** Priority date 3/1; no closing date. FAFSA required. Applicants notified on a rolling basis starting 3/1; must reply within 2 week(s) of notification.

Academics. Special study options: Accelerated study, combined bachelor's/graduate degree, distance learning, dual enrollment of high school students, ESL, honors, independent study, internships, study abroad. **Credit/placement by examination:** AP, CLEP, IB, ACT, institutional tests. 40 credit hours maximum toward associate degree, 40 toward bachelor's. **Support services:** Learning center, remedial instruction, tutoring, writing center.

Majors. Biology: Bioinformatics. **Business:** General, accounting, business admin, finance, human resources, international, marketing. **Communications technology:** Animation/special effects. **Computer sciences:** Information systems, networking, programming, security. **Health services:** Health care admin, health information management, management/clinical assistant, nursing (RN). **Parks/recreation:** Sports admin.

Most popular majors. Business/marketing 58%, computer/information sciences 13%, health sciences 33%.

Technology on campus. 3,556 workstations in dormitories, library, computer center, student center. Dormitories wired for high-speed internet access and linked to campus network. Commuter students can connect to campus network. Online course registration, online library, helpline, wireless network available.

Student life. Freshman orientation: Mandatory. Preregistration for classes offered. **Housing:** Coed dorms, wellness housing available. $150 fully refundable deposit. **Activities:** International student organizations, literary magazine, student government, student newspaper, Alternative Spring Break, black student union, Business Professionals of America, Collegiate DECA, Health Information Management student association, legal assistants club, residence hall community council, Society of Human Resource Management, student activities committee, Student Veterans of America.

Athletics. NAIA. **Intercollegiate:** Baseball M, basketball, bowling, cheerleading W, cross-country, golf, ice hockey M, lacrosse, rugby, soccer, softball, tennis, track and field, volleyball W, wrestling M. **Team name:** Panthers.

Student services. Career counseling, student employment services, financial aid counseling, personal counseling, veterans' counselor. **Physically disabled:** Services for visually impaired.

Contact. E-mail: gradmiss@davenport.edu
Phone: (616) 698-7111 Toll-free number: (866) 925-3884
Fax: (616) 555-5214
Malia Roberts, Executive Director of Admissions, Davenport University, 6191 Kraft Avenue SE, Grand Rapids, MI 49512-9396

Eastern Michigan University
Ypsilanti, Michigan
www.emich.edu

CB member
CB code: 1201

- Public 4-year university
- Residential campus in small city
- 17,284 degree-seeking undergraduates: 25% part-time, 59% women, 20% African American, 2% Asian American, 5% Hispanic/Latino, 4% Multi-racial, non-Hispanic, 2% international
- 3,334 degree-seeking graduate students
- 75% of applicants admitted
- SAT or ACT (ACT writing optional) required
- 40% graduate within 6 years

General. Founded in 1849. Regionally accredited. **Degrees:** 3,321 bachelor's awarded; master's, professional, doctoral offered. **ROTC:** Army, Naval, Air Force. **Location:** 7 miles from Ann Arbor, 35 miles from Detroit. **Calendar:** Semester, limited summer session. **Full-time faculty:** 753 total; 80% have terminal degrees, 19% minority, 52% women. **Part-time faculty:** 631 total; 17% have terminal degrees, 17% minority, 58% women. **Class size:** 41% < 20, 52% 20-39, 3% 40-49, 3% 50-99, less than 1% >100. **Special facilities:** Corporate education center, observatory, laser laboratory, textiles research and training institute.

Freshman class profile. 14,228 applied, 10,639 admitted, 2,888 enrolled.

Mid 50% test scores			
SAT critical reading:	440-590	GPA 2.0-2.99:	28%
SAT math:	450-590	Rank in top quarter:	39%
SAT writing:	430-580	Rank in top tenth:	13%
ACT composite:	19-25	Return as sophomores:	75%
GPA 3.75 or higher:	18%	Out-of-state:	16%
GPA 3.50-3.74:	20%	Live on campus:	65%
GPA 3.0-3.49:	34%	International:	1%

Basis for selection. School achievement record and test scores important. Grades and test results combined to predict academic success. Michigan English Language Assessment Battery accepted in place of TOEFL with minimum score 72 for unconditional acceptance. Essay recommended. Audition required of music majors. Portfolio required of art majors.

High school preparation. College-preparatory program recommended. 21 units recommended. Recommended units include English 4, mathematics 4, social studies 2, history 1, science 4 (laboratory 1), foreign language 2 and academic electives 4.

2015-2016 Annual costs. Tuition/fees: $10,417; $27,712 out-of-state. Room/board: $9,344. Books/supplies: $1,000. Personal expenses: $1,118. **Additional information:** Higher course levels charged at higher rates.

2014-2015 Financial aid. Need-based: 2,369 full-time freshmen applied for aid; 1,879 deemed to have need; 1,862 received aid. Average need met was 46%. Average scholarship/grant was $6,255; average loan $3,257. 50% of total undergraduate aid awarded as scholarships/grants, 50% as loans/jobs. **Non-need-based:** Awarded to 6,784 full-time undergraduates, including 2,143 freshmen. Scholarships awarded for academics, alumni affiliation, art, athletics, leadership, minority status, music/drama, ROTC, state residency.

Application procedures. Admission: Priority date 2/15; no deadline. $35 fee, may be waived for applicants with need. Admission notification on a rolling basis beginning on or about 10/1. **Financial aid:** No deadline. FAFSA required. Applicants notified on a rolling basis starting 3/1.

Academics. Special study options: Accelerated study, combined bachelor's/graduate degree, cooperative education, cross-registration, distance learning, double major, dual enrollment of high school students, ESL, exchange student, external degree, honors, independent study, internships, liberal arts/career combination, student-designed major, study abroad, teacher certification program, Washington semester, weekend college. Dual enrollment program requires students to apply for admission to EMU. **Credit/placement by examination:** AP, CLEP, IB, SAT, ACT, institutional tests. 30 credit hours maximum toward bachelor's degree. **Support services:** Learning center, reduced course load, remedial instruction, study skills assistance, tutoring, writing center. Conditionally-admit students may take Summer Incentive Program.

Honors college/program. Admission based on high school GPA, test scores, letters of recommendation. Approximately 250 freshmen admitted each year; reduced class size emphasizing student-professor interaction.

Majors. Architecture: Urban/community planning. **Area/ethnic studies:** African-American, women's. **Biology:** General, biochemistry, toxicology. **Business:** General, accounting, actuarial science, business admin, construction management, entrepreneurial studies, fashion, finance, hospitality admin, international, labor studies, logistics, management information systems, managerial economics, marketing, office management. **Communications:** Communications/speech/rhetoric, journalism, public relations. **Communications technology:** General, animation/special effects. **Computer sciences:** General, computer science. **Conservation:** Environmental studies. **Education:** Art, biology, business, chemistry, computer, Deaf/hearing impaired, early childhood, elementary, emotionally handicapped, English, foreign languages, French, German, history, mathematics, mentally handicapped, music, physical, physically handicapped, physics, reading, sales/marketing, science, secondary, social science, social studies, Spanish, speech impaired, technology/industrial arts, visually handicapped. **Engineering:** Applied physics. **English:** Creative writing, English lit, rhetoric/composition, technical writing, writing. **Foreign languages:** French, German, Germanic, Japanese, linguistics, Spanish. **Health services:** Athletic training, clinical lab science, dietetics, health care admin, music therapy, nursing (RN), occupational therapy, predental, premedicine, prepharmacy, preveterinary, recreational therapy, speech pathology. **History:** General. **Human services:** General, social work. **Math:** General, statistics. **Parks/recreation:** Exercise sciences, facilities management, health/fitness. **Philosophy/religion:** Philosophy. **Physical sciences:** Chemistry, geology, geophysics, physics. **Psychology:** General. **Social sciences:** General, anthropology, criminology, economics, geography, international relations, political science, sociology. **Visual/performing arts:** Art, art history/conservation, dance, directing/producing, dramatic, film/cinema/video, interior design, music, music performance, studio arts management. **Work/family studies:** Facilities/event planning.

Most popular majors. Business/marketing 20%, education 11%, health sciences 15%, interdisciplinary studies 7%, psychology 6%, public administration/social services 6%, social sciences 7%.

Technology on campus. 1,500 workstations in dormitories, library, computer center, student center. Dormitories wired for high-speed internet access and linked to campus network. Commuter students can connect to campus network. Online course registration, online library, helpline, student web hosting, wireless network available.

Student life. Freshman orientation: Mandatory, $310 fee. Preregistration for classes offered. Four-day orientation held Saturday-Tuesday. **Housing:** Coed dorms, special housing for disabled, apartments, cooperative housing, fraternity/sorority housing, themed housing, wellness housing available. $200 partly refundable deposit, deadline 5/1. **Activities:** Bands, campus ministries, choral groups, dance, drama, film society, international student organizations, literary magazine, music ensembles, Model UN, musical theater, opera, radio station, student government, student newspaper, symphony orchestra, TV station, over 300 student organizations.

Athletics. NCAA. **Intercollegiate:** Baseball M, basketball, cross-country, diving, football (tackle) M, golf, gymnastics W, rowing (crew) W, soccer W, softball W, swimming, tennis W, track and field, volleyball W, wrestling M. **Intramural:** Badminton, basketball, bowling, cross-country, football (non-tackle), golf, racquetball, soccer, softball, swimming, table tennis, track and field, ultimate frisbee, volleyball, weight lifting. **Team name:** Eagles.

Student services. Adult student services, alcohol/substance abuse counseling, chaplain/spiritual director, career counseling, student employment services, financial aid counseling, health services, minority student services, on-campus daycare, personal counseling, placement for graduates, veterans' counselor, women's services. **Physically disabled:** Services for visually, speech, hearing impaired.

Contact. E-mail: undergraduate.admissions@emich.edu
Phone: (734) 487-3060 Toll-free number: (800) 468-6368
Fax: (734) 487-6559
Brian Selfridge, Associate Director, Admissions, Eastern Michigan University, 400 Pierce Hall, Ypsilanti, MI 48197

Ferris State University
Big Rapids, Michigan
www.ferris.edu

CB member
CB code: 1222

- Public 4-year university
- Residential campus in large town
- 12,550 degree-seeking undergraduates: 28% part-time, 51% women, 8% African American, 2% Asian American, 4% Hispanic/Latino, 1% Native American, 3% Multi-racial, non-Hispanic, 1% international
- 1,375 degree-seeking graduate students
- 78% of applicants admitted
- SAT or ACT (ACT writing optional) required
- 51% graduate within 6 years

General. Founded in 1884. Regionally accredited. **Degrees:** 2,423 bachelor's, 697 associate awarded; master's, professional, doctoral offered. **ROTC:** Army. **Location:** 55 miles from Grand Rapids. **Calendar:** Semester, limited summer session. **Full-time faculty:** 590 total; 43% women. **Part-time faculty:** 393 total; 49% women. **Class size:** 42% < 20, 48% 20-39, 7% 40-49, 2% 50-99, 1% >100. **Special facilities:** Observatory, wildlife museum, Jim Crow museum, art walk, greenhouse.

Freshman class profile. 10,299 applied, 8,052 admitted, 1,967 enrolled.

Mid 50% test scores		Return as sophomores:	80%
ACT composite:	19-24	Out-of-state:	8%
GPA 3.75 or higher:	20%	Live on campus:	79%
GPA 3.50-3.74:	15%	Fraternities:	3%
GPA 3.0-3.49:	30%	Sororities:	2%
GPA 2.0-2.99:	35%		

Basis for selection. School achievement record most important. General admission requirements: 2.5 GPA (509 GED) or 17 ACT/1210 SAT. ACT and SAT scores used for admissions purposes for marginal applicants. Specific program requirements vary. Interview recommended. Portfolio recommended of visual communication majors. **Home schooled:** Statement describing home school structure and mission, transcript of courses and grades required. Course descriptions and grading scale, official ACT or SAT. **Learning Disabled:**

Submit documentation from professional psychologist or social worker to Disabilities Services Office in the Educational and Career Services Counseling Center.

High school preparation. College-preparatory program recommended. 18 units recommended. Recommended units include English 4, mathematics 4, social studies 3, science 3, foreign language 2 and visual/performing arts 1. 1 unit computer literacy recommended.

2015-2016 Annual costs. Tuition/fees: $11,460; $17,190 out-of-state. Room/board: $9,434. Books/supplies: $914. Personal expenses: $560.

2015-2016 Financial aid. Need-based: 1,796 full-time freshmen applied for aid; 1,476 deemed to have need; 1,473 received aid. Average need met was 71%. Average scholarship/grant was $4,560; average loan $3,640. 49% of total undergraduate aid awarded as scholarships/grants, 51% as loans/jobs. **Non-need-based:** Scholarships awarded for academics, alumni affiliation, art, athletics, job skills, leadership, minority status, music/drama, ROTC, state residency.

Application procedures. Admission: Closing date 8/1 (postmark date). $30 fee, may be waived for applicants with need, free for online applicants. Admission notification on a rolling basis. **Financial aid:** Priority date 2/1; no closing date. FAFSA required. Applicants notified on a rolling basis starting 3/15; must reply within 3 week(s) of notification.

Academics. Special study options: Accelerated study, combined bachelor's/graduate degree, cooperative education, distance learning, double major, dual enrollment of high school students, ESL, exchange student, external degree, honors, independent study, internships, liberal arts/career combination, student-designed major, study abroad, teacher certification program, weekend college. **Credit/placement by examination:** AP, CLEP, SAT, ACT, institutional tests. **Support services:** Learning center, remedial instruction, study skills assistance, tutoring, writing center.

Honors college/program. 3.4 GPA, 24 ACT/1120 SAT (Math & Reading only), essay required. 100-300 freshmen admitted annually, depending on space in Honors dorms.

Majors. Biology: General, biochemistry, biotechnology, environmental. **Business:** Accounting technology, accounting/finance, actuarial science, business admin, construction management, finance, hospitality admin, hospitality/recreation, hotel/motel admin, human resources, insurance, marketing, operations, statistics. **Communications:** Advertising, communications/speech/rhetoric, public relations, sports. **Communications technology:** Animation/special effects, printing management, radio/TV. **Computer sciences:** Information technology, networking, security. **Education:** Art, biology, business, chemistry, elementary, English, health, history, mathematics, social studies, voc/tech. **Engineering:** Surveying, systems. **English:** Rhetoric/composition, technical writing, writing. **Health services:** Clinical lab science, dental hygiene, health care admin, health information management, nuclear medical technology, nursing (RN). **History:** General. **Human services:** Social work. **Math:** Applied. **Parks/recreation:** Facilities management. **Physical sciences:** Chemistry. **Protective services:** Law enforcement admin, police science. **Psychology:** General. **Social sciences:** Political science, sociology. **Visual/performing arts:** Art history/conservation, design, drawing, fashion design, graphic design, illustration, industrial design, interior design, metal/jewelry, music management, painting, photography, printmaking, sculpture, studio arts. **Work/family studies:** Child care management.

Most popular majors. Business/marketing 20%, engineering/engineering technologies 12%, health sciences 20%, security/protective services 15%, visual/performing arts 9%.

Technology on campus. 1,875 workstations in dormitories, library, computer center, student center. Dormitories wired for high-speed internet access and linked to campus network. Commuter students can connect to campus network. Online course registration, online library, helpline, repair service, wireless network available.

Student life. Freshman orientation: Mandatory, $80 fee. Preregistration for classes offered. Held on 16 days in June & July. **Policies:** All students sign ethics statement during orientation. **Housing:** Guaranteed on-campus for all undergraduates. Coed dorms, special housing for disabled, apartments, themed housing, wellness housing available. $200 fully refundable deposit, deadline 6/1. Honors, substance free, first year experience, quiet house, sophomore leadership and graphic design housing available. **Activities:** Bands, campus ministries, choral groups, dance, drama, film society, international student organizations, music ensembles, musical theater, radio station, student government, student newspaper, symphony orchestra, TV station, Standing In the Gap, Circle K, Lutheran Student Fellowship, Colleges Against Cancer, Habitat for Humanity, Stars for Make-A-Wish Foundation, International Student Organization, National Organization for Women, Red Cross student chapter, Young Americans for Liberty, PetSavers, Indian Students Association.

Athletics. NCAA. **Intercollegiate:** Basketball, cross-country, football (tackle) M, golf, ice hockey M, soccer W, softball W, tennis, track and field, volleyball W. **Intramural:** Badminton, basketball, bowling, football (non-tackle), ice hockey, sand volleyball, soccer, softball, table tennis, ultimate frisbee, volleyball, water polo, weight lifting. **Team name:** Bulldogs.

Student services. Adult student services, alcohol/substance abuse counseling, chaplain/spiritual director, career counseling, services for economically disadvantaged, student employment services, financial aid counseling, health services, legal services, minority student services, on-campus daycare, personal counseling, placement for graduates, veterans' counselor. **Physically disabled:** Services for visually, speech, hearing impaired.

Contact. E-mail: admissions@ferris.edu
Phone: (231) 591-2100 Toll-free number: (800) 433-7747
Fax: (231) 591-3944
Charlotte Tetsworth, Associate Director of Admissions, Ferris State University, 1201 South State Street, CSS 201, Big Rapids, MI 49307-2714

Finlandia University
Hancock, Michigan
www.finlandia.edu   **CB code: 1743**

▶ Private 4-year university and liberal arts college affiliated with the Evangelical Lutheran Church in America
▶ Commuter campus in small town
▶ 570 undergraduates

General. Founded in 1896. Regionally accredited. **Degrees:** 69 bachelor's, 30 associate awarded. **ROTC:** Army, Naval, Air Force. **Location:** 100 miles from Marquette, 220 miles from Green Bay, WI. **Calendar:** Semester, limited summer session. **Full-time faculty:** 38 total. **Part-time faculty:** 42 total. **Class size:** 69% < 20, 27% 20-39, 4% 40-49. **Special facilities:** Finnish-American historical archive.

Freshman class profile.

GPA 3.75 or higher:	4%	GPA 2.0-2.99:	59%
GPA 3.50-3.74:	3%	Out-of-state:	19%
GPA 3.0-3.49:	33%	Live on campus:	28%

Basis for selection. Open admission, but selective for some programs. One unit of algebra and chemistry with grade of 3.0 and 2.5 cumulative GPA required for nursing. 1 unit of algebra and biology with grade of 3.0 and 3.0 cumulative GPA required for physical therapist assistant. 2.0 GPA required of all other programs. If GPA below 2.0, special consideration given in determining admission. Student may obtain admission into academic warning program based on placement test results. Nursing applicants should apply by 3/15, physical therapy assistant applicants by 4/15. SAT or ACT recommended. **Home schooled:** Transcript of courses and grades required. Placement tests required. **Learning Disabled:** Evaluation results and/or IEP that specifically states the disability is required for eligibility for accommodations, but not for admission to the university.

High school preparation. College-preparatory program recommended. Recommended units include English 4, mathematics 2, science 2 (laboratory 2).

2015-2016 Annual costs. Tuition/fees: $22,110. Room/board: $7,648. Books/supplies: $1,500. Personal expenses: $100.

Financial aid. Non-need-based: Scholarships awarded for academics, leadership, religious affiliation, state residency. **Additional information:** Work/study program; up to $2,800 per year.

Application procedures. Admission: Closing date 8/15 (postmark date). No application fee. Admission notification on a rolling basis. **Financial aid:** Priority date 3/1; no closing date. FAFSA, institutional form required. Applicants notified on a rolling basis starting 3/1; must reply within 2 week(s) of notification.

Academics. Special study options: Double major, dual enrollment of high school students, ESL, exchange student, honors, independent study, internships, liberal arts/career combination, student-designed major, study abroad, teacher certification program. **Credit/placement by examination:** AP, CLEP, IB, SAT, ACT, institutional tests. 18 credit hours maximum toward associate degree, 30 toward bachelor's. **Support services:** Learning center, remedial instruction, study skills assistance, tutoring, writing center.

Majors. Business: Accounting, business admin, international, marketing. **Education:** Elementary. **English:** English lit. **Health services:** Nursing (RN). **Liberal arts:** Arts/sciences. **Psychology:** General. **Social sciences:** General. **Visual/performing arts:** Art, ceramics, commercial/advertising art, design,

drawing, fashion design, fiber arts, graphic design, illustration, interior design, painting, studio arts.

Most popular majors. Business/marketing 19%, education 8%, health sciences 38%, liberal arts 8%, public administration/social services 8%, visual/performing arts 19%.

Technology on campus. 80 workstations in dormitories, library, computer center. Dormitories wired for high-speed internet access and linked to campus network. Online library, helpline, wireless network available.

Student life. Freshman orientation: Mandatory. Preregistration for classes offered. Three-day program includes testing, workshops, and special speakers. **Housing:** Guaranteed on-campus for all undergraduates. Coed dorms available. **Activities:** Pep band, campus ministries, choral groups, dance, drama, music ensembles, musical theater, student government, student newspaper, servant leadership program, local agency volunteer programs.

Athletics. NCAA. **Intercollegiate:** Baseball M, basketball, cross-country, football (tackle) M, golf, ice hockey, soccer, softball W, tennis, triathlon W, volleyball W, wrestling M. **Intramural:** Bowling, football (non-tackle), softball, swimming, table tennis, volleyball. **Team name:** Lions.

Student services. Alcohol/substance abuse counseling, chaplain/spiritual director, career counseling, services for economically disadvantaged, student employment services, financial aid counseling, personal counseling, placement for graduates, veterans' counselor.

Contact. E-mail: admissions@finlandia.edu
Phone: (906) 487-7274 Toll-free number: (877) 202-5491
Fax: (906) 487-7383
Julie Jennerjohn, Director of Enrollment, Finlandia University, 601 Quincy Street, Hancock, MI 49930-1882

Grace Bible College
Grand Rapids, Michigan
www.gbcol.edu   **CB code: 0809**

▶ Private 4-year Bible and liberal arts college affiliated with the Christian Church
▶ Residential campus in small city
▶ 303 degree-seeking undergraduates: 5% part-time, 50% women, 4% African American, 1% Asian American, 3% Hispanic/Latino, 1% Native American, 5% Multi-racial, non-Hispanic, 1% international
▶ 73% of applicants admitted
▶ SAT or ACT (ACT writing optional) required
▶ 61% graduate within 6 years

General. Founded in 1945. Regionally accredited; also accredited by ABHE. **Degrees:** 48 bachelor's, 10 associate awarded. **ROTC:** Army. **Location:** 50 miles from Kalamazoo. **Calendar:** Semester, limited summer session. **Full-time faculty:** 12 total; 58% have terminal degrees, 42% women. **Part-time faculty:** 24 total; 4% have terminal degrees, 17% minority, 42% women. **Class size:** 77% < 20, 20% 20-39, 1% 40-49, 1% 50-99.

Freshman class profile. 251 applied, 184 admitted, 89 enrolled.

Mid 50% test scores		GPA 2.0-2.99:	42%
SAT critical reading:	450-550	Rank in top quarter:	30%
SAT math:	410-550	Rank in top tenth:	4%
SAT writing:	420-570	End year in good standing:	75%
ACT composite:	18-23	Return as sophomores:	59%
GPA 3.75 or higher:	19%	Out-of-state:	9%
GPA 3.50-3.74:	17%	Live on campus:	66%
GPA 3.0-3.49:	22%		

Basis for selection. Evidence of personal salvation through Jesus Christ important. 2.5 GPA, 20 ACT, and rank in top half of class for regular admission. Probationary admission for those in third quarter of class. Interview may be recommended. **Learning Disabled:** Students may request academic accommodations with the assistant registrar who will co-ordinate their needs with faculty and the staff of the Academic Center for Excellence.

High school preparation. Recommended units include English 4, mathematics 3, social studies 3, science 3 and foreign language 1.

2015-2016 Annual costs. Tuition/fees: $17,850. Room/board: $7,400. Books/supplies: $600. Personal expenses: $1,150.

2014-2015 Financial aid. Need-based: 68 full-time freshmen applied for aid; 60 deemed to have need; 60 received aid. Average need met was 53%. Average scholarship/grant was $11,870; average loan $3,231. 71% of total undergraduate aid awarded as scholarships/grants, 29% as loans/jobs. **Non-need-based:** Awarded to 271 full-time undergraduates, including 72 freshmen. Scholarships awarded for academics, music/drama, religious affiliation.

Application procedures. Admission: Closing date 6/1 (receipt date). No application fee. Admission notification on a rolling basis. Must reply by May 1 or within 4 week(s) if notified thereafter. **Financial aid:** Priority date 3/1; no closing date. FAFSA required. Applicants notified on a rolling basis starting 5/15; must reply within 2 week(s) of notification.

Academics. All students major in Bible and theology in addition to degree major. **Special study options:** Combined bachelor's/graduate degree, cross-registration, double major, dual enrollment of high school students, independent study, internships, liberal arts/career combination. **Credit/placement by examination:** AP, CLEP, institutional tests. **Support services:** Reduced course load, remedial instruction, tutoring.

Majors. Business: General, accounting, business admin, finance, human resources, international, marketing. **Computer sciences:** General, information technology. **Education:** Early childhood, elementary, secondary. **Liberal arts:** Arts/sciences. **Theology:** Bible, missionary, pastoral counseling, religious ed, sacred music, theology, youth ministry.

Most popular majors. Business/marketing 8%, education 8%, interdisciplinary studies 6%, public administration/social services 21%, theological studies 34%, visual/performing arts 23%.

Technology on campus. 25 workstations in library, computer center. Dormitories wired for high-speed internet access and linked to campus network. Helpline, wireless network available.

Student life. Freshman orientation: Mandatory. Preregistration for classes offered. Five-day session held prior to start of fall classes. **Policies:** Religious observance required. **Housing:** Guaranteed on-campus for freshmen. Single-sex dorms, apartments, wellness housing available. $100 deposit, deadline 5/1. **Activities:** Jazz band, campus ministries, choral groups, drama, music ensembles, student government.

Athletics. NCCAA. **Intercollegiate:** Basketball, cross-country, soccer, volleyball W. **Intramural:** Basketball M, racquetball, soccer, volleyball. **Team name:** Tigers.

Student services. Chaplain/spiritual director, career counseling, student employment services, financial aid counseling, health services, personal counseling, placement for graduates.

Contact. E-mail: gbc@gbcol.edu
Phone: (616) 538-2330 Toll-free number: (800) 968-1887
Fax: (616) 538-0599
Kevin Gilliam, Enrollment Director, Grace Bible College, 1011 Aldon Street SW, PO Box 910, Grand Rapids, MI 49509

Grand Valley State University
Allendale, Michigan
www.gvsu.edu

CB member
CB code: 1258

- Public 4-year university
- Residential campus in large town
- 21,889 degree-seeking undergraduates: 11% part-time, 59% women, 5% African American, 2% Asian American, 5% Hispanic/Latino, 3% Multiracial, non-Hispanic, 1% international
- 3,146 degree-seeking graduate students
- 81% of applicants admitted
- SAT or ACT (ACT writing recommended) required
- 65% graduate within 6 years

General. Founded in 1960. Regionally accredited. **Degrees:** 4,328 bachelor's awarded; master's, professional offered. **Location:** 12 miles from Grand Rapids. **Calendar:** Semester, extensive summer session. **Full-time faculty:** 1,137 total; 76% have terminal degrees, 16% minority, 50% women. **Part-time faculty:** 612 total; 9% have terminal degrees, 7% minority, 56% women. **Class size:** 24% < 20, 57% 20-39, 13% 40-49, 5% 50-99, 1% >100. **Special facilities:** Cross-country fitness trail, recital hall, two Great Lakes research vessels, water resources research institute, center for presidential studies.

Freshman class profile. 16,987 applied, 13,784 admitted, 4,117 enrolled.

Mid 50% test scores			
		Rank in top quarter:	46%
ACT composite:	21-26	**Rank in top tenth:**	17%
GPA 3.75 or higher:	33%	**Return as sophomores:**	84%
GPA 3.50-3.74:	23%	**Out-of-state:**	8%
GPA 3.0-3.49:	38%	**Live on campus:**	88%
GPA 2.0-2.99:	6%	**International:**	1%

Basis for selection. Secondary school grades, courses, personal and academic data, ACT/SAT.

High school preparation. College-preparatory program recommended. Required units include English 4, mathematics 3, social studies 3, science 3 (laboratory 2) and foreign language 2.

2015-2016 Annual costs. Tuition/fees: $11,078; $15,744 out-of-state. Room/board: $8,360.

2015-2016 Financial aid. Need-based: 3,653 full-time freshmen applied for aid; 2,462 deemed to have need; 2,439 received aid. Average need met was 69%. Average scholarship/grant was $7,599; average loan $3,715. 55% of total undergraduate aid awarded as scholarships/grants, 45% as loans/jobs. **Non-need-based:** Awarded to 3,690 full-time undergraduates, including 937 freshmen. Scholarships awarded for academics, alumni affiliation, art, athletics, music/drama, state residency.

Application procedures. Admission: Closing date 5/1. $30 fee, may be waived for applicants with need. Admission notification on a rolling basis. Must reply by 5/1. Application closing date December 31 for scholarships. **Financial aid:** Priority date 3/1; no closing date. FAFSA required. Applicants notified on a rolling basis starting 3/3; must reply by 5/1 or within 4 week(s) of notification.

Academics. Special study options: Combined bachelor's/graduate degree, distance learning, double major, dual enrollment of high school students, ESL, honors, independent study, internships, student-designed major, study abroad, teacher certification program, Washington semester. Undergraduates may take graduate level classes as seniors; co-op programs in education, engineering, health professions. **Credit/placement by examination:** AP, CLEP, IB, SAT, ACT, institutional tests. 32 credit hours maximum toward bachelor's degree. **Support services:** Learning center, pre-admission summer program, remedial instruction, study skills assistance, tutoring, writing center.

Honors college/program. 3.5 GPA and 28 ACT required.

Majors. Architecture: Urban/community planning. **Area/ethnic studies:** Chinese, Russian/Slavic, women's. **Biology:** General, biochemistry, cellular/molecular, neuroscience. **Business:** Accounting, business admin, finance, human resources, international, logistics, management science, managerial economics, marketing, operations, tourism promotion, tourism/travel. **Communications:** Advertising, broadcast journalism, communications/speech/rhetoric, digital media, journalism, public relations, radio/TV. **Computer sciences:** General, computer science, information systems, programming. **Conservation:** Management/policy. **Education:** Art, music, physical, science, special ed. **Engineering:** General, computer, electrical, manufacturing, mechanical. **English:** Creative writing, English lit, technical writing, writing. **Foreign languages:** Ancient Greek, classics, French, German, Latin, Spanish. **Health services:** Athletic training, clinical lab science, medical radiologic technology/radiation therapy, nursing (RN), occupational health, predental, premedicine, prepharmacy, preveterinary, recreational therapy, sonography. **History:** General. **Human services:** General, social work. **Liberal arts:** Arts/sciences. **Math:** General, statistics. **Parks/recreation:** General, health/fitness. **Philosophy/religion:** Philosophy, religion. **Physical sciences:** Chemistry, geochemistry, geology, physics. **Protective services:** Law enforcement admin, security services. **Psychology:** General, social. **Social sciences:** General, anthropology, economics, geography, international relations, political science, sociology. **Visual/performing arts:** Art, art history/conservation, ceramics, commercial/advertising art, dance, dramatic, film/cinema/video, metal/jewelry, music, painting, photography, printmaking, sculpture, studio arts.

Most popular majors. Business/marketing 19%, communications/journalism 7%, education 8%, health sciences 18%, psychology 7%.

Technology on campus. 1,270 workstations in dormitories, library, computer center, student center. Dormitories wired for high-speed internet access and linked to campus network. Commuter students can connect to campus network. Online course registration, helpline, repair service, student web hosting, wireless network available.

Student life. Freshman orientation: Mandatory, $75 fee. Preregistration for classes offered. One-day program held for small groups on 50 possible dates from May-August. Students register for classes for full year. **Housing:** Guaranteed on-campus for freshmen. Coed dorms, apartments, fraternity/sorority housing, themed housing available. $150 fully refundable deposit, deadline 3/1. **Activities:** Bands, campus ministries, choral groups, dance, drama, international student organizations, literary magazine, music ensembles, Model UN, musical theater, radio station, student government, student newspaper, symphony orchestra, TV station, 143 registered organizations.

Athletics. NCAA. **Intercollegiate:** Baseball M, basketball, cheerleading, cross-country, diving, football (tackle) M, golf, soccer W, softball W, swimming, tennis, track and field, volleyball W. **Intramural:** Archery, badminton, basketball, bowling, cross-country, diving, fencing, field hockey, football (tackle) M, golf, gymnastics, racquetball, rowing (crew), skiing, skin diving, soccer, softball, squash, swimming, table tennis, tennis, volleyball, wrestling M. **Team name:** Lakers.

Student services. Adult student services, alcohol/substance abuse counseling, chaplain/spiritual director, career counseling, services for economically disadvantaged, student employment services, financial aid counseling, health services, minority student services, on-campus daycare, personal counseling, placement for graduates, women's services. **Physically disabled:** Services for visually, speech, hearing impaired.

Contact. E-mail: admissions@gvsu.edu
Phone: (616) 331-0246 Toll-free number: (800) 748-0246
Fax: (616) 331-2000
Jodi Chycinski, Director of Admissions, Grand Valley State University, 1 Campus Drive, Allendale, MI 49401-9403

Great Lakes Christian College
Lansing, Michigan
www.glcc.edu   CB code: 7320

- Private 4-year Bible college affiliated with the Christian Church
- Residential campus in small city
- 174 degree-seeking undergraduates
- SAT or ACT (ACT writing optional) required

General. Founded in 1949. Accredited by ABHE. **Degrees:** 17 bachelor's, 1 associate awarded. **Location:** 90 miles from Detroit, 65 miles from Grand Rapids. **Calendar:** Semester, limited summer session. **Full-time faculty:** 11 total. **Part-time faculty:** 17 total.

Basis for selection. Recommendations of character from applicant's minister and church leaders required. Students with GPA below 2.25 or ACT below 16 or SAT below 820 (exclusive of Writing) admitted on probation. **Home schooled:** Transcript of courses and grades, letter of recommendation (nonparent) required.

2015-2016 Annual costs. Tuition/fees: $14,540. Room/board: $8,500. Books/supplies: $1,000. Personal expenses: $722.

2015-2016 Financial aid. Need-based: 65% of total undergraduate aid awarded as scholarships/grants, 35% as loans/jobs. **Non-need-based:** Scholarships awarded for academics, alumni affiliation, music/drama.

Application procedures. Admission: Closing date 3/1 (receipt date). $30 fee, may be waived for applicants with need. Admission notification on a rolling basis. **Financial aid:** Closing date 8/1. FAFSA, institutional form required. Applicants notified on a rolling basis starting 5/1; must reply within 3 week(s) of notification.

Academics. Special study options: Combined bachelor's/graduate degree, cooperative education, double major, dual enrollment of high school students, internships. **Credit/placement by examination:** AP, CLEP. **Support services:** Remedial instruction, study skills assistance, tutoring.

Majors. History: General. **Theology:** Bible, religious ed, sacred music.

Technology on campus. 23 workstations in library, computer center, student center. Dormitories wired for high-speed internet access and linked to campus network. Commuter students can connect to campus network. Online library, helpline, repair service, wireless network available.

Student life. Freshman orientation: Mandatory. Preregistration for classes offered. **Policies:** Regular Christian service participation required of all graduates. Religious observance required. **Housing:** Single-sex dorms, apartments, wellness housing available. $200 fully refundable deposit, deadline 6/1. **Activities:** Campus ministries, choral groups, drama, music ensembles, musical theater, student government, student newspaper.

Athletics. NCCAA. **Intercollegiate:** Basketball M, soccer M. **Intramural:** Volleyball M. **Team name:** Crusaders.

Student services. Chaplain/spiritual director, financial aid counseling, personal counseling. **Physically disabled:** Services for visually, hearing impaired.

Contact. E-mail: admissions@glcc.edu
Phone: (517) 321-0242 ext. 221 Toll-free number: (800) 937-4522
Fax: (517) 321-5902
Lloyd Scharer, Vice President of Enrollment Management, Great Lakes Christian College, 6211 West Willow Highway, Lansing, MI 48917-1231

Hillsdale College
Hillsdale, Michigan   CB member
www.hillsdale.edu   CB code: 1295

- Private 4-year liberal arts college affiliated with the Christian Church
- Residential campus in small town
- 1,485 degree-seeking undergraduates: 2% part-time, 51% women
- 36 degree-seeking graduate students
- 50% of applicants admitted
- SAT or ACT (ACT writing optional), application essay required
- 77% graduate within 6 years

General. Founded in 1844. Regionally accredited. **Degrees:** 316 bachelor's awarded; master's, doctoral offered. **Location:** 120 miles from Detroit, 75 miles from Ann Arbor. **Calendar:** Semester, limited summer session. **Full-time faculty:** 135 total; 88% have terminal degrees, 24% women. **Part-time faculty:** 49 total; 51% have terminal degrees, 33% women. **Class size:** 73% < 20, 26% 20-39, less than 1% 40-49, less than 1% 50-99. **Special facilities:** Greenhouse, center for the arts, music hall, media center, K-8 private academy, arboretum, rare books library, shooting range, science center, preschool.

Freshman class profile. 1,859 applied, 930 admitted, 370 enrolled.

Mid 50% test scores		GPA 3.0-3.49:	11%
SAT critical reading:	620-750	GPA 2.0-2.99:	1%
SAT math:	580-660	Rank in top quarter:	82%
SAT writing:	610-730	Rank in top tenth:	50%
ACT composite:	27-31	Return as sophomores:	96%
GPA 3.75 or higher:	71%	Out-of-state:	66%
GPA 3.50-3.74:	17%	Live on campus:	99%

Basis for selection. 3.5 GPA, class rank in top quarter preferred. Test scores, recommendations, interview, personal essay important. SAT Subject Tests recommended. Portfolio recommended for art majors. Audition required for music scholarship applicants. **Home schooled:** Transcript of courses and grades required.

High school preparation. College-preparatory program recommended. 15 units required; 20 recommended. Required and recommended units include English 4, mathematics 3-4, social studies 2-4, history 3-4, science 3-4 (laboratory 2) and foreign language 3.

2015-2016 Annual costs. Tuition/fees: $24,592. Room/board: $9,760. Books/supplies: $1,200. Personal expenses: $1,000.

2014-2015 Financial aid. Need-based: 245 full-time freshmen applied for aid; 187 deemed to have need; 179 received aid. Average need met was 60%. Average scholarship/grant was $7,554; average loan $6,130. 64% of total undergraduate aid awarded as scholarships/grants, 36% as loans/jobs. **Non-need-based:** Awarded to 1,516 full-time undergraduates, including 381 freshmen. Scholarships awarded for academics, alumni affiliation, art, athletics, leadership, music/drama. **Additional information:** Campus employment available to all students.

Application procedures. Admission: Priority date 1/1; deadline 4/1 (postmark date). $35 fee. Admission notification on a rolling basis beginning on or about 12/15. Must reply by May 1 or within 3 week(s) if notified thereafter. **Financial aid:** Priority date 5/1; no closing date. Institutional form required. CSS PROFILE required for returning students only. Applicants notified on a rolling basis starting 12/1; must reply by 5/1 or within 4 week(s) of notification.

Academics. Highly qualified students may study at Oxford University, England for semester or summer. Summer business program at Regents College, London, England as well as study abroad programs in France, Germany and Spain. **Special study options:** Double major, dual enrollment of high school students, honors, independent study, internships, student-designed major, study abroad, Washington semester. **Credit/placement by examination:** AP, CLEP, IB, SAT, ACT, institutional tests. **Support services:** Reduced course load, study skills assistance, tutoring, writing center.

Majors. Area/ethnic studies: American, European. **Biology:** General, biochemistry. **Business:** Accounting, finance, international, marketing. **Communications:** Communications/speech/rhetoric. **English:** English lit. **Foreign languages:** Ancient Greek, classics, comparative lit, French, German, Latin, Spanish. **History:** General. **Math:** General, applied. **Parks/recreation:** Exercise sciences, health/fitness, sports admin, sports studies. **Philosophy/religion:** General, Christian, philosophy, religion. **Physical sciences:** Chemistry, physics. **Psychology:** General. **Social sciences:** Economics, political economy, political science, sociology. **Visual/performing arts:** Art, dramatic, music.

Most popular majors. Biology 9%, business/marketing 17%, English 11%, foreign language 9%, history 12%, social sciences 21%.

Technology on campus. 220 workstations in dormitories, library, computer center, student center. Dormitories wired for high-speed internet access and linked to campus network. Commuter students can connect to campus network. Online library, helpline, repair service, wireless network available.

Student life. Freshman orientation: Mandatory. Preregistration for classes offered. **Policies:** Honor Code signature required of all students each year. **Housing:** Guaranteed on-campus for all undergraduates. Single-sex dorms, cooperative housing, fraternity/sorority housing available. $300 nonrefundable deposit, deadline 5/1. **Activities:** Bands, campus ministries, choral groups, dance, drama, film society, international student organizations, literary magazine, music ensembles, musical theater, opera, radio station, student government, student newspaper, symphony orchestra, Catholic student council, Varsity H-Club, student federation, Students in Free Enterprise, Intervarsity Christian Fellowship, Fellowship of Christian Athletes, College Republicans, Young Life, Praxis, Charis.

Athletics. NCAA. **Intercollegiate:** Baseball M, basketball, cross-country, football (tackle) M, golf M, softball W, swimming W, tennis, track and field, volleyball W. **Intramural:** Basketball, football (tackle), sand volleyball, soccer, table tennis, volleyball. **Team name:** Chargers.

Student services. Chaplain/spiritual director, career counseling, student employment services, financial aid counseling, health services, personal counseling, placement for graduates, veterans' counselor. **Physically disabled:** Services for visually impaired.

Contact. E-mail: admissions@hillsdale.edu
Phone: (517) 607-2327 Fax: (517) 607-2223
Doug Banbury, Associate Vice President for Admissions, Hillsdale College, 33 East College Street, Hillsdale, MI 49242

Hope College
Holland, Michigan
www.hope.edu
CB member
CB code: 1301

- Private 4-year liberal arts college affiliated with the Reformed Church in America
- Residential campus in small city
- 3,238 degree-seeking undergraduates: 2% part-time, 60% women, 3% African American, 2% Asian American, 8% Hispanic/Latino, 2% Multiracial, non-Hispanic, 1% international
- 67% of applicants admitted
- SAT or ACT (ACT writing optional), application essay required
- 76% graduate within 6 years; 24% enter graduate study

General. Founded in 1862. Regionally accredited. **Degrees:** 736 bachelor's awarded. **ROTC:** Army. **Location:** 30 miles from Grand Rapids, 160 miles from Chicago. **Calendar:** Semester, limited summer session. **Full-time faculty:** 243 total; 81% have terminal degrees, 16% minority, 47% women. **Part-time faculty:** 145 total; 14% minority, 45% women. **Class size:** 54% < 20, 40% 20-39, 4% 40-49, 2% 50-99. **Special facilities:** Museum, Pelletron particle accelerator, biological field station, electron microscopes, laser research, cadaver lab.

Freshman class profile. 4,761 applied, 3,183 admitted, 771 enrolled.

Mid 50% test scores		GPA 2.0-2.99:	3%
SAT critical reading:	540-650	Rank in top quarter:	65%
SAT math:	550-670	Rank in top tenth:	34%
ACT composite:	24-29	Return as sophomores:	86%
GPA 3.75 or higher:	62%	Out-of-state:	32%
GPA 3.50-3.74:	18%	Live on campus:	100%
GPA 3.0-3.49:	17%		

Basis for selection. Strength of curriculum, performance in college prep courses, trends in performance, standardized test scores, and perceived ability to success are each important. Secondary factors include letters or recommendation and demonstrated interest. Interviews recommended. Auditions for Fine & Performing Arts are not required for admission, but are recommended and may play a significant role in the admissions decision for a student who is otherwise Waitlisted. **Home schooled:** Transcript of courses and grades, letter of recommendation (nonparent) required. School Report from Common Application. **Learning Disabled:** Students should consult the director of the academic success program to ensure available resources and personnel to accommodate the disability.

High school preparation. College-preparatory program recommended. 18 units recommended. Recommended units include English 4, mathematics 3, social studies 3, science 3 (laboratory 3), foreign language 2 and academic electives 3.

2015-2016 Annual costs. Tuition/fees: $30,550. Room/board: $9,390.

2015-2016 Financial aid. Need-based: Average need met was 80%. Average scholarship/grant was $19,996; average loan $4,039. 76% of total undergraduate aid awarded as scholarships/grants, 24% as loans/jobs. **Non-need-based:** Awarded to 2,244 full-time undergraduates, including 216 freshmen. Scholarships awarded for academics, art, minority status, music/drama, religious affiliation.

Application procedures. Admission: No deadline. $50 fee, may be waived for applicants with need. Application must be submitted online. Admission notification on a rolling basis beginning on or about 12/3. Must reply by May 1 or within 2 week(s) if notified thereafter. **Financial aid:** Priority date 3/1; no closing date. FAFSA, institutional form required. Applicants notified on a rolling basis starting 3/15.

Academics. Extensive undergraduate scientific research opportunities available. All fine arts divisions nationally accredited. **Special study options:** Double major, dual enrollment of high school students, exchange student, independent study, internships, New York semester, student-designed major, study abroad, teacher certification program, urban semester, Washington semester. **Credit/placement by examination:** AP, CLEP, IB, institutional tests. 32 credit hours maximum toward bachelor's degree. **Support services:** Reduced course load, study skills assistance, tutoring, writing center.

Majors. Area/ethnic studies: Japanese, women's. **Biology:** General. **Business:** Accounting, business admin, managerial economics. **Communications:** Communications/speech/rhetoric, journalism. **Computer sciences:** General. **Conservation:** Environmental science. **Education:** Art, biology, chemistry, drama/dance, emotionally handicapped, English, French, German, history, learning disabled, mathematics, music, physical, physics, science, social studies, Spanish. **Engineering:** General. **English:** English lit. **Foreign languages:** Classics, French, German, Spanish. **Health services:** Athletic training, nursing (RN). **History:** General. **Human services:** Social work. **Math:** General. **Parks/recreation:** Exercise sciences. **Philosophy/religion:** Philosophy, religion. **Physical sciences:** Chemistry, geology, physics. **Psychology:** General. **Social sciences:** Economics, political science, sociology. **Visual/performing arts:** Art history/conservation, dance, dramatic, jazz, music, music performance, music theory/composition, piano/keyboard, stringed instruments, studio arts, voice/opera.

Most popular majors. Biology 8%, business/marketing 12%, communications/journalism 7%, education 12%, psychology 9%, social sciences 7%.

Technology on campus. 350 workstations in dormitories, library, computer center, student center. Dormitories wired for high-speed internet access and linked to campus network. Commuter students can connect to campus network. Online library, helpline, repair service, student web hosting, wireless network available.

Student life. Freshman orientation: Mandatory. Preregistration for classes offered. Three-day orientation for students and parents begins Friday before school starts. **Policies:** Visitors of opposite gender not allowed after midnight on weekdays and 2 a.m. on weekends. No alcohol allowed on campus. **Housing:** Guaranteed on-campus for all undergraduates. Coed dorms, single-sex dorms, special housing for disabled, apartments, fraternity/sorority housing, themed housing, wellness housing available. $300 nonrefundable deposit, deadline 5/1. Cottages (houses on or near campus) available. **Activities:** Bands, campus ministries, choral groups, dance, drama, international student organizations, literary magazine, music ensembles, Model UN, radio station, student government, student newspaper, symphony orchestra, TV station, Fellowship of Christian Athletes, Inter-Varsity Christian Fellowship, Hope United for Justice, College Republicans, College Democrats, Hope's Asian Perspective Association, Black Student Union, La Raza Unida, Catholic Student Union, Engineers without Borders.

Athletics. NCAA. **Intercollegiate:** Baseball M, basketball, cheerleading, cross-country, diving, football (tackle) M, golf, lacrosse, soccer, softball W, swimming, tennis, track and field, volleyball W. **Intramural:** Badminton, basketball, football (non-tackle), racquetball, soccer, softball, tennis, ultimate frisbee, volleyball, water polo. **Team name:** Flying Dutchmen, Flying Dutch.

Student services. Adult student services, alcohol/substance abuse counseling, chaplain/spiritual director, career counseling, student employment services, financial aid counseling, health services, minority student services, personal counseling, placement for graduates, women's services. **Physically disabled:** Services for visually, speech, hearing impaired.

Contact. E-mail: admissions@hope.edu
Phone: (616) 395-7850 Toll-free number: (800) 968-7850
Fax: (616) 395-7130
William Vanderbilt, Vice President for Admissions, Hope College, 69 East 10th Street, Holland, MI 49422-9000

International Academy of Design and Technology: Detroit
Troy, Michigan
www.iadt.edu

- For-profit 4-year visual arts and technical college
- Commuter campus in small city
- 134 undergraduates

General. Accredited by ACICS. **Degrees:** 88 bachelor's, 9 associate awarded. **Calendar:** Semester. **Full-time faculty:** 5 total. **Part-time faculty:** 57 total.

Basis for selection. Open admission.

2015-2016 Annual costs. Books/supplies: $1,500. **Additional information:** Associate programs: $32,800. Bachelor's programs: $64,800.

Application procedures. Admission: No deadline. $50 fee. Admission notification on a rolling basis. **Financial aid:** No deadline.

Academics. Special study options: Distance learning. **Credit/placement by examination:** AP, CLEP.

Majors. Communications technology: Desktop publishing, graphics. **Visual/performing arts:** Fashion design, game design, graphic design, interior design.

Contact. Phone: (248) 457-2700
Roslyn White, Director of Admissions, International Academy of Design and Technology: Detroit, 1850 Research Drive, Troy, MI 48083

Kalamazoo College
Kalamazoo, Michigan   **CB member**
www.kzoo.edu   **CB code: 1365**

- Private 4-year liberal arts college
- Residential campus in small city
- 1,415 degree-seeking undergraduates: 1% part-time, 56% women, 6% African American, 7% Asian American, 10% Hispanic/Latino, 5% Multiracial, non-Hispanic, 7% international
- 72% of applicants admitted
- Application essay required
- 83% graduate within 6 years

General. Founded in 1833. Regionally accredited. Study abroad centers in Kenya, Senegal, Egypt, India, Thailand, Chile, Japan, Australia, UK, Ecuador, Spain, France, Germany, Mexico, Costa Rica, and China. **Degrees:** 348 bachelor's awarded. **ROTC:** Army. **Location:** 140 miles from Detroit, 140 miles from Chicago. **Calendar:** Quarter. **Full-time faculty:** 103 total; 91% have terminal degrees, 27% minority, 52% women. **Part-time faculty:** 23 total; 56% have terminal degrees, 22% minority, 70% women. **Class size:** 61% < 20, 37% 20-39, 2% 40-49, 1% 50-99. **Special facilities:** 3 theaters, rare books collection, science center, 100 acre arboretum.

Freshman class profile. 2,455 applied, 1,759 admitted, 365 enrolled.

Mid 50% test scores			
SAT critical reading:	530-660	Rank in top quarter:	79%
SAT math:	540-690	Rank in top tenth:	40%
SAT writing:	510-650	Return as sophomores:	92%
ACT composite:	26-30	Out-of-state:	34%
GPA 3.75 or higher:	60%	Live on campus:	100%
GPA 3.50-3.74:	20%	International:	7%
GPA 3.0-3.49:	19%		
GPA 2.0-2.99:	1%		

Basis for selection. Curriculum, grades, essay, recommendations, and special accomplishments influence decision. Interview recommended. **Home schooled:** Statement describing home school structure and mission, transcript of courses and grades, interview, letter of recommendation (nonparent) required.

High school preparation. College-preparatory program required. 17 units required; 20 recommended. Required and recommended units include English 4, mathematics 3-4, social studies 2, history 2, science 3-4 and foreign language 3-4.

2015-2016 Annual costs. Tuition/fees: $42,946. Room/board: $8,886. **Additional information:** $1,104 for health insurance if the student has no health insurance.

2015-2016 Financial aid. Need-based: 304 full-time freshmen applied for aid; 240 deemed to have need; 240 received aid. Average need met was 94%. Average scholarship/grant was $29,445; average loan $4,956. 80% of total undergraduate aid awarded as scholarships/grants, 20% as loans/jobs. **Non-need-based:** Awarded to 602 full-time undergraduates, including 185 freshmen. Scholarships awarded for academics, alumni affiliation, art, leadership, music/drama. **Additional information:** Paid career development internship and senior project experiences available on campus.

Application procedures. Admission: Priority date 11/15; deadline 2/15 (postmark date). No application fee. Application must be submitted online. Admission notification by 4/1. Admission notification on a rolling basis beginning on or about 12/1. Must reply by 5/1. **Financial aid:** Priority date 2/15; no closing date. FAFSA required. Applicants notified by 3/23; must reply by 5/1.

Academics. Most students participate in career internships and study abroad. College subsidizes most study abroad expenses. Students complete a senior individualized project as part of graduation requirements. **Special study options:** Accelerated study, combined bachelor's/graduate degree, cross-registration, double major, dual enrollment of high school students, ESL, exchange student, independent study, internships, New York semester, student-designed major, study abroad, urban semester. **Credit/placement by examination:** AP, CLEP, IB, institutional tests. 18 credit hours maximum toward bachelor's degree. **Support services:** Learning center, reduced course load, study skills assistance, tutoring, writing center.

Majors. Area/ethnic studies: Women's. **Biology:** General. **Business:** General. **Computer sciences:** General. **English:** Creative writing, English lit. **Foreign languages:** Classics, French, German, Spanish. **Health services:** Predental, premedicine, preveterinary. **History:** General. **Math:** General. **Philosophy/religion:** Philosophy, religion. **Physical sciences:** Chemistry, physics. **Psychology:** General. **Social sciences:** Anthropology, economics, political science, sociology. **Visual/performing arts:** Art, art history/conservation, dramatic, music.

Most popular majors. Biology 13%, business/marketing 11%, English 7%, foreign language 6%, physical sciences 8%, psychology 12%, social sciences 19%, visual/performing arts 6%.

Technology on campus. 250 workstations in library, computer center, student center. Dormitories wired for high-speed internet access and linked to campus network. Commuter students can connect to campus network. Online course registration, online library, helpline, student web hosting, wireless network available.

Student life. Freshman orientation: Mandatory. Preregistration for classes offered. Held on campus the week before fall classes begin. **Policies:** Freshmen not permitted cars on campus. **Housing:** Guaranteed on-campus for all undergraduates. Coed dorms, themed housing, wellness housing available. **Activities:** Bands, campus ministries, choral groups, dance, drama, international student organizations, literary magazine, music ensembles, Model UN, musical theater, radio station, student government, student newspaper, symphony orchestra, TV station, black student organization, Latino student organization, Caribbean Society, Young Persian Society, Jewish student organization, Christian student organization, College Democrats, College Republicans, K College for UNICEF, Habitat for Humanity.

Athletics. NCAA. **Intercollegiate:** Baseball M, basketball, cross-country, diving, football (tackle) M, golf, lacrosse W, soccer, softball W, swimming, tennis, volleyball W. **Intramural:** Basketball, racquetball, skiing, soccer, softball, squash, table tennis, tennis, volleyball. **Team name:** Hornets.

Student services. Alcohol/substance abuse counseling, chaplain/spiritual director, career counseling, student employment services, financial aid counseling, health services, minority student services, personal counseling, placement for graduates, women's services. **Physically disabled:** Services for visually, speech, hearing impaired.

Contact. E-mail: admission@kzoo.edu
Phone: (269) 337-7166 Toll-free number: (800) 253-3602
Fax: (269) 337-7390
Eric Staab, Dean of Admission & Financial Aid, Kalamazoo College, 1200 Academy Street, Kalamazoo, MI 49006

Kettering University
Flint, Michigan   **CB member**
www.kettering.edu   **CB code: 1246**

- Private 4-year university and engineering college
- Residential campus in small city
- 1,802 degree-seeking undergraduates: 3% part-time, 19% women, 4% African American, 4% Asian American, 4% Hispanic/Latino, 3% Multiracial, non-Hispanic, 5% international

- 391 degree-seeking graduate students
- 70% of applicants admitted
- SAT or ACT (ACT writing optional) required
- 54% graduate within 6 years

General. Founded in 1919. Regionally accredited. Formerly GMI Engineering and Management Institute. **Degrees:** 283 bachelor's awarded; master's offered. **Location:** 70 miles from Detroit. **Calendar:** Semester, extensive summer session. **Full-time faculty:** 120 total; 86% have terminal degrees, 23% minority, 28% women. **Part-time faculty:** 16 total; 6% minority, 44% women. **Class size:** 58% < 20, 35% 20-39, 5% 40-49, 2% 50-99. **Special facilities:** Computer-integrated manufacturing laboratory, GM-PACE e-design and e-manufacturing studio, acoustics laboratory, polymer optimization center, engine test center, SAE vehicle development laboratory, mechatronics laboratory, biomedical laboratories on campus and at nearby medical center, Ford design simulation studio, crash study lab, fuel cell research center.

Freshman class profile. 2,478 applied, 1,737 admitted, 434 enrolled.

Mid 50% test scores			
SAT critical reading:	520-630	GPA 2.0-2.99:	1%
SAT math:	580-670	Rank in top quarter:	65%
ACT composite:	24-29	Rank in top tenth:	32%
GPA 3.75 or higher:	45%	Out-of-state:	14%
GPA 3.50-3.74:	27%	Live on campus:	100%
GPA 3.0-3.49:	27%	International:	4%

Basis for selection. Strength of preparation, performance in school, test scores, nonscholastic activities and achievements most important. Accepted students encouraged to confirm enrollment plans early so co-op employment search process can begin. SAT Subject Tests (especially math level II, chemistry, and physics), while not required, are helpful when presented. Interview recommended. **Home schooled:** Laboratory science experience very important and may need to be documented.

High school preparation. College-preparatory program required. 10.5 units required; 21 recommended. Required and recommended units include English 3-4, mathematics 3.5-4, social studies 2, history 2, science 2-3 (laboratory 2-3), foreign language 2 and academic electives 1. At least 1 unit of either chemistry or physics with laboratory required. Both chemistry and physics strongly recommended. Algebra I and II, geometry and trigonometry required. Drafting or CAD recommended, especially for those considering engineering.

2015-2016 Annual costs. Tuition/fees: $38,430. Room/board: $7,510. Books/supplies: $1,200. Personal expenses: $2,955.

2015-2016 Financial aid. **Need-based:** 421 full-time freshmen applied for aid; 339 deemed to have need; 339 received aid. Average need met was 62%. Average scholarship/grant was $18,296; average loan $3,387. 78% of total undergraduate aid awarded as scholarships/grants, 22% as loans/jobs. **Non-need-based:** Awarded to 563 full-time undergraduates, including 130 freshmen. Scholarships awarded for academics.

Application procedures. **Admission:** No deadline. No application fee. Admission notification on a rolling basis beginning on or about 12/15. Must reply by May 1 or within 3 week(s) if notified thereafter. Enrollment may be postponed 1 year after admission. **Financial aid:** No deadline. FAFSA required. Applicants notified on a rolling basis starting 3/1.

Academics. **Special study options:** Accelerated study, combined bachelor's/graduate degree, cooperative education, distance learning, double major, dual enrollment of high school students, exchange student, external degree, independent study, study abroad. Paid professional co-op experience in industry required of all undergraduates. Co-op typically begins in first year. Each 24-week semester divided into 11 weeks of classes and 12 weeks of co-op. **Credit/placement by examination:** AP, CLEP, IB, institutional tests. **Support services:** Learning center, study skills assistance, tutoring.

Majors. **Biology:** Biochemistry. **Business:** Business admin. **Computer sciences:** Computer science. **Engineering:** Applied physics, chemical, computer, electrical, industrial, mechanical. **Math:** Applied. **Physical sciences:** Chemistry, physics.

Most popular majors. Computer/information sciences 8%, engineering/engineering technologies 84%.

Technology on campus. 450 workstations in dormitories, library, computer center, student center. Dormitories wired for high-speed internet access and linked to campus network. Commuter students can connect to campus network. Online library, helpline, wireless network available.

Student life. **Freshman orientation:** Mandatory, $150 fee. Preregistration for classes offered. Four-day program; begins Thursday before start of classes. **Policies:** Grade requirement to be eligible to join or maintain active membership in Greek letter organizations. **Housing:** Guaranteed on-campus for freshmen. Coed dorms, fraternity/sorority housing available. $100 fully refundable

deposit, deadline 5/1. **Activities:** Bands, campus ministries, dance, film society, international student organizations, Model UN, musical theater, radio station, student government, student newspaper, Christians in Action, Real Service, National Society of Black Engineers, Society of Hispanic Professional Engineers, Asian American association, Black Unity Congress, Crusade for Christ, India student organization.

Athletics. Intramural: Basketball, bowling, football (non-tackle), racquetball, soccer, softball, squash, tennis, volleyball, water polo. **Team name:** Bulldogs.

Student services. Alcohol/substance abuse counseling, career counseling, student employment services, financial aid counseling, health services, minority student services, personal counseling, placement for graduates, women's services. **Physically disabled:** Services for visually, speech, hearing impaired.

Contact. E-mail: admissions@kettering.edu
Phone: (810) 762-9865 Toll-free number: (800) 955-4464 ext. 7865
Fax: (810) 762-9837
Tracie Jones, Director of Admissions, Kettering University, 1700 University Avenue, Flint, MI 48504-6214

Kuyper College
Grand Rapids, Michigan
www.kuyper.edu   CB code: 1672

- Private 4-year Bible and liberal arts college affiliated with the Christian Reformed Church
- Residential campus in large city
- 252 degree-seeking undergraduates: 13% part-time, 57% women
- 1 degree-seeking graduate students
- 71% of applicants admitted
- SAT or ACT (ACT writing optional), application essay required
- 52% graduate within 6 years; 42% enter graduate study

General. Founded in 1939. Regionally accredited; also accredited by ABHE. **Degrees:** 62 bachelor's, 2 associate awarded. **ROTC:** Army. **Location:** 7 miles from downtown, 180 miles from Chicago. **Calendar:** Semester. **Full-time faculty:** 13 total; 62% have terminal degrees, 8% minority, 46% women. **Part-time faculty:** 28 total; 14% have terminal degrees, 4% minority, 54% women. **Class size:** 72% < 20, 27% 20-39, 2% 50-99.

Freshman class profile. 215 applied, 153 admitted, 67 enrolled.

Mid 50% test scores			
SAT math:	400-570	GPA 2.0-2.99:	22%
SAT writing:	370-530	End year in good standing:	89%
ACT composite:	19-24	Return as sophomores:	63%
GPA 3.75 or higher:	27%	Out-of-state:	10%
GPA 3.50-3.74:	12%	Live on campus:	65%
GPA 3.0-3.49:	36%	International:	2%

Basis for selection. Secondary school record, test scores important. Applicants with 2.0-2.5 GPA evaluated individually and possibly admitted on conditional acceptance. Kuyper College does not require test scores for students who are over the age of 21, or have at least 30 transferable credits. Interview required for borderline applicants. **Home schooled:** Transcript of courses and grades required.

High school preparation. College-preparatory program recommended. 17 units recommended. Recommended units include English 4, mathematics 3, social studies 3, science 3, foreign language 1 and academic electives 3.

2015-2016 Annual costs. Tuition/fees: $19,484. Room/board: $7,260. Books/supplies: $800. Personal expenses: $2,208.

2014-2015 Financial aid. **Need-based:** 45 full-time freshmen applied for aid; 38 deemed to have need; 38 received aid. Average need met was 78%. Average scholarship/grant was $14,013; average loan $3,989. 62% of total undergraduate aid awarded as scholarships/grants, 38% as loans/jobs. **Non-need-based:** Awarded to 41 full-time undergraduates, including 12 freshmen. Scholarships awarded for academics, alumni affiliation, leadership, minority status, music/drama.

Application procedures. **Admission:** Priority date 1/1; deadline 8/15. No application fee. Admission notification on a rolling basis beginning on or about 9/1. **Financial aid:** Priority date 3/1; no closing date. FAFSA required. Applicants notified on a rolling basis starting 3/15; must reply within 2 week(s) of notification.

Academics. **Special study options:** Accelerated study, combined bachelor's/graduate degree, cooperative education, double major, dual enrollment of high school students, ESL, independent study, internships, student-designed major, study abroad, teacher certification program. **Credit/placement by examination:** AP, CLEP, IB, SAT, ACT, institutional tests. 15 credit hours maximum toward associate degree, 30 toward bachelor's. **Support services:** Learning center, pre-admission summer program, reduced course load, remedial instruction, study skills assistance, tutoring, writing center.

Majors. Business: Accounting, business admin, international. **Communications:** Communications/speech/rhetoric, journalism, media studies, public relations. **Education:** Elementary, kindergarten/preschool, secondary. **Health services:** Prenursing. **Human services:** Social work. **Parks/recreation:** Exercise sciences. **Theology:** Bible, missionary, preministerial, religious ed, sacred music, youth ministry. **Visual/performing arts:** Dramatic.

Most popular majors. Business/marketing 7%, communications/journalism 8%, liberal arts 11%, public administration/social services 29%, theological studies 32%.

Technology on campus. 54 workstations in dormitories, library, computer center. Dormitories linked to campus network. Commuter students can connect to campus network. Online library, helpline, student web hosting, wireless network available.

Student life. Freshman orientation: Available. Preregistration for classes offered. Held for four days prior to the first week of fall semester. **Policies:** Smoke-, alcohol- and drug-free campus. Standards of conduct and housing policies in accordance with school's moral values. **Housing:** Guaranteed on-campus for freshmen. Coed dorms, special housing for disabled, apartments, wellness housing available. $200 fully refundable deposit. **Activities:** Campus ministries, choral groups, dance, international student organizations, music ensembles, student government, student newspaper, Bible studies, student activities committee, spiritual life committee, social work organization, intramurals committee, Street Team.

Athletics. Intramural: Basketball, soccer, table tennis, volleyball. **Team name:** Cougars.

Student services. Alcohol/substance abuse counseling, chaplain/spiritual director, career counseling, student employment services, financial aid counseling, health services, minority student services, personal counseling, placement for graduates, veterans' counselor. **Physically disabled:** Services for visually impaired.

Contact. E-mail: admissions@kuyper.edu
Phone: (616) 988-3621 Toll-free number: (800) 511-3749
Fax: (616) 988-3608
Dale Kuiper, Vice President for Enrollment, Kuyper College, 3333 East Beltline Avenue NE, Grand Rapids, MI 49525-9781

Lake Superior State University
Sault Ste. Marie, Michigan
www.lssu.edu   **CB code: 1421**

- Public 4-year university and engineering college
- Residential campus in large town
- 2,212 degree-seeking undergraduates: 13% part-time, 51% women, 1% African American, 1% Asian American, 2% Hispanic/Latino, 8% Native American, 7% international
- 1 graduate students
- 92% of applicants admitted
- SAT or ACT (ACT writing optional) required
- 37% graduate within 6 years

General. Founded in 1946. Regionally accredited. **Degrees:** 460 bachelor's, 171 associate awarded; master's offered. **Calendar:** Semester, limited summer session. **Full-time faculty:** 114 total; 57% have terminal degrees, 5% minority, 47% women. **Part-time faculty:** 90 total; 12% have terminal degrees, 7% minority, 60% women. **Class size:** 58% < 20, 32% 20-39, 4% 40-49, 6% 50-99. **Special facilities:** Aquatic research laboratory with fish hatchery and toxicology lab, planetarium, natural science museum, 200-acre biology station, robotic engineering laboratory, indoor rifle range, indoor ice arena, nursing simulation lab.

Freshman class profile. 1,504 applied, 1,388 admitted, 460 enrolled.

Mid 50% test scores		Return as sophomores:	65%
ACT composite:	19-24	Out-of-state:	7%
Rank in top quarter:	32%	Live on campus:	73%
Rank in top tenth:	8%	International:	9%

Basis for selection. Cumulative GPA, high school course curriculum, and ACT or SAT most important. Accepts the highest score sent out of all ACT and SAT scores sent. **Learning Disabled:** Students with learning disabilities referred to coordinator for Resource Center for Students with Disabilities.

High school preparation. College-preparatory program recommended. 18 units recommended. Recommended units include English 4, mathematics 4, social studies 2, history 1, science 3 (laboratory 3), foreign language 2, computer science 1 and visual/performing arts 1. Specific academic units required vary by college program.

2015-2016 Annual costs. Tuition/fees: $10,577; $10,577 out-of-state. Room/board: $9,290. Books/supplies: $1,100. Personal expenses: $1,000.

Financial aid. Non-need-based: Scholarships awarded for academics, athletics, state residency.

Application procedures. Admission: Priority date 3/1; deadline 9/2 (receipt date). $35 fee, may be waived for applicants with need. Admission notification on a rolling basis. **Financial aid:** Priority date 3/1; no closing date. FAFSA required. Applicants notified on a rolling basis starting 10/1; must reply by 5/1 or within 3 week(s) of notification.

Academics. Special study options: Accelerated study, combined bachelor's/graduate degree, cooperative education, distance learning, double major, dual enrollment of high school students, honors, independent study, internships, student-designed major, study abroad, teacher certification program. **Credit/placement by examination:** AP, CLEP, IB, SAT, ACT, institutional tests. **Support services:** Learning center, reduced course load, remedial instruction, study skills assistance, tutoring, writing center. Free tutoring offered to students in all academic departments.

Majors. Biology: General, biochemistry, conservation. **Business:** General, accounting, business admin, entrepreneurial studies, finance, managerial economics, marketing. **Communications:** Communications/speech/rhetoric. **Computer sciences:** General, LAN/WAN management. **Conservation:** General, environmental science, fisheries, wildlife/wilderness. **Education:** Chemistry, early childhood, earth science, elementary, mathematics, multi-level teacher, secondary. **Engineering:** Computer, electrical, industrial, mechanical. **English:** Creative writing, English lit. **Health services:** Clinical lab science, nursing (RN), recreational therapy. **History:** General. **Liberal arts:** Arts/sciences. **Math:** General. **Parks/recreation:** Exercise sciences, facilities management. **Physical sciences:** Chemistry, forensic chemistry, geology. **Protective services:** Corrections, criminal justice, criminalistics, fire safety technology, firefighting, forensics, homeland security, law enforcement admin, security services. **Psychology:** General. **Social sciences:** General, political science, sociology. **Visual/performing arts:** Studio arts.

Most popular majors. Biology 6%, business/marketing 15%, education 7%, engineering/engineering technologies 7%, health sciences 11%, security/protective services 24%.

Technology on campus. 450 workstations in library, computer center, student center. Dormitories wired for high-speed internet access and linked to campus network. Commuter students can connect to campus network. Online course registration, online library, helpline, repair service, wireless network available.

Student life. Freshman orientation: Mandatory, $125 fee. Preregistration for classes offered. One-day program held during the summer; 5 dates available. **Housing:** Guaranteed on-campus for freshmen. Coed dorms, single-sex dorms, apartments, fraternity/sorority housing, themed housing, wellness housing available. $300 partly refundable deposit, deadline 6/1. Honors housing, living learning communities available. **Activities:** Pep band, campus ministries, choral groups, dance, drama, international student organizations, literary magazine, radio station, student government, student newspaper, Campus Crusade for Christ, Christian fellowship, Newman Center, Native American students' council, political science club, environmental awareness club, professional organizations, Gay Straight Alliance (GSA).

Athletics. NCAA. **Intercollegiate:** Basketball, cross-country, golf, ice hockey M, softball W, tennis, track and field, volleyball W. **Intramural:** Basketball, football (non-tackle), handball, racquetball, soccer, softball, tennis, volleyball, water polo. **Team name:** Lakers.

Student services. Adult student services, alcohol/substance abuse counseling, chaplain/spiritual director, career counseling, services for economically disadvantaged, student employment services, financial aid counseling, health services, minority student services, on-campus daycare, personal counseling, placement for graduates, veterans' counselor. **Physically disabled:** Services for visually, speech, hearing impaired.

Contact. E-mail: admissions@lssu.edu
Phone: (906) 635-2231 Toll-free number: (888) 800-5778
Fax: (906) 635-6696
Allan Case, Director of Admissions, Lake Superior State University, 650 West Easterday Avenue, Sault Sainte Marie, MI 49783-1699

Lawrence Technological University
Southfield, Michigan
www.ltu.edu   CB code: 1399

- Private 4-year university
- Commuter campus in small city
- 1,967 degree-seeking undergraduates: 18% part-time, 26% women, 7% African American, 2% Asian American, 4% Hispanic/Latino, 2% Multiracial, non-Hispanic, 17% international
- 1,371 degree-seeking graduate students
- 55% of applicants admitted
- SAT or ACT (ACT writing optional), application essay required
- 45% graduate within 6 years; 12% enter graduate study

General. Founded in 1932. Regionally accredited. **Degrees:** 299 bachelor's, 15 associate awarded; master's, doctoral offered. **ROTC:** Air Force. **Location:** 20 miles from Detroit. **Calendar:** Semester, extensive summer session. **Full-time faculty:** 121 total; 69% have terminal degrees, 25% minority, 28% women. **Part-time faculty:** 295 total; 25% have terminal degrees, 17% minority, 32% women. **Class size:** 76% < 20, 24% 20-39, less than 1% 40-49, less than 1% >100. **Special facilities:** Frank Lloyd Wright-designed residence for academic study, center for innovative materials research.

Freshman class profile. 2,147 applied, 1,187 admitted, 350 enrolled.

Mid 50% test scores		Rank in top quarter:	50%
SAT critical reading:	460-590	Rank in top tenth:	24%
SAT math:	500-630	End year in good standing:	87%
SAT writing:	410-550	Return as sophomores:	82%
ACT composite:	22-29	Out-of-state:	14%
GPA 3.75 or higher:	28%	Live on campus:	68%
GPA 3.50-3.74:	18%	International:	7%
GPA 3.0-3.49:	32%	Fraternities:	18%
GPA 2.0-2.99:	22%	Sororities:	39%

Basis for selection. Previous academic record factors which demonstrate an aptitude for successful study. **Home schooled:** Transcript of courses and grades, letter of recommendation (nonparent) required.

High school preparation. College-preparatory program recommended. 12 units required; 16 recommended. Required and recommended units include English 4, mathematics 3-4, social studies 3, history 2, science 2-4 (laboratory 2).

2015-2016 Annual costs. Tuition/fees: $30,300. Room/board: $9,470.

2014-2015 Financial aid. Need-based: 315 full-time freshmen applied for aid; 247 deemed to have need; 246 received aid. Average need met was 69%. Average scholarship/grant was $16,867; average loan $6,440. 68% of total undergraduate aid awarded as scholarships/grants, 32% as loans/jobs. **Non-need-based:** Awarded to 1,250 full-time undergraduates, including 334 freshmen. Scholarships awarded for academics, alumni affiliation, minority status, ROTC, state residency. **Additional information:** March 1 state deadline for Michigan Competitive Scholarship and Michigan Tuition Grant.

Application procedures. Admission: No deadline. $30 fee, may be waived for applicants with need. Admission notification on a rolling basis. **Financial aid:** Priority date 4/1; no closing date. FAFSA required. Applicants notified on a rolling basis starting 4/1; must reply within 2 week(s) of notification.

Academics. Special study options: Combined bachelor's/graduate degree, cooperative education, distance learning, double major, ESL, honors, independent study, internships, study abroad. **Credit/placement by examination:** AP, CLEP, IB, institutional tests. 30 credit hours maximum toward associate degree, 90 toward bachelor's. **Support services:** Learning center, pre-admission summer program, reduced course load, remedial instruction, study skills assistance, tutoring, writing center. Macro for Math.

Majors. Architecture: Architecture, environmental design, history/criticism, interior, technology. **Biology:** Biochemistry, molecular. **Business:** Business admin, construction management. **Communications:** Communications/speech/rhetoric. **Computer sciences:** Computer science, information technology. **Engineering:** Architectural, biomedical, civil, computer, electrical, industrial, mechanical, robotics. **English:** English lit. **Liberal arts:** Humanities. **Math:** General. **Physical sciences:** Chemistry, environmental chemistry, physics. **Psychology:** General. **Visual/performing arts:** Design, digital arts, graphic design, illustration, industrial design.

Most popular majors. Architecture 32%, business/marketing 9%, computer/information sciences 9%, engineering/engineering technologies 37%, visual/performing arts 7%.

Technology on campus. PC or laptop required. Dormitories wired for high-speed internet access and linked to campus network. Commuter students can connect to campus network. Online course registration, online library, helpline, repair service, student web hosting, wireless network available.

Student life. Freshman orientation: Mandatory. Preregistration for classes offered. Held in late June. **Policies:** Student Code of Conduct. **Housing:** Special housing for disabled, apartments available. $200 fully refundable deposit. Pets allowed in dorm rooms. **Activities:** Pep band, dance, drama, international student organizations, literary magazine, music ensembles, student government, student newspaper, Alpha Sigma Phi, Delta Phi Epsilon, Delta Tau Sigma, black student union, Chi Omega Rho, artist's guild, Out! with Friends, Saudi student association, Hua Xia association, Indian student association.

Athletics. NAIA. **Intercollegiate:** Basketball, bowling, cross-country, golf, ice hockey M, lacrosse, soccer, tennis, volleyball W. **Intramural:** Badminton, basketball, football (non-tackle), golf, racquetball, skiing, soccer, softball, table tennis, tennis, volleyball. **Team name:** Blue Devils.

Student services. Alcohol/substance abuse counseling, career counseling, services for economically disadvantaged, student employment services, financial aid counseling, minority student services, personal counseling, placement for graduates, veterans' counselor, women's services. **Physically disabled:** Services for visually, speech, hearing impaired.

Contact. E-mail: admissions@ltu.edu
Phone: (248) 204-3160 Toll-free number: (800) 225-5588
Fax: (248) 204-2228
Jane Rohrback, Director of Admissions, Lawrence Technological University, 21000 West Ten Mile Road, Southfield, MI 48075-1058

Madonna University
Livonia, Michigan
www.madonna.edu   CB code: 1437

- Private 4-year university and liberal arts college affiliated with the Roman Catholic Church
- Commuter campus in small city
- 2,674 degree-seeking undergraduates: 47% part-time, 69% women, 12% African American, 1% Asian American, 4% Hispanic/Latino, 2% Multiracial, non-Hispanic, 17% international
- 823 graduate students
- 60% of applicants admitted
- SAT or ACT (ACT writing optional) required
- 61% graduate within 6 years

General. Founded in 1947. Regionally accredited. **Degrees:** 734 bachelor's, 149 associate awarded; master's, professional offered. **ROTC:** Army. **Location:** 6 miles from Detroit. **Calendar:** Semester, limited summer session. **Full-time faculty:** 105 total; 54% have terminal degrees, 11% minority, 66% women. **Part-time faculty:** 202 total; 31% have terminal degrees, 10% minority, 55% women. **Class size:** 69% < 20, 25% 20-39, 4% 40-49, 2% 50-99. **Special facilities:** Writing center, technology center, sign language lab, nursing simulation lab, television and radio studios, editing suites, science labs, gold-level LEED-Certified Franciscan Center.

Freshman class profile. 972 applied, 582 admitted, 182 enrolled.

Mid 50% test scores		Rank in top tenth:	19%
ACT composite:	20-24	End year in good standing:	80%
GPA 3.75 or higher:	27%	Return as sophomores:	82%
GPA 3.50-3.74:	16%	Out-of-state:	1%
GPA 3.0-3.49:	33%	Live on campus:	31%
GPA 2.0-2.99:	22%	International:	3%
Rank in top quarter:	43%		

Basis for selection. Rigor of secondary school record and academic GPA are very important. Some majors have more specific admission requirements. Campus visit recommended. **Learning Disabled:** Documentation required to be eligible for services.

High school preparation. College-preparatory program required. 19 units required; 22 recommended. Required and recommended units include English 3-4, mathematics 2-4, social studies 3-4, history 4, science 3-4 (laboratory 1) and foreign language 2. 1 biology, 1 chemistry, 1 algebra required for nursing applicants; biology, 1 chemistry, 2 algebra recommended for medical and radiologic technology program applicants.

2015-2016 Annual costs. Tuition/fees: $18,740. Room/board: $9,230. Books/supplies: $1,248. Personal expenses: $1,380.

2014-2015 Financial aid. Need-based: 132 full-time freshmen applied for aid; 110 deemed to have need; 110 received aid. Average need met was 66%. Average scholarship/grant was $10,894; average loan $2,994. 40% of total undergraduate aid awarded as scholarships/grants, 60% as loans/jobs. **Non-need-based:** Awarded to 373 full-time undergraduates, including 93 freshmen. Scholarships awarded for academics, alumni affiliation, art, athletics, leadership, minority status, music/drama, religious affiliation, state residency.

Application procedures. Admission: Priority date 4/1; no deadline. $25 fee, may be waived for applicants with need, free for online applicants. Admission notification on a rolling basis. **Financial aid:** Priority date 2/1; no closing date. FAFSA required. Applicants notified on a rolling basis starting 3/15; must reply by 9/1 or within 2 week(s) of notification.

Academics. Special study options: Accelerated study, cooperative education, cross-registration, distance learning, double major, dual enrollment of high school students, ESL, independent study, internships, liberal arts/career combination, student-designed major, study abroad, teacher certification program, weekend college. **Credit/placement by examination:** AP, CLEP, IB, institutional tests. 30 credit hours maximum toward associate degree, 60 toward bachelor's. **Support services:** Learning center, pre-admission summer program, reduced course load, study skills assistance, tutoring, writing center.

Majors. Biology: General, biochemistry, biomedical sciences. **Business:** Accounting, business admin, hospitality admin, human resources, international, management information systems, marketing. **Communications:** Journalism. **Computer sciences:** Computer science. **Conservation:** Environmental science. **Education:** Biology, chemistry, early childhood, elementary, English, mathematics, music, physical, physics, science, social studies. **English:** English lit, technical writing, writing. **Foreign languages:** American Sign Language, sign language interpretation, Spanish. **Health services:** Dietetics, health care admin, nursing (RN), palliative care nursing, predental, premedicine, prenursing, preoptometry, preveterinary. **History:** General. **Human services:** Social work. **Math:** General. **Parks/recreation:** Sports admin. **Philosophy/religion:** Religion. **Physical sciences:** Chemistry. **Protective services:** Criminal justice, firefighting, forensics. **Psychology:** General. **Social sciences:** Sociology. **Theology:** Sacred music. **Visual/performing arts:** Design, graphic design, music, music management, music performance, music theory/composition, piano/keyboard, studio arts, voice/opera. **Work/family studies:** General, aging, child development, food/nutrition, merchandising.

Most popular majors. Business/marketing 19%, health sciences 24%, security/protective services 20%.

Technology on campus. 266 workstations in dormitories, library, computer center. Dormitories wired for high-speed internet access and linked to campus network. Commuter students can connect to campus network. Online course registration, online library, helpline, wireless network available.

Student life. Freshman orientation: Mandatory. Preregistration for classes offered. Held all day in June, July and August for first-year students. **Policies:** Use of alcohol or drugs prohibited on campus; all buildings smoke-free; sexual assault, harassment policies in place. **Housing:** Single-sex dorms, wellness housing available. **Activities:** Pep band, campus ministries, choral groups, dance, film society, international student organizations, literary magazine, music ensembles, musical theater, radio station, student government, student newspaper, TV station, Red Cross club, Animal Awareness Organization, Ecological Volunteer Organization, Student United Way, Student Veterans Association, Franciscan Spirituality, Respect Life, Campus Crusade for Christ, Nursing Student Association, Broadcast and film club.

Athletics. NAIA. **Intercollegiate:** Baseball M, basketball, bowling, cross-country, golf, lacrosse, soccer, softball W, track and field, volleyball W. **Intramural:** Basketball, volleyball. **Team name:** Crusaders.

Student services. Adult student services, alcohol/substance abuse counseling, chaplain/spiritual director, career counseling, services for economically disadvantaged, student employment services, financial aid counseling, health services, minority student services, personal counseling, placement for graduates, women's services. **Physically disabled:** Services for visually, speech, hearing impaired.

Contact. E-mail: admissions@madonna.edu
Phone: (734) 432-5339 Toll-free number: (800) 852-4951
Director of Undergraduate Admissions, Madonna University, 36600 Schoolcraft Road, Livonia, MI 48150-1176

Manthano Christian College
Westland, Michigan
www.manthanochristian.org

- Private 4-year seminary college
- Very large city
- 24 degree-seeking undergraduates

General. Candidate for regional accreditation; also accredited by TRACS. Manthano admits Christian students who are planning to serve in Christian ministries. **Calendar:** Trimester. **Full-time faculty:** 4 total. **Part-time faculty:** 6 total.

Basis for selection. Open admission.

2015-2016 Annual costs. Tuition/fees: $5,500. Books/supplies: $800.

Financial aid. All financial aid based on need.

Application procedures. Admission: No deadline. $25 fee. **Financial aid:** No deadline. FAFSA required. Applicants notified on a rolling basis starting 9/1; must reply within 12 week(s) of notification.

Academics. Credit/placement by examination: AP.

Majors. Theology: Bible.

Student life. Freshman orientation: Available. Preregistration for classes offered.

Contact. Phone: (734) 895-3280 ext. 30
Bruce Snell, Director of Admissions, Manthano Christian College, 6420 North Newburgh, Westland, MI 48185

Marygrove College
Detroit, Michigan
www.marygrove.edu　　　　　　　　　　**CB code: 1452**

- Private 4-year liberal arts college affiliated with the Roman Catholic Church
- Commuter campus in very large city
- 676 degree-seeking undergraduates
- 57% of applicants admitted
- SAT or ACT (ACT writing recommended), application essay required

General. Founded in 1905. Regionally accredited. **Degrees:** 149 bachelor's, 10 associate awarded; master's offered. **Location:** 6 miles from downtown. **Calendar:** Semester, limited summer session.

Freshman class profile. 1,148 applied, 660 admitted, 102 enrolled.

Mid 50% test scores	ACT composite:	14-18

Basis for selection. School achievement record and test scores most important. Audition required of music, theater, dance majors. Portfolio required of art majors. Interview required of older applicants and academically weak applicants.

High school preparation. College-preparatory program recommended. 17 units recommended. Recommended units include English 4, mathematics 2, social studies 2, history 2, science 3 (laboratory 1), foreign language 2 and computer science 1.

2015-2016 Annual costs. Tuition/fees: $20,930. Room/board: $7,125. Books/supplies: $1,040. Personal expenses: $2,200.

Financial aid. All financial aid based on need.

Application procedures. Admission: Priority date 12/1; deadline 3/15 (postmark date). $25 fee, may be waived for applicants with need. Admission notification on a rolling basis. Must reply by 5/1. **Financial aid:** Priority date 3/15; no closing date. FAFSA, institutional form required. Applicants notified on a rolling basis starting 5/15; must reply within 2 week(s) of notification.

Academics. Special study options: Cooperative education, cross-registration, distance learning, double major, dual enrollment of high school students, honors, independent study, internships, student-designed major, study abroad, teacher certification program. **Credit/placement by examination:** AP, CLEP, SAT, ACT, institutional tests. 16 credit hours maximum toward associate degree, 32 toward bachelor's. Credit awarded for score of 3 or higher on AP exam. Credit hours awarded determined by faculty. **Support services:** Learning center, pre-admission summer program, reduced course load, remedial instruction, study skills assistance, tutoring, writing center.

Majors. Biology: General. **Business:** General, accounting, business admin, international. **Computer sciences:** General. **Conservation:** Environmental science. **Education:** General, early childhood, special ed. **English:** English lit. **Health services:** Art therapy. **History:** General. **Human services:** Social work. **Math:** General. **Philosophy/religion:** Religion. **Physical sciences:** Chemistry. **Psychology:** General. **Social sciences:** General, political science.

Visual/performing arts: Art, dance, music performance, music theory/composition, studio arts.

Technology on campus. 50 workstations in dormitories, library, computer center, student center. Dormitories wired for high-speed internet access and linked to campus network. Commuter students can connect to campus network. Online course registration, online library, helpline, wireless network available.

Student life. Freshman orientation: Mandatory. Preregistration for classes offered. **Housing:** Coed dorms, single-sex dorms available. $250 fully refundable deposit, deadline 8/1. **Activities:** Campus ministries, choral groups, dance, international student organizations, music ensembles, student government, student newspaper, Association of Black Social Workers, fraternities, honor societies, multicultural club, sororities.

Athletics. NAIA. **Intercollegiate:** Baseball M, basketball, cross-country, golf, soccer, track and field, volleyball W. **Intramural:** Badminton, basketball, bowling, football (non-tackle), golf, soccer, softball, table tennis, track and field, volleyball. **Team name:** Mustangs.

Student services. Alcohol/substance abuse counseling, chaplain/spiritual director, career counseling, services for economically disadvantaged, student employment services, financial aid counseling, health services, on-campus daycare, personal counseling, placement for graduates, veterans' counselor, women's services.

Contact. E-mail: info@marygrove.edu
Phone: (313) 927-1240 Fax: (313) 927-1345
Sharon Toles, Director of Admissions, Marygrove College, 8425 West McNichols Road, Detroit, MI 48221

Michigan Jewish Institute
West Bloomfield, Michigan
www.mji.edu   CB code: 1505

- Private 4-year liberal arts college affiliated with the Jewish faith
- Commuter campus in very large city
- 2,204 degree-seeking undergraduates

General. Accredited by ACICS. Extensive online (distance) learning to complete a Judaic Studies degree online (men and women) as well as a Certificate of Talmudic Law and Jurisprudence (men only). **Degrees:** 61 bachelor's awarded. **Location:** 25 miles from Detroit. **Calendar:** Semester, limited summer session. **Full-time faculty:** 5 total. **Part-time faculty:** 33 total; 36% have terminal degrees. **Special facilities:** Synagogue available on West Bloomfield campus.

Basis for selection. Open admission, but selective for some programs. 2.0 GPA required; applicants with less than 2.0 GPA or with GED may be accepted under provisional status. Certain programs require familiarity with Judaic studies. **Home schooled:** Statement describing home school structure and mission, transcript of courses and grades, state high school equivalency certificate, letter of recommendation (nonparent) required.

High school preparation. College-preparatory program recommended. Recommended units include English 3, mathematics 3, social studies 1, history 2, science 3 (laboratory 1), foreign language 2 and computer science 1.

2015-2016 Annual costs. Tuition/fees: $10,600. Books/supplies: $3,216. Personal expenses: $1,479.

2014-2015 Financial aid. All financial aid based on need.

Application procedures. Admission: No deadline. $50 fee. Admission notification on a rolling basis. High school students may enroll in dual studies program to earn high school and college credits for the same courses. Students may also be admitted into the college for up to 6 months before high school graduation. Should an admitted student not complete high school within the 6 months, they will not be able to continue until proof of high school graduation or GED is provided. **Financial aid:** No deadline. FAFSA required. Applicants notified on a rolling basis starting 1/1.

Academics. Special study options: Cooperative education, distance learning, double major, dual enrollment of high school students, independent study, internships, liberal arts/career combination, study abroad. **Credit/placement by examination:** AP, CLEP, IB, institutional tests. **Support services:** Learning center, reduced course load, remedial instruction, study skills assistance, tutoring.

Majors. Computer sciences: General. **Philosophy/religion:** Judaic.

Most popular majors. Philosophy/religious studies 96%.

Technology on campus. PC or laptop required. 16 workstations in library, student center. Online course registration, online library, helpline, wireless network available.

Student life. Freshman orientation: Available. Preregistration for classes offered. Scheduled onsite sessions and online tutorials available.

Student services. Adult student services, alcohol/substance abuse counseling, chaplain/spiritual director, career counseling, student employment services, financial aid counseling, personal counseling.

Contact. E-mail: info@mji.edu
Phone: (248) 414-6900 ext. 100 Toll-free number: (888) 463-6654
Fax: (248) 414-6907
Amy Herskovitz, Admissions Manager, Michigan Jewish Institute, 6888 West Maple Road, West Bloomfield, MI 48322

Michigan State University
East Lansing, Michigan   CB member
www.msu.edu   CB code: 1465

- Public 4-year university
- Residential campus in small city
- 38,853 degree-seeking undergraduates: 9% part-time, 50% women, 7% African American, 5% Asian American, 4% Hispanic/Latino, 3% Multiracial, non-Hispanic, 13% international
- 10,349 degree-seeking graduate students
- 66% of applicants admitted
- SAT or ACT with writing, application essay required
- 77% graduate within 6 years; 26% enter graduate study

General. Founded in 1855. Regionally accredited. **Degrees:** 8,299 bachelor's awarded; master's, professional, doctoral offered. **ROTC:** Army, Air Force. **Location:** 3 miles from Lansing, 80 miles from Detroit. **Calendar:** Semester, extensive summer session. **Full-time faculty:** 2,433 total; 90% have terminal degrees, 23% minority, 40% women. **Part-time faculty:** 406 total; 51% have terminal degrees, 14% minority, 60% women. **Class size:** 24% < 20, 45% 20-39, 7% 40-49, 10% 50-99, 13% >100. **Special facilities:** Planetarium, observatory, botanical garden, center for environmental toxicology, superconducting cyclotron laboratory, pesticide research center, experimental farms, 2 museums, center for performing arts, 2 golf courses, agricultural and livestock pavilion, children's garden.

Freshman class profile. 35,300 applied, 23,397 admitted, 8,173 enrolled.

Mid 50% test scores			
SAT critical reading:	450-580	GPA 2.0-2.99:	4%
SAT math:	530-680	Rank in top quarter:	67%
SAT writing:	460-580	Rank in top tenth:	31%
ACT composite:	23-28	Return as sophomores:	93%
GPA 3.75 or higher:	47%	Out-of-state:	16%
GPA 3.50-3.74:	27%	Live on campus:	95%
GPA 3.0-3.49:	22%	International:	12%

Basis for selection. Academic performance in high school, strength and quality of curriculum, recent trends in academic performance, class rank, test scores, leadership, talents, conduct, and diversity of experience. Audition required of music majors. **Home schooled:** Transcript of courses and grades required. Submit grades, list or provide information on curriculum and be prepared to answer questions. Test scores have stronger emphasis.

High school preparation. College-preparatory program required. Required and recommended units include English 4, mathematics 3-4, social studies 3, science 3 (laboratory 1) and foreign language 2.

2015-2016 Annual costs. Tuition/fees: $13,560; $36,360 out-of-state. Room/board: $9,474. Books/supplies: $1,068. Personal expenses: $1,532.

2015-2016 Financial aid. Need-based: 5,660 full-time freshmen applied for aid; 3,990 deemed to have need; 3,819 received aid. Average need met was 64%. Average scholarship/grant was $10,723; average loan $3,375. 69% of total undergraduate aid awarded as scholarships/grants, 31% as loans/jobs. **Non-need-based:** Awarded to 7,838 full-time undergraduates, including 2,450 freshmen. Scholarships awarded for academics, alumni affiliation, art, athletics, leadership, music/drama, ROTC, state residency.

Application procedures. Admission: Priority date 11/1; no deadline. $50 fee, may be waived for applicants with need. Admission notification on a rolling basis beginning on or about 10/7. Must reply by May 1 or within 2 week(s) if notified thereafter. **Financial aid:** No deadline. FAFSA required. Applicants notified on a rolling basis starting 3/15; must reply within 4 week(s) of notification.

Academics. Special study options: Accelerated study, combined bachelor's/graduate degree, cooperative education, distance learning, double major, dual enrollment of high school students, ESL, exchange student, honors, independent study, internships, liberal arts/career combination, student-designed major, study abroad, teacher certification program, weekend college. **Credit/placement by examination:** AP, CLEP, IB, SAT, ACT, institutional tests. 60 credit hours maximum toward bachelor's degree. **Support services:** Learning center, pre-admission summer program, reduced course load, remedial instruction, study skills assistance, tutoring, writing center.

Honors college/program. Selection criteria include test scores and class rank. Number admitted varies.

Majors. Architecture: Landscape, urban/community planning. **Area/ethnic studies:** Women's. **Biology:** General, Biochemistry/molecular biology, botany, entomology, environmental, microbiology, molecular genetics, neuroscience, physiology, zoology. **Business:** Accounting, apparel, business admin, construction management, fashion, finance, hospitality admin, human resources, logistics, marketing. **Communications:** Advertising, communications/speech/rhetoric, journalism, media studies, radio/TV. **Computer sciences:** General, IT project management. **Conservation:** Economics, environmental science, environmental studies, fisheries, forestry, wildlife/wilderness. **Education:** General, art, biology, chemistry, computer, early childhood, elementary, family/consumer sciences, French, geography, German, health, history, kindergarten/preschool, learning disabled, mathematics, middle, physical, physics, reading, science, secondary, social science, social studies, Spanish, special ed. **Engineering:** General, agricultural, chemical, civil, computer, electrical, materials, mechanical. **English:** English lit, technical writing. **Foreign languages:** Arabic, Chinese, French, German, Japanese, linguistics, Russian, Spanish. **Health services:** Athletic training, clinical lab science, dietetics, nursing (RN), premedicine, preveterinary, veterinary technology/assistant. **History:** General. **Human services:** Public policy, social work. **Liberal arts:** Humanities. **Math:** General, computational, statistics. **Parks/recreation:** Exercise sciences, facilities management. **Philosophy/religion:** Philosophy, religion. **Physical sciences:** General, astrophysics, chemical physics, chemistry, geology, physics. **Protective services:** Criminal justice, law enforcement admin. **Psychology:** General. **Social sciences:** General, anthropology, economics, geography, GIS/cartography, international relations, political science, sociology. **Visual/performing arts:** Acting, art, art history/conservation, dramatic, fashion design, graphic design, interior design, jazz, music, music pedagogy, music performance, music theory/composition, theater arts management. **Work/family studies:** Child care service, child development, clothing/textiles, family/community services.

Most popular majors. Biology 10%, business/marketing 18%, communications/journalism 12%, engineering/engineering technologies 9%, social sciences 11%.

Technology on campus. PC or laptop required. Dormitories wired for high-speed internet access and linked to campus network. Commuter students can connect to campus network. Online course registration, online library, helpline, repair service, student web hosting, wireless network available.

Student life. Freshman orientation: Mandatory. Preregistration for classes offered. One-and-a-half-day session in summer; includes placement tests. **Policies:** Freshmen not permitted cars on campus. **Housing:** Guaranteed on-campus for freshmen. Coed dorms, single-sex dorms, special housing for disabled, apartments, cooperative housing, fraternity/sorority housing, themed housing available. $250 fully refundable deposit. **Activities:** Bands, campus ministries, choral groups, dance, drama, film society, international student organizations, literary magazine, music ensembles, Model UN, musical theater, opera, radio station, student government, student newspaper, symphony orchestra, TV station.

Athletics. NCAA. **Intercollegiate:** Baseball M, basketball, cheerleading, cross-country, diving, field hockey W, football (tackle) M, golf, gymnastics W, ice hockey M, rowing (crew) W, soccer, softball W, swimming, tennis, track and field, volleyball W, wrestling M. **Intramural:** Archery, baseball M, basketball, cross-country, fencing, football (non-tackle) M, golf, gymnastics, ice hockey, lacrosse M, racquetball, rowing (crew) M, rugby, sailing, skiing, soccer, softball, squash, swimming, tennis, track and field, volleyball, water polo, wrestling M. **Team name:** Spartans.

Student services. Adult student services, alcohol/substance abuse counseling, career counseling, services for economically disadvantaged, student employment services, financial aid counseling, health services, legal services, minority student services, on-campus daycare, personal counseling, placement for graduates, veterans' counselor, women's services. **Physically disabled:** Services for visually, speech, hearing impaired.

Contact. E-mail: admis@msu.edu
Phone: (517) 355-8332 Fax: (517) 353-1647
James Cotter, Director of Admissions, Michigan State University, 250 Administration Building, East Lansing, MI 48824

Michigan Technological University
Houghton, Michigan CB member
www.mtu.edu CB code: 1464

- Public 4-year university
- Residential campus in small town
- 5,645 degree-seeking undergraduates: 5% part-time, 27% women, 1% African American, 1% Asian American, 2% Hispanic/Latino, 3% Multiracial, non-Hispanic, 4% international
- 1,494 degree-seeking graduate students
- 75% of applicants admitted
- SAT or ACT (ACT writing optional) required
- 65% graduate within 6 years; 8% enter graduate study

General. Founded in 1885. Regionally accredited. **Degrees:** 1,158 bachelor's awarded; master's, doctoral offered. **ROTC:** Army, Air Force. **Location:** 211 miles from Green Bay, WI; 325 miles from Milwaukee, WI. **Calendar:** Semester, limited summer session. **Full-time faculty:** 410 total; 88% have terminal degrees, 19% minority, 30% women. **Part-time faculty:** 41 total; 56% have terminal degrees, 5% minority, 58% women. **Class size:** 45% < 20, 31% 20-39, 8% 40-49, 13% 50-99, 3% >100. **Special facilities:** Mineral museum, center for the performing arts, theater, 4,000-acre forest, observatory, x-ray fluorescence spectrometer, process simulation and control center, sciences institute, engineering lab, micro fabrication lab, subsurface visualization lab, research center.

Freshman class profile. 5,386 applied, 4,063 admitted, 1,277 enrolled.

Mid 50% test scores			
SAT critical reading:	550-670	Rank in top quarter:	62%
SAT math:	570-690	Rank in top tenth:	28%
SAT writing:	510-630	End year in good standing:	82%
ACT composite:	24-29	Return as sophomores:	87%
GPA 3.75 or higher:	46%	Out-of-state:	23%
GPA 3.50-3.74:	23%	Live on campus:	92%
GPA 3.0-3.49:	25%	International:	2%
GPA 2.0-2.99:	6%	Fraternities:	5%
		Sororities:	7%

Basis for selection. Applicants are evaluated based on cumulative high school grade point average, high school courses taken and grades received, and ACT and/or SAT scores. Test scores should be received as soon as possible to process the application and for the student to be considered for merit-based scholarships. Applicants to Visual and Performing Arts Department degree programs are required to submit responses to essay questions as part of the application process. Applicants to select programs within the Visual and Performing Arts Department are also required to submit examples of creative work that demonstrate the applicant's interests and abilities.

High school preparation. College-preparatory program recommended. 8 units required; 19 recommended. Required and recommended units include English 3-4, mathematics 3-4, social studies 3, science 2-3, foreign language 2, computer science 1 and academic electives 2.

2015-2016 Annual costs. Tuition/fees: $14,286; $30,250 out-of-state. Room/board: $9,857. Books/supplies: $1,200. Personal expenses: $1,234.

2015-2016 Financial aid. Need-based: 1,151 full-time freshmen applied for aid; 857 deemed to have need; 857 received aid. Average need met was 81%. Average scholarship/grant was $9,417; average loan $3,218. 55% of total undergraduate aid awarded as scholarships/grants, 45% as loans/jobs. **Non-need-based:** Awarded to 4,144 full-time undergraduates, including 1,118 freshmen. Scholarships awarded for academics, alumni affiliation, athletics, job skills, leadership, ROTC, state residency.

Application procedures. Admission: Priority date 1/15; no deadline. No application fee. Admission notification on a rolling basis beginning on or about 6/15. Must reply by May 1 or within 4 week(s) if notified thereafter. **Financial aid:** Priority date 3/1; no closing date. FAFSA required. Applicants notified on a rolling basis starting 3/15; must reply by 5/1.

Academics. Special study options: Accelerated study, cooperative education, distance learning, double major, dual enrollment of high school students, ESL, honors, independent study, internships, semester at sea, study abroad, teacher certification program. **Credit/placement by examination:** AP, CLEP, IB, institutional tests. **Support services:** Learning center, reduced course load, study skills assistance, tutoring, writing center.

Majors. Biology: General, Biochemistry/molecular biology, bioinformatics. **Business:** Accounting, business admin, construction management, finance, management information systems, marketing. **Communications:** Intercultural, technical/scientific. **Communications technology:** Recording arts.

Computer sciences: Computer science, system admin. **Conservation:** Environmental science, forestry, management/policy, wildlife/wilderness. **Engineering:** General, biomedical, chemical, civil, computer, electrical, environmental, geological, materials, mechanical, software, surveying. **English:** English lit. **Health services:** Clinical lab science. **History:** General. **Liberal arts:** Arts/sciences. **Math:** General, statistics. **Parks/recreation:** Exercise sciences, sports admin. **Physical sciences:** Chemistry, geology, geophysics, physics. **Psychology:** General. **Social sciences:** General, anthropology, economics. **Visual/performing arts:** General, theater design.

Most popular majors. Business/marketing 7%, computer/information sciences 7%, engineering/engineering technologies 61%.

Technology on campus. 875 workstations in library, computer center, student center. Dormitories wired for high-speed internet access and linked to campus network. Commuter students can connect to campus network. Online course registration, online library, helpline, student web hosting, wireless network available.

Student life. Freshman orientation: Mandatory, $250 fee. Preregistration for classes offered. Week-long on-campus session. **Housing:** Guaranteed on-campus for freshmen. Coed dorms, special housing for disabled, apartments, cooperative housing, fraternity/sorority housing, themed housing, wellness housing available. **Activities:** Bands, campus ministries, choral groups, dance, drama, film society, international student organizations, literary magazine, music ensembles, musical theater, radio station, student government, student newspaper, symphony orchestra, Cru, Catholic Campus Ministries at St. Albert the Great University Parish, His House Christian Fellowship, International Fellowship Association, Book Club at Michigan Tech, Young Americans for Liberty, College Republicans, African Students Organization, Nosotros, and American Indian Science and Engineering Society.

Athletics. NCAA. **Intercollegiate:** Basketball, cross-country, football (tackle) M, ice hockey M, skiing, soccer W, tennis, track and field, volleyball W. **Intramural:** Badminton, basketball, bowling, football (non-tackle), golf, ice hockey, racquetball, rifle, sand volleyball, soccer, softball, swimming, table tennis, tennis, ultimate frisbee, volleyball, water polo. **Team name:** Huskies.

Student services. Alcohol/substance abuse counseling, career counseling, student employment services, financial aid counseling, health services, minority student services, on-campus daycare, personal counseling, placement for graduates, veterans' counselor, women's services. **Physically disabled:** Services for visually, hearing impaired.

Contact. E-mail: mtu4u@mtu.edu
Phone: (906) 487-2335 Toll-free number: (888) 688-1885
Fax: (906) 487-2125
Allison Carter, Director of Admissions, Michigan Technological University, 1400 Townsend Drive, Houghton, MI 49931-1295

Northern Michigan University
Marquette, Michigan
www.nmu.edu

CB member
CB code: 1560

◗ Public 4-year university
◗ Residential campus in large town
◗ 7,989 degree-seeking undergraduates
◗ 646 graduate students
◗ SAT or ACT (ACT writing optional) required

General. Founded in 1899. Regionally accredited. Every full-time student receives a ThinkPad or MacBook notebook computer as part of tuition and fees, which are replaced every 2 years. **Degrees:** 1,281 bachelor's, 222 associate awarded; master's, doctoral offered. **ROTC:** Army. **Location:** 300 miles from Milwaukee, 380 miles from Chicago. **Calendar:** Semester, limited summer session. **Full-time faculty:** 330 total; 75% have terminal degrees, 9% minority, 42% women. **Part-time faculty:** 151 total; 3% have terminal degrees, 4% minority, 49% women. **Class size:** 35% < 20, 51% 20-39, 4% 40-49, 8% 50-99, 2% >100. **Special facilities:** Education center, center for teaching and learning science and math, art and design studios, observatory with 12.5 F:6 Newtonian telescope, 120-acre nature preserve.

Freshman class profile.

GPA 3.75 or higher:	18%	GPA 2.0-2.99:	40%
GPA 3.50-3.74:	11%	Out-of-state:	22%
GPA 3.0-3.49:	24%	Live on campus:	75%

Basis for selection. High school record, test scores most important. Recommendations considered. Students who do not fulfill normal requirements for admission may be conditionally admitted for freshman probation and college transition programs. Applicants may re-take exams and submit new scores any time prior to the first day of fall classes. Some certificate, diploma

and associate degree programs do not require test scores. Audition recommended for music, drama majors. Portfolio recommended for art majors. Interview, extracurricular activities, talent/ability considered for borderline students. **Home schooled:** Transcript of courses and grades required.

High school preparation. College-preparatory program recommended. 19 units recommended. Recommended units include English 4, mathematics 4, social studies 4, science 4 and foreign language 2. Courses in the arts and information technology also encouraged.

2015-2016 Annual costs. Tuition/fees: $9,860; $15,260 out-of-state. Room/board: $9,286. Books/supplies: $800. Personal expenses: $1,234.

Financial aid. Non-need-based: Scholarships awarded for academics, art, athletics, leadership, music/drama, ROTC, state residency. **Additional information:** Audition or portfolio required for music, drama, and art scholarship applicants. Alumni Dependent Tuition Program gives resident tuition rates to nonresident dependents of NMU alumni who received master's, baccalaureate, or associate degree; renewable.

Application procedures. Admission: No deadline. $30 fee, may be waived for applicants with need. Admission notification on a rolling basis. Students may defer enrollment for one year. After one year, they must reapply. **Financial aid:** Priority date 3/1; no closing date. FAFSA required. Applicants notified on a rolling basis starting 4/1; must reply within 2 week(s) of notification.

Academics. Special study options: Accelerated study, combined bachelor's/graduate degree, distance learning, double major, dual enrollment of high school students, ESL, honors, independent study, internships, liberal arts/career combination, semester at sea, student-designed major, study abroad, teacher certification program, Washington semester. **Credit/placement by examination:** AP, CLEP, IB, SAT, ACT, institutional tests. 12 credit hours maximum toward associate degree, 32 toward bachelor's. 8 credits may be counted toward certificate. **Support services:** Learning center, pre-admission summer program, reduced course load, remedial instruction, study skills assistance, tutoring, writing center.

Honors college/program. Limited to 50 students; requires 3.5 GPA and 27 ACT or equivalent.

Majors. Area/ethnic studies: German. **Biology:** General, biochemistry, ecology, microbiology, physiology, zoology. **Business:** General, accounting, accounting/finance, business admin, entrepreneurial studies, finance, financial planning, hospitality admin, management information systems, marketing, small business admin. **Communications:** Communications/speech/rhetoric, digital media, public relations. **Computer sciences:** General, LAN/WAN management, networking, webmaster. **Conservation:** General, environmental science. **Education:** Art, biology, chemistry, elementary, emotionally handicapped, English, French, geography, health, history, mathematics, mentally handicapped, music, physical, physics, science, secondary, social science, social studies, Spanish, special ed, technology/industrial arts. **English:** Creative writing, English lit. **Foreign languages:** French, Spanish. **Health services:** Athletic training, clinical lab science, community health services, cytogenetics, histologic assistant, predental, premedicine, prepharmacy, prephysical therapy, preveterinary, radiologic technology/medical imaging, respiratory therapy assistant, respiratory therapy technology, speech pathology, surgical technology. **History:** General. **Human services:** General, social work. **Liberal arts:** Arts/sciences. **Math:** General. **Parks/recreation:** General, exercise sciences, health/fitness, sports admin. **Philosophy/religion:** Philosophy. **Physical sciences:** Chemistry, forensic chemistry, geology, physics. **Protective services:** Criminal justice, security services. **Psychology:** General, developmental, experimental. **Social sciences:** Economics, geography, GIS/cartography, international relations, political science, sociology. **Visual/performing arts:** Art, art history/conservation, ceramics, cinematography, digital arts, dramatic, drawing, graphic design, illustration, metal/jewelry, music, painting, photography, printmaking, sculpture. **Work/family studies:** Food/nutrition.

Most popular majors. Biology 9%, business/marketing 13%, education 9%, health sciences 13%, security/protective services 7%, visual/performing arts 10%.

Technology on campus. 9,500 workstations in library. Dormitories wired for high-speed internet access and linked to campus network. Commuter students can connect to campus network. Online course registration, online library, helpline, repair service, student web hosting, wireless network available.

Student life. Freshman orientation: Mandatory, $75 fee. Preregistration for classes offered. Three-day sessions held throughout the summer prior to start of classes. **Housing:** Guaranteed on-campus for all undergraduates. Coed dorms, single-sex dorms, special housing for disabled, apartments available. $125 partly refundable deposit. **Activities:** Bands, campus ministries, choral groups, dance, drama, film society, international student organizations, literary magazine, music ensembles, Model UN, musical theater, opera, radio station, student government, student newspaper, symphony orchestra,

TV station, Room at the Inn student chapter, Catholic campus ministry, Presque Isle Zen community, Amnesty International, Political Review, Native American student association, All Nations club, international dancers, Superior Edge citizen-leader program, student leader fellowship program.

Athletics. NCAA. **Intercollegiate:** Basketball, cheerleading, cross-country W, diving W, football (tackle) M, golf M, ice hockey M, skiing, soccer W, swimming W, track and field W, volleyball W. **Intramural:** Badminton, basketball, football (non-tackle), football (tackle), ice hockey, racquetball, soccer, table tennis, ultimate frisbee, volleyball, water polo. **Team name:** Wildcats.

Student services. Adult student services, chaplain/spiritual director, career counseling, student employment services, financial aid counseling, health services, minority student services, personal counseling, placement for graduates, veterans' counselor. **Physically disabled:** Services for visually, speech, hearing impaired.

Contact. E-mail: admiss@nmu.edu
Phone: (906) 227-2650 Toll-free number: (800) 682-9797
Fax: (906) 227-1747
Gerri Daniels, Director of Admissions, Northern Michigan University, 1401 Presque Isle Avenue, Marquette, MI 49855

Northwood University: Michigan
Midland, Michigan
www.northwood.edu   **CB code: 1568**

▶ Private 4-year university and business college

▶ Residential campus in large town

▶ 1,459 degree-seeking undergraduates: 3% part-time, 36% women, 7% African American, 3% Hispanic/Latino, 1% Native Hawaiian/Pacific islander, 2% Multi-racial, non-Hispanic, 6% international

▶ 397 degree-seeking graduate students

▶ 69% of applicants admitted

▶ SAT or ACT (ACT writing optional) required

▶ 57% graduate within 6 years; 12% enter graduate study

General. Founded in 1959. Regionally accredited. Specializes in business managerial and entrepreneurial education. **Degrees:** 332 bachelor's awarded; master's offered. **Location:** 125 miles from Detroit, 25 miles from Saginaw. **Calendar:** Semester, extensive summer session. **Full-time faculty:** 49 total; 45% have terminal degrees, 22% minority, 49% women. **Part-time faculty:** 81 total; 27% have terminal degrees, 10% minority, 52% women. **Class size:** 33% < 20, 58% 20-39, 8% 40-49, less than 1% 50-99. **Special facilities:** University operated hotel, business incubator.

Freshman class profile. 2,192 applied, 1,506 admitted, 334 enrolled.

Mid 50% test scores		Rank in top quarter:	31%
SAT critical reading:	420-530	Rank in top tenth:	11%
ACT composite:	20-24	End year in good standing:	87%
GPA 3.75 or higher:	23%	Return as sophomores:	80%
GPA 3.50-3.74:	20%	Out-of-state:	12%
GPA 3.0-3.49:	30%	Live on campus:	90%
GPA 2.0-2.99:	27%	International:	3%

Basis for selection. High school GPA and standardized test scores or transfer GPA, strong interest in business or related field important. Students with lower GPA and/or test scores admitted on probation. Interview recommended. **Home schooled:** Transcript of courses and grades, state high school equivalency certificate required.

High school preparation. College-preparatory program recommended. 17 units recommended. Recommended units include English 4, mathematics 3, social studies 3, science 3 (laboratory 2), foreign language 1 and academic electives 1.

2015-2016 Annual costs. Tuition/fees: $24,170. Room/board: $9,590. Books/supplies: $1,244.

2015-2016 Financial aid. Need-based: 291 full-time freshmen applied for aid; 232 deemed to have need; 232 received aid. Average need met was 67%. Average scholarship/grant was $5,657; average loan $3,379. 61% of total undergraduate aid awarded as scholarships/grants, 39% as loans/jobs. **Non-need-based:** Awarded to 764 full-time undergraduates, including 185 freshmen. Scholarships awarded for academics, alumni affiliation, athletics, leadership, minority status.

Application procedures. Admission: No deadline. $30 fee, may be waived for applicants with need, free for online applicants. Admission notification on a rolling basis. **Financial aid:** Priority date 3/1; no closing date.

FAFSA required. Applicants notified by 3/1; Applicants notified on a rolling basis starting 3/1.

Academics. Special study options: Accelerated study, distance learning, double major, dual enrollment of high school students, external degree, honors, internships, study abroad, weekend college. **Credit/placement by examination:** AP, CLEP, IB, SAT, ACT, institutional tests. 12 credit hours maximum toward bachelor's degree. Credit by exam and prior learning cannot exceed a total of 30 credits. **Support services:** Learning center, pre-admission summer program, reduced course load, remedial instruction, study skills assistance, tutoring.

Majors. Business: Accounting, business admin, entrepreneurial studies, fashion, finance, franchise operations, hospitality admin, insurance, international, logistics, management information systems, managerial economics, marketing, vehicle parts marketing. **Computer sciences:** General. **Parks/recreation:** General.

Most popular majors. Business/marketing 89%, parks/recreation 11%.

Technology on campus. 215 workstations in dormitories, library, computer center. Dormitories wired for high-speed internet access and linked to campus network. Commuter students can connect to campus network. Online course registration, online library, helpline, student web hosting, wireless network available.

Student life. Freshman orientation: Mandatory, $125 fee. Preregistration for classes offered. Several sessions held in the summer. **Housing:** Guaranteed on-campus for freshmen. Coed dorms, single-sex dorms, special housing for disabled, apartments available. $250 fully refundable deposit, deadline 5/1. **Activities:** Campus ministries, drama, international student organizations, student government, student newspaper, Business Professionals of America, American Marketing Association, ambassador club, Rotaract, law club, International Business Association, Minority Business Women, American Advertising Federation, The Church Reloaded, diversity club.

Athletics. NCAA. **Intercollegiate:** Baseball M, basketball, cheerleading, cross-country, football (tackle) M, golf, soccer, softball W, tennis, track and field, volleyball W. **Intramural:** Badminton, basketball, field hockey, football (non-tackle) M, soccer, tennis, volleyball. **Team name:** Timberwolves.

Student services. Adult student services, alcohol/substance abuse counseling, career counseling, student employment services, financial aid counseling, health services, minority student services, personal counseling, placement for graduates, veterans' counselor. **Physically disabled:** Services for visually, speech, hearing impaired.

Contact. E-mail: miadmit@northwood.edu
Phone: (989) 837-4273 Toll-free number: (800) 457-7878
Keri Nieto, Director of Admissions, Northwood University: Michigan, 4000 Whiting Drive, Midland, MI 48640

Oakland University
Rochester, Michigan   **CB member**
www.oakland.edu   **CB code: 1497**

▶ Public 4-year university

▶ Commuter campus in small city

▶ 16,733 degree-seeking undergraduates: 23% part-time, 57% women, 8% African American, 4% Asian American, 3% Hispanic/Latino, 3% Multi-racial, non-Hispanic, 2% international

▶ 3,460 degree-seeking graduate students

▶ 65% of applicants admitted

▶ SAT or ACT (ACT writing optional) required

▶ 44% graduate within 6 years

General. Founded in 1957. Regionally accredited. **Degrees:** 2,791 bachelor's awarded; master's, professional, doctoral offered. **ROTC:** Air Force. **Location:** 30 miles from Detroit. **Calendar:** Semester, limited summer session. **Full-time faculty:** 573 total; 91% have terminal degrees, 23% minority, 47% women. **Class size:** 37% < 20, 42% 20-39, 9% 40-49, 12% 50-99, less than 1% >100. **Special facilities:** Music pavilion, theater, engineering and science research laboratories, robotics laboratory, product development and manufacturing center, historic house, golf learning center, 2 golf courses.

Freshman class profile. 12,579 applied, 8,169 admitted, 2,713 enrolled.

Mid 50% test scores		Rank in top quarter:	46%
ACT composite:	20-26	Rank in top tenth:	15%
GPA 3.75 or higher:	28%	Return as sophomores:	76%
GPA 3.50-3.74:	18%	Out-of-state:	2%
GPA 3.0-3.49:	31%	Live on campus:	42%
GPA 2.0-2.99:	23%	International:	1%

Basis for selection. Rigor of secondary school record and academic GPA are very important; recommendations are important. Audition required of music, theater, dance majors. **Home schooled:** Transcript of courses and grades required. 20 ACT or 950 SAT required.

High school preparation. College-preparatory program required. Required and recommended units include English 4, mathematics 4, social studies 3, science 3 and foreign language 2.

2015-2016 Annual costs. Tuition/fees: $11,513; $23,873 out-of-state. Room/board: $9,250. Books/supplies: $912. Personal expenses: $1,716.

2014-2015 Financial aid. Need-based: 2,024 full-time freshmen applied for aid; 1,549 deemed to have need; 1,482 received aid. Average need met was 80%. Average scholarship/grant was $6,897; average loan $2,956. 51% of total undergraduate aid awarded as scholarships/grants, 49% as loans/jobs. **Non-need-based:** Awarded to 5,883 full-time undergraduates, including 1,508 freshmen. Scholarships awarded for academics, alumni affiliation, art, athletics, leadership, music/drama.

Application procedures. Admission: Closing date 8/1. No application fee. Application must be submitted online. Admission notification on a rolling basis beginning on or about 9/1. **Financial aid:** Priority date 2/15; no closing date. FAFSA required. Applicants notified on a rolling basis starting 3/8.

Academics. Special study options: Accelerated study, cooperative education, cross-registration, distance learning, double major, dual enrollment of high school students, ESL, exchange student, honors, independent study, internships, student-designed major, study abroad, teacher certification program. **Credit/placement by examination:** AP, CLEP, IB, SAT, ACT, institutional tests. 60 credit hours maximum toward bachelor's degree. **Support services:** Learning center, pre-admission summer program, reduced course load, remedial instruction, study skills assistance, tutoring, writing center.

Majors. Area/ethnic studies: East Asian, Latin American, women's. **Biology:** General, biochemistry, biophysics. **Business:** General, accounting, actuarial science, finance, human resources, management information systems, managerial economics, marketing, operations, training/development. **Communications:** Communications/speech/rhetoric, journalism. **Computer sciences:** General, information technology. **Conservation:** Environmental science. **Education:** Elementary, music. **Engineering:** Applied physics, computer, electrical, industrial, mechanical. **English:** Creative writing, English lit, writing. **Foreign languages:** General, French, German, Japanese, linguistics, Spanish. **Health services:** Clinical lab science, cytotechnology, environmental health, histologic technology, medical radiologic technology/radiation therapy, nuclear medical technology, nursing (RN), occupational health, radiologic technology/medical imaging. **History:** General. **Human services:** General, social work. **Liberal arts:** Arts/sciences. **Math:** General, statistics. **Philosophy/religion:** Philosophy. **Physical sciences:** Chemistry, physics. **Psychology:** General. **Social sciences:** Anthropology, economics, international relations, political science, sociology, sociology/anthropology. **Visual/performing arts:** Acting, art history/conservation, dance, dramatic, drawing, film/cinema/video, graphic design, music, music performance, musical theater, painting, photography, piano/keyboard, studio arts, theater design, voice/opera.

Most popular majors. Biology 6%, business/marketing 15%, communications/journalism 7%, health sciences 27%, psychology 6%.

Technology on campus. Dormitories linked to campus network. Commuter students can connect to campus network. Online course registration, online library, helpline, student web hosting, wireless network available.

Student life. Freshman orientation: Mandatory. Preregistration for classes offered. Held on weekdays from end of June through mid-July. One-and-a-half-day program requires overnight stay in residence halls. Condensed one-day program available. **Housing:** Guaranteed on-campus for freshmen. Coed dorms, special housing for disabled, apartments, fraternity/sorority housing, themed housing available. Residence halls easily accessible to handicapped persons. **Activities:** Bands, campus ministries, choral groups, dance, drama, film society, international student organizations, literary magazine, music ensembles, Model UN, musical theater, opera, radio station, student government, student newspaper, symphony orchestra, TV station, association of black students, Indian students association, Asian American association, College Democrats, College Republicans, Inter Varsity Christian Fellowship, Hillel, Muslim student association, Chinese friendship association, Gay/Straight Alliance.

Athletics. NCAA. **Intercollegiate:** Basketball, cross-country, diving, golf, soccer, softball W, swimming, tennis W, track and field, volleyball W. **Intramural:** Badminton, baseball, basketball, bowling, football (non-tackle), racquetball, soccer, softball, table tennis, triathlon, volleyball, water polo. **Team name:** Golden Grizzlies.

Student services. Adult student services, alcohol/substance abuse counseling, chaplain/spiritual director, career counseling, services for economically disadvantaged, student employment services, financial aid counseling, health services, minority student services, on-campus daycare, personal counseling, placement for graduates, veterans' counselor. **Physically disabled:** Services for visually, speech, hearing impaired.

Contact. E-mail: ouinfo@oakland.edu
Phone: (248) 370-3360 Toll-free number: (800) 625-8648
Fax: (248) 370-4462
Dawn Aubry, Director, Admissions, Oakland University, 101 North Foundation Hall, Rochester, MI 48309-4401

Olivet College	
Olivet, Michigan	**CB member**
www.olivetcollege.edu	**CB code: 1595**

- Private 4-year liberal arts college affiliated with the United Church of Christ
- Residential campus in rural community
- 912 degree-seeking undergraduates
- 24 degree-seeking graduate students
- 55% of applicants admitted
- SAT or ACT (ACT writing optional) required
- 45% graduate within 6 years

General. Founded in 1844. Regionally accredited. **Degrees:** 206 bachelor's awarded; master's offered. **ROTC:** Army, Air Force. **Location:** 30 miles from Lansing, 120 miles from Detroit. **Calendar:** Semester, limited summer session. **Full-time faculty:** 39 total; 64% have terminal degrees, 8% minority, 38% women. **Part-time faculty:** 58 total; 10% have terminal degrees, 5% minority, 43% women. **Class size:** 62% < 20, 36% 20-39, less than 1% 40-49, less than 1% 50-99, less than 1% >100. **Special facilities:** Observatory/planetarium, dynamic ecology laboratory, women's resource center, biological preserve.

Freshman class profile. 2,226 applied, 1,226 admitted, 246 enrolled.

Mid 50% test scores		ACT composite:	16-22
SAT critical reading:	400-500	Out-of-state:	8%
SAT math:	420-560	Live on campus:	88%

Basis for selection. GED not accepted. Minimum 2.6 GPA most important. Test scores, school achievement record, recommendations for those below 2.6 GPA important. Audition required for vocal/instrumental music majors. **Home schooled:** Transcript of courses and grades required. **Learning Disabled:** Interview and evaluation of IEP or 504 Plan by Academic Accommodations in the Student Resource Center required if disclosing disability.

2015-2016 Annual costs. Tuition/fees: $24,816. Room/board: $8,400. Books/supplies: $1,200. Personal expenses: $1,000.

2014-2015 Financial aid. All financial aid based on need. 212 full-time freshmen applied for aid; 205 deemed to have need; 205 received aid. Average need met was 68%. Average scholarship/grant was $11,500; average loan $3,410. 60% of total undergraduate aid awarded as scholarships/grants, 40% as loans/jobs.

Application procedures. Admission: Closing date 9/1 (receipt date). $25 fee, may be waived for applicants with need, free for online applicants. Admission notification on a rolling basis. **Financial aid:** No deadline. FAFSA required. Applicants notified on a rolling basis starting 2/1; must reply within 3 week(s) of notification.

Academics. Weekly seminars for major-specific career exploration and preparation; a service learning requirement to graduate; on- and off-campus experiential learning opportunities; internship and career services; domestic and international travel. **Special study options:** Cooperative education, double major, dual enrollment of high school students, honors, independent study, internships, liberal arts/career combination, student-designed major, teacher certification program. **Credit/placement by examination:** AP, CLEP, IB, ACT, institutional tests. 30 credit hours maximum toward bachelor's degree. **Support services:** Learning center, pre-admission summer program, study skills assistance, tutoring, writing center.

Majors. Biology: General, biochemistry. **Business:** Business admin, financial planning, insurance, managerial economics, marketing. **Communications:** Journalism, media studies. **Computer sciences:** Computer science. **Conservation:** Environmental science. **History:** General. **Liberal arts:** Arts/sciences. **Math:** General. **Parks/recreation:** Health/fitness, sports admin. **Physical sciences:** Chemistry. **Protective services:** Criminal justice. **Psychology:** General. **Social sciences:** General, sociology. **Visual/performing arts:** Art, music.

Most popular majors. Biology 11%, business/marketing 13%, education 9%, security/protective services 19%, social sciences 8%, visual/performing arts 12%.

Technology on campus. 140 workstations in dormitories, library, computer center, student center. Dormitories wired for high-speed internet access and linked to campus network. Commuter students can connect to campus network. Online course registration, helpline, repair service, student web hosting, wireless network available.

Student life. Freshman orientation: Mandatory, $75 fee. Preregistration for classes offered. One-day programs offered June through August. **Policies:** Alcohol Education for student clubs, organizations and Greek societies. Must be completed by all members of any organization that would like to host a registered party on campus. **Housing:** Guaranteed on-campus for all undergraduates. Coed dorms, single-sex dorms, apartments, fraternity/sorority housing, themed housing, wellness housing available. **Activities:** Bands, campus ministries, choral groups, drama, international student organizations, literary magazine, music ensembles, musical theater, radio station, student government, student newspaper, symphony orchestra, Phi Kappa Delta, Psi Chi, Earth Bound, black student union, NOW, Olivet gospel choir, Helping Hands, international club, Ladies of Excellence, Middle Ground, Olivet Chapter of NAACP, United Latino club.

Athletics. NCAA. **Intercollegiate:** Baseball M, basketball, bowling W, cheerleading, cross-country, diving, football (tackle) M, golf, lacrosse, soccer, softball W, swimming, tennis, track and field, volleyball, wrestling M. **Intramural:** Basketball, boxing M, football (non-tackle) M, football (tackle) M, sand volleyball, ultimate frisbee, volleyball, weight lifting. **Team name:** Comets.

Student services. Adult student services, alcohol/substance abuse counseling, chaplain/spiritual director, career counseling, services for economically disadvantaged, student employment services, financial aid counseling, health services, minority student services, personal counseling, placement for graduates, women's services.

Contact. E-mail: admissions@olivetcollege.edu
Phone: (269) 749-7635 Toll-free number: (800) 456-7189
Fax: (269) 749-6617
LIsa Lehman, Director of Admissions, Olivet College, 320 South Main Street, Olivet, MI 49076

Robert B. Miller College
Battle Creek, Michigan
www.millercollege.edu   CB code: 4801

◗ Private 4-year liberal arts college
◗ Commuter campus in small city
◗ 327 degree-seeking undergraduates

General. Regionally accredited. **Degrees:** 90 bachelor's awarded. **Location:** 64 miles from Grand Rapids, 122 miles from Detroit. **Calendar:** Semester, limited summer session. **Full-time faculty:** 6 total; 67% have terminal degrees, 67% women. **Part-time faculty:** 1 total; 100% women.

Basis for selection. Admission requirements vary by program.

2015-2016 Annual costs. Tuition/fees: $11,970.

Financial aid. Non-need-based: Scholarships awarded for academics, leadership.

Application procedures. Admission: No deadline. No application fee. **Financial aid:** No deadline.

Academics. Special study options: Distance learning, honors, independent study, internships, teacher certification program. **Credit/placement by examination:** AP, CLEP. Prior work and/or life experiences credit has no maximum limit. **Support services:** Tutoring.

Majors. Business: Business admin. **Education:** Adult/continuing, elementary. **Health services:** Health care admin, nursing (RN). **Liberal arts:** Arts/sciences.

Most popular majors. Business/marketing 26%, education 7%, health sciences 41%, liberal arts 23%.

Technology on campus. Online library, wireless network available.

Student services. Adult student services, student employment services.

Contact. E-mail: danielsonc@millercollege.edu
Phone: (269) 660-8021 ext. 2933
Chad Danielson, Director of Admissions, Robert B. Miller College, 450 North Avenue, Battle Creek, MI 49017

Rochester College
Rochester Hills, Michigan
www.rc.edu   CB code: 1516

◗ Private 4-year liberal arts college affiliated with the Church of Christ
◗ Residential campus in small city
◗ 960 degree-seeking undergraduates
◗ 12 graduate students
◗ ACT (writing optional), application essay required

General. Founded in 1959. Regionally accredited. **Degrees:** 207 bachelor's, 8 associate awarded; master's offered. **Location:** 25 miles from Detroit. **Calendar:** Semester, limited summer session. **Full-time faculty:** 38 total; 40% have terminal degrees, 5% minority, 50% women. **Part-time faculty:** 111 total; 20% have terminal degrees, 7% minority, 48% women. **Class size:** 85% < 20, 15% 20-39, less than 1% 40-49, less than 1% 50-99.

Freshman class profile.

GPA 3.75 or higher:	18%	Rank in top quarter:	28%
GPA 3.50-3.74:	15%	Rank in top tenth:	14%
GPA 3.0-3.49:	26%	Out-of-state:	5%
GPA 2.0-2.99:	38%	Live on campus:	53%

Basis for selection. ACT and GPA most important. Recommendations and interview considered. **Home schooled:** Transcript of courses and grades required.

High school preparation. College-preparatory program recommended.

2015-2016 Annual costs. Tuition/fees: $21,884. Room/board: $6,750. Books/supplies: $1,722. Personal expenses: $750.

Financial aid. Non-need-based: Scholarships awarded for academics, alumni affiliation, athletics, leadership, music/drama, religious affiliation, state residency.

Application procedures. Admission: No deadline. $35 fee. Admission notification on a rolling basis. **Financial aid:** Priority date 8/1; no closing date. FAFSA required. Applicants notified on a rolling basis starting 1/1; must reply within 2 week(s) of notification.

Academics. Special study options: Accelerated study, combined bachelor's/graduate degree, distance learning, dual enrollment of high school students, honors, independent study, internships, liberal arts/career combination, study abroad, teacher certification program. **Credit/placement by examination:** AP, CLEP, IB, SAT, ACT, institutional tests. 32 credit hours maximum toward associate degree, 64 toward bachelor's. Credit awarded for successful completion of selected DANTES Subject Standardized Testing Program. **Support services:** Learning center, reduced course load, remedial instruction, study skills assistance, tutoring, writing center.

Majors. Business: Accounting, business admin, management information systems, marketing. **Communications:** Communications/speech/rhetoric. **Computer sciences:** General. **Education:** General, early childhood, elementary, English, history, mathematics, middle, music, science, secondary. **English:** English lit. **History:** General. **Human services:** Social work. **Philosophy/religion:** Religion. **Psychology:** General. **Theology:** Bible, theology. **Visual/performing arts:** Music, music performance.

Most popular majors. Business/marketing 35%, communications/journalism 12%, education 14%, interdisciplinary studies 6%, psychology 21%.

Technology on campus. 34 workstations in dormitories, library, computer center. Dormitories wired for high-speed internet access and linked to campus network. Online library, helpline, student web hosting, wireless network available.

Student life. Freshman orientation: Mandatory, $100 fee. Preregistration for classes offered. **Housing:** Guaranteed on-campus for freshmen. Single-sex dorms, apartments available. $180 deposit, deadline 5/1. **Activities:** Concert band, campus ministries, choral groups, drama, international student organizations, literary magazine, musical theater, student government, student newspaper, service and mission organizations, social clubs, departmental organizations, honor societies.

Athletics. NCCAA. **Intercollegiate:** Baseball M, basketball, soccer, softball W, volleyball W. **Intramural:** Basketball, football (non-tackle), softball, volleyball. **Team name:** Warriors.

Student services. Adult student services, alcohol/substance abuse counseling, chaplain/spiritual director, career counseling, student employment services, financial aid counseling, minority student services, personal counseling, placement for graduates, veterans' counselor. **Physically disabled:** Services for visually, speech, hearing impaired.

Contact. E-mail: admissions@rc.edu
Phone: (248) 218-2031 Toll-free number: (800) 521-6010
Fax: (248) 218-2035
Scott Samuels, Admissions Director, Rochester College, 800 West Avon Road, Rochester Hills, MI 48307

Sacred Heart Major Seminary
Detroit, Michigan
www.shms.edu   CB code: 1686

- Private 4-year seminary college affiliated with the Roman Catholic Church
- Commuter campus in very large city
- 260 undergraduates
- SAT or ACT (ACT writing optional), application essay, interview required

General. Founded in 1919. Regionally accredited. **Degrees:** 24 bachelor's awarded; master's offered. **Calendar:** Semester, limited summer session. **Full-time faculty:** 25 total. **Part-time faculty:** 49 total. **Class size:** 70% < 20, 30% 20-39.

Freshman class profile.

GPA 3.75 or higher:	34%	Out-of-state:	67%
GPA 3.50-3.74:	33%	Live on campus:	100%
GPA 3.0-3.49:	33%		

Basis for selection. Recommendations of parish pastor, high school principal, and college counselor vital. School, community, and church-related activities viewed as important formative experiences. Religious commitment very important. Interview required for priesthood candidates. **Home schooled:** Transcript of courses and grades, interview, letter of recommendation (nonparent) required. **Learning Disabled:** Once admitted, students should contact the Office of the Dean of Studies for accommodations.

High school preparation. College-preparatory program recommended. 13 units required. Required and recommended units include English 4, mathematics 3, social studies 3, science 1 (laboratory 1) and foreign language 2.

2015-2016 Annual costs. Tuition/fees: $18,029. Room/board: $9,769. Books/supplies: $1,496. Personal expenses: $36. **Additional information:** Theology students pay additional tuition charges.

Financial aid. **Non-need-based:** Scholarships awarded for academics, religious affiliation.

Application procedures. **Admission:** Closing date 8/15 (postmark date). $30 fee. Application must be submitted online. Admission notification by 8/22. **Financial aid:** No deadline. FAFSA, institutional form required. Applicants notified on a rolling basis; must reply within 2 week(s) of notification.

Academics. 30 to 40% of undergraduate course work taken at other consortium colleges. **Special study options:** Double major, dual enrollment of high school students, ESL, independent study. **Credit/placement by examination:** AP, CLEP, institutional tests. 6 credit hours maximum toward associate degree, 12 toward bachelor's. Must accumulate 15 hours at SHMS before credit is recorded. **Support services:** Learning center, reduced course load, study skills assistance, tutoring.

Majors. **Liberal arts:** Arts/sciences. **Philosophy/religion:** Philosophy.

Most popular majors. Liberal arts 48%, philosophy/religious studies 39%, theological studies 13%.

Technology on campus. 12 workstations in library, computer center. Online library available.

Student life. Freshman orientation: Mandatory. Preregistration for classes offered. Three days for seminarians, 1 day for commuters at beginning of fall term. **Policies:** On-campus housing available and guaranteed to seminarians only. Religious observance required. **Activities:** Campus ministries, choral groups, music ensembles, student government, student newspaper.

Student services. Chaplain/spiritual director, financial aid counseling.

Contact. E-mail: IFM@shms.edu
Phone: (313) 883-8520 Fax: (313) 883-8530
Tamra Fromm, Director of Admissions and Enrollment Management, Sacred Heart Major Seminary, 2701 Chicago Boulevard, Detroit, MI 48206-1799

Saginaw Valley State University
University Center, Michigan
www.svsu.edu   CB code: 1766

- Public 4-year university
- Commuter campus in small city
- 8,434 degree-seeking undergraduates: 15% part-time, 57% women, 9% African American, 1% Asian American, 4% Hispanic/Latino, 2% Multiracial, non-Hispanic, 8% international
- 1,003 degree-seeking graduate students
- 76% of applicants admitted
- SAT or ACT (ACT writing optional) required
- 40% graduate within 6 years

General. Founded in 1963. Regionally accredited. **Degrees:** 1,438 bachelor's awarded; master's, professional offered. **Location:** 10 miles from Bay City and Saginaw. **Calendar:** Semester, limited summer session. **Full-time faculty:** 308 total; 83% have terminal degrees. **Part-time faculty:** 447 total. **Class size:** 33% < 20, 61% 20-39, 3% 40-49, 2% 50-99, less than 1% >100. **Special facilities:** Fine arts center, sculpture museum, observatory.

Freshman class profile. 7,021 applied, 5,348 admitted, 1,571 enrolled.

Mid 50% test scores		End year in good standing:	65%
ACT composite:	19-25	Return as sophomores:	72%
GPA 3.75 or higher:	30%	Out-of-state:	2%
GPA 3.50-3.74:	17%	Live on campus:	68%
GPA 3.0-3.49:	29%	International:	15%
GPA 2.0-2.99:	24%	Fraternities:	2%
Rank in top quarter:	7%	Sororities:	3%
Rank in top tenth:	2%		

Basis for selection. Minimum high school GPA of 2.5 preferred.

High school preparation. College-preparatory program recommended. Recommended units include English 4, mathematics 3, social studies 3, science 3 and foreign language 2.

2015-2016 Annual costs. Tuition/fees: $8,969; $21,062 out-of-state. Room/board: $8,600. Books/supplies: $1,250. Personal expenses: $1,114.

2015-2016 Financial aid. **Need-based:** 1,535 full-time freshmen applied for aid; 1,193 deemed to have need; 1,193 received aid. Average scholarship/grant was $4,100; average loan $3,286. 47% of total undergraduate aid awarded as scholarships/grants, 53% as loans/jobs. **Non-need-based:** Awarded to 3,691 full-time undergraduates, including 1,024 freshmen. Scholarships awarded for academics, art, athletics, leadership, minority status, music/drama.

Application procedures. **Admission:** No deadline. $30 fee, may be waived for applicants with need. Admission notification on a rolling basis. **Financial aid:** Priority date 1/1; no closing date. FAFSA required. Applicants notified on a rolling basis starting 3/1.

Academics. **Special study options:** Accelerated study, combined bachelor's/graduate degree, cooperative education, distance learning, double major, dual enrollment of high school students, ESL, honors, independent study, internships, student-designed major, study abroad, teacher certification program. **Credit/placement by examination:** AP, CLEP, IB, ACT, institutional tests. 62 credit hours maximum toward bachelor's degree. **Support services:** Learning center, reduced course load, remedial instruction, study skills assistance, tutoring, writing center.

Majors. **Biology:** General, biochemistry. **Business:** General, accounting, business admin, finance, international, managerial economics, marketing, operations. **Communications:** Communications/speech/rhetoric. **Computer sciences:** General, systems analysis. **Education:** Elementary, English, physical, science, secondary, special ed. **Engineering:** Electrical, mechanical. **English:** Creative writing, English lit, technical writing. **Foreign languages:** French, Spanish. **Health services:** Athletic training, clinical lab science, nurse practitioner, nursing (RN). **History:** General. **Human services:** General, social work. **Math:** General, applied. **Parks/recreation:** Exercise sciences. **Physical sciences:** Chemical physics, chemistry, optics, physics. **Protective services:** Criminal justice. **Psychology:** General. **Social sciences:** International relations, political science, sociology. **Visual/performing arts:** Art, dramatic, graphic design, music, studio arts.

Most popular majors. Business/marketing 17%, education 10%, health sciences 20%, public administration/social services 9%, security/protective services 6%.

Technology on campus. 1,100 workstations in library, computer center, student center. Dormitories wired for high-speed internet access and linked to campus network. Commuter students can connect to campus network. Online course registration, online library, helpline, student web hosting, wireless network available.

Student life. Freshman orientation: Mandatory, $95 fee. Preregistration for classes offered. One-day program includes advising and registering for fall classes. **Housing:** Coed dorms, special housing for disabled, apartments, themed housing available. $200 partly refundable deposit. **Activities:** Bands, campus ministries, choral groups, dance, drama, film society, international student organizations, literary magazine, music ensembles, Model UN, musical theater, student government, student newspaper, Adventist Students for Christ, God's Children of Integrity, His House Christian Fellowship, Muslim students association, Valley Voices Gospel Choir, Indian students association, Japanese Culture club, Chinese students and scholars association, Saudi club, College Democrats, College Republicans.

Athletics. NCAA. **Intercollegiate:** Baseball M, basketball, bowling M, cheerleading, cross-country, football (tackle) M, golf M, soccer, softball W, tennis W, track and field, volleyball W. **Intramural:** Badminton, basketball, football (non-tackle), golf, racquetball, soccer, softball, table tennis, tennis, volleyball, water polo. **Team name:** Cardinals.

Student services. Adult student services, alcohol/substance abuse counseling, career counseling, services for economically disadvantaged, student employment services, financial aid counseling, health services, minority student services, personal counseling, placement for graduates, veterans' counselor, women's services. **Physically disabled:** Services for visually, hearing impaired.

Contact. E-mail: admissions@svsu.edu
Phone: (989) 964-4200 Toll-free number: (800) 968-9500
Fax: (989) 790-0180
Jennifer Pahl, Director of Admissions, Saginaw Valley State University, 7400 Bay Road, University Center, MI 48710

Siena Heights University
Adrian, Michigan
www.sienaheights.edu
CB member
CB code: 1719

- Private 4-year university and liberal arts college affiliated with the Roman Catholic Church
- Residential campus in large town
- 2,266 degree-seeking undergraduates
- 240 graduate students
- SAT or ACT (ACT writing optional) required

General. Founded in 1919. Regionally accredited. Degree completion programs are offered in Battle Creek, Benton Harbor, Dearborn, Jackson, Lansing, Monroe, and Southfield. Completely online programs are also available. **Degrees:** 888 bachelor's, 10 associate awarded; master's offered. **Location:** 35 miles from Ann Arbor, MI, and Toledo, OH; 70 miles from downtown Detroit, MI. **Calendar:** Semester, extensive summer session. **Full-time faculty:** 81 total; 82% have terminal degrees, 5% minority, 51% women. **Part-time faculty:** 171 total; 55% women. **Class size:** 79% < 20, 20% 20-39, less than 1% 40-49, less than 1% 50-99.

Freshman class profile.

| Out-of-state: | 10% | Fraternities: | 1% |
| Live on campus: | 89% | Sororities: | 1% |

Basis for selection. GPA and standardized test scores most important. Core GPA is a very important consideration for admission. IB tests are also used for placement. ACT recommended. **Home schooled:** Transcript of courses and grades required.

High school preparation. College-preparatory program recommended. 21 units recommended. Recommended units include English 4, mathematics 3, social studies 4, science 3 (laboratory 2) and foreign language 2.

2015-2016 Annual costs. Tuition/fees: $23,750. Room/board: $9,710. Books/supplies: $2,556.

Application procedures. Admission: Priority date 3/1; deadline 8/1. No application fee. Admission notification on a rolling basis beginning on or about 7/1. Recommended reply by May 1 or within 2 weeks if notified thereafter. **Financial aid:** Priority date 3/15, closing date 8/15.

Academics. Special study options: Cooperative education, cross-registration, distance learning, double major, dual enrollment of high school students, ESL, external degree, independent study, internships, liberal arts/career combination, student-designed major, study abroad, teacher certification program, weekend college. **Credit/placement by examination:** AP, CLEP, IB, SAT, ACT, institutional tests. **Support services:** Learning center, pre-admission summer program, reduced course load, remedial instruction, study skills assistance, tutoring, writing center.

Majors. Area/ethnic studies: American. **Biology:** General. **Business:** General, accounting, hospitality/recreation. **Communications:** Communications/speech/rhetoric. **Computer sciences:** General. **Education:** Business, elementary, secondary. **English:** Creative writing, English lit. **Foreign languages:** Spanish. **Health services:** Nursing (RN), predental, premedicine, prenursing, prepharmacy. **History:** General. **Human services:** Social work. **Liberal arts:** Arts/sciences. **Math:** General. **Parks/recreation:** Sports admin. **Philosophy/religion:** Philosophy, religion. **Physical sciences:** Chemistry. **Protective services:** Criminal justice. **Psychology:** General. **Social sciences:** General. **Visual/performing arts:** Art, ceramics, commercial/advertising art, dramatic, drawing, metal/jewelry, music, painting, photography, sculpture, studio arts.

Most popular majors. Business/marketing 22%, health sciences 24%, liberal arts 6%, public administration/social services 7%, security/protective services 11%.

Technology on campus. Dormitories linked to campus network. Commuter students can connect to campus network. Online course registration, online library, helpline, student web hosting, wireless network available.

Student life. Freshman orientation: Mandatory. Preregistration for classes offered. **Housing:** Coed dorms, apartments available. $100 fully refundable deposit. Dorm floors exclusively for men and for women. **Activities:** Bands, campus ministries, choral groups, dance, drama, international student organizations, literary magazine, music ensembles, musical theater, student government, student newspaper, symphony orchestra, campus ministry scholars program, student programming and residence hall coalition, Men of Distinction, PRIDE, Students Embracing Experiences in Diversity, Green Light club, PSI CHI, Acappellicans (acappella group), Meaning in Colors, Siena Serves.

Athletics. NAIA. **Intercollegiate:** Baseball M, basketball, bowling, cheerleading, cross-country, football (tackle) M, golf, lacrosse, soccer, softball W, track and field, volleyball. **Intramural:** Basketball, bowling, softball, ultimate frisbee, volleyball. **Team name:** Saints.

Student services. Adult student services, alcohol/substance abuse counseling, chaplain/spiritual director, career counseling, services for economically disadvantaged, student employment services, financial aid counseling, health services, minority student services, personal counseling, placement for graduates, veterans' counselor. **Physically disabled:** Services for visually, hearing impaired.

Contact. E-mail: admissions@sienaheights.edu
Phone: (517) 264-7180 Toll-free number: (800) 521-0009 ext. 7180
Fax: (517) 264-7745
Trudy Mohre, Director of Undergraduate Admissions, Siena Heights University, 1247 East Siena Heights Drive, Adrian, MI 49221-1796

Spring Arbor University
Spring Arbor, Michigan
www.arbor.edu
CB code: 1732

- Private 4-year university and liberal arts college affiliated with the Free Methodist Church of North America
- Residential campus in rural community
- 2,307 degree-seeking undergraduates: 26% part-time, 69% women
- 969 degree-seeking graduate students
- 69% of applicants admitted
- SAT or ACT (ACT writing optional) required
- 52% graduate within 6 years

General. Founded in 1873. Regionally accredited. Adult degree completion offered through School of Graduate and Professional Studies. Nine degree completion programs available at 13 regional sites across Michigan (including one in Ohio). **Degrees:** 755 bachelor's, 24 associate awarded; master's offered. **ROTC:** Army, Air Force. **Location:** 8 miles from Jackson, 40 miles from Lansing. **Calendar:** Semester, limited summer session. **Full-time faculty:** 84 total; 74% have terminal degrees, 10% minority, 32% women. **Part-time faculty:** 51 total. **Class size:** 71% < 20, 24% 20-39, 3% 40-49, 1% 50-99. **Special facilities:** Trading center with high-tech trading room.

Freshman class profile. 1,546 applied, 1,065 admitted, 291 enrolled.

Mid 50% test scores		Rank in top quarter:	48%
ACT composite:	20-26	Rank in top tenth:	23%
GPA 3.75 or higher:	38%	Return as sophomores:	79%
GPA 3.50-3.74:	19%	Out-of-state:	12%
GPA 3.0-3.49:	23%	Live on campus:	95%
GPA 2.0-2.99:	19%		

Basis for selection. 20 ACT/950 SAT (exclusive of Writing) and 2.6 GPA recommended. Applicants whose scores are below recommendations may be admitted on a conditional basis. ACT recommended. Interview recommended for borderline applicants. **Home schooled:** Letter of recommendation from the parent/teacher and 2-3 page paper regarding applicant's home school experience required.

High school preparation. College-preparatory program required. 14 units required. Required and recommended units include English 4, mathematics 3, history 3, science 3 (laboratory 3), foreign language 2 and computer science 1.

2015-2016 Annual costs. Tuition/fees: $25,510. Room/board: $8,870. Books/supplies: $800. Personal expenses: $922.

Financial aid. **Non-need-based:** Scholarships awarded for academics, art, athletics, minority status, music/drama, religious affiliation.

Application procedures. Admission: Priority date 2/15; deadline 8/1 (receipt date). $30 fee, may be waived for applicants with need, free for online applicants. Admission notification on a rolling basis beginning on or about 9/1. **Financial aid:** Priority date 3/1; no closing date. FAFSA required. Applicants notified on a rolling basis starting 3/1; must reply within 2 week(s) of notification.

Academics. Special study options: Accelerated study, combined bachelor's/graduate degree, cross-registration, distance learning, double major, dual enrollment of high school students, ESL, honors, independent study, internships, student-designed major, study abroad, teacher certification program, Washington semester, weekend college. Environmental study semester offered at AuSable Trails Institute in northern Michigan; cross-cultural program with several foreign country destinations. **Credit/placement by examination:** AP, CLEP, IB, SAT, ACT, institutional tests. 10 credit hours maximum toward associate degree, 60 toward bachelor's. No more than 1/3 of credits for a major can be earned through credit by examination. **Support services:** Learning center, pre-admission summer program, reduced course load, remedial instruction, study skills assistance, tutoring, writing center.

Majors. Biology: General, biochemistry. **Business:** Accounting, actuarial science, business admin, finance, management information systems, managerial economics, operations. **Communications:** General, advertising, broadcast journalism, communications/speech/rhetoric, public relations. **Computer sciences:** Computer science. **Education:** Art, biology, chemistry, early childhood, elementary, English, history, mathematics, music, physical, secondary, social science, social studies, Spanish, special ed. **English:** Creative writing, English lit, rhetoric/composition. **Foreign languages:** Spanish. **Health services:** Health care admin. **History:** General. **Human services:** Social work. **Math:** General. **Parks/recreation:** General, health/fitness. **Philosophy/religion:** Christian, philosophy, religion. **Physical sciences:** Chemistry, theoretical physics. **Protective services:** Law enforcement admin. **Psychology:** General. **Social sciences:** General, political economy, sociology, urban studies. **Theology:** Bible, missionary, pastoral counseling, sacred music, theology, youth ministry. **Visual/performing arts:** Art, design, dramatic, film/cinema/video, graphic design, music, music performance. **Work/family studies:** Family studies.

Most popular majors. Biology 6%, business/marketing 11%, communications/journalism 7%, education 10%, history 7%, parks/recreation 10%, philosophy/religious studies 7%, psychology 9%, public administration/social services 10%, social sciences 7%.

Technology on campus. 362 workstations in dormitories, library, computer center, student center. Dormitories wired for high-speed internet access and linked to campus network. Commuter students can connect to campus network. Online course registration, helpline, repair service, student web hosting, wireless network available.

Student life. Freshman orientation: Mandatory. Preregistration for classes offered. Three-day session held at beginning of September. Parents encouraged to attend the first day. **Policies:** Emphasis placed on active commitment to Jesus Christ and His teachings. Chapel attendance required twice a week. Religious observance required. **Housing:** Guaranteed on-campus for freshmen. Single-sex dorms, special housing for disabled, apartments, wellness housing available. $200 fully refundable deposit, deadline 5/1. Community homes on campus. **Activities:** Bands, campus ministries, choral groups, drama, film society, international student organizations, literary magazine, music ensembles, Model UN, musical theater, radio station, student government, student newspaper, symphony orchestra, Inter-faith shelter ministries, Habitat for Humanity, Band of Brothers, Circle of Sisters, Bandfire, Heartside Homeless, Wellspring, multicultural organization.

Athletics. NAIA, NCCAA. **Intercollegiate:** Baseball M, basketball, cross-country, golf, soccer, softball W, tennis, track and field, volleyball W. **Intramural:** Basketball, field hockey M, football (non-tackle) M, golf M, soccer, softball, table tennis, tennis, ultimate frisbee, volleyball. **Team name:** Cougars.

Student services. Adult student services, chaplain/spiritual director, career counseling, student employment services, financial aid counseling, health services, minority student services, personal counseling, placement for graduates. **Physically disabled:** Services for visually, speech, hearing impaired.

Contact. E-mail: admissions@arbor.edu
Phone: (517) 750-6468 Toll-free number: (800) 968-0011
Fax: (517) 750-6620
Jill Raymond, Director of Enrollment Operations, Spring Arbor University, 106 East Main Street, Spring Arbor, MI 49283-9799

University of Detroit Mercy
Detroit, Michigan   **CB member**
www.udmercy.edu   **CB code: 1835**

▶ Private 4-year university affiliated with the Roman Catholic Church
▶ Commuter campus in very large city
▶ 2,586 degree-seeking undergraduates: 20% part-time, 65% women, 15% African American, 5% Asian American, 4% Hispanic/Latino, 3% Multiracial, non-Hispanic, 5% international
▶ 1,121 degree-seeking graduate students
▶ 73% of applicants admitted
▶ SAT or ACT (ACT writing optional), application essay required
▶ 63% graduate within 6 years

General. Founded in 1991. Regionally accredited. **Degrees:** 819 bachelor's awarded; master's, professional, doctoral offered. **Calendar:** Semester, extensive summer session. **Full-time faculty:** 322 total; 92% have terminal degrees, 10% minority, 49% women. **Part-time faculty:** 402 total; 66% have terminal degrees, 14% minority, 52% women. **Class size:** 53% < 20, 39% 20-39, 5% 40-49, 2% 50-99.

Freshman class profile. 4,453 applied, 3,247 admitted, 516 enrolled.

Mid 50% test scores		Rank in top quarter:	45%
SAT critical reading:	440-610	Rank in top tenth:	20%
SAT math:	460-630	End year in good standing:	88%
SAT writing:	430-610	Return as sophomores:	85%
ACT composite:	22-27	Out-of-state:	8%
GPA 3.75 or higher:	35%	Live on campus:	63%
GPA 3.50-3.74:	21%	International:	5%
GPA 3.0-3.49:	30%	Fraternities:	3%
GPA 2.0-2.99:	14%	Sororities:	9%

Basis for selection. A combination of standardized test scores and academic achievement as summarized on high school and/or college transcripts. Essays, personal statements, recommendation letters and evaluations are also required. Each college/major has its own requirement. For students who do not meet the minimum requirements for entry into a specific college or school of the University, but who show potential, a personal non-cognitive characteristic interview is conducted by admissions and/or student success staff and assessed using a rubric. International students are not required to submit the ACT or SAT. Interview required for University College applicants, recommended for all others. **Home schooled:** Documentation of academic progress and completion of high school from affiliated home schooling agency, local school district or State Department of Education required. More information may be requested during the evaluation process.

High school preparation. College-preparatory program recommended. 11 units required. Required and recommended units include English 4, mathematics 3, social studies 1, history 2, science 2, foreign language 1, visual/performing arts 1 and academic electives 1.

2015-2016 Annual costs. Tuition/fees: $38,626. Room/board: $8,870. Books/supplies: $880. Personal expenses: $3,382.

2015-2016 Financial aid. Need-based: 455 full-time freshmen applied for aid; 365 deemed to have need; 365 received aid. Average need met was 78%. Average scholarship/grant was $27,115; average loan $3,764. 69% of total undergraduate aid awarded as scholarships/grants, 31% as loans/jobs. **Non-need-based:** Awarded to 712 full-time undergraduates, including 174

freshmen. Scholarships awarded for academics, alumni affiliation, athletics, religious affiliation, state residency.

Application procedures. Admission: Priority date 12/1; deadline 3/1 (receipt date). No application fee. Application must be submitted online. Admission notification on a rolling basis beginning on or about 10/1. Must reply by May 1 or within 2 week(s) if notified thereafter. **Financial aid:** Priority date 4/1; no closing date. FAFSA required. Applicants notified on a rolling basis starting 3/1.

Academics. Special study options: Accelerated study, combined bachelor's/graduate degree, cooperative education, cross-registration, distance learning, double major, dual enrollment of high school students, ESL, honors, independent study, internships, study abroad, teacher certification program, Washington semester, weekend college. Bachelor's degree completion program and an accelerated second bachelor's program for registered nurses. Multiple programs that combine a bachelor's degree with a master's or professional level degree. **Credit/placement by examination:** AP, CLEP, IB, institutional tests. 30 credit hours maximum toward bachelor's degree. **Support services:** Learning center, reduced course load, remedial instruction, study skills assistance, tutoring, writing center.

Majors. Architecture: Architecture. **Biology:** General, biochemistry. **Business:** Accounting, business admin, management information systems. **Communications:** Communications/speech/rhetoric, digital media. **Computer sciences:** Computer science. **Education:** General, biology, elementary, emotionally handicapped, learning disabled, mathematics, secondary, social science, social studies, special ed. **Engineering:** General, architectural, civil, electrical, manufacturing, mechanical, robotics, software. **English:** English lit. **Health services:** Dental hygiene, health care admin, health information management, health services admin, nursing (RN), predental, premedicine, substance abuse counseling. **History:** General. **Human services:** Social work. **Liberal arts:** Arts/sciences. **Math:** General, applied. **Philosophy/religion:** Philosophy, religion. **Physical sciences:** Chemistry. **Protective services:** Criminal justice. **Psychology:** General, developmental, industrial. **Social sciences:** General, economics, political science, sociology. **Visual/performing arts:** Dramatic.

Most popular majors. Biology 12%, business/marketing 7%, health sciences 58%.

Technology on campus. 250 workstations in library, computer center. Dormitories wired for high-speed internet access and linked to campus network. Commuter students can connect to campus network. Online course registration, helpline, wireless network available.

Student life. Freshman orientation: Mandatory, $250 fee. Preregistration for classes offered. **Housing:** Guaranteed on-campus for all undergraduates. Coed dorms, themed housing available. $100 nonrefundable deposit, deadline 5/1. **Activities:** Pep band, campus ministries, choral groups, drama, film society, international student organizations, literary magazine, musical theater, radio station, student government, student newspaper, Campus Crusade for Christ, Muslim Student Association, Arab Cultural Society, Chinese Student Association, International Student Union, Chaldean American Student Association, Hispanic American Student Association, Indian Student Association, African-American Student Organization.

Athletics. NCAA. **Intercollegiate:** Basketball, cross-country, fencing, golf, lacrosse, soccer, softball W, tennis, track and field. **Intramural:** Basketball, cheerleading, field hockey, table tennis, volleyball. **Team name:** Detroit Titans.

Student services. Adult student services, alcohol/substance abuse counseling, chaplain/spiritual director, career counseling, student employment services, financial aid counseling, health services, personal counseling, placement for graduates. **Physically disabled:** Services for visually, speech, hearing impaired.

Contact. E-mail: admissions@udmercy.edu
Phone: (313) 993-1245 Toll-free number: (800) 635-5020
Fax: (313) 993-3326
Deborah Stieffel, Vice President for Enrollment Management & Student Affairs, University of Detroit Mercy, 4001 West McNichols Road, Detroit, MI 48221-3038

University of Michigan
Ann Arbor, Michigan
www.umich.edu

CB member
CB code: 1839

- Public 4-year university
- Residential campus in small city
- 28,120 degree-seeking undergraduates: 3% part-time, 50% women, 4% African American, 13% Asian American, 5% Hispanic/Latino, 3% Multiracial, non-Hispanic, 7% international

- 15,011 degree-seeking graduate students
- 26% of applicants admitted
- SAT or ACT with writing, application essay required
- 90% graduate within 6 years

General. Founded in 1817. Regionally accredited. **Degrees:** 7,091 bachelor's awarded; master's, professional, doctoral offered. **ROTC:** Army, Naval, Air Force. **Location:** 43 miles from Detroit. **Calendar:** Trimester, limited summer session. **Full-time faculty:** 2,735 total; 91% have terminal degrees, 23% minority, 40% women. **Part-time faculty:** 593 total; 76% have terminal degrees, 15% minority, 49% women. **Class size:** 57% < 20, 22% 20-39, 4% 40-49, 10% 50-99, 7% >100. **Special facilities:** Botanical gardens, biological station in northern Michigan, arboretum, planetarium, laboratories, observatory, field station in greater Yellowstone ecosystem, exhibit museum, art museum, herbarium.

Freshman class profile. 51,761 applied, 13,584 admitted, 6,071 enrolled.

Mid 50% test scores			
SAT critical reading:	630-730	GPA 3.0-3.49:	4%
SAT math:	660-770	End year in good standing:	97%
SAT writing:	640-730	Return as sophomores:	97%
ACT composite:	29-33	Out-of-state:	41%
GPA 3.75 or higher:	77%	Live on campus:	98%
GPA 3.50-3.74:	19%	International:	4%

Basis for selection. School achievement record, including quality of school and courses elected, and test scores. Talents and extracurricular activities considered. Audition, portfolio or interview required for music majors; portfolio required for art majors.

High school preparation. College-preparatory program recommended. 18 units required; 27 recommended. Required and recommended units include English 4, mathematics 3-4, social studies 3-4, history 3-4, science 3-4 (laboratory 1), foreign language 2-4, computer science 1 and visual/performing arts 2. Recommend AP, IB, honors, enriched, advanced, accelerated courses. Two units of foreign language required for College of LSA.

2015-2016 Annual costs. Tuition/fees: $13,856; $43,476 out-of-state. Room/board: $10,554. Books/supplies: $1,048. Personal expenses: $2,354.

2014-2015 Financial aid. Need-based: 3,415 full-time freshmen applied for aid; 2,539 deemed to have need; 2,359 received aid. Average need met was 86%. Average scholarship/grant was $15,006; average loan $4,254. 72% of total undergraduate aid awarded as scholarships/grants, 28% as loans/jobs. **Non-need-based:** Awarded to 11,566 full-time undergraduates, including 3,108 freshmen. Scholarships awarded for academics, alumni affiliation, art, athletics, leadership, music/drama, religious affiliation, ROTC, state residency.

Application procedures. Admission: Priority date 11/1; deadline 2/1 (postmark date). $75 fee, may be waived for applicants with need. Admission notification on a rolling basis beginning on or about 12/24. Must reply by May 1 or within 2 week(s) if notified thereafter. **Financial aid:** Priority date 4/30, closing date 4/30. FAFSA, CSS PROFILE required. Applicants notified by 4/30; Applicants notified on a rolling basis starting 3/15.

Academics. Over 150 first-year seminars and hundreds of undergraduate research opportunities. Small-scale, interdisciplinary instruction programs in residence halls; freshman and sophomore seminars, undergraduate research, study abroad opportunities. Numerous interdisciplinary undergraduate programs between Engineering, LSA, Business, and other schools/colleges. **Special study options:** Accelerated study, combined bachelor's/graduate degree, cooperative education, cross-registration, distance learning, double major, dual enrollment of high school students, ESL, exchange student, external degree, honors, independent study, internships, liberal arts/career combination, student-designed major, study abroad, teacher certification program, urban semester, Washington semester, weekend college. Dual and combined baccalaureate degree options in the College of Engineering; dual degree options in the Ross School of Business, College of Literature, Science and Arts, School of Kinesiology, and School of Music, Theater and Dance. **Credit/placement by examination:** AP, CLEP, IB, institutional tests. 60 credit hours maximum toward bachelor's degree. Policies on credit by examination vary by exam. **Support services:** Learning center, reduced course load, study skills assistance, tutoring, writing center. Library use workshops; software use workshops.

Honors college/program. Grades, test scores, recommendations, essay used in decision process. Roughly 500 members of each incoming freshman class admitted. Students must elect Honors courses, maintain minimum course load and GPA, and pursue an Honors major.

Majors. Architecture: Architecture. **Area/ethnic studies:** African-American, American, Asian, Chicano/Hispanic-American/Latino, Latin American/Caribbean, Near/Middle Eastern, Russian/Slavic, women's. **Biology:** General, biochemistry, biophysics, cellular/molecular, ecology/evolutionary, microbiology, molecular, neuroscience. **Business:** Business admin, organizational behavior. **Communications:** Communications/speech/rhetoric. **Computer sciences:** General, database management, informatics, information systems. **Conservation:** General, environmental studies. **Education:** Elementary, music, secondary. **Engineering:** General, aerospace, applied physics, biomedical, chemical, civil, computer, electrical, engineering science, environmental, geological, industrial, marine, materials, mechanical, nuclear. **English:** Creative writing, English lit. **Foreign languages:** Ancient Greek, classics, comparative lit, French, German, Hebrew, Italian, Latin, linguistics, modern Greek, Polish, Romance, Russian, Spanish. **Health services:** Athletic training, dental hygiene, nursing (RN), pharmaceutical sciences. **History:** General. **Human services:** Public policy. **Liberal arts:** Humanities. **Math:** General, statistics. **Parks/recreation:** Exercise sciences, health/fitness, sports admin. **Philosophy/religion:** Judaic, philosophy, religion. **Physical sciences:** Astronomy, atmospheric science, chemistry, geology, oceanography, physics. **Psychology:** Experimental, psychobiology. **Social sciences:** General, anthropology, economics, political science, sociology. **Visual/performing arts:** Art, art history/conservation, ceramics, dance, dramatic, drawing, fiber arts, film/cinema/video, graphic design, illustration, industrial design, jazz, metal/jewelry, music, music history, music performance, music technology, music theory/composition, musical theater, printmaking, sculpture, theater design, woodwind instruments.

Most popular majors. Biology 9%, business/marketing 7%, engineering/engineering technologies 15%, psychology 10%, social sciences 14%, visual/performing arts 6%.

Technology on campus. 2,564 workstations in dormitories, library, computer center, student center. Dormitories wired for high-speed internet access and linked to campus network. Commuter students can connect to campus network. Online course registration, online library, helpline, repair service, student web hosting, wireless network available.

Student life. Freshman orientation: Mandatory, $297 fee. Preregistration for classes offered. Numerous 3-day programs offered throughout summer. **Policies:** Expect Respect is a campaign aimed at creating a unified community and educating students on what it means to respect others. Smoke-free campus. **Housing:** Guaranteed on-campus for freshmen. Coed dorms, single-sex dorms, special housing for disabled, apartments, cooperative housing, fraternity/sorority housing, gender-neutral housing, themed housing, wellness housing available. Living-learning communities available. **Activities:** Bands, campus ministries, choral groups, dance, drama, film society, international student organizations, literary magazine, music ensembles, Model UN, musical theater, opera, radio station, student government, student newspaper, symphony orchestra, TV station, 1507 student organizations available.

Athletics. NCAA. **Intercollegiate:** Baseball M, basketball, cross-country, diving, fencing, field hockey W, football (tackle) M, golf, gymnastics, ice hockey M, lacrosse, rifle, rowing (crew) W, rugby, sailing, soccer, softball W, swimming, tennis, track and field, ultimate frisbee, volleyball, water polo, wrestling M. **Intramural:** Badminton, basketball, bowling, football (non-tackle), racquetball, sand volleyball, soccer, softball, squash, swimming, tennis, triathlon, ultimate frisbee, volleyball. **Team name:** Wolverines.

Student services. Adult student services, alcohol/substance abuse counseling, chaplain/spiritual director, career counseling, student employment services, financial aid counseling, health services, legal services, minority student services, on-campus daycare, personal counseling, placement for graduates, veterans' counselor, women's services. **Physically disabled:** Services for visually, speech, hearing impaired.

Contact. Phone: (734) 764-7433 Fax: (734) 936-0740
Erica Sanders, Director, Office of Undergraduate Admissions, University of Michigan, 1220 Student Activities Building, Ann Arbor, MI 48109-1316

University of Michigan: Dearborn

Dearborn, Michigan   CB member
www.umd.umich.edu   CB code: 1861

- Public 4-year university
- Commuter campus in small city
- 6,843 degree-seeking undergraduates: 29% part-time, 48% women, 10% African American, 7% Asian American, 6% Hispanic/Latino, 3% Multiracial, non-Hispanic, 2% international
- 1,834 degree-seeking graduate students
- 62% of applicants admitted
- SAT or ACT (ACT writing optional) required
- 53% graduate within 6 years

General. Founded in 1959. Regionally accredited. **Degrees:** 1,292 bachelor's awarded; master's, doctoral offered. **ROTC:** Army, Naval, Air Force.

Location: 10 miles from Detroit. **Calendar:** Semester, limited summer session. **Full-time faculty:** 322 total; 87% have terminal degrees, 34% minority, 41% women. **Part-time faculty:** 233 total; 38% have terminal degrees, 17% minority, 42% women. **Class size:** 30% < 20, 50% 20-39, 11% 40-49, 7% 50-99, less than 1% >100. **Special facilities:** Environmental study area, extensive rotating art collection, engineering CAD-CAM robotics laboratory, Armenian research center.

Freshman class profile. 5,312 applied, 3,318 admitted, 951 enrolled.

Mid 50% test scores			
ACT composite:	21-27	Rank in top quarter:	59%
GPA 3.75 or higher:	43%	Rank in top tenth:	28%
GPA 3.50-3.74:	19%	Return as sophomores:	81%
GPA 3.0-3.49:	28%	Out-of-state:	4%
GPA 2.0-2.99:	10%	International:	1%

Basis for selection. 3.0 GPA with 500 SAT verbal and math or 22 ACT preferred; class rank considered. Interview recommended for applicants with less than 3.0 GPA or 20 ACT/1000 SAT (exclusive of Writing). Essay recommended for all.

High school preparation. 15 units required; 20 recommended. Required and recommended units include English 4, mathematics 4, social studies 4, history 4, science 2 (laboratory 1) and foreign language 2. 1 unit information technology and 1 unit fine and performing arts recommended.

2015-2016 Annual costs. Tuition/fees: $11,304; $23,520 out-of-state. Books/supplies: $1,300. Personal expenses: $3,306.

2015-2016 Financial aid. Need-based: Average need met was 67%. Average scholarship/grant was $6,909; average loan $2,868. 46% of total undergraduate aid awarded as scholarships/grants, 54% as loans/jobs. **Non-need-based:** Scholarships awarded for academics, alumni affiliation, art, athletics, job skills, leadership, minority status, music/drama, ROTC, state residency.

Application procedures. Admission: Priority date 5/1; no deadline. $30 fee, may be waived for applicants with need, free for online applicants. Admission notification on a rolling basis beginning on or about 9/1. Must reply by 9/1. Must reply by May 1 or within 4 week(s) if notified thereafter. **Financial aid:** Priority date 3/1; no closing date. FAFSA required. Applicants notified on a rolling basis starting 3/5; must reply within 3 week(s) of notification.

Academics. Special study options: Cooperative education, cross-registration, distance learning, double major, dual enrollment of high school students, honors, independent study, internships, liberal arts/career combination, student-designed major, study abroad, teacher certification program, Washington semester. Professional development courses in education, engineering, liberal arts, and management. **Credit/placement by examination:** AP, CLEP, institutional tests. 30 credit hours maximum toward bachelor's degree. **Support services:** Learning center, pre-admission summer program, tutoring, writing center.

Majors. Area/ethnic studies: American. **Biology:** General, bacteriology, biochemistry, ecology. **Business:** Business admin, management science. **Communications:** Communications/speech/rhetoric. **Computer sciences:** General, programming. **Conservation:** General, environmental studies. **Education:** General, art, business, chemistry, early childhood, foreign languages, mathematics, science, secondary, social studies. **Engineering:** General, computer, electrical, manufacturing, mechanical. **English:** English lit. **Foreign languages:** French, Spanish. **Health services:** Health care admin. **History:** General. **Human services:** General. **Liberal arts:** Arts/sciences. **Math:** General. **Philosophy/religion:** Philosophy. **Physical sciences:** Chemistry, physics. **Psychology:** General. **Social sciences:** Anthropology, economics, political science, sociology. **Visual/performing arts:** Music, painting.

Most popular majors. Biology 9%, business/marketing 18%, communications/journalism 7%, education 7%, engineering/engineering technologies 12%, psychology 11%, social sciences 9%.

Technology on campus. 962 workstations in library, computer center, student center. Commuter students can connect to campus network. Online course registration, helpline, wireless network available.

Student life. Freshman orientation: Mandatory, $50 fee. Preregistration for classes offered. **Activities:** Campus ministries, choral groups, international student organizations, literary magazine, radio station, student government, student newspaper, Arab student union, African American association, campus engineers, Asian American association, student activities board, professional accounting society, Muslim student association.

Athletics. NAIA. **Intercollegiate:** Basketball, softball W, volleyball W. **Intramural:** Basketball, volleyball. **Team name:** Wolves.

Student services. Adult student services, alcohol/substance abuse counseling, career counseling, services for economically disadvantaged, student employment services, financial aid counseling, health services, on-campus daycare, personal counseling, placement for graduates, veterans' counselor, women's services. **Physically disabled:** Services for visually, speech, hearing impaired.

Contact. E-mail: admissions@umd.umich.edu
Phone: (313) 593-5100 Fax: (313) 436-9167
Deb Peffer, Director of Admissions and Orientation, University of Michigan: Dearborn, 4901 Evergreen Road, 1145 UC, Dearborn, MI 48128-1491

University of Michigan: Flint

Flint, Michigan   **CB member**
www.umflint.edu   **CB code: 1853**

- Public 4-year university and branch campus college
- Commuter campus in small city
- 6,255 degree-seeking undergraduates: 36% part-time, 60% women, 14% African American, 2% Asian American, 4% Hispanic/Latino, 1% Native American, 3% Multi-racial, non-Hispanic, 6% international
- 1,575 degree-seeking graduate students
- 74% of applicants admitted
- SAT or ACT (ACT writing optional) required
- 37% graduate within 6 years

General. Founded in 1956. Regionally accredited. Institution shares many resources of entire University of Michigan system. **Degrees:** 1,223 bachelor's awarded; master's, professional, doctoral offered. **ROTC:** Army. **Location:** 60 miles from Detroit. **Calendar:** Semester, limited summer session. **Full-time faculty:** 318 total; 70% have terminal degrees, 23% minority, 54% women. **Part-time faculty:** 266 total; 24% have terminal degrees, 15% minority, 65% women. **Class size:** 50% < 20, 44% 20-39, 5% 40-49, 1% 50-99.

Freshman class profile. 3,918 applied, 2,883 admitted, 642 enrolled.

Mid 50% test scores		Rank in top quarter:	24%
SAT critical reading:	470-530	Rank in top tenth:	16%
SAT math:	490-640	End year in good standing:	75%
SAT writing:	460-540	Return as sophomores:	72%
ACT composite:	18-24	Out-of-state:	1%
GPA 3.75 or higher:	20%	Live on campus:	24%
GPA 3.50-3.74:	17%	International:	6%
GPA 3.0-3.49:	31%	Fraternities:	3%
GPA 2.0-2.99:	32%	Sororities:	3%

Basis for selection. 2.7 GPA and test scores equaling national average recommended. Essay and interview recommended. Audition required for art and music majors. **Home schooled:** Transcript of courses and grades required.

High school preparation. College-preparatory program recommended. 17 units recommended. Recommended units include English 4, mathematics 4, history 3, science 3 and foreign language 3.

2015-2016 Annual costs. Tuition/fees: $10,458; $19,980 out-of-state. Room/board: $8,178. Books/supplies: $1,000. Personal expenses: $1,160.

2014-2015 Financial aid. Need-based: 536 full-time freshmen applied for aid; 451 deemed to have need; 430 received aid. Average need met was 70%. Average scholarship/grant was $6,526; average loan $3,275. 34% of total undergraduate aid awarded as scholarships/grants, 66% as loans/jobs. **Non-need-based:** Awarded to 736 full-time undergraduates, including 142 freshmen. Scholarships awarded for academics, art, leadership, music/drama.

Application procedures. Admission: Closing date 8/15 (receipt date). $30 fee, may be waived for applicants with need, free for online applicants. Admission notification on a rolling basis beginning on or about 12/1. Must reply by May 1 or within 2 week(s) if notified thereafter. **Financial aid:** Priority date 3/1; no closing date. FAFSA, institutional form required. Applicants notified on a rolling basis starting 3/15.

Academics. Special study options: Accelerated study, combined bachelor's/graduate degree, cooperative education, distance learning, double major, dual enrollment of high school students, ESL, honors, independent study, internships, student-designed major, study abroad, teacher certification program. **Credit/placement by examination:** AP, CLEP, SAT, ACT, institutional tests. 9 credit hours maximum toward bachelor's degree. Maximum of 3 courses may be passed by examination in Arts & Sciences, School of Education and Human Services, School of Management and Nursing. **Support services:** Learning center, reduced course load, remedial instruction, study skills assistance, tutoring, writing center.

Majors. Area/ethnic studies: African-American. **Biology:** General, biochemistry, biomedical sciences, ecology, molecular, wildlife. **Business:**

Accounting, actuarial science, business admin, entrepreneurial studies, finance, human resources, international, marketing, operations. **Communications:** General, journalism. **Computer sciences:** General, computer science, information systems. **Conservation:** Environmental science. **Education:** General, art, biology, chemistry, early childhood, earth science, elementary, English, French, history, mathematics, music, physics, psychology, secondary, social studies, Spanish, speech. **Engineering:** Engineering science, mechanical. **English:** English lit, general lit, writing. **Foreign languages:** French, Spanish. **Health services:** Clinical lab science, health care admin, medical radiologic technology/radiation therapy, nursing (RN), predental, premedicine, prenursing, prepharmacy, preveterinary. **History:** General. **Human services:** General, social work. **Liberal arts:** Arts/sciences. **Math:** General. **Philosophy/religion:** Ethics, philosophy, professional ethics. **Physical sciences:** General, chemistry, physics. **Psychology:** General, applied. **Social sciences:** General, anthropology, economics, geography, political science, sociology, urban studies. **Visual/performing arts:** Art history/conservation, dance, design, dramatic, music, music performance, painting, studio arts, theater design.

Most popular majors. Biology 6%, business/marketing 15%, education 7%, health sciences 35%, psychology 7%.

Technology on campus. 238 workstations in library, computer center, student center. Dormitories wired for high-speed internet access and linked to campus network. Commuter students can connect to campus network. Online course registration, online library, helpline, repair service, student web hosting, wireless network available.

Student life. Freshman orientation: Mandatory, $150 fee. Preregistration for classes offered. One-day program for students and parents before start of fall semester. **Housing:** Coed dorms available. $100 nonrefundable deposit, deadline 2/1. **Activities:** Bands, choral groups, dance, drama, international student organizations, literary magazine, music ensembles, musical theater, student government, student newspaper, College Democrats, College Republicans, Students for Life, Intervarsity Christian Fellowship, Muslim Student Association, Newman Catholic Fellowship, Black Student Union, International Student Organization, Student Veterans of America-Flint Chapter, Colleges Against Cancer.

Athletics. Intramural: Badminton, basketball, cricket, soccer, table tennis, volleyball.

Student services. Adult student services, alcohol/substance abuse counseling, career counseling, services for economically disadvantaged, student employment services, financial aid counseling, health services, minority student services, on-campus daycare, personal counseling, veterans' counselor, women's services. **Physically disabled:** Services for visually, speech, hearing impaired.

Contact. E-mail: admissions@umflint.edu
Phone: (810) 762-3300 Fax: (810) 762-3272
Jon Davidson, Admissions Director, University of Michigan: Flint, 303 East Kearsley Street, Flint, MI 48502-1950

University of Phoenix: Metro Detroit

Southfield, Michigan
www.phoenix.edu

- For-profit 4-year university
- Commuter campus in small city
- 1,126 undergraduates

General. Regionally accredited. **Degrees:** 297 bachelor's, 2 associate awarded; master's offered. **Calendar:** Differs by program. Other academic calendar. **Full-time faculty:** 24 total. **Part-time faculty:** 248 total.

Basis for selection. Open admission.

2015-2016 Annual costs. Per-credit-hour charge, $410 to $635, depending upon level and course of study. Books, material charges, and other fees vary by course and program. All fees are subject to change.

Application procedures. Admission: No deadline. No application fee. **Financial aid:** No deadline.

Academics. Credit/placement by examination: AP, CLEP.

Majors. Business: Accounting, accounting/business management, business admin, e-commerce, entrepreneurial studies, finance, human resources, marketing, operations. **Communications:** General. **Computer sciences:** General, database management, networking, programming, security, support specialist, system admin, systems analysis, web page design, webmaster. **Conservation:** Environmental studies. **Health services:** Facilities admin, health information management, long term care admin, nursing (RN). **Human services:** General.

Protective services: Disaster management, law enforcement admin, security management.

Student life. Freshman orientation: Mandatory. Preregistration for classes offered.

Contact. Toll-free number: (866) 766-0766
University of Phoenix: Metro Detroit, 26261 Evergreen Road, Southfield, MI 48076-4400

University of Phoenix: West Michigan
Walker, Michigan
www.phoenix.edu

- For-profit 4-year university
- Commuter campus in large town
- 660 degree-seeking undergraduates

General. Regionally accredited. **Degrees:** 30 bachelor's awarded; master's offered. **Calendar:** Differs by program. Other academic calendar. **Full-time faculty:** 12 total. **Part-time faculty:** 122 total.

Basis for selection. Open admission.

2015-2016 Annual costs. Per-credit-hour charge, $410 to $635, depending upon level and course of study. Books, material charges, and other fees vary by course and program. All fees are subject to change.

Application procedures. Admission: No deadline. No application fee. **Financial aid:** No deadline.

Academics. Credit/placement by examination: AP, CLEP.

Majors. Business: Accounting, accounting/business management, business admin, e-commerce, entrepreneurial studies, finance, human resources, marketing, operations. **Communications:** General. **Computer sciences:** Database management, networking, programming, security, system admin, systems analysis, web page design, webmaster. **English:** English lit. **Health services:** Facilities admin, health information management, long term care admin, nursing (RN). **Human services:** General. **Protective services:** Disaster management, law enforcement admin, security management.

Student life. Freshman orientation: Mandatory. Preregistration for classes offered.

Contact. Toll-free number: (866) 766-0766
University of Phoenix: West Michigan, 318 River Ridge Drive NW, Walker, MI 49544-1683

Walsh College of Accountancy and Business Administration
Troy, Michigan
www.walshcollege.edu   CB code: 0372

- Private two-year upper-division business college
- Commuter campus in large city

General. Founded in 1922. Regionally accredited. **Degrees:** 360 bachelor's awarded; master's, professional offered. **Articulation:** Agreements with Henry Ford CC, Oakland CC, Macomb CC, Mott CC, Schoolcraft College, Washtenaw CC, St. Clair County CC, Wayne County CC, Kellogg CC, Jackson CC, Lansing CC. **Location:** 17 miles from Detroit. **Calendar:** Semester, extensive summer session. **Full-time faculty:** 27 total; 63% have terminal degrees, 63% women. **Part-time faculty:** 163 total. **Class size:** 45% < 20, 54% 20-39, less than 1% 40-49. **Special facilities:** Finance lab.

Student profile. 939 degree-seeking undergraduates. 100% entered as juniors.

Basis for selection. Open admission. College transcript required. 30 transferred credits must be in liberal arts, including course in English composition or written communication. Transfer accepted as juniors.

2015-2016 Annual costs. Tuition/fees: $12,820. Books/supplies: $1,000.

Financial aid. Need-based: 26% of total undergraduate aid awarded as scholarships/grants, 74% as loans/jobs. **Non-need-based:** Scholarships awarded for academics.

Application procedures. Admission: Rolling admission. $35 fee, may be waived for applicants with need. **Financial aid:** Priority date 3/1, no deadline. Applicants notified on a rolling basis.

Academics. Special study options: Accelerated study, combined bachelor's/graduate degree, distance learning, double major, internships. Joint partnerships with area community colleges to offer 150-hour honors program in which students complete associate, bachelor and MBA degrees in 5 years. **Credit/placement by examination:** AP, CLEP, IB, institutional tests.

Majors. Business: General, accounting, business admin, finance. **Computer sciences:** Information technology.

Most popular majors. Business/marketing 96%.

Technology on campus. 200 workstations in library, computer center. Commuter students can connect to campus network. Online course registration, online library, helpline, wireless network available.

Student life. Activities: International student organizations, student government, American Marketing Association, finance/economics club, National Association of Black Accountants, accounting club, Association of Information Technology Professionals, international club.

Student services. Career counseling, student employment services, financial aid counseling, placement for graduates, veterans' counselor. **Physically disabled:** Services for visually, hearing impaired.

Contact. E-mail: admissions@walshcollege.edu
Phone: (248) 823-1610 Toll-free number: (800) 925-7401
Fax: (248) 823-1611
Heather Rigby, Director of Admissions and Academic Advising, Walsh College of Accountancy and Business Administration, PO Box 7006, Troy, MI 48007-7006

Wayne State University
Detroit, Michigan   CB member
www.wayne.edu   CB code: 1898

- Public 4-year university
- Commuter campus in very large city
- 16,728 degree-seeking undergraduates: 31% part-time, 55% women, 19% African American, 8% Asian American, 5% Hispanic/Latino, 3% Multi-racial, non-Hispanic, 2% international
- 9,457 degree-seeking graduate students
- 80% of applicants admitted
- SAT or ACT (ACT writing optional) required
- 35% graduate within 6 years

General. Founded in 1868. Regionally accredited. Five extension center locations. **Degrees:** 3,180 bachelor's awarded; master's, professional, doctoral offered. **ROTC:** Army, Air Force. **Location:** 3 miles from downtown. **Calendar:** Semester, extensive summer session. **Full-time faculty:** 1,024 total; 27% minority, 46% women. **Part-time faculty:** 775 total; 21% minority, 52% women. **Class size:** 52% < 20, 36% 20-39, 5% 40-49, 6% 50-99, 2% >100. **Special facilities:** Planetarium, museum of anthropology, theaters, several research centers.

Freshman class profile. 10,009 applied, 7,994 admitted, 2,562 enrolled.

Mid 50% test scores		Rank in top tenth:	22%
ACT composite:	20-26	End year in good standing:	80%
GPA 3.75 or higher:	26%	Return as sophomores:	77%
GPA 3.50-3.74:	18%	Out-of-state:	2%
GPA 3.0-3.49:	27%	Live on campus:	38%
GPA 2.0-2.99:	29%	International:	2%
Rank in top quarter:	51%		

Basis for selection. Combination of high school record/GPA, standardized test scores, and in some cases, other documentation as needed. Audition required for music, dance, and theater applicants. **Learning Disabled:** Students may register with Student Disability Services.

High school preparation. College-preparatory program recommended. 18 units recommended. Recommended units include English 4, mathematics 4, social studies 3, science 3, foreign language 2 and visual/performing arts 2.

2015-2016 Annual costs. Tuition/fees: $11,814; $25,254 out-of-state. Room/board: $10,061. Books/supplies: $1,196. Personal expenses: $2,020.

2014-2015 Financial aid. Need-based: 1,828 full-time freshmen applied for aid; 1,571 deemed to have need; 1,555 received aid. Average need met was 57%. Average scholarship/grant was $7,142; average loan $3,187. 41%

of total undergraduate aid awarded as scholarships/grants, 59% as loans/jobs. **Non-need-based:** Awarded to 6,450 full-time undergraduates, including 1,498 freshmen. Scholarships awarded for academics, art, athletics, leadership, music/drama. **Additional information:** Need-based institutional grants cover tuition and fees with grants and EFC (no loans).

Application procedures. Admission: Closing date 8/1. $25 fee, may be waived for applicants with need. Application must be submitted online. Admission notification by 9/15. Admission notification on a rolling basis. Must reply by May 1 or within 1 week(s) if notified thereafter. **Financial aid:** Priority date 3/31; no closing date. FAFSA required. Applicants notified on a rolling basis starting 3/31.

Academics. Special study options: Accelerated study, combined bachelor's/graduate degree, cooperative education, distance learning, double major, dual enrollment of high school students, ESL, honors, independent study, internships, liberal arts/career combination, study abroad, teacher certification program. Off-campus courses for credit, international exchange student programs. **Credit/placement by examination:** AP, CLEP, IB, SAT, ACT, institutional tests. 32 credit hours maximum toward bachelor's degree. No more than 16 credits by examination may be earned in any one subject. Credit will be recorded with grade to indicate level of performance in exam but will not be considered in computing GPA. Credit will not be considered residence credit. **Support services:** Learning center, pre-admission summer program, reduced course load, remedial instruction, study skills assistance, tutoring, writing center. Through Academic Success Center, Math Success Services and free study skills workshops are also available. Additionally, a range of first and second year courses have supplemental instruction available.

Honors college/program. Invitations to Honors College are based on admissions application. Some departments may require additional application to pursue Honors in the major. Current WSU students and transfer students with a minimum 3.3 or higher GPA may apply for membership in the Honors College.

Majors. Area/ethnic studies: African-American, East Asian, Russian/Eastern European/Eurasian. **Biology:** General. **Business:** Accounting, finance, international, labor relations, management information systems, marketing, organizational behavior. **Communications:** Communications/speech/rhetoric, journalism, public relations, radio/TV. **Computer sciences:** General, information systems. **Conservation:** Environmental science. **Education:** Educational technology, elementary, English, health, mathematics, physical, science, secondary, social studies, special ed, speech impaired. **Engineering:** Biomedical, chemical, civil, electrical, industrial, mechanical. **English:** English lit. **Foreign languages:** General, classics, German, linguistics, Slavic. **Health services:** Clinical lab science, communication disorders, dietetics, medical radiologic technology/radiation therapy, pathology assistant. **History:** General. **Human services:** General, social work. **Math:** General. **Philosophy/religion:** Philosophy. **Physical sciences:** Astronomy, chemistry, geology, physics. **Protective services:** Criminal justice. **Psychology:** General. **Social sciences:** Anthropology, economics, political science, sociology, urban studies. **Visual/performing arts:** Art, art history/conservation, cinematography, dance, dramatic, film/cinema/video, music. **Work/family studies:** Apparel marketing, food/nutrition.

Most popular majors. Biology 6%, business/marketing 16%, communications/journalism 6%, education 6%, engineering/engineering technologies 6%, health sciences 14%, psychology 12%, visual/performing arts 7%.

Technology on campus. Dormitories wired for high-speed internet access and linked to campus network. Commuter students can connect to campus network. Online course registration, online library, helpline, repair service, wireless network available.

Student life. Freshman orientation: Mandatory. Preregistration for classes offered. Held several times a year. **Housing:** Coed dorms, special housing for disabled, apartments, gender-neutral housing, themed housing available. $100 nonrefundable deposit. **Activities:** Bands, campus ministries, choral groups, dance, drama, international student organizations, music ensembles, Model UN, musical theater, radio station, student government, student newspaper, symphony orchestra, TV station, Indian Students Association, Black Student Union, Slavic Klub, Christians on Campus, Muslim Students' Association, Association of Students for Hinduism Awareness (ASHA), Student United Way for Southeastern Michigan, Wayne State University Global Brigades, Wayne State University College Democrats, College Republicans at Wayne State University.

Athletics. NCAA. **Intercollegiate:** Baseball M, basketball, cheerleading, cross-country, diving, fencing, football (tackle) M, golf, softball W, swimming, tennis, track and field W, volleyball W. **Intramural:** Baseball, basketball, football (non-tackle), sand volleyball, soccer, softball, table tennis, tennis, ultimate frisbee, volleyball, weight lifting. **Team name:** Warriors.

Student services. Adult student services, alcohol/substance abuse counseling, chaplain/spiritual director, career counseling, services for economically disadvantaged, student employment services, financial aid counseling, health services, legal services, minority student services, on-campus daycare, personal counseling, placement for graduates, veterans' counselor, women's services. **Physically disabled:** Services for visually, speech, hearing impaired.

Contact. E-mail: admissions@wayne.edu
Phone: (313) 577-2100
LaJoyce Brown, Senior Director of Undergraduate Admissions, Wayne State University, PO Box 02759, Detroit, MI 48202-0759

Western Michigan University
Kalamazoo, Michigan   CB member
www.wmich.edu   CB code: 1902

- Public 4-year university
- Residential campus in small city
- 18,179 degree-seeking undergraduates: 16% part-time, 49% women, 12% African American, 2% Asian American, 5% Hispanic/Latino, 3% Multi-racial, non-Hispanic, 4% international
- 4,423 degree-seeking graduate students
- 82% of applicants admitted
- SAT or ACT (ACT writing optional) required
- 54% graduate within 6 years

General. Founded in 1903. Regionally accredited. **Degrees:** 3,768 bachelor's awarded; master's, professional, doctoral offered. **ROTC:** Army. **Location:** 140 miles from Detroit, 140 miles from Chicago. **Calendar:** Semester, extensive summer session. **Full-time faculty:** 946 total; 78% have terminal degrees, 17% minority, 44% women. **Part-time faculty:** 494 total; 7% minority, 58% women. **Class size:** 38% < 20, 44% 20-39, 7% 40-49, 7% 50-99, 3% >100. **Special facilities:** Particle accelerator, pilot plant for manufacturing and printing of paper and fiber recovery, aviation flight simulators, business technology park, business incubator for student entrepreneurs and inventors, stock trading room with electronic ticker and terminals providing real-time data on market movement, 274-acre lakeside nature preserve dedicated to passive-use recreation and learning, historic farm sustainability living/learning community with permaculture landscape.

Freshman class profile. 15,175 applied, 12,501 admitted, 2,988 enrolled.

Mid 50% test scores		End year in good standing:	75%
ACT composite:	19-25	Return as sophomores:	79%
GPA 3.75 or higher:	26%	Out-of-state:	12%
GPA 3.50-3.74:	13%	Live on campus:	88%
GPA 3.0-3.49:	32%	International:	2%
GPA 2.0-2.99:	29%	Fraternities:	5%
Rank in top quarter:	36%	Sororities:	7%
Rank in top tenth:	13%		

Basis for selection. School achievement record, test scores most important. Trend of grades and number of solid high school academic subjects completed considered; students not meeting college-preparatory program requirements may be admitted conditionally if they meet other admission requirements. Audition required for dance, music, and theater applicants. Portfolio required for some art applicants. **Home schooled:** Transcript of courses and grades required. Applicants should present a transcript of course work and an ACT/SAT score. Must meet the same admission criteria as all other applicants; however, emphasis is placed on test scores.

High school preparation. College-preparatory program recommended. Recommended units include English 4, mathematics 3, social studies 3 and science 3. 2 units of foreign language recommended if going into Arts or Science major.

2015-2016 Annual costs. Tuition/fees: $11,029; $25,713 out-of-state. Room/board: $9,238.

2015-2016 Financial aid. Need-based: 2,614 full-time freshmen applied for aid; 2,064 deemed to have need; 2,064 received aid. Average need met was 75%. Average scholarship/grant was $5,075; average loan $3,170. 39% of total undergraduate aid awarded as scholarships/grants, 61% as loans/jobs. **Non-need-based:** Scholarships awarded for academics, alumni affiliation, art, athletics, minority status, music/drama, ROTC, state residency.

Application procedures. Admission: No deadline. $40 fee, may be waived for applicants with need. Admission notification on a rolling basis. **Financial aid:** Priority date 3/1; no closing date. FAFSA required. Applicants notified on a rolling basis starting 3/15.

Academics. Special study options: Accelerated study, combined bachelor's/graduate degree, cooperative education, cross-registration, distance learning, double major, dual enrollment of high school students, ESL, honors, independent study, internships, student-designed major, study abroad, teacher certification program, Washington semester. **Credit/placement by examination:** AP, CLEP, IB, SAT, ACT, institutional tests. Maximum semester hours of credit by examination which may be counted toward degree varies by department. Credit by examination may not be used to satisfy minimum residency requirement of 30 semester hours. **Support services:** Learning center, pre-admission summer program, reduced course load, remedial instruction, study skills assistance, tutoring, writing center.

Honors college/program. Incoming first year students are automatically invited to join the honors college if they have a 3.6 high school GPA on 4-point scale, 26 ACT or 1190 SAT composite. Students may also be admitted via an application process or may transfer into the honors college. Students from other institutions are invited to join the honors college if they have a 3.5 cumulative GPA at the transfer institution, and current students may join the college if they maintain at 3.5 cumulative GPA at WMU for two semesters. Approximately 400 freshmen join the honors college each year. Students in the honors college are required to complete an honors thesis, 18 honors credits (pro-rated for transfer students), 20 hours of community service per year and maintain a 3.5 GPA.

Majors. Architecture: Urban/community planning. **Area/ethnic studies:** African-American, women's. **Biology:** General, aquatic, biochemistry, biomedical sciences. **Business:** General, accounting, business admin, e-commerce, entrepreneurial studies, fashion, finance, financial planning, information resources management, logistics, managerial economics, marketing, travel services. **Communications:** Advertising, communications/speech/rhetoric, journalism, organizational. **Computer sciences:** General, computer science. **Conservation:** Environmental studies. **Education:** Art, biology, business, chemistry, early childhood, earth science, elementary, English, family/consumer sciences, French, geography, German, health, history, Latin, learning disabled, mathematics, music, physical, physics, sales/marketing, science, social science, social studies, Spanish, technology/industrial arts, trade/industrial. **Engineering:** Aerospace, chemical, civil, computer, electrical, industrial, manufacturing, mechanical, paper, structural. **English:** Creative writing, English lit, writing. **Foreign languages:** French, German, Japanese, Latin, Spanish. **Health services:** Athletic training, audiology/hearing, audiology/speech pathology, dietetics, medical informatics, music therapy, nursing (RN), occupational therapy. **History:** General, applied. **Human services:** Social work. **Math:** General, applied, statistics. **Parks/recreation:** General, exercise sciences, facilities management, sports admin. **Philosophy/religion:** Philosophy, professional ethics, religion. **Physical sciences:** Chemistry, geochemistry, geology, geophysics, hydrology, physics. **Protective services:** Criminal justice. **Psychology:** General, behavior analysis, social. **Social sciences:** Anthropology, economics, geography, political science, sociology, U.S. government. **Visual/performing arts:** Acting, art, art history/conservation, dance, fashion design, film/cinema/video, graphic design, interior design, jazz, music, music performance, music technology, music theory/composition, musical theater, piano/keyboard, studio arts, theater design, theater history, voice/opera. **Work/family studies:** Child development, family systems, institutional food production.

Most popular majors. Business/marketing 19%, education 8%, engineering/engineering technologies 6%, health sciences 10%, interdisciplinary studies 7%, psychology 7%, visual/performing arts 6%.

Technology on campus. 2,438 workstations in library, computer center, student center. Dormitories wired for high-speed internet access and linked to campus network. Commuter students can connect to campus network. Online course registration, online library, helpline, repair service, student web hosting, wireless network available.

Student life. Freshman orientation: Mandatory, $235 fee. Preregistration for classes offered. Two-day program in June; includes session for parents. **Housing:** Guaranteed on-campus for freshmen. Coed dorms, single-sex dorms, special housing for disabled, apartments, fraternity/sorority housing, themed housing, wellness housing available. Aviation house, business, education, engineering and applied sciences houses, fine arts house, health and human services house, honors community, second year experience, science scholars, transfer student communities. **Activities:** Bands, campus ministries, choral groups, dance, drama, film society, international student organizations, literary magazine, music ensembles, Model UN, musical theater, opera, radio station, student government, student newspaper, symphony orchestra, Alternative Bronco Break, International Programs Council, COEXIST, International Student Fellowship, Peace Center, Student Veterans of America, Broncos for Heroes.

Athletics. NCAA. **Intercollegiate:** Baseball M, basketball, cross-country W, football (tackle) M, golf W, gymnastics W, ice hockey M, soccer, softball W, tennis, track and field W, volleyball W. **Intramural:** Basketball, football (non-tackle), golf, ice hockey, racquetball, sand volleyball, soccer, softball, table tennis, tennis, ultimate frisbee, volleyball. **Team name:** Broncos.

Student services. Adult student services, alcohol/substance abuse counseling, chaplain/spiritual director, career counseling, student employment services, financial aid counseling, health services, minority student services, on-campus daycare, personal counseling, placement for graduates, veterans' counselor, women's services. **Physically disabled:** Services for visually, speech, hearing impaired.

Contact. E-mail: ask-wmu@wmich.edu
Phone: (269) 387-2000 Fax: (269) 387-2096
Dachea Hill, Director of Admissions, Western Michigan University, 1903 West Michigan Avenue, Kalamazoo, MI 49008-5211

Yeshiva Beth Yehuda-Yeshiva Gedolah of Greater Detroit
Oak Park, Michigan
CB code: 7010

- Private 5-year rabbinical college for men affiliated with the Jewish faith
- Residential campus in large town
- 57 degree-seeking undergraduates
- Interview required

General. Accredited by AARTS. **Degrees:** 2 bachelor's awarded; master's, doctoral offered. **Calendar:** Semester. **Full-time faculty:** 5 total.

Basis for selection. GED not accepted. Qualifications include independent comprehension of basic Talmudic text and completion of 150 folios of Talmud with commentary of Rashi, completion of Pentateuch and substantial parts of Prophets and Hagiography, ability to read and write classical Hebrew, working knowledge of Aramaic language of Talmud, and Yiddish.

2015-2016 Annual costs. Tuition/fees: $6,200. Room/board: $4,200. Books/supplies: $500. Personal expenses: $500.

Application procedures. Admission: No deadline. No application fee. **Financial aid:** Closing date 8/1. Applicants notified on a rolling basis.

Academics. Special study options: Independent study. **Credit/placement by examination:** AP, CLEP. **Support services:** Tutoring.

Majors. Theology: Talmudic.

Student life. Housing: Guaranteed on-campus for all undergraduates.

Student services. Adult student services, career counseling, health services, on-campus daycare, personal counseling, placement for graduates.

Contact. Phone: (248) 968-3360 Fax: (248) 968-8613
Yeshiva Beth Yehuda-Yeshiva Gedolah of Greater Detroit, 24600 Greenfield Road, Oak Park, MI 48237

Minnesota

Argosy University: Twin Cities
Eagan, Minnesota
www.argosy.edu/twincities   CB code: 6427

- For-profit 4-year university
- Commuter campus in very large city
- 1,072 degree-seeking undergraduates: 73% part-time, 82% women
- 421 graduate students

General. **Degrees:** 57 bachelor's, 269 associate awarded; master's, professional, doctoral offered. **Calendar:** Differs by program. **Full-time faculty:** 54 total. **Part-time faculty:** 173 total.

Basis for selection. Open admission.

2015-2016 Annual costs. Tuition/fees: $16,842. **Additional information:** Tuition indicated is for programs in the College of Arts and Sciences. College of Health Sciences programs range $450-$575 per credit-hour-hour. Additional program fees may apply. All costs are subject to change.

Application procedures. **Admission:** Closing date 9/14. $50 fee. **Financial aid:** No deadline.

Academics. **Credit/placement by examination:** AP, CLEP.

Majors. **Business:** Business admin. **Health services:** Clinical lab science. **Liberal arts:** Arts/sciences. **Protective services:** Police science. **Psychology:** General.

Contact. E-mail: autcadmissions@argosy.edu
Phone: (651) 846-3300
Janet Zimprich, Senior Director of Admissions, Argosy University: Twin Cities, 1515 Central Parkway, Eagan, MN 55121

Art Institutes International Minnesota
Minneapolis, Minnesota
www.artinstitutes.edu/minneapolis   CB code: 2332

- For-profit 4-year culinary school and visual arts college
- Commuter campus in large city
- 820 degree-seeking undergraduates
- Application essay, interview required

General. Accredited by ACICS. **Degrees:** 151 bachelor's, 47 associate awarded. **Calendar:** Quarter, extensive summer session. **Full-time faculty:** 69 total. **Part-time faculty:** 63 total. **Special facilities:** Student-run dining lab.

Basis for selection. Open admission. School tour required prior to admission. **Home schooled:** Transcript of courses and grades, interview required. **Learning Disabled:** Notify Dean of Student Affairs.

2015-2016 Annual costs. Tuition/fees: $23,088. Room only: $7,065. Books/supplies: $1,500.

Financial aid. **Non-need-based:** Scholarships awarded for academics.

Application procedures. **Admission:** No deadline. $50 fee. Admission notification on a rolling basis. **Financial aid:** FAFSA required.

Academics. **Special study options:** Cooperative education, distance learning, honors, independent study, internships, weekend college. **Credit/placement by examination:** AP, CLEP, institutional tests. **Support services:** Learning center, reduced course load, remedial instruction, study skills assistance, tutoring.

Majors. **Business:** Customer service, fashion, hospitality admin, hospitality/recreation, hotel/motel admin, marketing, merchandising, resort management, restaurant/food services, retailing, selling. **Communications:** Advertising, digital media, photojournalism. **Communications technology:** Animation/special effects, graphics, photo/film/video, recording arts. **Computer sciences:** Computer graphics, web page design, webmaster. **Visual/performing**

arts: Cinematography, commercial photography, commercial/advertising art, design, film/cinema/video, graphic design, interior design, multimedia, photography, studio arts management.

Most popular majors. Business/marketing 9%, communications/journalism 10%, computer/information sciences 21%, personal/culinary services 7%, visual/performing arts 51%.

Technology on campus. 320 workstations in dormitories, library, computer center, student center. Dormitories wired for high-speed internet access and linked to campus network. Online library, student web hosting, wireless network available.

Student life. **Freshman orientation:** Mandatory. Preregistration for classes offered. **Housing:** Apartments, wellness housing available. $250 deposit. **Activities:** Campus ministries, film society, student government, student newspaper.

Student services. Alcohol/substance abuse counseling, career counseling, student employment services, financial aid counseling, personal counseling, placement for graduates, veterans' counselor. **Physically disabled:** Services for hearing impaired.

Contact. E-mail: aimadm@aii.edu
Phone: (612) 332-3361 Toll-free number: (800) 777-3643
Fax: (612) 332-3934
Amanda Karlstad, Senior Director of Admissions, Art Institutes International Minnesota, 15 South Ninth Street, Minneapolis, MN 55402

Augsburg College
Minneapolis, Minnesota   CB member
www.augsburg.edu   CB code: 6014

- Private 4-year liberal arts college affiliated with the Evangelical Lutheran Church in America
- Residential campus in large city
- 2,492 degree-seeking undergraduates: 19% part-time, 53% women, 11% African American, 7% Asian American, 8% Hispanic/Latino, 2% Native American, 2% Multi-racial, non-Hispanic, 2% international
- 981 degree-seeking graduate students
- 59% of applicants admitted
- SAT or ACT with writing, application essay required
- 56% graduate within 6 years

General. Founded in 1869. Regionally accredited. **Degrees:** 608 bachelor's awarded; master's, professional offered. **ROTC:** Army, Naval, Air Force. **Location:** 2 miles from downtown Minneapolis. **Calendar:** Semester, extensive summer session. **Full-time faculty:** 171 total; 91% have terminal degrees, 14% minority, 53% women. **Part-time faculty:** 212 total; 45% have terminal degrees, 14% minority, 55% women. **Class size:** 64% < 20, 35% 20-39, less than 1% 40-49, less than 1% 50-99. **Special facilities:** Center for atmospheric research, ice arena complex, domed athletic field (seasonal).

Freshman class profile. 2,925 applied, 1,731 admitted, 478 enrolled.

Mid 50% test scores			
SAT critical reading:	460-650	GPA 3.0-3.49:	37%
SAT math:	440-560	GPA 2.0-2.99:	34%
SAT writing:	490-580	Return as sophomores:	79%
ACT composite:	19-24	Out-of-state:	13%
GPA 3.75 or higher:	13%	Live on campus:	78%
GPA 3.50-3.74:	15%	International:	2%

Basis for selection. School achievement record, class rank in top half, test scores, essays and recommendations very important; extracurricular activities important. Interview recommended. **Home schooled:** Interview required.

High school preparation. College-preparatory program recommended. 15 units required. Required and recommended units include English 4, mathematics 3-4, social studies 2-4, history 2, science 3 (laboratory 1) and foreign language 2-3.

2015-2016 Annual costs. Tuition/fees: $35,465. Room/board: $9,380. Books/supplies: $1,200. Personal expenses: $2,500.

2014-2015 Financial aid. **Need-based:** 358 full-time freshmen applied for aid; 329 deemed to have need; 328 received aid. Average need met was 73%. Average scholarship/grant was $22,567; average loan $3,894. 70% of total undergraduate aid awarded as scholarships/grants, 30% as loans/jobs. **Non-need-based:** Awarded to 395 full-time undergraduates, including 79 freshmen. Scholarships awarded for academics, alumni affiliation, art, leadership, music/drama, religious affiliation.

Application procedures. **Admission:** Priority date 5/1; deadline 8/1. No application fee. Admission notification on a rolling basis beginning on or about 11/1. Must reply by May 1 or within 2 week(s) if notified thereafter. **Financial aid:** Priority date 3/15, closing date 8/1. FAFSA required. Applicants notified on a rolling basis starting 3/1; must reply within 3 week(s) of notification.

Academics. **Special study options:** Combined bachelor's/graduate degree, cooperative education, cross-registration, double major, dual enrollment of high school students, ESL, honors, independent study, internships, liberal arts/career combination, student-designed major, study abroad, teacher certification program, urban semester. Metro-urban studies internship program; global education program in Central America, Mexico, Namibia and Norway. **Credit/placement by examination:** AP, CLEP, IB, institutional tests. 1 credit hours maximum toward bachelor's degree. **Support services:** Learning center, pre-admission summer program, reduced course load, remedial instruction, study skills assistance, tutoring, writing center.

Majors. **Area/ethnic studies:** Native American, Scandinavian, women's. **Biology:** General. **Business:** Accounting, business admin, finance, international, management information systems, marketing. **Communications:** Communications/speech/rhetoric. **Computer sciences:** Computer science. **Conservation:** Environmental studies. **Education:** General, early childhood, elementary, health, music, physical, secondary, special ed. **Engineering:** General. **English:** Creative writing, English lit. **Foreign languages:** French, German, Scandinavian, Spanish. **Health services:** Music therapy. **History:** General. **Human services:** Social work. **Liberal arts:** Arts/sciences. **Math:** General. **Parks/recreation:** Exercise sciences. **Philosophy/religion:** Philosophy, religion. **Physical sciences:** Chemistry, physics. **Psychology:** General, clinical, social. **Social sciences:** Applied economics, economics, international relations, political economy, political science, sociology, urban studies. **Theology:** Youth ministry. **Visual/performing arts:** Acting, art history/conservation, directing/producing, dramatic, film/cinema/video, graphic design, music, music management, music performance, studio arts, theater design, theater history.

Most popular majors. Business/marketing 28%, communications/journalism 6%, education 7%, health sciences 12%, psychology 7%, social sciences 8%.

Technology on campus. 260 workstations in dormitories, library, computer center, student center. Dormitories wired for high-speed internet access and linked to campus network. Commuter students can connect to campus network. Online course registration, online library, helpline, student web hosting, wireless network available.

Student life. **Freshman orientation:** Available, $100 fee. Preregistration for classes offered. Students attend in June or July; lasts Friday through Saturday morning. **Housing:** Guaranteed on-campus for freshmen. Coed dorms, special housing for disabled, apartments, wellness housing available. $200 partly refundable deposit, deadline 6/1. **Activities:** Bands, campus ministries, choral groups, drama, international student organizations, literary magazine, music ensembles, Model UN, radio station, student government, student newspaper, symphony orchestra, Auggie Ultimate Frisbee, art club, chemistry society, Spanish club, Muslim student association, Fellowship of Christian Athletes, Tri-Beta Biology honor society, cycling club, KAUG radio.

Athletics. NCAA. **Intercollegiate:** Baseball M, basketball, cross-country, diving W, football (tackle) M, golf, ice hockey, lacrosse W, soccer, softball W, swimming W, track and field, volleyball W, wrestling M. **Intramural:** Badminton, basketball, football (non-tackle), racquetball, sand volleyball, soccer, softball, tennis, volleyball. **Team name:** Auggies.

Student services. Adult student services, alcohol/substance abuse counseling, chaplain/spiritual director, career counseling, student employment services, financial aid counseling, health services, minority student services, personal counseling, placement for graduates. **Physically disabled:** Services for visually, speech, hearing impaired.

Contact. E-mail: admissions@augsburg.edu
Phone: (612) 330-1001 Toll-free number: (800) 788-5678
Fax: (612) 330-1590
Rick Ellis, Director of Undergraduate Admissions, Augsburg College, 2211 Riverside Avenue, Minneapolis, MN 55454

Bemidji State University
Bemidji, Minnesota
www.bemidjistate.edu   CB code: 6676

- Public 4-year university
- Residential campus in large town

- 4,393 degree-seeking undergraduates: 23% part-time, 57% women, 2% African American, 1% Asian American, 2% Hispanic/Latino, 3% Native American, 3% Multi-racial, non-Hispanic, 2% international
- 146 degree-seeking graduate students
- 94% of applicants admitted
- SAT or ACT (ACT writing optional) required
- 45% graduate within 6 years

General. Founded in 1919. Regionally accredited. Arrowhead University Center located on Minnesota's Mesabi Iron Range offers several degree programs. **Degrees:** 972 bachelor's, 51 associate awarded; master's offered. **Location:** 150 miles from Duluth, 230 miles from Minneapolis-St. Paul. **Calendar:** Semester, extensive summer session. **Full-time faculty:** 174 total; 68% have terminal degrees, 9% minority, 44% women. **Part-time faculty:** 93 total; 17% have terminal degrees, 6% minority, 62% women. **Class size:** 41% < 20, 47% 20-39, 4% 40-49, 5% 50-99, 2% >100. **Special facilities:** Freshwater aquatics laboratory, research center, forest and nature preserve.

Freshman class profile. 2,566 applied, 2,407 admitted, 748 enrolled.

Mid 50% test scores			
ACT composite:	19-24	Rank in top quarter:	23%
GPA 3.75 or higher:	15%	Rank in top tenth:	7%
GPA 3.50-3.74:	14%	Return as sophomores:	66%
GPA 3.0-3.49:	33%	Out-of-state:	12%
GPA 2.0-2.99:	36%	Live on campus:	87%
		International:	2%

Basis for selection. Rank in top half of class or test scores above 50th percentile preferred. ACT scores considered for applicants in bottom half of class. Composite score of 21 or higher preferred. ACT scores are required to be received by the university by the fifth day of classes from the beginning of the Fall term to be considered for acceptance. Interview recommended. Audition recommended for music applicants; portfolio recommended for art applicants. **Learning Disabled:** Students encouraged to identify themselves to Office of Disabilities to be apprised of services available.

High school preparation. 16 units required. Required units include English 4, mathematics 3, social studies 3, science 3, foreign language 2 and academic electives 1. 1 unit of art, music, world culture required.

2015-2016 Annual costs. Tuition/fees: $8,366; $8,366 out-of-state. Room/board: $7,690. Books/supplies: $890. Personal expenses: $1,600.

2014-2015 Financial aid. **Need-based:** 487 full-time freshmen applied for aid; 344 deemed to have need; 339 received aid. Average need met was 68%. Average scholarship/grant was $5,475; average loan $3,483. 52% of total undergraduate aid awarded as scholarships/grants, 48% as loans/jobs. **Non-need-based:** Awarded to 2,504 full-time undergraduates, including 435 freshmen. Scholarships awarded for academics, alumni affiliation, art, athletics, job skills, leadership, minority status, music/drama, ROTC.

Application procedures. **Admission:** Priority date 2/1; no deadline. $20 fee, may be waived for applicants with need. Admission notification on a rolling basis. **Financial aid:** Priority date 3/31, closing date 3/31. FAFSA, institutional form required. Applicants notified on a rolling basis starting 3/15.

Academics. **Special study options:** Combined bachelor's/graduate degree, cooperative education, cross-registration, distance learning, double major, dual enrollment of high school students, ESL, external degree, honors, independent study, internships, study abroad, teacher certification program. Exchange program with other Minnesota state universities, Euro-spring semester, Sino-summer semester. **Credit/placement by examination:** AP, CLEP, IB, ACT, institutional tests. Department defined number of hours of credit by examination may be counted towards degree. **Support services:** Learning center, reduced course load, remedial instruction, study skills assistance, tutoring, writing center.

Majors. **Area/ethnic studies:** Native American. **Biology:** General, aquatic. **Business:** Accounting, business admin, e-commerce, management information systems. **Communications:** Media studies. **Computer sciences:** Computer science, information systems. **Conservation:** Environmental studies, wildlife/wilderness. **Education:** Elementary, English, health, mathematics, music, physical, science, social studies, Spanish. **English:** Creative writing, English lit. **Foreign languages:** Spanish. **Health services:** Clinical lab science, community health, nursing (RN). **History:** General. **Human services:** Social work. **Liberal arts:** Arts/sciences, humanities. **Math:** General. **Parks/recreation:** Exercise sciences, sports admin. **Physical sciences:** Chemistry. **Protective services:** Criminal justice. **Psychology:** General. **Social sciences:** General, economics, geography, political science, sociology. **Visual/performing arts:** Commercial/advertising art, music.

Most popular majors. Biology 7%, business/marketing 20%, education 12%, engineering/engineering technologies 6%, health sciences 18%, security/protective services 7%.

Technology on campus. 1,600 workstations in dormitories, library, computer center, student center. Dormitories wired for high-speed internet access and linked to campus network. Commuter students can connect to campus network. Online course registration, online library, helpline, repair service, student web hosting, wireless network available.

Student life. Freshman orientation: Available, $25 fee. Preregistration for classes offered. One-day orientation for students and parents. Student orientation program is also scheduled the weekend prior to first day of class. **Policies:** Zero tolerance for discrimination, racism, sexual violence, illegal activities including drug use. **Housing:** Coed dorms, special housing for disabled, apartments, themed housing available. $150 nonrefundable deposit, deadline 8/1. Honors learning committee, first year residential experience, emerging leaders first year community housing available. **Activities:** Bands, campus ministries, choral groups, dance, drama, international student organizations, literary magazine, music ensembles, musical theater, opera, radio station, student government, student newspaper, symphony orchestra, TV station, Newman Center, Lutheran center, Young Republicans, Young Democrats, social service organization, veterans club, Council of Indian Students, Black Student Coalition.

Athletics. NCAA. **Intercollegiate:** Baseball M, basketball, cross-country, football (tackle) M, golf, ice hockey, soccer W, softball W, tennis W, track and field W, volleyball W. **Intramural:** Badminton, baseball, basketball, field hockey, football (non-tackle), golf, ice hockey, racquetball, skiing, soccer, softball, table tennis, tennis, triathlon, volleyball, weight lifting M, wrestling M. **Team name:** Beavers.

Student services. Adult student services, alcohol/substance abuse counseling, chaplain/spiritual director, career counseling, services for economically disadvantaged, student employment services, financial aid counseling, health services, minority student services, on-campus daycare, personal counseling, placement for graduates, veterans' counselor, women's services. **Physically disabled:** Services for visually, speech, hearing impaired.

Contact. E-mail: admissions@bemidjistate.edu
Phone: (218) 755-2040 Toll-free number: (877) 236-4354
Fax: (218) 755-2390
Michael Heitkamp, Associate VP for Admissions & Enrollment, Bemidji State University, 102 Deputy Hall #13, Bemidji, MN 56601-2699

Bethany Lutheran College
Mankato, Minnesota
www.blc.edu   CB code: 6035

- Private 4-year liberal arts college affiliated with the Evangelical Lutheran Synod
- Residential campus in small city
- 493 degree-seeking undergraduates: 3% part-time, 54% women, 3% African American, 3% Hispanic/Latino, 1% Multi-racial, non-Hispanic, 3% international
- 85% of applicants admitted
- SAT or ACT (ACT writing optional) required
- 55% graduate within 6 years; 34% enter graduate study

General. Founded in 1927. Regionally accredited. **Degrees:** 95 bachelor's awarded. **ROTC:** Army. **Location:** 80 miles from Minneapolis-St. Paul. **Calendar:** Semester. **Full-time faculty:** 40 total; 50% have terminal degrees, 5% minority, 25% women. **Part-time faculty:** 23 total; 4% have terminal degrees, 48% women. **Class size:** 75% < 20, 22% 20-39, less than 1% 40-49, 1% 50-99.

Freshman class profile. 347 applied, 296 admitted, 135 enrolled.

Mid 50% test scores		Rank in top quarter:	35%
ACT composite:	20-26	Rank in top tenth:	14%
GPA 3.75 or higher:	28%	End year in good standing:	87%
GPA 3.50-3.74:	15%	Return as sophomores:	73%
GPA 3.0-3.49:	30%	Out-of-state:	22%
GPA 2.0-2.99:	27%	Live on campus:	93%

Basis for selection. College-prep GPA, overall GPA, test scores most important. **Learning Disabled:** Students with learning disabilities must meet with head of Academic Resources Center.

High school preparation. College-preparatory program recommended. Recommended units include English 4, mathematics 3, social studies 3, history 3, science 3 (laboratory 1) and foreign language 2.

2015-2016 Annual costs. Tuition/fees: $25,300. Room/board: $7,910. Books/supplies: $800. Personal expenses: $1,500.

2014-2015 Financial aid. Need-based: 132 full-time freshmen applied for aid; 118 deemed to have need; 118 received aid. Average need met was 83%. Average scholarship/grant was $18,158; average loan $4,436. 69% of total undergraduate aid awarded as scholarships/grants, 31% as loans/jobs. **Non-need-based:** Awarded to 94 full-time undergraduates, including 25 freshmen. Scholarships awarded for academics, alumni affiliation, art, music/drama, ROTC.

Application procedures. Admission: Closing date 7/1 (postmark date). No application fee. Admission notification on a rolling basis beginning on or about 9/15. Early admission only through the Post Secondary Options Program by the State of Minnesota. **Financial aid:** Priority date 4/15; no closing date. FAFSA, institutional form required. Applicants notified on a rolling basis starting 3/1; must reply within 4 week(s) of notification.

Academics. Special study options: Combined bachelor's/graduate degree, double major, dual enrollment of high school students, independent study, internships, student-designed major, study abroad, teacher certification program. **Credit/placement by examination:** AP, CLEP, IB, SAT, ACT, institutional tests. There is currently no limit on the hours of credit examination that may be counted toward a bachelor's degree. **Support services:** Learning center, reduced course load, remedial instruction, study skills assistance, tutoring, writing center. Weekly one on one academic resource advising sessions, testing accommodations, and disability support services.

Majors. Biology: General, exercise physiology. **Business:** Business admin. **Communications:** Communications/speech/rhetoric. **Education:** Elementary. **English:** English lit. **History:** General. **Liberal arts:** Arts/sciences. **Math:** General. **Philosophy/religion:** Religion. **Physical sciences:** General, chemistry. **Psychology:** General. **Social sciences:** General, sociology. **Visual/performing arts:** Digital arts, dramatic, music, studio arts.

Most popular majors. Biology 17%, business/marketing 21%, communications/journalism 18%, education 8%, English 7%, visual/performing arts 19%.

Technology on campus. 100 workstations in dormitories, library, computer center, student center. Dormitories wired for high-speed internet access and linked to campus network. Commuter students can connect to campus network. Online course registration, online library, helpline, repair service, student web hosting, wireless network available.

Student life. Freshman orientation: Mandatory. Preregistration for classes offered. Orientation held weekly for 50 minutes during the first semester for first year, first time students. **Policies:** Freshmen and sophomores not living with family required to live on campus. **Housing:** Guaranteed on-campus for all undergraduates. Single-sex dorms, apartments, wellness housing available. **Activities:** Bands, campus ministries, choral groups, drama, international student organizations, literary magazine, music ensembles, musical theater, student government, student newspaper, Spiritual Life committee, Lutherans for Life, Student Senate, Lambda Pi Eta, Scholastic Leadership Society.

Athletics. NCAA. **Intercollegiate:** Baseball M, basketball, cross-country, golf, soccer, softball W, tennis, track and field, volleyball W. **Intramural:** Basketball, football (non-tackle), racquetball, sand volleyball, softball, tennis, volleyball. **Team name:** Vikings.

Student services. Chaplain/spiritual director, career counseling, financial aid counseling, health services, minority student services, personal counseling.

Contact. E-mail: admissions@blc.edu
Phone: (507) 344-7331 Toll-free number: (800) 944-3066
Fax: (507) 344-7376
Dan Tomhave, VP of Admissions & Enrollment Management, Bethany Lutheran College, 700 Luther Drive, Mankato, MN 56001-4490

Bethel University
St. Paul, Minnesota   CB member
www.bethel.edu   CB code: 6038

- Private 4-year university and liberal arts college affiliated with the Baptist General Conference
- Residential campus in large city
- 2,875 degree-seeking undergraduates: 17% part-time, 62% women, 5% African American, 4% Asian American, 4% Hispanic/Latino, 2% Multi-racial, non-Hispanic
- 1,800 degree-seeking graduate students
- 95% of applicants admitted
- SAT or ACT (ACT writing optional), application essay required
- 73% graduate within 6 years

General. Founded in 1871. Regionally accredited. **Degrees:** 862 bachelor's, 23 associate awarded; master's, professional, doctoral offered. **ROTC:** Army, Air Force. **Location:** 10 miles from Minneapolis-St. Paul. **Calendar:** Continuous, limited summer session. **Full-time faculty:** 215 total; 80% have terminal degrees, 7% minority, 46% women. **Part-time faculty:** 300 total; 37% have terminal degrees, 5% minority, 52% women. **Class size:** 58% < 20, 34% 20-39, 5% 40-49, 2% 50-99, less than 1% >100.

Freshman class profile. 1,531 applied, 1,453 admitted, 616 enrolled.

Mid 50% test scores		Rank in top quarter:	57%
ACT composite:	22-28	Rank in top tenth:	26%
GPA 3.75 or higher:	37%	Return as sophomores:	84%
GPA 3.50-3.74:	23%	Out-of-state:	21%
GPA 3.0-3.49:	27%	Live on campus:	94%
GPA 2.0-2.99:	13%	International:	1%

Basis for selection. Students must show academic ability based on standardized test scores and high school process toward graduation, must have high school diploma or GED, and have personal and character fit with the mission of BU. **Home schooled:** Letter of recommendation (nonparent) required. **Learning Disabled:** There are no special requirements or procedures for students prior to admission. After being admitted, an IEP or 504 plan is needed for university service assessment.

High school preparation. College-preparatory program required. 14 units required. Required and recommended units include English 4, mathematics 3, social studies 4, history 2, science 3 (laboratory 2), foreign language 2, computer science 1 and visual/performing arts 1.

2015-2016 Annual costs. Tuition/fees: $34,140. Room/board: $9,770. Books/supplies: $1,150. Personal expenses: $2,036.

2015-2016 Financial aid. Need-based: 565 full-time freshmen applied for aid; 451 deemed to have need; 451 received aid. Average need met was 83%. Average scholarship/grant was $22,123; average loan $3,988. 71% of total undergraduate aid awarded as scholarships/grants, 29% as loans/jobs. **Non-need-based:** Awarded to 832 full-time undergraduates, including 220 freshmen. Scholarships awarded for academics, alumni affiliation, art, leadership, music/drama, state residency.

Application procedures. Admission: Priority date 11/1; no deadline. No application fee. Admission notification on a rolling basis beginning on or about 10/1. **Financial aid:** Priority date 4/15; no closing date. FAFSA required. Applicants notified on a rolling basis starting 3/1.

Academics. Special study options: Combined bachelor's/graduate degree, cross-registration, distance learning, double major, dual enrollment of high school students, exchange student, honors, independent study, internships, liberal arts/career combination, semester at sea, student-designed major, study abroad, teacher certification program, urban semester, Washington semester. Dual degree program for engineering science with the University of Minnesota or other schools on individual basis. **Credit/placement by examination:** AP, CLEP, IB, institutional tests. 30 credit hours maximum toward associate degree, 30 toward bachelor's. **Support services:** Learning center, study skills assistance, tutoring, writing center. Individual support for multilingual students seeking to strengthen their academic English, with emphasis on research, writing and presentation skills. Tutoring labs offered in science (chemistry, biology, biokinetics, physics), math, business, modern world languages and general education courses. Academic counseling offered on a variety of study skill topics: managing time, managing stress, mastering motivation, assessing learning styles, increasing reading skills. Individual tutors available for any course at no additional cost to the student.

Majors. Biology: General, Biochemistry/molecular biology. **Business:** Accounting/finance, business admin, organizational behavior. **Communications:** General, journalism, media studies. **Computer sciences:** General. **Conservation:** Environmental science, environmental studies. **Education:** Art, early childhood, elementary, English, ESL, health, kindergarten/preschool, mathematics, middle, music, physical, secondary, social studies, Spanish. **Engineering:** Engineering science. **English:** English lit. **Foreign languages:** Linguistics, Spanish. **Health services:** Athletic training, nursing (RN). **History:** General. **Human services:** Social work. **Math:** General. **Parks/recreation:** Exercise sciences. **Philosophy/religion:** Philosophy. **Physical sciences:** Chemistry, physics. **Psychology:** General. **Social sciences:** General, economics, international relations, political science. **Theology:** Bible, lay ministry, youth ministry. **Visual/performing arts:** Art, dramatic, graphic design, music, music performance, studio arts.

Most popular majors. Business/marketing 15%, communications/journalism 10%, education 15%, health sciences 13%, psychology 6%, social sciences 6%.

Technology on campus. 420 workstations in dormitories, library, computer center, student center. Dormitories wired for high-speed internet access and linked to campus network. Commuter students can connect to campus network. Online course registration, online library, helpline, repair service, student web hosting, wireless network available.

Student life. Freshman orientation: Mandatory. Preregistration for classes offered. Two days prior to the start of classes. **Policies:** Freshmen not permitted cars on campus. **Housing:** Guaranteed on-campus for freshmen. Special housing for disabled, apartments, cooperative housing available. **Activities:** Bands, campus ministries, choral groups, dance, drama, film society, international student organizations, literary magazine, music ensembles, musical theater, radio station, student government, student newspaper, symphony orchestra, United Cultures of Bethel, College Republicans, College Democrats, Habitat for Humanity, dormitory discipleship programs, Mu Kappa (for students from missionary homes), Twin Cities Outreach.

Athletics. NCAA. **Intercollegiate:** Baseball M, basketball, cross-country, football (tackle) M, golf, ice hockey, soccer, softball W, tennis, track and field, volleyball W. **Intramural:** Badminton, basketball, football (non-tackle) M, ice hockey, softball, volleyball. **Team name:** Royals.

Student services. Adult student services, alcohol/substance abuse counseling, chaplain/spiritual director, career counseling, student employment services, financial aid counseling, health services, minority student services, on-campus daycare, personal counseling, placement for graduates, veterans' counselor, women's services. **Physically disabled:** Services for visually, speech, hearing impaired.

Contact. E-mail: buadmissions-cas@bethel.edu
Phone: (651) 638-6242 Toll-free number: (800) 255-8706 ext. 6242
Fax: (651) 635-1490
Bret Hyder, Director of Admissions, Bethel University, 3900 Bethel Drive, St. Paul, MN 55112-6999

Brown College: Brooklyn Center
Brooklyn Center, Minnesota
www.browncollege.edu

▶ For-profit 3-year branch campus college
▶ Commuter campus in very large city
▶ 169 undergraduates

General. Regionally accredited; also accredited by ACCSC. **Degrees:** 7 bachelor's, 40 associate awarded. **Calendar:** Quarter. **Part-time faculty:** 27 total.

Basis for selection. Open admission.

2015-2016 Annual costs. Tuition for Bachelor of Science in Criminal Justice program is $35,720. Associate degree programs range $18,500-$34,200. Costs are subject to change.

Academics. Credit/placement by examination: AP, CLEP.

Majors. BACHELOR'S. Business: Business admin. **Protective services:** Police science. **Visual/performing arts:** Game design. **ASSOCIATE. Computer sciences:** Information technology, networking. **Health services:** Medical assistant, pharmacy assistant. **Protective services:** Police science.

Contact. E-mail: jhuston@browncollege.edu
Phone: (763) 279-2549 Toll-free number: (877) 888-8888
Jennifer Huston, Director of Admissions, Brown College: Brooklyn Center, 5951 Earle Brown Dr., Brooklyn Center, MN 55430

Brown College: Mendota Heights
Mendota Heights, Minnesota
www.browncollege.edu   **CB code: 1210**

▶ For-profit 4-year career college
▶ Commuter campus in small city
▶ 308 undergraduates
▶ Interview required

General. Founded in 1946. Regionally accredited; also accredited by ACCSC. **Degrees:** 34 bachelor's, 50 associate awarded. **Location:** 14 miles from Minneapolis-St. Paul. **Calendar:** Differs by program, extensive summer session. **Full-time faculty:** 10 total. **Part-time faculty:** 50 total.

Basis for selection. Open admission, but selective for some programs. Additional requirements for radio broadcasting. ACCUPLACER required in lieu of other tests. **Home schooled:** Statement describing home school structure and mission, transcript of courses and grades required. **Learning Disabled:** IEP's and/or other requests for ADA-level accommodations accepted. Eligible students must complete brief Application for Auxiliary Aid and return with any supporting documentation available well in advance of enrollment.

High school preparation. Recommended units include English 4, mathematics 2 and science 1.

2015-2016 Annual costs. Tuition and fees for associate degree programs vary and range $18,500 to $34,200; bachelor degree programs range $63,000 to $69,160. Some programs have additional costs for books and supplies which vary by program. Costs are subject to change.

Financial aid. Non-need-based: Scholarships awarded for academics.

Application procedures. Admission: No deadline. $25 fee. Admission notification on a rolling basis beginning on or about 1/1. **Financial aid:** Priority date 7/1; no closing date. FAFSA, institutional form required. Applicants notified on a rolling basis starting 1/1; must reply within 2 week(s) of notification.

Academics. Special study options: Accelerated study, combined bachelor's/graduate degree, cooperative education, distance learning, honors, independent study, internships, liberal arts/career combination. **Credit/placement by examination:** AP, CLEP, institutional tests. **Support services:** Learning center, reduced course load, remedial instruction, study skills assistance, tutoring, writing center.

Majors. Business: General. **Communications technology:** Graphics. **Computer sciences:** Information technology. **Protective services:** Criminal justice. **Visual/performing arts:** Design.

Most popular majors. Business/marketing 7%, computer/information sciences 6%, security/protective services 6%, visual/performing arts 80%.

Technology on campus. 231 workstations in library, computer center, student center. Commuter students can connect to campus network. Online course registration, online library, helpline, repair service, wireless network available.

Student life. Freshman orientation: Mandatory. Preregistration for classes offered. **Housing:** Apartments available. **Activities:** Radio station, student government, student senate, Campus Crusade for Christ, minority students club.

Student services. Adult student services, career counseling, student employment services, financial aid counseling, personal counseling, placement for graduates.

Contact. E-mail: info@browncollege.edu
Phone: (651) 905-3400 Toll-free number: (800) 627-6966 ext. 240
Fax: (651) 905-3540
Jennifer Huston, Director of Admissions, Brown College: Mendota Heights, 1345 Mendota Heights Road, Mendota Heights, MN 55120

Capella University
Minneapolis, Minnesota
www.capella.edu   **CB code: 3829**

- For-profit 4-year virtual university
- Commuter campus in very large city
- 8,750 undergraduates
- 27,670 graduate students

General. Regionally accredited. **Degrees:** 1,280 bachelor's awarded; master's, professional, doctoral offered. **Calendar:** Quarter, extensive summer session. **Full-time faculty:** 256 total. **Part-time faculty:** 1,292 total.

Basis for selection. Open admission, but selective for some programs. Along with high school diploma or equivalent, applicants required to have at least one transferrable credit or complete and pass both a reading and writing assessment. Bachelor's programs are completion programs for students who have associate degree or at least 90 quarter credits of undergraduate coursework completed. Requirements vary by degree.

2015-2016 Annual costs. Books/supplies: $399. **Additional information:** Tuition varies by program and level. Per-credit-hour for Certificate programs: $387-$787; per-credit-hour for Bachelor's degrees: $315-$371. All costs are subject to change.

Application procedures. Admission: No deadline. $50 fee. Admission notification on a rolling basis. **Financial aid:** No deadline.

Academics. Special study options: Accelerated study, combined bachelor's/graduate degree, distance learning, double major, internships. **Credit/placement by examination:** AP, CLEP, IB. **Support services:** Learning center, tutoring, writing center.

Majors. Business: Accounting, business admin, e-commerce, finance, human resources, marketing, retailing. **Computer sciences:** Computer graphics, information technology, LAN/WAN management, security, web page design. **Health services:** Health care admin, medical informatics, nursing (RN). **Human services:** General. **Protective services:** Criminal justice, disaster management, homeland security. **Psychology:** General.

Most popular majors. Business/marketing 55%, computer/information sciences 22%, health sciences 6%, psychology 11%, security/protective services 6%.

Technology on campus. PC or laptop required.

Student life. Freshman orientation: Available. Preregistration for classes offered. Online seminar that provides students with knowledge, skills, and advice needed to be successful in Capella's online environment.

Student services. Adult student services, career counseling, financial aid counseling. **Physically disabled:** Services for visually, hearing impaired.

Contact. E-mail: info@capella.edu
Phone: (888) 227-2736 Toll-free number: (866) 679-9682
Tonia Teasley, VP Learner Services and Operations, Capella University, 225 South Sixth Street, Minneapolis, MN 55402

Carleton College
Northfield, Minnesota   **CB member**
www.carleton.edu   **CB code: 6081**

- Private 4-year liberal arts college
- Residential campus in large town
- 1,995 degree-seeking undergraduates: 51% women, 4% African American, 8% Asian American, 7% Hispanic/Latino, 5% Multi-racial, non-Hispanic, 10% international
- 21% of applicants admitted
- SAT or ACT with writing, application essay required
- 95% graduate within 6 years; 25% enter graduate study

General. Founded in 1866. Regionally accredited. Sustainability initiatives include green roofs, eco-building class, eco house built by students, 2 wind turbines. **Degrees:** 480 bachelor's awarded. **Location:** 35 miles from Minneapolis-St. Paul. **Calendar:** Trimester. **Full-time faculty:** 205 total; 97% have terminal degrees, 26% minority, 47% women. **Part-time faculty:** 40 total; 72% have terminal degrees, 22% minority, 55% women. **Class size:** 71% < 20, 26% 20-39, 2% 40-49, less than 1% 50-99. **Special facilities:** 880 acre arboretum, 35 acre virgin prairie, greenhouse, observatory, scanning and transmission electron microscope, refractor and reflector telescopes, nuclear magnet resonance spectrometer, center for creativity.

Freshman class profile. 6,722 applied, 1,388 admitted, 491 enrolled.

Mid 50% test scores		Rank in top tenth:	71%
SAT critical reading:	660-750	Return as sophomores:	96%
SAT math:	660-770	Out-of-state:	82%
SAT writing:	660-750	Live on campus:	100%
ACT composite:	29-33	International:	12%
Rank in top quarter:	96%		

Basis for selection. School achievement record and recommendations most important. Test scores, extracurricular school and community activities also important. SAT Subject Tests recommended. Interview recommended but not required. **Learning Disabled:** Untimed standardized tests and GED accepted.

High school preparation. College-preparatory program recommended. Recommended units include English 4, mathematics 3, social studies 3, science 3 (laboratory 1) and foreign language 3. 3 units distributed between history and social sciences recommended.

2015-2016 Annual costs. Tuition/fees: $49,263. Room/board: $12,783. Books/supplies: $800. Personal expenses: $799.

2014-2015 Financial aid. All financial aid based on need. 377 full-time freshmen applied for aid; 267 deemed to have need; 267 received aid. Average need met was 100%. Average scholarship/grant was $39,854; average loan $4,285. 82% of total undergraduate aid awarded as scholarships/grants, 18% as loans/jobs. **Additional information:** Full financial need of all admitted applicants met through combination of work, loans, grants.

Application procedures. Admission: Closing date 1/15 (postmark date). $30 fee, may be waived for applicants with need, free for online applicants. Admission notification by 3/30. Must reply by May 1 or within 2 week(s) if notified thereafter. **Financial aid:** Closing date 2/15. FAFSA, CSS PROFILE required. Applicants notified by 3/31; must reply by 5/1 or within 2 week(s) of notification.

Academics. **Special study options:** Accelerated study, combined bachelor's/graduate degree, cross-registration, double major, dual enrollment of high school students, independent study, internships, student-designed major, study abroad, teacher certification program. **Credit/placement by examination:** AP, CLEP, IB, institutional tests. 36 credit hours maximum toward bachelor's degree. **Support services:** Learning center, tutoring, writing center.

Majors. **Area/ethnic studies:** African-American, American, Asian, French, Latin American, women's. **Biology:** General. **Computer sciences:** Computer science. **Conservation:** Environmental studies. **English:** English lit. **Foreign languages:** Classics, German, linguistics, Romance, Russian, Spanish. **History:** General. **Math:** General, statistics. **Philosophy/religion:** Philosophy, religion. **Physical sciences:** Chemistry, geology, physics. **Psychology:** General. **Social sciences:** Anthropology, economics, international relations, political science, sociology. **Visual/performing arts:** Art history/conservation, dance, dramatic, film/cinema/video, music, studio arts.

Most popular majors. Biology 10%, computer/information sciences 10%, mathematics 7%, physical sciences 16%, psychology 6%, social sciences 17%, visual/performing arts 10%.

Technology on campus. 250 workstations in library, computer center, student center. Dormitories wired for high-speed internet access and linked to campus network. Online course registration, online library, helpline, repair service, student web hosting, wireless network available.

Student life. **Freshman orientation:** Mandatory. Preregistration for classes offered. Four days prior to start of fall classes. **Policies:** Freshmen not permitted cars on campus. **Housing:** Guaranteed on-campus for all undergraduates. Coed dorms, special housing for disabled, apartments, themed housing, wellness housing available. College-owned houses within 2 blocks of campus, some coeducational, with varying board options; several for special interest groups available. **Activities:** Bands, campus ministries, choral groups, dance, drama, film society, international student organizations, literary magazine, music ensembles, Model UN, musical theater, radio station, student government, student newspaper, symphony orchestra, Close to 200 registered student organizations.

Athletics. NCAA. **Intercollegiate:** Baseball M, basketball, cross-country, diving, football (tackle) M, golf, soccer, softball W, swimming, tennis, track and field, volleyball W. **Intramural:** Basketball, football (non-tackle), ice hockey, racquetball, sand volleyball, soccer, softball, squash, tennis, triathlon, ultimate frisbee, volleyball. **Team name:** Knights.

Student services. Alcohol/substance abuse counseling, chaplain/spiritual director, career counseling, student employment services, financial aid counseling, health services, minority student services, personal counseling, placement for graduates, women's services. **Physically disabled:** Services for visually, hearing impaired.

Contact. E-mail: Admissions@carleton.edu
Phone: (507) 222-4190 Toll-free number: (800) 995-2275
Fax: (507) 222-4526
Paul Thiboutot, Vice President and Dean of Admissions and Financial Aid, Carleton College, 100 South College Street, Northfield, MN 55057

College of St. Benedict

St. Joseph, Minnesota
www.csbsju.edu

CB member
CB code: 6104

▸ Private 4-year liberal arts college affiliated with the Roman Catholic Church

▸ Residential campus in small town

▸ 1,943 degree-seeking undergraduates: 1% part-time, 100% women, 3% African American, 6% Asian American, 6% Hispanic/Latino, 1% Native American, 1% Multi-racial, non-Hispanic, 4% international

▸ 75% of applicants admitted

▸ SAT or ACT (ACT writing optional) required

▸ 85% graduate within 6 years; 17% enter graduate study

General. Founded in 1887. Regionally accredited. Institution located six miles from St. John's University; students enrolled on both campuses have access to facilities, classes, activities and events held by the two institutions. **Degrees:** 479 bachelor's awarded. **ROTC:** Army. **Location:** 10 miles from St. Cloud, 70 miles from Minneapolis-St. Paul. **Calendar:** Semester, limited summer session. **Full-time faculty:** 144 total; 92% have terminal degrees, 11% minority, 52% women. **Part-time faculty:** 24 total; 38% have terminal degrees, 4% minority, 58% women. **Class size:** 59% < 20, 40% 20 39, less than 1% 40-49, less than 1% 50-99. **Special facilities:** Labyrinth, performing arts center, pottery studio, kiln, green house, observatory, ecumenical center, Hill Museum and Manuscript Library, liturgical press, nature preserve and herbarium, Saint John's Outdoor University, natural history museum.

Freshman class profile. 1,858 applied, 1,389 admitted, 476 enrolled.

Mid 50% test scores			
SAT critical reading:	490-590	GPA 2.0-2.99:	4%
SAT math:	450-570	Rank in top quarter:	61%
SAT writing:	480-560	Rank in top tenth:	31%
ACT composite:	22-27	End year in good standing:	97%
GPA 3.75 or higher:	43%	Return as sophomores:	91%
GPA 3.50-3.74:	26%	Out-of-state:	16%
GPA 3.0-3.49:	27%	Live on campus:	100%
		International:	4%

Basis for selection. College preparatory curriculum, college entrance exams (ACT or SAT), grade point average are important and carefully considered. In addition, institution seeks to enroll students who show promise of community contribution and productive participation in the classroom as evidenced by both their academic record and their participation in extracurricular activities. Interview recommended for conditionally accepted/academically weak applicants. **Home schooled:** Applicants are not required to have a high school diploma but are required to provide appropriate documentation of college preparatory curriculum. **Learning Disabled:** Diagnostic tests are required to determine the existence of most disabilities; we do not require specific exams. Accept documentation administered by qualified diagnosticians. Accommodations provided on case-by-case basis for students who provide adequate documentation of a disability. Individual tutoring available as needed. Academic and psychological counseling available on an unlimited basis.

High school preparation. College-preparatory program required. 15 units required. Required and recommended units include English 4, mathematics 3, social studies 2, science 2 (laboratory 2), foreign language 2 and academic electives 4.

2015-2016 Annual costs. Tuition/fees: $40,846. Room/board: $10,231. Books/supplies: $1,000. Personal expenses: $1,400. **Additional information:** Meal plan is flexible meal plan.

2015-2016 Financial aid. **Need-based:** 419 full-time freshmen applied for aid; 363 deemed to have need; 363 received aid. Average need met was 91%. Average scholarship/grant was $29,368; average loan $4,515. 68% of total undergraduate aid awarded as scholarships/grants, 32% as loans/jobs. **Non-need-based:** Awarded to 1,749 full-time undergraduates, including 441 freshmen. Scholarships awarded for academics, alumni affiliation, art, leadership, music/drama, ROTC. **Additional information:** Scholarship letters will be mailed on a rolling basis approximately two weeks from the time the admission acceptance letter is sent.

Application procedures. **Admission:** Priority date 11/15; no deadline. No application fee. Must reply by 5/1. A non-refundable enrollment deposit of $300 is due May 1. **Financial aid:** Priority date 3/15; no closing date. FAFSA, institutional form required. Applicants notified on a rolling basis starting 3/15; must reply by 5/1.

Academics. **Special study options:** Combined bachelor's/graduate degree, cross-registration, double major, dual enrollment of high school students, ESL, honors, independent study, internships, student-designed major, study abroad, teacher certification program. 3-1 program in dentistry with University of Minnesota, cross registration with St. Cloud State University. **Credit/placement by examination:** AP, CLEP, IB, SAT, ACT, institutional tests. **Support services:** Reduced course load, study skills assistance, tutoring, writing center. Math skills center; tutoring not available in all departments.

Majors. **Area/ethnic studies:** Asian, women's. **Biology:** General, biochemistry. **Business:** Accounting, business admin. **Computer sciences:** Computer science. **Conservation:** Environmental studies. **Education:** Elementary. **English:** English lit, rhetoric/composition. **Foreign languages:** Classics, French, German, Spanish. **Health services:** Dietetics, nursing (RN). **History:** General. **Liberal arts:** Arts/sciences, humanities. **Math:** General. **Philosophy/religion:** Philosophy. **Physical sciences:** Chemistry, physics. **Psychology:** General. **Social sciences:** General, economics, political science, sociology. **Theology:** Theology. **Visual/performing arts:** Art, dramatic, music.

Most popular majors. Biology 7%, business/marketing 14%, education 6%, English 14%, health sciences 8%, interdisciplinary studies 12%, psychology 13%, social sciences 7%.

Technology on campus. 989 workstations in dormitories, library, computer center, student center. Dormitories wired for high-speed internet access and linked to campus network. Commuter students can connect to campus network. Online course registration, online library, helpline, repair service, student web hosting, wireless network available.

Student life. **Freshman orientation:** Mandatory. Preregistration for classes offered. Fall orientation begins the evening of move-in day and concludes with convocation the first day of classes. **Policies:** There is a 4

year residency requirement. **Housing:** Guaranteed on-campus for freshmen. Single-sex dorms, special housing for disabled, apartments, themed housing, wellness housing available. Eco/environmental houses. **Activities:** Bands, campus ministries, choral groups, dance, drama, film society, international student organizations, literary magazine, music ensembles, Model UN, musical theater, opera, radio station, student government, student newspaper, symphony orchestra, TV station, Volunteers in Service to Others, College Republicans, College Democrats, Joint Events Council, Asia club, Alternative Spring Break, Students in Free Enterprise, Magis, Cultural Fusion club, Outdoor Leadership Center.

Athletics. NCAA. **Intercollegiate:** Basketball W, cross-country W, diving W, golf W, ice hockey W, soccer W, softball W, swimming W, tennis W, track and field W, volleyball W. **Intramural:** Basketball W, football (non-tackle) W, racquetball W, soccer W, softball W, tennis W, volleyball W. **Team name:** Blazers.

Student services. Alcohol/substance abuse counseling, chaplain/spiritual director, career counseling, financial aid counseling, health services, minority student services, personal counseling, placement for graduates, women's services. **Physically disabled:** Services for visually, hearing impaired.

Contact. E-mail: admissions@csbsju.edu
Phone: (320) 363-5060 Toll-free number: (800) 544-1489
Fax: (320) 363-5650
Calvin Mosley, Vice President for Admission and Financial Aid, College of St. Benedict, College of Saint Benedict/Saint John's University, Collegeville, MN 56321-7155

College of St. Scholastica
Duluth, Minnesota **CB member**
www.css.edu **CB code: 6107**

- Private 4-year liberal arts college affiliated with the Roman Catholic Church
- Residential campus in small city
- 2,782 degree-seeking undergraduates: 18% part-time, 71% women, 3% African American, 2% Asian American, 3% Hispanic/Latino, 2% Native American, 3% Multi-racial, non-Hispanic, 3% international
- 1,513 degree-seeking graduate students
- 61% of applicants admitted
- SAT or ACT (ACT writing optional) required
- 70% graduate within 6 years

General. Founded in 1912. Regionally accredited. **Degrees:** 924 bachelor's awarded; master's, professional offered. **ROTC:** Air Force. **Location:** 2 miles from downtown, 150 miles from Minneapolis-St. Paul. **Calendar:** Semester, limited summer session. **Full-time faculty:** 185 total; 56% have terminal degrees, 10% minority, 64% women. **Part-time faculty:** 202 total; 31% have terminal degrees, 6% minority, 59% women. **Class size:** 52% < 20, 43% 20-39, 2% 40-49, 2% 50-99, less than 1% >100. **Special facilities:** Wellness center with climbing wall.

Freshman class profile. 3,589 applied, 2,206 admitted, 439 enrolled.

Mid 50% test scores			
SAT critical reading:	380-470	**GPA 2.0-2.99:**	12%
SAT math:	340-540	**Rank in top quarter:**	48%
SAT writing:	370-490	**Rank in top tenth:**	23%
ACT composite:	20-26	**Return as sophomores:**	84%
GPA 3.75 or higher:	30%	**Out-of-state:**	12%
GPA 3.50-3.74:	27%	**Live on campus:**	89%
GPA 3.0-3.49:	31%	**International:**	3%

Basis for selection. School achievement record and test scores most important. Interview recommended. **Home schooled:** State high school equivalency certificate required.

High school preparation. College-preparatory program recommended. Recommended units include English 4, mathematics 2, social studies 3, history 3, science 3 and foreign language 3.

2015-2016 Annual costs. Tuition/fees: $33,994. Room/board: $8,932. Books/supplies: $1,150. Personal expenses: $1,188.

2015-2016 Financial aid. Need-based: 402 full-time freshmen applied for aid; 360 deemed to have need; 360 received aid. Average need met was 80%. Average scholarship/grant was $7,795; average loan $3,589. 58% of total undergraduate aid awarded as scholarships/grants, 42% as loans/jobs. **Non-need-based:** Awarded to 1,594 full-time undergraduates, including 402 freshmen. Scholarships awarded for academics, alumni affiliation, music/drama, religious affiliation, ROTC, state residency.

Application procedures. Admission: Priority date 3/1; no deadline. No application fee. Admission notification on a rolling basis beginning on or about 9/1. Must reply by May 1 or within 2 week(s) if notified thereafter. **Financial aid:** Priority date 3/1; no closing date. FAFSA required. Applicants notified on a rolling basis starting 3/1; must reply by 5/1 or within 2 week(s) of notification.

Academics. Special study options: Accelerated study, combined bachelor's/graduate degree, cross-registration, distance learning, double major, dual enrollment of high school students, honors, independent study, internships, liberal arts/career combination, student-designed major, study abroad, teacher certification program, Washington semester, weekend college. **Credit/placement by examination:** AP, CLEP, IB, ACT, institutional tests. 96 credit hours maximum toward bachelor's degree. All external credit meeting score expectations will be accepted; last 32 semester hours must be completed in residence. **Support services:** Pre-admission summer program, reduced course load, study skills assistance, tutoring, writing center.

Honors college/program. Should meet 2 of the following: top 15% of high school class, 26 ACT or 1100 (exclusive of Writing) SAT, GPA of 3.5; others may apply by contacting the honors director. Students must complete 20 honors credits, at least 8 of which are upper division level credits.

Majors. Biology: General, biochemistry, exercise physiology. **Business:** Accounting, business admin, finance, marketing, organizational behavior. **Communications:** Advertising, communications/speech/rhetoric, journalism. **Computer sciences:** General. **Education:** Elementary, multi-level teacher, Native American, school librarian, social science. **English:** English lit. **Foreign languages:** Spanish. **Health services:** Health information management, nursing (RN). **History:** General. **Human services:** Social work. **Liberal arts:** Humanities. **Math:** General. **Philosophy/religion:** Christian, philosophy, religion. **Physical sciences:** Chemistry. **Psychology:** General. **Social sciences:** General, applied economics. **Visual/performing arts:** Art, music performance.

Most popular majors. Biology 10%, business/marketing 18%, health sciences 44%, psychology 6%, public administration/social services 9%.

Technology on campus. 451 workstations in dormitories, library, computer center, student center. Dormitories wired for high-speed internet access and linked to campus network. Commuter students can connect to campus network. Online course registration, online library, helpline, student web hosting, wireless network available.

Student life. Freshman orientation: Mandatory. Preregistration for classes offered. **Housing:** Guaranteed on-campus for freshmen. Coed dorms, special housing for disabled, apartments available. $150 fully refundable deposit, deadline 5/1. Pets allowed in dorm rooms. Quiet or study wing; housing for students with dependent children available. **Activities:** Bands, campus ministries, choral groups, dance, drama, international student organizations, literary magazine, music ensembles, Model UN, musical theater, radio station, student government, student newspaper, TV station, Circle-K, InterVarsity Christian Fellowship, Indigenous Students' Association, Benedictine Friends, Volunteers Involved Through Action, Amnesty International, Kaleidoscope Multicultural Club, Habitat for Humanity, United for Africa, Earth Action.

Athletics. NCAA. **Intercollegiate:** Baseball M, basketball, cross-country, football (tackle) M, ice hockey, skiing, soccer, softball W, tennis, track and field, volleyball W. **Intramural:** Badminton, basketball, bowling, football (non-tackle), soccer, softball, tennis, volleyball. **Team name:** Saints.

Student services. Adult student services, alcohol/substance abuse counseling, chaplain/spiritual director, career counseling, student employment services, financial aid counseling, health services, minority student services, personal counseling, placement for graduates, veterans' counselor, women's services. **Physically disabled:** Services for visually, hearing impaired.

Contact. E-mail: admissions@css.edu
Phone: (218) 723-6046 Toll-free number: (800) 249-6412
Fax: (218) 723-5991
Eric Berg, Vice President for Enrollment Management, College of St. Scholastica, 1200 Kenwood Avenue, Duluth, MN 55811-4199

Concordia College: Moorhead
Moorhead, Minnesota **CB member**
www.concordiacollege.edu **CB code: 6113**

- Private 4-year liberal arts college affiliated with the Evangelical Lutheran Church in America
- Residential campus in large town

◆ 2,104 degree-seeking undergraduates: 1% part-time, 59% women, 2% African American, 2% Asian American, 2% Hispanic/Latino, 1% Native American, 2% Multi-racial, non-Hispanic, 3% international

◆ 15 degree-seeking graduate students

◆ 78% of applicants admitted

◆ SAT or ACT (ACT writing optional) required

◆ 73% graduate within 6 years

General. Founded in 1891. Regionally accredited. **Degrees:** 581 bachelor's awarded; master's offered. **ROTC:** Army, Air Force. **Location:** 234 miles from Minneapolis-St. Paul, 1 mile from Fargo, North Dakota. **Calendar:** Semester, limited summer session. **Full-time faculty:** 171 total; 86% have terminal degrees, 8% minority, 48% women. **Part-time faculty:** 77 total; 35% have terminal degrees, 1% minority, 53% women. **Class size:** 61% < 20, 37% 20-39, 1% 40-49. **Special facilities:** Observatory, 2MeV hypervelocity dust particle accelerator, language villages, television production studio, field biology research facility, nursing lab, laser facility.

Freshman class profile. 2,276 applied, 1,780 admitted, 519 enrolled.

Mid 50% test scores		Rank in top quarter:	59%
ACT composite:	22-28	Rank in top tenth:	31%
GPA 3.75 or higher:	45%	Return as sophomores:	82%
GPA 3.50-3.74:	23%	Out-of-state:	32%
GPA 3.0-3.49:	25%	Live on campus:	96%
GPA 2.0-2.99:	7%	International:	2%

Basis for selection. Academic record (types of courses and grades) most important, followed by test scores and recommendations. Interview recommended. **Home schooled:** Transcript of courses and grades, letter of recommendation (nonparent) required.

High school preparation. College-preparatory program recommended. Recommended units include English 4, mathematics 3, social studies 3, science 3, foreign language 2, computer science 1 and visual/performing arts 1.

2015-2016 Annual costs. Tuition/fees: $35,464. Room/board: $7,600. Books/supplies: $920. Personal expenses: $1,200.

2014-2015 Financial aid. **Need-based:** 503 full-time freshmen applied for aid; 416 deemed to have need; 416 received aid. Average need met was 91%. Average scholarship/grant was $22,242; average loan $4,637. 70% of total undergraduate aid awarded as scholarships/grants, 30% as loans/jobs. **Non-need-based:** Awarded to 800 full-time undergraduates, including 184 freshmen. Scholarships awarded for academics, art, leadership, minority status, music/drama.

Application procedures. **Admission:** No deadline. $20 fee, may be waived for applicants with need, free for online applicants. Admission notification on a rolling basis beginning on or about 6/15. **Financial aid:** Priority date 3/1; no closing date. FAFSA required. Applicants notified on a rolling basis starting 3/15.

Academics. **Special study options:** Cooperative education, cross-registration, double major, exchange student, honors, independent study, internships, liberal arts/career combination, student-designed major, study abroad, teacher certification program, urban semester, Washington semester. A wide variety of global education opportunities including exploration seminars, summer field studies, semester and year long programs, May seminars, summer school abroad, summer research abroad, music ensemble tours, global cooperative education, and student teacher placements. **Credit/placement by examination:** AP, CLEP, IB, institutional tests. 20 credit hours maximum toward bachelor's degree. **Support services:** Learning center, reduced course load, study skills assistance, tutoring, writing center.

Majors. **Area/ethnic studies:** Scandinavian. **Biology:** General. **Business:** Accounting, business admin, international. **Communications:** General, communications/speech/rhetoric. **Conservation:** Environmental studies. **Education:** General, art, biology, business, chemistry, elementary, foreign languages, French, German, health, Latin, mathematics, music, physical, physics, social studies, Spanish. **English:** English lit. **Foreign languages:** Chinese, classics, French, German, Latin, Spanish. **Health services:** Nursing (RN). **History:** General. **Human services:** Social work. **Liberal arts:** Humanities. **Math:** General, financial. **Parks/recreation:** Health/fitness. **Philosophy/religion:** Philosophy, religion. **Physical sciences:** Chemistry, physics. **Psychology:** General. **Social sciences:** General, political science, sociology. **Visual/performing arts:** Art, dramatic, music, music performance, music theory/composition.

Most popular majors. Biology 9%, business/marketing 12%, communications/journalism 8%, education 12%, foreign language 6%, health sciences 7%, social sciences 7%, visual/performing arts 8%.

Technology on campus. 405 workstations in dormitories, library, student center. Dormitories wired for high-speed internet access and linked to campus network. Commuter students can connect to campus network. Online course

registration, online library, helpline, repair service, wireless network available.

Student life. **Freshman orientation:** Mandatory. Preregistration for classes offered. Four-day program prior to the beginning of fall semester classes. **Housing:** Guaranteed on-campus for freshmen. Coed dorms, single-sex dorms, apartments, themed housing available. $200 fully refundable deposit, deadline 8/1. EcoHouse. **Activities:** Bands, campus ministries, choral groups, dance, drama, international student organizations, literary magazine, music ensembles, musical theater, radio station, student government, student newspaper, symphony orchestra, TV station, more than 100 student organizations reflecting interests in many different areas including academics, athletics, programming, religion, special interest, service and media.

Athletics. NCAA. **Intercollegiate:** Baseball M, basketball, cross-country, diving W, football (tackle) M, golf, ice hockey, soccer, softball W, swimming W, tennis, track and field, volleyball W, wrestling M. **Intramural:** Basketball, bowling, football (non-tackle) M, swimming, ultimate frisbee, volleyball. **Team name:** Cobbers.

Student services. Alcohol/substance abuse counseling, chaplain/spiritual director, career counseling, student employment services, financial aid counseling, health services, minority student services, on-campus daycare, personal counseling, placement for graduates. **Physically disabled:** Services for visually, speech, hearing impaired.

Contact. E-mail: admissions@cord.edu
Phone: (218) 299-3004 Toll-free number: (800) 699-9897
Fax: (218) 299-4720
Scott Ellingson, Dean of Admissions, Concordia College: Moorhead, 901 Eighth Street South, Moorhead, MN 56562

Concordia University St. Paul
Saint Paul, Minnesota — **CB member**
www.csp.edu — **CB code: 6114**

◆ Private 4-year university affiliated with the Lutheran Church - Missouri Synod

◆ Residential campus in large city

◆ 2,281 degree-seeking undergraduates: 43% part-time, 57% women, 13% African American, 7% Asian American, 4% Hispanic/Latino, 1% Native American, 4% Multi-racial, non-Hispanic, 5% international

◆ 1,813 degree-seeking graduate students

◆ 55% of applicants admitted

◆ SAT or ACT (ACT writing optional) required

◆ 46% graduate within 6 years

General. Founded in 1893. Regionally accredited. **Degrees:** 557 bachelor's, 5 associate awarded; master's, professional offered. **ROTC:** Army, Air Force. **Location:** 2 miles from the downtown Minneapolis and downtown St. Paul. **Calendar:** Semester, limited summer session. **Full-time faculty:** 96 total; 76% have terminal degrees, 8% minority, 48% women. **Part-time faculty:** 332 total; 38% have terminal degrees, 8% minority, 52% women. **Class size:** 75% < 20, 24% 20-39, less than 1% 40-49.

Freshman class profile. 1,483 applied, 822 admitted, 229 enrolled.

Mid 50% test scores		Rank in top tenth:	11%
ACT composite:	18-24	End year in good standing:	79%
GPA 3.75 or higher:	16%	Return as sophomores:	70%
GPA 3.50-3.74:	14%	Out-of-state:	21%
GPA 3.0-3.49:	28%	Live on campus:	74%
GPA 2.0-2.99:	41%	International:	5%
Rank in top quarter:	30%		

Basis for selection. School record, test scores, recommendations important. ACT preferred. Interview recommended.

High school preparation. 15 units required; 18 recommended. Required and recommended units include English 4, mathematics 2-3, social studies 2, history 2, science 2-3, foreign language 1 and visual/performing arts 2. 1 unit of health/physical education required.

2016-2017 Annual costs. Tuition/fees (projected): $21,250. Room/board: $8,500. Books/supplies: $2,000.

2015-2016 Financial aid. **Need-based:** 212 full-time freshmen applied for aid; 173 deemed to have need; 170 received aid. Average need met was 66%. Average scholarship/grant was $12,383; average loan $3,443. 62% of total undergraduate aid awarded as scholarships/grants, 38% as loans/jobs. **Non-need-based:** Awarded to 262 full-time undergraduates, including 66 freshmen. Scholarships awarded for academics, art, athletics, minority status, music/drama, religious affiliation. **Additional information:** Church districts and local congregations are major sources of aid for church-vocation students.

Application procedures. Admission: Priority date 12/1; deadline 8/1 (receipt date). $30 fee, may be waived for applicants with need. Admission notification on a rolling basis beginning on or about 1/3. Housing deposit refundable in full prior to May 1st. **Financial aid:** Priority date 5/1; no closing date. FAFSA required. Applicants notified on a rolling basis starting 3/1.

Academics. Offers a variety of non-traditional undergraduate degree completion programs designed for working adults in both face-to-face and distance education formats. Approximately 45% of the undergraduates fall into this non-traditional category. **Special study options:** Accelerated study, cross-registration, distance learning, double major, dual enrollment of high school students, honors, independent study, internships, student-designed major, study abroad, teacher certification program. **Credit/placement by examination:** AP, CLEP, IB, SAT, ACT, institutional tests. **Support services:** Learning center, reduced course load, remedial instruction, study skills assistance, tutoring, writing center.

Majors. Biology: General. **Business:** Accounting, business admin, finance, hospitality admin, human resources, marketing, sales/distribution. **Communications:** Media studies. **Computer sciences:** Computer science. **Education:** Art, bilingual, biology, chemistry, early childhood, elementary, English, ESL, health, history, kindergarten/preschool, mathematics, middle, music, physical, science, secondary, social studies. **Engineering:** Engineering science. **English:** Creative writing, English lit, general lit, technical writing. **Health services:** Athletic training, health care admin, nursing practice, orthotics/prosthetics, respiratory therapy technology. **History:** General. **Math:** General, applied. **Parks/recreation:** Exercise sciences, health/fitness, sports admin, sports studies. **Protective services:** Criminal justice. **Psychology:** General. **Social sciences:** Sociology. **Theology:** Missionary, religious ed, sacred music, theology. **Visual/performing arts:** Art, design, dramatic, graphic design, music, music management, studio arts. **Work/family studies:** Child development, family studies.

Most popular majors. Business/marketing 40%, education 8%, parks/recreation 11%, psychology 6%, security/protective services 7%.

Technology on campus. 8 workstations in library. Dormitories wired for high-speed internet access and linked to campus network. Commuter students can connect to campus network. Online library, helpline, repair service, wireless network available.

Student life. Freshman orientation: Mandatory. Preregistration for classes offered. Three-day program prior to start of fall semester. **Policies:** Two-year residence requirement for freshmen and sophomores, either in residence hall or with parents. Students over 21 may have alcohol in their room if they have completed an application and have been approved for alcohol privileges. **Housing:** Guaranteed on-campus for freshmen. Coed dorms, single-sex dorms, special housing for disabled, apartments available. $125 fully refundable deposit. **Activities:** Bands, campus ministries, choral groups, dance, drama, international student organizations, music ensembles, musical theater, student government, student newspaper, Art club, business club, criminal justice club, International Student Organization, Hmong United Student Association, STAGE (Theater), Teachers of Tomorrow, veterans club, Tri Pi (Math), United Minds of Joint Action.

Athletics. NCAA. **Intercollegiate:** Baseball M, basketball, cross-country, football (tackle) M, golf, lacrosse W, soccer W, softball W, track and field, volleyball W. **Intramural:** Basketball, cheerleading, racquetball, softball, volleyball. **Team name:** Golden Bears.

Student services. Adult student services, alcohol/substance abuse counseling, chaplain/spiritual director, career counseling, services for economically disadvantaged, student employment services, financial aid counseling, minority student services, on-campus daycare, personal counseling, veterans' counselor. **Physically disabled:** Services for visually, speech, hearing impaired.

Contact. E-mail: admissions@csp.edu
Phone: (651) 641-8230 Toll-free number: (800) 333-4705
Fax: (651) 603-6320
Kristin Vogel, Associate Vice President for Traditional Enrollment Management, Concordia University St. Paul, 1282 Concordia Avenue, Saint Paul, MN 55104-5494

Crossroads College
Rochester, Minnesota
www.crossroadscollege.edu
CB code: 6412

- Private 4-year Bible college affiliated with the Christian Church
- Residential campus in small city

- 96 degree-seeking undergraduates
- SAT or ACT (ACT writing optional), application essay required

General. Founded in 1913. Accredited by ABHE. Offers degree completion program with evening and online courses available. **Degrees:** 15 bachelor's, 2 associate awarded. **Location:** 85 miles from Minneapolis-St. Paul. **Calendar:** Semester, limited summer session. **Class size:** 95% < 20, 4% 20-39, 2% 40-49.

Freshman class profile.

Rank in top quarter: 10% **Out-of-state:** 50%

Basis for selection. High school rank, experience, aptitude for Christian ministry, character references, and personal statement of goals considered. High school GPA, rank and ACT/SAT scores determine number of credit hours a student may take during first semester if accepted. Interview recommended. **Home schooled:** Letter of recommendation (nonparent) required. **Learning Disabled:** Provide verification of learning disability.

2015-2016 Annual costs. Tuition/fees: $16,040. Room only: $4,150. Books/supplies: $1,000.

Financial aid. Non-need-based: Scholarships awarded for academics, leadership, music/drama, religious affiliation.

Application procedures. Admission: Closing date 8/15 (receipt date). No application fee. Admission notification on a rolling basis. **Financial aid:** Priority date 4/1, closing date 4/15. FAFSA, institutional form required. Applicants notified on a rolling basis starting 2/1; must reply within 4 week(s) of notification.

Academics. Minors in religious music, counseling psychology, biblical and classical languages, missions, youth ministries. **Special study options:** Accelerated study, distance learning, double major, independent study, internships, student-designed major. **Credit/placement by examination:** AP, CLEP, SAT, ACT, institutional tests. 30 credit hours maximum toward bachelor's degree. **Support services:** Reduced course load, remedial instruction, study skills assistance, tutoring, writing center.

Majors. Business: Business admin, nonprofit/public. **Psychology:** Counseling. **Theology:** Missionary, religious ed, sacred music, theology, youth ministry. **Visual/performing arts:** Music.

Technology on campus. 17 workstations in library, student center. Dormitories wired for high-speed internet access and linked to campus network. Commuter students can connect to campus network. Online library, repair service, wireless network available.

Student life. Freshman orientation: Mandatory. Preregistration for classes offered. Two-day session with some placement testing in August; one-day session in January. **Policies:** Attendance required at weekly Chapel and Spiritual Formation Group meetings; Field Service participation required. Religious observance required. **Housing:** Guaranteed on-campus for freshmen. Single-sex dorms, special housing for disabled, apartments, wellness housing available. $125 deposit. **Activities:** Campus ministries, choral groups, drama, international student organizations, music ensembles, student government, Ambassadors group, international students fellowship.

Athletics. NCCAA. **Intercollegiate:** Basketball, soccer, volleyball W. **Intramural:** Bowling, golf, racquetball, tennis, weight lifting. **Team name:** Knights.

Student services. Adult student services, chaplain/spiritual director, career counseling, student employment services, financial aid counseling, personal counseling, placement for graduates, veterans' counselor.

Contact. E-mail: admissions@crossroadscollege.edu
Phone: (507) 288-4563 Toll-free number: (800) 456-7651
Fax: (507) 288-9046
Todd Looney, Director of Admissions, Crossroads College, 920 Mayowood Road SW, Rochester, MN 55902

Crown College
Saint Bonifacius, Minnesota
www.crown.edu
CB code: 6639

- Private 4-year liberal arts college affiliated with the Christian and Missionary Alliance
- Residential campus in small town
- 885 full-time, degree-seeking undergraduates
- 185 graduate students
- SAT or ACT (ACT writing optional), application essay required

General. Founded in 1916. Regionally accredited. **Degrees:** 185 bachelor's, 10 associate awarded; master's offered. **ROTC:** Army. **Location:** 25 miles from Minneapolis-St. Paul. **Calendar:** Semester, limited summer session. **Full-time faculty:** 33 total. **Part-time faculty:** 127 total. **Class size:** 68% < 20, 25% 20-39, 5% 40-49, 3% 50-99. **Special facilities:** Nursing lab with SIM man and other mannequins, 18-hole disc golf course.

Freshman class profile.

GPA 3.75 or higher:	26%	Rank in top quarter:	38%
GPA 3.50-3.74:	20%	Rank in top tenth:	13%
GPA 3.0-3.49:	37%	Out-of-state:	43%
GPA 2.0-2.99:	16%	Live on campus:	94%

Basis for selection. Applicants must profess personal faith in Jesus Christ. Academic records and test scores important. **Learning Disabled:** Applicant should meet with director of academic support.

High school preparation. College-preparatory program recommended. Recommended units include English 4, mathematics 3, social studies 3, science 3 and foreign language 2.

2015-2016 Annual costs. Tuition/fees: $23,740. Room/board: $7,940. Books/supplies: $1,150. Personal expenses: $2,500.

Financial aid. Non-need-based: Scholarships awarded for academics, alumni affiliation, leadership, minority status, music/drama, religious affiliation.

Application procedures. Admission: No deadline. $20 fee, may be waived for applicants with need. Admission notification on a rolling basis. Within 30 days of acceptance notification. **Financial aid:** Priority date 4/1; no closing date. FAFSA required. Applicants notified on a rolling basis starting 4/1; must reply within 3 week(s) of notification.

Academics. Special study options: Accelerated study, distance learning, double major, dual enrollment of high school students, ESL, exchange student, honors, independent study, internships, liberal arts/career combination, study abroad, teacher certification program, urban semester, weekend college. 2-2 with non-accredited Bible colleges. **Credit/placement by examination:** AP, CLEP, IB, SAT, ACT. 30 credit hours maximum toward associate degree, 30 toward bachelor's. **Support services:** Learning center, reduced course load, remedial instruction, study skills assistance, tutoring, writing center.

Majors. Biology: General. **Business:** General, business admin, entrepreneurial studies, operations. **Communications:** General, advertising, digital media, persuasive communications. **Computer sciences:** System admin. **Education:** Early childhood, elementary, English, ESL, music, physical, science, secondary, social studies. **English:** English lit. **Foreign languages:** Linguistics. **Health services:** Nursing (RN). **History:** General. **Liberal arts:** Arts/sciences. **Parks/recreation:** Sports admin. **Psychology:** General, counseling. **Social sciences:** Urban studies. **Theology:** Bible, missionary, pastoral counseling, religious ed, theology, youth ministry. **Visual/performing arts:** Music, music performance.

Most popular majors. Business/marketing 8%, communications/journalism 9%, education 14%, health sciences 14%, psychology 14%, theological studies 34%.

Technology on campus. 105 workstations in library, computer center. Dormitories wired for high-speed internet access and linked to campus network. Commuter students can connect to campus network. Online library, helpline, repair service, wireless network available.

Student life. Freshman orientation: Mandatory. Preregistration for classes offered. Two-day orientation program at the beginning of the spring semester, four days prior to fall semester. **Policies:** Must abide by Crown College Covenant. Religious observance required. **Housing:** Guaranteed on-campus for all undergraduates. Single-sex dorms, special housing for disabled, apartments, wellness housing available. $150 fully refundable deposit. **Activities:** Bands, campus ministries, choral groups, dance, drama, film society, international student organizations, literary magazine, music ensembles, musical theater, radio station, student government, student newspaper, Hmong student fellowship, Hispanic/Spanish club, multi-cultural committee, African-American club, Team Managers' club, Student Family Association, outdoor adventure club, The Session (skiing & snowboarding), Students in Free Enterprise, College Conservatives.

Athletics. NCAA. **Intercollegiate:** Baseball M, basketball, cross-country, football (tackle) M, golf, soccer, softball W, volleyball W. **Intramural:** Basketball, soccer, softball, ultimate frisbee, volleyball. **Team name:** Storm.

Student services. Adult student services, chaplain/spiritual director, career counseling, student employment services, financial aid counseling, health services, personal counseling. **Physically disabled:** Services for visually, hearing impaired.

Contact. E-mail: admissions@crown.edu
Phone: (952) 446-4142 Toll-free number: (800) 682-7696
Fax: (952) 446-4149
Bret Hyder, Director of Admissions, Crown College, 8700 College View Drive, Saint Bonifacius, MN 55375-9001

Globe University: Minneapolis
Minneapolis, Minnesota
www.globeuniversity.edu

- For-profit 4-year university and career college
- Commuter campus in large city
- 164 undergraduates
- 79 graduate students
- Interview required

General. Regionally accredited; also accredited by ACICS. **Degrees:** 12 bachelor's, 1 associate awarded; master's, doctoral offered. **Location:** Located in the heart of downtown. **Calendar:** Quarter, extensive summer session. **Full-time faculty:** 4 total. **Part-time faculty:** 24 total.

Basis for selection. Open admission, but selective for some programs.

2015-2016 Annual costs. Tuition/fees: $18,702. Books/supplies: $1,260. **Additional information:** Per-credit hour charge for 1 to 11 hours, $460; for 12 to 16 hours, $390. Course fees: $10 to $400 per course.

Application procedures. Admission: No deadline. $50 fee. Admission notification on a rolling basis. **Financial aid:** No deadline. FAFSA, institutional form required. Applicants notified on a rolling basis starting 7/1; must reply within 2 week(s) of notification.

Academics. Special study options: Distance learning, independent study, internships, liberal arts/career combination. **Credit/placement by examination:** AP, CLEP. **Support services:** Remedial instruction, study skills assistance, tutoring, writing center.

Majors. Business: Accounting, business admin. **Computer sciences:** Information technology. **Health services:** Health care admin. **Protective services:** Financial forensics, law enforcement admin. **Visual/performing arts:** Arts management.

Most popular majors. Business/marketing 45%, computer/information sciences 9%, legal studies 18%, security/protective services 18%, visual/performing arts 9%.

Technology on campus. 60 workstations in library, computer center, student center. Commuter students can connect to campus network. Online library, helpline, student web hosting, wireless network available.

Student life. Freshman orientation: Mandatory. Preregistration for classes offered. Day and evening sessions available the week prior to start of classes. **Activities:** International student organizations, literary magazine.

Student services. Career counseling, student employment services, financial aid counseling, placement for graduates.

Contact. Phone: (612) 455-3000 Toll-free number: (877) 455-3697
Fax: (612) 455-3001
Mitch Ward, Director of Admissions, Globe University: Minneapolis, 80 South 8th Street, Minneapolis, MN 55402

Globe University: Moorhead
Moorhead, Minnesota
www.globeuniversity.edu

- For-profit 4-year university and career college
- Commuter campus in large town
- 220 undergraduates
- Interview required

General. Regionally accredited; also accredited by ACICS. **Degrees:** 14 bachelor's, 51 associate awarded. **Calendar:** Quarter, extensive summer session. **Full-time faculty:** 8 total. **Part-time faculty:** 18 total.

Basis for selection. Open admission.

2015-2016 Annual costs. Tuition/fees: $18,702. Books/supplies: $1,260. **Additional information:** Per-credit hour charge for 1 to 11 hours, $460; for 12 to 16 hours, $390. Course fees: $10 to $400 per course.

Application procedures. Admission: No deadline. $50 fee. Admission notification on a rolling basis. **Financial aid:** No deadline. FAFSA, institutional form required. Applicants notified on a rolling basis starting 7/1; must reply within 2 week(s) of notification.

Academics. Special study options: Distance learning, independent study, internships, liberal arts/career combination. **Credit/placement by examination:** AP, CLEP. **Support services:** Remedial instruction, study skills assistance, tutoring, writing center.

Majors. Business: Accounting, business admin. **Computer sciences:** Information technology. **Health services:** Health care admin.

Most popular majors. Business/marketing 79%, computer/information sciences 7%, legal studies 14%.

Technology on campus. 60 workstations in library, computer center, student center. Commuter students can connect to campus network. Online course registration, online library, helpline, student web hosting, wireless network available.

Student life. Freshman orientation: Mandatory. Preregistration for classes offered. Day and evening sessions available the week prior to classes starting. **Activities:** Literary magazine.

Student services. Career counseling, student employment services, financial aid counseling, placement for graduates.

Contact. Phone: (218) 422-1000 Toll-free number: (877) 373-7855 Melinda Rustad, Campus Director, Globe University: Moorhead, 2777 34th Street South, Moorhead, MN 56560

Globe University: Woodbury
Woodbury, Minnesota
www.globeuniversity.edu   **CB code: 2296**

- For-profit 4-year health science and career college
- Commuter campus in small city
- 717 undergraduates
- 50 graduate students
- Interview required

General. Accredited by ACICS. **Degrees:** 121 bachelor's, 145 associate awarded; master's offered. **Location:** 8 miles from Minneapolis-St. Paul. **Calendar:** Quarter, extensive summer session. **Full-time faculty:** 28 total. **Part-time faculty:** 92 total. **Special facilities:** Music business labs, medical assisting labs, health fitness labs, research vet tech facility with AVMA accreditation.

Basis for selection. Open admission, but selective for some programs.

2015-2016 Annual costs. Tuition/fees: $18,702. Books/supplies: $1,260. **Additional information:** Per-credit hour charge for 1 to 11 hours, $460; for 12 to 16 hours, $390. Course fees: $10 to $400 per course.

Application procedures. Admission: No deadline. $50 fee. Admission notification on a rolling basis. **Financial aid:** No deadline. FAFSA, institutional form required. Applicants notified on a rolling basis starting 7/1; must reply within 2 week(s) of notification.

Academics. Special study options: Combined bachelor's/graduate degree, distance learning, independent study, internships, liberal arts/career combination. **Credit/placement by examination:** AP, CLEP. **Support services:** Remedial instruction, study skills assistance, tutoring, writing center.

Majors. Business: Accounting, business admin. **Computer sciences:** Information technology. **Health services:** Health care admin, veterinary technology/assistant. **Parks/recreation:** Physical fitness technician. **Protective services:** Financial forensics, law enforcement admin. **Visual/performing arts:** Arts management.

Most popular majors. Business/marketing 43%, computer/information sciences 10%, health sciences 18%, legal studies 9%, parks/recreation 12%.

Technology on campus. 173 workstations in library, computer center, student center. Commuter students can connect to campus network. Online library, helpline, student web hosting, wireless network available.

Student life. Freshman orientation: Mandatory. Preregistration for classes offered. Day and evening sessions available the week prior to classes starting. **Activities:** Literary magazine.

Student services. Career counseling, student employment services, financial aid counseling, placement for graduates.

Contact. E-mail: admissions@globeuniversity.edu
Phone: (651) 730-5100 Toll-free number: (800) 231-0660
Fax: (651) 730-5151
Brian Saintey, Director of Admissions, Globe University: Woodbury, 8089 Globe Drive, Woodbury, MN 55125

Gustavus Adolphus College
St. Peter, Minnesota   **CB member**
www.gustavus.edu   **CB code: 6253**

- Private 4-year liberal arts college affiliated with the Evangelical Lutheran Church in America
- Residential campus in large town
- 2,376 degree-seeking undergraduates: 1% part-time, 53% women, 2% African American, 4% Asian American, 4% Hispanic/Latino, 3% Multiracial, non-Hispanic, 4% international
- 67% of applicants admitted
- Application essay required
- 83% graduate within 6 years

General. Founded in 1862. Regionally accredited. **Degrees:** 616 bachelor's awarded. **ROTC:** Army. **Location:** 65 miles from Minneapolis-St. Paul, 10 miles from Mankato. **Calendar:** 4-1-4. **Full-time faculty:** 189 total; 95% have terminal degrees, 18% minority, 54% women. **Part-time faculty:** 51 total; 45% have terminal degrees, 4% minority, 43% women. **Class size:** 64% < 20, 31% 20-39, 5% 40-49. **Special facilities:** Arboretum with walking and skiing paths, theme gardens, native woods and prairies, art museum, interpretive center, observatory.

Freshman class profile. 4,657 applied, 3,123 admitted, 614 enrolled.

Mid 50% test scores			
SAT critical reading:	550-620	Rank in top quarter:	65%
SAT math:	530-680	Rank in top tenth:	30%
ACT composite:	24-30	Return as sophomores:	89%
GPA 3.75 or higher:	42%	Out-of-state:	18%
GPA 3.50-3.74:	27%	Live on campus:	100%
GPA 3.0-3.49:	27%	International:	7%
GPA 2.0-2.99:	4%		

Basis for selection. School achievement record, test scores, recommendations, interview, essay or personal statement, school and community activities most important. Special consideration given to children of alumni and minority applicants. **Home schooled:** Statement describing home school structure and mission, interview, letter of recommendation (nonparent) required.

High school preparation. College-preparatory program recommended. 17 units required; 22 recommended. Required and recommended units include English 4, mathematics 3-4, social studies 2, history 2, science 2-3 (laboratory 2-3), foreign language 2-3 and academic electives 2.

2015-2016 Annual costs. Tuition/fees: $41,812. Room/board: $9,176. Books/supplies: $900. Personal expenses: $860.

2014-2015 Financial aid. Need-based: 524 full-time freshmen applied for aid; 464 deemed to have need; 464 received aid. Average need met was 93%. Average scholarship/grant was $28,974; average loan $3,267. 84% of total undergraduate aid awarded as scholarships/grants, 16% as loans/jobs. **Non-need-based:** Awarded to 812 full-time undergraduates, including 204 freshmen. Scholarships awarded for academics, alumni affiliation, art, minority status, music/drama, religious affiliation, state residency.

Application procedures. Admission: Closing date 4/1. No application fee. Admission notification by 4/15. Admission notification on a rolling basis beginning on or about 11/20. Must reply by May 1 or within 2 week(s) if notified thereafter. **Financial aid:** Priority date 3/15, closing date 5/1. FAFSA required. CSS PROFILE required of students applying for need-based assistance. Applicants notified on a rolling basis starting 3/15; must reply by 5/1 or within 2 week(s) of notification.

Academics. Special study options: Cooperative education, cross-registration, double major, dual enrollment of high school students, exchange student, honors, independent study, internships, liberal arts/career combination, student-designed major, study abroad, teacher certification program, Washington semester. **Credit/placement by examination:** AP, CLEP, IB, institutional tests. **Support services:** Reduced course load, study skills assistance, tutoring, writing center.

Majors. Area/ethnic studies: Japanese, Russian/Slavic, Scandinavian, women's. **Biology:** General, biochemistry. **Business:** General, accounting, international. **Communications:** Communications/speech/rhetoric. **Computer sciences:** General, computer science. **Conservation:** Environmental studies. **Education:** General, elementary, secondary. **English:** English lit. **Foreign languages:** Classics, French, German, Japanese, Russian, Scandinavian, Spanish. **Health services:** Athletic training, nursing (RN), predental, premedicine, preveterinary. **History:** General. **Math:** General. **Parks/recreation:** Health/fitness. **Philosophy/religion:** Philosophy, religion. **Physical sciences:** Chemistry, geology, physics. **Protective services:** Criminal justice. **Psychology:** General. **Social sciences:** Anthropology, economics, geography, political science, sociology. **Theology:** Sacred music. **Visual/performing arts:** Art, art history/conservation, dance, dramatic, music, music performance.

Most popular majors. Biology 12%, business/marketing 12%, education 6%, health sciences 6%, physical sciences 7%, psychology 9%, social sciences 12%.

Technology on campus. 500 workstations in dormitories, library, computer center, student center. Dormitories wired for high-speed internet access and linked to campus network. Commuter students can connect to campus network. Online course registration, online library, helpline, repair service, student web hosting, wireless network available.

Student life. Freshman orientation: Mandatory, $100 fee. Preregistration for classes offered. On-campus registration and pre-orientation sessions take place in June for students and families. Orientation program begins for first-year students four days prior to the beginning of classes. **Housing:** Guaranteed on-campus for all undergraduates. Coed dorms, special housing for disabled, apartments, wellness housing available. $300 nonrefundable deposit, deadline 5/1. **Activities:** Bands, campus ministries, choral groups, dance, drama, international student organizations, literary magazine, music ensembles, musical theater, radio station, student government, student newspaper, symphony orchestra, over 100 religious, political, ethnic, and social service organizations.

Athletics. NCAA. **Intercollegiate:** Baseball M, basketball, cross-country, diving, football (tackle) M, golf, gymnastics W, ice hockey, soccer, softball W, swimming, tennis, track and field, volleyball W. **Intramural:** Badminton, basketball, football (non-tackle) M, golf, handball, ice hockey, lacrosse M, racquetball, rugby, soccer, softball, swimming, table tennis, tennis, volleyball. **Team name:** Gusties.

Student services. Alcohol/substance abuse counseling, chaplain/spiritual director, career counseling, student employment services, financial aid counseling, health services, minority student services, personal counseling, placement for graduates, women's services. **Physically disabled:** Services for visually, hearing impaired.

Contact. E-mail: admission@gustavus.edu
Phone: (507) 933-7676 Toll-free number: (800) 487-8288
Fax: (507) 933-7474
Tom Crady, Vice-President for Enrollment Management, Gustavus Adolphus College, 800 West College Avenue, St. Peter, MN 56082

Hamline University
St. Paul, Minnesota
www.hamline.edu

CB member
CB code: 6265

♦ Private 4-year university and liberal arts college affiliated with the United Methodist Church
♦ Residential campus in very large city
♦ 2,141 degree-seeking undergraduates: 2% part-time, 58% women, 6% African American, 6% Asian American, 7% Hispanic/Latino, 6% Multiracial, non-Hispanic, 1% international
♦ 1,643 degree-seeking graduate students
♦ 72% of applicants admitted
♦ SAT or ACT (ACT writing recommended), application essay required
♦ 63% graduate within 6 years

General. Founded in 1854. Regionally accredited. **Degrees:** 484 bachelor's awarded; master's, professional, doctoral offered. **ROTC:** Army, Air Force. **Location:** 5 miles from downtown St. Paul, 5 miles from downtown Minneapolis. **Calendar:** 4-1-4, extensive summer session. **Full-time faculty:** 163 total; 85% have terminal degrees, 11% minority, 54% women. **Part-time faculty:** 226 total; 36% have terminal degrees, 9% minority, 56% women. **Class size:** 52% < 20, 40% 20-39, 5% 40-49, 3% 50-99.

Freshman class profile. 3,995 applied, 2,892 admitted, 512 enrolled.

Mid 50% test scores			
SAT critical reading:	480-660	GPA 3.0-3.49:	33%
SAT math:	500-650	GPA 2.0-2.99:	16%
SAT writing:	480-620	Rank in top quarter:	47%
ACT composite:	21-28	Rank in top tenth:	17%
GPA 3.75 or higher:	30%	Return as sophomores:	79%
GPA 3.50-3.74:	21%	Out-of-state:	21%
		Live on campus:	83%

Basis for selection. High school GPA, class rank, and selection of college-preparatory courses of primary importance. Test scores, extracurricular activities, recommendations of teacher and guidance counselor also emphasized. Interviews recommended. **Home schooled:** Transcript of courses and grades, letter of recommendation (nonparent) required.

High school preparation. College-preparatory program recommended. 21 units recommended. Recommended units include English 4, mathematics 4, social studies 4, science 3, foreign language 2 and academic electives 4.

2015-2016 Annual costs. Tuition/fees: $37,896. Room/board: $9,736. Books/supplies: $1,200. Personal expenses: $1,067. **Additional information:** Per credit hour charge is for part time (less than 12 credits).

2014-2015 Financial aid. Need-based: 484 full-time freshmen applied for aid; 437 deemed to have need; 437 received aid. Average need met was 85%. Average scholarship/grant was $24,164; average loan $4,013. 73% of total undergraduate aid awarded as scholarships/grants, 27% as loans/jobs. **Non-need-based:** Awarded to 501 full-time undergraduates, including 137 freshmen. Scholarships awarded for academics, alumni affiliation, art, leadership, minority status, music/drama, religious affiliation.

Application procedures. Admission: Priority date 1/15; no deadline. No application fee. Admission notification on a rolling basis beginning on or about 10/1. Must reply by May 1 or within 2 week(s) if notified thereafter. **Financial aid:** Priority date 3/15; no closing date. FAFSA required. Applicants notified on a rolling basis starting 3/15; must reply by 5/1 or within 2 week(s) of notification.

Academics. Special study options: Combined bachelor's/graduate degree, cross-registration, distance learning, double major, dual enrollment of high school students, ESL, exchange student, honors, independent study, internships, liberal arts/career combination, student-designed major, study abroad, teacher certification program, urban semester, Washington semester. **Credit/placement by examination:** AP, CLEP, IB, institutional tests. 64 credit hours maximum toward bachelor's degree. **Support services:** Learning center, pre-admission summer program, reduced course load, study skills assistance, tutoring, writing center.

Majors. Area/ethnic studies: East Asian, Latin American, women's. **Biology:** General, biochemistry. **Business:** Accounting, business admin, finance, international, management science, marketing. **Communications:** Communications/speech/rhetoric. **Conservation:** Environmental studies. **Education:** Elementary, multi-level teacher, secondary. **English:** Creative writing, English lit. **Foreign languages:** German, Spanish. **Health services:** Predental, premedicine, prepharmacy, preveterinary. **History:** General. **Math:** General. **Parks/recreation:** Exercise sciences. **Philosophy/religion:** Philosophy, religion. **Physical sciences:** Chemistry, physics. **Protective services:** Criminal justice, forensics. **Psychology:** General. **Social sciences:** Anthropology, economics, political science, sociology. **Visual/performing arts:** Art history/conservation, digital arts, dramatic, music, music performance, studio arts.

Most popular majors. Biology 7%, business/marketing 13%, English 8%, interdisciplinary studies 8%, legal studies 6%, psychology 11%, social sciences 13%.

Technology on campus. 300 workstations in dormitories, library, computer center, student center. Dormitories wired for high-speed internet access and linked to campus network. Commuter students can connect to campus network. Online course registration, online library, helpline, repair service, student web hosting, wireless network available.

Student life. Freshman orientation: Mandatory. Preregistration for classes offered. Fall orientation begins in September, the weekend before classes start, and lasts three days. Previews of orientation are held in June and July. **Housing:** Guaranteed on-campus for freshmen. Coed dorms, special housing for disabled, apartments, gender-neutral housing, themed housing, wellness housing available. PRIDE Black Student Alliance house, Hmong student house available. **Activities:** Bands, campus ministries, choral groups, dance, drama, film society, international student organizations, literary magazine, music ensembles, Model UN, musical theater, radio station, student government, student newspaper, symphony orchestra, TV station, Asian Pacific American Coalition, College Democrats, College Republicans, Habitat for Humanity, Hamline African Student Association, Hmong Student Association, Inter-Varsity Christian Fellowship, Minnesota Public Interest Research Group, PRIDE Black Student Alliance, Spectrum (awareness of LGBT issues).

Athletics. NCAA. **Intercollegiate:** Baseball M, basketball, cross-country, diving, football (tackle) M, gymnastics W, ice hockey, lacrosse W, soccer, softball W, swimming, tennis, track and field, volleyball W. **Intramural:** Basketball, football (non-tackle), soccer, volleyball. **Team name:** Pipers.

Student services. Chaplain/spiritual director, career counseling, student employment services, financial aid counseling, health services, minority student services, personal counseling, placement for graduates, women's services. **Physically disabled:** Services for visually, speech, hearing impaired.

Contact. E-mail: admission@hamline.edu
Phone: (651) 523-2207 Toll-free number: (800) 753-9753
Fax: (651) 523-2458
Holly Collins, Director of Admission, Hamline University, 1536 Hewitt Avenue, St. Paul, MN 55104-1284

Macalester College
St. Paul, Minnesota
www.macalester.edu

CB member
CB code: 6390

- Private 4-year liberal arts college affiliated with the Presbyterian Church (USA)
- Residential campus in very large city
- 2,149 degree-seeking undergraduates: 1% part-time, 60% women, 2% African American, 7% Asian American, 6% Hispanic/Latino, 5% Multi-racial, non-Hispanic, 14% international
- 39% of applicants admitted
- SAT or ACT (ACT writing optional), application essay required
- 90% graduate within 6 years

General. Founded in 1874. Regionally accredited. **Degrees:** 455 bachelor's awarded. **ROTC:** Army, Naval, Air Force. **Location:** 5 miles from Minneapolis and St. Paul. **Calendar:** Semester. **Full-time faculty:** 180 total; 93% have terminal degrees, 22% minority, 50% women. **Part-time faculty:** 77 total; 51% have terminal degrees, 21% minority, 56% women. **Class size:** 68% < 20, 30% 20-39, 1% 40-49, less than 1% 50-99. **Special facilities:** Observatory with DT-M 16 inch F/8 cassegrain telescope, nature preserve, nuclear accelerator, computer modeling facilities, laser spectroscopy laboratory, x-ray diffractometer and a nuclear magnetic spectrometer, fully-equipped animal operant chamber, international research center, econometrics lab, ethnographic lab, geographic information systems (GIS) lab, Bruker Dimension Edge Atomic Force Microscope.

Freshman class profile. 6,030 applied, 2,353 admitted, 583 enrolled.

Mid 50% test scores		Rank in top tenth:	65%
SAT critical reading:	620-730	Return as sophomores:	95%
SAT math:	620-740	Out-of-state:	86%
SAT writing:	630-720	Live on campus:	100%
ACT composite:	29-32	International:	18%
Rank in top quarter:	95%		

Basis for selection. Test scores and curriculum most important. Leadership potential and extracurricular involvements also important, with special attention given to service to others. Students whose native language is not English must also submit the results of the Test of English as a Foreign Language (TOEFL) or the International English Language Testing System (IELTS). Interview recommended. **Home schooled:** Transcript of courses and grades, letter of recommendation (nonparent) required.

High school preparation. College-preparatory program recommended. Recommended units include English 4, mathematics 3, social studies 3, science 3 (laboratory 3) and foreign language 3. Honors, AP, or IB level courses recommended.

2015-2016 Annual costs. Tuition/fees: $48,887. Room/board: $10,874. Books/supplies: $1,118. Personal expenses: $974.

2015-2016 Financial aid. Need-based: 455 full-time freshmen applied for aid; 399 deemed to have need; 399 received aid. Average need met was 100%. Average scholarship/grant was $37,273; average loan $3,849. 83% of total undergraduate aid awarded as scholarships/grants, 17% as loans/jobs. **Non-need-based:** Awarded to 280 full-time undergraduates, including 85 freshmen. Scholarships awarded for academics, minority status. **Additional information:** College constructs a financial aid package that meets full demonstrated need for all admitted students.

Application procedures. Admission: Closing date 1/15 (postmark date). $40 fee, may be waived for applicants with need. Admission notification by 3/30. Must reply by 5/1. **Financial aid:** Priority date 2/8, closing date 3/1. FAFSA, CSS PROFILE required. Applicants notified by 4/1; must reply by 5/1.

Academics. Special study options: Combined bachelor's/graduate degree, cross-registration, double major, honors, independent study, internships, student-designed major, study abroad, urban semester, Washington semester. BA/Master's in Architecture with Washington University, St. Louis, Missouri; BA/BS in Engineering with Washington University, St. Louis. **Credit/placement by examination:** AP, CLEP, IB, institutional tests. Limited to 8 semester credits. **Support services:** Learning center, study skills assistance, tutoring, writing center. Supplemental instruction, alternative tests, notetakers.

Majors. Area/ethnic studies: Asian, Latin American, women's. **Biology:** General, neuroscience. **Communications:** Media studies. **Computer sciences:** General. **Conservation:** Environmental studies. **Education:** General. **English:** English lit. **Foreign languages:** Chinese, classics, French, German, Japanese, linguistics, Russian, Spanish. **History:** General. **Math:** General. **Philosophy/religion:** Philosophy, religion. **Physical sciences:** Chemistry, geology, physics. **Psychology:** General. **Social sciences:** Anthropology, economics, geography, political science, sociology. **Visual/performing arts:** Art, dramatic, music.

Most popular majors. Biology 11%, foreign language 8%, interdisciplinary studies 10%, mathematics 6%, physical sciences 6%, psychology 7%, social sciences 24%.

Technology on campus. 550 workstations in dormitories, library, computer center, student center. Dormitories wired for high-speed internet access and linked to campus network. Commuter students can connect to campus network. Online course registration, online library, helpline, student web hosting, wireless network available.

Student life. Freshman orientation: Mandatory. Preregistration for classes offered. Five days prior to classes in September. **Policies:** Two-year residency requirement for first-year students. Freshmen not permitted cars on campus. **Housing:** Guaranteed on-campus for freshmen. Coed dorms, special housing for disabled, apartments, cooperative housing, gender-neutral housing, themed housing, wellness housing available. $300 nonrefundable deposit, deadline 5/1. Six language houses available (French, German, Russian, Spanish, Japanese, Chinese), EcoHous (green living), cultural house, Arabic Interest House, vegetarian co-op housing, single-sex floors within coed dorms, accommodations for disabled students. **Activities:** Bands, campus ministries, choral groups, dance, drama, international student organizations, literary magazine, music ensembles, Model UN, radio station, student government, student newspaper, symphony orchestra, Asian student alliance, Habitat for Humanity, Amnesty International, Multifaith Council, Christian Fellowship, Afrika, Queer Union, Adelante, Black Liberation Affairs Committee, Muslim Student Association.

Athletics. NCAA. **Intercollegiate:** Baseball M, basketball, cross-country, diving, football (tackle) M, golf, soccer, softball W, swimming, tennis, track and field, volleyball W, water polo W. **Intramural:** Basketball, racquetball, soccer, softball, table tennis, ultimate frisbee, volleyball. **Team name:** Scots.

Student services. Alcohol/substance abuse counseling, chaplain/spiritual director, career counseling, services for economically disadvantaged, student employment services, financial aid counseling, health services, minority student services, personal counseling, placement for graduates. **Physically disabled:** Services for visually, speech, hearing impaired.

Contact. E-mail: admissions@macalester.edu
Phone: (651) 696-6357 Toll-free number: (800) 231-7974
Fax: (651) 696-6724
Lorne Robinson, Dean of Admissions and Financial Aid, Macalester College, 1600 Grand Avenue, St. Paul, MN 55105-1899

Martin Luther College
New Ulm, Minnesota
www.mlc-wels.edu

CB code: 6435

- Private 4-year college of theology and education affiliated with the Wisconsin Evangelical Lutheran Synod
- Residential campus in large town
- 747 degree-seeking undergraduates: 6% part-time, 51% women, 1% African American, 1% Asian American, 1% Hispanic/Latino, 1% Multi-racial, non-Hispanic, 3% international
- 73 degree-seeking graduate students
- 78% of applicants admitted
- ACT with writing required
- 73% graduate within 6 years

General. Founded in 1995. Regionally accredited. Offers programs of study in early childhood education and staff ministry. **Degrees:** 137 bachelor's awarded; master's offered. **Location:** 90 miles from Minneapolis-St. Paul. **Calendar:** Semester, limited summer session. **Full-time faculty:** 50 total;

42% have terminal degrees, 2% minority, 16% women. **Part-time faculty:** 23 total; 30% have terminal degrees, 44% women. **Class size:** 46% < 20, 50% 20-39, 2% 40-49, 2% 50-99.

Freshman class profile. 262 applied, 204 admitted, 172 enrolled.

Mid 50% test scores			
ACT composite:	22-28	Rank in top quarter:	37%
GPA 3.75 or higher:	36%	Rank in top tenth:	15%
GPA 3.50-3.74:	24%	Return as sophomores:	83%
GPA 3.0-3.49:	22%	Out-of-state:	88%
GPA 2.0-2.99:	18%	Live on campus:	100%
		International:	2%

Basis for selection. Primarily pastor's letter of recommendation, high school transcript, and test scores required. Rating provided by student's high school considered.

High school preparation. College-preparatory program required. 14 units required. Required units include English 4, mathematics 3, social studies 2, science 3 (laboratory 2) and academic electives 2. 5 units in foreign language required for pastoral program.

2016-2017 Annual costs. Tuition/fees (projected): $13,980. Room/board: $5,510. Books/supplies: $800. Personal expenses: $2,400.

2014-2015 Financial aid. Need-based: 157 full-time freshmen applied for aid; 128 deemed to have need; 126 received aid. Average need met was 66%. Average scholarship/grant was $7,667; average loan $3,641. 58% of total undergraduate aid awarded as scholarships/grants, 42% as loans/jobs. **Non-need-based:** Awarded to 122 full-time undergraduates, including 29 freshmen. Scholarships awarded for academics, leadership, music/drama, religious affiliation.

Application procedures. Admission: Priority date 5/1; no deadline. No application fee. Admission notification on a rolling basis beginning on or about 9/15. **Financial aid:** Priority date 4/15, closing date 4/15. FAFSA, institutional form required. Applicants notified on a rolling basis starting 4/15; must reply by 9/1.

Academics. Special study options: Distance learning, double major, teacher certification program. **Credit/placement by examination:** AP, CLEP, ACT, institutional tests. **Support services:** Learning center, reduced course load, remedial instruction, study skills assistance, tutoring.

Majors. Education: Chemistry, early childhood, elementary, English, mathematics, multi-level teacher, music, physical, physics, science, social studies, Spanish, special ed. **Theology:** Preministerial.

Most popular majors. Education 82%, theological studies 18%.

Technology on campus. 129 workstations in dormitories, library, computer center. Dormitories linked to campus network. Helpline, repair service available.

Student life. Freshman orientation: Mandatory. Preregistration for classes offered. **Policies:** Religious observance required. **Housing:** Guaranteed on-campus for freshmen. Single-sex dorms, special housing for disabled, apartments available. $135 partly refundable deposit, deadline 5/15. **Activities:** Bands, campus ministries, choral groups, drama, international student organizations, music ensembles, musical theater, student newspaper, symphony orchestra.

Athletics. NAIA, NCAA. **Intercollegiate:** Baseball M, basketball, cross-country, football (tackle) M, golf M, soccer, softball W, tennis, track and field, volleyball W. **Intramural:** Badminton, basketball, bowling, football (tackle) M, soccer, softball, tennis, volleyball. **Team name:** Knights.

Student services. Chaplain/spiritual director, student employment services, financial aid counseling, health services, personal counseling.

Contact. E-mail: mlcadmit@mlc-wels.edu
Phone: (507) 354-8221 Toll-free number: (877) 652-1995
Fax: (507) 354-8225
Mark Stein, Director of Admissions, Martin Luther College, 1995 Luther Court, New Ulm, MN 56073-3965

McNally Smith College of Music
St. Paul, Minnesota
www.mcnallysmith.edu   CB code: 4194

- Private 4-year music and performing arts college
- Residential campus in large city

- 420 degree-seeking undergraduates: 13% part-time, 29% women, 9% African American, 4% Asian American, 5% Hispanic/Latino, 8% Multi-racial, non-Hispanic
- 18 degree-seeking graduate students
- 49% of applicants admitted
- Application essay required
- 47% graduate within 6 years

General. Candidate for regional accreditation. **Degrees:** 48 bachelor's, 18 associate awarded; master's offered. **Location:** Downtown Saint Paul. **Calendar:** Semester, limited summer session. **Full-time faculty:** 54 total; 7% have terminal degrees, 13% minority, 20% women. **Part-time faculty:** 108 total; less than 1% have terminal degrees, 14% minority, 21% women. **Class size:** 86% < 20, 12% 20-39, less than 1% 40-49, 1% 50-99. **Special facilities:** Ten recording studios, three live venues on campus.

Freshman class profile. 374 applied, 182 admitted, 70 enrolled.

GPA 3.75 or higher:	10%	End year in good standing:	3%
GPA 3.50-3.74:	15%	Return as sophomores:	53%
GPA 3.0-3.49:	19%	Out-of-state:	54%
GPA 2.0-2.99:	45%	Live on campus:	59%

Basis for selection. McNally Smith College of Music considers each applicant individually when determining admission. Listed standards and requirements are important indicators of an incoming student's potential, but are not the only factors controlling acceptance. McNally Smith takes a holistic approach to applicant review and makes offers of admission accordingly. **Home schooled:** Transcript of courses and grades, state high school equivalency certificate required.

2016-2017 Annual costs. Tuition/fees: $27,940. Room/board: $5,100. Books/supplies: $1,000. Personal expenses: $3,430.

2014-2015 Financial aid. Need-based: 53 full-time freshmen applied for aid; 46 deemed to have need; 46 received aid. Average need met was 27%. Average scholarship/grant was $5,726; average loan $1,653. 91% of total undergraduate aid awarded as scholarships/grants, 9% as loans/jobs. **Non-need-based:** Awarded to 135 full-time undergraduates, including 21 freshmen. Scholarships awarded for academics, music/drama.

Application procedures. Admission: No deadline. $75 fee. Application must be submitted online. Admission notification on a rolling basis beginning on or about 6/1. Must reply by May 1 or within 2 week(s) if notified thereafter. **Financial aid:** Priority date 5/1, closing date 8/1. FAFSA required. Applicants notified on a rolling basis starting 3/1; must reply within 3 week(s) of notification.

Academics. Special study options: Dual enrollment of high school students, exchange student, independent study, internships, study abroad. **Credit/placement by examination:** AP, institutional tests. **Support services:** Learning center, study skills assistance, tutoring.

Majors. Visual/performing arts: Brass instruments, music management, music technology, music theory/composition, percussion instruments, piano/keyboard, stringed instruments, voice/opera.

Technology on campus. Dormitories wired for high-speed internet access and linked to campus network. Commuter students can connect to campus network. Online library, helpline, wireless network available.

Student life. Freshman orientation: Mandatory. Preregistration for classes offered. **Housing:** Coed dorms, gender-neutral housing available. $225 partly refundable deposit. **Activities:** Jazz band, choral groups, film society, international student organizations, literary magazine, music ensembles, musical theater, Cru (Christ Revealed in Us); Gay-Straight Alliance; Project Heart.

Student services. Career counseling, student employment services, financial aid counseling, personal counseling.

Contact. E-mail: admissions@mcnallysmith.edu
Phone: (651) 361-3460 Toll-free number: (800) 594-9500
Matthew Edlund, Director of Admissions, McNally Smith College of Music, 19 Exchange Street East, St. Paul, MN 55101

Metropolitan State University
St. Paul, Minnesota
www.metrostate.edu   CB code: 1245

- Public 4-year university
- Commuter campus in very large city

- 7,244 degree-seeking undergraduates: 63% part-time, 56% women, 20% African American, 13% Asian American, 5% Hispanic/Latino, 1% Native American, 4% Multi-racial, non-Hispanic, 2% international
- 841 graduate students

General. Founded in 1971. Regionally accredited. **Degrees:** 1,844 bachelor's awarded; master's, doctoral offered. **Calendar:** Semester, extensive summer session. **Special facilities:** Collaborative University and Public Library, Gordon Parks Art Gallery, Meditation Labyrinth.

Freshman class profile. 114 enrolled.

Basis for selection. Consideration for freshman admission is based on some or all of the following criteria: High school class rank in the upper 50th percentile; ACT, PSAT or SAT composite score at or above national median, and a GED transcript with test scores. Interview and essays only used as part of the appeals process if admission was denied.

High school preparation. 16 units required. Required units include English 4, mathematics 3, social studies 3, science 3 (laboratory 1) and academic electives 3. 3 years of electives from language, world culture, or arts.

2015-2016 Annual costs. Tuition/fees: $7,492; $14,320 out-of-state.

2014-2015 Financial aid. Need-based: 33% of total undergraduate aid awarded as scholarships/grants, 67% as loans/jobs. **Non-need-based:** Scholarships awarded for academics, leadership, minority status, state residency.

Application procedures. Admission: Closing date 6/15. No application fee. Admission notification on a rolling basis. **Financial aid:** Priority date 3/1; no closing date. FAFSA required. Applicants notified on a rolling basis starting 5/1; must reply within 2 week(s) of notification.

Academics. Special study options: Cross-registration, distance learning, double major, dual enrollment of high school students, external degree, honors, independent study, internships, liberal arts/career combination, student-designed major, study abroad, teacher certification program, weekend college. **Credit/placement by examination:** AP, CLEP, IB, institutional tests. 90 credit hours maximum toward bachelor's degree. **Support services:** Learning center, reduced course load, remedial instruction, study skills assistance, tutoring, writing center.

Majors. Area/ethnic studies: General, women's. **Biology:** General. **Business:** Accounting, business admin, finance, hospitality admin, human resources, international, management information systems, marketing, nonprofit/public, operations, sales/distribution. **Communications:** Advertising. **Computer sciences:** Computer science, information systems, security. **Education:** Biology, early childhood, elementary, English, mathematics, social studies. **English:** Creative writing, English lit, technical writing. **Health services:** Dental hygiene, nursing (RN), substance abuse counseling. **History:** General. **Human services:** Social work. **Liberal arts:** Arts/sciences. **Math:** Applied. **Philosophy/religion:** Philosophy. **Physical sciences:** Chemistry. **Protective services:** Criminal justice, police science. **Psychology:** General, developmental. **Social sciences:** General, economics. **Visual/performing arts:** Dramatic, play/screenwriting.

Most popular majors. Business/marketing 34%, health sciences 8%, interdisciplinary studies 14%, psychology 6%, public administration/social services 8%, security/protective services 10%.

Technology on campus. 550 workstations in library, computer center. Commuter students can connect to campus network. Online course registration, online library, helpline, wireless network available.

Student life. Freshman orientation: Mandatory, $40 fee. Preregistration for classes offered. Orientation sessions of 3 hours are held several times each semester. **Policies:** Annual registration required of all student organizations. **Activities:** Drama, international student organizations, literary magazine, student government, student newspaper, Asian Student Organization, Lavender Bridge, African-American Student Association, Graduate Student Advisory Committee, Voice of Indian Council for Educational Success, Social Work Student Association, psychology club, Muslim Student Association, Urban Teachers Student Program Organization.

Student services. Adult student services, career counseling, minority student services, personal counseling, veterans' counselor, women's services. **Physically disabled:** Services for visually, speech, hearing impaired.

Contact. E-mail: admission.metro@metrostate.edu
Phone: (651) 793-1300 Fax: (651) 793-1310
Julio Vargas-Essex, Admissions Director, Metropolitan State University, 700 East Seventh Street, St. Paul, MN 55106-5000

Minneapolis College of Art and Design
Minneapolis, Minnesota   CB member
www.mcad.edu   CB code: 6411

- Private 4-year visual arts college
- Residential campus in very large city
- 668 degree-seeking undergraduates: 2% part-time, 66% women, 4% African American, 8% Asian American, 6% Hispanic/Latino, 1% Native American, 3% Multi-racial, non-Hispanic
- 118 degree-seeking graduate students
- 66% of applicants admitted
- SAT or ACT (ACT writing optional), application essay required
- 61% graduate within 6 years

General. Founded in 1886. Regionally accredited. 24/7 campus access to all students. **Degrees:** 119 bachelor's awarded; master's offered. **Location:** Within the city of Minneapolis. **Calendar:** Semester, limited summer session. **Full-time faculty:** 37 total; 62% have terminal degrees, 3% minority, 35% women. **Part-time faculty:** 91 total; 68% have terminal degrees, 7% minority, 54% women. **Class size:** 82% < 20, 17% 20-39, less than 1% 40-49, less than 1% 50-99. **Special facilities:** Art and design galleries, personal on-campus studio space, 3-D furniture/sculpture studios, animation studios, drawing studios, film studios, print/paper/book studios, painting studios, photo studios, on-campus professional design studio, extensive on-campus printing services, art and design focused library.

Freshman class profile. 556 applied, 367 admitted, 145 enrolled.

Mid 50% test scores			
SAT critical reading:	480-650	GPA 3.50-3.74:	22%
SAT math:	450-550	GPA 3.0-3.49:	33%
SAT writing:	450-560	GPA 2.0-2.99:	27%
ACT composite:	21-27	Return as sophomores:	82%
GPA 3.75 or higher:	18%	Out-of-state:	59%
		Live on campus:	84%

Basis for selection. Bachelor of Fine Arts applicants are required to submit a portfolio of visual art work. For all BFA and Bachelor of Science students, academic record and test scores reviewed. Level of interest and motivation determined through personal statement of interest, letter of recommendation, and essay requirement. Tests not required for transfer applicants who have completed 12 or more satisfactory credits (C or better) at the college level. Interview recommended. Personal statement essay required on specific topic for all applications. **Home schooled:** Transcript of courses and grades required. **Learning Disabled:** It is recommended that students disclose any learning disabilities for appropriate accommodations to be prepared.

High school preparation. College-preparatory program recommended. Recommended units include English 4, social studies 4, history 4 and visual/performing arts 6.

2015-2016 Annual costs. Tuition/fees: $35,326. Room only: $5,110. Books/supplies: $2,824. Personal expenses: $2,942. **Additional information:** Estimated expenses: food $2,130, books/supplies $2,870, personal $900, transportation $432, loan fees $72. Required laptop purchase of $1,500 may be waived if student has a laptop with appropriate specs.

2014-2015 Financial aid. Need-based: 118 full-time freshmen applied for aid; 103 deemed to have need; 103 received aid. Average need met was 68%. Average scholarship/grant was $19,639; average loan $4,506. 65% of total undergraduate aid awarded as scholarships/grants, 35% as loans/jobs. **Non-need-based:** Awarded to 155 full-time undergraduates, including 33 freshmen. Scholarships awarded for academics, alumni affiliation, art.

Application procedures. Admission: Priority date 2/15; deadline 4/1 (receipt date). $50 fee, may be waived for applicants with need. Application must be submitted online. Admission notification by 5/14. Admission notification on a rolling basis beginning on or about 9/1. Must reply by May 1 or within 2 week(s) if notified thereafter. **Financial aid:** Priority date 3/1, closing date 6/1. FAFSA required. Applicants notified on a rolling basis starting 3/1; must reply by 5/1 or within 2 week(s) of notification.

Academics. Special study options: Combined bachelor's/graduate degree, cooperative education, cross-registration, distance learning, exchange student, independent study, internships, New York semester, study abroad. **Credit/placement by examination:** AP, CLEP, IB. **Support services:** Learning center, reduced course load, study skills assistance, tutoring, writing center.

Majors. Business: Entrepreneurial studies, project management. **Communications:** Advertising, public relations. **Communications technology:** Animation/special effects. **Visual/performing arts:** Drawing, graphic design, illustration, painting, photography, printmaking, sculpture, studio arts.

Most popular majors. Visual/performing arts 98%.

Technology on campus. PC or laptop required. 160 workstations in library, computer center, student center. Dormitories wired for high-speed internet access and linked to campus network. Commuter students can connect to campus network. Online library, helpline, repair service, student web hosting, wireless network available.

Student life. Freshman orientation: Mandatory. Preregistration for classes offered. Held 3 days prior to first day of fall semester classes; includes 1 day for parent/guardian orientation. **Policies:** Freshmen not permitted cars on campus. **Housing:** Guaranteed on-campus for freshmen. Coed dorms, apartments available. $350 fully refundable deposit, deadline 5/1. **Activities:** Student government, animation club, anime club, bike club, Comic Heads, film club, musicians club, design club, green club, OH NO HOMO, recess club.

Student services. Alcohol/substance abuse counseling, career counseling, student employment services, financial aid counseling, personal counseling, placement for graduates.

Contact. E-mail: admissions@mcad.edu
Phone: (612) 874-3760 Toll-free number: (800) 874-6223 ext. 1
Fax: (612) 874-3701
Melissa Huybrecht, Associate Vice President, Enrollment Management, Minneapolis College of Art and Design, 2501 Stevens Avenue, Minneapolis, MN 55404

Minnesota School of Business: Blaine
Blaine, Minnesota
www.msbcollege.edu

- For-profit 4-year career college
- Commuter campus in small city
- 239 undergraduates
- Interview required

General. Regionally accredited; also accredited by ACICS. **Degrees:** 38 bachelor's, 68 associate awarded. **Location:** 20 miles from Minneapolis. **Calendar:** Quarter, extensive summer session. **Full-time faculty:** 12 total. **Part-time faculty:** 25 total.

Basis for selection. Open admission.

2015-2016 Annual costs. Tuition/fees: $18,702. Books/supplies: $1,260. **Additional information:** Per-credit hour charge for 1 to 11 hours, $460; for 12 to 16 hours, $390. Course fees: $10 to $400 per course.

Application procedures. Admission: No deadline. $50 fee. Admission notification on a rolling basis. **Financial aid:** No deadline. FAFSA, institutional form required. Applicants notified on a rolling basis starting 7/1; must reply within 2 week(s) of notification.

Academics. Special study options: Distance learning, independent study, internships, liberal arts/career combination. **Credit/placement by examination:** AP, CLEP. **Support services:** Remedial instruction, study skills assistance, tutoring, writing center.

Majors. Business: Accounting, business admin. **Computer sciences:** Information technology. **Health services:** Health care admin. **Protective services:** Financial forensics, law enforcement admin.

Most popular majors. Business/marketing 63%, computer/information sciences 17%, health sciences 8%, security/protective services 7%.

Technology on campus. 60 workstations in library, computer center, student center. Commuter students can connect to campus network. Online library, helpline, student web hosting, wireless network available.

Student life. Freshman orientation: Mandatory. Preregistration for classes offered. Day and evening sessions available the week prior to classes starting. **Activities:** Literary magazine.

Student services. Career counseling, student employment services, financial aid counseling, placement for graduates.

Contact. E-mail: jokoye@msbcollege.edu
Phone: (763) 225-8000 Toll-free number: (877) 655-7676
Janea Okoye, Director of Admissions, Minnesota School of Business: Blaine, 3680 Pheasant Ridge Dr. NE, Blaine, MN 55449

Minnesota School of Business: Elk River
Elk River, Minnesota
www.msbcollege.edu

- For-profit 4-year university and career college
- Commuter campus in large town
- 236 undergraduates
- Interview required

General. Regionally accredited; also accredited by ACICS. **Degrees:** 35 bachelor's, 39 associate awarded. **Location:** 35 miles from Minneapolis-St. Paul. **Calendar:** Quarter, extensive summer session. **Full-time faculty:** 7 total.

Basis for selection. Open admission.

2015-2016 Annual costs. Tuition/fees: $18,702. Books/supplies: $1,260. **Additional information:** Per-credit hour charge for 1 to 11 hours, $460; for 12 to 16 hours, $390. Course fees: $10 to $400 per course.

Application procedures. Admission: No deadline. $50 fee. Admission notification on a rolling basis. **Financial aid:** No deadline. FAFSA, institutional form required. Applicants notified on a rolling basis starting 7/1; must reply within 2 week(s) of notification.

Academics. Special study options: Distance learning, independent study, internships, liberal arts/career combination. **Credit/placement by examination:** AP, CLEP. **Support services:** Remedial instruction, study skills assistance, tutoring, writing center.

Majors. Business: Accounting, business admin. **Computer sciences:** Information technology. **Health services:** Health care admin. **Protective services:** Financial forensics, law enforcement admin.

Most popular majors. Business/marketing 74%, computer/information sciences 6%, health sciences 6%, legal studies 6%, security/protective services 9%.

Technology on campus. 60 workstations in library, computer center, student center. Commuter students can connect to campus network. Online library, helpline, student web hosting, wireless network available.

Student life. Freshman orientation: Mandatory. Preregistration for classes offered. Day and evening sessions available the week prior to classes starting. **Activities:** Literary magazine.

Student services. Career counseling, student employment services, financial aid counseling, placement for graduates.

Contact. Phone: (763) 367-7000 Toll-free number: (877) 333-9757
Tim Elliott, Director of Admissions, Minnesota School of Business: Elk River, 11500 193rd Avenue NW, Elk River, MN 55330

Minnesota School of Business: Lakeville
Lakeville, Minnesota
www.msbcollege.edu

- For-profit 4-year university and career college
- Commuter campus in small city
- 195 undergraduates
- Interview required

General. Regionally accredited; also accredited by ACICS. **Degrees:** 22 bachelor's, 43 associate awarded. **Location:** 25 minutes from Twin Cities. **Calendar:** Quarter, extensive summer session. **Full-time faculty:** 6 total. **Part-time faculty:** 23 total.

Basis for selection. Open admission.

2015-2016 Annual costs. Tuition/fees: $18,702. Books/supplies: $1,260. **Additional information:** Per-credit hour charge for 1 to 11 hours, $460; for 12 to 16 hours, $390. Course fees: $10 to $400 per course.

Application procedures. Admission: No deadline. $50 fee. Admission notification on a rolling basis. **Financial aid:** No deadline. FAFSA, institutional form required. Applicants notified on a rolling basis starting 7/1; must reply within 2 week(s) of notification.

Academics. Special study options: Distance learning, independent study, internships, liberal arts/career combination. **Credit/placement by examination:** AP, CLEP. **Support services:** Remedial instruction, study skills assistance, tutoring, writing center.

Majors. Business: Accounting, business admin. **Computer sciences:** Information technology. **Health services:** Health care admin. **Protective services:** Law enforcement admin.

Most popular majors. Business/marketing 73%, legal studies 14%, security/protective services 9%.

Technology on campus. 60 workstations in library, computer center, student center. Commuter students can connect to campus network. Online library, helpline, student web hosting, wireless network available.

Student life. Freshman orientation: Mandatory. Preregistration for classes offered. Day and evening sessions available the week prior to classes starting. **Activities:** Literary magazine.

Student services. Career counseling, student employment services, financial aid counseling, placement for graduates.

Contact. Phone: (952) 892-9000 Toll-free number: (877) 560-8777 Jennifer Pullin, Director of Admissions, Minnesota School of Business: Lakeville, 17685 Juniper Path, Lakeville, MN 55044

Minnesota School of Business: Plymouth
Plymouth, Minnesota
www.msbcollege.edu

- For-profit 4-year university and career college
- Commuter campus in small city
- 130 undergraduates
- Interview required

General. Accredited by ACICS. **Degrees:** 22 bachelor's, 40 associate awarded. **Location:** Downtown. **Calendar:** Quarter, extensive summer session. **Full-time faculty:** 6 total. **Part-time faculty:** 22 total. **Special facilities:** Several major lakes, parks and trails within walking distance.

Basis for selection. Open admission.

2015-2016 Annual costs. Tuition/fees: $18,702. Books/supplies: $1,260. **Additional information:** Per-credit hour charge for 1 to 11 hours, $460; for 12 to 16 hours, $390. Course fees: $10 to $400 per course.

Application procedures. Admission: No deadline. $50 fee. Admission notification on a rolling basis. **Financial aid:** No deadline. FAFSA, institutional form required. Applicants notified on a rolling basis starting 7/1; must reply within 2 week(s) of notification.

Academics. Special study options: Distance learning, independent study, internships, liberal arts/career combination. **Credit/placement by examination:** AP, CLEP, SAT, ACT, institutional tests. **Support services:** Remedial instruction, study skills assistance, tutoring, writing center.

Majors. Business: Accounting, business admin. **Computer sciences:** Information technology. **Health services:** Health care admin, veterinary technology/assistant. **Parks/recreation:** Physical fitness technician. **Protective services:** Financial forensics.

Most popular majors. Business/marketing 62%, health sciences 10%, parks/recreation 19%.

Technology on campus. 60 workstations in library, computer center, student center. Commuter students can connect to campus network. Online course registration, online library, helpline, student web hosting, wireless network available.

Student life. Freshman orientation: Mandatory. Preregistration for classes offered. Day and evening sessions available the week prior to classes starting. **Activities:** Literary magazine.

Student services. Career counseling, student employment services, financial aid counseling, placement for graduates.

Contact. Toll-free number: (866) 476-2121 Fax: (736) 476-1000 Charles Andria, Director of Admissions, Minnesota School of Business: Plymouth, 1455 County Road 101 North, Plymouth, MN 55447

Minnesota School of Business: Richfield
Richfield, Minnesota
www.msbcollege.edu

- For-profit 4-year university and career college
- Commuter campus in large town

- 693 undergraduates
- 80 graduate students
- Interview required

General. Accredited by ACICS. Minnesota School of Business-Richfield, a Globe education partner, is located in a bustling urban suburb of Minneapolis. We also operate a separate state-of-the-art facility in Edina for our creative media students. **Degrees:** 145 bachelor's, 91 associate awarded; master's offered. **Calendar:** Quarter, extensive summer session. **Full-time faculty:** 22 total. **Part-time faculty:** 96 total.

Basis for selection. Open admission, but selective for some programs.

2015-2016 Annual costs. Tuition/fees: $18,702. Books/supplies: $1,260. **Additional information:** Per-credit hour charge for 1 to 11 hours, $460; for 12 to 16 hours, $390. Course fees: $10 to $400 per course.

Application procedures. Admission: No deadline. $50 fee. Admission notification on a rolling basis. **Financial aid:** No deadline. FAFSA, institutional form required. Applicants notified on a rolling basis starting 7/1; must reply within 2 week(s) of notification.

Academics. Special study options: Combined bachelor's/graduate degree, distance learning, independent study, internships, liberal arts/career combination. **Credit/placement by examination:** AP, CLEP. **Support services:** Remedial instruction, study skills assistance, tutoring, writing center.

Majors. Business: Accounting, business admin. **Communications technology:** Animation/special effects. **Computer sciences:** Information technology, programming. **Health services:** Health care admin, nursing (RN). **Parks/recreation:** Physical fitness technician. **Protective services:** Financial forensics, law enforcement admin. **Visual/performing arts:** Arts management.

Most popular majors. Business/marketing 50%, computer/information sciences 11%, health sciences 26%.

Technology on campus. 60 workstations in library, computer center, student center. Commuter students can connect to campus network. Online library, helpline, student web hosting, wireless network available.

Student life. Freshman orientation: Mandatory. Preregistration for classes offered. Day and evening sessions available the week prior to classes starting. **Activities:** Literary magazine.

Student services. Career counseling, student employment services, financial aid counseling, placement for graduates.

Contact. Phone: (612) 861-2000 Toll-free number: (800) 752-4223 Fax: (612) 861-5548
Sonia Sultan, Director of Admissions, Minnesota School of Business: Richfield, 1401 West 76 Street, Suite 500, Richfield, MN 55423

Minnesota School of Business: Rochester
Rochester, Minnesota
www.msbcollege.edu

- For-profit 4-year university and career college
- Commuter campus in small city
- 183 undergraduates
- Interview required

General. Accredited by ACICS. **Degrees:** 34 bachelor's, 54 associate awarded. **Calendar:** Quarter, extensive summer session. **Full-time faculty:** 10 total. **Part-time faculty:** 34 total.

Basis for selection. Open admission.

2015-2016 Annual costs. Tuition/fees: $18,702. Books/supplies: $1,260. **Additional information:** Per-credit hour charge for 1 to 11 hours, $460; for 12 to 16 hours, $390. Course fees: $10 to $400 per course.

Application procedures. Admission: No deadline. $50 fee. Admission notification on a rolling basis. **Financial aid:** No deadline. FAFSA, institutional form required. Applicants notified on a rolling basis starting 7/1; must reply within 2 week(s) of notification.

Academics. Special study options: Distance learning, independent study, internships, liberal arts/career combination. **Credit/placement by examination:** AP, CLEP. **Support services:** Remedial instruction, study skills assistance, tutoring, writing center.

Majors. Business: Accounting, business admin. **Computer sciences:** Information technology. **Health services:** Health care admin. **Parks/recreation:**

Physical fitness technician. **Protective services:** Financial forensics, law enforcement admin.

Most popular majors. Business/marketing 49%, computer/information sciences 19%, health sciences 12%, legal studies 11%, security/protective services 9%.

Technology on campus. 60 workstations in library, computer center, student center. Commuter students can connect to campus network. Online course registration, online library, helpline, student web hosting, wireless network available.

Student life. Freshman orientation: Mandatory. Preregistration for classes offered. Day and evening sessions available the week prior to classes starting. **Activities:** Literary magazine.

Student services. Career counseling, student employment services, financial aid counseling, placement for graduates.

Contact. Phone: (507) 536-9500 Toll-free number: (888) 662-8772 Angie Helm, Director of Admissions, Minnesota School of Business: Rochester, 2521 Pennington Drive NW, Rochester, MN 55901

Minnesota School of Business: Shakopee
Shakopee, Minnesota
www.msbcollege.edu

- For-profit 4-year university and career college
- Commuter campus in large town
- 210 undergraduates
- Interview required

General. Accredited by ACICS. **Degrees:** 23 bachelor's, 29 associate awarded. **Calendar:** Quarter, extensive summer session. **Full-time faculty:** 6 total. **Part-time faculty:** 12 total.

Basis for selection. Open admission.

2015-2016 Annual costs. Tuition/fees: $18,702. Books/supplies: $1,260. **Additional information:** Per-credit hour charge for 1 to 11 hours, $460; for 12 to 16 hours, $390. Course fees: $10 to $400 per course.

Application procedures. Admission: No deadline. $50 fee. Admission notification on a rolling basis. **Financial aid:** No deadline. FAFSA, institutional form required. Applicants notified on a rolling basis starting 7/1; must reply within 2 week(s) of notification.

Academics. Special study options: Distance learning, independent study, internships, liberal arts/career combination. **Credit/placement by examination:** AP, CLEP. **Support services:** Remedial instruction, study skills assistance, tutoring, writing center.

Majors. Business: Accounting, business admin. **Computer sciences:** Information technology. **Health services:** Health care admin. **Protective services:** Financial forensics, law enforcement admin.

Most popular majors. Business/marketing 78%, legal studies 13%, security/protective services 9%.

Technology on campus. 60 workstations in library, computer center, student center. Commuter students can connect to campus network. Online library, helpline, student web hosting, wireless network available.

Student life. Freshman orientation: Mandatory. Preregistration for classes offered. Day and evening sessions available the week prior to classes starting. **Activities:** Literary magazine.

Student services. Career counseling, student employment services, financial aid counseling, placement for graduates.

Contact. Phone: (952) 345-1200 Toll-free number: (866) 776-1200 Ryan Kilpatrick, Director of Admissions, Minnesota School of Business: Shakopee, 1200 Shakopee Town Square, Shakopee, MN 55379

Minnesota School of Business: St. Cloud
Waite Park, Minnesota
www.msbcollege.edu

- For profit 4-year university and career college
- Commuter campus in small city
- 218 undergraduates
- Interview required

General. Accredited by ACICS. **Degrees:** 23 bachelor's, 73 associate awarded. **Location:** Located just outside the city in nearby Waite Park. **Calendar:** Quarter, extensive summer session. **Full-time faculty:** 10 total. **Part-time faculty:** 31 total.

Basis for selection. Open admission.

2015-2016 Annual costs. Tuition/fees: $18,702. Books/supplies: $1,260. **Additional information:** Per-credit hour charge for 1 to 11 hours, $460; for 12 to 16 hours, $390. Course fees: $10 to $400 per course.

Application procedures. Admission: No deadline. $50 fee. Admission notification on a rolling basis. **Financial aid:** No deadline. FAFSA, institutional form required. Applicants notified on a rolling basis starting 7/1; must reply within 2 week(s) of notification.

Academics. Special study options: Distance learning, independent study, internships, liberal arts/career combination. **Credit/placement by examination:** AP, CLEP. **Support services:** Remedial instruction, study skills assistance, tutoring, writing center.

Majors. Business: Accounting, business admin. **Computer sciences:** Information technology, programming. **Health services:** Health care admin. **Parks/recreation:** Physical fitness technician. **Protective services:** Law enforcement admin. **Visual/performing arts:** Arts management.

Most popular majors. Business/marketing 47%, computer/information sciences 25%, health sciences 8%, parks/recreation 6%, security/protective services 11%.

Technology on campus. 60 workstations in library, computer center, student center. Commuter students can connect to campus network. Online course registration, online library, helpline, student web hosting, wireless network available.

Student life. Freshman orientation: Mandatory. Preregistration for classes offered. Day and evening sessions available the week prior to classes starting. **Activities:** Literary magazine.

Student services. Career counseling, student employment services, financial aid counseling, placement for graduates.

Contact. E-mail: info@msbcollege.edu
Toll-free number: (866) 403-3333
Kim Plombon, Director of Admissions, Minnesota School of Business: St. Cloud, 1201 Second Street South, Waite Park, MN 56387

Minnesota State University Mankato
Mankato, Minnesota　　　　　　　　　**CB member**
www.mnsu.edu　　　　　　　　　　　**CB code: 6677**

- Public 4-year university
- Residential campus in small city
- 12,292 degree-seeking undergraduates
- 1,981 graduate students
- ACT (writing optional) required

General. Founded in 1867. Regionally accredited. **Degrees:** 2,424 bachelor's, 247 associate awarded; master's, doctoral offered. **ROTC:** Army. **Location:** 85 miles from Minneapolis-St. Paul. **Calendar:** Semester, extensive summer session. **Full-time faculty:** 444 total; 20% minority, 45% women. **Part-time faculty:** 317 total; 7% minority, 56% women. **Class size:** 26% < 20, 55% 20-39, 8% 40-49, 7% 50-99, 3% >100. **Special facilities:** 2 observatories, ropes course, indoor and outdoor rock climbing wall.

Freshman class profile.

Rank in top quarter:	25%	Out-of-state:	10%
Rank in top tenth:	7%	Live on campus:	85%

Basis for selection. Students must rank in top 50 percent of high school class or score 21 or better on the ACT. College preparatory courses also reviewed. ACT used only when admission cannot be achieved using high school rank and college preparatory courses. Essays and/or recommendations used only for contract/admission review by faculty committees. **Home schooled:** Must submit standardized test results in lieu of rank/record.

High school preparation. College-preparatory program required. 16 units required. Required units include English 4, mathematics 3, social studies 2,

653

history 1, science 3 (laboratory 3) and foreign language 2. One year world culture course or arts course.

2015-2016 Annual costs. Tuition/fees: $7,966; $16,110 out-of-state. Room/board: $8,430. Books/supplies: $910.

2015-2016 Financial aid. Need-based: Average need met was 70%. Average scholarship/grant was $5,658; average loan $3,810. 36% of total undergraduate aid awarded as scholarships/grants, 64% as loans/jobs. **Non-need-based:** Scholarships awarded for academics, art, athletics, leadership, minority status, music/drama.

Application procedures. Admission: No deadline. $20 fee, may be waived for applicants with need. Admission notification on a rolling basis. **Financial aid:** Priority date 3/15; no closing date. FAFSA required. Applicants notified on a rolling basis starting 3/30; must reply within 2 week(s) of notification.

Academics. Special study options: Combined bachelor's/graduate degree, cross-registration, distance learning, double major, dual enrollment of high school students, ESL, exchange student, external degree, honors, independent study, internships, semester at sea, student-designed major, study abroad, teacher certification program, weekend college. **Credit/placement by examination:** AP, CLEP, IB, ACT, institutional tests. **Support services:** Learning center, reduced course load, remedial instruction, study skills assistance, tutoring, writing center.

Majors. Architecture: Urban/community planning. **Area/ethnic studies:** French, German, Scandinavian, women's. **Biology:** General, anatomy, bacteriology, biochemistry, biotechnology, botany, ecology, genetics, toxicology, zoology. **Business:** General, accounting, banking/financial services, business admin, finance, financial planning, human resources, international, management information systems, management science, operations. **Communications:** Communications/speech/rhetoric, journalism, media studies, public relations. **Computer sciences:** General, computer science. **Conservation:** General, environmental studies. **Education:** General, art, biology, business, chemistry, computer, curriculum, drama/dance, early childhood, elementary, English, family/consumer sciences, foreign languages, French, German, health, health occupations, history, mathematics, middle, music, physical, physics, science, secondary, social science, social studies, Spanish, speech, technology/industrial arts, voc/tech. **Engineering:** General, civil, computer, electrical, mechanical. **English:** Creative writing, English lit, rhetoric/composition, technical writing. **Foreign languages:** French, German, Spanish. **General:** Maintenance. **Health services:** Communication disorders, cytotechnology, dental hygiene, health care admin, nursing (RN), predental, premedicine, preop/surgical nursing, prepharmacy, preveterinary, public health ed, recreational therapy. **History:** General. **Human services:** General, social work. **Math:** General. **Parks/recreation:** General, exercise sciences, facilities management, health/fitness, sports admin. **Philosophy/religion:** Philosophy. **Physical sciences:** Astronomy, chemistry, physics. **Protective services:** Corrections, law enforcement admin, police science. **Psychology:** General. **Social sciences:** Anthropology, economics, geography, international relations, political science, sociology, urban studies. **Visual/performing arts:** General, art, art history/conservation, ceramics, commercial/advertising art, dramatic, drawing, fiber arts, music, music management, music performance, painting, sculpture, studio arts, theater design. **Work/family studies:** General, clothing/textiles, family studies, family/community services, food/nutrition, housing.

Most popular majors. Business/marketing 19%, education 7%, health sciences 15%, parks/recreation 7%, security/protective services 7%, social sciences 6%.

Technology on campus. 900 workstations in dormitories, library, computer center, student center. Dormitories wired for high-speed internet access and linked to campus network. Commuter students can connect to campus network. Online course registration, online library, helpline, repair service, student web hosting, wireless network available.

Student life. Freshman orientation: Mandatory, $65 fee. Preregistration for classes offered. Includes overnight stay. **Housing:** Coed dorms, special housing for disabled, apartments, fraternity/sorority housing, wellness housing available. $250 partly refundable deposit. **Activities:** Bands, campus ministries, choral groups, dance, drama, international student organizations, literary magazine, music ensembles, musical theater, radio station, student government, student newspaper, symphony orchestra, African student association, Hmong student association, Asian Pacific student organization, Saudi student's club, Fellowship of Christian Athletes, InterVarsity Christian Fellowship, Muslim student association, Pagan Association for Growth and Neutrality, St. Thomas More Catholic Newman Center and Lutheran Campus Ministry-The Crossroads.

Athletics. NCAA. **Intercollegiate:** Baseball M, basketball, cheerleading, cross-country, diving, football (tackle) M, golf, ice hockey, soccer W, softball W, swimming W, tennis W, track and field, volleyball W, wrestling M. **Intramural:** Archery, basketball, bowling, football (non-tackle), golf, ice hockey, racquetball, rugby, soccer, softball, swimming, tennis, track and field, triathlon, volleyball, wrestling M. **Team name:** Mavericks.

Student services. Adult student services, alcohol/substance abuse counseling, chaplain/spiritual director, career counseling, services for economically disadvantaged, student employment services, financial aid counseling, health services, legal services, minority student services, on-campus daycare, personal counseling, placement for graduates, veterans' counselor, women's services. **Physically disabled:** Services for visually, speech, hearing impaired.

Contact. E-mail: admissions@mnsu.edu
Phone: (507) 389-1822 Toll-free number: (800) 722-0544
Fax: (507) 389-1511
Brian Jones, Director of Admissions, Minnesota State University Mankato, 122 Taylor Center, Mankato, MN 56001

Minnesota State University Moorhead
Moorhead, Minnesota
www.mnstate.edu　　　　　　　　　　**CB code: 6678**

▸ Public 4-year university
▸ Residential campus in small city
▸ 5,037 degree-seeking undergraduates: 15% part-time, 60% women, 3% African American, 1% Asian American, 3% Hispanic/Latino, 1% Native American, 3% Multi-racial, non-Hispanic, 7% international
▸ 515 degree-seeking graduate students
▸ 84% of applicants admitted
▸ SAT or ACT (ACT writing optional) required
▸ 42% graduate within 6 years

General. Founded in 1885. Regionally accredited. **Degrees:** 1,235 bachelor's, 15 associate awarded; master's offered. **ROTC:** Army, Air Force. **Location:** 240 miles from Minneapolis-St. Paul. **Calendar:** Semester, extensive summer session. **Full-time faculty:** 266 total; 79% have terminal degrees, 9% minority, 49% women. **Part-time faculty:** 150 total; 18% have terminal degrees, 4% minority, 57% women. **Class size:** 36% < 20, 49% 20-39, 8% 40-49, 6% 50-99, less than 1% >100. **Special facilities:** On-campus planetarium, 300-acre regional science center.

Freshman class profile. 2,992 applied, 2,519 admitted, 894 enrolled.

Mid 50% test scores			
SAT critical reading:	450-520	Rank in top tenth:	9%
SAT math:	480-570	Return as sophomores:	71%
ACT composite:	20-25	Out-of-state:	31%
Rank in top quarter:	31%	Live on campus:	83%
		International:	11%

Basis for selection. High school rank in the upper one-half of the graduating class with a minimum composite score of 17 on the ACT or 830 on the SAT or achieve the following score(s) on any one of the standardized college admissions tests (ACT is preferred): ACT Composite Score of 21 or above (ACT writing will not be required), SAT Verbal and Math combined re-centered score of 1000 or above and complete preparation standards. New entering freshmen who have met preparation standards for university admission in their respective states will be deemed to have met Minnesota preparation standards. ACT recommended. **Learning Disabled:** Contact Office of Disability Services to make sure appropriate accommodations can be provided.

High school preparation. College-preparatory program required. Required units include English 4, mathematics 3, social studies 3, science 3 (laboratory 1), foreign language 2 and academic electives 1. Minnesota preparation standards include 4 years of English (including composition and literature), 3 years of mathematics (2 years of algebra, of which one is intermediate or advanced algebra, and one year of geometry), 3 years of science (at least one year of a biological and a physical science and at least one course including significant laboratory experiences), 3 years of social studies (including U.S. history and at least one course that includes significant emphasis on geography), 2 years of world language, 1 year of world culture or the arts. One unit fine arts, .5 computer science recommended.

2015-2016 Annual costs. Tuition/fees: $8,092; $15,228 out-of-state. Room/board: $7,798. Books/supplies: $800. Personal expenses: $2,200.

2014-2015 Financial aid. Need-based: 758 full-time freshmen applied for aid; 512 deemed to have need; 505 received aid. Average scholarship/grant was $2,510; average loan $3,177. 47% of total undergraduate aid awarded as scholarships/grants, 53% as loans/jobs. **Non-need-based:** Awarded to 809 full-time undergraduates, including 294 freshmen. Scholarships awarded for academics, alumni affiliation, art, athletics, leadership, minority status, music/drama, state residency. **Additional information:** The financial aid application process consists of several steps. At each step institution may ask for information or additional documentation. The entire process can take 6-12 weeks.

Application procedures. Admission: Closing date 6/15 (postmark date). $20 fee, may be waived for applicants with need. Admission notification on a rolling basis beginning on or about 10/1. Students who may have attended post-secondary institutions while still in high school are classified as freshmen in the admission process. Students wishing to begin classes in the fall are encouraged to apply for admission as early as the previous fall. **Financial aid:** Priority date 2/15; no closing date. FAFSA required.

Academics. Special study options: Combined bachelor's/graduate degree, cross-registration, distance learning, double major, dual enrollment of high school students, exchange student, honors, independent study, internships, student-designed major, study abroad, teacher certification program. **Credit/ placement by examination:** AP, CLEP, IB, SAT, ACT, institutional tests. 12 credit hours maximum toward bachelor's degree. **Support services:** Learning center, pre-admission summer program, reduced course load, remedial instruction, study skills assistance, tutoring, writing center.

Majors. Area/ethnic studies: General, East Asian, women's. **Biology:** General, Biochemistry/molecular biology. **Business:** Accounting, business admin, construction management, finance, operations, project management. **Communications:** Advertising, broadcast journalism, communications/speech/ rhetoric, digital media, journalism, persuasive communications, photojournalism, public relations. **Computer sciences:** Computer science, information systems. **Conservation:** Environmental studies. **Education:** Art, biology, chemistry, early childhood, earth science, elementary, English, ESL, health, mathematics, music, physical, physics, social studies, Spanish, special ed. **English:** English lit. **Foreign languages:** Spanish. **Health services:** Athletic training, audiology/speech pathology, clinical lab science, community health, health care admin, nursing (RN). **History:** General. **Human services:** Social work. **Math:** General. **Parks/recreation:** Exercise sciences, health/fitness. **Philosophy/religion:** Philosophy. **Physical sciences:** Chemistry, geology, physics. **Protective services:** Criminal justice. **Psychology:** General. **Social sciences:** Anthropology, economics, political science, sociology. **Visual/performing arts:** Art, commercial/advertising art, dramatic, film/cinema/video, graphic design, jazz, music, music management, music performance, music theory/composition.

Most popular majors. Biology 6%, business/marketing 15%, communications/journalism 7%, education 16%, health sciences 10%, public administration/social services 6%, visual/performing arts 11%.

Technology on campus. 791 workstations in dormitories, library, computer center, student center. Dormitories wired for high-speed internet access and linked to campus network. Commuter students can connect to campus network. Online course registration, online library, helpline, repair service, student web hosting, wireless network available.

Student life. Freshman orientation: Available. Preregistration for classes offered. Four-day program typically held before classes begin. **Housing:** Guaranteed on-campus for freshmen. Coed dorms, single-sex dorms, special housing for disabled, apartments, fraternity/sorority housing, themed housing available. $250 partly refundable deposit, deadline 3/15. **Activities:** Bands, campus ministries, choral groups, dance, drama, film society, international student organizations, literary magazine, music ensembles, Model UN, musical theater, radio station, student government, student newspaper, symphony orchestra, TV station, Over 100 recognized student organizations.

Athletics. NCAA. **Intercollegiate:** Basketball, cheerleading, cross-country, diving W, football (tackle) M, golf W, soccer W, softball W, swimming W, tennis W, track and field, volleyball W, wrestling M. **Intramural:** Badminton, basketball, cricket, football (non-tackle), ice hockey, soccer, softball, tennis, ultimate frisbee, volleyball. **Team name:** Dragons.

Student services. Adult student services, alcohol/substance abuse counseling, career counseling, student employment services, financial aid counseling, health services, minority student services, on-campus daycare, personal counseling, placement for graduates, veterans' counselor, women's services. **Physically disabled:** Services for visually, speech, hearing impaired.

Contact. E-mail: admissions@mnstate.edu
Phone: (218) 477-2161 Toll-free number: (877) 678-6463
Fax: (218) 477-4374
Jim Anderson, Assistant Director of Admissions, Minnesota State University Moorhead, 1104 Seventh Avenue South, Moorhead, MN 56563

National American University: Bloomington
Bloomington, Minnesota
www.national.edu   CB code: 5358

▶ For-profit 4-year business and nursing college
▶ Commuter campus in very large city
▶ 422 undergraduates

General. Founded in 1974. Regionally accredited. Campuses in Bloomington/Mall of America, Brooklyn Center and Roseville. **Degrees:** 38 bachelor's, 43 associate awarded. **Calendar:** Quarter, extensive summer session. **Full-time faculty:** 8 total. **Part-time faculty:** 20 total. **Class size:** 95% < 20, 5% 20-39.

Basis for selection. Open admission.

2015-2016 Annual costs. Tuition/fees: $16,470. **Additional information:** Additional fees may apply.

Financial aid. Non-need-based: Scholarships awarded for academics.

Application procedures. Admission: No deadline. $25 fee. Admission notification on a rolling basis. **Financial aid:** Priority date 8/21; no closing date. FAFSA required. Applicants notified on a rolling basis.

Academics. Special study options: Accelerated study, distance learning, double major, independent study, internships. **Credit/placement by examination:** AP, CLEP, IB, institutional tests. **Support services:** Reduced course load, tutoring.

Majors. Business: General, accounting, business admin, hospitality admin, international, management information systems, marketing. **Computer sciences:** Information technology, LAN/WAN management, networking. **Health services:** Health care admin, nursing (RN). **Protective services:** Criminal justice.

Technology on campus. 112 workstations in library, computer center. Online library available.

Student life. Freshman orientation: Mandatory. Preregistration for classes offered. **Activities:** Student government, student business club, Southeast Asian student organization, student government, international student organizations.

Athletics. Team name: Mavericks.

Student services. Career counseling, student employment services, placement for graduates.

Contact. E-mail: moaadmissions@national.edu
Phone: (952) 356-3600 Toll-free number: (866) 628-6387
Fax: (952) 356-3605
Chris Celestino, Director of Admissions, National American University: Bloomington, 7801 Metro Parkway Suite 200, Bloomington, MN 55425

National American University: Roseville
Roseville, Minnesota
www.national.edu

▶ For-profit 4-year university and branch campus college
▶ Commuter campus in very large city
▶ 264 undergraduates

General. Regionally accredited. **Degrees:** 8 bachelor's, 35 associate awarded. **Calendar:** Quarter. **Full-time faculty:** 1 total. **Part-time faculty:** 17 total.

Basis for selection. Open admission.

2015-2016 Annual costs. Tuition/fees: $16,470. Books/supplies: $1,350. **Additional information:** Additional fees may apply.

Application procedures. Admission: $25 fee. **Financial aid:** Closing date 8/25.

Academics. Credit/placement by examination: AP, CLEP.

Majors. Business: Accounting, business admin, finance, human resources, marketing. **Computer sciences:** Information technology, LAN/WAN management, programming. **Health services:** Health care admin. **Protective services:** Criminal justice.

Contact. E-mail: rosadmissions@national.edu
Toll-free number: (866) 628-6387
Matt Smith, Director of Admissions, National American University: Roseville, 1550 West Highway 36, Roseville, MN 55113

North Central University
Minneapolis, Minnesota
www.northcentral.edu

CB code: 0051

- Private 4-year university affiliated with the Assemblies of God
- Residential campus in large city
- 1,301 degree-seeking undergraduates
- SAT or ACT (ACT writing optional), application essay required

General. Founded in 1930. Regionally accredited. **Degrees:** 203 bachelor's, 9 associate awarded. **ROTC:** Army, Air Force. **Calendar:** Semester, limited summer session. **Full-time faculty:** 42 total. **Part-time faculty:** 85 total. **Class size:** 63% < 20, 26% 20-39, 6% 40-49, 5% 50-99, less than 1% >100. **Special facilities:** Private recording studio on-campus, center for youth and leadership, children's literature library.

Freshman class profile.

Out-of-state:	61%	Live on campus:	93%

Basis for selection. School achievement record, essay character recommendation, and pastor's recommendation are most important. Conditional admission available for students not in good standing at previous institution. Applicants with GPA below 2.2 or ACT scores below 18 may be provisionally admitted. The writing portions of the ACT and SAT are not required and not taken into consideration for admission or scholarship. **Home schooled:** Statement describing home school structure and mission, transcript of courses and grades required. Must meet their state's requirements for graduation.

High school preparation. 9 units recommended. Recommended units include English 3, mathematics 1, social studies 2, history 1, science 1 and foreign language 1.

2015-2016 Annual costs. Tuition/fees: $21,586. Room/board: $6,584. Books/supplies: $1,160.

Financial aid. Non-need-based: Scholarships awarded for academics, leadership, music/drama.

Application procedures. Admission: Priority date 1/15; deadline 6/1 (postmark date). $25 fee, may be waived for applicants with need. Admission notification on a rolling basis. **Financial aid:** No deadline. FAFSA required. Applicants notified on a rolling basis starting 3/1; must reply within 2 week(s) of notification.

Academics. Special study options: Double major, dual enrollment of high school students, exchange student, independent study, internships, liberal arts/career combination, student-designed major, study abroad, teacher certification program, weekend college. **Credit/placement by examination:** AP, CLEP, SAT, ACT. **Support services:** Learning center, pre-admission summer program, reduced course load, remedial instruction, study skills assistance, tutoring, writing center.

Majors. Business: Business admin. **Communications:** Journalism, media studies. **Communications technology:** Recording arts. **Education:** Elementary, ESL, secondary. **English:** English lit. **Foreign languages:** American Sign Language, sign language interpretation. **Health services:** Substance abuse counseling. **Human services:** Social work. **Math:** General. **Parks/recreation:** Sports admin. **Philosophy/religion:** Christian, religion. **Psychology:** General. **Social sciences:** Urban studies. **Theology:** Bible, missionary; pastoral counseling, religious ed, sacred music, theology, youth ministry. **Visual/performing arts:** Dramatic, music, music management, music performance.

Most popular majors. Business/marketing 6%, education 12%, family/consumer sciences 11%, interdisciplinary studies 26%, theological studies 24%, visual/performing arts 7%.

Technology on campus. 120 workstations in dormitories, library, computer center, student center. Dormitories wired for high-speed internet access and linked to campus network. Commuter students can connect to campus network. Online course registration, online library, helpline, wireless network available.

Student life. Freshman orientation: Mandatory, $115 fee. Preregistration for classes offered. Four-five optional dates in the summer months. **Policies:** North Central requires all members of the community to refrain from any form of sexual immorality. Students must refrain from the possession, use or distribution of non-medical drugs, alcoholic beverages, and tobacco in any form. Religious observance required. **Housing:** Single-sex dorms, special housing for disabled, apartments, wellness housing available. $200 partly refundable deposit, deadline 6/1. **Activities:** Bands, campus ministries, choral groups, dance, drama, literary magazine, music ensembles, musical theater, student government, student newspaper, leadership development committee, student committee, the Northern Light, SIFE, Alpha Kai, deaf culture fellowship, student senate, student missions fellowship, student activities committee.

Athletics. NCAA, NCCAA. **Intercollegiate:** Baseball M, basketball, cross-country, golf M, soccer, softball W, track and field, volleyball W. **Intramural:** Basketball M, football (non-tackle). **Team name:** Rams.

Student services. Chaplain/spiritual director, career counseling, student employment services, financial aid counseling, health services, personal counseling, placement for graduates, women's services. **Physically disabled:** Services for visually, speech, hearing impaired.

Contact. E-mail: admissions@northcentral.edu
Phone: (612) 343-4460 Toll-free number: (800) 289-6222
Fax: (612) 343-4146
Troy Pearson, Executive Director of Admissions and Enrollment, North Central University, 910 Elliot Avenue, Minneapolis, MN 55404

Northwestern Health Sciences University
Bloomington, Minnesota
www.nwhealth.edu

CB code: 6516

- Private two-year upper-division university and health science college
- Commuter campus in very large city

General. Regionally accredited. **Degrees:** 54 bachelor's, 27 associate awarded; master's, professional offered. **Location:** Approximately 10 miles from downtown Minneapolis. **Calendar:** Trimester, limited summer session.

Student profile. 113 degree-seeking undergraduates, 791 graduate students.

Out-of-state:	17%	25 or older:	67%

Basis for selection. The College of Undergraduate Health Sciences and School of Massage Therapy require a high school GPA of 2.0 or above. Additionally, applicants to the School of Massage Therapy must pass a criminal background check. Applicants to the College of Acupuncture and Oriental Medicine must transfer with 60 credits at the baccalaureate level or above, with a minimum cumulative GPA of 2.5 or higher. Applicants to the College of Chiropractic must transfer with 90 credits at the baccalaureate level or above, with a minimum cumulative GPA of 2.75 or higher. Transfer accepted as sophomores, juniors, seniors.

2015-2016 Annual costs. Tuition/fees: $12,267. Books/supplies: $1,020.

Application procedures. Admission: Rolling admission. $50 fee, may be waived for applicants with need. **Financial aid:** FAFSA required.

Academics. Special study options: Internships, study abroad. **Credit/placement by examination:** AP, CLEP.

Technology on campus. Wireless network available.

Student life. Activities: Student government.

Contact. E-mail: admit@nwhealth.edu
Phone: (952) 888-4777 ext. 409
Kate DiAna, Director of Admissions, Northwestern Health Sciences University, 2501 West 84th Street, Bloomington, MN 55431

Oak Hills Christian College
Bemidji, Minnesota
www.oakhills.edu

CB code: 7247

- Private 4-year Bible college affiliated with the interdenominational tradition
- Residential campus in large town
- 114 degree-seeking undergraduates
- ACT (writing optional), application essay required

General. Founded in 1946. Accredited by ABHE. **Degrees:** 18 bachelor's, 3 associate awarded. **Location:** 4 miles from Bemidji, 230 miles from Minneapolis-St. Paul. **Calendar:** Semester. **Full-time faculty:** 4 total. **Part-time faculty:** 8 total. **Class size:** 60% < 20, 29% 20-39, 9% 40-49, 3% 50-99. **Special facilities:** Center for Indian ministries resource center.

Freshman class profile.

GPA 3.75 or higher:	14%	Rank in top quarter:	15%
GPA 3.50-3.74:	17%	Out-of-state:	15%
GPA 3.0-3.49:	20%	Live on campus:	80%
GPA 2.0-2.99:	45%		

Basis for selection. Applicants must have high school GPA of 2.0 or above and/or ACT score of 18 or above to be eligible for consideration. Applicants not meeting minimum requirements considered on individual basis. SAT/ACT scores must be received at latest 4 weeks after first day of classes. Not required if student has 24 college credits past high school or if 2 years out of high school. An essay or personal statement may generate an interview. **Home schooled:** Transcript of courses and grades, letter of recommendation (nonparent) required. Proof of graduation from high school. **Learning Disabled:** All special education or diagnostic (IEP) records required. Interview may be requested.

2015-2016 Annual costs. Tuition/fees: $16,165. Room/board: $5,816. Books/supplies: $500.

Financial aid. Non-need-based: Scholarships awarded for academics, alumni affiliation.

Application procedures. Admission: No deadline. No application fee. Admission notification on a rolling basis beginning on or about 9/1. Early Admission of high school students is allowed if they are PSEO students. **Financial aid:** No deadline. FAFSA, institutional form required. Applicants notified on a rolling basis starting 3/1.

Academics. Special study options: Combined bachelor's/graduate degree, double major, dual enrollment of high school students, independent study, internships, study abroad. **Credit/placement by examination:** AP, CLEP, ACT, institutional tests. **Support services:** Reduced course load, remedial instruction, study skills assistance, tutoring, writing center.

Majors. Psychology: General. **Theology:** Bible, missionary, sacred music, youth ministry.

Most popular majors. Liberal arts 24%, theological studies 76%.

Technology on campus. 8 workstations in library, computer center. Dormitories wired for high-speed internet access and linked to campus network. Commuter students can connect to campus network. Online course registration, wireless network available.

Student life. Freshman orientation: Mandatory. Preregistration for classes offered. Held first weekend prior to start of fall classes. **Policies:** Mandatory chapel, no alcohol, illegal drugs, gambling, or smoking on campus. Religious observance required. **Housing:** Guaranteed on-campus for freshmen. Single-sex dorms, apartments, wellness housing available. $100 nonrefundable deposit. Apartments for students with dependent children available. **Activities:** Campus ministries, student government, married students group, students older than average group, women's group, engaged couples group, many outreach programs, single student cell groups.

Athletics. Intercollegiate: Basketball M, volleyball W. **Intramural:** Basketball, football (non-tackle), table tennis. **Team name:** Wolfpack.

Student services. Adult student services, chaplain/spiritual director, career counseling, student employment services, financial aid counseling, health services, placement for graduates. **Physically disabled:** Services for visually, speech, hearing impaired.

Contact. E-mail: admissions@oakhills.edu
Phone: (218) 751-8671 ext. 1285 Toll-free number: (866) 307-6422
Fax: (218) 444-1311
Steven Ware, Dean of the College, Oak Hills Christian College, 1600 Oak Hills Road SW, Bemidji, MN 56601-8826

Rasmussen College: Blaine
Blaine, Minnesota
www.rasmussen.edu

- For-profit 4-year branch campus and career college
- Commuter campus in small city
- 770 degree-seeking undergraduates

General. Regionally accredited. **Degrees:** 47 bachelor's, 162 associate awarded. **Calendar:** Quarter. **Full-time faculty:** 9 total. **Part-time faculty:** 34 total.

Freshman class profile. 226 applied, 187 admitted, 187 enrolled.

Basis for selection. Open admission, but selective for some programs.

2016-2017 Annual costs. Tuition/fees (projected): $13,455.

Application procedures. Admission: No deadline. No application fee. Admission notification on a rolling basis. **Financial aid:** No deadline. FAFSA, institutional form required. Applicants notified on a rolling basis.

Academics. Credit/placement by examination: AP, CLEP.

Majors. Business: Accounting, accounting/business management, business admin, finance, human resources, information resources management, marketing. **Computer sciences:** Computer science, security, system admin, web page design. **Health services:** Health care admin, health information management, nursing (RN). **Protective services:** Criminal justice, special ops. **Visual/performing arts:** Digital arts, game design.

Contact. Phone: (763) 795-4720 Toll-free number: (888) 549-6755
Susan Hammerstrom, Director of Admissions, Rasmussen College: Blaine, 3629 95th Avenue NE, Blaine, MN 55014

Rasmussen College: Lake Elmo/Woodbury
Lake Elmo, Minnesota
www.rasmussen.edu

- For-profit 4-year career college
- Commuter campus in small city
- 586 degree-seeking undergraduates

General. Regionally accredited. **Degrees:** 74 bachelor's, 114 associate awarded. **Calendar:** Quarter. **Full-time faculty:** 6 total. **Part-time faculty:** 20 total.

Freshman class profile. 203 applied, 155 admitted, 155 enrolled.

Basis for selection. Open admission, but selective for some programs.

2016-2017 Annual costs. Tuition/fees (projected): $13,455. Personal expenses: $2,214.

Application procedures. Admission: No deadline. No application fee. Admission notification on a rolling basis. **Financial aid:** No deadline. FAFSA, institutional form required. Applicants notified on a rolling basis.

Academics. Credit/placement by examination: AP, CLEP.

Majors. Business: Accounting, accounting/business management, business admin, finance, human resources, information resources management, marketing. **Computer sciences:** Computer science, security, system admin, web page design. **Health services:** Health care admin, health information management, nursing (RN). **Protective services:** Criminal justice, special ops. **Visual/performing arts:** Digital arts, game design.

Student services. Adult student services, career counseling, services for economically disadvantaged, student employment services, financial aid counseling, minority student services, placement for graduates, veterans' counselor.

Contact. Phone: (651) 259-6600 Fax: (651) 259-6601
Susan Hammerstrom, Director of Admissions, Rasmussen College: Lake Elmo/Woodbury, 8565 Eagle Point Circle, Lake Elmo, MN 55042-8637

Rasmussen College: Moorhead
Moorhead, Minnesota
www.rasmussen.edu

- For-profit 4-year career college
- Small city
- 371 degree-seeking undergraduates

General. Degrees: 22 bachelor's, 97 associate awarded. **Calendar:** Quarter. **Full-time faculty:** 7 total. **Part-time faculty:** 42 total.

Freshman class profile. 152 applied, 116 admitted, 116 enrolled.

Basis for selection. Open admission, but selective for some programs.

2016-2017 Annual costs. Tuition/fees (projected): $13,455.

Application procedures. Admission: No deadline. No application fee. Admission notification on a rolling basis. **Financial aid:** No deadline. FAFSA, institutional form required. Applicants notified on a rolling basis.

Academics. Credit/placement by examination: AP, CLEP.

Majors. Business: Accounting, business admin, human resources. **Computer sciences:** General, computer science, security, system admin, web page design. **Health services:** Health care admin, health information management, nursing (RN). **Protective services:** Criminal justice, special ops. **Visual/performing arts:** Digital arts, game design.

Contact. Phone: (218) 304-6200 Fax: (218) 304-6201
Susan Hammerstrom, Director of Admissions, Rasmussen College: Moorhead, 1250 29th Avenue South, Moorhead, MN 56560

Saint Cloud State University
St. Cloud, Minnesota
www.stcloudstate.edu   CB code: 6679

- Public 4-year university
- Commuter campus in small city
- 10,620 degree-seeking undergraduates: 17% part-time, 51% women, 7% African American, 6% Asian American, 3% Hispanic/Latino, 3% Multiracial, non-Hispanic, 7% international
- 1,716 degree-seeking graduate students
- 86% of applicants admitted
- SAT or ACT (ACT writing optional) required
- 42% graduate within 6 years

General. Founded in 1869. Regionally accredited. **Degrees:** 2,239 bachelor's, 402 associate awarded; master's, doctoral offered. **ROTC:** Army. **Location:** 80 miles from Minneapolis-St. Paul. **Calendar:** Semester, limited summer session. **Full-time faculty:** 528 total; 84% have terminal degrees, 22% minority, 44% women. **Part-time faculty:** 235 total; 18% have terminal degrees, 14% minority, 59% women. **Class size:** 42% < 20, 48% 20-39, 6% 40-49, 2% 50-99, 2% >100. **Special facilities:** Planetarium, greenhouse, nature preserve, observatory, GIS cartographic center, aviation facilities, weather labs, hockey center, editing equipment.

Freshman class profile. 6,110 applied, 5,267 admitted, 1,863 enrolled.

Mid 50% test scores			
ACT composite:	19-25	Rank in top quarter:	20%
		Rank in top tenth:	5%
GPA 3.75 or higher:	16%	Return as sophomores:	72%
GPA 3.50-3.74:	17%	Out-of-state:	12%
GPA 3.0-3.49:	36%	Live on campus:	69%
GPA 2.0-2.99:	31%	International:	6%

Basis for selection. Each application individually reviewed and evaluated using a combination of high school rank, GPA, curriculum, test scores, and other indicators of academic performance and potential.

High school preparation. College-preparatory program recommended. 16 units required. Required units include English 4, mathematics 3, social studies 3, science 3, foreign language 2 and visual/performing arts 1.

2015-2016 Annual costs. Tuition/fees: $7,814; $15,732 out-of-state. Room/board: $7,930. Books/supplies: $1,200. Personal expenses: $2,700.

2015-2016 Financial aid. Need-based: 1,501 full-time freshmen applied for aid; 1,104 deemed to have need; 1,103 received aid. Average need met was 60%. Average scholarship/grant was $5,982; average loan $3,543. 49% of total undergraduate aid awarded as scholarships/grants, 51% as loans/jobs. **Non-need-based:** Awarded to 1,746 full-time undergraduates, including 1,054 freshmen. Scholarships awarded for academics, art, athletics, minority status, music/drama, ROTC.

Application procedures. Admission: Priority date 12/15; deadline 8/1 (receipt date). $20 fee, may be waived for applicants with need. Admission notification on a rolling basis beginning on or about 9/15. Early application recommended for those who want to live on-campus. **Financial aid:** Priority date 4/15; no closing date. FAFSA required. Applicants notified on a rolling basis starting 6/15.

Academics. Special study options: Accelerated study, cooperative education, cross-registration, distance learning, double major, dual enrollment of high school students, ESL, honors, independent study, internships, student-designed major, study abroad, teacher certification program, weekend college. **Credit/placement by examination:** AP, CLEP, IB, ACT, institutional tests. 32 credit hours maximum toward bachelor's degree. **Support services:** Learning center, pre-admission summer program, remedial instruction, study skills assistance, tutoring, writing center.

Majors. Area/ethnic studies: Latin American, women's. **Biology:** General, aquatic, biochemistry, biotechnology, cellular/anatomical, ecology, marine. **Business:** General, accounting, business admin, entrepreneurial studies, finance, human resources, insurance, international, management information systems, marketing, real estate, tourism/travel. **Communications:** General, advertising, broadcast journalism, communications/speech/rhetoric, journalism, media studies, public relations, radio/TV. **Computer sciences:** General, computer science, networking, security. **Conservation:** Environmental science, environmental studies. **Education:** Art, biology, chemistry, drama/dance, driver/safety, early childhood, educational technology, elementary, English, foreign languages, French, German, health, history, kindergarten/preschool, mathematics, multi-level teacher, music, physical, physics, psychology, reading, science, secondary, social science, social studies, Spanish, special ed, speech, technology/industrial arts, voc/tech. **Engineering:** Computer, electrical, manufacturing, mechanical. **English:** American lit, creative writing, English lit, rhetoric/composition, writing. **Foreign languages:** French, German, linguistics, Spanish. **Health services:** Audiology/speech pathology, clinical lab science, communication disorders, community health services, medical radiologic technology/radiation therapy, nuclear medical technology, nursing (RN), predental, premedicine, prepharmacy, preveterinary, public health ed, recreational therapy, substance abuse counseling. **History:** General. **Human services:** General, social work. **Liberal arts:** Arts/sciences, library science. **Math:** General, statistics. **Parks/recreation:** General, health/fitness. **Philosophy/religion:** Philosophy. **Physical sciences:** General, atmospheric science, chemistry, geology, hydrology, meteorology, physics, planetary. **Protective services:** Criminal justice. **Psychology:** General, community. **Social sciences:** General, anthropology, econometrics, economics, geography, international relations, political science, sociology, urban studies. **Visual/performing arts:** Acting, art, art history/conservation, ceramics, dramatic, drawing, film/cinema/video, jazz, music, music history, music performance, painting, piano/keyboard, printmaking, sculpture, stringed instruments, studio arts, voice/opera.

Most popular majors. Business/marketing 25%, communications/journalism 9%, education 10%, health sciences 8%, interdisciplinary studies 6%, psychology 8%.

Technology on campus. 1,465 workstations in dormitories, library, computer center, student center. Dormitories wired for high-speed internet access and linked to campus network. Commuter students can connect to campus network. Online course registration, online library, helpline, repair service, student web hosting, wireless network available.

Student life. Freshman orientation: Mandatory. Preregistration for classes offered. Includes assistance with fall term registration. **Housing:** Coed dorms, single-sex dorms, special housing for disabled, apartments, fraternity/sorority housing, themed housing available. $250 partly refundable deposit, deadline 8/1. **Activities:** Bands, campus ministries, choral groups, dance, drama, film society, international student organizations, music ensembles, Model UN, musical theater, radio station, student government, student newspaper, symphony orchestra, TV station, more than 240 clubs and departmental organizations.

Athletics. NCAA. **Intercollegiate:** Baseball M, basketball, cross-country, diving, football (tackle) M, golf, ice hockey, skiing W, soccer W, softball W, swimming, tennis, track and field, volleyball W, wrestling M. **Intramural:** Badminton, basketball, football (non-tackle), golf, ice hockey, racquetball, soccer, softball, tennis, volleyball, water polo. **Team name:** Huskies.

Student services. Adult student services, alcohol/substance abuse counseling, career counseling, student employment services, financial aid counseling, health services, legal services, minority student services, on-campus daycare, personal counseling, placement for graduates, veterans' counselor, women's services. **Physically disabled:** Services for visually, speech, hearing impaired.

Contact. E-mail: scsu4u@stcloudstate.edu
Phone: (320) 308-3981 Toll-free number: (877) 654-7278
Fax: (320) 308-2243
Amber Schultz, Asst Provost for Student Recruitment and Enrollment, Saint Cloud State University, 720 Fourth Avenue South, AS 115, St. Cloud, MN 56301

Southwest Minnesota State University
Marshall, Minnesota
www.smsu.edu   CB code: 6703

- Public 4-year university and liberal arts college
- Residential campus in large town
- 2,291 degree-seeking undergraduates: 20% part-time, 58% women, 6% African American, 3% Asian American, 2% Hispanic/Latino, 1% Native American, 5% international
- 391 degree-seeking graduate students

- 64% of applicants admitted
- SAT or ACT (ACT writing optional) required
- 40% graduate within 6 years

General. Founded in 1963. Regionally accredited. **Degrees:** 556 bachelor's, 16 associate awarded; master's offered. **Location:** 150 miles from Minneapolis-St. Paul, 92 miles from Sioux Falls, SD. **Calendar:** Semester, limited summer session. **Full-time faculty:** 108 total; 86% have terminal degrees, 11% minority, 49% women. **Part-time faculty:** 86 total; 33% have terminal degrees, 9% minority, 60% women. **Class size:** 46% < 20, 48% 20-39, 2% 40-49, 3% 50-99, less than 1% >100. **Special facilities:** Planetarium, greenhouse, museums, wildlife area, agronomy fields/test plots.

Freshman class profile. 2,013 applied, 1,289 admitted, 449 enrolled.

Mid 50% test scores			
SAT critical reading:	370-540	**GPA 2.0-2.99:**	32%
SAT math:	380-530	**Rank in top quarter:**	21%
SAT writing:	330-540	**Rank in top tenth:**	5%
ACT composite:	19-24	**Return as sophomores:**	68%
GPA 3.75 or higher:	16%	**Out-of-state:**	17%
GPA 3.50-3.74:	21%	**Live on campus:**	87%
GPA 3.0-3.49:	30%	**International:**	9%

Basis for selection. Class rank in top half of class or SAT combined score of 970 or ACT composite score of 21. Provisional admission may be granted to students who rank in top two-thirds of class or have ACT composite score of 19 or SAT combined score of 890. ACT recommended. PSAT/NMSQT may be submitted in place of SAT or ACT. Interview recommended for academically weak students; audition recommended for music students. **Home schooled:** Transcript of courses and grades required.

High school preparation. College-preparatory program required. 16 units required. Required units include English 4, mathematics 3, social studies 3, science 3, foreign language 2 and academic electives 1. Social studies units must include American history and geography.

2015-2016 Annual costs. Tuition/fees: $8,337; $8,337 out-of-state. Room/board: $7,572. Books/supplies: $1,200. Personal expenses: $1,578.

2015-2016 Financial aid. Need-based: 384 full-time freshmen applied for aid; 277 deemed to have need; 277 received aid. Average need met was 51%. Average scholarship/grant was $5,713; average loan $3,441. 50% of total undergraduate aid awarded as scholarships/grants, 50% as loans/jobs. **Non-need-based:** Awarded to 1,301 full-time undergraduates, including 390 freshmen. Scholarships awarded for academics, alumni affiliation, art, athletics, leadership, minority status, music/drama, state residency.

Application procedures. Admission: Priority date 8/15; no deadline. $20 fee. Admission notification on a rolling basis. **Financial aid:** Priority date 3/1; no closing date. FAFSA, institutional form required. Applicants notified on a rolling basis starting 5/1.

Academics. Special study options: Cooperative education, cross-registration, distance learning, double major, dual enrollment of high school students, external degree, honors, independent study, internships, student-designed major, study abroad, teacher certification program. 2+2 bachelor's programs with Community Colleges. Visiting Exchange Student Program. **Credit/placement by examination:** AP, CLEP, IB, ACT, institutional tests. 10 credit hours maximum toward associate degree, 20 toward bachelor's. **Support services:** Learning center, pre-admission summer program, reduced course load, remedial instruction, study skills assistance, tutoring, writing center.

Majors. Biology: General, cell/histology, ecology. **Business:** Accounting, business admin, finance, hospitality admin, marketing, nonprofit/public, restaurant/food services. **Communications:** Broadcast journalism, communications/speech/rhetoric, public relations, radio/TV. **Computer sciences:** General, information technology. **Conservation:** Environmental science. **Education:** General, agricultural, art, biology, chemistry, drama/dance, early childhood, elementary, ESL, health, mathematics, music, physical, science, special ed, speech. **English:** Creative writing, English lit, rhetoric/composition. **Foreign languages:** Spanish. **Health services:** Nursing (RN). **History:** General. **Human services:** General, social work. **Liberal arts:** Arts/sciences. **Math:** General. **Parks/recreation:** Exercise sciences, health/fitness. **Philosophy/religion:** Philosophy. **Physical sciences:** Chemistry. **Protective services:** Criminal justice, fire services admin, law enforcement admin. **Psychology:** General. **Social sciences:** Political science, sociology. **Visual/performing arts:** Art, dramatic, music, music management.

Most popular majors. Business/marketing 28%, education 16%, parks/recreation 9%.

Technology on campus. 300 workstations in dormitories, library, computer center, student center. Dormitories wired for high-speed internet access and linked to campus network. Commuter students can connect to campus network. Online course registration, online library, helpline, repair service, student web hosting, wireless network available.

Student life. Freshman orientation: Available, $135 fee. Preregistration for classes offered. **Housing:** Guaranteed on-campus for freshmen. Coed dorms, single-sex dorms, special housing for disabled, apartments, gender-neutral housing, themed housing available. $100 fully refundable deposit. **Activities:** Bands, campus ministries, choral groups, dance, drama, film society, international student organizations, literary magazine, music ensembles, Model UN, musical theater, radio station, student government, student newspaper, symphony orchestra, TV station, Black Student Union, Inter-Varsity Christian Fellowship, Lutheran Student Commission, student activities committee, Republican Speakers club, Young DFL, non-traditional students organization, Newman Club, GLBTA.

Athletics. NCAA. **Intercollegiate:** Baseball M, basketball, football (tackle) M, golf W, soccer W, softball W, tennis W, volleyball W, wrestling M. **Intramural:** Basketball, ice hockey M, racquetball, skiing, softball, tennis, track and field, volleyball, wrestling M. **Team name:** Mustangs.

Student services. Adult student services, alcohol/substance abuse counseling, chaplain/spiritual director, career counseling, student employment services, financial aid counseling, health services, minority student services, on-campus daycare, personal counseling, placement for graduates, veterans' counselor, women's services. **Physically disabled:** Services for visually, speech, hearing impaired.

Contact. E-mail: smsu.admissions@smsu.edu
Phone: (507) 537-6286 Toll-free number: (800) 642-0684
Fax: (507) 537-7154
Matt Suby, Director of Admissions, Southwest Minnesota State University, 1501 State Street, Marshall, MN 56258-1598

St. Catherine University
Saint Paul, Minnesota
www.stkate.edu

CB member
CB code: 6105

- Private 4-year health science and liberal arts college for women affiliated with the Roman Catholic Church
- Commuter campus in large city
- 3,243 degree-seeking undergraduates: 34% part-time, 97% women, 9% African American, 12% Asian American, 7% Hispanic/Latino, 1% Native American, 3% Multi-racial, non-Hispanic, 1% international
- 1,631 degree-seeking graduate students
- 67% of applicants admitted
- SAT or ACT (ACT writing optional) required
- 64% graduate within 6 years

General. Founded in 1905. Regionally accredited. St. Catherine University is organized into 4 schools: Humanities, Art & Science; Health; Business & Leadership; and Professional Studies. **Degrees:** 602 bachelor's, 189 associate awarded; master's, professional offered. **ROTC:** Army, Air Force. **Location:** 6 miles from downtown St. Paul and downtown Minneapolis. **Calendar:** 4-1-4, extensive summer session. **Full-time faculty:** 293 total; 79% have terminal degrees, 10% minority, 82% women. **Part-time faculty:** 232 total; 48% have terminal degrees, 12% minority, 79% women. **Class size:** 69% < 20, 26% 20-39, 3% 40-49, 1% 50-99. **Special facilities:** Center for women's research, observatory, art gallery.

Freshman class profile. 2,999 applied, 2,021 admitted, 429 enrolled.

Mid 50% test scores			
SAT critical reading:	510-610	**GPA 2.0-2.99:**	8%
SAT math:	490-550	**Rank in top quarter:**	68%
ACT composite:	21-26	**Rank in top tenth:**	25%
GPA 3.75 or higher:	38%	**Return as sophomores:**	86%
GPA 3.50-3.74:	27%	**Out-of-state:**	16%
GPA 3.0-3.49:	27%	**Live on campus:**	70%
		International:	1%

Basis for selection. School achievement record with rank in top half of class and test scores important. Extracurricular and community involvement also considered. Recommendations important. Interview recommended for all applicants, required for marginal students. Audition recommended for music students; portfolio recommended for art students. Essay recommended for marginal students.

High school preparation. College-preparatory program recommended. 15 units recommended. Recommended units include English 4, mathematics 3, social studies 2, science 2 and foreign language 4.

2015-2016 Annual costs. Tuition/fees: $35,629. Room/board: $8,750. Books/supplies: $1,000. Personal expenses: $2,350. **Additional information:**

Evening, weekend, and online baccalaureate students are $548 per credit; associate degree students are $664 per credit.

2015-2016 Financial aid. Need-based: 395 full-time freshmen applied for aid; 347 deemed to have need; 347 received aid. Average need met was 92%. Average scholarship/grant was $9,800; average loan $3,900. 57% of total undergraduate aid awarded as scholarships/grants, 43% as loans/jobs. **Non-need-based:** Scholarships awarded for academics, alumni affiliation, leadership, state residency. **Additional information:** Audition required for music scholarships.

Application procedures. Admission: Priority date 4/15; no deadline. No application fee. Admission notification on a rolling basis beginning on or about 4/15. Must reply by May 1 or within 2 week(s) if notified thereafter. Students must be accepted by 2/1 to be eligible to compete in merit scholarship competition. **Financial aid:** Priority date 4/15; no closing date. FAFSA, institutional form required. Applicants notified on a rolling basis starting 3/30; must reply within 2 week(s) of notification.

Academics. Special study options: Combined bachelor's/graduate degree, cross-registration, distance learning, double major, dual enrollment of high school students, exchange student, honors, independent study, internships, student-designed major, study abroad, teacher certification program, urban semester, Washington semester, weekend college. Cooperative program in fashion merchandising with Fashion Institute of Technology in New York City and Fashion Institute of Design in Los Angeles, academic year of study in New York City, exchange program with other Carondolet Colleges, internship program includes over 500 sites in Twin Cities area. **Credit/placement by examination:** AP, CLEP, IB, ACT, institutional tests. 32 credit hours maximum toward bachelor's degree. **Support services:** Learning center, reduced course load, remedial instruction, study skills assistance, tutoring, writing center.

Majors. Area/ethnic studies: Women's. **Biology:** General, biochemistry. **Business:** Accounting, business admin, fashion, international, management information systems, sales/distribution. **Communications:** Communications/speech/rhetoric. **Computer sciences:** General, information systems. **Education:** General, art, business, early childhood, elementary, English, family/consumer sciences, foreign languages, mathematics, middle, music, physical, secondary. **English:** English lit, rhetoric/composition. **Foreign languages:** American Sign Language, French, sign language interpretation, Spanish. **Health services:** Dietetics, health information management, nursing (RN), predental, premedicine, prepharmacy, preveterinary, respiratory therapy technology. **History:** General. **Human services:** Social work. **Math:** General. **Parks/recreation:** Exercise sciences. **Philosophy/religion:** Philosophy. **Physical sciences:** Chemistry, physics. **Psychology:** General. **Social sciences:** General, economics, international relations, political science, sociology. **Theology:** Theology. **Visual/performing arts:** Art history/conservation, dramatic, fashion design, music, music performance, studio arts. **Work/family studies:** General, food/nutrition.

Most popular majors. Business/marketing 12%, health sciences 43%, social sciences 6%.

Technology on campus. 350 workstations in dormitories, library, computer center, student center. Dormitories wired for high-speed internet access and linked to campus network. Commuter students can connect to campus network. Online course registration, online library, helpline, wireless network available.

Student life. Freshman orientation: Mandatory. Preregistration for classes offered. **Housing:** Guaranteed on-campus for freshmen. Apartments, themed housing available. $100 nonrefundable deposit. Apartments for student-parents available. **Activities:** Campus ministries, choral groups, dance, drama, international student organizations, literary magazine, music ensembles, musical theater, radio station, student government, student newspaper, Volunteers in Action, League of Women Voters, Minnesota Public Interest Research Group, Women of Color, clubs for majors, women's issues groups.

Athletics. NCAA. **Intercollegiate:** Basketball W, cross-country W, diving W, golf W, ice hockey W, soccer W, softball W, swimming W, tennis W, track and field W, volleyball W. **Intramural:** Basketball W, cheerleading W, football (non-tackle) W, golf W, lacrosse W, racquetball W, soccer W, softball W, tennis W, volleyball W. **Team name:** Wildcats.

Student services. Adult student services, chaplain/spiritual director, career counseling, student employment services, financial aid counseling, health services, minority student services, on-campus daycare, personal counseling, placement for graduates, women's services. **Physically disabled:** Services for visually, speech, hearing impaired.

Contact. E-mail: admissions@stkate.edu
Phone: (651) 690-8850 Toll-free number: (800) 945-4599
Fax: (651) 690-8868
Marlene Mohs, Associate Dean of Admissions, St. Catherine University, 2004 Randolph Avenue #F-02, St. Paul, MN 55105

St. John's University
Collegeville, Minnesota
www.csbsju.edu

CB member
CB code: 6624

- Private 4-year university and liberal arts college affiliated with the Roman Catholic Church
- Residential campus in rural community
- 1,742 degree-seeking undergraduates: 2% part-time, 3% African American, 3% Asian American, 6% Hispanic/Latino, 1% Native American, 1% Multi-racial, non-Hispanic, 5% international
- 127 graduate students
- 74% of applicants admitted
- SAT or ACT (ACT writing optional) required
- 77% graduate within 6 years; 15% enter graduate study

General. Founded in 1857. Regionally accredited. Located six miles from the College of Saint Benedict; students enrolled on both campuses have access to facilities, classes, activities and events held by the two institutions. **Degrees:** 402 bachelor's awarded; master's offered. **ROTC:** Army. **Location:** 75 miles from Minneapolis-St. Paul, 15 miles from St. Cloud. **Calendar:** Semester, limited summer session. **Full-time faculty:** 139 total; 88% have terminal degrees, 9% minority, 50% women. **Part-time faculty:** 29 total; 45% have terminal degrees, 3% minority, 59% women. **Class size:** 59% < 20, 40% 20-39, less than 1% 40-49, less than 1% 50-99. **Special facilities:** Observatory, ecumenical center, museum and manuscript library, Liturgical Press, Saint John's Outdoor University, natural history museum, pottery studio and kiln, greenhouse, nature preserve and herbarium; labyrinth.

Freshman class profile. 1,607 applied, 1,191 admitted, 451 enrolled.

Mid 50% test scores		GPA 2.0-2.99:	17%
SAT critical reading:	470-560	Rank in top quarter:	48%
SAT math:	450-580	Rank in top tenth:	21%
SAT writing:	460-540	End year in good standing:	90%
ACT composite:	23-28	Return as sophomores:	85%
GPA 3.75 or higher:	28%	Out-of-state:	22%
GPA 3.50-3.74:	22%	Live on campus:	100%
GPA 3.0-3.49:	33%	International:	3%

Basis for selection. College preparatory curriculum, college entrance exams (ACT or SAT) and grade point average are important and carefully considered. Applicants should show promise of community contribution and productive participation in the classroom as evidenced by both their academic record and their participation in extra-curricular activities. Interview recommended for conditionally accepted/academically weak students. **Home schooled:** Applicants are not required to have a high school diploma, but are required to provide appropriate documentation of college preparatory curriculum. **Learning Disabled:** Diagnostic tests are required to determine the existence of most disabilities; we do not require specific exams. Accept documentation administered by qualified diagnosticians. Accommodations provided on case-by-case basis for students who provide adequate documentation of a disability.

High school preparation. College-preparatory program required. 15 units required. Required and recommended units include English 4, mathematics 3, social studies 2, science 2 (laboratory 2), foreign language 2 and academic electives 4.

2015-2016 Annual costs. Tuition/fees: $40,226. **Room/board:** $9,604. **Books/supplies:** $1,000. **Personal expenses:** $1,400.

2015-2016 Financial aid. Need-based: 388 full-time freshmen applied for aid; 340 deemed to have need; 340 received aid. Average need met was 93%. Average scholarship/grant was $28,696; average loan $2,530. 71% of total undergraduate aid awarded as scholarships/grants, 29% as loans/jobs. **Non-need-based:** Awarded to 1,528 full-time undergraduates, including 411 freshmen. Scholarships awarded for academics, alumni affiliation, art, leadership, music/drama, ROTC, state residency. **Additional information:** Scholarship letters will be mailed on rolling basis approximately 2 weeks from the time admission acceptance letter is sent.

Application procedures. Admission: Priority date 11/15; no deadline. No application fee. Must reply by 5/1. A non-refundable enrollment deposit of $300 is due by May 1. **Financial aid:** Priority date 3/15; no closing date. FAFSA, institutional form required. Applicants notified on a rolling basis starting 3/15; must reply by 5/1.

Academics. The Writing Center has some evening and weekend hours. **Special study options:** Combined bachelor's/graduate degree, cross-registration, double major, dual enrollment of high school students, ESL, honors, independent study, internships, student-designed major, study abroad, teacher certification program. 3-2 program in engineering and 3-1 program in dentistry with University of Minnesota, cross registration with St. Cloud State University. **Credit/placement by examination:** AP, CLEP, IB, SAT,

ACT, institutional tests. **Support services:** Reduced course load, study skills assistance, tutoring, writing center. Math skills center. Tutoring is not available for all departments.

Majors. Area/ethnic studies: Asian, women's. **Biology:** General, biochemistry. **Business:** Accounting, business admin. **Computer sciences:** Computer science. **Conservation:** Environmental science. **Education:** Elementary. **English:** English lit, rhetoric/composition. **Foreign languages:** Classics, French, German, Spanish. **Health services:** Dietetics, nursing (RN). **History:** General. **Liberal arts:** Arts/sciences, humanities. **Math:** General. **Philosophy/religion:** Philosophy. **Physical sciences:** Chemistry, physics. **Psychology:** General. **Social sciences:** General, economics, political science, sociology. **Theology:** Preministerial, theology. **Visual/performing arts:** Art, dramatic, music.

Most popular majors. Biology 14%, business/marketing 30%, English 7%, physical sciences 6%, social sciences 14%.

Technology on campus. 989 workstations in dormitories, library, computer center, student center. Dormitories wired for high-speed internet access and linked to campus network. Commuter students can connect to campus network. Online course registration, online library, helpline, repair service, student web hosting, wireless network available.

Student life. Freshman orientation: Mandatory. Preregistration for classes offered. Fall orientation begins the evening of move-in day and concludes with convocation the first day of classes. **Policies:** Four year residency requirement. **Housing:** Guaranteed on-campus for freshmen. Single-sex dorms, special housing for disabled, apartments, themed housing available. Eco-environmental houses and Benedictine Living community-associated with a 2 credit class. **Activities:** Bands, campus ministries, choral groups, dance, drama, film society, international student organizations, literary magazine, music ensembles, Model UN, musical theater, opera, radio station, student government, student newspaper, symphony orchestra, TV station, Volunteers in Service to Others, College Republicans, College Democrats, Joint Events Council, Asia Club, Alternative Spring Break, Students in Free Enterprise, Magis, Cultural Fusion Club, Outdoor Leadership Center.

Athletics. NCAA. **Intercollegiate:** Baseball M, basketball M, cross-country M, diving M, football (tackle) M, golf M, ice hockey M, soccer M, swimming M, tennis M, track and field M, wrestling M. **Intramural:** Basketball M, football (tackle) M, ice hockey M, racquetball M, soccer M, softball M, tennis M, volleyball M. **Team name:** Johnnies.

Student services. Alcohol/substance abuse counseling, chaplain/spiritual director, career counseling, financial aid counseling, health services, minority student services, personal counseling, placement for graduates. **Physically disabled:** Services for visually, hearing impaired.

Contact. E-mail: admissions@csbsju.edu
Phone: (320) 363-5060 Toll-free number: (800) 544-1489
Fax: (320) 363-5650
Calvin Mosley, Vice President for Admission and Financial Aid, St. John's University, College of St Benedict/St John's University, Collegeville, MN 56321-7155

St. Mary's University of Minnesota

Winona, Minnesota
www.smumn.edu

CB member
CB code: 6632

- Private 4-year university affiliated with the Roman Catholic Church
- Residential campus in large town
- 1,718 degree-seeking undergraduates: 29% part-time, 54% women, 7% African American, 2% Asian American, 5% Hispanic/Latino, 1% Multiracial, non-Hispanic, 3% international
- 3,840 degree-seeking graduate students
- 78% of applicants admitted
- SAT or ACT (ACT writing optional), application essay required
- 61% graduate within 6 years; 10% enter graduate study

General. Founded in 1912. Regionally accredited. **Degrees:** 537 bachelor's awarded; master's, professional, doctoral offered. **ROTC:** Army. **Location:** 110 miles from Minneapolis-St. Paul, 45 miles from Rochester. **Calendar:** Semester, limited summer session. **Full-time faculty:** 99 total; 90% have terminal degrees, 6% minority, 40% women. **Part-time faculty:** 461 total; 42% have terminal degrees, 9% minority, 55% women. **Class size:** 67% < 20, 33% 20-39. **Special facilities:** Disc golf course, running, skiing and hiking trails, challenge ropes course, over 100 acres of forest with trails and creek.

Freshman class profile. 1,447 applied, 1,123 admitted, 277 enrolled.

Mid 50% test scores			
SAT critical reading:	450-550	GPA 2.0-2.99:	31%
SAT math:	420-550	Rank in top quarter:	39%
SAT writing:	420-540	Rank in top tenth:	17%
ACT composite:	19-26	Return as sophomores:	80%
GPA 3.75 or higher:	28%	Out-of-state:	39%
GPA 3.50-3.74:	15%	Live on campus:	99%
GPA 3.0-3.49:	26%	International:	3%

Basis for selection. Minimum 2.5 GPA, upper half of class, 50th percentile on standardized tests, essay, college prep coursework required. Recommendations, interview, school and community activities considered. Interview recommended for academically marginal students. **Home schooled:** Statement describing home school structure and mission, transcript of courses and grades required.

High school preparation. College-preparatory program required. 18 units required. Required and recommended units include English 4, mathematics 3, social studies 2, science 3 (laboratory 2), foreign language 2 and academic electives 6.

2016-2017 Annual costs. Tuition/fees (projected): $32,575. Room/board: $8,635. Books/supplies: $1,300. Personal expenses: $890.

2015-2016 Financial aid. Need-based: 243 full-time freshmen applied for aid; 214 deemed to have need; 214 received aid. Average need met was 81%. Average scholarship/grant was $23,138; average loan $2,216. 65% of total undergraduate aid awarded as scholarships/grants, 35% as loans/jobs. **Non-need-based:** Awarded to 291 full-time undergraduates, including 61 freshmen. Scholarships awarded for academics, alumni affiliation, art, leadership, minority status, music/drama.

Application procedures. Admission: Priority date 4/1; deadline 5/1 (postmark date). $25 fee, may be waived for applicants with need, free for online applicants. Admission notification by 5/1. Admission notification on a rolling basis. Must reply by May 1 or within 2 week(s) if notified thereafter. **Financial aid:** Priority date 3/15; no closing date. FAFSA required. Applicants notified on a rolling basis starting 2/1; must reply within 3 week(s) of notification.

Academics. Special study options: Cooperative education, cross-registration, distance learning, double major, dual enrollment of high school students, ESL, honors, independent study, internships, student-designed major, study abroad, teacher certification program, urban semester, Washington semester. **Credit/placement by examination:** AP, CLEP, IB, SAT, ACT, institutional tests. 15 credit hours maximum toward bachelor's degree. **Support services:** Learning center, reduced course load, remedial instruction, study skills assistance, tutoring, writing center.

Majors. Biology: General, biochemistry, environmental. **Business:** General, accounting, actuarial science, entrepreneurial studies, finance, human resources, international, management science, marketing, sales/distribution. **Communications:** Journalism, persuasive communications. **Communications technology:** Desktop publishing. **Computer sciences:** Computer science, information systems. **Education:** Biology, chemistry, elementary, English, mathematics, music, physics, social science, Spanish. **Engineering:** Applied physics. **English:** General lit. **Foreign languages:** Spanish. **Health services:** Clinical lab science, cytotechnology, electrocardiograph technology, nuclear medical technology, nursing (RN), prephysical therapy, radiologic technology/medical imaging. **History:** General. **Math:** General. **Philosophy/religion:** Christian, philosophy. **Physical sciences:** Chemistry, physics. **Protective services:** Police science. **Psychology:** General. **Social sciences:** General, political science, sociology. **Theology:** Lay ministry, religious ed, theology. **Visual/performing arts:** Dramatic, graphic design, music, music performance, studio arts.

Most popular majors. Biology 6%, business/marketing 42%, education 6%, health sciences 9%, security/protective services 6%, visual/performing arts 6%.

Technology on campus. 365 workstations in dormitories, library, computer center, student center. Dormitories wired for high-speed internet access and linked to campus network. Commuter students can connect to campus network. Online course registration, online library, helpline, student web hosting, wireless network available.

Student life. Freshman orientation: Mandatory. Preregistration for classes offered. Held during summer prior to fall enrollment. **Housing:** Guaranteed on-campus for all undergraduates. Coed dorms, single-sex dorms, special housing for disabled, apartments available. Living learning communities for freshmen. **Activities:** Bands, campus ministries, choral groups, dance, drama, international student organizations, literary magazine, music ensembles, musical theater, radio station, student government, student newspaper, Big and Little Pals, College Democrats, College Republicans, Serving Others United in Love, Intercultural Awareness Association, liturgical ministers, BUDDIES, Habitat for Humanity, Colleges Against Cancer.

Athletics. NCAA. **Intercollegiate:** Baseball M, basketball, cross-country, diving, golf, ice hockey, soccer, softball W, swimming, tennis, track and field, volleyball W. **Intramural:** Basketball, football (non-tackle), handball, ice hockey, soccer, softball, ultimate frisbee, volleyball. **Team name:** Cardinals.

Student services. Alcohol/substance abuse counseling, chaplain/spiritual director, career counseling, financial aid counseling, health services, personal counseling, veterans' counselor. **Physically disabled:** Services for visually, hearing impaired.

Contact. E-mail: admission@smumn.edu
Phone: (507) 457-1700 Toll-free number: (800) 635-5987
Fax: (507) 457-1722
Mark Kormann, Assistant Vice President Admission, St. Mary's University of Minnesota, 700 Terrace Heights #2, Winona, MN 55987-1399

St. Olaf College
Northfield, Minnesota　　　　　　　　　**CB member**
www.stolaf.edu　　　　　　　　　　**CB code: 6638**

- Private 4-year liberal arts college affiliated with the Evangelical Lutheran Church in America
- Residential campus in large town
- 3,005 degree-seeking undergraduates: 57% women, 2% African American, 6% Asian American, 5% Hispanic/Latino, 4% Multi-racial, non-Hispanic, 7% international
- 36% of applicants admitted
- SAT or ACT (ACT writing optional), application essay required
- 87% graduate within 6 years; 19% enter graduate study

General. Founded in 1874. Regionally accredited. **Degrees:** 677 bachelor's awarded. **Location:** 35 miles from Minneapolis-St. Paul. **Calendar:** 4-1-4, limited summer session. **Full-time faculty:** 213 total; 93% have terminal degrees, 13% minority, 46% women. **Part-time faculty:** 120 total; 56% have terminal degrees, 8% minority, 51% women. **Class size:** 54% < 20, 41% 20-39, 2% 40-49, 3% 50-99, less than 1% >100. **Special facilities:** 325 acres of restored wetlands, woodlands, and native tallgrass prairie, utility-grade wind turbine, student-run organic farm.

Freshman class profile. 7,571 applied, 2,723 admitted, 763 enrolled.

Mid 50% test scores			
SAT critical reading:	560-710	Rank in top quarter:	77%
SAT math:	580-700	Rank in top tenth:	43%
ACT composite:	26-31	End year in good standing:	95%
GPA 3.75 or higher:	46%	Return as sophomores:	93%
GPA 3.50-3.74:	20%	Out-of-state:	53%
GPA 3.0-3.49:	25%	Live on campus:	100%
GPA 2.0-2.99:	9%	International:	9%

Basis for selection. Academic achievement most important, with academic aptitude and personal qualifications, as well as leadership and significant involvement in school and community, strongly considered. Interview recommended. Audition required for music students. **Home schooled:** Statement describing home school structure and mission, letter of recommendation (nonparent) required. Interview preferred. **Learning Disabled:** Personal interview recommended. Untimed standardized tests accepted.

High school preparation. College-preparatory program required. 20 units recommended. Recommended units include English 4, mathematics 4, social studies 4, science 4 (laboratory 2) and foreign language 4.

2015-2016 Annual costs. Tuition/fees: $42,940. Room/board: $9,790. Books/supplies: $1,000.

2015-2016 Financial aid. Need-based: 633 full-time freshmen applied for aid; 515 deemed to have need; 515 received aid. Average need met was 99%. Average scholarship/grant was $32,224; average loan $3,674. 86% of total undergraduate aid awarded as scholarships/grants, 14% as loans/jobs. **Non-need-based:** Awarded to 1,114 full-time undergraduates, including 306 freshmen. Scholarships awarded for academics, art, leadership, music/drama. **Additional information:** Limited number of music lesson fee waivers available for music majors, awarded on audition basis only.

Application procedures. Admission: Closing date 1/15 (postmark date). No application fee. Admission notification by 3/20. Must reply by 5/1. **Financial aid:** Priority date 2/1, closing date 3/1. FAFSA required. CSS PROFILE due February 1. Applicants notified by 4/1; must reply by 5/1.

Academics. Students may propose self-designed integrative majors. **Special study options:** Cross-registration, double major, dual enrollment of high

school students, independent study, internships, student-designed major, study abroad, teacher certification program, urban semester, Washington semester. **Credit/placement by examination:** AP, CLEP, IB, SAT, ACT, institutional tests. Maximum of six St. Olaf-equivalent credits (one course = one credit) awarded from among all pre-college (PSEO/CIS/AP/IB) credits presented by matriculating first-year students. St. Olaf does not offer credit for any other exams. **Support services:** Learning center, pre-admission summer program, reduced course load, study skills assistance, tutoring, writing center.

Majors. Area/ethnic studies: General, American, Asian, Latin American, Russian/Slavic, women's. **Biology:** General. **Computer sciences:** Computer science. **Conservation:** Environmental studies. **Education:** Music, social studies. **English:** English lit. **Foreign languages:** Ancient Greek, classics, French, German, Latin, Norwegian, Russian, Spanish. **Health services:** Nursing (RN). **History:** General. **Human services:** Social work. **Liberal arts:** Arts/sciences. **Math:** General. **Parks/recreation:** Exercise sciences. **Philosophy/religion:** Philosophy, religion. **Physical sciences:** Chemistry, physics. **Psychology:** General. **Social sciences:** Economics, political science, sociology/anthropology. **Theology:** Sacred music. **Visual/performing arts:** Art, art history/conservation, dance, dramatic, music, music performance, music theory/composition.

Most popular majors. Area/ethnic studies 7%, biology 12%, English 7%, mathematics 8%, physical sciences 7%, psychology 8%, social sciences 17%, visual/performing arts 10%.

Technology on campus. 824 workstations in dormitories, library, computer center, student center. Dormitories wired for high-speed internet access and linked to campus network. Commuter students can connect to campus network. Online course registration, online library, helpline, student web hosting, wireless network available.

Student life. Freshman orientation: Mandatory. Preregistration for classes offered. Held 5 days before start of fall classes. **Policies:** Alcohol not permitted on campus. **Housing:** Guaranteed on-campus for freshmen. Coed dorms, special housing for disabled, themed housing available. Honor houses, language houses, quiet houses, first-year-only dorms available. **Activities:** Bands, campus ministries, choral groups, dance, drama, film society, international student organizations, literary magazine, music ensembles, Model UN, musical theater, opera, radio station, student government, student newspaper, symphony orchestra, 221 registered student organizations.

Athletics. NCAA. **Intercollegiate:** Baseball M, basketball, cross-country, diving, football (tackle) M, golf, ice hockey, skiing, soccer, softball W, swimming, tennis, track and field, volleyball W, wrestling M. **Intramural:** Basketball, bowling, football (non-tackle), golf, soccer, softball, swimming, table tennis, triathlon, ultimate frisbee, volleyball, wrestling. **Team name:** Oles.

Student services. Alcohol/substance abuse counseling, chaplain/spiritual director, career counseling, services for economically disadvantaged, student employment services, financial aid counseling, health services, minority student services, personal counseling. **Physically disabled:** Services for visually, hearing impaired.

Contact. E-mail: admissions@stolaf.edu
Phone: (507) 786-3025 Toll-free number: (800) 800-3025
Fax: (507) 786-3832
David Wagner, Director of Admissions, St. Olaf College, 1520 St. Olaf Avenue, Northfield, MN 55057

University of Minnesota: Crookston
Crookston, Minnesota
www.crk.umn.edu　　　　　　　　　**CB code: 6893**

- Public 4-year branch campus college
- Residential campus in small town
- 1,874 degree-seeking undergraduates: 37% part-time, 51% women, 7% African American, 2% Asian American, 4% Hispanic/Latino, 2% Multi-racial, non-Hispanic, 5% international
- 78% of applicants admitted
- SAT or ACT (ACT writing optional) required
- 45% graduate within 6 years

General. Founded in 1965. Regionally accredited. **Degrees:** 401 bachelor's awarded. **ROTC:** Air Force. **Location:** 25 miles from Grand Forks, ND; 70 miles from Fargo, ND. **Calendar:** Semester, limited summer session. **Full-time faculty:** 71 total; 46% have terminal degrees, 10% minority, 45% women. **Part-time faculty:** 45 total; 16% have terminal degrees, 9% minority, 53% women. **Class size:** 62% < 20, 35% 20-39, 2% 40-49, 1% 50-99. **Special facilities:** 85-acre Red River Valley Natural History Area containing prairie, marshes, and forests; visualization and informatics lab, telescope.

Freshman class profile. 1,073 applied, 839 admitted, 239 enrolled.

Mid 50% test scores		GPA 2.0-2.99:	32%
SAT critical reading:	430-530	Rank in top quarter:	37%
SAT math:	450-560	Rank in top tenth:	11%
SAT writing:	400-510	Return as sophomores:	65%
ACT composite:	19-25	Out-of-state:	32%
GPA 3.75 or higher:	25%	Live on campus:	90%
GPA 3.50-3.74:	14%	International:	5%
GPA 3.0-3.49:	26%	Fraternities:	1%

Basis for selection. High school class rank and ACT test scores most important. ACT recommended. **Learning Disabled:** Students encouraged to contact Disability Services early in the admissions process to insure availability of appropriate services.

High school preparation. College-preparatory program recommended. 13 units required. Required and recommended units include English 4, mathematics 3, social studies 3, science 3 (laboratory 2) and foreign language 2.

2015-2016 Annual costs. Tuition/fees: $11,646; $11,646 out-of-state. Room/board: $7,506. Books/supplies: $1,000. Personal expenses: $1,540.

2015-2016 Financial aid. Need-based: 196 full-time freshmen applied for aid; 151 deemed to have need; 150 received aid. Average need met was 76%. Average scholarship/grant was $9,760; average loan $3,300. 52% of total undergraduate aid awarded as scholarships/grants, 48% as loans/jobs. **Non-need-based:** Awarded to 193 full-time undergraduates, including 70 freshmen. Scholarships awarded for academics, alumni affiliation, athletics, leadership, minority status, music/drama, ROTC, state residency. **Additional information:** Under the University of Minnesota Promise Scholarship (U Promise), eligible new Minnesota resident undergraduates with a family income of up to $100,000 will be guaranteed a U Promise Scholarship. Eligible new freshman and transfer students enrolling for the first time will receive a guaranteed, multi-year, U Promise Scholarship. Eligible new freshmen will receive a guaranteed need-based scholarship, ranging from $500 to $3,500 each year, for four years. Eligible new transfer students will receive a guaranteed, need-based scholarship, ranging from $500 to $1,500 each year, for two years.

Application procedures. Admission: Priority date 2/1; no deadline. $30 fee, may be waived for applicants with need. Admission notification on a rolling basis beginning on or about 9/1. **Financial aid:** Priority date 3/1; no closing date. FAFSA required. Applicants notified on a rolling basis starting 3/1; must reply within 8 week(s) of notification.

Academics. Special study options: Cross-registration, distance learning, double major, dual enrollment of high school students, ESL, honors, independent study, internships, student-designed major, study abroad, teacher certification program. **Credit/placement by examination:** AP, CLEP, IB, ACT, institutional tests. Proficiency examinations are administered by appropriate academic department, require no fee, and yield no credit or grade but may fulfill prerequisites for advanced courses or satisfy requirements. Special Examinations for Credit have fee of $50 per credit. Credits earned by examination do not count as residence credits. Exams given at discretion of appropriate academic department. **Support services:** Learning center, reduced course load, remedial instruction, study skills assistance, tutoring, writing center.

Majors. Biology: General. **Business:** Accounting, business admin, entrepreneurial studies, hospitality admin, management information systems, marketing, operations. **Communications:** General. **Computer sciences:** Information technology. **Conservation:** General, enforcement, urban forestry, water/wetlands/marine. **Education:** Early childhood, environmental, kindergarten/preschool, technology/industrial arts. **Engineering:** Software. **Health services:** Health care admin, preveterinary. **Parks/recreation:** Facilities management, sports admin. **Protective services:** Corrections, law enforcement admin.

Most popular majors. Agriculture 20%, business/marketing 37%, health sciences 11%, interdisciplinary studies 6%, natural resources/environmental science 13%.

Technology on campus. PC or laptop required. 50 workstations in library. Dormitories wired for high-speed internet access and linked to campus network. Commuter students can connect to campus network. Online course registration, online library, helpline, repair service, student web hosting, wireless network available.

Student life. Freshman orientation: Mandatory, $75 fee. Preregistration for classes offered. The new student orientation program for the fall term begins three days before the first day of class; for the spring term begins the weekend before the first day of class. **Housing:** Coed dorms, special housing for disabled, apartments available. $100 nonrefundable deposit, deadline 9/1. **Activities:** Pep band, campus ministries, choral groups, drama, international student organizations, musical theater, student government, multicultural club, UMC Ambassadors, Students in Free Enterprise, Wildlife Society Chapter, Collegiate FFA, flying club, Habitat for Humanity, Rodeo Association, Student Athletic Advisory Committee.

Athletics. NCAA. **Intercollegiate:** Baseball M, basketball, equestrian W, football (tackle) M, golf, soccer W, softball W, tennis W, volleyball W. **Intramural:** Basketball, football (non-tackle), golf, racquetball, soccer, softball, table tennis, tennis, volleyball. **Team name:** Golden Eagles.

Student services. Adult student services, alcohol/substance abuse counseling, chaplain/spiritual director, career counseling, student employment services, financial aid counseling, health services, minority student services, on-campus daycare, personal counseling, placement for graduates, veterans' counselor, women's services. **Physically disabled:** Services for visually, hearing impaired.

Contact. E-mail: umcinfo@umn.edu
Phone: (218) 281-8569 Toll-free number: (800) 862-6466
Fax: (218) 281-8575 ext. 369
Carola Thorson, Director of Admissions, University of Minnesota: Crookston, 2900 University Avenue, Crookston, MN 56716-5001

University of Minnesota: Duluth
Duluth, Minnesota
www.d.umn.edu   CB code: 6873

▸ Public 4-year university
▸ Residential campus in small city
▸ 8,929 degree-seeking undergraduates: 5% part-time, 45% women, 2% African American, 3% Asian American, 3% Hispanic/Latino, 3% Multiracial, non-Hispanic, 2% international
▸ 1,007 degree-seeking graduate students
▸ 76% of applicants admitted
▸ SAT or ACT (ACT writing optional) required
▸ 60% graduate within 6 years

General. Founded in 1947. Regionally accredited. **Degrees:** 2,007 bachelor's awarded; master's, doctoral offered. **ROTC:** Air Force. **Location:** 150 miles from Minneapolis-St. Paul. **Calendar:** Semester, extensive summer session. **Full-time faculty:** 500 total; 72% have terminal degrees, 17% minority, 43% women. **Part-time faculty:** 111 total; 28% have terminal degrees, 8% minority, 45% women. **Class size:** 34% < 20, 45% 20-39, 4% 40-49, 11% 50-99, 6% >100. **Special facilities:** Planetarium, art museum, music performance hall, performing arts center, visual imaging laboratory, multicultural center, American Indian Learning Resource Center, nature center, Large Lakes Observatory and Blue Heron research vessel, natural resources research institute, coleraine minerals research lab, neutrino detector laboratory, farm and research center.

Freshman class profile. 7,491 applied, 5,696 admitted, 1,997 enrolled.

Mid 50% test scores		GPA 2.0-2.99:	9%
SAT critical reading:	470-610	Rank in top quarter:	44%
SAT math:	490-590	Rank in top tenth:	19%
SAT writing:	440-570	End year in good standing:	83%
ACT composite:	22-26	Return as sophomores:	76%
GPA 3.75 or higher:	26%	Out-of-state:	12%
GPA 3.50-3.74:	24%	Live on campus:	93%
GPA 3.0-3.49:	41%	International:	1%

Basis for selection. Overall assessment of each student's academic preparation and performance. Primary factors include completion of high school preparation requirements, high school grade point average, and ACT/SAT scores. Essays or personal statements considered in an admissions decision appeals process. Audition required for music students. **Learning Disabled:** Students must meet our general admission policy.

High school preparation. College-preparatory program required. 17 units required. Required units include English 4, mathematics 4, social studies 3, science 3, foreign language 2 and visual/performing arts 1. One year of physical and biological science required. Mathematics requirements: two years of algebra, one of which must be intermediate or advanced algebra, and one year of geometry. Social studies should include one year each of geography and American History. Visual and performing arts courses and computer skills courses strongly recommended.

2015-2016 Annual costs. Tuition/fees: $13,082; $17,032 out-of-state. Room/board: $7,210. Books/supplies: $1,200. Personal expenses: $2,000.

2014-2015 Financial aid. Need-based: 1,958 full-time freshmen applied for aid; 1,307 deemed to have need; 1,272 received aid. Average need met was 68%. Average scholarship/grant was $8,276; average loan $3,933. 48% of total undergraduate aid awarded as scholarships/grants, 52% as loans/jobs. **Non-need-based:** Awarded to 1,963 full-time undergraduates, including 568 freshmen. Scholarships awarded for academics, alumni affiliation, art, athletics, music/drama, ROTC, state residency.

Application procedures. Admission: Priority date 12/15; deadline 8/1 (receipt date). $40 fee, may be waived for applicants with need. Admission notification on a rolling basis beginning on or about 9/15. Must reply by May 1 or within 3 week(s) if notified thereafter. **Financial aid:** Priority date 3/1; no closing date. FAFSA required. Applicants notified on a rolling basis starting 3/1.

Academics. Special study options: Accelerated study, combined bachelor's/graduate degree, cooperative education, cross-registration, distance learning, double major, dual enrollment of high school students, ESL, exchange student, honors, independent study, internships, liberal arts/career combination, semester at sea, student-designed major, study abroad, teacher certification program, weekend college. **Credit/placement by examination:** AP, CLEP, IB, ACT, institutional tests. Less than 50% of total credits examination may be counted towards major, minor or liberal education program. **Support services:** Learning center, reduced course load, remedial instruction, study skills assistance, tutoring, writing center. Supplemental instruction, advising for underprepared students. The Learning Commons, a consortium of four academic support programs: Supportive Services Program (including tutoring), writers' workshop, reference librarians, and multimedia hub.

Majors. Area/ethnic studies: Chinese, Latin American, Native American, women's. **Biology:** General, biochemistry, biomedical sciences, cell/histology. **Business:** Accounting, business admin, entrepreneurial studies, finance, financial planning, marketing. **Communications:** General. **Communications technology:** Printing management. **Computer sciences:** Computer science, networking. **Conservation:** Environmental science, environmental studies. **Education:** Art, foreign languages, kindergarten/preschool, mathematics, music, physical, science, social studies. **Engineering:** Chemical, civil, electrical, industrial, mechanical. **English:** English lit. **Foreign languages:** French, German, linguistics, Spanish. **Health services:** Communication disorders, health care admin, public health ed. **History:** General. **Math:** General, statistics. **Parks/recreation:** General, exercise sciences. **Philosophy/religion:** Philosophy. **Physical sciences:** Chemistry, geology, physics. **Psychology:** General. **Social sciences:** Anthropology, criminology, economics, geography, GIS/cartography, international relations, political science, sociology, urban studies. **Visual/performing arts:** Art, art history/conservation, commercial/advertising art, dramatic, jazz, music, music performance, music theory/composition, studio arts.

Most popular majors. Biology 10%, business/marketing 18%, communications/journalism 6%, education 8%, engineering/engineering technologies 12%, psychology 8%, social sciences 9%.

Technology on campus. PC or laptop required. 468 workstations in library, computer center, student center. Dormitories wired for high-speed internet access and linked to campus network. Commuter students can connect to campus network. Online course registration, online library, helpline, repair service, student web hosting, wireless network available.

Student life. Freshman orientation: Mandatory, $80 fee. Preregistration for classes offered. Held in June, July and August. **Policies:** Smoke and alcohol free campus. **Housing:** Coed dorms, single-sex dorms, special housing for disabled, apartments, themed housing available. $200 nonrefundable deposit, deadline 5/1. Housing facilities are fully accessible to persons with physical disabilities. All facilities are smoke free. **Activities:** Bands, campus ministries, choral groups, dance, drama, film society, international student organizations, music ensembles, musical theater, opera, radio station, student government, student newspaper, symphony orchestra, Intervarsity Christian Fellowship, Minnesota Public Interest Research Group, Anishinabe club, Black student association, Queer and Allied Students Union, Spanish Club, Chinese Student and Scholar Association, Cru, College Democrats, veterans club.

Athletics. NCAA. **Intercollegiate:** Baseball M, basketball, cross-country, football (tackle) M, ice hockey, soccer W, softball W, tennis W, track and field, volleyball W. **Intramural:** Badminton, basketball, bowling, football (non-tackle), golf, ice hockey, soccer, softball, table tennis, tennis, volleyball, water polo. **Team name:** Bulldogs.

Student services. Adult student services, alcohol/substance abuse counseling, chaplain/spiritual director, career counseling, student employment services, financial aid counseling, health services, minority student services, on-campus daycare, personal counseling, placement for graduates, veterans' counselor, women's services. **Physically disabled:** Services for visually, speech, hearing impaired.

Contact. E-mail: umdadmis@d.umn.edu
Phone: (218) 726-7171 Toll-free number: (800) 232-1339
Fax: (218) 726-7040
Scott Schulz, Director of Undergraduate Recruitment, University of Minnesota: Duluth, Solon Campus Center 25, Duluth, MN 55812-3000

University of Minnesota: Morris
Morris, Minnesota
www.morris.umn.edu   CB code: 6890

▶ Public 4-year university and liberal arts college
▶ Residential campus in small town
▶ 1,741 degree-seeking undergraduates: 4% part-time, 54% women, 2% African American, 3% Asian American, 4% Hispanic/Latino, 6% Native American, 11% Multi-racial, non-Hispanic, 11% international
▶ 60% of applicants admitted
▶ SAT or ACT with writing required
▶ 67% graduate within 6 years; 22% enter graduate study

General. Founded in 1959. Regionally accredited. **Degrees:** 374 bachelor's awarded. **Location:** 150 miles from Minneapolis-St. Paul; 100 miles from Fargo, ND. **Calendar:** Semester, limited summer session. **Full-time faculty:** 126 total; 82% have terminal degrees, 13% minority, 42% women. **Part-time faculty:** 40 total; 22% have terminal degrees, 12% minority, 52% women. **Class size:** 66% < 20, 28% 20-39, 3% 40-49, 3% 50-99, less than 1% >100. **Special facilities:** Tropical conservatory, prairie gate press, historical center, experiment station, USDA soil laboratory, center for small towns, observatory.

Freshman class profile. 3,619 applied, 2,164 admitted, 416 enrolled.

Mid 50% test scores			
SAT critical reading:	500-660	GPA 2.0-2.99:	5%
SAT math:	510-640	Rank in top quarter:	55%
SAT writing:	490-620	Rank in top tenth:	24%
ACT composite:	22-28	End year in good standing:	90%
GPA 3.75 or higher:	42%	Return as sophomores:	77%
GPA 3.50-3.74:	24%	Out-of-state:	15%
GPA 3.0-3.49:	28%	Live on campus:	98%
		International:	5%

Basis for selection. Four primary factors: high school performance, ACT/SAT scores, extra-curricular involvement/leadership, experience/honors. Interview recommended. Audition required for music students receiving scholarships and for placement in bands/combos. **Home schooled:** Submit portfolio of works studied.

High school preparation. College-preparatory program required. 16 units required. Required units include English 4, mathematics 4, social studies 3, science 3 and foreign language 2. Science units must include 1 biological science and 1 physical science. Social Studies includes U.S. history.

2015-2016 Annual costs. Tuition/fees: $12,846; $12,846 out-of-state. Room/board: $7,804. Books/supplies: $900. Personal expenses: $1,600.

2015-2016 Financial aid. Need-based: 374 full-time freshmen applied for aid; 279 deemed to have need; 278 received aid. Average need met was 81%. Average scholarship/grant was $10,921; average loan $3,168. 68% of total undergraduate aid awarded as scholarships/grants, 32% as loans/jobs. **Non-need-based:** Awarded to 305 full-time undergraduates, including 106 freshmen. Scholarships awarded for academics. **Additional information:** Land-grant program waiving tuition for Native Americans.

Application procedures. Admission: Priority date 12/15; deadline 3/15 (postmark date). $35 fee, may be waived for applicants with need. Admission notification on a rolling basis beginning on or about 9/15. Must reply by May 1 or within 2 week(s) if notified thereafter. **Financial aid:** No deadline. FAFSA required. Applicants notified on a rolling basis starting 4/1.

Academics. Academic opportunities that allow students to assist faculty in research or teaching endeavors and receive a stipend or expense allowances include: The Undergraduate Research Opportunities Program, The Morris Academic Partnership, The Minority Mentorship Program, The Morris Administrative Internship, and The Student Internship Program. **Special study options:** Combined bachelor's/graduate degree, cross-registration, distance learning, double major, dual enrollment of high school students, ESL, exchange student, honors, independent study, internships, New York semester, semester at sea, student-designed major, study abroad, teacher certification program, United Nations semester, urban semester, Washington semester. **Credit/placement by examination:** AP, CLEP, IB, SAT, ACT, institutional tests. No limit for credit by exam, but the credit awarded does not count as resident credit; must have 30 resident credits. **Support services:** Learning center, pre-admission summer program, reduced course load, study skills assistance, tutoring, writing center.

Majors. Area/ethnic studies: European, Latin American, Native American, women's. **Biology:** General. **Business:** Management science. **Communications:** Communications/speech/rhetoric. **Computer sciences:** Computer science. **Conservation:** Environmental studies. **Education:** Elementary. **English:** English lit. **Foreign languages:** French, German, Spanish. **History:** General. **Human services:** Social work. **Liberal arts:** Humanities. **Math:**

General, statistics. **Philosophy/religion:** Philosophy. **Physical sciences:** Chemistry, geology, physics. **Psychology:** General. **Social sciences:** Anthropology, economics, political science, sociology. **Visual/performing arts:** Art history/conservation, dramatic, music, music performance, studio arts.

Most popular majors. Biology 11%, business/marketing 8%, education 6%, English 12%, physical sciences 10%, psychology 10%, social sciences 13%.

Technology on campus. 220 workstations in dormitories, library, computer center, student center. Dormitories wired for high-speed internet access and linked to campus network. Commuter students can connect to campus network. Online course registration, online library, helpline, repair service, wireless network available.

Student life. Freshman orientation: Mandatory. Preregistration for classes offered. Held 4 days prior to fall semester. **Housing:** Guaranteed on-campus for all undergraduates. Coed dorms, special housing for disabled, apartments, themed housing available. $50 nonrefundable deposit, deadline 5/1. **Activities:** Bands, campus ministries, choral groups, dance, drama, international student organizations, literary magazine, music ensembles, musical theater, radio station, student government, student newspaper, symphony orchestra, Amnesty International, Big Friend/Little Friend, Campus Aglow Outreach, E-Quality, Habitat for Humanity, Intervarsity Christian Fellowship, Minnesota Public Interest Research Group, Morris Campus Student Association, Positive Spirituality, Women of Color Association.

Athletics. NCAA. **Intercollegiate:** Baseball M, basketball, cross-country, diving W, football (tackle) M, golf, soccer, softball W, swimming W, tennis, track and field, volleyball W. **Intramural:** Baseball, basketball, bowling, field hockey, football (non-tackle), ice hockey, softball, triathlon, volleyball. **Team name:** Cougars.

Student services. Alcohol/substance abuse counseling, career counseling, student employment services, financial aid counseling, health services, minority student services, personal counseling, placement for graduates, veterans' counselor, women's services. **Physically disabled:** Services for visually, speech, hearing impaired.

Contact. Phone: (320) 589-6035 Toll-free number: (888) 866-3382 Fax: (320) 589-6051
Ben Iverson, Director of Admission, University of Minnesota: Morris, 600 E. 4th St., Morris, MN 56267

University of Minnesota: Rochester
Rochester, Minnesota
http://r.umn.edu   CB code: 5877

- Public 4-year university and health science college
- Residential campus in small city
- 402 degree-seeking undergraduates: 3% part-time, 72% women, 6% African American, 9% Asian American, 3% Hispanic/Latino, 2% Multiracial, non-Hispanic, 1% international
- 28% of applicants admitted
- SAT or ACT with writing, application essay required
- 60% graduate within 6 years

General. Regionally accredited. **Degrees:** 109 bachelor's awarded. **Location:** 90 miles from Minneapolis-St Paul. **Calendar:** Semester, limited summer session. **Full-time faculty:** 36 total; 64% have terminal degrees, 17% minority, 47% women. **Part-time faculty:** 1 total; 100% have terminal degrees, 100% women. **Class size:** 70% < 20, 27% 20-39, 3% 50-99.

Freshman class profile. 803 applied, 221 admitted, 88 enrolled.

Mid 50% test scores		Return as sophomores:	66%
ACT composite:	22-26	Out-of-state:	21%
Rank in top quarter:	63%	Live on campus:	83%
Rank in top tenth:	21%	International:	1%

Basis for selection. Applications are reviewed holistically. Review factors include high school and college GPA, GPA in STEM courses, ACT with Writing or SAT scores, application essay, and high school rank.

High school preparation. College-preparatory program required. Required and recommended units include English 4, mathematics 4, social studies 3, science 3-4 (laboratory 3).

2015-2016 Annual costs. Tuition/fees: $13,232; $13,232 out-of-state. Room/board: $9,440. Books/supplies: $1,000. Personal expenses: $2,000.

2015-2016 Financial aid. Need-based: 86 full-time freshmen applied for aid; 64 deemed to have need; 64 received aid. Average need met was 82%.

Average scholarship/grant was $10,270; average loan $3,332. 49% of total undergraduate aid awarded as scholarships/grants, 51% as loans/jobs. **Non-need-based:** Awarded to 58 full-time undergraduates, including 9 freshmen. Scholarships awarded for academics.

Application procedures. Admission: Priority date 12/15; no deadline. $35 fee, may be waived for applicants with need. Admission notification on a rolling basis beginning on or about 12/16. Must reply by May 1 or within 2 week(s) if notified thereafter. **Financial aid:** Priority date 3/1; no closing date. FAFSA required. Applicants notified on a rolling basis starting 3/15.

Academics. Special study options: Distance learning, exchange student, independent study, internships, study abroad. **Credit/placement by examination:** AP, CLEP, IB, institutional tests. **Support services:** Learning center, study skills assistance, tutoring, writing center.

Technology on campus. PC or laptop required. 12 workstations in library. Commuter students can connect to campus network. Online course registration, online library, repair service, wireless network available.

Student life. Freshman orientation: Mandatory. Preregistration for classes offered. **Housing:** Coed dorms, apartments, themed housing, wellness housing available. $100 nonrefundable deposit, deadline 5/1. **Activities:** Campus ministries, dance, international student organizations, student government, Helping Us Give Service, Active Minds, Chi Alpha, CRU - Rochester, intercultural club, Greek Exploratory Committee, Navigators, optimist club, Student Advocates for Public Health, pre-professional club.

Athletics. Intramural: Basketball, football (non-tackle), soccer, softball, table tennis, tennis, volleyball. **Team name:** Raptors.

Student services. Alcohol/substance abuse counseling, career counseling, student employment services, financial aid counseling, health services, legal services, personal counseling, veterans' counselor. **Physically disabled:** Services for visually, hearing impaired.

Contact. E-mail: applyumr@r.umn.edu
Phone: (507) 258-8686 Toll-free number: (877) 280-4699
Fax: (507) 258-8021
Director of Admissions, University of Minnesota: Rochester, 111 South Broadway, Suite 300, Rochester, MN 55904

University of Minnesota: Twin Cities
Minneapolis, Minnesota   CB member
www.umn.edu   CB code: 6874

- Public 4-year university
- Residential campus in very large city
- 30,511 degree-seeking undergraduates: 8% part-time, 51% women, 4% African American, 9% Asian American, 4% Hispanic/Latino, 4% Multiracial, non-Hispanic, 9% international
- 16,294 degree-seeking graduate students
- 45% of applicants admitted
- SAT or ACT with writing required
- 77% graduate within 6 years

General. Founded in 1851. Regionally accredited. Campuses in Minneapolis and St. Paul. **Degrees:** 7,553 bachelor's awarded; master's, professional, doctoral offered. **ROTC:** Army, Naval, Air Force. **Calendar:** Semester, extensive summer session. **Full-time faculty:** 2,589 total; 78% have terminal degrees, 17% minority, 42% women. **Part-time faculty:** 1,102 total; 49% have terminal degrees, 8% minority, 46% women. **Class size:** 38% < 20, 36% 20-39, 6% 40-49, 12% 50-99, 8% >100. **Special facilities:** West bank arts quarter, natural history museum, showboat, rehabilitation museum, arboretum, concert hall.

Freshman class profile. 46,165 applied, 20,579 admitted, 5,771 enrolled.

Mid 50% test scores		Rank in top tenth:	49%
SAT critical reading:	560-700	Return as sophomores:	93%
SAT math:	620-740	Out-of-state:	33%
SAT writing:	570-690	Live on campus:	89%
ACT composite:	26-31	International:	5%
Rank in top quarter:	85%		

Basis for selection. Successful completion of a college preparatory curriculum, high school rank percentile, grade point average, ACT or SAT scores, and strength of curriculum very important. Writing tests required. Results considered as secondary admission factor.

High school preparation. College-preparatory program required. 17 units required; 18 recommended. Required and recommended units include English 4, mathematics 4, social studies 3, science 3-4 (laboratory 1), foreign language

2 and visual/performing arts 1. Management, biological sciences, and technology applicants require a fourth year of mathematics and 3 years of science including 1 year each of biological science, chemistry, and physics.

2015-2016 Annual costs. Tuition/fees: $13,790; $22,210 out-of-state. Room/board: $9,314.

2015-2016 Financial aid. All financial aid based on need. 4,631 full-time freshmen applied for aid; 2,881 deemed to have need; 2,840 received aid. Average need met was 78%. Average scholarship/grant was $10,320; average loan $3,687. 57% of total undergraduate aid awarded as scholarships/grants, 43% as loans/jobs.

Application procedures. Admission: Priority date 12/15; no deadline. $55 fee, may be waived for applicants with need. Admission notification on a rolling basis. Must reply by 5/1. **Financial aid:** Priority date 3/1; no closing date. FAFSA, institutional form required. Applicants notified on a rolling basis starting 2/15.

Academics. Four year graduation guarantee offered. **Special study options:** Accelerated study, combined bachelor's/graduate degree, cooperative education, cross-registration, distance learning, double major, dual enrollment of high school students, ESL, exchange student, external degree, honors, independent study, internships, liberal arts/career combination, student-designed major, study abroad, teacher certification program. Qualified undergraduates may take graduate-level classes. **Credit/placement by examination:** AP, CLEP, IB, SAT, ACT, institutional tests. **Support services:** Learning center, pre-admission summer program, reduced course load, remedial instruction, study skills assistance, tutoring, writing center.

Majors. Architecture: Architecture, environmental design. **Area/ethnic studies:** African-American, American, Chicano/Hispanic-American/Latino, Native American, women's. **Biology:** General, bacteriology, biochemistry, cell/histology, ecology, exercise physiology, neuroscience, physiology. **Business:** Accounting, construction management, finance, human resources, insurance, international, labor relations, marketing, nonprofit/public, operations, retailing, sales/distribution. **Communications:** Journalism. **Computer sciences:** Computer science, networking, systems analysis. **Conservation:** Environmental science, fisheries. **Education:** Agricultural, biology, business, early childhood, elementary, kindergarten/preschool, music, special ed. **Engineering:** Aerospace, agricultural, biomedical, chemical, civil, computer, electrical, environmental, geological, industrial, materials, mechanical. **English:** English lit, rhetoric/composition. **Foreign languages:** General, classics, comparative lit, French, Italian, linguistics, Russian, Spanish. **Health services:** Audiology/speech pathology, dental hygiene, health care admin, music therapy, nursing (RN), predental, premedicine. **History:** General. **Math:** General, statistics. **Parks/recreation:** General, sports admin. **Philosophy/religion:** Judaic, philosophy, religion. **Physical sciences:** Astrophysics, chemistry, geology, physics. **Psychology:** General, developmental. **Social sciences:** Anthropology, applied economics, criminology, econometrics, economics, geography, international relations, political science, sociology, urban studies. **Theology:** Bible. **Visual/performing arts:** Art, art history/conservation, dance, dramatic, graphic design, interior design, music. **Work/family studies:** Clothing/textiles, housing.

Most popular majors. Biology 12%, business/marketing 9%, engineering/engineering technologies 11%, English 6%, psychology 7%, social sciences 11%.

Technology on campus. Dormitories wired for high-speed internet access and linked to campus network. Commuter students can connect to campus network. Online course registration, online library, helpline, repair service, student web hosting, wireless network available.

Student life. Freshman orientation: Mandatory. Preregistration for classes offered. **Housing:** Guaranteed on-campus for freshmen. Coed dorms, special housing for disabled, apartments, cooperative housing, fraternity/sorority housing available. $250 fully refundable deposit, deadline 5/1. Honors housing, 24 living and learning communities available. **Activities:** Bands, choral groups, dance, drama, film society, international student organizations, literary magazine, music ensembles, Model UN, musical theater, opera, radio station, student government, student newspaper, symphony orchestra, TV station, 600 student-run organizations.

Athletics. NCAA. **Intercollegiate:** Baseball, basketball, cheerleading, cross-country, diving, football (tackle), golf, gymnastics, ice hockey, rowing (crew) W, soccer W, softball W, swimming, tennis, track and field, volleyball W, wrestling M. **Intramural:** Badminton, baseball, basketball, bowling, fencing, football (tackle) M, golf, gymnastics, handball, ice hockey, judo, lacrosse, racquetball, rugby, sailing, skiing, soccer, softball, squash, swimming, synchronized swimming, tennis, volleyball, water polo, wrestling M. **Team name:** Golden Gophers.

Student services. Adult student services, alcohol/substance abuse counseling, chaplain/spiritual director, career counseling, services for economically disadvantaged, student employment services, financial aid counseling, health services, legal services, minority student services, on-campus daycare,

personal counseling, placement for graduates, veterans' counselor, women's services. **Physically disabled:** Services for visually, speech, hearing impaired.

Contact. Phone: (612) 625-2008 Toll-free number: (800) 752-1000 Fax: (612) 626-1693
Rachelle Hernandez, Associate Vice Provost and Director of Admission, University of Minnesota: Twin Cities, 240 Williamson Hall, Minneapolis, MN 55455-0213

University of Northwestern - St. Paul
Saint Paul, Minnesota
www.unwsp.edu   **CB code: 6489**

- Private 4-year university and liberal arts college affiliated with the non-denominational tradition
- Residential campus in very large city
- 1,945 degree-seeking undergraduates
- 205 graduate students
- SAT or ACT (ACT writing optional), application essay required

General. Founded in 1902. Regionally accredited. **Degrees:** 522 bachelor's, 17 associate awarded; master's offered. **ROTC:** Army, Air Force. **Location:** 9 miles from Minneapolis-St. Paul. **Calendar:** Semester, limited summer session. **Full-time faculty:** 97 total. **Part-time faculty:** 113 total. **Class size:** 57% < 20, 36% 20-39, 4% 40-49, 3% 50-99, less than 1% >100.

Freshman class profile.

GPA 3.75 or higher:	39%	Rank in top quarter:	55%
GPA 3.50-3.74:	21%	Rank in top tenth:	23%
GPA 3.0-3.49:	26%	Out-of-state:	27%
GPA 2.0-2.99:	14%	Live on campus:	96%

Basis for selection. Evidence that student will benefit from the education and contribute to the community is important. School record, recommendations, test scores, essay, character, and religious affiliation very important. ACT recommended. Audition required for music students. Portfolio recommended for art students. Interview recommended for borderline students. **Learning Disabled:** Students should contact the DOSS office to review specific needs for disability services.

High school preparation. College-preparatory program recommended. 16 units recommended. Recommended units include English 4, mathematics 3, social studies 3, science 3, foreign language 2 and academic electives 1.

2015-2016 Annual costs. Tuition/fees: $28,730. Room/board: $8,954. Books/supplies: $600. Personal expenses: $2,160. **Additional information:** Technology fee for commuting students is $150.

Financial aid. Non-need-based: Scholarships awarded for academics, alumni affiliation, leadership, music/drama. **Additional information:** Students enrolled at least half-time in the FOCUS or Distance Education degree programs may apply for financial aid from the same Federal and state sources as traditional undergraduates. However, their expense budgets and aid are less due to lower tuition.

Application procedures. Admission: Priority date 5/1; deadline 8/1 (receipt date). $25 fee, may be waived for applicants with need. Admission notification on a rolling basis beginning on or about 10/1. **Financial aid:** Priority date 3/1, closing date 8/1. FAFSA, institutional form required. Applicants notified on a rolling basis starting 3/1; must reply within 2 week(s) of notification.

Academics. Core curriculum built around a biblical worldview theme thoroughly integrates general education and biblical studies (64-68 credits). Transfer students meet core curriculum requirements on a proportional basis. **Special study options:** Combined bachelor's/graduate degree, distance learning, double major, dual enrollment of high school students, exchange student, honors, independent study, internships, liberal arts/career combination, student-designed major, study abroad, teacher certification program, urban semester, Washington semester. **Credit/placement by examination:** AP, CLEP, IB, SAT, ACT, institutional tests. 32 credit hours maximum toward associate degree, 32 toward bachelor's. **Support services:** Learning center, reduced course load, remedial instruction, study skills assistance, tutoring.

Majors. Biology: General, biochemistry. **Business:** Accounting, business admin, finance, human resources, international, management information systems, marketing, organizational behavior. **Communications:** Communications/speech/rhetoric, journalism, public relations, radio/TV. **Communications technology:** Animation/special effects. **Education:** Art, early childhood, elementary, English, ESL, health, mathematics, music, physical, social studies, Spanish. **Engineering:** General. **English:** English lit, technical writing. **Foreign languages:** Spanish. **Health services:** Prenursing. **History:** General. **Math:** General. **Parks/recreation:** Exercise sciences, health/fitness.

Protective services: Criminal justice. **Psychology:** General. **Social sciences:** General. **Theology:** Bible, missionary, preministerial, youth ministry. **Visual/performing arts:** Digital arts, dramatic, graphic design, music, music performance, music theory/composition, piano/keyboard, stringed instruments, studio arts, voice/opera. **Work/family studies:** Family studies.

Most popular majors. Business/marketing 19%, communications/journalism 9%, education 13%, psychology 10%, theological studies 17%, visual/performing arts 7%.

Technology on campus. PC or laptop required. 100 workstations in dormitories, library, computer center, student center. Dormitories wired for high-speed internet access and linked to campus network. Commuter students can connect to campus network. Online course registration, online library, helpline, student web hosting, wireless network available.

Student life. Freshman orientation: Mandatory. Preregistration for classes offered. Six one-day events during late spring and summer. General orientation: four days prior to start of classes. Multicultural orientation: four days prior to general orientation. **Policies:** Religious observance required. Freshmen not permitted cars on campus. **Housing:** Guaranteed on-campus for freshmen. Single-sex dorms, special housing for disabled, apartments, themed housing, wellness housing available. $200 fully refundable deposit, deadline 5/1. Some special housing accommodations for disabilities available. **Activities:** Bands, campus ministries, choral groups, dance, drama, film society, literary magazine, music ensembles, musical theater, opera, radio station, student government, student newspaper, symphony orchestra, TV station, Student Missions Fellowship, The Gathering, Transfer Student Organization, Guardian Angels, Mu Kappa, Inter-cultural Unity Organization, Young Republicans.

Athletics. NCAA, NCCAA. **Intercollegiate:** Baseball M, basketball, cross-country, football (tackle) M, golf, lacrosse W, soccer, softball W, tennis, track and field, volleyball W. **Intramural:** Basketball, football (non-tackle), softball, table tennis, tennis, ultimate frisbee, volleyball. **Team name:** Eagles.

Student services. Adult student services, chaplain/spiritual director, career counseling, student employment services, financial aid counseling, health services, minority student services, personal counseling, placement for graduates, veterans' counselor. **Physically disabled:** Services for visually impaired.

Contact. E-mail: admissions@unwsp.edu
Phone: (651) 631-5111 Toll-free number: (800) 827-6827
Fax: (651) 631-5680
Kenneth Faffler, Director of Admissions, University of Northwestern - St. Paul, 3003 Snelling Avenue North, Saint Paul, MN 55113-1598

University of Phoenix: Minneapolis-St. Paul
Saint Louis Park, Minnesota
www.phoenix.edu

◗ For-profit 4-year university
◗ Commuter campus in large town
◗ 132 undergraduates
◗ 34 graduate students

General. Regionally accredited. **Degrees:** 49 bachelor's awarded; master's offered. **Calendar:** Differs by program. **Full-time faculty:** 8 total. **Part-time faculty:** 50 total.

Basis for selection. Open admission.

2015-2016 Annual costs. Per-credit-hour charge, $395 to $635, depending upon level and course of study. Books, material charges, and other fees vary by course and program. All fees are subject to change.

Application procedures. Admission: No deadline. No application fee. **Financial aid:** No deadline.

Academics. Credit/placement by examination: AP, CLEP.

Majors. Business: Accounting, accounting/business management, business admin, e-commerce, entrepreneurial studies, finance, human resources, marketing, operations. **Computer sciences:** Database management, networking, programming, security, system admin, systems analysis, web page design, webmaster. **Conservation:** Environmental studies. **Health services:** Facilities admin, health information management, long term care admin, nursing (RN). **Human services:** General. **Protective services:** Disaster management, law enforcement admin, security management.

Student life. Freshman orientation: Mandatory. Preregistration for classes offered.

Contact. Toll-free number: (866) 766-0766
University of Phoenix: Minneapolis-St. Paul, 435 Ford Road, Saint Louis Park, MN 55426

University of St. Thomas
Saint Paul, Minnesota   **CB member**
www.stthomas.edu   **CB code: 6110**

◗ Private 4-year university affiliated with the Roman Catholic Church
◗ Residential campus in very large city
◗ 6,126 degree-seeking undergraduates: 3% part-time, 45% women, 3% African American, 3% Asian American, 5% Hispanic/Latino, 3% Multi-racial, non-Hispanic, 1% international
◗ 3,557 degree-seeking graduate students
◗ 84% of applicants admitted
◗ SAT or ACT (ACT writing optional), application essay required
◗ 76% graduate within 6 years

General. Founded in 1885. Regionally accredited. **Degrees:** 1,421 bachelor's awarded; master's, professional, doctoral offered. **ROTC:** Army, Naval, Air Force. **Calendar:** 4-1-4. **Full-time faculty:** 427 total. **Part-time faculty:** 465 total. **Class size:** 40% < 20, 57% 20-39, less than 1% 40-49, 2% 50-99.

Freshman class profile. 5,436 applied, 4,564 admitted, 1,421 enrolled.

Mid 50% test scores			
SAT critical reading:	520-630	GPA 2.0-2.99:	8%
SAT math:	510-620	Rank in top quarter:	56%
ACT composite:	24-29	Rank in top tenth:	24%
GPA 3.75 or higher:	38%	Return as sophomores:	89%
GPA 3.50-3.74:	21%	Out-of-state:	22%
GPA 3.0-3.49:	33%	Live on campus:	92%
		International:	2%

Basis for selection. Admissions decision by formula using combination of high school rank and standardized test scores, including consideration of the contributions the student has made to their school, community or church.

High school preparation. College-preparatory program recommended. Required and recommended units include English 4, mathematics 3-4, social studies 2, science 2 and foreign language 4. Some departments may require 3 units social studies (includes 1 geography), 1 US history, 1 unit visual or performing arts.

2015-2016 Annual costs. Tuition/fees: $38,105. Room/board: $9,750. Books/supplies: $1,000. Personal expenses: $3,718.

2015-2016 Financial aid. Need-based: 1,155 full-time freshmen applied for aid; 874 deemed to have need; 874 received aid. Average need met was 88%. Average scholarship/grant was $20,889; average loan $7,604. 69% of total undergraduate aid awarded as scholarships/grants, 31% as loans/jobs. **Non-need-based:** Awarded to 1,183 full-time undergraduates, including 431 freshmen. Scholarships awarded for academics, music/drama, ROTC.

Application procedures. Admission: No deadline. No application fee. Admission notification on a rolling basis beginning on or about 10/1. Must reply by 5/1. **Financial aid:** Priority date 4/1; no closing date. FAFSA required. Applicants notified on a rolling basis starting 3/1; must reply within 3 week(s) of notification.

Academics. Special study options: Cross-registration, double major, ESL, honors, independent study, internships, student-designed major, study abroad, teacher certification program. **Credit/placement by examination:** AP, CLEP, SAT, ACT. Typically credit by exam can be used for only 1/8 of a student's courses. CLEP credit awarded if student scores at 50th percentile or above for those examinations that have been approved by the department in which the subject is usually taught.

Majors. Area/ethnic studies: Women's. **Biology:** General, biochemistry, neuroscience. **Business:** Accounting, actuarial science, business admin, entrepreneurial studies, finance, human resources, international, marketing, operations, real estate. **Communications:** General. **Computer sciences:** Computer science, information systems, information technology, security. **Conservation:** Environmental science, environmental studies. **Education:** Chemistry, elementary, English, French, German, health, mathematics, middle, multi-level teacher, music, physical, physics, science, social studies, Spanish. **Engineering:** General, electrical, mechanical. **English:** Creative writing, English lit. **Foreign languages:** Classics, comparative lit, French, German, Latin, Spanish. **Health services:** Predental, prephysical therapy, preveterinary, public health ed. **History:** General. **Human services:** Social work. **Liberal arts:** Arts/sciences. **Math:** General, statistics. **Philosophy/religion:** Philosophy, religion. **Physical sciences:** Chemistry, geology, physics. **Psychology:** General. **Social sciences:** General, criminology, econometrics, economics, geography, international economics, international relations, political science, sociology. **Theology:** Preministerial. **Visual/performing arts:** Music, music performance.

Most popular majors. Biology 7%, business/marketing 41%, communications/journalism 6%, engineering/engineering technologies 6%, philosophy/religious studies 6%, social sciences 7%.

Student life. Housing: Single-sex dorms, special housing for disabled, apartments, themed housing, wellness housing available. $200 fully refundable deposit, deadline 5/1. Catholic women's and Catholic men's communities available. **Activities:** Bands, campus ministries, choral groups, dance, drama, international student organizations, literary magazine, music ensembles, Model UN, radio station, student government, student newspaper, TV station.

Contact. E-mail: admissions@stthomas.edu
Phone: (651) 962-6150 Toll-free number: (800) 328-6819 ext. 26150
Fax: (651) 962-6160
University of St. Thomas, 2115 Summit Avenue, Mail 5017, Saint Paul, MN 55105

Walden University
Minneapolis, Minnesota
www.waldenu.edu   CB code: 6755

- For-profit 4-year virtual university
- Large city
- 7,815 degree-seeking undergraduates: 90% part-time, 77% women, 30% African American, 2% Asian American, 6% Hispanic/Latino, 2% Multiracial, non-Hispanic, 1% international
- 44,436 degree-seeking graduate students

General. Walden University is a fully online institution accredited by the Higher Learning Commission's North Central Association offering programs in a variety of disciplines and degree levels, from undergraduate to doctorate. **Degrees:** 1,634 bachelor's awarded; master's, doctoral offered. **Calendar:** Continuous, extensive summer session. **Full-time faculty:** 210 total; 100% have terminal degrees. **Part-time faculty:** 2,544 total; 94% have terminal degrees.

Freshman class profile. 479 applied, 471 admitted, 66 enrolled.

Basis for selection. Open admission, but selective for some programs. Must meet one of the following criteria: at least 24 years of age, between the ages of 21-23 with at least 12 transferable college credit hours, at least 60 college credit hours completed, or an active member of the military or a veteran with documentation of service or be concurrently enrolled in an approved partner institution with an articulation agreement with Walden.

2015-2016 Annual costs. Tuition/fees: $14,970.

2014-2015 Financial aid. All financial aid based on need. 22% of total undergraduate aid awarded as scholarships/grants, 78% as loans/jobs.

Application procedures. Admission: No deadline. No application fee. Application must be submitted online. Admission notification on a rolling basis. Offer remains in effect for 12 months. **Financial aid:** No deadline. FAFSA required. Applicants notified on a rolling basis.

Academics. Special study options: Accelerated study, combined bachelor's/graduate degree, distance learning, honors, internships, student-designed major, study abroad, teacher certification program. **Credit/placement by examination:** AP, CLEP, IB. 30 credit hours maximum toward bachelor's degree. **Support services:** Remedial instruction, tutoring, writing center.

Majors. Business: Accounting, business admin, communications. **Communications:** General. **Computer sciences:** General. **Health services:** Health care admin, nursing (RN). **Human services:** General. **Protective services:** Law enforcement admin. **Psychology:** General, forensic. **Work/family studies:** Family studies.

Most popular majors. Business/marketing 13%, health sciences 52%, psychology 12%.

Technology on campus. PC or laptop required. Online course registration, online library, helpline available.

Student life. Freshman orientation: Available. Preregistration for classes offered.

Student services. Career counseling, financial aid counseling, personal counseling, veterans' counselor. **Physically disabled:** Services for visually, speech, hearing impaired.

Contact. E-mail: admissions@waldenu.edu
Phone: (800) 925-3368 Toll-free number: (866) 492-5336
Reena Lichtenfeld, Exec Dir Business Ops, Walden University, 100 Washington Ave South, Suite 900, Minneapolis, MN 55401

Winona State University
Winona, Minnesota
www.winona.edu   CB code: 6680

- Public 4-year university
- Residential campus in large town
- 7,816 degree-seeking undergraduates: 11% part-time, 62% women, 2% African American, 2% Asian American, 3% Hispanic/Latino, 2% Multiracial, non-Hispanic, 3% international
- 404 degree-seeking graduate students
- 62% of applicants admitted
- SAT or ACT (ACT writing optional) required
- 59% graduate within 6 years

General. Founded in 1858. Regionally accredited. **Degrees:** 1,790 bachelor's, 49 associate awarded; master's, doctoral offered. **ROTC:** Army. **Location:** 120 miles from Minneapolis-St. Paul. **Calendar:** Semester, extensive summer session. **Full-time faculty:** 324 total; 65% have terminal degrees, 14% minority, 50% women. **Part-time faculty:** 187 total; 16% have terminal degrees, 4% minority, 67% women. **Class size:** 26% < 20, 56% 20-39, 8% 40-49, 8% 50-99, 2% >100.

Freshman class profile. 6,780 applied, 4,235 admitted, 1,642 enrolled.

Mid 50% test scores		Rank in top quarter:	30%
ACT composite:	20-25	Rank in top tenth:	9%
GPA 3.75 or higher:	20%	Return as sophomores:	80%
GPA 3.50-3.74:	20%	Out-of-state:	33%
GPA 3.0-3.49:	38%	Live on campus:	94%
GPA 2.0-2.99:	22%	International:	2%

Basis for selection. 16 units of college prep high school courses and rank in top 2/3 of class and SAT combined score of 1000 (exclusive of Writing) or ACT composite score of 21 required; or top half of class with ACT 18 or higher for regular admission. Interview required for academically marginal students. **Home schooled:** Transcript of courses and grades required.

High school preparation. College-preparatory program required. 16 units required. Required units include English 4, mathematics 3, social studies 2, history 1, science 3 (laboratory 3), foreign language 2 and academic electives 1. One English unit may be speech.

2015-2016 Annual costs. Tuition/fees: $9,047; $14,744 out-of-state. Room/board: $8,120. Books/supplies: $1,200. Personal expenses: $2,420. **Additional information:** Fees include mandatory laptop and tablet lease ($970 / year) for full-time students.

2014-2015 Financial aid. Need-based: 1,458 full-time freshmen applied for aid; 1,021 deemed to have need; 999 received aid. Average need met was 50%. Average scholarship/grant was $5,133; average loan $3,466. 36% of total undergraduate aid awarded as scholarships/grants, 64% as loans/jobs. **Non-need-based:** Awarded to 2,504 full-time undergraduates, including 954 freshmen. Scholarships awarded for academics, alumni affiliation, art, athletics, leadership, minority status, music/drama, ROTC, state residency.

Application procedures. Admission: Closing date 7/12 (postmark date). $20 fee, may be waived for applicants with need. Admission notification on a rolling basis. **Financial aid:** Priority date 5/1; no closing date. FAFSA required. Applicants notified on a rolling basis starting 5/1; must reply within 3 week(s) of notification.

Academics. Special study options: Accelerated study, cross-registration, distance learning, double major, dual enrollment of high school students, ESL, external degree, independent study, internships, student-designed major, study abroad, teacher certification program. **Credit/placement by examination:** AP, CLEP, IB, ACT, institutional tests. **Support services:** Learning center, reduced course load, remedial instruction, study skills assistance, tutoring, writing center.

Majors. Area/ethnic studies: Women's. **Biology:** General, biochemistry. **Business:** Accounting, business admin, finance, human resources, management information systems, marketing. **Communications:** Advertising, communications/speech/rhetoric, health, journalism, media studies, persuasive communications, photojournalism. **Computer sciences:** Computer science.

Education: General, art, biology, business, chemistry, early childhood special, earth science, elementary, English, ESL, health, learning disabled, learning sciences, mathematics, music, physical, physics, science, social science, social studies, Spanish, special ed. **Engineering:** Materials. **English:** English lit. **Foreign languages:** Spanish. **Health services:** Athletic training, clinical lab science, cytotechnology, health care admin, nursing (RN), public health ed. **History:** General. **Human services:** General, social work. **Math:** General, statistics. **Parks/recreation:** Exercise sciences, facilities management. **Physical sciences:** Chemistry, physics. **Protective services:** Corrections. **Psychology:** General. **Social sciences:** Economics, political science, sociology. **Visual/performing arts:** Art, dramatic, music, music management, music performance.

Most popular majors. Biology 6%, business/marketing 19%, communications/journalism 7%, education 16%, health sciences 17%, parks/recreation 7%.

Technology on campus. PC or laptop required. 100 workstations in library, student center. Dormitories wired for high-speed internet access and linked to campus network. Commuter students can connect to campus network. Online course registration, online library, helpline, repair service, student web hosting, wireless network available.

Student life. Freshman orientation: Available, $25 fee. Preregistration for classes offered. **Policies:** Smoke and alcohol-free, sustainable campus. **Housing:** Guaranteed on-campus for freshmen. Coed dorms, single-sex dorms, special housing for disabled, apartments, themed housing available. $250 partly refundable deposit, deadline 3/1. Residence hall with classrooms and faculty offices available. **Activities:** Bands, campus ministries, choral groups, dance, drama, film society, international student organizations, literary magazine, music ensembles, Model UN, musical theater, radio station, student government, student newspaper, symphony orchestra, TV station, Over 200 student clubs and organizations.

Athletics. NCAA. **Intercollegiate:** Baseball M, basketball, cross-country, football (tackle) M, golf, gymnastics W, soccer W, softball W, tennis W, track and field W, volleyball W. **Intramural:** Badminton, basketball, football (non-tackle) M, racquetball, rugby, skiing, soccer, softball, swimming, volleyball. **Team name:** Warriors.

Student services. Adult student services, alcohol/substance abuse counseling, career counseling, services for economically disadvantaged, student employment services, financial aid counseling, health services, legal services, minority student services, on-campus daycare, personal counseling, placement for graduates, veterans' counselor, women's services. **Physically disabled:** Services for visually, speech, hearing impaired.

Contact. E-mail: admissions@winona.edu
Phone: (507) 457-5100 Toll-free number: (800) 342-5978 ext. 5100
Fax: (507) 457-5620
Carl Stange, Director of Admissions, Winona State University, Office of Admissions, Winona, MN 55987

Mississippi

Alcorn State University

Lorman, Mississippi
www.alcorn.edu

CB member
CB code: 1008

- Public 4-year university and agricultural college
- Residential campus in rural community
- 2,911 degree-seeking undergraduates: 12% part-time, 64% women, 93% African American, 2% Multi-racial, non-Hispanic, 1% international
- 598 degree-seeking graduate students
- 81% of applicants admitted
- SAT or ACT (ACT writing optional) required
- 34% graduate within 6 years; 39% enter graduate study

General. Founded in 1871. Regionally accredited. **Degrees:** 347 bachelor's, 34 associate awarded; master's offered. **ROTC:** Army. **Location:** 40 miles from Natchez, 45 miles from Vicksburg. **Calendar:** Semester, limited summer session. **Full-time faculty:** 157 total; 68% have terminal degrees, 81% minority, 48% women. **Part-time faculty:** 59 total; 58% have terminal degrees, 90% minority, 59% women. **Special facilities:** Nature trails, lakes, animal facility, bike trail, Mississippi River research center.

Freshman class profile. 3,010 applied, 2,425 admitted, 631 enrolled.

Mid 50% test scores			
SAT critical reading:	390-480	GPA 3.0-3.49:	29%
SAT math:	390-500	GPA 2.0-2.99:	46%
ACT composite:	16-20	Return as sophomores:	76%
GPA 3.75 or higher:	9%	Out-of-state:	38%
GPA 3.50-3.74:	13%	Live on campus:	87%

Basis for selection. Test scores, school achievement record important; specific academic units considered. Test score requirements depend upon high school GPA. Audition required for music majors. Interview required for students not meeting regular admission criteria. **Home schooled:** Statement describing home school structure and mission, transcript of courses and grades required.

High school preparation. College-preparatory program required. 15.5 units required; 19.5 recommended. Required and recommended units include English 4, mathematics 3-4, social studies 3-4, science 3-4 (laboratory 2), foreign language 1, computer science .5, visual/performing arts 1 and academic electives 1. 1 advanced elective must be in foreign language or world geography.

2015-2016 Annual costs. Tuition/fees: $6,384; $15,433 out-of-state. Room/board: $8,996. Books/supplies: $1,536. Personal expenses: $2,559.

2015-2016 Financial aid. **Need-based:** 601 full-time freshmen applied for aid; 594 deemed to have need; 581 received aid. Average need met was 91%. Average scholarship/grant was $6,139; average loan $3,373. 67% of total undergraduate aid awarded as scholarships/grants, 33% as loans/jobs. **Non-need-based:** Awarded to 492 full-time undergraduates, including 313 freshmen. Scholarships awarded for academics, athletics, leadership, ROTC.

Application procedures. **Admission:** No deadline. No application fee. Application must be submitted online. Admission notification on a rolling basis. **Financial aid:** Priority date 3/15; no closing date. FAFSA, institutional form required. Applicants notified on a rolling basis starting 4/1; must reply within 4 week(s) of notification.

Academics. Math center available to students. On-line tutoring is available 24/7. **Special study options:** Accelerated study, cooperative education, distance learning, double major, dual enrollment of high school students, honors, independent study, internships, liberal arts/career combination, study abroad, teacher certification program. **Credit/placement by examination:** AP, CLEP, SAT, ACT, institutional tests. 15 credit hours maximum toward associate degree, 30 toward bachelor's. Student must earn 12 hours in residence before credit by examination may be recorded on student's transcript. **Support services:** Pre-admission summer program, reduced course load, remedial instruction, tutoring, writing center. Offers honors, pre-professional and global programs.

Majors. Biology: General. **Business:** Accounting, business admin. **Communications:** Media studies. **Computer sciences:** General, LAN/WAN management. **Education:** Elementary. **English:** English lit. **Health services:** Nursing (RN). **History:** General. **Human services:** Social work. **Liberal arts:** Arts/sciences. **Math:** General. **Parks/recreation:** General, sports admin. **Physical sciences:** Chemistry. **Protective services:** Criminal justice. **Psychology:** General. **Social sciences:** Political science, sociology. **Visual/performing arts:** Music, music performance. **Work/family studies:** Child development, food/nutrition.

Most popular majors. Agriculture 8%, biology 15%, business/marketing 6%, family/consumer sciences 8%, health sciences 11%, liberal arts 10%, public administration/social services 6%, security/protective services 7%.

Technology on campus. 500 workstations in dormitories, library, computer center, student center. Dormitories wired for high-speed internet access and linked to campus network. Commuter students can connect to campus network. Online course registration, online library, helpline, repair service, wireless network available.

Student life. Freshman orientation: Mandatory. Preregistration for classes offered. Entrance and placement exams given. **Housing:** Guaranteed on-campus for all undergraduates. Single-sex dorms available. $75 fully refundable deposit. **Activities:** Bands, choral groups, dance, drama, music ensembles, radio station, student government, student newspaper, TV station, Wesley Foundation, NAACP, YWCA, PHA Masonic Order, heritage committee.

Athletics. NCAA. **Intercollegiate:** Baseball M, basketball, cross-country, football (tackle) M, golf, soccer W, softball W, tennis, track and field, volleyball W. **Intramural:** Basketball, football (tackle) M. **Team name:** Braves.

Student services. Alcohol/substance abuse counseling, chaplain/spiritual director, career counseling, student employment services, financial aid counseling, health services, on-campus daycare, personal counseling, placement for graduates, veterans' counselor.

Contact. E-mail: ksampson@alcorn.edu
Phone: (601) 877-6147 Toll-free number: (800) 222-6790
Fax: (601) 877-6347
Katangelia Tenner, Director of Admissions and Recruiting, Alcorn State University, 1000 ASU Drive #300, Lorman, MS 39096-7500

Belhaven University

Jackson, Mississippi
www.belhaven.edu

CB code: 1055

- Private 4-year university and liberal arts college affiliated with the Presbyterian Church (USA)
- Residential campus in large city
- 2,715 degree-seeking undergraduates: 47% part-time, 65% women, 47% African American, 2% Asian American, 5% Hispanic/Latino, 1% Native American, 2% Multi-racial, non-Hispanic, 2% international
- 1,628 degree-seeking graduate students
- 51% of applicants admitted
- SAT or ACT (ACT writing optional), application essay required
- 45% graduate within 6 years

General. Founded in 1883. Regionally accredited. Christian liberal arts college. **Degrees:** 504 bachelor's, 35 associate awarded; master's offered. **ROTC:** Army, Air Force. **Location:** 188 miles from New Orleans, 200 miles from Memphis, Tennessee. **Calendar:** Semester, extensive summer session. **Full-time faculty:** 113 total; 68% have terminal degrees, 44% women. **Part-time faculty:** 297 total; 48% women. **Class size:** 85% < 20, 12% 20-39, 2% 40-49, less than 1% 50-99. **Special facilities:** Museum, heritage room.

Freshman class profile. 3,053 applied, 1,551 admitted, 284 enrolled.

Mid 50% test scores			
SAT critical reading:	490-600	GPA 2.0-2.99:	28%
SAT math:	470-560	Rank in top quarter:	43%
ACT composite:	20-24	Rank in top tenth:	15%
GPA 3.75 or higher:	29%	Return as sophomores:	66%
GPA 3.50-3.74:	18%	Out-of-state:	56%
GPA 3.0-3.49:	23%	Live on campus:	82%

Basis for selection. Test scores, school record, recommendations, and character important. Interview recommended for art, dance, music, and theater majors; portfolio recommended for art majors. Audition required for dance, music, and theater majors.

High school preparation. 16 units required. Required and recommended units include English 4, mathematics 2, social studies 1, science 1, computer science 1 and academic electives 8.

2015-2016 Annual costs. Tuition/fees: $21,816. Room/board: $8,000. Books/supplies: $1,244. Personal expenses: $102.

2014-2015 Financial aid. Need-based: 265 full-time freshmen applied for aid; 246 deemed to have need; 246 received aid. Average need met was 80%. Average scholarship/grant was $16,000; average loan $3,400. 50% of total undergraduate aid awarded as scholarships/grants, 50% as loans/jobs. **Non-need-based:** Awarded to 1,365 full-time undergraduates, including 286 freshmen. Scholarships awarded for academics, alumni affiliation, art, athletics, job skills, leadership, music/drama.

Application procedures. Admission: No deadline. $25 fee, may be waived for applicants with need. Admission notification on a rolling basis. Accepted applicants must reply within 30 days. **Financial aid:** Priority date 1/31; no closing date. FAFSA required. Applicants notified on a rolling basis starting 2/1.

Academics. Special study options: Accelerated study, distance learning, double major, dual enrollment of high school students, ESL, honors, independent study, internships, student-designed major, study abroad, teacher certification program, weekend college. **Credit/placement by examination:** AP, CLEP, IB, SAT, ACT, institutional tests. 30 credit hours maximum toward bachelor's degree. **Support services:** Learning center, reduced course load, remedial instruction, study skills assistance, tutoring, writing center.

Majors. Biology: General. **Business:** Accounting, business admin. **Communications:** Communications/speech/rhetoric. **Computer sciences:** General. **Education:** Elementary. **English:** Creative writing, English lit. **Health services:** Health care admin. **History:** General. **Liberal arts:** Humanities. **Math:** General. **Parks/recreation:** Exercise sciences, sports admin. **Philosophy/religion:** Philosophy. **Physical sciences:** Chemistry. **Psychology:** General. **Social sciences:** General, political science. **Theology:** Bible. **Visual/performing arts:** Art, dance, dramatic, music, studio arts management.

Most popular majors. Business/marketing 32%, health sciences 8%, parks/recreation 9%, social sciences 13%, visual/performing arts 9%.

Technology on campus. 40 workstations in library, computer center. Dormitories wired for high-speed internet access and linked to campus network. Commuter students can connect to campus network. Online course registration, online library, wireless network available.

Student life. Freshman orientation: Mandatory. Preregistration for classes offered. Held 5 days before fall classes begin. **Policies:** Religious observance required. **Housing:** Single-sex dorms, apartments, wellness housing available. $100 fully refundable deposit, deadline 6/1. **Activities:** Bands, campus ministries, choral groups, dance, drama, international student organizations, literary magazine, music ensembles, musical theater, student government, student newspaper, symphony orchestra, College Republicans, Fellowship of Christian Athletes, Praise & Worship Fellowship, Reformed University Fellowship, Student Missions Fellowship.

Athletics. NCAA. **Intercollegiate:** Baseball M, basketball, cheerleading W, cross-country, football (tackle) M, golf, soccer, softball W, tennis, volleyball W. **Intramural:** Basketball, football (non-tackle), soccer W, softball, volleyball, weight lifting W. **Team name:** Blazers.

Student services. Adult student services, chaplain/spiritual director, career counseling, student employment services, financial aid counseling, health services, personal counseling.

Contact. E-mail: admission@belhaven.edu
Phone: (601) 968-5940 Toll-free number: (800) 960-5940
Fax: (601) 968-8946
Suzanne Sullivan, Assistant Vice-President of Traditional and Online Admission, Belhaven University, 1500 Peachtree Street, Jackson, MS 39202

Blue Mountain College
Blue Mountain, Mississippi
www.bmc.edu   **CB code: 1066**

- Private 4-year liberal arts college affiliated with the Southern Baptist Convention
- Residential campus in rural community
- 436 degree-seeking undergraduates: 9% part-time, 56% women, 10% African American, 1% Hispanic/Latino, 1% Multi-racial, non-Hispanic, 2% international
- 26 degree-seeking graduate students
- 38% of applicants admitted
- SAT or ACT (ACT writing optional) required
- 55% graduate within 6 years

General. Founded in 1873. Regionally accredited. **Degrees:** 125 bachelor's awarded; master's offered. **Location:** 65 miles from Memphis, TN. **Calendar:** Semester, limited summer session. **Full-time faculty:** 33 total; 79% have terminal degrees, 54% women. **Part-time faculty:** 16 total; 44% have terminal degrees, 44% women. **Class size:** 87% < 20, 11% 20-39, 1% 40-49, less than 1% 50-99.

Freshman class profile. 326 applied, 125 admitted, 56 enrolled.

Mid 50% test scores		Rank in top tenth:	17%
ACT composite:	18-24	End year in good standing:	89%
GPA 3.75 or higher:	34%	Return as sophomores:	69%
GPA 3.50-3.74:	20%	Out-of-state:	43%
GPA 3.0-3.49:	26%	Live on campus:	86%
GPA 2.0-2.99:	20%	International:	4%
Rank in top quarter:	37%		

Basis for selection. High school record, test scores, and individual motivation considered.

High school preparation. College-preparatory program recommended. 15 units recommended. Recommended units include English 4, mathematics 3, social studies 1, history 2, science 3 (laboratory 2) and foreign language 2.

2015-2016 Annual costs. Tuition/fees: $10,968. Room/board: $5,424. Books/supplies: $1,200. Personal expenses: $1,200.

2015-2016 Financial aid. Need-based: 53 full-time freshmen applied for aid; 44 deemed to have need; 44 received aid. Average need met was 63%. Average scholarship/grant was $6,788; average loan $3,140. 74% of total undergraduate aid awarded as scholarships/grants, 26% as loans/jobs. **Non-need-based:** Awarded to 218 full-time undergraduates, including 24 freshmen. Scholarships awarded for academics, alumni affiliation, art, athletics, leadership, music/drama, religious affiliation, state residency.

Application procedures. Admission: No deadline. $10 fee, may be waived for applicants with need, free for online applicants. Admission notification on a rolling basis beginning on or about 10/1. **Financial aid:** Priority date 3/1, closing date 7/31. FAFSA required. Applicants notified on a rolling basis starting 4/1; must reply within 4 week(s) of notification.

Academics. Special study options: Accelerated study, combined bachelor's/graduate degree, distance learning, double major, dual enrollment of high school students, honors, internships, teacher certification program. **Credit/placement by examination:** AP, CLEP, IB, SAT, ACT, institutional tests. 30 credit hours maximum toward bachelor's degree. **Support services:** Learning center, reduced course load, remedial instruction, tutoring.

Majors. Biology: General. **Business:** Business admin. **Education:** Biology, elementary, English, mathematics, music, physical, social science, Spanish. **English:** English lit. **Foreign languages:** Spanish. **Health services:** Clinical lab science, prephysical therapy. **History:** General. **Math:** General. **Parks/recreation:** Exercise sciences. **Protective services:** Criminal justice. **Psychology:** General. **Theology:** Bible, sacred music. **Visual/performing arts:** General, music.

Most popular majors. Biology 7%, business/marketing 11%, education 25%, psychology 21%, theological studies 19%.

Technology on campus. 52 workstations in library, computer center. Dormitories wired for high-speed internet access. Commuter students can connect to campus network. Online library, helpline, wireless network available.

Student life. Freshman orientation: Mandatory. Preregistration for classes offered. Held prior to fall semester; provides opportunities for learning methods that support college success. **Policies:** Smoking and alcoholic beverages forbidden. Chapel attendance is required of all full-time students. Unmarried full-time students under the age of 21 are required to live on campus unless they are independent students, or living at home with parents or immediate family and commuting to school. **Housing:** Single-sex dorms, wellness housing available. $50 fully refundable deposit. **Activities:** Choral groups, drama, literary magazine, music ensembles, musical theater, student government, Alpha Psi Omega, Baptist Student Union, Cap & Gown Honor Society, Mississippi Association of Educators Student Program, psychology club, Society of Mathematicians & Scientists, Vivace club, Ministerial Association, Koinonia, and Social Societies.

Athletics. NAIA. **Intercollegiate:** Baseball M, basketball, cross-country, golf, softball W. **Intramural:** Basketball, football (non-tackle) M, soccer M, softball, swimming W, table tennis W, tennis W, track and field, ultimate frisbee M, volleyball. **Team name:** Toppers.

Student services. Health services, placement for graduates. **Physically disabled:** Services for visually, hearing impaired.

Contact. E-mail: admissions@bmc.edu
Phone: (662) 685-4771 ext. 166 Toll-free number: (800) 235-0136
Fax: (662) 685-4776
Lynn Gibson, Vice President for Enrollment Services, Blue Mountain
College, PO Box 160, Blue Mountain, MS 38610-0160

Delta State University

Cleveland, Mississippi	CB member
www.deltastate.edu	CB code: 1163

- Public 4-year university
- Commuter campus in large town
- 2,441 degree-seeking undergraduates
- ACT (writing optional) required

General. Founded in 1924. Regionally accredited. Nursing school, only
CAV program in state, Delta Music Institute. **Degrees:** 452 bachelor's
awarded; master's, doctoral offered. **ROTC:** Army. **Location:** 40 miles from
Greenville, 110 miles from Memphis, Tennessee. **Calendar:** Semester, extensive summer session. **Full-time faculty:** 183 total; 69% have terminal degrees,
19% minority, 54% women. **Part-time faculty:** 73 total; 36% have terminal
degrees, 14% minority, 59% women. **Class size:** 64% < 20, 31% 20-39, 4%
40-49, less than 1% 50-99, less than 1% >100. **Special facilities:** Planetarium,
airport, archives and museum, music studio.

Freshman class profile.

GPA 3.75 or higher:	16%	Rank in top tenth:	14%
GPA 3.50-3.74:	19%	Out-of-state:	18%
GPA 3.0-3.49:	33%	Live on campus:	88%
GPA 2.0-2.99:	31%	Fraternities:	23%
Rank in top quarter:	38%	Sororities:	26%

Basis for selection. Combination of college preparatory curriculum, test
scores, class rank. Mississippi residents must take ACT for admission. Interview required for art, music majors. Audition recommended for music majors;
portfolio recommended for art majors.

High school preparation. College-preparatory program required. 15.5
units required. Required units include English 4, mathematics 3, social studies
3, science 3 (laboratory 2), computer science .5 and academic electives 2.

2015-2016 Annual costs. Tuition/fees: $6,112. Room/board: $7,592.
Books/supplies: $1,000.

Financial aid. Non-need-based: Scholarships awarded for academics,
alumni affiliation, art, athletics, leadership, music/drama, state residency.

Application procedures. Admission: Priority date 8/1; no deadline. $25
fee. Admission notification on a rolling basis. **Financial aid:** Priority date
3/1; no closing date. FAFSA, institutional form required. Applicants notified
on a rolling basis starting 5/1.

Academics. Special study options: Distance learning, double major, dual
enrollment of high school students, honors, independent study, internships,
student-designed major, teacher certification program. **Credit/placement by
examination:** AP, CLEP, SAT, ACT, institutional tests. 30 credit hours
maximum toward bachelor's degree. **Support services:** Learning center, pre-
admission summer program, remedial instruction, study skills assistance,
tutoring, writing center.

Majors. Biology: General. **Business:** General, accounting, business admin,
finance, hospitality admin, insurance, management information systems, marketing. **Communications:** Journalism. **Education:** Elementary, English,
mathematics, music, physical, social science. **English:** English lit. **Foreign
languages:** General. **Health services:** Athletic training, audiology/speech
pathology, nursing (RN). **History:** General. **Human services:** Social work.
Math: General. **Physical sciences:** Chemistry. **Protective services:** Criminal
justice. **Psychology:** General. **Social sciences:** General, political science.
Visual/performing arts: General, music. **Work/family studies:** General.

Most popular majors. Biology 9%, business/marketing 18%, education
20%, family/consumer sciences 11%, health sciences 13%, public administra-
tion/social services 7%, visual/performing arts 6%.

Technology on campus. 533 workstations in dormitories, library, computer center, student center. Dormitories wired for high-speed internet access
and linked to campus network. Commuter students can connect to campus
network. Online course registration, online library, helpline, repair service,
student web hosting, wireless network available.

Student life. Freshman orientation: Available, $35 fee. Preregistration
for classes offered. Provides opportunity for academic advisement. **Housing:**
Guaranteed on-campus for all undergraduates. Single-sex dorms, apartments,

fraternity/sorority housing available. $50 fully refundable deposit, deadline
8/1. **Activities:** Bands, campus ministries, choral groups, dance, drama, international student organizations, literary magazine, music ensembles, musical
theater, opera, student government, student newspaper, several religious,
ethnic, social, political organizations available on campus.

Athletics. NCAA. **Intercollegiate:** Baseball M, basketball, cross-country
W, diving, football (tackle) M, golf M, soccer, softball W, swimming, tennis.
Intramural: Badminton, basketball, bowling, cross-country, diving, football
(non-tackle), golf, racquetball, rifle, soccer, softball, swimming, table tennis,
tennis, triathlon, ultimate frisbee, volleyball. **Team name:** Statesmen;
Lady Statesmen.

Student services. Alcohol/substance abuse counseling, career counseling,
student employment services, financial aid counseling, health services, on-
campus daycare, personal counseling, placement for graduates. **Physically
disabled:** Services for speech, hearing impaired.

Contact. E-mail: admissions@deltastate.edu
Phone: (662) 846-4655 Toll-free number: (800) 468-6378
Fax: (662) 846-4684
Chris Gaines, Director of Admissions, Delta State University, 117 Kent
Wyatt Hall, Cleveland, MS 38733

Jackson State University

Jackson, Mississippi	CB member
www.jsums.edu	CB code: 1341

- Public 4-year university
- Commuter campus in small city
- 7,422 degree-seeking undergraduates: 10% part-time, 63% women, 92%
  African American, 1% Multi-racial, non-Hispanic, 2% international
- 2,327 degree-seeking graduate students
- 68% of applicants admitted
- SAT or ACT (ACT writing optional) required
- 43% graduate within 6 years

General. Founded in 1877. Regionally accredited. **Degrees:** 989 bachelor's
awarded; master's, doctoral offered. **ROTC:** Army, Air Force. **Location:**
210 miles from Memphis, TN; 190 miles from New Orleans. **Calendar:**
Semester, extensive summer session. **Full-time faculty:** 387 total; 76% have
terminal degrees, 79% minority, 46% women. **Part-time faculty:** 219 total;
35% have terminal degrees, 74% minority, 54% women. **Class size:** 39%
< 20, 40% 20-39, 11% 40-49, 9% 50-99, less than 1% >100. **Special facilities:**
National research center, science observatory, academic research and computing center, medical mall campus.

Freshman class profile. 8,035 applied, 5,425 admitted, 1,252 enrolled.

Mid 50% test scores		GPA 2.0-2.99:	45%
ACT composite:	17-21	Return as sophomores:	78%
GPA 3.75 or higher:	12%	Out-of-state:	39%
GPA 3.50-3.74:	13%	Live on campus:	75%
GPA 3.0-3.49:	28%	International:	2%

Basis for selection. Test scores and high school transcript important.
Audition recommended for music majors. **Home schooled:** Interview
required.

High school preparation. College-preparatory program required. 16.5
units required. Required units include English 4, mathematics 3, social studies
3, science 3, computer science .5, visual/performing arts 1 and academic
electives 2.

2015-2016 Annual costs. Tuition/fees: $6,866; $16,821 out-of-state.
Room/board: $8,226. Books/supplies: $2,300.

2014-2015 Financial aid. Need-based: 1,120 full-time freshmen applied
for aid; 1,038 deemed to have need; 1,033 received aid. Average need met
was 36%. Average scholarship/grant was $5,245; average loan $3,350. 51%
of total undergraduate aid awarded as scholarships/grants, 49% as loans/jobs.
Non-need-based: Awarded to 2,789 full-time undergraduates, including 735
freshmen. Scholarships awarded for academics, alumni affiliation, athletics,
leadership, minority status, music/drama, ROTC.

Application procedures. Admission: Priority date 8/1; deadline 9/2
(receipt date). No application fee. Admission notification on a rolling basis
beginning on or about 9/1. **Financial aid:** Priority date 4/15; no closing date.
FAFSA required. Applicants notified on a rolling basis starting 3/1.

Academics. Special study options: Distance learning, double major, dual
enrollment of high school students, ESL, honors, independent study, internships, study abroad, teacher certification program, weekend college. **Credit/**

placement by examination: AP, CLEP, IB, SAT, ACT. 30 credit hours maximum toward bachelor's degree. **Support services:** Learning center, pre-admission summer program, reduced course load, remedial instruction, study skills assistance, tutoring, writing center.

Honors college/program. Honors college membership is granted to students who have been admitted and would have completed a college preparatory curriculum, and have earned a composite score of 24 or higher on the ACT (SAT equivalent), possesses a minimum of 3.0, or rank as class Valedictorian or Salutatorian.

Majors. Biology: General. **Business:** Accounting, business admin, entrepreneurial studies, finance, managerial economics, marketing. **Communications:** Media studies. **Computer sciences:** General. **Education:** Elementary, mathematics, music, physical, social science, special ed. **Engineering:** Civil, computer, electrical. **English:** English lit, rhetoric/composition. **Foreign languages:** General. **Health services:** Health care admin, speech pathology. **History:** General. **Human services:** Social work. **Math:** General. **Physical sciences:** Atmospheric science, chemistry, geology, physics. **Protective services:** Criminal justice. **Psychology:** General. **Social sciences:** Political science, sociology, urban studies. **Visual/performing arts:** General, music performance.

Most popular majors. Biology 7%, business/marketing 14%, education 18%, engineering/engineering technologies 6%, interdisciplinary studies 12%, public administration/social services 8%, security/protective services 8%.

Technology on campus. 55 workstations in dormitories, library, computer center, student center. Dormitories wired for high-speed internet access and linked to campus network. Commuter students can connect to campus network. Online course registration, online library, helpline, repair service, wireless network available.

Student life. Freshman orientation: Mandatory. Preregistration for classes offered. All-day program held in summer, fall and spring. **Housing:** Single-sex dorms available. $100 nonrefundable deposit. **Activities:** Bands, campus ministries, choral groups, dance, drama, film society, international student organizations, literary magazine, music ensembles, opera, radio station, student government, student newspaper, symphony orchestra, TV station, Reform University Fellowship, Fellowship of Christian Athletes, Wesley Foundation, Young Life, Intervarsity Christian Fellwoship Church of God in Christ club.

Athletics. NCAA. **Intercollegiate:** Baseball M, basketball, bowling W, cheerleading, cross-country, football (tackle) M, golf, soccer, softball W, tennis, track and field, volleyball W. **Intramural:** Basketball, football (tackle), soccer, softball, tennis, volleyball. **Team name:** JSU Tigers.

Student services. Adult student services, alcohol/substance abuse counseling, career counseling, student employment services, financial aid counseling, health services, on-campus daycare, personal counseling, placement for graduates, veterans' counselor, women's services. **Physically disabled:** Services for visually, speech, hearing impaired.

Contact. E-mail: admapply@jsums.edu
Phone: (601) 979-0928 Toll-free number: (800) 848-6817
Fax: (601) 979-3445
Janieth Wilson-Adams, Director of Undergraduate Admissions, Jackson State University, 1400 John R. Lynch Street, Jackson, MS 39217

Millsaps College
Jackson, Mississippi
www.millsaps.edu

CB member
CB code: 1471

▸ Private 4-year business and liberal arts college affiliated with the United Methodist Church

▸ Residential campus in large city

▸ 756 degree-seeking undergraduates: 1% part-time, 49% women, 13% African American, 3% Asian American, 4% Hispanic/Latino, 1% Native American, 4% international

▸ 49 degree-seeking graduate students

▸ 53% of applicants admitted

▸ SAT or ACT (ACT writing optional), application essay required

▸ 66% graduate within 6 years

General. Founded in 1890. Regionally accredited. **Degrees:** 175 bachelor's awarded; master's offered. **ROTC:** Army, Air Force. **Location:** 190 miles from New Orleans, 210 miles from Memphis, Tennessee. **Calendar:** Semester, limited summer session. **Full-time faculty:** 87 total; 97% have terminal degrees, 13% minority, 49% women. **Part-time faculty:** 20 total; 75% have terminal degrees, 5% minority, 45% women. **Class size:** 83% < 20, 17%

20-39. **Special facilities:** Molecular biology/functional genomics research laboratory, fluorescence microscopy suite and imaging facility, GIS workstation, microsurgical lab for animal surgeries, hydrogeologic monitoring station, computational modeling laboratory, sorbent and environmental laboratory.

Freshman class profile. 3,657 applied, 1,925 admitted, 223 enrolled.

Mid 50% test scores			
SAT critical reading:	520-630	Rank in top quarter:	64%
SAT math:	530-630	Rank in top tenth:	34%
ACT composite:	23-28	Return as sophomores:	79%
GPA 3.75 or higher:	44%	Out-of-state:	57%
GPA 3.50-3.74:	21%	Live on campus:	97%
GPA 3.0-3.49:	24%	International:	3%
GPA 2.0-2.99:	11%	Fraternities:	65%
		Sororities:	42%

Basis for selection. Test scores, GPA in academic courses, recommendations, essays, and school and community activities are important. Advanced credit is awarded for A-Levels, International Baccalaureate, and some other systems. Students interested in fine and performing arts scholarships are required to submit a portfolio and/or audition for scholarships. **Learning Disabled:** No special admission requirements; students requesting accommodations are recommended to submit appropriate documentation to the Director of Disability Services prior to first semester.

High school preparation. College-preparatory program recommended. 14 units required; 20 recommended. Required and recommended units include English 4, mathematics 3-4, social studies 2, history 2, science 3-4 (laboratory 2), foreign language 1-2 and academic electives 1-2.

2015-2016 Annual costs. Tuition/fees: $35,510. Room/board: $12,412. Books/supplies: $1,100.

2015-2016 Financial aid. Need-based: 198 full-time freshmen applied for aid; 159 deemed to have need; 159 received aid. Average need met was 81%. Average scholarship/grant was $27,019; average loan $3,553. 80% of total undergraduate aid awarded as scholarships/grants, 20% as loans/jobs. **Non-need-based:** Awarded to 380 full-time undergraduates, including 96 freshmen. Scholarships awarded for academics, art, leadership, music/drama, religious affiliation.

Application procedures. Admission: Priority date 2/1; deadline 7/1 (postmark date). No application fee. Admission notification on a rolling basis beginning on or about 10/15. Must reply by 10/15. Must reply by May 1 or within 2 week(s) if notified thereafter. Early action notification two weeks after application is complete. **Financial aid:** Priority date 3/1; no closing date. FAFSA required. Applicants notified on a rolling basis starting 3/15; must reply by 5/1 or within 2 week(s) of notification.

Academics. 4,000-acre biocultural reserve and learning center in the state of Yucatan, Mexico, for anthropology and archaeology and courses in various other disciplines. **Special study options:** Accelerated study, combined bachelor's/graduate degree, double major, honors, independent study, internships, liberal arts/career combination, semester at sea, student-designed major, study abroad, teacher certification program, Washington semester, weekend college. Faith and work service-learning opportunities; undergraduate field research opportunities in the Pacific Northwest, Yellowstone, Mexico, and Europe; multi-disciplinary study, including socio-cultural anthropology in Yucatan Peninsula; study abroad programs in Albania, Cambodia, China, Costa Rica, England, France, Germany, Ghana, Greece, Israel, Italy, Japan, Scotland, Mexico (Yucatan), Tanzania and Viet Nam; direct exchange programs in Albania, Japan, Ireland and Liechtenstein; pre-professional programs in dentistry, engineering, law, medicine, ministry, and social work; dual degree programs in engineering, applied science or nursing through Auburn University, Columbia University, Vanderbilt University, Washington University, and University of Mississippi Medical Health Center. Ford Teaching Fellows research and internships for students interested in college teaching; Weiner pre-medical fellows program for summer research. **Credit/placement by examination:** AP, CLEP, IB, SAT, ACT, institutional tests. 28 credit hours maximum toward bachelor's degree. Limited to two courses in any discipline and seven courses overall. **Support services:** Pre-admission summer program, reduced course load, study skills assistance, tutoring, writing center.

Majors. Area/ethnic studies: European, Latin American. **Biology:** General, biochemistry. **Business:** Accounting, business admin. **Communications:** Communications/speech/rhetoric. **Education:** Elementary. **English:** English lit. **Foreign languages:** Classics, Spanish. **History:** General. **Human services:** General. **Math:** General, applied. **Philosophy/religion:** Philosophy, religion. **Physical sciences:** Chemistry, geology, physics. **Psychology:** General. **Social sciences:** Economics, political science, sociology/anthropology. **Visual/performing arts:** Art history/conservation, music, studio arts.

Most popular majors. Biology 22%, business/marketing 29%, psychology 9%, social sciences 9%.

Technology on campus. 150 workstations in dormitories, library, computer center, student center. Dormitories wired for high-speed internet access and linked to campus network. Commuter students can connect to campus

network. Online course registration, online library, helpline, student web hosting, wireless network available.

Student life. Freshman orientation: Mandatory. Preregistration for classes offered. Eight days of educational and social activities held four days prior to classes and 12-week Foundations course held once weekly. **Policies:** Students required to live on campus through sophomore year. Students with family in the area may be exempted. **Housing:** Guaranteed on-campus for freshmen. Coed dorms, single-sex dorms, special housing for disabled, fraternity/sorority housing, themed housing available. Community service theme housing available. **Activities:** Campus ministries, choral groups, dance, drama, international student organizations, literary magazine, music ensembles, Model UN, musical theater, student government, student newspaper, Circle K, Christian Fellowship, Black student association, Habitat for Humanity, Catholic student association, Fellowship of Christian Athletes, College Republicans, Young Democrats, Multicultural Affairs Diversity Group, E.A.R.T.H. (environmental service club), Jewish cultural organization.

Athletics. NCAA. **Intercollegiate:** Baseball M, basketball, cross-country, football (tackle) M, golf, lacrosse, soccer, softball W, tennis, track and field, volleyball W. **Intramural:** Basketball, bowling, football (non-tackle), golf, handball, racquetball, soccer, softball, table tennis, tennis, volleyball. **Team name:** Millsaps Majors, Lady Majors.

Student services. Adult student services, alcohol/substance abuse counseling, chaplain/spiritual director, career counseling, student employment services, financial aid counseling, health services, minority student services, personal counseling, placement for graduates.

Contact. E-mail: admissions@millsaps.edu
Phone: (601) 974-1050 Toll-free number: (800) 352-1050
Fax: (601) 974-1059
Robert Alexander, Vice President for Enrollment & Communications, Millsaps College, 1701 North State Street, Jackson, MS 39210-0001

Mississippi College
Clinton, Mississippi
www.mc.edu   CB code: 1477

- Private 4-year university affiliated with the Southern Baptist Convention
- Residential campus in large town
- 2,856 degree-seeking undergraduates
- SAT or ACT (ACT writing optional) required

General. Founded in 1826. Regionally accredited. **Degrees:** 621 bachelor's awarded; master's, professional, doctoral offered. **ROTC:** Army, Air Force. **Location:** 10 miles from Jackson. **Calendar:** Semester, limited summer session. **Full-time faculty:** 211 total. **Part-time faculty:** 245 total. **Class size:** 59% < 20, 35% 20-39, 5% 40-49, 1% 50-99, less than 1% >100. **Special facilities:** Baptist Healthplex, Choctaw Trails, Samuel Marshall Gore Art Gallery, Science Building with Cadaver Lab.

Freshman class profile.

GPA 3.75 or higher:	35%	Rank in top quarter:	57%
GPA 3.50-3.74:	19%	Rank in top tenth:	33%
GPA 3.0-3.49:	27%	Out-of-state:	39%
GPA 2.0-2.99:	17%	Live on campus:	94%

Basis for selection. ACT/SAT scores most important, followed by high school record. Recommendations considered in marginal cases. For placement purposes, provisional admission if ACT score is less than 18. Admission and advising affects course load and course selection. Audition recommended for music majors; portfolio recommended for art majors. **Home schooled:** Transcript of courses and grades required.

High school preparation. College-preparatory program recommended. 22 units recommended. Recommended units include English 4, mathematics 4, social studies 2, history 2, science 4 (laboratory 2), foreign language 1, computer science .5, visual/performing arts 1, academic electives 3.5. 2 units of advanced electives recommended.

2015-2016 Annual costs. Tuition/fees: $16,114. Room/board: $8,744. Books/supplies: $1,100. Personal expenses: $2,249.

2015-2016 Financial aid. Need-based: 513 full-time freshmen applied for aid; 312 deemed to have need; 312 received aid. Average need met was 39%. Average scholarship/grant was $6,627; average loan $2,856. 62% of total undergraduate aid awarded as scholarships/grants, 38% as loans/jobs. **Non-need-based:** Awarded to 1,129 full-time undergraduates, including 267 freshmen. Scholarships awarded for academics, alumni affiliation, art, athletics, leadership, music/drama, religious affiliation, ROTC. **Additional information:** Student reply date for institutional scholarships: May 1.

Application procedures. Admission: Priority date 5/1; no deadline. $25 fee, may be waived for applicants with need. Notified after all admission documents received and reviewed. Either SAT or ACT may be substituted for TOEFL scores for foreign students. **Financial aid:** Priority date 3/1; no closing date. FAFSA required. Applicants notified on a rolling basis starting 3/1; must reply by 5/1.

Academics. Special study options: Accelerated study, combined bachelor's/graduate degree, distance learning, double major, dual enrollment of high school students, ESL, honors, independent study, internships, study abroad, teacher certification program. **Credit/placement by examination:** AP, CLEP, IB, institutional tests. 30 credit hours maximum toward bachelor's degree. **Support services:** Reduced course load, remedial instruction, study skills assistance, tutoring, writing center.

Majors. Biology: General, biochemistry, biomedical sciences. **Business:** Accounting, business admin, finance, marketing. **Communications:** General, communications/speech/rhetoric, media studies. **Computer sciences:** General, computer science. **Education:** Art, biology, business, chemistry, elementary, English, mathematics, music, physical, social studies, special ed. **Engineering:** Applied physics. **English:** English lit, general lit, writing. **Foreign languages:** French, Spanish, translation. **Health services:** Nursing (RN). **History:** General. **Human services:** Social work. **Math:** General. **Parks/recreation:** Exercise sciences, sports admin. **Philosophy/religion:** Christian. **Physical sciences:** Chemical physics, chemistry, physics. **Protective services:** Law enforcement admin. **Psychology:** General. **Social sciences:** Political science, sociology. **Theology:** Sacred music. **Visual/performing arts:** Graphic design, interior design, music, music performance, music theory/composition, piano/keyboard, studio arts, voice/opera.

Most popular majors. Biology 9%, business/marketing 20%, communications/journalism 6%, education 13%, health sciences 10%, parks/recreation 7%.

Technology on campus. 350 workstations in dormitories, library, computer center, student center. Dormitories wired for high-speed internet access and linked to campus network. Commuter students can connect to campus network. Online course registration, helpline, repair service, student web hosting, wireless network available.

Student life. Freshman orientation: Mandatory, $180 fee. Preregistration for classes offered. Held on a Thursday, Friday, and Saturday in June and July. **Policies:** No alcohol or smoking on campus. **Housing:** Single-sex dorms, special housing for disabled, apartments, wellness housing available. $100 nonrefundable deposit, deadline 7/15. **Activities:** Bands, campus ministries, choral groups, dance, drama, international student organizations, literary magazine, music ensembles, musical theater, opera, radio station, student government, student newspaper, Baptist Student Union, Civitan, Circle-K, Rotoract, Young Democrats, Young Republicans, Black Student Association, 5 women's social/service clubs, Reformed University Fellowship, Habitat for Humanity.

Athletics. NCAA. **Intercollegiate:** Baseball M, basketball, cross-country, football (tackle) M, golf, soccer, softball W, tennis, track and field, volleyball W. **Intramural:** Badminton, basketball, field hockey, football (non-tackle), soccer, softball, table tennis, tennis, volleyball. **Team name:** Choctaws.

Student services. Adult student services, chaplain/spiritual director, career counseling, student employment services, financial aid counseling, health services, personal counseling, placement for graduates, veterans' counselor. **Physically disabled:** Services for visually, speech, hearing impaired.

Contact. E-mail: admissions@mc.edu
Phone: (601) 925-3800 Toll-free number: (800) 738-1236
Fax: (601) 925-3950
William Brantley, Director of Admissions, Mississippi College, Box 4026, Clinton, MS 39058-0001

Mississippi State University
Mississippi State, Mississippi   CB member
www.msstate.edu   CB code: 1480

- Public 4-year university and agricultural college
- Residential campus in large town
- 16,712 degree-seeking undergraduates: 7% part-time, 49% women, 20% African American, 1% Asian American, 2% Hispanic/Latino, 1% Native American, 2% Multi-racial, non-Hispanic, 1% international
- 3,320 degree-seeking graduate students
- 72% of applicants admitted
- SAT or ACT (ACT writing optional) required
- 60% graduate within 6 years

General. Founded in 1878. Regionally accredited. Branch campus located in Meridian; extension offices in all 82 counties; branch experiment stations and research units in 15 locations. **Degrees:** 3,211 bachelor's awarded; master's, professional, doctoral offered. **ROTC:** Army, Air Force. **Location:** 125 miles from Jackson, 23 miles from Columbus. **Calendar:** Semester, extensive summer session. **Full-time faculty:** 902 total; 80% have terminal degrees, 17% minority, 39% women. **Part-time faculty:** 151 total; 45% have terminal degrees, 11% minority, 59% women. **Class size:** 40% < 20, 39% 20-39, 7% 40-49, 10% 50-99, 4% >100. **Special facilities:** Clock museum, historic costume and textiles collection, archaeology museum, Mississippi entomological museum, arboretum, music museum, observatory, advanced vehicular systems center, computational sciences center, computer security research center, computational simulation and design center, geosystems research institute, high performance computing collaboratory, high voltage laboratory, industrial assessment center, industrial outreach service, clean energy technology institute, digital biology institute, neurocognitive science and technology institute, microsystems prototyping laboratory, Mississippi transportation research center, flight research laboratory, forensics training center, sustainable energy research center.

Freshman class profile. 12,701 applied, 9,113 admitted, 3,471 enrolled.

Mid 50% test scores		Rank in top quarter:	52%
SAT critical reading:	480-620	Rank in top tenth:	26%
SAT math:	480-640	Return as sophomores:	82%
ACT composite:	20-27	Out-of-state:	40%
GPA 3.75 or higher:	31%	Live on campus:	96%
GPA 3.50-3.74:	15%	International:	1%
GPA 3.0-3.49:	28%	Fraternities:	27%
GPA 2.0-2.99:	26%	Sororities:	38%

Basis for selection. Admission based on standardized test scores, GPA, class rank. Students with academic deficiencies may be admitted after additional review. Requirements may vary by department; student should contact department to ensure that requirements are met. Successful completion of summer developmental program results in admission for fall term with mandatory participation in academic support program freshmen year. Audition/portfolio required for specific majors or departments. Interview recommended for architecture, professional golf management, and veterinary medicine students. **Home schooled:** Transcript of courses and grades required.

High school preparation. College-preparatory program required. 17 units required; 20 recommended. Required and recommended units include English 4, mathematics 3-4, social studies 1-2, history 2, science 3-4 (laboratory 2), foreign language 1, computer science 1-2, visual/performing arts 1 and academic electives 1. One of the two academic electives must be a foreign language or world geography. Additional unit recommended.

2015-2016 Annual costs. Tuition/fees: $7,502; $20,142 out-of-state. Room/board: $9,068. Books/supplies: $1,200. Personal expenses: $2,972.

2014-2015 Financial aid. **Need-based:** 2,442 full-time freshmen applied for aid; 2,016 deemed to have need; 2,007 received aid. Average need met was 63%. Average scholarship/grant was $6,244; average loan $3,375. 38% of total undergraduate aid awarded as scholarships/grants, 62% as loans/jobs. **Non-need-based:** Awarded to 4,065 full-time undergraduates, including 1,170 freshmen. Scholarships awarded for academics, alumni affiliation, art, athletics, job skills, leadership, minority status, music/drama, ROTC, state residency.

Application procedures. **Admission:** No deadline. $40 fee, may be waived for applicants with need. Admission notification on a rolling basis beginning on or about 9/1. **Financial aid:** Priority date 3/1; no closing date. FAFSA required. Applicants notified on a rolling basis starting 12/1; must reply by 5/1.

Academics. **Special study options:** Combined bachelor's/graduate degree, cooperative education, cross-registration, distance learning, double major, dual enrollment of high school students, ESL, exchange student, honors, independent study, internships, liberal arts/career combination, semester at sea, student-designed major, study abroad, teacher certification program, weekend college. **Credit/placement by examination:** AP, CLEP, IB, SAT, ACT, institutional tests. Maximum of 25% of any curriculum may be earned by examination which includes correspondence and military. **Support services:** Learning center, pre-admission summer program, reduced course load, remedial instruction, study skills assistance, tutoring, writing center.

Honors college/program. 30 ACT/1230 SAT (exclusive of Writing) and 3.8 core GPA required; 470 freshmen admitted.

Majors. **Architecture:** Architecture, interior, landscape. **Biology:** General, bacteriology, biochemistry. **Business:** Accounting, business admin, construction management, finance, insurance, management information systems, managerial economics, marketing, real estate. **Communications:** Communications/speech/rhetoric. **Computer sciences:** General. **Conservation:** Forestry, wildlife/wilderness. **Education:** Agricultural, business, elementary, music, physical, secondary, special ed, voc/tech. **Engineering:** Aerospace, biomedical, chemical, civil, computer, electrical, industrial, mechanical. **English:**

English lit. **Foreign languages:** General. **Health services:** Clinical lab science. **History:** General. **Human services:** Social work. **Liberal arts:** Arts/sciences. **Math:** General. **Philosophy/religion:** Philosophy. **Physical sciences:** Chemistry, geology, physics. **Psychology:** General, educational. **Social sciences:** Anthropology, criminology, economics, political science, sociology. **Visual/performing arts:** General, music. **Work/family studies:** General.

Most popular majors. Business/marketing 19%, education 8%, engineering/engineering technologies 16%, interdisciplinary studies 6%, parks/recreation 9%.

Technology on campus. Dormitories wired for high-speed internet access and linked to campus network. Commuter students can connect to campus network. Online course registration, online library, helpline, repair service, student web hosting, wireless network available.

Student life. **Freshman orientation:** Available, $30 fee. Preregistration for classes offered. Half-day event held prior to start of classes. **Policies:** Freshmen required to live in residence hall and purchase meal plan. **Housing:** Guaranteed on-campus for freshmen. Single-sex dorms, special housing for disabled, fraternity/sorority housing, themed housing available. $75 nonrefundable deposit. Co-residential housing available. **Activities:** Bands, campus ministries, choral groups, dance, drama, film society, international student organizations, literary magazine, music ensembles, Model UN, musical theater, radio station, student government, student newspaper, TV station, more than 300 organizations on campus.

Athletics. NCAA. **Intercollegiate:** Baseball M, basketball, cross-country, football (tackle) M, golf, soccer W, softball W, tennis, track and field, volleyball W. **Intramural:** Badminton, basketball, bowling, cross-country, football (non-tackle), golf, racquetball, rifle, soccer, softball, swimming, table tennis, tennis, ultimate frisbee, volleyball, water polo, weight lifting. **Team name:** Bulldogs.

Student services. Alcohol/substance abuse counseling, chaplain/spiritual director, career counseling, services for economically disadvantaged, student employment services, financial aid counseling, health services, minority student services, on-campus daycare, personal counseling, veterans' counselor. **Physically disabled:** Services for visually, speech, hearing impaired.

Contact. E-mail: admit@msstate.edu
Phone: (662) 325-2224 Fax: (662) 325-1678
Phil Bonfanti, Director of Admissions and Scholarships, Mississippi State University, Box 6334, Mississippi State, MS 39762

Mississippi University for Women
Columbus, Mississippi
www.muw.edu CB code: 1481

‣ Public 4-year university and liberal arts college
‣ Commuter campus in large town
‣ 2,192 degree-seeking undergraduates
‣ 96% of applicants admitted

General. Founded in 1884. Regionally accredited. **Degrees:** 731 bachelor's, 46 associate awarded; master's, professional offered. **ROTC:** Army, Air Force. **Location:** 120 miles from Birmingham, AL; 160 miles from Memphis, TN. **Calendar:** Semester, limited summer session. **Full-time faculty:** 135 total. **Part-time faculty:** 80 total. **Class size:** 60% < 20, 33% 20-39, 4% 40-49, 2% 50-99, 2% >100. **Special facilities:** Environmental education center.

Freshman class profile. 671 applied, 645 admitted, 246 enrolled.

Mid 50% test scores		GPA 2.0-2.99:	30%
SAT critical reading:	410-490	Rank in top quarter:	61%
SAT math:	580-660	Rank in top tenth:	30%
ACT composite:	18-24	Out-of-state:	10%
GPA 3.75 or higher:	23%	Live on campus:	66%
GPA 3.50-3.74:	18%	Fraternities:	42%
GPA 3.0-3.49:	29%	Sororities:	43%

Basis for selection. Test scores, high school GPA, academic achievement considered in that order. SAT or ACT recommended. Students with a 3.2 GPA or higher not required to provide test scores. Interview required for students who are taking a placement test. **Home schooled:** Portfolio of work and/or transcript is required. Placement test may be required.

High school preparation. College-preparatory program recommended. 16 units required; 20 recommended. Required and recommended units include English 4, mathematics 3-4, social studies 3, science 3-4 (laboratory 2), foreign language 1, computer science .5 and academic electives 2. One elective of foreign language or world geography required; other elective must be in foreign language, world geography, 4th year mathematics, or 4th year laboratory science.

2015-2016 Annual costs. Tuition/fees: $5,781; $15,847 out-of-state. Room/board: $6,591. Books/supplies: $1,500. Personal expenses: $1,200.

Financial aid. Non-need-based: Scholarships awarded for academics, alumni affiliation, leadership, minority status, music/drama, ROTC, state residency.

Application procedures. Admission: No deadline. No application fee. Admission notification on a rolling basis. **Financial aid:** Priority date 3/1; no closing date. FAFSA required. Applicants notified on a rolling basis starting 3/15; must reply within 2 week(s) of notification.

Academics. Special study options: Cross-registration, distance learning, double major, dual enrollment of high school students, honors, independent study, internships, study abroad, teacher certification program, weekend college. **Credit/placement by examination:** AP, CLEP, SAT, ACT, institutional tests. 60 credit hours maximum toward bachelor's degree. **Support services:** Learning center, pre-admission summer program, remedial instruction, tutoring.

Majors. Area/ethnic studies: Women's. **Biology:** General, bacteriology. **Business:** Accounting, business admin. **Communications:** Communications/speech/rhetoric. **Education:** Art, elementary, music. **English:** English lit. **Foreign languages:** Spanish. **Health services:** Music therapy, nursing (RN), speech pathology. **History:** General. **Liberal arts:** Arts/sciences. **Math:** General. **Parks/recreation:** Health/fitness. **Physical sciences:** General, chemistry. **Psychology:** General. **Social sciences:** General, political science. **Visual/performing arts:** General, music. **Work/family studies:** Family systems.

Most popular majors. Business/marketing 9%, education 15%, health sciences 33%.

Technology on campus. 500 workstations in dormitories, library, computer center. Dormitories wired for high-speed internet access and linked to campus network. Commuter students can connect to campus network. Online course registration, online library, helpline, student web hosting available.

Student life. Freshman orientation: Available. Preregistration for classes offered. **Housing:** Guaranteed on-campus for all undergraduates. Single-sex dorms, apartments, wellness housing available. $100 partly refundable deposit. **Activities:** Jazz band, choral groups, drama, international student organizations, literary magazine, music ensembles, radio station, student government, student newspaper, Methodist/Presbyterian/Episcopal/Baptist/Catholic/student interfaith associations, black student organizations, College Republicans, Young Democrats.

Athletics. Intramural: Badminton, basketball, football (non-tackle), golf, racquetball, soccer, softball, table tennis, tennis, volleyball.

Student services. Adult student services, alcohol/substance abuse counseling, career counseling, student employment services, financial aid counseling, health services, on-campus daycare, personal counseling, placement for graduates, veterans' counselor. **Physically disabled:** Services for visually, speech, hearing impaired.

Contact. E-mail: admissions@muw.edu
Phone: (662) 329-7106 Toll-free number: (877) 462-8439
Fax: (662) 241-7481
Shelly Moss, Director of Admissions, Mississippi University for Women, 1100 College St. MUW-1613, Columbus, MS 39701

Mississippi Valley State University
Itta Bena, Mississippi   **CB member**
www.mvsu.edu   **CB code: 1482**

‣ Public 4-year university and liberal arts college
‣ Commuter campus in small town
‣ 1,767 degree-seeking undergraduates: 5% part-time, 57% women
‣ 361 degree-seeking graduate students
‣ SAT or ACT (ACT writing optional) required

General. Founded in 1946. Regionally accredited. **Degrees:** 323 bachelor's awarded; master's offered. **ROTC:** Army. **Location:** 100 miles from Jackson, 130 miles from Memphis, Tennessee. **Calendar:** Semester, extensive summer session. **Full-time faculty:** 115 total; 66% have terminal degrees, 31% minority, 47% women. **Part-time faculty:** 31 total; 36% have terminal degrees, 10% minority, 48% women. **Class size:** 62% < 20, 34% 20-39, 2% 40-49, 2% 50-99.

Freshman class profile.

GPA 3.75 or higher:	7%	GPA 2.0-2.99:	51%
GPA 3.50-3.74:	7%	Out-of-state:	38%
GPA 3.0-3.49:	28%	Live on campus:	89%

Basis for selection. High school curriculum and test scores very important. Audition required for music education majors. Interview required of some students, but recommended for all students.

High school preparation. 16 units required; 18 recommended. Required and recommended units include English 4, mathematics 3, social studies 3, science 3 (laboratory 2), foreign language 1 and academic electives 2. Mathematics requirement includes algebra I and II and geometry. Social sciences must include US government and US history. Sciences must be chosen from introductory and advanced biology, physics, and chemistry. Advanced science or mathematics may be substituted for a foreign language.

2015-2016 Annual costs. Tuition/fees: $5,936. Room/board: $7,756.

Financial aid. Non-need-based: Scholarships awarded for academics, athletics, minority status, ROTC.

Application procedures. Admission: Priority date 8/1; deadline 8/17 (receipt date). No application fee. Admission notification on a rolling basis. **Financial aid:** Priority date 3/1, closing date 5/1. FAFSA, institutional form required. Applicants notified on a rolling basis starting 4/1; must reply within 2 week(s) of notification.

Academics. Special study options: Cooperative education, distance learning, double major, dual enrollment of high school students, honors, independent study, internships, teacher certification program. **Credit/placement by examination:** AP, CLEP, ACT. 30 credit hours maximum toward bachelor's degree. **Support services:** Learning center, pre-admission summer program, reduced course load, remedial instruction, study skills assistance, tutoring, writing center.

Majors. Biology: General. **Business:** Accounting, business admin, office management. **Communications:** Communications/speech/rhetoric. **Computer sciences:** General. **Education:** Early childhood, elementary, music, physical, secondary. **English:** English lit, rhetoric/composition. **Health services:** Environmental health. **History:** General. **Human services:** General, social work. **Math:** General. **Physical sciences:** Chemistry. **Protective services:** Criminal justice. **Social sciences:** Political science, sociology. **Visual/performing arts:** Music, studio arts.

Most popular majors. Biology 8%, business/marketing 19%, education 27%, public administration/social services 12%, security/protective services 9%.

Technology on campus. 600 workstations in dormitories, library, computer center. Dormitories wired for high-speed internet access and linked to campus network. Commuter students can connect to campus network. Online course registration, online library, wireless network available.

Student life. Freshman orientation: Mandatory, $100 fee. Preregistration for classes offered. Three-day event held in late July. **Housing:** Single-sex dorms, apartments available. $50 nonrefundable deposit, deadline 7/31. **Activities:** Bands, choral groups, dance, drama, music ensembles, radio station, student government, student newspaper, TV station, numerous honor societies, political, social, religious organizations, prelaw club.

Athletics. NCAA. Intercollegiate: Baseball M, basketball, bowling, cross-country, football (tackle) M, golf, soccer W, softball W, tennis, track and field, volleyball W. **Intramural:** Baseball M, basketball, bowling, cross-country, softball W, swimming, tennis, volleyball. **Team name:** Delta Devils (M), Devilettes (W).

Student services. Adult student services, career counseling, student employment services, financial aid counseling, health services, on-campus daycare, personal counseling, placement for graduates, veterans' counselor.

Contact. E-mail: jawill@mvsu.edu
Phone: (662) 254-3347 Fax: (662) 254-3759
Jacqueline Williams, Director of Admissions, Mississippi Valley State University, 14000 Highway 82 West, Itta Bena, MS 38941-1400

Rust College
Holly Springs, Mississippi
www.rustcollege.edu   **CB code: 1669**

‣ Private 4-year liberal arts and teachers college affiliated with the United Methodist Church
‣ Residential campus in small town

♦ 856 degree-seeking undergraduates
♦ ACT (writing optional) required

General. Founded in 1866. Regionally accredited. **Degrees:** 139 bachelor's, 9 associate awarded. **Location:** 35 miles from Memphis, TN. **Calendar:** Semester, limited summer session. **Full-time faculty:** 48 total; 56% have terminal degrees, 83% minority, 44% women. **Part-time faculty:** 2 total; 100% minority, 50% women. **Class size:** 54% < 20, 44% 20-39, 2% 40-49. **Special facilities:** Library for ministers and ministerial students, Inuit and African art collections, international artifacts' collection.

Basis for selection. Recommendations most important; GPA and test scores important. Special requirements for teacher education program. **Home schooled:** State high school equivalency certificate, letter of recommendation (nonparent) required.

High school preparation. College-preparatory program recommended. 19 units required. Required units include English 4, mathematics 3, social studies 3, science 3 and academic electives 6.

2015-2016 Annual costs. Tuition/fees: $9,500. Room/board: $4,100. Books/supplies: $250. Personal expenses: $1,350.

Financial aid. Non-need-based: Scholarships awarded for academics, leadership, music/drama, religious affiliation, state residency.

Application procedures. Admission: Priority date 5/5; no deadline. $10 fee, may be waived for applicants with need. Admission notification on a rolling basis. Must reply by May 1 or within 2 week(s) if notified thereafter. **Financial aid:** Priority date 3/15, closing date 6/30. FAFSA, institutional form required. Applicants notified on a rolling basis starting 4/1; must reply within 2 week(s) of notification.

Academics. Special study options: Accelerated study, combined bachelor's/graduate degree, distance learning, double major, dual enrollment of high school students, honors, independent study, internships, liberal arts/career combination, study abroad, teacher certification program. **Credit/placement by examination:** AP, CLEP, SAT, ACT, institutional tests. 12 credit hours maximum toward associate degree, 12 toward bachelor's. **Support services:** Learning center, pre-admission summer program, reduced course load, remedial instruction, study skills assistance, tutoring, writing center.

Majors. Biology: General. **Business:** Business admin. **Communications:** Broadcast journalism, journalism. **Computer sciences:** Computer science. **Education:** Biology, business, elementary, English, mathematics, social science. **English:** English lit. **Human services:** Social work. **Math:** General. **Physical sciences:** Chemistry. **Social sciences:** General, political science, sociology. **Visual/performing arts:** Music. **Work/family studies:** Child care management.

Most popular majors. Biology 34%, business/marketing 7%, communications/journalism 12%, computer/information sciences 9%, mathematics 7%, public administration/social services 10%.

Technology on campus. 220 workstations in dormitories, library, computer center. Dormitories wired for high-speed internet access and linked to campus network. Commuter students can connect to campus network. Online library, helpline, wireless network available.

Student life. Freshman orientation: Mandatory. Preregistration for classes offered. Orientation and assessment program begins 1 week prior to registration. **Housing:** Guaranteed on-campus for freshmen. Single-sex dorms available. $50 fully refundable deposit. Housing for single parents available. **Activities:** Bands, campus ministries, choral groups, drama, international student organizations, music ensembles, radio station, student government, student newspaper, TV station, Methodist Student Movement, Baptist student union, Catholic student association, pre-law club, NAACP, social work club, Sunday School.

Athletics. NCAA. **Intercollegiate:** Baseball M, basketball, cheerleading, cross-country, softball W, tennis, track and field, volleyball. **Intramural:** Basketball, football (non-tackle), swimming, volleyball. **Team name:** Bearcats.

Student services. Adult student services, chaplain/spiritual director, career counseling, financial aid counseling, health services, on-campus daycare, personal counseling, placement for graduates, veterans' counselor.

Contact. E-mail: b_talley@rustcollege.edu
Phone: (662) 252-8000 ext. 4059
Toll-free number: (888) 886-8492 ext. 4059 Fax: (662) 252-8895
Braque Talley, Director of Enrollment Services, Rust College, 150 Rust Avenue, Holly Springs, MS 38635-2328

Southeastern Baptist College
Laurel, Mississippi
www.southeasternbaptist.edu   CB code: 1781

♦ Private 4-year Bible and business college affiliated with the Baptist faith
♦ Commuter campus in large town
♦ 52 undergraduates

General. Founded in 1949. Accredited by ABHE. **Degrees:** 5 associate awarded. **Location:** 90 miles from Jackson. **Calendar:** Semester, limited summer session. **Full-time faculty:** 2 total. **Part-time faculty:** 9 total. **Special facilities:** Game room, physical fitness room.

Basis for selection. Open admission. Home school friendly. ACT determines placement. High school or equivalent required. Interview, essay recommended for all students. Audition recommended for religious music majors.

High school preparation. In place of high school diploma or GED, 17 high school units including 2 natural/biological sciences, 1 English, 1 mathematics, 2 social sciences accepted.

2015-2016 Annual costs. Tuition/fees: $6,550. Room/board: $2,196. Books/supplies: $300. Personal expenses: $350.

Application procedures. Admission: Closing date 8/1 (receipt date). $50 fee. Application must be submitted on paper. Admission notification on a rolling basis beginning on or about 1/1. Students may attend classes for two weeks without enrollment. They must be enrolled the third week to attend classes. **Financial aid:** Priority date 7/1; no closing date. Institutional form required. Applicants notified on a rolling basis starting 7/15; must reply within 4 week(s) of notification.

Academics. Special study options: Distance learning, double major. **Credit/placement by examination:** AP, CLEP. **Support services:** Learning center, remedial instruction, tutoring.

Majors. Philosophy/religion: Religion. **Theology:** Bible, theology.

Technology on campus. 17 workstations in dormitories, library, computer center. Dormitories wired for high-speed internet access and linked to campus network. Commuter students can connect to campus network. Helpline, wireless network available.

Student life. Freshman orientation: Mandatory, $20 fee. Preregistration for classes offered. Offered as class taken during first semester. **Policies:** Student handbook for important policies. Religious observance required. **Housing:** Guaranteed on-campus for all undergraduates. Single-sex dorms, apartments available. $75 fully refundable deposit, deadline 8/1. **Activities:** Choral groups, music ensembles, student government, Association of Baptist Students, Ministerial Alliance.

Student services. Student employment services, financial aid counseling, personal counseling, placement for graduates, veterans' counselor.

Contact. E-mail: admissions@southeasternbaptist.edu
Phone: (601) 426-6346 Fax: (601) 426-6347
Ronnie Kitchens, Director of Admissions, Southeastern Baptist College, 4229 Highway 15 North, Laurel, MS 39440

Tougaloo College
Tougaloo, Mississippi   CB member
www.tougaloo.edu   CB code: 1807

♦ Private 4-year liberal arts college affiliated with the United Church of Christ
♦ Residential campus in large city
♦ 857 degree-seeking undergraduates: 5% part-time, 65% women, 99% African American
♦ 9 degree-seeking graduate students
♦ 39% of applicants admitted
♦ SAT or ACT (ACT writing optional) required
♦ 41% graduate within 6 years; 34% enter graduate study

General. Founded in 1869. Regionally accredited. Cooperative program with Brown University provides exchange of financial resources and students. Exchange opportunities available between New York and Boston universities in pre-med and other areas. **Degrees:** 141 bachelor's awarded; master's offered. **ROTC:** Army, Naval. **Calendar:** Semester, limited summer session. **Full-time faculty:** 76 total; 66% have terminal degrees, 64% minority, 54% women. **Part-time faculty:** 23 total. **Class size:** 70% < 20, 24% 20-39, 4%

40-49, 2% 50-99. **Special facilities:** Civil rights documents and prints, East and West African art and artifacts.

Freshman class profile. 2,321 applied, 908 admitted, 154 enrolled.

Mid 50% test scores		GPA 2.0-2.99:	44%
SAT critical reading:	350-450	Rank in top quarter:	24%
SAT math:	360-500	Rank in top tenth:	18%
ACT composite:	15-20	End year in good standing:	77%
GPA 3.75 or higher:	12%	Return as sophomores:	66%
GPA 3.50-3.74:	14%	Out-of-state:	27%
GPA 3.0-3.49:	24%	Live on campus:	80%

Basis for selection. Transcript, test scores important. Minimum 3.0 GPA and ACT composite score of 18 required of applicants in junior year of high school and dual enrolled high school students. Audition required for music majors. Portfolio recommended for art majors. **Home schooled:** Transcript of courses and grades, state high school equivalency certificate, letter of recommendation (nonparent) required.

High school preparation. College-preparatory program recommended. 16 units required. Required and recommended units include English 3, mathematics 2, social studies 2, science 2, foreign language 2 and academic electives 9.

2015-2016 Annual costs. Tuition/fees: $10,607. Room/board: $6,400. Books/supplies: $60. Personal expenses: $800.

Financial aid. Non-need-based: Scholarships awarded for academics, art, athletics, leadership, music/drama.

Application procedures. Admission: Priority date 4/15; no deadline. $25 fee, may be waived for applicants with need. Admission notification on a rolling basis. **Financial aid:** Priority date 4/15; no closing date. FAFSA, institutional form required. Applicants notified on a rolling basis starting 5/1; must reply within 2 week(s) of notification.

Academics. Special study options: Accelerated study, cooperative education, cross-registration, double major, dual enrollment of high school students, exchange student, honors, independent study, internships, liberal arts/career combination, New York semester, student-designed major, study abroad, teacher certification program, Washington semester. 3-2 program in pre-engineering and physical sciences with Brown University, Georgia Institute of Technology, University of Mississippi, University of Wisconsin Madison, Tuskegee Institute, Washington University St. Louis, Howard University, University of Memphis, Florida A&M. **Credit/placement by examination:** AP, CLEP, IB, SAT, ACT, institutional tests. 12 credit hours maximum toward bachelor's degree. **Support services:** Learning center, pre-admission summer program, reduced course load, remedial instruction, study skills assistance, tutoring, writing center.

Majors. Biology: General. **Business:** Hotel/motel/restaurant management. **Communications:** Media studies. **Education:** Elementary, health, kindergarten/preschool, secondary, special ed. **English:** English lit. **History:** General. **Liberal arts:** Arts/sciences. **Math:** General. **Physical sciences:** Chemistry, physics. **Psychology:** General. **Social sciences:** Economics, political science, sociology. **Visual/performing arts:** Art, music.

Most popular majors. Biology 16%, business/marketing 11%, history 8%, parks/recreation 6%, physical sciences 8%, psychology 7%, social sciences 23%.

Technology on campus. 4 workstations in dormitories, library, computer center, student center. Dormitories linked to campus network. Commuter students can connect to campus network. Helpline, repair service, wireless network available.

Student life. Freshman orientation: Mandatory. Preregistration for classes offered. **Policies:** Smoke-free campus, zero tolerance for weapons, drugs and alcohol. **Housing:** Single-sex dorms, wellness housing available. $50 nonrefundable deposit. **Activities:** Jazz band, choral groups, dance, drama, music ensembles, radio station, student government, student newspaper, Baptist student union, biology club, Afro-American studies group, College Republicans, foreign students club, French club, pre-health club, pre-law club, honor societies, human services clubs.

Athletics. NAIA. **Intercollegiate:** Baseball M, basketball, cross-country, golf, tennis. **Intramural:** Badminton, baseball M, basketball, cheerleading, cross-country M, football (non-tackle) M, golf, soccer M, softball, tennis, volleyball. **Team name:** Bulldogs.

Student services. Adult student services, chaplain/spiritual director, career counseling, student employment services, financial aid counseling, health services, personal counseling, placement for graduates, veterans' counselor.

Contact. E-mail: info@tougaloo.edu
Phone: (601) 977-7765 Toll-free number: (888) 424-2566
Fax: (601) 977-4501
Junoesque Jacobs, Director of Admissions, Tougaloo College, 500 West County Line Road, Tougaloo, MS 39174

University of Mississippi
University, Mississippi
www.olemiss.edu

CB member
CB code: 1840

- Public 4-year university
- Residential campus in large town
- 18,472 degree-seeking undergraduates: 7% part-time, 57% women, 14% African American, 2% Asian American, 3% Hispanic/Latino, 2% Multiracial, non-Hispanic, 1% international
- 4,427 graduate students
- 79% of applicants admitted
- 61% graduate within 6 years

General. Founded in 1844. Regionally accredited. **Degrees:** 3,659 bachelor's awarded; master's, professional, doctoral offered. **ROTC:** Army, Naval, Air Force. **Location:** 75 miles from Memphis, Tennessee. **Calendar:** Semester, extensive summer session. **Class size:** 44% < 20, 33% 20-39, 7% 40-49, 12% 50-99, 3% >100. **Special facilities:** Art museums with Southern folk art, Greek and Roman antiquities, 19th century scientific instruments and American fine art, William Faulkner's home and grounds, blues archive, world's largest collection of accountancy publications, university field station with 740 acres and more than 200 experimental ponds, factory with full manufacturing lines for wood, metal and plastic fabrication.

Freshman class profile. 18,059 applied, 14,217 admitted, 3,969 enrolled.

Mid 50% test scores		GPA 2.0-2.99:	12%
SAT critical reading:	490-600	Rank in top quarter:	49%
SAT math:	500-600	Rank in top tenth:	24%
ACT composite:	21-28	Out-of-state:	58%
GPA 3.75 or higher:	41%	Fraternities:	46%
GPA 3.50-3.74:	18%	Sororities:	64%
GPA 3.0-3.49:	29%		

Basis for selection. School achievement record and test scores are important. SAT/ACT required for students with core GPA under 3.2. Essay required for Croft Institute for International Studies, honors college; audition required for music, theater majors. Portfolio recommended for art majors. **Home schooled:** Transcript of courses and grades required. **Learning Disabled:** Report and document disabilities to student disabilities office.

High school preparation. College-preparatory program required. 16 units required; 20 recommended. Required and recommended units include English 4, mathematics 3-4, social studies 3-4, science 3-4 (laboratory 2), foreign language 2, computer science 1 and academic electives 1. Math must include algebra and 2 higher courses. Social sciences units must include U.S. history and U.S. government. Academic electives must include foreign language or advanced world geography; second unit can be fourth year math or fourth year lab science.

2015-2016 Annual costs. Tuition/fees: $7,444; $20,674 out-of-state. Books/supplies: $1,200.

2014-2015 Financial aid. Need-based: 2,779 full-time freshmen applied for aid; 1,842 deemed to have need; 1,793 received aid. Average need met was 75%. Average scholarship/grant was $8,532; average loan $3,192. 51% of total undergraduate aid awarded as scholarships/grants, 49% as loans/jobs. **Non-need-based:** Awarded to 5,354 full-time undergraduates, including 1,658 freshmen. Scholarships awarded for academics, alumni affiliation, art, athletics, leadership, music/drama, ROTC, state residency.

Application procedures. Admission: Priority date 4/1; deadline 9/1 (postmark date). $40 fee ($60 out-of-state), may be waived for applicants with need. Admission notification on a rolling basis beginning on or about 9/15. Online out-of-state application fee: $60. **Financial aid:** Priority date 3/1; no closing date. FAFSA required. Applicants notified on a rolling basis starting 4/1; must reply within 4 week(s) of notification.

Academics. Special study options: Accelerated study, combined bachelor's/graduate degree, cooperative education, distance learning, double major, dual enrollment of high school students, ESL, exchange student, honors, independent study, internships, study abroad, teacher certification program. **Credit/placement by examination:** AP, CLEP, IB, SAT, ACT, institutional tests. 63 credit hours maximum toward bachelor's degree. Student must earn 12 hours in residence before any credit-by-examination hours are recorded on transcript. **Support services:** Learning center, pre-admission summer program, reduced course load, remedial instruction, study skills assistance, tutoring, writing center.

Honors college/program. Requires test scores, transcript, essays, and recommendations. 120 students admitted each fall. Unique courses which meet general education requirements taught by senior/master faculty. Senior thesis required.

Majors. Area/ethnic studies: African-American, regional. **Biology:** General, biochemistry. **Business:** Accounting, business admin, finance, hospitality admin, insurance, management information systems, managerial economics, marketing, real estate. **Communications:** Digital media, journalism. **Computer sciences:** General. **Education:** Elementary, English, foreign languages, mathematics, science, social studies, special ed. **Engineering:** General, chemical, civil, electrical, geological, mechanical. **English:** English lit. **Foreign languages:** Arabic, Chinese, classics, French, German, linguistics, Spanish. **Health services:** Audiology/speech pathology, clinical lab science, communication disorders, cytotechnology, dental hygiene, dietetics, health information management, pharmaceutical sciences, radiologic technology/medical imaging. **History:** General. **Human services:** Public policy, social work. **Liberal arts:** Arts/sciences. **Math:** General. **Parks/recreation:** Exercise sciences, facilities management, sports admin. **Philosophy/religion:** Philosophy, religion. **Physical sciences:** Chemistry, forensic chemistry, geology, physics. **Protective services:** Law enforcement admin. **Psychology:** General. **Social sciences:** Anthropology, economics, international relations, political science, sociology. **Visual/performing arts:** General, art history/conservation, dramatic, music, studio arts.

Most popular majors. Business/marketing 23%, education 7%, health sciences 18%, liberal arts 6%.

Technology on campus. Dormitories wired for high-speed internet access and linked to campus network. Commuter students can connect to campus network. Online course registration, online library, helpline, repair service, student web hosting, wireless network available.

Student life. Freshman orientation: Mandatory, $115 fee. Preregistration for classes offered. Two days in June with additional session immediately before beginning of term. Additional fee of $75 if a parent attends. **Housing:** Guaranteed on-campus for freshmen. Single-sex dorms, apartments, fraternity/sorority housing, wellness housing available. $75 nonrefundable deposit. Intensive study floors available to honors and other students. Special interest, graduate/older students, substance-free, environmental interest housing available. **Activities:** Bands, campus ministries, choral groups, dance, drama, international student organizations, music ensembles, musical theater, opera, radio station, student government, student newspaper, symphony orchestra, TV station, Wesley Foundation, Baptist student union, black student union, Students for Environmental Awareness, Mortar Board, Habitat for Humanity, Students Envisioning Equality through Diversity, Engineers without Borders, One Mississippi.

Athletics. NCAA. **Intercollegiate:** Baseball M, basketball, cheerleading, cross-country, fencing, football (tackle) M, golf, lacrosse M, racquetball M, rifle W, rugby M, skiing M, soccer, softball W, tennis, track and field, volleyball W. **Intramural:** Badminton, basketball, bowling, football (tackle), golf, handball, rifle, soccer, softball, swimming, table tennis, tennis, track and field, volleyball, water polo. **Team name:** Rebels.

Student services. Adult student services, alcohol/substance abuse counseling, chaplain/spiritual director, career counseling, student employment services, financial aid counseling, health services, legal services, minority student services, personal counseling, placement for graduates, veterans' counselor, women's services. **Physically disabled:** Services for visually, speech, hearing impaired.

Contact. E-mail: admissions@olemiss.edu
Phone: (662) 915-7226 Toll-free number: (800) 653-6477
Fax: (662) 915-5869
Whitman Smith, Director of Admissions, University of Mississippi, 145 Martindale, University, MS 38677-1848

University of Mississippi Medical Center
Jackson, Mississippi
www.umc.edu   CB code: 0358

▸ Public two-year upper-division health science college
▸ Commuter campus in large city

General. Founded in 1955. Regionally accredited. **Degrees:** 406 bachelor's awarded; master's, professional, doctoral offered. **Location:** 200 miles from Memphis, TN. **Calendar:** Semester, limited summer session. **Full-time faculty:** 795 total. **Part-time faculty:** 168 total.

Student profile. 701 degree-seeking undergraduates.

Out-of-state:	1%	**25 or older:**	80%
Live on campus:	3%		

Basis for selection. College transcript required. Competitive admission to health science programs based on grades, recommendations, test scores, interviews. Transfer accepted as juniors.

2015-2016 Annual costs. Tuition/fees: $7,344; $20,574 out-of-state. Books/supplies: $1,380. Personal expenses: $4,050.

Application procedures. Admission: Deadline 2/11. $25 fee. Application must be submitted online. Admission notification 4/11. Must reply by 5/11. Application closing dates and reply dates vary by program. **Financial aid:** FAFSA, institutional form required.

Academics. Includes schools of medicine, nursing, health-related professions, and dentistry, graduate programs in medical and clinical health sciences, and 623-bed teaching hospital. Certificate programs in emergency medical technology and radiologic technology and clinical nuclear medicine offered. **Special study options:** Combined bachelor's/graduate degree, liberal arts/career combination. **Credit/placement by examination:** AP, CLEP. **Support services:** Pre-admission summer program, study skills assistance, tutoring.

Majors. Health services: Clinical lab science, cytotechnology, dental hygiene, health information management.

Technology on campus. 75 workstations in library, computer center. Online library available.

Student life. Housing: Single-sex dorms, apartments available. **Activities:** Student government, student newspaper, University Christian Fellowship, Catholic Student Organization.

Athletics. Intramural: Baseball, basketball, football (tackle) M, golf, soccer, softball, table tennis.

Student services. Alcohol/substance abuse counseling, chaplain/spiritual director, career counseling, financial aid counseling, health services, minority student services, personal counseling. **Physically disabled:** Services for speech, hearing impaired.

Contact. Phone: (601) 984-1080
Barbara Westerfield, Registrar, University of Mississippi Medical Center, 2500 North State Street, Jackson, MS 39216

University of Phoenix: Jackson
Flowood, Mississippi
www.phoenix.edu

▸ For-profit 4-year university
▸ Commuter campus in small town
▸ 49 undergraduates

General. Degrees: 2 bachelor's awarded; master's offered. **Calendar:** Differs by program. Other Academic Calendar. **Full-time faculty:** 3 total. **Part-time faculty:** 13 total.

Basis for selection. Open admission.

2015-2016 Annual costs. Per-credit-hour charge $410 to $635, depending upon level and course of study; electronic course materials fee $95-$200, if applicable. Book and material charges may vary by course and program. All fees are subject to change.

Application procedures. Admission: No deadline. No application fee.

Academics. Credit/placement by examination: AP, CLEP.

Majors. Business: Accounting/business management, business admin, e-commerce, entrepreneurial studies, finance, human resources, marketing, operations. **Communications:** General. **Computer sciences:** Programming, security, system admin, systems analysis, web page design, webmaster. **Human services:** General. **Protective services:** Law enforcement admin.

Student life. Freshman orientation: Mandatory. Preregistration for classes offered.

Contact. Toll-free number: (866) 766-0766
University of Phoenix: Jackson, 1625 W. Fountainhead Pkwy, Tempe, AZ 85282

University of Southern Mississippi

Hattiesburg, Mississippi
www.usm.edu

CB member
CB code: 1479

- Public 4-year university
- Commuter campus in small city
- 11,736 degree-seeking undergraduates: 13% part-time, 64% women, 30% African American, 1% Asian American, 3% Hispanic/Latino, 2% Multi-racial, non-Hispanic, 1% international
- 2,711 degree-seeking graduate students
- 58% of applicants admitted
- SAT or ACT (ACT writing optional) required
- 50% graduate within 6 years

General. Founded in 1910. Regionally accredited. Dual campus with main campus in Hattiesburg and nonresidential, nontraditional campus in Long Beach; other sites along Mississippi Gulf Coast. **Degrees:** 2,352 bachelor's awarded; master's, doctoral offered. **ROTC:** Army, Air Force. **Location:** 85 miles from Jackson, 110 miles from New Orleans. **Calendar:** Semester, extensive summer session. **Full-time faculty:** 689 total; 78% have terminal degrees, 16% minority, 48% women. **Part-time faculty:** 218 total; 38% have terminal degrees, 10% minority, 59% women. **Class size:** 44% < 20, 40% 20-39, 7% 40-49, 6% 50-99, 3% >100. **Special facilities:** Marine education center, aquarium.

Freshman class profile. 6,046 applied, 3,509 admitted, 1,527 enrolled.

Mid 50% test scores			
SAT critical reading:	450-560	End year in good standing:	77%
SAT math:	450-570	Return as sophomores:	73%
ACT composite:	19-26	Out-of-state:	27%
GPA 3.75 or higher:	26%	Live on campus:	92%
GPA 3.50-3.74:	15%	International:	2%
GPA 3.0-3.49:	26%	Fraternities:	7%
GPA 2.0-2.99:	32%	Sororities:	15%

Basis for selection. Test scores, GPA, class rank important. Applicants who don't meet criteria may be required to participate in screening process that includes testing.

High school preparation. College-preparatory program required. 16.5 units required; 20.5 recommended. Required and recommended units include English 4, mathematics 3-4, social studies 3-4, science 3-4 (laboratory 3), foreign language 1, computer science .5, visual/performing arts 1 and academic electives 2.

2015-2016 Annual costs. Tuition/fees: $7,224; $16,094 out-of-state. Room/board: $7,550. Books/supplies: $2,000. Personal expenses: $2,000.

2014-2015 Financial aid. Need-based: 1,493 full-time freshmen applied for aid; 1,247 deemed to have need; 1,244 received aid. Average need met was 74%. Average scholarship/grant was $4,794; average loan $4,304. 53% of total undergraduate aid awarded as scholarships/grants, 47% as loans/jobs. **Non-need-based:** Awarded to 5,254 full-time undergraduates, including 1,199 freshmen. Scholarships awarded for academics, alumni affiliation, art, athletics, leadership, music/drama, ROTC, state residency.

Application procedures. Admission: No deadline. $40 fee, may be waived for applicants with need. Admission notification on a rolling basis. Amount of housing deposit after 6/15 is $150. **Financial aid:** Priority date 3/15; no closing date. FAFSA required. Applicants notified on a rolling basis starting 3/15.

Academics. Special study options: Combined bachelor's/graduate degree, distance learning, double major, dual enrollment of high school students, ESL, exchange student, honors, internships, study abroad, teacher certification program. Certificate Programs. **Credit/placement by examination:** AP, CLEP, IB, institutional tests. 30 credit hours maximum toward bachelor's degree. **Support services:** Learning center, pre-admission summer program, remedial instruction, tutoring, writing center.

Honors college/program. Requires an ACT score of 26 or equivalent GPA requirement, and essay.

Majors. Architecture: Interior. **Area/ethnic studies:** American. **Biology:** General, marine. **Business:** Accounting, business admin, finance, hotel/motel admin, human resources, international, management information systems, managerial economics, marketing, tourism/travel. **Communications:** Advertising, communications/speech/rhetoric, journalism, radio/TV. **Computer sciences:** General, data processing. **Education:** Business, Deaf/hearing impaired, elementary, music, physical, special ed. **English:** English lit. **Foreign languages:** General. **Health services:** Athletic training, audiology/speech pathology, clinical lab science, dietetics, nursing (RN). **History:** General. **Human services:** Social work. **Liberal arts:** Library science. **Math:**

General. **Parks/recreation:** General, sports admin. **Philosophy/religion:** Philosophy, religion. **Physical sciences:** Chemistry, geology, oceanography, physics. **Protective services:** Criminal justice, forensics. **Psychology:** General. **Social sciences:** Anthropology, geography, international relations, political science, sociology. **Visual/performing arts:** General, dance, dramatic, music, music management. **Work/family studies:** Clothing/textiles, family systems.

Most popular majors. Business/marketing 18%, education 10%, health sciences 14%, psychology 7%.

Technology on campus. 550 workstations in dormitories, library, computer center. Dormitories wired for high-speed internet access and linked to campus network. Commuter students can connect to campus network. Online course registration, online library, helpline, student web hosting, wireless network available.

Student life. Freshman orientation: Mandatory, $100 fee. Preregistration for classes offered. **Policies:** Freshmen who reside in area may live at home. All freshmen who request campus housing required to live in freshman dormitories. **Housing:** Single-sex dorms, special housing for disabled, fraternity/sorority housing, themed housing available. $75 nonrefundable deposit, deadline 6/15. Honors available. **Activities:** Bands, campus ministries, choral groups, dance, drama, film society, international student organizations, literary magazine, music ensembles, musical theater, opera, radio station, student government, student newspaper, symphony orchestra, Honor societies, service and religious organizations, Young Republicans, Young Democrats.

Athletics. NCAA. **Intercollegiate:** Baseball M, basketball, cross-country, football (tackle) M, golf, rugby M, soccer W, softball W, tennis, track and field, volleyball W. **Intramural:** Badminton, basketball, bowling, football (non-tackle), golf, racquetball, soccer, softball, squash, swimming, table tennis, tennis, track and field, ultimate frisbee, volleyball, water polo, weight lifting. **Team name:** Golden Eagles.

Student services. Adult student services, career counseling, student employment services, health services, minority student services, on-campus daycare, personal counseling, placement for graduates, veterans' counselor, women's services. **Physically disabled:** Services for visually, speech, hearing impaired.

Contact. E-mail: admissions@usm.edu
Phone: (601) 266-5000 Fax: (601) 266-5148
Amanda King, Admissions Operations, University of Southern Mississippi, 118 College Drive #5166, Hattiesburg, MS 39406-0001

William Carey University

Hattiesburg, Mississippi
www.wmcarey.edu

CB code: 1907

- Private 4-year university and liberal arts college affiliated with the Baptist faith
- Commuter campus in small city
- 2,047 degree-seeking undergraduates

General. Founded in 1906. Regionally accredited. Additional campuses in Biloxi and New Orleans. **Degrees:** 554 bachelor's awarded; master's, professional, doctoral offered. **ROTC:** Army, Air Force. **Location:** 110 miles from New Orleans. **Calendar:** Trimester, extensive summer session. **Full-time faculty:** 169 total. **Part-time faculty:** 12 total. **Class size:** 57% < 20, 42% 20-39, less than 1% 40-49. **Special facilities:** Lucile Parker art collection and gallery, garden.

Freshman class profile. 842 applied, 479 admitted, 194 enrolled.

Mid 50% test scores			
SAT critical reading:	380-520	Out-of-state:	12%
SAT math:	430-560	Live on campus:	82%
ACT composite:	20-27	Fraternities:	1%
		Sororities:	1%

Basis for selection. Open admission, but selective for some programs. ACT of 20 or SAT of 950 (exclusive of Writing) required. Additional requirements for nursing and education majors. **Home schooled:** Transcript of courses and grades required.

High school preparation. College-preparatory program recommended. 16 units required. Required units include English 4, mathematics 3, social studies 2 and science 3.

2015-2016 Annual costs. Tuition/fees: $11,700. Room/board: $5,220. Books/supplies: $2,850. Personal expenses: $1,800.

Financial aid. Non-need-based: Scholarships awarded for academics, alumni affiliation, art, athletics, music/drama, religious affiliation.

Application procedures. Admission: Priority date 7/12; no deadline. $40 fee, may be waived for applicants with need. Application must be submitted online. Admission notification on a rolling basis. Admissions application priority date: 30 days prior to beginning of term. **Financial aid:** Priority date 4/1, closing date 9/1. FAFSA required. Applicants notified on a rolling basis starting 6/1; must reply within 2 week(s) of notification.

Academics. Special study options: Accelerated study, cross-registration, distance learning, double major, dual enrollment of high school students, honors, independent study, internships, study abroad, teacher certification program. **Credit/placement by examination:** AP, CLEP, IB, institutional tests. 30 credit hours maximum toward bachelor's degree. **Support services:** Reduced course load, remedial instruction, study skills assistance, tutoring.

Majors. Biology: General. **Business:** Business admin. **Communications:** Communications/speech/rhetoric, journalism. **Education:** Art, biology, drama/dance, elementary, English, mathematics, music, physical, social science, speech. **English:** English lit. **Health services:** Music therapy, nursing (RN). **History:** General. **Math:** General. **Parks/recreation:** Health/fitness. **Physical sciences:** Chemistry. **Psychology:** General. **Social sciences:** General. **Theology:** Bible, sacred music. **Visual/performing arts:** Art, dramatic, music, music performance, studio arts.

Most popular majors. Business/marketing 9%, education 15%, health sciences 28%, liberal arts 11%, psychology 13%.

Technology on campus. 50 workstations in library, computer center. Dormitories wired for high-speed internet access. Commuter students can connect to campus network. Online library, helpline, wireless network available.

Student life. Freshman orientation: Mandatory. Preregistration for classes offered. Orientation for new students is held prior to the start of the fall term. **Policies:** Religious observance required. **Housing:** Guaranteed on-campus for freshmen. Single-sex dorms, apartments, wellness housing available. $150 fully refundable deposit. **Activities:** Bands, campus ministries, choral groups, dance, drama, international student organizations, music ensembles, musical theater, student government, student newspaper, Baptist student union, Afro-American club, psychology club, Fellowship of Christian Athletes, honorary organizations, Church Related Vocations Fellowship, science society, student nurses association, music therapy association.

Athletics. NAIA. **Intercollegiate:** Baseball M, basketball, golf, soccer, softball W. **Intramural:** Basketball, bowling, football (non-tackle) M, football (tackle), soccer, softball, table tennis, tennis, volleyball. **Team name:** Crusaders.

Student services. Adult student services, alcohol/substance abuse counseling, chaplain/spiritual director, career counseling, services for economically disadvantaged, student employment services, financial aid counseling, personal counseling, placement for graduates, veterans' counselor. **Physically disabled:** Services for visually impaired.

Contact. E-mail: admissions@wmcarey.edu
Phone: (601) 318-6103 Toll-free number: (800) 962-5991
Fax: (601) 318-6765
Alissa King, Director of Admissions, William Carey University, 498 Tuscan Avenue, Hattiesburg, MS 39401

Missouri

Avila University
Kansas City, Missouri
www.avila.edu
CB code: 6109

- Private 4-year university and liberal arts college affiliated with the Roman Catholic Church
- Commuter campus in very large city
- 1,368 degree-seeking undergraduates: 16% part-time, 61% women, 19% African American, 2% Asian American, 8% Hispanic/Latino, 1% Native American, 3% Multi-racial, non-Hispanic, 8% international
- 435 degree-seeking graduate students
- 51% of applicants admitted
- SAT or ACT (ACT writing optional) required
- 55% graduate within 6 years

General. Founded in 1916. Regionally accredited. **Degrees:** 254 bachelor's awarded; master's offered. **ROTC:** Army. **Calendar:** Semester, extensive summer session. **Full-time faculty:** 73 total; 74% have terminal degrees, 10% minority, 59% women. **Part-time faculty:** 165 total; 38% have terminal degrees, 11% minority, 58% women. **Class size:** 65% < 20, 34% 20-39, less than 1% 40-49, less than 1% 50-99. **Special facilities:** Radiological laboratory, campus media production facilities, nursing learning resource center, photography lab, Santa Fe Trail walking path, learning commons.

Freshman class profile. 2,018 applied, 1,027 admitted, 199 enrolled.

Mid 50% test scores			
SAT critical reading:	410-490	Rank in top quarter:	23%
SAT math:	450-520	Rank in top tenth:	13%
ACT composite:	19-24	End year in good standing:	82%
GPA 3.75 or higher:	16%	Return as sophomores:	62%
GPA 3.50-3.74:	17%	Out-of-state:	26%
GPA 3.0-3.49:	38%	Live on campus:	71%
GPA 2.0-2.99:	29%	International:	2%

Basis for selection. Unconditional acceptance for applicants with minimum GPA of 2.5 and ACT composite of 20 or higher. Others may be considered. ACT subscores used for math and English placement. Audition recommended for drama, music students. **Home schooled:** Transcript of courses and grades required. GED may be requested.

High school preparation. 17 units required. Required and recommended units include English 4, mathematics 3, social studies 3, science 3 (laboratory 1), foreign language 3 and visual/performing arts 1.

2015-2016 Annual costs. Tuition/fees: $26,500. Room/board: $7,500. Books/supplies: $1,600. Personal expenses: $2,064.

2014-2015 Financial aid. Need-based: 482 full-time freshmen applied for aid; 441 deemed to have need; 441 received aid. Average need met was 70%. Average scholarship/grant was $16,486; average loan $3,443. 63% of total undergraduate aid awarded as scholarships/grants, 37% as loans/jobs. **Non-need-based:** Awarded to 659 full-time undergraduates, including 389 freshmen. Scholarships awarded for academics, alumni affiliation, art, athletics, music/drama, religious affiliation. **Additional information:** Financial aid adjusted based on need for increases in tuition.

Application procedures. Admission: No deadline. $25 fee, may be waived for applicants with need, free for online applicants. Admission notification on a rolling basis. **Financial aid:** Closing date 4/1. FAFSA, institutional form required. Applicants notified on a rolling basis starting 2/1; must reply within 2 week(s) of notification.

Academics. Outcome-based core curriculum; interdisciplinary course work at junior level required; unique senior experience bridges transition from college to community. **Special study options:** Accelerated study, combined bachelor's/graduate degree, cooperative education, cross-registration, distance learning, double major, dual enrollment of high school students, ESL, exchange student, independent study, internships, liberal arts/career combination, study abroad, teacher certification program, Washington semester, weekend college. **Credit/placement by examination:** AP, CLEP, IB, SAT, ACT, institutional tests. 30 credit hours maximum toward bachelor's degree. **Support services:** Learning center, reduced course load, remedial instruction, study skills assistance, tutoring, writing center.

Majors. Biology: General. **Business:** General, accounting, business admin, entrepreneurial studies, finance, human resources, international, sales/distribution. **Communications:** Communications/speech/rhetoric, media studies. **Computer sciences:** General. **Education:** General, business, elementary, learning disabled, middle. **English:** English lit. **Health services:** Facilities admin, medical radiologic technology/radiation therapy, nursing (RN), premedicine. **History:** General. **Human services:** Social work. **Math:** General. **Parks/recreation:** Exercise sciences. **Philosophy/religion:** Religion. **Psychology:** General. **Social sciences:** Criminology, political science, sociology. **Visual/performing arts:** Art, dramatic, music performance.

Most popular majors. Business/marketing 14%, health sciences 39%, psychology 8%, visual/performing arts 8%.

Technology on campus. 141 workstations in dormitories, library, computer center, student center. Dormitories wired for high-speed internet access and linked to campus network. Commuter students can connect to campus network. Online course registration, online library, helpline, wireless network available.

Student life. Freshman orientation: Mandatory. Preregistration for classes offered. Held 3 days prior to first day of classes; programs available for freshmen-adult transfer students and friends/family of new students. **Policies:** First-time, first-year students not living at home with parents/guardians required to live on campus through sophomore year. **Housing:** Guaranteed on-campus for freshmen. Coed dorms, apartments, wellness housing available. Single-sex floors available. **Activities:** Pep band, campus ministries, choral groups, dance, drama, film society, international student organizations, literary magazine, music ensembles, musical theater, student government, student newspaper, student nurses association, psychology club, black student union, premedical club, English club, education club, Association of Radiological Science, social work association, Society of Latinos.

Athletics. NAIA. **Intercollegiate:** Baseball M, basketball, cheerleading W, cross-country, football (tackle) M, golf, soccer, softball W, track and field, volleyball W. **Intramural:** Basketball, table tennis, volleyball. **Team name:** Eagles.

Student services. Adult student services, alcohol/substance abuse counseling, chaplain/spiritual director, career counseling, student employment services, financial aid counseling, health services, personal counseling, veterans' counselor, women's services. **Physically disabled:** Services for visually, speech, hearing impaired.

Contact. E-mail: admission@avila.edu
Phone: (816) 501-2400 Toll-free number: (800) 462-8452
Fax: (816) 501-2453
Brandon Johnson, VP for Enrollment Management, Avila University, 11901 Wornall Road, Kansas City, MO 64145-1007

Baptist Bible College
Springfield, Missouri
www.gobbc.edu
CB code: 0991

- Private 4-year Bible and seminary college affiliated with the Baptist faith
- Residential campus in small city
- 321 undergraduates
- 69 graduate students

General. Founded in 1950. Regionally accredited; also accredited by ABHE. **Degrees:** 52 bachelor's, 6 associate awarded; master's offered. **Location:** 180 miles from Kansas City, 225 miles from St. Louis. **Calendar:** Semester, limited summer session. **Full-time faculty:** 25 total. **Part-time faculty:** 10 total.

Basis for selection. Open admission. Pastor's recommendation required.

2015-2016 Annual costs. Tuition/fees: $12,850. Room/board: $6,550. Books/supplies: $840.

Application procedures. Admission: Priority date 8/1; no deadline. $40 fee. Admission notification on a rolling basis. **Financial aid:** Closing date 5/1. FAFSA, institutional form required. Applicants notified on a rolling basis; must reply within 2 week(s) of notification.

Academics. Special study options: Distance learning. **Credit/placement by examination:** AP, CLEP. **Support services:** Learning center, reduced course load, study skills assistance, tutoring.

Majors. Business: Administrative services. **Education:** Elementary, music. **Philosophy/religion:** Religion. **Theology:** Missionary, pastoral counseling, religious ed, sacred music, theology. **Visual/performing arts:** Music.

Technology on campus. 70 workstations in library, computer center, student center. Dormitories wired for high-speed internet access and linked to campus network. Online library, helpline, repair service, wireless network available.

Student life. Freshman orientation: Mandatory. Preregistration for classes offered. **Policies:** Religious observance required. **Housing:** Guaranteed on-campus for freshmen. Single-sex dorms, apartments available. **Activities:** Concert band, choral groups, music ensembles, radio station, student government.

Athletics. NCCAA. **Intercollegiate:** Basketball, volleyball W. **Intramural:** Basketball, volleyball. **Team name:** Patriots.

Student services. Chaplain/spiritual director, financial aid counseling, health services, on-campus daycare, personal counseling, veterans' counselor.

Contact. E-mail: rherrin@gobbc.edu
Phone: (417) 268-6000 Toll-free number: (800) 228-5754 ext. 6601
Fax: (417) 268-6694
Reuben Herrin, Director of Recruiting, Baptist Bible College, 628 East Kearney Street, Springfield, MO 65803

Calvary Bible College and Theological Seminary
Kansas City, Missouri
www.calvary.edu   CB code: 6331

- Private 4-year Bible and seminary college affiliated with the nondenominational tradition
- Residential campus in large city
- 226 degree-seeking undergraduates: 28% part-time, 50% women, 11% African American, 2% Asian American, 3% Hispanic/Latino, 1% Native American, 3% Multi-racial, non-Hispanic
- 57 degree-seeking graduate students
- 94% of applicants admitted
- SAT or ACT (ACT writing optional), application essay required
- 50% graduate within 6 years

General. Founded in 1932. Regionally accredited; also accredited by ABHE. **Degrees:** 45 bachelor's, 6 associate awarded; master's offered. **ROTC:** Army. **Location:** 20 miles from downtown Kansas City. **Calendar:** Semester, limited summer session. **Full-time faculty:** 17 total; 82% have terminal degrees, 12% minority, 41% women. **Part-time faculty:** 30 total; 10% have terminal degrees, 7% minority, 30% women. **Class size:** 95% < 20, 5% 20-39.

Freshman class profile. 52 applied, 49 admitted, 33 enrolled.

Mid 50% test scores			
		GPA 3.0-3.49:	19%
SAT critical reading:	450-520	GPA 2.0-2.99:	28%
SAT math:	500-520	Return as sophomores:	69%
ACT composite:	19-24	Out-of-state:	70%
GPA 3.75 or higher:	31%	Live on campus:	76%
GPA 3.50-3.74:	22%		

Basis for selection. Christian character stressed along with academic preparation. Pastor's and personal reference forms required. School achievement record and test scores considered. Applicants are required to submit a written Personal Testimony/Confirmation and Statement of Faith. If a student submits multiple scores for the same test, then only the test(s) with the highest composite score(s) is/are considered. Audition required for music students. **Home schooled:** Transcript of courses and grades required. Transcripts are required in compliance with state's home-school policies. **Learning Disabled:** Students should contact the Director of Admissions.

2015-2016 Annual costs. Tuition/fees: $11,640. Room/board: $5,200. Books/supplies: $794. Personal expenses: $1,262. **Additional information:** Visit web site for detailed information regarding tuition and expenses at Calvary Bible College.

2014-2015 Financial aid. **Need-based:** 30 full-time freshmen applied for aid; 27 deemed to have need; 27 received aid. Average need met was 74%. Average scholarship/grant was $6,014; average loan $3,472. 43% of total undergraduate aid awarded as scholarships/grants, 57% as loans/jobs. **Non-need-based:** Awarded to 18 full-time undergraduates, including 6 freshmen. Scholarships awarded for academics, alumni affiliation, music/drama, religious affiliation, ROTC.

Application procedures. **Admission:** No deadline. No application fee. Notified continually as accepted. **Financial aid:** Closing date 4/1. FAFSA

required. Applicants notified on a rolling basis starting 5/1; must reply within 2 week(s) of notification.

Academics. Each student carries a major in Bible and theology and second major in a professional area, which prepares them for vocational and/or volunteer involvement in Christian ministry. **Special study options:** Accelerated study, combined bachelor's/graduate degree, distance learning, double major, dual enrollment of high school students, independent study, internships, teacher certification program. **Credit/placement by examination:** AP, CLEP, IB, institutional tests. 16 credit hours maximum toward associate degree, 30 toward bachelor's. **Support services:** Learning center, reduced course load, remedial instruction, study skills assistance, tutoring.

Majors. **Business:** Business admin. **Communications:** Broadcast journalism. **Computer sciences:** Computer science. **Education:** Elementary, music, secondary. **English:** Creative writing, English lit. **History:** General. **Math:** General. **Protective services:** Law enforcement admin. **Social sciences:** Political science. **Theology:** Bible, pastoral counseling, theology, youth ministry. **Visual/performing arts:** Art, cinematography, dramatic, music performance, photography.

Most popular majors. Business/marketing 9%, theological studies 76%.

Technology on campus. 35 workstations in library, computer center, student center. Dormitories wired for high-speed internet access. Online course registration, online library, repair service, wireless network available.

Student life. Freshman orientation: Mandatory, $60 fee. Preregistration for classes offered. **Policies:** Weekly Christian ministry, chapel and church attendance required. Single students required to live in college housing unless living with parents or at least 23 years of age. Religious observance required. **Housing:** Guaranteed on-campus for all undergraduates. Single-sex dorms, apartments available. $150 fully refundable deposit, deadline 8/15. Duplexes for married students available. **Activities:** Concert band, campus ministries, choral groups, drama, music ensembles, musical theater, student government, Missionary Prayer Fellowship, Missions Committee, Calvary Veteran's Fellowship.

Athletics. NCCAA. **Intercollegiate:** Basketball, soccer M, volleyball W. **Intramural:** Sand volleyball, soccer. **Team name:** Warriors.

Student services. Adult student services, alcohol/substance abuse counseling, chaplain/spiritual director, career counseling, student employment services, financial aid counseling, health services, personal counseling, veterans' counselor, women's services.

Contact. E-mail: admissions@calvary.edu
Phone: (816) 322-3960 Toll-free number: (800) 326-3960
Fax: (816) 331-4474
Brian Mason, Dean of Assessment, Enrollment Management, Calvary Bible College and Theological Seminary, 15800 Calvary Road, Kansas City, MO 64147-1341

Central Christian College of the Bible
Moberly, Missouri
www.cccb.edu   CB code: 6145

- Private 4-year Bible college affiliated with the Christian Church
- Residential campus in large town
- 272 degree-seeking undergraduates: 17% part-time, 48% women
- ACT (writing recommended), application essay required

General. Founded in 1957. Accredited by ABHE. Every full-time student receives a full-tuition scholarship. **Degrees:** 47 bachelor's, 16 associate awarded. **Location:** 35 miles from Columbia. **Calendar:** Semester, limited summer session. **Full-time faculty:** 10 total. **Part-time faculty:** 11 total. **Special facilities:** 71,000 volume library with computer lab and foreign language lab.

Basis for selection. High school transcript, ACT/SAT scores and references very important. Students with GPA below 2.0 assigned reduced course load. **Home schooled:** Transcript of courses and grades required.

High school preparation. 15 units recommended. Recommended units include English 2, mathematics 2, social studies 1 and science 2.

2015-2016 Annual costs. Books/supplies: $325. Personal expenses: $3,237.

Application procedures. **Admission:** No deadline. $50 fee. Admission notification on a rolling basis beginning on or about 12/1. Admitted applicants must reply within 6 weeks of notification. **Financial aid:** Priority date 4/1; no closing date. Applicants notified on a rolling basis starting 3/1; must reply within 4 week(s) of notification.

Academics. **Special study options:** Cooperative education, distance learning, dual enrollment of high school students, internships, teacher certification program. **Credit/placement by examination:** AP, CLEP. 6 credit hours maximum toward bachelor's degree. **Support services:** Reduced course load, study skills assistance, tutoring.

Majors. **Philosophy/religion:** Religion. **Theology:** Pastoral counseling, religious ed, sacred music, theology. **Visual/performing arts:** Music.

Technology on campus. 30 workstations in library, student center. Dormitories wired for high-speed internet access and linked to campus network. Commuter students can connect to campus network. Wireless network available.

Student life. **Freshman orientation:** Mandatory, $250 fee. Preregistration for classes offered. **Policies:** Religious observance required. **Housing:** Guaranteed on-campus for all undergraduates. Single-sex dorms, wellness housing available. **Activities:** Campus ministries, choral groups, international student organizations, music ensembles, student government, Harvesters missions group, Gospel choir.

Athletics. NCCAA. **Intercollegiate:** Basketball, cross-country, soccer M, volleyball W. **Intramural:** Basketball, bowling, softball, table tennis, tennis, volleyball. **Team name:** Saints.

Student services. Chaplain/spiritual director, career counseling, financial aid counseling, personal counseling, placement for graduates, veterans' counselor.

Contact. E-mail: admissions@cccb.edu
Phone: (660) 263-3900 ext. 144 Toll-free number: (888) 263-3900
Rocky Christensen, Executive Director of Admission, Central Christian College of the Bible, 911 East Urbandale Drive, Moberly, MO 65270-1997

Central Methodist University
Fayette, Missouri
www.centralmethodist.edu   **CB code: 6089**

- Private 4-year university and liberal arts college affiliated with the United Methodist Church
- Residential campus in small town
- 1,091 degree-seeking undergraduates: 2% part-time, 52% women, 8% African American, 3% Hispanic/Latino, 3% Multi-racial, non-Hispanic, 4% international
- 58% of applicants admitted
- SAT or ACT (ACT writing optional) required
- 52% graduate within 6 years

General. Founded in 1854. Regionally accredited. **Degrees:** 254 bachelor's, 6 associate awarded. **ROTC:** Army, Air Force. **Location:** 25 miles from Columbia, 150 miles from St. Louis. **Calendar:** Semester, limited summer session. **Full-time faculty:** 64 total; 61% have terminal degrees, 5% minority, 50% women. **Part-time faculty:** 49 total; 24% have terminal degrees, 2% minority, 63% women. **Class size:** 65% < 20, 31% 20-39, 1% 40-49, 2% 50-99, less than 1% >100. **Special facilities:** Observatory, wildlife sanctuary outdoor learning center, natural history museum, conservatory.

Freshman class profile. 1,430 applied, 827 admitted, 286 enrolled.

Mid 50% test scores			
SAT critical reading:	450-500	GPA 2.0-2.99:	14%
SAT math:	410-570	Return as sophomores:	65%
SAT writing:	420-470	Out-of-state:	11%
ACT composite:	20-25	Live on campus:	88%
GPA 3.75 or higher:	31%	International:	5%
GPA 3.50-3.74:	19%	Fraternities:	11%
GPA 3.0-3.49:	36%	Sororities:	23%

Basis for selection. Full acceptance requires 2.5 GPA and 21 ACT or equivalent SAT. Students transferring with more than 15 hours of college credit are not required to submit scores. Interview required for nursing applicants; audition recommended for drama, music students.

High school preparation. College-preparatory program recommended. 26 units recommended. Recommended units include English 4, mathematics 3, social studies 3, science 3 and foreign language 1. 2 humanities recommended.

2016-2017 Annual costs. Tuition/fees (projected): $23,010. Room/board: $7,550. Books/supplies: $1,000. Personal expenses: $2,560.

2015-2016 Financial aid. **Need-based:** 262 full-time freshmen applied for aid; 237 deemed to have need; 237 received aid. Average need met was 69%. Average scholarship/grant was $5,086; average loan $3,471. 49% of total undergraduate aid awarded as scholarships/grants, 51% as loans/jobs. **Non-need-based:** Awarded to 1,658 full-time undergraduates, including 455 freshmen. Scholarships awarded for academics, alumni affiliation, athletics, leadership, music/drama, religious affiliation, ROTC.

Application procedures. **Admission:** No deadline. No application fee. Admission notification on a rolling basis beginning on or about 10/1. **Financial aid:** Priority date 3/15; no closing date. FAFSA required. Applicants notified on a rolling basis starting 1/1; must reply by 8/5 or within 2 week(s) of notification.

Academics. **Special study options:** Combined bachelor's/graduate degree, distance learning, double major, dual enrollment of high school students, honors, independent study, internships, liberal arts/career combination, student-designed major, study abroad, teacher certification program. 3-year bachelor's degree, 2-week January travel program. **Credit/placement by examination:** AP, CLEP, IB, SAT, ACT. 32 credit hours maximum toward associate degree, 32 toward bachelor's. **Support services:** Learning center, study skills assistance, tutoring, writing center.

Majors. **Biology:** General, marine. **Business:** General, accounting, banking/financial services, business admin, entrepreneurial studies, international, management science, marketing. **Communications:** Communications/speech/rhetoric. **Computer sciences:** Computer science. **Conservation:** Environmental science. **Education:** Biology, chemistry, early childhood, elementary, foreign languages, middle, music, physical, physics, science, secondary, social science, special ed. **English:** English lit. **Foreign languages:** Spanish. **Health services:** Athletic training, nursing (RN). **History:** General. **Math:** General. **Parks/recreation:** Facilities management. **Philosophy/religion:** Philosophy, religion. **Physical sciences:** Chemistry, physics. **Protective services:** Law enforcement admin. **Psychology:** General. **Social sciences:** Political science, sociology. **Visual/performing arts:** Dramatic, music, music performance. **Work/family studies:** Child development.

Most popular majors. Biology 11%, business/marketing 15%, education 17%, health sciences 18%, interdisciplinary studies 7%, psychology 6%, security/protective services 6%.

Technology on campus. 325 workstations in dormitories, library, computer center, student center. Dormitories wired for high-speed internet access and linked to campus network. Commuter students can connect to campus network. Online library, helpline, repair service, wireless network available.

Student life. **Freshman orientation:** Mandatory. Preregistration for classes offered. **Housing:** Guaranteed on-campus for freshmen. Coed dorms, single-sex dorms, apartments available. $100 partly refundable deposit, deadline 4/9. **Activities:** Bands, campus ministries, choral groups, dance, drama, international student organizations, literary magazine, music ensembles, opera, radio station, student government, student newspaper, various religious, service, business, music organizations.

Athletics. NAIA. **Intercollegiate:** Baseball M, basketball, cheerleading W, cross-country, football (tackle) M, golf, soccer, softball W, track and field, volleyball W. **Intramural:** Basketball, bowling, football (non-tackle), racquetball, sand volleyball, soccer, softball, table tennis, tennis, track and field, ultimate frisbee, volleyball, weight lifting. **Team name:** Eagles.

Student services. Alcohol/substance abuse counseling, chaplain/spiritual director, career counseling, student employment services, financial aid counseling, health services, personal counseling, placement for graduates.

Contact. E-mail: admissions@centralmethodist.edu
Phone: (660) 248-6374 Toll-free number: (877) 268-1854
Fax: (660) 248-1872
Adam Jenkins, Director of Admissions, Central Methodist University, 411 Central Methodist Square, Fayette, MO 65248-1198

Chamberlain College of Nursing: St. Louis
St Louis, Missouri
www.chamberlain.edu   **CB code: 3139**

- For-profit 4-year nursing college
- Commuter campus in very large city
- 510 degree-seeking undergraduates
- SAT or ACT with writing, application essay required

General. Founded in 1889. Regionally accredited. In addition to the St. Louis campus, there is a second campus in Columbus, OH. Affiliated with

Fontbonne College; general education requirements offered on both campuses. **Degrees:** 163 bachelor's awarded. **Calendar:** Semester, limited summer session. **Full-time faculty:** 21 total; 14% minority, 95% women. **Part-time faculty:** 40 total; 20% minority, 92% women. **Special facilities:** Hospital, archives.

Basis for selection. High school GPA of 2.5, rank in top third of class, ACT scores, personal statement important. Interview and reference may be considered.

2015-2016 Annual costs. Tuition/fees: $18,160. Books/supplies: $1,400. Personal expenses: $2,452. **Additional information:** Tuition quoted is for Nursing courses at $590 per credit. Tuition and fees vary by program.

Financial aid. Non-need-based: Scholarships awarded for academics.

Application procedures. Admission: No deadline. $95 fee, may be waived for applicants with need. Admission notification on a rolling basis. **Financial aid:** No deadline. FAFSA, institutional form required. Applicants notified on a rolling basis starting 4/1; must reply within 2 week(s) of notification.

Academics. Special study options: Accelerated study, cross-registration. **Credit/placement by examination:** AP, CLEP, institutional tests. 30 credit hours maximum toward bachelor's degree. **Support services:** Learning center, reduced course load, remedial instruction, tutoring.

Majors. Health services: Nursing (RN).

Technology on campus. 20 workstations in computer center.

Student life. Freshman orientation: Mandatory. Preregistration for classes offered. **Housing:** $50 deposit. **Activities:** Choral groups, student government, National Student Nurse Association.

Student services. Health services, on-campus daycare, personal counseling.

Contact. Phone: (314) 991-6200 Toll-free number: (800) 942-3410 Fax: (314) 768-5673
Chamberlain College of Nursing: St. Louis, 11830 Westline Industrial Drive, Suite 106, St. Louis, MO 63146

College of the Ozarks
Point Lookout, Missouri
www.cofo.edu   CB code: 6713

- Private 4-year liberal arts college affiliated with the interdenominational tradition
- Residential campus in small town
- 1,442 degree-seeking undergraduates: 1% part-time, 53% women, 1% African American, 1% Asian American, 2% Hispanic/Latino, 2% Multi-racial, non-Hispanic, 2% international
- 12% of applicants admitted
- SAT or ACT with writing, interview required
- 63% graduate within 6 years; 27% enter graduate study

General. Founded in 1906. Regionally accredited. Each full-time student's cost of education is met 100% by participating in the Work Education Program and a combination of private, institutional, and federal/state student aid, but without loans of any kind. **Degrees:** 321 bachelor's awarded. **ROTC:** Army. **Location:** 2 miles from Branson, 45 miles from Springfield. **Calendar:** Semester. **Full-time faculty:** 87 total; 59% have terminal degrees, 1% minority, 46% women. **Part-time faculty:** 56 total; 18% have terminal degrees, 2% minority, 48% women. **Class size:** 58% < 20, 37% 20-39, 2% 40-49, 2% 50-99. **Special facilities:** Grist mill, weaving studio, fire department, the Missouri Vietnam veterans memorial.

Freshman class profile. 3,122 applied, 386 admitted, 345 enrolled.

Mid 50% test scores			
SAT critical reading:	460-500	Rank in top quarter:	61%
SAT math:	500-560	Rank in top tenth:	23%
SAT writing:	490-530	End year in good standing:	83%
ACT composite:	21-25	Return as sophomores:	73%
GPA 3.75 or higher:	43%	Out-of-state:	21%
GPA 3.50-3.74:	23%	Live on campus:	92%
GPA 3.0-3.49:	33%		
GPA 2.0-2.99:	1%		

Basis for selection. High school record, financial need, test scores, class rank, recommendations, activities and interview important. Academic interest and growth, development of intellectual skills considered. ACT with writing required. Audition recommended for music students; portfolio recommended

for art students. **Home schooled:** Pass grades are not acceptable. Candidates must present a transcript with a letter or percentage grade.

High school preparation. College-preparatory program recommended. 24 units recommended. Required and recommended units include English 4, mathematics 3, social studies 3, history 3, science 2 (laboratory 1) and foreign language 2. Public speaking, visual and performing arts recommended.

2015-2016 Annual costs. Tuition/fees: $18,730. Room/board: $6,500. Books/supplies: $1,000. Personal expenses: $430.

2014-2015 Financial aid. Need-based: 246 full-time freshmen applied for aid; 236 deemed to have need; 236 received aid. Average need met was 86%. Average scholarship/grant was $14,336. 65% of total undergraduate aid awarded as scholarships/grants, 35% as loans/jobs. **Non-need-based:** Awarded to 268 full-time undergraduates, including 90 freshmen. Scholarships awarded for academics, art, athletics, leadership, music/drama, ROTC, state residency. **Additional information:** The College guarantees to meet 100% of total cost for each full-time student without loans of any kind. All full-time students work on campus in exchange for full financial assistance for tuition.

Application procedures. Admission: Priority date 2/15; no deadline. No application fee. Admission notification on a rolling basis beginning on or about 3/1. Must reply by May 1 or within 2 week(s) if notified thereafter. Acceptance fee due within two weeks of admission offer. **Financial aid:** Priority date 2/15; no closing date. FAFSA required. Applicants notified on a rolling basis starting 7/1.

Academics. Curriculum offers liberal arts foundation with intensive concentration in special areas. **Special study options:** Combined bachelor's/graduate degree, double major, dual enrollment of high school students, independent study, internships, student-designed major, teacher certification program. 3-2 engineering program, interdisciplinary programs, pre-professional programs, dietetics program. **Credit/placement by examination:** AP, CLEP, IB, ACT, institutional tests. 15 credit hours maximum toward bachelor's degree. Five "credits by exam" classes unless specific approval by academic dean. **Support services:** Learning center, reduced course load, remedial instruction, study skills assistance, tutoring, writing center.

Majors. Biology: Biomedical sciences, ecology, molecular. **Business:** Accounting, business admin, event planning, hospitality admin, international, managerial economics, marketing, restaurant/food services. **Communications:** General, journalism. **Communications technology:** Printing management, radio/TV. **Computer sciences:** Computer science, information technology. **Conservation:** Wildlife/wilderness. **Education:** Agricultural, art, biology, drama/dance, early childhood, elementary, English, history, mathematics, music, physical, Spanish. **English:** English lit. **Foreign languages:** Spanish. **Health services:** Dietetics, nursing (RN). **History:** General. **Human services:** Social work. **Math:** General. **Parks/recreation:** Facilities management, health/fitness. **Philosophy/religion:** General. **Physical sciences:** Chemistry. **Protective services:** Corrections, police science. **Psychology:** General. **Social sciences:** Sociology. **Theology:** Bible, sacred music. **Visual/performing arts:** Acting, ceramics, design, dramatic, fiber arts, graphic design, music, painting, piano/keyboard, studio arts, theater design. **Work/family studies:** General, child development, family/community services, food/nutrition.

Most popular majors. Agriculture 11%, business/marketing 14%, education 11%, health sciences 7%, security/protective services 7%.

Technology on campus. 225 workstations in dormitories, library. Dormitories wired for high-speed internet access and linked to campus network. Commuter students can connect to campus network. Online course registration, online library, helpline, wireless network available.

Student life. Freshman orientation: Mandatory. Preregistration for classes offered. Eight-day program held week before classes begin. **Policies:** Convocations and chapel attendance required for residential freshman, sophomore, and junior students. All full-time students must live in residence halls unless married or living with parents. Religious observance required. **Housing:** Guaranteed on-campus for all undergraduates. Single-sex dorms, wellness housing available. $100 fully refundable deposit. Living facilities at the fire department available for volunteer student members. **Activities:** Bands, campus ministries, choral groups, drama, film society, international student organizations, music ensembles, musical theater, radio station, student government, student newspaper, Young Americans For Freedom, Baptist Student Union, Rotaract, InterVarsity Christian Fellowship, Wilderness Activities Club, Business Undergraduate Society, College Republicans, Catholic Christian Newman Association, Chi Alpha.

Athletics. NAIA. **Intercollegiate:** Baseball M, basketball, cross-country, volleyball W. **Intramural:** Baseball M, basketball, football (non-tackle), racquetball, soccer, softball, table tennis, tennis, ultimate frisbee, volleyball. **Team name:** Bobcats.

Student services. Chaplain/spiritual director, career counseling, student employment services, financial aid counseling, health services, on-campus daycare, personal counseling, placement for graduates, veterans' counselor. **Physically disabled:** Services for visually, speech, hearing impaired.

Contact. E-mail: admiss4@cofo.edu
Phone: (417) 690-2636 Toll-free number: (800) 222-0525
Fax: (417) 690-2635
Marci Linson, Vice President for Patriotic Activities and Dean of Admissions, College of the Ozarks, PO Box 17, Point Lookout, MO 65726-0017

Columbia College
Columbia, Missouri
www.ccis.edu   CB code: 6095

- Private 4-year liberal arts college affiliated with the Christian Church (Disciples of Christ)
- Commuter campus in small city
- 805 degree-seeking undergraduates: 15% part-time, 59% women, 5% African American, 1% Asian American, 3% Hispanic/Latino, 1% Native American, 4% Multi-racial, non-Hispanic, 11% international
- 216 degree-seeking graduate students
- 60% of applicants admitted
- SAT or ACT (ACT writing optional) required
- 46% graduate within 6 years

General. Founded in 1851. Regionally accredited. Thirty-five locations in United States and Cuba. **Degrees:** 144 bachelor's, 16 associate awarded; master's offered. **ROTC:** Army, Naval, Air Force. **Location:** 120 miles from Kansas City, 120 miles from St. Louis. **Calendar:** Semester, extensive summer session. **Full-time faculty:** 72 total; 83% have terminal degrees, 8% minority, 46% women. **Part-time faculty:** 63 total; 29% have terminal degrees, 10% minority, 56% women. **Class size:** 87% < 20, 13% 20-39.

Freshman class profile. 724 applied, 437 admitted, 125 enrolled.

Mid 50% test scores			
SAT math:	470-540	**GPA 2.0-2.99:**	18%
SAT writing:	480-570	**Rank in top quarter:**	30%
ACT composite:	20-26	**Rank in top tenth:**	8%
GPA 3.75 or higher:	33%	**Return as sophomores:**	71%
GPA 3.50-3.74:	23%	**Out-of-state:**	18%
GPA 3.0-3.49:	26%	**Live on campus:**	81%
		International:	6%

Basis for selection. School achievement, class rank, test scores most important. **Home schooled:** Statement describing home school structure and mission, transcript of courses and grades required.

High school preparation. College-preparatory program recommended. Recommended units include English 4.

2015-2016 Annual costs. Tuition/fees: $20,963. Room/board: $8,221. Books/supplies: $1,380. Personal expenses: $4,120. **Additional information:** Entering students will pay a fixed rate that is good for five consecutive years. Lab fees may apply to some classes, all other fees are covered by cost of tuition.

2014-2015 Financial aid. Need-based: 92 full-time freshmen applied for aid; 77 deemed to have need; 77 received aid. Average need met was 64%. Average scholarship/grant was $4,473; average loan $2,932. 44% of total undergraduate aid awarded as scholarships/grants, 56% as loans/jobs. **Non-need-based:** Awarded to 582 full-time undergraduates, including 112 freshmen. Scholarships awarded for academics, alumni affiliation, art, athletics, leadership, minority status, music/drama, religious affiliation, ROTC, state residency.

Application procedures. Admission: No deadline. $35 fee, may be waived for applicants with need. Admission notification on a rolling basis beginning on or about 3/1. **Financial aid:** Priority date 3/1; no closing date. FAFSA required. Applicants notified on a rolling basis starting 5/1.

Academics. Evening degree program available based on 8-week ongoing terms. **Special study options:** Combined bachelor's/graduate degree, cooperative education, cross-registration, distance learning, double major, ESL, exchange student, honors, independent study, internships, liberal arts/career combination, student-designed major, study abroad, teacher certification program. **Credit/placement by examination:** AP, CLEP, IB, SAT, ACT, institutional tests. 45 credit hours maximum toward associate degree, 60 toward bachelor's. **Support services:** Tutoring, writing center.

Honors college/program. Must demonstrate academic achievement with two of the following: 3.5 GPA; 78th percentile on ACT or equivalent SAT; 78th percentile on GED. Fifty-one freshmen admitted.

Majors. Area/ethnic studies: American. **Biology:** General. **Business:** General, accounting, business admin, finance, human resources, international, management information systems, marketing. **Communications:** Communications/speech/rhetoric, persuasive communications. **Computer sciences:** General, computer science. **Conservation:** Environmental science. **English:** English lit. **History:** General. **Human services:** General. **Math:** General. **Parks/recreation:** Sports admin. **Philosophy/religion:** Philosophy. **Physical sciences:** Chemistry. **Protective services:** Forensics, law enforcement admin. **Psychology:** General. **Social sciences:** Political science, sociology. **Visual/performing arts:** Art, ceramics, graphic design, painting, photography, printmaking.

Most popular majors. Biology 6%, business/marketing 28%, liberal arts 8%, public administration/social services 6%, security/protective services 13%, visual/performing arts 9%.

Technology on campus. 121 workstations in dormitories, library, computer center, student center. Dormitories wired for high-speed internet access and linked to campus network. Commuter students can connect to campus network. Online course registration, online library, helpline, repair service, wireless network available.

Student life. Freshman orientation: Available. Preregistration for classes offered. Four-day orientation, including day trips; continuing activities throughout the first week of classes. **Policies:** Alcohol and illegal drugs forbidden on campus. Students with less than 52 credit hours must live on campus. **Housing:** Guaranteed on-campus for freshmen. Coed dorms, single-sex dorms, special housing for disabled, apartments, themed housing available. **Activities:** Pep band, campus ministries, choral groups, drama, international student organizations, Model UN, musical theater, student government, international club, College Democrats, Chi Alpha Christian Fellowship, human service organization, peace club, Crossfire, environmentally conscious organization, Committed and Serving Together, Student Veterans.

Athletics. NAIA. **Intercollegiate:** Basketball, cross-country, golf, soccer, softball W, volleyball W. **Intramural:** Basketball, football (non-tackle), soccer, softball, volleyball. **Team name:** Cougars.

Student services. Alcohol/substance abuse counseling, career counseling, services for economically disadvantaged, student employment services, financial aid counseling, health services, minority student services, personal counseling, placement for graduates, veterans' counselor. **Physically disabled:** Services for visually, speech, hearing impaired.

Contact. E-mail: admissions@ccis.edu
Phone: (573) 875-7352 Toll-free number: (800) 231-2391 ext. 7352
Fax: (573) 875-7506
Stephanie Johnson, Director of Admissions, Columbia College, 1001 Rogers Street, Columbia, MO 65216

Conception Seminary College
Conception, Missouri
www.conception.edu   CB code: 6112

- Private 4-year seminary college for men affiliated with the Roman Catholic Church
- Residential campus in rural community
- 106 degree-seeking undergraduates
- 100% of applicants admitted
- ACT (writing optional), application essay required

General. Founded in 1883. Regionally accredited. Operated by Benedictine Monks of Conception Abbey, for both independent seminary students and candidates affiliated with sponsoring diocese. Women may enroll on part-time basis. **Degrees:** 18 bachelor's awarded. **Location:** 100 miles from Kansas City, 45 miles from St. Joseph. **Calendar:** Semester. **Full-time faculty:** 12 total. **Part-time faculty:** 18 total. **Special facilities:** Abbey Basilica of the Immaculate Conception.

Freshman class profile. 19 applied, 19 admitted, 19 enrolled.

End year in good standing:	96%	**Out-of-state:**	81%
Return as sophomores:	10%	**Live on campus:**	100%

Basis for selection. ACT composite scores tend to count more heavily than high school grades. Class rank considered. Applicants must be sponsored. Interview recommended. **Home schooled:** State high school equivalency certificate required. ACT score of 24 or better.

High school preparation. College-preparatory program recommended.

2016-2017 Annual costs. Tuition/fees (projected): $20,706. Room/board: $12,316. Books/supplies: $650. Personal expenses: $850.

Financial aid. Non-need-based: Scholarships awarded for academics.

Application procedures. Admission: Priority date 6/1; deadline 7/31 (receipt date). No application fee. Admission notification on a rolling basis beginning on or about 2/1. Foreign applications require written certification of financial, ecclesiastical sponsorship. **Financial aid:** No deadline. FAFSA required. Applicants notified on a rolling basis starting 8/1; must reply by 8/20.

Academics. Curriculum combines liberal arts and pre-theology training to accommodate varying degrees of vocational commitment. **Special study options:** ESL, independent study. **Credit/placement by examination:** AP, CLEP, IB, ACT, institutional tests. 12 credit hours maximum toward bachelor's degree. **Support services:** Learning center, reduced course load, remedial instruction, study skills assistance, tutoring.

Majors. Philosophy/religion: Philosophy.

Technology on campus. 15 workstations in dormitories, library, computer center. Dormitories wired for high-speed internet access and linked to campus network. Online library, helpline, repair service, wireless network available.

Student life. Freshman orientation: Mandatory. Preregistration for classes offered. **Policies:** Religious observance required. **Housing:** Guaranteed on-campus for all undergraduates. Wellness housing available. $50 fully refundable deposit. **Activities:** Choral groups, drama, music ensembles, musical theater, student government, student newspaper, apostolic work, social concerns, community council, Inner-Life.

Athletics. Intercollegiate: Basketball M, soccer M, volleyball M. **Intramural:** Basketball M, football (non-tackle) M, racquetball M, soccer M, softball M, table tennis M, tennis M, track and field M, ultimate frisbee M, volleyball M, weight lifting M. **Team name:** Sons of Thunder.

Student services. Adult student services, alcohol/substance abuse counseling, chaplain/spiritual director, career counseling, financial aid counseling, health services, personal counseling.

Contact. E-mail: vocations@conception.edu
Phone: (660) 944-2886 Fax: (660) 944-2829
Br. Luke Kral, Director of Admissions, Conception Seminary College, Box 502, Conception, MO 64433-0502

Cox College
Springfield, Missouri
www.coxcollege.edu   **CB code: 3932**

◗ Private 4-year health science and nursing college
◗ Commuter campus in small city
◗ 747 degree-seeking undergraduates

General. Regionally accredited. **Degrees:** 51 bachelor's, 10 associate awarded; master's offered. **Calendar:** Semester, limited summer session. **Full-time faculty:** 66 total. **Special facilities:** Nursing resource center.

Basis for selection. Minimum GPA and ACT composite score required. TOEFL required of non-native English speakers and all international applicants. ACT or SAT scores required for early decision candidates. If ACT or SAT scores are less than 5 years old, student may be exempt from pre-entrance placement testing. **Home schooled:** Applicants must submit official transcript from a state accredited institution or official GED or high school equivalency score report.

High school preparation. Recommended units include English 4, mathematics 2 and science 2. Early Decision candidates must achieve grade of C or better in biology, chemistry, 4 units English, 2 units math, including algebra.

2015-2016 Annual costs. Tuition/fees: $13,248. Books/supplies: $1,500.

Application procedures. Admission: Closing date 8/1 (receipt date). $45 fee, may be waived for applicants with need. Application must be submitted on paper. Admission notification on a rolling basis. **Financial aid:** Priority date 3/1; no closing date.

Academics. Special study options: Accelerated study. **Credit/placement by examination:** AP, CLEP, SAT, ACT, institutional tests. 6 credit hours maximum toward associate degree, 6 toward bachelor's. **Support services:** Remedial instruction, study skills assistance, tutoring, writing center.

Majors. Health services: Nursing (RN).

Technology on campus. 34 workstations in dormitories, library, computer center.

Student life. Freshman orientation: Available. Preregistration for classes offered. **Housing:** Coed dorms available. $100 deposit. **Activities:** Student government, National Student Nurses Association, student council, residence hall council, Christian Fellowship.

Student services. Financial aid counseling.

Contact. E-mail: admissions@coxcollege.edu
Phone: (417) 269-3068 Toll-free number: (866) 898-5355
Fax: (417) 269-3586
Lindy Biglieni, Director of Admission, Cox College, 1423 North Jefferson Avenue, Springfield, MO 65802

Culver-Stockton College
Canton, Missouri   **CB member**
www.culver.edu   **CB code: 6123**

◗ Private 4-year liberal arts college affiliated with the Christian Church (Disciples of Christ)
◗ Residential campus in small town
◗ 973 degree-seeking undergraduates: 5% part-time, 51% women, 13% African American, 5% Hispanic/Latino, 2% Multi-racial, non-Hispanic, 8% international
◗ 17 degree-seeking graduate students
◗ 56% of applicants admitted
◗ SAT or ACT (ACT writing optional) required
◗ 53% graduate within 6 years; 14% enter graduate study

General. Founded in 1853. Regionally accredited. Blends traditional coursework and experiential opportunities. **Degrees:** 165 bachelor's awarded; master's offered. **Location:** 130 miles from St. Louis, 20 miles from Quincy, Illinois. **Calendar:** Semester, limited summer session. **Full-time faculty:** 49 total; 67% have terminal degrees, 6% minority, 41% women. **Part-time faculty:** 45 total; 18% have terminal degrees, 4% minority, 67% women. **Class size:** 60% < 20, 40% 20-39, less than 1% 40-49. **Special facilities:** Phage genomics research facility with DNA sequencer, astronomy observation deck, biological research station, collegiate teaching greenhouse, fine arts multi-media editing suite and recording studio, radio and television broadcast studios, mock trial courtroom with legal research library.

Freshman class profile. 2,913 applied, 1,628 admitted, 260 enrolled.

Mid 50% test scores			
SAT critical reading:	400-540	Rank in top tenth:	11%
SAT math:	430-520	End year in good standing:	96%
ACT composite:	18-23	Return as sophomores:	69%
GPA 3.75 or higher:	17%	Out-of-state:	47%
GPA 3.50-3.74:	9%	Live on campus:	91%
GPA 3.0-3.49:	31%	International:	9%
GPA 2.0-2.99:	43%	Fraternities:	38%
Rank in top quarter:	27%	Sororities:	40%

Basis for selection. Secondary school record and test scores most important; recommendations, application essay and alumni relation considered. **Home schooled:** Transcript of courses and grades, state high school equivalency certificate required. **Learning Disabled:** Must request accommodations and submit appropriate documentation.

High school preparation. College-preparatory program recommended. 15 units recommended. Recommended units include English 4, mathematics 2, social studies 3, history 3, science 2 and foreign language 1.

2015-2016 Annual costs. Tuition/fees: $24,900. Room/board: $7,950. Books/supplies: $1,100. Personal expenses: $400.

Financial aid. Non-need-based: Scholarships awarded for academics, alumni affiliation, art, athletics, leadership, music/drama, religious affiliation.

Application procedures. Admission: Priority date 5/1; deadline 8/1 (receipt date). No application fee. Admission notification on a rolling basis beginning on or about 9/15. **Financial aid:** Priority date 3/1, closing date 6/1. FAFSA required. Applicants notified on a rolling basis starting 2/15; must reply within 2 week(s) of notification.

Academics. Special study options: Combined bachelor's/graduate degree, distance learning, double major, dual enrollment of high school students, honors, independent study, internships, liberal arts/career combination, semester at sea, student-designed major, study abroad, teacher certification program, Washington semester. **Credit/placement by examination:** AP, CLEP, IB, SAT, ACT, institutional tests. 90 credit hours maximum toward bachelor's degree. **Support services:** Learning center, reduced course load, remedial instruction, study skills assistance, tutoring, writing center.

Majors. Biology: General, biochemistry. **Business:** Accounting, business admin, finance, marketing. **Communications:** Communications/speech/rhetoric, media studies, sports. **Education:** General, art, elementary, music, physical, speech. **English:** English lit. **Health services:** Athletic training, nursing (RN). **History:** General. **Liberal arts:** Arts/sciences. **Math:** General. **Parks/recreation:** Sports admin. **Philosophy/religion:** Religion. **Protective services:** Law enforcement admin. **Psychology:** General. **Social sciences:** Political science. **Visual/performing arts:** Art, dramatic, graphic design, music, musical theater, studio arts management.

Most popular majors. Business/marketing 21%, education 7%, health sciences 12%, liberal arts 8%, parks/recreation 10%, psychology 11%, security/protective services 8%, visual/performing arts 6%.

Technology on campus. 100 workstations in dormitories, library, computer center, student center. Dormitories wired for high-speed internet access and linked to campus network. Commuter students can connect to campus network. Online course registration, online library, helpline, repair service, student web hosting, wireless network available.

Student life. Freshman orientation: Mandatory, $200 fee. Preregistration for classes offered. Held 3 days prior to beginning of fall semester. **Policies:** All students under age 21 are required to live on campus unless living with parents or married. Students have voting representation on faculty committees. **Housing:** Guaranteed on-campus for all undergraduates. Coed dorms, fraternity/sorority housing, wellness housing available. **Activities:** Bands, campus ministries, choral groups, dance, drama, international student organizations, literary magazine, music ensembles, musical theater, radio station, student government, student newspaper, TV station, Disciples on Campus, Christians in Action, Men of Character, black student union, International & Domestic Events Awareness Society, psychology club, athletic trainers organization, Up 'Til Dawn, pre-law club.

Athletics. NAIA. Intercollegiate: Baseball M, basketball, bowling, cheerleading, cross-country, football (tackle) M, golf, soccer, softball W, track and field, volleyball. **Intramural:** Basketball, bowling, football (non-tackle), golf, racquetball, softball, volleyball. **Team name:** Wildcats.

Student services. Adult student services, alcohol/substance abuse counseling, chaplain/spiritual director, career counseling, student employment services, financial aid counseling, personal counseling, placement for graduates, veterans' counselor.

Contact. E-mail: admission@culver.edu
Phone: (573) 288-6331 Toll-free number: (800) 537-1883
Fax: (573) 288-6618
Misty McBee, Director of Admission, Culver-Stockton College, One College Hill, Canton, MO 63435-1299

DeVry University: Kansas City
Kansas City, Missouri
www.devry.edu   CB code: 6092

- For-profit 4-year university
- Commuter campus in large city
- 423 degree-seeking undergraduates
- Interview required

General. Founded in 1931. Regionally accredited. Additional locations: Kansas City Downtown, St. Louis West. **Degrees:** 139 bachelor's, 24 associate awarded; master's offered. **Location:** 15 miles from downtown. **Calendar:** Semester, extensive summer session. **Full-time faculty:** 24 total; 8% minority, 21% women. **Part-time faculty:** 52 total; 4% minority, 38% women.

Basis for selection. Applicants must have high school diploma or equivalent degree from accredited postsecondary institution and be at least 17 years of age on the first day of classes. New students may enter at beginning of any semester. CPT also accepted.

High school preparation. Required units include mathematics 1. Math unit must be algebra or higher.

2015-2016 Annual costs. Tuition/fees: $17,132. Books/supplies: $1,310. Personal expenses: $2,376.

Financial aid. All financial aid based on need.

Application procedures. Admission: No deadline. $40 fee, may be waived for applicants with need. Admission notification on a rolling basis. **Financial aid:** No deadline. FAFSA required. Applicants notified on a rolling basis.

Academics. Special study options: Accelerated study, distance learning, study abroad. **Credit/placement by examination:** AP, CLEP, institutional tests. **Support services:** Learning center, remedial instruction, tutoring.

Majors. Business: General, business admin, management information systems. **Communications:** General. **Computer sciences:** Networking, systems analysis, web page design.

Most popular majors. Business/marketing 41%, computer/information sciences 49%, engineering/engineering technologies 10%.

Technology on campus. 1,300 workstations in library, computer center. Online course registration, online library, helpline available.

Student life. Freshman orientation: Mandatory. Preregistration for classes offered. **Activities:** Association of Information Technology Professionals, Campus Crusade for Christ, Institute for Electrical & Electronics Engineers, Phi Beta Lambda, Tau Alpha Pi, professional certification club, drama club, Gamma Beta Phi.

Student services. Career counseling, student employment services, financial aid counseling, placement for graduates, veterans' counselor. **Physically disabled:** Services for visually, hearing impaired.

Contact. E-mail: ssmeed@kc.devry.edu
Phone: (816) 943-7300 Toll-free number: (800) 821-3766
Fax: (816) 941-0896
DeVry University: Kansas City, 11224 Holmes Street, Kansas City, MO 64131

Drury University
Springfield, Missouri
www.drury.edu   CB code: 6169

- Private 4-year university and liberal arts college affiliated with the United Church of Christ
- Residential campus in large city
- 1,313 degree-seeking undergraduates: 2% part-time, 55% women
- 243 degree-seeking graduate students
- 65% of applicants admitted
- SAT or ACT (ACT writing optional) required
- 67% graduate within 6 years; 34% enter graduate study

General. Founded in 1873. Regionally accredited. Drury Center in Aegina, Greece. **Degrees:** 737 bachelor's, 184 associate awarded; master's offered. **ROTC:** Army. **Location:** 220 miles from St. Louis, 170 miles from Kansas City. **Calendar:** Semester, limited summer session. **Full-time faculty:** 134 total; 82% have terminal degrees, 8% minority, 42% women. **Part-time faculty:** 24 total; 12% have terminal degrees, 67% women. **Class size:** 70% < 20, 29% 20-39, less than 1% 40-49, less than 1% 50-99. **Special facilities:** Science center, greenhouse, astronomical observation station, electronic music lab, Chalfant pipe organ, television and radio studios, outdoor student-built classroom, philosopher's table, Gold-LEED certified event center, platinum-LEED certified housing.

Freshman class profile. 1,423 applied, 927 admitted, 271 enrolled.

Mid 50% test scores			
ACT composite:	20-31	End year in good standing:	94%
GPA 3.75 or higher:	53%	Return as sophomores:	77%
GPA 3.50-3.74:	19%	Out-of-state:	19%
GPA 3.0-3.49:	20%	Live on campus:	88%
GPA 2.0-2.99:	8%	International:	7%
Rank in top quarter:	59%	Fraternities:	19%
Rank in top tenth:	28%	Sororities:	28%

Basis for selection. School achievement record, test scores, reference from high school counselor, essay important. Interview recommended for all. Audition recommended for music, theater students; portfolio recommended for architecture, art students. **Learning Disabled:** Encouraged to self-disclose early and seek resources and support of Disability Support Services office. Must present documentation outlining disability to receive accommodations. Documentation should be no more than 3 years old.

High school preparation. College-preparatory program recommended. 12 units required. Required and recommended units include English 4, mathematics 3-4, social studies 3, science 3 and foreign language 2.

2016-2017 Annual costs. Tuition/fees (projected): $25,905. Room/board: $8,256. Books/supplies: $1,200. Personal expenses: $1,500.

2014-2015 Financial aid. Need-based: 234 full-time freshmen applied for aid; 187 deemed to have need; 187 received aid. Average need met was

70%. Average scholarship/grant was $15,667; average loan $3,988. 67% of total undergraduate aid awarded as scholarships/grants, 33% as loans/jobs. **Non-need-based:** Awarded to 684 full-time undergraduates, including 164 freshmen. Scholarships awarded for academics, alumni affiliation, art, athletics, job skills, leadership, minority status, music/drama, religious affiliation.

Application procedures. Admission: Priority date 1/10; deadline 5/1 (postmark date). $50 fee, may be waived for applicants with need. Admission notification on a rolling basis beginning on or about 10/1. Must reply by May 1 or within 6 week(s) if notified thereafter. Application fee waived if applicant visits campus. **Financial aid:** Priority date 2/15, closing date 3/1. FAFSA, institutional form required. Applicants notified on a rolling basis starting 3/1; must reply within 2 week(s) of notification.

Academics. Special study options: Accelerated study, combined bachelor's/graduate degree, cooperative education, distance learning, double major, dual enrollment of high school students, ESL, honors, independent study, internships, liberal arts/career combination, student-designed major, study abroad, teacher certification program, Washington semester. Living-learning communities, leadership/community service communities available. **Credit/ placement by examination:** AP, CLEP, IB, SAT, ACT, institutional tests. 31 credit hours maximum toward associate degree, 31 toward bachelor's. Completion of the general examinations prior to completion of 30 semester hours of university work required to receive credits. CLEP test credits will not be recognized or awarded when current or previous coursework overlaps with the subject of the CLEP test(s). Scaled scores result in 6 hours credit for each general exam (total possible credits: 30 hours). AP is awarded on a minimum score, determined by department chairs. IB is awarded on either a diploma score or individual exam scores. A maximum of 30 hours can be earned. **Support services:** Pre-admission summer program, reduced course load, remedial instruction, study skills assistance, tutoring, writing center.

Majors. Architecture: Architecture. **Biology:** General, biochemistry, environmental, neuroscience. **Business:** Accounting, business admin, entrepreneurial studies, finance, marketing, organizational leadership. **Communications:** General, advertising, journalism, persuasive communications, public relations. **Computer sciences:** Computer science. **Conservation:** Environmental science, environmental studies. **Education:** General, educational technology, elementary, music, physical, secondary. **English:** English lit, writing. **Foreign languages:** French, Spanish. **Health services:** Community health, EMT paramedic, medical radiologic technology/radiation therapy, music therapy, nursing (RN), prechiropractic, predental, premedicine, prenursing, preoccupational therapy, preoptometry, prepharmacy, prephysical therapy, preveterinary, surgical technology. **History:** General. **Human services:** General. **Math:** General. **Parks/recreation:** Exercise sciences. **Philosophy/religion:** General, philosophy, religion. **Physical sciences:** Chemistry, physics. **Protective services:** Disaster management, law enforcement admin, police science. **Psychology:** General. **Social sciences:** Criminology, economics, political science, sociology. **Theology:** Preministerial. **Visual/performing arts:** Art history/conservation, arts management, design, dramatic, music, studio arts.

Most popular majors. Architecture 7%, biology 9%, business/marketing 13%, education 7%, psychology 14%, security/protective services 7%, social sciences 6%, visual/performing arts 6%.

Technology on campus. 389 workstations in dormitories, library, computer center, student center. Dormitories wired for high-speed internet access and linked to campus network. Commuter students can connect to campus network. Online course registration, online library, helpline, repair service, student web hosting, wireless network available.

Student life. Freshman orientation: Mandatory, $150 fee. Preregistration for classes offered. Four-day program including parent session and service projects. **Policies:** Smoke-free campus. **Housing:** Guaranteed on-campus for freshmen. Coed dorms, apartments, fraternity/sorority housing, themed housing available. $200 nonrefundable deposit, deadline 6/1. Pets allowed in dorm rooms. Living-learning, honors housing, leadership/service communities available. **Activities:** Bands, campus ministries, choral groups, dance, drama, film society, international student organizations, literary magazine, music ensembles, musical theater, opera, radio station, student government, student newspaper, symphony orchestra, TV station, The Vine, Catholic Campus Ministry, Disciples on Campus, Mortar Board, Habitat for Humanity, Enactus (SIFE), Volunteer Corps, Think Green, ONE Drury, Panthers for Prevention.

Athletics. NCAA. **Intercollegiate:** Baseball M, basketball, cheerleading W, cross-country, diving, golf, soccer, softball W, swimming, tennis, track and field, volleyball W, wrestling M. **Intramural:** Basketball, football (nontackle), racquetball, rugby M, soccer, softball, volleyball. **Team name:** Panthers.

Student services. Adult student services, alcohol/substance abuse counseling, chaplain/spiritual director, career counseling, services for economically disadvantaged, student employment services, financial aid counseling, health services, minority student services, personal counseling, placement for graduates, veterans' counselor, women's services. **Physically disabled:** Services for visually, speech, hearing impaired.

Contact. E-mail: druryad@drury.edu
Phone: (417) 873-7205 Toll-free number: (800) 922-2274
Fax: (417) 866-3873
Jay Fedje, Dean of Enrollment Management, Drury University, 900 North Benton Avenue, Springfield, MO 65802-3712

Evangel University
Springfield, Missouri
www.evangel.edu

CB code: 6198

- Private 4-year liberal arts college affiliated with the Assemblies of God
- Residential campus in small city
- 1,723 degree-seeking undergraduates: 10% part-time, 55% women, 4% African American, 2% Asian American, 4% Hispanic/Latino, 1% Native American, 3% Multi-racial, non-Hispanic, 1% international
- 223 degree-seeking graduate students
- 61% of applicants admitted
- SAT or ACT with writing required

General. Founded in 1955. Regionally accredited. **Degrees:** 394 bachelor's, 38 associate awarded; master's, doctoral offered. **ROTC:** Army. **Location:** 170 miles from Kansas City, 212 miles from St. Louis. **Calendar:** Semester, limited summer session. **Full-time faculty:** 108 total; 55% have terminal degrees, 3% minority, 33% women. **Part-time faculty:** 46 total; 13% have terminal degrees, 2% minority, 59% women. **Class size:** 65% < 20, 27% 20-39, 5% 40-49, 3% 50-99, less than 1% >100.

Freshman class profile. 1,483 applied, 912 admitted, 362 enrolled.

Mid 50% test scores			
SAT critical reading:	470-580	Rank in top quarter:	40%
SAT math:	440-580	Rank in top tenth:	18%
ACT composite:	20-26	Return as sophomores:	71%

Basis for selection. 2.0 high school GPA, acceptance of college's moral and religious standards, acceptable ACT/SAT, rank in top half of graduating class. Statement of Christian faith required. **Home schooled:** Letter of recommendation (nonparent) required. Admissions based upon ACT/SAT scores and letters of recommendation.

High school preparation. Recommended units include English 3, mathematics 1, social studies 2, science 1 (laboratory 1).

2015-2016 Annual costs. Tuition/fees: $21,416. Room/board: $7,582. Books/supplies: $1,000. Personal expenses: $2,358.

2014-2015 Financial aid. All financial aid based on need. 322 full-time freshmen applied for aid; 283 deemed to have need; 283 received aid. Average need met was 67%. Average scholarship/grant was $12,568; average loan $3,584. 52% of total undergraduate aid awarded as scholarships/grants, 48% as loans/jobs.

Application procedures. Admission: No deadline. No application fee. Admission notification on a rolling basis. **Financial aid:** Priority date 3/1, closing date 7/1. FAFSA required. Applicants notified on a rolling basis starting 3/1; must reply within 3 week(s) of notification.

Academics. Special study options: Distance learning, double major, internships, study abroad, teacher certification program, Washington semester, weekend college. **Credit/placement by examination:** AP, CLEP, IB, SAT, ACT, institutional tests. 30 credit hours maximum toward associate degree, 30 toward bachelor's. **Support services:** Learning center, reduced course load, remedial instruction, study skills assistance, tutoring, writing center.

Majors. Biology: General. **Business:** General, accounting, business admin, marketing. **Communications:** Broadcast journalism, communications/speech/rhetoric, journalism. **Communications technology:** General. **Computer sciences:** General. **Education:** Art, business, early childhood, elementary, English, foreign languages, mathematics, middle, music, physical, science, secondary, social studies, special ed. **English:** English lit, rhetoric/composition. **Foreign languages:** Spanish. **Health services:** Clinical lab technology, predental, premedicine, preveterinary. **History:** General. **Human services:** Social work. **Math:** General. **Parks/recreation:** General. **Physical sciences:** Chemistry. **Protective services:** Criminal justice. **Psychology:** General. **Social sciences:** General, criminology, political science, sociology. **Theology:** Bible, missionary, sacred music. **Visual/performing arts:** Dramatic, music, music performance, studio arts.

Technology on campus. 407 workstations in dormitories, library, computer center, student center. Dormitories wired for high-speed internet access and linked to campus network. Online library, helpline, wireless network available.

Student life. Freshman orientation: Mandatory, $50 fee. Preregistration for classes offered. **Policies:** Religious observance required. **Housing:** Guaranteed on-campus for freshmen. Coed dorms, single-sex dorms, apartments available. **Activities:** Bands, campus ministries, choral groups, dance, drama, film society, international student organizations, literary magazine, music ensembles, musical theater, opera, radio station, student government, student newspaper, symphony orchestra, TV station, honor fraternities, student ministries.

Athletics. NAIA. **Intercollegiate:** Baseball M, basketball, cross-country, football (tackle) M, golf, softball W, tennis, track and field, volleyball W. **Intramural:** Basketball, football (non-tackle), soccer, softball, volleyball W. **Team name:** Crusaders.

Student services. Chaplain/spiritual director, career counseling, student employment services, financial aid counseling, health services, personal counseling, placement for graduates, veterans' counselor. **Physically disabled:** Services for visually, hearing impaired.

Contact. E-mail: admission@evangel.edu
Phone: (417) 865-2815 ext. 7300 Toll-free number: (800) 382-6435
Fax: (417) 865-9599
Jeff Burnett, Director of Admissions, Evangel University, 1111 North Glenstone, Springfield, MO 65802

Fontbonne University
St. Louis, Missouri
www.fontbonne.edu

CB member
CB code: 6216

- Private 4-year university and liberal arts college affiliated with the Roman Catholic Church
- Commuter campus in large city
- 1,086 degree-seeking undergraduates: 18% part-time, 69% women, 15% African American, 1% Asian American, 2% Hispanic/Latino, 2% Multiracial, non-Hispanic, 7% international
- 596 degree-seeking graduate students
- 97% of applicants admitted
- SAT or ACT (ACT writing optional), application essay required
- 54% graduate within 6 years

General. Founded in 1923. Regionally accredited. **Degrees:** 309 bachelor's awarded; master's offered. **ROTC:** Army, Air Force. **Location:** 7 miles from downtown. **Calendar:** Semester, limited summer session. **Full-time faculty:** 69 total; 74% have terminal degrees, 10% minority, 74% women. **Part-time faculty:** 136 total; 12% minority, 68% women. **Class size:** 84% < 20, 16% 20-39. **Special facilities:** Chapel, commuter lounge, fine arts gallery, theater, speech, language, and hearing clinic, academic resource and ADA accommodations center.

Freshman class profile. 494 applied, 478 admitted, 178 enrolled.

Mid 50% test scores		End year in good standing:	91%
ACT composite:	20-25	Return as sophomores:	79%
GPA 3.75 or higher:	32%	Out-of-state:	27%
GPA 3.50-3.74:	16%	Live on campus:	56%
GPA 3.0-3.49:	32%	International:	4%
GPA 2.0-2.99:	19%		

Basis for selection. High school GPA, test scores considered. Recommendations may be requested. Student may be required to take the university subject-related placement tests. A portfolio is required for art students.

High school preparation. College-preparatory program required. 22 units required. Required units include English 4, mathematics 3, social studies 3, science 3 (laboratory 1), foreign language 1, visual/performing arts 1 and academic electives 5. 1 unit of practical arts and 1 unit of physical education.

2016-2017 Annual costs. Tuition/fees: $24,610. Room/board: $9,107. Books/supplies: $1,000. Personal expenses: $3,210.

2015-2016 Financial aid. Need-based: 46% of total undergraduate aid awarded as scholarships/grants, 54% as loans/jobs. **Non-need-based:** Scholarships awarded for academics, alumni affiliation, art, leadership, minority status, music/drama, religious affiliation, state residency.

Application procedures. Admission: Closing date 8/1 (receipt date). $25 fee, may be waived for applicants with need. Admission notification on a rolling basis. Must reply by May 1 or within 3 week(s) if notified thereafter. **Financial aid:** Priority date 3/15; no closing date. FAFSA, institutional form required. Applicants notified on a rolling basis starting 2/1; must reply within 2 week(s) of notification.

Academics. Special study options: Accelerated study, combined bachelor's/graduate degree, cooperative education, cross-registration, distance learning, double major, dual enrollment of high school students, ESL, exchange student, honors, independent study, internships, liberal arts/career combination, semester at sea, student-designed major, study abroad, teacher certification program, weekend college. Dual degree programs include: engineering (Washington University and University of Missouri Kansas City), Occupational Therapy (Washington University), Chiropractic (Logan University), and Social Work (St. Louis University). **Credit/placement by examination:** AP, CLEP, IB, institutional tests. 30 credit hours maximum toward bachelor's degree. Fontbonne will accept undergraduate credit by exam for non-standardized examinations given by accredited institutions. Course number, title, and credit hours must appear on official transcript. Determination as to fulfillment of certain course requirements will be reviewed and considered by department chairperson. **Support services:** Learning center, reduced course load, remedial instruction, study skills assistance, tutoring, writing center.

Majors. Biology: General. **Business:** Accounting, business admin, human resources, international marketing, organizational behavior, organizational leadership. **Communications:** Advertising, communications/speech/rhetoric. **Computer sciences:** General. **Education:** Deaf/hearing impaired, early childhood, elementary, family/consumer sciences, middle, special ed. **English:** English lit. **Health services:** Dietetics, speech pathology. **History:** General. **Human services:** Social work. **Liberal arts:** Arts/sciences. **Math:** General. **Parks/recreation:** Sports admin. **Psychology:** General. **Social sciences:** Sociology. **Visual/performing arts:** Art, dramatic, studio arts. **Work/family studies:** Clothing/textiles.

Most popular majors. Business/marketing 31%, education 16%, health sciences 11%, public administration/social services 10%.

Technology on campus. 210 workstations in dormitories, library, computer center. Dormitories wired for high-speed internet access and linked to campus network. Commuter students can connect to campus network. Online course registration, online library, helpline, repair service, wireless network available.

Student life. Freshman orientation: Mandatory, $150 fee. Preregistration for classes offered. Held during week prior to classes, includes community service. **Housing:** Coed dorms, special housing for disabled, apartments, wellness housing available. $150 fully refundable deposit. Apartment style residence halls available. **Activities:** Campus ministries, choral groups, dance, drama, international student organizations, literary magazine, music ensembles, musical theater, student government, student newspaper, Fontbonne in Service and Humility, Students for the Enhancement of Cultural Awareness, Gaming2Gether, LGBT Alliance For Respect and Equality.

Athletics. NCAA. **Intercollegiate:** Baseball M, basketball, cross-country, golf, lacrosse M, soccer, softball W, tennis, track and field, volleyball. **Intramural:** Badminton, basketball, bowling, football (non-tackle), sand volleyball, soccer, table tennis. **Team name:** Griffins.

Student services. Adult student services, alcohol/substance abuse counseling, chaplain/spiritual director, career counseling, student employment services, financial aid counseling, health services, minority student services, personal counseling, placement for graduates. **Physically disabled:** Services for speech, hearing impaired.

Contact. E-mail: fbyou@fontbonne.edu
Phone: (314) 889-1400 Toll-free number: (800) 205-5862
Fax: (314) 889-1451
Michelle Palumbo, Associate Vice President of Admissions, Fontbonne University, 6800 Wydown Boulevard, Saint Louis, MO 63105-3098

Global University
Springfield, Missouri
www.globaluniversity.edu

CB code: 4916

- Private 4-year Bible and seminary college affiliated with the Assemblies of God
- Commuter campus in small city

General. Founded in 1948. Accredited by DETC. **Location:** 200 miles from St. Louis, 170 miles from Kansas City. **Calendar:** Differs by program.

Annual costs/financial aid. Tuition/fees (2015-2016): $4,312. Books/supplies: $1,280.

Contact. Phone: (417) 862-9533
Registrar and Associate Dean of Student Services, 1211 South Glenstone Avenue, Springfield, MO 65804

Goldfarb School of Nursing at Barnes-Jewish College
St. Louis, Missouri
www.barnesjewishcollege.edu

CB code: 6329

- Private two-year upper-division nursing college
- Commuter campus in very large city
- 81% of applicants admitted

General. Regionally accredited. Affiliated with Barnes-Jewish Hospital and Washington University Medical Center. **Degrees:** 434 bachelor's awarded; master's, doctoral offered. **Location:** Downtown. **Calendar:** Trimester, extensive summer session. **Full-time faculty:** 48 total; 52% have terminal degrees, 6% minority, 90% women. **Part-time faculty:** 9 total. **Class size:** 9% < 20, 39% 20-39, 17% 40-49, 35% 50-99.

Student profile. 637 degree-seeking undergraduates, 89 degree-seeking graduate students. 542 applied as first time-transfer students, 439 admitted, 158 enrolled. 64% transferred from two-year, 36% transferred from four-year institutions.

Women:	88%	Multi-racial, non-Hispanic:	2%
African American:	6%	Part-time:	11%
Asian American:	3%	Out-of-state:	28%
Hispanic/Latino:	2%	25 or older:	43%

Basis for selection. Open admission. College transcript required. Transfer accepted as juniors, seniors.

2016-2017 Annual costs. Tuition/fees (projected): $19,423. Books/supplies: $1,600.

Financial aid. **Need-based:** 503 applied for aid; 478 deemed to have need; 478 received aid. 13% of total undergraduate aid awarded as scholarships/grants, 87% as loans/jobs. **Non-need-based:** Awarded to 66 undergraduates. Scholarships awarded for academics, leadership, minority status.

Application procedures. **Admission:** Rolling admission. $50 fee. Application must be submitted online. **Financial aid:** No deadline. Applicants notified on a rolling basis. FAFSA required.

Academics. **Special study options:** Accelerated study. **Credit/placement by examination:** AP, CLEP, IB.

Majors. **Health services:** Nursing (RN).

Technology on campus. 60 workstations in library, computer center. Commuter students can connect to campus network. Online library, helpline, wireless network available.

Student life. **Activities:** Student newspaper.

Student services. Alcohol/substance abuse counseling, chaplain/spiritual director, career counseling, services for economically disadvantaged, student employment services, financial aid counseling, minority student services, personal counseling, veterans' counselor, women's services.

Contact. E-mail: bjcon-admissions@bjc.org
Phone: (314) 454-7057 Toll-free number: (800) 832-9009
Fax: (314) 362-9250
Jason Crowe, Director of Enrollment Management, Goldfarb School of Nursing at Barnes-Jewish College, 4483 Duncan Avenue, St. Louis, MO 63110-1091

Hannibal-LaGrange University
Hannibal, Missouri
www.hlg.edu

CB code: 6266

- Private 4-year university and liberal arts college affiliated with the Southern Baptist Convention
- Residential campus in large town
- 881 full-time, degree-seeking undergraduates
- 74 graduate students
- 56% of applicants admitted
- SAT or ACT (ACT writing optional), interview required

General. Founded in 1858. Regionally accredited. **Degrees:** 173 bachelor's, 41 associate awarded; master's offered. **Location:** 100 miles from St. Louis. **Calendar:** Semester, limited summer session. **Full-time faculty:** 59 total; 19% have terminal degrees, 56% women. **Part-time faculty:** 39 total; 8% have terminal degrees, 3% minority, 64% women. **Class size:** 82% < 20, 17% 20-39, less than 1% 40-49, less than 1% 50-99. **Special facilities:** Nature trail, fine arts theater, mission center.

Freshman class profile. 581 applied, 324 admitted, 160 enrolled.

Out-of-state:	38%	Live on campus:	94%

Basis for selection. Most applicants admitted. Test scores important. 20 ACT required. Applicants with 16-19 ACT admitted provisionally. ACT administered on campus on registration day. Allied health programs acceptance involves academic and health screenings. Applications without English composition 1 and college algebra must submit ACT and take math placement exam. Interviews required for performance and honor students. **Home schooled:** Transcript of courses and grades required. ACT score required. **Learning Disabled:** Must provide appropriate ADA documentation.

High school preparation. College-preparatory program recommended. Recommended units include English 4, mathematics 3, history 3, science 2 (laboratory 1).

2015-2016 Annual costs. Tuition/fees: $20,560. Room/board: $3,804. Books/supplies: $950. Personal expenses: $2,698.

Financial aid. **Non-need-based:** Scholarships awarded for academics, art, athletics, music/drama, religious affiliation. **Additional information:** Work-study opportunities vary according to on-and off-campus needs.

Application procedures. **Admission:** No deadline. $25 fee. Admission notification on a rolling basis beginning on or about 9/1. **Financial aid:** No deadline. FAFSA, institutional form required. Applicants notified on a rolling basis; must reply by 8/31.

Academics. **Special study options:** Accelerated study, distance learning, double major, dual enrollment of high school students, ESL, honors, independent study, internships, student-designed major, study abroad, teacher certification program. **Credit/placement by examination:** AP, CLEP, SAT, ACT, institutional tests. 16 credit hours maximum toward associate degree, 30 toward bachelor's. No more than 8 credit hours in one discipline. **Support services:** Remedial instruction, study skills assistance, tutoring, writing center.

Honors college/program. 27 ACT, essay required. Additional 21 hours plus research project required, must maintain requirements for eligibility each semester. Approximately 9 freshmen enter the program each year.

Majors. **Biology:** General. **Business:** General, accounting, business admin, finance, marketing, organizational behavior. **Communications:** Communications/speech/rhetoric. **Computer sciences:** General. **Education:** General, art, business, early childhood, elementary, English, mathematics, music, physical, science, secondary, social studies. **English:** English lit. **Health services:** Nursing (RN), predental, preoptometry, prepharmacy. **History:** General. **Human services:** Social work. **Liberal arts:** Arts/sciences. **Math:** General. **Parks/recreation:** Facilities management. **Protective services:** Law enforcement admin. **Psychology:** General. **Social sciences:** Sociology. **Theology:** Bible, religious ed, sacred music. **Visual/performing arts:** Art, dramatic, music performance.

Most popular majors. Business/marketing 26%, education 37%, public administration/social services 6%, security/protective services 9%.

Technology on campus. 91 workstations in library, computer center, student center. Dormitories linked to campus network. Commuter students can connect to campus network. Online library, repair service, wireless network available.

Student life. **Freshman orientation:** Mandatory, $100 fee. Preregistration for classes offered. Conducted 4 days before classes begin. **Policies:** Students under 21 years of age at beginning of enrollment required to live in residence housing unless living with approved relative. Religious observance required. **Housing:** Guaranteed on-campus for freshmen. Single-sex dorms, special housing for disabled, apartments, wellness housing available. $100 fully refundable deposit, deadline 8/26. **Activities:** Campus ministries, choral groups, drama, international student organizations, music ensembles, student government, student newspaper, Democratic club, Fellowship of Christian Athletes, Phi Beta Delta (men's service), Phi Beta Lambda, Gatekeepers (mentoring), Students for Life, Natures Investigation Circulus, Missouri State Teachers Association, Society for the Behavioral Sciences, Republican club, art club.

Athletics. NAIA. **Intercollegiate:** Baseball M, basketball, cross-country, golf, soccer, softball W, track and field, volleyball, wrestling M. **Intramural:** Badminton, basketball, racquetball, table tennis, ultimate frisbee, volleyball. **Team name:** Trojans.

Student services. Adult student services, chaplain/spiritual director, career counseling, student employment services, financial aid counseling, health services. **Physically disabled:** Services for visually, hearing impaired.

Harris-Stowe State University
St. Louis, Missouri
www.hssu.edu   CB code: 6269

- Public 4-year university
- Commuter campus in large city
- 1,363 degree-seeking undergraduates: 24% part-time, 67% women

General. Founded in 1857. Regionally accredited. **Degrees:** 134 bachelor's awarded. **ROTC:** Army, Air Force. **Location:** Midtown. **Calendar:** Semester, limited summer session. **Full-time faculty:** 44 total; 57% minority, 43% women. **Part-time faculty:** 132 total; 88% minority, 60% women. **Class size:** 88% < 20, 12% 20-39. **Special facilities:** Jazz institute.

Freshman class profile. 2,573 applied, 1,321 admitted, 279 enrolled.

Mid 50% test scores		GPA 2.0-2.99:	63%
SAT critical reading:	360-450	Rank in top quarter:	20%
SAT math:	360-470	Rank in top tenth:	4%
ACT composite:	14-18	End year in good standing:	57%
GPA 3.75 or higher:	2%	Return as sophomores:	47%
GPA 3.50-3.74:	7%	Out-of-state:	17%
GPA 3.0-3.49:	21%	Live on campus:	62%

Basis for selection. Open admission. First-time freshmen with below 2.0 GPA required to complete summer enrichment program for admission. Institutional placement test required of applicants with scores below 18 on any section of the ACT or below 440 on any section of the SAT. Full-time, first-year freshmen encouraged to meet Missouri high school core curriculum requirements. **Learning Disabled:** Submit documentation of disability for review by Director of the Center for Retention and Student Success.

High school preparation. College-preparatory program recommended. Required units include English 4, mathematics 3, social studies 3, science 3 (laboratory 1), foreign language 2, visual/performing arts 1 and academic electives 5. 1 visual/performing arts and 1 practical art required. Finance, health and physical education also required. Social studies must include American government.

2015-2016 Annual costs. Tuition/fees: $5,220; $9,853 out-of-state. Room/board: $9,140. Books/supplies: $700. Personal expenses: $2,000.

2014-2015 Financial aid. **Need-based:** 55% of total undergraduate aid awarded as scholarships/grants, 45% as loans/jobs. **Non-need-based:** Scholarships awarded for academics, alumni affiliation, art, athletics, leadership, music/drama, state residency.

Application procedures. **Admission:** Priority date 12/1; no deadline. $20 fee. Admission notification on a rolling basis. **Financial aid:** Closing date 4/1. FAFSA, institutional form required. Applicants notified on a rolling basis starting 4/1; must reply within 3 week(s) of notification.

Academics. **Special study options:** Accelerated study, cooperative education, ESL, honors, internships, student-designed major, study abroad, teacher certification program. **Credit/placement by examination:** AP, CLEP, institutional tests. **Support services:** Learning center, pre-admission summer program, reduced course load, remedial instruction, study skills assistance, tutoring, writing center.

Majors. **Biology:** General. **Business:** Accounting, business admin, hospitality admin, management information systems. **Education:** General, early childhood, elementary, middle, secondary. **Health services:** Health care admin. **Math:** General. **Protective services:** Criminal justice. **Social sciences:** Urban studies.

Most popular majors. Business/marketing 34%, education 28%, security/protective services 19%.

Technology on campus. 272 workstations in dormitories, library, computer center, student center. Dormitories wired for high-speed internet access and linked to campus network. Commuter students can connect to campus network. Helpline, wireless network available.

Student life. Freshman orientation: Mandatory. Preregistration for classes offered. Program directed by counseling staff during semester. **Housing:** Guaranteed on-campus for freshmen. Coed dorms available. $500 fully refundable deposit. **Activities:** Choral groups, dance, drama, international student organizations, literary magazine, music ensembles, student government, student newspaper, African American Studies Society, multicultural council, 100 Strong, Organization for Cultural Progress, Student Ambassadors.

Athletics. NAIA. **Intercollegiate:** Baseball M, basketball, cheerleading, soccer, softball W, volleyball W. **Intramural:** Basketball, football (non-tackle), sand volleyball, volleyball. **Team name:** Hornets.

Student services. Career counseling, student employment services, financial aid counseling, health services, personal counseling, placement for graduates, veterans' counselor.

Hickey College
St. Louis, Missouri
www.hickeycollege.edu   CB code: 2308

- For-profit 4-year business and technical college
- Commuter campus in very large city
- 372 undergraduates

General. Founded in 1933. Accredited by ACICS. **Degrees:** 31 bachelor's, 160 associate awarded. **Location:** 15 miles from downtown. **Calendar:** Semester. **Full-time faculty:** 28 total. **Part-time faculty:** 28 total.

Basis for selection. Open admission, but selective for some programs. Selective enrollment for paralegal and veterinary technician programs.

2015-2016 Annual costs. Books/supplies: $1,000. **Additional information:** Diploma programs: $13,890-$21,620, books and supplies $1,810-$2,574, room and board $5,920-$8,880. Associate programs: $27,730-$31,710, books and supplies $2,434-$3,328, room and board $11,840-$13,320. Bachelor's program: $21,380, books and supplies $2,413, room and board $17,760.

Application procedures. **Admission:** No deadline. $50 fee. Admission notification on a rolling basis. **Financial aid:** No deadline. FAFSA required. Applicants notified on a rolling basis.

Academics. **Credit/placement by examination:** AP, CLEP.

Majors. **Business:** Management science.

Technology on campus. 134 workstations in library, computer center.

Student life. Freshman orientation: Mandatory. Preregistration for classes offered. **Housing:** Apartments available.

Student services. Student employment services, placement for graduates.

ITT Technical Institute: Arnold
Arnold, Missouri
www.itt-tech.edu   CB code: 2691

- For-profit 4-year technical college
- Commuter campus in large town
- 291 undergraduates
- Interview required

General. Accredited by ACICS. **Degrees:** 25 bachelor's, 76 associate awarded. **Calendar:** Quarter, extensive summer session. **Full-time faculty:** 12 total. **Part-time faculty:** 46 total.

Basis for selection. Satisfactory scores from on-site tests in English and mathematics required.

2015-2016 Annual costs. Per-credit-hour charge, $493, will vary depending on program level and course of study. Academic fee, $200. Some programs require purchase of tools, which could cost an additional $500. All costs subject to change.

Application procedures. Admission: No deadline. No application fee. Admission notification on a rolling basis. **Financial aid:** No deadline. FAFSA, institutional form required. Applicants notified on a rolling basis.

Academics. Credit/placement by examination: AP, CLEP. **Support services:** Learning center, tutoring.

Majors. Business: Business admin, construction management, e-commerce, project management. **Communications technology:** Animation/special effects. **Computer sciences:** Applications programming, IT project management, programming, security. **Protective services:** Law enforcement admin. **Visual/performing arts:** Game design.

Technology on campus. Online library available.

Student life. Freshman orientation: Available. Preregistration for classes offered.

Student services. Career counseling, student employment services, placement for graduates.

Contact. Phone: (636) 464-6600 Toll-free number: (888) 488-1082 Fax: (636) 464-6611
James Rowe, Director of Recruitment, ITT Technical Institute: Arnold, 1930 Meyer Drury Drive, Arnold, MO 63010

ITT Technical Institute: Earth City
Earth City, Missouri
www.itt-tech.edu   CB code: 1216

- For-profit 4-year technical college
- Commuter campus in large city
- 602 undergraduates
- Interview required

General. Founded in 1936. Accredited by ACICS. **Degrees:** 36 bachelor's, 172 associate awarded. **Location:** 15 miles from St. Louis. **Calendar:** Quarter, extensive summer session. **Full-time faculty:** 17 total. **Part-time faculty:** 57 total.

Basis for selection. Satisfactory scores from on-site tests in English and mathematics required.

2015-2016 Annual costs. Per-credit-hour charge, $493, will vary depending on program level and course of study. Academic fee, $200. Some programs require purchase of tools, which could cost an additional $500. All costs subject to change.

Application procedures. Admission: No deadline. No application fee. Admission notification on a rolling basis. **Financial aid:** No deadline. FAFSA, institutional form required. Applicants notified on a rolling basis.

Academics. Credit/placement by examination: AP, CLEP. **Support services:** Learning center, tutoring.

Majors. Business: Business admin, construction management, e-commerce, project management. **Communications technology:** Animation/special effects. **Computer sciences:** Applications programming, IT project management, programming, security. **Protective services:** Law enforcement admin.

Technology on campus. Online library available.

Student life. Freshman orientation: Available. Preregistration for classes offered.

Student services. Career counseling, student employment services, placement for graduates.

Contact. Phone: (314) 298-7800 Toll-free number: (800) 235-5488 Fax: (314) 298-0559
Arlen Freeman, Director of Recruitment, ITT Technical Institute: Earth City, 3640 Corporate Trail Drive, Earth City, MO 63045

Kansas City Art Institute
Kansas City, Missouri
www.kcai.edu   CB code: 6330

- Private 4-year visual arts college
- Residential campus in large city

- 636 degree-seeking undergraduates: 1% part-time, 67% women
- 58% of applicants admitted
- SAT or ACT (ACT writing optional), application essay required

General. Founded in 1885. Regionally accredited. **Degrees:** 184 bachelor's awarded. **Location:** 250 miles from St. Louis, 500 miles from Denver. **Calendar:** Semester, limited summer session. **Full-time faculty:** 51 total; 84% have terminal degrees, 6% minority, 45% women. **Part-time faculty:** 60 total; 40% have terminal degrees, 38% women. **Class size:** 83% < 20, 17% 20-39. **Special facilities:** Gallery for contemporary artists.

Freshman class profile. 683 applied, 393 admitted, 141 enrolled.

Mid 50% test scores			
SAT critical reading:	510-610	Rank in top quarter:	34%
SAT math:	480-570	Rank in top tenth:	12%
SAT writing:	490-570	Out-of-state:	66%
ACT composite:	20-26	Live on campus:	90%

Rank in top quarter and tenth shown: Rank in top quarter: 34%, Rank in top tenth: 12%, Out-of-state: 66%, Live on campus: 90%.

Basis for selection. High school or GED academic record and college transcripts, 2 letters of reference (recommended), ACT, SAT or TOEFL scores, and a statement of purpose. Portfolio with minimum of 15 pieces of artwork is required. **Home schooled:** Statement describing home school structure and mission, transcript of courses and grades required. **Learning Disabled:** Disclosure of special needs recommended but not required.

High school preparation. College-preparatory program recommended. 20 units recommended. Recommended units include English 4, mathematics 3, social studies 3, science 3, visual/performing arts 4 and academic electives 3.

2015-2016 Annual costs. Tuition/fees: $35,270. Room/board: $10,240. Books/supplies: $2,000. Personal expenses: $2,250.

2015-2016 Financial aid. Need-based: 74% of total undergraduate aid awarded as scholarships/grants, 26% as loans/jobs. **Non-need-based:** Scholarships awarded for academics, art.

Application procedures. Admission: Priority date 12/1; deadline 8/1 (postmark date). $45 fee, may be waived for applicants with need. Admission notification on a rolling basis beginning on or about 9/1. Must reply by May 1 or within 2 week(s) if notified thereafter. **Financial aid:** Priority date 3/15, closing date 4/1. FAFSA required. Applicants notified on a rolling basis starting 4/1; must reply within 2 week(s) of notification.

Academics. Special study options: Double major, exchange student, independent study, internships, New York semester, study abroad, teacher certification program. **Credit/placement by examination:** AP, CLEP, IB. 15 credit hours maximum toward bachelor's degree. **Support services:** Learning center, reduced course load, remedial instruction, study skills assistance, tutoring, writing center.

Majors. English: Creative writing. **Visual/performing arts:** Art history/conservation, ceramics, cinematography, digital arts, fiber arts, graphic design, illustration, painting, photography, printmaking, sculpture.

Technology on campus. 50 workstations in dormitories, library, computer center. Dormitories wired for high-speed internet access and linked to campus network. Commuter students can connect to campus network. Online course registration, online library, helpline, wireless network available.

Student life. Freshman orientation: Mandatory. Preregistration for classes offered. Three-day program held prior to start of academic year. **Housing:** Guaranteed on-campus for freshmen. Coed dorms, apartments, gender-neutral housing, wellness housing available. $230 nonrefundable deposit, deadline 6/1. **Activities:** Film society, international student organizations, student government, Black Artist's Culture and Community, LOCAL (Latino/Latina organization), Art and Faith.

Student services. Adult student services, career counseling, student employment services, financial aid counseling, minority student services, personal counseling, veterans' counselor. **Physically disabled:** Services for visually, speech, hearing impaired.

Contact. E-mail: admiss@kcai.edu
Phone: (816) 474-5224 Toll-free number: (800) 522-5224
Fax: (816) 802-3309
Julia Welles, Director of Admissions and Recruitment, Kansas City Art Institute, 4415 Warwick Boulevard, Kansas City, MO 64111

Lincoln University
Jefferson City, Missouri
www.lincolnu.edu   CB code: 6366

- Public 4-year university and liberal arts college
- Commuter campus in large town

◗ 2,247 degree-seeking undergraduates: 15% part-time, 55% women, 52% African American, 2% Hispanic/Latino, 4% Multi-racial, non-Hispanic, 2% international

◗ 112 degree-seeking graduate students

General. Founded in 1866. Regionally accredited. 1890 land-grant institution. Historically Black College and University (HBCU). **Degrees:** 287 bachelor's, 71 associate awarded; master's offered. **ROTC:** Army, Naval, Air Force. **Location:** 132 miles from St. Louis, 157 miles from Kansas City. **Calendar:** Semester, limited summer session. **Full-time faculty:** 124 total; 27% minority, 47% women. **Part-time faculty:** 60 total; 7% minority, 55% women. **Class size:** 47% < 20, 44% 20-39, 5% 40-49, 3% 50-99. **Special facilities:** Ethnic studies center and archives, 3 research farms, agriculture and extension information center, native plants outdoor laboratory.

Freshman class profile. 6,938 applied, 2,776 admitted, 600 enrolled.

Mid 50% test scores		Rank in top quarter:	23%
SAT math:	430-540	Rank in top tenth:	6%
ACT composite:	15-19	End year in good standing:	48%
GPA 3.75 or higher:	4%	Return as sophomores:	46%
GPA 3.50-3.74:	5%	Out-of-state:	26%
GPA 3.0-3.49:	20%	Live on campus:	78%
GPA 2.0-2.99:	58%	International:	1%

Basis for selection. Open admission, but selective for some programs and for out-of-state students. Special requirements for nursing and education programs. Audition required for sacred music and music education students. **Home schooled:** Transcript of courses and grades required. Must submit transcript with parent's notarized signature, demonstrating completion of Missouri Minimum Core Curriculum or its equivalency, as determined by the University. **Learning Disabled:** Comprehensive documentation of disability by qualified professional must be on file to request accommodations.

High school preparation. College-preparatory program recommended. 18 units required; 20 recommended. Required and recommended units include English 4, mathematics 3, social studies 3, science 3 (laboratory 1), foreign language 2 and visual/performing arts 1.

2015-2016 Annual costs. Tuition/fees: $7,042; $13,432 out-of-state. Room/board: $6,070. Books/supplies: $1,000. Personal expenses: $203.

2015-2016 Financial aid. Need-based: 566 full-time freshmen applied for aid; 530 deemed to have need; 530 received aid. Average need met was 62%. Average scholarship/grant was $6,483; average loan $6,418. 62% of total undergraduate aid awarded as scholarships/grants, 38% as loans/jobs. **Non-need-based:** Awarded to 198 full-time undergraduates, including 46 freshmen. Scholarships awarded for academics, art, athletics, job skills, leadership, minority status, music/drama, ROTC, state residency.

Application procedures. Admission: No deadline. No application fee. Admission notification on a rolling basis. **Financial aid:** Priority date 3/1; no closing date. FAFSA, institutional form required. Applicants notified on a rolling basis starting 3/15; must reply within 2 week(s) of notification.

Academics. Special study options: Accelerated study, cooperative education, cross-registration, distance learning, double major, dual enrollment of high school students, exchange student, honors, independent study, internships, study abroad, teacher certification program. Senior citizen program. **Credit/placement by examination:** AP, CLEP, IB, institutional tests. 18 credit hours maximum toward associate degree, 18 toward bachelor's. Total number of alternative credit hours cannot exceed 30. Students may receive credit only for courses numbered 100-299. Each examination may be taken only once. Students must be currently enrolled during the semester in which he/she elects to take the exam. **Support services:** Learning center, pre-admission summer program, reduced course load, remedial instruction, study skills assistance, tutoring, writing center.

Majors. Biology: General. **Business:** Accounting, business admin, marketing. **Communications:** Journalism. **Computer sciences:** Information systems. **Conservation:** Environmental science. **Education:** Art, biology, business, chemistry, elementary, English, mathematics, middle, music, physical, physics, social science, special ed. **English:** English lit. **Foreign languages:** Spanish. **Health services:** Clinical lab science, nursing (RN). **History:** General. **Human services:** General, social work. **Liberal arts:** Arts/sciences. **Math:** General. **Physical sciences:** Chemistry, physics. **Protective services:** Law enforcement admin. **Psychology:** General. **Social sciences:** Political science, sociology. **Theology:** Sacred music. **Visual/performing arts:** Studio arts. **Work/family studies:** Food/nutrition.

Most popular majors. Business/marketing 18%, computer/information sciences 6%, education 13%, liberal arts 15%, psychology 7%, security/protective services 7%.

Technology on campus. 365 workstations in dormitories, library, computer center, student center. Dormitories wired for high-speed internet access and linked to campus network. Online library, helpline, wireless network available.

Student life. Freshman orientation: Mandatory, $75 fee. Preregistration for classes offered. One-day program held several dates during the summer. **Policies:** Unmarried students under 21, whose primary domicile is beyond a 60-mile radius, are required to live in residence halls for four consecutive semesters. Armed Forces veterans and any student who has established a local primary domicile one year prior to entering are exempt. **Housing:** Coed dorms, wellness housing available. $125 fully refundable deposit, deadline 7/1. Honors housing available. **Activities:** Bands, campus ministries, choral groups, dance, drama, international student organizations, literary magazine, music ensembles, radio station, student government, student newspaper, TV station, Baptist Student Center, Wesley Foundation.

Athletics. NCAA. **Intercollegiate:** Baseball M, basketball, bowling W, cheerleading W, cross-country W, football (tackle) M, golf, softball W, tennis W, track and field. **Intramural:** Basketball, bowling, volleyball, weight lifting. **Team name:** Blue Tigers.

Student services. Alcohol/substance abuse counseling, career counseling, services for economically disadvantaged, student employment services, financial aid counseling, health services, personal counseling, placement for graduates, veterans' counselor, women's services. **Physically disabled:** Services for visually, speech, hearing impaired.

Contact. E-mail: enroll@lincolnu.edu
Phone: (573) 681-5599 Toll-free number: (800) 521-5052
Fax: (573) 681-5889
DeRecco Lynch, Director of Admissions, Lincoln University, 820 Chestnut Street, B7 Young Hall, Jefferson City, MO 65101

Lindenwood University
St. Charles, Missouri
www.lindenwood.edu   CB code: 6367

◗ Private 4-year university and liberal arts college affiliated with the Presbyterian Church (USA)

◗ Residential campus in small city

◗ 7,787 degree-seeking undergraduates: 7% part-time, 55% women, 13% African American, 1% Asian American, 4% Hispanic/Latino, 3% Multi-racial, non-Hispanic, 12% international

◗ 3,287 degree-seeking graduate students

◗ 55% of applicants admitted

◗ SAT or ACT (ACT writing optional), application essay required

◗ 49% graduate within 6 years

General. Founded in 1827. Regionally accredited. **Degrees:** 1,645 bachelor's awarded; master's, doctoral offered. **ROTC:** Army, Air Force. **Location:** 20 miles from St. Louis. **Calendar:** Continuous, limited summer session. **Full-time faculty:** 301 total; 72% have terminal degrees, 9% minority, 49% women. **Part-time faculty:** 1,377 total; 24% have terminal degrees, 12% minority, 51% women. **Class size:** 67% < 20, 32% 20-39, less than 1% 40-49, less than 1% 50-99. **Special facilities:** Greenhouse, wetland program facility, success center, natural history, professional theater, archeological sites.

Freshman class profile. 4,156 applied, 2,302 admitted, 1,221 enrolled.

Mid 50% test scores		Rank in top quarter:	33%
SAT critical reading:	430-540	Rank in top tenth:	13%
SAT math:	460-560	Return as sophomores:	66%
SAT writing:	400-500	Out-of-state:	50%
ACT composite:	20-25	Live on campus:	91%
GPA 3.75 or higher:	16%	International:	15%
GPA 3.50-3.74:	17%	Fraternities:	5%
GPA 3.0-3.49:	36%	Sororities:	11%
GPA 2.0-2.99:	31%		

Basis for selection. Class rank, school record, high school GPA very important. **Home schooled:** Transcript of courses and grades required.

High school preparation. College-preparatory program recommended. 20 units recommended. Recommended units include English 4, mathematics 3, social studies 3, history 1, science 3 (laboratory 1), foreign language 2 and visual/performing arts 1.

2015-2016 Annual costs. Tuition/fees: $16,022. Room/board: $7,934. Books/supplies: $1,800. Personal expenses: $2,800.

2015-2016 Financial aid. Need-based: 827 full-time freshmen applied for aid; 629 deemed to have need; 629 received aid. Average need met was 73%. Average scholarship/grant was $7,274; average loan $3,286. 58% of

total undergraduate aid awarded as scholarships/grants, 42% as loans/jobs. **Non-need-based:** Awarded to 4,540 full-time undergraduates, including 954 freshmen. Scholarships awarded for academics, art, athletics, leadership, minority status, music/drama, religious affiliation, state residency.

Application procedures. Admission: No deadline. $30 fee, may be waived for applicants with need. Admission notification on a rolling basis. **Financial aid:** Priority date 4/1; no closing date. FAFSA required. Applicants notified on a rolling basis.

Academics. Special study options: Accelerated study, combined bachelor's/graduate degree, distance learning, double major, dual enrollment of high school students, ESL, external degree, honors, independent study, internships, student-designed major, study abroad, teacher certification program. Study abroad semester at York St. John. **Credit/placement by examination:** AP, CLEP, IB, SAT, ACT, institutional tests. **Support services:** Learning center, reduced course load, remedial instruction, study skills assistance, tutoring, writing center.

Majors. Area/ethnic studies: Chinese. **Biology:** General, environmental. **Business:** General, accounting, business admin, entrepreneurial studies, finance, human resources, international, management information systems, marketing, nonprofit/public, personal/financial services, retailing. **Communications:** Advertising, communications/speech/rhetoric, digital media, journalism, media studies, organizational. **Computer sciences:** General, computer science, information technology. **Conservation:** Environmental science. **Education:** Art, biology, business, chemistry, early childhood, early childhood special, elementary, French, history, middle, physical, science, social studies, Spanish, technology/industrial arts, trade/industrial. **English:** Creative writing, English lit. **Foreign languages:** French, Spanish. **Health services:** Athletic training, health care admin, nursing (RN). **History:** General. **Human services:** General, social work. **Math:** General. **Parks/recreation:** General, exercise sciences, sports admin. **Philosophy/religion:** Christian, philosophy, religion. **Physical sciences:** Chemistry. **Protective services:** Criminal justice, fire services admin, law enforcement admin. **Psychology:** General. **Social sciences:** Anthropology, economics, international relations, political science, sociology. **Theology:** Pastoral counseling, youth ministry. **Visual/performing arts:** General, acting, art, art history/conservation, dance, directing/producing, dramatic, fashion design, multimedia, music, music management, music performance, music theory/composition, musical theater, studio arts, studio arts management, theater arts management, theater design.

Most popular majors. Business/marketing 33%, communications/journalism 8%, computer/information sciences 6%, education 11%, parks/recreation 7%, security/protective services 9%.

Technology on campus. 286 workstations in library, computer center, student center. Dormitories wired for high-speed internet access and linked to campus network. Commuter students can connect to campus network. Online course registration, online library, helpline, wireless network available.

Student life. Freshman orientation: Mandatory. Preregistration for classes offered. Held 5 days before start of fall semester. **Policies:** Zero tolerance of illegal substances. **Housing:** Single-sex dorms, special housing for disabled, apartments, fraternity/sorority housing available. $300 nonrefundable deposit. Single parent housing available. **Activities:** Bands, campus ministries, choral groups, dance, drama, international student organizations, literary magazine, music ensembles, musical theater, radio station, student government, student newspaper, symphony orchestra, TV station, Campus Crusade for Christ, intercultural club, American Humanics, Circle K, Reform Campus Fellowship, Lewis & Clark Historical Society, Eastern Debating Society, Christian Life Group, Fellowship of Christian Athletes.

Athletics. NCAA. **Intercollegiate:** Baseball M, basketball, cross-country, diving, field hockey W, football (tackle) M, golf, gymnastics W, ice hockey W, lacrosse, soccer, softball W, swimming, tennis, track and field, volleyball, wrestling M. **Intramural:** Basketball, football (non-tackle), sand volleyball, soccer, softball, volleyball. **Team name:** Lions.

Student services. Adult student services, alcohol/substance abuse counseling, chaplain/spiritual director, career counseling, student employment services, financial aid counseling, health services, personal counseling, placement for graduates, veterans' counselor, women's services.

Contact. E-mail: admissions@lindenwood.edu
Phone: (636) 949-4949 Fax: (636) 949-4989
Rachel South, Director of Day Admissions, Lindenwood University, 209 South Kingshighway, St. Charles, MO 63301

Logan University
Chesterfield, Missouri
www.logan.edu

CB code: 4965

- Private 3-year university
- Commuter campus in very large city

- 52 degree-seeking undergraduates: 35% part-time, 58% women, 2% African American, 2% Asian American, 4% Hispanic/Latino, 2% Native Hawaiian/Pacific islander, 2% Multi-racial, non-Hispanic, 2% international
- 860 graduate students

General. Founded in 1935. Regionally accredited. **Degrees:** 118 bachelor's awarded; master's, professional, doctoral offered. **Calendar:** Trimester. **Full-time faculty:** 61 total. **Part-time faculty:** 45 total.

Basis for selection. Applicants for bachelor's degree programs must have minimum of 30 semester hours from regionally accredited college or university; only credits for which grades of 2.0 and higher were received will be transferable.

2015-2016 Annual costs. Tuition/fees: $8,390. Books/supplies: $850. Personal expenses: $4,488.

2014-2015 Financial aid. Need-based: 28% of total undergraduate aid awarded as scholarships/grants, 72% as loans/jobs.

Application procedures. Admission: No deadline. $50 fee. **Financial aid:** No deadline.

Academics. Special study options: Accelerated study, distance learning, independent study. **Credit/placement by examination:** AP, CLEP. **Support services:** Learning center, study skills assistance, tutoring.

Majors. Biology: General.

Student life. Activities: Student government.

Athletics. Team name: Leopards.

Student services. Financial aid counseling.

Contact. E-mail: Admissions@logan.edu
Phone: (636) 230-1750 Toll-free number: (800) 533-9210
Stacey Till, Assistant Vice President-Admissions & Development, Logan University, 1851 Schoettler Road, Chesterfield, MO 63017

Maryville University of Saint Louis
St. Louis, Missouri
www.maryville.edu

CB member
CB code: 6399

- Private 4-year university
- Commuter campus in very large city
- 2,703 degree-seeking undergraduates: 29% part-time, 69% women, 8% African American, 2% Asian American, 3% Hispanic/Latino, 2% Multi-racial, non-Hispanic, 4% international
- 3,609 degree-seeking graduate students
- 72% of applicants admitted
- 71% graduate within 6 years

General. Founded in 1872. Regionally accredited. **Degrees:** 536 bachelor's awarded; master's, doctoral offered. **ROTC:** Army. **Location:** 20 miles from downtown. **Calendar:** Semester, limited summer session. **Full-time faculty:** 129 total; 79% have terminal degrees, 13% minority, 65% women. **Part-time faculty:** 465 total; 38% have terminal degrees, 12% minority, 70% women. **Class size:** 74% < 20, 25% 20-39, less than 1% 40-49, less than 1% 50-99. **Special facilities:** Observatory, walking trails, coffeehouse, teaching laboratory, clinical laboratories, communications laboratory, multi-media classrooms.

Freshman class profile. 1,457 applied, 1,053 admitted, 382 enrolled.

Mid 50% test scores			
SAT critical reading:	480-600	GPA 2.0-2.99:	8%
SAT math:	510-630	Rank in top quarter:	59%
ACT composite:	23-27	Rank in top tenth:	25%
GPA 3.75 or higher:	49%	Return as sophomores:	89%
GPA 3.50-3.74:	20%	Out-of-state:	34%
GPA 3.0-3.49:	23%	Live on campus:	65%
		International:	3%

Basis for selection. School record most important. Recommendations and extracurricular activities considered. ACT or SAT very important. Test-optional but is required under certain circumstances. Interview and 20 hours observation in clinical setting required for physical therapy students. Audition required for music therapy students; portfolio required for art education, graphic design, interior design, and studio art majors. **Home schooled:** Increased weight placed on ACT or SAT scores.

High school preparation. College-preparatory program recommended. 22 units required. Required units include English 4, mathematics 3, social studies 2 and science 2. 3 additional units required, either in foreign language or any of the above units. Applicants for actuarial science, art, education, interior design, clinical laboratory science, nursing, occupational therapy, and physical therapy must meet other specific requirements.

2015-2016 Annual costs. Tuition/fees: $26,958. Room/board: $10,240. Books/supplies: $1,800. Personal expenses: $3,600.

2015-2016 Financial aid. Need-based: 343 full-time freshmen applied for aid; 304 deemed to have need; 304 received aid. Average need met was 71%. Average scholarship/grant was $17,196; average loan $3,311. 62% of total undergraduate aid awarded as scholarships/grants, 38% as loans/jobs. **Non-need-based:** Awarded to 575 full-time undergraduates, including 83 freshmen. Scholarships awarded for academics, art, athletics, job skills, leadership, minority status, music/drama, ROTC, state residency.

Application procedures. Admission: Priority date 12/15; deadline 8/15. No application fee. Admission notification on a rolling basis. Must reply by May 1 or within 4 week(s) if notified thereafter. **Financial aid:** Priority date 3/1; no closing date. FAFSA required. Applicants notified on a rolling basis starting 3/1; must reply by 5/1 or within 2 week(s) of notification.

Academics. Special study options: Accelerated study, combined bachelor's/graduate degree, cooperative education, cross-registration, distance learning, double major, dual enrollment of high school students, ESL, honors, independent study, internships, liberal arts/career combination, semester at sea, student-designed major, study abroad, teacher certification program, Washington semester, weekend college. Online programs. **Credit/placement by examination:** AP, CLEP, IB, SAT, ACT, institutional tests. 30 credit hours maximum toward bachelor's degree. **Support services:** Learning center, reduced course load, study skills assistance, tutoring, writing center. Division of Student Success and Life Coaching.

Majors. Biology: General, biochemistry, biomedical sciences. **Business:** General, accounting, actuarial science, business admin, e-commerce, financial planning, international, management information systems, marketing. **Communications:** Media studies. **Conservation:** Environmental science, environmental studies. **Education:** Art, early childhood, elementary, middle, science. **English:** English lit. **Health services:** General, clinical lab science, communication disorders, health care admin, music therapy, nursing (RN), prechiropractic, predental, prepharmacy, preveterinary, vocational rehab counseling. **History:** General. **Liberal arts:** Arts/sciences. **Math:** General, applied. **Military:** Cyber ops. **Parks/recreation:** Sports admin. **Philosophy/religion:** Philosophy. **Physical sciences:** Chemistry, forensic chemistry. **Psychology:** General, forensic, industrial, social. **Social sciences:** Criminology, sociology. **Visual/performing arts:** Graphic design, interior design, studio arts.

Technology on campus. 575 workstations in dormitories, library, computer center, student center. Dormitories wired for high-speed internet access and linked to campus network. Commuter students can connect to campus network. Online course registration, online library, helpline, student web hosting, wireless network available.

Student life. Freshman orientation: Available. Preregistration for classes offered. Three-day program prior to start of classes. **Housing:** Guaranteed on-campus for all undergraduates. Coed dorms, apartments, themed housing, wellness housing available. $300 partly refundable deposit, deadline 5/1. **Activities:** Bands, campus ministries, choral groups, dance, international student organizations, literary magazine, music ensembles, student government, student newspaper, symphony orchestra, Association of Black Collegians, multicultural club, community service club, Catholic students club, Fellowship of Christian Athletes, Inclusion at Maryville, International Student Organization, Hillel, Green Maryville Student Association.

Athletics. NCAA. **Intercollegiate:** Baseball M, basketball, bowling W, cross-country, diving, golf, lacrosse M, soccer, softball W, swimming, tennis W, track and field, volleyball W, wrestling M. **Intramural:** Basketball, bowling, cheerleading, football (non-tackle), lacrosse, soccer, softball, table tennis, ultimate frisbee, volleyball. **Team name:** Saints.

Student services. Adult student services, alcohol/substance abuse counseling, chaplain/spiritual director, career counseling, student employment services, financial aid counseling, health services, minority student services, personal counseling, placement for graduates, veterans' counselor. **Physically disabled:** Services for visually, speech, hearing impaired.

Contact. E-mail: admissions@maryville.edu
Phone: (314) 529-9350 Toll-free number: (800) 627-9855 ext. 9350
Fax: (314) 529-9927
Shani Lenore-Jenkins, Associate Vice President of Enrollment, Maryville University of Saint Louis, 650 Maryville University Drive, St. Louis, MO 63141-7299

Midwest University
Wentzville, Missouri
www.midwest.edu

- Private two-year upper-division university and seminary college
- Large town

General. Candidate for regional accreditation. **Calendar:** Semester.

Annual costs/financial aid. Tuition/fees (2015-2016): $7,610. Books/supplies: $450.

Contact. Phone: (636) 327-4645
Registrar and Director of Admissions, 851 Parr Road, Wentzville, MO 63385

Missouri Baptist University
St. Louis, Missouri
www.mobap.edu   CB code: 2258

- Private 4-year university and liberal arts college affiliated with the Baptist faith
- Commuter campus in very large city
- 1,719 degree-seeking undergraduates: 23% part-time, 56% women, 11% African American, 1% Asian American, 2% Hispanic/Latino, 3% Multiracial, non-Hispanic, 2% international
- 1,034 degree-seeking graduate students
- 57% of applicants admitted
- SAT or ACT (ACT writing optional) required
- 44% graduate within 6 years

General. Founded in 1963. Regionally accredited. **Degrees:** 351 bachelor's, 10 associate awarded; master's, doctoral offered. **ROTC:** Army. **Location:** 20 miles from downtown. **Calendar:** Semester, limited summer session. **Full-time faculty:** 69 total; 64% have terminal degrees, 12% minority, 49% women. **Part-time faculty:** 221 total; 22% have terminal degrees, 8% minority, 47% women. **Special facilities:** Coffee house.

Freshman class profile. 910 applied, 522 admitted, 263 enrolled.

Mid 50% test scores		
SAT critical reading:	380-470	
SAT math:	360-510	
ACT composite:	19-23	

End year in good standing:	73%
Return as sophomores:	59%
International:	1%

Basis for selection. 2.0 GPA, 20 ACT/950 SAT (exclusive of Writing), class rank in upper 50% of graduating class required. Applicants with high school GPA below 2.0 may be admitted on a probationary status. Interview and/or essay required for academically weak students; audition required for music majors. **Home schooled:** Transcript of courses and grades required. **Learning Disabled:** Must self-identify to the Special Needs Access Office, provide current written documentation of disability from qualified professional or agency, and request accommodations. Documentation must meet institutional criteria, indicate substantial limitation, and be completed 6 weeks prior to start of class.

High school preparation. 24 units required. Required units include English 4, mathematics 3, social studies 3, science 3 (laboratory 1), visual/performing arts 1 and academic electives 7. 1 practical arts, 1 physical education, .5 health education, .5 personal finance required.

2015-2016 Annual costs. Tuition/fees: $23,750. Room/board: $9,510. Books/supplies: $1,200. Personal expenses: $1,505.

2014-2015 Financial aid. Need-based: 46% of total undergraduate aid awarded as scholarships/grants, 54% as loans/jobs. **Non-need-based:** Scholarships awarded for academics, alumni affiliation, athletics, leadership, music/drama, religious affiliation.

Application procedures. Admission: No deadline. $35 fee, may be waived for applicants with need, free for online applicants. Admission notification on a rolling basis. **Financial aid:** Priority date 4/1; no closing date. FAFSA, institutional form required. Applicants notified on a rolling basis starting 4/16; must reply within 2 week(s) of notification.

Academics. Special study options: Accelerated study, cooperative education, cross-registration, distance learning, double major, dual enrollment of high school students, honors, independent study, internships, liberal arts/career combination, student-designed major, study abroad, teacher certification program, urban semester, Washington semester. **Credit/placement by examination:** AP, CLEP, institutional tests. 45 credit hours maximum toward bachelor's degree. No single source may account for more than 30 of the 45 credit-hour maximum. **Support services:** Learning center, reduced course load, remedial instruction, study skills assistance, tutoring, writing center.

Majors. Biology: General, biochemistry, biotechnology. **Business:** Accounting, business admin, marketing, organizational leadership. **Communications:** Journalism, public relations, radio/TV. **Computer sciences:** Information technology. **Education:** General, business, drama/dance, early childhood, early childhood special, elementary, health, middle, multi-level teacher, multiple handicapped, music, physical, science, secondary. **English:** English lit. **Health services:** General, health care admin. **History:** General. **Liberal arts:** Arts/sciences. **Math:** General. **Parks/recreation:** Exercise sciences, sports admin. **Philosophy/religion:** Christian. **Physical sciences:** Chemistry, forensic chemistry. **Protective services:** Criminal justice. **Psychology:** General. **Social sciences:** General. **Theology:** Sacred music. **Visual/performing arts:** Dramatic, music, music management, music performance, musical theater. **Work/family studies:** Child development.

Technology on campus. 50 workstations in dormitories, library, computer center, student center. Dormitories wired for high-speed internet access and linked to campus network. Commuter students can connect to campus network. Online library, helpline, wireless network available.

Student life. Freshman orientation: Mandatory. Preregistration for classes offered. **Policies:** Religious observance required. **Housing:** Single-sex dorms, apartments, wellness housing available. $260 deposit, deadline 6/1. **Activities:** Bands, campus ministries, choral groups, drama, international student organizations, literary magazine, music ensembles, musical theater, opera, radio station, student government, student newspaper, Association of Black Collegians, A Mighty Passion, Ministerial Alliance, Gamma Delta Sigma, Students and Professors Exploring All Cultures, The MBU Institute for Leadership.

Athletics. NAIA. **Intercollegiate:** Baseball M, basketball, bowling, cheerleading, cross-country, football (tackle) M, golf, lacrosse, soccer, softball W, tennis, track and field, volleyball, wrestling. **Intramural:** Basketball, bowling, football (non-tackle), volleyball. **Team name:** Spartans.

Student services. Adult student services, chaplain/spiritual director, career counseling, student employment services, financial aid counseling, health services, personal counseling, placement for graduates, veterans' counselor. **Physically disabled:** Services for visually, hearing impaired.

Contact. E-mail: admissions@mobap.edu
Phone: (314) 392-2290 Toll-free number: (877) 434-1115
Fax: (314) 392-2292
Cynthia Sutton, Director of Admissions, Missouri Baptist University, One College Park Drive, St. Louis, MO 63141-8660

Missouri Southern State University
Joplin, Missouri
www.mssu.edu
CB code: 6322

- Public 4-year university and liberal arts college
- Commuter campus in small city
- 5,202 degree-seeking undergraduates: 21% part-time, 55% women, 6% African American, 2% Asian American, 5% Hispanic/Latino, 3% Native American, 1% Multi-racial, non-Hispanic, 3% international
- 51 degree-seeking graduate students
- 94% of applicants admitted
- SAT or ACT (ACT writing optional) required
- 36% graduate within 6 years

General. Founded in 1937. Regionally accredited. Extension courses offered in Crowder College (Neosho), Pineville, Jane, Nevada, Webb City School District R-7, Rolla, Sikeston (dental hygiene only). **Degrees:** 833 bachelor's, 183 associate awarded; master's offered. **ROTC:** Army. **Location:** 138 miles from Kansas City, 126 miles from Tulsa, Oklahoma. **Calendar:** Semester, extensive summer session. **Full-time faculty:** 202 total; 57% have terminal degrees, 8% minority, 50% women. **Part-time faculty:** 148 total; 19% have terminal degrees, 5% minority, 53% women. **Class size:** 49% < 20, 47% 20-39, 4% 40-49. **Special facilities:** Biology pond, crime lab, child development center, small business development center, indoor firearms range, performing arts center, greenhouse, law library, cyber coffee shop.

Freshman class profile. 2,333 applied, 2,196 admitted, 925 enrolled.

Mid 50% test scores		Rank in top tenth:	14%
ACT composite:	19-25	Return as sophomores:	63%
GPA 3.75 or higher:	29%	Out-of-state:	1%
GPA 3.50-3.74:	16%	Live on campus:	42%
GPA 3.0-3.49:	27%	International:	1%
GPA 2.0-2.99:	28%	Fraternities:	1%
Rank in top quarter:	39%	Sororities:	2%

Basis for selection. Minimum 18 ACT or rank in upper 50% of class. ACT recommended. **Home schooled:** Transcript of courses and grades required. Transcript with GPA; final transcript with date of graduation needed prior to enrollment; ACT composite score of 21 or GPA of 2.25. Must meet high school core requirements. **Learning Disabled:** Submission of documentation is not the same as the request for services. Request for services and/or accommodations must be initiated by the student after admission.

High school preparation. College-preparatory program recommended. 18 units required. Required units include English 4, mathematics 4, social studies 3, science 3 (laboratory 1), visual/performing arts 1 and academic electives 3.

2015-2016 Annual costs. Tuition/fees: $5,876; $11,186 out-of-state. Room/board: $6,622. Books/supplies: $804. Personal expenses: $2,157. **Additional information:** Transportation and miscellaneous expenses $3303.

2014-2015 Financial aid. Need-based: 683 full-time freshmen applied for aid; 402 deemed to have need; 400 received aid. Average need met was 69%. Average scholarship/grant was $4,822; average loan $4,735. 56% of total undergraduate aid awarded as scholarships/grants, 44% as loans/jobs. **Non-need-based:** Awarded to 1,195 full-time undergraduates, including 430 freshmen. Scholarships awarded for academics, alumni affiliation, art, athletics, job skills, leadership, minority status, music/drama, religious affiliation, state residency.

Application procedures. Admission: Priority date 8/1; no deadline. $25 fee, may be waived for applicants with need. Admission notification by 9/1. Admission notification on a rolling basis. **Financial aid:** No deadline. FAFSA required. Applicants notified on a rolling basis starting 3/15; must reply by 5/1.

Academics. Special study options: Accelerated study, combined bachelor's/graduate degree, cooperative education, distance learning, double major, dual enrollment of high school students, ESL, exchange student, honors, independent study, internships, liberal arts/career combination, study abroad, teacher certification program, weekend college. **Credit/placement by examination:** AP, CLEP, IB, SAT, ACT, institutional tests. After a student has taken a department examination, the professor will transmit the grade to the Vice President for Academic Affairs office. If performance is equated as a 'C' grade or above, the Registrar will record the credit. The credit granted will be based on applicability and will carry the grade of "CR". **Support services:** Learning center, reduced course load, remedial instruction, study skills assistance, tutoring, writing center.

Honors college/program. Entrance by invitation. Approximately 35-40 freshmen students admitted each year. Application closing date March 1. Require 28 ACT, 3.7 GPA. or be in the top 10% of High School class.

Majors. Biology: General, biochemistry. **Business:** General, logistics, managerial economics. **Communications:** Communications/speech/rhetoric. **Computer sciences:** General. **Education:** General, elementary, secondary. **English:** English lit. **Foreign languages:** French, Spanish. **Health services:** Clinical lab science, nursing (RN). **History:** General. **Human services:** Social work. **Liberal arts:** Arts/sciences. **Math:** General. **Physical sciences:** Chemistry, physics. **Protective services:** Juvenile corrections, law enforcement admin. **Psychology:** General. **Social sciences:** International relations, political science, sociology. **Visual/performing arts:** Art, dramatic, graphic design, music management, music performance, studio arts.

Most popular majors. Biology 6%, business/marketing 26%, education 13%, health sciences 11%, liberal arts 8%, security/protective services 11%, visual/performing arts 6%.

Technology on campus. 522 workstations in dormitories, library, computer center, student center. Dormitories wired for high-speed internet access and linked to campus network. Commuter students can connect to campus network. Online library, helpline, repair service, student web hosting, wireless network available.

Student life. Freshman orientation: Available, $50 fee. Preregistration for classes offered. Several sessions held throughout the year for freshmen. **Policies:** Freshmen must live in residence halls if space is available, unless married, residing with relatives, or excused by the Coordinator of Student Housing. **Housing:** Coed dorms, single-sex dorms, apartments available. $150 fully refundable deposit, deadline 5/29. **Activities:** Bands, campus ministries, choral groups, dance, drama, film society, international student organizations, literary magazine, music ensembles, Model UN, musical theater, opera, radio station, student government, student newspaper, symphony orchestra, TV station, over 90 clubs and organizations available.

Athletics. NCAA. **Intercollegiate:** Baseball M, basketball, cross-country, football (tackle) M, golf M, soccer W, softball W, track and field, volleyball W. **Intramural:** Basketball, bowling, football (non-tackle), sand volleyball, soccer, softball, tennis. **Team name:** Lions, Lady Lions.

Student services. Adult student services, alcohol/substance abuse counseling, career counseling, services for economically disadvantaged, student

employment services, financial aid counseling, health services, on-campus daycare, personal counseling, placement for graduates, veterans' counselor. **Physically disabled:** Services for visually, speech, hearing impaired.

Contact. E-mail: admissions@mssu.edu
Phone: (417) 625-9378 Toll-free number: (866) 818-6778
Fax: (417) 659-4429
Derek Skaggs, Director of Enrollment Services, Missouri Southern State University, 3950 East Newman Road, Joplin, MO 64801-1595

Missouri State University
Springfield, Missouri
www.missouristate.edu

CB code: 6665

- Public 4-year university
- Residential campus in small city
- 16,617 degree-seeking undergraduates: 13% part-time, 58% women, 5% African American, 1% Asian American, 3% Hispanic/Latino, 3% Multiracial, non-Hispanic, 5% international
- 2,930 degree-seeking graduate students
- 86% of applicants admitted
- SAT or ACT (ACT writing optional) required
- 52% graduate within 6 years

General. Founded in 1906. Regionally accredited. **Degrees:** 3,237 bachelor's awarded; master's, professional offered. **ROTC:** Army. **Location:** 180 miles from Kansas City. **Calendar:** Semester, extensive summer session. **Full-time faculty:** 734 total; 77% have terminal degrees, 12% minority, 47% women. **Part-time faculty:** 408 total; 22% have terminal degrees, 4% minority, 54% women. **Class size:** 27% < 20, 48% 20-39, 12% 40-49, 9% 50-99, 3% >100. **Special facilities:** Observatory, 125-acre agriculture research and demonstration center, summer tent theater, archaeological research center, social research center, agriculture research center.

Freshman class profile. 8,672 applied, 7,445 admitted, 3,244 enrolled.

Mid 50% test scores			
SAT critical reading:	480-610	Rank in top quarter:	52%
SAT math:	470-610	Rank in top tenth:	22%
ACT composite:	21-26	Return as sophomores:	78%
GPA 3.75 or higher:	44%	Out-of-state:	13%
GPA 3.50-3.74:	19%	Live on campus:	83%
GPA 3.0-3.49:	26%	International:	1%
GPA 2.0-2.99:	10%	Fraternities:	34%
		Sororities:	30%

Basis for selection. Applicant must have 108 or higher on selection index (sum of high school class rank percentile and test score percentile).

High school preparation. College-preparatory program recommended. 24 units required. Required units include English 4, mathematics 3, social studies 2, history 1, science 3 (laboratory 1), visual/performing arts 1 and academic electives 3.

2015-2016 Annual costs. Tuition/fees: $7,060; $13,930 out-of-state. Room/board: $7,868. Books/supplies: $1,000. Personal expenses: $3,974.

2015-2016 Financial aid. **Need-based:** 2,817 full-time freshmen applied for aid; 2,011 deemed to have need; 1,984 received aid. Average need met was 64%. Average scholarship/grant was $6,329; average loan $3,357. 46% of total undergraduate aid awarded as scholarships/grants, 54% as loans/jobs. **Non-need-based:** Awarded to 2,258 full-time undergraduates, including 765 freshmen. Scholarships awarded for academics, alumni affiliation, art, athletics, job skills, leadership, minority status, music/drama, ROTC, state residency. **Additional information:** Extensive scholarship program offered to freshmen and transfer students. Out-of-state fee stipends available. Student employment service available to assist students in securing employment on campus and in community.

Application procedures. Admission: Priority date 3/1; deadline 7/20 (postmark date). $35 fee, may be waived for applicants with need. Admission notification on a rolling basis beginning on or about 6/1. **Financial aid:** Priority date 3/31; no closing date. FAFSA required. Applicants notified on a rolling basis starting 3/31; must reply within 4 week(s) of notification.

Academics. Special study options: Accelerated study, combined bachelor's/graduate degree, cooperative education, distance learning, double major, dual enrollment of high school students, ESL, exchange student, honors, independent study, internships, liberal arts/career combination, student-designed major, study abroad, teacher certification program. **Credit/placement by examination:** AP, CLEP, IB, SAT, ACT, institutional tests. **Support services:** Learning center, pre-admission summer program, study skills assistance, tutoring, writing center.

Honors college/program. Minimum 27 ACT or 1220 (exclusive of Writing) SAT, rank in top 10th percentile of high school class or graduated high school with 3.9 GPA. Approximately 250 to 300 freshmen enroll each year. Program includes freshman honors seminar, honors general education courses, departmental honors courses, senior project, senior honors seminar.

Majors. Architecture: Urban/community planning. **Biology:** General, cellular/molecular. **Business:** General, accounting, business admin, construction management, entrepreneurial studies, finance, hospitality admin, insurance, logistics, management information systems, marketing. **Communications:** Communications/speech/rhetoric, journalism, media studies, organizational, political, public relations, radio/TV. **Computer sciences:** Computer science. **Conservation:** Wildlife/wilderness. **Education:** Agricultural, art, biology, business, chemistry, early childhood, elementary, English, family/consumer sciences, French, German, history, Latin, mathematics, middle, music, physical, physics, science, Spanish, special ed, technology/industrial arts. **English:** English lit, technical writing. **Foreign languages:** French, German, Latin, Spanish. **Health services:** Athletic training, audiology/speech pathology, clinical lab science, dietetics, nursing (RN), predental, premedicine, prepharmacy, preveterinary, radiologic technology/medical imaging, respiratory therapy technology. **History:** General. **Human services:** General, social work. **Liberal arts:** Humanities. **Math:** General. **Parks/recreation:** General, exercise sciences. **Philosophy/religion:** Philosophy, religion. **Physical sciences:** Chemistry, geology, physics. **Psychology:** General. **Social sciences:** Anthropology, criminology, economics, geography, political science, sociology. **Visual/performing arts:** General, art, art history/conservation, dance, design, dramatic, multimedia, music, music performance. **Work/family studies:** Clothing/textiles, facilities/event planning, family studies, housing.

Most popular majors. Business/marketing 30%, education 13%, health sciences 6%, psychology 6%, social sciences 7%.

Technology on campus. 2,000 workstations in dormitories, library, computer center, student center. Dormitories wired for high-speed internet access and linked to campus network. Commuter students can connect to campus network. Online library, helpline, student web hosting, wireless network available.

Student life. Freshman orientation: Mandatory, $40 fee. Preregistration for classes offered. Two-day program held during summer. **Housing:** Guaranteed on-campus for freshmen. Coed dorms, special housing for disabled, apartments, fraternity/sorority housing, themed housing available. $100 fully refundable deposit, deadline 5/1. **Activities:** Bands, campus ministries, choral groups, dance, drama, film society, international student organizations, literary magazine, music ensembles, Model UN, musical theater, opera, radio station, student government, student newspaper, symphony orchestra, TV station, nearly 300 student organizations available.

Athletics. NCAA. **Intercollegiate:** Baseball M, basketball, cross-country, field hockey W, football (tackle) M, golf, soccer, softball W, swimming, track and field, volleyball W. **Intramural:** Basketball, bowling, football (non-tackle), golf, racquetball, soccer, softball, table tennis, tennis, track and field, volleyball, weight lifting, wrestling. **Team name:** Bears.

Student services. Adult student services, alcohol/substance abuse counseling, chaplain/spiritual director, career counseling, services for economically disadvantaged, student employment services, financial aid counseling, health services, legal services, minority student services, on-campus daycare, personal counseling, placement for graduates, veterans' counselor. **Physically disabled:** Services for visually, speech, hearing impaired.

Contact. E-mail: info@missouristate.edu
Phone: (417) 836-5517 Toll-free number: (800) 492-7900
Fax: (417) 836-5137
Andrew Wright, Director of Admissions, Missouri State University, 901 South National Avenue, Springfield, MO 65897.

Missouri Tech
St. Charles, Missouri
www.motech.edu

CB code: 2383

- For-profit 4-year engineering and technical college
- Commuter campus in very large city
- 108 undergraduates
- Interview required

General. Founded in 1932. Accredited by ACCSC. **Degrees:** 10 bachelor's, 11 associate awarded. **Location:** 20 miles from downtown. **Calendar:** Semester, extensive summer session. **Full-time faculty:** 6 total; 83% have terminal degrees. **Part-time faculty:** 9 total.

Basis for selection. Test scores and interview most important.

High school preparation. Math and science courses recommended.

2015-2016 Annual costs. Books/supplies: $800. **Additional information:** Certificate program: $11,337, books and supplies $825. Diploma programs: $28,092-$32,350, books and supplies $2,075-$2,400. Associate programs: $42,882-$47,140, books and supplies $3,175-$3,500. Bachelor's programs: $82,995-$89,545, books and supplies $6,150-$6,650.

Financial aid. All financial aid based on need.

Application procedures. Admission: No deadline. $125 fee. Admission notification on a rolling basis. **Financial aid:** No deadline. FAFSA, institutional form required. Applicants notified on a rolling basis.

Academics. Classes held 4 days per week; academic year is three 17 week semesters of 2 segments each. **Special study options:** Accelerated study, double major, independent study, internships. **Credit/placement by examination:** AP, CLEP, IB, institutional tests. **Support services:** Reduced course load, remedial instruction, study skills assistance, tutoring.

Majors. Computer sciences: Computer graphics, computer science, information systems, LAN/WAN management, programming, systems analysis. **Engineering:** Computer, electrical, software. **Health services:** Substance abuse counseling.

Technology on campus. 120 workstations in library, computer center, student center. Commuter students can connect to campus network. Helpline, repair service available.

Student life. Freshman orientation: Mandatory. Preregistration for classes offered. Held for 2 hours on Saturday before the term starts. **Housing:** $175 deposit. Apartment housing available. **Activities:** Student government, student newspaper.

Student services. Adult student services, alcohol/substance abuse counseling, career counseling, student employment services, financial aid counseling, placement for graduates. **Physically disabled:** Services for visually, hearing impaired.

Contact. Toll-free number: (800) 960-8324
Director of Admissions, Missouri Tech, 1690 Country Club Plaza Drive, St. Charles, MO 63303

Missouri University of Science and Technology
Rolla, Missouri   **CB member**
www.mst.edu   **CB code: 6876**

- Public 4-year university
- Residential campus in large town
- 6,749 degree-seeking undergraduates: 10% part-time, 23% women, 4% African American, 3% Asian American, 3% Hispanic/Latino, 3% Multiracial, non-Hispanic, 6% international
- 1,805 degree-seeking graduate students
- 88% of applicants admitted
- SAT or ACT (ACT writing optional) required
- 65% graduate within 6 years

General. Founded in 1870. Regionally accredited. **Degrees:** 1,307 bachelor's awarded; master's, doctoral offered. **ROTC:** Army, Air Force. **Location:** 100 miles from St. Louis, 100 miles from Springfield. **Calendar:** Semester, extensive summer session. **Full-time faculty:** 367 total; 91% have terminal degrees, 31% minority, 26% women. **Part-time faculty:** 119 total; 44% have terminal degrees, 21% minority, 34% women. **Class size:** 27% < 20, 35% 20-39, 16% 40-49, 16% 50-99, 6% >100. **Special facilities:** Computerized manufacturing system, nuclear reactor, observatory, experimental mine, rocks, minerals, and gemstones museum, centers for environmental research, virtual reality laboratory; student design team center, wind tunnel, hot glass shop.

Freshman class profile. 3,592 applied, 3,164 admitted, 1,489 enrolled.

Mid 50% test scores			
SAT critical reading:	520-660	GPA 3.0-3.49:	13%
SAT math:	560-640	GPA 2.0-2.99:	5%
SAT writing:	490-640	Rank in top quarter:	74%
ACT composite:	25-31	Rank in top tenth:	44%
GPA 3.75 or higher:	66%	Out-of-state:	19%
GPA 3.50-3.74:	16%	International:	2%

Basis for selection. Admission based on secondary school record, class rank, and standardized test scores. Recommendations considered. ACT or SAT score percentage, plus high school class rank percentile should equal 120 (minimum). Exceptions may be made on individual basis. ACT recommended. Campus visit and personal statement encouraged. **Home schooled:**

Transcript of courses and grades required. **Learning Disabled:** Should submit voluntary declaration of disability to receive accommodation.

High school preparation. College-preparatory program required. 17 units required. Required units include English 4, mathematics 4, social studies 3, science 3 (laboratory 1), foreign language 2 and visual/performing arts 1. Foreign language units must be in same language.

2015-2016 Annual costs. Tuition/fees: $9,784; $26,308 out-of-state. Room/board: $9,464. Books/supplies: $878. Personal expenses: $2,502.

2014-2015 Financial aid. Need-based: 715 full-time freshmen applied for aid; 677 deemed to have need; 677 received aid. Average need met was 33%. Average scholarship/grant was $9,955; average loan $6,606. 28% of total undergraduate aid awarded as scholarships/grants, 72% as loans/jobs. **Non-need-based:** Awarded to 2,073 full-time undergraduates, including 556 freshmen. Scholarships awarded for academics, alumni affiliation, athletics, job skills, leadership, minority status, music/drama, religious affiliation, ROTC, state residency.

Application procedures. Admission: Priority date 12/1; deadline 7/1 (postmark date). $50 fee, may be waived for applicants with need. Admission notification on a rolling basis beginning on or about 10/1. Must reply by May 1 or within 3 week(s) if notified thereafter. **Financial aid:** Priority date 3/1; no closing date. FAFSA required. Applicants notified on a rolling basis starting 4/1; must reply within 3 week(s) of notification.

Academics. Special study options: Accelerated study, combined bachelor's/graduate degree, cooperative education, distance learning, double major, dual enrollment of high school students, ESL, honors, independent study, internships, study abroad, teacher certification program. **Credit/placement by examination:** AP, CLEP, IB, institutional tests. **Support services:** Learning center, pre-admission summer program, reduced course load, study skills assistance, tutoring, writing center.

Majors. Biology: General, biochemistry, biophysics. **Business:** General, business admin, management information systems. **Computer sciences:** General, computer science, information systems, information technology. **Engineering:** Aerospace, architectural, ceramic, chemical, civil, computer, electrical, engineering mechanics, environmental, geological, mechanical, metallurgical, mining, nuclear, petroleum. **English:** English lit, technical writing. **Health services:** Predental, premedicine. **History:** General. **Math:** Applied. **Philosophy/religion:** Philosophy. **Physical sciences:** Chemistry, geochemistry, geology, geophysics, physics. **Psychology:** General. **Social sciences:** Economics.

Most popular majors. Computer/information sciences 9%, engineering/engineering technologies 71%.

Technology on campus. 812 workstations in dormitories, library, computer center. Dormitories wired for high-speed internet access and linked to campus network. Commuter students can connect to campus network. Online course registration, online library, helpline, repair service, student web hosting, wireless network available.

Student life. Freshman orientation: Mandatory, $160 fee. Preregistration for classes offered. **Housing:** Guaranteed on-campus for freshmen. Coed dorms, special housing for disabled, apartments, cooperative housing, fraternity/sorority housing, themed housing, wellness housing available. $200 partly refundable deposit, deadline 5/31. Residential college available. **Activities:** Bands, campus ministries, choral groups, dance, drama, international student organizations, literary magazine, music ensembles, musical theater, radio station, student government, student newspaper, symphony orchestra, over 200 student groups available.

Athletics. NCAA. **Intercollegiate:** Baseball M, basketball, cheerleading, cross-country, football (tackle) M, soccer, softball W, swimming M, track and field, volleyball W. **Intramural:** Badminton, basketball, bowling, cross-country, football (non-tackle), golf, racquetball, soccer, softball, swimming, table tennis, tennis, track and field, ultimate frisbee, volleyball, weight lifting. **Team name:** Miners.

Student services. Adult student services, alcohol/substance abuse counseling, career counseling, student employment services, financial aid counseling, health services, minority student services, personal counseling, placement for graduates, women's services. **Physically disabled:** Services for visually, speech, hearing impaired.

Contact. E-mail: admissions@mst.edu
Phone: (573) 341-4165 Toll-free number: (800) 522-0938
Fax: (573) 341-4082
Lynn Stichnote, Director of Admissions, Missouri University of Science and Technology, 106 Parker Hall, Rolla, MO 65409-1060

Missouri Valley College
Marshall, Missouri
www.moval.edu   CB code: 6413

- Private 4-year liberal arts college affiliated with the Presbyterian Church (USA)
- Residential campus in large town
- 1,380 degree-seeking undergraduates: 2% part-time, 40% women
- 16 degree-seeking graduate students
- 46% of applicants admitted
- SAT or ACT (ACT writing optional) required

General. Founded in 1889. Regionally accredited. **Degrees:** 170 bachelor's, 7 associate awarded; master's offered. **ROTC:** Army. **Location:** 75 miles from Kansas City, 65 miles from Columbia. **Calendar:** Semester, limited summer session. **Full-time faculty:** 85 total. **Part-time faculty:** 87 total. **Class size:** 45% < 20, 54% 20-39, less than 1% 40-49, less than 1% 50-99. **Special facilities:** The Malcolm Center for Student Life.

Freshman class profile. 2,879 applied, 1,312 admitted, 395 enrolled.

GPA 3.75 or higher:	6%	Out-of-state:	25%
GPA 3.50-3.74:	9%	Live on campus:	79%
GPA 3.0-3.49:	28%	International:	9%
GPA 2.0-2.99:	53%	Fraternities:	25%
Rank in top quarter:	19%	Sororities:	25%
Rank in top tenth:	6%		

Basis for selection. Interview, recommendations, high school record, test scores important; extracurricular activities, personal attributes also important; class rank considered. Essay recommended for academically weak students. Audition recommended for drama majors; portfolio recommended for art majors. **Home schooled:** Transcript of courses and grades required. GED in addition to acceptable ACT/SAT score is sufficient.

High school preparation. College-preparatory program recommended. Recommended units include English 4, mathematics 3, social studies 1, history 3, science 3 and foreign language 1.

2015-2016 Annual costs. Tuition/fees: $19,750. Room/board: $8,400. Books/supplies: $1,530. Personal expenses: $1,800. **Additional information:** Fees include all required books.

Financial aid. Non-need-based: Scholarships awarded for academics, state residency.

Application procedures. Admission: Priority date 3/1; no deadline. No application fee. Admission notification on a rolling basis. Must reply by May 1 or within 4 week(s) if notified thereafter. **Financial aid:** Priority date 3/15; no closing date. FAFSA required. Applicants notified on a rolling basis starting 2/1; must reply within 6 week(s) of notification.

Academics. Special study options: Accelerated study, combined bachelor's/graduate degree, distance learning, double major, dual enrollment of high school students, ESL, external degree, honors, independent study, internships, liberal arts/career combination, student-designed major, study abroad, teacher certification program. **Credit/placement by examination:** AP, CLEP, SAT, ACT, institutional tests. 30 credit hours maximum toward bachelor's degree. **Support services:** Learning center, reduced course load, remedial instruction, study skills assistance, tutoring, writing center.

Majors. Biology: General. **Business:** Accounting, business admin. **Communications:** Media studies. **Computer sciences:** General. **Education:** Elementary, multiple handicapped, physical, secondary, social studies, special ed. **English:** English lit. **Health services:** Athletic training, nursing (RN), substance abuse counseling. **History:** General. **Human services:** General. **Liberal arts:** Arts/sciences. **Math:** General. **Parks/recreation:** Exercise sciences, facilities management. **Philosophy/religion:** Philosophy, religion. **Protective services:** Law enforcement admin. **Psychology:** General. **Social sciences:** Economics, political science, sociology. **Visual/performing arts:** Art, dance, dramatic, music.

Most popular majors. Business/marketing 15%, education 15%, health sciences 21%, psychology 6%, security/protective services 12%.

Technology on campus. 250 workstations in dormitories, library, computer center, student center. Dormitories wired for high-speed internet access and linked to campus network. Commuter students can connect to campus network. Online library, helpline, repair service, wireless network available.

Student life. Freshman orientation: Mandatory. Preregistration for classes offered. Early Registration Days held in summer. **Policies:** Dry campus, smoke free campus. **Housing:** Guaranteed on-campus for all undergraduates. Single-sex dorms, apartments, fraternity/sorority housing available. $250 nonrefundable deposit, deadline 8/1. **Activities:** Bands, campus ministries,

choral groups, dance, drama, film society, international student organizations, literary magazine, music ensembles, musical theater, radio station, student government, student newspaper, symphony orchestra, TV station, American Humanics, Minority Student Union, Fellowship of Christian Athletes, Student Council for Exceptional Children.

Athletics. NAIA. **Intercollegiate:** Baseball M, basketball, cheerleading, cross-country, football (tackle) M, golf, lacrosse, rodeo, soccer, softball W, tennis, track and field, volleyball, wrestling. **Intramural:** Badminton, baseball M, basketball, bowling, cross-country, football (non-tackle), soccer, softball, table tennis, track and field, ultimate frisbee, volleyball, weight lifting. **Team name:** Vikings.

Student services. Alcohol/substance abuse counseling, chaplain/spiritual director, career counseling, student employment services, financial aid counseling, health services, personal counseling, placement for graduates, veterans' counselor.

Contact. E-mail: admissions@moval.edu
Phone: (660) 831-4114 Fax: (660) 831-4233
Tennille Langdon, Director of Admissions, Missouri Valley College, 500 East College Street, Marshall, MO 65340

Missouri Western State University
St Joseph, Missouri
www.missouriwestern.edu   CB code: 6625

- Public 4-year university and liberal arts college
- Commuter campus in small city
- 4,420 degree-seeking undergraduates: 18% part-time, 60% women, 10% African American, 1% Asian American, 1% Hispanic/Latino, 3% Multiracial, non-Hispanic, 1% international
- 213 degree-seeking graduate students
- 35% graduate within 6 years

General. Founded in 1915. Regionally accredited. **Degrees:** 787 bachelor's, 40 associate awarded; master's offered. **ROTC:** Army. **Location:** 48 miles from Kansas City. **Calendar:** Semester, extensive summer session. **Full-time faculty:** 200 total; 84% have terminal degrees, 9% minority, 42% women. **Part-time faculty:** 207 total; 11% have terminal degrees, 4% minority, 60% women. **Class size:** 40% < 20, 53% 20-39, 3% 40-49, 4% 50-99, less than 1% >100. **Special facilities:** Biology nature study area, planetarium.

Freshman class profile. 3,341 applied, 2,528 admitted, 868 enrolled.

Mid 50% test scores		GPA 2.0-2.99:	28%
ACT composite:	18-24	Rank in top quarter:	32%
GPA 3.75 or higher:	27%	Rank in top tenth:	11%
GPA 3.50-3.74:	17%	Return as sophomores:	64%
GPA 3.0-3.49:	25%	International:	1%

Basis for selection. Open admission, but selective for some programs. Passing scores in all 5 sub-tests of the Missouri General Education Assessment (MOGEA) and ACT composite score. Nursing requires a minimum 2.7 overall GPA and must have completed all general studies and nursing support courses. The Craig School of Business requires either a 23 ACT composite or, with a lower ACT composite, completion of 8 select courses with a 2.0 or higher GPA and 2.5 GPA in 36 University hours. Interview required for education, nursing, social work programs. Portfolio recommended for art majors, audition recommended for music majors.

High school preparation. College-preparatory program recommended. 17 units required. Required and recommended units include English 4, mathematics 3, social studies 3, science 3 (laboratory 1), foreign language 2, visual/performing arts 1 and academic electives 2.

2015-2016 Annual costs. Tuition/fees: $6,652; $12,810 out-of-state. Room/board: $8,565. Books/supplies: $800. Personal expenses: $2,665.

Financial aid. Non-need-based: Scholarships awarded for academics, alumni affiliation, art, athletics, job skills, leadership, minority status, music/drama, state residency.

Application procedures. Admission: No deadline. No application fee. Admission notification on a rolling basis. **Financial aid:** Priority date 3/1; no closing date. FAFSA, institutional form required. Applicants notified on a rolling basis starting 4/5; must reply within 3 week(s) of notification.

Academics. Special study options: Accelerated study, cooperative education, distance learning, double major, dual enrollment of high school students, ESL, honors, independent study, internships, liberal arts/career combination, student-designed major, study abroad, teacher certification program. **Credit/placement by examination:** AP, CLEP, IB, institutional tests. **Support**

services: Learning center, pre-admission summer program, reduced course load, remedial instruction, study skills assistance, tutoring, writing center.

Majors. Biology: General, biochemistry, biotechnology. **Business:** Accounting, business admin, finance, marketing. **Communications:** Communications/speech/rhetoric. **Communications technology:** Animation/special effects. **Computer sciences:** General, information technology. **Conservation:** Wildlife/wilderness. **Education:** Art, early childhood, elementary, English, French, music, Spanish. **English:** English lit. **Foreign languages:** General. **Health services:** Clinical lab science, health information management, nursing (RN). **History:** General. **Human services:** Social work. **Math:** General. **Parks/recreation:** Facilities management, health/fitness. **Philosophy/religion:** Philosophy. **Physical sciences:** Chemistry. **Protective services:** Criminal justice. **Psychology:** General. **Social sciences:** Economics, political science, sociology. **Visual/performing arts:** Dramatic, graphic design, music, studio arts.

Most popular majors. Biology 6%, business/marketing 17%, education 12%, health sciences 15%, parks/recreation 7%, security/protective services 9%.

Technology on campus. Dormitories wired for high-speed internet access and linked to campus network. Commuter students can connect to campus network. Online course registration, online library, helpline, student web hosting, wireless network available.

Student life. Freshman orientation: Available, $60 fee. Preregistration for classes offered. **Housing:** Coed dorms, special housing for disabled, apartments, fraternity/sorority housing, wellness housing available. $100 fully refundable deposit. **Activities:** Bands, choral groups, dance, drama, international student organizations, literary magazine, music ensembles, musical theater, opera, student government, student newspaper, symphony orchestra, TV station.

Athletics. NCAA. **Intercollegiate:** Baseball M, basketball, football (tackle) M, golf, soccer W, softball W, tennis W, volleyball W, wrestling M. **Intramural:** Archery, badminton, baseball M, basketball, bowling, golf, handball, racquetball, rugby M, soccer M, softball, table tennis, tennis, volleyball. **Team name:** Griffons.

Student services. Adult student services, alcohol/substance abuse counseling, career counseling, student employment services, financial aid counseling, health services, minority student services, on-campus daycare, personal counseling, placement for graduates, veterans' counselor.

Contact. E-mail: admissions@missouriwestern.edu
Phone: (816) 271-4266 Toll-free number: (800) 662-7041
Fax: (816) 271-5833
Jamie Sweiger, Assistant Director Admissions/Operations, Missouri Western State University, 4525 Downs Drive, Saint Joseph, MO 64507

National American University: Kansas City
Independence, Missouri
www.national.edu
CB code: 5357

- For-profit 4-year university
- Commuter campus in large city
- 646 undergraduates
- Interview required

General. Founded in 1941. Regionally accredited. **Degrees:** 19 bachelor's, 48 associate awarded; master's offered. **Location:** 8 miles from downtown. **Calendar:** Quarter, extensive summer session. **Full-time faculty:** 2 total. **Part-time faculty:** 29 total.

Basis for selection. Open admission. Open enrollment policy, but students have to test out of entry-level English/math in order to be enrolled in algebra and English comp I.

2015-2016 Annual costs. Tuition/fees: $15,885. Books/supplies: $1,350. **Additional information:** Additional fees may apply.

Financial aid. All financial aid based on need.

Application procedures. Admission: No deadline. No application fee. Admission notification on a rolling basis. **Financial aid:** No deadline. FAFSA, institutional form required. Applicants notified on a rolling basis starting 6/4.

Academics. Special study options: Accelerated study, distance learning, double major, independent study, internships, liberal arts/career combination. **Credit/placement by examination:** AP, CLEP, institutional tests. **Support services:** Learning center, study skills assistance, tutoring.

Majors. Business: Accounting, business admin, management information systems, marketing. **Computer sciences:** Information systems. **Health services:** Nursing (RN).

Technology on campus. 50 workstations in computer center. Online library available.

Student life. Freshman orientation: Mandatory. Preregistration for classes offered. **Activities:** Student government, student newspaper.

Athletics. Team name: Mavericks.

Student services. Adult student services, career counseling, student employment services, financial aid counseling, placement for graduates.

Contact. Phone: (866) 628-1288 Fax: (816) 412-7705
Sharon Anderson, Director of Admissions, National American University; Kansas City, 3620 Arrowhead Avenue, Independence, MO 64057

National American University: Lee's Summit
Lee's Summit, Missouri
www.national.edu

- For-profit 3-year branch campus college
- Commuter campus in small city
- 360 undergraduates

General. Regionally accredited. **Degrees:** 24 bachelor's, 21 associate awarded. **Calendar:** Quarter. **Part-time faculty:** 3 total.

Basis for selection. Open admission.

2015-2016 Annual costs. Tuition/fees: $15,885. Books/supplies: $1,350. **Additional information:** Additional fees may apply.

Academics. Credit/placement by examination: AP, CLEP.

Majors. BACHELOR'S. Business: Accounting, business admin, finance, human resources, marketing, organizational leadership. **Computer sciences:** Information technology, networking, security, web page design. **Health services:** Health care admin, nursing (RN). **Protective services:** Criminal justice. **ASSOCIATE. Business:** Accounting technology, business admin. **Computer sciences:** Support specialist. **Health services:** Medical assistant, pharmacy assistant. **Protective services:** Criminal justice.

Contact. E-mail: lsadmissions@national.edu
Phone: (816) 600-3900
Joey Landara, Director of Admissions, National American University; Lee's Summit, 401 NW Murray Road, Lee's Summit, MO 64081

Northwest Missouri State University
Maryville, Missouri
www.nwmissouri.edu
CB code: 6488

- Public 4-year university
- Residential campus in large town
- 5,288 degree-seeking undergraduates: 7% part-time, 57% women, 7% African American, 1% Asian American, 4% Hispanic/Latino, 3% Multiracial, non-Hispanic, 6% international
- 927 degree-seeking graduate students
- 75% of applicants admitted
- SAT or ACT (ACT writing optional) required
- 49% graduate within 6 years

General. Founded in 1905. Regionally accredited. **Degrees:** 992 bachelor's, 47 associate awarded; master's offered. **ROTC:** Army. **Location:** 100 miles from Kansas City. **Calendar:** Trimester, extensive summer session. **Full-time faculty:** 260 total; 72% have terminal degrees, 14% minority, 45% women. **Part-time faculty:** 54 total; 32% minority, 65% women. **Class size:** 44% < 20, 44% 20-39, 4% 40-49, 8% 50-99, less than 1% >100. **Special facilities:** Arboretum, lake-front outdoor education recreation area, laboratory school, dairy operation, swine herd, horticulture complex, experimental farmland, center for innovation and entrepreneurship (incubator), studio/black box experimental theater, alternative energy learning center, observatory, online museum, science museum, agriculture museum, computing museum, museum of broadcasting, cricket pitch.

Freshman class profile. 5,009 applied, 3,754 admitted, 1,499 enrolled.

Mid 50% test scores			
SAT critical reading:	370-470	**Rank in top quarter:**	40%
SAT math:	480-630	**Rank in top tenth:**	16%
ACT composite:	20-25	**Return as sophomores:**	71%
GPA 3.75 or higher:	27%	**Out-of-state:**	33%
GPA 3.50-3.74:	21%	**Live on campus:**	94%
GPA 3.0-3.49:	31%	**Fraternities:**	19%
GPA 2.0-2.99:	21%	**Sororities:**	27%

Basis for selection. School achievement record and test scores most important. Index based on class rank and national test. Audition recommended for dramatic arts and music students; portfolio recommended for art students. **Home schooled:** Transcript of courses and grades, state high school equivalency certificate required.

High school preparation. College-preparatory program recommended. 24 units required. Required and recommended units include English 4, mathematics 3-4, social studies 3, science 3 (laboratory 1), foreign language 2, visual/performing arts 1 and academic electives 3. One fine arts required. Foreign language and additional math and science highly recommended.

2015-2016 Annual costs. Tuition/fees: $8,459; $14,779 out-of-state. Room/board: $9,538. Books/supplies: $400. Personal expenses: $1,575.

2014-2015 Financial aid. Need-based: 1,210 full-time freshmen applied for aid; 903 deemed to have need; 903 received aid. Average need met was 77%. Average scholarship/grant was $7,444; average loan $3,282. 48% of total undergraduate aid awarded as scholarships/grants, 52% as loans/jobs. **Non-need-based:** Awarded to 1,624 full-time undergraduates, including 695 freshmen. Scholarships awarded for academics, alumni affiliation, art, athletics, job skills, leadership, minority status, music/drama, ROTC, state residency.

Application procedures. Admission: No deadline. $25 fee, may be waived for applicants with need, free for online applicants. Admission notification on a rolling basis beginning on or about 7/1. **Financial aid:** Priority date 4/1; no closing date. FAFSA required. Applicants notified on a rolling basis starting 3/15.

Academics. Special study options: Cooperative education, cross-registration, distance learning, double major, dual enrollment of high school students, ESL, exchange student, honors, independent study, internships, liberal arts/career combination, study abroad, teacher certification program, Washington semester. Programs at satellite campuses that allow students to complete an MBA in 18 months. **Credit/placement by examination:** AP, CLEP, IB, SAT, ACT, institutional tests. **Support services:** Learning center, reduced course load, remedial instruction, study skills assistance, tutoring, writing center.

Majors. Biology: General, marine. **Business:** Accounting, administrative services, business admin, finance, international, management information systems, managerial economics, marketing. **Communications:** Advertising, communications/speech/rhetoric, journalism, organizational, public relations, radio/TV. **Computer sciences:** General, web page design. **Conservation:** Wildlife/wilderness. **Education:** Agricultural, art, biology, business, chemistry, curriculum, elementary, English, family/consumer sciences, mathematics, middle, multiple handicapped, music, physical, physics, science, social science, Spanish. **English:** English lit. **Foreign languages:** Spanish. **Health services:** Clinical lab science, dietetics, nursing (RN), premedicine, prenursing, preoccupational therapy, prepharmacy, prephysical therapy, preveterinary. **History:** General. **Human services:** General. **Liberal arts:** Arts/sciences, humanities. **Math:** General, statistics. **Parks/recreation:** Facilities management. **Philosophy/religion:** Philosophy. **Physical sciences:** Chemistry, geology, physics. **Psychology:** General, industrial, psychobiology, social. **Social sciences:** Economics, geography, GIS/cartography, political science, sociology. **Visual/performing arts:** Acting, dramatic, music, studio arts, theater design. **Work/family studies:** Family studies, institutional food production.

Most popular majors. Agriculture 9%, business/marketing 22%, communications/journalism 8%, education 19%, psychology 11%.

Technology on campus. 6,465 workstations in dormitories, library, computer center, student center. Dormitories wired for high-speed internet access and linked to campus network. Commuter students can connect to campus network. Online course registration, online library, helpline, repair service, student web hosting, wireless network available.

Student life. Freshman orientation: Mandatory, $100 fee. Preregistration for classes offered. One-day program in June plus 4-day program held before classes begin in August. **Policies:** Alcohol- and smoke-free campus. **Housing:** Guaranteed on-campus for freshmen. Coed dorms, special housing for disabled, apartments, fraternity/sorority housing, gender-neutral housing available. $150 nonrefundable deposit. Freshman and upper-class housing available. **Activities:** Bands, choral groups, dance, drama, film society, international student organizations, literary magazine, music ensembles, musical

theater, radio station, student government, student newspaper, symphony orchestra, TV station, over 150 organizations available.

Athletics. NCAA. **Intercollegiate:** Baseball M, basketball, cheerleading, cross-country, football (tackle) M, golf W, soccer W, softball W, tennis, track and field, volleyball W. **Intramural:** Badminton, basketball, cross-country, football (non-tackle), golf, racquetball, skiing, softball W, swimming, table tennis, tennis, track and field, volleyball. **Team name:** Bearcats.

Student services. Alcohol/substance abuse counseling, chaplain/spiritual director, career counseling, services for economically disadvantaged, student employment services, financial aid counseling, health services, minority student services, personal counseling, placement for graduates. **Physically disabled:** Services for visually, speech, hearing impaired.

Contact. E-mail: admissions@nwmissouri.edu
Phone: (660) 562-1148 Toll-free number: (800) 633-1175
Fax: (660) 562-1821
Tamera Grow, Associate Director, Admissions, Northwest Missouri State University, 800 University Drive, Maryville, MO 64468-6001

Ozark Christian College
Joplin, Missouri
www.occ.edu   **CB code: 6542**

▸ Private 4-year Bible college affiliated with the nondenominational tradition

▸ Residential campus in small city

▸ 742 degree-seeking undergraduates

▸ SAT or ACT (ACT writing optional), application essay required

General. Founded in 1942. Accredited by ABHE. **Degrees:** 101 bachelor's, 47 associate awarded. **Location:** 70 miles from Springfield, 100 miles from Tulsa, Oklahoma. **Calendar:** Semester, limited summer session. **Full-time faculty:** 27 total; 37% have terminal degrees, 4% minority, 15% women. **Part-time faculty:** 33 total; 21% have terminal degrees, 18% women. **Class size:** 64% < 20, 26% 20-39, 5% 40-49, 6% 50-99.

Basis for selection. Open admission. Audition required for music ministry students. **Home schooled:** Transcript of courses and grades required. Provide notarized transcript of grades signed by student and parents. **Learning Disabled:** Provides reasonable accommodations to qualified students with disabilities.

High school preparation. 15 units recommended. Recommended units include English 3, mathematics 2, history 1, science 2 and academic electives 7.

2015-2016 Annual costs. Tuition/fees: $11,110. Room/board: $4,820. Books/supplies: $800. Personal expenses: $1,558.

Financial aid. Non-need-based: Scholarships awarded for academics, leadership.

Application procedures. Admission: Closing date 8/5 (receipt date). $30 fee, may be waived for applicants with need. Admission notification on a rolling basis. Applicant must submit high school transcript through first half of senior year. **Financial aid:** Priority date 4/1; no closing date. FAFSA required. Applicants notified on a rolling basis starting 4/15; must reply within 3 week(s) of notification.

Academics. Special study options: Cooperative education, distance learning, double major, independent study, internships. 5-year bachelor's degree program in theology. **Credit/placement by examination:** AP, CLEP, ACT, institutional tests. **Support services:** Learning center, study skills assistance, tutoring, writing center.

Majors. Theology: Bible, missionary, religious ed, sacred music, theology.

Technology on campus. 23 workstations in library, student center. Dormitories wired for high-speed internet access and linked to campus network. Commuter students can connect to campus network. Online library, helpline, repair service, wireless network available.

Student life. Freshman orientation: Mandatory. Preregistration for classes offered. **Policies:** Religious observance required. **Housing:** Guaranteed on-campus for all undergraduates. Single-sex dorms, wellness housing available. $90 deposit, deadline 8/5. **Activities:** Choral groups, drama, music ensembles, musical theater, student government.

Athletics. NCCAA. **Intercollegiate:** Basketball, soccer M, volleyball W. **Intramural:** Basketball, racquetball, volleyball. **Team name:** Ambassadors.

Student services. Adult student services, chaplain/spiritual director, career counseling, student employment services, financial aid counseling, health services, personal counseling, placement for graduates, veterans' counselor. **Physically disabled:** Services for hearing impaired.

Contact. E-mail: admissions@occ.edu
Phone: (417) 624-2518 Toll-free number: (800) 299-4622
Fax: (417) 624-0090
Troy Nelson, Director of Admissions, Ozark Christian College, 1111 North Main Street, Joplin, MO 64801

Park University
Parkville, Missouri
www.park.edu

CB member
CB code: 6574

- Private 4-year university
- Commuter campus in small town
- 8,502 degree-seeking undergraduates
- 911 graduate students
- 40% of applicants admitted

General. Founded in 1875. Regionally accredited. MetroPark School for adult education in Kansas City offers bachelor's degree. School for Extended Learning (SEL) offers degree programs in 21 states. **Degrees:** 2,071 bachelor's, 413 associate awarded; master's offered. **ROTC:** Army. **Location:** 12 miles from downtown Kansas City. **Calendar:** Semester, extensive summer session. **Full-time faculty:** 82 total; 66% have terminal degrees, 4% minority, 38% women. **Part-time faculty:** 86 total. **Class size:** 82% < 20, 17% 20-39, less than 1% 40-49. **Special facilities:** 700 acres of woodland.

Freshman class profile. 998 applied, 403 admitted, 114 enrolled.

Mid 50% test scores		GPA 2.0-2.99:	30%
ACT composite:	16-27	Rank in top quarter:	37%
GPA 3.75 or higher:	20%	Rank in top tenth:	14%
GPA 3.50-3.74:	11%	Out-of-state:	27%
GPA 3.0-3.49:	37%	Live on campus:	88%

Basis for selection. Based on 6th semester transcript with 3.0 or higher GPA, or qualifying for Missouri's A-Plus program, or meet two of following three criteria: 2.0 GPA; ACT composite score of 20 or SAT of 940 (exclusive of Writing); top 50% of class. Admission may also be granted with total GED score of 2500, with no area less than 450, and ACT composite score of 20 or SAT of 940 (exclusive of Writing). Students not meeting criteria may be considered on individual basis. Students with 3.0 GPA not required to submit SAT/ACT for admission; however, institutional placement test must be substituted. Entering freshmen with GPA of 2.0 to 3.0 must either be in top half of graduating class or submit satisfactory SAT/ACT scores. Interview recommended for academically weak students; audition recommended for music and theater students; portfolio recommended for art students.

High school preparation. 19 units recommended. Recommended units include English 3, mathematics 2, social studies 3, history 1, science 2 (laboratory 1), foreign language 2 and academic electives 6.

2015-2016 Annual costs. Tuition/fees: $11,470. Room/board: $7,672. Books/supplies: $1,800. Personal expenses: $1,900. **Additional information:** Active-Duty Military and their dependents; $250 per-credit-hour. Veterans and their dependents; $310 per-credit-hour.

2014-2015 Financial aid. Non-need-based: Scholarships awarded for academics, alumni affiliation, art, athletics, music/drama.

Application procedures. Admission: Priority date 4/15; deadline 8/1. $25 fee, may be waived for applicants with need. Admission notification on a rolling basis. **Financial aid:** Priority date 4/1, closing date 8/1. FAFSA, institutional form required. Applicants notified on a rolling basis starting 4/1; must reply by 8/1 or within 4 week(s) of notification.

Academics. Special study options: Accelerated study, cross-registration, distance learning, double major, dual enrollment of high school students, ESL, honors, independent study, internships, student-designed major, study abroad, teacher certification program, Washington semester, weekend college. **Credit/placement by examination:** AP, CLEP, ACT, institutional tests. **Support services:** Learning center, reduced course load, remedial instruction, study skills assistance, tutoring, writing center.

Majors. Biology: General. **Business:** Accounting, accounting/business management, business admin, logistics, management information systems, managerial economics, marketing. **Communications:** Communications/ speech/rhetoric. **Computer sciences:** General, computer science. **Education:** Early childhood, elementary. **English:** English lit. **Foreign languages:** Spanish. **Health services:** Athletic training. **History:** General. **Human services:**

General, social work. **Liberal arts:** Arts/sciences. **Math:** General. **Physical sciences:** Chemistry. **Protective services:** Fire services admin, law enforcement admin. **Psychology:** General. **Social sciences:** Economics, geography, political science, sociology. **Visual/performing arts:** Dramatic, graphic design, interior design, music, studio arts. **Work/family studies:** Child development.

Most popular majors. Biology 14%, communications/journalism 27%, education 48%, English 8%, health sciences 85%, interdisciplinary studies 27%, parks/recreation 11%, public administration/social services 38%, social sciences 33%, trade and industry 6%, visual/performing arts 19%.

Technology on campus. 300 workstations in dormitories, library, computer center, student center. Dormitories linked to campus network. Commuter students can connect to campus network. Online course registration available.

Student life. Freshman orientation: Mandatory. Preregistration for classes offered. **Housing:** Guaranteed on-campus for freshmen. Coed dorms, apartments available. $100 deposit. **Activities:** Choral groups, drama, literary magazine, radio station, student government, student newspaper, symphony orchestra, service organizations, Christian Fellowship, World Student Union, Brothers and Sisters United, accounting society, Latin American student organization, marketing club, honors club, non-traditional student organization.

Athletics. NAIA. **Intercollegiate:** Baseball M, basketball, cross-country, golf W, soccer, softball W, track and field, volleyball. **Intramural:** Basketball, soccer, softball, volleyball. **Team name:** Pirates.

Student services. Career counseling, student employment services, financial aid counseling, health services, on-campus daycare, personal counseling, placement for graduates, veterans' counselor. **Physically disabled:** Services for visually, speech, hearing impaired.

Contact. E-mail: admissions@park.edu
Phone: (816) 584-6215 Toll-free number: (800) 745-7275
Fax: (816) 741-4462
Cathy Colapietro, Executive Director of Admissions and Student Financial Services, Park University, 8700 NW River Park Drive, Parkville, MO 64152

Research College of Nursing
Kansas City, Missouri
www.researchcollege.edu

CB code: 6612

- For-profit 4-year nursing college
- Residential campus in very large city
- 293 degree-seeking undergraduates: 2% part-time, 91% women, 3% African American, 1% Asian American, 3% Hispanic/Latino, 1% Native American, 1% Multi-racial, non-Hispanic
- 152 degree-seeking graduate students
- 87% of applicants admitted
- SAT or ACT (ACT writing optional) required
- 58% graduate within 6 years

General. Founded in 1905. Regionally accredited. Natural science, social science, and liberal arts courses taken at Rockhurst University. Students have access to facilities, organizations, sports and activities on both campuses. Bachelor of Science in Nursing is awarded jointly by Research College of Nursing and Rockhurst University. **Degrees:** 114 bachelor's awarded; master's offered. **ROTC:** Army. **Location:** 5 miles from downtown Kansas City, Missouri. **Calendar:** Semester, limited summer session. **Full-time faculty:** 34 total; 24% have terminal degrees, 3% minority, 97% women. **Part-time faculty:** 3 total; 100% women. **Class size:** 100% 50-99. **Special facilities:** Medical library, 532-bed research medical center.

Freshman class profile. 403 applied, 349 admitted, 57 enrolled.

Out-of-state:	25%	Live on campus:	77%

Basis for selection. Academic record, high school GPA, rank in top half of class, counselor's recommendation, test scores very important. ACT score of 21 required. Interview, high school activities considered. Interview recommended for all; strongly recommended for applicants with ACT scores below 20.

High school preparation. College-preparatory program recommended. 18 units recommended. Recommended units include English 4, mathematics 3, social studies 3, science 4 and foreign language 2. Visual or performing arts also recommended. Mathematics should include algebra II, science should include chemistry.

2015-2016 Annual costs. Tuition/fees: $34,790. Room/board: $9,055. Books/supplies: $800. Personal expenses: $915.

Financial aid. Non-need-based: Scholarships awarded for academics, leadership. **Additional information:** Financial aid handled by Rockhurst University for freshmen and sophomores.

Application procedures. Admission: Priority date 3/1; no deadline. $20 fee, may be waived for applicants with need, free for online applicants. Admission notification on a rolling basis beginning on or about 10/1. Must reply by May 1 or within 4 week(s) if notified thereafter. **Financial aid:** Priority date 3/15; no closing date. FAFSA, institutional form required. Applicants notified on a rolling basis starting 3/15.

Academics. Students admitted into nursing program in freshman year guaranteed place in upper-division nursing courses if academic requirements maintained. **Special study options:** Accelerated study, cross-registration, double major, dual enrollment of high school students, exchange student, honors, independent study, study abroad. **Credit/placement by examination:** AP, CLEP, IB, ACT, institutional tests. 32 credit hours maximum toward bachelor's degree. **Support services:** Learning center, tutoring.

Majors. Health services: Nursing (RN).

Technology on campus. 300 workstations in dormitories, library, computer center. Dormitories wired for high-speed internet access and linked to campus network. Commuter students can connect to campus network. Online course registration, helpline, wireless network available.

Student life. Freshman orientation: Mandatory, $60 fee. Preregistration for classes offered. Held for 4 days prior to the start of the fall semester. **Housing:** Guaranteed on-campus for freshmen. Coed dorms, single-sex dorms, apartments, fraternity/sorority housing available. $200 fully refundable deposit. Freshman nursing students not living at home must live on Rockhurst College campus. All other undergraduates may choose to live on Research College campus or at Rockhurst College. **Activities:** Campus ministries, choral groups, drama, music ensembles, musical theater, radio station, student government, student newspaper, Alpha Phi Omega, Black Student Union, Young Republicans, Young Democrats, Missouri Student Nurses Association, National Student Nurses Association, Rockhurst Organization of Collegiate Women.

Athletics. NCAA. **Intercollegiate:** Baseball M, basketball, golf, soccer, softball W, tennis, volleyball W. **Intramural:** Basketball, lacrosse, racquetball, rugby, table tennis, volleyball.

Student services. Chaplain/spiritual director, career counseling, student employment services, financial aid counseling, health services, on-campus daycare, personal counseling, placement for graduates, veterans' counselor.

Contact. E-mail: leslie.mendenhall@researchcollege.edu
Phone: (816) 995-2812 Toll-free number: (866) 855-0296
Fax: (816) 995-2813
Lane Ramey, Director of Freshmen Admission, Research College of Nursing, 2525 East Meyer Boulevard, Kansas City, MO 64132-1199

Rockhurst University
Kansas City, Missouri
ww2.rockhurst.edu

CB member
CB code: 6611

- Private 4-year business and liberal arts college affiliated with the Roman Catholic Church
- Residential campus in very large city
- 1,542 degree-seeking undergraduates: 7% part-time, 58% women, 4% African American, 3% Asian American, 8% Hispanic/Latino, 3% Multiracial, non-Hispanic, 2% international
- 719 degree-seeking graduate students
- 74% of applicants admitted
- SAT or ACT (ACT writing optional) required
- 72% graduate within 6 years

General. Founded in 1910. Regionally accredited. Students graduate with community service transcript in addition to academic transcript. **Degrees:** 402 bachelor's awarded; master's, professional offered. **ROTC:** Army. **Location:** 5 miles from downtown. **Calendar:** Semester, limited summer session. **Full-time faculty:** 131 total; 90% have terminal degrees, 9% minority, 54% women. **Part-time faculty:** 119 total; 34% have terminal degrees, 6% minority, 60% women. **Class size:** 41% < 20, 54% 20-39, 3% 40-49, 1% 50-99, less than 1% >100.

Freshman class profile. 2,774 applied, 2,041 admitted, 320 enrolled.

Mid 50% test scores			
SAT critical reading:	490-600	Rank in top quarter:	56%
SAT math:	520-610	Rank in top tenth:	28%
ACT composite:	23-28	Return as sophomores:	85%
GPA 3.75 or higher:	50%	Out-of-state:	28%
GPA 3.50-3.74:	19%	Live on campus:	86%
GPA 3.0-3.49:	24%	International:	1%
		GPA 2.0-2.99:	7%

Basis for selection. High school GPA, rigor of secondary school record, and test scores most important; recommendations, school and community activities considered. Interviews recommended for all students. Essay or personal statement may be required or requested. **Home schooled:** Transcript of courses and grades, state high school equivalency certificate required. GED requested depending on quality of grades presented on transcript.

High school preparation. College-preparatory program recommended. 16 units recommended. Recommended units include English 4, mathematics 3, social studies 3, history 2, science 3 (laboratory 3), foreign language 2 and academic electives 4.

2016-2017 Annual costs. Tuition/fees (projected): $34,790. Room/board: $9,056. Books/supplies: $1,485. Personal expenses: $1,894.

2014-2015 Financial aid. Need-based: 361 full-time freshmen applied for aid; 272 deemed to have need; 272 received aid. Average need met was 82%. Average scholarship/grant was $2,688; average loan $5,838. 79% of total undergraduate aid awarded as scholarships/grants, 21% as loans/jobs. **Non-need-based:** Awarded to 1,386 full-time undergraduates, including 399 freshmen. Scholarships awarded for academics, alumni affiliation, athletics, leadership, music/drama. **Additional information:** Auditions, portfolios required for some scholarships.

Application procedures. Admission: No deadline. $25 fee, may be waived for applicants with need, free for online applicants. Admission notification on a rolling basis beginning on or about 9/1. Must reply by May 1 or within 2 week(s) if notified thereafter. **Financial aid:** Priority date 3/1; no closing date. FAFSA required. Applicants notified on a rolling basis starting 3/1; must reply within 4 week(s) of notification.

Academics. Core curriculum based on 7 "modes of inquiry," different ways people approach reality to seek truth including artistic, literary, historical, scientific-causal, scientific-relational, philosophical, and theological. **Special study options:** Accelerated study, cooperative education, cross-registration, double major, dual enrollment of high school students, exchange student, honors, independent study, internships, liberal arts/career combination, study abroad, teacher certification program. **Credit/placement by examination:** AP, CLEP, IB, SAT, ACT, institutional tests. 32 credit hours maximum toward bachelor's degree. **Support services:** Learning center, study skills assistance, tutoring, writing center.

Majors. Biology: General, biochemistry. **Business:** Business admin, communications, nonprofit/public. **Communications:** Communications/speech/rhetoric. **Computer sciences:** Information technology, programming. **Education:** Elementary, secondary. **Engineering:** Civil, electrical, mechanical. **English:** English lit. **Foreign languages:** French, Spanish. **Health services:** Clinical lab science, nursing (RN), speech pathology. **History:** General. **Human services:** Community org/advocacy. **Math:** General, applied. **Parks/recreation:** Exercise sciences. **Philosophy/religion:** Philosophy, religion. **Physical sciences:** Chemistry, physics. **Protective services:** Law enforcement admin. **Psychology:** General. **Social sciences:** General, economics, political science.

Most popular majors. Biology 10%, business/marketing 17%, health sciences 29%, parks/recreation 6%, psychology 9%, social sciences 8%.

Technology on campus. 270 workstations in dormitories, library, computer center, student center. Dormitories wired for high-speed internet access and linked to campus network. Online course registration, online library, helpline, repair service, wireless network available.

Student life. Freshman orientation: Mandatory, $150 fee. Preregistration for classes offered. Programs held 4 days before fall semester begins. Includes participation in community service projects. **Policies:** Full-time unmarried freshmen and sophomores must live on campus if not living with family. **Housing:** Guaranteed on-campus for freshmen. Coed dorms, single-sex dorms, apartments, themed housing available. $200 nonrefundable deposit. **Activities:** Campus ministries, choral groups, dance, drama, international student organizations, literary magazine, music ensembles, Model UN, musical theater, student government, student newspaper, Alpha Phi Omega, black student union, multicultural affairs office, American Humanics, Student Senate, Delta Sigma Pi Business Fraternity, student activities board, student organization of Latinos, theatre troupe.

Athletics. NCAA. **Intercollegiate:** Baseball M, basketball, cross-country W, golf, lacrosse, soccer, softball W, tennis, volleyball W. **Intramural:**

Basketball, bowling, field hockey W, football (tackle), golf, soccer, softball, tennis, ultimate frisbee, volleyball. **Team name:** Hawks.

Student services. Alcohol/substance abuse counseling, chaplain/spiritual director, career counseling, student employment services, financial aid counseling, health services, personal counseling, placement for graduates. **Physically disabled:** Services for visually, speech, hearing impaired.

Contact. E-mail: admission@rockhurst.edu
Phone: (816) 501-4100 Toll-free number: (800) 842-6776
Fax: (816) 501-4241
Kyle Johnson, Director of Freshman Admission, Rockhurst University, 1100 Rockhurst Road, Kansas City, MO 64110-2561

Saint Louis University
Saint Louis, Missouri   **CB member**
www.slu.edu   **CB code: 6629**

- Private 4-year university affiliated with the Roman Catholic Church
- Residential campus in very large city
- 7,973 degree-seeking undergraduates: 9% part-time, 59% women, 6% African American, 9% Asian American, 6% Hispanic/Latino, 4% Multiracial, non-Hispanic, 5% international
- 4,599 degree-seeking graduate students
- 63% of applicants admitted
- SAT or ACT (ACT writing optional), application essay required
- 74% graduate within 6 years

General. Founded in 1818. Regionally accredited. Institution maintains campus in Madrid, Spain. **Degrees:** 1,988 bachelor's awarded; master's, professional, doctoral offered. **ROTC:** Army, Air Force. **Location:** Midtown. **Calendar:** Semester, extensive summer session. **Full-time faculty:** 749 total; 88% have terminal degrees, 17% minority, 49% women. **Part-time faculty:** 420 total; 20% have terminal degrees, 10% minority, 58% women. **Class size:** 54% < 20, 32% 20-39, 5% 40-49, 6% 50-99, 3% >100. **Special facilities:** Vatican manuscripts microfilm library, art museums, 3 student unions, LEED certified research facility, biological station, entrepreneurial studies center, earthquake research center, performing arts center, supersonic wind tunnel, water tunnel, shock tube, fabrication labs, flight simulators, airport, sculpture/ceramics studio, physiology and gait research labs, student media broadcasting (TV, radio).

Freshman class profile. 13,216 applied, 8,273 admitted, 1,618 enrolled.

Mid 50% test scores			
SAT critical reading:	540-670	Rank in top quarter:	70%
SAT math:	560-680	Rank in top tenth:	42%
ACT composite:	25-31	Return as sophomores:	90%
GPA 3.75 or higher:	64%	Out-of-state:	66%
GPA 3.50-3.74:	15%	Live on campus:	92%
GPA 3.0-3.49:	15%	International:	4%
GPA 2.0-2.99:	6%	Fraternities:	13%
		Sororities:	38%

Basis for selection. Secondary school record, standardized test scores important; recommendations, essay, extracurricular activities, character/personal qualities, volunteer work considered, and admission interview. Academic performance is most important for international applicants. However, for non-native English speakers, 550 on TOEFL or 6.5 on IELTS, or equivalent required for full-time enrollment. Audition required for music program. Portfolio required for art program. **Home schooled:** Applicants are strongly recommended to present 5 academic courses each semester for all four years. These should include 4 years of English, 4 years of mathematics (algebra I & II, and geometry), 3 years each of foreign language, natural science, social science and academic electives. **Learning Disabled:** Students with learning disabilities are responsible for contacting Disabilities Services in order to learn about the accommodation process on campus and to receive academic accommodations within the classroom.

High school preparation. College-preparatory program recommended. 20 units required. Required units include English 4, mathematics 4, social studies 3, science 3, foreign language 3 and academic electives 3.

2015-2016 Annual costs. Tuition/fees: $39,226. Room/board: $10,640. Books/supplies: $1,200. Personal expenses: $2,970.

2014-2015 Financial aid. Need-based: 1,329 full-time freshmen applied for aid; 1,055 deemed to have need; 1,055 received aid. Average need met was 76%. Average scholarship/grant was $23,362; average loan $3,691. 83% of total undergraduate aid awarded as scholarships/grants, 17% as loans/jobs. **Non-need-based:** Awarded to 2,815 full-time undergraduates, including 668 freshmen. Scholarships awarded for academics, art, athletics, leadership, music/drama, religious affiliation, ROTC. **Additional information:** Presidential Scholarship applications due 12/1. Martin Luther King Jr. Scholarship applications have priority date of 2/1. Emergency Scholarship Fund available to assist students and families with special circumstances. Loan program available to assist some students without other financing options. Will match, dollar for dollar, all qualified scholarship gifts of $100 and more.

Application procedures. Admission: Priority date 12/1; deadline 8/20 (receipt date). No application fee. Admission notification by 8/20. Admission notification on a rolling basis beginning on or about 11/1. Must reply by May 1 or within 2 week(s) if notified thereafter. **Financial aid:** Priority date 3/1; no closing date. FAFSA required. Applicants notified on a rolling basis starting 3/15; must reply by 5/1 or within 4 week(s) of notification.

Academics. Special study options: Accelerated study, combined bachelor's/graduate degree, cooperative education, cross-registration, distance learning, double major, dual enrollment of high school students, ESL, exchange student, honors, independent study, internships, liberal arts/career combination, student-designed major, study abroad, teacher certification program. Evening courses, learning disabilities services, summer session for credit. **Credit/placement by examination:** AP, CLEP, IB, SAT, ACT, institutional tests. 30 credit hours maximum toward bachelor's degree. **Support services:** Pre-admission summer program, reduced course load, study skills assistance, tutoring, writing center. Career planning, helpline/ombudservice, computer support, student employment and placement, commuter and transportation services, TRIO programs.

Honors college/program. 30 ACT/1330 SAT verbal and math/3.8 unweighted GPA. There are approximately 100-120 freshman admitted each year. Academic offerings: Honors core classes, honors opportunities in major, senior honors thesis.

Majors. Area/ethnic studies: African-American, American, Latin American, women's. **Biology:** General, biochemistry, biomedical sciences, biostatistics, neuroscience. **Business:** Accounting, entrepreneurial studies, finance, international, management information systems, managerial economics, marketing, organizational behavior, organizational leadership. **Communications:** General. **Computer sciences:** General, computer science. **Conservation:** Environmental science, environmental studies. **Education:** General, elementary, English, mathematics, middle, science, social science. **Engineering:** General, aerospace, applied physics, biomedical, civil, computer, electrical, mechanical. **English:** English lit. **Foreign languages:** French, German, Italian, Russian, Spanish. **Health services:** Clinical lab science, communication disorders, cytotechnology, dietetics, health care admin, health information management, medical radiologic technology/radiation therapy, MRI technology, nuclear medical technology, nursing (RN), occupational therapy. **History:** General. **Human services:** Social work. **Math:** General. **Parks/recreation:** Exercise sciences. **Philosophy/religion:** Philosophy. **Physical sciences:** Atmospheric science, chemistry, geology, physics. **Protective services:** Criminal justice, disaster management, forensics, security management. **Psychology:** General. **Social sciences:** Anthropology, international relations, political science, sociology, urban studies. **Theology:** Theology. **Visual/performing arts:** Art history/conservation, dramatic, music, studio arts, theater arts management.

Most popular majors. Biology 8%, business/marketing 23%, engineering/engineering technologies 6%, health sciences 24%, parks/recreation 6%, social sciences 6%.

Technology on campus. 1,091 workstations in library, computer center, student center. Dormitories wired for high-speed internet access and linked to campus network. Commuter students can connect to campus network. Online course registration, online library, helpline, student web hosting, wireless network available.

Student life. Freshman orientation: Mandatory, $200 fee. Preregistration for classes offered. Two-day program held 9 times in the summer before fall enrollment. **Housing:** Guaranteed on-campus for freshmen. Coed dorms, single-sex dorms, special housing for disabled, apartments, fraternity/sorority housing, themed housing available. $250 partly refundable deposit, deadline 5/1. Micah Program (learning community) houses. **Activities:** Bands, campus ministries, choral groups, dance, drama, international student organizations, literary magazine, music ensembles, Model UN, musical theater, radio station, student government, student newspaper, TV station, Black Student Alliance, Muslim Student Association, College Democrats, College Republicans, student activities board, Relay for Life, interfaith ministries, International Student Federation, student government association, Hispanic American Leadership Organization.

Athletics. NCAA. **Intercollegiate:** Baseball M, basketball, cross-country, diving, field hockey W, soccer, softball W, swimming, tennis, track and field, volleyball W. **Intramural:** Badminton, basketball, bowling, football (non-tackle), golf, handball, racquetball, sand volleyball, soccer, softball, squash, table tennis, tennis, track and field, triathlon, ultimate frisbee, volleyball. **Team name:** Billikens.

Student services. Adult student services, alcohol/substance abuse counseling, chaplain/spiritual director, career counseling, services for economically disadvantaged, student employment services, financial aid counseling, health services, minority student services, personal counseling, placement for graduates, veterans' counselor, women's services. **Physically disabled:** Services for visually, speech, hearing impaired.

Contact. E-mail: admission@slu.edu
Phone: (314) 977-2500 Toll-free number: (800) 758-3678
Fax: (314) 977-7136
Jean Gilman, Asst. V.P., Office of Admissions, Saint Louis University, One North Grand Boulevard, St. Louis, MO 63103

Southeast Missouri State University
Cape Girardeau, Missouri   **CB member**
www.semo.edu   **CB code: 6655**

- Public 4-year university
- Commuter campus in large town
- 9,098 degree-seeking undergraduates: 15% part-time, 55% women, 10% African American, 1% Asian American, 2% Hispanic/Latino, 7% international
- 1,300 degree-seeking graduate students
- 84% of applicants admitted
- SAT or ACT (ACT writing optional) required
- 48% graduate within 6 years

General. Founded in 1873. Regionally accredited. **Degrees:** 1,699 bachelor's, 25 associate awarded; master's offered. **ROTC:** Air Force. **Location:** 120 miles from St. Louis. **Calendar:** Semester, extensive summer session. **Full-time faculty:** 407 total; 75% have terminal degrees, 16% minority, 52% women. **Part-time faculty:** 169 total; 22% have terminal degrees, 6% minority, 60% women. **Class size:** 42% < 20, 50% 20-39, 3% 40-49, 4% 50-99, less than 1% >100. **Special facilities:** Demonstration farm, museum.

Freshman class profile. 4,622 applied, 3,896 admitted, 1,703 enrolled.

Mid 50% test scores			
SAT critical reading:	450-580	Rank in top tenth:	17%
SAT math:	470-600	End year in good standing:	80%
ACT composite:	20-25	Return as sophomores:	73%
GPA 3.75 or higher:	31%	Out-of-state:	21%
GPA 3.50-3.74:	16%	Live on campus:	66%
GPA 3.0-3.49:	29%	International:	5%
GPA 2.0-2.99:	23%	Fraternities:	15%
Rank in top quarter:	44%	Sororities:	19%

Basis for selection. A traditional beginning freshman applicant is evaluated on ACT/SAT score, high school cumulative grade point average, class rank (if available) and high school core curriculum. Non-traditional students may take the ASSET exam. ACT preferred; SAT accepted. BFA in Performing Arts and Art degree programs requires audition or portfolio for formal admittance. Bachelor of Music Education, Bachelor of Music, Bachelor of Arts in Music require audition prior to formal admittance.

High school preparation. College-preparatory program required. 17 units required. Required units include English 4, mathematics 3, social studies 2, history 1, science 3 (laboratory 1), visual/performing arts 1 and academic electives 3. Of social studies requirements, .5 units must be in U.S. government.

2016-2017 Annual costs. Tuition/fees (projected): $6,990; $12,375 out-of-state. Room/board: $8,285. Books/supplies: $499. Personal expenses: $2,590.

2014-2015 Financial aid. Need-based: 1,503 full-time freshmen applied for aid; 1,101 deemed to have need; 1,086 received aid. Average need met was 58%. Average scholarship/grant was $6,522; average loan $3,255. 50% of total undergraduate aid awarded as scholarships/grants, 50% as loans/jobs. Non-need-based: Awarded to 1,765 full-time undergraduates, including 549 freshmen. Scholarships awarded for academics, alumni affiliation, art, athletics, job skills, leadership, minority status, music/drama, ROTC, state residency.

Application procedures. Admission: Priority date 12/1; deadline 7/1 (postmark date). $30 fee, may be waived for applicants with need. Admission notification on a rolling basis beginning on or about 9/1. Must reply by 5/1. Financial aid: Priority date 3/1; no closing date. FAFSA required. Applicants notified on a rolling basis starting 4/1; must reply within 3 week(s) of notification.

Academics. Special study options: Accelerated study, distance learning, double major, dual enrollment of high school students, ESL, honors, independent study, internships, liberal arts/career combination, student-designed major, study abroad, teacher certification program. Credit/placement by examination: AP, CLEP, IB, SAT, ACT, institutional tests. 30 credit hours maximum

toward associate degree, 30 toward bachelor's. College credit earned by examination may be counted toward University Studies, major, minor or elective requirements. A maximum of 30 semester hours of combined credit from AP, CLEP, DANTES, DE, CPS, and IB options may be counted toward a single degree. Support services: Learning center, pre-admission summer program, reduced course load, remedial instruction, study skills assistance, tutoring, writing center.

Majors. Biology: General. **Business:** Accounting, business admin, finance, international, marketing. **Communications:** Communications/speech/rhetoric, health, organizational. **Computer sciences:** General, programming, security. **Conservation:** Environmental science. **Education:** Agricultural, art, business, early childhood, elementary, English, family/consumer sciences, foreign languages, mathematics, middle, music, physical, science, social studies, special ed, technology/industrial arts. **Engineering:** Applied physics. **English:** English lit, rhetoric/composition. **Health services:** Athletic training, clinical lab science, communication disorders, health care admin, nursing (RN). **History:** General. **Human services:** Social work. **Math:** General. **Parks/recreation:** General, health/fitness, sports admin. **Philosophy/religion:** Philosophy. **Physical sciences:** Chemistry, physics. **Protective services:** Corrections, disaster management. **Psychology:** General. **Social sciences:** General, economics, political science. **Visual/performing arts:** General, art, dramatic, music. **Work/family studies:** General.

Most popular majors. Business/marketing 13%, communications/journalism 7%, education 16%, engineering/engineering technologies 7%, health sciences 10%, liberal arts 9%.

Technology on campus. 1,241 workstations in dormitories, library, student center. Dormitories wired for high-speed internet access and linked to campus network. Online course registration, online library, helpline, wireless network available.

Student life. Freshman orientation: Mandatory, $65 fee. Preregistration for classes offered. One-day program offered many times throughout the semester. **Housing:** Coed dorms, special housing for disabled, apartments, fraternity/sorority housing, themed housing, wellness housing available. $150 partly refundable deposit. Apartments for students with dependents available. **Activities:** Bands, campus ministries, choral groups, dance, drama, film society, international student organizations, literary magazine, music ensembles, Model UN, musical theater, opera, radio station, student government, student newspaper, symphony orchestra, TV station, Lutheran Student Fellowship, Catholic Campus Ministry, Campus Outreach, Association of Black Collegians, College Democrats, Gay-Straight Alliance, Indian Subcontinent Student Association, Chinese Students & Scholars Association, Japanese Student Association, Club Red.

Athletics. NCAA. **Intercollegiate:** Baseball M, basketball, cheerleading, cross-country, football (tackle) M, gymnastics W, soccer W, softball W, tennis W, track and field, volleyball W. **Intramural:** Basketball, football (non-tackle), soccer, softball, table tennis, tennis, ultimate frisbee, volleyball. **Team name:** Redhawks.

Student services. Adult student services, alcohol/substance abuse counseling, career counseling, services for economically disadvantaged, student employment services, financial aid counseling, health services, minority student services, on-campus daycare, personal counseling, placement for graduates, veterans' counselor. **Physically disabled:** Services for visually, speech, hearing impaired.

Contact. E-mail: admissions@semo.edu
Phone: (573) 651-2590 Fax: (573) 651-5936
Lenell Hahn, Director of Admissions, Southeast Missouri State University, One University Plaza MS 3550, Cape Girardeau, MO 63701

Southwest Baptist University
Bolivar, Missouri
www.sbuniv.edu   **CB code: 6664**

- Private 4-year university affiliated with the Southern Baptist Convention
- Residential campus in large town
- 2,394 degree-seeking undergraduates: 21% part-time, 66% women
- 734 graduate students
- 51% graduate within 6 years

General. Founded in 1878. Regionally accredited. **Degrees:** 370 bachelor's, 198 associate awarded; master's, professional, doctoral offered. **ROTC:** Army. **Location:** 25 miles from Springfield, 120 miles from Kansas City. **Calendar:** Semester, extensive summer session. **Full-time faculty:** 148 total; 58% have terminal degrees. **Part-time faculty:** 157 total.

Freshman class profile.

GPA 3.75 or higher:	43%	Rank in top quarter:	49%
GPA 3.50-3.74:	17%	Rank in top tenth:	25%
GPA 3.0-3.49:	25%	Out-of-state:	29%
GPA 2.0-2.99:	14%	Live on campus:	93%

Basis for selection. Must meet 2 of 3 qualifiers: 2.50 GPA, 21 ACT or 990 SAT score (exclusive of Writing), top 50% high school class rank. Interview required for conditionally admitted applicants, recommended for all. Audition recommended for music, speech, and theater students.

High school preparation. College-preparatory program recommended. 13 units recommended. Recommended units include English 4, mathematics 3, social studies 2, science 2 and academic electives 2. 2 additional units of foreign language or computer science or 2 units of English, math, social studies or natural sciences recommended.

2015-2016 Annual costs. Tuition/fees: $21,840. Room/board: $7,160. Books/supplies: $1,500. Personal expenses: $1,000.

Financial aid. Non-need-based: Scholarships awarded for academics, alumni affiliation, art, athletics, minority status, music/drama, religious affiliation.

Application procedures. Admission: No deadline. $30 fee, may be waived for applicants with need. Admission notification on a rolling basis. **Financial aid:** Priority date 3/15; no closing date. FAFSA required. Applicants notified on a rolling basis starting 3/1; must reply within 2 week(s) of notification.

Academics. Special study options: Accelerated study, cross-registration, distance learning, double major, dual enrollment of high school students, exchange student, honors, independent study, internships, liberal arts/career combination, study abroad, teacher certification program. **Credit/placement by examination:** AP, CLEP, IB, SAT, ACT, institutional tests. 16 credit hours maximum toward associate degree, 32 toward bachelor's. **Support services:** Learning center, reduced course load, remedial instruction, study skills assistance, tutoring, writing center.

Majors. Biology: General. **Business:** Accounting, business admin, customer service, finance, international, marketing, office management. **Communications:** Communications/speech/rhetoric. **Computer sciences:** General, computer science. **Education:** Art, biology, chemistry, elementary, English, health, middle, music, physical, science, social science. **English:** English lit. **Foreign languages:** Spanish. **Health services:** Athletic training, clinical lab science, nursing (RN). **History:** General. **Math:** General. **Parks/recreation:** General, health/fitness, sports admin. **Philosophy/religion:** Religion. **Physical sciences:** Chemistry. **Protective services:** Law enforcement admin. **Psychology:** General. **Social sciences:** Political science, sociology. **Theology:** Bible, missionary, religious ed, sacred music, theology. **Visual/performing arts:** Art, commercial/advertising art, dramatic, music.

Technology on campus. 242 workstations in dormitories, library, computer center, student center. Dormitories linked to campus network. Commuter students can connect to campus network. Online library, helpline, wireless network available.

Student life. Freshman orientation: Available. Preregistration for classes offered. Three-days prior to start of the fall semester. **Policies:** Religious observance required. **Housing:** Guaranteed on-campus for freshmen. Single-sex dorms, apartments, wellness housing available. **Activities:** Bands, campus ministries, choral groups, drama, music ensembles, musical theater, opera, student government, student newspaper, symphony orchestra, University Missions, Habitat for Humanity, Christian Service organization, Theatrical Evangelism and Mission, Students in Free Enterprise, Discipleship-Now teams.

Athletics. NCAA. **Intercollegiate:** Baseball M, basketball, cheerleading, cross-country, football (tackle) M, golf M, soccer W, softball W, tennis, track and field, volleyball W. **Intramural:** Basketball, football (non-tackle), racquetball, soccer, softball, ultimate frisbee, volleyball. **Team name:** Bearcats.

Student services. Chaplain/spiritual director, career counseling, student employment services, financial aid counseling, health services, personal counseling, placement for graduates.

Contact. E-mail: dcrowder@sbuniv.edu
Phone: (417) 328-1810 Toll-free number: (800) 526-5859
Fax: (417) 328-1808
Darren Crowder, Director of Admissions, Southwest Baptist University, 1600 University Avenue, Bolivar, MO 65613-2597

St. Louis Christian College	
Florissant, Missouri	
www.stlchristian.edu	**CB code: 0334**

- Private 4-year Bible college affiliated with the Christian Church
- Residential campus in small city
- 153 degree-seeking undergraduates: 18% part-time, 44% women, 31% African American, 3% Hispanic/Latino, 1% Native American, 3% Multiracial, non-Hispanic
- 36% of applicants admitted
- SAT or ACT (ACT writing optional), application essay required
- 48% graduate within 6 years

General. Founded in 1956. Regionally accredited; also accredited by ABHE. Students highly involved in service and field education. **Degrees:** 27 bachelor's, 8 associate awarded. **Location:** 15 miles from downtown. **Calendar:** Semester, limited summer session. **Full-time faculty:** 8 total; 12% have terminal degrees, 25% minority, 25% women. **Part-time faculty:** 20 total; 5% have terminal degrees, 5% minority, 30% women.

Freshman class profile. 72 applied, 26 admitted, 16 enrolled.

Mid 50% test scores		Out-of-state:	40%
ACT composite:	18-22	Live on campus:	99%
Return as sophomores:	73%		

Basis for selection. ACT, class rank, and GPA very important. English and math placement based on ACT subscores or COMPASS tests. Interviews required for some. **Learning Disabled:** Students with learning disabilities encouraged to utilize on-campus tutoring center and to meet with director of 504 program to develop a 504.

High school preparation. Recommended units include English 4, mathematics 3, social studies 3, science 3, foreign language 2 and academic electives 4.

2015-2016 Annual costs. Tuition/fees: $9,750. Room/board: $4,600. Books/supplies: $600. Personal expenses: $2,780.

2015-2016 Financial aid. Need-based: 13 full-time freshmen applied for aid; 12 deemed to have need; 12 received aid. Average need met was 51%. Average scholarship/grant was $4,883; average loan $3,500. 35% of total undergraduate aid awarded as scholarships/grants, 65% as loans/jobs.

Application procedures. Admission: Priority date 12/15; deadline 8/7 (receipt date). $100 fee. Admission notification by 8/14. Admission notification on a rolling basis beginning on or about 6/1. **Financial aid:** Closing date 8/1. FAFSA required. Applicants notified on a rolling basis starting 7/20; must reply within 2 week(s) of notification.

Academics. Preparation for ministries in preaching, education, youth work, mission fields, music, worship and pre-seminary education. **Special study options:** Cross-registration, internships. **Credit/placement by examination:** AP, CLEP, SAT, ACT, institutional tests. 30 credit hours maximum toward associate degree, 30 toward bachelor's. **Support services:** Learning center, remedial instruction, study skills assistance, tutoring, writing center.

Majors. Education: General. **Theology:** Bible, missionary, religious ed, sacred music, theology.

Technology on campus. 10 workstations in library, computer center. Dormitories wired for high-speed internet access and linked to campus network. Student web hosting, wireless network available.

Student life. Freshman orientation: Mandatory. Preregistration for classes offered. Held weekend before first day of class. **Policies:** Students involved in evangelistic activities of area churches. Religious observance required. **Housing:** Guaranteed on-campus for all undergraduates. Single-sex dorms, apartments available. **Activities:** Campus ministries, choral groups, drama, music ensembles, student government, missions interest group.

Athletics. NCCAA. **Intercollegiate:** Basketball, cross-country W, volleyball W. **Intramural:** Basketball, cross-country, softball, tennis, volleyball. **Team name:** Soldiers.

Student services. Adult student services, chaplain/spiritual director, career counseling, student employment services, financial aid counseling, personal counseling, veterans' counselor. **Physically disabled:** Services for visually, hearing impaired.

Contact. E-mail: admissions@stlchristian.edu
Phone: (314) 837-6777 ext. 8110 Toll-free number: (800) 887-7522
Fax: (314) 837-8291
Bob Farrar, Admissions Director, St. Louis Christian College, 1360 Grandview Drive, Florissant, MO 63033

St. Luke's College
Kansas City, Missouri
www.saintlukescollege.edu

CB code: 7127

- Private two-year upper-division nursing college affiliated with the Episcopal Church
- Commuter campus in large city
- Test scores, application essay, interview required

General. Founded in 1903. Regionally accredited. **Degrees:** 185 bachelor's awarded; master's offered. **Calendar:** Semester, limited summer session. **Full-time faculty:** 25 total. **Class size:** 16% < 20, 42% 20-39, 5% 40-49, 32% 50-99, 5% >100. **Special facilities:** Hospital simulation center, learning exchange center with teleconferencing capability.

Student profile. 434 degree-seeking undergraduates. 100% entered as juniors.

Basis for selection. High school transcript, college transcript, application essay, interview, standardized test scores required. Recommendations required. Health care-related work and community service considered. Transfer accepted as juniors.

2015-2016 Annual costs. Tuition/fees: $15,164. Books/supplies: $1,300.

Application procedures. Admission: Deadline 1/15. $35 fee. Application must be submitted on paper. Admission notification 3/1. **Financial aid:** Priority date 4/1, no deadline. Applicants notified on a rolling basis; must reply within 3 weeks of notification.

Academics. Special study options: Combined bachelor's/graduate degree, distance learning. **Credit/placement by examination:** AP, CLEP. 15 credit hours maximum toward bachelor's degree. Exams must not be older than 10 years Only CLEP and AP exams accepted.

Majors. Health services: Nursing (RN).

Technology on campus. PC or laptop required. 10 workstations in library, computer center. Online library, helpline, wireless network available.

Student life. Activities: Student government.

Student services. Career counseling, financial aid counseling, health services, personal counseling.

Contact. E-mail: admissions@saintlukescollege.edu
Phone: (816) 936-8700 Fax: (816) 936-8700
Josh Richards, Director of Admissions, St. Luke's College, 624 Westport Road, Kansas City, MO 64111

Stephens College
Columbia, Missouri
www.stephens.edu

CB member
CB code: 6683

- Private 4-year liberal arts and career college for women
- Residential campus in small city
- 706 degree-seeking undergraduates: 16% part-time, 99% women, 15% African American, 1% Asian American, 5% Hispanic/Latino, 1% Native American, 1% Native Hawaiian/Pacific islander, 6% Multi-racial, non-Hispanic
- 185 degree-seeking graduate students
- 68% of applicants admitted
- SAT or ACT (ACT writing optional), application essay required

General. Founded in 1833. Regionally accredited. **Degrees:** 141 bachelor's awarded; master's offered. **ROTC:** Army, Naval, Air Force. **Location:** 120 miles from St. Louis and Kansas City. **Calendar:** Semester, limited summer session. **Full-time faculty:** 48 total; 79% have terminal degrees, 4% minority, 75% women. **Part-time faculty:** 67 total; 70% have terminal degrees, 6% minority, 67% women. **Class size:** 75% < 20, 24% 20-39, 1% 40-49. **Special facilities:** Professional theater, private elementary lab school and child study center; horse stables, historical costume collection.

Freshman class profile. 1,219 applied, 826 admitted, 193 enrolled.

Mid 50% test scores			
SAT critical reading:	520-600	Rank in top quarter:	45%
SAT math:	520-580	Rank in top tenth:	19%
SAT writing:	510-590	End year in good standing:	85%
ACT composite:	20-24	Return as sophomores:	71%
GPA 3.75 or higher:	25%	Out-of-state:	43%
GPA 3.50-3.74:	18%	Live on campus:	99%
GPA 3.0-3.49:	33%	International:	1%
GPA 2.0-2.99:	21%		

Basis for selection. Holistic review of application file including GPA, test scores, essay, resume, recommendations and student interaction with admissions office. Interview recommended for all students. Audition mandatory for dance, recommended for theater and musical theater students. **Home schooled:** Statement describing home school structure and mission, transcript of courses and grades, letter of recommendation (nonparent) required. Require short narrative by primary instructor describing secondary-level education. Examples of student's work may be provided as supplemental information. Narrative may be considered in lieu of transcript when transcript not available. Campus visit for individual meeting with admissions counselor encouraged.

High school preparation. College-preparatory program recommended. 12 units recommended. Recommended units include English 4, mathematics 3, social studies 1, science 2 and foreign language 2.

2015-2016 Annual costs. Tuition/fees: $29,176. Room/board: $9,818. Books/supplies: $900. Personal expenses: $1,300.

2014-2015 Financial aid. Need-based: 49% of total undergraduate aid awarded as scholarships/grants, 51% as loans/jobs. **Non-need-based:** Scholarships awarded for academics, alumni affiliation, athletics, leadership, music/drama, state residency.

Application procedures. Admission: Priority date 1/1; no deadline. $50 fee, may be waived for applicants with need, free for online applicants. Admission notification on a rolling basis beginning on or about 1/1. Must reply by May 1 or within 2 week(s) if notified thereafter. **Financial aid:** Priority date 3/15; no closing date. FAFSA required. Applicants notified on a rolling basis starting 3/1.

Academics. Academic Resource Center offers one-on-one and group sessions in many course subjects, as well as time management, study skills and writing. **Special study options:** Accelerated study, cross-registration, distance learning, double major, dual enrollment of high school students, external degree, honors, independent study, internships, liberal arts/career combination, semester at sea, student-designed major, study abroad, teacher certification program. **Credit/placement by examination:** AP, CLEP, IB, SAT, ACT. 15 credit hours maximum toward associate degree, 30 toward bachelor's. **Support services:** Learning center, pre-admission summer program, study skills assistance, tutoring, writing center.

Honors college/program. Honors living/learning community; members selected for invitation based on application materials and credentials. Limited number of positions available; only new incoming freshman are selected for invitation.

Majors. Biology: General. **Business:** Event planning. **Communications:** Media studies. **Communications technology:** Graphics. **Education:** Multi-level teacher. **English:** Creative writing, English lit. **Health services:** Health information management. **Liberal arts:** Arts/sciences. **Psychology:** General. **Visual/performing arts:** Acting, costume design, dance, fashion design, film/cinema/video, graphic design, interior design, musical theater, theater arts management, theater design. **Work/family studies:** Clothing/textiles, family studies.

Most popular majors. Agriculture 9%, business/marketing 19%, English 6%, health sciences 20%, visual/performing arts 31%.

Technology on campus. 120 workstations in dormitories, library, computer center, student center. Dormitories wired for high-speed internet access and linked to campus network. Commuter students can connect to campus network. Online course registration, online library, helpline, repair service, student web hosting, wireless network available.

Student life. Freshman orientation: Mandatory. Preregistration for classes offered. Typically held third week of August, one week prior to start of classes. Registration held mid-June on campus with academic adviser. **Policies:** Undergraduate students required to live on campus in college-sanctioned housing. **Housing:** Guaranteed on-campus for all undergraduates. Special housing for disabled, apartments, themed housing available. $200 partly refundable deposit, deadline 5/1. Pets allowed in dorm rooms. Freshman academic residence hall; designated housing available for students who bring pets. **Activities:** Campus ministries, choral groups, dance, drama, film society, literary magazine, music ensembles, musical theater, radio station, student government, student newspaper, TV station.

Athletics. NAIA. **Intercollegiate:** Basketball W, cross-country W, golf W, soccer W, softball W, tennis W, volleyball W. **Intramural:** Equestrian W. **Team name:** Stars.

Student services. Adult student services, career counseling, student employment services, financial aid counseling, health services, minority student services, personal counseling, placement for graduates, women's services.

Contact. E-mail: apply@stephens.edu
Phone: (573) 876-7207 Toll-free number: (800) 876-7207
Fax: (573) 876-7237
Tiffany Golder, Director of Undergraduate Admissions, Stephens College, 1200 East Broadway, Columbia, MO 65215

Truman State University
Kirksville, Missouri
www.truman.edu

CB member
CB code: 6483

- Public 4-year university and liberal arts college
- Residential campus in large town
- 5,290 degree-seeking undergraduates: 3% part-time, 58% women, 4% African American, 2% Asian American, 3% Hispanic/Latino, 3% Multiracial, non-Hispanic, 7% international
- 275 degree-seeking graduate students
- 79% of applicants admitted
- SAT or ACT (ACT writing optional), application essay required
- 73% graduate within 6 years; 41% enter graduate study

General. Founded in 1867. Regionally accredited. **Degrees:** 1,223 bachelor's awarded; master's offered. **ROTC:** Army. **Location:** 90 miles from Columbia,195 miles from St. Louis. **Calendar:** Semester, extensive summer session. **Full-time faculty:** 328 total; 82% have terminal degrees, 10% minority, 40% women. **Part-time faculty:** 68 total; 32% have terminal degrees, 3% minority, 56% women. **Class size:** 49% < 20, 48% 20-39, 1% 40-49, 1% 50-99, less than 1% >100. **Special facilities:** Planetarium, movement analysis lab, motor learning/biomechanics lab, observatory, greenhouse, local history museum, 400-acre farm, speech and hearing clinic, biofeedback laboratory, nursing simulation lab, radio station, television studio, publications technology lab, 24-hour art studio space, Apple/Mac labs, language learning lab, writing center, strength and conditioning center, large format printer, human anatomy laboratory, medical resource library, ROTC classrooms and training facilities, SMART Board classrooms and lecture capture technology.

Freshman class profile. 3,900 applied, 3,080 admitted, 1,262 enrolled.

Mid 50% test scores		Rank in top tenth:	47%
SAT critical reading:	580-730	End year in good standing:	91%
SAT math:	560-680	Return as sophomores:	89%
ACT composite:	25-30	Out-of-state:	22%
GPA 3.75 or higher:	64%	Live on campus:	98%
GPA 3.50-3.74:	18%	International:	6%
GPA 3.0-3.49:	16%	Fraternities:	25%
GPA 2.0-2.99:	2%	Sororities:	23%
Rank in top quarter:	79%		

Basis for selection. High school performance (class rank, GPA, college preparatory curriculum), test scores, and essay are most important; special ability, talent and achievement are considered. Portfolio recommended for fine arts students. Audition required for music students. Additional nursing-specific application required for all students interested in pursuing a Nursing degree. **Learning Disabled:** Students are welcome to provide additional documentation of their learning disability to the Office of Disability Services.

High school preparation. College-preparatory program recommended. 24 units required; 25 recommended. Required and recommended units include English 4, mathematics 3-4, social studies 2, history 1, science 3 (laboratory 2), foreign language 2, visual/performing arts 1 and academic electives 5. 1 practical arts, 1 physical education, .5 health education, .5 personal finance required.

2015-2016 Annual costs. Tuition/fees: $7,430; $13,654 out-of-state. Room/board: $8,480. Books/supplies: $1,000. Personal expenses: $2,500.

2014-2015 Financial aid. Need-based: 1,141 full-time freshmen applied for aid; 739 deemed to have need; 739 received aid. Average need met was 88%. Average scholarship/grant was $8,180; average loan $3,663. 57% of total undergraduate aid awarded as scholarships/grants, 43% as loans/jobs. **Non-need-based:** Awarded to 4,369 full-time undergraduates, including 1,350 freshmen. Scholarships awarded for academics, alumni affiliation, art, athletics, leadership, minority status, music/drama, ROTC, state residency.

Application procedures. Admission: Priority date 12/1; no deadline. No application fee. Admission notification on a rolling basis beginning on or about 9/1. Housing deposit not refundable after May 1. **Financial aid:** Priority date 4/1; no closing date. FAFSA required. Applicants notified on a rolling basis starting 3/1.

Academics. Special study options: Combined bachelor's/graduate degree, double major, dual enrollment of high school students, ESL, honors, independent study, internships, semester at sea, student-designed major, study abroad, teacher certification program, Washington semester. **Credit/placement by examination:** AP, CLEP, IB, ACT, institutional tests. Students who complete a CLEP exam must have an original College Grade Report sent from the College Board to Truman State University (our CEEB code is 6483). Credit will be awarded when the student scores at or above the ACE recommended credit-granting score. A grade of "T" is granted to indicate credit received. The "T" grade does not affect the grade point average (GPA), but does count toward total earned hours. **Support services:** Learning center, study skills assistance, tutoring, writing center.

Majors. Biology: General. **Business:** Accounting, business admin. **Communications:** Communications/speech/rhetoric. **Computer sciences:** Computer science. **English:** Creative writing, English lit. **Foreign languages:** Classics, French, German, linguistics, Romance, Russian, Spanish. **Health services:** Athletic training, communication disorders, nursing (RN). **History:** General. **Math:** General. **Parks/recreation:** Exercise sciences, health/fitness. **Philosophy/religion:** General. **Physical sciences:** Chemistry, physics. **Protective services:** Criminal justice. **Psychology:** General. **Social sciences:** Economics, political science, sociology. **Visual/performing arts:** Art, art history/conservation, dramatic, music, music performance.

Most popular majors. Biology 8%, business/marketing 15%, English 8%, health sciences 8%, parks/recreation 15%, psychology 9%, visual/performing arts 7%.

Technology on campus. 1,099 workstations in dormitories, library, computer center, student center. Dormitories wired for high-speed internet access and linked to campus network. Commuter students can connect to campus network. Online course registration, online library, helpline, student web hosting, wireless network available.

Student life. Freshman orientation: Mandatory, $315 fee. Preregistration for classes offered. Sessions held during June and August, with additional "Truman Week" program a few days before fall semester begins. **Policies:** Dry campus. First-time freshmen are required to live on campus. **Housing:** Guaranteed on-campus for freshmen. Coed dorms, special housing for disabled, apartments, fraternity/sorority housing, themed housing available. $150 partly refundable deposit, deadline 5/1. Pets allowed in dorm rooms. Spanish and French language (Romance languages), pre-med, service-learning, transfer student and sustainability housing available. **Activities:** Bands, campus ministries, choral groups, dance, drama, film society, international student organizations, literary magazine, music ensembles, Model UN, musical theater, opera, radio station, student government, student newspaper, symphony orchestra, TV station, Alpha Phi Omega, Association of Black Collegians, College Republicans, Campus Christian Fellowship, Blue Key, Cardinal Key, College Democrats, Baptist Student Union, Newman Center, Hispanic American Leadership Organization.

Athletics. NCAA. **Intercollegiate:** Baseball M, basketball, cross-country, football (tackle) M, golf W, soccer, softball W, swimming, tennis, track and field, volleyball W, wrestling M. **Intramural:** Badminton, basketball, football (non-tackle), soccer, softball, swimming, table tennis, tennis, track and field, triathlon, ultimate frisbee, volleyball. **Team name:** Bulldogs.

Student services. Alcohol/substance abuse counseling, career counseling, services for economically disadvantaged, student employment services, financial aid counseling, health services, minority student services, personal counseling, veterans' counselor, women's services. **Physically disabled:** Services for visually, speech, hearing impaired.

Contact. E-mail: admissions@truman.edu
Phone: (660) 785-4114 Toll-free number: (800) 892-7792
Fax: (660) 785-7456
Melody Chambers, Director of Admission, Truman State University, 100 East Normal Avenue, Kirksville, MO 63501

University of Central Missouri
Warrensburg, Missouri
www.ucmo.edu

CB code: 6090

- Public 4-year university
- Commuter campus in large town
- 9,017 degree-seeking undergraduates: 11% part-time, 55% women, 11% African American, 1% Asian American, 4% Hispanic/Latino, 4% Multiracial, non-Hispanic, 2% international
- 4,238 degree-seeking graduate students
- 79% of applicants admitted
- SAT or ACT (ACT writing optional) required
- 52% graduate within 6 years

General. Founded in 1871. Regionally accredited. **Degrees:** 1,839 bachelor's awarded; master's offered. **ROTC:** Army, Air Force. **Location:** 50 miles from Kansas City. **Calendar:** Semester, extensive summer session. **Full-time faculty:** 513 total; 8% have terminal degrees, 11% minority, 46% women. **Part-time faculty:** 201 total; 1% have terminal degrees, 7% minority, 66% women. **Class size:** 46% < 20, 46% 20-39, 4% 40-49, 4% 50-99, less than 1% >100. **Special facilities:** Airport, 260-acre farm, children's literature collection, musical instruments collection, child development lab, advanced technology library.

Freshman class profile. 4,818 applied, 3,828 admitted, 1,658 enrolled.

Mid 50% test scores		Rank in top tenth:	11%
ACT composite:	19-24	Out-of-state:	11%
GPA 3.75 or higher:	26%	Live on campus:	87%
GPA 3.50-3.74:	17%	International:	1%
GPA 3.0-3.49:	30%	Fraternities:	17%
GPA 2.0-2.99:	26%	Sororities:	17%
Rank in top quarter:	33%		

Basis for selection. Applicant must be in top two-thirds of high school class, complete 16-unit core curriculum and have 20 ACT. Essay required for some programs; audition recommended for music students. **Home schooled:** Transcript of courses and grades required. Recommend ACT, GED, or equivalent.

High school preparation. College-preparatory program required. 16 units required. Required units include English 4, mathematics 3, social studies 3, science 2 (laboratory 1), visual/performing arts 1 and academic electives 3. 1 fine/performing arts required.

2015-2016 Annual costs. Tuition/fees: $7,321; $13,767 out-of-state. Room/board: $8,102. Books/supplies: $800. Personal expenses: $2,400.

2014-2015 Financial aid. Need-based: 1,554 full-time freshmen applied for aid; 1,141 deemed to have need; 1,141 received aid. Average need met was 68%. Average scholarship/grant was $4,242. 58% of total undergraduate aid awarded as scholarships/grants, 42% as loans/jobs. **Non-need-based:** Awarded to 6,756 full-time undergraduates, including 1,536 freshmen. Scholarships awarded for academics, alumni affiliation, art, athletics, leadership, minority status, music/drama, religious affiliation, ROTC, state residency.

Application procedures. Admission: Priority date 6/1; no deadline. $30 fee, may be waived for applicants with need. Admission notification on a rolling basis beginning on or about 8/18. Deferred admission is allowed for one semester. **Financial aid:** Priority date 3/1; no closing date. FAFSA, institutional form required. Applicants notified on a rolling basis starting 3/1; must reply within 2 week(s) of notification.

Academics. Online services and resources include library, technical support, writing center and bookstore. Extensive international exchange program. **Special study options:** Accelerated study, combined bachelor's/graduate degree, cooperative education, cross-registration, distance learning, double major, dual enrollment of high school students, ESL, exchange student, honors, independent study, internships, liberal arts/career combination, student-designed major, study abroad, teacher certification program, weekend college. Engineering program with University of Missouri (Columbia, Rolla) and University of Indiana, Missouri University of Science & Technology at Rolla. **Credit/placement by examination:** AP, CLEP, IB, ACT, institutional tests. 15 credit hours maximum toward associate degree, 30 toward bachelor's. **Support services:** Learning center, remedial instruction, study skills assistance, tutoring, writing center.

Honors college/program. 25 ACT required; 319 freshmen admitted; requires 48 credit hours.

Majors. Biology: General. **Business:** Accounting, actuarial science, business admin, finance, hotel/motel admin, human resources, management information systems, marketing, office management, tourism promotion. **Communications:** Broadcast journalism, communications/speech/rhetoric, journalism, public relations. **Communications technology:** Graphic/printing. **Computer sciences:** General, data processing. **Education:** Agricultural, art, biology, business, chemistry, elementary, English, family/consumer sciences, foreign languages, French, German, mathematics, middle, music, physical, physics, science, secondary, social studies, Spanish, special ed, speech, technology/industrial arts. **English:** English lit, rhetoric/composition. **Foreign languages:** French, German, Spanish. **Health services:** Nursing (RN), public health nursing, speech pathology. **History:** General. **Human services:** Social work. **Math:** General. **Parks/recreation:** General, facilities management. **Physical sciences:** Chemistry, geology, physics, planetary. **Protective services:** Law enforcement admin. **Psychology:** General. **Social sciences:** Economics, geography, political science, sociology. **Visual/performing arts:** Art, commercial/advertising art, dramatic, interior design, music, photography, studio arts. **Work/family studies:** General, child development, clothing/textiles, family studies.

Most popular majors. Business/marketing 13%, education 14%, engineering/engineering technologies 9%, health sciences 15%, security/protective services 10%, visual/performing arts 6%.

Technology on campus. 2,826 workstations in dormitories, library, computer center, student center. Dormitories wired for high-speed internet access and linked to campus network. Commuter students can connect to campus network. Online course registration, online library, helpline, student web hosting, wireless network available.

Student life. Freshman orientation: Mandatory. Preregistration for classes offered. One-day sessions in early summer. **Policies:** First year freshmen required to live on campus. **Housing:** Guaranteed on-campus for all undergraduates. Coed dorms, single-sex dorms, special housing for disabled, apartments, fraternity/sorority housing available. $100 nonrefundable deposit, deadline 6/1. Honors hall, economy suites available. **Activities:** Bands, campus ministries, choral groups, dance, drama, film society, international student organizations, literary magazine, music ensembles, Model UN, musical theater, opera, radio station, student government, student newspaper, symphony orchestra, TV station, Association of Black Collegiates, nontraditional student association, student ambassadors, College Republicans, College Democrats, United Students for Equal Access, student government association.

Athletics. NCAA. **Intercollegiate:** Baseball M, basketball, bowling W, cross-country, football (tackle) M, golf M, soccer W, softball W, track and field, volleyball W, wrestling M. **Intramural:** Archery M, badminton M, basketball, bowling, cross-country, diving, football (tackle), golf, racquetball, rifle, rugby M, soccer, softball, swimming, table tennis, tennis, track and field, volleyball, water polo, weight lifting M, wrestling M. **Team name:** Mules (M), Jennies (W).

Student services. Adult student services, alcohol/substance abuse counseling, chaplain/spiritual director, career counseling, student employment services, financial aid counseling, health services, minority student services, on-campus daycare, personal counseling, placement for graduates, veterans' counselor, women's services. **Physically disabled:** Services for visually, speech, hearing impaired.

Contact. E-mail: admit@ucmovmb.ucmo.edu
Phone: (660) 543-4290 Toll-free number: (877) 729-8266
Fax: (660) 543-8517
Ann Nordyke, Chief Admissions Officer, University of Central Missouri, WDE 1400, Warrensburg, MO 64093

University of Missouri: Columbia

Columbia, Missouri	CB member
www.missouri.edu	CB code: 6875

- Public 4-year university
- Residential campus in small city
- 27,393 degree-seeking undergraduates: 5% part-time, 52% women, 8% African American, 2% Asian American, 4% Hispanic/Latino, 3% Multiracial, non-Hispanic, 4% international
- 7,374 degree-seeking graduate students
- 78% of applicants admitted
- SAT or ACT (ACT writing optional) required
- 69% graduate within 6 years

General. Founded in 1839. Regionally accredited. **Degrees:** 5,995 bachelor's awarded; master's, professional, doctoral offered. **ROTC:** Army, Naval, Air Force. **Location:** 125 miles from Kansas City, 125 miles from St. Louis. **Calendar:** Semester, limited summer session. **Full-time faculty:** 1,270 total; 91% have terminal degrees, 21% minority, 40% women. **Part-time faculty:** 107 total; 89% have terminal degrees, 13% minority, 38% women. **Class size:** 46% < 20, 35% 20-39, 4% 40-49, 8% 50-99, 7% >100. **Special facilities:** Life sciences center, observatory, research nuclear reactor, freedom of information center, engineering experiment station, center for research in social behavior, equine center, research farms, child development laboratory, black culture center, state historical society, botanical garden, art and archaeology museum.

Freshman class profile. 21,988 applied, 17,180 admitted, 6,191 enrolled.

Mid 50% test scores		Rank in top tenth:	28%
SAT critical reading:	530-650	Return as sophomores:	87%
SAT math:	530-650	Out-of-state:	37%
ACT composite:	24-29	Live on campus:	87%
Rank in top quarter:	58%	International:	3%

Basis for selection. Required core courses and combination of high school rank and test scores. Individual programs may have additional requirements. Trial summer admission open to Missouri residents. Students must complete math and English with C or better to continue enrollment on probation in fall. ACT recommended. ACT preferred. **Learning Disabled:** Must submit current (within 5 years) official documentation of disability.

High school preparation. College-preparatory program required. 17 units required. Required units include English 4, mathematics 4, social studies 3, science 3 (laboratory 1) and foreign language 2. 1 fine arts required. Math must include algebra I or higher.

Financial aid. Non-need-based: Scholarships awarded for academics, alumni affiliation, art, athletics, leadership, minority status, music/drama, ROTC, state residency. **Additional information:** Scholarship available for international students based on success during 1st semester.

Application procedures. Admission: Priority date 5/1; no deadline. $55 fee, may be waived for applicants with need. Admission notification on a rolling basis beginning on or about 9/1. Must reply by May 1 or within 4 week(s) if notified thereafter. **Financial aid:** Priority date 3/1; no closing date. FAFSA required. Applicants notified on a rolling basis starting 4/1; must reply within 4 week(s) of notification.

Academics. Special study options: Accelerated study, combined bachelor's/graduate degree, cooperative education, cross-registration, distance learning, double major, dual enrollment of high school students, ESL, exchange student, external degree, honors, independent study, internships, New York semester, student-designed major, study abroad, teacher certification program, Washington semester. **Credit/placement by examination:** AP, CLEP, IB, ACT, institutional tests. Credit by examination policy varies by school/college. **Support services:** Learning center, pre-admission summer program, reduced course load, study skills assistance, tutoring, writing center.

Honors college/program. 29 ACT or 1280 SAT and top 10% of high school graduating class required. If school does not rank, 3.71 core GPA necessary. Core GPA includes all English courses, all math courses Algebra I and higher, all science, social studies, and foreign language courses.

Majors. Area/ethnic studies: African-American, East Asian, European, Latin American, South Asian, women's. **Biology:** General, biochemistry, conservation, microbiology. **Business:** General, accounting, banking/financial services, business admin, hotel/motel admin, international, marketing, real estate, restaurant/food services, travel services. **Communications:** Advertising, broadcast journalism, communications/speech/rhetoric, journalism, photojournalism, radio/TV. **Computer sciences:** General, computer science, information technology. **Conservation:** Fisheries, forestry, wildlife/wilderness. **Education:** General, agricultural, art, biology, business, chemistry, early childhood, elementary, English, foreign languages, mathematics, middle, multiple handicapped, music, physics, science, secondary, social studies, Spanish, voc/tech. **Engineering:** Agricultural, biomedical, chemical, civil, computer, electrical, industrial, mechanical. **English:** English lit. **Foreign languages:** Classics, East Asian, French, German, linguistics, Russian, South Asian, Spanish. **Health services:** Audiology/speech pathology, dietetics, health services admin, medical radiologic technology/radiation therapy, nuclear medical technology, nursing (RN), premedicine, prepharmacy, preveterinary, radiologic technology/medical imaging, respiratory therapy technology, sonography. **History:** General. **Human services:** Social work. **Math:** General, statistics. **Parks/recreation:** General, exercise sciences. **Philosophy/religion:** Philosophy, religion. **Physical sciences:** Atmospheric science, chemistry, geology, physics. **Psychology:** General. **Social sciences:** Anthropology, archaeology, economics, geography, political science, sociology. **Visual/performing arts:** Art, dramatic, music. **Work/family studies:** Clothing/textiles, family resources, family studies, food/nutrition, housing, human nutrition.

Most popular majors. Biology 6%, business/marketing 15%, communications/journalism 11%, engineering/engineering technologies 8%, health sciences 14%.

Technology on campus. 1,200 workstations in dormitories, library, computer center, student center. Dormitories wired for high-speed internet access and linked to campus network. Commuter students can connect to campus network. Online course registration, online library, helpline, repair service, student web hosting, wireless network available.

Student life. Freshman orientation: Available. Preregistration for classes offered. Two-day sessions during summer. **Policies:** Alcohol- and smoke-free campus buildings, residence halls. **Housing:** Guaranteed on-campus for freshmen. Coed dorms, single-sex dorms, apartments, fraternity/sorority housing, themed housing, wellness housing available. $300 fully refundable deposit, deadline 4/1. Specialized living/learning communities and freshman interest groups in residence halls available. **Activities:** Bands, campus ministries, choral groups, dance, drama, film society, international student organizations, literary magazine, music ensembles, Model UN, musical theater, opera, radio station, student government, student newspaper, symphony orchestra, TV station, more than 600 organizations available.

Athletics. NCAA. **Intercollegiate:** Baseball M, basketball, cross-country, diving, football (tackle) M, golf, gymnastics W, soccer W, softball W, swimming, tennis W, track and field, volleyball W, wrestling M. **Intramural:** Basketball, football (non-tackle), golf, soccer, softball, volleyball. **Team name:** Tigers.

Student services. Alcohol/substance abuse counseling, chaplain/spiritual director, career counseling, services for economically disadvantaged, student employment services, financial aid counseling, health services, legal services, minority student services, on-campus daycare, personal counseling, placement for graduates, veterans' counselor, women's services. **Physically disabled:** Services for visually, speech, hearing impaired.

Contact. E-mail: mu4u@missouri.edu
Phone: (573) 882-7786 Toll-free number: (800) 225-6075
Fax: (573) 882-7887
Chuck May, Director of Admissions, University of Missouri: Columbia, 230 Jesse Hall, Columbia, MO 65211

University of Missouri: Kansas City

Kansas City, Missouri
www.umkc.edu

CB member
CB code: 6872

- Public 4-year university
- Commuter campus in large city
- 7,977 degree-seeking undergraduates: 19% part-time, 57% women, 15% African American, 7% Asian American, 8% Hispanic/Latino, 5% Multiracial, non-Hispanic, 4% international
- 5,263 degree-seeking graduate students
- 63% of applicants admitted
- SAT or ACT (ACT writing optional) required
- 52% graduate within 6 years

General. Founded in 1929. Regionally accredited. **Degrees:** 1,812 bachelor's awarded; master's, professional, doctoral offered. ROTC: Army. **Location:** 500 miles from Chicago, 250 miles from St. Louis. **Calendar:** Semester, extensive summer session. **Full-time faculty:** 731 total; 76% have terminal degrees, 22% minority, 46% women. **Part-time faculty:** 441 total; 33% have terminal degrees, 12% minority, 48% women. **Class size:** 59% < 20, 32% 20-39, 5% 40-49, 2% 50-99, 2% >100. **Special facilities:** Observatory, science and technology library, music conservatory, miniature toy museum.

Freshman class profile. 4,428 applied, 2,777 admitted, 1,049 enrolled.

Mid 50% test scores			
SAT critical reading:	510-680	Rank in top tenth:	32%
SAT math:	520-710	End year in good standing:	79%
ACT composite:	21-28	Return as sophomores:	73%
GPA 3.75 or higher:	31%	Out-of-state:	24%
GPA 3.50-3.74:	18%	Live on campus:	61%
GPA 3.0-3.49:	27%	International:	5%
GPA 2.0-2.99:	24%	Fraternities:	10%
Rank in top quarter:	57%	Sororities:	12%

Basis for selection. Class rank, test scores, and high school course requirements. Admission is very selective to combined arts and sciences/medical; highly selective to pharmacy program; and selective to Conservatory of Music. Interview required for six-year medicine applicants; audition required for Conservatory of Music and Dance applicants. **Home schooled:** Transcript of courses and grades required. ACT/SAT required.

High school preparation. College-preparatory program required. 17 units required. Required units include English 4, mathematics 4, social studies 3, science 3 (laboratory 1), foreign language 2 and visual/performing arts 1.

2015-2016 Annual costs. Tuition/fees: $9,559; $22,714 out-of-state. Room/board: $9,772. Books/supplies: $1,180. Personal expenses: $4,900.

2015-2016 Financial aid. Need-based: 887 full-time freshmen applied for aid; 692 deemed to have need; 675 received aid. Average need met was 62%. Average scholarship/grant was $8,510; average loan $5,937. 47% of total undergraduate aid awarded as scholarships/grants, 53% as loans/jobs. **Non-need-based:** Awarded to 1,075 full-time undergraduates, including 252 freshmen. Scholarships awarded for academics, alumni affiliation, art, athletics, leadership, minority status, music/drama, state residency. **Additional information:** Many automatic scholarships and non-resident fee waivers available for students who apply for admission by 2/1. Automatic awards range from $1,000 to a complete non-resident fee differential.

Application procedures. Admission: Priority date 4/1; deadline 6/15 (receipt date). $45 fee, may be waived for applicants with need. Admission notification on a rolling basis. Architecture, six-year medicine, conservatory and pharmacy programs have separate application deadlines and specific admissions requirements. **Financial aid:** Priority date 3/1; no closing date. FAFSA required. Applicants notified on a rolling basis starting 4/15; must reply within 2 week(s) of notification.

Academics. Special study options: Accelerated study, combined bachelor's/graduate degree, cooperative education, distance learning, double major, dual enrollment of high school students, ESL, honors, independent study, internships, liberal arts/career combination, student-designed major, study abroad, teacher certification program. **Credit/placement by examination:** AP, CLEP, IB, institutional tests. 30 credit hours maximum toward bachelor's degree. **Support services:** Learning center, reduced course load, study skills assistance, tutoring, writing center.

Majors. Architecture: Architecture, urban/community planning. **Area/ethnic studies:** American. **Biology:** General. **Business:** General, accounting, accounting/business management, accounting/finance, business admin, entrepreneurial studies, finance, market research. **Communications:** Communications/speech/rhetoric. **Computer sciences:** Computer science, information technology. **Conservation:** Environmental science, environmental studies. **Education:** General, art, bilingual, biology, chemistry, early childhood, elementary, English, foreign languages, French, geography, German, history, kindergarten/preschool, middle, music, physics, science, secondary, social science, social studies, Spanish. **Engineering:** Civil, electrical, mechanical. **English:** English lit. **Foreign languages:** French, German, Spanish. **Health services:** Clinical lab science, dental hygiene, ethics, music therapy, nursing (RN), pharmaceutical sciences, predental, premedicine, prenursing, prepharmacy. **History:** General. **Liberal arts:** Arts/sciences. **Math:** General, statistics. **Philosophy/religion:** Philosophy. **Physical sciences:** Chemistry, geology, physics. **Protective services:** Criminal justice, law enforcement admin, police science. **Psychology:** General. **Social sciences:** Criminology, economics, geography, political science, sociology, urban studies. **Visual/performing arts:** Art, art history/conservation, dance, dramatic, jazz, music, music performance, music theory/composition, piano/keyboard, stringed instruments, studio arts, voice/opera.

Most popular majors. Business/marketing 17%, communications/journalism 6%, health sciences 16%, liberal arts 10%, physical sciences 8%, psychology 6%.

Technology on campus. 680 workstations in dormitories, library, computer center, student center. Dormitories wired for high-speed internet access and linked to campus network. Commuter students can connect to campus network. Online course registration, online library, helpline, wireless network available.

Student life. Freshman orientation: Mandatory, $40 fee. Preregistration for classes offered. Several day-long orientations offered in spring and summer. **Housing:** Coed dorms, special housing for disabled, apartments, fraternity/sorority housing available. $300 partly refundable deposit. University owned houses available. **Activities:** Bands, campus ministries, choral groups, dance, drama, international student organizations, literary magazine, music ensembles, Model UN, musical theater, opera, radio station, student government, student newspaper, symphony orchestra, over 300 religious, political, ethnic, and social service organizations.

Athletics. NCAA. **Intercollegiate:** Basketball, cheerleading, cross-country, golf, soccer, softball W, tennis, track and field, volleyball W. **Intramural:** Badminton, basketball, football (tackle), handball, racquetball, soccer, softball, tennis, ultimate frisbee, volleyball. **Team name:** Kangaroos.

Student services. Adult student services, alcohol/substance abuse counseling, career counseling, student employment services, financial aid counseling, health services, minority student services, on-campus daycare, personal counseling, placement for graduates, veterans' counselor, women's services. **Physically disabled:** Services for visually, speech, hearing impaired.

Contact. E-mail: admit@umkc.edu
Phone: (816) 235-1111 Toll-free number: (800) 775-8652
Fax: (816) 235-5544
Tamara Byland, Director of Admissions, University of Missouri: Kansas City, 5100 Rockhill Road, AC120, Kansas City, MO 64110-2499

University of Missouri: St. Louis

St. Louis, Missouri	CB member
www.umsl.edu	CB code: 6889

- Public 4-year university
- Commuter campus in very large city
- 8,276 degree-seeking undergraduates: 33% part-time, 57% women, 19% African American, 5% Asian American, 3% Hispanic/Latino, 3% Multiracial, non-Hispanic, 3% international
- 3,077 degree-seeking graduate students
- 76% of applicants admitted
- SAT or ACT (ACT writing optional) required
- 41% graduate within 6 years; 32% enter graduate study

General. Founded in 1963. Regionally accredited. **Degrees:** 2,246 bachelor's awarded; master's, professional, doctoral offered. **ROTC:** Army, Air

Force. **Location:** 10 miles from downtown. **Calendar:** Semester, extensive summer session. **Full-time faculty:** 467 total; 74% have terminal degrees, 21% minority, 51% women. **Part-time faculty:** 492 total; 31% have terminal degrees, 17% minority, 60% women. **Class size:** 51% < 20, 35% 20-39, 8% 40-49, 5% 50-99, 1% >100. **Special facilities:** Galleries, observatory, on-campus pre-school, nonprofit management/leadership program, women in public life institute, centers for nanoscience, neurodynamics, emerging technologies, entrepreneurship and economic education, French, German, Greek cultural centers.

Freshman class profile. 1,770 applied, 1,343 admitted, 516 enrolled.

Mid 50% test scores			
SAT critical reading:	390-490	GPA 2.0-2.99:	15%
SAT math:	460-570	Rank in top quarter:	61%
SAT writing:	400-490	Rank in top tenth:	29%
ACT composite:	21-27	End year in good standing:	83%
GPA 3.75 or higher:	29%	Return as sophomores:	75%
GPA 3.50-3.74:	26%	Out-of-state:	20%
GPA 3.0-3.49:	30%	Live on campus:	53%
		International:	8%

Basis for selection. Class rank, test scores and high school course requirements most important. Audition required for music majors; not required for admission but for the purpose of placement with instrument. **Home schooled:** ACT is key factor in determining admission. Students should strive for score of 24 or higher.

High school preparation. College-preparatory program required. 17 units required. Required units include English 4, mathematics 4, social studies 3, science 3 (laboratory 1) and foreign language 2. 1 fine art required.

2015-2016 Annual costs. Tuition/fees: $10,065; $25,512 out-of-state. Room/board: $9,052. Books/supplies: $1,000. Personal expenses: $3,382.

2015-2016 Financial aid. Need-based: 429 full-time freshmen applied for aid; 366 deemed to have need; 363 received aid. Average need met was 79%. Average scholarship/grant was $11,204; average loan $3,285. 43% of total undergraduate aid awarded as scholarships/grants, 57% as loans/jobs. **Non-need-based:** Awarded to 847 full-time undergraduates, including 153 freshmen. Scholarships awarded for academics, alumni affiliation, art, athletics, music/drama, ROTC, state residency.

Application procedures. Admission: Closing date 9/15 (receipt date). $35 fee, may be waived for applicants with need. Admission notification on a rolling basis beginning on or about 9/1. **Financial aid:** Priority date 3/1; no closing date. FAFSA required. Applicants notified on a rolling basis starting 4/1; must reply within 2 week(s) of notification.

Academics. Special study options: Accelerated study, combined bachelor's/graduate degree, cooperative education, cross-registration, distance learning, double major, dual enrollment of high school students, ESL, exchange student, external degree, honors, independent study, internships, liberal arts/career combination, semester at sea, student-designed major, study abroad, teacher certification program. Engineering UMSL/WU, 2+3 B.S./M.A. Program in Economics, 2+3 B.A./B.S.-Ed and M.A. Program in History, 2+3 B.A./M.A. Program in Philosophy, 2+3 B.A./M.A. Program in Political Science, 2+3 B.A. in Psychology and M.S. in Gerontology Program, 2+3 B.A./M.A. Program in Sociology, Biology 3+4 Program for UMSL College of Optometry, Physics and Astronomy 3+4 Program for UMSL College of Optometry; Accounting Program for UMSL. Liberal Studies programs in the following: Biology 3+3 Program for Logan Chiropractic College, Kansas City University of Medicine and Biosciences 3+4, Kent State College of Podiatric Medicine 3+4, University of Missouri College of Veterinary Medicine 3+4, Washington University Program in Occupation Therapy 3+2, Physical Therapy. **Credit/placement by examination:** AP, CLEP, IB, SAT, ACT, institutional tests. 36 credit hours maximum toward bachelor's degree. **Support services:** Learning center, reduced course load, study skills assistance, tutoring, writing center. Student retention services, academic alert, multicultural relations, disability services.

Honors college/program. Selection based on scores, class rank, extracurricular activities, test scores, 2 recommendations, essay, interview with Dean. Approximately 50 freshmen admitted each fall. Academic program includes honors classes.

Majors. Biology: General, biochemistry. **Business:** General, accounting, business admin, finance, international, logistics, management information systems, marketing, operations, organizational behavior. **Communications:** Communications/speech/rhetoric, media studies. **Computer sciences:** Computer science. **Education:** General, art, early childhood, elementary, music, physical, secondary, special ed. **Engineering:** Civil, electrical, mechanical. **English:** English lit. **Foreign languages:** General, French, German, Spanish. **Health services:** Nursing (RN). **History:** General. **Human services:** General, social work. **Liberal arts:** Arts/sciences. **Math:** General. **Philosophy/religion:** Philosophy. **Physical sciences:** Chemistry, physics. **Psychology:** General. **Social sciences:** Anthropology, criminology, economics, political science, sociology. **Visual/performing arts:** Art, art history/conservation, dramatic, music, music history, studio arts.

Most popular majors. Business/marketing 23%, communications/journalism 7%, education 9%, health sciences 13%, psychology 7%, social sciences 11%.

Technology on campus. 1,300 workstations in dormitories, library, computer center, student center. Dormitories wired for high-speed internet access and linked to campus network. Commuter students can connect to campus network. Online course registration, online library, helpline, student web hosting, wireless network available.

Student life. Freshman orientation: Mandatory, $65 fee. Preregistration for classes offered. One-day program held several times throughout summer. Spring session offered in January. **Housing:** Guaranteed on-campus for all undergraduates. Coed dorms, special housing for disabled, apartments, fraternity/sorority housing, themed housing, wellness housing available. Pets allowed in dorm rooms. Apartments available for students over 21, and graduate/professional school housing available. **Activities:** Bands, campus ministries, choral groups, dance, drama, film society, international student organizations, literary magazine, music ensembles, Model UN, musical theater, opera, radio station, student government, student newspaper, TV station, Associated Black Collegians, Minority Student Nurses Association, HISLA, Jewish student association, Catholic Newman Center, Chi Alpha Christian Fellowship, Muslim student association, Pan-African student association, Alpha Phi Omega, Japan America students association.

Athletics. NCAA. **Intercollegiate:** Baseball M, basketball, golf, soccer, softball W, swimming, tennis, volleyball W. **Intramural:** Basketball, bowling, football (non-tackle), golf, racquetball, soccer, softball, table tennis, tennis, ultimate frisbee, volleyball, weight lifting. **Team name:** Tritons.

Student services. Adult student services, alcohol/substance abuse counseling, career counseling, student employment services, financial aid counseling, health services, minority student services, on-campus daycare, personal counseling, placement for graduates, veterans' counselor, women's services. **Physically disabled:** Services for visually, speech, hearing impaired.

Contact. E-mail: admissions@umsl.edu
Phone: (314) 516-5451 Toll-free number: (888) 462-8675
Fax: (314) 516-5310
Andrew Griffin, Director of Admissions, University of Missouri: St. Louis, One University Boulevard, St. Louis, MO 63121-4400

University of Phoenix: Kansas City
Kansas City, Missouri
www.phoenix.edu

⬧ For-profit 4-year university
⬧ Large city
⬧ 660 degree-seeking undergraduates

General. Regionally accredited. **Degrees:** 55 bachelor's awarded; master's offered. **Calendar:** Differs by program. **Full-time faculty:** 14 total. **Part-time faculty:** 121 total.

Basis for selection. Open admission.

2015-2016 Annual costs. Per-credit-hour charge $410 to $635, depending upon level and course of study; electronic course materials fee $95 and no more than $200, if applicable. Book and material charges may vary by course and program. All fees are subject to change.

Application procedures. Admission: No deadline. No application fee. **Financial aid:** No deadline.

Academics. Credit/placement by examination: AP, CLEP.

Majors. Business: Accounting/business management, business admin, e-commerce, entrepreneurial studies, finance, human resources, marketing, operations. **Communications:** General. **Computer sciences:** Programming, security, system admin, systems analysis, web page design, webmaster. **Education:** Elementary. **Health services:** Facilities admin, health information management, long term care admin. **Human services:** General. **Protective services:** Disaster management, law enforcement admin, security management.

Student life. Freshman orientation: Mandatory. Preregistration for classes offered.

Contact. Toll-free number: (866) 766-0766
University of Phoenix: Kansas City, 1625 W. Fountainhead Parkway, Tempe, AZ 85282

University of Phoenix: St. Louis
St. Louis, Missouri
www.phoenix.edu

⬧ For-profit 4-year university
⬧ Commuter campus in large city
⬧ 700 degree-seeking undergraduates
⬧ 30 graduate students

General. Regionally accredited. **Degrees:** 210 bachelor's awarded; master's offered. **Calendar:** Differs by program. Other Academic Calendar. **Full-time faculty:** 9 total. **Part-time faculty:** 116 total.

Basis for selection. Open admission.

2015-2016 Annual costs. Per-credit-hour charge $225 to $635, depending upon level and course of study; electronic course materials fee $95 but not more than $200, if applicable. Book and material charges may vary by course and program. All fees are subject to change.

Application procedures. Admission: No deadline. No application fee. **Financial aid:** No deadline.

Academics. Credit/placement by examination: AP, CLEP.

Majors. Business: Accounting, accounting/business management, business admin, e-commerce, entrepreneurial studies, finance, human resources, marketing, operations. **Communications:** General. **Computer sciences:** Programming, security, system admin, systems analysis, web page design, webmaster. **Conservation:** Environmental studies. **Education:** Elementary. **English:** English lit. **Health services:** Facilities admin, health information management, long term care admin, nursing (RN). **Human services:** General. **Protective services:** Disaster management, law enforcement admin, security management.

Student life. Freshman orientation: Mandatory. Preregistration for classes offered.

Student services. Career counseling.

Contact. Toll-free number: (866) 766-0766
University of Phoenix: St. Louis, 13801 Riverport Drive, St. Louis, MO 63043-4828

Washington University in St. Louis
St. Louis, Missouri   CB member
www.wustl.edu   CB code: 6929

⬧ Private 4-year university
⬧ Residential campus in large city
⬧ 7,032 degree-seeking undergraduates: 4% part-time, 52% women, 6% African American, 19% Asian American, 7% Hispanic/Latino, 4% Multiracial, non-Hispanic, 8% international
⬧ 7,051 degree-seeking graduate students
⬧ 17% of applicants admitted
⬧ SAT or ACT (ACT writing optional), application essay required
⬧ 92% graduate within 6 years

General. Founded in 1853. Regionally accredited. **Degrees:** 1,631 bachelor's, 3 associate awarded; master's, professional, doctoral offered. **ROTC:** Army, Air Force. **Location:** 7 miles from downtown St. Louis. **Calendar:** Semester, extensive summer session. **Full-time faculty:** 915 total; 94% have terminal degrees, 23% minority, 38% women. **Part-time faculty:** 362 total; 16% minority, 43% women. **Class size:** 63% < 20, 20% 20-39, 7% 40-49, 7% 50-99, 3% >100. **Special facilities:** Research center, 59-acre medical campus, observatory, plant growth facility, international writer's center, planetarium, business/economics experimental laboratory, laboratory science building, outdoor research center, theater, gallery of art.

Freshman class profile. 29,259 applied, 4,898 admitted, 1,731 enrolled.

Mid 50% test scores		Return as sophomores:	96%
SAT critical reading:	690-760	Out-of-state:	92%
SAT math:	710-790	Live on campus:	100%
SAT writing:	690-770	International:	7%
ACT composite:	32-34	Fraternities:	30%
Rank in top quarter:	100%	Sororities:	30%
Rank in top tenth:	89%		

Basis for selection. Rigor of high school curriculum and academic performance, GPA, test scores, extracurricular activities, essay, recommendations very important. Counselor and teacher recommendations required of all applicants. IELTS or TOEFL scores are required for students whose first language is not English. Portfolios required for students applying to College of Art. Portfolios strongly encouraged for students applying to College of Architecture. **Home schooled:** Letter of recommendation (nonparent) required. Recommendation should be from someone in the community who can give information on the student's background.

High school preparation. College-preparatory program recommended. 20 units recommended. Recommended units include English 4, mathematics 4, social studies 4, history 4, science 4 (laboratory 4) and foreign language 2.

2016-2017 Annual costs. Tuition/fees: $49,770. Room/board: $15,596. Books/supplies: $980. Personal expenses: $2,132.

2015-2016 Financial aid. Need-based: 865 full-time freshmen applied for aid; 685 deemed to have need; 678 received aid. Average need met was 100%. Average scholarship/grant was $40,752; average loan $4,926. 89% of total undergraduate aid awarded as scholarships/grants, 11% as loans/jobs. **Non-need-based:** Awarded to 871 full-time undergraduates, including 257 freshmen. Scholarships awarded for academics, art, leadership, ROTC. **Additional information:** Scholarship funds increased and a program offered to eliminate need-based loans to families of students with incomes of $75,000 or less.

Application procedures. Admission: Closing date 1/15. $75 fee, may be waived for applicants with need. Admission notification by 4/1. Must reply by 5/1. **Financial aid:** Closing date 2/1. FAFSA, institutional form, CSS PROFILE required. Applicants notified by 4/1; must reply by 5/1.

Academics. Special study options: Accelerated study, combined bachelor's/graduate degree, cooperative education, cross-registration, double major, dual enrollment of high school students, ESL, independent study, internships, liberal arts/career combination, student-designed major, study abroad, teacher certification program. University Scholars Program gives selected students the opportunity to be admitted to undergraduate study and the School of Medicine at the same time. **Credit/placement by examination:** AP, CLEP, IB, institutional tests. **Support services:** Learning center, pre-admission summer program, reduced course load, study skills assistance, tutoring, writing center.

Majors. Architecture: Architecture, technology. **Area/ethnic studies:** African-American, American, Asian, East Asian, European, German, Latin American, Near/Middle Eastern, Russian/Eastern European/Eurasian, women's. **Biology:** General, biochemistry, biophysics, ecology, environmental, neuroscience. **Business:** General, accounting, business admin, entrepreneurial studies, finance, human resources, international, international finance, managerial economics, marketing. **Communications:** Advertising, journalism. **Computer sciences:** General, computer science, data processing. **Conservation:** Environmental science, environmental studies, management/policy. **Education:** General, art, biology, chemistry, drama/dance, elementary, English, French, German, history, mathematics, middle, physics, science, secondary, social science, social studies, Spanish. **Engineering:** Biomedical, chemical, computer, electrical, mechanical, systems. **English:** American lit, British lit, creative writing, English lit, general lit. **Foreign languages:** General, ancient Greek, Arabic, Chinese, classics, comparative lit, French, German, Germanic, Hebrew, Italian, Japanese, Latin, linguistics, Romance, Spanish. **Health services:** Health care admin, predental, premedicine, prepharmacy, preveterinary. **History:** General. **Liberal arts:** Arts/sciences, humanities. **Math:** General, applied, statistics. **Philosophy/religion:** Islamic, Judaic, philosophy, religion. **Physical sciences:** Chemistry, geochemistry, geology, geophysics, physics, planetary. **Psychology:** General, industrial. **Social sciences:** General, anthropology, archaeology, economics, international relations, medical anthropology, political science, urban studies. **Visual/performing arts:** General, art, art history/conservation, ceramics, commercial/advertising art, dance, design, dramatic, drawing, fashion design, film/cinema/video, graphic design, illustration, music, music history, music theory/composition, painting, photography, printmaking, sculpture, studio arts, theater history, voice/opera.

Most popular majors. Biology 11%, business/marketing 13%, engineering/engineering technologies 19%, interdisciplinary studies 7%, psychology 6%, social sciences 14%, visual/performing arts 6%.

Technology on campus. 2,500 workstations in dormitories, library, computer center, student center. Dormitories wired for high-speed internet access and linked to campus network. Commuter students can connect to campus network. Online course registration, online library, helpline, repair service, student web hosting, wireless network available.

Student life. Freshman orientation: Mandatory. Preregistration for classes offered. **Housing:** Guaranteed on-campus for freshmen. Coed dorms, apartments, cooperative housing, fraternity/sorority housing, wellness housing available. $250 deposit, deadline 5/1. Special-interest suites, upper-class housing, and small-group housing for students who share common interests

and goals. **Activities:** Bands, campus ministries, choral groups, dance, drama, film society, international student organizations, literary magazine, music ensembles, Model UN, musical theater, opera, radio station, student government, student newspaper, symphony orchestra, TV station, approximately 350 social clubs and organizations available.

Athletics. NCAA. **Intercollegiate:** Baseball M, basketball, cross-country, diving, football (tackle) M, golf W, soccer, softball W, swimming, tennis, track and field, volleyball W. **Intramural:** Badminton, basketball, bowling, cross-country, football (non-tackle), golf, racquetball, soccer, softball, swimming, table tennis, tennis, track and field, ultimate frisbee, volleyball, water polo. **Team name:** Bears.

Student services. Adult student services, alcohol/substance abuse counseling, chaplain/spiritual director, career counseling, services for economically disadvantaged, student employment services, financial aid counseling, health services, minority student services, on-campus daycare, personal counseling, placement for graduates, veterans' counselor, women's services. **Physically disabled:** Services for visually, speech, hearing impaired.

Contact. E-mail: admissions@wustl.edu
Phone: (314) 935-6000 Toll-free number: (800) 638-0700
Fax: (314) 935-4290
Julie Shimabukuro, Director of Admissions, Washington University in St. Louis, Campus Box 1089, One Brookings Drive, St. Louis, MO 63130-4899

Webster University
St. Louis, Missouri   **CB member**
www.webster.edu   **CB code: 6933**

- Private 4-year university
- Residential campus in very large city
- 2,721 degree-seeking undergraduates: 15% part-time, 55% women, 13% African American, 2% Asian American, 5% Hispanic/Latino, 3% Multiracial, non-Hispanic, 5% international
- 1,641 degree-seeking graduate students
- 56% of applicants admitted
- SAT or ACT (ACT writing optional), application essay required
- 62% graduate within 6 years

General. Founded in 1915. Regionally accredited. Additional programs offered at five St. Louis area campuses. Undergraduate degrees offered at extended campus locations in Missouri, California, Colorado, Florida, South Carolina, Texas, and international campuses in Vienna, Austria; Leiden, The Netherlands; Geneva, Switzerland; Cha-am, Thailand; Athens, Greece; Accra, Ghana; as well as online. **Degrees:** 802 bachelor's awarded; master's, doctoral offered. **ROTC:** Army, Air Force. **Location:** 6 miles from St. Louis. **Calendar:** Semester, limited summer session. **Full-time faculty:** 200 total; 78% have terminal degrees, 16% minority, 48% women. **Part-time faculty:** 626 total; 33% have terminal degrees, 13% minority, 46% women. **Class size:** 87% < 20, 13% 20-39, less than 1% 40-49. **Special facilities:** Repertory theater, opera theater, community music school.

Freshman class profile. 1,994 applied, 1,119 admitted, 419 enrolled.

Mid 50% test scores		Rank in top tenth:	20%
ACT composite:	21-27	End year in good standing:	92%
GPA 3.75 or higher:	36%	Return as sophomores:	78%
GPA 3.50-3.74:	14%	Out-of-state:	36%
GPA 3.0-3.49:	30%	Live on campus:	67%
GPA 2.0-2.99:	20%	International:	2%
Rank in top quarter:	47%	Sororities:	5%

Basis for selection. Moderately selective admission based on overall academic record. Applicants most likely to be admitted will have 3.0 GPA, rank in top half of class and 21 ACT/1000 SAT (exclusive of Writing). Audition required for dance, music, music theater, and theater students; portfolio required for art and film students. **Home schooled:** Transcript of courses and grades required.

High school preparation. College-preparatory program recommended. 19 units recommended. Recommended units include English 4, mathematics 3, social studies 3, science 3 (laboratory 2), foreign language 2, visual/performing arts 1 and academic electives 3.

2015-2016 Annual costs. Tuition/fees: $25,500. Room/board: $10,860. Books/supplies: $1,000. Personal expenses: $1,200.

2015-2016 Financial aid. Need-based: 375 full-time freshmen applied for aid; 298 deemed to have need; 295 received aid. Average need met was 69%. Average scholarship/grant was $10,586; average loan $3,564. 64% of total undergraduate aid awarded as scholarships/grants, 36% as loans/jobs.

Non-need-based: Awarded to 1,825 full-time undergraduates, including 320 freshmen. Scholarships awarded for academics, art, leadership, music/drama, state residency.

Application procedures. Admission: Priority date 3/1; deadline 8/1 (postmark date). $35 fee, may be waived for applicants with need. Admission notification on a rolling basis beginning on or about 9/1. Must reply by May 1 or within 4 week(s) if notified thereafter. **Financial aid:** Priority date 4/1; no closing date. FAFSA, institutional form required. Applicants notified on a rolling basis starting 2/1; must reply within 2 week(s) of notification.

Academics. Special study options: Combined bachelor's/graduate degree, cooperative education, cross-registration, distance learning, double major, ESL, independent study, internships, liberal arts/career combination, student-designed major, study abroad, teacher certification program. Certificate programs and combination bachelor's/master's degree in many subject areas, student leadership development program, individualized majors. **Credit/placement by examination:** AP, CLEP, IB. 64 credit hours maximum toward bachelor's degree. **Support services:** Learning center, reduced course load, study skills assistance, tutoring, writing center. Institution's Transitions program offers support and resources to conditionally admitted freshmen and students who have 30 credit hours or fewer of college coursework completed at the time of their admission.

Majors. Area/ethnic studies: European, women's. **Biology:** General. **Business:** Accounting, accounting/finance, business admin, finance, human resources, marketing. **Communications:** Advertising, communications/speech/rhetoric, digital media, journalism, media studies, public relations. **Communications technology:** Animation/special effects. **Computer sciences:** General, computer science, information systems. **Education:** General, early childhood, elementary, middle, music, science, secondary, special ed. **English:** English lit. **Foreign languages:** General, French, German, Spanish. **Health services:** Nursing (RN). **History:** General. **Liberal arts:** Humanities. **Math:** General. **Parks/recreation:** Exercise sciences. **Philosophy/religion:** Ethics, philosophy, religion. **Psychology:** General. **Social sciences:** Cultural anthropology, economics, international relations, political science, sociology. **Visual/performing arts:** Acting, art, cinematography, costume design, dance, directing/producing, dramatic, film/cinema/video, jazz, music, music performance, music theory/composition, musical theater, photography.

Most popular majors. Business/marketing 21%, communications/journalism 15%, communication technologies 6%, computer/information sciences 6%, social sciences 6%, visual/performing arts 18%.

Technology on campus. 714 workstations in dormitories, library, computer center, student center. Dormitories wired for high-speed internet access and linked to campus network. Commuter students can connect to campus network. Online course registration, online library, helpline, repair service, student web hosting, wireless network available.

Student life. Freshman orientation: Mandatory, $125 fee. Preregistration for classes offered. Held the 4 days before classes begin; includes events for both students and parents. **Housing:** Coed dorms, special housing for disabled, apartments, themed housing available. $175 partly refundable deposit, deadline 4/1. **Activities:** Jazz band, campus ministries, choral groups, dance, drama, film society, international student organizations, literary magazine, music ensembles, musical theater, opera, radio station, student government, student newspaper, symphony orchestra, TV station, Amnesty International, Catholic Student Union, Cru, Encounter, Muslim Student Association, Society of International Languages & Cultures, Initiative for Land Development Gardeners, LGBTQ Alliance, Students for Environmental Sustainability, Japanese Student Association.

Athletics. NCAA. **Intercollegiate:** Baseball M, basketball, cross-country, golf M, soccer, softball W, tennis, track and field, volleyball W. **Intramural:** Basketball, bowling, football (non-tackle), volleyball. **Team name:** Gorloks.

Student services. Alcohol/substance abuse counseling, career counseling, student employment services, financial aid counseling, health services, minority student services, personal counseling, placement for graduates, veterans' counselor, women's services. **Physically disabled:** Services for visually, speech, hearing impaired.

Contact. E-mail: admit@webster.edu
Phone: (314) 246-7800 Toll-free number: (800) 753-6765
Fax: (314) 246-7116
James Myers, Assoc. VP Undergraduate Admission & Financial Aid, Webster University, 470 East Lockwood Avenue, St. Louis, MO 63119-3194

Westminster College
Fulton, Missouri
www.westminster-mo.edu

CB member
CB code: 6937

- Private 4-year liberal arts college affiliated with the Presbyterian Church (USA)
- Residential campus in large town

- 930 degree-seeking undergraduates: 1% part-time, 43% women, 9% African American, 3% Hispanic/Latino, 2% Native American, 1% Native Hawaiian/Pacific islander, 1% Multi-racial, non-Hispanic, 15% international
- 64% of applicants admitted
- SAT or ACT (ACT writing optional) required
- 66% graduate within 6 years

General. Founded in 1851. Regionally accredited. **Degrees:** 205 bachelor's awarded. **ROTC:** Army, Air Force. **Location:** 100 miles from St. Louis, 24 miles from Columbia. **Calendar:** Semester, limited summer session. **Full-time faculty:** 61 total; 88% have terminal degrees, 7% minority, 41% women. **Part-time faculty:** 35 total; 29% have terminal degrees, 6% minority, 57% women. **Class size:** 68% < 20, 32% 20-39. **Special facilities:** National Winston Churchill Museum and Library.

Freshman class profile. 1,789 applied, 1,139 admitted, 239 enrolled.

Mid 50% test scores			
SAT critical reading:	430-540	GPA 2.0-2.99:	22%
SAT math:	530-620	Rank in top quarter:	40%
SAT writing:	440-520	Rank in top tenth:	21%
ACT composite:	21-28	Out-of-state:	19%
GPA 3.75 or higher:	29%	Live on campus:	97%
GPA 3.50-3.74:	17%	International:	18%
GPA 3.0-3.49:	31%	Fraternities:	60%
		Sororities:	24%

Basis for selection. High school achievement (including class rank, involvement, ACT, curriculum, GPA) and recommendations most important. Interview recommended for borderline students. **Learning Disabled:** Learning Disabilities Program applicants must have completed application credentials and personal interview prior to 4/1, including untimed SAT/ACT results.

High school preparation. College-preparatory program recommended. 16 units required. Required and recommended units include English 4, mathematics 3, social studies 2, science 2 (laboratory 2), foreign language 2 and academic electives 2. Pre-med and pre-dental students should have at least 3 lab science, 1 advanced math.

2015-2016 Annual costs. Tuition/fees: $23,480. Room/board: $9,340. Books/supplies: $1,100. Personal expenses: $1,670.

2015-2016 Financial aid. Need-based: 184 full-time freshmen applied for aid; 157 deemed to have need; 157 received aid. Average need met was 92%. Average scholarship/grant was $18,524; average loan $3,087. 85% of total undergraduate aid awarded as scholarships/grants, 15% as loans/jobs. **Non-need-based:** Awarded to 314 full-time undergraduates, including 80 freshmen. Scholarships awarded for academics, alumni affiliation, leadership, minority status, music/drama.

Application procedures. Admission: Priority date 2/1; no deadline. No application fee. Admission notification on a rolling basis beginning on or about 10/1. Must reply by May 1 or within 3 week(s) if notified thereafter. **Financial aid:** Priority date 2/15; no closing date. FAFSA required. Applicants notified on a rolling basis starting 3/15.

Academics. Special study options: Combined bachelor's/graduate degree, cooperative education, cross-registration, distance learning, double major, dual enrollment of high school students, ESL, exchange student, honors, independent study, internships, liberal arts/career combination, New York semester, semester at sea, student-designed major, study abroad, teacher certification program, urban semester, Washington semester. **Credit/placement by examination:** AP, CLEP, IB, institutional tests. 30 credit hours maximum toward bachelor's degree. **Support services:** Learning center, reduced course load, remedial instruction, study skills assistance, tutoring, writing center.

Honors college/program. Selection based on the total student record. Application essay required; leadership skills, potential, and academic and professional goals considered. Strongest candidates will have 3.5 GPA. Provides highly specialized curriculum.

Majors. Biology: General, biochemistry. **Business:** Accounting, business admin, management information systems. **Communications:** Advertising, journalism, media studies. **Computer sciences:** General. **Conservation:** Environmental science, environmental studies. **Education:** Elementary, middle, physical, secondary. **English:** English lit. **Foreign languages:** French, Spanish. **History:** General. **Math:** General. **Parks/recreation:** Exercise sciences, sports admin. **Philosophy/religion:** Philosophy, religion. **Physical sciences:** Chemistry, physics. **Psychology:** General. **Social sciences:** Anthropology, economics, international relations, political science, sociology.

Most popular majors. Biology 11%, business/marketing 26%, education 10%, foreign language 7%, parks/recreation 7%, social sciences 9%.

Technology on campus. 200 workstations in library, computer center. Dormitories wired for high-speed internet access and linked to campus network. Commuter students can connect to campus network. Online course registration, online library, helpline, student web hosting, wireless network available.

Student life. Freshman orientation: Mandatory. Preregistration for classes offered. Held three days before classes start. **Housing:** Guaranteed on-campus for freshmen. Coed dorms, single-sex dorms, apartments, fraternity/sorority housing, themed housing available. **Activities:** Bands, campus ministries, choral groups, dance, drama, international student organizations, literary magazine, music ensembles, Model UN, student government, student newspaper, Young Democrats, Young Republicans, Big Brother-Big Sister program, Environmentally Concerned Students, Chapel Leadership Council, Habitat For Humanity, Fellowship of Christian Athletes.

Athletics. NCAA. **Intercollegiate:** Baseball M, basketball, cheerleading W, cross-country, football (tackle) M, golf, soccer, softball W, tennis, track and field, volleyball W. **Intramural:** Basketball, football (non-tackle), soccer, softball, volleyball. **Team name:** Blue Jays.

Student services. Alcohol/substance abuse counseling, chaplain/spiritual director, career counseling, student employment services, financial aid counseling, health services, minority student services, personal counseling, placement for graduates, veterans' counselor, women's services. **Physically disabled:** Services for visually, speech, hearing impaired.

Contact. E-mail: admissions@westminster-mo.edu
Phone: (573) 592-5251 Toll-free number: (800) 475-3361
Fax: (573) 592-5255
Robert Andrews, Vice President and Dean of Enrollment Services, Westminster College, 501 Westminster Avenue, Fulton, MO 65251-1299

William Jewell College

Liberty, Missouri
www.jewell.edu

CB member
CB code: 6941

▶ Private 4-year liberal arts college
▶ Residential campus in large town
▶ 1,053 degree-seeking undergraduates: 3% part-time, 58% women, 4% African American, 1% Asian American, 4% Hispanic/Latino, 6% Multiracial, non-Hispanic, 5% international
▶ 10 degree-seeking graduate students
▶ 54% of applicants admitted
▶ 62% graduate within 6 years; 26% enter graduate study

General. Founded in 1849. Regionally accredited. Campus in Harlaxton, England. **Degrees:** 258 bachelor's awarded; master's offered. **ROTC:** Army. **Location:** 14 miles from downtown Kansas City. **Calendar:** Semester, limited summer session. **Full-time faculty:** 80 total; 81% have terminal degrees, 2% minority, 46% women. **Part-time faculty:** 63 total; 14% have terminal degrees, 57% women. **Class size:** 73% < 20, 26% 20-39, 1% 40-49, less than 1% 50-99. **Special facilities:** Idea exchange, center for leadership development, observatory, flow cytometer, high and low ropes course, outdoor environmental learning lab, greenhouse, Quimby pipe organ.

Freshman class profile. 1,333 applied, 719 admitted, 245 enrolled.

Mid 50% test scores			
SAT critical reading:	500-640	Rank in top tenth:	30%
SAT math:	490-620	End year in good standing:	87%
ACT composite:	23-28	Return as sophomores:	82%
GPA 3.75 or higher:	55%	Out-of-state:	44%
GPA 3.50-3.74:	18%	Live on campus:	98%
GPA 3.0-3.49:	23%	International:	4%
GPA 2.0-2.99:	4%	Fraternities:	39%
Rank in top quarter:	59%	Sororities:	42%

Basis for selection. Secondary school record. Class rank, standardized test scores, and essay also important. SAT or ACT recommended. Test optional consideration for students with a core GPA of 3.0 or higher. Audition or portfolio required for scholarship seeking music, theater, or art students. **Home schooled:** Transcript of courses and grades, letter of recommendation (nonparent) required. High school transcript provided by a diploma-granting organization or completion of the Transcript Form by the person primarily responsible for student's educational experience. Official transcripts must be submitted from any two- or four-year colleges where a student has been enrolled in courses, even if credit was not awarded. Official standardized test score reports (ACT and/or SAT) required. One academic recommendation to be completed by a teacher or professor who can attest to the applicant's academic abilities. A separate page addressing questions specified by the institution.

High school preparation. College-preparatory program required. 15 units required; 19 recommended. Required and recommended units include English 4, mathematics 3-4, social studies 3, science 3 (laboratory 1), foreign language 2-3 and academic electives 2.

2016-2017 Annual costs. Tuition/fees (projected): $32,930. Room/board: $9,280. Books/supplies: $800. Personal expenses: $1,980.

2015-2016 Financial aid. Need-based: 217 full-time freshmen applied for aid; 181 deemed to have need; 181 received aid. Average need met was 80%. Average scholarship/grant was $22,452; average loan $4,166. 69% of total undergraduate aid awarded as scholarships/grants, 31% as loans/jobs. **Non-need-based:** Awarded to 1,091 full-time undergraduates, including 237 freshmen. Scholarships awarded for academics, alumni affiliation, athletics, music/drama.

Application procedures. Admission: No application fee. Admission notification on a rolling basis beginning on or about 7/1. Must reply by May 1 or within 2 week(s) if notified thereafter. **Financial aid:** Priority date 3/1; no closing date. FAFSA required. Applicants notified on a rolling basis starting 3/1; must reply within 2 week(s) of notification.

Academics. Interdisciplinary core curriculum required. **Special study options:** Accelerated study, combined bachelor's/graduate degree, distance learning, double major, honors, independent study, internships, liberal arts/career combination, semester at sea, student-designed major, study abroad, teacher certification program, Washington semester. Pryor Leadership Studies. **Credit/placement by examination:** AP, CLEP, IB, SAT, ACT, institutional tests. No limit to credit by examination, but student must complete a minimum of 30 hours in residence. **Support services:** Study skills assistance, tutoring, writing center.

Honors college/program. 3.8 GPA, 28 ACT required for admission. 30-35 enrolled in the Oxbridge Honors Program.

Majors. Biology: General, biochemistry, molecular. **Business:** Accounting, business admin, nonprofit/public. **Communications:** Communications/speech/rhetoric. **Computer sciences:** Web page design. **Education:** Elementary, music, secondary, speech. **Engineering:** Civil. **English:** English lit. **Foreign languages:** French, Romance, Spanish. **Health services:** Nursing (RN). **History:** General. **Liberal arts:** Arts/sciences. **Math:** General. **Parks/recreation:** General. **Philosophy/religion:** Philosophy, religion. **Physical sciences:** Chemistry, physics. **Psychology:** General. **Social sciences:** Economics, international relations, political science. **Theology:** Sacred music. **Visual/performing arts:** Art, dramatic, music, music performance, music theory/composition.

Most popular majors. Business/marketing 19%, education 7%, health sciences 33%, psychology 10%, social sciences 7%.

Technology on campus. PC or laptop required. 220 workstations in library, computer center, student center. Dormitories wired for high-speed internet access and linked to campus network. Commuter students can connect to campus network. Online course registration, online library, helpline, student web hosting, wireless network available.

Student life. Freshman orientation: Mandatory. Preregistration for classes offered. Four-day program prior to first day of classes. **Policies:** Honor code, alcohol education requirement for all entering students, 4-year campus residency requirement, annual Title IX training in effect. **Housing:** Guaranteed on-campus for all undergraduates. Coed dorms, single-sex dorms, special housing for disabled, fraternity/sorority housing, wellness housing available. $300 fully refundable deposit, deadline 5/1. First-year, upper class, fraternity/sorority housing available. **Activities:** Bands, campus ministries, choral groups, dance, drama, international student organizations, literary magazine, music ensembles, musical theater, opera, student government, student newspaper, symphony orchestra, Black Student Association, Christian Student Ministries, Independent Student Association, Inter-fraternity Council, International Student Association, Nonprofit Leadership Association, Panhellenic Council, residence hall councils, student senate, WJC Catholic Fellowship.

Athletics. NCAA. **Intercollegiate:** Baseball M, basketball, cheerleading, cross-country, football (tackle) M, golf, soccer, softball W, swimming, tennis, track and field, volleyball W. **Intramural:** Basketball, bowling, football (non-tackle), golf, sand volleyball, soccer, softball, table tennis, tennis, volleyball. **Team name:** Cardinals.

Student services. Alcohol/substance abuse counseling, chaplain/spiritual director, career counseling, student employment services, financial aid counseling, health services, minority student services, personal counseling, placement for graduates. **Physically disabled:** Services for visually, speech, hearing impaired.

Contact. E-mail: admission@william.jewell.edu
Phone: (816) 415-7511 Toll-free number: (888) 253-9355
Fax: (816) 415-5040
Cory Scheer, Dean of Admission, William Jewell College, 500 College Hill, Liberty, MO 64068

William Woods University
Fulton, Missouri
www.williamwoods.edu   CB code: 6944

- Private 4-year university and teachers college affiliated with the Christian Church (Disciples of Christ)
- Residential campus in large town
- 962 degree-seeking undergraduates: 13% part-time, 75% women, 4% African American, 2% Hispanic/Latino, 2% Multi-racial, non-Hispanic, 1% international
- 1,134 degree-seeking graduate students
- 93% of applicants admitted
- SAT or ACT (ACT writing recommended) required
- 51% graduate within 6 years

General. Founded in 1870. Regionally accredited. Students may enroll in courses offered at 4 other mid-Missouri colleges and universities. **Degrees:** 212 bachelor's, 7 associate awarded; master's, doctoral offered. **ROTC:** Army. **Location:** 100 miles from St. Louis, 30 miles from Columbia. **Calendar:** Semester, limited summer session. **Full-time faculty:** 70 total; 50% have terminal degrees, 6% minority, 47% women. **Part-time faculty:** 180 total; 42% have terminal degrees, 2% minority, 38% women. **Class size:** 78% < 20, 22% 20-39. **Special facilities:** Equestrian studies facilities, ASL interpreting laboratories.

Freshman class profile. 682 applied, 636 admitted, 184 enrolled.

Mid 50% test scores			
SAT critical reading:	430-540	Rank in top tenth:	38%
SAT math:	450-520	End year in good standing:	89%
ACT composite:	19-26	Return as sophomores:	75%
GPA 3.75 or higher:	34%	Out-of-state:	31%
GPA 3.50-3.74:	16%	Live on campus:	96%
GPA 3.0-3.49:	29%	International:	1%
GPA 2.0-2.99:	21%	Fraternities:	43%
Rank in top quarter:	57%	Sororities:	58%

Basis for selection. Secondary school record, class rank, and standardized test scores most important.

High school preparation. College-preparatory program recommended. 16 units required; 20 recommended. Required and recommended units include English 4, mathematics 3, social studies 2, history 3, science 3 (laboratory 3) and foreign language 2.

2015-2016 Annual costs. Tuition/fees: $22,160. Room/board: $8,960. Books/supplies: $1,200. Personal expenses: $3,000.

2014-2015 Financial aid. Need-based: 127 full-time freshmen applied for aid; 104 deemed to have need; 104 received aid. Average need met was 70%. Average scholarship/grant was $14,008; average loan $4,205. 61% of total undergraduate aid awarded as scholarships/grants, 39% as loans/jobs. **Non-need-based:** Awarded to 309 full-time undergraduates, including 74 freshmen. Scholarships awarded for academics, alumni affiliation, art, athletics, leadership, music/drama, religious affiliation.

Application procedures. Admission: Priority date 3/1; no deadline. No application fee. Application must be submitted online. Admission notification on a rolling basis. Must reply by May 1 or within 2 week(s) if notified thereafter. **Financial aid:** Priority date 3/1; no closing date. FAFSA required. Applicants notified on a rolling basis starting 3/15; must reply within 2 week(s) of notification.

Academics. Special study options: Accelerated study, combined bachelor's/graduate degree, cross-registration, distance learning, double major, dual enrollment of high school students, ESL, honors, independent study, internships, liberal arts/career combination, study abroad, teacher certification program. **Credit/placement by examination:** AP, CLEP, IB, SAT, ACT, institutional tests. 30 credit hours maximum toward bachelor's degree. **Support services:** Pre-admission summer program, reduced course load, remedial instruction, study skills assistance, tutoring, writing center. ASL interpreting available.

Majors. Biology: General. **Business:** Accounting, business admin, international, management information systems, managerial economics. **Communications:** Communications/speech/rhetoric. **Education:** General, art, elementary, English, mathematics, middle, physical, science, secondary, social science, special ed. **English:** English lit, writing. **Foreign languages:** American Sign Language, Spanish. **Health services:** Athletic training. **History:** General. **Human services:** Social work. **Math:** General. **Parks/recreation:** Sports admin. **Physical sciences:** General. **Psychology:** General. **Social sciences:** Political science. **Visual/performing arts:** Art, design, dramatic, graphic design, studio arts.

Most popular majors. Agriculture 16%, business/marketing 25%, education 13%, foreign language 13%, parks/recreation 9%.

Technology on campus. 152 workstations in dormitories, library, computer center, student center. Dormitories wired for high-speed internet access and linked to campus network. Commuter students can connect to campus network. Online course registration, online library, helpline, repair service, wireless network available.

Student life. Freshman orientation: Mandatory. Preregistration for classes offered. Five-day session held in the fall, 1-day session held in the spring prior to the start of classes. **Policies:** All residence halls non-smoking. Students under 23 must reside on campus unless married or living with parent or guardian; lottery offered in spring to students who wish to move off campus the following fall semester. **Housing:** Guaranteed on-campus for freshmen. Coed dorms, single-sex dorms, special housing for disabled, apartments, fraternity/sorority housing available. $250 fully refundable deposit, deadline 8/15. Single rooms available. **Activities:** Pep band, campus ministries, choral groups, drama, film society, literary magazine, musical theater, radio station, student government, Campus Crusade for Christ, Students of Social Work, Active Minds, International Justice Mission, Kindness Connection, Multicultural Affairs.

Athletics. NAIA. **Intercollegiate:** Baseball M, basketball, cheerleading W, cross-country, golf, soccer, softball W, tennis, track and field, volleyball W. **Intramural:** Basketball, equestrian. **Team name:** Owls.

Student services. Adult student services, chaplain/spiritual director, career counseling, student employment services, financial aid counseling, health services, minority student services, personal counseling. **Physically disabled:** Services for visually, speech, hearing impaired.

Contact. E-mail: admissions@williamwoods.edu
Phone: (573) 592-4221 Toll-free number: (800) 995-3159
Fax: (573) 592-1146
Kathy Groves, Vice President of Enrollment and Marketing, William Woods University, One University Avenue, Fulton, MO 65251-2388

Montana

Carroll College

Helena, Montana
www.carroll.edu

CB member
CB code: 4041

- Private 4-year liberal arts college affiliated with the Roman Catholic Church
- Residential campus in large town
- 1,428 degree-seeking undergraduates: 2% part-time, 58% women, 1% African American, 2% Asian American, 5% Hispanic/Latino, 1% Native American, 2% Multi-racial, non-Hispanic, 1% international
- 64% of applicants admitted
- SAT or ACT (ACT writing recommended) required
- 63% graduate within 6 years

General. Founded in 1909. Regionally accredited. **Degrees:** 276 bachelor's, 1 associate awarded. **ROTC:** Army. **Location:** 90 miles from Great Falls, 240 miles from Billings. **Calendar:** Semester, limited summer session. **Full-time faculty:** 88 total; 3% minority, 44% women. **Part-time faculty:** 76 total; 1% minority, 53% women. **Class size:** 65% < 20, 32% 20-39, 2% 40-49, less than 1% 50-99, less than 1% >100. **Special facilities:** Observatory, seismograph station, engineering lab, nursing lab including SimMan and Sim-Baby.

Freshman class profile. 3,513 applied, 2,252 admitted, 387 enrolled.

Mid 50% test scores			
SAT critical reading:	480-600	Rank in top quarter:	60%
SAT math:	490-600	Rank in top tenth:	23%
SAT writing:	460-590	Return as sophomores:	79%
ACT composite:	22-27	Out-of-state:	61%
GPA 3.75 or higher:	38%	Live on campus:	96%
GPA 3.50-3.74:	26%	International:	2%
GPA 3.0-3.49:	27%		
GPA 2.0-2.99:	9%		

Basis for selection. School achievement record, test scores, recommendations most important. SAT and SAT Subject Tests required of home schooled and nonaccredited high school graduates. Personal statement required. Interview recommended for academically weak students.

High school preparation. College-preparatory program recommended. Recommended units include English 4, mathematics 3, social studies 2, history 2, science 2 (laboratory 1), visual/performing arts 1 and academic electives 2. 1 technology recommended.

2015-2016 Annual costs. Tuition/fees: $30,754. Room/board: $9,218.

2014-2015 Financial aid. Need-based: 271 full-time freshmen applied for aid; 218 deemed to have need; 218 received aid. Average need met was 79%. Average scholarship/grant was $16,371; average loan $3,237. 77% of total undergraduate aid awarded as scholarships/grants, 23% as loans/jobs. **Non-need-based:** Awarded to 823 full-time undergraduates, including 203 freshmen. Scholarships awarded for academics, art, athletics, leadership, minority status, music/drama, religious affiliation, ROTC.

Application procedures. Admission: Priority date 2/15; deadline 5/1 (receipt date). $35 fee, may be waived for applicants with need, free for online applicants. Admission notification on a rolling basis beginning on or about 12/1. Must reply by May 1 or within 3 week(s) if notified thereafter. Housing deposit fully refundable prior to May 1; partially refundable prior to June 1. **Financial aid:** Priority date 3/1; no closing date. FAFSA required. Applicants notified on a rolling basis starting 3/1; must reply by 5/1 or within 2 week(s) of notification.

Academics. Special study options: Cooperative education, double major, dual enrollment of high school students, honors, independent study, internships, liberal arts/career combination, student-designed major, study abroad, teacher certification program. 3-2 engineering program with Notre Dame, Columbia University, USC, Gonzaga University, Montana State University-Bozeman, Montana Tech Butte. **Credit/placement by examination:** AP, CLEP, IB, SAT, ACT, institutional tests. 9 credit hours maximum toward associate degree, 18 toward bachelor's. **Support services:** Learning center, pre-admission summer program, reduced course load, study skills assistance, tutoring, writing center.

Majors. Biology: General. **Business:** Accounting, business admin. **Communications:** Communications/speech/rhetoric, public relations. **Computer sciences:** Computer science. **Conservation:** Environmental studies. **Education:** Biology, chemistry, elementary, English, ESL, history, mathematics, physical, social science, social studies, Spanish, speech. **Engineering:** Civil. **English:** English lit, writing. **Foreign languages:** Classics, French, Spanish. **Health services:** Community health services, nursing (RN). **History:** General. **Human services:** General. **Math:** General, applied. **Parks/recreation:** Sports admin. **Philosophy/religion:** Ethics, philosophy. **Physical sciences:** Chemistry. **Psychology:** General. **Social sciences:** International relations, political science, sociology. **Theology:** Theology. **Visual/performing arts:** General.

Most popular majors. Biology 13%, business/marketing 10%, communications/journalism 7%, education 6%, English 18%, health sciences 22%.

Technology on campus. 85 workstations in dormitories, library, computer center, student center. Dormitories wired for high-speed internet access and linked to campus network. Commuter students can connect to campus network. Online course registration, helpline, wireless network available.

Student life. Freshman orientation: Mandatory, $100 fee. Preregistration for classes offered. Four-day program. Fee includes cost of meals, entertainment, and various activities. **Policies:** Freshmen and sophomores required to live on campus. **Housing:** Guaranteed on-campus for freshmen. Coed dorms, special housing for disabled, apartments available. $200 partly refundable deposit, deadline 5/1. **Activities:** Bands, campus ministries, choral groups, dance, drama, film society, international student organizations, literary magazine, music ensembles, musical theater, radio station, student government, student newspaper, TV station, College Democrats, Circle K, cultural exchange club, Into the Streets service organization, peer mentors, social work club, sociology club, student community outreach experience, Young Republicans.

Athletics. NAIA. **Intercollegiate:** Basketball, cross-country, football (tackle) M, golf, soccer, softball W, swimming, volleyball W. **Intramural:** Badminton, basketball, bowling, cross-country, golf, handball, racquetball, skiing, soccer, softball M, swimming, table tennis, volleyball, water polo. **Team name:** Saints.

Student services. Adult student services, alcohol/substance abuse counseling, chaplain/spiritual director, career counseling, student employment services, financial aid counseling, health services, personal counseling, placement for graduates, veterans' counselor.

Contact. E-mail: admission@carroll.edu
Phone: (406) 447-4384 Toll-free number: (800) 992-3648
Fax: (406) 447-4533
Cynthia Thornquist, Director of Admissions and Enrollment, Carroll College, 1601 North Benton Avenue, Helena, MT 59625

Montana Bible College

Bozeman, Montana
www.montanabiblecollege.edu

CB code: 5955

- Private 4-year Bible college
- Residential campus in large town
- 84 degree-seeking undergraduates: 27% part-time, 48% women, 1% African American, 1% Hispanic/Latino, 1% international
- 100% of applicants admitted
- Application essay required
- 50% graduate within 6 years

General. Regionally accredited; also accredited by ABHE. **Degrees:** 11 bachelor's awarded. **Calendar:** Semester. **Full-time faculty:** 6 total; 17% have terminal degrees, 17% women. **Part-time faculty:** 13 total; 38% have terminal degrees, 15% women. **Class size:** 78% < 20, 22% 20-39.

Freshman class profile. 22 applied, 22 admitted, 19 enrolled.

Mid 50% test scores			
SAT critical reading:	630-700	Return as sophomores:	91%
SAT math:	470-490	Out-of-state:	43%
SAT writing:	510-550	Live on campus:	86%

Basis for selection. Applicants must have a standard diploma from an accredited high school (or its equivalent) or a GED. Those with no prior college experience must also provide a copy of their SAT or ACT test scores, and students transferring college credits must provide an official college transcript. The MBC admissions committee meets to ensure these qualifications are met and that applicants are compatible to our mission statement. **Home schooled:** Transcript of courses and grades required.

2016-2017 Annual costs. Tuition/fees: $7,540. Room only: $2,800. Books/supplies: $300.

Application procedures. Admission: Priority date 6/15; no deadline. $50 fee. Admission notification on a rolling basis.

Academics. Credit/placement by examination: AP, CLEP. 15 credit hours maximum toward bachelor's degree. **Support services:** Study skills assistance.

Majors. Theology: Missionary, pastoral counseling.

Technology on campus. 8 workstations in library. Dormitories wired for high-speed internet access. Commuter students can connect to campus network. Online course registration, wireless network available.

Student life. Housing: Guaranteed on-campus for freshmen. Single-sex dorms, apartments available. $200 fully refundable deposit. **Activities:** Choral groups.

Student services. Chaplain/spiritual director.

Contact. Phone: (406) 586-3585
Susan Jackson, Director of Admissions, Montana Bible College, 3625 South 19th Avenue, Bozeman, MT 59718

Montana State University

Bozeman, Montana   **CB member**
www.montana.edu   **CB code: 4488**

- Public 4-year university
- Residential campus in large town
- 13,527 degree-seeking undergraduates: 15% part-time, 45% women, 1% African American, 1% Asian American, 4% Hispanic/Latino, 2% Native American, 3% Multi-racial, non-Hispanic, 3% international
- 1,660 degree-seeking graduate students
- 83% of applicants admitted
- SAT or ACT (ACT writing recommended) required
- 52% graduate within 6 years

General. Founded in 1893. Regionally accredited. **Degrees:** 2,239 bachelor's, 57 associate awarded; master's, professional, doctoral offered. **ROTC:** Army, Air Force. **Location:** 139 miles from Billings; 90 miles from Yellowstone National Park. **Calendar:** Semester, limited summer session. **Full-time faculty:** 581 total; 82% have terminal degrees, 6% minority, 42% women. **Part-time faculty:** 403 total; 18% have terminal degrees, 6% minority, 57% women. **Class size:** 43% < 20, 33% 20-39, 11% 40-49, 8% 50-99, 6% >100. **Special facilities:** Animal bioscience facility, architecture fabrication laboratory, agricultural teach and research farm, center for undergraduate excellence, center for biofilm engineering (multidisciplinary), child development center, imaging and chemical analysis laboratory, mass spectrometry facility, microfabrication facility, music technology studios, movement science/human performance lab, multimedia language resource center, Museum of the Rockies, nursing simulation laboratory with 3G mannequin, nutrition lab, plant bio-containment facility, plant growth center, space science engineering lab, spectrum lab, subzero science and engineering research facility, math learning center, writing center, Western Transportation Institute.

Freshman class profile. 14,780 applied, 12,256 admitted, 3,015 enrolled.

Mid 50% test scores			
SAT critical reading:	510-630	Rank in top quarter:	42%
SAT math:	510-640	Rank in top tenth:	18%
ACT composite:	21-28	Return as sophomores:	77%
GPA 3.75 or higher:	29%	Out-of-state:	48%
GPA 3.50-3.74:	18%	Live on campus:	76%
GPA 3.0-3.49:	30%	International:	2%
GPA 2.0-2.99:	22%	Fraternities:	4%
		Sororities:	3%

Basis for selection. Interviews recommended. Students may use SAT/ACT math scores for placement or take departmental exam. Students with 27 ACT English or 640 SAT verbal can waive freshman composition. **Home schooled:** GED required.

High school preparation. College-preparatory program required. 14 units required. Required units include English 4, mathematics 3, social studies 3, science 2 (laboratory 2). 2 units.

2015-2016 Annual costs. Tuition/fees: $6,968; $21,961 out-of-state. Room/board: $8,650. Books/supplies: $1,250. Personal expenses: $2,040.

2014-2015 Financial aid. Need-based: 1,732 full-time freshmen applied for aid; 1,192 deemed to have need; 1,155 received aid. Average need met

was 91%. Average scholarship/grant was $5,192; average loan $3,829. 41% of total undergraduate aid awarded as scholarships/grants, 59% as loans/jobs. **Non-need-based:** Awarded to 552 full-time undergraduates, including 113 freshmen. Scholarships awarded for academics, alumni affiliation, art, athletics, job skills, leadership, minority status, music/drama, ROTC, state residency. **Additional information:** Tuition waiver for honorably discharged veterans, children of members of the United States armed forces who, at the time of entry into service, had legal residence in Montana and who were killed in action or who died as a result of injury, disease, or other disability incurred while in the service.

Application procedures. Admission: No deadline. $30 fee. Admission notification on a rolling basis. **Financial aid:** Priority date 3/1; no closing date. FAFSA required. Applicants notified on a rolling basis starting 4/1; must reply within 3 week(s) of notification.

Academics. Special study options: Combined bachelor's/graduate degree, cooperative education, cross-registration, distance learning, double major, dual enrollment of high school students, ESL, exchange student, honors, independent study, internships, student-designed major, study abroad, teacher certification program. Combined bachelor's/master's programs in environmental design/architecture and construction engineering technology/construction engineering management. **Credit/placement by examination:** AP, CLEP, IB, SAT, ACT, institutional tests. No more than 30 semester credits earned by correspondence, extension, or continuing education count toward bachelor's degree. **Support services:** Learning center, remedial instruction, study skills assistance, tutoring, writing center.

Majors. Architecture: Environmental design. **Biology:** General, bacteriology, biotechnology, cell/histology. **Business:** General, marketing. **Computer sciences:** Computer science. **Conservation:** General, environmental science, land use planning, wildlife/wilderness. **Education:** Agricultural, elementary, music, science. **Engineering:** Chemical, civil, computer, electrical, industrial, mechanical. **English:** English lit. **Foreign languages:** General. **Health services:** Nursing (RN), premedicine, preveterinary. **History:** General. **Liberal arts:** Arts/sciences. **Math:** General. **Philosophy/religion:** Philosophy, religion. **Physical sciences:** Chemistry, geology, physics. **Psychology:** General. **Social sciences:** Anthropology, economics, political science, sociology. **Visual/performing arts:** Art, cinematography, music, music technology. **Work/family studies:** General.

Most popular majors. Biology 7%, business/marketing 10%, engineering/engineering technologies 21%, family/consumer sciences 9%, health sciences 10%, social sciences 6%.

Technology on campus. 1,200 workstations in dormitories, library, computer center. Dormitories wired for high-speed internet access and linked to campus network. Commuter students can connect to campus network. Online course registration, online library, helpline, student web hosting, wireless network available.

Student life. Freshman orientation: Mandatory, $65 fee. Preregistration for classes offered. **Housing:** Guaranteed on-campus for freshmen. Coed dorms, single-sex dorms, special housing for disabled, apartments, fraternity/sorority housing, themed housing, wellness housing available. $200 nonrefundable deposit. Non-traditional age housing. **Activities:** Bands, campus ministries, choral groups, dance, drama, film society, international student organizations, literary magazine, music ensembles, Model UN, musical theater, opera, radio station, student government, student newspaper, symphony orchestra, TV station, several clubs and organizations.

Athletics. NCAA. **Intercollegiate:** Basketball, cheerleading, cross-country, football (tackle) M, golf W, rodeo, skiing, tennis, track and field, volleyball W. **Intramural:** Archery, badminton, basketball, bowling, cross-country, golf, gymnastics, handball, racquetball, rodeo, skiing, soccer, softball, swimming, table tennis, tennis, track and field, volleyball, water polo, weight lifting, wrestling M. **Team name:** Bobcats.

Student services. Adult student services, alcohol/substance abuse counseling, chaplain/spiritual director, career counseling, student employment services, financial aid counseling, health services, legal services, minority student services, on-campus daycare, personal counseling, placement for graduates, veterans' counselor, women's services. **Physically disabled:** Services for visually, speech, hearing impaired.

Contact. E-mail: admissions@montana.edu
Phone: (406) 994-2452 Toll-free number: (888) 678-2287
Fax: (406) 994-7360
Ronda Russell, Director of Admissions, Montana State University, PO Box 172190, Bozeman, MT 59717-2190

Montana State University: Billings

Billings, Montana

www.msubillings.edu

CB member
CB code: 4298

- Public 4-year university and technical college
- Commuter campus in small city
- 3,744 degree-seeking undergraduates: 29% part-time, 62% women, 1% African American, 1% Asian American, 5% Hispanic/Latino, 4% Native American, 3% Multi-racial, non-Hispanic, 3% international
- 313 degree-seeking graduate students
- 100% of applicants admitted

General. Founded in 1927. Regionally accredited. Montana State University Billings Downtown located in downtown Billings. **Degrees:** 582 bachelor's, 344 associate awarded; master's offered. **ROTC:** Army. **Location:** 224 miles from Helena, 560 miles from Denver. **Calendar:** Semester, limited summer session. **Full-time faculty:** 174 total; 59% have terminal degrees, 7% minority, 44% women. **Part-time faculty:** 151 total; 22% have terminal degrees, 5% minority, 60% women. **Class size:** 53% < 20, 39% 20-39, 5% 40-49, 4% 50-99. **Special facilities:** Biological station, center for business enterprise, Montana Center for Disabilities, special education learning center, center for gerontological studies, small business institute, urban institute, public radio, center for applied economic research.

Freshman class profile. 1,470 applied, 1,463 admitted, 689 enrolled.

Mid 50% test scores			
SAT critical reading:	420-540	Rank in top quarter:	31%
SAT math:	440-560	Rank in top tenth:	8%
ACT composite:	18-24	Return as sophomores:	53%
GPA 3.75 or higher:	16%	Out-of-state:	9%
GPA 3.50-3.74:	17%	Live on campus:	33%
GPA 3.0-3.49:	31%	International:	1%
GPA 2.0-2.99:	31%		

Basis for selection. Applicants must meet one of the following: 2.5 GPA, 22 ACT/1030 SAT (exclusive of Writing), or rank in upper half of graduating class. ACT or SAT required of students less than 3 years out of high school. **Home schooled:** Applicants may be admitted based on GED, ACT, or COMPASS scores.

High school preparation. College-preparatory program recommended. 14 units required. Required units include English 4, mathematics 3, social studies 3, science 2 (laboratory 2). 2 years foreign language, computer science, visual and performing arts, or vocational education also recommended.

2015-2016 Annual costs. Tuition/fees: $5,802; $17,712 out-of-state. Room/board: $7,214. Books/supplies: $1,460. Personal expenses: $2,130.

2014-2015 Financial aid. Need-based: 567 full-time freshmen applied for aid; 446 deemed to have need; 443 received aid. Average need met was 68%. Average scholarship/grant was $4,599; average loan $4,997. 42% of total undergraduate aid awarded as scholarships/grants, 58% as loans/jobs. **Non-need-based:** Awarded to 376 full-time undergraduates, including 125 freshmen. Scholarships awarded for academics, alumni affiliation, art, athletics, job skills, leadership, minority status, music/drama, ROTC, state residency. **Additional information:** Veterans and honors fee waivers offered.

Application procedures. Admission: Priority date 3/1; no deadline. $30 fee. Admission notification by 9/1. Admission notification on a rolling basis. **Financial aid:** Priority date 3/1; no closing date. FAFSA required. Applicants notified on a rolling basis starting 3/1; must reply within 3 week(s) of notification.

Academics. Full degree programs and many courses designed for working professionals. **Special study options:** Accelerated study, cooperative education, cross-registration, distance learning, double major, dual enrollment of high school students, ESL, external degree, honors, independent study, internships, liberal arts/career combination, student-designed major, study abroad, teacher certification program, weekend college. Evening College, with extensive online programs and courses. City College offers training and retraining for employment by combining academics and vocational opportunities. **Credit/placement by examination:** AP, CLEP, SAT, ACT, institutional tests. **Support services:** Learning center, reduced course load, remedial instruction, study skills assistance, tutoring, writing center.

Majors. Biology: General, microbiology. **Business:** General. **Communications:** Communications/speech/rhetoric, media studies, public relations. **Conservation:** Environmental studies. **Education:** General, art, biology, chemistry, curriculum, elementary, English, foreign languages, health, history, mathematics, music, physical, physics, science, secondary, social science, social studies, Spanish, special ed. **English:** English lit. **Foreign languages:** Spanish. **Health services:** Athletic training, health care admin, vocational rehab counseling. **History:** General. **Liberal arts:** Arts/sciences. **Math:** General.

Parks/recreation: Health/fitness, sports admin. **Physical sciences:** Chemistry. **Protective services:** Criminal justice. **Psychology:** General. **Social sciences:** Political science, sociology. **Visual/performing arts:** Art, dramatic, music, music performance.

Most popular majors. Business/marketing 28%, education 24%, liberal arts 8%, psychology 7%.

Technology on campus. 1,700 workstations in dormitories, library, computer center, student center. Dormitories wired for high-speed internet access and linked to campus network. Commuter students can connect to campus network. Online course registration, online library, helpline, student web hosting, wireless network available.

Student life. Freshman orientation: Mandatory, $75 fee. Preregistration for classes offered. Two-day orientation sessions held throughout summer. **Housing:** Coed dorms, special housing for disabled, apartments available. $150 partly refundable deposit. **Activities:** Bands, campus ministries, choral groups, drama, international student organizations, literary magazine, music ensembles, musical theater, radio station, student government, student newspaper, symphony orchestra, more than 50 student groups available.

Athletics. NCAA. **Intercollegiate:** Baseball M, basketball, cheerleading, cross-country, golf, soccer, softball W, tennis, track and field, volleyball W. **Intramural:** Archery, basketball, cross-country, golf, racquetball, skiing, softball, swimming, table tennis, tennis, volleyball. **Team name:** Yellowjackets.

Student services. Adult student services, alcohol/substance abuse counseling, chaplain/spiritual director, career counseling, services for economically disadvantaged, student employment services, financial aid counseling, health services, legal services, minority student services, on-campus daycare, personal counseling, placement for graduates, veterans' counselor. **Physically disabled:** Services for visually, speech, hearing impaired.

Contact. E-mail: cjohannes@msubillings.edu
Phone: (406) 657-2158 Toll-free number: (800) 656-6782
Fax: (406) 657-2051
Tammi Watson, Director of New Student Services, Montana State University: Billings, 1500 University Drive, Billings, MT 59101-0298

Montana State University: Northern

Havre, Montana

www.msun.edu

CB code: 4538

- Public 4-year university
- Residential campus in large town
- 1,218 undergraduates
- 116 graduate students
- SAT or ACT (ACT writing recommended) required

General. Founded in 1929. Regionally accredited. Extended campuses in Great Falls and Lewistown. **Degrees:** 166 bachelor's, 96 associate awarded; master's offered. **Location:** 115 miles from Great Falls. **Calendar:** Semester, extensive summer session. **Full-time faculty:** 62 total; 36% have terminal degrees, 2% minority, 34% women. **Part-time faculty:** 34 total; 6% minority, 50% women. **Class size:** 70% < 20, 27% 20-39, 1% 40-49, 1% 50-99.

Freshman class profile.

GPA 3.75 or higher:	6%	Rank in top quarter:	14%
GPA 3.50-3.74:	11%	Rank in top tenth:	4%
GPA 3.0-3.49:	23%	Out-of-state:	91%
GPA 2.0-2.99:	50%	Live on campus:	32%

Basis for selection. Bachelor degree-seeking admission requirements ONLY: 2.5 GPA or upper half of class, in conjunction with college preparatory program. Writing and math proficiency as scored on basis of ACT and/or writing assessment.

High school preparation. College-preparatory program required. 14 units required. Required units include English 4, mathematics 3, social studies 3, science 2 (laboratory 2) and academic electives 2.

2015-2016 Annual costs. Tuition/fees: $4,871; $16,841 out-of-state. Room/board: $6,525. **Additional information:** Out-of-state students pay an additional $106 in fees.

Financial aid. Non-need-based: Scholarships awarded for academics, athletics.

Application procedures. Admission: No deadline. $30 fee, may be waived for applicants with need. Admission notification on a rolling basis. **Financial aid:** Priority date 4/15; no closing date. FAFSA, institutional form required. Applicants notified on a rolling basis starting 5/1; must reply within 4 week(s) of notification.

Academics. Special study options: Combined bachelor's/graduate degree, cooperative education, distance learning, double major, dual enrollment of high school students, independent study, internships, liberal arts/career combination, study abroad, teacher certification program. **Credit/placement by examination:** AP, CLEP, IB, SAT, ACT, institutional tests. **Support services:** Learning center, pre-admission summer program, reduced course load, remedial instruction, study skills assistance, tutoring.

Majors. Biology: General. **Business:** Business admin. **Computer sciences:** Information systems. **Education:** Elementary, mathematics, physical, science, secondary, social science, technology/industrial arts. **English:** English lit. **Foreign languages:** French. **Health services:** Nursing (RN). **Human services:** Community org/advocacy. **Math:** General. **Physical sciences:** Chemistry. **Visual/performing arts:** Commercial/advertising art, graphic design, studio arts.

Most popular majors. Business/marketing 19%, education 22%, engineering/engineering technologies 8%, health sciences 16%, trade and industry 15%.

Technology on campus. 250 workstations in dormitories, library, computer center, student center. Dormitories wired for high-speed internet access and linked to campus network. Commuter students can connect to campus network. Online course registration, online library, helpline, repair service, wireless network available.

Student life. Freshman orientation: Mandatory, $40 fee. Preregistration for classes offered. **Housing:** Guaranteed on-campus for all undergraduates. Coed dorms, single-sex dorms, apartments available. $75 fully refundable deposit, deadline 9/1. Limited housing available for nontraditional students. **Activities:** Pep band, radio station, student government, student newspaper, Inter-Christian fellowship, Sweetgrass Society, community involvement association, Mental Mafia, residence hall association, SkillsUSA, student education association.

Athletics. NAIA. **Intercollegiate:** Basketball, football (tackle) M, golf W, rodeo, volleyball W, wrestling M. **Intramural:** Badminton, basketball, bowling, cheerleading, football (non-tackle), racquetball, rodeo, soccer, softball, table tennis, tennis, ultimate frisbee, volleyball. **Team name:** Lights, Skylights.

Student services. Adult student services, alcohol/substance abuse counseling, career counseling, services for economically disadvantaged, student employment services, financial aid counseling, health services, minority student services, personal counseling, placement for graduates, veterans' counselor. **Physically disabled:** Services for visually, speech, hearing impaired.

Contact. E-mail: admissions@msun.edu
Phone: (406) 265-3704 Toll-free number: (800) 662-6132 ext. 3704
Fax: (406) 265-3792
Director of Admissions, Montana State University: Northern, Box 7751, Havre, MT 59501-7751

Montana Tech of the University of Montana
Butte, Montana
www.mtech.edu   **CB code: 4487**

- Public 4-year engineering and technical college
- Commuter campus in large town
- 2,447 degree-seeking undergraduates: 9% part-time, 36% women, 1% African American, 1% Asian American, 2% Hispanic/Latino, 2% Native American, 11% international
- 205 degree-seeking graduate students
- 88% of applicants admitted
- SAT or ACT (ACT writing recommended) required

General. Founded in 1893. Regionally accredited. **Degrees:** 294 bachelor's, 111 associate awarded; master's, doctoral offered. **Location:** 82 miles from Bozeman, 65 miles from Helena. **Calendar:** Semester, extensive summer session. **Full-time faculty:** 138 total; 60% have terminal degrees, 10% minority, 36% women. **Part-time faculty:** 78 total; 5% minority, 45% women. **Class size:** 62% < 20, 21% 20-39, 7% 40-49, 9% 50-99, less than 1% >100. **Special facilities:** Mineral museum, earthquake studies office, underground mining laboratory.

Freshman class profile. 969 applied, 857 admitted, 425 enrolled.

Mid 50% test scores			
SAT critical reading:	520-600	GPA 2.0-2.99:	10%
SAT math:	530-640	Rank in top quarter:	56%
SAT writing:	460-550	Rank in top tenth:	23%
ACT composite:	23-27	Return as sophomores:	76%
GPA 3.75 or higher:	39%	Out-of-state:	16%
GPA 3.50-3.74:	25%	Live on campus:	50%
GPA 3.0-3.49:	26%	International:	5%

Basis for selection. Rank in top half of graduating class, or graduate with minimum cumulative GPA of 2.5, or achieve minimum composite score on ACT of 22, or minimum total score on SAT of 1540; meet math and English standards, and complete preparatory requirements. **Home schooled:** Students can satisfy the requirement of high school graduation by obtaining a high school equivalency diploma based on the GED. examination, or satisfactory performance on either the ACT or COMPASS examinations. Home schooled students must also submit a transcript summarizing their academic history.

High school preparation. College-preparatory program required. Required and recommended units include English 4, mathematics 3-4, social studies 3, science 2 (laboratory 2) and academic electives 2. Combined 2 years of foreign language, visual and performing arts, computer science, or vocational education required.

2015-2016 Annual costs. Tuition/fees: $6,539; $19,571 out-of-state. Room/board: $8,562. Books/supplies: $1,050. Personal expenses: $1,660.

2014-2015 Financial aid. Need-based: 369 full-time freshmen applied for aid; 260 deemed to have need; 260 received aid. Average need met was 66%. Average scholarship/grant was $5,575; average loan $3,017. 48% of total undergraduate aid awarded as scholarships/grants, 52% as loans/jobs. **Non-need-based:** Awarded to 454 full-time undergraduates, including 121 freshmen. Scholarships awarded for academics, alumni affiliation, athletics, leadership, minority status, music/drama, religious affiliation, state residency.

Application procedures. Admission: No deadline. $30 fee. Admission notification on a rolling basis. **Financial aid:** Priority date 3/1; no closing date. FAFSA required. Applicants notified on a rolling basis starting 3/15; must reply within 2 week(s) of notification.

Academics. Special study options: Combined bachelor's/graduate degree, cooperative education, cross-registration, distance learning, double major, dual enrollment of high school students, external degree, honors, independent study, internships, teacher certification program. 3-2 liberal arts-engineering program with Carroll College, dual enrollment agreement with Flathead Valley Community College, collaborative programs with UM Helena (BAS Business, BS BIT, BAS General Studies), UM Western (Elementary Education Certification and Secondary Education Certification in Biological Sciences, General Sciences, and Mathematical Sciences), and Missoula College (AAS Surgical Technology). **Credit/placement by examination:** AP, CLEP, IB, SAT, ACT, institutional tests. 10 credit hours maximum toward associate degree, 30 toward bachelor's. **Support services:** Learning center, pre-admission summer program, reduced course load, remedial instruction, study skills assistance, tutoring, writing center. Online, real time tutoring is available 24 hours a day, 7 days a week.

Majors. Biology: General. **Business:** General. **Computer sciences:** Computer science, networking. **Engineering:** General, electrical, environmental, geological, metallurgical, mining, petroleum, software. **English:** Technical writing. **Health services:** General, medical informatics, nursing (RN), occupational health. **Liberal arts:** Arts/sciences. **Math:** General, statistics. **Physical sciences:** General, chemistry.

Most popular majors. Business/marketing 13%, engineering/engineering technologies 60%, health sciences 14%.

Technology on campus. 708 workstations in dormitories, library, computer center, student center. Dormitories wired for high-speed internet access and linked to campus network. Commuter students can connect to campus network. Online course registration, online library, helpline, wireless network available.

Student life. Freshman orientation: Mandatory. Preregistration for classes offered. Held several days before semester start. **Housing:** Guaranteed on-campus for freshmen. Coed dorms, special housing for disabled, apartments available. $100 fully refundable deposit. **Activities:** Pep band, campus ministries, choral groups, international student organizations, radio station, student government, student newspaper, Baptist student union, Circle-K, American Indian Science and Engineering Society, Society of Women Engineers.

Athletics. NAIA. **Intercollegiate:** Basketball, football (tackle) M, golf, volleyball W. **Intramural:** Basketball, football (non-tackle), racquetball, softball, volleyball. **Team name:** Orediggers.

Student services. Adult student services, alcohol/substance abuse counseling, career counseling, services for economically disadvantaged, student employment services, financial aid counseling, health services, minority student services, personal counseling, placement for graduates, veterans' counselor, women's services. **Physically disabled:** Services for visually, speech, hearing impaired.

Contact. E-mail: enrollment@mtech.edu
Phone: (406) 496-4256 Toll-free number: (800) 445-8324
Fax: (406) 496-4710
Stephanie Crowe, Director of Recruiting, Montana Tech of the University of Montana, 1300 West Park Street, Butte, MT 59701-8997

Rocky Mountain College
Billings, Montana
www.rocky.edu   CB code: 4660

- Private 4-year liberal arts college affiliated with the United Church of Christ
- Residential campus in small city
- 906 degree-seeking undergraduates: 2% part-time, 47% women, 3% African American, 1% Asian American, 6% Hispanic/Latino, 2% Native American, 1% Native Hawaiian/Pacific islander, 4% Multi-racial, non-Hispanic, 4% international
- 97 degree-seeking graduate students
- 70% of applicants admitted
- SAT or ACT (ACT writing optional) required
- 44% graduate within 6 years; 15% enter graduate study

General. Founded in 1878. Regionally accredited. **Degrees:** 204 bachelor's awarded; master's offered. **ROTC:** Army. **Calendar:** Semester, limited summer session. **Full-time faculty:** 68 total; 81% have terminal degrees, 48% women. **Part-time faculty:** 58 total; 45% have terminal degrees, 45% women. **Class size:** 74% < 20, 23% 20-39, 2% 40-49, less than 1% 50-99. **Special facilities:** Outdoor recreation center, flight school, equestrian facilities, geology library, college-run art gallery.

Freshman class profile. 1,424 applied, 995 admitted, 240 enrolled.

Mid 50% test scores		GPA 2.0-2.99:	27%
SAT critical reading:	450-550	Rank in top quarter:	38%
SAT math:	450-550	Rank in top tenth:	13%
SAT writing:	440-540	End year in good standing:	88%
ACT composite:	20-25	Return as sophomores:	71%
GPA 3.75 or higher:	30%	Out-of-state:	45%
GPA 3.50-3.74:	16%	Live on campus:	90%
GPA 3.0-3.49:	27%	International:	4%

Basis for selection. 2.50 GPA, ACT 21, or combined critical reading/math SAT of 1000 meets requirement for regular admission. Test scores accepted on a rolling basis. An essay is recommended for all students, and an interview is recommended for students not meeting regular admission requirements. **Home schooled:** Applicants must either have GED or pass ACT/SAT based on college entrance standards.

High school preparation. 19 units recommended. Recommended units include English 4, mathematics 4, social studies 3, history 2, science 3 and academic electives 3.

2016-2017 Annual costs. Tuition/fees (projected): $26,665. Room/board: $8,133. Books/supplies: $1,300. Personal expenses: $1,500.

2015-2016 Financial aid. Need-based: 219 full-time freshmen applied for aid; 194 deemed to have need; 194 received aid. Average need met was 77%. Average scholarship/grant was $18,407; average loan $3,272. 76% of total undergraduate aid awarded as scholarships/grants, 24% as loans/jobs. **Non-need-based:** Awarded to 225 full-time undergraduates, including 80 freshmen. Scholarships awarded for academics, athletics.

Application procedures. Admission: No deadline. $35 fee, may be waived for applicants with need, free for online applicants. Admission notification on a rolling basis. **Financial aid:** Priority date 3/1; no closing date. FAFSA required. Applicants notified on a rolling basis starting 2/15; must reply within 4 week(s) of notification.

Academics. Special study options: Accelerated study, combined bachelor's/graduate degree, double major, dual enrollment of high school students, ESL, honors, independent study, internships, student-designed major, study abroad, teacher certification program. **Credit/placement by examination:** AP, CLEP, IB, SAT, ACT, institutional tests. 15 credit hours maximum toward associate degree, 31 toward bachelor's. **Support services:** Learning

center, reduced course load, remedial instruction, study skills assistance, tutoring, writing center.

Majors. Biology: General. **Business:** Accounting, accounting/business management, business admin, management science, small business admin. **Communications:** Communications/speech/rhetoric. **Computer sciences:** Computer science. **Conservation:** Environmental science, environmental studies, management/policy. **Education:** Art, biology, elementary, English, history, mathematics, music, physical, psychology, science, social studies. **English:** Creative writing, English lit. **Health services:** Athletic training. **History:** General. **Math:** General. **Parks/recreation:** Exercise sciences, health/fitness, sports admin. **Physical sciences:** Chemistry, geology. **Psychology:** General. **Social sciences:** Sociology. **Visual/performing arts:** Art, dramatic, music, music performance, theater design.

Most popular majors. Biology 13%, business/marketing 26%, parks/recreation 11%, trade and industry 7%, visual/performing arts 6%.

Technology on campus. 113 workstations in dormitories, library, computer center, student center. Dormitories wired for high-speed internet access and linked to campus network. Commuter students can connect to campus network. Online course registration, online library, helpline, student web hosting, wireless network available.

Student life. Freshman orientation: Mandatory. Preregistration for classes offered. Held during the 4 days before classes start. **Housing:** Guaranteed on-campus for freshmen. Coed dorms, special housing for disabled, apartments available. Suites available. **Activities:** Bands, campus ministries, choral groups, drama, international student organizations, literary magazine, music ensembles, musical theater, radio station, student government, student newspaper, symphony orchestra, Intervarsity Christian Fellowship, ENACTUS (international non-profit business association), Student Ambassadors, Bears and Cubs, Tobacco Free RMC, Gay-Straight Alliance, IHSA equestrian club, Alpha Eta Rho National Aviation Fraternity, environmental club, Amnesty International.

Athletics. NAIA. **Intercollegiate:** Basketball, cheerleading, cross-country, equestrian, football (tackle) M, golf, skiing, soccer, track and field, volleyball W. **Intramural:** Basketball, football (non-tackle), golf, racquetball, skiing, soccer, softball, swimming, table tennis, tennis, ultimate frisbee, volleyball. **Team name:** Battlin' Bears.

Student services. Chaplain/spiritual director, career counseling, student employment services, financial aid counseling, health services, personal counseling, placement for graduates. **Physically disabled:** Services for visually, speech, hearing impaired.

Contact. E-mail: admissions@rocky.edu
Phone: (406) 657-1026 Toll-free number: (800) 877-6259
Fax: (406) 657-1189
Austin Mapston, Dean of Enrollment Services, Rocky Mountain College, 1511 Poly Drive, Billings, MT 59102-1796

Salish Kootenai College
Pablo, Montana
www.skc.edu   CB code: 0898

- Private 4-year liberal arts college
- Commuter campus in rural community
- 818 degree-seeking undergraduates

General. Founded in 1977. Regionally accredited. Native American cultural heritage. **Degrees:** 62 bachelor's, 91 associate awarded. **Location:** 55 miles from Missoula, 65 miles from Kalispell. **Calendar:** Quarter, limited summer session. **Full-time faculty:** 69 total. **Part-time faculty:** 39 total.

Basis for selection. Open admission, but selective for some programs. Special requirements for highway construction worker training, social work, dental assisting technology and nursing. Highway construction worker training program has special application which includes drug testing. Third-year applicants to social work program must complete special application which includes background check. Dental assisting technology and nursing also require special applications.

2015-2016 Annual costs. Tuition/fees: $6,279; $11,463 out-of-state. Books/supplies: $1,050. Personal expenses: $2,000.

Application procedures. Admission: Priority date 7/1; no deadline. No application fee. Application must be submitted on paper. Admission notification on a rolling basis. **Financial aid:** Priority date 3/31; no closing date. FAFSA required. Applicants notified on a rolling basis starting 7/15; must reply within 6 week(s) of notification.

Academics. Special study options: Combined bachelor's/graduate degree, cooperative education, distance learning, double major, dual enrollment of high school students, independent study, internships. **Credit/placement by examination:** AP, CLEP, institutional tests. **Support services:** Learning center, remedial instruction, study skills assistance, tutoring, writing center.

Majors. Biology: Cell/histology. **Business:** Business admin. **Computer sciences:** Computer science, information technology. **Conservation:** Environmental science, forest technology, land use planning, water/wetlands/marine. **Education:** General, early childhood, elementary, mathematics. **Engineering:** Computer. **Health services:** Nursing (RN). **Human services:** Social work. **Physical sciences:** Hydrology. **Psychology:** General.

Most popular majors. Business/marketing 16%, computer/information sciences 8%, health sciences 20%, natural resources/environmental science 12%, public administration/social services 44%.

Technology on campus. 42 workstations in library, computer center, student center. Dormitories wired for high-speed internet access. Online course registration, online library, helpline, wireless network available.

Student life. Freshman orientation: Mandatory. Preregistration for classes offered. Held prior to registration day; one-half to one-day session. **Housing:** Single-sex dorms, special housing for disabled, apartments available. **Activities:** Student government, student newspaper, TV station.

Athletics. Intercollegiate: Basketball. **Intramural:** Basketball, skiing, softball, volleyball. **Team name:** Bison.

Student services. Career counseling, student employment services, on-campus daycare, personal counseling, placement for graduates, veterans' counselor. **Physically disabled:** Services for visually, speech, hearing impaired.

Contact. E-mail: raelyn_dumontier@skc.edu
Phone: (406) 275-4855 Fax: (406) 275-4801
Raelyn DuMontier, Admissions, Salish Kootenai College, PO Box 70, Pablo, MT 59855

University of Great Falls
Great Falls, Montana
www.ugf.edu   **CB code: 4058**

- Private 4-year university and liberal arts college affiliated with the Roman Catholic Church
- Residential campus in small city
- 1,052 degree-seeking undergraduates: 3% African American, 3% Asian American, 7% Hispanic/Latino, 2% Native American, 1% Native Hawaiian/Pacific islander
- 25 degree-seeking graduate students
- 84% of applicants admitted
- SAT or ACT (ACT writing optional), application essay required
- 41% graduate within 6 years

General. Founded in 1932. Regionally accredited. **Degrees:** 269 bachelor's, 7 associate awarded; master's offered. **Location:** 600 miles from Seattle, 370 miles from Spokane, Washington. **Calendar:** Semester, limited summer session. **Full-time faculty:** 44 total; 89% have terminal degrees, 9% minority, 46% women. **Part-time faculty:** 72 total; 15% have terminal degrees, 4% minority, 56% women. **Class size:** 66% < 20, 34% 20-39. **Special facilities:** Herbarium.

Freshman class profile. 828 applied, 693 admitted, 168 enrolled.

Mid 50% test scores			
		GPA 3.50-3.74:	22%
SAT critical reading:	410-520	GPA 3.0-3.49:	26%
SAT math:	410-530	GPA 2.0-2.99:	34%
SAT writing:	400-510	Return as sophomores:	65%
ACT composite:	17-22	Out-of-state:	66%
GPA 3.75 or higher:	18%	Live on campus:	85%

Basis for selection. High school record and character most important. ACT/SAT scores may be considered when making scholarship decisions. SAT and SAT Subject Tests or ACT, SAT Subject Tests recommended. Interview recommended. **Home schooled:** Transcript of courses and grades required. Applicants should submit SAT/ACT test scores, bibliography of school literature and essay describing and evaluating preparation for university-level work.

High school preparation. 20 units required; 22 recommended. Required and recommended units include mathematics 3, social studies 1-2, history 3, science 3 (laboratory 1) and academic electives 5.

2015-2016 Annual costs. Tuition/fees: $22,170. Room/board: $7,920. Books/supplies: $1,000. Personal expenses: $100.

2015-2016 Financial aid. Need-based: 144 full-time freshmen applied for aid; 125 deemed to have need; 125 received aid. Average need met was 75%. Average scholarship/grant was $11,047; average loan $3,343. 55% of total undergraduate aid awarded as scholarships/grants, 45% as loans/jobs. **Non-need-based:** Scholarships awarded for academics, alumni affiliation, art, athletics, music/drama, religious affiliation, state residency.

Application procedures. Admission: Priority date 5/5; deadline 9/1 (postmark date). $35 fee, may be waived for applicants with need. Admission notification on a rolling basis beginning on or about 10/1. Must reply by May 1 or within 2 week(s) if notified thereafter. Admission granted with 6th semester transcripts. **Financial aid:** Priority date 3/1; no closing date. FAFSA required. Applicants notified on a rolling basis starting 3/1; must reply within 3 week(s) of notification.

Academics. Trio Title IV Student Support Services program available to eligible students. **Special study options:** Combined bachelor's/graduate degree, cooperative education, distance learning, double major, dual enrollment of high school students, exchange student, honors, independent study, internships, liberal arts/career combination, study abroad, teacher certification program, weekend college. **Credit/placement by examination:** AP, CLEP, IB, SAT, ACT, institutional tests. 30 credit hours maximum toward associate degree, 30 toward bachelor's. **Support services:** Learning center, pre-admission summer program, reduced course load, remedial instruction, study skills assistance, tutoring, writing center.

Majors. Biology: General, botany. **Business:** Accounting, accounting/business management, business admin. **Computer sciences:** General, applications programming, computer graphics, computer science, data processing, LAN/WAN management, networking, programming, security, system admin, systems analysis. **Education:** Art, biology, chemistry, early childhood, elementary, English, gifted/talented, health, history, kindergarten/preschool, mathematics, middle, physical, psychology, reading, science, secondary, social science, social studies, special ed. **English:** English lit. **Health services:** Predental, premedicine, preveterinary, substance abuse counseling. **History:** General. **Math:** General. **Parks/recreation:** Health/fitness. **Philosophy/religion:** Religion. **Physical sciences:** Chemistry. **Protective services:** Corrections, criminal justice, forensics, juvenile corrections, police science. **Psychology:** General. **Social sciences:** General, political science, sociology. **Visual/performing arts:** Art.

Most popular majors. Biology 9%, business/marketing 8%, education 12%, health sciences 29%, legal studies 7%, psychology 10%, security/protective services 10%, social sciences 8%.

Technology on campus. 120 workstations in dormitories, library, computer center, student center. Dormitories wired for high-speed internet access and linked to campus network. Commuter students can connect to campus network. Online course registration, online library, helpline, repair service, student web hosting, wireless network available.

Student life. Freshman orientation: Mandatory, $75 fee. Preregistration for classes offered. Programs held 3 days prior to fall and spring semesters; includes float trip down Missouri River. **Policies:** No drugs, alcohol, firearms or weapons allowed on campus. **Housing:** Guaranteed on-campus for freshmen. Coed dorms, apartments, themed housing, wellness housing available. $150 fully refundable deposit, deadline 8/15. **Activities:** Bands, campus ministries, choral groups, dance, drama, film society, international student organizations, literary magazine, music ensembles, musical theater, student government, student newspaper, symphony orchestra, United Tribes Club, Americorps, drama club, art club, Students In Free Enterprise, international law and justice club, medical science club, student Montana education association, paralegal club.

Athletics. NAIA. **Intercollegiate:** Basketball, cross-country, golf, soccer W, softball W, volleyball W, wrestling M. **Intramural:** Baseball, basketball, bowling, cheerleading, football (non-tackle), softball, tennis, volleyball. **Team name:** Argonauts.

Student services. Adult student services, alcohol/substance abuse counseling, chaplain/spiritual director, career counseling, services for economically disadvantaged, student employment services, financial aid counseling, health services, minority student services, on-campus daycare, personal counseling, placement for graduates, veterans' counselor, women's services. **Physically disabled:** Services for visually, hearing impaired.

Contact. E-mail: enroll@ugf.edu
Phone: (406) 791-5200 Toll-free number: (800) 856-9544
Fax: (406) 791-5209
April Clutter, Assistant Director of Admissions, University of Great Falls, 1301 20th Street South, Great Falls, MT 59405

University of Montana
Missoula, Montana
www.umt.edu

CB member
CB code: 4489

- Public 4-year university and liberal arts college
- Residential campus in small city
- 10,632 degree-seeking undergraduates: 19% part-time, 54% women, 1% African American, 1% Asian American, 4% Hispanic/Latino, 3% Native American, 4% Multi-racial, non-Hispanic, 2% international
- 2,117 degree-seeking graduate students
- 91% of applicants admitted
- SAT or ACT (ACT writing recommended) required
- 46% graduate within 6 years

General. Founded in 1893. Regionally accredited. Two-year technical/community college provides technical and vocational training and education and postsecondary academic preparation through general associate programs. **Degrees:** 1,872 bachelor's, 365 associate awarded; master's, professional, doctoral offered. **ROTC:** Army. **Location:** 210 miles from Spokane, Washington. **Calendar:** Semester, extensive summer session. **Full-time faculty:** 569 total; 78% have terminal degrees, 10% minority, 39% women. **Part-time faculty:** 265 total; 42% have terminal degrees, 8% minority, 54% women. **Class size:** 51% < 20, 36% 20-39, 3% 40-49, 6% 50-99, 3% >100. **Special facilities:** Broadcast media center (public radio and TV) and performing arts facilities, 3 art galleries, wildlife biology museum, 29,000-acre experimental forest, biological research station, geology field camp, biological, biomedical, kinesiology, physiology, and forestry-related research centers and labs, environmental studies laboratory, primate colony, forensics lab, clinical psychology center, practical ethics center, Fort Missoula field research center, off-campus observatory, and media arts facilities (filmmaking, digital, animation and interactive, sonic).

Freshman class profile. 5,600 applied, 5,097 admitted, 1,750 enrolled.

Mid 50% test scores		Rank in top quarter:	39%
SAT critical reading:	490-620	Rank in top tenth:	18%
SAT math:	490-600	Return as sophomores:	73%
SAT writing:	480-600	Out-of-state:	37%
ACT composite:	20-27	Live on campus:	80%
GPA 3.75 or higher:	26%	International:	1%
GPA 3.50-3.74:	18%	Fraternities:	5%
GPA 3.0-3.49:	29%	Sororities:	6%
GPA 2.0-2.99:	26%		

Basis for selection. For traditional full-time students: high school graduation, 2.5 cumulative grade point average or score of 22 on the ACT or 1030 combined verbal/math on the SAT and successful completion of college prep program requirements. Nontraditional students, GED freshman, and summer-only students exempt from the above requirements. TOEFL or Michigan Test and statement of intent and personal contribution required for international students. Students must earn a minimum math score of 17 on ACT or 420 on SAT. Students who do not meet admissions requirements may be admitted on a provisional basis. Students will be granted full admission after completing 24 credits with a grade point average of at least 2.0.

High school preparation. College-preparatory program required. Required units include English 4, mathematics 3, social studies 3, history 2, science 2 (laboratory 2). Two years chosen from the following: foreign language, computer science, visual/performing arts, or approved vocational education units.

2015-2016 Annual costs. Tuition/fees: $6,158; $23,048 out-of-state. Room/board: $8,406. Books/supplies: $1,400. Personal expenses: $3,154.

Financial aid. **Non-need-based:** Scholarships awarded for academics, athletics, leadership, music/drama, ROTC, state residency. **Additional information:** Fee waivers for minority students available to American Indians with blood quantum eligibility for, or enrolled membership in, a Montana tribe.

Application procedures. **Admission:** Priority date 3/1; no deadline. $36 fee. Admission notification on a rolling basis beginning on or about 9/15. **Financial aid:** Priority date 2/15; no closing date. FAFSA required. Applicants notified on a rolling basis starting 4/1; must reply within 4 week(s) of notification.

Academics. **Special study options:** Combined bachelor's/graduate degree, cooperative education, cross-registration, distance learning, double major, dual enrollment of high school students, ESL, exchange student, external degree, honors, independent study, internships, study abroad, teacher certification program. English language institute, combined programs with other institutions for bachelor in nursing and master in public administration with Montana State University-Bozeman. **Credit/placement by examination:** AP, CLEP, SAT, ACT, institutional tests. 10 credit hours maximum toward associate degree. Credit hours awarded determined by academic department. **Support services:** Learning center, pre-admission summer program, reduced course load, remedial instruction, study skills assistance, tutoring, writing center.

Majors. Architecture: Urban/community planning. **Area/ethnic studies:** Asian, East Asian, Native American. **Biology:** General, biochemistry, botany, microbiology. **Business:** General, business admin, finance, international, management information systems, marketing. **Communications:** Communications/speech/rhetoric, journalism. **Computer sciences:** General, computer science. **Conservation:** General, environmental studies, forestry, wildlife/wilderness. **Education:** General, art, biology, business, elementary, English, mathematics, music, physical, secondary. **English:** English lit, rhetoric/composition. **Foreign languages:** Classics, French, German, Japanese, Latin, Russian, Spanish. **Health services:** Athletic training, clinical lab science, communication disorders. **History:** General, science/technology. **Human services:** Social work. **Liberal arts:** Arts/sciences. **Math:** General. **Parks/recreation:** Exercise sciences, facilities management, health/fitness. **Philosophy/religion:** Philosophy. **Physical sciences:** Chemistry, geology, physics. **Psychology:** General. **Social sciences:** Anthropology, criminology, economics, geography, GIS/cartography, international relations, political science, sociology. **Visual/performing arts:** General, art, art history/conservation, dance, dramatic, drawing, music performance, music theory/composition.

Most popular majors. Biology 6%, business/marketing 16%, communications/journalism 8%, natural resources/environmental science 8%, psychology 8%, social sciences 13%, visual/performing arts 9%.

Technology on campus. 1,800 workstations in dormitories, library, computer center, student center. Dormitories wired for high-speed internet access and linked to campus network. Commuter students can connect to campus network. Online course registration, online library, helpline, repair service, wireless network available.

Student life. Freshman orientation: Mandatory, $60 fee. Preregistration for classes offered. Three-day summer session which includes parent track. **Housing:** Guaranteed on-campus for freshmen. Coed dorms, single-sex dorms, special housing for disabled, apartments, fraternity/sorority housing, themed housing available. $120 partly refundable deposit, deadline 3/1. Apartments for students and families, Honors floors, international floors, quiet floors, activity dorms, personal development housing available. **Activities:** Bands, campus ministries, choral groups, dance, drama, international student organizations, literary magazine, music ensembles, Model UN, musical theater, opera, radio station, student government, student newspaper, symphony orchestra, TV station, Associated Students of University of Montana, University of Montana Advocates, Mortar Board, Spurs, Circle-K, forestry student association, honors student association, Kyi-Yo (Native American organization), environmental action club, American Indian Business Leaders.

Athletics. NCAA. **Intercollegiate:** Basketball, cheerleading, cross-country, football (tackle) M, golf W, soccer W, softball W, tennis, track and field, volleyball W. **Intramural:** Badminton, baseball M, basketball, football (non-tackle), football (tackle) M, golf, handball, racquetball, sand volleyball, soccer, softball, swimming, table tennis, tennis, track and field, triathlon, ultimate frisbee, volleyball, water polo. **Team name:** Grizzlies OR Griz / Lady Griz.

Student services. Adult student services, alcohol/substance abuse counseling, chaplain/spiritual director, career counseling, services for economically disadvantaged, student employment services, financial aid counseling, health services, legal services, minority student services, on-campus daycare, personal counseling, placement for graduates, veterans' counselor, women's services. **Physically disabled:** Services for visually, speech, hearing impaired.

Contact. E-mail: admiss@umontana.edu
Phone: (406) 243-6266 Toll-free number: (800) 462-8636
Fax: (406) 243-5711
Sharon O'Hare, Associate VP for Enrollment and Student Success, University of Montana, Lommasson Center 103, Missoula, MT 59812

University of Montana: Western
Dillon, Montana
www.umwestern.edu

CB member
CB code: 4945

- Public 4-year liberal arts and teachers college
- Residential campus in small town
- 1,410 degree-seeking undergraduates: 17% part-time, 61% women, 1% African American, 1% Asian American, 3% Hispanic/Latino, 2% Native American, 1% Multi-racial, non-Hispanic
- 43% graduate within 6 years

General. Founded in 1893. Regionally accredited. **Degrees:** 254 bachelor's, 129 associate awarded. **Location:** 65 miles from Butte, 115 miles from

Bozeman. **Calendar:** Semester, limited summer session. **Full-time faculty:** 67 total; 81% have terminal degrees, 46% women. **Part-time faculty:** 29 total; 21% have terminal degrees, 48% women. **Class size:** 71% < 20, 29% 20-39. **Special facilities:** Performing arts facility, outdoor education center, center for horsemanship, model classroom, office simulation center, computer labs, technology sandbox.

Freshman class profile. 721 applied, 532 admitted, 346 enrolled.

Mid 50% test scores			
SAT critical reading:	410-520	**GPA 2.0-2.99:**	40%
SAT math:	390-530	**Rank in top quarter:**	21%
ACT composite:	17-22	**Rank in top tenth:**	4%
GPA 3.75 or higher:	11%	**End year in good standing:**	92%
GPA 3.50-3.74:	13%	**Return as sophomores:**	69%
GPA 3.0-3.49:	33%	**Out-of-state:**	29%
		Live on campus:	72%

Basis for selection. Open admission, but selective for some programs. Students wishing to enter into 4 year degree programs are subject to minimum GPA, test score, and rank requirements. Students wishing to enter into the Natural Horsemanship degree must complete a secondary application process including resume, essay, references, and demonstrated ability. **Home schooled:** Transcript of courses and grades, state high school equivalency certificate required.

High school preparation. College-preparatory program required. 16 units recommended. Recommended units include English 4, mathematics 3, social studies 3, science 2 (laboratory 2) and academic electives 2. Vocational education, computer education, foreign language, visual or performing arts recommended.

2015-2016 Annual costs. Tuition/fees: $4,226; $15,711 out-of-state. Room/board: $6,994. Books/supplies: $925. Personal expenses: $2,350.

Financial aid. Non-need-based: Scholarships awarded for academics, alumni affiliation, art, athletics, leadership, minority status, music/drama, state residency. **Additional information:** Tuition waivers available for veterans, war orphans, Native Americans, senior citizens, and dependents of Montana University System employees.

Application procedures. Admission: Priority date 7/1; no deadline. $30 fee. Admission notification on a rolling basis. **Financial aid:** Priority date 3/1; no closing date. FAFSA, institutional form required. Applicants notified on a rolling basis starting 4/1; must reply within 4 week(s) of notification.

Academics. Block scheduling; students take 1 class at a time for 18 days before moving on to their next course; there is a 3-4 day break between classes. Classes are 3 hours daily, Monday-Friday. Most courses are valued at 4 credits. **Special study options:** Cooperative education, distance learning, double major, dual enrollment of high school students, honors, independent study, internships, liberal arts/career combination, study abroad, teacher certification program. **Credit/placement by examination:** AP, CLEP, IB, institutional tests. 30 credit hours maximum toward associate degree, 30 toward bachelor's. **Support services:** Learning center, reduced course load, remedial instruction, study skills assistance, tutoring.

Majors. Biology: General. **Business:** Business admin. **Conservation:** General, environmental science. **Education:** General, art, biology, business, chemistry, early childhood, elementary, English, health, history, mathematics, multi-level teacher, music, physical, school librarian, science, secondary, social studies. **English:** English lit. **History:** General. **Liberal arts:** Arts/sciences. **Math:** General. **Psychology:** General. **Social sciences:** General, anthropology, political science, sociology. **Visual/performing arts:** Art.

Most popular majors. Agriculture 7%, biology 9%, business/marketing 22%, education 35%, natural resources/environmental science 8%, parks/recreation 6%.

Technology on campus. 205 workstations in dormitories, library, computer center, student center. Dormitories wired for high-speed internet access and linked to campus network. Commuter students can connect to campus network. Online course registration, helpline, wireless network available.

Student life. Freshman orientation: Mandatory, $75 fee. Preregistration for classes offered. Three-day event at the end of August designed to help students connect with one another and the campus community. **Policies:** Students with fewer than 30 credits not living with family required to live in dormitory. Transfer students under 21 with fewer than 30 credits not living with parents required to live on campus. Tobacco free and dry campus. **Housing:** Guaranteed on-campus for freshmen. Coed dorms, single-sex dorms, special housing for disabled, apartments available. $200 partly refundable deposit. **Activities:** Campus ministries, choral groups, drama, music ensembles, musical theater, radio station, student government, Terra Verde, admissions ambassadors, UMW Libertine Party, College Democrats, College Republicans, Young Farmers and Ranchers, Catholic Campus Ministry, Chi Alpha-Christian fellowship, Polynesian club, rodeo club, IT club, academic clubs, humans in performance.

Athletics. NAIA. **Intercollegiate:** Basketball, cross-country, equestrian, football (tackle) M, rodeo, volleyball W. **Intramural:** Basketball, football (non-tackle), racquetball, soccer, softball, volleyball. **Team name:** Bulldogs.

Student services. Alcohol/substance abuse counseling, career counseling, services for economically disadvantaged, student employment services, financial aid counseling, health services, on-campus daycare, personal counseling, veterans' counselor. **Physically disabled:** Services for visually, speech, hearing impaired.

Contact. E-mail: admissions@umwestern.edu
Phone: (406) 683-7331 Toll-free number: (877) 683-7331
Fax: (406) 683-7493
Matthew Allen, Interium Director of Admissions, University of Montana: Western, 710 South Atlantic Street, Dillon, MT 59725

Nebraska

Bellevue University
Bellevue, Nebraska
www.bellevue.edu   CB code: 6053

‣ Private 4-year university and business college
‣ Commuter campus in large city
‣ 6,224 degree-seeking undergraduates: 40% part-time, 51% women
‣ 3,517 graduate students
‣ 32% graduate within 6 years

General. Founded in 1965. Regionally accredited. **Degrees:** 1,856 bachelor's awarded; master's, doctoral offered. **ROTC:** Army, Air Force. **Calendar:** Semester, extensive summer session. **Full-time faculty:** 89 total; 57% have terminal degrees, 12% minority, 42% women. **Part-time faculty:** 285 total; 18% have terminal degrees, 1% minority, 44% women. **Class size:** 77% < 20, 23% 20-39. **Special facilities:** Military veterans service center.

Freshman class profile. 1,893 enrolled.

Return as sophomores: 58% **Out-of-state:** 48%

Basis for selection. Open admission, but selective for some programs. Students suspended or dismissed from any post-secondary institution within the last five years may be accepted under the Academic Probation status. If it has been less than one year from the date of suspension or dismissal, a student may be admitted with approval from the Vice President of Community and Student Affairs. Admission to Professional Studies program requires roughly 60 transfer credit hours from an accredited institution. **Home schooled:** Students should submit official verification of completion.

High school preparation. Recommended units include English 3, mathematics 3, social studies 3, history 3, science 3 (laboratory 1), foreign language 3 and academic electives 3.

2015-2016 Annual costs. Tuition/fees: $8,700. Room/board: $7,285. Books/supplies: $1,350. **Additional information:** First year we are offering room and board on campus.

Financial aid. **Non-need-based:** Scholarships awarded for academics, athletics, leadership.

Application procedures. Admission: No deadline. $50 fee, may be waived for applicants with need. Admission notification on a rolling basis. **Financial aid:** No deadline. FAFSA, institutional form required. Applicants notified on a rolling basis starting 4/15; must reply within 2 week(s) of notification.

Academics. Special study options: Accelerated study, cross-registration, distance learning, double major, dual enrollment of high school students, independent study, internships, liberal arts/career combination, study abroad. **Credit/placement by examination:** AP, CLEP, IB, institutional tests. No limit to amount of credits by examination that can be counted towards degree as long as residency requirements are met. **Support services:** Learning center, remedial instruction, study skills assistance, tutoring, writing center.

Majors. Biology: General. **Business:** General, accounting, banking/financial services, business admin, customer service, human resources, international, logistics, management information systems, nonprofit/public, organizational leadership, project management, retailing, selling, traffic/customs clerk. **Communications:** General, health, organizational, persuasive communications. **Computer sciences:** General, information systems, information technology, programming, system admin, webmaster. **Education:** General. **Human services:** General. **Parks/recreation:** Sports admin. **Philosophy/religion:** Philosophy. **Protective services:** Correctional facilities, disaster management, intelligence analysis, police science. **Psychology:** General. **Social sciences:** General, international relations. **Visual/performing arts:** Graphic design.

Most popular majors. Business/marketing 52%, computer/information sciences 11%, health sciences 8%, security/protective services 7%, social sciences 14%.

Technology on campus. 464 workstations in library, computer center, student center. Dormitories wired for high-speed internet access. Commuter students can connect to campus network. Online course registration, online library, helpline, wireless network available.

Student life. Freshman orientation: Available. Preregistration for classes offered. 2-day programs held the beginning week of fall, winter and spring semesters. **Policies:** No alcohol at any student events. Any event must be coordinated through the Student Activities Office. **Housing:** Single-sex dorms, wellness housing available. **Activities:** Campus ministries, international student organizations, student government, Alpha Chi, Campus Crusade for Christ, institute of management accountants, order of the sword & shield, Pi Gamma Mu, Sigma Beta Delta, Student Veterans Association.

Athletics. NAIA. **Intercollegiate:** Baseball M, basketball M, golf, soccer, softball W, volleyball W. **Team name:** Bruins.

Student services. Career counseling, student employment services, financial aid counseling, veterans' counselor. **Physically disabled:** Services for visually, speech, hearing impaired.

Contact. E-mail: admissions@bellevue.edu
Phone: (402) 293-2000 Toll-free number: (800) 756-7920
Fax: (402) 557-7230
Jennifer Grossnicklaus, Director, Undergraduate Admissions, Bellevue University, 1000 Galvin Road South, Bellevue, NE 68005-3098

BryanLGH College of Health Sciences
Lincoln, Nebraska
www.bryanhealthcollege.edu   CB code: 6058

‣ Private 4-year health science college affiliated with the United Methodist Church
‣ Commuter campus in large city
‣ 590 degree-seeking undergraduates
‣ SAT or ACT (ACT writing optional), application essay, interview required

General. Regionally accredited. Affiliation with Bryan Health Medical Center and William Jennings Bryan home and museum. **Degrees:** 129 bachelor's, 1 associate awarded; master's offered. **ROTC:** Army, Naval. **Location:** 45 minutes from Omaha. **Calendar:** Semester, limited summer session. **Full-time faculty:** 30 total. **Part-time faculty:** 36 total. **Class size:** 66% < 20, 22% 20-39, 6% 40-49, 5% 50-99. **Special facilities:** Nine patient simulators, human cadavers for dissection.

Freshman class profile.

GPA 3.75 or higher:	54%	Rank in top quarter:	53%
GPA 3.50-3.74:	33%	Rank in top tenth:	17%
GPA 3.0-3.49:	10%	Out-of-state:	23%
GPA 2.0-2.99:	3%		

Basis for selection. Applicants are reviewed by a faculty admissions committee. Students scoring above a certain rubric level are admitted. **Home schooled:** Transcript of courses and grades required.

High school preparation. College-preparatory program recommended. 24 units recommended. Recommended units include English 4, mathematics 4, social studies 4, science 4 (laboratory 3), foreign language 4 and computer science 1.

2015-2016 Annual costs. Tuition/fees: $16,350. Books/supplies: $1,200. Personal expenses: $6,417.

Financial aid. Non-need-based: Scholarships awarded for academics, leadership.

Application procedures. Admission: Closing date 1/15 (postmark date). $50 fee, may be waived for applicants with need. Application must be submitted on paper. Admission notification on a rolling basis beginning on or about 3/1. Must reply by May 1 or within 4 week(s) if notified thereafter. **Financial aid:** Closing date 5/1. FAFSA, institutional form required. Applicants notified on a rolling basis starting 5/1; must reply within 3 week(s) of notification.

Academics. Special study options: Combined bachelor's/graduate degree, independent study. **Credit/placement by examination:** AP, CLEP, institutional tests. 3 credit hours maximum toward associate degree, 6 toward bachelor's. **Support services:** Learning center, pre-admission summer program, remedial instruction, study skills assistance, tutoring.

Majors. Health services: Cardiovascular technology, nursing (RN), sonography.

Technology on campus. 30 workstations in library, student center. Commuter students can connect to campus network. Online library, helpline, wireless network available.

Student life. Freshman orientation: Mandatory. Preregistration for classes offered. Held on-campus the Thursday and Friday before classes begin each term. **Activities:** Student government, Red Cross, Caring with Christ, Action for Students, student nurses association, health promotion organization.

Athletics. Team name: Blue Healers.

Student services. Alcohol/substance abuse counseling, chaplain/spiritual director, financial aid counseling, health services, personal counseling.

Contact. E-mail: briana.genetti@bryanhealth.org
Phone: (402) 481-8697 Toll-free number: (800) 742-7844 ext. 18697
Fax: (402) 481-8621
Kelli Backman, Dean of Students, BryanLGH College of Health Sciences, 5035 Everett Street, Lincoln, NE 68506

Chadron State College
Chadron, Nebraska
www.csc.edu   CB code: 6466

▶ Public 4-year business and liberal arts college
▶ Residential campus in small town
▶ 2,099 degree-seeking undergraduates: 18% part-time, 58% women, 5% African American, 8% Hispanic/Latino, 1% Native American, 1% Native Hawaiian/Pacific islander, 3% Multi-racial, non-Hispanic, 3% international
▶ 631 graduate students
▶ 42% graduate within 6 years

General. Founded in 1911. Regionally accredited. Limited distance education classes and programs offered online and at Scottsbluff, Alliance, Sidney, and throughout western Nebraska and eastern Wyoming. **Degrees:** 121 bachelor's awarded; master's offered. **ROTC:** Army. **Location:** 100 miles from Scottsbluff; 100 miles from Rapid City, SD. **Calendar:** Semester, limited summer session. **Full-time faculty:** 90 total. **Part-time faculty:** 60 total. **Class size:** 65% < 20, 30% 20-39, 4% 40-49, less than 1% 50-99. **Special facilities:** Planetarium, herbarium, geological museum, high plains heritage center.

Freshman class profile.

GPA 3.75 or higher:	20%	Rank in top tenth:	11%
GPA 3.50-3.74:	11%	Out-of-state:	29%
GPA 3.0-3.49:	22%	Live on campus:	90%
GPA 2.0-2.99:	28%	International:	3%
Rank in top quarter:	26%		

Basis for selection. Open admission, but selective for some programs. Test scores must be submitted for placement, but no minimum score required. Audition recommended for music program.

High school preparation. 12 units recommended. Recommended units include English 4, mathematics 3, social studies 3, science 2 (laboratory 2). Units in visual or performing arts, computer literacy, or foreign language recommended.

2015-2016 Annual costs. Tuition/fees: $6,204; $6,234 out-of-state. Room/board: $6,506. Books/supplies: $1,200. Personal expenses: $1,680.

Financial aid. Non-need-based: Scholarships awarded for academics, alumni affiliation, art, athletics, leadership, minority status, music/drama, state residency.

Application procedures. Admission: No deadline. $15 fee. Admission notification on a rolling basis. **Financial aid:** Priority date 6/1; no closing date. FAFSA, institutional form required. Applicants notified on a rolling basis starting 4/1; must reply within 2 week(s) of notification.

Academics. Special study options: Accelerated study, combined bachelor's/graduate degree, cooperative education, distance learning, double major, dual enrollment of high school students, honors, independent study, internships, student-designed major, study abroad, teacher certification program. **Credit/placement by examination:** AP, CLEP, SAT, ACT, institutional tests. 65 credit hours maximum toward bachelor's degree. **Support services:** Learning center, pre-admission summer program, reduced course load, remedial instruction, study skills assistance, tutoring, writing center.

Majors. Biology: General. **Business:** Accounting, business admin, finance, management information systems, management science, office management. **Computer sciences:** Information systems. **Education:** Art, biology, business, chemistry, drama/dance, elementary, English, family/consumer sciences, history, mathematics, middle, music, physical, physics, science, secondary,

social science, Spanish, technology/industrial arts, trade/industrial. **English:** English lit, rhetoric/composition. **Foreign languages:** Spanish. **History:** General. **Human services:** Social work. **Liberal arts:** Arts/sciences, library science. **Math:** General. **Parks/recreation:** General. **Physical sciences:** Chemistry. **Psychology:** General. **Social sciences:** General, sociology. **Visual/performing arts:** Art, dramatic, music. **Work/family studies:** General.

Most popular majors. Biology 11%, business/marketing 20%, education 27%.

Technology on campus. 120 workstations in dormitories, library, computer center, student center. Dormitories wired for high-speed internet access and linked to campus network. Commuter students can connect to campus network. Online course registration, online library, helpline, wireless network available.

Student life. Freshman orientation: Available, $100 fee. Preregistration for classes offered. Four or five 2-day weekend orientations held prior to start of fall term. **Housing:** Guaranteed on-campus for freshmen. Coed dorms, single-sex dorms, special housing for disabled, apartments, wellness housing available. $100 deposit, deadline 6/1. **Activities:** Bands, choral groups, dance, drama, international student organizations, music ensembles, musical theater, student government, student newspaper, Circle K, student education association, multicultural club, Intervarsity Christian Fellowship, White Buffalo Club.

Athletics. NCAA. **Intercollegiate:** Basketball, football (tackle) M, golf W, track and field, volleyball W, wrestling M. **Intramural:** Archery, badminton, basketball, bowling, golf, racquetball, rugby M, softball, track and field, volleyball, wrestling M. **Team name:** Eagles.

Student services. Adult student services, alcohol/substance abuse counseling, career counseling, services for economically disadvantaged, student employment services, financial aid counseling, health services, on-campus daycare, personal counseling, placement for graduates, veterans' counselor. **Physically disabled:** Services for visually, speech, hearing impaired.

Contact. E-mail: inquire@csc.edu
Phone: (308) 432-6263 Toll-free number: (800) 242-3766
Fax: (308) 432-6229
Tena Cook, Director of Admissions, Chadron State College, 1000 Main Street, Chadron, NE 69337

Clarkson College
Omaha, Nebraska
www.clarksoncollege.edu   CB code: 2250

▶ Private 4-year health science college affiliated with the Episcopal Church
▶ Commuter campus in large city
▶ 765 degree-seeking undergraduates
▶ Application essay required

General. Founded in 1888. Regionally accredited. **Degrees:** 142 bachelor's, 54 associate awarded; master's offered. **ROTC:** Army, Air Force. **Location:** 50 miles from Lincoln. **Calendar:** Semester, extensive summer session. **Full-time faculty:** 45 total. **Part-time faculty:** 55 total. **Class size:** 66% < 20, 30% 20-39, less than 1% 40-49, 3% 50-99. **Special facilities:** Health care clinical facilities for professional education (more than 180 clinical sites), fully energized radiologic technology lab.

Basis for selection. Open admission, but selective for some programs. GPA, class rank, test scores, essay important. **Home schooled:** Must take GED and submit ACT scores. Essay required. Transcript or portfolio recommended.

High school preparation. 9 units required. Required and recommended units include English 3-4, mathematics 2-4, social studies 2-3, history 2, science 2-4 (laboratory 1-2) and foreign language 2.

2015-2016 Annual costs. Tuition/fees: $15,210. Room only: $4,840. Books/supplies: $1,400. Personal expenses: $2,700.

Financial aid. Non-need-based: Scholarships awarded for academics, alumni affiliation, minority status, religious affiliation.

Application procedures. Admission: No deadline. $35 fee. Application must be submitted on paper. Admission notification on a rolling basis. Must reply by May 1 or within 4 week(s) if notified thereafter. Application deadlines may vary by program. Students should check with admissions office for program deadlines. **Financial aid:** Priority date 4/1; no closing date. FAFSA, institutional form required. Applicants notified on a rolling basis starting 4/13; must reply within 3 week(s) of notification.

Academics. Special study options: Accelerated study, combined bachelor's/graduate degree, cooperative education, cross-registration, distance learning, double major, dual enrollment of high school students, external degree, independent study, internships, study abroad. **Credit/placement by examination:** AP, CLEP, institutional tests. 40 credit hours maximum toward associate degree, 88 toward bachelor's. Unlimited number of hours of credit by examination may be counted toward degree if residency requirement of 40 hours is met. **Support services:** Learning center, reduced course load, study skills assistance, tutoring, writing center.

Majors. Business: General, business admin. **Health services:** Health care admin, medical radiologic technology/radiation therapy, nursing (RN), preop/surgical nursing, radiologic technology/medical imaging.

Technology on campus. 60 workstations in dormitories, library, computer center. Dormitories wired for high-speed internet access. Commuter students can connect to campus network. Online library, helpline, repair service available.

Student life. Freshman orientation: Mandatory. Preregistration for classes offered. One-day program held on Friday before classes begin. **Housing:** Guaranteed on-campus for freshmen. Coed dorms, apartments available. $250 deposit, deadline 6/30. Board plan not available, kitchens located in each apartment. **Activities:** Student government, student newspaper, Christian Fellowship, Red Cross, National Student Nurses Association, Fellows club, Ambassador club, student leadership council.

Athletics. Intercollegiate: Skiing M.

Student services. Adult student services, alcohol/substance abuse counseling, career counseling, student employment services, financial aid counseling, health services, minority student services, on-campus daycare, personal counseling, placement for graduates. **Physically disabled:** Services for visually, hearing impaired.

Contact. E-mail: admiss@clarksoncollege.edu
Phone: (402) 552-3041 Toll-free number: (800) 647-5500
Fax: (402) 552-6057
Denise Work, Director of Admission, Clarkson College, 101 South 42nd Street, Omaha, NE 68131-2739

College of Saint Mary
Omaha, Nebraska
www.csm.edu   CB code: 6106

- Private 4-year university and liberal arts college for women affiliated with the Roman Catholic Church
- Commuter campus in large city
- 705 degree-seeking undergraduates: 4% part-time, 100% women, 7% African American, 2% Asian American, 13% Hispanic/Latino, 1% Native American, 2% Multi-racial, non-Hispanic, 1% international
- 262 degree-seeking graduate students
- 61% of applicants admitted
- SAT or ACT (ACT writing optional) required
- 41% graduate within 6 years

General. Founded in 1923. Regionally accredited. **Degrees:** 140 bachelor's, 44 associate awarded; master's, doctoral offered. **ROTC:** Army, Air Force. **Location:** Downtown. **Calendar:** Semester, extensive summer session. **Full-time faculty:** 62 total; 64% have terminal degrees, 11% minority, 86% women. **Part-time faculty:** 150 total; 32% have terminal degrees, 5% minority, 81% women. **Class size:** 73% < 20, 27% 20-39, less than 1% 40-49. **Special facilities:** On-site child development center, green house, cadaver lab, digital piano lab, residence hall for single mothers and their children, fresh fish acquarium, extensive labs for nursing.

Freshman class profile. 314 applied, 193 admitted, 77 enrolled.

Mid 50% test scores		Rank in top quarter:	35%
ACT composite:	19-25	Rank in top tenth:	11%
GPA 3.75 or higher:	22%	End year in good standing:	79%
GPA 3.50-3.74:	21%	Return as sophomores:	83%
GPA 3.0-3.49:	31%	Out-of-state:	21%
GPA 2.0-2.99:	25%	Live on campus:	84%

Basis for selection. Test scores, secondary school record, class rank important factors. Recommendations also considered. Nursing program requires a specific minimum score on the TEAS test (Test of Essential Academic Skills).

High school preparation. College-preparatory program recommended. Required and recommended units include English 4, mathematics 2-3, social

studies 2 and science 2-3. Chemistry and biology required of nursing, occupational therapy, physician assistant students.

2015-2016 Annual costs. Tuition/fees: $28,964. Room/board: $7,400. Books/supplies: $1,024. Personal expenses: $1,085.

2015-2016 Financial aid. Need-based: Average need met was 75%. Average scholarship/grant was $19,031; average loan $2,785. 55% of total undergraduate aid awarded as scholarships/grants, 45% as loans/jobs. **Non-need-based:** Scholarships awarded for academics, athletics, music/drama.

Application procedures. Admission: No deadline. $30 fee, may be waived for applicants with need. Admission notification on a rolling basis. **Financial aid:** Priority date 3/15; no closing date. FAFSA required. Applicants notified on a rolling basis starting 3/15; must reply within 2 week(s) of notification.

Academics. Special study options: Accelerated study, combined bachelor's/graduate degree, cooperative education, distance learning, double major, dual enrollment of high school students, exchange student, honors, independent study, internships, liberal arts/career combination, study abroad, teacher certification program, weekend college. **Credit/placement by examination:** AP, CLEP, IB, SAT, ACT, institutional tests. 9 credit hours maximum toward associate degree, 9 toward bachelor's. 10 percent of program may be earned through credit by examination. **Support services:** Learning center, reduced course load, remedial instruction, study skills assistance, tutoring, writing center.

Majors. Biology: General. **Business:** Business admin. **Education:** Biology, chemistry, early childhood, earth science, elementary, English, mathematics, middle, science, secondary, social science, Spanish, special ed. **English:** English lit. **Health services:** Nursing (RN), predental, premedicine, preoccupational therapy, prepharmacy, preveterinary. **Liberal arts:** Arts/sciences. **Math:** General. **Physical sciences:** Chemistry. **Psychology:** General. **Theology:** Theology. **Visual/performing arts:** Studio arts.

Most popular majors. Business/marketing 11%, education 11%, health sciences 54%, legal studies 6%, psychology 7%.

Technology on campus. 90 workstations in dormitories, library, computer center, student center. Dormitories wired for high-speed internet access and linked to campus network. Commuter students can connect to campus network. Online course registration, online library, helpline, wireless network available.

Student life. Freshman orientation: Mandatory. Preregistration for classes offered. One-day program offered several times during late spring and summer. **Policies:** Several student organizations have GPA requirements. **Housing:** Guaranteed on-campus for freshmen. $125 fully refundable deposit. Residence hall for single student mothers with children available. **Activities:** Campus ministries, choral groups, drama, international student organizations, student government, Do Unto Others, residence hall council, campus activities board, Student Education Association of Nebraska, Student Occupational Therapy Association, Latinas Empowering Others, Student Nurse Association, Green Team, math/science club, student psychology club.

Athletics. NAIA. **Intercollegiate:** Basketball W, cross-country W, golf W, soccer W, softball W, swimming W, tennis W, volleyball W. **Team name:** Flames.

Student services. Adult student services, alcohol/substance abuse counseling, chaplain/spiritual director, career counseling, services for economically disadvantaged, student employment services, financial aid counseling, health services, minority student services, on-campus daycare, personal counseling, placement for graduates, veterans' counselor, women's services. **Physically disabled:** Services for visually, speech, hearing impaired.

Contact. E-mail: enroll@csm.edu
Phone: (402) 399-2355 Toll-free number: (800) 926-5534 ext. 2355
Fax: (402) 399-2412
Sara Hanson, Vice President for Enrollment Services, College of Saint Mary, 7000 Mercy Road, Omaha, NE 68106

Concordia University
Seward, Nebraska
www.cune.edu   CB code: 6116

- Private 4-year university affiliated with the Lutheran Church - Missouri Synod
- Residential campus in small town
- 1,255 degree-seeking undergraduates: 3% part-time, 52% women, 4% African American, 1% Asian American, 6% Hispanic/Latino, 2% international

- 979 degree-seeking graduate students
- 78% of applicants admitted
- SAT or ACT (ACT writing optional) required
- 59% graduate within 6 years; 17% enter graduate study

General. Founded in 1894. Regionally accredited. **Degrees:** 262 bachelor's awarded; master's offered. **ROTC:** Army, Air Force. **Location:** 25 miles from Lincoln, 75 miles from Omaha. **Calendar:** Semester, limited summer session. **Full-time faculty:** 63 total; 86% have terminal degrees, 2% minority, 36% women. **Part-time faculty:** 177 total; 41% have terminal degrees, 6% minority, 66% women. **Class size:** 51% < 20, 45% 20-39, 3% 40-49, 2% 50-99. **Special facilities:** Rock and mineral museum, observatory, arboretum.

Freshman class profile. 1,380 applied, 1,072 admitted, 347 enrolled.

Mid 50% test scores		GPA 2.0-2.99:	17%
SAT critical reading:	430-560	Rank in top quarter:	43%
SAT math:	470-560	Rank in top tenth:	17%
ACT composite:	20-27	Return as sophomores:	76%
GPA 3.75 or higher:	43%	Out-of-state:	55%
GPA 3.50-3.74:	14%	Live on campus:	98%
GPA 3.0-3.49:	26%	International:	1%

Basis for selection. High school GPA and SAT/ACT scores important in admissions decisions. Audition required for drama, music, and speech programs; portfolio required for art program. **Home schooled:** Statement describing home school structure and mission, transcript of courses and grades, state high school equivalency certificate required.

High school preparation. College-preparatory program recommended. 16 units recommended. Recommended units include English 4, mathematics 3, social studies 3, history 3, science 2, foreign language 1 and academic electives 3. One unit each in music, art, and physical education recommended.

2016-2017 Annual costs. Tuition/fees: $28,480. Room/board: $7,800. Books/supplies: $1,000. Personal expenses: $1,500.

2015-2016 Financial aid. Need-based: 324 full-time freshmen applied for aid; 280 deemed to have need; 280 received aid. Average need met was 81%. Average scholarship/grant was $18,413; average loan $3,450. 82% of total undergraduate aid awarded as scholarships/grants, 18% as loans/jobs. **Non-need-based:** Awarded to 473 full-time undergraduates, including 123 freshmen. Scholarships awarded for academics, alumni affiliation, art, athletics, leadership, music/drama, religious affiliation.

Application procedures. Admission: Priority date 7/1; deadline 8/1 (receipt date). No application fee. Admission notification on a rolling basis beginning on or about 9/1. Must reply within 30 days of receipt of acceptance letter or request extension. **Financial aid:** Priority date 3/1; no closing date. FAFSA required. Applicants notified on a rolling basis starting 3/1; must reply within 4 week(s) of notification.

Academics. Special study options: Accelerated study, distance learning, double major, exchange student, independent study, internships, study abroad. Undergraduate students may take graduate level classes. **Credit/placement by examination:** AP, CLEP, IB, SAT, ACT. **Support services:** Learning center, reduced course load, study skills assistance, tutoring, writing center.

Majors. Biology: General. **Business:** General, accounting, business admin, communications, management information systems, marketing. **Communications:** Communications/speech/rhetoric, organizational. **Computer sciences:** General, computer science. **Conservation:** Environmental science, environmental studies. **Education:** General, art, biology, business, chemistry, early childhood, elementary, elementary special ed, English, ESL, foreign languages, geography, health, history, junior high special ed, mathematics, middle, multi-level teacher, music, physical, physics, psychology, reading, science, secondary, social science, Spanish, special ed. **English:** English lit, rhetoric/composition. **Foreign languages:** Spanish. **Health services:** Nursing (RN), prechiropractic, predental, premedicine, prenursing, preoccupational therapy, prepharmacy, prephysical therapy, preveterinary. **History:** General. **Math:** General. **Parks/recreation:** Exercise sciences, health/fitness, sports admin. **Physical sciences:** General, chemistry, physics. **Psychology:** General. **Social sciences:** Geography, sociology. **Theology:** Preministerial, religious ed, sacred music, theology. **Visual/performing arts:** General, art, arts management, dramatic, graphic design, music, studio arts.

Most popular majors. Biology 10%, business/marketing 16%, education 30%, interdisciplinary studies 6%, psychology 7%.

Technology on campus. 220 workstations in dormitories, library, computer center, student center. Dormitories wired for high-speed internet access and linked to campus network. Commuter students can connect to campus network. Online course registration, online library, helpline, student web hosting, wireless network available.

Student life. Freshman orientation: Mandatory. Preregistration for classes offered. Three days before classes start. Includes community service events and community building. **Policies:** University responsibly maintains Christian standards of conduct among its students, faculty and staff. **Housing:** Guaranteed on-campus for all undergraduates. Single-sex dorms, special housing for disabled, apartments, wellness housing available. $200 fully refundable deposit, deadline 8/1. **Activities:** Bands, campus ministries, choral groups, dance, drama, international student organizations, literary magazine, music ensembles, musical theater, student government, student newspaper, symphony orchestra, Ongoing Ambassadors for Christ, multicultural awareness club, Peers and Leaders Serving, Habitat for Humanity, Leaders in Physical Health Education, Mission Minded Students, Students in Free Enterprise, Students with Families Association.

Athletics. NAIA. **Intercollegiate:** Baseball M, basketball, cheerleading W, cross-country, football (tackle) M, golf, soccer, softball W, tennis, track and field, volleyball W, wrestling M. **Intramural:** Badminton, basketball, bowling, cross-country, football (non-tackle), soccer, softball, table tennis, tennis, ultimate frisbee, volleyball. **Team name:** Bulldogs.

Student services. Adult student services, alcohol/substance abuse counseling, chaplain/spiritual director, career counseling, student employment services, financial aid counseling, health services, personal counseling, placement for graduates. **Physically disabled:** Services for visually, speech, hearing impaired.

Contact. E-mail: admiss@cune.edu
Toll-free number: (800) 535-5494 Fax: (402) 643-4073
Aaron Roberts, Director of Undergraduate Recruitment, Concordia University, 800 North Columbia Avenue, Seward, NE 68434-1556

Creative Center
Omaha, Nebraska
www.creativecenter.edu

- For-profit 4-year visual arts and career college
- Commuter campus in large city
- 64 degree-seeking undergraduates: 6% part-time, 66% women
- 94% of applicants admitted
- Application essay, interview required

General. Accredited by ACCSC. **Degrees:** 16 bachelor's, 23 associate awarded. **Calendar:** Semester, limited summer session. **Full-time faculty:** 3 total; 33% have terminal degrees, 33% women. **Part-time faculty:** 10 total; 10% have terminal degrees, 40% women. **Class size:** 67% < 20, 33% 20-39.

Freshman class profile. 50 applied, 47 admitted, 14 enrolled.

Basis for selection. Interview, campus visit, a letter of recommendation, letter of intent, high school transcript, and portfolio required. **Learning Disabled:** Students with learning disabilities must meet with Director of Admissions and Executive Director to communicate any needs before the semester begins.

2016-2017 Annual costs. Tuition/fees: $27,700.

Financial aid. Non-need-based: Scholarships awarded for academics, art.

Application procedures. Admission: No deadline. $100 fee. Application must be submitted on paper. Admission notification on a rolling basis. **Financial aid:** Closing date 7/15. FAFSA required. Applicants notified on a rolling basis starting 2/1.

Academics. Special study options: Accelerated study. **Credit/placement by examination:** AP, CLEP. **Support services:** Reduced course load, study skills assistance, tutoring.

Majors. Visual/performing arts: Graphic design.

Technology on campus. PC or laptop required. 8 workstations in library. Online library, helpline, student web hosting, wireless network available.

Student life. Freshman orientation: Mandatory. Preregistration for classes offered. Orientation is held throughout first week of regular classes.

Student services. Career counseling, financial aid counseling, placement for graduates.

Contact. E-mail: admissions@creativecenter.edu
Phone: (402) 898-1000 ext. 216
Toll-free number: (888) 898-1789 ext. 216 Fax: (402) 898-1301
Richard Caldwell, Director of Admissions, Creative Center, 10850 Emmet Street, Omaha, NE 68164-2911

Creighton University

Omaha, Nebraska

www.creighton.edu

CB member
CB code: 6121

- Private 4-year university affiliated with the Roman Catholic Church
- Residential campus in very large city
- 4,080 degree-seeking undergraduates: 4% part-time, 57% women, 2% African American, 10% Asian American, 8% Hispanic/Latino, 4% Multiracial, non-Hispanic, 3% international
- 4,176 degree-seeking graduate students
- 70% of applicants admitted
- SAT or ACT (ACT writing optional), application essay required
- 79% graduate within 6 years; 33% enter graduate study

General. Founded in 1878. Regionally accredited. **Degrees:** 909 bachelor's, 2 associate awarded; master's, professional, doctoral offered. **ROTC:** Army, Air Force. **Location:** 167 miles from Kansas City, 290 miles from Minneapolis. **Calendar:** Semester, extensive summer session. **Full-time faculty:** 560 total; 92% have terminal degrees, 11% minority, 44% women. **Part-time faculty:** 285 total; 54% have terminal degrees, 9% minority, 54% women. **Class size:** 48% < 20, 43% 20-39, 2% 40-49, 5% 50-99, 1% >100. **Special facilities:** Church, art gallery, wind energy collection system, solar array, trading room complete with a real-time stock ticker, interactive market boards, 11 Bloomberg terminals.

Freshman class profile. 9,747 applied, 6,870 admitted, 1,068 enrolled.

Mid 50% test scores			
SAT critical reading:	510-630	GPA 2.0-2.99:	5%
SAT math:	540-650	Rank in top quarter:	68%
SAT writing:	510-620	Rank in top tenth:	37%
ACT composite:	24-29	End year in good standing:	96%
GPA 3.75 or higher:	58%	Return as sophomores:	90%
GPA 3.50-3.74:	18%	Out-of-state:	81%
GPA 3.0-3.49:	19%	Live on campus:	95%
		International:	2%

Basis for selection. School record, high school GPA, test scores, and application essay important. Class rank, and recommendation(s) considered. **Home schooled:** Statement describing home school structure and mission, transcript of courses and grades, letter of recommendation (nonparent) required. Description of curriculum and texts used.

High school preparation. College-preparatory program recommended. 16 units required; 21 recommended. Required and recommended units include English 4, mathematics 3-4, social studies 2-4, science 2-3 (laboratory 1-2), foreign language 2-3 and academic electives 3.

2015-2016 Annual costs. Tuition/fees: $36,422. Room/board: $10,294. Books/supplies: $1,200. Personal expenses: $2,000.

2015-2016 Financial aid. Need-based: 853 full-time freshmen applied for aid; 645 deemed to have need; 645 received aid. Average need met was 85%. Average scholarship/grant was $21,566; average loan $5,120. 68% of total undergraduate aid awarded as scholarships/grants, 32% as loans/jobs. **Non-need-based:** Awarded to 2,025 full-time undergraduates, including 565 freshmen. Scholarships awarded for academics, alumni affiliation, art, athletics, leadership, minority status, music/drama, ROTC.

Application procedures. Admission: Priority date 12/1; deadline 2/15 (postmark date). $40 fee, may be waived for applicants with need, free for online applicants. Admission notification on a rolling basis beginning on or about 11/1. Must reply by May 1 or within 2 week(s) if notified thereafter. **Financial aid:** Priority date 3/1; no closing date. FAFSA, institutional form required. Applicants notified on a rolling basis starting 3/15; must reply by 3/15 or within 4 week(s) of notification.

Academics. Students are given admissions preference into all of university's professional schools. Core curriculum required (61 semester hours from 5 areas: cultures, ideas and civilizations; theology, philosophy and ethics; natural science; social and behavioral sciences; skills). **Special study options:** Accelerated study, combined bachelor's/graduate degree, cross-registration, distance learning, double major, dual enrollment of high school students, ESL, honors, independent study, internships, liberal arts/career combination, semester at sea, study abroad, teacher certification program. 3-3 Law (within Creighton University); Art-Engineering Program (with University of Detroit Mercy; with Marquette University). **Credit/placement by examination:** AP, CLEP, IB, SAT, ACT, institutional tests. CLEP Subject Examinations must be taken with essay where applicable. **Support services:** Learning center, reduced course load, remedial instruction, study skills assistance, tutoring, writing center.

Honors college/program. Admission by invitation only. 5% of entering freshmen were admitted.

Majors. Area/ethnic studies: American. **Biology:** General. **Business:** Accounting, business admin, entrepreneurial studies, finance, international, marketing, organizational leadership. **Communications:** Communications/speech/rhetoric, journalism. **Computer sciences:** Computer science, information technology, web page design. **Conservation:** Environmental science. **Education:** Elementary, secondary. **English:** Creative writing, English lit. **Foreign languages:** Ancient Greek, classics, French, German, Latin, Spanish. **Health services:** Dental hygiene, EMT paramedic, health care admin, nursing (RN). **History:** General. **Human services:** Social work. **Math:** General, applied. **Parks/recreation:** Exercise sciences. **Philosophy/religion:** Philosophy. **Physical sciences:** Atmospheric science, chemistry, physics. **Psychology:** General. **Social sciences:** Anthropology, economics, international relations, medical anthropology, political science, sociology. **Theology:** Theology. **Visual/performing arts:** Art, dramatic, graphic design, music, musical theater, studio arts.

Most popular majors. Biology 10%, business/marketing 18%, health sciences 23%, parks/recreation 6%, psychology 6%, social sciences 8%.

Technology on campus. Dormitories wired for high-speed internet access and linked to campus network. Commuter students can connect to campus network. Online course registration, online library, helpline, repair service, student web hosting, wireless network available.

Student life. Freshman orientation: Mandatory, $65 fee. Preregistration for classes offered. Four optional sessions held in summer. Ten-day welcome week held in fall. **Policies:** Student Code of Conduct in effect. **Housing:** Guaranteed on-campus for freshmen. Coed dorms, special housing for disabled, apartments, themed housing available. $100 nonrefundable deposit, deadline 5/1. Honors program, freshman leadership program, Cortina service community, and summer housing available. **Activities:** Pep band, campus ministries, choral groups, dance, drama, international student organizations, music ensembles, Model UN, musical theater, radio station, student government, student newspaper, symphony orchestra, College Democrats, College Republicans, Native American Association, Hawaiian student organization, Latino student association, Gender and Sexuality Alliance, Alpha Phi Omega Service Fraternity, Colleges Against Cancer, Justice without Borders, Muslim student association.

Athletics. NCAA. **Intercollegiate:** Baseball M, basketball, cross-country, golf, rowing (crew) W, soccer, softball W, tennis, volleyball W. **Intramural:** Basketball, football (non-tackle), golf, racquetball, soccer, softball, table tennis, tennis, ultimate frisbee, volleyball. **Team name:** Bluejays.

Student services. Adult student services, alcohol/substance abuse counseling, chaplain/spiritual director, career counseling, services for economically disadvantaged, student employment services, financial aid counseling, health services, minority student services, on-campus daycare, personal counseling, placement for graduates, veterans' counselor, women's services. **Physically disabled:** Services for visually, speech, hearing impaired.

Contact. E-mail: admissions@creighton.edu
Phone: (402) 280-2703 Toll-free number: (800) 282-5835
Fax: (402) 280-2685
Sarah Richardson, Director of Admissions and Scholarships, Creighton University, 2500 California Plaza, Omaha, NE 68178-0001

Doane College

Crete, Nebraska

www.doane.edu

CB member
CB code: 6165

- Private 4-year liberal arts college affiliated with the United Church of Christ
- Residential campus in small town
- 1,053 degree-seeking undergraduates: 1% part-time, 47% women, 3% African American, 1% Asian American, 7% Hispanic/Latino, 3% Multiracial, non-Hispanic, 2% international
- 77% of applicants admitted
- SAT or ACT (ACT writing optional) required
- 61% graduate within 6 years

General. Founded in 1872. Regionally accredited. Campuses also in Lincoln and Grand Island. **Degrees:** 235 bachelor's awarded; master's offered. **ROTC:** Army, Air Force. **Location:** 25 miles from Lincoln, 75 miles from Omaha. **Calendar:** Semester, limited summer session. **Full-time faculty:** 82 total; 83% have terminal degrees, 1% minority, 51% women. **Part-time faculty:** 38 total; 42% have terminal degrees, 3% minority, 66% women. **Class size:** 76% < 20, 23% 20-39, less than 1% 40-49, less than 1% 50-99. **Special facilities:** Arboretum, open-air theater, observatory, all-American rose test garden, ropes challenge course, fitness trail.

Freshman class profile. 1,892 applied, 1,449 admitted, 330 enrolled.

Mid 50% test scores		Rank in top quarter:	36%
ACT composite:	20-26	Rank in top tenth:	11%
GPA 3.75 or higher:	33%	Return as sophomores:	70%
GPA 3.50-3.74:	21%	Out-of-state:	20%
GPA 3.0-3.49:	32%	Live on campus:	96%
GPA 2.0-2.99:	14%	International:	2%

Basis for selection. Academic and personal record, recommendations, test scores important. Class rank considered. Interview required for academically marginal students; audition required for drama, music programs and forensics; portfolio required for art program. **Home schooled:** Transcript of courses and grades required. GED Required.

High school preparation. College-preparatory program recommended. 13 units recommended. Recommended units include English 4, mathematics 3, social studies 3 and science 3.

2015-2016 Annual costs. Tuition/fees: $28,790. Room/board: $8,350. Books/supplies: $900.

2015-2016 Financial aid. Need-based: 309 full-time freshmen applied for aid; 268 deemed to have need; 268 received aid. Average need met was 93%. Average scholarship/grant was $20,993; average loan $3,568. 76% of total undergraduate aid awarded as scholarships/grants, 24% as loans/jobs. **Non-need-based:** Awarded to 374 full-time undergraduates, including 122 freshmen. Scholarships awarded for academics, alumni affiliation, art, athletics, music/drama, religious affiliation.

Application procedures. Admission: No deadline. No application fee. Admission notification on a rolling basis beginning on or about 9/15. Must reply by May 1 or within 4 week(s) if notified thereafter. **Financial aid:** Priority date 2/25; no closing date. FAFSA required. Applicants notified on a rolling basis starting 3/15; must reply within 4 week(s) of notification.

Academics. Midwest Institute for International Students prepares students to meet English language requirement for admission to Doane and other American colleges. **Special study options:** Combined bachelor's/graduate degree, double major, ESL, honors, independent study, internships, student-designed major, study abroad, teacher certification program. 3-2 programs in engineering with Washington University, Columbia University, 3-2 program in environmental and forestry studies with Duke University. **Credit/placement by examination:** AP, CLEP, IB, SAT, ACT, institutional tests. 36 credit hours maximum toward bachelor's degree. International students who successfully complete Midwest Institute ESL program may be admitted without TOEFL scores. **Support services:** Learning center, reduced course load, remedial instruction, study skills assistance, tutoring, writing center.

Majors. Biology: General, biochemistry. **Business:** Accounting, business admin, human resources. **Communications:** Journalism, organizational. **Computer sciences:** General, computer science, information systems. **Conservation:** Environmental studies. **Education:** Elementary, ESL, physical, special ed. **English:** English lit. **Foreign languages:** French, German, Spanish. **History:** General. **Human services:** General. **Liberal arts:** Arts/sciences. **Math:** General. **Philosophy/religion:** Philosophy, religion. **Physical sciences:** Chemistry, physics. **Psychology:** General. **Social sciences:** General, economics, international relations, political science, sociology. **Visual/performing arts:** Art, dramatic, graphic design, music.

Most popular majors. Biology 12%, business/marketing 15%, education 21%, psychology 6%, social sciences 7%, visual/performing arts 11%.

Technology on campus. 400 workstations in dormitories, library, computer center, student center. Dormitories wired for high-speed internet access and linked to campus network. Commuter students can connect to campus network. Online course registration, online library, helpline, student web hosting, wireless network available.

Student life. Freshman orientation: Available. Preregistration for classes offered. **Policies:** Unmarried students under 22 not living with parents expected to live on campus. **Housing:** Guaranteed on-campus for freshmen. Coed dorms, single-sex dorms, themed housing available. $200 fully refundable deposit. **Activities:** Bands, campus ministries, choral groups, dance, drama, film society, literary magazine, music ensembles, musical theater, radio station, student government, student newspaper, TV station, student education association, Doane speakers, Club Internationale, Fellowship of Christian Athletes, American Minority Student Alliance, College Republicans, Young Democrats.

Athletics. NAIA. **Intercollegiate:** Baseball M, basketball, bowling, cheerleading W, cross-country, football (tackle) M, golf, soccer, softball W, tennis, track and field, volleyball W, wrestling M. **Intramural:** Basketball, cheerleading W, football (tackle) M, golf, softball, swimming, tennis, volleyball, wrestling M. **Team name:** Tigers.

Student services. Adult student services, chaplain/spiritual director, career counseling, student employment services, financial aid counseling, health services, personal counseling, placement for graduates, veterans' counselor.

Contact. E-mail: admissions@doane.edu
Phone: (402) 826-8222 Toll-free number: (800) 333-6263
Fax: (402) 826-8600
Kyle McMurray, Director of Admission, Doane College, 1014 Boswell Avenue, Crete, NE 68333

Grace University
Omaha, Nebraska
www.graceuniversity.edu   **CB code: 6248**

- Private 4-year university and Bible college affiliated with the interdenominational tradition
- Residential campus in large city
- 345 degree-seeking undergraduates
- ACT (writing optional), application essay required

General. Founded in 1943. Regionally accredited; also accredited by ABHE. **Degrees:** 67 bachelor's, 4 associate awarded; master's offered. **ROTC:** Air Force. **Calendar:** Semester, limited summer session. **Full-time faculty:** 30 total. **Part-time faculty:** 40 total.

Basis for selection. School achievement record, religious affiliation/commitment, test scores, and student profile important. Conditional admission for students who have not taken SAT/ACT. Audition required for music programs. **Home schooled:** Transcript of courses and grades required. ACT score of 20 or GED required.

High school preparation. College-preparatory program recommended. Teacher education program requires 4 language arts, 2 mathematics, 2 sciences, 2 social sciences.

2015-2016 Annual costs. Tuition/fees: $20,548. Room/board: $7,228. Books/supplies: $475.

Financial aid. Non-need-based: Scholarships awarded for academics, alumni affiliation, athletics, leadership, minority status, music/drama.

Application procedures. Admission: Priority date 3/1; no deadline. $35 fee, may be waived for applicants with need. Admission notification on a rolling basis. **Financial aid:** Priority date 3/1, closing date 4/1. FAFSA required. Applicants notified on a rolling basis starting 3/1; must reply within 3 week(s) of notification.

Academics. Special study options: Accelerated study, combined bachelor's/graduate degree, cooperative education, distance learning, double major, dual enrollment of high school students, independent study, internships, liberal arts/career combination, student-designed major, study abroad, teacher certification program, urban semester. **Credit/placement by examination:** AP, CLEP, ACT. 15 credit hours maximum toward bachelor's degree. **Support services:** Learning center, reduced course load, study skills assistance, tutoring, writing center.

Majors. Business: Business admin, management science. **Communications:** General, media studies. **Communications technology:** General. **Computer sciences:** General. **Education:** Business, early childhood, elementary, English, ESL, history, mathematics, middle, music, physical, secondary, social science, social studies. **Foreign languages:** Biblical. **Health services:** Nursing (RN). **History:** General. **Human services:** Social work. **Liberal arts:** Humanities. **Psychology:** General. **Theology:** Bible, missionary, religious ed, sacred music, theology, youth ministry. **Visual/performing arts:** Music, music performance, music theory/composition, piano/keyboard, voice/opera.

Technology on campus. Dormitories wired for high-speed internet access and linked to campus network. Commuter students can connect to campus network. Online library, helpline, wireless network available.

Student life. Freshman orientation: Mandatory. Preregistration for classes offered. **Policies:** All on campus housing is alcohol/drug/smoke-free. Religious observance required. **Housing:** Guaranteed on-campus for freshmen. Single-sex dorms, apartments, wellness housing available. $200 partly refundable deposit. **Activities:** Bands, campus ministries, choral groups, drama, international student organizations, music ensembles, musical theater, student government.

Athletics. NCCAA. **Intercollegiate:** Baseball M, basketball, soccer, softball W, volleyball W. **Intramural:** Basketball, soccer, volleyball W. **Team name:** Royals.

Student services. Adult student services, chaplain/spiritual director, career counseling, student employment services, financial aid counseling, health services, personal counseling, placement for graduates.

Contact. E-mail: admissions@graceuniversity.edu
Phone: (402) 449-2831 Toll-free number: (800) 383-1422
Fax: (402) 449-2999
Tara Koth, Director of Admissions, Grace University, 1311 South Ninth Street, Omaha, NE 68108-3629

Hastings College
Hastings, Nebraska
www.hastings.edu

CB code: 6270

- Private 4-year liberal arts college affiliated with the Presbyterian Church (USA)
- Residential campus in large town
- 1,103 degree-seeking undergraduates: 1% part-time, 48% women
- 31 degree-seeking graduate students
- SAT or ACT (ACT writing optional) required

General. Founded in 1882. Regionally accredited. **Degrees:** 235 bachelor's awarded; master's offered. **Location:** 100 miles from Lincoln, 150 miles from Omaha. **Calendar:** 4-1-4, limited summer session. **Full-time faculty:** 79 total; 78% have terminal degrees, 2% minority, 43% women. **Part-time faculty:** 40 total; 12% have terminal degrees, 38% women. **Class size:** 64% < 20, 35% 20-39, 1% 40-49, less than 1% 50-99. **Special facilities:** Glass blowing studio, observatory, music studios, communications center.

Freshman class profile.

GPA 3.75 or higher:	38%	Rank in top tenth:	20%
GPA 3.50-3.74:	20%	Out-of-state:	36%
GPA 3.0-3.49:	25%	Live on campus:	93%
GPA 2.0-2.99:	17%	Fraternities:	20%
Rank in top quarter:	45%	Sororities:	20%

Basis for selection. Academic achievement record most important; counselor recommendations, test scores, class ranking also important. Placement interview strongly recommended for all applicants; interview required for allied health program; audition required for forensics, music, theater programs; portfolio required for art program. **Home schooled:** ACT or SAT scores, satisfactory completion of high school graduation equivalency required. **Learning Disabled:** Interview recommended.

High school preparation. Required and recommended units include English 3-4, mathematics 3-4, social studies 4, history 4, science 3-4 (laboratory 3-4) and foreign language 2.

2015-2016 Annual costs. Tuition/fees: $27,300. Room/board: $8,080. Books/supplies: $170. Personal expenses: $2,670.

Financial aid. Non-need-based: Scholarships awarded for academics, alumni affiliation, art, athletics, leadership, music/drama.

Application procedures. Admission: No deadline. No application fee. Admission notification on a rolling basis beginning on or about 10/15. **Financial aid:** Closing date 5/1. FAFSA, institutional form required. Applicants notified on a rolling basis starting 2/15; must reply within 2 week(s) of notification.

Academics. Special study options: Combined bachelor's/graduate degree, double major, exchange student, independent study, internships, student-designed major, study abroad, teacher certification program, urban semester. 3-2 engineering programs with Columbia University, Georgia Institute of Technology, and Washington University, Missouri; International exchange program with colleges in England, Holland, Germany and Ireland; BA-BSN program with Creighton University. **Credit/placement by examination:** AP, CLEP, IB. 20 credit hours maximum toward bachelor's degree. All credit by examinations subject to approval of department. **Support services:** Learning center, reduced course load, study skills assistance, tutoring, writing center.

Majors. Biology: General. **Business:** Accounting, business admin, human resources, marketing. **Communications:** Advertising, broadcast journalism, communications/speech/rhetoric, journalism, media studies, public relations, radio/TV. **Communications technology:** General. **Computer sciences:** General, computer science. **Education:** General, art, biology, business, chemistry, drama/dance, early childhood, elementary, English, foreign languages, history, mathematics, music, physical, physics, science, secondary, social science, social studies, special ed, speech. **English:** Creative writing, English lit, rhetoric/composition. **Foreign languages:** General, German, Spanish. **Health services:** Health care admin, predental, premedicine, preveterinary. **History:** General. **Human services:** General. **Liberal arts:** Arts/sciences. **Math:** General. **Parks/recreation:** Exercise sciences, facilities management,

health/fitness, sports admin. **Philosophy/religion:** Philosophy, religion. **Physical sciences:** Chemistry, physics. **Protective services:** Corrections. **Psychology:** General. **Social sciences:** Economics, international relations, political science, sociology. **Visual/performing arts:** Art, art history/conservation, dramatic, music, music history, music pedagogy, music performance, piano/keyboard, stringed instruments, voice/opera.

Most popular majors. Biology 8%, business/marketing 16%, education 27%, psychology 7%, social sciences 8%, visual/performing arts 7%.

Technology on campus. 240 workstations in library, computer center, student center. Dormitories wired for high-speed internet access and linked to campus network. Commuter students can connect to campus network. Online course registration, online library, helpline, repair service, wireless network available.

Student life. Freshman orientation: Mandatory. Preregistration for classes offered. Weekend-long program, prior to the first day of class. Includes community service project. **Policies:** Alcohol not permitted on campus except in apartments for students of legal age; smoking forbidden in campus buildings. **Housing:** Guaranteed on-campus for all undergraduates. Coed dorms, single-sex dorms, apartments, wellness housing available. $200 fully refundable deposit, deadline 8/1. Honors housing, campus houses, apartments available to upperclass students. **Activities:** Bands, campus ministries, choral groups, drama, literary magazine, music ensembles, musical theater, radio station, student government, student newspaper, symphony orchestra, TV station, Fellowship of Christian Athletes, student health advisory council, religious programs committee, Religion in Life Committee, Multicultural Student Union, Peer HIV Education Organization, College Democrats, College Republicans, Habitat for Humanity, gay/straight alliance.

Athletics. NAIA. **Intercollegiate:** Baseball M, basketball, bowling, cheerleading W, cross-country, football (tackle) M, golf, soccer, softball W, tennis, track and field, volleyball W, wrestling M. **Intramural:** Basketball, bowling, football (non-tackle), racquetball, softball, table tennis, volleyball. **Team name:** Broncos.

Student services. Adult student services, chaplain/spiritual director, career counseling, student employment services, financial aid counseling, health services, minority student services, personal counseling, placement for graduates. **Physically disabled:** Services for hearing impaired.

Contact. E-mail: smeeske@hastings.edu
Phone: (402) 461-7403 Toll-free number: (800) 532-7642
Fax: (402) 461-7490
Chris Schukei, Director of Admissions, Hastings College, 710 North Turner Avenue, Hastings, NE 68901-7621

Herzing University: Omaha School of Massage Therapy and Healthcare
Omaha, Nebraska
www.osmhc.com

- For-profit 4-year health science college
- Very large city
- 168 degree-seeking undergraduates

General. Regionally accredited. **Degrees:** 12 associate awarded. **Calendar:** Semester. **Full-time faculty:** 4 total. **Part-time faculty:** 12 total.

Basis for selection. Secondary school record very important, test scores recommended.

2015-2016 Annual costs. Personal expenses: $2,665. **Additional information:** Certificate programs: $13,670 to $26,820. Associate programs: $26,180 to $53,640. Bachelor's programs: $61,515 to $88,065.

Application procedures. Admission: No deadline. **Financial aid:** No deadline.

Academics. Credit/placement by examination: AP, CLEP.

Majors. Business: Business admin. **Protective services:** Criminal justice. **Visual/performing arts:** Graphic design.

Contact. E-mail: info@osmhc.com
Angie Armstrong, Director of Admissions, Herzing University: Omaha School of Massage Therapy and Healthcare, 9748 Park Drive, Omaha, NE 68127

ITT Technical Institute: Omaha
Omaha, Nebraska
www.itt-tech.edu   CB code: 2740

- For-profit 4-year technical college
- Commuter campus in large city
- 395 undergraduates
- Interview required

General. Accredited by ACICS. **Degrees:** 21 bachelor's, 123 associate awarded. **Calendar:** Quarter, extensive summer session. **Full-time faculty:** 14 total. **Part-time faculty:** 61 total.

Basis for selection. Satisfactory scores from on-site tests in English and mathematics required.

2015-2016 Annual costs. Per-credit-hour charge, $493, will vary depending on program level and course of study. Academic fee, $200. Some programs require purchase of tools, which could cost an additional $100 to $655. All costs subject to change.

Application procedures. Admission: No deadline. No application fee. Admission notification on a rolling basis. **Financial aid:** No deadline. FAFSA, institutional form required. Applicants notified on a rolling basis.

Academics. Credit/placement by examination: AP, CLEP. **Support services:** Learning center, tutoring.

Majors. Business: Accounting/business management, business admin, construction management. **Communications technology:** Animation/special effects. **Computer sciences:** Networking, security.

Technology on campus. Online library available.

Student life. Freshman orientation: Available. Preregistration for classes offered.

Student services. Career counseling, student employment services, placement for graduates.

Contact. Phone: (402) 331-2900 Toll-free number: (800) 677-9260 Jacqueline Hawthorne, Director of Recruitment, ITT Technical Institute: Omaha, 1120 North 103rd Plaza, Suite 200, Omaha, NE 68114

Midland University
Fremont, Nebraska
www.midlandu.edu   CB code: 6406

- Private 4-year university and liberal arts college affiliated with the Evangelical Lutheran Church in America
- Residential campus in large town
- 1,224 degree-seeking undergraduates
- ACT (writing optional) required

General. Founded in 1883. Regionally accredited. **Degrees:** 230 bachelor's awarded; master's offered. **Location:** 25 miles from Omaha, 40 miles from Lincoln. **Calendar:** 4-1-4, limited summer session. **Full-time faculty:** 50 total. **Part-time faculty:** 28 total. **Class size:** 49% < 20, 47% 20-39, 3% 40-49, 2% 50-99. **Special facilities:** Planetarium/observatory, arboretum.

Freshman class profile.

Rank in top quarter:	14%	Out-of-state:	21%
Rank in top tenth:	9%	Live on campus:	80%

Basis for selection. School achievement record, test scores, recommendation by school official, rank in top half of class reviewed. Applicants with lesser qualifications considered by review of test scores and personal educational objectives. Interview recommended for all students; audition recommended for drama, music programs.

High school preparation. 12 units recommended. Recommended units include English 4, mathematics 2, social studies 2, history 1, science 2 and foreign language 1.

2015-2016 Annual costs. Tuition/fees: $29,400. Room/board: $7,484. Books/supplies: $1,020. Personal expenses: $1,934.

Financial aid. Non-need-based: Scholarships awarded for academics, alumni affiliation, art, athletics, leadership, minority status, music/drama, religious affiliation.

Application procedures. Admission: No deadline. $30 fee, may be waived for applicants with need, free for online applicants. Admission notification on a rolling basis beginning on or about 10/1. **Financial aid:** Priority date 4/15; no closing date. FAFSA, institutional form required. Applicants notified on a rolling basis starting 3/1; must reply within 2 week(s) of notification.

Academics. Special study options: Accelerated study, distance learning, double major, dual enrollment of high school students, independent study, internships, liberal arts/career combination, student-designed major, study abroad, teacher certification program. **Credit/placement by examination:** AP, CLEP, ACT, institutional tests. 32 credit hours maximum toward associate degree, 32 toward bachelor's. **Support services:** Learning center, reduced course load, study skills assistance, tutoring, writing center.

Majors. Area/ethnic studies: American. **Biology:** General. **Business:** General, accounting, business admin, management information systems, office management. **Communications:** Communications/speech/rhetoric, journalism, public relations. **Computer sciences:** General, computer science, programming. **Conservation:** General. **Education:** General, art, biology, business, chemistry, early childhood, elementary, English, German, history, mathematics, middle, multi-level teacher, music, physical, science, secondary, social science, social studies, Spanish, speech. **English:** English lit. **Foreign languages:** Spanish. **Health services:** Athletic training, predental, premedicine, preop/surgical nursing, prepharmacy, preveterinary, respiratory therapy technology. **History:** General. **Liberal arts:** Arts/sciences. **Math:** General. **Philosophy/religion:** Religion. **Physical sciences:** Chemistry. **Psychology:** General. **Social sciences:** General, criminology, economics, sociology. **Visual/performing arts:** Art, commercial/advertising art, dramatic, music, studio arts.

Most popular majors. Business/marketing 32%, communications/journalism 8%, education 27%, health sciences 20%, social sciences 10%.

Technology on campus. 190 workstations in dormitories, library, computer center, student center. Dormitories wired for high-speed internet access and linked to campus network. Commuter students can connect to campus network. Online course registration, online library, helpline, repair service, wireless network available.

Student life. Freshman orientation: Mandatory. Preregistration for classes offered. **Housing:** Guaranteed on-campus for freshmen. Coed dorms, single-sex dorms, special housing for disabled, apartments, wellness housing available. $100 nonrefundable deposit, deadline 8/1. **Activities:** Bands, campus ministries, choral groups, dance, drama, literary magazine, music ensembles, musical theater, student government, student newspaper, Fellowship of Christian Athletes, Circle K, Religious Life Council.

Athletics. NAIA. **Intercollegiate:** Baseball M, basketball, bowling, cheerleading, cross-country, football (tackle) M, golf, ice hockey, lacrosse W, soccer, softball W, tennis, track and field, volleyball W, wrestling. **Intramural:** Basketball, football (non-tackle), sand volleyball, soccer M, softball, table tennis, tennis, track and field, volleyball. **Team name:** Warriors.

Student services. Career counseling, student employment services, health services, personal counseling, placement for graduates, veterans' counselor.

Contact. E-mail: admissions@midlandu.edu
Phone: (402) 941-6503 Toll-free number: (800) 642-8382
Fax: (402) 721-0250
Nick Boone, Director of Admissions, Midland University, 900 North Clarkson, Fremont, NE 68025

Nebraska Christian College
Papillion, Nebraska
www.nechristian.edu   CB code: 1332

- Private 4-year Bible college affiliated with the Christian Church
- Residential campus in large town
- 130 degree-seeking undergraduates
- SAT or ACT (ACT writing optional), application essay required

General. Founded in 1944. Accredited by ABHE. Internships required. Local and international trips during Week of Ministry, job placement assistance, and study abroad in India available. **Degrees:** 18 bachelor's, 5 associate awarded. **Location:** 10 miles from Omaha. **Calendar:** Semester. **Full-time faculty:** 5 total; 60% have terminal degrees. **Part-time faculty:** 24 total; 21% have terminal degrees, 21% women. **Class size:** 77% < 20, 16% 20-39, 2% 40-49, 4% 50-99, 2% >100.

Freshman class profile.

Out-of-state:	45%	Live on campus:	90%

Basis for selection. Christian commitment, essays and references very important; high school transcript or GED required. Standardized test scores required. Transcript of any previous college work required. ACT recommended. **Home schooled:** Transcript of courses and grades, letter of recommendation (nonparent) required.

High school preparation. College-preparatory program recommended.

2015-2016 Annual costs. Tuition/fees: $600. Comprehensive fee: $22,900. Books/supplies: $600. Personal expenses: $1,900.

Financial aid. Non-need-based: Scholarships awarded for academics, leadership, religious affiliation.

Application procedures. Admission: No deadline. $30 fee, may be waived for applicants with need. Application must be submitted online. Admission notification on a rolling basis. Must reply by May 1 or within 4 week(s) if notified thereafter. **Financial aid:** Priority date 6/1; no closing date. FAFSA, institutional form required. Applicants notified on a rolling basis starting 5/5.

Academics. Special study options: Combined bachelor's/graduate degree, cooperative education, distance learning, double major, dual enrollment of high school students, independent study, internships, study abroad. **Credit/ placement by examination:** AP, CLEP, IB, ACT. **Support services:** Learning center, reduced course load, remedial instruction, study skills assistance, tutoring, writing center.

Majors. Theology: Bible, missionary, religious ed, sacred music, theology.

Technology on campus. 15 workstations in library, computer center. Dormitories wired for high-speed internet access and linked to campus network. Online course registration, helpline, repair service, wireless network available.

Student life. Freshman orientation: Mandatory. Preregistration for classes offered. Three-four-day session held the week before classes start. **Policies:** Religious observance required. **Housing:** Guaranteed on-campus for freshmen. Single-sex dorms, special housing for disabled, apartments, wellness housing available. $300 nonrefundable deposit. **Activities:** Campus ministries, choral groups, literary magazine, music ensembles, student government, ensembles, outreach team, running club, mountain climbing club, minority students association.

Athletics. Intercollegiate: Volleyball W. **Intramural:** Basketball, cross-country, football (non-tackle), golf, soccer, softball, volleyball. **Team name:** Parsons.

Student services. Adult student services, alcohol/substance abuse counseling, chaplain/spiritual director, career counseling, student employment services, financial aid counseling, health services, minority student services, personal counseling, placement for graduates.

Contact. E-mail: admissions@nechristian.edu
Phone: (402) 935-9400 Fax: (402) 935-9500
Kristin Miller, Director of Admissions, Nebraska Christian College, 12550 South 114th Street, Papillion, NE 68046

Nebraska Methodist College of Nursing and Allied Health
Omaha, Nebraska
www.methodistcollege.edu   CB code: 6510

◆ Private 4-year health science and nursing college affiliated with the United Methodist Church
◆ Commuter campus in large city
◆ 766 degree-seeking undergraduates: 38% part-time, 90% women, 4% African American, 1% Asian American, 5% Hispanic/Latino, 2% Multiracial, non-Hispanic
◆ 226 degree-seeking graduate students
◆ SAT or ACT (ACT writing optional), application essay, interview required
◆ 72% graduate within 6 years

General. Founded in 1891. Regionally accredited. **Degrees:** 182 bachelor's, 61 associate awarded; master's, doctoral offered. **ROTC:** Air Force. **Location:** 120 miles from Des Moines, Iowa, 180 miles from Kansas City, Missouri. **Calendar:** Semester, limited summer session. **Full-time faculty:** 60 total; 33% have terminal degrees, 5% minority, 97% women. **Part-time faculty:** 10 total; 20% have terminal degrees, 100% women. **Class size:** 52% < 20, 33% 20-39, 9% 40-49, 6% 50-99. **Special facilities:** Human cadaver lab, high-tech simulation labs, center for health partnerships.

Freshman class profile.

Mid 50% test scores			
ACT composite:	22-26	GPA 2.0-2.99:	17%
GPA 3.75 or higher:	32%	Return as sophomores:	81%
GPA 3.50-3.74:	24%	Out-of-state:	6%
GPA 3.0-3.49:	27%	Live on campus:	50%

Basis for selection. School achievement, test scores most important. Written personal statement important. Recommendations, school and community activities considered. Deadlines vary by program. ACT or SAT required of all current high school graduates and of students making application within two years of high school graduation. TEAS Math Assessment used for placement with traditional BSN students. **Home schooled:** Statement describing home school structure and mission, state high school equivalency certificate, interview required. ACT or SAT required for all applicants within two years of home school completion. Students with home school completion of more than two years and no results of ACT or SAT are required to show success in a minimum of 12 college credit hours. **Learning Disabled:** Educational transcript required.

High school preparation. College-preparatory program recommended. 10 units required. Required units include English 4, mathematics 2, social studies 2, history 1, science 4 (laboratory 2). Chemistry, biology, algebra, anatomy and physiology recommended. A background in physics is strongly recommended for applicants for radiologic technology, sonography, and physical therapist assistant.

2015-2016 Annual costs. Tuition/fees: $18,109. Room only: $6,460. Books/supplies: $1,300. Personal expenses: $1,506.

2015-2016 Financial aid. Need-based: 28 full-time freshmen applied for aid; 24 deemed to have need; 24 received aid. Average need met was 51%. Average scholarship/grant was $7,872; average loan $3,520. 32% of total undergraduate aid awarded as scholarships/grants, 68% as loans/jobs. **Non-need-based:** Awarded to 69 full-time undergraduates, including 5 freshmen. Scholarships awarded for academics, alumni affiliation, leadership, religious affiliation.

Application procedures. Admission: No deadline. $25 fee, may be waived for applicants with need. Application must be submitted online. Admission notification on a rolling basis. Required within two weeks of acceptance. Application deadlines vary by program. **Financial aid:** Priority date 3/1; no closing date. FAFSA, institutional form required. Applicants notified on a rolling basis starting 3/15; must reply within 3 week(s) of notification.

Academics. Peer tutoring available for most courses; supplemental instruction available for science and professional courses. **Special study options:** Accelerated study, combined bachelor's/graduate degree, distance learning, independent study, internships. **Credit/placement by examination:** AP, CLEP, institutional tests. 9 credit hours maximum toward associate degree, 9 toward bachelor's. Credit by examination considered on an individual basis. **Support services:** Learning center, pre-admission summer program, reduced course load, remedial instruction, study skills assistance, tutoring, writing center.

Majors. Health services: Cardiovascular technology, health care admin, nursing (RN), physical therapy assistant, public health ed, radiologic technology/medical imaging, respiratory therapy technology, sonography, surgical technology.

Technology on campus. 55 workstations in library, computer center, student center. Dormitories wired for high-speed internet access and linked to campus network. Commuter students can connect to campus network. Online course registration, online library, helpline, wireless network available.

Student life. Freshman orientation: Mandatory. Preregistration for classes offered. Two-day session held in August. One-day transfer orientation for health professions students held in May. **Housing:** Guaranteed on-campus for freshmen. Coed dorms, apartments, wellness housing available. $150 nonrefundable deposit, deadline 5/1. Family housing for students with children. **Activities:** Campus ministries, student government, student nurse association (state and national), allied health student association, College Ambassadors, minority student organization, residence hall council, military student organization.

Student services. Adult student services, alcohol/substance abuse counseling, chaplain/spiritual director, career counseling, student employment services, financial aid counseling, health services, minority student services, personal counseling, placement for graduates, veterans' counselor. **Physically disabled:** Services for hearing impaired.

Contact. E-mail: admissions@methodistcollege.edu
Phone: (402) 354-7200 Toll-free number: (800) 335-5510
Fax: (402) 354-7020
Megan Maryott, Director of Enrollment Services, Nebraska Methodist College of Nursing and Allied Health, 720 North 87th Street, Omaha, NE 68114-2852

Nebraska Wesleyan University
Lincoln, Nebraska
www.nebrwesleyan.edu   CB code: 6470

- Private 4-year liberal arts college affiliated with the United Methodist Church
- Residential campus in small city
- 1,788 degree-seeking undergraduates: 17% part-time, 61% women, 2% African American, 2% Asian American, 5% Hispanic/Latino, 2% Multiracial, non-Hispanic, 1% international
- 234 degree-seeking graduate students
- 79% of applicants admitted
- SAT or ACT (ACT writing optional) required
- 62% graduate within 6 years

General. Founded in 1887. Regionally accredited. **Degrees:** 465 bachelor's awarded; master's offered. **ROTC:** Army, Naval, Air Force. **Location:** 55 miles from Omaha, 200 miles from Kansas City, Missouri. **Calendar:** Semester, limited summer session. **Full-time faculty:** 107 total; 91% have terminal degrees, 2% minority, 53% women. **Part-time faculty:** 130 total; 8% minority. **Class size:** 75% < 20, 24% 20-39, 1% 40-49, less than 1% 50-99. **Special facilities:** Planetarium, laboratory theater, herbarium, nuclear magnetic resonance laboratory, sleep laboratory, art gallery, forensic science laboratory and crime house.

Freshman class profile. 1,689 applied, 1,331 admitted, 439 enrolled.

Mid 50% test scores			
SAT critical reading:	430-590	Rank in top quarter:	50%
SAT math:	510-600	Rank in top tenth:	18%
ACT composite:	22-27	Return as sophomores:	79%
GPA 3.75 or higher:	47%	Out-of-state:	15%
GPA 3.50-3.74:	21%	Live on campus:	91%
GPA 3.0-3.49:	24%	International:	1%
GPA 2.0-2.99:	8%	Fraternities:	24%
		Sororities:	34%

Basis for selection. Students with a cumulative GPA of 3.0 or above or achieve an ACT composite score of 20 or an SAT combined score of 950 (exclusive of Writing) are invited to apply for admission. Campus visit recommended for all students; audition required for drama, music scholarships; portfolio required for art scholarships. **Home schooled:** Transcript of courses and grades required. GED scores.

High school preparation. College-preparatory program recommended. Recommended units include English 4, mathematics 4, social studies 3, science 3 (laboratory 3) and foreign language 3.

2015-2016 Annual costs. Tuition/fees: $29,800. Room/board: $8,340. Books/supplies: $1,000. Personal expenses: $3,500.

2014-2015 Financial aid. Need-based: 332 full-time freshmen applied for aid; 294 deemed to have need; 293 received aid. Average need met was 81%. Average scholarship/grant was $17,683; average loan $4,956. 71% of total undergraduate aid awarded as scholarships/grants, 29% as loans/jobs. **Non-need-based:** Awarded to 451 full-time undergraduates, including 122 freshmen. Scholarships awarded for academics, alumni affiliation, art, leadership, music/drama.

Application procedures. Admission: Priority date 5/1; deadline 8/15. No application fee. Admission notification on a rolling basis beginning on or about 9/15. Must reply by May 1 or within 2 week(s) if notified thereafter. **Financial aid:** No deadline. FAFSA required. Applicants notified on a rolling basis starting 2/1; must reply by 5/1 or within 2 week(s) of notification.

Academics. Special study options: Combined bachelor's/graduate degree, distance learning, double major, dual enrollment of high school students, independent study, internships, liberal arts/career combination, semester at sea, study abroad, teacher certification program, United Nations semester, urban semester, Washington semester. 3-2 engineering with Washington University, Columbia University, and University of Nebraska-Lincoln; Capitol Hill Internship Program; Chicago Center for Urban Life and Culture; summer research fellowships in the natural sciences; faculty led international study tours. **Credit/placement by examination:** AP, CLEP, IB, SAT, ACT, institutional tests. **Support services:** Reduced course load, study skills assistance, tutoring, writing center. Academic success course; center for academic resources.

Majors. Biology: General, Biochemistry/molecular biology. **Business:** Accounting, business admin, international. **Communications:** Communications/speech/rhetoric, political. **Education:** Elementary, English, middle, music, physical, science, social science, special ed. **English:** English lit. **Foreign languages:** French, German, Spanish. **Health services:** Athletic training, nursing (RN). **History:** General. **Human services:** Social work. **Math:** General. **Parks/recreation:** Exercise sciences, health/fitness, sports admin. **Philosophy/religion:** Philosophy, religion. **Physical sciences:** Chemistry, physics. **Psychology:** General. **Social sciences:** Economics, political science, sociology. **Visual/performing arts:** Art, dramatic, music, music performance, studio arts.

Most popular majors. Biology 7%, business/marketing 13%, education 10%, health sciences 20%, parks/recreation 9%, psychology 6%.

Technology on campus. 360 workstations in dormitories, library, computer center, student center. Dormitories wired for high-speed internet access and linked to campus network. Commuter students can connect to campus network. Online course registration, online library, helpline, student web hosting, wireless network available.

Student life. Freshman orientation: Mandatory. Preregistration for classes offered. One-day sessions in summer; multi-day orientation program before fall classes begin. **Housing:** Guaranteed on-campus for all undergraduates. Coed dorms, single-sex dorms, special housing for disabled, apartments, fraternity/sorority housing, themed housing available. $95 fully refundable deposit, deadline 8/15. Residence hall suites and townhomes available. **Activities:** Bands, campus ministries, choral groups, dance, drama, international student organizations, literary magazine, music ensembles, Model UN, musical theater, opera, radio station, student government, student newspaper, symphony orchestra, Student Fellowship, Fellowship of Christian Athletes, Meeting of Students Addressing Intercultural Concerns (MOSAIC), College Republicans, Young Democrats, Nebraskans for Peace, International Relations Organization, Circle K, Environmental Action, Global Service Learning.

Athletics. NCAA. **Intercollegiate:** Baseball M, basketball, bowling W, cheerleading W, cross-country, football (tackle) M, golf, soccer, softball W, swimming, tennis, track and field, volleyball W, wrestling M. **Intramural:** Basketball, bowling, football (non-tackle), racquetball, soccer, softball, tennis, ultimate frisbee, volleyball, water polo. **Team name:** Prairie Wolves.

Student services. Adult student services, chaplain/spiritual director, career counseling, student employment services, financial aid counseling, health services, minority student services, personal counseling, placement for graduates, women's services. **Physically disabled:** Services for visually, speech, hearing impaired.

Contact. E-mail: admissions@nebrwesleyan.edu
Phone: (402) 465-2218 Toll-free number: (800) 541-3818
Fax: (402) 465-2177
Gordie Coffin, Director of Admissions, Nebraska Wesleyan University, 5000 St. Paul Avenue, Lincoln, NE 68504

Peru State College
Peru, Nebraska
www.peru.edu   CB code: 6468

- Public 4-year liberal arts and teachers college
- Commuter campus in rural community
- 1,472 degree-seeking undergraduates: 22% part-time, 57% women, 10% African American, 1% Asian American, 7% Hispanic/Latino, 1% Native American, 1% Multi-racial, non-Hispanic, 1% international
- 325 degree-seeking graduate students
- 33% graduate within 6 years

General. Founded in 1867. Regionally accredited. **Degrees:** 266 bachelor's awarded; master's offered. **Location:** 64 miles from Omaha, 67 miles from Lincoln. **Calendar:** Semester, limited summer session. **Full-time faculty:** 52 total; 73% have terminal degrees, 8% minority, 42% women. **Part-time faculty:** 56 total; 18% have terminal degrees, 59% women.

Freshman class profile. 945 applied, 316 admitted, 229 enrolled.

Mid 50% test scores			
		GPA 2.0-2.99:	40%
ACT composite:	17-23	Rank in top quarter:	22%
GPA 3.75 or higher:	14%	Rank in top tenth:	6%
GPA 3.50-3.74:	11%	Out-of-state:	29%
GPA 3.0-3.49:	31%	Live on campus:	85%

Basis for selection. Open admission. **Home schooled:** Transcript of courses and grades required.

High school preparation. College-preparatory program recommended. 16 units recommended. Recommended units include English 4, mathematics 2, social studies 3, science 2 and foreign language 1.

2015-2016 Annual costs. Tuition/fees: $6,397; $6,397 out-of-state. Room/board: $7,018.

Financial aid. Non-need-based: Scholarships awarded for academics, art, athletics, leadership, music/drama, state residency.

Application procedures. Admission: Priority date 12/1; no deadline. No application fee. Admission notification on a rolling basis beginning on or about 9/1. **Financial aid:** Priority date 3/1; no closing date. FAFSA required. Applicants notified on a rolling basis starting 3/1; must reply within 2 week(s) of notification.

Academics. Special study options: Cooperative education, cross-registration, distance learning, double major, dual enrollment of high school students, honors, independent study, internships, liberal arts/career combination, study abroad, teacher certification program. **Credit/placement by examination:** AP, CLEP, IB. 30 credit hours maximum toward bachelor's degree. **Support services:** Learning center, reduced course load, remedial instruction, study skills assistance, tutoring, writing center. Career services, counseling services, disability accommodations, probation counseling, summer bridge program (for incoming TRIO-SSS participants), TRIO-student support services.

Majors. Biology: General, biochemistry. **Business:** Accounting, business admin, entrepreneurial studies, management information systems, management science, marketing. **Education:** Art, biology, business, chemistry, early childhood, early childhood special, elementary, English, history, mathematics, middle, music, physical, science, social science, special ed. **Engineering:** Pre-engineering. **English:** English lit. **Health services:** Predental, premedicine, prenursing, preoptometry, prepharmacy, prephysical therapy, preveterinary. **History:** General. **Liberal arts:** Arts/sciences. **Math:** General. **Parks/recreation:** Exercise sciences. **Physical sciences:** Chemistry. **Protective services:** Criminal justice. **Psychology:** General. **Social sciences:** General. **Visual/performing arts:** Art, graphic design, music, music performance, studio arts.

Most popular majors. Business/marketing 34%, education 26%, psychology 13%, security/protective services 11%.

Technology on campus. 200 workstations in library, computer center, student center. Dormitories wired for high-speed internet access and linked to campus network. Commuter students can connect to campus network. Online course registration, online library, helpline, wireless network available.

Student life. Freshman orientation: Mandatory. Preregistration for classes offered. One-day sessions held in April, May, June, July, August. **Policies:** Drug/alcohol free and zero tolerance policy, smoke-free residential living. **Housing:** Guaranteed on-campus for freshmen. Coed dorms, single-sex dorms, special housing for disabled, apartments, themed housing, wellness housing available. $50 nonrefundable deposit. **Activities:** Bands, campus ministries, choral groups, dance, drama, film society, music ensembles, musical theater, student government, student newspaper, Peru's Individual Leaders of Today (PILOT), People Respecting Individual Differences and Equality (PRIDE), multicultural club, Black Student Union, Phi Beta Lambda, Student Senate, Riverside Ministries, student athlete advisory council, Students of Peru Accepting Responsible Choices (SPARC), Fellowship of Christian Athletes, Campus Crusade for Christ, Peru State Catholic Union.

Athletics. NAIA. **Intercollegiate:** Baseball M, basketball, cheerleading W, cross-country W, football (tackle) M, golf W, softball W, volleyball W. **Intramural:** Basketball, football (non-tackle), softball, volleyball. **Team name:** Bobcats.

Student services. Adult student services, alcohol/substance abuse counseling, chaplain/spiritual director, career counseling, services for economically disadvantaged, student employment services, financial aid counseling, health services, on-campus daycare, personal counseling, placement for graduates, veterans' counselor. **Physically disabled:** Services for visually, speech, hearing impaired.

Contact. E-mail: admissions@peru.edu
Phone: (402) 872-2221 Toll-free number: (800) 742-4412 ext. 2221
Fax: (402) 872-2296
Peru State College, P.O. Box 10, Peru, NE 68421-0010

Union College
Lincoln, Nebraska
www.ucollege.edu

CB code: 6865

- Private 4-year liberal arts college affiliated with the Seventh-day Adventists
- Residential campus in large city
- 762 degree-seeking undergraduates: 5% part-time, 60% women, 8% African American, 4% Asian American, 18% Hispanic/Latino, 1% Native American, 1% Native Hawaiian/Pacific islander, 5% Multi-racial, non-Hispanic, 8% international
- 89 degree-seeking graduate students

- 56% of applicants admitted
- SAT or ACT (ACT writing optional) required
- 52% graduate within 6 years

General. Founded in 1889. Regionally accredited. **Degrees:** 165 bachelor's, 15 associate awarded; master's offered. **Location:** 50 miles from Omaha. **Calendar:** Semester, limited summer session. **Full-time faculty:** 61 total; 48% have terminal degrees, 12% minority, 51% women. **Part-time faculty:** 53 total; 26% have terminal degrees, 15% minority, 57% women. **Class size:** 72% < 20, 24% 20-39, 2% 40-49, 3% 50-99. **Special facilities:** Arboretum.

Freshman class profile. 1,352 applied, 756 admitted, 171 enrolled.

Mid 50% test scores			
SAT math:	450-570	GPA 2.0-2.99:	17%
SAT writing:	460-570	Rank in top quarter:	8%
ACT composite:	19-26	Rank in top tenth:	8%
GPA 3.75 or higher:	34%	Return as sophomores:	71%
GPA 3.50-3.74:	23%	Out-of-state:	89%
GPA 3.0-3.49:	26%	Live on campus:	93%
		International:	7%

Basis for selection. GPA and ACT/SAT most important. Interview recommended for all students; audition recommended for music program; portfolio recommended for art program.

High school preparation. College-preparatory program recommended. Recommended units include English 4, mathematics 2, social studies 2, science 2 (laboratory 2) and computer science 1. 2 algebra, 1 geometry, trigonometry recommended for mathematics and science-related programs. Physics and chemistry recommended for nursing, biology, chemistry, physics, engineering, medical technology, pre-medicine, and pre-dental programs.

2016-2017 Annual costs. Tuition/fees: $22,538. Room/board: $6,766. Books/supplies: $1,100. Personal expenses: $2,800.

2014-2015 Financial aid. Need-based: 128 full-time freshmen applied for aid; 110 deemed to have need; 110 received aid. Average need met was 76%. Average scholarship/grant was $15,017; average loan $4,164. 56% of total undergraduate aid awarded as scholarships/grants, 44% as loans/jobs. **Non-need-based:** Awarded to 243 full-time undergraduates, including 63 freshmen. Scholarships awarded for academics, state residency. **Additional information:** Special institutional grants offered to all freshmen and sophomores demonstrating exceptional financial need.

Application procedures. Admission: Priority date 3/1; deadline 8/1. No application fee. Admission notification on a rolling basis beginning on or about 10/1. **Financial aid:** No deadline. FAFSA, institutional form required. Applicants notified on a rolling basis starting 12/1; must reply by 9/1.

Academics. Special study options: Double major, dual enrollment of high school students, honors, independent study, internships, student-designed major, study abroad, teacher certification program. **Credit/placement by examination:** AP, CLEP, SAT, ACT, institutional tests. **Support services:** Learning center, reduced course load, remedial instruction, study skills assistance, tutoring, writing center.

Majors. Biology: General, biochemistry. **Business:** Accounting, business admin, finance, international, international finance, organizational behavior. **Communications:** Communications/speech/rhetoric, journalism, public relations. **Computer sciences:** General, computer science, programming. **Education:** General, art, biology, business, chemistry, computer, elementary, English, ESL, history, mathematics, music, physical, physics, science, secondary, social science, technology/industrial arts. **English:** Creative writing, English lit. **Foreign languages:** General, German. **Health services:** General, clinical lab science, nursing (RN). **History:** General. **Human services:** Social work. **Math:** General. **Parks/recreation:** Exercise sciences, health/fitness, sports admin. **Philosophy/religion:** Religion. **Physical sciences:** Chemistry, physics. **Psychology:** General. **Social sciences:** General. **Theology:** Pastoral counseling, religious ed, theology. **Visual/performing arts:** General, commercial/advertising art, graphic design, music, music pedagogy, music performance, studio arts.

Technology on campus. 85 workstations in dormitories, library, computer center, student center. Dormitories wired for high-speed internet access and linked to campus network. Commuter students can connect to campus network. Online course registration, online library, helpline, student web hosting, wireless network available.

Student life. Freshman orientation: Mandatory. Preregistration for classes offered. One-week long sessions prior to classes start. **Policies:** Religious observance required. **Housing:** Guaranteed on-campus for all undergraduates. Single-sex dorms, special housing for disabled, apartments available. $105 fully refundable deposit, deadline 4/15. **Activities:** Concert band, campus ministries, choral groups, drama, international student organizations, music ensembles, student government, student newspaper, symphony orchestra, Collegiate Adventists for Better Living, Union for Kids, Amnesty International, Red Cross club.

Athletics. Intercollegiate: Basketball, golf M, volleyball W. **Intramural:** Basketball, football (non-tackle), softball, ultimate frisbee, volleyball. **Team name:** Warriors.

Student services. Chaplain/spiritual director, career counseling, student employment services, financial aid counseling, health services, minority student services, personal counseling, placement for graduates. **Physically disabled:** Services for visually, speech, hearing impaired.

Contact. E-mail: ucenroll@ucollege.edu
Phone: (402) 486-2504 Toll-free number: (800) 228-4600
Fax: (402) 486-2566
Kevin Erickson, Director of Admissions, Union College, 3800 South 48th Street, Lincoln, NE 68506-4300

University of Nebraska - Kearney
Kearney, Nebraska
www.unk.edu
CB code: 6467

- Public 4-year university
- Residential campus in large town
- 4,820 degree-seeking undergraduates: 10% part-time, 58% women, 2% African American, 1% Asian American, 11% Hispanic/Latino, 2% Multiracial, non-Hispanic, 5% international
- 1,225 degree-seeking graduate students
- 85% of applicants admitted
- SAT or ACT (ACT writing optional) required
- 57% graduate within 6 years

General. Founded in 1903. Regionally accredited. **Degrees:** 983 bachelor's awarded; master's offered. **ROTC:** Army. **Location:** 180 miles from Omaha. **Calendar:** Semester, extensive summer session. **Full-time faculty:** 333 total; 74% have terminal degrees, 10% minority, 46% women. **Part-time faculty:** 120 total; 18% have terminal degrees, 6% minority, 58% women. **Class size:** 48% < 20, 45% 20-39, 5% 40-49, 2% 50-99, less than 1% >100. **Special facilities:** Nebraska state art collection, state arboretum, planetarium.

Freshman class profile. 2,511 applied, 2,144 admitted, 938 enrolled.

Mid 50% test scores			
SAT critical reading:	440-540	Rank in top quarter:	41%
SAT math:	420-530	Rank in top tenth:	17%
ACT composite:	20-25	Return as sophomores:	80%
GPA 3.75 or higher:	38%	Out-of-state:	6%
GPA 3.50-3.74:	18%	Live on campus:	90%
GPA 3.0-3.49:	28%	International:	3%
GPA 2.0-2.99:	16%	Fraternities:	19%
		Sororities:	26%

Basis for selection. Test scores, school achievement record most important. Applicants who show promise of academic success, but do not meet admission requirements, may be admitted on conditional basis.

High school preparation. College-preparatory program recommended. 16 units required. Required units include English 4, mathematics 3, social studies 3, science 3 (laboratory 1), foreign language 2 and academic electives 1.

2015-2016 Annual costs. Tuition/fees: $6,724; $12,994 out-of-state. Room/board: $9,230. Books/supplies: $1,310. Personal expenses: $2,944.

2014-2015 Financial aid. Need-based: 852 full-time freshmen applied for aid; 695 deemed to have need; 689 received aid. Average need met was 74%. Average scholarship/grant was $8,200; average loan $3,386. 60% of total undergraduate aid awarded as scholarships/grants, 40% as loans/jobs. **Non-need-based:** Awarded to 1,225 full-time undergraduates, including 316 freshmen. Scholarships awarded for academics, alumni affiliation, art, athletics, leadership, minority status, music/drama, ROTC, state residency.

Application procedures. Admission: Closing date 9/1. $45 fee, may be waived for applicants with need. Admission notification on a rolling basis beginning on or about 9/1. **Financial aid:** Priority date 4/1; no closing date. FAFSA, institutional form required. Applicants notified on a rolling basis starting 3/15; must reply within 2 week(s) of notification.

Academics. Special study options: Combined bachelor's/graduate degree, cooperative education, distance learning, double major, dual enrollment of high school students, ESL, exchange student, honors, independent study, internships, study abroad, teacher certification program. International student exchange program with Sapporo University and Kansai Gaidai, Japan; Nebraska semester abroad. **Credit/placement by examination:** AP, CLEP, SAT, ACT, institutional tests. 45 credit hours maximum toward bachelor's degree. **Support services:** Learning center, study skills assistance, tutoring, writing center.

Majors. Biology: General. **Business:** Business admin, office management, office/clerical, operations, tourism/travel. **Communications:** Advertising, broadcast journalism, communications/speech/rhetoric, journalism, public relations, sports. **Computer sciences:** General, information systems. **Education:** General, art, biology, business, chemistry, early childhood, elementary, English, ESL, family/consumer sciences, foreign languages, French, German, health, history, learning disabled, mathematics, mentally handicapped, middle, multiple handicapped, music, physical, physically handicapped, physics, science, secondary, social science, Spanish, special ed, speech, speech impaired, technology/industrial arts, trade/industrial. **English:** English lit, rhetoric/composition. **Foreign languages:** French, German, Spanish, translation. **Health services:** Communication disorders, medical radiologic technology/radiation therapy, radiologic technology/medical imaging, respiratory therapy technology, speech pathology. **History:** General. **Human services:** Social work. **Liberal arts:** Arts/sciences. **Math:** General. **Parks/recreation:** Facilities management, sports admin. **Philosophy/religion:** Philosophy. **Physical sciences:** Chemistry, physics. **Protective services:** Criminal justice, police science. **Psychology:** General. **Social sciences:** General, economics, geography, international relations, political science, sociology. **Visual/performing arts:** General, art, art history/conservation, commercial/advertising art, dramatic, music, music performance, studio arts. **Work/family studies:** General, business, clothing/textiles, family studies, housing.

Most popular majors. Business/marketing 22%, education 20%, parks/recreation 9%.

Technology on campus. 800 workstations in dormitories, library, computer center, student center. Dormitories wired for high-speed internet access and linked to campus network. Commuter students can connect to campus network. Online course registration, helpline, repair service, wireless network available.

Student life. Freshman orientation: Available. Preregistration for classes offered. **Housing:** Guaranteed on-campus for freshmen. Coed dorms, apartments available. $50 nonrefundable deposit. **Activities:** Bands, campus ministries, choral groups, dance, drama, film society, international student organizations, literary magazine, music ensembles, Model UN, musical theater, opera, radio station, student government, student newspaper, symphony orchestra, TV station, Young Republicans, Young Democrats, Alpha Phi Omega, Fellowship of Christian Athletes, People of Color.

Athletics. NCAA. **Intercollegiate:** Baseball M, basketball, cross-country, diving W, football (tackle) M, golf, soccer W, softball W, swimming W, tennis, track and field, volleyball W, wrestling M. **Intramural:** Archery, badminton, basketball, bowling, cross-country, diving, football (non-tackle), golf, racquetball, soccer, softball, swimming, table tennis, tennis, track and field, volleyball, water polo, wrestling M. **Team name:** Lopers.

Student services. Alcohol/substance abuse counseling, career counseling, student employment services, financial aid counseling, health services, minority student services, on-campus daycare, personal counseling, placement for graduates, veterans' counselor, women's services. **Physically disabled:** Services for visually, hearing impaired.

Contact. E-mail: admissionsug@unk.edu
Phone: (308) 865-8526 Toll-free number: (800) 532-7639
Fax: (308) 865-8987
Dusty Newton, Director of Admissions, University of Nebraska - Kearney, 905 West 25th, Kearney, NE 68849

University of Nebraska - Lincoln
Lincoln, Nebraska
www.unl.edu
CB member
CB code: 6877

- Public 4-year university
- Residential campus in large city
- 20,182 degree-seeking undergraduates
- 76% of applicants admitted
- SAT or ACT (ACT writing optional) required

General. Founded in 1869. Regionally accredited. **Degrees:** 3,716 bachelor's, 6 associate awarded; master's, doctoral offered. **ROTC:** Army, Naval, Air Force. **Location:** 55 miles from Omaha. **Calendar:** Semester, extensive summer session. **Full-time faculty:** 1,083 total; 94% have terminal degrees, 18% minority, 31% women. **Part-time faculty:** 18 total; 100% have terminal degrees, 6% minority, 11% women. **Class size:** 39% < 20, 39% 20-39, 6% 40-49, 9% 50-99, 8% >100. **Special facilities:** Art museum, state natural science museum, planetarium, observatory, center for performing arts, arboretum, center for Great Plains studies, center for biomaterials and genetic research, international quilt study center and museum, diocles laser/extreme light lab, midwest roadside safety facility, food industries complex, center for mass spectrometry, animal science complex, veterinary animal research/diagnosis center, center for brain, biology and behavior.

Freshman class profile. 9,724 applied, 7,425 admitted, 2,368 enrolled.

Mid 50% test scores			
SAT critical reading:	500-630	GPA 2.0-2.99:	14%
SAT math:	500-660	Rank in top quarter:	51%
ACT composite:	22-28	Rank in top tenth:	24%
GPA 3.75 or higher:	39%	Out-of-state:	25%
GPA 3.50-3.74:	20%	Live on campus:	96%
GPA 3.0-3.49:	27%	Fraternities:	22%
		Sororities:	26%

Basis for selection. Students must meet minimum requirements of 20 ACT composite score, SAT combined score of 950 (exclusive of Writing) or rank in top half of class. ACT recommended. Audition or portfolio required for music, dance, and theater programs. **Home schooled:** Statement describing home school structure and mission required. Primary teacher/administrator must provide a copy of letter confirming registration with Nebraska State Department of Education, transcript and curriculum synopsis of the courses which parallel the University of Nebraska-Lincoln's 16 core course requirement, textbook information listed by course (including titles and authors). For courses in foreign language; must include description of how they learned the verbal component of the language. Administrator should also provide a detailed description of how the applicant fulfilled the natural science laboratory requirement. **Learning Disabled:** Students with disabilities are considered for admission on the same basis as all other applicants and must meet the same academic standards. If a student believes that a disability impacted his/her ability to successfully meet one of UNL's admission requirements, the student can submit an admission decision appeal to the Director of Admissions.

High school preparation. College-preparatory program required. 16 units required. Required units include English 4, mathematics 4, social studies 2, history 1, science 3 (laboratory 1) and foreign language 2. Mathematics must include algebra I and II, geometry, and 1 higher level math. 2 units of foreign language must be in same language. At least 1 social studies should be U.S. and/or world history and 1 additional unit should be history, American government, and/or geography. College of Engineering and Technology requires 1 pre-calculus/trigonometry, 1 physics and 1 chemistry. Architecture requires 0.5 trigonometry or pre-calculus for pre-architecture.

2015-2016 Annual costs. Tuition/fees: $8,279; $22,446 out-of-state. Room/board: $10,310. Books/supplies: $1,070. Personal expenses: $3,630.

Financial aid. Non-need-based: Scholarships awarded for academics, alumni affiliation, art, athletics, leadership, music/drama, state residency.

Application procedures. Admission: Priority date 1/15; deadline 5/1 (postmark date). $45 fee, may be waived for applicants with need. Application must be submitted online. Admission notification on a rolling basis beginning on or about 9/1. Must reply by 5/1. **Financial aid:** Priority date 4/1; no closing date. FAFSA required. Applicants notified on a rolling basis starting 4/1.

Academics. Research opportunities impacting state's economic development available to students. **Special study options:** Accelerated study, combined bachelor's/graduate degree, cooperative education, cross-registration, distance learning, double major, dual enrollment of high school students, ESL, exchange student, honors, independent study, internships, liberal arts/career combination, New York semester, semester at sea, student-designed major, study abroad, teacher certification program, United Nations semester, urban semester, Washington semester. **Credit/placement by examination:** AP, CLEP, IB, institutional tests. Individual colleges have different policies. **Support services:** Learning center, pre-admission summer program, reduced course load, study skills assistance, tutoring, writing center.

Honors college/program. Formal application required. Acceptance based on evaluation of the student's potential by the faculty committee.

Majors. Architecture: Architecture, interior, landscape. **Area/ethnic studies:** General, Latin American, women's. **Biology:** General, biochemistry, botany, entomology, microbiology. **Business:** Accounting, actuarial science, banking/financial services, business admin, finance, hospitality admin, insurance, international, investments/securities, logistics, managerial economics, marketing. **Communications:** Broadcast journalism, communications/speech/rhetoric, journalism, persuasive communications. **Computer sciences:** General. **Conservation:** General, environmental studies, management/policy. **Education:** Agricultural, biology, business, chemistry, computer, elementary, foreign languages, French, German, mathematics, multi-level teacher, music, physical, physics, science, social science, Spanish, trade/industrial. **Engineering:** General, agricultural, architectural, biological, chemical, civil, computer, construction, electrical, mechanical. **English:** English lit. **Foreign languages:** Classics, French, German, Russian, Spanish. **Health services:** Athletic training, predental, premedicine, prepharmacy, preveterinary, speech pathology, veterinary technology/assistant. **History:** General. **Liberal arts:** Arts/sciences. **Math:** General. **Philosophy/religion:** Philosophy. **Physical sciences:** Atmospheric science, chemistry, geology, physics. **Protective services:** Forensics. **Psychology:** General. **Social sciences:** Anthropology, economics, geography, political science, sociology. **Visual/performing arts:** Art history/conservation, dance, dramatic, film/cinema/video, music, studio arts. **Work/family studies:** Apparel marketing, clothing/textiles, food/nutrition, textile science.

Most popular majors. Agriculture 8%, business/marketing 23%, communications/journalism 6%, education 8%, engineering/engineering technologies 12%, family/consumer sciences 8%, psychology 6%.

Technology on campus. 650 workstations in dormitories, library, computer center, student center. Dormitories wired for high-speed internet access and linked to campus network. Commuter students can connect to campus network. Online course registration, online library, helpline, repair service, student web hosting, wireless network available.

Student life. Freshman orientation: Mandatory. Preregistration for classes offered. Day-long program conducted from mid-June to mid-July. **Policies:** No smoking allowed in University buildings. No alcohol or firearms on campus. Freshmen required to live on campus if not living with parents or close relatives. **Housing:** Guaranteed on-campus for freshmen. Coed dorms, single-sex dorms, special housing for disabled, apartments, cooperative housing, fraternity/sorority housing available. $400 partly refundable deposit. Special interest floors available. **Activities:** Bands, campus ministries, choral groups, dance, drama, film society, international student organizations, literary magazine, music ensembles, Model UN, musical theater, opera, radio station, student government, student newspaper, symphony orchestra, TV station, over 600 registered student organizations available.

Athletics. NCAA. **Intercollegiate:** Baseball M, basketball, bowling W, cross-country, diving W, football (tackle) M, golf, gymnastics, rifle W, soccer W, softball W, swimming W, tennis, track and field, volleyball W, wrestling M. **Intramural:** Basketball, bowling, cross-country, football (non-tackle), golf, rifle, sand volleyball, soccer, softball, tennis, track and field, ultimate frisbee, volleyball. **Team name:** Huskers.

Student services. Adult student services, alcohol/substance abuse counseling, chaplain/spiritual director, career counseling, services for economically disadvantaged, student employment services, financial aid counseling, health services, legal services, minority student services, on-campus daycare, personal counseling, placement for graduates, veterans' counselor, women's services. **Physically disabled:** Services for visually, speech, hearing impaired.

Contact. E-mail: admissions@unl.edu
Phone: (402) 472-2023 Toll-free number: (800) 742-8800
Fax: (402) 472-0670
Amber Williams, Associate Dean of Enrollment Management, University of Nebraska - Lincoln, 1410 Q Street, Lincoln, NE 68588-0417

University of Nebraska - Omaha
Omaha, Nebraska
www.unomaha.edu

CB member
CB code: 6420

- Public 4-year university
- Large city
- 12,287 degree-seeking undergraduates: 22% part-time, 52% women, 6% African American, 3% Asian American, 11% Hispanic/Latino, 4% Multiracial, non-Hispanic, 4% international
- 2,883 degree-seeking graduate students
- 76% of applicants admitted
- SAT or ACT (ACT writing optional) required
- 46% graduate within 6 years

General. Founded in 1908. Regionally accredited. Cooperative classes at Offutt Strategic Air Command. Cooperative programs with UNMC medical center. **Degrees:** 2,298 bachelor's awarded; master's, doctoral offered. **ROTC:** Army, Air Force. **Location:** 160 miles from Kansas City, Missouri. **Calendar:** Semester, limited summer session. **Full-time faculty:** 537 total; 79% have terminal degrees, 22% minority, 45% women. **Part-time faculty:** 546 total; 24% have terminal degrees, 11% minority, 49% women. **Class size:** 37% < 20, 44% 20-39, 9% 40-49, 9% 50-99, 2% >100. **Special facilities:** Outdoor venture center, nature preserve, planetarium, Nebraska Book Arts Center, community engagement center.

Freshman class profile. 5,581 applied, 4,238 admitted, 2,060 enrolled.

Mid 50% test scores			
ACT composite:	19-26	Rank in top tenth:	14%
GPA 3.75 or higher:	30%	Return as sophomores:	77%
GPA 3.50-3.74:	16%	Out-of-state:	10%
GPA 3.0-3.49:	29%	Live on campus:	42%
GPA 2.0-2.99:	24%	International:	4%
Rank in top quarter:	38%	Fraternities:	5%
		Sororities:	5%

Basis for selection. School achievement record, test scores important. Must have ACT score of 20, comparable SAT score or class rank in upper half of graduating class. Admitted for special talent consideration on case by case basis. Open admission for non-degree applicants and non-traditional adult freshman applicants. Audition required for music program. **Home schooled:** Applicants must submit official GED scores verifying successful completion of the GED. An ACT composite score of 25+ may be substituted in lieu of the GED score.

High school preparation. College-preparatory program required. 16 units required. Required units include English 4, mathematics 3, social studies 1, history 2, science 3 (laboratory 1), foreign language 2 and academic electives 1. Specific course requirements for programs in business administration, human resources and family services for College of Engineering and Technology.

2015-2016 Annual costs. Tuition/fees: $7,573; $20,368 out-of-state. Room/board: $8,848. Books/supplies: $1,080. Personal expenses: $2,366.

2014-2015 Financial aid. Need-based: 1,509 full-time freshmen applied for aid; 1,203 deemed to have need; 1,182 received aid. Average need met was 65%. Average scholarship/grant was $6,298; average loan $3,091. 71% of total undergraduate aid awarded as scholarships/grants, 29% as loans/jobs. **Non-need-based:** Awarded to 1,362 full-time undergraduates, including 323 freshmen. Scholarships awarded for academics, alumni affiliation, art, athletics, leadership, minority status, music/drama, ROTC, state residency.

Application procedures. Admission: Closing date 8/1 (postmark date). $45 fee. Admission notification on a rolling basis. **Financial aid:** Priority date 4/1; no closing date. FAFSA required. Applicants notified on a rolling basis starting 4/15; must reply within 2 week(s) of notification.

Academics. Associate degree program available on Omaha campus through University of Nebraska-Lincoln in construction, drafting and design technology, electronic technology, fire control and safety technology, fire protection, manufacturing technology. On-line courses in aviation studies also available. **Special study options:** Combined bachelor's/graduate degree, cooperative education, cross-registration, distance learning, double major, dual enrollment of high school students, ESL, exchange student, honors, independent study, internships, student-designed major, study abroad, teacher certification program. **Credit/placement by examination:** AP, CLEP, ACT, institutional tests. 30 credit hours maximum toward bachelor's degree. CLEP exams in American History and Western Civilization must be accompanied by essay. **Support services:** Reduced course load, study skills assistance, tutoring, writing center.

Majors. Area/ethnic studies: African-American, Latin American, Native American. **Biology:** General, bioinformatics, biotechnology, neuroscience. **Business:** General, accounting, banking/financial services, business admin, finance, human resources, international, investments/securities, logistics, managerial economics, marketing, organizational behavior, real estate, small business admin. **Communications:** Broadcast journalism, communications/speech/rhetoric, journalism. **Computer sciences:** Computer science, information systems, information technology, security. **Conservation:** Environmental science. **Education:** Art, early childhood special, elementary, music, secondary, secondary special ed, special ed, speech impaired. **English:** Creative writing, English lit. **Foreign languages:** General. **Health services:** Athletic training, health care admin. **History:** General. **Human services:** General, public policy, social work. **Liberal arts:** Library science. **Math:** General. **Parks/recreation:** General, exercise sciences. **Philosophy/religion:** Philosophy, religion. **Physical sciences:** Chemistry, geology, physics. **Protective services:** Criminal justice, disaster management, fire services admin. **Psychology:** General. **Social sciences:** Economics, geography, GIS/cartography, political science, sociology, urban studies. **Visual/performing arts:** Art, art history/conservation, dramatic, game design, graphic design, music, music performance, music theory/composition, piano/keyboard, stringed instruments, studio arts, voice/opera.

Most popular majors. Biology 7%, business/marketing 29%, education 9%, security/protective services 10%.

Technology on campus. 2,450 workstations in dormitories, library, computer center, student center. Dormitories wired for high-speed internet access and linked to campus network. Commuter students can connect to campus network. Online course registration, online library, helpline, student web hosting, wireless network available.

Student life. Freshman orientation: Mandatory. Preregistration for classes offered. Held every week April 15 thru August 1st. **Housing:** Coed dorms available. $260 partly refundable deposit. **Activities:** Bands, campus ministries, choral groups, dance, drama, film society, international student organizations, literary magazine, music ensembles, Model UN, musical theater, opera, radio station, student government, student newspaper, symphony orchestra, TV station, American multi-cultural students, chapter summary Bible study, Campus Crusade for Christ, honor societies, Greek letter organizations.

Athletics. NCAA. **Intercollegiate:** Baseball M, basketball, golf, ice hockey M, soccer, softball W, swimming W, tennis, track and field W, volleyball

W. Intramural: Basketball, field hockey, football (non-tackle), racquetball, soccer, ultimate frisbee, volleyball. **Team name:** Mavericks.

Student services. Adult student services, alcohol/substance abuse counseling, chaplain/spiritual director, career counseling, services for economically disadvantaged, student employment services, financial aid counseling, health services, minority student services, on-campus daycare, personal counseling, placement for graduates, veterans' counselor, women's services. **Physically disabled:** Services for visually, speech, hearing impaired.

Contact. E-mail: unoadm@unomaha.edu
Phone: (402) 554-2393 Toll-free number: (800) 858-8648
Fax: (402) 554-3472
Christina Liewer, Director of Admissions, University of Nebraska - Omaha, 6001 Dodge Street, Omaha, NE 68182-0005

University of Nebraska Medical Center
Omaha, Nebraska
www.unmc.edu · **CB code: 6896**

- Public two-year upper-division health science college
- Commuter campus in very large city

General. Founded in 1869. Regionally accredited. **Degrees:** 434 bachelor's awarded; master's, professional, doctoral offered. **ROTC:** Army, Air Force. **Calendar:** Semester, limited summer session. **Full-time faculty:** 1,023 total; 87% have terminal degrees, 21% minority, 41% women. **Part-time faculty:** 209 total; 85% have terminal degrees, 8% minority, 52% women.

Student profile. 739 degree-seeking undergraduates. 16% entered as juniors, 12% entered as seniors.

Basis for selection. College transcript required. Admissions requirements, application procedures, and closing dates vary by program. Health professions program applicants must have completed prerequisite courses at another institution. Transfer accepted as sophomores, juniors, seniors.

2015-2016 Annual costs. Books/supplies: $900. Personal expenses: $1,500. **Additional information:** College of Medicine: resident $28,000; nonresident $69,640; Books/Equipment $1,720. College of Dentistry: resident $28,700; nonresident $70,405; Books/Equipment $8,040. College of Pharmacy: resident $18,330; nonresident $37,770; Books/Equipment $1,130. Tuition is assessed on per semester not credit hour basis.

Application procedures. Admission: $45 fee, may be waived for applicants with need. Application must be submitted online. **Financial aid:** No deadline. Applicants notified on a rolling basis starting 5/1; must reply within 2 weeks of notification. FAFSA, institutional form required.

Academics. Special study options: Accelerated study, combined bachelor's/graduate degree, distance learning, honors. **Credit/placement by examination:** AP, CLEP, IB, institutional tests. 24 credit hours maximum toward bachelor's degree.

Majors. Health services: Clinical lab science, dental hygiene, medical radiologic technology/radiation therapy, nuclear medical technology, nursing (RN), radiologic technology/medical imaging, sonography.

Technology on campus. 108 workstations in library, computer center, student center. Commuter students can connect to campus network. Online library, helpline, repair service, wireless network available.

Student life. Housing: Apartments available. **Activities:** Student government, committee on minority concerns, American Academy of Physician Assistants, Religious Life Council, Christian Fellowship, student association for rural health, student services council, student professional organizations.

Student services. Alcohol/substance abuse counseling, career counseling, services for economically disadvantaged, financial aid counseling, health services, minority student services, on-campus daycare, personal counseling, veterans' counselor. **Physically disabled:** Services for hearing impaired.

Contact. Phone: (402) 559-6468
Toll-free number: (800) 626-8431 ext. 96468 Fax: (402) 559-6796
University of Nebraska Medical Center, 984230 Nebraska Medical Center, Omaha, NE 68198-4230

Wayne State College
Wayne, Nebraska
www.wsc.edu **CB code: 6469**

- Public 4-year liberal arts and teachers college
- Residential campus in small town

- 2,783 degree-seeking undergraduates: 6% part-time, 57% women, 3% African American, 1% Asian American, 7% Hispanic/Latino, 1% Native American, 2% Multi-racial, non-Hispanic, 1% international
- 435 degree-seeking graduate students
- 49% graduate within 6 years

General. Founded in 1909. Regionally accredited. **Degrees:** 577 bachelor's awarded; master's offered. **ROTC:** Army. **Location:** 45 miles from Sioux City, Iowa. **Calendar:** Semester, extensive summer session. **Full-time faculty:** 128 total; 82% have terminal degrees, 6% minority, 49% women. **Part-time faculty:** 89 total; 14% have terminal degrees, 1% minority, 73% women. **Class size:** 47% < 20, 49% 20-39, 3% 40-49, less than 1% 50-99, less than 1% >100. **Special facilities:** Planetarium, outdoor amphitheater.

Freshman class profile. 2,034 applied, 2,034 admitted, 631 enrolled.

Mid 50% test scores			
ACT composite:	18-25	Rank in top quarter:	29%
GPA 3.75 or higher:	23%	Rank in top tenth:	9%
GPA 3.50-3.74:	15%	Return as sophomores:	72%
GPA 3.0-3.49:	29%	Out-of-state:	14%
GPA 2.0-2.99:	29%	Live on campus:	95%
		International:	1%

Basis for selection. Open admission.

High school preparation. College-preparatory program recommended. 18 units recommended. Recommended units include English 4, mathematics 3, social studies 3, science 2, foreign language 2, computer science 2 and visual/performing arts 2.

2015-2016 Annual costs. Tuition/fees: $6,042; $10,632 out-of-state. Room/board: $6,760. Books/supplies: $1,120. Personal expenses: $1,062. **Additional information:** Additional Special Rates apply for residents of qualifying states.

2015-2016 Financial aid. **Need-based:** 573 full-time freshmen applied for aid; 418 deemed to have need; 407 received aid. Average need met was 54%. Average scholarship/grant was $4,323; average loan $3,242. 53% of total undergraduate aid awarded as scholarships/grants, 47% as loans/jobs. **Non-need-based:** Awarded to 1,531 full-time undergraduates, including 415 freshmen. Scholarships awarded for academics, art, athletics, leadership, minority status, music/drama, religious affiliation, ROTC, state residency.

Application procedures. Admission: No application fee. Admission notification on a rolling basis beginning on or about 9/15. **Financial aid:** Priority date 4/1; no closing date. FAFSA required. Applicants notified on a rolling basis starting 4/1; must reply within 4 week(s) of notification.

Academics. Special study options: Cooperative education, distance learning, double major, dual enrollment of high school students, ESL, honors, independent study, internships, study abroad, teacher certification program. Service Learning. **Credit/placement by examination:** AP, CLEP, institutional tests. **Support services:** Learning center, reduced course load, remedial instruction, study skills assistance, tutoring, writing center.

Majors. Biology: General. **Business:** Business admin. **Communications:** Communications/speech/rhetoric, journalism, media studies. **Computer sciences:** General, information systems. **Education:** Art, biology, business, chemistry, drama/dance, early childhood, elementary, English, family/consumer sciences, foreign languages, geography, history, mathematics, middle, music, physical, psychology, social science, special ed, speech, technology/industrial arts. **English:** English lit. **Foreign languages:** General, Spanish. **Health services:** Athletic training. **History:** General. **Math:** General. **Parks/recreation:** Health/fitness, physical fitness technician, sports admin. **Physical sciences:** Chemistry. **Protective services:** Criminal justice. **Psychology:** General, counseling. **Social sciences:** General, geography, political science, sociology. **Visual/performing arts:** Art, dramatic, graphic design, music. **Work/family studies:** General, child care service, food/nutrition.

Most popular majors. Business/marketing 14%, education 30%, engineering/engineering technologies 6%, parks/recreation 8%, psychology 8%, security/protective services 7%.

Technology on campus. 258 workstations in library, computer center, student center. Dormitories wired for high-speed internet access and linked to campus network. Commuter students can connect to campus network. Online course registration, helpline, wireless network available.

Student life. Freshman orientation: Available. Preregistration for classes offered. **Housing:** Guaranteed on-campus for freshmen. Coed dorms available. $50 nonrefundable deposit. **Activities:** Bands, campus ministries, choral groups, drama, international student organizations, literary magazine, music ensembles, musical theater, radio station, student government, student newspaper, TV station.

Athletics. NCAA. **Intercollegiate:** Baseball M, basketball, cross-country, football (tackle) M, soccer W, softball W, track and field, volleyball W.

Intramural: Archery, badminton, basketball, bowling, football (non-tackle), golf, handball, racquetball, softball, swimming, table tennis, tennis, track and field, volleyball, weight lifting M, wrestling M. **Team name:** Wildcats.

Student services. Alcohol/substance abuse counseling, chaplain/spiritual director, career counseling, services for economically disadvantaged, student employment services, financial aid counseling, health services, minority student services, personal counseling, placement for graduates, veterans' counselor. **Physically disabled:** Services for visually, speech, hearing impaired.

Contact. E-mail: admit1@wsc.edu
Phone: (402) 375-7234 Toll-free number: (800) 228-9972
Fax: (402) 375-7204
Kevin Halle, Director of Admissions, Wayne State College, 1111 Main Street, Wayne, NE 68787

York College
York, Nebraska
www.york.edu   CB code: 6984

- Private 4-year liberal arts and teachers college affiliated with the Church of Christ
- Residential campus in small town
- 392 degree-seeking undergraduates
- 3 graduate students
- 62% of applicants admitted
- SAT or ACT (ACT writing optional) required
- 37% graduate within 6 years

General. Founded in 1956. Regionally accredited. **Degrees:** 71 bachelor's, 23 associate awarded; master's offered. **ROTC:** Army, Naval, Air Force. **Location:** 50 miles from Lincoln. **Calendar:** Semester, limited summer session. **Full-time faculty:** 34 total. **Class size:** 85% < 20, 13% 20-39, 2% 40-49, less than 1% 50-99. **Special facilities:** 35,000 sq. ft. indoor sports practice facility, historic prayer chapel.

Freshman class profile. 850 applied, 523 admitted, 109 enrolled.

Mid 50% test scores			
SAT math:	390-510	GPA 2.0-2.99:	36%
SAT writing:	380-530	Rank in top quarter:	24%
ACT composite:	18-23	Rank in top tenth:	11%
GPA 3.75 or higher:	21%	Out-of-state:	66%
GPA 3.50-3.74:	10%	Live on campus:	95%
GPA 3.0-3.49:	30%	Fraternities:	66%
		Sororities:	76%

Basis for selection. ACT/SAT test scores, high school GPA, class rank very important. Essay recommended but not required. **Home schooled:** Transcript of courses and grades required. **Learning Disabled:** Submission of high school IEP is recommended for students who self-identify learning disabilities.

High school preparation. College-preparatory program recommended. 15 units required; 21 recommended. Required and recommended units include English 3-4, mathematics 2-4, social studies 1-4, history 1-4, science 2-4 and foreign language 3.

2016-2017 Annual costs. Tuition/fees: $17,700. Room/board: $6,600. Books/supplies: $200. Personal expenses: $1,750.

Financial aid. Non-need-based: Scholarships awarded for academics, alumni affiliation, athletics, leadership, music/drama.

Application procedures. Admission: Priority date 3/31; deadline 8/31 (receipt date). $20 fee, may be waived for applicants with need. Admission notification on a rolling basis. Must reply by 9/1. **Financial aid:** Priority date 4/1; no closing date. FAFSA required. Applicants notified on a rolling basis starting 3/1; must reply within 4 week(s) of notification.

Academics. Special study options: Accelerated study, double major, dual enrollment of high school students, independent study, internships, student-designed major, teacher certification program. **Credit/placement by examination:** AP, CLEP, IB, SAT, ACT, institutional tests. 12 credit hours maximum toward associate degree, 32 toward bachelor's. **Support services:** Reduced course load, remedial instruction, study skills assistance, tutoring.

Majors. Biology: General. **Business:** Accounting, business admin, finance, human resources. **Communications:** Communications/speech/rhetoric. **Education:** General, art, biology, business, drama/dance, elementary, English, history, mathematics, middle, multi-level teacher, music, physical, reading, secondary, social science, special ed, speech. **English:** English lit. **History:**

General. **Math:** General. **Philosophy/religion:** Religion. **Protective services:** Law enforcement admin. **Psychology:** General. **Social sciences:** Criminology. **Theology:** Bible, religious ed. **Visual/performing arts:** Voice/opera.

Most popular majors. Biology 7%, business/marketing 22%, communications/journalism 7%, education 17%, liberal arts 9%, psychology 19%, security/protective services 12%.

Technology on campus. 57 workstations in dormitories, library, computer center. Dormitories wired for high-speed internet access and linked to campus network. Online library, helpline, wireless network available.

Student life. Freshman orientation: Mandatory. Preregistration for classes offered. **Policies:** Students expected to conform to Christian norms. Alcohol and tobacco prohibited. Unmarried, full-time students under 21 required to live on campus or with relatives or staff off campus. **Housing:** Guaranteed on-campus for all undergraduates. Single-sex dorms, apartments, wellness housing available. $100 fully refundable deposit, deadline 8/31. **Activities:** Campus ministries, choral groups, drama, music ensembles, musical theater, student government, student newspaper, service clubs, Chi Rho, spiritual life committee.

Athletics. NAIA. **Intercollegiate:** Baseball M, basketball, cheerleading, cross-country, golf, soccer, softball W, track and field, volleyball W, wrestling M. **Intramural:** Basketball, football (non-tackle), soccer, softball, table tennis, volleyball. **Team name:** Panthers.

Student services. Adult student services, chaplain/spiritual director, career counseling, student employment services, financial aid counseling, personal counseling, placement for graduates, veterans' counselor.

Contact. E-mail: enroll@york.edu
Phone: (402) 363-5627 Toll-free number: (800) 950-9675
Fax: (402) 363-5623
David Odom, Director of Admissions, York College, 1125 East 8th Street, York, NE 68467

Nevada

Art Institute of Las Vegas
Henderson, Nevada
www.artinstitutes.edu/lasvegas   CB code: 3832

- For-profit 3-year culinary school and visual arts college
- Commuter campus in very large city
- 952 undergraduates
- Application essay, interview required

General. Regionally accredited; also accredited by ACICS, ACCSC. **Degrees:** 111 bachelor's, 56 associate awarded. **Location:** 10 miles from Las Vegas. **Calendar:** Quarter, extensive summer session. **Full-time faculty:** 26 total. **Part-time faculty:** 47 total. **Class size:** 77% < 20, 19% 20-39, 2% 40-49, 2% 50-99. **Special facilities:** Sound-mixing studio, control room, isolation chamber, student-run restaurant, print and service bureaus, photography lab, supply store, learning resource center.

Freshman class profile.

GPA 3.75 or higher:	2%	GPA 2.0-2.99:	60%
GPA 3.50-3.74:	4%	Out-of-state:	7%
GPA 3.0-3.49:	17%	Live on campus:	12%

Basis for selection. Open admission, but selective for some programs. 2.5 GPA required for game art & design and 2.0 for audio production applicants. Face-to-face or phone interview, an original essay of at least 150 words required. Personal portfolio may be required, depending upon the desired academic curriculum. Official transcripts for high school, GED, and/or college, ACCUPLACER test or satisfactory SAT or ACT scores required of all applicants. **Home schooled:** Program must be recognized by state or national department of education. **Learning Disabled:** Accommodations to qualified students with disabilities available through the Student Affairs office.

2015-2016 Annual costs. Tuition/fees: $22,645. Room only: $5,850.

Financial aid. Non-need-based: Scholarships awarded for academics, state residency.

Application procedures. Admission: No deadline. $50 fee. Application must be submitted on paper. Admission notification on a rolling basis. **Financial aid:** No deadline. Applicants notified on a rolling basis.

Academics. Special study options: Distance learning, honors, independent study, internships, liberal arts/career combination, study abroad. **Credit/placement by examination:** AP, CLEP, IB, institutional tests. 28 credit hours maximum toward associate degree, 48 toward bachelor's. **Support services:** Learning center, pre-admission summer program, reduced course load, remedial instruction, study skills assistance, tutoring, writing center.

Majors. Communications technology: Animation/special effects, recording arts. **Computer sciences:** Computer graphics. **Visual/performing arts:** General, cinematography, design, fashion design, game design, graphic design, interior design, multimedia, photography.

Most popular majors. Visual/performing arts 30%.

Technology on campus. 221 workstations in library, computer center. Commuter students can connect to campus network. Online course registration, online library, student web hosting, wireless network available.

Student life. Freshman orientation: Mandatory. Preregistration for classes offered. **Policies:** Resident Advisor available to on-campus students, apartment information and roommate referrals available to off-campus students. **Housing:** Apartments, wellness housing available. $150 partly refundable deposit. **Activities:** Film society.

Student services. Adult student services, alcohol/substance abuse counseling, career counseling, services for economically disadvantaged, student employment services, financial aid counseling, personal counseling, placement for graduates. **Physically disabled:** Services for visually, speech, hearing impaired.

Contact. Phone: (702) 369-9944
Laurie Perdue, Director of Admissions, Art Institute of Las Vegas, 2350 Corporate Circle, Henderson, NV 89074-7737

Great Basin College
Elko, Nevada
www.gbcnv.edu   CB code: 4293

- Public 4-year community and teachers college
- Commuter campus in large town
- 1,926 degree-seeking undergraduates

General. Founded in 1967. Regionally accredited. **Degrees:** 59 bachelor's, 289 associate awarded. **Location:** 280 miles from Reno, 220 miles from Salt Lake City. **Calendar:** Semester, limited summer session. **Full-time faculty:** 63 total; 25% have terminal degrees, 14% minority, 38% women. **Part-time faculty:** 120 total; 7% minority, 59% women. **Class size:** 80% < 20, 18% 20-39, less than 1% 40-49, 1% 50-99, less than 1% >100.

Freshman class profile.

Out-of-state:	16%	Live on campus:	15%

Basis for selection. Open admission, but selective for some programs. Placement test required for some English and math courses. Nursing applicants selected on basis of point system. Points given for courses completed, grades, current work experience in health field, certifications, letters of recommendation, and scores obtained on required entrance exam which measures math and reading comprehension skills. **Home schooled:** State high school equivalency certificate required.

2015-2016 Annual costs. Tuition/fees: $2,805; $9,450 out-of-state. Room only: $3,325. Books/supplies: $1,670. Personal expenses: $1,500.

Application procedures. Admission: No deadline. $10 fee. Application must be submitted online. Admission notification on a rolling basis. **Financial aid:** Priority date 6/1; no closing date. FAFSA required. Applicants notified on a rolling basis starting 7/1.

Academics. Special study options: Combined bachelor's/graduate degree, cooperative education, distance learning, dual enrollment of high school students, ESL, independent study, internships, liberal arts/career combination, teacher certification program. **Credit/placement by examination:** AP, CLEP, institutional tests. 15 credit hours maximum toward associate degree, 30 toward bachelor's. **Support services:** Learning center, reduced course load, remedial instruction, study skills assistance, tutoring, writing center.

Majors. Business: Business admin. **Computer sciences:** LAN/WAN management. **Conservation:** General. **Education:** Agricultural, biology, business, elementary, English, history, mathematics, science, secondary, social science, trade/industrial. **Engineering:** Surveying. **Health services:** Nursing (RN). **Social sciences:** General.

Most popular majors. Business/marketing 24%, education 19%, engineering/engineering technologies 18%, health sciences 24%, public administration/social services 10%.

Technology on campus. 200 workstations in dormitories, library, computer center, student center. Dormitories wired for high-speed internet access and linked to campus network. Commuter students can connect to campus network. Online course registration, online library, helpline, wireless network available.

Student life. Freshman orientation: Mandatory, $45 fee. Preregistration for classes offered. One-day program, held Saturday before school starts. Must compete assignment and receive passing grade. **Housing:** Coed dorms, apartments, wellness housing available. $250 partly refundable deposit. **Activities:** Drama, student government, Veterans club, vocational clubs, nursing club, rodeo, intramural sports, student ambassadors.

Athletics. Intramural: Rodeo.

Student services. Adult student services, career counseling, services for economically disadvantaged, student employment services, financial aid counseling, minority student services, personal counseling, placement for graduates, veterans' counselor. **Physically disabled:** Services for visually, speech, hearing impaired.

Contact. E-mail: admissions@gbcnv.edu
Phone: (775) 753-2311 Fax: (775) 738-8771
Janice King, Director of Admissions, Great Basin College, 1500 College Parkway, Elko, NV 89801

International Academy of Design and Technology: Henderson
Henderson, Nevada
www.iadtvegas.com   CB code: 5971

- For-profit 3-year visual arts and technical college
- Commuter campus in very large city
- 510 undergraduates

General. Accredited by ACICS. **Degrees:** 79 bachelor's, 10 associate awarded. **Location:** 10 miles from Las Vegas. **Calendar:** Quarter. **Full-time faculty:** 6 total. **Part-time faculty:** 54 total. **Class size:** 84% < 20, 16% 20-39.

Basis for selection. Open admission. **Home schooled:** ACT or SAT scores.

2015-2016 Annual costs. Total program tuition: certificates, $22,400; associate degrees, $32,800; bachelor's degrees, $64,800.

Application procedures. Admission: No deadline. $50 fee. **Financial aid:** No deadline.

Academics. Special study options: Accelerated study, distance learning, independent study, internships, study abroad. **Credit/placement by examination:** AP, CLEP. **Support services:** Tutoring.

Majors. BACHELOR'S. Business: Fashion, merchandising. **Communications technology:** Recording arts. **Visual/performing arts:** Fashion design, film/cinema/video, game design, graphic design, interior design. **ASSOCIATE. Business:** Merchandising. **Visual/performing arts:** Fashion design, graphic design.

Most popular majors. Communication technologies 17%, visual/performing arts 79%.

Technology on campus. Online course registration, online library, wireless network available.

Student life. Freshman orientation: Mandatory. Preregistration for classes offered.

Contact. E-mail: vegas_web@iadtvegas.com
Phone: (702) 990-0150 Toll-free number: (866) 400-4238
Fax: (702) 990-0161
Maggie Balderas, Director of Admissions, International Academy of Design and Technology: Henderson, 2495 Village View Drive, Henderson, NV 89074

ITT Technical Institute: Henderson
Henderson, Nevada
www.itt-tech.edu   CB code: 2710

- For-profit 4-year technical college
- Commuter campus in small city
- 412 undergraduates
- Interview required

General. Accredited by ACICS. **Degrees:** 23 bachelor's, 160 associate awarded. **Calendar:** Quarter, extensive summer session. **Full-time faculty:** 19 total. **Part-time faculty:** 51 total.

Basis for selection. Satisfactory scores from on-site tests in English and mathematics required.

2015-2016 Annual costs. Per-credit-hour charge, $493; academic fee, $100 per quarter. Certain programs require purchase of tools, which range from $150 to $500. All costs subject to change.

Application procedures. Admission: No deadline. No application fee. Admission notification on a rolling basis. **Financial aid:** FAFSA, institutional form required. Applicants notified on a rolling basis.

Academics. Credit/placement by examination: AP, CLEP. **Support services:** Learning center, tutoring.

Majors. Business: Business admin, construction management. **Communications technology:** Animation/special effects. **Computer sciences:** Security. **Protective services:** Law enforcement admin.

Technology on campus. Online library available.

Student life. Freshman orientation: Available. Preregistration for classes offered.

Student services. Career counseling, student employment services, placement for graduates.

Contact. Phone: (702) 558-5404 Toll-free number: (800) 488-8459
Fax: (702) 558-5412
Anne Buzak, Director of Recruitment, ITT Technical Institute: Henderson, 168 North Gibson Road, Henderson, NV 89014

Nevada State College
Henderson, Nevada
www.nsc.edu   CB code: 4572

- Public 4-year nursing, liberal arts and teachers college
- Commuter campus in large city
- 3,429 degree-seeking undergraduates: 61% part-time, 76% women
- 52% of applicants admitted

General. Regionally accredited. Offers dual enrollment programs with state community colleges. **Degrees:** 393 bachelor's awarded. **ROTC:** Air Force. **Location:** 15 miles from Las Vegas. **Calendar:** Semester, limited summer session. **Full-time faculty:** 66 total. **Part-time faculty:** 187 total. **Special facilities:** Smart classrooms, seismograph, weather center, anatomy and physiology cadaver laboratories, 16-inch telescope.

Freshman class profile. 1,503 applied, 775 admitted, 349 enrolled.

| End year in good standing: | 69% | Out-of-state: | 4% |
| Return as sophomores: | 69% | | |

Basis for selection. Academic record. SAT or ACT recommended. ACT/SAT used for placement in English and math. **Home schooled:** SAT/ACT required.

High school preparation. Required units include English 4, mathematics 3, social studies 3, science 2 (laboratory 1).

2015-2016 Annual costs. Tuition/fees: $5,033; $15,299 out-of-state. Books/supplies: $1,000. Personal expenses: $1,800.

Application procedures. Admission: Closing date 8/15 (receipt date). $30 fee, may be waived for applicants with need. Admission notification on a rolling basis. **Financial aid:** Priority date 3/1; no closing date. FAFSA, institutional form required. Applicants notified on a rolling basis starting 5/1.

Academics. Special study options: Accelerated study, distance learning, double major, dual enrollment of high school students, independent study, internships, liberal arts/career combination, student-designed major, study abroad, teacher certification program. **Credit/placement by examination:** AP, CLEP, SAT, ACT, institutional tests. 30 credit hours maximum toward bachelor's degree. **Support services:** Learning center, remedial instruction, study skills assistance, tutoring, writing center.

Majors. Biology: General. **Business:** Business admin, management science. **Communications technology:** Animation/special effects. **Conservation:** Environmental science. **Education:** General, autistic, bilingual, biology, Deaf/hearing impaired, elementary, elementary special ed, English, history, mathematics, science, secondary, secondary special ed. **English:** English lit. **Health services:** Nursing (RN), speech pathology. **History:** General. **Liberal arts:** Arts/sciences. **Math:** General. **Physical sciences:** Chemistry. **Protective services:** Law enforcement admin, police science. **Psychology:** General. **Social sciences:** Economics. **Visual/performing arts:** Design.

Technology on campus. 124 workstations in library, computer center, student center. Commuter students can connect to campus network. Online course registration, online library, helpline, wireless network available.

Student life. Freshman orientation: Mandatory. Preregistration for classes offered. One-day program held prior to start of classes; separate program for parents and family members offered concurrently. **Activities:** Drama, international student organizations, student government, student newspaper, American Sign Language Club, Kappa Delta Pi, Pre-Medical Society, Visual Media Club, African Student Association, Latino Scorpions Club, Prism-Straight Alliance, NSC Veterans & Allies, NSC Visionaries, and Nevada State Society of Psychology.

Athletics. Team name: Scorpions.

Student services. Career counseling, student employment services, financial aid counseling, minority student services. **Physically disabled:** Services for visually, speech, hearing impaired.

Contact. E-mail: admissions@nsc.edu
Phone: (702) 992-2130 Fax: (702) 992-2110
Adelfa Sullivan, Registrar, Nevada State College, 1125 Nevada State
Drive, Henderson, NV 89002

Roseman University of Health Sciences
Henderson, Nevada
www.roseman.edu

- Private two-year upper-division university
- Commuter campus in very large city
- Test scores, application essay, interview required

General. Regionally accredited. **Degrees:** 140 bachelor's awarded; master's, professional offered. **Articulation:** Agreements with Lake Tahoe Community College, Consumnes River College, San Diego Mesa College, San Diego City College, San Diego Mirimar College. **Location:** 9 miles from Las Vegas. **Calendar:** Continuous. **Full-time faculty:** 111 total; 77% have terminal degrees, 24% minority, 43% women. **Part-time faculty:** 134 total; 48% have terminal degrees, 20% minority, 49% women. **Class size:** 71% 20-39, 29% 50-99.

Student profile. 312 degree-seeking undergraduates, 1,135 degree-seeking graduate students. 45% transferred from two-year, 55% transferred from four-year institutions.

Women:	79%	Out-of-state:	39%
African American:	4%	25 or older:	65%

Basis for selection. College transcript, application essay, interview, standardized test scores required. Must complete specified courses - BSN and ABSN; ABSN must have a Bachelor's Degree in non-nursing field. Transfer accepted as juniors.

2016-2017 Annual costs. Tuition/fees (projected): $40,607. Books/supplies: $1,080. Personal expenses: $8,937.

Financial aid. **Need-based:** 278 applied for aid; 227 deemed to have need; 224 received aid. Average need met was 17%. 8% of total undergraduate aid awarded as scholarships/grants, 92% as loans/jobs. **Non-need-based:** Scholarships awarded for academics, leadership.

Application procedures. **Admission:** Rolling admission. $40 fee. Application must be submitted on paper. **Financial aid:** No deadline. Applicants notified on a rolling basis starting 1/1; must reply within 4 weeks of notification. FAFSA required.

Academics. **Special study options:** Accelerated study. **Credit/placement by examination:** AP, CLEP, IB.

Majors. **Health services:** Nursing (RN).

Technology on campus. PC or laptop required. 28 workstations in library. Commuter students can connect to campus network. Online library, helpline, repair service, wireless network available.

Student life. **Activities:** Student government.

Student services. Financial aid counseling, placement for graduates. **Physically disabled:** Services for visually, hearing impaired.

Contact. E-mail: bsnadmission@roseman.edu
Phone: (702) 968-2075 Fax: (702) 968-5279
Roseman University of Health Sciences, 11 Sunset Way, Henderson, NV
89014-2333

Sierra Nevada College
Incline Village, Nevada
www.sierranevada.edu   CB code: 4757

- Private 4-year liberal arts college
- Residential campus in small town
- 498 degree-seeking undergraduates: 2% part-time, 39% women, 3% African American, 4% Asian American, 5% Hispanic/Latino, 3% Native American, 1% Native Hawaiian/Pacific islander, 3% international
- 420 degree-seeking graduate students
- Application essay required

General. Founded in 1969. Regionally accredited. **Degrees:** 127 bachelor's awarded; master's offered. **Location:** 35 miles from Reno. **Calendar:** Semester, limited summer session. **Full-time faculty:** 39 total; 56% have terminal degrees, 10% minority, 56% women. **Part-time faculty:** 107 total; 32% have terminal degrees, 14% minority, 61% women. **Class size:** 74% < 20, 24% 20-39, 2% 40-49. **Special facilities:** Entertainment technology lab, LEED Platinum Certified Tahoe Center for Environmental Sciences, student-managed greenhouse, arts and media center.

Freshman class profile.

GPA 3.75 or higher:	5%	Rank in top quarter:	20%
GPA 3.50-3.74:	11%	Return as sophomores:	64%
GPA 3.0-3.49:	30%	Live on campus:	90%
GPA 2.0-2.99:	54%		

Basis for selection. Standard admission requirements include 2.6 GPA, 400 on each section of SAT (exclusive of Writing), or 19 ACT. Other factors, including leadership qualities, extracurricular activities, community involvement, and volunteer work, considered when evaluating application not meeting standard requirements. Interview not required. Campus visit and general meeting with Admissions Counselor highly encouraged. **Home schooled:** Letter of recommendation (nonparent) required. Considered on case by case basis. Must submit any documentation available regarding curriculum. **Learning Disabled:** Students may be admitted provisionally; academic support, tutoring, and other resources provided.

High school preparation. College-preparatory program recommended. 13 units recommended. Recommended units include English 4, mathematics 3, science 2 (laboratory 2) and foreign language 2.

2015-2016 Annual costs. Tuition/fees: $29,994. Room/board: $12,066. Books/supplies: $1,600. Personal expenses: $4,044.

2015-2016 Financial aid. **Need-based:** 77 full-time freshmen applied for aid; 66 deemed to have need; 66 received aid. Average need met was 53%. Average scholarship/grant was $26,237; average loan $3,299. 68% of total undergraduate aid awarded as scholarships/grants, 32% as loans/jobs. **Non-need-based:** Awarded to 459 full-time undergraduates, including 96 freshmen. Scholarships awarded for academics, alumni affiliation, art, athletics, state residency. **Additional information:** Institutional need-based grant provided based on remaining need after being awarded all scholarships and Federal Student Aid. First time freshmen awarded 50% of remaining need and 45% for continuing students.

Application procedures. **Admission:** Priority date 2/15; deadline 8/21 (receipt date). No application fee. Admission notification on a rolling basis beginning on or about 9/1. **Financial aid:** No deadline. FAFSA required. Applicants notified on a rolling basis starting 2/1.

Academics. **Special study options:** Accelerated study, combined bachelor's/graduate degree, distance learning, double major, dual enrollment of high school students, ESL, honors, independent study, internships, liberal arts/career combination, student-designed major, study abroad. Tuition exchange. **Credit/placement by examination:** AP, CLEP, IB, ACT, institutional tests. 30 credit hours maximum toward bachelor's degree. **Support services:** Reduced course load, remedial instruction, study skills assistance, tutoring, writing center.

Majors. **Biology:** General, ecology. **Business:** General, accounting, business admin, entrepreneurial studies, finance, managerial economics, marketing, nonprofit/public, resort management. **Communications:** Photojournalism. **Conservation:** Environmental science, management/policy. **English:** English lit. **Health services:** Premedicine, prenursing, prepharmacy. **Liberal arts:** Arts/sciences, humanities. **Parks/recreation:** Outdoor education. **Psychology:** General. **Social sciences:** Economics. **Visual/performing arts:** General, ceramics, drawing, painting, printmaking, sculpture, studio arts.

Most popular majors. Business/marketing 47%, English 7%, interdisciplinary studies 14%, liberal arts 8%, psychology 7%, visual/performing arts 7%.

Technology on campus. PC or laptop required. 30 workstations in library, computer center, student center. Dormitories wired for high-speed internet access and linked to campus network. Commuter students can connect to campus network. Online library, helpline, repair service, wireless network available.

Student life. **Freshman orientation:** Mandatory. Preregistration for classes offered. **Housing:** Guaranteed on-campus for freshmen. Coed dorms, special housing for disabled, themed housing available. $200 nonrefundable deposit, deadline 5/15. **Activities:** Choral groups, student government, First Generation club, clay club, gallery club, Tribe of Many Nations club, sustainability club, pride club.

Athletics. **Intercollegiate:** Lacrosse, skiing. **Intramural:** Lacrosse, skiing, soccer, volleyball. **Team name:** Eagles.

Student services. Adult student services, career counseling, student employment services, financial aid counseling, health services, personal counseling, placement for graduates, veterans' counselor.

Contact. E-mail: admissions@sierranevada.edu
Phone: (775) 831-1314 Toll-free number: (866) 412-4636
Fax: (775) 831-6223
Nick Anderson, Assistant Director of Admissions, Sierra Nevada College, 999 Tahoe Boulevard, Incline Village, NV 89451-4269

University of Nevada: Las Vegas

Las Vegas, Nevada | **CB member**
www.unlv.edu | **CB code: 4861**

- Public 4-year university
- Commuter campus in very large city
- 23,329 degree-seeking undergraduates: 25% part-time, 56% women, 8% African American, 15% Asian American, 26% Hispanic/Latino, 1% Native Hawaiian/Pacific islander, 9% Multi-racial, non-Hispanic, 4% international
- 4,307 degree-seeking graduate students
- 88% of applicants admitted
- SAT or ACT (ACT writing optional) required
- 41% graduate within 6 years

General. Founded in 1957. Regionally accredited. Credit courses available at Nellis Air Force Base. **Degrees:** 3,832 bachelor's awarded; master's, professional, doctoral offered. **ROTC:** Army, Air Force. **Location:** 268 miles from Los Angeles, 290 miles from Phoenix. **Calendar:** Semester, extensive summer session. **Special facilities:** National supercomputing center for energy and environment, natural history museum, arboretum, theaters, concert hall, international gaming institute, professional practice school for teachers, student recreation and wellness center.

Freshman class profile. 7,666 applied, 6,781 admitted, 3,784 enrolled.

Mid 50% test scores			
SAT critical reading:	440-560	**Rank in top quarter:**	52%
SAT math:	450-560	**Rank in top tenth:**	23%
SAT writing:	420-530	**Return as sophomores:**	74%
ACT composite:	18-25	**Out-of-state:**	16%
GPA 3.75 or higher:	16%	**Live on campus:**	24%
GPA 3.50-3.74:	18%	**International:**	2%
GPA 3.0-3.49:	42%	**Fraternities:**	8%
GPA 2.0-2.99:	23%	**Sororities:**	9%

Basis for selection. GED not accepted. 3.0 GPA required in core courses. ACT/SAT can waive GPA requirements, but all students must have core coursework. Recommendations, personal essay and test scores considered for students applying through alternate criteria program. Audition recommended for music, theater arts programs; portfolio recommended for art program. **Home schooled:** Transcript of courses and grades, letter of recommendation (nonparent) required. Two letters of recommendation, preferably from teachers, counselors, or an official who can address your academic abilities, or a copy of your ACT or SAT test scores.

High school preparation. College-preparatory program required. 13 units required. Required units include English 4, mathematics 3, social studies 3, science 3 (laboratory 2). High school mathematics must include Algebra I and Algebra II.

2015-2016 Annual costs. Tuition/fees: $6,823; $20,733 out-of-state. Room/board: $10,730. Books/supplies: $1,224. Personal expenses: $2,942.

2015-2016 Financial aid. **Need-based:** 3,194 full-time freshmen applied for aid; 2,561 deemed to have need; 2,439 received aid. Average need met was 72%. Average scholarship/grant was $6,193; average loan $3,179. 47% of total undergraduate aid awarded as scholarships/grants, 53% as loans/jobs. **Non-need-based:** Awarded to 6,777 full-time undergraduates, including 2,429 freshmen. Scholarships awarded for academics, alumni affiliation, athletics, music/drama. **Additional information:** Tuition reduction for state residents through consortium programs and for out-of-state students graduating from high schools in designated counties bordering Nevada, for military dependents residing in-state, and for dependents of children of alumni not residing in-state.

Application procedures. **Admission:** Priority date 2/1; deadline 7/1. $60 fee. Application must be submitted online. Admission notification on a rolling basis beginning on or about 7/1. Must reply by 8/26. Students may defer admission decisions within the academic year for which the student was admitted providing the student's academic record has not changed and the student has not attended another academic institution. **Financial aid:** Priority

date 2/1; no closing date. FAFSA required. Applicants notified on a rolling basis starting 3/20; must reply within 6 week(s) of notification.

Academics. **Special study options:** Accelerated study, combined bachelor's/graduate degree, cooperative education, cross-registration, distance learning, double major, dual enrollment of high school students, ESL, exchange student, honors, independent study, internships, study abroad, teacher certification program. **Credit/placement by examination:** AP, CLEP, IB, SAT, ACT, institutional tests. 30 credit hours maximum toward bachelor's degree. **Support services:** Learning center, pre-admission summer program, remedial instruction, study skills assistance, tutoring, writing center.

Honors college/program. Applicants must complete the honors application and provide letters of recommendation, test scores, personal statements, and essay response.

Majors. **Architecture:** Architecture, interior, landscape, urban/community planning. **Area/ethnic studies:** African-American, Asian, Latin American, women's. **Biology:** General, biochemistry. **Business:** Accounting, construction management, entrepreneurial studies, finance, hospitality admin, international, management information systems, marketing, real estate, restaurant/food services. **Communications:** Communications/speech/rhetoric, media studies. **Computer sciences:** Computer science. **Conservation:** General, environmental studies. **Education:** Early childhood, elementary, health, science, secondary, Spanish, special ed. **Engineering:** Civil, computer, electrical, mechanical. **English:** English lit. **Foreign languages:** French, German, linguistics, Spanish. **Health services:** Athletic training, health care admin, medical radiologic technology/radiation therapy, nuclear medical technology, nursing (RN), physics/radiologic health. **History:** General. **Human services:** General, social work. **Math:** General, applied. **Parks/recreation:** General, exercise sciences, health/fitness. **Philosophy/religion:** Philosophy. **Physical sciences:** Chemistry, physics. **Protective services:** Criminal justice. **Psychology:** General. **Social sciences:** Anthropology, economics, political science, sociology. **Visual/performing arts:** Acting, art, art history/conservation, dance, dramatic, film/cinema/video, graphic design, music, theater design.

Most popular majors. Biology 6%, business/marketing 33%, psychology 8%, security/protective services 6%, social sciences 6%.

Technology on campus. 1,550 workstations in dormitories, library, computer center, student center. Dormitories wired for high-speed internet access and linked to campus network. Commuter students can connect to campus network. Online course registration, online library, helpline, wireless network available.

Student life. **Freshman orientation:** Mandatory, $120 fee. Preregistration for classes offered. **Housing:** Guaranteed on-campus for freshmen. Coed dorms, special housing for disabled, themed housing available. $325 partly refundable deposit, deadline 7/1. **Activities:** Bands, campus ministries, choral groups, dance, drama, film society, international student organizations, literary magazine, music ensembles, Model UN, musical theater, opera, radio station, student government, student newspaper, symphony orchestra, TV station, Young Democrats/Republicans, Rebel Christian Fellowship, Hillel, ethnic student council, student organization of Latinos, black student association, Latter-day Saints student organization, Hawaii club, Circle K.

Athletics. NCAA. **Intercollegiate:** Baseball M, basketball, cheerleading, cross-country W, diving, football (tackle) M, golf, soccer, softball W, swimming, tennis, track and field W, volleyball W. **Intramural:** Badminton, basketball, bowling, cross-country, football (non-tackle), golf, racquetball, soccer, softball, swimming, table tennis, tennis, track and field, volleyball. **Team name:** Rebels.

Student services. Adult student services, alcohol/substance abuse counseling, career counseling, services for economically disadvantaged, student employment services, financial aid counseling, health services, legal services, minority student services, on-campus daycare, personal counseling, placement for graduates, veterans' counselor, women's services. **Physically disabled:** Services for visually, speech, hearing impaired.

Contact. E-mail: admissions@unlv.edu
Phone: (702) 774-8658 Fax: (702) 774-8008
Kris Shay, Executive Director of Admissions, University of Nevada: Las Vegas, 4505 Maryland Parkway, Box 451021, Las Vegas, NV 89154-1021

University of Nevada: Reno

Reno, Nevada | **CB member**
www.unr.edu | **CB code: 4844**

- Public 4-year university
- Commuter campus in small city

- 17,295 degree-seeking undergraduates: 14% part-time, 53% women, 4% African American, 7% Asian American, 19% Hispanic/Latino, 1% Native American, 1% Native Hawaiian/Pacific islander, 6% Multi-racial, non-Hispanic, 1% international
- 2,693 degree-seeking graduate students
- 86% of applicants admitted
- SAT or ACT (ACT writing optional) required
- 59% graduate within 6 years

General. Founded in 1874. Regionally accredited. **Degrees:** 2,974 bachelor's awarded; master's, professional, doctoral offered. **ROTC:** Army. **Location:** 225 miles from San Francisco, 35 miles from Lake Tahoe. **Calendar:** Semester, extensive summer session. **Full-time faculty:** 627 total; 84% have terminal degrees, 20% minority, 43% women. **Part-time faculty:** 539 total; 24% have terminal degrees, 22% minority, 53% women. **Class size:** 33% < 20, 40% 20-39, 7% 40-49, 11% 50-99, 8% >100. **Special facilities:** Mineral museum, planetarium, arboretum, disability resource center, ethnic student resource center, internship center.

Freshman class profile. 9,538 applied, 8,208 admitted, 3,851 enrolled.

Mid 50% test scores			
SAT critical reading:	480-590	GPA 2.0-2.99:	15%
SAT math:	490-600	Rank in top quarter:	56%
SAT writing:	460-570	Rank in top tenth:	24%
ACT composite:	21-26	Return as sophomores:	81%
GPA 3.75 or higher:	18%	Out-of-state:	33%
GPA 3.50-3.74:	22%	Live on campus:	77%
GPA 3.0-3.49:	45%	International:	1%

Basis for selection. GED not accepted. Secondary school record most important, with 3.0 GPA in academic core of English, math, social sciences and natural sciences. Students who do not meet Board of Regents admission requirements may appeal for special admission. If student does not meet GPA requirement, 1040 SAT/22 ACT may be used in place of GPA requirement. All students applying for scholarships must submit test scores. Interview recommended for nursing program; audition recommended for music program; portfolio recommended for fine arts program. **Home schooled:** Students who do not meet Board of Regents admission requirements may appeal for special admission.

High school preparation. College-preparatory program required. 13 units required. Required units include English 4, mathematics 3, social studies 3, science 3 (laboratory 2).

2015-2016 Annual costs. Tuition/fees: $6,882; $20,792 out-of-state. Room/board: $9,861. Books/supplies: $1,300. Personal expenses: $2,500.

2014-2015 Financial aid. **Need-based:** 2,690 full-time freshmen applied for aid; 1,892 deemed to have need; 1,892 received aid. Average need met was 62%. Average scholarship/grant was $5,490; average loan $3,365. 55% of total undergraduate aid awarded as scholarships/grants, 45% as loans/jobs. **Non-need-based:** Awarded to 7,868 full-time undergraduates, including 2,655 freshmen. Scholarships awarded for academics, alumni affiliation, art, athletics. **Additional information:** Reduced out-of-state tuition available for participants in WUE program.

Application procedures. **Admission:** Priority date 2/1; deadline 4/7 (receipt date). $60 fee. Admission notification on a rolling basis beginning on or about 9/15. Must reply by 6/1. **Financial aid:** Priority date 3/1; no closing date. FAFSA required. Applicants notified on a rolling basis starting 4/1; must reply by 6/1.

Academics. **Special study options:** Combined bachelor's/graduate degree, distance learning, double major, ESL, honors, independent study, internships, student-designed major, study abroad, teacher certification program. **Credit/placement by examination:** AP, CLEP, IB, SAT, ACT, institutional tests. 60 credit hours maximum toward bachelor's degree. **Support services:** Learning center, pre-admission summer program, reduced course load, remedial instruction, study skills assistance, tutoring, writing center.

Majors. **Area/ethnic studies:** Women's. **Biology:** General, biochemistry, biotechnology, neuroscience. **Business:** General, accounting, business admin, entrepreneurial studies, finance, international, managerial economics, marketing. **Communications:** Communications/speech/rhetoric, journalism. **Computer sciences:** General, computer science. **Conservation:** General, environmental science, forest management, wildlife/wilderness. **Education:** Music, secondary. **Engineering:** Applied physics, chemical, civil, computer, electrical, environmental, geological, mechanical, metallurgical, mining, water resource. **English:** English lit. **Foreign languages:** French, Spanish. **Health services:** Nursing (RN), preveterinary, speech pathology. **History:** General. **Human services:** Social work. **Math:** General. **Philosophy/religion:** Philosophy. **Physical sciences:** Atmospheric science, chemistry, geology, geophysics, physics. **Psychology:** General. **Social sciences:** Anthropology, criminology, geography, international relations, political science, sociology. **Visual/**

performing arts: Art, art history/conservation, dramatic, music, music performance. **Work/family studies:** Child development, family studies.

Most popular majors. Biology 11%, business/marketing 17%, engineering/engineering technologies 10%, health sciences 12%, psychology 7%, social sciences 11%.

Technology on campus. Dormitories wired for high-speed internet access and linked to campus network. Commuter students can connect to campus network. Online course registration, online library, helpline, repair service, student web hosting, wireless network available.

Student life. **Freshman orientation:** Mandatory, $110 fee. Preregistration for classes offered. Sessions held before each semester; family members welcome. **Housing:** Coed dorms, single-sex dorms, special housing for disabled, apartments, fraternity/sorority housing, themed housing, wellness housing available. $325 partly refundable deposit, deadline 5/1. Living-Learning Center. **Activities:** Bands, campus ministries, choral groups, dance, drama, film society, international student organizations, literary magazine, music ensembles, Model UN, musical theater, radio station, student government, student newspaper, symphony orchestra, Intervarsity Christian Fellowship, black student union, American Indian organization, Asian American Alliance, Chinese students association, Young Republicans, Young Democrats, Hillel, MEXA.

Athletics. NCAA. **Intercollegiate:** Baseball M, basketball, cross-country W, diving W, football (tackle) M, golf, rifle, soccer W, softball W, swimming W, tennis, track and field W, volleyball W. **Intramural:** Badminton, basketball, bowling, football (non-tackle), golf, racquetball, soccer, softball, swimming, table tennis, tennis, track and field, volleyball, water polo, weight lifting. **Team name:** Wolf Pack.

Student services. Adult student services, alcohol/substance abuse counseling, career counseling, services for economically disadvantaged, student employment services, financial aid counseling, health services, legal services, minority student services, on-campus daycare, personal counseling, placement for graduates, veterans' counselor, women's services. **Physically disabled:** Services for visually, speech, hearing impaired.

Contact. E-mail: asknevada@unr.edu
Phone: (775) 784-4700 Toll-free number: (866) 263-8232
Fax: (775) 784-4283
Steve Maples, Director of Admissions, University of Nevada: Reno, Mail Stop 120, Reno, NV 89557

University of Phoenix: Las Vegas
Las Vegas, Nevada
www.phoenix.edu

- For-profit 4-year university
- Commuter campus in very large city
- 2,000 degree-seeking undergraduates
- 510 graduate students

General. Regionally accredited. **Degrees:** 442 bachelor's awarded; master's offered. **Calendar:** Differs by program. Other academic calendar. **Full-time faculty:** 32 total. **Part-time faculty:** 225 total.

Basis for selection. Open admission, but selective for some programs.

2015-2016 Annual costs. Per-credit-hour charge, $410 to $635, depending upon level and course of study. Books, material charges, and other fees vary by course and program. All fees are subject to change.

Application procedures. **Admission:** No deadline. No application fee. **Financial aid:** No deadline.

Academics. **Credit/placement by examination:** AP, CLEP.

Majors. **Business:** Accounting, accounting/business management, business admin, e-commerce, entrepreneurial studies, finance, human resources, marketing, operations. **Computer sciences:** General, database management, networking, programming, security, system admin, systems analysis, web page design, webmaster. **Education:** Elementary. **English:** English lit. **Health services:** Facilities admin, health information management, long term care admin. **Human services:** General. **Protective services:** Disaster management, law enforcement admin, security management.

Student life. **Freshman orientation:** Mandatory. Preregistration for classes offered.

Contact. University of Phoenix: Las Vegas, 3755 Breakthrough Way, Las Vegas, NV 89135-3047

University of Phoenix: Northern Nevada
Reno, Nevada
www.phoenix.edu

- For-profit 4-year university
- Commuter campus in small city
- 300 degree-seeking undergraduates
- 80 graduate students

General. Regionally accredited. **Degrees:** 511 bachelor's awarded; master's offered. **Calendar:** Differs by program. Other academic calendar. **Full-time faculty:** 13 total. **Part-time faculty:** 80 total.

Basis for selection. Open admission, but selective for some programs.

2015-2016 Annual costs. Per-credit-hour charge, $410 to $635, depending upon level and course of study. Books, material charges, and other fees vary by course and program. All fees are subject to change.

Application procedures. Admission: No deadline. No application fee. **Financial aid:** No deadline.

Academics. Credit/placement by examination: AP, CLEP.

Majors. Business: Accounting, accounting/business management, business admin, finance, human resources, marketing. **Communications:** General. **Computer sciences:** Database management, networking, programming, security, systems analysis, web page design, webmaster. **Education:** Elementary. **English:** English lit. **Health services:** Facilities admin, health information management, long term care admin. **Human services:** General. **Protective services:** Disaster management, law enforcement admin.

Student life. Freshman orientation: Mandatory. Preregistration for classes offered.

Contact. Toll-free number: (866) 766-0766
University of Phoenix: Northern Nevada, 10345 Professional Circle, Reno, NV 89521-5862

New Hampshire

Colby-Sawyer College

New London, New Hampshire
www.colby-sawyer.edu

CB member
CB code: 3281

- Private 4-year liberal arts college
- Residential campus in small town
- 1,206 degree-seeking undergraduates: 4% part-time, 69% women, 7% African American, 2% Asian American, 3% Hispanic/Latino, 1% Native American, 9% international
- 75% of applicants admitted
- Application essay required
- 51% graduate within 6 years

General. Founded in 1837. Regionally accredited. **Degrees:** 310 bachelor's, 10 associate awarded. **ROTC:** Army, Air Force. **Location:** 30 miles from Hanover, 35 miles from Concord. **Calendar:** Semester, limited summer session. **Full-time faculty:** 81 total; 75% have terminal degrees, 7% minority, 49% women. **Part-time faculty:** 56 total; 29% have terminal degrees, 2% minority, 64% women. **Special facilities:** Fine arts center, laboratory school (preschool, K-3) library learning center, conservatory, sustainable classroom, maple sugaring shack.

Freshman class profile. 2,669 applied, 1,990 admitted, 289 enrolled.

GPA 3.75 or higher:	12%	Return as sophomores:	78%
GPA 3.50-3.74:	25%	Out-of-state:	70%
GPA 3.0-3.49:	36%	Live on campus:	96%
GPA 2.0-2.99:	27%	International:	5%

Basis for selection. High school transcript most important. Recommendations, school and community activities, essay also considered. Test scores considered if submitted. Nursing applicants must apply during early action and are strongly encouraged to have 3 years of college-preparatory lab sciences, including biology and chemistry, as well as math up to algebra 2. Interviews highly recommended. Portfolio recommended for art program.

High school preparation. College-preparatory program required. 15 units required. Required units include English 4, mathematics 3, social studies 3, science 3 (laboratory 3) and foreign language 2.

2016-2017 Annual costs. Tuition/fees (projected): $39,190. Room/board: $13,260. Books/supplies: $750. Personal expenses: $1,000.

2015-2016 Financial aid. Need-based: 70% of total undergraduate aid awarded as scholarships/grants, 30% as loans/jobs. **Non-need-based:** Scholarships awarded for academics, alumni affiliation, art, leadership, minority status, music/drama.

Application procedures. Admission: Priority date 3/1; no deadline. $45 fee, may be waived for applicants with need, free for online applicants. Admission notification on a rolling basis beginning on or about 12/1. **Financial aid:** Priority date 2/15, closing date 3/1. FAFSA required. Applicants notified on a rolling basis starting 2/1; must reply by 5/1.

Academics. Liberal arts and experiential education integrated. Internships or senior research projects required in all major programs. **Special study options:** Combined bachelor's/graduate degree, distance learning, double major, exchange student, honors, independent study, internships, semester at sea, study abroad, teacher certification program, Washington semester. **Credit/placement by examination:** AP, CLEP, IB, institutional tests. 15 credit hours maximum toward associate degree, 15 toward bachelor's. **Support services:** Learning center, reduced course load, study skills assistance, tutoring, writing center.

Majors. Biology: General. **Business:** Business admin. **Communications:** Media studies. **Conservation:** Environmental studies. **Education:** General, early childhood. **English:** Creative writing, English lit. **Health services:** Athletic training, health care admin, nursing (RN), public health ed. **History:** General. **Parks/recreation:** Exercise sciences, sports admin. **Philosophy/religion:** General, philosophy. **Psychology:** General, developmental. **Social sciences:** Sociology. **Visual/performing arts:** Art, art history/conservation, graphic design, studio arts.

Most popular majors. Biology 8%, business/marketing 11%, education 10%, health sciences 21%, interdisciplinary studies 8%, parks/recreation 13%, psychology 9%.

Technology on campus. 150 workstations in library, computer center. Dormitories wired for high-speed internet access and linked to campus network. Commuter students can connect to campus network. Online course registration, online library, helpline, wireless network available.

Student life. Freshman orientation: Mandatory. Preregistration for classes offered. Two days immediately preceding beginning of fall semester. **Housing:** Guaranteed on-campus for all undergraduates. Coed dorms, single-sex dorms, special housing for disabled, wellness housing available. $500 deposit, deadline 5/1. **Activities:** Choral groups, dance, drama, international student organizations, literary magazine, Model UN, musical theater, radio station, student government, student newspaper, community service club, Safe Zones, cross cultural club, Christian Fellowship, Coalition for Peace and Justice, Student Democrats.

Athletics. NCAA. **Intercollegiate:** Baseball M, basketball, cross-country, diving, equestrian, field hockey W, lacrosse W, skiing, soccer, swimming, tennis, track and field, volleyball W. **Intramural:** Basketball, football (non-tackle), golf, soccer, tennis, volleyball. **Team name:** Chargers.

Student services. Alcohol/substance abuse counseling, career counseling, student employment services, financial aid counseling, health services, personal counseling. **Physically disabled:** Services for visually, hearing impaired.

Contact. E-mail: admissions@colby-sawyer.edu
Phone: (603) 526-3700 Toll-free number: (800) 272-1015
Fax: (603) 526-3452
Anna Miner, Director of Admission, Colby-Sawyer College, 541 Main Street, New London, NH 03257-7835

Daniel Webster College

Nashua, New Hampshire
www.dwc.edu

CB member
CB code: 3648

- For-profit 4-year business and engineering college
- Residential campus in small city
- 636 degree-seeking undergraduates: 5% part-time, 17% women, 10% African American, 4% Asian American, 7% Hispanic/Latino, 5% Multiracial, non-Hispanic
- 47 degree-seeking graduate students
- 62% of applicants admitted
- 49% graduate within 6 years; 8% enter graduate study

General. Founded in 1965. Regionally accredited. Mechanical and Aeronautical Engineering programs are accredited by ABET (Accreditation Board for Engineering and Technology). **Degrees:** 87 bachelor's, 1 associate awarded; master's offered. **ROTC:** Army, Naval, Air Force. **Location:** 18 miles from Manchester, 47 miles from Boston. **Calendar:** Semester, limited summer session. **Full-time faculty:** 21 total; 48% have terminal degrees, 24% minority, 33% women. **Part-time faculty:** 65 total; 28% have terminal degrees, 2% minority, 38% women. **Class size:** 71% < 20, 29% 20-39. **Special facilities:** On campus aviation center, college-owned aircraft for aeronautical engineering research, air traffic control simulation laboratory, wind tunnel.

Freshman class profile. 817 applied, 504 admitted, 156 enrolled.

GPA 3.75 or higher:	6%	End year in good standing:	80%
GPA 3.50-3.74:	7%	Return as sophomores:	67%
GPA 3.0-3.49:	31%	Out-of-state:	70%
GPA 2.0-2.99:	50%	Live on campus:	67%

Basis for selection. High school or college achievement most important. Extracurricular activities, personal statement, recommendations helpful. SAT and ACT test scores are NOT required. Applicants may submit in support of their application. Interview highly recommended. Campus visit highly recommended, essay/personal statement highly recommended. **Home schooled:** Statement describing home school structure and mission, transcript of courses and grades, state high school equivalency certificate, interview, letter of recommendation (nonparent) required. Must submit portfolio of high school work.

High school preparation. College-preparatory program recommended. 16 units required. Required and recommended units include English 4, mathematics 3-4, social studies 2, history 2, science 3 (laboratory 2), foreign language 2 and computer science 1.

2015-2016 Annual costs. Tuition/fees: $15,630. Room/board: $10,970. Books/supplies: $1,800. Personal expenses: $900.

Financial aid. Non-need-based: Scholarships awarded for academics.

Application procedures. Admission: No deadline. No application fee. Admission notification on a rolling basis. Must reply by May 1 or within 2 week(s) if notified thereafter. **Financial aid:** Priority date 3/1; no closing date. FAFSA, institutional form required. Applicants notified on a rolling basis starting 3/15; must reply within 2 week(s) of notification.

Academics. Special study options: Combined bachelor's/graduate degree, distance learning, double major, independent study, internships, liberal arts/career combination, study abroad. **Credit/placement by examination:** AP, CLEP, IB, institutional tests. 30 credit hours maximum toward associate degree, 30 toward bachelor's. **Support services:** Learning center, preadmission summer program, reduced course load, remedial instruction, study skills assistance, tutoring, writing center.

Majors. Business: General, accounting, business admin, management information systems, marketing. **Computer sciences:** Computer science, modeling/simulation, systems analysis. **Engineering:** Aerospace, construction, electrical, mechanical. **Health services:** Health care admin. **Parks/recreation:** Sports admin. **Protective services:** Homeland security. **Psychology:** General. **Visual/performing arts:** Game design.

Most popular majors. Business/marketing 22%, engineering/engineering technologies 17%, parks/recreation 7%, security/protective services 14%, trade and industry 26%, visual/performing arts 6%.

Technology on campus. 182 workstations in library, computer center, student center. Dormitories wired for high-speed internet access and linked to campus network. Commuter students can connect to campus network. Online course registration, online library, helpline, repair service, student web hosting, wireless network available.

Student life. Freshman orientation: Mandatory. Preregistration for classes offered. **Housing:** Guaranteed on-campus for all undergraduates. Coed dorms, single-sex dorms, themed housing available. Townhouses and suites for 4 to 7 students available. Living/learning community option available. **Activities:** Drama, film society, music ensembles, student government, Kenya Connection, DWC Veterans Association, Big Brothers/Sisters, homeland security club.

Athletics. NCAA. **Intercollegiate:** Baseball M, basketball, cross-country, field hockey W, golf, ice hockey, lacrosse, soccer, softball W, volleyball, wrestling M. **Intramural:** Basketball, football (non-tackle), soccer, volleyball. **Team name:** Eagles.

Student services. Adult student services, alcohol/substance abuse counseling, career counseling, student employment services, financial aid counseling, health services, personal counseling, placement for graduates.

Contact. E-mail: admissions@dwc.edu
Phone: (603) 577-6600 Toll-free number: (800) 325-6876 ext. 3
Fax: (603) 577-6001
Cyndie Sylvester, Director of Enrollment Management, Daniel Webster College, 20 University Drive, Nashua, NH 03063

Dartmouth College
Hanover, New Hampshire
www.dartmouth.edu

CB member
CB code: 3351

▶ Private 4-year university and liberal arts college
▶ Residential campus in large town
▶ 4,214 degree-seeking undergraduates: 49% women, 7% African American, 15% Asian American, 8% Hispanic/Latino, 2% Native American, 5% Multi-racial, non-Hispanic, 8% international
▶ 2,001 degree-seeking graduate students
▶ 11% of applicants admitted
▶ SAT and SAT Subject Tests or ACT with writing, application essay required
▶ 94% graduate within 6 years

General. Founded in 1769. Regionally accredited. **Degrees:** 1,094 bachelor's awarded; master's, professional, doctoral offered. **ROTC:** Army. **Location:** 130 miles from Boston. **Calendar:** Quarter, extensive summer session. **Full-time faculty:** 582 total; 3% have terminal degrees, 18% minority, 36% women. **Part-time faculty:** 152 total; 6% have terminal degrees, 4% minority, 41% women. **Class size:** 64% < 20, 23% 20-39, 5% 40-49, 7% 50-99, less than 1% >100. **Special facilities:** Observatory, centers for humanities, social sciences, physical science, performing arts, museum of art, ethics, life science, computation.

Freshman class profile. 20,507 applied, 2,250 admitted, 1,116 enrolled.

Mid 50% test scores			
SAT critical reading:	660-780	Rank in top tenth:	91%
SAT math:	670-780	Return as sophomores:	97%
SAT writing:	670-780	Out-of-state:	98%
ACT composite:	30-34	Live on campus:	100%
Rank in top quarter:	97%	International:	8%

Basis for selection. Evidence of intellectual capability, motivation, and personal integrity of primary importance. Talent, accomplishment, and involvement in nonacademic areas also evaluated. Two SAT Subject Tests of student's choice required. Interview optional.

High school preparation. College-preparatory program recommended. Recommended units include English 4, mathematics 4, social studies 4, science 4 and foreign language 4. Strongest academic program available to applicant recommended.

2015-2016 Annual costs. Tuition/fees: $49,506. Room/board: $14,238. Books/supplies: $1,260. Personal expenses: $2,040. **Additional information:** First-Year Students have additional room charges and fees of $390.

2015-2016 Financial aid. All financial aid based on need. 679 full-time freshmen applied for aid; 553 deemed to have need; 553 received aid. Average need met was 100%. Average scholarship/grant was $46,917; average loan $4,312. 91% of total undergraduate aid awarded as scholarships/grants, 9% as loans/jobs.

Application procedures. Admission: Closing date 1/1 (postmark date). $80 fee, may be waived for applicants with need. Admission notification by 4/10. Must reply by 5/1. **Financial aid:** Closing date 2/1. FAFSA, CSS PROFILE required. Applicants notified by 4/2; must reply by 5/1.

Academics. Undergraduate research encouraged. **Special study options:** Combined bachelor's/graduate degree, double major, exchange student, honors, independent study, internships, semester at sea, student-designed major, study abroad, teacher certification program, Washington semester. Williams Mystic Seaport Maritime Studies program, study at Eugene O'Neill National Theater Institute, Twelve College Exchange, University of California-San Diego exchange program, McGill University exchange program, exchange programs with over 50 foreign universities, special academic programs in Washington, DC and Tucson, AZ. **Credit/placement by examination:** AP, CLEP, IB, SAT, ACT, institutional tests. **Support services:** Learning center, study skills assistance, tutoring, writing center.

Majors. Area/ethnic studies: African-American, Asian, Caribbean, Chicano/Hispanic-American/Latino, French, German, Italian, Latin American, Latin American/Caribbean, Native American, Near/Middle Eastern, Russian/Slavic, Spanish/Iberian, women's. **Biology:** General, biochemistry, Biochemistry/molecular biology, cell/histology, genetics, molecular. **Computer sciences:** Computer science. **Conservation:** Environmental studies. **Engineering:** Applied physics, biomedical, engineering science. **English:** English lit. **Foreign languages:** Arabic, Chinese, classics, comparative lit, French, German, Hebrew, Italian, Japanese, linguistics, Russian, South Asian, Spanish. **History:** General. **Math:** General. **Philosophy/religion:** Philosophy, religion. **Physical sciences:** Astronomy, chemistry, geology, physics. **Psychology:** General. **Social sciences:** Anthropology, economics, geography, political science, sociology. **Visual/performing arts:** Art history/conservation, dramatic, film/cinema/video, music, studio arts.

Most popular majors. Biology 12%, engineering/engineering technologies 6%, history 7%, psychology 6%, social sciences 39%.

Technology on campus. PC or laptop required. Dormitories wired for high-speed internet access and linked to campus network. Commuter students can connect to campus network. Online course registration, online library, helpline, repair service, student web hosting, wireless network available.

Student life. Freshman orientation: Mandatory. Preregistration for classes offered. Held week before fall classes begin; freshmen trips led by outing club. **Policies:** Freshmen not permitted cars on campus. **Housing:** Guaranteed on-campus for freshmen. Coed dorms, apartments, cooperative housing, fraternity/sorority housing, gender-neutral housing, themed housing, wellness housing available. Academic affinity housing, faculty-in-residence programs, special interest housing available. **Activities:** Bands, campus ministries, choral groups, dance, drama, film society, international student organizations, literary magazine, music ensembles, Model UN, musical theater, opera, radio station, student government, student newspaper, symphony orchestra, TV station, community and service programs, religious groups, and political and ethnic organizations available.

Athletics. NCAA. **Intercollegiate:** Baseball M, basketball, cross-country, diving, equestrian, field hockey W, football (tackle) M, golf, ice hockey, lacrosse, rowing (crew), sailing, skiing, soccer, softball W, squash, swimming, tennis, track and field, volleyball W. **Intramural:** Baseball M, basketball, bowling, cross-country, football (non-tackle), golf, handball, ice hockey, lacrosse, racquetball, skiing, soccer, softball, squash, swimming, table tennis, tennis, track and field, volleyball, water polo, wrestling M. **Team name:** Big Green.

Student services. Alcohol/substance abuse counseling, chaplain/spiritual director, career counseling, student employment services, financial aid counseling, health services, minority student services, on-campus daycare, personal counseling, placement for graduates, women's services. **Physically disabled:** Services for visually, speech, hearing impaired.

Contact. E-mail: admissions.office@dartmouth.edu
Phone: (603) 646-2875 Fax: (603) 646-1216
Paul Sunde, Intermim Dean of Admissions and Financial Aid, Dartmouth College, 6016 McNutt Hall, Hanover, NH 03755

Franklin Pierce University
Rindge, New Hampshire
www.franklinpierce.edu
CB member
CB code: 3395

- Private 4-year university and liberal arts college
- Residential campus in small town
- 1,657 degree-seeking undergraduates: 12% part-time, 55% women
- 593 degree-seeking graduate students
- 80% of applicants admitted
- Application essay required
- 48% graduate within 6 years

General. Founded in 1962. Regionally accredited. **Degrees:** 286 bachelor's, 7 associate awarded; master's, professional, doctoral offered. **ROTC:** Army, Air Force. **Location:** 20 miles from Keene, 60 miles from Boston. **Calendar:** Semester, limited summer session. **Full-time faculty:** 92 total; 48% women. **Part-time faculty:** 242 total; 53% women. **Special facilities:** Glass blowing studio, ceramic studio, graphic design workshop, costume design, archaeological dig site, television studio, media production studios, wood-pellet heating systems.

Freshman class profile. 3,740 applied, 2,981 admitted, 418 enrolled.

Mid 50% test scores		GPA 2.0-2.99:	57%
SAT critical reading:	420-520	Rank in top quarter:	22%
SAT math:	430-520	Rank in top tenth:	6%
SAT writing:	420-510	Return as sophomores:	67%
GPA 3.75 or higher:	4%	Out-of-state:	85%
GPA 3.50-3.74:	6%	Live on campus:	96%
GPA 3.0-3.49:	25%		

Basis for selection. School achievement record and difficulty of course work important. Community service, leadership and school involvement also primary considerations. Standardized test scores are required only for student-athletes and students applying for the Health Sciences to Doctorate in Physical Therapy Pathway Program. Interview and campus visit recommended for all. **Home schooled:** Letter of recommendation (nonparent) required. **Learning Disabled:** Students with disabilities invited to contact Center for Academic Excellence.

High school preparation. College-preparatory program required. Required units include English 4, mathematics 3, social studies 3 and science 3.

2015-2016 Annual costs. Tuition/fees: $33,320. Room/board: $12,546. Books/supplies: $1,200. Personal expenses: $400.

2015-2016 Financial aid. Need-based: 396 full-time freshmen applied for aid; 361 deemed to have need; 361 received aid. Average need met was 70%. Average scholarship/grant was $20,147; average loan $3,936. 70% of total undergraduate aid awarded as scholarships/grants, 30% as loans/jobs. **Non-need-based:** Awarded to 511 full-time undergraduates, including 171 freshmen. Scholarships awarded for academics, art, athletics, leadership.

Application procedures. Admission: No deadline. $40 fee, may be waived for applicants with need. Admission notification on a rolling basis beginning on or about 10/15. Must reply by May 1 or within 2 week(s) if notified thereafter. **Financial aid:** Priority date 3/1; no closing date. FAFSA required. Applicants notified on a rolling basis starting 3/1.

Academics. Special study options: Accelerated study, combined bachelor's/graduate degree, cross-registration, distance learning, double major, ESL, honors, independent study, internships, liberal arts/career combination, student-designed major, study abroad, teacher certification program, Washington semester. **Credit/placement by examination:** AP, CLEP, IB, institutional tests. 12 credit hours maximum toward associate degree, 30 toward

---

bachelor's. **Support services:** Learning center, reduced course load, remedial instruction, study skills assistance, tutoring, writing center.

Majors. Area/ethnic studies: American. **Biology:** General. **Business:** Accounting/finance, business admin, management information systems, management science, marketing. **Communications:** Media studies. **Computer sciences:** Information technology. **Conservation:** Environmental science. **Education:** General, elementary, secondary. **English:** English lit. **Health services:** Nursing (RN). **History:** General. **Human services:** Social work. **Liberal arts:** Arts/sciences. **Math:** General. **Parks/recreation:** Facilities management. **Protective services:** Criminal justice. **Psychology:** General. **Social sciences:** Anthropology, political science. **Visual/performing arts:** General, commercial/advertising art, dance, dramatic, graphic design, music, studio arts, studio arts management, theater arts management, theater design.

Most popular majors. Biology 7%, business/marketing 20%, health sciences 15%, parks/recreation 7%, psychology 8%, security/protective services 8%.

Technology on campus. 120 workstations in dormitories, library, computer center. Dormitories wired for high-speed internet access and linked to campus network. Commuter students can connect to campus network. Online course registration, online library, helpline, repair service, wireless network available.

Student life. Freshman orientation: Mandatory. Preregistration for classes offered. Held immediately before start of semester and lasts several days into semester. **Housing:** Guaranteed on-campus for all undergraduates. Coed dorms, apartments, wellness housing available. $250 nonrefundable deposit, deadline 7/15. **Activities:** Jazz band, campus ministries, choral groups, dance, drama, film society, international student organizations, literary magazine, music ensembles, radio station, student government, student newspaper, TV station, ALANA, Agape Christian club, black student alliance, College Democrats, College Republicans, gay/straight alliance, Jewish students alliance, Students for a Better Tomorrow, Students for a Sensible Drug Policy.

Athletics. NCAA. **Intercollegiate:** Baseball M, basketball, cross-country, field hockey W, golf M, ice hockey, lacrosse, rowing (crew), soccer, softball W, swimming W, tennis, track and field, volleyball W. **Intramural:** Baseball M, basketball, cross-country, field hockey W, sailing, skiing, soccer, softball, table tennis, tennis, volleyball. **Team name:** Ravens.

Student services. Alcohol/substance abuse counseling, chaplain/spiritual director, career counseling, student employment services, financial aid counseling, health services, minority student services, personal counseling, placement for graduates, women's services.

Contact. E-mail: admissions@franklinpierce.edu
Phone: (603) 899-4050 Toll-free number: (800) 437-0048
Fax: (603) 899-4394
Linda Quimby, Assistant Vice President of Enrollment, Franklin Pierce University, 40 University Drive, Rindge, NH 03461-0060

Granite State College
Concord, New Hampshire
www.granite.edu
CB code: 0458

- Public 4-year liberal arts college
- Commuter campus in large town
- 1,812 degree-seeking undergraduates: 44% part-time, 75% women, 2% African American, 1% Asian American, 3% Hispanic/Latino, 2% Multiracial, non-Hispanic
- 106 degree-seeking graduate students
- 53% graduate within 6 years; 37% enter graduate study

General. Founded in 1972. Regionally accredited. **Degrees:** 369 bachelor's, 145 associate awarded; master's offered. **ROTC:** Army, Air Force. **Calendar:** Trimester, extensive summer session. **Full-time faculty:** 4 total; 75% have terminal degrees, 75% women. **Part-time faculty:** 186 total; 52% have terminal degrees, 67% women. **Class size:** 80% < 20, 20% 20-39.

Freshman class profile. 233 applied, 233 admitted, 80 enrolled.

Return as sophomores:	75%	Out-of-state:	24%

Basis for selection. Open admission, but selective for some programs. Admission into the post-baccalaureate teacher certification program requires a bachelor's degree; candidates who earned their bachelor's with less than a 3.0 GPA will be considered for conditional admission. Accuplacer tests used for placement. **Home schooled:** State high school equivalency certificate required.

2015-2016 Annual costs. Tuition/fees: $8,940; $9,900 out-of-state. Books/supplies: $900. Personal expenses: $1,467.

Financial aid. All financial aid based on need.

Application procedures. Admission: No deadline. , may be waived for applicants with need. No application fee. Application must be submitted online. Admission notification on a rolling basis. **Financial aid:** No deadline. FAFSA, institutional form required. Applicants notified on a rolling basis starting 4/15.

Academics. Special study options: Accelerated study, cooperative education, cross-registration, distance learning, double major, dual enrollment of high school students, independent study, internships, liberal arts/career combination, student-designed major, teacher certification program. **Credit/placement by examination:** AP, CLEP, institutional tests. 30 credit hours maximum toward associate degree, 60 toward bachelor's. Exams must support degree program. **Support services:** Learning center, reduced course load, study skills assistance, tutoring, writing center.

Majors. Business: Accounting/finance, business admin, hospitality admin, human resources, marketing, nonprofit/public, operations. **Communications:** General, digital media. **Computer sciences:** Information technology. **Education:** Early childhood, elementary, English, ESL, mathematics, middle, secondary, social studies. **Health services:** General, health care admin, health information management, nursing (RN). **History:** General. **Liberal arts:** Arts/sciences. **Protective services:** Criminal justice. **Psychology:** General. **Social sciences:** General.

Most popular majors. Business/marketing 24%, education 8%, health sciences 11%, interdisciplinary studies 19%, liberal arts 6%, psychology 21%, security/protective services 6%.

Technology on campus. 150 workstations in computer center, student center. Commuter students can connect to campus network. Online course registration, online library, helpline, wireless network available.

Student life. Freshman orientation: Available. Preregistration for classes offered. **Activities:** Alumni Learner Association.

Student services. Adult student services, career counseling, financial aid counseling, placement for graduates, veterans' counselor. **Physically disabled:** Services for visually, speech, hearing impaired.

Contact. E-mail: gsc.admissions@granite.edu
Phone: (603) 228-3000 ext. 339
Toll-free number: (888) 228-3000 ext. 339 Fax: (603) 513-1386
Cortney Vachon, Associate Registrar, Granite State College, 25 Hall Street, Concord, NH 03301-7317

Keene State College
Keene, New Hampshire
www.keene.edu

CB member
CB code: 3472

- Public 4-year liberal arts college
- Residential campus in small city
- 4,186 degree-seeking undergraduates: 2% part-time, 56% women, 1% African American, 1% Asian American, 4% Hispanic/Latino, 2% Multiracial, non-Hispanic
- 91 degree-seeking graduate students
- 79% of applicants admitted
- SAT or ACT (ACT writing optional), application essay required
- 62% graduate within 6 years

General. Founded in 1909. Regionally accredited. **Degrees:** 1,073 bachelor's awarded; master's offered. **ROTC:** Army, Air Force. **Location:** 52 miles from Concord, 85 miles from Boston. **Calendar:** Semester, extensive summer session. **Class size:** 53% < 20, 43% 20-39, 3% 40-49, 1% 50-99. **Special facilities:** Arboretum and gardens, center for Holocaust studies, child development center, community research center, curriculum materials library, small business institute, college-owned camp, 400-acre preserve, theater complex, media arts center.

Freshman class profile. 5,674 applied, 4,464 admitted, 920 enrolled.

Mid 50% test scores			
SAT critical reading:	440-550	**GPA 2.0-2.99:**	46%
SAT math:	440-550	**Rank in top quarter:**	23%
SAT writing:	440-540	**Rank in top tenth:**	7%
GPA 3.75 or higher:	8%	**End year in good standing:**	93%
GPA 3.50-3.74:	11%	**Return as sophomores:**	73%
GPA 3.0-3.49:	35%	**Out-of-state:**	62%
		Live on campus:	94%

Basis for selection. High school record, including challenging courses, most important. SAT/ACT scores do not hold nearly as much weight as high school performance. Audition required for music education and music performance programs; portfolio required for art program. **Home schooled:** Transcript of courses and grades, letter of recommendation (nonparent) required. **Learning Disabled:** Documented proof of disability required for some services.

High school preparation. College-preparatory program recommended. 14 units required. Required units include English 4, mathematics 3, social studies 2, science 3 and academic electives 2.

2015-2016 Annual costs. Tuition/fees: $13,228; $21,408 out-of-state. Room/board: $9,712. Books/supplies: $900. Personal expenses: $750.

2014-2015 Financial aid. Need-based: 1,150 full-time freshmen applied for aid; 883 deemed to have need; 868 received aid. Average need met was 62%. Average scholarship/grant was $7,480; average loan $3,567. 32% of total undergraduate aid awarded as scholarships/grants, 68% as loans/jobs. **Non-need-based:** Awarded to 1,870 full-time undergraduates, including 684 freshmen. Scholarships awarded for academics, alumni affiliation, art, music/drama.

Application procedures. Admission: Closing date 4/1 (receipt date). $50 fee, may be waived for applicants with need. Admission notification on a rolling basis. Must reply by 5/1. **Financial aid:** Closing date 3/1. FAFSA required. Applicants notified on a rolling basis; must reply within 4 week(s) of notification.

Academics. Students majoring in the school of Arts and Humanities must complete a foreign language requirement. **Special study options:** Combined bachelor's/graduate degree, cooperative education, distance learning, double major, exchange student, honors, independent study, internships, liberal arts/career combination, semester at sea, student-designed major, study abroad, teacher certification program. **Credit/placement by examination:** AP, CLEP, IB. 60 credit hours maximum toward bachelor's degree. **Support services:** Learning center, pre-admission summer program, reduced course load, study skills assistance, tutoring, writing center.

Majors. Architecture: Architecture. **Area/ethnic studies:** American, women's. **Biology:** General. **Business:** Business admin. **Communications:** Communications/speech/rhetoric, digital media, journalism, public relations. **Computer sciences:** General. **Conservation:** Environmental studies. **Education:** Biology, chemistry, drama/dance, early childhood, elementary, English, French, history, mathematics, music, physical, science, secondary, social studies, Spanish. **English:** English lit. **Foreign languages:** French, Spanish. **Health services:** General, athletic training, dietetics, nursing (RN), substance abuse counseling. **History:** General, American, European. **Math:** General. **Parks/recreation:** Health/fitness. **Physical sciences:** Chemistry, geology. **Psychology:** General. **Social sciences:** Economics, geography, political science, sociology, sociology/anthropology. **Visual/performing arts:** Acting, cinematography, commercial/advertising art, dance, directing/producing, film/cinema/video, music, music performance, music technology, music theory/composition, studio arts, theater design.

Most popular majors. Business/marketing 6%, communications/journalism 7%, education 17%, engineering/engineering technologies 9%, health sciences 11%, psychology 10%, social sciences 9%, visual/performing arts 8%.

Technology on campus. 600 workstations in library, computer center, student center. Dormitories wired for high-speed internet access and linked to campus network. Commuter students can connect to campus network. Online course registration, online library, helpline, repair service, student web hosting, wireless network available.

Student life. Freshman orientation: Mandatory. Preregistration for classes offered. Orientation starts with Move-In Day, a students-only gathering where upperclassmen share their best advice and wisdom. **Policies:** Freshmen not permitted cars on campus. **Housing:** Guaranteed on-campus for freshmen. Coed dorms, single-sex dorms, apartments, fraternity/sorority housing, themed housing, wellness housing available. $300 nonrefundable deposit, deadline 5/1. Learning communities: Equity & Social Justice, Mind, Body & Character, Citizens & Service, Excellence in Teaching, Learning & Scholarship, Building Excellence in Science and Technology. **Activities:** Bands, campus ministries, choral groups, dance, drama, film society, international student organizations, literary magazine, music ensembles, musical theater, radio station, student government, student newspaper, TV station, Big Brothers/Big Sisters, campus ecology, Christian Impact, Circle K, feminist collective, Habitat for Humanity, Interfaith Voices, pride club, Republican club, Newman student organization.

Athletics. NCAA. **Intercollegiate:** Baseball M, basketball, cheerleading, cross-country, diving, field hockey W, lacrosse, soccer, softball W, swimming, track and field, volleyball W. **Intramural:** Badminton, basketball, bowling, football (non-tackle), racquetball, soccer, softball, table tennis, tennis, volleyball. **Team name:** Owls.

Student services. Adult student services, alcohol/substance abuse counseling, chaplain/spiritual director, career counseling, student employment services, financial aid counseling, health services, minority student services, on-campus daycare, personal counseling, placement for graduates, veterans' counselor, women's services. **Physically disabled:** Services for visually, speech, hearing impaired.

Contact. E-mail: kscadmissions@keene.edu
Phone: (603) 358-2276 Toll-free number: (800) 572-1909
Fax: (603) 358-2767
Margaret Richmond, Director of Admissions, Keene State College, 229 Main Street, Keene, NH 03435-2604

Mount Washington College
Manchester, New Hampshire
www.mountwashington.edu   CB code: 3452

- For-profit 4-year business and junior college
- Residential campus in small city
- 1,511 undergraduates
- Application essay, interview required

General. Founded in 1900. Regionally accredited. Courses also available at centers in Nashua, Salem, Portsmouth, and Concord. **Degrees:** 175 bachelor's, 225 associate awarded. **Location:** 50 miles from Boston. **Calendar:** Semester, limited summer session. **Full-time faculty:** 21 total. **Part-time faculty:** 219 total. **Class size:** 68% < 20, 32% 20-39.

Freshman class profile.

Out-of-state:	25%	Live on campus:	18%

Basis for selection. Open admission, but selective for some programs. Selective requirements for physical therapist and graphic design programs. Portfolio recommended for fashion design, interior design and graphic design programs. **Learning Disabled:** Must meet with director of center for teaching, learning and assessment.

2015-2016 Annual costs. Books/supplies: $1,200. Personal expenses: $450. **Additional information:** Degree program tuition: 8-week term tuition (per 3-credit course) $1,125; 8-week term tuition per credit $375. 20-week non-term tuition (textbooks included): full-time enrollment status (12-15 credit hours per payment period) $2,200.00, book fee $200; per 3 credit course (over 15 credit hours per payment period) $250, book fee $50. Enrollment fee: $10. Additional fees may apply.

Financial aid. All financial aid based on need. **Additional information:** Two private loans available to assist students in paying their balance; Tree Loan, SLM Loan.

Application procedures. Admission: No deadline. $10 fee, may be waived for applicants with need. Admission notification on a rolling basis. **Financial aid:** Priority date 5/1; no closing date. FAFSA, institutional form required. Applicants notified on a rolling basis starting 3/1; must reply within 3 week(s) of notification.

Academics. Special study options: Accelerated study, independent study, internships. **Credit/placement by examination:** AP, CLEP, IB, institutional tests. Max of 50% of total program credits awarded via CLEP, DSST, and AP exams. Max of 25% of total program credits awarded via institutional exams. **Support services:** Learning center, reduced course load, remedial instruction, tutoring, writing center.

Majors. Business: Accounting, business admin. **Protective services:** Law enforcement admin.

Technology on campus. 20 workstations in library, computer center. Dormitories wired for high-speed internet access. Helpline, repair service available.

Student life. Freshman orientation: Mandatory. Preregistration for classes offered. **Housing:** Guaranteed on-campus for freshmen. Single-sex dorms, wellness housing available. $125 deposit. **Activities:** Choral groups, radio station, student government, TV station, special interest organizations relating to accounting, business, travel, and retailing, community service club.

Athletics. NJCAA. **Intercollegiate:** Baseball M, basketball, soccer, softball W, volleyball. **Intramural:** Basketball, cheerleading W, football (non-tackle), soccer, volleyball. **Team name:** Blue Devils.

Student services. Alcohol/substance abuse counseling, career counseling, student employment services, financial aid counseling, health services, personal counseling, placement for graduates, veterans' counselor.

Contact. E-mail: admissions@hesser.edu
Phone: (603) 668-6660 ext. 2110 Toll-free number: (888) 971-2190
Fax: (603) 666-4722
Keith Scheib, Assistant Director of Admissions, Mount Washington College, 3 Sundial Avenue, Manchester, NH 03103

New England College
Henniker, New Hampshire
www.nec.edu   CB code: 3657

- Private 4-year liberal arts and teachers college
- Residential campus in small town
- 1,805 degree-seeking undergraduates: 2% part-time, 59% women, 24% African American, 1% Asian American, 7% Hispanic/Latino, 1% Native American, 1% Multi-racial, non-Hispanic, 3% international
- 588 degree-seeking graduate students
- 98% of applicants admitted
- Application essay required
- 31% graduate within 6 years; 20% enter graduate study

General. Founded in 1946. Regionally accredited. Environmental and Civic Environment is integrated throughout the curriculum. Experiential and problem based learning are the central focus of our pedagogy. **Degrees:** 207 bachelor's, 13 associate awarded; master's, professional offered. **ROTC:** Army, Air Force. **Location:** 18 miles from Concord. **Calendar:** Continuous, limited summer session. **Full-time faculty:** 44 total; 68% have terminal degrees, 4% minority, 50% women. **Part-time faculty:** 193 total; 44% have terminal degrees, 2% minority, 53% women. **Class size:** 80% < 20, 20% 20-39, less than 1% 40-49. **Special facilities:** Center for educational innovation.

Freshman class profile. 4,987 applied, 4,875 admitted, 430 enrolled.

Mid 50% test scores		Rank in top quarter:	16%
SAT critical reading:	390-520	Rank in top tenth:	4%
SAT math:	400-500	End year in good standing:	69%
SAT writing:	380-490	Return as sophomores:	59%
ACT composite:	18-24	Out-of-state:	83%
GPA 3.75 or higher:	3%	Live on campus:	74%
GPA 3.50-3.74:	4%	International:	3%
GPA 3.0-3.49:	22%	Fraternities:	3%
GPA 2.0-2.99:	58%	Sororities:	3%

Basis for selection. School achievement record most important, followed by recommendations, essay or personal statement, evidence of leadership and extracurricular activities. Interview recommended for all; portfolio recommended for art program. **Home schooled:** Transcript of courses and grades, state high school equivalency certificate, letter of recommendation (nonparent) required.

High school preparation. College-preparatory program recommended. 12 units required; 13 recommended. Required and recommended units include English 4, mathematics 2-3, social studies 2-3, science 2-3 (laboratory 1-2) and foreign language 2.

2016-2017 Annual costs. Tuition/fees (projected): $34,800. Room/board: $13,500. Books/supplies: $1,000. Personal expenses: $1,000.

2015-2016 Financial aid. Need-based: 340 full-time freshmen applied for aid; 321 deemed to have need; 320 received aid. Average need met was 79%. Average scholarship/grant was $19,440; average loan $13,151. 58% of total undergraduate aid awarded as scholarships/grants, 42% as loans/jobs. **Non-need-based:** Awarded to 1,458 full-time undergraduates, including 350 freshmen. Scholarships awarded for academics, alumni affiliation, art, job skills, leadership, music/drama, state residency. **Additional information:** Significant scholarship programs for veterans including non-Post 911 eligible veterans.

Application procedures. Admission: Priority date 5/1; no deadline. $35 fee, may be waived for applicants with need, free for online applicants. Admission notification on a rolling basis beginning on or about 11/1. **Financial aid:** Closing date 9/1. FAFSA, institutional form required. Applicants notified on a rolling basis starting 1/12; must reply within 4 week(s) of notification.

Academics. Special study options: Accelerated study, combined bachelor's/graduate degree, cross-registration, distance learning, double major, dual enrollment of high school students, ESL, exchange student, external degree, honors, independent study, internships, liberal arts/career combination, semester at sea, student-designed major, study abroad, teacher certification program, Washington semester. Exchange programs with Regent's College, London; American University of Paris; 18 colleges in Quebec, Canada; University of the Sunshine Coast, Australia. Students keep all financial aid when abroad. **Credit/placement by examination:** AP, CLEP, IB, institutional tests. 21 credit hours maximum toward associate degree, 21 toward bachelor's. **Support services:** Learning center, pre-admission summer program, reduced course load, remedial instruction, study skills assistance, tutoring, writing center.

Majors. Biology: General. **Business:** Accounting, business admin, entrepreneurial studies, finance, human resources, management information systems, marketing. **Communications:** Advertising, public relations. **Computer sciences:** General. **Conservation:** General, environmental science. **Education:** Biology, elementary, English, learning disabled, physical, science, secondary, social science, social studies, special ed. **English:** Creative writing. **Health services:** Health care admin, premedicine. **History:** General. **Liberal arts:** Arts/sciences. **Parks/recreation:** General, exercise sciences, facilities management, sports admin. **Philosophy/religion:** Philosophy. **Protective services:** Criminal justice. **Psychology:** General, clinical, developmental. **Social sciences:** Political science, sociology. **Visual/performing arts:** Art, dramatic, photography.

Most popular majors. Business/marketing 25%, communications/journalism 6%, education 9%, parks/recreation 11%, psychology 9%, security/protective services 11%.

Technology on campus. 250 workstations in library, computer center, student center. Dormitories wired for high-speed internet access and linked to campus network. Commuter students can connect to campus network. Online course registration, online library, helpline, wireless network available.

Student life. Freshman orientation: Available. Preregistration for classes offered. Held 3 days prior to first day of classes and 2 mid-summer options. **Housing:** Guaranteed on-campus for all undergraduates. Coed dorms, apartments, fraternity/sorority housing, themed housing, wellness housing available. $100 nonrefundable deposit, deadline 9/12. Quiet study options, special interest housing available. **Activities:** Dance, drama, international student organizations, literary magazine, radio station, student government, student newspaper, Hillel, Servcorps, environmental action committee, Women's Network, international diplomacy council, Adventure Bound, TEACH.

Athletics. NCAA. **Intercollegiate:** Baseball M, basketball, cross-country, field hockey W, ice hockey, lacrosse, soccer, softball W. **Intramural:** Baseball M, basketball, ice hockey, soccer, softball, table tennis, tennis, volleyball. **Team name:** Pilgrims.

Student services. Adult student services, alcohol/substance abuse counseling, career counseling, student employment services, financial aid counseling, health services, minority student services, personal counseling, placement for graduates, veterans' counselor.

Contact. E-mail: admission@nec.edu
Phone: (603) 428-2223 Toll-free number: (800) 521-7642
Fax: (603) 428-3155
Brad Posnanski, Director of Admissions, New England College, 15 Main Street, Henniker, NH 03242

New Hampshire Institute of Art
Manchester, New Hampshire
www.nhia.edu

CB member
CB code: 3868

- Private 4-year visual arts college
- Residential campus in small city
- 383 degree-seeking undergraduates: 8% part-time, 68% women
- 77 degree-seeking graduate students
- 52% of applicants admitted
- Application essay, interview required
- 52% graduate within 6 years

General. Regionally accredited. **Degrees:** 93 bachelor's awarded; master's offered. **Location:** 50 miles from Boston. **Calendar:** Semester, limited summer session. **Full-time faculty:** 14 total; 21% have terminal degrees, 7% minority, 43% women. **Part-time faculty:** 63 total; 8% have terminal degrees, 49% women. **Class size:** 96% < 20, 3% 20-39, less than 1% >100.

Freshman class profile. 573 applied, 298 admitted, 103 enrolled.

GPA 3.75 or higher:	9%	Return as sophomores:	85%
GPA 3.50-3.74:	9%	Out-of-state:	57%
GPA 3.0-3.49:	28%	Live on campus:	76%
GPA 2.0-2.99:	49%		

Basis for selection. A completed application includes: application, portfolio review, essay and high school transcripts. Letters of recommendation and SAT scores are optional. A completed application is reviewed and a student is accepted or denied based on the strength of application. SAT or ACT

---

recommended. Portfolio Review. **Home schooled:** Transcript of courses and grades required.

High school preparation. College-preparatory program recommended. Required and recommended units include English 4, mathematics 3, social studies 2, science 2 and visual/performing arts 3.

2016-2017 Annual costs. Tuition/fees (projected): $25,790. Room/board: $10,990. Books/supplies: $3,000. Personal expenses: $1,000.

2015-2016 Financial aid. Need-based: 58% of total undergraduate aid awarded as scholarships/grants, 42% as loans/jobs. **Non-need-based:** Scholarships awarded for academics, art.

Application procedures. Admission: Priority date 12/7; no deadline. $25 fee, may be waived for applicants with need, free for online applicants. Admission notification by 12/24. Admission notification on a rolling basis beginning on or about 12/15. Must reply by May 1 or within 4 week(s) if notified thereafter. **Financial aid:** Priority date 3/1; no closing date. FAFSA required. Applicants notified on a rolling basis starting 3/15; must reply within 2 week(s) of notification.

Academics. Special study options: Combined bachelor's/graduate degree, independent study, internships, New York semester, study abroad, teacher certification program. **Credit/placement by examination:** AP, IB. **Support services:** Learning center, reduced course load, study skills assistance, tutoring.

Majors. English: Creative writing. **Visual/performing arts:** Ceramics, design, illustration, photography, studio arts.

Most popular majors. Education 7%, visual/performing arts 93%.

Technology on campus. 100 workstations in library, computer center, student center. Dormitories wired for high-speed internet access. Online course registration, online library, helpline, wireless network available.

Student life. Freshman orientation: Mandatory. Preregistration for classes offered. **Policies:** The use of illegal drugs and the abuse of alcohol on the campus or in facilities are prohibited by college regulations and are incompatible with the goal of providing a healthy educational environment for students, faculty, staff, and guests. **Housing:** Guaranteed on-campus for freshmen. Coed dorms available. $200 fully refundable deposit, deadline 5/1. **Activities:** Literary magazine, student government.

Student services. Career counseling, financial aid counseling, health services, personal counseling.

Contact. E-mail: admissions@nhia.edu
Phone: (603) 836-2589 Toll-free number: (866) 241-4918 ext. 589
Bob Gielow, Vice President of Enrollment Services, New Hampshire Institute of Art, 148 Concord Street, Manchester, NH 03104

Northeast Catholic College
Warner, New Hampshire
www.northeastcatholic.edu

CB code: 3562

- Private 4-year liberal arts college affiliated with the Roman Catholic Church
- Residential campus in small town
- 89 degree-seeking undergraduates: 1% part-time, 55% women
- 30% of applicants admitted
- Application essay required

General. Regionally accredited. **Degrees:** 9 bachelor's, 4 associate awarded. **Location:** 15 miles from Concord. **Calendar:** Semester. **Full-time faculty:** 5 total; 100% have terminal degrees, 20% women. **Part-time faculty:** 11 total; 54% women. **Special facilities:** Observatory.

Freshman class profile. 204 applied, 61 admitted, 40 enrolled.

End year in good standing:	100%	Out-of-state:	93%
Return as sophomores:	100%	Live on campus:	100%

Basis for selection. Academic GPA, high school record very important. College prep courses recommended. SAT or ACT recommended. **Home schooled:** Transcript of courses and grades, letter of recommendation (nonparent) required.

High school preparation. College-preparatory program recommended. 24 units recommended. Recommended units include English 4, mathematics 4, social studies 3, history 2, science 3, foreign language 2 and academic electives 6.

2015-2016 Annual costs. Tuition/fees: $21,200. Room/board: $8,000. Books/supplies: $600. Personal expenses: $400.

Financial aid. All financial aid based on need.

Application procedures. Admission: Priority date 2/15; no deadline. No application fee. Rolling notification. **Financial aid:** Priority date 3/15; no closing date. Institutional form required. Applicants notified on a rolling basis starting 3/15.

Academics. Special study options: Honors, internships, study abroad. **Credit/placement by examination:** AP, CLEP. **Support services:** Study skills assistance, tutoring.

Majors. Liberal arts: Arts/sciences. **Philosophy/religion:** General, philosophy. **Theology:** Theology.

Technology on campus. Commuter students can connect to campus network. Online library, wireless network available.

Student life. Freshman orientation: Mandatory. Preregistration for classes offered. Two-day program in early September just prior to beginning of fall semester. **Policies:** Professional dress code for class. Curfews in dormitories. **Housing:** Guaranteed on-campus for all undergraduates. Single-sex dorms, wellness housing available. $500 nonrefundable deposit. Pets allowed in dorm rooms. **Activities:** Campus ministries, choral groups, drama, literary magazine, music ensembles, musical theater, student government, student newspaper, campus service organization, college choir, French club, pro-life club, polyphony choir.

Athletics. Intramural: Badminton, basketball, cross-country, equestrian, fencing, football (non-tackle), skiing, soccer, softball, table tennis, tennis, ultimate frisbee, volleyball. **Team name:** Norsemen.

Student services. Chaplain/spiritual director, career counseling, services for economically disadvantaged, student employment services, financial aid counseling. **Physically disabled:** Services for speech impaired.

Contact. E-mail: admissions@northeastcatholic.edu
Phone: (603) 456-2656 ext. 114 Toll-free number: (877) 498-1723
Fax: (603) 456-2660
Katie Moffett, Director of Admissions, Northeast Catholic College, 511 Kearsarge Mountain Road, Warner, NH 03278

Plymouth State University

Plymouth, New Hampshire **CB member**
www.plymouth.edu **CB code: 3690**

- Public 4-year university and teachers college
- Residential campus in small town
- 4,042 degree-seeking undergraduates: 5% part-time, 49% women, 2% African American, 2% Asian American, 2% Hispanic/Latino, 2% Multiracial, non-Hispanic, 2% international
- 851 degree-seeking graduate students
- 74% of applicants admitted
- SAT or ACT with writing, application essay required
- 58% graduate within 6 years

General. Founded in 1871. Regionally accredited. **Degrees:** 820 bachelor's awarded; master's, doctoral offered. **ROTC:** Army, Air Force. **Location:** 60 miles from Manchester, 110 miles from Boston. **Calendar:** Semester, limited summer session. **Full-time faculty:** 193 total; 84% have terminal degrees, 8% minority, 49% women. **Part-time faculty:** 297 total; 13% have terminal degrees, 1% minority, 62% women. **Class size:** 49% < 20, 48% 20-39, 1% 40-49, 1% 50-99. **Special facilities:** Planetarium, cultural arts center, child development and family center, geographic information systems lab, meteorology institute, center for the environment, ropes course, ice arena, museum of the white mountains, outdoor center.

Freshman class profile. 6,626 applied, 4,875 admitted, 1,349 enrolled.

Mid 50% test scores			
SAT critical reading:	440-530	Rank in top quarter:	21%
SAT math:	440-550	Rank in top tenth:	5%
SAT writing:	430-520	End year in good standing:	88%
ACT composite:	19-24	Return as sophomores:	77%
GPA 3.75 or higher:	6%	Out-of-state:	50%
GPA 3.50-3.74:	9%	Live on campus:	93%
GPA 3.0-3.49:	30%	International:	2%
GPA 2.0-2.99:	55%	Sororities:	1%

Basis for selection. Primary focus is on school performance (grades, course rigor, grade trends, etc.) while extracurricular involvement, the application essay, and recommendations are also taken into account. Standardized test scores for admission. When submitted, test scores are not considered to be an academic credential. Audition required for music, theater, and dance programs. Portfolio required for art program. **Home schooled:** Transcript of any work attempted in secondary school, GED or homeschool diploma, outline of homeschool curriculum required.

High school preparation. College-preparatory program required. 14 units required; 18 recommended. Required and recommended units include English 4, mathematics 3, social studies 3, science 3 (laboratory 1) and foreign language 2.

2015-2016 Annual costs. Tuition/fees: $13,128; $21,208 out-of-state. Room/board: $10,868. Books/supplies: $1,302.

2014-2015 Financial aid. Need-based: 697 full-time freshmen applied for aid; 539 deemed to have need; 538 received aid. Average need met was 56%. Average scholarship/grant was $4,581; average loan $3,429. 36% of total undergraduate aid awarded as scholarships/grants, 64% as loans/jobs. **Non-need-based:** Awarded to 1,586 full-time undergraduates, including 544 freshmen. Scholarships awarded for academics, art, leadership, music/drama.

Application procedures. Admission: Priority date 4/1; no deadline. $50 fee, may be waived for applicants with need. Application must be submitted online. Admission notification on a rolling basis beginning on or about 11/15. Must reply by May 1 or within 2 week(s) if notified thereafter. **Financial aid:** Priority date 3/1; no closing date. FAFSA required. Applicants notified on a rolling basis starting 3/1; must reply by 5/1.

Academics. Special study options: Combined bachelor's/graduate degree, cross-registration, distance learning, double major, exchange student, honors, independent study, internships, student-designed major, study abroad, teacher certification program. **Credit/placement by examination:** AP, CLEP, IB, institutional tests. 30 credit hours maximum toward bachelor's degree. **Support services:** Study skills assistance, tutoring, writing center.

Majors. Architecture: Urban/community planning. **Biology:** General, biotechnology, environmental. **Business:** General, accounting, business admin, finance, marketing, tourism/travel. **Communications:** Communications/speech/rhetoric. **Computer sciences:** Computer science, information technology. **Conservation:** Environmental studies. **Education:** Art, early childhood, elementary, English, health, mathematics, music, science, social studies. **English:** English lit. **Foreign languages:** General, French, Spanish. **Health services:** Athletic training, nursing (RN), public health ed. **History:** General. **Human services:** General, social work. **Math:** General. **Parks/recreation:** Exercise sciences, health/fitness, sports admin. **Philosophy/religion:** Philosophy. **Physical sciences:** Atmospheric science, chemistry. **Protective services:** Criminal justice. **Psychology:** General. **Social sciences:** General, anthropology, geography, political science, sociology. **Visual/performing arts:** Art, art history/conservation, dramatic, graphic design, music, studio arts.

Most popular majors. Business/marketing 24%, communications/journalism 7%, education 12%, health sciences 6%, parks/recreation 8%, security/protective services 7%.

Technology on campus. 500 workstations in dormitories, library, computer center, student center. Dormitories wired for high-speed internet access and linked to campus network. Commuter students can connect to campus network. Online course registration, online library, helpline, repair service, student web hosting, wireless network available.

Student life. Freshman orientation: Mandatory. Preregistration for classes offered. Held for five overnight sessions in June, one in September. **Housing:** Guaranteed on-campus for all undergraduates. Coed dorms, special housing for disabled, apartments, cooperative housing, themed housing available. $90 nonrefundable deposit, deadline 5/1. Music/theater/dance housing, honors housing, special interest housing, community service, non-traditional, and quiet study/academic housing available. **Activities:** Bands, campus ministries, choral groups, dance, drama, film society, international student organizations, literary magazine, music ensembles, Model UN, musical theater, radio station, student government, student newspaper, Chi Alpha Christian Fellowship, Nicaragua club, social work club, health and wellness club, Alternative Spring Break, PSU Democrats, PSU Republicans, Student Support Foundation, world language society, black student union.

Athletics. NCAA. Intercollegiate: Baseball M, basketball, cross-country, diving W, field hockey W, football (tackle) M, ice hockey, lacrosse, skiing, soccer, softball W, swimming W, tennis W, track and field, volleyball W, wrestling M. **Intramural:** Basketball, football (non-tackle), golf, soccer, softball, table tennis, volleyball, weight lifting. **Team name:** Panthers.

Student services. Adult student services, alcohol/substance abuse counseling, chaplain/spiritual director, career counseling, student employment services, financial aid counseling, health services, on-campus daycare, personal counseling, veterans' counselor, women's services. **Physically disabled:** Services for visually, hearing impaired.

Contact. E-mail: plymouthadmit@plymouth.edu
Phone: (603) 535-2237 Toll-free number: (800) 842-6900
Fax: (603) 535-2714
Tony Trodella, Director of Undergraduate Recruitment, Plymouth State University, 17 High Street MSC 52, Plymouth, NH 03264-1595

Rivier University
Nashua, New Hampshire
CB member
www.rivier.edu
CB code: 3728

- Private 4-year university and nursing college affiliated with the Roman Catholic Church
- Commuter campus in small city
- 1,344 degree-seeking undergraduates: 42% part-time, 81% women, 3% African American, 3% Asian American, 4% Hispanic/Latino, 3% Multiracial, non-Hispanic
- 1,072 degree-seeking graduate students
- 58% of applicants admitted
- Application essay required
- 58% graduate within 6 years

General. Founded in 1933. Regionally accredited. Founded by the Sisters of the Presentation of Mary Convent. **Degrees:** 351 bachelor's, 90 associate awarded; master's, professional, doctoral offered. **ROTC:** Army, Naval, Air Force. **Location:** 19 miles from Manchester, 45 miles from Boston. **Calendar:** Semester, limited summer session. **Full-time faculty:** 65 total; 68% have terminal degrees, 65% women. **Part-time faculty:** 144 total; 32% have terminal degrees, 65% women. **Special facilities:** Early childhood center/laboratory school, biology research lab, art gallery.

Freshman class profile. 1,725 applied, 992 admitted, 182 enrolled.

Mid 50% test scores			
		GPA 3.50-3.74:	11%
SAT critical reading:	450-530	GPA 3.0-3.49:	37%
SAT math:	440-550	GPA 2.0-2.99:	35%
SAT writing:	430-520	Return as sophomores:	77%
ACT composite:	17-27	Out-of-state:	48%
GPA 3.75 or higher:	16%	Live on campus:	55%

Basis for selection. High school academic record (course selection, course level, grades), test scores, extracurricular activities, application essay, and letters of recommendation considered. Interview recommended for all; portfolio required for art programs. **Home schooled:** Transcript of courses and grades, interview required. Portfolio required.

High school preparation. College-preparatory program recommended. 16 units recommended. Recommended units include English 4, mathematics 3, social studies 2, history 1, science 1 (laboratory 1), foreign language 2 and academic electives 3. Nursing program applicants must have completed chemistry, biology or anatomy and physiology as well as algebra in addition to a second higher math (geometry, precalc, calculus, algebra II).

2015-2016 Annual costs. Tuition/fees: $29,400. Room/board: $11,310. Books/supplies: $1,200. Personal expenses: $2,242.

Financial aid. **Non-need-based:** Scholarships awarded for academics, alumni affiliation.

Application procedures. **Admission:** Priority date 3/1; no deadline. $25 fee, may be waived for applicants with need, free for online applicants. Admission notification on a rolling basis beginning on or about 11/1. **Financial aid:** Priority date 3/1; no closing date. FAFSA required. Applicants notified on a rolling basis starting 3/1; must reply by 5/1 or within 2 week(s) of notification.

Academics. **Special study options:** Cross-registration, distance learning, double major, dual enrollment of high school students, honors, independent study, internships, liberal arts/career combination, student-designed major, study abroad, teacher certification program. **Credit/placement by examination:** AP, CLEP, IB, institutional tests. 12 credit hours maximum toward associate degree, 12 toward bachelor's. **Support services:** Learning center, reduced course load, study skills assistance, tutoring, writing center.

Majors. **Biology:** General. **Business:** Business admin, finance, management information systems, marketing. **Education:** General, biology, early childhood, elementary, English, foreign languages, history, mathematics, science, secondary, social science, social studies, Spanish. **English:** English lit. **Foreign languages:** Spanish. **Health services:** Nursing (RN), predental,

premedicine, preop/surgical nursing, preveterinary. **History:** General. **Liberal arts:** Arts/sciences. **Math:** General. **Psychology:** General. **Social sciences:** General, political science, sociology.

Most popular majors. Business/marketing 8%, education 10%, health sciences 56%, psychology 8%, social sciences 7%.

Technology on campus. 150 workstations in dormitories, library, computer center, student center. Dormitories linked to campus network. Commuter students can connect to campus network. Online course registration, online library, helpline, repair service, wireless network available.

Student life. **Freshman orientation:** Mandatory, $250 fee. Preregistration for classes offered. Two-day on-campus program in June; parallel program for parents. **Housing:** Guaranteed on-campus for all undergraduates. Coed dorms, special housing for disabled, wellness housing available. $400 partly refundable deposit, deadline 5/1. **Activities:** Campus ministries, choral groups, dance, drama, international student organizations, literary magazine, Model UN, musical theater, student government, environmental activists, Amnesty International, Chinese student association, America Reads, Americorps, Habitat for Humanity.

Athletics. NCAA. **Intercollegiate:** Baseball M, basketball, cross-country, field hockey W, lacrosse, soccer, softball W, volleyball. **Intramural:** Basketball, football (non-tackle), softball, volleyball. **Team name:** Raiders.

Student services. Adult student services, alcohol/substance abuse counseling, chaplain/spiritual director, career counseling, student employment services, financial aid counseling, health services, minority student services, on-campus daycare, personal counseling, placement for graduates, veterans' counselor.

Contact. E-mail: rivadmit@rivier.edu
Phone: (603) 897-8507 Toll-free number: (800) 447-4843
Fax: (603) 891-1799
Valerie Leclair, Director of Undergradaute Admissions, Rivier University, 420 South Main Street, Nashua, NH 03060-5086

Saint Anselm College
Manchester, New Hampshire
CB member
www.anselm.edu
CB code: 3748

- Private 4-year nursing and liberal arts college affiliated with the Roman Catholic Church
- Residential campus in small city
- 1,908 degree-seeking undergraduates: 2% part-time, 61% women, 2% African American, 1% Asian American, 3% Hispanic/Latino, 2% Multiracial, non-Hispanic, 1% international
- 73% of applicants admitted
- Application essay required
- 73% graduate within 6 years

General. Founded in 1889. Regionally accredited. Founded by Order of St. Benedict. **Degrees:** 476 bachelor's awarded. **ROTC:** Army. **Location:** 50 miles from Boston. **Calendar:** Semester, limited summer session. **Full-time faculty:** 147 total; 90% have terminal degrees, 10% minority, 54% women. **Part-time faculty:** 68 total; 31% have terminal degrees, 4% minority, 72% women. **Class size:** 68% < 20, 29% 20-39, less than 1% 40-49, 2% 50-99, less than 1% >100. **Special facilities:** Observatory, New Hampshire institute of politics and political library, art center, ice arena, center for the humanities and performing arts center, Abbey Church.

Freshman class profile. 3,955 applied, 2,883 admitted, 528 enrolled.

Mid 50% test scores			
		GPA 2.0-2.99:	24%
SAT critical reading:	530-620	Rank in top quarter:	62%
SAT math:	540-630	Rank in top tenth:	31%
SAT writing:	530-640	Return as sophomores:	90%
ACT composite:	24-28	Out-of-state:	80%
GPA 3.75 or higher:	14%	Live on campus:	93%
GPA 3.50-3.74:	19%	International:	1%
GPA 3.0-3.49:	43%		

Basis for selection. Strength of curriculum and performance, test scores (if submitted for non nursing applicants), involvement, leadership qualities, school counselor and teacher recommendations, and essay considered. SAT/ACT required for applicants to nursing; optional for all others. Interview recommended. **Home schooled:** Statement describing home school structure and mission, transcript of courses and grades, interview, letter of recommendation (nonparent) required.

High school preparation. College-preparatory program required. 16 units required; 22 recommended. Required and recommended units include English

4, mathematics 3-4, social studies 2-4, science 3-4 (laboratory 2) and foreign language 2-4.

2015-2016 Annual costs. Tuition/fees: $37,694. Room/board: $13,334. Books/supplies: $1,000. Personal expenses: $1,000.

2015-2016 Financial aid. Need-based: 483 full-time freshmen applied for aid; 389 deemed to have need; 389 received aid. Average need met was 81%. Average scholarship/grant was $22,396; average loan $2,828. 73% of total undergraduate aid awarded as scholarships/grants, 27% as loans/jobs. **Non-need-based:** Awarded to 849 full-time undergraduates, including 257 freshmen. Scholarships awarded for academics, alumni affiliation, athletics, leadership, music/drama, state residency.

Application procedures. Admission: Closing date 2/1 (postmark date). $50 fee, may be waived for applicants with need. Must reply by 5/1. **Financial aid:** Priority date 3/15, closing date 3/15. FAFSA, CSS PROFILE required. Applicants notified on a rolling basis starting 3/1; must reply by 5/1 or within 2 week(s) of notification.

Academics. Special study options: Accelerated study, cooperative education, cross-registration, distance learning, double major, dual enrollment of high school students, exchange student, honors, independent study, internships, liberal arts/career combination, semester at sea, study abroad, teacher certification program, Washington semester. **Credit/placement by examination:** AP, CLEP, IB, institutional tests. 30 credit hours maximum toward bachelor's degree. **Support services:** Learning center, reduced course load, study skills assistance, tutoring, writing center.

Majors. Biology: General, biochemistry. **Business:** General, accounting, finance, managerial economics. **Communications:** Media studies. **Computer sciences:** Computer science. **Conservation:** Environmental science, environmental studies. **Education:** Biology, chemistry, English, French, history, mathematics, science, secondary, social science, Spanish. **Engineering:** General, applied physics. **English:** English lit. **Foreign languages:** Classics, French, German, Spanish. **Health services:** Nursing (RN), predental, premedicine. **History:** General. **Liberal arts:** Arts/sciences. **Math:** General. **Philosophy/religion:** Philosophy. **Physical sciences:** Chemistry, physics. **Protective services:** Criminal justice. **Psychology:** General. **Social sciences:** Economics, international relations, political science, sociology. **Theology:** Theology. **Visual/performing arts:** Art.

Most popular majors. Business/marketing 16%, communications/journalism 7%, education 8%, health sciences 19%, psychology 7%, social sciences 16%.

Technology on campus. 400 workstations in dormitories, library, computer center, student center, student center. Dormitories wired for high-speed internet access and linked to campus network. Commuter students can connect to campus network. Online course registration, online library, helpline, repair service, wireless network available.

Student life. Freshman orientation: Mandatory. Preregistration for classes offered. Part 1 during the summer, Part 2 held 3 days prior to fall semester. Students must attend both parts. **Housing:** Guaranteed on-campus for all undergraduates. Coed dorms, single-sex dorms, special housing for disabled, apartments available. $250 nonrefundable deposit, deadline 5/1. Residential learning communities available (groups of students who devote a year to studying a topic and providing programming for their peers). **Activities:** Jazz band, campus ministries, choral groups, dance, drama, international student organizations, literary magazine, music ensembles, musical theater, student government, student newspaper, Muslim Student Associations, Multicultural Student Coalition, Knights of Columbus, Daughters of Saint Scholastica, College Republicans, College Democrat, French club, Irish/Celtic Society, King Edward Society, Red Key Society, STOP Campaign, Vietnamese Student Association.

Athletics. NCAA. **Intercollegiate:** Baseball M, basketball, cross-country, field hockey W, football (tackle) M, golf M, ice hockey, lacrosse, skiing, soccer, softball W, tennis, volleyball W. **Intramural:** Basketball, football (non-tackle), ice hockey, soccer, volleyball. **Team name:** Hawks.

Student services. Alcohol/substance abuse counseling, chaplain/spiritual director, career counseling, student employment services, financial aid counseling, health services, minority student services, personal counseling, placement for graduates, veterans' counselor.

Contact. E-mail: admission@anselm.edu
Phone: (603) 641-7500 Toll-free number: (888) 426-7356
Fax: (603) 641-7550
Eric Nichols, Dean of Admission, Saint Anselm College, 100 Saint Anselm Drive, Manchester, NH 03102-1310

Southern New Hampshire University
Manchester, New Hampshire   CB member
www.snhu.edu   CB code: 3649

- Private 4-year university and culinary school
- Residential campus in small city
- 3,027 degree-seeking undergraduates: 2% part-time, 52% women, 2% African American, 1% Asian American, 3% Hispanic/Latino, 2% Multiracial, non-Hispanic, 9% international
- 113 degree-seeking graduate students
- 92% of applicants admitted
- Application essay required
- 60% graduate within 6 years

General. Founded in 1932. Regionally accredited. Graduate programs and continuing education centers in Manchester, Nashua, Portsmouth, Salem, Brunswick, Burlington (Vermont), and online. **Degrees:** 595 bachelor's, 43 associate awarded; master's, doctoral offered. **ROTC:** Army. **Location:** 55 miles from Boston. **Calendar:** Continuous, extensive summer session. **Full-time faculty:** 122 total; 70% have terminal degrees, 8% minority, 48% women. **Part-time faculty:** 249 total; 20% have terminal degrees, 3% minority, 58% women. **Class size:** 55% < 20, 45% 20-39. **Special facilities:** Culinary institute, financial studies center, video game design lab, audiovisual studio, psychology observation lab, career development center, iMAC graphics lab.

Freshman class profile. 3,848 applied, 3,529 admitted, 794 enrolled.

Mid 50% test scores		Rank in top quarter:	24%
SAT critical reading:	440-540	Rank in top tenth:	6%
SAT math:	440-550	End year in good standing:	95%
SAT writing:	420-530	Return as sophomores:	73%
ACT composite:	20-25	Out-of-state:	61%
GPA 3.75 or higher:	9%	Live on campus:	82%
GPA 3.50-3.74:	13%	International:	4%
GPA 3.0-3.49:	34%	Fraternities:	2%
GPA 2.0-2.99:	43%	Sororities:	4%

Basis for selection. High school academic record weighed most heavily, including courses and course levels, grades, and class rank (if applicable). SAT/ACT, extracurricular activities, work experience, recommendations, and essay also considered. Test scores and interview required for 3-year bachelor's program. Interview recommended for all. Creative writing majors must submit samples of original writing. Music education majors must audition.

High school preparation. College-preparatory program required. 12 units required. Required units include English 4, mathematics 3, social studies 3, science 3 (laboratory 1).

2015-2016 Annual costs. Tuition/fees: $30,386. Room/board: $11,798. Books/supplies: $1,200. Personal expenses: $3,484.

2015-2016 Financial aid. Need-based: 707 full-time freshmen applied for aid; 639 deemed to have need; 637 received aid. Average need met was 70%. Average scholarship/grant was $4,220; average loan $3,247. 60% of total undergraduate aid awarded as scholarships/grants, 40% as loans/jobs. **Non-need-based:** Awarded to 2,604 full-time undergraduates, including 763 freshmen. Scholarships awarded for academics, alumni affiliation, art, athletics, job skills, leadership, music/drama, state residency.

Application procedures. Admission: Priority date 2/1; no deadline. $40 fee, may be waived for applicants with need, free for online applicants. Admission notification on a rolling basis beginning on or about 11/15. Must reply by May 1 or within 4 week(s) if notified thereafter. **Financial aid:** Priority date 3/15, closing date 6/30. FAFSA required. Applicants notified on a rolling basis starting 3/15; must reply within 3 week(s) of notification.

Academics. Special study options: Accelerated study, combined bachelor's/graduate degree, cooperative education, cross-registration, distance learning, double major, dual enrollment of high school students, ESL, honors, independent study, internships, student-designed major, study abroad, teacher certification program, Washington semester, weekend college. Three-year honors program in business administration. **Credit/placement by examination:** AP, CLEP, IB, institutional tests. 15 credit hours maximum toward associate degree, 15 toward bachelor's. **Support services:** Learning center, pre-admission summer program, reduced course load, remedial instruction, study skills assistance, tutoring.

Majors. Business: Accounting, accounting/finance, business admin, fashion, hospitality admin, international, marketing, operations. **Communications:** Organizational. **Computer sciences:** General, computer graphics. **Conservation:** Environmental science. **Education:** General, early childhood, elementary, English, mathematics, music, science, social studies. **English:** Creative writing, English lit. **History:** General. **Human services:** General.

Math: General. **Parks/recreation:** Sports admin. **Psychology:** General. **Social sciences:** General, economics, political science. **Visual/performing arts:** Graphic design.

Most popular majors. Business/marketing 40%, computer/information sciences 6%, education 10%, psychology 11%, security/protective services 7%.

Technology on campus. PC or laptop required. 674 workstations in library, computer center. Dormitories wired for high-speed internet access and linked to campus network. Commuter students can connect to campus network. Online course registration, online library, helpline, repair service, wireless network available.

Student life. Freshman orientation: Mandatory, $170 fee. Preregistration for classes offered. Five 1-day sessions held in June; 3-day program held at opening of fall term. **Housing:** Coed dorms, special housing for disabled, apartments, themed housing, wellness housing available. $500 fully refundable deposit, deadline 5/1. Women's floor, wellness housing available. **Activities:** Bands, campus ministries, choral groups, dance, drama, international student organizations, literary magazine, music ensembles, Model UN, musical theater, radio station, student government, student newspaper, symphony orchestra, TV station.

Athletics. NCAA. **Intercollegiate:** Baseball M, basketball, cheerleading, cross-country, golf M, ice hockey M, lacrosse, soccer, softball W, tennis, volleyball W. **Intramural:** Badminton, basketball, football (tackle), racquetball, skiing, soccer, softball, table tennis, tennis, volleyball W. **Team name:** Penmen.

Student services. Adult student services, alcohol/substance abuse counseling, chaplain/spiritual director, career counseling, student employment services, financial aid counseling, health services, personal counseling, placement for graduates, veterans' counselor. **Physically disabled:** Services for visually, speech, hearing impaired.

Contact. E-mail: admission@snhu.edu
Phone: (603) 645-9611 Toll-free number: (800) 642-4968
Fax: (603) 645-9693
Bethany Perkins, Director of Freshman Admissions, Southern New Hampshire University, 2500 North River Road, Manchester, NH 03106-1045

Thomas More College of Liberal Arts
Merrimack, New Hampshire
www.thomasmorecollege.edu   **CB code: 3892**

▸ Private 4-year liberal arts college affiliated with the Roman Catholic Church
▸ Residential campus in small city
▸ 89 degree-seeking undergraduates
▸ SAT or ACT (ACT writing optional), application essay required

General. Founded in 1978. Regionally accredited. **Degrees:** 23 bachelor's awarded. **Location:** 45 miles from Boston. **Calendar:** Semester. **Full-time faculty:** 9 total; 44% have terminal degrees. **Part-time faculty:** 7 total; 57% have terminal degrees, 43% women. **Class size:** 80% < 20, 10% 20-39, 10% 50-99.

Basis for selection. Evidence of student's desire to learn important. Complete application includes essay, 2 academic letters of recommendation, high school transcript, and SAT/ACT. Interviews and/or visits strongly recommended. **Home schooled:** Transcript of courses and grades required.

High school preparation. 17 units required. Required units include English 4, mathematics 3, social studies 2, history 2, science 2 (laboratory 2) and foreign language 2. Recommended languages: Latin, French, German, Greek. Recommended electives: music, art.

2015-2016 Annual costs. Tuition/fees: $20,400. Room/board: $9,500. Books/supplies: $700. Personal expenses: $150.

Financial aid. Non-need-based: Scholarships awarded for academics.

Application procedures. Admission: No deadline. No application fee. **Financial aid:** Priority date 5/1; no closing date. FAFSA required. Applicants notified on a rolling basis starting 5/15; must reply within 2 week(s) of notification.

Academics. Each student, regardless of major, takes 6-hour humanities course every semester throughout 4 years: philosophy, literature, politics, history, theology taught by faculty from various disciplines. **Special study options:** Independent study, internships, liberal arts/career combination, study

abroad. Sophomore semester in Rome, Italy, study abroad program in Oxford, England, internships in D.C., Rome, and Spain. **Credit/placement by examination:** AP, CLEP. **Support services:** Tutoring, writing center.

Majors. Liberal arts: Arts/sciences.

Technology on campus. 7 workstations in student center. Online course registration available.

Student life. Freshman orientation: Mandatory. Preregistration for classes offered. **Housing:** Guaranteed on-campus for all undergraduates. Single-sex dorms available. **Activities:** Campus ministries, choral groups, dance, drama, literary magazine, music ensembles, student government.

Athletics. Intramural: Baseball M, basketball, football (tackle), racquetball, skiing, soccer, swimming, table tennis, tennis, volleyball, weight lifting.

Student services. Chaplain/spiritual director, career counseling, financial aid counseling, personal counseling.

Contact. E-mail: admissions@thomasmorecollege.edu
Phone: (603) 880-8308 ext. 14 Toll-free number: (800) 880-8308 ext. 14
Fax: (603) 880-9280
Director of Admissions, Thomas More College of Liberal Arts, Six Manchester Street, Merrimack, NH 03054-4818

University of New Hampshire
Durham, New Hampshire   **CB member**
www.unh.edu   **CB code: 3918**

▸ Public 4-year university
▸ Residential campus in small town
▸ 12,788 degree-seeking undergraduates: 2% part-time, 54% women, 1% African American, 2% Asian American, 3% Hispanic/Latino, 2% Multiracial, non-Hispanic, 2% international
▸ 2,103 degree-seeking graduate students
▸ 79% of applicants admitted
▸ SAT or ACT with writing, application essay required
▸ 79% graduate within 6 years; 30% enter graduate study

General. Founded in 1866. Regionally accredited. **Degrees:** 2,832 bachelor's, 130 associate awarded; master's, professional, doctoral offered. **ROTC:** Army, Air Force. **Location:** 60 miles from Boston; 50 miles from Portland, ME. **Calendar:** Semester, extensive summer session. **Full-time faculty:** 618 total; 90% have terminal degrees, 14% minority, 43% women. **Part-time faculty:** 416 total; 33% have terminal degrees, 4% minority, 60% women. **Class size:** 40% < 20, 36% 20-39, 7% 40-49, 11% 50-99, 7% >100. **Special facilities:** Journalism laboratory, optical observatory, marine research laboratories (on Great Bay, coast of Atlantic and the Isle of Shoals), experiential learning center, child development center, agricultural and equine facilities, electron microscope, sawmill, nature preserve, radio station, research centers, survey center, writing center, interoperability lab, wind tunnel.

Freshman class profile. 19,255 applied, 15,137 admitted, 3,220 enrolled.

Mid 50% test scores		
SAT critical reading:	500-600	Rank in top quarter: 45%
SAT math:	500-610	Rank in top tenth: 18%
SAT writing:	490-590	End year in good standing: 92%
ACT composite:	22-27	Return as sophomores: 85%
GPA 3.75 or higher:	24%	Out-of-state: 62%
GPA 3.50-3.74:	16%	Live on campus: 94%
GPA 3.0-3.49:	39%	International: 1%
GPA 2.0-2.99:	21%	Fraternities: 8%
		Sororities: 8%

Basis for selection. School achievement record most important, followed by course selection, class rank, recommendations, test scores. Co-curricular activities, volunteer work, geographical residence, character/leadership considered. Audition required for music programs. **Home schooled:** Statement describing home school structure and mission, transcript of courses and grades, state high school equivalency certificate required. Supporting documents include GED scores, transcripts, education plans, syllabi, homeschool association information.

High school preparation. College-preparatory program required. 15 units required; 19 recommended. Required and recommended units include English 4, mathematics 3-4, social studies 3, science 3-4 (laboratory 2-3), foreign language 2-3 and visual/performing arts 1.

2015-2016 Annual costs. Tuition/fees: $16,986; $30,256 out-of-state. Room/board: $10,618. Books/supplies: $1,200. Personal expenses: $2,424. **Additional information:** Tuition rates are based on full-time registration

(12-20 credits). Students who register for fewer than 12 credits are charged per credit hour. Students who register for more than 20 credit hours are charged per credit hour for each credit over 20.

2014-2015 Financial aid. **Need-based:** 2,764 full-time freshmen applied for aid; 2,236 deemed to have need; 2,202 received aid. Average need met was 78%. Average scholarship/grant was $5,412; average loan $2,651. 59% of total undergraduate aid awarded as scholarships/grants, 41% as loans/jobs. **Non-need-based:** Awarded to 2,605 full-time undergraduates, including 703 freshmen. Scholarships awarded for academics, art, athletics, leadership, music/drama, ROTC.

Application procedures. **Admission:** Closing date 2/1 (postmark date). $50 fee ($65 out-of-state), may be waived for applicants with need. Admission notification on a rolling basis beginning on or about 1/15. Must reply by 5/1. **Financial aid:** Closing date 3/1. FAFSA required. Applicants notified on a rolling basis starting 3/1; must reply by 5/1.

Academics. All students must complete a set of writing intensive courses, including freshman composition and three additional courses, one of which must be in the student's major and one of which must be an upper-level course. Also required are 10-11 Discovery General Education courses from the following categories: 1 course in writing skills; 1 course in quantitative reasoning; 1 inquiry course; and 1 course from each of the following categories: Biological Science, Physical Science (one science must have a lab); Environment, Technology, and Society; Fine and Performing Arts; Historical Perspectives; Humanities; Social Science; World Cultures. In addition one senior capstone experience within a student's major is required. **Special study options:** Accelerated study, combined bachelor's/graduate degree, cooperative education, cross-registration, distance learning, double major, ESL, exchange student, honors, independent study, internships, semester at sea, student-designed major, study abroad, teacher certification program, United Nations semester, urban semester, Washington semester, weekend college. Research/creative opportunities, learning communities, service learning, experiential learning. **Credit/placement by examination:** AP, CLEP, IB, institutional tests. 32 credit hours maximum toward associate degree, 64 toward bachelor's. **Support services:** Learning center, reduced course load, study skills assistance, tutoring, writing center.

Majors. **Architecture:** Urban/community planning. **Area/ethnic studies:** European, French, women's. **Biology:** General, bacteriology, biochemistry, Biochemistry/molecular biology, biomedical sciences, botany, entomology, genetics, neurobiology/behavior, neuroscience, zoology. **Business:** General, business admin, hospitality admin. **Communications:** Communications/speech/rhetoric. **Computer sciences:** General, information technology. **Conservation:** General, economics, environmental science, forest technology, forestry, wildlife/wilderness. **Education:** Mathematics, physical. **Engineering:** Biomedical, chemical, civil, computer, electrical, environmental, mechanical, ocean. **English:** English lit. **Foreign languages:** Ancient Greek, classics, French, German, Latin, linguistics, Russian, Spanish. **Health services:** Athletic training, clinical lab science, health care admin, nursing (RN), recreational therapy. **History:** General. **Human services:** Social work. **Liberal arts:** Humanities. **Math:** General, applied. **Parks/recreation:** Exercise sciences, facilities management. **Philosophy/religion:** Philosophy. **Physical sciences:** Chemistry, geology, hydrology, materials science, physics. **Psychology:** General. **Social sciences:** Anthropology, criminology, economics, geography, international relations, political science, sociology. **Visual/performing arts:** Art, dramatic, music, studio arts. **Work/family studies:** Family studies.

Most popular majors. Biology 11%, business/marketing 19%, engineering/engineering technologies 10%, health sciences 7%, psychology 7%, social sciences 7%.

Technology on campus. 448 workstations in library, computer center, student center. Dormitories wired for high-speed internet access and linked to campus network. Commuter students can connect to campus network. Online course registration, online library, helpline, repair service, student web hosting, wireless network available.

Student life. **Freshman orientation:** Mandatory. Preregistration for classes offered. Two-day program held in June with additional session in fall. Special one week minority student orientation and one-week service-focused orientation offered in August. **Policies:** Student rights, rules, and responsibilities as outlined in the Student Handbook. Freshmen not permitted cars on campus. **Housing:** Guaranteed on-campus for freshmen. Coed dorms, special housing for disabled, apartments, themed housing available. $200 partly refundable deposit, deadline 5/1. **Activities:** Bands, campus ministries, choral groups, dance, drama, film society, international student organizations, literary magazine, music ensembles, Model UN, musical theater, radio station, student government, student newspaper, symphony orchestra, TV station, Diversity Support Coalition, Black Student Union, Indian student association, United Asian Coalition, Chinese students and scholars association, Intervarsity Christian Fellowship, Young Life, Catholic student organization, College Democrats, College Republicans.

Athletics. NCAA. **Intercollegiate:** Basketball, cross-country, diving W, field hockey W, football (tackle) M, gymnastics W, ice hockey, lacrosse W, skiing, soccer, swimming W, track and field, volleyball W. **Intramural:** Basketball, field hockey W, football (non-tackle), ice hockey, racquetball, soccer, softball, swimming, table tennis, tennis, ultimate frisbee, volleyball, water polo. **Team name:** Wildcats.

Student services. Adult student services, alcohol/substance abuse counseling, chaplain/spiritual director, career counseling, services for economically disadvantaged, student employment services, financial aid counseling, health services, legal services, minority student services, on-campus daycare, personal counseling, placement for graduates, veterans' counselor, women's services. **Physically disabled:** Services for visually, speech, hearing impaired.

Contact. E-mail: admissions@unh.edu
Phone: (603) 862-1360 Fax: (603) 862-0077
Robert McGann, Director of Admissions, University of New Hampshire, 3 Garrison Avenue, Durham, NH 03824

University of New Hampshire at Manchester
Manchester, New Hampshire   CB member
www.manchester.unh.edu   CB code: 2094

- Public 4-year university and liberal arts college
- Commuter campus in small city
- 719 degree-seeking undergraduates
- SAT or ACT with writing, application essay required

General. Founded in 1985. Regionally accredited. **Degrees:** 177 bachelor's, 14 associate awarded; master's offered. **Location:** 35 miles from Concord, 55 miles from Boston. **Calendar:** Semester, limited summer session. **Full-time faculty:** 39 total. **Part-time faculty:** 85 total.

Freshman class profile.

Rank in top quarter:	29%	Out-of-state:	1%
Rank in top tenth:	7%		

Basis for selection. Achievement in high school college preparatory program most important. SAT scores should be consistent with achievement. Recommendation, essay, interview very helpful for students of moderate achievement or in nontraditional cases. **Home schooled:** Transcript of courses and grades, state high school equivalency certificate, letter of recommendation (nonparent) required. GED, syllabus of curriculum encouraged; diploma from homeschool association requested if available. **Learning Disabled:** To be eligible for services, students must provide documentation of disability as determined by licensed physician and/or certified psychologist who is skilled in the diagnosis of disabilities. Documentation must be current (generally within 3 years).

High school preparation. College-preparatory program recommended. Required and recommended units include English 4, mathematics 3-4, social studies 3, science 3-4 (laboratory 1) and foreign language 2-3.

2015-2016 Annual costs. Tuition/fees: $14,955; $28,225 out-of-state. Books/supplies: $1,200. Personal expenses: $2,788. **Additional information:** New England Regional Student Program tuition is 175% of in-state tuition.

Financial aid. **Non-need-based:** Scholarships awarded for academics.

Application procedures. **Admission:** Closing date 4/1 (postmark date). $60 fee, may be waived for applicants with need. Application must be submitted online. Admission notification on a rolling basis. Must reply by May 1 or within 3 week(s) if notified thereafter. **Financial aid:** Closing date 3/1. FAFSA required. Applicants notified by 4/1; must reply within 2 week(s) of notification.

Academics. **Special study options:** Combined bachelor's/graduate degree, cross-registration, double major, ESL, exchange student, external degree, independent study, internships, student-designed major, study abroad, teacher certification program. **Credit/placement by examination:** AP, CLEP, IB, institutional tests. 48 credit hours maximum toward associate degree, 64 toward bachelor's. **Support services:** Learning center, pre-admission summer program, reduced course load, remedial instruction, study skills assistance, tutoring, writing center.

Majors. **Biology:** General. **Business:** Business admin. **Communications:** General. **Computer sciences:** General, computer science. **English:** English lit. **Foreign languages:** Sign language interpretation. **History:** General. **Liberal arts:** Arts/sciences, humanities. **Psychology:** General. **Social sciences:** Political science.

Technology on campus. 64 workstations in library, computer center. Commuter students can connect to campus network. Online library, helpline, wireless network available.

Student life. Freshman orientation: Mandatory, $30 fee. Preregistration for classes offered. Three-and-a-half-hour day or evening session held in June. **Housing:** Dormitories at New Hampshire Institute of Art available. **Activities:** Choral groups, dance, drama, music ensembles, musical theater, student government.

Athletics. Team name: Wildcats.

Student services. Career counseling, financial aid counseling, veterans' counselor. **Physically disabled:** Services for visually, speech, hearing impaired.

Contact. E-mail: unhm.admissions@unh.edu
Phone: (603) 641-4150 Fax: (603) 641-4342
University of New Hampshire at Manchester, 88 Commercial Street, Manchester, NH 03101-1113

New Jersey

Berkeley College
Woodland Park, New Jersey   CB member
www.berkeleycollege.edu   CB code: 2061

- For-profit 4-year business college
- Commuter campus in large town
- 3,806 degree-seeking undergraduates: 16% part-time, 73% women, 21% African American, 2% Asian American, 34% Hispanic/Latino
- 41 graduate students
- 99% of applicants admitted
- 30% graduate within 6 years

General. Founded in 1931. Regionally accredited. Additional locations in Paramus, Newark, Dover, and Woodbridge. **Degrees:** 494 bachelor's, 285 associate awarded; master's offered. **ROTC:** Army. **Location:** 20 miles from New York City. **Calendar:** Semester, limited summer session. **Full-time faculty:** 137 total; 47% minority. **Part-time faculty:** 198 total; 71% minority. **Class size:** 49% < 20, 51% 20-39.

Freshman class profile. 2,508 applied, 2,471 admitted, 978 enrolled.

End year in good standing:	93%	Out-of-state:	3%
Return as sophomores:	68%		

Basis for selection. Graduation from high school or the equivalent and an entrance exam or SAT/ACT scores are basic requirements for admission to degree and certificate programs. A personal interview is strongly recommended. Institutional entrance exam required of all applications. SAT or ACT accepted in lieu of institutional entrance exam. Interviews strongly recommended.

2015-2016 Annual costs. Tuition/fees: $24,300. Books/supplies: $960. Personal expenses: $6,780. **Additional information:** Certificate tuition varies from $14,800-$27,950 including books, background check where appropriate, and cost of first certification/licensure exam; fees are $1,200.

Financial aid. Non-need-based: Scholarships awarded for academics, alumni affiliation.

Application procedures. Admission: No deadline. $50 fee. Admission notification on a rolling basis. Admitted applicants must reply within 2 weeks of notification. **Financial aid:** FAFSA required.

Academics. Special study options: Accelerated study, distance learning, honors, internships, New York semester, study abroad. **Credit/placement by examination:** AP, CLEP, SAT, ACT, institutional tests. **Support services:** Learning center, pre-admission summer program, remedial instruction, study skills assistance, tutoring, writing center.

Majors. Business: Accounting, business admin, fashion, financial planning, international, marketing. **Health services:** Health care admin, nursing (RN). **Protective services:** Law enforcement admin. **Visual/performing arts:** Graphic design, interior design.

Most popular majors. Business/marketing 63%, health sciences 6%, security/protective services 23%.

Technology on campus. 358 workstations in library, computer center. Commuter students can connect to campus network. Online library, helpline, wireless network available.

Student life. Freshman orientation: Mandatory. Preregistration for classes offered. **Activities:** Choral groups, drama, literary magazine, student government, student newspaper, Phi Beta Lambda, interior design club, athletic club, fashion and marketing club, Phi Theta Kappa.

Athletics. USCAA. **Intercollegiate:** Cross-country, soccer M. **Team name:** Knights.

Student services. Adult student services, career counseling, student employment services, financial aid counseling, personal counseling, placement for graduates, veterans' counselor.

Contact. E-mail: info@berkeleycollege.edu
Phone: (973) 278-5400 ext. 1210 Toll-free number: (800) 446-5400
Fax: (973) 278-9141
Carol Covino, Director, High School Admissions, Berkeley College, 44 Rifle Camp Road, Woodland Park, NJ 07424-0440

Beth Medrash Govoha
Lakewood, New Jersey

CB code: 2166

- Private 4-year rabbinical college for men affiliated with the Jewish faith
- Residential campus in small city
- 2,747 degree-seeking undergraduates: 1% part-time
- 3,832 graduate students
- Interview required

General. Founded in 1943. Accredited by AARTS. Talmudical college. **Degrees:** 470 bachelor's awarded; master's offered. **Calendar:** Semester.

Basis for selection. Interviews required.

2015-2016 Annual costs. Tuition/fees: $19,240. Room/board: $4,172.

Application procedures. Admission: Closing date 7/17. $125 fee, may be waived for applicants with need. **Financial aid:** No deadline.

Academics. Special study options: Double major. **Credit/placement by examination:** AP, CLEP.

Majors. Theology: Talmudic.

Student life. Housing: Apartments available.

Student services. Career counseling, financial aid counseling, personal counseling, placement for graduates.

Contact. Phone: (732) 367-1060 ext. 4224 Fax: (732) 204-0673
Rabbi Abraham Feuer, Director of Admissions and Tuition, Beth Medrash Govoha, 617 Sixth Street, Lakewood, NJ 08701

Bloomfield College
Bloomfield, New Jersey   CB member
www.bloomfield.edu   CB code: 2044

- Private 4-year nursing and liberal arts college affiliated with the Presbyterian Church (USA)
- Commuter campus in large town
- 1,937 degree-seeking undergraduates: 10% part-time, 64% women, 50% African American, 3% Asian American, 26% Hispanic/Latino, 1% Multiracial, non-Hispanic, 4% international
- 1 degree-seeking graduate students
- 60% of applicants admitted
- SAT or ACT (ACT writing optional), application essay required
- 30% graduate within 6 years; 12% enter graduate study

General. Founded in 1868. Regionally accredited. **Degrees:** 288 bachelor's awarded; master's offered. **ROTC:** Army. **Location:** 7 miles from Newark, 15 miles from New York City. **Calendar:** Semester, limited summer session. **Full-time faculty:** 73 total; 75% have terminal degrees, 26% minority, 62% women. **Part-time faculty:** 146 total; 10% have terminal degrees, 34% minority, 46% women. **Class size:** 71% < 20, 28% 20-39, less than 1% 40-49. **Special facilities:** Technology and multimedia center, performing arts center, art gallery.

Freshman class profile. 3,027 applied, 1,807 admitted, 428 enrolled.

Mid 50% test scores		Rank in top quarter:	14%
SAT critical reading:	380-470	Rank in top tenth:	3%
SAT math:	390-480	End year in good standing:	54%
ACT composite:	15-19	Return as sophomores:	70%
GPA 3.75 or higher:	2%	Out-of-state:	3%
GPA 3.50-3.74:	7%	Live on campus:	47%
GPA 3.0-3.49:	24%	International:	5%
GPA 2.0-2.99:	60%		

Basis for selection. Bloomfield employs a holistic admission process, whereby High School performance, SAT/ACT scores, letters of recommendation, and essays are considered. Interviews strongly recommended. Essays must be self-recommendations or reflections on previous educational experiences. Recently graded term paper can be substituted for essay. Portfolios optional. **Home schooled:** Statement describing home school structure and mission, transcript of courses and grades, state high school equivalency certificate, interview, letter of recommendation (nonparent) required. Applicants must submit SAT and official transcript with information about organization that performed accreditation/conversion.

High school preparation. College-preparatory program recommended. 14 units required.

2016-2017 Annual costs. Tuition/fees: $28,600. Room/board: $11,500.

2015-2016 Financial aid. Need-based: 432 full-time freshmen applied for aid; 413 deemed to have need; 410 received aid. Average need met was 78%. Average scholarship/grant was $18,952. 78% of total undergraduate aid awarded as scholarships/grants, 22% as loans/jobs. **Non-need-based:** Awarded to 899 full-time undergraduates, including 244 freshmen. Scholarships awarded for academics, alumni affiliation, athletics, leadership.

Application procedures. Admission: Priority date 3/14; deadline 8/1 (postmark date). $40 fee, may be waived for applicants with need. Admission notification on a rolling basis beginning on or about 10/1. Must reply by May 1 or within 2 week(s) if notified thereafter. **Financial aid:** Priority date 3/15, closing date 6/1. FAFSA required. Applicants notified on a rolling basis starting 3/15; must reply within 2 week(s) of notification.

Academics. Special study options: Accelerated study, combined bachelor's/graduate degree, distance learning, double major, dual enrollment of high school students, ESL, honors, independent study, internships, liberal arts/career combination, student-designed major, study abroad, teacher certification program. Joint BS/MS in computer information systems program offered with NJIT; special programs offered by the Institute for Technology and Professional Studies. **Credit/placement by examination:** AP, CLEP, SAT, ACT, institutional tests. 16 credit hours maximum toward bachelor's degree. Maximum of 16 course units may be earned through combination of CLEP examinations, portfolio assessment, and nursing assessment. **Support services:** Learning center, pre-admission summer program, reduced course load, remedial instruction, study skills assistance, tutoring, writing center. Test preparation for GRE, TEAS, and Praxis. Services provided for adult students, transfers, and veterans. Academic support and counseling for at risk students. SSStar program is available for first generation students. McNair program offered for first generation and low income students.

Honors college/program. 3.3 GPA, participation in extracurricular activities, and recommendations from high school counselors or teachers required for pre-honors program; students eligible for induction into honors program upon completion of 3 college-level courses with 3.3 GPA.

Majors. Biology: General. **Business:** Accounting, business admin, e-commerce. **Computer sciences:** General, computer science, networking. **Education:** General. **English:** English lit. **Health services:** Nursing (RN). **History:** General. **Math:** Applied. **Philosophy/religion:** Philosophy, religion. **Physical sciences:** Chemistry. **Psychology:** General. **Social sciences:** Political science, sociology. **Visual/performing arts:** General.

Most popular majors. Business/marketing 14%, English 8%, health sciences 13%, psychology 14%, social sciences 15%, visual/performing arts 17%.

Technology on campus. 390 workstations in dormitories, library, computer center, student center. Commuter students can connect to campus network. Online course registration, online library, helpline, student web hosting, wireless network available.

Student life. Freshman orientation: Mandatory. Preregistration for classes offered. Multi-day sessions offered prior to beginning of fall semester. **Policies:** Statement of Shared Values adopted, addressing student conduct and standards for behavior. **Housing:** Coed dorms, apartments available. $100 fully refundable deposit, deadline 5/1. **Activities:** Campus ministries, dance, international student organizations, radio station, student government, Black Student Union, Team Infinite, Green Hearts Environmental Movement, Male Empowerment Network, Christian Fellowship, National Association of Black Accountants, Haitian Student Association, First Ladies of Bloomfield College.

Athletics. NCAA. **Intercollegiate:** Baseball M, basketball, cross-country, soccer, softball W, tennis M, volleyball W. **Intramural:** Basketball, volleyball. **Team name:** Bears.

Student services. Adult student services, alcohol/substance abuse counseling, chaplain/spiritual director, career counseling, student employment services, financial aid counseling, health services, personal counseling, placement for graduates, veterans' counselor. **Physically disabled:** Services for visually, speech, hearing impaired.

Contact. E-mail: admission@bloomfield.edu
Phone: (973) 748-9000 ext. 1230 Toll-free number: (800) 848-4555
Fax: (973) 748-0916
Nicole Cibelli, Director of Admissions, Bloomfield College, One Park Place, Bloomfield, NJ 07003

Caldwell University
Caldwell, New Jersey
www.caldwell.edu

CB member
CB code: 2072

- Private 4-year liberal arts college affiliated with the Roman Catholic Church
- Commuter campus in large town
- 1,595 degree-seeking undergraduates: 14% part-time, 71% women, 15% African American, 4% Asian American, 18% Hispanic/Latino, 1% Multiracial, non-Hispanic, 5% international
- 543 degree-seeking graduate students
- 64% of applicants admitted
- SAT or ACT (ACT writing recommended), application essay required
- 52% graduate within 6 years

General. Founded in 1939. Regionally accredited. **Degrees:** 362 bachelor's awarded; master's, professional, doctoral offered. **ROTC:** Army. **Location:** 20 miles from New York City. **Calendar:** Semester, limited summer session. **Full-time faculty:** 89 total. **Part-time faculty:** 178 total. **Class size:** 64% < 20, 35% 20-39, less than 1% 40-49.

Freshman class profile. 3,592 applied, 2,281 admitted, 330 enrolled.

Mid 50% test scores			
SAT critical reading:	420-520	GPA 2.0-2.99:	29%
SAT math:	430-550	Rank in top quarter:	37%
SAT writing:	420-530	Rank in top tenth:	7%
ACT composite:	18-24	Return as sophomores:	83%
GPA 3.75 or higher:	22%	Out-of-state:	9%
GPA 3.50-3.74:	17%	Live on campus:	45%
GPA 3.0-3.49:	31%	International:	8%

Basis for selection. School achievement record, test scores, interview, extracurricular activities very important. Counselor's recommendation, volunteer work important. Essay, interview recommended for all, audition required for music programs, portfolio required for art programs. **Home schooled:** Statement describing home school structure and mission required.

High school preparation. College-preparatory program required. 16 units required. Required units include English 4, mathematics 2, history 1, science 2 (laboratory 1), foreign language 2 and academic electives 5.

2015-2016 Annual costs. Tuition/fees: $31,200. Room/board: $10,965. Books/supplies: $2,000. Personal expenses: $1,000.

2014-2015 Financial aid. Need-based: 374 full-time freshmen applied for aid; 374 deemed to have need; 374 received aid. Average need met was 75%. Average scholarship/grant was $22,757; average loan $3,229. 76% of total undergraduate aid awarded as scholarships/grants, 24% as loans/jobs. **Non-need-based:** Awarded to 463 full-time undergraduates, including 135 freshmen. Scholarships awarded for academics, alumni affiliation, art, athletics, leadership, music/drama, religious affiliation.

Application procedures. Admission: Priority date 12/1; no deadline. $50 fee, may be waived for applicants with need. Admission notification on a rolling basis beginning on or about 12/31. Must reply by May 1 or within 2 week(s) if notified thereafter. **Financial aid:** Priority date 4/1; no closing date. FAFSA, institutional form required. Applicants notified on a rolling basis starting 3/1; must reply within 4 week(s) of notification.

Academics. Special study options: Accelerated study, combined bachelor's/graduate degree, cooperative education, distance learning, double major, dual enrollment of high school students, ESL, external degree, honors, independent study, internships, liberal arts/career combination, student-designed major, study abroad, teacher certification program, Washington semester, weekend college. **Credit/placement by examination:** AP, CLEP, IB, SAT, ACT, institutional tests. 30 credit hours maximum toward bachelor's degree. Credit by exam only available during first year (30 credits) of matriculation. Credit toward major dependent on departmental approval. Prior Learning Assessment (PLA) for adult students who must attend PLA workshop. **Support services:** Learning center, pre-admission summer program, reduced course load, remedial instruction, study skills assistance, tutoring, writing center.

Majors. Biology: General. **Business:** Accounting, business admin, international, marketing. **Communications:** Communications/speech/rhetoric.

Computer sciences: General, information technology. **Education:** Elementary, secondary. **English:** English lit. **Foreign languages:** Spanish. **Health services:** Clinical lab science, nursing (RN). **History:** General. **Math:** General. **Physical sciences:** Chemistry. **Protective services:** Criminal justice. **Psychology:** General. **Social sciences:** General, economics, political science, sociology. **Theology:** Theology. **Visual/performing arts:** Art, graphic design, music.

Most popular majors. Business/marketing 20%, education 8%, English 9%, health sciences 9%, psychology 19%, security/protective services 7%, social sciences 9%.

Technology on campus. 286 workstations in dormitories, library, computer center, student center. Dormitories wired for high-speed internet access and linked to campus network. Online course registration, online library, helpline, wireless network available.

Student life. Freshman orientation: Mandatory, $200 fee. Preregistration for classes offered. Two-day overnight program held in June; 3-day program prior to start of fall semester includes move in day and a day dedicated to community service. **Housing:** Guaranteed on-campus for freshmen. Coed dorms, wellness housing available. $200 nonrefundable deposit, deadline 6/1. **Activities:** Bands, campus ministries, choral groups, dance, drama, international student organizations, literary magazine, music ensembles, musical theater, student government, student newspaper, Caribbean student association, international student organization, French club, Spanish club, Socio-Political Society, Latin American student organization.

Athletics. NCAA. **Intercollegiate:** Baseball M, basketball, bowling W, cross-country, lacrosse W, soccer, softball W, tennis, track and field, volleyball W. **Intramural:** Basketball, football (non-tackle), soccer, tennis, ultimate frisbee, volleyball. **Team name:** Cougars.

Student services. Adult student services, alcohol/substance abuse counseling, chaplain/spiritual director, career counseling, services for economically disadvantaged, student employment services, financial aid counseling, health services, minority student services, personal counseling, placement for graduates, veterans' counselor, women's services. **Physically disabled:** Services for visually, hearing impaired.

Contact. E-mail: admissions@caldwell.edu
Phone: (973) 618-3500 Toll-free number: (888) 864-9516
Fax: (973) 618-3600
Stephen Quinn, Assistant Vice President, Enrollment Management, Caldwell University, 120 Bloomfield Avenue, Caldwell, NJ 07006-6195

Centenary College
Hackettstown, New Jersey   **CB member**
www.centenarycollege.edu   **CB code: 2080**

- Private 4-year liberal arts college affiliated with the United Methodist Church
- Residential campus in large town
- 1,548 degree-seeking undergraduates: 5% part-time, 61% women
- 736 graduate students
- 87% of applicants admitted
- SAT or ACT, application essay required
- 59% graduate within 6 years; 11% enter graduate study

General. Founded in 1867. Regionally accredited. **Degrees:** 433 bachelor's, 39 associate awarded; master's offered. **Location:** 55 miles from New York City. **Calendar:** Semester, limited summer session. **Full-time faculty:** 79 total; 62% have terminal degrees, 8% minority, 54% women. **Part-time faculty:** 147 total; 45% women. **Class size:** 82% < 20, 18% 20-39. **Special facilities:** Equestrian center.

Freshman class profile. 1,182 applied, 1,024 admitted, 227 enrolled.

Mid 50% test scores			
SAT critical reading:	410-510	GPA 3.0-3.49:	24%
SAT math:	420-510	GPA 2.0-2.99:	45%
SAT writing:	400-510	Rank in top quarter:	28%
ACT composite:	17-24	Rank in top tenth:	11%
GPA 3.75 or higher:	14%	Return as sophomores:	78%
GPA 3.50-3.74:	15%	Out-of-state:	24%
		Live on campus:	83%

Basis for selection. School achievement record, standardized test scores most important. Interview, recommendations, community activities also strongly considered. Interviews required for academically marginal students with special needs; recommended for others. Portfolio required for art and design, graphic arts majors. **Home schooled:** State high school equivalency certificate required. **Learning Disabled:** Interview with Director of Services,

documentation of psycho-education evaluation and IEP required for supportive services programs.

High school preparation. College-preparatory program recommended. 16 units required; 20 recommended. Required and recommended units include English 4, mathematics 3-4, social studies 4, science 2-3 (laboratory 1) and foreign language 2. Major-related courses on high school level recommended.

2015-2016 Annual costs. Tuition/fees: $31,654. Room/board: $10,730. Books/supplies: $1,400. Personal expenses: $1,200.

2014-2015 Financial aid. Need-based: 223 full-time freshmen applied for aid; 201 deemed to have need; 201 received aid. Average need met was 79%. Average scholarship/grant was $22,920; average loan $5,112. 69% of total undergraduate aid awarded as scholarships/grants, 31% as loans/jobs. **Non-need-based:** Awarded to 292 full-time undergraduates, including 59 freshmen. Scholarships awarded for academics, religious affiliation.

Application procedures. Admission: Priority date 3/1; no deadline. $30 fee, may be waived for applicants with need, free for online applicants. Admission notification on a rolling basis beginning on or about 12/15. Must reply by May 1 or within 4 week(s) if notified thereafter. **Financial aid:** Priority date 2/15, closing date 9/1. FAFSA required. Applicants notified on a rolling basis starting 3/1.

Academics. Core curriculum required. Educational program balances career and liberal arts. **Special study options:** Accelerated study, combined bachelor's/graduate degree, cross-registration, distance learning, double major, dual enrollment of high school students, ESL, exchange student, honors, independent study, internships, liberal arts/career combination, student-designed major, study abroad, teacher certification program, weekend college. **Credit/placement by examination:** AP, CLEP, IB. 15 credit hours maximum toward associate degree, 30 toward bachelor's. **Support services:** Learning center, pre-admission summer program, reduced course load, remedial instruction, study skills assistance, tutoring, writing center.

Majors. Biology: General, environmental. **Business:** Accounting, business admin. **Communications:** General. **Computer sciences:** General. **Education:** General. **English:** English lit. **Health services:** Clinical/medical social work. **History:** General. **Protective services:** Criminal justice. **Psychology:** General. **Social sciences:** Political science, sociology. **Visual/performing arts:** Commercial/advertising art, dramatic, fashion design.

Most popular majors. Business/marketing 39%, security/protective services 9%.

Technology on campus. PC or laptop required. 750 workstations in dormitories, library, computer center. Dormitories wired for high-speed internet access and linked to campus network. Commuter students can connect to campus network. Online course registration, online library, helpline, repair service, wireless network available.

Student life. Freshman orientation: Mandatory. Preregistration for classes offered. Three-day orientation prior to start of classes. **Housing:** Coed dorms available. $150 deposit, deadline 5/1. **Activities:** Campus ministries, dance, drama, film society, international student organizations, literary magazine, Model UN, musical theater, radio station, student government, student newspaper, TV station, art guild, student activities committee, service groups, fashion group, academic clubs, professional and honor societies, special interest clubs.

Athletics. NCAA. **Intercollegiate:** Baseball M, basketball, cross-country, equestrian, golf, lacrosse, soccer, softball W, volleyball W, wrestling M. **Intramural:** Basketball M, equestrian M. **Team name:** Cyclones.

Student services. Adult student services, alcohol/substance abuse counseling, chaplain/spiritual director, career counseling, services for economically disadvantaged, student employment services, financial aid counseling, health services, minority student services, personal counseling, placement for graduates, veterans' counselor, women's services.

Contact. E-mail: admissions@centenarycollege.edu
Phone: (908) 852-1400 ext. 2217 Toll-free number: (800) 236-8679
Fax: (908) 852-3454
Glenna Warren, Associate Dean of Freshman Enrollment, Centenary College, 400 Jefferson Street, Hackettstown, NJ 07840-9989

The College of New Jersey
Ewing, New Jersey   **CB member**
www.tcnj.edu   **CB code: 2519**

- Public 4-year liberal arts college
- Residential campus in large town

- 6,584 degree-seeking undergraduates: 3% part-time, 59% women, 6% African American, 10% Asian American, 12% Hispanic/Latino
- 596 degree-seeking graduate students
- 49% of applicants admitted
- SAT or ACT (ACT writing optional), application essay required
- 84% graduate within 6 years

General. Founded in 1855. Regionally accredited. **Degrees:** 1,538 bachelor's awarded; master's offered. **ROTC:** Army, Air Force. **Location:** 35 miles from Philadelphia. **Calendar:** Semester, limited summer session. **Full-time faculty:** 355 total; 91% have terminal degrees, 23% minority, 53% women. **Part-time faculty:** 498 total; 27% have terminal degrees, 9% minority, 55% women. **Class size:** 43% < 20, 55% 20-39, 3% 40-49, less than 1% 50-99. **Special facilities:** Concert hall, electron microscopy lab, nuclear magnetic resonance lab, optical spectroscopy lab, observatory, planetarium, greenhouse.

Freshman class profile. 11,290 applied, 5,495 admitted, 1,453 enrolled.

Mid 50% test scores		Rank in top tenth:	39%
SAT critical reading:	550-640	Return as sophomores:	95%
SAT math:	570-670	Out-of-state:	8%
SAT writing:	550-650	Live on campus:	94%
ACT composite:	26-30	International:	1%
Rank in top quarter:	79%		

Basis for selection. Standardized test scores, high school rank and choice of curriculum very important. Extracurricular service, activities and community involvement considered. Audition required for music; portfolio required for art. **Home schooled:** Statement describing home school structure and mission, transcript of courses and grades, state high school equivalency certificate required.

High school preparation. College-preparatory program recommended. 18 units required; 20 recommended. Required and recommended units include English 4, mathematics 4, social studies 2, science 4 (laboratory 2) and foreign language 2.

2015-2016 Annual costs. Tuition/fees: $15,466; $26,397 out-of-state. Room/board: $12,498. Books/supplies: $1,200. Personal expenses: $2,582.

2014-2015 Financial aid. Need-based: 1,229 full-time freshmen applied for aid; 788 deemed to have need; 719 received aid. Average need met was 42%. Average scholarship/grant was $14,316; average loan $3,632. 44% of total undergraduate aid awarded as scholarships/grants, 56% as loans/jobs. **Non-need-based:** Awarded to 1,376 full-time undergraduates, including 380 freshmen. Scholarships awarded for academics, art, music/drama. **Additional information:** Merit scholarships available to New Jersey high school graduates based on academic distinction. Limited number of scholarships available to out-of-state students who demonstrate exceptional academic achievement in high school and on SAT. The EOF Promise Award meets the direct cost of attendance freshman and sophomore years, with merit scholarship awards available in junior and senior years.

Application procedures. Admission: Priority date 11/15; deadline 2/1 (postmark date). $75 fee, may be waived for applicants with need. Application must be submitted online. Admission notification by 4/1. Admission notification on a rolling basis beginning on or about 2/1. Must reply by May 1 or within 3 week(s) if notified thereafter. **Financial aid:** Priority date 3/1, closing date 10/1. FAFSA required. Applicants notified on a rolling basis starting 6/1; must reply within 2 week(s) of notification.

Academics. Special study options: Accelerated study, combined bachelor's/graduate degree, double major, dual enrollment of high school students, ESL, exchange student, honors, independent study, internships, liberal arts/career combination, semester at sea, student-designed major, study abroad, teacher certification program, Washington semester. 7 year medical program with UMDNJ, 7 year BS/OD program with SUNY, Mentored Undergraduate Research Experience (MUSE). **Credit/placement by examination:** AP, CLEP, IB, SAT, institutional tests. 30 credit hours maximum toward bachelor's degree. **Support services:** Learning center, pre-admission summer program, reduced course load, remedial instruction, study skills assistance, tutoring, writing center.

Majors. Area/ethnic studies: Women's. **Biology:** General. **Business:** Accounting, business admin. **Communications:** General. **Computer sciences:** General. **Education:** Art, biology, chemistry, Deaf/hearing impaired, early childhood, elementary, English, history, kindergarten/preschool, mathematics, music, physical, physics, social studies, Spanish, special ed, technology/industrial arts. **Engineering:** Biomedical, civil, computer, electrical, engineering science, mechanical. **English:** English lit. **Foreign languages:** Spanish. **Health services:** Nursing (RN). **History:** General. **Math:** General. **Philosophy/religion:** Philosophy. **Physical sciences:** Chemistry, physics. **Protective services:** Law enforcement admin. **Psychology:** General. **Social sciences:** Economics, international relations, political science, sociology.

Visual/performing arts: General, art, commercial/advertising art, multimedia, music, studio arts.

Most popular majors. Business/marketing 20%, education 21%, engineering/engineering technologies 7%, psychology 7%, social sciences 7%, visual/performing arts 6%.

Technology on campus. 150 workstations in dormitories, library, computer center, student center. Dormitories wired for high-speed internet access and linked to campus network. Commuter students can connect to campus network. Online course registration, online library, helpline, repair service, student web hosting, wireless network available.

Student life. Freshman orientation: Mandatory, $192 fee. Preregistration for classes offered. Four-part program including June advisement week, summer readings, welcome week, college seminar. **Policies:** Freshmen not permitted cars on campus. **Housing:** Guaranteed on-campus for freshmen. Coed dorms, single-sex dorms, apartments, themed housing, wellness housing available. $600 nonrefundable deposit, deadline 5/1. Pets allowed in dorm rooms. Housing for transfer students available. **Activities:** Bands, campus ministries, choral groups, dance, drama, film society, international student organizations, literary magazine, music ensembles, Model UN, musical theater, opera, radio station, student government, student newspaper, TV station, black student union, Amnesty International, Circle K, EOF Alliance, PRISM, UNBOUND, Hillel, activist coalition, women in learning & leadership.

Athletics. NCAA. **Intercollegiate:** Baseball M, basketball, cross-country, diving, field hockey W, football (tackle) M, lacrosse W, soccer, softball W, swimming, tennis, track and field, wrestling M. **Intramural:** Basketball, bowling, football (non-tackle), ice hockey, rugby, skiing, soccer, softball, tennis, volleyball, water polo. **Team name:** Lions.

Student services. Alcohol/substance abuse counseling, chaplain/spiritual director, career counseling, services for economically disadvantaged, student employment services, financial aid counseling, health services, minority student services, personal counseling, placement for graduates, veterans' counselor, women's services. **Physically disabled:** Services for visually, speech, hearing impaired.

Contact. E-mail: tcnjinfo@tcnj.edu
Phone: (609) 771-2131 Fax: (609) 637-5174
Grecia Montero, Director of Admissions, The College of New Jersey, Office of Undergraduate Admissions PO Box 7718, Ewing, NJ 08628-0718

College of St. Elizabeth
Morristown, New Jersey **CB member**
www.cse.edu **CB code: 2090**

- Private 4-year liberal arts college for women affiliated with the Roman Catholic Church
- Residential campus in large town
- 769 degree-seeking undergraduates: 31% part-time, 95% women, 29% African American, 3% Asian American, 21% Hispanic/Latino, 2% Multiracial, non-Hispanic, 3% international
- 398 degree-seeking graduate students
- 63% of applicants admitted
- SAT or ACT (ACT writing optional), application essay required
- 49% graduate within 6 years

General. Founded in 1899. Regionally accredited. Men admitted to adult undergraduate programs and master's programs. **Degrees:** 252 bachelor's awarded; master's, professional offered. **Location:** 35 Miles from Midtown New York City. **Calendar:** Semester, limited summer session. **Full-time faculty:** 48 total; 81% have terminal degrees, 8% minority, 69% women. **Part-time faculty:** 108 total; 6% minority, 65% women. **Class size:** 88% < 20, 12% 20-39. **Special facilities:** Library of rare books and manuscripts, Greek theater, Shakespeare garden, Holocaust education resource center, Center for Catholic women's history, Center for theological and spiritual development.

Freshman class profile. 804 applied, 508 admitted, 101 enrolled.

Mid 50% test scores		Return as sophomores:	71%
SAT critical reading:	350-440	Out-of-state:	6%
SAT math:	360-460	Live on campus:	88%
SAT writing:	360-450	International:	1%
End year in good standing:	71%		

Basis for selection. School achievement record and recommendations most important, followed by test scores, class rank; interview recommended. **Home schooled:** Letter of recommendation (nonparent) required. Applicants processed on individual basis. Must provide approved curriculum guide.

Learning Disabled: Submit your High School IEP to the Director for Students with Special Needs.

High school preparation. College-preparatory program required. 16 units required; 18 recommended. Required and recommended units include English 3, mathematics 2-3, history 1, science 1-2 (laboratory 1) and academic electives 8.

2015-2016 Annual costs. Tuition/fees: $31,679. Room/board: $12,744. Books/supplies: $1,300. Personal expenses: $1,378.

2014-2015 Financial aid. Need-based: 134 full-time freshmen applied for aid; 134 deemed to have need; 134 received aid. Average need met was 61%. Average scholarship/grant was $24,726; average loan $3,476. 74% of total undergraduate aid awarded as scholarships/grants, 26% as loans/jobs. **Non-need-based:** Awarded to 678 full-time undergraduates, including 153 freshmen. Scholarships awarded for academics, alumni affiliation, art, leadership, state residency.

Application procedures. Admission: Priority date 3/1; no deadline. $35 fee, may be waived for applicants with need. Admission notification on a rolling basis beginning on or about 11/22. Must reply by May 1 or within 2 week(s) if notified thereafter. **Financial aid:** Closing date 10/1. FAFSA required. Applicants notified on a rolling basis starting 11/15; must reply by 5/1 or within 2 week(s) of notification.

Academics. Students with 60 undergraduate credits may take accelerated programs. **Special study options:** Accelerated study, combined bachelor's/graduate degree, cross-registration, distance learning, double major, dual enrollment of high school students, ESL, exchange student, honors, independent study, internships, liberal arts/career combination, student-designed major, study abroad, teacher certification program, weekend college. **Credit/placement by examination:** AP, CLEP, IB. 30 credit hours maximum toward bachelor's degree. Credit for prior work and/or life experience offered via portfolio. **Support services:** Learning center, pre-admission summer program, reduced course load, remedial instruction, study skills assistance, tutoring, writing center.

Majors. Area/ethnic studies: American, women's. **Biology:** General, biochemistry. **Business:** Business admin. **Communications:** Communications/speech/rhetoric. **Computer sciences:** Computer science. **Education:** Multilevel teacher. **English:** English lit. **Foreign languages:** Spanish. **Health services:** Clinical lab science, dietetics, nursing (RN). **History:** General. **Math:** General. **Philosophy/religion:** Philosophy. **Physical sciences:** Chemistry. **Psychology:** General. **Social sciences:** Economics, sociology. **Theology:** Theology. **Visual/performing arts:** Art, music.

Most popular majors. Business/marketing 8%, health sciences 51%, interdisciplinary studies 11%, psychology 10%.

Technology on campus. 127 workstations in dormitories, library, computer center. Dormitories wired for high-speed internet access and linked to campus network. Commuter students can connect to campus network. Online course registration, online library, helpline, wireless network available.

Student life. Freshman orientation: Mandatory, $200 fee. Preregistration for classes offered. Comprehensive program held before start of classes for Women's College students. **Housing:** Guaranteed on-campus for all undergraduates. Wellness housing available. $200 nonrefundable deposit, deadline 5/1. **Activities:** Campus ministries, choral groups, drama, literary magazine, music ensembles, student government, student newspaper, volunteer services center, international/intercultural club, Latin Roots, Students Take Action Committee, foreign language club, American Chemical Society Affiliates, psychology club, sociology club.

Athletics. NCAA. **Intercollegiate:** Basketball W, cross-country W, lacrosse W, soccer W, softball W, swimming W, tennis W, volleyball W. **Intramural:** Volleyball W. **Team name:** Eagles.

Student services. Adult student services, alcohol/substance abuse counseling, chaplain/spiritual director, career counseling, services for economically disadvantaged, student employment services, financial aid counseling, health services, minority student services, personal counseling, placement for graduates, women's services. **Physically disabled:** Services for visually, speech, hearing impaired.

Contact. E-mail: apply@cse.edu
Phone: (973) 290-4700 Toll-free number: (800) 210-7900
Fax: (973) 290-4710
Adriana Arroyo, Dean of Undergraduate Admission, College of St. Elizabeth, 2 Convent Road, Morristown, NJ 07960-6989

DeVry University: North Brunswick
North Brunswick, New Jersey
www.devry.edu   CB code: 2203

- For-profit 4-year university
- Commuter campus in small city
- 930 degree-seeking undergraduates
- Interview required

General. Founded in 1996. Regionally accredited. Additional location in Paramus. **Degrees:** 160 bachelor's, 77 associate awarded; master's offered. **Location:** 30 miles from New York City. **Calendar:** Semester, extensive summer session. **Full-time faculty:** 34 total; 26% minority, 35% women. **Part-time faculty:** 125 total; 18% minority, 51% women.

Basis for selection. Applicants must have high school diploma or equivalent, degree from an accredited postsecondary institution, or submit acceptable test scores and be at least 17 years of age on the first day of classes. New students may enter at beginning of any semester. SAT or ACT recommended. CPT also accepted.

High school preparation. Required units include mathematics 1. Math unit must be algebra or higher.

2015-2016 Annual costs. Tuition/fees: $17,132. Books/supplies: $1,320. Personal expenses: $2,376.

Financial aid. All financial aid based on need.

Application procedures. Admission: No deadline. $40 fee. Admission notification on a rolling basis. **Financial aid:** No deadline. FAFSA required. Applicants notified on a rolling basis.

Academics. Special study options: Accelerated study, cooperative education, distance learning, weekend college. **Credit/placement by examination:** AP, CLEP, institutional tests. **Support services:** Learning center, remedial instruction, tutoring.

Majors. Business: Business admin. **Computer sciences:** Networking, systems analysis, web page design.

Most popular majors. Business/marketing 51%, computer/information sciences 37%, engineering/engineering technologies 12%.

Technology on campus. 575 workstations in library, computer center. Online course registration, online library, helpline available.

Student life. Freshman orientation: Mandatory. Preregistration for classes offered. **Activities:** Student government, Phi Theta Kappa, Golden Key, Institution of Electrical and Electronics Engineers, cultural exchange club, chess club, art club, Crusade for Christ.

Student services. Career counseling, student employment services, financial aid counseling, on-campus daycare, placement for graduates, veterans' counselor. **Physically disabled:** Services for visually, hearing impaired.

Contact. E-mail: admissions@devry.edu
Phone: (732) 729-3960 Toll-free number: (800) 333-3879
Fax: (732) 435-4850
Director of Admissions, DeVry University: North Brunswick, 630 US Highway One, North Brunswick, NJ 08902-3362

Drew University
Madison, New Jersey   CB member
www.drew.edu   CB code: 2193

- Private 4-year university and liberal arts college affiliated with the United Methodist Church
- Residential campus in large town
- 1,346 degree-seeking undergraduates: 1% part-time, 62% women, 10% African American, 6% Asian American, 10% Hispanic/Latino, 4% Multiracial, non-Hispanic, 5% international
- 616 degree-seeking graduate students
- 71% of applicants admitted
- Application essay required
- 67% graduate within 6 years

General. Founded in 1867. Regionally accredited. Classes in NYC semester programs and internships. **Degrees:** 325 bachelor's awarded; master's, professional, doctoral offered. **Location:** 29 miles from New York City. **Calendar:**

Semester, limited summer session. **Full-time faculty:** 146 total; 97% have terminal degrees, 18% minority, 49% women. **Part-time faculty:** 107 total. **Class size:** 72% < 20, 27% 20-39, 1% 40-49, less than 1% 50-99. **Special facilities:** Eighty-acre forest preserve, arboretum, photography gallery, observatory, research greenhouse, laser holography laboratory, center for the arts, music hall.

Freshman class profile. 3,025 applied, 2,145 admitted, 357 enrolled.

Mid 50% test scores		GPA 2.0-2.99:	11%
SAT critical reading:	500-620	Rank in top quarter:	65%
SAT math:	490-620	Rank in top tenth:	27%
SAT writing:	490-610	Return as sophomores:	85%
ACT composite:	22-29	Out-of-state:	36%
GPA 3.75 or higher:	43%	Live on campus:	87%
GPA 3.50-3.74:	15%	International:	4%
GPA 3.0-3.49:	31%		

Basis for selection. Grades and strength of curriculum are important. Standardized test scores are considered when submitted and are required for the Baldwin and Presidential scholarships. Leadership in activities, evidence of civic engagement, and the ability to write well are considered. The interview is strongly encouraged, especially for students interested in academic scholarships. Standardized tests are not required for admission to Drew but will be considered along with other academic credentials when submitted. Students who elect not to submit scores must typically have strong high school transcripts in a college-prep or honors program with not grade below a B. Note: Some academic scholarships will require standardized test scores. Essay required; interview STRONGLY recommended. **Home schooled:** Statement describing home school structure and mission, transcript of courses and grades required.

High school preparation. College-preparatory program recommended. Recommended units include English 4, mathematics 3, social studies 2, history 2, science 2, foreign language 2 and academic electives 3.

2015-2016 Annual costs. Tuition/fees: $46,384. Room/board: $12,672. Books/supplies: $1,128. Personal expenses: $2,122.

2014-2015 Financial aid. **Need-based:** 245 full-time freshmen applied for aid; 220 deemed to have need; 220 received aid. Average need met was 79%. Average scholarship/grant was $32,459; average loan $3,417. 87% of total undergraduate aid awarded as scholarships/grants, 13% as loans/jobs. **Non-need-based:** Awarded to 379 full-time undergraduates, including 95 freshmen. Scholarships awarded for academics, art, leadership, minority status, music/drama.

Application procedures. **Admission:** Priority date 2/1; deadline 2/15 (postmark date). $60 fee, may be waived for applicants with need. Admission notification by 3/25. Must reply by 5/1. **Financial aid:** Closing date 2/15. FAFSA required. Applicants notified by 3/25; must reply by 5/1.

Academics. RISE program enables students to conduct scientific research with retired industrial scientists who are still active researchers in their field. **Special study options:** Accelerated study, combined bachelor's/graduate degree, cross-registration, double major, dual enrollment of high school students, ESL, exchange student, honors, independent study, internships, New York semester, student-designed major, study abroad, teacher certification program, United Nations semester, Washington semester. Civic Scholars program, five-year dual degree program (BA/MA in teaching) program, seven-year dual degree program (BA/MD) with Rutgers-New Jersey Medical School, five-year dual degree program (BA/BS in engineering) with Columbia University, six-year dual degree (BA/JD) program with Seton Hall Law School, six-year dual degree program with New York Law School, five-year dual degree program (BA/MEM or MF) in Environmental Management or Forestry with Duke University, five-year dual degree program (BA/MA in Management) with Wake Forest University. **Credit/placement by examination:** AP, CLEP, IB, institutional tests. **Support services:** Learning center, pre-admission summer program, reduced course load, study skills assistance, tutoring, writing center.

Majors. **Area/ethnic studies:** African-American, Chinese, women's. **Biology:** General, biochemistry, neuroscience. **Business:** Business admin. **Computer sciences:** Computer science. **Conservation:** Environmental studies. **English:** English lit. **Foreign languages:** Classics, French, German, Spanish. **History:** General. **Math:** General. **Philosophy/religion:** Philosophy, religion. **Physical sciences:** Chemistry, physics. **Psychology:** General. **Social sciences:** Anthropology, economics, international relations, political science, sociology. **Visual/performing arts:** Art history/conservation, dramatic, music, studio arts.

Most popular majors. Biology 12%, business/marketing 8%, foreign language 6%, psychology 9%, social sciences 29%, visual/performing arts 15%.

Technology on campus. PC or laptop required. Dormitories wired for high-speed internet access and linked to campus network. Commuter students can connect to campus network. Online course registration, online library, helpline, repair service, wireless network available.

Student life. **Freshman orientation:** Mandatory, $300 fee. Preregistration for classes offered. Held in July for one day. Second part of program occurs in August, immediately prior to the start of the fall term. **Policies:** Freshmen not permitted cars on campus. **Housing:** Guaranteed on-campus for all undergraduates. Coed dorms, special housing for disabled, themed housing, wellness housing available. $250 nonrefundable deposit, deadline 5/1. Single sex floors, substance-free floors. **Activities:** Jazz band, campus ministries, choral groups, dance, drama, film society, international student organizations, literary magazine, music ensembles, Model UN, musical theater, radio station, student government, student newspaper, symphony orchestra, Catholic Campus Ministry, Hillel, InterVarsity Christian Fellowship, Muslim Student Association, International Student Caucus, Black Ministerial Caucus, Ariel (Latin student cultural society), Environmental Action League, University Democrats, University Republicans.

Athletics. NCAA. **Intercollegiate:** Baseball M, basketball, cross-country, equestrian W, fencing, field hockey W, lacrosse, soccer, softball W, swimming, tennis. **Intramural:** Basketball, football (non-tackle), racquetball, soccer, softball, squash, table tennis, volleyball. **Team name:** Rangers.

Student services. Adult student services, alcohol/substance abuse counseling, chaplain/spiritual director, career counseling, services for economically disadvantaged, student employment services, financial aid counseling, health services, minority student services, on-campus daycare, personal counseling, placement for graduates, women's services. **Physically disabled:** Services for visually, hearing impaired.

Contact. E-mail: cadm@drew.edu
Phone: (973) 408-3739 Fax: (973) 408-3068
James Skiff, Executive Director of College Admissions, Drew University, 36 Madison Avenue, Madison, NJ 07940-4063

Fairleigh Dickinson University: College at Florham
Madison, New Jersey
www.fdu.edu   CB code: 2262

- Private 4-year university
- Residential campus in large town
- 2,505 degree-seeking undergraduates: 5% part-time, 54% women, 11% African American, 4% Asian American, 16% Hispanic/Latino, 2% Multiracial, non-Hispanic
- 848 degree-seeking graduate students
- 83% of applicants admitted
- SAT or ACT (ACT writing optional) required
- 53% graduate within 6 years

General. Regionally accredited. Additional campus locations: Wroxton College, England and Vancouver, Canada. **Degrees:** 448 bachelor's awarded; master's, professional offered. **ROTC:** Army, Air Force. **Location:** 27 miles from New York City. **Calendar:** Semester, extensive summer session. **Full-time faculty:** 160 total. **Part-time faculty:** 282 total. **Class size:** 65% < 20, 34% 20-39, less than 1% 40-49, less than 1% 50-99, less than 1% >100. **Special facilities:** ITV multimedia classrooms, web-lab, regional center for college students with learning disabilities.

Freshman class profile. 4,559 applied, 3,791 admitted, 698 enrolled.

Mid 50% test scores		GPA 2.0-2.99:	34%
SAT critical reading:	460-570	Rank in top quarter:	39%
SAT math:	460-570	Rank in top tenth:	13%
SAT writing:	450-560	Return as sophomores:	82%
GPA 3.75 or higher:	19%	Out-of-state:	25%
GPA 3.50-3.74:	14%	Live on campus:	82%
GPA 3.0-3.49:	33%	International:	1%

Basis for selection. GPA and test scores most important. **Learning Disabled:** Separate application along with admissions application.

High school preparation. College-preparatory program required. 16 units required; 18 recommended. Required and recommended units include English 4, mathematics 3, history 2, science 2-3 (laboratory 2), foreign language 2 and academic electives 3-4.

2015-2016 Annual costs. Tuition/fees: $39,092. Room/board: $12,632.

Application procedures. **Admission:** Priority date 1/15; no deadline. $40 fee, may be waived for applicants with need, free for online applicants. Admission notification on a rolling basis beginning on or about 11/28. Must reply by May 1 or within 2 week(s) if notified thereafter. **Financial aid:** Priority date 2/15; no closing date. FAFSA required. Applicants notified on a rolling basis starting 2/1; must reply by 5/1 or within 4 week(s) of notification.

Academics. Special study options: Accelerated study, combined bachelor's/graduate degree, cooperative education, cross-registration, distance learning, double major, dual enrollment of high school students, external degree, honors, independent study, internships, liberal arts/career combination, student-designed major, study abroad, teacher certification program, Washington semester, weekend college. **Credit/placement by examination:** AP, CLEP, SAT, institutional tests. 30 credit hours maximum toward bachelor's degree. **Support services:** Learning center, pre-admission summer program, reduced course load, remedial instruction, study skills assistance, tutoring, writing center.

Majors. Biology: General, biochemistry. **Business:** Accounting, business admin, entrepreneurial studies, hospitality admin, managerial economics, marketing. **Communications:** Communications/speech/rhetoric. **Computer sciences:** General. **English:** Creative writing, English lit. **Foreign languages:** French, Spanish. **Health services:** Clinical lab science, medical radiologic technology/radiation therapy, nursing (RN), respiratory therapy technology. **History:** General. **Liberal arts:** Humanities. **Math:** General. **Philosophy/religion:** Philosophy. **Physical sciences:** Chemistry. **Psychology:** General. **Social sciences:** Criminology, economics, political science, sociology. **Visual/performing arts:** General, cinematography, dramatic.

Most popular majors. Biology 7%, business/marketing 29%, communications/journalism 10%, English 6%, psychology 15%, social sciences 8%, visual/performing arts 8%.

Technology on campus. 150 workstations in library, computer center. Dormitories wired for high-speed internet access and linked to campus network. Commuter students can connect to campus network. Online library, helpline, wireless network available.

Student life. Freshman orientation: Mandatory. Preregistration for classes offered. **Policies:** Freshmen not permitted cars on campus. **Housing:** Guaranteed on-campus for freshmen. Coed dorms, special housing for disabled, themed housing available. $350 nonrefundable deposit, deadline 5/1. **Activities:** Campus ministries, choral groups, dance, drama, film society, international student organizations, literary magazine, musical theater, radio station, student government, student newspaper, Green club, Florham Programming Committee, Association of Black Collegians, Latin American student organization, Hillel, New Social Engine, Straight and Gay Alliance, Student Volunteer Association, Musician's Guild, animal rights club.

Athletics. NCAA. **Intercollegiate:** Baseball M, basketball, cross-country, field hockey W, football (tackle) M, golf, lacrosse, soccer, softball W, swimming, tennis, volleyball W. **Intramural:** Basketball, football (tackle), soccer, softball, volleyball, weight lifting. **Team name:** Devils.

Student services. Adult student services, alcohol/substance abuse counseling, chaplain/spiritual director, career counseling, services for economically disadvantaged, student employment services, financial aid counseling, health services, minority student services, personal counseling, placement for graduates, veterans' counselor, women's services. **Physically disabled:** Services for visually, speech, hearing impaired.

Contact. E-mail: admissions@fdu.edu
Toll-free number: (800) 338-8803 Fax: (973) 443-8088
Jonathan Wexler, Vice President of Enrollment Management, Fairleigh Dickinson University: College at Florham, 285 Madison Avenue, M-RI0-01, Madison, NJ 07940

Fairleigh Dickinson University: Metropolitan Campus

Teaneck, New Jersey
www.fdu.edu   CB code: 2263

- Private 4-year university
- Commuter campus in large town
- 3,705 degree-seeking undergraduates: 31% part-time, 56% women, 12% African American, 5% Asian American, 36% Hispanic/Latino, 2% Multiracial, non-Hispanic, 8% international
- 2,959 degree-seeking graduate students
- 80% of applicants admitted
- SAT or ACT (ACT writing optional) required
- 53% graduate within 6 years

General. Founded in 1942. Regionally accredited. Additional campus at Wroxton College, England and Vancouver, Canada. **Degrees:** 861 bachelor's, 45 associate awarded; master's, professional, doctoral offered. **ROTC:** Army, Air Force. **Location:** 13 miles from New York City. **Calendar:** Semester, extensive summer session. **Full-time faculty:** 197 total. **Part-time faculty:**

634 total. **Class size:** 69% < 20, 28% 20-39, 2% 40-49, less than 1% 50-99, less than 1% >100. **Special facilities:** ITV multimedia classrooms, photonics lab, regional center for college students with learning disabilities, psychological services center, marine biology lab, cyber crime lab.

Freshman class profile. 4,491 applied, 3,571 admitted, 579 enrolled.

Mid 50% test scores			
SAT critical reading:	440-540	GPA 2.0-2.99:	29%
SAT math:	460-560	Rank in top quarter:	45%
SAT writing:	430-520	Rank in top tenth:	18%
GPA 3.75 or higher:	18%	Return as sophomores:	74%
GPA 3.50-3.74:	18%	Out-of-state:	10%
GPA 3.0-3.49:	35%	Live on campus:	39%
		International:	6%

Basis for selection. Standardized test scores and GPA most important. **Learning Disabled:** Regional center for college students with learning disabilities requires additional application.

High school preparation. College-preparatory program required. 16 units required; 18 recommended. Required and recommended units include English 4, mathematics 3, history 2, science 2-3 (laboratory 2-3), foreign language 2 and academic electives 3-4.

2015-2016 Annual costs. Tuition/fees: $36,910. Room/board: $12,918.

Application procedures. Admission: Priority date 3/15; no deadline. $40 fee, may be waived for applicants with need, free for online applicants. Admission notification on a rolling basis beginning on or about 11/28. Must reply by May 1 or within 2 week(s) if notified thereafter. **Financial aid:** Priority date 2/15; no closing date. Applicants notified on a rolling basis starting 3/1; must reply by 5/1 or within 2 week(s) of notification.

Academics. Core curriculum consists of 4 interdisciplinary courses. **Special study options:** Accelerated study, combined bachelor's/graduate degree, cooperative education, cross-registration, distance learning, ESL, exchange student, honors, independent study, internships, liberal arts/career combination, student-designed major, study abroad, teacher certification program, Washington semester, weekend college. **Credit/placement by examination:** AP, CLEP, institutional tests. 30 credit hours maximum toward bachelor's degree. **Support services:** Learning center, pre-admission summer program, reduced course load, remedial instruction, study skills assistance, tutoring, writing center.

Majors. Biology: General, biochemistry, marine. **Business:** Accounting, business admin, entrepreneurial studies, finance, hospitality admin, managerial economics, marketing, nonprofit/public. **Communications:** Organizational. **Computer sciences:** Computer science, information technology. **Conservation:** Environmental science. **Engineering:** Electrical. **English:** English lit. **Foreign languages:** French, Spanish. **Health services:** Clinical lab science, health information management, nursing (RN), radiologic technology/medical imaging. **History:** General. **Liberal arts:** Humanities. **Math:** General. **Philosophy/religion:** Philosophy. **Physical sciences:** Chemistry, physics. **Protective services:** Law enforcement admin. **Psychology:** General. **Social sciences:** Economics, international relations, political science, sociology. **Visual/performing arts:** General.

Most popular majors. Business/marketing 7%, health sciences 9%, liberal arts 49%, psychology 6%, security/protective services 7%.

Technology on campus. 225 workstations in library, computer center. Dormitories wired for high-speed internet access and linked to campus network. Commuter students can connect to campus network. Online library, helpline, wireless network available.

Student life. Freshman orientation: Mandatory. Preregistration for classes offered. **Housing:** Coed dorms, single-sex dorms, themed housing available. $350 nonrefundable deposit, deadline 5/1. LIFE house, honor's house, global scholar's hall available. **Activities:** Campus ministries, choral groups, dance, drama, film society, international student organizations, literary magazine, music ensembles, musical theater, radio station, student government, student newspaper, over 70 organizations.

Athletics. NCAA. **Intercollegiate:** Baseball M, basketball, bowling W, cross-country, fencing W, golf, soccer, softball W, tennis, track and field, volleyball W. **Intramural:** Badminton, basketball, football (non-tackle), soccer, table tennis, volleyball. **Team name:** Knights.

Student services. Adult student services, alcohol/substance abuse counseling, chaplain/spiritual director, career counseling, services for economically disadvantaged, student employment services, financial aid counseling, health services, minority student services, personal counseling, placement for graduates, veterans' counselor, women's services. **Physically disabled:** Services for visually, speech, hearing impaired.

Contact. E-mail: globaleducation@fdu.edu
Phone: (201) 692-7308 Toll-free number: (800) 338-8803
Fax: (201) 692-7319
Jonathan Wexler, Associate Vice President for Admissions and Financial Aid, Fairleigh Dickinson University: Metropolitan Campus, 1000 River Road, H-DH3-10, Teaneck, NJ 07666-1996

Felician University
Lodi, New Jersey
www.felician.edu
CB code: 2321

- Private 4-year liberal arts college affiliated with the Roman Catholic Church
- Commuter campus in large town
- 1,600 degree-seeking undergraduates: 13% part-time, 72% women, 22% African American, 5% Asian American, 28% Hispanic/Latino, 1% Multiracial, non-Hispanic, 2% international
- 348 degree-seeking graduate students
- 79% of applicants admitted
- SAT or ACT (ACT writing optional) required
- 39% graduate within 6 years

General. Founded in 1942. Regionally accredited. Additional campus in Rutherford. All programs spread through both campuses. **Degrees:** 444 bachelor's, 7 associate awarded; master's, doctoral offered. **ROTC:** Army, Air Force. **Location:** 12 miles from New York City. **Calendar:** Semester, limited summer session. **Full-time faculty:** 86 total; 67% have terminal degrees, 10% minority, 62% women. **Part-time faculty:** 126 total; 18% have terminal degrees, 10% minority, 56% women. **Class size:** 72% < 20, 26% 20-39, 1% 40-49, less than 1% 50-99. **Special facilities:** Nursing skills laboratory, performance and theater facilities.

Freshman class profile. 1,763 applied, 1,389 admitted, 298 enrolled.

Mid 50% test scores			
SAT critical reading:	390-470	Rank in top quarter:	30%
SAT math:	400-500	Rank in top tenth:	12%
SAT writing:	390-480	Return as sophomores:	84%
GPA 3.75 or higher:	14%	Out-of-state:	11%
GPA 3.50-3.74:	12%	Live on campus:	62%
GPA 3.0-3.49:	32%	International:	1%
GPA 2.0-2.99:	42%		

Basis for selection. School achievement record, test scores most important. Interview, school and community activities, recommendations of high school counselor considered. SAT and SAT Subject Tests or ACT recommended. Nursing students should have SAT or ACT scores submitted by February 15th, Nursing application deadline. Interview recommended for all; portfolio recommended for art programs.

High school preparation. College-preparatory program required. 19 units recommended. Recommended units include English 4, mathematics 3, social studies 3, science 3 and academic electives 6. Biology, chemistry, algebra required for nursing and medical laboratory technology applicants.

2015-2016 Annual costs. Tuition/fees: $31,335. Room/board: $11,900. Books/supplies: $1,250. Personal expenses: $1,900.

2014-2015 Financial aid. Need-based: 265 full-time freshmen applied for aid; 265 deemed to have need; 265 received aid. Average need met was 45%. Average scholarship/grant was $14,534; average loan $3,260. 74% of total undergraduate aid awarded as scholarships/grants, 26% as loans/jobs. **Non-need-based:** Awarded to 1,171 full-time undergraduates, including 308 freshmen. Scholarships awarded for academics, athletics.

Application procedures. Admission: Priority date 4/1; no deadline. $30 fee, may be waived for applicants with need. Admission notification by 12/1. Admission notification on a rolling basis. Must reply by May 1 or within 2 week(s) if notified thereafter. **Financial aid:** Priority date 2/15; no closing date. FAFSA required. Applicants notified by 3/1; Applicants notified on a rolling basis starting 4/1; must reply within 2 week(s) of notification.

Academics. Post-baccalaureate certification available in elementary and secondary education. **Special study options:** Accelerated study, combined bachelor's/graduate degree, cooperative education, cross-registration, distance learning, double major, dual enrollment of high school students, ESL, honors, independent study, internships, liberal arts/career combination, student-designed major, study abroad, teacher certification program. **Credit/placement by examination:** AP, CLEP, IB, institutional tests. 15 credit hours maximum toward associate degree, 30 toward bachelor's. **Support services:** Learning center, tutoring, writing center.

Majors. Biology: General, toxicology. **Business:** Accounting, business admin, international, marketing. **Communications:** Broadcast journalism,

communications/speech/rhetoric, digital media, journalism. **Computer sciences:** General, computer science. **Education:** Early childhood, early childhood special, elementary, mathematics, multi-level teacher, secondary. **English:** English lit. **Health services:** Cytotechnology, health care admin, nuclear medical technology, nursing (RN), respiratory therapy technology. **History:** General. **Liberal arts:** Humanities. **Math:** General. **Philosophy/religion:** Philosophy, religion. **Protective services:** Law enforcement admin. **Psychology:** General. **Social sciences:** General, political science, sociology. **Visual/performing arts:** Art, music, studio arts.

Most popular majors. Biology 9%, business/marketing 15%, education 6%, health sciences 45%, security/protective services 7%.

Technology on campus. 140 workstations in dormitories, library, computer center. Dormitories wired for high-speed internet access and linked to campus network. Commuter students can connect to campus network. Online library, repair service, wireless network available.

Student life. Freshman orientation: Mandatory. Preregistration for classes offered. Three summer programs available. **Policies:** No drugs or alcohol on campus. **Housing:** Guaranteed on-campus for freshmen. Single-sex dorms, special housing for disabled available. $200 nonrefundable deposit, deadline 5/1. **Activities:** Jazz band, campus ministries, choral groups, drama, international student organizations, music ensembles, Model UN, radio station, student government, Angelicum club, history club, RCIA, Kappa Sigma Xi, aspiring authors, Students in Free Enterprise, Kappa Gamma Pi.

Athletics. NAIA, NCAA. **Intercollegiate:** Baseball M, basketball, cross-country, golf M, soccer, softball W, track and field, volleyball W. **Intramural:** Basketball M, bowling. **Team name:** Golden Falcons.

Student services. Chaplain/spiritual director, career counseling, financial aid counseling, health services.

Contact. E-mail: admissions@felician.edu
Phone: (201) 355-1465 Fax: (201) 355-1443
Collen Fuller, Director of Undergraduate Admissions, Felician University, 262 South Main Street, Lodi, NJ 07644-2198

Georgian Court University
Lakewood, New Jersey
www.georgian.edu
CB member
CB code: 2274

- Private 4-year university and liberal arts college affiliated with the Roman Catholic Church
- Residential campus in large town
- 1,352 degree-seeking undergraduates: 8% part-time, 77% women, 14% African American, 2% Asian American, 10% Hispanic/Latino, 2% Multiracial, non-Hispanic, 1% international
- 589 degree-seeking graduate students
- 96% of applicants admitted
- SAT or ACT (ACT writing optional) required
- 52% graduate within 6 years

General. Founded in 1908. Regionally accredited. **Degrees:** 348 bachelor's awarded; master's offered. **Location:** 60 miles from New York and Philadelphia. **Calendar:** Semester, limited summer session. **Full-time faculty:** 86 total; 92% have terminal degrees, 21% minority, 60% women. **Part-time faculty:** 161 total; 20% have terminal degrees, 11% minority, 64% women. **Class size:** 76% < 20, 24% 20-39. **Special facilities:** Estate and gardens, arboretum.

Freshman class profile. 1,004 applied, 963 admitted, 151 enrolled.

Mid 50% test scores			
SAT critical reading:	420-510	Rank in top quarter:	28%
SAT math:	420-540	Rank in top tenth:	7%
SAT writing:	410-520	Return as sophomores:	78%
GPA 3.75 or higher:	17%	Out-of-state:	11%
GPA 3.50-3.74:	19%	Live on campus:	64%
GPA 3.0-3.49:	39%	International:	1%
GPA 2.0-2.99:	23%		

Basis for selection. Completed high school program reviewed for rigor of courses and grades received. Students should be completing program of 16 academic units with grades of 2.5 or higher. Students not meeting criteria referred to faculty committee for review. **Home schooled:** Statement describing home school structure and mission required.

High school preparation. College-preparatory program required. 16 units required. Required units include English 4, mathematics 2, history 1, (laboratory 1), foreign language 2 and academic electives 6.

2015-2016 Annual costs. Tuition/fees: $31,618. Room/board: $10,808. Books/supplies: $1,350. Personal expenses: $1,200.

2015-2016 Financial aid. Need-based: 147 full-time freshmen applied for aid; 135 deemed to have need; 135 received aid. Average need met was 79%. Average scholarship/grant was $16,142; average loan $5,936. 70% of total undergraduate aid awarded as scholarships/grants, 30% as loans/jobs. **Non-need-based:** Awarded to 247 full-time undergraduates, including 26 freshmen. Scholarships awarded for academics, alumni affiliation, art, athletics, leadership, religious affiliation, state residency.

Application procedures. Admission: Closing date 8/1 (receipt date). $40 fee, may be waived for applicants with need. Admission notification on a rolling basis beginning on or about 10/1. Must reply by May 1 or within 2 week(s) if notified thereafter. **Financial aid:** Priority date 4/15, closing date 7/1. FAFSA required. Applicants notified on a rolling basis; must reply within 2 week(s) of notification.

Academics. Special study options: Accelerated study, combined bachelor's/graduate degree, distance learning, double major, dual enrollment of high school students, ESL, honors, independent study, internships, liberal arts/career combination, study abroad, teacher certification program. **Credit/placement by examination:** AP, CLEP, institutional tests. 30 credit hours maximum toward bachelor's degree. **Support services:** Learning center, reduced course load, remedial instruction, study skills assistance, tutoring, writing center.

Majors. Biology: General, biochemistry. **Business:** Accounting, business admin, hospitality admin. **Communications:** Communications/speech/rhetoric. **Education:** Elementary. **English:** English lit. **Foreign languages:** Spanish. **Health services:** Clinical lab science, nursing (RN). **History:** General. **Human services:** Social work. **Liberal arts:** Humanities. **Math:** General. **Parks/recreation:** Exercise sciences. **Philosophy/religion:** Religion. **Physical sciences:** Chemistry. **Protective services:** Criminal justice. **Psychology:** General, behavior analysis. **Visual/performing arts:** Art, dance.

Most popular majors. Business/marketing 11%, English 8%, health sciences 10%, psychology 30%, visual/performing arts 6%.

Technology on campus. 257 workstations in dormitories, library, computer center. Dormitories wired for high-speed internet access and linked to campus network. Commuter students can connect to campus network. Online course registration, online library, helpline, wireless network available.

Student life. Freshman orientation: Mandatory, $176 fee. Preregistration for classes offered. Two full days held before classes begin. **Housing:** Guaranteed on-campus for all undergraduates. Coed dorms, special housing for disabled available. $250 deposit, deadline 5/1. **Activities:** Bands, campus ministries, choral groups, dance, drama, international student organizations, literary magazine, music ensembles, Model UN, student government, student newspaper, Council for exceptional children, ODK, Black student union, Latin American student organization, ONE, Identity, Ink, nursing club, psychology club, Women in Leadership Development.

Athletics. NCAA. **Intercollegiate:** Basketball, cross-country, lacrosse, soccer, softball W, tennis W, track and field, volleyball W. **Team name:** Lions.

Student services. Alcohol/substance abuse counseling, chaplain/spiritual director, career counseling, services for economically disadvantaged, financial aid counseling, health services, personal counseling. **Physically disabled:** Services for visually, speech, hearing impaired.

Contact. E-mail: admissions@georgian.edu
Phone: (732) 987-2700 Toll-free number: (800) 458-8422 ext. 2760
Tracey Howard-Ubelhoer, Director of Admissions, Georgian Court University, 900 Lakewood Avenue, Lakewood, NJ 08701-2697

Kean University
Union, New Jersey
www.kean.edu
CB member
CB code: 2517

- Public 4-year university and liberal arts college
- Small city
- 11,755 degree-seeking undergraduates: 22% part-time, 60% women, 20% African American, 5% Asian American, 27% Hispanic/Latino, 2% Multi-racial, non-Hispanic, 2% international
- 2,138 degree-seeking graduate students
- 74% of applicants admitted
- SAT or ACT (ACT writing optional) required
- 50% graduate within 6 years

General. Founded in 1855. Regionally accredited. Additional locations in Toms River, NJ and Wenzhou, China. **Degrees:** 2,712 bachelor's awarded; master's, doctoral offered. **ROTC:** Army, Air Force. **Calendar:** Semester, extensive summer session. **Full-time faculty:** 336 total; 84% have terminal degrees, 27% minority, 53% women. **Part-time faculty:** 1,026 total; 22% minority, 53% women. **Class size:** 35% < 20, 64% 20-39, less than 1% 40-49, less than 1% 50-99. **Special facilities:** Holocaust resource center, ethnic studies center, center for science/technology/mathematics, museum.

Freshman class profile. 7,944 applied, 5,900 admitted, 1,518 enrolled.

Mid 50% test scores			
SAT critical reading:	410-500	GPA 2.0-2.99:	41%
SAT math:	430-520	Rank in top quarter:	28%
ACT composite:	17-21	Rank in top tenth:	11%
GPA 3.75 or higher:	9%	Return as sophomores:	74%
GPA 3.50-3.74:	13%	Out-of-state:	5%
GPA 3.0-3.49:	37%	Live on campus:	42%
		International:	2%

Basis for selection. Academic GPA and rigor of secondary school record very important; standardized test scores important. Non-US-educated applicants evaluated based on their academic record in home country. If needed, applicants are advised of specific additional requirements. SAT or ACT test not required for EPIC or Spanish Speaking Program (SSP) students. Essay/Personal statement and two (2) letters of recommendation are recommended, but not required. College of Visual & Performing Arts and Robert Busch School of Design require auditions and portfolio review, respectively. **Home schooled:** State high school equivalency certificate required.

High school preparation. College-preparatory program recommended. 16 units required; 20 recommended. Required and recommended units include English 4, mathematics 3, social studies 2, history 2, science 2 (laboratory 2), foreign language 2 and academic electives 5.

2015-2016 Annual costs. Tuition/fees: $11,581; $18,183 out-of-state. Room/board: $12,565.

2015-2016 Financial aid. Need-based: 1,332 full-time freshmen applied for aid; 1,165 deemed to have need; 1,096 received aid. Average need met was 82%. Average scholarship/grant was $8,555; average loan $3,387. 60% of total undergraduate aid awarded as scholarships/grants, 40% as loans/jobs. **Non-need-based:** Awarded to 791 full-time undergraduates, including 218 freshmen. Scholarships awarded for academics, art, leadership, music/drama.

Application procedures. Admission: Priority date 4/30; deadline 8/15 (postmark date). $75 fee, may be waived for applicants with need. Admission notification on a rolling basis beginning on or about 11/1. Must reply by May 1 or within 2 week(s) if notified thereafter. **Financial aid:** Closing date 4/17. FAFSA required. Applicants notified on a rolling basis starting 3/1; must reply by 5/1.

Academics. Special study options: Combined bachelor's/graduate degree, cooperative education, cross-registration, distance learning, double major, dual enrollment of high school students, ESL, honors, independent study, internships, liberal arts/career combination, study abroad, teacher certification program, weekend college. 2-year bachelor's degree program for RNs, foreign transfer programs, TraveLearn. **Credit/placement by examination:** AP, CLEP, IB, SAT, ACT, institutional tests. **Support services:** Learning center, pre-admission summer program, reduced course load, remedial instruction, study skills assistance, tutoring, writing center.

Majors. Architecture: Architecture. **Area/ethnic studies:** Asian. **Biology:** General. **Business:** Accounting, business admin, finance, international, marketing. **Communications:** Communications/speech/rhetoric. **Computer sciences:** General, networking. **Education:** Elementary, kindergarten/preschool, music, physical, special ed. **English:** English lit. **Foreign languages:** Spanish. **Health services:** Athletic training, clinical lab science, health information management. **History:** General. **Human services:** General. **Math:** General. **Parks/recreation:** Facilities management. **Physical sciences:** Chemistry, geology. **Protective services:** Law enforcement admin. **Psychology:** General. **Social sciences:** Economics, political science, sociology. **Visual/performing arts:** Acting, art, art history/conservation, design, dramatic, industrial design, interior design, music, music performance, studio arts, theater design.

Most popular majors. Biology 7%, business/marketing 16%, communications/journalism 6%, education 14%, health sciences 7%, psychology 17%, security/protective services 6%, visual/performing arts 6%.

Technology on campus. 1,700 workstations in dormitories, library, computer center, student center. Dormitories wired for high-speed internet access and linked to campus network. Commuter students can connect to campus network. Online course registration, online library, student web hosting, wireless network available.

Student life. Freshman orientation: Mandatory, $50 fee. Preregistration for classes offered. One-day program held prior to start of the fall semester. **Policies:** Freshmen not permitted cars on campus. **Housing:** Coed dorms, special housing for disabled, apartments available. $125 nonrefundable deposit, deadline 5/1. Freshmen housing, floor for women-only, floor for transfer students, floor for graduate students, living learning communities for SIMS (Success in Math & Science), and WELL (Women Empowered toward Leadership and Learning) available. **Activities:** Bands, campus ministries, choral groups, dance, drama, film society, international student organizations, literary magazine, music ensembles, musical theater, radio station, student government, student newspaper, symphony orchestra, TV station, Filipinos Uniting Nations at Kean, Haitian Student Association, Italian Cultural Experience, Pan-African Student Union, West Indian culture club, Catholic Newman club, Coptic Orthodox Christian Fellowship, Cru at Kean University, Equality for All.

Athletics. NCAA. **Intercollegiate:** Baseball M, basketball, field hockey W, football (tackle) M, lacrosse, soccer, softball W, tennis W, volleyball. **Intramural:** Basketball, football (non-tackle), sand volleyball, soccer, softball, tennis, ultimate frisbee, volleyball, weight lifting. **Team name:** Cougars.

Student services. Adult student services, alcohol/substance abuse counseling, chaplain/spiritual director, career counseling, services for economically disadvantaged, student employment services, financial aid counseling, health services, minority student services, on-campus daycare, personal counseling, placement for graduates, veterans' counselor, women's services. **Physically disabled:** Services for visually, speech, hearing impaired.

Contact. E-mail: admitme@kean.edu
Phone: (908) 737-7100 Fax: (908) 737-7105
Jennifer Kanellis, Director of University Admissions, Kean University, Office of Admissions - Kean Hall, Union, NJ 07083-0411

Monmouth University
West Long Branch, New Jersey — CB member
www.monmouth.edu — CB code: 2416

- Private 4-year university
- Residential campus in small town
- 4,661 degree-seeking undergraduates: 5% part-time, 58% women, 5% African American, 3% Asian American, 11% Hispanic/Latino, 2% Multiracial, non-Hispanic, 1% international
- 1,580 degree-seeking graduate students
- 78% of applicants admitted
- SAT or ACT (ACT writing optional), application essay required
- 67% graduate within 6 years; 33% enter graduate study

General. Founded in 1933. Regionally accredited. **Degrees:** 1,107 bachelor's, 1 associate awarded; master's, professional offered. **ROTC:** Army, Air Force. **Location:** 50 miles from New York City, 75 miles from Philadelphia. **Calendar:** Semester, extensive summer session. **Full-time faculty:** 288 total; 80% have terminal degrees, 17% minority, 54% women. **Part-time faculty:** 350 total; 25% have terminal degrees, 9% minority, 50% women. **Class size:** 39% < 20, 61% 20-39, less than 1% 40-49. **Special facilities:** Multimedia communications center with TV and radio station, sculpture garden, ice house-gallery, six lane indoor track, financial markets lab, community garden, bowling alley, vineyard, Center for Speech and Language Disorders.

Freshman class profile. 8,486 applied, 6,651 admitted, 1,128 enrolled.

Mid 50% test scores			
SAT critical reading:	480-570	GPA 2.0-2.99:	24%
SAT math:	470-550	Rank in top quarter:	39%
SAT writing:	440-560	Rank in top tenth:	14%
ACT composite:	20-25	End year in good standing:	98%
GPA 3.75 or higher:	19%	Return as sophomores:	83%
GPA 3.50-3.74:	19%	Out-of-state:	18%
GPA 3.0-3.49:	38%	Live on campus:	82%
		International:	1%

Basis for selection. School record, GPA, test scores important followed by recommendations and essay. Resume of activities including community involvement and leadership positions encouraged. One letter of recommendation required. Audition recommended for music programs; portfolio recommended for art programs; interview recommended for music. **Home schooled:** Transcript of courses and grades, letter of recommendation (nonparent) required. All students who submit portfolio of coursework in lieu of transcript must also complete institution's curriculum chart for homeschooled students. State certificate required only when required by state where home schooled.

High school preparation. College-preparatory program recommended. 16 units required; 20 recommended. Required and recommended units include English 4, mathematics 3, social studies 2, history 2, science 2 (laboratory 1), foreign language 2 and academic electives 5.

2015-2016 Annual costs. Tuition/fees: $33,728. Room/board: $12,506. Books/supplies: $1,184. Personal expenses: $2,197.

2015-2016 Financial aid. Need-based: 1,034 full-time freshmen applied for aid; 889 deemed to have need; 889 received aid. Average need met was

66%. Average scholarship/grant was $11,806; average loan $3,474. 60% of total undergraduate aid awarded as scholarships/grants, 40% as loans/jobs. **Non-need-based:** Awarded to 4,746 full-time undergraduates, including 1,128 freshmen. Scholarships awarded for academics, alumni affiliation, art, athletics, state residency.

Application procedures. Admission: Priority date 12/1; deadline 3/1 (postmark date). $50 fee, may be waived for applicants with need. Admission notification by 4/1. Must reply by 5/1. All deposits non-refundable after May 1. **Financial aid:** Priority date 2/15; no closing date. FAFSA required. Applicants notified on a rolling basis starting 3/1; must reply within 2 week(s) of notification.

Academics. Special study options: Accelerated study, combined bachelor's/graduate degree, cooperative education, cross-registration, distance learning, double major, dual enrollment of high school students, honors, independent study, internships, liberal arts/career combination, student-designed major, study abroad, teacher certification program, Washington semester. **Credit/placement by examination:** AP, CLEP, IB, SAT, ACT, institutional tests. AP credit awarded only for institutional course equivalents. **Support services:** Learning center, reduced course load, remedial instruction, study skills assistance, tutoring, writing center.

Honors college/program. SAT score and 3.5 GPA required for consideration. Honors has learning communities. Students in the Honors School must fulfill all the requirements of their major and successfully complete 25 credits of Honors courses including an Honors Thesis. The Honor Thesis is completed over the last two semesters and defended before a faculty committee.

Majors. Biology: General, environmental. **Business:** Business admin, international. **Communications:** Communications/speech/rhetoric. **Computer sciences:** General. **Education:** General, special ed. **Engineering:** Software. **English:** English lit. **Foreign languages:** General. **Health services:** Clinical lab science, nursing (RN). **History:** General. **Human services:** Social work. **Math:** General. **Parks/recreation:** Health/fitness. **Physical sciences:** Chemistry. **Protective services:** Criminal justice. **Psychology:** General. **Social sciences:** Anthropology, political science, sociology. **Visual/performing arts:** Art, graphic design, music, studio arts.

Most popular majors. Business/marketing 23%, communications/journalism 12%, education 11%, health sciences 6%, psychology 7%, security/protective services 7%, social sciences 6%.

Technology on campus. 1,000 workstations in dormitories, library, computer center, student center. Dormitories wired for high-speed internet access and linked to campus network. Commuter students can connect to campus network. Online library, helpline, student web hosting, wireless network available.

Student life. Freshman orientation: Mandatory, $200 fee. Preregistration for classes offered. Two-day session held in July. **Policies:** Must complete at least 12 credit hours to associate with a fraternity or sorority. Students must have 2.2 GPA and be registered full-time. Transfer students taking 12 or more credits may also associate. **Housing:** Guaranteed on-campus for freshmen. Coed dorms, apartments, themed housing available. $150 nonrefundable deposit, deadline 5/1. Honors residence available. **Activities:** Bands, campus ministries, choral groups, dance, drama, international student organizations, literary magazine, music ensembles, musical theater, radio station, student government, student newspaper, TV station, Hillel, Catholic Ministry, African-American Student Union, Latin American Student Organization, Circle K, All Lifestyles Included, Global Service Project, Students United Way, Muslim Student Association, Political Science Club.

Athletics. NCAA. **Intercollegiate:** Baseball M, basketball, bowling W, cross-country, field hockey W, football (tackle) M, golf, lacrosse, soccer, softball W, swimming, tennis, track and field. **Intramural:** Basketball, football (non-tackle), soccer, softball, volleyball. **Team name:** Hawks.

Student services. Alcohol/substance abuse counseling, chaplain/spiritual director, career counseling, services for economically disadvantaged, student employment services, financial aid counseling, health services, legal services, personal counseling, placement for graduates, veterans' counselor, women's services. **Physically disabled:** Services for visually, speech, hearing impaired.

Contact. E-mail: admission@monmouth.edu
Phone: (732) 571-3456 Toll-free number: (800) 543-9671
Fax: (732) 263-5166
Victoria Bobik, Director of Undergraduate Admission, Monmouth University, 400 Cedar Avenue, West Long Branch, NJ 07764-1898

Montclair State University
Montclair, New Jersey — CB member
www.montclair.edu — CB code: 2520

- Public 4-year university
- Residential campus in large town

- 16,129 degree-seeking undergraduates: 11% part-time, 62% women, 11% African American, 5% Asian American, 25% Hispanic/Latino, 3% Multi-racial, non-Hispanic, 2% international
- 3,567 degree-seeking graduate students
- 70% of applicants admitted
- 66% graduate within 6 years; 16% enter graduate study

General. Founded in 1908. Regionally accredited. **Degrees:** 3,392 bachelor's awarded; master's, professional, doctoral offered. **Location:** 14 miles from New York City. **Calendar:** Semester, limited summer session. **Full-time faculty:** 604 total; 91% have terminal degrees, 27% minority, 48% women. **Part-time faculty:** 1,210 total; 12% minority, 54% women. **Class size:** 34% < 20, 63% 20-39, 2% 40-49, 1% 50-99, less than 1% >100. **Special facilities:** Observatory, child care center, ice arena, train station, diner.

Freshman class profile. 11,990 applied, 8,401 admitted, 3,115 enrolled.

Mid 50% test scores		Rank in top quarter:	37%
SAT critical reading:	430-540	Rank in top tenth:	10%
SAT math:	440-550	End year in good standing:	90%
SAT writing:	430-540	Return as sophomores:	83%
GPA 3.75 or higher:	9%	Out-of-state:	4%
GPA 3.50-3.74:	15%	Live on campus:	45%
GPA 3.0-3.49:	52%	International:	1%
GPA 2.0-2.99:	24%		

Basis for selection. School achievement record most important. Extracurricular activities, test scores, community activities also important. Consideration given to disadvantaged applicants. SAT math used for placement testing exemption. Interview required for communication, speech; audition required for dance, music, speech, theater programs; portfolio required for art programs. **Home schooled:** Statement describing home school structure and mission, transcript of courses and grades, state high school equivalency certificate required.

High school preparation. College-preparatory program required. 16 units required. Required units include English 4, mathematics 3, social studies 2, science 2 (laboratory 2), foreign language 2 and academic electives 3. 4 math (including trigonometry) required of computer science majors. Algebra II required for business administration majors. 3 additional units in English, social studies, science, math, or foreign language required.

2015-2016 Annual costs. Tuition/fees: $11,773; $20,320 out-of-state. Room/board: $13,884. Books/supplies: $1,225. Personal expenses: $2,096.

2014-2015 Financial aid. **Need-based:** 2,625 full-time freshmen applied for aid; 2,174 deemed to have need; 1,950 received aid. Average scholarship/grant was $9,844; average loan $3,470. 57% of total undergraduate aid awarded as scholarships/grants, 43% as loans/jobs. **Non-need-based:** Awarded to 2,142 full-time undergraduates, including 141 freshmen. Scholarships awarded for academics, alumni affiliation, art.

Application procedures. Admission: Priority date 12/15; deadline 3/1 (postmark date). $65 fee, may be waived for applicants with need. Application must be submitted online. Admission notification on a rolling basis beginning on or about 12/15. Must reply by 5/1. Immediate decision process available to seniors at some local high schools. **Financial aid:** Priority date 3/15; no closing date. FAFSA required. Applicants notified on a rolling basis starting 4/1; must reply within 2 week(s) of notification.

Academics. Special study options: Combined bachelor's/graduate degree, cooperative education, double major, ESL, honors, independent study, internships, semester at sea, study abroad, teacher certification program, Washington semester. Joint admission with UMDNJ. **Credit/placement by examination:** AP, CLEP, IB, institutional tests. 24 credit hours maximum toward bachelor's degree. **Support services:** Learning center, pre-admission summer program, reduced course load, remedial instruction, tutoring, writing center.

Honors college/program. Two of the following required: rank in top 10% of high school class; 600 SAT verbal or math; 1200 SAT (exclusive of Writing); unusual ability in creative arts or exceptional leadership or other extraordinary accomplishment.

Majors. Area/ethnic studies: Women's. **Biology:** General, biochemistry, marine, molecular. **Business:** Accounting, business admin, hospitality admin. **Communications:** Journalism, organizational, radio/TV. **Computer sciences:** General, information technology. **Education:** Business, drama/dance, health, physical. **English:** English lit. **Foreign languages:** Classics, French, German, Italian, Latin, linguistics, Spanish. **Health services:** Athletic training, music therapy. **History:** General. **Human services:** Youth services. **Liberal arts:** Humanities. **Math:** General. **Parks/recreation:** Exercise sciences. **Philosophy/religion:** Philosophy, religion. **Physical sciences:** Chemistry, geology, physics. **Psychology:** General. **Social sciences:** Anthropology, economics, geography, political science, sociology. **Visual/performing arts:**

Art, cinematography, dance, dramatic, fashion design, graphic design, industrial design, music, music performance. **Work/family studies:** General, food/nutrition.

Most popular majors. Biology 6%, business/marketing 16%, family/consumer sciences 11%, interdisciplinary studies 6%, psychology 11%, social sciences 7%, visual/performing arts 13%.

Technology on campus. 700 workstations in dormitories, library, computer center, student center. Dormitories wired for high-speed internet access and linked to campus network. Commuter students can connect to campus network. Online course registration, online library, helpline, repair service, wireless network available.

Student life. Freshman orientation: Mandatory. Preregistration for classes offered. **Policies:** Freshmen not permitted cars on campus. **Housing:** Guaranteed on-campus for freshmen. Coed dorms, single-sex dorms, special housing for disabled, apartments, themed housing available. $300 nonrefundable deposit, deadline 5/1. **Activities:** Bands, campus ministries, choral groups, dance, drama, international student organizations, literary magazine, music ensembles, Model UN, musical theater, opera, radio station, student government, student newspaper, symphony orchestra, TV station, Newman Catholic Center, college life union board, Muslim student association, organization for students of African unity, Latin American student organization, Femvolution, Bonners, Hillel.

Athletics. NCAA. **Intercollegiate:** Baseball M, basketball, diving, field hockey W, football (tackle) M, lacrosse, soccer, softball W, swimming, track and field, volleyball W. **Intramural:** Badminton, basketball, bowling, football (tackle) M, golf, handball, racquetball, soccer, softball, table tennis, tennis, volleyball, water polo. **Team name:** Red Hawks.

Student services. Adult student services, alcohol/substance abuse counseling, chaplain/spiritual director, career counseling, services for economically disadvantaged, student employment services, financial aid counseling, health services, on-campus daycare, personal counseling, placement for graduates, veterans' counselor, women's services. **Physically disabled:** Services for visually, speech, hearing impaired.

Contact. E-mail: msuadm@mail.montclair.edu
Phone: (973) 655-4444 Toll-free number: (800) 331-9205
Fax: (973) 655-7700
Jeffrey Indiveri-Gant, Director of Admissions, Montclair State University, One Normal Avenue, Montclair, NJ 07043

New Jersey City University
Jersey City, New Jersey
CB member
www.njcu.edu
CB code: 2516

- Public 4-year university
- Commuter campus in small city
- 6,201 degree-seeking undergraduates: 23% part-time, 60% women, 21% African American, 7% Asian American, 35% Hispanic/Latino, 1% Native Hawaiian/Pacific islander, 2% Multi-racial, non-Hispanic, 3% international
- 1,471 degree-seeking graduate students
- 87% of applicants admitted
- Application essay required
- 30% graduate within 6 years

General. Founded in 1927. Regionally accredited. **Degrees:** 1,482 bachelor's awarded; master's, doctoral offered. **ROTC:** Army, Air Force. **Location:** 5 miles from New York City. **Calendar:** Semester, extensive summer session. **Full-time faculty:** 251 total; 38% minority, 52% women. **Part-time faculty:** 558 total; 26% minority. **Class size:** 49% < 20, 51% 20-39. **Special facilities:** Laboratory school for multihandicapped children, computer technology center, cooperative education, media studies center.

Freshman class profile. 2,789 applied, 2,419 admitted, 819 enrolled.

Mid 50% test scores		Rank in top quarter:	29%
SAT critical reading:	370-470	Rank in top tenth:	9%
SAT math:	390-500	Return as sophomores:	74%
GPA 3.75 or higher:	8%	Out-of-state:	1%
GPA 3.50-3.74:	8%	Live on campus:	31%
GPA 3.0-3.49:	25%	International:	4%
GPA 2.0-2.99:	58%		

Basis for selection. High school courses, grades, class rank, and test scores most important, followed by essay or personal statement. Special program for educationally disadvantaged applicants available with above criteria. SAT or ACT recommended. Interview recommended for all; audition required for music programs; portfolio recommended for art programs.

High school preparation. College-preparatory program recommended. 16 units required; 21 recommended. Required and recommended units include English 4, mathematics 4, social studies 4, science 4 (laboratory 2-3) and foreign language 2.

2015-2016 Annual costs. Tuition/fees: $11,179; $20,008 out-of-state. Room/board: $11,618. Books/supplies: $2,130. Personal expenses: $2,758.

2014-2015 Financial aid. Need-based: 609 full-time freshmen applied for aid; 553 deemed to have need; 530 received aid. Average scholarship/grant was $9,400; average loan $3,316. 68% of total undergraduate aid awarded as scholarships/grants, 32% as loans/jobs. **Non-need-based:** Awarded to 590 full-time undergraduates, including 113 freshmen. Scholarships awarded for academics.

Application procedures. Admission: Closing date 4/1. $50 fee, may be waived for applicants with need. Admission notification on a rolling basis beginning on or about 1/1. Must reply by May 1 or within 3 week(s) if notified thereafter. **Financial aid:** Priority date 4/15; no closing date. FAFSA required. Applicants notified by 5/15.

Academics. Cooperative education placement offered in all majors. Professional diploma in school psychology offered. **Special study options:** Accelerated study, cooperative education, cross-registration, distance learning, double major, dual enrollment of high school students, ESL, honors, independent study, internships, study abroad, teacher certification program, Washington semester, weekend college. **Credit/placement by examination:** AP, CLEP, IB, institutional tests. 30 credit hours maximum toward bachelor's degree. **Support services:** Learning center, pre-admission summer program, reduced course load, remedial instruction, tutoring, writing center.

Majors. Area/ethnic studies: Women's. **Biology:** General. **Business:** Business admin. **Communications:** Communications/speech/rhetoric. **Computer sciences:** General. **Education:** Early childhood, elementary, reading, special ed. **English:** English lit. **Foreign languages:** Spanish. **Health services:** Clinical lab science, nursing (RN). **History:** General. **Math:** General. **Philosophy/religion:** Philosophy. **Physical sciences:** Chemistry, geology, physics. **Protective services:** Firefighting, security services. **Psychology:** General. **Social sciences:** Economics, political science, sociology. **Visual/performing arts:** Art, music, studio arts.

Most popular majors. Business/marketing 20%, health sciences 16%, psychology 14%, security/protective services 17%, social sciences 8%.

Technology on campus. 704 workstations in dormitories, library, computer center, student center. Dormitories wired for high-speed internet access and linked to campus network. Commuter students can connect to campus network. Online course registration, online library, helpline, wireless network available.

Student life. Freshman orientation: Mandatory. Preregistration for classes offered. **Housing:** Coed dorms available. $150 nonrefundable deposit, deadline 8/13. **Activities:** Bands, campus ministries, choral groups, dance, drama, literary magazine, music ensembles, musical theater, opera, radio station, student government, student newspaper, symphony orchestra, Campus Christian fellowship, black freedom society, Latin power association, Africana journal.

Athletics. NCAA. **Intercollegiate:** Baseball M, basketball, bowling W, cross-country, soccer, softball W, track and field W, volleyball. **Intramural:** Basketball, bowling, racquetball, soccer, softball, swimming, table tennis, volleyball, weight lifting. **Team name:** Gothic Knights.

Student services. Chaplain/spiritual director, career counseling, student employment services, financial aid counseling, health services, on-campus daycare, personal counseling, placement for graduates, veterans' counselor, women's services. **Physically disabled:** Services for visually, speech, hearing impaired.

Contact. E-mail: admissions@njcu.edu
Phone: (201) 200-3234 Toll-free number: (888) 441-6528
Jose Balda, Director of Admissions, New Jersey City University, 2039 Kennedy Boulevard, Jersey City, NJ 07305-1597

New Jersey Institute of Technology
Newark, New Jersey   CB member
www.njit.edu   CB code: 2513

- Public 4-year university
- Residential campus in large city
- 7,049 degree-seeking undergraduates: 13% part-time, 21% women, 9% African American, 22% Asian American, 22% Hispanic/Latino, 3% Multi-racial, non-Hispanic, 4% international

- 3,112 degree-seeking graduate students
- 61% of applicants admitted
- SAT or ACT (ACT writing optional) required
- 61% graduate within 6 years

General. Founded in 1881. Regionally accredited. **Degrees:** 1,352 bachelor's awarded; master's, doctoral offered. **ROTC:** Army, Air Force. **Location:** 10 miles from New York City. **Calendar:** Semester, extensive summer session. **Full-time faculty:** 410 total; 29% minority, 20% women. **Part-time faculty:** 391 total. **Class size:** 28% < 20, 59% 20-39, 6% 40-49, 6% 50-99, less than 1% >100. **Special facilities:** Computer chip manufacturing laboratory, multi-lifecycle engineering center, government and industry-sponsored research laboratories, hazardous waste management research center, factory floor manufacturing center, observatory.

Freshman class profile. 6,045 applied, 3,673 admitted, 1,108 enrolled.

Mid 50% test scores			
SAT critical reading:	520-630	GPA 2.0-2.99:	10%
SAT math:	590-680	Rank in top quarter:	59%
SAT writing:	510-630	Rank in top tenth:	31%
GPA 3.75 or higher:	36%	Return as sophomores:	88%
GPA 3.50-3.74:	22%	Out-of-state:	21%
GPA 3.0-3.49:	32%	Live on campus:	51%
		International:	4%

Basis for selection. Class rank, test scores, secondary school record including grades and curriculum most important. Grades in math and science very important, especially for engineering, engineering science and computer science applicants. Essay and interview required for honors college; interview and portfolio required for architecture programs. Interview required for conditional admission, educational opportunity program.

High school preparation. College-preparatory program required. 16 units required. Required and recommended units include English 4, mathematics 4, social studies 1, history 1, science 2 (laboratory 2), foreign language 2 and academic electives 2. 3 math required of management majors and science, technology and society majors. One lab science required for management majors.

2015-2016 Annual costs. Tuition/fees: $16,108; $30,326 out-of-state. Room/board: $13,296. Books/supplies: $2,600. Personal expenses: $2,400.

2014-2015 Financial aid. Need-based: 880 full-time freshmen applied for aid; 725 deemed to have need; 725 received aid. Average need met was 61%. Average scholarship/grant was $12,902; average loan $3,801. 78% of total undergraduate aid awarded as scholarships/grants, 22% as loans/jobs. **Non-need-based:** Awarded to 2,314 full-time undergraduates, including 643 freshmen. Scholarships awarded for academics, alumni affiliation, athletics, job skills, leadership, minority status, religious affiliation, ROTC, state residency. **Additional information:** Extensive co-op program for all majors.

Application procedures. Admission: Closing date 3/1 (receipt date). $75 fee, may be waived for applicants with need. Admission notification on a rolling basis beginning on or about 11/15. Must reply by May 1 or within 2 week(s) if notified thereafter. **Financial aid:** Priority date 3/15; no closing date. FAFSA required. Applicants notified on a rolling basis starting 12/1; must reply by 5/1 or within 2 week(s) of notification.

Academics. Numerous research opportunities available. **Special study options:** Accelerated study, combined bachelor's/graduate degree, cooperative education, cross-registration, distance learning, double major, ESL, honors, independent study, internships, study abroad, teacher certification program, weekend college. Environmental Scholars Program, Career Advancement Plan, University Research Experience. **Credit/placement by examination:** AP, CLEP, SAT, institutional tests. **Support services:** Learning center, pre-admission summer program, reduced course load, remedial instruction, study skills assistance, tutoring.

Honors college/program. 1250 SAT required.

Majors. Architecture: Architecture. **Biology:** General, biochemistry, bioinformatics, biophysics. **Business:** Business admin, international. **Communications technology:** Animation/special effects. **Computer sciences:** General, computer science, information systems, information technology. **Conservation:** Environmental science. **Engineering:** Biomedical, chemical, civil, computer, electrical, engineering science, environmental, geological, industrial, manufacturing, mechanical. **English:** Technical writing. **History:** General. **Math:** General, applied. **Physical sciences:** Chemistry, physics. **Visual/performing arts:** Art, interior design.

Most popular majors. Architecture 10%, business/marketing 7%, computer/information sciences 18%, engineering/engineering technologies 53%.

Technology on campus. PC or laptop required. 1,500 workstations in dormitories, library, computer center, student center. Dormitories wired for high-speed internet access and linked to campus network. Commuter students can connect to campus network. Online course registration, online library, helpline, repair service, student web hosting, wireless network available.

Student life. Freshman orientation: Mandatory. Preregistration for classes offered. **Housing:** Guaranteed on-campus for freshmen. Coed dorms available. $50 nonrefundable deposit, deadline 6/2. **Activities:** Drama, international student organizations, musical theater, radio station, student government, student newspaper, Arab student association, black student engineers association, Caribbean student association, Chinese student association, Hispanic students in technology association, Intervarsity Christian Federation, Polish student association, Islamic student association, women engineers club.

Athletics. NCAA. **Intercollegiate:** Baseball M, basketball, cheerleading, cross-country, fencing, soccer, swimming, tennis, volleyball. **Intramural:** Badminton, basketball, bowling, cricket, fencing, racquetball, soccer, swimming, table tennis, tennis, track and field, volleyball, weight lifting. **Team name:** Highlanders.

Student services. Adult student services, alcohol/substance abuse counseling, career counseling, services for economically disadvantaged, student employment services, financial aid counseling, health services, minority student services, on-campus daycare, personal counseling, placement for graduates, veterans' counselor, women's services. **Physically disabled:** Services for visually, speech, hearing impaired.

Contact. E-mail: admissions@njit.edu
Phone: (973) 596-3300 Toll-free number: (800) 925-6548
Fax: (973) 596-3461
Stephen Eck, Director of Admissions, New Jersey Institute of Technology, University Heights, Newark, NJ 07102

Pillar College
Newark, New Jersey
www.pillar.edu
CB code: 3933

▶ Private 4-year Bible and liberal arts college affiliated with the Christian Church
▶ Commuter campus in large city
▶ 369 degree-seeking undergraduates
▶ SAT or ACT (ACT writing optional), application essay required

General. Regionally accredited; also accredited by ABHE. **Degrees:** 51 bachelor's, 27 associate awarded. **Calendar:** Semester, limited summer session. **Full-time faculty:** 11 total; 73% have terminal degrees, 64% minority, 36% women. **Part-time faculty:** 50 total.

Basis for selection. Recommendations most important. High school record, standardized test scores, essay also important. **Home schooled:** Transcript of courses and grades, interview, letter of recommendation (nonparent) required. Transcript of study including subjects, grades and GPA required. Students must send proof of graduation date or GED scores. **Learning Disabled:** Students must have documented diagnosis and portfolio of prior school collaboration in accommodating students' learning disabilities.

High school preparation. 15 units required. Required units include English 4, mathematics 1, social studies 3, science 2, foreign language 2 and academic electives 3.

2015-2016 Annual costs. Tuition/fees: $19,440. Books/supplies: $1,200. Personal expenses: $2,485.

Financial aid. All financial aid based on need.

Application procedures. Admission: Closing date 8/15 (postmark date). $50 fee, may be waived for applicants with need. Admission notification on a rolling basis. **Financial aid:** No deadline. FAFSA required. Applicants notified on a rolling basis starting 1/31.

Academics. Special study options: Accelerated study, distance learning, double major, dual enrollment of high school students, ESL, independent study, internships, weekend college. **Credit/placement by examination:** AP, CLEP, IB, institutional tests. 15 credit hours maximum toward associate degree, 30 toward bachelor's. **Support services:** Learning center, preadmission summer program, reduced course load, remedial instruction, study skills assistance, tutoring, writing center.

Majors. Business: Business admin. **Communications:** General. **Education:** Elementary. **Philosophy/religion:** Christian. **Psychology:** General. **Theology:** Bible.

Most popular majors. Business/marketing 22%, psychology 63%, theological studies 16%.

Technology on campus. 50 workstations in library, computer center, student center. Online library, wireless network available.

Student life. Freshman orientation: Mandatory. Preregistration for classes offered. **Activities:** Campus ministries, student government.

Athletics. Team name: Panthers.

Student services. Chaplain/spiritual director, career counseling, financial aid counseling.

Contact. E-mail: info@pillar.edu
Phone: (973) 803-5000 ext. 2001 Toll-free number: (800) 234-9305
Fax: (973) 230-3220
Dominic DiGioacchino, Director of Admissions, Pillar College, 60 Park Place, Suite 701, Newark, NJ 07102

Princeton University
Princeton, New Jersey
www.princeton.edu
CB member
CB code: 2672

▶ Private 4-year university
▶ Residential campus in large town
▶ 5,260 degree-seeking undergraduates: 48% women
▶ 2,704 degree-seeking graduate students
▶ 7% of applicants admitted
▶ SAT or ACT with writing, application essay required

General. Founded in 1746. Regionally accredited. **Degrees:** 1,282 bachelor's awarded; master's, doctoral offered. **ROTC:** Army, Naval, Air Force. **Location:** 50 miles from New York City, 45 miles from Philadelphia. **Calendar:** Semester. **Full-time faculty:** 919 total; 93% have terminal degrees, 22% minority, 31% women. **Part-time faculty:** 253 total; 59% have terminal degrees, 25% minority, 44% women. **Class size:** 72% < 20, 15% 20-39, 2% 40-49, 7% 50-99, 4% >100. **Special facilities:** Center for equality and cultural understanding, art museum, center for innovation in engineering education, center for the arts, center for human values, plasma physics laboratory, observatory, center for energy and the environment, international center, neuroscience research center.

Freshman class profile. 27,290 applied, 1,948 admitted, 1,325 enrolled.

Mid 50% test scores			
		GPA 3.50-3.74:	9%
SAT critical reading:	690-790	GPA 3.0-3.49:	3%
SAT math:	700-800	Rank in top quarter:	99%
SAT writing:	710-790	Rank in top tenth:	96%
ACT composite:	32-35	Out-of-state:	82%
GPA 3.75 or higher:	88%	Live on campus:	100%

Basis for selection. School achievement record and recommendations of guidance counselor and 2 teachers very important. SAT or ACT with Writing required along with 2 SAT Subject Test scores. For applicants pursuing BSE degree one of the SAT Subject Tests should be in either physics or chemistry; the other in mathematics (Level I or II). SAT Subject Tests recommended. All applicants required to take two SAT Subject tests; recommend prospective Engineering students take two SAT Subject Tests - math 1 or math 2 and either physics or chemistry. Interview recommended when possible. Submission of supplementary materials for the visual and performing arts considered. **Home schooled:** Statement describing home school structure and mission required.

High school preparation. College-preparatory program recommended. 21 units recommended. Recommended units include English 4, mathematics 4, social studies 2, history 2, science 4 (laboratory 2), foreign language 4 and visual/performing arts 1. 1 physics or chemistry (preferably both) and 4 math encouraged for prospective engineering majors.

2015-2016 Annual costs. Tuition/fees: $43,450. Room/board: $14,160. Books/supplies: $1,050. Personal expenses: $2,550.

2014-2015 Financial aid. All financial aid based on need. 882 full-time freshmen applied for aid; 770 deemed to have need; 770 received aid. Average need met was 100%. Average scholarship/grant was $44,115. 98% of total undergraduate aid awarded as scholarships/grants, 2% as loans/jobs. **Additional information:** All aid need-based; all aid grant money (no loans); institution meets full demonstrated need. FAFSA due 4/15; financial aid application due 11/15 for early action applicants.

Application procedures. Admission: Closing date 1/1 (postmark date). $65 fee, may be waived for applicants with need. Admission notification by 3/31. Must reply by May 1 or within 1 week(s) if notified thereafter. **Financial aid:** Closing date 2/1. FAFSA, institutional form required. Applicants notified by 3/31; must reply by 5/1.

Academics. Independent project in junior year and senior thesis required for graduation. **Special study options:** Cross-registration, exchange student, independent study, student-designed major, study abroad, teacher certification program. **Credit/placement by examination:** AP, CLEP, IB, SAT, ACT, institutional tests. **Support services:** Learning center, pre-admission summer program, study skills assistance, tutoring, writing center.

Majors. Architecture: Architecture. **Area/ethnic studies:** East Asian, Near/Middle Eastern. **Biology:** Ecology/evolutionary, molecular, neuroscience. **Engineering:** Chemical, civil, computer, electrical, mechanical, operations research. **English:** English lit. **Foreign languages:** Classics, comparative lit, French, German, Italian, Portuguese, Slavic, Spanish. **History:** General. **Human services:** General. **Math:** General. **Philosophy/religion:** Philosophy, religion. **Physical sciences:** Astrophysics, chemistry, geology, physics. **Psychology:** General. **Social sciences:** Anthropology, economics, political science, sociology. **Visual/performing arts:** Art history/conservation, music.

Most popular majors. Biology 8%, engineering/engineering technologies 26%, English 6%, history 6%, physical sciences 6%, psychology 6%, public administration/social services 12%, social sciences 17%.

Technology on campus. 650 workstations in dormitories, library, computer center, student center. Dormitories wired for high-speed internet access and linked to campus network. Commuter students can connect to campus network. Online course registration, online library, helpline, repair service, student web hosting, wireless network available.

Student life. Freshman orientation: Mandatory. Preregistration for classes offered. Three-day orientation. Optional 1-week trip with Outdoor Action or Student Volunteer Council. **Policies:** Freshmen not permitted cars on campus. **Housing:** Guaranteed on-campus for all undergraduates. Coed dorms, special housing for disabled, apartments, cooperative housing, wellness housing available. Residential colleges for freshmen and sophomores available. Kosher dining facilities available. **Activities:** Bands, campus ministries, choral groups, dance, drama, film society, international student organizations, literary magazine, music ensembles, Model UN, musical theater, opera, radio station, student government, student newspaper, symphony orchestra, over 300 student organizations available.

Athletics. NCAA. **Intercollegiate:** Baseball M, basketball, cross-country, diving, fencing, field hockey W, football (tackle) M, golf, ice hockey, lacrosse, rowing (crew), soccer, softball W, squash, swimming, tennis, track and field, volleyball, water polo, wrestling M. **Intramural:** Badminton, basketball, bowling, football (non-tackle), golf, ice hockey, judo, racquetball, soccer, softball, tennis, water polo. **Team name:** Tigers.

Student services. Alcohol/substance abuse counseling, chaplain/spiritual director, career counseling, student employment services, financial aid counseling, health services, minority student services, personal counseling, placement for graduates, women's services. **Physically disabled:** Services for visually, speech, hearing impaired.

Contact. E-mail: uaoffice@princeton.edu
Phone: (609) 258-3060 Fax: (609) 258-6743
Janet Rapelye, Dean of Admission, Princeton University, Princeton University, Princeton, NJ 08542-0430

Rabbi Jacob Joseph School
Edison, New Jersey

▶ Private 4-year rabbinical college
▶ Large town
▶ 86 degree-seeking undergraduates

General. Accredited by AARTS. **Degrees:** 1 bachelor's awarded. **Calendar:** Semester. **Full-time faculty:** 4 total. **Part-time faculty:** 2 total.

Basis for selection. Admission requirements will vary by program.

2015-2016 Annual costs. Tuition/fees: $11,200. Room/board: $3,300.

Academics. Credit/placement by examination: AP, CLEP.

Majors. Theology: Talmudic.

Contact. Phone: (732) 985-6533
Rabbi Jacob Joseph School, One Plainfield Avenue, Edison, NJ 08817

Rabbinical College of America
Morristown, New Jersey
www.rca.edu   CB code: 1546

▶ Private 4-year rabbinical college for men affiliated with the Jewish faith
▶ Residential campus in large town
▶ 249 degree-seeking undergraduates

General. Founded in 1956. Accredited by AARTS. Affiliate of world-wide Lubavitch movement. **Degrees:** 24 bachelor's awarded. **Location:** One mile from downtown, 35 miles from New York City. **Calendar:** Semester, extensive summer session. **Full-time faculty:** 16 total. **Part-time faculty:** 2 total.

Basis for selection. Applicants must demonstrate interest, ability, and perseverance necessary for successful completion of required courses. Recommendation required, preferably from local rabbi. Interview recommended.

2015-2016 Annual costs. Tuition/fees: $11,000. Room/board: $7,500.

Application procedures. Admission: Closing date 9/1. $150 fee. Admission notification on a rolling basis. **Financial aid:** Priority date 10/20; no closing date. Applicants notified on a rolling basis starting 10/31.

Academics. New Direction program for young Jewish men with little or no Jewish education. Program ranges from basics of Judaism to Talmud and Chassidic philosophy. **Special study options:** Internships. **Credit/placement by examination:** AP, CLEP. **Support services:** Pre-admission summer program, remedial instruction.

Majors. Philosophy/religion: Judaic, religion.

Student life. Policies: Religious observance required. **Housing:** Guaranteed on-campus for all undergraduates. Apartments available. **Activities:** Student newspaper, community activities.

Student services. Personal counseling.

Contact. Phone: (973) 267-9404 Fax: (973) 267-5208
Israel Teitelbaum, Registrar, Rabbinical College of America, 226 Sussex Avenue, CN 1996, Morristown, NJ 07962-1996

Ramapo College of New Jersey
Mahwah, New Jersey   CB member
www.ramapo.edu   CB code: 2884

▶ Public 4-year liberal arts college
▶ Residential campus in large town
▶ 5,425 degree-seeking undergraduates: 9% part-time, 54% women, 5% African American, 7% Asian American, 13% Hispanic/Latino, 1% Multiracial, non-Hispanic, 1% international
▶ 361 degree-seeking graduate students
▶ 53% of applicants admitted
▶ SAT or ACT (ACT writing optional), application essay required
▶ 74% graduate within 6 years

General. Founded in 1969. Regionally accredited. **Degrees:** 1,250 bachelor's awarded; master's offered. **ROTC:** Army, Air Force. **Location:** 35 miles from New York City. **Calendar:** Continuous, extensive summer session. **Full-time faculty:** 215 total; 91% have terminal degrees, 25% minority, 51% women. **Part-time faculty:** 280 total; 14% minority, 52% women. **Class size:** 36% < 20, 63% 20-39, 1% 40-49. **Special facilities:** International telecommunications center, electron microscope, Holocaust center, performing arts center, international and intercultural education office, environmental studies/sustainability education center, greenhouse center, astronomical observatory, global financial markets trading laboratory, spirituality center, center for nursing excellence.

Freshman class profile. 7,106 applied, 3,783 admitted, 918 enrolled.

Mid 50% test scores		GPA 2.0-2.99:	24%
SAT critical reading:	490-590	Rank in top quarter:	25%
SAT math:	500-610	Rank in top tenth:	10%
SAT writing:	480-590	Return as sophomores:	86%
GPA 3.75 or higher:	18%	Out-of-state:	4%
GPA 3.50-3.74:	18%	Live on campus:	75%
GPA 3.0-3.49:	40%	International:	2%

Basis for selection. School achievement record, test scores most important. Applicants should rank in top 25% of high school class. SAT Reading and ACT Reading/English may be used for academic advising. Certain majors have additional entrance requirements.

High school preparation. College-preparatory program required. 18 units required. Required units include English 4, mathematics 3, social studies 3, science 3 (laboratory 2), foreign language 2 and academic electives 3. Math must consist of algebra I, geometry, and algebra II.

2015-2016 Annual costs. Tuition/fees: $13,698; $22,563 out-of-state. Room/board: $11,640. Books/supplies: $1,400. Personal expenses: $2,432.

2014-2015 Financial aid. Need-based: 827 full-time freshmen applied for aid; 602 deemed to have need; 567 received aid. Average need met was 48%. Average scholarship/grant was $13,049; average loan $3,301. 55% of total undergraduate aid awarded as scholarships/grants, 45% as loans/jobs. **Non-need-based:** Awarded to 504 full-time undergraduates, including 267 freshmen. Scholarships awarded for academics, leadership, state residency.

Application procedures. Admission: Closing date 3/1. $60 fee, may be waived for applicants with need. Admission notification by 4/1. Must reply by 12/1. **Financial aid:** Priority date 3/1; no closing date. FAFSA required. Applicants notified on a rolling basis starting 4/1; must reply by 5/1 or within 2 week(s) of notification.

Academics. Thematic learning communities available. **Special study options:** Accelerated study, combined bachelor's/graduate degree, cooperative education, cross-registration, distance learning, double major, dual enrollment of high school students, exchange student, external degree, honors, independent study, internships, liberal arts/career combination, student-designed major, study abroad, teacher certification program, weekend college. **Credit/placement by examination:** AP, CLEP, IB, SAT. 65 credit hours maximum toward bachelor's degree. **Support services:** Learning center, pre-admission summer program, reduced course load, remedial instruction, study skills assistance, tutoring, writing center.

Majors. Area/ethnic studies: African-American, American. **Biology:** General, biochemistry, bioinformatics. **Business:** Accounting, business admin, international. **Communications:** Communications/speech/rhetoric. **Computer sciences:** General, information systems. **Conservation:** Environmental science, environmental studies. **Foreign languages:** Comparative lit, Spanish. **Health services:** Clinical lab science. **History:** General. **Human services:** Social work. **Liberal arts:** Arts/sciences, humanities. **Math:** General. **Physical sciences:** Chemistry, physics. **Psychology:** General. **Social sciences:** Economics, political science, sociology. **Visual/performing arts:** General, art, dramatic, multimedia, music.

Most popular majors. Biology 6%, business/marketing 23%, communications/journalism 10%, health sciences 8%, psychology 15%, visual/performing arts 7%.

Technology on campus. 1,058 workstations in dormitories, library, computer center, student center. Dormitories wired for high-speed internet access and linked to campus network. Commuter students can connect to campus network. Online course registration, online library, helpline, repair service, student web hosting, wireless network available.

Student life. Freshman orientation: Mandatory, $130 fee. Preregistration for classes offered. Several sessions held throughout summer. **Policies:** Smoking prohibited in all physical buildings on campus. Smokers must stand 25 feet away from buildings. Freshmen not permitted cars on campus. **Housing:** Guaranteed on-campus for freshmen. Coed dorms, themed housing, wellness housing available. $200 partly refundable deposit, deadline 5/1. Sustainability housing. **Activities:** Campus ministries, choral groups, dance, drama, international student organizations, literary magazine, music ensembles, Model UN, musical theater, radio station, student government, student newspaper, TV station, United Asian Americans, Haitian Organization for Progress, College Democrats, College Republicans, Hillel, Intervarsity Christian Fellowship, Muslim student association, Community Builders Coalition, culture club.

Athletics. NCAA. **Intercollegiate:** Baseball M, basketball, cross-country, field hockey W, lacrosse W, soccer, softball W, swimming, tennis, track and field, volleyball. **Intramural:** Archery, basketball, cheerleading, football (non-tackle), soccer, table tennis, volleyball. **Team name:** Roadrunners.

Student services. Adult student services, alcohol/substance abuse counseling, chaplain/spiritual director, career counseling, services for economically disadvantaged, student employment services, financial aid counseling, health services, minority student services, personal counseling, placement for graduates, veterans' counselor, women's services. **Physically disabled:** Services for visually, speech, hearing impaired.

Contact. E-mail: admissions@ramapo.edu
Phone: (201) 684-7300 Toll-free number: (800) 972-6276
Fax: (201) 684-7964
Peter Rice, Director of Admissions, Ramapo College of New Jersey, 505 Ramapo Valley Road, Mahwah, NJ 07430-1680

Rider University
Lawrenceville, New Jersey — CB member
www.rider.edu — CB code: 2758

◗ Private 4-year university
◗ Residential campus in small town
◗ 4,039 degree-seeking undergraduates: 9% part-time, 57% women, 12% African American, 5% Asian American, 12% Hispanic/Latino, 3% Multiracial, non-Hispanic, 3% international
◗ 872 degree-seeking graduate students
◗ 69% of applicants admitted
◗ SAT or ACT (ACT writing optional), application essay required
◗ 64% graduate within 6 years

General. Founded in 1865. Regionally accredited. Westminster College of the Arts, located in Lawrenceville and Princeton campuses. **Degrees:** 1,006 bachelor's, 7 associate awarded; master's offered. **ROTC:** Army. **Location:** 5 miles from Princeton, 3 miles from Trenton. **Calendar:** Semester, extensive summer session. **Full-time faculty:** 252 total; 98% have terminal degrees, 17% minority, 49% women. **Part-time faculty:** 338 total; 40% have terminal degrees, 11% minority, 53% women. **Class size:** 52% < 20, 45% 20-39, 3% 40-49, less than 1% 50-99. **Special facilities:** Holocaust/genocide center, teaching and learning center, art gallery.

Freshman class profile. 9,851 applied, 6,798 admitted, 862 enrolled.

Mid 50% test scores			
SAT critical reading:	450-550	GPA 2.0-2.99:	26%
SAT math:	460-560	Rank in top quarter:	37%
SAT writing:	450-540	Rank in top tenth:	14%
ACT composite:	19-25	Return as sophomores:	80%
GPA 3.75 or higher:	15%	Out-of-state:	26%
GPA 3.50-3.74:	21%	Live on campus:	82%
GPA 3.0-3.49:	38%	International:	1%

Basis for selection. High school curriculum most important, followed by GPA, test scores, essay, and recommendations. Extracurricular activities, interview considered. Deadline for SAT/ACT: 11/15 for Early Action; 1/15 for scholarship consideration. Interview recommended for all; audition required for music program with Westminster College of the Arts. **Home schooled:** Information about syllabi, reading lists, and/or course descriptions recommended.

High school preparation. College-preparatory program required. 16 units required. Required and recommended units include English 4, mathematics 3-4, social studies 2, history 2, science 4 (laboratory 4) and foreign language 2. Algebra I and II and geometry required for business administration, science, math majors.

2015-2016 Annual costs. Tuition/fees: $38,360. Room/board: $13,770. Books/supplies: $1,500. Personal expenses: $985.

2015-2016 Financial aid. Need-based: Average need met was 73%. Average scholarship/grant was $24,203; average loan $3,876. 69% of total undergraduate aid awarded as scholarships/grants, 31% as loans/jobs. **Non-need-based:** Scholarships awarded for academics, leadership.

Application procedures. Admission: Priority date 1/15; no deadline. $50 fee, may be waived for applicants with need. Admission notification on a rolling basis beginning on or about 12/15. Must reply by May 1 or within 4 week(s) if notified thereafter. Notification of admission decision sent within 3-4 weeks of receiving application. **Financial aid:** Priority date 3/1; no closing date. FAFSA required. Applicants notified on a rolling basis starting 3/1.

Academics. Special study options: Cooperative education, cross-registration, distance learning, double major, ESL, honors, independent study, internships, liberal arts/career combination, study abroad, teacher certification program, Washington semester, weekend college. **Credit/placement by examination:** AP, CLEP, IB, SAT, ACT, institutional tests. Policy varies by major. 30 hours of credit by general examination may be counted toward degree. No limit for subject examinations. Not acceptable for last 30 credits of degree program. 4-8 AP courses (24 credits) required for sophomore standing. **Support services:** Learning center, reduced course load, remedial instruction, study skills assistance, tutoring, writing center.

Majors. Area/ethnic studies: American. **Biology:** General, biochemistry. **Business:** Accounting, business admin, entrepreneurial studies, finance, human resources, international, management science, managerial economics, marketing, office management, organizational behavior. **Communications:** Advertising, communications/speech/rhetoric, journalism, public relations, radio/TV. **Computer sciences:** General, web page design. **Conservation:** Environmental studies. **Education:** Business, elementary, music, sales/marketing, science, secondary. **English:** English lit, rhetoric/composition. **Foreign languages:** French, German, Russian, Spanish. **History:** General.

Liberal arts: Arts/sciences. **Math:** General. **Philosophy/religion:** Philosophy. **Physical sciences:** Chemistry, geology, oceanography, physics. **Psychology:** General. **Social sciences:** Economics, international relations, political science, sociology. **Theology:** Sacred music. **Visual/performing arts:** Art, dance, directing/producing, graphic design, music, music history, music theory/composition, musical theater, piano/keyboard, studio arts, studio arts management, theater arts management, voice/opera.

Most popular majors. Business/marketing 34%, communications/journalism 10%, education 17%, psychology 10%, visual/performing arts 8%.

Technology on campus. 300 workstations in library, computer center, student center. Dormitories wired for high-speed internet access and linked to campus network. Commuter students can connect to campus network. Online course registration, online library, helpline, student web hosting, wireless network available.

Student life. Freshman orientation: Mandatory, $250 fee. Preregistration for classes offered. Two-day program for new students and family members. **Housing:** Guaranteed on-campus for freshmen. Coed dorms, single-sex dorms, special housing for disabled, apartments, fraternity/sorority housing, themed housing, wellness housing available. $200 nonrefundable deposit, deadline 5/1. **Activities:** Bands, campus ministries, choral groups, dance, drama, film society, international student organizations, literary magazine, music ensembles, Model UN, musical theater, opera, radio station, student government, student newspaper, TV station, student entertainment council, residence hall association, finance board, Asian student organization, interfraternity council, hunger and homelessness awareness, College Republicans, Latin American student organization.

Athletics. NCAA. **Intercollegiate:** Baseball M, basketball, cheerleading, cross-country, diving, field hockey W, golf M, soccer, softball W, swimming, tennis, track and field, volleyball W, wrestling M. **Intramural:** Basketball, football (non-tackle), ice hockey M, lacrosse, soccer, softball, track and field, volleyball. **Team name:** Broncs.

Student services. Adult student services, alcohol/substance abuse counseling, chaplain/spiritual director, career counseling, services for economically disadvantaged, student employment services, financial aid counseling, health services, minority student services, personal counseling, placement for graduates, veterans' counselor, women's services. **Physically disabled:** Services for visually, speech, hearing impaired.

Contact. E-mail: admissions@rider.edu
Phone: (609) 896-5042 Toll-free number: (800) 257-9026
Fax: (609) 895-6645
William Larrousse, Director of Undergraduate Admission, Rider University, 2083 Lawrenceville Road, Lawrenceville, NJ 08648-3099

Rowan University
Glassboro, New Jersey
www.rowan.edu

CB member
CB code: 2515

- Public 4-year university
- Residential campus in large town
- 13,003 degree-seeking undergraduates: 10% part-time, 46% women, 10% African American, 5% Asian American, 12% Hispanic/Latino, 3% Multi-racial, non-Hispanic, 1% international
- 2,933 degree-seeking graduate students
- 56% of applicants admitted
- SAT or ACT (ACT writing optional) required
- 66% graduate within 6 years

General. Founded in 1923. Regionally accredited. **Degrees:** 2,853 bachelor's awarded; master's, professional, doctoral offered. **ROTC:** Army. **Location:** 20 miles from Philadelphia. **Calendar:** Semester, extensive summer session. **Full-time faculty:** 428 total; 83% have terminal degrees, 20% minority, 48% women. **Part-time faculty:** 1,005 total; 24% have terminal degrees, 13% minority, 47% women. **Class size:** 40% < 20, 58% 20-39, 1% 40-49, less than 1% 50-99, less than 1% >100. **Special facilities:** Observatory, early childhood demonstration center, greenhouse for biological studies, concert hall, automated virtual environment, planetarium.

Freshman class profile. 12,156 applied, 6,860 admitted, 1,770 enrolled.

Mid 50% test scores			
SAT critical reading:	490-600	GPA 2.0-2.99:	14%
SAT math:	510-630	End year in good standing:	93%
SAT writing:	470-580	Return as sophomores:	88%
GPA 3.75 or higher:	42%	Out-of-state:	5%
GPA 3.50-3.74:	19%	Live on campus:	79%
GPA 3.0-3.49:	25%	International:	1%

Basis for selection. School achievement record and test scores most important, followed by recommendations. Audition required for music, theater programs; portfolio interview required for art program. **Home schooled:** Transcript of courses and grades required.

High school preparation. College-preparatory program required. 16 units required; 20 recommended. Required and recommended units include English 4, mathematics 3-4, social studies 2, history 2, science 2-3 (laboratory 2-3), foreign language 2, visual/performing arts 1 and academic electives 5. Engineering applicants should have 3 units of laboratory science including physics and chemistry, and 4 units of college preparatory math including precalculus. Calculus strongly recommended.

2016-2017 Annual costs. Tuition/fees (projected): $12,864; $20,978 out-of-state. Room/board: $11,627. Books/supplies: $1,500. Personal expenses: $1,000.

2014-2015 Financial aid. Need-based: 1,731 full-time freshmen applied for aid; 1,252 deemed to have need; 1,193 received aid. Average need met was 71%. Average scholarship/grant was $9,121; average loan $3,274. 39% of total undergraduate aid awarded as scholarships/grants, 61% as loans/jobs. **Non-need-based:** Awarded to 2,883 full-time undergraduates, including 912 freshmen. Scholarships awarded for academics, art, music/drama.

Application procedures. Admission: Closing date 3/1 (receipt date). $65 fee, may be waived for applicants with need. Admission notification on a rolling basis beginning on or about 10/15. Must reply by 5/1. **Financial aid:** Priority date 3/16; no closing date. FAFSA required. Applicants notified on a rolling basis starting 3/16.

Academics. Camden campus offers general education courses and major programs in elementary education, business administration, law/justice, and sociology. **Special study options:** Accelerated study, combined bachelor's/graduate degree, cooperative education, cross-registration, distance learning, double major, dual enrollment of high school students, ESL, honors, independent study, internships, liberal arts/career combination, study abroad, teacher certification program, weekend college. **Credit/placement by examination:** AP, CLEP, IB, SAT, ACT. 30 credit hours maximum toward bachelor's degree. The University recognizes CLEP and AP assessments. Assignment of credit based upon external evaluation is considered as transfer credit. Credit assessments made by Thomas Edison College are accepted as transfer credit. No more than 30 hours total semester credit may be attained for life experience. Courses taken in the armed services and recommended for credit by the American Council on Education may be accepted. When these courses are applied to meet the major requirements, the respective major department/program adviser and dean must approve. **Support services:** Pre-admission summer program, remedial instruction, study skills assistance, tutoring, writing center.

Majors. Area/ethnic studies: African, American. **Biology:** General, biochemistry. **Business:** Accounting, business admin, entrepreneurial studies, finance, human resources, management information systems, management science, marketing. **Communications:** Advertising, journalism, public relations, radio/TV. **Computer sciences:** Computer science. **Conservation:** Environmental studies. **Engineering:** Biochemical, chemical, civil, electrical, mechanical. **English:** English lit, writing. **Foreign languages:** Spanish. **Health services:** Athletic training. **History:** General. **Math:** General. **Parks/recreation:** Health/fitness, sports admin. **Philosophy/religion:** General. **Physical sciences:** General, chemistry, physics. **Protective services:** Criminal justice. **Psychology:** General. **Social sciences:** Economics, geography, GIS/cartography, political science, sociology. **Visual/performing arts:** Art, dance, jazz, music, studio arts.

Most popular majors. Biology 8%, business/marketing 14%, communications/journalism 9%, education 12%, engineering/engineering technologies 6%, psychology 9%, security/protective services 6%.

Technology on campus. 900 workstations in dormitories, library, computer center. Dormitories wired for high-speed internet access and linked to campus network. Commuter students can connect to campus network. Online course registration, online library, helpline, repair service, wireless network available.

Student life. Freshman orientation: Available. Preregistration for classes offered. Overnight program for freshmen and their families during summer. **Policies:** Freshmen not permitted cars on campus. **Housing:** Guaranteed on-campus for freshmen. Coed dorms, special housing for disabled, apartments, themed housing available. $200 nonrefundable deposit. **Activities:** Bands, campus ministries, choral groups, dance, drama, film society, music ensembles, musical theater, opera, radio station, student government, student newspaper, symphony orchestra, TV station, over 100 clubs and student organizations available.

Athletics. NCAA. **Intercollegiate:** Baseball M, basketball, cross-country, diving, field hockey W, football (tackle) M, lacrosse W, soccer, softball W, swimming, track and field, volleyball W. **Intramural:** Basketball, bowling, golf, handball, racquetball, soccer, softball, table tennis, tennis, volleyball. **Team name:** Profs.

Student services. Adult student services, alcohol/substance abuse counseling, chaplain/spiritual director, career counseling, services for economically disadvantaged, student employment services, financial aid counseling, health services, legal services, minority student services, on-campus daycare, personal counseling, placement for graduates, veterans' counselor, women's services. **Physically disabled:** Services for visually, speech, hearing impaired.

Contact. E-mail: admissions@rowan.edu
Phone: (856) 256-4200 Toll-free number: (877) 787-6926
Fax: (856) 256-4430
Albert Betts, Director of Admissions, Rowan University, Savitz Hall, 201 Mullica Hill Road, Glassboro, NJ 08028-1701

Rutgers, The State University of New Jersey: Camden Campus
Camden, New Jersey CB member
www.camden.rutgers.edu CB code: 2742

- Public 4-year university
- Commuter campus in small city
- 4,835 degree-seeking undergraduates: 19% part-time, 58% women, 16% African American, 9% Asian American, 13% Hispanic/Latino, 4% Multiracial, non-Hispanic, 1% international
- 1,438 degree-seeking graduate students
- 58% of applicants admitted
- SAT or ACT with writing required
- 57% graduate within 6 years

General. Founded in 1927. Regionally accredited. **Degrees:** 1,270 bachelor's awarded; master's, professional, doctoral offered. **ROTC:** Army, Air Force. **Location:** One mile from Philadelphia. **Calendar:** Semester, extensive summer session. **Full-time faculty:** 292 total; 98% have terminal degrees, 22% minority, 44% women. **Part-time faculty:** 342 total; 98% have terminal degrees, 11% minority, 51% women. **Class size:** 43% < 20, 39% 20-39, 8% 40-49, 8% 50-99, 2% >100. **Special facilities:** Fine arts center.

Freshman class profile. 7,518 applied, 4,389 admitted, 429 enrolled.

Mid 50% test scores		Rank in top tenth:	15%
SAT critical reading:	450-550	Return as sophomores:	83%
SAT math:	470-570	Out-of-state:	3%
SAT writing:	450-550	Live on campus:	44%
Rank in top quarter:	44%	International:	2%

Basis for selection. School achievement record (including grades, rank, strength of program, honors) and test scores most important. Extracurricular activities, talent, disadvantaged status considered. SAT Subject Tests required for applicants who will not have diploma from accredited high school by entrance date. May also be required of GED holders. **Home schooled:** SAT Subject Tests required for applicants who will not have diploma from accredited high school by entrance date.

High school preparation. College-preparatory program required. 16 units required. Required units include English 4, mathematics 3, science 2, foreign language 2 and academic electives 5.

2015-2016 Annual costs. Tuition/fees: $14,000; $28,890 out-of-state. Room/board: $11,710. Books/supplies: $1,350. Personal expenses: $2,863. **Additional information:** School of Business and School of Nursing tuition and fees are slightly higher.

2014-2015 Financial aid. Need-based: 377 full-time freshmen applied for aid; 314 deemed to have need; 314 received aid. Average need met was 61%. Average scholarship/grant was $11,513; average loan $3,849. 65% of total undergraduate aid awarded as scholarships/grants, 35% as loans/jobs. **Non-need-based:** Awarded to 370 full-time undergraduates, including 59 freshmen. Scholarships awarded for academics, alumni affiliation, art, athletics, leadership, music/drama, state residency.

Application procedures. Admission: Closing date 12/1. $65 fee, may be waived for applicants with need. Application must be submitted online. Admission notification on a rolling basis beginning on or about 2/28. Must reply by May 1 or within 2 week(s) if notified thereafter. May apply to up to 3 Rutgers colleges with 1 application. Students applying by 12/1 notified by 2/28. **Financial aid:** Priority date 3/15; no closing date. FAFSA required. Applicants notified on a rolling basis starting 3/1; must reply within 4 week(s) of notification.

Academics. Special study options: Accelerated study, combined bachelor's/graduate degree, cooperative education, cross-registration, distance learning, double major, dual enrollment of high school students, ESL, exchange student, honors, independent study, internships, liberal arts/career combination, student-designed major, study abroad, teacher certification program, weekend college. Cooperative baccalaureate program in Engineering with School of Engineering (New Brunswick Campus); interdisciplinary program in African-American studies, general science. Cooperative baccalaureate in medical technology with approved hospital. BA/MA in Childhood Studies; English, History, Liberal Studies or Psychology; BA/MS in Biology, Chemistry or Mathematics (with the Graduate School-Camden). BA in Economics or Political Science/Master of Public Administration (with the Graduate School-Camden); BS/Master of Business and Science (MBS). **Credit/placement by examination:** AP, CLEP, IB, institutional tests. No more than 8 credits given for elementary or intermediate levels of any foreign language. Graduating seniors may take no more than one examination in their final term. **Support services:** Learning center, pre-admission summer program, reduced course load, remedial instruction, study skills assistance, tutoring, writing center.

Majors. Area/ethnic studies: African-American. **Biology:** General, biomedical sciences, computational. **Business:** Accounting, business admin, finance, hospitality admin, human resources, marketing. **Computer sciences:** Computer science. **English:** English lit. **Foreign languages:** French, German, Spanish. **Health services:** Clinical lab science, nursing (RN), predental, premedicine. **History:** General. **Human services:** Social work. **Liberal arts:** Arts/sciences. **Math:** General. **Philosophy/religion:** Philosophy. **Physical sciences:** Chemistry, physics. **Protective services:** Criminal justice. **Psychology:** General. **Social sciences:** Economics, political science, sociology, urban studies. **Visual/performing arts:** Art, dramatic, music.

Most popular majors. Business/marketing 25%, health sciences 17%, psychology 11%, security/protective services 8%, social sciences 9%.

Technology on campus. 187 workstations in dormitories, library, computer center, student center. Dormitories linked to campus network. Commuter students can connect to campus network. Online course registration, helpline, repair service, wireless network available.

Student life. Freshman orientation: Available. Preregistration for classes offered. **Housing:** Coed dorms, special housing for disabled, apartments available. $200 nonrefundable deposit. **Activities:** Choral groups, drama, international student organizations, literary magazine, radio station, student government, student newspaper, accounting society, forensics society, political science association, black student union, Latin American students organization, physics society, Jewish student union, marketing association, psychology club.

Athletics. NCAA. **Intercollegiate:** Baseball M, basketball, cross-country, golf M, rowing (crew) W, soccer, softball W, tennis M, track and field, volleyball W. **Intramural:** Badminton, basketball, football (tackle) M, handball, racquetball, soccer, softball, squash, volleyball. **Team name:** Scarlet Raptors.

Student services. Career counseling, student employment services, health services, on-campus daycare, personal counseling, placement for graduates, veterans' counselor. **Physically disabled:** Services for visually, speech, hearing impaired.

Contact. E-mail: admissions@ugadm.rutgers.edu
Phone: (856) 225-6104 Fax: (856) 225-6498
Deborah Bowles, Director of Admissions, Rutgers, The State University of New Jersey: Camden Campus, 406 Penn Street, Camden, NJ 08102

Rutgers, The State University of New Jersey: New Brunswick/Piscataway Campus
Piscataway, New Jersey CB member
www.newbrunswick.rutgers.edu CB code: 2765

- Public 4-year university
- Residential campus in small city
- 35,102 degree-seeking undergraduates: 5% part-time, 50% women, 7% African American, 26% Asian American, 13% Hispanic/Latino, 3% Multi-racial, non-Hispanic, 7% international
- 13,297 degree-seeking graduate students
- 58% of applicants admitted
- SAT or ACT with writing required
- 80% graduate within 6 years

General. Founded in 1969. Regionally accredited. **Degrees:** 7,555 bachelor's, 105 associate awarded; master's, professional, doctoral offered. **ROTC:** Army, Naval, Air Force. **Location:** 33 miles from New York City. **Calendar:** Semester, extensive summer session. **Full-time faculty:** 2,027 total; 98% have terminal degrees, 20% minority, 46% women. **Part-time faculty:** 2,033 total; 98% have terminal degrees, 16% minority, 59% women. **Class size:** 37% < 20, 36% 20-39, 6% 40-49, 12% 50-99, 9% >100. **Special facilities:** Geology museum, ecological preserve, 2 theaters, center for urban policy research, institute for health, health care policy and aging research, journalism resources institute, laboratory for computer science research, center for math, science and computer education.

Freshman class profile. 35,340 applied, 20,657 admitted, 6,607 enrolled.

Mid 50% test scores		Rank in top tenth:	38%
SAT critical reading:	530-640	Return as sophomores:	93%
SAT math:	580-700	Out-of-state:	6%
SAT writing:	540-660	Live on campus:	87%
Rank in top quarter:	76%	International:	10%

Basis for selection. School achievement record (including grades, rank, strength of program, honors, AP) and test scores most important. Extracurricular activities, leadership talent, minority, disadvantaged status considered. State residents with educationally and economically disadvantaged backgrounds given consideration through state Educational Opportunity Fund program. SAT Subject Tests required of applicants who, by expected date of entrance, will not have diploma from accredited high school. May also be required of GED holders. Interview, audition, portfolio review required for School of the Arts. **Home schooled:** SAT Subject Tests required of graduates from non-accredited high schools.

High school preparation. College-preparatory program required. 16 units required. Required units include English 4, mathematics 3, science 2, foreign language 2 and academic electives 5.

2015-2016 Annual costs. Tuition/fees: $14,131; $29,521 out-of-state. Room/board: $12,054. Books/supplies: $1,350. Personal expenses: $2,863. **Additional information:** Tuition and Fees listed are for the School of Arts and Sciences. School of Engineering, School of Pharmacy, School of Environmental & Biological Sciences and School of Business tuition and fees are slightly higher.

2015-2016 Financial aid. **Need-based:** 4,368 full-time freshmen applied for aid; 3,489 deemed to have need; 3,489 received aid. Average need met was 56%. Average scholarship/grant was $12,575; average loan $4,036. 65% of total undergraduate aid awarded as scholarships/grants, 35% as loans/jobs. **Non-need-based:** Awarded to 4,270 full-time undergraduates, including 1,439 freshmen. Scholarships awarded for academics, alumni affiliation, art, athletics, leadership, music/drama, state residency.

Application procedures. **Admission:** Closing date 12/1. $65 fee, may be waived for applicants with need. Application must be submitted online. Admission notification on a rolling basis. Must reply by May 1 or within 2 week(s) if notified thereafter. May apply to up to 3 Rutgers colleges with 1 application. Applications received by 12/1 will be answered by 2/28. Candidates must respond by 5/1. **Financial aid:** Priority date 3/15; no closing date. FAFSA required. Applicants notified on a rolling basis starting 3/1; must reply within 4 week(s) of notification.

Academics. **Special study options:** Accelerated study, combined bachelor's/graduate degree, cooperative education, cross-registration, distance learning, double major, dual enrollment of high school students, ESL, exchange student, honors, independent study, internships, liberal arts/career combination, student-designed major, study abroad, teacher certification program, Washington semester, weekend college. 5-year BA or BS/MPA program in Rutgers Business School; BS in Business Discipline/MBA; BA or BS in Science Discipline/MBA; 8-year Bachelor/Medical Dual Degree program with Robert Wood Johnson Medical School; 5-year BS/BS in Bioenvironmental Engineering with the School of Engineering; 5-year accelerated BA or BS-MBA with RU Business School; exchange program between School of Engineering and the City University of London for qualified students majoring in civil, electrical, or mechanical engineering; 5-year BA/BS degree program in liberal arts and engineering; 5-year BA or BS/M.Ed. with the Graduate School of Education; BA in Religion/MA in Religious Studies; BA/Master of Communication and Information Studies (with SCI); BA/MLER with School of Management and Labor Relations; Baccalaureate/MCRP or MPP with EJB School of Planning and Public Policy; Baccalaureate in Business major/Master of Human Resources Management with School of Management and Labor Relations (SMLR); BS/Master of Business and Science (MBS), Pharm.D./MBA program with Rutgers Business School; Pharm.D./MPH; Pharm.D./Ph.D. in Pharmaceutical Science; Pharm.D./Ph.D. in Toxicology; Pharm.D./M.D. **Credit/placement by examination:** AP, CLEP, IB, institutional tests. 30 credit hours maximum toward bachelor's degree. **Support services:** Learning center, pre-admission summer program, reduced course load, remedial instruction, study skills assistance, tutoring, writing center.

Majors. **Architecture:** Environmental design, landscape, urban/community planning. **Area/ethnic studies:** African-American, American, Caribbean, Chicano/Hispanic-American/Latino, East Asian, European, Latin American, Near/Middle Eastern, women's. **Biology:** General, animal genetics, bacteriology, biochemistry, biometrics, biotechnology, cell/histology, genetics, marine, microbiology, molecular, molecular genetics. **Business:** Accounting,

business admin, finance, human resources, labor relations, logistics, management information systems, management science, marketing. **Communications:** Communications/speech/rhetoric, journalism. **Computer sciences:** General, information systems. **Conservation:** General, environmental science, environmental studies. **Engineering:** Agricultural, biomedical, ceramic, chemical, civil, electrical, engineering science, industrial, mechanical. **English:** English lit. **Foreign languages:** General, Chinese, classics, comparative lit, French, German, Italian, linguistics, Portuguese, Russian, Spanish. **Health services:** Clinical lab technology, dietetics, health information management, health services admin, nursing (RN), predental, premedicine. **History:** General. **Human services:** Social work. **Math:** General, statistics. **Parks/recreation:** Exercise sciences. **Philosophy/religion:** Judaic, philosophy, religion. **Physical sciences:** Astrophysics, atmospheric science, chemistry, climatology, geology, meteorology, physics. **Protective services:** Law enforcement admin. **Psychology:** General. **Social sciences:** Anthropology, economics, geography, political science, sociology, urban studies. **Visual/performing arts:** Art, art history/conservation, dance, dramatic, music, music performance.

Most popular majors. Biology 10%, business/marketing 14%, communications/journalism 8%, engineering/engineering technologies 10%, health sciences 10%, psychology 7%, social sciences 10%.

Technology on campus. 1,450 workstations in dormitories, library, computer center, student center. Dormitories linked to campus network. Commuter students can connect to campus network. Helpline, repair service, wireless network available.

Student life. **Freshman orientation:** Available. Preregistration for classes offered. **Housing:** Guaranteed on-campus for freshmen. Coed dorms, single-sex dorms, special housing for disabled, apartments, cooperative housing, fraternity/sorority housing, themed housing available. $200 nonrefundable deposit, deadline 6/15. **Activities:** Bands, campus ministries, choral groups, dance, drama, film society, international student organizations, literary magazine, music ensembles, musical theater, opera, radio station, student government, student newspaper, symphony orchestra, TV station, 400 organizations available.

Athletics. NCAA. **Intercollegiate:** Baseball M, basketball, cross-country, diving W, fencing M, field hockey W, football (tackle) M, golf, gymnastics W, lacrosse, rowing (crew), soccer, softball W, swimming W, tennis W, track and field, volleyball W, wrestling M. **Intramural:** Badminton, basketball, bowling, cross-country, golf, racquetball, soccer, softball, squash, swimming W, table tennis, tennis, track and field, volleyball, water polo, wrestling M. **Team name:** Scarlet Knights.

Student services. Adult student services, alcohol/substance abuse counseling, career counseling, student employment services, financial aid counseling, health services, minority student services, on-campus daycare, personal counseling, placement for graduates, veterans' counselor. **Physically disabled:** Services for visually, speech, hearing impaired.

Contact. E-mail: admissions@ugadm.rutgers.edu
Phone: (732) 932-4636 Fax: (732) 445-0237
Diane Harris, Director of Undergraduate Admissions, Rutgers, The State University of New Jersey: New Brunswick/Piscataway Campus, 65 Davidson Road, Room 202, Piscataway, NJ 08854-8097

Rutgers, The State University of New Jersey: Newark Campus

Newark, New Jersey
www.newark.rutgers.edu   CB code: 2753

- Public 4-year university
- Commuter campus in large city
- 7,208 degree-seeking undergraduates: 14% part-time, 53% women, 19% African American, 21% Asian American, 27% Hispanic/Latino, 2% Multi-racial, non-Hispanic, 4% international
- 3,887 degree-seeking graduate students
- 65% of applicants admitted
- SAT or ACT with writing required
- 68% graduate within 6 years

General. Founded in 1930. Regionally accredited. **Degrees:** 1,534 bachelor's awarded; master's, professional, doctoral offered. **ROTC:** Army, Naval, Air Force. **Location:** 10 miles from New York City. **Calendar:** Semester, extensive summer session. **Full-time faculty:** 515 total; 98% have terminal degrees, 23% minority, 33% women. **Part-time faculty:** 353 total; 98% have terminal degrees, 21% minority, 38% women. **Class size:** 28% < 20, 45% 20-39, 11% 40-49, 12% 50-99, 5% >100. **Special facilities:** Biology learning center, jazz institute, animal behavior institute, center for molecular and behavioral neuroscience, center for negotiation and conflict resolution.

Freshman class profile. 11,646 applied, 7,529 admitted, 1,200 enrolled.

Mid 50% test scores			
SAT critical reading:	450-550	Rank in top tenth:	19%
SAT math:	480-580	Return as sophomores:	86%
SAT writing:	460-550	Out-of-state:	3%
Rank in top quarter:	50%	Live on campus:	32%
		International:	5%

Basis for selection. School achievement record and test scores most important. Extracurricular activities, leadership talent, minority, disadvantaged status considered. State residents with educational and economically disadvantaged backgrounds given consideration through state Educational Opportunity Fund program. SAT Subject Tests required of applicants who, by expected date of entrance, will not have diploma from accredited high school. May also be required of GED holders.

High school preparation. College-preparatory program required. 16 units required. Required units include English 4, mathematics 3, science 2, foreign language 2 and academic electives 5.

2015-2016 Annual costs. Tuition/fees: $13,597; $28,987 out-of-state. Room/board: $12,841. Books/supplies: $1,350. Personal expenses: $2,863. **Additional information:** School of Business and School of Nursing tuition and fees are slightly higher.

2014-2015 Financial aid. Need-based: 797 full-time freshmen applied for aid; 736 deemed to have need; 736 received aid. Average need met was 62%. Average scholarship/grant was $12,235; average loan $4,262. 71% of total undergraduate aid awarded as scholarships/grants, 29% as loans/jobs. **Non-need-based:** Awarded to 388 full-time undergraduates, including 107 freshmen. Scholarships awarded for academics, alumni affiliation, art, athletics, leadership, music/drama, state residency.

Application procedures. Admission: Closing date 12/1. $65 fee, may be waived for applicants with need. Application must be submitted online. Admission notification on a rolling basis beginning on or about 2/28. Must reply by May 1 or within 2 week(s) if notified thereafter. May apply to up to 3 Rutgers colleges with 1 application. Applications completed by December 1 will be answered by February 28. **Financial aid:** Priority date 3/15; no closing date. FAFSA required. Applicants notified on a rolling basis starting 3/1; must reply within 2 week(s) of notification.

Academics. Special study options: Accelerated study, combined bachelor's/graduate degree, cooperative education, cross-registration, distance learning, double major, dual enrollment of high school students, ESL, exchange student, honors, independent study, internships, liberal arts/career combination, student-designed major, study abroad, teacher certification program, Washington semester, weekend college. 5-year baccalaureate-MBA with RU Business School; BS in Business Discipline/MBA; BA or BS in Science Discipline/MBA; Baccalaureate/MA in Criminal Justice; Baccalaureate/MPA with the School of Public Affairs and Administration; Cooperative baccalaureate program with the School of Engineering (New Brunswick campus); Cooperative baccalaureate in medical technology with affiliated hospitals; interdisciplinary program in archaeology, international affairs, legal studies, women's studies; continuing professional education; Baccalaureate in Business Major/Master of Human Resource Management (with School of Management and Labor Relations in New Brunswick); Baccalaureate-Master's dual degree programs with the School of Criminal Justice and Rutgers Business School; BA or BS in Biology/MS in Biology; BA in Chemistry/MS in Chemistry; BA in Economics/MA in Economics; BS in Environmental Sciences/MS in Environmental Geology; BS/MS in Environmental Sciences; BA in Political Science, Sociology or Anthropology/MS in Global Affairs; BA/MA in History; Sociology or Anthropology/MA in Jazz History and Research; BA/MA in Political Science; BA/MA in Peace and Conflict Studies; BS in Computer Science or Information Science/Master of Information Technology; BS in Accounting/Master of Accountancy (Governmental Accounting or Financial Accounting); BS in Accounting/MBA in Professional Accounting; BS in Finance/Master of Quantitative Finance; BS/MS in Nursing, Pharm.D./M.B.A. program with Rutgers Business School. **Credit/placement by examination:** AP, CLEP, IB, institutional tests. 24 credit hours maximum toward bachelor's degree. **Support services:** Learning center, pre-admission summer program, reduced course load, remedial instruction, study skills assistance, tutoring, writing center.

Majors. Area/ethnic studies: African, African-American, American, Chicano/Hispanic-American/Latino, Russian/Eastern European/Eurasian, women's. **Biology:** General, bacteriology, botany, microbiology, molecular genetics, zoology. **Business:** Accounting, business admin, finance, logistics, management information systems, marketing. **Communications:** Journalism. **Computer sciences:** General, information systems. **Conservation:** Environmental science. **Engineering:** Biomedical, geological. **English:** English lit. **Foreign languages:** French, German, Italian, Portuguese, Spanish. **Health services:** Clinical lab science, clinical lab technology, health information management, nursing (RN), predental, premedicine. **History:** General. **Human services:** Social work. **Math:** General, applied. **Philosophy/religion:** Philosophy. **Physical sciences:** Chemistry, geology, physics. **Protective services:** Criminal justice. **Psychology:** General. **Social sciences:** Anthropology,

economics, political science, sociology. **Visual/performing arts:** Art, cinematography, dramatic, music.

Most popular majors. Biology 7%, business/marketing 40%, psychology 13%, public administration/social services 8%, security/protective services 12%, social sciences 7%.

Technology on campus. 450 workstations in dormitories, library, computer center. Dormitories linked to campus network. Commuter students can connect to campus network. Helpline, repair service available.

Student life. Freshman orientation: Available. Preregistration for classes offered. **Housing:** Coed dorms, special housing for disabled, apartments, fraternity/sorority housing available. $200 deposit. **Activities:** Choral groups, drama, international student organizations, radio station, student government, student newspaper, black organization of students, Puerto Rican and Latin American student organizations, political organizations, religious organizations, service organizations.

Athletics. NCAA. **Intercollegiate:** Baseball M, basketball, soccer, softball W, tennis, volleyball. **Intramural:** Basketball, racquetball, soccer, tennis, volleyball. **Team name:** Scarlet Raiders.

Student services. Career counseling, student employment services, health services, personal counseling, placement for graduates, veterans' counselor. **Physically disabled:** Services for visually, speech, hearing impaired.

Contact. E-mail: newarkadmissions@ugadm.rutgers.edu
Phone: (973) 353-5205 Fax: (973) 353-1440
Director of Admissions at Newark, Rutgers, The State University of New Jersey: Newark Campus, 249 University Avenue, Newark, NJ 07102-1896

Saint Peter's University
Jersey City, New Jersey
www.saintpeters.edu

CB member
CB code: 2806

- Private 4-year university affiliated with the Roman Catholic Church
- Commuter campus in small city
- 2,424 degree-seeking undergraduates: 9% part-time, 61% women, 25% African American, 7% Asian American, 37% Hispanic/Latino, 1% Native American, 1% Native Hawaiian/Pacific islander, 2% Multi-racial, non-Hispanic, 2% international
- 840 degree-seeking graduate students
- 67% of applicants admitted
- Application essay required
- 55% graduate within 6 years

General. Founded in 1872. Regionally accredited. Extensive evening program for adult learners on main campus, branch campus at Englewood Cliffs and various other sites throughout metropolitan area. **Degrees:** 486 bachelor's, 20 associate awarded; master's, professional offered. **ROTC:** Army, Air Force. **Location:** 3 miles from New York City. **Calendar:** Semester, extensive summer session. **Full-time faculty:** 113 total; 85% have terminal degrees, 15% minority, 47% women. **Part-time faculty:** 201 total; 25% minority, 37% women. **Class size:** 59% < 20, 41% 20-39.

Freshman class profile. 4,528 applied, 3,048 admitted, 569 enrolled.

Mid 50% test scores			
		GPA 2.0-2.99:	36%
SAT critical reading:	400-500	Rank in top quarter:	28%
SAT math:	410-510	Rank in top tenth:	12%
SAT writing:	400-490	Return as sophomores:	82%
ACT composite:	16-21	Out-of-state:	15%
GPA 3.75 or higher:	18%	Live on campus:	46%
GPA 3.50-3.74:	18%	International:	2%
GPA 3.0-3.49:	28%		

Basis for selection. In rank order: school achievement record, test scores, essay, letters of recommendation, class activities. Interview recommended.

High school preparation. College-preparatory program recommended. 17 units required. Required units include English 4, mathematics 3, history 2, science 2 (laboratory 1), foreign language 2 and academic electives 3.

2015-2016 Annual costs. Tuition/fees: $34,198. Room/board: $14,468. Books/supplies: $1,000. Personal expenses: $600.

Financial aid. Non-need-based: Scholarships awarded for academics, athletics. **Additional information:** Cooperative education internships available in all majors, with average salaries exceeding $5,200.

Application procedures. Admission: Priority date 12/1; deadline 8/31. No application fee. Admission notification on a rolling basis beginning on or about 12/1. Must reply by May 1 or within 2 week(s) if notified thereafter. **Financial aid:** Priority date 3/15; no closing date. FAFSA required. Applicants notified on a rolling basis starting 2/15; must reply by 5/1 or within 2 week(s) of notification.

Academics. Joint Pre-Med/MD program with UMDNJ, joint Pre-Law/Law and Occupational Therapy program with Seton Hall University, joint Pharmacy and Physical Therapy program with Rutgers University, joint Engineering Program with New Jersey Institute of Technology. **Special study options:** Accelerated study, combined bachelor's/graduate degree, cooperative education, cross-registration, distance learning, double major, dual enrollment of high school students, ESL, exchange student, honors, independent study, internships, student-designed major, study abroad, teacher certification program, Washington semester, weekend college. Joint degree in clinical laboratory sciences with University of Medicine and Dentistry of New Jersey. **Credit/placement by examination:** AP, CLEP, IB, SAT, ACT, institutional tests. 30 credit hours maximum toward bachelor's degree. **Support services:** Learning center, pre-admission summer program, reduced course load, remedial instruction, study skills assistance, tutoring, writing center.

Majors. Area/ethnic studies: American. **Biology:** General, biochemistry, toxicology. **Business:** Accounting, banking/financial services, business admin, finance, international, management information systems, managerial economics, marketing. **Communications:** Communications/speech/rhetoric. **Computer sciences:** General, computer science, information systems, programming. **Education:** Elementary. **English:** English lit. **Foreign languages:** General, classics, Spanish. **Health services:** Clinical lab science, cytotechnology, nursing (RN). **History:** General. **Human services:** Public policy. **Math:** General. **Parks/recreation:** Health/fitness. **Philosophy/religion:** Philosophy, religion. **Physical sciences:** Chemistry, physics. **Protective services:** Law enforcement admin. **Psychology:** General. **Social sciences:** General, economics, political science, sociology, urban studies. **Visual/performing arts:** Studio arts.

Most popular majors. Biology 12%, business/marketing 22%, education 6%, health sciences 13%, security/protective services 9%, social sciences 7%.

Technology on campus. 225 workstations in dormitories, library, computer center, student center. Dormitories wired for high-speed internet access and linked to campus network. Commuter students can connect to campus network. Online library, helpline, student web hosting, wireless network available.

Student life. Freshman orientation: Mandatory, $200 fee. Preregistration for classes offered. Three-day sessions held throughout July. Program features academic advising, social activities, and introduction to community service. **Housing:** Guaranteed on-campus for all undergraduates. Coed dorms, special housing for disabled, apartments available. $250 nonrefundable deposit, deadline 5/1. **Activities:** Campus ministries, choral groups, drama, international student organizations, literary magazine, Model UN, musical theater, radio station, student government, student newspaper, Alpha Phi Omega, Emmaus Spiritual Retreats, Circle K, Young Republicans, Hispanic culture club, Irish American club, Asian American student union, Black Action Committee, Indo-Pak culture club.

Athletics. NCAA. **Intercollegiate:** Baseball M, basketball, bowling, cheerleading, cross-country, diving, golf M, soccer, softball W, swimming, tennis, track and field, volleyball W. **Intramural:** Baseball M, basketball, bowling, racquetball, soccer, softball, swimming, table tennis, tennis, volleyball, water polo. **Team name:** Peacocks.

Student services. Adult student services, alcohol/substance abuse counseling, chaplain/spiritual director, career counseling, services for economically disadvantaged, student employment services, financial aid counseling, health services, minority student services, personal counseling, placement for graduates, veterans' counselor. **Physically disabled:** Services for visually, speech, hearing impaired.

Contact. E-mail: admissions@saintpeters.edu
Phone: (201) 761-7100 Toll-free number: (888) 772-9933
Fax: (201) 761-7105
Elizabeth Sullivan, Assistant Vice President Enrollment/Dean of Undergraduate Admissions, Saint Peter's University, 2641 Kennedy Boulevard, Jersey City, NJ 07306

Seton Hall University
South Orange, New Jersey
www.shu.edu

CB member
CB code: 2811

- Private 4-year university affiliated with the Roman Catholic Church
- Residential campus in large town
- 5,818 degree-seeking undergraduates
- SAT or ACT (ACT writing optional), application essay required

General. Founded in 1856. Regionally accredited. Immaculate Conception Seminary and School of Theology located on campus. Off-campus sites for nursing and education. **Degrees:** 1,101 bachelor's awarded; master's, professional, doctoral offered. **ROTC:** Army. **Location:** 14 miles from New York City. **Calendar:** Semester, extensive summer session. **Full-time faculty:** 460 total. **Part-time faculty:** 520 total. **Class size:** 46% < 20, 50% 20-39, 2% 40-49, 2% 50-99, less than 1% >100. **Special facilities:** Computer graphics and communications laboratories, educational media center, nursing demonstration room, art center, music laboratories, special collections center.

Freshman class profile.

GPA 3.75 or higher:	31%	Rank in top quarter:	69%
GPA 3.50-3.74:	22%	Rank in top tenth:	38%
GPA 3.0-3.49:	34%	Out-of-state:	33%
GPA 2.0-2.99:	13%	Live on campus:	75%

Basis for selection. Holistic approach considering academic performance in high school, grades and the rigor of the curriculum, and SAT and/or ACT scores. A personal essay, recommendations, and extracurricular activities are also considerations. The typical student who entered the institution last year had an average GPA of 3.4 (B+), an average SAT score of 1130 (Critical Reading and Math), and/or an average ACT score of 25. Audition required for music majors. **Home schooled:** Statement describing home school structure and mission, transcript of courses and grades, state high school equivalency certificate, letter of recommendation (nonparent) required. Required to meet home state requirements and must submit supporting documentation. Students must submit transcript or portfolio of academic work completed.

High school preparation. College-preparatory program required. 16 units required. Required units include English 4, mathematics 3, social studies 2, science 1 (laboratory 1), foreign language 2 and academic electives 4. Nursing majors require additional units in science.

2015-2016 Annual costs. Tuition/fees: $38,272. Room/board: $14,154.

Financial aid. Non-need-based: Scholarships awarded for academics, alumni affiliation, athletics, leadership, music/drama, ROTC.

Application procedures. Admission: Priority date 3/1; no deadline. $55 fee, may be waived for applicants with need. Admission notification on a rolling basis beginning on or about 11/15. Must reply by May 1 or within 2 week(s) if notified thereafter. **Financial aid:** No deadline. FAFSA required.

Academics. Special study options: Accelerated study, combined bachelor's/graduate degree, cross-registration, distance learning, double major, dual enrollment of high school students, ESL, honors, independent study, internships, liberal arts/career combination, study abroad, teacher certification program, Washington semester. **Credit/placement by examination:** AP, CLEP, IB, SAT, ACT, institutional tests. 30 credit hours maximum toward bachelor's degree. **Support services:** Learning center, pre-admission summer program, reduced course load, remedial instruction, study skills assistance, tutoring, writing center.

Majors. Area/ethnic studies: African-American, Asian, Latin American. **Biology:** General, biochemistry. **Business:** Accounting, business admin, finance, information resources management, labor relations, management information systems, managerial economics, marketing. **Communications:** Communications/speech/rhetoric, journalism, public relations, radio/TV. **Computer sciences:** General. **Conservation:** Environmental studies. **Education:** Elementary, secondary, special ed. **English:** Creative writing, English lit. **Foreign languages:** General, classics, French, Italian, Spanish. **Health services:** Nursing (RN). **History:** General. **Human services:** Social work. **Liberal arts:** Arts/sciences, humanities. **Math:** General, financial. **Parks/recreation:** Sports admin. **Philosophy/religion:** Christian, philosophy, religion. **Physical sciences:** Chemistry, physics. **Protective services:** Criminal justice. **Psychology:** General. **Social sciences:** Anthropology, economics, international relations, political science, sociology. **Theology:** Theology. **Visual/performing arts:** General, art history/conservation, commercial/advertising art, dramatic, music, music performance.

Most popular majors. Biology 9%, business/marketing 16%, communications/journalism 8%, education 6%, health sciences 19%, liberal arts 7%, social sciences 12%.

Technology on campus. PC or laptop required. 5,000 workstations in dormitories, library, computer center, student center. Commuter students can connect to campus network. Online course registration, online library, helpline, repair service, student web hosting, wireless network available.

Student life. Freshman orientation: Mandatory, $300 fee. Preregistration for classes offered. Two-day program held at various times in June. **Policies:** 1.8 GPA housing requirement. Freshmen not permitted cars on campus. **Housing:** Coed dorms, special housing for disabled, apartments, themed housing, wellness housing available. $375 fully refundable deposit, deadline 5/1. **Activities:** Pep band, campus ministries, choral groups, drama, international student organizations, Model UN, radio station, student government, student newspaper, TV station, Adelante, black student union, Buddhists for

Peace, Jewish student union, Lusophone student association, SHU STAND, Kraut und Lederhosen, College Republicans, College Democrats, Students for Individual Liberty.

Athletics. NCAA. **Intercollegiate:** Baseball M, basketball, cross-country, golf, soccer, softball W, swimming, tennis W, volleyball W. **Intramural:** Basketball, football (non-tackle), racquetball, soccer, softball, tennis, volleyball. **Team name:** Pirates.

Student services. Alcohol/substance abuse counseling, chaplain/spiritual director, career counseling, services for economically disadvantaged, student employment services, financial aid counseling, health services, minority student services, personal counseling, placement for graduates. **Physically disabled:** Services for visually, speech, hearing impaired.

Contact. E-mail: thehall@shu.edu
Toll-free number: (800) 843-4255 Fax: (973) 275-2321
Mary Clare Cullum, Director of Undergraduate Admissions, Seton Hall University, 400 South Orange Avenue, South Orange, NJ 07079-2680

Stevens Institute of Technology
Hoboken, New Jersey
www.stevens.edu

CB member
CB code: 2819

- Private 4-year university and engineering college
- Residential campus in small city
- 2,956 degree-seeking undergraduates: 29% women, 2% African American, 10% Asian American, 9% Hispanic/Latino, 4% international
- 3,231 degree-seeking graduate students
- 44% of applicants admitted
- Application essay, interview required
- 82% graduate within 6 years; 6% enter graduate study

General. Founded in 1870. Regionally accredited. Approximately 90% of all students participate in internships, externships, cooperative education and research. **Degrees:** 541 bachelor's awarded; master's, doctoral offered. **ROTC:** Army, Air Force. **Location:** One mile from New York City. **Calendar:** Semester, extensive summer session. **Full-time faculty:** 255 total; 94% have terminal degrees, 25% minority, 25% women. **Part-time faculty:** 149 total; 20% minority, 20% women. **Class size:** 38% < 20, 46% 20-39, 8% 40-49, 8% 50-99, 1% >100. **Special facilities:** Laboratory for coastal, ocean and naval engineering, environmental laboratory, design and manufacturing institute, advanced telecommunications institute, geoenvironmental laboratory, optical communications lab, quantum cascade laser, center for mass spectrometry, center for microchemical systems, computer visualization laboratory.

Freshman class profile. 6,540 applied, 2,849 admitted, 686 enrolled.

Mid 50% test scores		Rank in top quarter:	92%
SAT critical reading:	590-680	Rank in top tenth:	62%
SAT math:	650-750	Return as sophomores:	94%
ACT composite:	29-32	Out-of-state:	36%
GPA 3.75 or higher:	80%	Live on campus:	91%
GPA 3.50-3.74:	11%	International:	5%
GPA 3.0-3.49:	8%	Fraternities:	28%
GPA 2.0-2.99:	1%	Sororities:	26%

Basis for selection. Admissions committee meets to review applicant's file once official transcript and standardized test scores are received and the interview requirement completed. Other information submitted considered as well. Applicants to Music and Technology or Visual Arts and Technology may submit a digital portfolio in place of standardized test scores. International applicants may submit 2 SAT II scores, 2 AP scores, or 2 IB scores in place of statndardized test scores. Students who live outside 250-mile radius and are unable to visit campus may schedule phone interview. Additional interview with departmental committee required of applicants to accelerated premed, predentistry, and prelaw programs. **Home schooled:** Letter of recommendation (nonparent) required.

High school preparation. College-preparatory program required. 16 units required. Required and recommended units include English 4, mathematics 4, social studies 2, history 2, science 3-4 (laboratory 3-4), foreign language 2 and academic electives 4. Business, engineering, computer science, and applied science programs require 2 algebra, 1 geometry, 1 pre-calculus or calculus, 1 chemistry, 1 physics, 1 biology.

2016-2017 Annual costs. Tuition/fees (projected): $48,838. Room/board: $13,500. Books/supplies: $1,000. Personal expenses: $1,250.

2014-2015 Financial aid. **Need-based:** 69% of total undergraduate aid awarded as scholarships/grants, 31% as loans/jobs. **Non-need-based:** Scholarships awarded for academics, leadership, music/drama, ROTC.

Application procedures. **Admission:** Closing date 2/1 (postmark date). $60 fee, may be waived for applicants with need. Admission notification by 4/1. Must reply by 5/1. **Financial aid:** Priority date 2/15; no closing date. FAFSA required. Applicants notified on a rolling basis starting 3/30; must reply by 5/1 or within 2 week(s) of notification.

Academics. **Special study options:** Accelerated study, combined bachelor's/graduate degree, cooperative education, cross-registration, distance learning, double major, dual enrollment of high school students, honors, independent study, internships, study abroad. 4-year bachelor's/master's programs in all engineering and science disciplines. **Credit/placement by examination:** AP, CLEP, IB. This option is open to students with a GPA of 3.0 or better either in the previous semester or overall, and is limited to one per semester. Permission to take a course by examination must be obtained on a Request for a Course by Examination form from the instructor, student advisor, and the Office of Undergraduate Academics. If the examination is successfully completed, the instructor who administered the examination issues a letter grade in the course. The examination must be taken prior to the start of a semester, and if the examination is not passed, the unsuccessful attempt is recorded as part of the student's permanent record, and the student must enroll in that course in the following semester. A course that has already been attempted by a student cannot subsequently be taken as a Course by Examination. **Support services:** Pre-admission summer program, reduced course load, remedial instruction, study skills assistance, tutoring, writing center.

Majors. **Biology:** Biochemistry, bioinformatics. **Business:** Business admin, management information systems. **Computer sciences:** General, networking, security. **Engineering:** General, applied physics, biomedical, chemical, civil, computer, electrical, environmental, mechanical. **English:** English lit. **History:** General. **Liberal arts:** Arts/sciences. **Math:** Applied. **Philosophy/religion:** Philosophy. **Physical sciences:** Chemistry, materials science, physics.

Most popular majors. Business/marketing 13%, computer/information sciences 9%, engineering/engineering technologies 67%.

Technology on campus. PC or laptop required. 500 workstations in dormitories, library, computer center, student center. Dormitories wired for high-speed internet access and linked to campus network. Commuter students can connect to campus network. Online course registration, online library, helpline, repair service, student web hosting, wireless network available.

Student life. **Freshman orientation:** Mandatory, $550 fee. Preregistration for classes offered. Three-day program. **Policies:** Honor system observed. Freshmen not living at home must live on campus. **Housing:** Guaranteed on-campus for all undergraduates. Coed dorms, single-sex dorms, apartments, fraternity/sorority housing, wellness housing available. $400 nonrefundable deposit, deadline 6/1. **Activities:** Bands, campus ministries, choral groups, dance, drama, film society, international student organizations, literary magazine, music ensembles, musical theater, radio station, student government, student newspaper, TV station, over 70 organizations.

Athletics. NCAA. **Intercollegiate:** Baseball M, basketball, cheerleading W, cross-country, equestrian W, fencing, field hockey W, golf M, lacrosse, soccer, softball W, swimming, tennis, track and field, volleyball, wrestling M. **Intramural:** Archery, badminton, basketball, bowling, cricket, football (non-tackle), lacrosse M, racquetball, soccer, softball, squash, tennis, ultimate frisbee, volleyball. **Team name:** Ducks.

Student services. Alcohol/substance abuse counseling, chaplain/spiritual director, career counseling, services for economically disadvantaged, student employment services, financial aid counseling, health services, minority student services, personal counseling, placement for graduates, veterans' counselor, women's services. **Physically disabled:** Services for visually, speech, hearing impaired.

Contact. E-mail: admissions@stevens.edu
Phone: (201) 216-5194 Toll-free number: (800) 458-5323
Fax: (201) 216-8348
Jackie Williams, Dean of Undergraduate Admissions, Stevens Institute of Technology, One Castle Point on Hudson, Hoboken, NJ 07030-5991

Stockton University
Galloway, New Jersey
www.stockton.edu

CB member
CB code: 2889

- Public 4-year liberal arts college
- Residential campus in large town
- 7,765 degree-seeking undergraduates: 5% part-time, 59% women, 7% African American, 5% Asian American, 11% Hispanic/Latino, 3% Multiracial, non-Hispanic
- 816 degree-seeking graduate students

- 64% of applicants admitted
- SAT or ACT (ACT writing recommended), application essay required
- 73% graduate within 6 years

General. Founded in 1969. Regionally accredited. 7-acre marine science field station located off-campus. **Degrees:** 1,989 bachelor's awarded; master's, professional offered. **Location:** 12 miles from Atlantic City, 50 miles from Philadelphia. **Calendar:** Semester, extensive summer session. **Full-time faculty:** 315 total; 95% have terminal degrees, 22% minority, 55% women. **Part-time faculty:** 361 total; 38% have terminal degrees, 11% minority, 50% women. **Class size:** 22% < 20, 74% 20-39, 2% 40-49, less than 1% 50-99, less than 1% >100. **Special facilities:** Nature path, arboretum, forestry nursery, ecologic succession plots and study preserve, child care center, interdisciplinary natural sciences laboratory, observatory, Holocaust center, geothermal plant, ITV classroom, performing arts theater, hospital located on college grounds, solar carport, learning lab of hotel, conference center and resort management.

Freshman class profile. 5,482 applied, 3,531 admitted, 1,151 enrolled.

Mid 50% test scores		Rank in top quarter:	54%
SAT critical reading:	480-580	Rank in top tenth:	21%
SAT math:	500-600	Return as sophomores:	87%
SAT writing:	470-560	Out-of-state:	1%
ACT composite:	19-25	Live on campus:	73%

Basis for selection. Secondary school record, class rank, test scores most important; essay, recommendations, extracurricular activities also important; interview, work experience considered. **Home schooled:** Statement describing home school structure and mission, transcript of courses and grades required.

High school preparation. College-preparatory program recommended. 16 units required; 18 recommended. Required and recommended units include English 4, mathematics 3, social studies 2, science 2 (laboratory 2), foreign language 2 and academic electives 5.

2015-2016 Annual costs. Tuition/fees: $12,820; $19,472 out-of-state. Room/board: $11,707. Books/supplies: $1,587. Personal expenses: $2,173.

2015-2016 Financial aid. **Need-based:** 1,083 full-time freshmen applied for aid; 845 deemed to have need; 831 received aid. Average need met was 76%. Average scholarship/grant was $9,681; average loan $3,360. 41% of total undergraduate aid awarded as scholarships/grants, 59% as loans/jobs. **Non-need-based:** Awarded to 1,991 full-time undergraduates, including 431 freshmen. Scholarships awarded for academics, art, leadership, minority status, music/drama, state residency. **Additional information:** Institutional grants are provided to the neediest incoming students.

Application procedures. **Admission:** Priority date 2/1; deadline 5/1 (postmark date). $50 fee, may be waived for applicants with need. Admission notification by 10/1. Admission notification on a rolling basis beginning on or about 10/1. Must reply by May 1 or within 2 week(s) if notified thereafter. **Financial aid:** Priority date 3/1; no closing date. FAFSA required. Applicants notified by 4/1; Applicants notified on a rolling basis starting 4/1; must reply within 2 week(s) of notification.

Academics. **Special study options:** Accelerated study, combined bachelor's/graduate degree, cross-registration, distance learning, double major, dual enrollment of high school students, ESL, honors, independent study, internships, liberal arts/career combination, semester at sea, student-designed major, study abroad, teacher certification program, Washington semester. Dual degree bachelor's program in engineering with Rutgers University and New Jersey Institute of Technology, preceptoral advising, opportunities for specialized research, extensive Washington internship available. Accelerated Health Professions Program. **Credit/placement by examination:** AP, CLEP, IB, SAT, ACT, institutional tests. 32 credit hours maximum toward bachelor's degree. **Support services:** Learning center, pre-admission summer program, reduced course load, remedial instruction, study skills assistance, tutoring, writing center.

Majors. **Biology:** General, biochemistry, marine. **Business:** Business admin, hospitality admin. **Communications:** Communications/speech/rhetoric. **Computer sciences:** Information systems. **Conservation:** Environmental studies. **Education:** Multi-level teacher. **English:** English lit. **Foreign languages:** General. **Health services:** Audiology/speech pathology, nursing (RN). **History:** General. **Human services:** Social work. **Liberal arts:** Arts/sciences. **Math:** General. **Philosophy/religion:** General. **Physical sciences:** Chemistry, geology, physics. **Psychology:** General. **Social sciences:** Criminology, economics, political science, sociology. **Visual/performing arts:** General, studio arts.

Most popular majors. Biology 12%, business/marketing 19%, health sciences 18%, psychology 11%, social sciences 12%.

Technology on campus. 1,112 workstations in dormitories, library, computer center, student center. Dormitories wired for high-speed internet access

and linked to campus network. Commuter students can connect to campus network. Online course registration, online library, helpline, student web hosting, wireless network available.

Student life. **Freshman orientation:** Mandatory, $100 fee. Preregistration for classes offered. **Housing:** Guaranteed on-campus for freshmen. Coed dorms, special housing for disabled, apartments, themed housing, wellness housing available. $150 partly refundable deposit, deadline 5/1. Academic units, living/learning communities include themes of diversity, global citizenship, sustainability and wellness available. **Activities:** Bands, campus ministries, choral groups, dance, drama, international student organizations, literary magazine, music ensembles, Model UN, musical theater, radio station, student government, student newspaper, TV station, Books Without Borders, unified black students society, Christian Fellowship, Jewish student union, Circle K International, Amnesty International, action volunteers for the environment, Water Watch, CHANGE, campus religious council.

Athletics. NCAA. **Intercollegiate:** Baseball M, basketball, cheerleading, cross-country, field hockey W, lacrosse M, rowing (crew) W, soccer, softball W, tennis W, track and field, volleyball W. **Intramural:** Basketball, football (non-tackle), lacrosse W, soccer, softball, table tennis, volleyball. **Team name:** Ospreys.

Student services. Adult student services, alcohol/substance abuse counseling, chaplain/spiritual director, career counseling, services for economically disadvantaged, student employment services, financial aid counseling, health services, on-campus daycare, personal counseling, placement for graduates, veterans' counselor, women's services. **Physically disabled:** Services for visually, speech, hearing impaired.

Contact. E-mail: admissions@stockton.edu
Phone: (609) 652-4261 Toll-free number: (866) 772-2885
Fax: (609) 748-5541
John Iacovelli, Dean of Enrollment Management, Stockton University, 101 Vera King Farris Drive, Galloway, NJ 08205

Talmudical Academy of New Jersey
Adelphia, New Jersey
CB code: 0686

- Private 4-year rabbinical college for men affiliated with the Jewish faith
- Large town
- 45 degree-seeking undergraduates

General. Founded in 1967. Accredited by AARTS. Ordination available. **Degrees:** 1 bachelor's awarded. **Calendar:** Semester. **Full-time faculty:** 4 total. **Part-time faculty:** 2 total.

Basis for selection. Personal interview most important.

2015-2016 Annual costs. Tuition/fees: $12,000. Room/board: $2,700.

Application procedures. **Admission:** No deadline. No application fee. Admission notification on a rolling basis. **Financial aid:** No deadline. Applicants notified on a rolling basis.

Academics. Credit/placement by examination: AP, CLEP.

Majors. Theology: Talmudic.

Student life. Activities: Choral groups, TV station.

Contact. Phone: (732) 431-1600
Rabbi Yeruchim Shain, Registrar and Admissions Director, Talmudical Academy of New Jersey, Route 524, PO Box 7, Adelphia, NJ 07710

Thomas Edison State University
Trenton, New Jersey
www.tesu.edu
CB member
CB code: 0682

- Public 4-year university
- Commuter campus in small city
- 17,590 degree-seeking undergraduates: 99% part-time, 46% women, 15% African American, 4% Asian American, 9% Hispanic/Latino, 1% Native American, 1% Native Hawaiian/Pacific islander, 2% Multi-racial, non-Hispanic, 1% international
- 1,093 graduate students

General. Founded in 1972. Regionally accredited. **Degrees:** 2,445 bachelor's, 587 associate awarded; master's offered. **Location:** 45 miles from Philadelphia, 76 miles from New York City. **Calendar:** Differs by program.

Basis for selection. Open admission, but selective for some programs. Applicants should be at least 21 years old. Certain programs in health professions limited to persons holding appropriate certification. Admission to bachelor's degree nursing program limited to registered nurses (RNs) currently licensed in the USA. Applicants under the age of 21 may be accepted on case-by-case basis, or if they are member of a special population such as a corporate partner or member of U.S. military. Admission to Accelerated 2nd Degree BSN program limited to applicants who already have a non-nursing bachelor's degree.

2015-2016 Annual costs. Tuition/fees: $6,266; $9,167 out-of-state. Books/supplies: $1,698. **Additional information:** Tuition provided represents the College's Comprehensive Tuition Plan, which enables students to take 36 credits over a 12 month period. The College offers several other tuition plans.

2014-2015 Financial aid. All financial aid based on need. 21% of total undergraduate aid awarded as scholarships/grants, 79% as loans/jobs. **Additional information:** Financial aid applications should be received two months before each new term begins.

Application procedures. **Admission:** No deadline. $75 fee. Admission notification on a rolling basis. **Financial aid:** No deadline. FAFSA, institutional form required. Applicants notified on a rolling basis starting 3/1; must reply within 4 week(s) of notification.

Academics. Provides flexibility to complete degree, including credit by examination, assessment of experiential learning, guided study, online courses and credit for licenses and certificates, corporate and military training. Contracts with subject matter experts to act as mentors to academic units of college. **Special study options:** Accelerated study, combined bachelor's/graduate degree, distance learning, dual enrollment of high school students, external degree, independent study, student-designed major. Bachelor of Science in Health Sciences program offered in partnership with the Rutgers School of Health Related Professions. Program designed for those employed in the allied health field and requires students to possess professional certifications and licensures. **Credit/placement by examination:** AP, CLEP. 60 credit hours maximum toward associate degree, 120 toward bachelor's.

Majors. **Biology:** General. **Business:** Accounting, business admin, entrepreneurial studies, finance, human resources, international, labor relations, marketing, operations, organizational leadership. **Communications:** General. **Computer sciences:** General. **Conservation:** Environmental studies. **English:** English lit. **Foreign languages:** General. **Health services:** Clinical lab science, dental hygiene, facilities admin, health information management, medical radiologic technology/radiation therapy, nuclear medical technology, nursing (RN), radiation protection, respiratory therapy technology. **History:** General. **Human services:** Social work. **Liberal arts:** Arts/sciences, humanities. **Math:** General. **Philosophy/religion:** Philosophy, religion. **Protective services:** Law enforcement admin. **Psychology:** General. **Social sciences:** General, anthropology, international relations, political science, sociology. **Visual/performing arts:** Art, dramatic, music, photography.

Technology on campus. Commuter students can connect to campus network. Online course registration, online library, wireless network available.

Student life. **Activities:** Student newspaper.

Student services. Adult student services, financial aid counseling, veterans' counselor. **Physically disabled:** Services for visually, hearing impaired.

Contact. E-mail: admissions@tesc.edu
Toll-free number: (888) 442-8372 Fax: (609) 984-8447
David Hoftiezer, Director, Admissions, Thomas Edison State University, 111 West State Street, Trenton, NJ 08608-1176

University of Phoenix: Jersey City
Jersey City, New Jersey
www.phoenix.edu

▸ For-profit 4-year university
▸ Commuter campus in small city
▸ 371 undergraduates

General. Regionally accredited. **Degrees:** 66 bachelor's awarded. **Calendar:** Differs by program. Other academic calendar. **Full-time faculty:** 29 total. **Part-time faculty:** 47 total.

Basis for selection. Open admission, but selective for some programs.

2015-2016 Annual costs. Per-credit-hour charge, $410 to $635, depending upon level and course of study. Books, material charges, and other fees vary by course and program. All fees are subject to change.

Application procedures. **Admission:** No deadline. No application fee. **Financial aid:** No deadline.

Academics. **Credit/placement by examination:** AP, CLEP.

Majors. **Business:** Accounting/business management, business admin, e-commerce, entrepreneurial studies, finance, human resources, marketing, operations. **Computer sciences:** Database management, networking, programming, security, support specialist, system admin, systems analysis, web page design, webmaster. **Human services:** General.

Student life. **Freshman orientation:** Mandatory. Preregistration for classes offered.

Contact. University of Phoenix: Jersey City, 100 Town Square Place, Jersey City, NJ 07310-1756

William Paterson University of New Jersey
Wayne, New Jersey   **CB member**
www.wpunj.edu   **CB code: 2518**

▸ Public 4-year university and liberal arts college
▸ Commuter campus in large town
▸ 9,272 degree-seeking undergraduates: 17% part-time, 55% women, 16% African American, 7% Asian American, 28% Hispanic/Latino, 3% Multiracial, non-Hispanic
▸ 946 degree-seeking graduate students
▸ 74% of applicants admitted
▸ SAT or ACT (ACT writing optional) required
▸ 48% graduate within 6 years

General. Founded in 1855. Regionally accredited. **Degrees:** 2,134 bachelor's awarded; master's, professional offered. **ROTC:** Air Force. **Location:** 20 miles from New York City. **Calendar:** Semester, limited summer session. **Full-time faculty:** 411 total; 93% have terminal degrees, 35% minority, 50% women. **Part-time faculty:** 653 total; 21% have terminal degrees, 21% minority, 53% women. **Class size:** 49% < 20, 50% 20-39, less than 1% 40-49, less than 1% 50-99, less than 1% >100. **Special facilities:** Global financial center, science complex, art gallery, green house/nature preserve.

Freshman class profile. 9,848 applied, 7,315 admitted, 1,340 enrolled.

Mid 50% test scores		Rank in top quarter:	31%
SAT critical reading:	440-540	Rank in top tenth:	10%
SAT math:	460-540	End year in good standing:	68%
GPA 3.75 or higher:	11%	Return as sophomores:	75%
GPA 3.50-3.74:	13%	Out-of-state:	2%
GPA 3.0-3.49:	31%	Live on campus:	47%
GPA 2.0-2.99:	45%	International:	1%

Basis for selection. School records and test scores are most important; recommendations are also important; class rank and essay are considered. Audition required for music programs; portfolio required for art programs. Essays recommended. **Home schooled:** Transcript of courses and grades, state high school equivalency certificate required.

High school preparation. College-preparatory program required. 16 units required. Required units include English 4, mathematics 3, social studies 2, science 2 (laboratory 2) and academic electives 5. 5 additional college preparatory courses (advanced math, literature, foreign language, social science) also required.

2015-2016 Annual costs. Tuition/fees: $12,365; $20,125 out-of-state. Room/board: $10,885. Books/supplies: $1,600. Personal expenses: $2,250.

2015-2016 Financial aid. **Need-based:** 1,267 full-time freshmen applied for aid; 1,052 deemed to have need; 1,035 received aid. Average scholarship/grant was $8,511; average loan $3,411. 56% of total undergraduate aid awarded as scholarships/grants, 44% as loans/jobs. **Non-need-based:** Awarded to 1,893 full-time undergraduates, including 436 freshmen. Scholarships awarded for academics, art, music/drama.

Application procedures. **Admission:** Priority date 12/1; deadline 6/1 (postmark date). $50 fee, may be waived for applicants with need. Admission notification on a rolling basis beginning on or about 1/15. Must reply by May 1 or within 2 week(s) if notified thereafter. **Financial aid:** Priority date 4/1; no closing date. FAFSA required. Applicants notified by 4/15; Applicants notified on a rolling basis.

Academics. **Special study options:** Accelerated study, combined bachelor's/graduate degree, cross-registration, distance learning, double major, dual enrollment of high school students, ESL, exchange student, honors, independent study, internships, liberal arts/career combination, study abroad, teacher certification program, Washington semester. Cluster courses (program that provides opportunities for students and faculty to study and learn together in courses grouped in interdisciplinary clusters of three). **Credit/placement by examination:** AP, CLEP, SAT, ACT, institutional tests. 60 credit hours maximum toward bachelor's degree. **Support services:** Learning center, preadmission summer program, reduced course load, remedial instruction, study skills assistance, tutoring, writing center.

Honors college/program. Average Honors students receive a 1206 SAT score (middle 50% range of 1160 to 1250- Critical Reading and Math only). Average Honors students have a 3.77 high school GPA (middle 50% range of 3.59 to 3.94). Students must have completed honors, AP, and/or IB courses in high school and are engaged learners.

Majors. **Area/ethnic studies:** African-American, Asian, Latin American, women's. **Biology:** General, biotechnology. **Business:** Accounting, business admin, finance, financial planning, international, management science, marketing, selling. **Communications:** Communications/speech/rhetoric. **Computer sciences:** General. **Conservation:** Environmental studies. **Education:** Early childhood, elementary, physical, secondary, special ed. **English:** English lit. **Foreign languages:** French, Spanish. **Health services:** Athletic training, communication disorders, community health services, nursing (RN). **History:** General. **Liberal arts:** Arts/sciences. **Math:** General. **Parks/recreation:** Exercise sciences, sports admin. **Philosophy/religion:** Philosophy. **Physical sciences:** Chemistry, geology. **Protective services:** Criminal justice. **Psychology:** General. **Social sciences:** Anthropology, economics, geography, political science, sociology. **Visual/performing arts:** Art, art history/conservation, dramatic, music, music performance.

Most popular majors. Business/marketing 19%, communications/journalism 11%, education 10%, English 6%, health sciences 9%, psychology 12%, social sciences 9%.

Technology on campus. 700 workstations in dormitories, library, computer center. Dormitories wired for high-speed internet access and linked to campus network. Commuter students can connect to campus network. Online course registration, online library, helpline, student web hosting, wireless network available.

Student life. **Freshman orientation:** Mandatory. Preregistration for classes offered. Two-day program held twice in early summer. Freshmen and parents invited to stay overnight for nominal fee. **Housing:** Guaranteed on-campus for all undergraduates. Coed dorms, special housing for disabled, apartments available. $150 nonrefundable deposit, deadline 5/1. Hall reserved for students 21-and-older, apartment-style housing, women's floor, academic interest housing available. **Activities:** Campus ministries, choral groups, dance, drama, film society, literary magazine, music ensembles, Model UN, musical theater, opera, radio station, student government, student newspaper, symphony orchestra, TV station, Black Student Association, Christian Fellowship club, Jewish Student Association, Feminist Collective, Organization of Latin American Students, United Asian Americans, Coalition of Lesbians/Gays/Friends, Muslim Student Association.

Athletics. NCAA. **Intercollegiate:** Baseball M, basketball, field hockey W, football (tackle) M, golf M, soccer, softball W, swimming, tennis W, volleyball W. **Intramural:** Basketball, field hockey W, soccer W, softball, volleyball. **Team name:** Pioneers.

Student services. Adult student services, alcohol/substance abuse counseling, chaplain/spiritual director, career counseling, services for economically disadvantaged, student employment services, financial aid counseling, health services, legal services, minority student services, personal counseling, placement for graduates, veterans' counselor, women's services. **Physically disabled:** Services for visually, speech, hearing impaired.

Contact. E-mail: admissions@wpunj.edu
Phone: (973) 720-2125 Toll-free number: (877) 978-3923
Fax: (973) 720-2910
Rohan Howell, Director of Admissions, William Paterson University of New Jersey, 300 Pompton Road, Wayne, NJ 07470

New Mexico

Eastern New Mexico University
Portales, New Mexico
www.enmu.edu   CB code: 4299

- Public 4-year university
- Residential campus in large town
- 3,627 degree-seeking undergraduates
- 50% of applicants admitted
- SAT or ACT (ACT writing optional) required

General. Founded in 1927. Regionally accredited. **Degrees:** 705 bachelor's, 103 associate awarded; master's offered. **Location:** 225 miles from Albuquerque,105 miles from Lubbock, TX. **Calendar:** Semester, extensive summer session. **Full-time faculty:** 156 total; 74% have terminal degrees, 8% minority, 49% women. **Part-time faculty:** 175 total; 17% have terminal degrees, 18% minority, 57% women. **Class size:** 53% < 20, 40% 20-39, 4% 40-49, 2% 50-99, less than 1% >100. **Special facilities:** Natural history museum, mineral museum, archaeological museum, scanning and transmission electron microscopes.

Freshman class profile. 2,382 applied, 1,187 admitted, 612 enrolled.

Mid 50% test scores			
SAT critical reading:	400-520	GPA 3.0-3.49:	37%
SAT math:	420-520	GPA 2.0-2.99:	32%
ACT composite:	17-23	Rank in top quarter:	29%
GPA 3.75 or higher:	15%	Rank in top tenth:	10%
GPA 3.50-3.74:	15%	Out-of-state:	20%
		Live on campus:	76%

Basis for selection. Admission based on either a national test score or a cumulative, unweighted grade point average. **Home schooled:** Transcript of courses and grades required. Recommend all in-state home-schooled students earn a GED no more than one semester before enrolling at ENMU.

High school preparation. College-preparatory program recommended. 12 units recommended. Recommended units include English 4, mathematics 4, social studies 2 and science 2.

2015-2016 Annual costs. Tuition/fees: $5,168; $10,943 out-of-state. Room/board: $6,718. Books/supplies: $950. Personal expenses: $2,397.

Financial aid. Non-need-based: Scholarships awarded for academics, alumni affiliation, art, athletics, leadership, music/drama, state residency.

Application procedures. Admission: Priority date 8/15; no deadline. No application fee. Admission notification on a rolling basis. Housing deposit refundable if requested before August 1st. **Financial aid:** No deadline. FAFSA required. Applicants notified on a rolling basis starting 5/1.

Academics. Special study options: Accelerated study, combined bachelor's/graduate degree, distance learning, double major, dual enrollment of high school students, ESL, independent study, internships, study abroad, teacher certification program. **Credit/placement by examination:** AP, CLEP, SAT, ACT, institutional tests. 32 credit hours maximum toward associate degree, 50 toward bachelor's. **Support services:** Learning center, pre-admission summer program, remedial instruction, tutoring, writing center.

Majors. Biology: General, biochemistry. **Business:** Accounting, business admin, finance, human resources, management information systems, managerial economics, marketing. **Communications:** Communications/speech/rhetoric. **Computer sciences:** General. **Conservation:** Environmental science, wildlife/wilderness. **Education:** Agricultural, business, early childhood, elementary, music, physical, sales/marketing, special ed, trade/industrial. **English:** English lit. **Foreign languages:** Spanish. **Health services:** Audiology/speech pathology, clinical lab science, clinical/medical social work, nursing (RN). **History:** General. **Liberal arts:** Arts/sciences. **Math:** General, computational/applied. **Parks/recreation:** Health/fitness. **Philosophy/religion:** Religion. **Physical sciences:** Chemistry, geology. **Protective services:** Criminal justice, forensics. **Psychology:** General. **Social sciences:** General, anthropology, political science, sociology. **Visual/performing arts:** Art, cinematography, dramatic, music. **Work/family studies:** General.

Most popular majors. Business/marketing 10%, education 9%, health sciences 13%, liberal arts 27%, security/protective services 6%, visual/performing arts 7%.

Technology on campus. 506 workstations in dormitories, library, computer center, student center. Dormitories wired for high-speed internet access and linked to campus network. Commuter students can connect to campus network. Online library, helpline, wireless network available.

Student life. Freshman orientation: Mandatory. Preregistration for classes offered. Incoming freshman are encouraged to take part in Dawg Days the week before the fall semester starts. **Policies:** All housing options are alcohol/drug/smoke-free facilities. All freshman are required to have on-campus housing and a meal plan for the first year unless already living within the immediate commuting area. **Housing:** Guaranteed on-campus for freshmen. Coed dorms, single-sex dorms, special housing for disabled, apartments, fraternity/sorority housing available. $150 nonrefundable deposit, deadline 8/1. **Activities:** Bands, campus ministries, choral groups, dance, drama, film society, international student organizations, literary magazine, music ensembles, musical theater, radio station, student government, student newspaper, TV station, Paradigm, Association to Help Our Race Advance, N.A.T.I.V.E. club, Muslim students association, College Republicans, Society of Political Scholars, Student Association for Voters Empowerment, Gay-Straight Alliance, Voices of Inclusive and Committed Education Students.

Athletics. NCAA. **Intercollegiate:** Baseball M, basketball, cross-country, football (tackle) M, rodeo, soccer, softball W, track and field, volleyball W. **Intramural:** Badminton, basketball, cross-country, football (non-tackle), golf, racquetball, soccer, softball, tennis, volleyball. **Team name:** Greyhounds.

Student services. Adult student services, alcohol/substance abuse counseling, career counseling, student employment services, financial aid counseling, health services, minority student services, on-campus daycare, personal counseling, placement for graduates, veterans' counselor. **Physically disabled:** Services for visually, speech, hearing impaired.

Contact. E-mail: enrollment.services@enmu.edu
Phone: (575) 562-2178 Toll-free number: (800) 367-3668
Fax: (575) 562-2118
Cody Spitz, Director of Enrollment Services, Eastern New Mexico University, 1500 South Avenue K, Portales, NM 88130

Institute of American Indian Arts
Santa Fe, New Mexico   CB member
www.iaia.edu   CB code: 0180

- Public 4-year visual arts and liberal arts college
- Residential campus in small city
- 263 degree-seeking undergraduates: 1% African American, 5% Hispanic/Latino, 83% Native American, 2% international
- 61 graduate students
- Application essay required

General. Founded in 1962. Regionally accredited. **Degrees:** 27 bachelor's, 3 associate awarded; master's offered. **Location:** 60 miles from Albuquerque. **Calendar:** Semester, limited summer session.

Basis for selection. Based on completion of high school or GED, college placement scores from ACT, SAT, ACCUPLACER, COMPASS. SAT or ACT recommended. Personal statement of educational intention required.

High school preparation. College-preparatory program required.

2015-2016 Annual costs. Tuition/fees: $4,440; $4,440 out-of-state. Room/board: $8,140. Books/supplies: $2,816. Personal expenses: $3,960.

Application procedures. Admission: Closing date 8/4 (receipt date). $25 fee, may be waived for applicants with need. Admission notification on a rolling basis beginning on or about 5/1. Must reply by May 1 or within 1 week(s) if notified thereafter. **Financial aid:** Priority date 3/15; no closing date. FAFSA, institutional form required. Applicants notified on a rolling basis starting 5/1.

Academics. Special study options: Cross-registration, distance learning, double major, dual enrollment of high school students, independent study, internships, study abroad. **Credit/placement by examination:** AP, CLEP, IB, SAT, ACT, institutional tests. **Support services:** Learning center, pre-admission summer program, remedial instruction, study skills assistance, tutoring.

Majors. Area/ethnic studies: Native American. **English:** Creative writing. **Visual/performing arts:** Cinematography, studio arts.

Technology on campus. 50 workstations in dormitories, library, computer center, student center. Dormitories wired for high-speed internet access and linked to campus network. Commuter students can connect to campus

network. Online course registration, online library, helpline, repair service, wireless network available.

Student life. Freshman orientation: Mandatory. Preregistration for classes offered. Conducted each semester one week before registration. **Housing:** Guaranteed on-campus for freshmen. Coed dorms, special housing for disabled, apartments available. $150 fully refundable deposit. **Activities:** Drama, film society, literary magazine, student government, student newspaper, TV station.

Student services. Alcohol/substance abuse counseling, career counseling, student employment services, financial aid counseling, health services, personal counseling, placement for graduates, veterans' counselor.

Contact. E-mail: admissions@iaia.edu
Phone: (505) 424-2300 Fax: (505) 424-4500
Mary Curley, Admissions and Recruitment Director, Institute of American Indian Arts, 83 Avan Nu Po Road, Santa Fe, NM 87508-1300

ITT Technical Institute: Albuquerque
Albuquerque, New Mexico
www.itt-tech.edu
CB code: 2690

- For-profit 4-year technical college
- Commuter campus in large city
- 402 undergraduates
- Interview required

General. Accredited by ACICS. **Degrees:** 25 bachelor's, 112 associate awarded. **Calendar:** Quarter, extensive summer session. **Full-time faculty:** 25 total. **Part-time faculty:** 78 total.

Basis for selection. Satisfactory scores from on-site tests in English and mathematics required.

2015-2016 Annual costs. Per-credit-hour charge, $529, will vary depending upon level and course of study; academic fee, $200. Certain programs of study require purchase of tools, which could cost an additional $150 to $655. All costs are subject to change.

Application procedures. Admission: No deadline. No application fee. Admission notification on a rolling basis. **Financial aid:** No deadline. FAFSA, institutional form required. Applicants notified on a rolling basis.

Academics. Credit/placement by examination: AP, CLEP. **Support services:** Learning center, tutoring.

Majors. Business: Business admin, construction management, e-commerce. **Communications technology:** Animation/special effects. **Computer sciences:** Security. **Protective services:** Law enforcement admin.

Most popular majors. Business/marketing 16%, computer/information sciences 29%, engineering/engineering technologies 19%, security/protective services 37%.

Technology on campus. Online library available.

Student life. Freshman orientation: Available. Preregistration for classes offered.

Student services. Career counseling, student employment services, placement for graduates.

Contact. Phone: (505) 828-1114 Toll-free number: (800) 636-1114
Fax: (505) 828-1849
John Crooks, Director of Recruitment, ITT Technical Institute: Albuquerque, 5100 Masthead Street NE, Albuquerque, NM 87109

National American University: Albuquerque
Rio Rancho, New Mexico
www.national.edu
CB code: 5360

- For-profit 4-year business college
- Commuter campus in large city
- 352 undergraduates

General. Founded in 1941. Regionally accredited. **Degrees:** 41 bachelor's, 47 associate awarded. **ROTC:** Naval, Air Force. **Calendar:** Quarter, extensive summer session. **Part-time faculty:** 60 total.

Basis for selection. Open admission.

2015-2016 Annual costs. Tuition/fees: $15,885. Books/supplies: $1,350. **Additional information:** Additional fees may apply.

Application procedures. Admission: No deadline. $25 fee. Admission notification on a rolling basis. **Financial aid:** No deadline. Institutional form required. Applicants notified on a rolling basis.

Academics. Special study options: Combined bachelor's/graduate degree, distance learning, independent study. **Credit/placement by examination:** AP, CLEP. 45 credit hours maximum toward associate degree, 95 toward bachelor's. **Support services:** Tutoring.

Majors. Business: Accounting, accounting/business management, business admin, finance, human resources, management information systems, organizational leadership. **Computer sciences:** Information technology, LAN/WAN management. **Health services:** Health care admin, nursing (RN). **Protective services:** Criminal justice.

Technology on campus. 15 workstations in library, computer center.

Student life. Activities: Choral groups, literary magazine, music ensembles, TV station.

Athletics. Team name: Mavericks.

Student services. Adult student services, career counseling, student employment services, placement for graduates, veterans' counselor.

Contact. E-mail: albadmissions@national.edu
Phone: (505) 348-3750 Toll-free number: (800) 895-9904
Fax: (505) 348-3755
Nancy Pointer-Meason, Director of Admissions, National American University: Albuquerque, 4775 Indian School Road NE, Suite 200, Albuquerque, NM 87110

New Mexico Highlands University
Las Vegas, New Mexico
www.nmhu.edu
CB member
CB code: 4532

- Public 4-year university
- Commuter campus in large town
- 2,128 degree-seeking undergraduates: 31% part-time, 61% women, 6% African American, 1% Asian American, 56% Hispanic/Latino, 8% Native American, 1% Native Hawaiian/Pacific islander, 1% Multi-racial, non-Hispanic, 6% international
- 1,112 degree-seeking graduate students

General. Founded in 1893. Regionally accredited. **Degrees:** 465 bachelor's, 1 associate awarded; master's offered. **Location:** 68 miles from Santa Fe, 120 miles from Albuquerque. **Calendar:** Semester, limited summer session. **Full-time faculty:** 137 total; 72% have terminal degrees, 33% minority, 44% women. **Part-time faculty:** 146 total; 8% have terminal degrees, 40% minority, 66% women. **Class size:** 70% < 20, 28% 20-39, 1% 40-49, less than 1% 50-99.

Freshman class profile. 993 applied, 993 admitted, 298 enrolled.

Mid 50% test scores			
SAT critical reading:	350-	GPA 3.50-3.74:	12%
SAT math:	390-480	GPA 3.0-3.49:	30%
SAT writing:	380-470	GPA 2.0-2.99:	46%
ACT composite:	15-20	Out-of-state:	30%
GPA 3.75 or higher:	9%	Live on campus:	76%
		International:	4%

Basis for selection. Open admission. **Home schooled:** Transcript of courses and grades, state high school equivalency certificate required.

2016-2017 Annual costs. Tuition/fees (projected): $4,800; $7,534 out-of-state. Room/board: $7,164. Books/supplies: $1,000. Personal expenses: $2,044.

2014-2015 Financial aid. Need-based: 251 full-time freshmen applied for aid; 214 deemed to have need; 210 received aid. Average scholarship/grant was $1,774; average loan $1,958. 84% of total undergraduate aid awarded as scholarships/grants, 16% as loans/jobs. **Non-need-based:** Awarded to 1,475 full-time undergraduates, including 453 freshmen. Scholarships awarded for academics, alumni affiliation, art, athletics, music/drama, state residency. **Additional information:** Work study funds available on no-need basis to state residents.

Application procedures. Admission: No deadline. $15 fee, may be waived for applicants with need. Admission notification on a rolling basis. **Financial aid:** No deadline. FAFSA required. Applicants notified on a rolling basis starting 3/15; must reply within 2 week(s) of notification.

Academics. Special study options: Combined bachelor's/graduate degree, cooperative education, distance learning, double major, dual enrollment of high school students, honors, independent study, internships, liberal arts/career combination, teacher certification program. **Credit/placement by examination:** AP, CLEP, SAT, ACT, institutional tests. As approved by appropriate department. **Support services:** Learning center, remedial instruction, study skills assistance, tutoring, writing center.

Majors. Biology: General. **Business:** Accounting, business admin, finance, international, management information systems, marketing. **Communications:** Media studies. **Computer sciences:** Computer science. **Conservation:** Forest management. **Education:** Art, biology, early childhood, elementary, mathematics, music, science, secondary, special ed. **English:** English lit. **Foreign languages:** Spanish. **Health services:** Nursing (RN). **History:** General. **Human services:** Social work. **Math:** General. **Parks/recreation:** Health/fitness, sports admin. **Physical sciences:** Chemistry, forensic chemistry, geology. **Protective services:** Criminal justice, forensics. **Psychology:** General. **Social sciences:** Anthropology, criminology, political science, sociology. **Visual/performing arts:** Art, music, music performance, studio arts.

Most popular majors. Business/marketing 16%, education 24%, health sciences 34%, security/protective services 6%.

Technology on campus. 250 workstations in dormitories, library, computer center, student center. Dormitories wired for high-speed internet access and linked to campus network. Commuter students can connect to campus network. Online library, helpline, repair service, wireless network available.

Student life. Freshman orientation: Mandatory, $50 fee. Preregistration for classes offered. **Housing:** Guaranteed on-campus for freshmen. Coed dorms, special housing for disabled, apartments available. $100 partly refundable deposit. **Activities:** Campus ministries, choral groups, dance, drama, international student organizations, literary magazine, music ensembles, musical theater, radio station, student government, social work club, several ethnic and religious groups.

Athletics. NAIA, NCAA. Intercollegiate: Baseball M, basketball, cross-country, football (tackle) M, rodeo, soccer W, softball W, track and field W, volleyball W, wrestling M. **Intramural:** Baseball M, basketball, golf, handball, racquetball, rifle, rugby, skiing, softball, swimming, table tennis, tennis, track and field. **Team name:** Cowboys, Cowgirls.

Student services. Adult student services, career counseling, services for economically disadvantaged, student employment services, financial aid counseling, health services, on-campus daycare, personal counseling. **Physically disabled:** Services for visually, speech, hearing impaired.

Contact. E-mail: mdbassett@nmhu.edu
Phone: (505) 454-3439 Toll-free number: (800) 338-6648
Fax: (505) 454-3552
John Coca, Director of Admissions, New Mexico Highlands University, Box 9000, Las Vegas, NM 87701

New Mexico Institute of Mining and Technology
Socorro, New Mexico   CB member
www.nmt.edu   CB code: 4533

- Public 4-year engineering and liberal arts college
- Residential campus in small town
- 1,502 degree-seeking undergraduates: 5% part-time, 27% women, 2% African American, 3% Asian American, 29% Hispanic/Latino, 3% Native American, 5% Multi-racial, non-Hispanic, 3% international
- 393 degree-seeking graduate students
- 24% of applicants admitted
- SAT or ACT (ACT writing optional) required
- 49% graduate within 6 years

General. Founded in 1889. Regionally accredited. Student employment opportunities in research facilities and in faculty research. **Degrees:** 247 bachelor's, 1 associate awarded; master's, doctoral offered. **Location:** 75 miles from Albuquerque. **Calendar:** Semester, limited summer session. **Full-time faculty:** 130 total; 95% have terminal degrees, 28% minority, 22% women. **Part-time faculty:** 42 total; 38% have terminal degrees, 14% minority, 33% women. **Class size:** 56% < 20, 31% 20-39, 7% 40-49, 5% 50-99, less than 1% >100. **Special facilities:** Experimental mine, mineral museum, laboratory for atmospheric physics and chemistry, energetic materials research, seismic research network, scanning electron microscope, scanning

transmission electron microscope, transmission electron microscope, observatory.

Freshman class profile. 1,628 applied, 398 admitted, 338 enrolled.

Mid 50% test scores			
		GPA 2.0-2.99:	9%
SAT critical reading:	520-650	Rank in top quarter:	66%
SAT math:	570-680	Rank in top tenth:	36%
ACT composite:	23-29	Return as sophomores:	75%
GPA 3.75 or higher:	50%	Out-of-state:	14%
GPA 3.50-3.74:	21%	Live on campus:	87%
GPA 3.0-3.49:	20%	International:	3%

Basis for selection. Test scores and high school GPA most important. Minimum 2.5 GPA required. Minimum 21 ACT or 970 SAT (exclusive of Writing) required. ACT recommended. Non-degree-seeking students do not need to take ACT or SAT. Interview and recommendations considered if GPA and test scores are borderline or if other issues need to be addressed. **Home schooled:** Transcript of courses and grades required. Must supply documentation of courses completed.

High school preparation. College-preparatory program recommended. 15 units required; 18 recommended. Required and recommended units include English 4, mathematics 3-4, social studies 2-3, history 1, science 2-4 (laboratory 2-3), foreign language 2 and academic electives 3. High school courses in pre-calculus and calculus are strongly recommended.

2015-2016 Annual costs. Tuition/fees: $6,613; $19,137 out-of-state. Room/board: $7,586. Books/supplies: $1,066. Personal expenses: $1,634.

2015-2016 Financial aid. Need-based: 324 full-time freshmen applied for aid; 180 deemed to have need; 178 received aid. Average need met was 84%. Average scholarship/grant was $4,582; average loan $2,939. 56% of total undergraduate aid awarded as scholarships/grants, 44% as loans/jobs. **Non-need-based:** Awarded to 984 full-time undergraduates, including 309 freshmen. Scholarships awarded for academics, alumni affiliation, minority status, state residency. **Additional information:** Campus research projects offer student employment based on abilities, interest, and merit.

Application procedures. Admission: Priority date 3/1; deadline 8/1. $15 fee, may be waived for applicants with need. Admission notification on a rolling basis beginning on or about 3/1. Must reply by May 1 or within 2 week(s) if notified thereafter. **Financial aid:** Priority date 5/1; no closing date. FAFSA, institutional form required. Applicants notified on a rolling basis starting 5/1; must reply within 2 week(s) of notification.

Academics. Special study options: Accelerated study, cooperative education, distance learning, double major, dual enrollment of high school students, exchange student, independent study, internships, student-designed major, teacher certification program. **Credit/placement by examination:** AP, CLEP, SAT, ACT, institutional tests. No limit to number of credits. Must have permission of instructor. **Support services:** Pre-admission summer program, reduced course load, study skills assistance, tutoring, writing center.

Majors. Biology: General, biochemistry, biomedical sciences. **Business:** Business admin. **Computer sciences:** General, computer science, information technology. **Conservation:** General, environmental studies. **Engineering:** General, chemical, civil, electrical, environmental, materials, mechanical, metallurgical, mining, petroleum. **English:** Technical writing. **Math:** General, applied. **Physical sciences:** Astrophysics, atmospheric physics, chemistry, geology, geophysics, physics. **Psychology:** General.

Most popular majors. Biology 7%, computer/information sciences 8%, engineering/engineering technologies 62%, physical sciences 15%.

Technology on campus. 225 workstations in dormitories, library, computer center, student center. Dormitories wired for high-speed internet access and linked to campus network. Commuter students can connect to campus network. Helpline, student web hosting, wireless network available.

Student life. Freshman orientation: Available, $40 fee. Preregistration for classes offered. Two-day event held weekend before classes start. **Policies:** Students living on-campus must purchase meal plan. **Housing:** Coed dorms, single-sex dorms, apartments, wellness housing available. $100 partly refundable deposit, deadline 6/1. **Activities:** Bands, choral groups, dance, drama, international student organizations, music ensembles, musical theater, student government, student newspaper.

Athletics. Intramural: Badminton, basketball, golf, racquetball, rifle, rugby, soccer, softball, tennis, volleyball.

Student services. Adult student services, career counseling, student employment services, health services, on-campus daycare, personal counseling, placement for graduates. **Physically disabled:** Services for visually, hearing impaired.

Contact. E-mail: admission@admin.nmt.edu
Phone: (575) 835-5424 Toll-free number: (800) 428-8324
Fax: (575) 835-5989
Tony Ortiz, Director of Admission, New Mexico Institute of Mining and
Technology, 801 Leroy Place, Socorro, NM 87801

New Mexico State University
Las Cruces, New Mexico
www.nmsu.edu   **CB code: 4531**

- Public 4-year university
- Commuter campus in small city
- 12,104 degree-seeking undergraduates: 15% part-time, 53% women,
  3% African American, 1% Asian American, 55% Hispanic/Latino, 2%
  Native American, 2% Multi-racial, non-Hispanic, 5% international
- 2,914 degree-seeking graduate students
- 66% of applicants admitted
- SAT or ACT (ACT writing optional) required
- 42% graduate within 6 years

General. Founded in 1888. Regionally accredited. **Degrees:** 2,616 bachelor's, 21 associate awarded; master's, professional, doctoral offered. **ROTC:** Army, Air Force. **Location:** 42 miles from El Paso, Texas. **Calendar:** Semester, extensive summer session. **Full-time faculty:** 690 total; 87% have terminal degrees, 30% minority, 45% women. **Part-time faculty:** 359 total; 40% have terminal degrees, 29% minority, 59% women. **Class size:** 47% < 20, 33% 20-39, 9% 40-49, 7% 50-99, 3% >100. **Special facilities:** Observatory, horse farm, rodeo grounds, electron microscope, sports medicine training clinic, farm, college operated museums, chile pepper institute, entrepreneurship institute, cafe for culinary training.

Freshman class profile. 7,427 applied, 4,884 admitted, 1,993 enrolled.

Mid 50% test scores		Rank in top quarter:	40%
SAT critical reading:	410-530	Rank in top tenth:	17%
SAT math:	430-540	Return as sophomores:	74%
SAT writing:	400-520	Out-of-state:	24%
ACT composite:	18-24	Live on campus:	48%
GPA 3.75 or higher:	28%	International:	4%
GPA 3.50-3.74:	17%	Fraternities:	7%
GPA 3.0-3.49:	34%	Sororities:	8%
GPA 2.0-2.99:	21%		

Basis for selection. School achievement record, test scores most important. **Home schooled:** Transcript of courses and grades required. The home school educator must submit a transcript or document that lists the courses completed and grades earned by the student. This transcript or document must also indicate the date the student completed or graduated from the home school program.

High school preparation. College-preparatory program recommended. 11 units required. Required units include English 4, mathematics 4, science 2 (laboratory 2) and foreign language 1. English must include at least 2 units of writing-intensive courses, one of which must be a junior- or senior-level course. Math must include completion of Algebra 1, Geometry, Algebra 2 and one additional math course. Will accept 1 unit foreign language or 1 unit fine arts.

2015-2016 Annual costs. Tuition/fees: $6,729; $21,234 out-of-state. Room/board: $7,572. Books/supplies: $1,084. Personal expenses: $3,216.

2014-2015 Financial aid. **Need-based:** 1,658 full-time freshmen applied for aid; 1,347 deemed to have need; 1,346 received aid. Average need met was 64%. Average scholarship/grant was $7,053; average loan $3,162. 56% of total undergraduate aid awarded as scholarships/grants, 44% as loans/jobs. **Non-need-based:** Awarded to 2,124 full-time undergraduates, including 494 freshmen. Scholarships awarded for academics, alumni affiliation, art, athletics, leadership, minority status, music/drama, ROTC, state residency.

Application procedures. **Admission:** No deadline. $20 fee. Admission notification on a rolling basis. **Financial aid:** Priority date 1/1, closing date 3/1. FAFSA required. Applicants notified on a rolling basis starting 4/1.

Academics. **Special study options:** Combined bachelor's/graduate degree, cooperative education, distance learning, double major, dual enrollment of high school students, ESL, exchange student, honors, independent study, internships, student-designed major, study abroad, teacher certification program. **Credit/placement by examination:** AP, CLEP, SAT, ACT, institutional tests. **Support services:** Learning center, reduced course load, study skills assistance, tutoring, writing center.

Majors. **Area/ethnic studies:** Women's. **Biology:** General, bacteriology, biochemistry, ecology, genetics, plant pathology. **Business:** General, accounting, business admin, finance, hospitality admin, international, marketing. **Communications:** General, journalism. **Communications technology:** Animation/special effects. **Computer sciences:** General, information technology. **Conservation:** Economics, environmental science, wildlife/wilderness. **Education:** General, agricultural, early childhood, elementary, family/consumer sciences, music, physical, secondary, special ed, speech impaired. **Engineering:** Aerospace, applied physics, chemical, civil, electrical, industrial, mechanical. **English:** English lit. **Foreign languages:** General. **Health services:** Athletic training, community health services, dietetics, nursing (RN), public health ed. **History:** General. **Human services:** Community org/advocacy, social work. **Liberal arts:** Arts/sciences. **Math:** General. **Parks/recreation:** Exercise sciences. **Philosophy/religion:** Philosophy. **Physical sciences:** Chemistry, geology, physics. **Protective services:** Criminal justice. **Psychology:** General. **Social sciences:** Anthropology, economics, geography, political science, sociology. **Visual/performing arts:** General, cinematography, dance, dramatic, music performance, studio arts. **Work/family studies:** Clothing/textiles, family resources, family studies, food/nutrition.

Most popular majors. Business/marketing 16%, education 7%, engineering/engineering technologies 13%, health sciences 7%, liberal arts 6%, security/protective services 7%.

Technology on campus. 371 workstations in library, computer center, student center. Dormitories wired for high-speed internet access and linked to campus network. Commuter students can connect to campus network. Online course registration, online library, helpline, repair service, student web hosting, wireless network available.

Student life. **Freshman orientation:** Mandatory, $40 fee. Preregistration for classes offered. All new, incoming freshmen and transfer students must complete orientation before registering. **Housing:** Guaranteed on-campus for freshmen. Coed dorms, apartments, fraternity/sorority housing available. $200 nonrefundable deposit. Upper division dorms available. **Activities:** Bands, campus ministries, choral groups, dance, drama, international student organizations, literary magazine, music ensembles, Model UN, musical theater, opera, radio station, student government, student newspaper, symphony orchestra, TV station, Baptist Student Union, Black Students Association, Cancer Aid Resource and Education, College Democrats, international club, Latinos for Exito, Newman Catholic Students, Rotaract club, United Native American Association, Young Americans for Liberty.

Athletics. NCAA. **Intercollegiate:** Baseball M, basketball, cross-country, diving W, equestrian W, football (tackle) M, golf, soccer W, softball W, swimming W, tennis, track and field W, volleyball W. **Intramural:** Badminton, basketball, cheerleading, football (non-tackle), golf, racquetball, soccer, softball, table tennis, tennis, ultimate frisbee, volleyball, water polo. **Team name:** Aggies.

Student services. Adult student services, alcohol/substance abuse counseling, career counseling, student employment services, financial aid counseling, health services, legal services, minority student services, on-campus daycare, personal counseling, placement for graduates, veterans' counselor, women's services. **Physically disabled:** Services for visually, speech, hearing impaired.

Contact. E-mail: admissions@nmsu.edu
Phone: (575) 646-3121 Toll-free number: (800) 662-6678
Fax: (575) 646-6330
Delia De Leon, Director of Admissions, New Mexico State University, Box 30001, MSC 3A, Las Cruces, NM 88003-8001

Northern New Mexico College
Espanola, New Mexico
www.nnmc.edu   **CB code: 0425**

- Public 4-year business and nursing college
- Commuter campus in small town
- 1,601 undergraduates

General. Founded in 1909. Regionally accredited. Off-site facilities in seven locations. **Degrees:** 59 bachelor's, 121 associate awarded. **Location:** 24 miles from Santa Fe. **Calendar:** Semester, limited summer session. **Full-time faculty:** 50 total. **Part-time faculty:** 142 total.

Freshman class profile.

GPA 3.75 or higher:	2%	GPA 2.0-2.99:	57%
GPA 3.50-3.74:	7%	Out-of-state:	1%
GPA 3.0-3.49:	27%	Live on campus:	1%

Basis for selection. Open admission, but selective for some programs and for out-of-state students. Nursing, radiography, massage therapy, engineering, business, environmental science, education, barbering, and cosmetology programs require separate applications subsequent to admission. 2-year nursing program requires 2.5 GPA and pre-admission test. Pre-requisite for BSN program is an RN. Limited number of out-of-state applicants considered. **Home schooled:** Transcript of courses and grades, state high school equivalency certificate required. Applicant must be at least 16. **Learning Disabled:** Students may provide an IEP and are offered accommodations for placement test.

2015-2016 Annual costs. Tuition/fees: $2,183. Books/supplies: $2,168. Personal expenses: $1,144.

Financial aid. All financial aid based on need.

Application procedures. Admission: Closing date 8/15 (receipt date). No application fee. Application must be submitted online. Admission notification on a rolling basis. **Financial aid:** Priority date 3/1; no closing date. FAFSA required. Applicants notified on a rolling basis starting 6/1; must reply within 2 week(s) of notification.

Academics. Special study options: Distance learning, double major, dual enrollment of high school students, ESL, internships, teacher certification program. **Credit/placement by examination:** AP, CLEP, IB, institutional tests. 15 credit hours maximum toward associate degree, 30 toward bachelor's. **Support services:** Learning center, remedial instruction, study skills assistance, tutoring, writing center.

Majors. Biology: General. **Business:** Business admin.

Technology on campus. 24 workstations in library, computer center. Dormitories wired for high-speed internet access and linked to campus network. Commuter students can connect to campus network. Online course registration, online library, wireless network available.

Student life. Freshman orientation: Mandatory. Preregistration for classes offered. Four hour sessions held on Tuesdays prior to term. **Housing:** Single-sex dorms, wellness housing available. **Activities:** Bands, dance, drama, film society, international student organizations, music ensembles, student government, student newspaper, Phi Theta Kappa, American Indian organization.

Athletics. NAIA. **Intercollegiate:** Basketball, cross-country, golf. **Intramural:** Basketball, soccer, softball, volleyball. **Team name:** Eagles.

Student services. Services for economically disadvantaged, student employment services, financial aid counseling, minority student services, veterans' counselor. **Physically disabled:** Services for visually, speech, hearing impaired.

Contact. E-mail: forona@nnmc.edu
Phone: (505) 747-2111 Fax: (505) 747-5449
Frank Orona, Director of Admissions, Northern New Mexico College, 921 Paseo de Onate, Espanola, NM 87532

Santa Fe University of Art and Design

Santa Fe, New Mexico   **CB member**
www.santafeuniversity.edu   **CB code: 4676**

◗ For-profit 4-year visual arts and liberal arts college
◗ Residential campus in small city
◗ 849 degree-seeking undergraduates: 51% women, 8% African American, 2% Asian American, 28% Hispanic/Latino, 3% Native American, 1% Native Hawaiian/Pacific islander, 8% Multi-racial, non-Hispanic, 4% international
◗ Application essay, interview required

General. Founded in 1947. Regionally accredited. Garson Studios is a professional film studio where students have interned on almost all commercial productions. **Degrees:** 115 bachelor's awarded; master's offered. **Location:** 60 miles from Albuquerque. **Calendar:** Semester, limited summer session. **Class size:** 75% < 20, 23% 20-39, less than 1% 40-49, less than 1% 50-99, less than 1% >100. **Special facilities:** Professional sound stages, visual arts center, theater center, digital arts laboratory, recording studios.

Freshman class profile.

Out-of-state: 81% **International:** 3%

Basis for selection. Admissions based on secondary school record, interview, talent, ability, character, and personal qualities. Class rank, recommendations, standardized test scores, essay, and volunteer work also important. **Home schooled:** Statement describing home school structure and mission, transcript of courses and grades, interview required.

High school preparation. 16 units required. Required and recommended units include English 4, mathematics 2, social studies 2, science 2 (laboratory 2) and foreign language 2.

2016-2017 Annual costs. Tuition/fees (projected): $32,346. Room/board: $9,546. Books/supplies: $1,400. Personal expenses: $1,500.

2015-2016 Financial aid. Need-based: 190 full-time freshmen applied for aid; 171 deemed to have need; 171 received aid. Average need met was 59%. Average scholarship/grant was $17,635; average loan $3,319. 67% of total undergraduate aid awarded as scholarships/grants, 33% as loans/jobs. **Non-need-based:** Awarded to 201 full-time undergraduates, including 43 freshmen. Scholarships awarded for academics, art, music/drama, state residency.

Application procedures. Admission: No deadline. $50 fee, may be waived for applicants with need. Admission notification on a rolling basis. **Financial aid:** Priority date 3/15; no closing date. FAFSA required. Applicants notified on a rolling basis starting 3/1.

Academics. Special study options: Distance learning, double major, dual enrollment of high school students, exchange student, honors, independent study, internships, New York semester, student-designed major, study abroad. Study abroad in Milan, Italy, New Zealand and several other locations through the Laureate International Universities network. **Credit/placement by examination:** AP, CLEP, IB, institutional tests. 64 credit hours maximum toward bachelor's degree. **Support services:** Learning center, reduced course load, remedial instruction, study skills assistance, tutoring, writing center.

Majors. Business: Business admin. **English:** Creative writing. **Visual/performing arts:** General, acting, art, art history/conservation, cinematography, dance, digital arts, dramatic, film/cinema/video, graphic design, multimedia, music, music performance, music theory/composition, musical theater, painting, photography, play/screenwriting, sculpture, studio arts, studio arts management, theater arts management, theater design.

Most popular majors. English 12%, visual/performing arts 86%.

Technology on campus. 120 workstations in library, computer center, student center. Dormitories wired for high-speed internet access and linked to campus network. Online course registration, online library, helpline, wireless network available.

Student life. Freshman orientation: Mandatory. Preregistration for classes offered. **Housing:** Guaranteed on-campus for freshmen. Coed dorms, single-sex dorms, special housing for disabled, apartments available. $200 nonrefundable deposit, deadline 8/13. **Activities:** Bands, campus ministries, choral groups, dance, drama, film society, international student organizations, literary magazine, music ensembles, musical theater, student government, student newspaper, Colors (LGBTs student club), recycling club, Feminist Collective club, United States Institute for Theatrical Technology club.

Athletics. Intercollegiate: Weight lifting. **Intramural:** Basketball, handball, racquetball, skiing, soccer, softball, table tennis, tennis, ultimate frisbee, volleyball, weight lifting.

Student services. Alcohol/substance abuse counseling, career counseling, financial aid counseling, health services, personal counseling. **Physically disabled:** Services for visually, speech, hearing impaired.

Contact. E-mail: admissions@santafeuniversity.edu
Phone: (505) 473-6937 Toll-free number: (800) 456-2673
Fax: (505) 473-6127
Melissa Lewis, Director of Student Services, Santa Fe University of Art and Design, 1600 Saint Michael's Drive, Santa Fe, NM 87505-7634

Southwest University of Visual Arts

Albuquerque, New Mexico
www.suva.edu   **CB code: 3039**

◗ For-profit 4-year visual arts college
◗ Commuter campus in very large city
◗ 209 degree-seeking undergraduates
◗ Application essay, interview required

General. Degrees: 35 bachelor's awarded. **ROTC:** Army. **Calendar:** Semester, extensive summer session. **Full-time faculty:** 24 total. **Part-time faculty:** 21 total.

Basis for selection. High school transcripts (GED accepted), ACT or SAT scores, essay, interview, personal statement form, and art work for illustration, animation, fine arts and graphic design programs. Applications accepted based on an evaluation of strengths, academic preparedness and communication skills. SAT or ACT recommended. **Home schooled:** Transcript of courses and grades required.

High school preparation. College-preparatory program recommended.

2015-2016 Annual costs. Tuition/fees: $22,944. Books/supplies: $2,500. Personal expenses: $3,204. **Additional information:** Estimated total costs for books and supplies for each program: $3,900-$4,750.

Financial aid. Non-need-based: Scholarships awarded for academics.

Application procedures. Admission: No deadline. $25 fee. Admission notification on a rolling basis. **Financial aid:** No deadline. FAFSA required.

Academics. Special study options: Double major, independent study, internships, liberal arts/career combination. **Credit/placement by examination:** AP, CLEP, IB, SAT, ACT, institutional tests. **Support services:** Learning center, reduced course load, remedial instruction, study skills assistance, tutoring, writing center.

Majors. Architecture: Landscape. **Business:** Marketing. **Communications:** Advertising. **Communications technology:** Animation/special effects. **Visual/performing arts:** Graphic design, illustration, interior design, photography, studio arts.

Most popular majors. Communications/journalism 11%, communication technologies 14%, visual/performing arts 75%.

Technology on campus. 50 workstations in library, computer center, student center. Online course registration, online library, student web hosting, wireless network available.

Student life. Freshman orientation: Mandatory, $100 fee. Preregistration for classes offered.

Student services. Adult student services, career counseling, student employment services, financial aid counseling, personal counseling, placement for graduates, veterans' counselor.

Contact. E-mail: inquire@suva.edu
Phone: (505) 254-7575 Toll-free number: (800) 825-8753
Fax: (505) 254-4754
Steve Dietzman, Director of Admissions, Southwest University of Visual Arts, 5000 Marble Avenue NE, Albuquerque, NM 87119

St. John's College
Santa Fe, New Mexico
www.sjc.edu

CB member
CB code: 4737

- Private 4-year liberal arts college
- Residential campus in small city
- 324 degree-seeking undergraduates: 2% part-time, 43% women
- 66 degree-seeking graduate students
- 81% of applicants admitted
- Application essay required
- 47% graduate within 6 years; 12% enter graduate study

General. Founded in 1964. Regionally accredited. Second campus in Annapolis, MD, where students may transfer. **Degrees:** 84 bachelor's awarded; master's offered. **Location:** 60 miles from Albuquerque. **Calendar:** Semester, limited summer session. **Full-time faculty:** 63 total; 75% have terminal degrees, 3% minority, 25% women. **Part-time faculty:** 11 total. **Class size:** 100% < 20. **Special facilities:** Forest with hiking trails.

Freshman class profile. 177 applied, 144 admitted, 77 enrolled.

Mid 50% test scores		GPA 2.0-2.99:	16%
SAT critical reading:	600-730	Rank in top quarter:	57%
SAT math:	560-690	Rank in top tenth:	26%
SAT writing:	570-680	End year in good standing:	94%
ACT composite:	26-31	Return as sophomores:	82%
GPA 3.75 or higher:	46%	Out-of-state:	94%
GPA 3.50-3.74:	19%	Live on campus:	98%
GPA 3.0-3.49:	19%		

Basis for selection. Three essays describing educational and personal background and goals are most important, along with 2 letters of reference from teachers; a secondary school reference from a guidance counselor or other school official is requested. High school achievement record considered. SAT or ACT required of early admission, homeschooled, and international applicants; optional for others. Interview and overnight campus visit are strongly encouraged, as are interviews off-campus when offered by admissions officers. **Home schooled:** Statement describing home school structure

and mission, transcript of courses and grades, letter of recommendation (nonparent) required. SAT or ACT scores.

High school preparation. College-preparatory program recommended. 5 units required; 20 recommended. Required and recommended units include English 4, mathematics 3-4, history 2, science 3 (laboratory 3) and foreign language 2-4. Math includes 2 algebra, 1 geometry required; precalculus or trigonometry recommended.

2015-2016 Annual costs. Tuition/fees: $49,269. Room/board: $10,890. Books/supplies: $630. Personal expenses: $1,000.

2015-2016 Financial aid. Need-based: 80 full-time freshmen applied for aid; 76 deemed to have need; 76 received aid. Average need met was 93%. Average scholarship/grant was $31,415; average loan $5,500. 87% of total undergraduate aid awarded as scholarships/grants, 13% as loans/jobs. **Non-need-based:** Scholarships awarded for academics. **Additional information:** FAFSA is the only application used to apply for financial aid. Priority filing date is 2/15 for entering students and 3/1 for continuing students. CSS profile is optional for domestic students but required for international students.

Application procedures. Admission: Priority date 11/15; no deadline. No application fee. Admission notification on a rolling basis beginning on or about 12/15. Must reply by May 1 or within 2 week(s) if notified thereafter. Early Action I deadline November 15; notification December 15. Early Action II deadline January 15; notification February 15. Regular rolling after February 15. **Financial aid:** Priority date 2/15; no closing date. FAFSA required. Applicants notified on a rolling basis starting 12/15; must reply by 5/1 or within 2 week(s) of notification.

Academics. Special study options: Exchange student, internships, study abroad. Outdoor leadership program. **Credit/placement by examination:** AP, CLEP. **Support services:** Study skills assistance, tutoring, writing center. Student academic assistants for all tutorial classes.

Majors. Liberal arts: Arts/sciences.

Technology on campus. 25 workstations in library, computer center. Dormitories wired for high-speed internet access and linked to campus network. Online library, helpline, wireless network available.

Student life. Freshman orientation: Mandatory. Preregistration for classes offered. Four-day program held twice a year. **Policies:** All undergraduates are required to live on campus. **Housing:** Guaranteed on-campus for freshmen. Coed dorms, single-sex dorms, special housing for disabled, apartments, gender-neutral housing, wellness housing available. **Activities:** Choral groups, dance, drama, film society, international student organizations, literary magazine, music ensembles, student government, student newspaper, Project Politae, Polity, Johnnie Community Board, Johnnies of Color, Gay-Straight Alliance.

Athletics. Intercollegiate: Archery. **Intramural:** Badminton, basketball, football (non-tackle), soccer, softball, ultimate frisbee, volleyball.

Student services. Alcohol/substance abuse counseling, career counseling, student employment services, financial aid counseling, health services, personal counseling, placement for graduates, women's services.

Contact. E-mail: SantaFe.Admissions@sjc.edu
Phone: (505) 984-6060 Toll-free number: (800) 331-5232
Fax: (505) 984-6162
Yvette Shafer, Director of Admissions, St. John's College, 1160 Camino Cruz Blanca, Santa Fe, NM 87505

University of New Mexico
Albuquerque, New Mexico
www.unm.edu

CB member
CB code: 4845

- Public 4-year university
- Commuter campus in very large city
- 19,886 degree-seeking undergraduates: 20% part-time, 55% women, 2% African American, 3% Asian American, 47% Hispanic/Latino, 6% Native American, 3% Multi-racial, non-Hispanic, 1% international
- 5,938 degree-seeking graduate students
- 50% of applicants admitted
- SAT or ACT (ACT writing optional) required

General. Founded in 1889. Regionally accredited. Campus in Rio Rancho; branch campuses in Valencia County, Los Alamos, Gallup, and Taos. **Degrees:** 3,667 bachelor's awarded; master's, professional, doctoral offered. **ROTC:** Army, Naval, Air Force. **Location:** 2 miles from downtown. **Calendar:** Semester, limited summer session. **Full-time faculty:** 1,070 total; 81% have terminal degrees, 25% minority, 48% women. **Part-time faculty:** 531

total; 20% have terminal degrees, 24% minority, 57% women. **Class size:** 55% < 20, 30% 20-39, 5% 40-49, 7% 50-99, 3% >100. **Special facilities:** Five museums, observatory, meteoritics institute, arboretum, teaching hospital, research facilities in ceramics, optoelectronics, space nuclear power, high power devices and systems, institute of lithography.

Freshman class profile. 13,517 applied, 6,780 admitted, 3,327 enrolled.

Mid 50% test scores			
SAT critical reading:	480-610	GPA 2.0-2.99:	22%
SAT math:	470-600	Return as sophomores:	80%
SAT writing:	460-590	Out-of-state:	15%
ACT composite:	19-25	Live on campus:	23%
GPA 3.75 or higher:	23%	International:	2%
GPA 3.50-3.74:	18%	Fraternities:	3%
GPA 3.0-3.49:	37%	Sororities:	3%

Basis for selection. School achievement record (2.5 GPA on a 4.0 scale) most important. Test scores important. Essays, recommendations considered. Essay is considered in student appeal process. **Home schooled:** Applicants must either pass GED, submit SAT Subject Test scores, or have 2.5 GPA and complete 16 college prep academic units. **Learning Disabled:** Student who is not admissible according to numerical admissions and self-discloses disability can be admitted after being approved by Special Admissions Committee.

High school preparation. College-preparatory program required. 16 units required. Required units include English 4, mathematics 4, social studies 2, history 1, science 3 (laboratory 2) and foreign language 2. Foreign language requirements must be in same language. 2 science must be laboratory in biology, chemistry or physics. Math must be algebra I, geometry, algebra II, trigonometry or higher. 1 English must be 11th or 12th grade composition.

2015-2016 Annual costs. Tuition/fees: $6,664; $21,304 out-of-state. Room/board: $8,690. Books/supplies: $1,064. Personal expenses: $3,286. **Additional information:** N/A.

Financial aid. Non-need-based: Scholarships awarded for academics, alumni affiliation, art, athletics, job skills, leadership, minority status, music/drama, religious affiliation, ROTC, state residency.

Application procedures. Admission: Priority date 5/1; no deadline. $20 fee, may be waived for applicants with need. Admission notification on a rolling basis. Must reply by 7/12. **Financial aid:** Priority date 3/1; no closing date. FAFSA required. Applicants notified on a rolling basis starting 3/31.

Academics. Special study options: Accelerated study, combined bachelor's/graduate degree, cooperative education, distance learning, double major, dual enrollment of high school students, ESL, exchange student, honors, independent study, internships, semester at sea, student-designed major, study abroad, teacher certification program, Washington semester, weekend college. **Credit/placement by examination:** AP, CLEP, IB, SAT, ACT, institutional tests. Credit granted to newly admitted and regularly enrolled (in undergraduate degree status) students who achieve passing scores on specified CLEP exams as approved by the appropriate academic departments. For all of these CLEP Examinations, the total semester hours to be accepted towards a student's degree is at the discretion of the pertinent degree-granting college. **Support services:** Learning center, reduced course load, remedial instruction, study skills assistance, tutoring, writing center.

Honors college/program. Cumulative GPA of 3.5 or higher, ACT composite 29 (or higher) or SAT score of 1860 (or higher).

Majors. Architecture: Architecture, environmental design. **Area/ethnic studies:** African-American, American, Asian, Chicano/Hispanic-American/Latino, European, Latin American, Native American, Russian/Slavic, women's. **Biology:** General, biochemistry. **Business:** Business admin. **Communications:** Journalism, media studies. **Computer sciences:** General. **Conservation:** Environmental science. **Education:** Art, early childhood, elementary, health, music, physical, secondary, special ed, technology/industrial arts. **Engineering:** Chemical, civil, computer, electrical, engineering science, mechanical, nuclear. **English:** English lit, rhetoric/composition. **Foreign languages:** General, classics, comparative lit, French, German, linguistics, Portuguese, sign language interpretation, Spanish. **Health services:** Audiology/speech pathology, clinical lab technology, dental hygiene, EMT paramedic, medical radiologic technology/radiation therapy, nursing (RN). **History:** General. **Human services:** Community org/advocacy. **Liberal arts:** Arts/sciences, humanities. **Math:** General, statistics. **Philosophy/religion:** Philosophy, religion. **Physical sciences:** Astrophysics, chemistry, geology, physics. **Protective services:** Corrections. **Psychology:** General. **Social sciences:** Anthropology, economics, geography, political science, sociology. **Visual/performing arts:** Art, art history/conservation, dance, digital arts, dramatic, film/cinema/video, music performance, theater design. **Work/family studies:** General, family studies, food/nutrition.

Most popular majors. Biology 8%, business/marketing 15%, education 10%, engineering/engineering technologies 6%, English 6%, health sciences 7%, liberal arts 6%, psychology 10%, social sciences 7%, visual/performing arts 6%.

Technology on campus. 766 workstations in dormitories, library, computer center, student center. Dormitories wired for high-speed internet access and linked to campus network. Commuter students can connect to campus network. Online course registration, online library, helpline, student web hosting, wireless network available.

Student life. Freshman orientation: Mandatory, $175 fee. Preregistration for classes offered. Two-day sessions held June-August. **Housing:** Coed dorms, special housing for disabled, apartments, fraternity/sorority housing, themed housing, wellness housing available. $50 nonrefundable deposit, deadline 7/12. Senior housing, academic floors, scholar's wing, global learning center, freshman living learning community, outdoors/wellness, major based housing available. **Activities:** Bands, campus ministries, choral groups, dance, drama, film society, international student organizations, literary magazine, music ensembles, Model UN, musical theater, opera, radio station, student government, student newspaper, symphony orchestra, TV station, World Student Alliance, Residence Hall Association, Best Buddies NM, Baha'i Student Association, Raza Graduate Student Association, Nourish International, American Indian Business Association.

Athletics. NCAA. **Intercollegiate:** Baseball M, basketball, cross-country, diving W, football (tackle) M, golf, skiing, soccer, softball W, swimming W, tennis, track and field, volleyball W. **Intramural:** Archery, badminton, basketball, fencing, football (non-tackle), football (tackle) M, golf, racquetball, skiing, soccer, softball, swimming, tennis, triathlon, volleyball, water polo. **Team name:** Lobos.

Student services. Adult student services, alcohol/substance abuse counseling, career counseling, services for economically disadvantaged, student employment services, financial aid counseling, health services, legal services, minority student services, on-campus daycare, personal counseling, placement for graduates, veterans' counselor, women's services. **Physically disabled:** Services for visually, speech, hearing impaired.

Contact. E-mail: apply@unm.edu
Phone: (505) 277-8900 Toll-free number: (800) 225-5866
Fax: (505) 277-6686
Matthew Hulett, Director of Admissions and Recruiting Services, University of New Mexico, Office of Admissions, Albuquerque, NM 87196-4895

University of Phoenix: New Mexico
Albuquerque, New Mexico
www.phoenix.edu

- For-profit 4-year career college
- Commuter campus in very large city
- 1,238 undergraduates
- 410 graduate students

General. Regionally accredited. **Degrees:** 702 bachelor's awarded; master's offered. **Calendar:** Differs by program. **Full-time faculty:** 33 total. **Part-time faculty:** 352 total.

Basis for selection. Open admission.

2015-2016 Annual costs. Per-credit-hour charge, $410 to $635, depending upon level and course of study. Books, material charges, and other fees vary by course and program. All fees are subject to change.

Application procedures. Admission: No deadline. No application fee. **Financial aid:** No deadline.

Academics. Credit/placement by examination: AP, CLEP.

Majors. Business: Accounting/business management, business admin, e-commerce, entrepreneurial studies, finance, human resources, marketing, operations. **Computer sciences:** General, database management, networking, programming, security, support specialist, system admin, systems analysis, web page design, webmaster. **Conservation:** Environmental studies. **Education:** Elementary. **English:** English lit. **Health services:** Facilities admin, nursing (RN). **Human services:** General. **Protective services:** Law enforcement admin.

Student life. Freshman orientation: Mandatory. Preregistration for classes offered.

Contact. Toll-free number: (866) 766-0766
University of Phoenix: New Mexico, 5700 Pasadena Avenue NE, Albuquerque, NM 87113-1570

University of the Southwest
Hobbs, New Mexico
www.usw.edu

CB code: 4116

- Private 4-year business, liberal arts and teachers college affiliated with the nondenominational tradition
- Commuter campus in large town
- 430 degree-seeking undergraduates: 40% part-time, 47% women
- 866 graduate students

General. Founded in 1956. Regionally accredited. Christ-centered educational community. **Degrees:** 48 bachelor's awarded; master's offered. **Location:** 110 miles from Lubbock, TX, 102 miles from Midland, TX. **Calendar:** Semester, limited summer session. **Full-time faculty:** 18 total; 61% have terminal degrees, 11% minority, 50% women. **Part-time faculty:** 52 total; 35% have terminal degrees, 14% minority, 56% women. **Class size:** 88% < 20, 12% 20-39.

Freshman class profile.

GPA 3.75 or higher:	17%	Rank in top quarter:	18%
GPA 3.50-3.74:	15%	Rank in top tenth:	7%
GPA 3.0-3.49:	36%	Out-of-state:	37%
GPA 2.0-2.99:	26%	Live on campus:	82%

Basis for selection. Open admission, but selective for some programs. First-time entering freshmen must be a graduate of an accredited high school, must have completed an accredited home school program, or must have earned a GED from an accredited program. **Home schooled:** Statement describing home school structure and mission, transcript of courses and grades, state high school equivalency certificate required. **Learning Disabled:** Required to submit diagnostic test results from last 3 years, Individual Education Plan (IEP), and other supporting documentation.

2015-2016 Annual costs. Tuition/fees: $15,660. Room/board: $7,303. Books/supplies: $1,200. Personal expenses: $1,000.

Financial aid. **Non-need-based:** Scholarships awarded for academics, athletics, leadership.

Application procedures. Admission: No deadline. No application fee. Admission notification on a rolling basis beginning on or about 7/1. **Financial aid:** Priority date 4/1, closing date 6/1. FAFSA required. Applicants notified on a rolling basis starting 4/1; must reply within 2 week(s) of notification.

Academics. 6 hours religious studies, 3 hours Ethics, Freedom and Free Enterprise is required of all students. **Special study options:** Combined bachelor's/graduate degree, distance learning, double major, dual enrollment of high school students, internships, teacher certification program. **Credit/placement by examination:** AP, CLEP, IB, institutional tests. 30 credit hours maximum toward bachelor's degree. **Support services:** Reduced course load, study skills assistance, tutoring.

Majors. Biology: General. **Business:** Accounting, business admin, management information systems, marketing. **Education:** General, bilingual, elementary, English, mathematics, multi-level teacher, physical, science, secondary, social science, special ed. **English:** English lit. **History:** General. **Liberal arts:** Arts/sciences, humanities. **Parks/recreation:** Health/fitness, sports admin. **Protective services:** Criminal justice. **Psychology:** General. **Social sciences:** General. **Theology:** Pastoral counseling.

Most popular majors. Biology 19%, business/marketing 22%, education 26%, liberal arts 10%, psychology 13%, security/protective services 9%.

Technology on campus. 35 workstations in library, computer center. Dormitories wired for high-speed internet access. Online course registration, online library, helpline, wireless network available.

Student life. Freshman orientation: Mandatory. Preregistration for classes offered. Two-day orientation, Saturday and Sunday prior to semester start. **Housing:** Guaranteed on-campus for all undergraduates. Single-sex dorms, apartments, wellness housing available. $125 fully refundable deposit. **Activities:** Campus ministries, dance, literary magazine, student government, B.E.S.T., Students in Free Enterprise, speech and debate, Catholic student association.

Athletics. NAIA. **Intercollegiate:** Baseball M, basketball, cross-country, golf, soccer, softball W, tennis, track and field, volleyball W. **Intramural:** Badminton, basketball, football (tackle), soccer, table tennis, volleyball. **Team name:** Mustangs.

Student services. Alcohol/substance abuse counseling, chaplain/spiritual director, financial aid counseling, personal counseling.

Contact. E-mail: admissions@usw.edu
Phone: (575) 392-6563 Toll-free number: (800) 530-4400
Fax: (575) 392-6006
Lissete Terrazas, Director of Admissions, University of the Southwest, 6610 North Lovington Highway, #506, Hobbs, NM 88240

Western New Mexico University
Silver City, New Mexico
www.wnmu.edu

CB member
CB code: 4535

- Public 4-year university
- Commuter campus in large town
- 1,869 degree-seeking undergraduates: 25% part-time, 64% women, 7% African American, 2% Asian American, 51% Hispanic/Latino, 3% Native American, 1% Multi-racial, non-Hispanic, 2% international
- 802 degree-seeking graduate students

General. Founded in 1893. Regionally accredited. **Degrees:** 240 bachelor's, 138 associate awarded; master's offered. **Location:** 155 miles from El Paso, Texas, 193 miles from Tucson, Arizona. **Calendar:** Semester, extensive summer session. **Full-time faculty:** 108 total; 82% have terminal degrees, 34% minority, 54% women. **Part-time faculty:** 121 total; 16% have terminal degrees, 35% minority, 60% women. **Class size:** 69% < 20, 30% 20-39, less than 1% 40-49, less than 1% 50-99. **Special facilities:** Cultures museum, fine arts center and gallery, amphitheater.

Freshman class profile. 954 applied, 954 admitted, 283 enrolled.

Return as sophomores:	52%	Live on campus:	43%
Out-of-state:	30%	International:	1%

Basis for selection. Open admission. New undergraduate students required to take the COMPASS placement test. Scores are used to place students in appropriate university or developmental writing, reading and mathematics courses. Standardized test scores considered if submitted. **Home schooled:** State high school equivalency certificate required. If state high school equivalency certificate not received, student must take GED.

High school preparation. College-preparatory program recommended. 12 units recommended. Recommended units include English 4, mathematics 3, social studies 2, history 1 and science 2.

2015-2016 Annual costs. Tuition/fees: $6,417; $15,035 out-of-state. Room/board: $7,010. Books/supplies: $810. Personal expenses: $2,060.

2014-2015 Financial aid. Need-based: 270 full-time freshmen applied for aid; 269 deemed to have need; 269 received aid. Average need met was 64%. Average scholarship/grant was $4,753; average loan $2,979. 31% of total undergraduate aid awarded as scholarships/grants, 69% as loans/jobs. **Non-need-based:** Awarded to 708 full-time undergraduates, including 161 freshmen. Scholarships awarded for academics, art, athletics, music/drama.

Application procedures. Admission: Priority date 4/1; deadline 8/1 (receipt date). $30 fee, may be waived for applicants with need. Admission notification on a rolling basis. **Financial aid:** Priority date 3/1; no closing date. FAFSA, institutional form required. Applicants notified on a rolling basis starting 3/1; must reply within 2 week(s) of notification.

Academics. Special study options: Cooperative education, distance learning, double major, dual enrollment of high school students, honors, independent study, internships, student-designed major, teacher certification program. **Credit/placement by examination:** AP, CLEP, IB. 12 credit hours maximum toward associate degree, 32 toward bachelor's. **Support services:** Learning center, remedial instruction, study skills assistance, tutoring, writing center.

Majors. Area/ethnic studies: Chicano/Hispanic-American/Latino. **Biology:** General, botany, cellular/molecular, zoology. **Business:** Accounting, business admin, operations. **Conservation:** Environmental studies, wildlife/wilderness. **Education:** Art, biology, business, chemistry, early childhood, elementary, ESL, health, mathematics, physical, science, secondary, social studies, Spanish, special ed, technology/industrial arts, voc/tech. **English:** English lit. **Foreign languages:** Spanish. **Health services:** Clinical lab technology, nursing (RN), rehabilitation science, substance abuse counseling. **History:** General. **Human services:** General, social work. **Liberal arts:** Arts/sciences. **Math:** General. **Physical sciences:** General, chemistry. **Protective services:** Criminal justice, law enforcement admin. **Psychology:** General. **Social sciences:** General, sociology. **Visual/performing arts:** Studio arts.

Most popular majors. Biology 6%, business/marketing 15%, education 10%, health sciences 9%, interdisciplinary studies 8%, psychology 8%, security/protective services 19%.

Technology on campus. 150 workstations in dormitories, library, computer center. Dormitories linked to campus network. Commuter students can connect to campus network. Online course registration, online library, helpline available.

Student life. Freshman orientation: Available, $10 fee. Preregistration for classes offered. Two-day sessions held once a month from late May through mid-August. **Housing:** Guaranteed on-campus for all undergraduates. Coed dorms, single-sex dorms, apartments available. $75 partly refundable deposit. **Activities:** Campus ministries, film society, international student organizations, student government, Baptist student union, Society for the Advancement of Management, St. Francis Newman Club, Chicano student organization, criminal justice, Native American club.

Athletics. NCAA. **Intercollegiate:** Basketball, cross-country, football (tackle) M, golf, softball W, tennis, volleyball W. **Intramural:** Basketball, racquetball, softball, swimming, tennis, volleyball. **Team name:** Mustangs.

Student services. Chaplain/spiritual director, career counseling, student employment services, financial aid counseling, health services, minority student services, on-campus daycare, personal counseling, placement for graduates. **Physically disabled:** Services for visually, speech, hearing impaired.

Contact. E-mail: admissions@wnmu.edu
Phone: (575) 538-6000 Toll-free number: (800) 872-9668
Fax: (575) 538-6127
Dan Tressler, Director of Admissions, Western New Mexico University, Castorena 106, Silver City, NM 88062

New York

Adelphi University
Garden City, New York
www.adelphi.edu

CB member
CB code: 2003

- Private 4-year university
- Commuter campus in large town
- 4,813 degree-seeking undergraduates: 9% part-time, 69% women, 9% African American, 10% Asian American, 15% Hispanic/Latino, 2% Multi-racial, non-Hispanic, 4% international
- 2,349 degree-seeking graduate students
- 72% of applicants admitted
- Application essay required
- 67% graduate within 6 years; 8% enter graduate study

General. Founded in 1896. Regionally accredited. **Degrees:** 1,219 bachelor's, 28 associate awarded; master's, professional, doctoral offered. **ROTC:** Army, Air Force. **Location:** 20 miles from New York City. **Calendar:** Semester, limited summer session. **Full-time faculty:** 317 total; 86% have terminal degrees, 24% minority, 54% women. **Part-time faculty:** 697 total; 25% have terminal degrees, 28% minority, 68% women. **Class size:** 51% < 20, 44% 20-39, 3% 40-49, 2% 50-99. **Special facilities:** Speech and hearing center, science library, observatory, arboretum, center for health innovation.

Freshman class profile. 9,367 applied, 6,762 admitted, 868 enrolled.

Mid 50% test scores			
SAT critical reading:	500-600	**GPA 2.0-2.99:**	15%
SAT math:	510-620	**Rank in top quarter:**	62%
SAT writing:	500-620	**Rank in top tenth:**	29%
ACT composite:	19-25	**End year in good standing:**	95%
GPA 3.75 or higher:	27%	**Return as sophomores:**	84%
GPA 3.50-3.74:	25%	**Out-of-state:**	10%
GPA 3.0-3.49:	32%	**Live on campus:**	42%
		International:	4%

Basis for selection. 3.0 cumulative GPA, and combined critical reading, math and writing SAT score of 1500 or higher very important. Rank in top third of class, school and community activities, references also important. SAT/ACT scores accepted on rolling basis. SAT recommended for General Studies entrants, not required for adult academic programs in University College. Applicants to dance, drama, music, or art require audition and portfolio review, education majors must have 2.75 minimum GPA. **Home schooled:** State high school equivalency certificate required. GED required if applicant not receiving diploma from accredited high school or academy. **Learning Disabled:** Fee-based learning disability program where students receive academic and counseling support, requires admission: interview required, SAT recommended, WAIS-III, WJ-III required.

High school preparation. College-preparatory program recommended. 16 units recommended. Recommended units include English 4, mathematics 3, science 3 and foreign language 2. 4 additional units recommended in either social studies, history, English, mathematics, science or foreign language.

2015-2016 Annual costs. Tuition/fees: $34,034. Room/board: $13,510. Books/supplies: $1,400. Personal expenses: $1,509.

2015-2016 Financial aid. Need-based: 750 full-time freshmen applied for aid; 636 deemed to have need; 614 received aid. Average need met was 18%. Average scholarship/grant was $7,417; average loan $3,902. 76% of total undergraduate aid awarded as scholarships/grants, 24% as loans/jobs. **Non-need-based:** Awarded to 3,396 full-time undergraduates, including 659 freshmen. Scholarships awarded for academics, alumni affiliation, art, athletics, leadership, minority status, music/drama, religious affiliation.

Application procedures. Admission: No deadline. $40 fee, may be waived for applicants with need. Admission notification on a rolling basis beginning on or about 10/1. **Financial aid:** Priority date 3/1; no closing date. FAFSA required. Applicants notified on a rolling basis starting 3/1.

Academics. Special study options: Accelerated study, combined bachelor's/graduate degree, cross-registration, distance learning, double major, dual enrollment of high school students, ESL, honors, independent study, internships, liberal arts/career combination, student-designed major, study abroad, teacher certification program, Washington semester, weekend college. Learning Disabilities program combining matriculation with support services; University College for adults 21 and over; 1-year intensive General Studies

program for freshmen with HS records/SAT scores that do not meet school standards. Students who successfully complete this program invited to enroll in other school programs in their sophomore year. **Credit/placement by examination:** AP, CLEP, IB. 30 credit hours maximum toward bachelor's degree. **Support services:** Learning center, pre-admission summer program, reduced course load, study skills assistance, tutoring, writing center.

Honors college/program. SAT, 3.5 GPA, evidence of academic or creative writing and interview required. 60-90 freshmen admitted.

Majors. Area/ethnic studies: Latin American. **Biology:** General, biochemistry. **Business:** Accounting, business admin, finance, marketing. **Communications:** Journalism, media studies. **Computer sciences:** General, information systems. **Conservation:** Environmental studies. **Education:** Art, health, physical. **English:** English lit. **Foreign languages:** French, Spanish. **Health services:** Audiology/speech pathology, nursing (RN). **History:** General. **Human services:** Social work. **Liberal arts:** Arts/sciences, humanities. **Math:** General. **Parks/recreation:** Health/fitness, sports admin. **Philosophy/religion:** Philosophy. **Physical sciences:** Chemistry, physics. **Protective services:** Criminal justice, disaster management. **Psychology:** General. **Social sciences:** General, anthropology, economics, political science, sociology. **Visual/performing arts:** Art history/conservation, dance, dramatic, music.

Most popular majors. Business/marketing 13%, health sciences 33%, psychology 8%, social sciences 8%, visual/performing arts 7%.

Technology on campus. 680 workstations in dormitories, library, computer center, student center. Dormitories wired for high-speed internet access and linked to campus network. Commuter students can connect to campus network. Online course registration, online library, helpline, repair service, student web hosting, wireless network available.

Student life. Freshman orientation: Mandatory, $275 fee. Preregistration for classes offered. Three-day orientation held on Garden City campus. **Housing:** Coed dorms, special housing for disabled, themed housing available. $300 nonrefundable deposit, deadline 5/1. Special housing available for students in Honors College, Performing Arts, and Excel Mentoring Program. **Activities:** Bands, campus ministries, choral groups, dance, drama, film society, international student organizations, literary magazine, music ensembles, Model UN, musical theater, opera, radio station, student government, student newspaper, symphony orchestra, approximately 80 activities are offered.

Athletics. NCAA. **Intercollegiate:** Baseball M, basketball, bowling W, cross-country, field hockey W, golf, lacrosse, soccer, softball W, swimming, tennis, track and field, volleyball W. **Intramural:** Badminton, basketball, cheerleading W, football (non-tackle), soccer, volleyball, water polo, weight lifting M. **Team name:** Panthers.

Student services. Adult student services, alcohol/substance abuse counseling, chaplain/spiritual director, career counseling, student employment services, financial aid counseling, health services, minority student services, on-campus daycare, personal counseling, placement for graduates, veterans' counselor. **Physically disabled:** Services for visually, speech, hearing impaired.

Contact. E-mail: admissions@adelphi.edu
Phone: (516) 877-3050 Toll-free number: (800) 233-5744
Fax: (516) 877-3039
Kristen Capezza, Executive Director for Admissions, Adelphi University, One South Avenue, Levermore 110, Garden City, NY 11530-0701

Albany College of Pharmacy and Health Sciences
Albany, New York
www.acphs.edu

CB code: 2013

- Private 4-year health science and pharmacy college
- Residential campus in small city
- 1,003 degree-seeking undergraduates: 1% part-time, 60% women, 4% African American, 14% Asian American, 4% Hispanic/Latino, 1% Multiracial, non-Hispanic, 7% international
- 476 degree-seeking graduate students
- 71% of applicants admitted
- SAT or ACT with writing, application essay required

General. Founded in 1881. Regionally accredited. **Degrees:** 28 bachelor's awarded; master's, professional offered. **Location:** 200 miles from New York City. **Calendar:** Semester, limited summer session. **Full-time faculty:** 99 total; 83% have terminal degrees, 14% minority, 46% women. **Part-time faculty:** 27 total; 56% have terminal degrees, 15% minority, 59% women. **Special facilities:** Antique pharmacy.

Freshman class profile. 1,311 applied, 936 admitted, 188 enrolled.

Mid 50% test scores		GPA 3.50-3.74:	36%
SAT critical reading:	510-620	GPA 3.0-3.49:	19%
SAT math:	560-650	GPA 2.0-2.99:	3%
SAT writing:	500-610	Out-of-state:	20%
ACT composite:	23-28	Live on campus:	94%
GPA 3.75 or higher:	42%	International:	2%

Basis for selection. High school record, test scores, essay, letters of recommendation, New York State Regents Examinations considered. Special emphasis on science and mathematics grades. Interviews required for certain programs.

High school preparation. College-preparatory program recommended. 21 units required; 22 recommended. Required and recommended units include English 4, mathematics 4, science 3-4 (laboratory 3-4) and academic electives 6. Chemistry, pre-calculus or calculus.

2015-2016 Annual costs. Tuition/fees: $31,081. Room/board: $10,410. Books/supplies: $1,000. Personal expenses: $800.

Financial aid. Non-need-based: Scholarships awarded for academics, alumni affiliation, athletics, state residency.

Application procedures. Admission: Priority date 2/1; deadline 7/16 (postmark date). $75 fee, may be waived for applicants with need. Admission notification by 7/11. Admission notification on a rolling basis beginning on or about 2/1. Must reply by May 1 or within 2 week(s) if notified thereafter. **Financial aid:** Priority date 2/1, closing date 5/1. FAFSA required. CSS PROFILE priority date November 15. Applicants notified by 3/1; must reply within 2 week(s) of notification.

Academics. Special study options: Combined bachelor's/graduate degree, cross-registration, double major, independent study, internships, study abroad. **Credit/placement by examination:** AP, CLEP, IB, SAT, ACT. **Support services:** Study skills assistance, tutoring, writing center. Science assistance center.

Majors. Biology: Microbiology. **Health services:** Clinical lab science, pharmaceutical sciences. **Physical sciences:** Chemistry.

Technology on campus. PC or laptop required. Dormitories wired for high-speed internet access and linked to campus network. Commuter students can connect to campus network. Online course registration, online library, helpline, repair service, wireless network available.

Student life. Freshman orientation: Mandatory, $250 fee. Preregistration for classes offered. Usually held over first weekend prior to class start. **Policies:** Residency required in first 2 years of study except for students living within 30-mile radius of campus. **Housing:** Guaranteed on-campus for freshmen. Coed dorms, apartments available. $250 nonrefundable deposit, deadline 7/7. **Activities:** Bands, campus ministries, choral groups, dance, international student organizations, literary magazine, music ensembles, student government, Academy of Student Pharmacists, Student Society of Health Systems Pharmacists, Rho Chi, Phi Lambda Sigma.

Athletics. USCAA. **Intercollegiate:** Basketball, cross-country, soccer. **Intramural:** Basketball, football (tackle), ultimate frisbee, volleyball. **Team name:** Panthers.

Student services. Alcohol/substance abuse counseling, chaplain/spiritual director, career counseling, student employment services, financial aid counseling, health services, personal counseling, placement for graduates.

Contact. E-mail: admissions@acphs.edu
Phone: (518) 694-7221 Toll-free number: (888) 203-8010
Fax: (518) 694-7322
Director of Admissions, Albany College of Pharmacy and Health Sciences, 106 New Scotland Avenue, Albany, NY 12208-3492

Alfred University
Alfred, New York
www.alfred.edu

CB member
CB code: 2005

▸ Private 4-year university
▸ Residential campus in rural community
▸ 1,754 degree-seeking undergraduates
▸ 68% of applicants admitted
▸ SAT or ACT (ACT writing optional), application essay required

General. Founded in 1836. Regionally accredited. **Degrees:** 388 bachelor's awarded; master's, doctoral offered. **ROTC:** Army. **Location:** 75 miles from Rochester, 65 miles from Elmira. **Calendar:** Semester, limited summer session. **Full-time faculty:** 159 total; 45% women. **Part-time faculty:** 59 total; 48% women. **Class size:** 59% <20, 35% 20-39, 3% 40-49, 2% 50-99, less than 1% >100. **Special facilities:** Observatory, memorial carillon, art galleries, ceramics museum and library, equestrian center.

Freshman class profile. 3,640 applied, 2,490 admitted, 455 enrolled.

Mid 50% test scores		GPA 3.0-3.49:	37%
SAT critical reading:	450-570	GPA 2.0-2.99:	32%
SAT math:	470-580	Rank in top quarter:	43%
SAT writing:	420-540	Rank in top tenth:	16%
ACT composite:	21-27	Out-of-state:	20%
GPA 3.75 or higher:	12%	Live on campus:	98%
GPA 3.50-3.74:	19%		

Basis for selection. Rigor of high school curriculum, grades, class rank, ACT/SAT, extracurricular involvement, letters of recommendation, and character are all factors. International students may submit the TOEFL or IELTS in lieu of SAT or ACT scores. Interview recommended. Portfolio required for students seeking admission to the School of Art and Design. **Home schooled:** Document courses taken and provide reading lists. SAT/ACT relied on heavily.

High school preparation. College-preparatory program required. 16 units required. Required units include English 4, mathematics 2, social studies 2, science 2 (laboratory 2). College of Professional Studies and School of Business: 3-4 units of social studies and history; 3-4 units of college prep math. College of Liberal Arts & Sciences: 3-4 units of social studies and history; 2-3 units of college prep math. School of Art and Design: 3-4 units of social studies and history. Inamori School of Engineering: 4 units of college prep math; 3 units of lab science.

2015-2016 Annual costs. Tuition/fees: $30,200. Room/board: $11,960. Books/supplies: $1,250. Personal expenses: $1,300. **Additional information:** Tuition figures provided are for the College of Liberal Arts & Sciences and Professional Studies. Tuition for the School of Art & Design and Biomaterials, Ceramic, Materials Science, and Glass Engineering is $23,664 for non-NYS residents and $17,200 for NYS residents. Tuition for Mechanical, Renewable, and Undecided Engineering is $23,664.

Financial aid. Non-need-based: Scholarships awarded for academics, art, leadership, music/drama.

Application procedures. Admission: Priority date 2/1; deadline 8/1 (postmark date). $50 fee, may be waived for applicants with need. Admission notification on a rolling basis beginning on or about 11/15. Must reply by May 1 or within 2 week(s) if notified thereafter. Application priority deadline is 2/1, however applications accepted through 8/1 on a space available basis. Art & Design applications rarely accepted after priority deadline. **Financial aid:** Closing date 3/15. FAFSA, institutional form required. Applicants notified on a rolling basis starting 2/15; must reply by 5/1 or within 2 week(s) of notification.

Academics. Credit hours needed for graduation vary from 120-138 depending on major. Physical education requirement for all students. Additional graduation requirements vary by college/school. Preadmission summer program is required for students enrolling at AU through Opportunity Programs (EOP or HEOP). **Special study options:** Combined bachelor's/graduate degree, cooperative education, cross-registration, double major, ESL, exchange student, honors, independent study, internships, liberal arts/career combination, New York semester, semester at sea, student-designed major, study abroad, teacher certification program, United Nations semester, Washington semester. **Credit/placement by examination:** AP, CLEP, IB, SAT, institutional tests. 75 credit hours maximum toward bachelor's degree. Credits awarded from AP, IB, CLEP or from any other standardized exam program are considered to be transfer credits. They count toward the 75 credit hour limit on total transfer credit, and they do not affect the AU GPA. **Support services:** Reduced course load, study skills assistance, tutoring, writing center. Special Academic Services provides services to students with documented learning, physical, or psychological disabilities.

Majors. Biology: General. **Business:** Accounting, business admin, finance, marketing. **Communications:** Communications/speech/rhetoric. **Conservation:** Environmental studies. **Education:** Art, biology, business, chemistry, elementary, English, French, mathematics, middle, physics, social studies, Spanish. **Engineering:** Biomedical, ceramic, materials, mechanical. **English:** English lit. **Foreign languages:** Spanish. **Health services:** Athletic training, predental, premedicine, preveterinary. **History:** General. **Liberal arts:** Arts/sciences. **Math:** General. **Philosophy/religion:** Philosophy. **Physical sciences:** Chemistry, geology, materials science, physics. **Protective services:** Criminal justice. **Psychology:** General. **Social sciences:** Economics, political science, sociology. **Visual/performing arts:** Ceramics, dramatic, studio arts.

Most popular majors. Biology 8%, business/marketing 8%, engineering/engineering technologies 17%, psychology 8%, visual/performing arts 31%.

Technology on campus. 450 workstations in dormitories, library, computer center, student center. Dormitories wired for high-speed internet access and linked to campus network. Commuter students can connect to campus network. Online course registration, online library, helpline, repair service, student web hosting, wireless network available.

Student life. Freshman orientation: Available. Preregistration for classes offered. Starts the Thursday before classes begin in the fall. **Policies:** Students must abide by Code of Honor. Policies against hazing and sexual harassment. All students required to live in residence halls 6 semesters. Students in poor academic standing required to live on campus. Exceptions granted for married students, students 23 and older, students living with parents/legal guardian and commuting from home, students with dependents, and veterans. **Housing:** Guaranteed on-campus for freshmen. Coed dorms, apartments, themed housing, wellness housing available. $300 nonrefundable deposit, deadline 5/1. **Activities:** Bands, campus ministries, choral groups, dance, drama, film society, international student organizations, literary magazine, music ensembles, musical theater, radio station, student government, student newspaper, TV station, Hillel, Brothers and Sisters in Christ, Spectrum, Student Volunteers for Community Action, Alpha Phi Omega, Habitat for Humanity, Students Acting for Equality, Umoja, Omicron Delta Kappa, Poder Latino.

Athletics. NCAA. **Intercollegiate:** Basketball, cross-country, diving, equestrian, football (tackle) M, lacrosse, skiing, soccer, softball W, swimming, tennis, track and field, volleyball W. **Intramural:** Basketball, football (non-tackle), lacrosse M, racquetball, skiing, soccer, softball, squash, tennis, volleyball. **Team name:** Saxons.

Student services. Alcohol/substance abuse counseling, chaplain/spiritual director, career counseling, services for economically disadvantaged, student employment services, financial aid counseling, health services, minority student services, personal counseling, placement for graduates, women's services. **Physically disabled:** Services for visually, speech, hearing impaired.

Contact. E-mail: admissions@alfred.edu
Phone: (607) 871-2115 Toll-free number: (800) 541-9229
Fax: (607) 871-2198
Corry Unis, Director of Admissions, Alfred University, Alumni Hall, Alfred, NY 14802-1205

Bard College
Annandale-on-Hudson, New York   CB member
www.bard.edu   CB code: 2037

- Private 4-year liberal arts college affiliated with the Episcopal Church
- Residential campus in small town
- 1,962 degree-seeking undergraduates: 2% part-time, 55% women, 8% African American, 6% Asian American, 1% Hispanic/Latino, 1% Native American, 10% international
- 237 degree-seeking graduate students
- 32% of applicants admitted
- Application essay required
- 78% graduate within 6 years

General. Founded in 1860. Regionally accredited. **Degrees:** 436 bachelor's awarded; master's, doctoral offered. **Location:** 90 miles from New York City, 50 miles from Albany. **Calendar:** Semester. **Full-time faculty:** 152 total; 96% have terminal degrees, 16% minority, 43% women. **Part-time faculty:** 121 total; 80% have terminal degrees, 17% minority, 39% women. **Class size:** 77% < 20, 22% 20-39, less than 1% 40-49, less than 1% 50-99. **Special facilities:** Ecology field station, curatorial studies and art center, museum of late 20th-century art, archaeological field school, economics institute, center for studies in decorative arts, design and culture; performing arts center, science center.

Freshman class profile. 7,044 applied, 2,266 admitted, 447 enrolled.

Mid 50% test scores		End year in good standing:	86%
SAT critical reading:	590-690	Return as sophomores:	85%
SAT math:	570-680	Live on campus:	99%
Rank in top quarter:	76%	International:	13%
Rank in top tenth:	49%		

Basis for selection. School transcripts and achievement record, rigor of high school program, essays, academic recommendations, talents and dedication to activities, love of learning, and personal ambition important. Campus tour and information session recommended. Tape or CD, brief musical autobiography, and audition required of conservatory applicants. **Home schooled:** Statement describing home school structure and mission, transcript of courses and grades required.

High school preparation. College-preparatory program required. 24 units recommended. Recommended units include English 4, mathematics 4, social studies 4, history 4, science 4 (laboratory 3) and foreign language 4.

2015-2016 Annual costs. Tuition/fees: $49,906. Room/board: $14,118. Books/supplies: $950. Personal expenses: $800.

2015-2016 Financial aid. Need-based: 307 full-time freshmen applied for aid; 285 deemed to have need; 285 received aid. Average need met was 81%. Average scholarship/grant was $38,766; average loan $5,649. 85% of total undergraduate aid awarded as scholarships/grants, 15% as loans/jobs. **Non-need-based:** Awarded to 29 full-time undergraduates, including 3 freshmen. Scholarships awarded for academics. **Additional information:** Excellence and Equal Cost Program for students who graduate in top 10 of public high school class lowers fees to levels equivalent to those at home state university or college.

Application procedures. Admission: Closing date 1/1 (receipt date). $50 fee, may be waived for applicants with need. Application must be submitted on paper. Admission notification on a rolling basis beginning on or about 4/1. Must reply by May 1 or within 2 week(s) if notified thereafter. Using the Common Application, candidates may apply through Regular Admission, Early Action, Early Decision, or through the Immediate Decision Plan. An alternative method of application is the Bard Entrance Examination, an online essay application. **Financial aid:** Closing date 2/15. FAFSA, CSS PROFILE required. Applicants notified by 4/1; must reply by 5/1.

Academics. Strong tradition of independent study and tutorial work with faculty member. Writing-intensive, multidisciplinary programs. Extensive programs in languages, human rights and globalization and international affairs. Unique collaboration with The Rockefeller University. **Special study options:** Combined bachelor's/graduate degree, cross-registration, double major, dual enrollment of high school students, ESL, independent study, internships, New York semester, student-designed major, study abroad, Washington semester. Intensive language studies in Italy, Germany, France, Mexico, Russia, China, program in International Education (Central and Eastern Europe and Southern Africa). **Credit/placement by examination:** AP, CLEP, IB. **Support services:** Learning center, reduced course load, remedial instruction, study skills assistance, tutoring, writing center.

Majors. Area/ethnic studies: African, American, Asian, French, German, Italian, Latin American, Near/Middle Eastern, Russian/Slavic, Spanish/Iberian. **Biology:** General, neuroscience. **Computer sciences:** Computer science. **Conservation:** Environmental studies. **English:** American lit, British lit, creative writing, English lit. **Foreign languages:** General, ancient Greek, Arabic, Chinese, comparative lit, French, German, Hebrew, Italian, Japanese, Latin, Russian, Sanskrit, Spanish, translation. **Health services:** Premedicine. **History:** General, American, Asian, European. **Liberal arts:** Arts/sciences. **Math:** General. **Philosophy/religion:** Judaic, philosophy, religion. **Physical sciences:** Chemistry, physics. **Psychology:** General. **Social sciences:** General, anthropology, economics, political science, sociology. **Visual/performing arts:** General, acting, art history/conservation, cinematography, conducting, dance, directing/producing, dramatic, film/cinema/video, jazz, multimedia, music, music history, music performance, music theory/composition, photography, piano/keyboard, play/screenwriting, stringed instruments, studio arts, theater history, voice/opera.

Most popular majors. English 14%, social sciences 16%, visual/performing arts 31%.

Technology on campus. 425 workstations in library, computer center, student center. Dormitories wired for high-speed internet access and linked to campus network. Commuter students can connect to campus network. Online course registration, online library, helpline, student web hosting, wireless network available.

Student life. Freshman orientation: Mandatory, $694 fee. Preregistration for classes offered. Three-week writing-intensive Language and Thinking program held on campus in August immediately prior to fall semester. **Policies:** All students members of the student government association, a democratic forum that allocates funds, takes action on campus issues, and provides student representation on administrative and faculty committees. **Housing:** Guaranteed on-campus for freshmen. Coed dorms, single-sex dorms, special housing for disabled, cooperative housing, themed housing, wellness housing available. Pets allowed in dorm rooms. Suites available. **Activities:** Bands, campus ministries, choral groups, dance, drama, film society, international student organizations, literary magazine, music ensembles, Model UN, musical theater, opera, radio station, student government, student newspaper, symphony orchestra, approximately 150 clubs and organizations available.

Athletics. NCAA. **Intercollegiate:** Baseball M, basketball, cross-country, lacrosse, soccer, squash M, swimming, tennis, track and field, volleyball. **Intramural:** Badminton, basketball, bowling, golf, softball, squash, tennis, volleyball. **Team name:** Raptors.

Student services. Adult student services, alcohol/substance abuse counseling, chaplain/spiritual director, career counseling, services for economically disadvantaged, student employment services, financial aid counseling, health services, minority student services, personal counseling, placement for graduates, women's services. **Physically disabled:** Services for visually, hearing impaired.

Contact. E-mail: admissions@bard.edu
Phone: (845) 758-7472 Fax: (845) 758-5208
Mary Backlund, Director of Admission, Bard College, 30 Campus Road, Annandale-on-Hudson, NY 12504-5000

Barnard College
New York, New York

CB member

www.barnard.edu

CB code: 2038

- Private 4-year liberal arts college for women
- Residential campus in very large city
- 2,536 degree-seeking undergraduates: 1% part-time, 100% women, 7% African American, 14% Asian American, 12% Hispanic/Latino, 6% Multi-racial, non-Hispanic, 8% international
- 20% of applicants admitted
- SAT and SAT Subject Tests or ACT with writing, application essay required
- 91% graduate within 6 years

General. Founded in 1889. Regionally accredited. Cross-registration and shared facilities with Columbia University. Students receive Columbia University degrees. **Degrees:** 692 bachelor's awarded. **ROTC:** Army, Naval, Air Force. **Calendar:** Semester. **Full-time faculty:** 214 total; 92% have terminal degrees, 23% minority, 62% women. **Part-time faculty:** 135 total; 73% have terminal degrees, 13% minority, 64% women. **Class size:** 70% < 20, 17% 20-39, 2% 40-49, 8% 50-99, 3% >100. **Special facilities:** Theater, center for toddler development, center for research on women, architecture and dance studios, access to 3,600-acre nature preserves, greenhouse, access to geological observatory.

Freshman class profile. 6,655 applied, 1,306 admitted, 635 enrolled.

Mid 50% test scores		GPA 3.0-3.49:	6%
SAT critical reading:	640-730	Rank in top quarter:	94%
SAT math:	620-720	Rank in top tenth:	81%
SAT writing:	650-740	Return as sophomores:	95%
ACT composite:	29-32	Out-of-state:	76%
GPA 3.75 or higher:	76%	Live on campus:	99%
GPA 3.50-3.74:	18%	International:	9%

Basis for selection. High school record most important. Depth and difficulty of high school program considered. Test scores, recommendations, involvement in school and community activities, special talents, skills considered. Interview recommended. **Home schooled:** Statement describing home school structure and mission, transcript of courses and grades, letter of recommendation (nonparent) required.

High school preparation. College-preparatory program recommended. Recommended units include English 4, mathematics 3, history 3, science 3 and foreign language 3.

2015-2016 Annual costs. Tuition/fees: $47,631. Room/board: $15,110.

2015-2016 Financial aid. All financial aid based on need. 357 full-time freshmen applied for aid; 287 deemed to have need; 287 received aid. Average need met was 100%. Average scholarship/grant was $44,840; average loan $3,258. 89% of total undergraduate aid awarded as scholarships/grants, 11% as loans/jobs.

Application procedures. Admission: Closing date 1/1 (postmark date). $65 fee, may be waived for applicants with need. Admission notification by 4/1. Must reply by May 1 or within 2 week(s) if notified thereafter. **Financial aid:** Closing date 2/15. FAFSA required. CSS Profile required for returning students, except those who had a parent contribution less than $2,000 in the prior academic year. Returning international students also not required to complete the CSS Profile. Applicants notified by 3/31; must reply by 5/1.

Academics. Interdisciplinary first-year seminar; coursework in global cultures, which may also fulfill other degree requirements. **Special study options:** Combined bachelor's/graduate degree, cross-registration, double major, dual enrollment of high school students, exchange student, independent study, internships, student-designed major, study abroad, teacher certification program. **Credit/placement by examination:** AP, CLEP, IB, institutional tests. **Support services:** Pre-admission summer program, tutoring, writing center.

Majors. Architecture: Architecture, history/criticism. **Area/ethnic studies:** African, American, Asian, European, French, German, Latin American, Near/Middle Eastern, Russian/Slavic, Slavic, Spanish/Iberian, women's. **Biology:** General, biochemistry, biophysics, environmental, neuroscience. **Computer sciences:** General, computer science. **Conservation:** Environmental science, environmental studies. **Engineering:** Applied physics. **English:** English lit. **Foreign languages:** Ancient Greek, classics, comparative lit, French, German, Italian, Latin, linguistics, modern Greek, Russian, Spanish. **History:** General. **Math:** General, applied, statistics. **Philosophy/religion:** Philosophy, religion. **Physical sciences:** Astronomy, astrophysics, chemistry, physics. **Psychology:** General. **Social sciences:** Anthropology, economics, geography, political science, sociology, urban studies. **Visual/performing arts:** General, art history/conservation, dance, dramatic, film/cinema/video, music.

Most popular majors. Area/ethnic studies 7%, biology 9%, English 10%, psychology 13%, social sciences 30%, visual/performing arts 10%.

Technology on campus. 162 workstations in dormitories, library, computer center, student center. Dormitories wired for high-speed internet access and linked to campus network. Commuter students can connect to campus network. Online course registration, online library, helpline, repair service, wireless network available.

Student life. Freshman orientation: Mandatory, $400 fee. Preregistration for classes offered. Held for a week-long beginning August 27. **Housing:** Guaranteed on-campus for all undergraduates. Special housing for disabled, fraternity/sorority housing available. $400 nonrefundable deposit, deadline 5/1. **Activities:** Bands, campus ministries, choral groups, dance, drama, film society, international student organizations, literary magazine, music ensembles, Model UN, musical theater, opera, radio station, student government, student newspaper, symphony orchestra, united students of color council, multicultural international student association, late night theater, Athena pre-law society, network of pre-medical students of color, women in politics, Barnard Earth club, feminist thought, smart women lead, V-Day.

Athletics. NCAA. **Intercollegiate:** Archery W, basketball W, cross-country W, diving W, fencing W, field hockey W, golf W, lacrosse W, rowing (crew) W, soccer W, softball W, swimming W, tennis W, track and field W, volleyball W. **Intramural:** Archery W, badminton W, basketball W, bowling W, cross-country W, fencing W, racquetball W, sailing W, soccer W, softball W, swimming W, tennis W, volleyball W. **Team name:** Lions.

Student services. Alcohol/substance abuse counseling, career counseling, student employment services, financial aid counseling, health services, personal counseling, placement for graduates, women's services. **Physically disabled:** Services for visually, speech, hearing impaired.

Contact. E-mail: admissions@barnard.edu
Phone: (212) 854-2014 Fax: (212) 854-6220
Carolyn Middleton, Director of Admissions, Barnard College, 3009 Broadway, New York, NY 10027-6598

Beis Medrash Heichal Dovid
Far Rockaway, New York

- Private 4-year rabbinical college for men affiliated with the Jewish faith
- Residential campus in large city
- 105 degree-seeking undergraduates

General. Accredited by AARTS. **Degrees:** 4 bachelor's awarded; doctoral offered. **Calendar:** Semester. **Full-time faculty:** 4 total. **Part-time faculty:** 6 total.

Basis for selection. Religious faith most important criteria. **Home schooled:** Transcript of courses and grades, state high school equivalency certificate, interview, letter of recommendation (nonparent) required.

2015-2016 Annual costs. Tuition/fees: $9,450. Room/board: $5,500.

Application procedures. Admission: No deadline. $100 fee. Admission notification on a rolling basis.

Academics. Credit/placement by examination: AP, CLEP.

Majors. Theology: Talmudic.

Contact. Phone: (718) 868-2300 ext. 360 Fax: (718) 406-8359
Aaron Steinberg, Admin. Assist., Beis Medrash Heichal Dovid, 257 Beach 17th Street, Far Rockaway, NY 11691

Berkeley College
White Plains, New York
www.berkeleycollege.edu   CB code: 2064

- For-profit 4-year branch campus and business college
- Commuter campus in small city
- 465 degree-seeking undergraduates: 8% part-time, 65% women, 29% African American, 2% Asian American, 23% Hispanic/Latino, 7% international
- 31% graduate within 6 years

General. Founded in 1945. Regionally accredited. **Degrees:** 81 bachelor's, 17 associate awarded. **Location:** 28 miles from New York City. **Calendar:** Semester, extensive summer session. **Full-time faculty:** 27 total. **Part-time faculty:** 29 total. **Class size:** 38% < 20, 62% 20-39.

Freshman class profile.

End year in good standing:	86%	Out-of-state:	39%
Return as sophomores:	54%	International:	7%

Basis for selection. Class rank, high school record, interview most important. Passing grade on school entrance examination required. SAT/ACT considered if submitted. Interviews strongly recommended.

2015-2016 Annual costs. Tuition/fees: $24,300. Room only: $9,000. Books/supplies: $960. Personal expenses: $3,984.

Financial aid. Non-need-based: Scholarships awarded for academics, alumni affiliation.

Application procedures. Admission: No deadline. $50 fee. Admission notification on a rolling basis. Admitted applicants must reply within two weeks of notification. **Financial aid:** No deadline. FAFSA required. Applicants notified on a rolling basis starting 3/1; must reply within 6 week(s) of notification.

Academics. Special study options: Accelerated study, distance learning, honors, internships, New York semester, study abroad. **Credit/placement by examination:** AP, CLEP, SAT, ACT, institutional tests. **Support services:** Learning center, pre-admission summer program, remedial instruction, study skills assistance, tutoring, writing center.

Majors. Business: Business admin, fashion, marketing. **Protective services:** Law enforcement admin.

Most popular majors. Business/marketing 52%, health sciences 10%, security/protective services 38%.

Technology on campus. 150 workstations in library, computer center. Dormitories linked to campus network. Commuter students can connect to campus network. Online library, helpline, wireless network available.

Student life. Freshman orientation: Mandatory. Preregistration for classes offered. **Housing:** Coed dorms available. $400 fully refundable deposit. **Activities:** International student organizations, student government, accounting club, Berkeley club, Phi Beta Lambda, Phi Theta Kappa, international club, fashion club, paralegal club.

Athletics. Intercollegiate: Basketball, cross-country, soccer, tennis. **Team name:** Knights.

Student services. Adult student services, career counseling, student employment services, financial aid counseling, personal counseling, placement for graduates, veterans' counselor.

Contact. E-mail: info@berkeleycollege.edu
Phone: (914) 694-1122 Toll-free number: (800) 446-5400
Fax: (914) 328-9469
Lynn Ovimeleh, Director, High School Admissions, Berkeley College, 99 Church Street, White Plains, NY 10601

Berkeley College of New York City
New York, New York
www.berkeleycollege.edu   CB code: 0954

- For-profit 4-year business college
- Commuter campus in very large city
- 3,935 degree-seeking undergraduates: 12% part-time, 64% women, 25% African American, 3% Asian American, 21% Hispanic/Latino, 16% international
- 31% graduate within 6 years

General. Founded in 1936. Regionally accredited. Additional locations in Brooklyn, and White Plains. **Degrees:** 777 bachelor's, 214 associate awarded. **Location:** Midtown Manhattan. **Calendar:** Semester, extensive summer session. **Full-time faculty:** 376 total. **Part-time faculty:** 382 total. **Class size:** 23% < 20, 77% 20-39.

Freshman class profile.

End year in good standing:	90%	Out-of-state:	9%
Return as sophomores:	59%	International:	20%

Basis for selection. Graduation from high school or the equivalent and an entrance exam or SAT/ACT scores are basic requirements for admission to degree and certificate programs. A personal interview is strongly recommended. Institutional entrance tests required of all applicants. SAT or ACT accepted in lieu of institutional entrance exam. Interviews strongly recommended.

2015-2016 Annual costs. Tuition/fees: $24,300. Books/supplies: $960. Personal expenses: $11,013.

Financial aid. Non-need-based: Scholarships awarded for academics, alumni affiliation.

Application procedures. Admission: No deadline. $50 fee. Admission notification on a rolling basis. Admitted applicants must reply within two weeks of notification. **Financial aid:** No deadline. FAFSA required. Applicants notified on a rolling basis starting 3/1; must reply within 6 week(s) of notification.

Academics. Special study options: Accelerated study, distance learning, ESL, honors, internships, study abroad. **Credit/placement by examination:** AP, CLEP, SAT, ACT, institutional tests. **Support services:** Learning center, pre-admission summer program, remedial instruction, study skills assistance, tutoring, writing center.

Majors. Business: Business admin, fashion, financial planning, international, marketing. **Health services:** Health care admin. **Protective services:** Law enforcement admin.

Most popular majors. Business/marketing 71%, health sciences 9%, security/protective services 17%.

Technology on campus. 200 workstations in library, computer center. Commuter students can connect to campus network. Online library, helpline, wireless network available.

Student life. Freshman orientation: Mandatory. Preregistration for classes offered. **Activities:** Student government, international club, multicultural club, fashion club, accounting club.

Athletics. Intercollegiate: Basketball, cross-country, soccer. **Team name:** Knights.

Student services. Adult student services, alcohol/substance abuse counseling, career counseling, student employment services, financial aid counseling, personal counseling, placement for graduates, veterans' counselor.

Contact. E-mail: info@berkeleycollege.edu
Phone: (212) 986-4343 Toll-free number: (800) 446-5400
Fax: (212) 818-1079
Michelle Gomez, Director, High School Admissions, Berkeley College of New York City, 3 East 43rd Street, New York, NY 10017

Beth Hamedrash Shaarei Yosher Institute
Brooklyn, New York
     CB code: 0731

- Private 5-year rabbinical college for men affiliated with the Jewish faith
- Very large city
- 49 degree-seeking undergraduates

General. Founded in 1962. Accredited by AARTS. First Talmudic degree and ordination available. **Degrees:** 6 bachelor's awarded; doctoral offered. **Calendar:** Semester. **Full-time faculty:** 4 total. **Part-time faculty:** 3 total.

Basis for selection. Test scores most important. High school record considered.

2015-2016 Annual costs. Tuition/fees: $8,250. Room/board: $1,800. Personal expenses: $2,000.

Application procedures. Admission: No deadline. $100 fee.

Academics. Credit/placement by examination: AP, CLEP.

Majors. Philosophy/religion: Judaic.

Contact. Phone: (718) 854-2290
Director of Student Financial Aid, Beth Hamedrash Shaarei Yosher
Institute, 4102 16th Avenue, Brooklyn, NY 11204

Beth Hatalmud Rabbinical College
Brooklyn, New York
CB code: 7317

- Private 4-year rabbinical college for men affiliated with the Jewish faith
- Very large city
- 47 degree-seeking undergraduates

General. Founded in 1950. Accredited by AARTS. Ordination and First
Rabbinic degree available. **Degrees:** 3 bachelor's awarded. **Calendar:** Semester. **Full-time faculty:** 6 total.

Basis for selection. Institutional examination.

2015-2016 Annual costs. Tuition/fees: $10,950.

Application procedures. Admission: Closing date 9/1. Admission notification on a rolling basis.

Academics. Credit/placement by examination: AP, CLEP.

Majors. Philosophy/religion: Judaic.

Student life. Policies: Religious observance required.

Contact. Phone: (718) 259-2525
Director of Admissions, Beth Hatalmud Rabbinical College, 2127 82nd
Street, Brooklyn, NY 11214

Boricua College
New York, New York
www.boricuacollege.edu
CB code: 2901

- Private 4-year liberal arts college
- Commuter campus in very large city
- 1,019 degree-seeking undergraduates
- 56 graduate students
- Application essay, interview required

General. Founded in 1974. Regionally accredited. Boricua College has four
centers: one each in Manhattan and the Bronx, and two in Brooklyn. **Degrees:**
141 bachelor's, 157 associate awarded; master's offered. **Calendar:** Semester,
limited summer session. **Full-time faculty:** 63 total; 33% have terminal
degrees, 51% women. **Part-time faculty:** 58 total; 22% women. **Class size:**
100% 20-39.

Basis for selection. Entrance examination, academic records, interview
by the faculty, 2 letters of recommendation. Institutional tests required for
admissions and placement. Final interview and approval by the faculty is
required. **Home schooled:** Transcript of courses and grades, interview, letter
of recommendation (nonparent) required. **Learning Disabled:** Evaluation is
done based on individual needs of the candidate.

2015-2016 Annual costs. Tuition/fees: $10,100. Books/supplies: $400.
Personal expenses: $3,625.

Application procedures. Admission: No deadline. $25 fee, may be
waived for applicants with need. Admission notification on a rolling basis.
Financial aid: Priority date 4/30; no closing date. FAFSA required. Applicants notified on a rolling basis; must reply within 3 week(s) of notification.

Academics. Academic load consists of 5 courses per semester: 3 applied
studies courses (individualized instruction, colloquium, experiential), 1 theoretical, and 1 cultural class. Academic support services are available at
different hours upon request. **Special study options:** Accelerated study,
independent study, internships, liberal arts/career combination, teacher certification program. **Credit/placement by examination:** AP, CLEP, institutional

tests. 30 credit hours maximum toward bachelor's degree. **Support services:**
Reduced course load, tutoring.

Majors. Area/ethnic studies: Latin American. **Business:** Business admin.
Education: Elementary. **Liberal arts:** Arts/sciences.

Technology on campus. 180 workstations in library, computer center,
student center. Online library, helpline, wireless network available.

Student life. Freshman orientation: Mandatory. Preregistration for
classes offered. Based on appointments. **Policies:** Student regulations include
a sexual harassment policy. **Activities:** Choral groups, dance, drama, opera,
student government, student newspaper.

Athletics. Intramural: Basketball, volleyball.

Student services. Adult student services, career counseling, student
employment services, personal counseling, placement for graduates.

Contact. E-mail: isanches@boricuacollege.edu
Phone: (212) 694-1000 ext. 675 Fax: (212) 694-1015
Brenda Rodriguez, Director of Admissions, Boricua College, 3755
Broadway, New York, NY 10032

Briarcliffe College
Bethpage, New York
www.briarcliffe.edu
CB code: 3108

- For-profit 4-year business and career college
- Commuter campus in large town
- 1,719 undergraduates

General. Founded in 1966. Regionally accredited. **Degrees:** 318 bachelor's,
351 associate awarded. **Location:** 20 miles from New York City. **Calendar:**
Semester, extensive summer session. **Full-time faculty:** 26 total. **Part-time
faculty:** 209 total.

Basis for selection. At minimum, an enrolling student must provide documentation of a high school diploma (meeting New York State regulations),
G.E.D., or college degree. Favorable applications for admission may include
previous academic achievement, participation in extracurricular activities,
work experience, and the demonstration of positive personal characteristics.
Interviews recommended. **Home schooled:** Not accepted.

High school preparation. Recommended units include English 4, mathematics 2, social studies 4 and science 1.

2015-2016 Annual costs. Associate programs: $23,280-$37,440. Bachelor's programs: $21,930-$74,880.

Financial aid. Non-need-based: Scholarships awarded for academics,
alumni affiliation.

Application procedures. Admission: No deadline. $35 fee. Admission
notification on a rolling basis. **Financial aid:** No deadline. FAFSA, institutional form required. Applicants notified on a rolling basis.

Academics. Special study options: Distance learning, independent study,
internships. **Credit/placement by examination:** AP, CLEP, IB, SAT, ACT,
institutional tests. 15 credit hours maximum toward associate degree, 15
toward bachelor's. **Support services:** Learning center, reduced course load,
remedial instruction, study skills assistance, tutoring.

Majors. Business: Accounting, business admin, marketing. **Computer sciences:** Information technology, networking, programming. **Visual/performing arts:** General.

Technology on campus. 400 workstations in library, computer center.
Commuter students can connect to campus network. Online library available.

Student life. Freshman orientation: Mandatory. Preregistration for
classes offered. **Activities:** Student government.

Athletics. USCAA. **Intercollegiate:** Baseball M, bowling, lacrosse M, soccer M, softball W. **Team name:** Bulldogs.

Student services. Financial aid counseling, placement for graduates.

Contact. E-mail: info@bcl.edu
Phone: (516) 918-3600 Fax: (516) 470-6020
Richard Kleinman, Director of Admissions, Briarcliffe College, 1055
Stewart Avenue, Bethpage, NY 11714

Canisius College

Buffalo, New York

CB member

www.canisius.edu

CB code: 2073

- Private 4-year liberal arts and teachers college affiliated with the Roman Catholic Church
- Residential campus in large city
- 2,552 degree-seeking undergraduates: 1% part-time, 54% women, 8% African American, 2% Asian American, 6% Hispanic/Latino, 1% Multiracial, non-Hispanic, 4% international
- 1,215 degree-seeking graduate students
- 87% of applicants admitted
- SAT or ACT (ACT writing optional) required
- 70% graduate within 6 years

General. Founded in 1870. Regionally accredited. Campus connected by underground tunnel system, rapid transit stations near campus. **Degrees:** 702 bachelor's, 13 associate awarded; master's offered. **ROTC:** Army. **Calendar:** Semester, limited summer session. **Full-time faculty:** 189 total; 96% have terminal degrees, 10% minority, 40% women. **Part-time faculty:** 242 total; 33% have terminal degrees, 10% minority, 47% women. **Class size:** 50% < 20, 47% 20-39, 2% 40-49, less than 1% 50-99. **Special facilities:** Miniplanetarium, seismograph station, rare book room, digital media lab, human performance lab, animal care unit.

Freshman class profile. 4,209 applied, 3,661 admitted, 605 enrolled.

Mid 50% test scores		GPA 2.0-2.99:	14%
SAT critical reading:	470-580	Rank in top quarter:	50%
SAT math:	480-600	Rank in top tenth:	18%
ACT composite:	21-27	Return as sophomores:	83%
GPA 3.75 or higher:	27%	Out-of-state:	10%
GPA 3.50-3.74:	26%	Live on campus:	71%
GPA 3.0-3.49:	32%	International:	4%

Basis for selection. Primary emphasis placed on strength of academic record, achievement, class rank and SAT/ACT scores. Essays, recommendations important. Extracurricular activities, alumni affiliation factors. Interview and essay recommended.

High school preparation. College-preparatory program required. 16 units required; 26 recommended. Required and recommended units include English 4, mathematics 3-4, social studies 4, science 3-4 (laboratory 2), foreign language 2-4 and academic electives 4.

2015-2016 Annual costs. Tuition/fees: $34,690. Room/board: $12,766.

2015-2016 Financial aid. Need-based: 561 full-time freshmen applied for aid; 508 deemed to have need; 508 received aid. Average need met was 84%. Average scholarship/grant was $25,939; average loan $3,922. 78% of total undergraduate aid awarded as scholarships/grants, 22% as loans/jobs. **Non-need-based:** Awarded to 1,084 full-time undergraduates, including 259 freshmen. Scholarships awarded for academics, alumni affiliation, art, athletics, job skills, minority status, music/drama, ROTC.

Application procedures. Admission: Priority date 11/1; deadline 5/1. $40 fee, may be waived for applicants with need, free for online applicants. Admission notification on a rolling basis beginning on or about 12/15. Must reply by May 1 or within 2 week(s) if notified thereafter. **Financial aid:** Priority date 2/15; no closing date. FAFSA required. Applicants notified on a rolling basis starting 3/1.

Academics. Special study options: Combined bachelor's/graduate degree, cross-registration, distance learning, double major, dual enrollment of high school students, ESL, exchange student, external degree, honors, independent study, internships, student-designed major, study abroad, teacher certification program, weekend college. Early assurance Dental school with SUNY (UB) Buffalo and Upstate Medical School in Syracuse, seven year joint degree with UB Dental and SUNY College of Optometry in NYC, AS/BS With Fashion Institute of Technology in NYC, 3+2. Dual degree in Physics Engineering programs in conjunction with UB and Penn state at Eerie. **Credit/placement by examination:** AP, CLEP, IB, SAT, ACT, institutional tests. 30 credit hours maximum toward bachelor's degree. **Support services:** Learning center, pre-admission summer program, reduced course load, remedial instruction, study skills assistance, tutoring, writing center.

Majors. Area/ethnic studies: European, Irish, Latin American. **Biology:** General, animal behavior, biochemistry, bioinformatics, zoology. **Business:** Accounting, entrepreneurial studies, finance, international, management information systems, management science, managerial economics, marketing. **Communications:** Communications/speech/rhetoric, digital media, journalism. **Computer sciences:** Computer science. **Conservation:** Environmental science, environmental studies. **Education:** Early childhood, early childhood special, elementary, elementary special ed, learning disabled, physical, secondary, secondary special ed. **Engineering:** Pre-engineering. **English:** Creative writing, English lit, general lit. **Foreign languages:** Ancient Greek, classics, French, Germanic, Latin, Spanish. **Health services:** General, athletic training, clinical lab science. **History:** General. **Liberal arts:** Arts/sciences, humanities. **Math:** General, mathematics/statistics. **Parks/recreation:** Sports admin. **Philosophy/religion:** Philosophy, religion. **Physical sciences:** Chemistry, physics. **Protective services:** Criminal justice, law enforcement admin. **Psychology:** General, forensic. **Social sciences:** General, anthropology, economics, international relations, political science, sociology, urban studies. **Visual/performing arts:** Art history/conservation, music, music performance, studio arts.

Most popular majors. Biology 14%, business/marketing 23%, communications/journalism 8%, education 9%, health sciences 7%, psychology 11%, social sciences 10%.

Technology on campus. 700 workstations in dormitories, library, computer center, student center. Dormitories wired for high-speed internet access and linked to campus network. Commuter students can connect to campus network. Online course registration, online library, helpline, repair service, student web hosting, wireless network available.

Student life. Freshman orientation: Mandatory, $200 fee. Preregistration for classes offered. **Housing:** Coed dorms, special housing for disabled, apartments, themed housing, wellness housing available. $200 partly refundable deposit, deadline 5/1. Honors student housing available. All college owned housing is handicapped accessible. **Activities:** Bands, campus ministries, choral groups, dance, drama, film society, international student organizations, literary magazine, music ensembles, Model UN, musical theater, radio station, student government, student newspaper, symphony orchestra, TV station, political science association, ethnic and social service organizations, international affairs society, social justice club, Circle K, Global Horizons, German club, Italian club, Little Theater.

Athletics. NCAA. **Intercollegiate:** Baseball M, basketball, cross-country, golf M, ice hockey M, lacrosse, rowing (crew) W, soccer, softball W, swimming, synchronized swimming W, volleyball W. **Intramural:** Basketball, football (non-tackle) M, golf M, handball, soccer, volleyball. **Team name:** Golden Griffins.

Student services. Adult student services, alcohol/substance abuse counseling, chaplain/spiritual director, career counseling, services for economically disadvantaged, student employment services, financial aid counseling, health services, minority student services, personal counseling, placement for graduates, veterans' counselor. **Physically disabled:** Services for visually, speech, hearing impaired.

Contact. E-mail: admissions@canisius.edu
Phone: (716) 888-2200 Toll-free number: (800) 843-1517
Fax: (716) 888-3230
Mollie Ballaro, Director of Admissions, Canisius College, 2001 Main Street, Buffalo, NY 14208-1098

Cazenovia College

Cazenovia, New York

www.cazenovia.edu

CB code: 2078

- Private 4-year liberal arts and career college
- Residential campus in small town
- 1,050 degree-seeking undergraduates: 10% part-time, 74% women, 8% African American, 1% Asian American, 6% Hispanic/Latino, 2% Multiracial, non-Hispanic
- 81% of applicants admitted
- 58% graduate within 6 years; 31% enter graduate study

General. Founded in 1824. Regionally accredited. **Degrees:** 208 bachelor's awarded. **ROTC:** Army, Air Force. **Location:** 20 miles from Syracuse. **Calendar:** Semester, limited summer session. **Full-time faculty:** 57 total; 81% have terminal degrees, 68% women. **Part-time faculty:** 72 total; 32% have terminal degrees, 57% women. **Class size:** 76% < 20, 24% 20-39. **Special facilities:** 160-acre farm and equine center, art and design facility and gallery.

Freshman class profile. 2,307 applied, 1,880 admitted, 250 enrolled.

Mid 50% test scores		Rank in top quarter:	35%
SAT critical reading:	420-530	Rank in top tenth:	12%
SAT math:	420-530	End year in good standing:	75%
GPA 3.75 or higher:	24%	Return as sophomores:	71%
GPA 3.50-3.74:	14%	Out-of-state:	13%
GPA 3.0-3.49:	30%	Live on campus:	99%
GPA 2.0-2.99:	31%		

Basis for selection. Rigor of secondary school record very important; interview, recommendations, school activities important. SAT or ACT recommended. Portfolio recommended for art, graphic and interior design, photography programs. **Learning Disabled:** Students who wish to utilize the services available through the Office of Special Services must provide appropriate documentation of their disability. Student identification must be voluntary and all documentation received is confidential. Documentation must identify the individual as a person with a disability as defined by the Rehabilitation Act of 1973, Chapter 504, and/or the Americans with Disabilities Act of 1990.

High school preparation. College-preparatory program recommended. 16 units recommended. Recommended units include English 4, mathematics 2, social studies 4 and science 2. Art courses recommended for art and design majors.

2015-2016 Annual costs. Tuition/fees: $31,754. Room/board: $12,826. Books/supplies: $1,000. Personal expenses: $100.

Financial aid. **Non-need-based:** Scholarships awarded for academics, leadership.

Application procedures. **Admission:** Priority date 3/1; no deadline. $30 fee, may be waived for applicants with need, free for online applicants. Admission notification on a rolling basis beginning on or about 11/1. Must reply by May 1 or within 2 week(s) if notified thereafter. **Financial aid:** Priority date 3/1; no closing date. FAFSA required. Applicants notified on a rolling basis starting 3/1; must reply by 5/1 or within 2 week(s) of notification.

Academics. **Special study options:** Combined bachelor's/graduate degree, distance learning, double major, honors, independent study, internships, liberal arts/career combination, student-designed major, study abroad, teacher certification program, Washington semester. **Credit/placement by examination:** AP, CLEP, IB, SAT, ACT, institutional tests. **Support services:** Learning center, pre-admission summer program, reduced course load, remedial instruction, study skills assistance, tutoring, writing center.

Majors. **Business:** Accounting, business admin, fashion. **Communications:** Communications/speech/rhetoric. **Conservation:** Environmental studies. **Education:** Early childhood, special ed. **English:** English lit. **Liberal arts:** Arts/sciences. **Parks/recreation:** Sports admin. **Protective services:** Criminal justice. **Psychology:** General. **Social sciences:** General. **Visual/performing arts:** Design, fashion design, interior design, photography, studio arts.

Most popular majors. Business/marketing 21%, psychology 8%, public administration/social services 21%, security/protective services 6%, visual/performing arts 27%.

Technology on campus. 400 workstations in dormitories, library, computer center, student center. Dormitories wired for high-speed internet access and linked to campus network. Commuter students can connect to campus network. Online course registration, online library, helpline, repair service, wireless network available.

Student life. **Freshman orientation:** Mandatory, $170 fee. Preregistration for classes offered. **Housing:** Guaranteed on-campus for freshmen. Coed dorms, single-sex dorms, special housing for disabled, apartments, themed housing, wellness housing available. $400 nonrefundable deposit, deadline 5/1. Single room suites available. **Activities:** Campus ministries, choral groups, dance, drama, international student organizations, musical theater, radio station, student government, student newspaper, human services club, overseas travel club, Young Democrats, Young Republicans, Cazventures outdoor club, Certified Peer Educators, You Are Not Alone-LGBT, Student Organization of Ethnic Diversity.

Athletics. NCAA. **Intercollegiate:** Baseball M, basketball, cheerleading, cross-country, equestrian, golf M, lacrosse, rowing (crew), soccer, softball W, tennis, volleyball. **Intramural:** Basketball, bowling, equestrian, football (non-tackle), ice hockey M, rowing (crew), skiing, soccer, softball, swimming, volleyball, weight lifting. **Team name:** Wildcats.

Student services. Alcohol/substance abuse counseling, chaplain/spiritual director, career counseling, services for economically disadvantaged, student employment services, financial aid counseling, health services, personal counseling, placement for graduates. **Physically disabled:** Services for visually, speech, hearing impaired.

Contact. E-mail: admission@cazenovia.edu
Phone: (315) 655-7208 Toll-free number: (800) 654-3210
Fax: (315) 655-4860
Christine Mandel, Dean of Enrollment Management, Cazenovia College, 3 Sullivan Street, Cazenovia, NY 13035

Central Yeshiva Tomchei Tmimim-Lubavitch
Brooklyn, New York

CB code: 0549

- Private 4-year rabbinical college for men affiliated with the Jewish faith
- Very large city
- 648 degree-seeking undergraduates

General. Accredited by AARTS. **Degrees:** 115 bachelor's awarded; master's offered. **Calendar:** Differs by program. **Full-time faculty:** 15 total. **Part-time faculty:** 6 total.

Basis for selection. Completion of college-preparatory program and recommendations required. Secondary school record recommended.

2015-2016 Annual costs. Tuition/fees: $6,700. Room/board: $2,500.

Application procedures. **Admission:** No deadline.

Academics. **Credit/placement by examination:** AP, CLEP.

Majors. **Philosophy/religion:** Judaic. **Theology:** Talmudic.

Contact. E-mail: uofiop@juno.com
Phone: (718) 859-7600
Central Yeshiva Tomchei Tmimim-Lubavitch, 841-853 Ocean Parkway, Brooklyn, NY 11230

City University of New York: Baruch College
New York, New York
www.baruch.cuny.edu

CB member
CB code: 2034

- Public 4-year business and liberal arts college
- Commuter campus in very large city
- 14,896 degree-seeking undergraduates: 25% part-time, 49% women, 9% African American, 32% Asian American, 22% Hispanic/Latino, 2% Multi-racial, non-Hispanic, 11% international
- 3,138 degree-seeking graduate students
- 32% of applicants admitted

General. Founded in 1919. Regionally accredited. **Degrees:** 3,054 bachelor's awarded; master's offered. **ROTC:** Army. **Location:** Located in New York City. **Calendar:** Semester, extensive summer session. **Full-time faculty:** 513 total; 95% have terminal degrees, 29% minority, 39% women. **Part-time faculty:** 711 total; 38% have terminal degrees, 31% minority, 42% women. **Class size:** 19% < 20, 58% 20-39, 7% 40-49, 12% 50-99, 4% >100. **Special facilities:** Performing arts center, black box theater, gallery, theaters, recital halls.

Freshman class profile. 19,864 applied, 6,443 admitted, 1,477 enrolled.

Mid 50% test scores			
SAT critical reading:	520-630	Rank in top quarter:	78%
SAT math:	580-690	Rank in top tenth:	48%
GPA 3.75 or higher:	21%	Return as sophomores:	91%
GPA 3.50-3.74:	20%	Out-of-state:	4%
GPA 3.0-3.49:	36%	Live on campus:	9%
GPA 2.0-2.99:	22%	International:	5%

Basis for selection. Average high school GPA is 3.3 and average SAT score (out of 1600) is 1170-1280. Applicants must apply through the City University of New York (CUNY) Application, exclusively online. Students who did not score a minimum of 480 on the verbal and math SAT are required to take a skills assessment test. Essays are optional but recommended. **Learning Disabled:** No special requirements; recommended that students call Disability Service Office to discuss available services.

High school preparation. 16 units required. Required and recommended units include English 4, mathematics 3, social studies 4, science 2 (laboratory 2), foreign language 2 and academic electives 1.

2015-2016 Annual costs. Tuition/fees: $6,861; $17,331 out-of-state. Books/supplies: $1,304. Personal expenses: $1,798. **Additional information:** Room / Housing Rates vary depending on room sizes among other factors, ranges from $12,152 to $12,990.

Financial aid. **Non-need-based:** Scholarships awarded for academics, state residency.

Application procedures. **Admission:** Priority date 12/1; deadline 2/1 (postmark date). $65 fee, may be waived for applicants with need. Application must be submitted online. Admission notification by 5/1. Admission notification on a rolling basis beginning on or about 2/1. Must reply by May 1 or within 2 week(s) if notified thereafter. All CUNY schools operate on a rolling admission basis; therefore colleges and programs may close before the deadline date. **Financial aid:** Priority date 4/15; no closing date. FAFSA required. Applicants notified on a rolling basis starting 4/15; must reply within 2 week(s) of notification:

Academics. 120 credit hours required for BA/BS degrees, 124 for BBA. Optional humanities seminar examining 2 or more disciplines in arts and sciences; joint business/liberal arts and science majors; programs in arts administration, management of musical enterprise, real estate, and metropolitan development. **Special study options:** Accelerated study, combined bachelor's/graduate degree, cross-registration, distance learning, double major, ESL, exchange student, honors, independent study, internships, liberal arts/career combination, student-designed major, study abroad. **Credit/placement by examination:** AP, CLEP, IB, SAT, institutional tests. 21 credit hours maximum toward bachelor's degree. No more than 21 credits through AP and/or college courses taken in high school. **Support services:** Learning center, pre-admission summer program, reduced course load, study skills assistance, tutoring, writing center.

Honors college/program. Applicants must have high standardized test scores (1300+ on the SAT, exclusive of Writing) and high school averages (90+). Leadership potential and community involvement sought. Applicants must supply teacher recommendations and essay.

Majors. Biology: General. **Business:** General, accounting, actuarial science, business admin, communications, finance, labor relations, management information systems, managerial economics, marketing, operations, real estate, statistics. **Communications:** Journalism. **Computer sciences:** General, computer science, information systems. **Engineering:** Operations research. **English:** English lit. **Foreign languages:** Spanish. **History:** General. **Human services:** General. **Liberal arts:** Arts/sciences. **Math:** General, statistics. **Philosophy/religion:** Philosophy, religion. **Psychology:** General. **Social sciences:** Economics, political science, sociology. **Visual/performing arts:** Music, music management, studio arts management.

Most popular majors. Business/marketing 79%.

Technology on campus. 1,300 workstations in library, computer center, student center. Dormitories wired for high-speed internet access. Online course registration, online library, helpline, wireless network available.

Student life. Freshman orientation: Mandatory. Preregistration for classes offered. Held over a half day long, on-campus session offered on multiple days. **Housing:** Coed dorms available. $300 nonrefundable deposit, deadline 4/15. **Activities:** Campus ministries, choral groups, dance, drama, literary magazine, Model UN, musical theater, radio station, student government, student newspaper, Hillel, National Association of Black Accountants, Golden Key International Honor Society, Asian student association, Muslim student association, United International Student Body, Pre-Law Society, Caribbean student association.

Athletics. NCAA. **Intercollegiate:** Baseball M, basketball, cheerleading, cross-country, diving W, soccer M, softball W, swimming, tennis, volleyball. **Intramural:** Badminton, basketball, cross-country, racquetball, swimming, table tennis, volleyball. **Team name:** Bearcats.

Student services. Adult student services, alcohol/substance abuse counseling, chaplain/spiritual director, career counseling, student employment services, financial aid counseling, health services, legal services, personal counseling, placement for graduates, veterans' counselor. **Physically disabled:** Services for visually, speech, hearing impaired.

Contact. E-mail: admissions@baruch.cuny.edu
Phone: (646) 312-1400 Fax: (646) 312-1363
Marisa Delacruz, Director, Undergraduate Admissions, City University of New York: Baruch College, One Bernard Baruch Way, Box H-0720, New York, NY 10010-5585

City University of New York: Brooklyn College
Brooklyn, New York
www.brooklyn.cuny.edu   **CB code: 2046**

- Public 4-year liberal arts college
- Commuter campus in very large city
- 13,172 degree-seeking undergraduates: 23% part-time, 58% women, 22% African American, 18% Asian American, 22% Hispanic/Latino, 2% Multi-racial, non-Hispanic, 4% international
- 3,114 degree-seeking graduate students
- 37% of applicants admitted

- SAT or ACT (ACT writing optional) required
- 54% graduate within 6 years

General. Founded in 1930. Regionally accredited. **Degrees:** 2,448 bachelor's awarded; master's offered. **Location:** 10 miles from Manhattan. **Calendar:** Semester, extensive summer session. **Full-time faculty:** 537 total; 93% have terminal degrees, 25% minority, 46% women. **Part-time faculty:** 711 total; 40% have terminal degrees, 24% minority, 54% women. **Class size:** 27% < 20, 58% 20-39, 10% 40-49, 4% 50-99, less than 1% >100. **Special facilities:** Astronomical observatory, greenhouse, applied sciences institute, institute for the humanities, infant study center, center for the performing arts, particle accelerator.

Freshman class profile. 20,324 applied, 7,583 admitted, 1,340 enrolled.

Mid 50% test scores		Rank in top quarter:	50%
SAT critical reading:	470-570	Rank in top tenth:	18%
SAT math:	500-610	Return as sophomores:	82%
GPA 3.75 or higher:	6%	Out-of-state:	3%
GPA 3.50-3.74:	22%	International:	4%
GPA 3.0-3.49:	58%	Fraternities:	1%
GPA 2.0-2.99:	14%	Sororities:	1%

Basis for selection. Students accepted based on SAT scores and academic average. Essay required for BA/MD, CHC and Scholars, interview recommended for scholars program. Audition required for music conservatory, theater programs; portfolio required for fine arts program.

High school preparation. College-preparatory program recommended. 21 units recommended. Recommended units include English 4, mathematics 3, social studies 4, science 3, foreign language 3 and academic electives 4.

2015-2016 Annual costs. Tuition/fees: $6,838; $17,308 out-of-state. Books/supplies: $1,364. Personal expenses: $1,816. **Additional information:** Room/Housing Rates range from $12,418 to $17,520, depending on room sizes among other factors.

Financial aid. Non-need-based: Scholarships awarded for academics, art, leadership, music/drama, state residency.

Application procedures. Admission: Priority date 2/1; no deadline. $65 fee. Admission notification on a rolling basis beginning on or about 2/1. Must reply by May 1 or within 3 week(s) if notified thereafter. All CUNY schools operate on a rolling admission basis; therefore colleges and programs may close before the deadline date. **Financial aid:** Priority date 4/11; no closing date. FAFSA required. Applicants notified on a rolling basis starting 5/11.

Academics. Special study options: Accelerated study, combined bachelor's/graduate degree, distance learning, double major, dual enrollment of high school students, ESL, honors, independent study, internships, liberal arts/career combination, student-designed major, study abroad, teacher certification program, Washington semester, weekend college. **Credit/placement by examination:** AP, CLEP, IB, SAT, ACT, institutional tests. 35 credit hours maximum toward bachelor's degree. **Support services:** Learning center, pre-admission summer program, reduced course load, study skills assistance, tutoring, writing center.

Honors college/program. Honors Academy offers interdisciplinary seminars, honors sections of Core curriculum classes, senior thesis colloquia, individual academic and professional advisement, monitored internships, small class sizes, a collaborative community of well-matched students.

Majors. Area/ethnic studies: African-American, American, Caribbean, Chicano/Hispanic-American/Latino, women's. **Biology:** General. **Business:** Accounting, business admin. **Communications:** Broadcast journalism, communications/speech/rhetoric, journalism, radio/TV. **Computer sciences:** General, information systems, web page design. **Conservation:** Environmental studies. **Education:** Biology, chemistry, early childhood, earth science, elementary, English, French, mathematics, music, physical, physics, social studies, Spanish. **English:** Creative writing, English lit. **Foreign languages:** Classics, comparative lit, French, Italian, linguistics, Russian, Spanish. **Health services:** Audiology/speech pathology. **History:** General. **Liberal arts:** Arts/sciences. **Math:** General, computational/applied, financial. **Parks/recreation:** Exercise sciences, health/fitness. **Philosophy/religion:** Judaic, philosophy, religion. **Physical sciences:** Chemistry, geology, physics. **Psychology:** General. **Social sciences:** Anthropology, economics, political science, sociology. **Visual/performing arts:** Art, art history/conservation, cinematography, dramatic, music, music performance, music theory/composition, studio arts. **Work/family studies:** Food/nutrition.

Most popular majors. Business/marketing 32%, communications/journalism 6%, education 8%, health sciences 8%, psychology 16%, visual/performing arts 6%.

Technology on campus. 2,000 workstations in library, computer center, student center. Online library, wireless network available.

Student life. Freshman orientation: Available. Preregistration for classes offered. **Activities:** Dance, drama, film society, international student organizations, literary magazine, music ensembles, musical theater, radio station, student government, student newspaper, symphony orchestra, TV station, Hillel, Newman Club, student Christian association, Alpha Phi Omega, Christian fellowship, Islamic society, Caribbean student union, accounting society, lesbian/gay/bisexual/transgender alliance.

Athletics. NCAA. **Intercollegiate:** Basketball, cross-country, diving, soccer, softball W, swimming, tennis, volleyball. **Intramural:** Basketball, soccer, tennis, volleyball. **Team name:** Bulldogs.

Student services. Adult student services, alcohol/substance abuse counseling, career counseling, services for economically disadvantaged, student employment services, financial aid counseling, health services, on-campus daycare, personal counseling, placement for graduates, veterans' counselor, women's services. **Physically disabled:** Services for visually, speech, hearing impaired.

Contact. E-mail: adminqry@brooklyn.cuny.edu
Phone: (718) 951-5001 Fax: (718) 951-4506
Penelope Terry, Director of Undergraduate Admissions, City University of New York: Brooklyn College, 2900 Bedford Avenue, Brooklyn, NY 11210

City University of New York: City College

New York, New York   **CB member**
www.ccny.cuny.edu   **CB code: 2083**

- Public 4-year university and liberal arts college
- Commuter campus in very large city
- 13,294 degree-seeking undergraduates: 27% part-time, 50% women
- 2,333 degree-seeking graduate students
- 40% of applicants admitted
- SAT required

General. Founded in 1847. Regionally accredited. **Degrees:** 2,156 bachelor's awarded; master's, doctoral offered. **ROTC:** Army. **Calendar:** Semester, extensive summer session. **Full-time faculty:** 881 total; 51% have terminal degrees, 10% minority, 38% women. **Part-time faculty:** 680 total; 24% have terminal degrees, 56% minority, 33% women. **Class size:** 44% < 20, 53% 20-39, 3% 40-49, less than 1% 50-99, less than 1% >100. **Special facilities:** Planetarium, weather station, ultra-fast laser spectroscopy laboratory, microwave laboratory, computer-aided design facilities, slide library, darkroom facilities, sonic music arts facility, structural biology center.

Freshman class profile. 24,735 applied, 9,794 admitted, 1,630 enrolled.

Mid 50% test scores			
SAT critical reading:	460-580	GPA 3.50-3.74:	29%
SAT math:	520-640	GPA 3.0-3.49:	35%
SAT writing:	450-580	GPA 2.0-2.99:	23%
GPA 3.75 or higher:	13%	Out-of-state:	1%

Basis for selection. Academic average and number of academic units achieved in high school, SAT, or GED score of 325 or better important. Units recommended for admission must be acquired before graduation from any CUNY senior college. Interview required for biomedical education, audition required for music program; portfolio required for electronic design and multimedia. **Home schooled:** Applicants must obtain GED or diploma through regionally accredited program.

High school preparation. 19 units required. Required units include English 4, mathematics 3, social studies 4, science 2 (laboratory 2), foreign language 3 and academic electives 1.

2015-2016 Annual costs. Tuition/fees: $6,740; $17,210 out-of-state. Books/supplies: $1,364. Personal expenses: $4,018. **Additional information:** Room/Housing Rates range from $12,370 to $18,086 depending on room sizes among other factors.

2015-2016 Financial aid. Need-based: 73% of total undergraduate aid awarded as scholarships/grants, 27% as loans/jobs. **Non-need-based:** Scholarships awarded for academics, alumni affiliation, art, leadership, music/drama, state residency.

Application procedures. Admission: Closing date 1/15 (postmark date). $65 fee. Admission notification on a rolling basis beginning on or about 3/1. All CUNY schools operate on a rolling admission basis; therefore colleges and programs may close before the deadline date. **Financial aid:** Priority date 3/15; no closing date. FAFSA required. Applicants notified on a rolling basis starting 4/1.

Academics. Special study options: Accelerated study, combined bachelor's/graduate degree, cooperative education, cross-registration, distance learning, double major, dual enrollment of high school students, ESL, honors, independent study, internships, study abroad, teacher certification program. **Credit/placement by examination:** AP, CLEP, IB, institutional tests. 32 credit hours maximum toward bachelor's degree. **Support services:** Learning center, pre-admission summer program, reduced course load, study skills assistance, tutoring, writing center.

Honors college/program. Admits only new first-year students, who must apply by special application. Application deadline November 1 for early admission, December 15 for regular admission. For the class admitted fall 2005 (Class of 2009), the average high school GPA was 93.7 (on a scale of 100) and the average SAT was 1371 (exclusive of Writing). Students are expected to achieve an overall 3.3 GPA by the end of their first year and a 3.5 GPA by the end of their second year, which must be maintained until graduation in four years.

Majors. Architecture: Architecture. **Area/ethnic studies:** African-American, Asian, Caribbean, Latin American. **Biology:** General, biochemistry. **Business:** General. **Communications:** Advertising, communications/speech/rhetoric, journalism, public relations. **Computer sciences:** Computer science. **Education:** Art, bilingual, biology, chemistry, early childhood, elementary, English, foreign languages, French, history, mathematics, music, physics, science, secondary, social studies, Spanish. **Engineering:** Biomedical, chemical, civil, computer, electrical, mechanical. **English:** English lit. **Foreign languages:** General, comparative lit, French, Spanish. **Health services:** Physician assistant, premedicine, prepharmacy, preveterinary. **History:** General. **Math:** General. **Philosophy/religion:** Judaic, philosophy. **Physical sciences:** Chemistry, geology, physics, planetary. **Psychology:** General. **Social sciences:** Anthropology, economics, international relations, political science, sociology. **Visual/performing arts:** General, art, art history/conservation, cinematography, commercial/advertising art, dramatic, film/cinema/video, graphic design, jazz, music, music performance, music theory/composition, studio arts.

Most popular majors. Biology 8%, engineering/engineering technologies 13%, English 7%, liberal arts 7%, psychology 15%, social sciences 11%, visual/performing arts 10%.

Technology on campus. 2,700 workstations in library, computer center, student center. Dormitories wired for high-speed internet access and linked to campus network. Commuter students can connect to campus network. Online course registration, online library, helpline, repair service, wireless network available.

Student life. Freshman orientation: Mandatory. Preregistration for classes offered. Full-day program, including registration, held in spring and summer. **Policies:** No smoking allowed. **Housing:** Apartments available. $400 nonrefundable deposit. **Activities:** Jazz band, choral groups, dance, drama, film society, international student organizations, literary magazine, music ensembles, Model UN, musical theater, radio station, student government, student newspaper, TV station, numerous religious, political, ethnic, and social service organizations.

Athletics. NCAA. **Intercollegiate:** Baseball M, basketball, cross-country, fencing, lacrosse M, soccer, tennis, track and field, volleyball. **Intramural:** Badminton M, basketball, fencing, soccer M, softball W, swimming, tennis, track and field, volleyball. **Team name:** Beavers.

Student services. Alcohol/substance abuse counseling, chaplain/spiritual director, career counseling, services for economically disadvantaged, student employment services, financial aid counseling, health services, minority student services, on-campus daycare, personal counseling, placement for graduates, veterans' counselor, women's services. **Physically disabled:** Services for visually, speech, hearing impaired.

Contact. E-mail: admissions@ccny.cuny.edu
Phone: (212) 650-6977 Fax: (212) 650-6417
Joseph Fatozzi, Executive Director of Enrollment Management, City University of New York: City College, 160 Convent Avenue, A100, New York, NY 10031

City University of New York: College of Staten Island

Staten Island, New York   **CB member**
www.csi.cuny.edu   **CB code: 2778**

- Public 4-year liberal arts college
- Commuter campus in large city
- 12,298 degree-seeking undergraduates: 21% part-time, 56% women, 9% African American, 9% Asian American, 11% Hispanic/Latino, 3% international

- 862 degree-seeking graduate students
- 100% of applicants admitted
- SAT or ACT (ACT writing optional) required
- 42% graduate within 6 years

General. Founded in 1955. Regionally accredited. **Degrees:** 1,486 bachelor's, 438 associate awarded; master's, professional offered. **Location:** 15 miles from downtown Manhattan. **Calendar:** Semester, extensive summer session. **Full-time faculty:** 364 total; 90% have terminal degrees, 27% minority, 47% women. **Part-time faculty:** 866 total; 35% have terminal degrees, 18% minority, 50% women. **Class size:** 17% < 20, 60% 20-39, 14% 40-49, 7% 50-99, 2% >100. **Special facilities:** Art gallery, radio station, astrophysical observatory, archives and special collections, center for engineered polymeric materials, center for study of Staten Island, center for the arts, center for developmental neuroscience, high performance computational facility, intelligent robotics lab.

Freshman class profile. 13,051 applied, 13,051 admitted, 2,569 enrolled.

Mid 50% test scores			
SAT critical reading:	440-540	GPA 3.0-3.49:	30%
SAT math:	470-560	GPA 2.0-2.99:	39%
SAT writing:	430-520	Return as sophomores:	81%
GPA 3.75 or higher:	5%	Out-of-state:	1%
GPA 3.50-3.74:	23%	Live on campus:	9%
		International:	3%

Basis for selection. Open admission for associates degree programs pending assessment test outcomes. Specific admission criteria for baccalaureate programs based primarily on high school average (college academic average), SAT Critical Reading and Math (or ACT equivalents), and in some cases academic units. **Home schooled:** State high school equivalency certificate required.

High school preparation. College-preparatory program required. 15 units required; 16 recommended. Required and recommended units include English 4, mathematics 3, social studies 4, science 2-3, foreign language 2-3, visual/performing arts .5.

2015-2016 Annual costs. Tuition/fees: $6,889; $17,359 out-of-state. Books/supplies: $1,364. Personal expenses: $1,816. **Additional information:** Room/Housing Rates range from $11,103 to $15,561 depending on room sizes among other factors.

2014-2015 Financial aid. **Need-based:** 2,036 full-time freshmen applied for aid; 1,882 deemed to have need; 1,394 received aid. Average need met was 69%. Average scholarship/grant was $5,622; average loan $3,598. 88% of total undergraduate aid awarded as scholarships/grants, 12% as loans/jobs. **Non-need-based:** Awarded to 5,080 full-time undergraduates, including 1,055 freshmen. Scholarships awarded for academics, alumni affiliation, art, leadership, minority status, music/drama, state residency.

Application procedures. **Admission:** Priority date 2/1; no deadline. $65 fee, may be waived for applicants with need. Application must be submitted online. Admission notification on a rolling basis beginning on or about 2/15. Must reply by May 1 or within 2 week(s) if notified thereafter. All CUNY schools operate on a rolling admission basis; therefore colleges and programs may close after the priority deadline. **Financial aid:** Priority date 3/30; no closing date. FAFSA required. Applicants notified by 6/1; Applicants notified on a rolling basis starting 6/1.

Academics. **Special study options:** Cross-registration, double major, ESL, honors, independent study, internships, semester at sea, study abroad, teacher certification program. **Credit/placement by examination:** AP, CLEP, IB, SAT, ACT, institutional tests. 30 credit hours maximum toward associate degree, 30 toward bachelor's. **Support services:** Learning center, pre-admission summer program, reduced course load, remedial instruction, study skills assistance, tutoring, writing center. Supplemental instruction in various courses, specialized review sessions for math, and a special retesting initiative for the Common Elementary Algebra Final Exam.

Honors college/program. Admission to Macaulay Honors College is based on a variety of leadership attributes: high school grades, SAT and ACT scores, extracurricular activities, community service, personal initiative and leadership, teacher recommendations.

Majors. **Area/ethnic studies:** African-American, American. **Biology:** General, biochemistry. **Business:** General, accounting. **Communications:** Communications/speech/rhetoric. **Computer sciences:** Computer science, information systems. **Education:** Biology, chemistry, elementary, English, foreign languages, history, mathematics, physics, Spanish. **Engineering:** General, electrical. **English:** English lit. **Foreign languages:** Italian, Spanish. **Health services:** Clinical lab science, nursing (RN). **History:** General. **Human services:** Social work. **Liberal arts:** Arts/sciences. **Math:** General. **Philosophy/religion:** Philosophy. **Physical sciences:** Chemistry, physics. **Psychology:** General. **Social sciences:** Economics, geography, international relations, political science, sociology/anthropology. **Visual/performing arts:** Cinematography, dramatic, film/cinema/video, music, studio arts.

Most popular majors. Business/marketing 18%, communications/journalism 6%, education 7%, health sciences 11%, psychology 18%, social sciences 10%.

Technology on campus. 1,600 workstations in library, computer center, student center. Dormitories wired for high-speed internet access. Online course registration, online library, helpline, wireless network available.

Student life. **Freshman orientation:** Mandatory. Preregistration for classes offered. The two-day NSO program takes place prior to the start of each semester. **Housing:** Coed dorms, special housing for disabled, apartments available. $400 nonrefundable deposit. **Activities:** Campus ministries, choral groups, dance, drama, film society, international student organizations, literary magazine, music ensembles, radio station, student government, student newspaper, Hillel club, Muslim Student Association, Chi Alpha Christian club, South Asian Nations club, Gay/Straight Alliance, United African Students, Students for Justice in Palestine.

Athletics. NCAA. **Intercollegiate:** Baseball M, basketball, cross-country, diving, soccer, softball W, swimming, tennis, volleyball. **Intramural:** Badminton, basketball, football (non-tackle), handball, racquetball, soccer, swimming, table tennis, tennis, ultimate frisbee, volleyball. **Team name:** Dolphins.

Student services. Adult student services, alcohol/substance abuse counseling, chaplain/spiritual director, career counseling, services for economically disadvantaged, student employment services, financial aid counseling, health services, minority student services, on-campus daycare, personal counseling, placement for graduates, veterans' counselor, women's services. **Physically disabled:** Services for visually, speech, hearing impaired.

Contact. E-mail: admissions@csi.cuny.edu
Phone: (718) 982-2010 Fax: (718) 982-2500
Emmanuel Esperance, Director of Recruitment & Admissions, City University of New York: College of Staten Island, 2800 Victory Boulevard 2A-103, Staten Island, NY 10314

City University of New York: CUNY Online
New York, New York
http://sps.cuny.edu/

- Public 4-year university
- Commuter campus in very large city
- 1,098 degree-seeking undergraduates
- 834 graduate students
- Application essay required

General. Regionally accredited. CUNY School of Professional Studies gives students instruction and academic support in programs offered online, in traditional classroom settings, and in the workplace. **Degrees:** 165 bachelor's awarded; master's offered. **Calendar:** Semester, extensive summer session. **Part-time faculty:** 210 total; 24% minority, 58% women. **Class size:** 72% < 20, 28% 20-39.

Basis for selection. Open admission, but selective for some programs. Applicants must have earned at least 24 transferable credits from an accredited college or university, maintained an overall minimum GPA of 2.5 and Demonstrate basic proficiency in reading, writing, and mathematics. Additional requirements for the Online Bachelor's Degree in Nursing. CUNY SPS does not admit first-time freshmen. The undergraduate degree programs at the CUNY School of Professional Studies (CUNY SPS) are degree completion programs. Applicants must have earned twenty-four or more credits to be considered for admission. **Home schooled:** State high school equivalency certificate required.

Financial aid. All financial aid based on need.

Application procedures. **Admission:** Priority date 2/1; deadline 8/1 (postmark date). $70 fee, may be waived for applicants with need. Application must be submitted online. Admission notification on a rolling basis beginning on or about 2/1. CUNY School of Professional Studies reviews applications on a rolling basis. Applicants are encouraged to complete the process as early as possible and should request to have an official transcript sent from each postsecondary institution previously attended as soon as they begin the application process. **Financial aid:** Closing date 8/1.

Academics. **Special study options:** Distance learning. **Credit/placement by examination:** AP, CLEP, IB. 45 credit hours maximum toward bachelor's degree. Bachelor's degree candidates are eligible to transfer up to 90 academic credits from previous educational institutions and from the options listed: Credit by Portfolio Evaluation; 18 credits maximum; Credit by Examination; 30 credits maximum; and Credit for Corporate or Military Training. **Support services:** Learning center, study skills assistance, tutoring, writing center.

Majors. Business: General. **Health services:** Health information management, nursing practice. **Psychology:** General. **Social sciences:** Sociology.

Most popular majors. Business/marketing 40%, communications/journalism 46%, psychology 6%.

Technology on campus. PC or laptop required. Commuter students can connect to campus network. Online course registration, online library, helpline, student web hosting, wireless network available.

Student life. Freshman orientation: Mandatory. Preregistration for classes offered. Orientation is strongly encouraged for online students.

Athletics. Team name: Lynx.

Student services. Adult student services, career counseling, student employment services, financial aid counseling, veterans' counselor. **Physically disabled:** Services for visually, speech, hearing impaired.

Contact. E-mail: information@sps.cuny.edu
Phone: (212) 652-2869
Jennifer Lee, Assistant Dean of Admissions and Enrollment Management, City University of New York: CUNY Online, 119 West 31st Street, New York, NY 10001-3507

City University of New York: Hunter College

New York, New York   **CB member**
www.hunter.cuny.edu/main/   **CB code: 2301**

- Public 4-year liberal arts college
- Commuter campus in very large city
- 15,465 degree-seeking undergraduates: 23% part-time, 65% women, 11% African American, 28% Asian American, 21% Hispanic/Latino, 6% international
- 6,040 degree-seeking graduate students
- 44% of applicants admitted
- SAT or ACT required
- 54% graduate within 6 years

General. Founded in 1870. Regionally accredited. **Degrees:** 2,778 bachelor's awarded; master's, professional, doctoral offered. **Calendar:** Semester, limited summer session. **Full-time faculty:** 734 total; 85% have terminal degrees, 27% minority, 52% women. **Part-time faculty:** 1,554 total; 29% have terminal degrees, 28% minority, 60% women. **Class size:** 43% < 20, 46% 20-39, 4% 40-49, 5% 50-99, 2% >100. **Special facilities:** Mathematics learning center, on-campus elementary and secondary schools.

Freshman class profile. 24,040 applied, 10,496 admitted, 2,200 enrolled.

Mid 50% test scores		GPA 3.0-3.49:	54%
SAT critical reading:	510-610	GPA 2.0-2.99:	7%
SAT math:	540-630	Return as sophomores:	82%
SAT writing:	490-600	Out-of-state:	3%
GPA 3.75 or higher:	7%	Live on campus:	2%
GPA 3.50-3.74:	32%	International:	4%

Basis for selection. Requirements vary by program. Indexing formula using weighted averages, high school academic units, and SAT scores for admission to some programs. SAT or ACT not required, but recommended, of first-time freshmen who graduated high school more than a year preceding admission.

High school preparation. 16 units recommended. Required and recommended units include English 2-4, mathematics 2-3, social studies 4, science 1-2 (laboratory 1), foreign language 2, visual/performing arts 1 and academic electives 1. 1 fine art or performing art recommended.

2015-2016 Annual costs. Tuition/fees: $6,780; $17,250 out-of-state. Books/supplies: $1,304. Personal expenses: $4,106. **Additional information:** Room/Housing Rates range from $4,407 to $14,096 depending on room sizes among other factors.

2015-2016 Financial aid. Need-based: 1,776 full-time freshmen applied for aid; 1,338 deemed to have need; 1,231 received aid. Average need met was 73%. Average scholarship/grant was $8,713; average loan $4,177. 86% of total undergraduate aid awarded as scholarships/grants, 14% as loans/jobs. **Non-need-based:** Awarded to 1,880 full-time undergraduates, including 1,281 freshmen. Scholarships awarded for academics.

Application procedures. Admission: $65 fee, may be waived for applicants with need. Admission notification on a rolling basis beginning on or about 2/1. All CUNY schools operate on a rolling admission basis; therefore colleges and programs may close before the deadline date. **Financial aid:**

Priority date 5/1; no closing date. FAFSA required. Applicants notified on a rolling basis starting 5/15.

Academics. Special study options: Accelerated study, combined bachelor's/graduate degree, cross-registration, distance learning, double major, dual enrollment of high school students, exchange student, honors, independent study, internships, liberal arts/career combination, student-designed major, study abroad, teacher certification program. BA/MA/MS programs in anthropology, biology/EOPS, economics, English, history, math, music, physics, social research (MS). **Credit/placement by examination:** AP, CLEP, IB, institutional tests. 30 credit hours maximum toward bachelor's degree. **Support services:** Learning center, reduced course load, remedial instruction, study skills assistance, tutoring, writing center.

Majors. Area/ethnic studies: African-American, Latin American, Near/Middle Eastern, women's. **Biology:** General, bioinformatics, biophysics, biotechnology, pharmacology. **Business:** Accounting. **Communications:** Media studies. **Computer sciences:** General. **Education:** General, art, biology, chemistry, drama/dance, early childhood, elementary, English, foreign languages, French, geography, German, health, history, Latin, mathematics, music, physical, physics, secondary, social studies, Spanish. **English:** British lit, creative writing, English lit. **Foreign languages:** General, ancient Greek, Chinese, classics, comparative lit, French, German, Hebrew, Italian, Latin, Romance, Russian, Spanish. **Health services:** Adult health nursing, clinical lab science, clinical lab technology, maternal/child health nursing, nurse practitioner, nursing (RN), pediatric nursing, psychiatric nursing, public health nursing, speech pathology. **History:** General. **Liberal arts:** Humanities. **Math:** General, statistics. **Philosophy/religion:** Judaic, philosophy, religion. **Physical sciences:** Chemistry, physics. **Psychology:** General. **Social sciences:** Anthropology, archaeology, economics, geography, international relations, political science, sociology, urban studies. **Visual/performing arts:** Art history/conservation, cinematography, dance, dramatic, film/cinema/video, music, music performance, music theory/composition, studio arts. **Work/family studies:** Food/nutrition.

Most popular majors. Communications/journalism 6%, English 11%, health sciences 8%, psychology 23%, social sciences 17%, visual/performing arts 8%.

Technology on campus. 1,280 workstations in dormitories, library, computer center, student center, student center. Commuter students can connect to campus network. Online course registration, online library, helpline, repair service, student web hosting, wireless network available.

Student life. Freshman orientation: Available. Preregistration for classes offered. **Housing:** Coed dorms available. **Activities:** Bands, choral groups, dance, drama, film society, literary magazine, music ensembles, Model UN, musical theater, radio station, student government, student newspaper, symphony orchestra, TV station, over 100 political, ethnic, social, and religious organizations.

Athletics. NCAA. **Intercollegiate:** Basketball, cross-country, fencing, football (non-tackle) W, soccer M, softball W, swimming W, tennis, track and field, volleyball, wrestling M. **Intramural:** Basketball, bowling, football (non-tackle), racquetball, swimming, table tennis, tennis, volleyball. **Team name:** Hawks.

Student services. Adult student services, alcohol/substance abuse counseling, chaplain/spiritual director, career counseling, services for economically disadvantaged, student employment services, financial aid counseling, health services, legal services, minority student services, on-campus daycare, personal counseling, placement for graduates, veterans' counselor, women's services. **Physically disabled:** Services for visually, speech, hearing impaired.

Contact. E-mail: admissions@hunter.cuny.edu
Phone: (212) 772-4490
Lori Janowski, Director of Admissions, City University of New York: Hunter College, 695 Park Avenue, New York, NY 10065

City University of New York: John Jay College of Criminal Justice

New York, New York   **CB member**
www.jjay.cuny.edu   **CB code: 2115**

- Public 4-year liberal arts college
- Commuter campus in very large city
- 12,545 degree-seeking undergraduates: 19% part-time, 57% women, 20% African American, 3% international
- 1,620 degree-seeking graduate students
- 52% of applicants admitted
- SAT or ACT with writing required
- 41% graduate within 6 years; 68% enter graduate study

General. Founded in 1964. Regionally accredited. **Degrees:** 2,667 bachelor's, 46 associate awarded; master's offered. **Calendar:** Semester, limited summer session. **Class size:** 32% < 20, 66% 20-39, less than 1% 40-49, less than 1% 50-99, less than 1% >100. **Special facilities:** Security laboratory, fire science laboratory, explosion-proof toxicology research laboratory.

Freshman class profile. 13,398 applied, 6,971 admitted, 1,499 enrolled.

Mid 50% test scores		GPA 3.0-3.49:	29%
SAT critical reading:	420-520	GPA 2.0-2.99:	55%
SAT math:	440-530	Return as sophomores:	78%
GPA 3.75 or higher:	4%	Out-of-state:	5%
GPA 3.50-3.74:	10%	International:	3%

Basis for selection. Admission to baccalaureate degree program requires minimum SAT score from 960 to 1020 and minimum high school average of 80. A minimum of 14 academic units with a total of 4 units in English and mathematics with at least 1 unit in each discipline. **Home schooled:** State high school equivalency certificate required. Applicants must have diploma issued by local registered high school, and minimum combined verbal and math SAT of 1100.

High school preparation. College-preparatory program required. 14 units required; 19 recommended. Required and recommended units include English 4, mathematics 3-4, social studies 2-4, (laboratory 2-3), foreign language 2-3 and visual/performing arts 1. One unit in fine arts required/recommended.

2015-2016 Annual costs. Tuition/fees: $6,810; $17,280 out-of-state. **Additional information:** Room/Housing Rates range from $14,550 to $22,100 depending on room sizes among other factors.

2014-2015 Financial aid. Need-based: 2,940 full-time freshmen applied for aid; 2,703 deemed to have need; 2,489 received aid. Average need met was 85%. Average scholarship/grant was $2,889; average loan $4,152. 89% of total undergraduate aid awarded as scholarships/grants, 11% as loans/jobs. **Non-need-based:** Awarded to 218 full-time undergraduates, including 206 freshmen.

Application procedures. Admission: Priority date 2/1; deadline 5/31 (postmark date). $65 fee. Application must be submitted online. Admission notification on a rolling basis beginning on or about 1/15. Admission to John Jay on space-available basis. Centralized application processing allows students to apply to 6 academic programs within CUNY system at same time. **Financial aid:** Priority date 4/30; no closing date. FAFSA required. Applicants notified on a rolling basis starting 4/1; must reply within 2 week(s) of notification.

Academics. Degree requirements and curriculum combine professional education with the liberal arts. The Baccalaureate for Unique and Interdisciplinary Studies (CUNY BA), is CUNY's individualized, university-wide BA/BS degree, where students formulate proposals for unique areas of concentration, then collaborate with CUNY faculty members to design their degrees. **Special study options:** Combined bachelor's/graduate degree, cooperative education, cross-registration, distance learning, dual enrollment of high school students, ESL, exchange student, honors, independent study, internships, liberal arts/career combination, student-designed major, study abroad, weekend college. **Credit/placement by examination:** AP, CLEP, IB, SAT, ACT, institutional tests. 30 credit hours maximum toward associate degree, 30 toward bachelor's. **Support services:** Learning center, pre-admission summer program, reduced course load, remedial instruction, tutoring, writing center.

Honors college/program. Based on high school average and ACT or SAT score with rank in top 10 percent of the freshmen cohort. Interview and personal statement required. Classes taught seminar style and the concept of justice is the foundational theme of the interdisciplinary curriculum.

Majors. Biology: Cellular/molecular. **English:** English lit. **Foreign languages:** Spanish. **History:** General. **Human services:** General. **Protective services:** Criminal justice, financial forensics, fire services admin, firefighting, forensics, law enforcement admin, police science. **Psychology:** Forensic. **Social sciences:** Anthropology, criminology, economics, political science.

Most popular majors. Psychology 17%, security/protective services 52%, social sciences 17%.

Technology on campus. 1,920 workstations in library, computer center. Commuter students can connect to campus network. Online course registration, helpline available.

Student life. Freshman orientation: Available. Preregistration for classes offered. **Policies:** Students represented on college committees. **Activities:** Choral groups, dance, drama, musical theater, radio station, student government, student newspaper, Law Society, Able Forces, ethnic organizations, Desi Club, Intern Criminal Justice, Intervarsity Christian Fellowship, Martial Arts Club, Student Technology Club, JJ Radio, Urban Culture Commission.

Athletics. NCAA. **Intercollegiate:** Baseball M, basketball, cross-country, rifle, soccer, softball W, swimming W, tennis, volleyball. **Intramural:** Basketball, soccer, swimming. **Team name:** Bloodhounds.

Student services. Career counseling, services for economically disadvantaged, student employment services, financial aid counseling, health services, minority student services, on-campus daycare, personal counseling, placement for graduates, veterans' counselor, women's services. **Physically disabled:** Services for visually, speech, hearing impaired.

Contact. E-mail: admiss@jjay.cuny.edu
Phone: (212) 237-8865 Fax: (212) 237-8777
City University of New York: John Jay College of Criminal Justice, 524 West 59th Street, New York, NY 10019

City University of New York: Lehman College
Bronx, New York   **CB member**
www.lehman.edu   **CB code: 2312**

- Public 4-year liberal arts college
- Commuter campus in very large city
- 9,874 degree-seeking undergraduates: 37% part-time, 68% women, 32% African American, 7% Asian American, 50% Hispanic/Latino, 3% international
- 1,909 degree-seeking graduate students
- 31% of applicants admitted
- SAT or ACT (ACT writing optional) required
- 37% graduate within 6 years

General. Founded in 1931. Regionally accredited. **Degrees:** 2,038 bachelor's awarded; master's offered. **ROTC:** Army. **Location:** 8 miles from Manhattan. **Calendar:** Semester, limited summer session. **Full-time faculty:** 376 total; 77% have terminal degrees, 31% minority. **Part-time faculty:** 415 total; 25% have terminal degrees, 40% minority. **Class size:** 37% < 20, 61% 20-39, less than 1% 40-49, 1% 50-99, less than 1% >100. **Special facilities:** 2,500-seat performing arts center.

Freshman class profile. 14,076 applied, 4,402 admitted, 632 enrolled.

Mid 50% test scores		Return as sophomores:	82%
SAT critical reading:	470-550	Out-of-state:	1%
SAT math:	470-550	International:	6%
SAT writing:	450-540		

Basis for selection. High school record, GPA, and college preparatory courses most important. Tests are used to exempt students from placement tests. **Home schooled:** State high school equivalency certificate required.

High school preparation. 16 units required. Required units include English 4, mathematics 3, social studies 4, science 2 (laboratory 1), foreign language 2 and visual/performing arts 1.

2015-2016 Annual costs. Tuition/fees: $6,759; $17,229 out-of-state. Books/supplies: $1,304. Personal expenses: $2,946. **Additional information:** Room/Housing Rates range from $9,432 to $11,142 depending on room sizes among other factors.

Financial aid. All financial aid based on need.

Application procedures. Admission: $65 fee. Admission notification on a rolling basis beginning on or about 2/1. All CUNY schools operate on a rolling admission basis; therefore colleges and programs may close before the deadline date. **Financial aid:** No deadline. FAFSA required. Applicants notified on a rolling basis starting 3/1.

Academics. Special study options: Accelerated study, cooperative education, cross-registration, distance learning, double major, dual enrollment of high school students, ESL, honors, independent study, internships, student-designed major, study abroad, teacher certification program. **Credit/placement by examination:** AP, CLEP, IB, institutional tests. 30 credit hours maximum toward bachelor's degree. **Support services:** Learning center, pre-admission summer program, reduced course load, remedial instruction, study skills assistance, tutoring, writing center.

Honors college/program. Criteria for selection include high school academic record, SAT/ACT scores, essay, 2 letters of recommendation and interview.

Majors. Area/ethnic studies: African-American, Latin American. **Biology:** General. **Business:** Accounting, business admin. **Communications:** Communications/speech/rhetoric. **Computer sciences:** General, information systems. **Education:** Health, mathematics, physical. **English:** English lit, rhetoric/composition. **Foreign languages:** Comparative lit, French, Italian, linguistics,

Spanish. **Health services:** Audiology/speech pathology, facilities admin, nursing (RN). **History:** General. **Human services:** Social work. **Liberal arts:** Arts/sciences. **Math:** General. **Philosophy/religion:** Philosophy. **Physical sciences:** Chemistry, geology, physics. **Psychology:** General. **Social sciences:** Anthropology, economics, geography, political science, sociology. **Visual/performing arts:** Art history/conservation, commercial/advertising art, music performance. **Work/family studies:** Food/nutrition.

Most popular majors. Business/marketing 19%, health sciences 31%, psychology 6%, public administration/social services 6%, social sciences 14%.

Technology on campus. 88 workstations in library, computer center, student center. Commuter students can connect to campus network. Online library, helpline, repair service, student web hosting, wireless network available.

Student life. Freshman orientation: Mandatory. Preregistration for classes offered. **Activities:** Bands, choral groups, dance, drama, film society, literary magazine, music ensembles, musical theater, opera, radio station, student government, student newspaper, symphony orchestra, TV station, various religious, political, ethnic, and social service organizations.

Athletics. NCAA. **Intercollegiate:** Baseball M, basketball, cross-country, diving, softball W, swimming, tennis, track and field, volleyball. **Intramural:** Badminton, basketball, racquetball, soccer, softball, swimming, table tennis, tennis, volleyball. **Team name:** Lightning.

Student services. Adult student services, chaplain/spiritual director, career counseling, services for economically disadvantaged, student employment services, financial aid counseling, health services, on-campus daycare, personal counseling, placement for graduates, veterans' counselor, women's services. **Physically disabled:** Services for visually, speech, hearing impaired.

Contact. E-mail: enroll@lehman.cuny.edu
Phone: (718) 960-8713 Toll-free number: (877) 534-6261
Fax: (718) 960-8712
Laurie Austin, Director of Admissions, City University of New York: Lehman College, 250 Bedford Park Boulevard West, Bronx, NY 10468

City University of New York: Medgar Evers College
Brooklyn, New York   **CB member**
www.mec.cuny.edu   **CB code: 2460**

- Public 4-year liberal arts college
- Commuter campus in very large city
- 6,257 degree-seeking undergraduates: 30% part-time, 73% women, 67% African American, 2% Asian American, 13% Hispanic/Latino, 1% Native American, 1% international

General. Founded in 1969. Regionally accredited. **Degrees:** 466 bachelor's, 396 associate awarded. **Calendar:** Semester, extensive summer session. **Full-time faculty:** 183 total; 64% have terminal degrees, 79% minority, 44% women. **Part-time faculty:** 307 total; 28% have terminal degrees, 86% minority, 46% women. **Class size:** 18% < 20, 78% 20-39, 3% 40-49, less than 1% 50-99.

Freshman class profile. 1,092 enrolled.

Mid 50% test scores		GPA 3.50-3.74:	1%
SAT critical reading:	350-430	GPA 3.0-3.49:	13%
SAT math:	340-430	GPA 2.0-2.99:	62%
SAT writing:	350-430	Out-of-state:	1%
GPA 3.75 or higher:	1%	International:	1%

Basis for selection. Open admission, but selective for some programs. Special requirements for nursing and baccalaureate programs with school record, class rank, and test scores considered. Discretionary policy admits 25 students each semester without high school diplomas. Must be 21 years old, legal residents of New York City.

High school preparation. 16 units recommended. Recommended units include English 4, mathematics 3, social studies 2, history 2, science 2, foreign language 2 and visual/performing arts 1.

2015-2016 Annual costs. Tuition/fees: $6,683; $17,153 out-of-state. Books/supplies: $1,304. Personal expenses: $2,946.

Financial aid. Non-need-based: Scholarships awarded for academics, leadership.

Application procedures. Admission: Priority date 7/8; no deadline. $65 fee, may be waived for applicants with need. Admission notification on a rolling basis beginning on or about 2/1. All CUNY schools operate on a rolling admission basis; therefore colleges and programs may close before the deadline date. **Financial aid:** Priority date 1/2, closing date 6/1. FAFSA required. Applicants notified on a rolling basis; must reply within 3 week(s) of notification.

Academics. Special study options: Accelerated study, cross-registration, distance learning, double major, honors, independent study, internships, study abroad, teacher certification program, weekend college. 2-year bachelor's program in nursing for RNs. **Credit/placement by examination:** AP, CLEP, IB, SAT, ACT, institutional tests. 15 credit hours maximum toward associate degree, 30 toward bachelor's. **Support services:** Learning center, remedial instruction, tutoring, writing center.

Majors. Biology: General. **Business:** General, accounting, business admin. **Computer sciences:** Information systems. **Conservation:** Environmental studies. **Education:** Elementary, special ed. **English:** English lit. **Health services:** Nursing (RN). **Human services:** General. **Liberal arts:** Arts/sciences. **Math:** General. **Psychology:** General.

Most popular majors. Biology 9%, business/marketing 37%, health sciences 16%, liberal arts 8%, psychology 14%, public administration/social services 7%.

Technology on campus. 200 workstations in library, computer center. Commuter students can connect to campus network. Online course registration, online library, wireless network available.

Student life. Freshman orientation: Available. Preregistration for classes offered. **Activities:** Jazz band, choral groups, dance, drama, literary magazine, radio station, student government, student newspaper, TV station, numerous religious, political, ethnic, and social service clubs.

Athletics. NCAA. **Intercollegiate:** Basketball, cross-country, soccer, softball W, track and field, volleyball. **Intramural:** Basketball, bowling, cheerleading W, soccer M, swimming, track and field W. **Team name:** Cougar.

Student services. Career counseling, student employment services, financial aid counseling, health services, on-campus daycare, personal counseling, placement for graduates, veterans' counselor, women's services. **Physically disabled:** Services for visually, speech, hearing impaired.

Contact. E-mail: enroll@mec.cuny.edu
Phone: (718) 270-6024 Fax: (718) 270-6411
Shannon Clark, Director of Admissions, City University of New York: Medgar Evers College, 1665 Bedford Avenue, Brooklyn, NY 11225-2201

City University of New York: New York City College of Technology
Brooklyn, New York   **CB member**
www.citytech.cuny.edu   **CB code: 2550**

- Public 4-year technical college
- Commuter campus in very large city
- 16,297 degree-seeking undergraduates: 34% part-time, 43% women, 29% African American, 20% Asian American, 32% Hispanic/Latino, 1% Multi-racial, non-Hispanic, 5% international
- 30% graduate within 6 years

General. Founded in 1946. Regionally accredited. Largest public college of technology in New York state. **Degrees:** 1,129 bachelor's, 1,073 associate awarded. **Location:** 1 mile from Manhattan. **Calendar:** Semester, extensive summer session. **Full-time faculty:** 445 total; 66% have terminal degrees, 37% minority, 48% women. **Part-time faculty:** 982 total; 22% have terminal degrees, 44% minority, 42% women. **Class size:** 28% < 20, 67% 20-39, 5% 40-49, less than 1% 50-99. **Special facilities:** Ophthalmic dispensing and dental clinics, laboratory kitchens and dining room, immigration clinic, theater.

Freshman class profile. 14,338 applied, 5,387 admitted, 3,404 enrolled.

Mid 50% test scores		Return as sophomores:	77%
SAT critical reading:	360-460	Out-of-state:	8%
SAT math:	380-490	International:	4%
SAT writing:	350-440		

Basis for selection. Open admission, but selective for some programs. **Home schooled:** Transcript of courses and grades, state high school equivalency certificate required. If NY State, letter from superintendent or comparable chief school administrator certifying completion of substantial equivalent of NYS 4 year high school program. Out of State students require a state-issued diploma.

High school preparation. College-preparatory program recommended. 15 units required; 18 recommended. Required and recommended units include English 4, mathematics 3-4, social studies 3-4, science 2-3 (laboratory 2-3), foreign language 2 and visual/performing arts 1.

2015-2016 Annual costs. Tuition/fees: $6,720; $17,190 out-of-state. Books/supplies: $1,364. Personal expenses: $1,816.

Financial aid. Non-need-based: Scholarships awarded for state residency. **Additional information:** Foreign students applying for aid must have resided in New York for at least 1 year.

Application procedures. Admission: Closing date 2/1 (postmark date). $65 fee, may be waived for applicants with need. Admission notification on a rolling basis beginning on or about 2/1. Must reply by 5/1. All CUNY schools operate on a rolling admission basis; therefore colleges and programs may close before the deadline date. **Financial aid:** Priority date 3/31; no closing date. FAFSA required.

Academics. Students in health science programs work under supervision with patients in clinical settings. Industry standard facilities used in hospitality management program. **Special study options:** Distance learning, dual enrollment of high school students, ESL, honors, independent study, internships, student-designed major, study abroad, teacher certification program, weekend college. Bridge programs to higher education or careers in engineering technology, alternate format program for those out of high school 5 years with or without diploma. **Credit/placement by examination:** AP, CLEP, IB, institutional tests. Students can earn credit by successfully completing examinations offered for certain courses. Eligibility and the nature, content and grading of each exam are determined by the departmental faculty and must be approved by the provost. **Support services:** Learning center, pre-admission summer program, remedial instruction, study skills assistance, tutoring, writing center.

Majors. Architecture: Technology. **Biology:** Bioinformatics. **Business:** Hospitality admin. **Computer sciences:** Information systems, web page design. **Education:** Mathematics, technology/industrial arts. **Health services:** Facilities admin, medical radiologic technology/radiation therapy, nursing (RN). **Liberal arts:** Arts/sciences. **Math:** Applied. **Visual/performing arts:** Commercial/advertising art, design, theater design. **Work/family studies:** Facilities/event planning.

Most popular majors. Agriculture 9%, business/marketing 14%, computer/information sciences 16%, engineering/engineering technologies 9%, health sciences 23%, public administration/social services 9%, visual/performing arts 13%.

Technology on campus. 340 workstations in library, computer center, student center. Commuter students can connect to campus network. Online course registration, online library, helpline, student web hosting, wireless network available.

Student life. Freshman orientation: Available. Preregistration for classes offered. Held the week before classes begin. **Housing:** Some housing available at nearby university. **Activities:** Drama, international student organizations, literary magazine, musical theater, student government, student newspaper, Muslim Student Association, Seekers Christian club, Women in Islam, Chinese Christian club, Inter Varsity Christian Organization, Caribbean club, Technically Jewish, Bangladeshi club, Desi club.

Athletics. NCAA. **Intramural:** Boxing, handball, table tennis. **Team name:** Yellow Jackets.

Student services. Adult student services, career counseling, services for economically disadvantaged, student employment services, financial aid counseling, health services, minority student services, on-campus daycare, personal counseling, veterans' counselor. **Physically disabled:** Services for visually, speech, hearing impaired.

Contact. E-mail: admissions@citytech.cuny.edu
Phone: (718) 260-5500 Fax: (718) 260-5504
Alexis Chaconis, Director of Admissions, City University of New York: New York City College of Technology, 300 Jay Street Namm G17, Brooklyn, NY 11201

City University of New York: Queens College
Flushing, New York
www.qc.cuny.edu

CB code: 2750

- Public 4-year liberal arts college
- Commuter campus in very large city
- 15,148 degree-seeking undergraduates: 24% part-time, 55% women, 9% African American, 27% Asian American, 29% Hispanic/Latino, 1% Multi-racial, non-Hispanic, 5% international

- 3,214 degree-seeking graduate students
- 40% of applicants admitted
- SAT or ACT (ACT writing optional) required
- 58% graduate within 6 years

General. Founded in 1937. Regionally accredited. **Degrees:** 3,018 bachelor's awarded; master's offered. **ROTC:** Army, Air Force. **Location:** 10 miles from Manhattan. **Calendar:** Semester, extensive summer session. **Full-time faculty:** 606 total; 22% minority, 44% women. **Part-time faculty:** 858 total; 23% minority, 51% women. **Class size:** 32% < 20, 55% 20-39, 5% 40-49, 6% 50-99, 2% >100. **Special facilities:** Louis Armstrong archives, center for performing arts, center for Byzantine and modern Greek studies, the center for Jewish studies, neuroscience research center, center for ethnic and racial understanding, Godwin-Ternbach museum, Louis Armstrong house museum, center for ethnic, racial and religious understanding.

Freshman class profile. 18,416 applied, 7,447 admitted, 1,547 enrolled.

Mid 50% test scores			
SAT critical reading:	490-580	GPA 3.0-3.49:	42%
SAT math:	530-620	GPA 2.0-2.99:	11%
SAT writing:	460-560	Return as sophomores:	85%
GPA 3.75 or higher:	20%	Out-of-state:	1%
GPA 3.50-3.74:	27%	Live on campus:	1%
		International:	6%

Basis for selection. Factors include high school grades, strength of academic program, and test scores. Successful candidates will have chosen well-rounded program of study and attained at least B+ average. SAT scores on Critical Reading and Mathematics are considered. SAT Subject Tests recommended. SAT and SAT Subject Test required of scholarship and honors college applicants. Essay and interview required for scholarship, honors program; audition recommended for music, performance; portfolio recommended for bachelor of fine arts. Other criteria considered for appeals. **Home schooled:** Transcript of courses and grades required. Students must submit a letter from the superintendent of their school district confirming that all high school graduation requirements of the district have been met through home schooling. If students cannot obtain the letter from the high school district, they must obtain a General Equivalency Development Diploma (GED). **Learning Disabled:** Untimed SAT/ACT accepted.

High school preparation. College-preparatory program required. 16 units required; 17 recommended. Required and recommended units include English 4, mathematics 3, social studies 4, science 2-3 (laboratory 2-3) and foreign language 3.

2015-2016 Annual costs. Tuition/fees: $6,777; $17,247 out-of-state. Books/supplies: $1,304. Personal expenses: $1,798. **Additional information:** Room/Housing Rates range from $11,330 to $16,900 depending on room sizes among other factors.

2015-2016 Financial aid. Need-based: 1,150 full-time freshmen applied for aid; 780 deemed to have need; 745 received aid. Average need met was 95%. Average scholarship/grant was $5,011; average loan $4,870. 84% of total undergraduate aid awarded as scholarships/grants, 16% as loans/jobs. **Non-need-based:** Awarded to 524 full-time undergraduates, including 103 freshmen. Scholarships awarded for academics, athletics, state residency.

Application procedures. Admission: $65 fee, may be waived for applicants with need. Application must be submitted online. Admission notification on a rolling basis beginning on or about 2/1. Must reply by May 1 or within 4 week(s) if notified thereafter. Admitted applicants must reply by May 1 for some programs, within 4 weeks after notification for others. All CUNY schools operate on a rolling admission basis; therefore colleges and programs may close before the deadline date. **Financial aid:** Priority date 2/15; no closing date. FAFSA, institutional form required. Applicants notified on a rolling basis starting 3/1; must reply within 3 week(s) of notification.

Academics. Special study options: Accelerated study, combined bachelor's/graduate degree, double major, dual enrollment of high school students, ESL, exchange student, honors, independent study, internships, liberal arts/career combination, student-designed major, study abroad, teacher certification program, weekend college. BA/MA degree offered in Chemistry and Biochemistry, Computer Science, Music, Philosophy, Political Science and Physics. Undergraduate research, service learning, work-based learning available. **Credit/placement by examination:** AP, CLEP, IB, SAT, ACT, institutional tests. Consult with the college advisors regarding this information. **Support services:** Pre-admission summer program, tutoring, writing center.

Honors college/program. 60 students, average SAT of 1300 (exclusive of Writing) or higher, high school average 95 or higher, required to submit SAT Subject Test scores, interview required.

Majors. Area/ethnic studies: African, American, East Asian, Latin American, women's. **Biology:** General, neuroscience. **Business:** Accounting, actuarial science, finance, international, labor studies. **Communications:** Media studies. **Computer sciences:** Computer science. **Conservation:** Environmental science, environmental studies. **Education:** General, art, biology, chemistry, early childhood, elementary, English, ESL, family/consumer sciences, French, mathematics, music, physical, physics, science, social studies, Spanish. **English:** English lit. **Foreign languages:** Ancient Greek, Chinese, comparative lit, French, German, Hebrew, Italian, Latin, linguistics, Russian, Spanish. **Health services:** Communication disorders. **History:** General. **Liberal arts:** Arts/sciences. **Math:** General. **Parks/recreation:** Exercise sciences. **Philosophy/religion:** Judaic, philosophy, religion. **Physical sciences:** Chemistry, geology, physics. **Psychology:** General. **Social sciences:** General, anthropology, economics, political science, sociology, urban studies. **Visual/performing arts:** Art history/conservation, dramatic, film/cinema/video, graphic design, music performance, studio arts. **Work/family studies:** General.

Most popular majors. Business/marketing 17%, education 7%, psychology 19%, social sciences 23%.

Technology on campus. Dormitories wired for high-speed internet access and linked to campus network. Commuter students can connect to campus network. Online library, repair service, wireless network available.

Student life. Freshman orientation: Mandatory. Preregistration for classes offered. Several orientation sessions available during June, July and August for freshmen and their families. **Policies:** Academic integrity and anti-bullying policies. **Housing:** Apartments available. $400 partly refundable deposit, deadline 6/1. Dormitories available on a first-come, first-served basis. **Activities:** Jazz band, campus ministries, choral groups, dance, drama, international student organizations, literary magazine, music ensembles, Model UN, musical theater, opera, radio station, student government, student newspaper, symphony orchestra, various political, religious, ethnic student associations, lesbian, and gay student organizations, honor societies, various clubs.

Athletics. NCAA. **Intercollegiate:** Baseball M, basketball, cross-country, diving, fencing W, lacrosse W, soccer, softball W, swimming, tennis, track and field, volleyball W. **Intramural:** Basketball, cross-country, football (non-tackle), soccer, softball, table tennis, tennis, track and field, volleyball. **Team name:** Knights.

Student services. Adult student services, career counseling, services for economically disadvantaged, student employment services, financial aid counseling, health services, minority student services, on-campus daycare, placement for graduates, veterans' counselor, women's services. **Physically disabled:** Services for visually, speech, hearing impaired.

Contact. E-mail: vincent.angrisani@qc.cuny.edu
Phone: (718) 997-5600 Fax: (718) 997-5617
Vincent Angrisani, Executive Director of Admissions and Enrollment Management, City University of New York: Queens College, 6530 Kissena Boulevard, Jefferson 117, Flushing, NY 11367-1597

City University of New York: York College
Jamaica, New York   **CB member**
www.york.cuny.edu   **CB code: 2992**

- Public 4-year liberal arts college
- Commuter campus in very large city
- 7,264 degree-seeking undergraduates: 29% part-time, 66% women, 42% African American, 24% Asian American, 20% Hispanic/Latino, 1% Native American, 5% international
- 65 degree-seeking graduate students
- SAT or ACT (ACT writing optional) required

General. Founded in 1966. Regionally accredited. **Degrees:** 1,163 bachelor's awarded; master's offered. **ROTC:** Army. **Location:** 14 miles from midtown Manhattan. **Calendar:** Semester, limited summer session. **Class size:** 28% < 20, 57% 20-39, 6% 40-49, 9% 50-99. **Special facilities:** Theater, cardio-pneumo-simulator, flight simulator, health promotion center, human performance laboratory, athletic training center.

Freshman class profile. 1,030 enrolled.

Mid 50% test scores			
SAT critical reading:	380-460	Return as sophomores:	74%
SAT math:	390-490	Out-of-state:	1%
SAT writing:	380-470	International:	4%

Basis for selection. Academic GPA and Standardized test scores most important. Rigor of secondary school record also important. Units recommended for admission must be acquired before graduation from any CUNY senior college. Admission requirements for CUNY senior colleges will be automatically satisfied with completion of our core requirement. Interview

required for occupational therapy, nursing, physician assistant, and social work or for appeal.

High school preparation. College-preparatory program required. 12 units required; 14 recommended. Required and recommended units include English 4, mathematics 2-3, social studies 3, history 1, science 2-3, foreign language 2-3 and visual/performing arts 1.

2015-2016 Annual costs. Tuition/fees: $6,747; $17,217 out-of-state. Books/supplies: $1,364. Personal expenses: $2,964.

Financial aid. Non-need-based: Scholarships awarded for academics.

Application procedures. Admission: Priority date 2/1; deadline 6/1 (postmark date). $65 fee, may be waived for applicants with need. Admission notification on a rolling basis beginning on or about 2/19. Must reply by 5/1. All CUNY schools operate on a rolling admission basis; therefore colleges and programs may close before the deadline date. Centralized application processing allows students to apply to 6 schools within CUNY system at same time. **Financial aid:** Priority date 4/1, closing date 5/30. FAFSA required. Applicants notified on a rolling basis starting 2/15; must reply within 4 week(s) of notification.

Academics. Special study options: Combined bachelor's/graduate degree, double major, ESL, honors, internships, liberal arts/career combination, study abroad, teacher certification program, weekend college. **Credit/placement by examination:** AP, CLEP, IB, SAT, ACT, institutional tests. 16 credit hours maximum toward bachelor's degree. Students with SAT/ACT scores exempt from CUNY skills assessment tests. **Support services:** Learning center, pre-admission summer program, remedial instruction, study skills assistance, tutoring, writing center.

Majors. Area/ethnic studies: African-American. **Biology:** General, biotechnology, pharmacology. **Business:** Accounting, business admin, management information systems, marketing. **Communications:** Communications/speech/rhetoric, journalism. **Communications technology:** General. **Computer sciences:** General, computer science. **Education:** Biology, chemistry, earth science, health, mathematics, physical. **English:** English lit, rhetoric/composition. **Foreign languages:** French, Spanish. **Health services:** Clinical lab science, clinical lab technology, environmental health, movement therapy, nursing (RN), pharmaceutical sciences, physician assistant, public health ed. **History:** General. **Human services:** Social work, youth services. **Liberal arts:** Arts/sciences. **Math:** General. **Philosophy/religion:** Philosophy. **Physical sciences:** Chemistry, geology, physics. **Psychology:** General. **Social sciences:** General, anthropology, economics, political science, sociology. **Visual/performing arts:** Art history/conservation, dramatic, music, studio arts.

Most popular majors. Business/marketing 16%, health sciences 19%, psychology 21%, public administration/social services 7%, social sciences 8%.

Technology on campus. 300 workstations in library, computer center. Commuter students can connect to campus network. Online library, helpline, repair service, wireless network available.

Student life. Freshman orientation: Available. Preregistration for classes offered. **Activities:** Choral groups, dance, drama, radio station, student government, student newspaper.

Athletics. NCAA. **Intercollegiate:** Basketball, cross-country, soccer, softball W, swimming, tennis, track and field, volleyball. **Intramural:** Badminton, basketball, soccer M, softball W, swimming, table tennis, tennis, track and field, volleyball, weight lifting. **Team name:** Cardinals.

Student services. Adult student services, chaplain/spiritual director, career counseling, student employment services, financial aid counseling, health services, on-campus daycare, personal counseling, placement for graduates, veterans' counselor, women's services. **Physically disabled:** Services for visually, speech, hearing impaired.

Contact. E-mail: Admissions@york.cuny.edu
Phone: (718) 262-2165
La Toro Yates, Director of Admissions, City University of New York: York College, 94-20 Guy R. Brewer Boulevard., Room 1B07, Jamaica, NY 11451

Clarkson University
Potsdam, New York   **CB member**
www.clarkson.edu   **CB code: 2084**

- Private 4-year university
- Residential campus in small town
- 3,153 degree-seeking undergraduates: 30% women, 2% African American, 2% Multi-racial, non-Hispanic, 3% international

- 640 degree-seeking graduate students
- 68% of applicants admitted
- SAT or ACT (ACT writing optional), application essay required
- 73% graduate within 6 years; 15% enter graduate study

General. Founded in 1896. Regionally accredited. **Degrees:** 703 bachelor's awarded; master's, professional, doctoral offered. **ROTC:** Army, Air Force. **Location:** 85 miles from Ottawa, Canada; 69 miles from Lake Placid. **Calendar:** Semester, extensive summer session. **Full-time faculty:** 229 total; 88% have terminal degrees, 28% minority, 29% women. **Part-time faculty:** 80 total; 42% have terminal degrees, 9% minority, 40% women. **Class size:** 42% < 20, 26% 20-39, 9% 40-49, 17% 50-99, 7% >100. **Special facilities:** Design, prototyping and testing facilities, institute for a sustainable environment, center for air resources engineering and science, center for advanced materials processing, institute for rivers and estuaries, center for rehabilitation engineering, center for innovation, wind turbine test site, wind turbine blade test facility, wind tunnel facility, water tunnel facility, greenhouse, observatory, nature preserve, food digester, solar power production facility.

Freshman class profile. 6,906 applied, 4,700 admitted, 792 enrolled.

Mid 50% test scores			
SAT critical reading:	520-630	GPA 2.0-2.99:	4%
SAT math:	560-660	Rank in top quarter:	72%
SAT writing:	490-600	Rank in top tenth:	36%
ACT composite:	24-30	End year in good standing:	79%
GPA 3.75 or higher:	46%	Return as sophomores:	90%
GPA 3.50-3.74:	29%	Out-of-state:	28%
GPA 3.0-3.49:	21%	Live on campus:	97%
		International:	2%

Basis for selection. Secondary school transcripts, test scores, recommendations, school and community involvement are all given strong consideration. SAT Subject Tests recommended. Interview recommended. **Home schooled:** Transcript of courses and grades required. **Learning Disabled:** Documented information on disabilities is necessary.

High school preparation. College-preparatory program recommended. 16 units required. Required and recommended units include English 4, mathematics 3-4 and science 1-4. Engineering and science majors require an additional 1 credit in math and 3-4 credits in science (including chemistry and physics).

2016-2017 Annual costs. Tuition/fees: $46,132. Room/board: $14,260. Books/supplies: $1,416. Personal expenses: $816.

2015-2016 Financial aid. **Need-based:** 713 full-time freshmen applied for aid; 637 deemed to have need; 636 received aid. Average need met was 89%. Average scholarship/grant was $31,060; average loan $3,417. 80% of total undergraduate aid awarded as scholarships/grants, 20% as loans/jobs. **Non-need-based:** Awarded to 891 full-time undergraduates, including 241 freshmen. Scholarships awarded for academics, alumni affiliation, leadership, minority status, ROTC.

Application procedures. Admission: Closing date 1/16 (postmark date). $50 fee, may be waived for applicants with need, free for online applicants. Admission notification on a rolling basis beginning on or about 2/1. Must reply by May 1 or within 2 week(s) if notified thereafter. Candidates encouraged to submit completed applications between October 1 and March 1 of their final year in high school. **Financial aid:** Priority date 2/15, closing date 3/1. FAFSA required. Applicants notified on a rolling basis starting 3/14; must reply by 5/1 or within 2 week(s) of notification.

Academics. All students must fulfill the learning outcomes of the Clarkson Common Experience; a BS degree may be earned in 3 years by motivated students. All students in the School of Business programs must complete a study-abroad experience. All business students provided entrepreneurship experineces. **Special study options:** Accelerated study, combined bachelor's/graduate degree, cooperative education, cross-registration, distance learning, double major, dual enrollment of high school students, ESL, honors, independent study, internships, liberal arts/career combination, semester at sea, student-designed major, study abroad, Washington semester. **Credit/placement by examination:** AP, CLEP, IB, institutional tests. 30 credit hours maximum toward bachelor's degree. Credit may be awarded by examinations specially prepared or approved by the Clarkson departments involved or by transfer of college courses taken elsewhere. AP credit may be counted toward graduation requirements, but it will not be used in computing a student's GPA. **Support services:** Learning center, pre-admission summer program, reduced course load, remedial instruction, study skills assistance, tutoring, writing center.

Majors. Biology: General, environmental toxicology, molecular biochemistry. **Business:** Accounting/finance, business admin, entrepreneurial studies, logistics, management information systems. **Communications:** Communications/speech/rhetoric, digital media. **Computer sciences:** Computer science. **Conservation:** Environmental science. **Engineering:** General, aerospace, chemical, civil, computer, electrical, environmental, mechanical, software. **History:** General. **Liberal arts:** Arts/sciences, humanities. **Math:** General,

applied. **Physical sciences:** Chemistry, physics. **Psychology:** General. **Social sciences:** General, political science, sociology.

Most popular majors. Biology 8%, business/marketing 10%, engineering/engineering technologies 63%.

Technology on campus. 350 workstations in library, computer center. Dormitories wired for high-speed internet access and linked to campus network. Commuter students can connect to campus network. Online course registration, online library, helpline, repair service, student web hosting, wireless network available.

Student life. Freshman orientation: Available. Preregistration for classes offered. **Policies:** Complies with all Title IX legislation and New York State's "Enough is Enough" law policies on alcohol mirror New York State law. All incoming students must participate in an alcohol and sexual assault education, a mentoring program with a staff member, and must complete the College Student Inventory (CSI), an advising tool. Students (First-year and Seniors) take the NSSE (National Survey of Student Engagement). **Housing:** Guaranteed on-campus for freshmen. Coed dorms, single-sex dorms, special housing for disabled, apartments, fraternity/sorority housing, gender-neutral housing, themed housing available. **Activities:** Bands, choral groups, dance, drama, international student organizations, Model UN, musical theater, radio station, student government, student newspaper, symphony orchestra, TV station, Alpha Phi Omega, Circle K, College Republicans, Hillel club, International Student Organization, Intervarsity Christian Fellowship, National Society of Black Engineers, Society of Hispanic Professional Engineers, Society of Asian Scientists and Engineers, Students Without Borders, College Liberals.

Athletics. NCAA. **Intercollegiate:** Baseball M, basketball, cross-country, diving, golf M, ice hockey, lacrosse, skiing, soccer, softball W, swimming, volleyball W. **Intramural:** Basketball, football (non-tackle), ice hockey, soccer, softball, volleyball. **Team name:** Golden Knights.

Student services. Alcohol/substance abuse counseling, career counseling, services for economically disadvantaged, student employment services, financial aid counseling, health services, legal services, minority student services, personal counseling, placement for graduates, veterans' counselor. **Physically disabled:** Services for visually, speech, hearing impaired.

Contact. E-mail: admission@clarkson.edu
Phone: (315) 268-6480 Toll-free number: (800) 527-6577
Fax: (315) 268-7647
Brian Grant, Dean of Admissions, Clarkson University, Holcroft House, Potsdam, NY 13699

Colgate University
Hamilton, New York   CB member
www.colgate.edu   CB code: 2086

- Private 4-year university and liberal arts college
- Residential campus in small town
- 2,834 degree-seeking undergraduates: 55% women, 4% African American, 4% Asian American, 9% Hispanic/Latino, 3% Multi-racial, non-Hispanic, 9% international
- 4 degree-seeking graduate students
- 27% of applicants admitted
- SAT or ACT (ACT writing optional), application essay required
- 90% graduate within 6 years

General. Founded in 1819. Regionally accredited. **Degrees:** 732 bachelor's awarded; master's offered. **ROTC:** Army. **Location:** 38 miles from Syracuse, 25 miles from Utica. **Calendar:** Semester. **Full-time faculty:** 295 total; 99% have terminal degrees, 23% minority, 41% women. **Part-time faculty:** 57 total; 61% have terminal degrees, 21% minority, 54% women. **Class size:** 71% < 20, 27% 20-39, less than 1% 40-49, 1% 50-99, less than 1% >100. **Special facilities:** Visualization laboratory, anthropology museum, center for learning, teaching, and research, life sciences complex, geology/fossil collection, observatory, electron microscopes, laser lab, weather lab, geographic information system, center for outreach volunteerism and education.

Freshman class profile. 8,724 applied, 2,387 admitted, 773 enrolled.

Mid 50% test scores			
SAT critical reading:	620-720	GPA 2.0-2.99:	3%
SAT math:	630-730	Rank in top quarter:	94%
ACT composite:	30-33	Rank in top tenth:	75%
GPA 3.75 or higher:	48%	Return as sophomores:	95%
GPA 3.50-3.74:	27%	Out-of-state:	74%
GPA 3.0-3.49:	22%	International:	7%

Basis for selection. School achievement record of primary importance. Teacher/counselor recommendations, test scores, and major talent or personal accomplishment considered. Disadvantaged, nontraditional, and minority applicants given special consideration. Colgate supplement required. **Home schooled:** Statement describing home school structure and mission, transcript of courses and grades, letter of recommendation (nonparent) required. **Learning Disabled:** Optional self-disclosure of disabilities in admissions process.

High school preparation. College-preparatory program recommended. 16 units required; 20 recommended. Required and recommended units include English 4, mathematics 3-4, social studies 3-4, science 3-4 (laboratory 2-4) and foreign language 3-4. Foreign language units should be in 1 language.

2015-2016 Annual costs. Tuition/fees: $49,970. Room/board: $12,570. Books/supplies: $2,260.

2015-2016 Financial aid. Need-based: 332 full-time freshmen applied for aid; 290 deemed to have need; 290 received aid. Average need met was 100%. Average scholarship/grant was $45,417; average loan $1,498. 92% of total undergraduate aid awarded as scholarships/grants, 8% as loans/jobs. **Non-need-based:** Awarded to 257 full-time undergraduates, including 80 freshmen. Scholarships awarded for athletics.

Application procedures. Admission: Closing date 1/15 (postmark date). $60 fee, may be waived for applicants with need. Admission notification by 4/1. Must reply by May 1 or within 2 week(s) if notified thereafter. **Financial aid:** Priority date 1/15, closing date 1/15. CSS PROFILE required. Applicants notified by 3/20; must reply by 5/1.

Academics. Special study options: Combined bachelor's/graduate degree, cross-registration, double major, honors, independent study, internships, semester at sea, student-designed major, study abroad, teacher certification program, urban semester, Washington semester. 3-4 architecture program with Washington University (MO), 3-2 program in engineering with Columbia University, Rensselaer Polytechnic Institute, and Washington University (MO); Early Assurance Medical School program with Washington University (MO) and University of Rochester; extended study program allows students to further academic work with a 3-5 week off-campus experience during the winter or summer breaks. Recent trips have included South Africa, Ireland, Mexico, and China. **Credit/placement by examination:** AP, CLEP, IB, institutional tests. **Support services:** Learning center, pre-admission summer program, reduced course load, study skills assistance, tutoring, writing center.

Majors. Area/ethnic studies: African, African-American, Asian, Latin American, Native American, Russian/Slavic, women's. **Biology:** General, biochemistry, molecular, neuroscience. **Computer sciences:** General, computer science. **Conservation:** General, environmental studies. **Education:** General. **English:** English lit. **Foreign languages:** Classics, French, German, Japanese, Latin, modern Greek, Russian, Spanish. **Health services:** Predental, premedicine, preveterinary. **History:** General. **Liberal arts:** Arts/sciences. **Math:** General. **Philosophy/religion:** Philosophy, religion. **Physical sciences:** Astronomy, astrophysics, chemistry, geology, physics. **Psychology:** General. **Social sciences:** General, anthropology, economics, geography, international economic development, international relations, political science, sociology. **Visual/performing arts:** Art, art history/conservation, dramatic, music, studio arts.

Most popular majors. Biology 15%, English 6%, foreign language 6%, history 7%, philosophy/religious studies 6%, social sciences 33%.

Technology on campus. 848 workstations in dormitories, library, computer center, student center. Dormitories wired for high-speed internet access and linked to campus network. Commuter students can connect to campus network. Online course registration, online library, helpline, repair service, student web hosting, wireless network available.

Student life. Freshman orientation: Mandatory. Preregistration for classes offered. Held 4 days before first day of classes. **Policies:** All students required to read, sign, and abide by Academic Honor Code. **Housing:** Guaranteed on-campus for all undergraduates. Coed dorms, special housing for disabled, apartments, cooperative housing, fraternity/sorority housing, themed housing, wellness housing available. $500 nonrefundable deposit, deadline 5/1. LOFT ,Peace Studies, La Casa Pan Latina, Harlem Renaissance Center, Art House, Asia House, Ciccone Commons available. **Activities:** Bands, campus ministries, choral groups, dance, drama, international student organizations, literary magazine, music ensembles, Model UN, musical theater, opera, radio station, student government, student newspaper, symphony orchestra, African student union, Asian awareness coalition, Brothers, Caribbean student association, aviation club, Christian fellowship, debate society, ballet company, Global Citizens for Peace, Colgate Dischords.

Athletics. NCAA. **Intercollegiate:** Basketball, cheerleading, cross-country, diving, field hockey W, football (tackle) M, golf M, ice hockey, lacrosse, rowing (crew), soccer, softball W, swimming, tennis, track and field, volleyball W. **Intramural:** Basketball, bowling, football (non-tackle), golf, ice hockey, racquetball, rifle, soccer, softball, squash, table tennis, tennis, volleyball. **Team name:** Raiders.

Student services. Alcohol/substance abuse counseling, chaplain/spiritual director, career counseling, services for economically disadvantaged, student employment services, financial aid counseling, health services, minority student services, personal counseling, placement for graduates, women's services. **Physically disabled:** Services for visually, hearing impaired.

Contact. E-mail: admission@colgate.edu
Phone: (315) 228-7401 Fax: (315) 228-7524
Gary Ross, Dean of Admission, Colgate University, 13 Oak Drive, Hamilton, NY 13346-1383

College of Mount St. Vincent
Riverdale, New York
www.mountsaintvincent.edu

CB member
CB code: 2088

- Private 4-year liberal arts college affiliated with the Roman Catholic Church
- Residential campus in very large city
- 1,585 degree-seeking undergraduates: 5% part-time, 69% women, 15% African American, 10% Asian American, 38% Hispanic/Latino, 5% Multi-racial, non-Hispanic, 2% international
- 162 degree-seeking graduate students
- 86% of applicants admitted
- SAT or ACT (ACT writing optional), application essay required
- 53% graduate within 6 years

General. Founded in 1847. Regionally accredited. Dual certification in elementary and special education and secondary and special education. 5-year program for master of science in education. **Degrees:** 357 bachelor's awarded; master's offered. **ROTC:** Army, Air Force. **Location:** 12 miles from midtown Manhattan. **Calendar:** Semester, limited summer session. **Full-time faculty:** 79 total; 87% have terminal degrees, 18% minority, 58% women. **Part-time faculty:** 102 total; 28% minority, 48% women. **Class size:** 47% < 20, 52% 20-39, 1% 40-49. **Special facilities:** NMR spectrometer, computer graphics and animation center, computer classrooms, forensic science equipment.

Freshman class profile. 2,734 applied, 2,353 admitted, 321 enrolled.

Mid 50% test scores			
SAT critical reading:	410-500	GPA 3.0-3.49:	33%
SAT math:	400-490	GPA 2.0-2.99:	49%
SAT writing:	410-490	Rank in top quarter:	19%
ACT composite:	17-21	Rank in top tenth:	5%
GPA 3.75 or higher:	9%	Out-of-state:	12%
GPA 3.50-3.74:	8%	Live on campus:	53%
		International:	1%

Basis for selection. School achievement record (3.0 high school GPA) most important, test scores and recommendations important, school and community activities considered. Interview recommended. **Home schooled:** Transcript of courses and grades required. **Learning Disabled:** Must submit IEP or other certification to receive service.

High school preparation. College-preparatory program required. 16 units required; 20 recommended. Required and recommended units include English 4, mathematics 3-4, social studies 3-4, science 2-3 (laboratory 2-3), foreign language 2-3 and academic electives 2-3. 3 math for nursing, science, and math majors; 3 science with lab for nursing and science majors.

2015-2016 Annual costs. Tuition/fees: $35,130. Room/board: $8,720. Books/supplies: $1,185. Personal expenses: $1,100.

Financial aid. Non-need-based: Scholarships awarded for academics, alumni affiliation, leadership.

Application procedures. Admission: Priority date 4/1; no deadline. $35 fee, may be waived for applicants with need, free for online applicants. Admission notification on a rolling basis beginning on or about 12/1. Must reply by May 1 or within 3 week(s) if notified thereafter. **Financial aid:** Priority date 3/1; no closing date. FAFSA required. Applicants notified on a rolling basis starting 3/1; must reply by 5/1 or within 3 week(s) of notification.

Academics. Special study options: Combined bachelor's/graduate degree, double major, honors, independent study, internships, liberal arts/career combination, study abroad, teacher certification program. 3-2 occupational therapy program with Columbia University, 3-2 physical therapy with New York Medical College. **Credit/placement by examination:** AP, CLEP, IB, SAT, ACT, institutional tests. 18 credit hours maximum toward bachelor's degree. **Support services:** Learning center, pre-admission summer program, reduced course load, remedial instruction, study skills assistance, tutoring, writing center.

Majors. Biology: General, biochemistry. **Business:** General, business admin. **Communications:** Communications/speech/rhetoric. **English:** English lit. **Foreign languages:** General, French, Spanish. **Health services:** Nursing (RN), preop/surgical nursing. **History:** General. **Liberal arts:** Arts/sciences. **Math:** General. **Philosophy/religion:** Philosophy, religion. **Physical sciences:** Chemistry. **Psychology:** General. **Social sciences:** Economics, sociology.

Most popular majors. Business/marketing 14%, communications/journalism 10%, health sciences 43%, psychology 10%, social sciences 8%.

Technology on campus. 323 workstations in library, computer center. Dormitories wired for high-speed internet access and linked to campus network. Commuter students can connect to campus network. Online course registration, online library, helpline, repair service, wireless network available.

Student life. Freshman orientation: Mandatory, $125 fee. Preregistration for classes offered. Held Two days with overnight for all freshmen. **Housing:** Guaranteed on-campus for all undergraduates. Coed dorms, special housing for disabled available. $200 fully refundable deposit, deadline 7/18. **Activities:** Campus ministries, choral groups, dance, drama, international student organizations, literary magazine, Model UN, radio station, student government, student newspaper, TV station, Culturally Aware Students of Today, Latino club, student nurses association, Circle-K, Student Action for Viable Earth, black student union, pep club, communications club.

Athletics. NCAA. **Intercollegiate:** Baseball M, basketball, cross-country, lacrosse, soccer, softball W, swimming, tennis, track and field W, volleyball. **Team name:** Dolphins.

Student services. Adult student services, chaplain/spiritual director, career counseling, student employment services, financial aid counseling, health services, personal counseling, placement for graduates. **Physically disabled:** Services for visually, hearing impaired.

Contact. E-mail: admissions.office@mountsaintvincent.edu
Phone: (718) 405-3267 Toll-free number: (800) 665-2678
Fax: (718) 549-7945
Jackie Williams, Director of Admission, College of Mount St. Vincent, 6301 Riverdale Avenue, Riverdale, NY 10471-1093

College of New Rochelle
New Rochelle, New York **CB member**
www.cnr.edu **CB code: 2089**

- Private 4-year nursing and liberal arts college affiliated with the Roman Catholic Church
- Residential campus in small city
- 570 degree-seeking undergraduates: 11% part-time, 94% women, 37% African American, 2% international
- 609 degree-seeking graduate students
- 32% of applicants admitted
- SAT or ACT (ACT writing optional) required
- 36% graduate within 6 years

General. Founded in 1904. Regionally accredited. **Degrees:** 115 bachelor's awarded; master's offered. **ROTC:** Army, Naval. **Location:** 14 miles from New York City. **Calendar:** Semester, limited summer session. **Full-time faculty:** 50 total; 90% have terminal degrees, 16% minority, 72% women. **Part-time faculty:** 36 total; 53% have terminal degrees, 28% minority, 58% women. **Class size:** 74% < 20, 23% 20-39, 2% 40-49, 2% 50-99. **Special facilities:** Nursing simulation lab, television studio, learning skills centers, electron microscope, computer graphics laboratory, model classroom, rare book collections, castle with an art gallery.

Freshman class profile. 1,727 applied, 546 admitted, 95 enrolled.

Mid 50% test scores		GPA 2.0-2.99:	20%
SAT critical reading:	450-520	Rank in top quarter:	47%
SAT math:	420-500	Rank in top tenth:	17%
ACT composite:	20-23	Return as sophomores:	78%
GPA 3.75 or higher:	10%	Out-of-state:	19%
GPA 3.50-3.74:	16%	Live on campus:	82%
GPA 3.0-3.49:	54%		

Basis for selection. Admissions based on secondary school record, class rank, standardized test scores, activities/ volunteer experience, and extra curricular activities. Essay, interview recommended; portfolio required for art program. Audition is required for the Choir Scholarship.

High school preparation. College-preparatory program recommended. 18 units required. Required and recommended units include English 4, mathematics 3, social studies 3, science 3 (laboratory 2) and foreign language 3. Biology, chemistry, 3 math required for nursing and physical therapy.

2016-2017 Annual costs. Tuition/fees (projected): $34,648. Room/board: $13,208. Books/supplies: $810. Personal expenses: $1,100.

Financial aid. Non-need-based: Scholarships awarded for academics, art, leadership, music/drama.

Application procedures. Admission: No deadline. $35 fee, may be waived for applicants with need, free for online applicants. Admission notification on a rolling basis beginning on or about 11/1. **Financial aid:** Priority date 2/1; no closing date. FAFSA, institutional form required. Applicants notified on a rolling basis starting 1/1; must reply within 2 week(s) of notification.

Academics. Special study options: Accelerated study, combined bachelor's/graduate degree, cooperative education, cross-registration, double major, exchange student, honors, independent study, internships, liberal arts/career combination, study abroad, teacher certification program, United Nations semester, Washington semester. **Credit/placement by examination:** AP, CLEP, IB, institutional tests. 15 credit hours maximum toward bachelor's degree. **Support services:** Learning center, reduced course load, remedial instruction, study skills assistance, tutoring, writing center.

Majors. Area/ethnic studies: American, women's. **Biology:** General. **Business:** General. **Communications:** Broadcast journalism, communications/speech/rhetoric, media studies. **Conservation:** Environmental studies. **Education:** General, art, elementary, special ed. **English:** English lit. **Foreign languages:** Classics, French, Latin, Spanish. **Health services:** Art therapy, nursing (RN). **History:** General. **Human services:** Social work. **Math:** General. **Philosophy/religion:** Philosophy, religion. **Physical sciences:** Chemistry. **Psychology:** General. **Social sciences:** Economics, political science, sociology. **Visual/performing arts:** Art history/conservation, studio arts.

Most popular majors. Health sciences 73%.

Technology on campus. 223 workstations in dormitories, library, computer center. Dormitories wired for high-speed internet access and linked to campus network. Commuter students can connect to campus network. Online course registration, online library, helpline, wireless network available.

Student life. Freshman orientation: Mandatory. Preregistration for classes offered. **Policies:** Freshmen not permitted cars on campus. **Housing:** Guaranteed on-campus for all undergraduates. Coed dorms, single-sex dorms, themed housing, wellness housing available. $100 nonrefundable deposit, deadline 5/1. **Activities:** Campus ministries, choral groups, dance, drama, film society, literary magazine, music ensembles, Model UN, musical theater, student government, student newspaper, community services, Latin American Women Society, black student union, CNR Drama, nurses gospel choir.

Athletics. NCAA. **Intercollegiate:** Basketball, cross-country W, soccer M, softball W, swimming, tennis W, volleyball. **Intramural:** Badminton, basketball, soccer, swimming, table tennis, ultimate frisbee, volleyball. **Team name:** Blue Angels.

Student services. Adult student services, alcohol/substance abuse counseling, chaplain/spiritual director, career counseling, services for economically disadvantaged, student employment services, financial aid counseling, health services, personal counseling, placement for graduates, women's services. **Physically disabled:** Services for visually, speech, hearing impaired.

Contact. E-mail: admission@cnr.edu
Phone: (914) 654-5452 Toll-free number: (800) 933-5923
Fax: (914) 654-5464
Michael DiPiazza, Director of Undergraduate Admissions, College of New Rochelle, 29 Castle Place, New Rochelle, NY 10805-2339

College of Saint Rose
Albany, New York **CB member**
www.strose.edu **CB code: 2091**

- Private 4-year liberal arts college
- Residential campus in small city
- 2,626 degree-seeking undergraduates: 3% part-time, 66% women, 10% African American, 2% Asian American, 6% Hispanic/Latino, 7% Multiracial, non-Hispanic, 2% international
- 1,657 degree-seeking graduate students
- 82% of applicants admitted

▶ Application essay, interview required

▶ 61% graduate within 6 years; 72% enter graduate study

General. Founded in 1920. Regionally accredited. **Degrees:** 569 bachelor's awarded; master's offered. **ROTC:** Army, Naval, Air Force. **Location:** 140 miles from New York City. **Calendar:** Semester, limited summer session. **Full-time faculty:** 204 total; 93% have terminal degrees, 12% minority, 54% women. **Part-time faculty:** 150 total; 9% minority, 51% women. **Class size:** 57% < 20, 42% 20-39, less than 1% 40-49, less than 1% 50-99. **Special facilities:** Club-atmosphere performance venue, recital hall, choral and orchestra rehearsal rooms, digital photography studio with 3-D printer, full recording studio, television studio, painting and sculpture studios, film screening classroom, visiting artist and student galleries, on-site pre-school, speech-hearing and special education clinic, curriculum library for pre-K-12 teachers, neuroscience, geology and earth science labs, veteran's center.

Freshman class profile. 5,599 applied, 4,578 admitted, 632 enrolled.

Mid 50% test scores			
SAT critical reading:	480-570	Rank in top quarter:	40%
SAT math:	470-560	Rank in top tenth:	14%
ACT composite:	20-25	Return as sophomores:	79%
GPA 3.75 or higher:	29%	Out-of-state:	15%
GPA 3.50-3.74:	18%	Live on campus:	81%
GPA 3.0-3.49:	30%	International:	2%
GPA 2.0-2.99:	23%		

Basis for selection. High school transcript is the most important. Strongly consider extracurricular activities, overall academic rigor of high school work (Honors, AP, University in the High School courses) and SAT/ACT scores are considered if submitted. SAT/ACT required for merit scholarships, athletics, dual degree programs and home schooled students. Portfolio review required for art majors, audition required for music majors. **Home schooled:** State high school equivalency certificate required. SAT/ACT required.

High school preparation. College-preparatory program required. 23 units required; 30 recommended. Required and recommended units include English 4, mathematics 3-4, social studies 4, history 4, science 3-4 (laboratory 2), foreign language 1-2 and academic electives 4.

2015-2016 Annual costs. Tuition/fees: $29,826. Room/board: $11,878. Books/supplies: $1,200. Personal expenses: $1,500.

2014-2015 Financial aid. Need-based: 511 full-time freshmen applied for aid; 470 deemed to have need; 470 received aid. Average need met was 79%. Average scholarship/grant was $11,463; average loan $3,725. 70% of total undergraduate aid awarded as scholarships/grants, 30% as loans/jobs. **Non-need-based:** Awarded to 2,039 full-time undergraduates, including 57 freshmen. Scholarships awarded for academics, alumni affiliation, art, athletics, music/drama.

Application procedures. Admission: Priority date 12/1; deadline 5/1 (postmark date). , may be waived for applicants with need, free for online applicants. No application fee. Admission notification by 5/1. Admission notification on a rolling basis beginning on or about 10/1. Must reply by May 1 or within 2 week(s) if notified thereafter. Students may be reviewed on a rolling basis after May 1. **Financial aid:** Priority date 2/1, closing date 4/1. FAFSA required. Applicants notified by 3/1; Applicants notified on a rolling basis starting 3/1; must reply by 5/1 or within 2 week(s) of notification.

Academics. Special study options: Accelerated study, combined bachelor's/graduate degree, cross-registration, distance learning, double major, ESL, exchange student, independent study, internships, liberal arts/career combination, student-designed major, study abroad, teacher certification program. Fourteen dual degree programs in which students can earn both their bachelor's and master's degrees in 5 years while maintaining all of their undergraduate financial aid. **Credit/placement by examination:** AP, CLEP, IB, institutional tests. 15 credit hours maximum toward bachelor's degree. Students can also earn credits by examination through AP, IB and University in High School programs. **Support services:** Learning center, pre-admission summer program, reduced course load, remedial instruction, study skills assistance, tutoring, writing center. Academic Support services for students with documented disabilities.

Majors. Biology: General, biochemistry, cell/histology. **Business:** Accounting, business admin, finance, financial planning, human resources, marketing. **Computer sciences:** Computer science, information technology. **Education:** Biology, early childhood, elementary, English, mathematics, music, social studies. **English:** English lit. **Health services:** Audiology/speech pathology, clinical lab science. **History:** General. **Human services:** Social work. **Liberal arts:** Arts/sciences. **Math:** General. **Physical sciences:** Chemistry. **Protective services:** Forensics, law enforcement admin. **Psychology:** General, forensic. **Social sciences:** Political science. **Visual/performing arts:** Commercial/advertising art, music, music technology.

Most popular majors. Business/marketing 15%, communications/journalism 9%, education 25%, health sciences 7%, psychology 8%, security/protective services 6%, visual/performing arts 10%.

Technology on campus. 733 workstations in dormitories, library, computer center, student center. Dormitories wired for high-speed internet access and linked to campus network. Commuter students can connect to campus network. Online course registration, online library, helpline, student web hosting, wireless network available.

Student life. Freshman orientation: Mandatory, $331 fee. Preregistration for classes offered. Two-part orientation: Two-day overnight summer program and week-long program that begins two days prior to start of fall classes. **Policies:** Sanctions for plagiarism, cheating, academic misconduct, or any other submission of another's work as one's own. Use of alcohol by underage students prohibited, with limits on amounts students 21 and over can possess. Use of drugs prohibited. Sexual violence not tolerated. No tobacco-use on college-owned or leased property or in any college-owned vehicle. Freshmen not permitted cars on campus. **Housing:** Guaranteed on-campus for freshmen. Coed dorms, single-sex dorms, special housing for disabled, apartments available. $150 fully refundable deposit, deadline 5/1. **Activities:** Bands, campus ministries, choral groups, dance, drama, international student organizations, literary magazine, music ensembles, musical theater, radio station, student government, student newspaper, symphony orchestra, TV station, Brothers and Sisters in Christ, ALANA Steppers, Best Buddies, Big Brothers/Big Sisters, Spectrum, gospel choir,.

Athletics. NCAA. **Intercollegiate:** Baseball M, basketball, cross-country, diving, golf, lacrosse M, soccer, softball W, swimming, tennis W, track and field, volleyball W. **Intramural:** Basketball, football (non-tackle) M, soccer, softball, ultimate frisbee, volleyball. **Team name:** Golden Knights.

Student services. Adult student services, alcohol/substance abuse counseling, chaplain/spiritual director, career counseling, services for economically disadvantaged, student employment services, financial aid counseling, health services, legal services, minority student services, personal counseling, placement for graduates. **Physically disabled:** Services for visually, speech, hearing impaired.

Contact. E-mail: admit@strose.edu
Phone: (518) 454-5150 Toll-free number: (800) 637-8556
Fax: (518) 454-2013
Mary Grondahl, Associate Vice President for Enrollment Planning and Undergraduate Admissions, College of Saint Rose, 432 Western Avenue, Albany, NY 12203

Columbia University

New York, New York   **CB member**
www.columbia.edu   **CB code: 2116**

▶ Private 4-year university

▶ Residential campus in very large city

▶ 6,102 degree-seeking undergraduates: 48% women, 12% African American, 22% Asian American, 12% Hispanic/Latino, 2% Native American, 14% international

▶ 6% of applicants admitted

▶ SAT or ACT (ACT writing optional), application essay required

▶ 96% graduate within 6 years

General. Founded in 1754. Regionally accredited. **Degrees:** 1,579 bachelor's awarded; master's, professional, doctoral offered. **ROTC:** Army, Naval, Air Force. **Calendar:** Semester, extensive summer session. **Special facilities:** Art and architecture galleries, cinemas, theaters, geological observatory, interactive graphics laboratory, telecommunications research center, plasma laboratory, materials laboratory, astronomical observatory.

Freshman class profile. 36,250 applied, 2,220 admitted, 1,398 enrolled.

Mid 50% test scores			
SAT critical reading:	700-790	Return as sophomores:	99%
SAT math:	700-800	Out-of-state:	78%
SAT writing:	700-790	Live on campus:	100%
ACT composite:	32-35	International:	15%

Basis for selection. Admission is highly selective using a holistic review process. Admission is not based on a simple formula of grades and test scores. Instead, a variety of factors are considered: academic record, extracurricular interests, intellectual achievements and personal background. TOEFL or IELTS exam required of all non-native speakers. Audition required for the Columbia-Juilliard Exchange Program. **Home schooled:** Common Application home-schooled supplement required.

High school preparation. College-preparatory program required. Required and recommended units include English 4, mathematics 3-4, history 3-4, science 3-4 (laboratory 3-4), foreign language 3-4 and academic electives 3-4.

2015-2016 Annual costs. Tuition/fees: $53,000. Room/board: $12,860. Books/supplies: $1,200. Personal expenses: $2,024.

2015-2016 Financial aid. All financial aid based on need. 879 full-time freshmen applied for aid; 730 deemed to have need; 730 received aid. Average need met was 100%. Average scholarship/grant was $48,172. **Additional information:** Institution has eliminated student loans for those receiving Columbia need-based aid and replaced them with additional University grants, and significantly reduced the parent contribution for families making less than $100,000 per year.

Application procedures. Admission: Closing date 1/1 (postmark date). $85 fee, may be waived for applicants with need. Admission notification by 4/1. Must reply by May 1 or within 2 week(s) if notified thereafter. **Financial aid:** Priority date 3/1; no closing date. FAFSA, CSS PROFILE required. Applicants notified by 4/1; must reply by 5/1 or within 2 week(s) of notification.

Academics. Special study options: Accelerated study, combined bachelor's/graduate degree, cooperative education, cross-registration, double major, dual enrollment of high school students, ESL, exchange student, independent study, internships, liberal arts/career combination, student-designed major, study abroad, teacher certification program. Combined 3-2 program with engineering with over 100 liberal arts colleges around the country. **Credit/placement by examination:** AP, CLEP, IB, institutional tests. 16 credit hours maximum toward bachelor's degree. **Support services:** Pre-admission summer program, study skills assistance, tutoring, writing center.

Majors. Architecture: Architecture. **Area/ethnic studies:** African, African-American, American, Asian, Asian-American, Chicano/Hispanic-American/Latino, Chinese, East Asian, European, French, German, Italian, Japanese, Korean, Latin American, Near/Middle Eastern, Polish, regional, Russian/Eastern European/Eurasian, Russian/Slavic, Slavic, Spanish/Iberian, women's. **Biology:** General, biochemistry, biophysics, ecology, environmental, evolutionary, neuroscience. **Computer sciences:** Computer science. **Conservation:** General, environmental science. **Education:** General. **Engineering:** Biomedical, chemical, civil, computer, electrical, engineering mechanics, environmental, geological, materials, mechanical, metallurgical, mining, operations research. **English:** American lit, British lit, creative writing, English lit. **Foreign languages:** Ancient Greek, Biblical, Chinese, classics, comparative lit, East Asian, French, German, Germanic, Italian, Japanese, Korean, Latin, linguistics, modern Greek, Russian, Slavic, Spanish. **History:** General. **Math:** General, applied, statistics. **Philosophy/religion:** Philosophy, religion. **Physical sciences:** Astronomy, astrophysics, chemical physics, chemistry, geochemistry, geology, geophysics, materials science, physics, planetary. **Psychology:** General. **Social sciences:** Anthropology, archaeology, economics, political science, sociology, urban studies. **Visual/performing arts:** General, art history/conservation, dance, dramatic, film/cinema/video, jazz, music, studio arts, theater history.

Most popular majors. Biology 9%, engineering/engineering technologies 22%, social sciences 22%.

Technology on campus. Dormitories wired for high-speed internet access and linked to campus network. Commuter students can connect to campus network. Online course registration, online library, helpline, student web hosting, wireless network available.

Student life. Freshman orientation: Mandatory, $420 fee. Preregistration for classes offered. A one-week program offering academic advising sessions, cultural events, parents orientation sessions, and more. Students may also choose to participate in pre-orientation programs like the Columbia Outdoor Orientation Program, International Student Orientation Program or the Columbia Urban Experience. **Housing:** Guaranteed on-campus for all undergraduates. Coed dorms, special housing for disabled, cooperative housing, fraternity/sorority housing, themed housing, wellness housing available. Special interest communities around shared interests available. **Activities:** Bands, campus ministries, choral groups, dance, drama, film society, international student organizations, literary magazine, music ensembles, Model UN, musical theater, opera, radio station, student government, student newspaper, symphony orchestra, TV station, African-American, Hispanic, Native American, Asian-American, LGBTQ student organizations, community service groups, religious groups of all denominations.

Athletics. NCAA. **Intercollegiate:** Archery W, baseball M, basketball, cross-country, diving, fencing, field hockey W, football (tackle) M, golf, lacrosse W, rowing (crew), soccer, softball W, squash, swimming, tennis, track and field, volleyball W, wrestling M. **Intramural:** Basketball, football (non-tackle), racquetball, soccer, softball, tennis, volleyball. **Team name:** Lions.

Student services. Alcohol/substance abuse counseling, chaplain/spiritual director, career counseling, services for economically disadvantaged, student employment services, financial aid counseling, health services, minority student services, personal counseling, placement for graduates, women's services. **Physically disabled:** Services for visually, speech, hearing impaired.

Contact. E-mail: ugrad-ask@columbia.edu
Phone: (212) 854-2522 Fax: (212) 854-1209
Jessica Marinaccio, Dean of Undergraduate Admissions and Financial Aid, Columbia University, 1130 Amsterdam Avenue, New York, NY 10027

Columbia University: School of General Studies
New York, New York
www.gs.columbia.edu   CB code: 2095

- Private 4-year university and liberal arts college
- Residential campus in very large city
- 2,005 degree-seeking undergraduates: 23% part-time, 41% women, 5% African American, 8% Asian American, 10% Hispanic/Latino, 18% international
- 36% of applicants admitted
- SAT or ACT (ACT writing optional), application essay required

General. Founded in 1947. Regionally accredited. Liberal arts division of university for nontraditional students whose undergraduate study has been interrupted or postponed for at least one year. For students who have not had a break in their education, joint degree programs are available with the Jewish Theological Seminary, Sciences Po, and City University of Hong Kong. The Postbaccalaureate Premedical Program is offered to students who have completed little or none of the required coursework for application to medical school. **Degrees:** 471 bachelor's awarded. **ROTC:** Army, Naval, Air Force. **Calendar:** Semester, extensive summer session. **Special facilities:** Earth institute, observatory.

Freshman class profile. 606 applied, 218 admitted, 129 enrolled.

Mid 50% test scores			
		GPA 3.50-3.74:	19%
SAT critical reading:	630-750	GPA 3.0-3.49:	25%
SAT math:	630-740	Out-of-state:	79%
SAT writing:	640-750	Live on campus:	15%
ACT composite:	29-32	International:	19%
GPA 3.75 or higher:	56%		

Basis for selection. Maturity and varied backgrounds of students considered. Aptitude and motivation important together with academic performance and test scores. Students who have not taken the SAT or ACT, or whose test scores are older than 8 years, may take the General Studies Admissions Exam. Interview requested when needed. **Home schooled:** State high school equivalency certificate required. **Learning Disabled:** Registration with the Office of Disability Services recommended.

2015-2016 Annual costs. Tuition/fees: $51,114. Room/board: $10,356. Books/supplies: $1,400.

2014-2015 Financial aid. Need-based: 34 full-time freshmen applied for aid; 28 deemed to have need; 27 received aid. Average need met was 34%. Average scholarship/grant was $16,007; average loan $7,760. 54% of total undergraduate aid awarded as scholarships/grants, 46% as loans/jobs. **Non-need-based:** Awarded to 53 full-time undergraduates, including 4 freshmen. Scholarships awarded for academics.

Application procedures. Admission: Priority date 3/1; deadline 6/1 (postmark date). $80 fee. Admission notification by 7/20. Admission notification on a rolling basis. The School of General Studies begins releasing admissions decisions in March for the summer and fall terms and in October for the spring term. **Financial aid:** Closing date 6/1. FAFSA, institutional form required. Applicants notified on a rolling basis; must reply within 3 week(s) of notification.

Academics. Special study options: Accelerated study, combined bachelor's/graduate degree, cross-registration, double major, dual enrollment of high school students, exchange student, honors, independent study, internships, student-designed major, study abroad, teacher certification program. Dual degree program with Jewish Theological Seminary, List College; dual BA program with Sciences Po, dual BA program with City University of Hong Kong. **Credit/placement by examination:** AP, CLEP, SAT, ACT, institutional tests. 30 credit hours maximum toward bachelor's degree. **Support services:** Learning center, pre-admission summer program, reduced course load, remedial instruction, study skills assistance, tutoring, writing center.

Majors. Architecture: Architecture, history/criticism. **Area/ethnic studies:** African, African-American, American, Asian, Caribbean, Chicano/Hispanic-American/Latino, East Asian, French, German, Italian, Latin American, Near/Middle Eastern, Russian/Eastern European/Eurasian, Russian/Slavic, South Asian, women's. **Biology:** General, biochemistry, biophysics, evolutionary. **Computer sciences:** General, computer science. **Conservation:** Environmental science. **English:** Creative writing, English lit. **Foreign languages:**

Classics, comparative lit, French, German, Italian, Portuguese, Russian, Spanish. **Health services:** Premedicine. **History:** General. **Math:** General, applied, mathematics/statistics, statistics. **Philosophy/religion:** Philosophy, religion. **Physical sciences:** Astronomy, astrophysics, chemistry, geology, geophysics, oceanography, physics. **Psychology:** General. **Social sciences:** Anthropology, archaeology, economics, political science, sociology, sociology/anthropology, urban studies. **Visual/performing arts:** Art history/conservation, dance, dramatic, film/cinema/video, music, studio arts.

Technology on campus. 347 workstations in dormitories, library, computer center, student center. Dormitories wired for high-speed internet access and linked to campus network. Commuter students can connect to campus network. Online course registration, online library, helpline, repair service, student web hosting, wireless network available.

Student life. Freshman orientation: Mandatory, $150 fee. Preregistration for classes offered. Held 1 week before classes start, and lasts two days. Optional orientation activities are held throughout the following week. Academic planning session (held prior to beginning of semester) required of all new students. **Policies:** Freshmen not permitted cars on campus. **Housing:** Coed dorms, special housing for disabled, apartments, cooperative housing, fraternity/sorority housing, themed housing available. Limited on-campus housing available. Off-campus housing registry provides listings of Columbia-affiliated apartments. **Activities:** Bands, campus ministries, choral groups, dance, drama, film society, international student organizations, literary magazine, music ensembles, Model UN, musical theater, opera, radio station, student government, student newspaper, TV station, many religious, political, and ethnic organizations.

Athletics. NCAA. **Intercollegiate:** Archery W, baseball M, basketball, cross-country, diving, fencing, field hockey W, football (tackle) M, golf, lacrosse W, rowing (crew), soccer, softball W, squash, swimming, tennis, track and field, volleyball W, wrestling M. **Intramural:** Basketball, boxing, diving, fencing, racquetball, skiing, soccer, swimming, tennis, volleyball, weight lifting. **Team name:** Lions.

Student services. Adult student services, alcohol/substance abuse counseling, chaplain/spiritual director, career counseling, services for economically disadvantaged, student employment services, financial aid counseling, health services, minority student services, personal counseling, placement for graduates, veterans' counselor, women's services. **Physically disabled:** Services for visually, hearing impaired.

Contact. E-mail: gsdegree@columbia.edu
Phone: (212) 854-2772 Toll-free number: (800) 895-1169
Fax: (212) 854-6316
Curtis Rodgers, Dean of Enrollment Management, Columbia University: School of General Studies, 408 Lewisohn Hall, Mail Code 4101, New York, NY 10027

Concordia College
Bronxville, New York — CB member
www.concordia-ny.edu — CB code: 2096

- Private 4-year liberal arts college affiliated with the Lutheran Church - Missouri Synod
- Residential campus in small town
- 886 degree-seeking undergraduates
- 93 graduate students
- SAT or ACT (ACT writing recommended), application essay required

General. Founded in 1881. Regionally accredited. **Degrees:** 188 bachelor's, 3 associate awarded; master's offered. **Location:** 14 miles from New York City. **Calendar:** Semester, limited summer session. **Full-time faculty:** 42 total. **Part-time faculty:** 95 total. **Class size:** 62% < 20, 37% 20-39, 1% 40-49. **Special facilities:** Music laboratory, distance learning classroom, media and digital production center, art gallery, art studio, nursing labs.

Freshman class profile.

GPA 3.75 or higher:	7%	Rank in top quarter:	21%
GPA 3.50-3.74:	11%	Rank in top tenth:	4%
GPA 3.0-3.49:	23%	Out-of-state:	11%
GPA 2.0-2.99:	56%	Live on campus:	62%

Basis for selection. Test scores, school achievement record, interview important; community and church involvement considered. Interview required for some, recommended for others. **Home schooled:** Statement describing home school structure and mission, transcript of courses and grades, state high school equivalency certificate, letter of recommendation (nonparent) required. Show explanation of all course work studied and grades obtained. **Learning Disabled:** Students required to meet with learning specialist and submit most recent psychological assessment.

High school preparation. College-preparatory program recommended. 15 units recommended. Recommended units include English 4, mathematics 3, social studies 2, science 2 (laboratory 2) and foreign language 2.

2015-2016 Annual costs. Tuition/fees: $29,700. Room/board: $11,024. Books/supplies: $1,000. Personal expenses: $950.

Financial aid. Non-need-based: Scholarships awarded for academics, athletics, leadership, music/drama, religious affiliation.

Application procedures. Admission: Priority date 3/15; no deadline. $50 fee, may be waived for applicants with need. Admission notification on a rolling basis beginning on or about 12/1. Must reply by May 1 or within 4 week(s) if notified thereafter. Student must interview with Admission Counselor and have approved plan of study for senior year completion. **Financial aid:** Priority date 4/1; no closing date. FAFSA required. Applicants notified on a rolling basis starting 2/15; must reply by 5/1 or within 3 week(s) of notification.

Academics. Special study options: Accelerated study, combined bachelor's/graduate degree, cooperative education, double major, ESL, exchange student, honors, independent study, internships, liberal arts/career combination, student-designed major, study abroad, teacher certification program. **Credit/placement by examination:** AP, CLEP, IB, institutional tests. 30 credit hours maximum toward associate degree, 30 toward bachelor's. **Support services:** Reduced course load, remedial instruction, study skills assistance, tutoring, writing center.

Majors. Biology: General, ecology. **Business:** General, accounting, business admin, finance, international. **Education:** General, elementary. **English:** English lit. **Foreign languages:** Comparative lit. **Health services:** Nursing (RN), premedicine, radiologic technology/medical imaging. **History:** General. **Human services:** Social work. **Liberal arts:** Arts/sciences. **Math:** General. **Philosophy/religion:** Religion. **Physical sciences:** Geology. **Psychology:** General. **Social sciences:** General. **Theology:** Religious ed, sacred music. **Visual/performing arts:** Art, arts management, design, music.

Technology on campus. 30 workstations in library, computer center. Dormitories wired for high-speed internet access and linked to campus network. Commuter students can connect to campus network. Online course registration, online library, helpline, repair service, wireless network available.

Student life. Freshman orientation: Mandatory. Preregistration for classes offered. Held at beginning of semester with adviser. **Policies:** Freshmen not permitted cars on campus. **Housing:** Guaranteed on-campus for all undergraduates. Single-sex dorms, themed housing available. $300 nonrefundable deposit, deadline 5/1. **Activities:** Jazz band, campus ministries, choral groups, drama, international student organizations, music ensembles, musical theater, student government, student newspaper, Christian service organizations, Afro-Latino American club, social work club, Prayer Partners, environmental club, In His Name, Lutheran Women League, Rotaract club.

Athletics. NCAA. **Intercollegiate:** Baseball M, basketball, cross-country, golf M, soccer, softball W, tennis, volleyball W. **Intramural:** Basketball, football (non-tackle), softball W, squash, tennis, volleyball. **Team name:** Clippers.

Student services. Adult student services, alcohol/substance abuse counseling, chaplain/spiritual director, career counseling, student employment services, financial aid counseling, health services, minority student services, personal counseling, placement for graduates.

Contact. E-mail: admission@concordia-ny.edu
Phone: (914) 337-9300 ext. 2155 Toll-free number: (800) 937-2655
Fax: (914) 395-4636
Donald Vos, Vice President for Enrollment Management, Concordia College, 171 White Plains Road, Bronxville, NY 10708-1923

Cooper Union for the Advancement of Science and Art
New York, New York — CB member
www.cooper.edu — CB code: 2097

- Private 4-year visual arts and engineering college
- Commuter campus in very large city
- 873 degree-seeking undergraduates: 33% women, 3% African American, 18% Asian American, 9% Hispanic/Latino, 9% Multi-racial, non-Hispanic, 16% international
- 73 degree-seeking graduate students
- 13% of applicants admitted

♦ SAT or ACT (ACT writing optional), application essay required
♦ 81% graduate within 6 years; 60% enter graduate study

General. Founded in 1859. Regionally accredited. **Degrees:** 191 bachelor's awarded; master's offered. **ROTC:** Army. **Location:** In New York City's East Village. **Calendar:** Semester, limited summer session. **Full-time faculty:** 49 total; 92% have terminal degrees, 12% minority, 24% women. **Part-time faculty:** 167 total; 34% have terminal degrees, 12% minority, 29% women. **Class size:** 70% < 20, 28% 20-39, less than 1% 40-49, less than 1% 50-99, 1% >100. **Special facilities:** Special labs in: biomechanics, materials, soils, hydraulics, design systems, computers, circuits, signal processing, acoustics and audio engineering, combustion research and demonstration, robotic theater studio, rapid prototyping, energy reclamation and innovation, materials and micro/nano engineering, mechatronics, thermal/fluid/engines, tissue engineering, two fully programmed galleries for art and architecture.

Freshman class profile. 3,258 applied, 426 admitted, 233 enrolled.

Mid 50% test scores		GPA 2.0-2.99:	18%
SAT critical reading:	610-720	Rank in top quarter:	90%
SAT math:	630-790	Rank in top tenth:	85%
SAT writing:	600-720	End year in good standing:	96%
ACT composite:	30-34	Return as sophomores:	96%
GPA 3.75 or higher:	20%	Out-of-state:	38%
GPA 3.50-3.74:	16%	Live on campus:	90%
GPA 3.0-3.49:	44%	International:	21%

Basis for selection. Engineering applicants reviewed on high school record and courses selected, essays, SAT, and required SAT Subject Test scores. (Math and Chemistry or Math and Physics SAT Subject Tests required.) Art and architecture applicants selected on basis of home test (art), studio test (architecture) high school record and program, SAT. For art and architecture applicants, please note that the home test and studio tests (and portfolios where applicable) are weighed significantly during the admissions process. These, even more so than standardized test scores and high school/college grades. Applicants with extensive college experience may be eligible for an ACT/SAT waiver. Please contact admissions office for additional information. Portfolios required for art applicants. All art applicants must complete a home test. All architecture applicants must complete a studio test. **Home schooled:** Statement describing home school structure and mission, transcript of courses and grades, letter of recommendation (nonparent) required. Must present proof of high school graduation certification (national) or equivalent.

High school preparation. College-preparatory program recommended. 16 units required; 18 recommended. Required and recommended units include English 4, mathematics 1-4, social studies 1-4, history 1, science 1-4 (laboratory 3), foreign language 2 and academic electives 8. 1 science required for architecture and art. 4 science and 4 math required for engineering including physics, chemistry, and precalculus; calculus preferred. 1 math required for art, 3 math for architecture including trigonometry and precalculus. 18 total units recommended for engineering.

2015-2016 Annual costs. Tuition/fees: $42,650. Room only: $11,560. Books/supplies: $1,650. Personal expenses: $1,575. **Additional information:** All incoming undergraduate students receive at a minimum, a half-tuition scholarship. Cooper Union provides to those that demonstrate need, additional assistance to cover the remaining costs of attending, including tuition, room and board, books and supplies, personal expenses and transportation.

2014-2015 Financial aid. Need-based: 150 full-time freshmen applied for aid; 135 deemed to have need; 135 received aid. Average need met was 92%. Average scholarship/grant was $20,143; average loan $2,842. 94% of total undergraduate aid awarded as scholarships/grants, 6% as loans/jobs. **Non-need-based:** Awarded to 857 full-time undergraduates, including 226 freshmen. Scholarships awarded for academics. **Additional information:** All Pell eligible students receive a full tuition scholarship. All undergraduate students receive at a minimum half-tuition merit scholarships. Late financial aid applications processed on rolling basis.

Application procedures. Admission: Priority date 12/1; deadline 1/11 (receipt date). $75 fee, may be waived for applicants with need. Admission notification by 4/1. Admission notification on a rolling basis beginning on or about 12/20. Must reply by May 1 or within 4 week(s) if notified thereafter. Early Decision closing date (art and engineering only) is December 1. Regular application closing date for undergraduates is January 11. **Financial aid:** Priority date 3/1, closing date 5/1. FAFSA, CSS PROFILE required. Applicants notified on a rolling basis starting 12/20; must reply by 6/30 or within 2 week(s) of notification.

Academics. Engineering tutorials and engineering mentor program available. All freshman engineering majors required to prove or acquire computer literacy. 128 credit hours required for graduation in art program, 135 in engineering, and 160 in architecture. Students may take classes in all 3 schools. Art students encouraged to take courses throughout 7 disciplines. Architecture students take 5 years of design culminating in thesis year. Engineering students encouraged to take coursework in other majors and

end their studies with a senior project. **Special study options:** Combined bachelor's/graduate degree, cross-registration, exchange student, independent study, internships, student-designed major, study abroad. Research opportunities. Students may take up to 1 year off between studies to pursue experiences related to their academic goals. **Credit/placement by examination:** AP, CLEP, IB, institutional tests. Varies depending upon school and department. **Support services:** Tutoring, writing center.

Majors. Architecture: Architecture. **Engineering:** General, chemical, civil, electrical, mechanical. **Visual/performing arts:** Graphic design, studio arts.

Most popular majors. Architecture 14%, engineering/engineering technologies 54%, visual/performing arts 32%.

Technology on campus. 100 workstations in dormitories, library, computer center. Dormitories wired for high-speed internet access and linked to campus network. Commuter students can connect to campus network. Online course registration, online library, helpline, repair service, student web hosting, wireless network available.

Student life. Freshman orientation: Available. Preregistration for classes offered. Held the week prior to the start of the fall semester and lasts 7 days. **Policies:** Residence hall primarily used by first-year students. Most if not all first-year students offered housing in the residence hall. **Housing:** Coed dorms, wellness housing available. $500 fully refundable deposit, deadline 6/1. **Activities:** Bands, choral groups, dance, drama, film society, music ensembles, musical theater, student government, student newspaper, symphony orchestra, Close to 100 registered clubs available.

Athletics. Intercollegiate: Basketball, cross-country, soccer, tennis, volleyball. **Intramural:** Badminton, basketball, bowling, cross-country, fencing, golf, judo, soccer, softball, table tennis, tennis, volleyball. **Team name:** Hawks, Pioneers.

Student services. Alcohol/substance abuse counseling, career counseling, student employment services, financial aid counseling, personal counseling, placement for graduates, veterans' counselor. **Physically disabled:** Services for visually, hearing impaired.

Contact. E-mail: admissions@cooper.edu
Phone: (212) 353-4120 Fax: (212) 353-4342
Mitchell Lipton, VP Enrollment Services and Dean of Admissions, Cooper Union for the Advancement of Science and Art, 30 Cooper Square, Suite 300, New York, NY 10003-7183

Cornell University	
Ithaca, New York	**CB member**
www.cornell.edu	**CB code: 2098**

♦ Private 4-year university
♦ Residential campus in large town
♦ 14,226 degree-seeking undergraduates: 52% women, 6% African American, 18% Asian American, 12% Hispanic/Latino, 4% Multi-racial, non-Hispanic, 10% international
♦ 7,491 degree-seeking graduate students
♦ 15% of applicants admitted
♦ SAT or ACT (ACT writing optional), application essay required
♦ 93% graduate within 6 years; 22% enter graduate study

General. Founded in 1865. Regionally accredited. Seven undergraduate colleges; four graduate/professional units; two medical graduate and professional units in New York City as well as one in Doha, Qatar; and the Cornell NYC Tech campus in New York City. **Degrees:** 3,674 bachelor's awarded; master's, professional, doctoral offered. **ROTC:** Army, Naval, Air Force. **Location:** 60 miles from Syracuse. **Calendar:** Semester, extensive summer session. **Full-time faculty:** 1,783 total; 92% have terminal degrees, 19% minority, 35% women. **Part-time faculty:** 356 total; 64% have terminal degrees, 10% minority, 36% women. **Class size:** 57% < 20, 21% 20-39, 4% 40-49, 10% 50-99, 7% >100. **Special facilities:** Art museum, studies/research center, arboretum, particle accelerator, biotechnology institute, supercomputer, national research centers, center for performing arts, optical observatory, marine laboratory, woods sanctuary, ornithology laboratory, vertebrates museum.

Freshman class profile. 41,900 applied, 6,315 admitted, 3,180 enrolled.

Mid 50% test scores			
		Return as sophomores:	97%
SAT critical reading:	650-750	Out-of-state:	68%
SAT math:	680-780	Live on campus:	100%
ACT composite:	30-34	International:	9%
Rank in top quarter:	97%	Fraternities:	35%
Rank in top tenth:	89%	Sororities:	32%

Basis for selection. School achievement record (difficulty of courses, grades earned), test scores, preparation and background for specific programs especially important. Essays, recommendations considered. Subject Test requirements depend upon college/school. Please consult admissions office. Interview required for architecture; portfolio required for design programs. **Home schooled:** Well-documented coursework required.

High school preparation. College-preparatory program recommended. 16 units required. Required and recommended units include English 4, mathematics 3, social studies 3, history 3, science 3 (laboratory 3) and foreign language 3.

2015-2016 Annual costs. Tuition/fees: $49,116. Room/board: $13,678.

2014-2015 Financial aid. All financial aid based on need. 1,718 full-time freshmen applied for aid; 1,431 deemed to have need; 1,431 received aid. Average need met was 100%. Average scholarship/grant was $39,787; average loan $4,031. 85% of total undergraduate aid awarded as scholarships/grants, 15% as loans/jobs.

Application procedures. Admission: Closing date 1/2 (postmark date). $80 fee, may be waived for applicants with need. Application must be submitted online. Early April. Must reply by May 1 or within 2 week(s) if notified thereafter. **Financial aid:** Closing date 2/15. FAFSA, CSS PROFILE required. Applicants notified by 4/1; must reply by 5/1.

Academics. Cornell/Hughes Scholars program for independent research in neurobiology, physiology, genetics and development, and biochemistry (molecular and cell biology), Cornell in Rome program for studies in architecture and fine arts, undergraduate research opportunities in traditional majors as well as in many interdisciplinary fields including American Indian studies, cognitive studies, agriculture, food and society, FALCON language programs. **Special study options:** Accelerated study, cooperative education, cross-registration, distance learning, double major, ESL, exchange student, honors, independent study, internships, liberal arts/career combination, New York semester, semester at sea, student-designed major, study abroad, teacher certification program, urban semester, Washington semester. **Credit/placement by examination:** AP, CLEP, IB, institutional tests. Policy varies by college and program. **Support services:** Learning center, pre-admission summer program, reduced course load, study skills assistance, tutoring, writing center.

Majors. Architecture: Architecture, environmental design, history/criticism, landscape, urban/community planning. **Area/ethnic studies:** African-American, American, Asian, gay/lesbian, German, Near/Middle Eastern. **Biology:** General, biometrics, entomology. **Business:** Hotel/motel admin, labor relations. **Communications:** General. **Computer sciences:** General, computer science, information technology. **Conservation:** General. **Engineering:** General, agricultural, applied physics, chemical, civil, electrical, environmental, materials, mechanical, operations research. **English:** English lit. **Foreign languages:** Classics, comparative lit, French, German, Italian, linguistics, Russian, Spanish. **Health services:** International public health. **History:** General. **Human services:** Public policy. **Liberal arts:** Arts/sciences. **Math:** General, statistics. **Philosophy/religion:** Philosophy, religion. **Physical sciences:** Astronomy, atmospheric science, chemistry, physics. **Psychology:** General. **Social sciences:** Anthropology, archaeology, economics, political science, sociology. **Visual/performing arts:** Art history/conservation, dramatic, fiber arts, film/cinema/video, music, studio arts. **Work/family studies:** Family studies.

Most popular majors. Agriculture 13%, biology 15%, business/marketing 13%, computer/information sciences 6%, engineering/engineering technologies 17%, social sciences 10%.

Technology on campus. 2,650 workstations in dormitories, library, computer center, student center. Dormitories wired for high-speed internet access and linked to campus network. Commuter students can connect to campus network. Online course registration, online library, helpline, repair service, wireless network available.

Student life. Freshman orientation: Mandatory. Preregistration for classes offered. Four days and nights immediately prior to start of classes in August. Over 500 upper-level student Orientation Volunteers participate. All seven undergraduate colleges/schools provide orientations that include academic advising, information sessions, and a number of other programs. **Housing:** Guaranteed on-campus for freshmen. Coed dorms, single-sex dorms, special housing for disabled, apartments, cooperative housing, fraternity/sorority housing, gender-neutral housing, themed housing available. **Activities:** Bands, campus ministries, choral groups, dance, drama, film society, international student organizations, literary magazine, music ensembles, Model UN, musical theater, radio station, student government, student newspaper, symphony orchestra, TV station, Hillel, Campus Crusade for Christ, La Asociacion Latina, various African, Native American, Caribbean, Vietnamese, international, and lesbian/gay/bisexual groups, debate club.

Athletics. NCAA. **Intercollegiate:** Baseball M, basketball, cross-country, diving, equestrian W, fencing W, field hockey W, football (tackle) M, golf

M, gymnastics W, ice hockey, lacrosse, rowing (crew), sailing W, soccer, softball W, squash, swimming, tennis, track and field, volleyball W, wrestling M. **Intramural:** Badminton, basketball, bowling, football (non-tackle), golf, sand volleyball, soccer, softball, squash, table tennis, tennis, ultimate frisbee, volleyball, water polo. **Team name:** Big Red.

Student services. Alcohol/substance abuse counseling, chaplain/spiritual director, career counseling, services for economically disadvantaged, student employment services, financial aid counseling, health services, minority student services, on-campus daycare, personal counseling, placement for graduates, veterans' counselor, women's services. **Physically disabled:** Services for visually, speech, hearing impaired.

Contact. E-mail: admissions@cornell.edu
Phone: (607) 255-5241 Fax: (607) 255-0659
Shawn Felton, Director of Undergraduate Admissions, Cornell University, 410 Thurston Avenue, Ithaca, NY 14850

Culinary Institute of America
Hyde Park, New York
www.ciachef.edu

CB member
CB code: 3301

▶ Private 4-year culinary school
▶ Residential campus in large town
▶ 2,859 degree-seeking undergraduates: 50% women
▶ 92% of applicants admitted
▶ Application essay required
▶ 74% graduate within 6 years

General. Founded in 1946. Regionally accredited. **Degrees:** 321 bachelor's, 1,101 associate awarded. **Location:** 80 miles from New York City. **Calendar:** Semester. **Class size:** 72% < 20, 28% 20-39, less than 1% 40-49, less than 1% 50-99. **Special facilities:** 41 teaching kitchens and bakeshops, 4 restaurants, theaters.

Freshman class profile. 1,431 applied, 1,319 admitted, 587 enrolled.

Mid 50% test scores			
SAT critical reading:	450-560	Out-of-state:	69%
SAT math:	450-570	Live on campus:	88%
SAT writing:	420-530	International:	8%

Basis for selection. School achievement record, 6 months work experience in the food service industry. SAT/ACT tests not required for admissions, but if taken it is recommended that students submit their scores. **Home schooled:** Transcript of courses and grades required.

High school preparation. Required and recommended units include English 4, mathematics 3, social studies 4, science 3 and foreign language 2.

2015-2016 Annual costs. Tuition/fees: $29,250. Room/board: $9,880.

2015-2016 Financial aid. Need-based: 510 full-time freshmen applied for aid; 467 deemed to have need; 467 received aid. Average need met was 80%. Average scholarship/grant was $11,277; average loan $3,268. 53% of total undergraduate aid awarded as scholarships/grants, 47% as loans/jobs. **Non-need-based:** Awarded to 2,082 full-time undergraduates, including 487 freshmen. Scholarships awarded for academics, alumni affiliation, job skills, leadership.

Application procedures. Admission: No deadline. $50 fee, may be waived for applicants with need. Admission notification on a rolling basis. Must reply by 5/1. **Financial aid:** No deadline. FAFSA required. Applicants notified on a rolling basis starting 3/5; must reply within 2 week(s) of notification.

Academics. Curriculum devoted exclusively to culinary arts and baking and pastry arts education. Freshmen may enroll in one of 4 enrollment seasons throughout the year. All students complete 15-week paid externship program; the vast majority are paid externships, though some students opt for an externship where they are compensated another way. Two-thirds of class time involves hands-on cooking, baking, table service, and dining room operations management in kitchens, bakeshops, and 5 student-staffed public restaurants. **Special study options:** Independent study, internships. **Credit/placement by examination:** AP, CLEP, IB, institutional tests. 6 credit hours maximum toward associate degree, 36 toward bachelor's. **Support services:** Learning center, reduced course load, remedial instruction, study skills assistance, tutoring, writing center.

Majors. Business: Restaurant/food services.

Most popular majors. Business/marketing 90%, personal/culinary services 10%.

Technology on campus. 250 workstations in dormitories, library, computer center, student center. Dormitories wired for high-speed internet access and linked to campus network. Commuter students can connect to campus network. Online library, helpline, repair service, wireless network available.

Student life. Freshman orientation: Mandatory. Preregistration for classes offered. **Housing:** Guaranteed on-campus for all undergraduates. Coed dorms, special housing for disabled available. Hearing impaired student housing available. **Activities:** International student organizations, student government, student newspaper, Alliance, Bacchus Wine Society, Eta Sigma Delta Honor Society, Black Culinarian Society, Culinary Christian Fellowship, Culinary Science, Fromage Friends, Jewish Culture & Community, Korean Association of the CIA, Veterans Association & Auxiliary.

Athletics. Intercollegiate: Basketball, cross-country, soccer, tennis. **Intramural:** Basketball, football (non-tackle), soccer, softball, tennis, volleyball, weight lifting. **Team name:** Flames.

Student services. Alcohol/substance abuse counseling, chaplain/spiritual director, career counseling, student employment services, financial aid counseling, health services, personal counseling, placement for graduates, veterans' counselor. **Physically disabled:** Services for visually, speech, hearing impaired.

Contact. E-mail: admissions@culinary.edu
Phone: (845) 452-9430 Toll-free number: (800) 285-4627
Fax: (845) 451-1068
Rachel Birchwood, Director of Admissions, Culinary Institute of America, 1946 Campus Drive, Hyde Park, NY 12538-1499

Daemen College
Amherst, New York
www.daemen.edu   CB code: 2762

- Private 4-year liberal arts college
- Residential campus in small city
- 1,968 degree-seeking undergraduates: 15% part-time, 72% women, 12% African American, 2% Asian American, 7% Hispanic/Latino, 1% Multiracial, non-Hispanic, 1% international
- 739 degree-seeking graduate students
- 50% of applicants admitted
- Application essay required
- 49% graduate within 6 years; 18% enter graduate study

General. Founded in 1947. Regionally accredited. **Degrees:** 492 bachelor's awarded; master's, professional offered. **ROTC:** Army. **Location:** 9 miles from downtown Buffalo. **Calendar:** Semester, limited summer session. **Full-time faculty:** 138 total; 76% have terminal degrees, 6% minority, 60% women. **Part-time faculty:** 159 total; 14% have terminal degrees, 6% minority, 57% women. **Class size:** 61% < 20, 37% 20-39, less than 1% 40-49, 2% 50-99. **Special facilities:** Natural and health science research center, center for sustainable communities and civic engagement, center for special education and after-school programs, international center for excellence in animation.

Freshman class profile. 3,047 applied, 1,514 admitted, 384 enrolled.

Mid 50% test scores			
SAT critical reading:	450-570	Rank in top quarter:	51%
SAT math:	470-570	Rank in top tenth:	19%
SAT writing:	440-550	Return as sophomores:	78%
ACT composite:	21-26	Out-of-state:	1%
GPA 3.75 or higher:	30%	Live on campus:	61%
GPA 3.50-3.74:	42%	International:	1%
GPA 3.0-3.49:	28%	Fraternities:	1%

Basis for selection. Emphasis on rigor of high school academic program and test scores with secondary consideration given to school activities and recommendations. Work experience also considered for entry into physician assistant program. 30 credit hour transfer limit on International Baccalaureate coursework. SAT or ACT recommended. Applicants who have been out of high school for more than 2 years not required to submit SAT or ACT scores. Submission of tests are optional for all. If opting out of tests, must provide high school transcript, grades and rigor of courses, class rank, writing sample, teacher/counselor recommendation, and extracurricular activities. Essay and interview required for physician assistant program; portfolio required for art program. High school counselor completes recommendation section of the application. **Home schooled:** State high school equivalency certificate required. Applicants should provide evidence of equivalency of high school education by GED or attestation of equivalency by superintendent of schools in student's public school district of residence. This documentation needed for financial aid eligibility. **Learning Disabled:** Bring to the attention of Admission Office need for special accommodations and submit current medical evidence of disability and limitations that require accommodations. Feasibility determined by nature and cost of accommodation, availability of funding, and whether accommodation will impact fundamental nature of course or program, among other factors.

High school preparation. College-preparatory program recommended. 16 units recommended. Recommended units include English 4, mathematics 4, social studies 2, science 4 (laboratory 1) and foreign language 2. All science and allied health programs require 3 math and 3 science units. Business program requires 3 math. Foreign language programs require 3 foreign language units.

2015-2016 Annual costs. Tuition/fees: $25,995. Room/board: $12,050. Books/supplies: $1,000. Personal expenses: $800.

2014-2015 Financial aid. Need-based: 377 full-time freshmen applied for aid; 342 deemed to have need; 342 received aid. Average need met was 83%. Average scholarship/grant was $11,205; average loan $3,942. 62% of total undergraduate aid awarded as scholarships/grants, 38% as loans/jobs. **Non-need-based:** Awarded to 1,413 full-time undergraduates, including 398 freshmen. Scholarships awarded for academics, art, athletics, leadership.

Application procedures. Admission: No deadline. $25 fee, may be waived for applicants with need, free for online applicants. Admission notification on a rolling basis beginning on or about 9/1. Must reply by May 1 or within 2 week(s) if notified thereafter. **Financial aid:** Priority date 2/1; no closing date. FAFSA required. Applicants notified on a rolling basis starting 2/1; must reply within 2 week(s) of notification.

Academics. All professional programs require internships or field placements. There is a general service-learning graduation requirement for all students. **Special study options:** Accelerated study, combined bachelor's/graduate degree, cross-registration, distance learning, double major, dual enrollment of high school students, exchange student, honors, independent study, internships, liberal arts/career combination, student-designed major, study abroad, teacher certification program, Washington semester. Post-RN BS program in nursing and the 1-2-1 nursing program with RN and BS degree. Dual degree (BS/MS) in Physician Assistant Studies and Accounting/Professional Accountancy. **Credit/placement by examination:** AP, CLEP, IB, SAT, ACT, institutional tests. Veterans may receive credit for military educational experiences. Freshmen with transfer credits must take 9 credits in writing intensive courses, 3 credits in service learning, and 3 credits in quantitative literacy. **Support services:** Learning center, pre-admission summer program, remedial instruction, study skills assistance, tutoring, writing center. Peer Step Mentor program: junior, senior level students work with groups or individuals.

Majors. Biology: General, biochemistry. **Business:** Accounting, business admin. **Education:** Art, early childhood, elementary, special ed. **English:** English lit. **Foreign languages:** French, Spanish. **Health services:** General, nursing (RN). **History:** General. **Human services:** Social work. **Liberal arts:** Arts/sciences. **Math:** General. **Philosophy/religion:** Religion. **Psychology:** General. **Social sciences:** General, political science. **Visual/performing arts:** Art, digital arts, dramatic, graphic design, studio arts, studio arts management.

Most popular majors. Biology 17%, business/marketing 10%, health sciences 56%.

Technology on campus. 156 workstations in library, computer center. Dormitories wired for high-speed internet access and linked to campus network. Commuter students can connect to campus network. Online course registration, online library, helpline, repair service, wireless network available.

Student life. Freshman orientation: Mandatory, $105 fee. Preregistration for classes offered. Held over two sessions (2 days each) offered in July for incoming freshmen. One day in mid-August for new transfer students. **Housing:** Guaranteed on-campus for freshmen. Coed dorms, wellness housing available. $200 fully refundable deposit, deadline 5/1. Coed dormitory for freshmen and coed apartment-style residence halls for upper classmen; some apartments are handicapped accessible. **Activities:** Choral groups, dance, drama, international student organizations, literary magazine, student government, student newspaper, Multicultural Association, Students without Borders, Enactus, environmental club, Voices of Zion, Sister2Sister, Student Veteran Alliance, Black Student Union, Hispanos y Latinos Unidos, Chinese culture club.

Athletics. NCAA. **Intercollegiate:** Basketball, bowling W, cross-country, golf M, soccer, tennis, track and field, triathlon W, volleyball W. **Intramural:** Basketball, football (non-tackle) M, sand volleyball, soccer, softball, ultimate frisbee, volleyball. **Team name:** Wildcats.

Student services. Alcohol/substance abuse counseling, chaplain/spiritual director, career counseling, financial aid counseling, personal counseling, veterans' counselor. **Physically disabled:** Services for hearing impaired.

Contact. E-mail: admissions@daemen.edu
Phone: (716) 839-8225 Toll-free number: (800) 462-7652
Fax: (716) 839-8229
Frank Williams, Dean of Enrollment Management, Daemen College, 4380 Main Street, Amherst, NY 14226-3592

Davis College
Johnson City, New York
www.davisny.edu   CB code: 2233

- Private 4-year Bible college affiliated with the nondenominational tradition
- Residential campus in large town
- 231 degree-seeking undergraduates
- SAT or ACT (ACT writing optional), application essay required

General. Regionally accredited; also accredited by ABHE. **Degrees:** 42 bachelor's, 9 associate awarded. **Location:** 2 miles from Binghamton. **Calendar:** Semester, limited summer session. **Full-time faculty:** 6 total. **Part-time faculty:** 12 total.

Basis for selection. Pastor recommendation and high school record most important. Must give evidence of personal knowledge of the Lord Jesus Christ as Savior. Applicant lifestyle consistency with biblical principles is important. **Home schooled:** Transcript of courses and grades required. Must submit evidence of completion of high school requirements such as a high school transcript, home school transcript or GED. **Learning Disabled:** Must submit IEP, a specialized plan will be developed based on the student's needs.

2015-2016 Annual costs. Tuition/fees: $12,390. Room/board: $7,200. Books/supplies: $600. Personal expenses: $750.

Financial aid. **Non-need-based:** Scholarships awarded for academics, alumni affiliation.

Application procedures. **Admission:** No deadline. $45 fee, may be waived for applicants with need, free for online applicants. Admission notification on a rolling basis. **Financial aid:** No deadline. FAFSA, institutional form required. Applicants notified on a rolling basis.

Academics. Dual credit opportunities for high school sophomores, juniors, and seniors through on-campus and online courses. Possible for high school students to complete all freshman requirements prior to high school graduation. **Special study options:** Distance learning, dual enrollment of high school students, independent study, internships, student-designed major. **Credit/placement by examination:** AP, CLEP, IB, SAT, ACT, institutional tests. **Support services:** Learning center, reduced course load, remedial instruction, study skills assistance, tutoring, writing center.

Majors. **Theology:** Religious ed.

Technology on campus. 2 workstations in library, student center. Dormitories wired for high-speed internet access and linked to campus network. Commuter students can connect to campus network. Online library, helpline, wireless network available.

Student life. **Freshman orientation:** Mandatory. Preregistration for classes offered. Held for three days directly prior to the start of the semester. **Policies:** Chapel and church attendance required of all students. Ministry credits mandatory for graduation. Religious observance required. **Housing:** Guaranteed on-campus for all undergraduates. Single-sex dorms, apartments available. $150 partly refundable deposit. **Activities:** Campus ministries, choral groups, drama, international student organizations, music ensembles, student government, student newspaper.

Athletics. NCCAA. **Intercollegiate:** Basketball, soccer M, volleyball W. **Intramural:** Soccer, volleyball. **Team name:** Falcons.

Student services. Chaplain/spiritual director, financial aid counseling, health services, personal counseling.

Contact. E-mail: admissions@davisny.edu
Phone: (607) 729-1581 ext. 406
Toll-free number: (800) 331-4137 ext. 406 Fax: (607) 770-6886
Charles Dresser, Vice President for Enrollment Management, Davis College, 400 Riverside Drive, Johnson City, NY 13790

DeVry College of New York: Midtown Campus
New York, New York
www.devry.edu   CB code: 4276

- For-profit 4-year business and technical college
- Commuter campus in very large city
- 936 degree-seeking undergraduates
- Interview required

General. Regionally accredited. Additional locations: Manhattan, Queens. **Degrees:** 165 bachelor's, 22 associate awarded; master's offered. **Calendar:** Semester, extensive summer session. **Full-time faculty:** 27 total; 37% minority, 15% women. **Part-time faculty:** 41 total; 24% minority, 46% women.

Basis for selection. Applicants must have high school diploma or equivalent, or degree from an accredited postsecondary institution. Must demonstrate proficiency in basic college-level skills through test scores and/or institutionally administered placement examinations, and be at least 17 years of age on the first day of classes. New students may enter at beginning of any semester.

High school preparation. College-preparatory program recommended.

2015-2016 Annual costs. Tuition/fees: $17,132. Books/supplies: $1,320. Personal expenses: $2,376. **Additional information:** Annual tuition: $10,810-$21,163; fees $50-$90.

Financial aid. All financial aid based on need.

Application procedures. **Admission:** No deadline. $40 fee. Admission notification on a rolling basis. **Financial aid:** No deadline.

Academics. **Special study options:** Accelerated study, distance learning. **Credit/placement by examination:** AP, CLEP, institutional tests. **Support services:** Learning center, remedial instruction, tutoring.

Majors. **Business:** Business admin. **Computer sciences:** Networking, systems analysis.

Most popular majors. Business/marketing 48%, computer/information sciences 39%, engineering/engineering technologies 13%.

Technology on campus. 394 workstations in library, computer center. Online course registration, online library, helpline available.

Student life. **Freshman orientation:** Mandatory. Preregistration for classes offered. **Activities:** Muslim student association, martial arts club.

Student services. Career counseling, student employment services, financial aid counseling, placement for graduates, veterans' counselor. **Physically disabled:** Services for visually, hearing impaired.

Contact. Phone: (718) 472-2728 Toll-free number: (866) 338-7941
DeVry College of New York: Midtown Campus, 180 Madison Avenue, Suite 900, New York, NY 10016

Dominican College of Blauvelt
Orangeburg, New York   CB member
www.dc.edu   CB code: 2190

- Private 4-year health science and liberal arts college
- Residential campus in small town
- 1,552 degree-seeking undergraduates: 13% part-time, 66% women, 17% African American, 7% Asian American, 29% Hispanic/Latino, 3% Multiracial, non-Hispanic, 1% international
- 509 graduate students
- 71% of applicants admitted
- SAT or ACT with writing required
- 44% graduate within 6 years

General. Founded in 1952. Regionally accredited. Private non-affiliated institution, Catholic in origin and Dominican in tradition. **Degrees:** 341 bachelor's, 6 associate awarded; master's, professional offered. **Location:** 17 miles from midtown Manhattan. **Calendar:** Continuous, limited summer session. **Full-time faculty:** 73 total; 67% have terminal degrees, 15% minority, 70% women. **Part-time faculty:** 155 total; 22% have terminal degrees, 14% minority, 64% women. **Class size:** 60% < 20, 40% 20-39.

Freshman class profile. 1,959 applied, 1,400 admitted, 365 enrolled.

Mid 50% test scores		GPA 3.0-3.49:	48%
SAT critical reading:	390-480	GPA 2.0-2.99:	37%
SAT math:	390-490	Return as sophomores:	76%
SAT writing:	390-480	Out-of-state:	26%
ACT composite:	17-21	Live on campus:	70%
GPA 3.75 or higher:	8%	International:	1%
GPA 3.50-3.74:	7%		

Basis for selection. Admissions based on secondary school records and standardized test scores. Interviews and written essays required in some cases. Meeting with admissions counselor not always required for admission but always desirable. Some applicants may be asked to meet with member of admissions staff. **Learning Disabled:** Students with current professional documentation of disabilities will be provided with reasonable accommodations to assure access to and full participation in mainstream of educational process.

High school preparation. College-preparatory program recommended. 16 units required; 18 recommended. Required and recommended units include English 4, mathematics 3, social studies 3-4, science 3 (laboratory 1), foreign language 1-2 and academic electives 2.

2015-2016 Annual costs. Tuition/fees: $26,450. Room/board: $12,120. Books/supplies: $1,450. Personal expenses: $950.

2015-2016 Financial aid. Need-based: 363 full-time freshmen applied for aid; 346 deemed to have need; 335 received aid. Average need met was 70%. Average scholarship/grant was $20,124; average loan $4,122. 70% of total undergraduate aid awarded as scholarships/grants, 30% as loans/jobs. **Non-need-based:** Awarded to 119 full-time undergraduates, including 79 freshmen. Scholarships awarded for academics, athletics. **Additional information:** Individual financial aid counseling available.

Application procedures. Admission: No deadline. $35 fee, may be waived for applicants with need. Admission notification on a rolling basis. **Financial aid:** Priority date 2/15; no closing date. FAFSA required. Applicants notified on a rolling basis starting 2/1; must reply within 2 week(s) of notification.

Academics. Special study options: Accelerated study, combined bachelor's/graduate degree, cooperative education, distance learning, dual enrollment of high school students, honors, independent study, internships, study abroad, teacher certification program, weekend college. Accelerated Bachelor of Science in Nursing for college graduates. **Credit/placement by examination:** AP, CLEP, IB, SAT, ACT, institutional tests. 30 credit hours maximum toward associate degree, 60 toward bachelor's. **Support services:** Learning center, remedial instruction, study skills assistance, tutoring, writing center.

Majors. Biology: General. **Business:** Accounting, business admin, finance, human resources, international, management information systems, marketing. **Communications:** Media studies. **Computer sciences:** General. **Education:** General, biology, elementary, English, mathematics, multiple handicapped, secondary, social science, special ed. **English:** English lit. **Foreign languages:** Spanish. **Health services:** Athletic training, nursing (RN). **History:** General. **Human services:** Social work. **Liberal arts:** Humanities. **Math:** General. **Psychology:** General. **Social sciences:** General, criminology, economics.

Most popular majors. Biology 6%, business/marketing 16%, education 7%, health sciences 33%, security/protective services 7%, social sciences 11%.

Technology on campus. 140 workstations in dormitories, library, computer center. Dormitories wired for high-speed internet access and linked to campus network. Commuter students can connect to campus network. Online library, repair service, wireless network available.

Student life. Freshman orientation: Mandatory. Preregistration for classes offered. Held end of August, early September. **Policies:** Alcohol-free campus. **Housing:** Guaranteed on-campus for all undergraduates. Coed dorms, wellness housing available. $250 fully refundable deposit. Suites with multiple bedrooms, a bathroom and kitchen available for upperclass students. **Activities:** Campus ministries, choral groups, dance, drama, literary magazine, Model UN, musical theater, radio station, student government, student newspaper, Dominicans Uniting Latinos for Cultural Education, Helping Hands, Bridges International Service Project, Campus Compact for Community Service and Civic Engagement, Students Against the Abuse of Women, United Nations Committee.

Athletics. NAIA, NCAA. **Intercollegiate:** Baseball M, basketball, cross-country, golf M, lacrosse, soccer, softball W, track and field, volleyball W. **Intramural:** Basketball, football (non-tackle), handball, rowing (crew), softball, volleyball. **Team name:** Chargers.

Student services. Alcohol/substance abuse counseling, chaplain/spiritual director, career counseling, student employment services, financial aid counseling, health services, personal counseling, placement for graduates. **Physically disabled:** Services for visually, hearing impaired.

Contact. E-mail: admissions@dc.edu
Phone: (845) 848-7901 Toll-free number: (866) 432-4636
Fax: (845) 365-3150
Director of Admissions, Dominican College of Blauvelt, 470 Western Highway, Orangeburg, NY 10962-1210

Dowling College
Oakdale, New York   CB member
www.dowling.edu   CB code: 2011

- Private 4-year business, liberal arts and teachers college
- Commuter campus in large town
- 1,152 degree-seeking undergraduates: 15% part-time, 51% women, 11% African American, 1% Asian American, 9% Hispanic/Latino, 4% international
- 556 degree-seeking graduate students
- 75% of applicants admitted
- Application essay required
- 36% graduate within 6 years

General. Founded in 1955. Regionally accredited. **Degrees:** 330 bachelor's awarded; master's, doctoral offered. **ROTC:** Army, Air Force. **Location:** 50 miles from New York City. **Calendar:** Semester, extensive summer session. **Full-time faculty:** 47 total; 89% have terminal degrees, 13% minority, 36% women. **Part-time faculty:** 187 total; 25% have terminal degrees, 11% minority, 68% women. **Class size:** 82% < 20, 18% 20-39. **Special facilities:** Flight simulators; virtual airport, athletic complex, center for estuarine.

Freshman class profile. 1,864 applied, 1,394 admitted, 216 enrolled.

GPA 3.75 or higher:	1%	Live on campus:	56%
GPA 3.50-3.74:	6%	International:	4%
GPA 3.0-3.49:	49%	Fraternities:	2%
GPA 2.0-2.99:	37%	Sororities:	1%
Out-of-state:	12%		

Basis for selection. Program of study, recent achievement, academic rank, school record, standardized test scores, counselor's recommendation considered. SAT or ACT recommended. Letter of recommendation required. **Home schooled:** Transcript of courses and grades, state high school equivalency certificate required.

High school preparation. 16 units required. Required units include English 4, mathematics 3, social studies 4, science 2, foreign language 2 and academic electives 1. 4 additional units recommended.

2015-2016 Annual costs. Tuition/fees: $29,100. Room/board: $11,120. Books/supplies: $1,000. Personal expenses: $1,302.

2014-2015 Financial aid. Need-based: 157 full-time freshmen applied for aid; 156 deemed to have need; 156 received aid. Average need met was 40%. Average scholarship/grant was $11,512; average loan $3,264. 63% of total undergraduate aid awarded as scholarships/grants, 37% as loans/jobs. **Non-need-based:** Awarded to 1,085 full-time undergraduates, including 260 freshmen. Scholarships awarded for academics, alumni affiliation, athletics.

Application procedures. Admission: No deadline. $35 fee, may be waived for applicants with need. Admission notification on a rolling basis beginning on or about 10/1. **Financial aid:** Priority date 2/15; no closing date. FAFSA required. Applicants notified on a rolling basis starting 3/15; must reply within 2 week(s) of notification.

Academics. Optional winter and summer terms. **Special study options:** Accelerated study, combined bachelor's/graduate degree, distance learning, double major, ESL, honors, independent study, internships, teacher certification program, weekend college. Federal Aviation Administration cooperative program, Higher Education Opportunity Program. **Credit/placement by examination:** AP, CLEP, IB, institutional tests. 30 credit hours maximum toward bachelor's degree. **Support services:** Learning center, pre-admission summer program, reduced course load, remedial instruction, study skills assistance, tutoring, writing center. Disability accommodations.

Majors. Biology: General. **Business:** Accounting, business admin, finance, marketing. **Communications:** Communications/speech/rhetoric. **Computer sciences:** General, computer science. **Education:** General, art, biology, business, chemistry, early childhood, elementary, English, ESL, foreign languages, mathematics, middle, multi-level teacher, music, physical, science, social science, social studies, Spanish, special ed. **English:** English lit.

Foreign languages: General. **History:** General. **Liberal arts:** Arts/sciences, humanities. **Math:** General, applied. **Parks/recreation:** Sports admin. **Philosophy/religion:** Philosophy. **Physical sciences:** Chemistry. **Psychology:** General. **Social sciences:** General, anthropology, economics, political science, sociology. **Visual/performing arts:** General, graphic design, music.

Most popular majors. Business/marketing 16%, education 19%, social sciences 9%, trade and industry 10%.

Technology on campus. 289 workstations in library, computer center. Dormitories wired for high-speed internet access and linked to campus network. Commuter students can connect to campus network. Online course registration, online library, helpline, wireless network available.

Student life. Freshman orientation: Available. Preregistration for classes offered. Approximately 1 full day. **Housing:** Coed dorms available. $200 fully refundable deposit. **Activities:** Jazz band, campus ministries, choral groups, dance, drama, international student organizations, literary magazine, music ensembles, musical theater, student government, student newspaper, 41 clubs and organizations related to academics, honor societies in business, education, economics, and psychology, Circle-K, computer science, scholarship society.

Athletics. NCAA. **Intercollegiate:** Baseball M, basketball, cross-country, field hockey W, golf M, lacrosse, soccer, softball W, volleyball W. **Intramural:** Basketball, football (non-tackle), handball, soccer, softball, ultimate frisbee, volleyball. **Team name:** Golden Lions.

Student services. Adult student services, career counseling, services for economically disadvantaged, student employment services, health services, minority student services, personal counseling, veterans' counselor. **Physically disabled:** Services for visually, speech, hearing impaired.

Contact. E-mail: admissions@dowling.edu
Phone: (631) 244-3030 Toll-free number: (800) 369-5464
Fax: (631) 244-1059
Jonathan White, Assistant Vice-President for Enrollment Services, Dowling College, 150 Idle Hour Boulevard, Oakdale, NY 11769-1999

D'Youville College
Buffalo, New York
www.dyc.edu

CB member
CB code: 2197

- Private 4-year health science and liberal arts college
- Commuter campus in large city
- 1,707 degree-seeking undergraduates: 17% part-time, 74% women, 7% African American, 3% Asian American, 4% Hispanic/Latino, 1% Native American, 2% Multi-racial, non-Hispanic, 5% international
- 1,092 degree-seeking graduate students
- 70% of applicants admitted
- SAT or ACT (ACT writing optional) required
- 44% graduate within 6 years

General. Founded in 1908. Regionally accredited. **Degrees:** 389 bachelor's awarded; master's, professional, doctoral offered. **ROTC:** Army. **Location:** 1 mile from downtown. **Calendar:** Semester, extensive summer session. **Full-time faculty:** 189 total; 68% have terminal degrees, 4% minority, 68% women. **Part-time faculty:** 109 total; 20% have terminal degrees, 7% minority, 65% women. **Class size:** 63% < 20, 34% 20-39, 1% 40-49, 2% 50-99. **Special facilities:** Professional theater, gross anatomy lab, equipment for blind and visually impaired including computer system with speech synthesizer, Braille printer, Versabraille and print enhancer.

Freshman class profile. 1,216 applied, 854 admitted, 233 enrolled.

Mid 50% test scores		Return as sophomores:	78%
SAT critical reading:	450-560	Out-of-state:	8%
SAT math:	450-570	Live on campus:	48%
SAT writing:	420-540	International:	1%
ACT composite:	20-27		

Basis for selection. High school GPA, class rank, test scores, type of high school program important. Interview, essay, letters of recommendation optional. 3 recommendations required for physician's assistant program. Interview required for physician's assistant and chiropractic programs. **Home schooled:** Transcript of courses and grades, state high school equivalency certificate, letter of recommendation (nonparent) required.

High school preparation. College-preparatory program recommended. 16 units recommended. Recommended units include English 4, mathematics 3, social studies 3, science 3 and foreign language 3. Biology and chemistry

required for nursing, occupational therapy, physical therapy, dietetics, chiropractic and physician's assistant programs. 3 units of math required for accounting.

2015-2016 Annual costs. Tuition/fees: $24,370. Room/board: $11,180. Books/supplies: $1,200. Personal expenses: $800.

2015-2016 Financial aid. Need-based: 218 full-time freshmen applied for aid; 196 deemed to have need; 196 received aid. Average need met was 73%. Average scholarship/grant was $15,650; average loan $3,609. 65% of total undergraduate aid awarded as scholarships/grants, 35% as loans/jobs. **Non-need-based:** Awarded to 201 full-time undergraduates, including 65 freshmen. Scholarships awarded for academics, leadership, religious affiliation, ROTC.

Application procedures. Admission: No deadline. No application fee. Admission notification on a rolling basis. Must reply by May 1 or within 2 week(s) if notified thereafter. **Financial aid:** Priority date 3/1; no closing date. FAFSA required. Applicants notified on a rolling basis starting 4/1; must reply within 2 week(s) of notification.

Academics. Special study options: Accelerated study, combined bachelor's/graduate degree, cross-registration, distance learning, double major, dual enrollment of high school students, exchange student, independent study, internships, liberal arts/career combination, study abroad, teacher certification program, weekend college. Career discovery program for undecided students; teacher certification at the graduate level only. **Credit/placement by examination:** AP, CLEP, IB, institutional tests. 15 credit hours maximum toward bachelor's degree. Life experience may be granted credit through local Challenge Examinations. Prior to entering D'Youville, up to 15 credits may be earned via standardized examinations; additional 15 credits may be earned via standardized examinations after enrolling. **Support services:** Learning center, pre-admission summer program, reduced course load, remedial instruction, study skills assistance, tutoring, writing center.

Majors. Biology: General. **Business:** General, accounting, business admin. **English:** Creative writing, English lit, technical writing. **Health services:** Health care admin, nursing (RN), physician assistant, predental, premedicine, preop/surgical nursing, prepharmacy, preveterinary. **History:** General. **Math:** General. **Philosophy/religion:** Philosophy. **Physical sciences:** Chemistry. **Psychology:** General. **Social sciences:** Sociology.

Most popular majors. Business/marketing 7%, education 10%, health sciences 71%, interdisciplinary studies 6%.

Technology on campus. 100 workstations in dormitories, library, computer center, student center. Dormitories wired for high-speed internet access and linked to campus network. Commuter students can connect to campus network. Online library, helpline, repair service, student web hosting, wireless network available.

Student life. Freshman orientation: Mandatory, $60 fee. Preregistration for classes offered. **Housing:** Guaranteed on-campus for freshmen. Coed dorms, special housing for disabled, apartments, wellness housing available. $100 fully refundable deposit. Quiet floors for upper level students available. **Activities:** Campus ministries, choral groups, drama, international student organizations, literary magazine, Model UN, student government, student newspaper, black student union, Latin American club, Lambda Sigma, writers club, student nurses association, Asian student union.

Athletics. NCAA. **Intercollegiate:** Baseball M, basketball, cross-country, golf, rowing (crew) W, soccer, softball W, tennis, volleyball. **Intramural:** Basketball, cheerleading W, table tennis, volleyball. **Team name:** Spartans.

Student services. Adult student services, alcohol/substance abuse counseling, chaplain/spiritual director, career counseling, services for economically disadvantaged, student employment services, financial aid counseling, health services, minority student services, personal counseling, placement for graduates, veterans' counselor. **Physically disabled:** Services for visually, speech, hearing impaired.

Contact. E-mail: admissions@dyc.edu
Phone: (716) 829-7600 Toll-free number: (800) 777-3921
Fax: (716) 829-7900
Steve Smith, Director of Admissions, D'Youville College, 320 Porter Avenue, Buffalo, NY 14201-1084

Eastman School of Music of the University of Rochester
Rochester, New York
www.esm.rochester.edu

CB code: 2224

- Private 4-year music and performing arts college
- Residential campus in small city

- 565 degree-seeking undergraduates: 48% women
- 371 degree-seeking graduate students
- 32% of applicants admitted
- Application essay, interview required

General. Founded in 1921. Regionally accredited. **Degrees:** 126 bachelor's awarded; master's, professional, doctoral offered. **ROTC:** Naval. **Location:** 357 miles from New York City, 80 miles from Niagara Falls. **Calendar:** Semester, limited summer session. **Full-time faculty:** 101 total; 27% women. **Part-time faculty:** 53 total; 47% women. **Class size:** 92% < 20, 4% 20-39, 2% 40-49, 2% 50-99, less than 1% >100. **Special facilities:** Five performance halls, three recital halls, computers for synthesis and analysis of music, complete analog and digital recording studios, music library, over 135 practice rooms.

Freshman class profile. 932 applied, 295 admitted, 131 enrolled.

Out-of-state:	75%	Fraternities:	7%
Live on campus:	99%	Sororities:	11%

Basis for selection. Demonstrated ability in major area (instrument or voice) most important, in addition to academic record, test scores, interview, recommendations. Composition majors submit portfolio of scores. Most instruments/majors require a pre-screening recording, which must be uploaded within application. Audition required for all; research/term paper required for theory majors; portfolio required for composition majors. Interview recommended for all, required for composition, music education, music theory majors. **Home schooled:** Statement describing home school structure and mission, transcript of courses and grades, letter of recommendation (nonparent) required. SAT or ACT scores, along with detailed documentation of texts, coursework, experiential learning, and transcripts of any college coursework. Taking college credit classes also encouraged. **Learning Disabled:** To facilitate a smooth audition day experience, Admissions Office requests advance notice of any special considerations.

High school preparation. College-preparatory program recommended. 16 units required. Required units include English 4.

2015-2016 Annual costs. Tuition/fees: $49,108. Room/board: $14,294. Books/supplies: $700. Personal expenses: $980.

Financial aid. Non-need-based: Scholarships awarded for academics, alumni affiliation, job skills, leadership, minority status, music/drama, state residency.

Application procedures. Admission: Priority date 11/1; deadline 12/1 (receipt date). $125 fee, may be waived for applicants with need. Application must be submitted online. Admission notification by 4/15. Admission notification on a rolling basis beginning on or about 3/15. Must reply by May 1 or within 2 week(s) if notified thereafter. Admission review occurs following candidate's audition/interview. Regional auditions in United States typically occur in January, auditions at Eastman School of Music take place in February; typically, admission review and decisions follow final audition date in Rochester. Separate (additional) application required for dual degree program with University of Rochester's College of Arts, Sciences and Engineering. **Financial aid:** Closing date 2/28. FAFSA, institutional form required. CSS Profile required for International students only. Applicants notified by 4/15; must reply by 5/1 or within 2 week(s) of notification.

Academics. Certificate programs in arts leadership, college and/or community music teaching, world music available to matriculated students; diploma programs in orchestral studies, ethnomusicology and sacred music also available. **Special study options:** Double major, dual enrollment of high school students, ESL, independent study, internships, student-designed major, study abroad, teacher certification program. **Credit/placement by examination:** AP, CLEP, institutional tests. **Support services:** Pre-admission summer program, remedial instruction, study skills assistance, tutoring, writing center.

Majors. Education: Music. **Visual/performing arts:** Jazz, music, music history, music performance, music theory/composition, piano/keyboard, voice/opera.

Most popular majors. Education 8%, visual/performing arts 43%.

Technology on campus. 50 workstations in dormitories, library, computer center, student center. Dormitories wired for high-speed internet access and linked to campus network. Commuter students can connect to campus network. Online course registration, online library, helpline, wireless network available.

Student life. Freshman orientation: Mandatory, $266 fee. Preregistration for classes offered. Includes mandatory placement testing. **Policies:** Undergraduates required to live in college housing for first 3 years unless released by Assistant Dean of Residential Life. **Housing:** Guaranteed on-campus for freshmen. Coed dorms, single-sex dorms, special housing for disabled, fraternity/sorority housing, wellness housing available. **Activities:** Bands,

campus ministries, choral groups, dance, drama, international student organizations, literary magazine, music ensembles, opera, radio station, student government, student newspaper, symphony orchestra, International students association, Catholic Newman community, Intervarsity Christian fellowship, Hillel, Mu Phi Epsilon, Sigma Alpha Iota, student association, graduate student association, musical organizations.

Student services. Adult student services, alcohol/substance abuse counseling, chaplain/spiritual director, career counseling, student employment services, financial aid counseling, health services, personal counseling, placement for graduates, veterans' counselor, women's services. **Physically disabled:** Services for visually, speech impaired.

Contact. E-mail: admissions@esm.rochester.edu
Phone: (585) 274-1060 Toll-free number: (800) 388-9695
Fax: (585) 232-8601
Matthew Ardizzone, Director of Admissions, Eastman School of Music of the University of Rochester, 26 Gibbs Street, Rochester, NY 14604-2599

Elmira College
Elmira, New York
www.elmira.edu

CB member
CB code: 2226

- Private 4-year liberal arts and teachers college
- Residential campus in large town
- 1,252 degree-seeking undergraduates: 10% part-time, 70% women, 4% African American, 2% Asian American, 3% Hispanic/Latino, 2% Multi-racial, non-Hispanic, 5% international
- 79 degree-seeking graduate students
- 76% of applicants admitted
- Application essay required
- 55% graduate within 6 years

General. Founded in 1855. Regionally accredited. **Degrees:** 286 bachelor's, 2 associate awarded; master's offered. **ROTC:** Army, Air Force. **Location:** 106 miles from Rochester, 90 miles from Syracuse, 50 miles from Binghamton. **Calendar:** 4-4-1. Limited summer session. **Full-time faculty:** 67 total; 91% have terminal degrees, 52% women. **Part-time faculty:** 103 total; 37% have terminal degrees, 61% women. **Class size:** 74% < 20, 24% 20-39, less than 1% 40-49, 1% 50-99. **Special facilities:** Center for Mark Twain studies, Mark Twain archives and his summer home.

Freshman class profile. 2,387 applied, 1,818 admitted, 258 enrolled.

Mid 50% test scores			
SAT critical reading:	450-560	Rank in top quarter:	61%
SAT math:	460-570	Rank in top tenth:	26%
ACT composite:	22-27	End year in good standing:	97%
GPA 3.75 or higher:	20%	Return as sophomores:	79%
GPA 3.50-3.74:	18%	Out-of-state:	45%
GPA 3.0-3.49:	31%	Live on campus:	96%
GPA 2.0-2.99:	31%	International:	6%

Basis for selection. GED not accepted. Academic record, extracurricular activities, and performance on standardized tests (SAT or ACT) that demonstrate his or her potential for succeeding. SAT or ACT recommended. Test optional policy. **Home schooled:** Statement describing home school structure and mission, transcript of courses and grades, interview, letter of recommendation (nonparent) required.

High school preparation. College-preparatory program recommended. 16 units required. Required and recommended units include English 4, mathematics 3, social studies 3, history 1, science 3 (laboratory 2), foreign language 2 and academic electives 2. 1 additional unit of foreign language is recommended for students pursuing majors in foreign language, education (teaching a language), or international business.

2015-2016 Annual costs. Tuition/fees: $39,950. Room/board: $12,000. Books/supplies: $600. Personal expenses: $550.

2015-2016 Financial aid. Need-based: 236 full-time freshmen applied for aid; 220 deemed to have need; 220 received aid. Average need met was 76%. Average scholarship/grant was $27,992; average loan $3,481. 78% of total undergraduate aid awarded as scholarships/grants, 22% as loans/jobs. **Non-need-based:** Awarded to 333 full-time undergraduates, including 61 freshmen. Scholarships awarded for academics, leadership, ROTC, state residency. **Additional information:** Sibling Scholarship program provides 50% discount on second immediate family member's room and board, regardless of need.

Application procedures. Admission: Priority date 2/1; no deadline., may be waived for applicants with need. No application fee. Admission notification on a rolling basis beginning on or about 10/15. Must reply by

Four-Year Colleges

May 1 or within 2 week(s) if notified thereafter. Students can defer enrollment for one year. **Financial aid:** Priority date 2/1; no closing date. FAFSA required. Applicants notified on a rolling basis starting 2/1; must reply by 5/1 or within 2 week(s) of notification.

Academics. Mandatory writing program for all freshmen. Internship/community service requirement, often done during 6 week spring term, required of all students. International study emphasized. **Special study options:** Accelerated study, combined bachelor's/graduate degree, double major, ESL, honors, independent study, internships, liberal arts/career combination, student-designed major, study abroad, teacher certification program. **Credit/placement by examination:** AP, CLEP, IB, SAT, ACT, institutional tests. 15 credit hours maximum toward associate degree, 30 toward bachelor's. **Support services:** Learning center, reduced course load, study skills assistance, tutoring, writing center.

Majors. Area/ethnic studies: American. **Biology:** General, biochemistry. **Business:** Accounting, business admin, finance, international, managerial economics, marketing. **Conservation:** Environmental studies. **Education:** Art, biology, chemistry, early childhood special, elementary, English, foreign languages, French, history, mathematics, middle, multi-level teacher, science, secondary, social studies, Spanish, speech, speech impaired. **English:** British lit, English lit. **Foreign languages:** General. **Health services:** Clinical lab science, nursing (RN), predental, premedicine, preveterinary, speech pathology. **History:** General. **Liberal arts:** Arts/sciences. **Math:** General. **Philosophy/religion:** General. **Physical sciences:** Chemistry. **Protective services:** Criminal justice. **Psychology:** General. **Social sciences:** General, economics, international relations, political science, sociology/anthropology. **Visual/performing arts:** Art, dramatic, music.

Most popular majors. Biology 6%, business/marketing 17%, education 16%, health sciences 23%, psychology 6%, social sciences 8%.

Technology on campus. 173 workstations in library, computer center. Dormitories wired for high-speed internet access and linked to campus network. Commuter students can connect to campus network. Online course registration, online library, helpline, wireless network available.

Student life. Freshman orientation: Mandatory. Preregistration for classes offered. Two-day summer registration program for taking placement exams, meeting an adviser, and registering for courses. There are separate activities for parents/guardians. Typically held in July. Two-day orientation program preceding the start of classes in the fall. **Housing:** Guaranteed on-campus for all undergraduates. Coed dorms, single-sex dorms, special housing for disabled, apartments, wellness housing available. Quiet floors available. All undergraduates required to live in college housing unless over the age of 25 or living with family. **Activities:** Concert band, campus ministries, choral groups, dance, drama, international student organizations, literary magazine, music ensembles, Model UN, musical theater, radio station, student government, student newspaper, Christian Fellowship, Hillel, Amnesty International, Red Cross club, College Democrats, College Republicans, Circle-K, Voices United of Elmira for Diversity, PRIDE, Colleges Against Cancer.

Athletics. NCAA. **Intercollegiate:** Baseball M, basketball, cheerleading W, cross-country, equestrian, field hockey W, golf, ice hockey, lacrosse, soccer, softball W, tennis, volleyball. **Intramural:** Badminton, basketball, bowling, equestrian, football (non-tackle), handball, ice hockey, racquetball, skiing, soccer, softball, squash, swimming, ultimate frisbee, volleyball. **Team name:** Soaring Eagles.

Student services. Adult student services, alcohol/substance abuse counseling, chaplain/spiritual director, career counseling, student employment services, financial aid counseling, health services, personal counseling, placement for graduates, veterans' counselor, women's services. **Physically disabled:** Services for visually, speech, hearing impaired.

Contact. E-mail: admissions@elmira.edu
Phone: (607) 735-1724 Toll-free number: (800) 935-6472
Fax: (607) 735-1718
Brett Moore, Dean of Admissions, Elmira College, One Park Place, Elmira, NY 14901

Eugene Lang College The New School for Liberal Arts
New York, New York
www.newschool.edu   CB code: 2521

- Private 4-year liberal arts college
- Commuter campus in very large city
- 1,506 degree-seeking undergraduates: 5% part-time, 73% women, 8% African American, 5% Asian American, 17% Hispanic/Latino, 6% Multiracial, non-Hispanic, 8% international
- 71% of applicants admitted

- Application essay required
- 53% graduate within 6 years

General. Founded in 1978. Regionally accredited. **Degrees:** 311 bachelor's awarded. **Calendar:** Semester, limited summer session. **Full-time faculty:** 71 total; 82% have terminal degrees, 22% minority, 49% women. **Part-time faculty:** 129 total; less than 1% have terminal degrees, 21% minority, 54% women. **Class size:** 88% < 20, 10% 20-39, 2% 40-49. **Special facilities:** Photography labs, screening rooms, art galleries, art and sound space, environment and design center, center for art and politics.

Freshman class profile. 3,449 applied, 2,436 admitted, 412 enrolled.

Mid 50% test scores			
SAT critical reading:	500-620	GPA 3.0-3.49:	45%
SAT math:	500-630	GPA 2.0-2.99:	11%
SAT writing:	500-620	Return as sophomores:	74%
ACT composite:	22-27	Out-of-state:	76%
GPA 3.75 or higher:	20%	Live on campus:	70%
GPA 3.50-3.74:	24%	International:	5%

Basis for selection. Success in college preparatory studies most important supplemented by writing ability, intellectual curiosity, interview. Extracurricular/community activities, evidence of special talents, recommendations important. Applicants may opt not to submit SAT/ACT scores. Additional requirements for BA/BFA with Parsons or The New School for Jazz.

High school preparation. College-preparatory program recommended. Required and recommended units include English 4, mathematics 4, social studies 4, history 4, science 4 and foreign language 4.

2015-2016 Annual costs. Tuition/fees: $43,006. Room/board: $17,235. Books/supplies: $920. Personal expenses: $1,550.

2014-2015 Financial aid. Need-based: 259 full-time freshmen applied for aid; 235 deemed to have need; 235 received aid. Average need met was 71%. Average scholarship/grant was $19,886; average loan $5,605. 74% of total undergraduate aid awarded as scholarships/grants, 26% as loans/jobs. **Non-need-based:** Awarded to 1,019 full-time undergraduates, including 281 freshmen. Scholarships awarded for academics, art, leadership, minority status, music/drama, state residency.

Application procedures. Admission: Priority date 1/15; deadline 8/1. $60 fee, may be waived for applicants with need. Admission notification on a rolling basis beginning on or about 4/1. Must reply by May 1 or within 2 week(s) if notified thereafter. **Financial aid:** Closing date 3/1. FAFSA required. Applicants notified on a rolling basis starting 4/1; must reply within 4 week(s) of notification.

Academics. Students map out individual program of study within 5 broad areas of concentration. Seminars rather than lecture classes. Students can select courses within The New School and Cooper Union. **Special study options:** Accelerated study, cross-registration, distance learning, double major, dual enrollment of high school students, ESL, exchange student, independent study, internships, liberal arts/career combination, student-designed major, study abroad, urban semester. Five year combined BA/BFA Studio Program, Global Citizen Year (First Year Abroad Program). **Credit/placement by examination:** AP, CLEP, IB. **Support services:** Tutoring, writing center.

Majors. Conservation: Environmental studies. **Education:** General, foundations. **English:** General lit. **Foreign languages:** General, comparative lit. **History:** General. **Liberal arts:** Arts/sciences. **Philosophy/religion:** Judaic, philosophy, religion. **Psychology:** General. **Social sciences:** General, economics, international relations, political science, urban studies. **Visual/performing arts:** General, studio arts.

Most popular majors. Architecture 25%, communications/journalism 6%, history 6%, liberal arts 19%, philosophy/religious studies 6%, psychology 19%, social sciences 19%.

Technology on campus. Dormitories wired for high-speed internet access and linked to campus network. Commuter students can connect to campus network. Online course registration, online library, helpline, student web hosting, wireless network available.

Student life. Freshman orientation: Mandatory. Preregistration for classes offered. Held one week before classes begin. **Housing:** Guaranteed on-campus for all undergraduates. Coed dorms, special housing for disabled, apartments, themed housing, wellness housing available. $500 nonrefundable deposit, deadline 7/1. **Activities:** Bands, choral groups, drama, film society, international student organizations, literary magazine, musical theater, opera, student government, student newspaper, symphony orchestra, TV station, Sustainable Design Review, New School Styling Club, Roots & Shoots, Radical student union, Global Health student organization, international club, PHOTOfeast, the Theatre Collective, Jewish student union, New School Remnant Christian Fellowship.

Athletics. Intercollegiate: Basketball M, cross-country. **Intramural:** Basketball, soccer, volleyball.

Student services. Career counseling, student employment services, financial aid counseling, health services, minority student services, personal counseling.

Contact. E-mail: admission@newschool.edu
Phone: (212) 229-5150 Toll-free number: (800) 292-3040
Karen Williams, Director of Admissions, Eugene Lang College The New School for Liberal Arts, 79 Fifth Avenue, New York, NY 10003

Excelsior College
Albany, New York
www.excelsior.edu   **CB code: 0759**

- Private 4-year virtual liberal arts college
- Commuter campus in small city
- 36,927 degree-seeking undergraduates: 100% part-time, 55% women, 22% African American, 3% Asian American, 10% Hispanic/Latino, 1% Native American, 1% Native Hawaiian/Pacific islander, 3% Multi-racial, non-Hispanic, 1% international
- 3,176 degree-seeking graduate students

General. Founded in 1970. Regionally accredited. The average age of a student at Excelsior College is 37. Nearly 40 percent of students are active duty or veteran status. **Degrees:** 2,746 bachelor's, 1,730 associate awarded; master's offered. **Location:** 1 mile from downtown. **Calendar:** Trimester, extensive summer session. **Part-time faculty:** 1,371 total; 37% have terminal degrees, 12% minority, 61% women. **Class size:** 71% < 20, 29% 20-39. **Special facilities:** Online writing lab, student success center.

Basis for selection. Open admission, but selective for some programs. Admission to associate degree nursing program is limited to students with experience in clinically oriented health care disciplines. Admission to bachelor's degree and RN-to-MS in nursing degree programs require candidates to have current RN license. **Home schooled:** State high school equivalency certificate required.

2016-2017 Annual costs. Undergraduate per credit hour charge: $490. For students committed to taking at least 12 Excelsior College credits prior to graduation the enrollment fee is waived. An enrollment fee of up to $1,065 may be charged for evaluation of credits earned elsewhere. Students enrolled via a partnership (academic, corporate, military) qualify for different fees, tuition, credit requirements and rules based on the individual partnership agreement. Students taking 12 credits annually are not subject to $495 annual student services fee.

2014-2015 Financial aid. All financial aid based on need. 32% of total undergraduate aid awarded as scholarships/grants, 68% as loans/jobs. **Additional information:** Excelsior College is Title IV eligible for its course-based degree programs; approved for all veterans' education benefit programs.

Application procedures. Admission: No deadline. $100 fee, may be waived for applicants with need. Admission notification on a rolling basis beginning on or about 1/1. **Financial aid:** No deadline. Applicants notified on a rolling basis; must reply within 2 week(s) of notification.

Academics. A portfolio assessment option is available via CAEL in subject areas where proficiency or performance examinations are unavailable. An online library is provided in collaboration with Sheridan Libraries at Johns Hopkins University. **Special study options:** Combined bachelor's/graduate degree, distance learning, dual enrollment of high school students, independent study, student-designed major, study abroad. **Credit/placement by examination:** AP, CLEP, IB. Some degrees may be earned entirely by examination. **Support services:** Study skills assistance, tutoring, writing center. Mentorship program, virtual library, coaching on non-academic skills, peer support groups, career center. Student Success Center offers newly-enrolled and at-risk students coaching on time management, study skills, learning, resources, etc.

Majors. Biology: General. **Business:** General, accounting, business admin. **Computer sciences:** Information systems. **Health services:** Nursing (RN). **History:** General. **Liberal arts:** Arts/sciences, humanities. **Physical sciences:** Chemistry, geology, optics, physics. **Protective services:** Computer forensics, law enforcement admin. **Psychology:** General. **Social sciences:** General, sociology.

Most popular majors. Business/marketing 12%, engineering/engineering technologies 8%, health sciences 20%, liberal arts 49%.

Technology on campus. PC or laptop required. Commuter students can connect to campus network. Online course registration, online library, helpline, wireless network available.

Student life. Freshman orientation: Available. Preregistration for classes offered. Orientation is conducted online for incoming students at all levels. **Activities:** Literary magazine.

Student services. Adult student services, career counseling, financial aid counseling, veterans' counselor.

Contact. E-mail: admissions@excelsior.edu
Phone: (518) 464-8500 ext. 21 Toll-free number: (888) 647-2388 ext. 21
Fax: (518) 464-8833
Shannon Easton, Director of Admissions, Excelsior College, 7 Columbia Circle, Albany, NY 12203

Fashion Institute of Technology
New York, New York
www.fitnyc.edu   **CB member**   **CB code: 2257**

- Public 4-year visual arts and business college
- Commuter campus in very large city
- 8,229 degree-seeking undergraduates: 11% part-time, 86% women, 9% African American, 10% Asian American, 17% Hispanic/Latino, 4% Multi-racial, non-Hispanic, 14% international
- 179 degree-seeking graduate students
- 41% of applicants admitted
- Application essay required

General. Founded in 1944. Regionally accredited. **Degrees:** 1,528 bachelor's, 2,113 associate awarded; master's offered. **Location:** Located in Manhattan. **Calendar:** Semester, extensive summer session. **Full-time faculty:** 232 total; 10% minority, 53% women. **Part-time faculty:** 738 total; 13% minority, 51% women. **Class size:** 43% < 20, 57% 20-39. **Special facilities:** Museum, toy design workshop, design/research lighting lab, stoll knitting lab, computer-aided design and communication center; cutting/sewing, textile testing, dyeing, and printing labs.

Freshman class profile. 4,753 applied, 1,948 admitted, 1,265 enrolled.

GPA 3.75 or higher:	31%	Return as sophomores:	90%
GPA 3.50-3.74:	23%	Out-of-state:	40%
GPA 3.0-3.49:	34%	Live on campus:	65%
GPA 2.0-2.99:	11%	International:	11%

Basis for selection. Academic history, portfolio, essay, community service, work experience, awards and honors considered. SAT and/or ACT scores are required for placement. Portfolio required for applicants to the School of Art and Design. **Home schooled:** Statement describing home school structure and mission, transcript of courses and grades, state high school equivalency certificate required.

High school preparation. College-preparatory program recommended.

2015-2016 Annual costs. Tuition/fees: $5,230; $14,230 out-of-state. Room/board: $13,291. Books/supplies: $1,750. Personal expenses: $1,500.

2014-2015 Financial aid. All financial aid based on need. 59% of total undergraduate aid awarded as scholarships/grants, 41% as loans/jobs.

Application procedures. Admission: Closing date 1/1 (receipt date). $50 fee, may be waived for applicants with need. Application must be submitted online. Admission notification by 4/1. Must reply by May 1 or within 3 week(s) if notified thereafter. The SUNY application must be filed by January 1 to receive priority consideration for the Fall semester. **Financial aid:** Priority date 2/15; no closing date. FAFSA required. Applicants notified on a rolling basis starting 4/15; must reply within 2 week(s) of notification.

Academics. Special study options: Distance learning, ESL, exchange student, honors, independent study, internships, liberal arts/career combination, study abroad. One-year AAS programs, evening/weekend degree programs. **Credit/placement by examination:** AP, CLEP, IB, SAT, ACT, institutional tests. 30 credit hours maximum toward associate degree, 30 toward bachelor's. **Support services:** Learning center, remedial instruction, study skills assistance, tutoring, writing center. The Educational Opportunity Program offers certain students supplemental academic, financial and personal student support services intended to encourage persistence and completion of studies.

Honors college/program. The Presidential Scholars Program accepts applications though February 1. Students accepted to the program enroll in honors courses, participate in the colloquia series and specially designed extracurricular activities.

Majors. Business: Fashion, international marketing, market research, special products marketing. **Communications:** Advertising. **Communications technology:** Animation/special effects. **Visual/performing arts:** Art history/conservation, cinematography, commercial photography, commercial/advertising art, fashion design, graphic design, illustration, industrial design, interior design, studio arts, studio arts management. **Work/family studies:** Clothing/textiles, textile manufacture.

Most popular majors. Business/marketing 39%, communications/journalism 16%, visual/performing arts 40%.

Technology on campus. 1,700 workstations in dormitories, library, computer center, student center. Dormitories wired for high-speed internet access and linked to campus network. Commuter students can connect to campus network. Online course registration, online library, helpline, wireless network available.

Student life. Freshman orientation: Mandatory. Preregistration for classes offered. Fall, spring, and transfer orientations are held the week prior to the beginning of school. Program includes academic advisement, campus tours, NYC tours, volunteer opportunities, and campus life information sessions. **Policies:** All clubs required to do community service. Student Government is part of the SUNY Student Assembly. Alcohol free campus, academic honor code, student code of conduct. Freshmen not permitted cars on campus. **Housing:** Coed dorms, single-sex dorms, special housing for disabled, apartments, wellness housing available. $300 nonrefundable deposit. **Activities:** Campus ministries, choral groups, dance, drama, international student organizations, literary magazine, musical theater, radio station, student government, student newspaper, TV station, approximately 70 clubs on campus, including black student union, Asian student network, fashion show club, gospel choir, Korean student organization, Latin American student association, Phi Theta Kappa.

Athletics. NJCAA. **Intercollegiate:** Cross-country, soccer W, swimming, table tennis, tennis, track and field, volleyball W. **Team name:** Tigers.

Student services. Alcohol/substance abuse counseling, career counseling, services for economically disadvantaged, student employment services, financial aid counseling, health services, personal counseling, placement for graduates, veterans' counselor. **Physically disabled:** Services for visually, speech, hearing impaired.

Contact. E-mail: fitinfo@fitnyc.edu
Phone: (212) 217-3760 Fax: (212) 217-3761
Magda Francois, Director of Admissions and Strategic Recruitment, Fashion Institute of Technology, 227 West 27th Street, New York, NY 10001-5992

Five Towns College
Dix Hills, New York
www.ftc.edu
CB code: 3142

- For-profit 4-year business and performing arts college
- Commuter campus in large town
- 630 degree-seeking undergraduates: 3% part-time, 32% women, 20% African American, 4% Asian American, 15% Hispanic/Latino, 1% Native American, 4% Multi-racial, non-Hispanic
- 24 degree-seeking graduate students
- 62% of applicants admitted
- Application essay required

General. Founded in 1972. Regionally accredited. **Degrees:** 125 bachelor's, 16 associate awarded; master's, doctoral offered. **Location:** 48 miles from New York City. **Calendar:** Semester, limited summer session. **Full-time faculty:** 22 total; 46% have terminal degrees, 14% minority, 36% women. **Part-time faculty:** 63 total; 22% have terminal degrees, 8% minority, 35% women. **Class size:** 79% < 20, 21% 20-39. **Special facilities:** 72-channel recording studios, Korg MIDI technology studio, AVID system, professional film/video arts studio, theater technology labs.

Freshman class profile. 382 applied, 238 admitted, 119 enrolled.

Mid 50% test scores		GPA 3.50-3.74:	2%
SAT critical reading:	390-490	GPA 3.0-3.49:	19%
SAT math:	380-490	GPA 2.0-2.99:	62%
SAT writing:	380-500	Return as sophomores:	74%
ACT composite:	16-24	Out-of-state:	8%
GPA 3.75 or higher:	2%	Live on campus:	40%

Basis for selection. Minimum 2.5 GPA required. Applicants for music and theater programs must pass audition and demonstrate competency in their field of study. SAT or ACT recommended. SAT/ACT recommended but not required for transfer students. Audition required for music, theater,

---

musical theater programs. Entrance exams and interviews required for some. **Home schooled:** Statement describing home school structure and mission, transcript of courses and grades, state high school equivalency certificate, interview, letter of recommendation (nonparent) required. **Learning Disabled:** Provide recent copy of individualized educational program and psychological report or 504 Plan.

High school preparation. 18 units required. Required units include English 4, mathematics 3, social studies 4, science 3 (laboratory 2), foreign language 2 and academic electives 4.

2015-2016 Annual costs. Tuition/fees: $21,870. Room/board: $12,270. Books/supplies: $1,400. Personal expenses: $3,200.

2014-2015 Financial aid. Need-based: 104 full-time freshmen applied for aid; 104 deemed to have need; 97 received aid. Average need met was 68%. Average scholarship/grant was $4,450; average loan $3,344. 57% of total undergraduate aid awarded as scholarships/grants, 43% as loans/jobs. **Non-need-based:** Awarded to 480 full-time undergraduates, including 108 freshmen. Scholarships awarded for academics, art, leadership, music/drama.

Application procedures. Admission: No deadline. $35 fee, may be waived for applicants with need, free for online applicants. Admission notification on a rolling basis beginning on or about 1/31. **Financial aid:** Priority date 4/30; no closing date. FAFSA required. Applicants notified on a rolling basis starting 3/1; must reply within 4 week(s) of notification.

Academics. Number of credit hours required for students in major field of study varies by program. **Special study options:** Distance learning, independent study, internships, liberal arts/career combination, teacher certification program. **Credit/placement by examination:** AP, CLEP, institutional tests. **Support services:** Learning center, pre-admission summer program, reduced course load, tutoring, writing center.

Majors. Business: Business admin. **Communications:** Broadcast journalism, journalism, media studies, radio/TV. **Communications technology:** Recording arts. **Education:** Elementary, music. **Visual/performing arts:** Acting, cinematography, dramatic, film/cinema/video, jazz, music, music performance, music theory/composition, piano/keyboard, stringed instruments, voice/opera.

Most popular majors. Business/marketing 45%, education 8%, visual/performing arts 43%.

Technology on campus. 84 workstations in library, computer center, student center. Dormitories wired for high-speed internet access and linked to campus network. Commuter students can connect to campus network. Helpline, wireless network available.

Student life. Freshman orientation: Mandatory. Preregistration for classes offered. **Policies:** Freshmen not permitted cars on campus. **Housing:** Coed dorms available. $250 fully refundable deposit. **Activities:** Bands, choral groups, dance, drama, film society, music ensembles, musical theater, radio station, student government, student newspaper.

Student services. Alcohol/substance abuse counseling, career counseling, services for economically disadvantaged, student employment services, financial aid counseling, personal counseling.

Contact. E-mail: admissions@ftc.edu
Phone: (631) 656-2110 Fax: (631) 656-2172
Ronnie MacDonald, Director of Admissions, Five Towns College, 305 North Service Road, Dix Hills, NY 11746-6055

Fordham University
Bronx, New York
www.fordham.edu
CB member
CB code: 2259

- Private 4-year university affiliated with the Roman Catholic Church
- Residential campus in very large city
- 8,701 degree-seeking undergraduates: 5% part-time, 56% women, 5% African American, 10% Asian American, 14% Hispanic/Latino, 4% Multi-racial, non-Hispanic, 7% international
- 6,234 degree-seeking graduate students
- 48% of applicants admitted
- SAT or ACT with writing, application essay required
- 81% graduate within 6 years; 18% enter graduate study

General. Founded in 1841. Regionally accredited. Fordham University has two primary undergraduate campuses: Rose Hill in the Bronx, and Lincoln Center in Manhattan. **Degrees:** 1,996 bachelor's awarded; master's, professional, doctoral offered. **ROTC:** Army, Naval, Air Force. **Location:** Rose

Hill campus is in the Bronx and the Lincoln Center campus is in Manhattan. **Calendar:** Semester, extensive summer session. **Full-time faculty:** 737 total; 92% have terminal degrees, 15% minority, 43% women. **Part-time faculty:** 861 total; 43% have terminal degrees, 20% minority, 50% women. **Class size:** 48% < 20, 49% 20-39, 1% 40-49, 1% 50-99, less than 1% >100. **Special facilities:** Louis Calder Center (biological field station); Museum of Greek, Roman and Etruscan Art.

Freshman class profile. 42,811 applied, 20,366 admitted, 2,211 enrolled.

Mid 50% test scores		GPA 2.0-2.99:	4%
SAT critical reading:	580-670	Rank in top quarter:	79%
SAT math:	590-680	Rank in top tenth:	46%
SAT writing:	590-680	Return as sophomores:	91%
ACT composite:	27-31	Out-of-state:	61%
GPA 3.75 or higher:	44%	Live on campus:	77%
GPA 3.50-3.74:	26%	International:	8%
GPA 3.0-3.49:	26%		

Basis for selection. School achievement record most important, followed by test scores, class rank, extracurricular activities, recommendations and essay. Personal characteristics, special talents and relationships to Fordham University also considered. Audition required for dance and theater programs. **Home schooled:** Statement describing home school structure and mission, transcript of courses and grades, letter of recommendation (nonparent) required.

High school preparation. College-preparatory program required. 15 units required; 20 recommended. Required and recommended units include English 4, mathematics 3-4, social studies 3-4, science 3-4 and foreign language 2-4.

2015-2016 Annual costs. Tuition/fees: $46,932. Room/board: $16,350. Books/supplies: $1,012. Personal expenses: $1,814.

2014-2015 Financial aid. Need-based: 1,959 full-time freshmen applied for aid; 1,465 deemed to have need; 1,465 received aid. Average need met was 82%. Average scholarship/grant was $25,614; average loan $5,337. 77% of total undergraduate aid awarded as scholarships/grants, 23% as loans/jobs. **Non-need-based:** Awarded to 2,643 full-time undergraduates, including 929 freshmen. Scholarships awarded for academics, athletics, ROTC.

Application procedures. Admission: Priority date 11/1; deadline 1/1 (postmark date). $70 fee, may be waived for applicants with need. Admission notification by 4/1. Must reply by 5/1. **Financial aid:** Closing date 2/10. FAFSA, CSS PROFILE required. Applicants notified by 3/31; Applicants notified on a rolling basis starting 3/31; must reply by 5/1 or within 2 week(s) of notification.

Academics. Special study options: Accelerated study, combined bachelor's/graduate degree, cross-registration, distance learning, double major, ESL, exchange student, honors, independent study, internships, liberal arts/career combination, student-designed major, study abroad, teacher certification program. **Credit/placement by examination:** AP, CLEP, IB, SAT, ACT, institutional tests. Credit for CLEP examination and prior work/life experience only offered for School of Continuing and Professional Studies. **Support services:** Pre-admission summer program, tutoring, writing center.

Majors. Area/ethnic studies: African, African-American, American, Latin American, Near/Middle Eastern, women's. **Biology:** General, neuroscience. **Business:** Accounting, accounting/finance, business admin, finance, international, management information systems, marketing. **Communications:** General. **Computer sciences:** General, information systems. **Conservation:** Environmental science, environmental studies. **Engineering:** Applied physics. **English:** English lit. **Foreign languages:** General, classics, French, German, Italian, Spanish. **Health services:** Predental, premedicine, preveterinary. **History:** General. **Human services:** Social work. **Liberal arts:** Humanities. **Math:** General. **Philosophy/religion:** Philosophy, religion. **Physical sciences:** Chemistry, physics. **Psychology:** General. **Social sciences:** Anthropology, economics, political economy, political science, sociology, urban studies. **Theology:** Theology. **Visual/performing arts:** Art, art history/conservation, dance, design, dramatic, music.

Most popular majors. Business/marketing 30%, communications/journalism 12%, psychology 7%, social sciences 19%.

Technology on campus. 1,400 workstations in dormitories, library, computer center, student center. Dormitories wired for high-speed internet access and linked to campus network. Commuter students can connect to campus network. Online course registration, online library, helpline, repair service, wireless network available.

Student life. Freshman orientation: Mandatory, $385 fee. Preregistration for classes offered. Comprehensive academic and social orientation held three days prior to start of classes. **Housing:** Coed dorms, apartments, themed housing, wellness housing available. $200 partly refundable deposit, deadline 5/1. **Activities:** Bands, campus ministries, choral groups, dance, drama, film society, international student organizations, literary magazine, music ensembles, musical theater, radio station, student government, student newspaper,

symphony orchestra, TV station, ASCEND, Campus Ministry, Colleges Against Cancer, Global Outreach, International Community of Fordham, Mock Trial, Muslim Students Association, PRIDE Alliance, Students for Fair Trade, UNICEF.

Athletics. NCAA. Intercollegiate: Baseball M, basketball, cheerleading W, cross-country, diving, football (tackle) M, golf M, rowing (crew) W, soccer, softball W, squash M, swimming, tennis, track and field, volleyball W, water polo M. **Intramural:** Basketball, football (non-tackle), soccer, softball, tennis, volleyball W. **Team name:** Rams.

Student services. Adult student services, alcohol/substance abuse counseling, chaplain/spiritual director, career counseling, services for economically disadvantaged, student employment services, financial aid counseling, health services, minority student services, personal counseling, placement for graduates, veterans' counselor, women's services. **Physically disabled:** Services for visually, hearing impaired.

Contact. E-mail: enroll@fordham.edu
Phone: (718) 817-4000 Toll-free number: (800) 367-3426
Fax: (718) 367-9404
Patricia Peek, Director of Undergraduate Admission, Fordham University, Office of Undergraduate Admission, Fordham University, Bronx, NY 10458-9993

Globe Institute of Technology
New York, New York
www.globe.edu   CB code: 3333

- For-profit 4-year university and business college
- Commuter campus in very large city
- 447 degree-seeking undergraduates: 2% part-time, 30% women

General. Regionally accredited. **Degrees:** 20 bachelor's, 98 associate awarded. **Calendar:** Trimester, extensive summer session. **Full-time faculty:** 12 total. **Part-time faculty:** 42 total. **Class size:** 55% < 20, 40% 20-39, 5% 40-49.

Freshman class profile. 540 applied, 262 admitted, 146 enrolled.

Basis for selection. Open admission, but selective for some programs. Special requirements for video game development program. Interviews strongly recommended. **Home schooled:** Transcript of courses and grades, state high school equivalency certificate required. **Learning Disabled:** Student should meet with school psychologist to discuss needs.

2015-2016 Annual costs. Books/supplies: $800. Personal expenses: $2,861.

2014-2015 Financial aid. Need-based: 73% of total undergraduate aid awarded as scholarships/grants, 27% as loans/jobs. **Non-need-based:** Scholarships awarded for academics, athletics.

Application procedures. Admission: No deadline. $50 fee, may be waived for applicants with need. Admission notification on a rolling basis. Housing deposit required 30 days before first day of the semester. **Financial aid:** No deadline. FAFSA, institutional form required. Applicants notified on a rolling basis.

Academics. Special study options: Combined bachelor's/graduate degree, distance learning, ESL, independent study, internships, liberal arts/career combination, weekend college. Video Game Development program admits only students in top 15% of graduating class and students with combined SAT score greater than 1950. **Credit/placement by examination:** AP, CLEP, institutional tests. 30 credit hours maximum toward associate degree, 60 toward bachelor's. **Support services:** Learning center, pre-admission summer program, reduced course load, remedial instruction, study skills assistance, tutoring, writing center.

Majors. Business: General, accounting, accounting technology, accounting/business management, accounting/finance, banking/financial services, business admin, customer service, finance, hospitality admin, hotel/motel admin, management information systems, nonprofit/public, office management, operations, resort management, restaurant/food services, small business admin, tourism/travel. **Computer sciences:** General, applications programming, artificial intelligence, computer graphics, computer science, database management, information technology, LAN/WAN management, networking, programming, security, system admin, systems analysis, vendor certification, web page design, webmaster. **Health services:** Facilities admin, health care admin, office admin.

Most popular majors. Business/marketing 60%, computer/information sciences 20%, health sciences 10%, legal studies 10%.

Technology on campus. 200 workstations in library, computer center, student center. Dormitories wired for high-speed internet access. Commuter students can connect to campus network. Online library, wireless network available.

Student life. Freshman orientation: Mandatory. Preregistration for classes offered. **Housing:** Apartments available. **Activities:** Choral groups, dance, student government, Women's Empowerment Group, Poetry Club, Caribbean Club.

Athletics. NJCAA. **Intercollegiate:** Baseball M, basketball, football (tackle) M, soccer, softball W, volleyball W. **Team name:** Knights.

Student services. Adult student services, career counseling, services for economically disadvantaged, student employment services, financial aid counseling, minority student services, placement for graduates, women's services.

Contact. E-mail: admissions@globe.edu
Phone: (212) 349-4330 Toll-free number: (877) 394-5623
Fax: (212) 302-9242
Sergey Byderman, Director, Globe Institute of Technology, 500 Seventh Avenue, 2nd Floor, New York, NY 10018

Hamilton College

Clinton, New York
www.hamilton.edu

CB member
CB code: 2286

- Private 4-year liberal arts college
- Residential campus in rural community
- 1,861 degree-seeking undergraduates: 51% women, 5% African American, 7% Asian American, 7% Hispanic/Latino, 3% Multi-racial, non-Hispanic, 6% international
- 25% of applicants admitted
- SAT and SAT Subject Tests or ACT (ACT writing optional), application essay required
- 92% graduate within 6 years; 11% enter graduate study

General. Founded in 1812. Regionally accredited. **Degrees:** 505 bachelor's awarded. **ROTC:** Army, Air Force. **Location:** 10 miles from Utica, 50 miles from Syracuse. **Calendar:** Semester. **Full-time faculty:** 189 total; 95% have terminal degrees, 18% minority, 46% women. **Part-time faculty:** 43 total; 44% have terminal degrees, 12% minority, 46% women. **Class size:** 76% < 20, 20% 20-39, 3% 40-49, less than 1% 50-99. **Special facilities:** Community garden, electron microscope, food coop, nature preserve, observatory, outdoor leadership center, supercomputer.

Freshman class profile. 5,434 applied, 1,348 admitted, 473 enrolled.

Mid 50% test scores			
SAT critical reading:	650-740	Rank in top tenth:	77%
SAT math:	650-730	Return as sophomores:	93%
SAT writing:	650-750	Out-of-state:	71%
ACT composite:	31-33	Live on campus:	100%
Rank in top quarter:	96%	International:	7%

Basis for selection. School achievement record, rank in high school class, school and community activities, application essay, recommendations important. Test scores and interview also considered. Some preference given to children of alumni. Special consideration given to students from minority groups, disadvantaged backgrounds, and certain geographic regions. Applicants a variety of ways to meet the standardized test requirement. They include: The SAT (Essay optional); ACT (Writing Section optional); or Three individual exams of your choice, selected from SAT sections (including Essay test), SAT subject tests, ACT writing, AP scores or IB final exams. One must be a verbal or writing/essay test, one must be a quantitative test, and the third is your choice. The following tests satisfy Hamilton's quantitative and verbal/writing requirements: Acceptable Quantitative Tests: SAT Math; SAT Subject Tests in Math, Chemistry, or Physics; AP Computer Science, Chemistry, Economics, Math, or Physics; IB final exam results for Chemistry, Computing Studies, Economics, Math, Physics, or Physical and Chemical Systems. Acceptable Verbal/Writing Tests: SAT Critical Reading; SAT Writing; SAT Essay; ACT Writing; AP English Language and Composition; IB final exam results for Language (A1, A2, or B English); TOEFL or IELTS (for International students ONLY). Applicants are encouraged to submit all testing to Hamilton and the best scores will be chosen. Interview strongly recommended for all; audition CD, videotape, or DVD recommended for music applicants; audition DVD recommended for theater and dance applicants; artist's statement and portfolio recommended for studio art applicants. **Home schooled:** Statement describing home school structure and mission required.

High school preparation. College-preparatory program recommended. 16 units recommended. Recommended units include English 4, mathematics 3, social studies 3, science 3 and foreign language 3.

2015-2016 Annual costs. Tuition/fees: $49,500. Room/board: $12,570. Books/supplies: $1,300. Personal expenses: $1,000.

2015-2016 Financial aid. All financial aid based on need. 267 full-time freshmen applied for aid; 253 deemed to have need; 253 received aid. Average need met was 100%. Average scholarship/grant was $40,802; average loan $3,226. 90% of total undergraduate aid awarded as scholarships/grants, 10% as loans/jobs.

Application procedures. Admission: Closing date 1/1 (postmark date). $50 fee, may be waived for applicants with need. Admission notification by 4/1. Must reply by 5/1. **Financial aid:** Closing date 2/15. FAFSA, institutional form, CSS PROFILE required. Applicants notified by 4/1; must reply by 5/1.

Academics. Students may participate in Williams College Mystic Seaport Program. Students must complete senior program or project in their concentration. **Special study options:** Accelerated study, combined bachelor's/graduate degree, cross-registration, double major, ESL, independent study, internships, New York semester, student-designed major, study abroad, Washington semester. 3-2 program in engineering with Columbia University, Rensselaer Polytechnic Institute, Washington University (St. Louis); 3-3 program in law at Columbia University; New England Center for Children Cooperative Learning Program. **Credit/placement by examination:** AP, CLEP, IB, institutional tests. **Support services:** Learning center, pre-admission summer program, reduced course load, study skills assistance, tutoring, writing center.

Majors. Area/ethnic studies: African-American, American, Asian, German, Russian/Slavic, women's. **Biology:** General, biochemistry, neuroscience. **Computer sciences:** General. **Conservation:** Environmental studies. **English:** Creative writing, English lit. **Foreign languages:** General, Chinese, classics, comparative lit, French, Hispanic and Latin American. **History:** General. **Human services:** Public policy. **Math:** General. **Philosophy/religion:** Philosophy, religion. **Physical sciences:** Chemical physics, chemistry, geology, physics. **Psychology:** General. **Social sciences:** Anthropology, archaeology, economics, international relations, political science, sociology. **Visual/performing arts:** Art history/conservation, dance, dramatic, music, studio arts.

Most popular majors. Biology 8%, English 6%, foreign language 11%, mathematics 8%, physical sciences 8%, psychology 6%, social sciences 28%, visual/performing arts 7%.

Technology on campus. 840 workstations in library, computer center, student center. Dormitories wired for high-speed internet access and linked to campus network. Commuter students can connect to campus network. Online course registration, online library, helpline, repair service, student web hosting, wireless network available.

Student life. Freshman orientation: Mandatory. Preregistration for classes offered. One week prior to start of classes. **Policies:** Honor code covers all examinations, papers, research, and use of library. Statement of Community promotes engagement in dialogue to create mutual understanding and expanded knowledge. Freshmen not permitted cars on campus. **Housing:** Guaranteed on-campus for all undergraduates. Coed dorms, special housing for disabled, apartments, cooperative housing, gender-neutral housing, wellness housing available. First-year residential program available. **Activities:** Jazz band, campus ministries, choral groups, dance, drama, film society, international student organizations, literary magazine, music ensembles, Model UN, musical theater, radio station, student government, student newspaper, symphony orchestra, TV station, Christian Fellowship, Newman Council, Hillel, Muslim Students Association, Black and Latino Student Union, Amnesty International, South Asian Students Association, Womyn's Center, Alternative Spring Break.

Athletics. NCAA. **Intercollegiate:** Baseball M, basketball, cross-country, diving, field hockey W, football (tackle) M, golf, ice hockey, lacrosse, rowing (crew), soccer, softball W, squash, swimming, tennis, track and field, volleyball W. **Intramural:** Badminton, basketball, football (non-tackle), golf, ice hockey, racquetball, skiing, soccer, softball, squash, tennis, volleyball, water polo. **Team name:** Continentals.

Student services. Adult student services, alcohol/substance abuse counseling, chaplain/spiritual director, career counseling, student employment services, financial aid counseling, health services, minority student services, personal counseling, placement for graduates, women's services. **Physically disabled:** Services for visually, speech, hearing impaired.

Contact. E-mail: admission@hamilton.edu
Phone: (315) 859-4421 Toll-free number: (800) 843-2655
Fax: (315) 859-4457
Monica Inzer, Vice President and Dean of Admission and Financial Aid, Hamilton College, 198 College Hill Road, Clinton, NY 13323-1293

Hartwick College
Oneonta, New York

CB member
CB code: 2288
www.hartwick.edu

- Private 4-year liberal arts college
- Residential campus in large town
- 1,383 degree-seeking undergraduates: 2% part-time, 60% women, 9% African American, 2% Asian American, 7% Hispanic/Latino, 3% international
- 81% of applicants admitted
- 56% graduate within 6 years; 21% enter graduate study

General. Founded in 1797. Regionally accredited. **Degrees:** 334 bachelor's awarded. **Location:** 75 miles from Albany. **Calendar:** 4-1-4, extensive summer session. **Full-time faculty:** 105 total; 87% have terminal degrees, 10% minority, 43% women. **Part-time faculty:** 82 total; 6% have terminal degrees, 10% minority, 65% women. **Class size:** 71% < 20, 28% 20-39, less than 1% 40-49, less than 1% 50-99. **Special facilities:** Environmental field station, museum, artifact and library collections, tissue culture laboratory, 16-inch telescope and observatory, nuclear magnetic resonance spectrometer, fine and performing arts center.

Freshman class profile. 2,692 applied, 2,174 admitted, 297 enrolled.

Mid 50% test scores			
SAT critical reading:	450-560	Rank in top quarter:	25%
SAT math:	460-550	Rank in top tenth:	6%
SAT writing:	420-540	Return as sophomores:	74%
ACT composite:	21-26	Out-of-state:	21%
GPA 3.75 or higher:	5%	Live on campus:	94%
GPA 3.50-3.74:	26%	International:	2%
GPA 3.0-3.49:	39%	Fraternities:	7%
GPA 2.0-2.99:	29%	Sororities:	9%

Basis for selection. School achievement record, class rank, personal qualities, extracurricular activities, recommendations considered. Test scores optional except for applicants applying to nursing program or those who were homeschooled. SAT/ACT score submission not required for admission except for nursing majors and homeschooled candidates. Audition required for music program; portfolio recommended for art program. **Home schooled:** Transcript of courses and grades, letter of recommendation (nonparent) required. Must meet all stated application requirements and submit SAT or ACT test score. At least 3 SAT Subject Tests strongly recommended. Transcripts should be submitted with course description and/or syllabi. **Learning Disabled:** Students are not obligated to self-disclose a disability. However, self-disclosure is required when the student anticipates a need for accommodations or services relating to a disability. A phone call, personal interview or the submission of the Voluntary Disclosure of a Disability Form will initiate the process.

High school preparation. College-preparatory program recommended. 19 units recommended. Recommended units include English 4, mathematics 3, social studies 2, history 2, science 3 (laboratory 2) and foreign language 3.

2015-2016 Annual costs. Tuition/fees: $41,440. Room/board: $11,120. Books/supplies: $700. Personal expenses: $400.

2015-2016 Financial aid. **Need-based:** 268 full-time freshmen applied for aid; 254 deemed to have need; 254 received aid. Average need met was 82%. Average scholarship/grant was $27,415; average loan $4,902. 71% of total undergraduate aid awarded as scholarships/grants, 29% as loans/jobs. **Non-need-based:** Awarded to 361 full-time undergraduates, including 70 freshmen. Scholarships awarded for academics, alumni affiliation, art, athletics, music/drama.

Application procedures. **Admission:** No deadline. No application fee. Admission notification on a rolling basis beginning on or about 10/15. Must reply by May 1 or within 2 week(s) if notified thereafter. **Financial aid:** Priority date 2/15; no closing date. FAFSA required. Applicants notified on a rolling basis starting 1/15; must reply by 5/1 or within 2 week(s) of notification.

Academics. Curriculum includes first-year seminar, core requirements and contemporary issues seminar. Senior thesis required. **Special study options:** Accelerated study, combined bachelor's/graduate degree, cooperative education, cross-registration, distance learning, honors, independent study, internships, semester at sea, student-designed major, study abroad, teacher certification program, urban semester, Washington semester. Off-campus January term changes yearly but has included programs in England, France, Ghana, Madagascar, South Africa; Philadelphia Urban Semester; Outward Bound, NOLS programs; cooperative program in law with Albany Law School; 3-2 engineering with Clarkson University, Columbia University; 3-year accelerated bachelor's degree. **Credit/placement by examination:** AP, CLEP, IB, institutional tests. **Support services:** Learning center, pre-admission summer program, reduced course load, study skills assistance, tutoring, writing center.

Majors. Biology: General, biochemistry. **Business:** Accounting, business admin. **Computer sciences:** General, information systems. **Education:** Music. **English:** English lit. **Foreign languages:** French, German, Spanish. **Health services:** Clinical lab science, nursing (RN). **History:** General. **Liberal arts:** Arts/sciences. **Math:** General. **Philosophy/religion:** Philosophy, religion. **Physical sciences:** Chemistry, geology, physics. **Psychology:** General. **Social sciences:** Anthropology, economics, political science, sociology. **Visual/performing arts:** Art, art history/conservation, dramatic, music.

Most popular majors. Biology 14%, business/marketing 17%, health sciences 16%, physical sciences 6%, psychology 8%, social sciences 18%, visual/performing arts 7%.

Technology on campus. 56 workstations in library, computer center. Dormitories wired for high-speed internet access and linked to campus network. Commuter students can connect to campus network. Online course registration, online library, helpline, repair service, student web hosting, wireless network available.

Student life. Freshman orientation: Mandatory. Preregistration for classes offered. 4-day pre-semester in-residence program. **Housing:** Guaranteed on-campus for freshmen. Coed dorms, wellness housing available. Housing at environmental campus available. **Activities:** Bands, campus ministries, choral groups, dance, drama, film society, international student organizations, literary magazine, music ensembles, Model UN, radio station, student government, student newspaper, symphony orchestra, 66 academic and social organizations available including Jewish Student Organization, Newman Club, Campus Ambassadors, Society of Sisters United/Brothers United, Latinos Unidos Con Honor Y Alma, Hartwick Identity Alliance.

Athletics. NCAA. **Intercollegiate:** Basketball, cheerleading W, cross-country, diving, equestrian W, field hockey W, football (tackle) M, lacrosse, soccer, swimming, tennis, volleyball W, water polo W. **Intramural:** Basketball, football (non-tackle), racquetball, soccer, volleyball. **Team name:** Hawks.

Student services. Alcohol/substance abuse counseling, career counseling, financial aid counseling, health services, personal counseling. **Physically disabled:** Services for visually impaired.

Contact. E-mail: admissions@hartwick.edu
Phone: (607) 431-4150 Toll-free number: (888) 427-8942
Fax: (607) 431-4102
Lisa Starkey-Wood, Director of Admissions, Hartwick College, 1 Hartwick Drive, Oneonta, NY 13820-4022

Hilbert College
Hamburg, New York

CB member
CB code: 2334
www.hilbert.edu

- Private 4-year liberal arts college affiliated with the Roman Catholic Church
- Commuter campus in small city
- 864 degree-seeking undergraduates: 9% part-time, 55% women, 8% African American, 3% Hispanic/Latino, 2% Native American, 5% Multi-racial, non-Hispanic, 1% international
- 58 degree-seeking graduate students
- 82% of applicants admitted
- 50% graduate within 6 years; 12% enter graduate study

General. Founded in 1957. Regionally accredited. Affiliated with Franciscan Sisters of St. Joseph. **Degrees:** 220 bachelor's, 13 associate awarded; master's offered. **ROTC:** Army. **Location:** 10 miles from Buffalo. **Calendar:** Semester, limited summer session. **Full-time faculty:** 43 total; 58% have terminal degrees, 7% minority, 51% women. **Part-time faculty:** 91 total; 31% have terminal degrees, 41% women. **Class size:** 77% < 20, 22% 20-39, less than 1% 50-99. **Special facilities:** Comprehensive law library.

Freshman class profile. 741 applied, 605 admitted, 153 enrolled.

Mid 50% test scores			
SAT critical reading:	420-520	GPA 3.0-3.49:	44%
SAT math:	440-530	GPA 2.0-2.99:	21%
SAT writing:	410-500	End year in good standing:	95%
ACT composite:	18-23	Return as sophomores:	77%
GPA 3.75 or higher:	9%	Out-of-state:	5%
GPA 3.50-3.74:	26%	Live on campus:	49%
		International:	1%

Basis for selection. School achievement record and course selection important. Candidates must meet minimum academic criteria including high school GPA. SAT or ACT recommended. Scores from national exams, such as the ACT and SAT, are not a requirement for admission to Hilbert, but if submitted will be used as an aid for course placement and scholarship consideration. Essay, interview recommended. **Home schooled:** Transcript of courses and grades, state high school equivalency certificate required. **Learning Disabled:** Separate statement directly to academic services required.

High school preparation. 16 units required; 21 recommended. Required and recommended units include English 4, mathematics 3-4, social studies 3-4, history 2, science 2-3 (laboratory 1-2) and foreign language 1-2.

2015-2016 Annual costs. Tuition/fees: $20,700. Room/board: $9,380. Books/supplies: $700. Personal expenses: $800.

2015-2016 Financial aid. Need-based: 89 full-time freshmen applied for aid; 80 deemed to have need; 80 received aid. Average need met was 72%. Average scholarship/grant was $14,081; average loan $3,777. 60% of total undergraduate aid awarded as scholarships/grants, 40% as loans/jobs. **Non-need-based:** Awarded to 129 full-time undergraduates, including 14 freshmen. Scholarships awarded for academics, alumni affiliation, leadership, minority status.

Application procedures. Admission: Priority date 6/30; deadline 8/15 (receipt date). $25 fee, may be waived for applicants with need, free for online applicants. Admission notification on a rolling basis beginning on or about 10/1. **Financial aid:** Priority date 3/1; no closing date. FAFSA required. Applicants notified on a rolling basis starting 3/1; must reply within 2 week(s) of notification.

Academics. Legal assistant program approved by American Bar Association. **Special study options:** Accelerated study, combined bachelor's/graduate degree, cooperative education, cross-registration, distance learning, dual enrollment of high school students, honors, independent study, internships, liberal arts/career combination, study abroad, Washington semester. Member of Western New York consortium. Accelerated BS degree programs offered in the evening: Organization Development; Conflict Studies and Dispute Resolution. Must have 24 credits transferred in to be eligible for these new accelerated degree completion programs. **Credit/placement by examination:** AP, CLEP, IB, SAT, ACT, institutional tests. 18 credit hours maximum toward associate degree, 32 toward bachelor's. **Support services:** Learning center, pre-admission summer program, reduced course load, remedial instruction, study skills assistance, tutoring, writing center.

Majors. Business: Accounting, business admin, organizational leadership. **Communications:** Digital media. **Computer sciences:** Information technology. **English:** English lit. **Liberal arts:** Arts/sciences. **Parks/recreation:** Sports admin. **Protective services:** Criminal justice, forensics. **Psychology:** General. **Social sciences:** Political science.

Most popular majors. Business/marketing 20%, legal studies 6%, public administration/social services 9%, security/protective services 49%.

Technology on campus. 146 workstations in dormitories, library, computer center, student center. Dormitories wired for high-speed internet access. Commuter students can connect to campus network. Online course registration, online library, helpline, wireless network available.

Student life. Freshman orientation: Mandatory, $50 fee. Preregistration for classes offered. One-day programs held in June, July or August. **Housing:** Coed dorms, apartments available. $125 nonrefundable deposit, deadline 8/1. **Activities:** Campus ministries, drama, literary magazine, radio station, student government, SADD, Human Service Association, Great Expectations, criminal justice club, Students in Free Enterprise, economic crime investigation club, Common Ground club, Oxfam America.

Athletics. NCAA. **Intercollegiate:** Baseball M, basketball, cross-country, golf M, lacrosse, soccer, softball W, volleyball. **Intramural:** Basketball, football (non-tackle), soccer, softball, table tennis, volleyball. **Team name:** Hawks.

Student services. Adult student services, alcohol/substance abuse counseling, chaplain/spiritual director, career counseling, student employment services, financial aid counseling, health services, minority student services, personal counseling, placement for graduates, veterans' counselor. **Physically disabled:** Services for visually, hearing impaired.

Contact. E-mail: admissions@hilbert.edu
Phone: (716) 649-7900 ext. 211 Toll-free number: (800) 649-8003
Fax: (716) 649-1152
Patrick Quinn, VP for Enrollment Management, Hilbert College, 5200 South Park Avenue, Hamburg, NY 14075-1597

Hobart and William Smith Colleges
Geneva, New York
www.hws.edu

CB member
CB code: 2294

◆ Private 4-year liberal arts college
◆ Residential campus in large town

◆ 2,257 degree-seeking undergraduates: 50% women, 5% African American, 3% Asian American, 6% Hispanic/Latino, 6% international
◆ 7 degree-seeking graduate students
◆ 57% of applicants admitted
◆ Application essay required
◆ 81% graduate within 6 years

General. Founded in 1822. Regionally accredited. **Degrees:** 578 bachelor's awarded; master's offered. **ROTC:** Army, Air Force. **Location:** 50 miles from Syracuse, 40 miles from Rochester, 45 miles from Ithaca. **Calendar:** Semester, limited summer session. **Full-time faculty:** 223 total; 98% have terminal degrees, 18% minority, 48% women. **Part-time faculty:** 7 total; 14% have terminal degrees, 14% minority, 29% women. **Class size:** 65% < 20, 34% 20-39, less than 1% 40-49. **Special facilities:** Finger Lakes institute, center for the performing arts, research vessel, farm, nature preserve, centennial center for leadership.

Freshman class profile. 4,488 applied, 2,549 admitted, 631 enrolled.

Mid 50% test scores			
SAT critical reading:	570-670	Rank in top quarter:	65%
SAT math:	600-670	Rank in top tenth:	30%
ACT composite:	26-30	End year in good standing:	86%
GPA 3.75 or higher:	28%	Return as sophomores:	86%
GPA 3.50-3.74:	19%	Out-of-state:	59%
GPA 3.0-3.49:	33%	Live on campus:	100%
GPA 2.0-2.99:	19%	International:	7%

Rank in top quarter: 65%

Basis for selection. High school record, school and community activities, recommendations, interview and talents are all considered. Economically and educationally disadvantaged New York State residents may apply through the Higher Education Oppoartunity Program. Standardized tests only required for those applying for the Trustee or Blackwell scholarships, those who come from a high school without a traditionally graded transcript, or those for whom English is not a first language (TOEFL exam is acceptable for non-native English speakers). Interview strongly encouraged for all and required for Trustee Scholar applicants. Candidates for Arts Scholars program must submit portfolio. **Home schooled:** Letter of recommendation (nonparent) required. Students without a traditional, graded transcript must submit standardized test scores.

High school preparation. College-preparatory program required. Required and recommended units include English 4, mathematics 3, social studies 2-3, science 3 (laboratory 2), foreign language 2-3 and academic electives 2-4. Mathematics must include algebra, geometry, and trigonometry sequence.

2015-2016 Annual costs. Tuition/fees: $49,677. Room/board: $12,583. Books/supplies: $1,300. Personal expenses: $600.

2014-2015 Financial aid. Need-based: 439 full-time freshmen applied for aid; 354 deemed to have need; 354 received aid. Average need met was 80%. Average scholarship/grant was $29,520; average loan $3,265. 81% of total undergraduate aid awarded as scholarships/grants, 19% as loans/jobs. **Non-need-based:** Awarded to 874 full-time undergraduates, including 283 freshmen. Scholarships awarded for academics, alumni affiliation, art, leadership, music/drama, religious affiliation.

Application procedures. Admission: Closing date 2/1 (postmark date). $45 fee, may be waived for applicants with need, free for online applicants. Admission notification by 4/1. Must reply by 5/1. **Financial aid:** Priority date 2/1, closing date 2/1. FAFSA, CSS PROFILE required. Applicants notified by 4/1; must reply by 5/1 or within 2 week(s) of notification.

Academics. All students must complete a major and a minor (or a second major), and must meet 8 broad academic goals. **Special study options:** Combined bachelor's/graduate degree, double major, ESL, honors, independent study, internships, student-designed major, study abroad, teacher certification program, Washington semester. **Credit/placement by examination:** AP, CLEP, IB, institutional tests. Credit by examination counted toward degree limited to equivalent of 7 courses. **Support services:** Learning center, pre-admission summer program, reduced course load, study skills assistance, tutoring, writing center.

Majors. Architecture: Architecture. **Area/ethnic studies:** African, African-American, American, Asian, Chicano/Hispanic-American/Latino, European, gay/lesbian, Latin American, Russian/Slavic, women's. **Biology:** General, biochemistry. **Communications:** Media studies. **Computer sciences:** General, computer science. **Conservation:** Environmental studies. **English:** English lit. **Foreign languages:** Chinese, classics, comparative lit, French, Japanese, Latin, Russian, Spanish. **Health services:** Predental, premedicine, preveterinary. **History:** General. **Human services:** Public policy. **Math:** General. **Philosophy/religion:** Philosophy, religion. **Physical sciences:** Chemistry, geology, physics. **Psychology:** General. **Social sciences:** Anthropology, economics, international relations, political science, sociology, urban studies. **Visual/performing arts:** Art history/conservation, dance, dramatic, music, studio arts.

Most popular majors. Biology 8%, communications/journalism 7%, natural resources/environmental science 6%, public administration/social services 6%, social sciences 26%, visual/performing arts 6%.

Technology on campus. 175 workstations in library, computer center. Dormitories wired for high-speed internet access and linked to campus network. Commuter students can connect to campus network. Online course registration, online library, helpline, repair service, student web hosting, wireless network available.

Student life. Freshman orientation: Mandatory. Preregistration for classes offered. Held three days in late August. **Housing:** Guaranteed on-campus for all undergraduates. Coed dorms, single-sex dorms, special housing for disabled, apartments, cooperative housing, fraternity/sorority housing, themed housing, wellness housing available. **Activities:** Bands, campus ministries, choral groups, dance, drama, film society, international student organizations, literary magazine, music ensembles, radio station, student government, student newspaper, International Student Association, Sankofa: Black Student Union, Pride Alliance, Mosaic NY, HWS Hillel, Geneva Heroes (service), Caribbean Student Association, Latin American Organization, Leadership League of Women, HWS Votes, Project Nur.

Athletics. NCAA. **Intercollegiate:** Basketball, cross-country, diving W, field hockey W, football (tackle) M, golf, ice hockey, lacrosse, rowing (crew), sailing, soccer, squash, swimming W, tennis. **Intramural:** Badminton, basketball, football (non-tackle), golf, soccer, softball, squash, table tennis, tennis, volleyball. **Team name:** Statesmen (Hobart); Herons (William Smith).

Student services. Alcohol/substance abuse counseling, chaplain/spiritual director, career counseling, services for economically disadvantaged, student employment services, financial aid counseling, health services, minority student services, personal counseling, placement for graduates, veterans' counselor, women's services. **Physically disabled:** Services for visually, speech, hearing impaired.

Contact. E-mail: admissions@hws.edu
Phone: (315) 781-3622 Toll-free number: (800) 852-2256
Fax: (315) 781-3914
John Young, Director of Admissions, Hobart and William Smith Colleges, 629 South Main Street, Geneva, NY 14456

Hofstra University
Hempstead, New York   **CB member**
www.hofstra.edu   **CB code: 2295**

- Private 4-year university
- Residential campus in large city
- 6,716 degree-seeking undergraduates: 5% part-time, 54% women, 8% African American, 9% Asian American, 14% Hispanic/Latino, 1% Native Hawaiian/Pacific islander, 2% Multi-racial, non-Hispanic, 4% international
- 3,871 degree-seeking graduate students
- 61% of applicants admitted
- Application essay required
- 60% graduate within 6 years; 25% enter graduate study

General. Founded in 1935. Regionally accredited. 100% wireless campus. **Degrees:** 1,522 bachelor's awarded; master's, professional, doctoral offered. **ROTC:** Army. **Location:** 25 miles from New York City. **Calendar:** Semester, extensive summer session. **Full-time faculty:** 498 total; 92% have terminal degrees, 22% minority, 45% women. **Part-time faculty:** 663 total; 44% have terminal degrees, 18% minority, 44% women. **Class size:** 50% < 20, 44% 20-39, 3% 40-49, 3% 50-99, less than 1% >100. **Special facilities:** Cell and tissue engineering lab, civil/environmental engineering lab, electrical and signal processing lab, engineering computer lab, aerodynamics and transport phenomena laboratory, first year engineering laboratory/technology and public policy forensic analysis laboratory, materials analysis laboratory, thermodynamics laboratory, big data lab at school of engineering and applied science.

Freshman class profile. 27,991 applied, 17,090 admitted, 1,651 enrolled.

Mid 50% test scores		Rank in top quarter:	63%
SAT critical reading:	540-620	Rank in top tenth:	27%
SAT math:	550-640	End year in good standing:	90%
ACT composite:	24-29	Return as sophomores:	80%
GPA 3.75 or higher:	42%	Out-of-state:	47%
GPA 3.50-3.74:	21%	Live on campus:	69%
GPA 3.0-3.49:	28%	International:	4%
GPA 2.0-2.99:	9%		

Basis for selection. Holistic review of each applicant's secondary school record. TOEFL or IELTS scores are required for international applicants. Personal essay and letters of recommendation are most important. For some, interview is required. Test optional, standardized test scores are not required for most programs with the exception of home schooled and international applicants. Interview required for New Opportunities at Hofstra (NOAH) and Program for Academic Learning Skills (PALS) applicants. Audition recommended for music theater programs; portfolio recommended for fine arts program. **Home schooled:** Statement describing home school structure and mission, transcript of courses and grades, state high school equivalency certificate required. Must provide at least 2 recommendations, including 1 from primary instructor or person who has primary responsibility for assessing applicant's academic performance. School is required to certify completion of secondary school for all enrolled students prior to graduation. **Learning Disabled:** Students may apply to the Program for Academic Learning Skills. Application includes copy of psychological testing, WAISR.

High school preparation. College-preparatory program required. 16 units required. Required and recommended units include English 4, mathematics 3-4, social studies 3-4, science 3-4 (laboratory 1-2) and foreign language 2-3. Social studies includes history; 4 math, 1 chemistry, and 1 physics required for engineering.

2015-2016 Annual costs. Tuition/fees: $40,460. Room/board: $13,330. Books/supplies: $1,000. Personal expenses: $1,650.

2014-2015 Financial aid. Need-based: 1,479 full-time freshmen applied for aid; 1,244 deemed to have need; 1,244 received aid. Average need met was 66%. Average scholarship/grant was $19,719; average loan $3,469. 64% of total undergraduate aid awarded as scholarships/grants, 36% as loans/jobs. **Non-need-based:** Awarded to 2,068 full-time undergraduates, including 607 freshmen. Scholarships awarded for academics, alumni affiliation, art, athletics, leadership, minority status, music/drama, ROTC, state residency.

Application procedures. Admission: No deadline. $70 fee, may be waived for applicants with need. Admission notification on a rolling basis beginning on or about 2/1. Must reply by May 1 or within 2 week(s) if notified thereafter. Notification of Early Action I begins December 15, notification for Early Action II begins January 15. **Financial aid:** Priority date 2/15; no closing date. FAFSA required. Applicants notified on a rolling basis starting 3/1; must reply by 5/1 or within 2 week(s) of notification.

Academics. Special study options: Accelerated study, combined bachelor's/graduate degree, cooperative education, cross-registration, distance learning, double major, dual enrollment of high school students, ESL, external degree, honors, independent study, internships, liberal arts/career combination, New York semester, student-designed major, study abroad, teacher certification program, Washington semester. **Credit/placement by examination:** AP, CLEP, IB, institutional tests. 30 credit hours maximum toward bachelor's degree. **Support services:** Learning center, pre-admission summer program, reduced course load, study skills assistance, tutoring, writing center.

Honors college/program. Students invited to join after acceptance to the University. Typically only the top 10% of all admits are offered invitation. During first year, students enroll in small multidisciplinary courses. After first year, students choose from wide range of honors-level courses in all academic areas of study.

Majors. Area/ethnic studies: African, American, Caribbean, East Asian, Japanese, Latin American, women's. **Biology:** General, biochemistry. **Business:** General, accounting, business admin, entrepreneurial studies, finance, international, labor studies, logistics, management information systems, managerial economics, marketing. **Communications:** Communications/speech/rhetoric, journalism, media studies, public relations, radio/TV. **Computer sciences:** Computer science. **Conservation:** Environmental studies. **Education:** Art, biology, business, chemistry, drama/dance, early childhood, elementary, English, foreign languages, French, German, health, mathematics, multi-level teacher, music, physical, physics, science, secondary, social studies, Spanish. **Engineering:** Biomedical, civil, computer, electrical, engineering science, industrial, manufacturing, mechanical. **English:** Creative writing, English lit. **Foreign languages:** Chinese, classics, comparative lit, French, German, Hebrew, Italian, Japanese, Latin, linguistics, Russian, Spanish. **Health services:** Athletic training, audiology/speech pathology, community health, predental, premedicine, preveterinary. **History:** General. **Liberal arts:** Arts/sciences. **Math:** General, financial. **Philosophy/religion:** Judaic, philosophy, religion. **Physical sciences:** Chemistry, geology, physics. **Protective services:** Forensics. **Psychology:** General. **Social sciences:** Anthropology, criminology, econometrics, economics, geography, political science, sociology. **Visual/performing arts:** Acting, art history/conservation, ceramics, dance, directing/producing, dramatic, jazz, metal/jewelry, music, music history, music management, music performance, music theory/composition, painting, photography, studio arts.

Most popular majors. Business/marketing 24%, communications/journalism 17%, education 6%, health sciences 8%, psychology 7%, social sciences 9%, visual/performing arts 6%.

Technology on campus. 1,501 workstations in dormitories, library, computer center. Dormitories wired for high-speed internet access and linked to campus network. Commuter students can connect to campus network. Online course registration, online library, helpline, repair service, student web hosting, wireless network available.

Student life. Freshman orientation: Mandatory, $250 fee. Preregistration for classes offered. Summer orientation is a 3-day/2-night program in which new students live on campus and begin preparation for the fall semester. The program extends into the entire first year beginning with the full array of programs five days prior to the start of classes and then throughout the year with programs and events designed to acclimate students to student life. **Housing:** Guaranteed on-campus for all undergraduates. Coed dorms, special housing for disabled, apartments, themed housing, wellness housing available. $300 nonrefundable deposit, deadline 5/1. Honors housing, living-learning community, quiet floors, women's floors available, and themed living communities. **Activities:** Bands, campus ministries, choral groups, dance, drama, film society, international student organizations, literary magazine, music ensembles, Model UN, musical theater, opera, radio station, student government, student newspaper, symphony orchestra, TV station, Adopt a Dream, She's the First, Black Student Union, Hofstra International, Hillel, H*INT, Organization of Latin Americans, Hofstra Pride Network, Habitat for Humanity, Newman Club, Hofstra NAACP.

Athletics. NCAA. **Intercollegiate:** Baseball M, basketball, cross-country, field hockey W, golf, lacrosse, soccer, softball W, tennis, volleyball W, wrestling M. **Intramural:** Basketball, football (non-tackle), soccer, softball, table tennis, ultimate frisbee, volleyball. **Team name:** Pride.

Student services. Adult student services, alcohol/substance abuse counseling, chaplain/spiritual director, career counseling, student employment services, financial aid counseling, health services, minority student services, on-campus daycare, personal counseling, placement for graduates, veterans' counselor. **Physically disabled:** Services for visually, speech, hearing impaired.

Contact. E-mail: admission@hofstra.edu
Phone: (516) 463-6700 Toll-free number: (800) 463-7872
Fax: (516) 463-5100
Sunil Samuel, Assistant Vice President of Admission, Hofstra University, Admissions Center, 100 Hofstra University, Hempstead, NY 11549-1450

Holy Trinity Orthodox Seminary
Jordanville, New York
www.hts.edu   **CB code: 2298**

◗ Private 5-year seminary college for men affiliated with the Russian Orthodox Church
◗ Residential campus in rural community
◗ 64 degree-seeking undergraduates
◗ Application essay required

General. Founded in 1948. Regionally accredited. **Degrees:** 2 bachelor's awarded. **Location:** 20 miles from Utica. **Calendar:** Semester, limited summer session. **Full-time faculty:** 14 total; 14% have terminal degrees, 7% women. **Part-time faculty:** 6 total. **Class size:** 100% < 20. **Special facilities:** Museum, archives, icon painting studio.

Freshman class profile.

Out-of-state:	50%	**Live on campus:**	100%

Basis for selection. Orthodoxy/Orthodox baptism, entrance exam required. Recommendation from spiritual father or parish priest necessary. **Home schooled:** Transcript of courses and grades, letter of recommendation (nonparent) required.

High school preparation. College-preparatory program required.

2015-2016 Annual costs. Tuition/fees: $3,100. Room/board: $2,500. Books/supplies: $200.

Financial aid. Additional information: Work-study program can reasonably pay for room and board over course of academic year.

Application procedures. Admission: Closing date 5/1 (postmark date). No application fee.

Academics. Special study options: Distance learning, ESL. **Credit/placement by examination:** AP, CLEP, institutional tests. **Support services:** Remedial instruction, tutoring.

Majors. Theology: Theology.

Technology on campus. 8 workstations in dormitories, library. Dormitories wired for high-speed internet access.

Student life. Freshman orientation: Mandatory. Preregistration for classes offered. **Policies:** Closed campus. Religious observance required. **Housing:** Guaranteed on-campus for all undergraduates. Wellness housing available. **Activities:** Choral groups, student newspaper.

Student services. Chaplain/spiritual director.

Contact. E-mail: info@hts.edu
Phone: (315) 858-0945
V. Rev. Luke Murianka, Rector, Holy Trinity Orthodox Seminary, PO Box 36, Jordanville, NY 13361

Houghton College
Houghton, New York   **CB member**
www.houghton.edu   **CB code: 2299**

◗ Private 4-year liberal arts college affiliated with the Wesleyan Church
◗ Residential campus in rural community
◗ 1,009 degree-seeking undergraduates: 2% part-time, 64% women, 3% African American, 2% Asian American, 2% Hispanic/Latino, 4% Multiracial, non-Hispanic, 11% international
◗ 20 degree-seeking graduate students
◗ 94% of applicants admitted
◗ SAT or ACT (ACT writing optional), application essay required
◗ 71% graduate within 6 years

General. Founded in 1883. Regionally accredited. **Degrees:** 260 bachelor's, 2 associate awarded; master's offered. **ROTC:** Army. **Location:** 60 miles from Buffalo, 70 miles from Rochester. **Calendar:** Semester, limited summer session. **Full-time faculty:** 73 total; 92% have terminal degrees, 4% minority, 38% women. **Part-time faculty:** 58 total; 34% have terminal degrees, 47% women. **Class size:** 69% < 20, 24% 20-39, 5% 40-49, 1% 50-99. **Special facilities:** Equestrian center, ropes/initiatives course, downhill and cross-country skiing facilities, media arts computer lab, hiking and biking trails, mini-cyclotron.

Freshman class profile. 737 applied, 696 admitted, 244 enrolled.

Mid 50% test scores		GPA 3.0-3.49:	24%
SAT critical reading:	500-630	GPA 2.0-2.99:	11%
SAT math:	490-620	Rank in top quarter:	61%
SAT writing:	480-600	Rank in top tenth:	27%
ACT composite:	21-29	Return as sophomores:	84%
GPA 3.75 or higher:	38%	Live on campus:	88%
GPA 3.50-3.74:	27%	International:	13%

Basis for selection. Student's high school transcript, standardized test scores of the utmost importance. Application essays, recommendation, other intangibles also considered. SAT/ACT not required for international applicants although highly recommended for scholarship consideration. Interview recommended for all applicants. Audition and separate application required for entrance into the School of Music. **Home schooled:** While state high school equivalency is not required for admission, it is required for matriculation and certain financial aid qualifications. **Learning Disabled:** There are no special admission requirements or procedures for students with learning disabilities, however students with learning disabilities are encouraged to consult with the Center for Academic Success and Advising prior to matriculation.

High school preparation. College-preparatory program recommended. 16 units recommended. Recommended units include English 4, mathematics 3, social studies 1, history 3, science 3 (laboratory 2) and foreign language 2.

2015-2016 Annual costs. Tuition/fees: $29,458. Room/board: $8,498. Books/supplies: $1,000. Personal expenses: $2,250.

2015-2016 Financial aid. Need-based: 243 full-time freshmen applied for aid; 227 deemed to have need; 226 received aid. Average need met was 81%. Average scholarship/grant was $12,334; average loan $4,067. 69% of total undergraduate aid awarded as scholarships/grants, 31% as loans/jobs. **Non-need-based:** Awarded to 776 full-time undergraduates, including 206 freshmen. Scholarships awarded for academics, alumni affiliation, art, minority status, music/drama, religious affiliation, ROTC, state residency. **Additional information:** Loan Repayment Assistance Program (LRAP) to all new students. Offered through a partnership with the LRAP Foundation, this program covers up to 100% of all federal, private, and parent PLUS loans at no cost to the student or parent.

Application procedures. Admission: Priority date 3/1; no deadline. $40 fee, may be waived for applicants with need. Admission notification on a rolling basis beginning on or about 11/1. Must reply by May 1 or within 4 week(s) if notified thereafter. **Financial aid:** Priority date 3/1; no closing date. FAFSA required. Applicants notified on a rolling basis starting 3/1.

Academics. **Special study options:** Combined bachelor's/graduate degree, cross-registration, distance learning, double major, dual enrollment of high school students, ESL, exchange student, honors, independent study, internships, liberal arts/career combination, student-designed major, study abroad, teacher certification program, urban semester. **Credit/placement by examination:** AP, CLEP, IB, SAT, ACT, institutional tests. 16 credit hours maximum toward associate degree, 32 toward bachelor's. **Support services:** Learning center, reduced course load, study skills assistance, tutoring, writing center.

Honors college/program. Requires separate application, academic reference, writing sample, and interview. Approximately 50 first-year students admitted.

Majors. **Area/ethnic studies:** Regional. **Biology:** General, biochemistry, environmental. **Business:** General, accounting, business admin. **Communications:** Communications/speech/rhetoric, digital media. **Computer sciences:** Computer science. **Education:** General, art, biology, chemistry, elementary, English, ESL, foreign languages, history, mathematics, music, physical, physics, secondary, social studies, Spanish. **Engineering:** Applied physics. **English:** English lit, writing. **Foreign languages:** Spanish. **Health services:** Predental, premedicine, prenursing, preoptometry, prepharmacy, prephysical therapy, preveterinary. **History:** General. **Liberal arts:** Humanities. **Math:** General. **Parks/recreation:** General. **Philosophy/religion:** Philosophy, religion. **Physical sciences:** Chemistry, physics. **Psychology:** General. **Social sciences:** International economic development, political science, sociology. **Theology:** Bible, preministerial. **Visual/performing arts:** Art, brass instruments, design, music, music performance, music theory/composition, percussion instruments, piano/keyboard, stringed instruments, studio arts, voice/opera, woodwind instruments.

Most popular majors. Biology 12%, business/marketing 22%, communications/journalism 7%, education 18%, psychology 6%, visual/performing arts 9%.

Technology on campus. 33 workstations in library, student center. Dormitories wired for high-speed internet access and linked to campus network. Commuter students can connect to campus network. Online library, helpline, repair service, wireless network available.

Student life. **Freshman orientation:** Mandatory. Preregistration for classes offered. **Policies:** Drinking of alcoholic beverages and smoking on or off campus is prohibited. The only pets allowed in dorm rooms are fish in tanks of 25 gallons and under. Religious observance required. **Housing:** Guaranteed on-campus for all undergraduates. Single-sex dorms, special housing for disabled, apartments, cooperative housing available. $300 nonrefundable deposit, deadline 5/1. Pets allowed in dorm rooms. **Activities:** Bands, campus ministries, choral groups, dance, drama, international student organizations, literary magazine, music ensembles, musical theater, opera, student government, student newspaper, symphony orchestra, Allegany County Outreach, Global Christian Fellowship, Habitat for Humanity, Youth for Christ, Fellowship of Christian Athletes, Intercultural Student Organization, Journey's End Refugee Tutoring, Black Heritage Club, Pre-Law Society.

Athletics. NCAA, NCCAA. **Intercollegiate:** Baseball M, basketball, cross-country, field hockey W, lacrosse, soccer, softball W, tennis, track and field, volleyball W. **Intramural:** Basketball, football (non-tackle) M, racquetball, soccer, table tennis, volleyball, water polo. **Team name:** Highlanders.

Student services. Alcohol/substance abuse counseling, chaplain/spiritual director, career counseling, student employment services, financial aid counseling, health services, personal counseling, placement for graduates, women's services. **Physically disabled:** Services for visually impaired.

Contact. E-mail: admission@houghton.edu
Phone: (585) 567-9353 Toll-free number: (800) 777-2556
Fax: (585) 567-9522
Ryan Spear, Associate Director of Admission, Houghton College, 1 Willard Avenue/PO Box 128, Houghton, NY 14744-0128

Iona College
New Rochelle, New York   **CB member**
www.iona.edu   **CB code: 2324**

- Private 4-year business and liberal arts college affiliated with the Roman Catholic Church
- Residential campus in small city

- 3,018 degree-seeking undergraduates: 2% part-time, 51% women, 8% African American, 2% Asian American, 22% Hispanic/Latino, 2% Multiracial, non-Hispanic, 3% international
- 702 degree-seeking graduate students
- 91% of applicants admitted
- SAT or ACT (ACT writing optional), application essay required
- 66% graduate within 6 years

General. Founded in 1940. Regionally accredited. **Degrees:** 738 bachelor's awarded; master's offered. **ROTC:** Army, Air Force. **Location:** 20 miles from New York City. **Calendar:** Semester, extensive summer session. **Full-time faculty:** 172 total; 89% have terminal degrees, 16% minority, 39% women. **Part-time faculty:** 169 total; 15% minority, 48% women. **Class size:** 38% < 20, 60% 20-39, 1% 40-49, less than 1% 50-99. **Special facilities:** Fine and performing art studios.

Freshman class profile. 9,587 applied, 8,744 admitted, 842 enrolled.

Mid 50% test scores		GPA 2.0-2.99:	43%
SAT critical reading:	450-550	Rank in top quarter:	29%
SAT math:	440-550	Rank in top tenth:	8%
ACT composite:	20-25	Return as sophomores:	77%
GPA 3.75 or higher:	10%	Out-of-state:	26%
GPA 3.50-3.74:	14%	Live on campus:	63%
GPA 3.0-3.49:	29%	International:	3%

Basis for selection. High school curriculum and GPA most important, followed by test scores, interview, extracurricular activities, essays, grade trends. Letters of recommendation considered but not required in most cases. Interviews recommended. **Home schooled:** Transcript of courses and grades, interview, letter of recommendation (nonparent) required.

High school preparation. College-preparatory program recommended. 16 units required; 20 recommended. Required and recommended units include English 4, mathematics 3-4, social studies 2, history 1-2, science 3 (laboratory 2), foreign language 2 and academic electives 1-3.

2015-2016 Annual costs. Tuition/fees: $35,324. Room/board: $13,980. Books/supplies: $1,500. Personal expenses: $1,250.

Financial aid. **Non-need-based:** Scholarships awarded for academics, alumni affiliation, athletics.

Application procedures. **Admission:** Closing date 2/15 (postmark date). $50 fee, may be waived for applicants with need. Admission notification on a rolling basis beginning on or about 12/5. Must reply by 5/1. **Financial aid:** Priority date 4/15; no closing date. FAFSA required. Applicants notified on a rolling basis starting 3/1; must reply by 5/1 or within 2 week(s) of notification.

Academics. **Special study options:** Accelerated study, combined bachelor's/graduate degree, distance learning, double major, dual enrollment of high school students, ESL, external degree, honors, independent study, internships, liberal arts/career combination, student-designed major, study abroad, teacher certification program, weekend college. **Credit/placement by examination:** AP, CLEP, IB, SAT, ACT. 60 credit hours maximum toward bachelor's degree. **Support services:** Learning center, reduced course load, study skills assistance, tutoring, writing center.

Honors college/program. 1200 SAT or 27 ACT/3.5 HS GPA. Additional honors essay, letter of recommendation, and resume. 5% of freshmen admitted.

Majors. **Biology:** General, biochemistry, environmental. **Business:** Accounting, business admin, finance, international, management information systems, marketing. **Communications:** Communications/speech/rhetoric, media studies. **Computer sciences:** General, computer science, networking, web page design. **Conservation:** Environmental studies. **Education:** Biology, elementary, English, foreign languages, French, mathematics, secondary, social studies, Spanish. **English:** English lit. **Foreign languages:** French, Italian, Spanish. **Health services:** Audiology/speech pathology. **History:** General. **Human services:** Social work. **Liberal arts:** Arts/sciences. **Math:** General, applied. **Philosophy/religion:** Philosophy, religion. **Physical sciences:** Chemistry, physics. **Protective services:** Law enforcement admin. **Psychology:** General. **Social sciences:** Economics, international relations, political science, sociology.

Most popular majors. Business/marketing 36%, communications/journalism 17%, health sciences 6%, psychology 8%, security/protective services 9%.

Technology on campus. 738 workstations in dormitories, library, computer center, student center. Dormitories wired for high-speed internet access and linked to campus network. Commuter students can connect to campus network. Online course registration, online library, helpline, wireless network available.

Student life. Freshman orientation: Mandatory, $200 fee. Preregistration for classes offered. Held overnight in June and July. **Policies:** Adherence to college code of conduct and regulations outlined in student handbook. Freshmen not permitted cars on campus. **Housing:** Coed dorms, special housing for disabled, apartments, gender-neutral housing, themed housing, wellness housing available. $250 nonrefundable deposit, deadline 5/1. Living-learning communities available. **Activities:** Bands, campus ministries, choral groups, dance, drama, film society, international student organizations, literary magazine, music ensembles, Model UN, musical theater, radio station, student government, student newspaper, TV station, Gaelic Society, Council of Multicultural Leaders, Italian Society, Students of Caribbean Ancestry, Hispanic Organization for Latin Awareness, Hellenic Society, Black Student Union, Gay Straight Alliance, Iona International Club, Middle Eastern Club.

Athletics. NCAA. **Intercollegiate:** Baseball M, basketball, cross-country, diving, golf M, lacrosse W, rowing (crew), soccer, softball W, swimming, track and field, volleyball W, water polo. **Intramural:** Badminton, basketball, football (non-tackle), handball, soccer, ultimate frisbee, volleyball. **Team name:** Gaels.

Student services. Adult student services, alcohol/substance abuse counseling, chaplain/spiritual director, career counseling, services for economically disadvantaged, student employment services, financial aid counseling, health services, minority student services, personal counseling, placement for graduates, veterans' counselor, women's services. **Physically disabled:** Services for visually, speech, hearing impaired.

Contact. E-mail: admissions@iona.edu
Phone: (914) 633-2502 Toll-free number: (800) 231-4662
Fax: (914) 633-2182
Alick Letang, Associate Vice President, Enrollment Management, Iona College, 715 North Avenue, New Rochelle, NY 10801-1890

Ithaca College
Ithaca, New York
www.ithaca.edu

CB member
CB code: 2325

- Private 4-year health science and liberal arts college
- Residential campus in large town
- 6,278 degree-seeking undergraduates: 1% part-time, 58% women, 6% African American, 4% Asian American, 8% Hispanic/Latino, 3% Multiracial, non-Hispanic, 2% international
- 443 degree-seeking graduate students
- 67% of applicants admitted
- Application essay required
- 76% graduate within 6 years; 28% enter graduate study

General. Founded in 1892. Regionally accredited. **Degrees:** 1,438 bachelor's awarded; master's, professional offered. **ROTC:** Army, Air Force. **Location:** 250 miles from New York City, 60 miles from Syracuse. **Calendar:** Semester, extensive summer session. **Full-time faculty:** 512 total; 90% have terminal degrees, 13% minority, 46% women. **Part-time faculty:** 278 total; 51% have terminal degrees, 7% minority, 52% women. **Class size:** 60% < 20, 34% 20-39, 2% 40-49, 3% 50-99, less than 1% >100. **Special facilities:** Digital audio/video labs, photography labs, cinematography postproduction studio, film animation lab, lighting studio, physical therapy and occupational therapy clinics, speech and hearing clinic, exercise science labs, human anatomy lab, movement analysis lab, financial trading room, recording and electroacoustic music studio, performance halls, psychology labs, observatory, natural lands, greenhouse, organic garden, apiary.

Freshman class profile. 16,519 applied, 11,072 admitted, 1,809 enrolled.

Mid 50% test scores		Rank in top tenth:	23%
SAT critical reading:	550-640	End year in good standing:	92%
SAT math:	550-630	Return as sophomores:	86%
SAT writing:	560-640	Out-of-state:	55%
ACT composite:	24-29	Live on campus:	99%
Rank in top quarter:	63%	International:	2%

Basis for selection. School achievement record most important. School and community activities, accomplishments, special talents, interview also important. SAT/ACT optional. Only students who are home-schooled or who attend high schools that provide only descriptive report cards (rather than alpha numeric grades) are required to submit SAT/ACT. Students who submit scores should have them sent directly from the testing agency. Audition required for music, theater arts programs; portfolio recommended for BFA program. **Home schooled:** Transcript of courses and grades, letter of recommendation (nonparent) required. SAT/ACT required.

High school preparation. College-preparatory program required. 16 units required; 20 recommended. Required and recommended units include English 4, mathematics 3-4, social studies 3-4, science 3-4, foreign language 2-3 and academic electives 1.

2015-2016 Annual costs. Tuition/fees: $40,658. Room/board: $14,674. Books/supplies: $1,537. Personal expenses: $1,929.

2015-2016 Financial aid. Need-based: 1,561 full-time freshmen applied for aid; 1,273 deemed to have need; 1,273 received aid. Average need met was 90%. Average scholarship/grant was $25,597; average loan $5,528. 76% of total undergraduate aid awarded as scholarships/grants, 24% as loans/jobs. **Non-need-based:** Awarded to 2,045 full-time undergraduates, including 806 freshmen. Scholarships awarded for academics, alumni affiliation, leadership, minority status, music/drama, ROTC.

Application procedures. Admission: Closing date 2/1 (receipt date). $60 fee, may be waived for applicants with need. Application must be submitted online. Admission notification by 4/15. Admission notification on a rolling basis beginning on or about 11/15. Must reply by May 1 or within 2 week(s) if notified thereafter. **Financial aid:** Priority date 2/1; no closing date. FAFSA, CSS PROFILE required. Applicants notified on a rolling basis starting 2/15; must reply by 5/1.

Academics. Integrative Core Curriculum (ICC) required of all students. Students take courses from natural science, creative arts, humanities, and social sciences, all focusing on a general theme such as "Inquiry, Imagination, and Innovation" or "Quest for a Sustainable Future". Additional elements of the ICC include coursework in writing, diversity, and quantitative literacy, as well as a capstone experience and learning portfolio. **Special study options:** Accelerated study, combined bachelor's/graduate degree, cross-registration, distance learning, double major, dual enrollment of high school students, honors, independent study, internships, liberal arts/career combination, New York semester, semester at sea, student-designed major, study abroad, teacher certification program, Washington semester. London Center (England), Los Angeles and New York (ICNYC) programs, study opportunities in more than 50 countries. **Credit/placement by examination:** AP, CLEP, IB, institutional tests. 36 credit hours maximum toward bachelor's degree. A limited number of CLEP credits may be applied toward general education requirements. **Support services:** Learning center, study skills assistance, tutoring, writing center. Academic Advising Center.

Honors college/program. Accepts approximately 100 high-achieving students every year into an integrated academic and co-curricular program. Honors students take a series of special interdisciplinary seminars open only to honor students. The co-curricular programming includes social events, travel opportunities and service projects.

Majors. Architecture: Architecture. **Biology:** General, biochemistry, exercise physiology. **Business:** General, accounting, business admin. **Communications:** Broadcast journalism, communications/speech/rhetoric, digital media, journalism, media studies, organizational, persuasive communications, radio/TV, sports. **Communications technology:** Recording arts. **Computer sciences:** General, computer science, programming. **Conservation:** Environmental science, environmental studies. **Education:** Art, biology, chemistry, Deaf/hearing impaired, English, foreign languages, French, German, health, history, mathematics, multi-level teacher, music, physical, science, secondary, social studies, Spanish, speech impaired. **English:** Creative writing, English lit, rhetoric/composition, writing. **Foreign languages:** General, French, German, Italian, Spanish. **Health services:** Athletic training, communication disorders, community health, facilities admin, health services admin, occupational therapy, physical therapy, predental, premedicine, preveterinary, recreational therapy, speech pathology. **History:** General. **Liberal arts:** Arts/sciences. **Math:** General. **Parks/recreation:** General, exercise sciences, health/fitness, sports admin, sports studies. **Philosophy/religion:** General, philosophy. **Physical sciences:** Chemistry, physics. **Psychology:** General, industrial. **Social sciences:** General, anthropology, applied economics, econometrics, economics, political science, sociology. **Visual/performing arts:** General, acting, art, art history/conservation, brass instruments, cinematography, dance, documentaries, dramatic, film/cinema/video, jazz, music, music performance, music theory/composition, musical theater, percussion instruments, photography, studio arts, studio arts management, theater arts management, theater design, woodwind instruments.

Most popular majors. Business/marketing 12%, communications/journalism 22%, health sciences 16%, visual/performing arts 17%.

Technology on campus. 640 workstations in library, computer center. Dormitories wired for high-speed internet access and linked to campus network. Commuter students can connect to campus network. Online course registration, online library, helpline, repair service, student web hosting, wireless network available.

Student life. Freshman orientation: Available, $265 fee. Preregistration for classes offered. 2.5 days in summer or 4 days before school begins. Separate parent orientation program offered in summer. **Housing:** Guaranteed on-campus for all undergraduates. Coed dorms, single-sex dorms, special housing for disabled, apartments, gender-neutral housing, themed housing, wellness housing available. **Activities:** Bands, campus ministries, choral groups, dance, drama, film society, international student organizations, literary magazine, music ensembles, Model UN, musical theater, opera, radio station, student government, student newspaper, symphony orchestra, TV station, Catholic, Buddhist, Protestant communities, Hillel, Spectrum, students for justice in Palestine, student alliance for Israel, IC human rights, IC Republicans, IC environmental society, African-Latino society, Habitat for Humanity.

Athletics. NCAA. **Intercollegiate:** Baseball M, basketball, cross-country, diving, field hockey W, football (tackle) M, golf W, gymnastics W, lacrosse, rowing (crew), soccer, softball W, swimming, tennis, track and field, volleyball W, wrestling M. **Intramural:** Badminton, basketball, football (non-tackle), soccer, tennis, ultimate frisbee, volleyball. **Team name:** Bombers.

Student services. Adult student services, alcohol/substance abuse counseling, chaplain/spiritual director, career counseling, student employment services, financial aid counseling, health services, minority student services, personal counseling, placement for graduates, veterans' counselor. **Physically disabled:** Services for visually, speech, hearing impaired.

Contact. E-mail: admission@ithaca.edu
Phone: (607) 274-3124 Toll-free number: (800) 429-4274
Fax: (607) 274-1900
Nicole Eversley Bradwell, Director of Admission, Ithaca College, 953 Danby Road, Ithaca, NY 14850-7002

Jewish Theological Seminary of America
New York, New York
www.jtsa.edu/list
CB code: 2339

- Private 4-year liberal arts college affiliated with the Jewish faith
- Residential campus in very large city
- 158 degree-seeking undergraduates: 53% women
- 208 degree-seeking graduate students
- 52% of applicants admitted
- SAT or ACT with writing, application essay required
- 86% graduate within 6 years

General. Founded in 1886. Regionally accredited. List College and its dual-degree programs with Columbia University and Barnard College provide a rigorous education in the liberal arts and Jewish Studies, preparing young Jewish scholars for leadership roles in a variety of venues within the Jewish community. **Degrees:** 32 bachelor's awarded; master's, doctoral offered. **Calendar:** Semester, extensive summer session. **Full-time faculty:** 46 total; 98% have terminal degrees, 30% women. **Part-time faculty:** 43 total; 84% have terminal degrees, 37% women. **Class size:** 82% < 20, 18% 20-39. **Special facilities:** Jewish museum containing over 27,000 objects (paintings, sculptures, works on paper, artifacts, etc.), library containing largest collection of Hebraica and Judaica outside of Israel.

Freshman class profile. 106 applied, 55 admitted, 39 enrolled.

Mid 50% test scores		Rank in top quarter:	60%
SAT critical reading:	660-750	Rank in top tenth:	40%
SAT math:	630-710	Out-of-state:	77%
SAT writing:	680-720	Live on campus:	100%
ACT composite:	28-32	Fraternities:	15%
GPA 3.75 or higher:	45%	Sororities:	15%
GPA 3.50-3.74:	55%		

Basis for selection. School achievement record, interest in Jewish studies, test scores, recommendations important; leadership potential considered. Interview recommended for residents in the New York area (within 100 mile radius).

High school preparation. College-preparatory program recommended. Required and recommended units include English 3-4, mathematics 3-4, social studies 3-4, history 3-4, science 3-4 (laboratory 4), foreign language 3-4, computer science 3-4, visual/performing arts 3-4 and academic electives 3-4. Additional courses in Judaic studies, when available.

2015-2016 Annual costs. Tuition/fees: $20,340. Room only: $11,720.

2014-2015 Financial aid. **Need-based:** 20 full-time freshmen applied for aid; 16 deemed to have need; 16 received aid. Average need met was 88%. Average scholarship/grant was $34,537; average loan $3,138. 96% of total undergraduate aid awarded as scholarships/grants, 4% as loans/jobs. **Non-need-based:** Awarded to 68 full-time undergraduates, including 18 freshmen. Scholarships awarded for academics, leadership.

Application procedures. **Admission:** Closing date 2/15 (postmark date). $65 fee, may be waived for applicants with need. Admission notification by 4/1. Must reply by 5/1. Application deadline January 1 for double degree

program with Barnard College, February 15 for joint program with Columbia University. **Financial aid:** Closing date 3/1. FAFSA, institutional form required. Applicants notified by 4/1; must reply within 2 week(s) of notification.

Academics. **Special study options:** Cross-registration, double major, dual enrollment of high school students, internships, New York semester, student-designed major, study abroad. **Credit/placement by examination:** AP, CLEP, IB, institutional tests. 6 credit hours maximum toward bachelor's degree. **Support services:** Pre-admission summer program, remedial instruction, tutoring, writing center.

Majors. **Foreign languages:** General. **Philosophy/religion:** Judaic. **Theology:** Sacred music. **Visual/performing arts:** Music performance, music theory/composition.

Technology on campus. 50 workstations in dormitories, library, computer center. Dormitories wired for high-speed internet access and linked to campus network. Commuter students can connect to campus network. Online course registration, online library, helpline, wireless network available.

Student life. **Freshman orientation:** Mandatory. Preregistration for classes offered. **Policies:** Student life centers around supportive Jewish community. Undergraduates enrolled in joint degree programs with Barnard and Columbia participate in their extracurricular activities. **Housing:** Coed dorms available. $500 nonrefundable deposit, deadline 5/1. **Activities:** Choral groups, dance, community service organization.

Athletics. **Intramural:** Basketball, bowling, field hockey W, lacrosse M, softball, volleyball.

Student services. Career counseling, student employment services, financial aid counseling, health services, personal counseling, placement for graduates.

Contact. E-mail: lcadmissions@jtsa.edu
Phone: (212) 678-8832 Fax: (212) 280-6022
Melissa Present, Director of Admissions, Jewish Theological Seminary of America, 3080 Broadway, New York, NY 10025

Juilliard School
New York, New York
www.juilliard.edu
CB code: 2340

- Private 4-year music and performing arts college
- Commuter campus in very large city
- 489 degree-seeking undergraduates: 48% women
- 364 degree-seeking graduate students
- 6% of applicants admitted
- Application essay, interview required

General. Founded in 1905. Regionally accredited. **Degrees:** 123 bachelor's awarded; master's, doctoral offered. **Calendar:** Semester. **Full-time faculty:** 131 total; 12% minority, 34% women. **Part-time faculty:** 220 total; 12% minority, 36% women. **Class size:** 89% < 20, 11% 20-39, less than 1% 50-99. **Special facilities:** Media center, over 100 practice rooms with over 200 pianos, scenery and costume shops, 15 2-story rehearsal studios, 5 theaters, 2 recital halls.

Freshman class profile. 2,551 applied, 164 admitted, 108 enrolled.

Out-of-state:	90%	Live on campus:	100%

Basis for selection. Quality of performance at audition most important. Foreign students given English proficiency examination at time of audition or may present TOEFL. In general, standardized test scores are requested of home schooled applicants. Audition required. **Home schooled:** Transcript of courses and grades, letter of recommendation (nonparent) required.

High school preparation. Recommended units include visual/performing arts 4.

2016-2017 Annual costs. Tuition/fees (projected): $41,460. Room/board: $15,380. Books/supplies: $580. Personal expenses: $2,860.

2015-2016 Financial aid. **Need-based:** 84% of total undergraduate aid awarded as scholarships/grants, 16% as loans/jobs. **Non-need-based:** Scholarships awarded for music/drama.

Application procedures. **Admission:** Closing date 12/1. $110 fee, may be waived for applicants with need. Admission notification by 4/1. Must reply by May 1 or within 2 week(s) if notified thereafter. Music auditions held in March. Drama auditions in January and February. Dance auditions in February and March. Application closing date December 1; notification by April 1 or one month after audition. **Financial aid:** Closing date 3/1. FAFSA, institutional form, CSS PROFILE required. Applicants notified by 4/1; must reply by 5/1.

Academics. 3-year diploma program available in performing arts. **Special study options:** Accelerated study. **Credit/placement by examination:** AP, CLEP, institutional tests. **Support services:** Tutoring.

Majors. Visual/performing arts: Dance, dramatic, jazz, music performance, music theory/composition, piano/keyboard, stringed instruments.

Technology on campus. 65 workstations in dormitories, library, computer center. Dormitories wired for high-speed internet access. Online library, wireless network available.

Student life. Freshman orientation: Mandatory, $200 fee. Preregistration for classes offered. Held 10 days before first day of classes for all new students. **Housing:** Guaranteed on-campus for freshmen. Coed dorms available. $150 fully refundable deposit, deadline 5/15. **Activities:** Jazz band, dance, drama, music ensembles, opera, student government, symphony orchestra, ArtREACH, Korea Campus Crusade for Christ, Christian Fellowship, Amnesty Juilliard.

Student services. Alcohol/substance abuse counseling, career counseling, student employment services, financial aid counseling, health services, minority student services, personal counseling, placement for graduates.

Contact. E-mail: admissions@juilliard.edu
Phone: (212) 799-5000 ext. 223
Lee Cioppa, Associate Director for Admissions, Juilliard School, 60 Lincoln Center Plaza, New York, NY 10023-6588

Kehilath Yakov Rabbinical Seminary
Ossining, New York
www.kehilathyakov.com   **CB code: 0619**

- Private 4-year rabbinical college for men affiliated with the Jewish faith
- Very large city
- 126 degree-seeking undergraduates

General. Accredited by AARTS. **Degrees:** 14 bachelor's awarded. **Calendar:** Differs by program. **Full-time faculty:** 6 total.

Basis for selection. Open admission.

2015-2016 Annual costs. Tuition/fees: $9,300. Room/board: $3,800.

Application procedures. Admission: No deadline.

Academics. Credit/placement by examination: AP, CLEP.

Majors. Philosophy/religion: Judaic. **Theology:** Talmudic.

Contact. Phone: (718) 963-1212
Kehilath Yakov Rabbinical Seminary, 340 Ilington Road, Ossining, NY 10562

Keuka College
Keuka Park, New York   **CB member**
www.keuka.edu   **CB code: 2350**

- Private 4-year liberal arts college affiliated with the American Baptist Churches in the USA
- Residential campus in rural community
- 1,717 degree-seeking undergraduates: 22% part-time, 74% women, 9% African American, 1% Asian American, 4% Hispanic/Latino, 1% Native American, 2% Multi-racial, non-Hispanic, 3% international
- 209 degree-seeking graduate students
- 77% of applicants admitted
- Application essay required
- 51% graduate within 6 years; 42% enter graduate study

General. Founded in 1890. Regionally accredited. Keuka offers an Accelerated Studies for Adults Program (ASAP). Also, Keuka offers programs in China and Vietnam. **Degrees:** 547 bachelor's awarded; master's offered. **Location:** 50 miles from Rochester, 60 miles from Syracuse. **Calendar:** 4-1-4, limited summer session. **Full-time faculty:** 91 total; 78% have terminal degrees, 7% minority, 60% women. **Part-time faculty:** 354 total; 14% have terminal degrees, 9% minority, 54% women.

Freshman class profile. 2,290 applied, 1,756 admitted, 318 enrolled.

Mid 50% test scores			
SAT critical reading:	430-520	GPA 2.0-2.99:	37%
SAT math:	420-560	Rank in top quarter:	26%
SAT writing:	410-520	Rank in top tenth:	8%
GPA 3.75 or higher:	16%	End year in good standing:	88%
GPA 3.50-3.74:	15%	Return as sophomores:	73%
GPA 3.0-3.49:	32%	Out-of-state:	8%
		Live on campus:	94%

Basis for selection. Overall GPA, extracurricular activities, community service, leadership experience, letter of recommendation, quality of essay, SAT/ACT scores considered by committee. Interview recommended for all, required for some.

High school preparation. 18 units recommended. Recommended units include English 4, mathematics 3, social studies 3, history 2, science 3 (laboratory 2) and foreign language 3.

2016-2017 Annual costs. Tuition/fees: $29,506. Room/board: $11,070. Books/supplies: $1,300. Personal expenses: $2,940.

2015-2016 Financial aid. Need-based: 312 full-time freshmen applied for aid; 293 deemed to have need; 293 received aid. Average scholarship/grant was $9,280; average loan $3,502. 62% of total undergraduate aid awarded as scholarships/grants, 38% as loans/jobs. **Non-need-based:** Awarded to 801 full-time undergraduates, including 303 freshmen. Scholarships awarded for academics, alumni affiliation, leadership, minority status.

Application procedures. Admission: No deadline. No application fee. Admission notification on a rolling basis beginning on or about 8/1. **Financial aid:** Priority date 3/15; no closing date. FAFSA required. Applicants notified on a rolling basis starting 2/1; must reply by 5/1 or within 2 week(s) of notification.

Academics. All students must complete 1 field period or internship each year, every 30 credit hours (experiential education). Field Period enables students to spend 4 weeks a year participating in an internship or international travel, or undertaking an independent project. **Special study options:** Accelerated study, combined bachelor's/graduate degree, cooperative education, cross-registration, double major, dual enrollment of high school students, independent study, internships, student-designed major, study abroad, teacher certification program. **Credit/placement by examination:** AP, CLEP, institutional tests. 12 credit hours maximum toward bachelor's degree. **Support services:** Learning center, reduced course load, remedial instruction, study skills assistance, tutoring, writing center.

Majors. Biology: General, biochemistry. **Business:** Accounting, business admin, marketing. **Communications:** Communications/speech/rhetoric. **Conservation:** Environmental science. **Education:** Biology, early childhood, English, mathematics, secondary, social studies, special ed. **English:** English lit. **Foreign languages:** American Sign Language, sign language interpretation. **Health services:** Clinical lab science, nursing (RN), occupational therapy. **History:** General. **Human services:** Social work. **Liberal arts:** Arts/sciences. **Math:** General. **Protective services:** Law enforcement admin. **Psychology:** General. **Social sciences:** General, criminology, sociology. **Visual/performing arts:** Art.

Most popular majors. Business/marketing 20%, education 7%, health sciences 34%, public administration/social services 22%, security/protective services 8%.

Technology on campus. 148 workstations in dormitories, library, computer center, student center. Dormitories wired for high-speed internet access and linked to campus network. Online course registration, online library, helpline, repair service, wireless network available.

Student life. Freshman orientation: Mandatory, $150 fee. Preregistration for classes offered. Two-session summer program. **Policies:** No smoking allowed in any campus building, including residence halls. **Housing:** Guaranteed on-campus for all undergraduates. Coed dorms, single-sex dorms, special housing for disabled, apartments, cooperative housing, themed housing, wellness housing available. $200 fully refundable deposit, deadline 5/1. Leadership and management housing available. **Activities:** Bands, campus ministries, choral groups, dance, drama, film society, international student organizations, literary magazine, musical theater, radio station, student government, student newspaper, social work club, Keuka Leaders club, Keuka Circle, Newman Club, minority support group, political action coalition, Student Nurse Association.

Athletics. NCAA. **Intercollegiate:** Baseball M, basketball, cross-country, field hockey W, golf, lacrosse, soccer, softball W, tennis, volleyball W. **Intramural:** Basketball, football (non-tackle), soccer, softball, volleyball. **Team name:** Wolf Pack.

Student services. Adult student services, alcohol/substance abuse counseling, chaplain/spiritual director, career counseling, student employment services, financial aid counseling, health services, minority student services, personal counseling, placement for graduates, women's services. **Physically disabled:** Services for visually, speech, hearing impaired.

Contact. E-mail: admissions@keuka.edu
Phone: (315) 279-5254 Toll-free number: (800) 335-3852
Fax: (315) 536-5386
Megan Ryan, Director of Admissions, Keuka College, 141 Central Avenue, Keuka Park, NY 14478-0098

The King's College
New York, New York
www.tkc.edu

CB code: 2871

- Private 4-year liberal arts college affiliated with the nondenominational tradition
- Residential campus in very large city
- 490 degree-seeking undergraduates: 2% part-time, 62% women, 3% African American, 3% Asian American, 8% Hispanic/Latino, 1% Native Hawaiian/Pacific islander, 3% Multi-racial, non-Hispanic, 3% international
- 40% of applicants admitted
- SAT or ACT (ACT writing recommended), interview required
- 45% graduate within 6 years

General. Regionally accredited. **Degrees:** 110 bachelor's awarded. **ROTC:** Army. **Location:** Located in New York City. **Calendar:** Semester, limited summer session. **Full-time faculty:** 26 total; 100% have terminal degrees, 8% minority, 15% women. **Part-time faculty:** 34 total; 53% have terminal degrees, 44% women. **Class size:** 47% < 20, 50% 20-39, less than 1% 40-49, 2% 50-99.

Freshman class profile. 2,529 applied, 1,001 admitted, 150 enrolled.

Mid 50% test scores			
SAT critical reading:	550-660	GPA 3.50-3.74:	20%
SAT math:	520-590	GPA 3.0-3.49:	24%
SAT writing:	530-640	GPA 2.0-2.99:	7%
ACT composite:	24-29	Return as sophomores:	66%
GPA 3.75 or higher:	49%	Out-of-state:	92%
		International:	1%

Basis for selection. Admissions based on academic preparedness and leadership qualities, primarily assessed through transcript, SAT or ACT scores, and entrance interview. **Home schooled:** Transcript should include all information regarding state requirements for high school graduation. SAT and ACT scores especially important to determine student's ability to succeed academically. Personal interview required during which student can elaborate on courses they have studied and activities they have participated in outside the home. **Learning Disabled:** Documentation required of any learning disabilities that will require special accommodation.

High school preparation. Required and recommended units include English 4, mathematics 3-4, social studies 2, history 2, science 3-4, foreign language 1-2 and academic electives 2.

2015-2016 Annual costs. Tuition/fees: $33,270. Room only: $13,000. Books/supplies: $800. Personal expenses: $2,625.

2014-2015 Financial aid. Need-based: 127 full-time freshmen applied for aid; 107 deemed to have need; 107 received aid. Average need met was 60%. Average scholarship/grant was $21,130; average loan $2,579. 73% of total undergraduate aid awarded as scholarships/grants, 27% as loans/jobs. **Non-need-based:** Awarded to 153 full-time undergraduates, including 40 freshmen. Scholarships awarded for academics, leadership.

Application procedures. Admission: Priority date 11/15; no deadline. $30 fee, may be waived for applicants with need. Admission notification on a rolling basis beginning on or about 9/15. Must reply by May 1 or within 4 week(s) if notified thereafter. **Financial aid:** Priority date 3/15; no closing date. FAFSA required. Applicants notified on a rolling basis starting 2/15.

Academics. Biblically-based curriculum with a common core in politics, philosophy, and economics. **Special study options:** Distance learning, dual enrollment of high school students, independent study, internships, study abroad. **Credit/placement by examination:** AP, CLEP, IB, SAT, ACT, institutional tests. 6 credit hours maximum toward bachelor's degree. Students may receive open elective credit for CLEP exams in French, German, or Spanish. To receive credit, score must be equal to the grade of B based on ACE guidelines. **Support services:** Learning center, tutoring.

Majors. Business: Business admin, finance. **Liberal arts:** Humanities. **Philosophy/religion:** Religion.

Most popular majors. Business/marketing 20%, liberal arts 80%.

Technology on campus. PC or laptop required. 12 workstations in library. Dormitories wired for high-speed internet access and linked to campus network. Commuter students can connect to campus network. Online course registration, online library, wireless network available.

Student life. Freshman orientation: Mandatory. Preregistration for classes offered. Held two days prior to first day of class. **Policies:** No alcoholic beverages/drug usage permitted on campus or in housing. **Housing:** Guaranteed on-campus for freshmen. Single-sex dorms, special housing for disabled, apartments available. $450 nonrefundable deposit, deadline 6/30. **Activities:** Campus ministries, choral groups, dance, drama, international student organizations, literary magazine, music ensembles, student government, student newspaper.

Athletics. USCAA, NCCAA. **Intercollegiate:** Soccer W. **Team name:** The Lions.

Student services. Chaplain/spiritual director, career counseling, student employment services, financial aid counseling, personal counseling.

Contact. E-mail: admissions@tkc.edu
Phone: (212) 659-3610 Toll-free number: (888) 969-7200 ext. 3610
Fax: (212) 659-3611
Luke Smith, Director of Admissions, The King's College, 56 Broadway, New York, NY 10004

Le Moyne College
Syracuse, New York
www.lemoyne.edu

CB member
CB code: 2366

- Private 4-year liberal arts college affiliated with the Roman Catholic Church
- Residential campus in small city
- 2,769 degree-seeking undergraduates: 10% part-time, 59% women
- 492 degree-seeking graduate students
- 62% of applicants admitted
- Application essay required
- 67% graduate within 6 years; 28% enter graduate study

General. Founded in 1946. Regionally accredited. **Degrees:** 636 bachelor's awarded; master's offered. **ROTC:** Army, Air Force. **Location:** 2 miles from downtown. **Calendar:** Semester, extensive summer session. **Full-time faculty:** 171 total; 92% have terminal degrees, 15% minority, 41% women. **Part-time faculty:** 175 total; 36% have terminal degrees, 9% minority, 52% women. **Class size:** 51% < 20, 44% 20-39, 3% 40-49, 1% 50-99, less than 1% >100. **Special facilities:** Performing arts center, art gallery.

Freshman class profile. 6,877 applied, 4,247 admitted, 634 enrolled.

Mid 50% test scores			
SAT critical reading:	480-580	Rank in top quarter:	55%
SAT math:	500-590	Rank in top tenth:	22%
ACT composite:	21-25	End year in good standing:	93%
GPA 3.75 or higher:	31%	Return as sophomores:	88%
GPA 3.50-3.74:	24%	Out-of-state:	6%
GPA 3.0-3.49:	30%	Live on campus:	83%
GPA 2.0-2.99:	15%	International:	1%

Basis for selection. High school courses and performance most important; class rank, test scores, recommendations, essay, interview, extracurricular activities also important. Students from underrepresented populations encouraged. Test optional. SAT or ACT still required for the following categories for students: A student who has been home schooled; An international student for whom English is not a first language, and whose educational instruction was not in English for the greater part of their educational experience; OR applying for Presidential or Dean Scholarship; Physician Assistant Studies Program; Dual Degree Nursing Program; Early Assurance Medical or Dental Programs; All Affiliated 3-3 and Affiliated 3-4 Medical Programs; Higher Education Opportunity Program (HEOP). Interview recommended. **Home schooled:** Statement describing home school structure and mission, transcript of courses and grades, interview, letter of recommendation (nonparent) required. **Learning Disabled:** Interview strongly recommended.

High school preparation. College-preparatory program recommended. 17 units required. Required and recommended units include English 4, mathematics 3-4, social studies 4, science 3-4 (laboratory 3) and foreign language 3. 4 math required for science and math majors.

2016-2017 Annual costs. Tuition/fees: $33,030. Room/board: $12,970. Books/supplies: $1,300. Personal expenses: $865.

2014-2015 Financial aid. Need-based: 647 full-time freshmen applied for aid; 570 deemed to have need; 570 received aid. Average need met was

80%. Average scholarship/grant was $20,903; average loan $3,573. 66% of total undergraduate aid awarded as scholarships/grants, 34% as loans/jobs. **Non-need-based:** Awarded to 640 full-time undergraduates, including 211 freshmen. Scholarships awarded for academics, alumni affiliation, athletics, leadership, minority status, ROTC. **Additional information:** Parent loan program at low interest, monthly payment plans and alternative loans for students.

Application procedures. Admission: Priority date 2/1; no deadline. $35 fee, may be waived for applicants with need, free for online applicants. Admission notification on a rolling basis beginning on or about 1/1. Must reply by May 1 or within 4 week(s) if notified thereafter. **Financial aid:** Priority date 2/15; no closing date. FAFSA required. Applicants notified by 3/15; must reply by 5/1 or within 2 week(s) of notification.

Academics. Academic accommodations and services for students with documented disabilities. **Special study options:** Accelerated study, combined bachelor's/graduate degree, distance learning, double major, dual enrollment of high school students, honors, independent study, internships, liberal arts/career combination, semester at sea, study abroad, teacher certification program, Washington semester. Certificate of Advanced Studies in Educational Leadership, Certificate of Advanced Studies in Nursing, Post-Baccalaureate RN to MS Certificate, Postbachelor's Certificate in Higher Education Leadership, Postbachelor's Certificate in Health Care Leadership, Postbachelor's Certificate in Adult Education, Postbachelor's Certificate in Health Information Systems, and Postbachelor's Certificate in Arts Administration. **Credit/placement by examination:** AP, CLEP, IB, institutional tests. **Support services:** Learning center, remedial instruction, study skills assistance, tutoring, writing center.

Majors. Biology: General, biochemistry, ecology. **Business:** Accounting, finance, human resources, management information systems, marketing, operations. **Communications:** General. **Computer sciences:** General, programming. **Conservation:** Environmental studies. **Engineering:** Pre-engineering. **English:** English lit. **Foreign languages:** French, Spanish. **Health services:** Nursing (RN), predental, premedicine, preoptometry, prepharmacy, preveterinary. **History:** General. **Math:** General. **Philosophy/religion:** Philosophy, religion. **Physical sciences:** Chemistry, physics. **Psychology:** General. **Social sciences:** Criminology, economics, political science, sociology. **Visual/performing arts:** Dramatic.

Most popular majors. Biology 17%, business/marketing 23%, communications/journalism 8%, health sciences 8%, psychology 14%, social sciences 11%.

Technology on campus. 330 workstations in dormitories, library, computer center, student center. Dormitories wired for high-speed internet access and linked to campus network. Commuter students can connect to campus network. Online course registration, online library, helpline, repair service, student web hosting, wireless network available.

Student life. Freshman orientation: Mandatory, $200 fee. Preregistration for classes offered. Four one-day summer welcome sessions and one three-day fall arrival session prior to the beginning of classes. **Housing:** Guaranteed on-campus for all undergraduates. Coed dorms, special housing for disabled, apartments, themed housing available. Living/Learning communities available. **Activities:** Bands, campus ministries, choral groups, dance, drama, film society, international student organizations, literary magazine, music ensembles, Model UN, musical theater, radio station, student government, student newspaper, TV station, international club, Amnesty International, Habitat for Humanity, Democrats club, Republican club, Gaelic Society, El Progreso, Pride in Our Work Ethnicity and Race, Muslim student association, Asian Students in Alliance.

Athletics. NCAA. **Intercollegiate:** Baseball M, basketball, cross-country, diving, golf, lacrosse, soccer, softball W, swimming, tennis, track and field, volleyball W. **Intramural:** Basketball, football (non-tackle), racquetball, soccer, softball, volleyball. **Team name:** Dolphins.

Student services. Adult student services, alcohol/substance abuse counseling, chaplain/spiritual director, career counseling, student employment services, financial aid counseling, health services, minority student services, personal counseling, placement for graduates, veterans' counselor. **Physically disabled:** Services for visually, speech, hearing impaired.

Contact. E-mail: admission@lemoyne.edu
Phone: (315) 445-4300 Toll-free number: (800) 333-4733
Fax: (315) 445-4711
Mary Chandler, Senior Director of Admission, Le Moyne College, 1419 Salt Springs Road, Syracuse, NY 13214-1301

LIM College
New York, New York   **CB member**
www.limcollege.edu   **CB code: 2380**

- For-profit 4-year business college
- Residential campus in very large city
- 1,515 degree-seeking undergraduates: 6% part-time, 93% women, 15% African American, 6% Asian American, 12% Hispanic/Latino, 1% Native American, 1% Native Hawaiian/Pacific islander, 1% Multi-racial, non-Hispanic, 4% international
- 185 degree-seeking graduate students
- 79% of applicants admitted
- SAT or ACT (ACT writing optional), application essay required
- 50% graduate within 6 years

General. Founded in 1939. Regionally accredited. **Degrees:** 320 bachelor's, 10 associate awarded; master's offered. **Calendar:** Semester, limited summer session. **Full-time faculty:** 32 total. **Part-time faculty:** 164 total. **Class size:** 52% < 20, 48% 20-39.

Freshman class profile. 1,242 applied, 983 admitted, 269 enrolled.

Mid 50% test scores			
		GPA 3.0-3.49:	35%
SAT critical reading:	430-520	GPA 2.0-2.99:	44%
SAT math:	410-510	Return as sophomores:	73%
SAT writing:	420-510	Out-of-state:	63%
GPA 3.75 or higher:	5%	Live on campus:	68%
GPA 3.50-3.74:	11%	International:	4%

Basis for selection. High school and college transcripts, SAT/ACT scores, letters of recommendation, interview when required or requested. Interviews required for a select group of students. **Home schooled:** Transcript of courses and grades, state high school equivalency certificate, interview, letter of recommendation (nonparent) required.

High school preparation. College-preparatory program recommended.

2016-2017 Annual costs. Tuition/fees: $25,725. Room/board: $20,350. Books/supplies: $900. Personal expenses: $1,500.

2014-2015 Financial aid. Need-based: 269 full-time freshmen applied for aid; 209 deemed to have need; 205 received aid. Average need met was 34%. Average scholarship/grant was $9,624; average loan $3,288. 62% of total undergraduate aid awarded as scholarships/grants, 38% as loans/jobs. **Non-need-based:** Awarded to 639 full-time undergraduates, including 163 freshmen. Scholarships awarded for academics, leadership, state residency.

Application procedures. Admission: Priority date 3/1; no deadline. $40 fee, may be waived for applicants with need. Admission notification on a rolling basis beginning on or about 11/15. **Financial aid:** Priority date 3/1, closing date 11/15. FAFSA required. Applicants notified on a rolling basis starting 2/25; must reply by 7/31 or within 2 week(s) of notification.

Academics. Special study options: Honors, internships, study abroad. 3-credit trip to Europe in winter/summer. **Credit/placement by examination:** AP, CLEP, SAT, ACT, institutional tests. **Support services:** Learning center, pre-admission summer program, reduced course load, remedial instruction, study skills assistance, tutoring, writing center.

Majors. Business: Business admin, fashion, management science, marketing.

Most popular majors. Business/marketing 95%.

Technology on campus. 270 workstations in dormitories, library, computer center, student center. Dormitories wired for high-speed internet access. Commuter students can connect to campus network. Online course registration, online library, helpline, wireless network available.

Student life. Freshman orientation: Mandatory. Preregistration for classes offered. **Housing:** Coed dorms, single-sex dorms, special housing for disabled available. $725 partly refundable deposit, deadline 6/1. **Activities:** Dance, international student organizations, literary magazine, student government.

Student services. Alcohol/substance abuse counseling, career counseling, student employment services, financial aid counseling, personal counseling.

Contact. E-mail: admissions@limcollege.edu
Phone: (212) 310-0639 Toll-free number: (800) 677-1323
Fax: (212) 750-3432
Kristina Ortiz, Dean of Admissions, LIM College, 12 East 53rd Street, New York, NY 10022

LIU Brooklyn

Brooklyn, New York — CB member
http://liu.edu/brooklyn — CB code: 2369

- Private 4-year university and liberal arts college
- Commuter campus in very large city
- 4,568 degree-seeking undergraduates: 12% part-time, 69% women, 28% African American, 16% Asian American, 15% Hispanic/Latino, 2% Multi-racial, non-Hispanic, 3% international
- 3,485 degree-seeking graduate students
- 91% of applicants admitted
- Application essay required

General. Founded in 1926. Regionally accredited. **Degrees:** 807 bachelor's, 22 associate awarded; master's, professional, doctoral offered. **ROTC:** Army. **Calendar:** Semester, extensive summer session. **Full-time faculty:** 238 total; 38% have terminal degrees, 37% minority, 54% women. **Part-time faculty:** 628 total; 46% minority, 57% women. **Class size:** 56% < 20, 40% 20-39, 2% 40-49, 1% 50-99, 1% >100.

Freshman class profile. 7,289 applied, 6,626 admitted, 834 enrolled.

Mid 50% test scores			
SAT critical reading:	400-520	GPA 3.0-3.49:	28%
SAT math:	410-560	GPA 2.0-2.99:	34%
SAT writing:	410-520	End year in good standing:	69%
ACT composite:	18-26	Return as sophomores:	66%
GPA 3.75 or higher:	17%	Out-of-state:	16%
GPA 3.50-3.74:	13%	Live on campus:	26%
		International:	5%

Basis for selection. Rigor of secondary school record, class rank, academic GPA, recommendations, test scores, essay considered. SAT is optional for most programs. Interview, audition, and/or personal statement may be required for particular programs.

High school preparation. College-preparatory program recommended. 15 units recommended. Recommended units include English 4, mathematics 3, social studies 1, history 2, science 3 (laboratory 3) and foreign language 2.

2015-2016 Annual costs. Tuition/fees: $35,546. Room/board: $12,600. Books/supplies: $2,000. Personal expenses: $1,500.

2015-2016 Financial aid. Need-based: 704 full-time freshmen applied for aid; 679 deemed to have need; 679 received aid. Average need met was 55%. Average scholarship/grant was $16,243; average loan $3,682. 74% of total undergraduate aid awarded as scholarships/grants, 26% as loans/jobs. **Non-need-based:** Awarded to 2,529 full-time undergraduates, including 296 freshmen. Scholarships awarded for academics, alumni affiliation, art, athletics, leadership, music/drama, ROTC.

Application procedures. Admission: Priority date 12/1; no deadline. $50 fee, may be waived for applicants with need. Admission notification on a rolling basis beginning on or about 9/1. Must reply by May 1 or within 2 week(s) if notified thereafter. Some programs have February 1 application deadline. **Financial aid:** Priority date 2/15; no closing date. FAFSA required. Applicants notified on a rolling basis starting 2/1; must reply within 4 week(s) of notification.

Academics. Special study options: Accelerated study, combined bachelor's/graduate degree, double major, ESL, honors, internships, student-designed major, study abroad, teacher certification program. **Credit/placement by examination:** AP, CLEP, IB, SAT, ACT, institutional tests. **Support services:** Pre-admission summer program, remedial instruction, tutoring, writing center.

Honors college/program. Selection is based on a student's academic record and the successful completion of an interview.

Majors. Biology: General, biochemistry. **Business:** Accounting, business admin, finance, sales/distribution. **Communications:** Communications/speech/rhetoric, journalism. **Computer sciences:** General. **Education:** Art, biology, chemistry, elementary, English, mathematics, music, physical, social studies, Spanish. **Engineering:** Operations research. **English:** English lit. **Foreign languages:** General. **Health services:** Adult health nursing, athletic training, audiology/speech pathology, clinical lab science, nursing (RN), occupational therapy, physician assistant, respiratory therapy technology, sonography. **History:** General. **Human services:** Social work. **Liberal arts:** Arts/sciences, humanities. **Math:** General. **Parks/recreation:** Exercise sciences, sports admin. **Philosophy/religion:** Philosophy. **Physical sciences:** Chemistry. **Psychology:** General. **Social sciences:** General, economics, political science, sociology. **Visual/performing arts:** Commercial/advertising art, dance, music performance, studio arts.

Most popular majors. Biology 8%, business/marketing 8%, health sciences 57%.

Technology on campus. 580 workstations in dormitories, library, computer center. Dormitories wired for high-speed internet access and linked to campus network. Commuter students can connect to campus network. Online library, helpline, repair service, wireless network available.

Student life. Freshman orientation: Mandatory, $55 fee. Preregistration for classes offered. **Policies:** All students living in the residence halls must be full-time and have a meal plan. Freshmen not permitted cars on campus. **Housing:** Guaranteed on-campus for freshmen. Coed dorms, themed housing available. $300 fully refundable deposit, deadline 8/15. **Activities:** Bands, campus ministries, choral groups, dance, drama, international student organizations, literary magazine, music ensembles, Model UN, radio station, student government, student newspaper, TV station, Activists for Social Justice, Black Students Union, Caribbean Students Movement, Christian Fellowship Club, Colleges Against Cancer, Helping Hands, Hillel, International Students Club, Muslim Students Association, Students for Environmental Action.

Athletics. NCAA. **Intercollegiate:** Baseball M, basketball, bowling W, cross-country W, field hockey W, golf, lacrosse W, soccer, softball W, swimming W, tennis W, track and field, volleyball W. **Team name:** Blackbirds.

Student services. Adult student services, chaplain/spiritual director, career counseling, student employment services, financial aid counseling, health services, personal counseling, placement for graduates, veterans' counselor, women's services. **Physically disabled:** Services for visually, speech, hearing impaired.

Contact. E-mail: bkln-admissions@liu.edu
Phone: (718) 488-1011 Toll-free number: (800) 548-7526
Fax: (718) 780-6110
Catherine Calame, Director of Undergraduate Admissions, LIU Brooklyn, 1 University Plaza, Brooklyn, NY 11201-8423

LIU Post

Brookville, New York — CB member
www.liu.edu/post — CB code: 2070

- Private 4-year university and liberal arts college
- Commuter campus in small town
- 3,443 degree-seeking undergraduates: 11% part-time, 61% women, 12% African American, 4% Asian American, 14% Hispanic/Latino, 2% Multi-racial, non-Hispanic, 9% international
- 2,397 degree-seeking graduate students
- 81% of applicants admitted
- SAT or ACT (ACT writing optional), application essay required
- 49% graduate within 6 years

General. Founded in 1954. Regionally accredited. **Degrees:** 918 bachelor's, 2 associate awarded; master's, doctoral offered. **ROTC:** Army. **Location:** 25 miles from New York City. **Calendar:** Semester, extensive summer session. **Full-time faculty:** 278 total; 90% have terminal degrees, 19% minority, 52% women. **Part-time faculty:** 652 total; 9% minority, 55% women. **Class size:** 69% < 20, 27% 20-39, 3% 40-49, 1% 50-99, less than 1% >100.

Freshman class profile. 6,371 applied, 5,134 admitted, 530 enrolled.

Mid 50% test scores			
SAT critical reading:	450-550	GPA 3.0-3.49:	35%
SAT math:	460-560	GPA 2.0-2.99:	33%
SAT writing:	440-550	End year in good standing:	77%
ACT composite:	19-24	Return as sophomores:	72%
GPA 3.75 or higher:	13%	Out-of-state:	14%
GPA 3.50-3.74:	17%	Live on campus:	57%
		International:	10%

Basis for selection. Rigor of secondary school record, class rank, GPA, recommendations, test scores, essay considered. Audition required for music, dance, and theater programs.

High school preparation. College-preparatory program recommended. 24 units recommended. Recommended units include English 4, mathematics 3, history 2, science 3 (laboratory 1) and foreign language 2.

2015-2016 Annual costs. Tuition/fees: $35,446. Room/board: $13,138. Books/supplies: $2,000. Personal expenses: $1,500.

2014-2015 Financial aid. Need-based: 440 full-time freshmen applied for aid; 371 deemed to have need; 371 received aid. Average need met was 58%. Average scholarship/grant was $10,335; average loan $3,468. 65% of total undergraduate aid awarded as scholarships/grants, 35% as loans/jobs. **Non-need-based:** Awarded to 1,925 full-time undergraduates, including 417 freshmen. Scholarships awarded for academics, alumni affiliation, art, athletics, leadership, music/drama, ROTC.

Application procedures. Admission: Priority date 12/1; no deadline. $50 fee, may be waived for applicants with need. Admission notification on a rolling basis beginning on or about 12/20. Must reply by May 1 or within 2 week(s) if notified thereafter. **Financial aid:** Priority date 2/15, closing date 2/15. FAFSA required. Applicants notified by 2/24; Applicants notified on a rolling basis starting 2/1; must reply by 5/1 or within 2 week(s) of notification.

Academics. Special study options: Accelerated study, combined bachelor's/graduate degree, cooperative education, distance learning, double major, dual enrollment of high school students, ESL, exchange student, honors, independent study, internships, liberal arts/career combination, student-designed major, study abroad, teacher certification program, weekend college. **Credit/placement by examination:** AP, CLEP, IB, SAT, ACT, institutional tests. **Support services:** Learning center, pre-admission summer program, reduced course load, remedial instruction, study skills assistance, tutoring, writing center.

Honors college/program. Entering freshmen applicants must have an average of 88 or above along with a combined SAT score of 1200 (1800 on the three-part exam) or ACT score of 24 or higher. Continuing LIU Post students must have a 3.2 G.P.A. or higher and transfer students are accepted with a 3.4 or higher G.P.A.

Majors. Area/ethnic studies: American. **Biology:** General, cell/histology. **Business:** Accounting, business admin. **Communications:** Journalism, public relations. **Communications technology:** Radio/TV. **Computer sciences:** Computer science, information systems, information technology. **Education:** Art, biology, chemistry, early childhood, earth science, elementary, English, foreign languages, French, health, history, kindergarten/preschool, mathematics, music, physical, social studies, Spanish. **English:** English lit. **Foreign languages:** General, French, Italian, Spanish. **Health services:** Art therapy, audiology/speech pathology, clinical lab science, clinical nutrition, health care admin, health information management, medical radiologic technology/radiation therapy, nursing (RN). **History:** General. **Human services:** General, social work. **Liberal arts:** Arts/sciences, humanities. **Math:** General, applied. **Philosophy/religion:** Philosophy. **Physical sciences:** Chemistry, geology, physics. **Protective services:** Forensics, law enforcement admin. **Psychology:** General. **Social sciences:** Economics, geography, political science, sociology. **Visual/performing arts:** Art history/conservation, arts management, cinematography, commercial/advertising art, dance, digital arts, dramatic, game design, music performance, photography, studio arts, voice/opera.

Most popular majors. Business/marketing 19%, education 12%, health sciences 21%, psychology 7%, security/protective services 7%, social sciences 6%, visual/performing arts 10%.

Technology on campus. 580 workstations in dormitories, library, computer center. Dormitories wired for high-speed internet access and linked to campus network. Commuter students can connect to campus network. Online library, helpline, repair service, wireless network available.

Student life. Freshman orientation: Mandatory, $150 fee. Preregistration for classes offered. Two night/three day sessions for freshmen held in July and August prior to the start of fall classes. **Housing:** Guaranteed on-campus for freshmen. Coed dorms, special housing for disabled, gender-neutral housing, themed housing available. $300 fully refundable deposit, deadline 5/1. 24-hour intensified study housing, 10-month housing available. **Activities:** Bands, campus ministries, choral groups, dance, drama, film society, international student organizations, literary magazine, music ensembles, Model UN, musical theater, radio station, student government, student newspaper, symphony orchestra, TV station, Black Students United, Chinese Student Scholars Association, Hillel, Inter-Greek Council, International Student Union, Korean Student Association, NAACP, Newman Club, Student Activities Board, Relay for Life Committee.

Athletics. NCAA. **Intercollegiate:** Baseball M, basketball, cheerleading, cross-country, fencing W, field hockey W, football (tackle) M, golf W, lacrosse, soccer, softball W, swimming W, tennis W, track and field, volleyball W, wrestling M. **Team name:** Pioneers.

Student services. Adult student services, alcohol/substance abuse counseling, chaplain/spiritual director, career counseling, student employment services, financial aid counseling, health services, minority student services, personal counseling, placement for graduates, veterans' counselor. **Physically disabled:** Services for visually, speech, hearing impaired.

Contact. E-mail: post-enroll@liu.edu
Phone: (516) 299-2900 Toll-free number: (800) 548-7526
Fax: (516) 299-2137
Marcelle Hicks, Director of Freshman Admissions, LIU Post, 720 Northern Boulevard, Brookville, NY 11548-1300

Machzikei Hadath Rabbinical College
Brooklyn, New York

CB code: 0726

- Private 5-year rabbinical and seminary college for men affiliated with the Jewish faith
- Commuter campus in very large city
- 148 degree-seeking undergraduates
- Interview required

General. Founded in 1956. Accredited by AARTS. First Talmudic degree and ordination available. **Degrees:** 14 bachelor's awarded. **Calendar:** Semester. **Full-time faculty:** 8 total. **Part-time faculty:** 4 total.

Basis for selection. Interview most important. Essay recommended.

2015-2016 Annual costs. Tuition/fees: $11,050.

Application procedures. Admission: Priority date 6/1; deadline 7/1. $150 fee, may be waived for applicants with need. Admission notification on a rolling basis. **Financial aid:** No deadline. Applicants notified on a rolling basis.

Academics. Special study options: Independent study, study abroad. **Credit/placement by examination:** AP, CLEP. **Support services:** Pre-admission summer program, remedial instruction.

Majors. Theology: Talmudic.

Student life. Policies: Religious observance required.

Contact. Phone: (718) 854-8777 ext. 23 Fax: (718) 851-1265
Rabbi A.M. Leizerowitz, Director of Admissions, Machzikei Hadath Rabbinical College, 5407 16th Avenue, Brooklyn, NY 11204

Manhattan College
Riverdale, New York
www.manhattan.edu

CB member
CB code: 2395

- Private 4-year engineering and liberal arts college affiliated with the Roman Catholic Church
- Residential campus in very large city
- 3,576 degree-seeking undergraduates: 5% part-time, 45% women, 4% African American, 5% Asian American, 21% Hispanic/Latino, 2% Multiracial, non-Hispanic, 3% international
- 495 degree-seeking graduate students
- 67% of applicants admitted
- SAT or ACT (ACT writing recommended) required
- 72% graduate within 6 years; 31% enter graduate study

General. Founded in 1853. Regionally accredited. Independent institution in the Roman Catholic tradition sponsored by De La Salle Christian Brothers. **Degrees:** 766 bachelor's awarded; master's offered. **ROTC:** Army, Air Force. **Location:** 10 miles from midtown Manhattan. **Calendar:** Semester, extensive summer session. **Full-time faculty:** 221 total; 97% have terminal degrees, 14% minority, 42% women. **Part-time faculty:** 217 total; 43% have terminal degrees, 20% minority, 44% women. **Class size:** 46% < 20, 53% 20-39, less than 1% 40-49, less than 1% 50-99. **Special facilities:** Interfaith education center, multicultural center, rooftop garden.

Freshman class profile. 8,313 applied, 5,557 admitted, 900 enrolled.

Mid 50% test scores			
SAT critical reading:	490-580	GPA 2.0-2.99:	17%
SAT math:	500-610	Rank in top quarter:	51%
SAT writing:	480-590	Rank in top tenth:	23%
ACT composite:	22-27	End year in good standing:	87%
GPA 3.75 or higher:	27%	Return as sophomores:	84%
GPA 3.50-3.74:	21%	Out-of-state:	36%
GPA 3.0-3.49:	35%	Live on campus:	76%
		International:	3%

Basis for selection. School achievement record and test scores most important. Essay, recommendations, and extracurricular activities also reviewed. Rolling Admissions. Interview recommended. **Home schooled:** State high school equivalency certificate, letter of recommendation (nonparent) required.

High school preparation. College-preparatory program required. Required and recommended units include English 4, mathematics 3-4, social studies 3-4, science 2-4 (laboratory 2-4), foreign language 2-3 and academic electives 2. 4 mathematics, 4 science (including precalculus, chemistry, and physics) recommended of engineering majors and most science majors.

2015-2016 Annual costs. Tuition/fees: $38,900. Room/board: $14,430. Books/supplies: $1,200. Personal expenses: $1,200.

2014-2015 Financial aid. All financial aid based on need. 839 full-time freshmen applied for aid; 830 deemed to have need; 795 received aid. Average need met was 80%. Average scholarship/grant was $21,362. 77% of total undergraduate aid awarded as scholarships/grants, 23% as loans/jobs.

Application procedures. Admission: Priority date 2/15; no deadline. $60 fee, may be waived for applicants with need. Application must be submitted on paper. Admission notification on a rolling basis beginning on or about 12/15. All accepted students must make enrollment deposit by 5/1. **Financial aid:** Priority date 3/1, closing date 4/15. FAFSA required. Applicants notified on a rolling basis starting 2/15; must reply by 5/1.

Academics. Special study options: Combined bachelor's/graduate degree, cross-registration, distance learning, double major, independent study, internships, study abroad, teacher certification program, Washington semester. **Credit/placement by examination:** AP, CLEP, IB, SAT, ACT, institutional tests. 30 credit hours maximum toward bachelor's degree. **Support services:** Learning center, reduced course load, remedial instruction, study skills assistance, tutoring, writing center. Center for academic success.

Majors. Biology: General, biochemistry. **Business:** General, accounting, finance, international, labor relations, management information systems, managerial economics, statistics. **Communications:** Broadcast journalism, communications/speech/rhetoric, journalism. **Computer sciences:** General, computer science, information systems. **Education:** General, biology, chemistry, computer, early childhood, elementary, English, foreign languages, French, health, history, mathematics, middle, physical, physics, science, secondary, social science, social studies, Spanish, special ed. **Engineering:** Chemical, civil, computer, electrical, mechanical. **English:** Writing. **Foreign languages:** French, Spanish. **Health services:** Medical radiologic technology/radiation therapy, nuclear medical technology, predental, premedicine, preveterinary. **History:** General. **Math:** General. **Philosophy/religion:** Philosophy, religion. **Physical sciences:** Chemistry, physics. **Psychology:** General. **Social sciences:** Economics, international relations, political science, sociology, urban studies.

Most popular majors. Business/marketing 22%, communications/journalism 11%, education 11%, engineering/engineering technologies 31%, psychology 7%.

Technology on campus. 450 workstations in library, computer center, student center. Dormitories wired for high-speed internet access and linked to campus network. Commuter students can connect to campus network. Online course registration, online library, helpline, repair service, student web hosting, wireless network available.

Student life. Freshman orientation: Mandatory, $285 fee. Preregistration for classes offered. **Policies:** Must be a full-time undergraduate student to participate in club offerings. **Housing:** Guaranteed on-campus for all undergraduates. Coed dorms, special housing for disabled, apartments, themed housing available. $400 nonrefundable deposit, deadline 5/1. Learning/living community for freshmen available. **Activities:** Bands, campus ministries, choral groups, dance, drama, film society, international student organizations, literary magazine, music ensembles, Model UN, musical theater, radio station, student government, student newspaper, symphony orchestra, TV station, Christ-centered community, Gaelic society, international student association, Just Peace, LaSallian Collegians, Italian club, French club, Society of Hispanic Engineers, College Republicans, Muslim student association.

Athletics. NCAA. **Intercollegiate:** Baseball M, basketball, cross-country, golf M, lacrosse, rowing (crew) W, soccer, softball W, swimming, track and field, volleyball W. **Intramural:** Basketball, cheerleading, football (tackle), golf, ice hockey, softball, volleyball. **Team name:** Jaspers.

Student services. Alcohol/substance abuse counseling, chaplain/spiritual director, career counseling, financial aid counseling, health services, personal counseling, veterans' counselor. **Physically disabled:** Services for visually, hearing impaired.

Contact. E-mail: admit@manhattan.edu
Phone: (718) 862-7200 Toll-free number: (800) 622-9235
Fax: (718) 862-8019
William Bisset, Vice President for Enrollment Management, Manhattan College, 4513 Manhattan College Parkway, Riverdale, NY 10471

Manhattan School of Music
New York, New York
www.msmnyc.edu   CB code: 2396

- Private 4-year music college
- Residential campus in very large city
- 410 degree-seeking undergraduates
- Application essay required

General. Founded in 1917. Regionally accredited. Extensive performance opportunities on and off campus. **Degrees:** 88 bachelor's awarded; master's, doctoral offered. **Calendar:** Semester. **Full-time faculty:** 78 total; 31% have terminal degrees, 10% minority, 36% women. **Part-time faculty:** 290 total; 11% have terminal degrees, 18% minority, 37% women. **Class size:** 85% < 20, 12% 20-39, less than 1% 40-49, 2% 50-99, less than 1% >100. **Special facilities:** Performance spaces, music library.

Freshman class profile.

GPA 3.75 or higher:	46%	GPA 2.0-2.99:	3%
GPA 3.50-3.74:	24%	Out-of-state:	71%
GPA 3.0-3.49:	27%	Live on campus:	90%

Basis for selection. Audition, availability of space in specific performance area, and academic record most important. Audition required. **Home schooled:** Statement describing home school structure and mission, transcript of courses and grades, letter of recommendation (nonparent) required. GED accepted, but if no GED, SAT or ACT required.

High school preparation. College-preparatory program recommended. Recommended units include English 4, mathematics 3, social studies 4, history 4, science 3 and foreign language 4. Extensive music training required.

2015-2016 Annual costs. Tuition/fees: $42,500. Room/board: $12,260. Books/supplies: $1,000. Personal expenses: $3,000.

Financial aid. Non-need-based: Scholarships awarded for academics, alumni affiliation, leadership, music/drama.

Application procedures. Admission: Closing date 12/1 (receipt date). $100 fee, may be waived for applicants with need. Application must be submitted online. Admission notification by 4/1. Must reply by May 1 or within 2 week(s) if notified thereafter. **Financial aid:** Closing date 3/1. FAFSA, institutional form required. Returning International students are required to complete the CSS Profile on a yearly basis. Applicants notified by 4/1; must reply by 5/1 or within 2 week(s) of notification.

Academics. Special study options: Cross-registration, distance learning, ESL, exchange student, independent study, internships, study abroad. **Credit/placement by examination:** AP, CLEP, institutional tests. 60 credit hours maximum toward bachelor's degree. **Support services:** Reduced course load, remedial instruction, tutoring.

Majors. Visual/performing arts: Music performance, music theory/composition.

Technology on campus. 20 workstations in library, computer center. Dormitories wired for high-speed internet access and linked to campus network. Wireless network available.

Student life. Freshman orientation: Mandatory. Preregistration for classes offered. One-two weeks before classes start. Placement exams, orchestra and opera auditions held. Convocation for students and their parents. **Policies:** Undergraduates required to live in residence hall for first 2 years. Alcohol allowed only for those over 21 and only in designated areas. No smoking in the building. Social network restrictions concerning bullying. **Housing:** Guaranteed on-campus for freshmen. Coed dorms available. $500 nonrefundable deposit, deadline 6/15. Housing guaranteed only to students who submit documents and pay deposit by set deadline. **Activities:** Bands, choral groups, international student organizations, music ensembles, musical theater, opera, student government, student newspaper, symphony orchestra, Pan-African student union, international student organization, resident community council, student council, GLBT student group, chess club, soccer club.

Student services. Alcohol/substance abuse counseling, career counseling, student employment services, financial aid counseling, health services, personal counseling. **Physically disabled:** Services for visually impaired.

Contact. E-mail: admission@msmnyc.edu
Phone: (917) 493-4436 Fax: (212) 749-3025
Amy Anderson, Dean for Enrollment Management, Manhattan School of Music, 120 Claremont Avenue, New York, NY 10027-4698

Manhattanville College

Purchase, New York
www.manhattanville.edu

CB member
CB code: 2397

- Private 4-year liberal arts and teachers college
- Residential campus in small town
- 1,744 degree-seeking undergraduates
- 74% of applicants admitted
- Application essay required

General. Founded in 1841. Regionally accredited. **Degrees:** 375 bachelor's awarded; master's, doctoral offered. **ROTC:** Army. **Location:** 25 miles from New York City. **Calendar:** Semester, extensive summer session. **Full-time faculty:** 105 total; 82% have terminal degrees, 13% minority, 51% women. **Part-time faculty:** 205 total; 18% have terminal degrees, 16% minority, 50% women. **Class size:** 59% < 20, 40% 20-39, less than 1% 40-49, less than 1% 50-99. **Special facilities:** Photography laboratory, heritage hall, digital media production, dance studio, e-Portfolio lab.

Freshman class profile. 4,033 applied, 2,989 admitted, 453 enrolled.

Mid 50% test scores			
		GPA 3.50-3.74:	17%
SAT critical reading:	480-580	GPA 3.0-3.49:	30%
SAT math:	480-570	GPA 2.0-2.99:	41%
SAT writing:	480-590	Out-of-state:	31%
ACT composite:	22-27	Live on campus:	72%
GPA 3.75 or higher:	12%		

Basis for selection. School achievement record, high school transcript, recommendations, test scores (when submitted) or samples of academic work most important. Essay, school and community activities also important. Interview strongly recommended. SAT or ACT recommended. Portfolio required for fine arts program; audition recommended for dance, music and theater programs.

High school preparation. 16 units required. Required units include English 4, mathematics 3, social studies 2, science 2 and academic electives 5.

2015-2016 Annual costs. Tuition/fees: $36,220. Room/board: $14,520. Books/supplies: $800. Personal expenses: $1,550.

2015-2016 Financial aid. Need-based: 391 full-time freshmen applied for aid; 355 deemed to have need; 355 received aid. Average need met was 68%. Average scholarship/grant was $5,889; average loan $3,468. 89% of total undergraduate aid awarded as scholarships/grants, 11% as loans/jobs. **Non-need-based:** Awarded to 1,718 full-time undergraduates, including 530 freshmen. Scholarships awarded for academics, alumni affiliation, art, music/drama. **Additional information:** Upper level students may earn additional money and academic credit through internship program.

Application procedures. Admission: Priority date 3/1; no deadline. $50 fee. Admission notification on a rolling basis beginning on or about 1/2. Must reply by May 1 or within 2 week(s) if notified thereafter. **Financial aid:** Closing date 3/1. FAFSA required. Applicants notified on a rolling basis starting 2/15; must reply by 5/1 or within 2 week(s) of notification.

Academics. Students must complete portfolio before graduation, which includes an individualized academic plan and a resume. **Special study options:** Accelerated study, combined bachelor's/graduate degree, cross-registration, double major, dual enrollment of high school students, honors, independent study, internships, liberal arts/career combination, student-designed major, study abroad, teacher certification program, weekend college. Study abroad programs in Oxford, Paris, Tokyo, Osaka, Madrid, Seville, Florence, Rome, Berlin, Galway and the world capitals program in Jerusalem, Santiago, Brussels, Buenos Aires, Prague, Moscow, and South Africa. Dual degree programs in Education, Creative Writing and Sport Business Management, providing interested students with the opportunity to complete combined undergraduate and graduate degrees at an accelerated pace. **Credit/placement by examination:** AP, CLEP, IB, institutional tests. Up to 90 credits allowed: up to 30 AP credits, up to 18 IB credits, no CLEP limit. **Support services:** Learning center, reduced course load, remedial instruction, study skills assistance, tutoring, writing center.

Majors. Area/ethnic studies: American, Asian. **Biology:** General, biochemistry. **Business:** Accounting, business admin, finance, marketing. **Communications:** Communications/speech/rhetoric, digital media. **Computer sciences:** General. **Conservation:** Environmental studies. **Education:** General, music. **English:** English lit. **Foreign languages:** French, Spanish. **History:** General. **Liberal arts:** Arts/sciences. **Math:** General. **Parks/recreation:** Sports studies. **Philosophy/religion:** Philosophy, religion. **Physical sciences:** Chemistry. **Psychology:** General. **Social sciences:** Anthropology, economics, political science, sociology. **Visual/performing arts:** Art history/conservation, dance, dramatic, music, studio arts.

Most popular majors. Business/marketing 18%, communications/journalism 9%, education 8%, history 6%, psychology 12%, social sciences 16%, visual/performing arts 12%.

Technology on campus. Dormitories wired for high-speed internet access and linked to campus network. Commuter students can connect to campus network. Online course registration, online library, helpline, repair service, student web hosting, wireless network available.

Student life. Freshman orientation: Mandatory. Preregistration for classes offered. Two-day event in which students meet with fellow classmates, student life staff, and faculty. **Policies:** The College adheres to its mission statement to educate ethically and socially responsible leaders for the global world. The College reaffirms its tenet that its community must be respectful of all differences including creeds, races, ethnic backgrounds, sexual orientations and genders. **Housing:** Guaranteed on-campus for freshmen. Coed dorms, special housing for disabled, wellness housing available. $500 nonrefundable deposit, deadline 5/1. Special interest housing options for upperclassmen, with the goal of providing interested students a living environment focused on community service and all aspects of health and wellness: physical, mental, emotional, and spiritual. **Activities:** Bands, campus ministries, choral groups, dance, drama, international student organizations, literary magazine, music ensembles, Model UN, musical theater, radio station, student government, student newspaper, Africa 57, Catholic student association, black student union, Christian Fellowship, Connie Hogarth Center for Social Justice, Gay Straight Alliance, Hui O Hawaii, Jewish student organization, Latin American student organization.

Athletics. NCAA. **Intercollegiate:** Baseball M, basketball, cross-country, field hockey W, golf, ice hockey, lacrosse, soccer, softball W, track and field, volleyball W. **Team name:** Valiants.

Student services. Adult student services, alcohol/substance abuse counseling, chaplain/spiritual director, career counseling, services for economically disadvantaged, student employment services, financial aid counseling, health services, personal counseling, veterans' counselor. **Physically disabled:** Services for visually, speech, hearing impaired.

Contact. E-mail: admissions@mville.edu
Phone: (914) 323-5464 Toll-free number: (800) 328-4553
Fax: (914) 694-1732
Joe Cosentino, VP Undergraduate Enrollment Management,
Manhattanville College, 2900 Purchase Street, Purchase, NY 10577

Mannes College The New School for Music

New York, New York
www.newschool.edu

CB code: 2398

- Private 4-year music college
- Commuter campus in very large city
- 519 degree-seeking undergraduates: 3% part-time, 40% women, 6% African American, 4% Asian American, 12% Hispanic/Latino, 3% Multiracial, non-Hispanic, 29% international
- 265 degree-seeking graduate students
- 59% of applicants admitted
- 64% graduate within 6 years

General. Founded in 1916. Regionally accredited. Division of The New School. **Degrees:** 86 bachelor's awarded; master's offered. **Calendar:** Semester, limited summer session. **Full-time faculty:** 20 total; 25% have terminal degrees, 15% minority, 55% women. **Part-time faculty:** 395 total; less than 1% have terminal degrees, 19% minority, 42% women. **Class size:** 91% < 20, 7% 20-39, less than 1% 40-49, 1% 50-99. **Special facilities:** Two concert halls.

Freshman class profile. 901 applied, 531 admitted, 126 enrolled.

Mid 50% test scores			
		GPA 3.0-3.49:	37%
SAT critical reading:	500-620	GPA 2.0-2.99:	40%
SAT math:	500-630	Return as sophomores:	71%
SAT writing:	500-620	Out-of-state:	84%
GPA 3.75 or higher:	9%	Live on campus:	66%
GPA 3.50-3.74:	14%	International:	32%

Basis for selection. GED not accepted. Talent, ability very important, application essay and recommendations important. Institutionally designed entrance examination, including major audition. Written examinations in music theory, dictation, ear training, and English usage. Placement exams and interviews required for all Bachelor of Music, Bachelor of Science, Undergraduate Diploma, and Master of Music applicants.

High school preparation. College-preparatory program recommended. Required and recommended units include English 4, mathematics 4, social studies 4, history 4, science 4 and foreign language 4.

2015-2016 Annual costs. Tuition/fees: $43,006. Room/board: $18,465. Books/supplies: $920. Personal expenses: $1,550.

2014-2015 Financial aid. Need-based: 94 full-time freshmen applied for aid; 83 deemed to have need; 83 received aid. Average need met was 63%. Average scholarship/grant was $10,086; average loan $5,594. 62% of total undergraduate aid awarded as scholarships/grants, 38% as loans/jobs. **Non-need-based:** Awarded to 270 full-time undergraduates, including 73 freshmen. Scholarships awarded for academics, art, leadership, minority status, music/drama, state residency.

Application procedures. Admission: Priority date 1/15; deadline 8/1 (postmark date). $50 fee, may be waived for applicants with need. Admission notification by 4/1. Admission notification on a rolling basis. Must reply by May 1 or within 2 week(s) if notified thereafter. **Financial aid:** Closing date 3/1. FAFSA required. Applicants notified on a rolling basis starting 4/1; must reply within 4 week(s) of notification.

Academics. Special study options: Cross-registration, double major, ESL, independent study, internships. **Credit/placement by examination:** AP, CLEP, institutional tests. **Support services:** Remedial instruction, tutoring, writing center.

Majors. Visual/performing arts: Conducting, music performance, music theory/composition, piano/keyboard, stringed instruments, voice/opera, woodwind instruments.

Technology on campus. Dormitories wired for high-speed internet access and linked to campus network. Commuter students can connect to campus network. Online course registration, helpline, student web hosting, wireless network available.

Student life. Freshman orientation: Mandatory. Preregistration for classes offered. **Housing:** Guaranteed on-campus for all undergraduates. Coed dorms, special housing for disabled, apartments, themed housing, wellness housing available. $500 nonrefundable deposit, deadline 7/1. **Activities:** Jazz band, choral groups, dance, drama, film society, international student organizations, literary magazine, music ensembles, musical theater, opera, radio station, student newspaper, symphony orchestra, Sustainable Design Review, New School Styling Club, Roots & Shoots, Radical student union, Global Health student organization, international club, PHOTOfeast, the Theatre Collective, Jewish student union, New School Remnant Christian Fellowship.

Athletics. Intercollegiate: Basketball M, cross-country. **Intramural:** Basketball, soccer, volleyball.

Student services. Career counseling, student employment services, financial aid counseling, health services, minority student services, personal counseling.

Contact. E-mail: admissions@newschool.edu
Phone: (212) 229-5150 Toll-free number: (800) 292-3040
Georgia Schmitt, Director of Admissions, Mannes College The New School for Music, 79 Fifth Avenue, Floor 5, New York, NY 10003

Marist College
Poughkeepsie, New York

CB member
CB code: 2400

www.marist.edu

- Private 4-year liberal arts college
- Residential campus in small city
- 5,205 degree-seeking undergraduates: 6% part-time, 59% women, 4% African American, 3% Asian American, 9% Hispanic/Latino, 2% Multiracial, non-Hispanic, 2% international
- 898 degree-seeking graduate students
- 45% of applicants admitted
- Application essay required
- 78% graduate within 6 years; 20% enter graduate study

General. Founded in 1929. Regionally accredited. Branch campus in Florence, Italy. **Degrees:** 1,335 bachelor's awarded; master's offered. **ROTC:** Army. **Location:** 75 miles from New York City, 75 miles from Albany. **Calendar:** Semester, limited summer session. **Full-time faculty:** 234 total; 77% have terminal degrees, 16% minority, 50% women. **Part-time faculty:** 385 total; 26% have terminal degrees, 11% minority, 45% women. **Class size:** 46% < 20, 54% 20-39, less than 1% 40-49. **Special facilities:** Center for cloud computing and analytics, environmental conditions monitoring station, arboretum, archives and special collections.

Freshman class profile. 9,213 applied, 4,142 admitted, 1,209 enrolled.

Mid 50% test scores			
SAT critical reading:	520-620	Rank in top quarter:	61%
SAT math:	530-630	Rank in top tenth:	26%
SAT writing:	520-630	End year in good standing:	92%
ACT composite:	23-28	Return as sophomores:	91%
GPA 3.75 or higher:	20%	Out-of-state:	53%
GPA 3.50-3.74:	16%	Live on campus:	97%
GPA 3.0-3.49:	40%	International:	2%
GPA 2.0-2.99:	24%	Fraternities:	1%
		Sororities:	1%

Basis for selection. Secondary school achievement record, rank in top third of class primary consideration. Recommendations, activities, personal and leadership qualities also important. Campus visits and information sessions with admission counselors strongly recommended. A portfolio or project is required for Fashion Design, Fashion Merchandising and BS Studio Art. Music and Theater programs offer scholarships that require auditions. **Home schooled:** Transcript of courses and grades, letter of recommendation (nonparent) required. Home school applicants required to submit SAT or ACT scores. **Learning Disabled:** A copy of psychological evaluation results to include WAIS subtest scores, narrative and diagnosis and current levels of achievement in reading, mathematics and written language as determined by individual achievement test scores. Scores must be within 3 years, a copy of most recent IEP/504 Plan, 2 Letters of recommendation from those familiar w/learning style in addition to regular admission requirements.

High school preparation. College-preparatory program required. 17 units required. Required and recommended units include English 4, mathematics 3-4, social studies 2, history 1, science 3-4 (laboratory 2-3), foreign language 2-3 and academic electives 2.

2015-2016 Annual costs. Tuition/fees: $32,750. Room/board: $14,100. Books/supplies: $1,000. Personal expenses: $900.

2015-2016 Financial aid. Need-based: 983 full-time freshmen applied for aid; 726 deemed to have need; 726 received aid. Average need met was 66%. Average scholarship/grant was $17,763; average loan $3,917. 59% of total undergraduate aid awarded as scholarships/grants, 41% as loans/jobs. **Non-need-based:** Awarded to 3,896 full-time undergraduates, including 1,126 freshmen. Scholarships awarded for academics, athletics, music/drama, ROTC, state residency.

Application procedures. Admission: Closing date 2/1 (postmark date). $50 fee, may be waived for applicants with need. Admission notification by 4/1. Must reply by 5/1. **Financial aid:** Priority date 2/15, closing date 5/1. FAFSA required. PROFILE required for early decision and early action applicants. Applicants notified on a rolling basis starting 4/1; must reply by 5/1 or within 2 week(s) of notification.

Academics. Paralegal certificates offered. Substantial internship opportunities for all majors. Students participate in community service program. **Special study options:** Accelerated study, combined bachelor's/graduate degree, cross-registration, distance learning, double major, dual enrollment of high school students, ESL, honors, independent study, internships, liberal arts/career combination, New York semester, study abroad, teacher certification program, United Nations semester, Washington semester, weekend college. Undergraduates may take graduate classes. Cooperative education in arts, business, computer science, education, humanities, natural science, social/behavioral science, technologies. **Credit/placement by examination:** AP, CLEP, IB, SAT, ACT, institutional tests. 60 credit hours maximum toward bachelor's degree. ACT-PEP accepted on individual basis. **Support services:** Learning center, reduced course load, remedial instruction, study skills assistance, tutoring, writing center.

Majors. Area/ethnic studies: American. **Biology:** General, biochemistry, biomedical sciences. **Business:** Accounting, business admin. **Communications:** General. **Computer sciences:** General, computer science. **Education:** Biology, chemistry, English, French, mathematics, social studies, Spanish. **English:** English lit. **Foreign languages:** French, Italian, Spanish. **Health services:** Athletic training, clinical lab science. **History:** General. **Human services:** Social work. **Liberal arts:** Arts/sciences. **Math:** General, applied. **Philosophy/religion:** General, philosophy. **Physical sciences:** Chemistry. **Protective services:** Law enforcement admin. **Psychology:** General. **Social sciences:** Economics, political science. **Visual/performing arts:** Art, art history/conservation, fashion design, interior design, multimedia, studio arts.

Most popular majors. Business/marketing 21%, communications/journalism 19%, psychology 15%, visual/performing arts 10%.

Technology on campus. 804 workstations in dormitories, library, computer center, student center. Dormitories wired for high-speed internet access and linked to campus network. Commuter students can connect to campus network. Online course registration, online library, helpline, repair service, student web hosting, wireless network available.

Student life. Freshman orientation: Mandatory, $90 fee. Preregistration for classes offered. One-day orientation in June. **Policies:** Freshmen not permitted cars on campus. **Housing:** Guaranteed on-campus for freshmen. Coed dorms, special housing for disabled, apartments, themed housing available. $500 nonrefundable deposit, deadline 5/1. Garden apartments, townhouses, suites available. **Activities:** Bands, campus ministries, choral groups, dance, drama, international student organizations, literary magazine, music ensembles, Model UN, musical theater, radio station, student government, student newspaper, symphony orchestra, TV station, Black Student Union, Asian Alliance, Circle K, ARCO, community service programs, Habitat for Humanity, Political Science Club, Literacy Arts Society, social action clubs.

Athletics. NCAA. **Intercollegiate:** Baseball M, basketball, cross-country, diving, football (tackle) M, lacrosse, rowing (crew), soccer, softball W, swimming, tennis, track and field, volleyball W, water polo W. **Intramural:** Basketball, field hockey W, football (non-tackle) M, soccer, softball, volleyball. **Team name:** Red Foxes.

Student services. Adult student services, alcohol/substance abuse counseling, chaplain/spiritual director, career counseling, services for economically disadvantaged, student employment services, financial aid counseling, health services, minority student services, personal counseling, placement for graduates, veterans' counselor. **Physically disabled:** Services for visually, hearing impaired.

Contact. E-mail: admission@marist.edu
Phone: (845) 575-3226 Toll-free number: (800) 436-5483
Fax: (845) 575-3215
Kent Rinehart, Dean of Undergraduate Admissions, Marist College, 3399 North Road, Poughkeepsie, NY 12601-1387

Marymount Manhattan College
New York, New York CB member
www.mmm.edu CB code: 2405

- Private 4-year liberal arts and performing arts college
- Residential campus in very large city
- 1,875 degree-seeking undergraduates: 9% part-time, 77% women, 10% African American, 4% Asian American, 18% Hispanic/Latino, 1% Native American, 1% Multi-racial, non-Hispanic, 5% international
- 84% of applicants admitted
- SAT or ACT (ACT writing optional), application essay required
- 42% graduate within 6 years; 11% enter graduate study

General. Founded in 1936. Regionally accredited. **Degrees:** 376 bachelor's, 13 associate awarded. **Location:** Located in New York City. **Calendar:** Semester, limited summer session. **Full-time faculty:** 94 total; 95% have terminal degrees, 10% minority, 62% women. **Part-time faculty:** 212 total; 3% minority, 53% women. **Class size:** 63% < 20, 37% 20-39. **Special facilities:** Communications and learning center, center for producing, communication arts multimedia suite, center for science education.

Freshman class profile. 4,459 applied, 3,737 admitted, 524 enrolled.

Mid 50% test scores			
SAT critical reading:	470-590	GPA 3.0-3.49:	38%
SAT math:	440-550	GPA 2.0-2.99:	24%
SAT writing:	480-580	Return as sophomores:	74%
ACT composite:	20-26	Out-of-state:	68%
GPA 3.75 or higher:	22%	Live on campus:	79%
GPA 3.50-3.74:	16%	International:	5%

Basis for selection. High school GPA of 3.0 and SAT verbal and math scores of 450 each recommended. Letters of recommendation from teachers and administrators, extracurricular and community activities important. Rolling deadline for SAT/ACT score receipt. Interview recommended for all; audition required for acting, dance, and theater programs; portfolio required for art program. **Home schooled:** Statement describing home school structure and mission, transcript of courses and grades, state high school equivalency certificate, letter of recommendation (nonparent) required. Must submit official high school transcripts if attended high school before withdrawing. **Learning Disabled:** Interview and Wechsler Delta Adult Intelligence Scale test required.

High school preparation. College-preparatory program recommended. 17 units required. Required and recommended units include English 4, mathematics 3, social studies 3, science 3 (laboratory 2), foreign language 2 and academic electives 4.

2015-2016 Annual costs. Tuition/fees: $28,700. Room/board: $15,500. Books/supplies: $1,000. Personal expenses: $5,300.

2014-2015 Financial aid. Need-based: 409 full-time freshmen applied for aid; 360 deemed to have need; 358 received aid. Average need met was 50%. Average scholarship/grant was $14,371; average loan $3,307. 77% of total undergraduate aid awarded as scholarships/grants, 23% as loans/jobs. **Non-need-based:** Awarded to 111 full-time undergraduates, including 48 freshmen. Scholarships awarded for academics, art, leadership, music/drama, state residency. **Additional information:** Limited international scholarships for top applicants and diplomats.

Application procedures. Admission: Priority date 8/1; no deadline. $60 fee, may be waived for applicants with need. Admission notification on a rolling basis beginning on or about 9/1. Must reply by May 1 or within 3 week(s) if notified thereafter. **Financial aid:** Priority date 3/15; no closing date. FAFSA required. Applicants notified on a rolling basis starting 3/15; must reply by 5/1 or within 2 week(s) of notification.

Academics. Special study options: Accelerated study, cross-registration, distance learning, double major, exchange student, honors, independent study, internships, liberal arts/career combination, student-designed major, study abroad. **Credit/placement by examination:** AP, CLEP, IB, SAT, ACT, institutional tests. 30 credit hours maximum toward bachelor's degree. Maximum of 12 credits for language proficiency. SAT Subject used for placement if submitted. **Support services:** Learning center, reduced course load, remedial instruction, study skills assistance, tutoring.

Majors. Biology: General, biomedical sciences. **Business:** General, business admin, entrepreneurial studies, fashion, finance, human resources, international, investments/securities, managerial economics, marketing. **Communications:** General, communications/speech/rhetoric, journalism. **Conservation:** Environmental studies. **English:** General lit. **Health services:** Audiology/speech pathology. **Liberal arts:** Arts/sciences. **Philosophy/religion:** General, philosophy. **Psychology:** General. **Social sciences:** International relations, sociology. **Visual/performing arts:** Acting, art, art history/conservation, ballet, costume design, dance, directing/producing, dramatic, graphic design, photography, play/screenwriting, studio arts, theater arts management, theater design, theater history.

Most popular majors. Business/marketing 12%, communications/journalism 18%, psychology 6%, social sciences 6%, visual/performing arts 40%.

Technology on campus. 215 workstations in library, computer center, student center. Dormitories wired for high-speed internet access and linked to campus network. Commuter students can connect to campus network. Online course registration, online library, helpline, wireless network available.

Student life. Freshman orientation: Mandatory, $150 fee. Preregistration for classes offered. 3 days of community building, informational sessions, activities, and social engagements followed by one day of academic department introductions all the week prior to the start of classes . **Housing:** Coed dorms, gender-neutral housing available. $500 nonrefundable deposit, deadline 5/1. **Activities:** Campus ministries, choral groups, dance, drama, international student organizations, musical theater, radio station, student government, student newspaper, Black and Latino Student Association, Hillel, Marymount Christian Fellowship, Student Government Association, Go Green Coalition, Debate Society, International Student Society, Club Mosaic-Untied Artists of Color Theater, Glamour Group, Club-Triple Fierce.

Student services. Alcohol/substance abuse counseling, chaplain/spiritual director, career counseling, student employment services, financial aid counseling, health services, personal counseling, placement for graduates. **Physically disabled:** Services for speech, hearing impaired.

Contact. E-mail: admissions@mmm.edu
Phone: (212) 517-0430 Toll-free number: (800) 627-9668
Fax: (212) 517-0448
Jim Rogers, Dean of Admission, Marymount Manhattan College, 221 East 71st Street, New York, NY 10021-4597

Medaille College
Buffalo, New York
www.medaille.edu CB code: 2422

- Private 4-year liberal arts college
- Commuter campus in large city
- 2,160 degree-seeking undergraduates
- 858 graduate students
- SAT or ACT with writing, application essay required

General. Founded in 1875. Regionally accredited. Medaille College's undergraduate campus is located in Buffalo, New York, on an attractive, tree-lined urban campus at the intersection of Route 198 (Scajaquada Expressway) and Parkside Avenue. The Campus is within the Olmsted Crescent, a historic area of parkways and landscape designed by Frederick Law Olmsted. **Degrees:** 237 bachelor's, 83 associate awarded; master's, professional offered. **ROTC:** Army. **Location:** Three miles from downtown. **Calendar:** Semester, limited summer session. **Full-time faculty:** 87 total; 74% have terminal degrees, 52% women. **Part-time faculty:** 207 total. **Class size:** 52% < 20, 46% 20-39, less than 1% 40-49, 1% 50-99.

Freshman class profile.

Out-of-state: 3% Live on campus: 40%

Basis for selection. Motivation and maturity, as well as academic record and test scores, considered. SAT recommended. Interview strongly recommended.

High school preparation. College-preparatory program recommended. 12 units required; 20 recommended. Required and recommended units include English 4, mathematics 2-3, social studies 4, history 2, science 2-3 (laboratory 2) and foreign language 2. 3 math, 3 science recommended for veterinary technology.

2015-2016 Annual costs. Tuition/fees: $26,252. Room/board: $12,460. Books/supplies: $1,100. Personal expenses: $1,100.

Financial aid. Non-need-based: Scholarships awarded for academics, leadership.

Application procedures. Admission: Priority date 8/1; no deadline. $25 fee, may be waived for applicants with need, free for online applicants. Admission notification on a rolling basis beginning on or about 10/1. Must reply by May 1 or within 4 week(s) if notified thereafter. **Financial aid:** Priority date 3/1; no closing date. FAFSA required. Applicants notified on a rolling basis starting 3/1; must reply within 2 week(s) of notification.

Academics. All pre-professional programs require participation in at least 1 internship. Branch campuses in Amherst and Rochester. **Special study options:** Accelerated study, combined bachelor's/graduate degree, cross-registration, distance learning, double major, honors, independent study, internships, liberal arts/career combination, student-designed major, teacher certification program, weekend college. Module system for full-time evening students and for full-time weekend students. **Credit/placement by examination:** AP, CLEP, IB, SAT. 30 credit hours maximum toward associate degree, 60 toward bachelor's. **Support services:** Learning center, reduced course load, remedial instruction, study skills assistance, tutoring.

Majors. Biology: General. **Business:** General, accounting, business admin, management information systems. **Communications:** Media studies. **Computer sciences:** General. **Education:** General, biology, elementary, English, mathematics, middle, secondary, social studies. **English:** English lit. **Health services:** Health information management, veterinary technology/assistant. **Liberal arts:** Arts/sciences. **Math:** General. **Parks/recreation:** Sports admin. **Protective services:** Homeland security, police science. **Psychology:** General. **Visual/performing arts:** General.

Most popular majors. Business/marketing 31%, communications/journalism 8%, education 12%, health sciences 10%, parks/recreation 6%, psychology 10%, security/protective services 9%.

Technology on campus. 120 workstations in dormitories, library, computer center, student center. Dormitories wired for high-speed internet access and linked to campus network. Commuter students can connect to campus network. Online library, helpline, wireless network available.

Student life. Freshman orientation: Mandatory. Preregistration for classes offered. **Housing:** Coed dorms, single-sex dorms, apartments, wellness housing available. $100 deposit, deadline 9/1. **Activities:** Drama, film society, literary magazine, musical theater, radio station, student government, student newspaper, TV station, African American student union, child and youth services club, student volunteer center, multicultural association, SADD, international student society, resident student council.

Athletics. NCAA. **Intercollegiate:** Baseball M, basketball, bowling W, cross-country, golf, lacrosse, soccer, softball W, volleyball. **Team name:** Mavericks.

Student services. Adult student services, career counseling, student employment services, financial aid counseling, health services, personal counseling, placement for graduates, veterans' counselor. **Physically disabled:** Services for visually, speech, hearing impaired.

Contact. E-mail: admissionsug@medaille.edu
Phone: (716) 880-2200 Toll-free number: (800) 292-1582
Fax: (716) 880-2007
Karen McGrath, Vice President for Enrollment Management and Undergraduate Admissions, Medaille College, 18 Agassiz Circle, Buffalo, NY 14214

Medaille College: Rochester
Rochester, New York
www.medaille.edu

- Private 4-year branch campus and liberal arts college
- Commuter campus in small city
- 138 degree-seeking undergraduates: 17% part-time, 83% women
- 45 degree-seeking graduate students
- 66% of applicants admitted

General. Branch campus of Medaille College. Financial aid data for this institution calculated on a system-wide basis and includes figures for all three Medaille campuses. The combined financial aid totals are reported under the main Medaille campus. **Degrees:** 239 bachelor's, 73 associate awarded; master's offered. **Calendar:** Semester.

Freshman class profile. 741 applied, 486 admitted, 295 enrolled.

Basis for selection. Motivation and maturity, as well as academic record and test scores considered.

High school preparation. 12 units required; 20 recommended. Required and recommended units include English 4, mathematics 2-3, social studies 4, history 2, science 2-3 (laboratory 2) and foreign language 2.

2015-2016 Annual costs. Tuition/fees: $26,252.

Application procedures. Admission: No deadline. $25 fee, may be waived for applicants with need, free for online applicants. Admission notification on a rolling basis. **Financial aid:** No deadline.

Academics. Special study options: Accelerated study, combined bachelor's/graduate degree, distance learning. **Credit/placement by examination:** AP, CLEP.

Majors. Business: General, business admin, management information systems.

Technology on campus. Online library, wireless network available.

Student life. Activities: Student newspaper.

Athletics. Team name: Mavericks.

Student services. Career counseling, financial aid counseling. **Physically disabled:** Services for visually, speech, hearing impaired.

Contact. E-mail: sageadmissions@medaille.edu
Phone: (585) 272-0030
Medaille College: Rochester, 1880 South Winton Road, Rochester, NY 14618

Mercy College
Dobbs Ferry, New York
www.mercy.edu   CB code: 2409

- Private 4-year liberal arts college
- Commuter campus in large town
- 6,410 degree-seeking undergraduates: 18% part-time, 69% women, 23% African American, 4% Asian American, 35% Hispanic/Latino, 1% Multiracial, non-Hispanic, 1% international
- 2,979 degree-seeking graduate students
- 66% of applicants admitted
- Application essay required
- 38% graduate within 6 years

General. Founded in 1950. Regionally accredited. Main campus in Dobbs Ferry plus additional branch campuses in Manhattan, Bronx, Yorktown Heights and Distance Learning. **Degrees:** 1,473 bachelor's, 68 associate awarded; master's, professional offered. **ROTC:** Army, Air Force. **Location:** 25 miles from New York City. **Calendar:** Semester, extensive summer session. **Full-time faculty:** 198 total; 86% have terminal degrees, 23% minority, 62% women. **Part-time faculty:** 857 total; 16% minority, 56% women. **Class size:** 50% < 20, 49% 20-39, less than 1% 40-49, less than 1% 50-99. **Special facilities:** Studio for animation studies, business program trading room, exercise science facility, music and recording studios, STEM biological research labs.

Freshman class profile. 5,573 applied, 3,661 admitted, 938 enrolled.

GPA 3.75 or higher:	8%	Return as sophomores:	76%
GPA 3.50-3.74:	11%	Out-of-state:	12%
GPA 3.0-3.49:	39%	Live on campus:	34%
GPA 2.0-2.99:	41%	International:	1%

Basis for selection. SAT/ACT optional. Additional interview with program director required for nursing, occupational therapy, physical therapy, social work, veterinary technology, computer arts programs. **Home schooled:** Transcript of courses and grades, state high school equivalency certificate, letter of recommendation (nonparent) required.

High school preparation. College-preparatory program recommended. 21 units required. Required units include English 4, mathematics 4, social studies 2, history 2, science 3 (laboratory 1), foreign language 3 and academic electives 3.

2015-2016 Annual costs. Tuition/fees: $18,076. Room/board: $13,200. Books/supplies: $1,492. Personal expenses: $1,784.

2014-2015 Financial aid. Need-based: 701 full-time freshmen applied for aid; 636 deemed to have need; 621 received aid. Average need met was 54%. Average scholarship/grant was $10,734; average loan $3,204. 69% of total undergraduate aid awarded as scholarships/grants, 31% as loans/jobs. **Non-need-based:** Awarded to 1,630 full-time undergraduates, including 429 freshmen. Scholarships awarded for academics, athletics.

Application procedures. Admission: No deadline. $40 fee, may be waived for applicants with need. Admission notification on a rolling basis beginning on or about 11/1. Must reply by May 1 or within 3 week(s) if notified thereafter. **Financial aid:** Priority date 2/15; no closing date. FAFSA required. Applicants notified on a rolling basis starting 2/20; must reply by 5/1 or within 2 week(s) of notification.

Academics. Programs leading to provisional state certification offered in education. **Special study options:** Accelerated study, combined bachelor's/graduate degree, cooperative education, distance learning, double major, dual enrollment of high school students, honors, independent study, internships, study abroad, teacher certification program, weekend college. **Credit/placement by examination:** AP, CLEP, SAT, ACT, institutional tests. 30 credit hours maximum toward associate degree, 30 toward bachelor's. **Support services:** Learning center, pre-admission summer program, reduced course load, study skills assistance, tutoring, writing center.

Honors college/program. Minimum 90 or above high school average required. Approximately 65 freshmen admitted. Students take honors English, speech and math freshmen year and additional four academic honors courses for total of 24 credits.

Majors. Biology: General. **Business:** Accounting, accounting/business management, business admin, entrepreneurial studies, marketing, nonprofit/public. **Communications:** Media studies. **Computer sciences:** General, computer science, information systems, security. **English:** English lit. **Foreign languages:** Spanish. **Health services:** Audiology/speech pathology, clinical lab science, nursing (RN), preveterinary. **History:** General. **Human services:** Social work. **Liberal arts:** Arts/sciences. **Math:** General. **Military:** Cyber ops. **Parks/recreation:** Exercise sciences. **Protective services:** Homeland security, law enforcement admin. **Psychology:** General. **Social sciences:** General, international relations, political science, sociology. **Visual/performing arts:** Commercial/advertising art, music technology.

Most popular majors. Business/marketing 14%, health sciences 22%, interdisciplinary studies 24%, psychology 14%, security/protective services 7%.

Technology on campus. 1,000 workstations in dormitories, library, computer center, student center. Dormitories wired for high-speed internet access and linked to campus network. Commuter students can connect to campus network. Online course registration, online library, helpline, repair service, wireless network available.

Student life. Freshman orientation: Available. Preregistration for classes offered. Various orientation dates offered beginning over the summer and running from June through October. **Policies:** Student services geared to commuter population with mid-day activities and programs available in evenings and weekends. Student Life creates dynamic programing utilizing close proximity to New York City and available sporting venues and opportunities like Broadway show tickets. Freshmen not permitted cars on campus. **Housing:** Coed dorms available. $300 fully refundable deposit, deadline 5/1. Off-campus college sponsored housing is available. **Activities:** Campus ministries, dance, international student organizations, Model UN, student government, student newspaper, Black Student Union, Caribbean student association, Colleges Against Cancer, GLOWUP: Gay Straight Alliance, campus ministry club, Military Veterans of Mercy club, ROTARACT Club for Community Volunteer Service, S.A.D.D. club, Student Government Association.

Athletics. NCAA. Intercollegiate: Baseball M, basketball, field hockey W, lacrosse, soccer, softball W, volleyball W. **Intramural:** Baseball M, basketball, field hockey W, softball W. **Team name:** Mavericks.

Student services. Adult student services, alcohol/substance abuse counseling, career counseling, services for economically disadvantaged, student employment services, financial aid counseling, health services, minority student services, personal counseling, placement for graduates, veterans' counselor. **Physically disabled:** Services for visually, speech, hearing impaired.

Contact. E-mail: admissions@mercy.edu
Phone: (877) 637-2946 Toll-free number: (877) 637-2946
Fax: (914) 674-7382
Deirdre Whitman, Vice President for Enrollment Management, Mercy College, 555 Broadway, Dobbs Ferry, NY 10522

Mesivta Torah Vodaath Seminary
Brooklyn, New York
independentrabbinicalcolleges.org/index.html CB code: 0636

- Private 5-year rabbinical college for men affiliated with the Jewish faith
- Very large city
- 210 degree-seeking undergraduates

General. Founded in 1918. Accredited by AARTS. First Talmudic degree and ordination available. **Degrees:** 23 bachelor's awarded. **ROTC:** Naval, Air Force. **Calendar:** Semester. **Full-time faculty:** 15 total. **Part-time faculty:** 3 total.

Basis for selection. Religious affiliation or commitment very important. Test scores, interview, school and community activities, recommendations, alumni relation important. School achievement record considered. Interview recommended.

2015-2016 Annual costs. Tuition/fees: $11,000. Room/board: $4,500.

Application procedures. Admission: No deadline. $200 fee.

Academics. Special study options: Independent study. **Credit/placement by examination:** AP, CLEP, institutional tests. **Support services:** Tutoring.

Majors. Theology: Talmudic.

Student life. Activities: Dance.

Student services. Career counseling, personal counseling, placement for graduates.

Contact. Phone: (718) 621-3651
Aaron Braun, Director of Admissions, Mesivta Torah Vodaath Seminary, 425 East Ninth Street, Brooklyn, NY 11218

Metropolitan College of New York
New York, New York   CB member
www.metropolitan.edu   CB code: 4802

- Private 4-year business and liberal arts college
- Commuter campus in very large city
- 779 degree-seeking undergraduates: 12% part-time, 74% women, 57% African American, 1% Native American, 3% international
- 416 degree-seeking graduate students
- 53% of applicants admitted
- Interview required
- 36% graduate within 6 years

General. Founded in 1964. Regionally accredited. **Degrees:** 220 bachelor's, 54 associate awarded; master's offered. **Location:** Downtown Manhattan. **Calendar:** Semester, extensive summer session. **Class size:** 89% < 20, 11% 20-39.

Freshman class profile. 333 applied, 176 admitted, 79 enrolled.

End year in good standing:	65%	Out-of-state:	6%
Return as sophomores:	57%	International:	13%

Basis for selection. Academic record, test scores, previous volunteer experience, school and community activities, motivation and communication skills as demonstrated in interviews considered. SAT or ACT recommended.

Combined SAT score of 1050 (exclusive of Writing) or higher can be substituted for institution-administered Test of Adult Basic Education or ACCUPLACER required for admission.

2016-2017 Annual costs. Tuition/fees: $18,730. Books/supplies: $1,000.

2015-2016 Financial aid. Need-based: 60 full-time freshmen applied for aid; 59 deemed to have need; 59 received aid. Average need met was 49%. Average scholarship/grant was $11,211; average loan $3,348. 48% of total undergraduate aid awarded as scholarships/grants, 52% as loans/jobs. **Non-need-based:** Awarded to 15 full-time undergraduates, including 7 freshmen. Scholarships awarded for academics. **Additional information:** Limited merit scholarships.

Application procedures. Admission: No deadline. $30 fee, may be waived for applicants with need, free for online applicants. Admission notification on a rolling basis. **Financial aid:** No deadline. FAFSA required.

Academics. Class work integrated with field work. Class learning applied, documented and assessed in internship or employment setting. **Special study options:** Accelerated study, distance learning, honors, independent study, internships, liberal arts/career combination, study abroad, teacher certification program, weekend college. **Credit/placement by examination:** AP, CLEP, IB, institutional tests. 35 credit hours maximum toward bachelor's degree. **Support services:** Learning center, remedial instruction, tutoring, writing center.

Majors. Business: General, business admin. **Human services:** General, community org/advocacy, social work. **Social sciences:** General, sociology, urban studies.

Most popular majors. Business/marketing 28%, health sciences 21%, public administration/social services 47%.

Technology on campus. 130 workstations in library, computer center. Wireless network available.

Student life. Freshman orientation: Mandatory. Preregistration for classes offered. **Activities:** Student government, student newspaper, honor societies, networking club, dance committee.

Student services. Adult student services, career counseling, student employment services, financial aid counseling, personal counseling, placement for graduates, veterans' counselor. **Physically disabled:** Services for visually, hearing impaired.

Contact. E-mail: admissions@mcny.edu
Phone: (212) 343-1234 ext. 5001 Toll-free number: (800) 338-4465
Fax: (212) 343-8470
Stephen Ostendorff, Director of Admissions, Metropolitan College of New York, 431 Canal Street, New York, NY 10013-1919

Mirrer Yeshiva Central Institute
Brooklyn, New York

CB code: 0661

- Private 4-year rabbinical college for men affiliated with the Jewish faith
- Very large city
- 161 degree-seeking undergraduates

General. Accredited by AARTS. **Degrees:** 9 bachelor's awarded; master's, doctoral offered. **Calendar:** Differs by program. **Full-time faculty:** 17 total.

Basis for selection. Secondary school record required, recommendations are recommended.

2015-2016 Annual costs. Tuition/fees: $6,650.

Application procedures. Admission: No deadline.

Academics. Credit/placement by examination: AP, CLEP.

Majors. Theology: Talmudic.

Contact. Phone: (718) 645-0536
Rabbi Pincus Hecht, Admissions Director, Mirrer Yeshiva Central Institute, 1795 Ocean Parkway, Brooklyn, NY 11223-2010

Molloy College
Rockville Centre, New York

CB member

www.molloy.edu

CB code: 2415

- Private 4-year liberal arts college affiliated with the Roman Catholic Church
- Commuter campus in large town
- 3,373 degree-seeking undergraduates: 19% part-time, 75% women, 12% African American, 7% Asian American, 15% Hispanic/Latino, 1% Multiracial, non-Hispanic
- 1,116 degree-seeking graduate students
- 76% of applicants admitted
- SAT or ACT with writing, application essay required
- 71% graduate within 6 years

General. Founded in 1955. Regionally accredited. Independent institution in Dominican tradition. **Degrees:** 759 bachelor's, 43 associate awarded; master's, doctoral offered. **ROTC:** Army, Naval. **Location:** 20 miles from New York City. **Calendar:** 4-1-4, limited summer session. **Full-time faculty:** 186 total; 77% have terminal degrees, 18% minority, 76% women. **Part-time faculty:** 518 total; 18% have terminal degrees, 18% minority, 66% women. **Class size:** 65% < 20, 33% 20-39, 2% 40-49, less than 1% 50-99. **Special facilities:** Weather station at Jones Beach, international business center.

Freshman class profile. 3,550 applied, 2,681 admitted, 539 enrolled.

Mid 50% test scores			
SAT critical reading:	480-570	Rank in top quarter:	56%
SAT math:	490-580	Rank in top tenth:	17%
SAT writing:	470-560	End year in good standing:	97%
ACT composite:	21-26	Return as sophomores:	88%
GPA 3.75 or higher:	12%	Out-of-state:	8%
GPA 3.50-3.74:	8%	Live on campus:	21%
GPA 3.0-3.49:	41%		
GPA 2.0-2.99:	33%		

Basis for selection. Secondary school achievement with particular attention to grade 11 performance most important. Test scores also important. Recommendations, school and community activities, interview considered. Audition required for music program; portfolio required for art program. **Home schooled:** State high school equivalency certificate required. **Learning Disabled:** Applicants reviewed by separate committee.

High school preparation. College-preparatory program required. 21 units required. Required and recommended units include English 4, mathematics 3-4, social studies 4, science 3-4, foreign language 3 and academic electives 4. Science, math, and nursing majors must have 1 biology, 1 chemistry, and 3 math.

2015-2016 Annual costs. Tuition/fees: $28,030. Room/board: $13,940. Books/supplies: $1,470. Personal expenses: $3,682.

2014-2015 Financial aid. Need-based: 465 full-time freshmen applied for aid; 408 deemed to have need; 407 received aid. Average need met was 60%. Average scholarship/grant was $13,966; average loan $3,242. 50% of total undergraduate aid awarded as scholarships/grants, 50% as loans/jobs. **Non-need-based:** Awarded to 377 full-time undergraduates, including 91 freshmen. Scholarships awarded for academics, alumni affiliation, art, athletics, leadership, music/drama, religious affiliation.

Application procedures. Admission: No deadline. $40 fee, may be waived for applicants with need. Admission notification on a rolling basis beginning on or about 10/15. Must reply by May 1 or within 2 week(s) if notified thereafter. **Financial aid:** Priority date 4/15, closing date 5/1. FAFSA required. Applicants notified on a rolling basis starting 2/1; must reply within 5 week(s) of notification.

Academics. Special study options: Combined bachelor's/graduate degree, double major, ESL, honors, independent study, internships, liberal arts/career combination, student-designed major, study abroad, teacher certification program. **Credit/placement by examination:** AP, CLEP, IB, SAT, ACT, institutional tests. 15 credit hours maximum toward associate degree, 30 toward bachelor's. **Support services:** Learning center, pre-admission summer program, reduced course load, remedial instruction, study skills assistance, tutoring, writing center.

Majors. Biology: General, ecology. **Business:** Accounting, business admin, finance, marketing. **Communications:** Communications/speech/rhetoric. **Computer sciences:** General, information systems. **Education:** Art, elementary, elementary special ed, multi-level teacher, music, secondary, secondary special ed. **English:** English lit. **Foreign languages:** Hispanic and Latin American. **Health services:** Music therapy, nuclear medical technology, nursing (RN), speech pathology. **History:** General. **Human services:** Social work. **Math:** General. **Philosophy/religion:** Philosophy, religion. **Protective**

services: Criminal justice. **Psychology:** General. **Social sciences:** Political science, sociology. **Visual/performing arts:** Dramatic, music, studio arts.

Most popular majors. Business/marketing 10%, education 11%, health sciences 54%.

Technology on campus. 713 workstations in dormitories, library, computer center, student center. Dormitories wired for high-speed internet access and linked to campus network. Commuter students can connect to campus network. Online course registration, online library, helpline, wireless network available.

Student life. Freshman orientation: Mandatory. Preregistration for classes offered. **Housing:** Coed dorms available. $500 nonrefundable deposit. **Activities:** Jazz band, campus ministries, choral groups, dance, drama, literary magazine, music ensembles, student government, student newspaper, African American and Caribbean organization, Gaelic society, Out for Acceptance, social work club, Union Hispana de Molloy, Youth for Christ, HOPE Team.

Athletics. NCAA. **Intercollegiate:** Baseball M, basketball, bowling W, cross-country, lacrosse, soccer, softball W, tennis W, track and field, volleyball W. **Team name:** Lions.

Student services. Adult student services, alcohol/substance abuse counseling, chaplain/spiritual director, career counseling, services for economically disadvantaged, student employment services, financial aid counseling, health services, personal counseling, veterans' counselor. **Physically disabled:** Services for visually, hearing impaired.

Contact. E-mail: admissions@molloy.edu
Phone: (516) 323-4000 Toll-free number: (888) 466-5569
Marguerite Lane, Dean of Admissions, Molloy College, PO Box 5002, Rockville Centre, NY 11571

Monroe College
Bronx, New York
www.monroecollege.edu   CB code: 2463

- For-profit 4-year business and health science college
- Commuter campus in very large city
- 6,178 degree-seeking undergraduates: 23% part-time, 64% women
- 500 degree-seeking graduate students
- Application essay, interview required

General. Founded in 1933. Regionally accredited. Branch campus in New Rochelle offers all programs, courses, and services available at main campus. **Degrees:** 1,096 bachelor's, 1,338 associate awarded; master's offered. **ROTC:** Army. **Calendar:** Semester, extensive summer session. **Full-time faculty:** 297 total; 66% minority, 52% women. **Part-time faculty:** 136 total; 61% minority, 46% women. **Class size:** 44% < 20, 55% 20-39, less than 1% 50-99.

Freshman class profile.

Out-of-state:	1%	Live on campus:	25%

Basis for selection. Interview, school achievement record, test scores required. Modified open admissions for students who pass admissions test.

2015-2016 Annual costs. Tuition/fees: $14,148. Room/board: $8,810. Books/supplies: $1,000. Personal expenses: $5,990.

Financial aid. All financial aid based on need.

Application procedures. Admission: No deadline. $35 fee. Admission notification on a rolling basis. **Financial aid:** Closing date 6/30. FAFSA required. Applicants notified on a rolling basis starting 7/1.

Academics. Special study options: Cooperative education, distance learning, dual enrollment of high school students, honors, internships, liberal arts/career combination, study abroad, teacher certification program, weekend college. **Credit/placement by examination:** AP, CLEP, IB, institutional tests. 12 credit hours maximum toward associate degree, 12 toward bachelor's. **Support services:** Learning center, pre-admission summer program, remedial instruction, study skills assistance, tutoring, writing center.

Majors. Business: Accounting, business admin, hospitality admin. **Computer sciences:** General, information technology. **Education:** Elementary. **Health services:** Health services admin, nursing (RN). **Protective services:** Law enforcement admin.

Most popular majors. Business/marketing 32%, computer/information sciences 11%, health sciences 38%, security/protective services 19%.

Technology on campus. 800 workstations in dormitories, library, computer center. Dormitories wired for high-speed internet access and linked to campus network. Commuter students can connect to campus network. Online course registration, online library, helpline, wireless network available.

Student life. Freshman orientation: Mandatory. Preregistration for classes offered. **Housing:** Coed dorms available. $100 partly refundable deposit. Assistance for foreign students in securing local housing. Student apartments available near New Rochelle campus. On-campus housing at New Rochelle campus. **Activities:** Dance, international student organizations, Students in Free Enterprise, National Association of Black Accountants, honors program.

Athletics. NJCAA. **Intercollegiate:** Baseball M, basketball, cross-country, football (tackle) M, soccer, softball W, track and field, volleyball W. **Intramural:** Basketball, softball W. **Team name:** Mustangs.

Student services. Adult student services, career counseling, services for economically disadvantaged, student employment services, financial aid counseling, health services, personal counseling, placement for graduates, veterans' counselor. **Physically disabled:** Services for visually, speech, hearing impaired.

Contact. E-mail: cwright@monroecollege.edu
Phone: (718) 933-6700 Toll-free number: (800) 556-6676
Fax: (718) 364-3552
Cecil Wright, Director of Admissions, Monroe College, 2501 Jerome Avenue, Bronx, NY 10468

Mount Saint Mary College
Newburgh, New York   CB member
www.msmc.edu   CB code: 2423

- Private 4-year liberal arts college affiliated with the Roman Catholic Church
- Residential campus in large town
- 2,140 degree-seeking undergraduates: 17% part-time, 71% women, 7% African American, 2% Asian American, 15% Hispanic/Latino, 1% Native American, 1% Multi-racial, non-Hispanic
- 347 degree-seeking graduate students
- 90% of applicants admitted
- SAT or ACT (ACT writing recommended) required
- 59% graduate within 6 years; 31% enter graduate study

General. Founded in 1954. Regionally accredited. Independent institution in Judeo-Christian tradition, founded by Dominican Sisters of Newburgh. **Degrees:** 476 bachelor's awarded; master's offered. **ROTC:** Army. **Location:** 58 miles from New York City. **Calendar:** Semester, limited summer session. **Full-time faculty:** 85 total; 88% have terminal degrees, 8% minority, 59% women. **Part-time faculty:** 192 total; 15% have terminal degrees, 17% minority, 64% women. **Class size:** 51% < 20, 45% 20-39, 3% 40-49, 1% 50-99. **Special facilities:** Elementary school on campus.

Freshman class profile. 3,628 applied, 3,249 admitted, 422 enrolled.

Mid 50% test scores		GPA 2.0-2.99:	25%
SAT critical reading:	450-530	Rank in top quarter:	32%
SAT math:	430-530	Rank in top tenth:	7%
SAT writing:	440-530	End year in good standing:	89%
ACT composite:	20-24	Return as sophomores:	78%
GPA 3.75 or higher:	11%	Out-of-state:	19%
GPA 3.50-3.74:	24%	Live on campus:	84%
GPA 3.0-3.49:	39%	International:	1%

Basis for selection. Total admission score weighs high school average, class rank, and test scores as well as teacher/counselor recommendations. Interviews are by invitation only after completed application is received. Personal essay required for transfer students. **Home schooled:** State high school equivalency certificate, interview required. Need SAT or ACT. **Learning Disabled:** Must include IEP with application. Must meet with Director of Counseling and Coordinator of Services for Persons with Disabilities.

High school preparation. College-preparatory program recommended. 20.5 units recommended. Recommended units include English 4, mathematics 3, social studies 4, science 3, foreign language 3, academic electives 3.5. Biology and chemistry required for nursing majors.

2016-2017 Annual costs. Tuition/fees: $29,048. Room/board: $14,104. Books/supplies: $1,200. Personal expenses: $1,000.

2015-2016 Financial aid. Need-based: 410 full-time freshmen applied for aid; 360 deemed to have need; 360 received aid. Average need met was 65%. Average scholarship/grant was $16,426; average loan $3,263. 59% of

total undergraduate aid awarded as scholarships/grants, 41% as loans/jobs. **Non-need-based:** Awarded to 450 full-time undergraduates, including 104 freshmen. Scholarships awarded for academics, alumni affiliation, leadership, ROTC, state residency.

Application procedures. Admission: Closing date 8/15 (postmark date). $45 fee, may be waived for applicants with need, free for online applicants. Admission notification on a rolling basis beginning on or about 9/15. Housing deposit refundable by May 1. **Financial aid:** Priority date 2/15, closing date 3/1. FAFSA required. Applicants notified on a rolling basis starting 3/1; must reply by 5/1.

Academics. Special study options: Accelerated study, combined bachelor's/graduate degree, cooperative education, cross-registration, distance learning, double major, dual enrollment of high school students, exchange student, honors, independent study, internships, liberal arts/career combination, student-designed major, study abroad, teacher certification program. **Credit/placement by examination:** AP, CLEP, IB, SAT, ACT, institutional tests. 45 credit hours maximum toward bachelor's degree. **Support services:** Learning center, pre-admission summer program, reduced course load, remedial instruction, study skills assistance, tutoring, writing center.

Majors. Biology: General. **Business:** Accounting, business admin. **Communications:** Media studies, public relations. **Computer sciences:** Information technology. **Education:** Early childhood, multi-level teacher, secondary. **English:** English lit. **Foreign languages:** Spanish. **Health services:** Clinical lab science, nursing (RN). **History:** General. **Math:** General. **Physical sciences:** Chemistry. **Psychology:** General. **Social sciences:** General, sociology.

Most popular majors. Business/marketing 18%, English 7%, health sciences 25%, history 8%, interdisciplinary studies 6%, psychology 10%, public administration/social services 7%.

Technology on campus. 470 workstations in dormitories, library, computer center, student center. Dormitories wired for high-speed internet access and linked to campus network. Commuter students can connect to campus network. Online course registration, online library, helpline, repair service, wireless network available.

Student life. Freshman orientation: Mandatory. Preregistration for classes offered. Held during two sessions in July. **Policies:** Freshmen not permitted cars on campus. **Housing:** Guaranteed on-campus for all undergraduates. Coed dorms, single-sex dorms, special housing for disabled available. $450 deposit, deadline 5/1. **Activities:** Bands, campus ministries, choral groups, dance, drama, film society, literary magazine, music ensembles, musical theater, radio station, student government, student newspaper, black student union, Habitat for Humanity, Big Brothers/Big Sisters, Christian fellowship, Latin student union.

Athletics. NCAA. **Intercollegiate:** Baseball M, basketball, cheerleading W, cross-country, golf M, lacrosse, soccer, softball W, swimming, tennis, track and field, volleyball W. **Intramural:** Basketball, bowling, football (non-tackle) M, golf, soccer, softball, swimming, table tennis, volleyball. **Team name:** Knights.

Student services. Adult student services, alcohol/substance abuse counseling, chaplain/spiritual director, career counseling, services for economically disadvantaged, student employment services, financial aid counseling, health services, personal counseling. **Physically disabled:** Services for visually impaired.

Contact. E-mail: admissions@msmc.edu
Phone: (845) 569-3488 Toll-free number: (888) 937-6762
Fax: (845) 562-3520
Nancy Scaffidi Clarke, Director of Undergraduate Admissions, Mount Saint Mary College, 330 Powell Avenue, Newburgh, NY 12550

Nazareth College
Rochester, New York
www.naz.edu

CB member
CB code: 2511

- Private 4-year liberal arts college
- Residential campus in large city
- 2,078 degree-seeking undergraduates: 5% part-time, 71% women, 7% African American, 3% Asian American, 5% Hispanic/Latino, 2% Multiracial, non-Hispanic, 2% international
- 743 degree-seeking graduate students
- 76% of applicants admitted
- Application essay required
- 73% graduate within 6 years; 27% enter graduate study

General. Founded in 1924. Regionally accredited. **Degrees:** 487 bachelor's awarded; master's, professional offered. **ROTC:** Army, Air Force. **Location:**

7 miles from downtown. **Calendar:** Semester, extensive summer session. **Full-time faculty:** 178 total; 82% have terminal degrees, 14% minority, 62% women. **Part-time faculty:** 308 total; 29% have terminal degrees, 9% minority, 59% women. **Class size:** 60% < 20, 39% 20-39, 1% 40-49. **Special facilities:** Arts center, psychology research facility, center for service learning, center for interfaith studies and dialogue, wellness and rehabilitation institute.

Freshman class profile. 3,677 applied, 2,778 admitted, 521 enrolled.

Mid 50% test scores			
SAT critical reading:	480-580	Rank in top quarter:	58%
SAT math:	490-590	Rank in top tenth:	27%
SAT writing:	460-580	Return as sophomores:	84%
ACT composite:	22-27	Out-of-state:	9%
GPA 3.75 or higher:	30%	Live on campus:	90%
GPA 3.50-3.74:	18%	International:	1%
GPA 3.0-3.49:	33%		
GPA 2.0-2.99:	19%		

Basis for selection. School achievement record, strength of high school academic program, class rank, standardized tests scores if available, recommendations, extracurricular activities most important. Standardized Test Optional in almost every case. The only exception is the Nursing program, which expects a minimum SAT score (CR & M) of 1100 or an ACT score of at least 24. Interview recommended for all; audition required for dance, music and theater arts programs; portfolio required for art programs.

High school preparation. College-preparatory program required. 17 units required; 20 recommended. Required and recommended units include English 4, mathematics 3-4, social studies 4, science 3-4 (laboratory 2) and foreign language 3-4.

2015-2016 Annual costs. Tuition/fees: $31,520. Room/board: $12,918. Books/supplies: $1,100. Personal expenses: $1,000.

2015-2016 Financial aid. Need-based: 497 full-time freshmen applied for aid; 444 deemed to have need; 444 received aid. Average need met was 84%. Average scholarship/grant was $18,752; average loan $3,598. 61% of total undergraduate aid awarded as scholarships/grants, 39% as loans/jobs. **Non-need-based:** Awarded to 916 full-time undergraduates, including 273 freshmen. Scholarships awarded for academics, art, minority status, music/drama.

Application procedures. Admission: Priority date 12/1; deadline 2/1 (postmark date). $45 fee, may be waived for applicants with need. Application must be submitted online. Notification begins March 1. **Financial aid:** Closing date 2/15. FAFSA required. Applicants notified on a rolling basis starting 2/1; must reply by 5/1.

Academics. Special study options: Combined bachelor's/graduate degree, cross-registration, distance learning, double major, dual enrollment of high school students, ESL, exchange student, honors, independent study, internships, liberal arts/career combination, study abroad, teacher certification program, Washington semester. **Credit/placement by examination:** AP, CLEP, IB, SAT, ACT. 30 credit hours maximum toward bachelor's degree. **Support services:** Pre-admission summer program, reduced course load, remedial instruction, study skills assistance, tutoring, writing center.

Majors. Area/ethnic studies: American, Asian. **Biology:** General, biochemistry, biomedical sciences, toxicology. **Business:** General, accounting, finance, international, marketing. **Communications:** Communications/speech/rhetoric. **Computer sciences:** Information systems. **Conservation:** Environmental science. **Education:** Art, biology, business, chemistry, elementary, English, foreign languages, history, mathematics, music, secondary, special ed, speech, speech impaired. **English:** English lit. **Foreign languages:** Chinese, French, German, Italian, Spanish. **Health services:** Clinical lab science, communication disorders, music therapy, nursing (RN), speech pathology. **History:** General. **Human services:** Social work. **Math:** General. **Philosophy/religion:** Philosophy, religion. **Physical sciences:** Chemistry. **Psychology:** General. **Social sciences:** General, anthropology, economics, political science, sociology. **Visual/performing arts:** Acting, art, art history/conservation, dance, design, dramatic, graphic design, music, music history, music management, music performance, music theory/composition, musical theater, studio arts.

Most popular majors. Business/marketing 13%, education 15%, health sciences 17%, psychology 8%, public administration/social services 6%, social sciences 6%, visual/performing arts 9%.

Technology on campus. 240 workstations in dormitories, library, computer center. Dormitories wired for high-speed internet access and linked to campus network. Commuter students can connect to campus network. Online course registration, online library, helpline, wireless network available.

Student life. Freshman orientation: Mandatory, $100 fee. Preregistration for classes offered. Orientation charge included in first-year fees. Three-day weekend program includes community service. **Policies:** First- and second-year students required to live on campus unless living with family within 30 miles of campus. **Housing:** Guaranteed on-campus for freshmen. Coed dorms, apartments, themed housing, wellness housing available. $100 nonrefundable deposit, deadline 5/1. Special interest housing available. **Activities:** Bands, campus ministries, choral groups, dance, drama, international student organizations, literary magazine, music ensembles, musical theater, opera, radio station, student government, student newspaper, symphony orchestra, Amnesty International, Inter-Ethnic Nazareth Coalition, Center for Spirituality Council, Go Green!, Undergraduate Association, Colleges Against Cancer, Students for Political Action and Awareness, French club, German club, ASL club.

Athletics. NCAA. **Intercollegiate:** Basketball, cross-country, diving, equestrian, field hockey W, golf, ice hockey, lacrosse, soccer, softball W, swimming, tennis, track and field, volleyball. **Intramural:** Basketball, racquetball, soccer, softball, swimming, tennis, volleyball. **Team name:** Golden Flyers.

Student services. Adult student services, alcohol/substance abuse counseling, chaplain/spiritual director, career counseling, services for economically disadvantaged, student employment services, financial aid counseling, health services, minority student services, personal counseling, placement for graduates, veterans' counselor, women's services. **Physically disabled:** Services for visually, speech, hearing impaired.

Contact. E-mail: admissions@naz.edu
Phone: (585) 389-2860 Toll-free number: (800) 462-3944
Fax: (585) 389-2826
John Mordaci, Director of Freshmen Admissions, Nazareth College, 4245 East Avenue, Rochester, NY 14618-3790

New York Institute of Technology
Old Westbury, New York
www.nyit.edu   CB code: 2561

- Private 4-year health science college
- Commuter campus in small town
- 3,950 degree-seeking undergraduates: 12% part-time, 36% women, 8% African American, 15% Asian American, 13% Hispanic/Latino, 1% Multi-racial, non-Hispanic, 18% international
- 3,988 degree-seeking graduate students
- 68% of applicants admitted
- SAT or ACT (ACT writing recommended), application essay required
- 45% graduate within 6 years; 35% enter graduate study

General. Founded in 1955. Regionally accredited. NYIT offers degree programs in more than 50 fields of study at campuses on Long Island and in Manhattan, online, and at sites in the Middle East, China, and Canada. **Degrees:** 1,031 bachelor's, 19 associate awarded; master's, professional offered. **ROTC:** Army, Air Force. **Location:** 20 miles from New York City. **Calendar:** Semester, extensive summer session. **Full-time faculty:** 298 total; 90% have terminal degrees, 26% minority, 38% women. **Part-time faculty:** 603 total; 20% minority, 42% women. **Class size:** 62% < 20, 36% 20-39, less than 1% 40-49, 1% 50-99. **Special facilities:** Gallery 61; NYIT Auditorium on Broadway; simulated trading floor; NYITCOM Health Care Clinic; financial technology center; motion capture lab.

Freshman class profile. 8,566 applied, 5,805 admitted, 742 enrolled.

Mid 50% test scores			
SAT critical reading:	460-570	Return as sophomores:	75%
SAT math:	500-610	Out-of-state:	10%
ACT composite:	21-26	Live on campus:	20%
GPA 3.75 or higher:	20%	International:	9%
GPA 3.50-3.74:	15%	Fraternities:	1%
GPA 3.0-3.49:	38%	Sororities:	1%
GPA 2.0-2.99:	25%		

Basis for selection. Special requirements for admission to specific programs in the School of Architecture and Design, School of Engineering and Computing Sciences, and the School of Health Professions. Proof of 100 hours of volunteer work experience required for admission to the B.S./ D.P.T. program in Physical Therapy and B.S./M.S. program in Occupational Therapy. Special program requirements for the Schools of Architecture and Design, Engineering and Computing Sciences, and Health Professions are available in the NYIT catalog.

High school preparation. College-preparatory program required. 17 units required. Required and recommended units include English 4, mathematics 3, social studies 3-4, science 3 (laboratory 1) and academic electives 7.

2015-2016 Annual costs. Tuition/fees: $33,480. Room/board: $13,090. Books/supplies: $936. Personal expenses: $2,080. **Additional information:** Room and board cost is for a double at the Old Westbury campus.

2014-2015 Financial aid. Need-based: 599 full-time freshmen applied for aid; 529 deemed to have need; 527 received aid. Average scholarship/ grant was $8,107; average loan $3,322. 66% of total undergraduate aid awarded as scholarships/grants, 34% as loans/jobs. **Non-need-based:** Awarded to 2,491 full-time undergraduates, including 607 freshmen. Scholarships awarded for academics, alumni affiliation, athletics.

Application procedures. Admission: Priority date 3/1; no deadline. $50 fee, may be waived for applicants with need. Admission notification on a rolling basis. Must reply by 1/15. Application closing date may vary by academic department; additional information is available at www.nyit.edu or by contacting the Admissions office. **Financial aid:** Priority date 3/1; no closing date. FAFSA required. Applicants notified on a rolling basis starting 3/1; must reply within 4 week(s) of notification.

Academics. School focuses on career-oriented professional education, applications-oriented research, and service in public interest. **Special study options:** Accelerated study, combined bachelor's/graduate degree, cooperative education, cross-registration, distance learning, double major, dual enrollment of high school students, ESL, honors, independent study, internships, liberal arts/career combination, study abroad, teacher certification program, weekend college. **Credit/placement by examination:** AP, CLEP, IB, institutional tests. 30 credit hours maximum toward associate degree, 60 toward bachelor's. Total hours of credit by examination includes all types of prior learning credits (including proficiency exams and prior work and/or life experience credits). **Support services:** Learning center, remedial instruction, study skills assistance, tutoring, writing center.

Majors. Architecture: Architecture, technology. **Biology:** General, biotechnology. **Business:** Accounting, business admin, finance, hotel/motel/ restaurant management, human resources, international, marketing. **Communications:** General, advertising, digital media, persuasive communications. **Computer sciences:** General, information technology. **Engineering:** Electrical, mechanical. **English:** English lit. **Health services:** General, nursing (RN). **Physical sciences:** Chemistry. **Psychology:** General. **Social sciences:** Political science, sociology, urban studies. **Visual/performing arts:** Commercial/advertising art, interior design.

Most popular majors. Architecture 13%, biology 11%, business/marketing 12%, communications/journalism 11%, computer/information sciences 10%, engineering/engineering technologies 20%, health sciences 10%.

Technology on campus. 1,250 workstations in dormitories, library, computer center, student center. Dormitories wired for high-speed internet access and linked to campus network. Commuter students can connect to campus network. Online course registration, online library, helpline, student web hosting, wireless network available.

Student life. Freshman orientation: Mandatory, $75 fee. Preregistration for classes offered. One-day orientations are held at the Old Westbury and Manhattan campuses before the start of the fall and spring semesters. **Housing:** Guaranteed on-campus for freshmen. Coed dorms, special housing for disabled, themed housing available. $300 nonrefundable deposit. **Activities:** Choral groups, dance, drama, film society, international student organizations, literary magazine, musical theater, radio station, student government, student newspaper, TV station, National Society of Black Engineers, Intervarsity Christian Fellowship, Jewish Student Union, International Students Association, Muslim Student Association, Students for Global Health Access, Asian Medical Humanitarian Association, Orthodox Christian Club, Woman's Association.

Athletics. NCAA. **Intercollegiate:** Baseball M, basketball, cross-country, lacrosse M, soccer, softball W, tennis, volleyball W. **Intramural:** Basketball, soccer, softball W, tennis, volleyball W. **Team name:** Bears.

Student services. Adult student services, alcohol/substance abuse counseling, career counseling, student employment services, financial aid counseling, health services, minority student services, personal counseling, placement for graduates, veterans' counselor, women's services. **Physically disabled:** Services for visually, speech, hearing impaired.

Contact. E-mail: admissions@nyit.edu
Phone: (516) 686-7520 Toll-free number: (800) 345-6948
Fax: (516) 686-7613
Karen Vahey, Dean, Admissions and Financial Aid, New York Institute of Technology, Box 8000, Old Westbury, NY 11568

New York School of Interior Design
New York, New York
www.nysid.edu   CB code: 0333

- Private 4-year visual arts college
- Commuter campus in very large city

- 335 degree-seeking undergraduates: 62% part-time, 90% women, 4% African American, 3% Asian American, 9% Hispanic/Latino, 2% Multi-racial, non-Hispanic, 14% international
- 157 degree-seeking graduate students
- 42% of applicants admitted
- Application essay required
- 100% graduate within 6 years

General. Founded in 1916. The college is devoted exclusively to interior design education. **Degrees:** 63 bachelor's, 29 associate awarded; master's offered. **Location:** Located in Manhattan. **Calendar:** Semester, extensive summer session. **Full-time faculty:** 5 total; 20% minority, 60% women. **Part-time faculty:** 115 total; 13% minority, 56% women. **Class size:** 92% < 20, 5% 20-39, 3% 50-99. **Special facilities:** Three galleries for architecture and interior design exhibits, lighting laboratory.

Freshman class profile. 155 applied, 65 admitted, 12 enrolled.

Return as sophomores:	80%	**Live on campus:**	25%
Out-of-state:	44%	**International:**	8%

Basis for selection. High school transcripts, 2 letters of recommendation, essay, and portfolio in art/design. Portfolio required, interview optional. **Home schooled:** State high school equivalency certificate required.

High school preparation. 16 units recommended. Recommended units include English 4, mathematics 2, social studies 2, history 2, science 2 and foreign language 2. Studio art or drafting is recommended.

2016-2017 Annual costs. Tuition/fees: $30,945. Room/board: $21,000. Books/supplies: $1,500. Personal expenses: $3,000.

2015-2016 Financial aid. Need-based: 4 full-time freshmen applied for aid; 4 deemed to have need; 3 received aid. Average need met was 5%. Average scholarship/grant was $2,560; average loan $3,500. 37% of total undergraduate aid awarded as scholarships/grants, 63% as loans/jobs. **Non-need-based:** Scholarships awarded for academics, art.

Application procedures. Admission: Priority date 2/1; no deadline. $60 fee, may be waived for applicants with need. Admission notification on a rolling basis beginning on or about 4/1. Must reply by May 1 or within 2 week(s) if notified thereafter. **Financial aid:** Priority date 8/1; no closing date. FAFSA required. Applicants notified on a rolling basis starting 4/15; must reply within 2 week(s) of notification.

Academics. Special study options: Distance learning, independent study, internships, study abroad, weekend college. **Credit/placement by examination:** AP, CLEP, IB, institutional tests. 17 credit hours maximum toward associate degree, 41 toward bachelor's. **Support services:** Study skills assistance, tutoring, writing center.

Majors. Visual/performing arts: Interior design.

Technology on campus. 125 workstations in library, computer center. Dormitories wired for high-speed internet access and linked to campus network. Commuter students can connect to campus network. Online course registration, helpline, wireless network available.

Student life. Freshman orientation: Available. Preregistration for classes offered. Held the week before classes begin. Additional orientation held for international students. **Housing:** Coed dorms available. $500 nonrefundable deposit. **Activities:** Student chapter of American Society of Interior Designers, student council.

Student services. Adult student services, career counseling, student employment services, financial aid counseling, personal counseling, placement for graduates.

Contact. E-mail: admissions@nysid.edu
Phone: (212) 472-1500 ext. 205
Toll-free number: (800) 336-9743 ext. 205 Fax: (212) 472-1867
Celeste Collins, Director of Admissions, New York School of Interior Design, 170 East 70th Street, New York, NY 10021-5110

New York University
New York, New York
www.nyu.edu

CB member
CB code: 2562

- Private 4-year university
- Residential campus in very large city
- 25,314 degree-seeking undergraduates: 4% part-time, 57% women

- 23,467 degree-seeking graduate students
- SAT and SAT Subject Tests or ACT with writing, application essay required

General. Founded in 1831. Regionally accredited. Degrees offered by campuses in New York City, Abu Dhabi, and Shanghai. **Degrees:** 5,552 bachelor's, 54 associate awarded; master's, professional, doctoral offered. **ROTC:** Army, Air Force. **Calendar:** Semester, extensive summer session. **Full-time faculty:** 2,843 total; 72% have terminal degrees, 24% minority, 41% women. **Part-time faculty:** 4,001 total; 20% have terminal degrees, 25% minority, 44% women. **Class size:** 61% < 20, 28% 20-39, 3% 40-49, 7% 50-99, 1% >100. **Special facilities:** Special academic facilities for arts, business, culture, education, international relations, language, law, media, music, public service, research, and social policy.

Freshman class profile.

GPA 3.75 or higher:	44%	**Out-of-state:**	71%
GPA 3.50-3.74:	15%	**Live on campus:**	85%
GPA 3.0-3.49:	38%	**Fraternities:**	4%
GPA 2.0-2.99:	3%	**Sororities:**	5%

Basis for selection. School achievement record most important. Standardized test scores, activities, essay, recommendations also important. Audition and/or submission of creative materials required for applicants to either Tisch School of the Arts or art and music programs within the School of Education. NYU has a flexible testing policy. A national examination for every freshman applicant is required but we are flexible about which examination must be submitted for eligibility. Audition required for dance, drama, and music programs; portfolio required for art, theater design, photography, cinema studies, film, television, radio, and dramatic writing programs. Portfolios may include writing, photography, film or other creative work. **Home schooled:** Transcript of courses and grades, letter of recommendation (nonparent) required. Applicants must submit official score reports from either the SAT (including the Writing section), or the ACT with the ACT Writing Test, and at least two SAT Subject Test scores or two Advanced Placement test scores. Students must either be able to provide a home school diploma or certificate of completion that is considered the equivalent of a high school diploma in the applicant's home state, or they must be willing, if admitted, to apply for a New York State equivalency diploma upon the completion of twenty-four college credits.

High school preparation. 16 units required; 20 recommended. Required and recommended units include English 4, mathematics 3-4, social studies 3-4, history 3-4, science 3-4 (laboratory 3-4) and foreign language 3-4.

2015-2016 Annual costs. Tuition/fees: $47,750. Room/board: $17,580. Books/supplies: $1,070. Personal expenses: $2,000.

Application procedures. Admission: Closing date 1/1 (postmark date). $70 fee, may be waived for applicants with need. Application must be submitted online. Admission notification by 4/1. Must reply by 5/1. **Financial aid:** Closing date 2/15. FAFSA, CSS PROFILE required. Applicants notified by 4/1; must reply by 5/1.

Academics. Special study options: Accelerated study, combined bachelor's/graduate degree, cooperative education, cross-registration, distance learning, double major, ESL, exchange student, external degree, honors, independent study, internships, liberal arts/career combination, student-designed major, study abroad, teacher certification program, Washington semester. Exchange program with several historically black colleges including Spelman College, Morehouse College, and Xavier University of Louisiana. **Credit/placement by examination:** AP, CLEP, IB. 32 credit hours maximum toward bachelor's degree. 8 to 32 hours of credit may be awarded for International Baccalaureate. **Support services:** Learning center, pre-admission summer program, reduced course load, study skills assistance, tutoring, writing center.

Majors. Area/ethnic studies: General, African-American, American, Asian, Chinese, East Asian, European, Latin American, Near/Middle Eastern, Spanish/Iberian. **Biology:** General, biochemistry, Biochemistry/molecular biology, ecology, neuroscience. **Business:** General, accounting, finance, hotel/motel admin, international, labor relations, managerial economics, real estate, sales/distribution. **Communications:** General, communications/speech/rhetoric, digital media, media studies, radio/TV, technical/scientific. **Communications technology:** Radio/TV. **Computer sciences:** General, computer science, information technology, webmaster. **Education:** Art, biology, business, chemistry, driver/safety, early childhood, earth science, elementary, English, ESL, family/consumer sciences, foreign languages, French, German, health, kindergarten/preschool, mathematics, music, physics, science, social studies, Spanish, special ed, speech impaired, trade/industrial. **Engineering:** General, applied physics, biomolecular, chemical, civil, computer, construction, electrical, environmental, mechanical, metallurgical, nuclear, operations research. **English:** American lit, British lit, English lit, rhetoric/composition. **Foreign languages:** General, ancient Greek, classics, comparative lit, French, German, Hebrew, Italian, Latin, linguistics, Portuguese, Russian, Spanish. **Health services:** Audiology/speech pathology, dental hygiene, nursing (RN), nursing practice, occupational therapy, orthotics/prosthetics, physical therapy. **History:** General. **Human services:** General, community org/advocacy, health policy, social work. **Liberal arts:** Arts/sciences, humanities. **Math:** General, applied. **Parks/recreation:** Facilities management. **Philosophy/religion:** Philosophy, religion. **Physical sciences:** Chemistry, physics. **Psychology:** General, clinical. **Social sciences:** General, anthropology, archaeology, economics, international relations, political science, sociology, urban studies. **Visual/performing arts:** General, art history/conservation, arts management, cinematography, commercial/advertising art, dance, dramatic, film/cinema/video, jazz, music, music performance, music technology, photography, studio arts, studio arts management, voice/opera, woodwind instruments. **Work/family studies:** General, food/nutrition.

Most popular majors. Business/marketing 13%, health sciences 7%, liberal arts 10%, social sciences 16%, visual/performing arts 21%.

Technology on campus. 595 workstations in dormitories, library, computer center, student center. Dormitories wired for high-speed internet access and linked to campus network. Commuter students can connect to campus network. Online course registration, online library, helpline, repair service, student web hosting, wireless network available.

Student life. Freshman orientation: Available. Preregistration for classes offered. Each undergraduate college handles its own. Charges and program vary by school. **Housing:** Guaranteed on-campus for all undergraduates. Coed dorms, special housing for disabled, apartments, fraternity/sorority housing, themed housing, wellness housing available. $1,000 nonrefundable deposit, deadline 5/1. First-year residential experience program, substance free communities, sophomore residential experience, learning communities, mixed sex housing available. **Activities:** Bands, campus ministries, choral groups, dance, drama, film society, international student organizations, literary magazine, music ensembles, Model UN, musical theater, opera, radio station, student government, student newspaper, symphony orchestra, TV station, over 500 clubs and organizations available.

Athletics. NCAA. **Intercollegiate:** Basketball, cross-country, diving, fencing, golf, soccer, softball W, swimming, tennis, track and field, volleyball, wrestling M. **Intramural:** Basketball, bowling, football (non-tackle), soccer, softball, tennis, triathlon, volleyball, weight lifting. **Team name:** Violets.

Student services. Adult student services, alcohol/substance abuse counseling, chaplain/spiritual director, career counseling, services for economically disadvantaged, student employment services, financial aid counseling, health services, minority student services, personal counseling, placement for graduates, veterans' counselor, women's services. **Physically disabled:** Services for visually, speech, hearing impaired.

Contact. E-mail: admissions@nyu.edu
Phone: (212) 998-4500 Fax: (212) 995-4902
Shawn Abbott, Assistant Vice President of Admissions, New York University, 665 Broadway, 11th floor, New York, NY 10012-2339

Niagara University
Niagara University, New York   **CB member**
www.niagara.edu   **CB code: 2558**

♦ Private 4-year university affiliated with the Roman Catholic Church
♦ Residential campus in small city
♦ 3,133 degree-seeking undergraduates: 10% part-time, 62% women, 5% African American, 1% Asian American, 4% Hispanic/Latino, 1% Native American, 2% Multi-racial, non-Hispanic, 13% international
♦ 870 degree-seeking graduate students
♦ 63% of applicants admitted
♦ SAT or ACT (ACT writing optional) required
♦ 63% graduate within 6 years; 28% enter graduate study

General. Founded in 1856. Regionally accredited. Independent institution in the Vincentian tradition. **Degrees:** 826 bachelor's, 2 associate awarded; master's, doctoral offered. **ROTC:** Army. **Location:** 4 miles from Niagara Falls, 20 miles from Buffalo; 90 miles from Toronto, Canada. **Calendar:** Semester, extensive summer session. **Full-time faculty:** 157 total; 96% have terminal degrees, 13% minority, 42% women. **Part-time faculty:** 211 total; 7% minority, 51% women. **Class size:** 52% < 20, 45% 20-39, 2% 40-49, less than 1% 50-99, less than 1% >100. **Special facilities:** Art museum, ice arena, theater, greenhouse, nursing simulation lab, family literacy center.

Freshman class profile. 3,926 applied, 2,479 admitted, 643 enrolled.

Mid 50% test scores			
SAT critical reading:	460-560	Rank in top tenth:	15%
SAT math:	470-570	End year in good standing:	85%
ACT composite:	20-25	Return as sophomores:	88%
GPA 3.75 or higher:	28%	Out-of-state:	8%
GPA 3.50-3.74:	20%	Live on campus:	74%
GPA 3.0-3.49:	31%	International:	3%
GPA 2.0-2.99:	20%	Fraternities:	3%
Rank in top quarter:	41%	Sororities:	3%

Basis for selection. School achievement record, class rank, test scores most important. School recommendation also important. Character, personality, and extracurricular activities considered. Alumni relationship also considered. Interview, essay recommended for all; audition recommended for theater program. **Home schooled:** Transcript of courses and grades required. Letter from district superintendent or local district official confirming that the student has received an education "substantially equivalent" to instruction given to students graduating from the public high school in that district.

High school preparation. College-preparatory program recommended. 16 units required. Required units include English 4, mathematics 2, social studies 2, science 2, foreign language 2 and academic electives 4. 3 science (biology, chemistry mandatory, physics recommended) for math, science, nursing applicants. 2 foreign language required of all except business applicants. 3 math required for math, biology, business, biochemistry, chemistry, computer and information sciences, natural sciences, and nursing applicants. 3 social studies required for prospective social studies majors.

2015-2016 Annual costs. Tuition/fees: $29,900. Room/board: $12,300. Books/supplies: $1,050. Personal expenses: $750.

2015-2016 Financial aid. Need-based: 589 full-time freshmen applied for aid; 532 deemed to have need; 532 received aid. Average need met was 84%. Average scholarship/grant was $23,059; average loan $4,568. 69% of total undergraduate aid awarded as scholarships/grants, 31% as loans/jobs. **Non-need-based:** Awarded to 2,295 full-time undergraduates, including 574 freshmen. Scholarships awarded for academics, athletics, music/drama, ROTC. **Additional information:** Opportunity program available for academically and economically disadvantaged students.

Application procedures. Admission: Closing date 8/1 (receipt date). No application fee. Admission notification on a rolling basis. Must reply by May 1 or within 4 week(s) if notified thereafter. **Financial aid:** Priority date 2/15; no closing date. FAFSA required. Applicants notified on a rolling basis starting 3/1; must reply within 3 week(s) of notification.

Academics. Academic exploration program for students undecided about their choice of major. **Special study options:** Accelerated study, combined bachelor's/graduate degree, cooperative education, cross-registration, distance learning, double major, dual enrollment of high school students, ESL, exchange student, honors, independent study, internships, liberal arts/career combination, New York semester, study abroad, teacher certification program, Washington semester. **Credit/placement by examination:** AP, CLEP, IB, institutional tests. 15 credit hours maximum toward associate degree, 15 toward bachelor's. **Support services:** Learning center, pre-admission summer program, reduced course load, remedial instruction, study skills assistance, tutoring, writing center.

Majors. Biology: General, biochemistry. **Business:** Accounting, finance, hospitality admin, hotel/motel admin, human resources, international, logistics, managerial economics, marketing, public finance, restaurant/food services, tourism/travel, training/development. **Communications:** Communications/speech/rhetoric. **Computer sciences:** General, computer science, information systems. **Education:** General, biology, business, chemistry, early childhood, elementary, English, French, mathematics, secondary, social studies, Spanish, special ed. **English:** English lit. **Foreign languages:** French, Spanish. **Health services:** Nursing (RN), predental, premedicine, preveterinary. **History:** General. **Human services:** Social work. **Liberal arts:** Arts/sciences. **Math:** General. **Philosophy/religion:** Philosophy, religion. **Physical sciences:** Chemistry. **Protective services:** Criminal justice. **Psychology:** General. **Social sciences:** General, criminology, political science, sociology. **Visual/performing arts:** Dramatic. **Work/family studies:** Family studies.

Most popular majors. Business/marketing 30%, education 27%, security/protective services 8%.

Technology on campus. 150 workstations in dormitories, library, computer center, student center. Dormitories wired for high-speed internet access and linked to campus network. Commuter students can connect to campus network. Online course registration, online library, helpline, repair service, wireless network available.

Student life. Freshman orientation: Mandatory. Preregistration for classes offered. **Policies:** Freshmen not within reasonable commuting distance are required to live on campus for 2 years. **Housing:** Guaranteed on-campus for all undergraduates. Coed dorms, apartments, themed housing available.

$100 nonrefundable deposit, deadline 5/1. **Activities:** Pep band, campus ministries, choral groups, dance, drama, international student organizations, literary magazine, musical theater, radio station, student government, Diversity Advocates; Circle K; Bienvenidos; Brothers & Sisters in Christ (BASIC); Pax Christi; College Democrats; College Republicans; Community Action Program; Model UN; Niagara University Helping Our Planet Earth (NUHOPE).

Athletics. NCAA. **Intercollegiate:** Baseball M, basketball, cross-country, diving, golf, ice hockey M, lacrosse W, soccer, softball W, swimming, tennis, track and field W, volleyball W. **Intramural:** Baseball M, basketball, bowling, football (non-tackle), golf, racquetball, sand volleyball, skiing, soccer, softball, volleyball, water polo. **Team name:** Purple Eagles.

Student services. Adult student services, alcohol/substance abuse counseling, chaplain/spiritual director, career counseling, services for economically disadvantaged, student employment services, financial aid counseling, health services, minority student services, personal counseling, placement for graduates, veterans' counselor.

Contact. E-mail: admissions@niagara.edu
Phone: (716) 286-8700 Toll-free number: (800) 462-2111
Fax: (716) 286-8710
Mark Wojnowski, Director of Undergraduate Admissions, Niagara University, Bailo Hall, Niagara University, NY 14109

Nyack College
Nyack, New York
www.nyack.edu   CB code: 2560

- Private 4-year liberal arts and seminary college affiliated with the Christian and Missionary Alliance
- Residential campus in large town
- 1,540 degree-seeking undergraduates: 16% part-time, 61% women, 30% African American, 8% Asian American, 31% Hispanic/Latino, 1% Native American, 2% Multi-racial, non-Hispanic, 6% international
- 1,111 degree-seeking graduate students
- 99% of applicants admitted
- Application essay required
- 46% graduate within 6 years

General. Founded in 1882. Regionally accredited. **Degrees:** 368 bachelor's, 13 associate awarded; master's, professional offered. **Location:** 25 miles from New York City. **Calendar:** Semester, limited summer session. **Full-time faculty:** 100 total; 82% have terminal degrees, 44% minority, 37% women. **Part-time faculty:** 184 total; 26% have terminal degrees, 50% minority, 51% women. **Class size:** 77% < 20, 19% 20-39, 3% 40-49, less than 1% 50-99.

Freshman class profile. 489 applied, 482 admitted, 239 enrolled.

Mid 50% test scores		GPA 2.0-2.99:	39%
SAT critical reading:	390-520	Rank in top quarter:	20%
SAT math:	380-510	Rank in top tenth:	6%
ACT composite:	16-22	Return as sophomores:	68%
GPA 3.75 or higher:	9%	Out-of-state:	32%
GPA 3.50-3.74:	13%	Live on campus:	90%
GPA 3.0-3.49:	23%	International:	8%

Basis for selection. Applicants must have a Christian commitment and sign an agreement to abide by community life standards. Academic record, class rank, and test scores are the most important considerations. A Pastor's recommendation is required for students applying to the traditional undergraduate program. Interview recommended for those with unsatisfactory recommendations or academic concerns; audition required for music program. **Learning Disabled:** Students should inform their admissions counselors.

High school preparation. College-preparatory program recommended. 15 units recommended. Recommended units include English 4, mathematics 3, social studies 3, science 3 and foreign language 2.

2016-2017 Annual costs. Tuition/fees: $24,850. Room/board: $9,200. Books/supplies: $1,000. Personal expenses: $3,100.

2014-2015 Financial aid. Need-based: 217 full-time freshmen applied for aid; 200 deemed to have need; 200 received aid. Average need met was 61%. Average scholarship/grant was $13,163; average loan $2,946. 61% of total undergraduate aid awarded as scholarships/grants, 39% as loans/jobs. **Non-need-based:** Awarded to 1,415 full-time undergraduates, including 272 freshmen. Scholarships awarded for academics, alumni affiliation, athletics, leadership, music/drama, religious affiliation, state residency.

Application procedures. Admission: No deadline. $25 fee, may be waived for applicants with need. Admission notification on a rolling basis beginning on or about 9/1. **Financial aid:** Priority date 3/31; no closing date. FAFSA required. Applicants notified on a rolling basis starting 3/1; must reply within 4 week(s) of notification.

Academics. Adult degree completion program offers accelerated study option for adult students, with classes held throughout the New York metropolitan and lower Hudson Valley regions. **Special study options:** Combined bachelor's/graduate degree, cross-registration, distance learning, double major, exchange student, honors, independent study, internships, liberal arts/career combination, student-designed major, study abroad, teacher certification program. **Credit/placement by examination:** AP, CLEP, SAT, ACT, institutional tests. 60 credit hours maximum toward bachelor's degree. **Support services:** Learning center, pre-admission summer program, reduced course load, remedial instruction, study skills assistance, tutoring, writing center.

Majors. Business: Accounting, business admin. **Communications:** General. **Computer sciences:** Computer science. **Education:** Early childhood, elementary, English, ESL, mathematics, multi-level teacher, music, social studies. **English:** English lit. **Health services:** Nursing (RN). **History:** General. **Human services:** Social work. **Math:** General. **Philosophy/religion:** Philosophy, religion. **Protective services:** Criminal justice. **Psychology:** General. **Social sciences:** Sociology. **Theology:** Bible, missionary, preministerial, sacred music, youth ministry. **Visual/performing arts:** Music, music performance, music theory/composition, piano/keyboard, voice/opera.

Most popular majors. Business/marketing 40%, health sciences 6%, interdisciplinary studies 11%, psychology 7%, theological studies 12%.

Technology on campus. 130 workstations in dormitories, library, computer center, student center. Dormitories wired for high-speed internet access and linked to campus network. Commuter students can connect to campus network. Online course registration, helpline, wireless network available.

Student life. Freshman orientation: Mandatory, $100 fee. Preregistration for classes offered. **Policies:** Alcohol, tobacco, and narcotic drug use and possession prohibited on and off campus. Religious observance required. **Housing:** Guaranteed on-campus for all undergraduates. Single-sex dorms, apartments available. $150 fully refundable deposit. **Activities:** Bands, campus ministries, choral groups, dance, drama, international student organizations, literary magazine, music ensembles, musical theater, opera, radio station, student government, student newspaper, Asian student fellowship, business club, international student union, Kingdom Praise dance team, Students Against Hunger, Hands of Compassion, social work organization, More than Conquerors gospel choir.

Athletics. NCAA, NCCAA. **Intercollegiate:** Baseball M, basketball, cheerleading, cross-country, golf M, lacrosse W, soccer, softball W, volleyball W. **Team name:** Warriors.

Student services. Adult student services, alcohol/substance abuse counseling, chaplain/spiritual director, career counseling, services for economically disadvantaged, student employment services, financial aid counseling, health services, personal counseling, placement for graduates, veterans' counselor. **Physically disabled:** Services for visually, speech impaired.

Contact. E-mail: admissions@nyack.edu
Phone: (845) 675-4401 Toll-free number: (800) 336-9225
Fax: (845) 358-3047
Dinesh Mahtani, Director of Undergraduate Admissions, Nyack College, 1 South Boulevard, Nyack, NY 10960-3698

Ohr Somayach Tanenbaum Education Center
Monsey, New York
www.os.edu   CB code: 3357

- Private 4-year rabbinical college for men affiliated with the Jewish faith
- Residential campus in large town
- 30 degree-seeking undergraduates
- Interview required

General. Founded in 1979. Accredited by AARTS. First and Second Talmudic degrees offered. **Degrees:** 2 bachelor's awarded; master's offered. **Location:** Half a mile from Spring Valley, 33 miles from New York City. **Calendar:** Semester, extensive summer session. **Full-time faculty:** 3 total. **Part-time faculty:** 3 total; 67% have terminal degrees.

Basis for selection. Potential for scholastic and character achievement evaluated through personal interview, recommendations, departmental examinations, and prior religious and secular studies. Essay recommended.

2015-2016 Annual costs. Tuition/fees: $7,750. Room/board: $9,000. Books/supplies: $300. Personal expenses: $725.

Application procedures. Admission: No deadline. $75 fee, may be waived for applicants with need. Admission notification on a rolling basis. **Financial aid:** No deadline. Applicants notified on a rolling basis starting 7/1; must reply within 4 week(s) of notification.

Academics. Special study options: Accelerated study, cross-registration, independent study, study abroad, teacher certification program. **Credit/placement by examination:** AP, CLEP, institutional tests. **Support services:** Preadmission summer program, reduced course load, tutoring.

Majors. Philosophy/religion: Judaic. **Theology:** Talmudic.

Technology on campus. 3 workstations in computer center. Repair service available.

Student life. Policies: Religious observance required. **Housing:** Apartments available. $100 deposit. Students above age 30 must arrange own housing off campus. Assistance provided in locating housing. **Activities:** Singing group, community volunteers.

Athletics. Intramural: Baseball M, basketball M, skiing M, swimming M.

Student services. Career counseling, student employment services, personal counseling, placement for graduates.

Contact. E-mail: ohr@os.edu
Phone: (845) 425-1370 Fax: (845) 425-8865
Avrohom Braun, Dean of Students, Ohr Somayach Tanenbaum Education Center, 244 Route 306, Monsey, NY 10952

Pace University
New York, New York

CB member

www.pace.edu

CB code: 2635

▶ Private 4-year university
▶ Residential campus in very large city
▶ 5,811 degree-seeking undergraduates: 9% part-time, 61% women, 9% African American, 9% Asian American, 13% Hispanic/Latino, 4% Multiracial, non-Hispanic, 13% international
▶ 2,610 degree-seeking graduate students
▶ 85% of applicants admitted
▶ Application essay required
▶ 49% graduate within 6 years; 10% enter graduate study

General. Founded in 1906. Regionally accredited. Three schools and two colleges of the University are located on the New York City campus: the Dyson College of Arts and Sciences, Lubin School of Business, College of Health Professions, School of Education, and Seidenberg School of Computer Science and Information Systems. **Degrees:** 1,081 bachelor's, 2 associate awarded; master's, professional, doctoral offered. **ROTC:** Army, Air Force. **Calendar:** Semester, limited summer session. **Full-time faculty:** 291 total; 88% have terminal degrees, 27% minority, 46% women. **Part-time faculty:** 517 total; 30% have terminal degrees, 24% minority, 50% women. **Class size:** 49% < 20, 47% 20-39, 1% 40-49, 2% 50-99, less than 1% >100. **Special facilities:** Art galleries, multimedia language laboratories, speech and hearing center, studio theater.

Freshman class profile. 13,552 applied, 11,580 admitted, 1,568 enrolled.

Mid 50% test scores			
SAT critical reading:	470-590	Rank in top quarter:	44%
SAT math:	480-580	Rank in top tenth:	17%
ACT composite:	22-27	Return as sophomores:	77%
GPA 3.75 or higher:	15%	Out-of-state:	58%
GPA 3.50-3.74:	20%	Live on campus:	68%
GPA 3.0-3.49:	45%	International:	16%
GPA 2.0-2.99:	20%		

Basis for selection. Rigor of secondary school record, standardized test scores, and the application essay are very important. GPA, class rank, and recommendations are also important. Non-native speakers of English are required to take TOEFL. Official scores must be sent directly to the school. Notarized copies are not acceptable. Audition required for dance, dramatic arts, and theater. Portfolio recommended for art programs. Applicants to nursing programs in the College of Health Professions must be certified in CPR. **Home schooled:** A transcript from a program and/or a detailed roster of academic course work at the secondary level. **Learning Disabled:** Diagnostic tests recommended.

High school preparation. College-preparatory program recommended. 16 units required. Required units include English 4, mathematics 3, history 3, science 2 (laboratory 2), foreign language 2 and academic electives 2.

2015-2016 Annual costs. Tuition/fees: $41,281. Room/board: $17,938.

2015-2016 Financial aid. Need-based: 1,151 full-time freshmen applied for aid; 1,043 deemed to have need; 1,041 received aid. Average need met was 70%. Average scholarship/grant was $26,608; average loan $3,639. 76% of total undergraduate aid awarded as scholarships/grants, 24% as loans/jobs. **Non-need-based:** Awarded to 1,561 full-time undergraduates, including 452 freshmen. Scholarships awarded for academics, alumni affiliation, athletics, music/drama.

Application procedures. Admission: Priority date 2/15; no deadline. $50 fee, may be waived for applicants with need. Admission notification on a rolling basis beginning on or about 12/15. Must reply by May 1 or within 2 week(s) if notified thereafter. **Financial aid:** Priority date 3/15; no closing date. FAFSA required. Applicants notified on a rolling basis starting 3/1; must reply by 5/1 or within 2 week(s) of notification.

Academics. Adult undergraduate degrees in liberal/general studies, business and computer science. **Special study options:** Accelerated study, combined bachelor's/graduate degree, cooperative education, cross-registration, distance learning, double major, dual enrollment of high school students, ESL, honors, independent study, internships, New York semester, semester at sea, study abroad, teacher certification program, United Nations semester, urban semester, Washington semester. Evening and freshman studies programs; pre-freshman summer program; learning communities and service learning. **Credit/placement by examination:** AP, CLEP, IB, SAT, ACT, institutional tests. 30 credit hours maximum toward associate degree, 96 toward bachelor's. **Support services:** Learning center, reduced course load, remedial instruction, study skills assistance, tutoring, writing center.

Honors college/program. Honors Program requires entering freshmen have 90 or higher high school GPA, SAT verbal minimum of 550, SAT math minimum of 550 and a combined SAT score of 1200 (exclusive of Writing). Honors program students may be enrolled in any of undergraduate schools/colleges at University.

Majors. Area/ethnic studies: American, Asian, Latin American, women's. **Biology:** General, biochemistry. **Business:** General, accounting, business admin, entrepreneurial studies, finance, hotel/motel admin, human resources, international, international marketing, managerial economics, marketing. **Communications:** Advertising, communications/speech/rhetoric, media studies. **Computer sciences:** General, computer science, information systems, IT project management. **Conservation:** Environmental science, environmental studies. **Education:** Biology, chemistry, early childhood, earth science, elementary, English, foreign languages, mathematics, social studies, Spanish, special ed, speech impaired. **Engineering:** Chemical. **English:** British lit. **Foreign languages:** General, Spanish. **Health services:** Communication disorders, nursing (RN), physical therapy, preoccupational therapy, preoptometry, prephysical therapy, speech pathology. **History:** General. **Liberal arts:** Arts/sciences. **Math:** General. **Parks/recreation:** Sports admin. **Philosophy/religion:** General. **Physical sciences:** Chemistry. **Protective services:** Forensics, law enforcement admin. **Psychology:** General, applied. **Social sciences:** General, economics, political science, sociology/anthropology. **Visual/performing arts:** Acting, art history/conservation, dance, directing/producing, film/cinema/video, musical theater, studio arts, theater arts management.

Most popular majors. Business/marketing 36%, communications/journalism 15%, health sciences 6%, psychology 7%, social sciences 7%, visual/performing arts 11%.

Technology on campus. 164 workstations in library, computer center, student center. Dormitories wired for high-speed internet access and linked to campus network. Commuter students can connect to campus network. Online course registration, online library, helpline, repair service, student web hosting, wireless network available.

Student life. Freshman orientation: Mandatory, $40 fee. Preregistration for classes offered. Two days held at different times during the summer. International students attend orientation for 2 days prior to the start of the fall term. One-day program for transfer students. **Policies:** No parking available on the New York City campus. **Housing:** Coed dorms, apartments, themed housing, wellness housing available. $500 partly refundable deposit, deadline 5/1. Apartment style housing for upperclassmen available. **Activities:** Dance, drama, film society, international student organizations, literary magazine, Model UN, musical theater, radio station, student government, student newspaper, TV station, Caribbean Student Association, Hillel, Muslim Students Association, Pace Christian Fellowship, SAMOSA, Stonewall Coalition, Black Student Union, Student Veterans Association.

Athletics. NCAA. **Intercollegiate:** Baseball M, basketball, cross-country, diving, field hockey W, football (tackle) M, lacrosse, soccer W, swimming, volleyball W. **Intramural:** Badminton, basketball, cheerleading W, football (non-tackle), soccer, ultimate frisbee, volleyball. **Team name:** Setters.

Student services. Adult student services, career counseling, student employment services, financial aid counseling, health services, personal counseling, placement for graduates, veterans' counselor. **Physically disabled:** Services for visually, speech, hearing impaired.

Contact. E-mail: ugnyc@pace.edu
Phone: (212) 346-1323 Toll-free number: (800) 874-7223
Fax: (212) 346-1040
Robina Schepp, Vice President of Enrollment Management, Pace University, 1 Pace Plaza, New York, NY 10038-1598

Pace University: Pleasantville/Briarcliff
Pleasantville, New York
www.pace.edu   **CB code: 2685**

▶ Private 4-year university
▶ Residential campus in small town
▶ 2,560 degree-seeking undergraduates: 13% part-time, 56% women, 14% African American, 6% Asian American, 17% Hispanic/Latino, 3% Multiracial, non-Hispanic, 2% international
▶ 893 degree-seeking graduate students
▶ 78% of applicants admitted
▶ SAT or ACT (ACT writing optional), application essay required
▶ 61% graduate within 6 years; 13% enter graduate study

General. Regionally accredited. Three schools and two colleges of the university are located on the Pleasantville campus: Dyson College of Arts and Sciences, College of Health Professions, School of Education, Lubin School of Business, and Seidenberg School of Computer Science and Information Systems. Pace School of Law is located in White Plains. **Degrees:** 613 bachelor's, 39 associate awarded; master's, professional, doctoral offered. **Location:** 7 miles from White Plains, 30 miles from New York City. **Calendar:** Semester, limited summer session. **Full-time faculty:** 162 total; 91% have terminal degrees, 15% minority, 54% women. **Part-time faculty:** 275 total; 18% have terminal degrees, 14% minority, 62% women. **Class size:** 49% < 20, 48% 20-39, 1% 40-49, 1% 50-99. **Special facilities:** Environmental center.

Freshman class profile. 3,486 applied, 2,703 admitted, 560 enrolled.

Mid 50% test scores		GPA 2.0-2.99:	23%
SAT critical reading:	460-560	Rank in top quarter:	39%
SAT math:	470-570	Rank in top tenth:	16%
ACT composite:	20-25	Out-of-state:	30%
GPA 3.75 or higher:	12%	Live on campus:	79%
GPA 3.50-3.74:	16%	International:	2%
GPA 3.0-3.49:	49%		

Basis for selection. Rigor of secondary school record, standardized test scores, and the application essay are very important. GPA, class rank, and recommendations are also important. Non-native speakers of English are required to take TOEFL. Official scores must be sent directly to school. Notarized copies are not acceptable. Applicants to the Lienhard School of Nursing in the College of Health Professions must be certified in CPR. **Home schooled:** The transcript should be from a program and/or a detailed roster of academic coursework at the secondary level. **Learning Disabled:** Diagnostic tests recommended.

High school preparation. College-preparatory program recommended. 16 units required. Required units include English 4, mathematics 3, history 3, science 2 (laboratory 2), foreign language 2 and academic electives 2.

2015-2016 Annual costs. Tuition/fees: $41,333. Room/board: $15,010.

2015-2016 Financial aid. Need-based: 516 full-time freshmen applied for aid; 475 deemed to have need; 475 received aid. Average need met was 82%. Average scholarship/grant was $31,432; average loan $3,612. 79% of total undergraduate aid awarded as scholarships/grants, 21% as loans/jobs. **Non-need-based:** Awarded to 578 full-time undergraduates, including 164 freshmen. Scholarships awarded for academics, alumni affiliation, athletics, music/drama.

Application procedures. Admission: Priority date 2/15; no deadline. $50 fee, may be waived for applicants with need. Admission notification on a rolling basis beginning on or about 12/15. Must reply by May 1 or within 2 week(s) if notified thereafter. **Financial aid:** Priority date 3/15; no closing date. FAFSA required. Applicants notified on a rolling basis starting 3/1; must reply by 5/1 or within 2 week(s) of notification.

Academics. Adult undergraduate degrees in liberal/general studies, business, and computer science. **Special study options:** Accelerated study, combined bachelor's/graduate degree, cooperative education, cross-registration, distance learning, double major, dual enrollment of high school students, ESL, honors, independent study, internships, New York semester, semester at sea, study abroad, teacher certification program, United Nations semester, urban semester, Washington semester. Evening and freshman studies programs, Pre-freshman summer program, Learning communities and service learning. **Credit/placement by examination:** AP, CLEP, IB, SAT, ACT, institutional tests. 30 credit hours maximum toward associate degree, 96 toward bachelor's. **Support services:** Learning center, reduced course load, remedial instruction, study skills assistance, tutoring, writing center.

Honors college/program. To be eligible for the Honors College, first-year students must have a high school average of 90 or higher, an SAT critical reading and math score of 550 or higher, and a combined SAT score (critical reading and math) of at least 1200. Students entering the Honors College as first-year students are required to take a total of eight Honors courses prior to graduation.

Majors. Area/ethnic studies: American. **Biology:** General, biochemistry. **Business:** General, accounting, business admin, entrepreneurial studies, finance, hotel/motel admin, human resources, international, international marketing, managerial economics, marketing. **Communications:** Advertising, communications/speech/rhetoric, media studies. **Computer sciences:** General, computer science, data processing, information systems, IT project management, systems analysis. **Conservation:** Environmental studies. **Education:** Biology, chemistry, computer, early childhood, elementary, English, foreign languages, history, mathematics, science, social science, social studies, special ed. **English:** English lit. **Foreign languages:** Spanish. **Health services:** Communication disorders, nursing (RN), physical therapy, preoptometry. **History:** General. **Liberal arts:** Arts/sciences. **Math:** General. **Parks/recreation:** Sports admin. **Philosophy/religion:** General. **Physical sciences:** Chemistry, geology, physics. **Protective services:** Forensics, law enforcement admin. **Psychology:** General, applied, personality, psychobiology. **Social sciences:** Economics, political science. **Visual/performing arts:** Film/cinema/video.

Most popular majors. Business/marketing 29%, communications/journalism 11%, computer/information sciences 6%, education 6%, health sciences 17%, psychology 11%.

Technology on campus. 130 workstations in library, computer center, student center. Dormitories wired for high-speed internet access and linked to campus network. Commuter students can connect to campus network. Online course registration, online library, helpline, repair service, student web hosting, wireless network available.

Student life. Freshman orientation: Mandatory, $40 fee. Preregistration for classes offered. Two days held at different times during the summer. International students attend orientation for 2 days before the start of the fall term. One-day program for transfer students. **Housing:** Coed dorms, apartments, themed housing, wellness housing available. $500 partly refundable deposit, deadline 5/1. Townhouses available for upperclassmen. Each unit houses 8 students in 4 double rooms. **Activities:** Dance, drama, international student organizations, literary magazine, Model UN, radio station, student government, student newspaper, Desi Heritage of Southeast Asia, Gay Straight Alliance, Muslim Student Association, Organization of Latin American Students, Students of Caribbean Awareness, Hillel at Pace, Black Student Union, Cru, Student Veterans Association.

Athletics. NCAA. **Intercollegiate:** Baseball M, basketball, cross-country, diving, field hockey W, football (tackle) M, lacrosse, soccer W, softball W, swimming, volleyball W. **Intramural:** Badminton, basketball, cheerleading W, football (non-tackle), soccer, ultimate frisbee, volleyball. **Team name:** Setters.

Student services. Adult student services, career counseling, student employment services, financial aid counseling, health services, personal counseling, placement for graduates, veterans' counselor. **Physically disabled:** Services for visually, speech, hearing impaired.

Contact. E-mail: ugplv@pace.edu
Phone: (914) 773-3746 Toll-free number: (800) 874-7223
Fax: (914) 773-3851
Robina Schepp, Vice President of Enrollment Management, Pace University: Pleasantville/Briarcliff, 861 Bedford Road, Pleasantville, NY 10570

Parsons The New School for Design
New York, New York
www.newschool.edu   **CB code: 2638**

▶ Private 4-year visual arts college
▶ Commuter campus in very large city

- 4,185 degree-seeking undergraduates: 11% part-time, 78% women, 5% African American, 13% Asian American, 9% Hispanic/Latino, 2% Multiracial, non-Hispanic, 44% international
- 918 degree-seeking graduate students
- 64% of applicants admitted
- 62% graduate within 6 years

General. Founded in 1896. Regionally accredited. Division of The New School. **Degrees:** 690 bachelor's, 233 associate awarded; master's offered. **Location:** Located in Manhattan. **Calendar:** Semester, extensive summer session. **Full-time faculty:** 155 total; 61% have terminal degrees, 14% minority, 49% women. **Part-time faculty:** 962 total; 2% have terminal degrees, 20% minority, 53% women. **Class size:** 94% < 20, 6% 20-39, less than 1% 40-49, less than 1% 50-99, less than 1% >100. **Special facilities:** Architecture studio, labs, galleries, institute for information mapping, environment and design center, center for art and politics.

Freshman class profile. 2,947 applied, 1,889 admitted, 738 enrolled.

Mid 50% test scores			
SAT critical reading:	500-620	GPA 3.0-3.49:	39%
SAT math:	500-630	GPA 2.0-2.99:	22%
SAT writing:	500-620	Return as sophomores:	87%
ACT composite:	22-27	Out-of-state:	76%
GPA 3.75 or higher:	16%	Live on campus:	71%
GPA 3.50-3.74:	23%	International:	44%

Basis for selection. Portfolio and home examination most important, followed by school achievement record and test scores. Activities, leadership, motivation considered.

High school preparation. College-preparatory program recommended. Required and recommended units include English 4, mathematics 4, social studies 4, history 4, science 4 and foreign language 4.

2015-2016 Annual costs. Tuition/fees: $44,486. Room/board: $17,235. Books/supplies: $2,050. Personal expenses: $1,550.

2014-2015 Financial aid. Need-based: 314 full-time freshmen applied for aid; 270 deemed to have need; 270 received aid. Average need met was 70%. Average scholarship/grant was $20,149; average loan $5,575. 72% of total undergraduate aid awarded as scholarships/grants, 28% as loans/jobs. **Non-need-based:** Awarded to 2,824 full-time undergraduates, including 557 freshmen. Scholarships awarded for academics, art, leadership, minority status, music/drama, state residency.

Application procedures. Admission: Priority date 1/15; deadline 8/1. $50 fee, may be waived for applicants with need. Admission notification on a rolling basis beginning on or about 4/1. Must reply by May 1 or within 2 week(s) if notified thereafter. **Financial aid:** Closing date 3/1. FAFSA required. Applicants notified on a rolling basis starting 4/1; must reply within 4 week(s) of notification.

Academics. Special study options: Accelerated study, cross-registration, distance learning, dual enrollment of high school students, ESL, independent study, internships, liberal arts/career combination, student-designed major, study abroad. Five-year combined BA/BFA, NY studio program. **Credit/placement by examination:** AP, CLEP, IB. **Support services:** Pre-admission summer program, remedial instruction, tutoring, writing center.

Majors. Architecture: Architecture. **Business:** Fashion. **Conservation:** Environmental studies. **Visual/performing arts:** Design, fashion design, illustration, industrial design, interior design, photography, studio arts.

Technology on campus. Dormitories wired for high-speed internet access and linked to campus network. Commuter students can connect to campus network. Online course registration, helpline, student web hosting, wireless network available.

Student life. Freshman orientation: Mandatory. Preregistration for classes offered. **Housing:** Guaranteed on-campus for all undergraduates. Coed dorms, special housing for disabled, apartments, themed housing, wellness housing available. $500 nonrefundable deposit, deadline 7/1. **Activities:** Jazz band, choral groups, dance, drama, film society, international student organizations, literary magazine, music ensembles, musical theater, opera, radio station, student government, student newspaper, symphony orchestra, Sustainable Design Review, New School Styling Club, Roots & Shoots, Radical student union, Global Health student organization, international club, PHOTOfeast, the Theatre Collective, Jewish student union, New School Remnant Christian Fellowship.

Athletics. Intercollegiate: Basketball M, cross-country. **Intramural:** Basketball, soccer, volleyball.

Student services. Career counseling, services for economically disadvantaged, student employment services, financial aid counseling, health services, minority student services, personal counseling, placement for graduates.

Contact. E-mail: admission@newschool.edu
Phone: (212) 229-5150 Toll-free number: (800) 292-3040
Carolina Wheat, Director of Undergraduate Admission, Parsons The New School for Design, 79 Fifth Avenue, Floor 5, New York, NY 10003

Paul Smith's College
Paul Smiths, New York
www.paulsmiths.edu

CB member
CB code: 2640

- Private 4-year culinary school and liberal arts college
- Residential campus in rural community
- 877 degree-seeking undergraduates
- SAT or ACT (ACT writing optional) required

General. Founded in 1937. Regionally accredited. Most classes have a strong hands-on, experiential component. **Degrees:** 186 bachelor's, 60 associate awarded. **Location:** 25 miles from Lake Placid, 143 miles from Albany. **Calendar:** Semester, limited summer session. **Full-time faculty:** 51 total. **Part-time faculty:** 35 total. **Class size:** 43% < 20, 48% 20-39, 6% 40-49, 2% 50-99, less than 1% >100. **Special facilities:** Sugar maple plantation, sawmill, on-campus restaurant, 14,200-acre forest, on-campus retail bakery, mini-palm training restaurant, woodman/lumberjack training area, student operated restaurant.

Freshman class profile.

GPA 3.75 or higher:	5%	Rank in top quarter:	18%
GPA 3.50-3.74:	11%	Rank in top tenth:	5%
GPA 3.0-3.49:	25%	Out-of-state:	38%
GPA 2.0-2.99:	52%	Live on campus:	99%

Basis for selection. Most consideration given to high school or college course work as well as SAT/ACT scores. Personal essays, letters of recommendation, relevant experience and SAT/ACT scores highly encouraged. Essay or personal statement and interview recommended. **Home schooled:** Statement describing home school structure and mission, transcript of courses and grades, interview, letter of recommendation (nonparent) required.

High school preparation. College-preparatory program recommended. 4 units required; 8 recommended. Required and recommended units include English 4, mathematics 2, science 2 (laboratory 2) and foreign language 2. High school subject requirements vary according to program.

2015-2016 Annual costs. Tuition/fees: $24,390. Room/board: $11,680. Books/supplies: $1,000. Personal expenses: $1,000.

Financial aid. Non-need-based: Scholarships awarded for academics. **Additional information:** Merit aid only for international students; no financial aid application required.

Application procedures. Admission: Priority date 5/1; no deadline. $30 fee, may be waived for applicants with need. Admission notification on a rolling basis beginning on or about 10/1. **Financial aid:** Priority date 3/31; no closing date. FAFSA required. Applicants notified on a rolling basis starting 3/5; must reply within 4 week(s) of notification.

Academics. Special study options: Combined bachelor's/graduate degree, double major, dual enrollment of high school students, independent study, internships, liberal arts/career combination. **Credit/placement by examination:** AP, CLEP, IB, institutional tests. 15 credit hours maximum toward associate degree, 15 toward bachelor's. **Support services:** Learning center, pre-admission summer program, reduced course load, remedial instruction, study skills assistance, tutoring, writing center.

Majors. Biology: General. **Business:** General, business admin, entrepreneurial studies, hospitality admin, hospitality/recreation, hotel/motel admin, resort management, restaurant/food services, tourism promotion, tourism/travel. **Conservation:** General, environmental science, fisheries, forest management, forest resources, forest sciences, forestry, wildlife/wilderness. **Health services:** Predental, premedicine, preveterinary. **Liberal arts:** Arts/sciences. **Parks/recreation:** General, facilities management.

Most popular majors. Business/marketing 18%, natural resources/environmental science 46%, parks/recreation 11%, personal/culinary services 19%.

Technology on campus. PC or laptop required. 140 workstations in library, computer center. Dormitories wired for high-speed internet access and linked to campus network. Commuter students can connect to campus

network. Online course registration, online library, helpline, student web hosting, wireless network available.

Student life. Freshman orientation: Mandatory, $125 fee. Preregistration for classes offered. **Housing:** Guaranteed on-campus for all undergraduates. Coed dorms, single-sex dorms, gender-neutral housing, wellness housing available. $100 nonrefundable deposit, deadline 5/1. **Activities:** Student government, gaming and Anime, conservation club, Junior American Culinary Federation, Christian Fellowship, fiber arts, campus council.

Athletics. USCAA. **Intercollegiate:** Cross-country, rugby, skiing, soccer, swimming, volleyball W. **Intramural:** Basketball, ice hockey M, rugby, soccer, volleyball, water polo. **Team name:** Bobcats.

Student services. Adult student services, alcohol/substance abuse counseling, chaplain/spiritual director, career counseling, services for economically disadvantaged, student employment services, financial aid counseling, health services, minority student services, personal counseling, placement for graduates, veterans' counselor. **Physically disabled:** Services for visually, hearing impaired.

Contact. E-mail: admissions@paulsmiths.edu
Phone: (518) 327-6227 Toll-free number: (800) 421-2605
Fax: (518) 327-6016
Sue MacGregor, Vice President of Enrollment Management, Paul Smith's College, PO Box 265, Routes 30 & 86, Paul Smiths, NY 12970-0265

Pratt Institute
Brooklyn, New York — CB member
www.pratt.edu — CB code: 2669

- Private 4-year university and visual arts college
- Residential campus in very large city
- 3,189 degree-seeking undergraduates: 3% part-time, 69% women, 4% African American, 15% Asian American, 10% Hispanic/Latino, 2% Multi-racial, non-Hispanic, 26% international
- 1,388 degree-seeking graduate students
- 66% of applicants admitted
- SAT or ACT with writing, application essay required
- 65% graduate within 6 years

General. Founded in 1887. Regionally accredited. Additional campus located in Manhattan with associate degree programs, bachelor's degree in construction management program, and various graduate programs. **Degrees:** 615 bachelor's, 35 associate awarded; master's offered. **ROTC:** Army. **Location:** 2 miles from Manhattan. **Calendar:** Semester, extensive summer session. **Full-time faculty:** 153 total; 75% have terminal degrees, 16% minority, 45% women. **Part-time faculty:** 960 total; 14% minority, 42% women. **Class size:** 74% < 20, 24% 20-39, 1% 40-49, less than 1% 50-99, less than 1% >100. **Special facilities:** Wood and metal workshops, ceramics kiln studios and casting foundry, digital arts labs, printmaking workshop, fine arts center, center for community development.

Freshman class profile. 4,819 applied, 3,186 admitted, 705 enrolled.

Mid 50% test scores		GPA 3.0-3.49:	25%
SAT critical reading:	520-630	GPA 2.0-2.99:	9%
SAT math:	530-660	Return as sophomores:	85%
SAT writing:	520-640	Out-of-state:	78%
ACT composite:	23-28	Live on campus:	90%
GPA 3.75 or higher:	45%	International:	29%
GPA 3.50-3.74:	21%		

Basis for selection. Admissions committee considers overall academic record which includes academic performance, portfolio, curriculum, test scores, recommendation, and essay. SAT Subject Test Math level 1 recommended for applicants to architecture program. Interview not required. Letter of recommendation required for all applicants. Portfolio required for architecture, art and design programs.

High school preparation. College-preparatory program recommended. 16 units recommended. Recommended units include English 4, mathematics 4, social studies 1, science 2 and academic electives 5.

2016-2017 Annual costs. Tuition/fees: $48,154. Room/board: $12,026. Books/supplies: $1,750. Personal expenses: $1,500.

Financial aid. Non-need-based: Scholarships awarded for academics.

Application procedures. Admission: Closing date 1/5 (postmark date). $50 fee, may be waived for applicants with need. Application must be submitted online. Admission notification by 4/1. **Financial aid:** Closing date

3/1. FAFSA required. Applicants notified on a rolling basis starting 4/15; must reply by 5/15.

Academics. Special study options: ESL, exchange student, independent study, internships, study abroad, teacher certification program. **Credit/placement by examination:** AP, CLEP, institutional tests. **Support services:** Learning center, pre-admission summer program, reduced course load, study skills assistance, tutoring, writing center.

Majors. Architecture: Architecture. **Business:** Construction management. **Communications technology:** Animation/special effects. **Computer sciences:** Computer graphics. **Education:** Art. **English:** Creative writing. **General:** Site management. **Visual/performing arts:** Art history/conservation, cinematography, design, digital arts, fashion design, industrial design, interior design, photography, studio arts.

Most popular majors. Architecture 19%, visual/performing arts 74%.

Technology on campus. 300 workstations in dormitories, library, computer center, student center. Dormitories wired for high-speed internet access and linked to campus network. Commuter students can connect to campus network. Online course registration, helpline, repair service, student web hosting, wireless network available.

Student life. Freshman orientation: Available. Preregistration for classes offered. **Housing:** Guaranteed on-campus for freshmen. Coed dorms, special housing for disabled, apartments, themed housing, wellness housing available. $300 partly refundable deposit, deadline 5/1. Global learning, healthy choice and quiet floors available. **Activities:** Campus ministries, film society, international student organizations, literary magazine, music ensembles, radio station, student government, student newspaper, TV station, Christian Fellowship, Jewish student union, Muslim student association, Asian student organization, The Agenda, Korean student association, environmental resource group, Gay/Lesbian at Pratt, New York Public Interest Research Group, Pratt Projects (socially conscious project design and creation).

Athletics. NCAA. **Intercollegiate:** Basketball M, cross-country, soccer, tennis, track and field, volleyball W. **Intramural:** Badminton, basketball, football (non-tackle) M, weight lifting. **Team name:** Canonneers.

Student services. Alcohol/substance abuse counseling, chaplain/spiritual director, career counseling, student employment services, financial aid counseling, health services, minority student services, personal counseling, placement for graduates, veterans' counselor. **Physically disabled:** Services for visually, speech, hearing impaired.

Contact. E-mail: visit@pratt.edu
Phone: (718) 636-3514 Toll-free number: (800) 331-0834
Fax: (718) 636-3670
William Swan, Director of Admissions, Pratt Institute, 200 Willoughby Avenue, Brooklyn, NY 11205-3817

Rabbinical Academy Mesivta Rabbi Chaim Berlin
Brooklyn, New York
CB code: 0719

- Private 4-year rabbinical college for men affiliated with the Jewish faith
- Very large city
- 177 degree-seeking undergraduates

General. Accredited by AARTS. **Degrees:** 25 bachelor's awarded; master's, doctoral offered. **Calendar:** Differs by program. **Full-time faculty:** 12 total. **Part-time faculty:** 1 total.

Basis for selection. Secondary school record, completion of college-preparatory program and recommendations required. Formal demonstration of competencies recommended.

2015-2016 Annual costs. Tuition/fees: $12,250. Room/board: $3,000.

Application procedures. Admission: No deadline. No application fee.

Academics. Credit/placement by examination: AP, CLEP.

Majors. Theology: Talmudic.

Contact. Phone: (718) 377-0777
Eli Rabinowitz, Admissions Director, Rabbinical Academy Mesivta Rabbi Chaim Berlin, 1593 Coney Island Avenue, Brooklyn, NY 11230

Rabbinical College Beth Shraga
Monsey, New York

‣ Private 4-year rabbinical college for men affiliated with the Jewish faith
‣ Commuter campus in large town
‣ 47 degree-seeking undergraduates

General. Degrees: 1 bachelor's awarded. **Calendar:** Differs by program. **Full-time faculty:** 4 total. **Part-time faculty:** 1 total.

Basis for selection. Completion of college-preparatory program and recommendations required. Secondary school record recommended.

2015-2016 Annual costs. Tuition/fees: $12,050. Room/board: $5,200.

Application procedures. Admission: No deadline.

Academics. Credit/placement by examination: AP, CLEP.

Majors. Theology: Talmudic.

Contact. Phone: (845) 356-1980
Schraga Schiff, Admissions Director, Rabbinical College Beth Shraga, PO Box 412, Monsey, NY 10952

Rabbinical College Bobover Yeshiva B'nei Zion
Brooklyn, New York
http://rabbinicalcollegeboboveryeshiva.edu/   CB code: 7011

‣ Private 5-year rabbinical college for men affiliated with the Jewish faith
‣ Very large city
‣ 232 degree-seeking undergraduates

General. Accredited by AARTS. **Degrees:** 63 bachelor's awarded; master's offered. **Calendar:** Differs by program. **Full-time faculty:** 5 total. **Part-time faculty:** 4 total.

Basis for selection. Approximately 150 folio pages of Talmud, courses on Pentateuch with commentaries, Orach Cham Codes of Jewish Law.

2015-2016 Annual costs. Tuition/fees: $7,750. Room/board: $4,500. Books/supplies: $400. Personal expenses: $500.

Application procedures. Admission: No deadline.

Academics. Credit/placement by examination: AP, CLEP.

Majors. Theology: Talmudic.

Contact. Phone: (718) 438-2018
Rabbinical College Bobover Yeshiva B'nei Zion, 1577 48th Street, Brooklyn, NY 11219

Rabbinical College Ch'san Sofer of New York
Brooklyn, New York
CB code: 0714

‣ Private 4-year rabbinical college for men affiliated with the Jewish faith
‣ Very large city
‣ 32 degree-seeking undergraduates
‣ Interview required

General. Founded in 1940. Accredited by AARTS. Ordination and First Talmudic degree available. **Degrees:** 6 bachelor's awarded; master's offered. **Calendar:** Semester. **Full-time faculty:** 4 total. **Part-time faculty:** 2 total.

Basis for selection. Religious commitment, school achievement record, and interview most important.

2015-2016 Annual costs. Tuition/fees: $8,500.

Application procedures. Admission: Closing date 9/1. Admission notification on a rolling basis.

Academics. Credit/placement by examination: AP, CLEP.

Majors. Theology: Talmudic.

Student life. Policies: Religious observance required.

Contact. Phone: (718) 236-1171
Rabbinical College Ch'san Sofer of New York, 1876 50th Street, Brooklyn, NY 11204

Rabbinical College of Long Island
Long Beach, New York
CB code: 0675

‣ Private 4-year rabbinical and teachers college for men affiliated with the Jewish faith
‣ Large town
‣ 96 degree-seeking undergraduates
‣ Interview required

General. Founded in 1965. Accredited by AARTS. Ordination and First Talmudic degree available. **Degrees:** 3 bachelor's awarded. **Calendar:** Trimester. **Full-time faculty:** 8 total.

Basis for selection. Religious commitment, interview, and recommendations most important.

2015-2016 Annual costs. Tuition/fees: $13,700. Room/board: $4,900.

Application procedures. Admission: No deadline. No application fee. Admission notification on a rolling basis.

Academics. Credit/placement by examination: AP, CLEP.

Majors. Theology: Talmudic.

Student life. Policies: Religious observance required.

Contact. Phone: (516) 431-7414
Rabbi Chaim Hoberman, Director of Admissions, Rabbinical College of Long Island, 205 West Beech Street, Long Beach, NY 11561

Rabbinical College of Ohr Shimon Yisroel
Brooklyn, New York

‣ Private 4-year rabbinical college for men
‣ Very large city
‣ 152 degree-seeking undergraduates

General. Accredited by AARTS. **Degrees:** 28 bachelor's awarded. **Calendar:** Semester. **Full-time faculty:** 14 total.

Basis for selection. Recommendations required. Secondary school record recommended.

2015-2016 Annual costs. Tuition/fees: $11,500.

Application procedures. Admission: No deadline.

Academics. Credit/placement by examination: AP, CLEP.

Majors. Theology: Talmudic.

Contact. Phone: (718) 855-4092
Rabbinical College of Ohr Shimon Yisroel, 215-217 Hewes Street, Brooklyn, NY 11211

Rabbinical Seminary of America
Flushing, New York
CB code: 2776

‣ Private 5-year rabbinical and seminary college for men affiliated with the Jewish faith
‣ Very large city
‣ 276 degree-seeking undergraduates
‣ Interview required

General. Founded in 1933. Accredited by AARTS. Ordination available. 4-and 5-year undergraduate programs as well as graduate study. Campus in Jerusalem enrolls 50 students. **Degrees:** 41 bachelor's awarded; master's, doctoral offered. **Calendar:** Semester. **Full-time faculty:** 10 total.

Freshman class profile.

Out-of-state: 40% Live on campus: 70%

Basis for selection. Interview most important. School record and test scores considered.

High school preparation. Diploma from Hebrew high school required.

2015-2016 Annual costs. Tuition/fees: $9,800. Room/board: $6,000.

Application procedures. Admission: Closing date 7/1. Admission notification on a rolling basis. **Financial aid:** No deadline. Applicants notified on a rolling basis.

Academics. Special study options: Independent study, internships. **Credit/placement by examination:** AP, CLEP.

Majors. Theology: Talmudic.

Contact. E-mail: registrar@rabbinical.org
Phone: (718) 268-4700 Fax: (718) 268-4684
Abraham Semmel, Registrar, Rabbinical Seminary of America, 76-01 147th Street, Flushing, NY 11367

Rensselaer Polytechnic Institute
Troy, New York CB member
www.rpi.edu CB code: 2757

- Private 4-year university
- Residential campus in small city
- 5,781 degree-seeking undergraduates: 31% women, 3% African American, 10% Asian American, 8% Hispanic/Latino, 7% Multi-racial, non-Hispanic, 11% international
- 1,238 degree-seeking graduate students
- 42% of applicants admitted
- SAT or ACT with writing, application essay required
- 81% graduate within 6 years; 18% enter graduate study

General. Founded in 1824. Regionally accredited. **Degrees:** 1,143 bachelor's awarded; master's, doctoral offered. **ROTC:** Army, Naval, Air Force. **Location:** 10 miles from Albany, 150 miles from New York City. **Calendar:** Semester, extensive summer session. **Full-time faculty:** 404 total; 96% have terminal degrees, 27% minority, 25% women. **Part-time faculty:** 74 total; 55% have terminal degrees, 16% minority, 31% women. **Class size:** 51% < 20, 28% 20-39, 8% 40-49, 10% 50-99, 3% >100. **Special facilities:** Spectrometer, performing arts center with concert hall, computational center for nanotechnology innovations, wind tunnel, geotechnical centrifuge, clean room, electron linear accelerator, plasma dynamics lab, lighting research center, athletic village, center for terahertz research, nanoscale science and engineering center, linear accelerator lab, astronomical observatory, business incubation center, fresh water institute, social and behavioral research lab, center for game studies research, artificial intelligence and reasoning lab, human-level intelligence lab.

Freshman class profile. 17,752 applied, 7,432 admitted, 1,379 enrolled.

Mid 50% test scores		Rank in top quarter:	94%
SAT critical reading:	610-720	Rank in top tenth:	72%
SAT math:	670-770	Return as sophomores:	94%
ACT composite:	28-32	Out-of-state:	71%
GPA 3.75 or higher:	66%	Live on campus:	100%
GPA 3.50-3.74:	23%	International:	12%
GPA 3.0-3.49:	10%	Fraternities:	23%
GPA 2.0-2.99:	1%	Sororities:	15%

Basis for selection. School achievement record important, test scores and essay required, activities considered. SAT Subject Tests in a math and a science required for accelerated program applicants only, or ACT (which must include the optional writing component in lieu of SAT and SAT Subject Tests); students applying from countries (such as China) that do not offer our required standardized tests will be considered without testing on a case-by-case basis. Portfolio required for electronic arts, highly recommended for architecture. **Home schooled:** Transcript of courses and grades, letter of recommendation (nonparent) required.

High school preparation. College-preparatory program required. 15 units required. Required and recommended units include English 4, mathematics 4, social studies 2-3 and science 3-4. Best suited applicants will have completed 4 math through pre-calculus, 3 science, and 2 social studies and/or history.

2015-2016 Annual costs. Tuition/fees: $49,341. Room/board: $14,095. Books/supplies: $2,736. **Additional information:** Freshmen are required to have a laptop. Students may purchase a university-subsidized laptop costing approximately $1,650, or they may bring one with them but it must contain the software and capabilities required to complete the coursework.

2015-2016 Financial aid. Need-based: 1,065 full-time freshmen applied for aid; 922 deemed to have need; 922 received aid. Average need met was 87%. Average scholarship/grant was $35,340; average loan $4,695. 81% of total undergraduate aid awarded as scholarships/grants, 19% as loans/jobs. **Non-need-based:** Awarded to 2,079 full-time undergraduates, including 488 freshmen. Scholarships awarded for academics, alumni affiliation, art, athletics, leadership, minority status, music/drama, ROTC.

Application procedures. Admission: Closing date 1/15 (postmark date). $70 fee, may be waived for applicants with need. Admission notification by 3/8. Must reply by 5/1. **Financial aid:** Closing date 2/1. FAFSA, CSS PROFILE required. Applicants notified by 3/12.

Academics. Extensive accelerated program offerings available in virtually all Science departments including Computer Science, Physics, Applied Physics, Biology, Biochemistry and Biophysics, Geology and Hydrology, leading to the BS-PhD. **Special study options:** Accelerated study, combined bachelor's/graduate degree, cooperative education, cross-registration, double major, dual enrollment of high school students, honors, independent study, internships, liberal arts/career combination, student-designed major, study abroad. BS/MD with Albany Medical College; BS/JD with Columbia University and Albany Law School. **Credit/placement by examination:** AP, CLEP, IB. **Support services:** Learning center, pre-admission summer program, reduced course load, remedial instruction, study skills assistance, tutoring, writing center.

Majors. Architecture: Architecture. **Biology:** General, Biochemistry/molecular biology, bioinformatics. **Business:** Business admin. **Communications:** Communications/speech/rhetoric, digital media. **Computer sciences:** Computer science, information technology. **Conservation:** Environmental science. **Engineering:** General, aerospace, applied physics, biomedical, chemical, civil, computer, electrical, engineering science, environmental, materials, mechanical, nuclear. **Health services:** Premedicine. **Math:** General. **Philosophy/religion:** Philosophy. **Physical sciences:** Chemistry, geology, hydrology, physics. **Psychology:** General. **Social sciences:** Economics. **Visual/performing arts:** Studio arts.

Most popular majors. Biology 6%, business/marketing 7%, computer/information sciences 10%, engineering/engineering technologies 59%.

Technology on campus. PC or laptop required. 400 workstations in dormitories, library, computer center, student center. Dormitories wired for high-speed internet access and linked to campus network. Commuter students can connect to campus network. Online course registration, online library, helpline, repair service, student web hosting, wireless network available.

Student life. Freshman orientation: Mandatory, $175 fee. Preregistration for classes offered. Held over 2-day period in July or August. **Policies:** College housing required of all freshmen unless student lives within 50-mile radius of campus with parent(s) or legal guardian(s). **Housing:** Guaranteed on-campus for freshmen. Coed dorms, special housing for disabled, apartments, fraternity/sorority housing, themed housing available. **Activities:** Bands, campus ministries, choral groups, dance, drama, film society, international student organizations, literary magazine, music ensembles, musical theater, radio station, student government, student newspaper, symphony orchestra, TV station, student-run union; more than 185 athletic, service, media, multicultural, performing arts, visual arts, religious clubs and organizations.

Athletics. NCAA. **Intercollegiate:** Baseball M, basketball, cross-country, diving, field hockey W, football (tackle) M, golf M, ice hockey, lacrosse, soccer, softball W, swimming, tennis, track and field. **Intramural:** Basketball, football (non-tackle), golf, racquetball, soccer, softball, swimming, tennis, track and field, volleyball. **Team name:** Redhawks, Engineers.

Student services. Alcohol/substance abuse counseling, chaplain/spiritual director, career counseling, services for economically disadvantaged, student employment services, financial aid counseling, health services, legal services, minority student services, personal counseling, placement for graduates, women's services. **Physically disabled:** Services for visually, speech, hearing impaired.

Contact. E-mail: admissions@rpi.edu
Phone: (518) 276-6216 Fax: (518) 276-4072
Jonathan David Wexler, VP, Enrollment Management, Rensselaer Polytechnic Institute, 110 Eighth Street, Troy, NY 12180-3590

Roberts Wesleyan College
Rochester, New York CB member
www.roberts.edu CB code: 2759

- Private 4-year liberal arts college affiliated with the Free Methodist Church of North America
- Residential campus in large city

◆ 1,282 degree-seeking undergraduates

◆ SAT or ACT (ACT writing recommended), application essay required

General. Founded in 1866. Regionally accredited. **Degrees:** 468 bachelor's awarded; master's offered. **ROTC:** Army, Air Force. **Location:** 8 miles from downtown. **Calendar:** Semester, limited summer session. **Full-time faculty:** 89 total; 67% have terminal degrees, 7% minority, 56% women. **Part-time faculty:** 174 total; 18% have terminal degrees, 6% minority, 58% women. **Class size:** 66% < 20, 26% 20-39, 5% 40-49, 3% 50-99. **Special facilities:** Art Gallery and theatre in the Howard Stowe Roberts Cultural Life Center.

Freshman class profile.

GPA 3.75 or higher:	27%	Rank in top quarter:	42%
GPA 3.50-3.74:	16%	Rank in top tenth:	18%
GPA 3.0-3.49:	33%	Out-of-state:	11%
GPA 2.0-2.99:	23%	Live on campus:	72%

Basis for selection. Rank in top 30% of high school class, 2.9 GPA, recommendations, test scores, and interview important. Students expected to recognize Christian perspectives and values college upholds. Audition required for music program; portfolio required for art program. **Home schooled:** Transcript of courses and grades, state high school equivalency certificate, letter of recommendation (nonparent) required. Strongly recommend applicants visit.

High school preparation. College-preparatory program recommended. 12 units required. Required and recommended units include English 4, mathematics 2-4, social studies 2-3, history 3, science 4 (laboratory 3) and foreign language 3. Biology and chemistry required of nursing applicants.

2015-2016 Annual costs. Tuition/fees: $29,036. Room/board: $10,038. Books/supplies: $1,100. Personal expenses: $1,886.

Financial aid. Non-need-based: Scholarships awarded for academics, alumni affiliation, art, athletics, music/drama, religious affiliation, ROTC. **Additional information:** Dollars for Scholars offer matching grants of up to $750.

Application procedures. Admission: Priority date 2/1; deadline 8/16 (postmark date). No application fee. Admission notification on a rolling basis. Must reply by May 1 or within 2 week(s) if notified thereafter. **Financial aid:** Priority date 3/15; no closing date. FAFSA required. Applicants notified on a rolling basis starting 2/28; must reply by 5/1 or within 2 week(s) of notification.

Academics. Special study options: Accelerated study, combined bachelor's/graduate degree, cross-registration, distance learning, double major, dual enrollment of high school students, ESL, honors, independent study, internships, student-designed major, study abroad, teacher certification program, Washington semester. **Credit/placement by examination:** AP, CLEP, IB, SAT, ACT. 30 credit hours maximum toward bachelor's degree. **Support services:** Learning center, reduced course load, remedial instruction, study skills assistance, tutoring, writing center.

Majors. Biology: General, biochemistry. **Business:** Accounting, business admin, human resources, marketing. **Communications:** Communications/ speech/rhetoric. **Education:** Biology, chemistry, early childhood, early childhood special, English, history, mathematics, music, physical, physics, science, social science, social studies, Spanish, special ed. **English:** English lit. **Foreign languages:** Spanish. **Health services:** Health care admin, nursing (RN), preop/surgical nursing. **History:** General. **Human services:** Social work. **Liberal arts:** Arts/sciences, humanities. **Math:** General. **Philosophy/ religion:** General. **Physical sciences:** Chemistry, physics. **Protective services:** Forensics, law enforcement admin. **Psychology:** General. **Social sciences:** General. **Theology:** Bible, preministerial. **Visual/performing arts:** Music, piano/keyboard, studio arts, voice/opera.

Most popular majors. Business/marketing 22%, education 12%, health sciences 34%, liberal arts 6%.

Technology on campus. 250 workstations in library, computer center, student center. Dormitories wired for high-speed internet access and linked to campus network. Commuter students can connect to campus network. Online course registration, online library, helpline, wireless network available.

Student life. Freshman orientation: Mandatory. Preregistration for classes offered. **Policies:** Religious observance required. **Housing:** Guaranteed on-campus for freshmen. Single-sex dorms, apartments available. $100 fully refundable deposit, deadline 5/1. **Activities:** Bands, campus ministries, choral groups, dance, drama, international student organizations, music ensembles, musical theater, student government, student newspaper, symphony orchestra, chapel, mission trips, At the Foot of the Cross service, Habitat for Humanity, In Jesus' Name, bible studies, ENACTUS, Acting on AIDS, senate, And He Made Me.

Athletics. NCAA, NCCAA. **Intercollegiate:** Basketball, cross-country, golf M, lacrosse, soccer, tennis, track and field, volleyball W. **Intramural:** Basketball, cross-country, field hockey, football (non-tackle), racquetball, skiing, soccer, softball, table tennis, tennis, track and field, ultimate frisbee, volleyball, water polo. **Team name:** Redhawks.

Student services. Adult student services, alcohol/substance abuse counseling, chaplain/spiritual director, career counseling, student employment services, financial aid counseling, health services, personal counseling, placement for graduates, veterans' counselor. **Physically disabled:** Services for visually, hearing impaired.

Contact. E-mail: admissions@roberts.edu
Phone: (585) 594-6400 Toll-free number: (800) 777-4792
Fax: (585) 594-6371
John Anderson, Associate VP of Undergraduate Admissions, Roberts Wesleyan College, 2301 Westside Drive, Rochester, NY 14624-1997

Rochester Institute of Technology
Rochester, New York   **CB member**
www.rit.edu   **CB code: 2760**

◆ Private 4-year university

◆ Residential campus in large city

◆ 12,874 degree-seeking undergraduates: 3% part-time, 32% women, 5% African American, 8% Asian American, 7% Hispanic/Latino, 3% Multiracial, non-Hispanic, 6% international

◆ 3,027 degree-seeking graduate students

◆ 57% of applicants admitted

◆ SAT or ACT (ACT writing recommended), application essay required

◆ 70% graduate within 6 years; 13% enter graduate study

General. Founded in 1829. Regionally accredited. The university has 10 degree-granting units including 9 colleges and the Golisano Institute of Sustainability. One of the colleges is the the National Technical Institute for the Deaf (NTID). RIT also maintains campuses in China, Croatia, Dubai, and Kosovo. **Degrees:** 2,732 bachelor's, 133 associate awarded; master's, doctoral offered. **ROTC:** Army, Naval, Air Force. **Location:** 5 miles from downtown Rochester, 70 miles from Buffalo. **Calendar:** Semester, extensive summer session. **Full-time faculty:** 1,015 total; 70% have terminal degrees, 19% minority, 36% women. **Part-time faculty:** 495 total; 1% have terminal degrees, 6% minority, 44% women. **Class size:** 47% < 20, 41% 20-39, 7% 40-49, 4% 50-99, less than 1% >100. **Special facilities:** Laser optics laboratory, observatory, animal care facility, photography darkrooms, electronic prepress and publishing equipment, ceramic kilns, glass furnaces, blacksmithing area, student-operated restaurant, computer graphics and robotic labs, microelectronic, telecommunications, and computer engineering facilities, access to Internet 2 research network.

Freshman class profile. 18,598 applied, 10,652 admitted, 2,905 enrolled.

Mid 50% test scores			
SAT critical reading:	550-660	Rank in top tenth:	34%
SAT math:	580-690	Return as sophomores:	89%
SAT writing:	520-630	Out-of-state:	50%
ACT composite:	26-31	Live on campus:	96%
Rank in top quarter:	69%	International:	5%

Basis for selection. Primary emphasis on high school grades in required courses, which vary by major. SAT or ACT given considerable weight. Class rank important. Admissions requirements vary from major to major. Students generally asked to apply directly to a specific major. Candidates allowed to apply for up to three majors. ACT preferred for applicants to National Technical Institute for the Deaf (NTID). Interview is required for admission to Physician Assistant program; Interview recommended for all; portfolio required for art, crafts, and design programs. **Home schooled:** Statement describing home school structure and mission, transcript of courses and grades required. Applicants should provide state certification of graduation if available.

High school preparation. College-preparatory program required. 16 units required; 18 recommended. Required and recommended units include English 4, mathematics 3, social studies 3, science 2-3 (laboratory 1-3), foreign language 2 and academic electives 4. Units required for social studies may be met with history courses. College of Engineering requires 4 math including precalculus.

2015-2016 Annual costs. Tuition/fees: $37,124. Room/board: $11,918. Books/supplies: $1,050. Personal expenses: $675.

2015-2016 Financial aid. Need-based: 2,613 full-time freshmen applied for aid; 2,247 deemed to have need; 2,247 received aid. Average need met was 87%. Average scholarship/grant was $22,000; average loan $3,600. 71%

of total undergraduate aid awarded as scholarships/grants, 29% as loans/jobs. **Non-need-based:** Awarded to 4,712 full-time undergraduates, including 1,179 freshmen. Scholarships awarded for academics, art, leadership, ROTC. **Additional information:** Most juniors and seniors participate in cooperative education program, earning an average $4,500-$6,500 per 3-month employment period through paid employment in jobs related to major.

Application procedures. Admission: Priority date 2/1; no deadline. $60 fee, may be waived for applicants with need. Admission notification on a rolling basis beginning on or about 3/1. Must reply by May 1 or within 2 week(s) if notified thereafter. Applications received after March 15 will be processed if space available. **Financial aid:** Priority date 3/1; no closing date. FAFSA required. Applicants notified on a rolling basis starting 3/15; must reply by 5/1.

Academics. Special study options: Accelerated study, combined bachelor's/graduate degree, cooperative education, cross-registration, distance learning, double major, ESL, exchange student, honors, independent study, internships, liberal arts/career combination, student-designed major, study abroad, teacher certification program, weekend college. Accelerated bachelor's/master's degree programs, England semester, Japan semester, summer program in Croatia. Teacher certification program is in art education. **Credit/placement by examination:** AP, CLEP, IB, SAT, ACT, institutional tests. 30 credit hours maximum toward associate degree. **Support services:** Learning center, pre-admission summer program, reduced course load, study skills assistance, tutoring, writing center.

Majors. Biology: General, biochemistry, bioinformatics, biomedical sciences, biotechnology. **Business:** Accounting, business admin, finance, hospitality admin, hotel/motel admin, management information systems, market research, marketing, resort management, restaurant/food services, sales/distribution, special products marketing, tourism promotion, tourism/travel, travel services. **Communications:** General, advertising, communications/speech/rhetoric, digital media, journalism, photojournalism, public relations. **Communications technology:** Animation/special effects, desktop publishing, graphics, photo/film/video, printing management. **Computer sciences:** General, computer graphics, computer science, database management, informatics, information technology, LAN/WAN management, modeling/simulation, networking, security, system admin, systems analysis, web page design, webmaster. **Conservation:** Environmental science. **Engineering:** Aerospace, biomedical, chemical, computer, electrical, industrial, mechanical, polymer, software, systems. **Foreign languages:** American Sign Language, sign language interpretation. **Health services:** Medical illustrating, medical informatics, physician assistant, predental, premedicine, prepharmacy, preveterinary, sonography. **Human services:** Public policy. **Math:** Applied, computational, probability, statistics. **Parks/recreation:** Exercise sciences. **Philosophy/religion:** Philosophy. **Physical sciences:** General, chemistry, physics. **Protective services:** Law enforcement admin. **Psychology:** General. **Social sciences:** Criminology, economics, international relations, urban studies. **Visual/performing arts:** Ceramics, cinematography, commercial/advertising art, graphic design, industrial design, interior design, metal/jewelry, multimedia, painting, photography, printmaking, sculpture, studio arts. **Work/family studies:** Food/nutrition.

Most popular majors. Biology 6%, business/marketing 9%, computer/information sciences 15%, engineering/engineering technologies 32%, visual/performing arts 15%.

Technology on campus. 2,750 workstations in dormitories, library, computer center, student center. Dormitories wired for high-speed internet access and linked to campus network. Commuter students can connect to campus network. Online course registration, online library, helpline, repair service, student web hosting, wireless network available.

Student life. Freshman orientation: Mandatory, $200 fee. Preregistration for classes offered. Orientation in late August prior to start of classes. **Housing:** Guaranteed on-campus for freshmen. Coed dorms, special housing for disabled, apartments, fraternity/sorority housing, themed housing, wellness housing available. $300 nonrefundable deposit, deadline 5/1. Special interest houses for students in selected majors or groups, single-sex floors within coed dorms, special honors program floor available. **Activities:** Bands, campus ministries, choral groups, dance, drama, film society, international student organizations, literary magazine, music ensembles, musical theater, radio station, student government, student newspaper, Asian Culture Society, Electronic Gaming Society, Gospel Ensemble, Society of Women Engineers, Society of Hispanic Engineers, National Society of Black Engineers, Emerging Black Artists, Feminist Action, Catholic Newman Network, Outing club.

Athletics. NCAA. **Intercollegiate:** Baseball M, basketball, cheerleading, cross-country, diving, ice hockey, lacrosse, rowing (crew), soccer, softball W, swimming, tennis, track and field, volleyball W, wrestling M. **Intramural:** Badminton, basketball, bowling, football (non-tackle) M, golf, ice hockey, racquetball, soccer, softball, table tennis, tennis, volleyball. **Team name:** Tigers.

Student services. Adult student services, alcohol/substance abuse counseling, chaplain/spiritual director, career counseling, services for economically disadvantaged, student employment services, financial aid counseling,

health services, legal services, minority student services, on-campus daycare, personal counseling, placement for graduates, veterans' counselor, women's services. **Physically disabled:** Services for visually, speech, hearing impaired.

Contact. E-mail: admissions@rit.edu
Phone: (585) 475-6631 Fax: (585) 475-7424
Daniel Shelley, Associate Vice President and Director of Undergraduate Admission, Rochester Institute of Technology, 60 Lomb Memorial Drive, Rochester, NY 14623-5604

The Sage Colleges
Troy, New York   **CB member**
www.sage.edu   **CB code: 2764**

- Private 4-year university
- Residential campus in small city
- 1,618 degree-seeking undergraduates: 12% part-time, 80% women, 13% African American, 3% Asian American, 9% Hispanic/Latino, 3% Multiracial, non-Hispanic
- 1,216 degree-seeking graduate students
- 54% of applicants admitted
- Application essay required
- 60% graduate within 6 years

General. Founded in 1916. Regionally accredited. The Sage Colleges include Russell Sage College in Troy, a 4-year college for women, and Sage College of Albany, a 4-year co-educational college specializing in professional fields of study. the School of Professional & Continuing Education is set apart from other schools at Sage because it is primarily focused on the unique needs of adult learners. SPCE also offers several online degree programs in a variety of areas. The graduate-level Esteves School of Education, School of Health Sciences and School of Management offer programs on both campuses, which include online programs in Business Administration, Health Services Administration and Organization Management. **Degrees:** 408 bachelor's, 2 associate awarded; master's, professional, doctoral offered. **ROTC:** Army, Naval, Air Force. **Location:** 10 miles from Albany, 150 miles from New York City. **Calendar:** Semester. **Full-time faculty:** 139 total; 81% have terminal degrees, 14% minority, 73% women. **Part-time faculty:** 166 total; 34% have terminal degrees, 9% minority, 59% women. **Class size:** 58% < 20, 38% 20-39, 4% 40-49: **Special facilities:** Center for women's studies, theater institute, nanotechnology business incubator, fine arts studio, graphic design and interior design studios.

Freshman class profile. 2,487 applied, 1,345 admitted, 263 enrolled.

Mid 50% test scores			
SAT critical reading:	430-540	Rank in top quarter:	48%
SAT math:	420-530	Rank in top tenth:	18%
ACT composite:	19-24	End year in good standing:	82%
GPA 3.75 or higher:	14%	Return as sophomores:	78%
GPA 3.50-3.74:	14%	Out-of-state:	11%
GPA 3.0-3.49:	42%	Live on campus:	86%
GPA 2.0-2.99:	30%	International:	1%

Basis for selection. High school record, recommendations of school officials, intended major, school and community activities considered. Applications reviewed on an individual basis. SAT scores required for some joint programs that are linked with another external institution. Interview recommended for all; portfolio required for art and design programs. **Home schooled:** Statement describing home school structure and mission, transcript of courses and grades, interview, letter of recommendation (nonparent) required. Students who have written evaluations must submit SAT or ACT scores. **Learning Disabled:** Students seeking accommodations are required to present a recent evaluation of their disability conducted by a licensed professional. Upon admission, those requesting accommodations must contact the Coordinator of Disability Services in the Campus Life Office.

High school preparation. College-preparatory program required. 16 units required. Required and recommended units include English 4, mathematics 3-4, social studies 4, science 3-4 (laboratory 2-3) and foreign language 2-3. Nursing program applicants must have 6 math/science combination including chemistry. Physical and occupational therapy students must have 4 math/science. Students applying to visual arts programs should have significant class experience.

2015-2016 Annual costs. Tuition/fees: $28,400. Room/board: $12,220. Books/supplies: $1,200. Personal expenses: $1,225.

2015-2016 Financial aid. Need-based: 257 full-time freshmen applied for aid; 246 deemed to have need; 246 received aid. Average scholarship/grant was $14,876; average loan $3,432. 72% of total undergraduate aid awarded as scholarships/grants, 28% as loans/jobs. **Non-need-based:**

Awarded to 1,298 full-time undergraduates, including 252 freshmen. Scholarships awarded for academics, alumni affiliation, art, leadership, minority status, music/drama, state residency.

Application procedures. Admission: Priority date 3/1; no deadline. $30 fee, may be waived for applicants with need, free for online applicants. Admission notification on a rolling basis beginning on or about 12/15. Must reply by May 1 or within 2 week(s) if notified thereafter. **Financial aid:** Priority date 3/1; no closing date. FAFSA required. Applicants notified on a rolling basis starting 3/1; must reply by 5/1 or within 2 week(s) of notification.

Academics. All students complete internship, field experience, or clinical experience. **Special study options:** Accelerated study, combined bachelor's/ graduate degree, cross-registration, distance learning, double major, honors, independent study, internships, liberal arts/career combination, student-designed major, study abroad, teacher certification program. Early College for high school juniors, combined bachelor's/master's, bachelor's/doctoral programs with Sage Graduate School, 3+3 BA/JD with Albany Law School, 3+2 BS/BSE with Rensselaer Polytechnic Institute, BA/MS Accelerated Physician Assistant Program, BA/MS Early Assurance Program and BA/MD Early Assurance Program with Albany Medical College. Discovery Degree Program (Your degree in 3). Sage Graduate Schools of Education, Health Sciences and Management offer a variety of master's degrees as well as several doctorates. **Credit/placement by examination:** AP, CLEP, IB, SAT, ACT, institutional tests. 30 credit hours maximum toward bachelor's degree. **Support services:** Learning center, pre-admission summer program, reduced course load, remedial instruction, study skills assistance, tutoring, writing center.

Majors. Biology: General, biochemistry, ecology. **Business:** Accounting, business admin. **Computer sciences:** Information systems. **Education:** Elementary, physical. **English:** English lit. **Health services:** Nursing (RN). **History:** General. **Human services:** General, public policy. **Liberal arts:** Arts/sciences, humanities. **Math:** General. **Physical sciences:** Chemistry. **Protective services:** Law enforcement admin. **Psychology:** General. **Social sciences:** General, political science, sociology. **Visual/performing arts:** Dramatic, graphic design, interior design, studio arts.

Most popular majors. Biology 10%, business/marketing 11%, education 6%, health sciences 27%, psychology 6%, social sciences 13%, visual/performing arts 9%.

Technology on campus. 437 workstations in library, computer center, student center. Dormitories wired for high-speed internet access and linked to campus network. Commuter students can connect to campus network. Online course registration, online library, helpline, wireless network available.

Student life. Freshman orientation: Mandatory, $250 fee. Preregistration for classes offered. One-day welcome programs offered in June. Four-day orientation in September. **Policies:** Zero tolerance for drugs, harassment, or violence on campus. **Housing:** Guaranteed on-campus for all undergraduates. Coed dorms, single-sex dorms, apartments, themed housing, wellness housing available. $100 partly refundable deposit, deadline 5/1. Special houses available for honor students and students interested in language/international awareness activities. Over-21 residence hall available for seniors. 19th-century brownstone residences available. **Activities:** Campus ministries, choral groups, dance, drama, literary magazine, music ensembles, musical theater, student government, student newspaper, Black and Latina Student Alliance, Gay and Lesbian Alliance, Christian students club, Muslim student association, Circle K, Habitat for Humanity, SALANA (African, Latino, Asian and Native American), Sage Votes, Sage SPECTRUMS, Campus Crusade for Christ.

Athletics. NCAA. **Intercollegiate:** Basketball, cross-country, golf M, lacrosse W, soccer, softball W, tennis, track and field, volleyball. **Intramural:** Badminton, football (non-tackle), volleyball W. **Team name:** Gators.

Student services. Adult student services, alcohol/substance abuse counseling, chaplain/spiritual director, career counseling, services for economically disadvantaged, student employment services, financial aid counseling, health services, minority student services, personal counseling, placement for graduates, women's services.

Contact. E-mail: tscadm@sage.edu
Phone: (518) 244-2217 Toll-free number: (888) 837-9724
Fax: (518) 244-6880
Thomas Breen, Senior Director of Undergraduate Admission, The Sage Colleges, 65 1st Street, Troy, NY 12180-4115

Saint Bonaventure University
St. Bonaventure, New York   **CB member**
www.sbu.edu   **CB code: 2793**

◆ Private 4-year university affiliated with the Roman Catholic Church
◆ Residential campus in large town

◆ 1,645 degree-seeking undergraduates: 1% part-time, 49% women, 6% African American, 4% Asian American, 7% Hispanic/Latino, 3% Multiracial, non-Hispanic, 2% international
◆ 314 degree-seeking graduate students
◆ 66% of applicants admitted
◆ SAT or ACT (ACT writing optional) required
◆ 64% graduate within 6 years

General. Founded in 1858. Regionally accredited. Catholic institution in Franciscan tradition. **Degrees:** 424 bachelor's awarded; master's offered. **ROTC:** Army. **Location:** 75 miles from Buffalo. **Calendar:** Semester, limited summer session. **Full-time faculty:** 129 total; 75% have terminal degrees, 6% minority, 37% women. **Part-time faculty:** 93 total; 22% have terminal degrees, 3% minority, 61% women. **Class size:** 57% < 20, 41% 20-39, 2% 40-49. **Special facilities:** Observatory, digital media laboratory, permanent art collection, retreat facility, rare books collection, art galleries and museum, remote television production studio, state-of-the-art science facilities, financial services lab, Allegheny Valley River Trail.

Freshman class profile. 2,985 applied, 1,969 admitted, 390 enrolled.

Mid 50% test scores			
SAT critical reading:	460-580	GPA 2.0-2.99:	23%
SAT math:	470-590	Rank in top quarter:	47%
SAT writing:	450-550	Rank in top tenth:	19%
ACT composite:	21-27	End year in good standing:	92%
GPA 3.75 or higher:	30%	Return as sophomores:	86%
GPA 3.50-3.74:	18%	Out-of-state:	60%
GPA 3.0-3.49:	29%	Live on campus:	97%
		International:	3%

Basis for selection. Interview, high school GPA and curriculum most important. Recommendation, class rank, test scores, extracurricular activities also considered. Applicants to dual admission premed program with George Washington University or SUNY Upstate Medical University must submit Biology SAT Subject Test score. Essay recommended for all. **Home schooled:** Statement describing home school structure and mission, transcript of courses and grades, letter of recommendation (nonparent) required. Course syllabus, book titles, and all course evaluations required to be considered for admission.

High school preparation. College-preparatory program recommended. 19 units recommended. Recommended units include English 4, mathematics 3, social studies 4, science 3 (laboratory 3) and foreign language 2. Science majors must have 4 science, 4 math. Recommend 3 science lab. Business majors need 4 math.

2015-2016 Annual costs. Tuition/fees: $31,389. Room/board: $11,728. Books/supplies: $800. Personal expenses: $700.

2014-2015 Financial aid. Need-based: 404 full-time freshmen applied for aid; 364 deemed to have need; 364 received aid. Average need met was 85%. Average scholarship/grant was $20,524; average loan $4,235. 66% of total undergraduate aid awarded as scholarships/grants, 34% as loans/jobs. **Non-need-based:** Awarded to 1,838 full-time undergraduates, including 480 freshmen. Scholarships awarded for academics, athletics, minority status, music/drama, religious affiliation, ROTC, state residency. **Additional information:** Families experiencing financial difficulties not adequately reflected by the FAFSA should contact the Office of Financial Assistance. Outside scholarships do not reduce other financial aid unless, when added to total aid, the new total exceeds need. If it exceeds need, then loans and work are reduced first.

Application procedures. Admission: Priority date 2/15; deadline 7/30 (postmark date). No application fee. Admission notification on a rolling basis beginning on or about 10/15. Must reply by May 1 or within 1 week(s) if notified thereafter. Applications considered until housing is closed. **Financial aid:** Priority date 2/15; no closing date. FAFSA required. Applicants notified on a rolling basis starting 3/1; must reply by 5/1 or within 2 week(s) of notification.

Academics. Special study options: Accelerated study, combined bachelor's/graduate degree, cross-registration, distance learning, double major, dual enrollment of high school students, exchange student, honors, independent study, internships, liberal arts/career combination, student-designed major, study abroad, teacher certification program, Washington semester. **Credit/ placement by examination:** AP, CLEP, IB, SAT, ACT. 30 credit hours maximum toward bachelor's degree. **Support services:** Learning center, pre-admission summer program, reduced course load, remedial instruction, study skills assistance, tutoring, writing center.

Majors. Area/ethnic studies: Women's. **Biology:** General, biochemistry, bioinformatics. **Business:** Accounting, finance, management information systems, management science. **Communications:** Digital media, journalism, media studies. **Computer sciences:** General, computer science. **Conservation:** Environmental science, environmental studies. **Education:** Elementary, physical, special ed. **English:** British lit, English lit. **Foreign languages:**

Classics, French, Latin, Spanish. **History:** General. **Math:** General. **Parks/ recreation:** Sports admin. **Philosophy/religion:** Philosophy. **Physical sciences:** Chemistry, physics. **Psychology:** General. **Social sciences:** General, political science, sociology. **Theology:** Theology. **Visual/performing arts:** General, art history/conservation, dramatic, music.

Most popular majors. Biology 8%, business/marketing 27%, communications/journalism 15%, education 9%, social sciences 8%.

Technology on campus. 320 workstations in dormitories, library, computer center. Dormitories wired for high-speed internet access and linked to campus network. Online course registration, online library, helpline, student web hosting, wireless network available.

Student life. Freshman orientation: Mandatory, $415 fee. Preregistration for classes offered. Two-day session held in July. **Housing:** Guaranteed on-campus for all undergraduates. Coed dorms, single-sex dorms, apartments, themed housing, wellness housing available. $200 partly refundable deposit, deadline 5/1. **Activities:** Campus ministries, choral groups, dance, drama, international student organizations, literary magazine, music ensembles, Model UN, radio station, student government, student newspaper, TV station, ENACTUS, College Republicans, College Democrats, Alpha Phi Omega, BonaResponds, Students for the Mountain, Center for Community Engagement.

Athletics. NCAA. **Intercollegiate:** Baseball M, basketball, cross-country, diving, golf M, lacrosse W, soccer, softball W, swimming, tennis. **Intramural:** Basketball, football (non-tackle), football (tackle) M, golf, racquetball, soccer, softball, table tennis, tennis, volleyball. **Team name:** Bonnies.

Student services. Alcohol/substance abuse counseling, chaplain/spiritual director, career counseling, services for economically disadvantaged, student employment services, financial aid counseling, health services, personal counseling, placement for graduates, veterans' counselor. **Physically disabled:** Services for visually, hearing impaired.

Contact. E-mail: admissions@sbu.edu
Phone: (716) 375-2400 Toll-free number: (800) 462-5050
Fax: (716) 375-4005
Bernard Valento, Vice President for Enrollment, Saint Bonaventure University, Box D, St. Bonaventure, NY 14778

Sarah Lawrence College
Bronxville, New York
www.sarahlawrence.edu

CB member
CB code: 2810

- Private 4-year liberal arts college
- Residential campus in small city
- 1,283 degree-seeking undergraduates: 1% part-time, 72% women, 4% African American, 5% Asian American, 10% Hispanic/Latino, 7% Multiracial, non-Hispanic, 13% international
- 295 degree-seeking graduate students
- 53% of applicants admitted
- Application essay required
- 77% graduate within 6 years

General. Founded in 1926. Regionally accredited. **Degrees:** 344 bachelor's awarded; master's offered. **Location:** 15 miles from midtown Manhattan. **Calendar:** Semester, limited summer session. **Full-time faculty:** 103 total; 18% minority, 48% women. **Part-time faculty:** 241 total; 14% minority, 64% women. **Class size:** 93% < 20, 4% 20-39, 2% 40-49, less than 1% 50-99. **Special facilities:** Visual arts center, student-run theater and radio station (WSLC), early childhood center, Center for the Urban River at Beczak.

Freshman class profile. 2,814 applied, 1,502 admitted, 353 enrolled.

Mid 50% test scores		GPA 2.0-2.99:	9%
SAT critical reading:	620-710	Rank in top quarter:	71%
SAT math:	550-680	Rank in top tenth:	36%
SAT writing:	600-700	End year in good standing:	91%
ACT composite:	27-31	Return as sophomores:	83%
GPA 3.75 or higher:	37%	Out-of-state:	80%
GPA 3.50-3.74:	27%	Live on campus:	100%
GPA 3.0-3.49:	27%	International:	14%

Basis for selection. Student writing, essays, and transcripts are most important. Letters of recommendation and extracurricular commitments are also important. Interview and test scores, if submitted, also considered. If on-campus interview not possible, applicant may arrange in-person or Skype interviews with an alumna/us or counselor. Interviews are recommended. Optional Visual Arts, Theater, Filmmaking, Dance, or Music portfolios must be submitted through Slideroom with the Common Application. Home

schooled: If unable to submit a paper with teacher's grades or comments, an ungraded research or analytical paper of 3-5 pages in length can satisfy the recommended analytical paper component of the application. High school transcript requirement should consist of a comprehensive lesson plan encompassing the past four years, including texts read, papers written, projects done, internships, etc. It is helpful if this can be divided by subject. Counselor recommendation requirement may be submitted by an educational supervisor or the student's parents, if they are acting in the capacity of the educational supervisor. Tutors, employers, internship or community service supervisors may submit recommendations as well. Ideally, these recommendations should come from people who have worked with the student in an academic or intellectual environment.

High school preparation. College-preparatory program recommended. 12 units required; 20 recommended. Required and recommended units include English 4, mathematics 2-4, social studies 4, history 2-4, science 2-4 and foreign language 2-4.

2015-2016 Annual costs. Tuition/fees: $51,030. Room/board: $14,700.

2015-2016 Financial aid. All financial aid based on need. 280 full-time freshmen applied for aid; 234 deemed to have need; 233 received aid. Average need met was 79%. Average scholarship/grant was $37,713; average loan $2,032. 89% of total undergraduate aid awarded as scholarships/grants, 11% as loans/jobs.

Application procedures. Admission: Closing date 1/15 (postmark date). $60 fee, may be waived for applicants with need. Application must be submitted online. Admission notification by 4/1. Must reply by 5/1. **Financial aid:** Closing date 2/15. FAFSA, CSS PROFILE required. Applicants notified by 4/1; must reply by 5/1.

Academics. Ninety percent of classes are seminars with 15 students. Individual biweekly conferences with professors related to independent study in all seminars. Students design their own courses of study and choose which classes to take with guidance from their academic advisors, based on the Oxford/Cambridge tradition. Although there are no formal majors, students may de facto create double majors. Course work required in 3 of 4 divisions: humanities, history and the social sciences, natural sciences and mathematics, creative and performing arts. **Special study options:** Combined bachelor's/ graduate degree, double major, exchange student, independent study, internships, student-designed major, study abroad, teacher certification program. Fall or Spring semester in Havana (Cuba). Spring semester in Lima (Peru) and Sub-Saharan Africa. Semester or year in Beijing, Paris and London. Full year of study in Oxford. Guest year or semester at Eugene Lang College The New School (NYC), Spelman College (GA), Pitzer College (CA), California Institute of Arts, University of Falmouth, England, Kansai Gaidai University, Osaka, Japan, Tusda College, Tokyo, Japan, and South India Term Abroad (SITA). **Credit/placement by examination:** AP, CLEP, IB. **Support services:** Tutoring, writing center.

Majors. Liberal arts: Arts/sciences.

Technology on campus. 110 workstations in library, computer center. Dormitories wired for high-speed internet access and linked to campus network. Commuter students can connect to campus network. Online library, helpline, student web hosting, wireless network available.

Student life. Freshman orientation: Mandatory. Preregistration for classes offered. A week-long period that involves interviewing, registering for classes, and social activities. **Policies:** Smoke-free campus. Freshmen not permitted cars on campus. **Housing:** Guaranteed on-campus for all undergraduates. Coed dorms, single-sex dorms, gender-neutral housing, themed housing, wellness housing available. $400 nonrefundable deposit, deadline 6/15. Designated sustainable living residences; students may petition for group housing. Students self-identify gender identity on the SLC housing questionnaire. **Activities:** Jazz band, campus ministries, choral groups, dance, drama, film society, international student organizations, literary magazine, music ensembles, Model UN, musical theater, radio station, student government, student newspaper, symphony orchestra, Trans Action, Christian Union, Hillel, SLC for Immigration Advocacy, Queer Voice Coalition, Cafe Latino, Disability Alliance, International Students Union, SLC Democrats.

Athletics. NCAA. **Intercollegiate:** Basketball, cross-country, equestrian, rowing (crew), soccer, softball W, swimming, tennis, volleyball. **Intramural:** Soccer, squash, volleyball. **Team name:** Gryphons.

Student services. Adult student services, alcohol/substance abuse counseling, career counseling, student employment services, financial aid counseling, health services, minority student services, personal counseling, placement for graduates. **Physically disabled:** Services for visually, speech, hearing impaired.

Contact. E-mail: slcadmit@sarahlawrence.edu
Phone: (914) 395-2510 Toll-free number: (800) 888-2858
Fax: (914) 395-2515
Kevin McKenna, Dean of Enrollment, Sarah Lawrence College, 1 Mead Way, Bronxville, NY 10708-5999

School of Visual Arts
New York, New York

www.sva.edu

CB member
CB code: 2835

- For-profit 4-year visual arts college
- Commuter campus in very large city
- 3,581 degree-seeking undergraduates: 4% part-time, 65% women, 6% African American, 14% Asian American, 5% Hispanic/Latino, 37% international
- 700 degree-seeking graduate students
- 74% of applicants admitted
- SAT or ACT (ACT writing optional), application essay required
- 69% graduate within 6 years

General. Founded in 1947. Regionally accredited. Faculty composed entirely of working professionals. **Degrees:** 751 bachelor's awarded; master's offered. **Calendar:** Semester, limited summer session. **Full-time faculty:** 196 total; 36% have terminal degrees, 9% minority, 33% women. **Part-time faculty:** 972 total; 18% have terminal degrees, 13% minority, 39% women. **Class size:** 74% < 20, 25% 20-39, less than 1% 40-49, less than 1% 50-99, less than 1% >100. **Special facilities:** Visual arts museum, Milton Glaser design study center and archives, 8 student galleries including 9,000-square-foot gallery.

Freshman class profile. 3,648 applied, 2,697 admitted, 698 enrolled.

Mid 50% test scores			
SAT critical reading:	460-590	GPA 3.0-3.49:	36%
SAT math:	460-610	GPA 2.0-2.99:	38%
SAT writing:	460-600	Return as sophomores:	84%
ACT composite:	21-27	Out-of-state:	59%
GPA 3.75 or higher:	11%	Live on campus:	70%
GPA 3.50-3.74:	14%	International:	38%

Basis for selection. Portfolio, academic record, interview important. Character and professional recommendations optional. Interview optional. Portfolio required for all programs. **Home schooled:** Statement describing home school structure and mission, transcript of courses and grades, state high school equivalency certificate, interview, letter of recommendation (non-parent) required. GED.

High school preparation. College-preparatory program recommended. Recommended units include English 4, history 4, foreign language 4 and visual/performing arts 2.

2016-2017 Annual costs. Tuition/fees: $36,500. Room only: $15,400. Books/supplies: $1,713. Personal expenses: $2,600.

2015-2016 Financial aid. Need-based: 364 full-time freshmen applied for aid; 335 deemed to have need; 318 received aid. Average need met was 45%. Average scholarship/grant was $14,447; average loan $3,197. 48% of total undergraduate aid awarded as scholarships/grants, 52% as loans/jobs. **Non-need-based:** Awarded to 701 full-time undergraduates, including 214 freshmen. Scholarships awarded for art.

Application procedures. Admission: No deadline. $50 fee, may be waived for applicants with need. Admission notification on a rolling basis beginning on or about 2/1. Admitted applicants are encouraged to reply by May 1. **Financial aid:** Priority date 2/1, closing date 3/1. FAFSA required. Applicants notified on a rolling basis starting 2/15; must reply within 4 week(s) of notification.

Academics. Curriculum designed to prepare students to graduate as working professionals in the arts. **Special study options:** ESL, exchange student, honors, independent study, internships, liberal arts/career combination, study abroad. **Credit/placement by examination:** AP, CLEP, IB. **Support services:** Learning center, pre-admission summer program, reduced course load, remedial instruction, study skills assistance, tutoring, writing center.

Honors college/program. Additional application component.

Majors. Communications technology: Animation/special effects. **Visual/performing arts:** Art history/conservation, commercial/advertising art, interior design, photography, studio arts.

Most popular majors. Computer/information sciences 8%, visual/performing arts 83%.

Technology on campus. 728 workstations in library, computer center, student center. Dormitories wired for high-speed internet access and linked to campus network. Commuter students can connect to campus network. Online library, helpline, wireless network available.

Student life. Freshman orientation: Mandatory. Preregistration for classes offered. Comprehensive 5-day program. **Housing:** Coed dorms, single-sex dorms, wellness housing available. $800 nonrefundable deposit, deadline 5/1. **Activities:** Film society, literary magazine, radio station, student government, student newspaper, Korean Christian, animal rights, international film club, Campus Crusade for Christ, political, anime film club, fine art club, MFA Speakers, wrestling club.

Athletics. Intramural: Baseball, tennis.

Student services. Alcohol/substance abuse counseling, career counseling, student employment services, financial aid counseling, health services, personal counseling, placement for graduates, veterans' counselor, women's services. **Physically disabled:** Services for hearing impaired.

Contact. E-mail: admissions@sva.edu
Phone: (212) 592-2100 Toll-free number: (800) 436-4204
Fax: (212) 592-2116
Adam Rogers, Director of Admissions, School of Visual Arts, 209 East 23rd Street, New York, NY 10010-3994

Shor Yoshuv Rabbinical College
Lawrence, New York

www.shoryoshuv.org

CB code: 7129

- Private 4-year rabbinical college for men affiliated with the Jewish faith
- Very large city
- 98 degree-seeking undergraduates
- 55 graduate students

General. Accredited by AARTS. **Degrees:** 26 bachelor's awarded; master's offered. **Calendar:** Differs by program. **Full-time faculty:** 14 total. **Part-time faculty:** 3 total.

Basis for selection. Recommendations and formal demonstration of competencies recommended.

2015-2016 Annual costs. Tuition/fees: $9,000. Room/board: $6,000.

Application procedures. Admission: Priority date 8/1; no deadline. $360 fee.

Academics. Credit/placement by examination: AP, CLEP.

Majors. Theology: Talmudic.

Contact. E-mail: info@shoryoshuv.org
Phone: (516) 239-9002
Sheila Fleischer, Admissions Director, Shor Yoshuv Rabbinical College, One Cedar Lawn Avenue, Lawrence, NY 11559

Siena College
Loudonville, New York

www.siena.edu

CB member
CB code: 2814

- Private 4-year liberal arts college affiliated with the Roman Catholic Church
- Residential campus in large town
- 3,062 degree-seeking undergraduates: 2% part-time, 51% women, 4% African American, 4% Asian American, 7% Hispanic/Latino, 2% Multiracial, non-Hispanic, 1% international
- 57 degree-seeking graduate students
- 59% of applicants admitted
- Application essay required
- 75% graduate within 6 years

General. Founded in 1937. Regionally accredited. **Degrees:** 825 bachelor's awarded; master's offered. **ROTC:** Army, Air Force. **Location:** 2 miles from Albany. **Calendar:** Semester, limited summer session. **Full-time faculty:** 220 total; 91% have terminal degrees, 12% minority, 45% women. **Part-time faculty:** 127 total; 35% have terminal degrees, 11% minority, 35% women. **Class size:** 40% < 20, 60% 20-39. **Special facilities:** Financial technology center featuring real-time capital market trading room, accounting lab, stock ticker, plasma data screens, 24 multimedia workstations, high-technology science instrumentation center, moot court/mock trial classroom.

Freshman class profile. 8,919 applied, 5,248 admitted, 755 enrolled.

Mid 50% test scores			
SAT critical reading:	480-590	GPA 2.0-2.99:	14%
SAT math:	500-610	Rank in top quarter:	50%
SAT writing:	470-590	Rank in top tenth:	21%
ACT composite:	21-27	End year in good standing:	92%
GPA 3.75 or higher:	34%	Return as sophomores:	90%
GPA 3.50-3.74:	21%	Out-of-state:	20%
GPA 3.0-3.49:	31%	Live on campus:	90%
		International:	1%

Basis for selection. Most important: Secondary school achievement record/academic GPA, priority given to students with challenging courses. Personal interview, standardized test scores, recommendations, and applicant activities also important. Interview required for Albany Medical School program finalists; recommended for all others. **Home schooled:** Transcript of courses and grades required.

High school preparation. College-preparatory program required. 15 units required; 19 recommended. Required and recommended units include English 4, mathematics 3-4, social studies 3-4, history 3-4, science 3-4 (laboratory 3-4) and foreign language 2-3.

2015-2016 Annual costs. Tuition/fees: $33,615. Room/board: $13,595. Books/supplies: $1,282. Personal expenses: $1,340.

2014-2015 Financial aid. Need-based: 646 full-time freshmen applied for aid; 564 deemed to have need; 564 received aid. Average need met was 81%. Average scholarship/grant was $23,060; average loan $3,290. 71% of total undergraduate aid awarded as scholarships/grants, 29% as loans/jobs. **Non-need-based:** Awarded to 2,800 full-time undergraduates, including 702 freshmen. Scholarships awarded for academics, athletics, leadership, minority status, ROTC, state residency.

Application procedures. Admission: Closing date 2/15 (postmark date). $50 fee, may be waived for applicants with need. Admission notification by 3/15. Must reply by 5/1. **Financial aid:** Priority date 2/15, closing date 5/1. FAFSA required. Applicants notified by 4/1; must reply by 5/1.

Academics. Extensive internship program in capital district with state legislature, businesses, social agencies, libraries, and museums. **Special study options:** Combined bachelor's/graduate degree, cooperative education, cross-registration, double major, ESL, honors, independent study, internships, liberal arts/career combination, student-designed major, study abroad, teacher certification program, Washington semester. Gettysburg semester. **Credit/placement by examination:** AP, CLEP, IB, SAT, institutional tests. 36 credit hours maximum toward bachelor's degree. 36 total credits permitted by proficiency examination, non-collegiate-sponsored instructional/experiential learning combined. **Support services:** Tutoring, writing center. Peer mentors.

Majors. Area/ethnic studies: American. **Biology:** General, biochemistry. **Business:** Accounting, actuarial science, business admin, finance, marketing. **Computer sciences:** General. **Conservation:** Environmental science, environmental studies. **English:** English lit. **Foreign languages:** Classics, French, Spanish. **Health services:** Premedicine. **History:** General. **Human services:** Social work. **Math:** General. **Philosophy/religion:** Philosophy, religion. **Physical sciences:** Chemistry, physics. **Psychology:** General. **Social sciences:** Economics, political science, sociology. **Visual/performing arts:** General.

Most popular majors. Biology 12%, business/marketing 40%, English 6%, psychology 13%, social sciences 9%.

Technology on campus. 456 workstations in library, computer center, student center. Dormitories wired for high-speed internet access and linked to campus network. Commuter students can connect to campus network. Online course registration, online library, helpline, wireless network available.

Student life. Freshman orientation: Mandatory, $220 fee. Preregistration for classes offered. Preregistration for classes takes place remotely during the summer. **Policies:** Non-smoking campus. Freshmen not permitted cars on campus. **Housing:** Guaranteed on-campus for freshmen. Coed dorms, special housing for disabled, apartments available. $350 nonrefundable deposit, deadline 5/1. On-campus townhouses, quiet living area available. **Activities:** Pep band, campus ministries, choral groups, dance, drama, film society, international student organizations, literary magazine, music ensembles, Model UN, musical theater, opera, radio station, student government, student newspaper, symphony orchestra, TV station, Siena College Entrepreneurship Organization; environmental policy and activism club; mentoring program; Volunteer Ministry Club, Democrats club; Republican club; Black and Latino Student Union; Gay Straight Alliance; International Students Association; Muslim Student Association; Spanish club.

Athletics. NCAA. **Intercollegiate:** Baseball M, basketball, cross-country, diving W, field hockey W, golf, lacrosse, soccer, softball W, swimming W, tennis, volleyball W, water polo W. **Intramural:** Basketball, football (non-tackle), handball, soccer, softball, volleyball. **Team name:** Saints.

Student services. Alcohol/substance abuse counseling, chaplain/spiritual director, career counseling, services for economically disadvantaged, student employment services, financial aid counseling, health services, minority student services, personal counseling, placement for graduates, veterans' counselor, women's services. **Physically disabled:** Services for visually, speech, hearing impaired.

Contact. E-mail: admissions@siena.edu
Phone: (518) 783-2423 Toll-free number: (888) 287-4362
Fax: (518) 783-2436
Mary Lawyer, Associate Vice President for Enrollment Management, Siena College, 515 Loudon Road, Loudonville, NY 12211-1462

Skidmore College
Saratoga Springs, New York
www.skidmore.edu

CB member
CB code: 2815

- Private 4-year liberal arts college
- Residential campus in large town
- 2,619 degree-seeking undergraduates: 1% part-time, 61% women, 4% African American, 6% Asian American, 8% Hispanic/Latino, 4% Multiracial, non-Hispanic, 10% international
- 8 degree-seeking graduate students
- 36% of applicants admitted
- SAT or ACT (ACT writing optional), application essay required
- 86% graduate within 6 years; 21% enter graduate study

General. Founded in 1903. Regionally accredited. **Degrees:** 608 bachelor's awarded; master's offered. **ROTC:** Army, Air Force. **Location:** 30 miles from Albany. **Calendar:** Semester, limited summer session. **Full-time faculty:** 277 total; 87% have terminal degrees, 16% minority, 55% women. **Part-time faculty:** 81 total; 22% have terminal degrees, 10% minority, 54% women. **Class size:** 72% < 20, 26% 20-39, less than 1% 40-49, 1% 50-99. **Special facilities:** Fine and performing arts facilities, equestrian center, 400 acres of woodlands and trails, teaching museum.

Freshman class profile. 8,508 applied, 3,105 admitted, 686 enrolled.

Mid 50% test scores			
SAT critical reading:	550-670	Rank in top tenth:	41%
SAT math:	560-670	Return as sophomores:	94%
SAT writing:	560-670	Out-of-state:	70%
ACT composite:	26-30	Live on campus:	100%
Rank in top quarter:	72%	International:	13%

Basis for selection. Rigor of school record very important. Class rank, GPA, recommendations, and test scores also important. 2 SAT Subject Tests recommended of all applicants (Subject Tests will be considered if submitted for those applying Fall 2017). Interview recommended for all.

High school preparation. College-preparatory program required. Recommended units include English 4, mathematics 4, social studies 4, science 4 (laboratory 3) and foreign language 4.

2015-2016 Annual costs. Tuition/fees: $49,120. Room/board: $13,072. Books/supplies: $1,300. Personal expenses: $1,058.

2015-2016 Financial aid. Need-based: 321 full-time freshmen applied for aid; 220 deemed to have need; 220 received aid. Average need met was 100%. Average scholarship/grant was $42,000; average loan $3,280. 93% of total undergraduate aid awarded as scholarships/grants, 7% as loans/jobs. **Non-need-based:** Awarded to 101 full-time undergraduates, including 20 freshmen. Scholarships awarded for music/drama.

Application procedures. Admission: Closing date 1/15 (postmark date). $65 fee, may be waived for applicants with need. Admission notification by 4/1. Must reply by 5/1. Enrollment deposit of $500 required on or before May 1 and is required whether the student requires housing or not. **Financial aid:** Closing date 2/1. CSS PROFILE required. Applicants notified by 4/1; must reply by 5/1.

Academics. Special study options: Accelerated study, combined bachelor's/graduate degree, cross-registration, distance learning, double major, dual enrollment of high school students, exchange student, honors, independent study, internships, liberal arts/career combination, student-designed major, study abroad, teacher certification program, Washington semester. 3+2 programs in engineering with Dartmouth College, Clarkson University and Rensselaer Polytechnic Institute; 4+1 MBA with Clarkson University, Union Graduate College, and Rochester Institute of Technology; Master of Science in Occupational Therapy 4+2 program and a Doctor of Physical Therapy 4+3 program with Sage College; second baccalaureate degree (BSN) in Nursing from NYU in either an accelerated 15-month program or an 18-month program; 4+1 MSA or MSF program with Syracuse University. **Credit/placement by examination:** AP, CLEP, IB, SAT, ACT, institutional tests. 16 credit hours maximum toward bachelor's degree. Up to 60 hours may be counted toward degree. Maximum of 12 semester hours may be granted in credit through CLEP subject examinations. **Support services:** Pre-admission summer program, reduced course load, study skills assistance, tutoring, writing center.

Majors. Area/ethnic studies: American, Asian, French. **Biology:** General, exercise physiology, neuroscience. **Business:** General. **Computer sciences:** General. **Conservation:** Environmental science, environmental studies. **Education:** General, elementary. **English:** English lit. **Foreign languages:** Classics, French, German, Spanish. **History:** General. **Human services:** Social work. **Liberal arts:** Arts/sciences. **Math:** General. **Philosophy/religion:** Philosophy, religion. **Physical sciences:** Chemistry, geology, physics. **Psychology:** General. **Social sciences:** Anthropology, economics, international relations, political science, sociology. **Visual/performing arts:** Art history/conservation, dance, dramatic, music history.

Most popular majors. Business/marketing 13%, English 8%, psychology 9%, social sciences 20%, visual/performing arts 14%.

Technology on campus. 600 workstations in library, computer center, student center. Dormitories wired for high-speed internet access and linked to campus network. Commuter students can connect to campus network. Online course registration, online library, helpline, student web hosting, wireless network available.

Student life. Freshman orientation: Mandatory. Preregistration for classes offered. Programs on and off campus. Fee for off-campus programs. **Housing:** Guaranteed on-campus for all undergraduates. Coed dorms, special housing for disabled, apartments, gender-neutral housing available. $500 nonrefundable deposit, deadline 5/1. Substance free, 24-hr quiet and women's floors available. **Activities:** Bands, campus ministries, choral groups, dance, drama, international student organizations, literary magazine, music ensembles, Model UN, musical theater, opera, radio station, student government, student newspaper, symphony orchestra, TV station, More than 110 clubs and organizations.

Athletics. NCAA. **Intercollegiate:** Baseball M, basketball, diving, equestrian W, field hockey W, golf M, ice hockey M, lacrosse, rowing (crew), soccer, softball W, swimming, tennis, volleyball W. **Intramural:** Basketball, football (non-tackle), racquetball, soccer, tennis, volleyball. **Team name:** Thoroughbreds.

Student services. Alcohol/substance abuse counseling, chaplain/spiritual director, career counseling, services for economically disadvantaged, student employment services, financial aid counseling, health services, minority student services, on-campus daycare, personal counseling, placement for graduates, veterans' counselor. **Physically disabled:** Services for visually, speech, hearing impaired.

Contact. E-mail: admissions@skidmore.edu
Phone: (518) 580-5570 Toll-free number: (800) 867-6007
Fax: (518) 580-5584
Mary Lou Bates, Dean of Admissions and Financial Aid, Skidmore College, 815 North Broadway, Saratoga Springs, NY 12866

St. Francis College

Brooklyn Heights, New York   **CB member**
www.sfc.edu   **CB code: 2796**

- Private 4-year liberal arts college affiliated with the Roman Catholic Church
- Commuter campus in very large city
- 2,578 degree-seeking undergraduates: 7% part-time, 58% women, 20% African American, 4% Asian American, 20% Hispanic/Latino, 1% Native Hawaiian/Pacific islander, 2% Multi-racial, non-Hispanic, 5% international
- 74 degree-seeking graduate students
- 79% of applicants admitted
- SAT, application essay required
- 52% graduate within 6 years

General. Founded in 1884. Regionally accredited. **Degrees:** 462 bachelor's, 17 associate awarded; master's offered. **ROTC:** Army, Air Force. **Calendar:** Semester, limited summer session. **Full-time faculty:** 86 total; 86% have terminal degrees, 21% minority, 48% women. **Part-time faculty:** 215 total; 32% have terminal degrees, 33% minority, 37% women. **Class size:** 56% < 20, 43% 20-39, less than 1% 40-49, less than 1% 50-99. **Special facilities:** Nursing lab with multiple simulators (SYMBaby, SYMMan), greenhouse.

Freshman class profile. 2,747 applied, 2,164 admitted, 534 enrolled.

Mid 50% test scores			
SAT critical reading:	410-500	GPA 3.0-3.49:	23%
SAT math:	400-500	GPA 2.0-2.99:	50%
SAT writing:	410-500	Return as sophomores:	76%
ACT composite:	17-22	Out-of-state:	6%
GPA 3.75 or higher:	6%	Live on campus:	3%
GPA 3.50-3.74:	12%	International:	4%

Basis for selection. Applicants should graduate from an accredited secondary school or have a GED. An entrance exam is required, as well as the submission of SAT scores and recommendation letters, official high school transcript or GED. Degree-seeking students who do not meet criteria may be admitted after review and assessment of their educational background. SAT/ACT scores must be received by first day of class for fall-term admission. Interview required of academically weak applicants. **Home schooled:** Statement describing home school structure and mission, state high school equivalency certificate required.

High school preparation. 18.5 units recommended. Required and recommended units include English 4, mathematics 2, social studies 4, science 2, visual/performing arts 1, academic electives 5.5.

2015-2016 Annual costs. Tuition/fees: $23,800. Room only: $13,600. Books/supplies: $1,000. Personal expenses: $5,500.

Financial aid. Non-need-based: Scholarships awarded for academics, athletics.

Application procedures. Admission: No deadline. $35 fee, may be waived for applicants with need. Admission notification on a rolling basis. Must reply by May 1 or within 2 week(s) if notified thereafter. **Financial aid:** Priority date 2/15; no closing date. FAFSA required. Applicants notified on a rolling basis starting 3/15; must reply within 2 week(s) of notification.

Academics. Special study options: Accelerated study, combined bachelor's/graduate degree, cooperative education, cross-registration, double major, dual enrollment of high school students, exchange student, honors, independent study, internships, student-designed major, study abroad, teacher certification program. Co-op programs in physical therapy, nursing and computer science. Work-study with Methodist Hospital or the borough president's office, pre-professional health programs with the State University of New York Health Science Center, Methodist Hospital and St. Vincent's Catholic Medical Center. Study abroad in several countries, dual majors, pass/fail options and credit for life experience are possible. **Credit/placement by examination:** AP, CLEP, IB, SAT, ACT, institutional tests. 32 credit hours maximum toward associate degree, 98 toward bachelor's. **Support services:** Learning center, pre-admission summer program, remedial instruction, study skills assistance, tutoring, writing center.

Majors. Biology: General, biomedical sciences. **Business:** Accounting, business admin. **Communications:** Communications/speech/rhetoric, digital media, public relations, radio/TV. **Computer sciences:** System admin. **Education:** Biology, chemistry, elementary, English, mathematics, physical, social studies, visually handicapped. **English:** English lit. **Foreign languages:** Spanish. **Health services:** Clinical lab science, medical radiologic technology/radiation therapy, nursing (RN), physician assistant. **History:** General. **Liberal arts:** Arts/sciences. **Math:** General. **Philosophy/religion:** Philosophy, religion. **Physical sciences:** Chemistry. **Protective services:** Criminal justice. **Psychology:** General. **Social sciences:** Economics, political science, sociology.

Most popular majors. Biology 6%, business/marketing 16%, communications/journalism 14%, education 10%, health sciences 12%, liberal arts 6%, psychology 8%, security/protective services 7%, social sciences 7%.

Technology on campus. 600 workstations in library, computer center, student center. Commuter students can connect to campus network. Helpline, wireless network available.

Student life. Freshman orientation: Mandatory. Preregistration for classes offered. **Housing:** St. Francis has partnered with Educational Housing Services and offers a limited amount of student housing. **Activities:** Campus ministries, choral groups, dance, drama, literary magazine, Model UN, student government, student newspaper, TV station, Latin American Society, Haitian Alliance, Caribbean student association, Christian club, Arab-American Society, French club, College Republicans, History and Political Science Society, Italian Historical Society.

Athletics. NCAA. **Intercollegiate:** Basketball, cross-country, diving, soccer M, swimming, tennis, track and field, volleyball W, water polo. **Intramural:** Basketball, football (tackle) M, soccer M, volleyball. **Team name:** Terriers.

Student services. Adult student services, chaplain/spiritual director, career counseling, services for economically disadvantaged, student employment services, financial aid counseling, health services, personal counseling, placement for graduates, veterans' counselor. **Physically disabled:** Services for visually, speech, hearing impaired.

Contact. E-mail: admissions@sfc.edu
Phone: (718) 489-3473 Fax: (718) 802-0453
Lisa Randazzo, Associate Director, St. Francis College, 180 Remsen Street, Brooklyn Heights, NY 11201-9902

St. John Fisher College
Rochester, New York — **CB member**
www.sjfc.edu — **CB code: 2798**

- Private 4-year liberal arts college affiliated with the Roman Catholic Church
- Residential campus in large town
- 2,791 degree-seeking undergraduates: 6% part-time, 60% women, 4% African American, 4% Asian American, 4% Hispanic/Latino, 2% Multi-racial, non-Hispanic
- 1,011 degree-seeking graduate students
- 62% of applicants admitted
- SAT or ACT (ACT writing optional), application essay required
- 70% graduate within 6 years; 40% enter graduate study

General. Founded in 1948. Regionally accredited. **Degrees:** 758 bachelor's awarded; master's, professional, doctoral offered. **ROTC:** Army, Naval, Air Force. **Location:** 6 miles from Rochester. **Calendar:** Semester, extensive summer session. **Full-time faculty:** 230 total; 89% have terminal degrees, 16% minority, 53% women. **Part-time faculty:** 217 total; 6% minority, 65% women. **Class size:** 44% < 20, 55% 20-39, less than 1% 40-49, less than 1% 50-99, less than 1% >100. **Special facilities:** Multimedia computer lab and TV studio.

Freshman class profile. 4,586 applied, 2,860 admitted, 553 enrolled.

Mid 50% test scores		GPA 2.0-2.99:	10%
SAT critical reading:	490-570	Rank in top quarter:	57%
SAT math:	510-600	Rank in top tenth:	22%
SAT writing:	470-560	End year in good standing:	93%
ACT composite:	21-26	Return as sophomores:	86%
GPA 3.75 or higher:	37%	Out-of-state:	5%
GPA 3.50-3.74:	26%	Live on campus:	90%
GPA 3.0-3.49:	27%		

Basis for selection. GED not accepted. Admission based primarily on student's high school academic record, SAT or ACT scores, course curriculum, extracurricular activities, counselor and teacher recommendations, and personal statement, essay or graded paper. Interview recommended for all. **Home schooled:** Transcript of courses and grades, letter of recommendation (nonparent) required. **Learning Disabled:** Admission standards and procedures for students with disabilities are the same as for all applicants.

High school preparation. College-preparatory program required. 16 units required. Required and recommended units include English 4, mathematics 4, social studies 4, science 4 and foreign language 3.

2015-2016 Annual costs. Tuition/fees: $30,690. Room/board: $11,460. Books/supplies: $1,100. Personal expenses: $900.

2014-2015 Financial aid. Need-based: 575 full-time freshmen applied for aid; 504 deemed to have need; 504 received aid. Average need met was 73%. Average scholarship/grant was $18,180; average loan $3,737. 61% of total undergraduate aid awarded as scholarships/grants, 39% as loans/jobs. **Non-need-based:** Awarded to 2,070 full-time undergraduates, including 481 freshmen. Scholarships awarded for academics, leadership.

Application procedures. Admission: Priority date 1/16; no deadline. , may be waived for applicants with need. No application fee. Admission notification on a rolling basis beginning on or about 12/1. Must reply by May 1 or within 3 week(s) if notified thereafter. **Financial aid:** Priority date 2/15; no closing date. FAFSA required. Applicants notified on a rolling basis starting 3/15; must reply by 5/1 or within 3 week(s) of notification.

Academics. All entering first-year students participate in an integrative learning community designed to examine a topic from multiple perspectives, discover connections between different disciplines and develop close working relationships with other students. **Special study options:** Accelerated study, cross-registration, distance learning, double major, exchange student, honors, independent study, internships, liberal arts/career combination, student-designed major, study abroad, teacher certification program, Washington semester, weekend college. 3+2 pre-engineering program with affiliated engineering schools; Columbia University, Rensselaer Polytechnic Institute, University of Rochester. **Credit/placement by examination:** AP, CLEP, IB,

institutional tests. 66 credit hours maximum toward bachelor's degree. **Support services:** Reduced course load, study skills assistance, tutoring, writing center. 24/7 access to online tutoring support services.

Majors. Area/ethnic studies: American. **Biology:** General. **Business:** Accounting, business admin, finance, human resources, marketing. **Communications:** General. **Computer sciences:** General. **Education:** General, biology, chemistry, elementary, English, French, history, mathematics, physics, secondary, social studies, Spanish, special ed. **English:** English lit. **Foreign languages:** French, Spanish. **Health services:** Nursing (RN). **History:** General. **Liberal arts:** Arts/sciences. **Math:** General, statistics. **Parks/recreation:** Sports admin. **Philosophy/religion:** Philosophy, religion. **Physical sciences:** Chemistry, physics. **Psychology:** General. **Social sciences:** Anthropology, criminology, economics, international relations, political science, sociology.

Most popular majors. Biology 8%, business/marketing 24%, education 10%, health sciences 22%, psychology 6%, social sciences 10%.

Technology on campus. 550 workstations in dormitories, library, computer center, student center. Dormitories wired for high-speed internet access and linked to campus network. Commuter students can connect to campus network. Online course registration, online library, helpline, student web hosting, wireless network available.

Student life. Freshman orientation: Available. Preregistration for classes offered. Three-day program in late August. **Policies:** All housing is smoke-free. Freshmen not permitted cars on campus. **Housing:** Guaranteed on-campus for freshmen. Coed dorms, single-sex dorms, special housing for disabled available. $300 nonrefundable deposit, deadline 5/1. All residence halls accessible to students with disabilities. **Activities:** Pep band, campus ministries, choral groups, dance, drama, literary magazine, musical theater, student government, student newspaper, TV station, Latino student union, Black student union, Asian student union, Muslim Student Association, Students of Multicultural Affairs, Students With A Vision, Fisher Players, Resident Student Association, Commuter Council, Student Activities Board.

Athletics. NCAA. **Intercollegiate:** Baseball M, basketball, cross-country, field hockey W, football (tackle) M, golf, lacrosse, rowing (crew) W, soccer, softball W, tennis, track and field, volleyball W. **Intramural:** Basketball, football (non-tackle) M, soccer, volleyball. **Team name:** Cardinals.

Student services. Adult student services, alcohol/substance abuse counseling, chaplain/spiritual director, career counseling, services for economically disadvantaged, student employment services, financial aid counseling, health services, minority student services, on-campus daycare, personal counseling, placement for graduates, veterans' counselor. **Physically disabled:** Services for visually, hearing impaired.

Contact. E-mail: admissions@sjfc.edu
Phone: (585) 385-8064 Toll-free number: (800) 444-4640
Fax: (585) 385-8386
Stacy Ledermann, Director of Freshman Admissions, St. John Fisher College, 3690 East Avenue, Rochester, NY 14618-3597

St. John's University
Queens, New York — **CB member**
www.stjohns.edu — **CB code: 2799**

- Private 4-year university affiliated with the Roman Catholic Church
- Commuter campus in very large city
- 11,248 degree-seeking undergraduates: 2% part-time, 55% women, 19% African American, 17% Asian American, 12% Hispanic/Latino, 5% Multi-racial, non-Hispanic, 5% international
- 4,540 degree-seeking graduate students
- 65% of applicants admitted
- SAT or ACT (ACT writing optional) required
- 58% graduate within 6 years

General. Founded in 1870. Regionally accredited. Full degree programs offered on four campuses: Queens, Staten Island, Manhattan, and Rome, Italy; selected degree programs offered through distance learning. Coursework, but not full degrees, are offered at Oakdale, Long Island, and at study abroad sites in Paris, France and Seville, Spain. **Degrees:** 2,035 bachelor's, 22 associate awarded; master's, professional, doctoral offered. **ROTC:** Army. **Location:** 10 miles from midtown Manhattan. **Calendar:** Semester, extensive summer session. **Full-time faculty:** 611 total; 93% have terminal degrees, 25% minority, 44% women. **Part-time faculty:** 820 total; 26% have terminal degrees, 23% minority, 45% women. **Class size:** 34% < 20, 53% 20-39, 6% 40-49, 5% 50-99, less than 1% >100. **Special facilities:** Speech and hearing clinic, instructional media center, health education resource center, writing institute, institute of Asian studies.

Freshman class profile. 36,086 applied, 23,429 admitted, 3,253 enrolled.

Mid 50% test scores			
SAT critical reading:	480-580	GPA 2.0-2.99:	19%
SAT math:	480-600	Rank in top quarter:	48%
ACT composite:	22-27	Rank in top tenth:	21%
GPA 3.75 or higher:	26%	Return as sophomores:	80%
GPA 3.50-3.74:	20%	Out-of-state:	33%
GPA 3.0-3.49:	35%	Live on campus:	50%
		International:	5%

Basis for selection. School achievement record, standardized test scores, counselor/teacher recommendations, extracurricular activities, personal essay used. All supporting documents must accompany the application, including an official high school transcript and official test scores (either SAT or ACT). Two letters of recommendation (one must be from a science or math teacher), an essay of 250 words describing extracurricular activities, and a signed copy of the program's Technical Standards are also required. International students may also have to submit TOEFL test scores, in addition to a high school transcript and either SAT or ACT scores. Writing section (ACT or SAT) required for applicants to the PharmD program. Writing section not required for any other program. For those out of school a number of years, or who have never taken the SAT/ACT, ACCUPLACER is necessary. Personal statement/essay recommended for all; portfolio required for creative photography, fine art, graphic design, illustration programs. Audition required for dramatic arts. Essay required for 3-year degree programs. Essay, letter of recommendation, resume of activities required for applicants to the 6-year Doctor of Pharmacy (PharmD) program. **Home schooled:** Statement describing home school structure and mission, transcript of courses and grades, state high school equivalency certificate required.

High school preparation. College-preparatory program recommended. 13 units required; 19 recommended. Required and recommended units include English 4, mathematics 2-3, history 1, science 1, foreign language 2 and academic electives 5-8.

2015-2016 Annual costs. Tuition/fees: $38,680. Room/board: $16,390. Books/supplies: $610. Personal expenses: $1,058. **Additional information:** Tuition may vary by program and class year. Full-time freshman or transfer students are provided with a laptop for their entire St. John's career.

Financial aid. Non-need-based: Scholarships awarded for academics, alumni affiliation, art, athletics, leadership, music/drama, religious affiliation, ROTC.

Application procedures. Admission: No deadline. $50 fee, may be waived for applicants with need, free for online applicants. Admission notification on a rolling basis beginning on or about 12/15. Must reply by May 1 or within 2 week(s) if notified thereafter. The latest date SAT or ACT scores must be received for fall-term admission to the PharmD program is 12/1 for the priority deadline with notification around 1/15, and 2/1 for the regular admission deadline with notification around 3/1; all other programs are rolling. **Financial aid:** Priority date 2/1; no closing date. FAFSA required. Must reply within 2 week(s) of notification.

Academics. Special study options: Accelerated study, combined bachelor's/graduate degree, cross-registration, distance learning, double major, dual enrollment of high school students, ESL, honors, independent study, internships, liberal arts/career combination, study abroad, teacher certification program, weekend college. Semester study abroad opportunities in Paris, France; Rome, Italy; Seville, Spain. Summer study abroad programs in Argentina, Austria, The Bahamas, China, France, Greece, Guatemala, Italy, Korea, and Spain. Available winter study abroad programs include Morocco and Dubai. 3-year degree programs offered at the Staten Island campus. **Credit/placement by examination:** AP, CLEP, IB, SAT, ACT, institutional tests. Students must complete at least 50 percent of major courses and at least 30 credits on campus. **Support services:** Learning center, pre-admission summer program, reduced course load, study skills assistance, tutoring, writing center. Student support services, Science & Technology Entry Program, and McNair Scholars Program.

Majors. Area/ethnic studies: Asian. **Biology:** General, toxicology. **Business:** Accounting, actuarial science, business admin, finance, hospitality admin, insurance, management information systems, marketing. **Communications:** Advertising, communications/speech/rhetoric, journalism, photojournalism. **Communications technology:** Photo/film/video. **Computer sciences:** General, security. **Conservation:** Environmental studies. **Education:** Biology, elementary, English, mathematics, physics, social studies, Spanish, special ed. **English:** English lit, rhetoric/composition. **Foreign languages:** French, Italian, Spanish. **Health services:** Audiology/speech pathology, clinical lab science, health information technology, physician assistant, radiologic technology/medical imaging. **History:** General. **Human services:** General. **Liberal arts:** Arts/sciences. **Math:** General. **Parks/recreation:** Sports admin. **Philosophy/religion:** Philosophy. **Physical sciences:** General, chemistry, physics. **Protective services:** Law enforcement admin, security management. **Psychology:** General. **Social sciences:** General, anthropology, economics, political science, sociology. **Theology:** Theology. **Visual/performing arts:** Dramatic, graphic design, illustration, photography.

Most popular majors. Biology 8%, business/marketing 19%, communications/journalism 12%, health sciences 10%, psychology 7%, security/protective services 9%, social sciences 6%.

Technology on campus. PC or laptop required. 1,295 workstations in dormitories, library, computer center, student center. Dormitories wired for high-speed internet access and linked to campus network. Commuter students can connect to campus network. Online course registration, online library, helpline, repair service, student web hosting, wireless network available.

Student life. Freshman orientation: Mandatory. Preregistration for classes offered. **Policies:** Policies outlined in online Student Handbook. Freshmen not permitted cars on campus. **Housing:** Coed dorms, apartments, themed housing available. $400 nonrefundable deposit, deadline 5/1. Limited off-campus apartments available. **Activities:** Bands, campus ministries, choral groups, dance, drama, literary magazine, Model UN, radio station, student government, student newspaper, over 180 organizations on all campuses.

Athletics. NCAA. **Intercollegiate:** Baseball M, basketball, cross-country W, fencing, golf, lacrosse M, soccer, softball W, tennis, track and field W, volleyball W. **Intramural:** Badminton, basketball, cheerleading, football (non-tackle), soccer, softball, table tennis, volleyball. **Team name:** Red Storm.

Student services. Adult student services, alcohol/substance abuse counseling, chaplain/spiritual director, career counseling, services for economically disadvantaged, student employment services, financial aid counseling, health services, minority student services, personal counseling, placement for graduates, veterans' counselor. **Physically disabled:** Services for visually, speech, hearing impaired.

Contact. E-mail: admission@stjohns.edu
Phone: (718) 990-2000 Toll-free number: (888) 978-5646
Fax: (718) 990-2096
Beth Evans, Vice President for Enrollment Management, St. John's University, 8000 Utopia Parkway, Queens, NY 11439

St. Joseph's College New York: Suffolk Campus
Patchogue, New York
www.sjcny.edu   CB code: 2841

- Private 4-year liberal arts and teachers college
- Commuter campus in large town
- 2,846 degree-seeking undergraduates: 16% part-time, 66% women, 5% African American, 2% Asian American, 11% Hispanic/Latino, 1% Native American, 1% Multi-racial, non-Hispanic
- 639 degree-seeking graduate students
- 75% of applicants admitted
- SAT or ACT (ACT writing optional), application essay required
- 68% graduate within 6 years; 34% enter graduate study

General. Founded in 1916. Regionally accredited. **Degrees:** 859 bachelor's awarded; master's offered. **Location:** 55 miles from midtown Manhattan. **Calendar:** Semester, limited summer session. **Full-time faculty:** 113 total; 77% have terminal degrees, 6% minority, 61% women. **Part-time faculty:** 280 total; 25% have terminal degrees, 7% minority, 49% women. **Class size:** 62% < 20, 38% 20-39, less than 1% 40-49. **Special facilities:** Playhouse, MVP center for performing arts.

Freshman class profile. 1,583 applied, 1,183 admitted, 361 enrolled.

Mid 50% test scores			
SAT critical reading:	480-560	GPA 3.50-3.74:	20%
SAT math:	470-570	GPA 3.0-3.49:	33%
SAT writing:	450-550	GPA 2.0-2.99:	10%
ACT composite:	19-25	End year in good standing:	98%
GPA 3.75 or higher:	37%	Return as sophomores:	88%

Basis for selection. Grades in high school academic classes, GPA and rank in class most important. Performance on standardized tests important. Strongly factored in are letters of recommendation, personal statement and school/community activities. Off-campus interview arranged with admissions representative. Transcripts, completed application, essay and 2 letters of recommendation are required. Campus visits are recommended. **Home schooled:** Statement describing home school structure and mission, transcript of courses and grades, state high school equivalency certificate, letter of recommendation (nonparent) required.

High school preparation. College-preparatory program required. 24 units required; 29 recommended. Required and recommended units include English

4, mathematics 3-4, social studies 4, science 3-4 (laboratory 3-4), foreign language 2-3, visual/performing arts 2 and academic electives 3-4.

2015-2016 Annual costs. Tuition/fees: $24,130. Books/supplies: $1,000. Personal expenses: $5,000.

2014-2015 Financial aid. Need-based: 308 full-time freshmen applied for aid; 242 deemed to have need; 240 received aid. Average need met was 71%. Average scholarship/grant was $12,518; average loan $3,245. 59% of total undergraduate aid awarded as scholarships/grants, 41% as loans/jobs. **Non-need-based:** Awarded to 1,878 full-time undergraduates, including 291 freshmen. Scholarships awarded for academics, alumni affiliation.

Application procedures. Admission: No deadline. $25 fee, may be waived for applicants with need. Admission notification on a rolling basis beginning on or about 11/1. Must reply by May 1 or within 2 week(s) if notified thereafter. **Financial aid:** Priority date 3/15; no closing date. FAFSA required. Applicants notified on a rolling basis starting 3/30; must reply by 5/1 or within 2 week(s) of notification.

Academics. Special study options: Accelerated study, combined bachelor's/graduate degree, distance learning, double major, honors, independent study, internships, liberal arts/career combination, study abroad, teacher certification program, weekend college. Continuing education, evening courses, learning communities, off-campus study, service members opportunity college, summer sessions for credit, first year experiences, service learning, senior capstone, undergraduate research/creative projects. **Credit/placement by examination:** AP, CLEP, IB, institutional tests. Up to 30 credits may be awarded for college courses taken while in high school and/or IBH and AP courses. **Support services:** Learning center, reduced course load, study skills assistance, tutoring, writing center.

Majors. Biology: General. **Business:** Accounting, business admin, hospitality admin, marketing. **Communications:** Communications/speech/rhetoric, journalism. **Computer sciences:** General. **Education:** General, biology, chemistry, early childhood, early childhood special, elementary, elementary special ed, English, mathematics, secondary, social studies, Spanish, special ed. **English:** English lit. **Foreign languages:** Spanish. **Health services:** Clinical lab science, facilities admin, nursing (RN). **History:** General. **Liberal arts:** Arts/sciences. **Math:** General. **Parks/recreation:** General, facilities management. **Philosophy/religion:** General. **Physical sciences:** Chemistry. **Protective services:** Law enforcement admin. **Psychology:** General. **Social sciences:** General, political science, sociology. **Work/family studies:** Family studies.

Most popular majors. Business/marketing 18%, education 28%, English 11%, health sciences 7%, psychology 8%.

Technology on campus. 343 workstations in library, computer center. Online course registration, online library, helpline, wireless network available.

Student life. Freshman orientation: Mandatory. Preregistration for classes offered. **Activities:** Campus ministries, choral groups, dance, drama, musical theater, opera, radio station, student government, student newspaper, Students Taking an Active Role in Society, Newman club, Brothers and Sisters in Christ, LGBTQA, Individual Needs Network, Diversity Union, latin dance club, Nicaragua project club.

Athletics. NCAA. **Intercollegiate:** Baseball M, basketball, cross-country, golf M, lacrosse, soccer, softball W, swimming W, tennis, track and field, volleyball. **Team name:** Golden Eagles.

Student services. Adult student services, chaplain/spiritual director, career counseling, student employment services, financial aid counseling, health services, personal counseling, veterans' counselor. **Physically disabled:** Services for visually, hearing impaired.

Contact. E-mail: longislandas@sjcny.edu
Phone: (631) 687-4500 Fax: (631) 447-3601
Gigi Lamens, Vice President for Enrollment Management, St. Joseph's College New York: Suffolk Campus, 155 West Roe Boulevard, Patchogue, NY 11772-2325

St. Joseph's College, New York

Brooklyn, New York   **CB member**
www.sjcny.edu   **CB code: 2802**

- Private 4-year liberal arts and teachers college
- Commuter campus in very large city
- 967 degree-seeking undergraduates: 22% part-time, 67% women, 25% African American, 7% Asian American, 17% Hispanic/Latino, 1% Multiracial, non-Hispanic
- 216 degree-seeking graduate students

- 61% of applicants admitted
- SAT or ACT (ACT writing optional), application essay required
- 66% graduate within 6 years; 37% enter graduate study

General. Founded in 1916. Regionally accredited. **Degrees:** 270 bachelor's awarded; master's offered. **Location:** 5 miles from midtown Manhattan. **Calendar:** Semester, limited summer session. **Full-time faculty:** 58 total; 84% have terminal degrees, 21% minority, 52% women. **Part-time faculty:** 131 total; 19% have terminal degrees, 31% minority, 57% women. **Class size:** 86% < 20, 14% 20-39. **Special facilities:** On-campus laboratory preschool for children 3-6 years old, model school for prospective teachers, outdoor theater, hill center.

Freshman class profile. 1,637 applied, 1,004 admitted, 155 enrolled.

Mid 50% test scores			
		GPA 3.50-3.74:	11%
SAT critical reading:	420-550	GPA 3.0-3.49:	28%
SAT math:	440-530	GPA 2.0-2.99:	31%
SAT writing:	420-510	End year in good standing:	95%
ACT composite:	18-23	Return as sophomores:	83%
GPA 3.75 or higher:	29%	Out-of-state:	5%

Basis for selection. High school achievement record, SAT/ACT scores, class rank, character and personal qualities, recommendations important. Personal statements required. Campus visits are recommended. Admission interview and off-campus admissions interview are recommended of some. Transcripts, essay and 2 letters of recommendation are required. **Home schooled:** State high school equivalency certificate, letter of recommendation (nonparent) required.

High school preparation. College-preparatory program recommended. 18 units required. Required units include English 4, mathematics 3, social studies 4, science 3 and foreign language 2.

2015-2016 Annual costs. Tuition/fees: $24,120. Books/supplies: $1,000. Personal expenses: $5,000.

2014-2015 Financial aid. Need-based: 181 full-time freshmen applied for aid; 153 deemed to have need; 152 received aid. Average need met was 64%. Average scholarship/grant was $15,341; average loan $2,953. 69% of total undergraduate aid awarded as scholarships/grants, 31% as loans/jobs. **Non-need-based:** Awarded to 703 full-time undergraduates, including 173 freshmen. Scholarships awarded for academics, alumni affiliation.

Application procedures. Admission: Closing date 8/31. $25 fee, may be waived for applicants with need. Admission notification on a rolling basis beginning on or about 11/1. Must reply by 5/1. Students admitted close to or after May 1 will be asked to reply within two weeks of their admission. Extensions may also be granted for all students on a case-by-case basis. **Financial aid:** Priority date 3/15; no closing date. FAFSA required. Applicants notified on a rolling basis starting 3/30; must reply within 2 week(s) of notification.

Academics. Special study options: Accelerated study, combined bachelor's/graduate degree, distance learning, double major, ESL, honors, independent study, internships, liberal arts/career combination, study abroad, teacher certification program. Certificate programs, continuing education, evening courses, learning communities, off-campus study, service members opportunity college, Summer sessions for credit, first year experiences, service learning, senior capstone, undergraduate research/creative projects. **Credit/placement by examination:** AP, CLEP, IB, institutional tests. 30 credit hours maximum toward bachelor's degree. **Support services:** Learning center, reduced course load, remedial instruction, study skills assistance, tutoring, writing center. Placement and credit by examination.

Majors. Biology: General. **Business:** Accounting, business admin, hospitality admin, marketing. **Communications:** Communications/speech/rhetoric, journalism. **Computer sciences:** General, information technology. **Education:** General, biology, chemistry, early childhood, early childhood special, elementary, elementary special ed, English, mathematics, secondary, social studies, Spanish, special ed. **English:** English lit. **Foreign languages:** Spanish. **Health services:** Clinical lab science, nursing (RN). **History:** General. **Liberal arts:** Arts/sciences. **Math:** General. **Parks/recreation:** General, facilities management. **Physical sciences:** Chemistry. **Protective services:** Law enforcement admin. **Psychology:** General. **Social sciences:** General, political science, sociology. **Work/family studies:** Family studies.

Most popular majors. Business/marketing 19%, education 18%, health sciences 17%, psychology 7%, security/protective services 10%.

Technology on campus. 322 workstations in library, computer center, student center. Dormitories wired for high-speed internet access and linked to campus network. Online course registration, online library, helpline, wireless network available.

Student life. Freshman orientation: Mandatory. Preregistration for classes offered. **Housing:** Coed dorms available. **Activities:** Campus ministries, dance, drama, film society, literary magazine, musical theater, student government, student newspaper, campus ministry and outreach club, Students Joined Through Christ, Asian Awareness club, Black Student Association, Desi Student Association, Gaelic Society, Paesanos Italian club, Poder Latino, Students for Justice in Palestine.

Athletics. NCAA. **Intercollegiate:** Baseball M, basketball, cross-country, soccer, softball W, swimming W, tennis, volleyball. **Intramural:** Basketball W. **Team name:** Bears.

Student services. Adult student services, chaplain/spiritual director, career counseling, student employment services, financial aid counseling, health services, personal counseling, veterans' counselor.

Contact. E-mail: brooklynas@sjcny.edu
Phone: (718) 940-5800 Fax: (718) 636-8303
Christine Murphy, Vice President for Enrollment Management, St. Joseph's College, New York, 245 Clinton Avenue, Brooklyn, NY 11205-3602

St. Lawrence University
Canton, New York
www.stlawu.edu

CB member
CB code: 2805

- Private 4-year liberal arts college
- Residential campus in small town
- 2,404 degree-seeking undergraduates: 55% women, 3% African American, 2% Asian American, 4% Hispanic/Latino, 2% Multi-racial, non-Hispanic, 9% international
- 87 degree-seeking graduate students
- 46% of applicants admitted
- Application essay required
- 87% graduate within 6 years

General. Founded in 1856. Regionally accredited. **Degrees:** 585 bachelor's awarded; master's offered. **ROTC:** Army, Air Force. **Location:** 70 miles from Ottawa, Canada. **Calendar:** Semester, limited summer session. **Full-time faculty:** 176 total; 5% have terminal degrees, 16% minority, 50% women. **Part-time faculty:** 31 total; 10% have terminal degrees, 16% minority, 58% women. **Class size:** 62% < 20, 37% 20-39, less than 1% 40-49, less than 1% 50-99, less than 1% >100. **Special facilities:** 1,000 contiguous acres include woods and river habitat for conducting primary research, modern science facility, center for arts technology, golf course, crew boathouse, Adirondack semester yurt village, sustainability semester site.

Freshman class profile. 5,835 applied, 2,713 admitted, 680 enrolled.

Mid 50% test scores			
SAT critical reading:	550-650	GPA 2.0-2.99:	10%
SAT math:	550-660	Rank in top quarter:	77%
SAT writing:	540-640	Rank in top tenth:	45%
ACT composite:	25-30	Return as sophomores:	89%
GPA 3.75 or higher:	42%	Out-of-state:	59%
GPA 3.50-3.74:	21%	Live on campus:	100%
GPA 3.0-3.49:	27%	International:	7%

Basis for selection. Academic record most important; test scores, extracurricular activities, seriousness of purpose and intellectual promise important. Although a Test Optional institution, international applicants must submit SAT's in order to be considered for admission. If SAT's are not offered in the student's home country, then TOEFL may be submitted instead. Interview recommended.

High school preparation. College-preparatory program required. 20 units recommended. Recommended units include English 4, mathematics 4, social studies 2, history 2, science 4 and foreign language 4.

2015-2016 Annual costs. Tuition/fees: $49,410. Room/board: $12,730. Books/supplies: $750. Personal expenses: $500.

2015-2016 Financial aid. Need-based: 495 full-time freshmen applied for aid; 429 deemed to have need; 429 received aid. Average need met was 87%. Average scholarship/grant was $37,312; average loan $3,410. 88% of total undergraduate aid awarded as scholarships/grants, 12% as loans/jobs. **Non-need-based:** Awarded to 1,914 full-time undergraduates, including 570 freshmen. Scholarships awarded for academics, alumni affiliation, athletics, leadership, minority status, ROTC, state residency.

Application procedures. Admission: Closing date 2/1 (postmark date). $60 fee, may be waived for applicants with need. Admission notification by 3/31. Must reply by May 1 or within 2 week(s) if notified thereafter. **Financial aid:** Priority date 2/1, closing date 2/1. FAFSA required. Applicants notified by 3/30; must reply by 5/1 or within 2 week(s) of notification.

Academics. The First-Year ProgramStudents live together and study in a team; developing the writing, speaking, and research skills needed for college. They continue to develop these skills in a spring First-Year Seminar. **Special study options:** Combined bachelor's/graduate degree, cross-registration, double major, ESL, exchange student, independent study, internships, New York semester, student-designed major, study abroad, teacher certification program, Washington semester. Community-based learning; 3-2 program in engineering with Clarkson University, Columbia University, Rensselaer Polytechnic Institute, University of Rochester, University of Southern California, Washington University in St. Louis; early assurance programs in medicine with SUNY Health Science Center at Syracuse, dentistry with SUNY Buffalo; a 3+4 combined bachelor's/doctorate in pharmacy with SUNY Buffalo's School of Pharmacy and Pharmaceutical Sciences; bachelor's/graduate degree program in business administration with Clarkson University, Union College and Rochester Institute of Technology; 25 off-campus programs in 19 countries in Europe, Kenya, Japan, Costa Rica, India, Jordan, Canada, Czech Republic, Trinidad and Tobago, China, Thailand, Australia and New Zealand. Domestic off-campus programs include yurt village 60-miles from campus for Adirondack Semester, farmstead 5-miles from campus for the Sustainability Semester, Liberal Arts in New York City semesters, and partnerships with The Washington Center, American University, and Fisk University. **Credit/placement by examination:** AP, CLEP, IB, institutional tests. 60 credit hours maximum toward bachelor's degree. **Support services:** Pre-admission summer program, reduced course load, study skills assistance, tutoring, writing center. Quantitative Resource Center for math assistance.

Majors. Area/ethnic studies: African, African-American, Asian, Canadian, European, Latin American/Caribbean. **Biology:** General, biochemistry, biophysics, conservation, neuroscience. **Communications:** Communications/speech/rhetoric. **Computer sciences:** General. **Conservation:** Environmental studies. **English:** American lit, British lit, creative writing. **Foreign languages:** French, Spanish. **History:** General. **Liberal arts:** Arts/sciences, humanities. **Math:** General, statistics. **Philosophy/religion:** Philosophy, religion. **Physical sciences:** Chemistry, geology, geophysics, physics. **Psychology:** General. **Social sciences:** Anthropology, econometrics, economics, political science, sociology. **Visual/performing arts:** Music, studio arts.

Most popular majors. Biology 12%, English 7%, psychology 10%, social sciences 32%.

Technology on campus. 675 workstations in dormitories, library, computer center, student center. Dormitories wired for high-speed internet access and linked to campus network. Commuter students can connect to campus network. Online course registration, online library, helpline, repair service, student web hosting, wireless network available.

Student life. Freshman orientation: Mandatory. Preregistration for classes offered. Orientation is three days preceding the start of fall classes. Programs are focused on academic introductions to the liberal arts, to the living-learning community concept, and St. Lawrence traditions. **Policies:** Residential living-learning program. First-year students live together in a residential college their first semester. Students required to live on campus all four years. **Housing:** Guaranteed on-campus for all undergraduates. Coed dorms, single-sex dorms, special housing for disabled, apartments, fraternity/sorority housing, gender-neutral housing, themed housing, wellness housing available. Townhouse apartments for senior leaders, some suites available. Students can petition to have quiet or single-sex halls within dormitory. **Activities:** Bands, campus ministries, choral groups, dance, drama, film society, international student organizations, literary magazine, music ensembles, Model UN, radio station, student government, student newspaper, Jewish student organization, black student union, Sociedad Hispana, Muslim students organization, environmental awareness organization, Habitat for Humanity, outing club, academic honorary societies, Circle K, Amnesty International.

Athletics. NCAA. **Intercollegiate:** Baseball M, basketball, cross-country, diving, equestrian, field hockey W, football (tackle) M, golf, ice hockey, lacrosse, rowing (crew), skiing, soccer, softball W, squash, swimming, tennis, track and field, volleyball W. **Intramural:** Basketball, football (non-tackle) M, football (tackle) M, ice hockey, soccer, softball W, triathlon, ultimate frisbee. **Team name:** Saints.

Student services. Alcohol/substance abuse counseling, chaplain/spiritual director, career counseling, services for economically disadvantaged, student employment services, financial aid counseling, health services, minority student services, personal counseling, placement for graduates, women's services. **Physically disabled:** Services for visually, hearing impaired.

Contact. E-mail: admissions@stlawu.edu
Phone: (315) 229-5261 Toll-free number: (800) 285-1856
Fax: (315) 229-5818
Jeffrey Rickey, Vice President and Dean of Admissions and Financial Aid, St. Lawrence University, Payson Hall, Canton, NY 13617

St. Thomas Aquinas College
Sparkill, New York
www.stac.edu   CB code: 2807

- Private 4-year liberal arts college
- Commuter campus in large town
- 1,170 degree-seeking undergraduates: 5% part-time, 51% women, 10% African American, 3% Asian American, 22% Hispanic/Latino, 1% Multiracial, non-Hispanic, 3% international
- 131 degree-seeking graduate students
- 79% of applicants admitted
- SAT or ACT (ACT writing optional) required
- 55% graduate within 6 years

General. Founded in 1952. Regionally accredited. **Degrees:** 282 bachelor's, 4 associate awarded; master's offered. **ROTC:** Air Force. **Location:** 15 miles from New York City. **Calendar:** Semester, extensive summer session. **Full-time faculty:** 57 total; 91% have terminal degrees, 5% minority, 54% women. **Part-time faculty:** 105 total; 24% have terminal degrees, 10% minority, 42% women. **Class size:** 59% < 20, 40% 20-39, less than 1% 40-49, less than 1% 50-99. **Special facilities:** Arts, sciences and technology center, digital imaging laboratory, professional laboratory.

Freshman class profile. 1,918 applied, 1,513 admitted, 276 enrolled.

Mid 50% test scores			
		GPA 3.50-3.74:	8%
SAT critical reading:	410-520	GPA 3.0-3.49:	30%
SAT math:	420-530	GPA 2.0-2.99:	47%
SAT writing:	410-510	Out-of-state:	18%
ACT composite:	18-22	Live on campus:	72%
GPA 3.75 or higher:	13%	International:	4%

Basis for selection. School achievement record, test scores, recommendation, and interview considered. Applicants should be in top half of class and have GPA above 3.0. Essay, interview recommended for all; portfolio recommended for art program. **Home schooled:** Statement describing home school structure and mission, transcript of courses and grades, state high school equivalency certificate, letter of recommendation (nonparent) required.

High school preparation. 20 units required. Required units include English 4, mathematics 3, social studies 4, science 3 (laboratory 2) and foreign language 3.

2015-2016 Annual costs. Tuition/fees: $28,740. Room/board: $12,030. Books/supplies: $1,000.

2015-2016 Financial aid. Need-based: 250 full-time freshmen applied for aid; 212 deemed to have need; 201 received aid. Average need met was 34%. Average scholarship/grant was $10,500; average loan $3,300. 65% of total undergraduate aid awarded as scholarships/grants, 35% as loans/jobs. **Non-need-based:** Awarded to 835 full-time undergraduates, including 189 freshmen. Scholarships awarded for academics, alumni affiliation, art, athletics, leadership, minority status, music/drama, religious affiliation.

Application procedures. Admission: No deadline. $30 fee. Admission notification on a rolling basis beginning on or about 10/1. **Financial aid:** Closing date 6/30. FAFSA required. Applicants notified on a rolling basis starting 11/1; must reply within 4 week(s) of notification.

Academics. Special study options: Accelerated study, combined bachelor's/graduate degree, cooperative education, cross-registration, double major, dual enrollment of high school students, ESL, exchange student, honors, independent study, internships, liberal arts/career combination, study abroad, teacher certification program, Washington semester. **Credit/placement by examination:** AP, CLEP, IB, SAT, ACT, institutional tests. 15 credit hours maximum toward associate degree, 30 toward bachelor's. **Support services:** Learning center, pre-admission summer program, reduced course load, remedial instruction, study skills assistance, tutoring, writing center.

Majors. Biology: General. **Business:** General, accounting, business admin, finance, international marketing, marketing. **Communications:** Broadcast journalism, communications/speech/rhetoric, journalism. **Computer sciences:** General. **Education:** General, art, biology, chemistry, elementary, English, foreign languages, history, mathematics, multi-level teacher, physics, science, secondary, social studies, Spanish, special ed. **English:** Creative writing, English lit. **Foreign languages:** General, French, Spanish. **Health services:** Art therapy, predental, premedicine, prenursing, prepharmacy, preveterinary. **History:** General. **Liberal arts:** Arts/sciences. **Math:** General, applied. **Parks/recreation:** Facilities management, golf management. **Philosophy/religion:** Philosophy, religion. **Physical sciences:** Chemistry, physics. **Protective services:** Forensics, law enforcement admin. **Psychology:** General. **Social sciences:** General. **Visual/performing arts:** Art, graphic design, studio arts.

Most popular majors. Biology 8%, business/marketing 29%, communications/journalism 7%, education 10%, legal studies 6%, parks/recreation 6%, psychology 10%, social sciences 7%, visual/performing arts 6%.

Technology on campus. 200 workstations in dormitories, library, computer center, student center. Dormitories wired for high-speed internet access and linked to campus network. Commuter students can connect to campus network. Online library, helpline, wireless network available.

Student life. Freshman orientation: Mandatory, $75 fee. Preregistration for classes offered. **Housing:** Guaranteed on-campus for freshmen. Single-sex dorms, apartments, wellness housing available. $250 nonrefundable deposit, deadline 5/1. **Activities:** Concert band, campus ministries, choral groups, dance, drama, literary magazine, music ensembles, musical theater, radio station, student government, student newspaper, political union, business association, community service organization.

Athletics. NCAA. **Intercollegiate:** Baseball M, basketball, cross-country, golf M, lacrosse W, soccer, softball W, tennis, track and field. **Intramural:** Basketball, football (tackle), handball, softball, tennis, ultimate frisbee. **Team name:** Spartans.

Student services. Adult student services, alcohol/substance abuse counseling, chaplain/spiritual director, career counseling, student employment services, financial aid counseling, health services, personal counseling, placement for graduates, veterans' counselor, women's services. **Physically disabled:** Services for visually, speech, hearing impaired.

Contact. E-mail: admissions@stac.edu
Phone: (845) 398-4100 Fax: (845) 398-4114
Samantha Bazile, Director of Admissions, St. Thomas Aquinas College, 125 Route 340, Sparkill, NY 10976-1050

SUNY College at Brockport
Brockport, New York   CB member
www.brockport.edu   CB code: 2537

- Public 4-year liberal arts college
- Residential campus in small town
- 6,993 degree-seeking undergraduates: 9% part-time, 55% women
- 1,046 degree-seeking graduate students
- 53% of applicants admitted
- SAT or ACT (ACT writing optional), application essay required
- 69% graduate within 6 years

General. Founded in 1867. Regionally accredited. **Degrees:** 1,865 bachelor's awarded; master's offered. **ROTC:** Army, Naval, Air Force. **Location:** 16 miles from Rochester, NY. **Calendar:** Semester, limited summer session. **Full-time faculty:** 335 total; 87% have terminal degrees, 18% minority, 52% women. **Part-time faculty:** 283 total; 18% have terminal degrees, 11% minority, 56% women. **Class size:** 33% < 20, 53% 20-39, 8% 40-49, 4% 50-99, 1% >100. **Special facilities:** Indoor track and event space, theater and black box performance space, modern dance facilities, art studios, greenhouse, planetarium, electron microscope, nuclear magnetic resonance spectrometer, Faraday Cage, geographic information systems lab with doppler radar station, aquaculture ponds, environmental science deciduous woodlot, 20 computer labs, smart classrooms, student learning center, weather information system, resolution germanium detector, research vessel on Lake Ontario, vacuum deposition lab, physics lab, 2 supercomputers.

Freshman class profile. 9,528 applied, 5,018 admitted, 1,145 enrolled.

Mid 50% test scores			
		GPA 2.0-2.99:	44%
SAT critical reading:	460-550	Rank in top quarter:	36%
SAT math:	470-570	Rank in top tenth:	11%
SAT writing:	440-530	End year in good standing:	87%
ACT composite:	20-25	Return as sophomores:	82%
GPA 3.75 or higher:	14%	Out-of-state:	4%
GPA 3.50-3.74:	12%	Live on campus:	89%
GPA 3.0-3.49:	28%	International:	2%

Basis for selection. Strength of academic program, course grades and high school average, standardized test scores (SAT and/or ACT), class rank, supplemental application information, anything additional supplied (letters of recommendation, resume, portfolio, etc) considered. Interview recommended in some cases; auditions required for dance major and dance minor. **Home schooled:** Statement describing home school structure and mission, transcript of courses and grades, state high school equivalency certificate, interview, letter of recommendation (nonparent) required. Outline of courses completed at high school level, official test scores (SAT/ACT), personal essay, 2 letters of recommendation, letter from local superintendent indicating local graduation requirements have been fulfilled, and bibliography of books read during high school program.

High school preparation. College-preparatory program recommended. 18 units required. Required and recommended units include English 4, mathematics 3, social studies 4, history 3, science 3 (laboratory 1) and foreign language 3.

2015-2016 Annual costs. Tuition/fees: $7,898; $17,748 out-of-state. Room/board: $11,910. Books/supplies: $1,150. Personal expenses: $1,126.

2014-2015 Financial aid. **Need-based:** 923 full-time freshmen applied for aid; 718 deemed to have need; 701 received aid. Average need met was 75%. Average scholarship/grant was $6,950; average loan $4,896. 54% of total undergraduate aid awarded as scholarships/grants, 46% as loans/jobs. **Non-need-based:** Awarded to 926 full-time undergraduates, including 334 freshmen. Scholarships awarded for academics, alumni affiliation, art, leadership, minority status, music/drama, ROTC.

Application procedures. **Admission:** Priority date 3/1; deadline 8/1 (postmark date). $50 fee, may be waived for applicants with need. Admission notification on a rolling basis beginning on or about 10/1. Must reply by May 1 or within 3 week(s) if notified thereafter. **Financial aid:** Priority date 3/15; no closing date. FAFSA required. Applicants notified on a rolling basis starting 3/1; must reply by 5/1.

Academics. **Special study options:** Accelerated study, combined bachelor's/graduate degree, cross-registration, distance learning, double major, dual enrollment of high school students, ESL, honors, independent study, internships, student-designed major, study abroad, teacher certification program, Washington semester. Time/credit-shortened B.S. degree, experiential learning, domestic and international internships through Delta College. 3-1-3 program allows 24 college credits to be earned during student's senior year of high school. **Credit/placement by examination:** AP, CLEP, IB, institutional tests. **Support services:** Learning center, pre-admission summer program, reduced course load, study skills assistance, tutoring, writing center.

Honors college/program. Each year approximately 90 students are admitted into the Honors College. Entering freshmen should have a minimum high school GPA of 94 and SAT scores of 1250 (or ACT scores of 28). Applications are evaluated holistically, including a review of AP courses, extra-curricular activities, and a required personal essay. For this reason students with slightly lower scores are also accepted into the Honors College.

Majors. **Area/ethnic studies:** African-American, women's. **Biology:** General, biochemistry. **Business:** Accounting, business admin, finance, international, marketing. **Communications:** Broadcast journalism, communications/speech/rhetoric. **Computer sciences:** General, information systems. **Conservation:** Environmental science. **Education:** Physical. **English:** English lit. **Foreign languages:** French, Spanish. **Health services:** Athletic training, clinical lab science, nursing (RN), predental, premedicine, preveterinary. **History:** General. **Human services:** Social work. **Liberal arts:** Arts/sciences. **Math:** General. **Parks/recreation:** Exercise sciences, facilities management, sports admin. **Philosophy/religion:** Philosophy. **Physical sciences:** Atmospheric science, chemistry, geology, hydrology, physics. **Protective services:** Criminal justice. **Psychology:** General. **Social sciences:** Anthropology, international relations, political science, sociology. **Visual/performing arts:** Art, dance, dramatic.

Most popular majors. Business/marketing 15%, communications/journalism 7%, health sciences 17%, parks/recreation 10%, psychology 8%, security/protective services 7%.

Technology on campus. 1,000 workstations in dormitories, library, computer center, student center. Dormitories wired for high-speed internet access and linked to campus network. Commuter students can connect to campus network. Online course registration, online library, helpline, student web hosting, wireless network available.

Student life. **Freshman orientation:** Available, $200 fee. Preregistration for classes offered. Held over the summer during a comprehensive overnight program. A parent/family program runs parallel to the student orientation. **Policies:** Student Code of Conduct. **Housing:** Guaranteed on-campus for freshmen. Coed dorms, special housing for disabled, apartments, gender-neutral housing, themed housing available. $100 nonrefundable deposit, deadline 5/1. Living learning communities available. **Activities:** Dance, drama, film society, international student organizations, literary magazine, Model UN, radio station, student government, student newspaper, symphony orchestra, TV station, African Student Union, Association of Latino American Students, Brockport Advocates for individuals with Disabilities, Brockport Muslim Student Association, Colleges Against Cancer, Habitat for Humanity, International Student Organization, Intervarsity Christian Fellowship/Brothers and Sisters in Christ, Korean Students Association, political science/pre-law club.

Athletics. NCAA. **Intercollegiate:** Baseball M, basketball, cross-country, diving, field hockey W, football (tackle) M, gymnastics W, ice hockey M, lacrosse, soccer, softball W, swimming, tennis W, track and field, volleyball

W, wrestling M. **Intramural:** Badminton, basketball, bowling, football (non-tackle), football (tackle), handball, soccer, table tennis, tennis, ultimate frisbee, volleyball. **Team name:** Golden Eagles.

Student services. Alcohol/substance abuse counseling, career counseling, services for economically disadvantaged, student employment services, financial aid counseling, health services, minority student services, on-campus daycare, personal counseling, placement for graduates, veterans' counselor, women's services. **Physically disabled:** Services for visually, speech, hearing impaired.

Contact. E-mail: admit@brockport.edu
Phone: (585) 395-2751 Fax: (585) 395-5452
Randall Langston, Assistant Vice President for Enrollment Management, SUNY College at Brockport, 350 New Campus Drive, Brockport, NY 14420-2915

SUNY College at Buffalo
Buffalo, New York **CB member**
www.buffalostate.edu **CB code: 2533**

- Public 4-year liberal arts and teachers college
- Commuter campus in large city
- 8,977 degree-seeking undergraduates: 10% part-time, 57% women, 28% African American, 3% Asian American, 12% Hispanic/Latino, 3% Multi-racial, non-Hispanic, 2% international
- 960 degree-seeking graduate students
- 62% of applicants admitted
- SAT and SAT Subject Tests or ACT (ACT writing optional) required
- 49% graduate within 6 years; 25% enter graduate study

General. Founded in 1867. Regionally accredited. **Degrees:** 1,841 bachelor's awarded; master's offered. **ROTC:** Army. **Location:** 450 miles from New York City, 250 miles from Cleveland. **Calendar:** Semester, limited summer session. **Full-time faculty:** 380 total; 87% have terminal degrees, 20% minority, 47% women. **Part-time faculty:** 468 total; 22% have terminal degrees, 10% minority, 52% women. **Class size:** 46% < 20, 43% 20-39, 4% 40-49, 7% 50-99, less than 1% >100. **Special facilities:** Planetarium, performing arts center, center for environmental research and education, child care center, art center, Great Lakes research facility.

Freshman class profile. 13,679 applied, 8,524 admitted, 1,859 enrolled.

Mid 50% test scores		Rank in top quarter:	32%
SAT critical reading:	400-500	Rank in top tenth:	3%
SAT math:	400-490	Return as sophomores:	71%
SAT writing:	390-480	Out-of-state:	4%
ACT composite:	16-22	Live on campus:	66%
GPA 3.75 or higher:	11%	International:	2%
GPA 3.50-3.74:	8%	Fraternities:	1%
GPA 3.0-3.49:	34%	Sororities:	1%
GPA 2.0-2.99:	47%		

Basis for selection. High school GPA, class rank, test scores important. Recommendations, essay, interview, volunteer work, work experience and extracurricular activities also considered. SAT recommended. Portfolio required for fine arts program.

High school preparation. College-preparatory program recommended. 17 units recommended. Required and recommended units include English 4, mathematics 2-3, science 2-3, foreign language 3 and academic electives 4.

2015-2016 Annual costs. Tuition/fees: $7,669; $17,519 out-of-state. Room/board: $12,332. Books/supplies: $1,037. Personal expenses: $1,236.

Financial aid. All financial aid based on need.

Application procedures. **Admission:** No deadline. $50 fee, may be waived for applicants with need. Admission notification on a rolling basis beginning on or about 12/15. Must reply by May 1 or within 4 week(s) if notified thereafter. **Financial aid:** Priority date 3/1, closing date 5/1. FAFSA required. Applicants notified on a rolling basis starting 5/1; must reply within 4 week(s) of notification.

Academics. **Special study options:** Cooperative education, cross-registration, distance learning, double major, dual enrollment of high school students, ESL, exchange student, honors, independent study, internships, liberal arts/career combination, New York semester, study abroad, teacher certification program, Washington semester. **Credit/placement by examination:** AP, CLEP, IB, institutional tests. 30 credit hours maximum toward bachelor's degree. **Support services:** Learning center, pre-admission summer program, reduced course load, remedial instruction, study skills assistance, tutoring.

Honors college/program. High school students must have GPA of 90 or higher (or rank within the top 10 percent of their graduating class) and SAT scores of 1100 (exclusive of Writing) or higher. Advanced Placement courses with grades of B or better, cocurricular activities, and community involvement also considered.

Majors. Architecture: Urban/community planning. **Biology:** General. **Business:** General, business admin, fashion, hospitality admin, hospitality/recreation, office management. **Communications:** Broadcast journalism, communications/speech/rhetoric, journalism, media studies. **Computer sciences:** General, information systems, programming. **Education:** General, art, biology, business, chemistry, early childhood, elementary, emotionally handicapped, English, foreign languages, French, health occupations, kindergarten/preschool, mathematics, mentally handicapped, music, physical, physically handicapped, physics, reading, sales/marketing, science, secondary, social studies, Spanish, speech impaired, technology/industrial arts, trade/industrial, voc/tech. **English:** English lit. **Foreign languages:** French, Spanish. **Health services:** Speech pathology. **History:** General. **Human services:** Social work. **Liberal arts:** Humanities. **Math:** General. **Parks/recreation:** Health/ fitness. **Philosophy/religion:** Philosophy. **Physical sciences:** Chemistry, geology, physics, planetary. **Protective services:** Criminal justice, forensics. **Psychology:** General. **Social sciences:** Anthropology, economics, geography, political science, sociology. **Visual/performing arts:** General, art history/ conservation, commercial/advertising art, dramatic, fashion design, fiber arts, interior design, metal/jewelry, music, painting, photography, printmaking, sculpture, studio arts, theater arts management. **Work/family studies:** Clothing/textiles, food/nutrition.

Most popular majors. Business/marketing 13%, communications/journalism 7%, education 13%, health sciences 6%, security/protective services 8%, social sciences 9%, visual/performing arts 7%.

Technology on campus. 1,700 workstations in dormitories, library, computer center, student center. Dormitories wired for high-speed internet access and linked to campus network. Commuter students can connect to campus network. Online course registration, online library, helpline, repair service, wireless network available.

Student life. Freshman orientation: Mandatory, $175 fee. Preregistration for classes offered. **Housing:** Coed dorms, apartments, wellness housing available. $100 fully refundable deposit, deadline 7/1. Apartments for students with dependent children available. **Activities:** Bands, campus ministries, choral groups, dance, drama, film society, international student organizations, literary magazine, music ensembles, radio station, student government, student newspaper, TV station, Newman Club, Amnesty International, public interest groups, African American student organization, Adelante Estudiantes, Native American student organization, Muslim student organization, Caribbean student organization.

Athletics. NCAA. **Intercollegiate:** Basketball, cross-country, diving, football (tackle) M, ice hockey M, lacrosse W, soccer, softball W, swimming, tennis W, track and field, volleyball W. **Intramural:** Basketball, football (tackle) M, racquetball, soccer, softball, volleyball. **Team name:** Bengals.

Student services. Adult student services, career counseling, student employment services, health services, minority student services, on-campus daycare, personal counseling, placement for graduates, veterans' counselor. **Physically disabled:** Services for visually, speech, hearing impaired.

Contact. E-mail: admissions@buffalostate.edu
Phone: (716) 878-4017 Fax: (716) 878-6100
Carmella Thompson, Director of Admissions, SUNY College at Buffalo, 1300 Elmwood Avenue, Moot Hall, Buffalo, NY 14222-1095

SUNY College at Cortland

Cortland, New York   **CB member**
www2.cortland.edu/home   **CB code: 2538**

- Public 4-year liberal arts and teachers college
- Residential campus in large town
- 6,276 degree-seeking undergraduates: 2% part-time, 57% women, 6% African American, 1% Asian American, 11% Hispanic/Latino, 2% Multiracial, non-Hispanic, 1% international
- 606 degree-seeking graduate students
- 51% of applicants admitted
- Application essay required
- 73% graduate within 6 years

General. Founded in 1868. Regionally accredited. **Degrees:** 1,583 bachelor's awarded; master's offered. **ROTC:** Army, Air Force. **Location:** 35 miles from Syracuse, 20 miles from Ithaca. **Calendar:** Semester, limited summer

session. **Full-time faculty:** 293 total; 78% have terminal degrees, 13% minority, 53% women. **Part-time faculty:** 330 total; 19% have terminal degrees, 6% minority, 53% women. **Class size:** 33% < 20, 54% 20-39, 7% 40-49, 5% 50-99, 1% >100. **Special facilities:** Raquette Lake outdoor education complex, education center (geology field station), nature preserve, science museum, ethnographic teaching museum, center for speech and hearing disorders.

Freshman class profile. 11,060 applied, 5,623 admitted, 1,214 enrolled.

Mid 50% test scores			
		GPA 3.0-3.49:	47%
SAT critical reading:	470-550	GPA 2.0-2.99:	14%
SAT math:	490-560	Rank in top quarter:	39%
ACT composite:	22-25	Rank in top tenth:	10%
GPA 3.75 or higher:	10%	Return as sophomores:	78%
GPA 3.50-3.74:	29%	Out-of-state:	5%

Basis for selection. Primary consideration given to course selection and performance. SAT/ACT scores, class rank, extracurricular activities, personal statement/essay, recommendations also enter into decision. Additional consideration for special talents, interview, alumni relation, geographical residence, minority status, volunteer work, work experience. Audition required for musical theater program; portfolio required for art studio program.

High school preparation. College-preparatory program required. Required and recommended units include English 4, mathematics 3-4, social studies 4, science 3-4 (laboratory 3-4) and foreign language 3-4.

2015-2016 Annual costs. Tuition/fees: $8,050; $17,900 out-of-state. Room/board: $12,200. Books/supplies: $1,000. Personal expenses: $1,904.

2014-2015 Financial aid. Need-based: 875 full-time freshmen applied for aid; 634 deemed to have need; 602 received aid. Average need met was 66%. Average scholarship/grant was $5,062; average loan $3,539. 49% of total undergraduate aid awarded as scholarships/grants, 51% as loans/jobs. **Non-need-based:** Awarded to 1,054 full-time undergraduates, including 246 freshmen. Scholarships awarded for academics, art, leadership, minority status, music/drama, state residency.

Application procedures. Admission: Priority date 12/1; no deadline. $50 fee, may be waived for applicants with need. Admission notification on a rolling basis beginning on or about 1/2. Must reply by May 1 or within 4 week(s) if notified thereafter. **Financial aid:** Priority date 3/1; no closing date. FAFSA required. Applicants notified on a rolling basis starting 3/15; must reply by 5/1 or within 4 week(s) of notification.

Academics. Special study options: Combined bachelor's/graduate degree, cooperative education, cross-registration, distance learning, double major, dual enrollment of high school students, exchange student, honors, independent study, internships, liberal arts/career combination, student-designed major, study abroad, teacher certification program, Washington semester. **Credit/placement by examination:** AP, CLEP, IB, institutional tests. 30 credit hours maximum toward bachelor's degree. **Support services:** Learning center, pre-admission summer program, reduced course load, study skills assistance, tutoring, writing center.

Honors college/program. Open to entering fall freshmen and rising sophomores. Applicants should have exceptional academic record based on grades, standardized tests, course selection and extracurricular activities. To complete Honors Program, students must take at least 24 credits of honors-level courses, by taking combination of specially designated honors courses, contract courses and a course in which they complete the required honors thesis. Students also may use maximum of 2 Writing Intensive (WRIT) courses beyond the all-college requirements toward completion of the honors program.

Majors. Area/ethnic studies: African-American. **Biology:** General, biomedical sciences. **Communications:** Communications/speech/rhetoric, organizational. **Education:** Biology, chemistry, elementary, English, ESL, French, health, kindergarten/preschool, mathematics, physical, physics, science, social studies, Spanish, special ed, speech impaired. **English:** English lit. **Foreign languages:** French, Spanish. **Health services:** Athletic training, audiology/speech pathology, recreational therapy. **History:** General. **Human services:** Community org/advocacy. **Math:** General. **Parks/recreation:** General, exercise sciences, facilities management, sports admin. **Philosophy/religion:** Philosophy. **Physical sciences:** Chemistry, geology, physics. **Psychology:** General. **Social sciences:** Anthropology, criminology, economics, geography, international relations, political science, sociology. **Visual/performing arts:** Art, commercial/advertising art, music, studio arts.

Most popular majors. Business/marketing 6%, communications/journalism 8%, education 27%, health sciences 8%, parks/recreation 17%, social sciences 10%.

Technology on campus. 838 workstations in dormitories, library, computer center, student center. Dormitories wired for high-speed internet access and linked to campus network. Commuter students can connect to campus

network. Online course registration, online library, helpline, repair service, wireless network available.

Student life. Freshman orientation: Mandatory, $140 fee. Preregistration for classes offered. Held for one and a half days during the summer. Includes overnight with faculty, staff and other students. **Policies:** All students must agree to abide by Code of Student Conduct. Freshmen, sophomores, transfers required to live on campus. **Housing:** Guaranteed on-campus for freshmen. Coed dorms, special housing for disabled, apartments, cooperative housing, wellness housing available. $150 deposit, deadline 5/1. Leadership house, quiet atmosphere, transfer floor available. **Activities:** Campus ministries, choral groups, dance, drama, film society, international student organizations, literary magazine, music ensembles, Model UN, musical theater, radio station, student government, student newspaper, symphony orchestra, TV station, Agape, Hillel, black student union, Caribbean student association, La Familia Latina, Habitat for Humanity, AIDS Prevention & Awareness, Colleges Against Cancer, Cortland Against All Rape, New York public interest research group.

Athletics. NCAA. **Intercollegiate:** Baseball M, basketball, cross-country, diving, field hockey W, football (non-tackle) M, football (tackle) M, golf W, gymnastics W, ice hockey, lacrosse, racquetball, soccer, softball W, swimming, tennis W, track and field, volleyball W, wrestling M. **Intramural:** Archery, badminton, basketball, bowling, football (non-tackle), golf, racquetball, soccer, softball, table tennis, tennis, volleyball, water polo, weight lifting. **Team name:** Red Dragons.

Student services. Adult student services, alcohol/substance abuse counseling, chaplain/spiritual director, career counseling, student employment services, financial aid counseling, health services, on-campus daycare, personal counseling, placement for graduates, veterans' counselor. **Physically disabled:** Services for visually, speech, hearing impaired.

Contact. E-mail: admissions@cortland.edu
Phone: (607) 753-4712 Fax: (607) 753-5998
Mark Yacavone, Director of Admissions, SUNY College at Cortland, PO Box 2000, Cortland, NY 13045-0900

SUNY College at Fredonia
Fredonia, New York
www.fredonia.edu

CB member
CB code: 2539

- Public 4-year liberal arts college
- Residential campus in large town
- 4,557 degree-seeking undergraduates: 2% part-time, 56% women, 6% African American, 2% Asian American, 7% Hispanic/Latino, 2% Multiracial, non-Hispanic, 2% international
- 253 degree-seeking graduate students
- 59% of applicants admitted
- SAT or ACT (ACT writing optional), application essay required
- 65% graduate within 6 years; 35% enter graduate study

General. Founded in 1826. Regionally accredited. **Degrees:** 1,126 bachelor's awarded; master's offered. **ROTC:** Army. **Location:** 45 miles from Buffalo, 50 miles from Erie, Pennsylvania. **Calendar:** Semester, limited summer session. **Full-time faculty:** 252 total; 87% have terminal degrees, 14% minority, 45% women. **Part-time faculty:** 236 total; 16% have terminal degrees, 7% minority, 51% women. **Class size:** 55% < 20, 37% 20-39, 3% 40-49, 4% 50-99, 1% >100. **Special facilities:** Sound recording technology studio, recital hall, technology incubator, nature preserve, science center with observatory and telescope.

Freshman class profile. 5,824 applied, 3,451 admitted, 926 enrolled.

Mid 50% test scores		Rank in top quarter:	38%
SAT critical reading:	460-580	Rank in top tenth:	15%
SAT math:	460-580	End year in good standing:	79%
ACT composite:	21-26	Out-of-state:	2%
GPA 3.75 or higher:	15%	Live on campus:	93%
GPA 3.50-3.74:	22%	International:	1%
GPA 3.0-3.49:	40%	Fraternities:	7%
GPA 2.0-2.99:	23%	Sororities:	10%

Basis for selection. Academic achievement, test results, and subjects taken given priority. Counselor recommendations, resume with supporting materials important when priority credentials marginal. Audition required for acting, music, musical performance, musical theater, production design. Portfolio required for all Visual Arts and New Media programs. **Home schooled:** State high school equivalency certificate required. Letter from superintendent of school district in which the student resides, attesting to the student's completion of program of home instruction meeting requirements of Section 100.10 of the Regulations of the Commission of Education.

High school preparation. College-preparatory program required. 20 units required; 24 recommended. Required and recommended units include English 4, mathematics 3-4, social studies 4, science 3-4 (laboratory 3-4), foreign language 3 and academic electives 1.

2015-2016 Annual costs. Tuition/fees: $8,074; $17,924 out-of-state. Room/board: $12,500. Books/supplies: $1,200. Personal expenses: $898.

2015-2016 Financial aid. Need-based: 853 full-time freshmen applied for aid; 654 deemed to have need; 644 received aid. Average need met was 62%. Average scholarship/grant was $5,781; average loan $5,472. 60% of total undergraduate aid awarded as scholarships/grants, 40% as loans/jobs. **Non-need-based:** Awarded to 1,149 full-time undergraduates, including 395 freshmen. Scholarships awarded for academics, alumni affiliation, art, minority status, music/drama, state residency. **Additional information:** More than 80% of students receive financial aid, and over $2 million in merit and need-based scholarships are available to academically qualified, new and returning students each year.

Application procedures. Admission: No deadline. $50 fee, may be waived for applicants with need. Admission notification on a rolling basis beginning on or about 11/15. Must reply by May 1 or within 4 week(s) if notified thereafter. **Financial aid:** No deadline. FAFSA required. Applicants notified on a rolling basis starting 3/1; must reply by 5/1.

Academics. Special study options: Accelerated study, combined bachelor's/graduate degree, cooperative education, cross-registration, distance learning, double major, ESL, exchange student, honors, independent study, internships, student-designed major, study abroad, teacher certification program, urban semester, Washington semester. Albany semester, over 90 exchange programs within SUNY system, 13 universities in engineering. **Credit/placement by examination:** AP, CLEP, IB. 30 credit hours maximum toward bachelor's degree. **Support services:** Learning center, study skills assistance, tutoring, writing center.

Majors. Area/ethnic studies: American, women's. **Biology:** General, biochemistry, molecular genetics. **Business:** Accounting, business admin, finance, management information systems, management science, marketing. **Communications:** General, journalism, media studies, persuasive communications, public relations, radio/TV. **Communications technology:** Recording arts. **Computer sciences:** General, computer science, systems analysis. **Conservation:** Environmental science. **Education:** General, biology, chemistry, early childhood, earth science, elementary, English, foreign languages, French, mathematics, music, physics, secondary, social studies, Spanish, speech impaired. **English:** English lit. **Foreign languages:** French, Spanish. **Health services:** Audiology/speech pathology, clinical lab technology, communication disorders, music therapy. **History:** General. **Human services:** Social work. **Math:** General, applied. **Parks/recreation:** Sports admin. **Philosophy/religion:** Philosophy. **Physical sciences:** Chemistry, geology, geophysics, physics, theoretical physics. **Protective services:** Criminal justice. **Psychology:** General. **Social sciences:** Economics, political science, sociology. **Visual/performing arts:** Acting, art, art history/conservation, ceramics, dance, dramatic, drawing, music, music management, music performance, music theory/composition, musical theater, painting, photography, sculpture, studio arts, theater design.

Most popular majors. Business/marketing 13%, communications/journalism 9%, education 15%, psychology 6%, visual/performing arts 13%.

Technology on campus. 500 workstations in dormitories, library, computer center. Dormitories wired for high-speed internet access and linked to campus network. Commuter students can connect to campus network. Online course registration, online library, helpline, repair service, wireless network available.

Student life. Freshman orientation: Available, $140 fee. Preregistration for classes offered. Two-day program with students and parents held late June and early July; attendance strongly recommended. Fee includes cost of program, meals, housing, entertainment, orientation materials. **Housing:** Guaranteed on-campus for all undergraduates. Coed dorms, single-sex dorms, apartments, themed housing, wellness housing available. $50 fully refundable deposit, deadline 5/1. **Activities:** Bands, campus ministries, choral groups, dance, drama, film society, international student organizations, literary magazine, music ensembles, Model UN, musical theater, opera, radio station, student government, student newspaper, symphony orchestra, TV station, Catholic student union, black student union, Young Republicans, service fraternities and sororities, Jewish student union/Hillel, Young Democrats, Native American student association, Latinos Unidos, intervarsity Christian fellowship, Strive ministries, Inner Room, Alpha Phi Omega, Compass College ministries.

Athletics. NCAA. **Intercollegiate:** Baseball M, basketball, cheerleading W, cross-country, diving, ice hockey M, lacrosse W, soccer, softball W, swimming, tennis W, track and field, volleyball W. **Intramural:** Basketball M, fencing M, field hockey M, football (non-tackle), ice hockey M, lacrosse M, rugby, soccer, softball, ultimate frisbee M, volleyball, water polo, wrestling M. **Team name:** Blue Devils.

Student services. Alcohol/substance abuse counseling, chaplain/spiritual director, career counseling, services for economically disadvantaged, student employment services, financial aid counseling, health services, legal services, minority student services, on-campus daycare, personal counseling, placement for graduates, veterans' counselor. **Physically disabled:** Services for visually, speech, hearing impaired.

Contact. E-mail: admissions@fredonia.edu
Phone: (716) 673-3251 Toll-free number: (800) 252-1212
Fax: (716) 673-3249
Cory Bezek, Director of Admissions, SUNY College at Fredonia, 280 Central Avenue, Fenner House, Fredonia, NY 14063-1136

SUNY College at Geneseo

Geneseo, New York	CB member
www.geneseo.edu	CB code: 2540

▶ Public 4-year liberal arts and teachers college
▶ Residential campus in small town
▶ 5,548 degree-seeking undergraduates: 2% part-time, 60% women, 3% African American, 6% Asian American, 7% Hispanic/Latino, 3% Multi-racial, non-Hispanic, 2% international
▶ 110 degree-seeking graduate students
▶ 73% of applicants admitted
▶ SAT or ACT (ACT writing optional), application essay required
▶ 82% graduate within 6 years; 33% enter graduate study

General. Founded in 1871. Regionally accredited. **Degrees:** 1,204 bachelor's awarded; master's offered. **ROTC:** Army, Air Force. **Location:** 30 miles from Rochester. **Calendar:** Semester, limited summer session. **Full-time faculty:** 250 total; 88% have terminal degrees, 15% minority, 43% women. **Part-time faculty:** 103 total; 28% have terminal degrees, 16% minority, 53% women. **Class size:** 29% < 20, 51% 20-39, 9% 40-49, 8% 50-99, 3% >100. **Special facilities:** Nuclear accelerator, planetarium, 4 theaters, ice arena, arboretum, wave tank.

Freshman class profile. 9,118 applied, 6,632 admitted, 1,330 enrolled.

Mid 50% test scores		Rank in top quarter:	74%
SAT critical reading:	550-640	Rank in top tenth:	36%
SAT math:	550-650	End year in good standing:	86%
ACT composite:	25-29	Return as sophomores:	89%
GPA 3.75 or higher:	42%	Out-of-state:	2%
GPA 3.50-3.74:	35%	Live on campus:	98%
GPA 3.0-3.49:	22%	International:	2%
GPA 2.0-2.99:	1%		

Basis for selection. Rigor of high school preparation, high school GPA, class rank, test scores, school and community activities, special talent, leadership, personal essay important. Special consideration given to minority applicants, children and grandchildren of alumni. Audition required for dramatic arts, music programs; portfolio required for art programs. **Home schooled:** Statement describing home school structure and mission, transcript of courses and grades, state high school equivalency certificate, letter of recommendation (nonparent) required.

High school preparation. College-preparatory program recommended. 20 units recommended. Recommended units include English 4, mathematics 4, social studies 4, science 4 and foreign language 4. Music, art also recommended. 4 math required for computer science and business majors.

2015-2016 Annual costs. Tuition/fees: $8,113; $17,963 out-of-state. Room/board: $11,980. Books/supplies: $1,000. Personal expenses: $1,500.

2015-2016 Financial aid. Need-based: 1,139 full-time freshmen applied for aid; 672 deemed to have need; 672 received aid. Average need met was 60%. Average scholarship/grant was $6,556; average loan $4,018. 55% of total undergraduate aid awarded as scholarships/grants, 45% as loans/jobs. **Non-need-based:** Awarded to 984 full-time undergraduates, including 212 freshmen. Scholarships awarded for academics, art, leadership, minority status, music/drama, religious affiliation, state residency.

Application procedures. Admission: Closing date 1/1 (postmark date). $50 fee, may be waived for applicants with need. Admission notification by 3/1. Must reply by May 1 or within 4 week(s) if notified thereafter. **Financial aid:** Closing date 2/15. FAFSA required. Applicants notified on a rolling basis starting 3/15; must reply by 5/1.

Academics. Special study options: Combined bachelor's/graduate degree, cross-registration, double major, dual enrollment of high school students, ESL, honors, independent study, internships, study abroad, teacher certification program, Washington semester. Albany semester, Washington semester, 3-2 engineering, 3-3 engineering, 4-1 MBA, 3-4 dentistry, 3-4 optometry,

3-4 osteopathic medicine, 3-2 or 3-1 nursing, 3-3 physical therapy, pre-med and pre-law advisory program. **Credit/placement by examination:** AP, CLEP, IB, SAT, ACT, institutional tests. 30 credit hours maximum toward bachelor's degree. **Support services:** Learning center, pre-admission summer program, reduced course load, study skills assistance, tutoring, writing center.

Majors. Area/ethnic studies: African-American, American. **Biology:** General, biochemistry, biophysics, neuroscience. **Business:** General, accounting, business admin. **Communications:** Communications/speech/rhetoric. **Education:** Biology, chemistry, early childhood, elementary, English, foreign languages, French, mathematics, physics, science, social studies, Spanish, special ed. **English:** English lit. **Foreign languages:** Comparative lit, French, Spanish. **History:** General. **Math:** General. **Philosophy/religion:** Philosophy. **Physical sciences:** Chemistry, geochemistry, geology, geophysics, physics. **Psychology:** General. **Social sciences:** Anthropology, economics, geography, international relations, political science, sociology. **Visual/performing arts:** Art history/conservation, dramatic, music performance.

Most popular majors. Biology 13%, business/marketing 13%, communications/journalism 7%, education 10%, English 8%, psychology 14%, social sciences 17%.

Technology on campus. PC or laptop required. 361 workstations in dormitories, library, computer center, student center. Dormitories wired for high-speed internet access and linked to campus network. Commuter students can connect to campus network. Online course registration, helpline, student web hosting, wireless network available.

Student life. Freshman orientation: Available, $150 fee. Preregistration for classes offered. Held for five sessions, 2 days each, during June and July. **Housing:** Guaranteed on-campus for all undergraduates. Coed dorms, special housing for disabled, themed housing available. $150 fully refundable deposit, deadline 5/1. Town houses and special interest housing available. **Activities:** Bands, campus ministries, choral groups, dance, drama, international student organizations, literary magazine, music ensembles, Model UN, musical theater, radio station, student government, student newspaper, symphony orchestra, TV station, 197 organizations and clubs, interfaith center.

Athletics. NCAA. **Intercollegiate:** Basketball, cross-country, diving, equestrian W, field hockey W, ice hockey M, lacrosse, soccer, softball W, swimming, tennis W, track and field, volleyball W. **Intramural:** Badminton, basketball, football (non-tackle), skiing, soccer M. **Team name:** Blue Knights, Lady Knights.

Student services. Alcohol/substance abuse counseling, career counseling, services for economically disadvantaged, student employment services, financial aid counseling, health services, legal services, minority student services, personal counseling, placement for graduates, veterans' counselor, women's services. **Physically disabled:** Services for visually, speech, hearing impaired.

Contact. E-mail: admissions@geneseo.edu
Phone: (585) 245-5571 Toll-free number: (866) 245-5211
Fax: (585) 245-5550
Kevin Reed, Director Of Admissions, SUNY College at Geneseo, 1 College Circle, Geneseo, NY 14454-1401

SUNY College at New Paltz

New Paltz, New York	CB member
www.newpaltz.edu	CB code: 2541

▶ Public 4-year liberal arts college
▶ Residential campus in large town
▶ 6,498 degree-seeking undergraduates: 6% part-time, 62% women, 6% African American, 6% Asian American, 17% Hispanic/Latino, 2% Multi-racial, non-Hispanic, 2% international
▶ 984 degree-seeking graduate students
▶ 42% of applicants admitted
▶ SAT or ACT (ACT writing optional), application essay required
▶ 73% graduate within 6 years; 21% enter graduate study

General. Founded in 1828. Regionally accredited. **Degrees:** 1,826 bachelor's awarded; master's offered. **Location:** 65 miles from Albany, 96 miles from New York City. **Calendar:** Semester, extensive summer session. **Full-time faculty:** 360 total; 82% have terminal degrees, 18% minority, 51% women. **Part-time faculty:** 304 total; 29% have terminal degrees, 12% minority, 58% women. **Class size:** 39% < 20, 55% 20-39, 4% 40-49, 2% 50-99, less than 1% >100. **Special facilities:** 3D printing initiative, Samuel Dorsky Museum of Art, 3 theaters, recital hall, speech and hearing clinical center, music therapy training center, observatory, planetarium.

Freshman class profile. 14,655 applied, 6,084 admitted, 1,079 enrolled.

Mid 50% test scores		GPA 2.0-2.99:	9%
SAT critical reading:	510-610	Rank in top quarter:	74%
SAT math:	520-600	Rank in top tenth:	30%
SAT writing:	500-600	End year in good standing:	90%
ACT composite:	23-27	Return as sophomores:	89%
GPA 3.75 or higher:	37%	Out-of-state:	4%
GPA 3.50-3.74:	27%	Live on campus:	92%
GPA 3.0-3.49:	27%	International:	2%

Basis for selection. Secondary school curriculum and achievement, standardized test scores most important. Applicants to all fine & performing arts programs must submit a portfolio or participate in an audition/interview after acceptance. Applicants selected to the 7-year medical program or 7-year optometry program must participate in an on-campus interview. One letter of recommendation required; audition required for music, music therapy, theater arts programs; portfolio required for art education, scenography, studio art, and visual arts programs. **Home schooled:** Must submit all data as required by NYS Commissioner of Education's regulations (Section 100.10).

High school preparation. College-preparatory program required. 17 units required; 21 recommended. Required and recommended units include English 4, mathematics 3-4, social studies 4, history 1, science 3-4 (laboratory 3-4) and foreign language 2-4.

2015-2016 Annual costs. Tuition/fees: $7,760; $17,610 out-of-state. Room/board: $11,480. Books/supplies: $1,600. Personal expenses: $900.

2015-2016 Financial aid. All financial aid based on need. 959 full-time freshmen applied for aid; 655 deemed to have need; 646 received aid. Average need met was 55%. Average scholarship/grant was $5,194; average loan $3,299. 56% of total undergraduate aid awarded as scholarships/grants, 44% as loans/jobs.

Application procedures. Admission: Closing date 4/1 (receipt date). $50 fee, may be waived for applicants with need. Admission notification on a rolling basis beginning on or about 1/15. Must reply by May 1 or within 2 week(s) if notified thereafter. Housing deposit refundable if requested by July 1. **Financial aid:** Priority date 3/15; no closing date. FAFSA required. Applicants notified by 3/30; Applicants notified on a rolling basis starting 4/1.

Academics. Special study options: Accelerated study, combined bachelor's/graduate degree, cross-registration, distance learning, double major, dual enrollment of high school students, ESL, honors, independent study, internships, New York semester, student-designed major, study abroad, teacher certification program, United Nations semester. **Credit/placement by examination:** AP, CLEP, IB, SAT, ACT, institutional tests. 30 credit hours maximum toward bachelor's degree. **Support services:** Learning center, reduced course load, remedial instruction, study skills assistance, tutoring, writing center.

Majors. Area/ethnic studies: African-American, Asian, Latin American, women's. **Biology:** General, biochemistry. **Business:** General, accounting, business admin, finance, international. **Communications:** Communications/speech/rhetoric, digital media, journalism, public relations. **Computer sciences:** General. **Education:** Art, biology, chemistry, elementary, English, French, learning disabled, mathematics, physics, science, social studies, Spanish. **Engineering:** Computer, electrical. **English:** English lit. **Foreign languages:** French, German, Spanish. **Health services:** Communication disorders. **History:** General. **Liberal arts:** Arts/sciences. **Math:** General. **Philosophy/religion:** Philosophy. **Physical sciences:** Astronomy, chemistry, geochemistry, geology, physics. **Psychology:** General. **Social sciences:** Anthropology, economics, geography, international relations, political science, sociology. **Visual/performing arts:** General, art history/conservation, ceramics, dramatic, graphic design, metal/jewelry, music, painting, photography, printmaking, sculpture.

Most popular majors. Business/marketing 14%, communications/journalism 13%, education 11%, English 6%, psychology 9%, social sciences 14%, visual/performing arts 11%.

Technology on campus. 950 workstations in dormitories, library, computer center, student center. Dormitories wired for high-speed internet access and linked to campus network. Commuter students can connect to campus network. Online course registration, online library, helpline, student web hosting, wireless network available.

Student life. Freshman orientation: Available, $215 fee. Preregistration for classes offered. Three-day academic and transition program in the summer. **Policies:** Freshmen not permitted cars on campus. **Housing:** Guaranteed on-campus for freshmen. Coed dorms, special housing for disabled, gender-neutral housing, themed housing, wellness housing available. $100 fully refundable deposit. First-year initiative, honors housing, art program housing, scholars mentorship program housing, East-West living/learning community. **Activities:** Bands, campus ministries, choral groups, dance, drama, international student organizations, literary magazine, music ensembles, Model UN, musical theater, opera, radio station, student government, student newspaper, symphony orchestra, TV station, black student union, queer student union, Asian student association, Latin American student union, Hillel, Student Christian Center, Muslim student association, Students for Sustainable Agriculture, recycling club, New Paltz Feminist Collective.

Athletics. NCAA. Intercollegiate: Baseball M, basketball, cross-country, field hockey W, lacrosse W, soccer, softball W, swimming, tennis W, volleyball. **Intramural:** Basketball, handball, lacrosse W, racquetball, soccer, softball, tennis, volleyball, water polo. **Team name:** Hawks.

Student services. Alcohol/substance abuse counseling, chaplain/spiritual director, career counseling, services for economically disadvantaged, student employment services, financial aid counseling, health services, minority student services, on-campus daycare, personal counseling, placement for graduates, veterans' counselor, women's services. **Physically disabled:** Services for visually, speech, hearing impaired.

Contact. E-mail: admissions@newpaltz.edu
Phone: (845) 257-3200 Toll-free number: (877) 696-7411
Fax: (845) 257-3209
Kimberly Strano, Director of Freshmen Admissions, SUNY College at New Paltz, 100 Hawk Drive, New Paltz, NY 12561-2443

SUNY College at Old Westbury
Old Westbury, New York
www.oldwestbury.edu

CB member
CB code: 2866

- Public 4-year business and liberal arts college
- Commuter campus in small city
- 3,998 degree-seeking undergraduates: 13% part-time, 58% women, 30% African American, 10% Asian American, 22% Hispanic/Latino, 3% Multi-racial, non-Hispanic, 1% international
- 212 degree-seeking graduate students
- 50% of applicants admitted
- SAT or ACT (ACT writing recommended), application essay required
- 40% graduate within 6 years

General. Founded in 1965. Regionally accredited. Curricular focus on interdisciplinary and multicultural academic programs. **Degrees:** 972 bachelor's awarded; master's offered. **ROTC:** Army, Air Force. **Location:** 25 miles from New York City. **Calendar:** Semester, extensive summer session. **Full-time faculty:** 166 total; 87% have terminal degrees, 40% minority, 57% women. **Part-time faculty:** 185 total; 29% have terminal degrees, 22% minority, 55% women. **Class size:** 34% < 20, 65% 20-39, less than 1% 40-49, less than 1% 50-99. **Special facilities:** Language lab, performing arts theater, recital hall, science laboratories, athletic center, writing center, math labs.

Freshman class profile. 4,474 applied, 2,241 admitted, 381 enrolled.

Mid 50% test scores		GPA 2.0-2.99:	39%
SAT critical reading:	460-530	Return as sophomores:	81%
SAT math:	450-550	Out-of-state:	1%
SAT writing:	430-510	Live on campus:	42%
GPA 3.75 or higher:	9%	International:	1%
GPA 3.50-3.74:	12%	Fraternities:	1%
GPA 3.0-3.49:	40%	Sororities:	1%

Basis for selection. High school GPA, SAT scores, letters of recommendation, interview, personal essay important. SAT Subject Tests recommended. Essay and interview recommended for academically weak students. **Home schooled:** Statement describing home school structure and mission required. Letter from superintendent of local school district verifying home schooling equivalent to high school curriculum required.

High school preparation. College-preparatory program recommended. 18 units required; 21 recommended. Required and recommended units include English 4, mathematics 3, social studies 3-4, science 3 (laboratory 2-3), foreign language 1-3, computer science 1, visual/performing arts 1, academic electives 3.5. Health and physical education.

2015-2016 Annual costs. Tuition/fees: $7,643; $17,493 out-of-state. Room/board: $10,390. Books/supplies: $2,500. Personal expenses: $1,960.

2015-2016 Financial aid. Need-based: 368 full-time freshmen applied for aid; 346 deemed to have need; 298 received aid. Average need met was 55%. Average scholarship/grant was $8,064; average loan $3,519. 42% of total undergraduate aid awarded as scholarships/grants, 58% as loans/jobs. **Non-need-based:** Awarded to 69 full-time undergraduates, including 19 freshmen. Scholarships awarded for academics, alumni affiliation, state residency.

Application procedures. Admission: Priority date 12/1; no deadline. $50 fee, may be waived for applicants with need. Admission notification on a rolling basis beginning on or about 11/15. Must reply by May 1 or within 2 week(s) if notified thereafter. **Financial aid:** Closing date 4/1. FAFSA, institutional form required. Applicants notified on a rolling basis starting 4/15; must reply within 2 week(s) of notification.

Academics. All freshmen enroll in First-Year Experience program. **Special study options:** Combined bachelor's/graduate degree, cross-registration, distance learning, double major, exchange student, honors, independent study, internships, liberal arts/career combination, study abroad, teacher certification program, Washington semester. Minority access to research centers, Minority biomedical research. **Credit/placement by examination:** AP, CLEP, IB, institutional tests. 30 credit hours maximum toward bachelor's degree. Each department has own policy for accepting credit by examination in fulfillment of departmental requirements. 8 credits awarded for minimum of 2 years of active duty in any branch of military service. Veterans may also apply for credit based on specific formal courses of instruction given by military services. **Support services:** Learning center, pre-admission summer program, reduced course load, remedial instruction, study skills assistance, tutoring, writing center.

Honors college/program. High school GPA 90 or above, SAT scores 1100 or higher. The Honors curriculum will be comprised of 24 credits: First-year Seminar; Gen Ed Linked Course; English Composition 2; Internship or Study Abroad or Directed Research (Independent Study) or Civic Engagement Honors Course; Major Course Requirement with Research Component and Capstone Honors Course.

Majors. Area/ethnic studies: American. **Biology:** General, biochemistry. **Business:** Accounting, business admin, finance, labor relations, marketing. **Communications:** Communications/speech/rhetoric. **Computer sciences:** General, information systems. **Education:** Bilingual, biology, chemistry, elementary, mathematics, middle, science, secondary, social studies, Spanish, special ed. **English:** English lit. **Foreign languages:** Comparative lit, Spanish. **Liberal arts:** Arts/sciences, humanities. **Math:** General. **Philosophy/religion:** Philosophy. **Physical sciences:** Chemistry. **Psychology:** General. **Social sciences:** General, criminology, sociology. **Visual/performing arts:** General.

Most popular majors. Business/marketing 26%, communications/journalism 8%, education 9%, psychology 16%, social sciences 23%.

Technology on campus. 640 workstations in library, computer center, student center. Dormitories wired for high-speed internet access and linked to campus network. Commuter students can connect to campus network. Online course registration, online library, helpline, wireless network available.

Student life. Freshman orientation: Mandatory, $150 fee. Preregistration for classes offered. Held prior to fall term for 2 days and 1 night; 1-day parent orientation. Three 1-day sessions held prior to spring term ($50). **Housing:** Guaranteed on-campus for all undergraduates. Coed dorms, wellness housing available. $50 fully refundable deposit, deadline 5/1. Honors wing available. **Activities:** Campus ministries, choral groups, dance, drama, film society, international student organizations, radio station, student government, student newspaper, women's center, Alianza Latina, African People's Organization, Big Brother/Big Sister club, Asian club, Access for All, Council for Unity, Shekinah Chorale.

Athletics. NCAA. **Intercollegiate:** Baseball M, basketball, cross-country, golf M, lacrosse W, soccer, softball W, swimming, volleyball W. **Intramural:** Badminton, basketball, racquetball, soccer, softball W, squash, ultimate frisbee, volleyball, weight lifting. **Team name:** Panthers.

Student services. Alcohol/substance abuse counseling, chaplain/spiritual director, career counseling, services for economically disadvantaged, student employment services, financial aid counseling, health services, on-campus daycare, personal counseling, women's services. **Physically disabled:** Services for visually, hearing impaired.

Contact. E-mail: enroll@oldwestbury.edu
Phone: (516) 876-3073 Fax: (516) 876-3307
Mary Marquez Bell, Vice President of Enrollment Services, SUNY College at Old Westbury, Box 307, Old Westbury, NY 11568-0307

SUNY College at Oneonta
Oneonta, New York
www.oneonta.edu/home/default.asp

CB member
CB code: 2542

- Public 4-year liberal arts college
- Residential campus in large town
- 5,825 degree-seeking undergraduates: 1% part-time, 60% women, 3% African American, 2% Asian American, 11% Hispanic/Latino, 2% Multiracial, non-Hispanic, 1% international

- 254 degree-seeking graduate students
- 40% of applicants admitted
- SAT or ACT (ACT writing optional), application essay required
- 72% graduate within 6 years

General. Founded in 1887. Regionally accredited. **Degrees:** 1,372 bachelor's awarded; master's offered. **Location:** 75 miles from Albany, 175 miles from New York City. **Calendar:** Semester, extensive summer session. **Full-time faculty:** 258 total; 86% have terminal degrees, 20% minority, 47% women. **Part-time faculty:** 172 total; 19% have terminal degrees, 6% minority, 56% women. **Class size:** 30% < 20, 53% 20-39, 11% 40-49, 6% 50-99, less than 1% >100. **Special facilities:** Digital planetarium, observatory, biological field station in Cooperstown, science discovery center, music recording studio with tunable walls, computer art lab, DNA computing and genomics lab, Center for Social Responsibility and Community.

Freshman class profile. 11,427 applied, 4,567 admitted, 1,130 enrolled.

Mid 50% test scores			
SAT critical reading:	490-580	GPA 3.0-3.49:	43%
SAT math:	510-590	Return as sophomores:	86%
ACT composite:	22-25	Out-of-state:	2%
GPA 3.75 or higher:	.32%	Live on campus:	98%
GPA 3.50-3.74:	25%	International:	1%

Basis for selection. School achievement record, curriculum, test scores most important. Personal experiences, motivations, awards, honors and recommendations considered. High school writing sample can be submitted in place of essay; interview recommended. **Home schooled:** Statement describing home school structure and mission, transcript of courses and grades, state high school equivalency certificate, interview, letter of recommendation (nonparent) required.

High school preparation. College-preparatory program required. 19 units required. Required and recommended units include English 4, mathematics 4, social studies 4, science 4 (laboratory 4) and foreign language 3-4.

2015-2016 Annual costs. Tuition/fees: $7,870; $17,720 out-of-state. Room/board: $11,842. Books/supplies: $1,200. Personal expenses: $1,100.

Financial aid. Non-need-based: Scholarships awarded for academics, leadership, minority status, music/drama, state residency.

Application procedures. Admission: No deadline. $50 fee, may be waived for applicants with need. Admission notification on a rolling basis beginning on or about 1/1. Must reply by May 1 or within 4 week(s) if notified thereafter. **Financial aid:** Priority date 3/1; no closing date. FAFSA required. Applicants notified on a rolling basis starting 3/1.

Academics. Special study options: Combined bachelor's/graduate degree, cross-registration, distance learning, double major, ESL, independent study, internships, liberal arts/career combination, New York semester, study abroad, teacher certification program, Washington semester. 3-1 program in fashion with Fashion Institute of Technology; 3-2 program in engineering with Alfred University, Clarkson University, Polytechnic Institute of New York, Rensselaer Polytechnic Institute, Binghamton University, University at Buffalo, Syracuse University; 2-2 programs in cardiovascular perfusion, medical imaging sciences, medical technology, radiation therapy and respiratory care with SUNY Upstate Medical University, 4-1 MBA program with Clarkson University, Rochester Institute of Technology, Union College. **Credit/placement by examination:** AP, CLEP, IB, SAT, ACT. **Support services:** Learning center, reduced course load, remedial instruction, study skills assistance, tutoring, writing center.

Majors. Area/ethnic studies: African-American, Chicano/Hispanic-American/Latino. **Biology:** General, biochemistry, cellular/molecular, ecology, human/medical genetics. **Business:** Accounting, accounting/finance, fashion, managerial economics. **Communications:** General, media studies. **Computer sciences:** Computer science. **Conservation:** Environmental science. **Education:** Biology, chemistry, early childhood, earth science, elementary, English, family/consumer sciences, French, mathematics, multi-level teacher, physics, social studies, Spanish. **English:** English lit. **Foreign languages:** French, Spanish. **History:** General. **Math:** General, statistics. **Philosophy/religion:** Philosophy. **Physical sciences:** Chemistry, geology, hydrology, meteorology, physics. **Protective services:** Criminal justice. **Psychology:** General. **Social sciences:** Anthropology, economics, geography, GIS/cartography, international economic development, international relations, political science, sociology. **Visual/performing arts:** Art history/conservation, design, digital arts, dramatic, drawing, music, music management, painting, photography, sculpture, studio arts. **Work/family studies:** General, clothing/textiles, family studies, food/nutrition, institutional food production.

Most popular majors. Biology 6%, business/marketing 9%, communications/journalism 11%, education 16%, family/consumer sciences 11%, psychology 8%, security/protective services 6%, social sciences 6%, visual/performing arts 12%.

Technology on campus. Dormitories wired for high-speed internet access and linked to campus network. Commuter students can connect to campus network. Online course registration, online library, helpline, wireless network available.

Student life. Freshman orientation: Available, $100 fee. Preregistration for classes offered. **Policies:** Freshmen not permitted cars on campus. **Housing:** Guaranteed on-campus for freshmen. Coed dorms, wellness housing available. $100 fully refundable deposit, deadline 5/1. **Activities:** Bands, campus ministries, choral groups, dance, drama, film society, international student organizations, literary magazine, music ensembles, Model UN, musical theater, opera, radio station, student government, student newspaper, symphony orchestra, TV station, Campus Ambassadors, Newman House, Hillel, HOLA Hispanic/Latino organization, Korean cultural club, Muslim student association, Students of Color Coalition, international student organization, Democracy Matters, Center for Social Responsibility and Community.

Athletics. NCAA. **Intercollegiate:** Baseball M, basketball, cross-country, field hockey W, lacrosse, soccer, softball W, swimming, tennis, track and field, volleyball W, wrestling M. **Intramural:** Basketball, football (non-tackle) W, soccer, softball, volleyball. **Team name:** Red Dragons.

Student services. Adult student services, alcohol/substance abuse counseling, career counseling, services for economically disadvantaged, student employment services, financial aid counseling, health services, minority student services, on-campus daycare, personal counseling, placement for graduates, women's services. **Physically disabled:** Services for visually, speech, hearing impaired.

Contact. E-mail: admissions@oneonta.edu
Phone: (607) 436-2524 Toll-free number: (800) 786-9123
Fax: (607) 436-3074
Karen Brown, Director of Admissions, SUNY College at Oneonta, Admissions Office, 116 Alumni Hall, Oneonta, NY 13820-4016

SUNY College at Oswego

Oswego, New York   **CB member**
www.oswego.edu   **CB code: 2543**

- Public 4-year university
- Residential campus in large town
- 7,046 degree-seeking undergraduates: 4% part-time, 50% women, 7% African American, 3% Asian American, 10% Hispanic/Latino, 2% Multiracial, non-Hispanic, 1% international
- 693 degree-seeking graduate students
- 51% of applicants admitted
- SAT or ACT (ACT writing optional), application essay required
- 66% graduate within 6 years

General. Founded in 1861. Regionally accredited. Only students in the School of Business are required to have a personal or laptop computer. **Degrees:** 1,710 bachelor's awarded; master's offered. **ROTC:** Army, Air Force. **Location:** 35 miles from Syracuse, 65 miles from Rochester. **Calendar:** Semester, limited summer session. **Full-time faculty:** 345 total; 88% have terminal degrees, 15% minority, 47% women. **Part-time faculty:** 255 total; 22% have terminal degrees, 6% minority, 52% women. **Class size:** 56% < 20, 30% 20-39, 9% 40-49, 4% 50-99, 2% >100. **Special facilities:** Weather facsimile machine, planetarium, cross-country ski facilities, advanced technology classrooms, biological field station.

Freshman class profile. 10,885 applied, 5,552 admitted, 1,490 enrolled.

Mid 50% test scores		Rank in top quarter:	52%
SAT critical reading:	500-590	Rank in top tenth:	14%
SAT math:	510-600	Return as sophomores:	80%
ACT composite:	22-26	Out-of-state:	4%
GPA 3.75 or higher:	29%	Live on campus:	96%
GPA 3.50-3.74:	20%	International:	1%
GPA 3.0-3.49:	42%	Fraternities:	6%
GPA 2.0-2.99:	9%	Sororities:	5%

Basis for selection. High school GPA and curriculum most important, followed by test scores, supplemental portion of application and letters of recommendation. Special talents considered. Applicants recommended to send both SAT and ACT; higher score accepted. Supplemental information and/or advanced credits supplant test scores for those out of High School for more than 3 years or for special consideration. Interview available for any who would like one; portfolio required for graphic design and fine arts (BFA). **Home schooled:** State high school equivalency certificate required. **Learning Disabled:** Advised to contact Office of Learning Services and/or Disability Services with copy of IEP if applicable. IEP is not considered, however, during admission process.

High school preparation. College-preparatory program required. 18 units required; 20 recommended. Required and recommended units include English 4, mathematics 3-4, social studies 4, science 3-4 (laboratory 2-3) and foreign language 2-4. Combined minimum of 7 units of college prep math and science recommended.

2015-2016 Annual costs. Tuition/fees: $7,934; $17,784 out-of-state. Room/board: $12,990. Books/supplies: $800. Personal expenses: $800.

2015-2016 Financial aid. Need-based: 1,353 full-time freshmen applied for aid; 1,026 deemed to have need; 1,018 received aid. Average need met was 86%. Average scholarship/grant was $8,121; average loan $4,169. 44% of total undergraduate aid awarded as scholarships/grants, 56% as loans/jobs. **Non-need-based:** Awarded to 2,411 full-time undergraduates, including 1,032 freshmen. Scholarships awarded for academics, state residency.

Application procedures. Admission: Priority date 1/15; no deadline. $50 fee, may be waived for applicants with need. Admission notification on a rolling basis beginning on or about 1/15. Must reply by May 1 or within 4 week(s) if notified thereafter. **Financial aid:** Priority date 2/15; no closing date. FAFSA required. Applicants notified on a rolling basis starting 2/15; must reply by 5/1 or within 3 week(s) of notification.

Academics. Special study options: Accelerated study, combined bachelor's/graduate degree, cooperative education, cross-registration, distance learning, double major, dual enrollment of high school students, ESL, exchange student, external degree, honors, independent study, internships, liberal arts/career combination, study abroad, teacher certification program, Washington semester. **Credit/placement by examination:** AP, CLEP, IB, SAT, institutional tests. 30 credit hours maximum toward bachelor's degree. **Support services:** Learning center, pre-admission summer program, reduced course load, remedial instruction, study skills assistance, tutoring, writing center.

Honors college/program. Approximately 80 freshmen enroll annually, distinct program of general education classes held in small class settings. Must meet or come very close to meeting requirements if Presidential Scholarship.

Majors. Area/ethnic studies: American, women's. **Biology:** General, zoology. **Business:** Accounting, business admin, finance, human resources, management science. **Communications:** Broadcast journalism, communications/speech/rhetoric, journalism, public relations. **Computer sciences:** Computer science, information systems. **Education:** Agricultural, biology, business, chemistry, elementary, English, French, German, health occupations, history, mathematics, physics, science, secondary, social studies, Spanish, technology/industrial arts, trade/industrial, voc/tech. **Engineering:** Electrical, software. **English:** English lit. **Foreign languages:** French, German, linguistics, Spanish. **Health services:** Medical radiologic technology/radiation therapy, perfusion technology, public health ed. **History:** General. **Math:** General, applied. **Philosophy/religion:** Philosophy. **Physical sciences:** Chemistry, geochemistry, geology, meteorology, physics. **Psychology:** General. **Social sciences:** Anthropology, econometrics, economics, political science, sociology. **Visual/performing arts:** Art, commercial/advertising art, dramatic, music. **Work/family studies:** Child development.

Most popular majors. Biology 8%, business/marketing 25%, communications/journalism 14%, education 13%, psychology 10%, security/protective services 6%, visual/performing arts 7%.

Technology on campus. 900 workstations in dormitories, library, computer center, student center. Dormitories wired for high-speed internet access and linked to campus network. Commuter students can connect to campus network. Online course registration, online library, helpline, student web hosting, wireless network available.

Student life. Freshman orientation: Mandatory, $196 fee. Preregistration for classes offered. Held over two days. **Housing:** Guaranteed on-campus for all undergraduates. Coed dorms, themed housing, wellness housing available. $100 fully refundable deposit, deadline 5/1. Pets allowed in dorm rooms. Global living and learning center, suites for upperclassmen, nontraditional student housing, first-year experience residence hall for incoming freshmen only, housing for 21 and over single suites available. **Activities:** Bands, choral groups, dance, drama, film society, international student organizations, literary magazine, music ensembles, musical theater, radio station, student government, student newspaper, symphony orchestra, TV station, Christian, Jewish, Catholic, and Baptist groups, Black student union, Latin student union, Caribbean student association, international student association, Native American Heritage Association, Students Educating Everyone About Disabilities.

Athletics. NCAA. **Intercollegiate:** Baseball M, basketball, cross-country, diving, field hockey W, golf M, ice hockey, lacrosse, soccer, softball W, swimming, tennis, track and field, volleyball W, wrestling M. **Intramural:** Badminton, basketball, football (non-tackle), golf, skiing, soccer, softball, swimming, table tennis, tennis, triathlon, volleyball, water polo. **Team name:** Lakers.

Student services. Adult student services, alcohol/substance abuse counseling, career counseling, services for economically disadvantaged, student employment services, financial aid counseling, health services, minority student services, on-campus daycare, personal counseling, placement for graduates, veterans' counselor, women's services. **Physically disabled:** Services for visually, speech, hearing impaired.

Contact. E-mail: admiss@oswego.edu
Phone: (315) 312-2250 Fax: (315) 312-3260
Daniel Griffin, Director of Admissions, SUNY College at Oswego, 229 Sheldon Hall, Oswego, NY 13126-3599

SUNY College at Plattsburgh
Plattsburgh, New York — **CB member**
www.plattsburgh.edu — **CB code: 2544**

- Public 4-year liberal arts and teachers college
- Residential campus in large town
- 5,272 degree-seeking undergraduates: 7% part-time, 56% women, 7% African American, 3% Asian American, 10% Hispanic/Latino, 2% Multiracial, non-Hispanic, 6% international
- 320 degree-seeking graduate students
- 50% of applicants admitted
- SAT or ACT (ACT writing optional), application essay required
- 65% graduate within 6 years

General. Founded in 1889. Regionally accredited. Residential satellite campus for biotechnology and environmental science majors. **Degrees:** 1,388 bachelor's awarded; master's offered. **ROTC:** Army. **Location:** 60 miles from Montreal, Canada, 30 miles from Burlington, Vermont. **Calendar:** Semester, extensive summer session. **Full-time faculty:** 283 total; 81% have terminal degrees, 10% minority, 45% women. **Part-time faculty:** 172 total; 26% have terminal degrees, 2% minority, 58% women. **Class size:** 42% < 20, 47% 20-39, 6% 40-49, 4% 50-99, less than 1% >100. **Special facilities:** Center for art, music and theater; wilderness and agricultural tract, planetarium, NMR spectrophotometer, computer-operated spectrophotometer, liquid scintillation counter, auditory research labs, speech and hearing clinic, Alzheimer's disease assistance center, program for children with Asperger's, literacy lab, traumatic brain injury lab, nursing skills lab with bedside computers and a high-fidelity simulator.

Freshman class profile. 8,261 applied, 4,105 admitted, 963 enrolled.

Mid 50% test scores			
SAT critical reading:	480-600	Rank in top quarter:	39%
SAT math:	500-600	Rank in top tenth:	11%
ACT composite:	21-25	Return as sophomores:	83%
GPA 3.75 or higher:	6%	Out-of-state:	6%
GPA 3.50-3.74:	19%	Live on campus:	99%
GPA 3.0-3.49:	45%	International:	6%
GPA 2.0-2.99:	30%	Fraternities:	5%
		Sororities:	4%

Basis for selection. Curriculum, high school GPA, class rank, test scores most important. Trend of grades, school and community activities, personal interview, and recommendations also considered. Educational opportunity program for academically and financially disadvantaged students. International applicants can submit TOEFL/IELTS in lieu of SAT/ACT. Interview recommended; portfolio required for bachelor of fine arts programs. **Home schooled:** Letter of recommendation (nonparent) required. Letter from superintendent of the school district in which the student resides attesting to the completion of program of home instruction meeting the requirements of the state of residence.

High school preparation. College-preparatory program required. 14 units required; 21 recommended. Required and recommended units include English 4, mathematics 3-4, social studies 3, history 1, science 3-4, foreign language 3 and academic electives 2.

2015-2016 Annual costs. Tuition/fees: $7,854; $17,704 out-of-state. Room/board: $11,270. Books/supplies: $1,220. Personal expenses: $1,810.

2014-2015 Financial aid. Need-based: 920 full-time freshmen applied for aid; 670 deemed to have need; 648 received aid. Average need met was 79%. Average scholarship/grant was $7,906; average loan $6,425. 47% of total undergraduate aid awarded as scholarships/grants, 53% as loans/jobs. **Non-need-based:** Awarded to 1,566 full-time undergraduates, including 407 freshmen. Scholarships awarded for academics, alumni affiliation, art, leadership, minority status, music/drama, state residency.

Application procedures. Admission: $50 fee, may be waived for applicants with need. Admission notification on a rolling basis beginning on or about 1/15. Must reply by May 1 or within 4 week(s) if notified thereafter.

Financial aid: Priority date 2/15; no closing date. FAFSA required. Applicants notified on a rolling basis starting 3/1; must reply by 5/1.

Academics. Credit for military experience, pass/fail option. **Special study options:** Accelerated study, combined bachelor's/graduate degree, cross-registration, distance learning, double major, dual enrollment of high school students, ESL, exchange student, honors, independent study, internships, student-designed major, study abroad, teacher certification program, Washington semester. Semester and academic year programs in Canada, study opportunities abroad in Australia, Chile, China, England, Italy, Mexico, Spain, and Switzerland. Students may also apply to more than 400 programs in more than 60 countries through other SUNY institutions. 3-4 BA/OD with SUNY College of Optometry, 4-1 BS/MBA with Clarkson University. **Credit/placement by examination:** AP, CLEP, IB, SAT, ACT, institutional tests. 30 credit hours maximum toward bachelor's degree. **Support services:** Learning center, pre-admission summer program, reduced course load, remedial instruction, study skills assistance, tutoring, writing center.

Majors. Area/ethnic studies: Latin American, women's. **Biology:** General, biochemistry, cell/histology, ecology. **Business:** General, accounting, business admin, entrepreneurial studies, finance, hotel/motel admin, international, management information systems, marketing, restaurant/food services, tourism/travel. **Communications:** Journalism, media studies, organizational, radio/TV. **Computer sciences:** General. **Conservation:** General, environmental science. **Education:** Biology, chemistry, computer, early childhood, elementary, English, foreign languages, French, history, mathematics, multi-level teacher, physics, science, social science, social studies, Spanish, special ed. **English:** English lit, rhetoric/composition. **Foreign languages:** French, Spanish. **Health services:** Audiology/speech pathology, clinical lab science, cytotechnology, nursing (RN). **History:** General. **Human services:** Social work. **Liberal arts:** Arts/sciences. **Math:** General. **Parks/recreation:** General. **Philosophy/religion:** Philosophy. **Physical sciences:** Chemistry, geology, physics. **Protective services:** Criminal justice. **Psychology:** General. **Social sciences:** Anthropology, economics, geography, political science, sociology. **Visual/performing arts:** General, art, dramatic, music. **Work/family studies:** Family studies, food/nutrition.

Most popular majors. Business/marketing 21%, communications/journalism 11%, education 7%, health sciences 9%, psychology 8%, security/protective services 8%.

Technology on campus. 566 workstations in dormitories, library, computer center, student center. Dormitories wired for high-speed internet access and linked to campus network. Commuter students can connect to campus network. Online course registration, online library, helpline, repair service, student web hosting, wireless network available.

Student life. Freshman orientation: Available, $135 fee. Preregistration for classes offered. Held over two nights with meals included; simultaneous program for parents and siblings. **Housing:** Guaranteed on-campus for all undergraduates. Coed dorms, special housing for disabled, apartments, gender-neutral housing, themed housing, wellness housing available. $250 fully refundable deposit, deadline 5/1. **Activities:** Bands, campus ministries, choral groups, dance, drama, film society, international student organizations, literary magazine, music ensembles, Model UN, musical theater, radio station, student government, student newspaper, TV station, Akeba, El Pueblo, environmental action committee, Hillel, inter-varsity Christian fellowship, Newman association, Project Help, College Democrats, College Republicans, Feurza.

Athletics. NCAA. **Intercollegiate:** Baseball M, basketball, cross-country, ice hockey, lacrosse M, soccer, softball W, tennis W, track and field, volleyball W. **Intramural:** Basketball, field hockey W, football (non-tackle) M, racquetball, soccer, softball, tennis, ultimate frisbee, volleyball. **Team name:** Cardinals.

Student services. Adult student services, alcohol/substance abuse counseling, chaplain/spiritual director, career counseling, services for economically disadvantaged, student employment services, financial aid counseling, health services, legal services, minority student services, on-campus daycare, personal counseling, placement for graduates, veterans' counselor, women's services. **Physically disabled:** Services for visually, speech, hearing impaired.

Contact. E-mail: admissions@plattsburgh.edu
Phone: (518) 564-2040 Toll-free number: (888) 673-0012
Fax: (518) 564-2045
Richard Higgins, Associate Vice President for Enrollment Management, SUNY College at Plattsburgh, Kehoe Administration Building, Plattsburgh, NY 12901

SUNY College at Potsdam
Potsdam, New York — **CB member**
www.potsdam.edu — **CB code: 2545**

- Public 4-year liberal arts and teachers college
- Residential campus in large town

- 3,595 degree-seeking undergraduates: 3% part-time, 57% women, 10% African American, 2% Asian American, 13% Hispanic/Latino, 2% Native American, 2% Multi-racial, non-Hispanic, 1% international
- 265 degree-seeking graduate students
- 74% of applicants admitted
- 55% graduate within 6 years; 49% enter graduate study

General. Founded in 1816. Regionally accredited. **Degrees:** 748 bachelor's awarded; master's offered. **ROTC:** Army, Air Force. **Location:** 105 miles from Montreal, 140 miles from Syracuse. **Calendar:** Semester, limited summer session. **Full-time faculty:** 249 total; 84% have terminal degrees, 12% minority, 45% women. **Part-time faculty:** 110 total; 28% have terminal degrees, 3% minority, 62% women. **Class size:** 68% < 20, 28% 20-39, 1% 40-49, 2% 50-99, less than 1% >100. **Special facilities:** Electronic music and recording studios, 6 performance halls, planetarium, seismographic laboratory, anthropology museum, art museum, dance studio and theater, fine arts studios, performing arts building.

Freshman class profile. 4,976 applied, 3,678 admitted, 854 enrolled.

Mid 50% test scores			
		GPA 2.0-2.99:	34%
SAT critical reading:	440-570	Rank in top quarter:	25%
SAT math:	440-580	Rank in top tenth:	15%
ACT composite:	22-28	End year in good standing:	94%
GPA 3.75 or higher:	16%	Return as sophomores:	75%
GPA 3.50-3.74:	17%	Out-of-state:	3%
GPA 3.0-3.49:	32%	Live on campus:	94%

Basis for selection. Secondary school record and standardized test scores important. Class rank, talent, ability, activities and community service also considered. Most applicants will not need to submit a standardized test score for admission consideration. Latest date which scores must be received is by the rolling start of the semester. Essays and interviews required for some. Auditions required for music majors. Auditions encouraged for dance and theater majors. Portfolios encouraged for art majors. **Home schooled:** Need either a letter of recommendation from local school superintendent that the curriculum is equal to high school diploma, or GED.

High school preparation. College-preparatory program required. 14 units required; 19 recommended. Required and recommended units include English 4, mathematics 2-3, social studies 4, science 2-3 (laboratory 1), foreign language 3 and visual/performing arts 1.

2015-2016 Annual costs. Tuition/fees: $7,908; $17,758 out-of-state. Room/board: $11,870. Books/supplies: $810. Personal expenses: $1,150.

2015-2016 Financial aid. Need-based: 821 full-time freshmen applied for aid; 680 deemed to have need; 676 received aid. Average need met was 90%. Average scholarship/grant was $10,710; average loan $3,674. 57% of total undergraduate aid awarded as scholarships/grants, 43% as loans/jobs. **Non-need-based:** Awarded to 1,179 full-time undergraduates, including 353 freshmen. Scholarships awarded for academics, art, leadership, music/drama. **Additional information:** Apply early to access limited, need-based awards.

Application procedures. Admission: No deadline. $50 fee, may be waived for applicants with need. Admission notification on a rolling basis beginning on or about 10/1. Must reply by May 1 for guaranteed enrollment. **Financial aid:** Priority date 3/1, closing date 5/1. FAFSA required. Applicants notified on a rolling basis starting 2/1; must reply by 5/1 or within 4 week(s) of notification.

Academics. Special study options: Combined bachelor's/graduate degree, cross-registration, distance learning, double major, dual enrollment of high school students, exchange student, honors, independent study, internships, liberal arts/career combination, self-designed major, study abroad, teacher certification program. Interdisciplinary program to study art, literature, science, and sociology of the Adirondacks; extension offers undergraduate and graduate courses with emphasis on teacher education; combined degree options in engineering with Clarkson University and SUNY Binghamton; engineering or management with SUNY Institute of Technology. **Credit/placement by examination:** AP, CLEP, IB. Credit awarded for International Baccalaureate on course-by-course evaluation. **Support services:** Learning center, pre-admission summer program, reduced course load, study skills assistance, tutoring, writing center. Academic advisors assist with transitions to college life and graduation from college. They also provide disability services.

Majors. Area/ethnic studies: Women's. **Biology:** General, biochemistry, exercise physiology. **Business:** Business admin, labor relations, managerial economics. **Communications:** Communications/speech/rhetoric. **Computer sciences:** General, computer science. **Conservation:** Environmental studies. **Education:** Biology, chemistry, drama/dance, early childhood, elementary, English, French, kindergarten/preschool, mathematics, music, physics, science, social studies, Spanish. **English:** Creative writing, English lit, rhetoric/composition, writing. **Foreign languages:** French, Spanish. **Health services:**

General. **History:** General. **Math:** General. **Philosophy/religion:** Philosophy. **Physical sciences:** Chemistry, geology, physics. **Protective services:** Criminal justice. **Psychology:** General. **Social sciences:** Anthropology, archaeology, economics, political science, sociology. **Visual/performing arts:** General, art, art history/conservation, dance, dramatic, music, music management, music performance, music theory/composition, musicology, studio arts.

Most popular majors. Biology 6%, business/marketing 8%, communications/journalism 6%, education 18%, English 8%, psychology 9%, social sciences 8%, visual/performing arts 14%.

Technology on campus. 608 workstations in dormitories, library, computer center, student center. Dormitories wired for high-speed internet access and linked to campus network. Commuter students can connect to campus network. Online course registration, online library, helpline, student web hosting, wireless network available.

Student life. Freshman orientation: Available, $195 fee. Preregistration for classes offered. Held June 30/July 1st, July 7/8, July 14/15, July 16/17, July 20/21 and July 23/24. **Policies:** Academic honor code outlines expectations for academic honesty and integrity; code of student rights, responsibilities, and conduct can be found in student handbook. **Housing:** Guaranteed on-campus for all undergraduates. Coed dorms, special housing for disabled, apartments, gender-neutral housing, themed housing, wellness housing available. $50 fully refundable deposit, deadline 5/1. Study-intensive housing, transfer student housing, gender inclusive housing and academic year housing available. **Activities:** Bands, campus ministries, choral groups, dance, drama, international student organizations, literary magazine, music ensembles, musical theater, opera, radio station, student government, student newspaper, symphony orchestra, inter-varsity Christian fellowship, black student alliance, Potsdam Association of Native Americans, Caribbean Latin American student society, political student association, Circle K, LGBT association, philosophy forum, pagan studies.

Athletics. NCAA. **Intercollegiate:** Basketball, cross-country, diving, golf M, ice hockey, lacrosse, rugby M, soccer, swimming, volleyball W. **Intramural:** Basketball, football (non-tackle) M, racquetball, soccer, softball, triathlon, volleyball. **Team name:** Bears.

Student services. Adult student services, alcohol/substance abuse counseling, chaplain/spiritual director, career counseling, services for economically disadvantaged, student employment services, financial aid counseling, health services, legal services, minority student services, on-campus daycare, personal counseling, placement for graduates, veterans' counselor, women's services. **Physically disabled:** Services for visually, speech, hearing impaired.

Contact. E-mail: admissions@potsdam.edu
Phone: (315) 267-2180 Toll-free number: (877) 768-7326
Fax: (315) 267-2163
Thomas Nesbitt, Director of Admissions, SUNY College at Potsdam, 44 Pierrepont Avenue, Potsdam, NY 13676

SUNY College at Purchase
Purchase, New York
www.purchase.edu   CB code: 2878

- Public 4-year university and liberal arts college
- Residential campus in large town
- 3,923 degree-seeking undergraduates: 6% part-time, 57% women, 10% African American, 4% Asian American, 18% Hispanic/Latino, 5% Multi-racial, non-Hispanic, 2% international
- 92 degree-seeking graduate students
- 41% of applicants admitted
- SAT or ACT (ACT writing optional) required
- 59% graduate within 6 years

General. Founded in 1967. Regionally accredited. **Degrees:** 970 bachelor's awarded; master's offered. **Location:** 25 miles from New York City, 5 miles from White Plains. **Calendar:** Semester, extensive summer session. **Full-time faculty:** 172 total; 49% have terminal degrees, 14% minority, 54% women. **Part-time faculty:** 266 total; 20% have terminal degrees, 13% minority, 50% women. **Class size:** 62% < 20, 33% 20-39, 1% 40-49, 3% 50-99, less than 1% >100. **Special facilities:** Performing arts center, children's center, electron microscope, Neuberger Museum of Art.

Freshman class profile. 7,928 applied, 3,235 admitted, 783 enrolled.

Mid 50% test scores			
		GPA 3.0-3.49:	34%
SAT critical reading:	490-610	GPA 2.0-2.99:	32%
SAT math:	470-570	Return as sophomores:	81%
ACT composite:	22-27	Out-of-state:	20%
GPA 3.75 or higher:	17%	Live on campus:	87%
GPA 3.50-3.74:	16%	International:	2%

Basis for selection. For liberal arts and sciences programs, high school achievement record or test scores important. For conservatory, performing arts and visual arts applicants, audition, interview, or portfolio most important. SAT recommended. Interview and essay required for film, theater design/technology programs; audition required for acting, dance, music programs; portfolio required for visual arts program.

High school preparation. College-preparatory program recommended. 20 units recommended. Recommended units include English 4, mathematics 4, social studies 4, science 3, foreign language 3 and computer science 2.

2015-2016 Annual costs. Tuition/fees: $8,267; $18,117 out-of-state. Room/board: $12,576. Books/supplies: $1,225. Personal expenses: $2,096.

2015-2016 Financial aid. Need-based: 686 full-time freshmen applied for aid; 480 deemed to have need; 478 received aid. Average need met was 44%. Average scholarship/grant was $8,586; average loan $3,387. 46% of total undergraduate aid awarded as scholarships/grants, 54% as loans/jobs. **Non-need-based:** Awarded to 846 full-time undergraduates, including 153 freshmen. Scholarships awarded for academics, art, minority status, music/drama. **Additional information:** All applicants automatically considered for scholarship upon review of applications, essays, auditions, and/or portfolio.

Application procedures. Admission: Priority date 3/1; deadline 7/15 (postmark date). $50 fee, may be waived for applicants with need. Admission notification on a rolling basis beginning on or about 5/1. Must reply by May 1 or within 2 week(s) if notified thereafter. Application deadlines vary by program. Priority date of 1/30 for students applying to acting, design/technology, and film programs. **Financial aid:** Priority date 2/1; no closing date. FAFSA required. Applicants notified on a rolling basis starting 3/1; must reply within 2 week(s) of notification.

Academics. Special study options: Cross-registration, distance learning, double major, ESL, independent study, internships, liberal arts/career combination, student-designed major, study abroad. Conservatory master-apprentice training in dance, music, acting, film, theater design technology, visual arts. **Credit/placement by examination:** AP, CLEP, institutional tests. 30 credit hours maximum toward bachelor's degree. **Support services:** Learning center, pre-admission summer program, remedial instruction, tutoring, writing center.

Majors. Area/ethnic studies: Women's. **Biology:** General, ecology. **Communications:** Journalism, media studies. **Conservation:** Environmental science, environmental studies. **English:** American lit, British lit, creative writing. **Foreign languages:** General. **History:** General. **Liberal arts:** Arts/sciences. **Math:** General. **Philosophy/religion:** Philosophy. **Physical sciences:** Chemistry. **Psychology:** General. **Social sciences:** Anthropology, economics, political science, sociology. **Visual/performing arts:** Art history/conservation, cinematography, commercial/advertising art, dance, dramatic, drawing, graphic design, music performance, music theory/composition, painting, photography, play/screenwriting, printmaking, sculpture, studio arts management, theater design, theater history.

Most popular majors. Communications/journalism 8%, liberal arts 15%, social sciences 11%, visual/performing arts 45%.

Technology on campus. 600 workstations in dormitories, library, computer center. Dormitories wired for high-speed internet access and linked to campus network. Commuter students can connect to campus network. Online course registration, online library, helpline, repair service, wireless network available.

Student life. Freshman orientation: Mandatory, $120 fee. Preregistration for classes offered. **Housing:** Coed dorms, special housing for disabled, apartments, themed housing, wellness housing available. $100 fully refundable deposit. Freshman residence, non-traditional age hall, presidential scholars, learning community available. **Activities:** Jazz band, choral groups, dance, drama, film society, international student organizations, literary magazine, music ensembles, musical theater, radio station, student government, student newspaper, TV station, philosophy club, chemistry society, literature club, dance club, ski club, Purchase Experimental Theatre, Organization of African People in America (OAPIA), Latinos Unidos, Gay/Lesbian/Bisexual and Transgendered Union.

Athletics. NCAA. **Intercollegiate:** Baseball M, basketball, cross-country, golf M, soccer, softball W, swimming W, tennis, volleyball. **Intramural:** Badminton, basketball, bowling, cross-country, fencing, golf, racquetball, skiing, soccer, softball, squash, swimming, table tennis, tennis, volleyball, water polo, weight lifting. **Team name:** Panthers.

Student services. Adult student services, alcohol/substance abuse counseling, career counseling, services for economically disadvantaged, student employment services, financial aid counseling, health services, on-campus daycare, personal counseling, placement for graduates, veterans' counselor, women's services. **Physically disabled:** Services for visually, hearing impaired.

Contact. E-mail: admissions@purchase.edu
Phone: (914) 251-6300 Fax: (914) 251-6314
Stephanie McCaine, Admissions Director, SUNY College at Purchase, 735 Anderson Hill Road, Purchase, NY 10577-1400

SUNY College of Agriculture and Technology at Morrisville
Morrisville, New York
www.morrisville.edu   **CB code: 2527**

- Public 4-year agricultural and technical college
- Residential campus in rural community
- 2,694 degree-seeking undergraduates: 8% part-time, 50% women, 18% African American, 1% Asian American, 8% Hispanic/Latino, 1% Native American, 2% Multi-racial, non Hispanic, 1% international
- 58% of applicants admitted
- Application essay required
- 37% graduate within 6 years

General. Founded in 1908. Regionally accredited. **Degrees:** 190 bachelor's, 460 associate awarded. **ROTC:** Army, Air Force. **Location:** 30 miles from Syracuse and Utica. **Calendar:** Semester, limited summer session. **Full-time faculty:** 140 total; 36% have terminal degrees, 9% minority, 45% women. **Part-time faculty:** 100 total; 11% have terminal degrees, 3% minority, 56% women. **Class size:** 51% < 20, 43% 20-39, 3% 40-49, 3% 50-99, less than 1% >100. **Special facilities:** Free-stall dairy complex, arboretum, greenhouses, aquaponics center, biodigester, wood technology center, equine rehabilitation center, four indoor riding rings, design center, cyber lab and student business center, police simulator, massage center, wellness center, automotive showroom and technology center, restaurant and farm market store, observatory/telescope.

Freshman class profile. 3,935 applied, 2,293 admitted, 811 enrolled.

Mid 50% test scores			
SAT critical reading:	380-490	GPA 2.0-2.99:	59%
SAT math:	390-500	Rank in top quarter:	16%
SAT writing:	370-460	Rank in top tenth:	3%
ACT composite:	17-21	End year in good standing:	75%
GPA 3.75 or higher:	5%	Return as sophomores:	69%
GPA 3.50-3.74:	7%	Out-of-state:	7%
GPA 3.0-3.49:	21%	Live on campus:	77%
		International:	2%

Basis for selection. Applicants are reviewed using a holistic approach. Overall high school GPA, state examinations, SAT/ACT scores (if provided/required), strength of courseload and college essay are reviewed in this process. Emphasis is placed on prerequisite coursework in relation to the applicants intended major. SAT or ACT required for bachelor's degree applicants, students seeking academic scholarship, or those seeking to participate in Division III athletics. Interviews not required, but recommended. **Home schooled:** State high school equivalency certificate required. GED required for students without supporting documentation. **Learning Disabled:** Submit documentation and any recommended individualized educational plan to the Office of Disability Services upon admission.

High school preparation. College-preparatory program recommended. 15 units required; 21 recommended. Required and recommended units include English 4, mathematics 3-4, social studies 4, history 4, science 3-4 (laboratory 2) and foreign language 1. Requirements vary depending on program. Math and science preparation important for technical majors.

2015-2016 Annual costs. Tuition/fees: $8,001; $12,171 out-of-state. Room/board: $13,488. Books/supplies: $1,400. Personal expenses: $1,000.

2014-2015 Financial aid. Need-based: 750 full-time freshmen applied for aid; 685 deemed to have need; 684 received aid. Average need met was 47%. Average scholarship/grant was $7,133; average loan $3,305. 63% of total undergraduate aid awarded as scholarships/grants, 37% as loans/jobs. **Non-need-based:** Awarded to 644 full-time undergraduates, including 247 freshmen. Scholarships awarded for academics, alumni affiliation, leadership, minority status, state residency.

Application procedures. Admission: Priority date 5/1; deadline 8/19. $50 fee, may be waived for applicants with need. Application must be submitted online. Admission notification on a rolling basis beginning on or about 10/1. Must reply by May 1 or within 4 week(s) if notified thereafter. Students apply to and are admitted to specific program areas. The tuition deposit secures a place in a particular program and is fully refundable prior to May 1. Should a program become oversubscribed, the admission offer to MSC is still honored but an alternate program may be offered. Housing preference is given on a first-come, first-served basis according to housing deposit date, and is fully refundable prior to June 30. **Financial aid:** Priority date 2/1; no closing date. FAFSA required. Applicants notified on a rolling basis starting 3/15; must reply by 5/1 or within 4 week(s) of notification.

Academics. Students interrested in programs not offered at the Norwich Campus may take general education or elective courses that can be applied to Morrisville State College (main campus) associate or bachelor's degree programs. **Special study options:** Accelerated study, combined bachelor's/graduate degree, cooperative education, cross-registration, distance learning, double major, dual enrollment of high school students, exchange student, independent study, internships, student-designed major, study abroad. **Credit/placement by examination:** AP, CLEP, IB, SAT, institutional tests. **Support services:** Learning center, pre-admission summer program, reduced course load, remedial instruction, study skills assistance, tutoring. OnCampus SUNY - value-added educational pathway for international students who do not meet direct admission requirements.

Majors. Business: Business admin, entrepreneurial studies, management information systems, resort management. **Communications:** Broadcast journalism. **Computer sciences:** LAN/WAN management, programming, web page design. **Conservation:** General. **Parks/recreation:** Exercise sciences. **Physical sciences:** General. **Protective services:** Law enforcement admin. **Psychology:** Applied.

Most popular majors. Agriculture 28%, business/marketing 21%, computer/information sciences 12%, security/protective services 17%, trade and industry 10%.

Technology on campus. PC or laptop required. 150 workstations in dormitories, library, computer center, student center. Commuter students can connect to campus network. Online course registration, online library, helpline, repair service, student web hosting, wireless network available.

Student life. Freshman orientation: Mandatory, $85 fee. Preregistration for classes offered. Freshmen and transfer students are welcomed to campus two days in advance of Welcome Weekend (general student move in). Special events and activities including orientation to campus life, first-year experience sessions, formal academic welcome, laptop and tech support orientation, and residence life sponsored social activities are held on Thursday and Friday as well as throughout the weekend. **Housing:** Guaranteed on-campus for all undergraduates. Coed dorms, special housing for disabled, apartments, gender-neutral housing, wellness housing available. $100 partly refundable deposit, deadline 5/1. **Activities:** Jazz band, choral groups, drama, international student organizations, literary magazine, musical theater, radio station, student government, student newspaper, African Student Union Black Alliance, Brothers and Sisters In Christ, Caribbean American Student Union, Latino American Student Organization, Pagan Alliance of Morrisville, Mustang Outreach and Volunteer Efforts.

Athletics. NCAA. **Intercollegiate:** Basketball, cross-country, equestrian, field hockey W, football (tackle) M, golf M, ice hockey, lacrosse, soccer, softball W, volleyball W. **Intramural:** Badminton, baseball, basketball, equestrian, football (non-tackle), handball, ice hockey, soccer, softball, table tennis, tennis, ultimate frisbee, volleyball. **Team name:** Mustangs.

Student services. Alcohol/substance abuse counseling, chaplain/spiritual director, career counseling, services for economically disadvantaged, student employment services, financial aid counseling, health services, minority student services, on-campus daycare, personal counseling, placement for graduates, veterans' counselor, women's services. **Physically disabled:** Services for visually, speech, hearing impaired.

Contact. E-mail: admissions@morrisville.edu
Phone: (315) 684-6046 Fax: (315) 684-6427
Robert Croot, Dean of Admission, SUNY College of Agriculture and Technology at Morrisville, PO Box 901, Morrisville, NY 13408-0901

SUNY College of Environmental Science and Forestry
Syracuse, New York   CB member
www.esf.edu   CB code: 2530

▸ Public 4-year university and liberal arts college
▸ Residential campus in small city
▸ 1,753 degree-seeking undergraduates: 2% part-time, 46% women, 1% African American, 3% Asian American, 5% Hispanic/Latino, 3% Multiracial, non-Hispanic, 2% international
▸ 469 degree-seeking graduate students
▸ 52% of applicants admitted
▸ SAT or ACT (ACT writing optional), application essay required
▸ 75% graduate within 6 years; 20% enter graduate study

General. Founded in 1911. Regionally accredited. Focused on the science, engineering, design and management of the environment and natural resources. Six regional campuses. Students may also take classes at adjacent Syracuse University. **Degrees:** 407 bachelor's, 50 associate awarded; master's, doctoral offered. **ROTC:** Army, Air Force. **Location:** 1 mile from downtown. **Calendar:** Semester, limited summer session. **Full-time faculty:** 132 total; 83% have terminal degrees, 11% minority, 32% women. **Part-time faculty:** 42 total; 29% have terminal degrees, 5% minority, 31% women. **Class size:** 51% < 20, 34% 20-39, 4% 40-49, 8% 50-99, 2% >100. **Special facilities:** Field stations for field study and research, 25,000-acre multi-campus forest system, ecological center, Roosevelt Wildlife Museum, semi-commercial paper mill.

Freshman class profile. 1,619 applied, 841 admitted, 318 enrolled.

Mid 50% test scores		GPA 2.0-2.99:	2%
SAT critical reading:	560-640	Rank in top quarter:	72%
SAT math:	560-660	Rank in top tenth:	34%
ACT composite:	25-29	End year in good standing:	95%
GPA 3.75 or higher:	69%	Return as sophomores:	85%
GPA 3.50-3.74:	18%	Out-of-state:	23%
GPA 3.0-3.49:	11%	Live on campus:	95%

Basis for selection. High school record most important, test scores, essay, and recommendations also important. Applicant should have strong college preparatory program with focus on mathematics and science for most programs and design background preferred for Landscape Architecture. Interview or participation in informational program recommended for all; portfolio required for some landscape architecture applicants. **Home schooled:** Statement describing home school structure and mission, transcript of courses and grades, state high school equivalency certificate required. If no superintendent's statement provided, student must have GED to enroll.

High school preparation. College-preparatory program required. 14 units required; 19 recommended. Required and recommended units include English 4, mathematics 3-4, social studies 3, history 1, science 3-4 (laboratory 3-4) and foreign language 3.

2015-2016 Annual costs. Tuition/fees: $7,717; $17,567 out-of-state. Room/board: $15,440. Books/supplies: $1,200. Personal expenses: $450.

2015-2016 Financial aid. Need-based: 295 full-time freshmen applied for aid; 262 deemed to have need; 262 received aid. Average need met was 82%. Average scholarship/grant was $6,000; average loan $4,100. 66% of total undergraduate aid awarded as scholarships/grants, 34% as loans/jobs. **Non-need-based:** Awarded to 861 full-time undergraduates, including 231 freshmen. Scholarships awarded for academics, alumni affiliation, leadership, minority status, ROTC, state residency.

Application procedures. Admission: Priority date 2/1; no deadline. $50 fee, may be waived for applicants with need. Application must be submitted online. Admission notification on a rolling basis beginning on or about 2/1. Must reply by May 1 or within 4 week(s) if notified thereafter. Applications submitted after the 2/1 priority date will be considered on a space-available basis. **Financial aid:** Priority date 3/1; no closing date. FAFSA required. Applicants notified on a rolling basis starting 3/15; must reply within 2 week(s) of notification.

Academics. Special study options: Combined bachelor's/graduate degree, cooperative education, cross-registration, distance learning, double major, honors, independent study, internships, semester at sea, study abroad, teacher certification program, Washington semester. Associate degree programs in forest technology, land surveying technology and environmental and natural resources conservation offered through The SUNY ESF Ranger School in Adirondack Park. **Credit/placement by examination:** AP, CLEP, IB, institutional tests. **Support services:** Learning center, pre-admission summer program, reduced course load, study skills assistance, tutoring, writing center.

Majors. Architecture: Landscape. **Biology:** Aquatic, biochemistry, biotechnology, conservation, environmental, wildlife. **Business:** Construction management. **Conservation:** General, environmental science, environmental studies, fisheries, forest management, forest resources, forest sciences, forestry, wildlife/wilderness. **Engineering:** General, environmental. **Physical sciences:** Chemistry.

Most popular majors. Architecture 9%, biology 38%, engineering/engineering technologies 15%, natural resources/environmental science 35%.

Technology on campus. 250 workstations in dormitories, library, computer center, student center. Dormitories wired for high-speed internet access and linked to campus network. Commuter students can connect to campus network. Online course registration, online library, helpline, repair service, student web hosting, wireless network available.

Student life. Freshman orientation: Mandatory, $60 fee. Preregistration for classes offered. Four-day program prior to start of fall classes. **Policies:** First-year students required to live on campus unless they live within commuting distance. Freshmen not permitted cars on campus. **Housing:** Guaranteed on-campus for freshmen. Coed dorms, special housing for disabled, apartments, fraternity/sorority housing, wellness housing available. $400 nonrefundable deposit, deadline 5/1. **Activities:** Bands, campus ministries, choral groups, dance, drama, film society, international student organizations, literary magazine, music ensembles, musical theater, radio station, student government, student newspaper, symphony orchestra, TV station, undergraduate student association, Alpha Xi Sigma honor society, Wildlife Society, multicultural student organization, Environmental Action Coalition, Woodsmen's Team, Creative Minds club, Green Campus Initiative, Habitat for Humanity, Alphi Chi Omega Service Fraternity.

Athletics. USCAA. **Intercollegiate:** Basketball M, cross-country, golf, soccer, track and field. **Intramural:** Basketball, football (non-tackle), racquetball, soccer, softball, tennis. **Team name:** The Mighty Oaks.

Student services. Alcohol/substance abuse counseling, chaplain/spiritual director, career counseling, services for economically disadvantaged, student employment services, financial aid counseling, health services, legal services, minority student services, on-campus daycare, personal counseling, placement for graduates, veterans' counselor, women's services.

Contact. E-mail: esfinfo@esf.edu
Phone: (315) 470-6600 Fax: (315) 470-6933
Susan Sanford, Director of Admissions & Inter-Institutional Relations, SUNY College of Environmental Science and Forestry, Gateway Center, Syracuse, NY 13210

SUNY Downstate Medical Center
Brooklyn, New York
www.downstate.edu
CB code: 2534

- Public two-year upper-division health science and nursing college
- Commuter campus in very large city
- 31% of applicants admitted
- Application essay, interview required

General. Founded in 1858. Regionally accredited. **Degrees:** 187 bachelor's awarded; master's, professional, doctoral offered. **Articulation:** Agreements with St. Francis College, CUNY Medgar Evers College. **Location:** 4 miles from downtown Brooklyn, 6 miles from downtown Manhattan. **Calendar:** Semester, limited summer session. **Full-time faculty:** 383 total. **Part-time faculty:** 98 total.

Student profile. 348 degree-seeking undergraduates, 1,513 graduate students. 959 applied as first time-transfer students, 299 admitted, 250 enrolled. 100% entered as juniors. 80% transferred from two-year, 20% transferred from four-year institutions.

Out-of-state:	4%	25 or older:	72%

Basis for selection. College transcript, application essay, interview required. College of Medicine applicants apply through AMCAS: $65 application fee. Rolling admissions for College of Nursing and College of Health-Related Professions: $30 fee. Each program has different admission requirements. RN/BS program requires New York State Registered Nurse license. Prerequisite courses vary by program. Transfer accepted as juniors.

2015-2016 Annual costs. Tuition/fees: $7,074; $16,924 out-of-state. Room only: $4,550. Books/supplies: $1,484.

Application procedures. Admission: Deadline 4/1. $50 fee, may be waived for applicants with need. Application must be submitted on paper. Closing dates for applications differ, depending on program, and begin December 15. **Financial aid:** FAFSA required.

Academics. Special study options: Accelerated study, combined bachelor's/graduate degree, liberal arts/career combination. **Credit/placement by examination:** AP, CLEP.

Majors. Health services: Nursing (RN), physician assistant, sonography.

Technology on campus. Dormitories wired for high-speed internet access and linked to campus network. Online library, wireless network available.

Student life. Housing: Coed dorms available. **Activities:** Student government, student newspaper.

Athletics. Intramural: Basketball M.

Student services. Health services.

Contact. E-mail: admissions@downstate.edu
Phone: (718) 270-2446 Fax: (718) 270-7592
Shushawna DeOliveira, Director of Admissions & Enrollment, SUNY Downstate Medical Center, 450 Clarkson Avenue, Box 60, Brooklyn, NY 11203-2098

SUNY Empire State College
Saratoga Springs, New York
www.esc.edu
CB member
CB code: 2214

- Public 4-year liberal arts college
- Commuter campus in large town
- 9,827 degree-seeking undergraduates: 57% part-time, 62% women, 17% African American, 2% Asian American, 12% Hispanic/Latino, 2% Multiracial, non-Hispanic
- 932 degree-seeking graduate students
- 84% of applicants admitted
- Application essay required

General. Founded in 1971. Regionally accredited. Empire State College has 34 locations in seven regions throughout New York state and abroad. Through the Center for Distance Learning (CDL), students can take a few courses or earn their entire degree online. **Degrees:** 2,651 bachelor's, 676 associate awarded; master's offered. **Calendar:** Differs by program. 5-term calendar. Extensive summer session. **Full-time faculty:** 190 total; 97% have terminal degrees, 17% minority, 66% women. **Part-time faculty:** 916 total; 26% have terminal degrees, 12% minority, 62% women.

Freshman class profile. 1,177 applied, 991 admitted, 335 enrolled.

Basis for selection. Requirements for undergraduate admission: completed application, possession of high school diploma or equivalent, ability to pursue college-level work, payment of nonrefundable orientation fee, and completion of the college's orientation process.

2015-2016 Annual costs. Tuition/fees: $6,985; $16,835 out-of-state. Books/supplies: $1,528.

Financial aid. All financial aid based on need.

Application procedures. Admission: No deadline. $50 fee. Admission notification on a rolling basis. **Financial aid:** Priority date 4/1; no closing date. FAFSA required. Applicants notified on a rolling basis; must reply within 3 week(s) of notification.

Academics. Special study options: Accelerated study, combined bachelor's/graduate degree, cross-registration, distance learning, double major, external degree, independent study, internships, student-designed major, teacher certification program, weekend college. **Credit/placement by examination:** AP, CLEP, IB. 40 credit hours maximum toward associate degree, 93 toward bachelor's. **Support services:** Reduced course load, study skills assistance, tutoring, writing center.

Majors. Business: General, labor relations. **Education:** General. **Health services:** Nursing (RN). **History:** General. **Human services:** Community org/advocacy. **Liberal arts:** Arts/sciences. **Psychology:** General. **Social sciences:** General, economics. **Visual/performing arts:** Studio arts.

Most popular majors. Business/marketing 37%, health sciences 6%, physical sciences 6%, psychology 7%, public administration/social services 25%.

Technology on campus. 100 workstations in computer center. Commuter students can connect to campus network. Online course registration, online library, helpline available.

Student life. Freshman orientation: Mandatory, $50 fee. Preregistration for classes offered.

Student services. Adult student services, career counseling, student employment services, financial aid counseling, veterans' counselor. **Physically disabled:** Services for visually, speech, hearing impaired.

Contact. E-mail: admissions@esc.edu
Toll-free number: (800) 847-3000 Fax: (518) 587-9759
Jennifer D'Agostino, Senior Director of Admissions, SUNY Empire State College, 1 Union Avenue, Saratoga Springs, NY 12866

SUNY Farmingdale State College

Farmingdale, New York
www.farmingdale.edu

CB member
CB code: 2526

- Public 4-year technical college
- Commuter campus in large town
- 7,977 degree-seeking undergraduates: 22% part-time, 42% women, 10% African American, 7% Asian American, 17% Hispanic/Latino, 2% Multiracial, non-Hispanic, 3% international
- 44% of applicants admitted
- SAT or ACT (ACT writing recommended) required
- 49% graduate within 6 years; 20% enter graduate study

General. Founded in 1912. Regionally accredited. **Degrees:** 1,373 bachelor's, 297 associate awarded. **ROTC:** Army, Naval, Air Force. **Location:** 30 miles from New York City. **Calendar:** Semester, extensive summer session. **Full-time faculty:** 212 total; 74% have terminal degrees, 48% women. **Part-time faculty:** 489 total; 43% women. **Class size:** 27% < 20, 64% 20-39, 8% 40-49, 1% 50-99. **Special facilities:** CAD/CAM laboratory, fleet of single-engine and multi-engine aircraft, sustainable gardens, dental and health care laboratories, bioscience labs, manufacturing labs with plasmajet and advanced robotic technology, solar cell and hydrogen fuel cell research.

Freshman class profile. 5,256 applied, 2,313 admitted, 1,021 enrolled.

Mid 50% test scores			
SAT critical reading:	450-530	Rank in top quarter:	25%
SAT math:	460-550	Rank in top tenth:	5%
ACT composite:	19-23	Return as sophomores:	79%
GPA 3.75 or higher:	13%	Live on campus:	11%
GPA 3.50-3.74:	20%	International:	2%
GPA 3.0-3.49:	42%	Fraternities:	3%
GPA 2.0-2.99:	25%	Sororities:	6%

Basis for selection. School achievement record of primary importance. Applicants apply to and are accepted into a specific curriculum. Requirements vary according to program. Requirements vary by program. **Home schooled:** Home schooled students must provide documentation of successful completion of the high school home school program. This can be done by providing an official notation of completion from the local school district; providing the official score report of the GED or TASC examination; or providing a college transcript indicating the student has taken and successfully completed 24 college credits in accordance with the NYS Education Commissioner's Regulations.

High school preparation. College-preparatory program recommended. 15 units required. Required and recommended units include English 4, mathematics 3, social studies 4, science 3 and foreign language 1. Requirements vary by curriculum.

2015-2016 Annual costs. Tuition/fees: $7,808; $17,658 out-of-state. Room/board: $12,500.

2014-2015 Financial aid. **Need-based:** 869 full-time freshmen applied for aid; 553 deemed to have need; 500 received aid. Average need met was 62%. Average scholarship/grant was $6,744; average loan $3,645. 69% of total undergraduate aid awarded as scholarships/grants, 31% as loans/jobs. **Non-need-based:** Awarded to 225 full-time undergraduates, including 44 freshmen. Scholarships awarded for academics, alumni affiliation, job skills, state residency.

Application procedures. **Admission:** Priority date 1/1; deadline 6/1. $50 fee, may be waived for applicants with need. Admission notification on a rolling basis beginning on or about 11/1. Must reply by May 1 or within 4 week(s) if notified thereafter. Certain programs may have additional requirements or deadlines. **Financial aid:** Priority date 4/1; no closing date. FAFSA required. Applicants notified on a rolling basis starting 3/1.

Academics. **Special study options:** Accelerated study, cross-registration, distance learning, double major, dual enrollment of high school students, ESL, independent study, internships, study abroad. **Credit/placement by examination:** AP, CLEP, SAT, ACT, institutional tests. Matriculated students may apply for and be granted a maximum of 18 credits through Credit-by-Evaluation. **Support services:** Learning center, remedial instruction, study skills assistance, tutoring, writing center.

Majors. **Biology:** General. **Business:** Business admin, international. **Computer sciences:** Programming. **Health services:** Clinical lab science, dental hygiene, nursing (RN). **Math:** Applied. **Parks/recreation:** Sports admin. **Protective services:** Forensics, security services. **Psychology:** Applied. **Social sciences:** Applied economics. **Visual/performing arts:** Design.

Most popular majors. Business/marketing 25%, computer/information sciences 6%, engineering/engineering technologies 14%, health sciences 11%, interdisciplinary studies 10%, security/protective services 11%.

Technology on campus. 367 workstations in dormitories, library, computer center, student center. Dormitories wired for high-speed internet access and linked to campus network. Commuter students can connect to campus network. Online course registration, online library, helpline, student web hosting, wireless network available.

Student life. **Freshman orientation:** Mandatory, $110 fee. Preregistration for classes offered. **Housing:** Coed dorms available. $50 fully refundable deposit. **Activities:** Dance, drama, international student organizations, Model UN, radio station, student government, student newspaper, African Heritage diversity club, Christian Fellowship club, Hugs Across America, Indian culture club, Latin-American Student Organization, Men in Action, Muslim Student Association, We Help Others.

Athletics. NCAA. **Intercollegiate:** Baseball M, basketball, cross-country, golf M, lacrosse, soccer, softball W, tennis, track and field, volleyball W. **Intramural:** Badminton, basketball, football (non-tackle), sand volleyball, soccer, softball, ultimate frisbee, volleyball. **Team name:** Rams.

Student services. Alcohol/substance abuse counseling, career counseling, services for economically disadvantaged, student employment services, financial aid counseling, health services, on-campus daycare, personal counseling, placement for graduates, veterans' counselor. **Physically disabled:** Services for visually, speech, hearing impaired.

Contact. E-mail: admissions@farmingdale.edu
Phone: (631) 420-2200 Fax: (631) 420-2633
Jim Hall, Director of Admissions, SUNY Farmingdale State College, 2350 Broadhollow Road, Farmingdale, NY 11735-1021

SUNY Maritime College

Throggs Neck, New York
www.sunymaritime.edu

CB member
CB code: 2536

- Public 4-year technical and maritime college
- Residential campus in very large city
- 1,667 degree-seeking undergraduates: 3% part-time, 10% women, 4% African American, 5% Asian American, 11% Hispanic/Latino, 2% Multiracial, non-Hispanic, 3% international
- 182 degree-seeking graduate students
- 68% of applicants admitted
- SAT or ACT (ACT writing recommended), application essay required
- 55% graduate within 6 years; 5% enter graduate study

General. Founded in 1874. Regionally accredited. Graduates eligible for commission as officers in Navy, Marine Corps, Coast Guard, Air Force, and commissioned Corps of the National Oceanic and Atmospheric Administration. 3 summer semesters at sea and regiment option required for students interested in obtaining U.S. Merchant Marine Officer's License. **Degrees:** 335 bachelor's, 10 associate awarded; master's offered. **ROTC:** Army, Naval. **Location:** 10 miles from New York City. **Calendar:** Semester, limited summer session. **Full-time faculty:** 87 total; 46% have terminal degrees, 7% minority, 23% women. **Part-time faculty:** 61 total; 16% have terminal degrees, 16% minority, 15% women. **Class size:** 32% < 20, 64% 20-39, 2% 40-49, 3% 50-99, less than 1% >100. **Special facilities:** 565-foot training ship, training tanker, Center for Simulated Marine Operations, bridge simulator, model basin and towing tank, CAD-CAM facilities, diesel propulsion simulators, maritime museum, sailing center including several 1-ton ocean racers.

Freshman class profile. 1,342 applied, 917 admitted, 334 enrolled.

Mid 50% test scores			
		GPA 2.0-2.99:	20%
SAT critical reading:	500-590	Rank in top quarter:	34%
SAT math:	530-610	Rank in top tenth:	13%
SAT writing:	470-550	End year in good standing:	87%
ACT composite:	22-26	Return as sophomores:	87%
GPA 3.75 or higher:	11%	Out-of-state:	29%
GPA 3.50-3.74:	22%	Live on campus:	96%
GPA 3.0-3.49:	47%	International:	1%

Basis for selection. Quality and strength of preparation, school achievement record, including first semester senior grades, class rank, test scores, extracurricular activities considered. Interview and essay recommended. SAT or ACT not required for international students if English is not native language, TOEFL or IELTS required. Interviews not required but are recommended. **Home schooled:** Statement describing home school structure and mission, transcript of courses and grades, state high school equivalency certificate, letter of recommendation (nonparent) required. Accreditation of home school.

High school preparation. College-preparatory program recommended. 18 units required. Required and recommended units include English 3-4, mathematics 3-4, social studies 3, history 3, science 3-4 (laboratory 1) and foreign language 1-3. Math requirement includes algebra, geometry, trigonometry; math beyond trigonometry recommended. Chemistry or physics required; both strongly recommended. Pre-calculus required for Bachelor of Engineering.

2015-2016 Annual costs. Tuition/fees: $7,809; $17,659 out-of-state. Room/board: $11,516. Books/supplies: $1,464. Personal expenses: $2,356.

2014-2015 Financial aid. Need-based: 198 full-time freshmen applied for aid; 190 deemed to have need; 161 received aid. Average need met was 43%. Average scholarship/grant was $5,732; average loan $3,255. 46% of total undergraduate aid awarded as scholarships/grants, 54% as loans/jobs. **Non-need-based:** Awarded to 341 full-time undergraduates, including 105 freshmen. Scholarships awarded for academics, leadership, minority status, ROTC, state residency. **Additional information:** The Strategic Sealift Officer Program is unique to the maritime schools. The program allows students earning unlimited licenses as Merchant Marine Deck or Engine Officers to be commissioned as an officer in the Navy Reserve upon graduation. Strategic Sealift Officers normally serve on inactive duty in the Individual Ready Reserve allowing them to work as civilians in the maritime industry. Qualified students may apply for the Student Incentive Payments funded by the U.S. Maritime Administration during their freshman year. SIP benefits amount to a maximum of $32,000; $4,000 per semester.

Application procedures. Admission: Closing date 1/31 (postmark date). $50 fee, may be waived for applicants with need. Application must be submitted online. Admission notification on a rolling basis beginning on or about 3/1. Must reply by May 1 or within 2 week(s) if notified thereafter. **Financial aid:** Priority date 3/15, closing date 7/15. FAFSA required. Applicants notified on a rolling basis starting 3/15; must reply by 5/1.

Academics. Cadets in U.S. Coastguard license programs acquire technical, professional, and leadership experience on training cruises to foreign and domestic ports during annual summer sea terms, while preparing for U.S. Merchant Marine Officer's License. All other students must complete an Internship related to their major. **Special study options:** Distance learning, double major, exchange student, independent study, internships, study abroad. United States Coast Guard-issued deck and engine license program. **Credit/placement by examination:** AP, CLEP, IB, SAT, ACT, institutional tests. 30 credit hours maximum toward associate degree, 30 toward bachelor's. **Support services:** Learning center, pre-admission summer program, reduced course load, remedial instruction, study skills assistance, tutoring.

Majors. Engineering: Electrical, industrial, marine, mechanical. **Physical sciences:** Atmospheric science.

Most popular majors. Business/marketing 20%, engineering/engineering technologies 38%, trade and industry 37%.

Technology on campus. 160 workstations in dormitories, library, computer center, student center. Dormitories wired for high-speed internet access and linked to campus network. Online course registration, online library, helpline, wireless network available.

Student life. Freshman orientation: Mandatory, $150 fee. Preregistration for classes offered. Held for one day in June and August. **Policies:** Students can choose from two lifestyle options on campus, either traditional college or Regiment of Cadets. All students governed by the College Code of Conduct and within that all Cadets are governed by the Regimental Rules and Regulations. All students have access to and can participate in student organizations, athletics, student government, and recreation facilities. Freshmen not permitted cars on campus. **Housing:** Coed dorms available. Most undergraduates required to live in on-campus housing if enrolled in degree program that includes USCG Mariner license. **Activities:** Marching band, campus ministries, choral groups, international student organizations, music ensembles, student government, Cadet Artillery, Campus Crusade for Christ, Billards Club, Divers Association, Jewish club, Newman club, Propeller Club, Fishing Club, Society of Naval Architects & Marine Engineers, Turkish club.

Athletics. NCAA. **Intercollegiate:** Baseball M, basketball M, cross-country, diving, football (tackle) M, lacrosse, rifle, rowing (crew), sailing, soccer, swimming, volleyball W. **Intramural:** Basketball, football (non-tackle), softball. **Team name:** Privateers.

Student services. Chaplain/spiritual director, career counseling, student employment services, financial aid counseling, health services, personal counseling, placement for graduates, veterans' counselor.

Contact. E-mail: admissions@sunymaritime.edu
Phone: (718) 409-7221
Rohan Howell, Dean of Admissions, SUNY Maritime College, 6 Pennyfield Avenue, Throggs Neck, NY 10465

SUNY Polytechnic Institute
Utica, New York   **CB member**
www.sunypoly.edu   **CB code: 0755**

- Public 4-year business and engineering college
- Commuter campus in small city
- 1,957 degree-seeking undergraduates: 12% part-time, 34% women, 7% African American, 4% Asian American, 7% Hispanic/Latino, 2% Multiracial, non-Hispanic, 1% international
- 643 degree-seeking graduate students
- 60% of applicants admitted
- SAT or ACT (ACT writing optional), application essay required
- 49% graduate within 6 years

General. Founded in 1966. Regionally accredited. **Degrees:** 425 bachelor's awarded; master's, doctoral offered. **ROTC:** Army, Air Force. **Location:** 50 miles from Syracuse, 90 miles from Albany. **Calendar:** Semester, limited summer session. **Full-time faculty:** 124 total; 86% have terminal degrees, 28% minority, 32% women. **Part-time faculty:** 120 total; 26% have terminal degrees, 8% minority, 48% women. **Class size:** 64% < 20, 34% 20-39, 2% 40-49.

Freshman class profile. 2,319 applied, 1,402 admitted, 347 enrolled.

Mid 50% test scores			
SAT critical reading:	470-640	Rank in top quarter:	59%
SAT math:	490-670	Rank in top tenth:	28%
ACT composite:	23-28	End year in good standing:	82%
GPA 3.75 or higher:	37%	Return as sophomores:	74%
GPA 3.50-3.74:	25%	Out-of-state:	3%
GPA 3.0-3.49:	28%	Live on campus:	72%
GPA 2.0-2.99:	10%	International:	1%

Basis for selection. All applicants must meet specific criteria for admission (GPA, test scores). International students without access to SAT/ACT testing may be admitted based on alternate criteria. Interview recommended for all. **Home schooled:** Transcript of courses and grades, letter of recommendation (nonparent) required. Statement from local public school superintendent that verifies home school curriculum matches NYS Regents Curriculum required. **Learning Disabled:** A student with a learning disability may choose to self disclose their interest in receiving accommodations and/or support with the Disability Services Office.

High school preparation. College-preparatory program required. 14 units required; 25 recommended. Required and recommended units include English 4, mathematics 3-4, social studies 2, history 2, science 3-4 (laboratory 3-4), foreign language 3 and academic electives 2. Engineering requires 4 units of math.

2015-2016 Annual costs. Tuition/fees: $7,739; $17,589 out-of-state. Room/board: $11,714. Books/supplies: $1,200. Personal expenses: $1,000.

2015-2016 Financial aid. Need-based: 308 full-time freshmen applied for aid; 235 deemed to have need; 235 received aid. Average need met was 100%. Average scholarship/grant was $8,242; average loan $3,357. 46% of total undergraduate aid awarded as scholarships/grants, 54% as loans/jobs. **Non-need-based:** Awarded to 607 full-time undergraduates, including 260 freshmen.

Application procedures. Admission: Priority date 3/1; deadline 7/1 (receipt date). $50 fee, may be waived for applicants with need. Admission notification on a rolling basis beginning on or about 1/15. Must reply by May 1 or within 4 week(s) if notified thereafter. **Financial aid:** Priority date 3/1; no closing date. FAFSA required. Applicants notified on a rolling basis starting 3/15; must reply within 2 week(s) of notification.

Academics. Five colleges: arts & sciences, health sciences and management, engineering, nanoscale sciences, nanoscale engineering and technology innovation. **Special study options:** Accelerated study, combined bachelor's/graduate degree, cross-registration, distance learning, double major, independent study, internships, study abroad. Study abroad is also coordinated through SUNY Study Abroad, offering 500 overseas programs in more than 51 countries. **Credit/placement by examination:** AP, CLEP, IB, SAT, ACT, institutional tests. 64 credit hours maximum toward bachelor's degree. Credit awarded for International Baccalaureate varies by academic department. **Support services:** Learning center, pre-admission summer program, reduced course load, study skills assistance, tutoring, writing center.

Majors. Biology: General. **Business:** Accounting, business admin. **Computer sciences:** General, information systems. **Engineering:** General, civil, electrical, mechanical. **Health services:** Health information management. **Math:** Applied. **Psychology:** General. **Social sciences:** Sociology.

Most popular majors. Business/marketing 21%, computer/information sciences 14%, engineering/engineering technologies 26%, health sciences 18%, psychology 7%, social sciences 6%.

Technology on campus. 380 workstations in library, computer center. Dormitories wired for high-speed internet access and linked to campus network. Commuter students can connect to campus network. Online course registration, online library, helpline, student web hosting, wireless network available.

Student life. Freshman orientation: Mandatory, $150 fee. Preregistration for classes offered. Held over the summer. There are three sessions during July with an Opening Weekend prior to classes beginning in August. **Housing:** Guaranteed on-campus for freshmen. Coed dorms, special housing for disabled available. $150 fully refundable deposit, deadline 5/1. **Activities:** Drama, international student organizations, literary magazine, radio station, student government, TV station, Black Latino American student union, Students of Christ, West Indian African club.

Athletics. NCAA. Intercollegiate: Baseball M, basketball, cross-country, lacrosse, soccer, softball W, volleyball. **Intramural:** Badminton, basketball, bowling, cricket, cross-country, football (tackle) M, racquetball, soccer, softball, volleyball. **Team name:** Wildcats.

Student services. Alcohol/substance abuse counseling, chaplain/spiritual director, career counseling, student employment services, financial aid counseling, health services, legal services, personal counseling, placement for graduates, veterans' counselor, women's services. **Physically disabled:** Services for visually, speech, hearing impaired.

Contact. E-mail: admissions@sunyit.edu
Phone: (315) 792-7500 Toll-free number: (866) 278-6948
Fax: (315) 792-7837
Gina Liscio, Director of Admissions, SUNY Polytechnic Institute, 100 Seymour Road, Utica, NY 13502

SUNY University at Albany
Albany, New York
http://albany.edu

CB member
CB code: 2532

- Public 4-year university
- Residential campus in small city
- 12,698 degree-seeking undergraduates: 4% part-time, 49% women, 16% African American, 8% Asian American, 15% Hispanic/Latino, 3% Multiracial, non-Hispanic, 6% international
- 4,070 degree-seeking graduate students
- 56% of applicants admitted
- SAT or ACT (ACT writing optional), application essay required
- 61% graduate within 6 years

General. Founded in 1844. Regionally accredited. **Degrees:** 2,976 bachelor's awarded; master's, doctoral offered. **ROTC:** Army, Air Force. **Location:** 4 miles from downtown. **Calendar:** Semester, extensive summer session. **Full-time faculty:** 675 total; 90% have terminal degrees, 24% minority, 41% women. **Part-time faculty:** 494 total; 42% have terminal degrees, 15% minority, 48% women. **Class size:** 30% < 20, 39% 20-39, 12% 40-49, 8% 50-99, 11% >100. **Special facilities:** Northeast Regional Forensic Institute, atmospheric science research center and Whiteface Mountain observation facility, microbeam analysis facility, large fine arts work areas, peptide synthesis facility, recombinant DNA sequencing laboratories.

Freshman class profile. 22,337 applied, 12,608 admitted, 2,592 enrolled.

Mid 50% test scores		GPA 2.0-2.99:	21%
SAT critical reading:	490-580	Rank in top quarter:	30%
SAT math:	510-590	Rank in top tenth:	16%
ACT composite:	22-26	Return as sophomores:	82%
GPA 3.75 or higher:	13%	Out-of-state:	7%
GPA 3.50-3.74:	19%	Live on campus:	92%
GPA 3.0-3.49:	47%	International:	4%

Basis for selection. High school record, class rank, GPA, standardized test scores very important; essay, recommendations important. Freshman applicants must submit the SUNY Online Academic Record (SOAR) or official high school transcript and SAT or ACT scores. In addition, all freshman applicants must submit a 250-500 word personal essay and one teacher or counselor letter of recommendation. **Home schooled:** Statement describing home school structure and mission, state high school equivalency certificate required.

High school preparation. College-preparatory program required. 18 units required. Required and recommended units include English 4, mathematics 2-4, social studies 3, history 2, science 2-3 (laboratory 2-3), foreign language 1-3 and academic electives 4.

2015-2016 Annual costs. Tuition/fees: $8,996; $22,116 out-of-state. Room/board: $12,426. Books/supplies: $1,200. Personal expenses: $1,065.

Financial aid. Non-need-based: Scholarships awarded for academics, athletics, state residency.

Application procedures. Admission: Closing date 3/1 (receipt date). $50 fee, may be waived for applicants with need. Decisions sent after 1/1. Must reply by May 1 or within 2 week(s) if notified thereafter. **Financial aid:** Priority date 3/15; no closing date. FAFSA required. Applicants notified on a rolling basis starting 3/20.

Academics. Special study options: Accelerated study, combined bachelor's/graduate degree, cross-registration, distance learning, double major, dual enrollment of high school students, ESL, honors, independent study, internships, liberal arts/career combination, student-designed major, study abroad, Washington semester. Accelerated 5-year Bachelors/Masters in 40 fields; internships with New York State Legislature; 3+3 Program with Albany Law School; Biology/Dental Program with Boston University Goldman School of Dental Medicine; bachelor's/Doctor of Optometry with SUNY State College; early assurance program with Albany Medical College and SUNY Upstate Medical University. **Credit/placement by examination:** AP, CLEP, IB. 60 credit hours maximum toward bachelor's degree. **Support services:** Pre-admission summer program, remedial instruction, study skills assistance, tutoring, writing center.

Honors college/program. Applicants admitted as Presidential Scholars & Frederick Douglass Scholars invited to apply to the Honors College. Approximately 125 freshmen will be admitted each fall. An additional 25 current University at Albany students will be admitted at the end of their first year.

Majors. Architecture: Urban/community planning. **Area/ethnic studies:** African-American, Asian, Caribbean, Chinese, East Asian, Japanese, Latin American, women's. **Biology:** General, biochemistry, molecular. **Business:** Accounting, business admin. **Communications:** Communications/speech/rhetoric, journalism. **Computer sciences:** General, information systems. **Conservation:** Environmental science. **Engineering:** Materials. **English:** English lit, rhetoric/composition. **Foreign languages:** Linguistics, Spanish. **Health services:** Predental, premedicine, prepharmacy, preveterinary. **History:** General. **Human services:** Public policy, social work. **Math:** General, applied. **Philosophy/religion:** Philosophy, religion. **Physical sciences:** Atmospheric science, chemistry, materials science, physics. **Protective services:** Criminal justice. **Psychology:** General. **Social sciences:** Anthropology, economics, geography, political science, sociology, urban studies. **Visual/performing arts:** Art history/conservation, music, music performance, music theory/composition, studio arts.

Most popular majors. Biology 11%, business/marketing 12%, English 14%, psychology 11%, social sciences 27%.

Technology on campus. 500 workstations in library. Dormitories wired for high-speed internet access and linked to campus network. Commuter students can connect to campus network. Online course registration, online library, helpline, student web hosting, wireless network available.

Student life. Freshman orientation: Mandatory, $210 fee. Preregistration for classes offered. Two days in summer with parental participation, 2 days in fall without parental participation. **Policies:** A parking permit may not be purchased by on-campus resident Freshman students, nor their family members. Exceptions exist for Sophomore level students, military obligations, or extenuating circumstances, still in their first year. **Housing:** Guaranteed on-campus for freshmen. Coed dorms, themed housing, wellness housing available. $125 fully refundable deposit. Disabled Student Services provies individualized services including information on accessible housing. **Activities:** Bands, campus ministries, choral groups, dance, drama, film society, international student organizations, literary magazine, music ensembles, Model UN, musical theater, radio station, student government, student newspaper, symphony orchestra, TV station, over 200 student groups.

Athletics. NCAA. Intercollegiate: Baseball M, basketball, cross-country, field hockey W, football (tackle) M, golf W, lacrosse, rugby, soccer, softball W, tennis W, track and field, volleyball W. **Intramural:** Basketball, football (non-tackle), racquetball, soccer, softball, tennis, track and field, volleyball. **Team name:** Great Danes.

Student services. Alcohol/substance abuse counseling, chaplain/spiritual director, career counseling, services for economically disadvantaged, student employment services, financial aid counseling, health services, legal services, minority student services, on-campus daycare, personal counseling, placement for graduates, women's services. **Physically disabled:** Services for visually, speech, hearing impaired.

Contact. E-mail: ugadmissions@albany.edu
Phone: (518) 442-5435 Fax: (518) 442-5383
Timothy Lee, Director of Undergraduate Admissions, SUNY University at Albany, Office of Undergraduate Admissions, University Hall, Albany, NY 12222

SUNY University at Binghamton

Binghamton, New York	CB member
www.binghamton.edu	CB code: 2535

- Public 4-year university
- Residential campus in small city
- 13,465 degree-seeking undergraduates: 3% part-time, 48% women, 5% African American, 14% Asian American, 10% Hispanic/Latino, 2% Multi-racial, non-Hispanic, 10% international
- 3,359 degree-seeking graduate students
- 42% of applicants admitted
- SAT or ACT with writing, application essay required
- 81% graduate within 6 years; 43% enter graduate study

General. Founded in 1946. Regionally accredited. We provide a small college atmosphere within the larger university, with our residential structure based on the Oxford collegiate model. **Degrees:** 3,170 bachelor's awarded; master's, professional, doctoral offered. **ROTC:** Army, Air Force. **Location:** 50 miles from Ithaca, 70 miles from Syracuse, 180 miles from New York City. **Calendar:** Semester, extensive summer session. **Full-time faculty:** 689 total; 94% have terminal degrees, 29% minority, 40% women. **Part-time faculty:** 289 total; 53% have terminal degrees, 16% minority, 46% women. **Class size:** 44% < 20, 36% 20-39, 6% 40-49, 7% 50-99, 7% >100. **Special facilities:** Nature preserve, 4-climate greenhouse, performing arts center (5 theaters), art/dance studios, sculpture foundry, research centers, electron microscopy laboratories, geographic information systems core facility, public archaeology facility, integrated electronics engineering center, institute for child development, kosher kitchen, innovative technologies complex, NYS Center of Excellence, art museum, 3D printing/scanning/design emerging technology studio.

Freshman class profile. 30,616 applied, 13,010 admitted, 2,661 enrolled.

Mid 50% test scores		GPA 3.0-3.49:	17%
SAT critical reading:	600-680	GPA 2.0-2.99:	2%
SAT math:	630-700	End year in good standing:	92%
SAT writing:	580-670	Return as sophomores:	91%
ACT composite:	27-31	Out-of-state:	8%
GPA 3.75 or higher:	64%	Live on campus:	98%
GPA 3.50-3.74:	17%	International:	10%

Basis for selection. Quality of courses, grades and grade trend, and test scores. Evidence of intellectual curiosity, interest in others, and nonacademic pursuits sought through application. Geographic, socioeconomic, and ethnic diversity considered. SAT or ACT scores accepted on a rolling basis for fall term admissions. Audition offered for music; portfolio review offered for art; theater, dance, speech and debate talent also considered. **Learning Disabled:** No special admission requirements or procedures for students with learning disabilities. Accepted students who anticipate a possible need for disability-related support services or equal access accommodations should contact the university's Services for Students with Disabilities office.

High school preparation. College-preparatory program required. 16 units required. Required and recommended units include English 4, mathematics 3-4, social studies 2-4, history 4, science 2-4 and foreign language 3. 3 units of 1 foreign language or 2 each of 2 foreign languages required of liberal arts applicants.

2015-2016 Annual costs. Tuition/fees: $9,053; $22,173 out-of-state. Room/board: $13,198. Books/supplies: $1,000. Personal expenses: $750.

2015-2016 Financial aid. Need-based: 2,129 full-time freshmen applied for aid; 1,245 deemed to have need; 1,242 received aid. Average need met was 66%. Average scholarship/grant was $9,032; average loan $3,695. 44% of total undergraduate aid awarded as scholarships/grants, 56% as loans/jobs. **Non-need-based:** Awarded to 1,123 full-time undergraduates, including 273 freshmen. Scholarships awarded for academics, art, athletics, leadership, minority status, music/drama, state residency. **Additional information:** Most institutional aid awarded on a first-come first-served basis while considering student's ability to pay (determined by use of the FAFSA application) and the student's academic achievement.

Application procedures. Admission: Priority date 1/15; no deadline. $50 fee, may be waived for applicants with need. Rolling notification: 2/1, 3/1, 4/1. Must reply by May 1 or within 3 week(s) if notified thereafter. **Financial aid:** Priority date 2/1; no closing date. FAFSA required. Applicants notified on a rolling basis starting 3/4; must reply within 2 week(s) of notification.

Academics. Special study options: Accelerated study, combined bachelor's/graduate degree, cross-registration, distance learning, double major, dual enrollment of high school students, ESL, exchange student, honors, independent study, internships, liberal arts/career combination, student-designed major, study abroad, teacher certification program, Washington semester. Individualized majors programs; early assurance program guarantees graduate admission at partner SUNY schools: Buffalo, Upstate Medical-Syracuse and College of Optometry; 3-2 and 4-1 combined BA or BS/MA, MS, MAT, MBA, or MPA degree programs; teacher certification program is graduate only. **Credit/placement by examination:** AP, CLEP, IB, institutional tests. 32 credit hours maximum toward bachelor's degree. **Support services:** Learning center, pre-admission summer program, study skills assistance, tutoring, writing center. Library research assistance, specialized ESL writing assistance, Student Athletic Success Center, Bridges to Baccalaureate Program, Howard Hughes Medical Institute STEM Interdisciplinary Research Program, Discovery Program.

Majors. Area/ethnic studies: African-American, Asian, Asian-American, East Asian, Latin American, South Asian. **Biology:** General, biochemistry, cellular/molecular, neuroscience. **Business:** Accounting, actuarial science, business admin, entrepreneurial studies, finance, international, logistics, management information systems, marketing. **Computer sciences:** General, computer science. **Conservation:** Environmental studies. **Engineering:** General, biomedical, computer, electrical, industrial, mechanical. **English:** Creative writing, English lit. **Foreign languages:** Arabic, classics, comparative lit, French, German, Hebrew, Italian, Latin, linguistics, Spanish. **Health services:** Nursing (RN), predental, premedicine, preoptometry, preveterinary. **History:** General. **Math:** General. **Philosophy/religion:** Judaic, philosophy. **Physical sciences:** Chemistry, geology, physics. **Psychology:** General, psychobiology. **Social sciences:** General, anthropology, applied economics, economics, GIS/cartography, international relations, political science, sociology. **Visual/performing arts:** Acting, art, art history/conservation, cinematography, directing/producing, dramatic, music, music performance, theater design.

Most popular majors. Biology 11%, business/marketing 15%, engineering/engineering technologies 10%, English 6%, health sciences 6%, psychology 12%, social sciences 14%.

Technology on campus. 1,589 workstations in dormitories, library, computer center, student center. Dormitories wired for high-speed internet access and linked to campus network. Commuter students can connect to campus network. Online course registration, online library, helpline, student web hosting, wireless network available.

Student life. Freshman orientation: Available, $225 fee. Preregistration for classes offered. Two-day session held in summer for fall semester. Parents invited to participate. Two-day session held in January for students entering spring semester. **Policies:** Freshmen not permitted cars on campus. **Housing:** Guaranteed on-campus for freshmen. Coed dorms, special housing for disabled, apartments, themed housing, wellness housing available. $350 nonrefundable deposit, deadline 5/1. Gender inclusive and family housing available; no special housing for international students, but housing is available over breaks. **Activities:** Bands, campus ministries, choral groups, dance, drama, film society, international student organizations, literary magazine, music ensembles, Model UN, musical theater, opera, radio station, student government, student newspaper, symphony orchestra, TV station, College Democrats/Republicans/Libertarians, Hillel Jewish Student Union, Chabad, Campus Bible Fellowship, Asian Student Union, Circle K, Rainbow Pride Union, Habitat for Humanity, Student Environmental Action Coalition, Colleges Against Cancer.

Athletics. NCAA. **Intercollegiate:** Baseball M, basketball, cross-country, diving, golf M, lacrosse, soccer, softball W, swimming, tennis, track and field, volleyball W, wrestling M. **Intramural:** Basketball, bowling, football (non-tackle), racquetball, soccer, softball, tennis, volleyball. **Team name:** Bearcats.

Student services. Adult student services, alcohol/substance abuse counseling, chaplain/spiritual director, career counseling, services for economically disadvantaged, student employment services, financial aid counseling, health services, legal services, minority student services, on-campus daycare, personal counseling, placement for graduates, veterans' counselor, women's services. **Physically disabled:** Services for visually, speech, hearing impaired.

Contact. E-mail: admit@binghamton.edu
Phone: (607) 777-2171 Fax: (607) 777-4445
Randall Edouard, Assistant Vice Provost and Director of Admissions and Enrollment, SUNY University at Binghamton, PO Box 6001, Binghamton, NY 13902-6001

SUNY University at Buffalo
Buffalo, New York
www.buffalo.edu

CB member
CB code: 2925

- Public 4-year university
- Residential campus in large city
- 19,692 degree-seeking undergraduates: 7% part-time, 44% women, 7% African American, 14% Asian American, 6% Hispanic/Latino, 2% Multi-racial, non-Hispanic, 16% international
- 9,435 degree-seeking graduate students
- 60% of applicants admitted
- SAT or ACT with writing required
- 74% graduate within 6 years; 36% enter graduate study

General. Founded in 1846. Regionally accredited. **Degrees:** 5,017 bachelor's awarded; master's, professional, doctoral offered. **ROTC:** Army. **Location:** 10 miles from downtown. **Calendar:** Semester, extensive summer session. **Full-time faculty:** 1,268 total; 100% have terminal degrees, 25% minority, 38% women. **Part-time faculty:** 579 total; 99% have terminal degrees, 9% minority, 46% women. **Class size:** 34% < 20, 37% 20-39, 8% 40-49, 13% 50-99, 8% >100. **Special facilities:** Concert hall, anthropology research museum, the school of pharmacy and pharmaceutical sciences apothecary and historical exhibits, the museum of radiology and medical physics, the museum of neuroanatomy, Anderson Gallery, New York State center in bioinformatics & life sciences, center for computational research, center for document analysis and recognition, center of excellence in materials informatics, electronic poetry center, the archaeological survey.

Freshman class profile. 23,629 applied, 14,175 admitted, 3,621 enrolled.

Mid 50% test scores			
SAT critical reading:	510-610	**Rank in top quarter:**	61%
SAT math:	550-650	**Rank in top tenth:**	27%
ACT composite:	24-29	**Return as sophomores:**	88%
GPA 3.75 or higher:	40%	**Out-of-state:**	3%
GPA 3.50-3.74:	25%	**Live on campus:**	75%
GPA 3.0-3.49:	30%	**International:**	12%
GPA 2.0-2.99:	5%		

Basis for selection. Secondary school performance, strength of curriculum, standardized test scores, and, in some cases, supplemental application. SAT Subject Test considered for placement for foreign language. Architecture requires a portfolio; dance, music theater, theater & music require an audition. **Home schooled:** Transcript of courses and grades, letter of recommendation (nonparent) required. Essay describing educational program, special projects, extracurricular activities, and special accomplishments required as well as 2 letters of recommendation: 1 from parent or other person providing education, 1 from person involved with other activities. If admitted, will need to submit letter from superintendent of local school district attesting to completion of program of home instruction meeting requirements of Section 100.10 of the Regulations of the Commissioner of Education, or passing score on GED. **Learning Disabled:** No separate admissions process: eligibility for services must be established by provision of disability documentation that meets institutional standards.

High school preparation. College-preparatory program recommended. 17 units recommended. Recommended units include English 4, mathematics 3, social studies 4, science 3 and foreign language 3.

2015-2016 Annual costs. Tuition/fees: $9,461; $24,541 out-of-state. Room/board: $13,061. Books/supplies: $1,196. Personal expenses: $1,230.

2014-2015 Financial aid. Need-based: 2,756 full-time freshmen applied for aid; 2,219 deemed to have need; 2,085 received aid. Average need met was 64%. Average scholarship/grant was $5,826; average loan $3,525. 42% of total undergraduate aid awarded as scholarships/grants, 58% as loans/jobs. **Non-need-based:** Awarded to 3,908 full-time undergraduates, including 623 freshmen. Scholarships awarded for academics, art, athletics, minority status, music/drama, state residency.

Application procedures. Admission: Priority date 11/15; no deadline. $50 fee, may be waived for applicants with need. Admission notification on a rolling basis beginning on or about 2/1. Must reply by May 1 or within 2 week(s) if notified thereafter. **Financial aid:** Priority date 3/1; no closing date. FAFSA required. Applicants notified on a rolling basis starting 2/1; must reply by 5/1.

Academics. Over 300 baccalaureate, master's and doctoral degree programs. **Special study options:** Accelerated study, combined bachelor's/graduate degree, cooperative education, cross-registration, distance learning, double major, dual enrollment of high school students, ESL, exchange student, honors, independent study, internships, liberal arts/career combination, student-designed major, study abroad, teacher certification program, Washington semester. Certificate programs, combined degree programs, early assurance program with School of Medicine and Dentistry, Honors College,

Learning Communities and The Academies. **Credit/placement by examination:** AP, CLEP, IB, SAT, ACT, institutional tests. Maximum of 30 credits from International Baccalaureate. **Support services:** Learning center, pre-admission summer program, reduced course load, study skills assistance, tutoring, writing center.

Honors college/program. Minimum 93 high school average, 1300 SAT combined reading and math, 29 ACT. Enroll approximately 325 freshmen a year. Program requirements include completion of colloquium and two honors seminars plus 16 credits of advanced study opportunities.

Majors. Architecture: Architecture, environmental design. **Area/ethnic studies:** African-American, American, Asian. **Biology:** General, biochemistry, bioinformatics, biomedical sciences, biophysics, biotechnology, exercise physiology, pharmacology/toxicology. **Business:** Accounting, business admin, international. **Communications:** Communications/speech/rhetoric. **Computer sciences:** Computer science, information systems. **Engineering:** General, aerospace, applied physics, biomedical, chemical, civil, computer, electrical, environmental, industrial, mechanical, structural. **English:** English lit. **Foreign languages:** Classics, French, German, Italian, linguistics, Spanish. **Health services:** Audiology/speech pathology, clinical lab science, nuclear medical technology, nursing (RN), occupational therapy, pharmaceutical sciences. **History:** General. **Liberal arts:** Humanities. **Math:** General, applied, statistics. **Philosophy/religion:** Judaic, philosophy. **Physical sciences:** Chemistry, geology, physics, theoretical physics. **Psychology:** General. **Social sciences:** General, anthropology, economics, geography, political science, sociology. **Visual/performing arts:** Art, art history/conservation, dance, dramatic, film/cinema/video, music, music performance, musical theater, studio arts.

Most popular majors. Biology 9%, business/marketing 17%, communications/journalism 8%, engineering/engineering technologies 14%, health sciences 6%, psychology 12%, social sciences 17%.

Technology on campus. 3,061 workstations in dormitories, library, computer center, student center. Dormitories wired for high-speed internet access and linked to campus network. Commuter students can connect to campus network. Online course registration, online library, helpline, repair service, student web hosting, wireless network available.

Student life. Freshman orientation: Available, $190 fee. Preregistration for classes offered. One-and-a-half-day program. **Policies:** University standards, administrative regulations and student conduct rules apply. **Housing:** Guaranteed on-campus for all undergraduates. Coed dorms, special housing for disabled, apartments, themed housing available. $300 fully refundable deposit, deadline 5/1. Academic interest, honors, freshman, shared interest housing available. **Activities:** Bands, campus ministries, choral groups, dance, drama, film society, international student organizations, literary magazine, music ensembles, Model UN, musical theater, opera, radio station, student government, student newspaper, symphony orchestra, TV station, over 450 registered organizations.

Athletics. NCAA. **Intercollegiate:** Baseball M, basketball, cross-country, diving, football (tackle) M, rowing (crew) W, soccer, softball W, swimming, tennis, track and field, volleyball W, wrestling M. **Intramural:** Basketball, football (non-tackle) W, ice hockey, soccer, volleyball. **Team name:** Bulls.

Student services. Adult student services, alcohol/substance abuse counseling, chaplain/spiritual director, career counseling, services for economically disadvantaged, student employment services, financial aid counseling, health services, legal services, minority student services, on-campus daycare, personal counseling, placement for graduates, veterans' counselor, women's services. **Physically disabled:** Services for visually, speech, hearing impaired.

Contact. E-mail: ub-admissions@buffalo.edu
Phone: (716) 645-6900 Toll-free number: (888) 822-3648
Fax: (716) 645-6411
Jose Aviles, Director of Admissions, SUNY University at Buffalo, 12 Capen Hall, Buffalo, NY 14260-1660

SUNY University at Stony Brook
Stony Brook, New York
www.stonybrook.edu

CB member
CB code: 2548

- Public 4-year university
- Residential campus in large town
- 16,583 degree-seeking undergraduates: 6% part-time, 45% women, 7% African American, 24% Asian American, 11% Hispanic/Latino, 2% Multi-racial, non-Hispanic, 13% international
- 7,849 degree-seeking graduate students
- 41% of applicants admitted
- SAT or ACT (ACT writing recommended), application essay required
- 68% graduate within 6 years

General. Founded in 1957. Regionally accredited. **Degrees:** 3,902 bachelor's awarded; master's, professional, doctoral offered. **ROTC:** Army, Air Force. **Location:** 60 miles from New York City. **Calendar:** Semester, limited summer session. **Full-time faculty:** 1,124 total; 91% have terminal degrees, 19% minority, 37% women. **Part-time faculty:** 580 total; 38% have terminal degrees, 13% minority, 53% women. **Class size:** 43% < 20, 31% 20-39, 5% 40-49, 12% 50-99, 9% >100. **Special facilities:** Brookhaven National Laboratory, supercomputer, Van de Graaf accelerator, Centers for Molecular Medicine and Biology Learning Laboratories, Museum of Long Island Natural Sciences, Stony Brook University Medical Center, observatory, marine station, marine and atmospheric sciences research vessel, nature preserve, Center for the Arts.

Freshman class profile. 34,146 applied, 13,995 admitted, 2,836 enrolled.

Mid 50% test scores		GPA 2.0-2.99:	1%
SAT critical reading:	550-660	Rank in top quarter:	79%
SAT math:	600-720	Rank in top tenth:	46%
SAT writing:	540-660	End year in good standing:	93%
ACT composite:	26-31	Return as sophomores:	90%
GPA 3.75 or higher:	54%	Out-of-state:	11%
GPA 3.50-3.74:	25%	Live on campus:	85%
GPA 3.0-3.49:	20%	International:	16%

Basis for selection. High school GPA, test scores and level of high school curriculum most important factors. One letter of recommendation and supplemental application, including an essay, are required. Class rank, interview, extracurricular activities, considered. Notification by 4/1. Applications accepted after priority deadline are on a space-available basis. Audition and musicianship examination required for major in music. Two essays required for admission to Scholars for Medicine, Engineering Scholars for Medicine, and Scholar for Dental Medicine. **Home schooled:** State high school equivalency certificate required. Applicants required to take 5 Regents exams through their home district or have their home district verify that they have fulfilled high school graduation requirements. **Learning Disabled:** Applicants required to submit documentation of learning disability. Psychological and educational evaluation also required.

High school preparation. College-preparatory program required. 16 units required; 19 recommended. Required and recommended units include English 4, mathematics 3-4, social studies 4, science 3-4 and foreign language 2-3. 4 math and 4 science recommended for applicants to science, engineering, and math programs.

2015-2016 Annual costs. Tuition/fees: $8,855; $23,935 out-of-state. Room/board: $12,032. Books/supplies: $900. Personal expenses: $1,368.

2014-2015 Financial aid. Need-based: 2,180 full-time freshmen applied for aid; 1,535 deemed to have need; 1,520 received aid. Average need met was 71%. Average scholarship/grant was $9,316; average loan $3,714. 48% of total undergraduate aid awarded as scholarships/grants, 52% as loans/jobs. **Non-need-based:** Awarded to 2,070 full-time undergraduates, including 689 freshmen. Scholarships awarded for academics, alumni affiliation, art, athletics, job skills, leadership, music/drama.

Application procedures. Admission: Priority date 1/15; deadline 2/1 (postmark date). $50 fee, may be waived for applicants with need. Admission notification on a rolling basis beginning on or about 4/1. Must reply by May 1 or within 2 week(s) if notified thereafter. **Financial aid:** Priority date 3/1; no closing date. FAFSA required. Applicants notified on a rolling basis starting 4/1; must reply by 5/1 or within 2 week(s) of notification.

Academics. Special study options: Combined bachelor's/graduate degree, cross-registration, distance learning, double major, dual enrollment of high school students, ESL, exchange student, honors, independent study, internships, New York semester, student-designed major, study abroad, teacher certification program, Washington semester. Sequential and combined Bachelor/Master degree programs. **Credit/placement by examination:** AP, CLEP, IB, SAT, ACT, institutional tests. 30 credit hours maximum toward bachelor's degree. **Support services:** Learning center, reduced course load, remedial instruction, tutoring, writing center.

Honors college/program. High grades in major subject areas, minimum cumulative unweighted high school average of 93, minimum combined SAT (exclusive of Writing) of 1300 or ACT score of 30, record of advanced or college-level course work, and evidence of writing ability required.

Majors. Architecture: Environmental design. **Area/ethnic studies:** African-American, American, Asian, European, women's. **Biology:** General, biochemistry, ecology, evolutionary, marine, pharmacology. **Business:** Business admin. **Communications:** Journalism. **Computer sciences:** General, information systems. **Conservation:** Environmental studies. **Engineering:** General, biomedical, biomolecular, civil, computer, computer hardware, electrical, mechanical. **English:** English lit. **Foreign languages:** Comparative lit, French, German, Italian, linguistics, Spanish. **Health services:** Athletic training, clinical lab science, clinical nutrition, nursing (RN), respiratory therapy technology. **History:** General. **Human services:** Social work. **Math:** General, applied. **Philosophy/religion:** Philosophy, religion. **Physical sciences:**

Astronomy, atmospheric science, chemistry, geology, physics. **Psychology:** General. **Social sciences:** Anthropology, economics, political science, sociology. **Visual/performing arts:** Art, art history/conservation, dramatic, music.

Most popular majors. Biology 13%, business/marketing 8%, engineering/engineering technologies 8%, health sciences 22%, psychology 12%, social sciences 10%.

Technology on campus. 1,746 workstations in dormitories, library, computer center, student center. Dormitories wired for high-speed internet access and linked to campus network. Commuter students can connect to campus network. Online course registration, online library, helpline, repair service, student web hosting, wireless network available.

Student life. Freshman orientation: Mandatory, $300 fee. Preregistration for classes offered. One-day session held June through August. One-day program prior to first day of classes. **Housing:** Coed dorms, special housing for disabled, apartments, wellness housing available. $200 partly refundable deposit, deadline 5/1. Single sex floors in coed dorms available. **Activities:** Bands, choral groups, dance, drama, film society, international student organizations, literary magazine, music ensembles, Model UN, musical theater, opera, radio station, student government, student newspaper, symphony orchestra, TV station, Jewish, Protestant, Catholic, Islamic Society, Baha'i religious organizations, Inter-Varsity Christian Fellowship, international club, Chinese association, Indian student association, Pakistan club, African students association.

Athletics. NCAA. **Intercollegiate:** Baseball M, basketball, cross-country, diving, football (tackle) M, lacrosse, soccer, softball W, swimming, tennis, track and field, volleyball W. **Intramural:** Badminton, basketball, racquetball, soccer, softball, table tennis, tennis, volleyball. **Team name:** Seawolves.

Student services. Adult student services, alcohol/substance abuse counseling, chaplain/spiritual director, career counseling, services for economically disadvantaged, student employment services, financial aid counseling, health services, minority student services, on-campus daycare, personal counseling, placement for graduates, veterans' counselor, women's services. **Physically disabled:** Services for visually, speech, hearing impaired.

Contact. E-mail: enroll@stonybrook.edu
Phone: (631) 632-6868 Toll-free number: (800) 872-7869
Fax: (631) 632-9898
Judith Burke-Berhannan, Dean of Admissions, SUNY University at Stony Brook, 118 Administration Building, Stony Brook, NY 11794-1901

SUNY Upstate Medical University
Syracuse, New York
www.upstate.edu   **CB code: 2547**

- Public two-year upper-division health science and nursing college
- Residential campus in small city
- Application essay, interview required

General. Founded in 1834. Regionally accredited. Undergraduate level consists of upper-division programs. Affiliated with Crouse-Irving Memorial Hospital, Veteran's Administration Medical Center, Community General Hospital of Greater Syracuse, St. Joseph's Hospital Health Center, Hutchings Psychiatric Center. **Degrees:** 106 bachelor's awarded; master's, professional, doctoral offered. **Articulation:** Agreements with SUNY Alfred, SUNY Canton, SUNY Cobleskill, SUNY Cortland, SUNY Delhi, SUNY Geneseo, SUNY Morrisville, SUNY Oswego, SUNY Oneonta, Cayuga CC, Columbia-Greene CC, Finger Lakes CC, Genesee CC, Jefferson CC, Mohawk Valley CC, Monroe CC, Niagara County CC, North Country CC, Onondaga CC, Sullivan CC, Tompkins Cortland CC. **ROTC:** Army. **Location:** 250 miles from New York City, 150 miles from Buffalo. **Calendar:** Semester, limited summer session. **Full-time faculty:** 47 total; 55% have terminal degrees, 4% minority, 68% women. **Part-time faculty:** 7 total; 71% women. **Class size:** 82% < 20, 14% 20-39, 3% 40-49, less than 1% 50-99. **Special facilities:** Institutionally owned and operated 350-bed teaching hospital and Level 1 trauma center.

Student profile. 217 degree-seeking undergraduates. 100% entered as juniors. 61% transferred from two-year, 39% transferred from four-year institutions.

Out-of-state:	9%	25 or older:	52%

Basis for selection. College transcript, application essay, interview required. Evaluation of academic performance in courses required for admission. Personal interviews, recommendations, essay also important. Applicants must complete admissions course requirements prior to enrolling. Final decision made at discretion of admissions committee, regardless of applicant's prior academic standing. Transfer accepted as juniors.

2015-2016 Annual costs. Tuition/fees: $7,279; $17,129 out-of-state. Books/supplies: $1,105. Personal expenses: $2,008.

Application procedures. Admission: Rolling admission. $50 fee, may be waived for applicants with need. Application must be submitted online. High school seniors may apply for admission two years prior to intended date of entry. Application deadline for 3+3 and 4+3 Physical Therapy (DPT) Early Admission program February 1. Early Admission deadline for bachelor's programs March 1. Preference to New York residents. Transfer students apply in fall one year prior to intended date of entry. **Financial aid:** Applicants notified on a rolling basis starting 4/15; must reply within 2 weeks of notification. FAFSA required.

Academics. Special study options: Accelerated study, combined bachelor's/graduate degree, distance learning, independent study, internships. Distance Learning available for the Respiratory Therapy program at the SUNY Jefferson Community College campus. Accelerated 3+3 Doctor of Physical Therapy program available in conjunction with SUNY Brockport, SUNY Oneonta, SUNY Geneseo, SUNY Oswego, SUNY ESF, Syracuse University and LeMoyne College. Accelerated RN to MS nursing program. **Credit/placement by examination:** AP, CLEP, institutional tests. 60 credit hours maximum toward bachelor's degree.

Majors. Health services: Clinical lab science, nursing (RN), perfusion technology, respiratory therapy technology, sonography.

Technology on campus. 150 workstations in dormitories, library, computer center, student center. Dormitories wired for high-speed internet access and linked to campus network. Commuter students can connect to campus network. Helpline, student web hosting, wireless network available.

Student life. Policies: Students under 21 required to live on campus unless living at home. **Housing:** Coed dorms, apartments available. $200 nonrefundable deposit, deadline 7/1. **Activities:** International student organizations, student government, student newspaper, campus activities governing board, Chinese student association, Adopt-a-School, Christian medical fellowship, Community Outreach Preventive Education (COPE), Jewish medical association, Muslim student association.

Athletics. Intramural: Basketball, racquetball, soccer, softball, table tennis, tennis, volleyball.

Student services. Alcohol/substance abuse counseling, career counseling, financial aid counseling, health services, minority student services, on-campus daycare, personal counseling, placement for graduates, veterans' counselor.

Contact. E-mail: admiss@upstate.edu
Phone: (315) 464-4570 Fax: (315) 464-8867
Jennifer Welch, Director of Admissions, SUNY Upstate Medical University, 766 Irving Avenue, Syracuse, NY 13210

Syracuse University
Syracuse, New York   **CB member**
www.syr.edu   **CB code: 2823**

- Private 4-year university
- Residential campus in small city
- 14,620 degree-seeking undergraduates: 3% part-time, 55% women, 8% African American, 8% Asian American, 11% Hispanic/Latino, 1% Native American, 3% Multi-racial, non-Hispanic, 12% international
- 6,390 degree-seeking graduate students
- 48% of applicants admitted
- SAT or ACT with writing, application essay required
- 81% graduate within 6 years; 19% enter graduate study

General. Founded in 1870. Regionally accredited. **Degrees:** 3,451 bachelor's, 6 associate awarded; master's, professional, doctoral offered. **ROTC:** Army, Air Force. **Location:** 150 miles from Albany, 250 miles from New York City. **Calendar:** Semester, extensive summer session. **Full-time faculty:** 1,077 total; 89% have terminal degrees, 20% minority, 38% women. **Part-time faculty:** 551 total; 16% have terminal degrees, 7% minority, 47% women. **Class size:** 87% < 20, 8% 20-39, 2% 40-49, 2% 50-99, 1% >100. **Special facilities:** Special collections research center, the global collaboratory, center of excellence in environmental and energy systems, center for science and technology, life sciences complex, Fidelity MODUS 622i flight simulator, the Dick Clark Studios, center for media innovation, digital news center, center for entrepreneurship, investment institute, architecture studios, technology center, child development laboratory, audio laboratory and archive, speech, language, and hearing clinic, humanities center.

Freshman class profile. 33,254 applied, 16,071 admitted, 3,481 enrolled.

Mid 50% test scores			
SAT critical reading:	530-630	Rank in top quarter:	70%
SAT math:	560-660	Rank in top tenth:	35%
SAT writing:	530-640	Return as sophomores:	91%
ACT composite:	24-29	Out-of-state:	67%
GPA 3.75 or higher:	43%	Live on campus:	99%
GPA 3.50-3.74:	22%	International:	13%
GPA 3.0-3.49:	29%	Fraternities:	29%
GPA 2.0-2.99:	6%	Sororities:	31%

Basis for selection. Important factors include: strong performance in a rigorous college preparatory curriculum, strength within applicable talent components (portfolio or audition when required), good citizenship, personal characteristics and talents. Other factors include: standardized test scores, academic recommendations and counselor evaluation. Applicants not admitted to their first-choice program may be considered for an alternate offer of admission on a space-available basis if second/third choice options are indicated on the Syracuse University-Common Application. Priority is given to those applying to first choice programs. Standardized test scores (SAT or ACT with writing section) are required if you are a domestic student or an international student studying in the U.S. or studying overseas in an American or international school. Syracuse University does not require or consider the SAT subject tests. Portfolio required for art and architecture programs; audition required for drama and music programs. Interviews are made available, but are not required. **Home schooled:** Transcript of courses and grades, interview, letter of recommendation (nonparent) required. Students without a GED are required to submit the following: Transcripts or the equivalent, signed by the parent, guardian, or home-school instructor that lists the courses completed for grades 9-12 and the student's performance in each course, SAT 1 or ACT with writing, two letters of recommendation from someone outside the student's household (teacher, community leader, or other individuals familiar with the student), proof of school completion by the state Department of Education or local school district. Specifically include an official document that attests that the home-schooled education meets the equivalency to what is taught in the high school district. This document may be provided by the state Department of Education (if provided by that state), the Homeschool liaison within the student's school district or from a school official in the high school district. **Learning Disabled:** There are no special admission requirements or procedures, but families are encouraged to contact the Office of Disability Services to learn more about supportive services.

High school preparation. College-preparatory program required. 23 units recommended. Recommended units include English 4, mathematics 4, social studies 4, history 4, science 4 and foreign language 3.

2015-2016 Annual costs. Tuition/fees: $43,318. Room/board: $14,880.

2015-2016 Financial aid. Need-based: 2,363 full-time freshmen applied for aid; 1,769 deemed to have need; 1,729 received aid. Average need met was 96%. Average scholarship/grant was $29,715; average loan $4,600. 74% of total undergraduate aid awarded as scholarships/grants, 26% as loans/jobs. **Non-need-based:** Awarded to 2,493 full-time undergraduates, including 747 freshmen. Scholarships awarded for academics, art, athletics, music/drama, ROTC.

Application procedures. Admission: Closing date 1/1 (postmark date). $75 fee, may be waived for applicants with need. Admission notification on a rolling basis beginning on or about 3/15. Must reply by May 1 or within 2 week(s) if notified thereafter. **Financial aid:** Closing date 2/1. FAFSA, CSS PROFILE required. Applicants notified by 3/15; must reply by 5/1.

Academics. Special study options: Accelerated study, combined bachelor's/graduate degree, cooperative education, cross-registration, distance learning, double major, dual enrollment of high school students, ESL, exchange student, honors, independent study, internships, liberal arts/career combination, New York semester, student-designed major, study abroad, teacher certification program, Washington semester. **Credit/placement by examination:** AP, CLEP, IB, institutional tests. 30 credit hours maximum toward associate degree, 30 toward bachelor's. For undergraduates, the student's school/college may accept a maximum of 30 semester hours from a combination of SU Advanced Credit exams and any other credit (e.g., AP exams, experiential learning). **Support services:** Learning center, pre-admission summer program, study skills assistance, tutoring, writing center.

Majors. Architecture: Architecture, history/criticism, interior. **Area/ethnic studies:** African-American, Latin American, Near/Middle Eastern, Russian/Slavic, women's. **Biology:** General, biochemistry, biophysics, biotechnology, neuroscience. **Business:** Accounting, business admin, entrepreneurial studies, finance, hospitality admin, knowledge management, logistics, marketing, organizational leadership, real estate, sales/distribution. **Communications:** Advertising, broadcast journalism, communications/speech/rhetoric, journalism, persuasive communications, photojournalism, public relations, radio/TV. **Computer sciences:** General, information systems. **Education:** General, art, biology, chemistry, early childhood special, earth science, elementary special ed, English, family/consumer sciences, mathematics, music, physical, physics, social studies, Spanish. **Engineering:** General, aerospace, applied physics, biomedical, chemical, civil, computer, electrical, environmental, mechanical. **English:** English lit. **Foreign languages:** General, classics, comparative lit, French, German, Italian, linguistics, Russian, Spanish. **Health services:** Communication disorders, predental, premedicine, preveterinary. **History:** General. **Human services:** General, social work. **Liberal arts:** Arts/sciences. **Math:** General, applied. **Parks/recreation:** Exercise sciences, health/fitness, sports admin. **Philosophy/religion:** Ethics, Judaic, philosophy, religion. **Physical sciences:** Chemistry, geology, physics. **Protective services:** Forensics. **Psychology:** General. **Social sciences:** Anthropology, economics, geography, international relations, political science, sociology. **Visual/performing arts:** Acting, art history/conservation, ceramics, cinematography, commercial/advertising art, design, dramatic, fashion design, fiber arts, illustration, industrial design, metal/jewelry, music, music history, music management, music performance, music technology, music theory/composition, musical theater, painting, percussion instruments, photography, piano/keyboard, printmaking, sculpture, stringed instruments, studio arts, theater arts management, theater design, voice/opera. **Work/family studies:** General, family studies, food/nutrition, human nutrition, merchandising.

Most popular majors. Business/marketing 14%, communications/journalism 13%, computer/information sciences 6%, engineering/engineering technologies 9%, social sciences 12%, visual/performing arts 11%.

Technology on campus. 3,500 workstations in dormitories, library, computer center, student center. Dormitories wired for high-speed internet access and linked to campus network. Commuter students can connect to campus network. Online course registration, online library, helpline, repair service, student web hosting, wireless network available.

Student life. Freshman orientation: Mandatory. Preregistration for classes offered. Held two times a year, August (4 to 5 days) and January (2 days). **Policies:** Freshmen and sophomores required to live on campus. Students must adhere to the Code of Student Conduct. Incoming students are required to complete Think About It, an interactive, online experience designed to help students make smart decisions in college around sex, alcohol, and drugs. Incoming students are required to attend certain mandatory events/trainings. Residence hall students must adhere to residence life policies. Students must adhere to academic integrity policies. Freshmen not permitted cars on campus. **Housing:** Guaranteed on-campus for freshmen. Coed dorms, special housing for disabled, apartments, fraternity/sorority housing, themed housing, wellness housing available. $450 partly refundable deposit, deadline 5/1. **Activities:** Bands, campus ministries, choral groups, dance, drama, film society, international student organizations, literary magazine, music ensembles, Model UN, musical theater, opera, radio station, student government, student newspaper, symphony orchestra, TV station, College Democrats, College Republicans, Pride Union, Student African American Society, Habitat For Humanity, Nourish International, SU Catholic Student Fellowship, Hillel Jewish Student Union, Muslim Students' Association, AMI: A Men's Issue.

Athletics. NCAA. **Intercollegiate:** Basketball, cheerleading, cross-country, field hockey W, football (tackle) M, ice hockey W, lacrosse, rowing (crew), soccer, softball W, tennis W, track and field, volleyball W. **Intramural:** Basketball, football (non-tackle), ice hockey, racquetball, soccer, softball, tennis, volleyball. **Team name:** Orange.

Student services. Adult student services, alcohol/substance abuse counseling, chaplain/spiritual director, career counseling, services for economically disadvantaged, student employment services, financial aid counseling, health services, legal services, minority student services, on-campus daycare, personal counseling, placement for graduates, veterans' counselor, women's services. **Physically disabled:** Services for visually, speech, hearing impaired.

Contact. E-mail: orange@syr.edu
Phone: (315) 443-3611 Fax: (315) 443-4226
Maurice Harris, Dean of Undergraduate Admissions, Syracuse University, 900 South Crouse Avenue, Syracuse, NY 13244-5040

Talmudical Institute of Upstate New York
Rochester, New York
www.tiuny.org
CB code: 1426

- Private 5-year rabbinical and seminary college for men affiliated with the Jewish faith
- Residential campus in large city
- 9 degree-seeking undergraduates
- Interview required

General. Founded in 1974. Accredited by AARTS. First Talmudic degree offered. **Degrees:** 4 bachelor's awarded; doctoral offered. **Calendar:** Semester. **Full-time faculty:** 2 total. **Part-time faculty:** 1 total.

Freshman class profile.

Out-of-state: 35% Live on campus: 100%

Basis for selection. Interview and school achievement record important.

2015-2016 Annual costs. Tuition/fees: $5,100. Room/board: $4,000.

Application procedures. Admission: Closing date 9/1. Admission notification on a rolling basis. **Financial aid:** No deadline. Applicants notified on a rolling basis.

Academics. Special study options: Dual enrollment of high school students. **Credit/placement by examination:** AP, CLEP.

Majors. Philosophy/religion: Judaic. **Theology:** Talmudic.

Technology on campus. 2 workstations in computer center.

Student life. Policies: Religious observance required. **Housing:** Guaranteed on-campus for all undergraduates.

Contact. Phone: (585) 473-2810 Fax: (585) 442-0417
Talmudical Institute of Upstate New York, 769 Park Avenue, Rochester, NY 14607

Talmudical Seminary Oholei Torah
Brooklyn, New York
www.tsot.edu
CB code: 0712

- Private 4-year rabbinical and seminary college for men affiliated with the Jewish faith
- Very large city
- 360 degree-seeking undergraduates
- Interview required

General. Founded in 1956. Accredited by AARTS. First Talmudic degree offered. **Degrees:** 8 bachelor's awarded. **ROTC:** Army, Naval. **Calendar:** Semester, limited summer session. **Full-time faculty:** 18 total. **Part-time faculty:** 5 total.

Basis for selection. Interview and institutional entrance examinations important.

2015-2016 Annual costs. Tuition/fees: $9,300. Room/board: $7,200.

Application procedures. Admission: No deadline. Admission notification on a rolling basis. **Financial aid:** No deadline. Applicants notified on a rolling basis starting 5/21.

Academics. Credit/placement by examination: AP, CLEP, institutional tests. **Support services:** Tutoring.

Majors. Theology: Talmudic.

Student life. Policies: Religious observance required. **Activities:** TV station, Lubavitcher Youth Organization.

Student services. Career counseling, personal counseling.

Contact. Phone: (718) 774-5215
Talmudical Seminary Oholei Torah, 667 Eastern Parkway, Brooklyn, NY 11213-3397

Torah Temimah Talmudical Seminary
Brooklyn, New York
CB code: 7132

- Private 4-year rabbinical and seminary college for men affiliated with the Jewish faith
- Very large city
- 178 degree-seeking undergraduates

General. Accredited by AARTS. **Degrees:** 5 bachelor's awarded; doctoral offered. **Calendar:** Differs by program. **Full-time faculty:** 9 total.

Basis for selection. Completion of college-preparatory program and recommendations required. Secondary school record recommended.

2015-2016 Annual costs. Tuition/fees: $10,750. Room/board: $3,500.

Application procedures. Admission: No deadline.

Academics. Credit/placement by examination: AP, CLEP.

Majors. Theology: Talmudic.

Contact. Phone: (718) 853-8500
Torah Temimah Talmudical Seminary, 507 Ocean Parkway, Brooklyn, NY 11218

Touro College
New York, New York
www.touro.edu CB code: 2902

- Private 4-year liberal arts college
- Commuter campus in very large city
- 6,036 degree-seeking undergraduates: 18% part-time, 68% women, 15% African American, 4% Asian American, 8% Hispanic/Latino, 4% international
- 4,662 degree-seeking graduate students
- 34% of applicants admitted
- 59% graduate within 6 years

General. Founded in 1970. Regionally accredited. School of General Studies provides programs for part-time and adult students. **Degrees:** 1,443 bachelor's, 608 associate awarded; master's, professional, doctoral offered. **Calendar:** Semester, limited summer session. **Full-time faculty:** 484 total; 15% minority, 49% women. **Part-time faculty:** 851 total; 21% minority, 51% women. **Class size:** 65% < 20, 22% 20-39, 5% 40-49, 7% 50-99, 1% >100.

Freshman class profile. 2,201 applied, 751 admitted, 381 enrolled.

Mid 50% test scores			
SAT critical reading:	480-630	GPA 3.0-3.49:	22%
SAT math:	470-610	GPA 2.0-2.99:	27%
SAT writing:	470-600	Return as sophomores:	66%
GPA 3.75 or higher:	13%	Out-of-state:	13%
GPA 3.50-3.74:	21%	International:	3%

Basis for selection. For College of Liberal Arts and Sciences, 3.0 high school GPA, SAT verbal and math scores of 500 preferred. Recommendations from high school teachers and counselors and motivation important. High school experience less important for applicants to associate degree programs who take institutional admissions test. SAT or ACT recommended. SAT/ACT scores are required in 90% of Admissions cases. Essay and interview recommended for College of Liberal Arts and Sciences.

High school preparation. College-preparatory program recommended. 16 units required. Required units include English 4, mathematics 2, history 2, science 2, foreign language 2 and academic electives 4. Requirements may vary by division.

2016-2017 Annual costs. Tuition/fees: $16,980. Room/board: $11,970. Books/supplies: $1,025. Personal expenses: $2,398.

2015-2016 Financial aid. Need-based: Average need met was 40%. Average scholarship/grant was $2,058; average loan $1,799. **Non-need-based:** Scholarships awarded for academics, alumni affiliation.

Application procedures. Admission: Priority date 4/15; no deadline. $50 fee, may be waived for applicants with need. Admission notification on a rolling basis beginning on or about 10/1. Must reply by May 1 or within 3 week(s) if notified thereafter. **Financial aid:** Priority date 5/15, closing date 8/15. FAFSA, institutional form required. Applicants notified on a rolling basis starting 5/1; must reply within 4 week(s) of notification.

Academics. Special study options: Accelerated study, combined bachelor's/graduate degree, cross-registration, distance learning, double major, dual enrollment of high school students, ESL, honors, independent study, internships, liberal arts/career combination, student-designed major, study abroad, teacher certification program. **Credit/placement by examination:** AP, CLEP, institutional tests. **Support services:** Learning center, reduced course load, remedial instruction, tutoring.

Majors. Biology: General. **Business:** General, accounting, business admin, management information systems, managerial economics, marketing. **Communications:** Communications/speech/rhetoric. **Computer sciences:** General. **Education:** Special ed. **English:** English lit, rhetoric/composition. **Foreign languages:** General, Hebrew. **Health services:** Communication disorders, health information technology, nursing (RN), physician assistant, predental, premedicine, prepharmacy, preveterinary. **History:** General. **Liberal arts:** Arts/sciences. **Math:** General. **Philosophy/religion:** Judaic, philosophy. **Physical sciences:** Chemistry. **Psychology:** General. **Social sciences:** General, economics, political science, sociology.

Most popular majors. Biology 9%, business/marketing 14%, health sciences 17%, interdisciplinary studies 17%, psychology 23%, public administration/social services 6%.

Technology on campus. 400 workstations in library, computer center.

Student life. Freshman orientation: Available. Preregistration for classes offered. **Housing:** Single-sex dorms available. $50 deposit. No board or meal plan available. Kitchen facilities in student housing. **Activities:** Campus ministries, dance, literary magazine, student government, student newspaper, accounting and business society, biology club, debating society, Jewish Affairs Committee, foreign students association, Omicron Delta.

Student services. Adult student services, career counseling, student employment services, personal counseling, placement for graduates, veterans' counselor.

Contact. E-mail: lasadmit@adminm.touro.edu
Phone: (718) 252-7800 ext. 299 Fax: (718) 253-9455
Arthur Wigfall, Director of Admissions, Touro College, 27 West 23rd Street, New York, NY 10010

U.T.A. Mesivta-Kiryas Joel
Monroe, New York

- Private 4-year rabbinical college for men affiliated with the Jewish faith
- Large town
- 1,527 degree-seeking undergraduates

General. Accredited by AARTS. **Degrees:** 293 bachelor's awarded. **Calendar:** Semester. **Full-time faculty:** 110 total.

Basis for selection. Religious commitment most important.

2015-2016 Annual costs. Tuition/fees: $9,000. Room/board: $4,000.

Application procedures. Admission: No deadline.

Academics. Credit/placement by examination: AP, CLEP.

Majors. Theology: Talmudic.

Contact. Phone: (845) 783-9901
U.T.A. Mesivta-Kiryas Joel, 48 Bakertown Road, Suite 501, Monroe, NY 10950-2169

Union College
Schenectady, New York CB member
www.union.edu CB code: 2920

- Private 4-year engineering and liberal arts college
- Residential campus in small city
- 2,206 degree-seeking undergraduates: 46% women, 4% African American, 6% Asian American, 7% Hispanic/Latino, 2% Multi-racial, non-Hispanic, 7% international
- 38% of applicants admitted
- Application essay required
- 88% graduate within 6 years

General. Founded in 1795. Regionally accredited. **Degrees:** 511 bachelor's awarded. **ROTC:** Army, Naval, Air Force. **Location:** 15 miles from Albany, 175 miles from New York City. **Calendar:** Trimester, limited summer session. **Full-time faculty:** 209 total; 98% have terminal degrees, 12% minority, 43% women. **Part-time faculty:** 25 total; 40% have terminal degrees, 8% minority, 60% women. **Class size:** 73% < 20, 23% 20-39, 2% 40-49, 1% 50-99. **Special facilities:** Horticultural garden, superconducting nuclear magnetic resonance spectrometer, electron scanning microscope, tandem pelletron positive ion accelerator, X-ray diffraction equipment, remote-controlled telescope.

Freshman class profile. 5,996 applied, 2,297 admitted, 568 enrolled.

Mid 50% test scores			
SAT critical reading:	610-680	GPA 2.0-2.99:	13%
SAT math:	630-720	Rank in top quarter:	87%
SAT writing:	600-680	Rank in top tenth:	71%
ACT composite:	29-32	End year in good standing:	99%
GPA 3.75 or higher:	24%	Return as sophomores:	93%
GPA 3.50-3.74:	20%	Out-of-state:	69%
GPA 3.0-3.49:	43%	Live on campus:	99%
		International:	9%

Basis for selection. GED not accepted. Strong course selection and grades closely considered along with recommendations from high school. Beyond the academic record, extracurricular activities, ethnicity and geographic diversity are taken into consideration. Testing is optional except for combined programs, required for homeschooled students. Leadership in Medicine program applicants must submit the SAT and two SAT Subject Tests or the ACT with writing component; Law and Public Policy program applicants must submit the SAT or the ACT. Applicants to these programs must complete the necessary tests no later than November of their senior year. It is recommended that international applicants submit the SAT or ACT. The TOEFL or IELTS is required if English is not the first language. Portfolio recommended for art programs. **Home schooled:** Interview required.

High school preparation. College-preparatory program required. 16 units required; 24 recommended. Required and recommended units include English 4, mathematics 3-4, social studies 1-2, history 1-2, science 2-4 (laboratory 2-4) and foreign language 2-4.

2015-2016 Annual costs. Tuition/fees: $50,013. Room/board: $12,261. Books/supplies: $1,500. Personal expenses: $471.

2015-2016 Financial aid. Need-based: 347 full-time freshmen applied for aid; 280 deemed to have need; 280 received aid. Average need met was 100%. Average scholarship/grant was $35,750; average loan $3,570. 87% of total undergraduate aid awarded as scholarships/grants, 13% as loans/jobs. **Non-need-based:** Awarded to 753 full-time undergraduates, including 258 freshmen. Scholarships awarded for academics, ROTC.

Application procedures. Admission: Closing date 1/15 (postmark date). No application fee. Application must be submitted online. Admission notification by 4/1. Must reply by 5/1. **Financial aid:** Priority date 2/1, closing date 2/1. FAFSA, CSS PROFILE required. Applicants notified by 3/25; must reply by 5/1.

Academics. Special study options: Accelerated study, combined bachelor's/graduate degree, cross-registration, double major, dual enrollment of high school students, honors, independent study, internships, liberal arts/career combination, student-designed major, study abroad, teacher certification program. **Credit/placement by examination:** AP, CLEP, IB, institutional tests. 4 credit hours maximum toward bachelor's degree. **Support services:** Study skills assistance, tutoring, writing center.

Majors. Area/ethnic studies: African, American, Asian, Latin American/Caribbean. **Biology:** General, biochemistry, neuroscience. **Business:** Managerial economics. **Computer sciences:** General. **Engineering:** Biomedical, electrical, mechanical. **English:** English lit. **Foreign languages:** General, Chinese, classics, French, German, Spanish. **History:** General. **Liberal arts:** Arts/sciences, humanities. **Math:** General. **Philosophy/religion:** Philosophy, religion. **Physical sciences:** Astronomy, chemistry, geology, physics. **Psychology:** General. **Social sciences:** General, anthropology, economics, political science, sociology. **Visual/performing arts:** General, studio arts.

Most popular majors. Biology 15%, engineering/engineering technologies 13%, liberal arts 6%, physical sciences 8%, psychology 8%, social sciences 30%.

Technology on campus. 554 workstations in dormitories, library, computer center, student center. Dormitories wired for high-speed internet access and linked to campus network. Commuter students can connect to campus network. Online course registration, online library, helpline, repair service, student web hosting, wireless network available.

Student life. Freshman orientation: Mandatory, $250 fee. Preregistration for classes offered. Begins Thursday and ends Sunday before classes begin. Orientation fee included in Admission and Security deposit. **Policies:** All students are expected to live on campus during undergraduate years, provided housing is available. Freshmen not permitted cars on campus. **Housing:** Guaranteed on-campus for freshmen. Coed dorms, apartments, fraternity/sorority housing, themed housing available. All students and faculty members have house affiliations. Each house contributes intellectual, cultural, and social events to the campus. **Activities:** Bands, campus ministries, choral groups, dance, drama, film society, international student organizations, literary magazine, music ensembles, Model UN, radio station, student government, student newspaper, symphony orchestra, TV station, African and Latino Alliance of Students, Asian Student Union, Big Brothers/Big Sisters, College Republicans, Intervarsity Christian Fellowship, Jewish Student Union, Middle Eastern Civilization and Culture Association, Newman Club, UCARE-a community action club, Union College Democrats.

Athletics. NCAA. **Intercollegiate:** Baseball M, basketball, cross-country, diving, equestrian W, field hockey W, football (tackle) M, golf W, ice hockey, lacrosse, rowing (crew), soccer, softball W, swimming, tennis, track and field, volleyball W. **Intramural:** Basketball, football (non-tackle), football (tackle), lacrosse, racquetball, soccer, softball, squash, tennis, ultimate frisbee, volleyball. **Team name:** Dutchmen, Dutchwomen.

Student services. Alcohol/substance abuse counseling, chaplain/spiritual director, career counseling, services for economically disadvantaged, student employment services, financial aid counseling, health services, minority student services, personal counseling, placement for graduates. **Physically disabled:** Services for visually, hearing impaired.

Contact. E-mail: admissions@union.edu
Phone: (518) 388-6112 Toll-free number: (888) 843-6688
Fax: (518) 388-6986
Ann Brown, Director of Admissions, Union College, Grant Hall, 807 Union Street, Schenectady, NY 12308-3107

United States Merchant Marine Academy
Kings Point, New York
www.usmma.edu   **CB code: 2923**

▶ Public 4-year military and maritime college
▶ Residential campus in large town
▶ 939 degree-seeking undergraduates: 16% women
▶ 22 degree-seeking graduate students
▶ SAT or ACT (ACT writing optional), application essay required

General. Founded in 1943. Regionally accredited. Accepted applicants appointed to academy as midshipmen, USNR. Unique Sea-Year experience. **Degrees:** 224 bachelor's awarded; master's offered. **ROTC:** Army, Naval, Air Force. **Location:** 20 miles from midtown Manhattan. **Calendar:** Trimester, limited summer session. **Full-time faculty:** 120 total. **Part-time faculty:** 25 total. **Class size:** 45% < 20, 54% 20-39, less than 1% 40-49, less than 1% 50-99. **Special facilities:** US Merchant Marine Museum, computer-aided operational research facility.

Freshman class profile.

Mid 50% test scores			
SAT critical reading:	570-660	Rank in top quarter:	57%
SAT math:	620-690	Rank in top tenth:	33%
ACT composite:	26-30	Live on campus:	100%

Basis for selection. Nomination by U.S. representatives or senators. Competitive standing determined by test scores, high school GPA, class rank, motivation, extracurricular activities, interest in academy, industry, citizenship, and recommendations from counselors, teachers, school principal. Must also meet medical requirements and pass physical fitness exercise regimen. Untimed test results not acceptable. **Home schooled:** Statement describing home school structure and mission, transcript of courses and grades, letter of recommendation (nonparent) required. Must have completed chemistry with lab or physics with lab through state-certified instructor.

High school preparation. College-preparatory program recommended. 18 units required. Required and recommended units include English 4, mathematics 3-4, science 3-4 (laboratory 1-2), foreign language 2 and academic electives 8.

2015-2016 Annual costs. Books/supplies: $990. **Additional information:** All costs for tuition, board, books, and uniforms paid for by Federal Government. Students are required to purchase a compliant laptop computer, academic equipment (as needed), and pay for license fees, transportation costs, laundry and barber services. Students are not paid a monthly salary/stipend, unless they are at sea.

2014-2015 Financial aid. All financial aid based on need. 105 full-time freshmen applied for aid; 63 deemed to have need; 63 received aid. Average need met was 75%. Average scholarship/grant was $4,285; average loan $3,500. **Additional information:** Financial Aid awarded on a rolling basis; all students regarded as full time, undergraduates. The academy does not have institutional aid. Only Title IV FSA is awarded. Students will spend a cumulative period of one year at sea, where they will be paid a monthly salary of about $950.

Application procedures. Admission: Closing date 3/1 (receipt date). No application fee. Admission notification on a rolling basis beginning on or about 11/1. Must reply by 5/1. **Financial aid:** No deadline. FAFSA, institutional form required. Applicants notified on a rolling basis starting 5/1; must reply within 8 week(s) of notification.

Academics. Special study options: Honors, independent study, internships, semester at sea, study abroad. Sea training on merchant vessels. **Credit/placement by examination:** AP, CLEP, IB, institutional tests. 12 credit hours maximum toward bachelor's degree. **Support services:** Learning center, remedial instruction, study skills assistance, tutoring.

Majors. Engineering: Marine, systems.

Most popular majors. Engineering/engineering technologies 49%, trade and industry 51%.

Technology on campus. PC or laptop required. 1,200 workstations in dormitories, library. Dormitories wired for high-speed internet access and linked to campus network. Helpline, wireless network available.

Student life. Freshman orientation: Mandatory. Preregistration for classes offered. Seventeen-day orientation starting in early July. **Policies:** All regulated within the Regiment of Midshipmen. Freshmen not permitted cars on campus. **Housing:** Guaranteed on-campus for all undergraduates. Coed dorms available. Students required to live on campus. **Activities:** Bands, campus ministries, choral groups, music ensembles, student government, student newspaper, Christian fellowship community, Newman club, Band of Sisters club (Christian women).

Athletics. NCAA. **Intercollegiate:** Baseball M, basketball, cross-country, diving, football (tackle) M, lacrosse, rowing (crew), sailing, soccer M, swimming, tennis, track and field, volleyball W, wrestling M. **Intramural:** Racquetball, sailing, water polo. **Team name:** Mariners.

Student services. Adult student services, alcohol/substance abuse counseling, chaplain/spiritual director, career counseling, services for economically disadvantaged, financial aid counseling, health services, legal services, minority student services, personal counseling, placement for graduates, women's services.

Contact. E-mail: admissions@usmma.edu
Phone: (516) 726-5646 Toll-free number: (866) 546-4778
Fax: (516) 773-5390
LCDR. Keith Watson, Admissions Specialist, United States Merchant Marine Academy, 300 Steamboat Road, Admissions Center, Kings Point, NY 11024-1699

United States Military Academy
West Point, New York   **CB member**
www.westpoint.edu   **CB code: 2924**

- Public 4-year military college
- Residential campus in small town
- 4,348 degree-seeking undergraduates: 19% women, 10% African American, 6% Asian American, 12% Hispanic/Latino, 1% Native American, 1% Native Hawaiian/Pacific islander, 3% Multi-racial, non-Hispanic, 1% international
- 10% of applicants admitted
- SAT or ACT with writing, application essay required
- 84% graduate within 6 years; 3% enter graduate study

General. Founded in 1802. Regionally accredited. Graduates are commissioned as second lieutenants in the United States Army. **Degrees:** 1,033 bachelor's awarded. **Location:** 50 miles from New York City. **Calendar:** Semester, limited summer session. **Full-time faculty:** 641 total; 44% have terminal degrees, 11% minority, 18% women. **Class size:** 97% < 20, 3% 20-39. **Special facilities:** West Point museum, American Revolutionary-era Fort Putnam, 4,500-seat Eisenhower Hall, 18-hole golf course, ski slope, 500,000 square-foot Arvin Cadet Physical Development Center, Jefferson Hall Library and learning center.

Freshman class profile. 14,635 applied, 1,486 admitted, 1,236 enrolled.

Mid 50% test scores			
SAT critical reading:	580-680	**Rank in top tenth:**	52%
SAT math:	610-710	**End year in good standing:**	95%
SAT writing:	560-670	**Return as sophomores:**	93%
ACT composite:	26-31	**Out-of-state:**	95%
Rank in top quarter:	78%	**Live on campus:**	100%
		International:	1%

Basis for selection. All applicants must obtain a nomination from an approved source (Congress, the President, Vice President, or Department of the Army). Applicants must be at least 17 but not yet 23 years of age by July 1 of year of entry. They must also be an unmarried U.S. citizen (foreign national with approval) in good health, with no parental obligations or responsibilities, and must demonstrate leadership ability. Applicants should seek nomination and submit Service Academies Pre-candidate Questionnaire in spring of junior year. Applicants advised to seek nominations from as many sources as possible and to contact Admissions office between July 1 and January 15 of senior year. All new cadets must pass Cadet Basic Training before being admitted into West Point. Interview recommended. **Learning Disabled:** All new incoming Plebe Cadets admitted are commissioned as officers in the United States Army upon graduation. Therefore, cadets must meet certain requirements specified by public law in order to be considered for admission. All cadets must be in good physical and mental health and pass a Department of Defense qualifying medical examination.

High school preparation. 19 units recommended. Recommended units include English 4, mathematics 4, social studies 1, history 1, science 4 (laboratory 2), foreign language 2 and academic electives 3. English units should have strong emphasis on composition, grammar, literature and speech; math should include algebra, geometry, intermediate algebra, and trigonometry; U.S. history should include courses in geography, government and economics. Precalculus, calculus and basic computing course helpful.

2016-2017 Annual costs. All Cadets are members of the United States Army and receive a full scholarship, room, board, and a monthly salary. However, an INITIAL DEPOSIT is required from all new incoming Cadets to cover the initial issue of uniforms, books, supplies, and equipment. Any Cadet who cannot meet the Initial Deposit will have their end of month pay reduced until their cadet account is in line.

Financial aid. Additional information: Scholarships can be accepted for a cadet to satisfy the requirement of the initial deposit. However, scholarships from any agency that states the scholarship is to be used for tuition and/or room and board will not be accepted since there is no charge for these items.

Application procedures. Admission: Closing date 2/28 (receipt date). No application fee. Application must be submitted online. Admission notification by 5/1. Admission notification on a rolling basis beginning on or about 2/26. Must reply within 45 days after receiving acceptance letter.

Academics. Standard academic courses provide an essential core of knowledge in the arts and sciences with emphasis on problem solving. Advanced and elective courses allow the individual cadet to concentrate or major in a specific area of interest. The Academic Program, Physical Program, and Military Program form the three major aspects of the academy's leader-development experience. **Special study options:** Double major, exchange student, honors, independent study, internships, study abroad. Opportunities to attend Army Schools (Airborne, Air Assault, etc.) to learn special skills and to intern with an Army organization during the summer. **Credit/placement by examination:** AP, CLEP, institutional tests. **Support services:** Learning center, reduced course load, remedial instruction, study skills assistance, tutoring. Academic Excellence Program (AEP) provides all cadets with a variety of hands-on, state of the art academic support resources and services to help at all stages of their education. Athletic Academic Support Coordinator Program (AASC) helps cadet athletes balance their academic and athletic requirements, and provides skills necessary for success.

Majors. Area/ethnic studies: African, East Asian, European, Latin American, Near/Middle Eastern, Russian/Slavic. **Biology:** General. **Business:** Business admin, organizational behavior. **Computer sciences:** General, information technology. **Conservation:** Environmental science, environmental studies. **Engineering:** Chemical, civil, electrical, environmental, mechanical, nuclear, operations research, systems. **English:** English lit. **Foreign languages:** Arabic, Chinese, French, German, Portuguese, Russian, Spanish. **History:** American, military. **Liberal arts:** Humanities. **Math:** General. **Parks/recreation:** Exercise sciences. **Philosophy/religion:** Philosophy. **Physical sciences:** General, chemistry, physics. **Psychology:** Applied. **Social sciences:** Economics, geography, GIS/cartography, international relations, political science, sociology, U.S. government.

Most popular majors. Business/marketing 7%, engineering/engineering technologies 30%, foreign language 7%, interdisciplinary studies 6%, social sciences 19%.

Technology on campus. PC or laptop required. 60 workstations in library, computer center. Dormitories wired for high-speed internet access and linked to campus network. Commuter students can connect to campus network. Online library, repair service, wireless network available.

Student life. Freshman orientation: Mandatory. Preregistration for classes offered. Cadet basic training (CBT) is an initial, 6-week cadet program held over the summer, designed to help new cadets make a rapid transition to the military lifestyle. CBT focuses on basic soldier skills and courtesies, discipline, personal appearance, military drill and ceremonies, and physical fitness. Extensive demands are made on new cadets as a test of their emotional stability, perseverance, and ability to organize and perform under stress. **Policies:** Through a formal system cadets enforce the Honor Code with power to recommend dismissal. Military dress required. All cadets participate in intercollegiate, club or intramural level sport each semester. Seniors and juniors (after spring break) permitted to maintain cars. Freshmen not permitted cars on campus. **Housing:** Guaranteed on-campus for all undergraduates. Coed dorms, wellness housing available. **Activities:** Pep band, campus ministries, choral groups, dance, drama, film society, international student organizations, literary magazine, music ensembles, Model UN, musical theater, radio station, student government, International Cadets of West Point, African-American Arts, Native American Heritage Forum, Jewish Chapel Group, Officers' Christian Fellowshp, Catholic Chapel Group, Big Brothers/Big Sister, Debate Council and Forum, Engineers and Scientist for a Sustainable World, Secular Student Alliance.

Athletics. NCAA. **Intercollegiate:** Baseball M, basketball, cheerleading, cross-country, diving, football (tackle) M, golf M, gymnastics M, ice hockey

M, lacrosse, rifle, soccer, softball W, swimming, tennis, track and field, volleyball W, wrestling M. **Intramural:** Basketball, football (non-tackle), rugby, soccer, squash, swimming, ultimate frisbee, wrestling. **Team name:** Black Knights.

Student services. Alcohol/substance abuse counseling, chaplain/spiritual director, career counseling, health services, legal services, personal counseling, placement for graduates, women's services.

Contact. E-mail: admissions@usma.edu
Phone: (845) 938-5760
Col. Deborah McDonald, Director of Admissions, United States Military Academy, 646 Swift Road, West Point, NY 10996-1905

United Talmudical Seminary
Brooklyn, New York
CB code: 0696

- Private 5-year rabbinical college for men affiliated with the Jewish faith
- Very large city
- 1,845 degree-seeking undergraduates

General. Founded in 1949. Accredited by AARTS. First Talmudic degree and ordination available. **Degrees:** 284 bachelor's awarded; master's offered. **Calendar:** Semester. **Full-time faculty:** 48 total. **Part-time faculty:** 127 total.

Basis for selection. Institutional examination.

2015-2016 Annual costs. Tuition/fees: $13,535. Room/board: $3,000.

Application procedures. Admission: No deadline.

Academics. Credit/placement by examination: AP, CLEP.

Majors. Theology: Talmudic.

Contact. Phone: (718) 963-9770
Moses Greenfield, Director of Admissions, United Talmudical Seminary, 191 Rodney Street, Brooklyn, NY 11211

University of Rochester
Rochester, New York
www.rochester.edu
CB member
CB code: 2928

- Private 4-year university
- Residential campus in large city
- 6,123 degree-seeking undergraduates: 2% part-time, 49% women, 5% African American, 11% Asian American, 7% Hispanic/Latino, 3% Multiracial, non-Hispanic, 18% international
- 4,507 degree-seeking graduate students
- 34% of applicants admitted
- Application essay required
- 88% graduate within 6 years; 34% enter graduate study

General. Founded in 1850. Regionally accredited. **Degrees:** 1,658 bachelor's awarded; master's, professional, doctoral offered. **ROTC:** Army, Naval, Air Force. **Location:** 2 miles from downtown. **Calendar:** Semester, extensive summer session. **Full-time faculty:** 606 total; 94% have terminal degrees. **Part-time faculty:** 234 total; 50% have terminal degrees. **Class size:** 71% < 20, 13% 20-39, 4% 40-49, 9% 50-99, 3% >100. **Special facilities:** Music library, laboratory for laser energetics, nuclear structure research laboratory, hospital, cancer center, children's hospital, dental center, center for visual sciences, institute for optics, VR lab, MRI scanner, digital media center.

Freshman class profile. 17,932 applied, 6,058 admitted, 1,400 enrolled.

Mid 50% test scores		Return as sophomores:	96%
SAT critical reading:	600-710	Out-of-state:	61%
SAT math:	640-760	Live on campus:	100%
SAT writing:	610-710	International:	19%
ACT composite:	29-33	Fraternities:	16%
Rank in top quarter:	92%	Sororities:	20%
Rank in top tenth:	66%		

Basis for selection. School achievement record, personal qualities, and recommendations are most important. Test scores, GPA, essay, interview, extracurricular activities are important. Unquantifiable strengths such as initiative, creativity, enthusiasm, and leadership are also valuable to ensure that the incoming class represents the full spectrum of diversity, including

hometowns, ideas, and experiences. SAT or ACT, SAT Subject Tests recommended. An audition is required for music programs at Eastman School of Music. **Home schooled:** Statement describing home school structure and mission, transcript of courses and grades, interview, letter of recommendation (nonparent) required. Must submit comprehensive description of the program of study (including syllabi with textbooks, where applicable), complete list of all literary texts completed, method of instruction (specifically for laboratory sciences) and assessment (written essays/multiple choice examinations, homework, etc.), and a personal statement reflecting on the value of the homeschooling experience. Most students who successfully gain admission have completed four years of English, four years of mathematics, four years of history/social studies, three years of laboratory science, and three years of foreign language study.

High school preparation. College-preparatory program required. 32 units required.

2015-2016 Annual costs. Tuition/fees: $48,290. Room/board: $14,366. Books/supplies: $1,310. Personal expenses: $1,080.

2014-2015 Financial aid. Need-based: 1,023 full-time freshmen applied for aid; 794 deemed to have need; 792 received aid. Average need met was 97%. Average scholarship/grant was $40,556; average loan $3,844. 84% of total undergraduate aid awarded as scholarships/grants, 16% as loans/jobs. **Non-need-based:** Awarded to 2,227 full-time undergraduates, including 553 freshmen. Scholarships awarded for academics, alumni affiliation, art, leadership, music/drama, ROTC. **Additional information:** Alternative loans and financing information available. Need-based aid available for eligible Mexican and Canadian citizens.

Application procedures. Admission: Closing date 1/5 (postmark date). $50 fee, may be waived for applicants with need. Application must be submitted online. Admission notification by 4/1. Must reply by 5/1. **Financial aid:** Closing date 2/15. FAFSA, CSS PROFILE required. Applicants notified by 4/1; must reply by 5/1.

Academics. Rochester Curriculum: imposes minimal requirements, students can take advantage of flexibility in the curriculum to complete an education that reflects their interests and passions. Senior Scholars Program: allows selected undergraduates to devote their entire final year to work on a single intellectual project as a year-long independent study. Take Five Scholars Program: provides additional semester or year, tuition-free, where students can explore offerings of another department. **Special study options:** Accelerated study, combined bachelor's/graduate degree, cooperative education, cross-registration, double major, dual enrollment of high school students, ESL, honors, independent study, internships, liberal arts/career combination, New York semester, semester at sea, student-designed major, study abroad, teacher certification program, urban semester, Washington semester. **Credit/placement by examination:** AP, CLEP, IB, institutional tests. Students who prepare a course by independent study without registering for it and who pass an examination in that course may receive degree credit for it upon petition to their Administrative Committee. A letter of support from the chair of the department, or from his or her authorized delegate, is required. **Support services:** Learning center, pre-admission summer program, reduced course load, study skills assistance, tutoring, writing center. Pre-major advisers, Office of Minority Student Affairs, CARE Network, International Student Services.

Majors. Area/ethnic studies: African-American, American, East Asian, Italian, Latin American, Russian/Slavic, women's. **Biology:** General, biochemistry, cell/histology, ecology, embryology, epidemiology, evolutionary, microbiology, molecular genetics, neuroscience. **Business:** General, business admin, marketing. **Communications:** Digital media, media studies. **Computer sciences:** Computer science. **Conservation:** Environmental science, environmental studies. **Engineering:** General, biomedical, chemical, electrical, engineering science, geological, laser/optical, mechanical. **English:** Creative writing, English lit. **Foreign languages:** General, American Sign Language, classics, comparative lit, French, German, Japanese, linguistics, Russian, Spanish. **Health services:** Environmental health, nursing (RN). **History:** General. **Liberal arts:** Arts/sciences. **Math:** General, applied, statistics. **Philosophy/religion:** Philosophy, religion. **Physical sciences:** Chemistry, geology, optics, physics. **Psychology:** General, experimental. **Social sciences:** Anthropology, economics, international relations, political science. **Visual/performing arts:** Art history/conservation, film/cinema/video, jazz, music, music performance, music theory/composition, studio arts, theater arts management.

Most popular majors. Biology 13%, engineering/engineering technologies 13%, health sciences 16%, psychology 9%, social sciences 16%, visual/performing arts 8%.

Technology on campus. 700 workstations in dormitories, library, computer center, student center. Dormitories wired for high-speed internet access. Commuter students can connect to campus network. Online course registration, online library, helpline, repair service, wireless network available.

Student life. Freshman orientation: Mandatory. Preregistration for classes offered. Held one week prior to first day of classes. **Policies:** Freshmen not permitted cars on campus. **Housing:** Guaranteed on-campus for freshmen. Coed dorms, single-sex dorms, special housing for disabled, apartments, fraternity/sorority housing, themed housing, wellness housing available. Freshman housing, special-interest floors, suite-style living, single-gender floors available. **Activities:** Bands, campus ministries, choral groups, dance, drama, film society, international student organizations, literary magazine, music ensembles, Model UN, musical theater, opera, radio station, student government, student newspaper, symphony orchestra, TV station, Campus Activities Board, Black Student Union, Grassroots (environmental group), Women's Caucus, Hillel, Catholic Newman Society, Debate Union, UR Bhangra, Charles Drew Pre-Health Society, Colleges Against Cancer.

Athletics. NCAA. **Intercollegiate:** Baseball M, basketball, cross-country, diving, field hockey W, football (tackle) M, golf M, lacrosse W, rowing (crew) W, soccer, softball W, squash M, swimming, tennis, track and field, volleyball W. **Intramural:** Basketball, boxing, football (non-tackle), football (tackle), judo, soccer, squash, ultimate frisbee, volleyball, weight lifting. **Team name:** Yellowjackets.

Student services. Adult student services, alcohol/substance abuse counseling, chaplain/spiritual director, career counseling, services for economically disadvantaged, student employment services, financial aid counseling, health services, minority student services, personal counseling, placement for graduates, veterans' counselor, women's services. **Physically disabled:** Services for visually, hearing impaired.

Contact. E-mail: admit@admissions.rochester.edu
Phone: (585) 275-3221 Toll-free number: (888) 822-2256
Fax: (585) 461-4595
Jonathan Burdick, Vice Provost and Dean of College Admission, University of Rochester, 300 Wilson Boulevard, Rochester, NY 14627-0251

Utica College
Utica, New York　　　　　　　　　　**CB member**
www.utica.edu　　　　　　　　　　**CB code: 2932**

▶ Private 4-year health science and liberal arts college
▶ Residential campus in small city
▶ 3,041 degree-seeking undergraduates: 21% part-time, 61% women, 11% African American, 3% Asian American, 8% Hispanic/Latino, 1% Native American, 3% Multi-racial, non-Hispanic, 2% international
▶ 1,365 degree-seeking graduate students
▶ 83% of applicants admitted
▶ Application essay required
▶ 42% graduate within 6 years

General. Founded in 1946. Regionally accredited. **Degrees:** 680 bachelor's awarded; master's, professional offered. **ROTC:** Army, Air Force. **Location:** 50 miles from Syracuse. **Calendar:** Semester, limited summer session. **Full-time faculty:** 141 total; 51% women. **Part-time faculty:** 271 total; 58% women. **Class size:** 66% < 20, 33% 20-39, less than 1% 40-49. **Special facilities:** Nursing laboratory, trading room, Center for Identity Management and Information Protection.

Freshman class profile. 5,151 applied, 4,270 admitted, 645 enrolled.

Mid 50% test scores		GPA 2.0-2.99:	32%
SAT critical reading:	440-540	Rank in top quarter:	33%
SAT math:	440-560	Rank in top tenth:	9%
SAT writing:	420-520	Return as sophomores:	70%
ACT composite:	20-24	Out-of-state:	16%
GPA 3.75 or higher:	15%	Live on campus:	79%
GPA 3.50-3.74:	14%	International:	2%
GPA 3.0-3.49:	39%		

Basis for selection. Academic record, high school course of study, rank in class most important. Extracurricular activities, essay, interview, and recommendations also important. SAT or ACT scores required only for freshmen applying to BS Health Studies/DPT Physical Therapy, BS Health Studies/MS Occupational Therapy, Nursing, or joint health professions programs, Higher Education Opportunity Program (HEOP), or for academic merit scholarships. Interview recommended. **Home schooled:** Applicants must receive GED within first year of attendance. **Learning Disabled:** Written evaluation required, including discrepancy analysis completed by licensed psychologist or certified learning disability specialist indicating specific learning disability or disabilities.

High school preparation. College-preparatory program recommended. 16 units required. Required units include English 4, mathematics 3, social studies 3, science 3, foreign language 2 and academic electives 1.

2016-2017 Annual costs. Tuition/fees: $19,996. Room/board: $10,434. Books/supplies: $1,400. Personal expenses: $1,134.

2015-2016 Financial aid. Need-based: 615 full-time freshmen applied for aid; 572 deemed to have need; 572 received aid. Average need met was 77%. Average scholarship/grant was $6,136; average loan $3,410. 65% of total undergraduate aid awarded as scholarships/grants, 35% as loans/jobs. **Non-need-based:** Awarded to 330 full-time undergraduates, including 109 freshmen. Scholarships awarded for academics, alumni affiliation.

Application procedures. Admission: No deadline. $40 fee, may be waived for applicants with need. Admission notification on a rolling basis beginning on or about 9/1. January 15 application deadline for all joint medical programs, BS in Health Studies/ MS in Occupational Therapy program, and BS in Health Studies/DPT in Physical Therapy program. February 15 application deadline for nursing program. **Financial aid:** Priority date 3/15; no closing date. FAFSA required. Applicants notified on a rolling basis starting 3/1; must reply by 5/1.

Academics. Special study options: Accelerated study, combined bachelor's/graduate degree, distance learning, double major, honors, independent study, internships, study abroad, teacher certification program, United Nations semester, Washington semester. Economic Crime Investigation online program for transfer students, accelerated second degree nursing program. **Credit/placement by examination:** AP, CLEP, IB, institutional tests. 30 credit hours maximum toward bachelor's degree. **Support services:** Learning center, pre-admission summer program, reduced course load, remedial instruction, study skills assistance, tutoring, writing center.

Majors. Biology: General. **Business:** Accounting, business admin, managerial economics. **Communications:** Communications/speech/rhetoric, journalism, public relations. **Computer sciences:** General. **Education:** Early childhood, elementary, ESL, secondary, special ed. **English:** English lit. **Foreign languages:** General. **General:** Site management. **Health services:** Facilities admin, nursing (RN), recreational therapy. **History:** General. **Liberal arts:** Arts/sciences. **Math:** General. **Philosophy/religion:** Philosophy. **Physical sciences:** Chemistry, physics. **Protective services:** Criminal justice. **Psychology:** General. **Social sciences:** Economics, international relations, political science, sociology.

Most popular majors. Business/marketing 9%, health sciences 47%, psychology 6%, security/protective services 21%.

Technology on campus. 430 workstations in library, computer center, student center. Dormitories wired for high-speed internet access and linked to campus network. Online course registration, online library, helpline, wireless network available.

Student life. Freshman orientation: Available, $50 fee. Preregistration for classes offered. Summer program for freshmen and parents held during the third week of July. **Policies:** All freshmen required to live in college residence for first 2 years, unless residing at home. **Housing:** Guaranteed on-campus for freshmen. Coed dorms, special housing for disabled, apartments, themed housing, wellness housing available. $100 fully refundable deposit, deadline 7/1. Separate floors for men and women available. **Activities:** Bands, campus ministries, choral groups, dance, drama, international student organizations, literary magazine, music ensembles, musical theater, radio station, student government, student newspaper, Latin American student union, Jewish student union, College Republicans, women's resource center, Asian association, gospel choir, Africa in Motion, Christian Fellowship, West Indian Connection, UC Pride.

Athletics. NCAA. **Intercollegiate:** Baseball M, basketball, cross-country, diving, field hockey W, football (tackle) M, golf M, ice hockey, lacrosse, soccer, softball W, swimming, tennis, track and field, volleyball W, water polo W. **Intramural:** Badminton, basketball, bowling, football (non-tackle), golf, racquetball, soccer, softball, tennis, ultimate frisbee, volleyball. **Team name:** Pioneers.

Student services. Adult student services, alcohol/substance abuse counseling, chaplain/spiritual director, career counseling, services for economically disadvantaged, student employment services, financial aid counseling, health services, minority student services, personal counseling, placement for graduates, veterans' counselor, women's services. **Physically disabled:** Services for visually, speech, hearing impaired.

Contact. E-mail: admiss@utica.edu
Phone: (315) 792-3006 Toll-free number: (800) 782-8884
Fax: (315) 792-3003
Donna Shaffner, Assistant Vice President for Enrollment Management, Utica College, 1600 Burrstone Road, Utica, NY 13502-4892

Vassar College
Poughkeepsie, New York
www.vassar.edu
CB member
CB code: 2956

- Private 4-year liberal arts college
- Residential campus in small city
- 2,414 degree-seeking undergraduates: 56% women, 5% African American, 11% Asian American, 11% Hispanic/Latino, 6% Multi-racial, non-Hispanic, 7% international
- 26% of applicants admitted
- SAT and SAT Subject Tests or ACT with writing, application essay required
- 91% graduate within 6 years; 33% enter graduate study

General. Founded in 1861. Regionally accredited. **Degrees:** 610 bachelor's awarded; master's offered. **Location:** 75 miles from New York City. **Calendar:** Semester, limited summer session. **Full-time faculty:** 275 total; 86% have terminal degrees, 24% minority, 46% women. **Part-time faculty:** 63 total; 57% have terminal degrees, 13% minority, 51% women. **Class size:** 66% < 20, 33% 20-39, less than 1% 40-49, less than 1% 50-99. **Special facilities:** Environmental nature center, observatory, electron microscope, nursery school, experimental theater, art center, geology museum, intercultural center, outdoor amphitheater, computer visualization laboratory, robotics laboratory, phytotron, herbarium.

Freshman class profile. 7,556 applied, 1,947 admitted, 667 enrolled.

Mid 50% test scores			
SAT critical reading:	670-750	Rank in top tenth:	72%
SAT math:	660-740	End year in good standing:	100%
SAT writing:	660-750	Return as sophomores:	94%
ACT composite:	30-33	Out-of-state:	71%
Rank in top quarter:	96%	Live on campus:	99%
		International:	7%

Basis for selection. Academic credentials most important. Personal achievements, essay, and recommendations also considered carefully. Evidence that students have elected most demanding program available crucial. Disadvantaged status considered. 2 SAT Subject Tests of student's choice required. Optional interviews available with alumni.

High school preparation. College-preparatory program recommended. 20 units recommended. Recommended units include English 4, mathematics 4, social studies 2, history 2, science 4 (laboratory 3) and foreign language 4. Advanced and accelerated courses recommended whenever possible. Minimum of 20 units recommended with additional unit in science, foreign language, and studies.

2015-2016 Annual costs. Tuition/fees: $51,300. Room/board: $11,980.

2015-2016 Financial aid. All financial aid based on need. 505 full-time freshmen applied for aid; 430 deemed to have need; 430 received aid. Average need met was 100%. Average scholarship/grant was $45,358; average loan $2,493. 91% of total undergraduate aid awarded as scholarships/grants, 9% as loans/jobs. **Additional information:** No loans in the initial financial aid packages for students from families with total income used in need analysis of $60,000 or less.

Application procedures. Admission: Closing date 1/1 (postmark date). $70 fee, may be waived for applicants with need. Admission notification by 4/1. Must reply by 5/1. **Financial aid:** Closing date 2/15. FAFSA, CSS PROFILE required. Applicants notified by 3/30; must reply by 5/1.

Academics. Introductory-level college course emphasizing written and oral communication required for freshmen. Majors declared through department, interdepartmental programs, multidisciplinary programs, and independent programs. Summer research with faculty. **Special study options:** Combined bachelor's/graduate degree, cooperative education, cross-registration, double major, exchange student, independent study, internships, liberal arts/career combination, semester at sea, student-designed major, study abroad, teacher certification program, urban semester, Washington semester. Independently designed junior year abroad programs; exchange programs with institutions in 12-college exchange as well as Fisk University, Hampton Institute, Howard University, Morehouse College, and Spelman College; 3-2 engineering program with Dartmouth College. **Credit/placement by examination:** AP, CLEP, IB, institutional tests. 4 credit hours maximum toward bachelor's degree. **Support services:** Learning center, reduced course load, study skills assistance, tutoring, writing center.

Majors. Area/ethnic studies: African, American, Asian, Latin American, women's. **Biology:** General, biochemistry, neuroscience. **Communications:** Media studies. **Computer sciences:** General. **Conservation:** Environmental studies. **English:** English lit. **Foreign languages:** Chinese, French, German, Italian, Japanese, Russian, Spanish. **History:** General. **Liberal arts:** Arts/sciences. **Math:** General. **Philosophy/religion:** Judaic, philosophy, religion.

Physical sciences: Astronomy, chemistry, geology, physics. **Psychology:** General. **Social sciences:** Anthropology, economics, geography, international relations, political science, sociology, urban studies. **Visual/performing arts:** Art, dramatic, film/cinema/video, music.

Most popular majors. Biology 12%, English 7%, foreign language 8%, psychology 7%, social sciences 26%, visual/performing arts 12%.

Technology on campus. 145 workstations in dormitories, library, computer center, student center. Dormitories wired for high-speed internet access and linked to campus network. Commuter students can connect to campus network. Online course registration, helpline, repair service, student web hosting, wireless network available.

Student life. Freshman orientation: Mandatory. Preregistration for classes offered. Held one week prior to start of classes. **Housing:** Guaranteed on-campus for all undergraduates. Coed dorms, single-sex dorms, special housing for disabled, apartments, cooperative housing, wellness housing available. Quiet housing available. **Activities:** Bands, campus ministries, choral groups, dance, film society, international student organizations, literary magazine, music ensembles, Model UN, musical theater, opera, radio station, student government, student newspaper, symphony orchestra, Catholic community, Jewish union, Promoting Equality and Community Everywhere, Amnesty International, Young Socialists, Republican/Libertarian Coalition, AIDS education committee, Habitat for Humanity, Step Beyond (community service), African students union, Buddhist Sangha.

Athletics. NCAA. **Intercollegiate:** Baseball M, basketball, cross-country, diving, fencing, field hockey W, golf W, lacrosse, rowing (crew), soccer, squash, swimming, tennis, track and field, volleyball. **Intramural:** Badminton, basketball, bowling, football (non-tackle), golf, handball, soccer, softball, squash, tennis, volleyball, water polo. **Team name:** Brewers.

Student services. Alcohol/substance abuse counseling, chaplain/spiritual director, career counseling, student employment services, financial aid counseling, health services, minority student services, on-campus daycare, personal counseling, placement for graduates, veterans' counselor, women's services. **Physically disabled:** Services for visually, hearing impaired.

Contact. E-mail: admissons@vassar.edu
Phone: (845) 437-7300 Toll-free number: (800) 827-7270
Fax: (845) 437-7063
Art Rodriguez, Dean of Admission and Financial Aid, Vassar College, Box 10, 124 Raymond Avenue, Poughkeepsie, NY 12604-0077

Vaughn College of Aeronautics and Technology
Flushing, New York
www.vaughn.edu
CB member
CB code: 2001

- Private 4-year engineering college
- Commuter campus in very large city
- 1,525 degree-seeking undergraduates: 20% part-time, 13% women, 19% African American, 10% Asian American, 34% Hispanic/Latino, 2% Native Hawaiian/Pacific islander, 3% Multi-racial, non-Hispanic, 4% international
- 11 degree-seeking graduate students
- 74% of applicants admitted
- SAT or ACT (ACT writing optional), application essay, interview required
- 56% graduate within 6 years

General. Founded in 1932. Regionally accredited. Partners with the Federal Aviation Administration in the Air Traffic Control Collegiate Training Initiative. **Degrees:** 109 bachelor's, 201 associate awarded; master's offered. **ROTC:** Army, Air Force. **Location:** 5 miles from Manhattan. **Calendar:** Semester, extensive summer session. **Full-time faculty:** 42 total; 50% have terminal degrees, 36% minority, 21% women. **Part-time faculty:** 162 total; 10% have terminal degrees, 48% minority, 18% women. **Class size:** 72% < 20, 28% 20-39, less than 1% 40-49. **Special facilities:** 65-foot observation tower overlooking LaGuardia Airport, two Redbird FMX full motion flight simulators, Frasca 241 flight simulator, Frasca 142 flight simulator, CRJ-200 flight simulator, radar and tower air traffic control simulator laboratory, mechatronic engineering laboratory, nondestructive testing laboratory, composite materials laboratory and computerized engine test-cell.

Freshman class profile. 748 applied, 553 admitted, 267 enrolled.

Mid 50% test scores			
SAT critical reading:	430-550	GPA 3.0-3.49:	32%
SAT math:	470-570	GPA 2.0-2.99:	43%
ACT composite:	19-24	Return as sophomores:	75%
GPA 3.75 or higher:	11%	Out-of-state:	14%
GPA 3.50-3.74:	12%	Live on campus:	22%
		International:	5%

Basis for selection. High school transcripts or GED scores most important followed by SAT, ACT, or TOEFL. B.S. programs require strong performance in high school math and sciences courses. Open admissions to associate degree programs. SAT and SAT Subject Tests or ACT, SAT Subject Tests recommended. Tests are required for all applicants to bachelor of science degree programs. Associates degrees and certificate programs do not require standardized tests. Interview required for all applicants to the Bachelor of Science program in Aircraft Operations (Flight). **Home schooled:** Statement describing home school structure and mission, transcript of courses and grades, state high school equivalency certificate required. **Learning Disabled:** IEP documentation required.

High school preparation. College-preparatory program recommended. 14 units required; 18 recommended. Required and recommended units include English 4, mathematics 3-4, social studies 2-4, history 1, science 2-4 (laboratory 2-3) and foreign language 2-3.

2016-2017 Annual costs. Tuition/fees (projected): $23,935. Room/board: $13,575. Books/supplies: $2,160. Personal expenses: $2,824.

2015-2016 Financial aid. Need-based: 230 full-time freshmen applied for aid; 209 deemed to have need; 209 received aid. Average need met was 92%. Average scholarship/grant was $11,354; average loan $2,851. 58% of total undergraduate aid awarded as scholarships/grants, 42% as loans/jobs. **Non-need-based:** Awarded to 368 full-time undergraduates, including 87 freshmen. Scholarships awarded for academics, alumni affiliation.

Application procedures. Admission: Priority date 4/1; no deadline. $40 fee, may be waived for applicants with need. Admission notification on a rolling basis. **Financial aid:** Priority date 3/15; no closing date. FAFSA required. Applicants notified on a rolling basis starting 4/15; must reply within 2 week(s) of notification.

Academics. Academic programs centered around engineering, engineering technology, aviation, and management. Engineering technology programs accredited by the Accreditation Board for Engineering and Technology. Management programs accredited by the International Assembly of Collegiate Business Education. **Special study options:** Distance learning, ESL, independent study, internships. **Credit/placement by examination:** AP, CLEP, IB, SAT, ACT, institutional tests. 30 credit hours maximum toward associate degree, 30 toward bachelor's. **Support services:** Learning center, pre-admission summer program, reduced course load, remedial instruction, study skills assistance, tutoring, writing center.

Majors. Business: General.

Most popular majors. Business/marketing 7%, engineering/engineering technologies 34%, trade and industry 59%.

Technology on campus. 50 workstations in dormitories, library, computer center, student center. Dormitories wired for high-speed internet access and linked to campus network. Commuter students can connect to campus network. Online library, helpline, repair service, wireless network available.

Student life. Freshman orientation: Mandatory, $160 fee. Preregistration for classes offered. Held during two-day orientation with one-night stay in residence hall. Offered on several dates throughout the summer. **Housing:** Guaranteed on-campus for freshmen. Coed dorms, special housing for disabled, themed housing, wellness housing available. $250 nonrefundable deposit, deadline 7/1. **Activities:** International student organizations, student government, robotics club, Society of Women Engineers, American Institute of Aeronautics and Astronautics, American Association of Airport Executives, Institute of Electrical and Electronics Engineers, Women in Aviation-International, Circle K, Gay-Straight Alliance.

Athletics. Intercollegiate: Basketball, cross-country, soccer M, tennis W. **Intramural:** Basketball, soccer, table tennis, tennis. **Team name:** Warriors.

Student services. Alcohol/substance abuse counseling, career counseling, student employment services, financial aid counseling, personal counseling, placement for graduates, veterans' counselor.

Contact. E-mail: admitme@vaughn.edu
Phone: (718) 429-6600 ext. 118
Toll-free number: (866) 682-8446 ext. 118 Fax: (718) 779-2231
David Griffey, Director of Admissions, Vaughn College of Aeronautics and Technology, 8601 23rd Avenue, Flushing, NY 11369

Wagner College
Staten Island, New York
www.wagner.edu
CB member
CB code: 2966

- Private 4-year liberal arts college affiliated with the Lutheran Church in America
- Residential campus in very large city

- 1,741 degree-seeking undergraduates: 2% part-time, 63% women, 7% African American, 3% Asian American, 11% Hispanic/Latino, 2% Multi-racial, non-Hispanic, 3% international
- 452 degree-seeking graduate students
- 68% of applicants admitted
- Application essay required
- 64% graduate within 6 years

General. Founded in 1883. Regionally accredited. **Degrees:** 445 bachelor's awarded; master's, professional offered. **ROTC:** Army. **Location:** 10 miles from New York City. **Calendar:** Semester, limited summer session. **Full-time faculty:** 96 total; 70% have terminal degrees, 12% minority, 52% women. **Part-time faculty:** 155 total; 16% have terminal degrees, 4% minority, 52% women. **Class size:** 62% < 20, 35% 20-39, 1% 40-49, 1% 50-99. **Special facilities:** Planetarium, electron microscopes.

Freshman class profile. 2,803 applied, 1,920 admitted, 421 enrolled.

Mid 50% test scores			
SAT critical reading:	520-610	GPA 3.0-3.49:	21%
SAT math:	510-620	GPA 2.0-2.99:	19%
SAT writing:	510-620	Return as sophomores:	86%
ACT composite:	22-27	Out-of-state:	55%
GPA 3.75 or higher:	40%	Live on campus:	71%
GPA 3.50-3.74:	20%	International:	4%

Basis for selection. School achievement, test scores, recommendations, interview, special talents, essay all considered. Test optional policy, but will consider scores when submitted. Interview recommended for all; audition required for music, theater programs; portfolio recommended for art programs. Interview required for Physician Assistant program. **Home schooled:** Transcript of courses and grades required.

High school preparation. College-preparatory program required. 21 units required. Required units include English 4, mathematics 3, history 3, science 2 (laboratory 1), foreign language 2 and academic electives 7. 4 economics, arts, computers, or other elective areas of study required.

2015-2016 Annual costs. Tuition/fees: $42,480. Room/board: $13,000. Books/supplies: $822. Personal expenses: $1,419.

2015-2016 Financial aid. Need-based: 348 full-time freshmen applied for aid; 305 deemed to have need; 305 received aid. Average need met was 78%. Average scholarship/grant was $16,866; average loan $2,197. 64% of total undergraduate aid awarded as scholarships/grants, 36% as loans/jobs. **Non-need-based:** Awarded to 498 full-time undergraduates, including 97 freshmen. Scholarships awarded for academics, athletics, music/drama.

Application procedures. Admission: Priority date 12/1; deadline 2/15 (postmark date). $60 fee, may be waived for applicants with need. Admission notification on a rolling basis beginning on or about 2/15. Must reply by May 1 or within 2 week(s) if notified thereafter. **Financial aid:** Priority date 2/15; no closing date. FAFSA required. Applicants notified on a rolling basis starting 3/1; must reply within 3 week(s) of notification.

Academics. Special study options: Accelerated study, combined bachelor's/graduate degree, double major, exchange student, honors, independent study, internships, New York semester, semester at sea, study abroad, teacher certification program, United Nations semester, Washington semester. Learning communities. **Credit/placement by examination:** AP, CLEP, IB, institutional tests. 9 credit hours maximum toward bachelor's degree. Up to 9 units may be awarded for credit by exam and prior experience. Each unit is equivalent to 3.3 credit hours. **Support services:** Reduced course load, study skills assistance, tutoring, writing center.

Majors. Biology: General, bacteriology. **Business:** Accounting, business admin, finance, international, managerial economics, marketing. **Computer sciences:** Computer science. **Education:** General, early childhood, middle, secondary. **English:** English lit. **Foreign languages:** French, Spanish. **Health services:** Nursing (RN), physician assistant, predental, premedicine, preoptometry, preveterinary. **History:** General. **Human services:** Public policy. **Liberal arts:** Arts/sciences. **Math:** General. **Philosophy/religion:** Philosophy. **Physical sciences:** Chemistry, physics. **Psychology:** General. **Social sciences:** Anthropology, economics, political science, sociology. **Visual/performing arts:** Dramatic, music performance, studio arts, studio arts management, theater design.

Most popular majors. Biology 7%, business/marketing 18%, education 6%, health sciences 27%, interdisciplinary studies 7%, psychology 9%, social sciences 10%, visual/performing arts 7%.

Technology on campus. 230 workstations in dormitories, library, computer center. Dormitories wired for high-speed internet access and linked to campus network. Commuter students can connect to campus network. Online course registration, online library, helpline, wireless network available.

Student life. Freshman orientation: Mandatory. Preregistration for classes offered. Held 3 days prior to start of fall semester. **Housing:** Guaranteed on-campus for all undergraduates. Coed dorms, fraternity/sorority housing, themed housing, wellness housing available. $300 nonrefundable deposit, deadline 5/1. Senior year housing. **Activities:** Bands, campus ministries, choral groups, dance, drama, international student organizations, literary magazine, music ensembles, Model UN, musical theater, radio station, student government, student newspaper, Lutheran student club, Newman Society, Hillel, national honor societies, Amnesty International, Young Democrats, Young Republicans, Nubian Society, Muslim student association, Habitat for Humanity.

Athletics. NCAA. **Intercollegiate:** Baseball M, basketball, cross-country, football (tackle) M, golf, lacrosse, soccer W, softball W, swimming W, tennis, track and field, water polo W. **Intramural:** Basketball, bowling, cheerleading W, football (non-tackle), football (tackle) M, soccer, softball, table tennis, tennis, volleyball. **Team name:** Seahawks.

Student services. Alcohol/substance abuse counseling, chaplain/spiritual director, career counseling, student employment services, financial aid counseling, health services, personal counseling, placement for graduates, women's services. **Physically disabled:** Services for visually, hearing impaired.

Contact. E-mail: adm@wagner.edu
Phone: (718) 390-3411 Toll-free number: (800) 221-1010
Fax: (718) 390-3105
Robert Herr, Dean of Admissions, Wagner College, One Campus Road, Staten Island, NY 10301

Webb Institute
Glen Cove, New York   **CB member**
www.webb.edu   **CB code: 2970**

- Private 4-year engineering college
- Residential campus in large town
- 91 degree-seeking undergraduates: 19% women, 11% Asian American, 8% Multi-racial, non-Hispanic, 1% international
- 36% of applicants admitted
- SAT or ACT (ACT writing optional), SAT Subject Tests, interview required
- 71% graduate within 6 years

General. Founded in 1889. Regionally accredited. All students participate in 2-month paid winter work program in marine industry each year. **Degrees:** 20 bachelor's awarded. **Location:** 22 miles from New York City. **Calendar:** Semester. **Full-time faculty:** 11 total; 73% have terminal degrees, 9% women. **Part-time faculty:** 3 total; 100% have terminal degrees. **Class size:** 20% < 20, 80% 20-39. **Special facilities:** Beach, adjoining nature preserve, model testing tank.

Freshman class profile. 105 applied, 38 admitted, 26 enrolled.

Mid 50% test scores			
		GPA 3.0-3.49:	8%
SAT critical reading:	670-730	Rank in top quarter:	88%
SAT math:	750-770	Rank in top tenth:	78%
SAT writing:	680-730	Return as sophomores:	83%
ACT composite:	30-33	Out-of-state:	77%
GPA 3.75 or higher:	92%	Live on campus:	100%

Basis for selection. GED not accepted. High school record, class rank, test scores, and interview with President of college most important. Character, motivation, and outside activities considered. **Home schooled:** Statement describing home school structure and mission, transcript of courses and grades, letter of recommendation (nonparent) required.

High school preparation. College-preparatory program recommended. 16 units required. Required units include English 4, mathematics 4, social studies 2, science 2 (laboratory 2) and academic electives 4.

2016-2017 Annual costs. Tuition/fees: $47,400. Room/board: $14,400. Books/supplies: $700. Personal expenses: $2,650. **Additional information:** All admitted students receive full-tuition scholarships.

2014-2015 Financial aid. All financial aid based on need. 11 full-time freshmen applied for aid; 11 deemed to have need; 11 received aid. Average need met was 80%. Average scholarship/grant was $2,000; average loan $3,340. 90% of total undergraduate aid awarded as scholarships/grants, 10% as loans/jobs. **Additional information:** Institutionally funded loans available.

Application procedures. Admission: Closing date 2/15 (postmark date). $25 fee, may be waived for applicants with need. Admission notification on a rolling basis beginning on or about 3/15. Must reply by May 1 or within 2 week(s) if notified thereafter. **Financial aid:** Closing date 7/1. FAFSA,

---

institutional form required. Applicants notified on a rolling basis starting 6/1; must reply within 2 week(s) of notification.

Academics. Intensive single curriculum program demands high career motivation. **Special study options:** Double major, independent study, internships, study abroad. **Credit/placement by examination:** AP, CLEP. **Support services:** Study skills assistance.

Majors. Engineering: Marine.

Technology on campus. PC or laptop required. 25 workstations in dormitories, library, computer center, student center. Dormitories wired for high-speed internet access and linked to campus network. Commuter students can connect to campus network. Repair service, wireless network available.

Student life. Freshman orientation: Mandatory. Preregistration for classes offered. Held 1 week before classes start. **Housing:** Guaranteed on-campus for all undergraduates. Coed dorms, single-sex dorms available. $150 deposit. **Activities:** Jazz band, choral groups, student government, American Society of Naval Engineers, WebbWomen, Society of Naval Architects and Marine Engineers, Marine Technology Society.

Athletics. Intercollegiate: Basketball, sailing, soccer, tennis, volleyball. **Intramural:** Basketball, cross-country, soccer, volleyball. **Team name:** Clippers.

Student services. Alcohol/substance abuse counseling, career counseling, student employment services, financial aid counseling, health services, personal counseling, placement for graduates.

Contact. E-mail: admissions@webb.edu
Phone: (516) 671-8355 ext. 1107 Fax: (516) 674-9838
William Murray, Director of Enrollment Management, Webb Institute, 298 Crescent Beach Road, Glen Cove, NY 11542-1398

Wells College
Aurora, New York   **CB member**
www.wells.edu   **CB code: 2971**

- Private 4-year liberal arts college
- Residential campus in rural community
- 572 degree-seeking undergraduates: 2% part-time, 67% women
- 63% of applicants admitted
- SAT or ACT (ACT writing optional), application essay required
- 58% graduate within 6 years; 26% enter graduate study

General. Founded in 1868. Regionally accredited. Cross registration with Cornell University and Ithaca College allows students to take up to four courses during their four years at Wells. **Degrees:** 82 bachelor's awarded. **Location:** 27 miles from Ithaca, 45 miles from Syracuse. **Calendar:** Semester. **Full-time faculty:** 39 total; 90% have terminal degrees, 15% minority, 62% women. **Part-time faculty:** 34 total; 35% have terminal degrees, 9% minority, 47% women. **Class size:** 88% < 20, 11% 20-39, 1% 40-49. **Special facilities:** Book arts center, lithography presses, digital imaging laboratory, darkroom, indoor tennis courts, 9-hole golf course, science facility with growth chamber, cold room, horse stables, SHARE farm, farmer's market, business and entrepreneurship center with active stock trading room and student run enterprise, center for sustainability.

Freshman class profile. 2,217 applied, 1,388 admitted, 169 enrolled.

GPA 3.75 or higher:	20%	Rank in top tenth:	35%
GPA 3.50-3.74:	30%	End year in good standing:	84%
GPA 3.0-3.49:	30%	Return as sophomores:	69%
GPA 2.0-2.99:	20%	Out-of-state:	24%
Rank in top quarter:	63%		

Basis for selection. Academic achievement, writing skills, and school/community involvement weighed heavily in the admissions process. Test scores, class rank, and teacher recommendations are also highly valuable. Evidence of leadership ability, intellectual curiosity, character fitness are considered. Require all students to submit their standardized test scores as part of their application. Interviews are highly recommended. **Home schooled:** Statement describing home school structure and mission, transcript of courses and grades, state high school equivalency certificate, letter of recommendation (nonparent) required. Please contact Admissions Office for additional information.

High school preparation. College-preparatory program recommended. 17 units required; 23 recommended. Required and recommended units include English 4, mathematics 3-4, social studies 1, history 3, science 2-3 (laboratory 2-3), foreign language 1-2 and academic electives 2-3. Students encouraged to complete 2 computer science, art, and/or music courses. AP and honors courses recommended.

2015-2016 Annual costs. Tuition/fees: $37,500. Room/board: $13,000. Books/supplies: $1,050. Personal expenses: $1,250.

2014-2015 Financial aid. Need-based: 161 full-time freshmen applied for aid; 155 deemed to have need; 155 received aid. Average need met was 83%. Average scholarship/grant was $29,177; average loan $3,768. 60% of total undergraduate aid awarded as scholarships/grants, 40% as loans/jobs. **Non-need-based:** Awarded to 94 full-time undergraduates, including 23 freshmen. Scholarships awarded for academics, alumni affiliation, leadership.

Application procedures. Admission: Priority date 12/15; deadline 3/1 (postmark date). $40 fee, may be waived for applicants with need. Admission notification by 4/1. Admission notification on a rolling basis beginning on or about 11/1. Must reply by 5/1. **Financial aid:** Priority date 2/15; no closing date. FAFSA required. Applicants notified on a rolling basis starting 3/10; must reply by 5/1.

Academics. Individualized majors offered. Experiential learning requirement fulfilled through internship and off-campus study programs, study abroad, research with professors, community service. January term. **Special study options:** Accelerated study, combined bachelor's/graduate degree, cross-registration, double major, independent study, internships, student-designed major, study abroad, teacher certification program, Washington semester. **Credit/placement by examination:** AP, CLEP, IB, SAT, ACT, institutional tests. 6 credit hours maximum toward bachelor's degree. **Support services:** Learning center, reduced course load, study skills assistance, tutoring, writing center.

Majors. Area/ethnic studies: Women's. **Biology:** General, biochemistry, molecular. **Business:** Managerial economics. **Computer sciences:** Computer science. **Conservation:** Environmental science. **Engineering:** Pre-engineering. **English:** English lit. **Foreign languages:** General, Spanish. **Health services:** Predental, premedicine, preoccupational therapy, prephysical therapy, preveterinary. **History:** General. **Math:** General. **Philosophy/religion:** Philosophy. **Physical sciences:** Chemistry, physics. **Psychology:** General. **Social sciences:** Anthropology, economics, international relations, political science, sociology. **Visual/performing arts:** General, art history/conservation, studio arts.

Most popular majors. Biology 7%, English 12%, history 10%, psychology 21%, social sciences 11%, visual/performing arts 10%.

Technology on campus. 100 workstations in dormitories, library, computer center. Dormitories wired for high-speed internet access and linked to campus network. Commuter students can connect to campus network. Online course registration, online library, helpline, wireless network available.

Student life. Freshman orientation: Mandatory. Preregistration for classes offered. Five-day program before classes begin. Incorporates traditions (bonfire, convocation, etc.) with integrating students into a rigorous academic environment. **Policies:** Honor code governs academic and co-curricular life. Student code of conduct. **Housing:** Guaranteed on-campus for all undergraduates. Coed dorms, single-sex dorms, apartments, themed housing, wellness housing available. $300 nonrefundable deposit, deadline 5/1. Social justice learning community available. **Activities:** Jazz band, choral groups, dance, drama, international student organizations, literary magazine, music ensembles, Model UN, student government, student newspaper, Amnesty International, American Red Cross club, College Democrats, College Republicans, Praising Our Work Ethnicity and Race, Spanish culture club, Japanese culture club, Women in Life-Long Learning, Inclusive and Intercultural Excellence Committee, international student association, Sexuality and Gender Activists, Sex Collective, Campus Greens, Students of Caribbean Ancestry.

Athletics. NCAA. **Intercollegiate:** Basketball, cross-country, field hockey W, lacrosse, soccer, swimming, tennis W, volleyball M. **Intramural:** Basketball, field hockey, sailing, skiing, soccer, tennis, volleyball. **Team name:** The Express.

Student services. Adult student services, alcohol/substance abuse counseling, career counseling, financial aid counseling, health services, minority student services, personal counseling, women's services. **Physically disabled:** Services for visually, hearing impaired.

Contact. E-mail: admissions@wells.edu
Phone: (315) 364-3264 Toll-free number: (800) 952-9355
Fax: (315) 364-3227
Susan Sloan, Director of Admissions, Wells College, 170 Main Street, Aurora, NY 13026

Yeshiva and Kolel Bais Medrash Elyon
Monsey, New York

‣ Private 4-year rabbinical college for men affiliated with the Jewish faith
‣ Small city
‣ 26 degree-seeking undergraduates

General. Accredited by AARTS. **Degrees:** 15 bachelor's awarded; doctoral offered. **Calendar:** Semester. **Full-time faculty:** 3 total. **Part-time faculty:** 1 total.

Basis for selection. Commitment to Jewish tenet.

2015-2016 Annual costs. Tuition/fees: $11,200. Room/board: $2,800.

Application procedures. Admission: No deadline. No application fee. Admission notification on a rolling basis.

Academics. Credit/placement by examination: AP, CLEP.

Majors. Theology: Talmudic.

Contact. Phone: (845) 356-7064
Rabbi Israel Falk, Admissions Director, Yeshiva and Kolel Bais Medrash Elyon, 73 Main Street, Monsey, NY 10952

Yeshiva and Kollel Harbotzas Torah
Brooklyn, New York

‣ Private 4-year rabbinical college for men affiliated with the Jewish faith
‣ Very large city
‣ 29 degree-seeking undergraduates

General. Accredited by AARTS. **Degrees:** 11 bachelor's awarded; doctoral offered. **Calendar:** Semester. **Full-time faculty:** 3 total.

Basis for selection. Selective admission to some programs.

2015-2016 Annual costs. Tuition/fees: $7,500.

Application procedures. Admission: No deadline.

Academics. Credit/placement by examination: AP, CLEP.

Majors. Theology: Talmudic.

Contact. Phone: (718) 692-0208
Yeshiva and Kollel Harbotzas Torah, 1049 East 15th Street, Brooklyn, NY 11230

Yeshiva Derech Chaim
Brooklyn, New York

CB code: 0552

‣ Private 5-year rabbinical college for men affiliated with the Jewish faith
‣ Very large city
‣ 103 degree-seeking undergraduates
‣ Interview required

General. Founded in 1975. Accredited by AARTS. First and advanced Talmudic degrees available. **Degrees:** 16 bachelor's awarded; doctoral offered. **Calendar:** Semester. **Full-time faculty:** 13 total. **Part-time faculty:** 8 total.

Basis for selection. Dean interviews each applicant. Recommendations very important. Applicants without high school diplomas may be admitted on basis of national AARTS exam.

2015-2016 Annual costs. Tuition/fees: $11,300. Books/supplies: $400.

Financial aid. Additional information: Financial aid interview held with each admitted student.

Application procedures. Admission: Priority date 8/20; no deadline. No application fee. Admission notification on a rolling basis. **Financial aid:** No deadline. Applicants notified on a rolling basis.

Academics. Credit/placement by examination: AP, CLEP.

Majors. Theology: Talmudic.

Student life. Policies: Religious observance required. **Activities:** Choral groups, TV station.

Contact. Phone: (718) 438-3070
Rabbi Mordechai Rennert, Admissions Director, Yeshiva Derech Chaim, 1573 39th Street, Brooklyn, NY 11218-4413

Yeshiva D'Monsey Rabbinical College
Monsey, New York

♦ Private 4-year rabbinical college for men affiliated with the Jewish faith
♦ Large town
♦ 49 degree-seeking undergraduates

General. Accredited by AARTS. **Degrees:** 4 bachelor's awarded; doctoral offered. **Calendar:** Semester. **Full-time faculty:** 4 total. **Part-time faculty:** 2 total.

Basis for selection. Formal demonstrations of competencies, recommendations and completion of college-preparatory program required. Secondary school record recommended.

2015-2016 Annual costs. Tuition/fees: $5,900. Room/board: $2,150.

Application procedures. Admission: No deadline.

Academics. Credit/placement by examination: AP, CLEP.

Majors. Theology: Talmudic.

Contact. Phone: (845) 352-5852
Yeshiva D'Monsey Rabbinical College, 2 Roman Boulevard, Monsey, NY 10952

Yeshiva Gedolah Imrei Yosef D'Spinka
Brooklyn, New York

♦ Private 4-year rabbinical college for men affiliated with the Jewish faith
♦ Very large city
♦ 130 degree-seeking undergraduates

General. Accredited by AARTS. **Degrees:** 17 bachelor's awarded. **Calendar:** Semester. **Full-time faculty:** 4 total. **Part-time faculty:** 2 total.

Basis for selection. Open admission.

2015-2016 Annual costs. Tuition/fees: $8,000.

Application procedures. Admission: Priority date 8/18; deadline 9/28. No application fee.

Academics. Credit/placement by examination: AP, CLEP.

Majors. Theology: Talmudic.

Contact. Phone: (718) 851-8721 ext. 2103
Yeshiva Gedolah Imrei Yosef D'Spinka, 1466 56th Street, Brooklyn, NY 11219

Yeshiva Gedolah Zichron Moshe
South Fallsburg, New York
CB code: 0750

♦ Private 4-year rabbinical college for men affiliated with the Jewish faith
♦ Small town
♦ 164 degree-seeking undergraduates

General. Founded in 1969. Accredited by AARTS. First Talmudic degree and ordination available. **Degrees:** 3 bachelor's awarded; doctoral offered. **Calendar:** Semester. **Full-time faculty:** 8 total.

Basis for selection. Institutional examination.

2015-2016 Annual costs. Tuition/fees: $11,500. Books/supplies: $200. Personal expenses: $2,000.

Application procedures. Admission: No deadline.

Academics. Credit/placement by examination: AP, CLEP.

Majors. Theology: Talmudic.

Contact. Phone: (845) 434-5240 Fax: (845) 434-1009
Abba Gorelick, Dean of Admissions, Yeshiva Gedolah Zichron Moshe, 84 Laurel Park Road, South Fallsburg, NY 12779

Yeshiva Karlin Stolin
Brooklyn, New York
CB code: 1582

♦ Private 4-year rabbinical college for men affiliated with the Jewish faith
♦ Very large city
♦ 115 degree-seeking undergraduates

General. Accredited by AARTS. **Degrees:** 16 bachelor's awarded. **Calendar:** Semester. **Full-time faculty:** 3 total. **Part-time faculty:** 2 total.

Basis for selection. Completion of college-preparatory program required. Secondary school record and recommendations recommended.

2015-2016 Annual costs. Tuition/fees: $9,650. Room/board: $4,000.

Application procedures. Admission: No deadline.

Academics. Credit/placement by examination: AP, CLEP.

Majors. Theology: Talmudic.

Contact. Phone: (718) 232-7800
Yeshiva Karlin Stolin, 1818 54th Street, Brooklyn, NY 11204-1545

Yeshiva of Nitra
Mount Kisco, New York
www.yeshivaofnitra.org
CB code: 7131

♦ Private 4-year rabbinical college for men affiliated with the Jewish faith
♦ Small city
♦ 216 degree-seeking undergraduates

General. Accredited by AARTS. **Degrees:** 21 bachelor's awarded; master's offered. **Calendar:** Differs by program. **Full-time faculty:** 20 total. **Part-time faculty:** 2 total.

Basis for selection. Open admission.

2015-2016 Annual costs. Tuition/fees: $8,200. Room/board: $4,200.

Application procedures. Admission: No deadline.

Academics. Credit/placement by examination: AP, CLEP.

Majors. Theology: Talmudic.

Contact. Phone: (718) 387-0423
Yeshiva of Nitra, Pines Bridge Road, Mount Kisco, NY 10549

Yeshiva of the Telshe Alumni
Riverdale, New York

♦ Private 4-year rabbinical college for men affiliated with the Jewish faith
♦ Very large city
♦ 115 degree-seeking undergraduates

General. Accredited by AARTS. **Calendar:** Semester. **Full-time faculty:** 4 total. **Part-time faculty:** 2 total.

Basis for selection. Completion of college-preparatory program and recommendations required. Secondary school record considered.

2015-2016 Annual costs. Tuition/fees: $9,100. Room/board: $5,400.

Application procedures. Admission: No deadline. $50 fee.

Academics. Credit/placement by examination: AP, CLEP.

Majors. Theology: Talmudic.

Contact. Phone: (718) 601-3523
Yeshiva of the Telshe Alumni, 4904 Independence Avenue, Riverdale, NY 10471

Yeshiva Shaar Hatorah
Kew Gardens, New York
www.shaarhatorah.edu
CB code: 0743

- Private 4-year rabbinical college for men affiliated with the Jewish faith
- Very large city
- 77 degree-seeking undergraduates
- Interview required

General. Founded in 1976. Accredited by AARTS. Ordination and first rabbinic degree available. **Degrees:** 8 bachelor's awarded; master's offered. **Calendar:** Semester. **Full-time faculty:** 5 total.

Basis for selection. Religious commitment, school achievement record, recommendations, and interview most important.

2015-2016 Annual costs. Tuition/fees: $16,850.

Application procedures. Admission: No deadline. $100 fee.

Academics. Special study options: Double major. **Credit/placement by examination:** AP, CLEP.

Majors. Theology: Talmudic.

Student life. Policies: Religious observance required.

Contact. Phone: (718) 846-1940
Yoel Yankelewitz, Admissions Director, Yeshiva Shaar Hatorah, 117-06 84th Avenue, Kew Gardens, NY 11418

Yeshiva Shaarei Torah of Rockland
Suffern, New York
www.yst.edu

- Private 4-year rabbinical college for men affiliated with the Jewish faith
- Commuter campus in large town
- 92 degree-seeking undergraduates

General. Accredited by AARTS. **Degrees:** 28 bachelor's awarded. **Calendar:** Semester. **Full-time faculty:** 8 total.

Basis for selection. Recommendations required.

2015-2016 Annual costs. Tuition/fees: $11,500. Room/board: $3,250.

Application procedures. Admission: No deadline. $250 fee.

Academics. Credit/placement by examination: AP, CLEP.

Majors. Theology: Talmudic.

Contact. Phone: (845) 352-3431
Rabbi Avraham Posner, Admissions Director, Yeshiva Shaarei Torah of Rockland, 91 West Carlton Road, Suffern, NY 10901

Yeshiva University
New York, New York
CB member
www.yu.edu
CB code: 2990

- Private 4-year university
- Residential campus in very large city
- 2,744 degree-seeking undergraduates: 2% part-time, 45% women, 5% international
- 3,459 degree-seeking graduate students
- 80% of applicants admitted
- SAT or ACT (ACT writing optional), application essay, interview required
- 92% graduate within 6 years

General. Founded in 1886. Regionally accredited. Campus locations in Manhattan and the Bronx. **Degrees:** 588 bachelor's, 266 associate awarded; master's, professional, doctoral offered. **Calendar:** Semester, limited summer session. **Full-time faculty:** 720 total; 68% have terminal degrees, 16% minority, 37% women. **Part-time faculty:** 308 total; 7% have terminal degrees, 3% minority, 45% women. **Class size:** 56% < 20, 37% 20-39, 6% 40-49, 1% 50-99, less than 1% >100.

Freshman class profile. 1,558 applied, 1,254 admitted, 776 enrolled.

Mid 50% test scores			
SAT critical reading:	580-700	GPA 3.50-3.74:	22%
SAT math:	570-710	GPA 3.0-3.49:	27%
SAT writing:	560-680	GPA 2.0-2.99:	14%
ACT composite:	23-29	Return as sophomores:	88%
GPA 3.75 or higher:	37%	Out-of-state:	67%
		International:	3%

Basis for selection. Equal weight given to high school GPA, test scores, ability and motivation as indicated in interview, school and community activities, recommendations of principal, guidance counselor, and/or employer. **Home schooled:** Statement describing home school structure and mission, transcript of courses and grades, state high school equivalency certificate, interview required.

High school preparation. College-preparatory program required. 16 units recommended. Recommended units include English 4, mathematics 2, social studies 2, science 2 and foreign language 2.

2015-2016 Annual costs. Tuition/fees: $39,530. Room/board: $11,250. Books/supplies: $1,224. Personal expenses: $5,351.

2015-2016 Financial aid. Need-based: 557 full-time freshmen applied for aid; 438 deemed to have need; 431 received aid. Average need met was 90%. Average scholarship/grant was $12,700; average loan $2,716. 89% of total undergraduate aid awarded as scholarships/grants, 11% as loans/jobs. **Non-need-based:** Awarded to 791 full-time undergraduates, including 322 freshmen. Scholarships awarded for academics, state residency. **Additional information:** Essays required of Distinguished Scholarship applicants.

Application procedures. Admission: Closing date 2/1 (postmark date). $65 fee, may be waived for applicants with need. Notification staggered: 12/15, 02/15, 04/01. Must reply by May 1 or within 2 week(s) if notified thereafter. **Financial aid:** Priority date 2/1; no closing date. FAFSA required. Applicants notified on a rolling basis starting 3/15; must reply by 5/1.

Academics. Special study options: Combined bachelor's/graduate degree, cross-registration, distance learning, double major, dual enrollment of high school students, honors, independent study, internships, liberal arts/career combination, student-designed major, study abroad, teacher certification program. **Credit/placement by examination:** AP, CLEP, institutional tests. 44 credit hours maximum toward bachelor's degree. **Support services:** Reduced course load, tutoring, writing center.

Honors college/program. 1400 SAT (exclusive of Writing) or ACT equivalent, 2 nominations, interview required.

Majors. Biology: General, biochemistry, molecular. **Business:** Accounting, business admin, finance, international, management information systems, marketing. **Computer sciences:** General. **Education:** Early childhood, elementary. **English:** Creative writing, English lit, general lit, technical writing. **Foreign languages:** Hebrew. **Health services:** Audiology/speech pathology. **History:** General. **Math:** General. **Philosophy/religion:** Philosophy. **Physical sciences:** General, chemistry, physics. **Psychology:** General. **Social sciences:** Economics, political science, sociology. **Visual/performing arts:** Music.

Most popular majors. Biology 18%, business/marketing 27%, English 6%, psychology 14%, social sciences 11%.

Technology on campus. 350 workstations in library, computer center, student center. Dormitories wired for high-speed internet access and linked to campus network. Online library, helpline, repair service, wireless network available.

Student life. Freshman orientation: Mandatory. Preregistration for classes offered. Held the week before classes. **Policies:** Students participate in university governance through college senates. **Housing:** Guaranteed on-campus for all undergraduates. Single-sex dorms, apartments available. $300 nonrefundable deposit, deadline 5/1. **Activities:** Bands, choral groups, dance, drama, film society, international student organizations, literary magazine, music ensembles, Model UN, musical theater, radio station, student government, student newspaper, neighborhood social service, pre-professional, special interest, and political clubs.

Athletics. NCAA. **Intercollegiate:** Baseball M, basketball, cross-country M, fencing M, soccer M, tennis M, volleyball M, wrestling M. **Intramural:** Basketball, tennis M, volleyball W. **Team name:** Macs.

Student services. Career counseling, student employment services, health services, personal counseling, placement for graduates.

Contact. E-mail: yuadmit@yu.edu
Phone: (212) 960-5277 Fax: (212) 960-0086
Geri Mansdorf, Director of Undergraduate Admissions, Yeshiva University, 500 West 185th Street, New York, NY 10033

Yeshivas Novominsk
Brooklyn, New York

- Private 4-year rabbinical college for men affiliated with the Jewish faith
- Very large city
- 130 degree-seeking undergraduates

General. Accredited by AARTS. **Calendar:** Semester. **Full-time faculty:** 6 total.

Basis for selection. Completion of college-preparatory program and recommendations required. Secondary school record recommended.

2015-2016 Annual costs. Tuition/fees: $14,400. Room/board: $3,500.

Application procedures. Admission: No deadline. $100 fee.

Academics. Credit/placement by examination: AP, CLEP.

Majors. Theology: Talmudic.

Contact. Phone: (718) 438-2727
Yeshivas Novominsk, 1690 60th Street, Brooklyn, NY 11204

Yeshivat Mikdash Melech
Brooklyn, New York
www.mikdashmelech.net   CB code: 1432

- Private 5-year rabbinical college for men affiliated with the Jewish faith
- Residential campus in very large city
- 17 degree-seeking undergraduates
- Interview required

General. Accredited by AARTS. **Degrees:** 4 bachelor's awarded; doctoral offered. **Calendar:** Semester, extensive summer session. **Full-time faculty:** 8 total. **Part-time faculty:** 2 total. **Class size:** 100% < 20.

Freshman class profile.

Out-of-state: 5%   **Live on campus:**   80%

Basis for selection. Open admission, but selective for some programs. Recommendations, school record, test scores, and class rank considered. **Home schooled:** Statement describing home school structure and mission required.

High school preparation. Required units include English 3, mathematics 3, social studies 1, history 1, science 2 (laboratory 1), foreign language 1 and academic electives 1.

2015-2016 Annual costs. Tuition/fees: $8,100. Room/board: $4,700. Personal expenses: $4,000.

Financial aid. Non-need-based: Scholarships awarded for academics, leadership, religious affiliation.

Application procedures. Admission: No deadline. $400 fee, may be waived for applicants with need. Application must be submitted on paper. Admission notification on a rolling basis. **Financial aid:** No deadline. FAFSA, institutional form required. Applicants notified on a rolling basis starting 5/1.

Academics. Special study options: Independent study, study abroad. **Credit/placement by examination:** AP, CLEP. **Support services:** Remedial instruction, tutoring.

Majors. Theology: Talmudic.

Technology on campus. Wireless network available.

Student life. Freshman orientation: Available. Preregistration for classes offered. **Policies:** Religious observance required. **Housing:** Guaranteed on-campus for freshmen. Wellness housing available.

Student services. Adult student services, chaplain/spiritual director, financial aid counseling.

Contact. E-mail: mikdashmelech@verizon.net
Phone: (718) 339-1090 Fax: (718) 998-9321
Rabbi Hillel Strouse, Admissions Director, Yeshivat Mikdash Melech, 1326 Ocean Parkway, Brooklyn, NY 11230-9963

Yeshivath Viznitz
Monsey, New York

- Private 4-year rabbinical college for men
- Large town
- 470 degree-seeking undergraduates

General. Accredited by AARTS. **Degrees:** 81 bachelor's awarded; doctoral offered. **Calendar:** Semester. **Full-time faculty:** 40 total. **Part-time faculty:** 5 total.

Basis for selection. Completion of college-preparatory program and recommendations required. Secondary school record recommended.

2015-2016 Annual costs. Tuition/fees: $8,600. Room/board: $2,100.

Application procedures. Admission: No deadline.

Academics. Credit/placement by examination: AP, CLEP.

Majors. Theology: Talmudic.

Contact. Phone: (845) 731-3700
Yeshivath Viznitz, 25 Phyllis Terrace, Monsey, NY 10952

North Carolina

Apex School of Theology
Durham, North Carolina
www.apexsot.edu

▶ Private 4-year Bible college
▶ Small city
▶ 682 degree-seeking undergraduates
▶ 202 graduate students

General. Regionally accredited; also accredited by TRACS. **Degrees:** 34 bachelor's, 7 associate awarded; master's, doctoral offered. **Calendar:** Semester. **Full-time faculty:** 16 total. **Part-time faculty:** 42 total.

Freshman class profile. 90 applied, 69 admitted, 69 enrolled.

Basis for selection. Open admission.

2015-2016 Annual costs. Tuition/fees: $6,200. Books/supplies: $300.

Application procedures. Admission: No deadline. $25 fee.

Academics. Special study options: Distance learning, dual enrollment of high school students, independent study, internships. **Credit/placement by examination:** AP, CLEP.

Majors. Theology: Theology.

Student life. Activities: Student newspaper.

Contact. E-mail: smanning@apexsot.edu
Phone: (919) 572-1625 ext. 7025
Sandra Manning, Director of Admissions, Apex School of Theology, 1701 TW Alexander Drive, Durham, NC 27703

Appalachian State University
Boone, North Carolina
www.appstate.edu

CB member
CB code: 5010

▶ Public 4-year university
▶ Residential campus in large town
▶ 16,126 degree-seeking undergraduates: 5% part-time, 54% women, 3% African American, 2% Asian American, 4% Hispanic/Latino, 3% Multiracial, non-Hispanic, 1% international
▶ 1,460 degree-seeking graduate students
▶ 66% of applicants admitted
▶ SAT or ACT (ACT writing optional) required
▶ 71% graduate within 6 years

General. Founded in 1899. Regionally accredited. **Degrees:** 3,713 bachelor's awarded; master's, doctoral offered. **ROTC:** Army. **Location:** 87 miles from Winston-Salem, 100 miles from Asheville, 100 miles from Charlotte. **Calendar:** Semester, extensive summer session. **Full-time faculty:** 930 total; 99% have terminal degrees, 7% minority, 48% women. **Part-time faculty:** 397 total; 82% have terminal degrees, 2% minority, 55% women. **Class size:** 35% < 20, 51% 20-39, 6% 40-49, 7% 50-99, 1% >100. **Special facilities:** Dark sky observatory, visual arts center, year round outdoor adventure camp, outdoor geology lab, looking glass gallery.

Freshman class profile. 13,083 applied, 8,684 admitted, 3,049 enrolled.

Mid 50% test scores			
SAT critical reading:	530-620	Rank in top quarter:	61%
SAT math:	530-620	Rank in top tenth:	21%
SAT writing:	500-600	End year in good standing:	92%
ACT composite:	23-28	Return as sophomores:	86%
GPA 3.75 or higher:	84%	Out-of-state:	10%
GPA 3.50-3.74:	10%	Live on campus:	99%
GPA 3.0-3.49:	5%	International:	1%
GPA 2.0-2.99:	1%	Fraternities:	8%
		Sororities:	14%

Basis for selection. Satisfactory combination of grades and/or class rank and required test scores. SAT Math used for placement. Audition required for music majors; portfolio required for art majors. **Home schooled:** Transcript of courses and grades required.

High school preparation. College-preparatory program required. 13 units required. Required units include English 4, mathematics 4, social studies 1, history 1, science 3 (laboratory 1) and foreign language 2. Specific math units required.

2015-2016 Annual costs. Tuition/fees: $6,852; $20,677 out-of-state. Room/board: $7,845.

2014-2015 Financial aid. Need-based: 1,602 full-time freshmen applied for aid; 1,570 deemed to have need; 1,465 received aid. Average need met was 73%. Average scholarship/grant was $8,203; average loan $3,322. 52% of total undergraduate aid awarded as scholarships/grants, 48% as loans/jobs. **Non-need-based:** Awarded to 3,387 full-time undergraduates, including 692 freshmen. Scholarships awarded for academics, alumni affiliation, art, athletics, job skills, leadership, minority status, music/drama, religious affiliation, ROTC, state residency.

Application procedures. Admission: Priority date 11/15; deadline 3/15. $55 fee, may be waived for applicants with need. Application must be submitted online. Admission notification on a rolling basis beginning on or about 1/25. Must reply by May 1 or within 3 week(s) if notified thereafter. Deferment allowed on individual basis for one term during academic year. **Financial aid:** Priority date 3/1; no closing date. FAFSA required. Applicants notified on a rolling basis starting 4/1; must reply within 3 week(s) of notification.

Academics. Special study options: Cross-registration, distance learning, double major, dual enrollment of high school students, ESL, exchange student, honors, independent study, internships, liberal arts/career combination, semester at sea, student-designed major, study abroad, teacher certification program. **Credit/placement by examination:** AP, CLEP, IB, SAT, ACT, institutional tests. Credit is determined by the appropriate department or program. **Support services:** Learning center, pre-admission summer program, study skills assistance, tutoring, writing center. Lead tutoring in chemistry class; academic advising for specific populations; academic coaching.

Honors college/program. Successful applicants will generally be in the top 5% of their high school class, with 1250 combined Math and Verbal SAT (29 ACT) on average. Application process includes 500-word essay, two letters of recommendation, and resume. 200 students matriculate.

Majors. Architecture: Urban/community planning. **Area/ethnic studies:** Women's. **Biology:** General. **Business:** Accounting, actuarial science, business admin, construction management, finance, hospitality admin, insurance, international, management information systems, marketing. **Communications:** Advertising, communications/speech/rhetoric, journalism, public relations, radio/TV. **Computer sciences:** Computer science. **Conservation:** Environmental science, environmental studies. **Education:** Art, elementary, English, history, learning disabled, middle, music, physical. **English:** English lit. **Health services:** Athletic training, communication disorders, dietetics, health care admin, music therapy, nursing (RN), public health ed. **History:** General. **Human services:** Social work. **Liberal arts:** Arts/sciences. **Math:** General. **Parks/recreation:** Exercise sciences, facilities management. **Philosophy/religion:** Philosophy, religion. **Physical sciences:** Chemistry, geology, physics. **Protective services:** Criminal justice. **Psychology:** General. **Social sciences:** Anthropology, economics, geography, political science, sociology. **Visual/performing arts:** Art, commercial photography, dance, dramatic, graphic design, industrial design, interior design, music management, music performance, studio arts. **Work/family studies:** Child development, clothing/textiles.

Most popular majors. Business/marketing 18%, communications/journalism 6%, education 12%, health sciences 9%, parks/recreation 7%, psychology 7%, social sciences 7%, visual/performing arts 7%.

Technology on campus. 2,500 workstations in library, computer center, student center. Dormitories wired for high-speed internet access and linked to campus network. Commuter students can connect to campus network. Online course registration, online library, helpline, repair service, wireless network available.

Student life. Freshman orientation: Mandatory, $115 fee. Preregistration for classes offered. 2-day program throughout summer and at beginning of each semester and summer school session. **Policies:** Student must be full-time and live on campus to join a fraternity or sorority. First semester students must enter with a 3.0 or higher high school GPA. Upper class men must have completed 12 hours at ASU and have at least a 2.5 GPA. Some organizations may have higher academic eligibility requirements. **Housing:** Guaranteed on-campus for freshmen. Coed dorms, single-sex dorms, special housing for disabled, apartments, themed housing available. Sorority housing available. **Activities:** Bands, campus ministries, choral groups, dance, drama, film society, international student organizations, literary magazine, music ensembles, Model UN, musical theater, opera, radio station, student government, student newspaper, symphony orchestra, TV station, Alliance College Connection, Collegians for Christ, College Republicans/ Democrats, prelaw society, Chinese culture club, Hispanic Student Organization, American Red Cross, Amnesty International, Habitat for Humanity, Wine to Water.

Athletics. NCAA. **Intercollegiate:** Baseball M, basketball, cross-country, field hockey W, football (tackle) M, golf, soccer, softball W, tennis, track and field, volleyball W, wrestling M. **Intramural:** Badminton, basketball, bowling, cross-country, football (non-tackle), golf, racquetball, soccer, softball, table tennis, tennis, ultimate frisbee, volleyball. **Team name:** Mountaineers.

Student services. Adult student services, alcohol/substance abuse counseling, chaplain/spiritual director, career counseling, services for economically disadvantaged, student employment services, financial aid counseling, health services, legal services, minority student services, on-campus daycare, personal counseling, placement for graduates, veterans' counselor, women's services. **Physically disabled:** Services for visually, speech, hearing impaired.

Contact. E-mail: admissions@appstate.edu
Phone: (828) 262-2000 Fax: (828) 262-3296
Alexis Pope, Director of Admissions, Appalachian State University, ASU Box 32004, Boone, NC 28608

Barton College
Wilson, North Carolina   CB member
www.barton.edu   CB code: 5016

- Private 4-year liberal arts college affiliated with the Christian Church (Disciples of Christ)
- Residential campus in large town
- 975 degree-seeking undergraduates: 7% part-time, 70% women
- 47 degree-seeking graduate students
- 42% of applicants admitted
- SAT or ACT (ACT writing optional) required
- 42% graduate within 6 years

General. Founded in 1902. Regionally accredited. **Degrees:** 285 bachelor's awarded; master's offered. **Location:** 45 miles from Raleigh. **Calendar:** Semester, limited summer session. **Full-time faculty:** 69 total; 77% have terminal degrees, 51% women. **Special facilities:** Barton Museum, greenhouse, TV and music recording studios, photo developing labs and darkroom, black box theater.

Freshman class profile. 2,920 applied, 1,220 admitted, 227 enrolled.

Mid 50% test scores		ACT composite:	18-23
SAT critical reading:	420-510	Rank in top quarter:	38%
SAT math:	430-540	Rank in top tenth:	11%

Basis for selection. High school GPA, test scores, and strong academic course study important. Interview recommended for marginal students; portfolio recommended for art students. **Home schooled:** State high school equivalency certificate required.

High school preparation. 13 units required. Required and recommended units include English 4, mathematics 3, social studies 2, science 2 (laboratory 1), foreign language 2 and academic electives 1.

2016-2017 Annual costs. Tuition/fees: $29,052. Room/board: $9,634. Books/supplies: $1,200. Personal expenses: $3,050.

Financial aid. Non-need-based: Scholarships awarded for academics, alumni affiliation, art, athletics, leadership, minority status, music/drama, religious affiliation, state residency.

Application procedures. Admission: No deadline. $25 fee, may be waived for applicants with need, free for online applicants. Admission notification on a rolling basis. Must reply by May 1 or within 2 week(s) if notified thereafter. **Financial aid:** Priority date 4/1; no closing date. FAFSA required. Applicants notified on a rolling basis starting 5/1; must reply within 2 week(s) of notification.

Academics. Special study options: Accelerated study, cooperative education, double major, honors, independent study, internships, liberal arts/career combination, study abroad, teacher certification program, Washington semester, weekend college. **Credit/placement by examination:** AP, CLEP, IB, SAT, ACT, institutional tests. 30 credit hours maximum toward bachelor's degree. **Support services:** Remedial instruction, study skills assistance, tutoring, writing center.

Majors. Biology: General. **Business:** Accounting, business admin, human resources. **Communications:** Media studies. **Computer sciences:** General. **Conservation:** Environmental science. **Education:** Art, Deaf/hearing impaired, elementary, learning disabled, middle, physical, social studies. **English:** English lit. **Foreign languages:** Spanish. **Health services:** Athletic training, nursing (RN). **History:** General. **Human services:** Social work. **Liberal arts:** Arts/sciences. **Math:** General. **Parks/recreation:** Health/fitness, sports admin. **Philosophy/religion:** Religion. **Physical sciences:** Chemistry. **Protective services:** Criminal justice. **Psychology:** General. **Social sciences:** Political science. **Visual/performing arts:** Dramatic, studio arts.

Most popular majors. Business/marketing 20%, education 8%, health sciences 20%, parks/recreation 9%, public administration/social services 11%, security/protective services 7%.

Technology on campus. 176 workstations in dormitories, library, computer center, student center. Dormitories wired for high-speed internet access and linked to campus network. Commuter students can connect to campus network. Online library, helpline, wireless network available.

Student life. Freshman orientation: Mandatory, $75 fee. Preregistration for classes offered. Two-day sessions held during June. **Policies:** Full-time freshmen and sophomores not living with parents required to live on campus. Special permission required for students under 23 to live off-campus. **Housing:** Guaranteed on-campus for freshmen. Coed dorms, single-sex dorms, special housing for disabled, fraternity/sorority housing, wellness housing available. $150 nonrefundable deposit, deadline 5/1. **Activities:** Pep band, campus ministries, choral groups, dance, drama, literary magazine, musical theater, student government, student newspaper, symphony orchestra, TV station, Disciples on Campus, Fellowship of Christian Athletes, Habitat for Humanity, Alpha Phi Omega, Campus Conservatives, College Democrats, diversity education team, political science club, Campus Crusade for Christ.

Athletics. NCAA. **Intercollegiate:** Baseball M, basketball, cross-country, golf, soccer, softball W, tennis, track and field, volleyball. **Intramural:** Badminton, basketball, football (non-tackle), soccer, softball, tennis, volleyball. **Team name:** Bulldogs.

Student services. Adult student services, chaplain/spiritual director, career counseling, student employment services, financial aid counseling, health services, personal counseling, placement for graduates. **Physically disabled:** Services for visually, speech, hearing impaired.

Contact. E-mail: enroll@barton.edu
Phone: (252) 399-6317 Toll-free number: (800) 345-4973
Fax: (252) 399-6572
Amanda Metts, Assistant Vice President for Admissions, Barton College, Box 5000, Wilson, NC 27893-7000

Belmont Abbey College
Belmont, North Carolina
www.belmontabbeycollege.edu   CB member
      CB code: 5055

- Private 4-year liberal arts college affiliated with the Roman Catholic Church
- Residential campus in small town
- 1,478 degree-seeking undergraduates: 7% part-time, 54% women, 22% African American, 1% Asian American, 1% Hispanic/Latino, 2% international
- 68% of applicants admitted
- SAT or ACT (ACT writing optional) required
- 43% graduate within 6 years

General. Founded in 1876. Regionally accredited. **Degrees:** 344 bachelor's awarded. **ROTC:** Army, Air Force. **Location:** 10 miles from Charlotte. **Calendar:** Semester, limited summer session. **Full-time faculty:** 75 total; 64% have terminal degrees, 9% minority, 48% women. **Part-time faculty:** 60 total; 20% have terminal degrees, 8% minority, 42% women. **Class size:** 65% < 20, 35% 20-39. **Special facilities:** Monastery, basilica, adoration chapel.

Freshman class profile. 1,967 applied, 1,335 admitted, 310 enrolled.

Return as sophomores:	60%	International:	3%
Out-of-state:	50%	Fraternities:	1%
Live on campus:	87%		

Basis for selection. GPA, class rank, high school curriculum, and test scores most important. Personal accomplishments, extracurricular activities, and letters of recommendation strongly considered. **Home schooled:** GED is accepted for home schooled applicants.

High school preparation. College-preparatory program recommended. 16 units required. Required units include English 4, mathematics 3, science 2 (laboratory 2), foreign language 2 and academic electives 3.

2015-2016 Annual costs. Tuition/fees: $18,500. Room/board: $10,390. Books/supplies: $1,200. Personal expenses: $1,600.

2015-2016 Financial aid. Need-based: 266 full-time freshmen applied for aid; 208 deemed to have need; 208 received aid. Average need met was 54%. Average scholarship/grant was $9,410; average loan $3,606. 47% of total undergraduate aid awarded as scholarships/grants, 53% as loans/jobs. **Non-need-based:** Awarded to 450 full-time undergraduates, including 171 freshmen. Scholarships awarded for academics, athletics.

Application procedures. Admission: Closing date 8/15 (receipt date). No application fee. Application must be submitted online. Admission notification on a rolling basis. **Financial aid:** Priority date 4/1; no closing date. FAFSA required. Applicants notified on a rolling basis starting 3/15; must reply within 2 week(s) of notification.

Academics. Special study options: Double major, dual enrollment of high school students, honors, independent study, internships, liberal arts/career combination, study abroad, teacher certification program, weekend college. **Credit/placement by examination:** AP, CLEP, IB. 30 credit hours maximum toward bachelor's degree. **Support services:** Learning center, study skills assistance, tutoring.

Honors college/program. High school seniors with a grade point average of 3.7 or higher and an SAT score (math and verbal) of at least 1200 (including a minimum verbal score of 600) will be considered for admission to the Honors Institute.

Majors. Biology: General. **Business:** Accounting, business admin. **Education:** General, elementary. **English:** English lit. **History:** General. **Liberal arts:** Arts/sciences. **Math:** General. **Parks/recreation:** Facilities management, sports admin. **Protective services:** Criminal justice. **Psychology:** General. **Social sciences:** U.S. government. **Theology:** Religious ed, theology.

Most popular majors. Business/marketing 31%, education 18%, liberal arts 11%, parks/recreation 6%, psychology 8%, security/protective services 6%.

Technology on campus. 100 workstations in library, computer center, student center. Dormitories wired for high-speed internet access and linked to campus network. Commuter students can connect to campus network. Online course registration, online library, helpline, wireless network available.

Student life. Freshman orientation: Mandatory. Preregistration for classes offered. 4 days prior to class start. **Policies:** All unmarried full-time students must live on-campus, unless they live within commuting distance with a parent/legal guardian or are an Adult Degree Program student. **Housing:** Guaranteed on-campus for all undergraduates. Single-sex dorms, special housing for disabled available. $400 nonrefundable deposit. 24-hour quiet (honors) dorm available. **Activities:** Campus ministries, choral groups, drama, international student organizations, literary magazine, musical theater, student government, student newspaper, Crusaders for Life, Abbey Volunteers, Improv Troupe, international club, Green Team, psychology club, Student Government Association, campus activities board, XCEL fitness club, Men's/Women's Household.

Athletics. NCAA. **Intercollegiate:** Baseball M, basketball, cheerleading W, cross-country, golf, lacrosse, soccer, softball W, tennis, track and field, volleyball, wrestling M. **Intramural:** Bowling, cheerleading W, football (non-tackle), sand volleyball, soccer, ultimate frisbee. **Team name:** Crusaders.

Student services. Adult student services, alcohol/substance abuse counseling, chaplain/spiritual director, career counseling, student employment services, financial aid counseling, health services, personal counseling, placement for graduates.

Contact. E-mail: admissions@bac.edu
Phone: (704) 461-6665 Toll-free number: (888) 222-0110
Fax: (704) 461-6220
Nicole Focareto, Executive Director of Admissions, Belmont Abbey College, 100 Belmont - Mt. Holly Road, Belmont, NC 28012-2795

Bennett College for Women
Greensboro, North Carolina
www.bennett.edu

CB member
CB code: 5058

- Private 4-year liberal arts college for women affiliated with the United Methodist Church
- Residential campus in large city

- 553 degree-seeking undergraduates: 1% part-time, 100% women
- SAT or ACT (ACT writing optional), application essay required

General. Founded in 1873. Regionally accredited. **Degrees:** 77 bachelor's awarded. **ROTC:** Army, Air Force. **Location:** 26 miles from Winston-Salem, 80 miles from Raleigh. **Calendar:** Semester, limited summer session. **Full-time faculty:** 58 total; 74% have terminal degrees, 79% minority, 62% women. **Part-time faculty:** 14 total; 14% have terminal degrees, 79% minority, 64% women. **Class size:** 75% < 20, 23% 20-39, 2% 40-49.

Freshman class profile.

Out-of-state: 55%	**Live on campus:**	84%

Basis for selection. Admission decisions are made by assessing school achievement record(s), test scores, recommendations and applicant's personal statement. Interview recommended for borderline students. **Home schooled:** Transcript of courses and grades required.

High school preparation. College-preparatory program recommended. 18 units required. Required units include English 4, mathematics 3, social studies 2, science 2 and foreign language 2.

2015-2016 Annual costs. Tuition/fees: $17,130. Room/board: $7,576. Books/supplies: $1,400. Personal expenses: $4,742.

Financial aid. Non-need-based: Scholarships awarded for academics, religious affiliation.

Application procedures. Admission: No deadline. $35 fee, may be waived for applicants with need. Admission notification on a rolling basis. **Financial aid:** Closing date 4/15. FAFSA, institutional form required. Applicants notified by 7/15.

Academics. Special study options: Cooperative education, cross-registration, double major, dual enrollment of high school students, exchange student, honors, independent study, internships, liberal arts/career combination, semester at sea, student-designed major, study abroad, teacher certification program, Washington semester. Dual degree programs in engineering with North Carolina Agricultural and Technical State University, Collaborative program in nursing with Howard University. **Credit/placement by examination:** AP, CLEP, IB, SAT, ACT, institutional tests. **Support services:** Learning center, pre-admission summer program, reduced course load, remedial instruction, study skills assistance, tutoring, writing center. Emerging Scholars Program provides advising for students who are admitted with a G.P.A. between 2.00 and 2.39.

Majors. Biology: General. **Business:** Business admin. **Communications:** Journalism. **Computer sciences:** General. **Education:** Elementary, English, mathematics, mentally handicapped, special ed. **Engineering:** Chemical, electrical, mechanical. **English:** English lit. **Human services:** Social work. **Math:** General. **Physical sciences:** Chemistry. **Psychology:** General. **Social sciences:** Political science. **Visual/performing arts:** General, arts management.

Most popular majors. Biology 14%, business/marketing 13%, communications/journalism 11%, education 7%, interdisciplinary studies 22%, psychology 15%, public administration/social services 9%, social sciences 7%.

Technology on campus. Dormitories wired for high-speed internet access and linked to campus network. Commuter students can connect to campus network. Online course registration, online library, helpline, repair service, wireless network available.

Student life. Freshman orientation: Mandatory, $125 fee. Preregistration for classes offered. **Policies:** Freshmen not permitted cars on campus. **Housing:** Guaranteed on-campus for all undergraduates. Wellness housing available. $250 nonrefundable deposit. Honors residence hall available. **Activities:** Campus ministries, choral groups, dance, drama, literary magazine, student government, American Civil Liberties club, Belles Against Domestic Violence, Belles of Peace, Belles Recognizing Individuality, Diversity and Empowering (B.R.I.D.E.), Campus Ministry, class governments (freshman, sophomore, junior and senior classes), Foster Friends club, Political Pacesetters, Pre-Alumnae Council (PAC)/UNCF.

Athletics. Team name: Belles.

Student services. Adult student services, chaplain/spiritual director, career counseling, student employment services, financial aid counseling, health services, on-campus daycare, personal counseling, placement for graduates, veterans' counselor.

Contact. E-mail: admiss@bennett.edu
Phone: (336) 370-5323 Toll-free number: (800) 413-5323
Fax: (336) 517-2166
Benita Corbin, Director of Admissions, Bennett College for Women, 900 East Washington Street, Greensboro, NC 27401-3239

Brevard College
Brevard, North Carolina

www.brevard.edu

CB member

CB code: 5067

- Private 4-year liberal arts college affiliated with the United Methodist Church
- Residential campus in small town
- 720 degree-seeking undergraduates
- Application essay required

General. Founded in 1853. Regionally accredited. **Degrees:** 110 bachelor's awarded. **Location:** 33 miles from Asheville. **Calendar:** Semester. **Full-time faculty:** 51 total; 84% have terminal degrees, 47% women. **Part-time faculty:** 44 total; 34% have terminal degrees, 46% women. **Class size:** 68% < 20, 32% 20-39. **Special facilities:** Fitness appraisal lab, performing arts center, academic enrichment center.

Freshman class profile.

GPA 3.75 or higher:	9%	Rank in top quarter:	24%
GPA 3.50-3.74:	14%	Rank in top tenth:	6%
GPA 3.0-3.49:	38%	Out-of-state:	43%
GPA 2.0-2.99:	39%	Live on campus:	87%

Basis for selection. High school record, class rank, SAT/ACT scores, references, extracurricular activities, recommendations, essay, interview, talent/ability, character/personal qualities, volunteer work important. Essay, interview recommended for all students; portfolio required for art students; audition required for music students. **Home schooled:** Statement describing home school structure and mission, transcript of courses and grades required. Legal documentation from home school agency, local school district, or State Department of Education and admissions interview required. **Learning Disabled:** Evaluation by licensed professional within past 3 years.

High school preparation. College-preparatory program recommended. 22 units recommended. Recommended units include English 4, mathematics 3, social studies 4, history 1, science 3 (laboratory 1), foreign language 2 and academic electives 4. Math units should include 2 algebra and 1 geometry.

2015-2016 Annual costs. Tuition/fees: $26,980. Room/board: $9,790. Books/supplies: $1,000. Personal expenses: $1,000.

Financial aid. Non-need-based: Scholarships awarded for academics, art, athletics, leadership, music/drama, religious affiliation, state residency.

Application procedures. Admission: No deadline. No application fee. Admission notification on a rolling basis beginning on or about 7/1. **Financial aid:** Priority date 2/1; no closing date. FAFSA required. Applicants notified on a rolling basis starting 2/1; must reply by 5/1 or within 4 week(s) of notification.

Academics. Special study options: Double major, dual enrollment of high school students, honors, independent study, internships, student-designed major, study abroad, teacher certification program. **Credit/placement by examination:** AP, CLEP, IB, SAT, ACT, institutional tests. 92 credit hours maximum toward bachelor's degree. **Support services:** Learning center, reduced course load, remedial instruction, study skills assistance, tutoring, writing center.

Majors. Biology: General. **Business:** Business admin. **Conservation:** Environmental studies. **Education:** Music. **English:** English lit. **Health services:** Predental, premedicine, prenursing, preveterinary. **History:** General. **Liberal arts:** Arts/sciences. **Math:** General. **Parks/recreation:** Exercise sciences, facilities management. **Philosophy/religion:** Religion. **Protective services:** Law enforcement admin. **Psychology:** General. **Visual/performing arts:** Art, dramatic, music, music performance.

Most popular majors. Business/marketing 16%, interdisciplinary studies 9%, natural resources/environmental science 8%, parks/recreation 26%, psychology 12%, visual/performing arts 12%.

Technology on campus. 100 workstations in library, computer center, student center. Dormitories wired for high-speed internet access and linked to campus network. Online library, helpline, wireless network available.

Student life. Freshman orientation: Mandatory. Preregistration for classes offered. Orientations held in summer prior to start of classes. **Housing:** Guaranteed on-campus for all undergraduates. Coed dorms, single-sex dorms, special housing for disabled, themed housing, wellness housing available. All non-county or non-adjacent-county residents required to live on campus until age 21. **Activities:** Bands, campus ministries, choral groups, dance, drama, literary magazine, music ensembles, musical theater, opera, student government, student newspaper, Recycling Club, Fellowship of Christian Athletes, Omicron Delta Kappa, Outing Club, Environmental Educators, History Club, Young Politicians of America, Business Club, Debate Society.

Athletics. NCAA. **Intercollegiate:** Baseball M, basketball, cheerleading W, cross-country, football (tackle) M, golf, lacrosse, soccer, softball W, tennis, track and field, volleyball W. **Intramural:** Archery, badminton, basketball, bowling, cross-country, equestrian, football (tackle) M, golf, skiing, soccer, softball, swimming, tennis, track and field, volleyball. **Team name:** Tornados.

Student services. Alcohol/substance abuse counseling, chaplain/spiritual director, career counseling, student employment services, financial aid counseling, health services, personal counseling, placement for graduates, veterans' counselor. **Physically disabled:** Services for visually, speech, hearing impaired.

Contact. E-mail: admissions@brevard.edu
Phone: (828) 883-8332 Toll-free number: (800) 527-9090
Fax: (828) 884-3790
Chad Holt, Vice President of Admissions & Financial Aid, Brevard College, One Brevard College Drive, Brevard, NC 28712

Cabarrus College of Health Sciences
Concord, North Carolina

www.cabarruscollege.edu

CB code: 5136

- Private 4-year health science and nursing college
- Commuter campus in small city
- 423 degree-seeking undergraduates: 63% part-time, 89% women
- 21 degree-seeking graduate students
- 94% of applicants admitted
- SAT or ACT (ACT writing optional), application essay required

General. Regionally accredited. **Degrees:** 23 bachelor's, 105 associate awarded; master's offered. **Location:** 25 miles from Charlotte. **Calendar:** Semester, limited summer session. **Full-time faculty:** 30 total. **Part-time faculty:** 37 total. **Class size:** 62% < 20, 30% 20-39, 4% 40-49, 4% 50-99.

Freshman class profile. 32 applied, 30 admitted, 25 enrolled.

GPA 3.75 or higher:	55%	GPA 2.0-2.99:	11%
GPA 3.50-3.74:	10%	Rank in top quarter:	28%
GPA 3.0-3.49:	24%	Rank in top tenth:	7%

Basis for selection. School record, class rank, essay, test scores, and recommendations most important.

High school preparation. Required units include English 4, mathematics 3 and science 2.

2015-2016 Annual costs. Tuition/fees: $12,526. Books/supplies: $1,400. Personal expenses: $1,600.

2015-2016 Financial aid. Need-based: 41% of total undergraduate aid awarded as scholarships/grants, 59% as loans/jobs. **Non-need-based:** Scholarships awarded for academics, leadership, state residency.

Application procedures. Admission: Priority date 2/1; no deadline. $50 fee. **Financial aid:** Closing date 4/15. FAFSA required. Applicants notified on a rolling basis starting 6/30.

Academics. Special study options: Accelerated study, cross-registration, distance learning, internships, liberal arts/career combination, weekend college. **Credit/placement by examination:** AP, CLEP, institutional tests. **Support services:** Learning center, study skills assistance.

Majors. Health services: Nursing (RN), physics/radiologic health.

Most popular majors. Health sciences 78%, interdisciplinary studies 22%.

Technology on campus. 23 workstations in library, computer center, student center. Commuter students can connect to campus network. Online course registration, online library, wireless network available.

Student life. Freshman orientation: Mandatory. Preregistration for classes offered. Online orientation is to be completed before the start of the semester. Some programs do have a face-to-face orientation on the first day of the semester, which usually last from half an hour to an hour. **Activities:** Student government, student newspaper, Christian Student Union, Association of Nursing Students, Rotaract.

Student services. Career counseling, financial aid counseling, on-campus daycare, personal counseling. **Physically disabled:** Services for hearing impaired.

Contact. E-mail: admissions@cabarruscollege.edu
Phone: (704) 403-1556 Fax: (704) 403-2077
Lorri Connor, Director of Recruitment and Retention, Cabarrus College of Health Sciences, 401 Medical Park Drive, Concord, NC 28025-2405

Campbell University

Buies Creek, North Carolina
www.campbell.edu

CB member
CB code: 5100

- Private 4-year university and liberal arts college affiliated with the Baptist faith
- Residential campus in rural community
- 4,217 degree-seeking undergraduates
- SAT or ACT (ACT writing recommended) required

General. Founded in 1887. Regionally accredited. **Degrees:** 904 bachelor's, 91 associate awarded; master's, professional, doctoral offered. **ROTC:** Army. **Location:** 30 miles from Raleigh, 30 miles from Fayetteville. **Calendar:** Semester, extensive summer session. **Full-time faculty:** 564 total; 99% have terminal degrees, 18% minority, 47% women. **Part-time faculty:** 145 total; 27% have terminal degrees, 28% minority, 32% women. **Class size:** 57% < 20, 30% 20-39, 6% 40-49, 7% 50-99, less than 1% >100. **Special facilities:** Golf course, animal museum, drug information center, nature trail.

Freshman class profile.

GPA 3.75 or higher:	56%	GPA 2.0-2.99:	10%
GPA 3.50-3.74:	13%	Out-of-state:	20%
GPA 3.0-3.49:	21%	Live on campus:	91%

Basis for selection. SAT, GPA, course selection, class rank, and standardized test scores considered. Candidates reviewed on an individual basis. Interview recommended on a case by case basis. Essay recommended for all students; audition recommended for music programs.

High school preparation. College-preparatory program recommended. 11 units required. Required and recommended units include English 4, mathematics 3, social studies 2, science 2 (laboratory 1) and foreign language 2. One social science should be U.S. History. Math units must include algebra I and II as well as geometry.

2015-2016 Annual costs. Tuition/fees: $28,635. Room/board: $10,050. Books/supplies: $1,500.

Financial aid. Non-need-based: Scholarships awarded for academics, athletics, music/drama, religious affiliation, ROTC, state residency.

Application procedures. Admission: No deadline. No application fee. Admission notification on a rolling basis. **Financial aid:** Priority date 2/15; no closing date. FAFSA required. Applicants notified on a rolling basis starting 2/1; must reply within 2 week(s) of notification.

Academics. Special study options: Accelerated study, combined bachelor's/graduate degree, distance learning, double major, exchange student, honors, independent study, internships, liberal arts/career combination, study abroad, teacher certification program, Washington semester. **Credit/placement by examination:** AP, CLEP, IB, SAT, ACT. **Support services:** Reduced course load, remedial instruction, study skills assistance, tutoring, writing center.

Majors. Biology: General, biochemistry. **Business:** General, accounting, business admin, financial planning, international, management information systems. **Communications:** Advertising, broadcast journalism, journalism, public relations, radio/TV. **Computer sciences:** Computer graphics, computer science, information systems. **Education:** General, biology, early childhood, elementary, English, French, history, mathematics, middle, music, physical, secondary, social studies, Spanish. **English:** English lit. **Foreign languages:** Spanish. **Health services:** Athletic training, predental, premedicine, prepharmacy, preveterinary. **History:** General. **Human services:** General, social work. **Math:** General. **Parks/recreation:** Exercise sciences, health/fitness, sports admin. **Philosophy/religion:** Religion. **Physical sciences:** Chemistry. **Protective services:** Criminal justice. **Psychology:** General. **Social sciences:** Economics, international relations, political science. **Theology:** Religious ed, theology. **Visual/performing arts:** Commercial/advertising art, dramatic, music, piano/keyboard, studio arts, voice/opera. **Work/family studies:** Child development, family studies.

Most popular majors. Business/marketing 27%, education 8%, health sciences 9%, parks/recreation 7%, psychology 8%, science technologies 11%, social sciences 9%.

Technology on campus. Dormitories wired for high-speed internet access and linked to campus network. Commuter students can connect to campus network. Online course registration, online library, helpline, repair service, wireless network available.

Student life. Freshman orientation: Mandatory, $50 fee. Preregistration for classes offered. Two weekend sessions in summer available to incoming freshmen and their families for students entering in Fall. Short program before classes start for students entering in Spring. **Policies:** Religious observance required. **Housing:** Guaranteed on-campus for all undergraduates. Single-sex dorms, special housing for disabled, apartments available. $100 fully refundable deposit. **Activities:** Bands, campus ministries, choral groups, drama, international student organizations, literary magazine, music ensembles, musical theater, student government, student newspaper, symphony orchestra, TV station, Baptist Student Union, College Democrats/Republicans, Fellowship of Christian Athletes, North Carolina Student Legislators, Campus Crusade, Christians in Action, Campbell Catholic Community, Circle K.

Athletics. NCAA. **Intercollegiate:** Baseball M, basketball, cheerleading, cross-country, football (tackle) M, golf, lacrosse W, soccer, softball W, swimming W, tennis, track and field, volleyball W, wrestling M. **Intramural:** Basketball, football (non-tackle), soccer, softball, table tennis, tennis, ultimate frisbee, volleyball. **Team name:** Fighting Camels.

Student services. Adult student services, alcohol/substance abuse counseling, chaplain/spiritual director, career counseling, student employment services, financial aid counseling, health services, personal counseling, placement for graduates, veterans' counselor. **Physically disabled:** Services for visually, speech, hearing impaired.

Contact. E-mail: admissions@campbell.edu
Phone: (910) 893-1290 ext. 1290
Toll-free number: (800) 334-4111 ext. 1290 Fax: (910) 893-1288
Jason Hall, Assistant Vice President for Admissions, Campbell University, PO Box 546, Buies Creek, NC 27506

Carolina Christian College

Winston-Salem, North Carolina
www.carolina.edu

- Private 4-year Bible college affiliated with the nondenominational tradition
- Commuter campus in large city
- 19 degree-seeking undergraduates
- Application essay required

General. Accredited by ABHE. **Degrees:** 8 bachelor's, 1 associate awarded; master's offered. **Calendar:** Semester, limited summer session. **Full-time faculty:** 1 total; 100% have terminal degrees, 100% minority. **Part-time faculty:** 14 total; 21% have terminal degrees, 50% minority, 50% women. **Class size:** 100% < 20.

Basis for selection. Open admission. COMPASS test required.

High school preparation. Specific distribution not required.

Financial aid. All financial aid based on need.

Application procedures. Admission: No deadline. $50 fee, may be waived for applicants with need. Admission notification on a rolling basis. **Financial aid:** No deadline. FAFSA required. Applicants notified on a rolling basis.

Academics. Special study options: Accelerated study, independent study. **Credit/placement by examination:** AP, CLEP. 12 credit hours maximum toward associate degree, 24 toward bachelor's. **Support services:** Remedial instruction.

Majors. Theology: Bible.

Technology on campus. PC or laptop required. 8 workstations in library. Commuter students can connect to campus network. Online course registration, wireless network available.

Student life. Freshman orientation: Mandatory. Preregistration for classes offered. **Activities:** Campus ministries, student government.

Contact. Phone: (336) 744-0900 Fax: (336) 744-0901
LaTanya Lucas, Academic Dean, Carolina Christian College, PO Box 777, Winston-Salem, NC 27102

Catawba College
Salisbury, North Carolina

www.catawba.edu

CB member
CB code: 5103

- Private 4-year liberal arts college affiliated with the United Church of Christ
- Residential campus in large town
- 1,256 degree-seeking undergraduates: 4% part-time, 52% women, 18% African American, 1% Asian American, 5% Hispanic/Latino, 3% Multi-racial, non-Hispanic, 3% international
- 5 degree-seeking graduate students
- 32% of applicants admitted
- Application essay required
- 47% graduate within 6 years

General. Founded in 1851. Regionally accredited. **Degrees:** 267 bachelor's awarded; master's offered. **ROTC:** Army, Air Force. **Location:** 40 miles from Charlotte, 45 miles from Greensboro. **Calendar:** Semester, limited summer session. **Full-time faculty:** 83 total; 86% have terminal degrees, 12% minority, 46% women. **Part-time faculty:** 96 total; 23% have terminal degrees, 10% minority, 46% women. **Class size:** 70% < 20, 29% 20-39, less than 1% 50-99. **Special facilities:** Three-manual Casavant pipe-organ, 189-acre outdoor ecological preserve, astronomical observatory.

Freshman class profile. 3,117 applied, 991 admitted, 308 enrolled.

Mid 50% test scores		GPA 3.0-3.49:	29%
SAT critical reading:	430-550	GPA 2.0-2.99:	12%
SAT math:	440-560	Rank in top quarter:	39%
SAT writing:	410-510	Rank in top tenth:	13%
ACT composite:	18-24	Return as sophomores:	73%
GPA 3.75 or higher:	47%	International:	2%
GPA 3.50-3.74:	12%		

Basis for selection. School achievement record, class rank, standardized test scores, school recommendations important. SAT preferred, but ACT also accepted. Interview recommended for all students; audition recommended for drama, music programs.

High school preparation. College-preparatory program required. 13 units required. Required and recommended units include English 4, mathematics 3, social studies 3, science 3 and foreign language 2. Required credits must be academic subjects at college preparatory level.

2016-2017 Annual costs. Tuition/fees: $29,333. Room/board: $10,487. Books/supplies: $1,400. Personal expenses: $1,623.

2014-2015 Financial aid. Need-based: 324 full-time freshmen applied for aid; 295 deemed to have need; 295 received aid. Average need met was 75%. Average scholarship/grant was $6,984; average loan $4,090. 58% of total undergraduate aid awarded as scholarships/grants, 42% as loans/jobs. **Non-need-based:** Awarded to 1,332 full-time undergraduates, including 428 freshmen. Scholarships awarded for academics, athletics, leadership, music/drama, religious affiliation, state residency.

Application procedures. Admission: Priority date 3/1; no deadline. No application fee. Admission notification on a rolling basis beginning on or about 10/1. Must reply by May 1 or within 2 week(s) if notified thereafter. **Financial aid:** Priority date 3/15; no closing date. FAFSA required. Applicants notified on a rolling basis starting 3/1; must reply within 2 week(s) of notification.

Academics. Special study options: Cross-registration, distance learning, double major, dual enrollment of high school students, honors, independent study, internships, student-designed major, study abroad, teacher certification program. **Credit/placement by examination:** AP, CLEP, IB, SAT, ACT. 30 credit hours maximum toward bachelor's degree. **Support services:** Study skills assistance, tutoring, writing center.

Majors. Biology: General. **Business:** Accounting, business admin, management information systems. **Communications:** Communications/speech/rhetoric. **Computer sciences:** General. **Conservation:** Environmental science, environmental studies. **Education:** Elementary, middle, music, physical. **English:** English lit. **Foreign languages:** Spanish. **Health services:** Athletic training, recreational therapy. **History:** General. **Human services:** General. **Math:** General. **Parks/recreation:** General, health/fitness, sports admin. **Philosophy/religion:** Religion. **Physical sciences:** Chemistry. **Protective services:** Law enforcement admin. **Psychology:** General. **Social sciences:** Political science, sociology. **Visual/performing arts:** Dramatic, music, music performance, studio arts management.

Most popular majors. Biology 8%, business/marketing 31%, education 17%, parks/recreation 8%, visual/performing arts 12%.

Technology on campus. 151 workstations in library, student center. Dormitories wired for high-speed internet access and linked to campus network. Commuter students can connect to campus network. Online course registration, online library, helpline, wireless network available.

Student life. Freshman orientation: Mandatory. Preregistration for classes offered. Held week prior to start of fall classes. **Housing:** Guaranteed on-campus for all undergraduates. Coed dorms, single-sex dorms, apartments available. $250 nonrefundable deposit, deadline 8/1. **Activities:** Bands, campus ministries, choral groups, dance, drama, literary magazine, music ensembles, musical theater, radio station, student government, student newspaper, Alpha program, Athenian society, Helen Foil Beard Society, political science associations, environmental service clubs, Fellowship of Christian Athletes, multi-cultural club, Philomathean club, volunteer club, music clubs.

Athletics. NCAA. **Intercollegiate:** Baseball M, basketball, cross-country, football (tackle) M, golf, lacrosse, soccer, softball W, swimming, tennis, volleyball W. **Intramural:** Badminton, basketball, bowling, football (non-tackle), football (tackle) M, racquetball, soccer, softball M, table tennis, tennis, ultimate frisbee, volleyball. **Team name:** Catawba Indians.

Student services. Adult student services, alcohol/substance abuse counseling, chaplain/spiritual director, career counseling, student employment services, financial aid counseling, health services, personal counseling, placement for graduates. **Physically disabled:** Services for visually, speech, hearing impaired.

Contact. E-mail: admission@catawba.edu
Phone: (704) 637-4402 Toll-free number: (800) 228-2922
Fax: (704) 637-4222
Cindy Barr, Vice President for Enrollment Services, Catawba College, 2300 West Innes Street, Salisbury, NC 28144-2488

Charlotte Christian College and Theological Seminary
Charlotte, North Carolina

www.nlts.edu

- Private 4-year university and seminary college
- Very large city
- 128 degree-seeking undergraduates

General. Regionally accredited; also accredited by TRACS. **Degrees:** 17 bachelor's, 5 associate awarded; master's offered. **Calendar:** Semester. **Full-time faculty:** 8 total. **Part-time faculty:** 19 total.

Basis for selection. Open admission, but selective for some programs. Admission requirements to the Undergraduate Degree Programs are considered on the basis of their Christian character and upon their testimony of faith in Jesus Christ as Lord and Savior. A high school equivalency diploma issued by the Department of Education or Satisfactory scores on the tests of General Education Development (GED). Admissions to the Master's Degree Program is restricted to students who hold a baccalaureate degree from an approved accredited institution operating legally within the state of the institution's physical location. The applicant will have to take the Miller Analogies Test (MAT) as part of the admissions process and submit a writing sample.

2015-2016 Annual costs. Tuition/fees: $9,125. Books/supplies: $1,280. Personal expenses: $2,187.

Application procedures. Admission: No deadline. $40 fee. **Financial aid:** No deadline.

Academics. Credit/placement by examination: AP.

Student life. Freshman orientation: Available. Preregistration for classes offered.

Contact. E-mail: chemphill@nlts.edu
Phone: (704) 334-6882 ext. 115
Constance Hemphill, Director of Admissions, Charlotte Christian College and Theological Seminary, PO Box 790106, Charlotte, NC 28206

Chowan University
Murfreesboro, North Carolina

www.chowan.edu

CB member
CB code: 5107

- Private 4-year university and liberal arts college affiliated with the Southern Baptist Convention
- Residential campus in rural community

907

- 1,513 degree-seeking undergraduates: 4% part-time, 54% women, 71% African American, 4% Hispanic/Latino, 5% Multi-racial, non-Hispanic, 2% international
- 10 degree-seeking graduate students
- 65% of applicants admitted
- SAT or ACT (ACT writing optional) required

General. Founded in 1848. Regionally accredited. **Degrees:** 191 bachelor's awarded; master's offered. **Location:** 40 miles from Hampton Roads, VA, 35 miles from Roanoke Rapids. **Calendar:** Semester, limited summer session. **Full-time faculty:** 66 total; 65% have terminal degrees, 14% minority, 42% women. **Part-time faculty:** 81 total; 35% have terminal degrees, 20% minority, 46% women. **Class size:** 51% < 20, 39% 20-39, 8% 40-49, 1% 50-99, less than 1% >100. **Special facilities:** Graphic communication center, fine arts center.

Freshman class profile. 4,612 applied, 2,982 admitted, 552 enrolled.

Mid 50% test scores		Rank in top tenth:	2%
SAT critical reading:	350-420	End year in good standing:	85%
SAT math:	350-430	Return as sophomores:	47%
GPA 3.75 or higher:	2%	Out-of-state:	53%
GPA 3.50-3.74:	3%	Live on campus:	90%
GPA 3.0-3.49:	16%	International:	2%
GPA 2.0-2.99:	62%	Fraternities:	1%
Rank in top quarter:	13%	Sororities:	1%

Basis for selection. School achievement record, standardized test score (SAT or ACT score), student "fit" with the institution as determined by information from the application for admission. Interview and campus visit is recommended for all students; audition required for music majors. **Home schooled:** State high school equivalency certificate required.

High school preparation. College-preparatory program recommended. Recommended units include English 4, mathematics 3, social studies 2, science 2 (laboratory 2) and academic electives 7.

2015-2016 Annual costs. Tuition/fees: $23,400. Room/board: $8,680. Books/supplies: $1,000. Personal expenses: $1,140.

2015-2016 Financial aid. Need-based: 71% of total undergraduate aid awarded as scholarships/grants, 29% as loans/jobs. **Non-need-based:** Scholarships awarded for academics, athletics, leadership, music/drama, religious affiliation, state residency.

Application procedures. Admission: No deadline. $20 fee, may be waived for applicants with need. Admission notification on a rolling basis. **Financial aid:** Priority date 3/1; no closing date. FAFSA required. Applicants notified on a rolling basis starting 3/1; must reply within 2 week(s) of notification.

Academics. Special study options: Combined bachelor's/graduate degree, distance learning, double major, dual enrollment of high school students, honors, independent study, internships, liberal arts/career combination, study abroad, teacher certification program. **Credit/placement by examination:** AP, CLEP, IB, SAT, ACT. 15 credit hours maximum toward associate degree, 15 toward bachelor's. **Support services:** Learning center, reduced course load, remedial instruction, study skills assistance, tutoring, writing center.

Majors. Biology: General. **Business:** Accounting/business management, business admin, information resources management, marketing, small business admin. **Communications technology:** Graphics. **Education:** General, elementary, English, history, music, physical, secondary. **English:** English lit. **Health services:** Athletic training, predental, premedicine, prenursing, prepharmacy, preveterinary. **History:** General. **Liberal arts:** Arts/sciences. **Parks/recreation:** Exercise sciences, health/fitness, sports admin. **Philosophy/religion:** Religion. **Physical sciences:** General. **Protective services:** Law enforcement admin. **Psychology:** General. **Social sciences:** General. **Visual/performing arts:** Graphic design, music performance, studio arts.

Most popular majors. Biology 8%, business/marketing 8%, education 11%, interdisciplinary studies 13%, parks/recreation 11%, psychology 12%, security/protective services 12%.

Technology on campus. 219 workstations in library, computer center. Dormitories wired for high-speed internet access and linked to campus network. Commuter students can connect to campus network. Online course registration, online library, helpline, repair service, wireless network available.

Student life. Freshman orientation: Mandatory. Preregistration for classes offered. **Policies:** No alcohol on campus, restricted dorm visitation, academic honor code. Religious observance required. **Housing:** Guaranteed on-campus for all undergraduates. Single-sex dorms, apartments, wellness housing available. $100 nonrefundable deposit. Apartments and suites available. **Activities:** Bands, campus ministries, choral groups, dance, drama,

international student organizations, literary magazine, music ensembles, student government, student newspaper, Instruments of Praise Gospel Choir, Student National Education Association, Fellowship of Christian Athletes, various academic area clubs.

Athletics. NCAA, NCCAA. **Intercollegiate:** Baseball M, basketball, bowling W, cheerleading, cross-country, football (tackle) M, golf M, lacrosse, soccer, softball W, swimming W, tennis, volleyball W. **Intramural:** Basketball, football (non-tackle), soccer, softball, table tennis, tennis, ultimate frisbee, volleyball W. **Team name:** Hawks.

Student services. Adult student services, alcohol/substance abuse counseling, chaplain/spiritual director, career counseling, student employment services, financial aid counseling, health services, personal counseling, placement for graduates, veterans' counselor.

Contact. E-mail: enroll@chowan.edu
Phone: (252) 398-1236 Toll-free number: (888) 424-6926
Fax: (252) 398-1190
Kim Bailey, Assistant VP & Dean of Enrollment Management, Chowan University, One University Place, Murfreesboro, NC 27855-9901

Davidson College
Davidson, North Carolina
www.davidson.edu

CB member
CB code: 5150

- Private 4-year liberal arts college affiliated with the Presbyterian Church (USA)
- Residential campus in small town
- 1,779 degree-seeking undergraduates: 50% women, 7% African American, 5% Asian American, 8% Hispanic/Latino, 1% Native American, 4% Multi-racial, non-Hispanic, 6% international
- 22% of applicants admitted
- SAT or ACT (ACT writing recommended), application essay required
- 93% graduate within 6 years

General. Founded in 1837. Regionally accredited. **Degrees:** 468 bachelor's awarded. **ROTC:** Army, Air Force. **Location:** 19 miles from Charlotte. **Calendar:** Semester. **Full-time faculty:** 176 total; 97% have terminal degrees, 19% minority, 42% women. **Part-time faculty:** 9 total; 89% have terminal degrees, 33% women. **Class size:** 73% < 20, 27% 20-39, less than 1% 40-49. **Special facilities:** Laser facility, electron microscope, campus arboretum.

Freshman class profile. 5,382 applied, 1,191 admitted, 510 enrolled.

Mid 50% test scores		GPA 3.0-3.49:	10%
SAT critical reading:	630-720	Rank in top quarter:	91%
SAT math:	630-720	Rank in top tenth:	55%
SAT writing:	610-720	Return as sophomores:	96%
ACT composite:	29-32	Out-of-state:	76%
GPA 3.75 or higher:	73%	Live on campus:	100%
GPA 3.50-3.74:	17%	International:	6%

Basis for selection. GED not accepted. Course selection, rigor of program, grades, recommendations, essays, test scores, class rank considered. SAT and SAT Subject Tests or ACT recommended. Campus visit strongly recommended.

High school preparation. College-preparatory program required. 16 units required. Required and recommended units include English 4, mathematics 3-4, science 2-4 and foreign language 2-4. Foreign language units should be in same language. 2 required, 4 recommended for social studies or history units.

2015-2016 Annual costs. Tuition/fees: $46,966. Room/board: $13,153. Books/supplies: $1,000. Personal expenses: $1,325.

2015-2016 Financial aid. Need-based: 361 full-time freshmen applied for aid; 265 deemed to have need; 265 received aid. Average need met was 100%. Average scholarship/grant was $37,846; average loan $3,071. 96% of total undergraduate aid awarded as scholarships/grants, 4% as loans/jobs. **Non-need-based:** Awarded to 587 full-time undergraduates, including 176 freshmen. Scholarships awarded for academics, alumni affiliation, art, athletics, leadership, minority status, music/drama, ROTC. **Additional information:** The college has increased the money it provides for grants in financial aid packages and eliminated mandatory loans, allowing all students, regardless of socio-economic background, to graduate debt-free.

Application procedures. Admission: Closing date 1/2 (postmark date). $50 fee, may be waived for applicants with need. Admission notification by 4/1. Must reply by 5/1. **Financial aid:** Closing date 2/15. FAFSA, CSS PROFILE required. Applicants notified by 4/1; must reply by 5/1.

Academics. 2-year interdisciplinary course in humanities available for freshmen and sophomores. Center for Special Studies supervises student-designed majors. **Special study options:** Cross-registration, double major, exchange student, independent study, internships, student-designed major, study abroad, Washington semester, weekend college. Visiting student program with Howard University and Morehouse College; Dean Rusk program in International Studies. **Credit/placement by examination:** AP, CLEP, IB, institutional tests. **Support services:** Learning center, tutoring, writing center.

Majors. Area/ethnic studies: African, East Asian, Latin American. **Biology:** General. **Conservation:** Environmental studies. **English:** English lit. **Foreign languages:** Chinese, classics, French, German, Spanish. **History:** General. **Math:** General. **Philosophy/religion:** Philosophy, religion. **Physical sciences:** Chemistry, physics. **Psychology:** General. **Social sciences:** Anthropology, economics, political science, sociology. **Visual/performing arts:** Art, dramatic, music.

Most popular majors. Biology 12%, English 7%, foreign language 6%, history 7%, mathematics 6%, physical sciences 6%, psychology 10%, social sciences 31%.

Technology on campus. 180 workstations in dormitories, library, computer center, student center. Dormitories wired for high-speed internet access and linked to campus network. Commuter students can connect to campus network. Online course registration, online library, helpline, repair service, wireless network available.

Student life. Freshman orientation: Mandatory, $100 fee. Preregistration for classes offered. **Housing:** Guaranteed on-campus for freshmen. Coed dorms, apartments, cooperative housing, themed housing, wellness housing available. Substance-free, suite/apartment-style housing available. **Activities:** Bands, campus ministries, choral groups, dance, drama, international student organizations, literary magazine, music ensembles, musical theater, radio station, student government, student newspaper, symphony orchestra, black student coalition, Amnesty International, Young Democrats, College Republicans, Habitat for Humanity, Asia 3D, gender resource center.

Athletics. NCAA. **Intercollegiate:** Baseball M, basketball, cross-country, diving, field hockey W, football (tackle) M, golf M, lacrosse W, soccer, swimming, tennis, track and field, volleyball W, wrestling M. **Intramural:** Basketball, football (non-tackle), soccer, softball, volleyball. **Team name:** Wildcats.

Student services. Alcohol/substance abuse counseling, chaplain/spiritual director, career counseling, financial aid counseling, health services, minority student services, personal counseling, placement for graduates. **Physically disabled:** Services for visually, hearing impaired.

Contact. E-mail: admission@davidson.edu
Phone: (704) 894-2230 Toll-free number: (800) 768-0380
Fax: (704) 894-2016
Christopher Gruber, Vice President and Dean of Admission and Financial Aid, Davidson College, Box 7156, Davidson, NC 28035-7156

Duke University
Durham, North Carolina
www.duke.edu

CB member
CB code: 5156

- Private 4-year university
- Residential campus in large city
- 6,501 degree-seeking undergraduates: 49% women, 10% African American, 22% Asian American, 7% Hispanic/Latino, 1% Native American, 2% Multi-racial, non-Hispanic, 10% international
- 9,152 degree-seeking graduate students
- 12% of applicants admitted
- SAT and SAT Subject Tests or ACT with writing, application essay required
- 95% graduate within 6 years

General. Founded in 1838. Regionally accredited. **Degrees:** 1,841 bachelor's awarded; master's, professional, doctoral offered. **ROTC:** Army, Naval, Air Force. **Location:** 30 miles from Raleigh, 170 miles from Richmond, VA. **Calendar:** Semester, extensive summer session. **Full-time faculty:** 1,462 total; 6% have terminal degrees, 19% minority, 39% women. **Part-time faculty:** 76 total; 8% have terminal degrees, 12% minority, 58% women. **Class size:** 73% < 20, 17% 20-39, 3% 40-49, 4% 50-99, 3% >100. **Special facilities:** Marine laboratory, museum of art, forest, teaching and research center, herbarium, science research center, French science center, global health institute, institute for genome sciences and policy, humanities institute, institute for ethics, phytotron, institute for environmental policy solutions, social science research institute, center for black culture.

Freshman class profile. 30,112 applied, 3,566 admitted, 1,745 enrolled.

Mid 50% test scores			
SAT critical reading:	670-760	Rank in top quarter:	98%
SAT math:	690-790	Rank in top tenth:	91%
SAT writing:	690-780	Out-of-state:	88%
ACT composite:	31-34	Live on campus:	100%
		International:	10%

Basis for selection. GED not accepted. Courses, school achievement record, school and community activities, essays, recommendations, test scores considered. Special consideration to alumni children and minority applicants. Applicants requesting alumni interview must submit Part I of application by 10/1 for Early Decision or by 12/1 for regular decision. Interview with alumnus/a in student's home area recommended, but not required; audition recommended for drama, music majors; portfolio recommended for art majors. **Home schooled:** Transcript of courses and grades, letter of recommendation (nonparent) required.

High school preparation. College-preparatory program required. Recommended units include English 4, mathematics 3, social studies 3, science 3 and foreign language 3. 4 math and 1 physics or chemistry required for engineering applicants, with calculus required before enrolling.

2016-2017 Annual costs. Tuition/fees (projected): $51,265. Room/board: $14,438. Books/supplies: $1,260. Personal expenses: $2,206.

Financial aid. Non-need-based: Scholarships awarded for academics, alumni affiliation, athletics, leadership, minority status, music/drama, religious affiliation, ROTC, state residency.

Application procedures. Admission: Closing date 1/3 (postmark date). $85 fee, may be waived for applicants with need. Admission notification by 4/1. Must reply by 5/1. **Financial aid:** Closing date 3/15. FAFSA, CSS PROFILE required. Applicants notified by 4/1; must reply by 5/1.

Academics. International comparative studies with an emphasis in one or more areas. Special Focus Program for freshmen: engineering frontiers, evolution and humankind, forging social ideals, genome revolution, global health, memory and invention, visions of freedom. **Special study options:** Combined bachelor's/graduate degree, cross-registration, double major, exchange student, independent study, internships, New York semester, semester at sea, student-designed major, study abroad, teacher certification program, Washington semester. **Credit/placement by examination:** AP, CLEP, IB, ACT. **Support services:** Learning center, pre-admission summer program, tutoring, writing center.

Majors. Area/ethnic studies: African-American, Asian, women's. **Biology:** General, anatomy, neuroscience. **Computer sciences:** General. **Conservation:** General. **Engineering:** Biomedical, civil, electrical, mechanical. **English:** British lit, English lit. **Foreign languages:** Ancient Greek, classics, East Asian, French, German, Italian, Latin, Russian, Slavic, Spanish. **History:** General. **Human services:** Public policy. **Math:** General, statistics. **Philosophy/religion:** Philosophy, religion. **Physical sciences:** Chemistry, geology, physics. **Psychology:** General. **Social sciences:** Anthropology, economics, political science, sociology. **Visual/performing arts:** Art history/conservation, dance, design, dramatic, music.

Most popular majors. Biology 15%, computer/information sciences 6%, engineering/engineering technologies 14%, health sciences 7%, psychology 6%, public administration/social services 9%, social sciences 17%.

Technology on campus. 450 workstations in dormitories, library, computer center, student center. Dormitories wired for high-speed internet access and linked to campus network. Commuter students can connect to campus network. Online course registration, online library, helpline, repair service, student web hosting, wireless network available.

Student life. Freshman orientation: Mandatory. Preregistration for classes offered. Held week prior to start of classes. **Housing:** Guaranteed on-campus for freshmen. Coed dorms, single-sex dorms, apartments, themed housing, wellness housing available. $300 nonrefundable deposit, deadline 5/1. Special interest housing available for students in women's studies, the arts, languages, service (Alpha Phi Omega). All first-year students live together on East Campus. Most first-year residence halls have a faculty member in residence. All sophomores must live on West Campus. **Activities:** Bands, campus ministries, choral groups, dance, drama, film society, international student organizations, literary magazine, music ensembles, Model UN, musical theater, opera, radio station, student government, student newspaper, symphony orchestra, TV station, Black Student Alliance, Asian Student Association, Duke Muslim Association, Arab Student Association, Mi Gente: La Asociacion de Estudiantes Latinos, Freeman Center for Jewish Life, Volunteers for Youth, Campus Crusade for Christ, Habitat for Humanity, Blue Devils United (the Alliance of Queer Undergraduates).

Athletics. NCAA. **Intercollegiate:** Baseball M, basketball, cross-country, diving, fencing, field hockey W, football (tackle) M, golf, lacrosse, rowing (crew) W, soccer, swimming, tennis, track and field, volleyball W, wrestling M. **Intramural:** Badminton, baseball, basketball, football (tackle) M, golf, racquetball, soccer M, softball, squash, swimming, table tennis, tennis, volleyball. **Team name:** Blue Devils.

Student services. Adult student services, alcohol/substance abuse counseling, chaplain/spiritual director, career counseling, student employment services, financial aid counseling, health services, minority student services, on-campus daycare, personal counseling, placement for graduates, veterans' counselor, women's services. **Physically disabled:** Services for visually, speech, hearing impaired.

Contact. E-mail: undergrad-admissions@duke.edu
Phone: (919) 684-3214 Fax: (919) 668-1661
Christoph Guttentag, Dean of Undergraduate Admissions, Duke University, 2138 Campus Drive, Durham, NC 27708

East Carolina University
Greenville, North Carolina **CB member**
www.ecu.edu **CB code: 5180**

- Public 4-year university
- Residential campus in small city
- 21,697 degree-seeking undergraduates: 11% part-time, 58% women, 16% African American, 3% Asian American, 6% Hispanic/Latino, 1% Native American, 3% Multi-racial, non-Hispanic
- 4,929 degree-seeking graduate students
- 69% of applicants admitted
- SAT or ACT (ACT writing optional) required
- 61% graduate within 6 years

General. Founded in 1907. Regionally accredited. **Degrees:** 4,431 bachelor's awarded; master's, professional, doctoral offered. **ROTC:** Army, Air Force. **Location:** 80 miles from Raleigh. **Calendar:** Semester, extensive summer session. **Full-time faculty:** 1,199 total; 81% have terminal degrees, 16% minority, 49% women. **Part-time faculty:** 262 total; 45% have terminal degrees, 8% minority, 62% women. **Class size:** 30% < 20, 42% 20-39, 10% 40-49, 12% 50-99, 6% >100. **Special facilities:** Particle accelerator, underwater archaeology, 3-D printing, multigenerational center, ropes course, global classroom, field station.

Freshman class profile. 16,871 applied, 11,647 admitted, 4,302 enrolled.

Mid 50% test scores		GPA 3.0-3.49:	25%
SAT critical reading:	470-550	GPA 2.0-2.99:	7%
SAT math:	490-560	Rank in top quarter:	44%
SAT writing:	450-540	Rank in top tenth:	16%
ACT composite:	20-24	Out-of-state:	15%
GPA 3.75 or higher:	51%	Live on campus:	96%
GPA 3.50-3.74:	17%		

Basis for selection. Class rank, high school GPA (unweighted), and standardized test scores. GED accepted for non-traditional freshmen. SAT and ACT scores may be used for math placement. SAT preferred, ACT also accepted. Audition, statement of purpose and letter of recommendation required for music programs. **Home schooled:** Transcript of courses and grades required.

High school preparation. College-preparatory program required. 16 units required; 18 recommended. Required and recommended units include English 4, mathematics 4, social studies 2, history 1, science 3 (laboratory 1), foreign language 2 and visual/performing arts 1.

2015-2016 Annual costs. Tuition/fees: $6,550; $22,124 out-of-state. Room/board: $9,319. Books/supplies: $1,254.

2015-2016 Financial aid. Need-based: 3,614 full-time freshmen applied for aid; 2,657 deemed to have need; 2,482 received aid. Average need met was 61%. Average scholarship/grant was $7,803; average loan $5,635. 45% of total undergraduate aid awarded as scholarships/grants, 55% as loans/jobs. **Non-need-based:** Awarded to 2,591 full-time undergraduates, including 779 freshmen. Scholarships awarded for academics, alumni affiliation, art, athletics, music/drama, ROTC.

Application procedures. Admission: Closing date 3/1 (postmark date). $70 fee, may be waived for applicants with need. Admission notification on a rolling basis beginning on or about 8/20. Must reply by 5/1. Out-of-state freshman enrollment limited to 18% of incoming freshman class, and processed on space-available basis. Applications received prior to December 31 receive priority. **Financial aid:** Priority date 3/1; no closing date. FAFSA required. Applicants notified on a rolling basis starting 4/1; must reply within 3 week(s) of notification.

Academics. Special study options: Accelerated study, combined bachelor's/graduate degree, cooperative education, cross-registration, distance learning, double major, dual enrollment of high school students, ESL, exchange student, honors, independent study, internships, student-designed major, study abroad, teacher certification program, Washington semester. **Credit/placement by examination:** AP, CLEP, IB, SAT, ACT, institutional tests. **Support services:** Learning center, reduced course load, remedial instruction, study skills assistance, tutoring, writing center.

Honors college/program. Admission is competitive and by invitation. Minimum eligibility criteria: Apply to (ECU) by December 1, minimum math/verbal combined SAT score of 1200 or minimum ACT score of 26, minimum un-weighted HS GPA of 3.5 or minimum weighted GPA of 4.0, completion of Honors College application.

Majors. Architecture: Urban/community planning. **Area/ethnic studies:** African-American. **Biology:** General, biochemistry, exercise physiology. **Business:** Accounting/business management, business admin, finance, hospitality admin, management information systems, marketing, office technology. **Communications:** Communications/speech/rhetoric. **Computer sciences:** Computer science, information systems, information technology. **Education:** Art, business, drama/dance, elementary, English, family/consumer sciences, German, health, kindergarten/preschool, mathematics, music, physical, science, social studies, special ed, visually handicapped. **Engineering:** General. **English:** English lit. **Foreign languages:** General. **Health services:** Athletic training, audiology/speech pathology, clinical lab science, dietetics, environmental health, health care admin, health information management, nursing (RN), public health ed, recreational therapy, vocational rehab counseling. **History:** General. **Human services:** Social work. **Liberal arts:** Arts/sciences. **Math:** General. **Parks/recreation:** General. **Philosophy/religion:** Philosophy. **Physical sciences:** Chemistry, geology, physics. **Protective services:** Criminal justice. **Psychology:** General. **Social sciences:** Anthropology, economics, geography, political science, sociology. **Visual/performing arts:** Dance, dramatic, interior design, music, studio arts. **Work/family studies:** Child development, clothing/textiles, family/community services.

Most popular majors. Biology 7%, business/marketing 17%, communications/journalism 6%, education 9%, engineering/engineering technologies 7%, health sciences 18%.

Technology on campus. 2,375 workstations in dormitories, library, computer center, student center. Dormitories wired for high-speed internet access and linked to campus network. Commuter students can connect to campus network. Online course registration, online library, helpline, repair service, student web hosting, wireless network available.

Student life. Freshman orientation: Mandatory, $100 fee. Preregistration for classes offered. Two-phase program: one summer session (overnight stay) and one session the day before the start of classes. **Housing:** Guaranteed on-campus for freshmen. Coed dorms, single-sex dorms, special housing for disabled, fraternity/sorority housing, themed housing, wellness housing available. $200 partly refundable deposit, deadline 5/1. Suite-style, summer on-campus, living-learning communities, honors housing available. **Activities:** Bands, campus ministries, choral groups, dance, drama, film society, international student organizations, literary magazine, music ensembles, Model UN, musical theater, opera, radio station, student government, student newspaper, symphony orchestra, TV station, 400 registered organizations.

Athletics. NCAA. **Intercollegiate:** Baseball M, basketball, cheerleading, cross-country, diving, football (tackle) M, golf, soccer W, softball W, swimming, tennis, track and field, volleyball. **Intramural:** Basketball, bowling, cross-country, football (non-tackle), golf, racquetball, sand volleyball, softball, table tennis, tennis, ultimate frisbee, volleyball. **Team name:** Pirates.

Student services. Adult student services, alcohol/substance abuse counseling, chaplain/spiritual director, career counseling, student employment services, financial aid counseling, health services, legal services, minority student services, personal counseling, placement for graduates, veterans' counselor. **Physically disabled:** Services for visually, speech, hearing impaired.

Contact. E-mail: admis@ecu.edu
Phone: (252) 328-6640 Fax: (252) 328-6945
David Meredith, Director of Undergraduate Admissions, East Carolina University, Office of Undergraduate Admissions, Greenville, NC 27858-4353

Elizabeth City State University
Elizabeth City, North Carolina **CB member**
www.ecsu.edu **CB code: 5629**

- Public 4-year liberal arts college
- Residential campus in large town
- 2,276 degree-seeking undergraduates
- 85 graduate students
- SAT or ACT (ACT writing optional) required

General. Founded in 1891. Regionally accredited. **Degrees:** 422 bachelor's awarded; master's offered. **ROTC:** Army. **Location:** 50 miles from Norfolk, VA. **Calendar:** Semester, extensive summer session. **Full-time faculty:** 143 total; 88% have terminal degrees, 74% minority, 42% women. **Part-time faculty:** 68 total; 87% have terminal degrees, 79% minority, 60% women. **Class size:** 66% < 20, 31% 20-39, 2% 40-49, less than 1% 50-99. **Special facilities:** Recording studio, boardwalk in nature preserves/wetlands, golf driving range.

Freshman class profile.

GPA 3.75 or higher:	16%	Rank in top quarter:	5%
GPA 3.50-3.74:	13%	Rank in top tenth:	2%
GPA 3.0-3.49:	32%	Out-of-state:	7%
GPA 2.0-2.99:	39%	Live on campus:	74%

Basis for selection. GPA and test scores considered. Special consideration given to residents from 21 neighboring counties. All applicants to any campus in the UNC system, except those exempted by current campus policies, must submit standardized test scores. SAT preferred, ACT accepted. **Home schooled:** Statement describing home school structure and mission, transcript of courses and grades, letter of recommendation (nonparent) required. **Learning Disabled:** Important to ascertain in advance the extent of the learning disability in order to provide the available service(s).

High school preparation. College-preparatory program recommended. 16 units required. Required units include English 4, mathematics 4, social studies 2, science 3 (laboratory 1) and foreign language 2.

2015-2016 Annual costs. Tuition/fees: $4,657; $17,010 out-of-state. Room/board: $7,844. Books/supplies: $363.

Financial aid. **Non-need-based:** Scholarships awarded for academics, athletics, minority status, ROTC, state residency.

Application procedures. **Admission:** Priority date 5/1; deadline 6/30. $30 fee. Admission notification on a rolling basis. **Financial aid:** Priority date 3/15, closing date 6/1. FAFSA required. Applicants notified on a rolling basis starting 6/1; must reply by 6/30 or within 3 week(s) of notification.

Academics. **Special study options:** Combined bachelor's/graduate degree, cooperative education, distance learning, double major, honors, independent study, internships, liberal arts/career combination, teacher certification program, weekend college. **Credit/placement by examination:** AP, CLEP, IB, SAT. 48 credit hours maximum toward bachelor's degree. **Support services:** Learning center, pre-admission summer program, reduced course load, remedial instruction, study skills assistance, tutoring, writing center.

Majors. Biology: General. **Business:** Accounting, business admin. **Communications:** Communications/speech/rhetoric. **Computer sciences:** Computer science. **Education:** Art, biology, chemistry, elementary, English, history, kindergarten/preschool, mathematics, middle, physical, special ed. **English:** English lit. **History:** General. **Human services:** Social work. **Math:** General. **Physical sciences:** Chemistry, geology, oceanography, physics. **Protective services:** Criminal justice. **Psychology:** General. **Social sciences:** Political science, sociology. **Visual/performing arts:** Graphic design, music management, studio arts.

Most popular majors. Business/marketing 15%, education 16%, English 6%, security/protective services 10%, trade and industry 18%.

Technology on campus. 350 workstations in dormitories, library, computer center, student center. Dormitories wired for high-speed internet access and linked to campus network. Commuter students can connect to campus network. Online course registration, online library, helpline, repair service, wireless network available.

Student life. Freshman orientation: Mandatory, $100 fee. Preregistration for classes offered. Three sessions held during summer months covering 2 1/2 days each. **Housing:** Guaranteed on-campus for freshmen. Coed dorms, single-sex dorms, apartments, wellness housing available. $125 nonrefundable deposit, deadline 8/1. College-leased housing available. **Activities:** Bands, choral groups, dance, drama, international student organizations, literary magazine, music ensembles, musical theater, radio station, student government, student newspaper, symphony orchestra, TV station, United Campus Religious Fellowship, honor and recognition societies in education, science, dramatics, journalism, student union program.

Athletics. NCAA. **Intercollegiate:** Baseball M, basketball, bowling M, cheerleading W, cross-country, football (tackle) M, golf M, softball W, tennis W, volleyball W. **Team name:** Vikings.

Student services. Alcohol/substance abuse counseling, chaplain/spiritual director, career counseling, student employment services, financial aid counseling, health services, personal counseling, placement for graduates, veterans' counselor. **Physically disabled:** Services for visually, speech, hearing impaired.

Contact. E-mail: mdwilliams2@mail.ecsu.edu
Phone: (252) 335-3305 Toll-free number: (800) 347-3278
Fax: (252) 335-3537
Monette Dutch, Director of Enrollment Management and Retention, Elizabeth City State University, 1704 Weeksville Road, Campus Box 901, Elizabeth City, NC 27909

Elon University
Elon, North Carolina   **CB member**
www.elon.edu   **CB code: 5183**

- Private 4-year university and liberal arts college
- Residential campus in large town
- 5,903 degree-seeking undergraduates: 3% part-time, 59% women, 6% African American, 2% Asian American, 5% Hispanic/Latino, 2% Multiracial, non-Hispanic, 2% international
- 728 degree-seeking graduate students
- 57% of applicants admitted
- SAT or ACT (ACT writing optional), application essay required
- 83% graduate within 6 years; 23% enter graduate study

General. Founded in 1889. Regionally accredited. **Degrees:** 1,315 bachelor's awarded; master's, professional offered. **ROTC:** Army, Air Force. **Location:** 15 miles from Greensboro. **Calendar:** 4-1-4, extensive summer session. **Full-time faculty:** 424 total; 88% have terminal degrees, 14% minority, 50% women. **Part-time faculty:** 161 total; 50% have terminal degrees, 9% minority, 48% women. **Class size:** 51% < 20, 48% 20-39, less than 1% 40-49. **Special facilities:** Fine arts center, science center, academic pavilions, global neighborhood, multi-faith center.

Freshman class profile. 10,256 applied, 5,866 admitted, 1,524 enrolled.

Mid 50% test scores			
SAT critical reading:	550-640	GPA 2.0-2.99:	5%
SAT math:	560-650	Rank in top quarter:	58%
SAT writing:	550-650	Rank in top tenth:	24%
ACT composite:	25-29	End year in good standing:	89%
GPA 3.75 or higher:	62%	Return as sophomores:	90%
GPA 3.50-3.74:	13%	Out-of-state:	81%
GPA 3.0-3.49:	20%	Live on campus:	99%
		International:	2%

Basis for selection. School achievement record most important, followed by test scores. Class rank, school and community activities, personal statement, recommendations also considered. Audition required for all performing arts programs. **Home schooled:** Statement describing home school structure and mission, transcript of courses and grades, state high school equivalency certificate, letter of recommendation (nonparent) required.

High school preparation. College-preparatory program required. 16 units required; 18 recommended. Required and recommended units include English 4, mathematics 3-4, social studies 1, history 2, science 3 (laboratory 1) and foreign language 2-3. Algebra I, II and Geometry required.

2015-2016 Annual costs. Tuition/fees: $32,172. Room/board: $10,998. Books/supplies: $900. Personal expenses: $1,500.

2015-2016 Financial aid. **Need-based:** 862 full-time freshmen applied for aid; 486 deemed to have need; 485 received aid. Average need met was 60%. Average scholarship/grant was $13,546; average loan $3,442. 59% of total undergraduate aid awarded as scholarships/grants, 41% as loans/jobs. **Non-need-based:** Awarded to 2,341 full-time undergraduates, including 611 freshmen. Scholarships awarded for academics, art, athletics, leadership, music/drama, religious affiliation.

Application procedures. **Admission:** Priority date 11/10; deadline 1/10 (postmark date). $50 fee, may be waived for applicants with need. Admission notification on a rolling basis beginning on or about 12/1. Must reply by May 1 or within 1 week(s) if notified thereafter. **Financial aid:** Priority date 2/15; no closing date. FAFSA, institutional form, CSS PROFILE required. Applicants notified on a rolling basis starting 3/30.

Academics. Study USA programs in Los Angeles, New York, D.C., and Alaska. **Special study options:** Accelerated study, combined bachelor's/graduate degree, cross-registration, distance learning, double major, dual enrollment of high school students, ESL, exchange student, honors, independent study, internships, liberal arts/career combination, New York semester, semester at sea, student-designed major, study abroad, teacher certification program, Washington semester. **Credit/placement by examination:** AP, CLEP, IB, SAT, ACT, institutional tests. **Support services:** Learning center, reduced course load, remedial instruction, study skills assistance, tutoring, writing center.

Majors. Biology: General, biochemistry, biophysics. **Business:** Accounting, business admin, entrepreneurial studies, finance, international, management information systems, marketing. **Communications:** General, broadcast journalism, journalism, radio/TV. **Communications technology:** Recording arts. **Computer sciences:** General, computer science, information systems. **Conservation:** Environmental science, environmental studies. **Education:** General, curriculum, early childhood, elementary, middle, secondary, special ed. **Engineering:** General, applied physics, biomedical, chemical, computer, environmental. **English:** Creative writing, English lit, general lit, rhetoric/composition. **Foreign languages:** General, French, Spanish. **Health services:** Predental, premedicine, public health ed. **History:** General. **Human services:** General, public policy. **Math:** General, applied, statistics. **Parks/recreation:** Exercise sciences, sports admin. **Philosophy/religion:** Philosophy, religion. **Physical sciences:** Chemistry, physics. **Protective services:** Criminal justice. **Psychology:** General. **Social sciences:** Anthropology, economics, international economics, international relations, political science, sociology. **Visual/performing arts:** Acting, art, art history/conservation, ceramics, dance, digital arts, directing/producing, dramatic, music, music performance, music technology, musical theater, painting, photography, theater design.

Most popular majors. Business/marketing 27%, communications/journalism 17%, parks/recreation 8%, psychology 6%, public administration/social services 6%, social sciences 10%, visual/performing arts 6%.

Technology on campus. 920 workstations in dormitories, library, computer center, student center. Dormitories wired for high-speed internet access and linked to campus network. Commuter students can connect to campus network. Online course registration, online library, helpline, repair service, student web hosting, wireless network available.

Student life. Freshman orientation: Mandatory. Preregistration for classes offered. Optional orientation during spring of high school senior year. Required orientation in August. **Policies:** Freshmen and sophomores are required to live on campus; housing is guaranteed. **Housing:** Guaranteed on-campus for freshmen. Coed dorms, single-sex dorms, apartments, fraternity/sorority housing, themed housing, wellness housing available. $500 fully refundable deposit, deadline 5/1. **Activities:** Bands, campus ministries, choral groups, dance, drama, film society, international student organizations, literary magazine, music ensembles, Model UN, musical theater, radio station, student government, student newspaper, symphony orchestra, TV station, Intervarsity Christian Fellowship, Young Democrats/Republicans, Black Cultural Society, Epsilon Sigma Alpha, Liberal Arts Forum, Hillel, student media, Habitat for Humanity.

Athletics. NCAA. **Intercollegiate:** Baseball M, basketball, cheerleading, cross-country, football (tackle) M, golf, lacrosse W, soccer, softball W, tennis, track and field W, volleyball W. **Intramural:** Basketball, bowling, football (non-tackle), handball, racquetball, soccer, softball, table tennis, volleyball. **Team name:** Phoenix.

Student services. Adult student services, alcohol/substance abuse counseling, chaplain/spiritual director, career counseling, student employment services, financial aid counseling, health services, minority student services, personal counseling, placement for graduates, veterans' counselor, women's services. **Physically disabled:** Services for visually, speech, hearing impaired.

Contact. E-mail: admissions@elon.edu
Phone: (336) 278-3566 Toll-free number: (800) 334-8448
Fax: (336) 278-7699
Greg Zaiser, Vice President of Admissions and Financial Planning, Elon University, 2700 Campus Box, Elon, NC 27244-2010

Fayetteville State University
Fayetteville, North Carolina   **CB member**
www.uncfsu.edu   **CB code: 5212**

▸ Public 4-year university
▸ Commuter campus in small city
▸ 5,087 degree-seeking undergraduates: 24% part-time, 68% women, 64% African American, 1% Asian American, 6% Hispanic/Latino, 3% Native American
▸ 400 degree-seeking graduate students
▸ 60% of applicants admitted
▸ SAT or ACT with writing, application essay required
▸ 32% graduate within 6 years

General. Founded in 1867. Regionally accredited. Courses leading to bachelor's degree also available at the Fort Bragg/Pope AFB Center, Seymour Johnson AFB, and online. **Degrees:** 911 bachelor's awarded; master's, doctoral offered. **ROTC:** Army, Air Force. **Location:** 60 miles from Raleigh. **Calendar:** Semester, limited summer session. **Full-time faculty:** 255 total; 83% have terminal degrees, 69% minority, 49% women. **Part-time faculty:**

87 total; 49% have terminal degrees, 69% minority, 63% women. **Class size:** 38% < 20, 57% 20-39, 5% 40-49, less than 1% 50-99. **Special facilities:** Greenhouse, observatory, planetarium, microprobe.

Freshman class profile. 3,945 applied, 2,383 admitted, 631 enrolled.

Mid 50% test scores			
SAT critical reading:	390-460	GPA 3.0-3.49:	32%
SAT math:	400-470	GPA 2.0-2.99:	33%
SAT writing:	360-430	Rank in top quarter:	26%
ACT composite:	16-19	Rank in top tenth:	9%
GPA 3.75 or higher:	21%	Return as sophomores:	79%
GPA 3.50-3.74:	13%	Out-of-state:	6%
		Live on campus:	80%

Basis for selection. 2.5 GPA, SAT scores, completion of 21 prescribed high school units required. All applicants, except those exempted by current campus policies, must submit a standardized test score. SAT preferred, ACT also accepted.

High school preparation. 22 units required. Required and recommended units include English 4, mathematics 4, social studies 2, history 1, science 3, foreign language 2 and academic electives 6. Foreign language units can be used as academic elective units.

2015-2016 Annual costs. Tuition/fees: $4,885; $16,493 out-of-state. Room/board: $7,130. Books/supplies: $1,000. Personal expenses: $750.

2014-2015 Financial aid. Need-based: 686 full-time freshmen applied for aid; 658 deemed to have need; 651 received aid. Average need met was 78%. Average scholarship/grant was $8,675; average loan $3,420. 47% of total undergraduate aid awarded as scholarships/grants, 53% as loans/jobs. **Non-need-based:** Awarded to 63 full-time undergraduates, including 28 freshmen. Scholarships awarded for academics, alumni affiliation, athletics, music/drama, ROTC, state residency.

Application procedures. Admission: Closing date 7/1 (postmark date). $40 fee, may be waived for applicants with need. Admission notification on a rolling basis beginning on or about 1/15. Must reply by 7/1. **Financial aid:** Closing date 3/1. FAFSA required. Applicants notified on a rolling basis starting 4/15; must reply within 2 week(s) of notification.

Academics. Special study options: Accelerated study, combined bachelor's/graduate degree, cooperative education, distance learning, double major, dual enrollment of high school students, honors, independent study, internships, study abroad, teacher certification program, weekend college. **Credit/placement by examination:** AP, CLEP, SAT, institutional tests. 30 credit hours maximum toward bachelor's degree. **Support services:** Learning center, pre-admission summer program, remedial instruction, tutoring.

Majors. Biology: General, biotechnology. **Business:** Accounting, business admin, finance, management information systems. **Communications:** Communications/speech/rhetoric. **Computer sciences:** General. **Education:** Art, early childhood, elementary, middle, music, physical. **English:** English lit. **Foreign languages:** Spanish. **Health services:** Health care admin, nursing (RN). **History:** General. **Human services:** Social work. **Math:** General. **Physical sciences:** Chemistry. **Protective services:** Criminal justice, fire services admin, forensics. **Psychology:** General. **Social sciences:** Geography, political science, sociology. **Visual/performing arts:** General, art, dramatic, music.

Most popular majors. Business/marketing 17%, education 6%, health sciences 16%, psychology 13%, security/protective services 17%, social sciences 9%.

Technology on campus. 600 workstations in dormitories, library, computer center, student center. Dormitories wired for high-speed internet access and linked to campus network. Commuter students can connect to campus network. Online course registration, online library, helpline, wireless network available.

Student life. Freshman orientation: Mandatory, $90 fee. Preregistration for classes offered. 3 Saturdays in July and August. **Policies:** Freshmen not permitted cars on campus. **Housing:** Coed dorms, single-sex dorms, apartments available. $125 nonrefundable deposit, deadline 7/1. **Activities:** Bands, choral groups, dance, drama, music ensembles, radio station, student government, student newspaper, symphony orchestra, TV station, Baptist student union, Federation of Young Democrats, NAACP, NCNW, Honda Campus All-Stars, art guild, Illusions modeling club.

Athletics. NCAA. **Intercollegiate:** Basketball, bowling W, cross-country, football (tackle) M, golf, softball W, tennis, track and field, volleyball W. **Intramural:** Baseball M, basketball, bowling, football (tackle) M, golf, gymnastics, swimming, tennis M, volleyball. **Team name:** Broncos.

Student services. Alcohol/substance abuse counseling, career counseling, student employment services, financial aid counseling, health services, on-campus daycare, personal counseling, placement for graduates, veterans' counselor. **Physically disabled:** Services for visually impaired.

Contact. E-mail: admissions@uncfsu.edu
Phone: (910) 672-1371 Toll-free number: (800) 222-2594
Fax: (910) 672-1414
Ulisa Bowles, Director of Admissions, Fayetteville State University, 1200
Murchison Road, Fayetteville, NC 28301-4298

Gardner-Webb University
Boiling Springs, North Carolina **CB member**
www.gardner-webb.edu **CB code: 5242**

- Private 4-year university and liberal arts college affiliated with the Southern Baptist Convention
- Residential campus in small town
- 2,617 degree-seeking undergraduates
- SAT or ACT (ACT writing optional) required

General. Founded in 1905. Regionally accredited. **Degrees:** 608 bachelor's, 41 associate awarded; master's, professional, doctoral offered. **ROTC:** Army, Air Force. **Location:** 55 miles from Charlotte, 60 miles from Greenville, SC. **Calendar:** Semester, extensive summer session. **Full-time faculty:** 165 total; 73% have terminal degrees, 7% minority, 48% women. **Part-time faculty:** 135 total; 9% minority, 52% women. **Class size:** 72% < 20, 28% 20-39. **Special facilities:** Observatory, adventure and ropes course, Lake Hollifield and Carillon, climbing wall, The Broad River Greenway.

Freshman class profile.

GPA 3.75 or higher:	52%	Rank in top quarter:	55%
GPA 3.50-3.74:	14%	Rank in top tenth:	23%
GPA 3.0-3.49:	19%	Out-of-state:	34%
GPA 2.0-2.99:	15%	Live on campus:	92%

Basis for selection. A student's school achievement record is most important, including GPA and class rank, followed by test scores, recommendations, and school and community activities. Expected 2.5 GPA. ACCUPLACER test required of students whose SAT or ACT scores fall below a certain minimum. This test will be used to determine whether the student is to be placed in remedial courses or college level English and Math courses. Interview, portfolio, essay recommended for all students; audition required for music scholarships. Interview may be required for conditionally admitted students.

High school preparation. College-preparatory program recommended. Recommended units include English 4, mathematics 3, social studies 1, science 3 (laboratory 2) and foreign language 2.

2015-2016 Annual costs. Tuition/fees: $28,280. Room/board: $9,280. Books/supplies: $1,000.

2015-2016 Financial aid. Need-based: 431 full-time freshmen applied for aid; 389 deemed to have need; 389 received aid. Average need met was 78%. Average scholarship/grant was $7,715; average loan $3,212. 69% of total undergraduate aid awarded as scholarships/grants, 31% as loans/jobs. **Non-need-based:** Awarded to 1,609 full-time undergraduates, including 488 freshmen. Scholarships awarded for academics, athletics, leadership, music/drama, religious affiliation, ROTC, state residency.

Application procedures. Admission: No deadline. $40 fee, may be waived for applicants with need, free for online applicants. Admission notification on a rolling basis. **Financial aid:** Priority date 3/1, closing date 6/30. FAFSA required. Applicants notified on a rolling basis starting 3/1; must reply within 2 week(s) of notification.

Academics. Special study options: Accelerated study, combined bachelor's/graduate degree, distance learning, double major, dual enrollment of high school students, honors, independent study, internships, liberal arts/career combination, study abroad, teacher certification program. Costa Rica and Quebec for language trips. **Credit/placement by examination:** AP, CLEP, IB, SAT, ACT, institutional tests. 64 credit hours maximum toward bachelor's degree. **Support services:** Learning center, pre-admission summer program, reduced course load, remedial instruction, study skills assistance, tutoring, writing center. Special program offerings possible (including interpreters, note takers) for students who have tested learning disabled or physically disabled.

Honors college/program. Students participating in the Honors program have an average SAT of 1850 and an average GPA of 3.8. Students must complete 24 semester hours of course work designated as honors (six of which is comprised of an Honors Thesis during the junior and/or senior year).

Majors. Biology: General, ecology. **Business:** General, accounting, business admin, finance, international, management information systems. **Communications:** Broadcast journalism, communications/speech/rhetoric, journalism, public relations. **Computer sciences:** General, computer science.

Conservation: Environmental science. **Education:** General, biology, chemistry, elementary, English, foreign languages, French, health, history, mathematics, middle, multi-level teacher, music, physical, science, secondary, social science, Spanish. **English:** Creative writing, English lit, technical writing, writing. **Foreign languages:** General, American Sign Language, French, sign language interpretation, Spanish. **Health services:** Athletic training, health care admin, nursing (RN), predental, premedicine, prepharmacy, prephysical therapy, preveterinary. **History:** General. **Math:** General. **Parks/recreation:** Exercise sciences, health/fitness, sports admin. **Philosophy/religion:** Philosophy, religion. **Physical sciences:** Chemistry. **Psychology:** General. **Social sciences:** General, political science, sociology. **Theology:** Missionary, religious ed, sacred music, youth ministry. **Visual/performing arts:** Art, ceramics, dramatic, drawing, music, music management, music performance, music theory/composition, painting, photography, piano/keyboard, printmaking, sculpture, stringed instruments, studio arts, voice/opera.

Most popular majors. Business/marketing 27%, health sciences 12%, psychology 6%, security/protective services 6%, social sciences 21%.

Technology on campus. 150 workstations in library, computer center, student center. Dormitories wired for high-speed internet access and linked to campus network. Commuter students can connect to campus network. Online library, helpline, wireless network available.

Student life. Freshman orientation: Mandatory, $100 fee. Preregistration for classes offered. One-day programs held throughout the summer months. **Policies:** Limited visitation hours: noon to midnight in dorm rooms. Lobbies open for visitation until 2:00 am., no alcohol or tobacco allowed on campus, quiet hours observed from 10 pm through 10 am. **Housing:** Guaranteed on-campus for all undergraduates. Single-sex dorms, special housing for disabled, apartments, wellness housing available. $300 nonrefundable deposit. Honors student residence hall available. **Activities:** Bands, campus ministries, choral groups, drama, international student organizations, literary magazine, music ensembles, musical theater, opera, radio station, student government, student newspaper, symphony orchestra, The Verge, Fellowship of Christian Athletes, student volunteer groups, prison ministry, student YMCA, gospel choir, Bible studies, College Republicans, College Democrats.

Athletics. NCAA. **Intercollegiate:** Baseball M, basketball, cheerleading, cross-country, football (tackle) M, golf, soccer, softball W, swimming, tennis, track and field, volleyball W, wrestling M. **Intramural:** Badminton, baseball, basketball, football (non-tackle), racquetball, skiing, soccer, softball, swimming, table tennis, tennis, ultimate frisbee, volleyball. **Team name:** Runnin' Bulldogs.

Student services. Alcohol/substance abuse counseling, chaplain/spiritual director, career counseling, student employment services, financial aid counseling, personal counseling, placement for graduates, veterans' counselor. **Physically disabled:** Services for visually, speech, hearing impaired.

Contact. E-mail: admissions@gardner-webb.edu
Phone: (704) 406-4498 Toll-free number: (800) 253-6472
Fax: (704) 406-4488
Angie Sundell, Associate Vice President of Undergraduate Admissions, Gardner-Webb University, PO Box 817, Boiling Springs, NC 28017

Greensboro College
Greensboro, North Carolina **CB member**
www.greensboro.edu **CB code: 5260**

- Private 4-year liberal arts college affiliated with the United Methodist Church
- Residential campus in large city
- 758 degree-seeking undergraduates: 3% part-time, 46% women, 34% African American, 3% Hispanic/Latino, 4% Multi-racial, non-Hispanic
- 44 degree-seeking graduate students
- 75% of applicants admitted
- SAT or ACT (ACT writing optional), application essay required
- 40% graduate within 6 years

General. Founded in 1838. Regionally accredited. **Degrees:** 47 bachelor's awarded; master's offered. **ROTC:** Army, Air Force. **Location:** 90 miles from Charlotte, 75 miles from Raleigh. **Calendar:** Semester, limited summer session. **Full-time faculty:** 41 total; 73% have terminal degrees, 10% minority, 39% women. **Part-time faculty:** 96 total; 18% have terminal degrees, 12% minority, 65% women. **Class size:** 82% < 20, 17% 20-39, 1% 40-49. **Special facilities:** Historical museum, computerized music laboratories.

Freshman class profile. 1,095 applied, 824 admitted, 226 enrolled.

Mid 50% test scores		GPA 2.0-2.99:	48%
SAT critical reading:	400-510	Rank in top quarter:	17%
SAT math:	400-510	Rank in top tenth:	1%
SAT writing:	380-470	End year in good standing:	55%
ACT composite:	16-20	Return as sophomores:	58%
GPA 3.75 or higher:	16%	Out-of-state:	27%
GPA 3.50-3.74:	14%	Live on campus:	95%
GPA 3.0-3.49:	22%		

Basis for selection. High school curriculum most important, followed by grades, class rank, test scores, personal statement, school and community activities, high school caliber. Recommendations, interview considered. Interview recommended for all students. Audition required for music, theater majors; portfolio required for art majors. **Home schooled:** Interview highly recommended and SAT/ACT required. **Learning Disabled:** Students wishing to receive accommodations facilitated by the Office of Disability Services are responsible for disclosure of physical, psychological, and learning disabilities. Accommodation of learning and psychological disabilities must be accompanied by appropriate documentation that includes professional evaluation, diagnosis, and recommendations.

High school preparation. College-preparatory program recommended. Recommended units include English 4, mathematics 4, history 3, science 3 (laboratory 1) and foreign language 2. Elective coursework in music, art and/or social science is recommended.

2015-2016 Annual costs. Tuition/fees: $26,900. Room/board: $10,100. Books/supplies: $1,400. Personal expenses: $1,200.

2015-2016 Financial aid. **Need-based:** 42% of total undergraduate aid awarded as scholarships/grants, 58% as loans/jobs. **Non-need-based:** Scholarships awarded for academics, alumni affiliation, art, leadership, music/drama, religious affiliation, state residency.

Application procedures. **Admission:** Priority date 12/15; no deadline. $35 fee, may be waived for applicants with need, free for online applicants. Admission notification on a rolling basis. Must reply by May 1 or within 4 week(s) if notified thereafter. **Financial aid:** Priority date 4/15; no closing date. FAFSA, institutional form required. Applicants notified on a rolling basis starting 2/1; must reply within 2 week(s) of notification.

Academics. **Special study options:** Accelerated study, cross-registration, distance learning, double major, dual enrollment of high school students, ESL, honors, independent study, internships, liberal arts/career combination, student-designed major, study abroad, teacher certification program, weekend college. Academic success program, minor in ethics across the curriculum, minor in women's and gender studies, minor in computer science. **Credit/placement by examination:** AP, CLEP, IB, institutional tests. 45 credit hours maximum toward bachelor's degree. **Support services:** Learning center, reduced course load, study skills assistance, tutoring, writing center.

Majors. **Biology:** General. **Business:** Accounting, managerial economics. **Education:** Art, biology, drama/dance, early childhood, elementary, emotionally handicapped, English, history, learning disabled, mathematics, mentally handicapped, middle, multiple handicapped, music, physical, social studies, Spanish, special ed. **English:** English lit. **Foreign languages:** Spanish. **Health services:** Athletic training. **History:** General. **Liberal arts:** Arts/sciences. **Math:** General. **Parks/recreation:** Exercise sciences, health/fitness, sports admin. **Philosophy/religion:** Religion. **Physical sciences:** Chemistry. **Psychology:** General. **Social sciences:** Political science, sociology. **Visual/performing arts:** Dramatic, music, music performance, studio arts, theater design.

Most popular majors. Biology 9%, business/marketing 21%, liberal arts 11%, parks/recreation 19%, psychology 11%, security/protective services 13%.

Technology on campus. 152 workstations in dormitories, library, computer center, student center. Dormitories wired for high-speed internet access and linked to campus network. Commuter students can connect to campus network. Online library, helpline, repair service, wireless network available.

Student life. **Freshman orientation:** Mandatory. Preregistration for classes offered. Orientations held in May, June, July and August. **Policies:** All students who have earned less than 58 credit hours required to live in college housing unless married, veterans, or residing with parents. All students encouraged to do so. **Housing:** Guaranteed on-campus for all undergraduates. Coed dorms, single-sex dorms, apartments, themed housing, wellness housing available. $200 partly refundable deposit. **Activities:** Bands, campus ministries, choral groups, dance, drama, international student organizations, literary magazine, music ensembles, Model UN, musical theater, opera, student government, student newspaper, Student Christian Fellowship, United African American Society, Student National Education Association, campus activity board, Fellowship of Christian Athletes, Los Amigos.

Athletics. NCAA. **Intercollegiate:** Baseball M, basketball, cheerleading, football (tackle) M, golf, lacrosse, soccer, softball W, swimming, tennis, volleyball W, wrestling M. **Intramural:** Baseball M, basketball, football (non-tackle), ice hockey M, softball W. **Team name:** The Pride.

Student services. Adult student services, alcohol/substance abuse counseling, chaplain/spiritual director, career counseling, student employment services, financial aid counseling, health services, personal counseling, placement for graduates. **Physically disabled:** Services for visually, speech, hearing impaired.

Contact. E-mail: admissions@greensboro.edu
Phone: (336) 217-7211 Toll-free number: (800) 346-8226
Fax: (336) 378-0154
Julie Schatz, Director of Admissions, Greensboro College, 815 West Market Street, Greensboro, NC 27401-1875

Guilford College
Greensboro, North Carolina **CB member**
www.guilford.edu **CB code: 5261**

- Private 4-year liberal arts college affiliated with the Society of Friends (Quaker)
- Residential campus in large city
- 1,767 degree-seeking undergraduates: 18% part-time, 53% women, 22% African American, 3% Asian American, 7% Hispanic/Latino, 3% Multiracial, non-Hispanic, 2% international
- 50% of applicants admitted
- Application essay required
- 56% graduate within 6 years; 26% enter graduate study

General. Founded in 1837. Regionally accredited. **Degrees:** 482 bachelor's awarded. **Location:** 87 miles from Raleigh, 95 miles from Charlotte. **Calendar:** Semester, limited summer session. **Full-time faculty:** 104 total; 92% have terminal degrees, 9% minority, 50% women. **Part-time faculty:** 48 total; 40% have terminal degrees, 21% minority, 50% women. **Class size:** 67% < 20, 33% 20-39, less than 1% 40-49. **Special facilities:** College woods, observatory, laboratory farm, community garden, walking and cross-country trails, computer modeling and visualization laboratory, photography studio, outdoor sculpture studio, telecommunications and multimedia learning centers.

Freshman class profile. 1,488 applied, 751 admitted, 311 enrolled.

Mid 50% test scores		GPA 2.0-2.99:	30%
SAT critical reading:	450-600	Rank in top quarter:	39%
SAT math:	460-570	Rank in top tenth:	14%
SAT writing:	430-570	End year in good standing:	91%
ACT composite:	18-22	Return as sophomores:	67%
GPA 3.75 or higher:	12%	Out-of-state:	45%
GPA 3.50-3.74:	16%	Live on campus:	93%
GPA 3.0-3.49:	41%	International:	1%

Basis for selection. School achievement record and essay most important. Test scores, interview, recommendations, interests, leadership ability also important. Minimum SAT composite score of 1000 or ACT score of 22 recommended. SAT or ACT recommended. Test-optional college, applicants have the option to submit an academic portfolio of written work (two additional writing samples) in lieu of SAT or ACT scores. Auditions and portfolios recommended in music, theater, and art. **Home schooled:** Interview required. Provide reason for homeschooling.

High school preparation. College-preparatory program required. 16 units recommended. Recommended units include English 4, mathematics 3, social studies 3, science 3 and foreign language 2.

2015-2016 Annual costs. Tuition/fees: $34,090. Room/board: $9,560. Books/supplies: $1,650. Personal expenses: $2,700.

2014-2015 Financial aid. **Need-based:** 308 full-time freshmen applied for aid; 256 deemed to have need; 256 received aid. Average need met was 74%. Average scholarship/grant was $7,204; average loan $4,184. 64% of total undergraduate aid awarded as scholarships/grants, 36% as loans/jobs. **Non-need-based:** Awarded to 1,220 full-time undergraduates, including 351 freshmen. Scholarships awarded for academics.

Application procedures. **Admission:** Priority date 12/1; no deadline. $25 fee, may be waived for applicants with need, free for online applicants. Admission notification on a rolling basis beginning on or about 1/1. Must reply by May 1 or within 3 week(s) if notified thereafter. **Financial aid:** Priority date 2/15; no closing date. FAFSA required. Applicants notified on a rolling basis starting 3/1; must reply within 2 week(s) of notification.

Academics. **Special study options:** Combined bachelor's/graduate degree, cross-registration, double major, honors, independent study, internships, student-designed major, study abroad, teacher certification program, Washington semester. 3-2 degree programs available in forestry and environmental studies with Duke University, and in physician assistant training with Bowman Gray School of Medicine at Wake Forest University. Many internships, work-study programs, accelerated degree programs in business management, computer information systems, psychology, and biology, dual majors, student-designed majors, study abroad in 9 countries, and cross-registration with members of the Greater Greensboro Consortium (8 colleges/universities). **Credit/placement by examination:** AP, CLEP, IB, SAT, ACT, institutional tests. 32 credit hours maximum toward bachelor's degree. **Support services:** Learning center, pre-admission summer program, reduced course load, remedial instruction, study skills assistance, tutoring, writing center.

Majors. **Area/ethnic studies:** African-American, women's. **Biology:** General. **Business:** Accounting, business admin. **Computer sciences:** General, information systems, information technology, security. **Conservation:** Environmental studies. **Education:** General, elementary, physical, secondary. **English:** Creative writing, English lit. **Foreign languages:** French, German, Germanic, Spanish. **Health services:** Athletic training. **History:** General. **Math:** General. **Parks/recreation:** Exercise sciences, sports admin. **Philosophy/religion:** Philosophy, religion. **Physical sciences:** Chemistry, geology, physics. **Protective services:** Criminal justice, forensics. **Psychology:** General. **Social sciences:** Anthropology, economics, political science, sociology. **Visual/performing arts:** Art, dramatic, music, theater arts management.

Most popular majors. Biology 8%, business/marketing 19%, parks/recreation 6%, psychology 9%, security/protective services 11%, social sciences 13%, visual/performing arts 6%.

Technology on campus. 371 workstations in dormitories, library, computer center, student center. Dormitories wired for high-speed internet access and linked to campus network. Commuter students can connect to campus network. Online course registration, online library, helpline, repair service, wireless network available.

Student life. **Freshman orientation:** Mandatory, $50 fee. Preregistration for classes offered. One-day event in Spring; parents invited. **Policies:** Consistent with its Quaker heritage, the College promotes and encourages student involvement in community service projects. **Housing:** Guaranteed on-campus for freshmen. Coed dorms, single-sex dorms, apartments, cooperative housing, themed housing available. $250 fully refundable deposit, deadline 5/1. Special interest housing and alternative houses with themes or community service project requirements available. **Activities:** Bands, campus ministries, choral groups, dance, drama, film society, international student organizations, literary magazine, music ensembles, Model UN, radio station, student government, student newspaper, Blacks Unifying Society (BUS), Community Senate, The Guilfordian, Campus Activities Board (CAB), Project Community, Omicron Delta Kappa, Hispanos Unidos de Guilford (HUG), Guilford Community of Religious Observants (GCRO), Pride.

Athletics. NCAA. **Intercollegiate:** Baseball, basketball, cheerleading W, cross-country, football (tackle) M, golf M, lacrosse, rugby, soccer, softball W, swimming W, tennis, track and field, volleyball W. **Intramural:** Basketball, football (non-tackle), sand volleyball, soccer, softball, table tennis, tennis, volleyball. **Team name:** Quakers.

Student services. Adult student services, alcohol/substance abuse counseling, chaplain/spiritual director, career counseling, student employment services, financial aid counseling, health services, minority student services, personal counseling, placement for graduates, veterans' counselor, women's services. **Physically disabled:** Services for visually, speech, hearing impaired.

Contact. E-mail: admission@guilford.edu
Phone: (336) 316-2100 Toll-free number: (800) 992-7759
Fax: (336) 316-2954
Arlene Cash, Vice President for Enrollment Management, Guilford College, Admissions, New Garden Hall, Greensboro, NC 27410-4108

High Point University
High Point, North Carolina
www.highpoint.edu

CB member
CB code: 5293

▶ Private 4-year university and liberal arts college affiliated with the United Methodist Church

▶ Residential campus in small city

▶ 4,362 degree-seeking undergraduates: 1% part-time, 60% women, 5% African American, 2% Asian American, 4% Hispanic/Latino, 5% Multiracial, non-Hispanic, 3% international

▶ 202 degree-seeking graduate students

▶ 72% of applicants admitted

▶ SAT or ACT (ACT writing recommended), application essay required

▶ 65% graduate within 6 years; 27% enter graduate study

General. Founded in 1924. Regionally accredited. **Degrees:** 896 bachelor's awarded; master's, doctoral offered. **ROTC:** Army, Air Force. **Location:** 15 miles from Greensboro, 15 miles from Winston Salem. **Calendar:** Semester, limited summer session. **Full-time faculty:** 276 total; 80% have terminal degrees, 11% minority, 48% women. **Part-time faculty:** 145 total; 35% have terminal degrees, 9% minority, 50% women. **Class size:** 61% < 20, 37% 20-39, less than 1% 40-49, less than 1% 50-99, less than 1% >100. **Special facilities:** Sports medicine center, MAC design labs, Linux labs, CAD labs, tutoring center, fine arts center, international home furnishings center.

Freshman class profile. 10,910 applied, 7,909 admitted, 1,362 enrolled.

Mid 50% test scores			
SAT critical reading:	500-590	GPA 2.0-2.99:	26%
SAT math:	510-600	Rank in top quarter:	54%
SAT writing:	490-590	Rank in top tenth:	25%
ACT composite:	22-27	Return as sophomores:	81%
GPA 3.75 or higher:	18%	Out-of-state:	78%
GPA 3.50-3.74:	19%	Live on campus:	98%
GPA 3.0-3.49:	37%	International:	4%

Basis for selection. The most important factors are the academic transcript, including grades received and course selection, followed by standardized test scores (SAT or ACT). Other important factors are demonstrated leadership, extracurricular and community involvement, and special talent. Test scores are required for all applicants. **Home schooled:** Transcript of courses and grades, letter of recommendation (nonparent) required.

High school preparation. College-preparatory program required. 15 units required; 17 recommended. Required and recommended units include English 4, mathematics 3-4, social studies 3, science 3 (laboratory 1) and foreign language 2-3.

2015-2016 Annual costs. Tuition/fees: $32,430. Room/board: $12,200. Books/supplies: $1,500. Personal expenses: $1,000.

2014-2015 Financial aid. **Non-need-based:** Scholarships awarded for academics, alumni affiliation, art, athletics, leadership, music/drama, religious affiliation, state residency.

Application procedures. **Admission:** Closing date 3/1 (postmark date). $50 fee, may be waived for applicants with need. Admission notification on a rolling basis beginning on or about 2/1. Must reply by 5/1. **Financial aid:** Priority date 3/1; no closing date. FAFSA required. Applicants notified on a rolling basis starting 4/1; must reply within 3 week(s) of notification.

Academics. **Special study options:** Accelerated study, combined bachelor's/graduate degree, cooperative education, cross-registration, double major, dual enrollment of high school students, ESL, honors, independent study, internships, liberal arts/career combination, student-designed major, study abroad, teacher certification program. Exchange programs in Austria, Belgium, Chile, China, Denmark, France, Germany, Italy, Netherlands, South Korea, Spain, Sweden, and United Kingdom. Opportunities for study abroad in Argentina, Australia, Austria, Czech Republic, Ecuador, Fiji, France, Germany, India, Italy, Japan, Russia, South Africa, Spain, and United Kingdom. **Credit/placement by examination:** AP, CLEP, IB, SAT, ACT, institutional tests. 32 credit hours maximum toward bachelor's degree. Credit by Examination is offered through 1) examinations written and administered by University faculty and 2) national test programs. A maximum of 32 credits may be earned by such examinations. If a student earns a significant number of credits through examination, no more than 8 of these credits will be applied to any given semester. **Support services:** Learning center, pre-admission summer program, reduced course load, study skills assistance, tutoring, writing center.

Majors. **Biology:** General, biochemistry. **Business:** Accounting, actuarial science, business admin, finance, international, managerial economics, marketing, nonprofit/public, organizational behavior, selling. **Communications:** General. **Computer sciences:** General. **Education:** Elementary, middle, physical, secondary, special ed. **English:** English lit, writing. **Foreign languages:** French, Spanish. **History:** General. **Math:** General. **Parks/recreation:** Exercise sciences. **Philosophy/religion:** Philosophy, religion. **Physical sciences:** Chemistry, physics. **Protective services:** Criminal justice. **Psychology:** General. **Social sciences:** Econometrics, international relations, political science, sociology/anthropology. **Visual/performing arts:** Documentaries, dramatic, graphic design, interior design, music, studio arts.

Most popular majors. Biology 6%, business/marketing 34%, communications/journalism 18%, education 7%, visual/performing arts 9%.

Technology on campus. 721 workstations in dormitories, library, computer center, student center. Dormitories wired for high-speed internet access and linked to campus network. Commuter students can connect to campus

network. Online course registration, online library, helpline, repair service, student web hosting, wireless network available.

Student life. Freshman orientation: Mandatory. Preregistration for classes offered. 3-5 days during move-in weekend and comprised of social activities, advising sessions, residence hall meetings and an activities fair. **Policies:** Outlined fully in Student Guide to Campus Life. **Housing:** Guaranteed on-campus for freshmen. Coed dorms, single-sex dorms, special housing for disabled, apartments, fraternity/sorority housing, themed housing, wellness housing available. $500 fully refundable deposit, deadline 5/1. **Activities:** Bands, campus ministries, choral groups, dance, drama, film society, international student organizations, literary magazine, music ensembles, Model UN, musical theater, opera, radio station, student government, student newspaper, symphony orchestra, TV station, College Democrats, College Republicans, debate club, Society for History and Political Awareness, BCA, Black Script, Alpha Phi Omega, Rotaract, Big Brothers Big Sisters, Habitat for Humanity.

Athletics. NCAA. **Intercollegiate:** Baseball M, basketball, cross-country, golf, lacrosse, soccer, track and field, volleyball W. **Intramural:** Badminton, basketball, bowling, football (non-tackle), racquetball, soccer, softball, tennis, ultimate frisbee, volleyball, water polo. **Team name:** Panthers.

Student services. Adult student services, alcohol/substance abuse counseling, chaplain/spiritual director, career counseling, student employment services, financial aid counseling, health services, personal counseling, placement for graduates, veterans' counselor.

Contact. E-mail: admiss@highpoint.edu
Phone: (336) 841-9216 Toll-free number: (800) 345-6993
Fax: (336) 888-6382
Andy Bills, Vice President for Enrollment, High Point University, One University Parkway, High Point, NC 27268-3598

Johnson and Wales University: Charlotte
Charlotte, North Carolina
www.jwu.edu   CB code: 4360

- Private 4-year university
- Residential campus in very large city
- 2,218 degree-seeking undergraduates: 2% part-time, 66% women, 37% African American, 1% Asian American, 6% Hispanic/Latino, 7% Multiracial, non-Hispanic, 1% international
- 72% of applicants admitted
- 49% graduate within 6 years

General. Degrees: 394 bachelor's, 428 associate awarded. **ROTC:** Army. **Calendar:** Trimester. **Full-time faculty:** 83 total. **Part-time faculty:** 34 total. **Class size:** 51% < 20, 44% 20-39, 5% 40-49.

Freshman class profile. 4,537 applied, 3,287 admitted, 641 enrolled.

GPA 3.75 or higher:	38%	Return as sophomores:	76%
GPA 3.50-3.74:	25%	Out-of-state:	62%
GPA 3.0-3.49:	21%	Live on campus:	84%
GPA 2.0-2.99:	16%	International:	1%

Basis for selection. Academic record, secondary school curriculum, class rank, GPA, test scores and interview important. Student motivation and interest given strong consideration. SAT or ACT required for applicants to the honors programs. **Home schooled:** Transcript of courses and grades, state high school equivalency certificate required. SAT (verbal and math) or ACT required.

High school preparation. College-preparatory program recommended. Required units include English 4, mathematics 3, social studies 2 and science 3.

2015-2016 Annual costs. Tuition/fees: $29,226. Room/board: $12,732. Books/supplies: $1,500. Personal expenses: $1,670.

2015-2016 Financial aid. Need-based: 655 full-time freshmen applied for aid; 601 deemed to have need; 601 received aid. Average need met was 68%. Average scholarship/grant was $9,159; average loan $3,381. 62% of total undergraduate aid awarded as scholarships/grants, 38% as loans/jobs. **Non-need-based:** Awarded to 1,963 full-time undergraduates, including 647 freshmen. Scholarships awarded for academics, alumni affiliation, leadership, state residency.

Application procedures. Admission: No deadline. No application fee. Admission notification on a rolling basis beginning on or about 11/1. Must reply by May 1 or within 2 week(s) if notified thereafter. **Financial aid:** No deadline. FAFSA required. Applicants notified on a rolling basis starting 3/1.

Academics. Math center. **Special study options:** Accelerated study, cooperative education, dual enrollment of high school students, ESL, exchange student, honors, independent study, internships, study abroad. **Credit/placement by examination:** AP, CLEP. **Support services:** Learning center, reduced course load, remedial instruction, study skills assistance, tutoring, writing center.

Majors. Business: General, accounting, accounting/business management, accounting/finance, apparel, auditing, business admin, event planning, fashion, hospitality admin, hospitality/recreation, hotel/motel admin, hotel/motel/restaurant management, marketing, merchandising, operations, personal/financial services, resort management, restaurant/food services, retail management, retailing. **Liberal arts:** Arts/sciences. **Parks/recreation:** General, facilities management, sports admin. **Work/family studies:** Clothing/textiles, food/nutrition, institutional food production.

Most popular majors. Business/marketing 34%, family/consumer sciences 55%, parks/recreation 11%.

Technology on campus. 160 workstations in library. Dormitories wired for high-speed internet access and linked to campus network. Commuter students can connect to campus network. Online library, helpline, wireless network available.

Student life. Freshman orientation: Available, $300 fee. Preregistration for classes offered. **Housing:** Coed dorms, special housing for disabled, apartments, wellness housing available. $300 deposit, deadline 5/1. **Activities:** Campus ministries, dance, international student organizations, student government, student newspaper.

Athletics. Intercollegiate: Basketball M, soccer, volleyball W. **Intramural:** Baseball M. **Team name:** Wildcats.

Student services. Career counseling, student employment services, financial aid counseling, health services, personal counseling, veterans' counselor. **Physically disabled:** Services for visually, speech, hearing impaired.

Contact. E-mail: clt@admissions.jwu.edu
Phone: (866) 598-2427 Toll-free number: (800) 342-5598
Fax: (980) 598-1111
Joseph Campos, Director of Admissions, Johnson and Wales University: Charlotte, 801 West Trade Street, Charlotte, NC 28202

Johnson C. Smith University
Charlotte, North Carolina   CB member
www.jcsu.edu   CB code: 5333

- Private 4-year university and liberal arts college
- Residential campus in very large city
- 1,371 degree-seeking undergraduates: 4% part-time, 61% women, 79% African American, 5% Hispanic/Latino, 2% Multi-racial, non-Hispanic, 4% international
- 63 degree-seeking graduate students
- 46% of applicants admitted
- SAT or ACT (ACT writing optional) required
- 46% graduate within 6 years

General. Founded in 1867. Regionally accredited. **Degrees:** 253 bachelor's awarded; master's offered. **Location:** 244 miles from Atlanta. **Calendar:** Semester, limited summer session. **Full-time faculty:** 92 total; 86% have terminal degrees, 67% minority, 58% women. **Part-time faculty:** 68 total; 25% have terminal degrees, 75% minority, 60% women. **Class size:** 74% < 20, 26% 20-39, less than 1% 40-49. **Special facilities:** Sustainablity Village which features a community garden as well as an aquaponic system.

Freshman class profile. 4,346 applied, 1,983 admitted, 334 enrolled.

Mid 50% test scores			
SAT critical reading:	350-440	Rank in top quarter:	15%
SAT math:	350-440	Rank in top tenth:	5%
ACT composite:	15-18	End year in good standing:	67%
GPA 3.75 or higher:	9%	Return as sophomores:	68%
GPA 3.50-3.74:	6%	Out-of-state:	42%
GPA 3.0-3.49:	22%	Live on campus:	95%
GPA 2.0-2.99:	54%	International:	1%

Basis for selection. Competitive test scores and grade point averages (GPA) are taken into account in admissions decisions. Two letters of recommendations and essay are considered. Essay or personal statement not required but highly recommended. **Home schooled:** Statement describing home school structure and mission, transcript of courses and grades, state high school equivalency certificate, letter of recommendation (nonparent) required.

High school preparation. 18 units required. Required units include English 4, mathematics 3, social studies 3, science 3 (laboratory 1), foreign language 2 and academic electives 3.

2016-2017 Annual costs. Tuition/fees: $18,236. Room/board: $7,100. Books/supplies: $1,700. Personal expenses: $3,350.

2015-2016 Financial aid. Need-based: 320 full-time freshmen applied for aid; 306 deemed to have need; 304 received aid. Average need met was 57%. Average scholarship/grant was $13,414; average loan $3,519. 58% of total undergraduate aid awarded as scholarships/grants, 42% as loans/jobs. **Non-need-based:** Awarded to 190 full-time undergraduates, including 34 freshmen. Scholarships awarded for academics, athletics, music/drama, ROTC.

Application procedures. Admission: No deadline. $25 fee, may be waived for applicants with need. Admission notification by 10/1. Must reply by May 1 or within 3 week(s) if notified thereafter. **Financial aid:** Priority date 3/1; no closing date. FAFSA required. Applicants notified on a rolling basis starting 3/1; must reply within 2 week(s) of notification.

Academics. Special study options: Accelerated study, combined bachelor's/graduate degree, cooperative education, cross-registration, double major, exchange student, independent study, internships, liberal arts/career combination, student-designed major, study abroad, teacher certification program. **Credit/placement by examination:** AP, CLEP, IB, institutional tests. **Support services:** Learning center, pre-admission summer program, reduced course load, study skills assistance, tutoring, writing center.

Majors. Biology: General. **Business:** Business admin. **Communications:** Media studies. **Computer sciences:** General, information technology. **Engineering:** Computer. **English:** English lit. **Foreign languages:** French, Spanish. **Health services:** Community health services. **History:** General. **Human services:** Social work. **Liberal arts:** Arts/sciences. **Math:** General. **Parks/recreation:** Sports admin. **Physical sciences:** Chemistry. **Psychology:** General. **Social sciences:** Criminology, economics, political science. **Visual/performing arts:** General, music.

Most popular majors. Biology 9%, business/marketing 21%, communications/journalism 8%, computer/information sciences 8%, parks/recreation 8%, psychology 6%, public administration/social services 8%, social sciences 15%.

Technology on campus. PC or laptop required. 125 workstations in dormitories, library, computer center. Dormitories wired for high-speed internet access and linked to campus network. Commuter students can connect to campus network. Online library, helpline, repair service, wireless network available.

Student life. Freshman orientation: Available. Preregistration for classes offered. **Policies:** Freshmen not permitted cars on campus. **Housing:** Guaranteed on-campus for freshmen. Coed dorms, single-sex dorms, apartments available. $150 nonrefundable deposit, deadline 5/1. **Activities:** Bands, campus ministries, choral groups, dance, drama, music ensembles, student government, Spiritual Life club, gospel choir, D.A.M.A.S (Determined Action through Multicultural Advancement and Service), L.E.O. (Latinos Empowering Others), National Society of Black Engineers (NSBE), Collegiate Sisters for Action, Lead with Pride.

Athletics. NCAA. **Intercollegiate:** Basketball, bowling W, cheerleading W, cross-country, football (tackle) M, golf M, softball W, tennis, track and field, volleyball W. **Intramural:** Basketball, football (non-tackle). **Team name:** Golden Bulls.

Student services. Adult student services, alcohol/substance abuse counseling, chaplain/spiritual director, career counseling, services for economically disadvantaged, student employment services, financial aid counseling, health services, minority student services, personal counseling, veterans' counselor. **Physically disabled:** Services for visually, speech, hearing impaired.

Contact. E-mail: admissions@jcsu.edu
Phone: (704) 378-1010 Toll-free number: (800) 782-7303
Fax: (704) 378-1242
James Burrell, Director of Admissions, Johnson C. Smith University, 100 Beatties Ford Road, Charlotte, NC 28216-5398

Laurel University
High Point, North Carolina
www.laureluniversity.edu
CB code: 5348

- Private 4-year university and Bible college affiliated with the interdenominational tradition
- Commuter campus in small city

- 125 degree-seeking undergraduates
- Application essay, interview required

General. Founded in 1932. Regionally accredited; also accredited by ABHE. **Degrees:** 33 bachelor's, 1 associate awarded; master's, doctoral offered. **Location:** 15 miles from Greensboro, 60 miles from Charlotte. **Calendar:** Semester, limited summer session. **Full-time faculty:** 3 total; 100% have terminal degrees. **Part-time faculty:** 34 total; 44% have terminal degrees, 32% women. **Class size:** 85% < 20, 15% 20-39.

Freshman class profile.

GPA 3.75 or higher:	30%	**GPA 2.0-2.99:**	35%
GPA 3.50-3.74:	12%	**Out-of-state:**	1%
GPA 3.0-3.49:	23%	**Live on campus:**	20%

Basis for selection. Future career in church-related vocations and motivation; religious commitment and personal statement very important. Positive personal testimony required. Finding and following God's will foremost. **Home schooled:** Transcript of courses and grades required. Junior or higher standing, GPA 3.2 or higher, 16 or older, and recommendation from high school administrator or guidance counselor required.

High school preparation. 20 units recommended. Recommended units include English 4, mathematics 4, social studies 4, science 3 (laboratory 2).

2015-2016 Annual costs. Tuition/fees: $13,030. Room only: $3,000. Books/supplies: $1,200. Personal expenses: $2,700.

Financial aid. Additional information: Early Acceptance Scholarships, Academic Honor Scholarships, Married Student Credit and Minister/Missionary Dependent Scholarship available.

Application procedures. Admission: Closing date 8/8 (postmark date). $20 fee, may be waived for applicants with need. Admission notification on a rolling basis. **Financial aid:** Priority date 3/15; no closing date. FAFSA required. Applicants notified on a rolling basis starting 6/1; must reply within 3 week(s) of notification.

Academics. Laurel U takes a Christian based approach to academics. Professional studies integrating faith and learning offered. **Special study options:** Accelerated study, cooperative education, distance learning, double major, dual enrollment of high school students, independent study, internships. **Credit/placement by examination:** AP, CLEP, IB, institutional tests. 15 credit hours maximum toward associate degree, 30 toward bachelor's. **Support services:** Reduced course load.

Majors. Business: Business admin. **Education:** Elementary. **Theology:** Pastoral counseling, religious ed, theology.

Most popular majors. Business/marketing 42%, philosophy/religious studies 50%.

Technology on campus. 6 workstations in library, computer center. Dormitories wired for high-speed internet access. Online library, wireless network available.

Student life. Freshman orientation: Mandatory. Preregistration for classes offered. Orientation activities held 2 business days before classes begin. **Policies:** Religious observance required. **Housing:** Apartments, wellness housing available. $50 deposit, deadline 7/15. **Activities:** Campus ministries, drama, student government, drama team, evangelistic ministries, urban ministry, foreign missions involvement team.

Athletics. Intercollegiate: Lacrosse M, soccer. **Team name:** Lions.

Student services. Chaplain/spiritual director, financial aid counseling, personal counseling, veterans' counselor.

Contact. E-mail: admissions@laureluniversity.edu
Phone: (336) 887-3000 ext. 127
Toll-free number: (855) 528-7358 ext. 127 Fax: (336) 889-2261
Mary Hancock, Director of Enrollment Management, Laurel University, 1215 Eastchester Drive, High Point, NC 27265-3115

Lees-McRae College
Banner Elk, North Carolina
www.lmc.edu
CB member
CB code: 5364

- Private 4-year liberal arts college affiliated with the Presbyterian Church (USA)
- Residential campus in rural community

♦ 1,032 degree-seeking undergraduates: 66% women, 7% African American, 1% Asian American, 4% Hispanic/Latino, 1% Multi-racial, non-Hispanic, 2% international

♦ 66% of applicants admitted

General. Founded in 1900. Regionally accredited. **Degrees:** 201 bachelor's awarded. **Location:** 17 miles from Boone, 40 miles from Johnson City, TN. **Calendar:** Semester, limited summer session. **Full-time faculty:** 48 total; 60% have terminal degrees, 50% women. **Part-time faculty:** 44 total; 30% have terminal degrees, 2% minority, 68% women. **Class size:** 75% < 20, 25% 20-39. **Special facilities:** Wireless campus, biology field station, Blue Ridge Wildlife Rehabilitation Institute.

Freshman class profile. 1,400 applied, 931 admitted, 198 enrolled.

GPA 3.75 or higher:	27%	Rank in top tenth:	6%
GPA 3.50-3.74:	12%	Out-of-state:	30%
GPA 3.0-3.49:	24%	Live on campus:	98%
GPA 2.0-2.99:	34%	International:	1%
Rank in top quarter:	22%		

Basis for selection. High school record and rank in top half of class preferred. Test scores optional. Recommendations considered. Interview recommended for all students; portfolio recommended for performing arts programs. Audition required for athletic, performing arts programs.

High school preparation. College-preparatory program recommended. Required and recommended units include English 4, mathematics 3, social studies 2, history 1, science 2 and foreign language 2.

2015-2016 Annual costs. Tuition/fees: $24,854. Room/board: $9,782. Books/supplies: $590. Personal expenses: $2,600.

2015-2016 Financial aid. Need-based: 181 full-time freshmen applied for aid; 166 deemed to have need; 166 received aid. Average need met was 71%. Average scholarship/grant was $9,993; average loan $3,500. 72% of total undergraduate aid awarded as scholarships/grants, 28% as loans/jobs. **Non-need-based:** Awarded to 1,203 full-time undergraduates, including 246 freshmen. Scholarships awarded for academics, athletics, leadership, music/drama, religious affiliation.

Application procedures. Admission: No deadline. $35 fee, may be waived for applicants with need. Admission notification on a rolling basis. **Financial aid:** Priority date 4/15; no closing date. FAFSA required. Applicants notified on a rolling basis starting 3/1; must reply within 2 week(s) of notification.

Academics. Special study options: Accelerated study, cross-registration, distance learning, double major, dual enrollment of high school students, exchange student, honors, independent study, internships, liberal arts/career combination, study abroad, teacher certification program. 3-2 program Environmental Science/Forestry with Duke University. **Credit/placement by examination:** AP, CLEP, IB, institutional tests. 16 credit hours maximum toward bachelor's degree. **Support services:** Learning center, remedial instruction, study skills assistance, tutoring, writing center.

Majors. Biology: General. **Business:** Business admin. **Communications:** Communications/speech/rhetoric. **Computer sciences:** Computer science, information systems. **Education:** Drama/dance, elementary, physical. **English:** English lit. **Health services:** Predental, premedicine, preveterinary. **Liberal arts:** Arts/sciences. **Math:** General. **Philosophy/religion:** Religion. **Protective services:** Criminal justice. **Psychology:** General. **Social sciences:** International relations. **Visual/performing arts:** General, art, dramatic, musical theater, studio arts management, theater design.

Most popular majors. Biology 16%, business/marketing 6%, education 12%, health sciences 37%, psychology 6%, security/protective services 10%.

Technology on campus. 125 workstations in dormitories, library, computer center, student center. Dormitories wired for high-speed internet access and linked to campus network. Commuter students can connect to campus network. Online course registration, online library, helpline, wireless network available.

Student life. Freshman orientation: Mandatory. Preregistration for classes offered. 6 summer Freshmen Experience sessions (1 required) followed by August orientation. **Housing:** Guaranteed on-campus for all undergraduates. Coed dorms, single-sex dorms, apartments, themed housing available. Pets allowed in dorm rooms. Pet-friendly student housing available. **Activities:** Campus ministries, dance, drama, music ensembles, musical theater, student government, Order of the Tower, student ambassadors, residence hall association, sports medicine club, Phi Beta Lambda, Circle K, campus after the class hours, EMS club.

Athletics. NCAA. **Intercollegiate:** Basketball, cheerleading, cross-country, lacrosse, soccer, softball W, tennis, track and field, volleyball. **Intramural:** Basketball, cross-country, football (non-tackle), golf, skiing, soccer, softball, table tennis, tennis, volleyball. **Team name:** Bobcats.

Student services. Alcohol/substance abuse counseling, chaplain/spiritual director, career counseling, student employment services, financial aid counseling, health services, personal counseling, veterans' counselor.

Contact. E-mail: admissions@lmc.edu
Phone: (828) 898-5241 Toll-free number: (800) 280-4562
Fax: (828) 898-8707
Ben Austin, Director of Admissions, Lees-McRae College, Box 128, Banner Elk, NC 28604

Lenoir-Rhyne University
Hickory, North Carolina **CB member**
www.lr.edu **CB code: 5365**

♦ Private 4-year university and liberal arts college affiliated with the Evangelical Lutheran Church in America

♦ Residential campus in large town

♦ 1,412 degree-seeking undergraduates: 4% part-time, 56% women, 15% African American, 1% Asian American, 5% Hispanic/Latino, 1% Native American, 3% Multi-racial, non-Hispanic, 2% international

♦ 703 degree-seeking graduate students

♦ 84% of applicants admitted

♦ SAT or ACT (ACT writing recommended) required

♦ 48% graduate within 6 years

General. Founded in 1891. Regionally accredited. **Degrees:** 296 bachelor's awarded; master's offered. **Location:** 50 miles from Charlotte. **Calendar:** Semester, limited summer session. **Full-time faculty:** 126 total; 87% have terminal degrees, 9% minority, 48% women. **Part-time faculty:** 143 total; 38% have terminal degrees, 4% minority, 52% women. **Class size:** 71% < 20, 29% 20-39. **Special facilities:** Observatory, multimedia classrooms, outdoor classroom, multimedia (TV) facilities.

Freshman class profile. 3,994 applied, 3,369 admitted, 448 enrolled.

Mid 50% test scores		GPA 2.0-2.99:	25%
SAT critical reading:	440-550	Return as sophomores:	64%
SAT math:	440-550	Out-of-state:	22%
SAT writing:	440-550	Live on campus:	80%
GPA 3.75 or higher:	20%	International:	4%
GPA 3.50-3.74:	18%	Fraternities:	11%
GPA 3.0-3.49:	37%	Sororities:	5%

Basis for selection. School achievement record, courses taken and scores on ACT or SAT are important. Audition required for music majors. **Learning Disabled:** Students with learning disabilities must meet the same requirements as any other student.

High school preparation. College-preparatory program recommended. Required and recommended units include English 4, mathematics 3-4, history 1-2, science 1-2 (laboratory 1) and foreign language 2-3. Chemistry required for nursing program. History refers to U.S. History; mathematics needs to include algebra I, algebra II, geometry.

2016-2017 Annual costs. Tuition/fees (projected): $33,730. Room/board: $11,600. Books/supplies: $1,160. Personal expenses: $1,850.

2014-2015 Financial aid. Need-based: 327 full-time freshmen applied for aid; 307 deemed to have need; 307 received aid. Average need met was 73%. Average scholarship/grant was $23,232; average loan $2,939. 47% of total undergraduate aid awarded as scholarships/grants, 53% as loans/jobs. **Non-need-based:** Awarded to 416 full-time undergraduates, including 108 freshmen. Scholarships awarded for academics, alumni affiliation, athletics, leadership, music/drama, religious affiliation.

Application procedures. Admission: No deadline. $35 fee, may be waived for applicants with need. Admission notification on a rolling basis. Students will not be put on the housing roster until the deposit is received. **Financial aid:** No deadline. FAFSA required. Applicants notified on a rolling basis; must reply by 5/1 or within 3 week(s) of notification.

Academics. Special study options: Accelerated study, cross-registration, distance learning, double major, dual enrollment of high school students, honors, independent study, internships, study abroad, teacher certification program, Washington semester. **Credit/placement by examination:** AP, CLEP, IB, SAT, ACT, institutional tests. 16 credit hours maximum toward bachelor's degree. **Support services:** Learning center, remedial instruction, study skills assistance, tutoring, writing center. Special program for deaf and hard of hearing students.

Majors. Area/ethnic studies: American. **Biology:** General. **Business:** Accounting, entrepreneurial studies, finance, international, management information systems, management science, marketing. **Communications:** General. **Computer sciences:** General, information systems. **Conservation:** Environmental studies, forestry. **Education:** Elementary, middle, music. **Engineering:** Pre-engineering. **English:** English lit. **Foreign languages:** German, Spanish. **Health services:** Athletic training, clinical lab science, nursing (RN), premedicine. **History:** General. **Liberal arts:** Arts/sciences. **Math:** General. **Parks/recreation:** Health/fitness, sports admin. **Philosophy/religion:** Philosophy, religion. **Physical sciences:** Chemistry, physics. **Protective services:** Criminal justice. **Psychology:** General. **Social sciences:** Economics, international relations, political science, sociology. **Theology:** Sacred music. **Visual/performing arts:** Dramatic, graphic design, music, music performance, studio arts management.

Most popular majors. Business/marketing 16%, education 7%, health sciences 22%, parks/recreation 17%, social sciences 7%.

Technology on campus. 150 workstations in library, computer center, student center. Dormitories wired for high-speed internet access and linked to campus network. Commuter students can connect to campus network. Online course registration, online library, helpline, wireless network available.

Student life. Freshman orientation: Mandatory. Preregistration for classes offered. Day-long orientation program held in June. On-campus orientation held 4 days before start of classes. **Housing:** Guaranteed on-campus for freshmen. Coed dorms, fraternity/sorority housing, themed housing available. $300 fully refundable deposit, deadline 8/1. Men or women only floors in dorms available. **Activities:** Bands, campus ministries, choral groups, dance, drama, film society, international student organizations, literary magazine, music ensembles, Model UN, musical theater, radio station, student government, student newspaper, symphony orchestra, Black Student Alliance, College Democrats, Lutheran Student Movement, Student Occupational Therapy Association, Gay Straight Alliance, College Republicans, El Club de Espanol, Fellowship of Christian Athletes, NC Student Legislature, Nu Generation gospel choir.

Athletics. NCAA. **Intercollegiate:** Baseball M, basketball, cheerleading, cross-country, football (tackle) M, golf, lacrosse, soccer, softball W, swimming, tennis, track and field, volleyball W. **Intramural:** Baseball M, basketball, football (non-tackle), sand volleyball, soccer, ultimate frisbee, volleyball. **Team name:** Bears.

Student services. Adult student services, chaplain/spiritual director, career counseling, student employment services, financial aid counseling, health services, minority student services, personal counseling, veterans' counselor. **Physically disabled:** Services for visually, hearing impaired.

Contact. E-mail: admissions@lr.edu
Phone: (828) 328-7300 Toll-free number: (800) 277-5721
Fax: (828) 328-7378
Nathanael Summer, Director of Undergraduate Recruiting, Lenoir-Rhyne University, LR Box 7227, Hickory, NC 28603

Livingstone College
Salisbury, North Carolina **CB member**
www.livingstone.edu **CB code: 5367**

- Private 4-year liberal arts college affiliated with the African Methodist Episcopal Zion Church
- Residential campus in large town
- 1,262 degree-seeking undergraduates
- 71% of applicants admitted
- SAT or ACT (ACT writing optional) required

General. Founded in 1879. Regionally accredited. **Degrees:** 149 bachelor's awarded. **ROTC:** Army. **Location:** 44 miles from Charlotte. **Calendar:** Semester. **Full-time faculty:** 71 total. **Part-time faculty:** 5 total. **Class size:** 64% < 20, 28% 20-39, 4% 40-49, 1% 50-99, 2% >100. **Special facilities:** Center for Negro and African life, literature and international studies.

Freshman class profile. 4,574 applied, 3,260 admitted, 421 enrolled.

Mid 50% test scores		Rank in top quarter:	6%
SAT critical reading:	320-400	Rank in top tenth:	4%
SAT math:	320-410	Out-of-state:	59%
ACT composite:	14-16	Live on campus:	85%

Basis for selection. School achievement record, test scores, recommendations important. College's placement test, instead of ELPT, used for advising and placement. Audition required for music majors; interview recommended for academically weak students.

High school preparation. 10 units required. Required and recommended units include English 4, mathematics 3, social studies 2, history 1, science 2 and foreign language 2.

2015-2016 Annual costs. Tuition/fees: $17,246. Room/board: $6,596. Books/supplies: $380. Personal expenses: $3,000.

Financial aid. Non-need-based: Scholarships awarded for academics, alumni affiliation, athletics, leadership, music/drama, religious affiliation, ROTC, state residency.

Application procedures. Admission: Priority date 5/15; no deadline. $25 fee, may be waived for applicants with need. Admission notification on a rolling basis. Must reply by May 1 or within 4 week(s) if notified thereafter. **Financial aid:** Priority date 3/15, closing date 6/30. FAFSA required. Applicants notified by 5/1; must reply within 4 week(s) of notification.

Academics. Special study options: Accelerated study, cross-registration, double major, independent study, internships, teacher certification program. **Credit/placement by examination:** AP, CLEP, institutional tests. **Support services:** Learning center, reduced course load, study skills assistance, tutoring.

Majors. Biology: General. **Business:** Accounting, business admin. **Computer sciences:** General. **Education:** Elementary. **Engineering:** General. **English:** English lit. **Health services:** Predental, prepharmacy. **History:** General. **Human services:** Social work. **Math:** General. **Parks/recreation:** Sports admin. **Physical sciences:** Chemistry. **Protective services:** Criminal justice. **Psychology:** General. **Social sciences:** General, political science, sociology. **Theology:** Theology. **Visual/performing arts:** Dramatic, music.

Most popular majors. Business/marketing 25%, parks/recreation 9%, psychology 18%, security/protective services 13%, social sciences 13%.

Technology on campus. 200 workstations in dormitories, library, computer center. Dormitories wired for high-speed internet access and linked to campus network.

Student life. Freshman orientation: Mandatory, $100 fee. Preregistration for classes offered. **Housing:** Single-sex dorms, special housing for disabled, apartments available. $100 deposit. **Activities:** Bands, choral groups, dance, drama, film society, music ensembles, musical theater, radio station, student government, pre-theological union, AME Zion Council.

Athletics. NCAA. **Intercollegiate:** Basketball, bowling, cross-country, football (tackle) M, softball W, tennis, track and field, volleyball W. **Intramural:** Basketball. **Team name:** Blue Bears.

Student services. Career counseling, student employment services, health services, personal counseling, placement for graduates, veterans' counselor.

Contact. E-mail: admissions@livingstone.edu
Phone: (704) 216-6001 Toll-free number: (800) 835-3435
Fax: (704) 216-6215
Tony Baldwin, Director of Enrollment Management and Admission, Livingstone College, 701 West Monroe Street, Salisbury, NC 28144-5213

Mars Hill University
Mars Hill, North Carolina **CB member**
www.mhu.edu **CB code: 5395**

- Private 4-year liberal arts college affiliated with the Baptist faith
- Residential campus in small town
- 1,351 degree-seeking undergraduates: 5% part-time, 51% women, 22% African American, 1% Asian American, 3% Hispanic/Latino, 1% Native American, 1% Multi-racial, non-Hispanic
- 15 degree-seeking graduate students
- 61% of applicants admitted
- SAT or ACT (ACT writing optional) required
- 37% graduate within 6 years

General. Founded in 1856. Regionally accredited. **Degrees:** 235 bachelor's awarded; master's offered. **Location:** 17 miles from Asheville, North Carolina. **Calendar:** Semester, extensive summer session. **Full-time faculty:** 91 total; 68% have terminal degrees, 2% minority, 50% women. **Part-time faculty:** 56 total; 50% women. **Class size:** 68% < 20, 31% 20-39, less than 1% 40-49, less than 1% 50-99. **Special facilities:** Appalachian archives.

Freshman class profile. 3,010 applied, 1,835 admitted, 387 enrolled.

Mid 50% test scores		GPA 2.0-2.99:	34%
SAT critical reading:	400-490	Rank in top quarter:	19%
SAT math:	410-500	Rank in top tenth:	5%
ACT composite:	17-22	Return as sophomores:	59%
GPA 3.75 or higher:	26%	Out-of-state:	30%
GPA 3.50-3.74:	11%	Live on campus:	95%
GPA 3.0-3.49:	29%		

Basis for selection. School achievement record, test scores, school and community activities, recommendations from school officials all important. Students interested in early admission must apply as full-time students, achieve A average in courses, minimum SAT 1000 (exclusive of Writing) or ACT 22, and submit 2 recommendations from high school personnel. Audition required for music, theater programs. Essay, portfolio recommended; interview recommended for students who do not meet other admissions criteria. **Home schooled:** Transcript of courses and grades required. **Learning Disabled:** Letter of documentation required.

High school preparation. College-preparatory program recommended. 11 units required. Required and recommended units include English 4, mathematics 3, social studies 2, history 2, science 2, foreign language 2 and computer science 1.

2015-2016 Annual costs. Tuition/fees: $29,382. Room/board: $8,234. Books/supplies: $1,500. Personal expenses: $1,300.

2015-2016 Financial aid. Need-based: 390 full-time freshmen applied for aid; 372 deemed to have need; 372 received aid. Average need met was 79%. Average scholarship/grant was $9,498; average loan $3,064. 60% of total undergraduate aid awarded as scholarships/grants, 40% as loans/jobs. **Non-need-based:** Awarded to 1,250 full-time undergraduates, including 436 freshmen. Scholarships awarded for academics, athletics, state residency.

Application procedures. Admission: No deadline. $25 fee, may be waived for applicants with need. Admission notification on a rolling basis. **Financial aid:** Priority date 3/15; no closing date. FAFSA required. Applicants notified on a rolling basis starting 1/15; must reply within 2 week(s) of notification.

Academics. Special study options: Accelerated study, cross-registration, distance learning, double major, dual enrollment of high school students, ESL, exchange student, honors, independent study, internships, liberal arts/career combination, study abroad, teacher certification program. **Credit/placement by examination:** AP, CLEP, IB, SAT, ACT, institutional tests. 32 credit hours maximum toward bachelor's degree. **Support services:** Learning center, reduced course load, remedial instruction, study skills assistance, tutoring, writing center.

Majors. Biology: General, botany, zoology. **Business:** General, accounting, business admin, finance, international. **Computer sciences:** Computer science. **Education:** General, art, elementary, English, middle, music, physical, secondary. **English:** English lit. **Foreign languages:** Spanish. **Health services:** Art therapy, athletic training, clinical lab assistant, physician assistant, predental, premedicine, prepharmacy, preveterinary. **History:** General. **Human services:** Social work. **Liberal arts:** Arts/sciences. **Math:** General. **Parks/recreation:** Facilities management, health/fitness. **Philosophy/religion:** Religion. **Physical sciences:** Chemistry. **Protective services:** Law enforcement admin. **Psychology:** General. **Social sciences:** International relations, political science, sociology. **Visual/performing arts:** Art, dramatic, fashion design, music, music performance.

Most popular majors. Business/marketing 20%, education 22%, history 6%, psychology 6%, public administration/social services 12%, visual/performing arts 6%.

Technology on campus. 180 workstations in library, computer center, student center. Dormitories wired for high-speed internet access and linked to campus network. Commuter students can connect to campus network. Online course registration, online library, helpline, repair service, wireless network available.

Student life. Freshman orientation: Mandatory. Preregistration for classes offered. **Housing:** Guaranteed on-campus for all undergraduates. Single-sex dorms, special housing for disabled, apartments available. $250 deposit. College townhouses and apartments available to upperclassmen. **Activities:** Bands, campus ministries, choral groups, dance, drama, literary magazine, music ensembles, musical theater, student government, Christian Student Movement, Fellowship of Christian Athletes, Ethos, Black student association, Bailey Mountain Cloggers, outdoor club, Blueprint, student ambassadors, SGA, Mars Hill Steppers.

Athletics. NCAA. **Intercollegiate:** Baseball M, basketball, cross-country, football (tackle) M, golf, lacrosse M, soccer, softball W, swimming, tennis, track and field, volleyball W. **Intramural:** Badminton, basketball, football (non-tackle), soccer, softball, tennis, ultimate frisbee, volleyball, water polo M. **Team name:** Lions.

Student services. Adult student services, chaplain/spiritual director, career counseling, services for economically disadvantaged, student employment services, financial aid counseling, health services, personal counseling, veterans' counselor.

Contact. E-mail: admissions@mhu.edu
Phone: (828) 689-1201 Toll-free number: (866) 642-4968
Fax: (828) 689-1473
Craig Goforth, Dean of Admissions, Mars Hill University, Mars Hill University Admissions Office, Mars Hill, NC 28754

Meredith College
Raleigh, North Carolina
www.meredith.edu
CB member
CB code: 5410

- Private 4-year liberal arts college for women
- Residential campus in large city
- 1,650 degree-seeking undergraduates: 2% part-time, 100% women, 10% African American, 3% Asian American, 3% Hispanic/Latino, 1% Native American, 4% Multi-racial, non-Hispanic, 5% international
- 198 degree-seeking graduate students
- 60% of applicants admitted
- SAT or ACT (ACT writing optional) required
- 62% graduate within 6 years

General. Founded in 1891. Regionally accredited. **Degrees:** 408 bachelor's awarded; master's offered. **ROTC:** Army, Air Force. **Location:** 250 miles from Washington, DC, 375 miles from Atlanta. **Calendar:** Semester, limited summer session. **Full-time faculty:** 126 total; 88% have terminal degrees, 10% minority, 73% women. **Part-time faculty:** 87 total; 29% have terminal degrees, 10% minority, 68% women. **Class size:** 62% < 20, 36% 20-39, 1% 40-49, less than 1% 50-99. **Special facilities:** Amphitheatre, child care laboratory, experimental and clinical psychology laboratories, autism laboratory, astronomy observation deck, electron microscope suite, 15 student/faculty research laboratories, greenhouse.

Freshman class profile. 1,721 applied, 1,033 admitted, 439 enrolled.

Mid 50% test scores		GPA 2.0-2.99:	22%
SAT critical reading:	460-560	Rank in top quarter:	48%
SAT math:	460-570	Rank in top tenth:	20%
ACT composite:	20-25	Return as sophomores:	79%
GPA 3.75 or higher:	17%	Out-of-state:	8%
GPA 3.50-3.74:	23%	Live on campus:	87%
GPA 3.0-3.49:	38%	International:	3%

Basis for selection. GED not accepted. School record (courses taken, grades on academic subjects, and class rank), test scores, and recommendations important. Meredith seeks to enroll qualified students of varying backgrounds, interests and talents and has a need-blind admission policy. Essay and/or interview may be required of some; audition recommended for music majors; portfolio recommended for art majors. **Home schooled:** Interview, letter of recommendation (nonparent) required.

High school preparation. College-preparatory program required. 16 units required. Required units include English 4, mathematics 3, science 3, foreign language 2 and academic electives 1. 3 units required in social studies or history. At least 1 elective required, preferably from core academic subjects.

2016-2017 Annual costs. Tuition/fees: $34,907. Room/board: $10,390. Books/supplies: $850. Personal expenses: $1,250.

Financial aid. Non-need-based: Scholarships awarded for academics, art, leadership, minority status, music/drama, religious affiliation, state residency.

Application procedures. Admission: No deadline. $40 fee, may be waived for applicants with need. Admission notification on a rolling basis beginning on or about 11/1. Must reply by May 1 or within 2 week(s) if notified thereafter. **Financial aid:** Priority date 2/15; no closing date. FAFSA required. Applicants notified on a rolling basis starting 3/15; must reply by 5/1 or within 2 week(s) of notification.

Academics. Undergraduate research program available to students in all disciplines. Post-baccalaureate dietetic internship program; post-baccalaureate certificate in paralegal studies; and pre-health post-baccalaureate certificate are available. **Special study options:** Accelerated study, cooperative education, cross-registration, double major, dual enrollment of high school students, honors, independent study, internships, student-designed major, study abroad, teacher certification program. Study Abroad includes summer programs, semester/year abroad opportunities, and individually-tailored semesters. 3-2 in engineering with NC State University. Sansepolcro, Italy. **Credit/placement by examination:** AP, CLEP, IB, SAT,

ACT, institutional tests. **Support services:** Learning center, reduced course load, remedial instruction, study skills assistance, tutoring, writing center.

Majors. Biology: General. **Business:** Accounting, business admin, fashion. **Communications:** Communications/speech/rhetoric, media studies. **Computer sciences:** Computer science. **Conservation:** Environmental studies. **Education:** Art, music, physical. **English:** English lit. **Foreign languages:** Spanish. **Health services:** Dietetics. **History:** General. **Human services:** Social work. **Math:** General. **Parks/recreation:** Exercise sciences, health/fitness. **Philosophy/religion:** Religion. **Physical sciences:** Chemistry. **Psychology:** General. **Social sciences:** Economics, international relations, political science, sociology, U.S. government. **Visual/performing arts:** Dance, dramatic, fashion design, graphic design, interior design, music, music pedagogy, studio arts. **Work/family studies:** General, child development, food/nutrition.

Most popular majors. Biology 14%, business/marketing 16%, communications/journalism 6%, family/consumer sciences 9%, psychology 9%, social sciences 7%, visual/performing arts 13%.

Technology on campus. Dormitories wired for high-speed internet access and linked to campus network. Commuter students can connect to campus network. Online course registration, online library, helpline, wireless network available.

Student life. Freshman orientation: Mandatory. Preregistration for classes offered. 4-day program before start of classes with extra day for athletes, international students, and students with disabilities. **Policies:** Honor Code is a longstanding tradition that requires individual integrity and community responsibility of all students. Traditional-aged freshmen and sophomores must live on campus except if married or living with parents or other relatives by special permission. **Housing:** Guaranteed on-campus for freshmen. Apartments available. $100 nonrefundable deposit, deadline 5/1. Campus housing available for all 4 years. All on-campus housing is wellness housing. **Activities:** Campus ministries, choral groups, dance, drama, international student organizations, literary magazine, music ensembles, Model UN, musical theater, student government, student newspaper, symphony orchestra, association for cultural awareness, unity council, service council, Habitat for Humanity, Interfaith Council, Angels for the Environment, College Democrats, College Republicans, Christian Association, Catholic Angels.

Athletics. NCAA. **Intercollegiate:** Basketball W, cross-country W, lacrosse W, soccer W, softball W, tennis W, track and field W, volleyball W. **Team name:** Avenging Angels.

Student services. Adult student services, alcohol/substance abuse counseling, chaplain/spiritual director, career counseling, student employment services, financial aid counseling, health services, minority student services, personal counseling, placement for graduates. **Physically disabled:** Services for visually, speech, hearing impaired.

Contact. E-mail: admissions@meredith.edu
Phone: (919) 760-8581 Toll-free number: (800) 637-3348
Fax: (919) 760-2348
Shery Boyles, Director of Admissions, Meredith College, 3800 Hillsborough Street, Raleigh, NC 27607-5298

Methodist University
Fayetteville, North Carolina
www.methodist.edu   CB code: 5426

- Private 4-year liberal arts college affiliated with the United Methodist Church
- Residential campus in small city
- 2,173 degree-seeking undergraduates
- SAT or ACT (ACT writing optional) required

General. Founded in 1956. Regionally accredited. **Degrees:** 328 bachelor's, 7 associate awarded; master's, professional offered. **ROTC:** Army, Air Force. **Location:** 50 miles from Raleigh-Durham. **Calendar:** Semester, extensive summer session. **Full-time faculty:** 157 total; 61% have terminal degrees, 15% minority, 47% women. **Part-time faculty:** 80 total; 20% minority, 44% women. **Class size:** 74% < 20, 25% 20-39, less than 1% 40-49, less than 1% 50-99. **Special facilities:** Computer-assisted English composition laboratory, psychology computer-experimental laboratory, nature trail, professional golf and tennis management center, 18-hole golf course and driving range, environmental simulation center (virtual reality laboratory).

Freshman class profile.

GPA 3.75 or higher:	31%	Rank in top tenth:	11%
GPA 3.50-3.74:	13%	Out-of-state:	40%
GPA 3.0-3.49:	32%	Live on campus:	84%
GPA 2.0-2.99:	24%	Fraternities:	8%
Rank in top quarter:	33%	Sororities:	10%

Basis for selection. High school record (GPA), curriculum, test scores carefully considered. All prospective student files reviewed on individual basis. Extracurricular achievements and teacher/counselor recommendations also considered. Students who transfer English 101 credits must take institutional English Placement Exam. SAT/ACT scores not required of transfer students with more than 31 semester hours of transferable credit. Essay and interview recommended for all students; audition recommended for drama and music majors; portfolio recommended for art majors. **Home schooled:** Transcript of courses and grades required.

High school preparation. College-preparatory program required. 16 units required. Required and recommended units include English 4, mathematics 3, history 2, science 2 and foreign language 2.

2015-2016 Annual costs. Tuition/fees: $30,530. Room/board: $11,344. Books/supplies: $1,400. Personal expenses: $5,265.

Financial aid. Non-need-based: Scholarships awarded for academics, alumni affiliation, leadership, music/drama, religious affiliation.

Application procedures. Admission: No deadline. $50 fee, may be waived for applicants with need, free for online applicants. Admission notification on a rolling basis beginning on or about 9/1. Must reply by May 1 or within 2 week(s) if notified thereafter. **Financial aid:** Priority date 8/1; no closing date. FAFSA required. Applicants notified on a rolling basis starting 3/6; must reply within 2 week(s) of notification.

Academics. Special study options: Distance learning, double major, dual enrollment of high school students, ESL, honors, independent study, internships, liberal arts/career combination, study abroad, teacher certification program, Washington semester, weekend college. **Credit/placement by examination:** AP, CLEP, IB, SAT, ACT, institutional tests. 45 credit hours maximum toward associate degree, 45 toward bachelor's. **Support services:** Learning center, reduced course load, remedial instruction, study skills assistance, tutoring, writing center.

Majors. Biology: General, botany, cellular/molecular, conservation, ecology, exercise physiology, microbiology, zoology. **Business:** Accounting, business admin, finance, hospitality admin, hospitality/recreation, management information systems, marketing, resort management, tourism/travel. **Communications:** Communications/speech/rhetoric, journalism, media studies, organizational. **Computer sciences:** General, computer graphics, computer science, web page design. **Education:** General, art, biology, chemistry, elementary, English, foreign languages, mathematics, middle, music, physical, secondary, social studies, special ed. **English:** English lit, rhetoric/composition. **Foreign languages:** French, Spanish. **Health services:** Athletic training, facilities admin, health care admin, nursing (RN), physician assistant, predental, premedicine, prenursing, prepharmacy, preveterinary. **History:** General. **Human services:** Social work. **Liberal arts:** Arts/sciences. **Math:** General. **Parks/recreation:** Exercise sciences, facilities management, golf management, health/fitness, sports admin. **Philosophy/religion:** Philosophy, religion. **Physical sciences:** Chemistry, forensic chemistry. **Protective services:** Criminal justice, forensics, homeland security, law enforcement admin. **Psychology:** General. **Social sciences:** Political science, sociology. **Theology:** Religious ed. **Visual/performing arts:** General, art, ceramics, graphic design, music, music performance, painting, printmaking, sculpture, studio arts.

Most popular majors. Biology 6%, business/marketing 33%, education 6%, health sciences 7%, public administration/social services 6%, security/protective services 7%, social sciences 8%.

Technology on campus. 220 workstations in library, computer center, student center. Dormitories wired for high-speed internet access and linked to campus network. Commuter students can connect to campus network. Online course registration, online library, helpline, wireless network available.

Student life. Freshman orientation: Available. Preregistration for classes offered. Typically held the weekend before classes begin in Fall. **Housing:** Guaranteed on-campus for all undergraduates. Coed dorms, single-sex dorms, special housing for disabled, apartments, fraternity/sorority housing, themed housing, wellness housing available. $100 nonrefundable deposit, deadline 5/1. Health/wellness hall, first-year experience hall available. **Activities:** Bands, campus ministries, choral groups, dance, drama, international student organizations, literary magazine, music ensembles, Model UN, musical theater, radio station, student government, student newspaper, symphony orchestra, Fellowship of Christian Athletes, Young Democrats/Republicans, African American culture society, student activities committee, commuting student organization.

Athletics. NCAA. **Intercollegiate:** Baseball M, basketball, cheerleading, cross-country, football (tackle) M, golf, lacrosse W, soccer, softball W, tennis, track and field, volleyball W. **Intramural:** Basketball, cheerleading W, football (non-tackle), golf, racquetball, soccer, softball, table tennis, tennis, volleyball. **Team name:** Monarchs.

Student services. Alcohol/substance abuse counseling, chaplain/spiritual director, career counseling, student employment services, financial aid counseling, health services, personal counseling, placement for graduates, veterans' counselor, women's services. **Physically disabled:** Services for visually impaired.

Contact. E-mail: admissions@methodist.edu
Phone: (910) 630-7027 Toll-free number: (800) 488-7110 ext. 7028
Fax: (910) 630-7285
Jamie Legg, Dean of Admissions, Methodist University, 5400 Ramsey Street, Fayetteville, NC 28311-1420

Mid-Atlantic Christian University
Elizabeth City, North Carolina
www.macuniversity.edu   CB code: 5597

▶ Private 4-year university and Bible college affiliated with the Church of Christ

▶ Residential campus in large town

▶ 204 degree-seeking undergraduates: 14% part-time, 58% women, 22% African American, 1% Asian American, 2% Hispanic/Latino, 1% Multi-racial, non-Hispanic

▶ 36% of applicants admitted

▶ SAT or ACT (ACT writing optional), application essay required

▶ 38% graduate within 6 years

General. Founded in 1948. Regionally accredited; also accredited by ABHE. **Degrees:** 18 bachelor's, 4 associate awarded. **ROTC:** Army. **Location:** 50 miles from Norfolk, Virginia. **Calendar:** Semester, limited summer session. **Full-time faculty:** 9 total; 67% have terminal degrees, 22% minority, 22% women. **Part-time faculty:** 28 total; 46% have terminal degrees, 7% minority, 36% women. **Class size:** 78% < 20, 17% 20-39, 4% 40-49.

Freshman class profile. 225 applied, 82 admitted, 55 enrolled.

Mid 50% test scores		GPA 3.50-3.74:	20%
SAT critical reading:	420-550	GPA 3.0-3.49:	24%
SAT math:	390-560	GPA 2.0-2.99:	34%
SAT writing:	360-520	Rank in top quarter:	38%
ACT composite:	16-23	Rank in top tenth:	18%
GPA 3.75 or higher:	22%	Return as sophomores:	74%

Basis for selection. Evidence of Christian character, school achievement record, test scores, school and community activities, recommendations important. Interview recommended if questions arise from references or academic record. **Home schooled:** Transcript of courses and grades, state high school equivalency certificate required.

High school preparation. 20 units required. Required and recommended units include English 4, mathematics 3, social studies 2, history 2, science 3 (laboratory 2), foreign language 6, computer science 1 and academic electives 4.

2015-2016 Annual costs. Tuition/fees: $12,600. Room/board: $8,200. Books/supplies: $1,000. Personal expenses: $2,500.

Financial aid. Non-need-based: Scholarships awarded for academics, alumni affiliation, leadership, music/drama, religious affiliation.

Application procedures. Admission: No deadline. $50 fee, may be waived for applicants with need. Admission notification on a rolling basis beginning on or about 9/1. Must reply by May 1 or within 2 week(s) if notified thereafter. **Financial aid:** Priority date 2/1; no closing date. FAFSA, institutional form required. Applicants notified on a rolling basis starting 5/1; must reply within 2 week(s) of notification.

Academics. Special study options: Cross-registration, distance learning, double major, dual enrollment of high school students, independent study, internships, teacher certification program. **Credit/placement by examination:** AP, CLEP, SAT, ACT, institutional tests. 8 credit hours maximum toward associate degree, 16 toward bachelor's. **Support services:** Learning center, reduced course load, remedial instruction, study skills assistance, writing center.

Majors. Business: Business admin. **Education:** Elementary. **Foreign languages:** Applied linguistics. **Psychology:** Counseling. **Theology:** Bible, missionary, pastoral counseling, preministerial, religious ed, theology, youth ministry. **Work/family studies:** Family systems.

Most popular majors. Business/marketing 13%, psychology 10%, theological studies 74%.

Technology on campus. 24 workstations in dormitories, library, computer center. Dormitories wired for high-speed internet access and linked to campus network. Commuter students can connect to campus network. Online course registration, online library, helpline, wireless network available.

Student life. Freshman orientation: Mandatory, $130 fee. Preregistration for classes offered. **Policies:** Religious observance required. **Housing:** Guaranteed on-campus for all undergraduates. Single-sex dorms, special housing for disabled, apartments, wellness housing available. $75 nonrefundable deposit, deadline 4/1. **Activities:** Campus ministries, choral groups, music ensembles, student government.

Athletics. USCAA. **Intercollegiate:** Basketball, golf, soccer M, volleyball W. **Intramural:** Basketball, bowling, football (non-tackle), golf, table tennis, tennis, volleyball. **Team name:** Mustangs.

Student services. Chaplain/spiritual director, career counseling, student employment services, financial aid counseling, personal counseling, placement for graduates. **Physically disabled:** Services for hearing impaired.

Contact. E-mail: admissions@macuniversity.edu
Phone: (252) 334-2028 Toll-free number: (866) 996-MACU
Fax: (252) 334-2064
Dan Smith, Director of Admissions, Mid-Atlantic Christian University, 715 North Poindexter Street, Elizabeth City, NC 27909

Miller-Motte College: Wilmington
Wilmington, North Carolina
www.miller-motte.edu   CB code: 3342

▶ For-profit 4-year technical college

▶ Commuter campus in small city

▶ 3,463 undergraduates

▶ Interview required

General. Accredited by ACICS. **Degrees:** 53 bachelor's, 389 associate awarded. **Location:** 145 miles from Raleigh. **Calendar:** Quarter, extensive summer session. **Full-time faculty:** 13 total. **Part-time faculty:** 29 total.

Basis for selection. Minimum test score of 15 on Wonderlic test for admission, 18 for Medical Assisting, 21 for Surgical Technology, 20 for Computer Systems Network Administrator, 18 for Criminal Justice, 18 for Paralegal, and 18 for Dental Assisting. **Home schooled:** Transcript of courses and grades required.

High school preparation. 17 units recommended. Recommended units include English 4, mathematics 4, social studies 4, science 4 (laboratory 1).

2015-2016 Annual costs. Books/supplies: $1,800. Personal expenses: $3,350. **Additional information:** Certificate programs: $9,660-$20,788, books and supplies $400-$3,900. Associate programs: $26,160-$29,136, books and supplies $4,550-$5,200. Bachelor's programs: $29,182-$31,048, books and supplies $3,900.

Financial aid. All financial aid based on need.

Application procedures. Admission: No deadline. $40 fee. Application must be submitted on paper. Admission notification on a rolling basis. **Financial aid:** No deadline. FAFSA, institutional form required.

Academics. Special study options: Distance learning, double major, internships. **Credit/placement by examination:** AP, CLEP, institutional tests. 46 credit hours maximum toward associate degree. **Support services:** Learning center, reduced course load, remedial instruction, study skills assistance, tutoring.

Majors. Business: Business admin. **Protective services:** Law enforcement admin.

Most popular majors. Business/marketing 50%, health sciences 50%.

Technology on campus. 120 workstations in library, computer center. Commuter students can connect to campus network. Online library, repair service, student web hosting available.

Student life. Freshman orientation: Mandatory. Preregistration for classes offered. **Activities:** Student newspaper.

Athletics. **Team name:** Marlin.

Student services. Career counseling, financial aid counseling, placement for graduates.

Four-Year Colleges

Contact. Phone: (910) 392-4660 Toll-free number: (800) 784-2110
Fax: (910) 799-6224
Adam Merritt, Director of Admissions, Miller-Motte College: Wilmington,
5000 Market Street, Wilmington, NC 28405

Montreat College
Montreat, North Carolina
www.montreat.edu   **CB code: 5423**

- Private 4-year liberal arts college affiliated with the Presbyterian Church Reformed and Independent
- Residential campus in small town
- 724 degree-seeking undergraduates: 30% part-time, 55% women, 16% African American, 2% Asian American, 3% Hispanic/Latino, 1% Native American, 3% Multi-racial, non-Hispanic, 5% international
- 200 degree-seeking graduate students
- 54% of applicants admitted
- SAT or ACT (ACT writing optional), application essay required

General. Founded in 1916. Regionally accredited. North Carolina's only member institute of the Council for Christian Colleges and Universities. **Degrees:** 112 bachelor's, 19 associate awarded; master's offered. **Location:** 16 miles from Asheville. **Calendar:** Semester, limited summer session. **Full-time faculty:** 31 total; 74% have terminal degrees, 6% minority, 23% women. **Part-time faculty:** 119 total; 52% have terminal degrees, 5% minority, 40% women. **Class size:** 81% < 20, 19% 20-39, less than 1% 40-49. **Special facilities:** Ropes course, climbing wall, chapel of the prodigal, Black Mountain Campus.

Freshman class profile. 819 applied, 442 admitted, 155 enrolled.

Mid 50% test scores		GPA 2.0-2.99:	39%
SAT critical reading:	430-540	Rank in top quarter:	26%
SAT math:	420-520	Rank in top tenth:	9%
ACT composite:	18-23	Return as sophomores:	59%
GPA 3.75 or higher:	14%	Out-of-state:	42%
GPA 3.50-3.74:	11%	Live on campus:	99%
GPA 3.0-3.49:	36%	International:	4%

Basis for selection. Decisions are criteria-based, using GPA and SAT/ACT scores as initial qualifiers. Essay, recommendation, and extracurricular activities also considered. Interview required for students who do not meet standard admission requirements. **Home schooled:** Transcript of courses and grades, letter of recommendation (nonparent) required. **Learning Disabled:** Students with documented learning disabilities are referred to the Director of Student Success before an admissions decision is made.

High school preparation. Required units include English 4, mathematics 3, social studies 3, science 3 and foreign language 1.

2015-2016 Annual costs. Tuition/fees: $24,240. Room/board: $8,266. Books/supplies: $1,236. Personal expenses: $1,180.

2014-2015 Financial aid. Need-based: 95 full-time freshmen applied for aid; 85 deemed to have need; 85 received aid. Average need met was 77%. Average scholarship/grant was $17,229; average loan $3,376. 54% of total undergraduate aid awarded as scholarships/grants, 46% as loans/jobs. **Non-need-based:** Awarded to 183 full-time undergraduates, including 62 freshmen. Scholarships awarded for academics, alumni affiliation, art, athletics, leadership, minority status, music/drama, religious affiliation, state residency.

Application procedures. Admission: No deadline. No application fee. Admission notification on a rolling basis beginning on or about 9/1. **Financial aid:** Priority date 3/1; no closing date. FAFSA required. Applicants notified on a rolling basis starting 3/1; must reply within 2 week(s) of notification.

Academics. Special study options: Accelerated study, distance learning, double major, dual enrollment of high school students, honors, internships, liberal arts/career combination, student-designed major, study abroad, teacher certification program, Washington semester. **Credit/placement by examination:** AP, CLEP, IB, SAT, ACT. 15 credit hours maximum toward associate degree, 30 toward bachelor's. **Support services:** Reduced course load, study skills assistance, tutoring, writing center.

Majors. Area/ethnic studies: American. **Biology:** General. **Business:** Business admin, international, marketing. **Communications:** Media studies. **Computer sciences:** General. **Conservation:** Environmental studies. **Education:** Elementary. **English:** English lit. **History:** General. **Parks/recreation:** General. **Philosophy/religion:** General, Christian. **Psychology:** General. **Theology:** Bible, missionary, religious ed, youth ministry. **Visual/performing arts:** Music management, music performance.

Most popular majors. Biology 9%, business/marketing 46%, psychology 24%, theological studies 6%.

Technology on campus. 60 workstations in library, computer center, student center. Dormitories wired for high-speed internet access and linked to campus network. Helpline, repair service, wireless network available.

Student life. Freshman orientation: Mandatory. Preregistration for classes offered. 5 days before classes start; pre-orientation program, Wilderness Journey, available at extra cost. **Policies:** No alcohol on campus. Religious observance required. **Housing:** Guaranteed on-campus for all undergraduates. Single-sex dorms, apartments available. $150 fully refundable deposit, deadline 8/15. 351 spaces available for undergraduate students. **Activities:** Concert band, campus ministries, choral groups, drama, literary magazine, music ensembles, student government, student newspaper, missions club, Fellowship of Christian Athletes, Young Life.

Athletics. NAIA. **Intercollegiate:** Baseball M, basketball, cross-country, golf, soccer, softball W, track and field, volleyball W. **Intramural:** Basketball, football (non-tackle), soccer, softball, table tennis, tennis, volleyball. **Team name:** Cavaliers.

Student services. Adult student services, alcohol/substance abuse counseling, chaplain/spiritual director, career counseling, student employment services, financial aid counseling, health services, personal counseling, placement for graduates, veterans' counselor. **Physically disabled:** Services for visually, speech, hearing impaired.

Contact. E-mail: admissions@montreat.edu
Phone: (800) 622-6968 Toll-free number: (800) 622-6968
Fax: (828) 669-0120
Tony Robinson, Director of Enrollment Development & Outreach,
Montreat College, P.O. Box 1267, Montreat, NC 28757

North Carolina Agricultural and Technical State University
Greensboro, North Carolina   **CB member**
www.ncat.edu   **CB code: 5003**

- Public 4-year university
- Residential campus in small city
- 9,036 degree-seeking undergraduates
- 60% of applicants admitted
- SAT or ACT with writing required

General. Founded in 1891. Regionally accredited. **Degrees:** 1,293 bachelor's awarded; master's, doctoral offered. **ROTC:** Army, Air Force. **Location:** 60 miles from Raleigh, 91 miles from Charlotte. **Calendar:** Semester. **Full-time faculty:** 472 total; 3% have terminal degrees, 54% minority, 43% women. **Part-time faculty:** 213 total; less than 1% have terminal degrees, 62% minority, 56% women. **Class size:** 40% < 20, 30% 20-39, 6% 40-49, 14% 50-99, 10% >100. **Special facilities:** University galleries (including African heritage collection and African American artists' collection), planetarium, Olympic track.

Freshman class profile. 6,010 applied, 3,635 admitted, 1,780 enrolled.

Mid 50% test scores		GPA 2.0-2.99:	85%
SAT critical reading:	410-490	Rank in top quarter:	34%
SAT math:	420-500	Rank in top tenth:	11%
SAT writing:	390-470	Out-of-state:	23%
ACT composite:	16-21	Live on campus:	98%
GPA 3.0-3.49:	9%		

Basis for selection. High school GPA, class rank, test scores, recommendations, course selection reviewed. SAT preferred, but ACT accepted. Audition recommended for music programs; portfolio recommended for art programs. **Home schooled:** State high school equivalency certificate required.

High school preparation. College-preparatory program required. 19 units required. Required units include English 4, mathematics 4, social studies 1, history 1, science 3 (laboratory 1), foreign language 2 and academic electives 4.

2015-2016 Annual costs. Tuition/fees: $5,972; $18,732 out-of-state. Room/board: $6,842. Books/supplies: $1,400. Personal expenses: $1,500.

Financial aid. Non-need-based: Scholarships awarded for academics.

Application procedures. Admission: Priority date 2/15; deadline 4/1. $55 fee. Application must be submitted on paper. Admission notification on a rolling basis. Must reply by May 1 or within 2 week(s) if notified thereafter. Please apply for housing immediately upon being accepted for admissions.

Housing is filled on a first-come, first-served basis. **Financial aid:** Priority date 3/1; no closing date. FAFSA required. Applicants notified on a rolling basis starting 4/15; must reply within 2 week(s) of notification.

Academics. Free tutoring in math, science, business, and more. Student Athlete Academic Enhancement Program (SAAE). **Special study options:** Accelerated study, cooperative education, cross-registration, distance learning, double major, dual enrollment of high school students, honors, internships, liberal arts/career combination, study abroad, teacher certification program. **Credit/placement by examination:** AP, CLEP, IB, institutional tests. **Support services:** Learning center, reduced course load, remedial instruction, study skills assistance, tutoring, writing center.

Majors. Architecture: Landscape. **Biology:** General. **Business:** Accounting, business admin, finance, marketing, transportation. **Communications:** Media studies. **Computer sciences:** Computer science. **Education:** General, agricultural, biology, business, chemistry, driver/safety, early childhood, elementary, English, family/consumer sciences, foreign languages, French, history, kindergarten/preschool, mathematics, music, physics, science, secondary, social science, Spanish, special ed, speech, technology/industrial arts, trade/industrial. **Engineering:** General, agricultural, architectural, biomedical, chemical, civil, computer, electrical, industrial, mechanical, surveying. **English:** English lit, rhetoric/composition. **Foreign languages:** French. **Health services:** Occupational health. **History:** General. **Human services:** Social work. **Liberal arts:** Arts/sciences. **Math:** General, applied. **Parks/recreation:** Facilities management, health/fitness, sports admin. **Physical sciences:** Atmospheric science, chemistry, physics. **Protective services:** Criminal justice. **Psychology:** General. **Social sciences:** General, economics, political science, sociology. **Visual/performing arts:** General, art, dramatic, graphic design, music. **Work/family studies:** General, child development, food/nutrition.

Most popular majors. Business/marketing 10%, communications/journalism 6%, engineering/engineering technologies 17%, liberal arts 9%, physical sciences 12%, psychology 8%.

Technology on campus. 675 workstations in library, computer center. Dormitories wired for high-speed internet access and linked to campus network. Commuter students can connect to campus network. Online course registration, online library, helpline, wireless network available.

Student life. Freshman orientation: Mandatory, $175 fee. Preregistration for classes offered. **Housing:** Guaranteed on-campus for freshmen. Coed dorms, single-sex dorms, wellness housing available. $150 deposit. Housing provided by North Carolina A&T University Foundation, Inc. **Activities:** Bands, campus ministries, choral groups, dance, drama, international student organizations, music ensembles, radio station, student government, student newspaper, symphony orchestra, TV station, National Society of Black Engineers, gospel choir, Toastmasters International, karate team, Caribbean student association, Chinese student association, environmental science club, Progressive Republicans, Students Against Driving Drunk, Young Democrats.

Athletics. NCAA. **Intercollegiate:** Baseball M, basketball, bowling W, cross-country, football (tackle) M, softball W, swimming W, tennis W, track and field, volleyball W. **Intramural:** Badminton, baseball M, basketball, bowling W, cross-country, football (tackle) M, golf, handball, racquetball, soccer, softball W, swimming, table tennis, tennis, track and field, volleyball. **Team name:** Aggies.

Student services. Adult student services, alcohol/substance abuse counseling, career counseling, student employment services, financial aid counseling, health services, minority student services, personal counseling, placement for graduates, veterans' counselor. **Physically disabled:** Services for visually, speech, hearing impaired.

Contact. E-mail: uadmit@ncat.edu
Phone: (336) 334-7946 Toll-free number: (800) 443-8964
Fax: (336) 334-7478
Cheryl Pollard-Burns, Director of Admissions, North Carolina Agricultural and Technical State University, Webb Hall, Greensboro, NC 27411-0002

North Carolina Central University
Durham, North Carolina   CB member
www.nccu.edu   CB code: 5495

- Public 4-year university
- Commuter campus in small city
- 5,797 degree-seeking undergraduates: 12% part-time, 67% women, 81% African American, 1% Asian American, 4% Hispanic/Latino, 5% Multiracial, non-Hispanic
- 1,763 degree-seeking graduate students
- 66% of applicants admitted

- SAT or ACT with writing required
- 42% graduate within 6 years

General. Founded in 1910. Regionally accredited. Historically, the majority of students have been African American. **Degrees:** 1,094 bachelor's awarded; master's, professional, doctoral offered. **ROTC:** Army, Air Force. **Location:** 23 miles from Raleigh. **Calendar:** Semester, extensive summer session. **Full-time faculty:** 391 total; 74% have terminal degrees, 74% minority, 51% women. **Part-time faculty:** 162 total; 41% have terminal degrees, 68% minority, 62% women. **Class size:** 39% < 20, 51% 20-39, 6% 40-49, 4% 50-99, less than 1% >100. **Special facilities:** Collection of primary resources on black life and culture, art museum with works of Afro-American culture.

Freshman class profile. 7,651 applied, 5,040 admitted, 1,108 enrolled.

Mid 50% test scores			
SAT critical reading:	400-470	GPA 3.0-3.49:	33%
SAT math:	400-470	GPA 2.0-2.99:	37%
SAT writing:	380-460	Rank in top quarter:	22%
ACT composite:	16-19	Rank in top tenth:	6%
GPA 3.75 or higher:	16%	Return as sophomores:	80%
GPA 3.50-3.74:	13%	Out-of-state:	13%
		Live on campus:	92%

Basis for selection. Academic achievement, class rank, test scores important. SAT and SAT Subject Tests or ACT recommended. SAT preferred, ACT also accepted. Audition required for music programs. **Home schooled:** Transcript of courses and grades, state high school equivalency certificate required.

High school preparation. College-preparatory program required. 20 units required. Required units include English 4, mathematics 4, social studies 2, history 1, science 3 (laboratory 1), foreign language 2 and academic electives 3. Social studies units must include 1 U.S. history. One foreign language, and 1 math recommended during 12th grade. Students who graduate high school in and after 2006 must have one additional math course from the following: pre-calculus, AP statistics, AP calculus, IB math level II, integrated math IV, discrete math, advanced models and functions.

2015-2016 Annual costs. Tuition/fees: $5,755; $17,793 out-of-state. Room/board: $8,165. Books/supplies: $1,500. Personal expenses: $2,611.

2014-2015 Financial aid. Need-based: 1,086 full-time freshmen applied for aid; 1,030 deemed to have need; 1,025 received aid. Average need met was 58%. Average scholarship/grant was $8,138; average loan $3,650. 50% of total undergraduate aid awarded as scholarships/grants, 50% as loans/jobs. **Non-need-based:** Awarded to 860 full-time undergraduates, including 233 freshmen. Scholarships awarded for academics, alumni affiliation, art, athletics, leadership, music/drama, ROTC. **Additional information:** Departmental grants based on need plus other available criteria.

Application procedures. Admission: Closing date 8/1. $40 fee. Admission notification on a rolling basis beginning on or about 10/15. Early admission available with permission from high school principal and academic dean. **Financial aid:** Closing date 3/1. FAFSA required. Applicants notified by 3/1; must reply within 2 week(s) of notification.

Academics. Special study options: Accelerated study, distance learning, double major, dual enrollment of high school students, ESL, exchange student, honors, independent study, internships, study abroad, teacher certification program, weekend college. **Credit/placement by examination:** AP, CLEP, institutional tests. 30 credit hours maximum toward bachelor's degree. **Support services:** Learning center, remedial instruction, study skills assistance, tutoring, writing center.

Majors. Biology: General. **Business:** Accounting, business admin, hospitality admin. **Communications:** Media studies. **Computer sciences:** Computer science, information systems. **Conservation:** Environmental science. **Education:** Art, biology, chemistry, drama/dance, elementary, English, family/consumer sciences, French, health, history, kindergarten/preschool, mathematics, middle, music, physical, physics, Spanish. **English:** English lit. **Foreign languages:** French, Spanish. **Health services:** Athletic training, nursing (RN), public health ed. **History:** General. **Human services:** Social work. **Math:** General. **Parks/recreation:** Facilities management, health/fitness. **Physical sciences:** Chemistry, physics. **Protective services:** Law enforcement admin. **Psychology:** General. **Social sciences:** Geography, political science, sociology. **Visual/performing arts:** Art, dramatic, jazz, music. **Work/family studies:** General.

Most popular majors. Biology 6%, business/marketing 13%, family/consumer sciences 12%, health sciences 11%, psychology 13%, security/protective services 12%.

Technology on campus. 400 workstations in dormitories, library, computer center. Dormitories wired for high-speed internet access and linked to campus network. Commuter students can connect to campus network. Online course registration, online library, helpline, repair service, wireless network available.

Student life. **Freshman orientation:** Mandatory, $125 fee. Preregistration for classes offered. **Housing:** Coed dorms, single-sex dorms available. $150 nonrefundable deposit, deadline 5/1. Coed honors dormitory available. **Activities:** Bands, campus ministries, choral groups, dance, drama, literary magazine, music ensembles, radio station, student government, student newspaper.

Athletics. NAIA, NCAA. **Intercollegiate:** Basketball, bowling, cheerleading M, cross-country, football (tackle) M, golf, softball W, tennis, track and field, volleyball W. **Team name:** Eagles.

Student services. Career counseling, student employment services, health services, on-campus daycare, personal counseling, placement for graduates, veterans' counselor.

Contact. E-mail: admissions@nccu.edu
Phone: (919) 560-6298 Toll-free number: (877) 667-7533
Fax: (919) 530-7625
Monica Leach, AVC for Enrollment Management, North Carolina Central University, PO Box 19717, Durham, NC 27707

North Carolina State University
Raleigh, North Carolina CB member
www.ncsu.edu CB code: 5496

- Public 4-year university
- Residential campus in large city
- 22,458 degree-seeking undergraduates: 7% part-time, 45% women, 6% African American, 5% Asian American, 5% Hispanic/Latino, 4% Multiracial, non-Hispanic, 4% international
- 9,036 degree-seeking graduate students
- 50% of applicants admitted
- SAT or ACT (ACT writing optional) required
- 76% graduate within 6 years

General. Founded in 1887. Regionally accredited. **Degrees:** 5,555 bachelor's, 173 associate awarded; master's, professional, doctoral offered. **ROTC:** Army, Naval, Air Force. **Location:** One mile from downtown. **Calendar:** Semester, extensive summer session. **Full-time faculty:** 1,706 total; 85% have terminal degrees, 18% minority, 35% women. **Part-time faculty:** 328 total; 74% have terminal degrees, 9% minority, 40% women. **Class size:** 35% < 20, 41% 20-39, 7% 40-49, 11% 50-99, 6% >100. **Special facilities:** Three electron microscopes, phytotron, research farms, 2 campus theaters, craft center, stable isotope laboratory, teaching forest, wood products laboratory, coastal marine science laboratory, arboretum, 80,000 acres of research forests and research farm lands, fiber, fabric, and garment manufacturing equipment.

Freshman class profile. 21,099 applied, 10,579 admitted, 4,212 enrolled.

Mid 50% test scores		Rank in top quarter:	87%
SAT critical reading:	570-650	Rank in top tenth:	51%
SAT math:	590-680	Return as sophomores:	94%
SAT writing:	540-630	Out-of-state:	12%
ACT composite:	27-31	Live on campus:	79%
GPA 3.75 or higher:	46%	International:	5%
GPA 3.50-3.74:	32%	Fraternities:	10%
GPA 3.0-3.49:	21%	Sororities:	18%
GPA 2.0-2.99:	1%		

Basis for selection. School academic record, standardized test scores important. Counselor evaluations, extracurricular activities also considered. Preference given to students with exceptionally strong high school record. Level and difficulty of courses considered. Weighted grades for advanced, honors, AP courses considered. All applicants to the UNC system, except those exempted by current campus policies, must submit SAT or ACT scores. Essay recommended for all students. Interview and portfolio required for College of Design applicants. Verification of golf playing ability required for Professional Golf Management Program.

High school preparation. College-preparatory program required. 16 units required. Required units include English 4, mathematics 4, social studies 1, history 1, science 3 (laboratory 1) and foreign language 2. Science units should include 1 life or biological science, 1 physical science, and 1 laboratory science. Honors, advanced, AP and IB courses given extra weight.

2015-2016 Annual costs. Tuition/fees: $8,581; $24,932 out-of-state. Room/board: $10,311. Books/supplies: $1,082. Personal expenses: $1,548.

2015-2016 Financial aid. **Need-based:** 3,342 full-time freshmen applied for aid; 2,010 deemed to have need; 1,972 received aid. Average need met was 80%. Average scholarship/grant was $10,186; average loan $2,862. 68% of total undergraduate aid awarded as scholarships/grants, 32% as loans/jobs. **Non-need-based:** Awarded to 2,642 full-time undergraduates, including 693

freshmen. Scholarships awarded for academics, alumni affiliation, athletics, leadership, ROTC, state residency. **Additional information:** Freshman Merit Scholarships; students submitting complete admissions application by the November 1 Early Action deadline automatically considered, additional information may be required after initial review.

Application procedures. **Admission:** Priority date 10/15; deadline 1/15 (receipt date). $80 fee, may be waived for applicants with need. Application must be submitted online. Admission notification by 3/30. Admission notification on a rolling basis beginning on or about 1/30. Must reply by May 1 or within 2 week(s) if notified thereafter. Students applying to College of Design studio majors must submit application by 11/1. Selected candidates will be invited to interview. **Financial aid:** Priority date 3/1; no closing date. FAFSA required. Applicants notified on a rolling basis starting 4/1.

Academics. **Special study options:** Accelerated study, combined bachelor's/graduate degree, cooperative education, cross-registration, distance learning, double major, dual enrollment of high school students, ESL, exchange student, honors, independent study, internships, liberal arts/career combination, student-designed major, study abroad, teacher certification program. **Credit/placement by examination:** AP, CLEP, IB, SAT, ACT, institutional tests. **Support services:** Learning center, pre-admission summer program, reduced course load, remedial instruction, study skills assistance, tutoring, writing center.

Majors. **Architecture:** Architecture, environmental design. **Area/ethnic studies:** German. **Biology:** General, biochemistry, botany, genetics, microbiology, zoology. **Business:** Accounting, business admin, managerial economics. **Communications:** Communications/speech/rhetoric. **Computer sciences:** Computer science. **Conservation:** General, environmental science, forest management, forestry, management/policy, wood science. **Education:** General, agricultural, elementary, mathematics, middle, science, technology/industrial arts. **Engineering:** General, aerospace, agricultural, biomedical, chemical, civil, computer, construction, electrical, environmental, industrial, materials, mechanical, nuclear, textile. **English:** English lit. **Foreign languages:** General, French, Spanish. **History:** General. **Human services:** Social work. **Liberal arts:** Arts/sciences. **Math:** General, applied, statistics. **Parks/recreation:** Facilities management, sports admin. **Philosophy/religion:** Philosophy, religion. **Physical sciences:** Atmospheric science, chemistry, geology, oceanography, physics. **Psychology:** General. **Social sciences:** Anthropology, criminology, geography, political science, sociology. **Visual/performing arts:** Art history/conservation, design, graphic design, industrial design, studio arts management.

Most popular majors. Agriculture 7%, biology 10%, business/marketing 14%, engineering/engineering technologies 25%.

Technology on campus. 3,000 workstations in dormitories, library, computer center, student center, student center. Dormitories wired for high-speed internet access and linked to campus network. Commuter students can connect to campus network. Online course registration, helpline, repair service, student web hosting, wireless network available.

Student life. **Freshman orientation:** Mandatory, $150 fee. Preregistration for classes offered. 2-day program. **Housing:** Coed dorms, single-sex dorms, special housing for disabled, apartments, fraternity/sorority housing, themed housing, wellness housing available. Living/learning villages available. **Activities:** Bands, campus ministries, choral groups, dance, drama, film society, international student organizations, literary magazine, music ensembles, Model UN, musical theater, radio station, student government, student newspaper, symphony orchestra, Alpha Phi Omega, Baptist Student Union, Campus Crusade for Christ, Circle-K, international student board, Young Democrats, Young Republicans, Society of Afro-American Culture, YMCA.

Athletics. NCAA. **Intercollegiate:** Baseball M, basketball, cheerleading, cross-country, diving, football (tackle) M, golf, gymnastics W, rifle, soccer, softball W, swimming, tennis, track and field, volleyball W, wrestling M. **Intramural:** Archery, badminton, baseball M, basketball, bowling, cross-country, fencing, field hockey W, football (non-tackle), golf, gymnastics, handball, ice hockey M, lacrosse M, racquetball, rugby M, sailing, skiing, skin diving, soccer, softball, squash, swimming, table tennis, tennis, track and field, volleyball, wrestling M. **Team name:** Wolfpack.

Student services. Adult student services, alcohol/substance abuse counseling, chaplain/spiritual director, career counseling, student employment services, financial aid counseling, health services, legal services, minority student services, on-campus daycare, personal counseling, placement for graduates, veterans' counselor, women's services. **Physically disabled:** Services for visually, speech, hearing impaired.

Contact. E-mail: undergrad-admissions@ncsu.edu
Phone: (919) 515-2434 Fax: (919) 515-5039
Thomas Griffin, Director of Undergraduate Admissions, North Carolina State University, Campus Box 7103, Raleigh, NC 27695-7103

North Carolina Wesleyan College
Rocky Mount, North Carolina
www.ncwc.edu   CB code: 5501

- Private 4-year liberal arts college affiliated with the United Methodist Church
- Residential campus in small city
- 2,119 degree-seeking undergraduates: 19% part-time, 59% women, 46% African American, 1% Asian American, 2% Hispanic/Latino, 1% Native American, 2% Multi-racial, non-Hispanic, 5% international
- 55% of applicants admitted
- SAT or ACT (ACT writing optional) required
- 35% graduate within 6 years

General. Founded in 1956. Regionally accredited. Adult students, 22 and older, can attend classes at sites in Raleigh, Goldsboro, Rocky Mount and several other locations. Silver Scholars program for age 60 and above. **Degrees:** 419 bachelor's awarded. **ROTC:** Army. **Location:** 57 miles from Raleigh. **Calendar:** Semester, extensive summer session. **Full-time faculty:** 58 total; 74% have terminal degrees. **Part-time faculty:** 191 total. **Class size:** 75% < 20, 25% 20-39, less than 1% 40-49. **Special facilities:** Black Mountain archival collection, center for the performing arts.

Freshman class profile. 3,102 applied, 1,720 admitted, 320 enrolled.

Mid 50% test scores			
SAT critical reading:	380-480	GPA 2.0-2.99:	46%
SAT math:	380-490	Rank in top quarter:	30%
GPA 3.75 or higher:	23%	Rank in top tenth:	10%
GPA 3.50-3.74:	9%	Return as sophomores:	52%
GPA 3.0-3.49:	21%	Out-of-state:	40%
		International:	13%

Basis for selection. High school GPA most important, followed by SAT or ACT score, rigor of high school curriculum, and recommendations. Essay, school and community activities considered. SAT preferred. Essay, interview recommended for all students. **Home schooled:** Statement describing home school structure and mission, interview required.

High school preparation. College-preparatory program recommended. Recommended units include English 4, mathematics 3, social studies 2, science 2 (laboratory 2) and foreign language 2.

2015-2016 Annual costs. Tuition/fees: $28,150. Room/board: $9,524. Books/supplies: $1,000. Personal expenses: $1,200.

Financial aid. Non-need-based: Scholarships awarded for academics, religious affiliation. **Additional information:** Scholarships based on GPA. Various scholarship and leadership awards available.

Application procedures. Admission: No deadline. No application fee. Admission notification on a rolling basis. **Financial aid:** Priority date 3/1; no closing date. FAFSA required. Applicants notified on a rolling basis starting 1/1; must reply within 2 week(s) of notification.

Academics. Special study options: Accelerated study, cooperative education, cross-registration, distance learning, double major, dual enrollment of high school students, honors, independent study, internships, liberal arts/career combination, teacher certification program, weekend college. **Credit/placement by examination:** AP, CLEP, institutional tests. **Support services:** Learning center, pre-admission summer program, reduced course load, remedial instruction, study skills assistance, tutoring, writing center.

Majors. Biology: General, biomedical sciences. **Business:** Accounting, business admin, marketing, organizational leadership. **Computer sciences:** General. **Conservation:** Environmental science. **Education:** General, elementary, middle, special ed. **English:** English lit. **History:** General. **Liberal arts:** Arts/sciences. **Math:** General. **Parks/recreation:** Exercise sciences. **Philosophy/religion:** Religion. **Physical sciences:** Chemistry. **Protective services:** Law enforcement admin. **Psychology:** General. **Social sciences:** Political science, sociology. **Visual/performing arts:** Dramatic.

Most popular majors. Business/marketing 40%, computer/information sciences 7%, legal studies 20%, psychology 16%.

Technology on campus. 223 workstations in dormitories, library, computer center, student center. Dormitories wired for high-speed internet access and linked to campus network. Commuter students can connect to campus network. Online course registration, online library, helpline, repair service, wireless network available.

Student life. Freshman orientation: Mandatory. Preregistration for classes offered. Takes place prior to start of fall classes. **Housing:** Guaranteed on-campus for freshmen. Coed dorms, single-sex dorms, special housing for disabled, wellness housing available. $100 deposit, deadline 7/15. **Activities:** Bands, choral groups, drama, literary magazine, music ensembles, student government, student newspaper, Black Student Association, Fellowship of Christian Athletes, College Republicans, Wesleyan Christian Fellowship.

Athletics. NCAA. **Intercollegiate:** Baseball M, basketball, cheerleading W, cross-country W, football (tackle) M, golf M, soccer, softball W, tennis, volleyball W. **Intramural:** Basketball, football (tackle) M, soccer, softball, table tennis, tennis, volleyball. **Team name:** Bishops.

Student services. Adult student services, alcohol/substance abuse counseling, chaplain/spiritual director, career counseling, student employment services, financial aid counseling, health services, personal counseling, placement for graduates, veterans' counselor. **Physically disabled:** Services for visually, hearing impaired.

Contact. E-mail: adm@ncwc.edu
Phone: (252) 985-5200 Toll-free number: (800) 488-6292
Fax: (252) 985-5295
Judy Rollins, Vice President, Enrollment Services, North Carolina Wesleyan College, 3400 North Wesleyan Boulevard, Rocky Mount, NC 27804

Pfeiffer University
Misenheimer, North Carolina   CB member
www.pfeiffer.edu   CB code: 5536

- Private 4-year university and liberal arts college affiliated with the United Methodist Church
- Residential campus in rural community
- 906 degree-seeking undergraduates: 10% part-time, 58% women, 21% African American, 1% Asian American, 3% Hispanic/Latino, 2% Multi-racial, non-Hispanic, 6% international
- 692 degree-seeking graduate students
- 47% of applicants admitted
- SAT or ACT (ACT writing optional) required
- 35% graduate within 6 years

General. Founded in 1885. Regionally accredited. **Degrees:** 199 bachelor's awarded; master's offered. **ROTC:** Army. **Location:** 42 miles from Charlotte, 55 miles from Winston-Salem, 60 miles from Greensboro. **Calendar:** Semester, limited summer session. **Full-time faculty:** 78 total; 83% have terminal degrees, 13% minority, 50% women. **Part-time faculty:** 45 total; 36% have terminal degrees, 24% minority, 40% women. **Class size:** 67% < 20, 32% 20-39, 1% 40-49. **Special facilities:** Francis Center for Servant Leadership.

Freshman class profile. 1,627 applied, 757 admitted, 160 enrolled.

Mid 50% test scores			
SAT critical reading:	410-530	GPA 2.0-2.99:	22%
SAT math:	400-530	Rank in top quarter:	28%
SAT writing:	380-500	Rank in top tenth:	8%
ACT composite:	17-22	End year in good standing:	76%
GPA 3.75 or higher:	36%	Return as sophomores:	69%
GPA 3.50-3.74:	15%	Out-of-state:	21%
GPA 3.0-3.49:	26%	Live on campus:	85%
		International:	6%

Basis for selection. Academic GPA, standardized test scores required. Level of interest in attending Pfeiffer, character considered. Essay tests for both SAT and ACT are used in scholarship/merit competitions. Interview recommended for all students; audition required for music programs.

High school preparation. College-preparatory program recommended. 12 units required; 16 recommended. Required and recommended units include English 4, mathematics 3, social studies 2-4, science 2-3 (laboratory 1) and foreign language 2. Math should include algebra. 2 units of either history or social studies required.

2015-2016 Annual costs. Tuition/fees: $27,125. Room/board: $10,525. Books/supplies: $2,100. Personal expenses: $1,400.

2014-2015 Financial aid. Need-based: 166 full-time freshmen applied for aid; 147 deemed to have need; 147 received aid. Average need met was 77%. Average scholarship/grant was $19,997; average loan $4,089. 75% of total undergraduate aid awarded as scholarships/grants, 25% as loans/jobs. **Non-need-based:** Awarded to 352 full-time undergraduates, including 121 freshmen. Scholarships awarded for academics, alumni affiliation, athletics, leadership, music/drama, religious affiliation, state residency.

Application procedures. Admission: No deadline. $50 fee, may be waived for applicants with need. Admission notification on a rolling basis. **Financial aid:** Priority date 4/15; no closing date. FAFSA required. Applicants notified on a rolling basis starting 3/1; must reply within 2 week(s) of notification.

Academics. **Special study options:** Combined bachelor's/graduate degree, cooperative education, cross-registration, distance learning, double major, dual enrollment of high school students, honors, independent study, internships, study abroad, teacher certification program, Washington semester. **Credit/placement by examination:** AP, CLEP, IB, SAT, ACT, institutional tests. **Support services:** Learning center, pre-admission summer program, reduced course load, remedial instruction, study skills assistance, tutoring, writing center.

Majors. **Biology:** General. **Business:** Accounting, business admin, international, management information systems. **Communications:** General. **Computer sciences:** General. **Conservation:** Environmental studies. **Education:** Biology, chemistry, elementary, English, mathematics, music, science, secondary, social studies, special ed. **English:** Creative writing, English lit. **Health services:** Health care admin, nursing (RN), premedicine. **History:** General. **Liberal arts:** Arts/sciences. **Math:** General. **Parks/recreation:** Exercise sciences, health/fitness, sports admin. **Philosophy/religion:** Religion. **Physical sciences:** Chemistry. **Protective services:** Criminal justice, financial forensics. **Psychology:** General. **Social sciences:** Economics, political science, sociology. **Theology:** Religious ed. **Visual/performing arts:** Music, studio arts. **Work/family studies:** Family studies.

Most popular majors. Biology 6%, business/marketing 21%, education 7%, health sciences 18%, parks/recreation 9%, psychology 7%, security/protective services 10%.

Technology on campus. 83 workstations in library, student center. Dormitories wired for high-speed internet access and linked to campus network. Online course registration, online library, helpline, wireless network available.

Student life. **Freshman orientation:** Mandatory, $65 fee. Preregistration for classes offered. **Policies:** Students who receive athletic scholarship are required to live on campus. Students have a residency requirement if they are under 21 years old or not living at home. **Housing:** Guaranteed on-campus for all undergraduates. Coed dorms, single-sex dorms, apartments, themed housing available. $150 fully refundable deposit. **Activities:** Bands, campus ministries, choral groups, film society, international student organizations, student government, student newspaper, Campus Crusade for Christ, Athletic Ministries at Pfeiffer, campus activities board, Student Government Association, Christians Engaged in Faith-formation, Francis Center for Servant Leadership, Spectrum, Sports Chaplains, Dance Ministry and Relay for Life.

Athletics. NCAA. **Intercollegiate:** Baseball M, basketball, cross-country, golf, lacrosse, soccer, softball W, tennis, track and field, volleyball. **Team name:** Falcons.

Student services. Adult student services, chaplain/spiritual director, career counseling, financial aid counseling, health services, personal counseling. **Physically disabled:** Services for visually, speech, hearing impaired.

Contact. E-mail: admissions@pfeiffer.edu
Phone: (704) 463-1360 ext. 2060 Toll-free number: (800) 338-2060
Fax: (704) 463-1363
Emily Carella, Director of Undergraduate Admissions, Pfeiffer University, PO Box 960, Misenheimer, NC 28109

Piedmont International University
Winston-Salem, North Carolina
www.piedmontu.edu CB code: 5555

- Private 4-year university and seminary college affiliated with the Baptist faith
- Small city
- 344 degree-seeking undergraduates
- ACT (writing optional), application essay required

General. Founded in 1945. Regionally accredited; also accredited by TRACS. **Degrees:** 39 bachelor's, 3 associate awarded; master's, doctoral offered. **Location:** 75 miles from Charlotte, 100 miles from Raleigh. **Calendar:** Semester, limited summer session. **Full-time faculty:** 20 total; 45% have terminal degrees, 35% women. **Part-time faculty:** 20 total; 40% have terminal degrees, 25% women. **Class size:** 77% < 20, 17% 20-39, 4% 40-49, 1% 50-99. **Special facilities:** Restored 18th Century Moravian community, Old Salem.

Basis for selection. Student's life objectives and previous academic record important. Interview recommended for all students; audition required for music program.

High school preparation. Recommended units include English 4, mathematics 3, social studies 3, science 3 and foreign language 2.

2015-2016 Annual costs. Tuition/fees: $9,580. Room/board: $6,410. Books/supplies: $600. Personal expenses: $4,095.

Financial aid. **Non-need-based:** Scholarships awarded for academics, alumni affiliation, leadership, minority status, religious affiliation.

Application procedures. **Admission:** Priority date 7/31; no deadline. $50 fee. Admission notification on a rolling basis beginning on or about 12/1. Must reply by May 1 or within 2 week(s) if notified thereafter. **Financial aid:** No deadline. FAFSA required. Applicants notified on a rolling basis starting 3/1.

Academics. **Special study options:** Cooperative education, distance learning, double major, dual enrollment of high school students, independent study, internships, teacher certification program. **Credit/placement by examination:** AP, CLEP, institutional tests. **Support services:** Learning center, reduced course load, remedial instruction, study skills assistance, tutoring.

Majors. **Education:** Elementary, English, music, physical. **Theology:** Bible, missionary, youth ministry. **Visual/performing arts:** Music.

Most popular majors. Education 33%, philosophy/religious studies 60%.

Technology on campus. 26 workstations in library, computer center, student center. Dormitories linked to campus network. Commuter students can connect to campus network. Online course registration, online library, helpline, wireless network available.

Student life. **Freshman orientation:** Mandatory. Preregistration for classes offered. Held 2 days prior to registration. **Policies:** Religious observance required. **Housing:** Guaranteed on-campus for freshmen. Single-sex dorms, apartments available. **Activities:** Choral groups, drama, music ensembles, student government, student newspaper, missions fellowship, preachers' fellowship, youth leaders' fellowship, educators' fellowship, music fellowship.

Athletics. NCCAA. **Intercollegiate:** Basketball, soccer M, volleyball W. **Team name:** Conquerors.

Student services. Chaplain/spiritual director, career counseling, financial aid counseling, health services, personal counseling, placement for graduates, veterans' counselor.

Contact. E-mail: admissions@piedmontu.edu
Phone: (336) 725-8344 ext. 7961 Toll-free number: (800) 937-5097
Fax: (336) 725-5522
Angela Hoover, Director of Enrollment Services, Piedmont International University, 420 South Boad Street, Winston-Salem, NC 27101-5133

Queens University of Charlotte
Charlotte, North Carolina CB member
www.queens.edu CB code: 5560

- Private 4-year university affiliated with the Presbyterian Church (USA)
- Residential campus in very large city
- 1,551 degree-seeking undergraduates: 13% part-time, 69% women, 17% African American, 3% Asian American, 8% Hispanic/Latino, 1% Native American, 1% Multi-racial, non-Hispanic, 7% international
- 637 degree-seeking graduate students
- 78% of applicants admitted
- SAT or ACT (ACT writing optional), application essay required
- 53% graduate within 6 years

General. Founded in 1857. Regionally accredited. **Degrees:** 395 bachelor's awarded; master's offered. **Calendar:** Semester, limited summer session. **Full-time faculty:** 127 total; 76% have terminal degrees, 9% minority, 63% women. **Part-time faculty:** 187 total; 34% have terminal degrees, 18% minority, 67% women. **Class size:** 68% < 20, 32% 20-39, less than 1% 40-49. **Special facilities:** Rare books museum, recital hall.

Freshman class profile. 1,958 applied, 1,536 admitted, 287 enrolled.

Mid 50% test scores			
SAT critical reading:	470-580	Rank in top quarter:	44%
SAT math:	470-570	Rank in top tenth:	15%
ACT composite:	21-26	Return as sophomores:	73%
GPA 3.75 or higher:	48%	Out-of-state:	47%
GPA 3.50-3.74:	16%	Live on campus:	87%
GPA 3.0-3.49:	27%	International:	8%
GPA 2.0-2.99:	9%	Fraternities:	8%
		Sororities:	31%

Basis for selection. Essay, official test scores and an official high school transcript. A letter of recommendation is also required. The rigor of the course load, the curriculum offered at the high school as well as extracurricular activities are also evaluated. Additional information may be considered for scholarship purposes. Students seeking direct admission into the nursing program must have a minimum 1100 SAT or 24 ACT and an un-weighted 3.5 GPA to be considered. Interview recommended for all students. Audition required for drama, music, music therapy programs; portfolio recommended for art program. **Home schooled:** Transcript of courses and grades required. Evidence of home school registration in the home state (copy of Home School License) required.

High school preparation. College-preparatory program required. 12 units required; 14 recommended. Required and recommended units include English 4, mathematics 3, social studies 2, science 2 (laboratory 1) and foreign language 2. Chemistry recommended for nursing majors.

2015-2016 Annual costs. Tuition/fees: $32,560. Room/board: $11,390. Books/supplies: $1,200. Personal expenses: $1,040.

2015-2016 Financial aid. Need-based: 228 full-time freshmen applied for aid; 173 deemed to have need; 173 received aid. Average need met was 74%. Average scholarship/grant was $8,183; average loan $3,405. 66% of total undergraduate aid awarded as scholarships/grants, 34% as loans/jobs. **Non-need-based:** Awarded to 1,267 full-time undergraduates, including 311 freshmen. Scholarships awarded for academics, art, athletics, leadership, minority status, music/drama, religious affiliation, state residency.

Application procedures. Admission: Priority date 3/1; deadline 9/6. No application fee. Admission notification on a rolling basis beginning on or about 12/15. Must reply by May 1 or within 3 week(s) if notified thereafter. Admission can be deferred up to one year. **Financial aid:** No deadline. FAFSA required. Applicants notified on a rolling basis starting 3/1; must reply by 5/1 or within 3 week(s) of notification.

Academics. 6 credit hours of internships required to enhance job placement and career opportunities. **Special study options:** Accelerated study, cross-registration, distance learning, double major, dual enrollment of high school students, exchange student, honors, independent study, internships, study abroad, teacher certification program, Washington semester. 3-week study tours in Europe and Asia; interdisciplinary core curriculum, Harvard Model UN, European internship program offered. **Credit/placement by examination:** AP, CLEP, IB, institutional tests. 43 credit hours maximum toward bachelor's degree. **Support services:** Learning center, reduced course load, study skills assistance, tutoring, writing center.

Majors. Biology: General, biochemistry. **Business:** Accounting, business admin, finance. **Communications:** General. **Conservation:** Environmental science, environmental studies. **Education:** Elementary. **English:** Creative writing, English lit. **Foreign languages:** French, Spanish. **Health services:** Music therapy, nursing (RN), public health ed. **History:** General. **Math:** General. **Parks/recreation:** Exercise sciences, sports admin. **Philosophy/religion:** Philosophy, religion. **Physical sciences:** Chemistry, environmental chemistry. **Psychology:** General. **Social sciences:** International relations, political science, sociology. **Visual/performing arts:** Art history/conservation, dramatic, graphic design, interior design, music, studio arts, studio arts management.

Most popular majors. Business/marketing 15%, communications/journalism 8%, health sciences 29%, social sciences 6%, visual/performing arts 9%.

Technology on campus. Dormitories wired for high-speed internet access and linked to campus network. Commuter students can connect to campus network. Online library, helpline, wireless network available.

Student life. Freshman orientation: Mandatory. Preregistration for classes offered. 1.5-day sessions held in June. **Housing:** Guaranteed on-campus for all undergraduates. Coed dorms, special housing for disabled, apartments, themed housing available. $150 nonrefundable deposit, deadline 7/1. Apartment style residence hall available for traditional undergraduates only. All residence hall facilities are smoke-free. **Activities:** Campus ministries, choral groups, dance, drama, international student organizations, literary magazine, music ensembles, radio station, student government, student newspaper, Students for Black Awareness, College Republicans, College Democrats, North Carolina Student Legislature, Justinian Society.

Athletics. NCAA. **Intercollegiate:** Basketball, cross-country, golf, lacrosse, soccer, softball W, swimming, tennis, track and field, volleyball W. **Intramural:** Basketball, field hockey, soccer, ultimate frisbee, volleyball. **Team name:** Royals.

Student services. Alcohol/substance abuse counseling, chaplain/spiritual director, career counseling, student employment services, financial aid counseling, health services, minority student services, personal counseling, placement for graduates. **Physically disabled:** Services for visually impaired.

Contact. E-mail: admissions@queens.edu
Phone: (704) 337-2212 Toll-free number: (800) 849-0202 ext. 2212
Fax: (704) 337-2403
Jazmane Brown, Director of Undergraduate Admissions, Queens University of Charlotte, 1900 Selwyn Avenue, Charlotte, NC 28274-0001

Saint Augustine's University
Raleigh, North Carolina
www.st-aug.edu

CB member
CB code: 5596

- Private 4-year liberal arts college affiliated with the Episcopal Church
- Residential campus in large city
- 810 degree-seeking undergraduates: 1% part-time, 47% women, 95% African American, 1% Hispanic/Latino, 1% Native American, 1% international
- 58% of applicants admitted
- SAT or ACT (ACT writing optional) required

General. Founded in 1867. Regionally accredited. **Degrees:** 208 bachelor's awarded. **ROTC:** Army. **Location:** One mile from downtown. **Calendar:** Semester, limited summer session. **Full-time faculty:** 58 total; 47% have terminal degrees, 78% minority, 45% women. **Part-time faculty:** 33 total; 36% have terminal degrees, 79% minority, 39% women. **Special facilities:** Archival collection (tracing history of African-Americans in North Carolina and the university's founding Delany family).

Freshman class profile. 2,581 applied, 1,488 admitted, 211 enrolled.

Return as sophomores:	40%	Live on campus:	100%
Out-of-state:	25%		

Basis for selection. High school record (GPA and rank), standardized test scores and letters of recommendation reviewed. Institutionally administered ACCUPLACER test is used for pre- and post-testing evaluation and placement purposes. Essay recommended. Auditions and interviews required of music majors. **Home schooled:** Transcript of courses and grades required. **Learning Disabled:** Students must self-identify. ADA Coordinator will assess level of disability and arrange for student to access the needed equipment or tutorials.

High school preparation. College-preparatory program recommended. 20 units required. Required units include English 4, mathematics 3, social studies 2, science 2 and academic electives 9. One unit of algebra required, 2 units of laboratory recommended.

2015-2016 Annual costs. Tuition/fees: $17,890. Room/board: $7,692. Books/supplies: $1,500. Personal expenses: $5,280.

2015-2016 Financial aid. Need-based: 138 full-time freshmen applied for aid; 138 deemed to have need; 138 received aid. Average need met was 65%. Average scholarship/grant was $4,769; average loan $6,160. 61% of total undergraduate aid awarded as scholarships/grants, 39% as loans/jobs. **Non-need-based:** Awarded to 44 full-time undergraduates, including 10 freshmen. Scholarships awarded for academics, art, athletics, leadership, minority status, music/drama, religious affiliation, ROTC, state residency.

Application procedures. Admission: No deadline. $50 fee, may be waived for applicants with need. Application must be submitted online. Admission notification on a rolling basis beginning on or about 11/1. **Financial aid:** Priority date 3/15; no closing date. FAFSA, institutional form required. Applicants notified on a rolling basis starting 3/1; must reply within 2 week(s) of notification.

Academics. Required Learning Community program for all new freshmen and transfers. First-year program includes skills enhancement, college survival tips. Community service requirement part of course. **Special study options:** Accelerated study, cooperative education, cross-registration, double major, dual enrollment of high school students, honors, independent study, internships, liberal arts/career combination, semester at sea, student-designed major, study abroad, teacher certification program, weekend college. **Credit/placement by examination:** AP, CLEP, IB, institutional tests. 15 credit hours maximum toward bachelor's degree. **Support services:** Learning center, pre-admission summer program, reduced course load, remedial instruction, study skills assistance, tutoring, writing center.

Majors. Biology: General. **Business:** Accounting, business admin, management science, real estate. **Communications:** Communications/speech/rhetoric. **Computer sciences:** General, computer science. **Education:** Elementary. **Engineering:** General. **English:** English lit. **Health services:** Public health ed. **Math:** General. **Parks/recreation:** Health/fitness, sports admin. **Philosophy/religion:** Religion. **Physical sciences:** Chemistry. **Protective services:** Criminal justice. **Psychology:** General. **Social sciences:** Political science, sociology. **Visual/performing arts:** General, art, cinematography, music performance.

Most popular majors. Business/marketing 15%, communications/journalism 6%, computer/information sciences 6%, health sciences 13%, library sciences 6%, physical sciences 7%, psychology 8%, security/protective services 12%, social sciences 9%, visual/performing arts 6%.

Technology on campus. 250 workstations in dormitories, library, computer center, student center. Dormitories wired for high-speed internet access

and linked to campus network. Commuter students can connect to campus network. Online course registration, online library, helpline, repair service, wireless network available.

Student life. Freshman orientation: Mandatory, $75 fee. Preregistration for classes offered. 2-day sessions held in June, July, and August with students and parents. **Policies:** Smoking is not allowed within the administrative buildings and dorms. There is an alcohol, drug and firearm free policy. Students may be accountable to both civil authorities and to the College for their conduct. Freshmen not permitted cars on campus. **Housing:** Guaranteed on-campus for freshmen. Coed dorms, single-sex dorms, wellness housing available. $200 nonrefundable deposit, deadline 7/15. **Activities:** Bands, campus ministries, choral groups, dance, drama, film society, international student organizations, literary magazine, music ensembles, musical theater, radio station, student government, student newspaper, symphony orchestra, TV station, Christian Fellowship Organization, Young Democrats of America, Falcons for the Cause, NAACP, Foreign Language Club, Falcon Battalion/Army ROTC, Student Service Corps, SAC Association for Black Journalists, International Student Association, Latin American Students Organization.

Athletics. NCAA. **Intercollegiate:** Baseball M, basketball, bowling W, cheerleading W, cross-country, football (tackle) M, golf M, softball W, tennis, track and field, volleyball W. **Intramural:** Basketball, football (non-tackle). **Team name:** Falcons.

Student services. Adult student services, alcohol/substance abuse counseling, chaplain/spiritual director, career counseling, services for economically disadvantaged, student employment services, financial aid counseling, health services, minority student services, personal counseling, placement for graduates, veterans' counselor. **Physically disabled:** Services for visually, hearing impaired.

Contact. E-mail: admissions@st-aug.edu
Phone: (919) 516-4012 Toll-free number: (800) 948-1126
Fax: (919) 516-5805
Chris Withers, Dean of Enrollment, Saint Augustine's University, 1315 Oakwood Avenue, Raleigh, NC 27610-2298

Salem College
Winston-Salem, North Carolina   **CB member**
www.salem.edu   **CB code: 5607**

- Private 4-year liberal arts college for women affiliated with the Moravian Church in America
- Residential campus in small city
- 917 degree-seeking undergraduates
- SAT or ACT (ACT writing optional), application essay required

General. Founded in 1772. Regionally accredited. Male students age 23 and over may enroll in adult program only; male students may not reside at the college. **Degrees:** 206 bachelor's awarded; master's offered. **ROTC:** Army. **Location:** 80 miles from Charlotte, 25 miles from Greensboro. **Calendar:** 4-1-4, limited summer session. **Full-time faculty:** 60 total; 83% have terminal degrees, 8% minority. **Part-time faculty:** 47 total; 38% have terminal degrees, 13% minority. **Class size:** 84% < 20, 16% 20-39. **Special facilities:** Center for women writers.

Freshman class profile.

GPA 3.75 or higher:	48%	Rank in top quarter:	67%
GPA 3.50-3.74:	22%	Rank in top tenth:	39%
GPA 3.0-3.49:	24%	Out-of-state:	35%
GPA 2.0-2.99:	6%	Live on campus:	98%

Basis for selection. School achievement record, essay or personal statement, test scores important. Recommendations, interview, extracurricular and community activities, talent, minority status considered. Interview recommended for all students. Audition required for music program; portfolio recommended for art program.

High school preparation. College-preparatory program required. 16 units required. Required units include English 4, mathematics 3, social studies 2, science 3, foreign language 2 and academic electives 3. Math requirement includes 2 algebra and 1 geometry. On a case by case basis, a portion of this requirement may be waived for adult students.

2015-2016 Annual costs. Tuition/fees: $25,930. Room/board: $11,824. Books/supplies: $1,000. Personal expenses: $985.

Financial aid. Non-need-based: Scholarships awarded for academics, alumni affiliation, leadership, minority status, music/drama, state residency.

Application procedures. Admission: Priority date 3/1; no deadline. $30 fee, may be waived for applicants with need, free for online applicants.

Admission notification on a rolling basis beginning on or about 10/1. Must reply by May 1 or within 2 week(s) if notified thereafter. **Financial aid:** Priority date 3/1; no closing date. FAFSA required. Applicants notified on a rolling basis starting 3/1; must reply by 5/1 or within 2 week(s) of notification.

Academics. Special study options: Accelerated study, cross-registration, double major, dual enrollment of high school students, exchange student, honors, independent study, internships, liberal arts/career combination, student-designed major, study abroad, teacher certification program, Washington semester. 3-1 clinical laboratory sciences/medical technology program with Wake Forest University's Baptist Medical Center; various study abroad options available through Brethren Colleges of America (BCA); St. Peters, Oxford; and St. Clare's, Oxford. **Credit/placement by examination:** AP, CLEP, IB, SAT, institutional tests. **Support services:** Learning center, reduced course load, study skills assistance, tutoring, writing center.

Majors. Area/ethnic studies: American. **Biology:** General. **Business:** Accounting, business admin, international, nonprofit/public. **Communications:** Communications/speech/rhetoric. **Education:** Elementary, music, secondary. **English:** Creative writing, English lit, writing. **Foreign languages:** French, Spanish. **Health services:** Clinical lab technology. **History:** General. **Math:** General. **Philosophy/religion:** Philosophy, religion. **Physical sciences:** Chemistry. **Psychology:** General. **Social sciences:** Economics, international relations, sociology. **Visual/performing arts:** Art history/conservation, interior design, music, music performance, studio arts, studio arts management.

Most popular majors. Biology 9%, business/marketing 12%, communications/journalism 9%, English 12%, foreign language 7%, psychology 9%, social sciences 18%, visual/performing arts 9%.

Technology on campus. 54 workstations in library, computer center. Dormitories wired for high-speed internet access and linked to campus network. Commuter students can connect to campus network. Online library, helpline, wireless network available.

Student life. Freshman orientation: Mandatory. Preregistration for classes offered. 3 days before fall term begins. Separate orientation program for adult students. **Policies:** All full-time students under 23 years required to reside on-campus unless they reside with family within a 30 mile radius of the college. **Housing:** Guaranteed on-campus for freshmen. Apartments, wellness housing available. $250 nonrefundable deposit, deadline 5/1. **Activities:** Marching band, campus ministries, choral groups, dance, drama, international student organizations, literary magazine, music ensembles, Model UN, musical theater, student government, student newspaper, College Democrats, College Republicans, Green Party, Catholic Student Association, Campus Activities Council, Intervarsity Fellowship, Habitat for Humanity.

Athletics. NCAA. **Intercollegiate:** Basketball W, cross-country W, soccer W, swimming W, tennis W, volleyball W. **Team name:** Spirits.

Student services. Adult student services, chaplain/spiritual director, career counseling, financial aid counseling, health services, personal counseling, placement for graduates, women's services.

Contact. E-mail: admissions@salem.edu
Phone: (336) 721-2621 Toll-free number: (800) 327-2536
Fax: (336) 917-5572
Katherine Watts, Dean of Admissions and Financial Aid, Salem College, 601 South Church Street, Winston-Salem, NC 27108

Shaw University
Raleigh, North Carolina   **CB member**
www.shawu.edu   **CB code: 5612**

- Private 4-year university and liberal arts college affiliated with the Baptist faith
- Residential campus in large city
- 1,503 degree-seeking undergraduates: 6% part-time, 57% women, 58% African American, 2% international
- 137 degree-seeking graduate students
- 60% of applicants admitted
- Application essay required

General. Founded in 1865. Regionally accredited. **Degrees:** 231 bachelor's awarded; master's offered. **ROTC:** Army. **Location:** 150 miles from Charlotte. **Calendar:** Semester, limited summer session. **Full-time faculty:** 93 total; 75% have terminal degrees, 76% minority, 50% women. **Part-time faculty:** 78 total; 35% have terminal degrees, 80% minority, 50% women. **Class size:** 52% < 20, 46% 20-39, less than 1% 40-49, less than 1% 50-99.

Freshman class profile. 5,030 applied, 3,042 admitted, 402 enrolled.

Mid 50% test scores		GPA 2.0-2.99:	76%
SAT critical reading:	320-410	Rank in top quarter:	5%
SAT math:	310-400	Rank in top tenth:	1%
SAT writing:	310-400	Return as sophomores:	49%
ACT composite:	13-17	Out-of-state:	31%
GPA 3.75 or higher:	1%	Live on campus:	91%
GPA 3.50-3.74:	1%	International:	1%
GPA 3.0-3.49:	10%		

Basis for selection. Academic GPA, recommendations, level of interest are very important. SAT or ACT recommended. Interview, portfolio recommended for some. **Home schooled:** Transcript of courses and grades, state high school equivalency certificate required.

High school preparation. College-preparatory program recommended. 18 units required. Required units include English 3, mathematics 2, social studies 2, science 2 and academic electives 9.

2015-2016 Annual costs. Tuition/fees: $14,840. Room/board: $8,158. Books/supplies: $1,100. Personal expenses: $2,040.

Financial aid. Non-need-based: Scholarships awarded for academics, athletics, music/drama.

Application procedures. Admission: Closing date 7/30 (receipt date). $25 fee, may be waived for applicants with need. Admission notification by 8/1. **Financial aid:** Priority date 3/1, closing date 6/30. FAFSA required. Applicants notified on a rolling basis starting 3/15.

Academics. Special study options: Accelerated study, cross-registration, distance learning, double major, dual enrollment of high school students, honors, independent study, internships, liberal arts/career combination, student-designed major, study abroad, teacher certification program. **Credit/placement by examination:** AP, CLEP, institutional tests. 60 credit hours maximum toward bachelor's degree. **Support services:** Learning center, reduced course load, study skills assistance, tutoring, writing center.

Majors. Biology: General. **Business:** Business admin. **Communications:** Media studies. **Computer sciences:** General, computer science. **Education:** Elementary, English. **English:** English lit. **Health services:** Athletic training, communication disorders, kinesiotherapy, recreational therapy. **Human services:** General, social work. **Liberal arts:** Arts/sciences. **Math:** General. **Parks/recreation:** General, exercise sciences. **Philosophy/religion:** Religion. **Physical sciences:** Chemistry. **Protective services:** Criminal justice. **Psychology:** General. **Social sciences:** Political science, sociology. **Visual/performing arts:** Music.

Most popular majors. Business/marketing 15%, communications/journalism 9%, computer/information sciences 6%, parks/recreation 9%, psychology 6%, public administration/social services 19%, security/protective services 9%, social sciences 7%.

Technology on campus. Dormitories wired for high-speed internet access and linked to campus network. Commuter students can connect to campus network. Online course registration, online library, helpline, repair service, student web hosting, wireless network available.

Student life. Freshman orientation: Available. Preregistration for classes offered. **Policies:** Religious observance required. Freshmen not permitted cars on campus. **Housing:** Single-sex dorms available. $150 nonrefundable deposit, deadline 7/1. **Activities:** Bands, campus ministries, choral groups, dance, drama, international student organizations, music ensembles, musical theater, radio station, student government, student newspaper, NAACP, business, sociology, criminal justice, accounting clubs, Christian Fellowship, northern exposure, Order of the Eastern Star.

Athletics. NCAA. **Intercollegiate:** Basketball, bowling W, cross-country, football (tackle) M, softball W, tennis, track and field, volleyball W. **Intramural:** Basketball, tennis, volleyball. **Team name:** Bears.

Student services. Adult student services, alcohol/substance abuse counseling, chaplain/spiritual director, career counseling, student employment services, financial aid counseling, health services, personal counseling, placement for graduates, veterans' counselor. **Physically disabled:** Services for visually, speech, hearing impaired.

Contact. E-mail: admissions@shawu.edu
Phone: (919) 546-8275 Toll-free number: (800) 214-6683
Fax: (919) 546-8271
Stacey Sowell, Director of Admissions, Shaw University, 118 East South Street, Raleigh, NC 27601

Southeastern Baptist Theological Seminary
Wake Forest, North Carolina
www.sebts.edu   CB code: 7050

- Private 4-year Bible and seminary college affiliated with the Southern Baptist Convention
- Residential campus in large town
- 418 degree-seeking undergraduates: 43% part-time, 32% women, 5% African American, 3% Asian American, 3% Hispanic/Latino
- 1,844 degree-seeking graduate students
- Application essay required
- 32% graduate within 6 years; 85% enter graduate study

General. Founded in 1950. Regionally accredited. Many of the theology and religious studies classes at the undergraduate level are cross-listed with the seminary, which allows undergraduates to get the same high quality content as the graduate students. **Degrees:** 57 bachelor's, 8 associate awarded; master's, professional, doctoral offered. **Location:** 20 miles from Raleigh, 30 miles from Durham. **Calendar:** Semester, limited summer session. **Full-time faculty:** 65 total; 86% have terminal degrees, 5% minority, 3% women. **Part-time faculty:** 73 total; 96% have terminal degrees, 3% minority, 16% women. **Class size:** 85% < 20, 14% 20-39, less than 1% 40-49.

Freshman class profile. 126 applied, 124 admitted, 86 enrolled.

End year in good standing:	66%	Live on campus:	82%
Return as sophomores:	72%	International:	1%
Out-of-state:	35%		

Basis for selection. Open admission, but selective for some programs. **Home schooled:** Transcript of courses and grades, letter of recommendation (nonparent) required.

2015-2016 Annual costs. Tuition/fees: $10,020. Room only: $2,196. Books/supplies: $840. Personal expenses: $3,789. **Additional information:** Non-Southern Baptist: $630 per credit hour + Student Enrollment Fee of $270 per semester. Military Discount Rate: $316 per credit hour + Student Enrollment Fee of $270 per semester.

Application procedures. Admission: Closing date 7/21 (receipt date). $40 fee, may be waived for applicants with need. Admission notification on a rolling basis. Students may be enrolled concurrently while in high school, but only on a part time basis.

Academics. Special study options: Distance learning, double major, independent study, internships, study abroad. **Credit/placement by examination:** AP, CLEP. 30 credit hours maximum toward associate degree, 30 toward bachelor's. **Support services:** Reduced course load, writing center.

Majors. English: English lit. **History:** General. **Philosophy/religion:** General, Christian, religion. **Theology:** Bible, missionary, preministerial, sacred music, theology.

Technology on campus. 40 workstations in library, computer center. Commuter students can connect to campus network. Online course registration, online library, wireless network available.

Student life. Freshman orientation: Mandatory, $130 fee. Preregistration for classes offered. **Policies:** Religious observance required. **Housing:** Single-sex dorms, apartments, wellness housing available. $200 fully refundable deposit. **Activities:** Concert band, choral groups, music ensembles, student government, student newspaper.

Athletics. Intramural: Basketball, football (non-tackle), racquetball, ultimate frisbee, volleyball.

Student services. Chaplain/spiritual director, career counseling, student employment services, financial aid counseling, health services, personal counseling, placement for graduates, veterans' counselor, women's services.

Contact. E-mail: admissions@sebts.edu
Phone: (919) 761-2280 Toll-free number: (800) 284-6317
Fax: (919) 556-0998
Larry Lyon, Director of Admissions, Southeastern Baptist Theological Seminary, PO Box 1889, Wake Forest, NC 27588

St. Andrews University
Laurinburg, North Carolina   CB member
www.sa.edu   CB code: 5214

- Private 4-year liberal arts college affiliated with the Presbyterian Church (USA)
- Residential campus in large town

- 601 degree-seeking undergraduates: 7% part-time, 54% women
- 33 degree-seeking graduate students

General. Founded in 1958. Regionally accredited. **Degrees:** 99 bachelor's awarded; master's offered. **Location:** 40 miles from Fayetteville, 20 miles from Pinehurst. **Calendar:** Semester, limited summer session. **Full-time faculty:** 30 total; 73% have terminal degrees, 3% minority, 47% women. **Part-time faculty:** 27 total; 26% have terminal degrees, 7% minority, 59% women. **Class size:** 70% < 20, 27% 20-39, 3% 40-49. **Special facilities:** Psychology laboratory complex, equestrian facilities, nature preserve, electronic fine arts center.

Freshman class profile.

GPA 3.75 or higher:	20%	Rank in top quarter:	30%
GPA 3.50-3.74:	10%	Rank in top tenth:	7%
GPA 3.0-3.49:	38%	Out-of-state:	43%
GPA 2.0-2.99:	29%	Live on campus:	99%

Basis for selection. High school GPA, test scores, curriculum, type of high school very important. Recommendations important. Interview required for academically weak students, recommended for all other applicants. **Home schooled:** Transcript of courses and grades, state high school equivalency certificate required. Standardized test scores and interview required.

High school preparation. College-preparatory program recommended. Required units include English 3, mathematics 3, social studies 3, science 3 and foreign language 1.

2015-2016 Annual costs. Tuition/fees: $24,390. Room/board: $10,194. Books/supplies: $1,800. Personal expenses: $1,800.

Financial aid. **Non-need-based:** Scholarships awarded for academics, alumni affiliation, art, athletics, job skills, leadership, music/drama, religious affiliation.

Application procedures. **Admission:** Priority date 5/1; no deadline. $35 fee, may be waived for applicants with need. Admission notification on a rolling basis beginning on or about 8/1. Housing deposit fully refundable until May 1st. **Financial aid:** Priority date 5/1; no closing date. Applicants notified on a rolling basis starting 3/1.

Academics. Academic programs include St. Andrew's General Education. **Special study options:** Double major, ESL, honors, independent study, internships, student-designed major, study abroad, teacher certification program. Courses offered abroad during winter or summer in Britain, Greece, India, Switzerland, Venezuela, China, Hawaii, former Soviet Union; exchange programs with Stirling University, Scotland and Kansai Gaidai University, Japan; study at Brunnenburg Castle, Italy, and Beijing Normal College of Foreign Languages. **Credit/placement by examination:** AP, CLEP, IB. 30 credit hours maximum toward bachelor's degree. **Support services:** Reduced course load, tutoring, writing center.

Majors. **Area/ethnic studies:** Asian. **Biology:** General. **Business:** General, business admin, international. **Communications:** Media studies. **Education:** Elementary, physical. **English:** Creative writing, English lit. **Health services:** Premedicine, preveterinary, recreational therapy. **History:** General, applied. **Liberal arts:** Arts/sciences. **Math:** General. **Parks/recreation:** Health/fitness. **Philosophy/religion:** Philosophy, religion. **Physical sciences:** Chemistry. **Psychology:** General. **Social sciences:** Political science. **Visual/performing arts:** General, art.

Most popular majors. Biology 20%, business/marketing 27%, education 10%, English 7%, parks/recreation 15%, psychology 13%.

Technology on campus. 100 workstations in library, computer center, student center. Dormitories wired for high-speed internet access and linked to campus network. Online library, repair service available.

Student life. **Freshman orientation:** Mandatory, $100 fee. Preregistration for classes offered. 3 days prior to start of fall term. **Policies:** Honor code enforced. **Housing:** Guaranteed on-campus for all undergraduates. Coed dorms, single-sex dorms available. $250 deposit, deadline 8/25. **Activities:** Choral groups, literary magazine, student government, student newspaper, Christian Student Fellowship, Black student union, women's issues group, writer's forum, world culture club, Eco-Action, student activities union.

Athletics. NAIA. **Intramural:** Basketball, bowling, racquetball, soccer, softball W, table tennis, volleyball. **Team name:** Knights.

Student services. Adult student services, alcohol/substance abuse counseling, career counseling, student employment services, financial aid counseling, health services, personal counseling, placement for graduates, women's services. **Physically disabled:** Services for visually, speech, hearing impaired.

Contact. E-mail: admissions@sapc.edu
Phone: (910) 277-5555 Toll-free number: (800) 763-0198
Fax: (910) 277-5020
Kirsten Simmons, Director of Admission, St. Andrews University, 1700 Dogwood Mile, Laurinburg, NC 28352

University of Mount Olive
Mount Olive, North Carolina
www.mou.edu

CB member
CB code: 5435

- Private 4-year university affiliated with the Free Will Baptists
- Residential campus in small town
- 3,152 degree-seeking undergraduates
- 49% of applicants admitted

General. Founded in 1951. Regionally accredited. **Degrees:** 575 bachelor's, 195 associate awarded; master's offered. **ROTC:** Air Force. **Location:** 13 miles from Goldsboro. **Calendar:** Semester, extensive summer session. **Full-time faculty:** 90 total; 87% have terminal degrees, 27% minority, 36% women. **Part-time faculty:** 212 total; 31% have terminal degrees, 13% minority, 45% women. **Class size:** 70% < 20, 30% 20-39, less than 1% 40-49.

Freshman class profile. 2,220 applied, 1,085 admitted, 302 enrolled.

Mid 50% test scores		ACT composite:	17-21
SAT critical reading:	400-500	Out-of-state:	18%
SAT math:	400-520	Live on campus:	40%

Basis for selection. School record, test scores, class rank important. Personal recommendations considered. Interview recommended for all students; portfolio recommended for art majors. Audition required for music majors.

High school preparation. College-preparatory program recommended. 13 units required. Required and recommended units include English 4, mathematics 3-4, social studies 3, science 3 and foreign language 2. 1 Health/Physical Education required.

2015-2016 Annual costs. Tuition/fees: $18,400. Room/board: $7,400. Books/supplies: $1,350. Personal expenses: $1,000.

Financial aid. **Non-need-based:** Scholarships awarded for academics, art, athletics, leadership, music/drama, religious affiliation.

Application procedures. **Admission:** No deadline. No application fee. Admission notification on a rolling basis beginning on or about 1/9. Must reply by May 1 or within 2 week(s) if notified thereafter. **Financial aid:** No deadline. FAFSA required. Applicants notified on a rolling basis starting 3/1; must reply within 2 week(s) of notification.

Academics. **Special study options:** Accelerated study, distance learning, double major, dual enrollment of high school students, honors, independent study, internships, teacher certification program. **Credit/placement by examination:** AP, CLEP, SAT, ACT, institutional tests. 15 credit hours maximum toward associate degree, 30 toward bachelor's. **Support services:** Reduced course load, remedial instruction, study skills assistance, tutoring, writing center.

Majors. **Biology:** General. **Business:** Accounting/business management, business admin, human resources, management information systems. **Education:** Agricultural, early childhood, elementary, English, mathematics, music, physical, science, secondary, social studies. **English:** English lit. **Health services:** Health care admin, nursing (RN). **History:** General. **Math:** General. **Parks/recreation:** General, exercise sciences, health/fitness, sports admin. **Philosophy/religion:** Religion. **Physical sciences:** Chemistry. **Protective services:** Criminal justice. **Psychology:** General. **Theology:** Sacred music. **Visual/performing arts:** Art, design, piano/keyboard, stringed instruments, voice/opera.

Most popular majors. Business/marketing 33%, education 18%, health sciences 20%, security/protective services 13%.

Technology on campus. 50 workstations in library, computer center. Dormitories wired for high-speed internet access and linked to campus network. Commuter students can connect to campus network. Online library, repair service, wireless network available.

Student life. **Freshman orientation:** Available. Preregistration for classes offered. **Housing:** Guaranteed on-campus for freshmen. Single-sex dorms, apartments available. $100 nonrefundable deposit, deadline 2/26. **Activities:** Concert band, campus ministries, choral groups, international student organizations, music ensembles, musical theater, student government, student newspaper, Collegiate Young Farmers and Ranchers, International club, martial arts club, music club, New Directions Ministries, Phi Beta Lambda.

Athletics. NCAA. **Intercollegiate:** Baseball M, basketball, cross-country, golf, lacrosse, soccer, softball W, tennis, track and field, volleyball. **Intramural:** Badminton, baseball M, basketball, football (tackle) M, handball, racquetball, softball, table tennis, tennis, volleyball. **Team name:** Trojans.

Student services. Adult student services, chaplain/spiritual director, career counseling, student employment services, financial aid counseling, health services, personal counseling, placement for graduates, veterans' counselor. **Physically disabled:** Services for visually, hearing impaired.

Contact. E-mail: admissions@moc.edu
Phone: (800) 653-0854 Toll-free number: (800) 653-0854
Fax: (919) 658-9816
Tim Woodard, Director of Admissions, University of Mount Olive, 634 Henderson Street, Mount Olive, NC 28365

University of North Carolina at Asheville
Asheville, North Carolina   CB member
www.unca.edu   CB code: 5013

- Public 4-year university and liberal arts college
- Residential campus in small city
- 3,505 degree-seeking undergraduates: 9% part-time, 55% women, 4% African American, 2% Asian American, 5% Hispanic/Latino, 1% Native American, 4% Multi-racial, non-Hispanic, 1% international
- 31 degree-seeking graduate students
- 79% of applicants admitted
- SAT or ACT with writing, application essay required
- 64% graduate within 6 years

General. Founded in 1927. Regionally accredited. **Degrees:** 746 bachelor's awarded; master's offered. **Location:** 130 miles from Charlotte, 200 miles from Atlanta. **Calendar:** Semester, limited summer session. **Full-time faculty:** 216 total; 86% have terminal degrees, 18% minority, 45% women. **Part-time faculty:** 100 total; 44% have terminal degrees, 9% minority, 59% women. **Class size:** 50% < 20, 47% 20-39, 2% 40-49, 1% 50-99. **Special facilities:** Electric music studio, N.C. center for health and wellness, National Environmental Modeling and Analysis Center, Renaissance Computing Institute, Pisgah Astronomical Research Institute (radio telescopes), optical telescope observatory, botanical gardens.

Freshman class profile. 3,324 applied, 2,617 admitted, 736 enrolled.

Mid 50% test scores			
SAT critical reading:	530-640	Rank in top quarter:	52%
SAT math:	520-610	Rank in top tenth:	21%
SAT writing:	510-610	Return as sophomores:	79%
ACT composite:	23-28	Out-of-state:	13%
GPA 3.75 or higher:	19%	Live on campus:	96%
GPA 3.50-3.74:	27%	International:	1%
GPA 3.0-3.49:	42%	Fraternities:	7%
GPA 2.0-2.99:	12%	Sororities:	6%

Basis for selection. GED not accepted. High school curriculum, GPA, and class rank (top third), most important. Test scores important. Counselor recommendation and essay question required. Interview, extracurricular activities that support academic achievement considered. Students expected to have completed advanced coursework. Personal statements helpful. Interviews recommended. **Home schooled:** Transcript of courses and grades, letter of recommendation (nonparent) required. Must provide a transcript documenting all courses taken, particularly UNC system minimum admissions requirements, units of credit received. Transcript must be signed by home school administrator, and notarized. For North Carolina residents, a copy of the school's registration with the North Carolina Department of Non-Public Instruction is required. **Learning Disabled:** Untimed SAT accepted.

High school preparation. College-preparatory program required. 15 units required. Required and recommended units include English 4, mathematics 4, social studies 1, history 1, science 3 (laboratory 1), foreign language 2 and academic electives 4. Science units should include biology and physical science such as chemistry or physics. One unit US history, 1 unit other social studies required. Math must include algebra I, II and geometry and 1 math course with algebra II as pre-requisite.

2015-2016 Annual costs. Tuition/fees: $6,605; $22,219 out-of-state. Room/board: $8,332. Books/supplies: $1,200. Personal expenses: $1,300.

2014-2015 Financial aid. **Need-based:** 525 full-time freshmen applied for aid; 344 deemed to have need; 341 received aid. Average need met was 70%. Average scholarship/grant was $5,995; average loan $4,221. 56% of total undergraduate aid awarded as scholarships/grants, 44% as loans/jobs. **Non-need-based:** Awarded to 512 full-time undergraduates, including 106 freshmen. Scholarships awarded for academics, alumni affiliation, art, athletics, job skills, leadership, music/drama, state residency.

Application procedures. **Admission:** Priority date 11/15; deadline 2/15 (postmark date). $60 fee, may be waived for applicants with need. Admission notification on a rolling basis beginning on or about 12/15. Must reply by 5/1. **Financial aid:** Priority date 3/1; no closing date. FAFSA required. Applicants notified on a rolling basis starting 3/15.

Academics. **Special study options:** Cross-registration, distance learning, double major, dual enrollment of high school students, exchange student, honors, independent study, internships, liberal arts/career combination, semester at sea, student-designed major, study abroad, teacher certification program. **Credit/placement by examination:** AP, CLEP, IB, institutional tests. 30 credit hours maximum toward bachelor's degree. AP and CLEP exam grades required for credit are subject to change. **Support services:** Learning center, reduced course load, study skills assistance, tutoring, writing center.

Majors. **Area/ethnic studies:** Women's. **Biology:** General. **Business:** Accounting, business admin, operations. **Communications:** Media studies. **Computer sciences:** Computer science, web page design. **Conservation:** Environmental studies. **Engineering:** General. **English:** English lit. **Foreign languages:** Classics, French, German, Spanish. **Health services:** Public health ed. **History:** General. **Liberal arts:** Arts/sciences. **Math:** General. **Philosophy/religion:** Philosophy, religion. **Physical sciences:** Atmospheric science, chemistry, physics. **Psychology:** General. **Social sciences:** Anthropology, economics, political science, sociology. **Visual/performing arts:** Art, dramatic, music, music technology, studio arts.

Most popular majors. Biology 6%, business/marketing 9%, health sciences 6%, natural resources/environmental science 7%, psychology 12%, social sciences 9%, visual/performing arts 13%.

Technology on campus. 477 workstations in dormitories, library, computer center, student center. Dormitories wired for high-speed internet access and linked to campus network. Commuter students can connect to campus network. Online course registration, online library, helpline, repair service, student web hosting, wireless network available.

Student life. **Freshman orientation:** Mandatory, $55 fee. Preregistration for classes offered. 2-day orientation program for freshmen and a 1-day orientation program for transfer students held in June. 1-day make-up orientation session for all incoming students held in August. 3-day orientation program begins the Friday before fall semester classes begin, for all incoming students. **Policies:** Freshmen not permitted cars on campus. **Housing:** Guaranteed on-campus for freshmen. Coed dorms, special housing for disabled, themed housing available. $300 deposit, deadline 5/1. Substance free floors available. **Activities:** Bands, campus ministries, choral groups, dance, drama, international student organizations, literary magazine, music ensembles, musical theater, radio station, student government, student newspaper, Baptist student union, InterVarsity Christian Fellowship, Black student association, Campus Crusade for Christ, Active Students for a Healthy Environment, university ambassadors, Jewish student association, Asian Students in Asheville, Students for a Democratic Society.

Athletics. NCAA. **Intercollegiate:** Baseball M, basketball, cheerleading W, cross-country, soccer, swimming W, tennis, track and field, volleyball W. **Intramural:** Badminton, football (non-tackle), racquetball, soccer, volleyball. **Team name:** Bulldogs.

Student services. Adult student services, alcohol/substance abuse counseling, chaplain/spiritual director, career counseling, student employment services, financial aid counseling, health services, minority student services, personal counseling, placement for graduates, veterans' counselor, women's services. **Physically disabled:** Services for visually, hearing impaired.

Contact. E-mail: admissions@unca.edu
Phone: (828) 251-6481 Toll-free number: (800) 531-9842
Fax: (828) 251-6482
Shannon Earle, Director of Admissions, University of North Carolina at Asheville, CPO#1320, UNCA, Asheville, NC 28804-8502

University of North Carolina at Chapel Hill
Chapel Hill, North Carolina   CB member
www.unc.edu   CB code: 5816

- Public 4-year university
- Residential campus in small city
- 17,951 degree-seeking undergraduates: 2% part-time, 58% women, 8% African American, 10% Asian American, 8% Hispanic/Latino, 1% Native American, 4% Multi-racial, non-Hispanic, 2% international
- 10,100 degree-seeking graduate students

- 30% of applicants admitted
- SAT or ACT (ACT writing optional), application essay required
- 91% graduate within 6 years; 28% enter graduate study

General. Founded in 1789. Regionally accredited. **Degrees:** 4,624 bachelor's awarded; master's, professional, doctoral offered. **ROTC:** Army, Naval, Air Force. **Location:** 8 miles from Durham, 26 miles from Raleigh. **Calendar:** Semester, extensive summer session. **Class size:** 42% < 20, 37% 20-39, 7% 40-49, 7% 50-99, 7% >100. **Special facilities:** Planetarium, observatory, arboretum, botanical garden, art museum.

Freshman class profile. 31,953 applied, 9,510 admitted, 4,076 enrolled.

Mid 50% test scores			
SAT critical reading:	590-690	Rank in top tenth:	77%
SAT math:	610-700	End year in good standing:	97%
SAT writing:	590-700	Return as sophomores:	97%
ACT composite:	27-32	Out-of-state:	17%
GPA 3.75 or higher:	98%	Live on campus:	100%
GPA 3.50-3.74:	1%	International:	3%
GPA 3.0-3.49:	1%	Fraternities:	18%
Rank in top quarter:	96%	Sororities:	18%

Basis for selection. GED not accepted. Course selection, high school grades, test scores, essays, extracurricular activities, and letters of recommendation required. For SAT, ACT, and SAT Subject Tests, the November test date is for early notification and the December test date is for regular notification. Audition required for music programs; portfolio recommended for art program. **Home schooled:** Detailed description of home-school curriculum required. **Learning Disabled:** Students may voluntarily supply documentation regarding disability and impact on educational experiences with application.

High school preparation. College-preparatory program required. 16 units required. Required units include English 4, mathematics 4, social studies 1, history 1, science 3 (laboratory 1), foreign language 2 and academic electives 1. History course must be U.S. history. Both foreign language units must be for the same language.

2015-2016 Annual costs. Tuition/fees: $8,591; $33,673 out-of-state. Room/board: $10,902. Books/supplies: $1,442. Personal expenses: $2,552. **Additional information:** Fees may be higher for selected programs.

2014-2015 Financial aid. Need-based: 3,000 full-time freshmen applied for aid; 1,789 deemed to have need; 1,789 received aid. Average need met was 100%. Average scholarship/grant was $16,972; average loan $4,643. 78% of total undergraduate aid awarded as scholarships/grants, 22% as loans/jobs. **Non-need-based:** Awarded to 1,486 full-time undergraduates, including 294 freshmen. Scholarships awarded for academics, alumni affiliation, art, athletics, leadership, music/drama, religious affiliation, state residency. **Additional information:** 100% of all documented need met for both resident and non-resident undergraduates who qualify for need based aid, with a favorable mix of approximately 60% grants and scholarships and 40% loans and work study. A no-loans program available for qualifying low-income students (in-state or out-of-state) whose family's adjusted gross income does not exceed 200% of the federal poverty standard, indexed by family size.

Application procedures. Admission: Priority date 10/15; deadline 1/15 (postmark date). $80 fee, may be waived for applicants with need. Notification on or around 1/31 for early notification; on or around 3/31 for regular notification. Must reply by 5/1. **Financial aid:** Priority date 3/1; no closing date. FAFSA, CSS PROFILE required. Applicants notified by 3/15; must reply by 5/1.

Academics. Entering first-year students are required to own laptop meeting university specifications, as a part of the Carolina Computing Initiative; qualified students will receive special loans or grants. **Special study options:** Combined bachelor's/graduate degree, cross-registration, distance learning, double major, dual enrollment of high school students, honors, independent study, internships, student-designed major, study abroad, teacher certification program, Washington semester. **Credit/placement by examination:** AP, CLEP, IB, SAT, ACT, institutional tests. Credit by examination varies by department. **Support services:** Learning center, pre-admission summer program, reduced course load, study skills assistance, tutoring, writing center.

Honors college/program. Students were chosen based on their academic merits, intellectual curiosity, and desire to embrace challenges and solve problems. Honors Carolina students are required to complete the same General Education requirements as other students. To remain members in good standing of Honors Carolina, students must maintain at least a 3.0 cumulative grade point average.

Majors. Area/ethnic studies: African-American, American, Asian, European, Latin American, women's. **Biology:** General, biostatistics. **Business:** Business admin, human resources. **Communications:** Communications/speech/rhetoric, journalism, media studies. **Computer sciences:** Computer

science, information systems. **Conservation:** Environmental science, environmental studies. **Education:** Early childhood, elementary, middle. **English:** English lit. **Foreign languages:** General, classics, comparative lit, linguistics, Romance. **Health services:** Clinical lab science, dental hygiene, environmental health, health care admin, medical radiologic technology/radiation therapy, nursing (RN), pharmaceutical sciences. **History:** General. **Human services:** Public policy. **Liberal arts:** Arts/sciences. **Math:** General, applied. **Parks/recreation:** Health/fitness. **Philosophy/religion:** Philosophy, religion. **Physical sciences:** Chemistry, geology, physics. **Psychology:** General. **Social sciences:** Anthropology, archaeology, economics, geography, political science, sociology. **Visual/performing arts:** Art history/conservation, dramatic, music, music performance, studio arts. **Work/family studies:** Food/nutrition.

Most popular majors. Area/ethnic studies 6%, biology 10%, business/marketing 7%, communications/journalism 10%, health sciences 6%, parks/recreation 6%, psychology 8%, social sciences 18%.

Technology on campus. PC or laptop required. 800 workstations in dormitories, library, computer center, student center. Dormitories wired for high-speed internet access and linked to campus network. Commuter students can connect to campus network. Online course registration, online library, helpline, repair service, student web hosting, wireless network available.

Student life. Freshman orientation: Mandatory, $215 fee. Preregistration for classes offered. 2-day required program (14 sessions) for freshmen, 1-day program (4 sessions) for transfer students, and parent/family program held throughout June, July, and August. **Policies:** Policies exist regarding: illegal drugs, honor code, student organizations, non-discrimination policy, no smoking policy, student possession and consumption of alcoholic beverages in facilities, harassment, facilities use policy, student grievance policy, and FERPA. Freshmen not permitted cars on campus. **Housing:** Guaranteed on-campus for freshmen. Coed dorms, single-sex dorms, special housing for disabled, apartments, fraternity/sorority housing, themed housing, wellness housing available. $250 nonrefundable deposit, deadline 5/15. Living-learning communities such as Language Houses, The Carolina Experience, W.E.L.L. (Women Experiencing Learning and Leadership), Service and Leadership, Substance Free Environments, Sustainability, UNITAS, SYNC (Sophomore Year Navigating Carolina), and Transfer United available. **Activities:** Bands, campus ministries, choral groups, dance, drama, film society, international student organizations, literary magazine, music ensembles, Model UN, musical theater, opera, radio station, student government, student newspaper, symphony orchestra, TV station, Alpha Phi Omega co-ed service fraternity, Asian students association, Black Student Movement, Campus Crusade for Christ (Cru at UCN-CH), College Republicans, Habitat for Humanity, Young Democrats, Carolina Indian Circle, Carolina Hispanic Student Association, Student Government.

Athletics. NCAA. **Intercollegiate:** Baseball M, basketball, cross-country, diving, fencing, field hockey W, football (tackle) M, golf, gymnastics W, lacrosse, rowing (crew) W, soccer, softball W, swimming, tennis, track and field, volleyball W, wrestling M. **Intramural:** Badminton, basketball, football (non-tackle), golf, racquetball, sand volleyball, soccer, softball, swimming, table tennis, tennis, triathlon, ultimate frisbee, volleyball, water polo. **Team name:** Tar Heels.

Student services. Alcohol/substance abuse counseling, career counseling, services for economically disadvantaged, student employment services, financial aid counseling, health services, legal services, minority student services, on-campus daycare, personal counseling, placement for graduates, veterans' counselor, women's services. **Physically disabled:** Services for visually, speech, hearing impaired.

Contact. E-mail: unchelp@admissions.unc.edu
Phone: (919) 966-3621 Fax: (919) 962-3045
Stephen Farmer, Vice Provost for Enrollment and Undergraduate Admissions, University of North Carolina at Chapel Hill, Jackson Hall, Chapel Hill, NC 27599-2200

University of North Carolina at Charlotte
Charlotte, North Carolina
www.uncc.edu

CB member
CB code: 5105

- Public 4-year university
- Residential campus in very large city
- 22,686 degree-seeking undergraduates: 13% part-time, 48% women, 17% African American, 6% Asian American, 9% Hispanic/Latino, 4% Multi-racial, non-Hispanic, 2% international
- 4,217 degree-seeking graduate students
- 63% of applicants admitted
- SAT or ACT with writing required
- 53% graduate within 6 years; 20% enter graduate study

General. Founded in 1946. Regionally accredited. Located 8 miles north of Uptown Charlotte. Internships and research opportunities throughout campus and the city. **Degrees:** 4,513 bachelor's awarded; master's, professional, doctoral offered. **ROTC:** Army, Air Force. **Location:** 8 miles from downtown. **Calendar:** Semester, limited summer session. **Full-time faculty:** 1,080 total; 83% have terminal degrees, 18% minority, 46% women. **Part-time faculty:** 471 total; 37% have terminal degrees, 13% minority, 58% women. **Class size:** 25% <20, 40% 20-39, 11% 40-49, 16% 50-99, 8% >100. **Special facilities:** Bioinformatics and genomics research center and core laboratories, performing arts theater, botanical gardens, greenhouse, architecture lighting lab, energy production and infrastructure center labs, motorsports laboratory, movie theater, billiard lounge.

Freshman class profile. 16,383 applied, 10,372 admitted, 3,452 enrolled.

Mid 50% test scores			
SAT critical reading:	500-580	Rank in top quarter:	57%
SAT math:	510-600	Rank in top tenth:	22%
SAT writing:	470-560	End year in good standing:	85%
ACT composite:	22-25	Return as sophomores:	83%
GPA 3.75 or higher:	65%	Out-of-state:	6%
GPA 3.50-3.74:	17%	Live on campus:	78%
GPA 3.0-3.49:	16%	International:	2%
GPA 2.0-2.99:	2%	Fraternities:	9%
		Sororities:	13%

Basis for selection. Overall performance in high school academic courses and SAT scores are considered. The SAT is preferred, but ACT is also accepted. SAT and/or ACT may not be required of international applicants or non-traditional adult students. To become an art major, students must be accepted into the institution, must submit a digital portfolio of work, and must be accepted into the major pending a review of the portfolio submission. Portfolios are accepted and reviewed in mid-Spring. **Learning Disabled:** Students can submit documentation of their learning disability in the admissions process if they choose to disclose.

High school preparation. College-preparatory program required. 16 units required. Required and recommended units include English 4, mathematics 4, social studies 1, history 1, science 3 (laboratory 1) and foreign language 2-3. English should emphasize grammar, composition & literature; science should include at least 1 unit in a life or biological science and at least 1 unit in a physical science and 1 lab; foreign language units should be in same language. 2 social studies unit includes 1 U.S. history. Health education and a computer course are also recommended.

2015-2016 Annual costs. Tuition/fees: $6,531; $19,702 out-of-state. Room/board: $9,840. Books/supplies: $1,200. Personal expenses: $1,500.

2014-2015 Financial aid. **Need-based:** 2,511 full-time freshmen applied for aid; 1,896 deemed to have need; 1,801 received aid. Average need met was 63%. Average scholarship/grant was $9,181; average loan $3,697. 44% of total undergraduate aid awarded as scholarships/grants, 56% as loans/jobs. **Non-need-based:** Awarded to 1,501 full-time undergraduates, including 397 freshmen. Scholarships awarded for academics, alumni affiliation, art, athletics, job skills, leadership, minority status, music/drama, religious affiliation, ROTC, state residency.

Application procedures. **Admission:** Closing date 6/1 (receipt date). $60 fee, may be waived for applicants with need. Admission notification on a rolling basis beginning on or about 11/1. Must reply by 5/1. **Financial aid:** Priority date 3/1; no closing date. FAFSA required. Applicants notified on a rolling basis starting 3/1; must reply within 3 week(s) of notification.

Academics. **Special study options:** Accelerated study, cooperative education, cross-registration, distance learning, double major, dual enrollment of high school students, ESL, honors, independent study, internships, study abroad, teacher certification program, Washington semester. **Credit/placement by examination:** AP, CLEP, IB, SAT, ACT, institutional tests. 23 credit hours maximum toward bachelor's degree. **Support services:** Learning center, pre-admission summer program, reduced course load, study skills assistance, tutoring, writing center.

Honors college/program. Students apply directly to this program before their freshmen year and will graduate with honors upon completion of the honors curriculum and capstone project or thesis. The Honors Program continues throughout all four years of the student's college career. The institution accepts students in their first two or three semesters, as well as transfer students.

Majors. Architecture: Architecture. **Area/ethnic studies:** African-American, Latin American. **Biology:** General. **Business:** Accounting, business admin, finance, international, management information systems, managerial economics, marketing, operations. **Communications:** Communications/speech/rhetoric. **Computer sciences:** Computer science. **Education:** Elementary, kindergarten/preschool, middle, special ed. **Engineering:** Civil,

computer, electrical, mechanical, systems. **English:** English lit. **Foreign languages:** French, German, Japanese, Spanish. **Health services:** Athletic training, clinical lab science, nursing (RN), respiratory therapy technology. **History:** General. **Human services:** Social work. **Math:** General. **Parks/recreation:** Health/fitness. **Philosophy/religion:** Philosophy, religion. **Physical sciences:** Chemistry, geology, meteorology, physics. **Protective services:** Criminal justice, fire services admin. **Psychology:** General. **Social sciences:** Anthropology, economics, geography, political science, sociology. **Visual/performing arts:** Art, art history/conservation, dance, dramatic, music, music performance, studio arts. **Work/family studies:** Family studies.

Most popular majors. Business/marketing 18%, communications/journalism 6%, education 6%, engineering/engineering technologies 10%, health sciences 8%, psychology 7%, security/protective services 6%, social sciences 9%.

Technology on campus. 1,600 workstations in dormitories, library, computer center, student center. Dormitories wired for high-speed internet access and linked to campus network. Commuter students can connect to campus network. Online course registration, online library, helpline, repair service, student web hosting, wireless network available.

Student life. **Freshman orientation:** Available, $120 fee. Preregistration for classes offered. 2-day program. **Policies:** Students must follow a Code of Student Responsibility, Code of Student Academic Integrity, and University Policy Statements. **Housing:** Coed dorms, special housing for disabled, apartments, fraternity/sorority housing, wellness housing available. Housing for disabled students is limited. Suite housing, honors housing, learning communities, Freshman-exclusive housing, non-traditional student housing, transfer student community housing, and Greek village housing is available. **Activities:** Bands, campus ministries, choral groups, dance, drama, international student organizations, literary magazine, music ensembles, Model UN, musical theater, radio station, student government, student newspaper, symphony orchestra, TV station, Mission 28, Hillel, College Democrats, College Republicans, Feminist Union, Black Student Union, Latin American Student Organization, Habitat for Humanity, Asian Student Association, Spectrum.

Athletics. NCAA. **Intercollegiate:** Baseball M, basketball, cheerleading, cross-country, football (tackle) M, golf M, soccer, softball W, tennis, track and field, volleyball W. **Intramural:** Badminton, basketball, bowling, football (non-tackle), golf, racquetball, soccer, softball, table tennis, tennis, ultimate frisbee, volleyball, water polo. **Team name:** Fortyniners.

Student services. Adult student services, alcohol/substance abuse counseling, career counseling, services for economically disadvantaged, student employment services, financial aid counseling, health services, minority student services, personal counseling, placement for graduates, veterans' counselor, women's services. **Physically disabled:** Services for visually, speech, hearing impaired.

Contact. E-mail: admissions@uncc.edu
Phone: (704) 687-5507 Fax: (704) 687-1664
Claire Kirby, Director of Admissions, University of North Carolina at Charlotte, Undergraduate Admissions- Cato Hall, Charlotte, NC 28223-0001

University of North Carolina at Greensboro

Greensboro, North Carolina **CB member**
www.uncg.edu **CB code: 5913**

- Public 4-year university
- Residential campus in large city
- 15,158 degree-seeking undergraduates: 12% part-time, 66% women, 28% African American, 5% Asian American, 8% Hispanic/Latino, 4% Multi-racial, non-Hispanic, 2% international
- 2,926 degree-seeking graduate students
- 59% of applicants admitted
- SAT or ACT with writing required
- 56% graduate within 6 years

General. Founded in 1891. Regionally accredited. **Degrees:** 2,832 bachelor's awarded; master's, doctoral offered. **ROTC:** Army, Air Force. **Location:** 90 miles from Raleigh. **Calendar:** Semester, extensive summer session. **Full-time faculty:** 739 total; 80% have terminal degrees, 20% minority, 55% women. **Part-time faculty:** 33 total; 76% have terminal degrees, 9% minority, 46% women. **Class size:** 41% <20, 39% 20-39, 7% 40-49, 11% 50-99, 4% >100. **Special facilities:** Weatherspoon art museum, Silva cello music collection, Randall Jarrell collection, women's studies collection.

Freshman class profile. 10,566 applied, 6,192 admitted, 2,773 enrolled.

Mid 50% test scores			
SAT critical reading:	470-560	**GPA 2.0-2.99:**	8%
SAT math:	470-550	**Rank in top quarter:**	41%
SAT writing:	440-540	**Rank in top tenth:**	13%
ACT composite:	20-25	**Return as sophomores:**	77%
GPA 3.75 or higher:	48%	**Out-of-state:**	5%
GPA 3.50-3.74:	17%	**Live on campus:**	81%
GPA 3.0-3.49:	27%	**International:**	2%

Basis for selection. GED not accepted. Combined test scores and high school GPA based on academic courses most important. High school recommendations and activities considered. SAT preferred, but ACT accepted. Audition required for music program.

High school preparation. College-preparatory program recommended. 15 units required. Required units include English 4, mathematics 4, social studies 2, science 3 (laboratory 1) and foreign language 2.

2015-2016 Annual costs. Tuition/fees: $6,733; $21,595 out-of-state. Room/board: $7,950. Books/supplies: $916. Personal expenses: $1,570.

2015-2016 Financial aid. **Need-based:** 2,483 full-time freshmen applied for aid; 2,286 deemed to have need; 2,277 received aid. Average need met was 57%. Average scholarship/grant was $6,194; average loan $3,376. 91% of total undergraduate aid awarded as scholarships/grants, 9% as loans/jobs. **Non-need-based:** Awarded to 8,177 full-time undergraduates, including 1,864 freshmen. Scholarships awarded for academics, athletics, music/drama, religious affiliation, ROTC, state residency.

Application procedures. **Admission:** Priority date 11/1; deadline 3/1 (postmark date). $55 fee, may be waived for applicants with need. Admission notification on a rolling basis beginning on or about 9/15. Must reply by 5/1. **Financial aid:** Priority date 3/1; no closing date. FAFSA required. Applicants notified on a rolling basis starting 3/15; must reply within 3 week(s) of notification.

Academics. **Special study options:** Accelerated study, combined bachelor's/graduate degree, cross-registration, distance learning, double major, dual enrollment of high school students, ESL, honors, independent study, internships, student-designed major, study abroad, teacher certification program, Washington semester. **Credit/placement by examination:** AP, CLEP, IB, SAT, institutional tests. Up to 64 semester hours of any combination of transfer, correspondence, examination or other will be accepted. SAT Subject Test scores in some subjects may qualify for credit. **Support services:** Learning center, reduced course load, remedial instruction, study skills assistance, tutoring, writing center.

Majors. **Area/ethnic studies:** African-American, women's. **Biology:** General, biochemistry. **Business:** Accounting, business admin, finance, hospitality admin, international, managerial economics. **Communications:** Communications/speech/rhetoric, media studies. **Computer sciences:** Computer science, networking. **Education:** Art, biology, Deaf/hearing impaired, drama/dance, early childhood, elementary, English, French, mathematics, middle, music, physical, social science, social studies, Spanish, special ed. **English:** English lit. **Foreign languages:** Classics, French, German, Spanish. **Health services:** Audiology/speech pathology, clinical lab science, nursing (RN), public health ed. **History:** General. **Human services:** Social work. **Liberal arts:** Arts/sciences. **Math:** General. **Parks/recreation:** General, exercise sciences. **Philosophy/religion:** Philosophy, religion. **Physical sciences:** Chemistry, physics. **Psychology:** General. **Social sciences:** Anthropology, economics, geography, political science, sociology. **Visual/performing arts:** Art, dance, dramatic, interior design, jazz, music, music performance, music theory/composition, studio arts. **Work/family studies:** Child development, clothing/textiles, family studies.

Most popular majors. Biology 6%, business/marketing 18%, communications/journalism 6%, education 9%, health sciences 8%, parks/recreation 6%, psychology 6%, social sciences 8%, visual/performing arts 7%.

Technology on campus. 600 workstations in dormitories, library, computer center, student center. Dormitories wired for high-speed internet access and linked to campus network. Commuter students can connect to campus network. Online course registration, online library, helpline, wireless network available.

Student life. **Freshman orientation:** Mandatory. Preregistration for classes offered. Two-day sessions held prior to beginning of fall and spring semesters. **Housing:** Coed dorms, single-sex dorms, special housing for disabled, apartments, themed housing available. $200 fully refundable deposit, deadline 5/1. Residential college (academic/residential program), International House available. **Activities:** Bands, campus ministries, choral groups, dance, drama, film society, international student organizations, literary magazine, music ensembles, Model UN, musical theater, opera, radio station, student government, student newspaper, symphony orchestra, neo-Black society, environmental awareness foundation, political awareness club, Habitat for Humanity, Rotaract Club, gay, lesbian and bisexual student association.

Athletics. NCAA. **Intercollegiate:** Baseball M, basketball, cross-country, golf, soccer, softball W, tennis, volleyball W. **Intramural:** Badminton, basketball, bowling, golf, racquetball, soccer, softball, swimming, table tennis, tennis, track and field, volleyball. **Team name:** Spartans.

Student services. Adult student services, chaplain/spiritual director, career counseling, services for economically disadvantaged, student employment services, financial aid counseling, health services, minority student services, personal counseling, placement for graduates, veterans' counselor. **Physically disabled:** Services for visually, speech, hearing impaired.

Contact. E-mail: admissions@uncg.edu
Phone: (336) 334-5243 Fax: (336) 334-4180
Lise Keller, Director of Admissions, University of North Carolina at Greensboro, PO Box 26170, Greensboro, NC 27402-6170

University of North Carolina at Pembroke
Pembroke, North Carolina CB member
www.uncp.edu CB code: 5534

▶ Public 4-year university and liberal arts college
▶ Commuter campus in small town
▶ 5,508 degree-seeking undergraduates: 18% part-time, 60% women, 36% African American, 2% Asian American, 6% Hispanic/Latino, 15% Native American, 2% Multi-racial, non-Hispanic, 1% international
▶ 737 degree-seeking graduate students
▶ 74% of applicants admitted
▶ SAT or ACT with writing required
▶ 34% graduate within 6 years

General. Founded in 1887. Regionally accredited. **Degrees:** 907 bachelor's awarded; master's offered. **ROTC:** Army, Air Force. **Location:** 31 miles from Fayetteville, 100 miles from Raleigh. **Calendar:** Semester, limited summer session. **Full-time faculty:** 295 total; 79% have terminal degrees, 25% minority, 51% women. **Part-time faculty:** 96 total; 38% have terminal degrees, 29% minority, 49% women. **Class size:** 47% < 20, 44% 20-39, 8% 40-49, 2% 50-99. **Special facilities:** Native American resource center, performing arts center, clinical learning center.

Freshman class profile. 4,596 applied, 3,418 admitted, 1,233 enrolled.

Mid 50% test scores			
SAT critical reading:	410-490	**GPA 2.0-2.99:**	22%
SAT math:	420-500	**Rank in top quarter:**	34%
SAT writing:	390-470	**Rank in top tenth:**	11%
ACT composite:	18-22	**Return as sophomores:**	67%
GPA 3.75 or higher:	30%	**Out-of-state:**	2%
GPA 3.50-3.74:	16%	**Live on campus:**	82%
GPA 3.0-3.49:	32%	**Fraternities:**	42%
		Sororities:	58%

Basis for selection. High school record, class standing, GPA, test scores, and college preparatory courses are important. Auditions and interviews may be required for acceptance to obtain entry into certain programs.

High school preparation. College-preparatory program recommended. 16 units required. Required units include English 4, mathematics 4, social studies 1, history 1, science 3 (laboratory 1) and foreign language 2.

2015-2016 Annual costs. Tuition/fees: $5,534; $15,982 out-of-state. Room/board: $8,502. Books/supplies: $1,505. Personal expenses: $1,434.

2015-2016 Financial aid. **Need-based:** Average need met was 66%. Average scholarship/grant was $7,144; average loan $3,361. 44% of total undergraduate aid awarded as scholarships/grants, 56% as loans/jobs. **Non-need-based:** Scholarships awarded for academics, alumni affiliation, art, athletics, minority status, music/drama.

Application procedures. **Admission:** Priority date 7/15; deadline 7/31 (receipt date). $45 fee, may be waived for applicants with need. Admission notification on a rolling basis beginning on or about 9/15. **Financial aid:** Priority date 3/15; no closing date. FAFSA required. Applicants notified on a rolling basis starting 4/15; must reply within 2 week(s) of notification.

Academics. Certification on secondary teaching level in English, biology, mathematics, social studies, and science education. **Special study options:** Accelerated study, combined bachelor's/graduate degree, cross-registration, distance learning, double major, dual enrollment of high school students, ESL, honors, internships, study abroad, teacher certification program, Washington semester. **Credit/placement by examination:** AP, CLEP, SAT, ACT, institutional tests. 30 credit hours maximum toward bachelor's degree. **Support**

services: Learning center, pre-admission summer program, reduced course load, remedial instruction, tutoring, writing center.

Honors college/program. Students selected based on academic achievement, leadership, and community involvement. SAT score of 1150 and GPA above 3.5 required. Approximately 35 students are chosen yearly to participate. Academic program offers interdisciplinary educational opportunities that enhance the general curriculum as well as social and cultural opportunities.

Majors. **Area/ethnic studies:** Native American. **Biology:** General, biotechnology. **Business:** Accounting, business admin. **Communications:** Media studies. **Computer sciences:** Computer science, information technology. **Conservation:** Environmental science, environmental studies. **Education:** Art, elementary, English, kindergarten/preschool, mathematics, middle, music, physical, science, social studies, special ed. **English:** English lit. **Foreign languages:** Spanish. **Health services:** Athletic training, nursing (RN). **History:** General. **Human services:** Social work. **Math:** General. **Parks/recreation:** Health/fitness. **Physical sciences:** Chemistry, physics. **Protective services:** Criminal justice. **Psychology:** General. **Social sciences:** Political science, sociology. **Visual/performing arts:** Dramatic, music, music performance, studio arts.

Most popular majors. Biology 9%, business/marketing 11%, education 10%, health sciences 6%, public administration/social services 7%, security/protective services 11%, social sciences 11%.

Technology on campus. 875 workstations in dormitories, library, computer center, student center. Dormitories wired for high-speed internet access and linked to campus network. Commuter students can connect to campus network. Online course registration, online library, helpline, wireless network available.

Student life. **Freshman orientation:** Mandatory, $50 fee. Preregistration for classes offered. 3-day orientation session held in Fall, Spring, Summer with campus tours, advising. **Housing:** Coed dorms, single-sex dorms, apartments available. $150 fully refundable deposit, deadline 5/29. Freshmen given preference for on-campus housing. Apartments available. **Activities:** Bands, campus ministries, choral groups, dance, drama, international student organizations, music ensembles, musical theater, radio station, student government, student newspaper, TV station, Native American Organization, African American Student Organization, Baptist Student Union, Methodist Campus Ministry, Fellowship of Christian Athletes, Campus Association of Social Workers, American Medical Student Association, criminal justice club.

Athletics. NCAA. **Intercollegiate:** Baseball M, basketball, cross-country, football (tackle) M, golf, soccer, softball W, tennis W, track and field, volleyball W, wrestling M. **Intramural:** Cheerleading, rugby M, tennis W. **Team name:** Braves.

Student services. Alcohol/substance abuse counseling, chaplain/spiritual director, career counseling, student employment services, financial aid counseling, health services, personal counseling, veterans' counselor. **Physically disabled:** Services for visually, hearing impaired.

Contact. E-mail: admissons@uncp.edu
Phone: (910) 521-6262 Toll-free number: (800) 949-8627
Fax: (910) 521-6497
Lela Clark, Director of Admissions, University of North Carolina at Pembroke, Box 1510, Pembroke, NC 28372

University of North Carolina at Wilmington
Wilmington, North Carolina   **CB member**
www.uncw.edu   **CB code: 5907**

- Public 4-year university
- Residential campus in small city
- 12,982 degree-seeking undergraduates: 11% part-time, 61% women, 5% African American, 2% Asian American, 7% Hispanic/Latino, 1% Native American, 3% Multi-racial, non-Hispanic, 1% international
- 1,574 degree-seeking graduate students
- 61% of applicants admitted
- SAT or ACT with writing, application essay required
- 71% graduate within 6 years

General. Founded in 1947. Regionally accredited. **Degrees:** 3,074 bachelor's awarded; master's, doctoral offered. **Location:** 125 miles from Raleigh. **Calendar:** Semester, extensive summer session. **Full-time faculty:** 635 total; 81% have terminal degrees, 19% minority, 50% women. **Part-time faculty:** 381 total; 28% have terminal degrees, 29% minority, 61% women. **Class size:** 30% < 20, 54% 20-39, 6% 40-49, 8% 50-99, 1% >100. **Special facilities:**

108-acre coastal forest research and teaching station, wildflower preserve, shellfish research hatchery.

Freshman class profile. 11,444 applied, 6,976 admitted, 2,029 enrolled.

Mid 50% test scores			
SAT critical reading:	560-630	Rank in top quarter:	62%
SAT math:	560-630	Rank in top tenth:	24%
SAT writing:	520-620	Return as sophomores:	85%
ACT composite:	23-27	Out-of-state:	15%
GPA 3.75 or higher:	81%	Live on campus:	89%
GPA 3.50-3.74:	11%	International:	1%
GPA 3.0-3.49:	7%	Fraternities:	5%
GPA 2.0-2.99:	1%	Sororities:	13%

Basis for selection. High school record; rank in class, if provided; standardized test scores; and rigor of courses completed in high school are very important. SAT or ACT with writing required. Auditions for Music majors required. **Home schooled:** Statement describing home school structure and mission, transcript of courses and grades, letter of recommendation (nonparent) required.

High school preparation. College-preparatory program required. Required units include English 4, mathematics 4, social studies 1, history 1, science 3 (laboratory 1) and foreign language 2. History must be US History.

2015-2016 Annual costs. Tuition/fees: $6,690; $20,556 out-of-state. Room/board: $9,466. Books/supplies: $1,082. Personal expenses: $3,222.

2014-2015 Financial aid. **Need-based:** 1,759 full-time freshmen applied for aid; 1,179 deemed to have need; 1,118 received aid. Average need met was 62%. Average scholarship/grant was $6,531; average loan $3,461. 63% of total undergraduate aid awarded as scholarships/grants, 37% as loans/jobs. **Non-need-based:** Awarded to 836 full-time undergraduates, including 295 freshmen. Scholarships awarded for academics, alumni affiliation, art, athletics, leadership, minority status, music/drama.

Application procedures. **Admission:** Priority date 11/1; deadline 2/1 (postmark date). $75 fee, may be waived for applicants with need. Admission notification by 4/1. Admission notification on a rolling basis beginning on or about 1/20. Must reply by May 1 or within 4 week(s) if notified thereafter. **Financial aid:** Priority date 3/1; no closing date. FAFSA required. Applicants notified on a rolling basis starting 3/15; must reply within 3 week(s) of notification.

Academics. **Special study options:** Accelerated study, combined bachelor's/graduate degree, distance learning, double major, dual enrollment of high school students, ESL, exchange student, honors, independent study, internships, study abroad, teacher certification program. 2+2 Pre-Engineering programs. **Credit/placement by examination:** AP, CLEP, IB, institutional tests. **Support services:** Learning center, reduced course load, remedial instruction, study skills assistance, tutoring, writing center.

Honors college/program. Average SAT is 1300 (exclusive of Writing), average ACT composite is 29, and average weighted high school GPA is 4.20. 132 students (freshmen) admitted. Letter of recommendation from a teacher required.

Majors. **Biology:** General, marine. **Business:** Accounting, business admin. **Communications:** Communications/speech/rhetoric. **Computer sciences:** Computer science, information technology. **Conservation:** Environmental science, environmental studies. **Education:** Biology, chemistry, elementary, English, French, kindergarten/preschool, mathematics, middle, multiple handicapped, music, physical, Spanish, special ed. **English:** Creative writing, English lit. **Foreign languages:** French, German, Spanish. **Health services:** Athletic training, nursing (RN), public health ed, recreational therapy. **History:** General. **Human services:** Social work. **Math:** General, statistics. **Parks/recreation:** Exercise sciences, facilities management, health/fitness. **Physical sciences:** Chemistry, geology, oceanography, physics. **Psychology:** General. **Social sciences:** Anthropology, criminology, economics, geography, political science, sociology. **Visual/performing arts:** Art history/conservation, cinematography, dramatic, music, music performance, studio arts.

Most popular majors. Biology 9%, business/marketing 19%, communications/journalism 6%, education 8%, health sciences 10%, psychology 7%, social sciences 9%, visual/performing arts 6%.

Technology on campus. PC or laptop required. 1,161 workstations in dormitories, library, computer center, student center. Dormitories wired for high-speed internet access and linked to campus network. Commuter students can connect to campus network. Online course registration, online library, helpline, repair service, student web hosting, wireless network available.

Student life. **Freshman orientation:** Mandatory, $130 fee. Preregistration for classes offered. **Housing:** Coed dorms, single-sex dorms, apartments, fraternity/sorority housing, wellness housing available. $105 nonrefundable deposit, deadline 5/1. **Activities:** Bands, campus ministries, choral groups, dance, drama, film society, international student organizations, literary magazine, music ensembles, Model UN, radio station, student government, student newspaper, TV station, Habitat for Humanity, Model UN Association, Young Life, Hillel, PRIDE, environmental concerns organization, Veteran Education and Transition Support, Black Student Union, Surfrider Foundation, International Student Organization.

Athletics. NCAA. **Intercollegiate:** Baseball M, basketball, cheerleading, cross-country, diving, golf, sand volleyball W, soccer, softball W, swimming, tennis, track and field, volleyball W. **Intramural:** Badminton, basketball, football (non-tackle), racquetball, sand volleyball, soccer, softball, tennis, volleyball, water polo. **Team name:** Seahawks.

Student services. Adult student services, alcohol/substance abuse counseling, career counseling, student employment services, financial aid counseling, health services, legal services, minority student services, personal counseling, veterans' counselor, women's services. **Physically disabled:** Services for visually, speech, hearing impaired.

Contact. E-mail: admissions@uncw.edu
Phone: (910) 962-3243 Fax: (910) 962-3038
Marcio Moreno, Director, University of North Carolina at Wilmington, 601 South College Road, Wilmington, NC 28403-5904

University of North Carolina School of the Arts
Winston-Salem, North Carolina   CB member
www.uncsa.edu/   CB code: 5512

- Public 4-year visual arts and performing arts college
- Residential campus in small city
- 850 degree-seeking undergraduates: 1% part-time, 50% women, 9% African American, 2% Asian American, 8% Hispanic/Latino, 5% Multiracial, non-Hispanic, 2% international
- 114 degree-seeking graduate students
- 34% of applicants admitted
- SAT or ACT with writing, interview required
- 68% graduate within 6 years

General. Founded in 1963. Regionally accredited. State conservatory with high school, undergraduate and graduate facilities. **Degrees:** 164 bachelor's awarded; master's offered. **Location:** 75 miles from Charlotte, 95 miles from Raleigh. **Calendar:** Semester, limited summer session. **Full-time faculty:** 137 total; 42% have terminal degrees, 4% minority, 38% women. **Part-time faculty:** 50 total; 34% have terminal degrees, 2% minority, 48% women. **Class size:** 90% < 20, 8% 20-39, less than 1% 40-49, less than 1% 50-99, less than 1% >100. **Special facilities:** Stage production shop, film village with sound and recording stages, new media facilities.

Freshman class profile. 887 applied, 305 admitted, 199 enrolled.

Mid 50% test scores		GPA 2.0-2.99:	9%
SAT critical reading:	510-630	Rank in top quarter:	43%
SAT math:	480-600	Rank in top tenth:	16%
SAT writing:	470-620	Return as sophomores:	83%
ACT composite:	21-27	Out-of-state:	57%
GPA 3.75 or higher:	49%	Live on campus:	89%
GPA 3.50-3.74:	21%	International:	3%
GPA 3.0-3.49:	21%		

Basis for selection. Talent, achievement, career potential are most important. Admission heavily dependent on audition. SAT combined score of 800 (exclusive of Writing) or ACT composite score of 19, school record, recommendations are important. Interview recommended for all students. Audition required for dance, drama, music programs; portfolio required for design, filmmaking, production programs.

High school preparation. College-preparatory program required. 16 units required. Required and recommended units include English 4, mathematics 3-4, social studies 2, history 1, science 3 (laboratory 1) and foreign language 2.

2015-2016 Annual costs. Tuition/fees: $8,917; $24,337 out-of-state. Room/board: $8,570. Books/supplies: $1,250. Personal expenses: $2,345.

2015-2016 Financial aid. Need-based: 163 full-time freshmen applied for aid; 126 deemed to have need; 125 received aid. Average need met was 56%. Average scholarship/grant was $8,100; average loan $3,693. 52% of total undergraduate aid awarded as scholarships/grants, 48% as loans/jobs. **Non-need-based:** Awarded to 294 full-time undergraduates, including 79 freshmen. Scholarships awarded for academics, art, leadership, music/drama, state residency.

Application procedures. Admission: Closing date 3/15. $95 fee, may be waived for applicants with need. Admission notification on a rolling basis

beginning on or about 4/1. Must reply by May 1 or within 3 week(s) if notified thereafter. Application closing date dependent upon audition. Applications must be submitted at least 2 weeks before audition date. Dance, drama and filmmaking interviews begin in January and end in early March. Music and technical theater auditions begin in November and end in early March. Decisions generally are made by April 1, or about 2 weeks after audition if later than April 1. **Financial aid:** Priority date 3/1; no closing date. FAFSA required. Applicants notified on a rolling basis starting 4/1; must reply within 2 week(s) of notification.

Academics. Professional training supplemented by strong general studies curriculum. **Special study options:** Independent study, internships. **Credit/placement by examination:** AP, CLEP, SAT, ACT. **Support services:** Learning center, study skills assistance, tutoring, writing center.

Majors. Liberal arts: Arts/sciences. **Visual/performing arts:** Cinematography, dance, dramatic, music performance, theater design.

Technology on campus. 117 workstations in dormitories, library, student center. Dormitories wired for high-speed internet access and linked to campus network. Commuter students can connect to campus network. Online course registration, online library, helpline, repair service, wireless network available.

Student life. Freshman orientation: Mandatory, $80 fee. Preregistration for classes offered. Orientation is the first three days in the academic year. All art schools have separate orientations which include academic assessment. **Housing:** Guaranteed on-campus for freshmen. Coed dorms available. $300 fully refundable deposit, deadline 5/20. **Activities:** Student government, student newspaper, A.R.T.S. Initiative, Artist Underground, Art & Soul, UNCSA Artists of Color.

Athletics. Team name: Fighting Pickles.

Student services. Alcohol/substance abuse counseling, career counseling, student employment services, financial aid counseling, health services, personal counseling.

Contact. E-mail: admission@uncsa.edu
Phone: (336) 770-3290 Fax: (336) 770-3370
Sheeler Lawson, Director of Admissions, University of North Carolina School of the Arts, 1533 South Main Street, Winston-Salem, NC 27127-2738

University of Phoenix: Charlotte
Charlotte, North Carolina
www.phoenix.edu

- For-profit 4-year career college
- Very large city
- 684 undergraduates

General. Regionally accredited. **Degrees:** 204 bachelor's awarded; master's offered. **Calendar:** Differs by program.

Basis for selection. Open admission, but selective for some programs.

2015-2016 Annual costs. Per-credit-hour charge, $410 to $635, depending upon level and course of study. Books, material charges, and other fees vary by course and program. All fees are subject to change.

Application procedures. Admission: No deadline. No application fee. **Financial aid:** No deadline.

Academics. Credit/placement by examination: AP, CLEP.

Majors. Business: Business admin, e-commerce, marketing. **Computer sciences:** General, programming, security, system admin, systems analysis, web page design, webmaster.

Student life. Freshman orientation: Mandatory. Preregistration for classes offered.

Contact. University of Phoenix: Charlotte, 3800 Arco Corporate Drive, Charlotte, NC 28273-3409

University of Phoenix: Raleigh
Raleigh, North Carolina
www.phoenix.edu

- For-profit 4-year career college
- Large city
- 402 undergraduates

General. Regionally accredited. **Degrees:** 54 bachelor's awarded; master's offered. **Calendar:** Differs by program. **Full-time faculty:** 11 total. **Part-time faculty:** 77 total.

Basis for selection. Open admission, but selective for some programs.

2015-2016 Annual costs. Per-credit-hour charge, $410 to $635, depending upon level and course of study. Books, material charges, and other fees vary by course and program. All fees are subject to change.

Application procedures. Admission: No deadline. No application fee. **Financial aid:** No deadline.

Academics. Credit/placement by examination: AP, CLEP.

Majors. Business: Business admin, e-commerce, marketing. **Computer sciences:** Programming, security, system admin, systems analysis, web page design, webmaster.

Student life. Freshman orientation: Mandatory. Preregistration for classes offered.

Contact. Toll-free number: (866) 766-0766
University of Phoenix: Raleigh, 5511 Capital Center Drive, Suite 390, Raleigh, NC 27606-3380

Wake Forest University
Winston-Salem, North Carolina   CB member
www.wfu.edu   CB code: 5885

- Private 4-year university
- Residential campus in small city
- 4,866 degree-seeking undergraduates: 1% part-time, 53% women, 6% African American, 5% Asian American, 7% Hispanic/Latino, 3% Multi-racial, non-Hispanic, 7% international
- 2,948 degree-seeking graduate students
- 29% of applicants admitted
- Application essay required
- 88% graduate within 6 years

General. Founded in 1834. Regionally accredited. First-year students receive a notebook computer. **Degrees:** 1,152 bachelor's awarded; master's, professional, doctoral offered. **ROTC:** Army. **Location:** 4 miles from downtown. **Calendar:** Semester, limited summer session. **Full-time faculty:** 573 total; 93% have terminal degrees, 16% minority, 43% women. **Part-time faculty:** 239 total; 51% women. **Class size:** 58% < 20, 36% 20-39, 5% 40-49, less than 1% 50-99. **Special facilities:** Museum of anthropology, center for nanotechnology and molecular materials, Reynolda house museum of American art, Charlotte and Philip Hanes art gallery, archaeology laboratory, biomechanics laboratory, laser physics laboratory, Reynolda gardens.

Freshman class profile. 13,281 applied, 3,903 admitted, 1,284 enrolled.

Mid 50% test scores		Return as sophomores:	93%
SAT critical reading:	590-690	Out-of-state:	79%
SAT math:	610-720	Live on campus:	100%
SAT writing:	600-700	International:	10%
Rank in top quarter:	93%	Fraternities:	35%
Rank in top tenth:	77%	Sororities:	57%

Basis for selection. High school curriculum and classroom performance combined with the student's writing ability, extracurricular activities, and evidence of character and talent are the most important criteria for admission. The admissions office strongly encourages personal interviews. Audition recommended for those competing for a Presidential Scholarship (for students with special talents in music, theater, art, dance, and debate).

High school preparation. College-preparatory program required. 16 units required; 20 recommended. Required and recommended units include English 4, mathematics 3-4, social studies 2-4, science 1-4 and foreign language 2-4.

2015-2016 Annual costs. Tuition/fees: $47,682. Room/board: $12,996. Books/supplies: $1,400. Personal expenses: $1,500.

2015-2016 Financial aid. Need-based: 574 full-time freshmen applied for aid; 441 deemed to have need; 441 received aid. Average need met was 100%. Average scholarship/grant was $42,212; average loan $8,521. 77% of total undergraduate aid awarded as scholarships/grants, 23% as loans/jobs. **Non-need-based:** Awarded to 1,363 full-time undergraduates, including 308 freshmen. Scholarships awarded for academics, alumni affiliation, art, athletics, leadership, music/drama, religious affiliation, ROTC, state residency. **Additional information:** First-year students with an annual family income of less than $40,000 will have their student loans capped at $4,000 per year

during their college years. Other financial aid to the students will come from grant and scholarship increases and work-study opportunities.

Application procedures. Admission: Closing date 1/1. $50 fee, may be waived for applicants with need. Admission notification by 4/1. Must reply by 5/1. **Financial aid:** Priority date 2/15, closing date 3/1. FAFSA, CSS PROFILE required. Applicants notified on a rolling basis starting 4/1; must reply by 5/1 or within 4 week(s) of notification.

Academics. Language courses at all levels in Russian, Greek, Italian, Hebrew; elementary and intermediate courses in Chinese, Japanese and Arabic; elementary courses in Hindi, Portuguese. **Special study options:** Combined bachelor's/graduate degree, cross-registration, distance learning, double major, dual enrollment of high school students, honors, independent study, internships, study abroad, teacher certification program, Washington semester. Semester in London, Venice, or Vienna and semester at universities in Dijon, Salamanca, Berlin, Moscow, Beijing, and Japan. **Credit/placement by examination:** AP, CLEP, IB, institutional tests. **Support services:** Learning center, reduced course load, study skills assistance, tutoring, writing center.

Majors. Area/ethnic studies: Women's. **Biology:** General, bacteriology. **Business:** General, accounting, finance, management science. **Communications:** Communications/speech/rhetoric. **Computer sciences:** Computer science. **Education:** Elementary, social studies. **English:** English lit. **Foreign languages:** Ancient Greek, Chinese, classics, French, German, Japanese, Latin, Russian, Spanish. **Health services:** Clinical lab science. **History:** General. **Math:** General. **Parks/recreation:** Exercise sciences. **Philosophy/religion:** Philosophy, religion. **Physical sciences:** Chemistry, physics. **Psychology:** General. **Social sciences:** Anthropology, econometrics, economics, political science, sociology. **Visual/performing arts:** Art history/conservation, dramatic, music history, music performance, studio arts.

Most popular majors. Biology 8%, business/marketing 19%, communications/journalism 8%, parks/recreation 6%, psychology 7%, social sciences 22%.

Technology on campus. PC or laptop required. Dormitories wired for high-speed internet access and linked to campus network. Commuter students can connect to campus network. Online course registration, online library, helpline, repair service, student web hosting, wireless network available.

Student life. Freshman orientation: Mandatory. Preregistration for classes offered. **Policies:** First-, second-, and third-year students with residential status required to live on campus. **Housing:** Guaranteed on-campus for all undergraduates. Coed dorms, apartments, fraternity/sorority housing, themed housing, wellness housing available. $500 nonrefundable deposit, deadline 5/1. ADA accommodations for disabled students available. **Activities:** Bands, campus ministries, choral groups, dance, drama, film society, international student organizations, literary magazine, music ensembles, Model UN, radio station, student government, student newspaper, symphony orchestra, TV station, Black Student Alliance, College Democrats, College Republicans, Alpha Phi Omega, InterVarsity Christian Fellowship, Amnesty International, Habitat for Humanity, volunteer service corps.

Athletics. NCAA. **Intercollegiate:** Baseball M, basketball, cheerleading, cross-country, field hockey W, football (tackle) M, golf, soccer, tennis, track and field, volleyball W. **Intramural:** Basketball, bowling, cross-country, diving, equestrian W, football (non-tackle), golf, racquetball, soccer, softball, table tennis, tennis, ultimate frisbee, volleyball, water polo, wrestling M. **Team name:** Demon Deacons.

Student services. Alcohol/substance abuse counseling, chaplain/spiritual director, career counseling, student employment services, financial aid counseling, health services, minority student services, personal counseling, placement for graduates. **Physically disabled:** Services for visually, speech, hearing impaired.

Contact. E-mail: admissions@wfu.edu
Phone: (336) 758-5201 Fax: (336) 758-4324
Martha Allman, Director of Admissions, Wake Forest University, PO Box 7305, Winston-Salem, NC 27109-7305

Warren Wilson College
Asheville, North Carolina   CB member
www.warren-wilson.edu   CB code: 5886

- Private 4-year liberal arts college
- Residential campus in small city
- 749 degree-seeking undergraduates: 2% part-time, 60% women, 4% African American, 1% Asian American, 9% Hispanic/Latino, 1% Native American, 3% Multi-racial, non-Hispanic, 2% international
- 59 degree-seeking graduate students
- 84% of applicants admitted

◆ SAT or ACT (ACT writing optional), application essay required

◆ 53% graduate within 6 years

General. Founded in 1894. Regionally accredited. **Degrees:** 163 bachelor's awarded; master's offered. **Location:** 5 miles from Asheville, NC. **Calendar:** Semester, limited summer session. **Full-time faculty:** 63 total; 10% minority, 49% women. **Part-time faculty:** 40 total; 10% minority, 70% women. **Class size:** 85% < 20, 15% 20-39. **Special facilities:** 276-acre sustainably managed college farm, 6-acre pesticide-free college garden, 776-acre sustainably managed college forest, an outdoor adventure learning lab, archaeology site, GIS laboratory, visual arts center and gallery, hiking trails.

Freshman class profile. 809 applied, 678 admitted, 195 enrolled.

Mid 50% test scores		Rank in top tenth:	17%
SAT critical reading:	520-650	Return as sophomores:	63%
SAT math:	470-590	Out-of-state:	71%
ACT composite:	21-28	Live on campus:	100%
Rank in top quarter:	18%	International:	2%

Basis for selection. Admission based on both the potential and academic qualifications. All available information is considered, including previous academic records, evidence of academic and social maturity, extracurricular activities, community service, SAT/ACT, interview, essay, references, recent grade trends and general contributions to school and community. All records of examinations taken overseas plus TOEFL required of international applicants. Interview, portfolio recommended. **Home schooled:** Transcript of courses and grades, interview, letter of recommendation (nonparent) required. Submit transcript listing course titles and content, partial portfolio of sample work completed (graded papers), document that serves as diploma, copy of state rules under which school was formed or is recognized, and interview (phone or in person).

High school preparation. College-preparatory program required. 14 units required. Required and recommended units include English 4, mathematics 3, social studies 3, science 2 (laboratory 2) and foreign language 2. Math requirement includes algebra I, algebra II and geometry. Sciences must include 2 laboratories.

2015-2016 Annual costs. Tuition/fees: $32,560. Room/board: $9,900. Books/supplies: $850. Personal expenses: $3,950. **Additional information:** All resident students are required to work a total of 480 hours per year in the college's work program (15 hours per week, on average). For this, $3,480 earnings are credited toward tuition costs.

2014-2015 Financial aid. Need-based: 211 full-time freshmen applied for aid; 191 deemed to have need; 191 received aid. Average need met was 85%. Average scholarship/grant was $6,161; average loan $3,436. 66% of total undergraduate aid awarded as scholarships/grants, 34% as loans/jobs. **Non-need-based:** Awarded to 295 full-time undergraduates, including 96 freshmen. Scholarships awarded for academics, art, athletics, leadership, religious affiliation, state residency.

Application procedures. Admission: Priority date 2/1; no deadline. No application fee. Application must be submitted online. Admission notification on a rolling basis beginning on or about 1/1. Must reply by May 1 or within 2 week(s) if notified thereafter. **Financial aid:** Priority date 3/1; no closing date. FAFSA required. Applicants notified on a rolling basis starting 3/1; must reply by 5/1 or within 3 week(s) of notification.

Academics. Special study options: Cross-registration, double major, ESL, honors, independent study, internships, liberal arts/career combination, student-designed major, study abroad. **Credit/placement by examination:** AP, CLEP, IB, institutional tests. **Support services:** Reduced course load, study skills assistance, tutoring, writing center.

Majors. Area/ethnic studies: Women's. **Biology:** General. **Conservation:** Environmental studies. **English:** Creative writing, English lit. **Foreign languages:** Spanish. **History:** General. **Human services:** Social work. **Philosophy/religion:** Philosophy, religion. **Physical sciences:** Chemistry. **Psychology:** General. **Social sciences:** Sociology. **Visual/performing arts:** General.

Most popular majors. Biology 6%, English 11%, history 7%, interdisciplinary studies 8%, natural resources/environmental science 21%, psychology 8%, public administration/social services 7%, social sciences 9%, visual/performing arts 9%.

Technology on campus. 91 workstations in library, computer center, student center. Dormitories wired for high-speed internet access and linked to campus network. Commuter students can connect to campus network. Online course registration, online library, helpline, wireless network available.

Student life. Freshman orientation: Mandatory, $260 fee. Preregistration for classes offered. 4-day orientation (immediately before classes begin, late August) includes academic advising, registration, introduction to Triad Education Program requirements, introduction to campus policies and resources, full day of community service, residence hall and social programming, dinner/discussions with faculty, staff and peer group. **Policies:** Freshmen not permitted cars on campus. **Housing:** Guaranteed on-campus for freshmen. Coed dorms, single-sex dorms, apartments, cooperative housing, themed housing, wellness housing available. **Activities:** Jazz band, campus ministries, choral groups, dance, drama, international student organizations, literary magazine, music ensembles, musical theater, student government, student newspaper, Amnesty International, Emmaus Christian Gathering, Interfaith, Christians in Action, Quaker Meeting, Jewish student group, Buddhist experience, earth first, sustainable living, Activist-in-residence.

Athletics. USCAA. **Intercollegiate:** Basketball, cross-country, soccer, swimming. **Intramural:** Basketball, soccer, table tennis, tennis. **Team name:** Owls.

Student services. Alcohol/substance abuse counseling, chaplain/spiritual director, career counseling, student employment services, financial aid counseling, health services, minority student services, personal counseling, placement for graduates, women's services. **Physically disabled:** Services for visually, speech, hearing impaired.

Contact. E-mail: admit@warren-wilson.edu
Phone: (828) 771-2073 Toll-free number: (800) 934-3536
Fax: (828) 298-1440
Sharon Lytle, Sr. Associate Director of Admission, Warren Wilson College, PO Box 9000, Asheville, NC 28815-9000

Western Carolina University
Cullowhee, North Carolina
www.wcu.edu

CB member
CB code: 5897

◆ Public 4-year university

◆ Residential campus in small town

◆ 8,652 degree-seeking undergraduates

◆ SAT or ACT with writing required

General. Founded in 1889. Regionally accredited. **Degrees:** 2,077 bachelor's awarded; master's, professional, doctoral offered. **Location:** 53 miles from Asheville, 157 miles from Atlanta, GA. **Calendar:** Semester, extensive summer session. **Full-time faculty:** 493 total; 76% have terminal degrees, 5% minority, 48% women. **Part-time faculty:** 183 total; 33% have terminal degrees, 3% minority, 57% women. **Class size:** 28% < 20, 55% 20-39, 12% 40-49, 5% 50-99, less than 1% >100. **Special facilities:** Center for applied technology, fine and performing arts center, collection of historical Native American artifacts and documents, center for the advancement of teaching, public policy institute, mountain heritage center.

Freshman class profile.

GPA 3.75 or higher:	50%	Rank in top quarter:	39%
GPA 3.50-3.74:	17%	Rank in top tenth:	13%
GPA 3.0-3.49:	27%	Out-of-state:	8%
GPA 2.0-2.99:	6%	Live on campus:	98%

Basis for selection. The most important admission factors are secondary school record, class rank, GPA, standardized test scores, talent/ability, and applicant's interest. All applicants, except those exempted by current campus policies, must submit standardized test scores. SAT preferred, ACT also accepted. Essays not required but will be considered if submitted. Auditions and/or portfolios are required for some art/music/theater programs. **Home schooled:** Must submit official transcript of all work completed and meet standards equivalent to those used for applicants from approved secondary schools.

High school preparation. College-preparatory program required. 20 units required; 24 recommended. Required and recommended units include English 4, mathematics 4, social studies 2, history 1, science 3 (laboratory 3), foreign language 2 and academic electives 4-8.

2015-2016 Annual costs. Tuition/fees: $6,903; $17,296 out-of-state. Room/board: $8,131. Books/supplies: $753. Personal expenses: $1,482.

2014-2015 Financial aid. Need-based: 1,588 full-time freshmen applied for aid; 1,226 deemed to have need; 1,200 received aid. Average need met was 64%. Average scholarship/grant was $6,371; average loan $5,403. 52% of total undergraduate aid awarded as scholarships/grants, 48% as loans/jobs. **Non-need-based:** Awarded to 509 full-time undergraduates, including 132 freshmen. Scholarships awarded for academics, art, athletics, leadership, music/drama, state residency.

Application procedures. Admission: Priority date 11/15; deadline 3/1 (postmark date). $55 fee, may be waived for applicants with need. Admission notification on a rolling basis beginning on or about 9/1. Must reply by 5/1. Housing deposit due upon receipt of student's acceptance. **Financial aid:**

Priority date 3/15; no closing date. FAFSA, institutional form required. Applicants notified on a rolling basis starting 4/1.

Academics. Special study options: Combined bachelor's/graduate degree, cooperative education, distance learning, double major, dual enrollment of high school students, ESL, honors, independent study, internships, student-designed major, study abroad, teacher certification program. Service learning. **Credit/placement by examination:** AP, CLEP, IB, institutional tests. Student may apply to be examined in any course identified by department head as available for credit by exam. Credit by exam attempts must be completed prior to semester of graduation. Catalog does not specify maximum number of hours. **Support services:** Learning center, pre-admission summer program, reduced course load, study skills assistance, tutoring, writing center.

Honors college/program. For first-year students to be considered, must meet at least one of the following: 1875 SAT or 30 ACT, 4.0 weighted cumulative high school GPA, rank in the top 10% of class. Other requirements apply to transfer students and students currently enrolled.

Majors. Biology: General. **Business:** Accounting, business admin, entrepreneurial studies, finance, hospitality admin, international, management information systems, marketing. **Communications:** Communications/speech/rhetoric. **Computer sciences:** Computer science. **Conservation:** Environmental science, management/policy. **Education:** Art, elementary, English, German, kindergarten/preschool, mathematics, middle, music, physical, science, social studies, Spanish, special ed. **Engineering:** Electrical. **English:** English lit. **Foreign languages:** French, German, Spanish. **Health services:** Athletic training, clinical lab science, communication disorders, dietetics, EMT paramedic, environmental health, health care admin, health information management, nursing (RN), recreational therapy. **History:** General. **Human services:** General, social work. **Liberal arts:** Arts/sciences. **Math:** General. **Parks/recreation:** Facilities management, sports admin. **Philosophy/religion:** Philosophy. **Physical sciences:** Chemistry, geology. **Protective services:** Criminal justice, forensics. **Psychology:** General. **Social sciences:** General, anthropology, geography, political science, sociology. **Visual/performing arts:** Art, dramatic, interior design, music, music performance, studio arts.

Most popular majors. Business/marketing 16%, education 10%, health sciences 19%, psychology 6%, security/protective services 8%, social sciences 6%.

Technology on campus. PC or laptop required. 115 workstations in library, computer center, student center. Dormitories wired for high-speed internet access and linked to campus network. Commuter students can connect to campus network. Online course registration, online library, helpline, repair service, student web hosting, wireless network available.

Student life. Freshman orientation: Mandatory, $125 fee. Preregistration for classes offered. 2-day orientation sessions held in June and July. Sessions for both students and parents. **Housing:** Guaranteed on-campus for freshmen. Coed dorms, single-sex dorms, special housing for disabled, apartments, fraternity/sorority housing, themed housing, wellness housing available. $150 nonrefundable deposit, deadline 5/1. **Activities:** Bands, campus ministries, choral groups, dance, drama, film society, international student organizations, literary magazine, music ensembles, Model UN, musical theater, radio station, student government, student newspaper, TV station, Amped Lifeway, Campus Mediation Society, campus outreach, Eco Campus Awareness Team for Sustainability, PeaceJam Scholars, UNITY, College Democrats, College Republicans, international studies club, The Leadership Institute.

Athletics. NCAA. **Intercollegiate:** Baseball M, basketball, cheerleading, cross-country, football (tackle) M, golf, soccer W, softball W, tennis W, track and field, volleyball W. **Intramural:** Badminton, basketball, bowling, cross-country, football (non-tackle), football (tackle), racquetball, soccer, softball, swimming, table tennis, tennis, ultimate frisbee, volleyball, water polo, weight lifting, wrestling. **Team name:** Catamounts.

Student services. Alcohol/substance abuse counseling, chaplain/spiritual director, career counseling, services for economically disadvantaged, student employment services, financial aid counseling, health services, minority student services, on-campus daycare, personal counseling, placement for graduates, veterans' counselor, women's services. **Physically disabled:** Services for visually, speech, hearing impaired.

Contact. E-mail: admiss@wcu.edu
Phone: (828) 227-7317 Toll-free number: (877) 928-4968
Fax: (828) 227-7319
Philip Cauley, Director of Admissions, Western Carolina University, 102 Camp Building, Cullowhee, NC 28723

William Peace University
Raleigh, North Carolina   **CB member**
www.peace.edu   **CB code: 5533**

- Private 4-year liberal arts college affiliated with the Presbyterian Church (USA)
- Residential campus in large city
- 1,038 degree-seeking undergraduates: 15% part-time, 62% women, 36% African American, 2% Asian American, 5% Hispanic/Latino, 1% Native American, 2% Multi-racial, non-Hispanic
- 50% of applicants admitted
- SAT or ACT (ACT writing optional) required
- 43% graduate within 6 years

General. Founded in 1857. Regionally accredited. **Degrees:** 170 bachelor's awarded. **ROTC:** Army, Air Force. **Location:** Less than a mile from downtown. **Calendar:** Semester, limited summer session. **Full-time faculty:** 26 total; 73% have terminal degrees, 12% minority, 54% women. **Part-time faculty:** 103 total; 42% have terminal degrees, 12% minority, 59% women. **Class size:** 34% < 20, 66% 20-39, less than 1% 50-99.

Freshman class profile. 1,829 applied, 918 admitted, 216 enrolled.

Mid 50% test scores			
SAT critical reading:	380-490	GPA 2.0-2.99:	37%
SAT math:	380-490	Rank in top quarter:	26%
ACT composite:	15-21	Rank in top tenth:	6%
GPA 3.75 or higher:	24%	Out-of-state:	11%
GPA 3.50-3.74:	15%	Live on campus:	97%
GPA 3.0-3.49:	23%	International:	2%

Basis for selection. A holistic approach is used to look at academic records and scores in addition to the person. Interview recommended for all students. Essay or personal statement recommended. Audition required for theater, drama, and music majors; portfolio required for art programs. Essay and interview required for honors program. **Home schooled:** Statement describing home school structure and mission required. **Learning Disabled:** Students with learning disabilities are encouraged to contact disabilities resource center regarding their needs.

High school preparation. College-preparatory program required. 14 units required; 17 recommended. Required and recommended units include English 4, mathematics 4, science 3 (laboratory 2).

2015-2016 Annual costs. Tuition/fees: $25,850. Room/board: $9,900. Books/supplies: $1,300. Personal expenses: $3,000.

2015-2016 Financial aid. Need-based: 199 full-time freshmen applied for aid; 191 deemed to have need; 191 received aid. Average need met was 61%. Average scholarship/grant was $11,256; average loan $4,284. 61% of total undergraduate aid awarded as scholarships/grants, 39% as loans/jobs. **Non-need-based:** Awarded to 646 full-time undergraduates, including 201 freshmen. Scholarships awarded for academics, leadership, music/drama.

Application procedures. Admission: No deadline. $35 fee, may be waived for applicants with need. Admission notification on a rolling basis beginning on or about 9/1. Must reply by May 1 or within 4 week(s) if notified thereafter. Prefer early admission candidates with SAT 1100 or above, 3.5 GPA in college preparatory courses, and rank in top 25% of class. On-campus interview required. **Financial aid:** Priority date 2/15; no closing date. FAFSA required. Applicants notified by 2/3; Applicants notified on a rolling basis starting 2/15.

Academics. Special study options: Cross-registration, distance learning, double major, honors, independent study, internships, liberal arts/career combination, study abroad, teacher certification program, weekend college. Adult degree evening program in Business, Liberal Studies and Psychology. **Credit/placement by examination:** AP, CLEP, IB, SAT, ACT, institutional tests. 6 credit hours maximum toward bachelor's degree. CLEP credit is granted to students who have achieved the minimum score in designated subject tests. Students may petition program coordinators for additional or alternative credit, if warranted. **Support services:** Learning center, reduced course load, remedial instruction, study skills assistance, tutoring, writing center.

Majors. Biology: General. **Business:** Business admin, human resources. **Communications:** Communications/speech/rhetoric. **Education:** Early childhood, multi-level teacher. **English:** English lit. **Foreign languages:** Spanish. **History:** General. **Liberal arts:** Arts/sciences. **Psychology:** General. **Social sciences:** Anthropology, political science. **Visual/performing arts:** Design, music performance, theater arts management. **Work/family studies:** Child development.

Most popular majors. Biology 6%, business/marketing 33%, communications/journalism 8%, education 11%, liberal arts 14%, psychology 19%.

Technology on campus. 180 workstations in dormitories, library, computer center, student center. Dormitories wired for high-speed internet access and linked to campus network. Commuter students can connect to campus network. Online course registration, online library, helpline, repair service, student web hosting, wireless network available.

Student life. Freshman orientation: Mandatory. Preregistration for classes offered. 2-day program offered prior to start of classes, during the summer and a four day program at the beginning with move-in. **Policies:** Freshmen required to live on campus unless living with relatives within a 30-mile radius. Honor Code and Student Code of Conduct. **Housing:** Guaranteed on-campus for freshmen. Coed dorms, single-sex dorms, apartments available. **Activities:** Campus ministries, choral groups, dance, drama, literary magazine, music ensembles, musical theater, student government, student newspaper, Christian Association, honor societies, recreation association, Young Democrats/Republicans, Phi Theta Kappa, Green Team, Helping Hands, Home Sweet Homes, politics club.

Athletics. NCAA. **Intercollegiate:** Basketball W, cross-country W, soccer W, softball W, tennis W, volleyball W. **Intramural:** Tennis W. **Team name:** Peace Pacers.

Student services. Adult student services, chaplain/spiritual director, career counseling, financial aid counseling, health services, minority student services, personal counseling, placement for graduates.

Contact. E-mail: admissions@peace.edu
Phone: (919) 508-2214 Toll-free number: (800) 732-2347
Fax: (919) 508-2306
Amber Stenbeck, Vice President of Enrollment, William Peace University, 15 East Peace Street, Raleigh, NC 27604-1194

Wingate University
Wingate, North Carolina
www.wingate.edu
CB member
CB code: 5908

- Private 4-year university
- Residential campus in small town
- 2,015 degree-seeking undergraduates: 2% part-time, 60% women, 15% African American, 2% Asian American, 4% Hispanic/Latino, 5% Multiracial, non-Hispanic, 4% international
- 1,088 degree-seeking graduate students
- 70% of applicants admitted
- SAT or ACT (ACT writing optional) required
- 54% graduate within 6 years

General. Founded in 1896. Regionally accredited. **Degrees:** 359 bachelor's awarded; master's, professional, doctoral offered. **ROTC:** Army, Air Force. **Location:** 25 miles from Charlotte. **Calendar:** Semester, limited summer session. **Full-time faculty:** 169 total; 94% have terminal degrees, 8% minority, 57% women. **Part-time faculty:** 110 total; 26% have terminal degrees, 16% minority, 44% women. **Class size:** 51% < 20, 46% 20-39, 3% 40-49, less than 1% 50-99. **Special facilities:** Lake, performing arts center.

Freshman class profile. 8,018 applied, 5,597 admitted, 664 enrolled.

Mid 50% test scores			
SAT critical reading:	460-560	**GPA 2.0-2.99:**	11%
		Rank in top quarter:	50%
SAT math:	470-570	**Rank in top tenth:**	22%
SAT writing:	440-550	**Out-of-state:**	22%
ACT composite:	20-25	**Live on campus:**	84%
GPA 3.75 or higher:	21%	**International:**	2%
GPA 3.50-3.74:	30%	**Fraternities:**	3%
GPA 3.0-3.49:	38%	**Sororities:**	17%

Basis for selection. Decisions based on secondary school record (GPA, class rank) and the rigor of secondary school record. Test scores are considered. SAT/ACT not required, but strongly recommended. Interview recommended for all students; portfolio recommended for art majors; audition required for music majors.

High school preparation. College-preparatory program recommended. 13 units recommended. Recommended units include English 4, mathematics 3, social studies 2, science 2 (laboratory 1) and foreign language 2.

2016-2017 Annual costs. Tuition/fees (projected): $29,170. Room/board: $10,780. Books/supplies: $1,400. Personal expenses: $1,874.

2014-2015 Financial aid. Need-based: 537 full-time freshmen applied for aid; 485 deemed to have need; 444 received aid. Average need met was 68%. Average scholarship/grant was $20,657, average loan $3,076. 74% of total undergraduate aid awarded as scholarships/grants, 26% as loans/jobs. **Non-need-based:** Awarded to 889 full-time undergraduates, including 252 freshmen. Scholarships awarded for academics, alumni affiliation, art, athletics, music/drama, religious affiliation. **Additional information:** Institutional aid may not be available after June 1.

Application procedures. Admission: Priority date 4/1; no deadline. $30 fee, may be waived for applicants with need. Admission notification on a rolling basis beginning on or about 9/15. Must reply by May 1 or within 4 week(s) if notified thereafter. **Financial aid:** Priority date 5/1; no closing date. FAFSA required. Applicants notified on a rolling basis starting 3/15; must reply within 2 week(s) of notification.

Academics. Attendance at cultural events required as part of Lyceum program. Travel abroad available. Internships and undergraduate research under faculty supervision available. **Special study options:** Combined bachelor's/graduate degree, double major, honors, independent study, internships, study abroad, teacher certification program. Adult Completion Program at the Wingate University School of Graduate Programs and Adult Education in downtown Matthews, NC. The program offers undergraduate courses in the evening for working adults. **Credit/placement by examination:** AP, CLEP, IB, institutional tests. 30 credit hours maximum toward bachelor's degree. **Support services:** Learning center, reduced course load, study skills assistance, tutoring, writing center.

Majors. Biology: General, environmental. **Business:** Accounting, business admin, finance, marketing. **Communications:** Communications/speech/rhetoric, journalism, public relations, sports. **Education:** Art, biology, elementary, English, mathematics, middle, music, physical, reading, social studies. **English:** English lit. **Health services:** Athletic training, predental, premedicine, prenursing, prepharmacy, preveterinary. **History:** General. **Math:** General. **Parks/recreation:** Facilities management, sports admin. **Philosophy/religion:** Religion. **Physical sciences:** Chemistry. **Protective services:** Law enforcement admin. **Psychology:** General. **Social sciences:** Political science, sociology. **Visual/performing arts:** Music, music performance.

Most popular majors. Biology 14%, business/marketing 15%, communications/journalism 11%, education 9%, health sciences 8%, parks/recreation 11%, psychology 11%, public administration/social services 7%.

Technology on campus. 75 workstations in library, computer center, student center. Dormitories wired for high-speed internet access and linked to campus network. Commuter students can connect to campus network. Online course registration, wireless network available.

Student life. Freshman orientation: Mandatory. Preregistration for classes offered. Held over the summer and right before classes begin. **Policies:** Honor Code. **Housing:** Guaranteed on-campus for all undergraduates. Single-sex dorms, apartments, themed housing available. **Activities:** Bands, campus ministries, choral groups, drama, international student organizations, literary magazine, music ensembles, musical theater, opera, student government, student newspaper, TV station, academic honors societies, Greek life, Christian Student Union, minority student association, university and community assistance network, gospel choir, College Republicans, outdoor recreation and adventure club, running club.

Athletics. NCAA. **Intercollegiate:** Baseball M, basketball, cross-country, football (tackle) M, golf, lacrosse, soccer, softball W, swimming, tennis, track and field, volleyball W. **Intramural:** Basketball, bowling, diving, football (tackle) M, golf, lacrosse, racquetball, soccer, softball, swimming, table tennis, tennis, volleyball, water polo. **Team name:** Bulldogs.

Student services. Chaplain/spiritual director, career counseling, student employment services, financial aid counseling, health services, minority student services, personal counseling, placement for graduates.

Contact. E-mail: admit@wingate.edu
Phone: (704) 233-8200 Toll-free number: (800) 755-5550
Fax: (704) 233-8199
Gabe Hollingsworth, Director of Admissions, Wingate University, 220 N. Camden Drive, Wingate, NC 28174-0157

Winston-Salem State University
Winston-Salem, North Carolina
www.wssu.edu
CB member
CB code: 5909

- Public 4-year university and health science college
- Commuter campus in small city
- 4,686 degree-seeking undergraduates: 14% part-time, 71% women, 72% African American, 1% Asian American, 3% Hispanic/Latino, 1% Native American, 4% Multi-racial, non-Hispanic, 2% international
- 421 degree-seeking graduate students
- 59% of applicants admitted
- SAT or ACT with writing required

General. Founded in 1892. Regionally accredited. **Degrees:** 1,291 bachelor's awarded; master's, professional offered. **ROTC:** Army. **Location:** 28 miles from Greensboro, 75 miles from Charlotte. **Calendar:** Semester, limited summer session. **Full-time faculty:** 310 total; 75% have terminal degrees, 61% minority, 56% women. **Part-time faculty:** 136 total; 21% have terminal degrees, 57% minority, 82% women. **Class size:** 47% < 20, 40% 20-39, 9% 40-49, 3% 50-99, 1% >100.

Freshman class profile. 4,478 applied, 2,621 admitted, 887 enrolled.

Mid 50% test scores			
		ACT composite:	17-19
SAT critical reading:	400-460	Rank in top quarter:	5%
SAT math:	410-470	Rank in top tenth:	1%
SAT writing:	370-440	Out-of-state:	5%

Basis for selection. Admission consideration based on submission of completed application, SAT or ACT scores, and high school transcript. Students must meet minimum course requirements, have minimum of 2.5 cumulative weighted GPA and minimum 800 SAT (Critical Reading and Math only). Interview recommended for all students; audition required for music program.

High school preparation. College-preparatory program recommended. 15 units required. Required units include English 4, mathematics 4, social studies 2, history 1, science 3 and foreign language 2. Mathematics units must include or exceed algebra I, geometry and algebra II. 1 science must be Biology, 1 must be a Physical Science. One Social Studies must be US History.

2015-2016 Annual costs. Tuition/fees: $5,707; $15,523 out-of-state. Room/board: $8,715. Books/supplies: $1,200. Personal expenses: $1,500.

Financial aid. Non-need-based: Scholarships awarded for academics, athletics, ROTC, state residency.

Application procedures. Admission: Closing date 3/7. $50 fee, may be waived for applicants with need. Admission notification on a rolling basis. Must reply by May 1 or within 2 week(s) if notified thereafter. **Financial aid:** Priority date 5/1; no closing date. FAFSA required. Must reply within 2 week(s) of notification.

Academics. Special study options: Accelerated study, cross-registration, distance learning, double major, ESL, honors, independent study, internships, study abroad, Washington semester. **Credit/placement by examination:** AP, CLEP, IB, institutional tests. 33 credit hours maximum toward bachelor's degree. **Support services:** Learning center, reduced course load, remedial instruction, study skills assistance, tutoring, writing center.

Majors. Area/ethnic studies: African-American. **Biology:** General, biotechnology. **Business:** Accounting, business admin, finance, marketing. **Communications:** Media studies. **Computer sciences:** Computer science, information systems, information technology. **Education:** Elementary, English, kindergarten/preschool, mathematics, middle, music, physical, special ed. **English:** English lit. **Foreign languages:** Spanish. **Health services:** Clinical lab science, health care admin, nursing (RN), recreational therapy, vocational rehab counseling. **History:** General. **Human services:** Social work. **Math:** General. **Parks/recreation:** Exercise sciences, facilities management, sports admin. **Physical sciences:** Chemistry. **Protective services:** Criminal justice. **Psychology:** General. **Social sciences:** Economics, political science, sociology. **Visual/performing arts:** Art, music.

Most popular majors. Business/marketing 6%, health sciences 59%, psychology 6%.

Technology on campus. PC or laptop required. 500 workstations in dormitories, library, computer center, student center. Dormitories wired for high-speed internet access and linked to campus network. Commuter students can connect to campus network. Online course registration, online library, wireless network available.

Student life. Freshman orientation: Available. Preregistration for classes offered. Held on a summer weekend. **Housing:** Coed dorms, single-sex dorms, apartments available. $135 nonrefundable deposit, deadline 5/1. **Activities:** Bands, campus ministries, choral groups, dance, drama, international student organizations, music ensembles, musical theater, opera, radio station, student government, student newspaper, symphony orchestra, TV station, student religious council.

Athletics. NCAA. **Intercollegiate:** Basketball, bowling W, cheerleading W, cross-country, football (tackle) M, golf M, softball W, tennis, track and field, volleyball W. **Intramural:** Basketball M. **Team name:** Rams.

Student services. Adult student services, career counseling, student employment services, financial aid counseling, health services, personal counseling, veterans' counselor. **Physically disabled:** Services for visually impaired.

Contact. E-mail: admissions@wssu.edu
Phone: (336) 750-2074 Toll-free number: (800) 257-4052
Fax: (336) 750-2079
Adrianne Freeman, Director/Dual Admission Program Coordinator, Winston-Salem State University, 601 Martin Luther King Jr Drive, Winston-Salem, NC 27110

North Dakota

Dickinson State University
Dickinson, North Dakota
www.dickinsonstate.edu   CB code: 6477

‣ Public 4-year university
‣ Residential campus in large town
‣ 1,134 degree-seeking undergraduates: 22% part-time, 59% women
‣ 7 graduate students

General. Founded in 1918. Regionally accredited. **Degrees:** 261 bachelor's, 38 associate awarded. **Location:** 100 miles from Bismarck, 300 miles from Billings, Montana. **Calendar:** Semester, limited summer session. **Full-time faculty:** 84 total; 52% have terminal degrees, 7% minority, 50% women. **Part-time faculty:** 54 total; 9% have terminal degrees, 6% minority, 67% women.

Freshman class profile. 521 applied, 321 admitted, 209 enrolled.

Mid 50% test scores			
ACT composite:	18-22	Out-of-state:	42%
Return as sophomores:	57%	Live on campus:	49%

Basis for selection. Open admission, but selective for some programs. Minimum 20 ACT composite or minimum 2.0 GPA required for nursing program. **Home schooled:** Transcript of courses and grades, letter of recommendation (nonparent) required.

High school preparation. College-preparatory program required. 13 units recommended. Recommended units include English 4, mathematics 3, social studies 3 and science 3. One algebra, 1 chemistry required for nursing program.

2015-2016 Annual costs. Tuition/fees: $6,173; $8,680 out-of-state. Room/board: $6,480. Books/supplies: $1,200. Personal expenses: $1,750.

2015-2016 Financial aid. **Need-based:** Average need met was 59%. Average scholarship/grant was $6,125; average loan $5,436. 48% of total undergraduate aid awarded as scholarships/grants, 52% as loans/jobs. **Non-need-based:** Scholarships awarded for academics, alumni affiliation, art, athletics, leadership, minority status, music/drama.

Application procedures. **Admission:** $35 fee ($35 out-of-state), may be waived for applicants with need. Admission notification on a rolling basis. **Financial aid:** Priority date 4/15; no closing date. FAFSA required. Applicants notified on a rolling basis starting 5/15; must reply within 4 week(s) of notification.

Academics. Limited evening classes available. **Special study options:** Accelerated study, combined bachelor's/graduate degree, cooperative education, distance learning, double major, dual enrollment of high school students, ESL, honors, independent study, internships, liberal arts/career combination, student-designed major, study abroad, teacher certification program. **Credit/placement by examination:** AP, CLEP, institutional tests. 8 credit hours maximum toward associate degree, 15 toward bachelor's. **Support services:** Learning center, remedial instruction, study skills assistance, tutoring, writing center.

Honors college/program. Must have a 3.5 high school GPA and/or a 26 on ACT; submit resume, essay and two letters of recommendation; 25 freshmen admitted each fall; includes special academic track that concludes with a leadership minor.

Majors. **Biology:** General. **Business:** General, accounting, business admin, finance. **Communications:** Communications/speech/rhetoric. **Computer sciences:** Computer science. **Education:** Art, biology, business, chemistry, computer, drama/dance, early childhood, elementary, English, history, mathematics, middle, music, physical, reading, science, secondary, social science, Spanish, speech. **English:** Creative writing, English lit. **Foreign languages:** Spanish. **Health services:** Nursing (RN), predental, premedicine, prepharmacy, preveterinary. **History:** General. **Liberal arts:** Arts/sciences. **Math:** General. **Parks/recreation:** Health/fitness. **Physical sciences:** Chemistry. **Psychology:** General. **Social sciences:** General, political science. **Visual/performing arts:** Art, dramatic, music, studio arts.

Most popular majors. Business/marketing 36%, education 21%, interdisciplinary studies 6%, parks/recreation 9%.

Technology on campus. 235 workstations in dormitories, library, computer center, student center. Dormitories wired for high-speed internet access and linked to campus network. Commuter students can connect to campus network. Online course registration, online library, helpline, repair service, wireless network available.

Student life. **Freshman orientation:** Mandatory, $35 fee. Preregistration for classes offered. **Housing:** Guaranteed on-campus for all undergraduates. Coed dorms, single-sex dorms, special housing for disabled, apartments, wellness housing available. $200 nonrefundable deposit. **Activities:** Bands, choral groups, dance, drama, film society, literary magazine, music ensembles, musical theater, student government, student newspaper.

Athletics. NAIA. **Intercollegiate:** Baseball M, basketball, cross-country, football (tackle) M, golf, rodeo, softball W, track and field, volleyball W, wrestling M. **Intramural:** Basketball, football (non-tackle), soccer, softball, volleyball. **Team name:** Blue Hawks.

Student services. Adult student services, career counseling, services for economically disadvantaged, student employment services, financial aid counseling, health services, minority student services, personal counseling, placement for graduates. **Physically disabled:** Services for visually, speech, hearing impaired.

Contact. E-mail: dsu.hawk@dickinsonstate.edu
Phone: (701) 483-2175 Toll-free number: (800) 279-4295
Fax: (701) 483-2409
Melanie Tucker, Vice President of Student Affairs and Enrollment Management, Dickinson State University, 291 Campus Drive, Dickinson, ND 58601-4896

Mayville State University
Mayville, North Dakota
www.mayvillestate.edu   CB code: 6478

‣ Public 4-year business and teachers college
‣ Residential campus in small town
‣ 819 degree-seeking undergraduates: 22% part-time, 56% women
‣ 19 graduate students
‣ 42% graduate within 6 years; 8% enter graduate study

General. Founded in 1889. Regionally accredited. **Degrees:** 148 bachelor's, 6 associate awarded. **ROTC:** Army, Air Force. **Location:** 60 miles from Fargo, 40 miles from Grand Forks. **Calendar:** Semester, limited summer session. **Full-time faculty:** 49 total; 41% have terminal degrees, 2% minority, 49% women. **Part-time faculty:** 35 total; 3% have terminal degrees, 6% minority, 57% women. **Class size:** 78% < 20, 20% 20-39, 1% 40-49, 2% 50-99. **Special facilities:** Head start and child development center, undergraduate research labs.

Freshman class profile. 336 applied, 180 admitted, 137 enrolled.

Mid 50% test scores			
ACT composite:	17-22	GPA 2.0-2.99:	45%
GPA 3.75 or higher:	15%	End year in good standing:	85%
GPA 3.50-3.74:	11%	Return as sophomores:	49%
GPA 3.0-3.49:	27%	Out-of-state:	42%
		Live on campus:	84%

Basis for selection. Open admission, but selective for some programs. Admission to teacher education programs based on meeting GPA criteria, completion of PPST, and specific prerequisites. ACT math and English scores used for placement. Interview recommended. **Home schooled:** Transcript of courses and grades required. Must provide documentation equivalent to high school diploma.

High school preparation. College-preparatory program required. 17 units required; 18 recommended. Required and recommended units include English 4, mathematics 3, social studies 3, science 3 (laboratory 2) and foreign language 2. One unit of computer studies recommended.

2015-2016 Annual costs. Tuition/fees: $6,380; $8,845 out-of-state. Room/board: $5,904. Books/supplies: $1,000. Personal expenses: $1,550. **Additional information:** Full-time tuition for South Dakota, Montana, Kansas, Michigan, Missouri, Nebraska, Wisconsin, Indiana, Illinois, Manitoba, and Saskatchewan residents: $6163. All other states, except MN, and Canadian provinces: $7395. Tuition for Minnesota residents estimated at $5522.

2015-2016 Financial aid. **Need-based:** 121 full-time freshmen applied for aid; 87 deemed to have need; 87 received aid. Average need met was 73%. Average scholarship/grant was $5,666; average loan $5,881. 43% of total undergraduate aid awarded as scholarships/grants, 57% as loans/jobs. **Non-need-based:** Awarded to 160 full-time undergraduates, including 45 freshmen. Scholarships awarded for academics, athletics, leadership, minority status, music/drama, state residency.

Application procedures. Admission: No deadline. $35 fee, may be waived for applicants with need. Admission notification on a rolling basis beginning on or about 1/1. **Financial aid:** Priority date 2/15; no closing date. FAFSA required. Applicants notified on a rolling basis starting 5/1; must reply within 2 week(s) of notification.

Academics. Special study options: Cooperative education, distance learning, double major, dual enrollment of high school students, independent study, internships, student-designed major, teacher certification program. **Credit/placement by examination:** AP, CLEP, IB, institutional tests. 30 credit hours maximum toward bachelor's degree. **Support services:** Learning center, pre-admission summer program, remedial instruction, study skills assistance, tutoring, writing center.

Majors. Biology: General. **Business:** Business admin. **Communications:** Communications/speech/rhetoric. **Computer sciences:** General. **Education:** Biology, chemistry, early childhood, elementary, English, geography, health, history, mathematics, physical, social science, special ed, teacher assistance. **English:** English lit. **Health services:** Clinical lab science, nursing (RN), predental, premedicine, prenursing, prepharmacy, preveterinary. **Math:** General. **Parks/recreation:** Health/fitness, sports admin. **Physical sciences:** Chemistry. **Psychology:** General. **Social sciences:** General. **Work/family studies:** Child care management.

Most popular majors. Business/marketing 28%, education 32%, family/consumer sciences 6%, liberal arts 10%, parks/recreation 8%.

Technology on campus. PC or laptop required. Dormitories wired for high-speed internet access and linked to campus network. Commuter students can connect to campus network. Online course registration, online library, helpline, repair service, wireless network available.

Student life. Freshman orientation: Mandatory, $35 fee. Preregistration for classes offered. Held in June and July. **Policies:** All freshmen and sophomore who are under 21 years of age or who have completed less than 60 credits are required to live in university owned housing facilities and are required to participate in an approved board plan. **Housing:** Guaranteed on-campus for all undergraduates. Coed dorms, single-sex dorms, apartments, wellness housing available. $25 nonrefundable deposit, deadline 8/25. **Activities:** Bands, choral groups, drama, international student organizations, music ensembles, musical theater, radio station, student government, student newspaper, Campus Crusade, student education association, residence hall association, health and physical education club, student activities council, alumni ambassadors, minority/international student association, business administration club, student volunteer organization, swim club.

Athletics. NAIA. **Intercollegiate:** Baseball M, basketball, football (tackle) M, softball W, volleyball W. **Intramural:** Badminton, basketball, football (non-tackle), golf, ice hockey M, racquetball, soccer, softball, table tennis, tennis, track and field, volleyball, weight lifting. **Team name:** Comets.

Student services. Adult student services, career counseling, student employment services, financial aid counseling, health services, minority student services, on-campus daycare, personal counseling, placement for graduates, veterans' counselor. **Physically disabled:** Services for visually, hearing impaired.

Contact. E-mail: MASU.admissions@mayvillestate.edu
Phone: (701) 788-4667 Toll-free number: (800) 437-4104
Fax: (701) 788-4656
Misti Wuori, Director of Admissions and Extended Learning, Mayville State University, 330 Third Street, NE, Mayville, ND 58257-1299

Minot State University
Minot, North Dakota
www.minotstateu.edu   CB code: 6479

- Public 4-year university and liberal arts college
- Commuter campus in large town
- 2,559 degree-seeking undergraduates: 21% part-time, 63% women, 6% African American, 2% Asian American, 6% Hispanic/Latino, 1% Native American, 4% Multi-racial, non-Hispanic, 13% international
- 284 degree-seeking graduate students
- 57% of applicants admitted
- SAT or ACT (ACT writing optional) required
- 40% graduate within 6 years

General. Founded in 1913. Regionally accredited. **Degrees:** 657 bachelor's, 3 associate awarded; master's offered. **Location:** 105 miles from Bismarck, 225 miles from Grand Forks. **Calendar:** Semester, limited summer session. **Full-time faculty:** 167 total; 59% have terminal degrees, 7% minority, 51% women. **Part-time faculty:** 112 total; 4% minority, 66% women. **Special**

facilities: Natural history museum, center for persons with disabilities, Native American collection, observatory, rural crime and justice center, Center for Extended Teaching and Learning.

Freshman class profile. 840 applied, 477 admitted, 341 enrolled.

Mid 50% test scores			
SAT critical reading:	430-510	Rank in top quarter:	20%
SAT math:	440-520	Rank in top tenth:	6%
ACT composite:	19-24	End year in good standing:	40%
GPA 3.75 or higher:	25%	Return as sophomores:	75%
GPA 3.50-3.74:	17%	Out-of-state:	23%
GPA 3.0-3.49:	33%	Live on campus:	52%
GPA 2.0-2.99:	25%	International:	13%

Basis for selection. Secondary school record very important; ACT/SAT test scores, ACT composite score must be no less than 17; those below the recommended composite score are reviewed on an individual basis.

High school preparation. 13 units required. Required units include English 4, mathematics 3, social studies 3, (laboratory 3). Science should include at least 3 units of biology, chemistry, physics, or physical science. Social science should not include consumer education, cooperative marketing, orientation to social science, or marriage/family. Math must be algebra I or above.

2015-2016 Annual costs. Tuition/fees: $6,391; $6,391 out-of-state. Room/board: $6,008. Books/supplies: $1,000. Personal expenses: $2,230.

2014-2015 Financial aid. Need-based: 234 full-time freshmen applied for aid; 131 deemed to have need; 130 received aid. Average need met was 71%. Average scholarship/grant was $5,255; average loan $3,529. 70% of total undergraduate aid awarded as scholarships/grants, 30% as loans/jobs. **Non-need-based:** Awarded to 396 full-time undergraduates, including 107 freshmen. Scholarships awarded for academics, alumni affiliation, art, athletics, minority status, music/drama, state residency. **Additional information:** Scholarship application deadline is 2/15.

Application procedures. Admission: Priority date 5/1; no deadline. $35 fee. Admission notification on a rolling basis. **Financial aid:** Priority date 3/15; no closing date. FAFSA required. Applicants notified on a rolling basis starting 5/1; must reply within 2 week(s) of notification.

Academics. Wide variety of distance courses offered. **Special study options:** Cooperative education, distance learning, double major, dual enrollment of high school students, ESL, external degree, honors, independent study, internships, liberal arts/career combination, student-designed major, study abroad, teacher certification program. **Credit/placement by examination:** AP, CLEP, SAT, ACT, institutional tests. **Support services:** Learning center, reduced course load, remedial instruction, study skills assistance, tutoring, writing center.

Majors. Biology: General. **Business:** Accounting, business admin, finance, international, management information systems, marketing. **Communications:** Broadcast journalism, radio/TV. **Communications technology:** General. **Computer sciences:** General. **Education:** Art, biology, business, chemistry, Deaf/hearing impaired, elementary, English, foreign languages, French, German, history, mathematics, mentally handicapped, music, physical, physics, science, social science, Spanish, speech impaired. **English:** English lit, rhetoric/composition. **Foreign languages:** General, French, German, Spanish. **Health services:** Clinical lab science, communication disorders, health care admin, medical radiologic technology/radiation therapy, nursing (RN), substance abuse counseling. **History:** General. **Human services:** Social work. **Liberal arts:** Arts/sciences. **Math:** General. **Parks/recreation:** Sports admin. **Physical sciences:** General, chemistry, geology, physics. **Protective services:** Criminal justice. **Psychology:** General. **Social sciences:** General, economics, geography, sociology. **Visual/performing arts:** Art, dramatic, music, music performance, studio arts management.

Most popular majors. Business/marketing 22%, education 20%, health sciences 17%, public administration/social services 12%, security/protective services 6%.

Technology on campus. 300 workstations in dormitories, library, computer center, student center. Dormitories wired for high-speed internet access and linked to campus network. Commuter students can connect to campus network. Online course registration, online library, helpline, repair service, wireless network available.

Student life. Freshman orientation: Mandatory, $35 fee. Preregistration for classes offered. **Policies:** First-year students required to live in university housing (exceptions exist). **Housing:** Guaranteed on-campus for freshmen. Coed dorms, single-sex dorms, special housing for disabled, apartments, wellness housing available. $100 deposit. **Activities:** Marching band, campus ministries, drama, international student organizations, musical theater, radio station, student government, student newspaper, TV station, disability awareness organization, Democratic Party, Republican Party, Intervarsity Christian

Fellowship, Native American cultural awareness club, United Campus Ministries, Catholic student association, international awareness club, Student Education of Hard of Hearing/Deaf, National Student Speech/Hearing Association.

Athletics. NCAA. **Intercollegiate:** Baseball M, basketball, cheerleading W, cross-country, football (tackle) M, golf, soccer W, softball W, track and field, volleyball W, wrestling M. **Intramural:** Basketball, bowling, ice hockey M, racquetball, softball, track and field, volleyball. **Team name:** Beavers.

Student services. Adult student services, alcohol/substance abuse counseling, chaplain/spiritual director, career counseling, services for economically disadvantaged, student employment services, financial aid counseling, health services, minority student services, personal counseling, placement for graduates, veterans' counselor, women's services. **Physically disabled:** Services for visually, speech, hearing impaired.

Contact. E-mail: askmsu@minotstateu.edu
Phone: (701) 858-3350 Toll-free number: (800) 777-0750
Fax: (701) 839-6933
Kevin Harmon, Dean of Admissions, Minot State University, 500 University Avenue West, Minot, ND 58707-5002

North Dakota State University

Fargo, North Dakota
www.ndsu.edu

CB member
CB code: 6474

- Public 4-year university
- Residential campus in small city
- 11,609 degree-seeking undergraduates: 9% part-time, 45% women
- 2,304 degree-seeking graduate students
- 94% of applicants admitted
- SAT or ACT (ACT writing optional) required

General. Founded in 1890. Regionally accredited. **Degrees:** 2,354 bachelor's awarded; master's, professional, doctoral offered. **ROTC:** Army, Air Force. **Location:** 250 miles from Minneapolis-St. Paul. **Calendar:** Semester, limited summer session. **Full-time faculty:** 712 total; 86% have terminal degrees, 17% minority, 40% women. **Part-time faculty:** 141 total; 33% have terminal degrees, 6% minority, 52% women. **Class size:** 30% < 20, 43% 20-39, 6% 40-49, 12% 50-99, 9% >100. **Special facilities:** Fine arts center, regional studies institute, biotechnology institute, engineering computer center, center for writers, wellness center, technology park, downtown campus for art and architecture, business and agribusiness, equine center.

Freshman class profile. 5,311 applied, 4,974 admitted, 2,552 enrolled.

GPA 3.75 or higher:	28%	Rank in top tenth:	16%
GPA 3.50-3.74:	21%	Out-of-state:	64%
GPA 3.0-3.49:	32%	Live on campus:	93%
GPA 2.0-2.99:	19%	Fraternities:	5%
Rank in top quarter:	40%	Sororities:	4%

Basis for selection. All applicants must have completed college preparatory program in high school. Admission based on overall performance in high school, performance in college preparatory courses and standardized test scores. Admission to electrical engineering and mechanical engineering programs based on academic record and test scores. Scores required of all applicants unless applicant is 25 or older on the first day of class or has 24 or more transferable credits. Campus visit recommended for all students. Audition required for music programs. Secondary admission requirements for many programs. **Home schooled:** Transcript of courses and grades required. Applicants advised to work with local school district for issuance of a Certificate of Graduation.

High school preparation. College-preparatory program required. 13 units required. Required units include English 4, mathematics 3, social studies 3, science 3 (laboratory 3).

2015-2016 Annual costs. Tuition/fees: $7,978; $19,272 out-of-state. Room/board: $7,502. Books/supplies: $1,100. **Additional information:** Full-time annual tuition for residents of South Dakota, Montana, Manitoba, Saskatchewan: $10,144. Full-time annual tuition for residents of Minnesota: $7,574.

2014-2015 Financial aid. **Need-based:** 2,069 full-time freshmen applied for aid; 1,311 deemed to have need; 1,272 received aid. Average need met was 70%. Average scholarship/grant was $5,124; average loan $6,504. 35% of total undergraduate aid awarded as scholarships/grants, 65% as loans/jobs. **Non-need-based:** Awarded to 959 full-time undergraduates, including 350 freshmen. Scholarships awarded for academics, alumni affiliation, art, athletics, leadership, minority status, music/drama, ROTC, state residency.

Application procedures. **Admission:** Closing date 8/1 (receipt date). $35 fee. Application must be submitted online. Admission notification on a rolling basis. **Financial aid:** Closing date 3/15. FAFSA required. Applicants notified on a rolling basis starting 4/20.

Academics. **Special study options:** Accelerated study, combined bachelor's/graduate degree, cooperative education, cross-registration, distance learning, double major, dual enrollment of high school students, ESL, exchange student, honors, independent study, internships, student-designed major, study abroad, teacher certification program. Tri-college, collaborative enrollment (ND University System), Pathway program with ND partner institution with remedial coursework for students not meeting admission requirements. **Credit/placement by examination:** AP, CLEP, IB, SAT, ACT, institutional tests. **Support services:** Reduced course load, remedial instruction, study skills assistance, tutoring, writing center.

Majors. **Architecture:** Environmental design, landscape. **Area/ethnic studies:** Women's. **Biology:** General, Biochemistry/molecular biology, biotechnology, botany, microbiology, zoology. **Business:** Accounting, business admin, communications, construction management, finance, hospitality admin, management information systems, marketing. **Communications:** Digital media, health, journalism, persuasive communications, public relations. **Computer sciences:** Computer science. **Conservation:** Management/policy. **Education:** Agricultural, biology, chemistry, earth science, English, family/consumer sciences, French, health, history, mathematics, music, physical, physics, science, social studies, Spanish. **Engineering:** Agricultural, civil, computer, construction, electrical, industrial, manufacturing, mechanical. **English:** English lit. **Foreign languages:** Classics, French, Spanish. **Health services:** Clinical lab science, dietetics, nursing (RN), pharmaceutical sciences, radiologic technology/medical imaging, respiratory therapy technology, veterinary technology/assistant. **History:** General, applied. **Math:** General, statistics. **Parks/recreation:** Exercise sciences, sports admin. **Philosophy/religion:** Philosophy. **Physical sciences:** Chemistry, geology, physics. **Protective services:** Criminal justice, disaster management. **Psychology:** General, psychometrics. **Social sciences:** General, anthropology, economics, political science, sociology. **Visual/performing arts:** Art, dramatic, interior design, music. **Work/family studies:** Clothing/textiles, family studies.

Most popular majors. Agriculture 7%, biology 7%, business/marketing 17%, engineering/engineering technologies 14%, family/consumer sciences 6%, health sciences 11%.

Technology on campus. 500 workstations in dormitories, library, computer center, student center. Dormitories wired for high-speed internet access. Online course registration, online library, helpline, repair service, student web hosting, wireless network available.

Student life. **Freshman orientation:** Available. Preregistration for classes offered. Offered in June, July or August and day before classes. **Policies:** No alcoholic beverages allowed on campus, code of student conduct. **Housing:** Guaranteed on-campus for freshmen. Coed dorms, single-sex dorms, apartments, fraternity/sorority housing, wellness housing available. $50 partly refundable deposit. Housing is handicap accessible. **Activities:** Bands, campus ministries, choral groups, dance, drama, international student organizations, music ensembles, musical theater, radio station, student government, student newspaper, TV station, Newman Center, Lutheran Student Fellowship, United Campus Ministry, College Republicans, College Democrats, Circle-K, Mortar Board, Black Student Alliance, Native American student association.

Athletics. NCAA. **Intercollegiate:** Baseball M, basketball, cross-country, football (tackle) M, golf, soccer W, softball W, track and field, volleyball W, wrestling M. **Intramural:** Basketball, football (non-tackle), softball, volleyball. **Team name:** Bison.

Student services. Adult student services, alcohol/substance abuse counseling, career counseling, services for economically disadvantaged, student employment services, financial aid counseling, health services, minority student services, on-campus daycare, personal counseling, veterans' counselor. **Physically disabled:** Services for visually, speech, hearing impaired.

Contact. E-mail: ndsu.admission@ndsu.edu
Phone: (701) 231-8643 Toll-free number: (800) 488-6378
Fax: (701) 231-8802
Merideth Sherlin, Director of Admission, North Dakota State University, Dept. 2832, PO Box 6050, Fargo, ND 58108-6050

Rasmussen College: Fargo

Fargo, North Dakota
www.rasmussen.edu

CB code: 3343

- For-profit 4-year career college
- Commuter campus in small city
- 395 degree-seeking undergraduates

General. Degrees: 45 bachelor's, 56 associate awarded. **Calendar:** Quarter. **Full-time faculty:** 4 total. **Part-time faculty:** 7 total.

Freshman class profile. 163 applied, 120 admitted, 120 enrolled.

Basis for selection. Open admission, but selective for some programs. Some programs require placement examinations and/or background checks.

2015-2016 Annual costs. Tuition/fees: $13,455. Personal expenses: $2,214.

Application procedures. Admission: No deadline. No application fee. Admission notification on a rolling basis. **Financial aid:** No deadline. FAFSA, institutional form required. Applicants notified on a rolling basis.

Academics. Special study options: Distance learning, double major, independent study, internships, liberal arts/career combination. **Credit/placement by examination:** AP, CLEP, IB, institutional tests. 45 credit hours maximum toward associate degree, 90 toward bachelor's. 50% of a student's program must be completed through coursework at Rasmussen College. **Support services:** Learning center, remedial instruction, study skills assistance, tutoring, writing center.

Majors. Business: Accounting, accounting/business management, business admin, finance, human resources, information resources management, marketing. **Computer sciences:** Computer science, security, system admin, web page design. **Health services:** Health care admin, health information management. **Protective services:** Criminal justice, special ops. **Visual/performing arts:** Digital arts, game design.

Technology on campus. 100 workstations in library, computer center, student center. Online course registration, online library, helpline, wireless network available.

Student life. Freshman orientation: Mandatory. Preregistration for classes offered. **Activities:** Student government.

Student services. Adult student services, career counseling, services for economically disadvantaged, student employment services, financial aid counseling, placement for graduates.

Contact. Phone: (701) 277-3889 Toll-free number: (800) 817-0009
Fax: (701) 277-5604
Susan Hammerstrom, Director of Admissions, Rasmussen College: Fargo, 4012 19th Avenue SW, Fargo, ND 58103

Trinity Bible College
Ellendale, North Dakota
www.trinitybiblecollege.edu   CB code: 0356

- Private 4-year Bible college affiliated with the Assemblies of God
- Residential campus in rural community
- 204 degree-seeking undergraduates
- 18 graduate students
- SAT or ACT (ACT writing optional), application essay required

General. Founded in 1948. Regionally accredited; also accredited by ABHE. **Degrees:** 36 bachelor's, 10 associate awarded. **Location:** 60 miles from Jamestown, 38 miles from Aberdeen. **Calendar:** Semester, limited summer session. **Full-time faculty:** 13 total. **Part-time faculty:** 17 total. **Special facilities:** Pentecostal heritage collection of rare and out-of-print works, teacher education laboratory.

Basis for selection. Test scores and GPA references, school record, evidence of Christian testimony and lifestyle. Interview recommended. **Home schooled:** Statement describing home school structure and mission, transcript of courses and grades, letter of recommendation (nonparent) required. Minimum ACT scores of 14 English, 15 math required.

2016-2017 Annual costs. Tuition/fees (projected): $15,508. Room/board: $5,746. Books/supplies: $800. Personal expenses: $1,950.

Financial aid. Non-need-based: Scholarships awarded for academics, alumni affiliation, art, leadership, music/drama, religious affiliation.

Application procedures. Admission: No deadline. $25 fee, may be waived for applicants with need. Admission notification on a rolling basis. **Financial aid:** Priority date 3/1, closing date 9/1. FAFSA required. Applicants notified on a rolling basis starting 3/1; must reply within 3 week(s) of notification.

Academics. All students major in Biblical studies in conjunction with another major or minor of their choice. **Special study options:** Distance

learning, double major, dual enrollment of high school students, independent study, internships, liberal arts/career combination, teacher certification program. **Credit/placement by examination:** AP, CLEP, IB, SAT, ACT, institutional tests. 30 credit hours maximum toward associate degree, 30 toward bachelor's. **Support services:** Learning center, reduced course load, remedial instruction, tutoring, writing center.

Majors. Business: General. **Education:** Elementary. **Philosophy/religion:** Religion. **Theology:** Bible, missionary, religious ed, theology. **Visual/performing arts:** Music.

Technology on campus. 30 workstations in dormitories, library, computer center, student center. Dormitories wired for high-speed internet access and linked to campus network. Online library, helpline, wireless network available.

Student life. Freshman orientation: Mandatory. Preregistration for classes offered. **Policies:** Chapel and student ministry required each semester. Drug, smoking and alcohol free environment. Religious observance required. **Housing:** Single-sex dorms, wellness housing available. $150 deposit, deadline 8/31. **Activities:** Campus ministries, choral groups, music ensembles, student government, missions, ministry clubs, mission trips.

Athletics. NCCAA. **Intercollegiate:** Basketball, cross-country, football (tackle) M, volleyball M. **Intramural:** Basketball, football (tackle) M, weight lifting. **Team name:** Lions.

Student services. Chaplain/spiritual director, career counseling, student employment services, financial aid counseling, personal counseling, placement for graduates, veterans' counselor.

Contact. E-mail: admissions@trinitybiblecollege.edu
Phone: (701) 349-5399 Toll-free number: (800) 523-1603
Fax: (701) 349-5786
Jordy Nunez, Dean of Students, Trinity Bible College, 50 6th Avenue South, Ellendale, ND 58436-7150

University of Jamestown
Jamestown, North Dakota
www.uj.edu   CB code: 6318

- Private 4-year liberal arts college affiliated with the Presbyterian Church (USA)
- Residential campus in large town
- 860 degree-seeking undergraduates: 2% part-time, 52% women, 5% African American, 2% Asian American, 7% Hispanic/Latino, 1% Native American, 1% Native Hawaiian/Pacific islander, 6% international
- 118 degree-seeking graduate students
- 65% of applicants admitted
- SAT or ACT (ACT writing optional) required
- 45% graduate within 6 years; 13% enter graduate study

General. Founded in 1883. Regionally accredited. **Degrees:** 196 bachelor's awarded; master's offered. **Location:** 100 miles from Fargo and Bismarck. **Calendar:** Semester, limited summer session. **Full-time faculty:** 68 total; 54% have terminal degrees, 4% minority, 56% women. **Part-time faculty:** 31 total; 16% have terminal degrees, 61% women. **Class size:** 60% < 20, 34% 20-39, 4% 40-49, 2% 50-99, less than 1% >100.

Freshman class profile. 1,131 applied, 735 admitted, 231 enrolled.

Mid 50% test scores			
SAT critical reading:	370-580	GPA 2.0-2.99:	18%
SAT math:	390-580	Rank in top quarter:	41%
ACT composite:	18-28	Rank in top tenth:	20%
GPA 3.75 or higher:	34%	Return as sophomores:	78%
GPA 3.50-3.74:	18%	Out-of-state:	43%
GPA 3.0-3.49:	30%	Live on campus:	95%
		International:	7%

Basis for selection. Applicants with minimum 2.5 high school GPA or 18 ACT or 850 SAT (exclusive of Writing) generally accepted. Applicants may be admitted on standard, conditional, or probationary basis. Audition required for music program; portfolio recommended for art program.

High school preparation. College-preparatory program recommended. Recommended units include English 4, mathematics 3, social studies 3, science 4 and foreign language 2.

2016-2017 Annual costs. Tuition/fees (projected): $20,510. Room/board: $7,022. Books/supplies: $1,000. Personal expenses: $1,500.

2014-2015 Financial aid. Need-based: 178 full-time freshmen applied for aid; 140 deemed to have need; 140 received aid. Average need met was

78%. Average scholarship/grant was $13,183; average loan $3,297. 60% of total undergraduate aid awarded as scholarships/grants, 40% as loans/jobs. **Non-need-based:** Awarded to 596 full-time undergraduates, including 172 freshmen. Scholarships awarded for academics, alumni affiliation, art, athletics, job skills, leadership, music/drama, religious affiliation. **Additional information:** FAFSA must be received by April 15th for residents to be given first consideration for North Dakota state grants.

Application procedures. Admission: Priority date 5/1; no deadline. No application fee. Application must be submitted online. Admission notification on a rolling basis. **Financial aid:** Priority date 3/15; no closing date. FAFSA required. Applicants notified on a rolling basis starting 2/1; must reply within 2 week(s) of notification.

Academics. Special study options: Combined bachelor's/graduate degree, cooperative education, double major, dual enrollment of high school students, ESL, honors, independent study, internships, liberal arts/career combination, student-designed major, study abroad, teacher certification program. **Credit/placement by examination:** AP, CLEP, IB, SAT, ACT, institutional tests. Unlimited number of hours of credit by examination may be counted toward degree. **Support services:** Learning center, reduced course load, remedial instruction, study skills assistance, tutoring, writing center.

Majors. Biology: General, biochemistry. **Business:** Accounting, business admin, finance, financial planning, hospitality admin, international, management information systems, managerial economics, marketing, tourism/travel. **Communications:** Communications/speech/rhetoric. **Computer sciences:** Computer science, information technology. **Education:** Biology, chemistry, early childhood, elementary, English, history, mathematics, music, physical, secondary, special ed. **Engineering:** Mechanical. **English:** English lit, writing. **Foreign languages:** French, German, Spanish. **Health services:** Clinical lab science, nursing (RN), radiologic technology/medical imaging. **History:** General. **Math:** General, applied. **Parks/recreation:** General, exercise sciences, sports admin. **Philosophy/religion:** Religion. **Physical sciences:** Chemistry. **Protective services:** Criminal justice. **Psychology:** General. **Social sciences:** Political science. **Visual/performing arts:** Dramatic, music, music performance, studio arts.

Most popular majors. Biology 6%, business/marketing 16%, computer/information sciences 7%, education 10%, health sciences 19%, history 7%, parks/recreation 13%, security/protective services 6%.

Technology on campus. 200 workstations in dormitories, library, computer center, student center. Dormitories wired for high-speed internet access and linked to campus network. Commuter students can connect to campus network. Online course registration, online library, helpline, repair service, student web hosting, wireless network available.

Student life. Freshman orientation: Mandatory. Preregistration for classes offered. Held 3 days prior to the start of the fall semester. **Policies:** Weekly chapel service available on campus. **Housing:** Guaranteed on-campus for all undergraduates. Coed dorms, special housing for disabled, apartments, wellness housing available. **Activities:** Bands, campus ministries, choral groups, dance, drama, international student organizations, music ensembles, musical theater, radio station, student government, student newspaper, TV station, honor societies, Students of Service, Fellowship of Christian Athletes, Jimmie Janes, Jimmie Ambassadors, Ignition.

Athletics. NAIA. **Intercollegiate:** Baseball M, basketball, cross-country, football (tackle) M, golf, soccer, softball W, track and field, volleyball W, wrestling. **Intramural:** Basketball, bowling, football (non-tackle), volleyball. **Team name:** Jimmies.

Student services. Alcohol/substance abuse counseling, chaplain/spiritual director, career counseling, student employment services, financial aid counseling, personal counseling, placement for graduates, veterans' counselor.

Contact. E-mail: admissions@uj.edu
Phone: (701) 252-3467 ext. 5562 Toll-free number: (800) 336-2554
Fax: (701) 253-4318
Mike Heitkamp, Vice President of Enrollment Management, University of Jamestown, 6081 College Lane, Jamestown, ND 58405

University of Mary
Bismarck, North Dakota
www.umary.edu

CB code: 6428

- Private 4-year university affiliated with the Roman Catholic Church
- Residential campus in small city
- 1,928 degree-seeking undergraduates
- 773 graduate students
- SAT or ACT (ACT writing optional) required

General. Founded in 1959. Regionally accredited. Additional centers in Bismarck, Fargo, Grand Forks; Billings, Montana; Kansas City, Missouri; Phoenix, Arizona. **Degrees:** 377 bachelor's awarded; master's, professional offered. **Location:** 6 miles from downtown. **Calendar:** Semester, extensive summer session. **Full-time faculty:** 100 total. **Part-time faculty:** 160 total. **Class size:** 66% < 20, 28% 20-39, 3% 40-49, 3% 50-99, less than 1% >100. **Special facilities:** Climbing wall, 3 art galleries.

Freshman class profile.

GPA 3.75 or higher:	32%	Rank in top quarter:	42%
GPA 3.50-3.74:	18%	Rank in top tenth:	16%
GPA 3.0-3.49:	27%	Out-of-state:	37%
GPA 2.0-2.99:	22%	Live on campus:	88%

Basis for selection. Automatic acceptance for applicants in top half of class with 2.5 GPA and 19 ACT. Applicants not meeting these standards may be admitted with specific conditions for enrollment. Audition required for music program; interview recommended for academically weak students. **Home schooled:** State high school equivalency certificate required.

High school preparation. College-preparatory program recommended. Recommended units include English 4, mathematics 3, social studies 4 and science 3.

2015-2016 Annual costs. Tuition/fees: $16,490. Room/board: $6,246. Books/supplies: $1,202. Personal expenses: $1,056.

Financial aid. Non-need-based: Scholarships awarded for academics, athletics, music/drama, religious affiliation, state residency.

Application procedures. Admission: No deadline. $30 fee, may be waived for applicants with need. Admission notification on a rolling basis. Must reply by May 1 or within 4 week(s) if notified thereafter. **Financial aid:** Priority date 3/1; no closing date. FAFSA required. Applicants notified on a rolling basis starting 2/1; must reply within 2 week(s) of notification.

Academics. Special study options: Accelerated study, combined bachelor's/graduate degree, distance learning, double major, dual enrollment of high school students, honors, independent study, internships, semester at sea, student-designed major, study abroad, teacher certification program. **Credit/placement by examination:** AP, CLEP, IB, SAT, ACT. **Support services:** Learning center, reduced course load, remedial instruction, study skills assistance, tutoring, writing center.

Majors. Biology: General. **Business:** Accounting, business admin, communications, finance, information resources management, management information systems, management science, marketing. **Communications:** Media studies. **Computer sciences:** General, information systems. **Education:** Biology, business, early childhood, elementary, English, history, mathematics, mentally handicapped, music, physical, reading, social science. **Engineering:** General. **English:** English lit. **Health services:** Athletic training, clinical lab science, nursing (RN), radiologic technology/medical imaging, respiratory therapy technology, substance abuse counseling. **Human services:** Social work. **Liberal arts:** Arts/sciences. **Math:** General. **Parks/recreation:** Exercise sciences, sports admin. **Philosophy/religion:** Religion. **Protective services:** Correctional facilities, criminal justice. **Psychology:** General. **Social sciences:** General. **Theology:** Sacred music, theology. **Visual/performing arts:** Music performance.

Most popular majors. Biology 6%, business/marketing 41%, education 9%, health sciences 18%, liberal arts 6%, parks/recreation 6%.

Technology on campus. 100 workstations in dormitories, library, computer center. Dormitories wired for high-speed internet access and linked to campus network. Commuter students can connect to campus network. Online course registration, online library, helpline, student web hosting, wireless network available.

Student life. Freshman orientation: Mandatory, $130 fee. Preregistration for classes offered. Three-day program immediately prior to the first day of classes. **Policies:** Freshmen and sophomores have an on-campus residency requirement. **Housing:** Guaranteed on-campus for freshmen. Coed dorms, single-sex dorms, special housing for disabled, apartments, wellness housing available. $100 fully refundable deposit. **Activities:** Bands, campus ministries, choral groups, dance, drama, international student organizations, literary magazine, music ensembles, musical theater, student government, student newspaper, Circle-K, Young Democrats, College Republicans, Fellowship of Christian Athletes, Lions Club, Spanish Club, Collegians for Life, Optimist Club.

Athletics. NCAA. **Intercollegiate:** Baseball M, basketball, cross-country, football (tackle) M, golf W, soccer, softball W, tennis W, track and field, volleyball W, wrestling M. **Intramural:** Badminton, basketball, football (non-tackle), golf, racquetball, soccer, softball, swimming, table tennis, tennis, triathlon, ultimate frisbee, volleyball, water polo, weight lifting. **Team name:** Marauders.

Student services. Adult student services, chaplain/spiritual director, career counseling, services for economically disadvantaged, student employment services, financial aid counseling, health services, minority student services, personal counseling, placement for graduates, veterans' counselor. **Physically disabled:** Services for visually, hearing impaired.

Contact. E-mail: marauder@umary.edu
Phone: (701) 355-8030 Toll-free number: (800) 288-6279
Fax: (701) 255-7687
Michael Mcmahon, Director of Admissions, University of Mary, 7500 University Drive, Bismarck, ND 58504-9652

University of North Dakota
Grand Forks, North Dakota
www.und.edu

CB code: 6878

- Public 4-year university
- Residential campus in small city
- 10,809 degree-seeking undergraduates: 16% part-time, 44% women, 2% African American, 2% Asian American, 3% Hispanic/Latino, 1% Native American, 3% Multi-racial, non-Hispanic, 4% international
- 3,229 degree-seeking graduate students
- 82% of applicants admitted
- SAT or ACT (ACT writing optional) required
- 53% graduate within 6 years; 14% enter graduate study

General. Founded in 1883. Regionally accredited. **Degrees:** 1,948 bachelor's awarded; master's, professional, doctoral offered. **ROTC:** Army, Air Force. **Location:** 320 miles from Minneapolis-St. Paul, 150 miles from Winnipeg, Canada. **Calendar:** Semester, extensive summer session. **Full-time faculty:** 683 total; 75% have terminal degrees, 15% minority, 43% women. **Part-time faculty:** 53 total; 42% have terminal degrees, 2% minority, 55% women. **Class size:** 40% < 20, 45% 20-39, 7% 40-49, 5% 50-99, 3% >100. **Special facilities:** Native media center, American Indian center, biomedical research center, climate change and CO_2 center, rural health center, children and family services training center, clinical education center, environmental training institute, ecological studies institute, hydrogen technology center, Native American aging resource center, behavioral research center, Indian law center, wellness center, unmanned serial systems center, observatory.

Freshman class profile. 4,920 applied, 4,029 admitted, 1,900 enrolled.

GPA 3.75 or higher:	28%	Return as sophomores:	81%
GPA 3.50-3.74:	20%	Out-of-state:	61%
GPA 3.0-3.49:	34%	Live on campus:	92%
GPA 2.0-2.99:	18%	International:	3%
Rank in top quarter:	41%	Fraternities:	12%
Rank in top tenth:	17%	Sororities:	11%
End year in good standing:	85%		

Basis for selection. High school record and test scores most important. **Home schooled:** Transcript of courses and grades required.

High school preparation. College-preparatory program required. 13 units required. Required and recommended units include English 4, mathematics 3, social studies 3, science 3 (laboratory 3) and foreign language 1. Math must be algebra I and above.

2015-2016 Annual costs. Tuition/fees: $7,965; $18,899 out-of-state. Room/board: $7,236. Books/supplies: $1,000. Personal expenses: $2,222.

Application procedures. Admission: Priority date 3/1; no deadline. $35 fee, may be waived for applicants with need. Admission notification on a rolling basis beginning on or about 9/1. **Financial aid:** No deadline. FAFSA required. Applicants notified on a rolling basis.

Academics. Special study options: Accelerated study, combined bachelor's/graduate degree, cooperative education, cross-registration, distance learning, double major, dual enrollment of high school students, ESL, exchange student, external degree, honors, independent study, internships, liberal arts/career combination, semester at sea, student-designed major, study abroad, teacher certification program, weekend college. **Credit/placement by examination:** AP, CLEP, IB, ACT, institutional tests. **Support services:** Learning center, pre-admission summer program, reduced course load, remedial instruction, study skills assistance, tutoring, writing center.

Majors. Area/ethnic studies: Chinese, Native American. **Biology:** General, molecular. **Business:** Accounting, accounting/finance, business admin, entrepreneurial studies, finance, human resources, investments/securities, managerial economics, marketing, operations. **Communications:** General. **Communications technology:** Graphics. **Computer sciences:** General, systems analysis. **Conservation:** Environmental studies. **Education:** Early childhood, elementary, middle, music, science, secondary, social science. **Engineering:** Chemical, civil, electrical, environmental, geological, mechanical, petroleum. **English:** English lit. **Foreign languages:** General, classics, French, German, Norwegian, Spanish. **Health services:** Athletic training, clinical lab science, clinical nutrition, communication disorders, cytotechnology, dietetics, music therapy, nursing (RN), public health ed, rehabilitation science. **History:** General. **Human services:** General, social work. **Math:** General. **Parks/recreation:** Exercise sciences, facilities management. **Philosophy/religion:** Philosophy, religion. **Physical sciences:** General, atmospheric science, chemistry, geology, physics. **Protective services:** Criminal justice, forensics. **Psychology:** General. **Social sciences:** General, anthropology, economics, geography, political science, sociology. **Visual/performing arts:** Art, dramatic, graphic design, music, music performance, musical theater.

Most popular majors. Business/marketing 14%, engineering/engineering technologies 13%, health sciences 13%, liberal arts 6%, psychology 6%, trade and industry 10%.

Technology on campus. 1,000 workstations in dormitories, library, computer center, student center. Dormitories wired for high-speed internet access and linked to campus network. Commuter students can connect to campus network. Online course registration, online library, helpline, repair service, student web hosting, wireless network available.

Student life. Freshman orientation: Available, $15 fee. Preregistration for classes offered. Held weekend before school opens in August. **Policies:** Code of Conduct, Code of Ethics, Code of Student Life. **Housing:** Coed dorms, single-sex dorms, special housing for disabled, apartments, fraternity/sorority housing, themed housing, wellness housing available. $250 partly refundable deposit, deadline 5/1. **Activities:** Bands, campus ministries, choral groups, dance, drama, film society, international student organizations, literary magazine, music ensembles, musical theater, opera, radio station, student government, student newspaper, symphony orchestra, TV station, over 275 organizations available.

Athletics. NCAA. **Intercollegiate:** Baseball M, basketball, cross-country, diving, football (tackle) M, golf, ice hockey, soccer W, softball W, swimming, tennis W, track and field, volleyball W. **Intramural:** Badminton, basketball, golf, ice hockey, racquetball, soccer W, softball W, tennis W, ultimate frisbee, volleyball W. **Team name:** North Dakota.

Student services. Adult student services, alcohol/substance abuse counseling, chaplain/spiritual director, career counseling, services for economically disadvantaged, student employment services, financial aid counseling, health services, legal services, minority student services, on-campus daycare, personal counseling, placement for graduates, veterans' counselor, women's services. **Physically disabled:** Services for visually, speech, hearing impaired.

Contact. E-mail: UND.admissions@UND.edu
Phone: (701) 777-3000 ext. 3000 Toll-free number: (800) 225-5863
Fax: (701) 777-2721
Jason Trainer, Director of Admissions, University of North Dakota, 2901 University Avenue Stop 8264, Grand Forks, ND 58202-8264

Valley City State University
Valley City, North Dakota
www.vcsu.edu

CB code: 6480

- Public 4-year liberal arts and teachers college
- Residential campus in small town
- 1,085 degree-seeking undergraduates: 28% part-time, 59% women
- 121 degree-seeking graduate students
- 86% of applicants admitted
- SAT or ACT (ACT writing optional) required

General. Founded in 1889. Regionally accredited. All full-time undergraduate students are provided a laptop computer. **Degrees:** 275 bachelor's awarded; master's offered. **Location:** 60 miles from Fargo. **Calendar:** Semester, limited summer session. **Full-time faculty:** 70 total; 60% have terminal degrees, 13% minority, 49% women. **Part-time faculty:** 42 total; 36% have terminal degrees, 5% minority, 52% women. **Class size:** 78% < 20, 20% 20-39, less than 1% 40-49, less than 1% 50-99. **Special facilities:** Planetarium, medicine wheel, undergraduate research labs.

Freshman class profile. 403 applied, 348 admitted, 209 enrolled.

Mid 50% test scores			
		GPA 2.0-2.99:	36%
SAT critical reading:	380-480	Rank in top quarter:	25%
SAT math:	360-480	Rank in top tenth:	7%
SAT writing:	350-450	Out-of-state:	22%
ACT composite:	18-23	Live on campus:	95%
GPA 3.75 or higher:	21%	Fraternities:	1%
GPA 3.50-3.74:	12%	Sororities:	1%
GPA 3.0-3.49:	29%		

Basis for selection. School achievement record and test scores important. **Home schooled:** Transcript of courses and grades required.

High school preparation. College-preparatory program required. 13 units required. Required and recommended units include English 4, mathematics 3, social studies 3, science 3 (laboratory 3) and foreign language 2.

2015-2016 Annual costs. Tuition/fees: $6,800; $15,406 out-of-state. Room/board: $6,000. Books/supplies: $1,200.

2015-2016 Financial aid. Need-based: 49% of total undergraduate aid awarded as scholarships/grants, 51% as loans/jobs. **Non-need-based:** Scholarships awarded for academics, athletics, minority status, music/drama.

Application procedures. Admission: No deadline. $35 fee. Admission notification on a rolling basis. **Financial aid:** Priority date 3/15; no closing date. FAFSA required. Applicants notified on a rolling basis starting 2/15; must reply within 4 week(s) of notification.

Academics. Special study options: Accelerated study, combined bachelor's/graduate degree, cross-registration, distance learning, double major, dual enrollment of high school students, ESL, independent study, internships, liberal arts/career combination, student-designed major, study abroad, teacher certification program. **Credit/placement by examination:** AP, CLEP, SAT, ACT, institutional tests. **Support services:** Learning center, reduced course load, study skills assistance, tutoring, writing center.

Majors. Biology: General. **Business:** Business admin, human resources, office management. **Communications:** Communications/speech/rhetoric. **Computer sciences:** General. **Conservation:** Wildlife/wilderness. **Education:** Art, biology, business, chemistry, educational technology, elementary, English, health, history, mathematics, music, physical, science, secondary, social science, Spanish, technology/industrial arts, trade/industrial, voc/tech. **Engineering:** Software. **English:** English lit. **Foreign languages:** Spanish. **Health services:** Athletic training, predental, premedicine, prenursing, prepharmacy, preveterinary. **History:** General. **Liberal arts:** Arts/sciences. **Math:** General. **Parks/recreation:** Health/fitness. **Physical sciences:** Chemistry. **Psychology:** General. **Social sciences:** General. **Visual/performing arts:** Art, music.

Most popular majors. Business/marketing 11%, education 55%, natural resources/environmental science 8%.

Technology on campus. 995 workstations in dormitories, library, computer center, student center. Dormitories wired for high-speed internet access and linked to campus network. Commuter students can connect to campus network. Online course registration, online library, helpline, repair service, student web hosting, wireless network available.

Student life. Freshman orientation: Available, $15 fee. Preregistration for classes offered. Half-day sessions for students with concurrent sessions for parents; held on 2 separate days in both April and June. **Policies:** Tobacco-free campus. **Housing:** Guaranteed on-campus for freshmen. Coed dorms, single-sex dorms, apartments available. $50 fully refundable deposit. Apartments for students with children available. **Activities:** Bands, campus ministries, choral groups, drama, international student organizations, literary magazine, music ensembles, student government, student newspaper, inter-residence hall council, inter-fraternity/sorority council, inter-varsity Christian fellowship, Music Educators National Conference, Student National Education Association, Newman Club, Association of Information Technology Professionals, Faith Lutheran student club.

Athletics. NAIA. **Intercollegiate:** Baseball M, basketball, cross-country, football (tackle) M, golf, softball W, track and field, volleyball W. **Intramural:** Basketball, bowling, football (non-tackle), golf, ice hockey, racquetball, softball, track and field, volleyball. **Team name:** Vikings.

Student services. Career counseling, student employment services, financial aid counseling, health services, on-campus daycare, personal counseling, placement for graduates, veterans' counselor.

Contact. E-mail: enrollment.services@vcsu.edu
Phone: (701) 845-7101 Toll-free number: (800) 532-8641 ext. 7101
Fax: (701) 845-7104
Charlene Stenson, Director of Enrollment Services, Valley City State University, 101 College Street SW, Valley City, ND 58072-4098

Ohio

Allegheny Wesleyan College
Salem, Ohio
www.awc.edu
CB code: 4120

- Private 4-year Bible college affiliated with the Allegheny Wesleyan Methodist Connection
- Residential campus in small town
- 43 degree-seeking undergraduates

General. Accredited by ABHE. Beautiful country setting on 45 acres. **Degrees:** 4 bachelor's, 1 associate awarded. **Location:** 2 miles from Salem. **Calendar:** Semester. **Full-time faculty:** 8 total. **Part-time faculty:** 5 total.

Basis for selection. Open admission.

2015-2016 Annual costs. Tuition/fees: $6,000. Room/board: $3,600. Books/supplies: $550. Personal expenses: $800.

Application procedures. Admission: Priority date 4/25; deadline 8/26. No application fee. Admission notification on a rolling basis. **Financial aid:** Priority date 8/26; no closing date.

Academics. Special study options: Double major, internships. **Credit/placement by examination:** AP, CLEP, institutional tests. 12 credit hours maximum toward associate degree, 12 toward bachelor's. **Support services:** Reduced course load, remedial instruction, tutoring.

Majors. Theology: Theology.

Technology on campus. 10 workstations in library, computer center. Online library, repair service available.

Student life. Housing: Coed dorms available. **Activities:** Student newspaper.

Contact. E-mail: college@awc.edu
Phone: (330) 337-6403 Toll-free number: (800) 292-3153 ext. 10
Fax: (330) 337-6255
Jeanne Zvaritch, Director of Admissions, Allegheny Wesleyan College, 2161 Woodside Road, Salem, OH 44460-9598

Antioch University Midwest
Yellow Springs, Ohio
www.antiochmidwest.edu
CB code: 4527

- Private 4-year university and branch campus college
- Commuter campus in small town
- 116 degree-seeking undergraduates
- 194 graduate students
- Application essay, interview required

General. Founded in 1988. Regionally accredited. **Degrees:** 17 bachelor's awarded; master's offered. **Location:** 18 miles from Dayton. **Calendar:** Semester, limited summer session. **Full-time faculty:** 20 total. **Part-time faculty:** 30 total. **Special facilities:** Nature reserve.

Basis for selection. Applicants must be over 21.

2015-2016 Annual costs. Tuition/fees: $16,210.

Application procedures. Admission: $45 fee, may be waived for applicants with need. Admission notification on a rolling basis. **Financial aid:** No deadline. FAFSA, institutional form required. Applicants notified on a rolling basis starting 3/1; must reply within 2 week(s) of notification.

Academics. Special study options: Combined bachelor's/graduate degree, cross-registration, distance learning, double major, independent study, student-designed major, teacher certification program, weekend college. **Credit/placement by examination:** AP, CLEP. 30 credit hours maximum toward bachelor's degree. **Support services:** Reduced course load, writing center.

Majors. Business: Business admin, human resources. **Education:** General, early childhood. **Liberal arts:** Arts/sciences, humanities. **Math:** General.

Most popular majors. Business/marketing 21%, education 27%, health sciences 9%, liberal arts 17%, psychology 11%, public administration/social services 15%.

Technology on campus. PC or laptop required. 35 workstations in computer center. Commuter students can connect to campus network. Online course registration, online library, helpline, wireless network available.

Student life. Freshman orientation: Mandatory, $25 fee. Preregistration for classes offered. **Activities:** Radio station.

Student services. Adult student services, financial aid counseling.

Contact. E-mail: sas.aum@antioch.edu
Phone: (937) 769-1818 Fax: (937) 769-1804
Oscar Robinson, Director of Admissions, Antioch University Midwest, 900 Dayton Street, Yellow Springs, OH 45387

Art Academy of Cincinnati
Cincinnati, Ohio
www.artacademy.edu
CB code: 1002

- Private 4-year visual arts college
- Commuter campus in large city
- 206 degree-seeking undergraduates
- 7 graduate students
- SAT or ACT (ACT writing optional), application essay required

General. Founded in 1869. Regionally accredited. **Degrees:** 53 bachelor's awarded; master's offered. **Location:** One mile from downtown. **Calendar:** Semester, limited summer session. **Full-time faculty:** 14 total; 57% women. **Part-time faculty:** 30 total. **Special facilities:** Glass-blowing facility, three art galleries.

Freshman class profile.

Out-of-state:	36%	Live on campus:	51%

Basis for selection. Academic background based upon GPA and ACT/SAT scores; portfolio review and interview very important; 1-page artist statement and 1 letter of recommendation required. Portfolio required for all; interview required for those within 150 miles of campus. **Home schooled:** Transcript of courses and grades, state high school equivalency certificate required.

High school preparation. 12 units recommended. Recommended units include English 4, mathematics 3, social studies 1 and science 2. 3-4 units art recommended.

2015-2016 Annual costs. Tuition/fees: $27,758. Room/board: $6,500. Books/supplies: $1,500.

Financial aid. Non-need-based: Scholarships awarded for academics, art.

Application procedures. Admission: Priority date 3/1; deadline 6/30 (postmark date). No application fee. Admission notification on a rolling basis. **Financial aid:** Priority date 4/1; no closing date. FAFSA required. Applicants notified on a rolling basis starting 4/1.

Academics. Special study options: Cross-registration, double major, exchange student, independent study, internships, New York semester, student-designed major, study abroad. **Credit/placement by examination:** AP, CLEP, institutional tests. **Support services:** Learning center, study skills assistance, tutoring, writing center.

Majors. Visual/performing arts: Art history/conservation, design, digital arts, drawing, illustration, painting, photography, printmaking, sculpture, studio arts.

Technology on campus. 40 workstations in computer center. Dormitories wired for high-speed internet access.

Student life. Freshman orientation: Mandatory. Preregistration for classes offered. Held five days before school begins. **Housing:** Coed dorms available. $250 nonrefundable deposit, deadline 6/1. **Activities:** Film society, literary magazine, student government.

Athletics. Team name: Stinks.

Student services. Career counseling, student employment services, financial aid counseling, personal counseling, placement for graduates, veterans' counselor. **Physically disabled:** Services for hearing impaired.

Contact. E-mail: admissions@artacademy.edu
Phone: (513) 562-8740 Toll-free number: (800) 323-5692
Fax: (513) 562-8778
John Cooper, Vice President of Enrollment Management, Art Academy of Cincinnati, 1212 Jackson Street, Cincinnati, OH 45202

Ashland University
Ashland, Ohio
www.ashland.edu   **CB code: 1021**

◆ Private 4-year university and liberal arts college affiliated with the Brethren Church

◆ Residential campus in large town

◆ 3,215 degree-seeking undergraduates: 22% part-time, 51% women, 5% African American, 1% Asian American, 3% Hispanic/Latino, 2% Multiracial, non-Hispanic, 2% international

◆ 1,642 degree-seeking graduate students

◆ 76% of applicants admitted

◆ SAT or ACT (ACT writing optional) required

General. Founded in 1878. Regionally accredited. **Degrees:** 584 bachelor's, 3 associate awarded; master's, professional, doctoral offered. **ROTC:** Army, Air Force. **Location:** 60 miles from Cleveland, 80 miles from Columbus. **Calendar:** Semester, extensive summer session. **Full-time faculty:** 218 total; 76% have terminal degrees. **Part-time faculty:** 342 total. **Class size:** 66% < 20, 34% 20-39, less than 1% 50-99. **Special facilities:** Center for public affairs, nature preserves.

Freshman class profile. 3,089 applied, 2,335 admitted, 587 enrolled.

Mid 50% test scores		Rank in top quarter:	48%
SAT critical reading:	450-550	Rank in top tenth:	18%
SAT math:	460-540	Out-of-state:	15%
ACT composite:	20-25	Live on campus:	86%
GPA 3.75 or higher:	28%	International:	1%
GPA 3.50-3.74:	23%	Fraternities:	7%
GPA 3.0-3.49:	27%	Sororities:	20%
GPA 2.0-2.99:	22%		

Basis for selection. School college prep curriculum and achievement record most important; test scores also important. Counselor's recommendation considered. Audition required for music, recommended for theater programs; portfolio recommended for art. Interview required for Ashbrook Scholars Program.

High school preparation. College-preparatory program recommended. Required and recommended units include English 3-4, mathematics 3-4, social studies 2-3, history 1-3, science 3-4, foreign language 2, computer science 1 and academic electives 1.

2016-2017 Annual costs. Tuition/fees (projected): $20,872. Room/board: $9,602. Books/supplies: $900. Personal expenses: $1,801.

2015-2016 Financial aid. **Need-based:** 546 full-time freshmen applied for aid; 468 deemed to have need; 468 received aid. Average scholarship/grant was $13,176; average loan $4,119. 48% of total undergraduate aid awarded as scholarships/grants, 52% as loans/jobs. **Non-need-based:** Scholarships awarded for academics, alumni affiliation, art, athletics, job skills, leadership, minority status, music/drama, religious affiliation, state residency.

Application procedures. **Admission:** Priority date 1/1; no deadline. , may be waived for applicants with need. No application fee. Admission notification on a rolling basis beginning on or about 8/1. Must reply by May 1 or within 4 week(s) if notified thereafter. **Financial aid:** Priority date 3/15; no closing date. FAFSA required. Applicants notified on a rolling basis starting 3/1.

Academics. Online coursework and programs available. **Special study options:** Accelerated study, combined bachelor's/graduate degree, distance learning, double major, dual enrollment of high school students, ESL, exchange student, honors, independent study, internships, New York semester, student-designed major, study abroad, teacher certification program, urban semester, Washington semester. Bachelor's degree completion program for RNs, teacher licensure for those with non-teaching degrees, pre-seminary, pre-med, pre-dental, pre-law. **Credit/placement by examination:** AP, CLEP, IB, SAT, ACT, institutional tests. 32 credit hours maximum toward associate degree, 32 toward bachelor's. **Support services:** Learning center, study skills assistance, tutoring, writing center.

Majors. Biology: General, biochemistry, biotechnology, environmental, exercise physiology, toxicology. **Business:** General, accounting, accounting/business management, accounting/finance, actuarial science, business admin, entrepreneurial studies, fashion, finance, hospitality admin, hospitality/recreation, hotel/motel admin, international, logistics, management information systems, management science, managerial economics, market research, marketing. **Communications:** General, advertising, broadcast journalism, digital media, health, journalism, media studies, organizational, persuasive communications, photojournalism, political, public relations, radio/TV, sports. **Computer sciences:** Computer science. **Conservation:** Environmental science. **Education:** Art, autistic, bilingual, biology, chemistry, developmentally delayed, early childhood, early childhood special, earth science, emotionally handicapped, English, French, gifted/talented, history, learning disabled, mathematics, mentally handicapped, middle, multiple handicapped, music, science, secondary, social studies, Spanish, special ed, speech impaired. **Engineering:** Pre-engineering. **English:** Creative writing, English lit. **Foreign languages:** French, Spanish. **Health services:** Athletic training, communication disorders, dietetics, prechiropractic, predental, premedicine, preoccupational therapy, preoptometry, prepharmacy, prephysical therapy, preveterinary. **History:** General. **Human services:** General, social work. **Math:** General, computational. **Parks/recreation:** Exercise sciences, sports admin. **Philosophy/religion:** Philosophy, religion. **Physical sciences:** Chemistry, environmental chemistry, forensic chemistry, geology, physics. **Protective services:** Forensics, law enforcement admin. **Psychology:** General. **Social sciences:** Economics, international relations, political science. **Theology:** Theology. **Visual/performing arts:** Acting, art, brass instruments, ceramics, commercial/advertising art, digital arts, dramatic, drawing, game design, graphic design, music, music performance, music theory/composition, painting, percussion instruments, piano/keyboard, play/screenwriting, sculpture, stringed instruments, studio arts, voice/opera, woodwind instruments. **Work/family studies:** Apparel marketing.

Most popular majors. Business/marketing 21%, education 26%, health sciences 21%.

Technology on campus. 500 workstations in dormitories, library, computer center, student center. Dormitories wired for high-speed internet access and linked to campus network. Commuter students can connect to campus network. Online course registration, online library, helpline, repair service, student web hosting, wireless network available.

Student life. **Freshman orientation:** Mandatory, $100 fee. Preregistration for classes offered. One-day program usually held in June and July. **Housing:** Guaranteed on-campus for all undergraduates. Coed dorms, single-sex dorms, special housing for disabled, apartments, fraternity/sorority housing, themed housing, wellness housing available. $300 fully refundable deposit, deadline 8/15. Scholar hall available. Apartments available to seniors. **Activities:** Bands, campus ministries, choral groups, dance, drama, international student organizations, literary magazine, music ensembles, musical theater, opera, radio station, student government, student newspaper, symphony orchestra, TV station, The Well Christian Fellowship, Newman Catholic club, Fellowship of Christian Athletes, international club, Diversity on Campus (D.O.C.), campus activities board, community care, tutoring/mentoring club, Republican club, Democratic club.

Athletics. NCAA. **Intercollegiate:** Baseball M, basketball, cheerleading W, cross-country, diving, football (tackle) M, golf, sand volleyball, soccer, softball W, swimming, tennis W, track and field, volleyball W, wrestling M. **Intramural:** Badminton, basketball, bowling, football (non-tackle), golf, lacrosse, racquetball, rugby, sand volleyball, skiing, soccer, softball, table tennis, triathlon, ultimate frisbee, volleyball, weight lifting. **Team name:** Eagles.

Student services. Alcohol/substance abuse counseling, chaplain/spiritual director, career counseling, student employment services, financial aid counseling, health services, minority student services, personal counseling, placement for graduates, veterans' counselor. **Physically disabled:** Services for visually, speech, hearing impaired.

Contact. E-mail: enrollme@ashland.edu
Phone: (419) 289-5052 Toll-free number: (800) 882-1548 ext. 5052
Fax: (419) 289-5999
W.C. Vance, Director of Admissions, Ashland University, 401 College Avenue, Ashland, OH 44805-9981

Baldwin Wallace University
Berea, Ohio   **CB member**
www.bw.edu   **CB code: 1050**

◆ Private 4-year university affiliated with the United Methodist Church

◆ Residential campus in large town

- 3,310 degree-seeking undergraduates: 8% part-time, 55% women, 9% African American, 1% Asian American, 5% Hispanic/Latino, 5% Multiracial, non-Hispanic, 1% international
- 584 degree-seeking graduate students
- 60% of applicants admitted
- Application essay required
- 67% graduate within 6 years; 16% enter graduate study

General. Founded in 1845. Regionally accredited. Campus in Warrensville Heights, offering evening and Saturday classes for bachelor's and master's degrees in business, professional development and executive education. **Degrees:** 666 bachelor's awarded; master's offered. **ROTC:** Army, Air Force. **Location:** 15 miles from Cleveland. **Calendar:** Semester, limited summer session. **Full-time faculty:** 201 total; 75% have terminal degrees, 8% minority, 47% women. **Part-time faculty:** 253 total; 10% have terminal degrees, 10% minority, 53% women. **Class size:** 60% < 20, 38% 20-39, 1% 40-49, less than 1% 50-99. **Special facilities:** Observatory, two art galleries, two theaters, conservatory of music, two dance studios, cybercafe, arboretum, Lyceum Square (historical site).

Freshman class profile. 4,363 applied, 2,626 admitted, 768 enrolled.

Mid 50% test scores			
SAT critical reading:	480-600	Rank in top quarter:	45%
SAT math:	480-600	Rank in top tenth:	19%
SAT writing:	450-580	End year in good standing:	91%
ACT composite:	20-27	Return as sophomores:	83%
GPA 3.75 or higher:	31%	Out-of-state:	26%
GPA 3.50-3.74:	18%	Live on campus:	87%
GPA 3.0-3.49:	32%	International:	1%
		Fraternities:	12%
GPA 2.0-2.99:	19%	Sororities:	18%

Basis for selection. Academic achievement (preferably 3.0 GPA) and class rank (preferably top 30%) most important. Test scores used to support data from high school record. 24 ACT, 550 SAT verbal, 550 SAT math recommended. Test optional for full-time, first-time, first year applicants who are US residents not home-schooled with a cumulative 3.0 GPA or higher. In lieu of test scores, a copy of a recently graded school writing paper is required. Pre-screen process for Music Theater applicants required. **Home schooled:** Statement describing home school structure and mission, transcript of courses and grades, letter of recommendation (nonparent) required. Must provide SAT/ACT.

High school preparation. College-preparatory program required. 15 units required; 21 recommended. Required and recommended units include English 4, mathematics 4, social studies 2-3, history 1, science 3-4 (laboratory 2), foreign language 1-2 and academic electives 3. Some flexibility in choice of subjects permitted.

2015-2016 Annual costs. Tuition/fees: $29,908. Room/board: $8,370. Books/supplies: $1,514. Personal expenses: $3,540.

2015-2016 Financial aid. **Need-based:** 707 full-time freshmen applied for aid; 614 deemed to have need; 614 received aid. Average need met was 86%. Average scholarship/grant was $21,883; average loan $4,083. 83% of total undergraduate aid awarded as scholarships/grants, 17% as loans/jobs. **Non-need-based:** Awarded to 969 full-time undergraduates, including 267 freshmen. Scholarships awarded for academics, alumni affiliation, art, minority status, music/drama, religious affiliation, state residency.

Application procedures. Admission: Priority date 3/1; no deadline. $25 fee, may be waived for applicants with need, free for online applicants. Admission notification on a rolling basis beginning on or about 10/15. Must reply by May 1 or within 3 week(s) if notified thereafter. New Student Fee of $200 refundable until May 1. **Financial aid:** Priority date 8/15; no closing date. FAFSA required. Applicants notified on a rolling basis starting 2/15.

Academics. Weekend classes limited to nontraditional students. **Special study options:** Accelerated study, combined bachelor's/graduate degree, cross-registration, distance learning, double major, dual enrollment of high school students, ESL, exchange student, honors, independent study, internships, liberal arts/career combination, semester at sea, student-designed major, study abroad, teacher certification program, weekend college. 3-2 in engineering with Case Western Reserve University and Columbia University (NY); 3-2 in Social Work with Case Western Reserve University; 3/2 Accounting MBA, 3/2 Human Resources MBA and 3/2 Computer Science/Info. Systems MBA Programs. **Credit/placement by examination:** AP, CLEP, IB, SAT, ACT, institutional tests. **Support services:** Learning center, remedial instruction, study skills assistance, tutoring, writing center. Reduced course load offered as an academic accommodation for students with documented disabilities.

Majors. Biology: General, exercise physiology, neuroscience. **Business:** Accounting, business admin, entrepreneurial studies, finance, human resources, international, marketing. **Communications:** Communications/speech/rhetoric, digital media, media studies, public relations. **Computer sciences:** Computer science, networking, systems analysis. **Conservation:** Economics. **Education:** Early childhood, learning disabled, middle, music. **Engineering:** Pre-engineering, software. **English:** Creative writing, English lit. **Foreign languages:** French, German, Spanish. **Health services:** Athletic training, communication disorders, health care admin, music therapy, nursing (RN), predental, premedicine, prepharmacy, preveterinary. **History:** General, applied. **Human services:** General. **Math:** General. **Parks/recreation:** Health/fitness, sports admin. **Philosophy/religion:** Philosophy, religion. **Physical sciences:** Chemistry, physics. **Protective services:** Criminal justice. **Psychology:** General, industrial. **Social sciences:** Econometrics, economics, national security policy, political science, sociology. **Visual/performing arts:** Acting, art, directing/producing, film/cinema/video, graphic design, music, music history, music performance, music theory/composition, piano/keyboard, studio arts, studio arts management, theater design, voice/opera.

Most popular majors. Biology 8%, business/marketing 22%, communications/journalism 7%, education 9%, health sciences 11%, psychology 6%, visual/performing arts 11%.

Technology on campus. PC or laptop required. 524 workstations in dormitories, library, computer center, student center. Dormitories wired for high-speed internet access and linked to campus network. Commuter students can connect to campus network. Online course registration, online library, helpline, repair service, student web hosting, wireless network available.

Student life. Freshman orientation: Mandatory, $100 fee. Preregistration for classes offered. Two-day program held on Friday and Saturday in June, July, and August. **Policies:** All full-time students required to live on campus first and second year. Residency exemptions made for commuting students living with families. **Housing:** Guaranteed on-campus for freshmen. Coed dorms, special housing for disabled, apartments, fraternity/sorority housing, themed housing available. Housing for single mothers and children, student-directed learning communities, living and learning center available. **Activities:** Bands, campus ministries, choral groups, dance, drama, film society, literary magazine, music ensembles, Model UN, musical theater, opera, radio station, student government, student newspaper, symphony orchestra, TV station, Cru, Hillel, Newman Catholic Campus Ministry, College Democrats, College Republicans, Black Student Alliance, Hispanic American Student Association, Middle Eastern culture club, Circle K International, Habitat for Humanity.

Athletics. NCAA. **Intercollegiate:** Baseball M, basketball, cross-country, diving, football (tackle) M, golf, lacrosse, soccer, softball W, swimming, tennis, track and field, volleyball W, wrestling M. **Intramural:** Badminton, basketball, football (non-tackle), football (tackle) M, golf, racquetball, soccer, softball, table tennis, tennis, ultimate frisbee, volleyball, wrestling M. **Team name:** Yellow Jackets.

Student services. Adult student services, alcohol/substance abuse counseling, chaplain/spiritual director, career counseling, student employment services, financial aid counseling, health services, minority student services, personal counseling, veterans' counselor. **Physically disabled:** Services for visually, speech, hearing impaired.

Contact. E-mail: admission@bw.edu
Phone: (440) 826-2222 Toll-free number: (877) 292-7759
Fax: (440) 826-3830
Scott Schulz, Vice President of Enrollment Management, Baldwin Wallace University, 275 Eastland Road, Berea, OH 44017-2088

Bluffton University
Bluffton, Ohio
www.bluffton.edu

CB code: 1067

- Private 4-year university and liberal arts college affiliated with the Mennonite Church
- Residential campus in small town
- 833 degree-seeking undergraduates: 11% part-time, 51% women, 6% African American, 4% Hispanic/Latino, 3% Multi-racial, non-Hispanic
- 93 degree-seeking graduate students
- 54% of applicants admitted
- SAT or ACT (ACT writing optional) required
- 46% graduate within 6 years; 14% enter graduate study

General. Founded in 1899. Regionally accredited. **Degrees:** 213 bachelor's awarded; master's offered. **Location:** 15 miles from Lima, 65 miles from Toledo, 88 miles to Dayton. **Calendar:** Semester, limited summer session. **Full-time faculty:** 56 total; 80% have terminal degrees, 2% minority, 39% women. **Part-time faculty:** 40 total; 32% have terminal degrees, 8% minority, 45% women. **Class size:** 63% < 20, 32% 20-39, 5% 40-49. **Special facilities:** Nature preserve, arts center.

Freshman class profile. 1,652 applied, 885 admitted, 218 enrolled.

Mid 50% test scores			
SAT critical reading:	410-580	GPA 3.0-3.49:	31%
SAT math:	430-560	GPA 2.0-2.99:	32%
SAT writing:	420-550	Rank in top quarter:	25%
ACT composite:	18-23	Rank in top tenth:	12%
GPA 3.75 or higher:	23%	Return as sophomores:	72%
GPA 3.50-3.74:	11%	Out-of-state:	14%
		Live on campus:	93%

Basis for selection. Class rank, school achievement record, and test scores very important. Campus visit and interview strongly recommended. Essay required for academically weak students; audition and portfolio required for scholarships in music and art. **Home schooled:** Interview required.

High school preparation. College-preparatory program recommended. 16 units recommended. Recommended units include English 4, mathematics 3, social studies 3, science 3 and foreign language 3.

2015-2016 Annual costs. Tuition/fees: $30,168. Room/board: $9,890. Books/supplies: $1,400. Personal expenses: $1,600.

2015-2016 Financial aid. Need-based: 205 full-time freshmen applied for aid; 192 deemed to have need; 192 received aid. Average need met was 75%. Average scholarship/grant was $21,248; average loan $4,363. 68% of total undergraduate aid awarded as scholarships/grants, 32% as loans/jobs. **Non-need-based:** Awarded to 163 full-time undergraduates, including 47 freshmen. Scholarships awarded for academics, alumni affiliation, art, job skills, leadership, minority status, music/drama, religious affiliation, state residency. **Additional information:** Tuition Equalization Program erases the difference between Bluffton's tuition and academic fees and that of the top state schools.

Application procedures. Admission: Priority date 5/1; deadline 8/15 (receipt date). $20 fee, may be waived for applicants with need, free for online applicants. Admission notification on a rolling basis beginning on or about 6/1. **Financial aid:** Priority date 5/1, closing date 10/1. FAFSA required. Applicants notified on a rolling basis starting 3/1; must reply within 3 week(s) of notification.

Academics. Cross-cultural experiences. **Special study options:** Accelerated study, distance learning, double major, dual enrollment of high school students, honors, independent study, internships, liberal arts/career combination, student-designed major, study abroad, teacher certification program, Washington semester. Degree-completion program for working adults 25 years and older. **Credit/placement by examination:** AP, CLEP, SAT, ACT, institutional tests. 20 credit hours maximum toward bachelor's degree. **Support services:** Learning center, reduced course load, remedial instruction, study skills assistance, tutoring, writing center.

Majors. Biology: General. **Business:** Accounting, business admin, marketing, organizational behavior. **Communications:** Broadcast journalism, communications/speech/rhetoric, persuasive communications, sports. **Computer sciences:** Information technology. **Education:** General, art, biology, chemistry, early childhood, elementary, English, ESL, history, kindergarten/preschool, mathematics, middle, music, physics, science, social studies, special ed. **English:** English lit, writing. **Foreign languages:** Spanish. **Health services:** Art therapy, health care admin, nursing (RN), premedicine. **History:** General. **Human services:** Social work. **Math:** General. **Parks/recreation:** Facilities management, health/fitness, sports admin. **Physical sciences:** Chemistry, physics. **Protective services:** Criminal justice. **Psychology:** General. **Social sciences:** General, economics, sociology. **Theology:** Bible, youth ministry. **Visual/performing arts:** Art, graphic design, music. **Work/family studies:** Child development, food/nutrition.

Most popular majors. Business/marketing 29%, education 10%, family/consumer sciences 6%, parks/recreation 15%, public administration/social services 14%.

Technology on campus. 125 workstations in dormitories, library, computer center, student center. Dormitories wired for high-speed internet access and linked to campus network. Commuter students can connect to campus network. Online course registration, online library, helpline, repair service, student web hosting, wireless network available.

Student life. Freshman orientation: Mandatory. Preregistration for classes offered. Fall orientation begins Friday before classes and continues through first week of classes. Additional one-day event held over summer; students can choose one of four dates. **Policies:** No alcoholic beverages or tobacco allowed on campus. Honor system applies to all student activities. Students should feel comfortable with emphasis on faith and values. All traditional undergraduate students required to live on campus or commute from home. **Housing:** Guaranteed on-campus for all undergraduates. Coed dorms, single-sex dorms, themed housing available. **Activities:** Bands, campus ministries, choral groups, drama, film society, international student organizations, literary magazine, music ensembles, musical theater, radio station, student government, student newspaper, departmental clubs, P.E.A.C.E. club, Habitat for Humanity, Fellowship of Christian Athletes, multicultural student organization, International Connection, Peer Awareness Leaders, College Republicans, Young Democrats.

Athletics. NCAA. **Intercollegiate:** Baseball M, basketball, cross-country, football (tackle) M, soccer, softball W, track and field, volleyball W. **Intramural:** Basketball, bowling, football (non-tackle), softball, tennis, volleyball. **Team name:** Beavers.

Student services. Alcohol/substance abuse counseling, chaplain/spiritual director, career counseling, student employment services, financial aid counseling, health services, minority student services, personal counseling, placement for graduates. **Physically disabled:** Services for visually, hearing impaired.

Contact. E-mail: admissions@bluffton.edu
Phone: (419) 358-3257 Toll-free number: (800) 488-3257
Fax: (419) 358-3081
Robin Hopkins, Director of Admissions, Bluffton University, 1 University Drive, Bluffton, OH 45817-2104

Bowling Green State University
Bowling Green, Ohio   CB member
www.bgsu.edu   CB code: 1069

- Public 4-year university
- Residential campus in large town
- 13,901 degree-seeking undergraduates: 5% part-time, 57% women, 10% African American, 1% Asian American, 4% Hispanic/Latino, 3% Multiracial, non-Hispanic, 2% international
- 2,431 degree-seeking graduate students
- 76% of applicants admitted
- SAT or ACT (ACT writing optional) required
- 56% graduate within 6 years

General. Founded in 1910. Regionally accredited. **Degrees:** 2,893 bachelor's awarded; master's, doctoral offered. **ROTC:** Army, Air Force. **Location:** 23 miles from Toledo. **Calendar:** Semester, limited summer session. **Full-time faculty:** 679 total; 81% have terminal degrees, 13% minority, 48% women. **Part-time faculty:** 328 total; 24% have terminal degrees, 6% minority, 65% women. **Class size:** 41% < 20, 45% 20-39, 5% 40-49, 7% 50-99, 2% >100. **Special facilities:** Planetarium, film theater, sound recording archives, popular culture library, marine biology laboratory, educational memorabilia center, student union.

Freshman class profile. 14,887 applied, 11,240 admitted, 3,392 enrolled.

Mid 50% test scores			
SAT critical reading:	460-580	Rank in top quarter:	36%
SAT math:	460-580	Rank in top tenth:	12%
SAT writing:	420-550	End year in good standing:	86%
ACT composite:	20-25	Return as sophomores:	78%
GPA 3.75 or higher:	24%	Out-of-state:	13%
GPA 3.50-3.74:	16%	Live on campus:	90%
GPA 3.0-3.49:	32%	International:	1%
GPA 2.0-2.99:	28%	Fraternities:	11%
		Sororities:	9%

Basis for selection. High school coursework/curriculum, cumulative grade point average, test scores, class rank very important. Audition required for music/theater; portfolio required for art programs. Essays required for honors program/college. **Home schooled:** Transcript of courses and grades required. **Learning Disabled:** Prospective students encouraged to arrange an interview with Disability Services.

High school preparation. College-preparatory program recommended. Recommended units include English 4, mathematics 3, social studies 3, science 3 (laboratory 2), foreign language 2 and visual/performing arts 1.

2015-2016 Annual costs. Tuition/fees: $10,726; $18,262 out-of-state. Room/board: $8,496. Books/supplies: $1,020. Personal expenses: $2,598.

2014-2015 Financial aid. Need-based: 2,747 full-time freshmen applied for aid; 2,135 deemed to have need; 2,104 received aid. Average need met was 78%. Average scholarship/grant was $7,030; average loan $3,509. 45% of total undergraduate aid awarded as scholarships/grants, 55% as loans/jobs. **Non-need-based:** Awarded to 3,424 full-time undergraduates, including 944 freshmen. Scholarships awarded for academics, alumni affiliation, art, athletics, leadership, minority status, music/drama, ROTC, state residency.

Application procedures. Admission: Priority date 2/1; deadline 7/15 (postmark date). $45 fee, may be waived for applicants with need. Admission notification on a rolling basis beginning on or about 8/1. Must reply by 6/1. **Financial aid:** No deadline. FAFSA required. Applicants notified on a rolling basis starting 4/15; must reply within 3 week(s) of notification.

Academics. Special study options: Accelerated study, combined bachelor's/graduate degree, cooperative education, cross-registration, distance learning, double major, dual enrollment of high school students, ESL, exchange student, honors, independent study, internships, liberal arts/career combination, student-designed major, study abroad, teacher certification program, Washington semester. **Credit/placement by examination:** AP, CLEP, IB, SAT, ACT, institutional tests. Students must be enrolled for at least 2 credit hours during the semester of the exam, have permission of the department and dean, the student must not have enrolled in the course previously and must present sufficient evidence of prior study or experience, and the (credit by exam) course cannot be a prerequisite for any course the student has completed. **Support services:** Learning center, remedial instruction, study skills assistance, tutoring, writing center.

Majors. Architecture: Environmental design, interior. **Area/ethnic studies:** African, African-American, American, Asian, Chicano/Hispanic-American/Latino, European, Latin American, Russian/Slavic, women's. **Biology:** General, bacteriology, biochemistry, microbiology, neuroscience, parasitology. **Business:** General, accounting, actuarial science, business admin, executive assistant, fashion, finance, hospitality admin, human resources, insurance, international, labor relations, logistics, management information systems, managerial economics, market research, marketing, office management, operations, organizational behavior, real estate, retailing, sales/distribution, tourism promotion, tourism/travel. **Communications:** Advertising, broadcast journalism, communications/speech/rhetoric, journalism, public relations, radio/TV. **Computer sciences:** General, information systems. **Conservation:** Environmental studies, management/policy. **Education:** General, art, biology, business, chemistry, college student counseling, computer, Deaf/hearing impaired, early childhood special, educational technology, elementary, English, family/consumer sciences, foreign languages, health, history, kindergarten/preschool, learning disabled, mathematics, mentally handicapped, middle, multi-level teacher, multiple handicapped, music, physical, physics, sales/marketing, school counseling, science, social science, social studies, special ed, speech, technology/industrial arts, trade/industrial, voc/tech. **Engineering:** Computer, construction, operations research, software: **English:** Creative writing, English lit, rhetoric/composition, technical writing. **Foreign languages:** Classics, French, German, Latin, Russian, Spanish. **Health services:** General, art therapy, athletic training, audiology/speech pathology, clinical lab science, communication disorders, community health, dietetics, environmental health, health care admin, health information management, long term care admin, nursing (RN), physical therapy, predental, premedicine, respiratory therapy technology, vocational rehab counseling. **History:** General. **Human services:** General, social work. **Liberal arts:** Arts/sciences. **Math:** General, statistics. **Parks/recreation:** General, sports admin. **Philosophy/religion:** Philosophy. **Physical sciences:** Chemistry, forensic chemistry, geochemistry, geology, geophysics, paleontology, physics. **Protective services:** Corrections, criminal justice, fire services admin, law enforcement admin, police science. **Psychology:** General. **Social sciences:** General, applied economics, economics, geography, international relations, political science, sociology. **Theology:** Sacred music. **Visual/performing arts:** Art, art history/conservation, ceramics, commercial/advertising art, crafts, dance, design, digital arts, dramatic, drawing, fashion design, fiber arts, film/cinema/video, metal/jewelry, music, music history, music performance, music theory/composition, musicology, painting, photography, piano/keyboard, printmaking, sculpture, studio arts, voice/opera. **Work/family studies:** General, aging, child development, clothing/textiles, family studies, family systems, family/community services, food/nutrition.

Most popular majors. Business/marketing 11%, education 18%, health sciences 12%, visual/performing arts 8%.

Technology on campus. 1,500 workstations in dormitories, library, computer center, student center. Dormitories wired for high-speed internet access and linked to campus network. Commuter students can connect to campus network. Online course registration, online library, helpline, repair service, student web hosting, wireless network available.

Student life. Freshman orientation: Available. Preregistration for classes offered. **Housing:** Guaranteed on-campus for freshmen. Coed dorms, single-sex dorms, special housing for disabled, fraternity/sorority housing, gender-neutral housing available. $200 nonrefundable deposit, deadline 6/1. Honors housing, no-alcohol wings available, residential learning/theme communities. **Activities:** Bands, campus ministries, choral groups, dance, drama, film society, international student organizations, literary magazine, music ensembles, Model UN, musical theater, opera, radio station, student government, student newspaper, symphony orchestra, TV station, Active Christians Today, African Peoples Association, Chinese culture club, College Democrats, College Republicans, Environmental Action Group, Habitat for Humanity, Latino Student Union, World Student Association, Vision.

Athletics. NCAA. **Intercollegiate:** Baseball M, basketball, cross-country, football (tackle) M, golf, gymnastics W, ice hockey M, soccer, softball W, swimming W, tennis W, track and field W, volleyball W. **Intramural:** Badminton, basketball, cross-country, football (non-tackle), football (tackle), golf, gymnastics W, ice hockey M, soccer, softball W, tennis, ultimate frisbee, volleyball. **Team name:** Falcons.

Student services. Adult student services, alcohol/substance abuse counseling, career counseling, services for economically disadvantaged, student employment services, financial aid counseling, health services, legal services, minority student services, personal counseling, placement for graduates, veterans' counselor, women's services. **Physically disabled:** Services for visually, speech, hearing impaired.

Contact. E-mail: choosebgsu@bgsu.edu
Phone: (419) 372-2478 Toll-free number: (866) 246-6732
Fax: (419) 372-6955
Adrea Spoon, Director of Admissions, Bowling Green State University, 110 McFall Center, Bowling Green, OH 43403-0085

Bryant & Stratton College: Eastlake
Eastlake, Ohio
www.bryantstratton.edu   CB code: 3251

- For-profit 4-year business college
- Commuter campus in small town
- 231 degree-seeking undergraduates
- Interview required

General. Degrees: 40 bachelor's, 122 associate awarded. **Location:** 15 miles from downtown Cleveland. **Calendar:** Differs by program, limited summer session. **Full-time faculty:** 21 total. **Part-time faculty:** 44 total.

Basis for selection. Open admission. Student's evaluation and diagnostic tests must show qualification for at least pre-college, preparatory math and English courses. **Learning Disabled:** Students with learning disability must provide instructional effectiveness plan from high school counselor.

2015-2016 Annual costs. Tuition/fees: $17,190. Books/supplies: $1,800. Personal expenses: $300. **Additional information:** Tuition and fees may vary by program.

Financial aid. Non-need-based: Scholarships awarded for academics.

Application procedures. Admission: Closing date 9/22 (receipt date). $35 fee. Admission notification on a rolling basis. **Financial aid:** No deadline. FAFSA required. Applicants notified on a rolling basis.

Academics. ACTIVUM learning system facilitates students in developing technical and career-based skills through field trips, portfolio presentations, computer simulations and internship opportunities. **Special study options:** Accelerated study, distance learning, double major, dual enrollment of high school students, independent study, internships. Professional skills center offers medical coding courses and computer certification. **Credit/placement by examination:** AP, CLEP, institutional tests. 12 credit hours maximum toward associate degree, 12 toward bachelor's. **Support services:** Remedial instruction, study skills assistance, tutoring.

Majors. Business: Business admin.

Technology on campus. 400 workstations in library, computer center. Commuter students can connect to campus network. Online library, helpline, repair service, wireless network available.

Student life. Freshman orientation: Mandatory. Preregistration for classes offered. Various four-hour sessions over one-two days prior to start of each term. **Activities:** Student government, student newspaper, student council, Institute of Management Accountants, PC users group, campus ambassador society.

Athletics. NJCAA. **Intercollegiate:** Soccer M. **Team name:** Bobcats.

Student services. Adult student services, student employment services, financial aid counseling, placement for graduates. **Physically disabled:** Services for visually, speech, hearing impaired.

Contact. E-mail: mejohnson@bryantstratton.edu
Phone: (440) 510-1112 Fax: (440) 306-2015
Melanie Johnson, Director of Admissions, Bryant & Stratton College: Eastlake, 35350 Curtis Boulevard, Eastlake, OH 44095

Bryant & Stratton College: Parma
Parma, Ohio
www.bryantstratton.edu   CB code: 0577

- For-profit 4-year nursing and junior college
- Commuter campus in small city

◗ 281 degree-seeking undergraduates

◗ Application essay, interview required

General. Founded in 1854. Regionally accredited. On-line classes available. **Degrees:** 28 bachelor's, 90 associate awarded. **Location:** 10 miles from Cleveland. **Calendar:** Semester, extensive summer session. **Full-time faculty:** 23 total. **Part-time faculty:** 50 total. **Class size:** 78% < 20, 21% 20-39, less than 1% 40-49.

Basis for selection. Open admission, but selective for some programs. Nursing program requires either a high school transcript or a GED. Portfolio recommended. **Home schooled:** Transcript of courses and grades required. **Learning Disabled:** IEP plan required.

2015-2016 Annual costs. Tuition/fees: $17,190. Books/supplies: $1,600. Personal expenses: $3,111.

Financial aid. All financial aid based on need.

Application procedures. Admission: Closing date 9/22. $35 fee. Application must be submitted on paper. Admission notification on a rolling basis. **Financial aid:** Closing date 9/22. FAFSA required. Applicants notified on a rolling basis starting 6/1.

Academics. Special study options: Distance learning, internships. **Credit/placement by examination:** AP, CLEP, IB, institutional tests. 30 credit hours maximum toward associate degree, 30 toward bachelor's. Students must pass Proficiency Exams with a score of 90% or higher. **Support services:** Learning center, reduced course load, study skills assistance, tutoring.

Majors. Business: Business admin. **Protective services:** Law enforcement admin.

Most popular majors. Business/marketing 50%.

Technology on campus. 107 workstations in library, computer center. Commuter students can connect to campus network. Online library, helpline, wireless network available.

Student life. Freshman orientation: Mandatory. Preregistration for classes offered. Three hour program held week prior to start of classes.

Student services. Career counseling, student employment services, financial aid counseling, placement for graduates.

Contact. E-mail: atinman@bryantstratton.edu
Phone: (216) 265-3151 ext. 229 Fax: (216) 265-0325
Andrea Inman, Director of Admissions, Bryant & Stratton College:
Parma, 12955 Snow Road, Parma, OH 44130-1013

Capital University
Columbus, Ohio
www.capital.edu

CB member
CB code: 1099

◗ Private 4-year university affiliated with the Evangelical Lutheran Church in America

◗ Residential campus in very large city

◗ 2,654 degree-seeking undergraduates: 7% part-time, 58% women, 10% African American, 1% Asian American, 4% Hispanic/Latino, 5% Multiracial, non-Hispanic, 2% international

◗ 663 degree-seeking graduate students

◗ 72% of applicants admitted

◗ SAT or ACT (ACT writing optional) required

◗ 63% graduate within 6 years

General. Founded in 1830. Regionally accredited. **Degrees:** 560 bachelor's awarded; master's, professional offered. **ROTC:** Army, Air Force. **Location:** 5 miles from downtown. **Calendar:** Semester, limited summer session. **Full-time faculty:** 159 total; 77% have terminal degrees, 9% minority, 49% women. **Part-time faculty:** 263 total; 33% have terminal degrees, 16% minority, 56% women. **Class size:** 56% < 20, 41% 20-39, 1% 40-49, 2% 50-99.

Freshman class profile. 3,718 applied, 2,685 admitted, 671 enrolled.

Mid 50% test scores			
SAT critical reading:	480-610	Rank in top quarter:	47%
SAT math:	480-580	Rank in top tenth:	16%
SAT writing:	460-590	Return as sophomores:	76%
ACT composite:	22-28	Out-of-state:	13%
GPA 3.75 or higher:	36%	Live on campus:	88%
GPA 3.50-3.74:	21%	International:	1%
GPA 3.0-3.49:	26%	Fraternities:	3%
GPA 2.0-2.99:	17%	Sororities:	7%

Basis for selection. Academic achievement in college-preparatory curriculum most important. Recommendations, test scores, and extracurricular activities considered. Talent/ability very important for admission into the Conservatory of Music. Interview recommended for all; audition required for music program; portfolio recommended for art, art therapy programs. **Home schooled:** Statement describing home school structure and mission, transcript of courses and grades, letter of recommendation (nonparent) required.

High school preparation. College-preparatory program recommended. 16 units recommended. Recommended units include English 4, mathematics 3, social studies 3, science 3 (laboratory 2), foreign language 2 and visual/performing arts 1. Chemistry and algebra II for nursing applicants. One fine arts recommended.

2015-2016 Annual costs. Tuition/fees: $32,830. Room/board: $9,422. Books/supplies: $1,550. Personal expenses: $1,508.

2014-2015 Financial aid. Need-based: 665 full-time freshmen applied for aid; 601 deemed to have need; 601 received aid. Average need met was 84%. Average scholarship/grant was $23,151; average loan $3,821. 85% of total undergraduate aid awarded as scholarships/grants, 15% as loans/jobs. **Non-need-based:** Awarded to 2,264 full-time undergraduates, including 698 freshmen. Scholarships awarded for academics, alumni affiliation, art, leadership, minority status, music/drama, religious affiliation, state residency.

Application procedures. Admission: Priority date 12/1; deadline 5/1 (postmark date). $25 fee, may be waived for applicants with need, free for online applicants. Admission notification on a rolling basis. Must reply by May 1 or within 2 week(s) if notified thereafter. **Financial aid:** Priority date 3/1; no closing date. FAFSA required. Applicants notified on a rolling basis starting 3/15; must reply by 5/1.

Academics. Teacher certification for learning disabilities and reading. Paralegal certification available from law school. **Special study options:** Accelerated study, combined bachelor's/graduate degree, cooperative education, cross-registration, double major, dual enrollment of high school students, ESL, exchange student, external degree, honors, independent study, internships, liberal arts/career combination, student-designed major, study abroad, teacher certification program, Washington semester. Dual degree engineering program with Washington University, St. Louis, and Case Western Reserve; 3-2 occupational therapy program with Washington University, St. Louis. **Credit/placement by examination:** AP, CLEP, IB, SAT, ACT, institutional tests. 27 credit hours maximum toward bachelor's degree. **Support services:** Learning center, reduced course load, remedial instruction, study skills assistance, tutoring, writing center.

Majors. Biology: General, biochemistry. **Business:** Accounting, business admin, managerial economics, marketing. **Communications:** Communications/speech/rhetoric, organizational, public relations, radio/TV. **Computer sciences:** Computer science. **Conservation:** Environmental science. **Education:** Early childhood, middle, music, physical, special ed. **Engineering:** Computer. **English:** Creative writing, English lit, technical writing. **Foreign languages:** French, Spanish. **Health services:** Art therapy, athletic training, nursing (RN). **History:** General. **Human services:** General, social work. **Math:** General. **Parks/recreation:** Exercise sciences, health/fitness. **Philosophy/religion:** Philosophy, religion. **Physical sciences:** Chemistry. **Psychology:** General. **Social sciences:** Criminology, economics, political science, sociology. **Visual/performing arts:** Art, dramatic, jazz, music, music management, music performance, music theory/composition, piano/keyboard, voice/opera.

Most popular majors. Business/marketing 12%, education 11%, health sciences 18%, psychology 6%, public administration/social services 7%, social sciences 9%, visual/performing arts 10%.

Technology on campus. 415 workstations in dormitories, library, computer center, student center. Dormitories wired for high-speed internet access and linked to campus network. Commuter students can connect to campus network. Online course registration, online library, helpline, wireless network available.

Student life. Freshman orientation: Mandatory. Preregistration for classes offered. One-day program in summer, five-day program before start of classes. **Housing:** Guaranteed on-campus for freshmen. Coed dorms, special housing for disabled, apartments, gender-neutral housing, themed housing, wellness housing available. $100 fully refundable deposit, deadline 5/1. Gender inclusive. **Activities:** Bands, campus ministries, choral groups, dance, drama, film society, international student organizations, literary magazine, music ensembles, musical theater, radio station, student government, student newspaper, symphony orchestra, TV station, black student union, Young Republicans, Campus Democrats, Circle K, Ebony Brotherhood Association, international student association, Capateers (volunteers), Habitat for Humanity, university programming.

Athletics. NCAA. **Intercollegiate:** Baseball M, basketball, cross-country, football (tackle) M, golf, lacrosse, soccer, softball W, tennis, track and field, volleyball W. **Intramural:** Basketball, football (non-tackle), racquetball, ultimate frisbee, volleyball. **Team name:** Crusaders.

Student services. Chaplain/spiritual director, career counseling, student employment services, financial aid counseling, health services, minority student services, personal counseling, placement for graduates, veterans' counselor.

Contact. E-mail: admission@capital.edu
Phone: (614) 236-6101 Toll-free number: (866) 544-6175
Fax: (614) 236-6926
Amanda Sohl, Director of Admission, Capital University, 1 College and Main, Columbus, OH 43209-2394

Case Western Reserve University

Cleveland, Ohio — CB member
www.case.edu — CB code: 1105

- Private 4-year university
- Residential campus in very large city
- 5,039 degree-seeking undergraduates: 1% part-time, 45% women, 5% African American, 20% Asian American, 6% Hispanic/Latino, 4% Multiracial, non-Hispanic, 11% international
- 6,014 degree-seeking graduate students
- 36% of applicants admitted
- SAT or ACT with writing, application essay required
- 81% graduate within 6 years; 41% enter graduate study

General. Founded in 1826. Regionally accredited. **Degrees:** 902 bachelor's awarded; master's, professional, doctoral offered. **ROTC:** Army, Air Force. **Location:** 4 miles from downtown. **Calendar:** Semester, extensive summer session. **Full-time faculty:** 759 total; 91% have terminal degrees, 17% minority, 43% women. **Part-time faculty:** 230 total; 56% have terminal degrees, 10% minority, 53% women. **Class size:** 59% < 20, 22% 20-39, 6% 40-49, 9% 50-99, 4% >100. **Special facilities:** Biology field station, observatory, interdisciplinary research centers, natural history museum, historical society, and botanical garden.,.

Freshman class profile. 22,807 applied, 8,271 admitted, 1,259 enrolled.

Mid 50% test scores			
SAT critical reading:	620-720	Return as sophomores:	94%
SAT math:	680-770	Out-of-state:	73%
SAT writing:	620-720	Live on campus:	99%
ACT composite:	30-33	International:	15%
Rank in top quarter:	91%	Fraternities:	47%
Rank in top tenth:	71%	Sororities:	41%

Basis for selection. School achievement record and test scores most important. School and community activities, essays, recommendations, and interview also considered. Special consideration to applicants from culturally, educationally, or economically disadvantaged backgrounds. IELTS, AP International English test, or TOEFL required for all international students. Interview recommended for all; audition required for music, music education programs; portfolio required for art education program. **Home schooled:** Transcript of courses and grades, interview required. At least 3 SAT Subject Tests highly recommended. Students encouraged to submit at least 2 letters from outside instructors or employers.

High school preparation. College-preparatory program required. 16 units required. Required and recommended units include English 4, mathematics 3-4, social studies 3-4, science 3 (laboratory 2-3) and foreign language 2-3. 3 laboratory science recommended. 4 math, 1 chemistry and physics recommended for engineering. 3 laboratory science (1 chemistry) recommended for science, math, and premedical.

2015-2016 Annual costs. Tuition/fees: $44,550. Room/board: $13,850.

2015-2016 Financial aid. Need-based: 857 full-time freshmen applied for aid; 665 deemed to have need; 665 received aid. Average need met was 87%. Average scholarship/grant was $29,932; average loan $4,357. 77% of total undergraduate aid awarded as scholarships/grants, 23% as loans/jobs. **Non-need-based:** Awarded to 1,915 full-time undergraduates, including 531 freshmen. Scholarships awarded for academics, alumni affiliation, art, leadership, music/drama.

Application procedures. Admission: Closing date 1/15 (postmark date). No application fee. Application must be submitted online. Admission notification by 3/20. Must reply by 5/1. **Financial aid:** Priority date 2/15, closing date 5/15. FAFSA, institutional form, CSS PROFILE required. Applicants notified on a rolling basis starting 3/15; must reply by 5/1 or within 2 week(s) of notification.

Academics. Preprofessional Scholars Program gives conditional acceptances to graduate schools of medicine, dentistry, law, and social work. Most programs allow students to pursue combined bachelor's/master's degrees. **Special study options:** Accelerated study, combined bachelor's/graduate degree, cooperative education, cross-registration, double major, dual enrollment of high school students, ESL, exchange student, honors, independent study, internships, liberal arts/career combination, student-designed major, study abroad, teacher certification program, Washington semester. Exchange program with Fisk University; global programs in engineering with Waseda University (Japan), Tianjin University (China), Universität Stuttgart (Germany); and 3-2 binary program in engineering. **Credit/placement by examination:** AP, CLEP, IB, institutional tests. **Support services:** Learning center, pre-admission summer program, reduced course load, study skills assistance, tutoring, writing center.

Majors. Area/ethnic studies: American, Asian, French, German, Japanese, women's. **Biology:** General, biochemistry, computational, evolutionary. **Business:** Accounting, business admin, finance, marketing. **Computer sciences:** General, computer science. **Conservation:** Environmental studies. **Education:** Art, music. **Engineering:** General, aerospace, applied physics, biomedical, chemical, civil, computer, electrical, materials, mechanical, polymer, systems. **English:** English lit. **Foreign languages:** Classics, comparative lit, French, German, Spanish. **Health services:** Communication disorders, dietetics, nursing (RN). **History:** General, science/technology. **Math:** General, applied, statistics. **Philosophy/religion:** Philosophy, religion. **Physical sciences:** Astronomy, chemistry, geology, materials science, physics. **Psychology:** General. **Social sciences:** Anthropology, economics, international relations, political science, sociology. **Visual/performing arts:** Art history/conservation, dance, dramatic, music. **Work/family studies:** Human nutrition.

Most popular majors. Biology 13%, business/marketing 8%, engineering/engineering technologies 27%, health sciences 9%, psychology 7%, social sciences 10%.

Technology on campus. 307 workstations in dormitories, library, computer center, student center. Dormitories wired for high-speed internet access and linked to campus network. Commuter students can connect to campus network. Online course registration, online library, helpline, repair service, student web hosting, wireless network available.

Student life. Freshman orientation: Mandatory, $495 fee. Preregistration for classes offered. One-week session held in August. **Policies:** Only approved small caged, nonpoisonous animals or fish permitted in residence halls. Dogs, cats, and ferrets strictly prohibited. **Housing:** Guaranteed on-campus for freshmen. Coed dorms, apartments, fraternity/sorority housing, wellness housing available. **Activities:** Bands, campus ministries, choral groups, dance, drama, film society, international student organizations, literary magazine, music ensembles, Model UN, musical theater, radio station, student government, student newspaper, symphony orchestra, Christians on Campus, Hillel Foundation, Cru, Muslim Student Association, African-American Society, Democrats, College Republicans, Habitat for Humanity, International Student Fellowship, Global Medical Initiative.

Athletics. NCAA. **Intercollegiate:** Baseball M, basketball, cross-country, diving, football (tackle) M, soccer, softball W, swimming, tennis, track and field, volleyball W, wrestling M. **Intramural:** Badminton, basketball, bowling, cross-country, football (non-tackle), golf, racquetball, soccer, softball, swimming, table tennis, tennis, track and field, ultimate frisbee, volleyball. **Team name:** Spartans.

Student services. Adult student services, alcohol/substance abuse counseling, chaplain/spiritual director, career counseling, student employment services, financial aid counseling, health services, legal services, minority student services, personal counseling, placement for graduates, veterans' counselor, women's services. **Physically disabled:** Services for visually, speech, hearing impaired.

Contact. E-mail: admission@case.edu
Phone: (216) 368-4450 Fax: (216) 368-5111
Robert McCullough, Director, Case Western Reserve University, Wolstein Hall, Cleveland, OH 44106-7055

Cedarville University

Cedarville, Ohio
www.cedarville.edu — CB code: 1151

- Private 4-year university and liberal arts college affiliated with the Baptist faith
- Residential campus in small town
- 3,061 degree-seeking undergraduates: 2% part-time, 52% women, 2% African American, 2% Asian American, 3% Hispanic/Latino, 3% Multiracial, non-Hispanic, 2% international

- 295 degree-seeking graduate students
- 74% of applicants admitted
- SAT or ACT (ACT writing optional), application essay required
- 72% graduate within 6 years

General. Founded in 1887. Regionally accredited. **Degrees:** 701 bachelor's awarded; master's, professional offered. **ROTC:** Army, Air Force. **Location:** 12 miles from Springfield, 20 miles from Dayton. **Calendar:** Semester, limited summer session. **Full-time faculty:** 193 total; 66% have terminal degrees, 8% minority, 36% women. **Part-time faculty:** 187 total; 32% have terminal degrees, 6% minority, 51% women. **Class size:** 63% < 20, 25% 20-39, 6% 40-49, 4% 50-99, 1% >100.

Freshman class profile. 3,159 applied, 2,344 admitted, 819 enrolled.

Mid 50% test scores			
SAT critical reading:	540-650	GPA 2.0-2.99:	5%
SAT math:	520-640	Rank in top quarter:	61%
SAT writing:	520-630	Rank in top tenth:	30%
ACT composite:	23-28	Return as sophomores:	86%
GPA 3.75 or higher:	52%	Out-of-state:	63%
GPA 3.50-3.74:	20%	Live on campus:	97%
GPA 3.0-3.49:	22%	International:	1%

Basis for selection. Clear testimony of personal faith in Jesus Christ, evidence of consistent Christian lifestyle, above-average academic performance (academic records, class rank, test scores), personal references considered. Applications reviewed on a rolling basis. Audition required for music majors; interview recommended for academically marginal students. Interview required for pre-pharmacy students. **Home schooled:** Statement describing home school structure and mission required. Applicants must provide an explanation of their course of study and their educator's teaching methods along with answers to the following: Who is ultimately responsible for setting up curriculum and selecting materials? What type of curriculum and materials did the student's educator(s) use? Who was responsible for providing instruction? Did the student have tutors in some areas and not in others, etc? Who recorded grades and how? What type of independent, standardized testing was used to measure the student's progress against a larger population? (Include copies of this information with the student's transcript.). **Learning Disabled:** Students encouraged to contact Coordinator of Disabilities Services.

High school preparation. College-preparatory program recommended. Required and recommended units include English 4, mathematics 4, social studies 2, history 2, science 3-4 (laboratory 2) and foreign language 3. Additional math and science recommended for nursing, science, engineering, and math applicants.

2015-2016 Annual costs. Tuition/fees: $27,206. Room/board: $6,542. Books/supplies: $1,200. Personal expenses: $1,700.

2014-2015 Financial aid. Need-based: 694 full-time freshmen applied for aid; 570 deemed to have need; 568 received aid. Average need met was 28%. Average scholarship/grant was $4,199; average loan $4,560. 61% of total undergraduate aid awarded as scholarships/grants, 39% as loans/jobs. **Non-need-based:** Awarded to 2,796 full-time undergraduates, including 790 freshmen. Scholarships awarded for academics, alumni affiliation, athletics, leadership, minority status, music/drama, ROTC, state residency.

Application procedures. Admission: Priority date 11/1; deadline 8/1. $30 fee, may be waived for applicants with need. Admission notification on a rolling basis beginning on or about 9/1. Must reply by May 1 or within 2 week(s) if notified thereafter. **Financial aid:** Priority date 3/1; no closing date. FAFSA required. Applicants notified on a rolling basis starting 3/1; must reply within 3 week(s) of notification.

Academics. Special study options: Combined bachelor's/graduate degree, cooperative education, cross-registration, distance learning, double major, dual enrollment of high school students, honors, independent study, internships, student-designed major, study abroad, teacher certification program, Washington semester. Academic enrichment. **Credit/placement by examination:** AP, CLEP, IB, SAT, ACT, institutional tests. 40 credit hours maximum toward bachelor's degree. **Support services:** Learning center, reduced course load, remedial instruction, study skills assistance, tutoring, writing center.

Honors college/program. 29 ACT/1290 SAT, 3.0 unweighted GPA in college-preparatory curriculum required.

Majors. Biology: General, cellular/molecular. **Business:** Accounting, business admin, finance, international, management information systems, marketing. **Communications:** Communications/speech/rhetoric, journalism, media studies, radio/TV. **Communications technology:** General. **Computer sciences:** Computer science, information technology. **Conservation:** Environmental science. **Education:** Biology, chemistry, early childhood, English, mathematics, middle, music, physical, physics, science, social studies, Spanish, special ed. **Engineering:** Computer, electrical, mechanical. **English:**

English lit, technical writing. **Foreign languages:** Linguistics, Spanish. **Health services:** Athletic training, clinical lab science, nursing (RN), pharmaceutical sciences, predental, premedicine, preveterinary. **History:** General. **Human services:** General, social work. **Math:** General. **Parks/recreation:** Exercise sciences, health/fitness, sports admin. **Philosophy/religion:** Philosophy. **Physical sciences:** Chemistry, geology, physics. **Protective services:** Forensics, law enforcement admin. **Psychology:** General. **Social sciences:** General, economics, political science. **Theology:** Missionary, religious ed, sacred music, theology, youth ministry. **Visual/performing arts:** Design, dramatic, graphic design, industrial design, music, music pedagogy, music performance, music theory/composition, studio arts.

Most popular majors. Business/marketing 8%, communications/journalism 7%, engineering/engineering technologies 11%, health sciences 20%, security/protective services 10%, social sciences 10%, theological studies 7%, visual/performing arts 7%.

Technology on campus. 3,000 workstations in dormitories, library, student center. Dormitories wired for high-speed internet access and linked to campus network. Commuter students can connect to campus network. Online course registration, online library, helpline, repair service, wireless network available.

Student life. Freshman orientation: Mandatory, $105 fee. Preregistration for classes offered. **Policies:** Alcohol, tobacco, and drugs prohibited. Religious observance required. **Housing:** Guaranteed on-campus for all undergraduates. Single-sex dorms, apartments available. $250 nonrefundable deposit, deadline 5/1. **Activities:** Bands, campus ministries, choral groups, dance, drama, film society, international student organizations, music ensembles, Model UN, musical theater, radio station, student government, student newspaper, symphony orchestra, emergency medical squad, Earth stewardship organization, Fellowship for World Missions, students for social justice, Society for Technical Communicators, Society of Automotive Engineers International, College Democrats, College Republicans, student films organization, branch of National Social Work Honor Society.

Athletics. NCAA. **Intercollegiate:** Baseball M, basketball, cheerleading, cross-country, golf M, soccer, softball W, tennis, track and field, volleyball W. **Intramural:** Badminton, basketball, bowling, cross-country, football (tackle) M, golf, racquetball, soccer, softball, table tennis, tennis, volleyball. **Team name:** Yellow Jackets.

Student services. Chaplain/spiritual director, career counseling, student employment services, financial aid counseling, health services, personal counseling, placement for graduates, veterans' counselor. **Physically disabled:** Services for visually, speech, hearing impaired.

Contact. E-mail: admissions@cedarville.edu
Phone: (937) 766-7700 Toll-free number: (800) 233-2784
Fax: (937) 766-7575
Roscoe Smth, Assoc VP for University Admissions, Cedarville University, 251 North Main Street, Cedarville, OH 45314-0601

Central State University
Wilberforce, Ohio   **CB member**
www.centralstate.edu   **CB code: 1107**

- Public 4-year university and liberal arts college
- Residential campus in rural community
- 1,775 degree-seeking undergraduates: 7% part-time, 55% women, 95% African American, 1% Hispanic/Latino, 1% Multi-racial, non-Hispanic, 1% international
- 12 degree-seeking graduate students
- 39% of applicants admitted
- SAT or ACT (ACT writing optional) required

General. Founded in 1887. Regionally accredited. Ohio's only public historically black university. **Degrees:** 287 bachelor's awarded; master's offered. **ROTC:** Army, Air Force. **Location:** 18 miles from Dayton. **Calendar:** Semester, limited summer session. **Full-time faculty:** 94 total; 76% have terminal degrees, 78% minority, 43% women. **Part-time faculty:** 106 total; 15% have terminal degrees, 79% minority, 48% women. **Class size:** 59% < 20, 39% 20-39, 2% 40-49, less than 1% 50-99. **Special facilities:** Afro-American museum, hydraulics laboratory, computer numerically controlled equipment for machining and robotic welding, business incubator.

Freshman class profile. 6,502 applied, 2,568 admitted, 519 enrolled.

Mid 50% test scores			
SAT critical reading:	330-410	GPA 3.0-3.49:	13%
SAT math:	340-420	GPA 2.0-2.99:	70%
ACT composite:	14-18	End year in good standing:	53%
GPA 3.75 or higher:	2%	Return as sophomores:	54%
GPA 3.50-3.74:	3%	Out-of-state:	56%
		Live on campus:	95%

Basis for selection. Test scores and GPA very important. Interview recommended. Personal essay required for admissions appeal process. **Home schooled:** Transcript of courses and grades, state high school equivalency certificate, interview, letter of recommendation (nonparent) required. Ohio students need ONGP test results or OGT.

High school preparation. 16 units recommended. Recommended units include English 4, mathematics 3, social studies 3, science 3 and foreign language 2. 1 art recommended.

2015-2016 Annual costs. Tuition/fees: $6,246; $13,928 out-of-state. Room/board: $9,318. Books/supplies: $1,200. Personal expenses: $1,500.

Financial aid. Non-need-based: Scholarships awarded for academics, alumni affiliation, art, athletics, leadership, music/drama, religious affiliation, ROTC.

Application procedures. Admission: No deadline. $20 fee, may be waived for applicants with need. Admission notification on a rolling basis. **Financial aid:** Priority date 2/15; no closing date. FAFSA, institutional form required. Applicants notified by 4/15; must reply by 5/1.

Academics. Special study options: Cooperative education, cross-registration, double major, honors, independent study, internships, study abroad, teacher certification program. **Credit/placement by examination:** AP, CLEP, SAT, ACT, institutional tests. 30 credit hours maximum toward bachelor's degree. **Support services:** Learning center, pre-admission summer program, reduced course load, remedial instruction, study skills assistance, tutoring, writing center.

Majors. Biology: General. **Business:** General, accounting. **Communications:** Broadcast journalism, journalism. **Computer sciences:** Computer science. **Education:** Art, early childhood, middle, multi-level teacher, music, secondary, special ed. **Engineering:** Environmental, manufacturing, water resource. **English:** English lit. **History:** General. **Human services:** Social work. **Math:** General. **Parks/recreation:** General. **Physical sciences:** Chemistry, geology. **Protective services:** Criminal justice. **Psychology:** General. **Social sciences:** Economics, geography, political science, sociology. **Visual/performing arts:** Art, jazz, music performance.

Most popular majors. Business/marketing 27%, communications/journalism 10%, education 13%, psychology 14%, security/protective services 11%.

Technology on campus. 400 workstations in library, computer center, student center. Dormitories wired for high-speed internet access and linked to campus network. Online course registration, online library, helpline, repair service, wireless network available.

Student life. Freshman orientation: Mandatory, $125 fee. Preregistration for classes offered. **Housing:** Guaranteed on-campus for freshmen. Coed dorms, single-sex dorms available. $195 fully refundable deposit, deadline 8/1. **Activities:** Bands, campus ministries, choral groups, dance, drama, music ensembles, radio station, student government, student newspaper, TV station.

Athletics. NCAA. **Intercollegiate:** Basketball, cross-country, football (tackle) M, golf W, tennis, track and field, volleyball. **Intramural:** Basketball, cross-country, football (non-tackle) M, racquetball, tennis. **Team name:** Marauders.

Student services. Alcohol/substance abuse counseling, chaplain/spiritual director, career counseling, services for economically disadvantaged, student employment services, financial aid counseling, health services, on-campus daycare, personal counseling, placement for graduates.

Contact. E-mail: admissions@centralstate.edu
Phone: (937) 376-6348 Toll-free number: (800) 388-2781
Fax: (937) 376-6648
Stephen Williams, Director of Admissions, Central State University, PO Box 1004, Wilberforce, OH 45384-1004

Chamberlain College of Nursing: Cleveland
Cleveland, Ohio
www.chamberlain.edu   CB code: 7251

- For-profit 4-year nursing college
- Large city
- 175 degree-seeking undergraduates
- SAT or ACT required

General. Calendar: Semester.

Basis for selection. Admission decisions based on interview, proof of high school diploma/GED, and satisfactory test scores.

2015-2016 Annual costs. Tuition/fees: $18,160.

Application procedures. Admission: No deadline. $95 fee. Admission notification on a rolling basis.

Academics. Special study options: Accelerated study, distance learning. **Credit/placement by examination:** AP, CLEP.

Majors. Health services: Nursing (RN).

Contact. Chamberlain College of Nursing: Cleveland, 6700 Euclid Avenue, Suite 201, Cleveland, OH 44103

Chamberlain College of Nursing: Columbus
Columbus, Ohio
www.chamberlain.edu

- For-profit 4-year nursing college
- Large city
- 555 degree-seeking undergraduates
- SAT or ACT required

General. Regionally accredited. **Degrees:** 111 bachelor's, 67 associate awarded. **Calendar:** Semester. **Full-time faculty:** 18 total. **Part-time faculty:** 68 total.

Basis for selection. Test scores, GPA, class rank very important.

2015-2016 Annual costs. Tuition/fees: $18,160. Books/supplies: $1,400. Personal expenses: $3,718. **Additional information:** Tuition quoted is for Nursing courses at $590 per credit. Tuition and fees vary by program.

Application procedures. Admission: No deadline. $95 fee. Admission notification on a rolling basis.

Academics. Special study options: Accelerated study, distance learning. **Credit/placement by examination:** AP, CLEP.

Majors. Health services: Nursing (RN).

Contact. Chamberlain College of Nursing: Columbus, 1350 Alum Creek Drive, Columbus, OH 43209

Cincinnati Christian University
Cincinnati, Ohio
www.ccuniversity.edu   CB code: 1091

- Private 4-year university affiliated with the Christian Church
- Residential campus in very large city
- 569 degree-seeking undergraduates: 13% part-time, 46% women, 16% African American, 1% Asian American, 2% Hispanic/Latino, 2% Multiracial, non-Hispanic, 1% international
- 199 degree-seeking graduate students
- 95% of applicants admitted
- SAT or ACT (ACT writing optional), application essay required
- 31% graduate within 6 years

General. Founded in 1924. Regionally accredited; also accredited by ABHE. Member of Greater Cincinnati Consortium of Colleges and Universities. **Degrees:** 124 bachelor's, 4 associate awarded; master's offered. **Location:** 10 miles from downtown. **Calendar:** Semester, limited summer session. **Full-time faculty:** 27 total; 82% have terminal degrees. **Part-time faculty:** 57 total; 28% have terminal degrees. **Class size:** 80% < 20, 13% 20-39, 3% 40-49, 4% 50-99, less than 1% >100.

Freshman class profile. 227 applied, 216 admitted, 105 enrolled.

Mid 50% test scores		GPA 3.0-3.49:	30%
SAT critical reading:	440-620	GPA 2.0-2.99:	38%
SAT math:	450-570	Rank in top quarter:	17%
SAT writing:	470-540	Rank in top tenth:	8%
ACT composite:	18-24	Return as sophomores:	74%
GPA 3.75 or higher:	18%	Out-of-state:	45%
GPA 3.50-3.74:	12%	Live on campus:	82%

Basis for selection. High school academic record and standardized test scores important. 2.5 GPA, 17 ACT/1215 SAT required for unconditional admission. Applicants age 25 or older can substitute English proficiency test and essay for SAT/ACT requirement. Audition required for music programs.

2015-2016 Annual costs. Tuition/fees: $15,966. Room/board: $7,860. Books/supplies: $900. Personal expenses: $2,400.

2014-2015 Financial aid. Need-based: 93 full-time freshmen applied for aid; 82 deemed to have need; 82 received aid. Average need met was 60%. Average scholarship/grant was $9,295; average loan $2,886. 48% of total undergraduate aid awarded as scholarships/grants, 52% as loans/jobs. **Non-need-based:** Awarded to 134 full-time undergraduates, including 27 freshmen. Scholarships awarded for academics, athletics, leadership, minority status, music/drama, religious affiliation, state residency.

Application procedures. Admission: Priority date 3/1; deadline 7/1 (postmark date). $40 fee, may be waived for applicants with need. Admission notification on a rolling basis. **Financial aid:** Priority date 3/1; no closing date. FAFSA required. Applicants notified on a rolling basis starting 4/1.

Academics. Special study options: Accelerated study, cooperative education, cross-registration, distance learning, double major, dual enrollment of high school students, honors, independent study, internships, teacher certification program. Adult degree completion program. **Credit/placement by examination:** AP, CLEP, IB. 15 credit hours maximum toward associate degree, 30 toward bachelor's. **Support services:** Learning center, reduced course load, remedial instruction, study skills assistance, tutoring, writing center.

Majors. Computer sciences: Data processing, information technology, LAN/WAN management, programming. **Education:** Early childhood, elementary, middle, secondary, special ed. **Philosophy/religion:** Christian. **Psychology:** General. **Theology:** Bible, missionary, religious ed, sacred music.

Most popular majors. Business/marketing 17%, education 8%, psychology 9%, theological studies 66%.

Technology on campus. 57 workstations in dormitories, library, computer center, student center. Dormitories wired for high-speed internet access and linked to campus network. Online library, helpline, repair service, wireless network available.

Student life. Freshman orientation: Mandatory. Preregistration for classes offered. **Policies:** Religious observance required. **Housing:** Guaranteed on-campus for all undergraduates. Single-sex dorms, apartments available. $35 nonrefundable deposit, deadline 7/1. **Activities:** Concert band, campus ministries, choral groups, drama, international student organizations, literary magazine, music ensembles, musical theater, student government, student newspaper.

Athletics. NCCAA. **Intercollegiate:** Baseball M, basketball, soccer, volleyball W. **Intramural:** Basketball, cheerleading, football (tackle) M, soccer, track and field, volleyball. **Team name:** Eagles.

Student services. Career counseling, student employment services, financial aid counseling, health services, personal counseling. **Physically disabled:** Services for hearing impaired.

Contact. E-mail: cbcadmission@ccuniversity.edu
Phone: (513) 244-8141 Toll-free number: (800) 949-4228
Fax: (513) 244-8140
Carrie Bouldin, Admissions Director, Cincinnati Christian University, 2700 Glenway Avenue, Cincinnati, OH 45204-3200

Cleveland Institute of Art

Cleveland, Ohio	CB member
www.cia.edu	CB code: 1152

▶ Private 4-year visual arts college
▶ Commuter campus in large city
▶ 600 degree-seeking undergraduates: 1% part-time, 57% women, 8% African American, 4% Asian American, 5% Hispanic/Latino, 4% Multiracial, non-Hispanic, 10% international
▶ 65% of applicants admitted
▶ SAT or ACT (ACT writing optional), application essay required
▶ 69% graduate within 6 years

General. Founded in 1882. Regionally accredited. **Degrees:** 93 bachelor's awarded. **ROTC:** Army, Naval, Air Force. **Location:** 4 miles from downtown. **Calendar:** Semester, limited summer session. **Full-time faculty:** 46 total; 63% have terminal degrees, 9% minority, 33% women. **Part-time faculty:** 58 total; 36% have terminal degrees, 5% minority, 40% women. **Class size:** 82% < 20, 18% 20-39. **Special facilities:** Individual studio spaces, exhibition spaces, ceramics studio, wood shop, green screen room, metal shop, glass shop, cinematheque, rapid 3-D prototype machines, blau kiln, lunchbox capture system.

Freshman class profile. 738 applied, 479 admitted, 168 enrolled.

Mid 50% test scores			
SAT critical reading:	480-620	Rank in top quarter:	36%
SAT math:	480-580	Rank in top tenth:	17%
SAT writing:	450-600	End year in good standing:	83%
ACT composite:	20-27	Return as sophomores:	83%
GPA 3.75 or higher:	25%	Out-of-state:	35%
GPA 3.50-3.74:	16%	Live on campus:	66%
GPA 3.0-3.49:	31%	International:	8%
GPA 2.0-2.99:	25%		

Basis for selection. Portfolio of 12 to 20 pieces, high school transcripts, statement of purpose, test scores, and 1 letter of recommendation required. Interview strongly recommended. **Home schooled:** Statement describing home school structure and mission, transcript of courses and grades required.

High school preparation. 20 units recommended. Recommended units include English 4, mathematics 3, social studies 3, science 3 and academic electives 6. 2 years of art recommended.

2015-2016 Annual costs. Tuition/fees: $38,487. Room/board: $11,454. Books/supplies: $2,170. Personal expenses: $2,010.

2014-2015 Financial aid. Need-based: 133 full-time freshmen applied for aid; 128 deemed to have need; 128 received aid. Average need met was 57%. Average scholarship/grant was $21,357; average loan $3,958. 69% of total undergraduate aid awarded as scholarships/grants, 31% as loans/jobs. **Non-need-based:** Awarded to 114 full-time undergraduates, including 30 freshmen. Scholarships awarded for academics, art.

Application procedures. Admission: Priority date 7/1; no deadline. $40 fee, may be waived for applicants with need. Admission notification on a rolling basis beginning on or about 10/1. Must reply by May 1 or within 2 week(s) if notified thereafter. **Financial aid:** Closing date 3/15. FAFSA required. Applicants notified on a rolling basis starting 3/16; must reply within 2 week(s) of notification.

Academics. Special study options: Cross-registration, double major, exchange student, independent study, internships, New York semester, study abroad. Study for up to 2 semesters at any Association of Independent Colleges of Art and Design. **Credit/placement by examination:** AP, CLEP, IB. 63 credit hours maximum toward bachelor's degree. **Support services:** Learning center, reduced course load, study skills assistance, tutoring, writing center. Professional Advisors and Programming throughout the year to support student success.

Majors. Health services: Medical illustrating. **Visual/performing arts:** Ceramics, drawing, game design, graphic design, illustration, industrial design, interior design, metal/jewelry, painting, photography, printmaking, sculpture.

Technology on campus. PC or laptop required. 313 workstations in dormitories, library, computer center, student center. Dormitories wired for high-speed internet access and linked to campus network. Commuter students can connect to campus network. Online course registration, online library, wireless network available.

Student life. Freshman orientation: Available, $175 fee. Preregistration for classes offered. The first part of the program is held online in early summer and the second part is held in-person immediately before the start of school. **Policies:** Freshmen not permitted cars on campus. **Housing:** Coed dorms, apartments, fraternity/sorority housing, wellness housing available. $150 nonrefundable deposit, deadline 5/1. **Activities:** Marching band, campus ministries, student government, Student Artist Association, Student Leadership Council, student activities program board, Student Independent Exhibition Committee, Gay/Lesbian Association, Artists for Christ, cinema club, community service club, video game club, gaffers club.

Athletics. Intramural: Badminton, basketball, bowling, football (non-tackle), golf, racquetball, soccer, softball, swimming, tennis, ultimate frisbee, volleyball, weight lifting.

Student services. Alcohol/substance abuse counseling, chaplain/spiritual director, career counseling, student employment services, financial aid counseling, health services, personal counseling, veterans' counselor, women's services. **Physically disabled:** Services for visually impaired.

Contact. E-mail: admissions@cia.edu
Phone: (216) 421-7418 Toll-free number: (800) 223-4700
Fax: (216) 754-3634
Eric Reitz, Associate Director of Enrollment & Financial Aid, Cleveland Institute of Art, 11610 Euclid Avenue, Cleveland, OH 44106-1710

Cleveland Institute of Music
Cleveland, Ohio
www.cim.edu   CB code: 1124

- Private 4-year music college
- Residential campus in very large city
- 247 degree-seeking undergraduates
- SAT or ACT (ACT writing optional), application essay required

General. Founded in 1920. Regionally accredited. **Degrees:** 47 bachelor's awarded; master's, doctoral offered. **Location:** 5 miles from downtown. **Calendar:** Semester, limited summer session. **Full-time faculty:** 39 total. **Part-time faculty:** 61 total. **Special facilities:** Electronic music studios, audio recording and distance learning facilities.

Freshman class profile.

Out-of-state: 75% Live on campus: 100%

Basis for selection. Audition most important. High school record, test scores, and letters of recommendation also reviewed. Required institutional examinations include ear training and theory. Additional testing includes sight singing and keyboard proficiency. Audition required. **Home schooled:** Transcript of courses and grades required.

High school preparation. 16 units recommended. Recommended units include English 4, mathematics 3, social studies 3, science 3 and foreign language 3.

2015-2016 Annual costs. Tuition/fees: $47,565. Room/board: $13,890. Books/supplies: $600. Personal expenses: $675.

2014-2015 Financial aid. **Need-based:** 49 full-time freshmen applied for aid; 40 deemed to have need; 40 received aid. Average need met was 78%. Average scholarship/grant was $26,321; average loan $3,653. 83% of total undergraduate aid awarded as scholarships/grants, 17% as loans/jobs. **Non-need-based:** Awarded to 126 full-time undergraduates, including 31 freshmen. Scholarships awarded for academics, music/drama.

Application procedures. **Admission:** Closing date 12/1 (receipt date). $110 fee. Application must be submitted online. Admission notification by 4/1. Must reply by 5/1. Deferred admission from fall to spring semesters is dependent upon space availability. **Financial aid:** Priority date 3/1, closing date 3/1. FAFSA, institutional form required. Applicants notified by 4/1; must reply by 5/1 or within 2 week(s) of notification.

Academics. **Special study options:** Cross-registration, double major, ESL, independent study, study abroad. **Credit/placement by examination:** AP, CLEP, IB, SAT, ACT, institutional tests. **Support services:** Learning center, reduced course load, remedial instruction, study skills assistance, tutoring, writing center.

Majors. **Communications technology:** Recording arts. **Visual/performing arts:** Music performance, music theory/composition, voice/opera.

Technology on campus. 36 workstations in dormitories, library, computer center, student center. Dormitories wired for high-speed internet access and linked to campus network. Commuter students can connect to campus network. Online course registration, online library, helpline, repair service, wireless network available.

Student life. **Freshman orientation:** Mandatory, $100 fee. Preregistration for classes offered. Held the week before the start of classes. **Policies:** Library privileges available through Case Western Reserve University. **Housing:** Guaranteed on-campus for freshmen. Coed dorms, wellness housing available. **Activities:** Jazz band, choral groups, dance, drama, music ensembles, opera, student government, symphony orchestra, student government association, most of student organizations are also accessible at Case Western Reserve University.

Student services. Alcohol/substance abuse counseling, career counseling, student employment services, financial aid counseling, health services, personal counseling, placement for graduates, veterans' counselor. **Physically disabled:** Services for visually impaired.

Contact. E-mail: admission@cim.edu
Phone: (216) 795-3107
Lynn Johnson, Director of Admission and Enrollment Management, Cleveland Institute of Music, 11021 East Boulevard, Cleveland, OH 44106

Cleveland State University
Cleveland, Ohio
www.csuohio.edu   CB member
                                                         CB code: 1221

- Public 4-year university
- Commuter campus in large city
- 11,669 degree-seeking undergraduates: 22% part-time, 53% women
- 4,294 degree-seeking graduate students
- 91% of applicants admitted
- SAT or ACT (ACT writing optional) required

General. Founded in 1964. Regionally accredited. **Degrees:** 2,317 bachelor's awarded; master's, professional, doctoral offered. **ROTC:** Army, Air Force. **Location:** Downtown. **Calendar:** Semester, extensive summer session. **Full-time faculty:** 524 total; 89% have terminal degrees, 14% minority, 43% women. **Part-time faculty:** 595 total; 8% minority, 50% women. **Class size:** 34% < 20, 46% 20-39, 11% 40-49, 8% 50-99, 1% >100. **Special facilities:** Poetry center, bioethics center, rooftop garden, Center for Healing Across Cultures, Center for Poverty Studies.

Freshman class profile. 7,544 applied, 6,876 admitted, 1,926 enrolled.

Mid 50% test scores			
SAT critical reading:	440-570	GPA 2.0-2.99:	33%
SAT math:	450-570	Rank in top quarter:	34%
ACT composite:	19-25	Rank in top tenth:	12%
GPA 3.75 or higher:	19%	Out-of-state:	7%
GPA 3.50-3.74:	15%	Live on campus:	29%
GPA 3.0-3.49:	33%	Fraternities:	1%
		Sororities:	1%

Basis for selection. 2.3 GPA, 16 ACT/750 SAT, and successful completion of 13 core academic units required. 2.5 GPA and 20 ACT/950 SAT required for education applicants; 2.7 GPA and 23 ACT/1070 SAT required for engineering applicants. SAT scores exclusive of Writing. Audition required for music majors.

High school preparation. College-preparatory program required. 13 units required. Required and recommended units include English 4, mathematics 3, social studies 3, science 3, foreign language 2 and visual/performing arts 1.

2016-2017 Annual costs. Tuition/fees (projected): $9,696; $12,938 out-of-state. Room/board: $12,500. Books/supplies: $800. Personal expenses: $3,160.

2015-2016 Financial aid. **Need-based:** 41% of total undergraduate aid awarded as scholarships/grants, 59% as loans/jobs. **Non-need-based:** Scholarships awarded for academics, alumni affiliation, art, athletics, leadership, music/drama, ROTC.

Application procedures. **Admission:** Priority date 7/15; deadline 8/15. $30 fee, may be waived for applicants with need. Admission notification on a rolling basis beginning on or about 9/1. **Financial aid:** Priority date 2/15; no closing date. FAFSA required. Applicants notified on a rolling basis starting 3/15; must reply within 4 week(s) of notification.

Academics. **Special study options:** Accelerated study, combined bachelor's/graduate degree, cooperative education, cross-registration, distance learning, double major, dual enrollment of high school students, ESL, exchange student, honors, independent study, internships, liberal arts/career combination, study abroad, teacher certification program, weekend college. **Credit/placement by examination:** AP, CLEP, IB, SAT, ACT, institutional tests. 90 credit hours maximum toward bachelor's degree. Unlimited AP exam credits accepted. **Support services:** Learning center, reduced course load, remedial instruction, study skills assistance, tutoring, writing center.

Majors. **Area/ethnic studies:** Women's. **Biology:** General. **Business:** Accounting, finance, international, labor relations, management information systems, managerial economics, marketing, statistics. **Communications:** Communications/speech/rhetoric, public relations. **Computer sciences:** General. **Conservation:** Environmental science, environmental studies. **Education:** General, early childhood, elementary, kindergarten/preschool, middle, physical, special ed. **Engineering:** Chemical, civil, computer, electrical, engineering science, mechanical, metallurgical. **English:** English lit. **Foreign languages:** French, linguistics, Spanish. **Health services:** Audiology/hearing, music therapy, nursing (RN), physician assistant. **History:** General. **Human services:** Social work. **Liberal arts:** Arts/sciences. **Math:** General. **Philosophy/religion:** Philosophy, religion. **Physical sciences:** Chemistry, physics. **Psychology:** General. **Social sciences:** General, anthropology, criminology, economics, international economic development, international relations, political science, sociology, urban studies. **Visual/performing arts:** Art, cinematography, dramatic, music.

Most popular majors. Business/marketing 17%, communications/journalism 6%, education 6%, engineering/engineering technologies 7%, health sciences 18%, psychology 11%, social sciences 11%.

Technology on campus. 711 workstations in dormitories, library, computer center, student center. Dormitories wired for high-speed internet access and linked to campus network. Commuter students can connect to campus network. Online course registration, online library, helpline, repair service, wireless network available.

Student life. Freshman orientation: Available, $25 fee. Preregistration for classes offered. All-day program during summer. **Housing:** Coed dorms, special housing for disabled available. $150 nonrefundable deposit, deadline 1/19. **Activities:** Bands, campus ministries, choral groups, dance, drama, international student organizations, literary magazine, music ensembles, Model UN, radio station, student government, student newspaper, symphony orchestra, Newman Center, Los Latinos Unidos, Hillel, University Christian Movement, Organization for Afro-American Unity, NAACP, environmental action group, College Democrats and Republicans.

Athletics. NCAA. **Intercollegiate:** Basketball, cross-country W, diving, fencing, golf, soccer, softball W, swimming, tennis, track and field W, volleyball W, wrestling M. **Intramural:** Badminton, basketball, bowling, cross-country, fencing, field hockey W, golf, handball, racquetball, rowing (crew), sailing, soccer, squash, swimming, table tennis, tennis, track and field, volleyball, water polo, wrestling M. **Team name:** Vikings.

Student services. Adult student services, alcohol/substance abuse counseling, career counseling, services for economically disadvantaged, student employment services, financial aid counseling, health services, legal services, minority student services, on-campus daycare, personal counseling, placement for graduates, veterans' counselor, women's services. **Physically disabled:** Services for visually, speech, hearing impaired.

Contact. E-mail: admissions@csuohio.edu
Phone: (216) 523-7416 Toll-free number: (888) 278-6446
Robert Spademan, Assistant Vice-President, Marketing & Admissions, Cleveland State University, 2121 Euclid Avenue, Cleveland, OH 44115-2214

College of Wooster
Wooster, Ohio
www.wooster.edu

CB member
CB code: 1134

- Private 4-year liberal arts college
- Residential campus in large town
- 2,026 degree-seeking undergraduates: 55% women, 8% African American, 5% Asian American, 5% Hispanic/Latino, 1% Native American, 9% international
- 55% of applicants admitted
- SAT or ACT (ACT writing recommended), application essay required
- 82% graduate within 6 years; 24% enter graduate study

General. Founded in 1866. Regionally accredited. **Degrees:** 449 bachelor's awarded. **Location:** 55 miles from Cleveland, 30 miles from Akron. **Calendar:** Semester, limited summer session. **Full-time faculty:** 165 total; 95% have terminal degrees, 17% minority, 48% women. **Part-time faculty:** 45 total; 62% have terminal degrees, 2% minority, 44% women. **Class size:** 70% < 20, 28% 20-39, 2% 40-49, less than 1% 50-99.

Freshman class profile. 5,748 applied, 3,178 admitted, 566 enrolled.

Mid 50% test scores		GPA 2.0-2.99:	9%
SAT critical reading:	540-670	Rank in top quarter:	70%
SAT math:	560-680	Rank in top tenth:	46%
SAT writing:	540-650	End year in good standing:	92%
ACT composite:	25-30	Return as sophomores:	88%
GPA 3.75 or higher:	30%	Out-of-state:	66%
GPA 3.50-3.74:	29%	Live on campus:	100%
GPA 3.0-3.49:	32%	International:	11%

Basis for selection. Course pattern and academic performance most important. Recommendations, extracurricular activities, class rank, test scores, interview important. Auditions required for music programs. **Home schooled:** Statement describing home school structure and mission, transcript of courses and grades, interview, letter of recommendation (nonparent) required. Submit detailed course descriptions and/or syllabi for academic work completed and 2 letters of recommendation, including 1 from a person who has provided academic instruction and at least 1 from someone outside student's home.

High school preparation. College-preparatory program required. 16 units required. Required units include English 4, mathematics 3, social studies 3, science 3 (laboratory 2), foreign language 2 and academic electives 1.

2015-2016 Annual costs. Tuition/fees: $44,950. Room/board: $10,650. Books/supplies: $1,000. Personal expenses: $600.

2015-2016 Financial aid. Need-based: 431 full-time freshmen applied for aid; 356 deemed to have need; 356 received aid. Average need met was 95%. Average scholarship/grant was $29,714; average loan $6,490. 81% of total undergraduate aid awarded as scholarships/grants, 19% as loans/jobs. **Non-need-based:** Awarded to 979 full-time undergraduates, including 285 freshmen. Scholarships awarded for academics, minority status, music/drama, religious affiliation.

Application procedures. Admission: Closing date 2/15 (postmark date). $45 fee, may be waived for applicants with need, free for online applicants. Admission notification by 4/1. Must reply by 5/1. **Financial aid:** Priority date 2/15; no closing date. FAFSA, institutional form required. Either CSS PROFILE or institution application for prospective students. Applicants notified on a rolling basis starting 3/1; must reply by 5/1 or within 2 week(s) of notification.

Academics. Special study options: Combined bachelor's/graduate degree, double major, exchange student, independent study, internships, New York semester, student-designed major, study abroad, teacher certification program, United Nations semester, urban semester, Washington semester. **Credit/placement by examination:** AP, CLEP, IB, institutional tests. **Support services:** Learning center, study skills assistance, tutoring, writing center.

Majors. Area/ethnic studies: African, African-American, East Asian, Latin American, Near/Middle Eastern, Russian/Slavic, South Asian, Western European, women's. **Biology:** General, Biochemistry/molecular biology, neuroscience. **Business:** Managerial economics. **Communications:** Communications/speech/rhetoric. **Computer sciences:** General. **Education:** Music. **English:** English lit. **Foreign languages:** General, classics, comparative lit, French, German, Russian, Spanish. **Health services:** Audiology/speech pathology, music therapy. **History:** General. **Math:** General. **Philosophy/religion:** Philosophy, religion. **Physical sciences:** Chemical physics, chemistry, geology, physics. **Psychology:** General. **Social sciences:** Anthropology, archaeology, economics, international relations, political science, sociology, urban studies. **Visual/performing arts:** Art history/conservation, dance, dramatic, music, music history, music performance, music theory/composition, studio arts.

Most popular majors. Biology 13%, history 8%, philosophy/religious studies 8%, physical sciences 7%, psychology 6%, social sciences 24%, visual/performing arts 7%.

Technology on campus. PC or laptop required. Dormitories wired for high-speed internet access and linked to campus network. Commuter students can connect to campus network. Online course registration, online library, helpline, student web hosting, wireless network available.

Student life. Freshman orientation: Mandatory. Preregistration for classes offered. Two-day program, held during summer prior to start of classes. **Housing:** Guaranteed on-campus for all undergraduates. Coed dorms, special housing for disabled, apartments, fraternity/sorority housing, themed housing available. Service related housing, cultural living experiences housing, housing for foreign language programs available. **Activities:** Bands, campus ministries, choral groups, dance, drama, film society, international student organizations, literary magazine, music ensembles, Model UN, musical theater, radio station, student government, student newspaper, symphony orchestra, variety of organizations available.

Athletics. NCAA. **Intercollegiate:** Baseball M, basketball, cross-country, diving, field hockey W, football (tackle) M, golf, lacrosse, soccer, softball W, swimming, tennis, track and field, volleyball W. **Intramural:** Basketball, bowling, football (non-tackle), soccer, softball, tennis, volleyball. **Team name:** Fighting Scots.

Student services. Alcohol/substance abuse counseling, chaplain/spiritual director, career counseling, student employment services, financial aid counseling, health services, minority student services, personal counseling, placement for graduates. **Physically disabled:** Services for visually impaired.

Contact. E-mail: admissions@wooster.edu
Phone: (330) 263-2322 Toll-free number: (800) 877-9905
Fax: (330) 263-2621
Jennifer Winge, Dean of Admissions, College of Wooster, Gault Admissions Center, Wooster, OH 44691-2363

Columbus College of Art and Design
Columbus, Ohio
www.ccad.edu

CB code: 1085

- Private 4-year visual arts college
- Commuter campus in very large city
- 1,081 degree-seeking undergraduates. 4% part-time, 64% women, 10% African American, 3% Asian American, 5% Hispanic/Latino, 5% Multiracial, non-Hispanic, 8% international

- 28 degree-seeking graduate students
- 38% of applicants admitted
- Application essay required
- 56% graduate within 6 years

General. Founded in 1879. Regionally accredited. **Degrees:** 299 bachelor's awarded; master's offered. **Location:** Downtown. **Calendar:** Semester, limited summer session. **Full-time faculty:** 69 total; 77% have terminal degrees, 9% minority, 44% women. **Part-time faculty:** 124 total; 37% have terminal degrees, 14% minority, 44% women. **Class size:** 78% < 20, 21% 20-39, less than 1% >100. **Special facilities:** Student exhibition hall.

Freshman class profile. 1,048 applied, 401 admitted, 241 enrolled.

Mid 50% test scores			
SAT critical reading:	500-520	GPA 3.0-3.49:	29%
SAT math:	540-550	GPA 2.0-2.99:	37%
SAT writing:	470-500	End year in good standing:	92%
ACT composite:	21-22	Return as sophomores:	76%
GPA 3.75 or higher:	12%	Out-of-state:	18%
GPA 3.50-3.74:	21%	Live on campus:	72%
		International:	5%

Basis for selection. Portfolio and 2.0 GPA important. SAT or ACT recommended. Test are required for home schooled first time freshmen. Portfolio required; interview recommended. **Home schooled:** Letter of recommendation (nonparent) required. ACT or SAT test scores. **Learning Disabled:** Student can self report & submit letter from doctor & IEP report to disabilities office for personalized learning plan.

High school preparation. Recommended units include English 4, mathematics 2, science 2 and foreign language 2. 4 units art recommended.

2015-2016 Annual costs. Tuition/fees: $30,840. Room/board: $8,390. Books/supplies: $4,000. Personal expenses: $200.

2015-2016 Financial aid. **Need-based:** Average need met was 59%. Average scholarship/grant was $18,416; average loan $5,999. 65% of total undergraduate aid awarded as scholarships/grants, 35% as loans/jobs. **Non-need-based:** Scholarships awarded for academics, art, ROTC, state residency.

Application procedures. **Admission:** Priority date 2/15; deadline 8/22 (receipt date). $50 fee, may be waived for applicants with need. Application must be submitted online. Admission notification on a rolling basis beginning on or about 12/15. Must reply by 8/15. **Financial aid:** Closing date 3/1. FAFSA required. Applicants notified on a rolling basis starting 3/15; must reply within 2 week(s) of notification.

Academics. **Special study options:** Cross-registration, distance learning, double major, ESL, exchange student, honors, independent study, internships, New York semester, study abroad. **Credit/placement by examination:** AP, CLEP, IB, SAT, ACT, institutional tests. **Support services:** Learning center, reduced course load, remedial instruction, study skills assistance, tutoring, writing center.

Majors. **Communications technology:** Animation/special effects. **Visual/performing arts:** Cinematography, commercial/advertising art, fashion design, illustration, industrial design, interior design, photography, studio arts.

Technology on campus. PC or laptop required. 485 workstations in dormitories, library, student center. Dormitories wired for high-speed internet access and linked to campus network. Online course registration, online library, helpline, wireless network available.

Student life. **Freshman orientation:** Mandatory. Preregistration for classes offered. Three two-day sessions held in June, one-day session in August, five-day session for international students, half day session for transfer students. **Housing:** Guaranteed on-campus for freshmen. Coed dorms, special housing for disabled, apartments, gender-neutral housing available. $250 fully refundable deposit, deadline 5/9. **Activities:** Film society, international student organizations, literary magazine, student government, Give Back, academic organizations, Sanctuary, Campus Crusade for Christians, Student Government Association, Girl talk, Queen Alliance, black student leadership association.

Student services. Alcohol/substance abuse counseling, career counseling, student employment services, financial aid counseling, minority student services, personal counseling, veterans' counselor. **Physically disabled:** Services for visually, speech, hearing impaired.

Contact. E-mail: admissions@ccad.edu
Phone: (614) 224-9101 ext. 3261 Toll-free number: (877) 997-2223
Fax: (614) 232-8344
Ramya Ravisankar, Senior Director of Admissions, Columbus College of Art and Design, 60 Cleveland Avenue, Columbus, OH 43215-3875

Defiance College
Defiance, Ohio
www.defiance.edu

CB code: 1162

- Private 4-year liberal arts college affiliated with the United Church of Christ
- Residential campus in large town
- 666 degree-seeking undergraduates: 14% part-time, 47% women, 8% African American, 1% Asian American, 6% Hispanic/Latino, 3% Multiracial, non-Hispanic, 2% international
- 66 degree-seeking graduate students
- 66% of applicants admitted
- SAT or ACT (ACT writing optional) required
- 41% graduate within 6 years

General. Founded in 1850. Regionally accredited. **Degrees:** 180 bachelor's, 8 associate awarded; master's offered. **Location:** 55 miles from Toledo; 45 miles from Fort Wayne, Indiana. **Calendar:** Semester, limited summer session. **Full-time faculty:** 38 total; 66% have terminal degrees, 13% minority, 50% women. **Part-time faculty:** 49 total; 20% have terminal degrees, 2% minority, 47% women. **Class size:** 75% < 20, 25% 20-39, less than 1% 40-49. **Special facilities:** Wildlife sanctuary, greenhouse/genetics center.

Freshman class profile. 1,197 applied, 787 admitted, 181 enrolled.

Mid 50% test scores			
SAT critical reading:	400-490	Rank in top quarter:	19%
SAT math:	390-520	Rank in top tenth:	11%
SAT writing:	380-440	End year in good standing:	85%
ACT composite:	19-24	Return as sophomores:	56%
GPA 3.75 or higher:	18%	Out-of-state:	36%
GPA 3.50-3.74:	14%	Live on campus:	84%
GPA 3.0-3.49:	35%	International:	1%
GPA 2.0-2.99:	32%	Fraternities:	3%
		Sororities:	5%

Basis for selection. School achievement record, test scores, college preparatory curriculum important. 2.25 GPA, 18 ACT or 860 SAT (exclusive of Writing) required. **Home schooled:** Transcript of courses and grades required.

High school preparation. College-preparatory program recommended. 16 units recommended. Recommended units include English 4, mathematics 3, social studies 2, science 3, foreign language 2 and visual/performing arts 2. One unit fine arts and 1 unit of computer proficiency recommended.

2015-2016 Annual costs. Tuition/fees: $31,082. Room/board: $9,850. Books/supplies: $1,350. Personal expenses: $1,600.

Financial aid. **Non-need-based:** Scholarships awarded for academics, leadership, minority status, music/drama.

Application procedures. **Admission:** No deadline. $25 fee, may be waived for applicants with need, free for online applicants. Admission notification on a rolling basis beginning on or about 9/1. Must reply by May 1 or within 4 week(s) if notified thereafter. **Financial aid:** Priority date 4/1; no closing date. FAFSA required. Applicants notified on a rolling basis starting 2/15; must reply by 5/1 or within 2 week(s) of notification.

Academics. Weekend college program for nontraditional and traditional students to pursue bachelor's or master's degree in several business majors. **Special study options:** Accelerated study, cooperative education, distance learning, double major, dual enrollment of high school students, honors, independent study, internships, liberal arts/career combination, student-designed major, study abroad, teacher certification program, weekend college. **Credit/placement by examination:** AP, CLEP, IB, institutional tests. 15 credit hours maximum toward associate degree, 30 toward bachelor's. Maximum of 30 credits of non-traditional credit may be earned toward graduation through armed forces service or assessment of prior learning (including testing and portfolio development). **Support services:** Learning center, reduced course load, study skills assistance, tutoring, writing center.

Majors. **Biology:** General, ecology, molecular. **Business:** General, accounting, business admin, management information systems. **Communications:** Communications/speech/rhetoric, journalism, public relations. **Computer sciences:** Security. **Conservation:** General, environmental science, environmental studies. **Education:** General, art, biology, business, chemistry, early childhood, elementary, elementary special ed, English, health, history, junior high special ed, mathematics, middle, multi-level teacher, physical, science, secondary, secondary special ed, social science, social studies, speech. **English:** English lit, rhetoric/composition. **Health services:** Athletic training, clinical lab technology, predental, premedicine, preveterinary. **History:** General. **Human services:** Social work. **Liberal arts:** Arts/sciences. **Math:**

General. **Parks/recreation:** Health/fitness, sports admin. **Philosophy/religion:** Religion. **Protective services:** Computer forensics, forensics. **Psychology:** General. **Social sciences:** General, criminology. **Theology:** Religious ed. **Visual/performing arts:** Art, commercial/advertising art, graphic design.

Most popular majors. Business/marketing 23%, education 17%, health sciences 6%, parks/recreation 14%, public administration/social services 8%, security/protective services 12%.

Technology on campus. 150 workstations in dormitories, library, computer center, student center. Dormitories wired for high-speed internet access and linked to campus network. Commuter students can connect to campus network. Online library, helpline, wireless network available.

Student life. Freshman orientation: Mandatory. Preregistration for classes offered. One-day sessions held in April, May, June, July, and August. **Policies:** Students must live and take meals on campus unless they are seniors, married, veterans, or living with parents or close relatives within approved commuting distance. **Housing:** Guaranteed on-campus for all undergraduates. Coed dorms, apartments, themed housing, wellness housing available. ADA-compliant rooms available. **Activities:** Bands, campus ministries, choral groups, dance, drama, literary magazine, music ensembles, musical theater, student government, student newspaper, black action student association, Catholics on Campus, criminal justice society, Fellowship of Christian Athletes, student ecology club, Habitat for Humanity, Alpha Phi Omega Service Fraternity, social work organization.

Athletics. NCAA. **Intercollegiate:** Baseball M, basketball, cross-country, football (tackle) M, golf, lacrosse M, soccer, softball W, tennis, track and field, volleyball W. **Intramural:** Basketball, bowling, football (non-tackle), racquetball, softball, table tennis, volleyball. **Team name:** Yellow Jackets.

Student services. Adult student services, alcohol/substance abuse counseling, chaplain/spiritual director, career counseling, student employment services, financial aid counseling, health services, minority student services, personal counseling, placement for graduates, veterans' counselor. **Physically disabled:** Services for hearing impaired.

Contact. E-mail: admissions@defiance.edu
Phone: (419) 783-2359 Toll-free number: (800) 520-4632
Fax: (419) 783-2468
Brad Harsha, Director of Admissions, Defiance College, 701 North Clinton Street, Defiance, OH 43512-1695

Denison University
Granville, Ohio | **CB member**
www.denison.edu | **CB code: 1164**

- Private 4-year liberal arts college
- Residential campus in small town
- 2,255 degree-seeking undergraduates: 57% women, 7% African American, 4% Asian American, 10% Hispanic/Latino, 4% Multi-racial, non-Hispanic, 8% international
- 48% of applicants admitted
- Application essay required
- 80% graduate within 6 years

General. Founded in 1831. Regionally accredited. **Degrees:** 551 bachelor's awarded. **ROTC:** Army. **Location:** 27 miles from Columbus. **Calendar:** Semester, limited summer session. **Full-time faculty:** 216 total; 100% have terminal degrees, 21% minority, 45% women. **Part-time faculty:** 30 total; 60% have terminal degrees, 17% minority, 47% women. **Class size:** 69% < 20, 31% 20-39, less than 1% 40-49, less than 1% 50-99. **Special facilities:** Field research station in 350-acre biological reserve, high resolution spectrometer lab, nuclear magnetic resonance spectrometer, planetarium, economics computer lab, harmonic systems lab, digital media lab, fine and performing arts MIX lab (intermedia experimental lab), geographic information systems lab.

Freshman class profile. 6,110 applied, 2,932 admitted, 632 enrolled.

Mid 50% test scores			
SAT critical reading:	580-680	GPA 2.0-2.99:	3%
SAT math:	580-680	Out-of-state:	71%
ACT composite:	26-31	Live on campus:	99%
GPA 3.75 or higher:	35%	International:	8%
GPA 3.50-3.74:	27%	Fraternities:	25%
GPA 3.0-3.49:	35%	Sororities:	42%

Basis for selection. Academic record, recommendations, talent and ability, character and personal qualities most important. School and community activities, essay and personal potential also important. Test scores considered. Test scores optional for admission consideration, but required for research

---

purposes upon matriculation. Interview recommended for all; audition required for visual and performing arts program; portfolio recommended for studio art programs.

High school preparation. College-preparatory program required. 19 units required. Required units include English 4, mathematics 4, social studies 2, history 1, science 4, foreign language 3 and academic electives 1.

2015-2016 Annual costs. Tuition/fees: $47,290. Room/board: $11,570. Books/supplies: $650. Personal expenses: $300.

2015-2016 Financial aid. Need-based: 435 full-time freshmen applied for aid; 357 deemed to have need; 357 received aid. Average need met was 90%. Average scholarship/grant was $33,696; average loan $3,464. 71% of total undergraduate aid awarded as scholarships/grants, 29% as loans/jobs. **Non-need-based:** Awarded to 2,116 full-time undergraduates, including 596 freshmen. Scholarships awarded for academics, alumni affiliation, art, leadership, minority status, music/drama, state residency.

Application procedures. Admission: Priority date 11/15; deadline 1/15 (postmark date). No application fee. Admission notification by 3/15. Must reply by May 1 or within 2 week(s) if notified thereafter. **Financial aid:** Priority date 3/15; no closing date. FAFSA required. Applicants notified on a rolling basis starting 3/28.

Academics. Special study options: Double major, independent study, internships, New York semester, semester at sea, student-designed major, study abroad, teacher certification program, Washington semester. 3-2 Duke U. Environmental Management; 3-2 U. of Michigan Natural Resources; 3-4 Case Western Reserve Dental; 3-2 Rensselaer Poly., Washington U. (St. Louis), Case Western Reserve, Columbia U. Engineering; Washington U. (St. Louis) Occupational Therapy. **Credit/placement by examination:** AP, CLEP, IB, institutional tests. **Support services:** Learning center, reduced course load, study skills assistance, tutoring, writing center.

Majors. Area/ethnic studies: African-American, East Asian, gay/lesbian, Latin American, Western European, women's. **Biology:** General, biochemistry. **Business:** International. **Communications:** Communications/speech/rhetoric, digital media. **Computer sciences:** General. **Conservation:** General. **Education:** General, physical. **English:** British lit, English lit. **Foreign languages:** Classics, French, German, Spanish. **History:** General. **Math:** General. **Philosophy/religion:** Philosophy, religion. **Physical sciences:** Chemistry, geology, physics. **Psychology:** General. **Social sciences:** Anthropology, economics, political science, sociology/anthropology. **Visual/performing arts:** Art history/conservation, dance, dramatic, film/cinema/video, music, studio arts.

Most popular majors. Biology 11%, communications/journalism 8%, education 9%, English 6%, history 6%, psychology 8%, social sciences 29%, visual/performing arts 7%.

Technology on campus. Dormitories wired for high-speed internet access and linked to campus network. Commuter students can connect to campus network. Online library, helpline, student web hosting, wireless network available.

Student life. Freshman orientation: Mandatory. Preregistration for classes offered. Mandatory no-fee August orientation program and optional but highly recommended June program costing $175. **Housing:** Guaranteed on-campus for all undergraduates. Coed dorms, single-sex dorms, apartments, cooperative housing, themed housing, wellness housing available. $300 non-refundable deposit, deadline 5/1. **Activities:** Jazz band, campus ministries, choral groups, dance, drama, film society, international student organizations, literary magazine, music ensembles, musical theater, radio station, student government, student newspaper, TV station, over 160 organizations available.

Athletics. NCAA. **Intercollegiate:** Baseball M, basketball, cross-country, diving, field hockey W, football (tackle) M, golf, lacrosse, soccer, softball W, swimming, tennis, track and field, volleyball W. **Intramural:** Basketball, equestrian, football (non-tackle), ice hockey M, lacrosse M, racquetball, rifle, rugby, skiing, soccer, softball, squash, tennis, volleyball, water polo, wrestling M. **Team name:** Big Red.

Student services. Alcohol/substance abuse counseling, chaplain/spiritual director, career counseling, student employment services, financial aid counseling, health services, minority student services, personal counseling, placement for graduates.

Contact. E-mail: admissions@denison.edu
Phone: (740) 587-6276 Toll-free number: (800) 336-4766
Fax: (740) 587-6306
Perry Robinson, Vice President and Director of Admissions, Denison University, 100 West College, Granville, OH 43023

DeVry University: Columbus

Columbus, Ohio	CB member
www.devry.edu	CB code: 1605

- For-profit 4-year university
- Commuter campus in very large city
- 1,676 degree-seeking undergraduates
- Interview required

General. Founded in 1952. Regionally accredited. Additional locations: Columbus North, Cincinnati, Dayton, Cleveland; Indianapolis (IN); Louisville (KY); Southfield (MI). **Degrees:** 377 bachelor's, 131 associate awarded; master's offered. **ROTC:** Army. **Location:** 5 miles from downtown. **Calendar:** Semester, extensive summer session. **Full-time faculty:** 36 total; 14% minority, 22% women. **Part-time faculty:** 71 total; 11% minority, 42% women.

Basis for selection. Applicants must have high school diploma or equivalent, demonstrate proficiency in basic college-level skills through SAT or ACT scores or institution-administered placement examinations, and be 17 years of age. New students may enter at beginning of any semester. SAT or ACT recommended. CPT also accepted.

High school preparation. Required units include mathematics 1. Math unit must be algebra or higher.

2015-2016 Annual costs. Tuition/fees: $17,132. Books/supplies: $1,320. Personal expenses: $2,376.

Financial aid. All financial aid based on need.

Application procedures. Admission: No deadline. $40 fee. Admission notification on a rolling basis. **Financial aid:** No deadline. FAFSA required. Applicants notified on a rolling basis.

Academics. Special study options: Accelerated study, distance learning, study abroad. **Credit/placement by examination:** AP, CLEP, institutional tests. **Support services:** Learning center, tutoring.

Majors. Business: Business admin. **Computer sciences:** Networking, systems analysis, web page design.

Most popular majors. Business/marketing 54%, computer/information sciences 33%, engineering/engineering technologies 13%.

Technology on campus. 408 workstations in library, computer center, student center. Online course registration, online library, helpline available.

Student life. Freshman orientation: Mandatory. Preregistration for classes offered. **Housing:** Private apartments, student-plan housing, private rooms available. **Activities:** Student association, Tau Alpha Pi, Christian Alliance, Asian American student association, Future Accounting Society, Institute of Electrical and Electronics Engineers, Association of IT Professionals, minority student union.

Athletics. Intramural: Basketball, soccer, volleyball.

Student services. Career counseling, student employment services, financial aid counseling, placement for graduates, veterans' counselor. **Physically disabled:** Services for visually, hearing impaired.

Contact. E-mail: admissions@devry.edu
Phone: (614) 253-1525 Toll-free number: (800) 426-2206
Fax: (614) 253-0843
DeVry University: Columbus, 1350 Alum Creek Drive, Columbus, OH 43209-2705

Franciscan University of Steubenville

Steubenville, Ohio	CB member
www.franciscan.edu	CB code: 1133

- Private 4-year university affiliated with the Roman Catholic Church
- Residential campus in large town
- 2,036 degree-seeking undergraduates: 2% part-time, 61% women, 1% African American, 2% Asian American, 10% Hispanic/Latino, 2% Multiracial, non-Hispanic, 1% international
- 593 degree-seeking graduate students
- 79% of applicants admitted
- SAT or ACT (ACT writing optional) required
- 79% graduate within 6 years

General. Founded in 1946. Regionally accredited. **Degrees:** 501 bachelor's, 42 associate awarded; master's offered. **ROTC:** Army, Air Force. **Location:** 40 miles from Pittsburgh. **Calendar:** Semester, limited summer session. **Full-time faculty:** 116 total. **Part-time faculty:** 128 total. **Class size:** 48% < 20, 40% 20-39, 11% 40-49, 1% 50-99. **Special facilities:** Replica of Portiuncula (St. Mary of the Angels) Chapel as rebuilt by St. Francis of Assisi in 1207, Tomb of the Unborn Child.

Freshman class profile. 1,741 applied, 1,368 admitted, 456 enrolled.

Mid 50% test scores			
SAT critical reading:	540-650	GPA 2.0-2.99:	7%
SAT math:	520-620	Rank in top quarter:	55%
SAT writing:	510-620	Rank in top tenth:	25%
ACT composite:	23-28	Return as sophomores:	86%
GPA 3.75 or higher:	55%	Out-of-state:	78%
GPA 3.50-3.74:	19%	Live on campus:	90%
GPA 3.0-3.49:	19%	International:	1%

Basis for selection. Admission requirements include 2.4 GPA, recommendations, interview when available, 1000 SAT (exclusive of Writing) or 21 ACT. Interview recommended. **Home schooled:** Applicants should contact Admissions Office for requirements.

High school preparation. College-preparatory program recommended. 15 units required. Required and recommended units include English 4, mathematics 3, social studies 2, history 1, science 3 (laboratory 3) and foreign language 2. 10 units in 4 of the following fields: English, foreign language, social science, math, natural sciences. Remaining 5 units may be in other subjects counted toward graduation. Majors in chemistry, engineering science, or math should have 2 units algebra and 2 units geometry/trigonometry.

2015-2016 Annual costs. Tuition/fees: $24,780. Room/board: $8,300. Books/supplies: $1,200. Personal expenses: $1,230.

Financial aid. Non-need-based: Scholarships awarded for academics, alumni affiliation, leadership, religious affiliation.

Application procedures. Admission: Priority date 1/31; no deadline. $20 fee, may be waived for applicants with need, free for online applicants. Admission notification on a rolling basis beginning on or about 9/1. **Financial aid:** Priority date 4/1; no closing date. FAFSA required. Applicants notified on a rolling basis starting 2/15; must reply within 3 week(s) of notification.

Academics. Special study options: Accelerated study, combined bachelor's/graduate degree, distance learning, double major, dual enrollment of high school students, honors, independent study, internships, study abroad, teacher certification program. **Credit/placement by examination:** AP, CLEP, IB, institutional tests. 30 credit hours maximum toward associate degree, 30 toward bachelor's. **Support services:** Learning center, reduced course load, study skills assistance, tutoring, writing center.

Honors college/program. 1180 SAT (exclusive of Writing) or 26 ACT, 3.4 GPA, and series of essays required. 40 freshmen admitted. Academic program consists of a great books seminar sequence.

Majors. Biology: General. **Business:** Accounting, business admin. **Communications:** Communications/speech/rhetoric. **Computer sciences:** General, computer science. **Education:** Elementary. **English:** English lit. **Foreign languages:** Classics, French, German, Spanish. **Health services:** Nursing (RN). **History:** General. **Human services:** Social work. **Liberal arts:** Humanities. **Math:** General. **Philosophy/religion:** Philosophy. **Physical sciences:** Chemistry. **Psychology:** General. **Social sciences:** Anthropology, economics, political science, sociology. **Theology:** Religious ed, sacred music, theology. **Visual/performing arts:** Dramatic.

Most popular majors. Business/marketing 10%, education 9%, health sciences 10%, philosophy/religious studies 6%, theological studies 31%.

Technology on campus. 126 workstations in library, computer center. Dormitories wired for high-speed internet access and linked to campus network. Commuter students can connect to campus network. Online course registration, online library, helpline available.

Student life. Freshman orientation: Available. Preregistration for classes offered. Held the weekend before fall classes begin, from Friday morning to Sunday afternoon. **Policies:** Freshmen not permitted cars on campus. **Housing:** Guaranteed on-campus for freshmen. Single-sex dorms, apartments available. $300 nonrefundable deposit. Household groups of 10-20 students in residence halls may develop distinctive environment for their group within the context of Christian and Franciscan perspective. **Activities:** Campus ministries, choral groups, drama, international student organizations, literary magazine, music ensembles, radio station, student government, student newspaper, international student organization, Human Life Concerns (pro-life), Works of Mercy Program (social justice), leadership development.

Athletics. NCAA. **Intercollegiate:** Basketball, cross-country, diving W, lacrosse, rugby M, soccer, softball W, swimming W, tennis, track and field, volleyball W. **Intramural:** Basketball, football (non-tackle), racquetball, soccer, softball, ultimate frisbee, volleyball, weight lifting. **Team name:** Barons.

Student services. Chaplain/spiritual director, career counseling, student employment services, financial aid counseling, health services, personal counseling, veterans' counselor. **Physically disabled:** Services for visually, speech, hearing impaired.

Contact. E-mail: admissions@franciscan.edu
Phone: (740) 283-6226 Toll-free number: (800) 783-6220
Fax: (740) 284-5456
Margaret Weber, Director of Admissions, Franciscan University of Steubenville, 1235 University Boulevard, Steubenville, OH 43952-1763

Franklin University
Columbus, Ohio
www.franklin.edu
CB code: 1229

- Private 4-year university and business college
- Commuter campus in very large city
- 4,049 degree-seeking undergraduates: 68% part-time, 56% women, 19% African American, 2% Asian American, 3% Hispanic/Latino, 4% Multiracial, non-Hispanic, 1% international
- 989 degree-seeking graduate students

General. Founded in 1902. Regionally accredited. Credit courses offered at suburban campuses, numerous co-locations, and online. **Degrees:** 1,575 bachelor's, 80 associate awarded; master's offered. **ROTC:** Army. **Location:** Downtown. **Calendar:** Trimester, extensive summer session. **Class size:** 83% < 20, 17% 20-39. **Special facilities:** Student learning center.

Basis for selection. Open admission, but selective for some programs. Admission tests not required but considered for placement if submitted. Selective admission for international (nonresident alien) students.

2015-2016 Annual costs. Tuition/fees: $14,545. Books/supplies: $1,080. Personal expenses: $2,754.

Financial aid. Non-need-based: Scholarships awarded for academics, leadership, minority status.

Application procedures. Admission: No deadline. No application fee. Admission notification on a rolling basis. **Financial aid:** Priority date 6/15; no closing date. FAFSA required. Applicants notified on a rolling basis; must reply within 2 week(s) of notification.

Academics. Accelerated 6-week course offerings in addition to 12- and 15-week formats. **Special study options:** Accelerated study, combined bachelor's/graduate degree, cooperative education, cross-registration, distance learning, double major, dual enrollment of high school students, ESL, independent study, internships, study abroad, weekend college. **Credit/placement by examination:** AP, CLEP, IB, institutional tests. 32 credit hours maximum toward associate degree, 84 toward bachelor's. **Support services:** Learning center, reduced course load, remedial instruction, study skills assistance, tutoring, writing center.

Majors. Business: Accounting, business admin, entrepreneurial studies, finance, financial planning, human resources, insurance, management information systems, marketing, operations. **Communications:** Digital media, organizational, public relations. **Computer sciences:** Computer science, information technology, security, web page design. **Health services:** Health care admin, health information technology. **Human services:** General. **Protective services:** Law enforcement admin. **Psychology:** Applied. **Social sciences:** General, economics. **Visual/performing arts:** Game design.

Most popular majors. Business/marketing 35%.

Technology on campus. 370 workstations in library, computer center, student center. Commuter students can connect to campus network. Online course registration, online library, helpline, wireless network available.

Student life. Freshman orientation: Available. Preregistration for classes offered. **Activities:** International student association.

Student services. Adult student services, career counseling, financial aid counseling, veterans' counselor. **Physically disabled:** Services for visually, speech, hearing impaired.

Contact. E-mail: info@franklin.edu
Phone: (614) 797-4700 Toll-free number: (877) 341-6300
Fax: (614) 224-8027
Lynne Hull, Assistant Director of New Student Enrollment, Franklin University, 201 South Grant Avenue, Columbus, OH 43215-5399

God's Bible School and College
Cincinnati, Ohio
www.gbs.edu
CB code: 1238

- Private 4-year Bible college affiliated with the interdenominational tradition
- Residential campus in large city
- 304 undergraduates

General. Founded in 1900. Accredited by ABHE. **Degrees:** 33 bachelor's, 13 associate awarded. **Location:** One mile from downtown. **Calendar:** Semester. **Full-time faculty:** 20 total. **Part-time faculty:** 5 total.

Basis for selection. Three references recommended (two required); SAT required for placement.

High school preparation. 17 units recommended. Recommended units include English 3, mathematics 2, social studies 2 and science 2.

2015-2016 Annual costs. Tuition/fees: $7,040. Room/board: $4,050. Books/supplies: $725. Personal expenses: $2,700.

Financial aid. Non-need-based: Scholarships awarded for academics, leadership, music/drama, religious affiliation. **Additional information:** Institutional work scholarships available.

Application procedures. Admission: Priority date 6/1; no deadline. $25 fee. Application must be submitted on paper. Admission notification on a rolling basis. **Financial aid:** Priority date 4/30; no closing date. FAFSA required. Applicants notified on a rolling basis.

Academics. Special study options: Distance learning, double major, independent study, internships, liberal arts/career combination. **Credit/placement by examination:** AP, CLEP, SAT, institutional tests. **Support services:** Learning center.

Majors. Education: Elementary, English, music. **Theology:** Missionary, pastoral counseling, religious ed, sacred music, theology, youth ministry.

Technology on campus. Dormitories wired for high-speed internet access. Wireless network available.

Student life. Freshman orientation: Mandatory. Preregistration for classes offered. Takes place week before classes begin, lasting for several days. **Policies:** Students agree to follow all rules, policies and regulations by matriculating. Please contact Office of Student Affairs for specific information. Religious observance required. **Housing:** Guaranteed on-campus for freshmen. Single-sex dorms, wellness housing available. **Activities:** Choral groups, drama, music ensembles, student government, student newspaper, symphony orchestra.

Athletics. Intramural: Basketball, volleyball.

Student services. Chaplain/spiritual director, student employment services, financial aid counseling, health services, personal counseling, placement for graduates, veterans' counselor.

Contact. E-mail: spouzar@gbs.edu
Phone: (513) 721-7944 ext. 205
Toll-free number: (800) 486-4637 ext. 205 Fax: (513) 721-1357
Steve Buckland, Director of Admissions, God's Bible School and College, 1810 Young Street, Cincinnati, OH 45202-6838

Heidelberg University
Tiffin, Ohio
www.heidelberg.edu
CB member
CB code: 1292

- Private 4-year liberal arts college affiliated with the United Church of Christ
- Residential campus in large town
- 1,026 degree-seeking undergraduates: 2% part-time, 48% women, 7% African American, 1% Asian American, 2% Hispanic/Latino, 4% Multiracial, non-Hispanic
- 100 degree-seeking graduate students
- 79% of applicants admitted
- SAT or ACT (ACT writing optional) required
- 39% graduate within 6 years

General. Founded in 1850. Regionally accredited. **Degrees:** 176 bachelor's awarded; master's offered. **ROTC:** Army, Air Force. **Location:** 52 miles from Toledo, 80 miles from Cleveland. **Calendar:** Semester, limited summer session. **Full-time faculty:** 61 total; 85% have terminal degrees, 12% minority, 49% women. **Part-time faculty:** 91 total; 23% have terminal degrees, 11% minority, 53% women. **Class size:** 66% < 20, 31% 20-39, 2% 40-49, less than 1% 50-99. **Special facilities:** National center for water quality research, cadaver laboratory, four wooded lots for science research, archaeology laboratory, historic and military archaeology center.

Freshman class profile. 1,147 applied, 905 admitted, 274 enrolled.

Mid 50% test scores				
SAT critical reading:	460-580	GPA 2.0-2.99:		26%
SAT math:	490-580	Return as sophomores:		64%
ACT composite:	19-25	Out-of-state:		22%
GPA 3.75 or higher:	22%	Live on campus:		93%
GPA 3.50-3.74:	15%	Fraternities:		11%
GPA 3.0-3.49:	37%	Sororities:		23%

Basis for selection. School achievement record most important, followed by test scores. Positive trend in grades and college prep coursework also important. Special talents, community activities, and leadership qualities considered. Audition required for music; interview recommended for academically challenged students. **Learning Disabled:** Students with learning disabilities are strongly encouraged to self-report to the Academic Success Center after acceptance to the University. Appointments to discuss possible services/accommodations are welcome.

High school preparation. College-preparatory program recommended. 21 units recommended. Recommended units include English 4, mathematics 3, social studies 3, history 2, science 3 (laboratory 1), foreign language 2 and academic electives 3.

2015-2016 Annual costs. Tuition/fees: $28,500. Room/board: $9,600. Books/supplies: $1,500. Personal expenses: $750.

2015-2016 Financial aid. **Need-based:** 266 full-time freshmen applied for aid; 249 deemed to have need; 249 received aid. Average need met was 79%. Average scholarship/grant was $19,240; average loan $4,000. 64% of total undergraduate aid awarded as scholarships/grants, 36% as loans/jobs. **Non-need-based:** Scholarships awarded for academics, alumni affiliation, music/drama, religious affiliation, state residency.

Application procedures. **Admission:** Priority date 6/1; deadline 8/1. No application fee. Admission notification on a rolling basis beginning on or about 10/15. **Financial aid:** Priority date 3/1; no closing date. FAFSA required. Applicants notified on a rolling basis starting 3/15; must reply by 5/1 or within 2 week(s) of notification.

Academics. **Special study options:** Combined bachelor's/graduate degree, cross-registration, double major, dual enrollment of high school students, ESL, honors, independent study, internships, liberal arts/career combination, student-designed major, study abroad, teacher certification program, Washington semester. **Credit/placement by examination:** AP, CLEP, IB, SAT, ACT, institutional tests. 30 credit hours maximum toward bachelor's degree. **Support services:** Learning center, reduced course load, study skills assistance, tutoring.

Majors. **Biology:** General. **Business:** Accounting, business admin, management science. **Communications:** Communications/speech/rhetoric. **Computer sciences:** General, computer science. **Education:** Music, physical. **English:** English lit. **Foreign languages:** German, Spanish. **Health services:** Athletic training, health care admin, predental, premedicine, prenursing, preveterinary. **History:** General. **Math:** General. **Parks/recreation:** Sports admin. **Philosophy/religion:** Religion. **Physical sciences:** Chemistry, physics. **Protective services:** Law enforcement admin. **Psychology:** General. **Social sciences:** Economics, political science. **Visual/performing arts:** Music, music management, music performance, music theory/composition, musical theater.

Most popular majors. Business/marketing 12%, parks/recreation 6%, personal/culinary services 7%, psychology 6%, security/protective services 7%, social sciences 43%.

Technology on campus. 125 workstations in dormitories, library, computer center, student center. Dormitories wired for high-speed internet access and linked to campus network. Online course registration, helpline, repair service, wireless network available.

Student life. **Freshman orientation:** Mandatory. Preregistration for classes offered. Five two-day summer sessions offered. **Housing:** Guaranteed on-campus for all undergraduates. Coed dorms, single-sex dorms, special housing for disabled, apartments, cooperative housing, fraternity/sorority housing, themed housing available. $250 fully refundable deposit. Undergraduate specialty houses by major, interest, service groups available. **Activities:** Bands, campus ministries, choral groups, dance, drama, film society, international student organizations, literary magazine, music ensembles, Model UN, musical theater, radio station, student government, student newspaper, symphony orchestra, TV station, campus fellowship, Black student union, Young

Democrats, Young Republicans, world student union, Alpha Phi Omega, political science organization, Amigos de ARISE.

Athletics. NCAA. **Intercollegiate:** Baseball M, basketball, cheerleading, cross-country, football (tackle) M, golf, soccer, softball W, tennis, track and field, volleyball W, wrestling M. **Intramural:** Archery, baseball M, basketball, bowling, golf, soccer, softball, table tennis, volleyball. **Team name:** Student Princes.

Student services. Adult student services, alcohol/substance abuse counseling, chaplain/spiritual director, career counseling, student employment services, financial aid counseling, health services, minority student services, personal counseling, placement for graduates, women's services. **Physically disabled:** Services for visually, hearing impaired.

Contact. E-mail: adminfo@heidelberg.edu
Phone: (419) 448-2330 Toll-free number: (800) 434-3352
Fax: (419) 448-2334
Jason Miller, Director of Admissions, Heidelberg University, 310 East Market Street, Tiffin, OH 44883-2462

Herzing University: Toledo
Toledo, Ohio
www.herzing.edu

- For-profit 4-year business and technical college
- Large city
- 193 undergraduates

General. Regionally accredited. **Degrees:** 13 bachelor's, 64 associate awarded. **Calendar:** Semester. **Full-time faculty:** 10 total. **Part-time faculty:** 15 total.

Basis for selection. Wonderlic exam required for some programs.

2015-2016 Annual costs. Certificate programs: $13,670 to $26,820. Associate programs: $26,180 to $53,640. Bachelor's programs: $61,515 to $88,065.

Academics. **Credit/placement by examination:** AP, CLEP.

Majors. **Business:** Accounting, business admin.

Contact. E-mail: info@tol.herzing.edu
Joe Guziolek, Director of Admissions, Herzing University: Toledo, 5212 Hill Avenue, Toledo, OH 43615

Hiram College
Hiram, Ohio
www.hiram.edu
CB member
CB code: 1297

- Private 4-year liberal arts college affiliated with the Christian Church (Disciples of Christ)
- Residential campus in rural community
- 1,063 degree-seeking undergraduates: 15% part-time, 52% women, 17% African American, 1% Asian American, 4% Hispanic/Latino, 3% Multiracial, non-Hispanic, 2% international
- 22 degree-seeking graduate students
- 58% of applicants admitted
- SAT or ACT (ACT writing optional), application essay required
- 60% graduate within 6 years

General. Founded in 1850. Regionally accredited. **Degrees:** 258 bachelor's awarded; master's offered. **ROTC:** Army, Air Force. **Location:** 35 miles from Cleveland. **Calendar:** Semester, limited summer session. **Full-time faculty:** 79 total; 90% have terminal degrees, 11% minority, 57% women. **Part-time faculty:** 55 total. **Class size:** 81% < 20, 19% 20-39. **Special facilities:** 2 nature/science field research stations, observatory, center for literature and medicine.

Freshman class profile. 1,864 applied, 1,074 admitted, 161 enrolled.

Mid 50% test scores				
SAT critical reading:	450-590	Rank in top quarter:		45%
SAT math:	430-580	Rank in top tenth:		17%
SAT writing:	430-580	Return as sophomores:		66%
ACT composite:	20-27	Out-of-state:		23%
GPA 3.75 or higher:	32%	Live on campus:		93%
GPA 3.50-3.74:	15%	International:		1%
GPA 3.0-3.49:	30%	Fraternities:		7%
GPA 2.0-2.99:	23%	Sororities:		13%

Basis for selection. School record, test scores, counselor and teacher recommendations emphasized. Extracurricular participation, alumni relationship considered. Interview required for scholarship candidates or academically marginal applicants; strongly recommended for all others.

High school preparation. College-preparatory program recommended. 16 units required; 18 recommended. Required and recommended units include English 4, mathematics 4, social studies 1, history 1, science 3 (laboratory 1), foreign language 1-2 and academic electives 1-2.

2015-2016 Annual costs. Tuition/fees: $31,530. Room/board: $10,190. Books/supplies: $700. Personal expenses: $1,408.

Financial aid. Non-need-based: Scholarships awarded for academics, alumni affiliation, art, music/drama, religious affiliation.

Application procedures. Admission: Priority date 12/15; no deadline. $25 fee, may be waived for applicants with need. Admission notification on a rolling basis beginning on or about 9/15. Must reply by May 1 or within 2 week(s) if notified thereafter. **Financial aid:** Priority date 2/15; no closing date. FAFSA required. Not require for domestic applicants. Applicants notified on a rolling basis starting 3/1; must reply by 5/1 or within 2 week(s) of notification.

Academics. Special study options: Accelerated study, combined bachelor's/graduate degree, cross-registration, distance learning, double major, dual enrollment of high school students, ESL, exchange student, honors, independent study, internships, liberal arts/career combination, student-designed major, study abroad, teacher certification program, Washington semester, weekend college. **Credit/placement by examination:** AP, CLEP, IB, institutional tests. 75 credit hours maximum toward bachelor's degree. **Support services:** Study skills assistance, tutoring, writing center.

Majors. Biology: General, biochemistry, biomedical sciences. **Business:** Accounting/finance, business admin. **Communications:** Communications/speech/rhetoric. **Computer sciences:** General, computer science. **Conservation:** Environmental studies. **Education:** General, biology, chemistry, early childhood, English, mathematics, middle, physics, reading, science, secondary, social studies. **English:** Creative writing, English lit. **Foreign languages:** Classics, French, Spanish. **History:** General. **Math:** General. **Philosophy/religion:** Philosophy, religion. **Physical sciences:** Chemistry, physics. **Psychology:** General. **Social sciences:** General, economics, political science, sociology. **Visual/performing arts:** Art history/conservation, dramatic, music, studio arts.

Most popular majors. Biology 12%, business/marketing 30%, education 6%, health sciences 9%, social sciences 10%.

Technology on campus. PC or laptop required. 75 workstations in dormitories, library, computer center, student center. Dormitories wired for high-speed internet access and linked to campus network. Commuter students can connect to campus network. Online course registration, online library, helpline, student web hosting, wireless network available.

Student life. Freshman orientation: Mandatory. Preregistration for classes offered. Several orientation sessions held throughout late spring and summer. **Housing:** Guaranteed on-campus for all undergraduates. Coed dorms, single-sex dorms, special housing for disabled, apartments, themed housing, wellness housing available. $100 nonrefundable deposit. Pets allowed in dorm rooms. Dormitories include 12-hour quiet floors. **Activities:** Concert band, campus ministries, choral groups, dance, drama, international student organizations, literary magazine, music ensembles, musical theater, radio station, student government, Disciples on Campus, The Net, Intercultural Forum, Latinos Unidos for Networking Awareness, Africana Cultural Collective, African American Students United, Gender Equality Student Alliance, Hiram College Students for Liberty, political science club.

Athletics. NCAA. **Intercollegiate:** Baseball M, basketball, diving, football (tackle) M, golf, lacrosse, soccer, softball W, swimming, volleyball W. **Intramural:** Basketball, football (non-tackle), soccer, softball, ultimate frisbee, volleyball. **Team name:** Terriers.

Student services. Chaplain/spiritual director, career counseling, student employment services, financial aid counseling, health services, minority student services, personal counseling, placement for graduates, veterans' counselor.

Contact. E-mail: admission@hiram.edu
Phone: (330) 569-5169 Toll-free number: (800) 362-5280
Fax: (330) 569-5944
Lindajean Western, Vice President of Enrollment, Hiram College, P.O. Box 96, Hiram, OH 44234

John Carroll University
University Heights, Ohio — CB member
www.jcu.edu — CB code: 1342

- Private 4-year university affiliated with the Roman Catholic Church
- Residential campus in large town
- 2,994 degree-seeking undergraduates
- 82% of applicants admitted
- SAT or ACT (ACT writing recommended), application essay required

General. Founded in 1886. Regionally accredited. **Degrees:** 701 bachelor's awarded; master's offered. **ROTC:** Army, Air Force. **Location:** 10 miles from Cleveland. **Calendar:** Semester, extensive summer session. **Full-time faculty:** 277 total; 69% have terminal degrees, 12% minority, 30% women. **Part-time faculty:** 198 total; 11% minority, 50% women. **Class size:** 49% < 20, 50% 20-39, less than 1% 40-49. **Special facilities:** Communications TV studio.

Freshman class profile. 4,087 applied, 3,346 admitted, 762 enrolled.

Mid 50% test scores			
SAT critical reading:	490-590	GPA 3.0-3.49:	31%
SAT math:	500-600	GPA 2.0-2.99:	16%
SAT writing:	480-590	Rank in top quarter:	41%
ACT composite:	22-28	Rank in top tenth:	19%
GPA 3.75 or higher:	34%	Out-of-state:	38%
GPA 3.50-3.74:	19%	Live on campus:	87%

Basis for selection. High school academic record, rigor of curricula most important. Other criteria include test scores, extracurricular activities, essay. **Home schooled:** State high school equivalency certificate, letter of recommendation (nonparent) required. Extra emphasis placed on standardized testing. Encourage SAT subject testing if possible.

High school preparation. College-preparatory program recommended. 16 units required; 21 recommended. Required and recommended units include English 4, mathematics 3-4, social studies 2-4, science 2-3 (laboratory 2-3), foreign language 2-3 and academic electives 3. 2-4 units among social studies, history, social science, or religion.

2016-2017 Annual costs. Tuition/fees: $38,490. Room/board: $11,250. Books/supplies: $1,000. Personal expenses: $1,000.

2014-2015 Financial aid. Need-based: 76% of total undergraduate aid awarded as scholarships/grants, 24% as loans/jobs. **Non-need-based:** Scholarships awarded for academics, alumni affiliation, leadership, minority status, ROTC, state residency. **Additional information:** John Carroll grant combined with federal and state grant aid, and the Federal Stafford Loan program to meet the published flat, full-time tuition cost for Pell-eligible Ohio families.

Application procedures. Admission: Priority date 12/1; no deadline. No application fee. Application must be submitted online. Admission notification on a rolling basis beginning on or about 12/15. Must reply by May 1 or within 4 week(s) if notified thereafter. **Financial aid:** Priority date 2/15, closing date 3/15. FAFSA required. Applicants notified on a rolling basis starting 2/15; must reply by 5/1 or within 4 week(s) of notification.

Academics. Special study options: Accelerated study, combined bachelor's/graduate degree, cross-registration, double major, dual enrollment of high school students, exchange student, honors, independent study, internships, liberal arts/career combination, student-designed major, study abroad, teacher certification program, Washington semester. Undergraduates may take graduate level classes. **Credit/placement by examination:** AP, CLEP, IB, SAT, ACT, institutional tests. 30 credit hours maximum toward bachelor's degree. **Support services:** Learning center, reduced course load, study skills assistance, tutoring, writing center.

Majors. Area/ethnic studies: East Asian, women's. **Biology:** General, biochemistry, cellular/molecular. **Business:** Accounting, business admin, finance, human resources, international, logistics, managerial economics, marketing. **Communications:** General. **Computer sciences:** General, computer science. **Conservation:** Environmental science, environmental studies. **Education:** Elementary, mathematics, physical. **Engineering:** Applied physics. **English:** Creative writing, English lit, technical writing, writing. **Foreign languages:** Ancient Greek, comparative lit, French, German, Latin, Spanish. **Health services:** Predental, premedicine, prepharmacy, preveterinary. **History:** General. **Liberal arts:** Arts/sciences. **Math:** General. **Philosophy/religion:** Philosophy, religion. **Physical sciences:** Chemistry, physics. **Psychology:** General. **Social sciences:** Criminology, economics, political science, sociology. **Visual/performing arts:** Art history/conservation.

Most popular majors. Biology 8%, business/marketing 28%, communications/journalism 12%, education 7%, English 6%, psychology 9%, social sciences 13%.

Technology on campus. 200 workstations in dormitories, library, computer center, student center. Dormitories wired for high-speed internet access and linked to campus network. Commuter students can connect to campus network. Online course registration, online library, helpline, repair service, student web hosting, wireless network available.

Student life. Freshman orientation: Mandatory, $325 fee. Preregistration for classes offered. Two-day, one overnight for parents and students. Variety of dates offered throughout June and July. **Policies:** Students must adhere to Student Code of Conduct. All incoming freshman not commuting from home required to live on campus freshman and sophomore years. **Housing:** Guaranteed on-campus for all undergraduates. Coed dorms, special housing for disabled, apartments, fraternity/sorority housing, themed housing, wellness housing available. $300 fully refundable deposit, deadline 5/1. **Activities:** Bands, campus ministries, choral groups, dance, drama, film society, international student organizations, literary magazine, music ensembles, musical theater, radio station, student government, student newspaper, TV station, Christian Life Community, African American Alliance, EMS Association, Habitat for Humanity, Labre Project, Students in Free Enterprise, Public Relations Student Society of America.

Athletics. NCAA. **Intercollegiate:** Baseball M, basketball, cheerleading W, cross-country, diving, football (tackle) M, golf, lacrosse, soccer, softball W, swimming, tennis, track and field, volleyball W, wrestling M. **Intramural:** Basketball, football (non-tackle), golf, racquetball, soccer, softball, table tennis, tennis, volleyball, water polo. **Team name:** Blue Streaks.

Student services. Adult student services, alcohol/substance abuse counseling, chaplain/spiritual director, career counseling, student employment services, financial aid counseling, health services, minority student services, personal counseling, placement for graduates, veterans' counselor, women's services. **Physically disabled:** Services for visually, speech, hearing impaired.

Contact. E-mail: enrollment@jcu.edu
Phone: (216) 397-4294 Toll-free number: (888) 335-6800
Fax: (216) 397-4981
Steve Vitatoe, Executive Director of Enrollment, John Carroll University, Office of Admission, University Heights, OH 44118-4581

Kent State University

Kent, Ohio	**CB member**
www.kent.edu	**CB code: 1367**

- Public 4-year university
- Residential campus in large town
- 22,779 degree-seeking undergraduates: 11% part-time, 60% women, 9% African American, 1% Asian American, 3% Hispanic/Latino, 3% Multiracial, non-Hispanic, 6% international
- 5,935 degree-seeking graduate students
- 85% of applicants admitted
- SAT or ACT (ACT writing optional) required
- 56% graduate within 6 years

General. Founded in 1910. Regionally accredited. **Degrees:** 4,747 bachelor's awarded; master's, professional, doctoral offered. **ROTC:** Army, Air Force. **Location:** 50 miles from Cleveland, 11 miles from Akron. **Calendar:** Semester, extensive summer session. **Full-time faculty:** 962 total; 12% minority, 54% women. **Part-time faculty:** 800 total; 9% minority, 56% women. **Class size:** 54% < 20, 34% 20-39, 4% 40-49, 6% 50-99, 3% >100. **Special facilities:** 287-acre airport, liquid crystal institute, fashion museum, planetarium, ice arena, 18-hole golf course, May 4th visitor's center.

Freshman class profile. 15,772 applied, 13,369 admitted, 4,334 enrolled.

Mid 50% test scores		GPA 2.0-2.99:	21%
SAT critical reading:	480-580	Rank in top quarter:	39%
SAT math:	470-580	Rank in top tenth:	14%
SAT writing:	460-560	Return as sophomores:	81%
ACT composite:	21-25	Out-of-state:	19%
GPA 3.75 or higher:	20%	Live on campus:	84%
GPA 3.50-3.74:	20%	International:	3%
GPA 3.0-3.49:	39%		

Basis for selection. Academic record, course work, test scores important. Varying criteria for nursing, education, speech pathology and audiology, flight, fashion design and merchandising, architecture, interior design, journalism and mass communication, 6-year medical program, music, dance, and honors college applicants. Interview required for 6-year medical program, recommended for all others. Audition required for dance, music, and musical theater students. **Home schooled:** State high school equivalency certificate required. Submit an equivalent diploma through a successful GED examination and an ACT/SAT score, or submit the following information for admission consideration: written verification from the appropriate school district

that the student has been excused from compulsory attendance for home education, ACT or SAT test scores, portfolio reflecting all secondary coursework completed.

High school preparation. College-preparatory program recommended. 17 units recommended. Recommended units include English 4, mathematics 4, social studies 3, science 3 (laboratory 2), foreign language 2 and visual/performing arts 1.

2015-2016 Annual costs. Tuition/fees: $10,012; $18,212 out-of-state. Room/board: $10,334.

2015-2016 Financial aid. Need-based: 3,727 full-time freshmen applied for aid; 2,940 deemed to have need; 2,925 received aid. Average need met was 60%. Average scholarship/grant was $5,813; average loan $4,062. 57% of total undergraduate aid awarded as scholarships/grants, 43% as loans/jobs. **Non-need-based:** Awarded to 10,010 full-time undergraduates, including 3,202 freshmen. Scholarships awarded for academics, alumni affiliation, art, athletics, leadership, minority status, music/drama, ROTC, state residency. **Additional information:** Participant in US Department of Education's Quality Assurance Program and Experimental Sites Program.

Application procedures. Admission: Priority date 3/1; deadline 5/1 (postmark date). $45 fee, may be waived for applicants with need. Admission notification on a rolling basis beginning on or about 10/1. Must reply by 5/1. **Financial aid:** Priority date 3/1; no closing date. FAFSA required. Applicants notified by 3/15; must reply within 2 week(s) of notification.

Academics. Special study options: Accelerated study, combined bachelor's/graduate degree, cooperative education, cross-registration, distance learning, double major, dual enrollment of high school students, ESL, exchange student, honors, independent study, internships, liberal arts/career combination, New York semester, student-designed major, study abroad, teacher certification program, Washington semester. **Credit/placement by examination:** AP, CLEP, IB, SAT, ACT, institutional tests. 15 credit hours maximum toward associate degree, 30 toward bachelor's. Certificate limit 50%. Limits are combined for CBE, CLEP, and AP. Students can petition college dean for a waiver of maximum limit. Credit must be completed by the semester preceding the semester in which a student plans to graduate. CBE credit does not fulfill the residency requirement. **Support services:** Learning center, pre-admission summer program, reduced course load, remedial instruction, study skills assistance, tutoring, writing center. Academic coaching.

Honors college/program. Approximately 400 incoming freshman admitted; 3.60 GPA; 27 ACT (24 minimum English)/1210 SAT Critical Reading & Math (510 Critical Reading); honors advising; small interactive classes (20 maximum); eight courses culminating with thesis project, portfolio, or course; two study abroad programs; Living-Learning Community available.

Majors. Architecture: Architecture. **Area/ethnic studies:** African-American. **Biology:** General, biotechnology, botany, zoology. **Business:** Accounting, business admin, construction management, entrepreneurial studies, fashion, finance, hospitality admin, managerial economics, marketing. **Communications:** Advertising, communications/speech/rhetoric, digital media, journalism, public relations. **Computer sciences:** General, systems analysis. **Conservation:** General. **Education:** General, art, chemistry, early childhood, ESL, health, mathematics, middle, music, physical, science, social studies, special ed. **Engineering:** Aerospace, industrial. **English:** English lit. **Foreign languages:** French, German, Russian, sign language interpretation, Spanish, translation. **Health services:** Athletic training, audiology/speech pathology, clinical lab science, clinical nutrition, nursing (RN). **History:** General. **Liberal arts:** Humanities. **Math:** General, applied. **Parks/recreation:** Exercise sciences, facilities management, sports admin. **Philosophy/religion:** Philosophy. **Physical sciences:** Chemistry, geology, physics. **Protective services:** Criminal justice. **Psychology:** General. **Social sciences:** Anthropology, geography, international relations, political science, sociology. **Visual/performing arts:** General, art history/conservation, commercial/advertising art, crafts, dance, dramatic, fashion design, interior design, music, painting. **Work/family studies:** Family studies.

Most popular majors. Business/marketing 20%, education 9%, health sciences 18%, psychology 7%, visual/performing arts 6%.

Technology on campus. Dormitories wired for high-speed internet access and linked to campus network. Commuter students can connect to campus network. Online course registration, online library, helpline, repair service, student web hosting, wireless network available.

Student life. Freshman orientation: Mandatory. Preregistration for classes offered. **Housing:** Guaranteed on-campus for freshmen. Coed dorms, single-sex dorms, special housing for disabled, apartments, cooperative housing, fraternity/sorority housing, gender-neutral housing, themed housing, wellness housing available. $200 fully refundable deposit, deadline 5/1. **Activities:** Bands, campus ministries, choral groups, dance, drama, international student organizations, literary magazine, music ensembles, Model UN, musical theater, opera, radio station, student government, student newspaper, symphony orchestra, TV station.

Athletics. NCAA. **Intercollegiate:** Baseball M, basketball, cross-country, field hockey W, football (tackle) M, golf, gymnastics W, soccer W, softball W, track and field, volleyball W, wrestling M. **Intramural:** Basketball, football (non-tackle), sand volleyball, soccer, softball, tennis. **Team name:** Golden Flashes.

Student services. Adult student services, alcohol/substance abuse counseling, career counseling, services for economically disadvantaged, student employment services, financial aid counseling, health services, legal services, minority student services, personal counseling, placement for graduates, veterans' counselor, women's services. **Physically disabled:** Services for visually, speech, hearing impaired.

Contact. E-mail: kentadm@kent.edu
Phone: (330) 672-2444 Toll-free number: (800) 988-5368
Fax: (330) 672-2499
Nancy DellaVecchia, Director of Admissions, Kent State University, 161 Schwartz Center, Kent, OH 44242-0001

Kenyon College
Gambier, Ohio   **CB member**
www.kenyon.edu   **CB code: 1370**

- Private 4-year liberal arts college affiliated with the nondenominational tradition
- Residential campus in rural community
- 1,698 degree-seeking undergraduates: 55% women, 4% African American, 4% Asian American, 7% Hispanic/Latino, 4% Multi-racial, non-Hispanic, 5% international
- 24% of applicants admitted
- SAT or ACT (ACT writing optional), application essay required
- 88% graduate within 6 years

General. Founded in 1824. Regionally accredited. **Degrees:** 431 bachelor's awarded. **Location:** 50 miles from Columbus. **Calendar:** Semester. **Full-time faculty:** 156 total; 99% have terminal degrees, 24% minority, 45% women. **Part-time faculty:** 44 total; 80% have terminal degrees, 16% minority, 50% women. **Class size:** 68% < 20, 31% 20-39, less than 1% 40-49, less than 1% 50-99, less than 1% >100. **Special facilities:** Observatory, environmental center and nature preserve, science center.

Freshman class profile. 7,076 applied, 1,703 admitted, 492 enrolled.

Mid 50% test scores		GPA 2.0-2.99:	1%
SAT critical reading:	630-730	Rank in top quarter:	84%
SAT math:	610-690	Rank in top tenth:	61%
SAT writing:	620-720	Return as sophomores:	93%
ACT composite:	28-32	Out-of-state:	81%
GPA 3.75 or higher:	68%	Live on campus:	100%
GPA 3.50-3.74:	15%	International:	4%
GPA 3.0-3.49:	16%		

Basis for selection. Secondary school record and personal character most important followed by test scores, class rank, recommendations, essay, talent, activities and interview. Alumni relationship, ethnicity, geographical residence and work experience considered. **Home schooled:** Provide complete curriculum with texts and books used.

High school preparation. College-preparatory program required. 20 units required; 23 recommended. Required and recommended units include English 4, mathematics 4, social studies 3, science 3-4 (laboratory 3), foreign language 3-4 and academic electives 3. 1 fine arts recommended.

2015-2016 Annual costs. Tuition/fees: $49,140. Room/board: $11,890. Books/supplies: $1,900. Personal expenses: $560.

2015-2016 Financial aid. Need-based: 319 full-time freshmen applied for aid; 224 deemed to have need; 224 received aid. Average need met was 100%. Average scholarship/grant was $40,319; average loan $2,602. 88% of total undergraduate aid awarded as scholarships/grants, 12% as loans/jobs. **Non-need-based:** Scholarships awarded for academics, art, minority status, music/drama. **Additional information:** Financial aid incentive guarantees a loan-free education for 25 students with the greatest need who bring the qualities of creativity, community service, and leadership.

Application procedures. Admission: Closing date 1/15 (postmark date). , may be waived for applicants with need, free for online applicants. No application fee. Admission notification by 4/1. Must reply by 5/1. **Financial aid:** Closing date 2/15. FAFSA, CSS PROFILE required. Applicants notified by 4/1; must reply by 5/1.

Academics. Special study options: Accelerated study, combined bachelor's/graduate degree, double major, honors, independent study, internships, semester at sea, student-designed major, study abroad, Washington semester. Departmental senior honors program. **Credit/placement by examination:** AP, CLEP, IB, institutional tests. 3 credit hours maximum toward bachelor's degree. Credit determined for AP, IB or School Articulation Program (SCAP) counts toward 16 units required for graduation. No diversification requirements may be satisfied with AP credit. Maximum of 3 units of Advanced Placement credit is accepted by Kenyon. **Support services:** Study skills assistance, tutoring, writing center.

Majors. Area/ethnic studies: American, Asian, women's. **Biology:** General, biochemistry, molecular, neuroscience. **English:** English lit. **Foreign languages:** General, ancient Greek, classics, French, German, Latin, Spanish. **History:** General. **Math:** General. **Philosophy/religion:** Philosophy, religion. **Physical sciences:** Chemistry, physics. **Psychology:** General. **Social sciences:** Anthropology, economics, political science, sociology. **Visual/performing arts:** Art history/conservation, dance, dramatic, film/cinema/video, music, studio arts.

Most popular majors. Biology 10%, English 14%, foreign language 7%, history 10%, interdisciplinary studies 7%, psychology 9%, social sciences 21%, visual/performing arts 13%.

Technology on campus. 400 workstations in dormitories, library, computer center. Dormitories wired for high-speed internet access and linked to campus network. Commuter students can connect to campus network. Online library, helpline, student web hosting, wireless network available.

Student life. Freshman orientation: Mandatory. Preregistration for classes offered. Held four days prior to start of classes. **Housing:** Guaranteed on-campus for all undergraduates. Coed dorms, single-sex dorms, special housing for disabled, apartments, fraternity/sorority housing, themed housing, wellness housing available. $350 nonrefundable deposit, deadline 5/1. Special accommodations can be made for married, international and disabled students. Fraternity and sorority housing available in room blocks only. Wellness and community service and social group halls on campus available. **Activities:** Bands, campus ministries, choral groups, dance, drama, film society, international student organizations, literary magazine, music ensembles, Model UN, musical theater, opera, radio station, student government, student newspaper, symphony orchestra, Black student union, Saturday Night Fellowship, Hillel, Asian awareness club, community service organization, allied sexual orientations, Amnesty International, political affairs clubs, Circle K.

Athletics. NCAA. **Intercollegiate:** Baseball M, basketball, cross-country, diving, field hockey W, football (tackle) M, golf M, lacrosse, soccer, softball W, swimming, tennis, track and field, volleyball W. **Intramural:** Basketball, football (non-tackle), racquetball, soccer, softball W, squash, tennis, volleyball. **Team name:** Lords/Ladies.

Student services. Alcohol/substance abuse counseling, chaplain/spiritual director, career counseling, student employment services, financial aid counseling, health services, minority student services, personal counseling, placement for graduates, women's services. **Physically disabled:** Services for visually, hearing impaired.

Contact. E-mail: admissions@kenyon.edu
Phone: (740) 427-5776 Toll-free number: (800) 848-2468
Fax: (740) 427-5770
Jennifer Delahunty, Dean of Admissions, Kenyon College, Kenyon College Admissions Office, Ransom Hall, Gambier, OH 43022-9623

Kettering College .
Kettering, Ohio
www.kc.edu   **CB code: 0602**

- Private 4-year health science and nursing college affiliated with the Seventh-day Adventists
- Commuter campus in large city
- 626 degree-seeking undergraduates: 48% part-time, 83% women, 4% African American, 3% Asian American, 3% Hispanic/Latino, 2% Multi-racial, non-Hispanic
- 99 degree-seeking graduate students
- Application essay required
- 68% graduate within 6 years

General. Founded in 1967. Regionally accredited. **Degrees:** 141 bachelor's, 38 associate awarded; master's offered. **Location:** 5 miles from Dayton. **Calendar:** Semester, limited summer session. **Full-time faculty:** 58 total; 60% have terminal degrees, 10% minority, 74% women. **Part-time faculty:** 16 total; 19% have terminal degrees, 19% minority, 81% women. **Class size:** 54% < 20, 34% 20-39, 8% 40-49, 4% 50-99.

Freshman class profile.

GPA 3.75 or higher:	27%	Return as sophomores:	60%
GPA 3.50-3.74:	28%	Out-of-state:	11%
GPA 3.0-3.49:	28%	Live on campus:	33%
GPA 2.0-2.99:	17%	International:	2%
End year in good standing:	88%		

Basis for selection. High school GPA, test scores, academic transcripts, personal statements. Interview required for physician assistant applicants. **Home schooled:** A student who presents a transcript issued by their parent(s) and/or an unaccredited source may be admitted upon presentation of an acceptable test score.

High school preparation. 14 units recommended. Recommended units include English 4, mathematics 2 and science 3. Strong mathematics and science background recommended.

2015-2016 Annual costs. Tuition/fees: $13,680. Room only: $3,800. Books/supplies: $1,530. Personal expenses: $1,604.

Financial aid. Non-need-based: Scholarships awarded for academics.

Application procedures. Admission: No deadline. No application fee. Application must be submitted online. Admission notification on a rolling basis. **Financial aid:** Priority date 3/31; no closing date. FAFSA, institutional form required. Applicants notified on a rolling basis starting 5/15; must reply within 3 week(s) of notification.

Academics. Special study options: Distance learning, double major, honors. **Credit/placement by examination:** AP, CLEP, SAT, ACT, institutional tests. **Support services:** Learning center, reduced course load, study skills assistance, tutoring, writing center.

Majors. Health services: Nursing (RN), predental, premedicine, respiratory therapy technology, sonography.

Technology on campus. 52 workstations in library, computer center. Dormitories wired for high-speed internet access and linked to campus network. Online library, helpline, wireless network available.

Student life. Freshman orientation: Mandatory. Preregistration for classes offered. **Policies:** Religious observance required. **Housing:** Single-sex dorms, wellness housing available. $200 nonrefundable deposit. **Activities:** Campus ministries, religious life organizations.

Athletics. Intramural: Basketball, volleyball.

Student services. Chaplain/spiritual director, financial aid counseling, health services, personal counseling, veterans' counselor.

Contact. E-mail: studentadmissions@kc.edu
Phone: (937) 395-8628 Fax: (937) 395-8338
Katrina Hill, Director of Enrollment Services, Kettering College, 3737 Southern Boulevard, Kettering, OH 45429-1299

Lake Erie College
Painesville, Ohio — CB member
www.lec.edu — CB code: 1391

- Private 4-year liberal arts college
- Residential campus in large town
- 804 degree-seeking undergraduates
- 56% of applicants admitted
- Application essay required

General. Founded in 1856. Regionally accredited. **Degrees:** 156 bachelor's awarded; master's offered. **Location:** 30 miles from Cleveland. **Calendar:** Semester, limited summer session. **Full-time faculty:** 44 total; 75% have terminal degrees, 59% women. **Part-time faculty:** 69 total; 1% have terminal degrees. **Class size:** 66% < 20, 34% 20-39. **Special facilities:** Equestrian center, hall for the fine and performing arts, airport and museum.

Freshman class profile. 1,712 applied, 964 admitted, 214 enrolled.

Mid 50% test scores			
		GPA 3.50-3.74:	11%
SAT critical reading:	440-540	GPA 3.0-3.49:	29%
SAT math:	450-540	GPA 2.0-2.99:	48%
SAT writing:	430-520	Out-of-state:	36%
ACT composite:	19-23	Live on campus:	89%
GPA 3.75 or higher:	11%		

Basis for selection. School achievement record, test scores, essay, reference letters and interview strongly considered. Special consideration of test

scores for some applicants. Interview strongly recommended. **Home schooled:** Statement describing home school structure and mission, transcript of courses and grades, interview, letter of recommendation (nonparent) required. **Learning Disabled:** Documentation of learning disability required.

High school preparation. College-preparatory program recommended. 17 units required. Required units include English 4, mathematics 3, social studies 3, science 3 (laboratory 2) and foreign language 2.

2015-2016 Annual costs. Tuition/fees: $29,162. Room/board: $9,178. Books/supplies: $1,100. Personal expenses: $2,110.

Financial aid. Non-need-based: Scholarships awarded for academics, art, athletics, leadership, music/drama, state residency.

Application procedures. Admission: Priority date 5/1; deadline 8/1. $30 fee, may be waived for applicants with need, free for online applicants. Admission notification on a rolling basis beginning on or about 9/1. Must reply by 8/1. **Financial aid:** No deadline. FAFSA required. Applicants notified on a rolling basis starting 2/15; must reply by 5/1 or within 4 week(s) of notification.

Academics. Special study options: Accelerated study, combined bachelor's/graduate degree, cross-registration, double major, dual enrollment of high school students, honors, independent study, internships, liberal arts/career combination, student-designed major, study abroad, teacher certification program. **Credit/placement by examination:** AP, CLEP, IB, SAT, ACT, institutional tests. 32 credit hours maximum toward bachelor's degree. **Support services:** Learning center, reduced course load, study skills assistance, tutoring, writing center.

Majors. Biology: General. **Business:** Accounting, business admin, entrepreneurial studies, finance, human resources, international, marketing. **Communications:** Persuasive communications. **Education:** Early childhood, secondary, special ed. **English:** English lit. **Foreign languages:** French, German, Italian, Spanish. **History:** General. **Math:** General. **Parks/recreation:** Sports admin, sports studies. **Physical sciences:** Chemistry. **Protective services:** Law enforcement admin. **Psychology:** General. **Social sciences:** General, political science. **Visual/performing arts:** Digital arts.

Most popular majors. Agriculture 10%, business/marketing 35%, communications/journalism 6%, education 17%, psychology 6%.

Technology on campus. 75 workstations in dormitories, library, computer center, student center. Dormitories wired for high-speed internet access and linked to campus network. Online course registration, wireless network available.

Student life. Freshman orientation: Available, $200 fee. Preregistration for classes offered. One-day program during summer; extended three-day orientation for freshmen a week prior to start of classes. **Housing:** Guaranteed on-campus for freshmen. Coed dorms, single-sex dorms, apartments available. $150 fully refundable deposit, deadline 5/1. Residence halls equipped with laundry and kitchen areas available. **Activities:** Choral groups, dance, drama, international student organizations, music ensembles, student government, honor association, academic association, athletic association, foreign language clubs, professional organizations, equestrian clubs, student activities council.

Athletics. NCAA. Intercollegiate: Baseball M, basketball, cross-country, equestrian, football (tackle) M, golf, lacrosse, soccer, softball W, swimming, track and field, volleyball W, wrestling M. **Intramural:** Basketball, football (tackle), soccer, softball, ultimate frisbee, volleyball. **Team name:** Storm.

Student services. Career counseling, student employment services, financial aid counseling, placement for graduates. **Physically disabled:** Services for visually, hearing impaired.

Contact. E-mail: admissions@lec.edu
Phone: (440) 375-7050 Toll-free number: (855) 467-8676
Fax: (440) 375-7005
Steve Lazowski, V.P. for Enrollment Management, Lake Erie College, 391 West Washington Street, Painesville, OH 44077-3389

Lourdes University
Sylvania, Ohio — CB member
www.lourdes.edu — CB code: 1427

- Private 4-year university affiliated with the Roman Catholic Church
- Commuter campus in large town
- 1,666 degree-seeking undergraduates
- 379 graduate students

General. Founded in 1958. Regionally accredited. **Degrees:** 290 bachelor's, 9 associate awarded; master's offered. **ROTC:** Army, Air Force. **Location:** 10 miles from Toledo. **Calendar:** Semester, limited summer session. **Full-time faculty:** 100 total; 59% have terminal degrees, 10% minority, 67% women. **Part-time faculty:** 177 total; 24% have terminal degrees, 7% minority, 62% women. **Class size:** 68% < 20, 32% 20-39. **Special facilities:** Planetarium.

Freshman class profile.

GPA 3.75 or higher:	9%	Rank in top quarter:	27%
GPA 3.50-3.74:	14%	Rank in top tenth:	8%
GPA 3.0-3.49:	26%	Out-of-state:	24%
GPA 2.0-2.99:	46%	Live on campus:	55%

Basis for selection. Academic GPA, test scores very important, interview considered. Conditional admission may be granted at the discretion of the Director of Admissions. **Home schooled:** Transcript of courses and grades required.

High school preparation. College-preparatory program recommended. 17 units recommended. Recommended units include English 4, mathematics 3, social studies 3, science 3, foreign language 2 and visual/performing arts 1. 1 unit Physical Education/Health recommended.

2015-2016 Annual costs. Tuition/fees: $18,970. Room/board: $9,800. Books/supplies: $1,275. Personal expenses: $1,174.

Financial aid. Non-need-based: Scholarships awarded for academics, art, athletics, minority status, religious affiliation, ROTC, state residency.

Application procedures. Admission: Priority date 1/15; no deadline. $25 fee, may be waived for applicants with need, free for online applicants. Admission notification on a rolling basis beginning on or about 2/1. Must reply by 5/1. **Financial aid:** Priority date 3/1; no closing date. FAFSA required. Applicants notified on a rolling basis starting 3/1; must reply within 4 week(s) of notification.

Academics. Special study options: Distance learning, double major, dual enrollment of high school students, independent study, internships, liberal arts/career combination, student-designed major, study abroad, teacher certification program. **Credit/placement by examination:** AP, CLEP, institutional tests. 15 credit hours maximum toward associate degree, 30 toward bachelor's. **Support services:** Learning center, reduced course load, remedial instruction, study skills assistance, tutoring, writing center.

Majors. Biology: General. **Business:** Accounting/finance, business admin, human resources, management science, marketing. **Conservation:** Environmental science. **Education:** Early childhood, middle, secondary. **English:** English lit. **Health services:** Health care admin, nursing (RN). **History:** General. **Human services:** Social work. **Philosophy/religion:** Religion. **Protective services:** Criminal justice. **Psychology:** General. **Social sciences:** Sociology. **Visual/performing arts:** Art, art history/conservation.

Most popular majors. Business/marketing 21%, education 7%, health sciences 38%, interdisciplinary studies 13%.

Technology on campus. 181 workstations in dormitories, library, computer center, student center. Dormitories wired for high-speed internet access and linked to campus network. Commuter students can connect to campus network. Online course registration, online library, helpline, wireless network available.

Student life. Freshman orientation: Mandatory, $250 fee. Preregistration for classes offered. **Housing:** Guaranteed on-campus for freshmen. Coed dorms, apartments available. $100 fully refundable deposit. **Activities:** Pep band, campus ministries, choral groups, dance, drama, literary magazine, student government, Latino student union, LINK.

Athletics. NAIA. **Intercollegiate:** Baseball M, basketball, cheerleading, cross-country, golf, lacrosse, softball W, volleyball. **Intramural:** Basketball, bowling, football (non-tackle), ice hockey, soccer, tennis, track and field, volleyball, wrestling M. **Team name:** Gray Wolves.

Student services. Adult student services, alcohol/substance abuse counseling, chaplain/spiritual director, career counseling, services for economically disadvantaged, financial aid counseling, personal counseling, veterans' counselor. **Physically disabled:** Services for visually, speech, hearing impaired.

Contact. E-mail: AdmissionsLCAdmits@lourdes.edu
Phone: (419) 885-5291 ext. 3680
Toll-free number: (800) 878-3210 ext. 3680 Fax: (419) 824-3916
Amy Houston, Associate Director of Admissions, Lourdes University, 6832 Convent Boulevard, Sylvania, OH 43560-2898

Malone University
Canton, Ohio
www.malone.edu   **CB code: 1439**

- Private 4-year university affiliated with the Evangelical Friends Church-Eastern Region
- Residential campus in small city
- 1,293 degree-seeking undergraduates: 10% part-time, 60% women, 9% African American, 1% Asian American, 2% Hispanic/Latino, 3% Multiracial, non-Hispanic, 1% international
- 355 degree-seeking graduate students
- 69% of applicants admitted
- SAT or ACT (ACT writing optional) required
- 57% graduate within 6 years; 27% enter graduate study

General. Founded in 1892. Regionally accredited. Interdenominational Christian environment. **Degrees:** 393 bachelor's awarded; master's offered. **Location:** 55 miles from Cleveland. **Calendar:** Semester, limited summer session. **Full-time faculty:** 89 total; 76% have terminal degrees, 6% minority, 51% women. **Part-time faculty:** 81 total; 16% have terminal degrees, 5% minority, 58% women. **Class size:** 63% < 20, 31% 20-39, 4% 40-49, 2% 50-99.

Freshman class profile. 1,168 applied, 804 admitted, 245 enrolled.

Mid 50% test scores		GPA 2.0-2.99:	27%
SAT critical reading:	480-560	Rank in top quarter:	42%
SAT math:	460-550	Rank in top tenth:	13%
ACT composite:	19-25	End year in good standing:	92%
GPA 3.75 or higher:	29%	Return as sophomores:	70%
GPA 3.50-3.74:	22%	Out-of-state:	14%
GPA 3.0-3.49:	22%	Live on campus:	86%

Basis for selection. Rigor of high school record, GPA, and test scores most important. Interview considered and encouraged. Audition required for entrance into music programs; portfolio required during first semester for art programs. **Home schooled:** Transcript of courses and grades required. **Learning Disabled:** Students disclosing learning disabilities must interview with Director of Student Accessibility Services.

High school preparation. College-preparatory program required. 18 units required. Required units include English 4, mathematics 3, social studies 2, history 1, science 3 (laboratory 1), foreign language 2, visual/performing arts 1 and academic electives 2.

2015-2016 Annual costs. Tuition/fees: $27,440. Room/board: $9,266.

2015-2016 Financial aid. Need-based: 239 full-time freshmen applied for aid; 224 deemed to have need; 224 received aid. Average need met was 80%. Average scholarship/grant was $20,667; average loan $4,434. 68% of total undergraduate aid awarded as scholarships/grants, 32% as loans/jobs. **Non-need-based:** Awarded to 317 full-time undergraduates, including 65 freshmen. Scholarships awarded for academics, alumni affiliation, athletics, leadership, music/drama, religious affiliation. **Additional information:** Prepayment discounts and employer deferred payments available for students in adult degree-completion programs. Employer deferred payment plan is available for traditional undergraduate students.

Application procedures. Admission: No deadline. $20 fee, may be waived for applicants with need, free for online applicants. Admission notification on a rolling basis beginning on or about 9/1. College Credit Plus enrollment on a part-time basis is allowed. **Financial aid:** Priority date 3/1, closing date 7/31. FAFSA required. Applicants notified on a rolling basis starting 3/1; must reply within 2 week(s) of notification.

Academics. 41-43 hours of general education courses organized under the 3 areas of Foundations of Faith and Learning, Foundational Skills, and Engaging God's World. **Special study options:** Accelerated study, cross-registration, distance learning, double major, dual enrollment of high school students, exchange student, honors, independent study, internships, student-designed major, study abroad, teacher certification program, Washington semester. American Studies Program (Washington, D.C.), Australia Studies Centre (Sydney), China Studies Program (Shanghai), Latin American Studies Program (San Jose, Costa Rica), Middle East Studies Program (Cairo, Egypt), Ugandan Studies Program, Los Angeles Film Studies Center, Contemporary Music Center (Nashville), Daystar University in Kenya. Some co-op credit hours are available (but not an entire program). **Credit/placement by examination:** AP, CLEP, SAT, ACT, institutional tests. 62 credit hours maximum toward bachelor's degree. External credit by exam limit is 20, excluding AP credit for which an additional 30 credits are available. Other credits available by in-house exams. **Support services:** Reduced course load, remedial instruction, study skills assistance, tutoring, writing center.

Majors. Biology: General, zoology. **Business:** Accounting, business admin, finance, marketing. **Communications:** Communications/speech/rhetoric, digital media, public relations. **Communications technology:** Recording arts. **Computer sciences:** Computer science. **Conservation:** Economics. **Education:** Early childhood, English, learning disabled, middle, music, science, social studies. **English:** Creative writing, English lit. **Health services:** Clinical lab science, health care admin, nursing (RN), public health ed. **History:** General. **Human services:** Social work. **Liberal arts:** Arts/sciences. **Math:** General. **Parks/recreation:** Exercise sciences, sports admin. **Philosophy/religion:** Philosophy. **Physical sciences:** Chemistry. **Psychology:** General. **Social sciences:** Political science. **Theology:** Bible, sacred music, theology, youth ministry. **Visual/performing arts:** Art history/conservation, crafts, digital arts, dramatic, film/cinema/video, graphic design, music.

Most popular majors. Business/marketing 26%, education 16%, health sciences 20%, theological studies 7%.

Technology on campus. 304 workstations in dormitories, library, computer center. Dormitories wired for high-speed internet access and linked to campus network. Commuter students can connect to campus network. Online course registration, online library, helpline, student web hosting, wireless network available.

Student life. Freshman orientation: Mandatory. Preregistration for classes offered. Held five days prior to start of semester; some on-campus events, community service, relationship-building activities. **Policies:** Christian institution with conservative campus lifestyle. Full-time students required to live on campus unless 22 or older, holding senior status, married, or commuting from home; exceptions considered. Religious observance required. **Housing:** Single-sex dorms, special housing for disabled, themed housing, wellness housing available. $100 nonrefundable deposit, deadline 8/15. **Activities:** Bands, campus ministries, choral groups, drama, film society, international student organizations, literary magazine, music ensembles, musical theater, opera, student government, student newspaper, Multicultural Student Union, Nurses Christian Fellowship, Spiritual Life Committee, gospel choir, Worldview Forum Council, be:Justice, Students Committed to Outreach for Persons with Exceptionalities, Wellness Council, Fellowship of Christian Athletes.

Athletics. NCAA. **Intercollegiate:** Baseball M, basketball, cheerleading, cross-country, diving, football (tackle) M, golf, soccer, softball W, swimming, track and field, volleyball W. **Intramural:** Basketball, football (non-tackle), sand volleyball, soccer, volleyball. **Team name:** Pioneers.

Student services. Adult student services, chaplain/spiritual director, career counseling, student employment services, financial aid counseling, health services, minority student services, personal counseling, placement for graduates. **Physically disabled:** Services for visually, speech, hearing impaired.

Contact. E-mail: admissions@malone.edu
Phone: (330) 471-8145 Toll-free number: (800) 521-1146
Fax: (330) 471-8149
Linda Kurtz Hoffman, Director of Admissions-Undergraduate and Graduate, Malone University, 2600 Cleveland Avenue NW, Canton, OH 44709-3308

Marietta College

Marietta, Ohio   CB member
www.marietta.edu   CB code: 1444

- Private 4-year liberal arts college
- Residential campus in large town
- 1,215 degree-seeking undergraduates: 3% part-time, 37% women, 6% African American, 1% Asian American, 2% Hispanic/Latino, 3% Multiracial, non-Hispanic, 14% international
- 83 degree-seeking graduate students
- 72% of applicants admitted
- SAT or ACT (ACT writing optional) required
- 66% graduate within 6 years

General. Founded in 1835. Regionally accredited. **Degrees:** 282 bachelor's, 4 associate awarded; master's offered. **Location:** 120 miles from Columbus, 110 miles from Pittsburgh. **Calendar:** Semester, limited summer session. **Full-time faculty:** 105 total; 87% have terminal degrees, 8% minority, 53% women. **Part-time faculty:** 55 total; 20% have terminal degrees, 4% minority, 40% women. **Class size:** 80% < 20, 19% 20-39, less than 1% 40-49, less than 1% 50-99. **Special facilities:** Observatory, center for leadership development, greenhouse, cadaver lab, extensive fossil collection, many historically important documents from the beginning of the old Northwest Territory, planetarium.

Freshman class profile. 2,863 applied, 2,062 admitted, 284 enrolled.

Mid 50% test scores		Rank in top tenth:	30%
SAT critical reading:	480-600	End year in good standing:	85%
SAT math:	470-620	Return as sophomores:	73%
ACT composite:	21-27	Out-of-state:	48%
GPA 3.75 or higher:	31%	Live on campus:	93%
GPA 3.50-3.74:	19%	International:	11%
GPA 3.0-3.49:	28%	Fraternities:	4%
GPA 2.0-2.99:	22%	Sororities:	20%
Rank in top quarter:	56%		

Basis for selection. High school curriculum, GPA, test scores most important. Recommendations and essay important. Interview recommended for all. Portfolio recommended for arts programs. Auditions required for some music programs. **Home schooled:** Statement describing home school structure and mission, transcript of courses and grades, interview required. Chronicle of study required.

High school preparation. College-preparatory program recommended. 16 units required. Required units include English 4, mathematics 3, social studies 2, history 2, science 3 (laboratory 2), foreign language 2 and academic electives 1.

2016-2017 Annual costs. Tuition/fees: $35,330. Room/board: $11,100. Books/supplies: $1,208. Personal expenses: $776.

2015-2016 Financial aid. Need-based: 243 full-time freshmen applied for aid; 216 deemed to have need; 216 received aid. Average need met was 79%. Average scholarship/grant was $19,944; average loan $3,759. 68% of total undergraduate aid awarded as scholarships/grants, 32% as loans/jobs. **Non-need-based:** Awarded to 826 full-time undergraduates, including 227 freshmen. Scholarships awarded for academics, alumni affiliation, art, music/drama. **Additional information:** Auditions/portfolios for art, creative writing, music and theater required for competitive fine art scholarships.

Application procedures. Admission: Priority date 3/1; deadline 5/1 (postmark date). $25 fee, may be waived for applicants with need, free for online applicants. Admission notification on a rolling basis beginning on or about 9/1. Must reply by May 1 or within 2 week(s) if notified thereafter. **Financial aid:** Priority date 2/15; no closing date. FAFSA required. Applicants notified on a rolling basis starting 3/15; must reply by 5/1 or within 2 week(s) of notification.

Academics. Early Alert Program whereby professors can contact the Academic Resource Center to assist those students demonstrating need for additional academic support. **Special study options:** Combined bachelor's/graduate degree, double major, dual enrollment of high school students, ESL, exchange student, honors, independent study, internships, liberal arts/career combination, student-designed major, study abroad, teacher certification program, Washington semester. Leadership program, investigative studies. **Credit/placement by examination:** AP, CLEP, IB, SAT, ACT, institutional tests. 36 credit hours maximum toward bachelor's degree. **Support services:** Learning center, reduced course load, remedial instruction, study skills assistance, tutoring, writing center.

Majors. Area/ethnic studies: Asian. **Biology:** General, biochemistry. **Business:** Accounting, communications, finance, human resources, international, management information systems, marketing. **Communications:** Advertising, broadcast journalism, communications/speech/rhetoric, journalism, organizational, public relations, radio/TV. **Computer sciences:** General, computer science, information systems. **Conservation:** Environmental science, environmental studies. **Education:** General, early childhood, elementary, middle, multi-level teacher, music, secondary. **Engineering:** Petroleum. **English:** English lit. **Foreign languages:** Spanish. **Health services:** Athletic training. **History:** General. **Math:** General. **Parks/recreation:** Sports admin. **Physical sciences:** Chemistry, geology, physics. **Psychology:** General. **Social sciences:** Economics, political science. **Visual/performing arts:** Commercial/advertising art, dramatic, music, studio arts.

Most popular majors. Biology 6%, business/marketing 12%, communications/journalism 9%, engineering/engineering technologies 26%, physical sciences 6%, psychology 6%, social sciences 7%, visual/performing arts 7%.

Technology on campus. 400 workstations in library, computer center, student center. Dormitories wired for high-speed internet access and linked to campus network. Commuter students can connect to campus network. Online library, helpline, wireless network available.

Student life. Freshman orientation: Mandatory, $385 fee. Preregistration for classes offered. Four-and-one-half day program. **Policies:** Student code of conduct, judicial system, no alcohol policy for students under age of 21. **Housing:** Guaranteed on-campus for freshmen. Coed dorms, single-sex dorms, special housing for disabled, apartments, fraternity/sorority housing, themed housing, wellness housing available. $200 fully refundable deposit, deadline 5/1. Special interest theme housing (honors, arts and humanities house) available. **Activities:** Bands, campus ministries, choral groups, dance, drama, international student organizations, literary magazine, music ensembles, Model UN, musical theater, radio station, student government, student newspaper, TV station, InterVarsity Christian Fellowship, Circle K, MC Democrats, MC Republicans, Rotoract, Feminist Rainbow Alliance, VOICE, American International Association, student global AIDS campaign.

Athletics. NCAA. **Intercollegiate:** Baseball M, basketball, cross-country, football (tackle) M, rowing (crew), soccer, softball W, tennis, track and field, volleyball W. **Intramural:** Badminton, basketball, bowling, football (non-tackle), golf, handball, racquetball, soccer, softball, table tennis, tennis, volleyball. **Team name:** Pioneers.

Student services. Adult student services, alcohol/substance abuse counseling, career counseling, student employment services, financial aid counseling, health services, minority student services, personal counseling, placement for graduates. **Physically disabled:** Services for visually, speech, hearing impaired.

Contact. E-mail: admit@marietta.edu
Phone: (740) 376-4600 Toll-free number: (800) 331-7896
Fax: (740) 376-8888
Scott McVicar, Director of Admission, Marietta College, 215 Fifth Street, Marietta, OH 45750-4005

Mercy College of Ohio
Toledo, Ohio
www.mercycollege.edu　　　　　　　　　**CB code: 4685**

▶ Private 4-year health science and nursing college affiliated with the Roman Catholic Church
▶ Commuter campus in large city
▶ 1,239 degree-seeking undergraduates: 63% part-time, 86% women, 9% African American, 1% Asian American, 5% Hispanic/Latino, 4% Multiracial, non-Hispanic
▶ 52% of applicants admitted
▶ 44% graduate within 6 years

General. **Degrees:** 142 bachelor's, 188 associate awarded. **Calendar:** Semester, limited summer session. **Full-time faculty:** 62 total; 24% have terminal degrees, 8% minority, 84% women. **Part-time faculty:** 153 total; 8% have terminal degrees, 7% minority, 84% women. **Class size:** 67% < 20, 28% 20-39, 3% 40-49, 3% 50-99.

Freshman class profile. 254 applied, 132 admitted, 69 enrolled.

GPA 3.75 or higher:	8%	GPA 2.0-2.99:	33%
GPA 3.50-3.74:	20%	Return as sophomores:	53%
GPA 3.0-3.49:	39%	Out-of-state:	25%

Basis for selection. A 2.0 GPA is required for entrance to the general college. Admission to programs of study may have higher GPA and specific course grade requirements. Standardized test scores and rigor of secondary school record is also taken into consideration. SAT or ACT recommended. ACT or SAT required for some programs of study.

High school preparation. College-preparatory program required. 11 units required. Required units include English 3, mathematics 2, social studies 2, science 2 (laboratory 2).

2015-2016 Annual costs. Tuition/fees: $12,530. Books/supplies: $1,660. Personal expenses: $3,490.

2014-2015 Financial aid. **Need-based:** 47% of total undergraduate aid awarded as scholarships/grants, 53% as loans/jobs. **Non-need-based:** Awarded to 12 full-time undergraduates, including 2 freshmen. Scholarships awarded for academics, alumni affiliation, leadership, minority status.

Application procedures. **Admission:** No deadline. $25 fee, may be waived for applicants with need. Admission notification on a rolling basis. Must reply by May 1 or within 2 week(s) if notified thereafter. **Financial aid:** Priority date 3/1; no closing date. FAFSA required. Applicants notified on a rolling basis starting 3/1; must reply within 2 week(s) of notification.

Academics. **Special study options:** Accelerated study, combined bachelor's/graduate degree, distance learning, double major, independent study, internships. **Credit/placement by examination:** AP, CLEP, SAT, ACT, institutional tests. **Support services:** Learning center, reduced course load, remedial instruction, study skills assistance, tutoring, writing center.

Majors. Biology: General. **Health services:** Health care admin, nursing (RN).

Most popular majors. Health sciences 97%.

Technology on campus. 84 workstations in library, computer center, student center. Online course registration, online library, wireless network available.

Student life. **Freshman orientation:** Mandatory. Preregistration for classes offered. **Housing:** Apartments available. $100 fully refundable deposit. **Activities:** Campus ministries, student government, Student Senate, Phi Theta Kappa, National Student Nurses Association, Sigma Theta Tau, College Ambassadors, American Society of Radiologic Technologists.

Student services. Adult student services, alcohol/substance abuse counseling, chaplain/spiritual director, career counseling, services for economically disadvantaged, student employment services, financial aid counseling, personal counseling. **Physically disabled:** Services for visually, speech, hearing impaired.

Contact. E-mail: admissions@mercycollege.edu
Phone: (419) 251-1313 Toll-free number: (888) 806-3729
Fax: (419) 251-1462
Lori Edgeworth, VP of Enrollment Services, Mercy College of Ohio, 2221 Madison Avenue, Toledo, OH 43604

Miami University: Oxford
Oxford, Ohio　　　　　　　　　**CB member**
www.MiamiOH.edu　　　　　　　　　**CB code: 1463**

▶ Public 4-year university
▶ Residential campus in large town
▶ 15,975 degree-seeking undergraduates: 2% part-time, 51% women, 3% African American, 2% Asian American, 4% Hispanic/Latino, 3% Multiracial, non-Hispanic, 10% international
▶ 2,114 degree-seeking graduate students
▶ 65% of applicants admitted
▶ SAT or ACT (ACT writing optional), application essay required
▶ 80% graduate within 6 years

General. Founded in 1809. Regionally accredited. Certificate, associate degree, and bachelor degree programs offered at regional campuses in Hamilton and Middletown. **Degrees:** 4,388 bachelor's, 182 associate awarded; master's, doctoral offered. **ROTC:** Army, Naval, Air Force. **Location:** 35 miles from Cincinnati, 46 miles from Dayton. **Calendar:** Semester, extensive summer session. **Full-time faculty:** 949 total; 86% have terminal degrees, 20% minority, 44% women. **Part-time faculty:** 243 total; 31% have terminal degrees, 8% minority, 45% women. **Class size:** 32% < 20, 51% 20-39, 8% 40-49, 6% 50-99, 4% >100. **Special facilities:** Geology, art, anthropology, zoology museums, herbarium, ecology research center, electron microscope center.

Freshman class profile. 27,454 applied, 17,980 admitted, 3,811 enrolled.

Mid 50% test scores			
SAT critical reading:	550-650	GPA 2.0-2.99:	4%
SAT math:	590-690	Rank in top quarter:	68%
SAT writing:	540-650	Rank in top tenth:	36%
ACT composite:	26-30	Return as sophomores:	90%
GPA 3.75 or higher:	52%	Out-of-state:	39%
GPA 3.50-3.74:	23%	Live on campus:	98%
GPA 3.0-3.49:	21%	International:	8%

Basis for selection. Admission based upon academic performance, test scores, secondary school experience, and recommendations from the high school. Applicants' talents, achievements, and character or personal qualities are also considered. Audition and/or portfolio required for the following majors in the School of Creative Arts: Architecture, Interior Design, Art, Art Education, Graphic Design, Music, Music Education, Music Performance, and Theater. **Home schooled:** Submit a list of educational resources and a curriculum description in addition to transcript.

High school preparation. College-preparatory program required. 16 units recommended. Recommended units include English 4, mathematics 3, social studies 2, history 1, science 3, foreign language 2 and visual/performing arts 1.

2015-2016 Annual costs. Tuition/fees: $14,287; $30,987 out-of-state. Room/board: $11,644. Books/supplies: $1,250. Personal expenses: $1,657.

2014-2015 Financial aid. **Need-based:** 2,522 full-time freshmen applied for aid; 1,421 deemed to have need; 1,388 received aid. Average need met was 60%. Average scholarship/grant was $10,176; average loan $4,318. 66% of total undergraduate aid awarded as scholarships/grants, 34% as loans/jobs. **Non-need-based:** Awarded to 673 full-time undergraduates, including 253 freshmen. Scholarships awarded for academics, art, athletics, leadership, minority status, music/drama, ROTC, state residency. **Additional information:** The Miami Access Initiative guarantees eligible students with scholarships and/or grants that meet or exceed the cost of tuition and academic fees. Academically competitive Ohio residents entering the Miami University Oxford campus as first-time, full-time freshmen in the fall semester and who have a total family income equal to or less than $35,000 will be considered.

Application procedures. Admission: Priority date 12/1; deadline 2/1 (postmark date). $50 fee, may be waived for applicants with need. Admission notification by 3/15. Must reply by 5/1. **Financial aid:** Priority date 2/15; no closing date. FAFSA required. Applicants notified on a rolling basis starting 3/20; must reply by 5/1 or within 3 week(s) of notification.

Academics. Special study options: Combined bachelor's/graduate degree, cooperative education, cross-registration, distance learning, double major, ESL, exchange student, honors, independent study, internships, liberal arts/career combination, semester at sea, student-designed major, study abroad, teacher certification program, Washington semester. Undergraduate associates, undergraduate research program, science and engineering research semester, 3-2 engineering with Case Western Reserve University and Columbia University, 3-2 forestry/environmental studies with Duke University, 3-1 and 4-1 in Clinical Laboratory Science, 3-1 Arts/Professional AB/Professional degree. **Credit/placement by examination:** AP, CLEP, IB, institutional tests. 32 credit hours maximum toward associate degree, 32 toward bachelor's. **Support services:** Learning center, study skills assistance, tutoring, writing center.

Majors. Architecture: Architecture, interior, urban/community planning. **Area/ethnic studies:** African-American, American, East Asian, Italian, Latin American, women's. **Biology:** General, biochemistry, biophysics, botany, microbiology, zoology. **Business:** Accounting, business admin, finance, management information systems, management science, managerial economics, marketing, operations. **Communications:** Digital media, journalism, media studies, public relations. **Computer sciences:** General, information technology. **Conservation:** Environmental science. **Education:** Art, biology, chemistry, early childhood, English, foreign languages, French, German, Latin, mathematics, middle, music, science, social studies, Spanish, special ed. **Engineering:** General, applied physics, biomedical, chemical, computer, electrical, manufacturing, mechanical, software. **English:** Creative writing, English lit, rhetoric/composition, technical writing. **Foreign languages:** Classics, French, German, linguistics, Spanish. **Health services:** Athletic training, audiology/speech pathology, clinical lab science, dietetics, nursing (RN), premedicine. **History:** General. **Human services:** General, social work. **Liberal arts:** Arts/sciences. **Math:** General, statistics. **Parks/recreation:** Exercise sciences, health/fitness, sports admin. **Philosophy/religion:** Philosophy, religion. **Physical sciences:** Chemistry, geology, physics. **Protective services:** Law enforcement admin. **Psychology:** General. **Social sciences:** Anthropology, economics, geography, international relations, political science, sociology. **Visual/performing arts:** Art, art history/conservation, commercial/advertising art, dramatic, music, music performance. **Work/family studies:** Family studies.

Most popular majors. Biology 6%, business/marketing 27%, communications/journalism 7%, education 8%, engineering/engineering technologies 6%, parks/recreation 7%, social sciences 8%.

Technology on campus. 1,200 workstations in dormitories, library, computer center, student center, student center. Dormitories wired for high-speed internet access and linked to campus network. Commuter students can connect to campus network. Online course registration, online library, helpline, repair service, student web hosting, wireless network available.

Student life. Freshman orientation: Mandatory, $95 fee. Preregistration for classes offered. One-and-a-half day program held throughout June. **Policies:** Freshmen not permitted cars on campus. **Housing:** Guaranteed on-campus for freshmen. Coed dorms, single-sex dorms, special housing for disabled, apartments, cooperative housing, fraternity/sorority housing, gender-neutral housing, themed housing, wellness housing available. $425 nonrefundable deposit, deadline 5/1. Special arrangements include sorority suites in residence halls. **Activities:** Bands, campus ministries, choral groups, dance, drama, film society, international student organizations, literary magazine, music ensembles, Model UN, musical theater, opera, radio station, student government, student newspaper, symphony orchestra, TV station, Cru (formerly Campus Crusade for Christ), Hillel: Association of Jewish Students, College Democrats/College Republicans, Asian-American association, Alpha Phi Omega, Black Student Action Association, Oxfam Miami University, Green Oxford.

Athletics. NCAA. **Intercollegiate:** Baseball M, basketball, cross-country, diving, field hockey W, football (tackle) M, golf M, ice hockey M, soccer W, softball W, swimming, tennis W, track and field, volleyball W. **Intramural:** Baseball, basketball, football (non-tackle), ice hockey, racquetball, soccer, softball, tennis, volleyball. **Team name:** RedHawks.

Student services. Alcohol/substance abuse counseling, career counseling, services for economically disadvantaged, student employment services, financial aid counseling, health services, legal services, minority student services,

on-campus daycare, personal counseling, placement for graduates, veterans' counselor, women's services. **Physically disabled:** Services for visually, speech, hearing impaired.

Contact. E-mail: admission@miamioh.edu
Phone: (513) 529-2531 Fax: (513) 529-1550
Ann Larson, Director of Admission, Miami University: Oxford, 301 South Campus Avenue, Oxford, OH 45056

Mount Carmel College of Nursing
Columbus, Ohio   CB member
www.mccn.edu   CB code: 1502

- Private 4-year nursing college affiliated with the Roman Catholic Church
- Very large city
- 897 degree-seeking undergraduates: 30% part-time, 90% women, 7% African American, 2% Asian American, 2% Hispanic/Latino, 2% Multiracial, non-Hispanic
- 164 degree-seeking graduate students
- 83% of applicants admitted
- 71% graduate within 6 years

General. Regionally accredited. **Degrees:** 343 bachelor's awarded; master's, professional offered. **ROTC:** Army, Naval, Air Force. **Location:** Downtown. **Calendar:** Semester, limited summer session. **Full-time faculty:** 49 total; 22% have terminal degrees, 8% minority, 94% women. **Part-time faculty:** 45 total; 11% have terminal degrees, 9% minority, 89% women. **Class size:** 20% < 20, 51% 20-39, 18% 40-49, 9% 50-99, 1% >100.

Freshman class profile. 171 applied, 142 admitted, 95 enrolled.

Mid 50% test scores		Rank in top quarter:	46%
ACT composite:	20-23	Rank in top tenth:	16%
GPA 3.75 or higher:	27%	Return as sophomores:	85%
GPA 3.50-3.74:	20%	Out-of-state:	1%
GPA 3.0-3.49:	51%	Live on campus:	41%
GPA 2.0-2.99:	2%		

Basis for selection. High school record and standardized test score most important. **Home schooled:** Transcript of courses and grades required.

High school preparation. College-preparatory program required. 3 units required. Required units include English 4, mathematics 3, science 3 (laboratory 3), foreign language 2 and visual/performing arts 1.

2015-2016 Annual costs. Tuition/fees: $12,425. Books/supplies: $1,500. Personal expenses: $3,240.

2015-2016 Financial aid. Need-based: 80 full-time freshmen applied for aid; 65 deemed to have need; 59 received aid. Average need met was 38%. Average scholarship/grant was $6,036; average loan $3,378. 39% of total undergraduate aid awarded as scholarships/grants, 61% as loans/jobs. **Non-need-based:** Scholarships awarded for academics.

Application procedures. Admission: Closing date 4/1. $30 fee, may be waived for applicants with need. Admission notification by 10/30. Must reply by 5/1. **Financial aid:** Priority date 3/1; no closing date. FAFSA required. Applicants notified on a rolling basis starting 5/31; must reply within 2 week(s) of notification.

Academics. Special study options: Accelerated study, cross-registration, distance learning, honors. **Credit/placement by examination:** AP, CLEP.

Majors. Health services: Nursing (RN).

Student life. Housing: Coed dorms, apartments available. $200 nonrefundable deposit. **Activities:** Campus ministries, student government.

Contact. E-mail: mccnadmissions@mchs.com
Phone: (614) 234-1085 Toll-free number: (800) 556-6942
Fax: (614) 234-2875
Kim Campbell, Director of Admissions, Mount Carmel College of Nursing, 127 South Davis Avenue, Columbus, OH 43222-1589

Mount St. Joseph University
Cincinnati, Ohio   CB member
www.msj.edu   CB code: 1129

- Private 4-year liberal arts college affiliated with the Roman Catholic Church
- Commuter campus in very large city

- 1,405 degree-seeking undergraduates: 22% part-time, 57% women, 11% African American, 1% Asian American, 1% Hispanic/Latino, 4% Multi-racial, non-Hispanic
- 551 degree-seeking graduate students
- 85% of applicants admitted
- SAT or ACT (ACT writing recommended) required
- 54% graduate within 6 years; 28% enter graduate study

General. Founded in 1920. Regionally accredited. **Degrees:** 321 bachelor's, 6 associate awarded; master's, doctoral offered. **ROTC:** Army, Air Force. **Location:** 7 miles from downtown. **Calendar:** Semester, extensive summer session. **Full-time faculty:** 103 total; 59% have terminal degrees, 4% minority, 62% women. **Part-time faculty:** 115 total; 22% have terminal degrees, 2% minority, 80% women. **Class size:** 56% < 20, 37% 20-39, 7% 40-49. **Special facilities:** Flats gallery.

Freshman class profile. 1,345 applied, 1,138 admitted, 330 enrolled.

Mid 50% test scores			
SAT critical reading:	430-530	GPA 2.0-2.99:	25%
SAT math:	430-530	Rank in top quarter:	36%
ACT composite:	19-24	Rank in top tenth:	9%
GPA 3.75 or higher:	25%	Return as sophomores:	71%
GPA 3.50-3.74:	20%	Out-of-state:	20%
GPA 3.0-3.49:	29%	Live on campus:	57%

Basis for selection. Criteria for admission include college prep high school curriculum, strong GPA, standardized test scores, evidence of leadership and extracurricular involvement, and personal background. Essays, recommendations and interviews may be required for some students. Audition required for music programs. Portfolio recommended for art programs. **Home schooled:** Letter of recommendation (nonparent) required. Transcripts required along with any documentation from state or national home schooling accreditation agency. Description of completed courses required.

High school preparation. College-preparatory program recommended. 19 units required; 21 recommended. Required and recommended units include English 4, mathematics 3-4, social studies 3, history 3, science 3-4 (laboratory 1-2), foreign language 2, visual/performing arts 1 and academic electives 1. May substitute 2 additional credits from other subjects in place of foreign language.

2015-2016 Annual costs. Tuition/fees: $27,500. Room/board: $8,810. Books/supplies: $1,000. Personal expenses: $600.

2015-2016 Financial aid. Need-based: 316 full-time freshmen applied for aid; 284 deemed to have need; 284 received aid. Average need met was 83%. Average scholarship/grant was $18,454; average loan $3,915. 68% of total undergraduate aid awarded as scholarships/grants, 32% as loans/jobs. **Non-need-based:** Awarded to 322 full-time undergraduates, including 80 freshmen. Scholarships awarded for academics, alumni affiliation, art, leadership, music/drama, ROTC, state residency.

Application procedures. Admission: Priority date 4/1; deadline 8/1 (postmark date). $25 fee, may be waived for applicants with need. Admission notification on a rolling basis beginning on or about 10/1. Must reply by May 1 or within 4 week(s) if notified thereafter. **Financial aid:** Priority date 3/1; no closing date. FAFSA required. Applicants notified on a rolling basis starting 1/31; must reply by 5/1 or within 4 week(s) of notification.

Academics. Special study options: Accelerated study, combined bachelor's/graduate degree, cooperative education, cross-registration, distance learning, double major, dual enrollment of high school students, honors, independent study, internships, liberal arts/career combination, study abroad, teacher certification program. **Credit/placement by examination:** AP, CLEP, IB, SAT, ACT, institutional tests. 32 credit hours maximum toward associate degree, 64 toward bachelor's. **Support services:** Learning center, reduced course load, remedial instruction, study skills assistance, tutoring, writing center.

Majors. Biology: General, biochemistry, neuroscience. **Business:** Accounting, business admin, organizational behavior. **Communications:** General. **Computer sciences:** Informatics. **Education:** Art, early childhood, middle, special ed. **English:** English lit. **Health services:** Athletic training, medical informatics, nursing (RN). **History:** General. **Human services:** Social work. **Liberal arts:** Arts/sciences. **Math:** General. **Parks/recreation:** Sports admin. **Philosophy/religion:** Religion. **Physical sciences:** Chemistry. **Psychology:** General. **Social sciences:** Criminology, sociology. **Theology:** Religious ed. **Visual/performing arts:** Art, design, graphic design, music, studio arts.

Most popular majors. Business/marketing 19%, education 7%, health sciences 19%, liberal arts 9%, parks/recreation 9%, visual/performing arts 9%.

Technology on campus. 190 workstations in library, computer center, student center. Commuter students can connect to campus network. Online course registration, online library, helpline, repair service, student web hosting, wireless network available.

Student life. Freshman orientation: Mandatory, $150 fee. Preregistration for classes offered. Two-part orientation: summer session, which includes a two-day, one-night stay in dorms, and welcome weekend consisting of service learning event and river cruise over the weekend before start of classes. **Policies:** Smoke-free campus. All unmarried freshmen and sophomores under age 21 who live outside 35-mile radius of college required to live on campus and participate in meal program. **Housing:** Guaranteed on-campus for freshmen. Coed dorms, special housing for disabled available. $100 fully refundable deposit, deadline 8/15. **Activities:** Bands, campus ministries, choral groups, dance, drama, international student organizations, literary magazine, music ensembles, musical theater, student government, student newspaper, Active Minds, Japanese cultural appreciation club, Black Student Union, Lions for Life, Habitat for Humanity, Mount Gaming League, Mount birding club, drama club, The Excel Crew, Veterans in Communities (VIC).

Athletics. NCAA. **Intercollegiate:** Baseball M, basketball, cheerleading W, cross-country, football (tackle) M, golf, lacrosse, soccer, softball W, tennis, track and field, volleyball, wrestling M. **Intramural:** Basketball, football (non-tackle), handball, racquetball, soccer, softball, tennis, volleyball. **Team name:** Lions.

Student services. Adult student services, alcohol/substance abuse counseling, chaplain/spiritual director, career counseling, services for economically disadvantaged, student employment services, financial aid counseling, health services, minority student services, on-campus daycare, personal counseling, placement for graduates, veterans' counselor, women's services. **Physically disabled:** Services for visually, speech, hearing impaired.

Contact. E-mail: admissions@msj.edu
Phone: (513) 244-4531 Toll-free number: (800) 654-9314
Fax: (513) 244-4629
Peggy Minnich, Director of Admission, Mount St. Joseph University, 5701 Delhi Road, Cincinnati, OH 45233-1670

Mount Vernon Nazarene University
Mount Vernon, Ohio — CB member
www.mvnu.edu — CB code: 1531

- Private 4-year university affiliated with the Church of the Nazarene
- Residential campus in large town
- 1,697 degree-seeking undergraduates: 15% part-time, 62% women, 5% African American, 2% Hispanic/Latino, 2% Multi-racial, non-Hispanic, 1% international
- 339 degree-seeking graduate students
- 78% of applicants admitted
- SAT or ACT (ACT writing optional), application essay required
- 59% graduate within 6 years; 4% enter graduate study

General. Founded in 1964. Regionally accredited. **Degrees:** 528 bachelor's, 9 associate awarded; master's offered. **Location:** 45 miles from Columbus. **Calendar:** Semester, limited summer session. **Full-time faculty:** 61 total; 74% have terminal degrees, 3% minority, 38% women. **Part-time faculty:** 181 total; 24% have terminal degrees, 2% minority, 52% women. **Class size:** 71% < 20, 22% 20-39, 4% 40-49, 3% 50-99. **Special facilities:** Weather station.

Freshman class profile. 1,059 applied, 822 admitted, 358 enrolled.

Mid 50% test scores			
SAT critical reading:	450-550	GPA 2.0-2.99:	21%
SAT math:	460-580	Rank in top quarter:	30%
ACT composite:	20-25	Rank in top tenth:	15%
GPA 3.75 or higher:	29%	Return as sophomores:	80%
GPA 3.50-3.74:	19%	Out-of-state:	10%
GPA 3.0-3.49:	30%	Live on campus:	92%
		International:	1%

Basis for selection. High school record, ACT or SAT scores, recommendations important. Interview recommended. **Home schooled:** Transcript of courses and grades, letter of recommendation (nonparent) required. Family members cannot complete either academic or character references. Employer can complete academic reference. Students who participate in accredited program must provide transcript from accrediting agency; otherwise, must provide a list of classes completed.

High school preparation. College-preparatory program recommended. 21 units recommended. Required and recommended units include English 4, mathematics 4, social studies 3, science 3 (laboratory 3), foreign language 2-3, visual/performing arts 1 and academic electives 2. 1 health and physical education.

2016-2017 Annual costs. Tuition/fees (projected): $26,950. Room/board: $7,550. Books/supplies: $1,400. Personal expenses: $2,416.

2015-2016 Financial aid. Need-based: 340 full-time freshmen applied for aid; 303 deemed to have need; 297 received aid. Average need met was 69%. Average scholarship/grant was $20,801; average loan $2,526. 44% of total undergraduate aid awarded as scholarships/grants, 56% as loans/jobs. **Non-need-based:** Scholarships awarded for academics, art, athletics, minority status, music/drama, religious affiliation, state residency. **Additional information:** Transfer students are not awarded the same amount of academic scholarship.

Application procedures. Admission: Priority date 3/15; deadline 7/15 (receipt date). $25 fee, may be waived for applicants with need. Admission notification on a rolling basis beginning on or about 9/1. **Financial aid:** Priority date 3/1; no closing date. FAFSA required. Applicants notified on a rolling basis starting 3/4.

Academics. Special study options: Combined bachelor's/graduate degree, cooperative education, cross-registration, distance learning, double major, dual enrollment of high school students, honors, independent study, internships, liberal arts/career combination, New York semester, study abroad, teacher certification program, Washington semester. Cooperative preoccupational therapy/physical therapy/physician's assistant programs with Chatham College, and articulation agreements with Zane State College, Central Ohio Technical College, Logan College of Chiropractic, Columbus State Community College, Marion Technical College, and North Central State College. Opportunities for service learning or mission trips in one of the following: Germany, Hungary, Venezuela, Costa Rica, Nicaragua, Belize, Benin, Romania, or several out-of-state US locations. **Credit/placement by examination:** AP, CLEP, IB, SAT, ACT, institutional tests. 30 credit hours maximum toward bachelor's degree. **Support services:** Learning center, pre-admission summer program, remedial instruction, study skills assistance, tutoring, writing center.

Majors. Biology: General. **Business:** Accounting, business admin, finance, international, management information systems, marketing. **Communications:** Broadcast journalism, communications/speech/rhetoric, journalism, public relations. **Computer sciences:** General, networking. **Education:** General, art, biology, business, chemistry, early childhood, English, family/consumer sciences, health, history, mathematics, middle, music, physical, physics, science, social studies, Spanish, special ed. **English:** English lit. **Foreign languages:** Spanish. **Health services:** Clinical lab science, communication disorders, nursing (RN). **History:** General. **Human services:** Social work. **Math:** General. **Parks/recreation:** Exercise sciences, health/fitness, sports admin. **Philosophy/religion:** Philosophy, religion. **Physical sciences:** General, chemistry, physics. **Protective services:** Criminal justice, law enforcement admin. **Psychology:** General. **Social sciences:** Political science, sociology. **Theology:** Bible, missionary, pastoral counseling, religious ed, sacred music, theology, youth ministry. **Visual/performing arts:** Art, dramatic, graphic design, music, music performance. **Work/family studies:** General.

Most popular majors. Business/marketing 33%, education 11%, health sciences 7%, public administration/social services 15%.

Technology on campus. 209 workstations in dormitories, library, computer center, student center. Dormitories wired for high-speed internet access and linked to campus network. Commuter students can connect to campus network. Online library, helpline, wireless network available.

Student life. Freshman orientation: Mandatory. Preregistration for classes offered. Sessions held in June and July. **Policies:** Students expected to comply with university's published lifestyle guidelines. Religious observance required. **Housing:** Guaranteed on-campus for freshmen. Single-sex dorms, special housing for disabled, apartments, wellness housing available. $150 fully refundable deposit, deadline 5/1. **Activities:** Bands, campus ministries, choral groups, drama, international student organizations, literary magazine, music ensembles, musical theater, radio station, student government, student newspaper, Enactus, Fellowship of Christian Athletes, Young Republicans club, Young Democratic club, men's association, women's association, computing machinery association, American Sign Language club, Students with Concern, Mandate.

Athletics. NAIA. **Intercollegiate:** Baseball M, basketball, cross-country, golf, soccer, softball W, track and field, volleyball W. **Intramural:** Basketball, bowling, football (non-tackle), soccer, softball, ultimate frisbee, volleyball. **Team name:** Cougars.

Student services. Adult student services, alcohol/substance abuse counseling, chaplain/spiritual director, career counseling, student employment services, financial aid counseling, health services, minority student services, personal counseling, placement for graduates. **Physically disabled:** Services for visually, speech, hearing impaired.

Contact. E-mail: admissions@mvnu.edu
Phone: (740) 392-6868 ext. 4510 Toll-free number: (866) 462-6868
Fax: (740) 393-0511
Tracy Waal, Director of Admissions, Mount Vernon Nazarene University, 800 Martinsburg Road, Mount Vernon, OH 43050

Muskingum University

New Concord, Ohio   **CB member**
www.muskingum.edu   **CB code: 1496**

- Private 4-year university and liberal arts college affiliated with the Presbyterian Church (USA)
- Residential campus in small town
- 1,580 degree-seeking undergraduates: 12% part-time, 55% women, 5% African American, 1% Asian American, 2% Hispanic/Latino, 3% Multiracial, non-Hispanic, 3% international
- 225 degree-seeking graduate students
- 74% of applicants admitted
- SAT or ACT (ACT writing optional) required
- 52% graduate within 6 years; 22% enter graduate study

General. Founded in 1837. Regionally accredited. **Degrees:** 350 bachelor's awarded; master's offered. **Location:** 70 miles from Columbus, 125 miles from Pittsburgh. **Calendar:** Semester, extensive summer session. **Full-time faculty:** 92 total; 96% have terminal degrees, 12% minority, 45% women. **Part-time faculty:** 87 total; 17% have terminal degrees, 3% minority, 63% women. **Class size:** 72% < 20, 27% 20-39, less than 1% 40-49, less than 1% 50-99. **Special facilities:** Biology field station, conservation facility.

Freshman class profile. 1,977 applied, 1,461 admitted, 360 enrolled.

Mid 50% test scores		Rank in top quarter:	33%
SAT critical reading:	400-550	Rank in top tenth:	12%
SAT math:	400-520	End year in good standing:	77%
SAT writing:	380-480	Return as sophomores:	74%
ACT composite:	18-24	Out-of-state:	9%
GPA 3.75 or higher:	14%	Live on campus:	85%
GPA 3.50-3.74:	15%	International:	2%
GPA 3.0-3.49:	31%	Fraternities:	7%
GPA 2.0-2.99:	37%	Sororities:	20%

Basis for selection. School achievement record most important. Strength of curriculum, standardized test scores, recommendations, extracurricular activities, interview considered. Special consideration to children of alumni. Essay and interview recommended for all; audition recommended for music programs; portfolio recommended for art programs. **Home schooled:** Transcript of courses and grades, state high school equivalency certificate required. Portfolio of curriculum; statement of compliance with state truancy laws in cases where state certificate is not issued. **Learning Disabled:** PLUS Program available for students with learning differences. Students must indicate interest in program when applying for admission, and must submit psychoeducational evaluations to complete application process. Preferred application filing date of March 1.

High school preparation. College-preparatory program required. 12 units required; 15 recommended. Required and recommended units include English 4, mathematics 2-3, social studies 2-3, science 2-3 (laboratory 2) and foreign language 2-3.

2015-2016 Annual costs. Tuition/fees: $26,082. Room/board: $10,190. Books/supplies: $1,100. Personal expenses: $900.

Financial aid. Non-need-based: Scholarships awarded for academics, alumni affiliation, art, leadership, minority status, music/drama, religious affiliation, state residency. **Additional information:** Scholarship priority date February 1.

Application procedures. Admission: Closing date 8/1 (receipt date). No application fee. Admission notification on a rolling basis beginning on or about 10/1. Must reply by May 1 or within 2 week(s) if notified thereafter. **Financial aid:** Priority date 3/1; no closing date. FAFSA required. Applicants notified on a rolling basis starting 3/1; must reply by 5/1 or within 2 week(s) of notification.

Academics. Special study options: Accelerated study, distance learning, double major, dual enrollment of high school students, ESL, exchange student, honors, independent study, internships, liberal arts/career combination, student-designed major, study abroad, teacher certification program, United Nations semester, Washington semester, weekend college. **Credit/placement by examination:** AP, CLEP, IB, SAT, ACT, institutional tests. **Support services:** Learning center, pre-admission summer program, reduced course load, study skills assistance, tutoring, writing center.

Majors. Biology: General, conservation, molecular, neuroscience. **Business:** Accounting, business admin, international, managerial economics, marketing. **Communications:** Communications/speech/rhetoric, digital media, journalism. **Computer sciences:** General, computer science, information systems. **Conservation:** Environmental science. **Education:** Early childhood, elementary, middle, secondary, special ed. **Engineering:** General, engineering science. **English:** English lit. **Foreign languages:** French, German, Spanish. **Health services:** General, clinical lab technology, community health services, health care admin, nursing (RN), predental, premedicine, prepharmacy, prephysical therapy, preveterinary, speech pathology. **History:** General. **Human services:** General. **Liberal arts:** Humanities. **Math:** General. **Parks/recreation:** Health/fitness, sports admin. **Philosophy/religion:** Philosophy, religion. **Physical sciences:** Chemistry, geology, physics, planetary. **Protective services:** Police science. **Psychology:** General. **Social sciences:** Anthropology, economics, international relations, political science, sociology. **Theology:** Religious ed. **Visual/performing arts:** Art, dramatic, music. **Work/family studies:** General.

Most popular majors. Business/marketing 19%, communications/journalism 7%, education 14%, health sciences 18%, psychology 9%, security/protective services 6%.

Technology on campus. 223 workstations in dormitories, library, computer center, student center. Dormitories wired for high-speed internet access and linked to campus network. Commuter students can connect to campus network. Online course registration, online library, helpline, repair service, student web hosting, wireless network available.

Student life. Freshman orientation: Available. Preregistration for classes offered. Five one-day sessions held on weekdays in June. **Housing:** Guaranteed on-campus for freshmen. Coed dorms, single-sex dorms, apartments, fraternity/sorority housing, themed housing, wellness housing available. $200 fully refundable deposit, deadline 5/1. **Activities:** Bands, campus ministries, choral groups, dance, drama, international student organizations, literary magazine, music ensembles, Model UN, musical theater, radio station, student government, student newspaper, symphony orchestra, TV station, Christian Fellowship, Fellowship of Christian Athletes, political awareness program, SADD, Habitat for Humanity, Young Democrats, Young Republicans, Animal Rights and Environmental Awareness.

Athletics. NCAA. **Intercollegiate:** Baseball M, basketball, cheerleading, cross-country, football (tackle) M, golf, lacrosse, soccer, softball W, tennis, track and field, volleyball W, wrestling M. **Intramural:** Basketball, bowling, cross-country, football (non-tackle), golf, lacrosse, racquetball, rugby, soccer, softball, table tennis M, tennis, track and field, volleyball, wrestling M. **Team name:** Muskies.

Student services. Adult student services, alcohol/substance abuse counseling, chaplain/spiritual director, career counseling, student employment services, financial aid counseling, health services, minority student services, on-campus daycare, personal counseling, placement for graduates, veterans' counselor. **Physically disabled:** Services for visually, hearing impaired.

Contact. E-mail: adminfo@muskingum.edu
Phone: (740) 826-8137 Toll-free number: (800) 752-6082
Fax: (740) 826-8100
Beth DaLonzo, Senior Director of Admissions and Student Financial Services, Muskingum University, 163 Stormont Street, New Concord, OH 43762-1199

Notre Dame College
Cleveland, Ohio
www.notredamecollege.edu

CB member
CB code: 1566

▶ Private 4-year nursing and liberal arts college affiliated with the Roman Catholic Church
▶ Residential campus in large town
▶ 1,792 degree-seeking undergraduates
▶ SAT or ACT (ACT writing optional), application essay required

General. Founded in 1922. Regionally accredited. **Degrees:** 278 bachelor's awarded; master's offered. **ROTC:** Army. **Location:** 10 miles from downtown Cleveland. **Calendar:** Semester, limited summer session. **Full-time faculty:** 57 total. **Part-time faculty:** 165 total. **Class size:** 55% < 20, 45% 20-39, less than 1% 40-49, less than 1% 50-99.

Freshman class profile.

GPA 3.75 or higher:	10%	Rank in top quarter:	23%
GPA 3.50-3.74:	9%	Rank in top tenth:	4%
GPA 3.0-3.49:	31%	Out-of-state:	9%
GPA 2.0-2.99:	46%	Live on campus:	84%

Basis for selection. School achievement record and test scores most important. Applicants should be in top half of class and have 2.5 high school GPA for unconditional admission. Extracurricular activities also considered. Interview recommended.

High school preparation. College-preparatory program recommended. Recommended units include English 4, mathematics 3, social studies 2, history 1, science 3 (laboratory 3) and foreign language 3.

2015-2016 Annual costs. Tuition/fees: $27,520. Room/board: $9,180. Books/supplies: $2,258. Personal expenses: $1,351.

Financial aid. Non-need-based: Scholarships awarded for academics, athletics, state residency.

Application procedures. Admission: No deadline. No application fee. Admission notification on a rolling basis. **Financial aid:** Closing date 5/1. FAFSA required. Applicants notified on a rolling basis starting 1/1; must reply within 2 week(s) of notification.

Academics. Special study options: Cooperative education, cross-registration, distance learning, double major, dual enrollment of high school students, exchange student, honors, independent study, internships, liberal arts/career combination, student-designed major, study abroad, teacher certification program. **Credit/placement by examination:** AP, CLEP, SAT, ACT, institutional tests. **Support services:** Learning center, reduced course load, remedial instruction, study skills assistance, tutoring, writing center.

Honors college/program. Students are selected on the basis of ACT/SAT scores and high school GPA placing them in the top 5% of the entering freshman class.

Majors. Biology: General, biochemistry, environmental. **Business:** Accounting, business admin, human resources, international, management information systems, marketing. **Communications:** Communications/speech/rhetoric, digital media, public relations. **Communications technology:** Graphics. **Education:** Early childhood, elementary, secondary. **English:** English lit. **Health services:** Nursing (RN), prenursing. **History:** General. **Math:** General. **Physical sciences:** Chemistry. **Psychology:** General. **Social sciences:** Criminology, political science. **Theology:** Theology. **Visual/performing arts:** General, graphic design, studio arts.

Most popular majors. Business/marketing 36%, education 22%, health sciences 15%.

Technology on campus. 100 workstations in dormitories, library, computer center. Dormitories wired for high-speed internet access. Wireless network available.

Student life. Freshman orientation: Mandatory, $100 fee. Preregistration for classes offered. One-day program held from May through July. **Housing:** Coed dorms, single-sex dorms, wellness housing available. $200 fully refundable deposit, deadline 5/1. **Activities:** Bands, campus ministries, choral groups, drama, literary magazine, music ensembles, musical theater, student government, student newspaper, campus ministry board, Black Scholars, multicultural student advisory board, St. Julie Scholars, psychology council, science and business clubs, Achievement in Research and Scholarship.

Athletics. NCAA. **Intercollegiate:** Baseball M, basketball, cross-country, diving, football (tackle) M, golf, lacrosse W, soccer, softball W, swimming, track and field, volleyball W, water polo, wrestling M. **Intramural:** Water polo. **Team name:** Falcons.

Student services. Adult student services, alcohol/substance abuse counseling, chaplain/spiritual director, career counseling, student employment services, financial aid counseling, health services, personal counseling, placement for graduates, veterans' counselor.

Contact. E-mail: admissions@ndc.edu
Phone: (216) 373-5355 Toll-free number: (877) 632-6446 ext. 5355
Fax: (216) 381-3802
Beth Ford, Dean of Admissions, Notre Dame College, 4545 College Road, Cleveland, OH 44121-4293

Oberlin College
Oberlin, Ohio
www.oberlin.edu

CB member
CB code: 1587

▶ Private 4-year music and liberal arts college
▶ Residential campus in small town
▶ 2,912 degree-seeking undergraduates: 1% part-time, 56% women, 5% African American, 4% Asian American, 8% Hispanic/Latino, 6% Multiracial, non-Hispanic, 8% international
▶ 17 degree-seeking graduate students
▶ 29% of applicants admitted
▶ SAT or ACT (ACT writing optional), application essay required
▶ 88% graduate within 6 years

General. Founded in 1833. Regionally accredited. **Degrees:** 712 bachelor's awarded; master's offered. **Location:** 35 miles from Cleveland, OH. **Calendar:** 4-1-4. **Full-time faculty:** 336 total. **Part-time faculty:** 36 total. **Class size:** 77% < 20, 19% 20-39, 2% 40-49, 1% 50-99, less than 1% >100. **Special facilities:** Observatory, art museum, environmental studies building, arboretum.

Freshman class profile. 7,815 applied, 2,249 admitted, 778 enrolled.

Mid 50% test scores		GPA 2.0-2.99:	4%
SAT critical reading:	640-740	Rank in top quarter:	85%
SAT math:	620-710	Rank in top tenth:	61%
SAT writing:	630-730	Return as sophomores:	92%
ACT composite:	29-32	Out-of-state:	96%
GPA 3.75 or higher:	36%	Live on campus:	100%
GPA 3.50-3.74:	29%	International:	9%
GPA 3.0-3.49:	31%		

Basis for selection. GED not accepted. For college of arts and sciences: school achievement record, test scores, school and community leadership activities, recommendations, and interview important. Special consideration to applicants from minority and first generation college families and to foreign applicants. For conservatory: audition most important factor; admission highly selective. Interview required for early admission and home schooled candidates; recommended for all others. Audition required of applicants to conservatory; essay required of applicants to college of arts and sciences. **Home schooled:** Interview, letter of recommendation (nonparent) required. SAT Subject Tests, interview, and detailed portfolio also required. Students who do not submit ACT scores must submit scores from the SAT I and two SAT II subject exams.

High school preparation. College-preparatory program required. Required and recommended units include English 4, mathematics 3-4, social studies 3, science 3-4 and foreign language 3.

2015-2016 Annual costs. Tuition/fees: $50,594. Room/board: $13,630. Books/supplies: $930. Personal expenses: $978.

2015-2016 Financial aid. Need-based: 460 full-time freshmen applied for aid; 388 deemed to have need; 388 received aid. Average need met was 100%. Average scholarship/grant was $33,033; average loan $3,154. 82% of total undergraduate aid awarded as scholarships/grants, 18% as loans/jobs. **Non-need-based:** Awarded to 2,107 full-time undergraduates, including 616 freshmen. Scholarships awarded for academics, music/drama.

Application procedures. Admission: Closing date 1/15 (postmark date). No application fee. Application must be submitted online. Admission notification by 4/1. Must reply by May 1 or within 2 week(s) if notified thereafter. 12/1 application closing date for Conservatory of Music with $100 application fee. 1/15 application closing date for College of Arts and Sciences, Regular Decision. No application fee. **Financial aid:** Closing date 2/1. FAFSA, institutional form, CSS PROFILE required. Applicants notified by 4/1; must reply by 5/1 or within 2 week(s) of notification.

Academics. No core, but a curriculum exploration requirement: two academic courses in each of the 3 divisions of the college (Arts and Humanities, Social Sciences, and Math and Natural Science), plus 2 courses outside their major division. Students must also complete 3 Winter Term projects, 2 writing courses, 2 quantitative and formal reasoning courses, and 3 courses related to cultural diversity. **Special study options:** Combined bachelor's/graduate degree, double major, ESL, honors, independent study, internships, New York semester, student-designed major, study abroad, teacher certification program. 5-year dual degree program with music conservatory and liberal arts college, 3-2 engineering with affiliations at Case Western Reserve University, Columbia University, Cal Poly, and Washington University in St. Louis. Many departments and programs offer Honors Programs to students of proven ability and independence. Students wishing to enter the Honors Program should consult the chairperson of their major department no later than the beginning of the second semester of the junior year. **Credit/placement by examination:** AP, CLEP, IB, institutional tests. 20 credit hours maximum toward bachelor's degree. Individual departments in which AP/IB credit is being requested decide standards and grant credit, within the overall limit of five full courses/20 credits. **Support services:** Learning center, reduced course load, remedial instruction, study skills assistance, tutoring, writing center.

Majors. Area/ethnic studies: African, African-American, American, East Asian, Latin American, Russian/Slavic, women's. **Biology:** General, biochemistry, neuroscience. **Computer sciences:** General. **Conservation:** Environmental studies. **English:** Creative writing, English lit. **Foreign languages:** Ancient Greek, classics, comparative lit, French, German, Latin, Russian, Spanish. **Health services:** Predental, premedicine, preveterinary. **History:** General. **Math:** General. **Philosophy/religion:** Judaic, philosophy, religion. **Psychology:** General. **Social sciences:** Anthropology, economics, political science, sociology. **Visual/performing arts:** Art history/conservation, conducting, dance, dramatic, film/cinema/video, jazz, music, music history, music theory/composition, piano/keyboard, stringed instruments, studio arts, voice/opera.

Most popular majors. Area/ethnic studies 6%, biology 14%, English 10%, social sciences 19%, visual/performing arts 13%.

Technology on campus. 340 workstations in dormitories, library, computer center. Dormitories wired for high-speed internet access and linked to campus network. Commuter students can connect to campus network. Online course registration, online library, helpline, repair service, student web hosting, wireless network available.

Student life. Freshman orientation: Mandatory. Preregistration for classes offered. Held week prior to fall classes. Includes day of service. **Policies:** Students agree to follow honor code. **Housing:** Guaranteed on-campus for all undergraduates. Coed dorms, single-sex dorms, special housing for disabled, apartments, cooperative housing, gender-neutral housing, themed housing, wellness housing available. **Activities:** Bands, campus ministries, choral groups, dance, drama, film society, international student organizations, literary magazine, music ensembles, musical theater, opera, radio station, student government, student newspaper, symphony orchestra, religious organizations, political organizations, inter-cultural organizations, ethnic organizations, social service club, LGBT club.

Athletics. NCAA. **Intercollegiate:** Baseball M, basketball, cross-country, diving, field hockey W, football (tackle) M, lacrosse, soccer, softball W, swimming, tennis, track and field, volleyball W. **Intramural:** Baseball M, basketball, bowling, football (non-tackle), handball, racquetball, rugby M, skin diving, soccer, softball, squash, table tennis, tennis, track and field, volleyball, weight lifting. **Team name:** Yeomen & Yeowomen.

Student services. Alcohol/substance abuse counseling, chaplain/spiritual director, career counseling, services for economically disadvantaged, student employment services, financial aid counseling, health services, minority student services, personal counseling, placement for graduates, women's services. **Physically disabled:** Services for visually, speech, hearing impaired.

Contact. E-mail: college.admissions@oberlin.edu
Phone: (440) 775-8411 Toll-free number: (800) 622-6243
Fax: (440) 775-6905
Debra Chermonte, Vice President and Dean of Admissions and Financial Aid, Oberlin College, Carnegie Building, 101 North Professor Street, Oberlin, OH 44074-1075

Ohio Christian University
Circleville, Ohio
www.ohiochristian.edu   **CB code: 1088**

- Private 4-year university and Bible college affiliated with the Church of Christ
- Residential campus in large town
- 3,306 degree-seeking undergraduates
- 65% of applicants admitted
- SAT or ACT (ACT writing optional), application essay required

General. Founded in 1948. Regionally accredited; also accredited by ABHE. **Degrees:** 305 bachelor's, 175 associate awarded; master's offered. **ROTC:** Air Force. **Location:** 30 miles from Columbus. **Calendar:** Semester, limited summer session. **Full-time faculty:** 154 total; 23% have terminal degrees. **Part-time faculty:** 248 total; 11% have terminal degrees. **Class size:** 93% < 20, 5% 20-39, less than 1% 40-49, less than 1% 50-99, less than 1% >100.

Freshman class profile. 844 applied, 552 admitted, 350 enrolled.

Out-of-state:	51%	International:	2%

Basis for selection. Positive Christian testimony, potential for Christian service, sound academic performance, and personal character references important. Students without SAT or ACT may be admitted conditionally but must meet test requirement at earliest opportunity. Interview recommended for all; audition required for music majors. **Home schooled:** Transcript of courses and grades, letter of recommendation (nonparent) required.

High school preparation. 15 units recommended. Recommended units include English 4, mathematics 3, social studies 3, science 3 and foreign language 2.

2015-2016 Annual costs. Tuition/fees: $18,165. Room/board: $7,498. Books/supplies: $2,000. Personal expenses: $6,700.

Financial aid. Non-need-based: Scholarships awarded for academics, alumni affiliation, religious affiliation, state residency. **Additional information:** Religious affiliation tuition discount.

Application procedures. Admission: No deadline. $25 fee, may be waived for applicants with need. Admission notification on a rolling basis.

Must reply by May 1 or within 2 week(s) if notified thereafter. **Financial aid:** Closing date 5/7. FAFSA, institutional form required. Applicants notified on a rolling basis starting 5/1; must reply within 2 week(s) of notification.

Academics. Every student required to complete minimum of 30 hours in Bible and theology courses. **Special study options:** Combined bachelor's/ graduate degree, distance learning, double major, independent study, internships, study abroad. **Credit/placement by examination:** AP, CLEP, SAT, ACT, institutional tests. 30 credit hours maximum toward associate degree, 30 toward bachelor's. **Support services:** Reduced course load, remedial instruction, study skills assistance, tutoring, writing center.

Majors. **Business:** General, business admin. **Education:** Early childhood, elementary, music, secondary. **Philosophy/religion:** Religion. **Psychology:** General. **Theology:** Missionary, pastoral counseling, religious ed, sacred music, theology, youth ministry.

Most popular majors. Business/marketing 43%, interdisciplinary studies 6%, psychology 22%, theological studies 25%.

Technology on campus. 75 workstations in dormitories, library, computer center, student center. Dormitories wired for high-speed internet access and linked to campus network. Commuter students can connect to campus network. Online library, helpline, repair service, wireless network available.

Student life. Freshman orientation: Mandatory. Preregistration for classes offered. Held two days prior to start of classes. **Policies:** Curfew of midnight (Sunday-Wednesday), 1:00 am (Thursday-Saturday); dress code. Religious observance required. **Housing:** Guaranteed on-campus for freshmen. Single-sex dorms, apartments, wellness housing available. $50 nonrefundable deposit, deadline 8/1. **Activities:** Concert band, campus ministries, choral groups, drama, international student organizations, music ensembles, student government, ministerial association, prison ministries, S.H.I.N.E., World Gospel Mission Global Cafe, summer camp ministries, drama team.

Athletics. NCCAA. **Intercollegiate:** Baseball M, basketball, cross-country, golf M, soccer, softball W, track and field, volleyball W. **Intramural:** Basketball, table tennis, ultimate frisbee. **Team name:** Trailblazers.

Student services. Adult student services, chaplain/spiritual director, career counseling, student employment services, financial aid counseling, health services, minority student services, veterans' counselor. **Physically disabled:** Services for visually impaired.

Contact. E-mail: enroll@ohiochristian.edu
Phone: (740) 477-7701 Toll-free number: (877) 762-8669
Fax: (740) 420-5921
Mike Egenreider, Vice President for Enrollment, Ohio Christian University, 1476 Lancaster Pike, Circleville, OH 43113

Ohio Dominican University
Columbus, Ohio
www.ohiodominican.edu

CB member
CB code: 1131

- Private 4-year university and liberal arts college affiliated with the Roman Catholic Church
- Commuter campus in very large city
- 1,213 degree-seeking undergraduates: 8% part-time, 53% women, 23% African American, 1% Asian American, 4% Hispanic/Latino, 5% Multiracial, non-Hispanic, 1% international
- 576 degree-seeking graduate students
- 81% of applicants admitted
- SAT or ACT (ACT writing optional), application essay required

General. Founded in 1911. Regionally accredited. **Degrees:** 348 bachelor's, 45 associate awarded; master's offered. **ROTC:** Army. **Location:** 4 miles from downtown. **Calendar:** Semester, limited summer session. **Full-time faculty:** 70 total; 91% have terminal degrees, 7% minority, 47% women. **Part-time faculty:** 173 total; 27% have terminal degrees, 8% minority, 46% women. **Class size:** 63% < 20, 37% 20-39.

Freshman class profile. 1,409 applied, 1,140 admitted, 249 enrolled.

Mid 50% test scores			
SAT critical reading:	400-580	GPA 3.0-3.49:	34%
SAT math:	450-570	GPA 2.0-2.99:	31%
SAT writing:	420-530	Rank in top quarter:	34%
ACT composite:	19-24	Rank in top tenth:	11%
GPA 3.75 or higher:	18%	Return as sophomores:	72%
GPA 3.50-3.74:	17%	Out-of-state:	4%
		Live on campus:	71%

Basis for selection. High school GPA, curriculum most important, followed by test scores, class rank, interview, recommendations, and activities.

Interview required for in-state applicants; recommended for out-of-state. **Home schooled:** Transcript of courses and grades, state high school equivalency certificate required.

High school preparation. College-preparatory program recommended. 18 units recommended. Recommended units include English 4, mathematics 4, social studies 3, science 4 and foreign language 3.

2015-2016 Annual costs. Tuition/fees: $30,270. Room/board: $10,600. Books/supplies: $1,100. Personal expenses: $2,100.

2014-2015 Financial aid. Non-need-based: Scholarships awarded for academics, athletics, state residency.

Application procedures. Admission: Priority date 4/1; no deadline. $25 fee, may be waived for applicants with need, free for online applicants. Admission notification on a rolling basis beginning on or about 1/1. **Financial aid:** Priority date 4/1; no closing date. FAFSA required. Applicants notified on a rolling basis starting 3/1; must reply within 2 week(s) of notification.

Academics. Special study options: Accelerated study, combined bachelor's/graduate degree, cross-registration, distance learning, double major, dual enrollment of high school students, ESL, honors, independent study, internships, liberal arts/career combination, student-designed major, study abroad, teacher certification program, Washington semester, weekend college. **Credit/placement by examination:** AP, CLEP, IB, ACT, institutional tests. No limit on credit hours by examination, but residency requirement must be met. **Support services:** Learning center, reduced course load, study skills assistance, tutoring, writing center.

Majors. Biology: General. **Business:** Accounting, business admin, finance, insurance, international. **Communications:** Communications/speech/rhetoric, public relations. **Computer sciences:** Information systems. **Conservation:** Environmental science. **Education:** General, art, biology, chemistry, elementary, English, mathematics, middle, multiple handicapped, physics, science, secondary, social studies, special ed. **Engineering:** Software. **English:** English lit. **History:** General. **Human services:** Social work. **Liberal arts:** Arts/sciences. **Math:** General. **Parks/recreation:** Exercise sciences, sports admin. **Philosophy/religion:** Philosophy. **Physical sciences:** Chemistry. **Protective services:** Criminal justice. **Psychology:** General. **Social sciences:** Economics, political science, sociology. **Theology:** Theology, youth ministry. **Visual/performing arts:** Art, graphic design.

Most popular majors. Biology 6%, business/marketing 47%, education 21%, social sciences 7%.

Technology on campus. 380 workstations in dormitories, library, computer center, student center. Dormitories wired for high-speed internet access and linked to campus network. Commuter students can connect to campus network. Online course registration, online library, helpline, student web hosting, wireless network available.

Student life. Freshman orientation: Mandatory, $175 fee. Preregistration for classes offered. Held 2 days in May, June or July. **Housing:** Coed dorms available. $150 fully refundable deposit, deadline 8/15. **Activities:** Bands, campus ministries, choral groups, drama, international student organizations, literary magazine, music ensembles, Model UN, musical theater, radio station, student government, student newspaper, Black Student Union, resident student association, commuter student association, Social Work Action Taskforce, psychology club, PhiAlpha Club, SigmaTau Delta, St. Alberts Society, Bands, Panther Players, St. Pauls's Outreach, and others.

Athletics. NCAA. **Intercollegiate:** Baseball M, basketball, cross-country, football (tackle) M, golf, soccer, softball W, tennis, track and field, volleyball W. **Intramural:** Basketball, football (non-tackle), sand volleyball, table tennis, ultimate frisbee, volleyball. **Team name:** Panthers.

Student services. Adult student services, alcohol/substance abuse counseling, chaplain/spiritual director, career counseling, student employment services, financial aid counseling, health services, minority student services, personal counseling, placement for graduates, veterans' counselor.

Contact. E-mail: admissions@ohiodominican.edu
Phone: (614) 251-4507 Toll-free number: (800) 955-6446
Fax: (614) 251-0156
Kevin Brinkman, Director of Admissions, Ohio Dominican University, 1216 Sunbury Road, Columbus, OH 43219

Ohio Northern University
Ada, Ohio
www.onu.edu

CB member
CB code: 1591

- Private 4-year university affiliated with the United Methodist Church
- Residential campus in small town

◗ 1,974 degree-seeking undergraduates: 2% part-time, 43% women, 4% African American, 1% Asian American, 1% Hispanic/Latino, 3% Multi-racial, non-Hispanic, 4% international

◗ 979 degree-seeking graduate students

◗ 69% of applicants admitted

◗ SAT or ACT (ACT writing optional) required

◗ 66% graduate within 6 years

General. Founded in 1871. Regionally accredited. **Degrees:** 444 bachelor's awarded; master's, professional offered. **ROTC:** Army, Air Force. **Location:** 15 miles from Lima, 80 miles from Columbus. **Calendar:** Semester, limited summer session. **Full-time faculty:** 211 total; 84% have terminal degrees, 14% minority, 41% women. **Part-time faculty:** 77 total; 29% have terminal degrees, 5% minority, 53% women. **Class size:** 60% < 20, 36% 20-39, 2% 40-49, 1% 50-99. **Special facilities:** Nature center, drug information center (College of Pharmacy), pharmacy museum.

Freshman class profile. 3,108 applied, 2,146 admitted, 586 enrolled.

Mid 50% test scores			
SAT critical reading:	480-600	**GPA 2.0-2.99:**	13%
SAT math:	530-640	**Rank in top quarter:**	60%
SAT writing:	510-590	**Rank in top tenth:**	32%
ACT composite:	23-28	**Return as sophomores:**	86%
GPA 3.75 or higher:	44%	**Out-of-state:**	23%
GPA 3.50-3.74:	20%	**Live on campus:**	96%
GPA 3.0-3.49:	23%	**International:**	3%

Basis for selection. Each file is reviewed individually in regards to high school curriculum, GPA, test scores, class rank, activities and community service. Secondary school record is very important. Colleges of Pharmacy and Engineering have higher test score credentials for consideration. Interview recommended for all. Audition required for music, music education, musical theater, and performance. **Home schooled:** Statement describing home school structure and mission, transcript of courses and grades required.

High school preparation. College-preparatory program required. 16 units required; 24 recommended. Required and recommended units include English 4, mathematics 2-4, social studies 2-3, history 2, science 2-3 (laboratory 2), foreign language 2, computer science 1, visual/performing arts 1 and academic electives 4. 4 units math and science required for engineering and pharmacy applicants.

2016-2017 Annual costs. Tuition/fees: $29,820. Room/board: $11,050. Books/supplies: $1,800.

Financial aid. Non-need-based: Scholarships awarded for academics, alumni affiliation, art, leadership, minority status, music/drama, ROTC, state residency.

Application procedures. Admission: Priority date 12/1; deadline 8/15 (receipt date). No application fee. Application must be submitted online. Admission notification on a rolling basis. Must reply by 5/1. Priority date for scholarship eligibility is December 1 of senior year. Pharmacy deadline is December 1 of senior year. **Financial aid:** No deadline. FAFSA required.

Academics. Pharmacy students admitted directly to 6-year PharmD. program. **Special study options:** Combined bachelor's/graduate degree, cooperative education, distance learning, double major, dual enrollment of high school students, ESL, exchange student, honors, independent study, internships, liberal arts/career combination, semester at sea, study abroad, teacher certification program, Washington semester. **Credit/placement by examination:** AP, CLEP, IB, SAT, ACT, institutional tests. 30 credit hours maximum toward bachelor's degree. **Support services:** Pre-admission summer program, reduced course load, remedial instruction, study skills assistance, tutoring, writing center.

Majors. Biology: General, biochemistry, exercise physiology, molecular. **Business:** General, accounting, accounting/business management, business admin, construction management, insurance, management science, marketing. **Communications:** Advertising, communications/speech/rhetoric, journalism, organizational, persuasive communications, radio/TV. **Computer sciences:** Computer science. **Conservation:** Environmental studies. **Education:** General, art, biology, chemistry, early childhood, English, foreign languages, French, German, history, kindergarten/preschool, mathematics, middle, multi-level teacher, music, physics, reading, science, social studies, Spanish, technology/industrial arts. **Engineering:** General, civil, computer, electrical, mechanical. **English:** British lit, creative writing, English lit, technical writing. **Foreign languages:** French, German, Germanic, Spanish. **General:** Site management. **Health services:** Athletic training, clinical lab science, nursing education, pediatric nursing, pharmaceutical marketing/management, predental, premedicine, preveterinary. **History:** General. **Liberal arts:** Arts/sciences. **Math:** General, applied, probability, statistics. **Parks/recreation:** Exercise sciences, sports admin. **Philosophy/religion:** Philosophy, religion. **Physical sciences:** Chemistry, physics. **Protective services:** Criminal justice, forensics, law enforcement admin. **Psychology:** General. **Social sciences:**

Political science, sociology. **Theology:** Youth ministry. **Visual/performing arts:** General, art, commercial/advertising art, dramatic, music, music management, music performance, music theory/composition, studio arts.

Most popular majors. Biology 9%, business/marketing 17%, engineering/engineering technologies 17%, health sciences 14%, visual/performing arts 6%.

Technology on campus. Dormitories wired for high-speed internet access and linked to campus network. Commuter students can connect to campus network. Online course registration, online library, helpline, repair service, wireless network available.

Student life. Freshman orientation: Mandatory. Preregistration for classes offered. Three 1-day sessions held in May and June on Fridays. **Policies:** All students must reside on campus until senior status reached. No smoking in residence halls. **Housing:** Guaranteed on-campus for freshmen. Coed dorms, single-sex dorms, special housing for disabled, apartments, fraternity/sorority housing, themed housing available. $200 fully refundable deposit. Pets allowed in dorm rooms. Honors residence halls available. **Activities:** Bands, campus ministries, choral groups, dance, drama, international student organizations, literary magazine, music ensembles, Model UN, musical theater, radio station, student government, student newspaper, symphony orchestra, TV station, Fellowship of Christian Athletes, Black Student Union, College Democrats, College Republicans, Habitat for Humanity, World Student Organization, Latino Student Organization, Northern Christian Fellowship, Volunteers in Mission, Ada Friends.

Athletics. NCAA. **Intercollegiate:** Baseball M, basketball, cross-country, diving, football (tackle) M, golf, lacrosse, soccer, softball W, swimming, tennis, track and field, volleyball W, wrestling M. **Intramural:** Basketball, football (non-tackle) M, racquetball, soccer, softball, swimming, table tennis M, tennis, track and field, volleyball. **Team name:** Polar Bears.

Student services. Alcohol/substance abuse counseling, chaplain/spiritual director, career counseling, student employment services, financial aid counseling, health services, legal services, minority student services, on-campus daycare, personal counseling, placement for graduates. **Physically disabled:** Services for visually, speech, hearing impaired.

Contact. E-mail: admissions-ug@onu.edu
Phone: (419) 772-2260 Toll-free number: (888) 408-4668
Fax: (419) 772-2821
Deborah Miller, Director of Admissions, Ohio Northern University, 525 South Main Street, Ada, OH 45810

Ohio State University: Columbus Campus
Columbus, Ohio   **CB member**
www.osu.edu   **CB code: 1592**

◗ Public 4-year university

◗ Residential campus in very large city

◗ 44,131 degree-seeking undergraduates: 7% part-time, 48% women, 6% African American, 6% Asian American, 4% Hispanic/Latino, 3% Multi-racial, non-Hispanic, 7% international

◗ 12,854 degree-seeking graduate students

◗ 49% of applicants admitted

◗ SAT or ACT (ACT writing optional), application essay required

◗ 83% graduate within 6 years

General. Founded in 1870. Regionally accredited. Additional campuses in Wooster, Marion, Lima, Newark, Mansfield. **Degrees:** 10,788 bachelor's, 696 associate awarded; master's, professional, doctoral offered. **ROTC:** Army, Naval, Air Force. **Location:** 2 miles from downtown Columbus. **Calendar:** Semester, extensive summer session. **Full-time faculty:** 3,722 total; 24% minority, 38% women. **Part-time faculty:** 1,575 total; 16% minority, 54% women. **Class size:** 30% < 20, 38% 20-39, 10% 40-49, 14% 50-99, 9% >100. **Special facilities:** Radio telescope, dance notation bureau, extension center for educational research, biological science laboratory on Lake Erie, campus airport, environmental studies center, research vessel on Lake Erie, nuclear research reactor, supercomputer facility, arts center, cultural center, public service and public policy institute, polar research center, health policy studies center, mapping center, materials research center.

Freshman class profile. 40,249 applied, 19,872 admitted, 7,032 enrolled.

Mid 50% test scores			
SAT critical reading:	560-670	**End year in good standing:**	94%
SAT math:	610-720	**Return as sophomores:**	94%
SAT writing:	560-660	**Out-of-state:**	27%
ACT composite:	27-31	**Live on campus:**	94%
Rank in top quarter:	95%	**International:**	5%
Rank in top tenth:	62%	**Fraternities:**	6%
		Sororities:	6%

Basis for selection. Secondary school record, class rank, test scores most important. Test scores not required for applicants more than two years removed from high school. Audition required for dance, music programs; portfolio required for art programs. **Home schooled:** May be required to provide GED.

High school preparation. College-preparatory program recommended. 19 units required; 22 recommended. Required and recommended units include English 4, mathematics 3-4, social studies 2-3, science 3 (laboratory 3), foreign language 2-3, computer science 1 and academic electives 1.

2015-2016 Annual costs. Tuition/fees: $10,037; $27,365 out-of-state. Room/board: $11,666. Books/supplies: $1,234. Personal expenses: $2,272.

2015-2016 Financial aid. **Need-based:** 5,632 full-time freshmen applied for aid; 3,398 deemed to have need; 3,381 received aid. Average need met was 74%. Average scholarship/grant was $11,071; average loan $3,601. 55% of total undergraduate aid awarded as scholarships/grants, 45% as loans/jobs. **Non-need-based:** Awarded to 9,174 full-time undergraduates, including 2,719 freshmen. Scholarships awarded for academics, alumni affiliation, art, athletics, job skills, leadership, minority status, music/drama, ROTC, state residency.

Application procedures. **Admission:** Closing date 2/1 (receipt date). $60 fee, may be waived for applicants with need. Application must be submitted online. Admission notification by 3/31. Admission notification on a rolling basis. Must reply by May 1 or within 3 week(s) if notified thereafter. **Financial aid:** Priority date 2/15; no closing date. FAFSA required. Applicants notified by 3/31; must reply by 5/1 or within 4 week(s) of notification.

Academics. **Special study options:** Accelerated study, combined bachelor's/graduate degree, cooperative education, cross-registration, distance learning, double major, dual enrollment of high school students, ESL, exchange student, honors, independent study, internships, liberal arts/career combination, semester at sea, student-designed major, study abroad, teacher certification program, Washington semester. **Credit/placement by examination:** AP, CLEP, IB, SAT, ACT, institutional tests. 30 credit hours maximum toward bachelor's degree. **Support services:** Learning center, pre-admission summer program, reduced course load, remedial instruction, study skills assistance, tutoring, writing center.

Majors. **Architecture:** Architecture, landscape, urban/community planning. **Area/ethnic studies:** African-American, women's. **Biology:** General, biochemistry, biomedical sciences, botany, entomology, microbiology, molecular genetics, neuroscience, plant pathology, zoology. **Business:** General, accounting, actuarial science, business admin, finance, hotel/motel admin, human resources, insurance, international, logistics, management information systems, managerial economics, marketing, operations, real estate, transportation. **Communications:** Communications/speech/rhetoric, journalism. **Computer sciences:** General. **Conservation:** General, environmental science, fisheries, urban forestry. **Education:** General, agricultural, art, English, family/consumer sciences, foreign languages, music, physical, special ed, technology/industrial arts, voc/tech. **Engineering:** Aerospace, agricultural, applied physics, biomedical, chemical, civil, computer, electrical, environmental, industrial, materials, mechanical, metallurgical, systems. **English:** English lit, writing. **Foreign languages:** Arabic, Chinese, comparative lit, French, German, Hebrew, Italian, Japanese, Korean, linguistics, modern Greek, Portuguese, Russian, Spanish. **Health services:** Athletic training, audiology/hearing, clinical lab science, dental hygiene, dietetics, health information management, medical radiologic technology/radiation therapy, nursing (RN), occupational therapy, perfusion technology, respiratory therapy technology. **History:** General. **Human services:** General, social work. **Liberal arts:** Humanities. **Math;** General. **Parks/recreation:** Exercise sciences, health/fitness, sports admin. **Philosophy/religion:** Islamic, Judaic, philosophy, religion. **Physical sciences:** Astronomy, atmospheric science, chemistry, geology, optics, physics. **Psychology:** General. **Social sciences:** Anthropology, criminology, economics, geography, GIS/cartography, international relations, political science, sociology, urban studies. **Visual/performing arts:** Art, art history/conservation, dance, design, dramatic, film/cinema/video, industrial design, interior design, jazz, music, music history, music performance, music theory/composition. **Work/family studies:** Clothing/textiles, family resources, family studies, food/nutrition, human nutrition.

Most popular majors. Biology 8%, business/marketing 17%, engineering/engineering technologies 14%, health sciences 9%, psychology 6%, social sciences 10%.

Technology on campus. 399 workstations in dormitories, library, computer center, student center. Dormitories wired for high-speed internet access and linked to campus network. Commuter students can connect to campus network. Online course registration, online library, helpline, wireless network available.

Student life. **Freshman orientation:** Mandatory, $50 fee. Preregistration for classes offered. Two-day programs throughout the summer (June-August) prior to enrollment. **Policies:** Student organizations need to have 5 student members, an OSU faculty or staff advisor, a constitution, and purpose statement to register. Freshmen not permitted cars on campus. **Housing:** Guaranteed on-campus for freshmen. Coed dorms, single-sex dorms, special housing for disabled, apartments, cooperative housing, fraternity/sorority housing, wellness housing available. $300 nonrefundable deposit, deadline 6/16. **Activities:** Bands, choral groups, dance, drama, film society, international student organizations, literary magazine, music ensembles, Model UN, musical theater, opera, radio station, student government, student newspaper, symphony orchestra, TV station, John Glenn Civic Leadership Council, College Democrats, College Republicans, Habitat for Humanity, Students for Recycling, SERV Team, Intergroup Council, Universitywide Council of Hispanic Organizations, Campus Crusade for Christ, Muslim Students Association.

Athletics. NCAA. **Intercollegiate:** Baseball M, basketball, cheerleading W, cross-country, diving, fencing, field hockey W, football (tackle) M, golf, gymnastics, ice hockey, lacrosse, rifle, rowing (crew) W, soccer, softball W, swimming, synchronized swimming W, tennis, track and field, volleyball, wrestling M. **Intramural:** Badminton, baseball, basketball, cricket, football (non-tackle), golf, ice hockey, racquetball, soccer, softball, table tennis, tennis, volleyball, water polo, weight lifting, wrestling. **Team name:** Buckeyes.

Student services. Adult student services, alcohol/substance abuse counseling, career counseling, services for economically disadvantaged, student employment services, financial aid counseling, health services, legal services, minority student services, on-campus daycare, personal counseling, veterans' counselor, women's services. **Physically disabled:** Services for visually, speech, hearing impaired.

Contact. E-mail: askabuckeye@osu.edu
Phone: (614) 292-3980 Fax: (614) 292-4818
Office of Undergraduate Admission, Ohio State University: Columbus Campus, Student Academic Services Building, 281 West Lane Avenue, Columbus, OH 43210

Ohio State University: Lima Campus
Lima, Ohio
http://lima.osu.edu/   CB code: 1541

- Public 4-year university and branch campus college
- Commuter campus in small city
- 928 degree-seeking undergraduates: 13% part-time, 56% women, 5% African American, 2% Asian American, 3% Hispanic/Latino, 3% Multiracial, non-Hispanic
- 7 degree-seeking graduate students
- 32% graduate within 6 years

General. Founded in 1960. Regionally accredited. Additional campuses in Wooster, Marion, Columbus, Newark, Mansfield. **Degrees:** 71 bachelor's, 79 associate awarded; master's offered. **ROTC:** Army, Naval, Air Force. **Location:** 78 miles from Toledo. **Calendar:** Semester, limited summer session. **Full-time faculty:** 34 total; 15% minority, 38% women. **Part-time faculty:** 49 total; 10% minority, 59% women. **Class size:** 61% < 20, 33% 20-39, 3% 40-49, 3% 50-99. **Special facilities:** Observatory, geology museum, nature preserve, nature trails, art gallery.

Freshman class profile. 1,078 applied, 1,064 admitted, 349 enrolled.

Mid 50% test scores			
SAT critical reading:	430-590	Rank in top quarter:	34%
SAT math:	510-620	Rank in top tenth:	5%
SAT writing:	410-610	End year in good standing:	73%
ACT composite:	20-25	Return as sophomores:	67%
		Out-of-state:	1%

Basis for selection. Open admission, but selective for out-of-state students. Out of state applicants evaluated on the basis of secondary school record, class rank, and test scores. **Home schooled:** May be required to provide GED.

High school preparation. College-preparatory program recommended. 19 units required; 22 recommended. Required and recommended units include English 4, mathematics 3-4, social studies 2-3, science 3 (laboratory 3), foreign language 2-3, computer science 1 and academic electives 1.

2015-2016 Annual costs. Tuition/fees: $7,140; $24,468 out-of-state. Books/supplies: $1,234. Personal expenses: $3,846.

2015-2016 Financial aid. **Need-based:** 314 full-time freshmen applied for aid; 238 deemed to have need; 235 received aid. Average need met was 55%. Average scholarship/grant was $4,708; average loan $3,534. 38% of total undergraduate aid awarded as scholarships/grants, 62% as loans/jobs. **Non-need-based:** Awarded to 89 full-time undergraduates, including 56 freshmen. Scholarships awarded for academics, alumni affiliation, art, athletics, job skills, leadership, minority status, music/drama, ROTC, state residency.

Application procedures. **Admission:** Closing date 6/1 (receipt date). $60 fee, may be waived for applicants with need. Admission notification on a rolling basis beginning on or about 11/15. Must reply by May 1 or within 3 week(s) if notified thereafter. **Financial aid:** Priority date 2/15; no closing date. FAFSA required. Applicants notified by 3/15; must reply by 5/1 or within 4 week(s) of notification.

Academics. Students often leave campus after 1-3 years and complete bachelor's degree on Columbus campus. **Special study options:** Accelerated study, cooperative education, cross-registration, distance learning, double major, dual enrollment of high school students, ESL, exchange student, honors, independent study, internships, liberal arts/career combination, semester at sea, student-designed major, study abroad, teacher certification program, Washington semester, weekend college. **Credit/placement by examination:** AP, CLEP, IB, institutional tests. 30 credit hours maximum toward bachelor's degree. **Support services:** Learning center, remedial instruction, tutoring, writing center.

Majors. **Biology:** General. **Business:** General, financial planning, hospitality admin. **Education:** General, elementary. **English:** English lit. **History:** General. **Math:** General. **Psychology:** General. **Visual/performing arts:** Dramatic. **Work/family studies:** Family resources.

Technology on campus. 150 workstations in library, computer center. Commuter students can connect to campus network. Online course registration, online library, helpline, wireless network available.

Student life. **Freshman orientation:** Mandatory, $50 fee. Preregistration for classes offered. 1-day programs throughout the summer prior to enrollment. **Policies:** Student organizations need to have 5 student members, an OSU faculty or staff advisor, a constitution, and purpose statement to register. **Activities:** Choral groups, dance, drama, literary magazine, music ensembles, musical theater, student government, Bible club, College Republicans, College Democrats, Newman Catholic Association, Stars and stripes vet club, outreach and engagement, Human Trafficking Awareness club, Multi cultural club, French and Japanese club, Global club.

Athletics. **Intramural:** Basketball, football (non-tackle), soccer, volleyball. **Team name:** Barons.

Student services. Adult student services, career counseling, services for economically disadvantaged, student employment services, financial aid counseling, health services, legal services, minority student services, on-campus daycare, personal counseling, placement for graduates, veterans' counselor. **Physically disabled:** Services for visually, speech, hearing impaired.

Contact. E-mail: lima-askabuckeye@osu.edu
Phone: (419) 995-8434 Fax: (419) 995-8483
Ohio State University: Lima Campus, 4240 Campus Drive, Lima, OH 45804-3596

Ohio State University: Mansfield Campus
Mansfield, Ohio
www.mansfield.ohio-state.edu CB code: 0744

- Public 4-year university and branch campus college
- Commuter campus in large town
- 1,115 degree-seeking undergraduates: 12% part-time, 54% women, 11% African American, 2% Asian American, 3% Hispanic/Latino, 3% Multi-racial, non-Hispanic
- 9 degree-seeking graduate students
- 43% graduate within 6 years

General. Founded in 1958. Regionally accredited. Additional campuses in Wooster, Marion, Lima, Newark, Columbus. **Degrees:** 89 bachelor's, 158 associate awarded; master's offered. **ROTC:** Army, Naval, Air Force. **Location:** 67 miles from Columbus. **Calendar:** Semester, limited summer session. **Full-time faculty:** 38 total; 10% minority, 50% women. **Part-time faculty:** 54 total; 13% minority, 67% women. **Class size:** 52% < 20, 42% 20-39, 5% 40-49, less than 1% 50-99. **Special facilities:** Wetlands, nature trails.

Freshman class profile. 1,607 applied, 1,595 admitted, 522 enrolled.

Mid 50% test scores		Rank in top quarter:	27%
SAT critical reading:	470-580	Rank in top tenth:	6%
SAT math:	470-610	End year in good standing:	77%
SAT writing:	450-570	Return as sophomores:	69%
ACT composite:	20-25	Live on campus:	32%

Basis for selection. Open admission, but selective for out-of-state students. Out-of-state applicants evaluated on basis of GPA, class rank, principal/counselor recommendations and SAT/ACT. **Home schooled:** May be required to provide GED.

High school preparation. College-preparatory program recommended. 19 units required; 22 recommended. Required and recommended units include English 4, mathematics 3-4, social studies 2-3, science 3 (laboratory 3), foreign language 2-3, computer science 1 and academic electives 1.

2015-2016 Annual costs. Tuition/fees: $7,140; $24,468 out-of-state. Room only: $5,970. Books/supplies: $1,234. Personal expenses: $2,272.

2015-2016 Financial aid. **Need-based:** 471 full-time freshmen applied for aid; 394 deemed to have need; 390 received aid. Average need met was 52%. Average scholarship/grant was $5,049; average loan $3,828. 39% of total undergraduate aid awarded as scholarships/grants, 61% as loans/jobs. **Non-need-based:** Awarded to 76 full-time undergraduates, including 57 freshmen. Scholarships awarded for academics, alumni affiliation, art, athletics, job skills, leadership, minority status, music/drama, ROTC, state residency.

Application procedures. **Admission:** Closing date 6/1 (receipt date). $60 fee, may be waived for applicants with need. Admission notification on a rolling basis beginning on or about 11/15. Must reply by May 1 or within 3 week(s) if notified thereafter. **Financial aid:** Priority date 2/15; no closing date. FAFSA required. Applicants notified by 3/15; must reply by 5/1 or within 4 week(s) of notification.

Academics. Students often leave campus after 1-3 years and complete bachelor's degree on Columbus campus. **Special study options:** Accelerated study, cooperative education, cross-registration, distance learning, double major, dual enrollment of high school students, ESL, exchange student, honors, independent study, internships, liberal arts/career combination, student-designed major, study abroad, teacher certification program, weekend college. **Credit/placement by examination:** AP, CLEP, institutional tests. 45 credit hours maximum toward bachelor's degree. **Support services:** Learning center, remedial instruction, tutoring, writing center.

Majors. **Business:** Business admin. **Education:** Elementary. **English:** English lit. **History:** General. **Psychology:** General.

Technology on campus. 260 workstations in library, computer center, student center. Commuter students can connect to campus network. Online course registration, online library, helpline, wireless network available.

Student life. **Freshman orientation:** Mandatory, $50 fee. Preregistration for classes offered. 1-day programs throughout the summer prior to enrollment. **Housing:** Special housing for disabled, apartments, wellness housing available. $350 partly refundable deposit. **Activities:** Pep band, campus ministries, choral groups, drama, international student organizations, student government, African American Student Union, campus activities board, Campus crusade for Christ, College Democrats/Republicans, Diversity Alliance, economics and business club, Habitat for Humanity, Single Parent Network, Spanish club, Theta Alpha Phi, Catholic Young Adults, Paralegal Association.

Athletics. **Intramural:** Basketball, equestrian W, football (non-tackle), softball, table tennis, tennis, volleyball. **Team name:** Mavericks.

Student services. Adult student services, career counseling, student employment services, financial aid counseling, minority student services, personal counseling, placement for graduates. **Physically disabled:** Services for visually, speech, hearing impaired.

Contact. E-mail: admissions@mansfield.ohio-state.edu
Phone: (419) 755-4011 Fax: (419) 755-4241
Ohio State University: Mansfield Campus, 1760 University Drive, Mansfield, OH 44906

Ohio State University: Marion Campus
Marion, Ohio
www.osumarion.osu.edu CB code: 0752

- Public 4-year university and branch campus college
- Commuter campus in large town
- 1,016 degree-seeking undergraduates: 16% part-time, 52% women, 4% African American, 3% Asian American, 4% Hispanic/Latino, 3% Multi-racial, non-Hispanic
- 2 graduate students
- 43% graduate within 6 years

General. Founded in 1958. Regionally accredited. Additional campuses in Wooster, Columbus, Lima, Newark, Mansfield. **Degrees:** 113 bachelor's,

86 associate awarded; master's offered. **ROTC:** Army, Naval, Air Force. **Location:** 44 miles from Columbus. **Calendar:** Semester, limited summer session. **Full-time faculty:** 35 total; 11% minority, 46% women. **Part-time faculty:** 61 total; 2% minority, 51% women. **Class size:** 53% < 20, 45% 20-39, 2% 40-49.

Freshman class profile. 873 applied, 860 admitted, 388 enrolled.

Mid 50% test scores			
SAT critical reading:	470-590	Rank in top tenth:	10%
SAT math:	490-620	End year in good standing:	72%
SAT writing:	470-560	Return as sophomores:	64%
ACT composite:	19-25	Out-of-state:	1%
Rank in top quarter:	29%	International:	1%

Basis for selection. Open admission, but selective for out-of-state students. Secondary school record, class rank, test scores most important. Out of state applicants evaluated on the basis of secondary school record, class rank, and test scores. **Home schooled:** May be required to provide GED.

High school preparation. College-preparatory program recommended. 19 units required; 22 recommended. Required and recommended units include English 4, mathematics 3-4, social studies 2-3, science 3 (laboratory 3), foreign language 2-3, computer science 1 and academic electives 1.

2015-2016 Annual costs. Tuition/fees: $7,140; $24,468 out-of-state. Books/supplies: $1,234. Personal expenses: $3,846.

2015-2016 Financial aid. Need-based: 345 full-time freshmen applied for aid; 256 deemed to have need; 253 received aid. Average need met was 58%. Average scholarship/grant was $5,050; average loan $3,578. 41% of total undergraduate aid awarded as scholarships/grants, 59% as loans/jobs. **Non-need-based:** Awarded to 129 full-time undergraduates, including 78 freshmen. Scholarships awarded for academics, alumni affiliation, art, athletics, job skills, leadership, minority status, music/drama, ROTC, state residency.

Application procedures. Admission: Closing date 6/1 (receipt date). $60 fee, may be waived for applicants with need. Admission notification on a rolling basis beginning on or about 11/15. Must reply by May 1 or within 3 week(s) if notified thereafter. **Financial aid:** Priority date 2/15; no closing date. FAFSA required. Applicants notified by 3/15; must reply by 5/1 or within 4 week(s) of notification.

Academics. Students often leave campus after 1-3 years and complete bachelor's degree on Columbus campus. **Special study options:** Accelerated study, cooperative education, cross-registration, distance learning, double major, dual enrollment of high school students, ESL, exchange student, honors, independent study, internships, liberal arts/career combination, student-designed major, study abroad, teacher certification program, weekend college. **Credit/placement by examination:** AP, CLEP, IB, institutional tests. 30 credit hours maximum toward bachelor's degree. **Support services:** Learning center, remedial instruction, tutoring, writing center.

Majors. Business: Business admin. **Education:** Elementary. **English:** English lit. **History:** General. **Psychology:** General.

Technology on campus. 163 workstations in library, computer center. Commuter students can connect to campus network. Online course registration, online library, helpline, wireless network available.

Student life. Freshman orientation: Mandatory, $50 fee. Preregistration for classes offered. 1-day programs throughout the summer prior to enrollment. **Housing:** $350 partly refundable deposit. **Activities:** Student government.

Athletics. USCAA. **Intercollegiate:** Basketball M, golf M, volleyball W. **Team name:** Scarlet Wave.

Student services. Career counseling, student employment services, financial aid counseling, legal services, on-campus daycare, personal counseling, placement for graduates. **Physically disabled:** Services for visually, speech, hearing impaired.

Contact. E-mail: askabuckeye@osu.edu
Phone: (740) 725-6337 Fax: (740) 386-2439
Matt Moreau, Coordinator of Admissions, Ohio State University: Marion Campus, 1465 Mount Vernon Avenue, Marion, OH 43302

Ohio State University: Newark Campus
Newark, Ohio
www.newark.osu.edu   CB code: 0824

- Public 4-year university and branch campus college
- Commuter campus in large town

- 2,362 degree-seeking undergraduates: 14% part-time, 50% women, 13% African American, 4% Asian American, 3% Hispanic/Latino, 4% Multiracial, non-Hispanic
- 13 degree-seeking graduate students
- 33% graduate within 6 years

General. Founded in 1957. Regionally accredited. Additional campuses in Columbus, Wooster, Marion, Lima, Mansfield. **Degrees:** 101 bachelor's, 370 associate awarded; master's offered. **ROTC:** Army, Naval, Air Force. **Location:** 40 miles from Columbus. **Calendar:** Semester, limited summer session. **Full-time faculty:** 50 total; 20% minority, 34% women. **Part-time faculty:** 100 total; 11% minority, 59% women. **Class size:** 34% < 20, 55% 20-39, 6% 40-49, 5% 50-99.

Freshman class profile. 2,831 applied, 2,793 admitted, 1,242 enrolled.

Mid 50% test scores			
SAT critical reading:	440-560	Rank in top tenth:	5%
SAT math:	470-570	End year in good standing:	67%
SAT writing:	440-550	Return as sophomores:	63%
ACT composite:	20-25	Out-of-state:	1%
Rank in top quarter:	23%	Live on campus:	13%

Basis for selection. Open admission, but selective for out-of-state students. Out of state applicants evaluated on the basis of secondary school record, class rank, and test scores. **Home schooled:** May be required to provide GED.

High school preparation. College-preparatory program recommended. 19 units required; 22 recommended. Required and recommended units include English 4, mathematics 3-4, social studies 2-3, science 3 (laboratory 3), foreign language 2-3, computer science 1 and academic electives 1.

2015-2016 Annual costs. Tuition/fees: $7,140; $24,468 out-of-state. Room only: $6,690. Books/supplies: $1,234. Personal expenses: $2,272.

2015-2016 Financial aid. Need-based: 1,056 full-time freshmen applied for aid; 810 deemed to have need; 794 received aid. Average need met was 52%. Average scholarship/grant was $4,851; average loan $3,640. 36% of total undergraduate aid awarded as scholarships/grants, 64% as loans/jobs. **Non-need-based:** Awarded to 55 full-time undergraduates, including 30 freshmen. Scholarships awarded for academics, alumni affiliation, art, athletics, job skills, leadership, minority status, music/drama, ROTC, state residency.

Application procedures. Admission: Closing date 6/1 (receipt date). $60 fee, may be waived for applicants with need. Admission notification on a rolling basis beginning on or about 11/15. Must reply by May 1 or within 3 week(s) if notified thereafter. **Financial aid:** Priority date 2/15; no closing date. FAFSA required. Applicants notified by 3/15; must reply by 5/1 or within 4 week(s) of notification.

Academics. Students often leave campus after 1-3 years and complete bachelor's degree on Columbus campus. **Special study options:** Accelerated study, cooperative education, cross-registration, distance learning, double major, dual enrollment of high school students, ESL, exchange student, honors, independent study, internships, liberal arts/career combination, student-designed major, study abroad, teacher certification program, weekend college. **Credit/placement by examination:** AP, CLEP, IB, institutional tests. **Support services:** Learning center, remedial instruction, tutoring, writing center.

Majors. Business: Business admin. **Education:** General, multicultural. **English:** English lit. **History:** General. **Psychology:** General.

Technology on campus. 399 workstations in dormitories, library, computer center. Dormitories wired for high-speed internet access and linked to campus network. Commuter students can connect to campus network. Online course registration, online library, helpline, wireless network available.

Student life. Freshman orientation: Mandatory, $50 fee. Preregistration for classes offered. 1-day programs throughout the summer prior to enrollment. **Housing:** Apartments, wellness housing available. $200 partly refundable deposit. **Activities:** Campus ministries, choral groups, drama, international student organizations, literary magazine, music ensembles, student government, support groups, minority organization. international multicultural association, ski club, gay/straight alliance, academic and honors organizations.

Athletics. Team name: Titans.

Student services. Career counseling, student employment services, financial aid counseling, minority student services, personal counseling, placement for graduates. **Physically disabled:** Services for visually, speech, hearing impaired.

Contact. E-mail: askabuckeye@osu.edu
Phone: (740) 366-9333 Fax: (740) 364-9645
Diane Kanney, Director of Enrollment, Ohio State University: Newark Campus, 1179 University Drive, Newark, OH 43055

Ohio University
Athens, Ohio
CB member
www.ohio.edu
CB code: 1593

- Public 4-year university
- Residential campus in large town
- 23,335 degree-seeking undergraduates: 26% part-time, 59% women, 5% African American, 1% Asian American, 3% Hispanic/Latino, 3% Multiracial, non-Hispanic, 3% international
- 5,662 degree-seeking graduate students
- 74% of applicants admitted
- SAT or ACT (ACT writing recommended) required
- 67% graduate within 6 years; 22% enter graduate study

General. Founded in 1804. Regionally accredited. **Degrees:** 6,338 bachelor's, 133 associate awarded; master's, professional, doctoral offered. **ROTC:** Army, Air Force. **Location:** 75 miles from Columbus. **Calendar:** Semester, extensive summer session. **Full-time faculty:** 939 total; 78% have terminal degrees, 16% minority, 40% women. **Part-time faculty:** 384 total; 33% have terminal degrees, 8% minority, 55% women. **Class size:** 31% < 20, 42% 20-39, 9% 40-49, 11% 50-99, 7% >100. **Special facilities:** University airport, academic and research center, nuclear accelerator, biotechnology research center, greenhouse, ridges land lab, innovation center, museum of American art, cartography and meteorology centers, contemporary history institute, fieldhouse, Athena theater.

Freshman class profile. 21,000 applied, 15,628 admitted, 4,423 enrolled.

Mid 50% test scores			
SAT critical reading:	490-600	Rank in top quarter:	43%
SAT math:	500-610	Rank in top tenth:	16%
SAT writing:	470-590	End year in good standing:	90%
ACT composite:	22-26	Return as sophomores:	79%
GPA 3.75 or higher:	25%	Out-of-state:	14%
GPA 3.50-3.74:	22%	Live on campus:	96%
GPA 3.0-3.49:	41%	International:	1%
GPA 2.0-2.99:	12%	Fraternities:	13%
		Sororities:	24%

Basis for selection. High school record as represented by class rank, GPA, and curriculum completed most important. Test scores and recommendation considered. Rank in top third of class preferred. Audition required for dance and music programs. Interview required of selected Honors Tutorial College candidates. **Home schooled:** Statement describing home school structure and mission, transcript of courses and grades, interview required. Copy of academic assessment report, curriculum outline, personal statement and documentation from school district.

High school preparation. College-preparatory program recommended. 21 units required. Required and recommended units include English 4, mathematics 4, social studies 3, science 3, foreign language 2, visual/performing arts 1 and academic electives 5. All other state core curriculum minimums, health .5, physical education .5.

2015-2016 Annual costs. Tuition/fees: $11,548; $20,512 out-of-state. Room/board: $10,864. Books/supplies: $990. Personal expenses: $1,152.

2015-2016 Financial aid. **Need-based:** 3,672 full-time freshmen applied for aid; 2,750 deemed to have need; 2,750 received aid. Average need met was 51%. Average scholarship/grant was $6,768; average loan $2,801. 36% of total undergraduate aid awarded as scholarships/grants, 64% as loans/jobs. **Non-need-based:** Awarded to 2,923 full-time undergraduates, including 718 freshmen. Scholarships awarded for academics, art, athletics, minority status, music/drama, religious affiliation, ROTC.

Application procedures. **Admission:** Closing date 2/1 (receipt date). $50 fee, may be waived for applicants with need. Admission notification on a rolling basis beginning on or about 9/15. Must reply by 5/1. Housing deposit is refundable if request is made in writing by May 1. **Financial aid:** Closing date 3/15. FAFSA required. Applicants notified on a rolling basis starting 4/1; must reply within 3 week(s) of notification.

Academics. Extensive learning community opportunities, writing center, academic advancement center. **Special study options:** Accelerated study, combined bachelor's/graduate degree, cooperative education, cross-registration, distance learning, double major, dual enrollment of high school students, ESL, external degree, honors, independent study, internships, liberal arts/career combination, student-designed major, study abroad, teacher certification program. **Credit/placement by examination:** AP, CLEP, IB, SAT, ACT, institutional tests. **Support services:** Learning center, pre-admission summer program, study skills assistance, tutoring, writing center.

Honors college/program. Honors Tutorial College application deadline December 1, interview required.

Majors. Area/ethnic studies: African, African-American, Asian, European, Latin American, women's. **Biology:** General, botany, cellular/molecular, ecology, microbiology, neuroscience, wildlife, zoology. **Business:** Accounting, actuarial science, business admin, customer service, finance, human resources, international, management information systems, managerial economics, marketing. **Communications:** Broadcast journalism, communications/speech/rhetoric, digital media, journalism, photojournalism, radio/TV. **Computer sciences:** General, computer science, networking. **Conservation:** Environmental studies. **Education:** Early childhood, family/consumer sciences, French, German, physical, secondary, Spanish, special ed. **Engineering:** Chemical, civil, electrical, industrial, mechanical. **English:** Creative writing, English lit, rhetoric/composition. **Foreign languages:** Classics, French, German, linguistics, Russian, Spanish. **Health services:** Athletic training, audiology/speech pathology, community health services, dietetics, environmental health, health care admin, nursing (RN), occupational health. **History:** General. **Human services:** Social work. **Math:** General, applied. **Parks/recreation:** General, exercise sciences, health/fitness. **Philosophy/religion:** Philosophy, religion. **Physical sciences:** Astrophysics, atmospheric science, chemistry, geology, physics. **Psychology:** General. **Social sciences:** Anthropology, criminology, economics, geography, international relations, political science, sociology, urban studies. **Visual/performing arts:** Acting, art, art history/conservation, ceramics, cinematography, dance, dramatic, graphic design, music history, music performance, music theory/composition, photography, piano/keyboard, play/screenwriting, printmaking, sculpture, studio arts, theater arts management, voice/opera. **Work/family studies:** Clothing/textiles, family resources, family studies, food/nutrition, housing, institutional food production.

Most popular majors. Business/marketing 10%, communications/journalism 10%, health sciences 43%.

Technology on campus. 1,000 workstations in library, computer center, student center. Dormitories wired for high-speed internet access and linked to campus network. Commuter students can connect to campus network. Online course registration, online library, helpline, repair service, student web hosting, wireless network available.

Student life. Freshman orientation: Mandatory. Preregistration for classes offered. One-and-a-half day program held in June. **Policies:** Student organizations required to register annually. Freshmen not permitted cars on campus. **Housing:** Guaranteed on-campus for freshmen. Coed dorms, single-sex dorms, special housing for disabled, gender-neutral housing, wellness housing available. $200 nonrefundable deposit, deadline 5/1. Scholarship housing and Intensive-study residence halls available. **Activities:** Bands, campus ministries, choral groups, dance, drama, film society, international student organizations, literary magazine, music ensembles, musical theater, opera, radio station, student government, student newspaper, symphony orchestra, TV station, Hillel at OU, Newman Catholic Community, Interfaith Impact, College Democrats, College Republicans, second amendment club, Alpha Phi Omega, combat veterans club, Colleges Against Cancer.

Athletics. NCAA. **Intercollegiate:** Baseball M, basketball, cheerleading, cross-country, diving W, field hockey W, football (tackle) M, golf, soccer W, softball W, swimming W, track and field W, volleyball W, wrestling M. **Intramural:** Badminton, basketball, football (non-tackle), sand volleyball, soccer, softball, tennis, volleyball, water polo. **Team name:** Bobcats.

Student services. Adult student services, alcohol/substance abuse counseling, career counseling, services for economically disadvantaged, student employment services, financial aid counseling, health services, legal services, minority student services, personal counseling, placement for graduates, veterans' counselor, women's services. **Physically disabled:** Services for visually, speech, hearing impaired.

Contact. E-mail: admissions@ohio.edu
Phone: (740) 593-4100 Fax: (740) 593-0560
Candace Boeninger, Assistant Vice President & Director of Undergraduate Admissions, Ohio University, 120 Chubb Hall, Athens, OH 45701-2979

Ohio University: Chillicothe Campus
Chillicothe, Ohio
www.chillicothe.ohiou.edu
CB code: 0775

- Public 4-year branch campus college
- Commuter campus in large town
- 2,236 degree-seeking undergraduates

General. Founded in 1946. Regionally accredited. **Degrees:** 139 associate awarded; master's offered. **Location:** 45 miles from Columbus. **Calendar:** Semester, limited summer session. **Full-time faculty:** 46 total. **Part-time faculty:** 100 total. **Special facilities:** Child development center, business incubator.

Basis for selection. Open admission, but selective for some programs. Business, communications, education, and engineering colleges require high school GPA and ACT/SAT test scores. **Home schooled:** State high school equivalency certificate required. Passing scores on Ohio graduation test or GED required.

High school preparation. College-preparatory program recommended. Recommended units include English 4, mathematics 3, social studies 3, science 3 and foreign language 2. College-preparatory program strongly recommended including 1 visual or performing art.

2015-2016 Annual costs. Tuition/fees: $5,048; $9,530 out-of-state. Books/supplies: $848.

Application procedures. Admission: No deadline. $20 fee, may be waived for applicants with need. Admission notification on a rolling basis. **Financial aid:** No deadline. FAFSA required. Applicants notified on a rolling basis.

Academics. Bachelor's programs in management, elementary education, criminal justice, nursing, technical and applied studies and self-designed major. Degree granted by Ohio University main campus. **Special study options:** Distance learning, double major, dual enrollment of high school students, external degree, independent study, internships, student-designed major, study abroad, teacher certification program. **Credit/placement by examination:** AP, CLEP, institutional tests. **Support services:** Learning center, pre-admission summer program, remedial instruction, study skills assistance, tutoring, writing center.

Majors. Business: Business admin. **Communications:** Organizational. **Education:** Early childhood, middle. **Health services:** Nursing (RN). **Protective services:** Criminal justice. **Psychology:** General.

Technology on campus. 275 workstations in library, computer center, student center. Commuter students can connect to campus network. Online course registration, online library, helpline, student web hosting, wireless network available.

Student life. Freshman orientation: Mandatory. Preregistration for classes offered. One-day session held prior to fall, spring and summer semesters. **Activities:** Drama, student government, student newspaper, National Communication Association, Ross County Association of Future Teachers, anime club, nursing student club, student programming club, human services association, law enforcement association, psychology club.

Athletics. Team name: Hilltoppers.

Student services. Adult student services, career counseling, services for economically disadvantaged, student employment services, financial aid counseling, personal counseling. **Physically disabled:** Services for visually, hearing impaired.

Contact. E-mail: lowej@ohio.edu
Phone: (740) 774-7240 Toll-free number: (877) 462-6824 ext. 240
Fax: (740) 774-7295
Jaime Lowe, Coordinator of Enrollment Services, Ohio University: Chillicothe Campus, 101 University Drive, Chillicothe, OH 45601

Ohio University: Eastern Campus
St. Clairsville, Ohio
www.eastern.ohiou.edu   CB code: 0828

▶ Public 4-year branch campus college
▶ Commuter campus in small town
▶ 1,010 degree-seeking undergraduates

General. Founded in 1957. Regionally accredited. **Degrees:** 23 associate awarded; master's offered. **Location:** 7 miles from downtown; 14 miles from Wheeling, West Virginia. **Calendar:** Quarter, limited summer session. **Full-time faculty:** 17 total. **Part-time faculty:** 44 total. **Special facilities:** Primeval oak forest laboratory, Great Western School (Little Red Schoolhouse).

Basis for selection. Open admission, but selective for some programs. Special requirements for education, business, communication programs. SAT/ACT scores required for admission to education program.

High school preparation. Recommended units include English 4, mathematics 4, social studies 3, science 3 and foreign language 2.

2015-2016 Annual costs. Tuition/fees: $4,806; $6,652 out-of-state.

Financial aid. Non-need-based: Scholarships awarded for academics, alumni affiliation, minority status.

Application procedures. Admission: No deadline. $20 fee, may be waived for applicants with need. Admission notification on a rolling basis. **Financial aid:** Priority date 3/15; no closing date. FAFSA required.

Academics. Several degree programs offered through cross-registration with main campus. **Special study options:** Accelerated study, cooperative education, cross-registration, distance learning, double major, dual enrollment of high school students, external degree, independent study, internships, student-designed major, teacher certification program. **Credit/placement by examination:** AP, CLEP, institutional tests. **Support services:** Learning center, reduced course load, remedial instruction, study skills assistance, tutoring, writing center.

Majors. Education: Elementary. **Liberal arts:** Arts/sciences.

Technology on campus. 11 workstations in library, computer center. Online course registration available.

Student life. Freshman orientation: Available. Preregistration for classes offered. **Activities:** Drama.

Athletics. Intercollegiate: Basketball, golf M, volleyball W. **Intramural:** Basketball. **Team name:** Panthers.

Student services. Adult student services, career counseling, on-campus daycare, personal counseling.

Contact. E-mail: admissions@ohio.edu
Phone: (740) 695-1720 Fax: (740) 695-7077
Kevin Chenoweth, Student Services Manager, Ohio University: Eastern Campus, 45425 National Road West, St. Clairsville, OH 43950-9724

Ohio University: Lancaster Campus
Lancaster, Ohio
www.lancaster.ohiou.edu   CB code: 0826

▶ Public 4-year branch campus college
▶ Large town
▶ 2,596 degree-seeking undergraduates

General. Founded in 1968. Regionally accredited. Some bachelor's and master's degrees available, awarded through Athens campus. **Degrees:** 132 associate awarded; master's offered. **ROTC:** Army, Naval, Air Force. **Location:** 30 miles from Columbus. **Calendar:** Quarter, extensive summer session. **Full-time faculty:** 31 total. **Part-time faculty:** 20 total.

Basis for selection. Open admission, but selective for some programs. Special requirements for business, education, engineering and communication programs. ACT or SAT scores used in admission decisions to colleges of education, engineering. International students must take English fluency test through Ohio Program of Intensive English.

2015-2016 Annual costs. Tuition/fees: $4,994; $9,530 out-of-state. Books/supplies: $500.

Financial aid. Additional information: Scholarship application deadline April 1.

Application procedures. Admission: No deadline. $20 fee, may be waived for applicants with need. Admission notification on a rolling basis. **Financial aid:** Priority date 2/15; no closing date. FAFSA required. Applicants notified on a rolling basis; must reply within 2 week(s) of notification.

Academics. Special study options: Combined bachelor's/graduate degree, cross-registration, double major, independent study, internships, student-designed major. **Credit/placement by examination:** AP, CLEP, institutional tests. **Support services:** Learning center, remedial instruction, tutoring.

Technology on campus. 98 workstations in library, computer center, student center. Online course registration, online library, helpline, student web hosting available.

Student life. Freshman orientation: Available. Preregistration for classes offered. **Activities:** Choral groups, drama, student government, outdoor club, Young Democrats, Young Republicans, Christian Fellowship, adult support group.

Athletics. Intercollegiate: Baseball M, basketball, golf, softball W, tennis. **Intramural:** Skiing, table tennis, volleyball. **Team name:** Cougars.

Student services. Career counseling, student employment services, financial aid counseling, on-campus daycare, placement for graduates, veterans' counselor. **Physically disabled:** Services for visually, speech, hearing impaired.

Contact. E-mail: admissions@ohio.edu
Phone: (740) 654-6711 ext. 215 Toll-free number: (888) 446-4468
Fax: (740) 687-9497
Pat Fox, Enrollment Manager, Ohio University: Lancaster Campus, 1570 Granville Pike, Lancaster, OH 43130

Ohio University: Southern Campus at Ironton
Ironton, Ohio
www.southern.ohiou.edu   CB code: 1912

+ Public 4-year branch campus college
+ Commuter campus in large town
+ 2,072 undergraduates

General. Founded in 1956. Regionally accredited. Student body reflects both traditional (65%) and non-traditional (45%) students who commute to classes from 3-state area (OH, KY, WV). **Degrees:** 122 associate awarded; master's offered. **Location:** 20 miles from Huntington, WV. **Calendar:** Semester, limited summer session. **Full-time faculty:** 45 total. **Part-time faculty:** 105 total. **Special facilities:** Microwave link with main campus and other regional campuses, Ohio horse park, nature center, Proctorville center.

Basis for selection. Open admission. **Home schooled:** Transcript of courses and grades, state high school equivalency certificate required. Written verification from appropriate school district excusing attendance, personal statement discussing academic preparation for college, ACT, SAT required.

High school preparation. College-preparatory program recommended.

2015-2016 Annual costs. Tuition/fees: $4,806; $6,652 out-of-state. Books/supplies: $873. Personal expenses: $1,257.

Financial aid. Non-need-based: Scholarships awarded for academics, state residency.

Application procedures. Admission: No deadline. $20 fee, may be waived for applicants with need. Admission notification on a rolling basis. **Financial aid:** Priority date 3/1, closing date 3/15. FAFSA required. Applicants notified on a rolling basis starting 4/1.

Academics. Special study options: Distance learning, double major, dual enrollment of high school students, teacher certification program. **Credit/placement by examination:** AP, CLEP, institutional tests. **Support services:** Learning center, remedial instruction, study skills assistance, tutoring, writing center.

Majors. Business: Business admin. **Communications:** Communications/speech/rhetoric, health, organizational, political. **Health services:** Nursing (RN). **History:** General. **Protective services:** Criminal justice. **Psychology:** General.

Technology on campus. Commuter students can connect to campus network. Online course registration, online library, helpline, repair service, wireless network available.

Student life. Freshman orientation: Mandatory. Preregistration for classes offered. Summer and online orientations available. **Activities:** Concert band, international student organizations, literary magazine, music ensembles, radio station, student government, TV station, Phi Alpha Xi service honor society, Los Amigos Internacionales club, diversity student council, student nurses association, psychology club, art club.

Athletics. Intercollegiate: Equestrian.

Student services. Adult student services, career counseling, services for economically disadvantaged, student employment services, financial aid counseling, minority student services, personal counseling, veterans' counselor. **Physically disabled:** Services for visually, speech, hearing impaired.

Contact. E-mail: askousc@ohiou.edu
Phone: (740) 533-4600 Toll-free number: (800) 626-0513
Fax: (740) 533-4632
Kim Keffer, Director of Enrollment and Student Services, Ohio University: Southern Campus at Ironton, 1804 Liberty Avenue, Ironton, OH 45638

Ohio University: Zanesville Campus
Zanesville, Ohio
www.ohio.edu/zanesville   CB code: 0846

+ Public 4-year branch campus college
+ Commuter campus in large town
+ 1,992 degree-seeking undergraduates

General. Founded in 1946. Regionally accredited. **Degrees:** 83 associate awarded. **Location:** 55 miles from Columbus. **Calendar:** Semester, limited summer session. **Full-time faculty:** 35 total. **Part-time faculty:** 75 total.

Basis for selection. Open admission, but selective for some programs. Nursing admissions based on National League for Nursing test scores, high school GPA, and class rank. Admission to Colleges of Business, Engineering, and Communication based on high school rank and ACT scores. **Home schooled:** Transcript of courses and grades required.

High school preparation. College-preparatory program recommended. Recommended units include English 4, mathematics 3, social studies 3, science 3, foreign language 2 and visual/performing arts 1. One year of visual or performing arts recommended.

2015-2016 Annual costs. Tuition/fees: $4,994; $9,530 out-of-state. Books/supplies: $1,200. Personal expenses: $879.

Financial aid. Non-need-based: Scholarships awarded for academics, minority status.

Application procedures. Admission: Priority date 3/1; no deadline. $20 fee, may be waived for applicants with need. Admission notification on a rolling basis. **Financial aid:** Priority date 3/15; no closing date. FAFSA required. Applicants notified on a rolling basis starting 4/15; must reply within 2 week(s) of notification.

Academics. Special study options: Cross-registration, distance learning, double major, dual enrollment of high school students, independent study, internships, student-designed major, study abroad, teacher certification program. **Credit/placement by examination:** AP, CLEP, institutional tests. **Support services:** Learning center, reduced course load, remedial instruction, study skills assistance, tutoring, writing center.

Majors. Biology: General. **Communications:** Health, organizational. **Education:** Early childhood, middle. **Health services:** Health services admin, nursing (RN). **History:** General. **Human services:** Social work. **Protective services:** Police science. **Psychology:** General.

Technology on campus. 200 workstations in library, computer center. Commuter students can connect to campus network. Online course registration, online library, wireless network available.

Student life. Freshman orientation: Mandatory. Preregistration for classes offered. **Activities:** Campus ministries, choral groups, literary magazine, radio station, student government, cultural events committee, student nursing association.

Athletics. Intercollegiate: Baseball M, basketball, golf, volleyball W. **Team name:** Tracers.

Student services. Career counseling, student employment services, financial aid counseling, personal counseling, placement for graduates, veterans' counselor.

Contact. E-mail: ouzservices@ohio.edu
Phone: (740) 588-1439 Fax: (740) 588-1444
Jason Howard, Associate Director of Student Services, Ohio University: Zanesville Campus, 1425 Newark Road, Zanesville, OH 43701

Ohio Wesleyan University
Delaware, Ohio   CB member
www.owu.edu   CB code: 1594

+ Private 4-year liberal arts college affiliated with the United Methodist Church
+ Residential campus in large town
+ 1,668 degree-seeking undergraduates: 1% part-time, 52% women, 8% African American, 3% Asian American, 5% Hispanic/Latino, 5% Multiracial, non-Hispanic, 6% international
+ 75% of applicants admitted
+ Application essay required
+ 71% graduate within 6 years

General. Founded in 1842. Regionally accredited. **Degrees:** 356 bachelor's awarded. **ROTC:** Army, Air Force. **Location:** 25 miles from Columbus. **Calendar:** Semester, limited summer session. **Full-time faculty:** 137 total; 100% have terminal degrees, 6% minority, 39% women. **Part-time faculty:** 79 total; 8% minority, 40% women. **Class size:** 72% < 20, 27% 20-39, 1% 40-49, less than 1% 50-99. **Special facilities:** 2 observatories, US Department of Agriculture laboratories, 2 nature field study preserves, science center, art museum, large pipe organ with 4,644 pipes.

Freshman class profile. 3,949 applied, 2,955 admitted, 435 enrolled.

Mid 50% test scores			
		GPA 2.0-2.99:	24%
SAT critical reading:	510-630	Rank in top quarter:	52%
SAT math:	510-620	Rank in top tenth:	23%
SAT writing:	480-610	Return as sophomores:	78%
ACT composite:	22-28	Out-of-state:	50%
GPA 3.75 or higher:	30%	Live on campus:	95%
GPA 3.50-3.74:	17%	International:	4%
GPA 3.0-3.49:	29%		

Basis for selection. High school record (level of challenge and success) most important, followed by class rank, recommendations, test scores, essay, extracurricular activities, general aptitude, character, volunteerism, alumni affiliation. Special consideration given to music, fine art and theater talent. Interview recommended for all. Audition required for music programs. Portfolio recommended for art programs. Essay required of all applicants. **Home schooled:** Statement describing home school structure and mission, transcript of courses and grades, state high school equivalency certificate, letter of recommendation (nonparent) required.

High school preparation. College-preparatory program required. 15 units required; 19 recommended. Required and recommended units include English 4, mathematics 3-4, social studies 3-4, science 3-4 and foreign language 2-3.

2015-2016 Annual costs. Tuition/fees: $43,230. Room/board: $11,540. Books/supplies: $1,300. Personal expenses: $1,700.

2014-2015 Financial aid. **Need-based:** 404 full-time freshmen applied for aid; 344 deemed to have need; 344 received aid. Average need met was 79%. Average scholarship/grant was $28,970; average loan $3,558. 77% of total undergraduate aid awarded as scholarships/grants, 23% as loans/jobs. **Non-need-based:** Awarded to 742 full-time undergraduates, including 206 freshmen. Scholarships awarded for academics, alumni affiliation, art, minority status, music/drama, religious affiliation, state residency.

Application procedures. **Admission:** Priority date 1/15; deadline 3/1 (postmark date). No application fee. Admission notification on a rolling basis beginning on or about 1/30. Must reply by May 1 or within 2 week(s) if notified thereafter. $400 enrollment deposit is due by 5/01. **Financial aid:** Priority date 2/15; no closing date. FAFSA required. Applicants notified on a rolling basis starting 2/15; must reply by 5/1 or within 2 week(s) of notification.

Academics. **Special study options:** Combined bachelor's/graduate degree, double major, dual enrollment of high school students, exchange student, honors, independent study, internships, New York semester, student-designed major, study abroad, teacher certification program, United Nations semester, urban semester, Washington semester. 3-2 engineering programs with Washington University (MO), Case Western Reserve University, California Institute of Technology (CA), Rensselaer Polytechnic Institute (NY), Alfred College of Ceramics (NY), and Polytechnic Institute of New York. **Credit/placement by examination:** AP, CLEP, IB, SAT, ACT, institutional tests. International Baccalaureate credit given for specific performance levels on higher exams. Students may receive exemption from certain requirements for test scores on SAT, SAT Subject Tests or ACT. **Support services:** Learning center, reduced course load, study skills assistance, tutoring, writing center. Quantitative Skills Center provides individualized and alternative modes of instruction and tutoring to students who need assistance with math skills in any area of study.

Majors. **Area/ethnic studies:** African-American, East Asian, women's. **Biology:** General, bacteriology, biochemistry, botany, genetics, microbiology, neuroscience, zoology. **Business:** Accounting, international, managerial economics. **Communications:** General, broadcast journalism, journalism, media studies. **Computer sciences:** General, computer science. **Conservation:** Environmental studies. **Education:** General, art, biology, chemistry, drama/dance, early childhood, elementary, foreign languages, French, German, health, kindergarten/preschool, Latin, mathematics, middle, multi-level teacher, music, physical, physics, science, secondary, social science, social studies, Spanish. **Engineering:** Pre-engineering. **English:** American lit, British lit, creative writing, English lit, writing. **Foreign languages:** Biblical, classics, comparative lit, French, German, Latin, Spanish. **Health services:** Predental, premedicine, preveterinary. **History:** General. **Liberal arts:** Arts/sciences. **Math:** General, statistics. **Philosophy/religion:** Philosophy, religion. **Physical sciences:** Astronomy, chemistry, geology, physics. **Psychology:** General. **Social sciences:** Anthropology, economics, geography, international relations, political science, sociology, U.S. government, urban studies.

Theology: Preministerial. **Visual/performing arts:** Art history/conservation, dance, dramatic, music, music performance, studio arts.

Most popular majors. Biology 14%, business/marketing 12%, English 7%, parks/recreation 7%, psychology 9%, social sciences 14%, visual/performing arts 9%.

Technology on campus. 300 workstations in dormitories, library, computer center, student center. Dormitories wired for high-speed internet access and linked to campus network. Commuter students can connect to campus network. Online course registration, online library, helpline, repair service, student web hosting, wireless network available.

Student life. **Freshman orientation:** Mandatory. Preregistration for classes offered. Two-day session held in June and during the week before classes begin in August. **Housing:** Guaranteed on-campus for all undergraduates. Coed dorms, single-sex dorms, apartments, fraternity/sorority housing, themed housing available. Pets allowed in dorm rooms. Small living units offer unique living opportunities to groups of (10-15 students). **Activities:** Bands, campus ministries, choral groups, dance, drama, international student organizations, literary magazine, music ensembles, Model UN, musical theater, opera, radio station, student government, student newspaper, symphony orchestra, B'nai B'rith Hillel Chapter, Christian Fellowship, Young Democrats, College Republicans, student union on black awareness, Sisters United, Tauheed, gay/lesbian/bisexual/transgender center, women's resource center, Habitat for Humanity.

Athletics. NCAA. **Intercollegiate:** Baseball M, basketball, cross-country, diving, field hockey W, football (tackle) M, golf, lacrosse, soccer, softball W, swimming, tennis, track and field, volleyball W. **Intramural:** Basketball, football (non-tackle), racquetball, soccer, tennis, volleyball. **Team name:** Battling Bishops.

Student services. Alcohol/substance abuse counseling, chaplain/spiritual director, career counseling, student employment services, financial aid counseling, health services, minority student services, on-campus daycare, personal counseling.

Contact. E-mail: owuadmit@owu.edu
Phone: (740) 368-3020 Toll-free number: (800) 922-8953
Fax: (740) 368-3314
Susan Dileno, Vice President for Enrollment, Ohio Wesleyan University, 61 South Sandusky Street, Delaware, OH 43015-2398

Otterbein University

Westerville, Ohio   **CB member**
www.otterbein.edu   **CB code: 1597**

- Private 4-year university and liberal arts college affiliated with the United Methodist Church
- Residential campus in large town
- 2,343 degree-seeking undergraduates: 9% part-time, 61% women, 6% African American, 2% Asian American, 2% Hispanic/Latino, 4% Multiracial, non-Hispanic, 2% international
- 465 degree-seeking graduate students
- 72% of applicants admitted
- SAT or ACT (ACT writing optional), application essay required
- 59% graduate within 6 years

General. Founded in 1847. Regionally accredited. **Degrees:** 497 bachelor's awarded; master's, professional offered. **ROTC:** Army, Air Force. **Location:** 12 miles from Columbus. **Calendar:** 4-1-4, limited summer session. **Full-time faculty:** 181 total; 90% have terminal degrees, 10% minority, 57% women. **Part-time faculty:** 155 total; 5% minority, 64% women. **Class size:** 70% < 20, 27% 20-39, less than 1% 40-49, 2% 50-99. **Special facilities:** Horse stables and riding facility, 3 performance stages, 3 art galleries.

Freshman class profile. 2,196 applied, 1,590 admitted, 561 enrolled.

Mid 50% test scores			
		GPA 2.0-2.99:	21%
SAT critical reading:	500-610	Rank in top quarter:	55%
SAT math:	490-610	Rank in top tenth:	26%
SAT writing:	470-600	Return as sophomores:	81%
ACT composite:	21-27	Out-of-state:	12%
GPA 3.75 or higher:	30%	Live on campus:	84%
GPA 3.50-3.74:	21%	International:	1%
GPA 3.0-3.49:	28%		

Basis for selection. School achievement record most important; test scores also important. Recommendations, essay, interview, and extracurricular activities considered. ACT used for placement in Nursing and Education. Visit recommended for all; audition required for music and theater programs;

portfolio recommended for visual art program. Essays required for scholarships. **Home schooled:** Statement describing home school structure and mission, transcript of courses and grades required. Submit written documentation of successful completion of college preparatory high school equivalency. Transcripts from cooperating school district preferred. **Learning Disabled:** Students with diagnosed learning disabilities recommended to send documentation with admission application.

High school preparation. College-preparatory program recommended. 17 units required; 22 recommended. Required and recommended units include English 4, mathematics 3, social studies 3, history 2, science 3 and foreign language 2. One unit in fine arts recommended.

2016-2017 Annual costs. Tuition/fees (projected): $31,624. Room/board: $10,006. Books/supplies: $1,258. Personal expenses: $1,624.

2014-2015 Financial aid. Need-based: 65% of total undergraduate aid awarded as scholarships/grants, 35% as loans/jobs. **Non-need-based:** Scholarships awarded for academics, alumni affiliation, art, leadership, minority status, music/drama, state residency.

Application procedures. Admission: Priority date 1/15; no deadline. $25 fee, may be waived for applicants with need. Admission notification on a rolling basis beginning on or about 10/1. Must reply by May 1 or within 4 week(s) if notified thereafter. Students applying between May 1 and June 1 accepted on space-available basis. **Financial aid:** Priority date 2/15; no closing date. FAFSA required. Applicants notified on a rolling basis starting 2/15.

Academics. Special study options: Combined bachelor's/graduate degree, cross-registration, double major, dual enrollment of high school students, ESL, exchange student, honors, independent study, internships, liberal arts/career combination, student-designed major, study abroad, teacher certification program, Washington semester. BA/BS in engineering with Washington University (MO) or Case Western Reserve University. **Credit/placement by examination:** AP, CLEP, IB, SAT, ACT, institutional tests. 60 credit hours maximum toward bachelor's degree. **Support services:** Learning center, reduced course load, remedial instruction, study skills assistance, tutoring, writing center.

Honors college/program. Presidential Scholars or must be in top 10% of high school class and have 25 ACT.

Majors. Biology: General, biochemistry, molecular. **Business:** General, accounting, actuarial science, business admin, finance, managerial economics. **Communications:** Broadcast journalism, communications/speech/rhetoric, journalism, organizational, public relations. **Computer sciences:** Computer science. **Conservation:** General, environmental studies, wildlife/wilderness. **Education:** General, art, biology, chemistry, early childhood, elementary, English, foreign languages, French, health, history, mathematics, middle, multi-level teacher, music, physical, physics, science, secondary, social studies, Spanish, special ed. **English:** Creative writing, English lit, writing. **Foreign languages:** French, Spanish. **Health services:** Athletic training, nursing (RN), predental, premedicine, prepharmacy, preveterinary. **History:** General. **Math:** General. **Parks/recreation:** Health/fitness, sports admin. **Philosophy/religion:** Philosophy, religion. **Physical sciences:** Chemistry, physics. **Psychology:** General. **Social sciences:** Economics, international relations, political science, sociology. **Visual/performing arts:** General, acting, art, dramatic, music, music history, music performance, music theory/composition, theater design.

Most popular majors. Business/marketing 12%, communications/journalism 8%, education 12%, health sciences 16%, parks/recreation 6%, psychology 7%, visual/performing arts 11%.

Technology on campus. 124 workstations in dormitories, library, computer center. Dormitories wired for high-speed internet access and linked to campus network. Commuter students can connect to campus network. Online course registration, online library, helpline, wireless network available.

Student life. Freshman orientation: Mandatory, $150 fee. Preregistration for classes offered. One-day program held in July or August. **Housing:** Guaranteed on-campus for freshmen. Coed dorms, single-sex dorms, apartments, fraternity/sorority housing, themed housing available. Pets allowed in dorm rooms. **Activities:** Bands, campus ministries, choral groups, dance, drama, international student organizations, music ensembles, musical theater, radio station, student government, symphony orchestra, TV station, Fellowship of Christian Athletes, Christian support group, Afro-American student union, Asian American student union, international students association, religious life council.

Athletics. NCAA. **Intercollegiate:** Baseball M, basketball, cheerleading, cross-country, equestrian, football (tackle) M, golf, lacrosse, soccer, softball W, tennis, track and field, volleyball W. **Intramural:** Basketball, bowling, football (non-tackle), handball, racquetball, soccer, softball, volleyball. **Team name:** Cardinals.

Student services. Adult student services, alcohol/substance abuse counseling, chaplain/spiritual director, career counseling, student employment services, financial aid counseling, health services, minority student services, personal counseling, veterans' counselor.

Contact. E-mail: uotterb@otterbein.edu
Phone: (614) 823-1500 Toll-free number: (800) 488-8144
Fax: (614) 823-1200
Ben Shoemaker, Director of Admission, Otterbein University, One Otterbein College, Westerville, OH 43081

Pontifical College Josephinum
Columbus, Ohio
www.pcj.edu   CB code: 1348

- Private 4-year liberal arts and seminary college for men affiliated with the Roman Catholic Church
- Residential campus in very large city
- 110 undergraduates
- SAT or ACT (ACT writing optional), application essay, interview required

General. Founded in 1892. Regionally accredited; also accredited by ATS. **Degrees:** 36 bachelor's awarded; master's offered. **Location:** 11 miles from downtown. **Calendar:** Semester. **Full-time faculty:** 22 total. **Part-time faculty:** 10 total. **Class size:** 80% < 20, 19% 20-39, 2% 50-99.

Freshman class profile.

Out-of-state: 64% Live on campus: 100%

Basis for selection. School achievement record, recommendations from pastor and director of vocations required. **Home schooled:** Transcript of courses and grades required.

High school preparation. College-preparatory program recommended. 10 units required; 18 recommended. Required and recommended units include English 4, mathematics 2-4, social studies 2-4, science 1-4 and foreign language 1-2.

2015-2016 Annual costs. Tuition/fees: $21,038. Room/board: $9,300. Books/supplies: $1,000.

Financial aid. All financial aid based on need.

Application procedures. Admission: Priority date 8/1; no deadline. $25 fee, may be waived for applicants with need. Application must be submitted on paper. Admission notification on a rolling basis beginning on or about 5/1. **Financial aid:** Priority date 9/2; no closing date. FAFSA, institutional form required. Applicants notified on a rolling basis starting 8/15; must reply within 2 week(s) of notification.

Academics. Students participate in supervised field experience and clinical pastoral education. **Special study options:** Double major, ESL, honors, independent study. **Credit/placement by examination:** AP, CLEP, IB, institutional tests. 30 credit hours maximum toward bachelor's degree. **Support services:** Learning center, reduced course load, remedial instruction, tutoring, writing center.

Majors. Area/ethnic studies: Chicano/Hispanic-American/Latino, Latin American. **English:** English lit. **History:** General. **Liberal arts:** Humanities. **Philosophy/religion:** Philosophy, religion.

Most popular majors. Philosophy/religious studies 83%.

Technology on campus. 16 workstations in library, computer center. Dormitories wired for high-speed internet access and linked to campus network. Commuter students can connect to campus network. Online course registration, online library, helpline, wireless network available.

Student life. Freshman orientation: Mandatory. Preregistration for classes offered. **Policies:** Daily chapel, morning and evening prayer. Religious observance required. **Activities:** Choral groups, music ensembles, student government.

Athletics. Intramural: Basketball M, soccer M, softball M.

Student services. Chaplain/spiritual director, career counseling, financial aid counseling, health services, personal counseling.

Contact. E-mail: acrawford@pcj.edu
Phone: (614) 985-2241 Toll-free number: (888) 252-5812
Fax: (614) 885-2307
V. Rev. James Wehner, Director of Admissions, Pontifical College
Josephinum, 7625 North High Street, Columbus, OH 43235-1499

Rabbinical College of Telshe
Wickliffe, Ohio

CB code: 1660

- Private 4-year rabbinical and teachers college for men affiliated with the Jewish faith
- Small city
- 52 undergraduates

General. Founded in 1941. Accredited by AARTS. **Degrees:** 11 bachelor's awarded; master's offered. **Calendar:** Semester. **Full-time faculty:** 10 total. **Part-time faculty:** 15 total.

Basis for selection. GED not accepted. Personal interview and religious commitment most important. **Home schooled:** Interview required.

2015-2016 Annual costs. Tuition/fees: $9,900. Room/board: $3,000. Books/supplies: $300. Personal expenses: $1,000.

Application procedures. Admission: Closing date 8/15. $100 fee.

Academics. Credit/placement by examination: AP, CLEP.

Majors. Theology: Theology.

Student life. Freshman orientation: Mandatory. Preregistration for classes offered.

Contact. Phone: (440) 943-5300 ext. 17 Fax: (440) 943-5303
Rabbi Abraham Matitia, Registrar, Rabbinical College of Telshe, 28400
Euclid Avenue, Wickliffe, OH 44092-2584

Shawnee State University
Portsmouth, Ohio
www.shawnee.edu

CB member
CB code: 1790

- Public 4-year university
- Commuter campus in large town
- 3,461 degree-seeking undergraduates: 13% part-time, 56% women, 6% African American, 1% Hispanic/Latino, 1% Native American, 2% Multiracial, non-Hispanic, 1% international
- 152 degree-seeking graduate students

General. Founded in 1986. Regionally accredited. **Degrees:** 434 bachelor's, 267 associate awarded; master's offered. **Location:** 90 miles from Columbus, 115 miles from Cincinnati. **Calendar:** Semester, extensive summer session. **Full-time faculty:** 153 total; 60% have terminal degrees, 10% minority, 43% women. **Part-time faculty:** 181 total; 3% minority, 56% women. **Class size:** 54% < 20, 40% 20-39, 4% 40-49, 1% 50-99, less than 1% >100. **Special facilities:** Planetarium, motion capture studio, center for the arts.

Freshman class profile. 3,694 applied, 2,765 admitted, 914 enrolled.

Mid 50% test scores		Rank in top quarter:	35%
SAT critical reading:	410-580	Rank in top tenth:	15%
SAT math:	400-560	End year in good standing:	66%
SAT writing:	390-500	Return as sophomores:	64%
ACT composite:	18-24	Out-of-state:	12%
GPA 3.75 or higher:	18%	Live on campus:	41%
GPA 3.50-3.74:	15%	International:	1%
GPA 3.0-3.49:	29%	Fraternities:	1%
GPA 2.0-2.99:	28%	Sororities:	1%

Basis for selection. Open admission, but selective for some programs. ACT required, interview recommended for admission to allied health programs. SAT/ACT may be used in lieu of university-developed placement test. **Home schooled:** State high school equivalency certificate required. GED required.

High school preparation. College-preparatory program recommended. 16 units recommended. Recommended units include English 4, mathematics 3, social studies 3, science 3, foreign language 2 and visual/performing arts 1. Algebra, biology, chemistry required for allied health programs.

2015-2016 Annual costs. Tuition/fees: $7,364; $12,761 out-of-state. Room/board: $9,766. Books/supplies: $1,440. Personal expenses: $2,642.

Financial aid. Additional information: ACT recommended for scholarship applicants.

Application procedures. Admission: No deadline. No application fee. Admission notification on a rolling basis. **Financial aid:** Priority date 2/16; no closing date. FAFSA required. Applicants notified on a rolling basis starting 3/15; must reply within 4 week(s) of notification.

Academics. Special study options: Accelerated study, combined bachelor's/graduate degree, distance learning, double major, dual enrollment of high school students, ESL, honors, independent study, internships, student-designed major, study abroad, teacher certification program. **Credit/placement by examination:** AP, CLEP, institutional tests. **Support services:** Learning center, reduced course load, remedial instruction, study skills assistance, tutoring, writing center.

Majors. Biology: General. **Business:** Business admin. **Education:** General, art, early childhood, elementary special ed, mathematics, multi-level teacher, science, social science, special ed. **English:** English lit. **Health services:** Athletic training, nursing (RN). **History:** General. **Math:** General. **Parks/recreation:** Health/fitness, sports admin. **Philosophy/religion:** General. **Physical sciences:** Chemistry. **Psychology:** General. **Social sciences:** General, international relations, sociology. **Visual/performing arts:** Game design, studio arts.

Most popular majors. Biology 9%, business/marketing 21%, education 11%, engineering/engineering technologies 6%, health sciences 7%, parks/recreation 7%, psychology 10%, social sciences 10%, visual/performing arts 7%.

Technology on campus. 620 workstations in library, computer center, student center. Dormitories wired for high-speed internet access. Commuter students can connect to campus network. Online course registration, online library, helpline, wireless network available.

Student life. Freshman orientation: Mandatory. Preregistration for classes offered. One-day programs held throughout the summer. **Housing:** Coed dorms, themed housing available. $150 partly refundable deposit. **Activities:** Campus ministries, choral groups, drama, international student organizations, literary magazine, music ensembles, musical theater, student government, student newspaper.

Athletics. NAIA. **Intercollegiate:** Baseball M, basketball, cross-country, golf M, soccer, softball W, tennis W, volleyball W. **Intramural:** Basketball, bowling, golf, racquetball, softball M, swimming, table tennis, tennis, volleyball. **Team name:** Bears.

Student services. Alcohol/substance abuse counseling, career counseling, services for economically disadvantaged, student employment services, financial aid counseling, health services, on-campus daycare, personal counseling, placement for graduates, veterans' counselor. **Physically disabled:** Services for visually, speech, hearing impaired.

Contact. E-mail: to_ssu@shawnee.edu
Phone: (740) 351-4778 Toll-free number: (800) 959-2778
Fax: (740) 351-3111
Rick Merb, Director of Admissions, Shawnee State University, 940
Second Street, Portsmouth, OH 45662

Tiffin University
Tiffin, Ohio
www.tiffin.edu

CB member
CB code: 1817

- Private 4-year university and liberal arts college
- Residential campus in large town
- 2,309 degree-seeking undergraduates: 22% part-time, 51% women, 14% African American, 3% Hispanic/Latino, 3% Multi-racial, non-Hispanic, 10% international
- 1,052 degree-seeking graduate students
- 93% of applicants admitted
- SAT or ACT (ACT writing optional) required
- 43% graduate within 6 years

General. Founded in 1888. Regionally accredited. Off-campus courses offered in Cleveland, Lorain, Columbus, Elyria, Toledo, Fremont, and Cincinnati. **Degrees:** 483 bachelor's, 102 associate awarded; master's offered. **ROTC:** Army, Air Force. **Location:** 50 miles from Toledo, 90 miles from Columbus. **Calendar:** Semester, limited summer session. **Full-time faculty:** 84 total; 61% have terminal degrees, 16% minority, 48% women. **Part-time**

Four-Year Colleges

faculty: 281 total; 35% have terminal degrees, 46% women. **Class size:** 56% < 20, 42% 20-39, 2% 40-49, less than 1% 50-99. **Special facilities:** Nature preserve.

Freshman class profile. 2,668 applied, 2,485 admitted, 487 enrolled.

Mid 50% test scores		Rank in top quarter:	23%
SAT critical reading:	400-530	Rank in top tenth:	8%
SAT math:	390-510	Return as sophomores:	62%
ACT composite:	18-23	Out-of-state:	25%
GPA 3.75 or higher:	9%	Live on campus:	83%
GPA 3.50-3.74:	16%	International:	8%
GPA 3.0-3.49:	32%	Fraternities:	2%
GPA 2.0-2.99:	42%	Sororities:	2%

Basis for selection. Test scores, GPA very important. Students with below 2.0 GPA may be admitted conditionally into Learning Assistance Program. Interview required for academically weak applicants.

High school preparation. College-preparatory program recommended. Required units include English 4, mathematics 4, social studies 3, history 0.5, science 3 (laboratory 1), visual/performing arts 1 and academic electives 5.

2015-2016 Annual costs. Tuition/fees: $22,165. Room/board: $10,196. Books/supplies: $2,000. Personal expenses: $1,000.

2015-2016 Financial aid. **Need-based:** Average need met was 67%. Average scholarship/grant was $14,690. 54% of total undergraduate aid awarded as scholarships/grants, 46% as loans/jobs. **Non-need-based:** Scholarships awarded for academics, art, athletics, leadership, music/drama, state residency.

Application procedures. **Admission:** No deadline. $20 fee, may be waived for applicants with need, free for online applicants. Admission notification on a rolling basis beginning on or about 9/1. **Financial aid:** No deadline. FAFSA required. Applicants notified on a rolling basis starting 2/1; must reply within 2 week(s) of notification.

Academics. **Special study options:** Accelerated study, cross-registration, distance learning, double major, dual enrollment of high school students, ESL, exchange student, honors, independent study, internships, student-designed major, study abroad, Washington semester. **Credit/placement by examination:** AP, CLEP, IB, SAT, ACT, institutional tests. 15 credit hours maximum toward associate degree, 30 toward bachelor's. **Support services:** Learning center, pre-admission summer program, reduced course load, remedial instruction, study skills assistance, tutoring, writing center.

Majors. **Business:** Accounting, business admin, e-commerce, finance, hospitality admin, human resources, international, logistics, marketing, nonprofit/public, operations, organizational behavior. **Communications:** Communications/speech/rhetoric, digital media, journalism, media studies, public relations. **Computer sciences:** General, information systems, information technology. **Education:** General, English, history, science. **English:** English lit. **Health services:** Health care admin, health services admin, long term care admin, substance abuse counseling. **History:** General. **Liberal arts:** Arts/sciences. **Parks/recreation:** Sports admin. **Protective services:** Computer forensics, corrections, counterterrorism, forensics, homeland security, law enforcement admin, special ops. **Psychology:** General, experimental, forensic, industrial. **Social sciences:** Criminology, international relations. **Visual/performing arts:** Art, music, music management, studio arts management.

Most popular majors. Business/marketing 36%, psychology 13%, security/protective services 37%.

Technology on campus. 300 workstations in dormitories, library, computer center, student center. Dormitories wired for high-speed internet access and linked to campus network. Commuter students can connect to campus network. Online course registration, online library, helpline, repair service, wireless network available.

Student life. **Freshman orientation:** Available. Preregistration for classes offered. Three-part program; first part occurs on a Saturday in April or May, or on a Friday in June; second part is a weekend in late July; third part occurs during first weekend of classes. **Policies:** Lower-division residential students required to be on meal plan. All undergraduates complete 26 hours of co-curricular credit. **Housing:** Guaranteed on-campus for freshmen. Coed dorms, single-sex dorms, special housing for disabled, apartments, fraternity/sorority housing, themed housing available. $100 partly refundable deposit, deadline 8/20. Theme housing, performing arts, leadership society, junior/senior house units available. **Activities:** Bands, campus ministries, choral groups, dance, drama, international student organizations, Model UN, musical theater, opera, radio station, student government, student newspaper, Black United Students, World Student Organization, Greek Council, H2O, Delta Sigma Kappa, gospel choir, Circle K, residence life council, Student African-American Brotherhood, Student African-American Sisterhood for Excellence.

Athletics. NCAA. **Intercollegiate:** Baseball M, basketball, cross-country, equestrian, football (tackle) M, golf, lacrosse W, soccer, softball W, tennis, track and field, volleyball W, wrestling M. **Intramural:** Basketball, cross-country. **Team name:** Dragons.

Student services. Adult student services, career counseling, student employment services, financial aid counseling, health services, minority student services, personal counseling, placement for graduates, veterans' counselor, women's services.

Contact. E-mail: admissions@tiffin.edu
Phone: (419) 447-6443 ext. 3423
Toll-free number: (800) 968-6446 ext. 3423 Fax: (419) 443-5006
Ronald Schumacher, Vice President for Enrollment Management, Tiffin University, 155 Miami Street, Tiffin, OH 44883

Tri-State Bible College
South Point, Ohio
www.tsbc.edu

- Private 4-year Bible college
- Commuter campus in rural community
- 49 degree-seeking undergraduates
- 3 graduate students
- Interview required

General. Accredited by ABHE. Main campus is located in South Point, Ohio; additional location in Akron, Ohio. Offering a biblically oriented program. **Degrees:** 3 bachelor's, 2 associate awarded. **Location:** 150 miles from Cincinnati, 150 miles from Columbus. **Calendar:** Semester, limited summer session. **Full-time faculty:** 6 total. **Part-time faculty:** 16 total. **Special facilities:** Bible research center, chapel.

Freshman class profile. 18 applied, 18 admitted, 18 enrolled.

Basis for selection. Open admission. **Home schooled:** State high school equivalency certificate required.

2015-2016 Annual costs. Tuition/fees: $9,600. Books/supplies: $540.

Application procedures. **Admission:** No deadline. $25 fee. **Financial aid:** No deadline.

Academics. **Special study options:** Distance learning. **Credit/placement by examination:** AP, CLEP. **Support services:** Learning center, remedial instruction, study skills assistance, tutoring.

Technology on campus. 3 workstations in library, student center. Commuter students can connect to campus network. Online course registration, wireless network available.

Student life. **Activities:** Student government.

Student services. Chaplain/spiritual director, financial aid counseling.

Contact. E-mail: tsbc@zoominternet.net
Phone: (740) 377-2520 ext. 10 Fax: (740) 377-0001
Bobby Mercer, Director of Admissions, Tri-State Bible College, Office of Admissions, South Point, OH 45680-0445

Union Institute & University
Cincinnati, Ohio
CB member
www.myunion.edu

- Private 4-year university
- Commuter campus in very large city
- 1,027 degree-seeking undergraduates: 46% part-time, 51% women, 18% African American, 1% Asian American, 32% Hispanic/Latino, 1% Native Hawaiian/Pacific islander, 2% Multi-racial, non-Hispanic
- 350 degree-seeking graduate students
- Application essay required

General. Founded in 1964. Regionally accredited. Academic centers in Brattleboro, VT; North Miami Beach, FL; Los Angeles and Sacramento, CA. **Degrees:** 597 bachelor's awarded; master's, doctoral offered. **Location:** 2 miles from downtown. **Calendar:** Continuous, extensive summer session. **Full-time faculty:** 34 total; 76% have terminal degrees, 29% minority, 44% women. **Part-time faculty:** 264 total; 36% have terminal degrees, 33% minority, 52% women. **Class size:** 94% < 20, 6% 20-39.

Basis for selection. Maturity and evidence of ability to engage in self-directed learning is important. Programs designed for adult learners; majority are over age 25. Students whose native language is not English are required to take the TOEFL.

2015-2016 Annual costs. Tuition/fees: $15,144. Books/supplies: $1,000. Personal expenses: $2,200.

Financial aid. Non-need-based: Scholarships awarded for academics, state residency.

Application procedures. Admission: No deadline. No application fee. Admission notification on a rolling basis. **Financial aid:** No deadline. FAFSA required. Must reply within 4 week(s) of notification.

Academics. All undergraduate courses are available through online learning or tutorials. **Special study options:** Accelerated study, cross-registration, distance learning, double major, independent study, internships, weekend college. Some majors offer courses at students' place of employment. **Credit/placement by examination:** AP, CLEP, IB. 30 credit hours maximum toward bachelor's degree. **Support services:** Reduced course load, study skills assistance, tutoring, writing center.

Majors. Business: Business admin, organizational leadership. **Education:** Elementary, ESL, secondary, special ed. **Health services:** Maternal/child health. **Human services:** Social work. **Protective services:** Disaster management, law enforcement admin. **Psychology:** General. **Work/family studies:** Child development.

Most popular majors. Family/consumer sciences 21%, security/protective services 62%.

Technology on campus. 74 workstations in computer center. Commuter students can connect to campus network. Online course registration, online library, helpline, wireless network available.

Student life. Freshman orientation: Available. Preregistration for classes offered.

Student services. Adult student services, career counseling, financial aid counseling, veterans' counselor. **Physically disabled:** Services for visually, speech, hearing impaired.

Contact. E-mail: admissions@myunion.edu
Phone: (800) 861-6400 Toll-free number: (800) 861-6400
Fax: (513) 861-3218
Kimbrea Browning, V.P. Enrollment Management, Union Institute & University, 440 East McMillan Street, Cincinnati, OH 45206

University of Akron

Akron, Ohio
www.uakron.edu

CB member
CB code: 1829

- Public 4-year university
- Commuter campus in small city
- 17,176 degree-seeking undergraduates: 15% part-time, 46% women, 12% African American, 2% Asian American, 2% Hispanic/Latino, 4% Multi-racial, non-Hispanic, 2% international
- 3,884 degree-seeking graduate students
- 97% of applicants admitted
- SAT or ACT (ACT writing recommended) required
- 40% graduate within 6 years

General. Founded in 1870. Regionally accredited. **Degrees:** 3,265 bachelor's, 663 associate awarded; master's, professional, doctoral offered. **ROTC:** Army, Air Force. **Location:** 40 miles from Cleveland. **Calendar:** Semester, limited summer session. **Full-time faculty:** 757 total; 80% have terminal degrees, 22% minority, 43% women. **Part-time faculty:** 748 total; 31% have terminal degrees, 9% minority, 54% women. **Class size:** 43% < 20, 43% 20-39, 6% 40-49, 5% 50-99, 2% >100. **Special facilities:** Polymer training center, bath nature preserve field station, gas turbine testing facility, training center for fire and hazardous materials.

Freshman class profile. 15,166 applied, 14,650 admitted, 3,919 enrolled.

Mid 50% test scores			
SAT critical reading:	440-580	**GPA 2.0-2.99:**	36%
SAT math:	450-610	**Rank in top quarter:**	38%
ACT composite:	19-26	**Rank in top tenth:**	16%
GPA 3.75 or higher:	17%	**Return as sophomores:**	74%
GPA 3.50-3.74:	17%	**Out-of-state:**	9%
GPA 3.0-3.49:	29%	**Live on campus:**	55%
		International:	1%

Basis for selection. School record, class rank, GPA, test scores most important. Open access to Applied Science and Technology Student Success Program and Wayne College. Essay, interview required for honors program; audition required for dance, music programs. **Home schooled:** Students required to obtain letter of exemption from school district.

High school preparation. College-preparatory program recommended. 15 units recommended. Recommended units include English 4, mathematics 3, social studies 3, science 3 and foreign language 2.

2015-2016 Annual costs. Tuition/fees: $10,509; $19,040 out-of-state. Room/board: $11,322. Books/supplies: $1,000. Personal expenses: $1,520.

2014-2015 Financial aid. Need-based: 3,476 full-time freshmen applied for aid; 2,796 deemed to have need; 2,796 received aid. Average need met was 53%. Average scholarship/grant was $4,915; average loan $3,255. 47% of total undergraduate aid awarded as scholarships/grants, 53% as loans/jobs. **Non-need-based:** Awarded to 9,003 full-time undergraduates, including 2,900 freshmen. Scholarships awarded for academics, art, athletics, leadership, music/drama, ROTC, state residency.

Application procedures. Admission: Priority date 3/15; deadline 7/1 (receipt date). $45 fee, may be waived for applicants with need. Admission notification on a rolling basis beginning on or about 9/15. **Financial aid:** Priority date 3/1; no closing date. FAFSA, institutional form required. Applicants notified on a rolling basis starting 3/15; must reply within 2 week(s) of notification.

Academics. Special study options: Accelerated study, combined bachelor's/graduate degree, cooperative education, distance learning, double major, ESL, external degree, honors, independent study, internships, student-designed major, study abroad, teacher certification program, weekend college. Undergraduates may take graduate level classes. Co-op programs in arts, business, computer science, engineering, family & consumer sciences, humanities, natural science, technologies. Dual enrollment offered for select graduate level programs. **Credit/placement by examination:** AP, CLEP, IB, SAT, ACT, institutional tests. 38 credit hours maximum toward associate degree, 38 toward bachelor's. **Support services:** Learning center, reduced course load, remedial instruction, study skills assistance, tutoring, writing center.

Honors college/program. Must have 2 out of 3 of following criteria: 3.5 GPA; high school class rank in highest 10%; 27 ACT or 1800 SAT. Some students with other unique qualifications may be admitted.

Majors. Architecture: Urban/community planning. **Biology:** General, animal physiology, bacteriology, biochemistry, biophysics, botany, ecology, microbiology, zoology. **Business:** General, accounting, business admin, e-commerce, finance, financial planning, hotel/motel admin, human resources, insurance, international, international finance, international marketing, logistics, management information systems, marketing, operations, real estate, retailing, sales/distribution. **Communications:** Broadcast journalism, communications/speech/rhetoric, media studies, organizational, public relations, radio/TV. **Computer sciences:** Computer science, networking, programming, systems analysis. **Education:** Art, bilingual, biology, business, chemistry, computer, drama/dance, early childhood, early childhood special, elementary, English, family/consumer sciences, foreign languages, foundations, French, German, health, history, kindergarten/preschool, leadership, learning disabled, mathematics, mentally handicapped, middle, multi-level teacher, multiple handicapped, music, physical, physically handicapped, physics, reading, school counseling, science, secondary, social science, social studies, Spanish, special ed, speech, voc/tech. **Engineering:** General, aerospace, applied physics, biomedical, chemical, civil, computer, electrical, mechanical, polymer. **English:** English lit. **Foreign languages:** Ancient Greek, classics, French, German, Latin, Russian, Spanish. **Health services:** Athletic training, audiology/speech pathology, clinical lab science, communication disorders, cytotechnology, dietetics, nursing (RN), physical therapy, premedicine, recreational therapy, respiratory therapy technology, speech pathology. **History:** General. **Human services:** Social work. **Liberal arts:** Arts/sciences, humanities. **Math:** General, applied, statistics. **Parks/recreation:** Exercise sciences, sports admin. **Philosophy/religion:** Philosophy. **Physical sciences:** Chemistry, geology, geophysics, molecular physics, physics, polymer chemistry. **Protective services:** Corrections, criminal justice, law enforcement admin. **Psychology:** General. **Social sciences:** General, anthropology, applied economics, criminology, economics, geography, GIS/cartography, international relations, political science, sociology, U.S. government. **Visual/performing arts:** Acting, art history/conservation, ceramics, crafts, dance, dramatic, drawing, graphic design, interior design, jazz, metal/jewelry, music, music history, music performance, music theory/composition, musicology, painting, photography, piano/keyboard, printmaking, sculpture, stringed instruments, studio arts, theater design, voice/opera. **Work/family studies:** General, child development, clothing/textiles, family systems, food/nutrition, housing.

Most popular majors. Business/marketing 20%, education 11%, engineering/engineering technologies 14%, health sciences 15%.

Technology on campus. 3,150 workstations in dormitories, library, student center. Dormitories wired for high-speed internet access and linked to campus network. Commuter students can connect to campus network. Online course registration, online library, helpline, repair service, student web hosting, wireless network available.

Student life. Freshman orientation: Mandatory, $125 fee. Preregistration for classes offered. One-day program over the summer and weekend before classes begin. **Policies:** All student organizations make own criteria for members, but some criteria stipulated through university, such as 2.0 GPA requirement and good standing within university. **Housing:** Coed dorms, single-sex dorms, special housing for disabled, fraternity/sorority housing available. $150 nonrefundable deposit, deadline 5/15. Honors student dormitory available. **Activities:** Bands, campus ministries, choral groups, dance, drama, international student organizations, music ensembles, musical theater, radio station, student government, student newspaper, symphony orchestra, TV station, Chinese students and scholars association, Indian students association, Muslim students association, black united students, H.O.L.A., Hillel, College Republicans, College Democrats, Campus Focus, gospel choir.

Athletics. NCAA. **Intercollegiate:** Basketball, cheerleading, cross-country, diving W, football (tackle) M, golf M, rifle, soccer, softball W, swimming W, tennis W, track and field, volleyball W. **Intramural:** Badminton, basketball, bowling, cross-country, golf, racquetball, skiing, soccer, softball, swimming, table tennis, track and field, volleyball W, wrestling M. **Team name:** Zips.

Student services. Adult student services, alcohol/substance abuse counseling, career counseling, student employment services, financial aid counseling, health services, minority student services, on-campus daycare, personal counseling, placement for graduates, veterans' counselor, women's services. **Physically disabled:** Services for visually, speech, hearing impaired.

Contact. E-mail: admissions@uakron.edu
Phone: (330) 972-7100 Toll-free number: (800) 655-4884
Fax: (330) 972-7022
Diane Raybuck, Director of Admissions, University of Akron, Simmons Hall, Akron, OH 44325-2001

University of Cincinnati
Cincinnati, Ohio
www.uc.edu

CB member
CB code: 1833

- Public 4-year university
- Commuter campus in large city
- 24,111 degree-seeking undergraduates: 13% part-time, 50% women, 7% African American, 3% Asian American, 3% Hispanic/Latino, 3% Multiracial, non-Hispanic, 4% international
- 10,531 degree-seeking graduate students
- 86% of applicants admitted
- SAT or ACT with writing, application essay required
- 66% graduate within 6 years

General. Founded in 1819. Regionally accredited. **Degrees:** 5,022 bachelor's, 73 associate awarded; master's, professional, doctoral offered. **ROTC:** Army, Air Force. **Location:** 2 miles from downtown. **Calendar:** Semester, extensive summer session. **Full-time faculty:** 1,296 total; 17% minority, 46% women. **Part-time faculty:** 987 total; 9% minority, 56% women. **Class size:** 41% < 20, 36% 20-39, 8% 40-49, 12% 50-99, 3% >100. **Special facilities:** Nipper Football Stadium (In the middle of campus, renovated in 2015), Dorothy & Reed Art Gallery, Astronomy Observatory (founded in 1842, the country's oldest), Mayne's Recreation Center (student housing, classrooms, athletic facilities - including a lazy river and six-court gymnasium, and dining hall), Vontz Center for Molecular Studies, Aronoff Center for Design and Art, College Conservatory of Music Village, CARE/Crawley research facilities, and Child Care Facility.

Freshman class profile. 15,286 applied, 13,081 admitted, 4,435 enrolled.

Mid 50% test scores			
SAT critical reading:	510-630	GPA 2.0-2.99:	12%
SAT math:	530-660	Rank in top quarter:	47%
SAT writing:	490-620	Rank in top tenth:	21%
ACT composite:	23-28	Return as sophomores:	88%
GPA 3.75 or higher:	31%	Out-of-state:	11%
GPA 3.50-3.74:	21%	Live on campus:	79%
GPA 3.0-3.49:	36%	International:	4%

Basis for selection. Secondary school record, test scores most important. Interview required for music programs; audition required for dance, music programs. **Home schooled:** Transcript of courses and grades required. Release for home schooling from local Board of Education required.

High school preparation. College-preparatory program required. 19 units required. Required and recommended units include English 4, mathematics 4, social studies 3, science 3 and foreign language 2. Specific requirements may vary for each college.

2015-2016 Annual costs. Tuition/fees: $11,000; $26,334 out-of-state. Room/board: $10,750. Books/supplies: $1,500. Personal expenses: $4,040.

2015-2016 Financial aid. Need-based: 3,706 full-time freshmen applied for aid; 2,694 deemed to have need; 2,546 received aid. Average need met was 48%. Average scholarship/grant was $6,894; average loan $3,718. 39% of total undergraduate aid awarded as scholarships/grants, 61% as loans/jobs. **Non-need-based:** Awarded to 8,121 full-time undergraduates, including 2,288 freshmen. Scholarships awarded for academics, alumni affiliation, art, athletics, leadership, minority status, music/drama, ROTC, state residency.

Application procedures. Admission: Priority date 12/1; deadline 3/1 (postmark date). $50 fee, may be waived for applicants with need. Admission notification on a rolling basis beginning on or about 10/1. Must reply by 5/1. **Financial aid:** No deadline. FAFSA required. Applicants notified on a rolling basis starting 3/15; must reply within 2 week(s) of notification.

Academics. Some engineering programs require students to acquire personal computers. **Special study options:** Accelerated study, combined bachelor's/graduate degree, cooperative education, distance learning, double major, dual enrollment of high school students, ESL, honors, independent study, internships, liberal arts/career combination, study abroad, teacher certification program, Washington semester, weekend college. Learning at Large (students earn college credit without attending regularly scheduled classes). **Credit/placement by examination:** AP, CLEP, IB, SAT, ACT, institutional tests. **Support services:** Learning center, pre-admission summer program, remedial instruction, study skills assistance, tutoring, writing center.

Majors. Architecture: Architecture, urban/community planning. **Area/ethnic studies:** African-American, Asian, women's. **Biology:** General, biochemistry, neuroscience. **Business:** Accounting, business admin, finance, insurance, international, marketing, operations, organizational behavior, real estate. **Communications:** Communications/speech/rhetoric, journalism, radio/TV. **Computer sciences:** General, information systems, information technology, security. **Education:** Early childhood, health, middle, music, secondary, special ed. **Engineering:** General, aerospace, architectural, biomedical, chemical, civil, computer, electrical, environmental, mechanical. **English:** Creative writing, English lit, rhetoric/composition. **Foreign languages:** Classics, French, German, Hebrew, sign language interpretation, Spanish. **Health services:** Athletic training, clinical lab science, communication disorders, dietetics, health information management, nuclear medical technology, nursing (RN), respiratory therapy technology, substance abuse counseling. **History:** General. **Human services:** Social work. **Liberal arts:** Arts/sciences. **Math:** General, financial. **Parks/recreation:** Sports admin. **Philosophy/religion:** Philosophy. **Physical sciences:** Astrophysics, chemistry, geology, physics. **Protective services:** Criminal justice, fire services admin. **Psychology:** General. **Social sciences:** Anthropology, archaeology, economics, geography, GIS/cartography, international relations, political science, sociology, urban studies. **Visual/performing arts:** Art history/conservation, commercial/advertising art, dance, design, dramatic, fashion design, industrial design, interior design, music, music history, music performance, music theory/composition, piano/keyboard, studio arts, theater design, voice/opera.

Most popular majors. Business/marketing 18%, communications/journalism 7%, engineering/engineering technologies 11%, health sciences 17%, visual/performing arts 7%.

Technology on campus. 560 workstations in library, computer center, student center. Dormitories wired for high-speed internet access and linked to campus network. Commuter students can connect to campus network. Online course registration, helpline, repair service, student web hosting, wireless network available.

Student life. Freshman orientation: Mandatory. Preregistration for classes offered. Held between June and July. **Housing:** Guaranteed on-campus for freshmen. Coed dorms, single-sex dorms, apartments, fraternity/sorority housing available. **Activities:** Bands, choral groups, dance, drama, film society, music ensembles, musical theater, opera, radio station, student government, student newspaper, symphony orchestra, women's initiative network, College Democrats, College Republicans.

Athletics. NCAA. **Intercollegiate:** Baseball M, basketball, cross-country, diving, football (tackle) M, golf, lacrosse W, soccer, swimming, tennis W, track and field, volleyball W. **Intramural:** Basketball, football (non-tackle), racquetball, soccer, softball, volleyball. **Team name:** Bearcats.

Student services. Adult student services, alcohol/substance abuse counseling, career counseling, services for economically disadvantaged, student employment services, financial aid counseling, health services, minority student services, personal counseling, placement for graduates, veterans' counselor, women's services. **Physically disabled:** Services for visually, speech, hearing impaired.

Contact. E-mail: admissions@uc.edu
Phone: (513) 556-1100 Toll-free number: (800) 827-8728
Fax: (513) 556-1105
Thomas Canepa, Associate Vice President, Admissions, University of
Cincinnati, PO Box 210091, Cincinnati, OH 45221-0091

University of Dayton
Dayton, Ohio   **CB member**
www.udayton.edu   **CB code: 1834**

- Private 4-year university affiliated with the Roman Catholic Church
- Residential campus in small city
- 8,556 degree-seeking undergraduates: 4% part-time, 47% women, 3% African American, 1% Asian American, 3% Hispanic/Latino, 2% Multiracial, non-Hispanic, 11% international
- 2,274 degree-seeking graduate students
- 58% of applicants admitted
- SAT or ACT (ACT writing optional), application essay required
- 79% graduate within 6 years

General. Founded in 1850. Regionally accredited. **Degrees:** 1,924 bachelor's awarded; master's, professional, doctoral offered. **ROTC:** Army, Air Force. **Location:** 2 miles from downtown Dayton, 50 miles from Cincinnati. **Calendar:** Semester, extensive summer session. **Full-time faculty:** 535 total; 87% have terminal degrees, 16% minority, 42% women. **Part-time faculty:** 482 total; 9% minority, 42% women. **Class size:** 31% < 20, 55% 20-39, 8% 40-49, 4% 50-99, 1% >100. **Special facilities:** Research institute, portfolio management center, learning-teaching center, information sciences center, student-operated stores and coffee shops, RISE Symposium, University of Dayton China Institute, entrepreneurial center.

Freshman class profile. 16,968 applied, 9,760 admitted, 2,138 enrolled.

Mid 50% test scores		GPA 2.0-2.99:	7%
SAT critical reading:	510-620	Rank in top quarter:	58%
SAT math:	520-630	Rank in top tenth:	25%
SAT writing:	520-610	Return as sophomores:	91%
ACT composite:	24-29	Out-of-state:	54%
GPA 3.75 or higher:	44%	Live on campus:	94%
GPA 3.50-3.74:	20%	International:	6%
GPA 3.0-3.49:	29%		

Basis for selection. Selection of courses in preparation for college, grade record and pattern in high school, class rank, SAT or ACT, character, record of leadership and service. Will review PAA if presented. Interview recommended for all; audition required for all music programs. **Home schooled:** Transcript of courses and grades required. Description of courses taken required, including bibliography of texts used for instruction. Examples of projects, homework or writing samples helpful. **Learning Disabled:** Prefer applicant provide documentation explaining disability for assessment.

High school preparation. College-preparatory program required. 16 units recommended. Recommended units include English 4, mathematics 4, social studies 4, history 4, science 4 (laboratory 1), foreign language 2, computer science 4 and visual/performing arts 4. 2 units of foreign language required for admission to the College of Arts and Sciences.

2015-2016 Annual costs. Tuition/fees: $39,090. Room/board: $12,190. Books/supplies: $1,000. Personal expenses: $1,750.

2014-2015 Financial aid. Need-based: 1,880 full-time freshmen applied for aid; 1,359 deemed to have need; 1,359 received aid. Average need met was 76%. Average scholarship/grant was $23,014; average loan $3,387. 78% of total undergraduate aid awarded as scholarships/grants, 22% as loans/jobs. **Non-need-based:** Awarded to 3,925 full-time undergraduates, including 952 freshmen. Scholarships awarded for academics, alumni affiliation, art, athletics, job skills, leadership, minority status, music/drama, religious affiliation, ROTC, state residency. **Additional information:** Guaranteed net-tuition for up to eight semesters of study. Students who visit campus and file the FAFSA prior to March 1st of their senior year in high school are eligible to receive up to $1,000 per year toward their textbooks.

Application procedures. Admission: Priority date 12/15; deadline 3/1 (postmark date). No application fee. Application must be submitted online. Admission notification on a rolling basis beginning on or about 2/15. Must reply by 5/1. **Financial aid:** Priority date 3/1; no closing date. FAFSA required. Applicants notified by 3/15; Applicants notified on a rolling basis starting 3/15; must reply within 2 week(s) of notification.

Academics. Special study options: Accelerated study, combined bachelor's/graduate degree, cooperative education, cross-registration, distance learning, double major, dual enrollment of high school students, ESL, exchange student, honors, independent study, internships, liberal arts/career combination, semester at sea, student-designed major, study abroad, teacher certification program, Washington semester. University of Dayton China Institute (located in Suzhou, China), domestic exchange program with other Marianist institutions; student-designed major in general studies only. **Credit/placement by examination:** AP, CLEP, IB, SAT, ACT, institutional tests. 24 credit hours maximum toward bachelor's degree. **Support services:** Learning center, pre-admission summer program, reduced course load, remedial instruction, study skills assistance, tutoring, writing center.

Majors. Area/ethnic studies: American. **Biology:** General, biochemistry, environmental. **Business:** General, accounting, business admin, entrepreneurial studies, finance, international, management information systems, managerial economics, marketing, operations. **Communications:** Digital media, journalism, media studies, public relations. **Computer sciences:** General, computer science. **Conservation:** Environmental science. **Education:** Art, early childhood, foreign languages, French, German, middle, multi-level teacher, music, physical, secondary, Spanish, special ed. **Engineering:** Chemical, civil, computer, electrical, mechanical. **English:** English lit. **Foreign languages:** French, German, Spanish. **Health services:** Dietetics, music therapy, predental, premedicine. **History:** General. **Math:** General. **Parks/recreation:** Exercise sciences, facilities management, sports admin. **Philosophy/religion:** Philosophy, religion. **Physical sciences:** General, chemistry, geology, physics. **Protective services:** Criminal justice. **Psychology:** General. **Social sciences:** Econometrics, economics, political science, sociology. **Visual/performing arts:** Art history/conservation, dramatic, graphic design, music, music performance, music theory/composition, photography, studio arts. **Work/family studies:** Food/nutrition.

Most popular majors. Business/marketing 29%, communications/journalism 7%, education 8%, engineering/engineering technologies 18%, health sciences 7%, psychology 6%.

Technology on campus. PC or laptop required. Dormitories wired for high-speed internet access and linked to campus network. Commuter students can connect to campus network. Online course registration, online library, helpline, repair service, student web hosting, wireless network available.

Student life. Freshman orientation: Mandatory. Preregistration for classes offered. Held 2-3 days preceding the first day of classes. Virtual orientation also available online. **Policies:** Freshmen not permitted cars on campus. **Housing:** Guaranteed on-campus for freshmen. Coed dorms, special housing for disabled, apartments, cooperative housing, fraternity/sorority housing, themed housing, wellness housing available. $400 deposit, deadline 5/1. University-owned houses available. **Activities:** Bands, campus ministries, choral groups, dance, drama, international student organizations, literary magazine, music ensembles, Model UN, musical theater, opera, radio station, student government, student newspaper, symphony orchestra, TV station, Catholic Life, Campus Crusade for Christ, College Democrats, College Republicans, diversity discussion group, Indian student association, NAACP, Irish club, Italian club.

Athletics. NCAA. **Intercollegiate:** Baseball M, basketball, cheerleading, cross-country, football (tackle) M, golf, rowing (crew) W, soccer, softball W, tennis, track and field W, volleyball W. **Intramural:** Badminton, basketball, bowling, football (non-tackle), golf, racquetball, soccer, softball, tennis, volleyball, water polo, wrestling. **Team name:** Flyers.

Student services. Adult student services, alcohol/substance abuse counseling, chaplain/spiritual director, career counseling, services for economically disadvantaged, student employment services, financial aid counseling, health services, minority student services, on-campus daycare, personal counseling, placement for graduates, veterans' counselor, women's services. **Physically disabled:** Services for visually, speech, hearing impaired.

Contact. E-mail: admission@udayton.edu
Phone: (937) 229-4411 Toll-free number: (800) UD-PRIDE
Fax: (937) 229-4729
Kathy McEuen Harmon, Dean of Admission and Financial Aid,
University of Dayton, 300 College Park, Dayton, OH 45469-1310

University of Findlay
Findlay, Ohio
www.findlay.edu   **CB code: 1223**

- Private 4-year university and health science college affiliated with the Church of God
- Residential campus in small city
- 2,882 degree-seeking undergraduates: 7% part-time, 63% women, 4% African American, 1% Asian American, 2% Hispanic/Latino, 2% Multiracial, non-Hispanic, 10% international
- 1,284 degree-seeking graduate students
- 76% of applicants admitted

▶ SAT or ACT (ACT writing recommended), application essay required

▶ 55% graduate within 6 years; 79% enter graduate study

General. Founded in 1882. Regionally accredited. **Degrees:** 469 bachelor's, 26 associate awarded; master's, professional offered. **ROTC:** Army, Air Force. **Location:** 45 miles from Toledo, 90 miles from Columbus. **Calendar:** Semester, limited summer session. **Full-time faculty:** 209 total; 65% have terminal degrees, 10% minority, 47% women. **Part-time faculty:** 69 total; 33% have terminal degrees, 6% minority, 55% women. **Class size:** 52% < 20, 44% 20-39, 2% 40-49, 2% 50-99. **Special facilities:** Two equestrian farms, animal science facility, cadaver lab, environmental resource training center, planetarium, habitat studies center, museum.

Freshman class profile. 3,106 applied, 2,357 admitted, 715 enrolled.

Mid 50% test scores		Rank in top quarter:	45%
SAT critical reading:	470-560	Rank in top tenth:	43%
SAT math:	470-480	End year in good standing:	92%
SAT writing:	470-480	Return as sophomores:	79%
ACT composite:	20-25	Out-of-state:	22%
GPA 3.75 or higher:	33%	Live on campus:	70%
GPA 3.50-3.74:	19%	Fraternities:	1%
GPA 3.0-3.49:	32%	Sororities:	1%
GPA 2.0-2.99:	16%		

Basis for selection. School achievement record, curriculum, class rank, and recommendations. Interview required for special admission programs. **Home schooled:** Statement describing home school structure and mission, state high school equivalency certificate, letter of recommendation (nonparent) required. Greater weight placed on standardized entrance exam scores for admission, evaluation of GED if taken. **Learning Disabled:** Strongly encourage interview or campus visit.

High school preparation. College-preparatory program recommended. 13 units required; 26 recommended. Required and recommended units include English 4, mathematics 4, social studies 4, history 2, science 3-4, foreign language 2, computer science 4 and visual/performing arts 2. One fine arts unit recommended. Additional 1 math and 1 science for preveterinary and environmental programs.

2015-2016 Annual costs. Tuition/fees: $31,508. Room/board: $9,442. Books/supplies: $1,900.

2014-2015 Financial aid. Need-based: 672 full-time freshmen applied for aid; 538 deemed to have need; 538 received aid. Average need met was 82%. Average scholarship/grant was $20,654; average loan $3,248. 51% of total undergraduate aid awarded as scholarships/grants, 49% as loans/jobs. **Non-need-based:** Awarded to 3,064 full-time undergraduates, including 794 freshmen. Scholarships awarded for academics, alumni affiliation, athletics, music/drama, state residency.

Application procedures. Admission: No deadline. No application fee. Admission notification on a rolling basis beginning on or about 9/1. Part-time applicants may be admitted year round to any of the six different program start dates. **Financial aid:** Priority date 8/1, closing date 9/1. FAFSA required. Applicants notified on a rolling basis starting 3/1; must reply within 2 week(s) of notification.

Academics. Special study options: Accelerated study, combined bachelor's/graduate degree, cooperative education, distance learning, double major, dual enrollment of high school students, ESL, external degree, honors, independent study, internships, liberal arts/career combination, semester at sea, student-designed major, study abroad, teacher certification program, Washington semester, weekend college. **Credit/placement by examination:** AP, CLEP, IB, SAT, ACT, institutional tests. 15 credit hours maximum toward associate degree, 30 toward bachelor's. **Support services:** Learning center, reduced course load, remedial instruction, study skills assistance, tutoring, writing center.

Majors. Biology: General. **Business:** General, accounting, business admin, entrepreneurial studies, finance, hospitality admin, hospitality/recreation, human resources, international, marketing. **Communications:** Communications/speech/rhetoric, journalism, public relations. **Computer sciences:** General, computer science, systems analysis. **Education:** General, art, bilingual, biology, curriculum, developmentally delayed, drama/dance, driver/safety, early childhood, early childhood special, emotionally handicapped, English, ESL, evaluation, foreign languages, foundations, geography, health, history, kindergarten/preschool, learning disabled, mathematics, mentally handicapped, middle, multi-level teacher, multicultural, multiple handicapped, physical, psychology, reading, science, secondary, social science, social studies, Spanish, special ed, speech, testing/assessment. **English:** Creative writing, English lit. **Foreign languages:** Japanese, Spanish. **Health services:** Athletic training, environmental health, health care admin, nuclear medical technology, nursing (RN), occupational health, prenursing, preveterinary, sonography. **History:** General. **Human services:** Social work. **Math:** General. **Parks/recreation:** Exercise sciences, health/fitness, sports admin. **Philosophy/religion:** Philosophy, religion. **Protective services:** Law enforcement admin.

Psychology: General. **Social sciences:** General, economics, political science, sociology. **Theology:** Theology. **Visual/performing arts:** Art, commercial/advertising art, dramatic, theater design.

Most popular majors. Agriculture 13%, business/marketing 16%, education 8%, health sciences 30%, parks/recreation 6%.

Technology on campus. 400 workstations in dormitories, library, computer center, student center. Dormitories wired for high-speed internet access and linked to campus network. Commuter students can connect to campus network. Online library, helpline, repair service, student web hosting, wireless network available.

Student life. Freshman orientation: Mandatory, $100 fee. Preregistration for classes offered. One-day registrations for students and orientation for parents during summer. 2-day program for students 2 days before classes begin. **Policies:** All freshmen, sophomores, under the age of 22 required to live on-campus. **Housing:** Guaranteed on-campus for freshmen. Coed dorms, single-sex dorms, special housing for disabled, apartments, fraternity/sorority housing, wellness housing available. $150 nonrefundable deposit, deadline 8/1. Honors house and special interest houses. **Activities:** Bands, campus ministries, choral groups, dance, drama, international student organizations, literary magazine, music ensembles, musical theater, opera, radio station, student government, student newspaper, symphony orchestra, TV station, Habitat for Humanity, Black Student Union, wilderness club, Anointed Worship, campus program board, College Republicans, Fellowship of Christian Athletes, Spanish club, Taiwanese Student Association, Student Government Association.

Athletics. NCAA. **Intercollegiate:** Baseball M, basketball, cross-country, diving, football (tackle) M, golf, lacrosse W, soccer, softball W, swimming, tennis, track and field, volleyball W, wrestling M. **Intramural:** Basketball, bowling, cheerleading, cricket, football (non-tackle), football (tackle), golf, racquetball, skiing, soccer, table tennis, tennis, volleyball. **Team name:** Oilers.

Student services. Adult student services, alcohol/substance abuse counseling, chaplain/spiritual director, career counseling, services for economically disadvantaged, student employment services, financial aid counseling, health services, minority student services, personal counseling, placement for graduates, veterans' counselor, women's services. **Physically disabled:** Services for visually, speech, hearing impaired.

Contact. E-mail: admissions@findlay.edu
Phone: (419) 434-4732 Toll-free number: (800) 472-9502
Fax: (419) 434-4898
Christopher Harris, Director of Admissions, University of Findlay, 1000 North Main Street, Findlay, OH 45840-3653

University of Mount Union

Alliance, Ohio   CB member
www.mountunion.edu   CB code: 1492

▶ Private 4-year university affiliated with the United Methodist Church

▶ Residential campus in large town

▶ 2,061 degree-seeking undergraduates: 1% part-time, 50% women, 6% African American, 1% Asian American, 2% Hispanic/Latino, 1% Native American, 3% Multi-racial, non-Hispanic, 2% international

▶ 97 degree-seeking graduate students

▶ 75% of applicants admitted

▶ SAT or ACT (ACT writing optional), application essay required

▶ 61% graduate within 6 years; 26% enter graduate study

General. Founded in 1846. Regionally accredited. **Degrees:** 436 bachelor's awarded; master's offered. **ROTC:** Army, Air Force. **Location:** 55 miles from Cleveland, 75 miles from Pittsburgh. **Calendar:** Semester, limited summer session. **Full-time faculty:** 135 total; 87% have terminal degrees, 14% minority, 46% women. **Part-time faculty:** 113 total; 8% minority, 50% women. **Class size:** 52% < 20, 44% 20-39, 3% 40-49, less than 1% 50-99. **Special facilities:** 2 astronomical observatories, nature center for ecological studies, bird observatory, scanning electron microscope facility.

Freshman class profile. 2,289 applied, 1,717 admitted, 545 enrolled.

Mid 50% test scores		Rank in top quarter:	50%
SAT critical reading:	460-540	Rank in top tenth:	22%
SAT math:	440-590	End year in good standing:	95%
ACT composite:	21-26	Return as sophomores:	78%
GPA 3.75 or higher:	31%	Out-of-state:	18%
GPA 3.50-3.74:	18%	Live on campus:	93%
GPA 3.0-3.49:	33%	Fraternities:	6%
GPA 2.0-2.99:	18%	Sororities:	12%

Basis for selection. Class rank, rigor of secondary school record, standardized test scores, academic GPA very important. Rolling deadline for SAT/ACT scores. Interview recommended for all. Audition recommended for communications, music, and theater programs. Portfolio recommended for art and communications programs. **Home schooled:** Statement describing home school structure and mission required.

High school preparation. 18 units recommended. Recommended units include English 4, mathematics 3, social studies 3, science 3 (laboratory 2), foreign language 2 and academic electives 1.

2015-2016 Annual costs. Tuition/fees: $28,550. Room/board: $9,540. Books/supplies: $1,100. Personal expenses: $800.

2014-2015 Financial aid. Need-based: 626 full-time freshmen applied for aid; 551 deemed to have need; 551 received aid. Average need met was 78%. Average scholarship/grant was $17,016; average loan $5,827. 66% of total undergraduate aid awarded as scholarships/grants, 34% as loans/jobs. **Non-need-based:** Awarded to 534 full-time undergraduates, including 161 freshmen. Scholarships awarded for academics, alumni affiliation, art, job skills, leadership, minority status, music/drama, religious affiliation, ROTC, state residency.

Application procedures. Admission: Priority date 3/1; no deadline. No application fee. Admission notification on a rolling basis beginning on or about 10/1. Admission determined by space availability after May 1. **Financial aid:** No deadline. FAFSA required. Applicants notified on a rolling basis starting 3/15; must reply within 4 week(s) of notification.

Academics. All freshmen must take First Year Seminar course. **Special study options:** Accelerated study, combined bachelor's/graduate degree, cooperative education, double major, dual enrollment of high school students, ESL, honors, independent study, internships, student-designed major, study abroad, teacher certification program, Washington semester. **Credit/placement by examination:** AP, CLEP, IB, institutional tests. 15 credit hours maximum toward bachelor's degree. **Support services:** Learning center, reduced course load, study skills assistance, tutoring, writing center.

Majors. Area/ethnic studies: African, American, Asian. **Biology:** General, biochemistry, neuroscience. **Business:** Accounting, actuarial science, business admin, finance, human resources, international, marketing. **Communications:** Communications/speech/rhetoric, digital media, media studies, organizational, persuasive communications. **Computer sciences:** Programming, web page design. **Conservation:** Environmental science. **Education:** Early childhood, health, middle, music, physical, special ed. **Engineering:** Civil, mechanical. **English:** Creative writing, English lit, writing. **Foreign languages:** French, German, Japanese, Spanish. **Health services:** Athletic training, clinical lab science, health care admin. **History:** General. **Math:** General, financial. **Parks/recreation:** Exercise sciences, sports admin. **Philosophy/religion:** Philosophy, religion. **Physical sciences:** Chemistry, geology, physics. **Protective services:** Criminal justice, criminalistics. **Psychology:** General. **Social sciences:** Criminology, economics, international relations, political science, sociology. **Visual/performing arts:** Dramatic, game design, music, music performance, studio arts.

Most popular majors. Biology 7%, business/marketing 22%, communications/journalism 6%, education 11%, parks/recreation 12%, psychology 6%.

Technology on campus. 200 workstations in dormitories, library, computer center, student center. Dormitories wired for high-speed internet access and linked to campus network. Commuter students can connect to campus network. Online course registration, online library, helpline, repair service, student web hosting, wireless network available.

Student life. Freshman orientation: Available. Preregistration for classes offered. Two-day summer orientation includes program for parents. Fall orientation held week before registration for students only. **Housing:** Guaranteed on-campus for all undergraduates. Coed dorms, single-sex dorms, special housing for disabled, apartments, fraternity/sorority housing, themed housing, wellness housing available. **Activities:** Bands, campus ministries, choral groups, dance, drama, literary magazine, music ensembles, Model UN, musical theater, radio station, student government, student newspaper, academic clubs, academic honoraries, religious clubs, service organizations, Alpha Phi Omega, black student union, international students association, women students association, religious life council, student activities council.

Athletics. NCAA. **Intercollegiate:** Baseball M, basketball, cheerleading, cross-country, diving, football (tackle) M, golf, lacrosse, soccer, softball W, swimming, tennis, track and field, volleyball W, wrestling M. **Intramural:** Badminton, basketball, bowling, diving, football (non-tackle), golf, lacrosse, racquetball, soccer, softball, swimming, tennis, volleyball, water polo, weight lifting. **Team name:** Purple Raiders.

Student services. Adult student services, alcohol/substance abuse counseling, chaplain/spiritual director, career counseling, student employment services, financial aid counseling, health services, minority student services,

personal counseling, placement for graduates, women's services. **Physically disabled:** Services for visually, hearing impaired.

Contact. E-mail: admission@mountunion.edu
Phone: (330) 823-2590 Toll-free number: (800) 334-6682
Fax: (330) 823-5097
Jess Canavan, Director of Admissions, University of Mount Union, 1972 Clark Avenue, Alliance, OH 44601-3993

University of Phoenix: Cleveland
Beachwood, Ohio
www.phoenix.edu

‣ For-profit 4-year university
‣ Large town
‣ 455 degree-seeking undergraduates

General. Regionally accredited. **Degrees:** 124 bachelor's awarded; master's offered. **Calendar:** Differs by program. **Full-time faculty:** 9 total. **Part-time faculty:** 69 total.

Basis for selection. Open admission.

2015-2016 Annual costs. Per-credit-hour charge, $410 to $610, depending upon level and course of study. Books, material charges, and other fees vary by course and program. All fees are subject to change.

Application procedures. Admission: No deadline. No application fee. **Financial aid:** No deadline.

Academics. Credit/placement by examination: AP, CLEP.

Majors. Business: Accounting/business management, business admin, e-commerce, entrepreneurial studies, finance, human resources, marketing, operations. **Computer sciences:** Database management, programming, security, system admin, systems analysis, web page design, webmaster. **Health services:** Facilities admin, health information management, long term care admin, nursing (RN). **Human services:** General. **Protective services:** Disaster management.

Student life. Freshman orientation: Mandatory. Preregistration for classes offered.

Contact. University of Phoenix: Cleveland, 3401 Enterprise Pkway, Beachwood, OH 44122-7343

University of Rio Grande
Rio Grande, Ohio
www.rio.edu   **CB code: 1663**

‣ Private 4-year community and liberal arts college
‣ Commuter campus in rural community
‣ 1,165 degree-seeking undergraduates: 21% part-time, 65% women, 5% African American, 1% Hispanic/Latino, 2% international
‣ 48 graduate students
‣ 39% graduate within 6 years

General. Founded in 1876. Regionally accredited. Institution is both public and private. First 2 years are state subsidized, second 2 years are private, with higher tuition. Affiliated with Rio Grande Community College. **Degrees:** 127 bachelor's, 246 associate awarded; master's offered. **Location:** 12 miles from Gallipolis. **Calendar:** Semester, limited summer session. **Full-time faculty:** 77 total; 46% have terminal degrees, 4% minority, 44% women. **Part-time faculty:** 85 total; 6% have terminal degrees, 2% minority, 69% women. **Class size:** 70% < 20, 28% 20-39, less than 1% 40-49, less than 1% 50-99. **Special facilities:** Early childhood care center.

Freshman class profile. 1,909 applied, 1,325 admitted, 461 enrolled.

Mid 50% test scores		Rank in top quarter:	20%
ACT composite:	17-22	Rank in top tenth:	5%
GPA 3.75 or higher:	7%	Out-of-state:	4%
GPA 3.50-3.74:	11%	Live on campus:	26%
GPA 3.0-3.49:	25%	International:	2%
GPA 2.0-2.99:	49%		

Basis for selection. Open admission, but selective for some programs. ACT required for nursing, medical laboratory technician, radiologic technology, diagnostic medical sonography, respiratory therapy, and education programs. Deferred admission for students demonstrating need for remedial work. COMPASS test required for all incoming students prior to scheduling. Acceptance to Education department occurs at end of sophomore year. **Learning Disabled:** Students with any kind of special needs asked to meet with Director of Accessibility to determine education plan and for academic advising purposes.

High school preparation. College-preparatory program recommended. 21 units recommended. Recommended units include English 4, mathematics 3, social studies 3, history 2, science 3 (laboratory 2), foreign language 2 and academic electives 9. Chemistry, algebra, biology required for nursing applicants.

2015-2016 Annual costs. Tuition/fees: $23,860. Room/board: $9,920. Books/supplies: $1,200. Personal expenses: $1,750.

2015-2016 Financial aid. Need-based: 253 full-time freshmen applied for aid; 253 deemed to have need; 238 received aid. Average need met was 81%. Average scholarship/grant was $3,248; average loan $268. 98% of total undergraduate aid awarded as scholarships/grants, 2% as loans/jobs. **Non-need-based:** Awarded to 871 full-time undergraduates, including 379 freshmen. Scholarships awarded for academics, alumni affiliation, athletics, leadership, music/drama, state residency.

Application procedures. Admission: No deadline. $25 fee, may be waived for applicants with need, free for online applicants. Admission notification on a rolling basis. **Financial aid:** No deadline. FAFSA required.

Academics. Special study options: Accelerated study, cooperative education, distance learning, double major, dual enrollment of high school students, ESL, honors, independent study, internships, liberal arts/career combination, student-designed major, study abroad, teacher certification program. **Credit/placement by examination:** AP, CLEP, IB, institutional tests. **Support services:** Learning center, pre-admission summer program, reduced course load, remedial instruction, tutoring, writing center. The college participates in Ohio's etutoring program for online tutoring.

Majors. Area/ethnic studies: American. **Biology:** General. **Business:** Accounting, business admin, marketing, office technology, retailing. **Communications:** Communications/speech/rhetoric, journalism, media studies, public relations. **Computer sciences:** General, applications programming, computer science. **Conservation:** General, environmental studies, wildlife/wilderness. **Education:** General, art, biology, business, chemistry, early childhood, elementary, English, health, history, mathematics, middle, multi-level teacher, music, physical, physics, reading, science, secondary, social science, special ed, speech. **English:** English lit. **Foreign languages:** Spanish. **Health services:** Facilities admin, health care admin, nursing (RN), prenursing, sonography. **History:** General. **Human services:** General, social work. **Liberal arts:** Humanities. **Math:** General. **Parks/recreation:** Sports admin. **Physical sciences:** Chemistry. **Psychology:** General. **Social sciences:** General, archaeology, economics. **Visual/performing arts:** General, graphic design, multimedia, music, music management.

Most popular majors. Business/marketing 19%, education 24%, health sciences 16%, natural resources/environmental science 8%.

Technology on campus. 300 workstations in library, computer center, student center. Dormitories wired for high-speed internet access and linked to campus network. Online course registration, online library, repair service, student web hosting, wireless network available.

Student life. Freshman orientation: Mandatory, $50 fee. Preregistration for classes offered. One-day program held in April, June, July, and August. **Policies:** Smoke free dorms and buildings. **Housing:** Guaranteed on-campus for all undergraduates. Coed dorms, single-sex dorms, wellness housing available. $200 fully refundable deposit, deadline 7/15. **Activities:** Bands, campus ministries, choral groups, dance, drama, literary magazine, music ensembles, musical theater, radio station, student government, student newspaper, symphony orchestra, TV station, international student organization, Valley Artist Services, Handicapped Coalition, Young Republicans, Rio Christian Fellowship, Student Ambassadors, Students in Free Enterprise.

Athletics. NAIA. **Intercollegiate:** Baseball M, basketball, cheerleading, cross-country, soccer, softball W, track and field, volleyball W. **Intramural:** Archery, badminton, basketball, equestrian, handball, racquetball, softball, swimming, tennis, water polo. **Team name:** Redstorm.

Student services. Career counseling, student employment services, financial aid counseling, health services, on-campus daycare, personal counseling, placement for graduates, veterans' counselor. **Physically disabled:** Services for visually, speech, hearing impaired.

Contact. E-mail: admissions@rio.edu
Phone: (740) 245-7208 Toll-free number: (800) 282-7201
Fax: (740) 245-7260
Kristie Russell, Admissions Director, University of Rio Grande, 218 North College Avenue, Rio Grande, OH 45674

University of Toledo
Toledo, Ohio — CB member
www.utoledo.edu — CB code: 1845

- Public 4-year university
- Commuter campus in large city
- 14,990 degree-seeking undergraduates: 16% part-time, 47% women, 12% African American, 2% Asian American, 5% Hispanic/Latino, 3% Multi-racial, non-Hispanic, 6% international
- 4,239 degree-seeking graduate students
- 41% graduate within 6 years

General. Founded in 1872. Regionally accredited. **Degrees:** 2,800 bachelor's, 69 associate awarded; master's, professional, doctoral offered. **ROTC:** Army, Air Force. **Location:** 6 miles from downtown. **Calendar:** Semester, extensive summer session. **Full-time faculty:** 804 total; 79% have terminal degrees, 20% minority, 43% women. **Part-time faculty:** 239 total; 22% have terminal degrees, 12% minority, 48% women. **Class size:** 27% < 20, 45% 20-39, 12% 40-49, 12% 50-99, 3% >100. **Special facilities:** 2 observatories, ion accelerator, Center for Drug Design and Development, Plant Science Research Center, Center for Agal Engineering Research and Commercialization.

Freshman class profile. 10,678 applied, 9,952 admitted, 3,341 enrolled.

Mid 50% test scores			
SAT critical reading:	450-580	GPA 2.0-2.99:	25%
SAT math:	470-620	Rank in top quarter:	42%
SAT writing:	430-560	Rank in top tenth:	16%
ACT composite:	20-26	Return as sophomores:	72%
GPA 3.75 or higher:	29%	Out-of-state:	23%
GPA 3.50-3.74:	16%	Live on campus:	56%
GPA 3.0-3.49:	26%	International:	4%

Basis for selection. Open admission, but selective for some programs and for out-of-state students. Unconditional general admission requires 15 ACT/740 SAT. Information Technology program: 2.5 GPA or 480 GED and 21 ACT/990 SAT. College of Communication and the Arts: 2.5 GPA or 20 ACT/950 SAT. Music Program: audition required. Engineering Science Programs: 3.0 GPA or 510 GED, and 22 ACT/1030 SAT, and 4 years of high school math. Engineering Technology programs: 2.5 GPA or 480 GED, and 21 ACT/990 SAT. College of Health Science: 2.7 GPA or 21 ACT/990 SAT. Exercise Science: 3.0 GPA or 21 ACT/990 SAT and 20 ACT math/480 SAT math and high school biology and chemistry with grade of C or better. College of Languages, Literature, and Social Sciences: 2.5 GPA or 20 ACT/950 SAT. College of Pharmacy and Pharmaceutical Sciences: 2.5 GPA or GED or 20 ACT/950 SAT. College of Social Justice and Human Service: 2.5 GPA or 19 ACT/910 SAT. Judith Herb College of Education: 2.7 GPA or 21 ACT/990 SAT. Audition required for music program. **Learning Disabled:** Registering with the Office of Accessibility recommended.

High school preparation. College-preparatory program required. Required and recommended units include English 4, mathematics 4, social studies 3, science 3 and foreign language 2.

2015-2016 Annual costs. Tuition/fees: $9,560; $18,898 out-of-state. Room/board: $11,494. Books/supplies: $1,245. Personal expenses: $3,900.

2015-2016 Financial aid. Need-based: 3,004 full-time freshmen applied for aid; 2,385 deemed to have need; 2,377 received aid. Average need met was 63%. Average scholarship/grant was $9,708; average loan $3,498. 56% of total undergraduate aid awarded as scholarships/grants, 44% as loans/jobs. **Non-need-based:** Awarded to 4,709 full-time undergraduates, including 1,439 freshmen. Scholarships awarded for academics, alumni affiliation, art, athletics, leadership, music/drama, ROTC, state residency. **Additional information:** March priority date for federal aid. Students encouraged to apply as early as December for priority consideration for institutional aid.

Application procedures. Admission: Priority date 3/1; no deadline. $40 fee, may be waived for applicants with need. Admission notification on a rolling basis beginning on or about 10/1. Freshman applicants desiring on-campus housing encouraged to apply early. **Financial aid:** Priority date 3/1; no closing date. FAFSA required. Applicants notified on a rolling basis starting 3/1; must reply within 8 week(s) of notification.

Academics. Special study options: Accelerated study, combined bachelor's/graduate degree, cooperative education, cross-registration, distance learning, double major, dual enrollment of high school students, ESL, exchange student, honors, independent study, internships, liberal arts/career combination, semester at sea, student-designed major, study abroad, teacher certification program. **Credit/placement by examination:** AP, CLEP, IB, institutional tests. 30 credit hours maximum toward associate degree, 30 toward bachelor's. **Support services:** Learning center, pre-admission summer program, reduced course load, remedial instruction, study skills assistance, tutoring, writing center.

Majors. Area/ethnic studies: African-American, American, Asian, European, Latin American, Near/Middle Eastern, women's. **Biology:** General, biochemistry. **Business:** General, accounting, business admin, e-commerce, entrepreneurial studies, finance, human resources, international, logistics, market research, marketing, office management, operations, organizational behavior. **Communications:** Communications/speech/rhetoric, journalism, media studies. **Computer sciences:** Information systems, information technology. **Conservation:** Environmental science, environmental studies. **Education:** Art, business, English, French, German, health, kindergarten/preschool, mathematics, multi-level teacher, music, physical, science, secondary, social studies, Spanish, trade/industrial. **Engineering:** Biomedical, chemical, civil, computer, electrical, mechanical. **English:** English lit. **Foreign languages:** French, German, linguistics, Spanish. **Health services:** Athletic training, facilities admin, health information management, nursing (RN), pharmaceutical sciences, public health ed, recreational therapy, respiratory therapy technology. **History:** General. **Human services:** Social work. **Liberal arts:** Arts/sciences, humanities. **Math:** General. **Parks/recreation:** General, exercise sciences. **Philosophy/religion:** Philosophy, religion. **Physical sciences:** Astronomy, chemistry, geology, physics. **Protective services:** Criminal justice. **Psychology:** General. **Social sciences:** Anthropology, economics, geography, international relations, political science, sociology, urban studies. **Visual/performing arts:** Art, art history/conservation, dramatic, film/cinema/video, music.

Most popular majors. Business/marketing 21%, engineering/engineering technologies 15%, health sciences 18%, interdisciplinary studies 7%.

Technology on campus. 5,000 workstations in dormitories, library, computer center, student center. Dormitories wired for high-speed internet access and linked to campus network. Commuter students can connect to campus network. Online course registration, online library, helpline, repair service, wireless network available.

Student life. Freshman orientation: Mandatory, $110 fee. Preregistration for classes offered. **Housing:** Guaranteed on-campus for freshmen. Coed dorms, special housing for disabled, fraternity/sorority housing, themed housing available. $50 partly refundable deposit, deadline 5/1. **Activities:** Bands, campus ministries, choral groups, dance, drama, film society, international student organizations, literary magazine, music ensembles, musical theater, radio station, student government, student newspaper, symphony orchestra, TV station, black student union, Campus Crusade for Christ, Hillel, Latino student union, University YMCA, gay and lesbian student union, international student association, Habitat for Humanity, Toledo Campus Ministry Fellowship.

Athletics. NCAA. **Intercollegiate:** Baseball M, basketball, cross-country, diving W, football (tackle) M, golf, soccer W, softball W, swimming W, tennis, track and field W, volleyball W. **Intramural:** Badminton, basketball, bowling, cheerleading W, diving W, fencing, football (tackle), golf, lacrosse, racquetball, soccer, softball, swimming, table tennis, tennis, track and field, volleyball, water polo, weight lifting. **Team name:** Rockets.

Student services. Adult student services, alcohol/substance abuse counseling, chaplain/spiritual director, career counseling, services for economically disadvantaged, student employment services, financial aid counseling, health services, legal services, minority student services, on-campus daycare, personal counseling, placement for graduates, veterans' counselor, women's services. **Physically disabled:** Services for visually, speech, hearing impaired.

Contact. E-mail: enroll@utoledo.edu
Phone: (419) 530-8888 Toll-free number: (800) 586-5336
Fax: (419) 530-5872
William Pierce, Director of Admission, University of Toledo, 2801 West Bancroft Street, Toledo, OH 43606-3390

Urbana University
Urbana, Ohio
www.urbana.edu   CB code: 1847

- Private 4-year university
- Commuter campus in large town
- 787 degree-seeking undergraduates
- 202 graduate students
- SAT or ACT (ACT writing optional) required

General. Founded in 1850. Regionally accredited. **Degrees:** 137 bachelor's, 3 associate awarded; master's offered. **ROTC:** Army. **Location:** 42 miles from Columbus, 49 miles from Dayton. **Calendar:** Semester, limited summer session. **Full-time faculty:** 50 total; 64% have terminal degrees, 10% minority. **Part-time faculty:** 55 total. **Special facilities:** Johnny Appleseed museum.

Basis for selection. School achievement record, class rank, GPA, test scores, extra-curricular activities and honors important. Special consideration

given to children of alumni. Recommendations and interviews encouraged. **Home schooled:** Transcript of courses and grades, state high school equivalency certificate required.

High school preparation. College-preparatory program required. 15 units recommended. Required and recommended units include English 4, mathematics 2, social studies 2, science 2, foreign language 1 and academic electives 2.

2015-2016 Annual costs. Tuition/fees: $22,012. Room/board: $8,938. Books/supplies: $1,080. Personal expenses: $3,160.

Financial aid. Non-need-based: Scholarships awarded for academics, alumni affiliation, athletics, music/drama.

Application procedures. Admission: No deadline. $25 fee, may be waived for applicants with need. Admission notification on a rolling basis. **Financial aid:** Priority date 4/1, closing date 8/15. FAFSA required. Applicants notified on a rolling basis starting 3/1; must reply within 4 week(s) of notification.

Academics. Special study options: Accelerated study, combined bachelor's/graduate degree, cooperative education, cross-registration, distance learning, double major, dual enrollment of high school students, ESL, honors, independent study, internships, liberal arts/career combination, student-designed major, study abroad, teacher certification program. **Credit/placement by examination:** AP, CLEP, SAT, ACT, institutional tests. 15 credit hours maximum toward associate degree, 15 toward bachelor's. **Support services:** Learning center, pre-admission summer program, reduced course load, remedial instruction, study skills assistance, tutoring, writing center.

Majors. Biology: General. **Business:** Accounting, accounting/business management, business admin, communications, entrepreneurial studies, finance, human resources, management science, managerial economics, marketing, organizational behavior. **Communications:** Communications/speech/rhetoric, journalism. **Computer sciences:** Information systems. **Education:** General, biology, elementary, English, mathematics, middle, science, secondary, social studies, special ed. **English:** English lit. **Health services:** Athletic training, predental, premedicine. **History:** General. **Human services:** Community org/advocacy. **Liberal arts:** Arts/sciences. **Math:** General. **Parks/recreation:** General, exercise sciences, sports admin. **Philosophy/religion:** Philosophy, religion. **Protective services:** Criminal justice, law enforcement admin. **Psychology:** General. **Social sciences:** General, political science, sociology. **Work/family studies:** General.

Technology on campus. 60 workstations in dormitories, library, computer center, student center. Dormitories wired for high-speed internet access and linked to campus network. Commuter students can connect to campus network. Online course registration, online library, helpline, repair service, wireless network available.

Student life. Freshman orientation: Mandatory. Preregistration for classes offered. Held during the summer. **Housing:** Guaranteed on-campus for freshmen. Single-sex dorms available. $125 deposit, deadline 5/1. **Activities:** Bands, choral groups, drama, literary magazine, music ensembles, musical theater, student government, student newspaper, black student union, College Against Cancer, commuter club, gay/straight alliance, Knights for Christ, sports medicine association, student activities committee, student business association, University Players theatre group, University Singers.

Athletics. NCAA. **Intercollegiate:** Baseball M, basketball, cross-country, football (tackle) M, golf, soccer, softball W, swimming, volleyball W. **Intramural:** Basketball, racquetball, swimming, table tennis, volleyball, weight lifting. **Team name:** Blue Knights.

Student services. Adult student services, alcohol/substance abuse counseling, career counseling, student employment services, financial aid counseling, health services, personal counseling, placement for graduates, veterans' counselor.

Contact. E-mail: admissions@urbana.edu
Phone: (937) 772-9239 Toll-free number: (800) 787-2262 ext. 9239
Steffi Lybeck, Associate Director of Admissions, Urbana University, 579 College Way, Urbana, OH 43078

Ursuline College
Pepper Pike, Ohio   CB member
www.ursuline.edu   CB code: 1848

- Private 4-year liberal arts college for women affiliated with the Roman Catholic Church
- Commuter campus in small town

♦ 641 degree-seeking undergraduates: 31% part-time, 93% women, 26% African American, 1% Asian American, 3% Hispanic/Latino, 3% Multiracial, non-Hispanic, 2% international

♦ 517 degree-seeking graduate students

♦ 88% of applicants admitted

♦ SAT or ACT (ACT writing optional) required

♦ 44% graduate within 6 years

General. Founded in 1871. Regionally accredited. Primarily women's college, but some men admitted. **Degrees:** 216 bachelor's awarded; master's, professional offered. **ROTC:** Army. **Location:** 10 miles from Cleveland. **Calendar:** Semester, limited summer session. **Full-time faculty:** 65 total; 69% have terminal degrees, 8% minority, 85% women. **Part-time faculty:** 129 total; 20% have terminal degrees, 9% minority, 78% women. **Class size:** 90% < 20, 10% 20-39.

Freshman class profile. 723 applied, 636 admitted, 115 enrolled.

Mid 50% test scores			
		GPA 2.0-2.99:	27%
SAT critical reading:	430-590	Rank in top quarter:	45%
SAT math:	440-540	Rank in top tenth:	16%
SAT writing:	420-570	Return as sophomores:	59%
ACT composite:	19-24	Out-of-state:	11%
GPA 3.75 or higher:	22%	Live on campus:	72%
GPA 3.50-3.74:	18%	International:	1%
GPA 3.0-3.49:	33%		

Basis for selection. Secondary school record and standardized test scores are very important. Interview recommended for all. **Home schooled:** Transcript of courses and grades, state high school equivalency certificate required. Official transcript from accrediting agency needed.

High school preparation. College-preparatory program recommended. 17 units recommended. Recommended units include English 4, mathematics 3, social studies 3, science 3 (laboratory 2) and foreign language 2. One physical education unit recommended. Nursing students should have chemistry.

2015-2016 Annual costs. Tuition/fees: $28,580. Room/board: $9,490. Books/supplies: $1,200. Personal expenses: $800.

2015-2016 Financial aid. Need-based: 111 full-time freshmen applied for aid; 103 deemed to have need; 103 received aid. Average need met was 84%. Average scholarship/grant was $22,271; average loan $4,407. 57% of total undergraduate aid awarded as scholarships/grants, 43% as loans/jobs. **Non-need-based:** Awarded to 142 full-time undergraduates, including 50 freshmen. Scholarships awarded for academics, alumni affiliation, art, athletics, minority status.

Application procedures. Admission: Priority date 2/1; no deadline. No application fee. Applicants notified within 3 weeks of application. Must reply by May 1 or within 4 week(s) if notified thereafter. **Financial aid:** Priority date 2/15; no closing date. FAFSA required. Applicants notified on a rolling basis starting 2/15; must reply within 3 week(s) of notification.

Academics. Special study options: Accelerated study, combined bachelor's/graduate degree, cross-registration, double major, dual enrollment of high school students, independent study, internships, New York semester, teacher certification program. Optional junior year program in fashion merchandising or design at Fashion Institute of Technology in New York City for enrichment electives only. **Credit/placement by examination:** AP, CLEP, institutional tests. 43 credit hours maximum toward bachelor's degree. **Support services:** Learning center, reduced course load, remedial instruction, study skills assistance, tutoring, writing center.

Majors. Biology: General, biotechnology. **Business:** Accounting, business admin, fashion, human resources, management information systems, marketing. **Communications:** Public relations. **Education:** Art, early childhood, English, mathematics, middle, science, social studies, special ed. **English:** English lit. **Health services:** Facilities admin, health care admin, nursing (RN), prenursing, preop/surgical nursing. **History:** General. **Human services:** Social work. **Liberal arts:** Humanities. **Math:** General. **Philosophy/religion:** Christian, philosophy. **Psychology:** General. **Social sciences:** Sociology. **Visual/performing arts:** Art history/conservation, fashion design, graphic design, interior design, studio arts.

Most popular majors. Business/marketing 16%, health sciences 53%, psychology 6%.

Technology on campus. 72 workstations in dormitories, library, computer center, student center. Dormitories wired for high-speed internet access and linked to campus network. Online library, wireless network available.

Student life. Freshman orientation: Available. Preregistration for classes offered. Three-day program offered prior to start of fall semester. **Housing:**

Coed dorms, themed housing available. $100 fully refundable deposit. **Activities:** Campus ministries, dance, drama, literary magazine, student government, student nurses, education association, campus service and spiritual life committees, ethnic groups, public relations society, peer mentors.

Athletics. NCAA. **Intercollegiate:** Basketball W, bowling W, cross-country W, golf W, lacrosse W, soccer W, softball W, swimming W, tennis W, track and field W, volleyball W. **Team name:** Arrows.

Student services. Adult student services, chaplain/spiritual director, career counseling, student employment services, financial aid counseling, minority student services, personal counseling. **Physically disabled:** Services for visually, speech, hearing impaired.

Contact. E-mail: admission@ursuline.edu
Phone: (440) 449-4203 Toll-free number: (888) 877-8456
Fax: (440) 684-6138
Carolyn Sorg, Director of Admission, Ursuline College, 2550 Lander Road, Pepper Pike, OH 44124-4398

Walsh University
North Canton, Ohio
www.walsh.edu
CB code: 1926

♦ Private 4-year university and liberal arts college affiliated with the Roman Catholic Church

♦ Residential campus in small city

♦ 2,157 degree-seeking undergraduates: 13% part-time, 61% women, 6% African American, 1% Asian American, 3% Hispanic/Latino, 2% Multiracial, non-Hispanic, 4% international

♦ 575 degree-seeking graduate students

♦ 80% of applicants admitted

♦ 55% graduate within 6 years; 23% enter graduate study

General. Founded in 1958. Regionally accredited. **Degrees:** 541 bachelor's, 3 associate awarded; master's, professional offered. **Location:** 20 miles from Akron, 55 miles from Cleveland. **Calendar:** Semester, limited summer session. **Full-time faculty:** 132 total; 67% have terminal degrees, 7% minority, 54% women. **Part-time faculty:** 150 total; 11% have terminal degrees, 5% minority, 45% women. **Class size:** 74% < 20, 26% 20-39. **Special facilities:** Bioinformatics laboratory, prayer garden, environmental education center.

Freshman class profile. 1,447 applied, 1,162 admitted, 439 enrolled.

Mid 50% test scores			
		Rank in top quarter:	43%
SAT critical reading:	450-630	Rank in top tenth:	17%
SAT math:	430-620	End year in good standing:	87%
ACT composite:	18-27	Return as sophomores:	80%
GPA 3.75 or higher:	34%	Out-of-state:	13%
GPA 3.50-3.74:	17%	Live on campus:	76%
GPA 3.0-3.49:	29%	International:	5%
GPA 2.0-2.99:	20%		

Basis for selection. Secondary school record very important; class rank, recommendations, essay, character important. Essay, interview recommended for all. **Home schooled:** Transcript of courses and grades required.

High school preparation. College-preparatory program recommended. 16 units recommended. Recommended units include English 4, mathematics 3, social studies 3, science 3, foreign language 2 and academic electives 1. Algebra, biology, and chemistry required for nursing applicants.

2015-2016 Annual costs. Tuition/fees: $27,710. Room/board: $9,920. Books/supplies: $1,104. Personal expenses: $1,386.

2015-2016 Financial aid. Need-based: 406 full-time freshmen applied for aid; 382 deemed to have need; 382 received aid. Average need met was 66%. Average scholarship/grant was $4,505; average loan $3,472. 63% of total undergraduate aid awarded as scholarships/grants, 37% as loans/jobs. **Non-need-based:** Awarded to 1,796 full-time undergraduates, including 519 freshmen. Scholarships awarded for academics, alumni affiliation, athletics, music/drama, religious affiliation, state residency.

Application procedures. Admission: Priority date 11/15; deadline 8/15 (postmark date). $25 fee, may be waived for applicants with need, free for online applicants. Admission notification on a rolling basis beginning on or about 9/15. **Financial aid:** Priority date 5/1; no closing date. FAFSA required. Applicants notified on a rolling basis starting 2/15.

Academics. Accelerated degree completion program for adults with evening and weekend classes. **Special study options:** Accelerated study, combined bachelor's/graduate degree, distance learning, double major, dual enrollment of high school students, ESL, exchange student, external degree, honors, independent study, internships, liberal arts/career combination, study abroad, teacher certification program, Washington semester. CCSA Consortium for Study Abroad, Rome Experience, Uganda experience. **Credit/placement by examination:** AP, CLEP, IB, SAT, ACT, institutional tests. 45 credit hours maximum toward bachelor's degree. Credit and placement are based on each division's evaluation of test information. **Support services:** Learning center, remedial instruction, study skills assistance, tutoring, writing center.

Honors college/program. Admissions based on 3.75 GPA, 27 ACT or 1200 SAT (exclusive of Writing), graduation in top 10% of class. Writing sample and interview required. 35 freshmen admitted each fall.

Majors. Biology: General, biochemistry, bioinformatics, environmental, exercise physiology. **Business:** General, accounting, business admin, communications, finance, international, management information systems, marketing. **Communications:** Communications/speech/rhetoric. **Computer sciences:** Computer graphics, computer science, programming, system admin, web page design. **Conservation:** Environmental science. **Education:** Early childhood, elementary, emotionally handicapped, English, mathematics, mentally handicapped, middle, multiple handicapped, physical, reading, science, secondary, social science, social studies. **English:** English lit, technical writing. **Foreign languages:** French, Spanish. **Health services:** Clinical lab science, nursing (RN), predental, premedicine, preoptometry, prepharmacy, preveterinary. **History:** General. **Math:** General. **Parks/recreation:** Health/fitness. **Philosophy/religion:** Philosophy. **Physical sciences:** Chemistry. **Psychology:** General. **Social sciences:** Criminology, international relations, political science, sociology. **Theology:** Theology. **Visual/performing arts:** Art history/conservation, graphic design, music.

Most popular majors. Biology 12%, business/marketing 37%, education 14%, health sciences 18%.

Technology on campus. 330 workstations in dormitories, library, student center. Dormitories wired for high-speed internet access and linked to campus network. Commuter students can connect to campus network. Online course registration, online library, helpline, repair service, wireless network available.

Student life. Freshman orientation: Mandatory. Preregistration for classes offered. Held on 5 separate weekends during the summer before classes begin in August. $15 charge for parents and other attendees. **Policies:** All full-time undergraduate students 23 and younger must live on campus (some exceptions permitted). **Housing:** Guaranteed on-campus for all undergraduates. Coed dorms, apartments, wellness housing available. $200 nonrefundable deposit, deadline 8/15. Special housing for honors students and global scholars; summer housing for honors students available. **Activities:** Bands, campus ministries, choral groups, dance, drama, international student organizations, literary magazine, music ensembles, radio station, student government, student newspaper, Black student union, Habitat for Humanity, College Democrats, College Republicans, World Student Organization, Students for Life, Walsh University Student Government, University Programming Board, Lean-in Club.

Athletics. NCAA. **Intercollegiate:** Baseball M, basketball, cross-country, football (tackle) M, golf, lacrosse, soccer, softball W, tennis, track and field, volleyball W. **Intramural:** Basketball, bowling, football (non-tackle), golf, soccer, softball, table tennis, tennis, ultimate frisbee, volleyball. **Team name:** Cavaliers.

Student services. Adult student services, alcohol/substance abuse counseling, chaplain/spiritual director, career counseling, student employment services, financial aid counseling, health services, minority student services, personal counseling, placement for graduates, veterans' counselor. **Physically disabled:** Services for visually, speech, hearing impaired.

Contact. E-mail: admissions@walsh.edu
Phone: (330) 490-7172 Toll-free number: (800) 362-9846
Fax: (330) 490-7165
Rebecca Coneglio, Director of Freshman Admission, Walsh University, 2020 East Maple Street, North Canton, OH 44720-3396

Wilberforce University
Wilberforce, Ohio
www.wilberforce.edu   **CB code: 1906**

- Private 4-year university and liberal arts college affiliated with the African Methodist Episcopal Church
- Residential campus in rural community
- 594 degree-seeking undergraduates
- 26 graduate students
- 44% of applicants admitted
- SAT or ACT (ACT writing recommended), application essay required

General. Founded in 1856. Regionally accredited. Cooperative education program required of all students. **Degrees:** 138 bachelor's awarded; master's offered. **ROTC:** Army, Air Force. **Location:** 18 miles from Dayton. **Calendar:** Semester, extensive summer session. **Full-time faculty:** 36 total. **Part-time faculty:** 42 total. **Special facilities:** African Methodist Episcopal Church archives.

Freshman class profile. 1,585 applied, 698 admitted, 181 enrolled.

Out-of-state: 66% **Live on campus:** 94%

Basis for selection. Minimum 2.0 GPA and submission of test scores. **Home schooled:** Letter of recommendation (nonparent) required. Essay required.

High school preparation. College-preparatory program recommended. 15 units required. Required and recommended units include English 4, mathematics 3-4, social studies 2, science 3 and foreign language 2.

2015-2016 Annual costs. Tuition/fees: $13,250. Room/board: $6,456. Books/supplies: $1,200. Personal expenses: $2,000.

2015-2016 Financial aid. Need-based: 195 full-time freshmen applied for aid; 193 deemed to have need; 193 received aid. Average need met was 79%. Average scholarship/grant was $13,282; average loan $2,784. 58% of total undergraduate aid awarded as scholarships/grants, 42% as loans/jobs. **Non-need-based:** Awarded to 6 full-time undergraduates, including 4 freshmen. Scholarships awarded for academics, alumni affiliation.

Application procedures. Admission: Priority date 1/1; deadline 5/1. $25 fee, may be waived for applicants with need. Admission notification on a rolling basis. **Financial aid:** Priority date 3/15, closing date 6/30. FAFSA, institutional form, CSS PROFILE required. Applicants notified on a rolling basis starting 3/15; must reply within 2 week(s) of notification.

Academics. Special study options: Accelerated study, combined bachelor's/graduate degree, cooperative education, cross-registration, distance learning, dual enrollment of high school students, honors, internships, study abroad. **Credit/placement by examination:** AP, CLEP, SAT, ACT, institutional tests. 30 credit hours maximum toward bachelor's degree. **Support services:** Study skills assistance, tutoring, writing center.

Majors. Biology: General. **Business:** Accounting, business admin, management science, market research. **Communications:** Media studies. **Computer sciences:** General, information systems, information technology. **Engineering:** Chemical, civil, electrical, mechanical, nuclear. **English:** English lit. **Health services:** Health care admin. **Human services:** Social work. **Liberal arts:** Arts/sciences. **Protective services:** Law enforcement admin. **Psychology:** General. **Social sciences:** Economics, political science, sociology. **Visual/performing arts:** Music.

Most popular majors. Business/marketing 41%, communications/journalism 8%, computer/information sciences 7%, health sciences 19%.

Technology on campus. 60 workstations in dormitories, library, computer center. Dormitories linked to campus network. Helpline, wireless network available.

Student life. Freshman orientation: Mandatory, $100 fee. Preregistration for classes offered. **Housing:** Guaranteed on-campus for freshmen. Single-sex dorms available. $225 nonrefundable deposit. **Activities:** Campus ministries, choral groups, dance, drama, music ensembles, radio station, student government, student newspaper, TV station, Inter-Faith Fellowship, Interdenominational Ministerial Alliance, Alpha-Omega.

Athletics. NAIA. **Intercollegiate:** Basketball. **Intramural:** Basketball. **Team name:** Bulldogs.

Student services. Adult student services, alcohol/substance abuse counseling, chaplain/spiritual director, career counseling, student employment services, financial aid counseling, health services, personal counseling, placement for graduates, veterans' counselor.

Contact. E-mail: admission@wilberforce.edu
Phone: (937) 708-5721 Toll-free number: (844) 849-2402
Fax: (937) 376-4751
Kenielle Morris, Admissions Director, Wilberforce University, 1055 North Bickett Road, Wilberforce, OH 45384-1001

Wilmington College
Wilmington, Ohio   **CB member**
www.wilmington.edu   **CB code: 1909**

- Private 4-year agricultural and liberal arts college affiliated with the Society of Friends (Quaker)
- Residential campus in large town

- 1,200 degree-seeking undergraduates
- 4 graduate students
- SAT or ACT (ACT writing optional) required

General. Founded in 1870. Regionally accredited. Affiliated with Wilmington Yearly Meeting of the Religious Society of Friends. Branch campuses in Cincinnati and other locations. BA in business offered at Cincinnati branch. **Degrees:** 288 bachelor's awarded; master's offered. **Location:** 50 miles from Cincinnati, 60 miles from Columbus. **Calendar:** Semester, limited summer session. **Full-time faculty:** 66 total. **Part-time faculty:** 53 total. **Class size:** 71% < 20, 28% 20-39, less than 1% 40-49, less than 1% 50-99. **Special facilities:** Greenhouse, herbarium, observatory, electron microscope, live animal area, sports medicine center, Peace Resource Center containing Hiroshima/Nagasaki Memorial collection.

Freshman class profile.

GPA 3.75 or higher:	20%	Rank in top quarter:	36%
GPA 3.50-3.74:	16%	Rank in top tenth:	11%
GPA 3.0-3.49:	31%	Out-of-state:	9%
GPA 2.0-2.99:	33%	Live on campus:	80%

Basis for selection. Previous academic record, test scores, counselor recommendation, and interview important. Essay, interview recommended for all.

High school preparation. College-preparatory program recommended. 16 units required. Required and recommended units include English 4, mathematics 2, social studies 2, science 2 (laboratory 2), foreign language 2 and academic electives 4. 6 art units recommended.

2015-2016 Annual costs. Tuition/fees: $24,500. Room/board: $9,500. Books/supplies: $1,100. Personal expenses: $1,400.

Financial aid. Non-need-based: Scholarships awarded for academics, alumni affiliation, religious affiliation, state residency.

Application procedures. Admission: Closing date 8/1. No application fee. Admission notification on a rolling basis beginning on or about 11/1. Online application does not require application fee. **Financial aid:** Priority date 3/31, closing date 6/1. FAFSA required. Applicants notified on a rolling basis starting 3/1; must reply by 5/1 or within 2 week(s) of notification.

Academics. Special study options: Cross-registration, double major, dual enrollment of high school students, honors, independent study, internships, liberal arts/career combination, student-designed major, study abroad, teacher certification program, weekend college. **Credit/placement by examination:** AP, CLEP, IB, SAT, ACT, institutional tests. 30 credit hours maximum toward bachelor's degree. **Support services:** Learning center, reduced course load, remedial instruction, study skills assistance, tutoring, writing center.

Majors. Biology: General, bacteriology, biochemistry, environmental. **Business:** Accounting, business admin, management science, marketing, sales/distribution. **Communications:** Communications/speech/rhetoric, journalism, media studies, public relations. **Computer sciences:** General, computer science. **Education:** General, agricultural, biology, chemistry, early childhood, elementary, English, health, history, mathematics, middle, multi-level teacher, physical, science, secondary, social science, social studies. **English:** English lit. **Foreign languages:** Spanish. **History:** General. **Human services:** Social work. **Liberal arts:** Arts/sciences. **Math:** General. **Parks/recreation:** Sports admin. **Physical sciences:** Astronomy, chemistry, geology, planetary. **Protective services:** Criminal justice. **Psychology:** General. **Social sciences:** General, economics, political science, sociology. **Visual/performing arts:** Art, commercial/advertising art, dramatic, music.

Most popular majors. Agriculture 9%, business/marketing 30%, education 18%, parks/recreation 6%, psychology 6%.

Technology on campus. 156 workstations in library, computer center. Dormitories wired for high-speed internet access and linked to campus network. Commuter students can connect to campus network. Online course registration, helpline, student web hosting, wireless network available.

Student life. Freshman orientation: Mandatory. Preregistration for classes offered. Held three days prior to start of fall semester. **Housing:** Guaranteed on-campus for all undergraduates. Coed dorms, single-sex dorms, apartments, fraternity/sorority housing available. $100 nonrefundable deposit, deadline 8/1. Living/learning units available. **Activities:** Pep band, campus ministries, choral groups, drama, international student organizations, music ensembles, musical theater, student government, student newspaper, social service, international club, education club, agriculture club, Christian Students, Young Friends (Quaker-Christian group), sports medicine association.

Athletics. NCAA. **Intercollegiate:** Baseball M, basketball, cheerleading, cross-country, football (tackle), golf, soccer, softball W, swimming, tennis, track and field, volleyball W, wrestling M. **Intramural:** Basketball, football (non-tackle), racquetball, soccer, softball, squash, table tennis, tennis, volleyball, weight lifting. **Team name:** Quakers.

Student services. Adult student services, alcohol/substance abuse counseling, chaplain/spiritual director, career counseling, student employment services, financial aid counseling, health services, minority student services, personal counseling, placement for graduates, veterans' counselor.

Contact. E-mail: admissions@wilmington.edu
Phone: (800) 341-9318 ext. 260 Fax: (937) 382-7077
Tina Garland, Director of Admission, Wilmington College, Box 1325 Pyle Center, Wilmington, OH 45177

Wittenberg University
Springfield, Ohio   CB member
www.wittenberg.edu   CB code: 1922

- Private 4-year liberal arts college affiliated with the Evangelical Lutheran Church in America
- Residential campus in small city
- 1,706 degree-seeking undergraduates: 56% women
- 8 degree-seeking graduate students
- 77% of applicants admitted
- Application essay required
- 64% graduate within 6 years

General. Founded in 1845. Regionally accredited. **Degrees:** 432 bachelor's awarded; master's offered. **ROTC:** Army, Air Force. **Location:** 25 miles from Dayton, 45 miles from Columbus. **Calendar:** Semester, limited summer session. **Full-time faculty:** 122 total; 97% have terminal degrees, 13% minority, 43% women. **Part-time faculty:** 57 total; 35% have terminal degrees, 14% minority, 53% women. **Class size:** 53% < 20, 45% 20-39, 1% 40-49, less than 1% 50-99, less than 1% >100. **Special facilities:** Observatory, East Asian art collection, Martin Luther library collection, humanities and technology center.

Freshman class profile. 6,487 applied, 4,986 admitted, 493 enrolled.

Mid 50% test scores			
SAT critical reading:	490-610	GPA 2.0-2.99:	20%
SAT math:	490-610	Rank in top quarter:	45%
SAT writing:	460-560	Rank in top tenth:	19%
ACT composite:	22-28	End year in good standing:	75%
GPA 3.75 or higher:	32%	Return as sophomores:	75%
GPA 3.50-3.74:	16%	Out-of-state:	23%
GPA 3.0-3.49:	32%	Live on campus:	92%

Basis for selection. In order of importance: school achievement record, courses taken, school attended, trend in work, test scores, counselor recommendation, extracurricular activities, and interview. Special consideration for children of alumni, minorities, Lutherans, residents of Clark County, and international students. University math and foreign language placement tests required. Submission of ACT/SAT scores is optional. Interview recommended for all; portfolio required for art program; audition recommended for dance, music, theater programs. **Home schooled:** On-campus interview. **Learning Disabled:** Students with disabilities are responsible for providing the Academic Services Office with appropriate documentation of their disability and arranging an appointment to assess their needs.

High school preparation. College-preparatory program recommended. 16 units required; 21 recommended. Required and recommended units include English 4, mathematics 3-4, history 2-3, science 3-5 (laboratory 2) and foreign language 2-3.

2016-2017 Annual costs. Tuition/fees (projected): $38,090. Room/board: $10,126. Books/supplies: $1,000. Personal expenses: $1,600.

2015-2016 Financial aid. Need-based: 466 full-time freshmen applied for aid; 411 deemed to have need; 411 received aid. Average need met was 67%. Average scholarship/grant was $27,177; average loan $5,212. 70% of total undergraduate aid awarded as scholarships/grants, 30% as loans/jobs. **Non-need-based:** Awarded to 343 full-time undergraduates, including 82 freshmen. Scholarships awarded for academics, alumni affiliation, art, minority status, music/drama, religious affiliation, state residency. **Additional information:** Auditions required of applicants for music, theater, and dance scholarships. Portfolio required of applicants for art scholarships.

Application procedures. Admission: Priority date 3/15; no deadline. $40 fee, may be waived for applicants with need, free for online applicants. Admission notification on a rolling basis. Must reply by May 1 or within 2 week(s) if notified thereafter. **Financial aid:** Priority date 3/1; no closing date. FAFSA required. Applicants notified on a rolling basis starting 3/1; must reply by 5/1 or within 2 week(s) of notification.

Academics. **Special study options:** Combined bachelor's/graduate degree, cross-registration, double major, dual enrollment of high school students, honors, independent study, internships, liberal arts/career combination, student-designed major, study abroad, teacher certification program, urban semester, Washington semester. Semester programs with Duke University (marine biology), School of Visual Arts in New York, Camarillo Hospital in California, National Institutes of Health in Washington, D.C., Washington University (MO) (occupational therapy), Johns Hopkins Nursing Program, 3-2 engineering with Washington University (MO), Case Western Reserve University. **Credit/placement by examination:** AP, CLEP, IB, institutional tests. A student seeking to gain credit by examination must first submit information to the chair of the department and the instructor of the course in which credit is to be earned. The petition must also be approved by the Academic Services Office. After all approvals are granted, the student must then pay the appropriate fee (cost of one overload credit) before taking the exam. The grade for the examination appears on the student's transcript. Important note: Credit can not be received for courses already taken and a grade has been received. **Support services:** Learning center, pre-admission summer program, reduced course load, study skills assistance, tutoring, writing center.

Majors. **Area/ethnic studies:** American, East Asian, Russian/Eastern European/Eurasian. **Biology:** General, Biochemistry/molecular biology. **Business:** General, accounting, entrepreneurial studies, finance, marketing. **Communications:** Communications/speech/rhetoric. **Conservation:** Environmental science. **Education:** General. **English:** English lit. **Foreign languages:** French, German, Spanish. **Health services:** Nursing (RN). **History:** General. **Liberal arts:** Arts/sciences. **Math:** General. **Parks/recreation:** Exercise sciences, sports admin. **Philosophy/religion:** Philosophy, religion. **Physical sciences:** Chemistry, geology, physics. **Psychology:** General. **Social sciences:** Criminology, economics, international relations, political science, sociology. **Visual/performing arts:** General, art, dance, music.

Most popular majors. Biology 10%, business/marketing 14%, education 7%, English 6%, physical sciences 6%, psychology 8%, social sciences 18%, visual/performing arts 6%.

Technology on campus. 900 workstations in dormitories, library, computer center, student center. Dormitories wired for high-speed internet access and linked to campus network. Commuter students can connect to campus network. Online course registration, online library, helpline, wireless network available.

Student life. **Freshman orientation:** Available, $55 fee. Preregistration for classes offered. Four-day program held before classes begin. **Housing:** Guaranteed on-campus for all undergraduates. Coed dorms, single-sex dorms, apartments, fraternity/sorority housing, themed housing, wellness housing available. $500 nonrefundable deposit. Pets allowed in dorm rooms. Substance-free residence hall, honors residence hall, special theme halls available. **Activities:** Bands, campus ministries, choral groups, dance, drama, film society, international student organizations, literary magazine, music ensembles, Model UN, musical theater, opera, radio station, student government, student newspaper, symphony orchestra, TV station, Newman club, Concerned Black Students, community volunteer service, Weaver Chapel Association, Project Woman, East Asian studies club, Hillel, Amnesty International, Habitat for Humanity.

Athletics. NCAA. **Intercollegiate:** Baseball M, basketball, cheerleading, cross-country, diving, field hockey W, football (tackle) M, golf, lacrosse, soccer, softball W, swimming, tennis, track and field, volleyball. **Intramural:** Badminton, basketball, football (non-tackle), soccer, softball, ultimate frisbee, volleyball. **Team name:** Tigers.

Student services. Adult student services, alcohol/substance abuse counseling, chaplain/spiritual director, career counseling, student employment services, financial aid counseling, health services, minority student services, personal counseling, placement for graduates, veterans' counselor, women's services.

Contact. E-mail: admission@wittenberg.edu
Phone: (937) 327-6314 Toll-free number: (877) 206-0332 ext. 6314
Fax: (937) 327-6345
Karen Hunt, Director of Admission, Wittenberg University, Ward Street and North Wittenberg, Springfield, OH 45501-0720

Wright State University
Dayton, Ohio
www.wright.edu

CB member
CB code: 1179

- Public 4-year university
- Commuter campus in small city
- 12,040 degree-seeking undergraduates: 18% part-time, 52% women, 12% African American, 2% Asian American, 3% Hispanic/Latino, 4% Multi-racial, non-Hispanic, 5% international

---

- 4,139 degree-seeking graduate students
- 96% of applicants admitted
- SAT or ACT (ACT writing optional) required
- 40% graduate within 6 years

General. Founded in 1964. Regionally accredited. **Degrees:** 2,312 bachelor's awarded; master's, professional, doctoral offered. **ROTC:** Army, Air Force. **Location:** 10 miles from downtown. **Calendar:** Semester, extensive summer session. **Full-time faculty:** 626 total; 16% minority, 45% women. **Class size:** 41% < 20, 36% 20-39, 8% 40-49, 12% 50-99, 2% >100. **Special facilities:** Biological preserve, disabled-accessible, garden of the senses, military/veteran center.

Freshman class profile. 5,560 applied, 5,336 admitted, 2,399 enrolled.

Mid 50% test scores			
SAT critical reading:	460-590	Rank in top quarter:	37%
SAT math:	450-590	Rank in top tenth:	17%
SAT writing:	430-560	End year in good standing:	79%
ACT composite:	19-25	Return as sophomores:	67%
GPA 3.75 or higher:	25%	Out-of-state:	3%
GPA 3.50-3.74:	14%	Live on campus:	53%
GPA 3.0-3.49:	26%	International:	2%
GPA 2.0-2.99:	34%	Fraternities:	4%
		Sororities:	8%

Basis for selection. Liberal admission policy. College-preparatory curriculum, 2.0 GPA required. Test scores important for selected programs. Audition required for acting, dance, directing/stage management, music programs; portfolio required for art, art education programs. **Home schooled:** Statement describing home school structure and mission required. Each applicant should clearly articulate all secondary coursework completed while providing written verification from the appropriate school district excusing the student from compulsory attendance. **Learning Disabled:** Students encouraged to contact Office of Disability Services to fill out application to qualify for support services.

High school preparation. College-preparatory program recommended. 16 units required. Required units include English 4, mathematics 3, social studies 3, science 3 (laboratory 3), foreign language 2 and visual/performing arts 1. Math requirement includes 2 algebra. Art, music or theater recommended. Students not meeting course recommendations must make up deficiency prior to admission to program.

2015-2016 Annual costs. Tuition/fees: $8,730; $17,098 out-of-state. Room/board: $9,304. Books/supplies: $1,392. Personal expenses: $1,070.

2015-2016 Financial aid. **Need-based:** 38% of total undergraduate aid awarded as scholarships/grants, 62% as loans/jobs. **Non-need-based:** Scholarships awarded for academics, alumni affiliation, art, athletics, leadership, minority status, music/drama, ROTC, state residency.

Application procedures. **Admission:** No deadline. $30 fee. Admission notification on a rolling basis beginning on or about 9/9. Application by January recommended for students desiring on-campus housing. **Financial aid:** Priority date 3/1; no closing date. FAFSA required. Applicants notified on a rolling basis starting 3/15.

Academics. **Special study options:** Cooperative education, cross-registration, distance learning, double major, dual enrollment of high school students, ESL, honors, independent study, internships, semester at sea, student-designed major, study abroad, teacher certification program, weekend college. **Credit/placement by examination:** AP, CLEP, SAT, ACT, institutional tests. **Support services:** Learning center, pre-admission summer program, reduced course load, remedial instruction, study skills assistance, tutoring, writing center. For students with learning disabilities additional services available such as testing accomodations; typists/scribe; note taking services; reading machines; remedial courses; texts on tape; LD specialists.

Honors college/program. First-year students direct from high school should meet at least two of the following criteria: 1) GPA of 3.25 or better in high school. 2) Rank in top 10 percent of the graduating class. 3) Score at 90th percentile on the ACT (approximately 27 Composite) or the SAT (approximately 1210 Critical Reading and Math).

Majors. **Area/ethnic studies:** African-American, women's. **Biology:** General. **Business:** Accounting, business admin, finance, human resources, international, logistics, management information systems, managerial economics, marketing. **Communications:** Communications/speech/rhetoric, media studies. **Computer sciences:** General. **Conservation:** Environmental science. **Education:** Early childhood, health, middle, multiple handicapped, music, physical, science, voc/tech. **Engineering:** General, applied physics, biomedical, computer, electrical, engineering science, materials, mechanical. **English:** English lit. **Foreign languages:** General, classics, French, German, Latin, modern Greek, sign language interpretation, Spanish. **Health services:** Clinical lab science, nursing (RN), vocational rehab counseling. **History:** General. **Human services:** Social work. **Liberal arts:** Arts/sciences. **Math:** General, statistics. **Parks/recreation:** Exercise sciences, health/fitness. **Philosophy/**

religion: Philosophy, religion. **Physical sciences:** Chemistry, geology, physics. **Psychology:** General. **Social sciences:** Anthropology, criminology, economics, geography, international relations, political science, sociology, urban studies. **Visual/performing arts:** Acting, art, art history/conservation, dance, dramatic, film/cinema/video, music, music history, music performance, studio arts, theater design.

Most popular majors. Business/marketing 27%, engineering/engineering technologies 10%, health sciences 11%, psychology 8%, social sciences 9%.

Technology on campus. 1,700 workstations in dormitories, library, computer center, student center. Dormitories wired for high-speed internet access and linked to campus network. Commuter students can connect to campus network. Online course registration, online library, helpline, repair service, student web hosting, wireless network available.

Student life. Freshman orientation: Mandatory, $20 fee. Preregistration for classes offered. All students under the age of 23 who have never attended college are required to attend orientation. **Housing:** Coed dorms, special housing for disabled, apartments, themed housing available. $150 fully refundable deposit. Honors dorm, institutional apartments available, STEM Living Learning Community available. **Activities:** Bands, campus ministries, choral groups, dance, drama, international student organizations, literary magazine, music ensembles, Model UN, musical theater, opera, radio station, student government, student newspaper, symphony orchestra, TV station, Veteran's Affairs Office, black student union, Baptist student union, student association for escorts, College Students for Special Wish, Fellowship of Christian Students, Circle-K, Campus Crusade for Christ, Ohio College Democrats, Jewish student union.

Athletics. NCAA. **Intercollegiate:** Baseball M, basketball, cheerleading, cross-country, diving, golf M, soccer, softball W, swimming, tennis, track and field, volleyball. **Intramural:** Baseball M, basketball, bowling, diving, football (tackle) M, golf, gymnastics, racquetball, sand volleyball, soccer, softball, table tennis, tennis, ultimate frisbee, volleyball. **Team name:** Raiders.

Student services. Adult student services, chaplain/spiritual director, career counseling, student employment services, financial aid counseling, health services, legal services, minority student services, on-campus daycare, personal counseling, placement for graduates, veterans' counselor, women's services. **Physically disabled:** Services for visually, speech, hearing impaired.

Contact. E-mail: admissions@wright.edu
Phone: (937) 775-5700 Toll-free number: (800) 247-1770
Fax: (937) 775-4410
Dani Heeter, Director of Undergraduate Admissions, Wright State University, 3640 Colonel Glenn Highway, 108 SU, Dayton, OH 45435

Xavier University
Cincinnati, Ohio
CB member
www.xavier.edu
CB code: 1965

- Private 4-year university affiliated with the Roman Catholic Church
- Residential campus in large city
- 4,461 degree-seeking undergraduates: 5% part-time, 54% women, 10% African American, 3% Asian American, 5% Hispanic/Latino, 4% Multi-racial, non-Hispanic, 2% international
- 1,571 degree-seeking graduate students
- 72% of applicants admitted
- SAT or ACT (ACT writing optional), application essay required
- 74% graduate within 6 years; 32% enter graduate study

General. Founded in 1831. Regionally accredited. **Degrees:** 948 bachelor's, 21 associate awarded; master's, professional offered. **ROTC:** Army, Air Force. **Location:** 5 miles from downtown. **Calendar:** Semester, limited summer session. **Full-time faculty:** 342 total; 76% have terminal degrees, 15% minority, 52% women. **Part-time faculty:** 362 total; 19% have terminal degrees, 10% minority, 58% women. **Class size:** 40% < 20, 56% 20-39, 3% 40-49, less than 1% 50-99. **Special facilities:** Observatory, business school trading terminal lab, center for innovation, library makerspace.

Freshman class profile. 10,661 applied, 7,631 admitted, 1,150 enrolled.

Mid 50% test scores			
SAT critical reading:	490-590	GPA 2.0-2.99:	15%
SAT math:	490-590	Rank in top quarter:	53%
SAT writing:	480-590	Rank in top tenth:	23%
ACT composite:	22-27	End year in good standing:	93%
GPA 3.75 or higher:	38%	Return as sophomores:	83%
GPA 3.50-3.74:	20%	Out-of-state:	56%
GPA 3.0-3.49:	27%	Live on campus:	91%
		International:	2%

Basis for selection. Rigor of curriculum, class rank, grades, ACT/SAT, counselor recommendations, an essay, and activities. Music applicants required to submit audition application and one music teacher recommendation, as well as attend a music audition to be considered for admission to the Music or Music Education majors. Home schooled: Transcript of courses and grades, letter of recommendation (nonparent) required. May require applicants submit to an on-campus or phone interview. Submit standardized test scores (ACT or SAT).

High school preparation. College-preparatory program recommended. 21 units recommended. Recommended units include English 4, mathematics 3, social studies 3, science 3, foreign language 2 and academic electives 5. 1 health/physical education recommended.

2015-2016 Annual costs. Tuition/fees: $35,080. Room/board: $11,380. Books/supplies: $1,000. Personal expenses: $1,000.

2014-2015 Financial aid. Need-based: Average scholarship/grant was $17,783; average loan $3,843. 69% of total undergraduate aid awarded as scholarships/grants, 31% as loans/jobs. **Non-need-based:** Scholarships awarded for academics, alumni affiliation, art, athletics, leadership, music/drama, religious affiliation.

Application procedures. Admission: Priority date 2/1; no deadline. $35 fee, may be waived for applicants with need, free for online applicants. Admission notification on a rolling basis beginning on or about 10/15. Must reply by 5/1. Tuition and housing deposits are refundable up until May 1. Admission to the Nursing program is competitive so deposits are non-refundable. **Financial aid:** Priority date 2/15; no closing date. FAFSA required. Applicants notified on a rolling basis starting 3/1; must reply by 5/1.

Academics. Strong emphasis on ethics and values in core curriculum. **Special study options:** Combined bachelor's/graduate degree, cooperative education, cross-registration, distance learning, double major, dual enrollment of high school students, ESL, exchange student, honors, independent study, internships, semester at sea, study abroad, teacher certification program, urban semester, Washington semester, weekend college. Cooperative science-engineering program (physics and chemistry) with University of Cincinnati, forestry program and environmental management programs with Duke University, Service Learning Semester. **Credit/placement by examination:** AP, CLEP, IB, institutional tests. 30 credit hours maximum toward associate degree, 60 toward bachelor's. University awards credit to veterans based on credit recommendations from the American Council on Education. ACE credit award is considered as prior work experience since most of the credit awarded is for training experiences. **Support services:** Learning center, pre-admission summer program, reduced course load, remedial instruction, study skills assistance, tutoring, writing center.

Majors. Biology: General. **Business:** General, accounting, actuarial science, business admin, entrepreneurial studies, finance, human resources, international, management information systems, managerial economics, marketing. **Communications:** General, advertising, public relations, radio/TV. **Computer sciences:** Computer science. **Conservation:** Environmental science, management/policy. **Education:** Biology, chemistry, drama/dance, early childhood, elementary, middle, Montessori teacher, music, physics, science, special ed. **Engineering:** Applied physics, chemical. **English:** English lit. **Foreign languages:** Classics, French, German, Spanish. **Health services:** Athletic training, nursing (RN). **History:** General. **Human services:** Social work. **Liberal arts:** Arts/sciences. **Math:** General. **Parks/recreation:** Sports admin. **Philosophy/religion:** Philosophy, religion. **Physical sciences:** Chemistry, physics. **Protective services:** Criminal justice. **Psychology:** General. **Social sciences:** Economics, international relations, political science, sociology. **Visual/performing arts:** Art, dramatic, graphic design, music, studio arts.

Most popular majors. Biology 7%, business/marketing 26%, communications/journalism 6%, health sciences 10%, liberal arts 12%, psychology 6%, social sciences 6%.

Technology on campus. 450 workstations in dormitories, library, computer center, student center. Dormitories wired for high-speed internet access and linked to campus network. Commuter students can connect to campus network. Online course registration, online library, helpline, repair service, wireless network available.

Student life. Freshman orientation: Mandatory, $190 fee. Preregistration for classes offered. Held the weekend before the start of classes. **Policies:** Student handbook, responsible computer use, university alcohol policy, harassment code accountability procedures. **Housing:** Guaranteed on-campus for freshmen. Coed dorms, special housing for disabled, apartments, themed housing available. $200 fully refundable deposit, deadline 5/1. **Activities:** Bands, campus ministries, choral groups, dance, drama, international student organizations, literary magazine, music ensembles, Model UN, musical theater, student government, student newspaper, TV station, Life after Sunday, Xavier Interfaith, Asian Pacific Society, X Change, African Student Association, College Republicans, College Democrats, Muslim Student Association, Voices of Solidarity, Latino Student Organization.

Athletics. NCAA. **Intercollegiate:** Baseball M, basketball, cheerleading, cross-country, golf, soccer, swimming, tennis, track and field, volleyball W. **Intramural:** Basketball, bowling, football (non-tackle), racquetball, sand volleyball, soccer, softball, tennis, volleyball. **Team name:** Musketeers.

Student services. Adult student services, alcohol/substance abuse counseling, chaplain/spiritual director, career counseling, services for economically disadvantaged, student employment services, financial aid counseling, health services, minority student services, personal counseling, placement for graduates, veterans' counselor, women's services. **Physically disabled:** Services for visually, speech, hearing impaired.

Contact. E-mail: xuadmit@xavier.edu
Phone: (513) 745-3301 Toll-free number: (877) 982-3648
Fax: (513) 745-4319
Aaron Meis, Dean of Admissions, Xavier University, 3800 Victory Parkway, Cincinnati, OH 45207-5311

Youngstown State University
Youngstown, Ohio
www.ysu.edu

CB member
CB code: 1975

- Public 4-year university
- Commuter campus in small city
- 10,255 degree-seeking undergraduates: 17% part-time, 52% women, 11% African American, 1% Asian American, 4% Hispanic/Latino, 3% Multi-racial, non-Hispanic, 1% international
- 1,241 degree-seeking graduate students
- 71% of applicants admitted
- SAT or ACT (ACT writing optional) required
- 30% graduate within 6 years

General. Founded in 1908. Regionally accredited. **Degrees:** 1,682 bachelor's, 202 associate awarded; master's, professional, doctoral offered. **ROTC:** Army, Air Force. **Location:** 65 miles from Cleveland, 60 miles from Pittsburgh. **Calendar:** Semester, limited summer session. **Full-time faculty:** 408 total; 90% have terminal degrees, 18% minority, 45% women. **Part-time faculty:** 639 total; 8% minority, 52% women. **Class size:** 39% < 20, 48% 20-39, 8% 40-49, 4% 50-99, 1% >100. **Special facilities:** Planetarium, historic preservation center, art museum, medical museum.

Freshman class profile. 7,281 applied, 5,152 admitted, 2,008 enrolled.

Mid 50% test scores		Rank in top quarter:	30%
SAT critical reading:	400-530	Rank in top tenth:	12%
SAT math:	410-540	End year in good standing:	78%
SAT writing:	380-510	Return as sophomores:	75%
ACT composite:	18-24	Out-of-state:	16%
GPA 3.75 or higher:	17%	Live on campus:	28%
GPA 3.50-3.74:	14%	International:	1%
GPA 3.0-3.49:	30%	Fraternities:	2%
GPA 2.0-2.99:	38%	Sororities:	3%

Basis for selection. Test scores, GPA, secodary school record very Important. Interview required for BS/MD program; audition required for music, BFA theater programs. **Home schooled:** Transcript of courses and grades required. ACT/SAT required unless out of high school 2 or more years. Official transcript showing documentation of coursework completed for grades 9-12 and indicating date of completion of studies or graduation must be sent to Admissions. Any relevant supporting documents required by applicant's home state verifying home school curriculum required. Curriculum outline, detailing course content, textbooks used, any other relevant information regarding coursework must be submitted. Copy of the Superintendent's Exemption Notice showing the student is excused to receive home schooling also required for Ohio students. Out of state admission requirements are based on the individual state requirements for home schooling.

High school preparation. College-preparatory program recommended. 16 units recommended. Recommended units include English 4, mathematics 4, social studies 3, science 3 (laboratory 1), foreign language 2 and visual/performing arts 1.

2015-2016 Annual costs. Tuition/fees: $8,327; $14,327 out-of-state. Room/board: $8,990. Books/supplies: $1,100. Personal expenses: $2,395.

2014-2015 Financial aid. **Need-based:** 1,513 full-time freshmen applied for aid; 1,298 deemed to have need; 1,297 received aid. Average need met was 33%. Average scholarship/grant was $5,050; average loan $3,013. 55% of total undergraduate aid awarded as scholarships/grants, 45% as loans/jobs. **Non-need-based:** Awarded to 3,512 full-time undergraduates, including 966 freshmen. Scholarships awarded for academics, alumni affiliation, athletics, ROTC, state residency.

Application procedures. Admission: Priority date 2/15; deadline 8/1 (postmark date). $45 fee, may be waived for applicants with need. Admission notification on a rolling basis beginning on or about 7/1. Students who apply by February 15 eligible for early registration and orientation. **Financial aid:** Priority date 2/15; no closing date. FAFSA, institutional form required. Applicants notified on a rolling basis starting 4/1; must reply within 2 week(s) of notification.

Academics. Special study options: Accelerated study, combined bachelor's/graduate degree, cooperative education, cross-registration, distance learning, double major, dual enrollment of high school students, ESL, exchange student, honors, independent study, internships, semester at sea, student-designed major, study abroad, teacher certification program, urban semester, Washington semester. Off-campus study with Lorain County Community College, Cuyahoga Community College, Lakeland Community College, Stark State Community College, Butler Community College, Belmont Technical College, Eastern Gateway CC, North Central State College. **Credit/placement by examination:** AP, CLEP, IB, SAT, ACT, institutional tests. In select CLEP and AP tests, higher grade may make student eligible for more credits. **Support services:** Learning center, pre-admission summer program, reduced course load, remedial instruction, study skills assistance, tutoring, writing center.

Majors. Area/ethnic studies: African-American, American. **Biology:** General, biochemistry. **Business:** General, accounting, apparel, banking/financial services, business admin, fashion, finance, financial planning, hospitality admin, hospitality/recreation, human resources, information resources management, management information systems, managerial economics, marketing, merchandising, operations, public finance, retailing, sales/distribution, selling, tourism promotion, tourism/travel. **Communications:** Advertising, communications/speech/rhetoric, journalism, public relations, radio/TV, sports. **Computer sciences:** General, computer science, information technology, programming. **Conservation:** Environmental science. **Education:** General, art, autistic, biology, business, chemistry, computer, early childhood, elementary, emotionally handicapped, English, family/consumer sciences, foreign languages, French, health, history, kindergarten/preschool, learning disabled, mathematics, mentally handicapped, middle, multi-level teacher, multiple handicapped, music, physical, physics, science, secondary, social science, social studies, Spanish, special ed, speech. **Engineering:** General, biomedical, chemical, civil, computer, electrical, industrial, mechanical. **English:** English lit, rhetoric/composition, technical writing. **Foreign languages:** General, French, Italian, Spanish. **Health services:** Athletic training, clinical lab science, community health, community health services, dental hygiene, dietetics, facilities admin, nursing (RN), predental, premedicine, prepharmacy, preveterinary, public health ed, respiratory therapy technology. **History:** General. **Human services:** General, social work. **Liberal arts:** Arts/sciences. **Math:** General, applied, mathematics/statistics, statistics. **Parks/recreation:** Exercise sciences, health/fitness, sports admin. **Philosophy/religion:** Philosophy, religion. **Physical sciences:** General, astronomy, chemistry, geology, physics, planetary. **Protective services:** Corrections, criminal justice, forensics, law enforcement admin, security services. **Psychology:** General. **Social sciences:** General, anthropology, econometrics, economics, geography, international economics, political science, sociology. **Visual/performing arts:** General, acting, art, art history/conservation, brass instruments, commercial/advertising art, dance, dramatic, graphic design, jazz, music, music history, music performance, music theory/composition, painting, percussion instruments, photography, piano/keyboard, printmaking, stringed instruments, studio arts, theater design, voice/opera, woodwind instruments. **Work/family studies:** General, clothing/textiles, family/community services, food/nutrition.

Most popular majors. Business/marketing 15%, education 11%, engineering/engineering technologies 11%, health sciences 12%, liberal arts 6%, public administration/social services 6%, security/protective services 7%.

Technology on campus. 170 workstations in dormitories, library, computer center, student center. Dormitories wired for high-speed internet access and linked to campus network. Commuter students can connect to campus network. Online course registration, online library, helpline, repair service, student web hosting, wireless network available.

Student life. Freshman orientation: Mandatory, $80 fee. Preregistration for classes offered. Held in March, June, July, and August. **Policies:** Student conduct policy, student grievance policy, basic student rights and responsibilities, student organization policy. **Housing:** Guaranteed on-campus for all undergraduates. Coed dorms, single-sex dorms, apartments, wellness housing available. $200 nonrefundable deposit. Honors college facility available. **Activities:** Bands, campus ministries, choral groups, dance, drama, film society, international student organizations, literary magazine, music ensembles, Model UN, musical theater, opera, radio station, student government, student newspaper, symphony orchestra, American Medical Student Association, African Student Union, Greek Campus Life, Student Social Workers Association, Catholic Student Association, Rotaract, College Democrats, College Republicans, YSUnity: LGBTQIA, Campus Crusade for Christ.

Athletics. NCAA. **Intercollegiate:** Baseball M, basketball, cross-country, diving W, football (tackle) M, golf, soccer W, softball W, swimming W, tennis, track and field, volleyball W. **Intramural:** Basketball, football (non-tackle), racquetball, soccer, softball, table tennis, ultimate frisbee, volleyball. **Team name:** Penguins.

Student services. Adult student services, alcohol/substance abuse counseling, chaplain/spiritual director, career counseling, student employment services, financial aid counseling, health services, minority student services, on-campus daycare, personal counseling, placement for graduates, veterans' counselor, women's services. **Physically disabled:** Services for visually, speech, hearing impaired.

Contact. E-mail: enroll@ysu.edu
Phone: (330) 941-2000 Toll-free number: (877) 468-6978
Fax: (330) 941-3674
Sue Davis, Director of Admissions, Youngstown State University, One University Plaza, Youngstown, OH 44555-0001

Oklahoma

Bacone College
Muskogee, Oklahoma
www.bacone.edu

CB code: 6030

▶ Private 4-year liberal arts college affiliated with the American Baptist Churches in the USA
▶ Residential campus in large town
▶ 968 undergraduates
▶ SAT or ACT required

General. Founded in 1880. Regionally accredited. American Indian heritage and commitment to serving Native Americans. Guided by Christian principles. **Degrees:** 71 bachelor's, 31 associate awarded. **Location:** 50 miles from Tulsa. **Calendar:** Semester, limited summer session. **Full-time faculty:** 79 total. **Part-time faculty:** 10 total. **Class size:** 70% < 20, 25% 20-39, 5% 40-49. **Special facilities:** Native American museum and collection.

Freshman class profile.

GPA 3.75 or higher:	6%	Rank in top quarter:	17%
GPA 3.50-3.74:	10%	Rank in top tenth:	5%
GPA 3.0-3.49:	26%	Out-of-state:	39%
GPA 2.0-2.99:	56%	Live on campus:	78%

Basis for selection. Student must meet two of the following: 2.0 GPA, top 50% of graduating class and/or 18 ACT. Additional standards for admission to nursing and radiography programs applied after student has been admitted. ACT used for counseling. Interview recommended for nursing, radiologic technology programs. **Home schooled:** Official transcript from accredited homeschool organization or GED required.

High school preparation. College-preparatory program recommended. Recommended units include English 4, mathematics 3, history 2, science 2 (laboratory 2).

2015-2016 Annual costs. Tuition/fees: $14,500. Room/board: $10,000. Books/supplies: $1,400. Personal expenses: $500.

Financial aid. All financial aid based on need.

Application procedures. Admission: No deadline. No application fee. Admission notification on a rolling basis. **Financial aid:** Priority date 3/31; no closing date. FAFSA required. Applicants notified on a rolling basis starting 4/1; must reply within 2 week(s) of notification.

Academics. Special study options: Accelerated study, cross-registration, double major, dual enrollment of high school students, independent study, internships, liberal arts/career combination, student-designed major, teacher certification program. **Credit/placement by examination:** AP, CLEP, SAT, ACT, institutional tests. 15 credit hours maximum toward associate degree. **Support services:** Learning center, pre-admission summer program, remedial instruction, study skills assistance, tutoring.

Majors. Area/ethnic studies: Native American. **Business:** Business admin. **Education:** Early childhood, elementary, health, physical. **Health services:** Medical radiologic technology/radiation therapy, nursing (RN). **Parks/recreation:** Exercise sciences, facilities management, sports admin. **Protective services:** Criminal justice.

Most popular majors. Business/marketing 12%, education 61%, parks/recreation 13%, social sciences 11%.

Technology on campus. 84 workstations in library, computer center. Dormitories wired for high-speed internet access and linked to campus network. Commuter students can connect to campus network. Online library, wireless network available.

Student life. Freshman orientation: Mandatory, $100 fee. Preregistration for classes offered. **Policies:** No alcohol or tobacco products allowed on campus. **Housing:** Single-sex dorms available. $100 deposit. **Activities:** Campus ministries, choral groups, dance, drama, student government, student newspaper, Native learning work community, Native American students of promise, journalism club, praise team club, praise band, American Indian stickball club, criminal justice studies club, Native American student association, black student association, American Indian dance and song.

Athletics. NAIA. **Intercollegiate:** Baseball M, basketball, cheerleading, cross-country, football (tackle) M, golf, rodeo, soccer, softball W, tennis, track and field, volleyball W, wrestling M. **Intramural:** Basketball, football (tackle) M, soccer, softball, table tennis. **Team name:** Warriors.

Student services. Chaplain/spiritual director, career counseling, student employment services, financial aid counseling, health services, personal counseling, placement for graduates. **Physically disabled:** Services for visually, speech, hearing impaired.

Contact. E-mail: admissionsoffice@bacone.edu
Phone: (918) 683-4581 ext. 7342
Toll-free number: (888) 682-5514 ext. 7342 Fax: (918) 781-7416
Aaron Jordan, Director of Admissions, Bacone College, 2299 Old Bacone Road, Muskogee, OK 74403

Cameron University
Lawton, Oklahoma
www.cameron.edu

CB member
CB code: 6080

▶ Public 4-year university
▶ Commuter campus in small city
▶ 4,361 degree-seeking undergraduates: 27% part-time, 60% women, 15% African American, 2% Asian American, 12% Hispanic/Latino, 6% Native American, 1% Native Hawaiian/Pacific islander, 8% Multi-racial, non-Hispanic, 5% international
▶ 416 degree-seeking graduate students
▶ 100% of applicants admitted

General. Founded in 1909. Regionally accredited. **Degrees:** 529 bachelor's, 616 associate awarded; master's offered. **ROTC:** Army. **Location:** 90 miles from Oklahoma City. **Calendar:** Semester, limited summer session. **Full-time faculty:** 174 total; 72% have terminal degrees, 23% minority, 41% women. **Part-time faculty:** 136 total; 12% have terminal degrees, 15% minority, 54% women. **Class size:** 47% < 20, 49% 20-39, 3% 40-49, less than 1% 50-99.

Freshman class profile. 1,047 applied, 1,045 admitted, 787 enrolled.

Mid 50% test scores		Rank in top tenth:	3%
ACT composite:	17-22	End year in good standing:	60%
GPA 3.75 or higher:	15%	Return as sophomores:	65%
GPA 3.50-3.74:	14%	Out-of-state:	11%
GPA 3.0-3.49:	35%	Live on campus:	21%
GPA 2.0-2.99:	33%	International:	6%
Rank in top quarter:	11%	Fraternities:	2%

Basis for selection. All applicants must be graduates of an accredited high school or possess a GED (student's high school class must have graduated). Baccalaureate degree requirements: 20 ACT/890 SAT OR rank in top 50% of high school class with 2.7 GPA. AS requirements: Meet minimum high school curriculum requirements and completed the ACT or SAT. AAS requirements: Completed the ACT or SAT.

High school preparation. College-preparatory program recommended. 15 units required. Required and recommended units include English 4, mathematics 3, history 3, science 3 (laboratory 3) and academic electives 2-4.

2015-2016 Annual costs. Tuition/fees: $5,580; $14,190 out-of-state. Room/board: $4,888. Books/supplies: $1,418. Personal expenses: $1,676.

2014-2015 Financial aid. Need-based: 595 full-time freshmen applied for aid; 486 deemed to have need; 467 received aid. Average need met was 56%. Average scholarship/grant was $6,005; average loan $2,895. 68% of total undergraduate aid awarded as scholarships/grants, 32% as loans/jobs. **Non-need-based:** Awarded to 687 full-time undergraduates, including 193 freshmen. Scholarships awarded for academics, alumni affiliation, art, athletics, leadership, minority status, music/drama, ROTC, state residency.

Application procedures. Admission: No deadline. $15 fee, may be waived for applicants with need. Admission notification on a rolling basis. **Financial aid:** Priority date 4/1; no closing date. Applicants notified on a rolling basis starting 4/1; must reply within 2 week(s) of notification.

Academics. Special study options: Accelerated study, distance learning, double major, dual enrollment of high school students, honors, independent study, internships, liberal arts/career combination, student-designed major, study abroad, teacher certification program. **Credit/placement by examination:** AP, CLEP, IB, ACT, institutional tests. **Support services:** Learning center, remedial instruction, study skills assistance, tutoring, writing center.

Majors. Biology: General. **Business:** Accounting, business admin. **Communications:** Broadcast journalism. **Computer sciences:** Computer science, information technology. **Education:** Early childhood, educational technology, elementary, English, mathematics, music, social studies. **English:** English lit. **Foreign languages:** General. **Health services:** Clinical lab science. **History:** General. **Math:** General. **Parks/recreation:** Health/fitness. **Physical sciences:** Chemistry, physics. **Psychology:** General. **Social sciences:** Political science, sociology. **Visual/performing arts:** Art, music. **Work/family studies:** Child development.

Most popular majors. Business/marketing 16%, communications/journalism 6%, computer/information sciences 9%, education 14%, parks/recreation 6%, psychology 9%, security/protective services 9%.

Technology on campus. 240 workstations in dormitories, library, computer center. Dormitories wired for high-speed internet access and linked to campus network. Commuter students can connect to campus network. Online library, helpline, student web hosting, wireless network available.

Student life. Freshman orientation: Available. Preregistration for classes offered. Held before classes start. **Policies:** Student code of conduct; no alcohol on campus. **Housing:** Single-sex dorms, special housing for disabled, apartments, gender-neutral housing available. $200 partly refundable deposit. Quiet areas available. **Activities:** Bands, campus ministries, choral groups, dance, drama, film society, international student organizations, literary magazine, music ensembles, musical theater, opera, student government, student newspaper, symphony orchestra, TV station, Student Government Association, Nepalese Association, Black Student Association, Nigerian Students Association, Baptist Collegiate Ministries, International Club, PRIDE, Campus Ministry, Circle K International, Student Advocates for Political Action.

Athletics. NCAA. **Intercollegiate:** Baseball M, basketball, cross-country M, golf, softball W, tennis, volleyball W. **Intramural:** Badminton, basketball, bowling, football (non-tackle), racquetball, soccer, softball, table tennis, tennis, volleyball, weight lifting. **Team name:** Aggies.

Student services. Adult student services, alcohol/substance abuse counseling, career counseling, services for economically disadvantaged, student employment services, financial aid counseling, health services, personal counseling, veterans' counselor. **Physically disabled:** Services for visually, speech, hearing impaired.

Contact. E-mail: admissions@cameron.edu
Phone: (580) 581-2289 Toll-free number: (888) 454-7600
Fax: (580) 581-5416
Zoe DuRant, Director of Admissions, Cameron University, 2800 West Gore Boulevard, Lawton, OK 73505-6377

East Central University
Ada, Oklahoma
www.ecok.edu   **CB code: 6186**

- Public 4-year university
- Residential campus in large town
- 3,637 degree-seeking undergraduates
- 791 graduate students
- SAT or ACT (ACT writing optional) required

General. Founded in 1909. Regionally accredited. **Degrees:** 724 bachelor's awarded; master's offered. **Location:** 86 miles from Oklahoma City. **Calendar:** Semester, extensive summer session. **Full-time faculty:** 168 total; 64% have terminal degrees, 14% minority, 47% women. **Part-time faculty:** 117 total; 13% have terminal degrees, 24% minority, 61% women. **Class size:** 40% < 20, 49% 20-39, 9% 40-49, 2% 50-99. **Special facilities:** Fine arts center, business center, outdoor sculpture garden, 2 theatres, TV studio, photography studio.

Freshman class profile.

GPA 3.75 or higher:	29%	Rank in top quarter:	47%
GPA 3.50-3.74:	16%	Rank in top tenth:	22%
GPA 3.0-3.49:	32%	Out-of-state:	11%
GPA 2.0-2.99:	22%	Live on campus:	93%

Basis for selection. Rank in top 50% of graduating class, 20 ACT or SAT equivalent, 2.7 GPA and required course work important.

High school preparation. 15 units required. Required units include English 4, mathematics 3, social studies 2, history 1, science 3 (laboratory 1) and academic electives 2. Additional courses from English, math, science, history, social sciences, foreign language, or computer science.

2015-2016 Annual costs. Tuition/fees: $5,824; $14,132 out-of-state. Room/board: $5,350. Books/supplies: $1,200. Personal expenses: $1,216.

Financial aid. Non-need-based: Scholarships awarded for academics, athletics.

Application procedures. Admission: No deadline. $20 fee. Admission notification on a rolling basis. **Financial aid:** Closing date 3/1. FAFSA required. Applicants notified on a rolling basis starting 4/15; must reply within 2 week(s) of notification.

Academics. Special study options: Distance learning, double major, dual enrollment of high school students, ESL, exchange student, honors, independent study, internships, study abroad, teacher certification program. **Credit/placement by examination:** AP, CLEP, ACT, institutional tests. 94 credit hours maximum toward bachelor's degree. Students do not receive CLEP or AP credit until 12 hours completed in residence with 2.0 GPA. **Support services:** Learning center, pre-admission summer program, reduced course load, remedial instruction, study skills assistance, tutoring, writing center.

Majors. Area/ethnic studies: Native American. **Biology:** General. **Business:** General, accounting, business admin, finance, human resources. **Communications:** Communications/speech/rhetoric, journalism, media studies. **Computer sciences:** General. **Education:** Art, biology, chemistry, drama/dance, early childhood, elementary, English, family/consumer sciences, history, mathematics, music, physical, physics, science, social studies, special ed, speech. **English:** English lit, rhetoric/composition. **Health services:** Athletic training, clinical lab science, environmental health, nursing (RN), vocational rehab counseling. **History:** General. **Human services:** Social work. **Math:** General, applied. **Parks/recreation:** General, exercise sciences. **Physical sciences:** Chemistry, physics. **Protective services:** Police science. **Psychology:** General. **Social sciences:** GIS/cartography, political science, sociology. **Theology:** Sacred music. **Visual/performing arts:** Art, dramatic, graphic design, music, piano/keyboard, voice/opera.

Most popular majors. Business/marketing 16%, education 9%, health sciences 15%, parks/recreation 6%, public administration/social services 12%, security/protective services 6%.

Technology on campus. 677 workstations in library, computer center, student center. Online course registration, online library, helpline, repair service, wireless network available.

Student life. Freshman orientation: Mandatory. Preregistration for classes offered. **Housing:** Coed dorms, single-sex dorms, special housing for disabled, apartments, fraternity/sorority housing available. $40 nonrefundable deposit. Pets allowed in dorm rooms. **Activities:** Bands, choral groups, dance, drama, film society, literary magazine, music ensembles, musical theater, student government, student newspaper, association of black students, Native American student association, Baptist student union, united campus ministry, students with disabilities, Church of Christ Bible Chair, Life House, Sigma Society, Panhellenic, silent friends club.

Athletics. NCAA. **Intercollegiate:** Baseball M, basketball, cross-country, football (tackle) M, golf, soccer W, softball W, tennis, volleyball W. **Intramural:** Basketball, soccer, softball, volleyball. **Team name:** Tigers.

Student services. Adult student services, alcohol/substance abuse counseling, career counseling, student employment services, financial aid counseling, health services, minority student services, on-campus daycare, personal counseling, placement for graduates, veterans' counselor. **Physically disabled:** Services for visually, speech, hearing impaired.

Contact. E-mail: parmstro@ecok.edu
Phone: (580) 559-5239 Fax: (580) 559-5432
Pamla Armstrong, Registrar and Director of Admissions, East Central University, PMBJ8, 1100 East 14th Street, Ada, OK 74820

Family of Faith College
Shawnee, Oklahoma
www.familyoffaithcollege.edu

- Private 4-year Bible college
- Residential campus in rural community
- 17 degree-seeking undergraduates
- Application essay required

General. Regionally accredited; also accredited by ABHE. **Degrees:** 10 bachelor's awarded. **Location:** 6 miles from Shawnee, 30 miles from Oklahoma City. **Calendar:** Semester, limited summer session. **Full-time faculty:** 5 total. **Part-time faculty:** 6 total.

Basis for selection. SAT/ACT not required for certificate programs. Academic and personal references required. **Home schooled:** Transcript of courses and grades, state high school equivalency certificate, letter of recommendation (nonparent) required.

2015-2016 Annual costs. Tuition/fees: $6,070. Room only: $2,400.

Application procedures. Admission: Closing date 4/1 (receipt date). $25 fee. **Financial aid:** Priority date 3/1, closing date 11/1.

Academics. Credit/placement by examination: AP, CLEP.

Majors. Education: Multi-level teacher. **Theology:** Bible, theology.

Student life. Freshman orientation: Mandatory. Preregistration for classes offered. **Policies:** Religious observance required. **Housing:** Single-sex dorms available. $50 fully refundable deposit. **Activities:** Campus ministries, choral groups, student government.

Athletics. Intramural: Volleyball.

Student services. Adult student services, alcohol/substance abuse counseling, chaplain/spiritual director, financial aid counseling, personal counseling.

Contact. E-mail: info@familyoffaithcollege.edu
Phone: (405) 273-5331 Fax: (405) 273-8535
Dara Gilliam, Vice President of Student Affairs, Family of Faith College, PO Box 1805, Shawnee, OK 74802-1805

Hillsdale Free Will Baptist College
Moore, Oklahoma
www.hc.edu   CB code: 0927

- Private 4-year liberal arts college
- Residential campus in small city
- 307 degree-seeking undergraduates
- 51% of applicants admitted
- SAT or ACT (ACT writing recommended) required

General. Regionally accredited; also accredited by TRACS. **Degrees:** 25 bachelor's, 13 associate awarded; master's offered. **Location:** 2 miles from Oklahoma City, 2 miles from Norman. **Calendar:** Semester, limited summer session. **Full-time faculty:** 19 total. **Part-time faculty:** 34 total.

Freshman class profile. 244 applied, 125 admitted, 64 enrolled.

Basis for selection. Academic GPA and test scores most important.

High school preparation. Required units include English 4, mathematics 3, history 3, science 2 (laboratory 2).

2015-2016 Annual costs. Tuition/fees: $11,720. Room/board: $6,400.

Application procedures. Admission: No deadline. $25 fee. **Financial aid:** No deadline.

Academics. Special study options: Distance learning, double major, independent study. **Credit/placement by examination:** AP, CLEP, ACT. **Support services:** Remedial instruction, tutoring.

Majors. Biology: Exercise physiology. **Business:** General. **Education:** Multi-level teacher. **Psychology:** General. **Theology:** Bible, missionary, theology. **Visual/performing arts:** Music.

Most popular majors. Business/marketing 14%, education 13%, interdisciplinary studies 20%, liberal arts 34%, psychology 14%, visual/performing arts 6%.

Technology on campus. Dormitories wired for high-speed internet access and linked to campus network. Commuter students can connect to campus network. Online library, helpline, wireless network available.

Student life. Freshman orientation: Mandatory, $210 fee. Preregistration for classes offered. **Housing:** Single-sex dorms, apartments available. **Activities:** Campus ministries, drama, music ensembles, student government.

Athletics. NCCAA. **Intercollegiate:** Baseball M, basketball, cross-country, soccer M, softball W, volleyball W. **Team name:** Saints.

Contact. E-mail: recruitment@hc.edu
Phone: (405) 912-9011
Lyndsey Braisher, Admissions Counselor, Hillsdale Free Will Baptist College, PO Box 7208, Moore, OK 73153

ITT Technical Institute: Tulsa
Tulsa, Oklahoma
www.itt-tech.edu   CB code: 7998

- For-profit 4-year business and technical college
- Large city
- 519 undergraduates
- Interview required

General. Accredited by ACICS. **Degrees:** 19 bachelor's, 156 associate awarded. **Calendar:** Quarter. **Full-time faculty:** 15 total. **Part-time faculty:** 80 total.

Basis for selection. Satisfactory scores from on-site tests in English and math required.

2015-2016 Annual costs. Per-credit-hour charge, $493, depending upon level and course of study; academic fee, $200. Certain programs of study require purchase of tools, which ranges between $150 and $655.

Application procedures. Admission: No deadline. No application fee. Admission notification on a rolling basis. **Financial aid:** No deadline.

Academics. Credit/placement by examination: AP, CLEP.

Majors. Business: Business admin, construction management. **Computer sciences:** Programming, security. **Protective services:** Law enforcement admin.

Contact. ITT Technical Institute: Tulsa, 8421 East 61st Street, Suite U, Tulsa, OK 74133

Langston University
Langston, Oklahoma   CB member
www.langston.edu   CB code: 6361

- Public 4-year university and liberal arts college
- Residential campus in rural community
- 2,159 degree-seeking undergraduates: 2% part-time, 64% women
- 203 degree-seeking graduate students
- 60% of applicants admitted
- SAT or ACT (ACT writing optional) required

General. Founded in 1897. Regionally accredited. Urban campuses in Oklahoma City, Tulsa. **Degrees:** 276 bachelor's, 12 associate awarded; master's, professional offered. **ROTC:** Army, Air Force. **Location:** 40 miles from Oklahoma City, 90 miles from Tulsa. **Calendar:** Semester, limited summer session. **Full-time faculty:** 141 total; 70% have terminal degrees, 70% minority, 43% women. **Part-time faculty:** 50 total; 60% have terminal degrees, 70% minority, 42% women. **Class size:** 72% < 20, 23% 20-39, 2% 40-49, 3% 50-99. **Special facilities:** International dairy goat research facility.

Freshman class profile. 9,318 applied, 5,590 admitted, 692 enrolled.

GPA 3.75 or higher:	4%	Rank in top tenth:	12%
GPA 3.50-3.74:	7%	End year in good standing:	66%
GPA 3.0-3.49:	24%	Return as sophomores:	47%
GPA 2.0-2.99:	61%	Out-of-state:	58%
Rank in top quarter:	31%	Live on campus:	98%

Basis for selection. 2.7 GPA, 20 ACT or SAT equivalent required. 3/1 priority date for SAT/ACT. Audition recommended for music program. **Home schooled:** Transcript of courses and grades, state high school equivalency certificate required.

High school preparation. College-preparatory program recommended. Required units include English 4, mathematics 3, history 3, science 3 (laboratory 3) and academic electives 2.

2015-2016 Annual costs. Tuition/fees: $5,043; $12,372 out-of-state. Room/board: $8,982. Books/supplies: $1,600. Personal expenses: $2,400.

2015-2016 Financial aid. All financial aid based on need. 608 full-time freshmen applied for aid; 560 deemed to have need; 560 received aid. Average need met was 60%. Average scholarship/grant was $13,413; average loan $11,550. 99% of total undergraduate aid awarded as scholarships/grants, 1% as loans/jobs.

Application procedures. Admission: Priority date 6/15; deadline 6/30. $25 fee. Admission notification on a rolling basis beginning on or about 8/11. **Financial aid:** Priority date 3/1, closing date 5/1. FAFSA required.

Applicants notified on a rolling basis starting 7/15; must reply within 2 week(s) of notification.

Academics. Special study options: Accelerated study, distance learning, double major, dual enrollment of high school students, ESL, exchange student, honors, independent study, internships, liberal arts/career combination, study abroad, weekend college. **Credit/placement by examination:** AP, CLEP, SAT, ACT, institutional tests. 16 credit hours maximum toward associate degree, 30 toward bachelor's. **Support services:** Learning center, pre-admission summer program, reduced course load, remedial instruction, study skills assistance, tutoring, writing center.

Majors. Biology: General, zoology. **Business:** Accounting, business admin, human resources. **Communications:** Broadcast journalism, communications/speech/rhetoric, journalism. **Communications technology:** General. **Computer sciences:** General. **Education:** General, elementary, family/consumer sciences, mathematics, music, physical, secondary, social studies, special ed, technology/industrial arts. **English:** English lit. **Health services:** Health care admin. **Math:** General. **Physical sciences:** Chemistry. **Protective services:** Corrections, police science. **Psychology:** General. **Social sciences:** General, economics, geography, sociology, urban studies. **Visual/performing arts:** Art, music, music performance. **Work/family studies:** General, clothing/textiles, family studies, food/nutrition.

Most popular majors. Biology 6%, business/marketing 15%, health sciences 32%, psychology 8%.

Technology on campus. 300 workstations in library, computer center, student center. Dormitories wired for high-speed internet access and linked to campus network. Commuter students can connect to campus network. Online course registration, online library, helpline, repair service, wireless network available.

Student life. Freshman orientation: Mandatory. Preregistration for classes offered. Held four days prior to fall enrollment. **Policies:** All freshman and sophomore students required to live on campus. Students must have 2.0 GPA to join student organizations. Students must have 2.5 GPA to be in student government, campus royalty, or fraternities and sororities. **Housing:** Guaranteed on-campus for all undergraduates. Single-sex dorms, special housing for disabled, apartments available. $200 fully refundable deposit. **Activities:** Bands, campus ministries, choral groups, dance, drama, film society, international student organizations, literary magazine, music ensembles, Model UN, musical theater, opera, radio station, student government, student newspaper, symphony orchestra, TV station, Pan Hellenic fraternities and sororities, NAACP, NCNW.

Athletics. NAIA. **Intercollegiate:** Basketball, cheerleading, cross-country, football (tackle) M, softball W, track and field, volleyball W. **Intramural:** Basketball, football (non-tackle), track and field, volleyball. **Team name:** Lions.

Student services. Alcohol/substance abuse counseling, chaplain/spiritual director, career counseling, services for economically disadvantaged, student employment services, financial aid counseling, health services, on-campus daycare, personal counseling, placement for graduates, veterans' counselor. **Physically disabled:** Services for visually, speech, hearing impaired.

Contact. E-mail: mavaughn@langston.edu
Phone: (405) 466-3428 Fax: (405) 466-3391
Chauncey Jackson, Executive Director of Enrollment Management, Langston University, Box 728, Langston, OK 73050

Mid-America Christian University
Oklahoma City, Oklahoma
www.macu.edu   CB code: 0918

▶ Private 4-year university and liberal arts college affiliated with the Church of God
▶ Residential campus in very large city
▶ 2,688 degree-seeking undergraduates

General. Founded in 1953. Regionally accredited. Free YMCA membership for all students. **Degrees:** 336 bachelor's, 56 associate awarded; master's offered. **Location:** 10 miles from downtown. **Calendar:** Semester, limited summer session. **Full-time faculty:** 38 total. **Part-time faculty:** 153 total. **Class size:** 67% < 20, 26% 20-39, 2% 40-49, 4% 50-99. **Special facilities:** On-campus nature reserve.

Basis for selection. Open admission. Two references required. Interview, audition recommended. **Home schooled:** Transcript of courses and grades, letter of recommendation (nonparent) required. Applicants without GED must have 15 ACT English and 14 ACT math.

2015-2016 Annual costs. Tuition/fees: $16,798. Room/board: $7,380. Books/supplies: $1,300. Personal expenses: $2,240.

Financial aid. Non-need-based: Scholarships awarded for academics, athletics, leadership, minority status, music/drama, religious affiliation.

Application procedures. Admission: Priority date 8/1; no deadline. $25 fee, may be waived for applicants with need, free for online applicants. Admission notification on a rolling basis beginning on or about 2/1. Students may provisionally enroll without graduation posted in senior year. **Financial aid:** Priority date 5/1; no closing date. FAFSA required. Applicants notified on a rolling basis starting 5/1.

Academics. Special study options: Combined bachelor's/graduate degree, double major, dual enrollment of high school students, external degree, independent study, internships, liberal arts/career combination, teacher certification program, weekend college. **Credit/placement by examination:** AP, CLEP, SAT, ACT, institutional tests. **Support services:** Remedial instruction, tutoring, writing center.

Majors. Business: Business admin, marketing. **Communications:** Persuasive communications. **Education:** Early childhood, elementary, English, mathematics, music, secondary, social science, social studies. **English:** English lit. **Math:** General. **Philosophy/religion:** Religion. **Physical sciences:** Physics. **Psychology:** General. **Social sciences:** General. **Theology:** Bible, pastoral counseling, sacred music, theology. **Visual/performing arts:** Music performance.

Technology on campus. 40 workstations in library, computer center, student center. Dormitories wired for high-speed internet access and linked to campus network. Online library, wireless network available.

Student life. Freshman orientation: Mandatory. Preregistration for classes offered. Held several consecutive days prior to start of classes. **Policies:** No smoking or drinking allowed on campus. Students under 22 must live on-campus unless they are married or live with parent/guardian within 40-mile radius. Students who are 22 and older must have lived on campus for at least 6 semesters, maintain 2.5 GPA, and have clean discipline history with Student Life. Maximum age for living on campus is 26. Religious observance required. **Housing:** Guaranteed on-campus for freshmen. Single-sex dorms, wellness housing available. $50 nonrefundable deposit. **Activities:** Concert band, campus ministries, choral groups, drama, music ensembles, musical theater, student government, missions club, Student Ministerial Fellowship, Ministry Refresher Institute.

Athletics. NAIA, NCCAA. **Intercollegiate:** Baseball M, basketball, cheerleading, golf M, soccer, softball W, volleyball W. **Intramural:** Basketball, bowling, softball W, table tennis, volleyball. **Team name:** Evangels.

Student services. Chaplain/spiritual director, career counseling, student employment services, financial aid counseling, health services, personal counseling, placement for graduates, veterans' counselor. **Physically disabled:** Services for speech impaired.

Contact. E-mail: info@macu.edu
Toll-free number: (888) 436-3035 Fax: (405) 692-3165
Mike Wilkinson, Director of Admissions, Mid-America Christian University, 3500 SW 119th Street, Oklahoma City, OK 73170

Northeastern State University
Tahlequah, Oklahoma
www.nsuok.edu   CB code: 6485

▶ Public 4-year university
▶ Commuter campus in large town
▶ 7,036 degree-seeking undergraduates: 29% part-time, 61% women, 4% African American, 2% Asian American, 5% Hispanic/Latino, 20% Native American, 17% Multi-racial, non-Hispanic, 2% international
▶ 1,232 degree-seeking graduate students
▶ 92% of applicants admitted
▶ ACT (writing optional) required
▶ 31% graduate within 6 years

General. Founded in 1851. Regionally accredited. **Degrees:** 1,379 bachelor's awarded; master's, professional offered. **ROTC:** Army. **Location:** 60 miles from Tulsa, 30 miles from Muskogee. **Calendar:** Semester, extensive summer session. **Full-time faculty:** 306 total; 77% have terminal degrees, 21% minority, 51% women. **Part-time faculty:** 205 total; 34% have terminal degrees, 17% minority, 52% women. **Class size:** 50% < 20, 41% 20-39, 6% 40-49, 3% 50-99. **Special facilities:** Literacy study center, tribal studies center, Oklahoma Institute for Learning Styles.

Freshman class profile. 1,397 applied, 1,292 admitted, 811 enrolled.

Mid 50% test scores		End year in good standing:	71%
ACT composite:	19-23	Return as sophomores:	62%
GPA 3.75 or higher:	28%	Out-of-state:	7%
GPA 3.50-3.74:	19%	Live on campus:	70%
GPA 3.0-3.49:	33%	International:	2%
GPA 2.0-2.99:	20%	Fraternities:	12%
Rank in top quarter:	47%	Sororities:	22%
Rank in top tenth:	20%		

Basis for selection. Admissions based on secondary school record, class rank, and standardized test scores. Audition required, interview recommended for music program. Interview recommended for drama program; portfolio recommended for graphic art program. Interview required for alternative admission. **Home schooled:** Transcript of courses and grades required.

High school preparation. College-preparatory program required. 15 units required. Required units include English 4, mathematics 3, social studies 2, history 1, science 3 (laboratory 3). 2 from English, lab science, math, history, social studies, computer science, or foreign language.

2015-2016 Annual costs. Tuition/fees: $5,547; $12,897 out-of-state. Room/board: $6,490. Books/supplies: $1,200. Personal expenses: $1,350.

2015-2016 Financial aid. Need-based: 735 full-time freshmen applied for aid; 497 deemed to have need; 497 received aid. Average need met was 98%. Average scholarship/grant was $7,507; average loan $4,993. 44% of total undergraduate aid awarded as scholarships/grants, 56% as loans/jobs. **Non-need-based:** Awarded to 820 full-time undergraduates, including 244 freshmen. Scholarships awarded for academics, alumni affiliation, art, athletics, leadership, minority status, music/drama, religious affiliation, ROTC, state residency. **Additional information:** Off-campus job location and development program introduced to assist students with finding off-campus employers to earn money for college expenses.

Application procedures. Admission: Priority date 8/1; no deadline. $25 fee, may be waived for applicants with need. Admission notification on a rolling basis. **Financial aid:** Priority date 3/1; no closing date. FAFSA required. Applicants notified on a rolling basis starting 3/1.

Academics. NSU College of Optometry on campus. **Special study options:** Distance learning, double major, dual enrollment of high school students, honors, independent study, internships, student-designed major, teacher certification program, weekend college. **Credit/placement by examination:** AP, CLEP, IB, ACT, institutional tests. 30 credit hours maximum toward bachelor's degree. **Support services:** Learning center, pre-admission summer program, reduced course load, remedial instruction, study skills assistance, tutoring, writing center.

Majors. Area/ethnic studies: Native American. **Biology:** General. **Business:** Accounting, business admin, entrepreneurial studies, finance, international, logistics, management information systems, marketing, operations, tourism/travel. **Communications:** Communications/speech/rhetoric, media studies. **Computer sciences:** Computer science. **Education:** Art, early childhood, elementary, English, learning disabled, mathematics, music, Native American, physical, science, social studies, Spanish. **English:** English lit. **Foreign languages:** Spanish. **Health services:** Audiology/speech pathology, clinical lab science, health services admin, nursing (RN). **History:** General. **Human services:** Social work. **Math:** General. **Parks/recreation:** Exercise sciences. **Physical sciences:** Chemistry. **Protective services:** Law enforcement admin. **Psychology:** General. **Social sciences:** Geography, political science, sociology. **Visual/performing arts:** Art, design, dramatic, music.

Most popular majors. Business/marketing 16%, education 19%, health sciences 8%, psychology 8%, security/protective services 6%.

Technology on campus. 1,160 workstations in dormitories, library, computer center, student center. Dormitories wired for high-speed internet access and linked to campus network. Commuter students can connect to campus network. Online library, helpline, student web hosting, wireless network available.

Student life. Freshman orientation: Mandatory, $22 fee. Preregistration for classes offered. **Housing:** Guaranteed on-campus for freshmen. Coed dorms, single-sex dorms, special housing for disabled, apartments, fraternity/sorority housing, themed housing available. $75 nonrefundable deposit. Living learning communities available. **Activities:** Bands, campus ministries, choral groups, dance, drama, international student organizations, literary magazine, music ensembles, Model UN, musical theater, student government, student newspaper, symphony orchestra, TV station, Native American student association, American Indian Business Leaders, Association of Black Collegians, gospel choir, Campus Christian Fellowship, Baptist campus ministries, Chi Alpha campus ministries, RiverHawk Prayer Walk, Indian Student Association, Oklahoma Intercollegiate Legislature.

Athletics. NCAA. **Intercollegiate:** Baseball M, basketball, football (tackle) M, golf, soccer, softball W, tennis W. **Intramural:** Basketball, football (nontackle), golf, racquetball, soccer, softball, tennis, volleyball. **Team name:** RiverHawks.

Student services. Adult student services, alcohol/substance abuse counseling, career counseling, services for economically disadvantaged, student employment services, financial aid counseling, health services, personal counseling, placement for graduates, veterans' counselor. **Physically disabled:** Services for visually, speech, hearing impaired.

Contact. E-mail: nsuinfo@nsuok.edu
Phone: (918) 444-2200 Toll-free number: (800) 722-9614
Fax: (918) 458-2342
Jennifer McClendon, Director Admission and Recruitment, Northeastern State University, 600 North Grand Avenue, Tahlequah, OK 74464-2399

Northwestern Oklahoma State University
Alva, Oklahoma
www.nwosu.edu   **CB code: 6493**

▸ Public 4-year university and teachers college
▸ Commuter campus in small town
▸ 1,799 degree-seeking undergraduates
▸ 64% of applicants admitted
▸ SAT or ACT (ACT writing optional) required

General. Founded in 1897. Regionally accredited. **Degrees:** 305 bachelor's awarded; master's offered. **Location:** 114 miles from Wichita, KS; 162 miles from Oklahoma City. **Calendar:** Semester, limited summer session. **Class size:** 63% < 20, 23% 20-39, 5% 40-49, 5% 50-99, 4% >100. **Special facilities:** Institute for citizenship studies, Green space area, wellness center, museum of natural history, academic success center, amphitheater, agriculture farm complex, nursing lab.

Freshman class profile. 871 applied, 558 admitted, 310 enrolled.

Out-of-state:	22%	International:	11%
Live on campus:	44%		

Basis for selection. First-time applicants with 2.7 GPA and in top 50% of class or with 20 ACT admitted unconditionally. Others admitted provisionally. Audition recommended for music program. **Home schooled:** Transcript of courses and grades required.

High school preparation. 15 units required. Required and recommended units include English 4, mathematics 3, social studies 1, history 2, science 3 (laboratory 3), foreign language 2, computer science 2 and academic electives 3. 1 unit required from either government, economics, geography or non-Western culture.

2015-2016 Annual costs. Tuition/fees: $5,821; $12,271 out-of-state. Room/board: $4,530. Books/supplies: $1,200. Personal expenses: $2,000.

Financial aid. Non-need-based: Scholarships awarded for academics, alumni affiliation, art, athletics, leadership, music/drama.

Application procedures. Admission: No deadline. $15 fee. Admission notification on a rolling basis. **Financial aid:** No deadline. FAFSA required. Applicants notified on a rolling basis starting 5/1; must reply by 8/15.

Academics. Special study options: Combined bachelor's/graduate degree, distance learning, double major, dual enrollment of high school students, honors, independent study, internships, study abroad, teacher certification program. 2-2 programs in many professional fields. **Credit/placement by examination:** AP, CLEP, SAT, ACT, institutional tests. **Support services:** Learning center, reduced course load, remedial instruction, tutoring, writing center.

Majors. Biology: General. **Business:** Accounting, business admin, e-commerce. **Communications:** Media studies. **Computer sciences:** General. **Education:** General, agricultural, early childhood, elementary, English, health, mathematics, middle, music, physical, science, secondary, social science, special ed. **English:** English lit. **Foreign languages:** Spanish. **Health services:** Nursing (RN). **History:** General. **Human services:** Social work. **Math:** General. **Parks/recreation:** Health/fitness. **Physical sciences:** Chemistry. **Protective services:** Police science. **Psychology:** General. **Social sciences:** General, political science, sociology. **Visual/performing arts:** Dramatic, music.

Most popular majors. Agriculture 7%, biology 6%, business/marketing 15%, education 18%, health sciences 12%, psychology 11%.

Technology on campus. 218 workstations in library, computer center, student center. Commuter students can connect to campus network. Online library, helpline, wireless network available.

Student life. Freshman orientation: Mandatory. Preregistration for classes offered. Held the Saturday before classes begin. **Housing:** Single-sex dorms, special housing for disabled available. $75 fully refundable deposit. **Activities:** Bands, campus ministries, choral groups, drama, international student organizations, music ensembles, radio station, student government, student newspaper, TV station, Conserving Our Ranger Environment, Spanish club, social sciences organization, Baptist student union, Wesley House, art society, Oklahoma Broadcast Education Association, Aggie club.

Athletics. NCAA. **Intercollegiate:** Baseball M, basketball, cross-country, football (tackle) M, golf, rodeo, soccer W, softball W, volleyball. **Intramural:** Basketball, bowling, football (non-tackle), racquetball, softball, volleyball. **Team name:** Rangers.

Student services. Adult student services, career counseling, student employment services, financial aid counseling, health services, personal counseling, placement for graduates, veterans' counselor, women's services. **Physically disabled:** Services for visually, speech, hearing impaired.

Contact. E-mail: recruit@nwosu.edu
Phone: (580) 327-8546 Fax: (580) 327-8413
Paige Fischer, Director of Recruitment, Northwestern Oklahoma State University, 709 Oklahoma Boulevard, Alva, OK 73717-2799

Oklahoma Baptist University
Shawnee, Oklahoma
www.okbu.edu   **CB code: 6541**

▶ Private 4-year university and liberal arts college affiliated with the Southern Baptist Convention

▶ Residential campus in large town

▶ 1,847 degree-seeking undergraduates: 4% part-time, 60% women, 7% African American, 1% Asian American, 3% Hispanic/Latino, 6% Native American, 8% Multi-racial, non-Hispanic, 3% international

▶ 79 degree-seeking graduate students

▶ 75% of applicants admitted

▶ SAT or ACT (ACT writing optional) required

▶ 53% graduate within 6 years

General. Founded in 1910. Regionally accredited. Each summer approximately 250 students, faculty and staff serve in projects around the world. About 300 students participate in local service projects during the year. **Degrees:** 339 bachelor's awarded; master's offered. **ROTC:** Air Force. **Location:** 35 miles from Oklahoma City, 90 miles from Tulsa. **Calendar:** Semester, limited summer session. **Full-time faculty:** 127 total; 71% have terminal degrees, 10% minority, 37% women. **Part-time faculty:** 60 total; 25% have terminal degrees, 53% women. **Class size:** 67% < 20, 27% 20-39, 2% 40-49, 3% 50-99. **Special facilities:** Planetarium (operated by students), greenhouse, music technology laboratory, biblical research library.

Freshman class profile. 4,785 applied, 3,590 admitted, 556 enrolled.

Mid 50% test scores		End year in good standing:	86%
ACT composite:	20-25	Return as sophomores:	75%
GPA 3.75 or higher:	53%	Out-of-state:	40%
GPA 3.50-3.74:	18%	Live on campus:	94%
GPA 3.0-3.49:	23%	International:	2%
GPA 2.0-2.99:	6%	Fraternities:	5%
Rank in top quarter:	49%	Sororities:	27%
Rank in top tenth:	23%		

Basis for selection. 20 ACT or 950 SAT (exclusive of Writing), 3.0 GPA or class rank in top half required. Interview recommended for borderline applicants; audition recommended for drama, music programs; portfolio recommended for art program. **Home schooled:** Transcript of courses and grades required.

High school preparation. 17 units recommended. Recommended units include English 4, mathematics 3, social studies 2, history 1, science 3 (laboratory 2), foreign language 2 and academic electives 2. Math recommendation includes 2 algebra and 1 plane geometry.

2016-2017 Annual costs. Tuition/fees: $25,310. Room/board: $7,010. Books/supplies: $1,300. Personal expenses: $2,100.

2014-2015 Financial aid. Need-based: 429 full-time freshmen applied for aid; 378 deemed to have need; 378 received aid. Average need met was 81%. Average scholarship/grant was $8,557; average loan $3,145. 77% of total undergraduate aid awarded as scholarships/grants, 23% as loans/jobs.

Non-need-based: Awarded to 2,125 full-time undergraduates, including 581 freshmen. Scholarships awarded for academics, art, athletics, leadership, minority status, music/drama, religious affiliation, ROTC.

Application procedures. Admission: Priority date 4/1; deadline 8/1 (postmark date). No application fee. Admission notification on a rolling basis beginning on or about 6/1. **Financial aid:** Priority date 3/1; no closing date. FAFSA required. Applicants notified on a rolling basis starting 2/1; must reply within 2 week(s) of notification.

Academics. Opportunities for January-term travel to Europe, Russia, South America; also opportunity to teach English in China and Hungary. **Special study options:** Accelerated study, combined bachelor's/graduate degree, cooperative education, distance learning, double major, ESL, exchange student, honors, independent study, internships, liberal arts/career combination, student-designed major, study abroad, teacher certification program. Exchange program with Seinan Gakuin University, Japan, and Hong Kong Baptist College. **Credit/placement by examination:** AP, CLEP, IB, SAT, ACT, institutional tests. 32 credit hours maximum toward bachelor's degree. Essay required for English, government, history exams; oral exam required for French, German and Spanish; lab exam required for information systems. **Support services:** Learning center, reduced course load, remedial instruction, study skills assistance, tutoring, writing center.

Majors. Biology: General, biochemistry. **Business:** General, accounting, business admin, entrepreneurial studies, finance, international, international finance, management information systems, management science, marketing. **Communications:** Broadcast journalism, communications/speech/rhetoric, journalism, public relations. **Communications technology:** Animation/special effects. **Computer sciences:** General, applications programming, computer science, information systems, systems analysis. **Education:** Biology, chemistry, early childhood, early childhood special, elementary, elementary special ed, English, history, learning disabled, mathematics, mentally handicapped, music, physical, physics, science, secondary, social science, special ed, speech. **English:** Creative writing, English lit, rhetoric/composition. **Foreign languages:** General, Biblical, Spanish. **Health services:** Athletic training, nursing (RN). **History:** General. **Human services:** Social work. **Liberal arts:** Arts/sciences. **Math:** General. **Parks/recreation:** Exercise sciences, facilities management, health/fitness, outdoor education, sports admin. **Philosophy/religion:** Philosophy, religion. **Physical sciences:** Chemistry, physics. **Psychology:** General, counseling. **Social sciences:** General, anthropology, political science, sociology. **Theology:** Bible, missionary, pastoral counseling, religious ed, sacred music, theology, women's ministry, youth ministry. **Visual/performing arts:** Art, dramatic, graphic design, music, music performance, music theory/composition, piano/keyboard, studio arts, voice/opera. **Work/family studies:** Family/community services.

Most popular majors. Business/marketing 9%, education 16%, health sciences 22%, psychology 6%, theological studies 12%.

Technology on campus. 200 workstations in dormitories, library, computer center, student center. Dormitories wired for high-speed internet access and linked to campus network. Commuter students can connect to campus network. Online course registration, online library, helpline, wireless network available.

Student life. Freshman orientation: Mandatory. Preregistration for classes offered. Held during the 3 days immediately prior to start of fall semester. **Policies:** Campus is alcohol/drug/smoke free. **Housing:** Guaranteed on-campus for all undergraduates. Single-sex dorms, apartments, themed housing, wellness housing available. $125 partly refundable deposit, deadline 8/1. **Activities:** Bands, campus ministries, choral groups, dance, drama, international student organizations, literary magazine, music ensembles, Model UN, musical theater, opera, student government, student newspaper, symphony orchestra, TV station, Campus Crusade, FCA, Baptist Collegiate Ministries, Collegiate Republicans, Young Democrats, black student fellowship, international student union, Native American heritage association, residence hall association.

Athletics. NAIA. **Intercollegiate:** Baseball M, basketball, cheerleading W, cross-country, diving, football (tackle) M, golf, lacrosse W, soccer, softball W, swimming, tennis, track and field, volleyball W. **Intramural:** Badminton, basketball, bowling, football (non-tackle), racquetball, soccer, softball, swimming, table tennis, tennis, ultimate frisbee, volleyball. **Team name:** Bison.

Student services. Alcohol/substance abuse counseling, chaplain/spiritual director, career counseling, student employment services, financial aid counseling, health services, minority student services, personal counseling, placement for graduates, veterans' counselor. **Physically disabled:** Services for visually, hearing impaired.

Contact. E-mail: admissions@okbu.edu
Phone: (405) 585-5000 Toll-free number: (800) 654-3285
Fax: (405) 585-5017
Will Brantley, Director of Admission, Oklahoma Baptist University, 500 West University, Shawnee, OK 74804

Oklahoma Christian University

Oklahoma City, Oklahoma
www.oc.edu

CB member
CB code: 6086

- Private 4-year university affiliated with the Church of Christ
- Residential campus in very large city
- 1,956 degree-seeking undergraduates: 3% part-time, 50% women, 5% African American, 1% Asian American, 6% Hispanic/Latino, 2% Native American, 6% Multi-racial, non-Hispanic, 8% international
- 582 degree-seeking graduate students
- 59% of applicants admitted
- SAT or ACT (ACT writing optional) required
- 49% graduate within 6 years

General. Founded in 1950. Regionally accredited. **Degrees:** 337 bachelor's awarded; master's offered. **ROTC:** Army, Air Force. **Calendar:** Semester, extensive summer session. **Full-time faculty:** 106 total; 66% have terminal degrees, 33% women. **Part-time faculty:** 127 total; 23% have terminal degrees, 39% women. **Class size:** 54% < 20, 36% 20-39, 3% 40-49, 6% 50-99, 1% >100.

Freshman class profile. 2,597 applied, 1,535 admitted, 452 enrolled.

Mid 50% test scores			
SAT critical reading:	480-610	GPA 2.0-2.99:	11%
SAT math:	490-620	Rank in top quarter:	49%
SAT writing:	490-580	Rank in top tenth:	25%
ACT composite:	21-28	Return as sophomores:	82%
GPA 3.75 or higher:	38%	Out-of-state:	55%
GPA 3.50-3.74:	26%	Live on campus:	94%
GPA 3.0-3.49:	24%	International:	4%

Basis for selection. Students evaluated on both merit and character. Students admitted scoring 18 or below on the ACT or the SAT equivalent participate in the University's Bridge Program. Interview/campus visit strongly recommended.

High school preparation. College-preparatory program recommended. 15 units recommended. Required and recommended units include English 4, mathematics 4, social studies 3, science 4 (laboratory 2) and foreign language 2.

2015-2016 Annual costs. Tuition/fees: $19,890. Room/board: $7,030. Books/supplies: $1,000. Personal expenses: $1,700.

2014-2015 Financial aid. Need-based: 376 full-time freshmen applied for aid; 305 deemed to have need; 302 received aid. Average need met was 70%. Average scholarship/grant was $3,261; average loan $2,306. 65% of total undergraduate aid awarded as scholarships/grants, 35% as loans/jobs. **Non-need-based:** Awarded to 1,790 full-time undergraduates, including 461 freshmen. Scholarships awarded for academics, art, athletics, music/drama, religious affiliation, ROTC.

Application procedures. Admission: Priority date 5/1; no deadline. $25 fee, may be waived for applicants with need. Admission notification on a rolling basis beginning on or about 9/1. **Financial aid:** Priority date 4/1, closing date 8/31. FAFSA required. Applicants notified on a rolling basis starting 1/15; must reply within 4 week(s) of notification.

Academics. Special study options: Accelerated study, combined bachelor's/graduate degree, cross-registration, double major, dual enrollment of high school students, ESL, honors, independent study, internships, liberal arts/career combination, student-designed major, study abroad, teacher certification program. **Credit/placement by examination:** AP, CLEP, IB, SAT, ACT, institutional tests. 60 credit hours maximum toward bachelor's degree. **Support services:** Learning center, reduced course load, remedial instruction, study skills assistance, tutoring, writing center.

Majors. Biology: General, biochemistry. **Business:** General, accounting, business admin, finance, international, management science, market research, marketing, merchandising. **Communications:** Advertising, broadcast journalism, communications/speech/rhetoric, journalism, media studies, public relations. **Communications technology:** Animation/special effects. **Computer sciences:** General, computer science, information systems, programming. **Education:** Art, early childhood, elementary, English, ESL, mathematics, middle, music, physical, science, secondary, social studies, speech. **Engineering:** Computer, electrical, mechanical. **English:** Creative writing, English lit, writing. **Foreign languages:** Spanish. **Health services:** Clinical lab science, nursing (RN), predental, premedicine, prenursing, prepharmacy, preveterinary. **History:** General. **Liberal arts:** Arts/sciences. **Math:** General. **Parks/recreation:** Health/fitness. **Philosophy/religion:** Christian, religion. **Physical sciences:** Chemistry, physics. **Psychology:** General. **Social sciences:** Political science. **Theology:** Bible, missionary, religious ed, theology, youth ministry. **Visual/performing arts:** Art, commercial/advertising art, design, dramatic, game design, graphic design, interior design, music, music performance, piano/keyboard, studio arts, voice/opera. **Work/family studies:** Family studies.

Most popular majors. Business/marketing 19%, communications/journalism 6%, education 10%, engineering/engineering technologies 15%, health sciences 6%, liberal arts 6%, parks/recreation 7%, visual/performing arts 7%.

Technology on campus. PC or laptop required. Dormitories wired for high-speed internet access and linked to campus network. Commuter students can connect to campus network. Online course registration, online library, helpline, repair service, student web hosting, wireless network available.

Student life. Freshman orientation: Mandatory. Preregistration for classes offered. Two-part program includes one-day summer event and week-long event the week before school starts. **Policies:** Single students must live on campus or with parents. Special arrangements considered. Religious observance required. **Housing:** Guaranteed on-campus for all undergraduates. Single-sex dorms, special housing for disabled, apartments, wellness housing available. $250 partly refundable deposit, deadline 5/1. Honors living/learning. **Activities:** Bands, campus ministries, choral groups, drama, international student organizations, literary magazine, music ensembles, musical theater, opera, radio station, student government, student newspaper, symphony orchestra, TV station.

Athletics. NCAA. **Intercollegiate:** Baseball M, basketball, cheerleading, cross-country, golf M, soccer, softball W, track and field. **Intramural:** Basketball, bowling, cross-country, football (non-tackle), golf M, soccer, softball, swimming, table tennis, tennis, track and field, volleyball. **Team name:** Eagles.

Student services. Alcohol/substance abuse counseling, chaplain/spiritual director, career counseling, student employment services, financial aid counseling, health services, minority student services, personal counseling, placement for graduates, veterans' counselor, women's services. **Physically disabled:** Services for visually, speech, hearing impaired.

Contact. E-mail: info@oc.edu
Phone: (405) 425-5050 Toll-free number: (800) 877-5050
Fax: (405) 425-5069
Michael Mitchell, Director of Admissions, Oklahoma Christian University, Box 11000, Oklahoma City, OK 73136-1100

Oklahoma City University

Oklahoma City, Oklahoma
www.okcu.edu

CB member
CB code: 6543

- Private 4-year university and liberal arts college affiliated with the United Methodist Church
- Residential campus in very large city
- 1,783 degree-seeking undergraduates: 9% part-time, 65% women, 6% African American, 2% Asian American, 9% Hispanic/Latino, 3% Native American, 7% Multi-racial, non-Hispanic, 12% international
- 1,270 degree-seeking graduate students
- 72% of applicants admitted
- SAT or ACT (ACT writing optional), application essay required
- 58% graduate within 6 years

General. Founded in 1904. Regionally accredited. **Degrees:** 531 bachelor's awarded; master's, professional, doctoral offered. **ROTC:** Army, Air Force. **Location:** 180 miles from Dallas, 350 miles from Kansas City. **Calendar:** Semester, limited summer session. **Full-time faculty:** 195 total; 67% have terminal degrees, 12% minority, 49% women. **Part-time faculty:** 137 total; 2% have terminal degrees, 16% minority, 49% women. **Class size:** 76% < 20, 22% 20-39, less than 1% 40-49, 1% 50-99, less than 1% >100. **Special facilities:** Art center, entrepreneurship center.

Freshman class profile. 1,448 applied, 1,037 admitted, 310 enrolled.

Mid 50% test scores			
SAT critical reading:	480-600	Rank in top quarter:	61%
SAT math:	480-590	Rank in top tenth:	36%
SAT writing:	470-580	End year in good standing:	92%
ACT composite:	22-28	Return as sophomores:	86%
GPA 3.75 or higher:	57%	Out-of-state:	55%
GPA 3.50-3.74:	16%	Live on campus:	71%
GPA 3.0-3.49:	21%	International:	12%
GPA 2.0-2.99:	6%	Fraternities:	24%
		Sororities:	38%

Basis for selection. School achievement record, including unweighted GPA and test scores, most important. Counselor recommendations, essays, and activities also considered. Interview recommended for all; audition required for dance and arts management, music and theater programs; portfolio required for studio art and photography programs. **Home schooled:** Must demonstrate that individual is graduating no earlier than their class in the public school system.

High school preparation. College-preparatory program recommended. 15 units required. Required units include English 4, mathematics 3, social studies 3, science 3 (laboratory 1) and foreign language 2. Math requirement includes 2 units algebra and 1 unit geometry, trigonometry, math analysis, or calculus. Social studies requirement includes 1 unit world history, 1 unit state history or civics, and 1 unit U.S. history.

2015-2016 Annual costs. Tuition/fees: $30,726. Room/board: $9,682. Books/supplies: $1,500. Personal expenses: $1,000.

2015-2016 Financial aid. **Need-based:** Average need met was 65%. Average scholarship/grant was $17,717; average loan $3,381. 38% of total undergraduate aid awarded as scholarships/grants, 62% as loans/jobs. **Non-need-based:** Scholarships awarded for academics, alumni affiliation, art, athletics, leadership, music/drama, religious affiliation, ROTC, state residency.

Application procedures. **Admission:** Priority date 3/3; deadline 8/15 (postmark date). $55 fee, may be waived for applicants with need. Admission notification on a rolling basis beginning on or about 10/1. Must reply by May 1 or within 2 week(s) if notified thereafter. **Financial aid:** Priority date 3/1; no closing date. FAFSA required. Applicants notified on a rolling basis starting 3/1; must reply within 2 week(s) of notification.

Academics. **Special study options:** Accelerated study, combined bachelor's/graduate degree, cooperative education, distance learning, double major, dual enrollment of high school students, ESL, exchange student, external degree, honors, independent study, internships, liberal arts/career combination, student-designed major, study abroad, teacher certification program, Washington semester. **Credit/placement by examination:** AP, CLEP, IB, SAT, ACT. **Support services:** Learning center, pre-admission summer program, reduced course load, remedial instruction, study skills assistance, tutoring, writing center.

Majors. **Biology:** General, biomedical sciences, cellular/molecular. **Business:** Accounting, business admin, finance, management information systems, managerial economics, marketing. **Communications:** Advertising, broadcast journalism, journalism, public relations. **Computer sciences:** General. **Conservation:** Environmental studies. **Education:** Art, biology, drama/dance, early childhood, elementary, English, history, mathematics, music. **Engineering:** Software. **English:** English lit. **Foreign languages:** Spanish. **Health services:** Adult health nursing, predental, premedicine, prepharmacy, preveterinary. **History:** General. **Liberal arts:** Arts/sciences, humanities. **Math:** General. **Parks/recreation:** Exercise sciences. **Philosophy/religion:** Philosophy, religion. **Physical sciences:** General, chemistry, physics. **Protective services:** Corrections, law enforcement admin. **Psychology:** General. **Social sciences:** Political science, sociology. **Theology:** Religious ed, sacred music, youth ministry. **Visual/performing arts:** Acting, art, cinematography, dance, dramatic, film/cinema/video, music, music management, music performance, music theory/composition, photography, piano/keyboard, theater arts management, theater design, voice/opera.

Most popular majors. Business/marketing 8%, health sciences 26%, liberal arts 23%, visual/performing arts 25%.

Technology on campus. 378 workstations in dormitories, library, computer center, student center. Dormitories wired for high-speed internet access and linked to campus network. Commuter students can connect to campus network. Online course registration, online library, helpline, repair service, student web hosting, wireless network available.

Student life. **Freshman orientation:** Mandatory, $300 fee. Preregistration for classes offered. Six-day event held the week before classes start in the Fall. **Housing:** Guaranteed on-campus for all undergraduates. Coed dorms, single-sex dorms, special housing for disabled, apartments, fraternity/sorority housing, wellness housing available. $250 nonrefundable deposit, deadline 6/15. Learning communities available. **Activities:** Bands, campus ministries, choral groups, dance, drama, international student organizations, literary magazine, music ensembles, musical theater, opera, student government, student newspaper, symphony orchestra, TV station, Kappa Phi, Sigma Theta Epsilon, Association for People of Color, United Methodist Student Fellowship, Students of Arts Management, Alpha Phi sorority, Gamma Phi Beta sorority, Lambda Chi Alpha fraternity, Kappa Sigma fraternity.

Athletics. NAIA. **Intercollegiate:** Baseball M, basketball, cheerleading, cross-country, golf, rowing (crew), soccer, softball W, track and field, volleyball W, wrestling. **Intramural:** Basketball, football (non-tackle), soccer, softball, table tennis, volleyball. **Team name:** Stars.

Student services. Adult student services, chaplain/spiritual director, career counseling, services for economically disadvantaged, student employment services, financial aid counseling, health services, minority student services, personal counseling, placement for graduates, veterans' counselor. **Physically disabled:** Services for visually, hearing impaired.

Contact. E-mail: uadmissions@okcu.edu
Phone: (405) 208-5050 Toll-free number: (800) 633-7242
Fax: (405) 208-5916
Michelle Cook, Senior Director of Admissions, Oklahoma City University, 2501 North Blackwelder Avenue, Oklahoma City, OK 73106-1493

Oklahoma Panhandle State University
Goodwell, Oklahoma
www.opsu.edu   CB code: 6571

- Public 4-year university and liberal arts college
- Residential campus in rural community
- 1,261 degree-seeking undergraduates

General. Founded in 1909. Regionally accredited. **Degrees:** 236 bachelor's, 86 associate awarded. **Location:** 110 miles from Amarillo, Texas; 10 miles from Guymon. **Calendar:** Semester, limited summer session. **Full-time faculty:** 70 total. **Part-time faculty:** 35 total. **Class size:** 72% < 20, 23% 20-39, 2% 40-49, 3% 50-99, less than 1% >100. **Special facilities:** Agronomy experiment station, historical museum, livestock facilities, farming area, rodeo arena, meat lab.

Freshman class profile.

GPA 3.75 or higher:	18%	**GPA 2.0-2.99:**	37%
GPA 3.50-3.74:	9%	**Out-of-state:**	54%
GPA 3.0-3.49:	33%	**Live on campus:**	90%

Basis for selection. School record, ACT/SAT, and class rank most important. SAT or ACT recommended. Incoming students without ACT, or with score of 19 or below, must take ACCUPLACER test. **Home schooled:** Transcript of courses and grades required.

High school preparation. 15 units required. Required units include English 4, mathematics 3, social studies 2, history 1, science 2 (laboratory 2) and academic electives 3.

2015-2016 Annual costs. Tuition/fees: $7,421; $12,980 out-of-state. Room/board: $4,708. Books/supplies: $582. Personal expenses: $3,744.

2014-2015 Financial aid. All financial aid based on need. 97% of total undergraduate aid awarded as scholarships/grants, 3% as loans/jobs.

Application procedures. **Admission:** No deadline. No application fee. Admission notification on a rolling basis. **Financial aid:** Priority date 3/15; no closing date. FAFSA, institutional form required.

Academics. **Special study options:** Cooperative education, distance learning, double major, ESL, independent study, internships, teacher certification program. **Credit/placement by examination:** AP, CLEP, SAT, ACT, institutional tests. 34 credit hours maximum toward associate degree, 60 toward bachelor's. **Support services:** Learning center, reduced course load, remedial instruction, study skills assistance, tutoring, writing center.

Majors. **Biology:** General. **Business:** Accounting, business admin. **Computer sciences:** General. **Education:** Agricultural, business, elementary. **English:** English lit. **Health services:** Nursing (RN). **History:** General. **Liberal arts:** Arts/sciences. **Math:** General. **Parks/recreation:** Health/fitness. **Physical sciences:** Chemistry. **Psychology:** General. **Social sciences:** General. **Visual/performing arts:** Art, music.

Most popular majors. Agriculture 20%, biology 12%, business/marketing 17%, health sciences 12%, parks/recreation 6%, psychology 9%, visual/performing arts 6%.

Technology on campus. 150 workstations in dormitories, library, computer center, student center. Dormitories wired for high-speed internet access. Online library, wireless network available.

Student life. **Freshman orientation:** Mandatory. Preregistration for classes offered. **Housing:** Guaranteed on-campus for freshmen. Single-sex dorms, apartments available. **Activities:** Bands, choral groups, drama, music ensembles, musical theater, radio station, student government, student newspaper, Wesley Foundation, Baptist student union, Church of Christ student center, Circle-K, Newman club, Methodist student center.

Athletics. NCAA. **Intercollegiate:** Baseball M, basketball, cheerleading, cross-country, football (tackle) M, golf, softball W, volleyball W. **Intramural:** Basketball, football (non-tackle), golf, soccer, softball, table tennis, volleyball. **Team name:** Aggies.

Student services. Adult student services, alcohol/substance abuse counseling, career counseling, student employment services, financial aid counseling, health services, minority student services, personal counseling, placement for graduates. **Physically disabled:** Services for visually, speech, hearing impaired.

Contact. E-mail: opsu@opsu.edu
Phone: (580) 349-2611 Toll-free number: (800) 664-6778
Fax: (580) 349-1371
Bobby Jenkins, Registrar and Director of Admissions, Oklahoma Panhandle State University, OPSU Admissions, Goodwell, OK 73939-0430

Oklahoma State University
Stillwater, Oklahoma
go.okstate.edu

CB member
CB code: 6546

- Public 4-year university
- Residential campus in large town
- 20,752 degree-seeking undergraduates: 12% part-time, 49% women, 5% African American, 1% Asian American, 6% Hispanic/Latino, 5% Native American, 9% Multi-racial, non-Hispanic, 3% international
- 4,593 degree-seeking graduate students
- 75% of applicants admitted
- SAT or ACT (ACT writing optional) required
- 62% graduate within 6 years

General. Founded in 1890. Regionally accredited. Campuses in Stillwater and Tulsa. Stillwater campus includes the Center for Veterinary Health Sciences. **Degrees:** 4,162 bachelor's awarded; master's, professional, doctoral offered. **ROTC:** Army, Air Force. **Location:** 65 miles from Oklahoma City, 65 miles from Tulsa. **Calendar:** Semester, extensive summer session. **Full-time faculty:** 1,048 total; 92% have terminal degrees, 20% minority, 35% women. **Part-time faculty:** 306 total; 14% have terminal degrees, 12% minority, 62% women. **Class size:** 35% < 20, 39% 20-39, 10% 40-49, 10% 50-99, 6% >100. **Special facilities:** Advanced technology research center, biotechnology and genetic engineering research center, telecommunication center, botanical garden.

Freshman class profile. 12,458 applied, 9,390 admitted, 4,177 enrolled.

Mid 50% test scores			
SAT critical reading:	470-590	Rank in top quarter:	56%
SAT math:	500-620	Rank in top tenth:	27%
ACT composite:	22-27	Return as sophomores:	81%
GPA 3.75 or higher:	36%	Out-of-state:	33%
GPA 3.50-3.74:	22%	Live on campus:	93%
GPA 3.0-3.49:	33%	International:	1%
GPA 2.0-2.99:	9%	Fraternities:	24%
		Sororities:	36%

Basis for selection. Students qualify for assured admission if they meet ONE of the following criteria: 3.0 GPA or better unweighted cumulative AND top 33.3% rank in high school graduating class, OR 3.0 GPA or better in 15-unit core AND 21 ACT/980 SAT or better, OR 24 ACT/1090 SAT or better. Early application encouraged. Interview recommended for academically borderline students.

High school preparation. College-preparatory program recommended. 15 units required. Required units include English 4, mathematics 3, social studies 2, history 1, science 3 (laboratory 3).

2015-2016 Annual costs. Tuition/fees: $7,778; $20,978 out-of-state. Room/board: $7,450. Books/supplies: $1,030. Personal expenses: $2,530.

2014-2015 Financial aid. **Need-based:** 3,104 full-time freshmen applied for aid; 2,153 deemed to have need; 2,089 received aid. Average need met was 78%. Average scholarship/grant was $7,337; average loan $3,255. 53% of total undergraduate aid awarded as scholarships/grants, 47% as loans/jobs. **Non-need-based:** Awarded to 5,997 full-time undergraduates, including 1,355 freshmen. Scholarships awarded for academics, alumni affiliation, art, athletics, leadership, minority status, music/drama, ROTC, state residency. **Additional information:** In-state students who file the FAFSA and who have financial need may receive additional funding through the Academic Opportunity Scholarship program.

Application procedures. **Admission:** No deadline. $40 fee, may be waived for applicants with need. Admission notification on a rolling basis. Deferred admission allowed based on military deployments. **Financial aid:** Priority date 2/1; no closing date. FAFSA required. Applicants notified on a rolling basis starting 4/1; must reply by 5/1 or within 2 week(s) of notification.

Academics. **Special study options:** Accelerated study, combined bachelor's/graduate degree, cross-registration, distance learning, double major, dual enrollment of high school students, ESL, exchange student, honors, independent study, internships, semester at sea, student-designed major, study abroad, teacher certification program. **Credit/placement by examination:** AP, CLEP, IB, SAT, ACT, institutional tests. Maximum number of credit hours towards degree is subject to university "residence credit" policy. **Support services:** Learning center, pre-admission summer program, reduced course load, study skills assistance, tutoring, writing center.

Honors college/program. 27 ACT/1220 SAT (exclusive of Writing) and 3.75 GPA required.

Majors. **Architecture:** Architecture, landscape. **Area/ethnic studies:** American. **Biology:** General, biochemistry, botany, ecology, entomology, microbiology, physiology, zoology. **Business:** Accounting, business admin, entrepreneurial studies, finance, hospitality admin, international, managerial economics, marketing. **Communications:** Journalism, sports. **Computer sciences:** General, information technology. **Conservation:** Environmental science. **Education:** Agricultural, elementary, music, physical, secondary, voc/tech. **Engineering:** Aerospace, agricultural, architectural, chemical, civil, computer, electrical, industrial, mechanical. **English:** English lit. **Foreign languages:** French, German, Russian, Spanish. **Health services:** Athletic training, public health ed, speech pathology. **History:** General. **Liberal arts:** Arts/sciences. **Math:** General, statistics. **Parks/recreation:** General. **Philosophy/religion:** Philosophy. **Physical sciences:** Chemistry, geology, physics. **Protective services:** Fire safety technology. **Psychology:** General. **Social sciences:** Economics, geography, political science, sociology. **Visual/performing arts:** Art, dramatic, music. **Work/family studies:** Family studies, food/nutrition, housing.

Most popular majors. Agriculture 9%, business/marketing 27%, education 6%, engineering/engineering technologies 13%, family/consumer sciences 7%.

Technology on campus. Dormitories wired for high-speed internet access and linked to campus network. Commuter students can connect to campus network. Online course registration, online library, helpline, repair service, wireless network available.

Student life. **Freshman orientation:** Mandatory, $75 fee. Preregistration for classes offered. One-day programs in June. Additional program held week before classes begin each fall semester. **Housing:** Guaranteed on-campus for freshmen. Coed dorms, single-sex dorms, special housing for disabled, apartments, fraternity/sorority housing, themed housing, wellness housing available. $150 fully refundable deposit. **Activities:** Bands, campus ministries, choral groups, dance, drama, international student organizations, literary magazine, music ensembles, musical theater, opera, radio station, student government, student newspaper, symphony orchestra, TV station, Flying Aggies, Young Democrats, College Republicans, Fire Protection Society, Alpha Pi Omega, Women's Resource Center Student Alliance, African American Student Association, Hispanic Student Association, Habitat for Humanity.

Athletics. NCAA. **Intercollegiate:** Baseball M, basketball, cross-country, equestrian W, football (tackle) M, golf, soccer W, softball W, tennis, track and field, wrestling M. **Intramural:** Archery, badminton, basketball, football (non-tackle), golf, racquetball, rowing (crew), soccer, softball, swimming, table tennis, tennis, triathlon, ultimate frisbee, volleyball, weight lifting, wrestling. **Team name:** Cowboys, Cowgirls.

Student services. Adult student services, alcohol/substance abuse counseling, career counseling, student employment services, financial aid counseling, health services, legal services, minority student services, personal counseling, placement for graduates, veterans' counselor. **Physically disabled:** Services for visually, speech, hearing impaired.

Contact. E-mail: admissions@okstate.edu
Phone: (405) 744-5358 Toll-free number: (800) 233-5019 ext. 1
Fax: (405) 744-7092
Christine Crenshaw, Director of Undergraduate Admissions, Oklahoma State University, 219 Student Union, Stillwater, OK 74078

Oklahoma Wesleyan University
Bartlesville, Oklahoma
www.okwu.edu

CB code: 6135

- Private 4-year university and liberal arts college affiliated with the Wesleyan Church
- Residential campus in large town
- 1,157 degree-seeking undergraduates: 48% part-time, 62% women, 8% African American, 1% Asian American, 8% Hispanic/Latino, 9% Native American, 5% international
- 274 degree-seeking graduate students
- 67% of applicants admitted

- SAT or ACT (ACT writing optional) required
- 45% graduate within 6 years

General. Founded in 1909. Regionally accredited. Strong emphasis in a Biblical foundation. Mission includes focus on Four Pillars: primacy of Jesus Christ, priority of Scripture, pursuit of Truth, and practice of Wisdom. **Degrees:** 345 bachelor's, 50 associate awarded; master's offered. **Location:** 45 mile from Tulsa. **Calendar:** Semester, limited summer session. **Full-time faculty:** 34 total; 59% have terminal degrees, 41% women.

Freshman class profile. 726 applied, 486 admitted, 202 enrolled.

Mid 50% test scores		End year in good standing:	90%
SAT critical reading:	410-500	Return as sophomores:	50%
SAT math:	430-540	Out-of-state:	60%
SAT writing:	420-500	Live on campus:	89%
ACT composite:	18-25	International:	4%

Basis for selection. In addition to required high school study, students must fulfill 2 of the following: rank in top half of class, 2.0 GPA, 18 ACT. **Home schooled:** Statement describing home school structure and mission, transcript of courses and grades required.

High school preparation. College-preparatory program recommended. 15 units required. Required units include English 4, mathematics 2, social studies 2, science 1 (laboratory 1) and academic electives 6.

2015-2016 Annual costs. Tuition/fees: $24,108. Room/board: $7,862. Books/supplies: $900. Personal expenses: $1,690.

Financial aid. **Non-need-based:** Scholarships awarded for academics, alumni affiliation, athletics, leadership, music/drama, religious affiliation, state residency.

Application procedures. **Admission:** No deadline. $25 fee, may be waived for applicants with need, free for online applicants. Admission notification on a rolling basis. Students must be accepted prior to beginning classes. **Financial aid:** Priority date 3/1; no closing date. FAFSA, institutional form required. Applicants notified on a rolling basis starting 3/1; must reply by 5/1 or within 2 week(s) of notification.

Academics. **Special study options:** Accelerated study, combined bachelor's/graduate degree, distance learning, double major, dual enrollment of high school students, independent study, internships, student-designed major, study abroad, teacher certification program, Washington semester. **Credit/ placement by examination:** AP, CLEP, SAT, ACT, institutional tests. 30 credit hours maximum toward associate degree, 36 toward bachelor's. **Support services:** Reduced course load, remedial instruction, study skills assistance, tutoring.

Majors. **Biology:** General. **Business:** General, business admin. **Communications:** Communications/speech/rhetoric. **Computer sciences:** General, computer science. **Education:** Business, elementary, English, mathematics, music, physical, science, social studies. **English:** English lit. **Health services:** Nursing (RN). **History:** General. **Math:** General. **Parks/recreation:** Exercise sciences. **Philosophy/religion:** Christian. **Physical sciences:** Chemistry. **Psychology:** General. **Social sciences:** General, political science. **Theology:** Bible, missionary, sacred music, theology.

Most popular majors. Business/marketing 31%, health sciences 38%, theological studies 11%.

Technology on campus. 40 workstations in library, student center. Dormitories wired for high-speed internet access and linked to campus network. Commuter students can connect to campus network. Online course registration, online library, helpline, repair service, wireless network available.

Student life. **Freshman orientation:** Mandatory, $100 fee. Preregistration for classes offered. **Policies:** Required Chapel attendance. Religious observance required. **Housing:** Guaranteed on-campus for all undergraduates. Single-sex dorms, apartments available. $250 partly refundable deposit. **Activities:** Bands, campus ministries, choral groups, music ensembles, student government, student newspaper, campus missionary fellowship, theology fellowship, Fellowship of Christian Athletes, Operation Saturation, Sudan fellowship, College Republicans.

Athletics. NAIA, NCCAA. **Intercollegiate:** Baseball M, basketball, cross-country, golf, soccer, softball W, tennis, track and field, volleyball W. **Intramural:** Basketball, football (non-tackle), racquetball, softball W, table tennis, volleyball. **Team name:** Eagles.

Student services. Adult student services, chaplain/spiritual director, career counseling, student employment services, financial aid counseling, health services, placement for graduates, veterans' counselor.

Contact. E-mail: admissions@okwu.edu
Phone: (918) 335-6219 Toll-free number: (800) 468-6292
Fax: (918) 335-6229
Samantha Peterson, Assistant Vice President of Enrollment Services, Oklahoma Wesleyan University, 2201 Silver Lake Road, Bartlesville, OK 74006

Oral Roberts University
Tulsa, Oklahoma
www.oru.edu

CB member
CB code: 6552

- Private 4-year university and liberal arts college affiliated with the non-denominational tradition
- Residential campus in large city
- 2,805 degree-seeking undergraduates: 10% part-time, 58% women, 15% African American, 2% Asian American, 9% Hispanic/Latino, 3% Native American, 6% Multi-racial, non-Hispanic, 8% international
- 557 degree-seeking graduate students
- 22% of applicants admitted
- SAT or ACT (ACT writing optional), application essay required
- 55% graduate within 6 years

General. Founded in 1965. Regionally accredited. Integrated math and science academy sponsored by Oklahoma State Regents for Higher Education. **Degrees:** 592 bachelor's awarded; master's, doctoral offered. **ROTC:** Air Force. **Location:** 7 miles from downtown. **Calendar:** Semester, limited summer session. **Full-time faculty:** 158 total; 66% have terminal degrees, 20% minority, 35% women. **Part-time faculty:** 116 total; 27% have terminal degrees, less than 1% minority, 63% women. **Class size:** 62% < 20, 29% 20-39, 5% 40-49, 3% 50-99, less than 1% >100. **Special facilities:** Prayer tower, mineralogical museum.

Freshman class profile. 2,378 applied, 522 admitted, 437 enrolled.

Mid 50% test scores		GPA 2.0-2.99:	18%
SAT critical reading:	460-550	Rank in top quarter:	38%
SAT math:	450-560	Rank in top tenth:	19%
ACT composite:	19-24	Return as sophomores:	80%
GPA 3.75 or higher:	36%	Out-of-state:	56%
GPA 3.50-3.74:	18%	Live on campus:	87%
GPA 3.0-3.49:	27%	International:	7%

Basis for selection. Academic record, test scores, personal essay, minister's recommendation, other recommendations, extracurricular activities considered. Students must provide immunization records. Interview recommended for all; audition required for music program; portfolio recommended for art program. **Home schooled:** Under special circumstances, applicants may be required to submit additional curricular information and/or proof of high school equivalency.

High school preparation. 16 units recommended. Recommended units include English 4, mathematics 2, social studies 2, science 2 (laboratory 1), foreign language 2 and academic electives 4. Students matriculating in bachelor of science program may substitute additional math units for foreign language.

2015-2016 Annual costs. Tuition/fees: $24,792. Room/board: $10,348. Books/supplies: $1,848. Personal expenses: $1,848.

2015-2016 Financial aid. **Need-based:** Average need met was 91%. Average scholarship/grant was $17,314; average loan $7,077. 70% of total undergraduate aid awarded as scholarships/grants, 30% as loans/jobs. **Non-need-based:** Scholarships awarded for academics, alumni affiliation, art, athletics, leadership, music/drama.

Application procedures. **Admission:** No deadline. $35 fee, may be waived for applicants with need, free for online applicants. Admission notification on a rolling basis beginning on or about 9/1. Must reply by May 1 or within 3 week(s) if notified thereafter. **Financial aid:** Priority date 3/15, closing date 4/19. FAFSA required. Applicants notified on a rolling basis starting 3/15; must reply by 5/1.

Academics. **Special study options:** Accelerated study, combined bachelor's/graduate degree, distance learning, double major, dual enrollment of high school students, ESL, external degree, honors, independent study, internships, liberal arts/career combination, student-designed major, study abroad, teacher certification program, Washington semester. **Credit/placement by examination:** AP, CLEP, SAT, ACT, institutional tests. 30 credit hours maximum toward associate degree, 30 toward bachelor's. **Support services:** Learning center, reduced course load, remedial instruction, study skills assistance, tutoring.

Majors. Biology: General, biochemistry. **Business:** Accounting, business admin, finance, international, international marketing, management information systems, management science, marketing, organizational behavior, organizational leadership. **Communications:** Communications/speech/rhetoric. **Computer sciences:** General, computer science. **Education:** Art, business, early childhood, elementary, English, foreign languages, health, mathematics, music, physical, science, social studies, Spanish, special ed. **Engineering:** General, applied physics, biomedical, computer, electrical, environmental, mechanical. **English:** English lit, writing. **Foreign languages:** French, Spanish. **Health services:** Clinical lab science, nursing (RN). **History:** General. **Human services:** Social work. **Liberal arts:** Arts/sciences. **Math:** General. **Parks/recreation:** Exercise sciences, facilities management, health/fitness. **Physical sciences:** Chemistry, physics. **Psychology:** General. **Social sciences:** International relations, political science. **Theology:** Bible, missionary, pastoral counseling, preministerial, religious ed, sacred music, theology. **Visual/performing arts:** Acting, art, commercial/advertising art, dance, design, dramatic, graphic design, music, music performance, music theory/composition, piano/keyboard, studio arts, theater design, voice/opera.

Most popular majors. Business/marketing 22%, communications/journalism 11%, education 8%, health sciences 8%, parks/recreation 6%, theological studies 13%, visual/performing arts 7%.

Technology on campus. 382 workstations in library, computer center. Dormitories linked to campus network. Commuter students can connect to campus network. Online course registration, online library, wireless network available.

Student life. Freshman orientation: Mandatory. Preregistration for classes offered. **Policies:** Single undergraduate students under 25 years of age must live in university housing or with parents. Religious observance required. **Housing:** Guaranteed on-campus for all undergraduates. Single-sex dorms, special housing for disabled available. $200 nonrefundable deposit, deadline 5/1. **Activities:** Bands, campus ministries, choral groups, dance, drama, international student organizations, literary magazine, music ensembles, Model UN, musical theater, opera, radio station, student government, student newspaper, symphony orchestra, TV station, Community Outreach, missions club, Young Republicans, Young Democrats, student activist society, Students in Free Enterprise, Oklahoma Intercollegiate Legislature.

Athletics. NCAA. **Intercollegiate:** Baseball M, basketball, cross-country, golf, soccer, tennis, track and field, volleyball W. **Intramural:** Badminton, basketball, bowling, cross-country, football (non-tackle), golf, racquetball, softball, swimming, table tennis, tennis, volleyball, wrestling M. **Team name:** Golden Eagles.

Student services. Chaplain/spiritual director, career counseling, student employment services, financial aid counseling, health services, personal counseling, placement for graduates, veterans' counselor. **Physically disabled:** Services for visually, speech, hearing impaired.

Contact. E-mail: admissions@oru.edu
Phone: (918) 496-6518 Toll-free number: (800) 678-8876
Fax: (918) 495-6222
Chris Belcher, Director of Admissions, Oral Roberts University, 7777 South Lewis Avenue, Tulsa, OK 74171

Rogers State University
Claremore, Oklahoma
www.rsu.edu   CB code: 6545

- Public 4-year university
- Commuter campus in large town
- 4,029 degree-seeking undergraduates: 39% part-time, 62% women
- 17 degree-seeking graduate students
- 82% of applicants admitted
- SAT or ACT (ACT writing optional) required

General. Founded in 1909. Regionally accredited. **Degrees:** 324 bachelor's, 254 associate awarded; master's offered. **Location:** 25 miles from Tulsa. **Calendar:** Semester, limited summer session. **Full-time faculty:** 104 total; 58% have terminal degrees, 14% minority, 45% women. **Part-time faculty:** 157 total; 20% have terminal degrees, 13% minority, 65% women. **Class size:** 51% < 20, 46% 20-39, 3% 40-49, less than 1% 50-99. **Special facilities:** Conservation education reserve, Oklahoma military academy museum.

Freshman class profile. 1,057 applied, 865 admitted, 739 enrolled.

Mid 50% test scores		Rank in top quarter:	33%
ACT composite:	16-18	Rank in top tenth:	11%
GPA 3.75 or higher:	20%	Return as sophomores:	65%
GPA 3.50-3.74:	14%	Out-of-state:	4%
GPA 3.0-3.49:	31%	Live on campus:	30%
GPA 2.0-2.99:	33%	Sororities:	1%

Basis for selection. Bachelor degree programs require 20 ACT and no curricular deficiencies. Open admission for associate degree programs only. ACT recommended. Essay required for returning suspension students only.

High school preparation. College-preparatory program recommended. 15 units required; 19 recommended. Required and recommended units include English 4, mathematics 3-4, history 3, science 3 (laboratory 3), foreign language 2, computer science 1, visual/performing arts 2 and academic electives 2. Math should include algebra I and II; 1 computer science also recommended; history should include 1 unit of U.S. history and 1 of citizenship (government, geography, etc.).

2015-2016 Annual costs. Tuition/fees: $6,309; $13,599 out-of-state. Room/board: $7,705. Books/supplies: $2,120. Personal expenses: $1,350.

2015-2016 Financial aid. Need-based: Average need met was 48%. Average scholarship/grant was $6,437; average loan $3,358. 53% of total undergraduate aid awarded as scholarships/grants, 47% as loans/jobs. **Non-need-based:** Scholarships awarded for academics, alumni affiliation, art, athletics, leadership, music/drama, state residency.

Application procedures. Admission: No deadline. $20 fee, may be waived for applicants with need. Admission notification on a rolling basis beginning on or about 8/1. Housing deposit refundable through July 1. **Financial aid:** Priority date 6/15; no closing date. FAFSA required. Applicants notified on a rolling basis starting 4/1; must reply within 1 week(s) of notification.

Academics. Special study options: Distance learning, honors, independent study, internships, study abroad, Washington semester. **Credit/placement by examination:** AP, CLEP, IB, SAT, ACT, institutional tests. 30 credit hours maximum toward associate degree, 45 toward bachelor's. **Support services:** Learning center, reduced course load, remedial instruction, study skills assistance, tutoring, writing center.

Majors. Biology: General. **Business:** Business admin, nonprofit/public. **Computer sciences:** Computer graphics. **Health services:** Nursing (RN). **History:** Military. **Human services:** General. **Liberal arts:** Arts/sciences. **Parks/recreation:** Sports admin. **Protective services:** Law enforcement admin. **Psychology:** Community. **Social sciences:** General. **Visual/performing arts:** General.

Most popular majors. Biology 10%, business/marketing 28%, communications/journalism 6%, health sciences 11%, interdisciplinary studies 10%, psychology 12%, visual/performing arts 6%.

Technology on campus. 254 workstations in dormitories, library, student center. Dormitories wired for high-speed internet access and linked to campus network. Online library, helpline, wireless network available.

Student life. Freshman orientation: Available. Preregistration for classes offered. **Housing:** Coed dorms, apartments available. $200 fully refundable deposit. **Activities:** Bands, campus ministries, choral groups, dance, drama, international student organizations, music ensembles, radio station, student government, TV station, Native American student association, Baptist collegiate ministry, student art association, student nursing association, Campus Crusade for Christ, College Republicans.

Athletics. NCAA. **Intercollegiate:** Baseball M, basketball, cross-country, golf, soccer, softball W, track and field. **Intramural:** Cheerleading, football (non-tackle), volleyball. **Team name:** Hillcats.

Student services. Adult student services, alcohol/substance abuse counseling, career counseling, services for economically disadvantaged, financial aid counseling, health services, personal counseling, veterans' counselor. **Physically disabled:** Services for visually, speech, hearing impaired.

Contact. E-mail: admissions@rsu.edu
Phone: (918) 343-7546 Toll-free number: (800) 256-7511
Fax: (918) 343-7595
Heidi Hoskinson, Vice President of Enrollment Management & Registrar, Rogers State University, 1701 West Will Rogers Boulevard, Claremore, OK 74017-3252

Southeastern Oklahoma State University
Durant, Oklahoma
www.se.edu   CB code: 6657

- Public 4-year liberal arts and teachers college
- Commuter campus in large town
- 3,209 degree-seeking undergraduates. 24% part-time, 54% women, 7% African American, 1% Asian American, 6% Hispanic/Latino, 30% Native American

◆ 466 degree-seeking graduate students
◆ 72% of applicants admitted
◆ SAT or ACT (ACT writing optional) required

General. Founded in 1909. Regionally accredited. Degree programs offered through satellite campus at Idabel and Higher Education Centers at Ardmore, McAlester, Tinker Air Force Base, Oklahoma City Community College, Grayson County College. **Degrees:** 655 bachelor's awarded; master's offered. **Location:** 90 miles from Dallas. **Calendar:** Semester, extensive summer session. **Full-time faculty:** 138 total; less than 1% have terminal degrees, 16% minority, 41% women. **Part-time faculty:** 132 total; less than 1% have terminal degrees, 27% minority, 59% women. **Class size:** 58% < 20, 36% 20-39, 3% 40-49, 3% 50-99. **Special facilities:** Herbarium, equestrian facilities.

Freshman class profile. 1,051 applied, 759 admitted, 476 enrolled.

Mid 50% test scores			
ACT composite:	18-23	Rank in top tenth:	13%
GPA 3.75 or higher:	21%	Return as sophomores:	61%
GPA 3.50-3.74:	22%	Out-of-state:	28%
GPA 3.0-3.49:	32%	Live on campus:	52%
GPA 2.0-2.99:	24%	Fraternities:	33%
Rank in top quarter:	41%	Sororities:	32%

Basis for selection. High school transcript and test scores important. Must have 2.7 GPA and rank in top half of class, 20 ACT or 940 SAT (exclusive of Writing), score in top half of applicants on ACT scores, or attain 2.7 GPA in 15 core units. Audition required for drama, music programs. Interview required for alternative admissions. **Home schooled:** 20 ACT required.

High school preparation. College-preparatory program recommended. 15 units required. Required and recommended units include English 4, mathematics 3, history 3, science 3 (laboratory 3), foreign language 1, computer science 1 and academic electives 2.

2015-2016 Annual costs. Tuition/fees: $6,075; $14,713 out-of-state. Room/board: $6,030. Books/supplies: $800. Personal expenses: $1,447.

2014-2015 Financial aid. **Need-based:** 418 full-time freshmen applied for aid; 343 deemed to have need; 338 received aid. Average need met was 50%. Average scholarship/grant was $1,879; average loan $1,393. 63% of total undergraduate aid awarded as scholarships/grants, 37% as loans/jobs. **Non-need-based:** Awarded to 884 full-time undergraduates, including 197 freshmen. Scholarships awarded for academics, alumni affiliation, art, athletics, leadership, minority status, music/drama, state residency.

Application procedures. **Admission:** No deadline. $20 fee. Admission notification on a rolling basis. Open admission for adults over 21. **Financial aid:** Priority date 3/1; no closing date. FAFSA, institutional form required. Applicants notified on a rolling basis starting 4/1.

Academics. Programs in aviation, ecology, energy, health-related sciences, and criminology. **Special study options:** Combined bachelor's/graduate degree, distance learning, double major, honors, independent study, internships, teacher certification program. **Credit/placement by examination:** AP, CLEP, IB, SAT, ACT, institutional tests. 60 credit hours maximum toward bachelor's degree. **Support services:** Learning center, pre-admission summer program, reduced course load, remedial instruction, study skills assistance, tutoring, writing center.

Majors. **Biology:** General, biotechnology. **Business:** Accounting, business admin, finance, management science, marketing, organizational leadership. **Communications:** Communications/speech/rhetoric. **Computer sciences:** General, information systems. **Conservation:** General. **Education:** Art, elementary, English, mathematics, music, physical, science, social studies, Spanish, special ed. **Engineering:** Aerospace. **English:** English lit. **Foreign languages:** Spanish. **History:** General. **Math:** General. **Parks/recreation:** General. **Physical sciences:** Chemistry. **Protective services:** Criminal justice. **Psychology:** General. **Social sciences:** Political science, sociology. **Visual/performing arts:** Art, dramatic, graphic design, music, music performance.

Most popular majors. Area/ethnic studies 7%, business/marketing 10%, education 12%, engineering/engineering technologies 20%, liberal arts 13%, psychology 10%, trade and industry 7%.

Technology on campus. 2,138 workstations in dormitories, library, computer center, student center. Dormitories wired for high-speed internet access and linked to campus network. Commuter students can connect to campus network. Online course registration, online library, helpline, student web hosting, wireless network available.

Student life. **Freshman orientation:** Available, $80 fee. Preregistration for classes offered. **Policies:** No alcohol at university events on/off campus. **Housing:** Coed dorms, apartments available. $100 nonrefundable deposit. **Activities:** Bands, campus ministries, choral groups, dance, drama, international student organizations, literary magazine, music ensembles, Model UN, musical theater, opera, radio station, student government, student newspaper, Black American society, Wesley Center, student Bible center, Chi Alpha, Young Democrats, College Republicans, Muslim student association.

Athletics. NCAA. **Intercollegiate:** Baseball M, basketball, cross-country W, football (tackle) M, golf M, rodeo, softball W, tennis, volleyball W. **Intramural:** Basketball, football (non-tackle), football (tackle) M, soccer, softball, ultimate frisbee, volleyball. **Team name:** Savage Storm.

Student services. Adult student services, alcohol/substance abuse counseling, chaplain/spiritual director, career counseling, student employment services, financial aid counseling, health services, minority student services, personal counseling, placement for graduates, veterans' counselor. **Physically disabled:** Services for visually, speech, hearing impaired.

Contact. E-mail: admissions@se.edu
Phone: (580) 745-2052 Toll-free number: (800) 435-1327
Fax: (580) 745-7502
Shelly Key, Director of Admissions and Recruitment, Southeastern Oklahoma State University, 1405 North Fourth Avenue, PMB 4225, Durant, OK 74701-0607

Southern Nazarene University
Bethany, Oklahoma   **CB member**
www.snu.edu   **CB code: 6036**

◆ Private 4-year university and liberal arts college affiliated with the Church of the Nazarene
◆ Residential campus in large town
◆ 1,639 degree-seeking undergraduates: 3% part-time, 53% women, 12% African American, 1% Asian American, 9% Hispanic/Latino, 3% Native American, 5% Multi-racial, non-Hispanic, 2% international
◆ 609 degree-seeking graduate students
◆ 33% of applicants admitted
◆ SAT or ACT required

General. Founded in 1899. Regionally accredited. **Degrees:** 483 bachelor's awarded; master's offered. **ROTC:** Army, Air Force. **Location:** 5 miles from Oklahoma City. **Calendar:** Semester, limited summer session. **Full-time faculty:** 74 total; 53% women. **Part-time faculty:** 80 total; 59% women. **Class size:** 70% < 20, 25% 20-39, 3% 40-49, 2% 50-99. **Special facilities:** Human cadaver laboratory, physics laser laboratory, laboratory school for children.

Freshman class profile. 979 applied, 322 admitted, 283 enrolled.

GPA 3.75 or higher:	35%	Out-of-state:	42%
GPA 3.50-3.74:	18%	Live on campus:	84%
GPA 3.0-3.49:	23%	International:	2%
GPA 2.0-2.99:	22%		

Basis for selection. 2.0 GPA and 19 ACT or SAT equivalent required for unconditional admissions. Students who do not meet requirements may be granted provisional acceptance by committee review. Interview recommended for all; audition recommended for music program. **Home schooled:** Transcript of courses and grades required.

High school preparation. College-preparatory program recommended. 13 units recommended. Recommended units include English 4, mathematics 3, social studies 2, science 2 and foreign language 2. One computer course recommended.

2016-2017 Annual costs. Tuition/fees (projected): $24,468. Room/board: $8,330. Books/supplies: $1,200. Personal expenses: $1,200.

2014-2015 Financial aid. **Need-based:** 83% of total undergraduate aid awarded as scholarships/grants, 17% as loans/jobs. **Non-need-based:** Scholarships awarded for academics, athletics, ROTC, state residency.

Application procedures. **Admission:** Priority date 5/1; deadline 8/1. $35 fee, may be waived for applicants with need, free for online applicants. Admission notification on a rolling basis. **Financial aid:** Priority date 3/1; no closing date. FAFSA, institutional form required. Applicants notified on a rolling basis starting 5/1; must reply within 2 week(s) of notification.

Academics. **Special study options:** Combined bachelor's/graduate degree, distance learning, double major, dual enrollment of high school students, external degree, honors, independent study, internships, liberal arts/career combination, student-designed major, study abroad, teacher certification program, urban semester, Washington semester. **Credit/placement by examination:** AP, CLEP, IB, institutional tests. 30 credit hours maximum toward bachelor's degree. **Support services:** Learning center, remedial instruction, study skills assistance, tutoring, writing center.

Majors. Area/ethnic studies: American. **Biology:** General, biochemistry. **Business:** General, accounting, business admin, finance, marketing. **Communications:** Communications/speech/rhetoric, journalism. **Communications technology:** General. **Computer sciences:** General, networking. **Conservation:** General. **Education:** General, early childhood, elementary, English, history, mathematics, music, physical, reading, science, secondary, Spanish, speech. **English:** English lit, rhetoric/composition. **Foreign languages:** Spanish. **Health services:** Athletic training, clinical lab technology. **History:** General. **Liberal arts:** Arts/sciences. **Math:** General. **Parks/recreation:** Exercise sciences. **Philosophy/religion:** Philosophy, religion. **Physical sciences:** Chemistry, physics. **Protective services:** Criminal justice. **Psychology:** General. **Social sciences:** General, political science, sociology. **Theology:** Missionary, religious ed, sacred music, theology. **Visual/performing arts:** General, graphic design, music.

Most popular majors. Biology 8%, business/marketing 23%, education 18%, family/consumer sciences 8%, health sciences 7%, psychology 7%, social sciences 12%, theological studies 6%.

Technology on campus. PC or laptop required. 120 workstations in library, computer center. Dormitories wired for high-speed internet access and linked to campus network. Online course registration, helpline, repair service, wireless network available.

Student life. Freshman orientation: Mandatory. Preregistration for classes offered. **Policies:** Single students under 23 required to live on campus or with relatives. Religious observance required. **Housing:** Guaranteed on-campus for freshmen. Single-sex dorms, apartments available. $50 deposit, deadline 8/1. **Activities:** Bands, campus ministries, choral groups, drama, film society, music ensembles, student government, student newspaper, symphony orchestra, TV station, Gospel team, Mission Crusaders, Circle-K, Spanish club, Mortar Board.

Athletics. NCAA, NCCAA. **Intercollegiate:** Baseball M, basketball, cheerleading, cross-country, equestrian, football (tackle) M, golf, soccer, softball W, tennis, track and field, volleyball W. **Intramural:** Basketball, football (non-tackle), soccer, softball, volleyball. **Team name:** Crimson Storm.

Student services. Alcohol/substance abuse counseling, chaplain/spiritual director, career counseling, services for economically disadvantaged, student employment services, financial aid counseling, health services, personal counseling, placement for graduates. **Physically disabled:** Services for visually, speech, hearing impaired.

Contact. E-mail: lcantwell@snu.edu
Phone: (405) 491-6324 Toll-free number: (800) 648-9899
Fax: (405) 491-6320
Linda Cantwell, Director of Admissions, Southern Nazarene University, 6729 NW 39th Expressway, Bethany, OK 73008

Southwestern Christian University
Bethany, Oklahoma
www.swcu.edu   **CB code: 1433**

▶ Private 4-year university and liberal arts college affiliated with the Pentecostal Holiness Church

▶ Residential campus in large town

▶ 713 degree-seeking undergraduates: 25% African American, 1% Asian American, 8% Hispanic/Latino, 4% Native American, 1% Native Hawaiian/Pacific islander, 3% Multi-racial, non-Hispanic, 10% international

▶ 27 graduate students

▶ SAT or ACT with writing, application essay, interview required

General. Founded in 1946. Regionally accredited. Adult degree-completion program offered. Lockstep program allows for degree completion in 18 months or less. **Degrees:** 87 bachelor's, 7 associate awarded; master's offered. **Location:** 10 miles from Oklahoma City. **Calendar:** Semester, limited summer session. **Full-time faculty:** 16 total. **Part-time faculty:** 42 total.

Freshman class profile.

GPA 3.75 or higher:	5%	Rank in top tenth:	8%
GPA 3.50-3.74:	25%	Out-of-state:	4%
GPA 3.0-3.49:	32%	Live on campus:	48%
GPA 2.0-2.99:	36%	International:	17%
Rank in top quarter:	27%		

Basis for selection. 2.5 GPA or 19 ACT required. Additional materials and interview may be requested.

High school preparation. Required units include English 4, mathematics 2, social studies 2, history 2, science 2 (laboratory 2).

2015-2016 Annual costs. Tuition/fees: $15,630. Room/board: $6,200. Books/supplies: $1,400. Personal expenses: $880.

2014-2015 Financial aid. Need-based: Average need met was 82%. Average scholarship/grant was $7,208; average loan $3,321. 57% of total undergraduate aid awarded as scholarships/grants, 43% as loans/jobs. **Non-need-based:** Awarded to 345 full-time undergraduates, including 102 freshmen. Scholarships awarded for academics, alumni affiliation, music/drama, religious affiliation, ROTC.

Application procedures. Admission: No deadline. No application fee. Application must be submitted on paper. Admission notification on a rolling basis. **Financial aid:** Priority date 3/1; no closing date. FAFSA, institutional form required. Applicants notified on a rolling basis starting 4/1; must reply within 2 week(s) of notification.

Academics. Applied Biblical Leadership Education (ABLE), an adult studies completion program. **Special study options:** Combined bachelor's/graduate degree, distance learning, double major, dual enrollment of high school students, independent study, internships. **Credit/placement by examination:** AP, CLEP. 30 credit hours maximum toward bachelor's degree. **Support services:** Learning center, reduced course load, remedial instruction, tutoring.

Majors. Business: Business admin. **Education:** General. **English:** English lit. **History:** General. **Liberal arts:** Arts/sciences. **Parks/recreation:** Sports admin. **Philosophy/religion:** Religion. **Psychology:** General. **Theology:** Bible, missionary, pastoral counseling, sacred music, theology, youth ministry. **Visual/performing arts:** Music performance. **Work/family studies:** General.

Most popular majors. Business/marketing 18%, interdisciplinary studies 6%, parks/recreation 13%, philosophy/religious studies 19%, psychology 6%, public administration/social services 30%, theological studies 12%.

Technology on campus. 9 workstations in library. Dormitories wired for high-speed internet access and linked to campus network. Online library, wireless network available.

Student life. Freshman orientation: Mandatory. Preregistration for classes offered. Held the week prior to classes; includes academic, financial aid and spiritual life orientation. **Policies:** Extracurricular Christian programs and activities emphasized. Mandatory dress code. Students sign lifestyle covenant agreeing to certain behaviors. Religious observance required. **Housing:** Single-sex dorms available. $100 nonrefundable deposit, deadline 8/15. **Activities:** Campus ministries, choral groups, drama, music ensembles, musical theater, student government, Southwestern Ministerial Association, missionary society.

Athletics. NCCAA. **Intercollegiate:** Baseball M, basketball M, cross-country, golf M, soccer M, softball, volleyball W. **Intramural:** Baseball M, basketball, cheerleading, football (non-tackle) M, softball, table tennis, volleyball. **Team name:** Eagles.

Student services. Adult student services, chaplain/spiritual director, career counseling, student employment services, financial aid counseling, personal counseling, veterans' counselor.

Contact. E-mail: admissions@swcu.edu
Phone: (405) 789-7661 ext. 3442
Toll-free number: (888) 418-9272 ext. 3442 Fax: (405) 495-0078
Joe Blackwell, Director of Admissions, Southwestern Christian University, Box 340, Bethany, OK 73008

Southwestern Oklahoma State University
Weatherford, Oklahoma   **CB member**
www.swosu.edu   **CB code: 6673**

▶ Public 4-year university

▶ Residential campus in large town

▶ 4,348 degree-seeking undergraduates

▶ SAT or ACT (ACT writing optional) required

General. Founded in 1901. Regionally accredited. Campus at Sayre offers lower division and remedial courses, as well as associate degrees. **Degrees:** 626 bachelor's, 162 associate awarded; master's, professional offered. **Location:** 75 miles from Oklahoma City. **Calendar:** Semester, extensive summer session. **Full-time faculty:** 216 total; 64% have terminal degrees, 12% minority, 50% women. **Part-time faculty:** 66 total. **Class size:** 45% < 20, 40% 20-39, 8% 40-49, 7% 50-99.

Freshman class profile.

GPA 3.75 or higher:	30%	**Rank in top quarter:**	44%
GPA 3.50-3.74:	16%	**Rank in top tenth:**	20%
GPA 3.0-3.49:	30%	**Out-of-state:**	10%
GPA 2.0-2.99:	22%	**Live on campus:**	56%

Basis for selection. Bachelor degree programs require 19 ACT and no curricular deficiencies. Open admission for associate degree programs. Last date to submit test scores is first day of classes. Essay required for returning suspension students only.

High school preparation. College-preparatory program required. 15 units required; 17 recommended. Required and recommended units include English 4, mathematics 3, social studies 1, history 2, science 2 (laboratory 2), computer science 1 and academic electives 2-4. Social studies unit must be citizenship. Academic electives should be in fine arts. 3 units computer science or foreign language required.

2015-2016 Annual costs. Tuition/fees: $5,820; $12,270 out-of-state. Room/board: $5,220. Books/supplies: $1,230. Personal expenses: $996.

Financial aid. Non-need-based: Scholarships awarded for academics, alumni affiliation, art, athletics, leadership, music/drama, state residency.

Application procedures. Admission: No deadline. $15 fee. Admission notification on a rolling basis. **Financial aid:** Closing date 3/1. FAFSA, institutional form required. Applicants notified by 3/15.

Academics. Special study options: Accelerated study, combined bachelor's/graduate degree, distance learning, double major, independent study, internships, student-designed major, study abroad, teacher certification program. **Credit/placement by examination:** AP, CLEP, IB, ACT, institutional tests. 62 credit hours maximum toward bachelor's degree. **Support services:** Pre-admission summer program, reduced course load, remedial instruction, study skills assistance, tutoring, writing center.

Majors. Biology: General, biophysics. **Business:** General, accounting, business admin, human resources, management information systems. **Communications:** Communications/speech/rhetoric. **Computer sciences:** General, computer science, information systems. **Education:** Art, early childhood, elementary, English, health, history, learning disabled, mathematics, mentally handicapped, music, physical, science, social science, special ed, technology/industrial arts. **Engineering:** General, applied physics. **English:** English lit. **Health services:** Athletic training, clinical lab technology, health care admin, health information management, music therapy, nursing (RN). **History:** General. **Human services:** Social work. **Math:** General. **Parks/recreation:** General, facilities management. **Physical sciences:** Chemistry, physics. **Protective services:** Criminal justice. **Psychology:** General. **Social sciences:** Political science, sociology. **Theology:** Sacred music. **Visual/performing arts:** Commercial/advertising art, music, music management, music performance, music theory/composition, piano/keyboard, voice/opera.

Most popular majors. Business/marketing 17%, education 14%, health sciences 24%, parks/recreation 9%.

Technology on campus. 200 workstations in library, computer center. Dormitories wired for high-speed internet access. Commuter students can connect to campus network. Online library, wireless network available.

Student life. Freshman orientation: Mandatory, $60 fee. Preregistration for classes offered. **Housing:** Guaranteed on-campus for all undergraduates. Single-sex dorms, apartments available. $100 fully refundable deposit, deadline 8/1. **Activities:** Bands, campus ministries, choral groups, drama, international student organizations, literary magazine, music ensembles, Model UN, musical theater, opera, student government, student newspaper, symphony orchestra, seven religious organizations, four political organizations, and approximately 75 social and professional clubs.

Athletics. NCAA. **Intercollegiate:** Baseball M, basketball, cheerleading, cross-country W, football (tackle) M, golf, rodeo, soccer, softball W. **Intramural:** Basketball, bowling, football (non-tackle), golf, racquetball, soccer, softball, swimming, tennis, volleyball. **Team name:** Bulldogs.

Student services. Adult student services, alcohol/substance abuse counseling, career counseling, student employment services, financial aid counseling, health services, personal counseling, placement for graduates, veterans' counselor. **Physically disabled:** Services for visually, hearing impaired.

Contact. E-mail: admissions@swosu.edu
Phone: (580) 774-3009 Fax: (580) 774-3795
Todd Boyd, Director of Admissions, Southwestern Oklahoma State University, 100 Campus Drive, Weatherford, OK 73096

Spartan College of Aeronautics and Technology
Tulsa, Oklahoma
www.spartan.edu   CB code: 0336

◆ For-profit 4-year technical college
◆ Commuter campus in large city
◆ 849 undergraduates
◆ 374 graduate students
◆ Interview required

General. Founded in 1928. Accredited by ACCSC. Multi-campus institution with technical campuses at Tulsa International Airport and R.L Jones Airport in South Tulsa. **Degrees:** 39 bachelor's, 219 associate awarded. **Location:** Downtown. **Calendar:** Continuous, extensive summer session. **Full-time faculty:** 65 total; 2% have terminal degrees, 14% women. **Part-time faculty:** 34 total; 3% have terminal degrees, 12% women. **Class size:** 60% < 20, 40% 20-39.

Freshman class profile.

Out-of-state:	83%	**Live on campus:**	25%

Basis for selection. Applicants must demonstrate proficiency in college-level skills by submission of examination scores deemed appropriate for the chosen program of study. Students wishing to attend flight training must obtain FAA Class II flight certificate and pass TSA screening. SAT or ACT recommended. **Home schooled:** Statement describing home school structure and mission, transcript of courses and grades, state high school equivalency certificate, interview required. Any student graduating from a non-accredited high school must submit ACT/SAT.

2015-2016 Annual costs. Tuition/fees: $16,150. **Additional information:** Annual cost shown is for Aviation Maintenance Technology program. Full program costs vary by program ranging from $20,060 to $73,209.

Application procedures. Admission: No deadline. $100 fee. Admission notification on a rolling basis. **Financial aid:** No deadline. FAFSA, institutional form required. Applicants notified on a rolling basis starting 2/1; must reply within 2 week(s) of notification.

Academics. Special study options: Distance learning, independent study. **Credit/placement by examination:** AP, CLEP, institutional tests. No more than half of credits required for degree may be earned through examination. **Support services:** Remedial instruction, tutoring.

Technology on campus. 100 workstations in library, student center. Dormitories wired for high-speed internet access. Online library, wireless network available.

Student life. Freshman orientation: Mandatory. Preregistration for classes offered. Usually held on Friday immediately preceding start of classes. **Policies:** All students subject to random drug testing. **Housing:** Apartments, wellness housing available. **Activities:** Student government.

Student services. Career counseling, student employment services, financial aid counseling, personal counseling, placement for graduates, veterans' counselor.

Contact. E-mail: spartan@spartan.edu
Phone: (918) 836-6886 ext. 242
Toll-free number: (800) 331-1204 ext. 242 Fax: (918) 831-8609
Scott Murphy, Vice President Marketing, Spartan College of Aeronautics and Technology, 8820 East Pine Street, Tulsa, OK 74158-2833

St. Gregory's University
Shawnee, Oklahoma
www.stgregorys.edu   CB code: 6621

◆ Private 4-year university and liberal arts college affiliated with the Roman Catholic Church
◆ Residential campus in large town
◆ 580 degree-seeking undergraduates: 18% part-time, 57% women, 8% African American, 1% Asian American, 12% Hispanic/Latino, 10% Native American, 8% Multi-racial, non-Hispanic, 3% international
◆ 45 degree-seeking graduate students
◆ 61% of applicants admitted
◆ SAT or ACT (ACT writing optional), application essay required
◆ 45% graduate within 6 years

General. Founded in 1875. Regionally accredited. Roman Catholic and Benedictine tradition. **Degrees:** 137 bachelor's, 27 associate awarded; master's offered. **ROTC:** Air Force. **Location:** 30 miles from Oklahoma City. **Calendar:** Semester, limited summer session. **Full-time faculty:** 24 total. **Part-time faculty:** 149 total. **Class size:** 92% < 20, 8% 20-39. **Special facilities:** Benedictine abbey, art museum.

Freshman class profile. 382 applied, 234 admitted, 90 enrolled.

GPA 3.75 or higher:	21%	Rank in top quarter:	41%
GPA 3.50-3.74:	18%	Rank in top tenth:	18%
GPA 3.0-3.49:	35%	Return as sophomores:	50%
GPA 2.0-2.99:	25%		

Basis for selection. Core classes, GPA most important; test scores, class rank important. Interview required for students admitted on probation; audition required for dance, drama, and choral scholarships; portfolio required for art scholarships. **Home schooled:** Interview required. **Learning Disabled:** Students with need beyond ADA standards may apply to Partners in Learning Program. Additional fee of approximately $7,000 required if admitted.

High school preparation. 17 units recommended. Recommended units include English 4, mathematics 3, social studies 2, history 2, science 2 (laboratory 1) and foreign language 2.

2015-2016 Annual costs. Tuition/fees: $24,480. Books/supplies: $900. Personal expenses: $1,500.

2014-2015 Financial aid. Need-based: 90% of total undergraduate aid awarded as scholarships/grants, 10% as loans/jobs. **Non-need-based:** Scholarships awarded for academics, alumni affiliation, art, athletics, job skills, leadership, music/drama, religious affiliation.

Application procedures. Admission: Priority date 8/1; no deadline. No application fee. Admission notification on a rolling basis beginning on or about 9/1. **Financial aid:** Priority date 4/1; no closing date. FAFSA, institutional form required. Applicants notified on a rolling basis starting 2/15; must reply within 3 week(s) of notification.

Academics. Discussion-based seminars on Western and Catholic intellectual traditions required of all freshmen and sophomore students. Special accelerated programs for non-traditional students in Shawnee, Oklahoma City, and Tulsa. **Special study options:** Accelerated study, cross-registration, double major, dual enrollment of high school students, honors, independent study, internships. **Credit/placement by examination:** AP, CLEP, IB, SAT, ACT. 12 credit hours maximum toward associate degree, 30 toward bachelor's. Course proficiency exams available in areas where no CLEP exams offered. **Support services:** Remedial instruction, study skills assistance, tutoring.

Majors. Biology: General, biomedical sciences. **Business:** Accounting, business admin, finance. **Communications:** Communications/speech/rhetoric. **Education:** General, elementary, secondary. **English:** English lit. **Health services:** Nursing (RN). **History:** General. **Liberal arts:** Arts/sciences. **Math:** General. **Parks/recreation:** Exercise sciences. **Philosophy/religion:** Philosophy. **Physical sciences:** Chemistry. **Protective services:** Criminal justice. **Psychology:** General. **Social sciences:** General, political science. **Theology:** Pastoral counseling, theology. **Visual/performing arts:** General, art, dance.

Most popular majors. Business/marketing 54%, social sciences 13%, theological studies 9%.

Technology on campus. 35 workstations in computer center. Dormitories wired for high-speed internet access and linked to campus network. Online library, helpline, wireless network available.

Student life. Freshman orientation: Mandatory, $150 fee. Preregistration for classes offered. Three-day program held prior to start of fall term, plus evenings in first week of fall semester. **Policies:** Smoke-free; alcohol/drug-free; on-campus residency required under age 22. **Housing:** Guaranteed on-campus for freshmen. Single-sex dorms available. $100 fully refundable deposit. **Activities:** Campus ministries, choral groups, dance, drama, international student organizations, student government, Knights of Columbus, Fellowship of Christian Athletes, history club, student alumni council, Students in Free Enterprise, Hispanic awareness student association, human rights action committee, pro-life team.

Athletics. NAIA. **Intercollegiate:** Baseball M, basketball, cheerleading, cross-country, golf W, soccer, softball W, track and field, volleyball W. **Intramural:** Basketball, football (non-tackle), football (tackle) M, racquetball, soccer, softball, table tennis, tennis, volleyball. **Team name:** Cavaliers.

Student services. Adult student services, alcohol/substance abuse counseling, chaplain/spiritual director, career counseling, services for economically disadvantaged, student employment services, financial aid counseling, minority student services, personal counseling, placement for graduates, veterans' counselor.

Contact. E-mail: admissions@stgregorys.edu
Phone: (405) 878-5444 Toll-free number: (888) 784-7347
Fax: (405) 878-5198
Sean Brown, Assistant Director of Admissions, St. Gregory's University, 1900 West MacArthur Drive, Shawnee, OK 74804

University of Central Oklahoma
Edmond, Oklahoma — CB member
www.uco.edu — CB code: 6091

- Public 4-year university
- Commuter campus in small city
- 14,788 degree-seeking undergraduates: 29% part-time, 58% women, 9% African American, 3% Asian American, 9% Hispanic/Latino, 4% Native American, 9% Multi-racial, non-Hispanic, 7% international
- 1,754 degree-seeking graduate students
- 70% of applicants admitted
- SAT or ACT (ACT writing optional) required
- 39% graduate within 6 years

General. Founded in 1890. Regionally accredited. **Degrees:** 2,578 bachelor's, 58 associate awarded; master's offered. **ROTC:** Army. **Location:** 12 miles from Oklahoma City. **Calendar:** Semester, extensive summer session. **Full-time faculty:** 513 total; 78% have terminal degrees, 13% minority, 50% women. **Part-time faculty:** 598 total; 22% have terminal degrees, 15% minority, 57% women. **Class size:** 37% < 20, 55% 20-39, 6% 40-49, 1% 50-99, less than 1% >100. **Special facilities:** Jazz lab, boathouse, labyrinth, fine arts theater, museums, forensic science institute.

Freshman class profile. 5,122 applied, 3,581 admitted, 2,474 enrolled.

Mid 50% test scores		End year in good standing:	75%
ACT composite:	19-24	Return as sophomores:	62%
GPA 3.75 or higher:	24%	Out-of-state:	1%
GPA 3.50-3.74:	20%	Live on campus:	31%
GPA 3.0-3.49:	35%	International:	6%
GPA 2.0-2.99:	21%	Fraternities:	2%
Rank in top quarter:	35%	Sororities:	4%
Rank in top tenth:	11%		

Basis for selection. 2.7 GPA and rank in top 50% of class, or 2.7 GPA in 15 unit high school core curriculum, or 20 ACT required. **Home schooled:** Admissions based on ACT/SAT only. **Learning Disabled:** To receive services, students with disabilities who require accommodations must apply, with proper documentation, to the Disability Support Services Office.

High school preparation. College-preparatory program recommended. 15 units required; 21 recommended. Required and recommended units include English 4, mathematics 3-4, social studies 1, history 2-3, science 3 (laboratory 3), foreign language 2, computer science 1 and academic electives 2. 2 additional units of math, science, English, history or 2 units computer science and/or foreign language required.

2015-2016 Annual costs. Tuition/fees: $6,096; $14,972 out-of-state. Room/board: $7,470. Books/supplies: $1,200. Personal expenses: $5,346.

2014-2015 Financial aid. Need-based: Average need met was 62%. Average scholarship/grant was $6,867; average loan $3,125. 49% of total undergraduate aid awarded as scholarships/grants, 51% as loans/jobs. **Non-need-based:** Scholarships awarded for academics, alumni affiliation, art, athletics, leadership, minority status, music/drama, ROTC, state residency.

Application procedures. Admission: No deadline. $90 fee, may be waived for applicants with need. Admission notification on a rolling basis beginning on or about 4/1. **Financial aid:** Priority date 5/31; no closing date. FAFSA, institutional form required. Applicants notified on a rolling basis.

Academics. Special study options: Accelerated study, cooperative education, distance learning, double major, dual enrollment of high school students, ESL, independent study, internships, study abroad, teacher certification program, weekend college. **Credit/placement by examination:** AP, CLEP, ACT, institutional tests. 94 credit hours maximum toward bachelor's degree. **Support services:** Learning center, reduced course load, remedial instruction, tutoring, writing center.

Majors. Biology: General. **Business:** Accounting, actuarial science, apparel, business admin, finance, human resources, insurance, international, management information systems, managerial economics, marketing, nonprofit/public, operations, organizational leadership, selling. **Communications:** General, broadcast journalism, persuasive communications, photojournalism. **Computer sciences:** General, information technology. **Education:** General, art, biology, business, chemistry, curriculum, drama/dance, early childhood, educational technology, elementary, ESL, family/consumer sciences, French, German, health occupations, history, mathematics, music, physical, physics, reading, science, social studies, Spanish, special ed, technology/industrial arts. **Engineering:** Applied physics, biomedical, electrical, mechanical. **English:** Creative writing, English lit, rhetoric/composition, writing. **Foreign languages:** French, German, Spanish. **Health services:** Athletic training, audiology/speech pathology, clinical lab science, nursing (RN), occupational health, public health ed, speech pathology, substance abuse counseling. **History:** General. **Liberal arts:** Arts/sciences, humanities. **Math:** General, applied, statistics. **Parks/recreation:** General, exercise sciences. **Philosophy/religion:** Philosophy. **Physical sciences:** Chemistry, physics. **Protective services:** Corrections, criminal justice, forensics, juvenile corrections, law enforcement admin, police science. **Psychology:** General. **Social sciences:** Applied economics, economics, geography, political science, sociology, urban studies. **Visual/performing arts:** Art, art history/conservation, dance, dramatic, graphic design, interior design, music, music performance, piano/keyboard, stringed instruments, studio arts, theater design, voice/opera. **Work/family studies:** General, aging, child development, family systems, food/nutrition, human nutrition.

Most popular majors. Business/marketing 24%, communications/journalism 7%, education 9%, health sciences 10%, liberal arts 14%, security/protective services 6%.

Technology on campus. 839 workstations in dormitories, library, computer center, student center. Dormitories wired for high-speed internet access and linked to campus network. Commuter students can connect to campus network. Online course registration, online library, wireless network available.

Student life. Freshman orientation: Available, $50 fee. Preregistration for classes offered. Three-day orientation held the week before classes start in August. **Housing:** Coed dorms, single-sex dorms, apartments, fraternity/sorority housing, wellness housing available. $100 fully refundable deposit. **Activities:** Bands, campus ministries, choral groups, dance, drama, international student organizations, music ensembles, Model UN, musical theater, radio station, student government, student newspaper, symphony orchestra, TV station, Baptist Collegiate Ministry, Fellowship of Christian Athletes, Young Democrats, Collegiate Republicans, Black student association, President's Leadership Council, premed club, ethics clubs, marketing club, Asian American student association.

Athletics. NCAA. **Intercollegiate:** Baseball M, basketball, cheerleading, cross-country W, football (tackle) M, golf, rowing (crew) W, soccer W, softball W, tennis W, track and field W, volleyball W, wrestling M. **Intramural:** Badminton, baseball M, basketball, football (non-tackle), handball, soccer, softball, table tennis, tennis, ultimate frisbee, volleyball, water polo. **Team name:** Bronchos.

Student services. Alcohol/substance abuse counseling, career counseling, student employment services, financial aid counseling, health services, personal counseling, placement for graduates, veterans' counselor, women's services. **Physically disabled:** Services for visually, speech, hearing impaired.

Contact. E-mail: onestop@uco.edu
Phone: (405) 974-2727 Fax: (405) 974-3841
Dallas Caldwell, Director of Undergraduate Admissions, University of Central Oklahoma, 100 North University Drive, Edmond, OK 73034-0151

University of Oklahoma
Norman, Oklahoma
www.ou.edu

CB member
CB code: 6879

- Public 4-year university
- Residential campus in small city
- 21,525 degree-seeking undergraduates: 13% part-time, 50% women, 5% African American, 6% Asian American, 9% Hispanic/Latino, 4% Native American, 7% Multi-racial, non-Hispanic, 4% international
- 8,615 graduate students
- 78% of applicants admitted
- SAT or ACT (ACT writing optional), application essay required
- 70% graduate within 6 years

General. Founded in 1890. Regionally accredited. Faculty-in-residence program has faculty live in student dorms and mix with students. **Degrees:** 4,729 bachelor's awarded; master's, professional, doctoral offered. **ROTC:** Army, Naval, Air Force. **Location:** 20 miles from Oklahoma City, 200 miles from Dallas. **Calendar:** Semester, extensive summer session. **Full-time faculty:** 1,511 total; 85% have terminal degrees, 21% minority, 44%

women. **Part-time faculty:** 380 total; 57% have terminal degrees, 15% minority, 42% women. **Class size:** 43% < 20, 40% 20-39, 7% 40-49, 6% 50-99, 4% >100. **Special facilities:** Art museum, natural history museum, national weather center, national severe storms laboratory, biological station, history of science collection, western history collection, Oklahoma geological survey.

Freshman class profile. 12,002 applied, 9,318 admitted, 4,200 enrolled.

Mid 50% test scores			
SAT critical reading:	520-670	Rank in top quarter:	68%
SAT math:	540-670	Rank in top tenth:	37%
ACT composite:	24-29	Return as sophomores:	86%
GPA 3.75 or higher:	43%	Out-of-state:	40%
GPA 3.50-3.74:	26%	Live on campus:	87%
GPA 3.0-3.49:	28%	International:	3%
GPA 2.0-2.99:	3%	Fraternities:	33%
		Sororities:	41%

Basis for selection. All applicants evaluated using a holistic admission process which includes review of standardized test scores, secondary school records, responses to essay questions, leadership experience, and course rigor. ACT or SAT not required for first-time entering freshmen who are 21 years or older or are active duty military. Audition required for dance, drama and music programs, portfolio for art. **Learning Disabled:** Students must self-identify after admission and provide documentation to receive special services.

High school preparation. College-preparatory program required. 15 units required. Required and recommended units include English 4, mathematics 3-4, social studies 1, history 2, science 3-4 (laboratory 3), foreign language 2, computer science 1 and academic electives 2. Must have 1 U.S. history and 2 additional units from history, economics, geography, government, or non-western culture.

2015-2016 Annual costs. Tuition/fees: $10,090; $23,476 out-of-state. Room/board: $9,368. Books/supplies: $714. Personal expenses: $3,411.

2014-2015 Financial aid. Need-based: 2,809 full-time freshmen applied for aid; 1,831 deemed to have need; 1,788 received aid. Average need met was 76%. Average scholarship/grant was $6,662; average loan $3,597. 48% of total undergraduate aid awarded as scholarships/grants, 52% as loans/jobs. **Non-need-based:** Awarded to 7,129 full-time undergraduates, including 1,903 freshmen. Scholarships awarded for academics, alumni affiliation, art, athletics, leadership, music/drama, ROTC.

Application procedures. Admission: Priority date 12/15; deadline 2/1 (receipt date). $40 fee, may be waived for applicants with need. Admission notification on a rolling basis. Must reply by May 1 or within 3 week(s) if notified thereafter. Admitted applicants should reply as soon as possible. Financial commitment is not refundable after 5/1. Applicants encouraged to apply by scholarship deadline of 12/15. **Financial aid:** Priority date 3/1; no closing date. FAFSA required. Applicants notified on a rolling basis starting 3/15.

Academics. College of Liberal Studies, through distance learning, provides non-traditional students with interdisciplinary liberal arts programs. **Special study options:** Accelerated study, combined bachelor's/graduate degree, cooperative education, distance learning, double major, dual enrollment of high school students, ESL, external degree, honors, independent study, internships, liberal arts/career combination, semester at sea, student-designed major, study abroad, teacher certification program, Washington semester, weekend college. **Credit/placement by examination:** AP, CLEP, IB, SAT, ACT, institutional tests. Credit for prior work/life experience awarded according to recommendations of American Council on Education. Applicability of credits toward a degree vary depending on the college. Credit by examination may be counted toward bachelor's degree, but total number of hours that may be applied vary depending on college. **Support services:** Learning center, pre-admission summer program, remedial instruction, study skills assistance, tutoring, writing center.

Honors college/program. Must have 30 ACT or 1330 SAT AND rank in top 10% of high school class or have a 3.75 GPA. Approximately 500 freshmen are admitted each year.

Majors. Architecture: Architecture, environmental design. **Area/ethnic studies:** African-American, Native American, women's. **Biology:** Biochemistry, botany, microbiology, zoology. **Business:** Accounting, business admin, construction management, finance, management information systems, managerial economics, marketing, organizational behavior. **Communications:** Advertising, broadcast journalism, communications/speech/rhetoric, journalism. **Computer sciences:** Computer science, information systems. **Conservation:** Environmental science, environmental studies. **Education:** Early childhood, elementary, English, foreign languages, mathematics, music, science, social studies, special ed. **Engineering:** General, aerospace, applied physics, architectural, chemical, civil, computer, electrical, environmental, industrial, mechanical, petroleum. **English:** English lit. **Foreign languages:** Arabic, Chinese, classics, French, Germanic, Italian, Japanese, linguistics, Russian,

Spanish. **Health services:** Communication disorders, dental hygiene, facilities admin; medical radiologic technology/radiation therapy, nuclear medical technology, nursing (RN), sonography. **History:** General, science/technology. **Human services:** General, social work. **Liberal arts:** Arts/sciences, humanities. **Math:** General. **Parks/recreation:** Exercise sciences. **Philosophy/religion:** Judaic, philosophy, religion. **Physical sciences:** Astronomy, astrophysics, chemistry, geology, geophysics, meteorology, physics. **Protective services:** Law enforcement admin. **Psychology:** General. **Social sciences:** Anthropology, economics, geography, GIS/cartography, political science, sociology. **Visual/performing arts:** Art history/conservation, dance, design, dramatic, film/cinema/video, interior design, music, music pedagogy, musical theater, studio arts.

Most popular majors. Business/marketing 19%, communications/journalism 9%, engineering/engineering technologies 10%, health sciences 9%, interdisciplinary studies 8%, liberal arts 8%, social sciences 6%.

Technology on campus. 4,500 workstations in dormitories, library, computer center, student center. Dormitories wired for high-speed internet access and linked to campus network. Commuter students can connect to campus network. Online course registration, online library, helpline, repair service, student web hosting, wireless network available.

Student life. Freshman orientation: Mandatory. Preregistration for classes offered. Mid-May to the end of July with two half-day sessions everyday. Informational videos, assessment tests, academic advisor, course enrollment available. **Housing:** Guaranteed on-campus for freshmen. Coed dorms, single-sex dorms, special housing for disabled, apartments, fraternity/sorority housing available. Honors house, cultural housing, National Merit, scholastic floors and quiet lifestyle communities. **Activities:** Bands, campus ministries, choral groups, dance, drama, film society, international student organizations, literary magazine, music ensembles, Model UN, musical theater, opera, radio station, student government, student newspaper, symphony orchestra, TV station, American Indian student association, black student association, Hispanic American student association, Asian American student association, College Republicans, Young Democrats, Hillel Jewish student organization, Chi Alpha campus ministries, Muslim student association, Alpha Phi Omega.

Athletics. NCAA. **Intercollegiate:** Baseball M, basketball, cheerleading, cross-country, football (tackle) M, golf, gymnastics, rowing (crew) W, soccer W, softball W, tennis, track and field, volleyball W, wrestling M. **Intramural:** Badminton, basketball, cross-country, football (non-tackle), golf, racquetball, soccer, softball, table tennis, tennis, volleyball. **Team name:** Sooners.

Student services. Adult student services, alcohol/substance abuse counseling, career counseling, services for economically disadvantaged, student employment services, financial aid counseling, health services, legal services, minority student services, on-campus daycare, personal counseling, placement for graduates, veterans' counselor, women's services. **Physically disabled:** Services for visually, speech, hearing impaired.

Contact. E-mail: admrec@ou.edu
Phone: (405) 325-2151 Toll-free number: (800) 234-6868
Fax: (405) 325-7124
Jeff Blahnik, Director of Admissions, University of Oklahoma, 1000 Asp Avenue, Room 127, Norman, OK 73019-4076

University of Phoenix: Oklahoma City
Oklahoma City, Oklahoma
www.phoenix.edu

- For-profit 4-year university
- Very large city
- 428 undergraduates

General. Regionally accredited. **Degrees:** 147 bachelor's awarded; master's offered. **Calendar:** Differs by program. **Full-time faculty:** 9 total. **Part-time faculty:** 95 total.

Basis for selection. Open admission, but selective for some programs.

2015-2016 Annual costs. Per-credit-hour charge $395 to $635, depending upon level and course of study; electronic course materials fee range between $95-$200, if applicable. Book and material charges may vary by course and program. All fees are subject to change.

Application procedures. Admission: No deadline. No application fee. **Financial aid:** No deadline.

Academics. Credit/placement by examination: AP, CLEP.

Majors. Business: Accounting/business management, business admin, e-commerce, finance, human resources, marketing. **Computer sciences:** Database management, networking, programming, security, system admin, systems analysis. **English:** English lit. **Health services:** Facilities admin, nursing (RN). **Human services:** General. **Protective services:** Law enforcement admin.

Student life. Freshman orientation: Mandatory. Preregistration for classes offered.

Contact. Toll-free number: (866) 766-0766
University of Phoenix: Oklahoma City, 1625 W. Fountainhead Pkwy, Tempe, AZ 85282

University of Phoenix: Tulsa
Tulsa, Oklahoma
www.phoenix.edu

- For-profit 4-year university
- Large city
- 500 degree-seeking undergraduates
- 57 graduate students

General. Regionally accredited. **Degrees:** 64 bachelor's awarded; master's offered. **Calendar:** Differs by program. **Full-time faculty:** 11 total. **Part-time faculty:** 91 total.

Basis for selection. Open admission, but selective for some programs.

2015-2016 Annual costs. Per-credit-hour charge $395 to $635, depending upon level and course of study; electronic course materials fee $95/$200, if applicable. Book and material charges may vary by course and program. All fees are subject to change.

Application procedures. Admission: No deadline. No application fee. **Financial aid:** No deadline.

Academics. Credit/placement by examination: AP, CLEP.

Majors. Business: Accounting/business management, business admin, finance, human resources, marketing. **Computer sciences:** Database management, networking, programming, security, systems analysis, web page design, webmaster. **Conservation:** Environmental studies. **English:** English lit. **Health services:** Facilities admin, health information management, long term care admin. **Human services:** General. **Protective services:** Disaster management, law enforcement admin.

Student life. Freshman orientation: Mandatory. Preregistration for classes offered.

Contact. Toll-free number: (866) 766-0766
University of Phoenix: Tulsa, 1625 W. Fountainhead Pkwy, Tempe, AZ 85282

University of Science and Arts of Oklahoma
Chickasha, Oklahoma   CB member
www.usao.edu   CB code: 6544

- Public 4-year university and liberal arts college
- Residential campus in large town
- 845 degree-seeking undergraduates
- SAT or ACT (ACT writing optional) required

General. Founded in 1908. Regionally accredited. Offers trimester system classes, allowing for graduation in 3 years. **Degrees:** 171 bachelor's awarded. **Location:** 45 miles from Oklahoma City. **Calendar:** Trimester, extensive summer session. **Full-time faculty:** 55 total; 82% have terminal degrees, 13% minority, 54% women. **Part-time faculty:** 28 total; 14% have terminal degrees, 7% minority, 50% women. **Class size:** 74% < 20, 22% 20-39, 2% 40-49, 1% 50-99. **Special facilities:** Speech and hearing clinic, herbarium, child development center, school for the deaf, art gallery.

Freshman class profile.

GPA 3.75 or higher:	29%	Rank in top quarter:	49%
GPA 3.50-3.74:	18%	Rank in top tenth:	27%
GPA 3.0-3.49:	39%	Out-of-state:	3%
GPA 2.0-2.99:	14%		

Basis for selection. One of the following required: 24 ACT/1090 SAT with 3.0 GPA or ranking in top 50% of high school graduating class; 3.0

GPA with rank in top 25% of class; 3.0 GPA in core curriculum with 22 ACT/1020 SAT. All SAT scores exclusive of Writing. **Home schooled:** Transcript of courses and grades required.

High school preparation. College-preparatory program required. 15 units required; 19 recommended. Required and recommended units include English 4, mathematics 3-4, social studies 2, history 1, science 3 (laboratory 3-4), visual/performing arts 2 and academic electives 2. 2 units of fine arts, drama and/or speech recommended.

2015-2016 Annual costs. Tuition/fees: $6,570; $16,020 out-of-state. Room/board: $5,800. Books/supplies: $1,200. Personal expenses: $1,730.

Financial aid. Non-need-based: Scholarships awarded for academics, art, athletics, leadership, music/drama, state residency.

Application procedures. Admission: Closing date 9/2 (postmark date). $40 fee, may be waived for applicants with need, free for online applicants. Admission notification on a rolling basis beginning on or about 1/2. **Financial aid:** Priority date 3/1; no closing date. FAFSA required. Applicants notified on a rolling basis starting 3/1.

Academics. Special study options: Accelerated study, double major, dual enrollment of high school students, independent study, internships, student-designed major, study abroad, teacher certification program. Interdisciplinary studies. **Credit/placement by examination:** AP, CLEP, SAT, ACT, institutional tests. 62 credit hours maximum toward bachelor's degree. **Support services:** Learning center, pre-admission summer program, reduced course load, remedial instruction, study skills assistance, tutoring, writing center.

Majors. Area/ethnic studies: Native American. **Biology:** General. **Business:** Business admin. **Communications:** Communications/speech/rhetoric. **Education:** Deaf/hearing impaired, early childhood, elementary. **English:** English lit. **Health services:** Speech pathology. **History:** General. **Math:** General. **Parks/recreation:** Health/fitness. **Physical sciences:** Chemistry, physics. **Psychology:** General. **Social sciences:** Economics, political science, sociology. **Visual/performing arts:** Art, dramatic, music, studio arts.

Most popular majors. Business/marketing 22%, education 19%, health sciences 7%, history 12%, psychology 10%, visual/performing arts 9%.

Technology on campus. 174 workstations in dormitories, library, computer center, student center. Dormitories wired for high-speed internet access and linked to campus network. Online library, helpline, repair service, student web hosting, wireless network available.

Student life. Freshman orientation: Available, $25 fee. Preregistration for classes offered. Held the week prior to start of fall trimester. **Housing:** Guaranteed on-campus for freshmen. Coed dorms, special housing for disabled, apartments available. $200 nonrefundable deposit, deadline 5/1. **Activities:** Bands, campus ministries, choral groups, dance, drama, international student organizations, literary magazine, music ensembles, musical theater, student government, student newspaper, TV station, inter-tribal heritage club, student activities board, Chi Alpha, Colleges Against Cancer, gay straight alliance, NNSSLHA, Student National Education Association, university musicians, Young Democrats, Baptist collegiate ministries, Young Conservatives of Oklahoma.

Athletics. NAIA. **Intercollegiate:** Baseball M, basketball, cheerleading, cross-country, soccer, softball W. **Intramural:** Basketball, golf, softball M, volleyball. **Team name:** Drovers.

Student services. Alcohol/substance abuse counseling, career counseling, services for economically disadvantaged, student employment services, financial aid counseling, health services, minority student services, personal counseling, placement for graduates, veterans' counselor. **Physically disabled:** Services for visually, hearing impaired.

Contact. E-mail: usao-admissions@usao.edu
Phone: (405) 574-1357 Toll-free number: (800) 933-8726
Fax: (405) 574-1220
Monica Trevino, Director of Admissions, University of Science and Arts of Oklahoma, 1727 West Alabama, Chickasha, OK 73018-5322

University of Tulsa
Tulsa, Oklahoma

www.utulsa.edu

CB member
CB code: 6883

- Private 4-year university affiliated with the Presbyterian Church (USA)
- Residential campus in large city
- 3,452 degree-seeking undergraduates: 3% part-time, 42% women, 5% African American, 4% Asian American, 5% Hispanic/Latino, 3% Native American, 1% Multi-racial, non-Hispanic, 26% international

- 1,187 degree-seeking graduate students
- 44% of applicants admitted
- SAT or ACT (ACT writing optional) required
- 68% graduate within 6 years; 32% enter graduate study

General. Founded in 1894. Regionally accredited. **Degrees:** 675 bachelor's awarded; master's, professional, doctoral offered. **ROTC:** Air Force. **Location:** Downtown. **Calendar:** Semester, limited summer session. **Full-time faculty:** 344 total; 96% have terminal degrees, 17% minority, 33% women. **Part-time faculty:** 99 total; 96% have terminal degrees, 9% minority, 46% women. **Class size:** 61% < 20, 28% 20-39, 7% 40-49, 3% 50-99. **Special facilities:** Center for American research, center for the humanities, center for communicative disorders, tallgrass prairie preserve, institute of trauma, abuse, and neglect, hurricane motorworks, institute of nanotechnology, institute of bioinformatics and computational biology, institute of alternative energy, risk management center.

Freshman class profile. 6,762 applied, 2,973 admitted, 713 enrolled.

Mid 50% test scores		Rank in top tenth:	73%
SAT critical reading:	560-700	End year in good standing:	84%
SAT math:	570-700	Return as sophomores:	87%
ACT composite:	26-32	Out-of-state:	48%
GPA 3.75 or higher:	63%	Live on campus:	83%
GPA 3.50-3.74:	19%	International:	17%
GPA 3.0-3.49:	14%	Fraternities:	19%
GPA 2.0-2.99:	4%	Sororities:	21%
Rank in top quarter:	91%		

Basis for selection. Primary requirements are strong record of scholastic achievement and test scores. High school guidance counselor recommendation required. Extracurricular activities, community involvement, and talents considered. SAT and ACT are not required for international students. Essays and interviews strongly recommended for all; audition required for music, musical theater, and theater programs; portfolio required for art program. **Home schooled:** Statement describing home school structure and mission, transcript of courses and grades, letter of recommendation (nonparent) required.

High school preparation. College-preparatory program recommended. 18 units recommended. Recommended units include English 4, mathematics 4, social studies 3, science 3 (laboratory 3), foreign language 2, computer science 1 and visual/performing arts 1.

2015-2016 Annual costs. Tuition/fees: $38,906. Room/board: $10,630. Books/supplies: $1,200. Personal expenses: $3,016.

2015-2016 Financial aid. Need-based: 520 full-time freshmen applied for aid; 391 deemed to have need; 390 received aid. Average need met was 86%. Average scholarship/grant was $6,508; average loan $4,263. 56% of total undergraduate aid awarded as scholarships/grants, 44% as loans/jobs. **Non-need-based:** Awarded to 2,910 full-time undergraduates, including 694 freshmen. Scholarships awarded for academics, alumni affiliation, art, athletics, leadership, minority status, music/drama, religious affiliation, ROTC.

Application procedures. Admission: Priority date 2/1; no deadline. $50 fee, may be waived for applicants with need. Admission notification on a rolling basis beginning on or about 12/15. Must reply by May 1 or within 2 week(s) if notified thereafter. **Financial aid:** Priority date 3/1; no closing date. FAFSA required. Applicants notified on a rolling basis starting 3/1; must reply by 5/1 or within 2 week(s) of notification.

Academics. Special study options: Accelerated study, combined bachelor's/graduate degree, double major, ESL, honors, independent study, internships, liberal arts/career combination, student-designed major, study abroad, teacher certification program. **Credit/placement by examination:** AP, CLEP, IB, SAT, ACT, institutional tests. 36 credit hours maximum toward bachelor's degree. **Support services:** Learning center, reduced course load, study skills assistance, tutoring, writing center.

Majors. Area/ethnic studies: Chinese, Russian/Slavic, women's. **Biology:** General, biochemistry. **Business:** Accounting, business admin, finance, international, management information systems, marketing, organizational behavior. **Communications:** Communications/speech/rhetoric. **Computer sciences:** General, computer science, information technology, modeling/simulation. **Conservation:** Environmental studies. **Education:** Chemistry, Deaf/hearing impaired, early childhood, elementary, mathematics, music. **Engineering:** Applied physics, chemical, electrical, mechanical, petroleum. **English:** English lit. **Foreign languages:** Chinese, French, German, Spanish. **Health services:** Athletic training, audiology/speech pathology, communication disorders, nursing (RN). **History:** General. **Liberal arts:** Arts/sciences. **Math:** General, applied. **Parks/recreation:** Exercise sciences. **Philosophy/religion:** Philosophy, religion. **Physical sciences:** Chemistry, geology, geophysics, physics. **Psychology:** General. **Social sciences:** Anthropology, economics, political science, sociology. **Visual/performing arts:** Art, art history/conservation, dramatic, film/cinema/video, music, music performance, music theory/composition, piano/keyboard, studio arts management, voice/opera.

Most popular majors. Biology 6%, business/marketing 23%, engineering/engineering technologies 27%, health sciences 6%, visual/performing arts 6%.

Technology on campus. 728 workstations in dormitories, library, computer center. Dormitories wired for high-speed internet access and linked to campus network. Commuter students can connect to campus network. Online course registration, online library, helpline, student web hosting, wireless network available.

Student life. Freshman orientation: Available. Preregistration for classes offered. Held the week prior to fall term for the entire week. **Policies:** All first-year students are required to live in university residence halls and second-year students are required to live on campus and both must participate in a university-provided meal plan. Exemptions to this requirement are granted for students who live with parents or guardians within a 20-mile radius of campus. **Housing:** Guaranteed on-campus for freshmen. Coed dorms, single-sex dorms, special housing for disabled, apartments, fraternity/sorority housing, themed housing, wellness housing available. $250 partly refundable deposit, deadline 5/1. International living community, honors, and language houses available. **Activities:** Bands, campus ministries, choral groups, dance, drama, film society, international student organizations, literary magazine, music ensembles, musical theater, opera, radio station, student government, student newspaper, symphony orchestra, TV station, True Blue Neighbors, Muslim student association, Fellowship of Christian Athletes, Jewish student association, Young Democrats, women's law caucus, Hispanic student association, College Republicans, International Fellowship House, Association of Black Collegians.

Athletics. NCAA. **Intercollegiate:** Basketball, cheerleading, cross-country, football (tackle) M, golf, rowing (crew) W, soccer, softball W, tennis, track and field, volleyball W. **Intramural:** Badminton, basketball, bowling, cross-country, football (non-tackle), golf, racquetball, sand volleyball, soccer, softball, squash, table tennis, tennis, track and field, ultimate frisbee, volleyball, wrestling M. **Team name:** Golden Hurricane.

Student services. Adult student services, alcohol/substance abuse counseling, chaplain/spiritual director, career counseling, student employment services, financial aid counseling, health services, legal services, minority student services, personal counseling, placement for graduates, veterans' counselor, women's services. **Physically disabled:** Services for visually, speech, hearing impaired.

Contact. E-mail: admission@utulsa.edu
Phone: (918) 631-2307 Toll-free number: (800) 331-3050
Fax: (918) 631-5003
Casey Reed, Dean of Admission, University of Tulsa, Office of Admission, Tulsa, OK 74104-3189

Oregon

Art Institute of Portland
Portland, Oregon
http://new.artinstitutes.edu/portland   CB code: 4231

◊ For-profit 4-year visual arts and liberal arts college
◊ Commuter campus in large city
◊ 1,111 undergraduates
◊ Application essay, interview required

General. Founded in 1963. Regionally accredited. **Degrees:** 180 bachelor's, 29 associate awarded. **Calendar:** Quarter, extensive summer session. **Full-time faculty:** 33 total. **Part-time faculty:** 128 total. **Special facilities:** Specialized library, design laboratories, audio/visual laboratory.

Basis for selection. Proof of graduation from secondary school/GED required. Interview, essay, college transcripts, and/or English/math placement exam considered.

2015-2016 Annual costs. Tuition/fees: $21,695. Room only: $6,570. Books/supplies: $2,208. Personal expenses: $4,020.

Financial aid. Non-need-based: Scholarships awarded for art. **Additional information:** Applicants encouraged to apply early for financial aid. Scholarship deadlines range from January 1 to March 1.

Application procedures. Admission: No deadline. $50 fee. Admission notification on a rolling basis. **Financial aid:** Priority date 3/1; no closing date. FAFSA required. Applicants notified on a rolling basis starting 1/1; must reply within 5 week(s) of notification.

Academics. Special study options: Accelerated study, distance learning, honors, independent study, internships, liberal arts/career combination, study abroad. **Credit/placement by examination:** AP, CLEP, IB, SAT, ACT, institutional tests. Credit by examination only offered for courses in writing, computing, graphics, drawing, and math. **Support services:** Learning center, reduced course load, remedial instruction, study skills assistance, tutoring.

Majors. Business: Fashion. **Computer sciences:** Applications programming, computer graphics, web page design. **Visual/performing arts:** Art history/conservation, cinematography, commercial/advertising art, design, fashion design, graphic design, industrial design, interior design, multimedia, studio arts management.

Most popular majors. Computer/information sciences 24%, visual/performing arts 76%.

Technology on campus. 240 workstations in library, computer center. Dormitories wired for high-speed internet access. Commuter students can connect to campus network. Student web hosting, wireless network available.

Student life. Freshman orientation: Mandatory. Preregistration for classes offered. Held before each quarter-registration, advising and community services available. **Policies:** Student code of conduct published in catalog. No alcohol or drugs on campus or in housing. **Housing:** Special housing for disabled, apartments, wellness housing available. $250 partly refundable deposit. Apartments for 2 or 4 students available. **Activities:** Film society, student government, student newspaper.

Student services. Alcohol/substance abuse counseling, career counseling, student employment services, financial aid counseling, personal counseling, placement for graduates, veterans' counselor. **Physically disabled:** Services for visually, speech, hearing impaired.

Contact. E-mail: aipdadm@aii.edu
Phone: (503) 228-6528 Toll-free number: (888) 228-6528
Fax: (503) 227-1945
Hector Verdugo, Senior Director of Admissions, Art Institute of Portland, 1122 Northwest Davis Street, Portland, OR 97209-2911

Concordia University
Portland, Oregon
www.cu-portland.edu   CB member   CB code: 4079

◊ Private 4-year liberal arts and teachers college affiliated with the Lutheran Church - Missouri Synod
◊ Commuter campus in very large city
◊ 1,168 degree-seeking undergraduates: 13% part-time, 66% women, 5% African American, 5% Asian American, 6% Hispanic/Latino, 1% Native American, 1% Native Hawaiian/Pacific islander, 7% Multi-racial, non-Hispanic, 2% international
◊ 5,991 degree-seeking graduate students
◊ 51% of applicants admitted
◊ SAT or ACT (ACT writing optional) required
◊ 48% graduate within 6 years

General. Founded in 1905. Regionally accredited. **Degrees:** 282 bachelor's awarded; master's, professional offered. **ROTC:** Air Force. **Location:** 5 miles from downtown. **Calendar:** Semester, limited summer session. **Full-time faculty:** 69 total. **Part-time faculty:** 355 total. **Class size:** 58% < 20, 41% 20-39, less than 1% 40-49, 1% 50-99. **Special facilities:** Environmental research center, children's literature center, Shakespeare authorship research center.

Freshman class profile. 2,336 applied, 1,181 admitted, 197 enrolled.

Mid 50% test scores			
SAT critical reading:	430-550	GPA 2.0-2.99:	16%
SAT math:	430-550	Rank in top quarter:	44%
ACT composite:	19-24	Rank in top tenth:	16%
GPA 3.75 or higher:	34%	Return as sophomores:	74%
GPA 3.50-3.74:	22%	Out-of-state:	47%
GPA 3.0-3.49:	28%	Live on campus:	78%
		International:	2%

Basis for selection. 2.5 GPA, 480 SAT verbal, or 18 ACT required. **Home schooled:** Statement describing home school structure and mission, state high school equivalency certificate, letter of recommendation (nonparent) required. Interview may be required.

High school preparation. College-preparatory program recommended. 19 units recommended. Recommended units include English 4, mathematics 3, social studies 3, science 3, foreign language 2 and academic electives 3. One computer/keyboarding recommended.

2015-2016 Annual costs. Tuition/fees: $28,420. Room/board: $8,810. Books/supplies: $900. Personal expenses: $1,674.

2014-2015 Financial aid. Need-based: 187 full-time freshmen applied for aid; 149 deemed to have need; 149 received aid. Average scholarship/grant was $9,461; average loan $3,261. 60% of total undergraduate aid awarded as scholarships/grants, 40% as loans/jobs. **Non-need-based:** Awarded to 1,120 full-time undergraduates, including 239 freshmen. Scholarships awarded for academics, athletics, leadership, music/drama, religious affiliation.

Application procedures. Admission: Priority date 3/1; deadline 7/1 (postmark date). $40 fee, may be waived for applicants with need, free for online applicants. Admission notification on a rolling basis beginning on or about 1/1. Must reply by May 1 or within 2 week(s) if notified thereafter. Official high school transcripts, 2 letters of recommendation required. **Financial aid:** No deadline. FAFSA required. Applicants notified on a rolling basis starting 3/1.

Academics. Special study options: Accelerated study, cross-registration, distance learning, double major, dual enrollment of high school students, ESL, exchange student, honors, independent study, internships, liberal arts/career combination, semester at sea, student-designed major, study abroad, teacher certification program. **Credit/placement by examination:** AP, CLEP, institutional tests. **Support services:** Learning center, remedial instruction, tutoring, writing center.

Majors. Biology: General. **Business:** General, business admin, international. **Education:** General, biology, business, chemistry, early childhood, elementary, English, health, history, mathematics, middle, multi-level teacher, physical, science, secondary, social studies. **English:** English lit. **Health services:** Athletic training, health care admin, nursing (RN), premedicine. **History:** General. **Human services:** Social work. **Parks/recreation:** Health/fitness, sports admin. **Philosophy/religion:** Religion. **Physical sciences:** Chemistry. **Protective services:** Homeland security. **Psychology:** General. **Social sciences:** General. **Theology:** Religious ed, theology. **Visual/performing arts:** Music.

Most popular majors. Business/marketing 33%, education 15%, health sciences 21%, parks/recreation 6%.

Technology on campus. PC or laptop required. 100 workstations in dormitories, library, computer center, student center. Dormitories wired for high-speed internet access and linked to campus network. Commuter students can connect to campus network. Online course registration, online library, helpline, repair service, wireless network available.

Student life. Freshman orientation: Mandatory. Preregistration for classes offered. Usually held the day before classes begin. **Policies:** Optional attendance for chapel services. Lutheran format, mixture of traditional and contemporary services offered. **Housing:** Guaranteed on-campus for freshmen. Coed dorms, single-sex dorms, special housing for disabled, apartments, wellness housing available. $50 nonrefundable deposit, deadline 5/1. Homestay option for international students. **Activities:** Concert band, campus ministries, choral groups, drama, international student organizations, literary magazine, music ensembles, student government, student newspaper, Christian Life Ministries, Teacher Corps, Hawaii club, Invisible Children, missions club, multi-cultural club, ONE Voice, peace club, Stop Human Trafficking, world club.

Athletics. NAIA. **Intercollegiate:** Baseball M, basketball, cross-country, golf, soccer, softball W, track and field, volleyball W. **Intramural:** Basketball, bowling, football (non-tackle), soccer, softball, table tennis, tennis, ultimate frisbee, volleyball. **Team name:** Cavaliers.

Student services. Adult student services, alcohol/substance abuse counseling, chaplain/spiritual director, career counseling, financial aid counseling, health services, personal counseling, placement for graduates, veterans' counselor.

Contact. E-mail: admission@cu-portland.edu
Phone: (503) 280-8501 Toll-free number: (800) 321-9371
Fax: (503) 280-8531
Bobi Swan, Dean of Admission, Concordia University, 2811 Northeast Holman Street, Portland, OR 97211-6099

Corban University
Salem, Oregon
www.corban.edu   CB code: 4956

- Private 4-year liberal arts college affiliated with the Baptist faith
- Residential campus in small city
- 985 degree-seeking undergraduates: 5% part-time, 62% women
- 166 degree-seeking graduate students
- 31% of applicants admitted
- SAT or ACT (ACT writing recommended), application essay required
- 57% graduate within 6 years

General. Founded in 1935. Regionally accredited. **Degrees:** 194 bachelor's, 11 associate awarded; master's, doctoral offered. **ROTC:** Army, Air Force. **Location:** 45 miles from Portland. **Calendar:** Semester, limited summer session. **Full-time faculty:** 52 total; 75% have terminal degrees, 6% minority, 23% women. **Part-time faculty:** 63 total; 14% have terminal degrees, 43% women. **Class size:** 53% < 20, 35% 20-39, 10% 40-49, 2% 50-99, less than 1% >100. **Special facilities:** Archaeological museum.

Freshman class profile. 3,108 applied, 949 admitted, 275 enrolled.

Mid 50% test scores			
SAT critical reading:	480-600	GPA 3.0-3.49:	27%
SAT math:	460-560	GPA 2.0-2.99:	10%
SAT writing:	460-590	Rank in top quarter:	60%
ACT composite:	21-27	Rank in top tenth:	33%
GPA 3.75 or higher:	46%	Return as sophomores:	80%
GPA 3.50-3.74:	17%	Out-of-state:	57%
		Live on campus:	88%

Basis for selection. Commitment to Christianity, GPA, test scores, recommendations, essays, school and community activities considered. Audition required for music program. **Home schooled:** Transcript of courses and grades required.

High school preparation. College-preparatory program recommended. 14 units recommended. Recommended units include English 4, mathematics 3, social studies 3, science 2 and foreign language 2.

2015-2016 Annual costs. Tuition/fees: $29,640. Room/board: $9,240. Books/supplies: $900. Personal expenses: $1,500.

2014-2015 Financial aid. Need-based: 235 full-time freshmen applied for aid; 217 deemed to have need; 217 received aid. Average need met was 67%. Average scholarship/grant was $17,989; average loan $3,872. 76% of total undergraduate aid awarded as scholarships/grants, 24% as loans/jobs. **Non-need-based:** Awarded to 272 full-time undergraduates, including 75 freshmen. Scholarships awarded for academics, alumni affiliation, athletics,

leadership, music/drama, ROTC. **Additional information:** The Corban Promise is a policy to retire student debt. After graduation, students who work at least 30 hours a week with incomes below $37,000 will qualify for assistance which increases proportionately as income decreases. Incomes below $20,000 will be eligible for 100% reimbursement.

Application procedures. Admission: Closing date 8/1 (receipt date). $40 fee, may be waived for applicants with need. Admission notification on a rolling basis beginning on or about 12/1. **Financial aid:** Priority date 2/1; no closing date. FAFSA required. Applicants notified on a rolling basis starting 2/20.

Academics. Special study options: Accelerated study, combined bachelor's/graduate degree, distance learning, double major, dual enrollment of high school students, ESL, honors, independent study, internships, liberal arts/career combination, student-designed major, study abroad, teacher certification program, Washington semester. **Credit/placement by examination:** AP, CLEP, IB, institutional tests. 32 credit hours maximum toward associate degree, 32 toward bachelor's. **Support services:** Learning center, reduced course load, tutoring, writing center.

Majors. Business: Accounting, accounting/business management, business admin. **Communications:** Communications/speech/rhetoric, journalism. **Education:** Biology, elementary, English, history, mathematics, middle, multi-level teacher, music, physical, secondary, social studies. **English:** English lit. **History:** General. **Liberal arts:** Arts/sciences, humanities. **Math:** General. **Parks/recreation:** Health/fitness, sports admin. **Protective services:** Criminal justice. **Psychology:** General. **Theology:** Bible, missionary, pastoral counseling, religious ed, sacred music, theology, women's ministry, youth ministry. **Visual/performing arts:** Music, music performance.

Most popular majors. Business/marketing 27%, education 12%, English 6%, health sciences 6%, psychology 24%, theological studies 7%.

Technology on campus. Dormitories wired for high-speed internet access and linked to campus network. Commuter students can connect to campus network. Online library, helpline, repair service, wireless network available.

Student life. Freshman orientation: Mandatory. Preregistration for classes offered. **Policies:** Religious observance required. **Housing:** Guaranteed on-campus for freshmen. Single-sex dorms, apartments available. $100 nonrefundable deposit, deadline 8/1. **Activities:** Bands, campus ministries, choral groups, drama, film society, literary magazine, music ensembles, radio station, student government, student newspaper, Christian fellowships.

Athletics. NAIA, NCCAA. **Intercollegiate:** Baseball M, basketball, cross-country, golf, soccer, softball W, track and field, volleyball W. **Intramural:** Badminton, basketball, soccer, table tennis, ultimate frisbee. **Team name:** Warriors.

Student services. Adult student services, chaplain/spiritual director, career counseling, student employment services, financial aid counseling, personal counseling, placement for graduates. **Physically disabled:** Services for visually, hearing impaired.

Contact. E-mail: admissions@corban.edu
Phone: (503) 375-7005 Toll-free number: (800) 845-3005
Fax: (503) 585-4316
Heidi Stowman, Director of Undergraduate Admissions, Corban University, 5000 Deer Park Drive SE, Salem, OR 97317-9392

Eastern Oregon University
La Grande, Oregon   CB member
www.eou.edu   CB code: 4300

- Public 4-year university and liberal arts college
- Residential campus in large town
- 2,765 degree-seeking undergraduates: 37% part-time, 63% women
- 3,488 graduate students
- 97% of applicants admitted

General. Founded in 1929. Regionally accredited. **Degrees:** 703 bachelor's, 3 associate awarded; master's offered. **ROTC:** Army. **Location:** 260 miles from Portland; 180 miles from Boise, Idaho. **Calendar:** Quarter, limited summer session. **Full-time faculty:** 106 total; 76% have terminal degrees, 8% minority, 42% women. **Part-time faculty:** 6 total; 50% have terminal degrees, 83% women. **Class size:** 74% < 20, 22% 20-39, 1% 40-49, 3% 50-99. **Special facilities:** Wildlife habitat laboratory, agriculture experiment station.

Freshman class profile. 994 applied, 967 admitted, 325 enrolled.

Mid 50% test scores			
SAT critical reading:	420-530	GPA 3.0-3.49:	31%
SAT math:	420-520	GPA 2.0-2.99:	31%
SAT writing:	400-490	Rank in top quarter:	36%
ACT composite:	18-23	Rank in top tenth:	9%
GPA 3.75 or higher:	17%	Out-of-state:	29%
GPA 3.50-3.74:	19%	Live on campus:	61%

Basis for selection. Secondary school record most important; 2.75 GPA in 15 subject areas required. Students not meeting requirements must submit documents for individual review including essay and 2 letters of recommendation. Limited number of students not meeting requirements may be admitted. **Home schooled:** State high school equivalency certificate, letter of recommendation (nonparent) required. Applicants must present certificate of completion and portfolio including essay, letters of recommendation, standardized test scores.

High school preparation. College-preparatory program required. Required and recommended units include English 4, mathematics 3, social studies 3, science 3 (laboratory 1) and foreign language 2.

2015-2016 Annual costs. Tuition/fees: $7,756.5; $17,994 out-of-state. Room/board: $9,642. Books/supplies: $1,425. Personal expenses: $1,758.

Financial aid. Non-need-based: Scholarships awarded for academics, art, leadership, minority status, music/drama, state residency.

Application procedures. Admission: Priority date 2/1; deadline 9/1 (postmark date). No application fee. Admission notification on a rolling basis beginning on or about 10/1. **Financial aid:** Priority date 1/1; no closing date. FAFSA required. Applicants notified on a rolling basis starting 4/1; must reply within 4 week(s) of notification.

Academics. Regional advisers for distance education students. **Special study options:** Combined bachelor's/graduate degree, cooperative education, cross-registration, distance learning, double major, dual enrollment of high school students, exchange student, external degree, honors, independent study, internships, liberal arts/career combination, semester at sea, student-designed major, study abroad, teacher certification program, weekend college. **Credit/placement by examination:** AP, CLEP, IB, SAT, institutional tests. 45 credit hours maximum toward bachelor's degree. **Support services:** Learning center, study skills assistance, tutoring, writing center.

Majors. Biology: General, biomedical sciences. **Business:** General, business admin. **Communications:** Media studies. **Computer sciences:** General. **Education:** Health. **English:** English lit. **History:** General. **Human services:** General. **Liberal arts:** Arts/sciences. **Math:** General. **Parks/recreation:** Health/fitness. **Physical sciences:** Chemistry. **Protective services:** Fire services admin. **Psychology:** General. **Visual/performing arts:** Art, dramatic, music.

Most popular majors. Business/marketing 34%, education 12%, liberal arts 17%.

Technology on campus. 150 workstations in dormitories, library, computer center, student center. Dormitories wired for high-speed internet access and linked to campus network. Commuter students can connect to campus network. Online course registration, online library, helpline, repair service, wireless network available.

Student life. Freshman orientation: Available. Preregistration for classes offered. **Housing:** Guaranteed on-campus for freshmen. Coed dorms, apartments available. **Activities:** Bands, choral groups, dance, drama, international student organizations, literary magazine, music ensembles, musical theater, radio station, student government, student newspaper, symphony orchestra, international relations club, outdoor club, biology club, Fellowship of Christian Athletes, Latter-day Saints student association.

Athletics. NAIA. **Intercollegiate:** Basketball, cheerleading, cross-country, football (tackle) M, rodeo, soccer W, softball W, track and field, volleyball W. **Intramural:** Badminton, basketball, football (non-tackle), racquetball, softball, swimming, tennis, volleyball. **Team name:** Mountaineers.

Student services. Alcohol/substance abuse counseling, career counseling, financial aid counseling, health services, minority student services, personal counseling, placement for graduates, veterans' counselor, women's services. **Physically disabled:** Services for visually, hearing impaired.

Contact. E-mail: admissions@eou.edu
Phone: (541) 962-3393 Toll-free number: (800) 452-8639
Fax: (541) 962-3418
Gina Galaviz, Director of Admissions, Eastern Oregon University, One University Boulevard, La Grande, OR 97850

George Fox University
Newberg, Oregon
www.georgefox.edu

CB member
CB code: 4325

- Private 4-year university and seminary college affiliated with the Society of Friends (Quaker)
- Residential campus in large town
- 2,558 degree-seeking undergraduates: 8% part-time, 56% women, 2% African American, 4% Asian American, 11% Hispanic/Latino, 1% Native American, 6% Multi-racial, non-Hispanic, 4% international
- 1,224 degree-seeking graduate students
- 78% of applicants admitted
- SAT or ACT (ACT writing optional), application essay required
- 71% graduate within 6 years

General. Founded in 1891. Regionally accredited. Volunteer service encouraged through all-campus Serve Day and serve trips during school breaks. **Degrees:** 596 bachelor's awarded; master's, professional, doctoral offered. **ROTC:** Air Force. **Location:** 23 miles from Portland. **Calendar:** Semester, limited summer session. **Full-time faculty:** 195 total; 80% have terminal degrees, 9% minority, 42% women. **Part-time faculty:** 401 total; 2% have terminal degrees, 3% minority, 52% women. **Class size:** 63% < 20, 30% 20-39, 4% 40-49, 2% 50-99, less than 1% >100. **Special facilities:** Electron microscope, art galleries, creek canyon.

Freshman class profile. 3,001 applied, 2,346 admitted, 637 enrolled.

Mid 50% test scores			
SAT critical reading:	480-600	GPA 2.0-2.99:	11%
SAT math:	480-600	Rank in top quarter:	55%
SAT writing:	460-590	Rank in top tenth:	25%
ACT composite:	21-27	Return as sophomores:	80%
GPA 3.75 or higher:	44%	Out-of-state:	49%
GPA 3.50-3.74:	20%	Live on campus:	90%
GPA 3.0-3.49:	25%	International:	2%

Basis for selection. Decision based on grade transcript; test scores; recommendations from teacher and counselor; church, school, and community activities. Interview recommended for all; audition recommended for drama, music programs. **Home schooled:** Transcript of courses and grades, letter of recommendation (nonparent) required.

High school preparation. College-preparatory program recommended. 16 units recommended. Recommended units include English 4, mathematics 2, social studies 3, history 2, science 2 (laboratory 2) and foreign language 2. 1 unit health and physical education recommended.

2016-2017 Annual costs. Tuition/fees: $33,730. Room/board: $10,528. Books/supplies: $950. Personal expenses: $1,320.

Financial aid. Non-need-based: Scholarships awarded for academics, alumni affiliation, art, job skills, leadership, minority status, music/drama, religious affiliation. **Additional information:** Audition required for music and drama scholarships.

Application procedures. Admission: Priority date 2/1; no deadline. $40 fee, may be waived for applicants with need. Admission notification on a rolling basis beginning on or about 11/15. Must reply by May 1 or within 2 week(s) if notified thereafter. **Financial aid:** Priority date 2/1; no closing date. FAFSA required. Applicants notified on a rolling basis starting 3/1; must reply within 6 week(s) of notification.

Academics. Special study options: Accelerated study, cross-registration, distance learning, double major, dual enrollment of high school students, ESL, exchange student, honors, independent study, internships, New York semester, student-designed major, study abroad, teacher certification program, Washington semester. **Credit/placement by examination:** AP, CLEP, IB, SAT, ACT, institutional tests. 32 credit hours maximum toward bachelor's degree. **Support services:** Learning center, reduced course load, remedial instruction, study skills assistance, tutoring, writing center.

Honors college/program. Program specific application and writing sample required followed by on-campus interview. 30 freshmen admitted per year. The William Penn Honors Program is an alternative liberal arts general education program for undergraduate students. Modeled on the Socratic tutorial style, the program is designed to hone students' critical thinking skills by exposing them to classical texts and using discussion as the primary mode of instruction.

Majors. Biology: General. **Business:** Accounting/business management, business admin, entrepreneurial studies, finance, international, management information systems, marketing. **Communications:** Communications/speech/rhetoric, journalism, organizational. **Computer sciences:** General, information systems. **Education:** Elementary, music. **Engineering:** General, civil, computer, electrical, mechanical. **English:** English lit. **Foreign languages:** Spanish. **Health services:** Athletic training, nursing (RN). **History:** General. **Human services:** Social work. **Math:** General. **Parks/recreation:** Health/fitness. **Philosophy/religion:** Philosophy. **Physical sciences:** Chemistry. **Psychology:** General. **Social sciences:** Economics, political science, sociology. **Theology:** Bible. **Visual/performing arts:** Art, cinematography, dramatic, music. **Work/family studies:** General.

Most popular majors. Biology 8%, business/marketing 14%, engineering/ engineering technologies 6%, health sciences 11%, interdisciplinary studies 8%, psychology 6%, visual/performing arts 12%.

Technology on campus. 186 workstations in dormitories, library, computer center, student center. Dormitories wired for high-speed internet access and linked to campus network. Commuter students can connect to campus network. Online course registration, online library, helpline, repair service, wireless network available.

Student life. Freshman orientation: Mandatory. Preregistration for classes offered. Held for one day during summer. New students attend separate three-day program at the start of the semester. **Policies:** Three-year residency requirement for undergraduates. Required spiritual formation program and chapel program. Religious observance required. **Housing:** Single-sex dorms, special housing for disabled, apartments, themed housing, wellness housing available. Pets allowed in dorm rooms. Houses available. **Activities:** Bands, campus ministries, choral groups, drama, international student organizations, literary magazine, music ensembles, musical theater, radio station, student government, student newspaper, symphony orchestra, Christian services committee, Associated Student Community, international club, Young Life, Advance Leadership Development Program, Little Bruin, Urban Services, International Justice Mission, College Republicans, Young Democrats.

Athletics. NCAA. **Intercollegiate:** Baseball M, basketball, cross-country, football (tackle) M, golf, lacrosse W, soccer, softball W, tennis, track and field, volleyball W. **Intramural:** Badminton, basketball, football (non-tackle), golf, racquetball, skiing, soccer, table tennis, tennis, volleyball. **Team name:** Bruins.

Student services. Adult student services, alcohol/substance abuse counseling, chaplain/spiritual director, career counseling, student employment services, financial aid counseling, health services, minority student services, personal counseling, veterans' counselor. **Physically disabled:** Services for visually, speech, hearing impaired.

Contact. E-mail: admissions@georgefox.edu
Phone: (503) 554-2240 Toll-free number: (800) 765-4369 ext. 2240
Fax: (503) 554-3110
Lindsay Knox, Director of Undergraduate Admissions, George Fox University, 414 North Meridian Street #6089, Newberg, OR 97132-2697

Gutenberg College
Eugene, Oregon
www.gutenberg.edu
CB code: 2605

- Private 4-year liberal arts college
- Residential campus in small city
- 22 degree-seeking undergraduates
- SAT, application essay required

General. Regionally accredited; also accredited by TRACS. "Great Books" education from a biblical worldview. **Degrees:** 4 bachelor's awarded. **Calendar:** Quarter. **Full-time faculty:** 8 total. **Part-time faculty:** 2 total.

Basis for selection. Admissions decision based on application, essays, 2 references (academic and character), SAT, transcripts, and course of study. 2 written essays required.

2015-2016 Annual costs. Tuition/fees: $12,650. Books/supplies: $650. Personal expenses: $500.

Application procedures. Admission: Closing date 3/1 (postmark date). $40 fee. Application must be submitted on paper. Late applications after 3/1 may be considered; application fee is $60 for late applicants. **Financial aid:** Closing date 6/1.

Academics. Credit/placement by examination: AP, CLEP.

Majors. Liberal arts: Arts/sciences.

Technology on campus. 1 workstations in library, computer center. Dormitories linked to campus network. Commuter students can connect to campus network. Online library, helpline, repair service, wireless network available.

Student life. Freshman orientation: Mandatory. Preregistration for classes offered. **Housing:** Single-sex dorms available.

Contact. E-mail: admissions@gutenberg.edu
Phone: (541) 683-5141
Tim McIntosh, Director of Admissions, Gutenberg College, 1883 University Street, Eugene, OR 97403

ITT Technical Institute: Portland
Portland, Oregon
www.itt-tech.edu
CB code: 0947

- For-profit 4-year technical college
- Commuter campus in large city
- 365 undergraduates
- Interview required

General. Founded in 1979. Accredited by ACICS. **Degrees:** 41 bachelor's, 180 associate awarded. **Location:** 10 miles from downtown. **Calendar:** Quarter, extensive summer session. **Full-time faculty:** 18 total. **Part-time faculty:** 59 total.

Basis for selection. Satisfactory scores from on-site tests in English and math required.

2015-2016 Annual costs. Per-credit-hour charge, $493. Academic fee, $200. Some programs require purchase of tools, which could cost an additional $150 to $655. All costs subject to change.

Application procedures. Admission: No deadline. No application fee. Admission notification on a rolling basis. **Financial aid:** No deadline. FAFSA, institutional form required. Applicants notified on a rolling basis.

Academics. Credit/placement by examination: AP, CLEP. **Support services:** Learning center, tutoring.

Majors. Business: Business admin, construction management. **Communications technology:** Animation/special effects. **Computer sciences:** Security, system admin. **Protective services:** Law enforcement admin.

Technology on campus. Online library available.

Student life. Freshman orientation: Available. Preregistration for classes offered.

Student services. Career counseling, student employment services, placement for graduates.

Contact. Phone: (503) 255-6500 Toll-free number: (800) 234-5488
Fax: (503) 255-6500
Cliff Custer, Director of Recruitment, ITT Technical Institute: Portland, 9500 NE Cascades Parkway, Portland, OR 97220

Lewis & Clark College
Portland, Oregon
www.lclark.edu
CB member
CB code: 4384

- Private 4-year liberal arts college
- Residential campus in very large city
- 2,085 degree-seeking undergraduates: 62% women, 2% African American, 6% Asian American, 10% Hispanic/Latino, 1% Native American, 4% Multi-racial, non-Hispanic, 5% international
- 1,299 degree-seeking graduate students
- 63% of applicants admitted
- Application essay required
- 73% graduate within 6 years

General. Founded in 1867. Regionally accredited. **Degrees:** 568 bachelor's awarded; master's, professional offered. **ROTC:** Army. **Location:** 6 miles from Portland City Center. **Calendar:** Semester, limited summer session. **Full-time faculty:** 206 total; 86% have terminal degrees, 19% minority, 54% women. **Part-time faculty:** 204 total; 14% have terminal degrees, 17% minority, 54% women. **Class size:** 67% < 20, 30% 20-39, 2% 40-49, 1% 50-99, less than 1% >100. **Special facilities:** DIC and fluorescence microscopes, time-lapse deconvolution microscope, high-resolution oxygen analyzer, carbon dioxide gas exchange analyzer, end-point and real-time PCR equipment, multi-capacity lyophilizer, gel electrophoresis and imaging facilities, solar telescope with spectrograph, imaging laboratory with high resolution optical microscope, research astronomical observatory, holographic laboratory, electro-acoustic music studio, 85-rank Casavant organ, multi-media foreign language lab, human-computer interaction laboratory, climate-controlled greenhouse, GIS lab running ArcGIS for environmental research.

Freshman class profile. 7,368 applied, 4,629 admitted, 654 enrolled.

Mid 50% test scores			
SAT critical reading:	600-720	GPA 2.0-2.99:	2%
SAT math:	590-670	Rank in top quarter:	82%
SAT writing:	580-630	Rank in top tenth:	48%
ACT composite:	27-31	End year in good standing:	95%
GPA 3.75 or higher:	64%	Return as sophomores:	83%
GPA 3.50-3.74:	17%	Out-of-state:	91%
GPA 3.0-3.49:	17%	Live on campus:	98%
		International:	6%

Basis for selection. School curriculum and achievement most important. Standardized tests, recommendations, extracurricular involvement, essay, and interview also considered. Students may apply using Test-Optional Portfolio Path, where test scores are optional. In addition to the Common Application, Test-Optional Portfolio Path applicants submit 2 academic teacher recommendations and academic portfolio. Applicants may choose whether to submit standardized test scores. All other admission requirements remain the same. SAT or ACT required of first year (freshman) applicants unless student chooses to apply via portfolio path. Interviews optional. Audition required for music scholarships (in person or via recording). **Home schooled:** Statement describing home school structure and mission, letter of recommendation (nonparent) required. School's Test-Optional Portfolio Path for admissions recommended. Interview recommended.

High school preparation. College-preparatory program recommended. Recommended units include English 4, mathematics 4, social studies 3, science 3 (laboratory 2), foreign language 2 and visual/performing arts 1.

2015-2016 Annual costs. Tuition/fees: $45,104. Room/board: $11,314. Books/supplies: $1,050. Personal expenses: $1,062.

2015-2016 Financial aid. Need-based: 515 full-time freshmen applied for aid; 390 deemed to have need; 389 received aid. Average need met was 90%. Average scholarship/grant was $29,808; average loan $6,568. 76% of total undergraduate aid awarded as scholarships/grants, 24% as loans/jobs. **Non-need-based:** Awarded to 694 full-time undergraduates, including 252 freshmen. Scholarships awarded for academics, leadership, music/drama.

Application procedures. Admission: Priority date 1/15; deadline 3/1 (postmark date). No application fee. Application must be submitted online. Admission notification by 4/1. Must reply by May 1 or within 2 week(s) if notified thereafter. **Financial aid:** Priority date 2/15; no closing date. FAFSA, CSS PROFILE required. Applicants notified on a rolling basis starting 3/15; must reply by 7/1 or within 2 week(s) of notification.

Academics. Special study options: Cross-registration, double major, dual enrollment of high school students, ESL, exchange student, honors, independent study, internships, New York semester, student-designed major, study abroad, Washington semester. 3-2 engineering program with Columbia University, University of Southern California, Oregon Graduate Institute of Science and Engineering at OHSU, Washington University (St. Louis). **Credit/placement by examination:** AP, CLEP, IB, institutional tests. 32 credit hours maximum toward bachelor's degree. AP and IB will also consider the following types of advanced standing coursework for evaluation and potential credit award: British A Level (GCE-A), Caribbean Advanced Proficiency Examination (CAPE), French Baccalaureat, or other similar international examination. Official documentation should be submitted to the Office of the Registrar for review. **Support services:** Learning center, reduced course load, study skills assistance, tutoring, writing center.

Majors. Area/ethnic studies: General, Chicano/Hispanic-American/Latino, East Asian, French, German. **Biology:** General, biochemistry. **Communications:** Communications/speech/rhetoric. **Computer sciences:** Computer science. **Conservation:** Environmental studies. **English:** English lit. **Foreign languages:** General, classics. **History:** General. **Liberal arts:** Arts/sciences. **Math:** General. **Philosophy/religion:** Philosophy, religion. **Physical sciences:** Chemistry, physics. **Psychology:** General. **Social sciences:** Anthropology, economics, international relations, political science, sociology. **Visual/performing arts:** Art, dramatic, music, music theory/composition, studio arts.

Most popular majors. Area/ethnic studies 7%, biology 11%, English 6%, physical sciences 6%, psychology 15%, social sciences 18%, visual/performing arts 9%.

Technology on campus. 428 workstations in library, computer center, student center. Dormitories wired for high-speed internet access and linked to campus network. Commuter students can connect to campus network. Online course registration, online library, helpline, repair service, student web hosting, wireless network available.

Student life. Freshman orientation: Mandatory. Preregistration for classes offered. Held four-five days preceding first day of class for fall semester (late August). **Policies:** Students required to live on-campus for four semesters. Freshmen not permitted cars on campus. **Housing:** Guaranteed on-campus for freshmen. Coed dorms, single-sex dorms, apartments, gender-neutral housing, themed housing, wellness housing available. $500 nonrefundable deposit, deadline 5/1. **Activities:** Bands, campus ministries, choral groups, dance, drama, international student organizations, literary magazine, music ensembles, Model UN, musical theater, radio station, student government, student newspaper, symphony orchestra, Ray Warren Symposium on Race and Ethnic Studies, Black Student Union, Hawaii Club, International Students of Lewis & Clark, Multicultural Organization Seeking An Inclusive Community, Pluralism and Unity Board, Third Culture Kids, Students Engaged in Eco-Defense, Hillel, Interfaith Council.

Athletics. NCAA. **Intercollegiate:** Baseball M, basketball, cross-country, football (tackle) M, golf, rowing (crew), soccer W, softball W, swimming, tennis, track and field, volleyball W. **Intramural:** Badminton, basketball, cross-country, softball, swimming, table tennis, tennis, volleyball, water polo. **Team name:** Pioneers, Pios.

Student services. Alcohol/substance abuse counseling, chaplain/spiritual director, career counseling, services for economically disadvantaged, student employment services, financial aid counseling, health services, legal services, minority student services, personal counseling, veterans' counselor, women's services. **Physically disabled:** Services for visually, speech, hearing impaired.

Contact. E-mail: admissions@lclark.edu
Phone: (503) 768-7040 Toll-free number: (800) 444-4111
Fax: (503) 768-7055
Erica Johnson, Director of Admissions, Lewis & Clark College, 0615 SW Palatine Hill Road, Portland, OR 97219-7899

Linfield College

McMinnville, Oregon **CB member**
www.linfield.edu **CB code:** 4387

- Private 4-year nursing and liberal arts college affiliated with the American Baptist Churches in the USA
- Residential campus in large town
- 1,663 degree-seeking undergraduates: 2% part-time, 60% women, 2% African American, 5% Asian American, 13% Hispanic/Latino, 1% Native American, 1% Native Hawaiian/Pacific islander, 13% Multiracial, non-Hispanic, 3% international
- 94% of applicants admitted
- SAT or ACT (ACT writing optional), application essay required
- 63% graduate within 6 years; 13% enter graduate study

General. Founded in 1849. Regionally accredited. Students interested in nursing may begin on the McMinnville Campus and then complete the nursing program on the Portland Campus. If you have completed college coursework but not yet earned a degree, you may complete a bachelor's degree online through the Online and Continuing Education Program. Online and Continuing Education also offers shorter certificate programs as well as personal enrichment opportunities. **Degrees:** 372 bachelor's awarded. **ROTC:** Air Force. **Location:** 38 miles from Portland. **Calendar:** 4-1-4, limited summer session. **Full-time faculty:** 119 total; 92% have terminal degrees, 11% minority, 52% women. **Part-time faculty:** 85 total; 39% have terminal degrees, 8% minority, 51% women. **Class size:** 71% < 20, 25% 20-39, 2% 40-49, 2% 50-99. **Special facilities:** Cadaver lab, anthropology display, music technology lab, interactive writing laboratory, speaking center.

Freshman class profile. 2,083 applied, 1,955 admitted, 475 enrolled.

Mid 50% test scores			
SAT critical reading:	470-580	GPA 2.0-2.99:	7%
SAT math:	480-580	Rank in top quarter:	59%
SAT writing:	460-560	Rank in top tenth:	26%
ACT composite:	20-26	End year in good standing:	94%
GPA 3.75 or higher:	39%	Return as sophomores:	87%
GPA 3.50-3.74:	24%	Out-of-state:	54%
GPA 3.0-3.49:	30%	Live on campus:	95%
		International:	2%

Basis for selection. High school academic performance, writing sample, recommendations from teachers and counselors, and pre-college test results important. Non-academic community and school activities considered. Interview recommended. **Home schooled:** Transcript of courses and grades required. Home school supplement to the Common Application required.

High school preparation. College-preparatory program recommended. 17 units recommended. Recommended units include English 4, mathematics 4, social studies 3, science 3 and foreign language 2.

2015-2016 Annual costs. Tuition/fees: $38,654. Room/board: $11,410. Books/supplies: $900. Personal expenses: $1,070. **Additional information:** The room and board costs in 2015-2016 reflect board costs for entering first year students who will be required to attend January term.

2015-2016 Financial aid. Need-based: 440 full-time freshmen applied for aid; 380 deemed to have need; 380 received aid. Average need met was 81%. Average scholarship/grant was $28,864; average loan $3,633. 76% of total undergraduate aid awarded as scholarships/grants, 24% as loans/jobs. **Non-need-based:** Awarded to 1,494 full-time undergraduates, including 457 freshmen. Scholarships awarded for academics, leadership, minority status, music/drama.

Application procedures. Admission: Priority date 2/15; no deadline. No application fee. Must reply by May 1 or within 2 week(s) if notified thereafter. **Financial aid:** Priority date 2/1; no closing date. FAFSA required. Applicants notified on a rolling basis starting 4/1; must reply by 5/1 or within 2 week(s) of notification.

Academics. Special study options: Cross-registration, distance learning, double major, ESL, external degree, independent study, internships, liberal arts/career combination, semester at sea, student-designed major, study abroad, teacher certification program, Washington semester. Semester abroad programs at Linfield centers in Australia, Austria, China (Beijing and Hong Kong), Costa Rica, Ecuador, England, France, Ireland, Japan, Korea, Mexico, New Zealand, Norway, and Senegal; shorter term study abroad opportunities through one-month January term. **Credit/placement by examination:** AP, CLEP, IB, institutional tests. 30 credit hours maximum toward bachelor's degree. **Support services:** Learning center, reduced course load, study skills assistance, tutoring, writing center.

Majors. Area/ethnic studies: French, German, Japanese, Latin American/Caribbean. **Biology:** General, Biochemistry/molecular biology. **Business:** Accounting, business admin, finance, international, marketing. **Communications:** Communications/speech/rhetoric, intercultural, media studies. **Computer sciences:** Computer science. **Conservation:** Environmental studies. **Education:** Elementary, health, music, physical. **Engineering:** Applied physics. **English:** Creative writing, English lit, general lit. **Foreign languages:** French, German, Japanese, Spanish. **Health services:** Athletic training, nursing (RN). **History:** General. **Math:** General. **Parks/recreation:** Exercise sciences, health/fitness. **Philosophy/religion:** Philosophy, religion. **Physical sciences:** General, chemistry, physics. **Psychology:** General. **Social sciences:** Anthropology, economics, international relations, political science, sociology. **Visual/performing arts:** Art, design, dramatic, music, studio arts.

Most popular majors. Biology 7%, business/marketing 19%, communications/journalism 6%, education 11%, psychology 8%, social sciences 13%, visual/performing arts 7%.

Technology on campus. 209 workstations in dormitories, library, computer center. Dormitories wired for high-speed internet access and linked to campus network. Commuter students can connect to campus network. Online course registration, online library, helpline, repair service, student web hosting, wireless network available.

Student life. Freshman orientation: Mandatory. Preregistration for classes offered. Four-day program held at beginning of fall semester; includes advising, peer mentoring. **Policies:** All students required to live on-campus unless they are of senior standing, married, or living with parents locally. **Housing:** Guaranteed on-campus for all undergraduates. Coed dorms, single-sex dorms, special housing for disabled, apartments, fraternity/sorority housing, wellness housing available. **Activities:** Bands, campus ministries, choral groups, dance, drama, international student organizations, literary magazine, music ensembles, Model UN, musical theater, opera, radio station, student government, student newspaper, symphony orchestra, American Sign Language club, Asian American Alliance, black student union, Change Corps, Fellowship of Christian Athletes, Fusion (gay/straight alliance), Hawaiian club, Japanese club, meditation club, Movimiemto Estudiantil Chicano/a de Aztlan, Native American student association.

Athletics. NCAA. **Intercollegiate:** Baseball M, basketball, cross-country, football (tackle) M, golf, lacrosse W, soccer, softball, swimming, tennis, track and field, volleyball W. **Intramural:** Basketball, bowling, soccer, softball, volleyball. **Team name:** Wildcats.

Student services. Adult student services, alcohol/substance abuse counseling, chaplain/spiritual director, career counseling, student employment services, financial aid counseling, health services, minority student services, personal counseling, placement for graduates, veterans' counselor, women's services. **Physically disabled:** Services for visually, speech, hearing impaired.

Contact. E-mail: admission@linfield.edu
Phone: (503) 883-2213 Toll-free number: (800) 640-2287
Fax: (503) 883-2472
Lisa Knodle-Bragiel, Director of Admission, Linfield College, 900 Southeast Baker Street, McMinnville, OR 97128-6894

Marylhurst University
Marylhurst, Oregon
www.marylhurst.edu   **CB code: 0440**

- Private 4-year university and liberal arts college affiliated with the Roman Catholic Church
- Commuter campus in large town
- 503 degree-seeking undergraduates: 71% part-time, 73% women, 3% African American, 3% Asian American, 7% Hispanic/Latino, 1% Native American, 3% Multi-racial, non-Hispanic, 3% international
- 468 degree-seeking graduate students
- 100% of applicants admitted
- Application essay, interview required
- 40% graduate within 6 years

General. Founded in 1893. Regionally accredited. **Degrees:** 170 bachelor's awarded; master's offered. **Location:** 10 miles from Portland. **Calendar:** Quarter, extensive summer session. **Full-time faculty:** 43 total. **Part-time faculty:** 175 total. **Special facilities:** Art gym.

Freshman class profile. 5 applied, 5 admitted, 5 enrolled.

Basis for selection. Bachelor's programs with special requirements include all music degree programs and accelerated online degree programs.

2015-2016 Annual costs. Tuition/fees: $20,835. Books/supplies: $2,475. Personal expenses: $1,950.

2015-2016 Financial aid. Need-based: 4 full-time freshmen applied for aid; 4 deemed to have need; 4 received aid. Average need met was 63%. Average scholarship/grant was $9,359; average loan $3,791. 37% of total undergraduate aid awarded as scholarships/grants, 63% as loans/jobs. **Non-need-based:** Scholarships awarded for academics.

Application procedures. Admission: No deadline. $50 fee, may be waived for applicants with need. Admission notification on a rolling basis. **Financial aid:** Priority date 3/1; no closing date. FAFSA, institutional form required. Applicants notified on a rolling basis starting 5/1.

Academics. Special study options: Accelerated study, cooperative education, cross-registration, distance learning, double major, ESL, independent study, internships, liberal arts/career combination, student-designed major, study abroad, teacher certification program, weekend college. **Credit/placement by examination:** AP, CLEP, IB, institutional tests. 45 credit hours maximum toward bachelor's degree. **Support services:** Reduced course load, writing center.

Majors. Business: General, business admin, communications, real estate. **Communications:** General. **Conservation:** Environmental studies. **Health services:** Music therapy. **Liberal arts:** Arts/sciences. **Philosophy/religion:** Religion. **Psychology:** General. **Social sciences:** General. **Visual/performing arts:** Art, interior design, music, studio arts.

Most popular majors. Business/marketing 38%, communications/journalism 6%, English 10%, interdisciplinary studies 18%, psychology 9%, visual/performing arts 9%.

Technology on campus. Online course registration, online library, helpline, wireless network available.

Student life. Freshman orientation: Available. Preregistration for classes offered. **Activities:** Campus ministries, choral groups, literary magazine, music ensembles, student government, student newspaper.

Student services. Adult student services, career counseling, financial aid counseling, personal counseling, veterans' counselor. **Physically disabled:** Services for visually, speech, hearing impaired.

Contact. E-mail: admissions@marylhurst.edu
Phone: (503) 699-6268 Toll-free number: (800) 634-9982 ext. 6268
Fax: (503) 699-6320
Ryan Clark, Director of Admissions, Marylhurst University, PO Box 261, Marylhurst, OR 97036-0261

Mount Angel Seminary
St. Benedict, Oregon
www.mountangelabbey.org   **CB code: 4491**

- Private 4-year seminary college for men affiliated with the Roman Catholic Church
- Residential campus in small town

- 75 degree-seeking undergraduates
- 87% of applicants admitted

General. Founded in 1887. Regionally accredited; also accredited by ATS. All undergraduates candidates for Roman Catholic priesthood. **Degrees:** 13 bachelor's awarded; master's offered. **Location:** 40 miles from Portland. **Calendar:** Semester. **Full-time faculty:** 22 total. **Part-time faculty:** 12 total.

Freshman class profile. 15 applied, 13 admitted, 13 enrolled.

Out-of-state: 55% **Live on campus:** 100%

Basis for selection. Primarily recommendations from sponsoring dioceses or clergymen, personal interview important. Test scores considered. Interview recommended. **Home schooled:** State high school equivalency certificate required.

2015-2016 Annual costs. Tuition/fees: $16,789. Room/board: $11,422. Books/supplies: $900. Personal expenses: $1,000. **Additional information:** Formation fee of $3,787.

Application procedures. Admission: Closing date 7/1 (postmark date). $29 fee, may be waived for applicants with need. Admission notification on a rolling basis beginning on or about 7/31. **Financial aid:** Priority date 4/30, closing date 6/30. FAFSA, institutional form required. Applicants notified on a rolling basis; must reply within 2 week(s) of notification.

Academics. Special study options: Cross-registration, double major, ESL. Inter-divisional program, 3-week full-time pursuit of single approved course of study. **Credit/placement by examination:** AP, CLEP, institutional tests. **Support services:** Study skills assistance, tutoring, writing center.

Majors. Liberal arts: Arts/sciences. **Philosophy/religion:** Philosophy. **Theology:** Theology.

Technology on campus. 10 workstations in dormitories, library, computer center. Dormitories wired for high-speed internet access and linked to campus network. Online library, helpline, wireless network available.

Student life. Freshman orientation: Mandatory. Preregistration for classes offered. One-week program held the week before classes begin. **Policies:** All full-time students working toward priesthood required to live on campus. Religious observance required. **Housing:** Guaranteed on-campus for all undergraduates. **Activities:** Student government.

Athletics. Intramural: Basketball M, racquetball M, soccer M, swimming M, volleyball M.

Student services. Chaplain/spiritual director, financial aid counseling, health services, personal counseling.

Contact. Phone: (503) 845-3951 Fax: (503) 845-3128
Rev. Ralph Recker, Admissions Director, Mount Angel Seminary, One Abbey Drive, St. Benedict, OR 97373

Multnomah University
Portland, Oregon
www.multnomah.edu CB code: 4496

- Private 4-year university and seminary college affiliated with the inter-denominational tradition
- Residential campus in very large city
- 405 degree-seeking undergraduates: 17% part-time, 45% women, 4% African American, 2% Asian American, 9% Hispanic/Latino, 1% Native American, 1% Native Hawaiian/Pacific islander, 6% Multi-racial, non-Hispanic
- 322 degree-seeking graduate students
- 61% of applicants admitted
- Application essay required
- 56% graduate within 6 years

General. Founded in 1936. Regionally accredited; also accredited by ABHE. Emphasis on preparation for Christian ministries. **Degrees:** 138 bachelor's awarded; master's, doctoral offered. **Location:** 5 miles from downtown. **Calendar:** Continuous, limited summer session. **Full-time faculty:** 31 total; 58% have terminal degrees, 32% women. **Part-time faculty:** 63 total; 32% have terminal degrees, 29% women. **Class size:** 82% < 20, 17% 20-39, 1% 40-49.

Freshman class profile. 211 applied, 128 admitted, 62 enrolled.

Mid 50% test scores			
SAT critical reading:	440-600	GPA 3.0-3.49:	33%
SAT math:	430-580	GPA 2.0-2.99:	18%
SAT writing:	440-570	Rank in top quarter:	48%
ACT composite:	20-28	Rank in top tenth:	28%
GPA 3.75 or higher:	30%	Return as sophomores:	77%
GPA 3.50-3.74:	19%	Out-of-state:	47%
		Live on campus:	60%

Basis for selection. School achievement record, test scores, recommendations most important. SAT or ACT recommended. Not required for international students. **Home schooled:** If official transcript cannot be supplied, parental statement verifying student has met high school graduation requirements for home schoolers for their home state or GED test scores required.

High school preparation. College-preparatory program recommended. 14 units recommended. Required and recommended units include English 2-4, mathematics 3, social studies 3, science 2 (laboratory 1) and academic electives 2.

2016-2017 Annual costs. Tuition/fees: $23,680. Room/board: $7,820. Books/supplies: $1,000. Personal expenses: $3,200.

2014-2015 Financial aid. Need-based: 87 full-time freshmen applied for aid; 73 deemed to have need; 65 received aid. Average need met was 43%. Average scholarship/grant was $10,847; average loan $3,312. 58% of total undergraduate aid awarded as scholarships/grants, 42% as loans/jobs. **Non-need-based:** Awarded to 40 full-time undergraduates, including 9 freshmen. Scholarships awarded for academics, alumni affiliation, athletics.

Application procedures. Admission: Priority date 3/1; no deadline. $40 fee, may be waived for applicants with need. Admission notification on a rolling basis beginning on or about 9/1. **Financial aid:** Priority date 4/1, closing date 8/1. FAFSA required. Applicants notified on a rolling basis starting 3/1; must reply within 2 week(s) of notification.

Academics. Special study options: Double major, teacher certification program. **Credit/placement by examination:** AP, CLEP, IB, institutional tests. 20 credit hours maximum toward bachelor's degree. **Support services:** Learning center, reduced course load, study skills assistance, tutoring, writing center.

Majors. Education: Elementary. **English:** English lit. **Foreign languages:** Ancient Greek, Hebrew. **History:** General. **Psychology:** General. **Theology:** Bible, missionary, pastoral counseling, religious ed, sacred music, theology, youth ministry.

Most popular majors. Education 6%, foreign language 6%, psychology 12%, theological studies 65%.

Technology on campus. 42 workstations in dormitories, library, computer center, student center. Dormitories wired for high-speed internet access and linked to campus network. Commuter students can connect to campus network. Online course registration, online library, helpline, wireless network available.

Student life. Freshman orientation: Mandatory. Preregistration for classes offered. Held three days before start of classes. **Policies:** No alcohol, smoking, gambling. Religious observance required. **Housing:** Guaranteed on-campus for freshmen. Single-sex dorms, special housing for disabled, apartments available. $100 nonrefundable deposit, deadline 7/15. Houses for students with spouses or dependents available. **Activities:** Campus ministries, choral groups, student government.

Athletics. NCCAA. Intercollegiate: Basketball, cross-country, golf, soccer M, volleyball W. **Intramural:** Basketball, volleyball. **Team name:** Lions.

Student services. Chaplain/spiritual director, career counseling, student employment services, financial aid counseling, personal counseling, placement for graduates.

Contact. E-mail: admiss@multnomah.edu
Phone: (503) 251-6485 Toll-free number: (800) 275-4672
Fax: (503) 254-1268
Palmer Muntz, Director of Admissions, Multnomah University, 8435 Northeast Glisan Street, Portland, OR 97220

New Hope Christian College
Eugene, Oregon
www.newhope.edu CB code: 4274

- Private 4-year Bible college affiliated with the nondenominational tradition
- Residential campus in small city

- 137 degree-seeking undergraduates
- Application essay required

General. Founded in 1925. Regionally accredited; also accredited by ABHE. **Degrees:** 20 bachelor's awarded. **Location:** 100 miles from Portland. **Calendar:** Semester, limited summer session. **Full-time faculty:** 9 total; 44% have terminal degrees, 33% minority, 33% women. **Part-time faculty:** 16 total; 19% have terminal degrees, 12% minority, 38% women. **Class size:** 76% < 20, 18% 20-39, 4% 40-49, 2% 50-99. **Special facilities:** Pentecostal historical archives.

Freshman class profile.

GPA 3.75 or higher:	10%	Rank in top quarter:	25%
GPA 3.50-3.74:	20%	Rank in top tenth:	5%
GPA 3.0-3.49:	45%	Out-of-state:	40%
GPA 2.0-2.99:	25%		

Basis for selection. School achievement and activities, test scores, recommendations, personal essay most important. Religious affiliation or commitment important factor. **Home schooled:** Transcript of courses and grades required.

2015-2016 Annual costs. Tuition/fees: $17,530. Room/board: $6,100. Books/supplies: $900. Personal expenses: $2,052.

Financial aid. **Non-need-based:** Scholarships awarded for academics, art, athletics, job skills, leadership, music/drama, religious affiliation, state residency. **Additional information:** Some early acceptance awards possible for those admitted by May 15. Distance awards to those coming from over 1,000 miles away. Some awards for husbands and wives enrolled at same time.

Application procedures. **Admission:** Priority date 1/1; deadline 8/1 (receipt date). $35 fee. Admission notification on a rolling basis beginning on or about 10/1. **Financial aid:** Priority date 4/1, closing date 8/1. FAFSA, institutional form required. Applicants notified on a rolling basis starting 2/1; must reply within 4 week(s) of notification.

Academics. Transfer-track programs available in elementary education: first two years at college, final two-three years at other institutions. **Special study options:** Accelerated study, distance learning, double major, dual enrollment of high school students, independent study, internships. **Credit/placement by examination:** AP, CLEP, institutional tests. **Support services:** Reduced course load, remedial instruction, study skills assistance, tutoring.

Majors. **Business:** Business admin. **Philosophy/religion:** Christian, religion. **Theology:** Bible, missionary, pastoral counseling, religious ed, sacred music, theology, youth ministry.

Technology on campus. 18 workstations in dormitories, library, computer center, student center. Dormitories wired for high-speed internet access. Repair service available.

Student life. **Freshman orientation:** Mandatory. Preregistration for classes offered. Week-long program ends with camping retreat to mountains with fellow students and faculty. **Policies:** Students required to sign Code of Conduct agreement. Student ministry/community service required. Religious observance required. **Housing:** Guaranteed on-campus for freshmen. Single-sex dorms, apartments available. $150 fully refundable deposit, deadline 8/1. **Activities:** Campus ministries, choral groups, dance, drama, music ensembles, musical theater, student government, student newspaper.

Athletics. NCCAA. **Intramural:** Basketball, soccer, volleyball. **Team name:** Deacons.

Student services. Chaplain/spiritual director, student employment services, financial aid counseling, personal counseling, placement for graduates, veterans' counselor.

Contact. E-mail: admissions@newhope.edu
Phone: (541) 485-1780 Toll-free number: (800) 322-2638
Fax: (541) 343-5801
Crystie Rios, Director of Enrollment, New Hope Christian College, 2155 Bailey Hill Road, Eugene, OR 97405

Northwest Christian University
Eugene, Oregon
www.nwcu.edu   CB code: 4543

- Private 4-year university affiliated with the Christian Church (Disciples of Christ)
- Commuter campus in small city

- 528 degree-seeking undergraduates: 20% part-time, 60% women, 3% African American, 2% Asian American, 9% Hispanic/Latino, 3% Native American, 1% Native Hawaiian/Pacific islander, 3% Multi-racial, non-Hispanic
- 206 degree-seeking graduate students
- 68% of applicants admitted
- SAT or ACT (ACT writing recommended), application essay required
- 49% graduate within 6 years

General. Founded in 1895. Regionally accredited. Northwest Christian University is located in the city of Eugene, Oregon (population 159,000), approximately one hour from the Coast, one hour from the Cascade Mountains, and ninety minutes south of Portland. **Degrees:** 115 bachelor's, 2 associate awarded; master's offered. **Location:** 70 miles from Salem, 110 miles from Portland. **Calendar:** Semester, limited summer session. **Full-time faculty:** 26 total; 77% have terminal degrees, 15% minority, 50% women. **Part-time faculty:** 62 total; 11% minority, 47% women. **Class size:** 67% < 20, 32% 20-39, 2% 50-99.

Freshman class profile. 369 applied, 251 admitted, 84 enrolled.

Mid 50% test scores			
SAT critical reading:	460-540	GPA 3.50-3.74:	20%
SAT math:	450-540	GPA 3.0-3.49:	35%
SAT writing:	430-540	GPA 2.0-2.99:	20%
ACT composite:	19-23	Return as sophomores:	84%
GPA 3.75 or higher:	25%	Out-of-state:	28%
		Live on campus:	79%

Basis for selection. Overall grade performance; adherence to College Preparation Standards; content and difficulty of courses taken; standardized test scores; quality of involvement in applicant's church, community, and school activities important. Additional information may be requested, including updated transcripts, additional essays, and interview. Interview recommended, personal statement required. **Home schooled:** Transcript of courses and grades required. A minimum score of 21 on the ACT or a combined score of 1020 on the Math and Critical Reading sections of the SAT I is strongly encouraged. A minimum 2.50 grade point average (GPA) in all high school subjects taken toward graduation is also required. Transcripts prepared in conjunction with a diploma program through a local secondary school or by an agency that assesses home school curricula are preferred. If a conventional transcript is not available, a typed list of all home courses studied with grades assigned is acceptable. An official transcript must also be submitted from each high school or college from which classes have been taken.

High school preparation. College-preparatory program recommended. 14 units recommended. Recommended units include English 4, mathematics 3, social studies 3, science 2 (laboratory 1) and foreign language 2. Other university preparatory coursework such as computer literacy, humanities, and social science, combined with participation in art, drama, or music.

2015-2016 Annual costs. Tuition/fees: $27,490. Room/board: $8,600. Books/supplies: $900. Personal expenses: $1,170.

2015-2016 Financial aid. **Need-based:** 78 full-time freshmen applied for aid; 65 deemed to have need; 65 received aid. Average need met was 77%. Average scholarship/grant was $19,767; average loan $2,808. 62% of total undergraduate aid awarded as scholarships/grants, 38% as loans/jobs. **Non-need-based:** Awarded to 132 full-time undergraduates, including 42 freshmen. Scholarships awarded for academics, alumni affiliation, athletics, leadership, music/drama, religious affiliation.

Application procedures. **Admission:** Priority date 7/1; no deadline. No application fee. Admission notification on a rolling basis. **Financial aid:** Priority date 3/1; no closing date. FAFSA required. Applicants notified on a rolling basis starting 3/1; must reply within 2 week(s) of notification.

Academics. **Special study options:** Accelerated study, distance learning, double major, ESL, exchange student, independent study, internships, study abroad, teacher certification program. **Credit/placement by examination:** AP, CLEP, IB, SAT, ACT. No limit on credit by examination. **Support services:** Reduced course load, remedial instruction, study skills assistance, tutoring, writing center. Career development.

Majors. **Biology:** General, exercise physiology. **Business:** Accounting, business admin, marketing. **Communications:** General, communications/speech/rhetoric. **Education:** Elementary, multi-level teacher, secondary. **English:** English lit. **History:** General. **Math:** General. **Protective services:** Law enforcement admin. **Psychology:** General. **Theology:** Missionary, pastoral counseling, sacred music, youth ministry. **Visual/performing arts:** Music management, music technology.

Most popular majors. Biology 6%, business/marketing 36%, education 25%, interdisciplinary studies 7%, psychology 17%.

Technology on campus. 16 workstations in library. Dormitories wired for high-speed internet access and linked to campus network. Commuter

Four-Year Colleges

students can connect to campus network. Online library, helpline, repair service, wireless network available.

Student life. Freshman orientation: Mandatory. Preregistration for classes offered. Four-day program; includes excursion trip. **Policies:** Chapel attendance is required. Religious observance required. **Housing:** Guaranteed on-campus for freshmen. Single-sex dorms, apartments available. $100 fully refundable deposit, deadline 5/1. **Activities:** Pep band, campus ministries, choral groups, dance, literary magazine, music ensembles, student government, student newspaper, Parable, Circle K, Believers Building Bonds through Boardgames, community life groups.

Athletics. NAIA. Intercollegiate: Basketball, cross-country, golf, soccer, softball W, track and field, volleyball W. **Intramural:** Basketball, football (non-tackle) W, volleyball. **Team name:** Beacons.

Student services. Adult student services, alcohol/substance abuse counseling, chaplain/spiritual director, career counseling, student employment services, financial aid counseling, personal counseling, placement for graduates, veterans' counselor. **Physically disabled:** Services for hearing impaired.

Contact. E-mail: admissions@nwcu.edu
Phone: (541) 684-7201 Toll-free number: (877) 463-6622
Fax: (541) 684-7317
Kacie Gerdrum, Executive Director of Admissions, Northwest Christian University, 828 East 11th Avenue, Eugene, OR 97401-3745

Oregon College of Art & Craft
Portland, Oregon
www.ocac.edu

CB code: 4236

- Private 4-year visual arts college
- Commuter campus in very large city
- 111 degree-seeking undergraduates
- Application essay required

General. Regionally accredited. **Degrees:** 37 bachelor's awarded; master's offered. **Calendar:** Semester, limited summer session. **Full-time faculty:** 9 total; 100% have terminal degrees, 22% minority, 56% women. **Part-time faculty:** 25 total; 96% have terminal degrees, 60% women. **Class size:** 97% < 20, 3% 20-39. **Special facilities:** Galleries and gift shop.

Freshman class profile.

GPA 3.75 or higher:	46%	Rank in top quarter:	60%
GPA 3.50-3.74:	28%	Rank in top tenth:	27%
GPA 3.0-3.49:	10%	Out-of-state:	68%
GPA 2.0-2.99:	16%	Live on campus:	55%

Basis for selection. Talent and ability, GPA, essay, interview, letters of recommendation, and test scores are all considered. SAT or ACT recommended. Portfolio required. **Home schooled:** Statement describing home school structure and mission required.

High school preparation. Recommended units include English 4, mathematics 3, social studies 1, history 3, science 3, foreign language 2 and visual/performing arts 4.

2015-2016 Annual costs. Tuition/fees: $28,730. Books/supplies: $1,400. Personal expenses: $1,000.

Financial aid. Non-need-based: Scholarships awarded for academics, art.

Application procedures. Admission: No deadline. $35 fee, may be waived for applicants with need. Admission notification on a rolling basis beginning on or about 1/1. Must reply by May 1 or within 4 week(s) if notified thereafter. **Financial aid:** Priority date 3/1; no closing date. FAFSA required. Applicants notified on a rolling basis starting 3/1.

Academics. Special study options: Cross-registration, exchange student, independent study, internships. **Credit/placement by examination:** AP, CLEP, IB, institutional tests. **Support services:** Study skills assistance, tutoring.

Majors. Visual/performing arts: Ceramics, crafts, drawing, fiber arts, metal/jewelry, painting, photography.

Technology on campus. 15 workstations in library, computer center. Dormitories wired for high-speed internet access. Helpline, wireless network available.

Student life. Freshman orientation: Mandatory, $20 fee. Preregistration for classes offered. A pre-event and one full day of orientation, followed by "first week" events. **Housing:** Coed dorms available. $150 nonrefundable

deposit, deadline 5/15. Small number of on-campus housing units available for first-time freshman, students from out of the area, and those under 21. **Activities:** Film society, student government.

Student services. Career counseling, student employment services, financial aid counseling, personal counseling.

Contact. E-mail: admissions@ocac.edu
Phone: (971) 255-4192 Toll-free number: (800) 390-0632
Fax: (503) 297-9651
Anne Boerner, Chief Enrollment Officer and Director of Admissions, Oregon College of Art & Craft, 8245 SW Barnes Road, Portland, OR 97225-6349

Oregon Health & Science University
Portland, Oregon
www.ohsu.edu

CB member
CB code: 4900

- Public 3-year university and health science college
- Commuter campus in very large city
- 827 degree-seeking undergraduates: 75% part-time, 85% women, 5% Asian American, 9% Hispanic/Latino, 4% Multi-racial, non-Hispanic, 1% international
- 2,036 degree-seeking graduate students

General. Founded in 1887. Regionally accredited. Primarily a transfer institution. We do not have first time, full-time, freshmen. **Degrees:** 354 bachelor's awarded; master's, professional, doctoral offered. **Calendar:** Quarter, limited summer session.

Basis for selection. Admission requirements vary by program.

2015-2016 Annual costs. Tuition/fees: $21,345; $34,620 out-of-state, Books/supplies: $900. **Additional information:** Tuition shown is for new 2015-2016 undergraduate nursing program; costs for other programs vary. The Required Fees amount includes student health insurance since it is required for all students.

2015-2016 Financial aid. Need-based: 21% of total undergraduate aid awarded as scholarships/grants, 79% as loans/jobs.

Application procedures. Admission: Closing date 1/15 (postmark date). $120 fee, may be waived for applicants with need. Application must be submitted online. Admission notification on a rolling basis. Must reply by 5/1. **Financial aid:** No deadline.

Academics. Special study options: Accelerated study, combined bachelor's/graduate degree, distance learning, dual enrollment of high school students. **Credit/placement by examination:** AP, CLEP. **Support services:** Pre-admission summer program, study skills assistance, tutoring.

Majors. Health services: Clinical lab science, EMT paramedic, medical radiologic technology/radiation therapy, nursing (RN).

Technology on campus. 60 workstations in library, computer center, student center. Commuter students can connect to campus network. Online library, helpline, wireless network available.

Student life. Freshman orientation: Mandatory. Preregistration for classes offered. Orientation varies by program. **Activities:** Student government, student newspaper.

Athletics. Intramural: Basketball, soccer, swimming, table tennis, tennis, volleyball.

Student services. Alcohol/substance abuse counseling, career counseling, financial aid counseling, health services, minority student services, on-campus daycare, personal counseling.

Contact. E-mail: proginfo@ohsu.edu
Phone: (503) 494-7800 Toll-free number: (800) 775-5460
Fax: (503) 494-4629
Tami Buedefeldt, Manager for the Office of Admission, Oregon Health & Science University, 3181 SW Sam Jackson Park Road, Portland, OR 97239-3098

Oregon Institute of Technology
Klamath Falls, Oregon
www.oit.edu

CB member
CB code: 4587

- Public 4-year career college
- Commuter campus in small city

- 3,446 degree-seeking undergraduates
- 41 graduate students
- SAT or ACT with writing required

General. Founded in 1947. Regionally accredited. Upper-division courses offered in electronics engineering technology, manufacturing engineering technology. Software engineering technology offered at OIT Portland West in Beaverton area. **Degrees:** 595 bachelor's, 67 associate awarded; master's offered. **Location:** 280 miles from Portland; 270 miles from Reno, Nevada. **Calendar:** Quarter, limited summer session. **Full-time faculty:** 134 total; 8% minority, 40% women. **Part-time faculty:** 113 total; 8% minority, 34% women. **Class size:** 54% < 20, 38% 20-39, 4% 40-49, 4% 50-99. **Special facilities:** Center for research on geothermal energy, renewable energy center, center for health professions.

Freshman class profile.

GPA 3.75 or higher:	28%	Rank in top quarter:	51%
GPA 3.50-3.74:	20%	Rank in top tenth:	23%
GPA 3.0-3.49:	39%	Out-of-state:	9%
GPA 2.0-2.99:	13%	Live on campus:	57%

Basis for selection. Secondary school record and standardized test scores very important. Class rank, recommendations, essay, interview, character/personal qualities and work experience all considered. Applicants from nonstandard or unaccredited high schools must take 3 SAT Subject Tests: 1 English, 1 math, 1 other of student's choice. **Learning Disabled:** Tech opportunities available.

High school preparation. College-preparatory program required. 14 units required. Required units include English 4, mathematics 3, social studies 3, science 2 (laboratory 1) and foreign language 2.

2015-2016 Annual costs. Tuition/fees: $8,839; $24,826 out-of-state. Room/board: $8,530. Books/supplies: $1,000. Personal expenses: $2,438.

Financial aid. Non-need-based: Scholarships awarded for academics, athletics, leadership.

Application procedures. Admission: Priority date 2/1; deadline 10/1. $50 fee, may be waived for applicants with need. Admission notification on a rolling basis beginning on or about 10/15. Must reply by May 1 or within 4 week(s) if notified thereafter. Housing deposit refundable in full if received by deadline; $100 refundable if cancellation received in writing by 7/15; not refundable if received after 7/15. Application deadline for dual enrollment is 3 weeks before term starts. **Financial aid:** Priority date 2/1; no closing date. FAFSA required. Applicants notified on a rolling basis starting 4/1.

Academics. Special study options: Combined bachelor's/graduate degree, cooperative education, cross-registration, distance learning, double major, dual enrollment of high school students, external degree, internships, liberal arts/career combination, study abroad. **Credit/placement by examination:** AP, CLEP, SAT, ACT, institutional tests. No more than 25% of credits submitted for graduation may be credit by examination. **Support services:** Learning center, reduced course load, remedial instruction, study skills assistance, tutoring.

Majors. Biology: General. **Business:** Accounting, management information systems, marketing, operations, small business admin. **Communications:** Communications/speech/rhetoric. **Computer sciences:** Information technology. **Conservation:** Environmental science. **Engineering:** Civil, electrical, mechanical. **Health services:** Clinical lab science, dental hygiene, health care admin, health information management, nuclear medical technology, radiologic technology/medical imaging, respiratory therapy technology, sonography. **Math:** Applied. **Psychology:** General.

Most popular majors. Business/marketing 7%, computer/information sciences 6%, engineering/engineering technologies 35%, health sciences 41%.

Technology on campus. 656 workstations in dormitories, library, computer center. Dormitories wired for high-speed internet access. Commuter students can connect to campus network. Online course registration, online library, helpline, repair service, student web hosting, wireless network available.

Student life. Freshman orientation: Mandatory. Preregistration for classes offered. **Housing:** Coed dorms available. $150 deposit, deadline 5/1. **Activities:** Pep band, choral groups, radio station, student government, student newspaper, symphony orchestra, TV station, Newman club, Latter-day Saints, Christian Fellowship, Native American club, international student club, Circle K, Latin American club, residence hall association, Phi Delta Theta, College Republicans.

Athletics. NAIA. **Intercollegiate:** Baseball M, basketball, cross-country, soccer W, softball W, track and field, volleyball W. **Intramural:** Basketball, cheerleading, cross-country, football (tackle) M, lacrosse M, soccer, softball, track and field, volleyball. **Team name:** Owls.

Student services. Adult student services, alcohol/substance abuse counseling, career counseling, student employment services, financial aid counseling, health services, personal counseling, placement for graduates, veterans' counselor. **Physically disabled:** Services for visually, hearing impaired.

Contact. E-mail: oit@oit.edu
Phone: (541) 885-1150 Toll-free number: (800) 422-2017
Fax: (541) 885-1024
Ginny Gardiner, Director of Admissions, Oregon Institute of Technology, 3201 Campus Drive, Klamath Falls, OR 97601

Oregon State University
Corvallis, Oregon — **CB member**
www.oregonstate.edu — **CB code: 4586**

- Public 4-year university
- Residential campus in small city
- 23,656 degree-seeking undergraduates: 24% part-time, 46% women, 1% African American, 7% Asian American, 9% Hispanic/Latino, 1% Native American, 7% Multi-racial, non-Hispanic, 6% international
- 4,050 degree-seeking graduate students
- 78% of applicants admitted
- SAT or ACT with writing, application essay required
- 64% graduate within 6 years

General. Founded in 1868. Regionally accredited. **Degrees:** 4,803 bachelor's awarded; master's, professional, doctoral offered. **ROTC:** Army, Naval, Air Force. **Location:** 80 miles from Portland, 45 miles from Eugene. **Calendar:** Quarter, extensive summer session. **Full-time faculty:** 1,161 total; 87% have terminal degrees, 16% minority, 37% women. **Part-time faculty:** 460 total; 56% have terminal degrees, 12% minority, 54% women. **Class size:** 28% < 20, 42% 20-39, 8% 40-49, 13% 50-99, 9% >100. **Special facilities:** Arboretum, 13,429-acre forest, radiation center (with TRIGA Mark II Nuclear Reactor), wave research facility, marine science center museum and aquarium.

Freshman class profile. 14,058 applied, 11,016 admitted, 3,593 enrolled.

Mid 50% test scores			
SAT critical reading:	480-610	Rank in top quarter:	54%
SAT math:	490-630	Rank in top tenth:	24%
SAT writing:	470-590	End year in good standing:	92%
ACT composite:	21-28	Return as sophomores:	85%
GPA 3.75 or higher:	40%	Out-of-state:	23%
GPA 3.50-3.74:	22%	Live on campus:	91%
GPA 3.0-3.49:	33%	International:	1%
GPA 2.0-2.99:	5%	Fraternities:	11%
		Sororities:	17%

Basis for selection. Secondary school record, GPA, essay most important. Students not meeting admission requirements may petition for exception. Students with a GED must have achieved an average score of at least 580 with no subtest score less than 410. Applicants admitted on basis of GED not required to submit SAT/ACT. **Home schooled:** 1540 SAT (including Writing) or 23 ACT; average of 470 with minimum total of 940 on two SAT Subject Tests (Math Level I or II required plus second test of student's choice).

High school preparation. College-preparatory program required. 15 units required. Required and recommended units include English 4, mathematics 3, social studies 3, science 3 (laboratory 2-3) and foreign language 2.

2015-2016 Annual costs. Tuition/fees: $10,107.33; $28,767.33 out-of-state. Room/board: $12,156. Books/supplies: $1,950. Personal expenses: $2,484.

2014-2015 Financial aid. Need-based: 2,950 full-time freshmen applied for aid; 2,038 deemed to have need; 2,018 received aid. Average need met was 67%. Average scholarship/grant was $7,265; average loan $3,749. 42% of total undergraduate aid awarded as scholarships/grants, 58% as loans/jobs. **Non-need-based:** Awarded to 2,793 full-time undergraduates, including 687 freshmen. Scholarships awarded for academics, alumni affiliation, athletics, job skills, leadership, minority status, ROTC, state residency.

Application procedures. Admission: Priority date 2/1; deadline 6/1. $60 fee. Admission notification on a rolling basis beginning on or about 10/15. Must reply by May 1 or within 3 week(s) if notified thereafter. **Financial aid:** Priority date 2/28; no closing date. FAFSA required. Applicants notified on a rolling basis starting 4/1; must reply within 4 week(s) of notification.

Academics. Special study options: Accelerated study, combined bachelor's/graduate degree, cooperative education, cross-registration, distance learning, double major, dual enrollment of high school students, ESL, exchange student, honors, independent study, internships, liberal arts/career combination, student-designed major, study abroad, teacher certification program. **Credit/placement by examination:** AP, CLEP, IB, institutional tests.

Support services: Learning center, remedial instruction, study skills assistance, tutoring.

Majors. Area/ethnic studies: General, American, women's. **Biology:** General, Biochemistry/molecular biology, biotechnology, botany, microbiology, zoology. **Business:** Accounting, business admin, finance, hospitality admin, management information systems, marketing, operations, R&D management. **Communications:** Communications/speech/rhetoric, digital media. **Computer sciences:** Computer science. **Conservation:** Environmental science, fisheries, management/policy, wildlife/wilderness, wood science. **Education:** General. **Engineering:** Agricultural, applied physics, biomedical, chemical, civil, computer, construction, electrical, environmental, forest, industrial, manufacturing, mechanical, nuclear. **English:** English lit. **Foreign languages:** French, German, Spanish. **Health services:** Environmental health, physics/radiologic health. **History:** General. **Liberal arts:** Arts/sciences. **Math:** General. **Parks/recreation:** General, exercise sciences. **Philosophy/religion:** Philosophy, religion. **Physical sciences:** Chemistry, physics. **Psychology:** General. **Social sciences:** General, anthropology, economics, political science, sociology. **Visual/performing arts:** General, art, design, interior design, music. **Work/family studies:** Clothing/textiles, family studies, food/nutrition, merchandising.

Most popular majors. Agriculture 7%, biology 6%, business/marketing 13%, engineering/engineering technologies 15%, family/consumer sciences 10%, health sciences 6%, natural resources/environmental science 6%, social sciences 6%.

Technology on campus. 2,179 workstations in dormitories, library, computer center, student center. Dormitories wired for high-speed internet access and linked to campus network. Commuter students can connect to campus network. Online course registration, online library, helpline, repair service, student web hosting, wireless network available.

Student life. Freshman orientation: Mandatory. Preregistration for classes offered. 2-day orientation, advising, and registration program with sessions offered June through September. Program for parents and family members offered. **Policies:** Incoming freshmen required to live on campus during their first year. OSU is a smoke-free campus. **Housing:** Guaranteed on-campus for freshmen. Coed dorms, special housing for disabled, apartments, fraternity/sorority housing, gender-neutral housing, themed housing available. **Activities:** Bands, campus ministries, choral groups, dance, drama, film society, international student organizations, literary magazine, music ensembles, Model UN, musical theater, opera, radio station, student government, student newspaper, symphony orchestra, TV station, 253 student organizations, 47 student honor and recognition societies.

Athletics. NCAA. **Intercollegiate:** Baseball M, basketball, cheerleading, cross-country W, football (tackle) M, golf, gymnastics W, rowing (crew), soccer, softball W, swimming W, track and field W, volleyball W, wrestling M. **Intramural:** Badminton, basketball, bowling, cross-country, football (tackle) M, golf, racquetball, skiing, soccer, softball, swimming, tennis, track and field, volleyball, water polo, wrestling M. **Team name:** Beavers.

Student services. Adult student services, alcohol/substance abuse counseling, career counseling, services for economically disadvantaged, student employment services, financial aid counseling, health services, legal services, minority student services, on-campus daycare, personal counseling, placement for graduates, veterans' counselor, women's services. **Physically disabled:** Services for visually, speech, hearing impaired.

Contact. E-mail: osuadmit@oregonstate.edu
Phone: (541) 737-4411 Toll-free number: (800) 291-4192
Fax: (541) 737-2482
Noah Buckley, Director of Admissions, Oregon State University, 104 Kerr Administration Building, Corvallis, OR 97331-2130

Pacific Northwest College of Art
Portland, Oregon
www.pnca.edu
CB code: 4504

♦ Private 4-year visual arts college
♦ Commuter campus in very large city
♦ 399 degree-seeking undergraduates: 8% part-time, 69% women, 1% African American, 3% Asian American, 6% Hispanic/Latino, 1% Native American, 12% Multi-racial, non-Hispanic, 2% international
♦ 94 degree-seeking graduate students
♦ 81% of applicants admitted
♦ Application essay required

General. Founded in 1909. Regionally accredited. **Degrees:** 73 bachelor's awarded; master's offered. **Calendar:** Semester, limited summer session. **Full-time faculty:** 33 total; 58% have terminal degrees, 15% minority, 48% women. **Part-time faculty:** 75 total; 43% have terminal degrees, 5% minority,

52% women. **Class size:** 97% < 20, 3% 20-39. **Special facilities:** Contemporary craft museum, student art galleries, printmaking center, individual studio spaces for seniors.

Freshman class profile. 295 applied, 238 admitted, 70 enrolled.

Return as sophomores:	68%	Live on campus:	81%
Out-of-state:	69%	International:	3%

Basis for selection. Portfolio, essays important. 2.0 GPA recommended for academic courses. Greater emphasis on portfolio. **Home schooled:** Statement describing home school structure and mission, transcript of courses and grades, state high school equivalency certificate, letter of recommendation (nonparent) required. SAT/ACT exam recommended.

High school preparation. College-preparatory program recommended. Recommended units include English 4, mathematics 3, social studies 3 and science 3. Visual arts classes recommended.

2015-2016 Annual costs. Tuition/fees: $33,120. Room only: $8,772. Books/supplies: $1,000. Personal expenses: $2,000.

Financial aid. Non-need-based: Scholarships awarded for academics, art.

Application procedures. Admission: Priority date 2/15; no deadline. $45 fee. Admission notification on a rolling basis. Must reply by May 1 or within 4 week(s) if notified thereafter. **Financial aid:** Priority date 3/1; no closing date. FAFSA required. Applicants notified on a rolling basis starting 4/1; must reply by 5/1 or within 4 week(s) of notification.

Academics. Thesis required during senior year. **Special study options:** Cooperative education, cross-registration, dual enrollment of high school students, exchange student, independent study, internships, New York semester, student-designed major, study abroad. 5-year BA/BFA program with Reed College. **Credit/placement by examination:** AP, CLEP. **Support services:** Learning center, study skills assistance, tutoring, writing center.

Majors. Visual/performing arts: Digital arts, graphic design, illustration, multimedia, painting, photography, printmaking, sculpture, studio arts.

Technology on campus. 233 workstations in dormitories, library, computer center, student center. Dormitories wired for high-speed internet access and linked to campus network. Commuter students can connect to campus network. Online course registration, online library, helpline, wireless network available.

Student life. Freshman orientation: Available, $50 fee. Preregistration for classes offered. Held during the week prior to the start of Fall and Spring semester. **Housing:** Guaranteed on-campus for freshmen. Coed dorms available. $450 partly refundable deposit, deadline 6/15. Pets allowed in dorm rooms. **Activities:** Film society, student government.

Student services. Career counseling, financial aid counseling, personal counseling.

Contact. E-mail: admissions@pnca.edu
Phone: (503) 821-8972 Fax: (503) 821-8978
Jean Hester, Director of Admissions, Pacific Northwest College of Art, 511 NW Broadway, Portland, OR 97209

Pacific University
Forest Grove, Oregon
www.pacificu.edu
CB code: 4601

♦ Private 4-year university affiliated with the United Church of Christ
♦ Residential campus in large town
♦ 1,884 degree-seeking undergraduates: 1% part-time, 60% women, 2% African American, 12% Asian American, 13% Hispanic/Latino, 1% Native American, 3% Native Hawaiian/Pacific islander, 12% Multi-racial, non-Hispanic, 2% international
♦ 1,825 degree-seeking graduate students
♦ 79% of applicants admitted
♦ SAT or ACT (ACT writing optional), application essay required
♦ 71% graduate within 6 years

General. Founded in 1849. Regionally accredited. Branch campuses in Hillsboro, Portland, and Eugene for selected professional programs. **Degrees:** 379 bachelor's awarded; master's, professional, doctoral offered. **ROTC:** Army, Air Force. **Location:** 25 miles from Portland. **Calendar:** Semester, limited summer session. **Full-time faculty:** 271 total; 88% have terminal degrees, 16% minority, 52% women. **Part-time faculty:** 143 total; 15% have terminal degrees, 13% minority, 61% women. **Class size:** 60% < 20, 35% 20-39, 2% 40-49, 3% 50-99, less than 1% >100. **Special facilities:** Permaculture project, wildlife refuge, performing arts center, arboretum, center for Internet studies, English language institute, humanitarian center, institute for ethics and social policy, center for gender equity.

Freshman class profile. 3,004 applied, 2,374 admitted, 479 enrolled.

Mid 50% test scores		Rank in top quarter:	66%
SAT critical reading:	490-590	Rank in top tenth:	34%
SAT math:	500-600	Return as sophomores:	77%
ACT composite:	21-26	Out-of-state:	63%
GPA 3.75 or higher:	42%	Live on campus:	94%
GPA 3.50-3.74:	24%	International:	1%
GPA 3.0-3.49:	27%	Fraternities:	8%
GPA 2.0-2.99:	7%	Sororities:	8%

Basis for selection. Strength of high school program, GPA, test scores, course selection, interview most important. 1000 SAT (exclusive of Writing) plus 3.0 GPA recommended. Recommendation, essay, extracurricular activities, leadership involvement also important. Audition required for music program; portfolio recommended for art program. **Home schooled:** Statement describing home school structure and mission, transcript of courses and grades, state high school equivalency certificate, interview, letter of recommendation (nonparent) required.

High school preparation. College-preparatory program recommended. 21 units recommended. Recommended units include English 4, mathematics 3, social studies 3, history 1, science 3 (laboratory 1), foreign language 2 and academic electives 4.

2016-2017 Annual costs. Tuition/fees: $41,054. Room/board: $11,822. Books/supplies: $1,050. Personal expenses: $960.

2015-2016 Financial aid. **Need-based:** 447 full-time freshmen applied for aid; 393 deemed to have need; 393 received aid. Average need met was 77%. Average scholarship/grant was $11,440; average loan $4,341. 73% of total undergraduate aid awarded as scholarships/grants, 27% as loans/jobs. **Non-need-based:** Awarded to 1,687 full-time undergraduates, including 463 freshmen. Scholarships awarded for academics, alumni affiliation, art, music/drama.

Application procedures. **Admission:** Priority date 2/15; deadline 8/15. $40 fee, may be waived for applicants with need. Admission notification on a rolling basis beginning on or about 11/1. Must reply by May 1 or within 2 week(s) if notified thereafter. **Financial aid:** Priority date 3/1; no closing date. FAFSA required. Applicants notified on a rolling basis starting 3/15.

Academics. **Special study options:** Accelerated study, combined bachelor's/graduate degree, cross-registration, distance learning, double major, dual enrollment of high school students, ESL, independent study, internships, student-designed major, study abroad, Washington semester. **Credit/placement by examination:** AP, CLEP, IB, SAT, ACT, institutional tests. **Support services:** Learning center, reduced course load, tutoring, writing center.

Majors. **Area/ethnic studies:** American, Asian, Latin American, Western European, women's. **Biology:** General, biochemistry, bioinformatics. **Business:** Business admin. **Communications:** Communications/speech/rhetoric, journalism. **Computer sciences:** General. **Conservation:** Environmental science, environmental studies. **Education:** General. **English:** Creative writing, English lit. **Foreign languages:** General, Chinese, French, German, Japanese, Spanish. **History:** General. **Human services:** Social work. **Liberal arts:** Arts/sciences. **Math:** General. **Parks/recreation:** Exercise sciences. **Philosophy/religion:** Philosophy. **Physical sciences:** Chemistry, physics. **Psychology:** General. **Social sciences:** Economics, international relations, political science, sociology. **Visual/performing arts:** General, art, dramatic, multimedia, music, music performance.

Most popular majors. Education 8%, English 6%, health sciences 41%, psychology 15%.

Technology on campus. 200 workstations in dormitories, library, computer center, student center. Dormitories wired for high-speed internet access and linked to campus network. Commuter students can connect to campus network. Online library, helpline, repair service, student web hosting, wireless network available.

Student life. **Freshman orientation:** Mandatory. Preregistration for classes offered. **Policies:** Unmarried freshmen and sophomores under age 21 must live on campus unless living near campus with family. **Housing:** Guaranteed on-campus for freshmen. Coed dorms, special housing for disabled, apartments available. $100 fully refundable deposit, deadline 5/1. 1 wing designated for females. **Activities:** Bands, campus ministries, choral groups, dance, drama, film society, international student organizations, literary magazine, music ensembles, radio station, student government, student newspaper, symphony orchestra, Hawaii club, Christian Fellowship, politics and law forum, Circle K, humanitarian center, gay and lesbian support group, ethnic diversity appreciation club, United Church of Christ student organization.

Athletics. NCAA. **Intercollegiate:** Baseball M, basketball, cheerleading, cross-country, golf, lacrosse W, soccer, softball W, swimming, tennis, track and field, volleyball W, wrestling. **Intramural:** Basketball, football (tackle), golf, handball, racquetball, soccer, softball, tennis, volleyball. **Team name:** Boxers.

Student services. Alcohol/substance abuse counseling, career counseling, student employment services, financial aid counseling, health services, minority student services, personal counseling, placement for graduates, veterans' counselor.

Contact. E-mail: admissions@pacificu.edu
Phone: (503) 352-2218 Toll-free number: (800) 677-6712
Fax: (503) 352-2975
Karen Dunston, Executive Director of Undergraduate Admission, Pacific University, 2043 College Way, Forest Grove, OR 97116-1797

Portland State University
Portland, Oregon CB member
www.pdx.edu CB code: 4610

▸ Public 4-year university
▸ Commuter campus in very large city
▸ 19,674 degree-seeking undergraduates: 28% part-time, 53% women, 3% African American, 8% Asian American, 11% Hispanic/Latino, 1% Native American, 1% Native Hawaiian/Pacific islander, 5% Multi-racial, non-Hispanic, 7% international
▸ 4,946 degree-seeking graduate students
▸ 86% of applicants admitted
▸ 41% graduate within 6 years

General. Founded in 1946. Regionally accredited. Courses offered at off-campus locations. **Degrees:** 4,116 bachelor's awarded; master's, doctoral offered. **ROTC:** Army, Air Force. **Calendar:** Quarter, extensive summer session. **Class size:** 33% < 20, 37% 20-39, 14% 40-49, 13% 50-99, 3% >100. **Special facilities:** Native American student and community center.

Freshman class profile. 6,299 applied, 5,397 admitted, 1,744 enrolled.

Mid 50% test scores		GPA 2.0-2.99:	14%
SAT critical reading:	470-590	Rank in top quarter:	36%
SAT math:	460-570	Rank in top tenth:	11%
SAT writing:	440-560	Return as sophomores:	70%
ACT composite:	19-25	Out-of-state:	34%
GPA 3.75 or higher:	20%	International:	9%
GPA 3.50-3.74:	21%	Fraternities:	1%
GPA 3.0-3.49:	45%	Sororities:	1%

Basis for selection. 3.0 GPA required. If GPA requirement is not met, specific combination of test scores and GPA may qualify under special action by admissions committee. Interview recommended for those who do not meet regular admission requirement. **Home schooled:** State high school equivalency certificate required.

High school preparation. 14 units required. Required and recommended units include English 4, mathematics 3, social studies 2, history 1, science 2 (laboratory 1) and foreign language 2. One unit laboratory science recommended.

2015-2016 Annual costs. Tuition/fees: $8,124; $24,009 out-of-state. Room/board: $10,260. Books/supplies: $1,263. Personal expenses: $2,130.

Financial aid. **Non-need-based:** Scholarships awarded for academics, alumni affiliation, art, athletics, leadership, minority status, music/drama, state residency.

Application procedures. **Admission:** Priority date 12/1; no deadline. $50 fee. Admission notification on a rolling basis. **Financial aid:** Priority date 2/28; no closing date. FAFSA required. Applicants notified on a rolling basis starting 3/15.

Academics. Community based service and research projects offered in Portland area. All students required to complete 45 credit hour multidisciplinary core curriculum, including community service learning experience. Teaching certification only offered at graduate level. **Special study options:** Accelerated study, combined bachelor's/graduate degree, cooperative education, distance learning, double major, dual enrollment of high school students, ESL, exchange student, honors, independent study, internships, liberal arts/career combination, study abroad, teacher certification program. **Credit/placement by examination:** AP, CLEP, institutional tests. 45 credit hours maximum toward bachelor's degree. **Support services:** Pre-admission summer program, reduced course load, remedial instruction, tutoring, writing center.

Honors college/program. 1200 SAT (exclusive of Writing) or 3.5 GPA or 26 ACT required. Limited to 200 participants.

Majors. Architecture: Architecture, urban/community planning. **Area/ethnic studies:** African, East Asian, European, Latin American, Near/Middle Eastern, Russian/Eastern European/Eurasian, women's. **Biology:** General, biochemistry. **Business:** General, accounting, business admin, finance, human resources, logistics, management information systems, marketing. **Computer sciences:** Computer science. **Conservation:** General. **Education:** Health. **Engineering:** Civil, computer, electrical, mechanical. **English:** English lit, rhetoric/composition. **Foreign languages:** Chinese, French, German, Japanese, linguistics, Russian, Spanish. **Health services:** Audiology/hearing, public health ed. **History:** General. **Human services:** Social work. **Liberal arts:** Arts/sciences. **Math:** General. **Philosophy/religion:** Philosophy. **Physical sciences:** Chemistry, geology, physics. **Protective services:** Criminal justice, law enforcement admin. **Psychology:** General. **Social sciences:** General, anthropology, economics, geography, international relations, political science, sociology, urban studies. **Visual/performing arts:** Art, art history/conservation, commercial/advertising art, design, dramatic, drawing, music, music performance, painting, printmaking, sculpture, studio arts. **Work/family studies:** Family studies.

Most popular majors. Business/marketing 17%, health sciences 8%, liberal arts 6%, psychology 8%, social sciences 15%, visual/performing arts 6%.

Technology on campus. 925 workstations in dormitories, library, computer center, student center. Dormitories wired for high-speed internet access and linked to campus network. Commuter students can connect to campus network. Online course registration, online library, helpline, repair service, student web hosting, wireless network available.

Student life. Freshman orientation: Mandatory. Preregistration for classes offered. **Housing:** Coed dorms, special housing for disabled, apartments, cooperative housing, fraternity/sorority housing available. $150 nonrefundable deposit. Pets allowed in dorm rooms. **Activities:** Bands, campus ministries, choral groups, dance, drama, film society, international student organizations, literary magazine, music ensembles, Model UN, musical theater, opera, radio station, student government, student newspaper, symphony orchestra, TV station, student public interest research group, black cultural affairs board, United Indian Students in Higher Education, women's union, outdoor program, disabled student union, Hispanic student union.

Athletics. NCAA. **Intercollegiate:** Baseball M, basketball, cross-country, football (tackle) M, golf W, soccer W, softball W, tennis, track and field, volleyball W. **Intramural:** Archery, basketball, football (tackle) M, golf, racquetball, soccer W, softball, volleyball. **Team name:** Vikings.

Student services. Adult student services, alcohol/substance abuse counseling, chaplain/spiritual director, career counseling, student employment services, financial aid counseling, health services, legal services, minority student services, on-campus daycare, personal counseling, placement for graduates, veterans' counselor, women's services. **Physically disabled:** Services for visually, speech, hearing impaired.

Contact. E-mail: admissions@pdx.edu
Phone: (503) 725-3511 Toll-free number: (800) 547-8887 ext. 3511
Fax: (503) 725-5525
Portland State University, PO Box 751-ADM, Portland, OR 97207-0751

Reed College
Portland, Oregon
www.reed.edu

CB member
CB code: 4654

- Private 4-year liberal arts college
- Residential campus in very large city
- 1,396 degree-seeking undergraduates: 1% part-time, 54% women, 2% African American, 5% Asian American, 11% Hispanic/Latino, 8% Multiracial, non-Hispanic, 7% international
- 23 degree-seeking graduate students
- 35% of applicants admitted
- SAT or ACT (ACT writing optional), application essay required
- 82% graduate within 6 years

General. Founded in 1909. Regionally accredited. **Degrees:** 314 bachelor's awarded; master's offered. **Location:** 5 miles from downtown city center. **Calendar:** Semester. **Full-time faculty:** 161 total; 92% have terminal degrees, 18% minority, 42% women. **Part-time faculty:** 6 total; 83% have terminal degrees, 33% minority, 33% women. **Class size:** 80% < 20, 18% 20-39, less than 1% 40-49, 1% 50-99, less than 1% >100. **Special facilities:** Performing arts building, nuclear research reactor, wildlife refuge, fish ladder, biodiversity center, thesis tower.

Freshman class profile. 5,396 applied, 1,888 admitted, 421 enrolled.

Mid 50% test scores			
SAT critical reading:	670-760	Rank in top quarter:	87%
SAT math:	620-720	Rank in top tenth:	53%
SAT writing:	640-730	Return as sophomores:	88%
ACT composite:	29-33	Out-of-state:	92%
GPA 3.75 or higher:	70%	Live on campus:	99%
GPA 3.50-3.74:	16%	International:	5%
GPA 3.0-3.49:	13%		
GPA 2.0-2.99:	1%		

Basis for selection. Academic achievement, level of curriculum, grades earned, essays, recommendations, and test scores are most important. Qualities of character, such as motivation, intellectual curiosity, individual responsibility, social consciousness, and community involvement are also important. SAT Subject Tests recommended. Priority given to applicants with scores received by 2/1. Interview recommended. **Home schooled:** Transcript of courses and grades, letter of recommendation (nonparent) required. The Common Application Home School Supplement or detailed outline of home-school curriculum, including subject areas studied, texts used, and time spent on each discipline.

High school preparation. College-preparatory program recommended. Recommended units include English 4, mathematics 3, social studies 3, science 3 and foreign language 3.

2016-2017 Annual costs. Tuition/fees: $52,150. Room/board: $13,150. Books/supplies: $1,050. Personal expenses: $900.

Financial aid. All financial aid based on need. **Additional information:** College meets demonstrated need of continuing students who have attended Reed minimum of 2 semesters, who file financial aid applications on time, and who maintain satisfactory academic progress. Institutional aid consideration is for total of 8 semesters.

Application procedures. Admission: Closing date 1/15 (postmark date). No application fee. Admission notification by 4/1. Must reply by 5/1. **Financial aid:** Closing date 2/1. FAFSA, CSS PROFILE required. Applicants notified by 4/1; must reply by 5/1.

Academics. All students take a one-year course in the humanities. After declaring their major, students must pass a junior qualifying examination prior to senior year. Seniors engage in a one-year research project in their major field writing a senior thesis and orally defending it before a committee of faculty members. **Special study options:** Combined bachelor's/graduate degree, cross-registration, double major, dual enrollment of high school students, exchange student, independent study, internships, liberal arts/career combination, student-designed major, study abroad. Computer Science, Engineering, Forestry/Environmental Sciences, Pre-medical and Pre-Veterinary, Visual Arts. **Credit/placement by examination:** AP, CLEP, IB, institutional tests. 30 credit hours maximum toward bachelor's degree. **Support services:** Learning center, study skills assistance, tutoring, writing center. Academic workshops on topics such as time management, reading effectively, note taking, etc. Language scholars who are native speakers assist students in foreign languages.

Majors. Area/ethnic studies: American. **Biology:** General, biochemistry, molecular. **Computer sciences:** Computer science. **Conservation:** Environmental studies. **English:** Creative writing, English lit. **Foreign languages:** Chinese, classics, comparative lit, French, German, linguistics, Russian, Spanish. **History:** General. **Math:** General, computational, computational/applied. **Philosophy/religion:** Philosophy, religion. **Physical sciences:** Chemistry, physics. **Psychology:** General. **Social sciences:** Anthropology, economics, international relations, political science, sociology. **Visual/performing arts:** Art, dance, dramatic, music.

Most popular majors. Biology 13%, English 9%, foreign language 9%, history 7%, physical sciences 12%, psychology 8%, social sciences 15%, visual/performing arts 11%.

Technology on campus. 434 workstations in dormitories, library, computer center, student center. Dormitories wired for high-speed internet access and linked to campus network. Commuter students can connect to campus network. Online course registration, online library, helpline, repair service, student web hosting, wireless network available.

Student life. Freshman orientation: Mandatory. Preregistration for classes offered. Held five days before the start of classes. **Policies:** Governed by an honor principle. First-year students are required to live on campus. **Housing:** Guaranteed on-campus for freshmen. Coed dorms, single-sex dorms, special housing for disabled, apartments, cooperative housing, themed housing, wellness housing available. $100 partly refundable deposit, deadline 6/15. Pets allowed in dorm rooms. Language houses accommodate upper-division students studying Chinese, French, Arabic, German, Russian, and Spanish. **Activities:** Jazz band, campus ministries, choral groups, dance, drama, film society, international student organizations, literary magazine, music ensembles, Model UN, musical theater, radio station, student government, student newspaper, symphony orchestra, Chaverim, Ecumenical Christian group, Blue Heron Collective, Amnesty International, Canyon Day, Greenboard, Black/Caribbean/Latino student union, feminist student union, Queer Alliance, Ecuador service project.

Athletics. Team name: Griffins.

Student services. Adult student services, alcohol/substance abuse counseling, career counseling, student employment services, financial aid counseling, health services, minority student services, personal counseling, placement for graduates. **Physically disabled:** Services for visually, speech, hearing impaired.

Contact. E-mail: admission@reed.edu
Phone: (503) 777-7511 Toll-free number: (800) 547-4750
Fax: (503) 777-7553
Milyon Trulove, Vice President of Admission and Financial Aid, Reed College, 3203 SE Woodstock Boulevard, Portland, OR 97202-8199

Southern Oregon University
Ashland, Oregon **CB member**
www.sou.edu **CB code: 4702**

- Public 4-year university and liberal arts college
- Residential campus in large town
- 4,203 degree-seeking undergraduates: 16% part-time, 58% women
- 324 degree-seeking graduate students
- 95% of applicants admitted
- SAT or ACT (ACT writing recommended), application essay required

General. Founded in 1926. Regionally accredited. **Degrees:** 774 bachelor's awarded; master's offered. **ROTC:** Army. **Location:** 180 miles from Eugene, 285 miles from Portland. **Calendar:** Quarter, extensive summer session. **Full-time faculty:** 163 total; 77% have terminal degrees, 12% minority, 43% women. **Part-time faculty:** 144 total; 19% have terminal degrees, 10% minority, 61% women. **Class size:** 44% < 20, 47% 20-39, 5% 40-49, 3% 50-99, less than 1% >100. **Special facilities:** Herbarium, U.S. Fish and Wildlife forensics laboratory, public radio network studios, preschool and kindergarten, community television studio, center for visual arts, biotechnology center, institute for environmental economic and civic studies.

Freshman class profile. 2,411 applied, 2,296 admitted, 823 enrolled.

Mid 50% test scores			
SAT critical reading:	460-590	GPA 3.50-3.74:	18%
SAT math:	450-560	GPA 3.0-3.49:	44%
SAT writing:	430-550	GPA 2.0-2.99:	21%
ACT composite:	20-25	Out-of-state:	43%
GPA 3.75 or higher:	17%	Live on campus:	78%

Basis for selection. Admission based on 2.75 GPA from regionally accredited high school, 21 ACT, 1010 SAT (exclusive of Writing), and 14 required high school academic units. Requests for special admission for undergraduates reviewed individually. **Home schooled:** 1010 combined scores on SAT Critical Reading and Math, 470 on SAT Writing, and 2 SAT Subject Tests (Math Level I or Math Level II and one other subject area of student's choice) required.

High school preparation. College-preparatory program required. 15 units required. Required units include English 4, mathematics 3, social studies 3, science 2 (laboratory 1) and foreign language 2.

2015-2016 Annual costs. Tuition/fees: $8,145; $22,365 out-of-state. Room/board: $12,105. Books/supplies: $999. Personal expenses: $3,252.

2015-2016 Financial aid. Need-based: 47% of total undergraduate aid awarded as scholarships/grants, 53% as loans/jobs. **Non-need-based:** Scholarships awarded for academics, athletics.

Application procedures. Admission: Priority date 2/15; no deadline. $50 fee. Admission notification on a rolling basis beginning on or about 9/15. **Financial aid:** Priority date 3/1; no closing date. FAFSA required. Applicants notified on a rolling basis starting 3/2; must reply within 4 week(s) of notification.

Academics. Designated by National Aeronautical and Space Administration to cooperate in NASA-directed joint space research by undergraduates. **Special study options:** Accelerated study, combined bachelor's/graduate degree, cross-registration, distance learning, double major, dual enrollment of high school students, ESL, exchange student, honors, independent study, internships, student-designed major, study abroad, teacher certification program. Online degree completion programs. **Credit/placement by examination:** AP, CLEP, IB, institutional tests. 24 credit hours maximum toward

bachelor's degree. **Support services:** Learning center, reduced course load, remedial instruction, study skills assistance, tutoring, writing center.

Majors. Biology: General. **Business:** General, accounting, business admin, hospitality admin, marketing. **Communications:** Communications/speech/rhetoric, digital media, journalism, public relations. **Computer sciences:** General, computer science, programming, security. **Conservation:** Environmental studies. **Education:** General. **English:** Creative writing, English lit, rhetoric/composition. **Foreign languages:** General, Spanish. **Health services:** Athletic training, nursing (RN), predental, premedicine, preop/surgical nursing, prepharmacy, preveterinary. **History:** General. **Math:** General. **Parks/recreation:** Health/fitness, sports admin. **Physical sciences:** Chemistry, geology. **Protective services:** Criminal justice, law enforcement admin, police science. **Psychology:** General. **Social sciences:** General, anthropology, criminology, economics, geography, political science, sociology. **Visual/performing arts:** Art, dramatic, music, music management.

Most popular majors. Business/marketing 18%, communications/journalism 7%, education 7%, parks/recreation 8%, psychology 10%, security/protective services 7%, social sciences 6%, visual/performing arts 15%.

Technology on campus. 750 workstations in dormitories, library, computer center, student center. Dormitories wired for high-speed internet access and linked to campus network. Commuter students can connect to campus network. Online course registration, online library, helpline, student web hosting, wireless network available.

Student life. Freshman orientation: Mandatory. Preregistration for classes offered. Early registration in July; orientation few days before start of classes. **Housing:** Guaranteed on-campus for freshmen. Coed dorms, special housing for disabled, apartments, themed housing, wellness housing available. $50 partly refundable deposit. 900 room housing complex featuring suite and apartment style rooms. Separate quiet, nonsmoking, older student or freshmen residence halls available. **Activities:** Bands, campus ministries, choral groups, dance, drama, film society, international student organizations, literary magazine, music ensembles, musical theater, radio station, student government, student newspaper, symphony orchestra, TV station, 100 clubs available.

Athletics. NAIA. **Intercollegiate:** Basketball, cross-country, football (tackle) M, soccer W, softball W, tennis W, track and field, volleyball W, wrestling M. **Intramural:** Badminton, baseball M, basketball, bowling, golf, racquetball, rugby, sailing, skiing, soccer, softball, swimming, table tennis, tennis, track and field, volleyball, water polo. **Team name:** Raiders.

Student services. Adult student services, alcohol/substance abuse counseling, career counseling, services for economically disadvantaged, student employment services, financial aid counseling, health services, legal services, minority student services, on-campus daycare, personal counseling, placement for graduates, veterans' counselor, women's services. **Physically disabled:** Services for visually, speech, hearing impaired.

Contact. E-mail: admissions@sou.edu
Phone: (541) 552-6411 Toll-free number: (800) 482-7672 ext. 6411
Fax: (541) 552-8403
Mark Bottorff, Director of Admissions, Southern Oregon University, 1250 Siskiyou Boulevard, Ashland, OR 97520-5032

University of Oregon
Eugene, Oregon **CB member**
www.uoregon.edu **CB code: 4846**

- Public 4-year university
- Residential campus in small city
- 20,220 degree-seeking undergraduates: 8% part-time, 53% women, 2% African American, 6% Asian American, 10% Hispanic/Latino, 7% Multiracial, non-Hispanic, 14% international
- 3,229 degree-seeking graduate students
- 74% of applicants admitted
- SAT or ACT (ACT writing optional), application essay required
- 72% graduate within 6 years

General. Founded in 1876. Regionally accredited. **Degrees:** 4,715 bachelor's awarded; master's, professional, doctoral offered. **ROTC:** Army, Air Force. **Location:** 110 miles from Portland. **Calendar:** Quarter, extensive summer session. **Full-time faculty:** 1,080 total; 96% have terminal degrees, 17% minority, 45% women. **Part-time faculty:** 595 total; 82% have terminal degrees, 8% minority, 48% women. **Class size:** 44% < 20, 30% 20-39, 5% 40-49, 13% 50-99, 9% >100. **Special facilities:** Art museum, natural and cultural history museum, sports marketing center, entrepreneurship center, Many Nations Longhouse, green chemistry laboratory, mountain observatory, marine biology institute.

Freshman class profile. 22,000 applied, 16,328 admitted, 4,133 enrolled.

Mid 50% test scores			
SAT critical reading:	500-620	GPA 2.0-2.99:	1%
SAT math:	500-610	Rank in top quarter:	64%
SAT writing:	490-600	Rank in top tenth:	29%
ACT composite:	22-27	End year in good standing:	87%
GPA 3.75 or higher:	35%	Return as sophomores:	88%
GPA 3.50-3.74:	27%	Out-of-state:	48%
GPA 3.0-3.49:	37%	Live on campus:	80%
		International:	9%

Basis for selection. Graduation from accredited high school, C- or higher in 15 college preparatory courses, submission of SAT or ACT scores, and application essay. Applications will be evaluated based on strength of academic course work, grades earned, grade trend, class rank, standardized test scores, senior course load, academic motivation as demonstrated in application essay, extracurricular activities, ability to enhance the diversity of the university, academic potential, and special talents. Applicants to architecture or interior architecture must submit SAT Reasoning Test or ACT scores regardless of class level. SAT Subject Tests in Math I or II, and a second test of choice are required for home schooled and students from non-accredited high schools. Also for these students, a second language subject test is strongly recommended to meet the second language proficiency requirements. Audition required for music programs. Portfolio required for arts, architecture, and interior architecture programs. **Home schooled:** SAT required with minimum score of 1540 for critical reading, mathematics and writing scores combined or submit ACT with optional writing , minimum score of 22. SAT Subject Tests in Math I or II, and second test of student's choice in subject other than math required. Must earn minimum score of 470 on each of the two tests, with a total score of at least 940. Standardized test in language strongly recommended to meet second language proficiency requirements. **Learning Disabled:** If student does not meet admission requirements and has self-identified a documented disability, a secondary review will take place by disability review committee.

High school preparation. College-preparatory program required. 15 units required. Required and recommended units include English 4, mathematics 3, social studies 3, science 3 (laboratory 1) and foreign language 2.

2015-2016 Annual costs. Tuition/fees: $10,289; $32,024 out-of-state. Room/board: $11,785.

Financial aid. Non-need-based: Scholarships awarded for academics, athletics, leadership, minority status, music/drama, ROTC, state residency.

Application procedures. Admission: Closing date 1/15 (postmark date). $65 fee, may be waived for applicants with need. Admission notification on a rolling basis beginning on or about 4/1. Must reply by May 1 or within 4 week(s) if notified thereafter. **Financial aid:** Priority date 3/1; no closing date. FAFSA required. Applicants notified on a rolling basis starting 4/15; must reply within 4 week(s) of notification.

Academics. Special study options: Distance learning, double major, ESL, exchange student, honors, independent study, internships, liberal arts/career combination, semester at sea, student-designed major, study abroad, teacher certification program. Dual enrollment program with Lane Community College and Southwestern Oregon Community College. Professional distinctions program (certificate program) in which students gain direct professional preparation through internships, special courses, professional mentor, and development of electronic resume and portfolio. **Credit/placement by examination:** AP, CLEP, IB, SAT, ACT, institutional tests. For some courses, departments have authorized the use of subject examinations prepared by the College Level Examination Program (CLEP). Once a student is admitted, successfully completed CLEP subject exams are accepted as transfer credit. **Support services:** Learning center, remedial instruction, study skills assistance, tutoring.

Honors college/program. Admissions based on short self-introduction, admission essay, two teacher recommendations, description of accomplishments, SAT or ACT, GPA, depth and breadth of high school curriculum, and ways in which applicant will add to diversity of honors community. Around 200 freshmen admitted each year.

Majors. Architecture: Architecture, interior, landscape. **Area/ethnic studies:** General, Asian, folklore, Latin American, Russian/Slavic, women's. **Biology:** General, biochemistry, marine, physiology. **Business:** General, accounting. **Communications:** Advertising, journalism, public relations. **Computer sciences:** General. **Conservation:** Environmental science, environmental studies. **Education:** General, music. **English:** English lit. **Foreign languages:** Chinese, classics, comparative lit, French, German, Italian, Japanese, linguistics, Romance, Spanish. **Health services:** Communication disorders. **History:** General. **Human services:** General. **Liberal arts:** Humanities. **Math:** General. **Philosophy/religion:** Judaic, philosophy, religion. **Physical sciences:** Chemistry, geology, physics. **Psychology:** General. **Social sciences:** General, anthropology, economics, geography, political science, sociology. **Visual/performing arts:** Art, art history/conservation, ceramics, dance, digital arts, dramatic, fiber arts, film/cinema/video, jazz, metal/jewelry, music, music performance, music theory/composition, painting, photography, printmaking, sculpture, studio arts.

Most popular majors. Biology 9%, business/marketing 15%, communications/journalism 12%, psychology 7%, social sciences 22%, visual/performing arts 7%.

Technology on campus. 1,118 workstations in dormitories, library, computer center, student center. Dormitories wired for high-speed internet access and linked to campus network. Commuter students can connect to campus network. Online course registration, online library, helpline, repair service, student web hosting, wireless network available.

Student life. Freshman orientation: Mandatory. Preregistration for classes offered. 2-day session held during summer for students and family members. **Housing:** Coed dorms, apartments, cooperative housing, fraternity/sorority housing, themed housing, wellness housing available. $350 partly refundable deposit. Residence halls have separate men's and women's floors. Gender inclusive hall, graduate student, and family housing available. **Activities:** Bands, campus ministries, choral groups, dance, drama, film society, international student organizations, literary magazine, music ensembles, musical theater, opera, radio station, student government, student newspaper, symphony orchestra, TV station, Jewish student union, Muslim student association, College Democrats, College Republicans, Black student union, Asian/Pacific American student union, non-traditional student union, coalition against environmental racism, service based fraternities and sororities.

Athletics. NCAA. **Intercollegiate:** Baseball M, basketball, cross-country, football (tackle) M, golf, lacrosse W, sand volleyball W, soccer W, softball W, tennis, track and field, volleyball W. **Intramural:** Basketball, football (non-tackle), soccer, softball, tennis, volleyball. **Team name:** Ducks.

Student services. Adult student services, alcohol/substance abuse counseling, career counseling, services for economically disadvantaged, student employment services, financial aid counseling, health services, legal services, minority student services, on-campus daycare, personal counseling, veterans' counselor, women's services. **Physically disabled:** Services for visually, speech, hearing impaired.

Contact. E-mail: uoadmit@uoregon.edu
Phone: (541) 346-3201 Toll-free number: (800) 232-3825
Fax: (541) 346-5815
Jim Rawlins, Director of Admissions, University of Oregon, 1217 University of Oregon, Eugene, OR 97403-1217

University of Phoenix: Oregon
Tigard, Oregon
www.phoenix.edu   **CB code: 7856**

- For-profit 4-year university
- Commuter campus in large town
- 496 undergraduates
- 73 graduate students

General. Regionally accredited. **Degrees:** 152 bachelor's awarded; master's offered. **Calendar:** Differs by program. **Full-time faculty:** 13 total. **Part-time faculty:** 164 total.

Basis for selection. Open admission.

2015-2016 Annual costs. Per-credit-hour charge, $410 to $635, depending upon level and course of study; electronic course materials fee, $95, if applicable. Book and material charges may vary by course and program. All fees are subject to change.

Application procedures. Admission: No deadline. No application fee. **Financial aid:** No deadline.

Academics. Credit/placement by examination: AP, CLEP.

Majors. Business: Accounting/business management, business admin, marketing. **Communications:** General. **Computer sciences:** Programming. **Health services:** Facilities admin. **Human services:** General. **Protective services:** Law enforcement admin.

Student life. Freshman orientation: Mandatory. Preregistration for classes offered.

Contact. Toll-free number: (866) 766-0766
University of Phoenix: Oregon, 13221 Southwest 68th Parkway, Tigard, OR 97223-8328

University of Portland
Portland, Oregon   **CB member**
www.up.edu   **CB code: 4847**

- Private 4-year university affiliated with the Roman Catholic Church
- Residential campus in large city
- 3,741 degree-seeking undergraduates: 1% part-time, 59% women, 1% African American, 12% Asian American, 11% Hispanic/Latino, 2% Native Hawaiian/Pacific islander, 8% Multi-racial, non-Hispanic, 3% international
- 509 degree-seeking graduate students
- 62% of applicants admitted
- SAT or ACT (ACT writing optional), application essay required
- 78% graduate within 6 years

General. Founded in 1901. Regionally accredited. **Degrees:** 854 bachelor's awarded; master's, professional offered. **ROTC:** Army, Air Force. **Calendar:** Semester, limited summer session. **Full-time faculty:** 223 total; 90% have terminal degrees, 8% minority, 50% women. **Part-time faculty:** 140 total; 5% have terminal degrees, 7% minority, 46% women. **Class size:** 30% < 20, 63% 20-39, 6% 40-49, less than 1% 50-99, less than 1% >100.

Freshman class profile. 11,202 applied, 6,939 admitted, 941 enrolled.

Mid 50% test scores			
SAT critical reading:	540-660	Rank in top quarter:	77%
SAT math:	550-640	Rank in top tenth:	45%
GPA 3.75 or higher:	48%	Return as sophomores:	92%
GPA 3.50-3.74:	25%	Out-of-state:	75%
GPA 3.0-3.49:	24%	Live on campus:	94%
GPA 2.0-2.99:	3%	International:	3%

Basis for selection. School achievement record, test scores, counselor recommendation, essay important. **Home schooled:** Transcript of courses and grades required. Interview strongly encouraged.

High school preparation. College-preparatory program required. Required and recommended units include English 3-4, mathematics 2-3, social studies 2, history 2, science 2 and academic electives 7. Engineering, math, and some science majors require additional math and science courses.

2015-2016 Annual costs. Tuition/fees: $40,250. Room/board: $11,902. Books/supplies: $960. Personal expenses: $1,680.

2015-2016 Financial aid. Need-based: 794 full-time freshmen applied for aid; 626 deemed to have need; 624 received aid. Average need met was 69%. Average scholarship/grant was $23,025; average loan $3,636. 75% of total undergraduate aid awarded as scholarships/grants, 25% as loans/jobs. **Non-need-based:** Awarded to 3,450 full-time undergraduates, including 920 freshmen. Scholarships awarded for academics, athletics, leadership, minority status, music/drama, ROTC.

Application procedures. Admission: Closing date 2/1 (postmark date). $50 fee, may be waived for applicants with need. Admission notification on a rolling basis beginning on or about 10/1. Must reply by May 1 or within 2 week(s) if notified thereafter. **Financial aid:** Priority date 3/1; no closing date. FAFSA required. Applicants notified by 3/1; Applicants notified on a rolling basis starting 3/1; must reply by 5/1.

Academics. Special study options: Cross-registration, double major, honors, independent study, internships, liberal arts/career combination, study abroad, teacher certification program, Washington semester. **Credit/placement by examination:** AP, CLEP, IB, institutional tests. 45 credit hours maximum toward bachelor's degree. **Support services:** Learning center, study skills assistance, tutoring, writing center.

Majors. Biology: General. **Business:** Accounting, business admin, finance, international, marketing. **Communications:** Media studies, organizational. **Computer sciences:** Computer science. **Conservation:** Environmental science, environmental studies. **Education:** Elementary, music, secondary. **Engineering:** Civil, computer, electrical, environmental, mechanical. **English:** English lit. **Foreign languages:** French, German, Spanish. **Health services:** Nursing (RN). **History:** General. **Human services:** Social work. **Math:** General. **Philosophy/religion:** Philosophy. **Physical sciences:** Chemistry, physics. **Psychology:** General. **Social sciences:** Political science, sociology. **Theology:** Theology. **Visual/performing arts:** Dramatic, music, theater arts management.

Most popular majors. Biology 10%, business/marketing 15%, engineering/engineering technologies 14%, foreign language 8%, health sciences 20%.

Technology on campus. 450 workstations in dormitories, library, computer center, student center. Dormitories wired for high-speed internet access and linked to campus network. Commuter students can connect to campus network. Online course registration, online library, helpline, student web hosting, wireless network available.

Student life. Freshman orientation: Available. Preregistration for classes offered. Held 3 days before classes begin. **Policies:** Freshmen not permitted cars on campus. **Housing:** Guaranteed on-campus for freshmen. Coed dorms, single-sex dorms, themed housing available. $100 nonrefundable deposit, deadline 5/1. Rental houses in neighborhood. **Activities:** Bands, campus ministries, choral groups, dance, drama, film society, international student organizations, literary magazine, music ensembles, musical theater, radio station, student government, student newspaper, symphony orchestra, volunteer services, black student union, Hawaiian club, Engineers Without Borders, feminist discussion group, Bible study group, Movimiento Estudiantil de Chicanos de Astlan, ecology club, student-led unity garden.

Athletics. NCAA. **Intercollegiate:** Baseball M, basketball, cross-country, rowing (crew), soccer, tennis, track and field, volleyball W. **Intramural:** Basketball, bowling, football (non-tackle), skiing, soccer, softball, swimming, table tennis, tennis, ultimate frisbee, volleyball, weight lifting. **Team name:** Pilots.

Student services. Adult student services, alcohol/substance abuse counseling, chaplain/spiritual director, career counseling, student employment services, financial aid counseling, health services, personal counseling, placement for graduates, veterans' counselor. **Physically disabled:** Services for visually, speech, hearing impaired.

Contact. E-mail: admissions@up.edu
Phone: (503) 943-7147 Toll-free number: (888) 627-5601
Fax: (503) 943-7315
Jason McDonald, Dean of Admissions, University of Portland, 5000 North Willamette Boulevard, Portland, OR 97203-5798

Warner Pacific College
Portland, Oregon
www.warnerpacific.edu   **CB code: 4595**

- Private 4-year liberal arts college affiliated with the Church of God
- Residential campus in very large city
- 519 degree-seeking undergraduates: 6% part-time, 56% women, 12% African American, 7% Asian American, 23% Hispanic/Latino, 2% Native American, 1% Native Hawaiian/Pacific islander, 4% Multi-racial, non-Hispanic, 2% international
- 51% of applicants admitted
- SAT or ACT (ACT writing optional), application essay required
- 55% graduate within 6 years

General. Founded in 1937. Regionally accredited. **Degrees:** 121 bachelor's awarded; master's offered. **ROTC:** Air Force. **Calendar:** Semester, limited summer session. **Full-time faculty:** 27 total; 70% have terminal degrees, 11% minority, 41% women. **Part-time faculty:** 58 total; 21% have terminal degrees, 5% minority, 47% women. **Class size:** 74% < 20, 25% 20-39, less than 1% 50-99. **Special facilities:** Field station for wildlife observation and study.

Freshman class profile. 1,418 applied, 728 admitted, 101 enrolled.

Mid 50% test scores			
		GPA 2.0-2.99:	28%
SAT critical reading:	390-550	Rank in top quarter:	25%
SAT math:	410-520	Rank in top tenth:	9%
SAT writing:	390-500	End year in good standing:	62%
ACT composite:	16-21	Return as sophomores:	63%
GPA 3.75 or higher:	9%	Out-of-state:	30%
GPA 3.50-3.74:	14%	Live on campus:	55%
GPA 3.0-3.49:	49%	International:	1%

Basis for selection. High school GPA important; test scores, essay, and signed lifestyle agreement required. **Home schooled:** Statement describing home school structure and mission, transcript of courses and grades, state high school equivalency certificate, interview, letter of recommendation (non-parent) required. **Learning Disabled:** Students are extended extra services to assist them to be successful.

High school preparation. College-preparatory program recommended. Recommended units include English 4, mathematics 2, social studies 3, science 2 (laboratory 2).

2016-2017 Annual costs. Tuition/fees: $22,710. Room/board: $8,900. Books/supplies: $1,300. Personal expenses: $1,794.

2015-2016 Financial aid. Need-based: 84 full-time freshmen applied for aid; 75 deemed to have need; 75 received aid. Average need met was 59%. Average scholarship/grant was $6,461; average loan $3,607. 54% of total undergraduate aid awarded as scholarships/grants, 46% as loans/jobs. **Non-need-based:** Awarded to 477 full-time undergraduates, including 95 freshmen. Scholarships awarded for academics, alumni affiliation, athletics, leadership, music/drama, religious affiliation.

Application procedures. Admission: No deadline. $50 fee, may be waived for applicants with need. Admission notification on a rolling basis. Housing deposit fully refundable by May 15. **Financial aid:** Priority date 3/1; no closing date. FAFSA required. Applicants notified on a rolling basis starting 3/1; must reply within 2 week(s) of notification.

Academics. Special study options: Combined bachelor's/graduate degree, double major, exchange student, independent study, internships, liberal arts/career combination, student-designed major, study abroad, teacher certification program, Washington semester. **Credit/placement by examination:** AP, CLEP, SAT, ACT, institutional tests. 30 credit hours maximum toward associate degree, 30 toward bachelor's. No more than 45 total alternative credits (maximum 30 of any one type). **Support services:** Learning center, reduced course load, remedial instruction, study skills assistance, tutoring.

Majors. Area/ethnic studies: American. **Biology:** General. **Business:** Business admin, international. **Communications:** Communications/speech/rhetoric. **Education:** Elementary, music, physical, secondary. **English:** English lit. **History:** General. **Human services:** Social work. **Liberal arts:** Arts/sciences. **Parks/recreation:** Exercise sciences, health/fitness, sports admin. **Philosophy/religion:** Religion. **Physical sciences:** General. **Psychology:** General, developmental. **Social sciences:** General, urban studies. **Theology:** Preministerial. **Visual/performing arts:** Music. **Work/family studies:** Family studies.

Most popular majors. Biology 8%, business/marketing 18%, communication technologies 9%, family/consumer sciences 13%, parks/recreation 7%, psychology 8%, public administration/social services 8%, social sciences 6%, theological studies 11%.

Technology on campus. 30 workstations in dormitories, library, computer center. Dormitories wired for high-speed internet access and linked to campus network. Online library, helpline, wireless network available.

Student life. Freshman orientation: Available. Preregistration for classes offered. **Policies:** Religious observance required. **Housing:** Guaranteed on-campus for freshmen. Single-sex dorms, special housing for disabled, apartments available. $250 fully refundable deposit, deadline 5/15. On-campus houses, duplexes available. **Activities:** Bands, campus ministries, choral groups, drama, international student organizations, literary magazine, music ensembles, student government, student newspaper.

Athletics. NAIA, NCCAA. **Intercollegiate:** Basketball, cross-country, golf, soccer, track and field, volleyball W, wrestling. **Intramural:** Badminton, basketball, football (non-tackle), volleyball. **Team name:** Knights.

Student services. Adult student services, chaplain/spiritual director, career counseling, student employment services, financial aid counseling, health services, minority student services, personal counseling, placement for graduates.

Contact. E-mail: admissions@warnerpacific.edu
Phone: (503) 517-1020 Toll-free number: (800) 804-1510
Fax: (503) 517-1540
Dale Seipp, Vice President for Enrollment and Marketing, Warner Pacific College, 2219 SE 68th Avenue, Portland, OR 97215-4026

Western Oregon University
Monmouth, Oregon
www.wou.edu

CB member
CB code: 4585

- Public 4-year liberal arts and teachers college
- Residential campus in small town
- 4,788 degree-seeking undergraduates: 15% part-time; 60% women, 4% African American, 4% Asian American, 11% Hispanic/Latino, 2% Native American, 2% Native Hawaiian/Pacific islander, 5% international
- 586 degree-seeking graduate students
- 88% of applicants admitted
- SAT or ACT with writing required
- 45% graduate within 6 years

General. Founded in 1856. Regionally accredited. **Degrees:** 1,014 bachelor's awarded; master's offered. **ROTC:** Army, Naval, Air Force. **Location:** 15 miles from Salem, 60 miles from Portland. **Calendar:** Quarter, limited summer session. **Full-time faculty:** 191 total; 77% have terminal degrees, 11% minority, 46% women. **Part-time faculty:** 215 total; 24% have terminal degrees, 11% minority, 54% women. **Class size:** 49% < 20, 41% 20-39, 6%

40-49, 3% 50-99, less than 1% >100. **Special facilities:** Teaching research institute, early childhood and training development center.

Freshman class profile. 3,327 applied, 2,920 admitted, 944 enrolled.

Mid 50% test scores			
SAT critical reading:	420-540	Rank in top quarter:	35%
SAT math:	420-530	Rank in top tenth:	11%
SAT writing:	410-510	Out-of-state:	20%
ACT composite:	17-22	Live on campus:	85%
GPA 3.75 or higher:	16%	Fraternities:	1%
GPA 3.50-3.74:	16%	Sororities:	1%
GPA 3.0-3.49:	37%		
GPA 2.0-2.99:	31%		

Basis for selection. 2.75 GPA required. 1000 SAT (exclusive of Writing) strongly recommended, but only used in admissions decision if applicant does not meet GPA or college preparation requirements. If applicant does not meet academic requirements, other evidence of potential in the form of interviews, portfolios, auditions, and essays considered. **Home schooled:** 1000 SAT (exclusive of Writing) or 21 ACT or 1410 SAT Subject Tests combined score in 3 subjects required; must take 1 SAT Reasoning Test, 1 SAT Subject Test in math, and second exam in foreign language.

High school preparation. College-preparatory program required. 14 units required. Required and recommended units include English 4, mathematics 3, social studies 2, history 1, science 3 (laboratory 2) and foreign language 2.

2015-2016 Annual costs. Tuition/fees: $8,433; $22,728 out-of-state. Room/board: $9,672. Books/supplies: $1,350. Personal expenses: $2,482. **Additional information:** Full participant in the Western Undergraduate Exchange (WUE) WUE Tuition is $10,215. Resident students can also select a Tuition Promise base tuition rate that is not subject to annual adjustments for 4 years.

2014-2015 Financial aid. Need-based: 616 full-time freshmen applied for aid; 520 deemed to have need; 520 received aid. Average need met was 56%. Average scholarship/grant was $7,589; average loan $3,071. 44% of total undergraduate aid awarded as scholarships/grants, 56% as loans/jobs. **Non-need-based:** Awarded to 312 full-time undergraduates, including 72 freshmen. Scholarships awarded for academics, alumni affiliation, art, athletics, leadership, minority status, music/drama.

Application procedures. Admission: No deadline. $50 fee. Admission notification on a rolling basis. **Financial aid:** Priority date 2/1; no closing date. FAFSA required. Applicants notified on a rolling basis starting 3/25; must reply within 3 week(s) of notification.

Academics. Special study options: Combined bachelor's/graduate degree, cooperative education, distance learning, double major, dual enrollment of high school students, ESL, exchange student, honors, independent study, internships, semester at sea, student-designed major, study abroad, teacher certification program. Pre-professional studies, interdisciplinary studies, non-degree licensure programs, service learning and career development. **Credit/placement by examination:** AP, CLEP, IB, SAT, ACT, institutional tests. 48 credit hours maximum toward bachelor's degree. **Support services:** Learning center, pre-admission summer program, remedial instruction, study skills assistance, tutoring, writing center.

Majors. Area/ethnic studies: Deaf. **Biology:** General. **Business:** General. **Communications:** Communications/speech/rhetoric. **Computer sciences:** General. **Education:** General, biology, chemistry, early childhood, educational technology, elementary, health, middle, multi-level teacher, physical, reading, science, secondary, social studies, Spanish. **English:** English lit, rhetoric/composition. **Foreign languages:** Sign language interpretation, Spanish. **Health services:** Nursing (RN). **History:** General. **Human services:** General. **Liberal arts:** Arts/sciences, humanities. **Math:** General. **Philosophy/religion:** Philosophy. **Physical sciences:** Chemistry, geology, planetary. **Protective services:** Corrections, fire services admin, law enforcement admin. **Psychology:** General, geropsychology. **Social sciences:** General, anthropology, economics, geography, international relations, political science, sociology. **Visual/performing arts:** General, art, dance, dramatic, music, studio arts, theater arts management.

Most popular majors. Business/marketing 15%, education 10%, foreign language 6%, interdisciplinary studies 11%, psychology 8%, security/protective services 8%, social sciences 9%.

Technology on campus. 411 workstations in dormitories, library, computer center, student center. Dormitories wired for high-speed internet access and linked to campus network. Commuter students can connect to campus network. Online course registration, online library, helpline, repair service, wireless network available.

Student life. Freshman orientation: Available. Preregistration for classes offered. Held last weekend in June and 2nd and 3rd weekends in July on Friday and/or Saturday. **Policies:** No alcohol permitted in residence halls. **Housing:** Guaranteed on-campus for freshmen. Coed dorms, single-sex dorms, special housing for disabled, apartments, gender-neutral housing, themed housing, wellness housing available. Family housing, housing by learning communities, community living options available. **Activities:** Bands, campus ministries, choral groups, dance, drama, international student organizations, literary magazine, music ensembles, Model UN, musical theater, radio station, student government, student newspaper, symphony orchestra, TV station, Baptist student union, Big Brother/Big Sister, multicultural student union, Campus Crusade for Christ, Circle K, environmental action committee.

Athletics. NCAA. **Intercollegiate:** Baseball M, basketball, cheerleading, cross-country, football (tackle) M, soccer W, softball W, track and field, volleyball W. **Intramural:** Badminton, basketball, bowling, cross-country, football (non-tackle), football (tackle) M, golf, racquetball, rifle, skiing, soccer, softball, swimming, table tennis, tennis, track and field, triathlon, volleyball, water polo, weight lifting, wrestling. **Team name:** Wolves.

Student services. Adult student services, alcohol/substance abuse counseling, chaplain/spiritual director, career counseling, services for economically disadvantaged, student employment services, financial aid counseling, health services, minority student services, on-campus daycare, personal counseling, placement for graduates, veterans' counselor, women's services. **Physically disabled:** Services for visually, speech, hearing impaired.

Contact. E-mail: wolfgram@wou.edu
Phone: (503) 838-8211 Toll-free number: (877) 877-1593
Fax: (503) 838-8067
Rob Findtner, Director of Admissions, Western Oregon University, 345 North Monmouth Avenue, Monmouth, OR 97361

Willamette University

Salem, Oregon	**CB member**
www.willamette.edu	**CB code: 4954**

- Private 4-year university and liberal arts college affiliated with the United Methodist Church
- Residential campus in small city
- 1,938 degree-seeking undergraduates: 1% part-time, 57% women, 2% African American, 9% Asian American, 12% Hispanic/Latino, 1% Native American, 10% Multi-racial, non-Hispanic, 1% international
- 579 degree-seeking graduate students
- 78% of applicants admitted
- SAT or ACT with writing, application essay required
- 79% graduate within 6 years

General. Founded in 1842. Regionally accredited. Sister school to Tokyo International University of America. **Degrees:** 502 bachelor's awarded; master's, professional offered. **ROTC:** Army, Air Force. **Location:** 45 miles from Portland. **Calendar:** Semester. **Full-time faculty:** 217 total; 95% have terminal degrees, 22% minority, 45% women. **Part-time faculty:** 63 total; 81% have terminal degrees, 19% minority, 41% women. **Class size:** 56% < 20, 43% 20-39, less than 1% 40-49. **Special facilities:** Art museum, American headquarters for International Debate Education Association, papers and memorabilia of Senator Mark O. Hatfield, botanical gardens, Japanese gardens, rose gardens, rural retreat center, wildlife refuge field station, digital art and music studios, two electron microscopes (scanning and transmission), 500 MHz Nuclear Magnetic Resonance spectrometer, 305-acre Zena research forest.

Freshman class profile. 6,332 applied, 4,935 admitted, 521 enrolled.

Mid 50% test scores		GPA 2.0-2.99:	1%
SAT critical reading:	550-670	Rank in top quarter:	73%
SAT math:	550-660	Rank in top tenth:	40%
SAT writing:	550-650	Return as sophomores:	87%
ACT composite:	25-30	Out-of-state:	84%
GPA 3.75 or higher:	58%	Live on campus:	99%
GPA 3.50-3.74:	20%	International:	1%
GPA 3.0-3.49:	21%	Fraternities:	1%

Basis for selection. School record most important, followed by test scores, essay, recommendations, school and community activities, and interview. Audition recommended for music, theater programs; portfolio recommended for art program. **Home schooled:** Recommend submission of accredited transcript from governing agency, if available.

High school preparation. College-preparatory program recommended. 20 units recommended. Recommended units include English 4, mathematics 4, social studies 1, history 2, science 3 (laboratory 3), foreign language 4 and academic electives 2.

2015-2016 Annual costs. Tuition/fees: $45,616. Room/board: $11,200. Books/supplies: $950.

2015-2016 Financial aid. Need-based: 456 full-time freshmen applied for aid; 363 deemed to have need; 363 received aid. Average need met was 84%. Average scholarship/grant was $29,199; average loan $3,742. 76% of total undergraduate aid awarded as scholarships/grants, 24% as loans/jobs. **Non-need-based:** Awarded to 872 full-time undergraduates, including 245 freshmen. Scholarships awarded for academics, alumni affiliation, leadership, minority status, music/drama, religious affiliation.

Application procedures. Admission: Priority date 2/1; no deadline. $50 fee, may be waived for applicants with need, free for online applicants. Admission notification on a rolling basis beginning on or about 10/1. Must reply by May 1 or within 2 week(s) if notified thereafter. **Financial aid:** Priority date 2/1; no closing date. FAFSA required. Applicants notified on a rolling basis starting 4/1; must reply by 5/1 or within 2 week(s) of notification.

Academics. Special study options: Accelerated study, combined bachelor's/graduate degree, cross-registration, double major, dual enrollment of high school students, exchange student, independent study, internships, student-designed major, study abroad, teacher certification program, urban semester, Washington semester. Interdisciplinary freshman study program, undergraduate research grants, field studies program in ecology in Hawaii, Ecuador, American Southwest, Oregon; 3-2 program, master's degree in management; 3-2 program, bachelor's degree in computer science with Oregon Graduate Institute, University of Oregon; 3-2 program, master's degree in forestry with Duke University. **Credit/placement by examination:** AP, CLEP, IB, institutional tests. 32 credit hours maximum toward bachelor's degree. **Support services:** Learning center, reduced course load, study skills assistance, tutoring, writing center.

Majors. Area/ethnic studies: General, African, American, Asian, Chinese, East Asian, Japanese, Latin American, Western European, women's. **Biology:** General, neuroscience. **Communications:** Communications/speech/rhetoric. **Computer sciences:** General. **Conservation:** Environmental science. **English:** English lit, rhetoric/composition. **Foreign languages:** Classics, comparative lit, French, German, Russian, Spanish. **Health services:** Environmental health, music therapy. **History:** General. **Human services:** General. **Liberal arts:** Arts/sciences, humanities. **Math:** General. **Parks/recreation:** Exercise sciences. **Philosophy/religion:** Philosophy, religion. **Physical sciences:** Chemistry, physics. **Psychology:** General. **Social sciences:** Anthropology, archaeology, economics, political science, sociology. **Visual/performing arts:** Art, art history/conservation, dramatic, film/cinema/video, music, music pedagogy, music performance, music theory/composition, piano/keyboard, stringed instruments, voice/opera.

Most popular majors. Biology 12%, English 10%, foreign language 7%, psychology 6%, social sciences 29%, visual/performing arts 8%.

Technology on campus. 400 workstations in dormitories, library, computer center, student center. Dormitories wired for high-speed internet access and linked to campus network. Commuter students can connect to campus network. Online course registration, online library, helpline, repair service, student web hosting, wireless network available.

Student life. Freshman orientation: Mandatory. Preregistration for classes offered. 5 day program held prior to start of fall semester. **Housing:** Guaranteed on-campus for freshmen. Coed dorms, apartments, fraternity/sorority housing, wellness housing available. $400 nonrefundable deposit, deadline 5/1. Environmental, intensive study residences available. **Activities:** Bands, campus ministries, choral groups, dance, drama, film society, international student organizations, literary magazine, music ensembles, Model UN, musical theater, opera, student government, student newspaper, symphony orchestra, more than 100 student organizations available.

Athletics. NCAA. **Intercollegiate:** Baseball M, basketball, cross-country, football (tackle) M, golf, rowing (crew) W, soccer, softball W, swimming, tennis, track and field, volleyball W. **Intramural:** Badminton, basketball, football (non-tackle), golf, racquetball, soccer, softball, table tennis, tennis, ultimate frisbee, volleyball, weight lifting. **Team name:** Bearcats.

Student services. Alcohol/substance abuse counseling, chaplain/spiritual director, career counseling, student employment services, financial aid counseling, health services, minority student services, personal counseling, veterans' counselor, women's services. **Physically disabled:** Services for visually, speech, hearing impaired.

Contact. E-mail: libarts@willamette.edu
Phone: (503) 370-6303 Toll-free number: (877) 542-2787
Fax: (503) 375-5363
Michael Beseda, Vice President for Enrollment, Willamette University, 900 State Street, Salem, OR 97301-3922

Pennsylvania

Albright College

Reading, Pennsylvania   **CB member**
www.albright.edu   **CB code: 2004**

- Private 4-year liberal arts college affiliated with the United Methodist Church
- Residential campus in small city
- 2,228 degree-seeking undergraduates: 60% women, 18% African American, 3% Asian American, 10% Hispanic/Latino, 1% Native American, 1% Multi-racial, non-Hispanic, 2% international
- 17 degree-seeking graduate students
- 49% of applicants admitted
- Application essay required
- 58% graduate within 6 years; 18% enter graduate study

General. Founded in 1856. Regionally accredited. **Degrees:** 513 bachelor's awarded; master's offered. **ROTC:** Army. **Location:** 50 miles from Philadelphia. **Calendar:** 4-1-4, limited summer session. **Full-time faculty:** 109 total; 79% have terminal degrees, 15% minority, 50% women. **Part-time faculty:** 71 total; 32% have terminal degrees, 6% minority, 58% women. **Class size:** 60% < 20, 39% 20-39, less than 1% 40-49, less than 1% 50-99. **Special facilities:** LEED-certified science center includes atomic force, fluorescent and scanning tunneling microscopes, flow cytometer, thermocycler and gel electrophoreses imaging station, CD spectrometer, rapid-scan UV-VIS spectrophotometer, spectrofluorometers, variety of gas chromatographs, refrigerated superspeed and ultraspeed centrifuges, glove-box and solvent purification systems, GIS lab, and large meade telescope. Holocaust Resource Center, Center for Excellence in Local Government, Center for Cultural Ecology, Center for Latin American Studies, community garden, global media lounge.

Freshman class profile. 7,645 applied, 3,759 admitted, 493 enrolled.

Mid 50% test scores			
SAT critical reading:	450-580	Rank in top quarter:	38%
SAT math:	480-570	Rank in top tenth:	16%
ACT composite:	20-25	End year in good standing:	89%
GPA 3.75 or higher:	26%	Return as sophomores:	78%
GPA 3.50-3.74:	12%	Out-of-state:	41%
GPA 3.0-3.49:	34%	Live on campus:	89%
GPA 2.0-2.99:	28%	International:	3%

Basis for selection. High school performance (with emphasis on difficulty of curriculum pursued), personal statement, and recommendations most important. Community service, extracurricular activity and test scores considered. Albright is a test optional college; we will use test scores in the application review process for those who wish to submit their scores. Standardized test scores are not needed to make informed admission decisions, so applicants have the option of not submitting their scores. Those who choose to not submit standardized test scores will be reviewed equally with those who do submit scores. This equality extends to all programs and opportunities, including merit scholarships and awards. Interview recommended.

High school preparation. College-preparatory program required. 16 units required; 20 recommended. Required and recommended units include English 4, mathematics 3, social studies 2, history 1, science 3-4 (laboratory 1-2), foreign language 2-3 and academic electives 1. Bachelor of science applicants should have one additional unit in science and one in math. Two units of laboratory science recommended.

2015-2016 Annual costs. Tuition/fees: $39,850. Room/board: $10,770. Books/supplies: $1,000. Personal expenses: $1,860.

2015-2016 Financial aid. Need-based: 473 full-time freshmen applied for aid; 445 deemed to have need; 445 received aid. Average need met was 82%. Average scholarship/grant was $30,490; average loan $4,782. 76% of total undergraduate aid awarded as scholarships/grants, 24% as loans/jobs. **Non-need-based:** Scholarships awarded for academics, art, music/drama, religious affiliation, state residency. **Additional information:** If student's financial aid and admission application is complete by 3/1, college will meet 100% of the family's institutionally determined need.

Application procedures. Admission: Priority date 3/1; no deadline. $35 fee, may be waived for applicants with need. Admission notification on a rolling basis beginning on or about 10/1. Must reply by May 1 or within 2 week(s) if notified thereafter. **Financial aid:** Priority date 3/1; no closing date. FAFSA required. The CSS Profile can be optionally completed in the fall prior to the start of student's college experience for early awarding. Applicants notified on a rolling basis starting 11/20; must reply by 5/1 or within 2 week(s) of notification.

Academics. Curriculum is firmly grounded in the liberal arts, conferring the skills employers say they seek in new graduates. **Special study options:** Accelerated study, combined bachelor's/graduate degree, cross-registration, distance learning, double major, exchange student, honors, independent study, internships, liberal arts/career combination, semester at sea, student-designed major, study abroad, teacher certification program, Washington semester. Undergraduate research program, student-faculty projects. **Credit/placement by examination:** AP, CLEP, IB, SAT, institutional tests. 28 credit hours maximum toward bachelor's degree. **Support services:** Learning center, pre-admission summer program, reduced course load, study skills assistance, tutoring, writing center.

Majors. Area/ethnic studies: American, Latin American, women's. **Biology:** General, biochemistry. **Business:** Accounting, accounting/finance, business admin, fashion, finance, international, marketing. **Communications:** General, communications/speech/rhetoric, digital media, journalism, persuasive communications. **Computer sciences:** General, computer science, information systems, modeling/simulation, web page design. **Conservation:** Environmental science, environmental studies. **Education:** Art, early childhood, elementary, secondary. **English:** English lit. **Foreign languages:** French, Spanish. **Health services:** Predental, premedicine, preveterinary. **History:** General. **Math:** General. **Philosophy/religion:** Philosophy, religion. **Physical sciences:** Chemistry, optics, physics. **Psychology:** General, psychobiology. **Social sciences:** Anthropology, criminology, economics, international relations, political science, sociology. **Visual/performing arts:** Art, arts management, costume design, digital arts, dramatic, fashion design, game design, music management, studio arts, studio arts management, theater arts management.

Most popular majors. Business/marketing 33%, psychology 16%, social sciences 13%, visual/performing arts 8%.

Technology on campus. 450 workstations in dormitories, library, computer center, student center. Dormitories wired for high-speed internet access and linked to campus network. Online course registration, online library, helpline, wireless network available.

Student life. Freshman orientation: Mandatory. Preregistration for classes offered. Held four days prior to start of fall classes. **Housing:** Guaranteed on-campus for freshmen. Coed dorms, special housing for disabled, apartments, themed housing available. Honors housing, break housing suite, all freshmen housing, all-female floors, all-male floors, single rooms, single-sex suites/apartments/wings available. **Activities:** Bands, campus ministries, choral groups, dance, drama, film society, international student organizations, literary magazine, music ensembles, radio station, student government, student newspaper, Alpha Phi Omega, Caribbean culture club, South Asian students association, Albright Christian Fellowship, Chinese students association, African student association, African American student association.

Athletics. NCAA. **Intercollegiate:** Baseball M, basketball, cheerleading, cross-country, field hockey W, football (tackle) M, golf, lacrosse, soccer, softball W, swimming, tennis, track and field, volleyball W. **Intramural:** Basketball, bowling, football (non-tackle), soccer, softball, triathlon, volleyball. **Team name:** Lions.

Student services. Adult student services, alcohol/substance abuse counseling, chaplain/spiritual director, career counseling, student employment services, financial aid counseling, health services, minority student services, personal counseling, women's services. **Physically disabled:** Services for visually, hearing impaired.

Contact. E-mail: admission@albright.edu
Phone: (610) 921-7700 Toll-free number: (800) 252-1856
Fax: (610) 921-7729
Gregory Eichhorn, Vice-President for Enrollment Management and Dean of Admission, Albright College, North 13th and Bern Streets, Reading, PA 19612-5234

Allegheny College

Meadville, Pennsylvania   **CB member**
www.allegheny.edu   **CB code: 2006**

- Private 4-year liberal arts college affiliated with the United Methodist Church
- Residential campus in large town

- 1,896 degree-seeking undergraduates: 1% part-time, 54% women, 6% African American, 2% Asian American, 7% Hispanic/Latino, 5% Multi-racial, non-Hispanic, 3% international
- 68% of applicants admitted
- Application essay required
- 75% graduate within 6 years; 24% enter graduate study

General. Founded in 1815. Regionally accredited. **Degrees:** 461 bachelor's awarded. **Location:** 2 hours from Pittsburgh and Cleveland. **Calendar:** Semester. **Full-time faculty:** 173 total; 91% have terminal degrees, 17% minority, 50% women. **Part-time faculty:** 24 total; 29% have terminal degrees, 8% minority, 42% women. **Class size:** 70% < 20, 28% 20-39, 2% 40-49, less than 1% 50-99. **Special facilities:** Planetarium, observatory, Geographic Information Systems learning lab, 283-acre environmental research reserve, 80-acre protected forest, seismographic network station, art studios, art galleries, dance studio and performance area, Center for Political Participation, environmental roof garden, theater and communication arts center, language learning center, Center for Environmental Science, Center for Business & Economics, Augmented Reality Sandbox,.

Freshman class profile. 4,324 applied, 2,955 admitted, 492 enrolled.

Mid 50% test scores			
SAT critical reading:	500-630	Rank in top quarter:	65%
SAT math:	510-620	Rank in top tenth:	35%
SAT writing:	480-620	End year in good standing:	97%
ACT composite:	22-29	Return as sophomores:	84%
GPA 3.75 or higher:	47%	Out-of-state:	54%
GPA 3.50-3.74:	24%	Live on campus:	98%
GPA 3.0-3.49:	20%	International:	4%
GPA 2.0-2.99:	9%	Fraternities:	16%
		Sororities:	29%

Basis for selection. Rigor of high school program most important, followed by high school achievement. Standardized test scores are optional but will be considered if submitted. Essay, minority status, alumni ties, geography, first generation to attend college, and volunteer work considered. One recommendation from guidance counselor and one from teacher required. SAT or ACT recommended. Test optional college. Test scores will be considered if submitted. Interview recommended. **Home schooled:** Campus visit and individual interview with admissions counselor to discuss portfolios recommended. Recommendation from a non-family member. Description of the level of instruction. **Learning Disabled:** Recommended interview with Director of Disability Services.

High school preparation. College-preparatory program required. 16 units required. Required units include English 4, mathematics 3, social studies 3, science 3, foreign language 2 and academic electives 1.

2016-2017 Annual costs. Tuition/fees: $44,250. Room/board: $11,170. Books/supplies: $1,000. Personal expenses: $1,000.

2015-2016 Financial aid. Need-based: 423 full-time freshmen applied for aid; 375 deemed to have need; 375 received aid. Average need met was 92%. Average scholarship/grant was $32,544; average loan $4,033. 82% of total undergraduate aid awarded as scholarships/grants, 18% as loans/jobs. **Non-need-based:** Awarded to 710 full-time undergraduates, including 186 freshmen. Scholarships awarded for academics, leadership, minority status, state residency. **Additional information:** Non need-based financial aid also determined by extra-curricular and co-curricular involvement and special achievement or activities. Daytime work-study programs available.

Application procedures. Admission: Closing date 2/15 (postmark date). No application fee. Admission notification by 4/1. Must reply by 5/1. **Financial aid:** Priority date 2/15; no closing date. FAFSA required. Applicants notified on a rolling basis starting 3/1; must reply by 5/1 or within 4 week(s) of notification.

Academics. Special study options: Combined bachelor's/graduate degree, double major, dual enrollment of high school students, ESL, independent study, internships, student-designed major, study abroad, Washington semester. Graduate school partnerships, marine biology study program, combined engineering degree program (3-2), Experiential Learning Term (summer study seminars), double minor, service learning, pre-professional programs, domestic off-campus semester away study programs, accelerated master's and doctorate programs, New York Arts Program, Oak Ridge Science Semester, The Philadelphia Center, Newberry Seminar Research in the Humanities, Ecosystems Center. **Credit/placement by examination:** AP, CLEP, IB, institutional tests. 20 credit hours maximum toward bachelor's degree. Up to 32 prematriculation credits, includes credit by examination, may be earned for college-level courses offered at high schools by accredited colleges or universities. **Support services:** Learning center, reduced course load, study skills assistance, tutoring, writing center. Speech consultations, test taking strategies, time management.

Majors. Biology: General, biochemistry, neuroscience. **Business:** Managerial economics. **Communications:** Communications/speech/rhetoric, media studies. **Computer sciences:** Computer science. **Conservation:** Environmental science, environmental studies. **Engineering:** Software. **English:** Creative writing, English lit. **Foreign languages:** French, German, Spanish. **Health services:** International public health, predental, premedicine, prenursing, prepharmacy, preveterinary. **History:** General. **Human services:** Community org/advocacy. **Math:** General. **Philosophy/religion:** Philosophy, religion. **Physical sciences:** Chemistry, geology, physics. **Psychology:** General. **Social sciences:** Applied economics, economics, international relations, political science. **Visual/performing arts:** Art, art history/conservation, dramatic, music, music performance, studio arts.

Most popular majors. Biology 17%, English 7%, natural resources/environmental science 10%, physical sciences 7%, psychology 13%, social sciences 18%.

Technology on campus. 207 workstations in library, student center. Dormitories wired for high-speed internet access and linked to campus network. Commuter students can connect to campus network. Online course registration, online library, helpline, repair service, student web hosting, wireless network available.

Student life. Freshman orientation: Mandatory. Preregistration for classes offered. Three-day session held three days directly before fall classes begin. **Policies:** Honor code. **Housing:** Guaranteed on-campus for all undergraduates. Coed dorms, single-sex dorms, special housing for disabled, apartments, fraternity/sorority housing, gender-neutral housing, themed housing, wellness housing available. Townhouses: environmentally-sensitive, LEED certified, low fume material; quiet study floors, living/learning residential communities available. **Activities:** Bands, campus ministries, choral groups, dance, drama, international student organizations, literary magazine, music ensembles, Model UN, musical theater, radio station, student government, student newspaper, symphony orchestra, TV station, Advancement of Black Culture, Union Latina, Newman Association, Hillel, Christian Outreach, Alpha Phi Omega, Americorps Bonner Leaders, College Democrats, College Republicans, international club.

Athletics. NCAA. **Intercollegiate:** Baseball M, basketball, cross-country, diving, football (tackle) M, golf, lacrosse W, soccer, softball W, swimming, tennis, track and field, volleyball W. **Intramural:** Basketball, football (non-tackle), soccer, volleyball. **Team name:** Gators.

Student services. Adult student services, chaplain/spiritual director, career counseling, student employment services, financial aid counseling, health services, minority student services, personal counseling, placement for graduates. **Physically disabled:** Services for visually, hearing impaired.

Contact. E-mail: admissions@allegheny.edu
Phone: (814) 332-4351 Toll-free number: (800) 521-5293
Fax: (814) 337-0431
Cornell LeSane, V.P. for Enrollment & Dean of Admissions, Allegheny College, Box 5, 520 North Main Street, Meadville, PA 16335

Alvernia University
Reading, Pennsylvania
www.alvernia.edu

CB member
CB code: 2431

- Private 4-year university and liberal arts college affiliated with the Roman Catholic Church
- Residential campus in small city
- 2,177 degree-seeking undergraduates: 19% part-time, 71% women, 13% African American, 2% Asian American, 7% Hispanic/Latino, 1% Multi-racial, non-Hispanic
- 460 degree-seeking graduate students
- 74% of applicants admitted
- SAT or ACT (ACT writing optional), application essay required
- 51% graduate within 6 years

General. Founded in 1958. Regionally accredited. Affiliated with Bernardine Sisters, Third Order of St. Francis. **Degrees:** 469 bachelor's, 27 associate awarded; master's, professional, doctoral offered. **ROTC:** Army. **Location:** 60 miles from Philadelphia. **Calendar:** Semester, limited summer session. **Full-time faculty:** 107 total; 72% have terminal degrees, 8% minority, 53% women. **Part-time faculty:** 230 total; 29% have terminal degrees, 19% minority, 50% women. **Class size:** 71% < 20, 28% 20-39, less than 1% 40-49, 1% 50-99.

Freshman class profile. 1,670 applied, 1,240 admitted, 401 enrolled.

Mid 50% test scores			
SAT critical reading:	450-540	GPA 2.0-2.99:	20%
SAT math:	450-550	Rank in top quarter:	35%
SAT writing:	420-530	Rank in top tenth:	10%
ACT composite:	19-24	End year in good standing:	93%
GPA 3.75 or higher:	23%	Return as sophomores:	76%
GPA 3.50-3.74:	24%	Out-of-state:	25%
GPA 3.0-3.49:	33%	Live on campus:	78%

Basis for selection. Important factors include academic performance, standardized test scores, class rank, extracurricular activities, and community involvement. GPA requirement is higher for Nursing, Occupational Therapy, and Education majors. Interview recommended for all. Interview required of nursing, occupational therapy and physical therapist assistant applicants. Recommendation letters required of nursing applicants.

High school preparation. College-preparatory program recommended. 16 units recommended. Recommended units include English 4, mathematics 4, social studies 3, science 2, foreign language 2 and computer science 1.

2016-2017 Annual costs. Tuition/fees: $32,270. Room/board: $11,430. Books/supplies: $1,500. Personal expenses: $1,250.

2015-2016 Financial aid. **Need-based:** 387 full-time freshmen applied for aid; 341 deemed to have need; 340 received aid. Average need met was 70%. Average scholarship/grant was $18,979; average loan $3,206. 60% of total undergraduate aid awarded as scholarships/grants, 40% as loans/jobs. **Non-need-based:** Awarded to 341 full-time undergraduates, including 101 freshmen. Scholarships awarded for academics, ROTC.

Application procedures. **Admission:** No deadline. $25 fee, may be waived for applicants with need. Admission notification on a rolling basis beginning on or about 10/1. Must reply by May 1 or within 2 week(s) if notified thereafter. **Financial aid:** Priority date 5/1; no closing date. FAFSA required. Applicants notified on a rolling basis starting 3/1; must reply by 5/1.

Academics. **Special study options:** Accelerated study, combined bachelor's/graduate degree, cross-registration, distance learning, double major, dual enrollment of high school students, ESL, honors, independent study, internships, student-designed major, study abroad, teacher certification program, Washington semester. **Credit/placement by examination:** AP, CLEP, IB, institutional tests. 30 credit hours maximum toward associate degree, 30 toward bachelor's. Total of 30 credits allowed for all experiential credit, CLEP, life experience, challenge exam. **Support services:** Learning center, pre-admission summer program, reduced course load, remedial instruction, study skills assistance, tutoring, writing center.

Majors. **Biology:** General, biochemistry, environmental. **Business:** General, accounting, business admin, finance, human resources, marketing. **Communications:** Communications/speech/rhetoric. **Education:** General, biology, chemistry, early childhood, elementary, elementary special ed, English, mathematics, middle, science, secondary, social studies, special ed. **English:** English lit. **Health services:** Athletic training, health care admin, nursing (RN), substance abuse counseling. **History:** General. **Human services:** Social work. **Liberal arts:** Arts/sciences. **Math:** General. **Parks/recreation:** Sports admin. **Philosophy/religion:** Philosophy, religion. **Physical sciences:** Chemistry. **Protective services:** Forensics, law enforcement admin. **Psychology:** General. **Social sciences:** Political science. **Visual/performing arts:** Dramatic.

Most popular majors. Business/marketing 16%, education 6%, health sciences 36%, public administration/social services 6%, security/protective services 13%.

Technology on campus. 426 workstations in dormitories, library, computer center, student center. Dormitories wired for high-speed internet access and linked to campus network. Commuter students can connect to campus network. Online course registration, online library, helpline, wireless network available.

Student life. **Freshman orientation:** Mandatory. Preregistration for classes offered. Held weekend before classes start. **Housing:** Guaranteed on-campus for freshmen. Coed dorms, special housing for disabled, apartments, themed housing available. $250 nonrefundable deposit, deadline 6/15. Single-sex townhouses, single-sex floors in dorms available. **Activities:** Concert band, campus ministries, choral groups, dance, drama, literary magazine, music ensembles, student government, student newspaper.

Athletics. NCAA. **Intercollegiate:** Baseball M, basketball, cross-country, field hockey W, golf M, ice hockey M, lacrosse, soccer, softball W, tennis, track and field, volleyball W. **Intramural:** Basketball, cheerleading W, football (non-tackle), soccer. **Team name:** Crusaders.

Student services. Adult student services, alcohol/substance abuse counseling, chaplain/spiritual director, career counseling, services for economically disadvantaged, student employment services, financial aid counseling,

health services, minority student services, personal counseling, placement for graduates, veterans' counselor. **Physically disabled:** Services for visually, speech, hearing impaired.

Contact. E-mail: admissions@alvernia.edu
Phone: (610) 796-8269 Toll-free number: (888) 258-3764
Fax: (610) 790-2873
Dan Hartzman, Director of Undergraduate Admissions, Alvernia University, 400 St. Bernardine Street, Reading, PA 19607-1799

Arcadia University
Glenside, Pennsylvania
www.arcadia.edu

CB member
CB code: 2039

- Private 4-year university affiliated with the Presbyterian Church (USA)
- Residential campus in large town
- 2,501 degree-seeking undergraduates: 5% part-time, 69% women, 9% African American, 5% Asian American, 8% Hispanic/Latino, 4% Multiracial, non-Hispanic, 3% international
- 1,239 degree-seeking graduate students
- SAT or ACT with writing, application essay required

General. Founded in 1853. Regionally accredited. **Degrees:** 496 bachelor's awarded; master's, professional, doctoral offered. **ROTC:** Army. **Location:** 10 miles from Philadelphia. **Calendar:** Semester, limited summer session. **Full-time faculty:** 163 total; 12% minority, 60% women. **Part-time faculty:** 312 total; 15% minority, 61% women. **Class size:** 72% < 20, 23% 20-39, 1% 40-49, 3% 50-99. **Special facilities:** Observatory housing 14-inch Schmidt-Cassegrain telescope with extensive astrophotography capabilities, Grey Towers Castle (national historic landmark) used as residence hall.

Freshman class profile.

GPA 3.75 or higher:	43%	Rank in top tenth:	28%
GPA 3.50-3.74:	27%	Out-of-state:	42%
GPA 3.0-3.49:	21%	Live on campus:	77%
GPA 2.0-2.99:	9%	International:	1%
Rank in top quarter:	60%		

Basis for selection. Emphasis placed on academic records, including type of program followed, courses taken, grades earned, class rank. Standardized test scores, counselor/ teacher recommendations, participation in school and community activities important. Character references also considered. Supplementary materials demonstrating student's talents and potential recommended. Portfolio review required for fine arts department. Auditions required for BFA in acting. **Home schooled:** Statement describing home school structure and mission, letter of recommendation (nonparent) required. Portfolio representing academic record/work and level of achievement for grades 9-12 required.

High school preparation. College-preparatory program required. 19 units recommended. Recommended units include English 4, mathematics 3, social studies 2, history 2, science 3 (laboratory 3) and foreign language 2. Additional units in foreign language, math, and/or laboratory science recommended. Math includes algebra II and geometry.

2015-2016 Annual costs. Tuition/fees: $39,560. Room/board: $13,200. Books/supplies: $1,500. Personal expenses: $850.

Financial aid. **Non-need-based:** Scholarships awarded for academics, alumni affiliation, art, leadership, music/drama. **Additional information:** Automatic $1,000 renewable FAFSA Early Filer Grant for new incoming full-time undergraduates who file FAFSA by March 1, listing Arcadia as a recipient school on the form, and have a completed admissions application on file by March 1.

Application procedures. **Admission:** Priority date 1/15; deadline 3/1. $30 fee, may be waived for applicants with need, free for online applicants. Admission notification on a rolling basis beginning on or about 9/1. Must reply by May 1 or within 2 week(s) if notified thereafter. **Financial aid:** Priority date 3/1; no closing date. FAFSA, institutional form required. Applicants notified on a rolling basis starting 2/1; must reply by 5/1.

Academics. **Special study options:** Accelerated study, combined bachelor's/graduate degree, cooperative education, cross-registration, distance learning, double major, dual enrollment of high school students, exchange student, honors, independent study, internships, liberal arts/career combination, student-designed major, study abroad, teacher certification program, Washington semester. Combined programs leading to graduate degrees in physical therapy, physician assistant studies (option to combine with public health), forensic science, international peace and conflict resolution. Combined with other universities for degrees in engineering, nursing, optometry. **Credit/placement by examination:** AP, CLEP, IB, institutional tests. 64

credit hours maximum toward bachelor's degree. **Support services:** Learning center, pre-admission summer program, reduced course load, remedial instruction, study skills assistance, tutoring, writing center.

Majors. Area/ethnic studies: French, Italian, Spanish/Iberian. **Biology:** General. **Business:** General, accounting, actuarial science, business admin, finance, human resources, international, management information systems, management science, marketing. **Communications:** Communications/speech/rhetoric, media studies, radio/TV. **Computer sciences:** General, computer science, programming. **Conservation:** Environmental studies. **Education:** General, art, biology, chemistry, early childhood, elementary, English, mathematics, multi-level teacher, science, secondary, social science, social studies, special ed. **Engineering:** General. **English:** Creative writing, English lit. **Foreign languages:** French, Spanish. **Health services:** Art therapy, facilities admin, health care admin, health services admin, medical illustrating. **History:** General. **Liberal arts:** Arts/sciences. **Math:** General. **Philosophy/religion:** Philosophy, religion. **Physical sciences:** Chemistry, physics. **Psychology:** General. **Social sciences:** Criminology, cultural anthropology, international relations, political science, sociology. **Visual/performing arts:** General, acting, art, art history/conservation, ceramics, commercial/advertising art, dramatic, graphic design, illustration, interior design, metal/jewelry, painting, photography, printmaking, studio arts, theater history.

Most popular majors. Biology 15%, business/marketing 13%, interdisciplinary studies 6%, psychology 11%, social sciences 11%, visual/performing arts 9%.

Technology on campus. 400 workstations in library, computer center. Dormitories wired for high-speed internet access and linked to campus network. Commuter students can connect to campus network. Online course registration, helpline, repair service, wireless network available.

Student life. Freshman orientation: Mandatory. Preregistration for classes offered. **Housing:** Guaranteed on-campus for all undergraduates. Coed dorms, single-sex dorms, special housing for disabled, apartments, wellness housing available. $400 nonrefundable deposit, deadline 5/1. Living and learning community available. **Activities:** Choral groups, dance, drama, literary magazine, music ensembles, musical theater, radio station, student government, student newspaper, TV station, approximately 45 clubs and organizations.

Athletics. NCAA. **Intercollegiate:** Baseball M, basketball, equestrian, field hockey W, golf, lacrosse, soccer, softball W, swimming, tennis, volleyball W. **Intramural:** Basketball, field hockey W, football (non-tackle), skiing, soccer, softball, swimming M, tennis, volleyball, weight lifting. **Team name:** Scarlet Knights.

Student services. Adult student services, alcohol/substance abuse counseling, career counseling, services for economically disadvantaged, student employment services, financial aid counseling, health services, minority student services, personal counseling, placement for graduates. **Physically disabled:** Services for visually, speech, hearing impaired.

Contact. E-mail: admiss@arcadia.edu
Phone: (215) 572-2910 Toll-free number: (877) 272-2342
Fax: (215) 881-8767
Mark Lapreziosa, Associate Vice President of Enrollment Management, Arcadia University, 450 South Easton Road, Glenside, PA 19038-3295

Art Institute of Philadelphia
Philadelphia, Pennsylvania
www.artinstitutes.edu/Philadelphia   **CB code: 2033**

‣ For-profit 4-year visual arts college
‣ Commuter campus in very large city
‣ 1,953 undergraduates
‣ Application essay, interview required

General. Founded in 1966. Regionally accredited. **Degrees:** 242 bachelor's, 145 associate awarded. **Calendar:** Quarter, extensive summer session. **Full-time faculty:** 91 total. **Part-time faculty:** 89 total. **Special facilities:** Recording studio utilizing Pro-tools software, digital photography laboratory, nonlinear digital editing suites, full-service chef instructor/student-run restaurant.

Basis for selection. High school transcript most important. Essay and interview required. Portfolio recommended. **Home schooled:** Transcript of courses and grades, state high school equivalency certificate required.

High school preparation. Background or strong interest in chosen major preferred.

2015-2016 Annual costs. Tuition/fees: $22,375. Room only: $8,673. Books/supplies: $2,094. Personal expenses: $3,354. **Additional information:** Additional fees may be apply. All costs are subject to change.

Financial aid. Additional information: Institute-sponsored scholarships available. May 1st application deadline for Pennsylvania State Grant.

Application procedures. Admission: No deadline. $50 fee. Admission notification on a rolling basis. **Financial aid:** No deadline. FAFSA, institutional form required. Applicants notified on a rolling basis starting 3/1; must reply within 2 week(s) of notification.

Academics. Academic program designed to simulate working environment, focusing course work on job-related skills. **Special study options:** Independent study, internships. **Credit/placement by examination:** AP, CLEP, IB, SAT, ACT, institutional tests. **Support services:** Learning center, reduced course load, remedial instruction, study skills assistance, tutoring.

Majors. Business: Apparel. **Communications:** Advertising. **Communications technology:** Animation/special effects, recording arts. **Computer sciences:** Computer graphics, web page design. **Visual/performing arts:** Cinematography, commercial photography, fashion design, graphic design, industrial design, interior design.

Most popular majors. Business/marketing 21%, communication technologies 6%, computer/information sciences 15%, visual/performing arts 51%.

Technology on campus. 507 workstations in dormitories, library, computer center. Dormitories wired for high-speed internet access. Online library, student web hosting available.

Student life. Freshman orientation: Mandatory. Preregistration for classes offered. **Housing:** Guaranteed on-campus for all undergraduates. Coed dorms, apartments available. **Activities:** Student government.

Student services. Career counseling, student employment services, financial aid counseling, personal counseling, placement for graduates.

Contact. E-mail: aiphadm@aii.edu
Phone: (215) 567-7080 Toll-free number: (800) 275-2474
Fax: (215) 405-6399
Steven Cohen, Director of Admissions, Art Institute of Philadelphia, 1622 Chestnut Street, Philadelphia, PA 19103-5198

Art Institute of Pittsburgh
Pittsburgh, Pennsylvania
www.artinstitutes.edu/pittsburgh   **CB code: 2029**

‣ For-profit 4-year culinary school and visual arts college
‣ Commuter campus in large city
‣ 900 degree-seeking undergraduates
‣ Application essay, interview required

General. Founded in 1921. Regionally accredited. **Degrees:** 193 bachelor's, 117 associate awarded. **Calendar:** Differs by program, extensive summer session. **Full-time faculty:** 20 total. **Part-time faculty:** 80 total. **Special facilities:** Photography laboratory, art gallery, traveling exhibits, 24-track recording studio.

Freshman class profile.

Out-of-state:	50%	Live on campus:	50%

Basis for selection. High school transcript most important. Limited portfolio required for some programs. **Home schooled:** Statement describing home school structure and mission, transcript of courses and grades, state high school equivalency certificate, letter of recommendation (nonparent) required.

High school preparation. Prefer students with demonstrated interest in chosen major.

2016-2017 Annual costs. Tuition/fees (projected): $23,476. Room only: $7,956. Books/supplies: $1,626.

Application procedures. Admission: $50 fee. Admission notification on a rolling basis. **Financial aid:** No deadline. FAFSA, institutional form required. Applicants notified on a rolling basis starting 4/15.

Academics. Special study options: Distance learning, internships. **Credit/placement by examination:** AP, CLEP, IB, institutional tests. **Support services:** Learning center, remedial instruction, tutoring, writing center.

Majors. Business: Fashion. **Communications:** Advertising. **Communications technology:** Animation/special effects. **Computer sciences:** Computer graphics, web page design. **Visual/performing arts:** Cinematography, commercial photography, commercial/advertising art, design, game design, graphic design, industrial design, interior design.

Technology on campus. 447 workstations in dormitories, library, computer center. Dormitories wired for high-speed internet access and linked to campus network. Commuter students can connect to campus network. Online course registration, online library, helpline, student web hosting, wireless network available.

Student life. Freshman orientation: Mandatory. Preregistration for classes offered. One-day program held before start of classes. **Housing:** Coed dorms, apartments, wellness housing available. $100 deposit. **Activities:** Drama, film society, international student organizations, student government, community relations activities, student success task force, student council.

Student services. Alcohol/substance abuse counseling, career counseling, student employment services, financial aid counseling, personal counseling, placement for graduates, veterans' counselor. **Physically disabled:** Services for visually, speech, hearing impaired.

Contact. E-mail: aipadm@aii.edu
Phone: (412) 263-6600 Toll-free number: (800) 275-2470
Fax: (412) 263-6667
Jennifer O'Brien, Senior Director of Admissions, Art Institute of Pittsburgh, 420 Boulevard of the Allies, Pittsburgh, PA 15219-1328

Bloomsburg University of Pennsylvania
Bloomsburg, Pennsylvania — CB member
www.bloomu.edu — CB code: 2646

- Public 4-year university
- Residential campus in large town
- 8,931 degree-seeking undergraduates: 6% part-time, 57% women, 9% African American, 1% Asian American, 6% Hispanic/Latino, 3% Multiracial, non-Hispanic, 1% international
- 594 degree-seeking graduate students
- 88% of applicants admitted
- SAT or ACT (ACT writing optional) required
- 62% graduate within 6 years

General. Founded in 1839. Regionally accredited. **Degrees:** 1,926 bachelor's awarded; master's, professional offered. **ROTC:** Army, Air Force. **Location:** 40 miles from Wilkes-Barre, 80 miles from Harrisburg. **Calendar:** Semester, extensive summer session. **Full-time faculty:** 414 total; 84% have terminal degrees, 12% minority, 43% women. **Part-time faculty:** 80 total; 12% have terminal degrees, 4% minority, 65% women. **Class size:** 23% < 20, 66% 20-39, 5% 40-49, 3% 50-99, 3% >100.

Freshman class profile. 9,795 applied, 8,592 admitted, 2,109 enrolled.

Mid 50% test scores			
SAT critical reading:	440-540	Rank in top quarter:	26%
		Rank in top tenth:	8%
SAT math:	440-540	Return as sophomores:	77%
SAT writing:	420-520	Out-of-state:	11%
ACT composite:	18-23	Live on campus:	90%

Basis for selection. Acceptance is determined after evaluation of high school work, achievement, SAT or ACT test scores, personal characteristics and enrollment capacity. To be considered for nursing, application must be complete by 11/15 of your senior year. Applications received by 12/1 will get priority consideration. All freshmen (including international students) are required to complete the ACCUPLACER Placement Test at Bloomsburg University. **Home schooled:** Statement describing home school structure and mission, transcript of courses and grades, state high school equivalency certificate required.

High school preparation. College-preparatory program recommended. 16 units required; 21 recommended. Required and recommended units include English 4, mathematics 3-4, social studies 2, history 2, science 3-4, foreign language 2, computer science 1 and academic electives 2.

2015-2016 Annual costs. Tuition/fees: $9,326; $19,916 out-of-state. Room/board: $8,480. Books/supplies: $1,200. Personal expenses: $2,530.

2015-2016 Financial aid. Need-based: 1,979 full-time freshmen applied for aid; 1,375 deemed to have need; 1,339 received aid. Average need met was 50%. Average scholarship/grant was $6,053; average loan $3,196. 47% of total undergraduate aid awarded as scholarships/grants, 53% as loans/jobs. **Non-need-based:** Awarded to 1,321 full-time undergraduates, including 460 freshmen. Scholarships awarded for academics, art, athletics, job skills, leadership, minority status, music/drama, ROTC, state residency.

Application procedures. Admission: Priority date 12/1; no deadline. $35 fee, may be waived for applicants with need. Admission notification on a rolling basis beginning on or about 9/18. Must reply by May 1 or within 2 week(s) if notified thereafter. **Financial aid:** Priority date 3/15; no closing date. FAFSA required. Applicants notified on a rolling basis starting 4/1.

Academics. The Department of Alumni and Professional Engagement works in collaboration with Global Education, Undergraduate Research and professional institutes in the College of Business and the College of Education. Professional U programs complement classroom learning by providing students with professional development and career experiences each year until graduation. **Special study options:** Combined bachelor's/graduate degree, cooperative education, cross-registration, distance learning, double major, dual enrollment of high school students, ESL, exchange student, honors, independent study, internships, liberal arts/career combination, student-designed major, study abroad, teacher certification program. **Credit/placement by examination:** AP, CLEP, institutional tests. 64 credit hours maximum toward bachelor's degree. **Support services:** Learning center, pre-admission summer program, reduced course load, remedial instruction, study skills assistance, tutoring, writing center.

Majors. Biology: General. **Business:** General, accounting, business admin. **Communications:** Communications/speech/rhetoric, media studies. **Computer sciences:** General, computer science. **Education:** Early childhood, middle, special ed. **Engineering:** Electrical. **English:** English lit. **Foreign languages:** General, sign language interpretation. **Health services:** Audiology/speech pathology, clinical lab science, medical radiologic technology/radiation therapy, nursing (RN), physics/radiologic health. **History:** General. **Human services:** Social work. **Math:** General. **Philosophy/religion:** Philosophy. **Physical sciences:** Chemistry, geology, physics. **Protective services:** Computer forensics, criminal justice. **Psychology:** General. **Social sciences:** Anthropology, economics, political science, sociology. **Visual/performing arts:** Art history/conservation, dramatic, music, studio arts.

Most popular majors. Business/marketing 22%, communications/journalism 11%, education 10%, health sciences 12%, psychology 6%, security/protective services 8%, social sciences 9%.

Technology on campus. 1,571 workstations in dormitories, library, computer center, student center. Dormitories wired for high-speed internet access and linked to campus network. Commuter students can connect to campus network. Online course registration, online library, helpline, wireless network available.

Student life. Freshman orientation: Mandatory, $95 fee. Preregistration for classes offered. Preview day program in summer and a 3-day program prior to start of classes. **Housing:** Guaranteed on-campus for freshmen. Coed dorms, apartments, cooperative housing, wellness housing available. $100 partly refundable deposit, deadline 5/1. Ten living and learning communities available: business, Compass, education, Frederick Douglass, health sciences, honors, Presidential Leadership, Quest Outdoor Leadership, ROTC, visual and performing arts. **Activities:** Bands, campus ministries, choral groups, dance, drama, international student organizations, literary magazine, music ensembles, Model UN, radio station, student government, student newspaper, symphony orchestra, TV station, Catholic Campus Ministry, Protestant Campus Ministry, Hillel, University Democrats, College Republicans, Black Cultural Society, Student Organization of Latinos, International Students Association, Student Veterans Association.

Athletics. NCAA. **Intercollegiate:** Baseball M, basketball, cross-country, field hockey W, football (tackle) M, lacrosse W, soccer, softball W, swimming, tennis, track and field, wrestling M. **Intramural:** Basketball, field hockey W, football (non-tackle) M, sand volleyball, soccer, softball, ultimate frisbee, volleyball. **Team name:** Huskies.

Student services. Adult student services, alcohol/substance abuse counseling, chaplain/spiritual director, career counseling, services for economically disadvantaged, student employment services, financial aid counseling, health services, legal services, minority student services, on-campus daycare, personal counseling, placement for graduates, veterans' counselor, women's services. **Physically disabled:** Services for visually, speech, hearing impaired.

Contact. E-mail: buadmiss@bloomu.edu
Phone: (570) 389-4316 Fax: (570) 389-4741
Christopher Lapos, Director of Admissions, Bloomsburg University of Pennsylvania, 104 Student Service Center, Bloomsburg, PA 17815

Bryn Athyn College
Bryn Athyn, Pennsylvania — CB member
www.brynathyn.edu — CB code: 2002

- Private 4-year liberal arts college affiliated with the Christian Church
- Residential campus in small town
- 273 degree-seeking undergraduates: 3% part-time, 47% women, 20% African American, 3% Asian American, 10% Hispanic/Latino, 4% international

♦ 4 degree-seeking graduate students
♦ 87% of applicants admitted
♦ SAT or ACT (ACT writing recommended), application essay required
♦ 77% graduate within 6 years

General. Founded in 1876. Regionally accredited. Religious college. **Degrees:** 50 bachelor's, 8 associate awarded; master's offered. **ROTC:** Army, Air Force. **Location:** 15 miles from Philadelphia. **Calendar:** Trimester. **Full-time faculty:** 28 total; 61% have terminal degrees, 4% minority, 39% women. **Part-time faculty:** 22 total; 46% have terminal degrees, 9% minority, 54% women. **Class size:** 86% < 20, 14% 20-39. **Special facilities:** Performing arts center, local and church archives, ecological restoration trust, cathedral, ice rink and pavilion, social center, Cairnwood Estate, outdoor sanctuary, Glencairn Museum.

Freshman class profile. 213 applied, 186 admitted, 78 enrolled.

Mid 50% test scores			
SAT critical reading:	390-560	GPA 3.0-3.49:	41%
SAT math:	400-550	GPA 2.0-2.99:	32%
SAT writing:	390-530	Return as sophomores:	64%
ACT composite:	18-23	Out-of-state:	30%
GPA 3.75 or higher:	14%	Live on campus:	63%
GPA 3.50-3.74:	13%	International:	1%

Basis for selection. Holistic approach to reviewing admissions. Students who want strong academics based on spiritual principles important. TOEFL required of non-native English speakers. SAT may be required of some Canadian applicants. Interview recommended; may be required. **Home schooled:** SAT Subject Tests in literature and math recommended.

High school preparation. College-preparatory program recommended. 15 units required. Required and recommended units include English 4, mathematics 3, social studies 3, history 3, science 3 (laboratory 3) and foreign language 2.

2015-2016 Annual costs. Tuition/fees: $19,353. Room/board: $11,202. Books/supplies: $750. Personal expenses: $1,000.

2015-2016 Financial aid. **Need-based:** 77 full-time freshmen applied for aid; 69 deemed to have need; 69 received aid. Average need met was 68%. Average scholarship/grant was $11,288; average loan $3,414. 68% of total undergraduate aid awarded as scholarships/grants, 32% as loans/jobs. **Non-need-based:** Awarded to 156 full-time undergraduates, including 47 freshmen. Scholarships awarded for academics, religious affiliation.

Application procedures. **Admission:** Priority date 2/1; no deadline. No application fee. Admission notification on a rolling basis beginning on or about 9/15. Must reply by May 1 or within 2 week(s) if notified thereafter. **Financial aid:** Priority date 2/15; no closing date. FAFSA required. Applicants notified by 2/18; Applicants notified on a rolling basis starting 3/15; must reply within 3 week(s) of notification.

Academics. **Special study options:** Accelerated study, cooperative education, cross-registration, dual enrollment of high school students, ESL, independent study, internships, student-designed major, study abroad, teacher certification program. Students can combine multiple curricular areas to design an educational program tailored to meet their particular interests, abilities, and needs. We do not have an ESL program, but we do have classes designed for international students. **Credit/placement by examination:** AP, CLEP, IB, institutional tests. Advanced standing and various types of credit at the 100-level for some AP and IB tests. **Support services:** Learning center, reduced course load, study skills assistance, tutoring, writing center. Math center and a research center, peer tutoring program, Academic Center of Excellence.

Majors. **Biology:** General. **Business:** General. **Education:** General, English. **English:** English lit. **History:** General. **Math:** General. **Philosophy/religion:** Religion. **Psychology:** General. **Theology:** Theology.

Most popular majors. Biology 10%, education 16%, history 14%, interdisciplinary studies 27%, psychology 23%.

Technology on campus. PC or laptop required. 24 workstations in dormitories, library, computer center, student center. Dormitories wired for high-speed internet access and linked to campus network. Commuter students can connect to campus network. Helpline, repair service, wireless network available.

Student life. **Freshman orientation:** Mandatory. Preregistration for classes offered. Held the weekend before classes begin. **Policies:** No alcohol on campus, restricted dorm visiting, required chapel attendance. Religious observance required. **Housing:** Guaranteed on-campus for all undergraduates. Single-sex dorms available. $250 fully refundable deposit, deadline 7/1. On campus housing (cottages) for upper classmen. **Activities:** Concert band, choral groups, dance, drama, international student organizations, literary magazine, music ensembles, student newspaper, Active Minds, community

service organization, dance ensemble, multicultural student services organization, outing club, peer listening group, social committee, student-athlete advisory committee, women's A Cappella.

Athletics. **Intercollegiate:** Basketball, ice hockey M, lacrosse, soccer M, tennis, volleyball W. **Team name:** Lions.

Student services. Alcohol/substance abuse counseling, chaplain/spiritual director, career counseling, student employment services, financial aid counseling, health services, minority student services, personal counseling.

Contact. E-mail: admissions@brynathyn.edu
Phone: (267) 502-6073 Toll-free number: (800) 767-9552
Fax: (267) 502-2593
Matthew McCaffrey, Director of Admissions, Bryn Athyn College, PO Box 462, Bryn Athyn, PA 19009-0462

Bryn Mawr College
Bryn Mawr, Pennsylvania
www.brynmawr.edu
CB member
CB code: 2049

♦ Private 4-year liberal arts college for women
♦ Residential campus in very large city
♦ 1,341 degree-seeking undergraduates: 1% part-time, 100% women, 6% African American, 12% Asian American, 9% Hispanic/Latino, 5% Multiracial, non-Hispanic, 23% international
♦ 343 degree-seeking graduate students
♦ 39% of applicants admitted
♦ Application essay required
♦ 85% graduate within 6 years; 20% enter graduate study

General. Founded in 1885. Regionally accredited. Academic exchange with Haverford College, Swarthmore College, and University of Pennsylvania. Extracurricular and social coordination with Haverford College. **Degrees:** 322 bachelor's awarded; master's, doctoral offered. **ROTC:** Air Force. **Location:** 11 miles from Philadelphia. **Calendar:** Semester, limited summer session. **Full-time faculty:** 154 total; 95% have terminal degrees, 20% minority, 55% women. **Part-time faculty:** 60 total; 73% have terminal degrees, 7% minority, 67% women. **Class size:** 73% < 20, 21% 20-39, 2% 40-49, 4% 50-99. **Special facilities:** Collections of mineral, archaeological, and anthropological artifacts.

Freshman class profile. 2,890 applied, 1,113 admitted, 385 enrolled.

Mid 50% test scores			
SAT critical reading:	620-730	Rank in top tenth:	63%
SAT math:	620-730	Return as sophomores:	94%
SAT writing:	630-730	Out-of-state:	89%
ACT composite:	28-32	Live on campus:	100%
Rank in top quarter:	88%	International:	21%

Basis for selection. School achievement record, recommendations, essay most important. Test scores (if provided), school and community activities, extracurricular achievements important. SAT I or ACT scores are optional for US citizens and US permanent residents. Non-US citizens and Non-US permanent residents are required to submit standardized test scores (SAT I or ACT). Interview recommended. **Home schooled:** Statement describing home school structure and mission, transcript of courses and grades, state high school equivalency certificate, interview, letter of recommendation (nonparent) required. Interview required, but may be completed with admissions officer or alumna.

High school preparation. College-preparatory program recommended. 16 units recommended. Recommended units include English 4, mathematics 3, social studies 2, history 2, science 2 (laboratory 1), foreign language 3 and academic electives 2.

2015-2016 Annual costs. Tuition/fees: $47,140. Room/board: $14,850. Books/supplies: $1,000. Personal expenses: $1,000.

2015-2016 Financial aid. All financial aid based on need. 244 full-time freshmen applied for aid; 198 deemed to have need; 198 received aid. Average need met was 100%. Average scholarship/grant was $38,885; average loan $4,291. 89% of total undergraduate aid awarded as scholarships/grants, 11% as loans/jobs.

Application procedures. **Admission:** Closing date 1/15 (postmark date). $50 fee, may be waived for applicants with need, free for online applicants. Admission notification by 4/1. Must reply by 5/1. **Financial aid:** Priority date 2/5, closing date 3/1. FAFSA, CSS PROFILE required. Applicants notified by 3/23; must reply by 5/1.

Academics. **Special study options:** Accelerated study, combined bachelor's/graduate degree, cross-registration, double major, dual enrollment of high school students, exchange student, independent study, internships, liberal arts/career combination, student-designed major, study abroad, teacher certification program. A.B./M.A. City Planning 3-2 Program in City and Regional Planning with the University of Pennsylvania. A.B./B.S. 3-2 engineering programs with University of Pennsylvania. **Credit/placement by examination:** AP, CLEP, IB, institutional tests. 32 credit hours maximum toward bachelor's degree. **Support services:** Pre-admission summer program, reduced course load, study skills assistance, tutoring, writing center.

Majors. **Architecture:** Urban/community planning. **Area/ethnic studies:** East Asian. **Biology:** General, Biochemistry/molecular biology. **Computer sciences:** Computer science. **English:** English lit. **Foreign languages:** Ancient Greek, classics, comparative lit, French, German, Italian, Latin, Russian, Spanish. **History:** General. **Math:** General. **Philosophy/religion:** Philosophy, religion. **Physical sciences:** Astronomy, chemistry, geology, physics. **Psychology:** General. **Social sciences:** Anthropology, archaeology, economics, political science, sociology, urban studies. **Visual/performing arts:** Art history/conservation, music, studio arts.

Most popular majors. Biology 10%, English 7%, foreign language 9%, interdisciplinary studies 7%, mathematics 9%, physical sciences 6%, psychology 15%, social sciences 24%, visual/performing arts 6%.

Technology on campus. 200 workstations in dormitories, library, computer center, student center. Dormitories linked to campus network. Commuter students can connect to campus network. Online course registration, online library, helpline, repair service, student web hosting, wireless network available.

Student life. **Freshman orientation:** Mandatory. Preregistration for classes offered. Week-long program; students divided into groups of 10-20 students based on residence hall assignments. **Policies:** Self-governing student body, academic and social honor code, Customs and Traditions programs. **Housing:** Guaranteed on-campus for all undergraduates. Coed dorms, apartments, cooperative housing available. $200 fully refundable deposit, deadline 6/1. Students may live at Haverford. Foreign language houses available (Chinese, French, German, Hebrew, Italian, Russian, Spanish). Special housing available for non-traditional-aged students. Co-ops, such as Vegan House, are available as well. **Activities:** Jazz band, choral groups, dance, drama, film society, international student organizations, literary magazine, music ensembles, Model UN, musical theater, radio station, student government, student newspaper, Mujeres, Rainbow Alliance, investment group, Jewish student union.

Athletics. NCAA. **Intercollegiate:** Badminton W, basketball W, cross-country W, field hockey W, lacrosse W, rowing (crew) W, soccer W, swimming W, tennis W, track and field W, volleyball W. **Intramural:** Tennis W, volleyball W. **Team name:** Owls.

Student services. Adult student services, alcohol/substance abuse counseling, chaplain/spiritual director, career counseling, services for economically disadvantaged, student employment services, financial aid counseling, health services, minority student services, personal counseling, placement for graduates, women's services. **Physically disabled:** Services for visually, speech, hearing impaired.

Contact. E-mail: admissions@brynmawr.edu
Phone: (610) 526-5152 Toll-free number: (800) 262-1885
Fax: (610) 526-7471
Peaches Valdes, Director of Admissions, Bryn Mawr College, 101 North Merion Avenue, Bryn Mawr, PA 19010-2899

Bucknell University
Lewisburg, Pennsylvania   CB member
www.bucknell.edu   CB code: 2050

- Private 4-year university
- Residential campus in small town
- 3,522 degree-seeking undergraduates: 52% women, 3% African American, 4% Asian American, 6% Hispanic/Latino, 4% Multi-racial, non-Hispanic, 5% international
- 47 degree-seeking graduate students
- 25% of applicants admitted
- SAT or ACT (ACT writing optional), application essay required
- 90% graduate within 6 years; 20% enter graduate study

General. Founded in 1846. Regionally accredited. **Degrees:** 868 bachelor's awarded; master's offered. **ROTC:** Army. **Location:** 75 miles from Harrisburg; 195 miles from Philadelphia. **Calendar:** Semester, limited summer

session. **Full-time faculty:** 375 total; 96% have terminal degrees, 16% minority, 41% women. **Part-time faculty:** 50 total; 74% have terminal degrees, 14% minority, 60% women. **Class size:** 59% < 20, 38% 20-39, 1% 40-49, 1% 50-99, less than 1% >100. **Special facilities:** Observatory, 63-acre nature preserve, center for performing arts, poetry center, greenhouse, outdoor naturalistic primate facility, engineering structural test lab, gas chromatograph/mass spectrometer, nuclear magnetic resonance spectrometer, herbarium, 18-hole golf course, small business development center, environmental center, center for public policy, high ropes course.

Freshman class profile. 10,967 applied, 2,718 admitted, 938 enrolled.

Mid 50% test scores			
SAT critical reading:	590-680	GPA 2.0-2.99:	6%
SAT math:	620-710	Rank in top quarter:	91%
SAT writing:	590-690	Rank in top tenth:	65%
ACT composite:	28-32	End year in good standing:	92%
GPA 3.75 or higher:	31%	Return as sophomores:	93%
GPA 3.50-3.74:	25%	Out-of-state:	79%
GPA 3.0-3.49:	38%	Live on campus:	100%
		International:	5%

Basis for selection. Emphasis on school achievement. Test scores, recommendations, special talents and abilities, evidence of volunteer work, personal qualities important. If English is not student's first language and student submits SAT scores with Critical Reading score below 550, TOEFL required. Audition required for music program; portfolio recommended for art program. **Home schooled:** Statement describing home school structure and mission required. SAT, graded English paper, writing sample (not from English class), program description or certification from home schooler's accrediting agency or school district, name/address/phone number of home school supervisor required. Important: personal qualities, extracurriculars, and evidence of volunteer work.

High school preparation. College-preparatory program required. 16 units required; 20 recommended. Required and recommended units include English 4, mathematics 3-4, social studies 2, history 2, science 2 (laboratory 2), foreign language 2-4 and academic electives 1.

2016-2017 Annual costs. Tuition/fees: $51,960. Room/board: $12,656. Books/supplies: $900. Personal expenses: $2,000.

2015-2016 Financial aid. **Need-based:** 528 full-time freshmen applied for aid; 417 deemed to have need; 417 received aid. Average need met was 91%. Average scholarship/grant was $27,400; average loan $3,500. 81% of total undergraduate aid awarded as scholarships/grants, 19% as loans/jobs. **Non-need-based:** Awarded to 795 full-time undergraduates, including 214 freshmen. Scholarships awarded for academics, art, athletics, leadership, music/drama, ROTC.

Application procedures. **Admission:** Closing date 1/15 (postmark date). $40 fee, may be waived for applicants with need. Admission notification by 4/1. Must reply by 5/1. **Financial aid:** Closing date 1/15. FAFSA, CSS PROFILE required. Applicants notified by 4/1; must reply by 5/1.

Academics. **Special study options:** Combined bachelor's/graduate degree, double major, dual enrollment of high school students, honors, independent study, internships, liberal arts/career combination, semester at sea, student-designed major, study abroad, teacher certification program, Washington semester. Pass/Fail option. **Credit/placement by examination:** AP, CLEP, IB, institutional tests. No policy limit on number of credits; only a few courses offer this option. **Support services:** Learning center, study skills assistance, tutoring, writing center.

Majors. **Area/ethnic studies:** African, East Asian, Italian, Latin American, women's. **Biology:** General, animal behavior, biochemistry, cellular/molecular, neuroscience. **Business:** Accounting/finance, business admin, international, marketing. **Computer sciences:** General. **Conservation:** Environmental science, environmental studies. **Education:** General, early childhood, music. **Engineering:** Biomedical, chemical, civil, computer, electrical, environmental, mechanical. **English:** Creative writing, English lit. **Foreign languages:** Classics, French, German, linguistics, Russian, Spanish. **History:** General. **Liberal arts:** Humanities. **Math:** General. **Philosophy/religion:** Philosophy, religion. **Physical sciences:** Chemistry, geology, physics. **Psychology:** General. **Social sciences:** Anthropology, econometrics, economics, geography, international relations, political science, sociology. **Visual/performing arts:** General, art history/conservation, dramatic, music, music history, music performance, music theory/composition, studio arts, voice/opera.

Most popular majors. Biology 11%, business/marketing 13%, engineering/engineering technologies 14%, foreign language 6%, psychology 6%, social sciences 27%.

Technology on campus. 1,031 workstations in dormitories, library, computer center, student center. Dormitories wired for high-speed internet access and linked to campus network. Commuter students can connect to campus network. Online course registration, online library, helpline, repair service, wireless network available.

Student life. Freshman orientation: Mandatory, $175 fee. Preregistration for classes offered. Held during the 5 days prior to start of classes. **Policies:** All first-year students must sign statement of student responsibility. Freshmen not permitted cars on campus. **Housing:** Guaranteed on-campus for all undergraduates. Coed dorms, single-sex dorms, special housing for disabled, apartments, cooperative housing, fraternity/sorority housing, themed housing, wellness housing available. Eight residential colleges with themes: arts, discovery, humanities, global, environment, social justice, technology and society, language and culture. Quiet floors available. **Activities:** Bands, campus ministries, choral groups, dance, drama, film society, international student organizations, literary magazine, music ensembles, Model UN, musical theater, opera, radio station, student government, student newspaper, symphony orchestra, Hillel, Chinese Culture Association, Japan society, Muslim student association, LACOS (Hispanic), College Democrats, College Republicans, Habitat for Humanity, Bucknell Brigade, Rooke Chapel Congregation.

Athletics. NCAA. **Intercollegiate:** Baseball M, basketball, cross-country, diving, field hockey W, football (tackle) M, golf, lacrosse, rowing (crew) W, soccer, softball W, swimming, tennis, track and field, volleyball W, water polo, wrestling M. **Intramural:** Basketball, football (non-tackle), golf, racquetball, soccer, softball, squash, table tennis, tennis, ultimate frisbee, volleyball, weight lifting M. **Team name:** Bison.

Student services. Alcohol/substance abuse counseling, chaplain/spiritual director, career counseling, financial aid counseling, health services, minority student services, personal counseling, placement for graduates, women's services. **Physically disabled:** Services for visually, hearing impaired.

Contact. E-mail: admissions@bucknell.edu
Phone: (570) 577-3000 Fax: (570) 577-3538
Robert Springall, Dean of Admissions, Bucknell University, Office of Admissions, Bucknell University, Lewisburg, PA 17837-9988

Cabrini College

Radnor, Pennsylvania	
www.cabrini.edu	CB member
	CB code: 2071

- Private 4-year liberal arts college affiliated with the Roman Catholic Church
- Residential campus in large town
- 1,377 degree-seeking undergraduates: 5% part-time, 63% women, 20% African American, 1% Asian American, 7% Hispanic/Latino, 4% Multiracial, non-Hispanic
- 727 degree-seeking graduate students
- 72% of applicants admitted
- Application essay required
- 54% graduate within 6 years; 15% enter graduate study

General. Founded in 1957. Regionally accredited. College sponsored by Missionary Sisters of the Sacred Heart of Jesus (international religious order). **Degrees:** 251 bachelor's awarded; master's offered. **ROTC:** Army, Air Force. **Location:** 18 miles from Philadelphia, 5 miles from King of Prussia. **Calendar:** Semester, limited summer session. **Full-time faculty:** 84 total; 92% have terminal degrees, 11% minority, 61% women. **Part-time faculty:** 201 total; 11% minority, 64% women. **Class size:** 79% < 20, 20% 20-39, less than 1% 40-49, less than 1% 50-99, less than 1% >100. **Special facilities:** College-operated preschool (off-campus), human performance lab, TV studio, graphic design lab, radio station.

Freshman class profile. 2,544 applied, 1,843 admitted, 401 enrolled.

Mid 50% test scores			
SAT critical reading:	380-500	GPA 3.0-3.49:	39%
SAT math:	370-500	GPA 2.0-2.99:	39%
SAT writing:	380-500	End year in good standing:	91%
GPA 3.75 or higher:	9%	Return as sophomores:	76%
GPA 3.50-3.74:	12%	Out-of-state:	34%
		Live on campus:	82%

Basis for selection. High school achievement record, standardized test scores, academic potential, and personal interest are most important. Some scholarships, such as the Honors Scholarship, require standardized test scores to be submitted. Institution has a test-optional admission policy. Students can choose whether or not to submit their individual test scores. Test scores that are submitted may be used in admissions decisions. SAT or ACT recommended. Non-English-speaking international students may take TOEFL instead of SAT/ACT. Interview recommended for all incoming students. **Home schooled:** Transcript of courses and grades, state high school equivalency certificate required. Provide as much high school academic achievement data as possible.

High school preparation. College-preparatory program required. 17 units required; 21 recommended. Required and recommended units include English 4, mathematics 3, social studies 3, science 3, foreign language 2 and academic electives 2-6. Two arts and humanities also recommended. Additional math and science units recommended for science students.

2016-2017 Annual costs. Tuition/fees: $30,588. Room/board: $12,026. Books/supplies: $1,200. Personal expenses: $1,568.

2014-2015 Financial aid. Need-based: 284 full-time freshmen applied for aid; 253 deemed to have need; 253 received aid. Average scholarship/grant was $7,757; average loan $3,663. 67% of total undergraduate aid awarded as scholarships/grants, 33% as loans/jobs. **Non-need-based:** Awarded to 1,265 full-time undergraduates, including 291 freshmen. Scholarships awarded for academics, alumni affiliation, religious affiliation, ROTC, state residency.

Application procedures. Admission: Priority date 5/1; no deadline. $35 fee, may be waived for applicants with need. Admission notification on a rolling basis. **Financial aid:** Priority date 2/15; no closing date. FAFSA required. Applicants notified on a rolling basis starting 3/1; must reply by 5/1.

Academics. Education fieldwork opportunities provided to education majors from sophomore to senior years. Students participate in community service. Internship or co-op programs offered in all majors. **Special study options:** Accelerated study, combined bachelor's/graduate degree, cooperative education, cross-registration, double major, honors, independent study, internships, liberal arts/career combination, semester at sea, student-designed major, study abroad, teacher certification program, Washington semester. Exchange programs with Eastern University, Rosemont College, Valley Forge Military College; cross-registration with Southeastern Pennsylvania Consortium for Higher Education (8-member consortium of private colleges/universities). **Credit/placement by examination:** AP, CLEP, IB, SAT, institutional tests. 30 credit hours maximum toward bachelor's degree. DANTES. **Support services:** Learning center, reduced course load, remedial instruction, study skills assistance, tutoring, writing center.

Majors. Area/ethnic studies: African-American, American, women's. **Biology:** General. **Business:** Accounting, business admin, finance, human resources, international, marketing, organizational leadership. **Communications:** Communications/speech/rhetoric, digital media. **Computer sciences:** General. **Education:** General, biology, chemistry, elementary, English, French, kindergarten/preschool, mathematics, social studies, Spanish, special ed. **English:** English lit. **Foreign languages:** French, Italian, Spanish. **History:** General. **Human services:** Social work. **Liberal arts:** Arts/sciences. **Math:** General. **Parks/recreation:** Exercise sciences. **Philosophy/religion:** Philosophy, religion. **Physical sciences:** Chemistry. **Psychology:** General. **Social sciences:** Criminology, political science, sociology. **Visual/performing arts:** Graphic design.

Most popular majors. Business/marketing 25%, communications/journalism 12%, education 12%, psychology 11%, social sciences 11%.

Technology on campus. 469 workstations in dormitories, library, computer center. Dormitories wired for high-speed internet access and linked to campus network. Commuter students can connect to campus network. Online course registration, online library, helpline, student web hosting, wireless network available.

Student life. Freshman orientation: Mandatory, $220 fee. Preregistration for classes offered. 1-day summer programs, 3-day full program prior to beginning of fall semester. **Policies:** Freshmen not permitted cars on campus. **Housing:** Guaranteed on-campus for freshmen. Coed dorms, single-sex dorms, special housing for disabled, apartments, themed housing available. $200 fully refundable deposit, deadline 5/1. Special interest housing options designated for intensified study, honors, Hispanic culture, community service, and for students participating in living and learning communities. **Activities:** Campus ministries, choral groups, dance, drama, film society, international student organizations, literary magazine, musical theater, radio station, student government, student newspaper, TV station, Black Student Union, Habitat for Humanity, Cavaliers for Life, La Raza, campus ministry activities council, search club, CRS ambassadors, sanctuary.

Athletics. NCAA. **Intercollegiate:** Basketball, cross-country, field hockey W, golf M, lacrosse, soccer, softball W, swimming, tennis, volleyball W. **Intramural:** Basketball, cricket, football (non-tackle), soccer, squash, ultimate frisbee, volleyball. **Team name:** Cavaliers.

Student services. Adult student services, alcohol/substance abuse counseling, chaplain/spiritual director, career counseling, services for economically disadvantaged, student employment services, financial aid counseling, health services, minority student services, personal counseling, placement for graduates, veterans' counselor. **Physically disabled:** Services for visually, hearing impaired.

Contact. E-mail: admit@cabrini.edu
Phone: (610) 902-8552 Toll-free number: (800) 848-1003
Fax: (610) 902-8508
Shannon Zottola, Executive Director of Admissions, Cabrini College, 610 King of Prussia Road, Radnor, PA 19087-3698

Cairn University
Langhorne, Pennsylvania
www.cairn.edu

CB code: 2661

- Private 4-year university and Bible college affiliated with the Christian Church
- Residential campus in small town
- 772 degree-seeking undergraduates: 6% part-time, 54% women, 14% African American, 4% Asian American, 7% Hispanic/Latino, 2% Multiracial, non-Hispanic, 2% international
- 233 degree-seeking graduate students
- 99% of applicants admitted
- SAT or ACT (ACT writing optional), application essay, interview required
- 57% graduate within 6 years; 37% enter graduate study

General. Founded in 1913. Regionally accredited; also accredited by ABHE. **Degrees:** 246 bachelor's awarded; master's offered. **ROTC:** Air Force. **Location:** 17 miles from Philadelphia; 5 miles from Trenton, New Jersey. **Calendar:** Semester, limited summer session. **Full-time faculty:** 38 total; 68% have terminal degrees, 16% minority, 26% women. **Part-time faculty:** 80 total; 35% have terminal degrees, 12% minority, 44% women. **Class size:** 73% < 20, 24% 20-39, 2% 40-49, 1% 50-99, less than 1% >100.

Freshman class profile. 390 applied, 385 admitted, 161 enrolled.

Mid 50% test scores			
SAT critical reading:	430-560	GPA 2.0-2.99:	32%
SAT math:	420-540	Rank in top quarter:	27%
SAT writing:	430-550	Rank in top tenth:	7%
ACT composite:	18-24	Return as sophomores:	69%
GPA 3.75 or higher:	23%	Out-of-state:	48%
GPA 3.50-3.74:	20%	Live on campus:	87%
GPA 3.0-3.49:	23%	International:	2%

Basis for selection. High school GPA, pastor's references, writing sample, SAT or ACT scores required for some. Audition required for music program. **Home schooled:** Letter of recommendation (nonparent) required.

High school preparation. College-preparatory program recommended. 15 units recommended. Recommended units include English 4, mathematics 1, social studies 3, science 2 and foreign language 2.

2015-2016 Annual costs. Tuition/fees: $23,920. Room/board: $9,350. Books/supplies: $1,000. Personal expenses: $1,060.

2015-2016 Financial aid. Need-based: 148 full-time freshmen applied for aid; 130 deemed to have need; 130 received aid. Average need met was 77%. Average scholarship/grant was $17,771; average loan $3,860. 66% of total undergraduate aid awarded as scholarships/grants, 34% as loans/jobs. **Non-need-based:** Awarded to 182 full-time undergraduates, including 34 freshmen. Scholarships awarded for academics, leadership, music/drama.

Application procedures. Admission: No deadline. $25 fee, may be waived for applicants with need. Admission notification on a rolling basis beginning on or about 7/1. Housing deposit refundable in full if requested before May 1. **Financial aid:** Priority date 3/1; no closing date. FAFSA required. Applicants notified on a rolling basis starting 2/1; must reply within 2 week(s) of notification.

Academics. Students may participate in semester studies in Israel or in the 'Best Semester' program. **Special study options:** Accelerated study, combined bachelor's/graduate degree, double major, dual enrollment of high school students, honors, internships, study abroad, teacher certification program. **Credit/placement by examination:** AP, CLEP, IB, SAT, ACT, institutional tests. 12 credit hours maximum toward bachelor's degree. **Support services:** Learning center, reduced course load, remedial instruction, study skills assistance, tutoring, writing center.

Majors. Business: Business admin. **Education:** Early childhood, elementary, English, mathematics, music, physical, social studies. **Human services:** Social work. **Parks/recreation:** Health/fitness. **Theology:** Bible, missionary, pastoral counseling, religious ed, sacred music, theology. **Visual/performing arts:** Music, music performance, music theory/composition.

Most popular majors. Business/marketing 9%, education 13%, philosophy/religious studies 59%, public administration/social services 13%.

Technology on campus. 68 workstations in dormitories, library, student center. Dormitories wired for high-speed internet access and linked to campus network. Commuter students can connect to campus network. Online course registration, online library, helpline, wireless network available.

Student life. Freshman orientation: Mandatory. Preregistration for classes offered. **Policies:** Religious observance required. **Housing:** Guaranteed on-campus for freshmen. Single-sex dorms, special housing for disabled, apartments available. $100 fully refundable deposit. **Activities:** Concert band, campus ministries, choral groups, drama, international student organizations, music ensembles, musical theater, opera, student government, student newspaper, symphony orchestra, Student Theological Society, Student Government Association, Student Visual Arts Society, Student Missionary Fellowship, Enactus, Chi Beta Sigma.

Athletics. NCAA, NCCAA. **Intercollegiate:** Baseball M, basketball, cross-country, golf M, soccer, softball W, tennis W, volleyball. **Intramural:** Badminton, basketball, football (non-tackle), handball, soccer, table tennis, tennis, ultimate frisbee, volleyball. **Team name:** Highlanders.

Student services. Alcohol/substance abuse counseling, chaplain/spiritual director, career counseling, student employment services, financial aid counseling, health services, personal counseling, placement for graduates. **Physically disabled:** Services for visually, hearing impaired.

Contact. E-mail: admissions@cairn.edu
Phone: (215) 702-4235 Toll-free number: (800) 366-0049
Fax: (215) 702-4248
Rebecca Lippert, Director of Admissions, Cairn University, 200 Manor Avenue, Langhorne, PA 19047-2990

California University of Pennsylvania
California, Pennsylvania
www.calu.edu

CB member
CB code: 2647

- Public 4-year university
- Residential campus in small town
- 5,715 degree-seeking undergraduates: 13% part-time, 53% women, 12% African American, 1% Asian American, 3% Hispanic/Latino, 3% Multiracial, non-Hispanic, 1% international
- 1,962 degree-seeking graduate students
- 83% of applicants admitted
- SAT required
- 52% graduate within 6 years

General. Founded in 1852. Regionally accredited. Green-oriented; utilizes geothermal technologies to reduce energy consumption. **Degrees:** 1,411 bachelor's, 45 associate awarded; master's offered. **ROTC:** Army. **Location:** 38 miles from Pittsburgh. **Calendar:** Semester, limited summer session. **Full-time faculty:** 255 total; 88% have terminal degrees, 14% minority, 50% women. **Part-time faculty:** 145 total; 50% have terminal degrees, 10% minority, 41% women. **Class size:** 28% < 20, 48% 20-39, 13% 40-49, 11% 50-99, less than 1% >100. **Special facilities:** International corporate art collection, 98-acre farm with recreational facilities.

Freshman class profile. 3,691 applied, 3,049 admitted, 937 enrolled.

Mid 50% test scores			
SAT critical reading:	410-510	GPA 2.0-2.99:	43%
SAT math:	410-510	Rank in top quarter:	23%
SAT writing:	390-490	Rank in top tenth:	8%
ACT composite:	17-22	Return as sophomores:	76%
GPA 3.75 or higher:	12%	Out-of-state:	8%
GPA 3.50-3.74:	12%	Live on campus:	70%
GPA 3.0-3.49:	31%	International:	1%

Basis for selection. School achievement record, test scores, activities, recommendations, interview considered. Essay recommended. **Home schooled:** Transcript of courses and grades required.

High school preparation. College-preparatory program recommended. 19 units required; 21 recommended. Required and recommended units include English 4, mathematics 3, social studies 2, history 2, science 1 (laboratory 1), foreign language 2 and academic electives 6.

2015-2016 Annual costs. Tuition/fees: $9,936; $13,466 out-of-state. Room/board: $10,238. Books/supplies: $1,000. Personal expenses: $2,850.

2014-2015 Financial aid. Need-based: 953 full-time freshmen applied for aid; 809 deemed to have need; 809 received aid. Average need met was 52%. Average scholarship/grant was $6,678; average loan $3,340. 53% of total undergraduate aid awarded as scholarships/grants, 47% as loans/jobs. **Non-need-based:** Awarded to 901 full-time undergraduates, including 281 freshmen. Scholarships awarded for academics, athletics, leadership, minority status, music/drama, state residency.

Application procedures. Admission: Closing date 8/22. $25 fee, may be waived for applicants with need. Admission notification on a rolling basis.

Financial aid: Priority date 3/1; no closing date. FAFSA required. Applicants notified on a rolling basis starting 4/1; must reply within 2 week(s) of notification.

Academics. Special study options: Accelerated study, combined bachelor's/graduate degree, cooperative education, cross-registration, distance learning, double major, exchange student, honors, independent study, internships, liberal arts/career combination, study abroad, teacher certification program, urban semester, Washington semester. **Credit/placement by examination:** AP, CLEP, IB, SAT, institutional tests. **Support services:** Learning center, pre-admission summer program, reduced course load, remedial instruction, study skills assistance, tutoring, writing center.

Honors college/program. Minimum 1100 SAT (exclusive of Writing), 3.0 GPA, letter of recommendation required. Admitted students work with adviser and dean to design course of study.

Majors. Biology: General. **Business:** Business admin. **Communications:** Communications/speech/rhetoric. **Computer sciences:** General. **Conservation:** Environmental science. **Education:** General, elementary, kindergarten/preschool, middle, special ed. **Engineering:** Robotics. **English:** English lit. **Foreign languages:** General, Arabic, French, German, Russian, Spanish. **Health services:** Athletic training, clinical lab technology, communication disorders, nursing (RN). **History:** General. **Human services:** Social work. **Liberal arts:** Arts/sciences. **Math:** General. **Parks/recreation:** Facilities management, sports admin. **Philosophy/religion:** Philosophy. **Physical sciences:** General, chemistry, geology, physics. **Protective services:** Criminal justice. **Psychology:** General. **Social sciences:** General, anthropology, geography, political science. **Visual/performing arts:** Art, commercial/advertising art, dramatic, graphic design, music management.

Most popular majors. Business/marketing 14%, education 7%, health sciences 13%, parks/recreation 12%, security/protective services 7%.

Technology on campus. 1,220 workstations in dormitories, library, computer center, student center. Dormitories wired for high-speed internet access and linked to campus network. Commuter students can connect to campus network. Online course registration, online library, helpline available.

Student life. Freshman orientation: Mandatory. Preregistration for classes offered. One-day session held in July or August. **Policies:** Freshman students under 21 and not commuting from parental home required to live in dormitory. **Housing:** Coed dorms, single-sex dorms, special housing for disabled, apartments, fraternity/sorority housing, themed housing, wellness housing available. $200 nonrefundable deposit. **Activities:** Bands, campus ministries, choral groups, dance, drama, international student organizations, literary magazine, music ensembles, musical theater, opera, radio station, student government, student newspaper, symphony orchestra, TV station.

Athletics. NCAA. **Intercollegiate:** Baseball M, basketball, cheerleading, cross-country, football (tackle) M, golf, rugby, soccer, softball, swimming W, tennis W, track and field, volleyball. **Intramural:** Archery, badminton, baseball M, basketball, bowling, cheerleading, cross-country, fencing, football (non-tackle), football (tackle), golf, gymnastics, handball, ice hockey, judo, lacrosse, racquetball, rugby, skiing, skin diving M, soccer, softball W, swimming W, table tennis, tennis W, track and field, triathlon, volleyball, weight lifting, wrestling M. **Team name:** Vulcans.

Student services. Adult student services, alcohol/substance abuse counseling, chaplain/spiritual director, career counseling, services for economically disadvantaged, student employment services, financial aid counseling, health services, legal services, minority student services, personal counseling, placement for graduates, veterans' counselor, women's services. **Physically disabled:** Services for visually, speech, hearing impaired.

Contact. E-mail: inquiry@calu.edu
Phone: (724) 938-4404 Toll-free number: (888) 412-0479
Fax: (724) 938-4564
William Edmonds, Dean of Admissions, California University of Pennsylvania, 250 University Avenue, California, PA 15419-1394

Carlow University
Pittsburgh, Pennsylvania
www.carlow.edu

CB member
CB code: 2421

▶ Private 4-year university affiliated with the Roman Catholic Church
▶ Commuter campus in large city
▶ 1,377 degree-seeking undergraduates: 25% part-time, 89% women, 22% African American, 1% Asian American, 2% Hispanic/Latino, 5% Multiracial, non-Hispanic
▶ 872 degree-seeking graduate students
▶ 81% of applicants admitted

▶ SAT or ACT (ACT writing optional) required
▶ 50% graduate within 6 years

General. Founded in 1929. Regionally accredited. Member of the Conference for Mercy Higher Education. **Degrees:** 296 bachelor's awarded; master's, professional offered. **ROTC:** Army, Naval, Air Force. **Location:** 3 miles from downtown. **Calendar:** Semester, limited summer session. **Full-time faculty:** 97 total; 73% have terminal degrees, 3% minority, 72% women. **Part-time faculty:** 169 total; 26% have terminal degrees, 4% minority, 75% women. **Class size:** 75% < 20, 25% 20-39, less than 1% >100. **Special facilities:** Early learning center, campus school (pre K-8), science and technology research labs, cadaver lab, communications lab, math lab, greenhouse, herbarium, biochamber, tissue culture lab, children's science lab.

Freshman class profile. 945 applied, 763 admitted, 223 enrolled.

Mid 50% test scores			
SAT critical reading:	440-540	Rank in top quarter:	38%
SAT math:	430-520	Rank in top tenth:	12%
SAT writing:	420-530	Return as sophomores:	77%
ACT composite:	19-23	Out-of-state:	8%
GPA 3.75 or higher:	23%	Live on campus:	77%
GPA 3.50-3.74:	21%	International:	1%
GPA 3.0-3.49:	35%	Fraternities:	11%
GPA 2.0-2.99:	21%	Sororities:	4%

Basis for selection. Secondary school GPA, rank, record, course work SAT/ACT most important. 2.5 GPA and class ranking in upper two-fifths of graduating class strengthen the application. International students must take TOEFL and ACT or SAT exams. Essay, interview recommended for all and in some cases required. Portfolio recommended for all art programs. **Home schooled:** Transcript of courses and grades required. Personal interview and portfolio from most recent year highly recommended.

High school preparation. College-preparatory program recommended. 18 units required. Required and recommended units include English 4, mathematics 3-4, social studies 2, history 2, science 3-4 (laboratory 2) and academic electives 4. Applicants to professional nursing programs must have 4 units English, 3 units social sciences, 2 units math (1 must be algebra), and 2 units laboratory science, including chemistry.

2015-2016 Annual costs. Tuition/fees: $26,832. Room/board: $10,572. Books/supplies: $1,020. Personal expenses: $1,382. **Additional information:** Part-time traditionally-aged undergraduates pay $846 per-credit-hour. Both full-time and part-time non-traditionally-aged undergraduates pay $642 per-credit-hour. RN-to-BSN students pay $495 per-credit-hour.

Application procedures. Admission: No deadline. No application fee. Application must be submitted online. Admission notification on a rolling basis. Must reply by May 1 or within 4 week(s) if notified thereafter. **Financial aid:** Priority date 5/1; no closing date. FAFSA required. Applicants notified on a rolling basis starting 2/15; must reply within 4 week(s) of notification.

Academics. Special study options: Accelerated study, combined bachelor's/graduate degree, cross-registration, distance learning, double major, honors, independent study, internships, liberal arts/career combination, study abroad, teacher certification program, weekend college. 3+2 program: BS Biology from Carlow/MS Environmental Science and Management at Duquesne. 3+3 program: BA/BS from Carlow/JD from University of Pittsburgh. **Credit/placement by examination:** AP, CLEP, IB, institutional tests. 30 credit hours maximum toward bachelor's degree. **Support services:** Learning center, remedial instruction, study skills assistance, tutoring, writing center. Full range of disability services available.

Majors. Biology: General. **Business:** Accounting, auditing, business admin. **Communications:** General, media studies. **Education:** Art, early childhood, middle. **English:** Creative writing, English lit. **Health services:** Art therapy, health care admin, nursing (RN), perfusion technology. **History:** General. **Human services:** Social work. **Liberal arts:** Arts/sciences. **Math:** General. **Philosophy/religion:** Philosophy. **Physical sciences:** Chemistry. **Psychology:** General. **Social sciences:** Criminology, political science, sociology. **Theology:** Theology. **Visual/performing arts:** Studio arts.

Most popular majors. Biology 9%, business/marketing 20%, education 9%, health sciences 33%, psychology 8%, public administration/social services 8%.

Technology on campus. 192 workstations in dormitories, library, computer center. Dormitories wired for high-speed internet access and linked to campus network. Commuter students can connect to campus network. Online library, helpline, wireless network available.

Student life. Freshman orientation: Mandatory. Preregistration for classes offered. Held for several days prior to Fall semester, includes seminars, team-building activities, social events. **Housing:** Coed dorms, single-sex dorms, themed housing available. $100 fully refundable deposit, deadline 5/1. **Activities:** Campus ministries, choral groups, dance, drama, literary magazine, student government, student newspaper, Alpha Phi Omega, American Chemical Society, Commuter Student Organization, Student Nurses Association of Pennsylvania, Black Student Union, LGBT and Allies, Kappa Delta Epsilon, Women in Communications, Pennsylvania State Education Association (PSEA), Strong Women Strong Girls.

Athletics. NAIA, USCAA. **Intercollegiate:** Basketball, cross-country, golf, soccer, softball W, tennis W, volleyball W. **Team name:** Celtics.

Student services. Adult student services, alcohol/substance abuse counseling, chaplain/spiritual director, career counseling, student employment services, financial aid counseling, health services, minority student services, on-campus daycare, personal counseling, placement for graduates, veterans' counselor, women's services. **Physically disabled:** Services for visually, speech, hearing impaired.

Contact. E-mail: admissions@carlow.edu
Phone: (412) 578-6059 Toll-free number: (800) 333-2275
Fax: (412) 578-6321
Wivina Chmura, Director of Undergraduate Admisssions, Carlow University, 3333 Fifth Avenue, Pittsburgh, PA 15213-3165

Carnegie Mellon University
Pittsburgh, Pennsylvania
www.cmu.edu

CB member
CB code: 2074

- Private 4-year university
- Residential campus in large city
- 6,362 degree-seeking undergraduates: 2% part-time, 46% women, 4% African American, 27% Asian American, 8% Hispanic/Latino, 4% Multiracial, non-Hispanic, 22% international
- 7,194 degree-seeking graduate students
- 24% of applicants admitted
- SAT or ACT (ACT writing recommended), application essay required
- 88% graduate within 6 years

General. Founded in 1900. Regionally accredited. **Degrees:** 1,483 bachelor's awarded; master's, doctoral offered. **ROTC:** Army, Naval, Air Force. **Location:** 5 miles from downtown. **Calendar:** Semester, limited summer session. **Full-time faculty:** 986 total; 93% have terminal degrees, 19% minority, 27% women. **Part-time faculty:** 27 total; 59% have terminal degrees, 4% minority, 37% women. **Class size:** 64% < 20, 21% 20-39, 4% 40-49, 7% 50-99, 5% >100. **Special facilities:** Botanical institute, rare books collection, recording studios, design studios, photo shoot studio, music halls.

Freshman class profile. 20,547 applied, 4,873 admitted, 1,576 enrolled.

Mid 50% test scores		GPA 3.0-3.49:	13%
SAT critical reading:	650-740	Rank in top quarter:	95%
SAT math:	710-800	Rank in top tenth:	78%
SAT writing:	670-760	Return as sophomores:	98%
ACT composite:	31-34	Out-of-state:	87%
GPA 3.75 or higher:	62%	Live on campus:	99%
GPA 3.50-3.74:	25%	International:	20%

Basis for selection. Academic and artistic potential, standardized tests, activities, jobs, interests, and other personalized information important. Applicants to art, architecture, design, drama, and music programs should submit Common Application and Carnegie Mellon Supplement by regular decision fine arts deadline of 12/1. SAT subject tests not required for drama, design, art, or music applicants. All other applicants must take appropriate tests, preferably by November, but no later than December. Interview recommended for all; audition required for drama, music programs; portfolio required for art, design programs. **Home schooled:** Transcript of courses and grades, letter of recommendation (nonparent) required. Submit an academic portfolio/transcript consistent with state guidelines and a list of all textbooks used for coursework. Provide proof the student will have met, by the end of May of the year of graduation, all requirements for an official high school diploma and submit an official final transcript, a GED or a certificate of completion from local school district or state board of education by the end of July of the year of matriculation.

High school preparation. College-preparatory program required. Required units include English 4, mathematics 4, science 3 (laboratory 3), foreign language 2 and academic electives 3. Requirements vary by program.

2015-2016 Annual costs. Tuition/fees: $50,665. Room/board: $12,830.

2015-2016 Financial aid. Need-based: 1,010 full-time freshmen applied for aid; 737 deemed to have need; 729 received aid. Average need met was 84%. Average scholarship/grant was $31,926; average loan $4,055. 80% of total undergraduate aid awarded as scholarships/grants, 20% as loans/jobs. **Non-need-based:** Awarded to 549 full-time undergraduates, including 218

freshmen. Scholarships awarded for academics, art, leadership, minority status, music/drama, state residency. **Additional information:** Early need analysis offered; merit awards available. Financial aid applicants will receive financial aid notification shortly after notification of admission or a spot on the waiting list.

Application procedures. Admission: Closing date 1/1 (postmark date). $75 fee, may be waived for applicants with need. Application must be submitted online. Admission notification by 4/15. Admission notification on a rolling basis. Must reply by 5/1. **Financial aid:** Priority date 2/15, closing date 4/15. FAFSA, institutional form required. Required for institutional financial aid programs only. Not required if applying only for federal financial aid. Applicants notified by 4/15; must reply by 5/1.

Academics. Special study options: Accelerated study, combined bachelor's/graduate degree, cooperative education, cross-registration, distance learning, double major, dual enrollment of high school students, independent study, internships, liberal arts/career combination, student-designed major, study abroad, teacher certification program, Washington semester. **Credit/placement by examination:** AP, CLEP, IB, institutional tests. **Support services:** Learning center, pre-admission summer program, study skills assistance, tutoring, writing center.

Majors. Architecture: Architecture. **Biology:** General, biometrics, neuroscience. **Business:** Actuarial science, business admin, management information systems. **Computer sciences:** Computer science. **Engineering:** Chemical, civil, electrical, mechanical. **English:** Creative writing, English lit, technical writing. **Foreign languages:** Chinese, French, Japanese, linguistics, Russian, Spanish. **History:** General. **Human services:** Public policy. **Liberal arts:** Arts/sciences. **Math:** General, financial, statistics. **Philosophy/religion:** Logic, philosophy, professional ethics. **Physical sciences:** Chemistry, materials science, physics. **Psychology:** General. **Social sciences:** Econometrics, economics, international relations. **Visual/performing arts:** Art, design, dramatic, music performance, music theory/composition, stringed instruments, voice/opera.

Most popular majors. Business/marketing 10%, computer/information sciences 15%, engineering/engineering technologies 25%, interdisciplinary studies 10%, mathematics 6%, physical sciences 6%, visual/performing arts 9%.

Technology on campus. 362 workstations in dormitories, library, computer center, student center. Dormitories wired for high-speed internet access and linked to campus network. Commuter students can connect to campus network. Online course registration, online library, helpline, repair service, student web hosting, wireless network available.

Student life. Freshman orientation: Mandatory, $270 fee. Preregistration for classes offered. Week-long program held one week before start of classes. **Policies:** Freshmen required to live on campus. **Housing:** Guaranteed on-campus for freshmen. Coed dorms, single-sex dorms, special housing for disabled, apartments, fraternity/sorority housing, themed housing, wellness housing available. $800 nonrefundable deposit, deadline 5/1. Special interest group housing available. **Activities:** Bands, campus ministries, choral groups, dance, drama, film society, international student organizations, literary magazine, music ensembles, Model UN, musical theater, radio station, student government, student newspaper, symphony orchestra, Alpha Phi Omega, Hillel, service clubs, National Society of Black Engineers, Society of Women Engineers, Phi Beta Kappa, Minority Association of Pre-health Studies.

Athletics. NCAA. **Intercollegiate:** Basketball, cross-country, diving, football (tackle) M, golf, soccer, swimming, tennis, track and field, volleyball W. **Intramural:** Badminton, basketball, football (non-tackle), golf, racquetball, soccer, softball, squash, table tennis, tennis, ultimate frisbee, volleyball, water polo. **Team name:** Tartans.

Student services. Alcohol/substance abuse counseling, chaplain/spiritual director, career counseling, student employment services, financial aid counseling, health services, minority student services, on-campus daycare, personal counseling, placement for graduates, women's services. **Physically disabled:** Services for visually, speech, hearing impaired.

Contact. E-mail: undergraduate-admissions@andrew.cmu.edu
Phone: (412) 268-2082 Fax: (412) 268-7838
Michael Steidel, Director of Admissions, Carnegie Mellon University, 5000 Forbes Avenue, Pittsburgh, PA 15213-3890

Cedar Crest College
Allentown, Pennsylvania
www.cedarcrest.edu

CB member
CB code: 2079

- Private 4-year liberal arts college for women
- Residential campus in small city

- 1,360 degree-seeking undergraduates: 43% part-time, 90% women, 10% African American, 3% Asian American, 15% Hispanic/Latino, 1% Multiracial, non-Hispanic, 5% international
- 203 degree-seeking graduate students
- 67% of applicants admitted
- SAT or ACT (ACT writing optional), application essay required
- 58% graduate within 6 years

General. Founded in 1867. Regionally accredited. Men admitted to evening and weekend classes and daytime programs in nursing and nuclear medicine. **Degrees:** 268 bachelor's awarded; master's offered. **Location:** 55 miles from Philadelphia, 100 miles from New York City. **Calendar:** Semester, extensive summer session. **Full-time faculty:** 76 total; 71% have terminal degrees, 8% minority, 72% women. **Part-time faculty:** 112 total; 38% have terminal degrees, 6% minority, 66% women. **Class size:** 75% < 20, 22% 20-39, less than 1% 40-49, less than 1% 50-99, 2% >100. **Special facilities:** Wildlife sanctuary, outdoor Greek theater, arboretum, sculpture garden, aquatic center, college-operated museums, media convergence lab.

Freshman class profile. 1,086 applied, 733 admitted, 179 enrolled.

Mid 50% test scores			
SAT critical reading:	420-550	GPA 2.0-2.99:	25%
SAT math:	410-530	Rank in top quarter:	45%
SAT writing:	410-520	Rank in top tenth:	16%
ACT composite:	19-26	End year in good standing:	79%
GPA 3.75 or higher:	24%	Return as sophomores:	79%
GPA 3.50-3.74:	18%	Out-of-state:	16%
GPA 3.0-3.49:	33%	Live on campus:	73%

Basis for selection. Secondary school curriculum and grades most important. Test scores important. Special talents, potential for academic and personal growth considered. Interview and essay recommended for all. **Home schooled:** Transcript of courses and grades, letter of recommendation (non-parent) required.

High school preparation. 20 units required. Required units include English 4, mathematics 3, social studies 3, history 3, science 2 (laboratory 2), foreign language 2 and academic electives 3. Special natural science requirements for nuclear medicine and nursing.

2015-2016 Annual costs. Tuition/fees: $35,400. Room/board: $10,765. Books/supplies: $1,000. Personal expenses: $850.

2015-2016 Financial aid. Need-based: 174 full-time freshmen applied for aid; 164 deemed to have need; 164 received aid. Average need met was 78%. Average scholarship/grant was $27,930; average loan $3,364. 75% of total undergraduate aid awarded as scholarships/grants, 25% as loans/jobs. **Non-need-based:** Scholarships awarded for academics, alumni affiliation, art, music/drama.

Application procedures. Admission: Priority date 2/15; no deadline. $30 fee, may be waived for applicants with need, free for online applicants. Admission notification on a rolling basis beginning on or about 9/15. Must reply by May 1 or within 2 week(s) if notified thereafter. **Financial aid:** Priority date 5/1; no closing date. FAFSA required. Applicants notified on a rolling basis starting 9/15; must reply within 2 week(s) of notification.

Academics. Special study options: Accelerated study, combined bachelor's/graduate degree, cooperative education, cross-registration, distance learning, double major, dual enrollment of high school students, honors, independent study, internships, liberal arts/career combination, student-designed major, study abroad, teacher certification program, weekend college. **Credit/placement by examination:** AP, CLEP, IB, SAT, ACT, institutional tests. 18 credit hours maximum toward bachelor's degree. **Support services:** Learning center, pre-admission summer program, remedial instruction, study skills assistance, tutoring, writing center.

Majors. Area/ethnic studies: Chicano/Hispanic-American/Latino. **Biology:** General, biochemistry, environmental, genetics, neuroscience. **Business:** Accounting, business admin, marketing. **Communications:** Communications/speech/rhetoric, digital media, media studies. **Computer sciences:** General. **Conservation:** Environmental science. **Education:** Early childhood, elementary, secondary. **English:** English lit. **Foreign languages:** Spanish. **Health services:** Art therapy, nuclear medical technology, nursing (RN). **History:** General. **Human services:** Social work. **Math:** General. **Physical sciences:** Chemistry. **Protective services:** Forensics. **Psychology:** General. **Social sciences:** Criminology, political science. **Visual/performing arts:** General, art, dance, dramatic, music, studio arts. **Work/family studies:** Food/nutrition.

Most popular majors. Business/marketing 6%, health sciences 44%, psychology 7%, public administration/social services 12%.

Technology on campus. 287 workstations in dormitories, library, computer center, student center. Dormitories wired for high-speed internet access and linked to campus network. Online course registration, online library, helpline, repair service, wireless network available.

Student life. Freshman orientation: Mandatory. Preregistration for classes offered. 5-day academic and social program in August mandatory. 2-day academic testing and advising program in June mandatory. **Policies:** Drinking under age 21 prohibited; honor philosophy exists. **Housing:** Guaranteed on-campus for all undergraduates. $100 nonrefundable deposit, deadline 7/1. **Activities:** Campus ministries, choral groups, dance, drama, international student organizations, literary magazine, music ensembles, musical theater, radio station, student government, student newspaper, Amnesty International, Black Student Union, Best Buddies, Cedar Crest Christian Fellowship, Hillel Society, Muslim student association, Sisters Inc, Global Eyes, Take Back the Night.

Athletics. NCAA. **Intercollegiate:** Basketball W, cheerleading W, cross-country W, equestrian W, field hockey W, lacrosse W, soccer W, softball W, swimming W, tennis W, volleyball W. **Intramural:** Badminton W, basketball W, football (non-tackle) W, soccer W, softball W, table tennis W, triathlon W. **Team name:** Falcons.

Student services. Adult student services, alcohol/substance abuse counseling, chaplain/spiritual director, career counseling, services for economically disadvantaged, student employment services, financial aid counseling, health services, minority student services, personal counseling, placement for graduates, women's services. **Physically disabled:** Services for visually, hearing impaired.

Contact. E-mail: admissions@cedarcrest.edu
Phone: (610) 740-3780 Toll-free number: (800) 360-1222
Fax: (610) 606-4647
Mary Alice Ozechoski, VP Student Affairs and Admissions, Cedar Crest College, 100 College Drive, Allentown, PA 18104-6196

Central Penn College
Summerdale, Pennsylvania   **CB member**
www.centralpenn.edu   **CB code: 1061**

- For-profit 4-year technical and career college
- Commuter campus in rural community
- 1,286 degree-seeking undergraduates: 44% part-time, 65% women
- 48 degree-seeking graduate students
- Application essay, interview required

General. Founded in 1881. Regionally accredited. **Degrees:** 287 bachelor's, 118 associate awarded; master's offered. **Location:** 5 miles from Harrisburg. **Calendar:** Quarter, extensive summer session. **Full-time faculty:** 28 total; 7% minority, 57% women. **Part-time faculty:** 105 total; 13% minority, 42% women. **Special facilities:** Student-staffed restaurant, mock courtroom, multimedia lab, advanced technology education center, conference and convention facility, crime lab.

Freshman class profile.

Out-of-state:	17%	Live on campus:	58%

Basis for selection. High school achievement record very important and minimum high school GPA of 3.0, SAT, 20 observation hours, two references required for admission to Physical Therapist Assistant program. Similar requirements also necessary for Occupational Therapist Assistant program. SAT required for entry into the Physical Therapy Assistant program, strongly recommended for Occupational Therapy Assistant program. Not required for other academic programs. **Home schooled:** Provide transcript of courses completed with grades and include parent/teacher/academy signatures. **Learning Disabled:** Students meet with academic dean to discuss provisions needed for individual learning experience.

High school preparation. One unit of biology, chemistry or physics required, two units of math (one must be algebra) all with 2.0 GPA required for Physical Therapist program. One unit of high school biology and algebra with a GPA of 2.0 or higher required for Occupational Therapist program.

2015-2016 Annual costs. Tuition/fees: $22,868. Room/board: $8,736. Books/supplies: $1,500. Personal expenses: $600.

Financial aid. Non-need-based: Scholarships awarded for academics, alumni affiliation, job skills, leadership, minority status, state residency.

Application procedures. Admission: Priority date 5/1; no deadline. No application fee. Admission notification on a rolling basis. **Financial aid:** Priority date 3/15; no closing date. FAFSA, institutional form required. Applicants notified on a rolling basis starting 2/1; must reply within 2 week(s) of notification.

Academics. Emphasis on hands on, career focused education; internship and community service hours are required for graduation. **Special study options:** Distance learning, double major, dual enrollment of high school students, honors, independent study, internships, study abroad. **Credit/placement by examination:** AP, CLEP, IB, institutional tests. 15 credit hours maximum toward associate degree, 15 toward bachelor's. **Support services:** Learning center, reduced course load, remedial instruction, study skills assistance, tutoring, writing center.

Majors. Business: Accounting, business admin, organizational leadership. **Communications:** Communications/speech/rhetoric. **Computer sciences:** Computer science. **Protective services:** Criminal justice, homeland security.

Most popular majors. Business/marketing 51%, computer/information sciences 14%, security/protective services 28%.

Technology on campus. 150 workstations in library, computer center. Dormitories wired for high-speed internet access and linked to campus network. Commuter students can connect to campus network. Online course registration, online library, helpline, wireless network available.

Student life. Freshman orientation: Mandatory. Preregistration for classes offered. **Policies:** Dress code, mandatory attendance, ethics policies, no alcohol or drugs. **Housing:** Guaranteed on-campus for freshmen. Apartments, wellness housing available. $250 deposit. All resident housing is either single-gender townhouses or apartments. **Activities:** Campus ministries, choral groups, literary magazine, student government, student newspaper, Gamma Beta Phi, Delta Epsilon Chi, technology club, Club MED, Toastmasters, Young Republicans.

Athletics. USCAA. **Intercollegiate:** Baseball M, basketball, cross-country, soccer, volleyball. **Intramural:** Basketball, football (non-tackle), softball, tennis, volleyball. **Team name:** Silver Knights.

Student services. Adult student services, alcohol/substance abuse counseling, chaplain/spiritual director, career counseling, student employment services, financial aid counseling, on-campus daycare, personal counseling, placement for graduates, veterans' counselor.

Contact. E-mail: admissions@centralpenn.edu
Phone: (717) 728-2201 Toll-free number: (800) 759-2727
Fax: (717) 732-5254
Stacey Obi, Vice President for Enrollment Management, Central Penn College, College Hill and Valley Roads, Summerdale, PA 17093-0309

Chatham University
Pittsburgh, Pennsylvania   **CB member**
www.chatham.edu   **CB code: 2081**

- Private 4-year university and liberal arts college
- Residential campus in large city
- 695 degree-seeking undergraduates: 12% part-time, 87% women, 10% African American, 2% Asian American, 5% Hispanic/Latino, 1% Native American, 2% Multi-racial, non-Hispanic, 3% international
- 1,176 degree-seeking graduate students
- 75% of applicants admitted
- Application essay required
- 56% graduate within 6 years; 21% enter graduate study

General. Founded in 1869. Regionally accredited. **Degrees:** 195 bachelor's awarded; master's, professional offered. **ROTC:** Army, Naval, Air Force. **Location:** 5 miles from downtown. **Calendar:** Semester, limited summer session. **Full-time faculty:** 114 total; 89% have terminal degrees, 68% women. **Part-time faculty:** 202 total; 75% women. **Class size:** 78% < 20, 18% 20-39, 2% 40-49, less than 1% 50-99. **Special facilities:** Broadcast studio, science complex and greenhouse, proscenium theater, arboretum.

Freshman class profile. 1,086 applied, 816 admitted, 211 enrolled.

Mid 50% test scores			
SAT critical reading:	490-590	GPA 2.0-2.99:	14%
SAT math:	470-560	Rank in top quarter:	53%
SAT writing:	460-580	Rank in top tenth:	23%
ACT composite:	21-26	Return as sophomores:	77%
GPA 3.75 or higher:	37%	Out-of-state:	24%
GPA 3.50-3.74:	20%	Live on campus:	87%
GPA 3.0-3.49:	28%	International:	3%

Basis for selection. School achievement record, essays, and test scores most important, though test scores are not required. Students who do not submit SAT/ACT scores required to submit a graded writing sample and resume/list of activities. Portfolios may also be submitted. Activities, talents, volunteer work, paid work, alumnae relationship, class rank, recommendations considered. TOEFL or IELTS required for international students. Campus visit or interviews recommended for all.

High school preparation. College-preparatory program required. 11 units required; 15 recommended. Required and recommended units include English 4, mathematics 2-3, social studies 3, science 2-3 and foreign language 2. 3 units of social science required.

2015-2016 Annual costs. Tuition/fees: $34,440. Room/board: $10,720. Books/supplies: $1,000. Personal expenses: $2,862.

2015-2016 Financial aid. Need-based: 197 full-time freshmen applied for aid; 163 deemed to have need; 163 received aid. Average need met was 82%. Average scholarship/grant was $9,487; average loan $3,572. 83% of total undergraduate aid awarded as scholarships/grants, 17% as loans/jobs. **Non-need-based:** Awarded to 563 full-time undergraduates, including 178 freshmen. Scholarships awarded for academics, alumni affiliation, art, music/drama.

Application procedures. Admission: Priority date 3/15; deadline 8/1. $35 fee, may be waived for applicants with need, free for online applicants. Admission notification on a rolling basis beginning on or about 10/15. Must reply by May 1 or within 2 week(s) if notified thereafter. **Financial aid:** Priority date 3/1; no closing date. FAFSA required. Applicants notified by 3/1; Applicants notified on a rolling basis starting 3/1; must reply within 3 week(s) of notification.

Academics. All students eligible through PACE Center to receive free tutoring in every course offered. Specialized courses offered for students having academic difficulties, as well as career preparation courses to help students choose a career path. **Special study options:** Accelerated study, combined bachelor's/graduate degree, cooperative education, cross-registration, distance learning, double major, dual enrollment of high school students, ESL, exchange student, honors, independent study, internships, liberal arts/career combination, semester at sea, student-designed major, study abroad, teacher certification program, Washington semester. Five-year bachelor's/master's programs on campus and with other institutions. **Credit/placement by examination:** AP, CLEP, IB. 12 credit hours maximum toward bachelor's degree. **Support services:** Learning center, reduced course load, remedial instruction, study skills assistance, tutoring, writing center.

Majors. Architecture: Interior. **Area/ethnic studies:** Women's. **Biology:** General, biochemistry. **Business:** Accounting, business admin, international, managerial economics, marketing. **Communications:** Broadcast journalism, communications/speech/rhetoric, journalism, public relations. **Conservation:** Environmental science, environmental studies. **Education:** Early childhood, elementary. **Engineering:** General. **English:** Creative writing, English lit. **Health services:** Nursing (RN). **History:** General. **Human services:** Public policy, social work. **Liberal arts:** Arts/sciences. **Math:** General. **Parks/recreation:** Exercise sciences. **Physical sciences:** Chemistry, physics. **Protective services:** Forensics. **Psychology:** General. **Social sciences:** Economics, international relations, political science. **Visual/performing arts:** Art history/conservation, music, photography, studio arts, studio arts management.

Most popular majors. Biology 12%, business/marketing 11%, English 6%, health sciences 26%, psychology 9%, social sciences 6%, visual/performing arts 10%.

Technology on campus. PC or laptop required. 300 workstations in dormitories, library, computer center. Dormitories wired for high-speed internet access and linked to campus network. Commuter students can connect to campus network. Online course registration, online library, helpline, repair service, student web hosting, wireless network available.

Student life. Freshman orientation: Mandatory. Preregistration for classes offered. Held immediately before classes begin in late August. Mini-orientations held during late spring and summer when students can register for courses. **Policies:** Honor code. **Housing:** Guaranteed on-campus for all undergraduates. Coed dorms, single-sex dorms, apartments, themed housing, wellness housing available. $150 nonrefundable deposit, deadline 5/1. Intercultural residence hall, community service floor and environmental floor within larger residence hall available. **Activities:** Campus ministries, choral groups, drama, film society, international student organizations, literary magazine, musical theater, student government, student newspaper, symphony orchestra, Black student union, Christian Fellowship, Jewish organization, Feminist collective, Gateway student association, Green Horizons, Mortar Board, Students Against Sexual Oppression, Chinese Student and Scholar Association.

Athletics. NCAA. **Intercollegiate:** Basketball, cross-country, diving W, ice hockey W, soccer W, softball W, swimming, tennis W, track and field, volleyball W. **Intramural:** Badminton, basketball, bowling, football (non-tackle), soccer, squash, volleyball. **Team name:** Cougars.

Student services. Adult student services, chaplain/spiritual director, career counseling, services for economically disadvantaged, student employment services, financial aid counseling, health services, personal counseling, placement for graduates, women's services. **Physically disabled:** Services for visually, speech, hearing impaired.

Contact. E-mail: admissions@chatham.edu
Phone: (412) 365-1825 Toll-free number: (800) 837-1290
Fax: (412) 365-1609
Amy Becher, VP for Enrollment Management, Chatham University, Woodland Road, Pittsburgh, PA 15232

Chestnut Hill College
Philadelphia, Pennsylvania   **CB member**
www.chc.edu   **CB code: 2082**

‣ Private 4-year liberal arts college affiliated with the Roman Catholic Church

‣ Residential campus in very large city

‣ 1,383 degree-seeking undergraduates: 37% African American, 2% Asian American, 9% Hispanic/Latino, 3% Multi-racial, non-Hispanic, 3% international

‣ 508 degree-seeking graduate students

‣ 93% of applicants admitted

‣ SAT or ACT (ACT writing optional) required

‣ 49% graduate within 6 years

General. Founded in 1924. Regionally accredited. Extended campus at adjacent Sugar Loaf Hill. **Degrees:** 349 bachelor's awarded; master's, professional offered. **Location:** 17 miles from Center City. **Calendar:** Semester, limited summer session. **Full-time faculty:** 92 total; 84% have terminal degrees, 8% minority, 66% women. **Part-time faculty:** 232 total; 24% have terminal degrees, 16% minority, 60% women. **Class size:** 85% < 20, 15% 20-39, less than 1% 40-49. **Special facilities:** Observatory, planetarium, Irish literature collection, multimedia center, smart classrooms, nearby stables.

Freshman class profile. 1,215 applied, 1,125 admitted, 205 enrolled.

Mid 50% test scores		GPA 2.0-2.99:	33%
SAT critical reading:	430-550	Rank in top quarter:	28%
SAT math:	420-530	Rank in top tenth:	9%
SAT writing:	420-530	End year in good standing:	63%
ACT composite:	17-24	Return as sophomores:	66%
GPA 3.75 or higher:	18%	Out-of-state:	40%
GPA 3.50-3.74:	20%	Live on campus:	83%
GPA 3.0-3.49:	29%	International:	2%

Basis for selection. Secondary school record, essay very important. Standardized test scores, recommendations, character, interview, extracurricular activities important. Alumni connection, talent, volunteer activity, work experience considered. Open admissions to accelerated program in the School of Continuing and Professional Studies only. Students are placed in writing, math, and language courses on basis of placement tests administered by the college. **Home schooled:** Must subscribe to a homeschool agency.

High school preparation. College-preparatory program recommended. 16 units recommended. Recommended units include English 4, mathematics 3, social studies 4, history 4, science 3 and foreign language 2.

2015-2016 Annual costs. Tuition/fees: $33,120. Room/board: $10,200. Books/supplies: $1,200. Personal expenses: $3,200.

2015-2016 Financial aid. **Need-based:** Average need met was 73%. Average scholarship/grant was $23,712; average loan $3,557. 64% of total undergraduate aid awarded as scholarships/grants, 36% as loans/jobs. **Non-need-based:** Scholarships awarded for academics, art, athletics.

Application procedures. Admission: No deadline. $35 fee, may be waived for applicants with need. Admission notification on a rolling basis beginning on or about 10/1. Housing deposit refunded if requested in writing prior to May 1. **Financial aid:** Priority date 2/15; no closing date. FAFSA required. Applicants notified on a rolling basis starting 2/16.

Academics. Many teacher certification preparation programs: Montessori, Early Education, Elementary/Middle Education, Secondary Education with a variety of academic specializations, Special Education, School Principal. Interdisciplinary bachelor's degree in international business, language, and culture. Combined program with Arcadia University in Physician Assistant. Combined program with Thomas Jefferson University in Biotechnology, Cytotechnology, Medical Laboratory Science, or Radiologic Sciences. Interdisciplinary Honors Program. Double majors. Individualized Majors. **Special study options:** Combined bachelor's/graduate degree, cross-registration, distance learning, double major, dual enrollment of high school students, ESL,

exchange student, honors, independent study, internships, student-designed major, study abroad, teacher certification program. 3-2 BS/MS instructional technology; 5-year BS/MS Administration of Human Services; 5-year BS/MEd early education with emphasis in special education; 3-2 BA/MS psychology; dual degree in biology or molecular biology or chemistry, articulation agreement with masters in Physician Assistant at Arcadia University; dual degree in biology and in radiologic science at Thomas Jefferson University; dual degree in biology or chemistry. **Credit/placement by examination:** AP, CLEP, IB, SAT, ACT, institutional tests. 15 credit hours maximum toward associate degree, 15 toward bachelor's. **Support services:** Learning center, reduced course load, remedial instruction, study skills assistance, tutoring, writing center. Math center, language center.

Majors. Biology: General, biochemistry, molecular. **Business:** Accounting, accounting/business management, business admin, communications, human resources, information resources management, international, marketing. **Communications:** Media studies. **Computer sciences:** General. **Conservation:** Environmental science. **Education:** Early childhood, elementary, music. **English:** English lit. **Foreign languages:** French, Spanish. **Health services:** Health care admin. **History:** General. **Liberal arts:** Arts/sciences. **Math:** General. **Physical sciences:** Chemistry, forensic chemistry. **Protective services:** Forensics, law enforcement admin. **Psychology:** General. **Social sciences:** Political science, sociology. **Visual/performing arts:** Music, studio arts. **Work/family studies:** Child care management.

Most popular majors. Business/marketing 16%, education 15%, psychology 7%, public administration/social services 22%, security/protective services 16%.

Technology on campus. 53 workstations in library, computer center. Dormitories wired for high-speed internet access and linked to campus network. Commuter students can connect to campus network. Online course registration, helpline, wireless network available.

Student life. Freshman orientation: Available. Preregistration for classes offered. Held two or three times during the summer. **Policies:** First and second year students may not park a car on campus. Freshmen not permitted cars on campus. **Housing:** Coed dorms, apartments available. $500 partly refundable deposit. **Activities:** Bands, campus ministries, choral groups, dance, drama, international student organizations, literary magazine, music ensembles, musical theater, radio station, student government, student newspaper, TV station, 37 organizations include: Black Student Union, computer club, Council for Exceptional Children, Global Student Association, history club, Mask and Foil (theater), Saudi student club, Harry Potter Alliance, film club, Unified for Uganda.

Athletics. NCAA. **Intercollegiate:** Baseball M, basketball, bowling W, cross-country, football (tackle) M, golf, lacrosse, soccer, softball W, tennis, track and field, volleyball W. **Team name:** Griffins.

Student services. Adult student services, alcohol/substance abuse counseling, chaplain/spiritual director, career counseling, financial aid counseling, health services, personal counseling, veterans' counselor. **Physically disabled:** Services for visually impaired.

Contact. E-mail: chcapply@chc.edu
Phone: (215) 248-7100 Toll-free number: (800) 248-0052
Fax: (215) 248-7082
Alaina Costa, Director of Admissions, School of Undergraduate Studies, Chestnut Hill College, 9601 Germantown Avenue, Philadelphia, PA 19118-2693

Cheyney University of Pennsylvania
Cheyney, Pennsylvania   **CB member**
www.cheyney.edu   **CB code: 2648**

‣ Public 4-year university

‣ Residential campus in small town

‣ 686 degree-seeking undergraduates: 10% part-time, 50% women, 82% African American, 5% Hispanic/Latino, 4% Multi-racial, non-Hispanic

‣ 24 degree-seeking graduate students

‣ 40% of applicants admitted

‣ SAT or ACT (ACT writing recommended), application essay required

General. Founded in 1837. Regionally accredited. Courses offered at Philadelphia Urban Center. **Degrees:** 147 bachelor's awarded; master's offered. **ROTC:** Army. **Location:** 25 miles from Philadelphia. **Calendar:** Semester, limited summer session. **Full-time faculty:** 40 total; 72% minority, 48% women. **Part-time faculty:** 45 total; 53% minority, 42% women. **Class size:** 44% < 20, 48% 20-39, 8% 40-49, less than 1% 50-99. **Special facilities:** Planetarium, weather station, theater arts center.

Freshman class profile. 1,700 applied, 685 admitted, 101 enrolled.

Mid 50% test scores			
SAT critical reading:	350-430	GPA 3.0-3.49:	20%
SAT math:	350-450	GPA 2.0-2.99:	67%
SAT writing:	340-420	Rank in top quarter:	23%
ACT composite:	14-16	Rank in top tenth:	10%
GPA 3.75 or higher:	4%	Return as sophomores:	44%
GPA 3.50-3.74:	2%	Out-of-state:	40%
		Live on campus:	95%

Basis for selection. Test scores, class rank, GPA, counselor recommendation, extracurricular activities important. 830 SAT (exclusive of Writing) or 17 ACT required. Interview recommended.

High school preparation. College-preparatory program recommended. 14 units required. Required units include English 4, mathematics 3, social studies 3 and science 3.

2015-2016 Annual costs. Tuition/fees: $9,344; $13,934 out-of-state. Room/board: $10,748. Books/supplies: $1,300.

Financial aid. **Non-need-based:** Scholarships awarded for academics, athletics.

Application procedures. **Admission:** Priority date 2/15; no deadline. $24 fee, may be waived for applicants with need. Admission notification on a rolling basis. **Financial aid:** Priority date 3/15; no closing date. FAFSA required. Applicants notified on a rolling basis starting 4/1; must reply within 2 week(s) of notification.

Academics. Health and physical education courses required of most students. **Special study options:** Cross-registration, distance learning, double major, honors, independent study, internships, study abroad, teacher certification program. **Credit/placement by examination:** AP, CLEP, SAT, institutional tests. 23 credit hours maximum toward bachelor's degree. **Support services:** Learning center, pre-admission summer program, reduced course load, remedial instruction, study skills assistance, tutoring, writing center.

Majors. **Biology:** General. **Business:** Business admin, hospitality admin. **Communications:** Communications/speech/rhetoric. **Computer sciences:** General. **Education:** Early childhood, elementary, special ed. **English:** English lit. **Foreign languages:** French, Spanish. **Health services:** Clinical lab science. **Math:** General. **Parks/recreation:** Facilities management. **Physical sciences:** Chemistry. **Psychology:** General. **Social sciences:** General, economics, political science, sociology. **Visual/performing arts:** Art, dramatic, music. **Work/family studies:** Clothing/textiles.

Most popular majors. Biology 7%, business/marketing 7%, liberal arts 7%, parks/recreation 7%, psychology 17%, social sciences 32%, visual/performing arts 14%.

Technology on campus. 296 workstations in dormitories, library, computer center, student center. Dormitories wired for high-speed internet access and linked to campus network. Online course registration, helpline, repair service, wireless network available.

Student life. **Freshman orientation:** Mandatory. Preregistration for classes offered. **Policies:** Ecumenical services held on campus. **Housing:** Guaranteed on-campus for freshmen. Coed dorms, themed housing available. $200 nonrefundable deposit, deadline 4/1. Honors dorm available. **Activities:** Marching band, choral groups, dance, international student organizations, literary magazine, Model UN, musical theater, radio station, student government, Shades of Unity, Toastmasters, business club, education club, NAACP, Latino Students in Action, LaOriginale, Commuter Students Association.

Athletics. NCAA. **Intercollegiate:** Basketball, bowling W, cross-country, football (tackle) M, tennis W, track and field, volleyball W. **Intramural:** Basketball, football (tackle) M. **Team name:** Wolves.

Student services. Adult student services, career counseling, student employment services, health services, personal counseling, placement for graduates, veterans' counselor.

Contact. E-mail: admissions@cheyney.edu
Phone: (610) 399-2275 Toll-free number: (800) 243-9639 ext. 2275
Fax: (610) 399-2099
Eric Hilton, Director of Admissions, Cheyney University of Pennsylvania, 1837 University Circle, Cheyney, PA 19319-0019

Clarion University of Pennsylvania
Clarion, Pennsylvania **CB member**
www.clarion.edu **CB code: 2649**

- Public 4-year business and teachers college
- Residential campus in small town

- 4,401 degree-seeking undergraduates
- SAT or ACT (ACT writing optional) required

General. Founded in 1867. Regionally accredited. **Degrees:** 922 bachelor's, 151 associate awarded; master's offered. **ROTC:** Army. **Location:** 80 miles from Pittsburgh, 90 miles from Erie. **Calendar:** Semester, limited summer session. **Full-time faculty:** 218 total; 84% have terminal degrees, 12% minority, 50% women. **Part-time faculty:** 76 total; 17% have terminal degrees, 4% minority, 71% women. **Class size:** 26% < 20, 53% 20-39, 13% 40-49, 7% 50-99, 1% >100. **Special facilities:** Planetarium.

Freshman class profile.

GPA 3.75 or higher:	15%	Rank in top quarter:	27%
GPA 3.50-3.74:	23%	Rank in top tenth:	10%
GPA 3.0-3.49:	30%	Out-of-state:	5%
GPA 2.0-2.99:	31%	Live on campus:	68%

Basis for selection. School achievement record, class rank, GPA, test scores considered. Audition required of music program applicants; Nursing students must complete NLN entrance exam. **Home schooled:** Transcript of courses and grades required.

High school preparation. College-preparatory program required. 13 units required; 20 recommended. Required and recommended units include English 4, mathematics 3-4, social studies 3-4, history 1, science 3-4 (laboratory 1) and foreign language 2.

2015-2016 Annual costs. Tuition/fees: $10,190; $13,720 out-of-state. Room/board: $9,792. Books/supplies: $1,000. Personal expenses: $3,000.

Financial aid. **Non-need-based:** Scholarships awarded for academics, alumni affiliation, art, athletics, job skills, leadership, minority status, music/drama, state residency.

Application procedures. **Admission:** Priority date 2/15; deadline 8/1. $40 fee, may be waived for applicants with need. Admission notification on a rolling basis beginning on or about 1/7. **Financial aid:** Priority date 5/1; no closing date. FAFSA required. Applicants notified on a rolling basis starting 3/30.

Academics. **Special study options:** Accelerated study, combined bachelor's/graduate degree, cooperative education, distance learning, double major, dual enrollment of high school students, ESL, honors, independent study, internships, liberal arts/career combination, student-designed major, study abroad, teacher certification program. Co-op program in engineering with two participating schools; co-op in speech pathology and audiology with Gallaudet University. Joint and collaborative programs in MSLS/JD, pharmacy, osteopathic medicine, nanotechnology, master of nursing, language, radiologic science, respiratory care and industrial technology. **Credit/placement by examination:** AP, CLEP, IB, SAT, ACT, institutional tests. 38 credit hours maximum toward bachelor's degree. **Support services:** Learning center, pre-admission summer program, remedial instruction, study skills assistance, tutoring, writing center.

Majors. **Biology:** General, ecology, environmental, molecular. **Business:** Business admin, finance, international, labor relations, managerial economics, marketing, real estate. **Communications:** Journalism, media studies. **Computer sciences:** General, information systems. **Conservation:** Environmental science. **Education:** Early childhood, elementary, special ed. **English:** English lit. **Foreign languages:** French, Spanish. **Health services:** Clinical lab technology, medical radiologic technology/radiation therapy, nursing (RN), rehabilitation science, speech pathology. **History:** General. **Liberal arts:** Arts/sciences, library science. **Math:** General. **Philosophy/religion:** Philosophy. **Physical sciences:** Chemistry, geology, physics. **Psychology:** General, social. **Social sciences:** Anthropology, economics, political science, sociology. **Visual/performing arts:** Art, dramatic, music.

Most popular majors. Business/marketing 14%, communications/journalism 8%, education 10%, health sciences 23%, liberal arts 12%, social sciences 6%.

Technology on campus. 1,143 workstations in dormitories, library, computer center, student center. Dormitories wired for high-speed internet access and linked to campus network. Commuter students can connect to campus network. Online course registration, online library, helpline, student web hosting, wireless network available.

Student life. **Freshman orientation:** Mandatory, $150 fee. Preregistration for classes offered. One-day session held in January, spring and summer. **Policies:** Students who live on campus have first option of returning to their same housing following year. **Housing:** Guaranteed on-campus for freshmen. Coed dorms, single-sex dorms, special housing for disabled, apartments, fraternity/sorority housing available. $200 nonrefundable deposit, deadline 7/18. Pets allowed in dorm rooms. **Activities:** Bands, campus ministries, choral groups, dance, drama, international student organizations, literary magazine, music ensembles, Model UN, musical theater, radio station, student government, student newspaper, symphony orchestra, TV station, Koinonia Christian Fellowship, African American Caucus, Newman Association, Hip Hop Dance Team, NAACP, Young Democrats, Eagle Ambassadors, People Reaching Out and Understanding Disabilities, Students Together Against Rape, University Activities Board.

Athletics. NCAA. **Intercollegiate:** Baseball M, basketball, cross-country, diving, football (tackle) M, golf M, soccer W, softball W, swimming, tennis W, track and field W, volleyball M. **Intramural:** Badminton, basketball, bowling, football (non-tackle), golf, racquetball, soccer, softball, swimming, table tennis, tennis, track and field, volleyball, water polo, wrestling. **Team name:** Golden Eagles.

Student services. Adult student services, alcohol/substance abuse counseling, chaplain/spiritual director, career counseling, services for economically disadvantaged, student employment services, financial aid counseling, health services, minority student services, personal counseling, placement for graduates, veterans' counselor, women's services. **Physically disabled:** Services for visually, speech, hearing impaired.

Contact. E-mail: admissions@clarion.edu
Phone: (814) 393-2306 Toll-free number: (800) 672-7171
Fax: (814) 393-2030
William Bailey, Dean of Enrollment Management, Clarion University of Pennsylvania, 840 Wood Street, Clarion, PA 16214

Curtis Institute of Music
Philadelphia, Pennsylvania
www.curtis.edu   **CB code: 2100**

⧫ Private 4-year music college
⧫ Residential campus in very large city

General. Founded in 1924. Regionally accredited. **Calendar:** Semester.

Annual costs/financial aid. All students receive a full-tuition scholarship. All students pay $2,525 in required fees. Students who do not have comprehensive health insurance are required to purchase insurance through the institution; the approximate cost is $3,200 for 12 months of coverage. Room/board: $14,710. Books/supplies: $1,640. Personal expenses: $1,648. Need-based financial aid available to full-time and part-time students.

Contact. Phone: (215) 717-3117
Director of Admissions, 1726 Locust Street, Philadelphia, PA 19103-6187

Delaware Valley University
Doylestown, Pennsylvania   **CB member**
www.delval.edu   **CB code: 2510**

⧫ Private 4-year university
⧫ Residential campus in large town
⧫ 1,879 degree-seeking undergraduates: 6% part-time, 60% women, 8% African American, 2% Asian American, 9% Hispanic/Latino, 1% Native American, 1% international
⧫ 220 degree-seeking graduate students
⧫ 69% of applicants admitted
⧫ SAT or ACT (ACT writing optional), application essay required
⧫ 57% graduate within 6 years

General. Founded in 1896. Regionally accredited. **Degrees:** 354 bachelor's, 3 associate awarded; master's, professional offered. **Location:** 20 miles from Philadelphia, 70 miles from New York City. **Calendar:** Semester, extensive summer session. **Full-time faculty:** 89 total; 66% have terminal degrees, 10% minority, 43% women. **Part-time faculty:** 107 total. **Class size:** 60% < 20, 35% 20-39, 3% 40-49, 2% 50-99. **Special facilities:** Equine facility with indoor and outdoor arenas, animal farms, dairy, farm market, arboretum greenhouses, tissue culture laboratories.

Freshman class profile. 2,594 applied, 1,782 admitted, 492 enrolled.

Mid 50% test scores			
SAT critical reading:	430-550	GPA 3.0-3.49:	27%
SAT math:	440-560	GPA 2.0-2.99:	27%
SAT writing:	410-540	Return as sophomores:	70%
ACT composite:	18-25	Out-of-state:	47%
GPA 3.75 or higher:	27%	Live on campus:	89%
GPA 3.50-3.74:	18%	Fraternities:	4%
		Sororities:	5%

Basis for selection. Academic achievement, class rank, test scores, letters of recommendation from math or science teacher and guidance counselor,

grades in math and science considered. Interview, essay recommended. **Home schooled:** State high school equivalency certificate required.

High school preparation. College-preparatory program required. 15 units required. Required units include English 3, mathematics 2, social studies 2, science 2 (laboratory 1) and academic electives 6. Business administration computer information systems management, criminal justice, or English majors and students applying for the equine science program need only one unit of science: biology, chemistry or physics.

2015-2016 Annual costs. Tuition/fees: $35,256. Room/board: $12,618. Books/supplies: $1,000. Personal expenses: $1,200.

2015-2016 Financial aid. Need-based: 438 full-time freshmen applied for aid; 406 deemed to have need; 406 received aid. Average need met was 68%. Average scholarship/grant was $21,898; average loan $3,720. 70% of total undergraduate aid awarded as scholarships/grants, 30% as loans/jobs. **Non-need-based:** Awarded to 419 full-time undergraduates, including 103 freshmen. Scholarships awarded for academics, alumni affiliation, leadership, music/drama, state residency.

Application procedures. Admission: Closing date 5/1. $50 fee, may be waived for applicants with need, free for online applicants. Admission notification on a rolling basis beginning on or about 10/31. Must reply by May 1 or within 4 week(s) if notified thereafter. **Financial aid:** Priority date 4/15; no closing date. FAFSA required. Applicants notified on a rolling basis starting 3/31; must reply by 5/1 or within 2 week(s) of notification.

Academics. Students complete 500-hour employment program related to major. **Special study options:** Accelerated study, combined bachelor's/graduate degree, distance learning, double major, dual enrollment of high school students, honors, independent study, internships, study abroad, teacher certification program. **Credit/placement by examination:** AP, CLEP, SAT, ACT, institutional tests. Credit for 5 courses may be granted through examination. **Support services:** Learning center, pre-admission summer program, reduced course load, remedial instruction, study skills assistance, tutoring, writing center.

Majors. Biology: General, zoology. **Business:** Accounting, business admin, management information systems, marketing. **Computer sciences:** General. **Conservation:** Wildlife/wilderness. **Education:** Secondary. **English:** English lit. **Math:** General. **Physical sciences:** Chemistry. **Protective services:** Law enforcement admin. **Psychology:** Counseling.

Most popular majors. Agriculture 44%, biology 14%, business/marketing 16%, natural resources/environmental science 12%.

Technology on campus. 150 workstations in dormitories, library, computer center, student center. Dormitories wired for high-speed internet access and linked to campus network. Commuter students can connect to campus network. Online course registration, online library, helpline, repair service, wireless network available.

Student life. Freshman orientation: Mandatory. Preregistration for classes offered. **Policies:** Freshmen not permitted cars on campus. **Housing:** Coed dorms, single-sex dorms, special housing for disabled, apartments available. $200 fully refundable deposit, deadline 5/1. **Activities:** Concert band, choral groups, drama, literary magazine, music ensembles, radio station, student government, Intervarsity Christian Fellowship, Hillel, Students for Diversity, Lions Club, Alpha Phi Omega, Habitat for Humanity, Project EARTH, Students in Free Enterprise, Animal Lifeline, Positive Awareness of Wildlife and Zoos.

Athletics. NCAA. **Intercollegiate:** Baseball M, basketball, cheerleading W, cross-country, equestrian, field hockey W, football (tackle) M, golf, lacrosse, soccer, softball W, tennis, track and field, volleyball W, wrestling M. **Intramural:** Equestrian, football (tackle) M, softball, ultimate frisbee, volleyball. **Team name:** Aggies.

Student services. Adult student services, career counseling, student employment services, financial aid counseling, health services, personal counseling, placement for graduates, veterans' counselor. **Physically disabled:** Services for visually, speech, hearing impaired.

Contact. E-mail: AdmitMe@delval.edu
Phone: (215) 489-2211 Toll-free number: (800) 233-5825
Fax: (215) 230-2968
Arthur Goon, Vice President for Enrollment Management, Delaware Valley University, 700 East Butler Avenue, Doylestown, PA 18901-2697

DeSales University
Center Valley, Pennsylvania   **CB member**
www.desales.edu   **CB code: 2021**

⧫ Private 4-year university affiliated with the Roman Catholic Church
⧫ Residential campus in large town

- 2,291 degree-seeking undergraduates: 24% part-time, 60% women, 4% African American, 2% Asian American, 12% Hispanic/Latino, 1% Native American
- 845 degree-seeking graduate students
- 78% of applicants admitted
- SAT or ACT (ACT writing optional) required
- 70% graduate within 6 years

General. Founded in 1964. Regionally accredited. **Degrees:** 602 bachelor's awarded; master's, professional offered. **ROTC:** Army. **Location:** 7 miles from Allentown and Bethlehem; 50 miles from Philadelphia. **Calendar:** Semester, extensive summer session. **Full-time faculty:** 125 total; 87% have terminal degrees, 10% minority, 50% women. **Part-time faculty:** 241 total; 8% minority, 51% women. **Class size:** 59% < 20, 38% 20-39, less than 1% 40-49, 2% 50-99.

Freshman class profile. 2,706 applied, 2,100 admitted, 428 enrolled.

Mid 50% test scores		GPA 3.0-3.49:	32%
SAT critical reading:	450-590	GPA 2.0-2.99:	26%
SAT math:	440-590	Rank in top quarter:	47%
SAT writing:	450-580	Rank in top tenth:	21%
ACT composite:	21-28	Return as sophomores:	79%
GPA 3.75 or higher:	20%	Out-of-state:	33%
GPA 3.50-3.74:	19%	Live on campus:	81%

Basis for selection. University is especially interested in students who have demonstrated significant achievement within a demanding curriculum. Quality of academic performance is the single most important factor in the decision-making process. Essay, interview recommended for all; audition required for dance and theater programs. Interview required for physician assistant program (medical studies), and physical therapy program (health sciences).

High school preparation. College-preparatory program required. 16 units required; 21 recommended. Required and recommended units include English 4, mathematics 3-4, social studies 3, science 2-3 (laboratory 2-3) and foreign language 2-4. Biology, chemistry, 3 math recommended for biology major. 3 math, including 2 algebra, recommended for business major. Chemistry, physics, 3 math recommended for chemistry major. Biology, chemistry, physics, 2 math recommended for nursing major. 2 biology, chemistry, or physics, and 3 math recommended for pre-med major. 4 math recommended for math major.

2015-2016 Annual costs. Tuition/fees: $33,350. Room/board: $12,050. Books/supplies: $992. Personal expenses: $1,586.

2015-2016 Financial aid. Need-based: 407 full-time freshmen applied for aid; 348 deemed to have need; 348 received aid. Average need met was 77%. Average scholarship/grant was $20,533; average loan $3,518. 64% of total undergraduate aid awarded as scholarships/grants, 36% as loans/jobs. **Non-need-based:** Awarded to 1,424 full-time undergraduates, including 400 freshmen. Scholarships awarded for academics, alumni affiliation, art, leadership, music/drama, religious affiliation, ROTC.

Application procedures. Admission: Priority date 3/1; deadline 8/1. No application fee. Admission notification on a rolling basis beginning on or about 10/6. Must reply by May 1 or within 2 week(s) if notified thereafter. **Financial aid:** Priority date 2/1, closing date 5/1. FAFSA required. Applicants notified on a rolling basis starting 2/15; must reply by 5/1 or within 2 week(s) of notification.

Academics. Special study options: Accelerated study, combined bachelor's/graduate degree, cross-registration, distance learning, double major, dual enrollment of high school students, exchange student, external degree, honors, independent study, internships, liberal arts/career combination, student-designed major, study abroad, teacher certification program, weekend college. BS in medical studies, MS in physician assistant studies; 5 year BS/MBA in accounting, 5 year BA/MACJ in criminal justice, cross-registration at consortium schools: Cedar Crest, Moravian, Muhlenberg, Lafayette, Lehigh. **Credit/placement by examination:** AP, CLEP, institutional tests. 24 credit hours maximum toward bachelor's degree. For AP credit for Physics B must complete lab component. Must submit research paper for CLEP English Composition with Essay to obtain 6 credits. **Support services:** Learning center, pre-admission summer program, reduced course load, study skills assistance, tutoring.

Majors. Biology: General, biochemistry, molecular. **Business:** General, accounting, business admin, e-commerce, finance, human resources, international, logistics, management information systems, marketing, personal/financial services. **Communications:** General. **Computer sciences:** General, information technology. **Education:** Early childhood, elementary, special ed. **English:** English lit. **Foreign languages:** Spanish. **Health services:** Clinical lab science, nursing (RN), pharmaceutical marketing/management. **History:** General. **Liberal arts:** Arts/sciences. **Math:** General. **Parks/recreation:** Exercise sciences, sports admin. **Philosophy/religion:** Philosophy. **Physical**

sciences: Chemistry. **Protective services:** Criminal justice, homeland security. **Psychology:** General. **Social sciences:** Economics, political science. **Theology:** Theology. **Visual/performing arts:** Dance, dramatic, film/cinema/video.

Most popular majors. Business/marketing 23%, health sciences 22%, parks/recreation 7%, psychology 10%, security/protective services 7%, visual/performing arts 10%.

Technology on campus. 200 workstations in library, computer center, student center. Dormitories wired for high-speed internet access and linked to campus network. Commuter students can connect to campus network. Online course registration, online library, helpline, student web hosting, wireless network available.

Student life. Freshman orientation: Mandatory, $200 fee. Preregistration for classes offered. One-day academic orientation in May or June; 3-day social and academic orientation in August. **Policies:** Students under 21 cannot possess or be in presence of alcohol. Access to dorm rooms of opposite sex restricted during certain hours (overnight), social gathering policy. **Housing:** Guaranteed on-campus for all undergraduates. Coed dorms, single-sex dorms, special housing for disabled, themed housing available. $400 fully refundable deposit, deadline 5/1. In Village and Town houses for upperclassmen. DeChantal residence hall, men and women live in separate wings of the buildings. **Activities:** Bands, campus ministries, choral groups, dance, drama, film society, international student organizations, literary magazine, music ensembles, Model UN, musical theater, radio station, student government, student newspaper, TV station, Pro-Life club, Habitat For Humanity, Best Buddies, Esto Vir, Lion's club, natural science club, Rotoract, St. Thomas More Society, American Marketing Association, Criminal Justice Association.

Athletics. NCAA. **Intercollegiate:** Baseball M, basketball, cross-country, field hockey W, golf M, lacrosse M, soccer, softball W, track and field, volleyball W. **Team name:** Bulldogs.

Student services. Adult student services, alcohol/substance abuse counseling, chaplain/spiritual director, career counseling, services for economically disadvantaged, student employment services, financial aid counseling, health services, minority student services, personal counseling, veterans' counselor. **Physically disabled:** Services for visually, speech, hearing impaired.

Contact. E-mail: admiss@desales.edu
Phone: (610) 282-4443 Toll-free number: (877) 433-7253
Fax: (610) 282-0131
Derrick Wetzel, Director of Admissions, DeSales University, 2755 Station Avenue, Center Valley, PA 18034-9568

DeVry University: Fort Washington
Fort Washington, Pennsylvania
www.devry.edu **CB code: 3866**

- For-profit 4-year university
- Commuter campus in large town
- 436 degree-seeking undergraduates
- Interview required

General. Additional locations: Philadelphia, King of Prussia, Pittsburgh. **Degrees:** 147 bachelor's, 20 associate awarded; master's offered. **Location:** 35 miles from Philadelphia. **Calendar:** Semester, extensive summer session. **Full-time faculty:** 19 total; 32% minority, 32% women. **Part-time faculty:** 131 total; 10% minority, 45% women.

Basis for selection. Applicants must have high school diploma or equivalent, or a degree from accredited postsecondary institution, demonstrate proficiency in basic college-level skills through SAT or ACT scores or institution-administered placement exams, and be at least 17 years of age on the first day of classes. New students may enter at beginning of any semester. CPT also accepted.

High school preparation. College-preparatory program recommended. Math unit must be algebra or higher.

2015-2016 Annual costs. Tuition/fees: $13,380. Books/supplies: $1,320. Personal expenses: $2,376.

Financial aid. All financial aid based on need.

Application procedures. Admission: No deadline. $40 fee. Admission notification on a rolling basis. **Financial aid:** No deadline. FAFSA required. Applicants notified on a rolling basis.

Academics. Special study options: Accelerated study, distance learning, study abroad. **Credit/placement by examination:** AP, CLEP. **Support services:** Learning center, remedial instruction, tutoring.

Majors. Business: Business admin. **Communications:** General. **Computer sciences:** Networking, systems analysis, web page design. **Engineering:** Software.

Most popular majors. Business/marketing 66%, computer/information sciences 17%, engineering/engineering technologies 17%.

Technology on campus. 407 workstations in library, computer center. Online course registration, online library, helpline available.

Student life. Freshman orientation: Mandatory. Preregistration for classes offered. **Activities:** Campus Crusade for Christ, electronic gamers club, creative arts club.

Athletics. Intramural: Volleyball.

Student services. Career counseling, student employment services, financial aid counseling, placement for graduates, veterans' counselor. **Physically disabled:** Services for visually, hearing impaired.

Contact. E-mail: admissions@phi.devry.edu
Phone: (215) 591-5701 Toll-free number: (866) 303-3879
Fax: (215) 591-5745
DeVry University: Fort Washington, 1140 Virginia Drive, Fort Washington, PA 19034-3204

Dickinson College

Carlisle, Pennsylvania
www.dickinson.edu

CB member
CB code: 2186

- Private 4-year liberal arts college
- Residential campus in large town
- 2,381 degree-seeking undergraduates: 58% women, 4% African American, 3% Asian American, 6% Hispanic/Latino, 4% Multi-racial, non-Hispanic, 10% international
- 47% of applicants admitted
- Application essay required
- 85% graduate within 6 years; 38% enter graduate study

General. Founded in 1783. Regionally accredited. **Degrees:** 562 bachelor's awarded. **ROTC:** Army. **Location:** 20 miles from Harrisburg, 90 miles from Washington, DC. **Calendar:** Semester. **Full-time faculty:** 222 total; 94% have terminal degrees, 13% minority, 48% women. **Part-time faculty:** 42 total; 60% have terminal degrees, 2% minority, 55% women. **Class size:** 75% < 20, 24% 20-39, 1% 40-49. **Special facilities:** Arts center with gallery and studios, planetarium and multiple telescope observatory, intercontinental satellite communications for study-abroad programs, study of contemporary issues center, research-quality greenhouse, certified organic farm.

Freshman class profile. 6,031 applied, 2,841 admitted, 731 enrolled.

Mid 50% test scores		End year in good standing:	99%
SAT critical reading:	590-680	Return as sophomores:	92%
SAT math:	600-700	Out-of-state:	78%
SAT writing:	590-690	Live on campus:	100%
ACT composite:	27-30	International:	11%

Basis for selection. Academic potential as shown by school achievement record most important. Extracurricular activities very important. Counselor recommendation required. Motivation, personal character very important. Important consideration given to applicants of color. Preference given to academically qualified children of alumni if they satisfy above criteria. Standardized tests optional. SAT or ACT recommended. Submission of standardized tests scores is optional. Interview recommended. **Home schooled:** Transcript of courses and grades, state high school equivalency certificate, letter of recommendation (nonparent) required.

High school preparation. College-preparatory program recommended. 16 units required. Required and recommended units include English 4, mathematics 3, social studies 2, science 3 (laboratory 2), foreign language 2-3 and academic electives 2.

2015-2016 Annual costs. Tuition/fees: $49,489. Room/board: $12,362. Books/supplies: $1,130. Personal expenses: $1,350.

2015-2016 Financial aid. Need-based: 451 full-time freshmen applied for aid; 396 deemed to have need; 396 received aid. Average need met was 99%. Average scholarship/grant was $36,639; average loan $4,237. 84% of total undergraduate aid awarded as scholarships/grants, 16% as loans/jobs.

Non-need-based: Awarded to 455 full-time undergraduates, including 166 freshmen. Scholarships awarded for academics, leadership, ROTC.

Application procedures. Admission: Closing date 2/1 (postmark date). $65 fee, may be waived for applicants with need. Admission notification by 3/20. Must reply by May 1 or within 2 week(s) if notified thereafter. **Financial aid:** Priority date 11/15, closing date 2/1. FAFSA, CSS PROFILE required. Applicants notified by 3/20; must reply by 5/1 or within 2 week(s) of notification.

Academics. Certificates offered in ballet, health studies, ROTC Global Preparedness, security studies and in Social Innovation & Entrepreneurship. Prebusiness, prelaw and premedical preparation available in conjunction with majors listed. **Special study options:** Accelerated study, combined bachelor's/graduate degree, cross-registration, double major, ESL, exchange student, independent study, internships, liberal arts/career combination, student-designed major, study abroad, teacher certification program, Washington semester. 3-2 engineering programs with University of Pennsylvania, Case Western Reserve University, Rensselaer Polytechnic Institute, Columbia School of Engineering. 3-3 law degree with Dickinson School of Law of Penn State University. 3-2 John Hopkins School of Advanced International Studies (SAIS). **Credit/placement by examination:** AP, CLEP, IB, institutional tests. **Support services:** Tutoring, writing center.

Majors. Area/ethnic studies: African, American, East Asian, Italian, Latin American, Near/Middle Eastern, women's. **Biology:** General, biochemistry, neuroscience. **Business:** International. **Computer sciences:** General. **Conservation:** Environmental science, environmental studies. **Education:** Foundations. **English:** English lit. **Foreign languages:** Classics, French, German, Italian, Russian, Spanish. **History:** General. **Human services:** Public policy. **Math:** General. **Philosophy/religion:** Judaic, philosophy, religion. **Physical sciences:** Chemistry, geology, physics. **Psychology:** General. **Social sciences:** Anthropology, archaeology, economics, international relations, political science, sociology. **Visual/performing arts:** Dance, dramatic, music, studio arts.

Most popular majors. Area/ethnic studies 7%, biology 10%, business/marketing 9%, English 6%, foreign language 8%, psychology 7%, social sciences 27%.

Technology on campus. 1,989 workstations in dormitories, library, computer center, student center. Dormitories wired for high-speed internet access and linked to campus network. Commuter students can connect to campus network. Online course registration, online library, helpline, repair service, wireless network available.

Student life. Freshman orientation: Mandatory. Preregistration for classes offered. **Policies:** Freshmen not permitted cars on campus. **Housing:** Guaranteed on-campus for all undergraduates. Coed dorms, special housing for disabled, apartments, fraternity/sorority housing, themed housing, wellness housing available. **Activities:** Bands, choral groups, dance, drama, film society, international student organizations, literary magazine, music ensembles, Model UN, musical theater, radio station, student government, student newspaper, symphony orchestra, public affairs, social service, religious, multicultural, College Democrats, College Republicans, mock trial, foreign language.

Athletics. NCAA. **Intercollegiate:** Baseball M, basketball, cross-country, field hockey W, football (tackle) M, golf, lacrosse, soccer, softball W, squash, swimming, tennis, track and field, volleyball W. **Intramural:** Badminton, basketball, field hockey W, football (non-tackle), racquetball, sand volleyball, soccer, softball M, squash, tennis, volleyball. **Team name:** Red Devils.

Student services. Adult student services, alcohol/substance abuse counseling, career counseling, student employment services, financial aid counseling, health services, minority student services, on-campus daycare, personal counseling, placement for graduates. **Physically disabled:** Services for visually, speech, hearing impaired.

Contact. E-mail: admissions@dickinson.edu
Phone: (717) 245-1231 Toll-free number: (800) 644-1773
Fax: (717) 245-1442
Catherine Davenport, Dean of Admissions, Dickinson College, PO Box 1773, Carlisle, PA 17013-2896

Drexel University

Philadelphia, Pennsylvania
www.drexel.edu

CB member
CB code: 2194

- Private 5-year university
- Residential campus in very large city

- 16,050 degree-seeking undergraduates: 12% part-time, 46% women, 6% African American, 14% Asian American, 6% Hispanic/Latino, 1% Native Hawaiian/Pacific islander, 3% Multi-racial, non-Hispanic, 13% international
- 8,763 degree-seeking graduate students
- 75% of applicants admitted
- SAT or ACT (ACT writing optional) required
- 68% graduate within 6 years

General. Founded in 1891. Regionally accredited. Most undergraduate programs require up to 18 months work experience within 5-year program of study. **Degrees:** 3,515 bachelor's, 23 associate awarded; master's, professional, doctoral offered. **ROTC:** Army, Naval, Air Force. **Calendar:** Quarter, extensive summer session. **Full-time faculty:** 1,143 total; 79% have terminal degrees, 19% minority, 45% women. **Part-time faculty:** 1,004 total; 79% have terminal degrees, 16% minority, 53% women. **Class size:** 58% < 20, 29% 20-39, 4% 40-49, 7% 50-99, 2% >100. **Special facilities:** Anthony J. Drexel Picture Gallery, observatory, Academy of Natural Sciences.

Freshman class profile. 28,757 applied, 21,494 admitted, 2,730 enrolled.

Mid 50% test scores			
SAT critical reading:	530-630	Rank in top quarter:	69%
SAT math:	570-680	Rank in top tenth:	42%
SAT writing:	520-640	Return as sophomores:	85%
ACT composite:	25-30	Out-of-state:	60%
GPA 3.75 or higher:	39%	Live on campus:	91%
GPA 3.50-3.74:	22%	International:	12%
GPA 3.0-3.49:	28%	Fraternities:	9%
GPA 2.0-2.99:	11%	Sororities:	12%

Basis for selection. Academic average, counselor's recommendation and test scores most important, followed by class rank, school, community and church activities. Employment also considered. Essay required for most majors for media arts and design programs. Portfolio required for graphic design, music industry, photography and fashion design. Audition required for dance.

High school preparation. College-preparatory program recommended. Required and recommended units include mathematics 3, science 1 (laboratory 1) and foreign language 1. Engineering applicants required to have 4 units math (including algebra I and II, geometry, trigonometry, and precalculus) and 2 units lab science (including chemistry and physics). Science applicants required to have 4 units math (including algebra I and II, geometry, and trigonometry) and 2 units lab science (including biology, chemistry, or physics). Most other applicants must have algebra I and II and geometry as required math units and one lab science.

2016-2017 Annual costs. Tuition/fees (projected): $51,065. Room/board: $14,367. Books/supplies: $2,053. Personal expenses: $2,514.

Financial aid. Non-need-based: Scholarships awarded for academics, art, athletics, music/drama, ROTC, state residency.

Application procedures. Admission: Closing date 1/15 (postmark date). $50 fee, may be waived for applicants with need. Admission notification on a rolling basis. Must reply by May 1 or within 2 week(s) if notified thereafter. **Financial aid:** Closing date 1/28. FAFSA, CSS PROFILE required.

Academics. Special study options: Accelerated study, combined bachelor's/graduate degree, cooperative education, distance learning, double major, dual enrollment of high school students, ESL, honors, independent study, internships, semester at sea, student-designed major, study abroad, teacher certification program, weekend college. 3-3 programs in engineering with Lincoln University and Indiana University of Pennsylvania. **Credit/placement by examination:** AP, CLEP, IB, institutional tests. 30 credit hours maximum toward bachelor's degree. **Support services:** Learning center, preadmission summer program, reduced course load, remedial instruction, study skills assistance, tutoring, writing center.

Majors. Architecture: Architecture. **Biology:** General. **Business:** General, accounting, construction management, customer service, entrepreneurial studies, finance, international, management information systems, management science, marketing, operations, real estate. **Communications:** General. **Communications technology:** Radio/TV. **Computer sciences:** Computer science, informatics, information systems, security, web page design. **Conservation:** Environmental science, environmental studies. **Education:** Elementary, secondary, special ed. **Engineering:** General, architectural, biomedical, chemical, civil, computer, electrical, environmental, materials, mechanical, software. **English:** English lit. **Health services:** Cardiovascular technology, health care admin, nursing (RN), physician assistant, substance abuse counseling. **History:** General. **Liberal arts:** Arts/sciences, humanities. **Math:** General. **Parks/recreation:** Sports admin. **Philosophy/religion:** Philosophy. **Physical sciences:** Chemistry, geology, physics. **Protective services:** Law enforcement admin. **Psychology:** General. **Social sciences:** Anthropology, criminology, economics, political science, sociology. **Visual/performing**

arts: General, arts management, cinematography, dance, fashion design, graphic design, industrial design, interior design, music management, photography, play/screenwriting.

Most popular majors. Business/marketing 23%, engineering/engineering technologies 20%, health sciences 23%, visual/performing arts 7%.

Technology on campus. PC or laptop required. Dormitories wired for high-speed internet access and linked to campus network. Commuter students can connect to campus network. Online course registration, online library, helpline, repair service, student web hosting, wireless network available.

Student life. Freshman orientation: Available. Preregistration for classes offered. 2-day overnight sessions held in July; 3-day program prior to start of classes. **Policies:** Freshmen required to live on campus unless living with parents. **Housing:** Guaranteed on-campus for freshmen. Coed dorms, special housing for disabled, apartments, fraternity/sorority housing available. $200 nonrefundable deposit, deadline 5/1. **Activities:** Bands, campus ministries, choral groups, dance, drama, film society, literary magazine, music ensembles, musical theater, radio station, student government, student newspaper, TV station, Newman Center, Hillel, Alpha Phi Omega, NAACP, Eye Openers, Disciples in Deed, Drexel Christian Fellowship, Jewish Heritage Program.

Athletics. NCAA. **Intercollegiate:** Basketball, diving, field hockey W, golf M, lacrosse, rowing (crew), soccer, softball W, squash, swimming, tennis, wrestling M. **Intramural:** Basketball, football (non-tackle), sand volleyball, soccer, softball, table tennis, tennis, volleyball. **Team name:** Dragons.

Student services. Adult student services, alcohol/substance abuse counseling, career counseling, student employment services, financial aid counseling, health services, legal services, minority student services, personal counseling, placement for graduates, veterans' counselor, women's services. **Physically disabled:** Services for visually, speech, hearing impaired.

Contact. E-mail: enroll@drexel.edu
Phone: (215) 895-2400 Toll-free number: (800) 237-3935
Fax: (215) 895-1285
Christopher Ferguson, VP, Dean of Admissions, Drexel University, 3141 Chestnut Street, Philadelphia, PA 19104-2876

Duquesne University
Pittsburgh, Pennsylvania
www.duq.edu   CB code: 2196

- Private 4-year university affiliated with the Roman Catholic Church
- Residential campus in large city
- 5,943 degree-seeking undergraduates: 4% part-time, 62% women, 5% African American, 2% Asian American, 3% Hispanic/Latino, 3% Multi-racial, non-Hispanic, 4% international
- 3,443 graduate students
- 76% of applicants admitted
- 76% graduate within 6 years; 35% enter graduate study

General. Founded in 1878. Regionally accredited. **Degrees:** 1,289 bachelor's awarded; master's, professional, doctoral offered. **ROTC:** Army, Naval, Air Force. **Calendar:** Semester, extensive summer session. **Full-time faculty:** 497 total; 94% have terminal degrees, 7% minority, 48% women. **Part-time faculty:** 512 total; 8% minority, 51% women. **Class size:** 40% < 20, 47% 20-39, 5% 40-49, 5% 50-99, 3% >100. **Special facilities:** Recording complex, music technology center, music control lab, center for performance/innovation, over 60 performance/rehearsal spaces, cadaver lab, patient simulation lab, exercise physiology lab, bio mechanics lab, digital media center, phenomenology center, writing center, center for pharmaceutical technology, center for student learning, center for research for underserved and vulnerable populations, curriculum center, confocal microscope live-cell and real-time imaging system, two-dimensional gel electrophoresis system, multi-color fluorescence, phosphorescence, and chemiluminescence imager, confocal fluorescence microscope, 400- and 500-MHz nuclear magnetic resonance spectrometers, single crystal x-ray diffractometer, powder x-ray diffractometer, cell culture facility, DNA sequencing facilities, center of excellence for mass spectrometry, scanning electron microscope with EBS detector, transmission electron microscope (TEM), supercomputing facilities.

Freshman class profile. 7,354 applied, 5,562 admitted, 1,435 enrolled.

Mid 50% test scores			
SAT critical reading:	520-600	Rank in top quarter:	54%
SAT math:	520-610	Rank in top tenth:	23%
SAT writing:	500-600	End year in good standing:	97%
ACT composite:	23-28	Return as sophomores:	87%
GPA 3.75 or higher:	50%	Out-of-state:	27%
GPA 3.50-3.74:	21%	Live on campus:	92%
GPA 3.0-3.49:	23%	International:	3%
GPA 2.0-2.99:	6%	Fraternities:	20%
		Sororities:	25%

Basis for selection. School achievement record, standardized test scores, recommendations, and essay. Decisions based on overall GPA, standardized test scores, curriculum, volunteer activities, and leadership roles. Business, Liberal Arts, and Music applicants with a minimum GPA of 3.0 can be considered for standardized test (SAT/ACT) optional admission. Interview recommended for all, audition required for music program, 40 hours shadowing for physical therapy. **Learning Disabled:** Documentation of learning disabilities may be required if accommodations requested.

High school preparation. College-preparatory program required. 16 units recommended. Recommended units include English 4, mathematics 2, social studies 2, science 2, foreign language 2 and academic electives 4.

2015-2016 Annual costs. Tuition/fees: $33,778. Room/board: $11,418. Books/supplies: $1,400. Personal expenses: $1,000.

2014-2015 Financial aid. Need-based: 1,165 full-time freshmen applied for aid; 964 deemed to have need; 964 received aid. Average need met was 76%. Average scholarship/grant was $18,586; average loan $4,111. 55% of total undergraduate aid awarded as scholarships/grants, 45% as loans/jobs. **Non-need-based:** Awarded to 5,609 full-time undergraduates, including 1,380 freshmen. Scholarships awarded for academics, alumni affiliation, athletics, music/drama, ROTC.

Application procedures. Admission: Priority date 11/1; deadline 7/1 (receipt date). $50 fee, may be waived for applicants with need. Admission notification on a rolling basis beginning on or about 10/1. Must reply by May 1 or within 2 week(s) if notified thereafter. **Financial aid:** Closing date 5/1. FAFSA, institutional form required. Applicants notified on a rolling basis starting 3/1; must reply by 5/1 or within 3 week(s) of notification.

Academics. Special study options: Accelerated study, combined bachelor's/graduate degree, cross-registration, distance learning, double major, dual enrollment of high school students, ESL, exchange student, external degree, honors, independent study, internships, liberal arts/career combination, semester at sea, student-designed major, study abroad, teacher certification program, Washington semester, weekend college. **Credit/placement by examination:** AP, CLEP, IB, institutional tests. 60 credit hours maximum toward bachelor's degree. **Support services:** Learning center, pre-admission summer program, reduced course load, remedial instruction, study skills assistance, tutoring, writing center.

Honors college/program. Admissions based on a number of factors; generally the top 5-7% of applicants invited. Students not receiving an invitation letter from University Honors College after general application may apply via our website.

Majors. Area/ethnic studies: Women's. **Biology:** General, biochemistry. **Business:** Accounting, communications, entrepreneurial studies, finance, international, logistics, management science, managerial economics, marketing, nonprofit/public, organizational leadership. **Communications:** Communications/speech/rhetoric, journalism. **Computer sciences:** Computer science, information technology, web page design. **Conservation:** Environmental science. **Education:** General, early childhood, English, Latin, mathematics, middle, music, social studies. **Engineering:** Biomedical. **English:** English lit, general lit, rhetoric/composition. **Foreign languages:** General, ancient Greek, classics, Latin, Spanish. **Health services:** Athletic training, health information management, music therapy, pharmaceutical sciences. **History:** General. **Liberal arts:** Arts/sciences. **Math:** General. **Philosophy/religion:** Philosophy. **Physical sciences:** Chemistry, physics. **Psychology:** General. **Social sciences:** Economics, international relations, political science, sociology. **Theology:** Theology. **Visual/performing arts:** Art history/conservation, dramatic, music performance.

Most popular majors. Biology 9%, business/marketing 28%, communications/journalism 6%, education 6%, health sciences 25%.

Technology on campus. 1,000 workstations in dormitories, library, computer center, student center. Dormitories wired for high-speed internet access and linked to campus network. Commuter students can connect to campus network. Online course registration, online library, helpline, repair service, student web hosting, wireless network available.

Student life. Freshman orientation: Mandatory, $200 fee. Preregistration for classes offered. 5 day educational and social program in August; includes volunteer opportunities. **Policies:** All students must abide by the Student Code of Rights, Responsibilities, and Conduct. **Housing:** Guaranteed on-campus for freshmen. Coed dorms, special housing for disabled, apartments, fraternity/sorority housing, wellness housing available. $500 nonrefundable deposit, deadline 5/1. Liberal Arts Learning Community, group/club wings, fraternity and sorority wings, and international wings available. **Activities:** Bands, campus ministries, choral groups, dance, drama, film society, international student organizations, literary magazine, music ensembles, Model UN, musical theater, opera, radio station, student government, student newspaper, symphony orchestra, TV station, Black Student Union, Duquesne University Volunteers, Latin American student association, Evergreen, Indian student

association, St. Vincent de Paul Society, College Republicans, Asian student association, Young Democrats, Knights of Columbus.

Athletics. NCAA. **Intercollegiate:** Basketball, bowling W, cross-country, football (tackle) M, lacrosse W, rowing (crew) W, soccer, swimming W, tennis, track and field, volleyball W. **Intramural:** Basketball, football (non-tackle), racquetball, soccer, ultimate frisbee, volleyball. **Team name:** Dukes.

Student services. Adult student services, alcohol/substance abuse counseling, chaplain/spiritual director, career counseling, services for economically disadvantaged, student employment services, financial aid counseling, health services, minority student services, on-campus daycare, personal counseling, placement for graduates, veterans' counselor, women's services. **Physically disabled:** Services for visually, speech, hearing impaired.

Contact. E-mail: admissions@duq.edu
Phone: (412) 396-6222 Toll-free number: (800) 456-0590
Fax: (412) 396-5644
Debra Zugates, Director, Admissions, Duquesne University, 600 Forbes Avenue, Administration Building, Pittsburgh, PA 15282-0201

East Stroudsburg University of Pennsylvania

East Stroudsburg, Pennsylvania **CB member**
www.esu.edu **CB code: 2650**

‣ Public 4-year university
‣ Residential campus in large town
‣ 6,100 degree-seeking undergraduates: 8% part-time, 56% women, 14% African American, 2% Asian American, 12% Hispanic/Latino, 4% Multiracial, non-Hispanic, 1% international
‣ 606 degree-seeking graduate students
‣ 55% graduate within 6 years

General. Founded in 1893. Regionally accredited. **Degrees:** 1,293 bachelor's awarded; master's offered. **ROTC:** Army, Air Force. **Location:** 40 miles from Allentown and Scranton. **Calendar:** Semester, extensive summer session. **Full-time faculty:** 281 total; 78% have terminal degrees, 17% minority, 51% women. **Part-time faculty:** 59 total; 24% have terminal degrees, 12% minority, 56% women. **Class size:** 30% < 20, 48% 20-39, 13% 40-49, 6% 50-99, 3% >100. **Special facilities:** Hearing clinic, exercise science performance lab, athletic training care center, 30-acre ecological studies area, center for research and economic development, planetarium, museum, applied DNA sciences facility, center for research and economic development, speech and hearing clinic, G3Design lab.

Freshman class profile. 6,516 applied, 5,026 admitted, 1,313 enrolled.

Mid 50% test scores			
SAT critical reading:	420-510	GPA 2.0-2.99:	38%
SAT math:	420-520	Rank in top quarter:	23%
SAT writing:	400-500	Rank in top tenth:	7%
ACT composite:	17-22	Return as sophomores:	72%
GPA 3.75 or higher:	13%	Out-of-state:	25%
GPA 3.50-3.74:	15%	Live on campus:	72%
GPA 3.0-3.49:	34%	International:	1%

Basis for selection. Open admission, but selective for some programs. The selection process places an emphasis on each applicant's college preparatory courses selected, the grades earned in those courses, class rank complimented by SAT/ACT scores, attendance and their intended college major.

High school preparation. College-preparatory program required. 13 units required. Required and recommended units include English 3, mathematics 3, social studies 3, history 3, science 3 (laboratory 1) and foreign language 1.

2015-2016 Annual costs. Tuition/fees: $9,684; $20,274 out-of-state. Room/board: $8,126. Books/supplies: $1,200. Personal expenses: $2,350. **Additional information:** Out-of-State tuition is $10,590 for domestic out-of-state students with high school GPA of at least 3.2 out of 4.0 and a combined Math and Critical Reading score on the SAT of at least 1,100 or a score of at least 24 on the ACT. Out-of-State tuition is $12,356 for transferring students with a minimum of 30 transferable credits and a GPA of 3.2 from higher education institutions attended.

2014-2015 Financial aid. Need-based: 1,204 full-time freshmen applied for aid; 980 deemed to have need; 927 received aid. Average need met was 45%. Average scholarship/grant was $5,149; average loan $3,239. 30% of total undergraduate aid awarded as scholarships/grants, 70% as loans/jobs. **Non-need-based:** Awarded to 128 full-time undergraduates, including 38 freshmen. Scholarships awarded for academics, alumni affiliation, art, athletics, job skills, leadership, minority status, music/drama, state residency.

Application procedures. Admission: Priority date 4/1; deadline 5/1 (postmark date). $25 fee, may be waived for applicants with need. Admission notification on a rolling basis beginning on or about 7/1. Must reply by May 1 or within 3 week(s) if notified thereafter. **Financial aid:** Priority date 2/14; no closing date. FAFSA required. Applicants notified on a rolling basis starting 3/15; must reply by 5/1.

Academics. Special study options: Accelerated study, combined bachelor's/graduate degree, distance learning, double major, dual enrollment of high school students, honors, independent study, internships, student-designed major, study abroad, teacher certification program. **Credit/placement by examination:** AP, CLEP, IB, institutional tests. 24 credit hours maximum toward bachelor's degree. **Support services:** Learning center, pre-admission summer program, reduced course load, remedial instruction, study skills assistance, tutoring, writing center.

Majors. Biology: General, biochemistry, biotechnology, ecology, environmental, marine. **Business:** Business admin, hospitality admin. **Communications:** Communications/speech/rhetoric. **Communications technology:** General. **Computer sciences:** General, security. **Education:** Early childhood, elementary, health, middle, physical, special ed. **English:** English lit. **Foreign languages:** French, Spanish. **Health services:** Athletic training, clinical lab science, nursing (RN), speech pathology. **History:** General. **Human services:** Social work. **Liberal arts:** Arts/sciences, humanities. **Math:** General. **Parks/recreation:** Exercise sciences, facilities management, sports admin. **Philosophy/religion:** Philosophy. **Physical sciences:** General, chemistry, geology, physics. **Protective services:** Criminal justice. **Psychology:** General. **Social sciences:** General, economics, geography, political science, sociology. **Visual/performing arts:** General, dramatic, graphic design.

Most popular majors. Biology 9%, business/marketing 15%, education 9%, health sciences 15%, parks/recreation 11%, psychology 9%.

Technology on campus. 500 workstations in dormitories, library, computer center, student center. Dormitories wired for high-speed internet access and linked to campus network. Commuter students can connect to campus network. Online course registration, online library, helpline, repair service, student web hosting, wireless network available.

Student life. Freshman orientation: Mandatory. Preregistration for classes offered. 1-day event during summer with joint and separate sessions for parents. **Policies:** Freshmen not permitted cars on campus. **Housing:** Guaranteed on-campus for freshmen. Coed dorms, special housing for disabled, apartments available. Living-learning community and Honors housing available. **Activities:** Bands, choral groups, dance, drama, international student organizations, literary magazine, music ensembles, Model UN, musical theater, radio station, student government, student newspaper, symphony orchestra, Latin American Students Association, Campus Democrats, Young Republicans, Stroud Courier, National Broadcasting Society, television production club, WESS FM Radio, chemistry club, athletic training student club, Pre-medicine club.

Athletics. NCAA. **Intercollegiate:** Baseball M, basketball, cross-country, field hockey W, football (tackle) M, soccer, softball W, swimming W, tennis W, track and field, volleyball W, wrestling M. **Intramural:** Basketball, football (non-tackle), racquetball, soccer, softball W. **Team name:** Warriors.

Student services. Adult student services, alcohol/substance abuse counseling, chaplain/spiritual director, career counseling, student employment services, financial aid counseling, health services, minority student services, on-campus daycare, personal counseling, placement for graduates, veterans' counselor, women's services. **Physically disabled:** Services for visually, speech, hearing impaired.

Contact. E-mail: jjones@esu.edu
Phone: (570) 422-3542 Toll-free number: (877) 230-5547
Fax: (570) 422-3933
Jeff Jones, Director of Admissions, East Stroudsburg University of Pennsylvania, 200 Prospect Street, East Stroudsburg, PA 18301-2999

Eastern University
St. Davids, Pennsylvania
www.eastern.edu

CB code: 2220

- Private 4-year university affiliated with the American Baptist Churches in the USA
- Residential campus in small town
- 2,163 degree-seeking undergraduates: 14% part-time, 70% women, 23% African American, 2% Asian American, 17% Hispanic/Latino, 1% Multiracial, non-Hispanic, 2% international
- 1,078 degree-seeking graduate students
- 52% of applicants admitted
- SAT or ACT (ACT writing optional), application essay required
- 63% graduate within 6 years

General. Founded in 1952. Regionally accredited. **Degrees:** 508 bachelor's, 105 associate awarded; master's, professional, doctoral offered. **ROTC:** Army, Air Force. **Location:** 10 miles from Philadelphia. **Calendar:** Semester, limited summer session. **Full-time faculty:** 151 total; 77% have terminal degrees, 20% minority, 46% women. **Part-time faculty:** 413 total. **Class size:** 85% < 20, 14% 20-39, less than 1% 40-49, less than 1% 50-99, less than 1% >100. **Special facilities:** Planetarium, observatory.

Freshman class profile. 2,941 applied, 1,536 admitted, 393 enrolled.

Mid 50% test scores			
SAT critical reading:	460-580	GPA 3.0-3.49:	32%
SAT math:	460-590	GPA 2.0-2.99:	21%
SAT writing:	440-540	Rank in top quarter:	51%
ACT composite:	18-28	Rank in top tenth:	20%
GPA 3.75 or higher:	30%	Return as sophomores:	74%
GPA 3.50-3.74:	17%	Live on campus:	95%
		International:	2%

Basis for selection. SAT, GPA, and class rank most important. Interest in school mission, slope of grades, attendance, interviews also evaluated. Interview recommended.

High school preparation. Recommended units include English 4, mathematics 3, history 3, science 3 and foreign language 2.

2016-2017 Annual costs. Tuition/fees: $31,020. Room/board: $10,674. Books/supplies: $1,200. Personal expenses: $2,205.

2014-2015 Financial aid. Need-based: 285 full-time freshmen applied for aid; 252 deemed to have need; 252 received aid. Average need met was 76%. Average scholarship/grant was $6,572; average loan $3,771. 57% of total undergraduate aid awarded as scholarships/grants, 43% as loans/jobs. **Non-need-based:** Awarded to 1,642 full-time undergraduates, including 277 freshmen. Scholarships awarded for academics, alumni affiliation, leadership, music/drama.

Application procedures. Admission: No deadline. $35 fee, may be waived for applicants with need, free for online applicants. Admission notification on a rolling basis beginning on or about 9/1. **Financial aid:** No deadline. FAFSA required. Applicants notified on a rolling basis starting 4/1.

Academics. Special study options: Accelerated study, cross-registration, distance learning, double major, dual enrollment of high school students, ESL, exchange student, honors, independent study, internships, liberal arts/career combination, student-designed major, study abroad, teacher certification program, Washington semester. **Credit/placement by examination:** AP, CLEP, IB, SAT, ACT. 30 credit hours maximum toward associate degree, 60 toward bachelor's. **Support services:** Pre-admission summer program, remedial instruction, study skills assistance, tutoring, writing center.

Honors college/program. Students must be in top 9% of class and have 1300 SAT (exclusive of Writing) or 30 ACT, or have extraordinary leadership abilities with significant academic achievements.

Majors. Biology: General, biochemistry. **Business:** Accounting/finance, business admin, entrepreneurial studies, international, organizational leadership. **Communications:** Communications/speech/rhetoric. **Conservation:** Environmental science. **Education:** Early childhood, middle, secondary. **Foreign languages:** Spanish. **Health services:** Athletic training, nursing (RN), nursing practice. **History:** General. **Human services:** Social work. **Math:** General. **Parks/recreation:** Exercise sciences. **Philosophy/religion:** Philosophy. **Physical sciences:** Chemistry. **Psychology:** General. **Social sciences:** Criminology, political science, sociology. **Theology:** Bible, missionary, theology, youth ministry. **Visual/performing arts:** Dance, music.

Most popular majors. Business/marketing 23%, education 20%, health sciences 12%, psychology 6%, public administration/social services 7%, theological studies 7%.

Technology on campus. 131 workstations in dormitories, library, computer center, student center. Dormitories wired for high-speed internet access and linked to campus network. Commuter students can connect to campus network. Repair service, wireless network available.

Student life. Freshman orientation: Mandatory. Preregistration for classes offered. Held three days before fall semester. **Policies:** Smoke-free campus. Freshmen not permitted cars on campus. **Housing:** Special housing for disabled, apartments available. $150 nonrefundable deposit, deadline 3/1. Men and women are housed in the same building but on separate floors. Students required to live on campus unless they receive permission from Dean of Students Office. **Activities:** Campus ministries, choral groups, dance, drama, international student organizations, literary magazine, music ensembles, Model UN, musical theater, radio station, student government, student newspaper, Black student league, Penn State Education Association, yacht club, gospel outreach, Fellowship of Christian Athletes, Habitat for Humanity, Evangelicals for Social Action, students organized against racism, prison ministry, Latinos Unidos.

Athletics. NCAA. **Intercollegiate:** Baseball M, basketball, cross-country, field hockey W, golf, lacrosse, soccer, softball W, tennis, volleyball W. **Intramural:** Basketball, soccer, volleyball. **Team name:** Eagles.

Student services. Adult student services, alcohol/substance abuse counseling, chaplain/spiritual director, career counseling, financial aid counseling, health services, legal services, minority student services, personal counseling, veterans' counselor, women's services. **Physically disabled:** Services for visually, speech, hearing impaired.

Contact. E-mail: ugadm@eastern.edu
Phone: (610) 341-5967 Toll-free number: (800) 452-0996
Fax: (610) 341-1723
Michael Dziedziak, Director of Admissions, Eastern University, 1300 Eagle Road, St. Davids, PA 19087-3696

Edinboro University of Pennsylvania

Edinboro, Pennsylvania
www.edinboro.edu

CB member
CB code: 2651

- Public 4-year university
- Commuter campus in small town
- 5,142 degree-seeking undergraduates: 8% part-time, 58% women, 8% African American, 1% Asian American, 3% Hispanic/Latino, 4% Multiracial, non-Hispanic, 2% international
- 1,290 degree-seeking graduate students
- 96% of applicants admitted
- SAT or ACT (ACT writing optional) required
- 49% graduate within 6 years

General. Founded in 1857. Regionally accredited. **Degrees:** 1,031 bachelor's, 91 associate awarded; master's, professional offered. **ROTC:** Army. **Location:** 18 miles from Erie. **Calendar:** Semester, extensive summer session. **Full-time faculty:** 286 total; 85% have terminal degrees, 7% minority, 46% women. **Part-time faculty:** 56 total; 32% have terminal degrees, 4% minority, 68% women. **Class size:** 29% < 20, 52% 20-39, 9% 40-49, 8% 50-99, less than 1% >100. **Special facilities:** Observatory, planetarium, natural wildlife museum, robotics laboratory, center for performing arts, speech and hearing clinic.

Freshman class profile. 3,509 applied, 3,358 admitted, 1,211 enrolled.

Mid 50% test scores			
SAT critical reading:	430-580	Rank in top quarter:	24%
SAT math:	430-530	Rank in top tenth:	6%
SAT writing:	400-500	Return as sophomores:	70%
ACT composite:	17-23	Out-of-state:	19%
GPA 3.75 or higher:	21%	Live on campus:	77%
GPA 3.50-3.74:	20%	International:	1%
GPA 3.0-3.49:	30%	Fraternities:	4%
GPA 2.0-2.99:	28%	Sororities:	6%

Basis for selection. High school curriculum, SAT/ACT test scores, GPA, and class rank most important. Recommendations and activities record also reviewed. Interview and essay considered; audition required for music program. **Home schooled:** Transcript of courses and grades, interview, letter of recommendation (nonparent) required. Students out of high school less than two years also need test scores.

High school preparation. College-preparatory program recommended. Required units include English 4, mathematics 3, social studies 3 and science 3.

2015-2016 Annual costs. Tuition/fees: $9,506; $9,860 out-of-state. Room/board: $10,166. Books/supplies: $1,000. Personal expenses: $1,300.

2014-2015 Financial aid. **Need-based:** 1,168 full-time freshmen applied for aid; 1,030 deemed to have need; 1,016 received aid. Average need met was 47%. Average scholarship/grant was $4,711; average loan $3,098. 55% of total undergraduate aid awarded as scholarships/grants, 45% as loans/jobs. **Non-need-based:** Scholarships awarded for academics, alumni affiliation, art, athletics, leadership, minority status, music/drama, ROTC, state residency.

Application procedures. **Admission:** No deadline. $30 fee, may be waived for applicants with need. Admission notification on a rolling basis beginning on or about 9/1. Must reply by May 1 or within 4 week(s) if notified thereafter. **Financial aid:** Priority date 3/15; no closing date. FAFSA required. Applicants notified on a rolling basis starting 2/15; must reply by 8/1.

Academics. 42 credits of general education electives required for bachelor's degree. **Special study options:** Combined bachelor's/graduate degree, cooperative education, cross-registration, distance learning, double major,

dual enrollment of high school students, honors, independent study, internships, liberal arts/career combination, student-designed major, study abroad, teacher certification program. Credit courses, continuing education, workshops, and seminars offered at Porreco Extension Center in Erie and Buba Center in Meadville. **Credit/placement by examination:** AP, CLEP, institutional tests. 30 credit hours maximum toward associate degree, 30 toward bachelor's. **Support services:** Learning center, pre-admission summer program, reduced course load, remedial instruction, study skills assistance, tutoring, writing center. Associate degree counseling, peer tutoring, peer mentors, academic advising center, trial admissions program, extensive programs and services for physically and learning disabled students available.

Majors. **Biology:** General. **Business:** Business admin. **Communications:** Broadcast journalism, communications/speech/rhetoric, journalism, media studies. **Computer sciences:** General. **Conservation:** Environmental science. **Education:** Early childhood, elementary, middle, special ed. **English:** English lit. **Foreign languages:** German, Spanish. **Health services:** Clinical lab assistant, communication disorders, nuclear medical technology, nursing (RN), prepharmacy. **History:** General. **Human services:** Social work. **Liberal arts:** Arts/sciences, humanities. **Math:** General. **Philosophy/religion:** Philosophy. **Physical sciences:** Chemistry, geology, physics, planetary. **Protective services:** Criminal justice. **Psychology:** General. **Social sciences:** General, anthropology, economics, geography, political science, sociology. **Visual/performing arts:** Art, art history/conservation, dramatic, music, studio arts.

Most popular majors. Business/marketing 8%, communications/journalism 8%, education 9%, health sciences 11%, parks/recreation 6%, psychology 6%, security/protective services 7%, social sciences 8%, visual/performing arts 17%.

Technology on campus. 1,000 workstations in dormitories, library, computer center, student center. Dormitories wired for high-speed internet access and linked to campus network. Commuter students can connect to campus network. Online course registration, online library, helpline, repair service, student web hosting, wireless network available.

Student life. **Freshman orientation:** Mandatory, $125 fee. Preregistration for classes offered. Summer and spring programs. **Policies:** Zero tolerance policy for alcohol and drugs on campus. **Housing:** Guaranteed on-campus for freshmen. Coed dorms, special housing for disabled available. $75 nonrefundable deposit, deadline 5/1. Living-learning and suite style housing available. **Activities:** Bands, campus ministries, choral groups, dance, drama, film society, international student organizations, literary magazine, music ensembles, Model UN, musical theater, opera, radio station, student government, student newspaper, symphony orchestra, TV station.

Athletics. NCAA. **Intercollegiate:** Basketball, cross-country, football (tackle) M, lacrosse W, soccer W, softball W, swimming, tennis, track and field, volleyball W, wrestling M. **Intramural:** Basketball, football (non-tackle), racquetball, soccer, softball, volleyball, wrestling M. **Team name:** The Fighting Scots.

Student services. Adult student services, alcohol/substance abuse counseling, chaplain/spiritual director, career counseling, student employment services, financial aid counseling, health services, minority student services, personal counseling, placement for graduates, veterans' counselor. **Physically disabled:** Services for visually, speech, hearing impaired.

Contact. E-mail: eup_admissions@edinboro.edu
Phone: (814) 732-2761 Toll-free number: (888) 846-2676
Fax: (814) 732-2420
Chris LaRusso, Assistant Vice President-Enrollment Services, Edinboro University of Pennsylvania, 200 East Normal Street, Edinboro, PA 16444

Elizabethtown College

Elizabethtown, Pennsylvania
www.etown.edu

CB code: 2225

- Private 4-year liberal arts college affiliated with the Brethren Church
- Residential campus in large town
- 1,762 degree-seeking undergraduates: 1% part-time, 62% women, 3% African American, 2% Asian American, 4% Hispanic/Latino, 2% Multiracial, non-Hispanic, 3% international
- 46 degree-seeking graduate students
- 71% of applicants admitted
- SAT or ACT (ACT writing optional), application essay required
- 76% graduate within 6 years

General. Founded in 1899. Regionally accredited. **Degrees:** 404 bachelor's awarded; master's offered. **Location:** 20 miles from Harrisburg, 90 miles from Philadelphia. **Calendar:** Semester, limited summer session. **Full-time**

faculty: 129 total; 92% have terminal degrees, 10% minority, 45% women. **Part-time faculty:** 51 total; 31% have terminal degrees, 4% minority, 55% women. **Class size:** 64% < 20, 34% 20-39, 1% 40-49, less than 1% 50-99. **Special facilities:** Center for Community and Civic Engagement, Center for Global Understanding and Peacemaking, Young Center for Anabaptist and Pietist Studies, mineral gallery, Bowers Writers House, and Center for Excellence in Teaching and Learning.

Freshman class profile. 3,453 applied, 2,442 admitted, 504 enrolled.

Mid 50% test scores			
SAT critical reading:	500-610	Rank in top tenth:	31%
SAT math:	500-620	Return as sophomores:	82%
SAT writing:	470-600	Out-of-state:	36%
ACT composite:	23-28	Live on campus:	97%
Rank in top quarter:	63%	International:	1%

Basis for selection. School achievement record is most important. College preparatory program is strongly recommended. Co-curricular activities are also considered, particularly service-oriented activities. Applicants should be in top quarter of class. Students may waive SAT/ACT score from admissions and merit-based scholarship decisions if they are ranked in top 10% of class or have 3.5 GPA if school does not rank. Interview required for occupational therapy and honors program. For international business applicants, essay must demonstrate interest in that subject area. Audition required for music, music education, and music therapy programs.

High school preparation. College-preparatory program recommended. 15 units required; 20 recommended. Required and recommended units include English 4, mathematics 3-4, social studies 2, history 2, science 2-4 (laboratory 2-3), foreign language 2 and academic electives 2.

2015-2016 Annual costs. Tuition/fees: $41,710. Room/board: $10,140. Books/supplies: $1,100. Personal expenses: $800.

2015-2016 Financial aid. Need-based: 493 full-time freshmen applied for aid; 441 deemed to have need; 441 received aid. Average need met was 82%. Average scholarship/grant was $27,128; average loan $3,806. 78% of total undergraduate aid awarded as scholarships/grants, 22% as loans/jobs. **Non-need-based:** Awarded to 610 full-time undergraduates, including 171 freshmen. Scholarships awarded for academics, alumni affiliation, art, music/ drama, religious affiliation.

Application procedures. Admission: Priority date 3/1; no deadline. $30 fee, may be waived for applicants with need, free for online applicants. Admission notification on a rolling basis beginning on or about 9/15. Must reply by May 1 or within 2 week(s) if notified thereafter. December 15 closing date for occupational therapy program. March 1 closing date for international business. January 15 closing date for honors program. **Financial aid:** Priority date 3/15; no closing date. FAFSA required. Applicants notified on a rolling basis starting 3/1; must reply by 5/1 or within 2 week(s) of notification.

Academics. Special study options: Combined bachelor's/graduate degree, distance learning, double major, dual enrollment of high school students, ESL, exchange student, honors, independent study, internships, study abroad, teacher certification program, Washington semester. Premedical Primary Care Program with Penn State University College of Medicine; Allied Health 3+3 with Thomas Jefferson University; Allied Health 3+3 with Widener University; 3+2 with Duke University Master of Forestry; 3+2 with Duke University; 3+4 with Philadelphia College of Osteopathic Medicine; 4+4 with Philadelphia College of Osteopathic Medicine; 3+4 with Temple University's School of Dentistry; Doctor of Optometry/B.S. 3+4 Program with Pennsylvania College of Optometry at Salus University; 3+1 with Lancaster General College of Nursing and Health Services Diploma in Cardiovascular Invasive Specialty; 4+1 with Drexel University College of Medicine MS in Molecular Medicine. **Credit/placement by examination:** AP, CLEP, IB, SAT, ACT, institutional tests. Credit by examination unlimited provided student is able to fulfill residency requirement. Credit for International Baccalaureate awarded only for subject exams and only for earned scores from 4-7. **Support services:** Learning center, reduced course load, study skills assistance, tutoring, writing center.

Majors. Biology: General, biochemistry, biotechnology, environmental. **Business:** Accounting, business admin, international. **Computer sciences:** General, information systems. **Conservation:** Forest management. **Education:** Early childhood, middle, science. **Engineering:** General, computer, industrial. **English:** English lit, technical writing. **Foreign languages:** French, German, Japanese, Spanish. **Health services:** Music therapy, occupational therapy. **History:** General. **Human services:** Social work. **Math:** General, applied. **Philosophy/religion:** Philosophy, religion. **Physical sciences:** Chemistry, physics. **Psychology:** General. **Social sciences:** General, economics, political science, sociology. **Visual/performing arts:** Dramatic, music, studio arts.

Most popular majors. Biology 12%, business/marketing 19%, communications/journalism 7%, education 9%, engineering/engineering technologies 6%, health sciences 13%, social sciences 8%.

Technology on campus. 200 workstations in dormitories, library, computer center, student center. Dormitories wired for high-speed internet access and linked to campus network. Commuter students can connect to campus network. Online course registration, online library, helpline, student web hosting, wireless network available.

Student life. Freshman orientation: Mandatory. Preregistration for classes offered. One-day summer program in June and multi-day program at beginning of fall semester. **Policies:** All residence halls are smoke-free. **Housing:** Guaranteed on-campus for all undergraduates. Coed dorms, special housing for disabled, apartments, gender-neutral housing, themed housing, wellness housing available. $300 nonrefundable deposit, deadline 5/1. Special housing available for students involved in service learning and community service, and FY Honors Learning Community. **Activities:** Bands, campus ministries, choral groups, dance, drama, international student organizations, literary magazine, music ensembles, musical theater, radio station, student government, student newspaper, symphony orchestra, TV station, Newman club, Intervarsity Christian Fellowship, Hillel, Habitat for Humanity, Republican club, Campus Crusades for Christ, Act for Humanity, Allies, Best Buddies, K-9 club.

Athletics. NCAA. Intercollegiate: Baseball M, basketball, cross-country, field hockey W, golf M, lacrosse, soccer, softball W, swimming, tennis, track and field, volleyball W, wrestling M. **Intramural:** Badminton, basketball, golf, racquetball, soccer, softball, tennis, volleyball, water polo. **Team name:** Blue Jays.

Student services. Adult student services, alcohol/substance abuse counseling, chaplain/spiritual director, career counseling, student employment services, financial aid counseling, health services, minority student services, personal counseling, placement for graduates, veterans' counselor, women's services. **Physically disabled:** Services for visually, hearing impaired.

Contact. E-mail: admissions@etown.edu
Phone: (717) 361-1400 Fax: (717) 361-1365
Lauren Deibler, Director of Admissions, Elizabethtown College, One Alpha Drive, Elizabethtown, PA 17022-2298

Franklin & Marshall College
Lancaster, Pennsylvania   CB member
www.fandm.edu   CB code: 2261

- Private 4-year liberal arts college
- Residential campus in small city
- 2,219 degree-seeking undergraduates: 52% women, 6% African American, 5% Asian American, 8% Hispanic/Latino, 2% Multi-racial, non-Hispanic, 14% international
- 32% of applicants admitted
- Application essay required
- 87% graduate within 6 years

General. Founded in 1787. Regionally accredited. **Degrees:** 553 bachelor's awarded. **Location:** 60 miles from Philadelphia, 120 miles from Washington, DC. **Calendar:** Semester, limited summer session. **Full-time faculty:** 234 total; 94% have terminal degrees, 11% minority, 47% women. **Part-time faculty:** 48 total; 58% have terminal degrees, 8% minority, 50% women. **Class size:** 62% < 20, 37% 20-39, less than 1% 40-49, less than 1% 50-99. **Special facilities:** Observatory, science library, retail sales complex, bronze casting foundry, field house, planetarium, museum of art, concert hall, performing arts center, Writers House.

Freshman class profile. 7,146 applied, 2,305 admitted, 592 enrolled.

Mid 50% test scores			
SAT critical reading:	580-670	GPA 2.0-2.99:	5%
SAT math:	630-730	Rank in top quarter:	80%
ACT composite:	28-31	Rank in top tenth:	48%
GPA 3.75 or higher:	51%	Return as sophomores:	92%
GPA 3.50-3.74:	21%	Out-of-state:	75%
GPA 3.0-3.49:	23%	Live on campus:	100%
		International:	16%

Basis for selection. School achievement record, test scores or graded writing samples, extracurricular activities, recommendations, essay considered. Submission of standardized test scores optional for all students. If student chooses to omit scores, two recent graded writing samples must be submitted instead. Interview required for early decision applicants, strongly recommended for others. Auditions and portfolios recommended for all students who wish to demonstrate particular talent. **Home schooled:** Transcript of courses and grades required. Students should present a transcript from either a parent or outside evaluating agency. If a parent serves as the primary source of evaluation, he or she may submit the School Report and Counselor Recommendation. Students should also submit a reading list and have an on-campus interview. It is strongly recommended that students submit standardized test scores for best admission consideration.

High school preparation. College-preparatory program required. Required and recommended units include English 4, mathematics 3-4, social studies 1-3, history 2-3, science 2-3 (laboratory 2-3), foreign language 2-4 and visual/performing arts 1.

2015-2016 Annual costs. Tuition/fees: $50,400. Room/board: $12,770. Books/supplies: $1,200. Personal expenses: $1,270.

2015-2016 Financial aid. All financial aid based on need. 373 full-time freshmen applied for aid; 298 deemed to have need; 298 received aid. Average need met was 100%. Average scholarship/grant was $43,342; average loan $2,868. 88% of total undergraduate aid awarded as scholarships/grants, 12% as loans/jobs.

Application procedures. Admission: Closing date 1/15 (postmark date). $60 fee, may be waived for applicants with need. Admission notification by 4/1. Must reply by May 1 or within 2 week(s) if notified thereafter. **Financial aid:** Priority date 2/15, closing date 2/15. FAFSA, CSS PROFILE required. Applicants notified by 4/1; must reply by 5/1.

Academics. Special study options: Accelerated study, combined bachelor's/graduate degree, cross-registration, double major, dual enrollment of high school students, ESL, exchange student, honors, independent study, internships, liberal arts/career combination, New York semester, student-designed major, study abroad, teacher certification program, Washington semester. 3-2 programs in forestry, engineering, environmental studies; Columbia University's New York/Paris program. **Credit/placement by examination:** AP, CLEP, IB, institutional tests. 64 credit hours maximum toward bachelor's degree. **Support services:** Pre-admission summer program, reduced course load, study skills assistance, tutoring, writing center.

Majors. Area/ethnic studies: African, American. **Biology:** General, animal behavior, biochemistry, neuroscience. **Business:** Business admin. **Computer sciences:** Computer science. **Conservation:** Environmental science, environmental studies. **English:** Creative writing, English lit. **Foreign languages:** Ancient Greek, classics, French, German, Latin, Spanish. **History:** General. **Math:** General. **Philosophy/religion:** Philosophy, religion. **Physical sciences:** Astrophysics, chemistry, geology, physics. **Psychology:** General. **Social sciences:** Anthropology, economics, political science, sociology. **Visual/performing arts:** Art history/conservation, dance, dramatic, film/cinema/video, music, studio arts.

Most popular majors. Biology 11%, business/marketing 12%, English 7%, interdisciplinary studies 9%, social sciences 23%.

Technology on campus. 125 workstations in library, computer center. Dormitories wired for high-speed internet access and linked to campus network. Commuter students can connect to campus network. Online course registration, online library, helpline, student web hosting, wireless network available.

Student life. Freshman orientation: Mandatory, $200 fee. Preregistration for classes offered. 5 days prior to start of classes. **Policies:** All students required to live in college-approved housing. Freshmen not permitted cars on campus. **Housing:** Guaranteed on-campus for freshmen. Coed dorms, special housing for disabled, apartments, fraternity/sorority housing, themed housing, wellness housing available. French house, arts house, international house, community outreach house, sustainability house, and men's and women's floors available. **Activities:** Bands, campus ministries, choral groups, dance, drama, film society, international student organizations, literary magazine, music ensembles, musical theater, opera, radio station, student government, student newspaper, symphony orchestra, TV station, East Asian society, Catholic Campus Community, Hillel, Christian Fellowship, Habitat for Humanity, Voices for Women, Coalition for Choice, Environmental Action Alliance, Black student union, Mi Gente Latina.

Athletics. NCAA. **Intercollegiate:** Baseball M, basketball, cross-country, field hockey W, football (tackle) M, golf, lacrosse, rowing (crew), soccer, softball W, squash, swimming, tennis, track and field, volleyball W, wrestling M. **Intramural:** Basketball, football (non-tackle), soccer, softball. **Team name:** Diplomats.

Student services. Alcohol/substance abuse counseling, chaplain/spiritual director, career counseling, student employment services, financial aid counseling, health services, minority student services, personal counseling, placement for graduates, women's services. **Physically disabled:** Services for visually, hearing impaired.

Contact. E-mail: admission@fandm.edu
Phone: (717) 291-3953 Toll-free number: (877) 678-9111
Fax: (717) 291-4389
Eric Maguire, Vice President and Dean of Admission and Financial Aid, Franklin & Marshall College, PO Box 3003, Lancaster, PA 17604-3003

Gannon University
Erie, Pennsylvania — CB member
www.gannon.edu — CB code: 2270

- Private 4-year university affiliated with the Roman Catholic Church
- Residential campus in small city
- 2,661 degree-seeking undergraduates: 5% part-time, 56% women, 5% African American, 2% Asian American, 3% Hispanic/Latino, 2% Multiracial, non-Hispanic, 9% international
- 1,299 degree-seeking graduate students
- 76% of applicants admitted
- SAT or ACT (ACT writing optional) required
- 66% graduate within 6 years; 40% enter graduate study

General. Founded in 1925. Regionally accredited. **Degrees:** 580 bachelor's, 33 associate awarded; master's, professional, doctoral offered. **ROTC:** Army. **Location:** 128 miles from Pittsburgh, 99 miles from Cleveland, 106 miles from Buffalo. **Calendar:** Semester, extensive summer session. **Full-time faculty:** 227 total; 71% have terminal degrees, 12% minority, 48% women. **Part-time faculty:** 168 total; 28% have terminal degrees, 4% minority, 53% women. **Class size:** 53% < 20, 46% 20-39, 1% 40-49. **Special facilities:** Floating laboratory providing hands-on environmental study on Lake Erie, patient simulation center and human performance center for health sciences, archaeology museum.

Freshman class profile. 4,213 applied, 3,192 admitted, 619 enrolled.

Mid 50% test scores		GPA 2.0-2.99:	15%
SAT critical reading:	460-560	Rank in top quarter:	50%
SAT math:	460-570	Rank in top tenth:	24%
SAT writing:	430-550	Return as sophomores:	84%
ACT composite:	20-25	Out-of-state:	31%
GPA 3.75 or higher:	44%	Live on campus:	71%
GPA 3.50-3.74:	17%	International:	7%
GPA 3.0-3.49:	24%		

Basis for selection. Specific courses in math and science required for some majors in health science and engineering. Admission requirements vary by program. Limited number of students who do not meet all requirements may be accepted into General Studies program. Essay required for some programs, recommended for all. **Home schooled:** Statement describing home school structure and mission, state high school equivalency certificate required. **Learning Disabled:** Students must submit official documentation of disability.

High school preparation. College-preparatory program recommended. 16 units required; 25 recommended. Required and recommended units include English 4, mathematics 2-4, social studies 2, history 1, science 2-4 (laboratory 2-3), foreign language 2, computer science 1, visual/performing arts 1 and academic electives 3.

2015-2016 Annual costs. Tuition/fees: $29,258. Room/board: $11,710. Books/supplies: $1,050. Personal expenses: $1,302. **Additional information:** $25 fee per-credit hour for part-time students.

2015-2016 Financial aid. Need-based: 546 full-time freshmen applied for aid; 496 deemed to have need; 496 received aid. Average need met was 76%. Average scholarship/grant was $21,000; average loan $3,388. 75% of total undergraduate aid awarded as scholarships/grants, 25% as loans/jobs. **Non-need-based:** Awarded to 820 full-time undergraduates, including 208 freshmen. Scholarships awarded for academics, athletics, leadership, music/drama, religious affiliation, ROTC.

Application procedures. Admission: No deadline. $25 fee, may be waived for applicants with need, free for online applicants. Admission notification on a rolling basis. Applicants notified on a rolling basis beginning the second week of September. Housing deposit refundable if requested before May 1. Early application especially recommended for health science programs since space is limited. Most accelerated and 5 year Master's programs have an application deadline of November 1. **Financial aid:** Priority date 3/15; no closing date. FAFSA required. Applicants notified on a rolling basis starting 11/1.

Academics. Preferred admission to doctorate physical therapy program granted to students with bachelor's degree from Gannon in physical therapy. Occupational therapy and physician assistant programs are 5-year master's degree programs. **Special study options:** Accelerated study, combined bachelor's/graduate degree, cooperative education, distance learning, double major, dual enrollment of high school students, ESL, honors, independent study, internships, liberal arts/career combination, study abroad, teacher certification program, Washington semester. **Credit/placement by examination:** AP, CLEP, IB, institutional tests. CLEP exams offered at Gannon through the Career Development and Employment Services Department. **Support services:** Learning center, reduced course load, remedial instruction, study skills assistance, tutoring, writing center. Speech communication center, STEM Center, TRIO Student Support Services Program.

Honors college/program. 1200 SAT, 3.3 GPA, 550V SAT or 23 Reading ACT, extracurricular activities required, essay, letter of recommendation; approximately 60 students admitted per year.

Majors. Biology: General, aquatic, biochemistry, bioinformatics. **Business:** Accounting, business admin, entrepreneurial studies, finance, insurance, international, logistics, management information systems, marketing. **Communications:** Advertising, journalism. **Communications technology:** Radio/TV. **Computer sciences:** General, programming. **Conservation:** Environmental science. **Education:** Early childhood, middle, multi-level teacher, social studies. **Engineering:** Biomedical, electrical, environmental, industrial, mechanical. **English:** British lit. **Foreign languages:** General. **Health services:** Clinical lab science, health care admin, nursing (RN), occupational therapy, physician assistant, respiratory therapy technology. **History:** General. **Human services:** Social work. **Liberal arts:** Arts/sciences. **Math:** General. **Parks/recreation:** Exercise sciences, sports admin. **Philosophy/religion:** Philosophy. **Physical sciences:** Chemistry. **Protective services:** Criminal justice, forensics. **Psychology:** General. **Social sciences:** Political science. **Theology:** Theology. **Visual/performing arts:** General, dramatic.

Most popular majors. Biology 9%, business/marketing 15%, health sciences 34%, parks/recreation 10%.

Technology on campus. 386 workstations in dormitories, library, computer center, student center. Dormitories wired for high-speed internet access and linked to campus network. Commuter students can connect to campus network. Online library, helpline, wireless network available.

Student life. Freshman orientation: Mandatory, $65 fee. Preregistration for classes offered. 4 sessions during summer; open to parents and students. One fall session held prior to first day of classes. Fee includes overnight accommodations; students who commute to campus during orientation charged $40. **Policies:** All first through fourth semester students whose parents/guardians' primary residence is outside the 25-mile radius of University must reside in university housing. **Housing:** Guaranteed on-campus for freshmen. Coed dorms, special housing for disabled, apartments, fraternity/sorority housing, themed housing, wellness housing available. $100 fully refundable deposit, deadline 9/1. **Activities:** Bands, campus ministries, choral groups, dance, drama, international student organizations, literary magazine, Model UN, radio station, student government, student newspaper, Active Minds, Center for Social Concerns, Catholic Relief Services Ambassadors, Gannon Goes Green Committee, Gannon Goodwill Garden, Global Unity at Gannon University (GU Squared), Habitat for Humanity GU Chapter, International Student Office, Love Is For Everyone, Team U.

Athletics. NCAA. **Intercollegiate:** Baseball M, basketball, cross-country, football (tackle) M, golf, lacrosse W, soccer, softball W, swimming, volleyball W, water polo, wrestling M. **Intramural:** Basketball, football (non-tackle), handball, racquetball, soccer, ultimate frisbee, volleyball. **Team name:** Golden Knights.

Student services. Adult student services, alcohol/substance abuse counseling, chaplain/spiritual director, career counseling, services for economically disadvantaged, student employment services, financial aid counseling, health services, minority student services, personal counseling, placement for graduates, veterans' counselor. **Physically disabled:** Services for speech, hearing impaired.

Contact. E-mail: admissions@gannon.edu
Phone: (814) 871-7240 Toll-free number: (800) 426-6668
Fax: (814) 871-5803
Thomas Camillo, Director of Undergraduate Admissions, Gannon University, 109 University Square, Erie, PA 16541-0001

Geneva College
Beaver Falls, Pennsylvania CB member
www.geneva.edu CB code: 2273

◆ Private 4-year liberal arts college affiliated with the Reformed Presbyterian Church of North America

◆ Residential campus in large town

◆ 1,458 degree-seeking undergraduates: 9% African American, 1% Hispanic/Latino, 3% Multi-racial, non-Hispanic, 1% international

◆ 249 degree-seeking graduate students

◆ 73% of applicants admitted

◆ SAT or ACT (ACT writing optional), application essay required

◆ 65% graduate within 6 years

General. Founded in 1848. Regionally accredited. **Degrees:** 427 bachelor's, 17 associate awarded; master's offered. **ROTC:** Army. **Location:** 35 miles

from Pittsburgh. **Calendar:** Semester, limited summer session. **Full-time faculty:** 81 total; 78% have terminal degrees, 5% minority, 35% women. **Part-time faculty:** 110 total; 9% have terminal degrees, 8% minority, 39% women. **Class size:** 68% < 20, 26% 20-39, 2% 40-49, 3% 50-99, 1% >100. **Special facilities:** Collection of artifacts and records of Pittsburgh steel industry, technology development center, high adventure ropes course, Covenanter collection of original documents about the Reformed Presbyterian church.

Freshman class profile. 1,678 applied, 1,230 admitted, 329 enrolled.

Mid 50% test scores			
SAT critical reading:	420-660	GPA 2.0-2.99:	12%
SAT math:	410-650	Rank in top quarter:	51%
SAT writing:	390-640	Rank in top tenth:	21%
ACT composite:	18-27	Return as sophomores:	83%
GPA 3.75 or higher:	48%	Out-of-state:	34%
GPA 3.50-3.74:	17%	Live on campus:	88%
GPA 3.0-3.49:	23%	International:	1%

Basis for selection. Academic performance and test scores most important. Recommendations and extracurricular activities considered. Placement tests in English and math required if the student does not perform well enough on the relevant SAT or ACT examinations. For students with high SAT or ACT scores, placement tests used to determine if students should be placed in more advanced courses. Interview recommended for all; audition required for music program. **Home schooled:** Transcript of courses and grades required. Help in preparing homeschooler's transcript available if necessary.

High school preparation. College-preparatory program required. 16 units required. Required units include English 4, mathematics 2, social studies 3, science 1, foreign language 2 and academic electives 4. Engineering students should have 1 unit of chemistry and physics, 4 units of college-preparatory mathematics including trigonometry or precalculus.

2015-2016 Annual costs. Tuition/fees: $25,450. Room/board: $9,630. Books/supplies: $900. Personal expenses: $1,150. **Additional information:** Some lab and practicum courses require additional fees.

2014-2015 Financial aid. Need-based: 300 full-time freshmen applied for aid; 267 deemed to have need; 266 received aid. Average need met was 77%. Average scholarship/grant was $16,855; average loan $3,473. 70% of total undergraduate aid awarded as scholarships/grants, 30% as loans/jobs. **Non-need-based:** Awarded to 302 full-time undergraduates, including 75 freshmen. Scholarships awarded for academics, alumni affiliation, music/drama, religious affiliation.

Application procedures. Admission: No deadline. $40 fee, may be waived for applicants with need, free for online applicants. Admission notification on a rolling basis beginning on or about 9/1. Must reply by May 1 or within 3 week(s) if notified thereafter. **Financial aid:** Priority date 3/15; no closing date. FAFSA required. Applicants notified on a rolling basis starting 3/1; must reply by 5/1 or within 4 week(s) of notification.

Academics. Special study options: Accelerated study, cooperative education, cross-registration, double major, dual enrollment of high school students, honors, independent study, internships, liberal arts/career combination, student-designed major, study abroad, teacher certification program, Washington semester. **Credit/placement by examination:** AP, CLEP, IB, SAT, ACT, institutional tests. 30 credit hours maximum toward bachelor's degree. **Support services:** Reduced course load, remedial instruction, study skills assistance, tutoring, writing center.

Majors. Biology: General, biochemistry. **Business:** Accounting, business admin. **Communications:** Communications/speech/rhetoric. **Computer sciences:** General. **Conservation:** Environmental science. **Education:** Elementary, mathematics, middle, multi-level teacher, music, special ed. **Engineering:** General, chemical. **English:** English lit, writing. **Foreign languages:** Biblical. **Health services:** Speech pathology. **History:** General. **Math:** Applied. **Parks/recreation:** Sports admin. **Philosophy/religion:** Philosophy. **Physical sciences:** Chemistry, physics. **Psychology:** General. **Social sciences:** Criminology, political science, sociology. **Theology:** Bible, youth ministry. **Visual/performing arts:** Music, music management, music performance.

Most popular majors. Business/marketing 15%, education 9%, engineering/engineering technologies 13%, public administration/social services 7%, theological studies 8%.

Technology on campus. 150 workstations in dormitories, library, computer center, student center. Dormitories wired for high-speed internet access and linked to campus network. Commuter students can connect to campus network. Online course registration, online library, helpline, repair service, wireless network available.

Student life. Freshman orientation: Mandatory. Preregistration for classes offered. Held 5 days prior to start of classes. **Policies:** Smoking, drinking, social or ballroom dancing not permitted on campus. Students must live on campus unless married, part-time, commuting, or over age 24. Religious observance required. **Housing:** Guaranteed on-campus for all undergraduates. Single-sex dorms, apartments, wellness housing available. $150 fully refundable deposit. **Activities:** Bands, campus ministries, choral groups, drama, international student organizations, literary magazine, music ensembles, student government, student newspaper, American Society of Civil Engineering, American Society of Mechanical Engineers, Black student organization, Business and Professional Women, Creation Stewardship club, International Justice Mission, College Republicans, Reformed Campus Ministry, God Led, COMPASS club.

Athletics. NCAA, NCCAA. **Intercollegiate:** Baseball M, basketball, cross-country, football (tackle) M, golf, soccer, softball W, tennis, track and field, volleyball W. **Intramural:** Basketball, football (non-tackle), racquetball, soccer, softball, ultimate frisbee, volleyball. **Team name:** Golden Tornadoes.

Student services. Alcohol/substance abuse counseling, chaplain/spiritual director, career counseling, student employment services, financial aid counseling, health services, minority student services, personal counseling, placement for graduates. **Physically disabled:** Services for visually, hearing impaired.

Contact. E-mail: admissions@geneva.edu
Phone: (724) 847-6500 Toll-free number: (800) 847-8255
Fax: (724) 847-6776
Dave Layton, Dean of Undergraduate Enrollment, Geneva College, 3200 College Avenue, Beaver Falls, PA 15010

Gettysburg College
Gettysburg, Pennsylvania   **CB member**
www.gettysburg.edu   **CB code: 2275**

▶ Private 4-year liberal arts college affiliated with the Evangelical Lutheran Church in America

▶ Residential campus in large town

▶ 2,441 degree-seeking undergraduates: 53% women, 3% African American, 2% Asian American, 5% Hispanic/Latino, 2% Multi-racial, non-Hispanic, 5% international

▶ 40% of applicants admitted

▶ SAT or ACT (ACT writing optional), application essay required

▶ 84% graduate within 6 years

General. Founded in 1832. Regionally accredited. **Degrees:** 613 bachelor's awarded. **ROTC:** Army. **Location:** 36 miles from Harrisburg, 80 miles from Washington, DC. **Calendar:** Semester. **Full-time faculty:** 222 total; 96% have terminal degrees, 17% minority, 43% women. **Part-time faculty:** 86 total; 52% have terminal degrees, 4% minority, 34% women. **Class size:** 66% < 20, 32% 20-39, 2% 40-49, less than 1% 50-99. **Special facilities:** Sunderman Conservatory of Music, women's resource center, child study center, public service center, optics and plasma physics laboratories, infrared and NMR spectrometers, proton accelerator, science center, observatory, planetarium.

Freshman class profile. 6,386 applied, 2,540 admitted, 699 enrolled.

Mid 50% test scores		Return as sophomores:	91%
SAT critical reading:	600-670	Out-of-state:	78%
SAT math:	610-680	Live on campus:	100%
Rank in top quarter:	82%	International:	8%
Rank in top tenth:	56%		

Basis for selection. Academic record, recommendations, activities are most important. Audition required for the Sunderman Conservatory of Music; portfolio recommended for art program. Interview strongly recommended. **Home schooled:** Statement describing home school structure and mission, transcript of courses and grades, interview, letter of recommendation (nonparent) required.

High school preparation. College-preparatory program required. Required and recommended units include English 4, mathematics 3-4, social studies 3-4, history 3-4, science 3-4 (laboratory 3-4) and foreign language 3-4.

2015-2016 Annual costs. Tuition/fees: $49,140. Room/board: $11,730. Books/supplies: $1,000.

2015-2016 Financial aid. **Need-based:** 449 full-time freshmen applied for aid; 379 deemed to have need; 372 received aid. Average need met was 90%. Average scholarship/grant was $33,314; average loan $5,223. 86% of total undergraduate aid awarded as scholarships/grants, 14% as loans/jobs. **Non-need-based:** Awarded to 1,158 full-time undergraduates, including 326 freshmen. Scholarships awarded for academics, music/drama.

Application procedures. **Admission:** Closing date 1/15 (postmark date). $60 fee, may be waived for applicants with need. Admission notification by 4/1. Must reply by May 1 or within 2 week(s) if notified thereafter. **Financial aid:** Closing date 2/1. FAFSA, CSS PROFILE required. Applicants notified by 3/18; must reply by 5/1.

Academics. **Special study options:** Combined bachelor's/graduate degree, double major, independent study, internships, semester at sea, student-designed major, study abroad, teacher certification program, United Nations semester, Washington semester. 3-2 programs in engineering with Columbia University, Rensselaer Polytechnic Institute, University of Pittsburgh, and Washington University in St. Louis; 4-1 program in nursing with Johns Hopkins University; pre-law and health professions advising available. **Credit/placement by examination:** AP, CLEP, IB, SAT, institutional tests. **Support services:** Study skills assistance, tutoring, writing center.

Majors. **Area/ethnic studies:** African-American, American, Asian, Asian-American, East Asian, gay/lesbian, Japanese, Latin American, Latin American/Caribbean, women's. **Biology:** General, biochemistry, conservation, molecular, neuroscience. **Business:** Business admin, finance, international, management science, marketing, nonprofit/public. **Communications:** Communications/speech/rhetoric, journalism. **Computer sciences:** General, computer science. **Conservation:** General, environmental science, environmental studies, forestry, water/wetlands/marine. **Education:** Music. **English:** American lit, British lit, creative writing, English lit. **Foreign languages:** Arabic, Chinese, classics, comparative lit, French, German, Italian, Japanese, Latin, Spanish. **Health services:** Nursing (RN), predental, premedicine, prepharmacy, preveterinary. **History:** General, American, Asian, European. **Liberal arts:** Arts/sciences. **Math:** General. **Parks/recreation:** Exercise sciences, health/fitness, sports admin. **Philosophy/religion:** Philosophy, religion. **Physical sciences:** Astronomy, chemistry, physics. **Psychology:** General. **Social sciences:** Anthropology, economics, international relations, political science, sociology, U.S. government. **Theology:** Preministerial. **Visual/performing arts:** General, art, art history/conservation, dramatic, film/cinema/video, music, music performance, music theory/composition, piano/keyboard, studio arts, theater arts management, voice/opera.

Most popular majors. Biology 13%, business/marketing 7%, English 8%, history 7%, psychology 8%, social sciences 24%.

Technology on campus. 295 workstations in library, computer center, student center. Dormitories wired for high-speed internet access and linked to campus network. Commuter students can connect to campus network. Online course registration, online library, helpline, repair service, student web hosting, wireless network available.

Student life. **Freshman orientation:** Mandatory. Preregistration for classes offered. Held 5 days prior to the start of fall semester. **Policies:** Freshmen not permitted cars on campus. **Housing:** Guaranteed on-campus for all undergraduates. Coed dorms, single-sex dorms, apartments, fraternity/sorority housing, gender-neutral housing, themed housing, wellness housing available. $500 nonrefundable deposit, deadline 5/1. **Activities:** Bands, campus ministries, choral groups, dance, drama, film society, international student organizations, literary magazine, music ensembles, Model UN, musical theater, radio station, student government, student newspaper, symphony orchestra, TV station, over 120 clubs available.

Athletics. NCAA. **Intercollegiate:** Baseball M, basketball, cheerleading, cross-country, field hockey W, football (tackle) M, golf, lacrosse, soccer, softball W, swimming, tennis, track and field, volleyball W, wrestling M. **Intramural:** Basketball, field hockey, football (non-tackle), soccer, softball, volleyball, water polo. **Team name:** Bullets.

Student services. Chaplain/spiritual director, career counseling, student employment services, financial aid counseling, health services, minority student services, personal counseling, placement for graduates, women's services.

Contact. E-mail: admiss@gettysburg.edu
Phone: (717) 337-6100 Toll-free number: (800) 431-0803
Fax: (717) 337-6145
Gail Sweezey, Director of Admissions, Gettysburg College, 300 North Washington Street, Gettysburg, PA 17325-1400

Gratz College
Melrose Park, Pennsylvania
www.gratz.edu   **CB code: 2280**

▶ Private 4-year liberal arts college affiliated with the Jewish faith

▶ Commuter campus in very large city

▶ 14 degree-seeking undergraduates

▶ Application essay required

General. Founded in 1895. Regionally accredited. **Degrees:** 3 bachelor's awarded; master's, professional offered. **Location:** 6 miles from Philadelphia. **Calendar:** Semester, limited summer session. **Full-time faculty:** 6 total. **Part-time faculty:** 6 total. **Special facilities:** Jewish music library and rare book collection, oral history Holocaust archives.

Basis for selection. Application, personal statement, transcripts, and two recommendations are used in evaluating applicants. Interviews may also be required for selected applicants. Interview recommended. **Learning Disabled:** Students seeking accommodations should submit written documentation to the Office of Disability Services.

2015-2016 Annual costs. Books/supplies: $1,200. **Additional information:** Undergraduate tuition is $775 per credit or $2,325 per course for the Bachelor of Arts in Jewish Studies.

Application procedures. Admission: No deadline. $50 fee, may be waived for applicants with need. Admission notification on a rolling basis. **Financial aid:** Priority date 6/1; no closing date. FAFSA, institutional form required. Applicants notified on a rolling basis starting 11/1.

Academics. Special study options: Cross-registration, distance learning, double major, independent study, internships, study abroad, teacher certification program. **Credit/placement by examination:** AP, CLEP, institutional tests. **Support services:** Reduced course load.

Majors. Philosophy/religion: Judaic, religion.

Technology on campus. 4 workstations in library, student center. Commuter students can connect to campus network. Wireless network available.

Student life. Freshman orientation: Available. Preregistration for classes offered. **Activities:** Student government.

Student services. Adult student services, career counseling, financial aid counseling, personal counseling, placement for graduates.

Contact. E-mail: admissions@gratz.edu
Phone: (215) 635-7300 ext. 140
Toll-free number: (800) 475-4635 ext. 140 Fax: (215) 635-7399
Ann Perazzelli, Director of Admissions, Gratz College, 7605 Old York Road, Melrose Park, PA 19027

Grove City College

Grove City, Pennsylvania

www.gcc.edu

CB member
CB code: 2277

- Private 4-year liberal arts college affiliated with the nondenominational tradition
- Residential campus in small town
- 2,409 degree-seeking undergraduates: 1% part-time, 50% women, 1% African American, 2% Asian American, 1% Hispanic/Latino, 3% Multiracial, non-Hispanic, 1% international
- 81% of applicants admitted
- SAT or ACT (ACT writing optional); application essay required
- 85% graduate within 6 years; 14% enter graduate study

General. Founded in 1876. Regionally accredited. **Degrees:** 543 bachelor's awarded. **Location:** 60 miles from Pittsburgh. **Calendar:** Semester, limited summer session. **Full-time faculty:** 154 total; 82% have terminal degrees, 6% minority, 33% women. **Part-time faculty:** 79 total; 20% have terminal degrees, 5% minority, 52% women. **Class size:** 51% < 20, 39% 20-39, 6% 40-49, 3% 50-99, less than 1% >100. **Special facilities:** Off-campus research-grade observatory.

Freshman class profile. 1,541 applied, 1,248 admitted, 547 enrolled.

Mid 50% test scores			
SAT critical reading:	540-660	Rank in top quarter:	68%
SAT math:	540-650	Rank in top tenth:	40%
ACT composite:	24-29	End year in good standing:	91%
GPA 3.75 or higher:	52%	Return as sophomores:	89%
GPA 3.50-3.74:	24%	Out-of-state:	45%
GPA 3.0-3.49:	21%	Live on campus:	98%
GPA 2.0-2.99:	3%	International:	1%

Basis for selection. High school GPA, rigor of curriculum, class rank, test scores, recommendations, interview, essay, character, and extracurricular activities are all considered. An interview is highly recommended. An audition is required for the music program. **Home schooled:** Letter of recommendation (nonparent) required. Extracurricular activities are important.

High school preparation. College-preparatory program recommended. 18 units recommended. Recommended units include English 4, mathematics 3, social studies 3, history 2, science 3 (laboratory 2) and foreign language 3. Engineering, science, and math applicants must have 4 math and 4 science.

2015-2016 Annual costs. Tuition/fees: $16,154. Room/board: $8,802. Books/supplies: $1,000. Personal expenses: $350.

2015-2016 Financial aid. Need-based: 346 full-time freshmen applied for aid; 259 deemed to have need; 258 received aid. Average need met was 56%. Average scholarship/grant was $7,594. 61% of total undergraduate aid awarded as scholarships/grants, 39% as loans/jobs. **Non-need-based:** Awarded to 556 full-time undergraduates, including 95 freshmen. Scholarships awarded for academics, leadership, music/drama. **Additional information:** Institutional aid applications required for institutional need-based scholarships. Federal monies are not accepted (Pell Grant, Stafford Loan, Parent Plus Loan, GI Bill, or any other government scholarship or loan program).

Application procedures. Admission: Closing date 2/1 (postmark date). $50 fee, may be waived for applicants with need. Decision letters mailed 3/15. Must reply by 5/1. **Financial aid:** Closing date 4/15. Institutional form required. Applicants notified on a rolling basis starting 3/15; must reply by 5/1.

Academics. Students are required to complete a minimum of 128 credit hours. All students must complete the 40-46 semester hour general education curriculum, which includes 15 hours of humanities; a 3-hour writing course; 8 hours of natural science; 3 hours of science, faith, and technology; 3 hours of social science; 6 hours of quantitative and logical reasoning; and 2 hours of physical/wellness education. Students must also demonstrate intermediate level proficiency in a foreign language. A minimum 2.0 GPA is required. **Special study options:** Accelerated study, combined bachelor's/graduate degree, distance learning, double major, dual enrollment of high school students, independent study, internships, study abroad, teacher certification program, Washington semester. **Credit/placement by examination:** AP, CLEP, IB. **Support services:** Reduced course load, study skills assistance, tutoring, writing center.

Majors. Biology: General, biochemistry. **Business:** Accounting, business admin, entrepreneurial studies, finance, international, managerial economics, marketing. **Communications:** Communications/speech/rhetoric. **Computer sciences:** Computer science. **Education:** Biology, chemistry, early childhood, English, French, mathematics, middle, music, physics, social studies, Spanish, special ed. **Engineering:** Electrical, mechanical. **English:** General lit. **Foreign languages:** French, Spanish. **History:** General. **Math:** General. **Parks/recreation:** Exercise sciences. **Philosophy/religion:** Philosophy, religion. **Physical sciences:** Chemistry, physics. **Psychology:** General. **Social sciences:** Economics, political science, sociology. **Visual/performing arts:** Music, music management, music performance.

Most popular majors. Biology 10%, business/marketing 22%, communications/journalism 7%, education 8%, engineering/engineering technologies 11%, English 8%, social sciences 9%.

Technology on campus. PC or laptop required. 50 workstations in library, computer center. Dormitories wired for high-speed internet access and linked to campus network. Commuter students can connect to campus network. Online course registration, online library, helpline, repair service, student web hosting, wireless network available.

Student life. Freshman orientation: Mandatory. Preregistration for classes offered. One-day Summer Preview programs in June strongly recommended and a mandatory 3-1/2-day program in August prior to the beginning of the fall semester. **Policies:** Drugs and alcohol are not permitted on campus. Chapel program consists of lectures, Sunday vespers, and seminars. Students must attend 16 chapels per semester from over 50 opportunities. Religious observance required. Freshmen not permitted cars on campus. **Housing:** Guaranteed on-campus for all undergraduates. Single-sex dorms, apartments, wellness housing available. $250 nonrefundable deposit. **Activities:** Bands, campus ministries, choral groups, dance, drama, international student organizations, literary magazine, music ensembles, musical theater, opera, radio station, student government, student newspaper, symphony orchestra, TV station, Fellowship of Christian Athletes, Salt Company, Warriors for Christ, Young Life, Newman Club, College Republicans, College Democrats, Koinonia/Gospel Team, Orientation Board, Life Advocates.

Athletics. NCAA. **Intercollegiate:** Baseball M, basketball, cross-country, diving, football (tackle) M, golf, soccer, softball W, swimming, tennis, track and field, volleyball W, water polo W. **Intramural:** Badminton, basketball, bowling, football (non-tackle), football (tackle), racquetball, soccer, softball, table tennis, tennis, ultimate frisbee, volleyball. **Team name:** Wolverines.

Student services. Alcohol/substance abuse counseling, chaplain/spiritual director, career counseling, student employment services, financial aid counseling, health services, minority student services, personal counseling, placement for graduates.

Contact. E-mail: admissions@gcc.edu
Phone: (724) 458-2100 Fax: (724) 458-3395
Sarah Gibbs, Director of Admissions, Grove City College, 100 Campus Drive, Grove City, PA 16127-2104

Gwynedd Mercy University
Gwynedd Valley, Pennsylvania   **CB member**
www.gmercyu.edu   **CB code: 2278**

- Private 4-year nursing and liberal arts college affiliated with the Roman Catholic Church
- Residential campus in large town
- 1,935 degree-seeking undergraduates: 7% part-time, 75% women, 23% African American, 5% Asian American, 5% Hispanic/Latino
- 556 degree-seeking graduate students
- 92% of applicants admitted
- SAT or ACT (ACT writing optional) required
- 60% graduate within 6 years

General. Founded in 1948. Regionally accredited. Sponsored by the Sisters of Mercy of the Americas. **Degrees:** 422 bachelor's, 209 associate awarded; master's, professional offered. **Location:** 20 miles from Philadelphia. **Calendar:** Semester, limited summer session. **Full-time faculty:** 75 total; 47% have terminal degrees, 4% minority, 69% women. **Part-time faculty:** 224 total; 20% have terminal degrees, 12% minority, 70% women. **Class size:** 61% < 20, 35% 20-39, less than 1% 40-49, 3% 50-99, less than 1% >100. **Special facilities:** Nursery laboratory school for early childhood education, interactive patient simulators used in the Clinical Nursing Laboratory.

Freshman class profile. 850 applied, 785 admitted, 241 enrolled.

Mid 50% test scores		GPA 3.0-3.49:	36%
SAT critical reading:	410-500	GPA 2.0-2.99:	24%
SAT math:	420-510	Rank in top quarter:	25%
SAT writing:	400-500	Rank in top tenth:	8%
ACT composite:	18-22	Return as sophomores:	80%
GPA 3.75 or higher:	16%	Out-of-state:	20%
GPA 3.50-3.74:	22%	Live on campus:	69%

Basis for selection. School achievement record most important, followed by test scores and recommendations. Extracurricular activities considered. Nursing program very competitive.

High school preparation. College-preparatory program recommended. 16 units required. Required units include English 4, mathematics 3, history 1, science 3 and academic electives 3. Chemistry required for applicants to nursing, cardiovascular, biology, medical technology programs. Biology required for cardiovascular, health information technology programs. Physics required for radiation therapy, medical technology, biology programs. Chemistry or physics required for respiratory therapy.

2016-2017 Annual costs. Tuition/fees: $34,380. Room/board: $11,300. Books/supplies: $1,000. Personal expenses: $500. **Additional information:** Cost reported is annual tuition for allied health and nursing programs; tuition for other programs, $31,780.

2015-2016 Financial aid. **Need-based:** 228 full-time freshmen applied for aid; 217 deemed to have need; 217 received aid. Average need met was 73%. Average scholarship/grant was $20,419; average loan $3,245. 62% of total undergraduate aid awarded as scholarships/grants, 38% as loans/jobs. **Non-need-based:** Scholarships awarded for academics, alumni affiliation, leadership, minority status, religious affiliation, state residency.

Application procedures. **Admission:** Priority date 4/1; deadline 8/20 (receipt date). No application fee. Application must be submitted online. Admission notification on a rolling basis beginning on or about 9/15. Must reply by May 1 or within 3 week(s) if notified thereafter. Nursing program usually filled by May 1. **Financial aid:** Priority date 3/15, closing date 5/1. FAFSA, institutional form required. Applicants notified on a rolling basis starting 2/15; must reply by 5/1 or within 2 week(s) of notification.

Academics. 8-week evening sessions available for business and accounting majors. Adult accelerated degree completion programs available for business, graduate education and nursing (RN to BSN). **Special study options:** Accelerated study, combined bachelor's/graduate degree, cross-registration, distance learning, double major, dual enrollment of high school students, honors, independent study, internships, liberal arts/career combination, study abroad, teacher certification program, weekend college. **Credit/placement by examination:** AP, CLEP, SAT, ACT, institutional tests. Credit by examination cannot be applied to open electives. **Support services:** Learning center, reduced course load, remedial instruction, study skills assistance, tutoring, writing center.

Majors. **Biology:** General. **Business:** Accounting, business admin, human resources. **Communications:** Communications/speech/rhetoric. **Computer sciences:** Web page design. **Education:** Business, early childhood special, elementary, history, mathematics, multi-level teacher. **English:** English lit. **Health services:** Health information management, medical radiologic technology/radiation therapy, nursing (RN), radiologic technology/medical imaging, respiratory therapy technology. **History:** General. **Math:** General. **Philosophy/religion:** Philosophy. **Protective services:** Police science. **Psychology:** General.

Most popular majors. Business/marketing 30%, health sciences 46%.

Technology on campus. 217 workstations in library, computer center, student center. Dormitories wired for high-speed internet access and linked to campus network. Commuter students can connect to campus network. Online course registration, online library, helpline, wireless network available.

Student life. **Freshman orientation:** Available. Preregistration for classes offered. Multiple full-day sessions offered during the summer. **Housing:** Coed dorms available. $250 partly refundable deposit, deadline 5/1. **Activities:** Campus ministries, choral groups, literary magazine, student government, student newspaper, Kappa Delta Pi, business society, honor societies, resident council, student nurses' association, education club, peer counseling, psychology/sociology club, biology student association, Sigma Phi Sigma.

Athletics. NCAA. **Intercollegiate:** Baseball M, basketball, cheerleading W, cross-country, field hockey W, golf M, lacrosse, soccer, softball W, tennis, track and field, volleyball W. **Intramural:** Volleyball. **Team name:** Griffins.

Student services. Adult student services, chaplain/spiritual director, career counseling, student employment services, financial aid counseling, health services, minority student services, personal counseling.

Contact. E-mail: admissions@gmercyu.edu
Phone: (215) 646-7300 ext. 530 Toll-free number: (800) 342-5462
Fax: (215) 641-5556
Michele Diehl, Director of Undergraduate Admissions, Gwynedd Mercy University, 1325 Sumneytown Pike, Gwynedd Valley, PA 19437-0901

Harrisburg University of Science and Technology
Harrisburg, Pennsylvania
www.harrisburgu.edu   **CB code: 4511**

- Private 4-year university
- Commuter campus in small city
- 278 degree-seeking undergraduates
- 55 graduate students

General. Regionally accredited. **Degrees:** 35 bachelor's awarded; master's offered. **Location:** Located in Central Pennsylvania. **Calendar:** Trimester, limited summer session. **Full-time faculty:** 10 total; 90% have terminal degrees, 40% minority, 50% women. **Part-time faculty:** 25 total; 20% have terminal degrees, 28% women. **Class size:** 95% < 20, 5% 20-39.

Freshman class profile.

GPA 3.75 or higher:	11%	GPA 2.0-2.99:	32%
GPA 3.50-3.74:	25%	Out-of-state:	30%
GPA 3.0-3.49:	32%	Live on campus:	85%

Basis for selection. Admissions based on high school record. SAT or ACT recommended. Interview and essay or personal statement strongly recommended. **Home schooled:** Statement describing home school structure and mission, transcript of courses and grades, letter of recommendation (nonparent) required.

2015-2016 Annual costs. Tuition/fees: $23,900. Books/supplies: $1,500. Personal expenses: $1,700.

Financial aid. **Non-need-based:** Scholarships awarded for academics, leadership, state residency.

Application procedures. **Admission:** No deadline. No application fee. Admission notification on a rolling basis. **Financial aid:** No deadline. FAFSA required. Applicants notified on a rolling basis; must reply within 2 week(s) of notification.

Academics. **Special study options:** Double major, dual enrollment of high school students, internships, student-designed major. **Credit/placement by examination:** AP, CLEP, IB, institutional tests. 18 credit hours maximum toward bachelor's degree. **Support services:** Reduced course load, remedial instruction, study skills assistance, tutoring.

Majors. Biology: Biotechnology. **Business:** E-commerce. **Computer sciences:** General, information technology. **Conservation:** Environmental science. **Physical sciences:** General, chemistry. **Social sciences:** Geography.

Most popular majors. Computer/information sciences 37%, physical sciences 48%, science technologies 15%.

Technology on campus. PC or laptop required. 12 workstations in computer center. Commuter students can connect to campus network. Online library, repair service, wireless network available.

Student life. Freshman orientation: Mandatory. Preregistration for classes offered. **Housing:** Guaranteed on-campus for freshmen. Coed dorms available. **Activities:** Student government, student newspaper.

Student services. Financial aid counseling.

Contact. E-mail: admissions@HarrisburgU.edu
Phone: (717) 901-5101 Fax: (717) 901-3101
Steven Infanti, Director of Admissions, Harrisburg University of Science and Technology, 326 Market Street, Harrisburg, PA 17101-2208

Haverford College
Haverford, Pennsylvania
www.haverford.edu
CB member
CB code: 2289

- Private 4-year liberal arts college
- Residential campus in large town
- 1,229 degree-seeking undergraduates: 51% women, 7% African American, 10% Asian American, 10% Hispanic/Latino, 4% Multi-racial, non-Hispanic, 7% international
- 25% of applicants admitted
- SAT and SAT Subject Tests or ACT (ACT writing optional), application essay required
- 90% graduate within 6 years; 17% enter graduate study

General. Founded in 1833. Regionally accredited. Founded by the Society of Friends (Quakers), but now independent. **Degrees:** 298 bachelor's awarded. **Location:** 8 miles from Philadelphia. **Calendar:** Semester. **Full-time faculty:** 125 total; 98% have terminal degrees, 24% minority, 46% women. **Part-time faculty:** 38 total; 95% have terminal degrees, 13% minority, 58% women. **Class size:** 71% < 20, 22% 20-39, 4% 40-49, 3% 50-99. **Special facilities:** Observatory, arboretum, fine arts foundry.

Freshman class profile. 3,467 applied, 852 admitted, 346 enrolled.

Mid 50% test scores		Rank in top tenth:	96%
SAT critical reading:	660-760	Return as sophomores:	97%
SAT math:	660-770	Out-of-state:	88%
SAT writing:	660-750	Live on campus:	100%
ACT composite:	31-34	International:	10%
Rank in top quarter:	100%		

Basis for selection. School record, test scores, extracurricular achievements, and recommendations important. College seeks diversity of social, economic, and geographic backgrounds. Two standardized testing options. The first is to submit results of the three-part SAT Critical Reasoning Test and two SAT Subject Tests (in any two subjects). The other is to submit results of the ACT with the optional writing test. Interview required of applicants living within 150 miles of college, recommended for others. **Home schooled:** Statement describing home school structure and mission, transcript of courses and grades, interview, letter of recommendation (nonparent) required.

High school preparation. College-preparatory program recommended. 20 units recommended. Recommended units include English 4, mathematics 3, social studies 3, science 3 (laboratory 3) and foreign language 3.

2015-2016 Annual costs. Tuition/fees: $49,098. Room/board: $14,888. Personal expenses: $1,468.

2015-2016 Financial aid. All financial aid based on need. 183 full-time freshmen applied for aid; 176 deemed to have need; 176 received aid. Average need met was 100%. Average scholarship/grant was $47,009; average loan $813. 97% of total undergraduate aid awarded as scholarships/grants, 3% as loans/jobs.

Application procedures. Admission: Closing date 1/15. $65 fee, may be waived for applicants with need. Admission notification by 4/1. Must reply by May 1 or within 1 week(s) if notified thereafter. **Financial aid:** Closing date 2/1. FAFSA, CSS PROFILE required. Applicants notified by 4/1; must reply by 5/1.

Academics. Academic Flexibility Program allows for advanced independent work and interdepartmental majors. Ample opportunity for student-faculty research. Senior seminars, comprehensive examination and/or senior thesis required for completion of all major programs. **Special study options:** Combined bachelor's/graduate degree, cross-registration, double major, exchange student, independent study, internships, liberal arts/career combination, student-designed major, study abroad, teacher certification program. Exchange program with University of Pennsylvania, Swarthmore College, and Bryn Mawr College; Noncredit internships also available; 3-2 Engineering program with California Institute of Technology; 4+1 Bioethics program with University of Pennsylvania; 4+1 Engineering program with University of Pennsylvania; 3/2 City Planning program with University of Pennsylvania; 1-yr Master's in Finance program with Claremont McKenna College; 5-yr Latin American Studies program with Georgetown University; 2-yr China Studies Master's program at Zhejiang Univeristy. **Credit/placement by examination:** AP, CLEP, IB. **Support services:** Learning center, study skills assistance, tutoring, writing center.

Majors. Architecture: Urban/community planning. **Area/ethnic studies:** East Asian. **Biology:** General. **Computer sciences:** General. **English:** English lit. **Foreign languages:** Ancient Greek, classics, comparative lit, French, German, Italian, Latin, Russian, Spanish. **History:** General. **Liberal arts:** Arts/sciences. **Math:** General. **Philosophy/religion:** Philosophy, religion. **Physical sciences:** Astronomy, chemistry, geology, physics. **Psychology:** General. **Social sciences:** Anthropology, archaeology, economics, political science, sociology, urban studies. **Visual/performing arts:** Art history/conservation, music, studio arts.

Most popular majors. Biology 9%, English 10%, foreign language 7%, history 7%, mathematics 7%, physical sciences 15%, psychology 9%, social sciences 24%.

Technology on campus. 300 workstations in dormitories, library, computer center, student center. Dormitories wired for high-speed internet access and linked to campus network. Commuter students can connect to campus network. Online course registration, online library, helpline, student web hosting, wireless network available.

Student life. Freshman orientation: Mandatory, $230 fee. Preregistration for classes offered. Directly precedes the start of the fall semester. **Policies:** Student conduct regulated by academic and social honor code, which allows for unsupervised examinations. Students serve on campus governance and policy-making committees. Freshmen not permitted cars on campus. **Housing:** Guaranteed on-campus for all undergraduates. Coed dorms, single-sex dorms, special housing for disabled, apartments, themed housing, wellness housing available. Students may live at Bryn Mawr College through dormitory exchange program. Students at both colleges may eat meals on either campus. **Activities:** Campus ministries, choral groups, dance, drama, international student organizations, literary magazine, music ensembles, musical theater, radio station, student government, student newspaper, Quaker activities committee, Hillel, Christian Fellowship, environmental action committee, black students league, Puerto Rican students association, Asian students association, Bisexual/Gay/Lesbian alliance, Eighth Dimension Volunteer Service Program.

Athletics. NCAA. **Intercollegiate:** Baseball M, basketball, cricket, cross-country, fencing, field hockey W, lacrosse, soccer, softball W, squash, tennis, track and field, volleyball W. **Intramural:** Basketball, soccer, tennis.

Student services. Alcohol/substance abuse counseling, career counseling, student employment services, financial aid counseling, health services, minority student services, personal counseling, placement for graduates, women's services. **Physically disabled:** Services for visually, speech, hearing impaired.

Contact. E-mail: admission@haverford.edu
Phone: (610) 896-1350 Fax: (610) 896-1338
Jess Lord, Dean of Admissions and Financial Aid, Haverford College, 370 Lancaster Avenue, Haverford, PA 19041-1392

Holy Family University
Philadelphia, Pennsylvania
www.holyfamily.edu
CB member
CB code: 2297

- Private 4-year university affiliated with the Roman Catholic Church
- Commuter campus in very large city
- 1,825 degree-seeking undergraduates: 22% part-time, 74% women, 9% African American, 4% Asian American, 7% Hispanic/Latino
- 652 degree-seeking graduate students
- 74% of applicants admitted
- SAT or ACT (ACT writing optional) required
- 57% graduate within 6 years; 20% enter graduate study

General. Founded in 1954. Regionally accredited. Additional instructional sites in Newtown and Bensalem. **Degrees:** 485 bachelor's, 12 associate awarded; master's, doctoral offered. **ROTC:** Army. **Location:** 12 miles from downtown. **Calendar:** Semester, extensive summer session. **Full-time faculty:** 74 total; 80% have terminal degrees, 11% minority, 70% women. **Part-time faculty:** 207 total; 25% have terminal degrees, 9% minority, 47% women. **Class size:** 55% < 20, 45% 20-39. **Special facilities:** Early childhood center with nursery and kindergarten classes, art museum.

Freshman class profile. 1,328 applied, 982 admitted, 342 enrolled.

Mid 50% test scores		GPA 2.0-2.99:	43%
SAT critical reading:	410-510	Rank in top quarter:	25%
SAT math:	410-500	Rank in top tenth:	10%
SAT writing:	410-500	End year in good standing:	86%
GPA 3.75 or higher:	16%	Return as sophomores:	77%
GPA 3.50-3.74:	11%	Out-of-state:	16%
GPA 3.0-3.49:	28%	Live on campus:	27%

Basis for selection. High school record most important, followed by recommendations, the interview, and test scores. Motivation, school work and community activities considered. Students may enroll as non-matriculated students but are not admitted into any degree program. Essay and interview recommended. **Home schooled:** State high school equivalency certificate required. **Learning Disabled:** Students encouraged to meet with the Counseling Center to determine how the necessary accommodations required by the student can be met.

High school preparation. College-preparatory program recommended. 16 units required. Required units include English 4, mathematics 3, history 2, science 2, foreign language 2 and academic electives 3. All students must have algebra I, algebra II, and geometry. Math majors need trigonometry. Nursing requires biology, chemistry, and science electives. Science requires biology, chemistry, and trigonometry.

2015-2016 Annual costs. Tuition/fees: $29,168. Room/board: $13,576. Books/supplies: $1,060. Personal expenses: $682.

2015-2016 Financial aid. Need-based: 329 full-time freshmen applied for aid; 303 deemed to have need; 303 received aid. Average need met was 83%. Average scholarship/grant was $19,706; average loan $1,550. 61% of total undergraduate aid awarded as scholarships/grants, 39% as loans/jobs. **Non-need-based:** Awarded to 1,387 full-time undergraduates, including 373 freshmen. Scholarships awarded for academics, athletics, leadership.

Application procedures. Admission: No deadline. $25 fee, may be waived for applicants with need. Admission notification on a rolling basis. **Financial aid:** Priority date 3/1, closing date 4/1. FAFSA required. Applicants notified on a rolling basis starting 3/15; must reply within 4 week(s) of notification.

Academics. Special study options: Accelerated study, combined bachelor's/graduate degree, cooperative education, cross-registration, distance learning, honors, independent study, internships, liberal arts/career combination, study abroad, teacher certification program, weekend college. RN to BSN program at Fox Chase Cancer Center. **Credit/placement by examination:** AP, CLEP, IB, SAT, ACT, institutional tests. 30 credit hours maximum toward bachelor's degree. **Support services:** Learning center, pre-admission summer program, reduced course load, remedial instruction, study skills assistance, tutoring, writing center. Center for Academic Enhancement. One-to-one tutoring is available and student study groups.

Majors. Biology: General, biochemistry. **Business:** Accounting, accounting/finance, business admin, finance, human resources, international, management information systems, marketing. **Communications:** Media studies. **Education:** Art, biology, chemistry, early childhood, elementary, English, French, history, mathematics, social science, social studies, Spanish, special ed. **English:** English lit. **Health services:** Clinical lab science, nursing (RN), radiologic technology/medical imaging. **History:** General. **Liberal arts:** Humanities. **Math:** General. **Parks/recreation:** Sports admin. **Philosophy/religion:** Religion. **Protective services:** Criminal justice, financial forensics, fire services admin. **Psychology:** General, industrial, psychobiology. **Visual/performing arts:** Graphic design, studio arts.

Most popular majors. Business/marketing 18%, education 9%, health sciences 46%, psychology 8%, security/protective services 8%.

Technology on campus. 350 workstations in dormitories, library, computer center. Dormitories wired for high-speed internet access and linked to campus network. Commuter students can connect to campus network. Online course registration, online library, helpline, repair service, wireless network available.

Student life. Freshman orientation: Mandatory, $75 fee. Preregistration for classes offered. One-day on campus during the summer, offered on three different dates. **Policies:** Mature and intelligent student conduct expected in accordance with college's interests, standards, and ideals. **Housing:** Guaranteed on-campus for freshmen. Coed dorms, special housing for disabled,

apartments available. $300 nonrefundable deposit, deadline 3/15. On-campus housing available for some athletes. **Activities:** Campus ministries, choral groups, dance, drama, international student organizations, literary magazine, musical theater, student government, student newspaper, TV station, Habitat for Humanity, Alliance for Student Equality, Campus Ministry, environmental club, Fusion, Rotoact, social and behavioral sciences club, Students at Your Service, Veritas.

Athletics. NCAA. **Intercollegiate:** Basketball, cross-country, lacrosse W, soccer, softball W, tennis W, track and field, volleyball W. **Intramural:** Basketball, football (non-tackle), skiing, volleyball. **Team name:** Tigers.

Student services. Adult student services, alcohol/substance abuse counseling, chaplain/spiritual director, career counseling, student employment services, financial aid counseling, health services, minority student services, personal counseling, placement for graduates. **Physically disabled:** Services for visually, speech, hearing impaired.

Contact. E-mail: admissions@holyfamily.edu
Phone: (215) 637-3050 Fax: (215) 281-1022
Lauren Campbell, Director of Admissions, Holy Family University, 9801 Frankford Avenue, Philadelphia, PA 19114-2009

Immaculata University
Immaculata, Pennsylvania CB member
www.immaculata.edu CB code: 2320

- Private 4-year university and liberal arts college affiliated with the Roman Catholic Church
- Residential campus in large town
- 1,694 degree-seeking undergraduates: 40% part-time, 73% women, 14% African American, 2% Asian American, 5% Hispanic/Latino, 2% Multiracial, non-Hispanic, 1% international
- 1,126 degree-seeking graduate students
- 79% of applicants admitted
- SAT or ACT (ACT writing recommended), application essay required
- 70% graduate within 6 years

General. Founded in 1920. Regionally accredited. **Degrees:** 589 bachelor's, 16 associate awarded; master's, professional, doctoral offered. **ROTC:** Army. **Location:** 20 miles from Philadelphia. **Calendar:** Semester, limited summer session. **Full-time faculty:** 71 total; 78% have terminal degrees, 3% minority, 79% women. **Part-time faculty:** 218 total; 30% have terminal degrees, 6% minority, 58% women. **Class size:** 86% < 20, 13% 20-39, less than 1% 40-49, less than 1% 50-99.

Freshman class profile. 1,586 applied, 1,250 admitted, 187 enrolled.

Mid 50% test scores		GPA 3.0-3.49:	28%
SAT critical reading:	440-530	GPA 2.0-2.99:	29%
SAT math:	420-550	Return as sophomores:	83%
SAT writing:	430-550	Out-of-state:	34%
ACT composite:	20-23	Live on campus:	83%
GPA 3.75 or higher:	23%	International:	2%
GPA 3.50-3.74:	19%		

Basis for selection. Class rank, academic program, test scores, counselor recommendation important. Minimum 2.3 GPA preferred. Interviews, essay recommended. Audition required for music program. **Home schooled:** Transcript of courses and grades required. **Learning Disabled:** Proof of psychological or educational testing date must be supplied.

High school preparation. College-preparatory program required. 16 units required. Required units include English 4, mathematics 2, social studies 2, science 2 (laboratory 1) and foreign language 2. 4 electives required; music required for music majors.

2016-2017 Annual costs. Tuition/fees: $35,210. Room/board: $12,500. Books/supplies: $1,974. Personal expenses: $2,664.

Financial aid. Non-need-based: Scholarships awarded for academics, alumni affiliation, art, job skills, leadership, minority status, music/drama, religious affiliation, state residency.

Application procedures. Admission: No deadline. $35 fee, may be waived for applicants with need, free for online applicants. Admission notification on a rolling basis beginning on or about 9/15. Must reply by May 1 or within 2 week(s) if notified thereafter. **Financial aid:** Priority date 2/15, closing date 4/15. FAFSA required. Applicants notified on a rolling basis starting 2/1; must reply within 2 week(s) of notification.

Academics. Special study options: Accelerated study, combined bachelor's/graduate degree, cross-registration, distance learning, double major, dual enrollment of high school students, honors, independent study, internships, liberal arts/career combination, semester at sea, study abroad, teacher certification program, Washington semester. **Credit/placement by examination:** AP, CLEP, IB, SAT, ACT, institutional tests. 30 credit hours maximum toward associate degree, 63 toward bachelor's. **Support services:** Learning center, reduced course load, remedial instruction, study skills assistance, tutoring, writing center.

Majors. Biology: General. **Business:** Accounting, business admin, fashion, finance, human resources, marketing. **Communications:** Communications/speech/rhetoric. **Computer sciences:** Information systems. **Conservation:** Environmental studies. **Education:** Business, elementary, family/consumer sciences, mathematics, music. **English:** English lit. **Foreign languages:** French, German, Spanish. **Health services:** Dietetics, health care admin, music therapy, nursing (RN), premedicine. **History:** General. **Human services:** Public policy. **Liberal arts:** Arts/sciences. **Math:** General. **Parks/recreation:** Exercise sciences. **Physical sciences:** Chemistry. **Protective services:** Criminal justice. **Psychology:** General. **Social sciences:** Economics, international relations, political science, sociology. **Theology:** Theology. **Visual/performing arts:** Music, music performance.

Most popular majors. Business/marketing 14%, health sciences 65%.

Technology on campus. 326 workstations in dormitories, library, computer center, student center. Dormitories wired for high-speed internet access and linked to campus network. Commuter students can connect to campus network. Online course registration, online library, helpline, wireless network available.

Student life. Freshman orientation: Mandatory. Preregistration for classes offered. 2-day session held in summer. **Housing:** Coed dorms, single-sex dorms, special housing for disabled, apartments, themed housing, wellness housing available. $250 partly refundable deposit, deadline 5/1. **Activities:** Bands, campus ministries, choral groups, dance, drama, international student organizations, literary magazine, music ensembles, musical theater, student government, student newspaper, symphony orchestra, African American cultural society, American Music Therapy Association, Modern Foreign Language Association.

Athletics. NCAA. **Intercollegiate:** Basketball, cross-country W, field hockey W, golf, lacrosse, soccer, softball W, tennis, track and field M, volleyball W. **Intramural:** Basketball, cross-country W, field hockey W, lacrosse W, soccer W, softball W, swimming W, tennis W, volleyball W. **Team name:** Mighty Macs.

Student services. Adult student services, alcohol/substance abuse counseling, chaplain/spiritual director, career counseling, student employment services, financial aid counseling, health services, minority student services, personal counseling, placement for graduates. **Physically disabled:** Services for visually, hearing impaired.

Contact. E-mail: admiss@immaculata.edu
Phone: (610) 647-4400 ext. 3060 Toll-free number: (877) 428-6329
Fax: (610) 640-0836
Nicola DiFronzo-Heitzer, Director of Admission, Immaculata University, 1145 King Road, Immaculata, PA 19345

Indiana University of Pennsylvania

Indiana, Pennsylvania	CB member
www.iup.edu	CB code: 2652

- Public 4-year university
- Residential campus in large town
- 11,237 degree-seeking undergraduates: 5% part-time, 55% women, 12% African American, 1% Asian American, 4% Hispanic/Latino, 4% Multi-racial, non-Hispanic, 4% international
- 2,155 degree-seeking graduate students.
- 88% of applicants admitted
- SAT or ACT (ACT writing optional) required
- 53% graduate within 6 years

General. Founded in 1875. Regionally accredited. Branch campuses located in Punxsutawney and Northpointe in Armstrong County. Additional sites are Monroevile Graduate and Professional Center in Wilkins Township; IUP Academy of Culinary Arts in Punxsutawney; Offer courses through the State System's Dixon Center in Harrisburg via distance education. **Degrees:** 2,566 bachelor's, 8 associate awarded; master's, professional, doctoral offered. **ROTC:** Army. **Location:** 50 miles from Pittsburgh. **Calendar:** Semester, extensive summer session. **Full-time faculty:** 603 total; 15% minority, 47% women. **Part-time faculty:** 113 total; 5% minority, 60% women. **Class size:** 34% < 20, 44% 20-39, 9% 40-49, 11% 50-99, 2% >100. **Special facilities:**

Museums, ski slopes, nature preserve, lodge, co-generation plant and sailing base.

Freshman class profile. 9,566 applied, 8,451 admitted, 2,540 enrolled.

Mid 50% test scores			
		Rank in top tenth:	8%
SAT critical reading:	430-530	**Return as sophomores:**	76%
SAT math:	430-530	**Out-of-state:**	6%
SAT writing:	410-520	**Live on campus:**	87%
Rank in top quarter:	26%	**International:**	1%

Basis for selection. School achievement record, recommendations and extracurricular activities considered, test scores, and high school rank important. SAT/ACT scores are not required for student who graduated more than two years ago, transfer, or second bachelor's degree students. Audition required for music program; portfolio required for art program. **Home schooled:** Transcript of courses and grades required.

High school preparation. College-preparatory program required. Required and recommended units include English 4, mathematics 3, social studies 3, history 2, science 3 (laboratory 2) and foreign language 2.

2015-2016 Annual costs. Tuition/fees: $9,936; $20,526 out-of-state. Room/board: $11,880. Books/supplies: $1,100. Personal expenses: $1,650. **Additional information:** Out-of-state tuition is $9,884 for students in the Southwestern University of Finance and Economics (China) partnership. Tuition is $12,002 for first-time freshmen admitted to main campus from Indiana, Maryland, Michigan, New Jersey, New York, Ohio, Virginia, and West Virginia or for first-time freshmen with a high school GPA of at least 3.0 out of 4.0.

2014-2015 Financial aid. Need-based: 2,544 full-time freshmen applied for aid; 2,067 deemed to have need; 2,032 received aid. Average need met was 62%. Average scholarship/grant was $6,645; average loan $3,755. 47% of total undergraduate aid awarded as scholarships/grants, 53% as loans/jobs. **Non-need-based:** Awarded to 2,395 full-time undergraduates, including 1,046 freshmen. Scholarships awarded for academics, alumni affiliation, art, athletics, job skills, leadership, music/drama, ROTC, state residency.

Application procedures. Admission: No deadline. $50 fee, may be waived for applicants with need. Admission notification on a rolling basis beginning on or about 9/1. Must reply by May 1 or within 2 week(s) if notified thereafter. **Financial aid:** Priority date 4/15; no closing date. FAFSA required. Applicants notified on a rolling basis starting 3/14.

Academics. Special study options: Accelerated study, combined bachelor's/graduate degree, cooperative education, cross-registration, distance learning, double major, dual enrollment of high school students, ESL, exchange student, external degree, honors, independent study, internships, liberal arts/career combination, semester at sea, student-designed major, study abroad, teacher certification program, urban semester, Washington semester, weekend college. **Credit/placement by examination:** AP, CLEP, IB, institutional tests. Unlimited number of hours of credit by examination may be counted toward degree. **Support services:** Learning center, pre-admission summer program, remedial instruction, study skills assistance, tutoring, writing center.

Honors college/program. Application, essay and a questionnaire. The number typically admitted is approximately 100. The typical student is in the top 10% of their class. The average SAT is 1300 and GPA is 3.8/4.0.

Majors. Architecture: Urban/community planning. **Area/ethnic studies:** Asian. **Biology:** General, biochemistry. **Business:** General, business admin, fashion, finance, hospitality admin, human resources, international, management information systems, marketing. **Communications:** Communications/speech/rhetoric, journalism. **Computer sciences:** General. **Education:** Early childhood special, middle, special ed, trade/industrial. **English:** English lit. **Foreign languages:** Spanish. **Health services:** Athletic training, audiology/speech pathology, clinical lab science, nuclear medical technology, nursing (RN), respiratory therapy technology. **History:** General. **Liberal arts:** Arts/sciences. **Math:** General. **Parks/recreation:** Health/fitness. **Philosophy/religion:** Philosophy, religion. **Physical sciences:** Chemistry, geology, physics. **Psychology:** General. **Social sciences:** Anthropology, criminology, economics, geography, international relations, political science, sociology. **Visual/performing arts:** General, art, dramatic, interior design, multimedia, music, music performance, studio arts. **Work/family studies:** General, family studies, food/nutrition.

Most popular majors. Business/marketing 24%, communications/journalism 6%, health sciences 9%, parks/recreation 6%, social sciences 17%, visual/performing arts 6%.

Technology on campus. 2,363 workstations in dormitories, library, computer center, student center. Dormitories wired for high-speed internet access and linked to campus network. Commuter students can connect to campus network. Online course registration, online library, helpline, repair service, student web hosting, wireless network available.

Student life. Freshman orientation: Mandatory, $190 fee. Preregistration for classes offered. **Housing:** Guaranteed on-campus for freshmen. Coed dorms, special housing for disabled, apartments, fraternity/sorority housing, themed housing, wellness housing available. $80 nonrefundable deposit, deadline 5/15. Honors college dormitory, substance-free housing, academic specialty floors available. Affiliated housing for fraternities/sororities. **Activities:** Bands, campus ministries, choral groups, dance, drama, film society, international student organizations, literary magazine, music ensembles, Model UN, musical theater, opera, radio station, student government, student newspaper, symphony orchestra, TV station, Alpha Phi Omega national service fraternity (coeducational), Gamma Sigma Sigma service sorority, African American cultural center, Campus Crusade for Christ, Coalition for Christian Outreach, Panhellenic Association, NAACP.

Athletics. NCAA. **Intercollegiate:** Baseball M, basketball, cross-country, field hockey W, football (tackle) M, golf M, lacrosse W, soccer W, softball W, swimming, tennis W, track and field, volleyball W. **Intramural:** Badminton, basketball, softball, volleyball. **Team name:** Crimson Hawks.

Student services. Adult student services, alcohol/substance abuse counseling, chaplain/spiritual director, career counseling, services for economically disadvantaged, student employment services, financial aid counseling, health services, legal services, minority student services, on-campus daycare, personal counseling, placement for graduates, veterans' counselor, women's services. **Physically disabled:** Services for visually, speech, hearing impaired.

Contact. E-mail: admissions-inquiry@iup.edu
Phone: (724) 357-2230 Toll-free number: (800) 442-6830
Fax: (724) 357-6281
Heather Andring, Director of Admissions Operations, Indiana University of Pennsylvania, 120 Sutton Hall, 1011 South Drive, Indiana, PA 15705-1088

Juniata College
Huntingdon, Pennsylvania
www.juniata.edu

CB member
CB code: 2341

- Private 4-year liberal arts college
- Residential campus in small town
- 1,470 degree-seeking undergraduates: 56% women, 3% African American, 4% Asian American, 4% Hispanic/Latino, 2% Multi-racial, non-Hispanic, 8% international
- 12 degree-seeking graduate students
- 77% of applicants admitted
- Application essay required
- 73% graduate within 6 years; 25% enter graduate study

General. Founded in 1876. Regionally accredited. **Degrees:** 322 bachelor's awarded; master's offered. **Location:** 30 miles from Altoona and State College. **Calendar:** Semester, limited summer session. **Full-time faculty:** 108 total; 90% have terminal degrees, 7% minority, 42% women. **Part-time faculty:** 41 total; 54% women. **Class size:** 72% < 20, 24% 20-39, 3% 40-49, 2% 50-99. **Special facilities:** Nature preserve, environmental studies field station, observatory, early childhood education center.

Freshman class profile. 2,604 applied, 2,003 admitted, 356 enrolled.

Mid 50% test scores		Rank in top quarter:	58%
SAT critical reading:	510-630	Rank in top tenth:	30%
SAT math:	510-620	End year in good standing:	99%
ACT composite:	23-29	Return as sophomores:	86%
GPA 3.75 or higher:	52%	Out-of-state:	32%
GPA 3.50-3.74:	19%	Live on campus:	99%
GPA 3.0-3.49:	24%	International:	6%
GPA 2.0-2.99:	5%		

Basis for selection. School achievement record most important. Standardized test scores, school and community activities, recommendations and essay also important. SAT or ACT recommended. Scores used for fall admission must be taken at the latest by the January test date of the same year. Interview recommended.

High school preparation. College-preparatory program required. 16 units required. Required units include English 4, mathematics 3, social studies 1, history 3, science 3 (laboratory 2).

2015-2016 Annual costs. Tuition/fees: $40,600. Room/board: $11,140.

2014-2015 Financial aid. Need-based: 309 full-time freshmen applied for aid; 278 deemed to have need; 276 received aid. Average need met was 83%. Average scholarship/grant was $26,702; average loan $4,688. 78% of total undergraduate aid awarded as scholarships/grants, 22% as loans/jobs. **Non-need-based:** Awarded to 553 full-time undergraduates, including 128

freshmen. Scholarships awarded for academics, alumni affiliation, art, minority status, music/drama.

Application procedures. Admission: Priority date 11/15; deadline 2/15 (postmark date). No application fee. Admission notification by 2/1. Must reply by May 1 or within 2 week(s) if notified thereafter. **Financial aid:** Closing date 2/15. FAFSA required. Applicants notified on a rolling basis starting 3/1; must reply by 5/1.

Academics. Special study options: Combined bachelor's/graduate degree, double major, dual enrollment of high school students, ESL, exchange student, honors, independent study, internships, student-designed major, study abroad, teacher certification program, urban semester, Washington semester. Marine biology with Oregon Marine Program; 3-3 law with Duquesne University; 3-2 engineering with Columbia University, Pennsylvania State University, Clarkson University, Washington University; 3-4 dentistry with Temple University, 4-4 LECOM School of Dental Medicine; 4-4 medicine with Temple University School of Medicine, Lake Erie College of Osteopathic Medicine, 3-4 optometry with Pennsylvania College of Optometry at Salus University; nursing with Johns Hopkins University, Case Western Reserve University; biotechnology, cytotechnology with Jefferson School of Health Professions; physical therapy with Widener University, Drexel University, Jefferson School of Health Professions; medical technology with Jefferson College of Health Professions; chiropractic medicine with New York Chiropractic College; pharmacy with Lake Erie College of Osteopathic Medicine School of Pharmacy at Erie Campus, and Lake Erie College of Osteopathic Medicine School of Pharmacy at Bradenton Campus; occupational Therapy, Jefferson School of Health Professions, radiological sciences, Jefferson School of Health Professions; podiatric medicine with Temple University. **Credit/placement by examination:** AP, CLEP, IB, institutional tests. Unlimited number of hours of credit by examination may be counted toward degree. **Support services:** Reduced course load, study skills assistance, tutoring, writing center.

Majors. Biology: General, biochemistry. **Business:** Accounting, business admin, entrepreneurial studies, finance, human resources, information resources management, international, marketing. **Communications:** Communications/speech/rhetoric, digital media, health. **Computer sciences:** General, information technology. **Conservation:** Economics, environmental science, environmental studies. **Education:** General, biology, chemistry, early childhood special, English, environmental, mathematics, physics, science, social studies, Spanish. **Engineering:** Applied physics. **English:** English lit, technical writing. **Foreign languages:** General, French, German, Russian, Spanish. **History:** General. **Human services:** Social work. **Liberal arts:** Arts/sciences, humanities. **Math:** General. **Philosophy/religion:** Philosophy, religion. **Physical sciences:** Chemistry, geology, physics. **Psychology:** General. **Social sciences:** General, anthropology, economics, international relations, political science, sociology. **Visual/performing arts:** Art history/conservation, directing/producing, dramatic, studio arts.

Most popular majors, Biology 12%, business/marketing 6%, natural resources/environmental science 6%, physical sciences 7%, social sciences 43%.

Technology on campus. PC or laptop required. 170 workstations in library, computer center, student center. Dormitories wired for high-speed internet access and linked to campus network. Commuter students can connect to campus network. Online course registration, online library, helpline, repair service, wireless network available.

Student life. Freshman orientation: Available. Preregistration for classes offered. 2 days in summer, parallel programs for new students and their parents. **Housing:** Guaranteed on-campus for all undergraduates. Coed dorms, single-sex dorms, apartments available. $400 nonrefundable deposit, deadline 5/1. Special interest housing available. **Activities:** Bands, campus ministries, choral groups, dance, drama, international student organizations, music ensembles, Model UN, musical theater, radio station, student government, student newspaper, symphony orchestra, Habitat for Humanity, PRISM, Power Up Gambia, Muslim Student Association, Catholic Council, Circle K, Chinese club, College Against Cancer, Amigo de Guanin,.

Athletics. NCAA. **Intercollegiate:** Baseball M, basketball, cross-country, field hockey W, football (tackle) M, soccer, softball W, swimming W, tennis, track and field, volleyball. **Intramural:** Basketball, bowling, football (tackle), racquetball, soccer, swimming, volleyball. **Team name:** Eagles.

Student services. Adult student services, alcohol/substance abuse counseling, chaplain/spiritual director, career counseling, student employment services, financial aid counseling, health services, minority student services, personal counseling, placement for graduates. **Physically disabled:** Services for visually, hearing impaired.

Contact. E-mail: admissions@juniata.edu
Phone: (814) 641-3420 Toll-free number: (877) 586-4282
Fax: (814) 641-3100
Michelle Bartol, Dean of Admission, Juniata College, 1700 Moore Street, Huntingdon, PA 16652-2196

Keystone College
La Plume, Pennsylvania
www.keystone.edu

CB member
CB code: 2351

- Private 4-year business and liberal arts college
- Residential campus in rural community
- 1,360 degree-seeking undergraduates
- 98% of applicants admitted
- SAT or ACT (ACT writing optional), application essay required

General. Founded in 1868. Regionally accredited. **Degrees:** 270 bachelor's, 70 associate awarded; master's offered. **ROTC:** Army, Air Force. **Location:** Northeastern region of Pennsylvania; 15 miles from the city of Scranton. **Calendar:** Semester, limited summer session. **Full-time faculty:** 65 total; 77% have terminal degrees, 2% minority, 66% women. **Part-time faculty:** 168 total; 4% minority, 51% women. **Class size:** 73% < 20, 26% 20-39, less than 1% 40-49. **Special facilities:** Astronomical observatory, children's center, art gallery, restaurant operated by culinary students, conservancy, nature trails, maple sugar shack.

Freshman class profile. 999 applied, 977 admitted, 293 enrolled.

Mid 50% test scores		GPA 3.0-3.49:	27%
SAT critical reading:	400-510	GPA 2.0-2.99:	45%
SAT math:	400-500	Rank in top quarter:	17%
SAT writing:	380-480	Rank in top tenth:	5%
ACT composite:	16-22	Out-of-state:	29%
GPA 3.75 or higher:	7%	Live on campus:	61%
GPA 3.50-3.74:	18%		

Basis for selection. School achievement record, extracurricular activities, standardized test scores, recommendations, class rank, preparation in proposed major area of study considered. Portfolio and interview required for all art and art education applications. Admissions interview required for some on a case-by-case basis. **Home schooled:** Interview required. Portfolio of high school level work and homeschool supplement to the Common Application's secondary school report required. **Learning Disabled:** Current psychological report and Individualized Educational Program or 504 plan should be submitted at time of application. On-campus interview generally required to ensure that the college provides a level of support needed for the student to be academically successful.

High school preparation. College-preparatory program recommended. 16 units required; 23 recommended. Required and recommended units include English 4, mathematics 3, social studies 2, history 2, science 2-3 (laboratory 1), foreign language 2, computer science 1, visual/performing arts 1 and academic electives 4. Foreign language recommended for art, communications, and liberal arts curricula. 4 math and 3 science (including 2 lab) recommended for allied health, environmental sciences, biology, pre-medical tracks, and forensic biology.

2015-2016 Annual costs. Tuition/fees: $24,700. Room/board: $10,050. Books/supplies: $1,900. Personal expenses: $2,000.

Financial aid. Non-need-based: Scholarships awarded for academics, alumni affiliation, art.

Application procedures. Admission: Priority date 4/1; deadline 6/1 (receipt date). $30 fee, may be waived for applicants with need. Admission notification on a rolling basis beginning on or about 10/1. Must reply by May 1 or within 3 week(s) if notified thereafter. **Financial aid:** Priority date 4/1, closing date 5/1. FAFSA required. Applicants notified on a rolling basis starting 2/1; must reply within 3 week(s) of notification.

Academics. Students in good academic and financial standing who have not received at least 1 job offer or acceptance into a transfer or graduate program within 6 months after graduating and fulfilling requirements of Career Development Center will be provided with additional courses and career counseling at no extra charge. **Special study options:** Combined bachelor's/graduate degree, distance learning, double major, dual enrollment of high school students, ESL, honors, independent study, internships, semester at sea, study abroad, teacher certification program, weekend college. 2+2, 2+3, 3+3, 4+3 programs with various 4-year institutions and graduate programs for students studying allied health, health sciences, and environmental sciences. **Credit/placement by examination:** AP, CLEP, IB, SAT, ACT, institutional tests. 12 credit hours maximum toward associate degree, 18 toward bachelor's. Maximum of 32 credits for associate degree-seekers and 64 credits for bachelor's degree-seekers awarded for prior work and/or life experience. **Support services:** Learning center, reduced course load, remedial instruction, study skills assistance, tutoring, writing center.

Majors. Biology: General, environmental, wildlife. **Business:** Accounting, business admin, hospitality admin, organizational behavior. **Communications:** General. **Computer sciences:** Information technology. **Conservation:**

Management/policy. Education: Art, early childhood, early childhood special, English, mathematics, social studies. **Health services:** Prechiropractic, predental, premedicine, prepharmacy, prephysical therapy, preveterinary. **Parks/recreation:** Sports admin. **Physical sciences:** Geology. **Protective services:** Forensics, law enforcement admin. **Psychology:** General. **Social sciences:** General. **Visual/performing arts:** Studio arts. **Work/family studies:** General.

Most popular majors. Business/marketing 20%, communications/journalism 6%, education 10%, family/consumer sciences 6%, parks/recreation 10%, psychology 9%, security/protective services 12%, visual/performing arts 7%.

Technology on campus. 120 workstations in dormitories, library, computer center, student center. Dormitories wired for high-speed internet access and linked to campus network. Commuter students can connect to campus network. Online course registration, online library, helpline, repair service, wireless network available.

Student life. Freshman orientation: Mandatory, $150 fee. Preregistration for classes offered. One-day program during summer for scheduling classes. Three-day program on-campus prior to the start of classes. **Policies:** Alcohol and drug-free campus. **Housing:** Guaranteed on-campus for freshmen. Coed dorms, single-sex dorms, special housing for disabled, apartments, themed housing available. $200 fully refundable deposit, deadline 5/1. Independent living. **Activities:** Bands, campus ministries, choral groups, drama, international student organizations, literary magazine, music ensembles, musical theater, radio station, student government, student newspaper, Multicultural Affairs Student Association, Opposing Prejudice Ending Negativity, service club, Key Choices club, Winner's Circle.

Athletics. NCAA. **Intercollegiate:** Baseball M, basketball, cross-country, field hockey W, golf M, lacrosse, soccer, softball W, tennis, track and field, volleyball W. **Intramural:** Basketball, football (non-tackle), soccer, volleyball. **Team name:** Giants.

Student services. Adult student services, alcohol/substance abuse counseling, chaplain/spiritual director, career counseling, services for economically disadvantaged, student employment services, financial aid counseling, health services, minority student services, on-campus daycare, personal counseling, placement for graduates, veterans' counselor, women's services.

Contact. E-mail: admissions@keystone.edu
Phone: (570) 945-8111 Toll-free number: (800) 824-2764 ext. 1
Fax: (570) 945-7916
Kara Stone, Dean of Enrollment, Keystone College, One College Green, La Plume, PA 18440-1099

King's College
Wilkes-Barre, Pennsylvania
www.kings.edu

CB member
CB code: 2353

- Private 4-year business and liberal arts college affiliated with the Roman Catholic Church
- Residential campus in small city
- 1,859 degree-seeking undergraduates: 3% part-time, 47% women, 3% African American, 2% Asian American, 7% Hispanic/Latino, 2% Multiracial, non-Hispanic, 2% international
- 237 degree-seeking graduate students
- 72% of applicants admitted
- 66% graduate within 6 years; 25% enter graduate study

General. Founded in 1946. Regionally accredited. **Degrees:** 445 bachelor's awarded; master's offered. **ROTC:** Army, Air Force. **Location:** 110 miles from Philadelphia, 140 miles from New York City. **Calendar:** Semester, extensive summer session. **Full-time faculty:** 139 total; 87% have terminal degrees, 4% minority, 46% women. **Part-time faculty:** 77 total; 21% have terminal degrees, 49% women. **Class size:** 58% < 20, 42% 20-39, less than 1% 40-49, less than 1% 50-99. **Special facilities:** Rooftop greenhouse, molecular biology laboratory.

Freshman class profile. 3,244 applied, 2,322 admitted, 522 enrolled.

Mid 50% test scores		GPA 2.0-2.99:	21%
SAT critical reading:	460-550	Rank in top quarter:	42%
SAT math:	470-580	Rank in top tenth:	15%
SAT writing:	440-540	Return as sophomores:	72%
ACT composite:	20-24	Out-of-state:	35%
GPA 3.75 or higher:	35%	Live on campus:	69%
GPA 3.50-3.74:	9%	International:	2%
GPA 3.0-3.49:	34%		

Basis for selection. Class rank and academic GPA very important. Standardized test scores important. SAT or ACT recommended. Students may choose a standardized test option/essay choice in which an official graded writing sample from either junior or senior year is submitted and notarized by the high school guidance office. Students choosing this option are required to notify the Office of Admission on the application. A student's decision is non-reversible and must be made prior to application review. Interview recommended. **Home schooled:** Transcript of courses and grades, state high school equivalency certificate required. **Learning Disabled:** Must submit supplemental application with appropriate documentation, contact Director of Academic Skills Center.

High school preparation. College-preparatory program required. 16 units required; 24 recommended. Required and recommended units include English 4, mathematics 3-4, social studies 3, history 1, science 3-4 (laboratory 2), foreign language 2-4 and computer science 2.

2015-2016 Annual costs. Tuition/fees: $33,090. Room/board: $11,958.

2015-2016 Financial aid. Need-based: 498 full-time freshmen applied for aid; 434 deemed to have need; 434 received aid. Average need met was 71%. Average scholarship/grant was $19,092; average loan $3,471. 71% of total undergraduate aid awarded as scholarships/grants, 29% as loans/jobs. **Non-need-based:** Awarded to 466 full-time undergraduates, including 119 freshmen. Scholarships awarded for academics, leadership, ROTC. **Additional information:** Any minority student with financial need may receive some aid in the form of a diversity scholarship.

Application procedures. Admission: No deadline. $30 fee, may be waived for applicants with need, free for online applicants. Admission notification on a rolling basis beginning on or about 10/1. Must reply by May 1 or within 2 week(s) if notified thereafter. **Financial aid:** Priority date 2/15; no closing date. FAFSA required. Applicants notified on a rolling basis starting 3/1; must reply within 2 week(s) of notification.

Academics. Special study options: Accelerated study, cross-registration, distance learning, double major, dual enrollment of high school students, ESL, honors, independent study, internships, student-designed major, study abroad, teacher certification program, Washington semester, weekend college. Dual degree program in engineering with the University of Notre Dame. **Credit/placement by examination:** AP, CLEP, IB, SAT, ACT, institutional tests. 15 credit hours maximum toward associate degree, 30 toward bachelor's. **Support services:** Learning center, pre-admission summer program, reduced course load, study skills assistance, tutoring, writing center.

Majors. Biology: General, neuroscience. **Business:** Accounting, business admin, finance, human resources, international, marketing. **Communications:** Media studies. **Computer sciences:** General, computer science. **Conservation:** Environmental science, environmental studies. **Education:** Early childhood, elementary, special ed. **English:** English lit. **Foreign languages:** French, Spanish. **Health services:** Athletic training, clinical lab science, predental, premedicine, prepharmacy, preveterinary. **History:** General. **Math:** General. **Parks/recreation:** Exercise sciences. **Philosophy/religion:** Philosophy. **Physical sciences:** Chemistry, physics. **Protective services:** Criminal justice. **Psychology:** General. **Social sciences:** Economics, political science, sociology. **Theology:** Theology. **Visual/performing arts:** Dramatic.

Most popular majors. Biology 11%, business/marketing 31%, education 8%, health sciences 12%, psychology 6%, security/protective services 9%.

Technology on campus. 470 workstations in dormitories, library, computer center, student center. Dormitories wired for high-speed internet access and linked to campus network. Commuter students can connect to campus network. Online course registration, helpline, repair service, student web hosting, wireless network available.

Student life. Freshman orientation: Mandatory, $165 fee. Preregistration for classes offered. Held the 4 days prior to start of fall classes. **Housing:** Guaranteed on-campus for all undergraduates. Coed dorms, single-sex dorms, apartments available. $200 nonrefundable deposit. **Activities:** Campus ministries, choral groups, dance, drama, literary magazine, music ensembles, radio station, student government, student newspaper, association of campus events, organizations of various majors, Campion Society, Blood Council, Circle K, politics society, environmental awareness and outdoors club, residence hall council, service fraternity and sorority.

Athletics. NCAA. **Intercollegiate:** Baseball M, basketball, cross-country, field hockey W, football (tackle) M, golf M, lacrosse, soccer, softball W, swimming, tennis, track and field, volleyball W, wrestling M. **Intramural:** Basketball, football (non-tackle) M, soccer. **Team name:** Monarchs.

Student services. Adult student services, chaplain/spiritual director, career counseling, student employment services, financial aid counseling, health services, on-campus daycare, personal counseling, placement for graduates.

Contact. E-mail: admissions@kings.edu
Phone: (570) 208-5858 Toll-free number: (888) 546-4772
Fax: (570) 208-5971
James Anderson, Director of Admission, King's College, 133 North River Street, Wilkes-Barre, PA 18711

Kutztown University of Pennsylvania
Kutztown, Pennsylvania
www.kutztown.edu

CB member
CB code: 2653

- Public 4-year university
- Residential campus in small town
- 8,249 degree-seeking undergraduates: 5% part-time, 54% women, 8% African American, 1% Asian American, 7% Hispanic/Latino, 3% Multiracial, non-Hispanic, 1% international
- 667 degree-seeking graduate students
- 82% of applicants admitted
- SAT or ACT (ACT writing optional) required
- 54% graduate within 6 years; 21% enter graduate study

General. Founded in 1866. Regionally accredited. **Degrees:** 1,952 bachelor's awarded; master's offered. **ROTC:** Army. **Location:** 20 miles from Allentown and Reading. **Calendar:** Semester, extensive summer session. **Full-time faculty:** 417 total; 84% have terminal degrees, 18% minority, 50% women. **Part-time faculty:** 33 total; 33% have terminal degrees, 6% minority, 42% women. **Class size:** 26% < 20, 63% 20-39, 2% 40-49, 6% 50-99, 3% >100. **Special facilities:** Observatory, Pennsylvania German heritage cultural center, planetarium.

Freshman class profile. 8,023 applied, 6,599 admitted, 1,863 enrolled.

Mid 50% test scores			
SAT critical reading:	430-530	Rank in top quarter:	19%
SAT math:	430-520	Rank in top tenth:	5%
SAT writing:	410-510	End year in good standing:	70%
ACT composite:	17-22	Return as sophomores:	73%
GPA 3.75 or higher:	14%	Out-of-state:	14%
GPA 3.50-3.74:	16%	Live on campus:	92%
GPA 3.0-3.49:	32%	International:	1%
GPA 2.0-2.99:	38%	Fraternities:	4%
		Sororities:	15%

Basis for selection. School records and academic aptitude tests most important. Recommendations, essays, extracurricular activities considered. SAT Subject Tests (biology and chemistry) required for medical technology program. Audition required for music program; portfolio and/or art test required for art education, communication design, crafts, and fine arts programs. **Home schooled:** Applicants must submit supporting data from Pennsylvania Home Schooling Association.

High school preparation. College-preparatory program required. 13 units required. Required units include English 4, mathematics 3, social studies 3 and science 3. Course recommendations vary for specific programs.

2015-2016 Annual costs. Tuition/fees: $9,145; $19,735 out-of-state. Room/board: $9,070. Books/supplies: $1,107. Personal expenses: $2,600. **Additional information:** Out-of-State tuition is $10,590 for domestic out-of-state students with a high school GPA of at least 3.25 out of 4.0 and a combined Math and Critical Reading score on the SAT of at least 1,100. Tuition is $14,120 for domestic out-of-state students with a high school GPA of at least 3.0 out of 4.0 and a combined Math and Critical Reading score on the SAT of at least 1,000.

2014-2015 Financial aid. Need-based: 1,654 full-time freshmen applied for aid; 1,324 deemed to have need; 1,288 received aid. Average need met was 44%. Average scholarship/grant was $5,889; average loan $3,575. 31% of total undergraduate aid awarded as scholarships/grants, 69% as loans/jobs. **Non-need-based:** Awarded to 1,661 full-time undergraduates, including 914 freshmen. Scholarships awarded for academics, art, athletics, leadership, minority status, music/drama.

Application procedures. Admission: Priority date 12/1; no deadline. $35 fee, may be waived for applicants with need. Admission notification on a rolling basis beginning on or about 10/1. Must reply by 5/1. Must reply by May 1 or by date stated on notification letter. **Financial aid:** Priority date 3/1; no closing date. FAFSA required. Applicants notified on a rolling basis starting 3/30; must reply by 5/1 or within 4 week(s) of notification.

Academics. Special study options: Combined bachelor's/graduate degree, cross-registration, distance learning, double major, dual enrollment of high school students, honors, independent study, internships, liberal arts/career combination, student-designed major, study abroad, teacher certification program. **Credit/placement by examination:** AP, CLEP, IB, SAT, ACT, institutional tests. **Support services:** Learning center, pre-admission summer program, remedial instruction, study skills assistance, tutoring, writing center.

Majors. Area/ethnic studies: German. **Biology:** General, biochemistry. **Business:** Business admin. **Communications:** Digital media. **Computer sciences:** General. **Conservation:** Environmental science. **Education:** Art, early childhood, elementary special ed, middle, music, secondary, secondary special ed, special ed, visually handicapped. **English:** English lit. **Foreign**

languages: Spanish. **History:** General. **Human services:** General, social work. **Liberal arts:** Arts/sciences, library science. **Math:** General. **Parks/ recreation:** General. **Philosophy/religion:** Philosophy. **Physical sciences:** Chemistry, geology, oceanography, physics. **Protective services:** Criminal justice. **Psychology:** General. **Social sciences:** General, anthropology, geography, political science, sociology. **Visual/performing arts:** Commercial/ advertising art, crafts, digital arts, music, studio arts.

Most popular majors. Business/marketing 19%, education 14%, English 9%, psychology 11%, public administration/social services 6%, security/ protective services 6%, social sciences 6%, visual/performing arts 7%.

Technology on campus. 800 workstations in dormitories, library, computer center, student center. Dormitories wired for high-speed internet access and linked to campus network. Commuter students can connect to campus network. Online course registration, online library, helpline, student web hosting, wireless network available.

Student life. Freshman orientation: Mandatory. Preregistration for classes offered. 2-day, one overnight session in June, plus 1-day informational program preceding fall semester. **Policies:** No alcohol or drugs. **Housing:** Guaranteed on-campus for freshmen. Coed dorms, single-sex dorms, apartments, cooperative housing available. $75 nonrefundable deposit. **Activities:** Bands, campus ministries, choral groups, dance, drama, film society, international student organizations, literary magazine, music ensembles, Model UN, musical theater, radio station, student government, student newspaper, symphony orchestra, TV station, Student Alliance for Learning, Success and Achievement, black student union, Minority Achievement Coalition, Brothers and Sisters Seeking Excellence, Feminist Majority Leadership Alliance, Circle K, volunteer center, social work club.

Athletics. NCAA. **Intercollegiate:** Baseball M, basketball, bowling W, cheerleading W, cross-country, field hockey W, football (tackle) M, golf W, lacrosse W, soccer W, softball W, swimming W, tennis, track and field, volleyball W, wrestling M. **Intramural:** Basketball, football (non-tackle), racquetball, soccer, softball, table tennis, tennis, volleyball. **Team name:** Golden Bears.

Student services. Adult student services, alcohol/substance abuse counseling, career counseling, services for economically disadvantaged, student employment services, financial aid counseling, health services, minority student services, on-campus daycare, personal counseling, veterans' counselor, women's services. **Physically disabled:** Services for visually, speech, hearing impaired.

Contact. E-mail: admissions@kutztown.edu
Phone: (610) 683-4060 Toll-free number: (877) 628-1915
Fax: (610) 683-1375
Nancy Wunderly, Director of Admissions, Kutztown University of Pennsylvania, Admissions Office, Kutztown, PA 19530-0730

La Roche College
Pittsburgh, Pennsylvania   **CB member**
www.laroche.edu   **CB code: 2379**

- Private 4-year liberal arts college affiliated with the Roman Catholic Church
- Commuter campus in large city
- 1,359 degree-seeking undergraduates: 14% part-time, 55% women, 8% African American, 1% Asian American, 2% Hispanic/Latino, 2% Multiracial, non-Hispanic, 16% international
- 125 degree-seeking graduate students
- 95% of applicants admitted
- SAT or ACT (ACT writing optional) required
- 45% graduate within 6 years

General. Founded in 1963. Regionally accredited. Founded and sponsored by Sisters of Divine Providence. **Degrees:** 314 bachelor's, 20 associate awarded; master's offered. **ROTC:** Army, Air Force. **Calendar:** Semester, limited summer session. **Full-time faculty:** 62 total; 81% have terminal degrees, 11% minority, 58% women. **Part-time faculty:** 139 total; 24% have terminal degrees, less than 1% minority, 51% women. **Class size:** 62% < 20, 37% 20-39, less than 1% 40-49.

Freshman class profile. 1,167 applied, 1,114 admitted, 291 enrolled.

Mid 50% test scores			
SAT critical reading:	420-520	GPA 2.0-2.99:	26%
SAT math:	410-520	Rank in top quarter:	29%
SAT writing:	400-510	Rank in top tenth:	7%
ACT composite:	17-23	End year in good standing:	83%
GPA 3.75 or higher:	25%	Return as sophomores:	78%
GPA 3.50-3.74:	19%	Out-of-state:	19%
GPA 3.0-3.49:	29%	Live on campus:	73%
		International:	22%

Basis for selection. Depth and rigor of curriculum considered. Standardized test scores considered in relation to other factors. Recommendation from guidance counselor important. Extracurricular involvement considered. Essay, interview recommended.

High school preparation. College-preparatory program recommended. 15 units required; 21 recommended. Required and recommended units include English 4, mathematics 2-3, social studies 2, history 2, science 3-4 (laboratory 2-3), foreign language 2, computer science 1 and academic electives 2-3.

2015-2016 Annual costs. Tuition/fees: $26,250. Room/board: $10,630. Books/supplies: $1,200. Personal expenses: $1,530.

2015-2016 Financial aid. Need-based: 179 full-time freshmen applied for aid; 168 deemed to have need; 168 received aid. Average need met was 86%. Average scholarship/grant was $9,275; average loan $3,945. 60% of total undergraduate aid awarded as scholarships/grants, 40% as loans/jobs. **Non-need-based:** Awarded to 842 full-time undergraduates, including 179 freshmen. Scholarships awarded for academics.

Application procedures. Admission: No deadline. $50 fee, may be waived for applicants with need. Admission notification on a rolling basis beginning on or about 10/15. **Financial aid:** Priority date 5/1; no closing date. FAFSA required. Applicants notified on a rolling basis starting 2/15; must reply within 2 week(s) of notification.

Academics. Special study options: Accelerated study, combined bachelor's/graduate degree, cross-registration, distance learning, double major, dual enrollment of high school students, ESL, honors, independent study, internships, student-designed major, study abroad, teacher certification program. **Credit/placement by examination:** AP, CLEP, IB, institutional tests. 60 credit hours maximum toward bachelor's degree. **Support services:** Learning center, pre-admission summer program, reduced course load, remedial instruction, study skills assistance, tutoring, writing center.

Honors college/program. Minimum 3.5 high school GPA on a 4.0 scale in a college preparatory program and a minimum SAT score of 1100 (Math and Critical Reading) or an ACT score of 24.

Majors. Architecture: Interior. **Biology:** General, biochemistry. **Business:** Accounting, finance, international, management science, marketing. **Communications:** Media studies. **Computer sciences:** General, computer science, information technology. **Education:** Early childhood, English. **English:** English lit, writing. **Health services:** Medical radiologic technology/radiation therapy, nursing (RN). **History:** General. **Liberal arts:** Arts/sciences. **Math:** General. **Parks/recreation:** Exercise sciences. **Philosophy/religion:** Religion. **Physical sciences:** Chemistry. **Protective services:** Criminal justice. **Psychology:** General. **Social sciences:** International relations, national security policy, political science, sociology. **Visual/performing arts:** Dance, design, film/cinema/video. **Work/family studies:** Family/community services.

Most popular majors. Business/marketing 28%, computer/information sciences 7%, health sciences 20%, psychology 11%, security/protective services 7%.

Technology on campus. 200 workstations in library, computer center. Dormitories wired for high-speed internet access and linked to campus network. Commuter students can connect to campus network. Online course registration, online library, helpline, wireless network available.

Student life. Freshman orientation: Mandatory. Preregistration for classes offered. **Policies:** No alcohol permitted in residence halls. Smoking only in designated areas. **Housing:** Coed dorms available. $100 nonrefundable deposit, deadline 5/1. **Activities:** Campus ministries, choral groups, dance, drama, international student organizations, literary magazine, radio station, student government, student newspaper, professional organizations, environment club, black student coalition, African Student Forum, Rotaract club, community service, Asian club.

Athletics. NCAA. **Intercollegiate:** Baseball M, basketball, cross-country, golf M, lacrosse M, soccer, softball W, tennis W, volleyball W. **Intramural:** Basketball, racquetball, soccer, softball, table tennis, tennis, volleyball. **Team name:** Redhawks.

Student services. Adult student services, alcohol/substance abuse counseling, chaplain/spiritual director, career counseling, services for economically disadvantaged, student employment services, financial aid counseling, health services, minority student services, personal counseling, placement for graduates, veterans' counselor. **Physically disabled:** Services for visually impaired.

Contact. E-mail: admissions@laroche.edu
Phone: (412) 536-1271 Toll-free number: (800) 838-4572
Fax: (412) 536-1048
Terrance Kizina, Director of Admissions, La Roche College, 9000 Babcock Boulevard, Pittsburgh, PA 15237

La Salle University
Philadelphia, Pennsylvania
www.lasalle.edu

CB member
CB code: 2363

- Private 4-year university and liberal arts college affiliated with the Roman Catholic Church
- Residential campus in very large city
- 3,801 degree-seeking undergraduates: 12% part-time, 62% women, 18% African American, 5% Asian American, 10% Hispanic/Latino, 6% Multi-racial, non-Hispanic, 2% international
- 1,704 degree-seeking graduate students
- 75% of applicants admitted
- SAT or ACT (ACT writing optional), application essay required
- 63% graduate within 6 years

General. Founded in 1863. Regionally accredited. **Degrees:** 933 bachelor's, 39 associate awarded; master's, professional offered. **ROTC:** Army, Air Force. **Location:** 6 miles from Center City Philadelphia. **Calendar:** Semester, extensive summer session. **Full-time faculty:** 242 total; 84% have terminal degrees, 11% minority, 56% women. **Part-time faculty:** 197 total; 13% minority, 46% women. **Class size:** 48% < 20, 51% 20-39, 1% 40-49, less than 1% 50-99. **Special facilities:** Art museum, cable television station.

Freshman class profile. 6,163 applied, 4,606 admitted, 815 enrolled.

Mid 50% test scores		Rank in top quarter:	38%
SAT critical reading:	440-550	Rank in top tenth:	18%
SAT math:	450-550	Return as sophomores:	78%
ACT composite:	18-23	Out-of-state:	43%
GPA 3.75 or higher:	27%	Live on campus:	81%
GPA 3.50-3.74:	19%	International:	2%
GPA 3.0-3.49:	31%	Fraternities:	10%
GPA 2.0-2.99:	23%	Sororities:	15%

Basis for selection. Criteria include college preparatory high school curriculum, SAT and/or ACT score, involvement in extracurricular high school athletics/clubs/activities. Other factors include evidence of commitment and maturity. Interview recommended. **Home schooled:** Statement describing home school structure and mission required.

High school preparation. College-preparatory program required. 16 units required. Required units include English 4, mathematics 3, history 1, science 1 (laboratory 1), foreign language 2 and academic electives 5.

2015-2016 Annual costs. Tuition/fees: $41,100. Room/board: $14,490. Books/supplies: $1,000. Personal expenses: $1,000.

2014-2015 Financial aid. Need-based: 863 full-time freshmen applied for aid; 811 deemed to have need; 809 received aid. Average need met was 74%. Average scholarship/grant was $24,997; average loan $3,576. 73% of total undergraduate aid awarded as scholarships/grants, 27% as loans/jobs. **Non-need-based:** Awarded to 910 full-time undergraduates, including 199 freshmen. Scholarships awarded for academics, athletics, ROTC.

Application procedures. Admission: Priority date 11/15; no deadline. $35 fee, may be waived for applicants with need, free for online applicants. Admission notification on a rolling basis beginning on or about 12/15. Must reply by May 1 or within 2 week(s) if notified thereafter. **Financial aid:** Priority date 2/15; no closing date. FAFSA required. Applicants notified on a rolling basis starting 3/15; must reply by 5/1 or within 2 week(s) of notification.

Academics. Special study options: Accelerated study, combined bachelor's/graduate degree, cooperative education, cross-registration, double major, dual enrollment of high school students, ESL, honors, independent study, internships, study abroad, teacher certification program. 2+3 Program with Thomas Jefferson University in Medical Technology and Occupational Therapy. **Credit/placement by examination:** AP, CLEP, SAT, ACT, institutional tests. **Support services:** Pre-admission summer program, reduced course load, remedial instruction, study skills assistance, tutoring, writing center. Supplemental instruction, facilitated study groups, academic coaching, learning instruction, early alert system for students at risk, freshmen advising program, and academic skills workshops.

Honors college/program. Admission to the University Honors Program is typically offered to students who present a combined critical reading and math SAT score of 1200 or greater (ACT 26 or greater), and a cumulative high school GPA of 3.5 or greater. Approximately 600 students are offered admission to the University Honors Program. In their first year, students enter into a learning community, living together as they take the Freshman Triple-linked courses in history, literature, and philosophy. Upperclassmen build on this foundational liberal arts education through interdisciplinary electives and the honors project, a research project of the student's own design. Students in the freshman triple explore the educational and cultural offerings of Philadelphia through the weekly labs while upperclassmen explore the world through travel study courses and study abroad.

Majors. Area/ethnic studies: American, Russian/Eastern European/Eurasian. **Biology:** General, biochemistry. **Business:** General, accounting, business admin, finance, international, labor relations, management information systems, management science, marketing, organizational leadership. **Communications:** General. **Communications technology:** Desktop publishing, radio/TV. **Computer sciences:** Computer science, information technology. **Conservation:** Environmental science, environmental studies. **Education:** General, early childhood, elementary special ed, junior high special ed, middle, secondary. **English:** English lit. **Foreign languages:** French, German, Italian, Russian, Spanish. **Health services:** Clinical nutrition, communication disorders, nursing (RN), prenursing, speech pathology. **History:** General. **Human services:** General, social work. **Liberal arts:** Arts/sciences. **Math:** General. **Philosophy/religion:** Philosophy, religion. **Physical sciences:** Chemistry, geology. **Protective services:** Criminal justice. **Psychology:** General. **Social sciences:** Economics, international economics, international relations, political economy, political science, sociology, U.S. government. **Visual/performing arts:** Art history/conservation, digital arts.

Most popular majors. Business/marketing 24%, communications/journalism 8%, health sciences 34%, psychology 6%, social sciences 6%.

Technology on campus. 344 workstations in library, computer center, student center. Dormitories wired for high-speed internet access and linked to campus network. Commuter students can connect to campus network. Online course registration, online library, helpline, repair service, student web hosting, wireless network available.

Student life. Freshman orientation: Mandatory. Preregistration for classes offered. Incoming freshmen and their parents attend a one-day program offered on select dates during the summer prior to their enrollment. **Policies:** Freshmen not permitted cars on campus. **Housing:** Guaranteed on-campus for all undergraduates. Coed dorms, special housing for disabled, apartments, themed housing, wellness housing available. $200 nonrefundable deposit, deadline 5/1. Campus owned and operated townhouses available. **Activities:** Jazz band, campus ministries, choral groups, dance, drama, film society, international student organizations, literary magazine, musical theater, radio station, student government, student newspaper, TV station, American/Asian Student Intercultural Assoc, African American Student League, Cross Cultural Assoc, Caribbean Student Assoc, Organization of Latino-American Students, South Asian Student Alliance, College Republican, College Democrats, The Alliance, and Neighbor to Neighbor.

Athletics. NCAA. **Intercollegiate:** Baseball M, basketball, cheerleading, cross-country, diving, field hockey W, golf, lacrosse W, rowing (crew), soccer, softball W, swimming, tennis, track and field, volleyball W, water polo. **Intramural:** Basketball, football (non-tackle), rugby M, softball, volleyball. **Team name:** Explorers.

Student services. Adult student services, alcohol/substance abuse counseling, chaplain/spiritual director, career counseling, services for economically disadvantaged, student employment services, financial aid counseling, health services, minority student services, on-campus daycare, personal counseling, placement for graduates, veterans' counselor.

Contact. E-mail: admiss@lasalle.edu
Phone: (215) 951-1500 Toll-free number: (800) 328-1910
Fax: (215) 951-1656
James Plunkett, Executive Director of Admission, La Salle University, 1900 West Olney Avenue, Philadelphia, PA 19141-1199

Lafayette College
Easton, Pennsylvania
www.lafayette.edu

CB member
CB code: 2361

- Private 4-year engineering and liberal arts college
- Residential campus in large town
- 2,505 degree-seeking undergraduates: 1% part-time, 49% women, 5% African American, 4% Asian American, 6% Hispanic/Latino, 2% Multi-racial, non-Hispanic, 9% international
- 30% of applicants admitted
- SAT or ACT (ACT writing optional), application essay required
- 90% graduate within 6 years; 7% enter graduate study

General. Founded in 1826. Regionally accredited. **Degrees:** 615 bachelor's awarded. **ROTC:** Army. **Location:** 70 miles from New York City, 60 miles from Philadelphia. **Calendar:** Semester, limited summer session. **Full-time faculty:** 220 total; 98% have terminal degrees, 16% minority, 36% women. **Part-time faculty:** 59 total; 64% have terminal degrees, 7% minority, 39% women. **Class size:** 61% < 20, 37% 20-39, 1% 40-49, 1% 50-99. **Special facilities:** Advanced computer-aided design laboratory, satellite downlink capability, advanced language labs, 3-D printer, film and media production studio.

Freshman class profile. 7,465 applied, 2,258 admitted, 672 enrolled.

Mid 50% test scores		GPA 2.0-2.99:	6%
SAT critical reading:	580-670	Rank in top quarter:	93%
SAT math:	620-710	Rank in top tenth:	70%
SAT writing:	590-690	Return as sophomores:	95%
ACT composite:	27-31	Out-of-state:	81%
GPA 3.75 or higher:	29%	Live on campus:	100%
GPA 3.50-3.74:	25%	International:	11%
GPA 3.0-3.49:	40%		

Basis for selection. Academic performance, class rank, quality of courses taken, personal qualities, extracurricular record, recommendations, and standardized test results important. Special consideration to applicants who will contribute diversity to student body. SAT Subject Tests recommended. SAT Subject Tests, if submitted, may be considered for placement in math and foreign languages. Interview highly recommended for all and is expected for candidates interested in the Marquis Scholarship; portfolio recommended for art program.

High school preparation. College-preparatory program recommended. 18 units recommended. Recommended units include English 4, mathematics 3, science 2 (laboratory 2), foreign language 2 and academic electives 5. 4 math, chemistry, physics required of bachelor of science degree candidates.

2015-2016 Annual costs. Tuition/fees: $47,010. Room/board: $13,920. Books/supplies: $1,000.

2015-2016 Financial aid. Need-based: 389 full-time freshmen applied for aid; 204 deemed to have need; 204 received aid. Average need met was 100%. Average scholarship/grant was $39,316; average loan $4,438. 84% of total undergraduate aid awarded as scholarships/grants, 16% as loans/jobs. **Non-need-based:** Awarded to 583 full-time undergraduates, including 173 freshmen. Scholarships awarded for academics, athletics, leadership, ROTC. **Additional information:** Parent loans, up to $7,500 annually, available with college absorbing interest while student is enrolled. Family has 8 years after graduation to repay. Not limited to those demonstrating need.

Application procedures. Admission: Closing date 1/15 (postmark date). $65 fee, may be waived for applicants with need. Admission notification by 4/1. Must reply by 5/1. **Financial aid:** Priority date 1/15, closing date 3/1. FAFSA, CSS PROFILE required. Applicants notified by 4/1; must reply by 5/1.

Academics. Examples of students' self-designed interdisciplinary majors include Management Science, Studies in Human Rights, Asian Studies, Computational Biology, and Community Development among many others. Interdisciplinary minors also offered. **Special study options:** Cross-registration, double major, dual enrollment of high school students, exchange student, honors, independent study, internships, New York semester, semester at sea, student-designed major, study abroad, urban semester, Washington semester. Interim-session courses abroad and on campus. **Credit/placement by examination:** AP, CLEP, IB, institutional tests. **Support services:** Reduced course load, study skills assistance, tutoring, writing center.

Majors. Area/ethnic studies: African, American, Asian, Russian/Slavic. **Biology:** General, biochemistry, neuroscience. **Computer sciences:** General. **Engineering:** General, chemical, civil, electrical, mechanical. **English:** English lit. **Foreign languages:** French, German, Spanish. **History:** General. **Human services:** Public policy. **Math:** General. **Philosophy/religion:** Philosophy, religion. **Physical sciences:** Chemistry, geology, physics. **Psychology:** General. **Social sciences:** Anthropology, econometrics, economics, international economics, international relations, political science, sociology. **Visual/performing arts:** Art, music, music history, studio arts, theater arts management.

Most popular majors. Biology 12%, engineering/engineering technologies 19%, psychology 7%, social sciences 32%, visual/performing arts 7%.

Technology on campus. 600 workstations in library, computer center, student center. Dormitories wired for high-speed internet access and linked to campus network. Commuter students can connect to campus network. Online course registration, online library, helpline, repair service, student web hosting, wireless network available.

Student life. Freshman orientation: Mandatory. Preregistration for classes offered. 4-day program before fall classes begin. **Policies:** Freshmen not permitted cars on campus. **Housing:** Guaranteed on-campus for all undergraduates. Coed dorms, single-sex dorms, special housing for disabled, apartments, fraternity/sorority housing, themed housing, wellness housing available. Scholars houses, Hillel House, arts houses available. **Activities:** Bands, campus ministries, choral groups, dance, drama, film society, international student organizations, literary magazine, music ensembles, Model UN, musical theater, radio station, student government, student newspaper, symphony orchestra, TV station, Hillel Society, Muslim student association,

Newman Association, Association of Black Collegians, Association for Lafayette Feminists, Lafayette Environmental Awareness and Protection, College Democrats, College Republicans, Students for Social Justice.

Athletics. NCAA. **Intercollegiate:** Baseball M, basketball, cheerleading, cross-country, diving, fencing, field hockey W, football (tackle) M, golf, lacrosse, soccer, softball W, swimming, tennis, track and field, volleyball W. **Intramural:** Badminton, basketball, bowling, football (non-tackle), golf, racquetball, soccer, softball, squash, table tennis, tennis, volleyball, water polo. **Team name:** Leopards.

Student services. Adult student services, alcohol/substance abuse counseling, chaplain/spiritual director, career counseling, services for economically disadvantaged, student employment services, financial aid counseling, health services, minority student services, personal counseling, placement for graduates, women's services. **Physically disabled:** Services for visually, hearing impaired.

Contact. E-mail: admissions@lafayette.edu
Phone: (610) 330-5100 Fax: (610) 330-5355
Matthew Hyde, Director of Admissions, Lafayette College, 118 Markle Hall, Easton, PA 18042

Lancaster Bible College
Lancaster, Pennsylvania
www.lbc.edu   CB code: 2388

- Private 4-year Bible college affiliated with the nondenominational tradition
- Residential campus in small city
- 1,254 degree-seeking undergraduates
- SAT or ACT (ACT writing recommended), application essay required

General. Founded in 1933. Regionally accredited; also accredited by ABHE. **Degrees:** 262 bachelor's, 17 associate awarded; master's, doctoral offered. **Location:** 64 miles from Philadelphia. **Calendar:** Semester, limited summer session. **Full-time faculty:** 47 total. **Part-time faculty:** 61 total. **Class size:** 65% < 20, 29% 20-39, 5% 40-49, less than 1% 50-99.

Freshman class profile.

Out-of-state:	17%	Live on campus:	78%

Basis for selection. Application must include personal spiritual testimony, academic transcripts, SAT or ACT scores, and 3 references. Interview recommended for all; audition required for music program. **Home schooled:** Yearly evaluations should be included with application.

2015-2016 Annual costs. Tuition/fees: $19,980. Room/board: $8,350. Books/supplies: $1,000. Personal expenses: $1,500.

2015-2016 Financial aid. Need-based: 65% of total undergraduate aid awarded as scholarships/grants, 35% as loans/jobs. **Non-need-based:** Scholarships awarded for academics, alumni affiliation, leadership, music/drama.

Application procedures. Admission: Priority date 8/1; no deadline. $25 fee, may be waived for applicants with need. Admission notification on a rolling basis. **Financial aid:** Priority date 5/1; no closing date. FAFSA required. Applicants notified on a rolling basis starting 3/1; must reply within 3 week(s) of notification.

Academics. Special study options: Accelerated study, distance learning, double major, independent study, internships, study abroad, teacher certification program. **Credit/placement by examination:** AP, CLEP, SAT, ACT, institutional tests. 15 credit hours maximum toward associate degree, 30 toward bachelor's. **Support services:** Learning center, reduced course load, remedial instruction, study skills assistance, tutoring, writing center.

Majors. Education: Elementary, physical. **Theology:** Bible.

Most popular majors. Education 7%, theological studies 93%.

Technology on campus. 35 workstations in dormitories, library, computer center, student center. Dormitories wired for high-speed internet access and linked to campus network. Commuter students can connect to campus network. Online course registration, online library, helpline, repair service, wireless network available.

Student life. Freshman orientation: Mandatory, $239 fee. Preregistration for classes offered. 2 days prior to start of classes. **Policies:** Religious observance required. **Housing:** Guaranteed on-campus for freshmen. Single-sex dorms available. **Activities:** Bands, choral groups, drama, international student organizations, music ensembles, musical theater, student government, student newspaper, Christian Counseling Fellowship, married couples fellowship, Journey teams, student missionary fellowship, resident affairs council, commuter affairs council.

Athletics. NCAA, NCCAA. **Intercollegiate:** Baseball M, basketball, cheerleading, cross-country, lacrosse W, soccer, tennis, volleyball. **Intramural:** Basketball, football (non-tackle) M, soccer, softball, table tennis, tennis, volleyball. **Team name:** Chargers.

Student services. Chaplain/spiritual director, career counseling, student employment services, financial aid counseling, health services, personal counseling, placement for graduates.

Contact. E-mail: admissions@lbc.edu
Phone: (717) 560-8271 Toll-free number: (800) 544-7335
Fax: (717) 560-8213
David Burge, Director of Admissions, Lancaster Bible College, 901 Eden Road, Lancaster, PA 17601-5036

Lebanon Valley College
Annville, Pennsylvania
www.lvc.edu

CB member
CB code: 2364

- Private 4-year liberal arts college affiliated with the United Methodist Church
- Residential campus in small town
- 1,651 degree-seeking undergraduates: 3% part-time, 53% women, 3% African American, 2% Asian American, 5% Hispanic/Latino, 2% Multiracial, non-Hispanic
- 191 degree-seeking graduate students
- 72% of applicants admitted
- 74% graduate within 6 years; 29% enter graduate study

General. Founded in 1866. Regionally accredited. **Degrees:** 416 bachelor's awarded; master's, professional offered. **Location:** 7 miles from Hershey, 25 miles from Harrisburg. **Calendar:** Semester, limited summer session. **Full-time faculty:** 108 total; 89% have terminal degrees, 9% minority, 40% women. **Part-time faculty:** 135 total; 29% have terminal degrees, 4% minority, 50% women. **Class size:** 58% < 20, 39% 20-39, 2% 40-49, less than 1% 50-99. **Special facilities:** Audio and music production studios, biotechnology suite, microscopy suite, two greenhouses, biology wetlands, physical therapy and sports rehabilitation clinic, center for global education, art studios, learning resource center.

Freshman class profile. 3,329 applied, 2,413 admitted, 456 enrolled.

Mid 50% test scores			
SAT critical reading:	490-590	Rank in top quarter:	69%
SAT math:.	510-620	Rank in top tenth:	35%
SAT writing:	480-580	End year in good standing:	85%
ACT composite:	19-25	Out-of-state:	21%
		Live on campus:	88%

Basis for selection. Record of high school achievement in challenging college prep courses is most important. Recommendations, test scores (optional), school and community activities evaluated. Submission of standardized test scores is optional for all applicants. Interview recommended for all; audition required for music program.

High school preparation. College-preparatory program required. 16 units required. Required and recommended units include English 4, mathematics 3, social studies 3, history 2, science 3 (laboratory 2), foreign language 2-3 and academic electives 1.

2015-2016 Annual costs. Tuition/fees: $39,030. Room/board: $10,510. Books/supplies: $1,100. Personal expenses: $1,400.

2015-2016 Financial aid. Need-based: 444 full-time freshmen applied for aid; 420 deemed to have need; 420 received aid. Average need met was 83%. Average scholarship/grant was $25,445; average loan $3,984. 81% of total undergraduate aid awarded as scholarships/grants, 19% as loans/jobs. **Non-need-based:** Awarded to 358 full-time undergraduates, including 96 freshmen. Scholarships awarded for academics, alumni affiliation, music/drama.

Application procedures. Admission: Priority date 3/1; no deadline. No application fee. Application must be submitted online. Admission notification on a rolling basis beginning on or about 12/15. Must reply by May 1 or within 2 week(s) if notified thereafter. **Financial aid:** Priority date 3/1; no closing date. FAFSA required. Applicants notified on a rolling basis starting 3/1; must reply by 5/1 or within 2 week(s) of notification.

Academics. Special study options: Combined bachelor's/graduate degree, double major, dual enrollment of high school students, ESL, independent study, internships, liberal arts/career combination, student-designed major, study abroad, teacher certification program, urban semester, Washington semester. **Credit/placement by examination:** AP, CLEP, IB, institutional tests. 30 credit hours maximum toward bachelor's degree. **Support services:** Learning center, reduced course load, study skills assistance, tutoring, writing center.

Majors. Area/ethnic studies: American. **Biology:** General, Biochemistry/molecular biology, neuroscience. **Business:** Accounting, actuarial science, business admin. **Communications:** Digital media. **Communications technology:** Recording arts. **Computer sciences:** Computer science. **Education:** Early childhood, music, special ed. **English:** English lit. **Foreign languages:** French, German, Spanish. **Health services:** Clinical lab science, health care admin. **History:** General. **Math:** General. **Parks/recreation:** Exercise sciences. **Philosophy/religion:** Philosophy, religion. **Physical sciences:** Chemistry, physics. **Psychology:** General. **Social sciences:** Criminology, economics, political science, sociology. **Visual/performing arts:** Art, music management, music performance, music technology, studio arts.

Most popular majors. Biology 8%, business/marketing 13%, education 27%, health sciences 10%, psychology 8%, social sciences 9%, visual/performing arts 8%.

Technology on campus. 199 workstations in library, computer center, student center. Dormitories wired for high-speed internet access and linked to campus network. Commuter students can connect to campus network. Online course registration, online library, helpline, student web hosting, wireless network available.

Student life. Freshman orientation: Mandatory. Preregistration for classes offered. 2 programs in May and July; 3-day program in August. **Housing:** Guaranteed on-campus for all undergraduates. Coed dorms, special housing for disabled, apartments, themed housing, wellness housing available. Suite style and small houses available. **Activities:** Bands, campus ministries, choral groups, dance, drama, literary magazine, music ensembles, musical theater, student government, student newspaper, symphony orchestra, College Conservatives, College Democrats, Servants of Christ, Circle K, Colleges Against Cancer, Hispanic Alliance, LVC mini-thon, ASIA, Habitat for Humanity, Alpha Phi Omega.

Athletics. NCAA. **Intercollegiate:** Baseball M, basketball, cross-country, field hockey W, football (tackle) M, golf, ice hockey, lacrosse, soccer, softball W, swimming, tennis, track and field, volleyball W. **Intramural:** Basketball, football (non-tackle), volleyball. **Team name:** Flying Dutchmen.

Student services. Adult student services, alcohol/substance abuse counseling, chaplain/spiritual director, career counseling, student employment services, financial aid counseling, health services, minority student services, personal counseling, placement for graduates, women's services. **Physically disabled:** Services for visually, speech, hearing impaired.

Contact. E-mail: admission@lvc.edu
Phone: (717) 867-6181 Toll-free number: (866) 582-4236
Fax: (717) 867-6026
Edwin Wright, Vice President of Enrollment, Lebanon Valley College, 101 North College Avenue, Annville, PA 17003-1400

Lehigh University
Bethlehem, Pennsylvania
www.lehigh.edu

CB member
CB code: 2365

- Private 4-year university
- Residential campus in small city
- 5,054 degree-seeking undergraduates: 1% part-time, 44% women, 4% African American, 9% Asian American, 9% Hispanic/Latino, 3% Multiracial, non-Hispanic, 8% international
- 1,886 degree-seeking graduate students
- 30% of applicants admitted
- SAT or ACT with writing, application essay required
- 88% graduate within 6 years; 23% enter graduate study

General. Founded in 1865. Regionally accredited. **Degrees:** 1,232 bachelor's awarded; master's, doctoral offered. **ROTC:** Army. **Location:** 50 miles from Philadelphia, 75 miles from New York City. **Calendar:** Semester, limited summer session. **Full-time faculty:** 521 total; 96% have terminal degrees, 21% minority, 32% women. **Part-time faculty:** 160 total; 36% have terminal degrees, 12% minority, 49% women. **Class size:** 47% < 20, 36% 20-39, 5% 40-49, 9% 50-99, 3% >100. **Special facilities:** Two aberration-corrected electron microscopes, financial service laboratory, broadband seismic station, multi-directional experimental laboratory, electron optical labs, particle accelerator, rock climbing wall, golf driving range, STEPS green building.

Freshman class profile. 12,843 applied, 3,905 admitted, 1,261 enrolled.

Mid 50% test scores			
SAT critical reading:	590-680	Rank in top tenth:	60%
SAT math:	640-740	Return as sophomores:	95%
ACT composite:	29-32	Out-of-state:	75%
Rank in top quarter:	89%	Live on campus:	99%
		International:	10%

Basis for selection. Recommendations and school record very important. All submitted material considered. SAT Subject Tests recommended. Applicants whose native language is not English must take the TOEFL. Minimum target score of 570 on the paper-pencil test, or 90 on the Internet-based TOEFL is recommended for admission. IELTS results accepted in place of TOEFL with a recommended minimum score of 7.0. Students scoring 570 or higher on the Critical Reading section of the SAT not required to submit TOEFL/IELTS scores, but it is highly recommended. Campus visit recommended. **Home schooled:** Statement describing home school structure and mission, transcript of courses and grades, state high school equivalency certificate, letter of recommendation (nonparent) required.

High school preparation. 16 units required. Required units include English 4, mathematics 3, social studies 2, science 2 (laboratory 2), foreign language 2 and academic electives 3. Chemistry required, physics recommended for engineering and science candidates. Waivers in math granted by some departments to well-qualified candidates.

2015-2016 Annual costs. Tuition/fees: $46,230. Room/board: $12,280. Books/supplies: $1,000. Personal expenses: $1,065.

2015-2016 Financial aid. Need-based: 770 full-time freshmen applied for aid; 502 deemed to have need; 502 received aid. Average need met was 95%. Average scholarship/grant was $34,998; average loan $3,996. 84% of total undergraduate aid awarded as scholarships/grants, 16% as loans/jobs. **Non-need-based:** Awarded to 805 full-time undergraduates, including 193 freshmen. Scholarships awarded for academics, art, athletics, leadership, music/drama, ROTC. **Additional information:** Loans eliminated in financial aid packages for students eligible for financial aid and whose calculated total family income is less than $50,000. Loans limited to $3,000 in financial aid packages for students eligible for financial aid and who have a calculated total family income between $50,000 and $75,000.

Application procedures. Admission: Closing date 1/1 (postmark date). $70 fee, may be waived for applicants with need. Admission notification by 4/1. Must reply by 5/1. **Financial aid:** Closing date 2/15. FAFSA, CSS PROFILE required. Applicants notified by 3/30; must reply by 5/1 or within 3 week(s) of notification.

Academics. Special study options: Accelerated study, combined bachelor's/graduate degree, cooperative education, cross-registration, distance learning, double major, ESL, exchange student, external degree, honors, independent study, internships, liberal arts/career combination, study abroad, urban semester, Washington semester. **Credit/placement by examination:** AP, CLEP. **Support services:** Learning center, study skills assistance, tutoring, writing center.

Majors. Architecture: Architecture. **Area/ethnic studies:** African, Asian, women's. **Biology:** General, biochemistry, molecular, neuroscience. **Business:** Accounting, finance, logistics, management science, managerial economics, marketing. **Communications:** Journalism, technical/scientific. **Computer sciences:** Computer science, information technology. **Conservation:** Environmental studies. **Engineering:** Applied physics, biomedical, chemical, civil, computer, electrical, engineering mechanics, environmental, industrial, materials, mechanical. **English:** English lit. **Foreign languages:** Chinese, classics, French, German, Spanish. **History:** General. **Math:** General, applied, statistics. **Philosophy/religion:** Philosophy, religion. **Physical sciences:** Astronomy, astrophysics, chemistry, physics. **Psychology:** General. **Social sciences:** Anthropology, international relations, political science, sociology. **Visual/performing arts:** Art, art history/conservation, design, dramatic, music, music history.

Most popular majors. Biology 7%, business/marketing 29%, computer/information sciences 7%, engineering/engineering technologies 29%, social sciences 6%.

Technology on campus. 586 workstations in dormitories, library, computer center, student center. Dormitories wired for high-speed internet access and linked to campus network. Commuter students can connect to campus network. Online course registration, online library, helpline, repair service, student web hosting, wireless network available.

Student life. Freshman orientation: Mandatory, $306 fee. Preregistration for classes offered. 4-day program held prior to first day of classes. **Policies:** Freshmen not permitted cars on campus. **Housing:** Guaranteed on-campus for freshmen. Coed dorms, special housing for disabled, apartments, fraternity/sorority housing, gender-neutral housing, themed housing, wellness housing available. $500 nonrefundable deposit, deadline 5/1. **Activities:** Bands, campus ministries, choral groups, dance, drama, film society, international student organizations, literary magazine, music ensembles, Model UN, musical theater, radio station, student government, student newspaper, symphony orchestra, Global Union, Asian Cultural Society, Fellowship of Christian Athletes, Chinese cultural club, Black Students Union, Muslim Students Association, Student Senate, Best Buddies, Habitat for Humanity.

Athletics. NCAA. **Intercollegiate:** Baseball M, basketball, cross-country, diving, field hockey W, football (tackle) M, golf, lacrosse, rowing (crew) W, soccer, softball W, swimming, tennis, track and field, volleyball W, wrestling M. **Intramural:** Basketball, cross-country, football (non-tackle), soccer, softball, ultimate frisbee, volleyball. **Team name:** Mountain Hawks.

Student services. Alcohol/substance abuse counseling, chaplain/spiritual director, career counseling, student employment services, financial aid counseling, health services, minority student services, on-campus daycare, personal counseling, placement for graduates, women's services. **Physically disabled:** Services for visually, speech, hearing impaired.

Contact. E-mail: admissions@lehigh.edu
Phone: (610) 758-3100 Fax: (610) 758-4361
Bruce Bunnick, Director of Admissions, Lehigh University, 27 Memorial Drive West, Bethlehem, PA 18015

Lincoln University
Lincoln University, Pennsylvania   CB member
www.lincoln.edu   CB code: 2367

- Public 4-year university and liberal arts college
- Residential campus in small town
- 1,628 degree-seeking undergraduates: 5% part-time, 63% women
- 204 degree-seeking graduate students
- 91% of applicants admitted
- SAT or ACT (ACT writing optional) required
- 42% graduate within 6 years

General. Founded in 1854. Regionally accredited. **Degrees:** 265 bachelor's awarded; master's offered. **ROTC:** Army, Air Force. **Location:** 45 miles from Philadelphia; 55 miles from Baltimore. **Calendar:** Semester, limited summer session. **Full-time faculty:** 97 total; 80% have terminal degrees, 57% minority, 39% women. **Part-time faculty:** 54 total. **Class size:** 53% < 20, 45% 20-39, 1% 40-49. **Special facilities:** Museum.

Freshman class profile. 3,318 applied, 3,032 admitted, 455 enrolled.

Mid 50% test scores			
SAT critical reading:	370-470	GPA 3.0-3.49:	32%
SAT math:	370-460	GPA 2.0-2.99:	57%
SAT writing:	360-450	End year in good standing:	81%
ACT composite:	16-21	Return as sophomores:	77%
GPA 3.75 or higher:	2%	Out-of-state:	55%
GPA 3.50-3.74:	9%	Live on campus:	99%

Basis for selection. Admissions is based on secondary school record (or GED) and class rank; standardized test scores (SAT and/or ACT) and recommendations. Essay recommended. **Home schooled:** Statement describing home school structure and mission, transcript of courses and grades, state high school equivalency certificate, letter of recommendation (nonparent) required.

High school preparation. College-preparatory program recommended. 21 units required. Required units include English 4, mathematics 3, social studies 3, science 3 and academic electives 5. 2 units of arts and/or humanities required; 1 unit of health and physical education required.

2015-2016 Annual costs. Tuition/fees: $10,289; $15,081 out-of-state. Room/board: $8,904. Books/supplies: $2,000. Personal expenses: $1,280.

Financial aid. Non-need-based: Scholarships awarded for academics, alumni affiliation, leadership, music/drama.

Application procedures. Admission: Priority date 4/1; no deadline. $20 fee, may be waived for applicants with need. Admission notification on a rolling basis beginning on or about 2/15. **Financial aid:** Closing date 5/1. FAFSA required. Applicants notified on a rolling basis starting 4/1; must reply within 3 week(s) of notification.

Academics. Special study options: Exchange student, honors, independent study, internships, study abroad. **Credit/placement by examination:** AP, CLEP, IB, SAT, institutional tests. **Support services:** Learning center, reduced course load, remedial instruction, study skills assistance, tutoring, writing center.

Majors. Biology: General. **Business:** Accounting, business admin, finance, human resources. **Communications:** Broadcast journalism, communications/

speech/rhetoric, journalism. **Computer sciences:** General, information technology. **Conservation:** Environmental science. **Engineering:** General. **English:** English lit. **Foreign languages:** French, Spanish. **Health services:** Recreational therapy. **History:** General. **Human services:** General. **Math:** General. **Parks/recreation:** Health/fitness. **Philosophy/religion:** Philosophy, religion. **Physical sciences:** General, chemistry, physics. **Protective services:** Criminal justice. **Psychology:** General, industrial, psychobiology. **Social sciences:** Anthropology, economics, international relations, political science, sociology. **Visual/performing arts:** Music, studio arts.

Most popular majors. Biology 9%, business/marketing 13%, communications/journalism 6%, health sciences 8%, public administration/social services 12%, security/protective services 13%, social sciences 13%.

Technology on campus. 200 workstations in dormitories, library, computer center. Dormitories wired for high-speed internet access and linked to campus network. Commuter students can connect to campus network. Online course registration, online library, helpline, repair service, wireless network available.

Student life. Freshman orientation: Mandatory. Preregistration for classes offered. **Policies:** Freshmen not permitted cars on campus. **Housing:** Guaranteed on-campus for freshmen. Coed dorms, single-sex dorms, apartments available. $200 deposit. **Activities:** Bands, campus ministries, choral groups, dance, drama, international student organizations, music ensembles, Model UN, musical theater, opera, radio station, student government, student newspaper, TV station, International student association, Pre-law society, Pre-med club, Rotaract club, National Council of Negro Women, Phi Iota Sigma, Pi Sigma Alpha honor society, fashion club, religious organizations, social clubs.

Athletics. NCAA. **Intercollegiate:** Baseball M, basketball, cross-country, football (tackle) M, soccer W, softball W, track and field, volleyball W. **Intramural:** Baseball M, basketball, cheerleading W, football (non-tackle) M, softball, swimming, tennis, track and field, volleyball. **Team name:** Lions.

Student services. Alcohol/substance abuse counseling, chaplain/spiritual director, career counseling, student employment services, financial aid counseling, health services, personal counseling, placement for graduates, veterans' counselor, women's services.

Contact. E-mail: admissions@lincoln.edu
Phone: (484) 365-7206 Toll-free number: (800) 790-0191
Fax: (484) 365-8109
Kimberly Taylor-Benns, Associate Vice President for Enrollment Management, Lincoln University, 1570 Baltimore Pike, Lincoln University, PA 19352-0999

Lock Haven University of Pennsylvania

| Lock Haven, Pennsylvania | **CB member** |
| www.lhup.edu | **CB code: 2654** |

- Public 4-year university and liberal arts college
- Residential campus in small town
- 4,158 degree-seeking undergraduates: 7% part-time, 57% women, 9% African American, 1% Asian American, 2% Hispanic/Latino, 1% Multiracial, non-Hispanic, 1% international
- 378 degree-seeking graduate students
- 92% of applicants admitted
- SAT or ACT (ACT writing optional) required
- 50% graduate within 6 years

General. Founded in 1870. Regionally accredited. Branch campus in Clearfield. **Degrees:** 895 bachelor's, 81 associate awarded; master's offered. **ROTC:** Army. **Location:** 26 miles from Williamsport, 35 miles from State College. **Calendar:** Semester, limited summer session. **Full-time faculty:** 214 total; 14% minority, 50% women. **Part-time faculty:** 20 total; 5% minority, 65% women. **Class size:** 34% < 20, 45% 20-39, 11% 40-49, 10% 50-99, less than 1% >100. **Special facilities:** Rural retreat conference center, cadaver dissection laboratory, electron microscope, primate laboratory.

Freshman class profile. 3,415 applied, 3,133 admitted, 854 enrolled.

Mid 50% test scores		GPA 2.0-2.99:	27%
SAT critical reading:	420-520	Rank in top quarter:	29%
SAT math:	430-530	Rank in top tenth:	9%
SAT writing:	400-510	End year in good standing:	73%
ACT composite:	17-22	Return as sophomores:	70%
GPA 3.75 or higher:	20%	Out-of-state:	5%
GPA 3.50-3.74:	24%	Live on campus:	79%
GPA 3.0-3.49:	28%	International:	1%

Basis for selection. Course selection, grades received, and test scores most important. Preferred test score report date February 1. Interview required for nursing program; audition required for music programs. **Home schooled:** Provide as much documentation as possible.

High school preparation. College-preparatory program required. 16 units required; 21 recommended. Required and recommended units include English 4, mathematics 3-4, social studies 2, history 2, science 3-4 (laboratory 2-3) and foreign language 2. 4 units math required for math, computer science, biology, physics, and chemistry majors. 1 unit each biology, chemistry, physics required for health science majors. 1 unit each biology, anatomy and physiology, chemistry recommended for health and physical education majors.

2015-2016 Annual costs. Tuition/fees: $9,665; $18,255 out-of-state. Room/board: $9,344. Books/supplies: $1,313. Personal expenses: $2,575. **Additional information:** Out-of-State tuition is $14,120 for domestic out-of-state students with a high school GPA of at least 3.25 out of 4.0.

2015-2016 Financial aid. Need-based: 834 full-time freshmen applied for aid; 711 deemed to have need; 692 received aid. Average need met was 85%. Average scholarship/grant was $7,519; average loan $3,225. 56% of total undergraduate aid awarded as scholarships/grants, 44% as loans/jobs. **Non-need-based:** Awarded to 603 full-time undergraduates, including 283 freshmen. Scholarships awarded for academics, art, athletics, leadership, minority status, music/drama, ROTC, state residency.

Application procedures. Admission: Priority date 3/1; no deadline. $25 fee, may be waived for applicants with need. Admission notification on a rolling basis beginning on or about 10/1. Must reply by May 1 or within 2 week(s) if notified thereafter. **Financial aid:** Closing date 3/15. FAFSA required. Applicants notified on a rolling basis starting 3/15; must reply within 2 week(s) of notification.

Academics. Special study options: Cross-registration, distance learning, double major, dual enrollment of high school students, honors, independent study, internships, student-designed major, study abroad, teacher certification program. **Credit/placement by examination:** AP, CLEP, IB, SAT, institutional tests.

Majors. Biology: General. **Business:** Accounting, business admin. **Communications:** Media studies. **Computer sciences:** General. **Education:** Early childhood special, middle. **English:** English lit. **Foreign languages:** General. **Health services:** Athletic training, nursing (RN). **History:** General. **Human services:** Social work. **Liberal arts:** Arts/sciences. **Math:** General. **Parks/recreation:** Facilities management, sports admin. **Physical sciences:** Chemistry, geology, physics. **Protective services:** Law enforcement admin. **Psychology:** General. **Social sciences:** General, international relations, political science, sociology. **Visual/performing arts:** Art, dramatic, music, studio arts.

Most popular majors. Business/marketing 11%, education 6%, health sciences 17%, parks/recreation 17%, security/protective services 10%.

Technology on campus. PC or laptop required.

Student life. Freshman orientation: Available. Preregistration for classes offered. **Housing:** Coed dorms, apartments available. $100 nonrefundable deposit, deadline 5/1. **Activities:** Bands, campus ministries, choral groups, dance, drama, international student organizations, literary magazine, music ensembles, musical theater, radio station, student government, student newspaper, symphony orchestra, TV station.

Athletics. NCAA. **Intercollegiate:** Baseball M, basketball, boxing, cheerleading, cross-country, field hockey W, football (tackle) M, lacrosse W, soccer, softball W, swimming W, track and field, volleyball W, wrestling M. **Intramural:** Badminton, basketball, cross-country, field hockey W, golf, racquetball, skiing, soccer, softball, tennis, volleyball, water polo, wrestling M. **Team name:** Bald Eagles, Lady Eagles.

Contact. E-mail: admissions@lhup.edu
Phone: (570) 484-2027 Fax: (570) 484-2201
Donna Tatarka, Director of Admissions, Lock Haven University of Pennsylvania, LHU Office of Admissions, Lock Haven, PA 17745

Lycoming College

| Williamsport, Pennsylvania | **CB member** |
| www.lycoming.edu | **CB code: 2372** |

- Private 4-year liberal arts college affiliated with the United Methodist Church
- Residential campus in small city

- 1,260 degree-seeking undergraduates: 53% women, 9% African American, 1% Asian American, 6% Hispanic/Latino, 3% Multi-racial, non-Hispanic, 5% international
- 71% of applicants admitted
- Application essay required
- 64% graduate within 6 years

General. Founded in 1812. Regionally accredited. **Degrees:** 308 bachelor's awarded. **ROTC:** Army. **Location:** 90 miles from Harrisburg, 170 miles from Philadelphia. **Calendar:** Semester, limited summer session. **Full-time faculty:** 86 total; 96% have terminal degrees, 7% minority, 42% women. **Part-time faculty:** 36 total; 47% have terminal degrees, 3% minority, 47% women. **Class size:** 65% < 20, 31% 20-39, 2% 40-49, 2% 50-99. **Special facilities:** Science center and planetarium, clean water institute, graphics computer lab, polling institute.

Freshman class profile. 1,845 applied, 1,314 admitted, 347 enrolled.

Mid 50% test scores		GPA 2.0-2.99:	18%
SAT critical reading:	460-570	Rank in top quarter:	37%
SAT math:	460-570	Rank in top tenth:	17%
SAT writing:	440-540	Return as sophomores:	79%
ACT composite:	20-25	Out-of-state:	42%
GPA 3.75 or higher:	22%	Live on campus:	93%
GPA 3.50-3.74:	26%	International:	7%
GPA 3.0-3.49:	34%		

Basis for selection. Academic achievement as reflected in school record, class rank, and test scores most important. Curriculum, counselor and teacher recommendations also considered. SAT or ACT recommended. Interview recommended for all; portfolio recommended for art program and creative writing program; audition recommended for music and theater programs.

High school preparation. College-preparatory program required. 17 units required; 21 recommended. Required and recommended units include English 4, mathematics 3-4, social studies 3-4, science 3, foreign language 2-3 and academic electives 2-3.

2015-2016 Annual costs. Tuition/fees: $35,900. Room/board: $10,884. Books/supplies: $1,000. Personal expenses: $1,000.

2015-2016 Financial aid. **Need-based:** 318 full-time freshmen applied for aid; 301 deemed to have need; 301 received aid. Average met was 84%. Average scholarship/grant was $29,434; average loan $3,816. 81% of total undergraduate aid awarded as scholarships/grants, 19% as loans/jobs. **Non-need-based:** Awarded to 335 full-time undergraduates, including 85 freshmen. Scholarships awarded for academics, art, minority status, music/drama, ROTC.

Application procedures. **Admission:** Priority date 12/1; deadline 3/1 (receipt date). $35 fee, may be waived for applicants with need, free for online applicants. Admission notification on a rolling basis beginning on or about 12/15. Must reply by May 1 or within 4 week(s) if notified thereafter. **Financial aid:** Priority date 5/1; no closing date. FAFSA required. Applicants notified on a rolling basis starting 3/1; must reply by 5/1.

Academics. Teacher certification offered on elementary and secondary levels; special education certification as part of bachelor of arts program. **Special study options:** Accelerated study, combined bachelor's/graduate degree, cooperative education, cross-registration, double major, dual enrollment of high school students, exchange student, honors, independent study, internships, student-designed major, study abroad, teacher certification program, United Nations semester, urban semester, Washington semester. **Credit/placement by examination:** AP, CLEP, IB, institutional tests. 64 credit hours maximum toward bachelor's degree. **Support services:** Learning center, study skills assistance, tutoring, writing center.

Majors. **Area/ethnic studies:** American, women's. **Biology:** General, anatomy, ecology, molecular. **Business:** Accounting, actuarial science, business admin, communications, finance, international, international finance, managerial economics, marketing. **Communications:** General, communications/speech/rhetoric, digital media. **English:** Creative writing, English lit. **Foreign languages:** French, German, Spanish. **History:** General, American, European. **Math:** General. **Philosophy/religion:** Philosophy, religion. **Physical sciences:** Astronomy, astrophysics, chemistry, physics. **Protective services:** Criminal justice. **Psychology:** General. **Social sciences:** Archaeology, criminology, econometrics, economics, political science, sociology/anthropology. **Visual/performing arts:** General, acting, art, art history/conservation, commercial/advertising art, directing/producing, dramatic, music, painting, photography, printmaking, sculpture, studio arts.

Most popular majors. Biology 11%, business/marketing 21%, psychology 11%, social sciences 19%, visual/performing arts 8%.

Technology on campus. 180 workstations in library, computer center, student center. Dormitories wired for high-speed internet access and linked to campus network. Commuter students can connect to campus network. Online course registration, online library, helpline, repair service, student web hosting, wireless network available.

Student life. **Freshman orientation:** Mandatory, $225 fee. Preregistration for classes offered. 1-day event for students and parents; choose 1 of 3 dates in June. 5-day event for international students the week before classes begin. 3-day event for outer territory students and their parents the week before classes begin. 3-day event for all new students beginning on Friday leading up to the first day of classes. **Policies:** Students must live in college-owned residence halls or apartments. **Housing:** Guaranteed on-campus for all undergraduates. Coed dorms, single-sex dorms, special housing for disabled, apartments, fraternity/sorority housing, themed housing, wellness housing available. $100 nonrefundable deposit, deadline 5/1. Living-learning community, study-intensive housing, Creative Arts Society housing available. **Activities:** Bands, campus ministries, choral groups, dance, drama, film society, international student organizations, literary magazine, music ensembles, musical theater, radio station, student government, student newspaper, symphony orchestra, TV station, Circle K, Habitat for Humanity, College Democrats, College Republicans, environmental awareness foundation, Black Student Union, Big Brothers/Big Sisters, Colleges Against Cancer, Religious Experiences at Lycoming.

Athletics. NCAA. **Intercollegiate:** Basketball, cross-country, football (tackle) M, golf, lacrosse, soccer, softball W, swimming, tennis, volleyball W, wrestling M. **Intramural:** Basketball, football (non-tackle), soccer, ultimate frisbee, volleyball. **Team name:** Warriors.

Student services. Alcohol/substance abuse counseling, chaplain/spiritual director, career counseling, student employment services, financial aid counseling, health services, personal counseling, placement for graduates, women's services. **Physically disabled:** Services for visually, hearing impaired.

Contact. E-mail: admissions@lycoming.edu
Phone: (570) 321-4026 Toll-free number: (800) 345-3920 ext. 4026
Fax: (570) 321-4317
Mike Konopski, Vice President for Enrollment Management, Lycoming College, 700 College Place, Williamsport, PA 17701

Mansfield University of Pennsylvania
Mansfield, Pennsylvania
www.mansfield.edu   **CB code: 2655**

- Public 4-year university
- Residential campus in small town
- 2,194 degree-seeking undergraduates: 7% part-time, 59% women, 9% African American, 1% Asian American, 3% Hispanic/Latino, 2% Multi-racial, non-Hispanic
- 118 degree-seeking graduate students
- 86% of applicants admitted
- 50% graduate within 6 years

General. Founded in 1857. Regionally accredited. **Degrees:** 553 bachelor's, 38 associate awarded; master's offered. **ROTC:** Army. **Location:** 50 miles from Williamsport, 30 miles from Corning, New York. **Calendar:** Semester, limited summer session. **Full-time faculty:** 113 total; 83% have terminal degrees, 11% minority, 50% women. **Part-time faculty:** 44 total; 23% have terminal degrees, 4% minority, 61% women. **Class size:** 42% < 20, 43% 20-39, 8% 40-49, 7% 50-99, less than 1% >100. **Special facilities:** Planetarium, solar collector, science museum, animal collection, fisheries research boat, leadership institute.

Freshman class profile. 2,017 applied, 1,742 admitted, 416 enrolled.

Mid 50% test scores		GPA 2.0-2.99:	27%
SAT critical reading:	420-540	Rank in top quarter:	30%
SAT math:	430-530	Rank in top tenth:	9%
SAT writing:	390-510	Return as sophomores:	76%
GPA 3.75 or higher:	33%	Out-of-state:	15%
GPA 3.50-3.74:	11%	Live on campus:	81%
GPA 3.0-3.49:	28%		

Basis for selection. Class rank, high school curriculum, test scores important; counselor's recommendation, extracurricular activities considered. Special consideration given to applicants eligible for Equal Education Opportunity Program. Entry competitive in X-ray technology, respiratory therapy, fisheries, music, art programs, premed, nursing, biology, chemistry. Essay recommended for all; interview required for radiology program; audition required for music program; portfolio required for art program. **Home schooled:** Statement describing home school structure and mission, transcript of courses and grades required.

High school preparation. College-preparatory program recommended. 21 units required; 25 recommended. Required and recommended units include English 4, mathematics 3-4, history 4, science 2-3 (laboratory 2-3), foreign language 2-4 and academic electives 6.

2015-2016 Annual costs. Tuition/fees: $9,806; $20,396 out-of-state. Room/board: $11,912. Books/supplies: $1,600. Personal expenses: $950. **Additional information:** Out-of-State tuition is $11,650 for all out-of-state students from New York and New Jersey.

2014-2015 Financial aid. Need-based: 557 full-time freshmen applied for aid; 485 deemed to have need; 485 received aid. Average need met was 93%. Average scholarship/grant was $2,721; average loan $2,286. 49% of total undergraduate aid awarded as scholarships/grants, 51% as loans/jobs. **Non-need-based:** Awarded to 783 full-time undergraduates, including 365 freshmen. Scholarships awarded for academics, alumni affiliation, art, athletics, job skills, leadership, minority status, music/drama, religious affiliation, ROTC, state residency.

Application procedures. Admission: Priority date 11/30; no deadline. $25 fee, may be waived for applicants with need. Admission notification on a rolling basis beginning on or about 8/1. Must reply by May 1 or within 2 week(s) if notified thereafter. Applicants to competitive programs should apply by January 15. **Financial aid:** Priority date 2/15, closing date 6/30. FAFSA required. Applicants notified on a rolling basis starting 2/17; must reply within 4 week(s) of notification.

Academics. Special study options: Cross-registration, distance learning, double major, dual enrollment of high school students, ESL, exchange student, honors, independent study, internships, liberal arts/career combination, student-designed major, study abroad, teacher certification program. Online programs. **Credit/placement by examination:** AP, CLEP, IB, SAT, ACT, institutional tests. **Support services:** Learning center, pre-admission summer program, reduced course load, remedial instruction, study skills assistance, tutoring, writing center.

Majors. Biology: General. **Business:** Business admin. **Communications:** Communications/speech/rhetoric, media studies. **Computer sciences:** General. **Conservation:** Environmental studies. **Education:** Early childhood, history, music, social studies, special ed. **English:** English lit. **Health services:** Clinical nutrition, community health, nursing (RN). **History:** General. **Human services:** Social work. **Liberal arts:** Arts/sciences. **Math:** General. **Philosophy/religion:** Philosophy. **Physical sciences:** Chemistry. **Protective services:** Law enforcement admin. **Psychology:** General. **Social sciences:** Political science. **Visual/performing arts:** Art history/conservation, graphic design, music, music management, music performance, piano/keyboard, voice/opera.

Most popular majors. Business/marketing 9%, health sciences 13%, liberal arts 8%, psychology 7%, public administration/social services 6%, security/protective services 10%, social sciences 12%, visual/performing arts 14%.

Technology on campus. 840 workstations in dormitories, library, computer center, student center. Dormitories wired for high-speed internet access and linked to campus network. Commuter students can connect to campus network. Online course registration, online library, helpline, wireless network available.

Student life. Freshman orientation: Mandatory, $65 fee. Preregistration for classes offered. **Housing:** Guaranteed on-campus for all undergraduates. Coed dorms, fraternity/sorority housing available. $200 nonrefundable deposit. **Activities:** Bands, campus ministries, choral groups, dance, drama, international student organizations, literary magazine, music ensembles, musical theater, radio station, student government, student newspaper, symphony orchestra, TV station, Black Awareness Association, Inter-Varsity Christian Fellowship, Commonwealth Association of Students.

Athletics. NCAA. **Intercollegiate:** Baseball M, basketball, cross-country, diving W, field hockey W, football (tackle) M, soccer W, softball W, swimming W, track and field. **Intramural:** Basketball, football (non-tackle) M, racquetball, soccer, softball, tennis, ultimate frisbee, volleyball, water polo. **Team name:** Mounties.

Student services. Adult student services, alcohol/substance abuse counseling, chaplain/spiritual director, career counseling, services for economically disadvantaged, student employment services, financial aid counseling, health services, minority student services, on-campus daycare, personal counseling, placement for graduates, veterans' counselor, women's services. **Physically disabled:** Services for visually, speech, hearing impaired.

Contact. E-mail: admissions@mansfield.edu
Phone: (570) 662-4243 Toll-free number: (800) 577-6826
Fax: (570) 662-4121
Rachel Green, Admissions Director, Mansfield University of Pennsylvania, 71 Academy Street, Mansfield, PA 16933

Marywood University
Scranton, Pennsylvania **CB member**
www.marywood.edu **CB code: 2407**

♦ Private 4-year university affiliated with the Roman Catholic Church
♦ Residential campus in small city
♦ 1,817 degree-seeking undergraduates: 5% part-time, 68% women, 2% African American, 2% Asian American, 6% Hispanic/Latino, 2% Multiracial, non-Hispanic, 1% international
♦ 1,041 degree-seeking graduate students
♦ 67% of applicants admitted
♦ SAT or ACT (ACT writing optional), application essay required
♦ 70% graduate within 6 years; 38% enter graduate study

General. Founded in 1915. Regionally accredited. Institution has four colleges and three schools: Insalaco College of Creative and Performing Arts, Reap College of Education and Human Development, College of Health and Human Services, Munley College of Liberal Arts and Sciences, the School of Architecture, the School of Business, the School of Social Work and the Center for Interdisciplinary Studies. **Degrees:** 478 bachelor's awarded; master's, professional, doctoral offered. **ROTC:** Army, Air Force. **Location:** 110 miles from Philadelphia, 120 miles from New York City. **Calendar:** Semester, extensive summer session. **Full-time faculty:** 160 total; 91% have terminal degrees, 14% minority, 56% women. **Part-time faculty:** 244 total; 6% minority. **Class size:** 57% < 20, 40% 20-39, 2% 40-49, less than 1% 50-99. **Special facilities:** Human physiology lab, human development laboratories, biotechnology lab, communication sciences and disorders clinic, nutrition and dietetics lab, learning technology center, outpatient mental health clinic, "smart" classrooms, computer labs, center for architectural studies studios, television studio and editing suites, radio station and studio, studio arts center, visual arts center, performance theater, black box theater, arena, fitness center, NCAA regulation competition pool and aquatic center, dance/aerobics studio, hydro-therapy room.

Freshman class profile. 2,389 applied, 1,602 admitted, 376 enrolled.

Mid 50% test scores			
SAT critical reading:	460-560	Rank in top quarter:	48%
SAT math:	470-560	Rank in top tenth:	13%
SAT writing:	450-550	Return as sophomores:	83%
GPA 3.75 or higher:	19%	Out-of-state:	34%
GPA 3.50-3.74:	40%	Live on campus:	63%
GPA 3.0-3.49:	34%	International:	2%
GPA 2.0-2.99:	7%	Sororities:	2%

Basis for selection. Class rank, high school achievement weighed alongside SAT/ACT scores. Course selection, achievement outside classroom, involvement in activities in and out of school, and letters of recommendations also considered. TOEFL or IELTS used for admission of non-native English speakers. Applicants are expected to be graduates of an accredited secondary school or have the GED. A minimum of 17 academic credits is required, including 4 in English, 3 each in Social Studies and Science (1 as lab), 2 in Mathematics and 6 academic electives. A letter of support is required in selected majors, as is a portfolio or an audition where appropriate. A personal interview is strongly recommended. Students wishing to major in art must submit a portfolio. Music students required to audition. **Home schooled:** Transcript of courses and grades, letter of recommendation (nonparent) required. **Learning Disabled:** Students may request accommodation by submitting documentation to admissions office or coordinator of services for students with disabilities.

High school preparation. College-preparatory program recommended. Required units include English 4, mathematics 2, social studies 3, science 1 (laboratory 1) and academic electives 6. Biological science must be laboratory science.

2015-2016 Annual costs. Tuition/fees: $32,692. Room/board: $13,900. Books/supplies: $1,000. Personal expenses: $700.

2015-2016 Financial aid. Need-based: 346 full-time freshmen applied for aid; 309 deemed to have need; 307 received aid. Average need met was 83%. Average scholarship/grant was $22,362; average loan $3,637. 71% of total undergraduate aid awarded as scholarships/grants, 29% as loans/jobs. **Non-need-based:** Awarded to 438 full-time undergraduates, including 96 freshmen. Scholarships awarded for academics, alumni affiliation, art, leadership, music/drama, ROTC.

Application procedures. Admission: No deadline. $35 fee, may be waived for applicants with need, free for online applicants. Admission notification on a rolling basis beginning on or about 9/1. Must reply by May 1 or within 2 week(s) if notified thereafter. Students applying for early admission must submit letter from their high school principal recommending them for early admission. **Financial aid:** Priority date 2/15; no closing date. FAFSA required. Applicants notified by 3/15; Applicants notified on a rolling basis starting 3/15; must reply by 5/1 or within 3 week(s) of notification.

Academics. Healthy Family Center provides opportunities for study and research in nutrition, dietetics, and athletic performance; Center for Athletics and Wellness provides full support for athletic training program. **Special study options:** Combined bachelor's/graduate degree, cross-registration, distance learning, double major, dual enrollment of high school students, ESL, honors, independent study, internships, student-designed major, study abroad, teacher certification program. Students may study in any accredited school in any country that is approved by Marywood, or Marywood also has faculty-led, short-term study abroad programs. **Credit/placement by examination:** AP, CLEP, IB. 66 credit hours maximum toward bachelor's degree. **Support services:** Learning center, pre-admission summer program, reduced course load, study skills assistance, tutoring, writing center.

Majors. **Architecture:** Architecture, environmental design. **Biology:** General, biotechnology. **Business:** Accounting, business admin, financial planning, hospitality admin, international, marketing. **Communications:** Broadcast journalism, digital media. **Computer sciences:** Computer science, security. **Conservation:** Environmental science. **Education:** Art, biology, elementary, English, mathematics, music, physical, science, secondary, social science, Spanish, special ed. **English:** English lit. **Foreign languages:** Spanish. **Health services:** Art therapy, athletic training, audiology/speech pathology, clinical lab science, dietetics, health care admin, music therapy, nursing (RN). **History:** General. **Human services:** Social work. **Math:** General. **Parks/recreation:** Health/fitness. **Philosophy/religion:** Philosophy, religion. **Protective services:** Criminal justice. **Psychology:** General, industrial. **Social sciences:** General, sociology. **Visual/performing arts:** Art history/conservation, ceramics, dramatic, graphic design, illustration, interior design, music performance, musical theater, painting, photography, sculpture, studio arts, studio arts management.

Most popular majors. Biology 7%, business/marketing 14%, education 7%, health sciences 24%, psychology 9%, visual/performing arts 11%.

Technology on campus. Dormitories wired for high-speed internet access and linked to campus network. Commuter students can connect to campus network. Online course registration, online library, helpline, student web hosting, wireless network available.

Student life. **Freshman orientation:** Available, $225 fee. Preregistration for classes offered. 2-day program held in July, for student and family. Additional 2-day program prior to start of classes. **Policies:** First- and second-year students under 21 not living at home with families in area required to live on campus. **Housing:** Guaranteed on-campus for freshmen. Coed dorms, special housing for disabled, apartments, themed housing available. $300 nonrefundable deposit. **Activities:** Bands, campus ministries, choral groups, dance, drama, international student organizations, literary magazine, music ensembles, musical theater, opera, radio station, student government, student newspaper, symphony orchestra, TV station, environmental club, volunteers in action, peer educators, education club, criminal justice club, social work club, students to uphold life, Irish dancers club, diversity united, politically active students united.

Athletics. NCAA. **Intercollegiate:** Baseball M, basketball, cross-country, diving, field hockey W, golf, lacrosse, soccer, softball W, swimming, tennis, track and field, volleyball W. **Intramural:** Badminton, basketball, football (non-tackle), racquetball, soccer, softball, table tennis, tennis, volleyball, water polo. **Team name:** Pacers.

Student services. Adult student services, alcohol/substance abuse counseling, chaplain/spiritual director, career counseling, services for economically disadvantaged, student employment services, financial aid counseling, health services, minority student services, on-campus daycare, personal counseling, veterans' counselor, women's services. **Physically disabled:** Services for visually, speech, hearing impaired.

Contact. E-mail: yourfuture@marywood.edu
Phone: (570) 348-6234 Toll-free number: (866) 279-9663
Fax: (570) 961-4763
Christian DiGregorio, Director of University Admissions, Marywood University, 2300 Adams Avenue, Scranton, PA 18509-1598

Mercyhurst University
Erie, Pennsylvania
www.mercyhurst.edu

CB member
CB code: 2410

◗ Private 4-year university and liberal arts college affiliated with the Roman Catholic Church
◗ Residential campus in small city
◗ 2,457 degree-seeking undergraduates

◗ 80% of applicants admitted
◗ Application essay required

General. Founded in 1926. Regionally accredited. **Degrees:** 564 bachelor's awarded; master's offered. **ROTC:** Army. **Location:** 100 miles from Pittsburgh, 90 miles from Buffalo, NY. **Calendar:** 4-1-4, limited summer session. **Full-time faculty:** 201 total; 54% have terminal degrees, 7% minority, 50% women. **Part-time faculty:** 115 total; 6% have terminal degrees, 6% minority, 47% women. **Class size:** 60% < 20, 39% 20-39, less than 1% 40-49. **Special facilities:** Observatory, archaeological materials preservation laboratory, principal center for forensic geoarchaeological studies for various federal agencies managing Archaeological Resources Protection Act cases.

Freshman class profile. 2,749 applied, 2,210 admitted, 606 enrolled.

GPA 3.75 or higher:	27%	Rank in top quarter:	16%
GPA 3.50-3.74:	15%	Rank in top tenth:	15%
GPA 3.0-3.49:	38%	Out-of-state:	56%
GPA 2.0-2.99:	20%	Live on campus:	91%

Basis for selection. Admissions based on secondary school record. Class rank, standardized test scores, talent, ability, character, and personal qualities also important. Audition required for dance and music programs; portfolio required for art program. **Home schooled:** SAT/ACT and transcript preferred.

High school preparation. College-preparatory program recommended. 16 units required; 21 recommended. Required and recommended units include English 4, mathematics 2-4, social studies 5, science 2-3 (laboratory 1-2) and foreign language 2-3.

2015-2016 Annual costs. Tuition/fees: $33,314. Room/board: $11,232. Books/supplies: $1,200. Personal expenses: $811.

Financial aid. **Non-need-based:** Scholarships awarded for academics, alumni affiliation, art, athletics, leadership, minority status, music/drama, religious affiliation, ROTC.

Application procedures. **Admission:** Priority date 3/15; no deadline. No application fee. Admission notification on a rolling basis beginning on or about 11/15. Must reply by May 1 or within 3 week(s) if notified thereafter. **Financial aid:** Priority date 3/1; no closing date. FAFSA required. Applicants notified on a rolling basis starting 2/15; must reply by 5/1 or within 2 week(s) of notification.

Academics. Education department offers graduate student-taught special education programs for learning disabled students. Asperger Initiative program offered. **Special study options:** Combined bachelor's/graduate degree, cross-registration, distance learning, double major, ESL, honors, independent study, internships, liberal arts/career combination, New York semester, semester at sea, student-designed major, study abroad, teacher certification program, Washington semester. **Credit/placement by examination:** AP, CLEP, IB, SAT, ACT, institutional tests. 30 credit hours maximum toward bachelor's degree. **Support services:** Learning center, pre-admission summer program, reduced course load, remedial instruction, study skills assistance, tutoring, writing center.

Majors. **Area/ethnic studies:** Russian/Slavic. **Biology:** General, biochemistry, exercise physiology. **Business:** Accounting, business admin, fashion, finance, hospitality admin, human resources, international, managerial economics, market research, marketing. **Communications:** Communications/speech/rhetoric. **Computer sciences:** General. **Education:** Art, biology, business, chemistry, early childhood, elementary, English, foreign languages, mathematics, music, science, secondary, social science, special ed. **English:** English lit. **Foreign languages:** General, French, Spanish. **Health services:** Art therapy, athletic training, health information technology, nursing (RN), prechiropractic, predental, premedicine, preoccupational therapy, prepharmacy, prephysical therapy, preveterinary. **History:** General. **Human services:** Health policy, social work. **Liberal arts:** Arts/sciences. **Math:** General. **Military:** "intel, generally". **Philosophy/religion:** Philosophy, religion. **Physical sciences:** Chemistry, geology. **Protective services:** Criminal justice, forensics. **Psychology:** General, behavior analysis. **Social sciences:** Anthropology, political science, sociology. **Theology:** Religious ed. **Visual/performing arts:** Dance, graphic design, interior design, music, music performance, studio arts.

Most popular majors. Biology 9%, business/marketing 21%, education 7%, health sciences 9%, interdisciplinary studies 14%, security/protective services 8%, visual/performing arts 8%.

Technology on campus. 375 workstations in dormitories, library, computer center, student center. Dormitories wired for high-speed internet access and linked to campus network. Commuter students can connect to campus network. Online course registration, online library, helpline, repair service, student web hosting, wireless network available.

Student life. **Freshman orientation:** Mandatory, $150 fee. Preregistration for classes offered. 3 days prior to start of classes. **Policies:** Freshmen not permitted cars on campus. **Housing:** Guaranteed on-campus for all undergraduates. Coed dorms, single-sex dorms, apartments, wellness housing available. $350 fully refundable deposit, deadline 8/1. **Activities:** Bands, campus ministries, choral groups, dance, drama, international student organizations, literary magazine, music ensembles, Model UN, musical theater, opera, radio station, student government, student newspaper, symphony orchestra, Association of Black Collegians, Habitat for Humanity, Amnesty International, ambassadors club.

Athletics. NCAA. **Intercollegiate:** Baseball M, basketball, cheerleading, cross-country, field hockey W, football (tackle) M, golf, ice hockey, lacrosse, rowing (crew), soccer, softball W, tennis, volleyball W, water polo, wrestling M. **Intramural:** Basketball, bowling, football (non-tackle) M, ice hockey, skiing, soccer, softball, ultimate frisbee. **Team name:** Lakers.

Student services. Adult student services, alcohol/substance abuse counseling, chaplain/spiritual director, career counseling, services for economically disadvantaged, student employment services, financial aid counseling, health services, personal counseling, placement for graduates, veterans' counselor. **Physically disabled:** Services for hearing impaired.

Contact. E-mail: admissions@mercyhurst.edu
Phone: (814) 824-2202 Toll-free number: (800) 825-1926
Fax: (814) 824-2071
Christian Byer, Director of Undergraduate Admissions, Mercyhurst University, 501 East 38th Street, Erie, PA 16546-0001

Messiah College
Mechanicsburg, Pennsylvania — CB member
www.messiah.edu — CB code: 2411

- Private 4-year liberal arts college affiliated with the interdenominational tradition
- Residential campus in small town
- 2,723 degree-seeking undergraduates: 2% part-time, 61% women, 3% African American, 2% Asian American, 4% Hispanic/Latino, 3% Multiracial, non-Hispanic, 4% international
- 482 degree-seeking graduate students
- 79% of applicants admitted
- SAT or ACT (ACT writing optional), application essay required
- 77% graduate within 6 years; 15% enter graduate study

General. Founded in 1909. Regionally accredited. **Degrees:** 632 bachelor's awarded; master's, professional offered. **Location:** 10 miles from Harrisburg, 20 miles from Gettysburg. **Calendar:** Semester, limited summer session. **Full-time faculty:** 192 total; 81% have terminal degrees, 7% minority, 42% women. **Part-time faculty:** 149 total; 18% have terminal degrees, 5% minority, 60% women. **Class size:** 46% < 20, 51% 20-39, 2% 40-49, 1% 50-99, less than 1% >100. **Special facilities:** Historical library and archives, natural history museum, service and learning center, community-supported agriculture, solar panel array and pavilion.

Freshman class profile. 2,469 applied, 1,950 admitted, 691 enrolled.

Mid 50% test scores		GPA 2.0-2.99:	5%
SAT critical reading:	500-620	Rank in top quarter:	63%
SAT math:	510-630	Rank in top tenth:	32%
SAT writing:	490-600	End year in good standing:	98%
ACT composite:	21-28	Return as sophomores:	88%
GPA 3.75 or higher:	59%	Out-of-state:	38%
GPA 3.50-3.74:	18%	Live on campus:	96%
GPA 3.0-3.49:	18%	International:	4%

Basis for selection. Admitted students normally in top third of class and have B average or better. **Home schooled:** Comprehensive transcript of senior year academic program as well as courses and course evaluations of 9th through 11th grades required. Include independent evaluation by qualified educator if available. **Learning Disabled:** After admitted, documentation required to qualify for disability services.

High school preparation. College-preparatory program required. 16 units required; 20 recommended. Required and recommended units include English 4, mathematics 2-3, social studies 2, history 2, science 2-3 (laboratory 2-3), foreign language 2 and academic electives 4.

2015-2016 Annual costs. Tuition/fees: $32,240. Room/board: $9,630. Books/supplies: $1,280. Personal expenses: $1,410.

2015-2016 Financial aid. **Need-based:** 603 full-time freshmen applied for aid; 524 deemed to have need; 524 received aid. Average need met was 73%. Average scholarship/grant was $18,943; average loan $3,769. 68% of total undergraduate aid awarded as scholarships/grants, 32% as loans/jobs. **Non-need-based:** Awarded to 939 full-time undergraduates, including 240 freshmen. Scholarships awarded for academics, art, leadership, music/drama, religious affiliation.

Application procedures. **Admission:** No deadline. $20 fee, may be waived for applicants with need. Admission notification by 9/15. Admission notification on a rolling basis. **Financial aid:** Priority date 4/1; no closing date. FAFSA required. Applicants notified on a rolling basis starting 3/15; must reply by 5/1 or within 4 week(s) of notification.

Academics. Supplemental instructional support available. **Special study options:** Accelerated study, combined bachelor's/graduate degree, double major, dual enrollment of high school students, ESL, exchange student, honors, independent study, internships, student-designed major, study abroad, teacher certification program, urban semester, Washington semester. Pass/Fail option for classes. **Credit/placement by examination:** AP, CLEP, IB, institutional tests. 32 credit hours maximum toward bachelor's degree. **Support services:** Learning center, pre-admission summer program, reduced course load, remedial instruction, study skills assistance, tutoring, writing center.

Majors. **Area/ethnic studies:** General. **Biology:** General, biochemistry, molecular. **Business:** Accounting, business admin, international, marketing, restaurant/food services. **Communications:** Communications/speech/rhetoric, digital media, journalism, persuasive communications. **Communications technology:** General. **Computer sciences:** Computer science. **Conservation:** Environmental science. **Education:** Art, biology, chemistry, early childhood, elementary, English, family/consumer sciences, foreign languages, French, German, mathematics, middle, music, physical, physics, social studies, Spanish. **Engineering:** General. **English:** English lit. **Foreign languages:** Chinese, French, German, Spanish. **Health services:** Athletic training, clinical nutrition, nursing (RN). **History:** General. **Human services:** Social work. **Liberal arts:** Humanities. **Math:** General. **Parks/recreation:** General, outdoor education, sports admin. **Philosophy/religion:** Philosophy. **Physical sciences:** Chemistry, physics. **Protective services:** Criminal justice. **Psychology:** General. **Social sciences:** Economics, international economic development, political science, sociology. **Theology:** Bible, religious ed. **Visual/performing arts:** Art history/conservation, cinematography, dance, dramatic, music, music management, music performance, musical theater, studio arts, studio arts management, theater arts management. **Work/family studies:** Child care management, family/community services.

Most popular majors. Business/marketing 13%, education 15%, engineering/engineering technologies 6%, health sciences 14%, psychology 6%, visual/performing arts 6%.

Technology on campus. 571 workstations in dormitories, library, computer center, student center. Dormitories wired for high-speed internet access and linked to campus network. Commuter students can connect to campus network. Online course registration, online library, helpline, repair service, student web hosting, wireless network available.

Student life. **Freshman orientation:** Mandatory. Preregistration for classes offered. 4-day program for students and parents during fall welcome weekend; includes placement exams and service day. **Policies:** Students generally required to live on campus unless married or living with relatives. Religious observance required. **Housing:** Guaranteed on-campus for all undergraduates. Coed dorms, single-sex dorms, special housing for disabled, apartments, themed housing available. $200 partly refundable deposit. **Activities:** Bands, campus ministries, choral groups, dance, drama, film society, international student organizations, literary magazine, music ensembles, musical theater, radio station, student government, student newspaper, symphony orchestra, outreach teams, World Christian Fellowship, Nurses Christian Fellowship, Newman Club, Powerhouse band, Acclamation dance, Alliance of Confessing Theologies.

Athletics. NCAA. **Intercollegiate:** Baseball M, basketball, cross-country, field hockey W, golf M, lacrosse, soccer, softball W, swimming, tennis, track and field, volleyball W, wrestling M. **Intramural:** Basketball, football (non-tackle), soccer, softball, volleyball. **Team name:** Falcons.

Student services. Chaplain/spiritual director, career counseling, student employment services, financial aid counseling, health services, minority student services, personal counseling, veterans' counselor. **Physically disabled:** Services for visually, speech, hearing impaired.

Contact. E-mail: admiss@messiah.edu
Phone: (717) 691-6000 Toll-free number: (800) 233-4220
Fax: (717) 691-2307
John Chopka, Vice President of Enrollment Management, Messiah College, One College Avenue, Suite 3005, Mechanicsburg, PA 17055

Millersville University of Pennsylvania

Millersville, Pennsylvania **CB member**
www.millersville.edu **CB code: 2656**

- Public 4-year university and liberal arts college
- Residential campus in small town
- 6,981 degree-seeking undergraduates: 12% part-time, 56% women, 9% African American, 3% Asian American, 8% Hispanic/Latino, 3% Multiracial, non-Hispanic
- 724 degree-seeking graduate students
- 73% of applicants admitted
- SAT or ACT (ACT writing recommended), application essay required
- 62% graduate within 6 years

General. Founded in 1855. Regionally accredited. **Degrees:** 1,498 bachelor's, 3 associate awarded; master's, doctoral offered. **ROTC:** Army. **Location:** 5 miles from Lancaster, 40 miles from Harrisburg. **Calendar:** 4-1-4, limited summer session. **Full-time faculty:** 291 total; 97% have terminal degrees, 19% minority, 47% women. **Part-time faculty:** 161 total; 30% have terminal degrees, 8% minority, 57% women. **Class size:** 27% < 20, 57% 20-39, 9% 40-49, 5% 50-99, 2% >100. **Special facilities:** Art galleries, recording studio, teleconferencing center, weather information center, foreign language lab, two performing arts centers, atmospheric research and aerostat facility, center for disaster research and education, Foucault pendulum, field station at marine science consortium, aircraft flight simulators, safety engineering and training modules.

Freshman class profile. 6,053 applied, 4,422 admitted, 1,336 enrolled.

Mid 50% test scores		Rank in top quarter:	29%
SAT critical reading:	450-550	Rank in top tenth:	9%
SAT math:	450-550	Return as sophomores:	77%
SAT writing:	430-530	Out-of-state:	8%
ACT composite:	19-24	Live on campus:	79%

Basis for selection. High school record most important, followed by class rank, test scores, and recommendations. Special consideration to students with special talents. All students required to take Basic Skills Test for placement purposes. All incoming students must take at least one math course; math placement test required. Some students may also be required to take a foreign language placement test. Educationally and economically disadvantaged students may be admitted to the enrichment program, known as the Millersville Scholars Program, if they demonstrate potential for college success. Applicants without SAT scores may enroll as non-degree students and be admitted to degree-seeking status after completing 12 credits in at least two subject areas with a 2.0 GPA. Secondary screening (letters of reference, essay, and family financial information) and interview required for Millersville Scholars Program. Audition required for music applicants; portfolio required for art applicant; Associate degree in Nursing or Diploma and RN license required for nursing program. Letters of reference and personal statement are recommended. **Home schooled:** Applicant should be a graduate of an approved home school association program. A GED issued by the Pennsylvania Department of Education is preferred if the student has not completed an approved program of study. Also required are satisfactory scores on the SAT or ACT.

High school preparation. College-preparatory program required. 15 units required; 21 recommended. Required and recommended units include English 4, mathematics 3, social studies 3, history 2, science 3 (laboratory 2), foreign language 2 and academic electives 4.

2015-2016 Annual costs. Tuition/fees: $10,918; $20,108 out-of-state. Room/board: $12,188. Books/supplies: $1,000. Personal expenses: $1,676. **Additional information:** There is a out-of-state tuition reduction program; depending on academic major and qualifications, some students may qualify for a reduced tuition rate of $12,356 or $14,120 for STEM majors.

2014-2015 Financial aid. **Need-based:** 1,249 full-time freshmen applied for aid; 949 deemed to have need; 914 received aid. Average need met was 60%. Average scholarship/grant was $5,483; average loan $3,295. 54% of total undergraduate aid awarded as scholarships/grants, 46% as loans/jobs. **Non-need-based:** Awarded to 642 full-time undergraduates, including 207 freshmen. Scholarships awarded for academics, athletics, minority status.

Application procedures. **Admission:** No deadline. $50 fee, may be waived for applicants with need. Admission notification on a rolling basis beginning on or about 9/15. Must reply by May 1 or within 2 week(s) if notified thereafter. Enrollment deposits are due May 1. **Financial aid:** Priority date 3/15; no closing date. FAFSA required. Applicants notified on a rolling basis starting 3/19; must reply within 2 week(s) of notification.

Academics. **Special study options:** Accelerated study, combined bachelor's/graduate degree, cooperative education, cross-registration, distance learning, double major, dual enrollment of high school students, honors, independent study, internships, student-designed major, study abroad, teacher certification program. Academic remediation, advanced placement credit, off-campus study, learning disabilities services, continuing education, online/blended courses, summer/winter sessions for credit. **Credit/placement by examination:** AP, CLEP, IB, institutional tests. No limit to the hours of credit examination that may be counted toward a degree. Students may challenge most courses in which they have not received a grade, and which have not been waived because of demonstrated competency or advanced placement. Because of content and structure, some courses may not be challenged by examination. **Support services:** Learning center, pre-admission summer program, reduced course load, remedial instruction, study skills assistance, tutoring, writing center.

Honors college/program. Students with combined SAT scores in Reading and Math of 1200 or higher and who have graduated in the top 10% of their high school class.

Majors. Biology: General. **Business:** Business admin. **Communications:** Communications/speech/rhetoric. **Computer sciences:** General. **Education:** Early childhood, middle, special ed. **English:** English lit. **Foreign languages:** French, German, Spanish. **History:** General. **Human services:** Social work. **Math:** General. **Philosophy/religion:** Philosophy. **Physical sciences:** Atmospheric science, chemistry, geology, oceanography, physics. **Psychology:** General. **Social sciences:** Anthropology, economics, geography, political science, sociology. **Visual/performing arts:** Art, design, music.

Most popular majors. Biology 7%, business/marketing 10%, communications/journalism 9%, education 11%, engineering/engineering technologies 7%, psychology 8%, public administration/social services 7%, social sciences 9%.

Technology on campus. 430 workstations in dormitories, library, computer center, student center. Dormitories wired for high-speed internet access and linked to campus network. Commuter students can connect to campus network. Online course registration, online library, helpline, repair service, wireless network available.

Student life. Freshman orientation: Mandatory, $335 fee. Preregistration for classes offered. 4-day program in June or August. Parents are invited to attend a separate session. **Policies:** All residence hall students are required to purchase a meal plan, have 24 hour visitation, and must adhere to housing guidelines. **Housing:** Guaranteed on-campus for freshmen. Coed dorms, special housing for disabled, apartments, themed housing, wellness housing available. $200 nonrefundable deposit, deadline 5/1. Academic interest housing available for several subject areas. University-affiliated apartments and dormitories for single students adjacent to campus. **Activities:** Bands, campus ministries, choral groups, dance, drama, film society, literary magazine, music ensembles, musical theater, radio station, student government, student newspaper, symphony orchestra, TV station, National Association for the Advancement of Colored People, Black Student Union, Society on Latino Affairs, Allies: the Gender and Sexuality Alliance at MU, Best Buddies, Circle K, Student Senate, Volunteer Central, Bible Campus Ministries, MU Hillel.

Athletics. NCAA. **Intercollegiate:** Baseball M, basketball, cross-country W, field hockey W, football (tackle) M, golf, lacrosse W, soccer, softball W, swimming W, tennis, track and field W, volleyball W, wrestling M. **Intramural:** Badminton, basketball, field hockey, football (non-tackle), golf, handball, soccer, softball, table tennis, tennis, ultimate frisbee, volleyball, water polo. **Team name:** Marauders.

Student services. Adult student services, alcohol/substance abuse counseling, chaplain/spiritual director, career counseling, services for economically disadvantaged, student employment services, financial aid counseling, health services, minority student services, personal counseling, placement for graduates, veterans' counselor, women's services. **Physically disabled:** Services for visually, speech, hearing impaired.

Contact. E-mail: admissions@millersville.edu
Phone: (717) 871-4625 Toll-free number: (800) 682-3648
Fax: (717) 871-2147
Katy Ferrier, Director of Admissions, Millersville University of Pennsylvania, PO Box 1002, Millersville, PA 17551-0302

Misericordia University

Dallas, Pennsylvania **CB member**
www.misericordia.edu **CB code: 2087**

- Private 4-year health science and liberal arts college affiliated with the Roman Catholic Church
- Residential campus in large town
- 2,298 degree-seeking undergraduates: 22% part-time, 68% women, 2% African American, 1% Asian American, 3% Hispanic/Latino, 1% Multiracial, non-Hispanic
- 563 degree-seeking graduate students

♦ 71% of applicants admitted

♦ SAT or ACT (ACT writing optional) required

♦ 72% graduate within 6 years; 33% enter graduate study

General. Founded in 1924. Regionally accredited. Guaranteed Placement Program (within six months of graduation); Women with Children program for single women. **Degrees:** 517 bachelor's awarded; master's, professional offered. **ROTC:** Army, Air Force. **Location:** 9 miles from Wilkes-Barre, 20 miles from Scranton. **Calendar:** Semester, extensive summer session. **Full-time faculty:** 134 total; 78% have terminal degrees, 7% minority, 60% women. **Part-time faculty:** 183 total; 18% have terminal degrees, 3% minority, 57% women. **Class size:** 44% < 20, 56% 20-39.

Freshman class profile. 1,956 applied, 1,398 admitted, 434 enrolled.

Mid 50% test scores		GPA 2.0-2.99:	16%
SAT critical reading:	480-570	Rank in top quarter:	56%
SAT math:	490-570	Rank in top tenth:	24%
ACT composite:	22-27	End year in good standing:	92%
GPA 3.75 or higher:	24%	Return as sophomores:	85%
GPA 3.50-3.74:	25%	Out-of-state:	32%
GPA 3.0-3.49:	35%	Live on campus:	82%

Basis for selection. In order of importance: high school achievement, test scores, character, recommendations from school teachers or counselors. Test scores weighed more heavily for health science programs. Essay required for occupational therapy and speech language pathology applicants. **Home schooled:** Transcript of courses and grades required. If applicant not affiliated with specific organization, college will accept transcript from home schooling parent that shows course work completed and grades achieved. GED not required. **Learning Disabled:** Essay, 3 letters of recommendation, documentation of disability, test results (i.e., WAIS) required. SAT/ACT not required.

High school preparation. College-preparatory program recommended. 16 units required. Required units include English 4, mathematics 4, social studies 4 and science 4. 2 units science and algebra required for allied health applicants. Strong math background required for computer science, physical therapy, chemistry and biology applicants.

2016-2017 Annual costs. Tuition/fees: $30,740. Room/board: $13,150. Books/supplies: $1,250. Personal expenses: $500.

2015-2016 Financial aid. **Need-based:** 425 full-time freshmen applied for aid; 366 deemed to have need; 366 received aid. Average need met was 82%. Average scholarship/grant was $17,497; average loan $7,102. 64% of total undergraduate aid awarded as scholarships/grants, 36% as loans/jobs. **Non-need-based:** Awarded to 445 full-time undergraduates, including 133 freshmen. Scholarships awarded for academics, alumni affiliation, leadership, minority status, state residency.

Application procedures. **Admission:** No deadline. $35 fee, may be waived for applicants with need. Admission notification on a rolling basis beginning on or about 9/1. Must reply by May 1 or within 4 week(s) if notified thereafter. **Financial aid:** Priority date 3/1, closing date 5/1. FAFSA required. Applicants notified on a rolling basis starting 3/15.

Academics. **Special study options:** Accelerated study, combined bachelor's/graduate degree, cross-registration, distance learning, double major, dual enrollment of high school students, honors, independent study, internships, student-designed major, study abroad, teacher certification program, weekend college. **Credit/placement by examination:** AP, CLEP, IB, SAT, ACT, institutional tests. 40 credit hours maximum toward bachelor's degree. **Support services:** Learning center, pre-admission summer program, study skills assistance, tutoring, writing center.

Majors. **Biology:** General, biochemistry. **Business:** Accounting, business admin, management information systems, marketing. **Communications:** General. **Computer sciences:** General. **Education:** Biology, chemistry, early childhood, elementary, English, mathematics, middle, social studies, special ed. **English:** English lit. **Health services:** Clinical lab science, health care admin, medical radiologic technology/radiation therapy, nursing (RN), nursing practice, sonography. **History:** General. **Human services:** Social work. **Liberal arts:** Arts/sciences. **Math:** General. **Parks/recreation:** Sports admin. **Philosophy/religion:** Philosophy. **Physical sciences:** Chemistry. **Psychology:** General. **Social sciences:** General, U.S. government.

Most popular majors. Business/marketing 21%, health sciences 41%, psychology 7%, social sciences 6%.

Technology on campus. 100 workstations in dormitories, library, computer center, student center. Dormitories wired for high-speed internet access and linked to campus network. Commuter students can connect to campus network. Online course registration, online library, helpline, repair service, wireless network available.

Student life. **Freshman orientation:** Mandatory, $200 fee. Preregistration for classes offered. One-day testing for math and English placement. **Policies:**

Freshmen not permitted cars on campus. **Housing:** Coed dorms, wellness housing available. $100 nonrefundable deposit, deadline 5/1. Leadership house, 3 apartment buildings for women with children located adjacent to campus. **Activities:** Jazz band, campus ministries, choral groups, dance, drama, literary magazine, music ensembles, radio station, student government, student newspaper, TV station, student nurses association, Council for Exceptional Children, Circle-K, Peer Associates, Diversity Institute.

Athletics. NCAA. **Intercollegiate:** Baseball M, basketball, cross-country, field hockey W, football (tackle) M, golf, lacrosse, soccer, softball W, swimming, tennis, track and field, volleyball W. **Intramural:** Basketball, cross-country, football (non-tackle), racquetball, soccer, softball, tennis, ultimate frisbee, volleyball. **Team name:** Cougars.

Student services. Adult student services, alcohol/substance abuse counseling, chaplain/spiritual director, career counseling, services for economically disadvantaged, student employment services, financial aid counseling, health services, minority student services, personal counseling, placement for graduates, veterans' counselor, women's services. **Physically disabled:** Services for visually, speech, hearing impaired.

Contact. E-mail: admiss@misericordia.edu
Phone: (570) 674-6264 Toll-free number: (866) 262-6363
Fax: (570) 675-2441
Glenn Bozinski, Director of Admissions, Misericordia University, 301 Lake Street, Dallas, PA 18612-1098

Moore College of Art and Design
Philadelphia, Pennsylvania
www.moore.edu   **CB code: 2417**

♦ Private 4-year visual arts college for women

♦ Commuter campus in very large city

♦ 406 degree-seeking undergraduates: 3% part-time, 100% women, 21% African American, 3% Asian American, 7% Hispanic/Latino, 6% Multiracial, non-Hispanic, 1% international

♦ 34 degree-seeking graduate students

♦ 56% of applicants admitted

♦ Interview required

♦ 67% graduate within 6 years

General. Founded in 1848. Regionally accredited. **Degrees:** 95 bachelor's awarded; master's offered. **Location:** Located in center city Philadelphia, 90 miles from New York City. **Calendar:** Semester, limited summer session. **Full-time faculty:** 23 total; 56% have terminal degrees, 9% minority, 61% women. **Part-time faculty:** 84 total; 66% have terminal degrees, 19% minority, 52% women. **Class size:** 83% < 20, 17% 20-39. **Special facilities:** Professional and student-run galleries.

Freshman class profile. 708 applied, 398 admitted, 97 enrolled.

GPA 3.75 or higher:	20%	Return as sophomores:	73%
GPA 3.50-3.74:	14%	Out-of-state:	42%
GPA 3.0-3.49:	36%	International:	1%
GPA 2.0-2.99:	30%		

Basis for selection. High school record, interview, portfolio, and test scores important. SAT optional, and 2.5 GPA required. SAT or ACT recommended. First-time degree seeking students must complete writing placement essay. Transfer students may participate in the Directed Self-Placement program for Writing courses. Portfolio required; essay recommended for all. **Home schooled:** State high school equivalency certificate required. **Learning Disabled:** Students who request accommodations must provide qualifying documentation on professional letterhead and contain dates of assessment, signatures, titles, and license/certification numbers of diagnosing professionals. Documentation should be no more than 5 years old.

High school preparation. College-preparatory program recommended. 14 units recommended. Recommended units include English 4, mathematics 2, social studies 4, science 2, foreign language 2 and visual/performing arts 3. Portfolio review required.

2015-2016 Annual costs. Tuition/fees: $37,098. Room/board: $13,836. Books/supplies: $2,400. Personal expenses: $2,000.

Financial aid. **Non-need-based:** Scholarships awarded for academics, art, leadership.

Application procedures. **Admission:** $60 fee, may be waived for applicants with need. Admission notification on a rolling basis beginning on or about 11/15. Must reply by May 1 or within 3 week(s) if notified thereafter. **Financial aid:** Priority date 3/1, closing date 5/1. FAFSA required. Applicants notified on a rolling basis starting 2/15; must reply within 2 week(s) of notification.

Academics. Special study options: Double major, exchange student, honors, independent study, internships, study abroad, teacher certification program. Dual enrollment available for the post-baccalaureate and graduate degree program for Art Education only. **Credit/placement by examination:** AP, CLEP, IB, institutional tests. 6 credit hours maximum toward bachelor's degree. **Support services:** Pre-admission summer program, reduced course load, study skills assistance, tutoring, writing center. Students who need support services on the weekends and in the evenings can get assistance via email.

Majors. Education: Art. **Visual/performing arts:** Art history/conservation, digital arts, fashion design, graphic design, illustration, interior design, photography, studio arts.

Most popular majors. Visual/performing arts 88%.

Technology on campus. PC or laptop required. 127 workstations in dormitories, library, computer center. Dormitories wired for high-speed internet access. Commuter students can connect to campus network. Online course registration, wireless network available.

Student life. Freshman orientation: Mandatory, $98 fee. Preregistration for classes offered. Held 4 days prior to beginning of semester. **Housing:** Guaranteed on-campus for freshmen. $250 partly refundable deposit, deadline 7/15. **Activities:** Student government, student-run gallery, student orientation staff, Visionary Woman Honors Program, student judiciary committee, residence life staff, Moore Magazine.

Student services. Adult student services, career counseling, financial aid counseling, health services, personal counseling.

Contact. E-mail: admiss@moore.edu
Phone: (215) 965-4014 Toll-free number: (800) 523-2025
Fax: (215) 568-3547
Elizabeth Mathis, Director of Admissions, Moore College of Art and Design, The Parkway at 20th Street, Philadelphia, PA 19103-1179

Moravian College
Bethlehem, Pennsylvania
www.moravian.edu

CB member
CB code: 2418

- Private 4-year liberal arts and seminary college affiliated with the Moravian Church in America
- Residential campus in small city
- 1,765 degree-seeking undergraduates: 5% part-time, 55% women, 4% African American, 1% Asian American, 9% Hispanic/Latino, 2% Multiracial, non-Hispanic, 6% international
- 386 degree-seeking graduate students
- 75% of applicants admitted
- SAT or ACT (ACT writing optional), application essay required
- 69% graduate within 6 years; 4% enter graduate study

General. Founded in 1742. Regionally accredited. Member of Lehigh Valley Association of Independent Colleges Consortium. **Degrees:** 342 bachelor's awarded; master's offered. **ROTC:** Army. **Location:** 60 miles from Philadelphia, 90 miles from New York City. **Calendar:** Semester, extensive summer session. **Full-time faculty:** 113 total; 86% have terminal degrees, 8% minority, 62% women. **Part-time faculty:** 84 total; 40% have terminal degrees, 5% minority, 40% women. **Class size:** 61% < 20, 36% 20-39, 2% 40-49, less than 1% 50-99. **Special facilities:** Outdoor laboratory, concert hall.

Freshman class profile. 2,737 applied, 2,041 admitted, 523 enrolled.

Mid 50% test scores		GPA 2.0-2.99:	19%
SAT critical reading:	570-580	Rank in top quarter:	38%
SAT math:	460-510	Rank in top tenth:	10%
SAT writing:	430-550	Return as sophomores:	80%
ACT composite:	19-23	Out-of-state:	38%
GPA 3.75 or higher:	28%	Live on campus:	80%
GPA 3.50-3.74:	17%	International:	6%
GPA 3.0-3.49:	36%		

Basis for selection. High school record and standardized test scores important. Academic credentials, character, extracurricular involvement, volunteer work and potential for contribution considered. Nursing program has higher admission standards. Interviews strongly recommended; audition required for music applicants; portfolio required for art applicants.

High school preparation. College-preparatory program recommended. 16 units required; 18 recommended. Required and recommended units include English 4, mathematics 3-4, social studies 4, science 3 (laboratory 2) and foreign language 2.

2015-2016 Annual costs. Tuition/fees: $38,832. Room/board: $11,636.

2015-2016 Financial aid. Need-based: Average need met was 77%. Average scholarship/grant was $25,311; average loan $3,957. 68% of total undergraduate aid awarded as scholarships/grants, 32% as loans/jobs. **Non-need-based:** Scholarships awarded for academics, alumni affiliation, art, leadership, music/drama, religious affiliation, ROTC, state residency.

Application procedures. Admission: Closing date 3/1. No application fee. Application must be submitted online. Admission notification on a rolling basis beginning on or about 10/15. Must reply by May 1 or within 2 week(s) if notified thereafter. **Financial aid:** Priority date 3/1; no closing date. FAFSA, institutional form required. Applicants notified on a rolling basis starting 2/25; must reply by 5/1.

Academics. Special study options: Accelerated study, combined bachelor's/graduate degree, cooperative education, cross-registration, distance learning, double major, dual enrollment of high school students, honors, independent study, internships, student-designed major, study abroad, teacher certification program, Washington semester. **Credit/placement by examination:** AP, CLEP, IB, SAT, ACT, institutional tests. **Support services:** Learning center, pre-admission summer program, study skills assistance, tutoring, writing center. Learning center offers a responsive program for students with learning disabilities.

Majors. Area/ethnic studies: French, German. **Biology:** General, biochemistry, neuroscience. **Business:** Accounting, business admin, international, nonprofit/public. **Computer sciences:** Computer science. **Conservation:** Environmental science, environmental studies. **English:** English lit. **Foreign languages:** French, German, Spanish. **Health services:** Community health, nursing (RN). **History:** General. **Math:** General. **Philosophy/religion:** Philosophy, religion. **Physical sciences:** Chemistry, geology, physics. **Psychology:** General. **Social sciences:** Economics, political science, sociology. **Visual/performing arts:** Art, music.

Most popular majors. Biology 11%, business/marketing 23%, English 7%, psychology 9%, social sciences 21%, visual/performing arts 10%.

Technology on campus. 227 workstations in dormitories, library, computer center, student center. Dormitories wired for high-speed internet access and linked to campus network. Commuter students can connect to campus network. Online course registration, online library, helpline, repair service, student web hosting, wireless network available.

Student life. Freshman orientation: Mandatory, $140 fee. Preregistration for classes offered. 3-day program held immediately prior to fall semester. **Policies:** Freshmen not permitted cars on campus. **Housing:** Guaranteed on-campus for all undergraduates. Coed dorms, single-sex dorms, special housing for disabled, apartments, fraternity/sorority housing, themed housing available. $400 nonrefundable deposit, deadline 5/1. **Activities:** Bands, campus ministries, choral groups, dance, drama, international student organizations, literary magazine, music ensembles, Model UN, opera, radio station, student government, student newspaper, symphony orchestra, Christian Fellowship, Hillel Society, Middle Eastern Club, Muslim Students Association, Newman Association, Religious Studies Society, Student Christian Community (Reformed Univ. Fellowship), Campus Community Connection, Habitat for Humanity, The Learning Connection.

Athletics. NCAA. **Intercollegiate:** Baseball M, basketball, cross-country, field hockey W, football (tackle) M, golf M, lacrosse, soccer, softball W, tennis, track and field, volleyball W. **Intramural:** Badminton, basketball, football (non-tackle), soccer, softball, tennis, volleyball. **Team name:** Greyhounds.

Student services. Adult student services, alcohol/substance abuse counseling, chaplain/spiritual director, career counseling, student employment services, financial aid counseling, health services, minority student services, personal counseling, placement for graduates. **Physically disabled:** Services for visually, speech, hearing impaired.

Contact. E-mail: admission@moravian.edu
Phone: (610) 861-1320 Toll-free number: (800) 441-3191
Fax: (610) 625-7930
Steven Soba, Vice President for Enrollment Management, Moravian College, 1200 Main Street, Bethlehem, PA 18018

Mount Aloysius College
Cresson, Pennsylvania
www.mtaloy.edu

CB member
CB code: 2420

- Private 4-year liberal arts college affiliated with the Roman Catholic Church
- Residential campus in small town

- 1,472 degree-seeking undergraduates: 21% part-time, 73% women, 3% African American, 1% Hispanic/Latino, 2% international
- 74 degree-seeking graduate students
- SAT or ACT (ACT writing optional), application essay required

General. Founded in 1939. Regionally accredited. **Degrees:** 213 bachelor's, 228 associate awarded; master's offered. **Location:** 12 miles from Altoona, 90 miles from Pittsburgh. **Calendar:** Semester, limited summer session. **Full-time faculty:** 72 total; 49% have terminal degrees, 3% minority, 72% women. **Part-time faculty:** 131 total; less than 1% minority, 60% women. **Class size:** 75% < 20, 25% 20-39. **Special facilities:** Health and science center with mock operating room, telehealth/telenursing, ecumenical library.

Freshman class profile. 1,485 applied, 1,082 admitted, 376 enrolled.

Mid 50% test scores			
		GPA 3.50-3.74:	20%
SAT critical reading:	430-510	GPA 3.0-3.49:	36%
SAT math:	430-510	GPA 2.0-2.99:	25%
SAT writing:	400-500	Out-of-state:	10%
ACT composite:	17-21	Live on campus:	55%
GPA 3.75 or higher:	17%	International:	5%

Basis for selection. Open admission, but selective for some programs. School record, test scores, activities, talent, and character most important. Nursing entrance test not required for students with SAT of 900 or higher. Placement test waived if student scores 500 or higher in either section. Application priority date for health and nursing applicants for the fall semester is June 1st. Interview required for students with lower SAT scores and GPA. Interviews and essays required for physical therapist assistant majors. **Learning Disabled:** Admission interview required.

High school preparation. College-preparatory program recommended. 16 units required. Required and recommended units include English 4, mathematics 3, social studies 3, history 3, science 3, foreign language 2 and academic electives 3. Algebra and 2 lab sciences required for nursing. Algebra, chemistry required for physical therapist assistant, radiography and medical imaging applicants. Biology required for occupational therapy assistant applicants.

2015-2016 Annual costs. Tuition/fees: $21,360. Room/board: $9,552. Books/supplies: $2,500. Personal expenses: $3,000.

2015-2016 Financial aid. **Need-based:** 364 full-time freshmen applied for aid; 296 deemed to have need; 296 received aid. Average need met was 35%. Average scholarship/grant was $6,400; average loan $3,500. 58% of total undergraduate aid awarded as scholarships/grants, 42% as loans/jobs. **Non-need-based:** Scholarships awarded for academics, art, leadership, music/drama, religious affiliation.

Application procedures. **Admission:** No deadline. $30 fee, may be waived for applicants with need. Admission notification on a rolling basis beginning on or about 8/1. Must reply by May 1 or within 4 week(s) if notified thereafter. **Financial aid:** Priority date 4/1; no closing date. FAFSA required. Applicants notified on a rolling basis starting 3/15; must reply within 2 week(s) of notification.

Academics. **Special study options:** Accelerated study, combined bachelor's/graduate degree, distance learning, double major, dual enrollment of high school students, honors, independent study, internships, student-designed major, study abroad, teacher certification program. **Credit/placement by examination:** AP, CLEP, SAT, institutional tests. 15 credit hours maximum toward associate degree, 30 toward bachelor's. **Support services:** Learning center, pre-admission summer program, reduced course load, remedial instruction, study skills assistance, tutoring, writing center.

Majors. Biology: General. **Business:** Accounting, business admin. **Computer sciences:** Information technology. **Education:** Early childhood, middle, secondary. **English:** English lit. **Foreign languages:** Sign language interpretation. **Health services:** Medical radiologic technology/radiation therapy, nursing (RN). **History:** General. **Liberal arts:** Arts/sciences. **Protective services:** Law enforcement admin. **Psychology:** General.

Most popular majors. Biology 10%, business/marketing 17%, health sciences 38%, liberal arts 11%, security/protective services 8%.

Technology on campus. 175 workstations in dormitories, library, computer center, student center. Dormitories linked to campus network. Helpline, repair service available.

Student life. Freshman orientation: Mandatory. Preregistration for classes offered. **Housing:** Guaranteed on-campus for all undergraduates. Coed dorms available. $125 nonrefundable deposit. **Activities:** Campus ministries, choral groups, dance, drama, international student organizations, student government, student newspaper, nursing, occupational therapy assistant, business, Phi Theta Kappa, student programming council.

Athletics. NCAA. **Intercollegiate:** Baseball M, basketball, bowling W, cross-country, golf, soccer, softball W, tennis, volleyball W. **Intramural:** Baseball M, basketball, bowling, football (non-tackle), golf, skiing, soccer, softball, table tennis, tennis, ultimate frisbee, volleyball. **Team name:** Mounties.

Student services. Alcohol/substance abuse counseling, chaplain/spiritual director, career counseling, student employment services, financial aid counseling, health services, on-campus daycare, personal counseling, placement for graduates, veterans' counselor. **Physically disabled:** Services for hearing impaired.

Contact. E-mail: admissions@mtaloy.edu
Phone: (814) 886-6383 Toll-free number: (888) 823-2220
Fax: (814) 886-6441
Frank Crouse, Vice President for Enrollment Management/Dean of Admissions, Mount Aloysius College, 7373 Admiral Peary Highway, Cresson, PA 16630

Muhlenberg College
Allentown, Pennsylvania
www.muhlenberg.edu

CB member
CB code: 2424

- Private 4-year liberal arts college affiliated with the Evangelical Lutheran Church in America
- Residential campus in small city
- 2,302 degree-seeking undergraduates: 2% part-time, 60% women, 3% African American, 3% Asian American, 7% Hispanic/Latino, 2% Multiracial, non-Hispanic, 3% international
- 48% of applicants admitted
- Application essay required
- 90% graduate within 6 years; 8% enter graduate study

General. Founded in 1848. Regionally accredited. **Degrees:** 614 bachelor's, 3 associate awarded. **ROTC:** Army. **Location:** 55 miles from Philadelphia, 90 miles from New York City. **Calendar:** Semester, limited summer session. **Full-time faculty:** 177 total; 85% have terminal degrees, 7% minority, 51% women. **Part-time faculty:** 108 total; 27% have terminal degrees, 6% minority, 47% women. **Class size:** 78% < 20, 21% 20-39, less than 1% 40-49, less than 1% 50-99, less than 1% >100. **Special facilities:** 3-theater complex, electronic music studio, natural history museum, 38-acre environmental field station, greenhouse, two electron microscopes, isolation laboratories, DNA sequencer, 20-foot boat for marine studies, 60-acre arboretum.

Freshman class profile. 5,015 applied, 2,426 admitted, 582 enrolled.

Mid 50% test scores			
		GPA 2.0-2.99:	22%
SAT critical reading:	550-660	Rank in top quarter:	71%
SAT math:	560-660	Rank in top tenth:	41%
SAT writing:	550-660	End year in good standing:	97%
ACT composite:	25-31	Return as sophomores:	93%
GPA 3.75 or higher:	17%	Out-of-state:	76%
GPA 3.50-3.74:	20%	Live on campus:	98%
GPA 3.0-3.49:	41%	International:	6%

Basis for selection. High school courses, grades, class rank, test scores, personal qualities, essay, recommendations, special talents and activities important. Interview strongly recommended. Test-optional for admission, but ACT or SAT exams are required to be considered for merit scholarships, honors programs, and cooperative programs (i.e., 4-4 medical, 3-4 dental, etc.). Audition recommended for dance, drama, music programs; portfolio recommended for art program. **Home schooled:** Statement describing home school structure and mission, transcript of courses and grades, state high school equivalency certificate, letter of recommendation (nonparent) required. Interview strongly recommended.

High school preparation. College-preparatory program required. 16 units required; 20 recommended. Required and recommended units include English 4, mathematics 3-4, social studies 2, history 2, science 2-3 (laboratory 2-3), foreign language 2-4 and academic electives 1. Advanced placement and accelerated courses encouraged.

2015-2016 Annual costs. Tuition/fees: $46,160. Room/board: $10,770. Books/supplies: $1,300. Personal expenses: $1,250.

2015-2016 Financial aid. **Need-based:** 372 full-time freshmen applied for aid; 273 deemed to have need; 273 received aid. Average need met was 93%. Average scholarship/grant was $32,445; average loan $3,852. 80% of total undergraduate aid awarded as scholarships/grants, 20% as loans/jobs. **Non-need-based:** Awarded to 1,586 full-time undergraduates, including 448 freshmen. Scholarships awarded for academics, art, leadership, music/drama, ROTC.

Application procedures. Admission: Closing date 2/15 (postmark date). $50 fee, may be waived for applicants with need. Admission notification by 3/15. Must reply by 5/1. **Financial aid:** Closing date 2/15. FAFSA, institutional form, CSS PROFILE required. Applicants notified by 4/1; must reply by 5/1.

Academics. Special study options: Accelerated study, combined bachelor's/graduate degree, cross-registration, double major, exchange student, honors, independent study, internships, student-designed major, study abroad, teacher certification program, Washington semester. Study abroad with Lehigh Valley Association of Independent Colleges; over 60 agreements with foreign universities for study abroad; 3-2 or 4-2 combined Degree Program in Engineering with Columbia University or Washington University. MC/Penn Dental Program-University of Pennsylvania. Combined program with Drexel University College of Medicine. 7-year Optometry Program-State University of New York 3-2 or 4-2. Combined Degree Program in Environmental Science or Forestry. **Credit/placement by examination:** AP, CLEP, IB, SAT, ACT, institutional tests. 68 credit hours maximum toward bachelor's degree. 68 credit hours equivalent to 17 course units. **Support services:** Learning center, reduced course load, study skills assistance, tutoring, writing center.

Majors. Area/ethnic studies: American, French, Russian/Slavic. **Biology:** General, biochemistry, neuroscience. **Business:** Accounting, business admin, finance, human resources, management information systems. **Communications:** Communications/speech/rhetoric. **Computer sciences:** General. **Conservation:** Environmental science. **English:** English lit. **Foreign languages:** Spanish. **History:** General. **Math:** General. **Philosophy/religion:** Judaic, philosophy, religion. **Physical sciences:** General, chemistry, physics. **Psychology:** General. **Social sciences:** Anthropology, economics, international relations, political science, sociology. **Visual/performing arts:** Art, dance, dramatic, film/cinema/video, music.

Most popular majors. Biology 10%, business/marketing 26%, communications/journalism 7%, psychology 11%, social sciences 10%, visual/performing arts 16%.

Technology on campus. 240 workstations in dormitories, library, computer center, student center. Dormitories wired for high-speed internet access and linked to campus network. Commuter students can connect to campus network. Online course registration, helpline, repair service, wireless network available.

Student life. Freshman orientation: Mandatory, $120 fee. Preregistration for classes offered. 3-day program prior to start of classes in August. **Policies:** Students share responsibility for maintaining high standards and must pledge to abide by Academic Behavior Code. Freshmen not permitted cars on campus. **Housing:** Guaranteed on-campus for all undergraduates. Coed dorms, single-sex dorms, special housing for disabled, apartments, fraternity/sorority housing available. $400 nonrefundable deposit, deadline 5/1. College-owned houses in neighborhood surrounding campus. **Activities:** Bands, campus ministries, choral groups, dance, drama, film society, international student organizations, literary magazine, music ensembles, musical theater, radio station, student government, student newspaper, symphony orchestra, over 100 clubs and organizations.

Athletics. NCAA. **Intercollegiate:** Baseball M, basketball, cheerleading, cross-country, field hockey W, football (tackle) M, golf, lacrosse, soccer, softball W, tennis, track and field, volleyball W, wrestling M. **Intramural:** Basketball, cross-country, football (non-tackle) M, racquetball, soccer, softball, swimming, tennis, volleyball. **Team name:** Mules.

Student services. Adult student services, alcohol/substance abuse counseling, chaplain/spiritual director, career counseling, student employment services, financial aid counseling, health services, minority student services, personal counseling, placement for graduates, women's services. **Physically disabled:** Services for visually, speech, hearing impaired.

Contact. E-mail: admissions@muhlenberg.edu
Phone: (484) 664-3200 Fax: (484) 664-3234
Christopher Hooker-Haring, Dean of Admission and Financial Aid, Muhlenberg College, 2400 Chew Street, Allentown, PA 18104

Neumann University
Aston, Pennsylvania   **CB member**
www.neumann.edu   **CB code: 2628**

- Private 4-year university affiliated with the Roman Catholic Church
- Residential campus in large town
- 2,358 degree-seeking undergraduates: 24% part-time, 64% women, 22% African American, 1% Asian American, 2% Hispanic/Latino, 2% Multiracial, non-Hispanic, 1% international
- 475 degree-seeking graduate students

- 91% of applicants admitted
- SAT or ACT (ACT writing optional) required
- 49% graduate within 6 years

General. Founded in 1965. Regionally accredited. **Degrees:** 558 bachelor's, 9 associate awarded; master's, professional, doctoral offered. **ROTC:** Army, Air Force. **Location:** 24 miles from Philadelphia. **Calendar:** Semester, limited summer session. **Full-time faculty:** 97 total; 75% have terminal degrees, 64% women. **Part-time faculty:** 206 total; 27% have terminal degrees, 61% women. **Class size:** 63% < 20, 35% 20-39, less than 1% 40-49, 1% 50-99. **Special facilities:** Institute for sport, spirituality and character development. Neumann Institute for Franciscan Studies.

Freshman class profile. 2,253 applied, 2,046 admitted, 401 enrolled.

Mid 50% test scores			
SAT critical reading:	410-490	GPA 3.0-3.49:	29%
SAT math:	410-500	GPA 2.0-2.99:	41%
SAT writing:	390-480	End year in good standing:	89%
ACT composite:	17-21	Return as sophomores:	70%
GPA 3.75 or higher:	11%	Out-of-state:	34%
GPA 3.50-3.74:	16%	Live on campus:	72%
		International:	1%

Basis for selection. Acceptance depends on major applied for, SAT scores, and high school GPA. Interview recommended. **Home schooled:** State high school equivalency certificate required.

High school preparation. College-preparatory program recommended. 16 units required; 17 recommended. Required and recommended units include English 4, mathematics 2, social studies 2, science 2-3, foreign language 2 and academic electives 4.

2015-2016 Annual costs. Tuition/fees: $26,918. Room/board: $11,754. Books/supplies: $1,488. Personal expenses: $1,020.

2014-2015 Financial aid. All financial aid based on need. 401 full-time freshmen applied for aid; 377 deemed to have need; 377 received aid. Average need met was 70%. Average scholarship/grant was $6,738; average loan $3,500. 77% of total undergraduate aid awarded as scholarships/grants, 23% as loans/jobs.

Application procedures. Admission: No deadline. $35 fee, may be waived for applicants with need, free for online applicants. Admission notification on a rolling basis beginning on or about 9/15. Must reply by May 1 or within 2 week(s) if notified thereafter. **Financial aid:** No deadline. FAFSA required. Applicants notified on a rolling basis; must reply within 2 week(s) of notification.

Academics. Combined bachelor's/graduate program for chiropractic medicine. **Special study options:** Accelerated study, combined bachelor's/graduate degree, cooperative education, cross-registration, distance learning, double major, dual enrollment of high school students, honors, independent study, internships, liberal arts/career combination, study abroad, teacher certification program. Leadership development, service learning. **Credit/placement by examination:** AP, CLEP, SAT, ACT, institutional tests. 15 credit hours maximum toward associate degree, 30 toward bachelor's. University grants credit for those scores which are at or above the C level as set forth in equivalency tables which are prepared and published by the testing agencies. The applicability of accepted credits toward general degree requirements and/or specific program requirements is determined by the Registrar, in consultation with the appropriate Dean. A maximum of 15 semester hours of either AP, ACT, CLEP, or DANTES credit may be applied toward the associate degree, and a maximum of 30 semester hours toward the bachelor's degree, provided that the maximum number of transfer credits has not been exceeded. **Support services:** Learning center, pre-admission summer program, reduced course load, remedial instruction, study skills assistance, tutoring, writing center.

Majors. Biology: General. **Business:** Accounting, business admin, international, marketing, organizational behavior. **Computer sciences:** General. **Education:** Elementary, elementary special ed. **English:** English lit. **Health services:** Athletic training. **Human services:** Social work. **Liberal arts:** Arts/sciences. **Parks/recreation:** Sports admin. **Protective services:** Criminal justice. **Psychology:** General. **Social sciences:** Political science. **Visual/performing arts:** Dramatic.

Most popular majors. Business/marketing 13%, education 8%, health sciences 20%, liberal arts 19%, parks/recreation 7%, psychology 12%, security/protective services 8%.

Technology on campus. 205 workstations in dormitories, library, computer center. Dormitories wired for high-speed internet access and linked to campus network. Commuter students can connect to campus network. Online library, helpline, wireless network available.

Student life. Freshman orientation: Mandatory. Preregistration for classes offered. Held the last weekend before classes begin. **Housing:** Coed dorms, special housing for disabled, apartments available. $300 nonrefundable deposit, deadline 8/1. **Activities:** Jazz band, campus ministries, choral groups, dance, drama, literary magazine, music ensembles, musical theater, radio station, student government, student newspaper, symphony orchestra, TV station, Black Student Union, Active Minds (mental health awareness group), Coffee and Conversation Club, Fashion for a Cause, mock trial club, personal finance club, Knights for Education, environmental awareness club, Student Peace Alliance, Wellness Educators.

Athletics. NCAA. **Intercollegiate:** Baseball M, basketball, cross-country, field hockey W, golf, ice hockey, lacrosse, soccer, softball W, tennis, track and field, volleyball W. **Intramural:** Basketball, football (non-tackle), sand volleyball, soccer, softball, table tennis, ultimate frisbee, volleyball. **Team name:** Knights.

Student services. Adult student services, alcohol/substance abuse counseling, chaplain/spiritual director, career counseling, services for economically disadvantaged, student employment services, financial aid counseling, health services, on-campus daycare, personal counseling, placement for graduates, veterans' counselor. **Physically disabled:** Services for visually, speech, hearing impaired.

Contact. E-mail: neumann@neumann.edu
Phone: (610) 558-5616 Toll-free number: (800) 963-8626
Fax: (610) 361-2548
Christopher Mayerski, Director of Admissions, Neumann University, Office of Admissions, Aston, PA 19014-1298

Peirce College

Philadelphia, Pennsylvania
www.peirce.edu

CB member
CB code: 2674

- Private 4-year business and technical college
- Commuter campus in very large city
- 1,622 degree-seeking undergraduates: 81% part-time, 72% women, 69% African American, 2% Asian American, 8% Hispanic/Latino
- 65 degree-seeking graduate students

General. Founded in 1865. Regionally accredited. Peirce College is located in the heart of Philadelphia's business district, adjacent to the Avenue of the Arts, and within the Historic Rittenhouse district. **Degrees:** 201 bachelor's, 98 associate awarded; master's offered. **Calendar:** Semester, limited summer session. **Full-time faculty:** 30 total; 77% have terminal degrees, 13% minority, 60% women. **Part-time faculty:** 91 total; 24% have terminal degrees, 25% minority, 50% women. **Class size:** 82% < 20, 18% 20-39.

Freshman class profile.

Return as sophomores: 50% Out-of-state: 1%

Basis for selection. Open admission, but selective for some programs. Official high school transcript or copy of GED scores, cumulative GPA of 2.0 or higher, and minimum of 30 transferable credits required for Business Administration with a concentration in Professional Studies for Bachelor of Science degree program. Nonmatriculated students may take up to 15 credits while waiting for official transcripts and other documents to be evaluated.

2015-2016 Annual costs. Tuition/fees: $17,580.

2014-2015 Financial aid. **Need-based:** 32 full-time freshmen applied for aid; 30 deemed to have need; 30 received aid. Average need met was 51%. Average scholarship/grant was $6,128; average loan $2,798. 34% of total undergraduate aid awarded as scholarships/grants, 66% as loans/jobs. **Non-need-based:** Awarded to 137 full-time undergraduates, including 27 freshmen. Scholarships awarded for academics, alumni affiliation, leadership, state residency. **Additional information:** Tuition discounts available for US students serving in US military and in protect-and-serve fields.

Application procedures. **Admission:** No deadline. $50 fee, may be waived for applicants with need. Admission notification on a rolling basis. **Financial aid:** Priority date 5/1; no closing date. FAFSA required. Applicants notified on a rolling basis starting 5/1.

Academics. Through the Walker Center for Academic Excellence, students are able to participate in workshops on campus or online. In addition, students can participate in tutoring services on campus, via telephone or online through Smarthinking. **Special study options:** Accelerated study, cooperative education, cross-registration, distance learning, dual enrollment of high school students, internships. **Credit/placement by examination:** AP, CLEP, institutional tests. 30 credit hours maximum toward associate degree, 90 toward bachelor's. **Support services:** Learning center, study skills assistance, tutoring.

Majors. Business: Accounting, business admin, human resources. **Computer sciences:** Information technology. **Health services:** Health care admin, health information management.

Most popular majors. Business/marketing 58%, computer/information sciences 15%, health sciences 8%, legal studies 18%.

Technology on campus. PC or laptop required. 46 workstations in library, student center. Commuter students can connect to campus network. Online course registration, online library, helpline, repair service, wireless network available.

Student life. Freshman orientation: Mandatory. Preregistration for classes offered. **Activities:** Chi Alpha Epsilon Honor Society, Delta Mu Delta Honor Society, Lambda Epsilon Chi Honor Society, paralegal student association, information technology student association, health program student association, Students for Free Enterprise and student leadership program.

Student services. Adult student services, career counseling, services for economically disadvantaged, student employment services, financial aid counseling, health services. **Physically disabled:** Services for visually, hearing impaired.

Contact. E-mail: info@peirce.edu
Phone: (215) 670-9214 Toll-free number: (888) 467-3472 ext. 9214
Fax: (215) 670-9366
Paul Ballentine, Director, Admissions, Peirce College, 1420 Pine Street, Philadelphia, PA 19102-4699

Penn State Abington

Abington, Pennsylvania
www.abington.psu.edu

CB code: 2660

- Public 4-year branch campus college
- Commuter campus in small city
- 3,490 degree-seeking undergraduates: 12% part-time, 51% women, 13% African American, 17% Asian American, 10% Hispanic/Latino, 2% Multi-racial, non-Hispanic, 5% international
- 5 graduate students
- 82% of applicants admitted
- SAT or ACT (ACT writing optional) required
- 48% graduate within 6 years

General. Founded in 1950. Regionally accredited. Applicants may choose from 20 campuses. Students may transfer between campuses after meeting entrance requirements for selected major. **Degrees:** 602 bachelor's, 29 associate awarded. **ROTC:** Army, Air Force. **Location:** 15 miles from Philadelphia. **Calendar:** Semester, extensive summer session. **Full-time faculty:** 136 total; 65% have terminal degrees, 17% minority, 50% women. **Part-time faculty:** 168 total; 31% have terminal degrees, 11% minority, 44% women. **Class size:** 52% < 20, 42% 20-39, 2% 40-49, 3% 50-99, less than 1% >100.

Freshman class profile. 3,946 applied, 3,251 admitted, 872 enrolled.

Mid 50% test scores			
		GPA 3.0-3.49:	37%
SAT critical reading:	420-520	GPA 2.0-2.99:	39%
SAT math:	430-570	Rank in top quarter:	27%
SAT writing:	410-520	Rank in top tenth:	8%
ACT composite:	19-25	Return as sophomores:	80%
GPA 3.75 or higher:	7%	Out-of-state:	12%
GPA 3.50-3.74:	17%	International:	9%

Basis for selection. High school GPA as well as other factors, including standardized test scores, class rank, personal statements, activities lists. Essay considered if submitted; portfolios required for select majors. **Home schooled:** Provide complete documentation showing courses studied and all evaluations presented from home school evaluator or supervisor assigned to student in cooperation with local school district or evaluator approved through program.

High school preparation. College-preparatory program required. Required and recommended units include English 4, mathematics 3, social studies 3, science 3 and foreign language 2-3.

2015-2016 Annual costs. Tuition/fees: $13,954; $21,266 out-of-state. Books/supplies: $1,840. Personal expenses: $1,854.

2014-2015 Financial aid. **Need-based:** 747 full-time freshmen applied for aid; 614 deemed to have need; 596 received aid. Average need met was 57%. Average scholarship/grant was $7,747; average loan $3,320. 51% of total undergraduate aid awarded as scholarships/grants, 49% as loans/jobs. **Non-need-based:** Awarded to 782 full-time undergraduates, including 279 freshmen. Scholarships awarded for academics, alumni affiliation, ROTC.

Application procedures. Admission: Priority date 11/30; no deadline. $50 fee, may be waived for applicants with need. Admission notification on a rolling basis beginning on or about 10/15. Must reply by May 1 or within 2 week(s) if notified thereafter. **Financial aid:** Priority date 2/15; no closing date. FAFSA required. Applicants notified on a rolling basis.

Academics. Special study options: Accelerated study, cooperative education, distance learning, double major, dual enrollment of high school students, ESL, exchange student, external degree, honors, independent study, internships, liberal arts/career combination, student-designed major, study abroad, teacher certification program, weekend college. **Credit/placement by examination:** AP, CLEP, IB, SAT, ACT, institutional tests. 60 credit hours maximum toward bachelor's degree. **Support services:** Learning center, preadmission summer program, remedial instruction, study skills assistance, tutoring, writing center.

Honors college/program. Candidates will be assessed based on the academic and extracurricular documents submitted with the application, as well as responses to essay questions and letters of recommendation.

Majors. Area/ethnic studies: African-American, American, Asian, Latin American, women's. **Biology:** General, bacteriology, biochemistry, toxicology. **Business:** General, accounting, communications, finance, labor relations, management information systems, marketing, organizational behavior. **Communications:** Advertising, communications/speech/rhetoric, journalism. **Computer sciences:** General, information systems. **Conservation:** General, environmental studies, forest sciences. **Education:** Adult ed admin, agricultural, art, early childhood, elementary, foreign languages, secondary, special ed. **Engineering:** General, aerospace, agricultural, architectural, biomedical, chemical, civil, computer, electrical, engineering science, environmental, industrial, mechanical, mining, nuclear, petroleum. **English:** English lit. **Foreign languages:** Chinese, classics, comparative lit, French, German, Italian, Japanese, Russian, Spanish. **Health services:** Athletic training, communication disorders, health care admin, nursing (RN), premedicine, preveterinary. **History:** General. **Liberal arts:** Arts/sciences. **Math:** General, statistics. **Parks/recreation:** Exercise sciences, facilities management. **Philosophy/religion:** Judaic, philosophy. **Physical sciences:** Astronomy, atmospheric science, chemistry, geology, materials science, physics. **Protective services:** Criminal justice, forensics, law enforcement admin. **Psychology:** General, social. **Social sciences:** Anthropology, archaeology, economics, geography, international relations, political science, sociology. **Visual/performing arts:** General, acting, art, art history/conservation, film/cinema/video, graphic design, music, theater design. **Work/family studies:** Family studies, human nutrition.

Most popular majors. Business/marketing 24%, computer/information sciences 7%, health sciences 23%, interdisciplinary studies 6%, psychology 17%, security/protective services 10%.

Technology on campus. 150 workstations in library, computer center, student center. Commuter students can connect to campus network. Online course registration, online library, helpline, repair service, student web hosting, wireless network available.

Student life. Freshman orientation: Mandatory. Preregistration for classes offered. Held for two days in May, June, July and August. **Policies:** Acts of intolerance and high-risk drinking discouraged at all locations. All facilities designated as smoke-free. Students expected to abide by The Penn State Principles. **Activities:** Jazz band, campus ministries, choral groups, dance, drama, film society, international student organizations, literary magazine, music ensembles, student government, student newspaper.

Athletics. USCAA. **Intercollegiate:** Baseball M, basketball, golf, lacrosse W, soccer, softball W, tennis, volleyball W. **Intramural:** Basketball, cross-country, football (non-tackle) M, soccer, softball, tennis, volleyball. **Team name:** Nittany Lions.

Student services. Adult student services, alcohol/substance abuse counseling, chaplain/spiritual director, career counseling, services for economically disadvantaged, student employment services, financial aid counseling, health services, minority student services, personal counseling, placement for graduates, veterans' counselor. **Physically disabled:** Services for visually, hearing impaired.

Contact. E-mail: abingtonadmissions@psu.edu
Phone: (215) 881-7600 Fax: (215) 881-7655
Clark Brigger, Executive Director for Undergraduate Admissions, Penn State Abington, 1600 Woodland Road, Abington, PA 19001

Penn State Altoona
Altoona, Pennsylvania
www.altoona.psu.edu   **CB code: 2660**

- Public 4-year branch campus college
- Residential campus in small city

- 3,772 degree-seeking undergraduates: 3% part-time, 44% women, 7% African American, 3% Asian American, 6% Hispanic/Latino, 2% Multiracial, non-Hispanic, 5% international
- 1 graduate students
- 89% of applicants admitted
- SAT or ACT (ACT writing optional) required
- 69% graduate within 6 years

General. Founded in 1929. Regionally accredited. Applicants may choose from 20 campuses. Students may transfer between campuses after meeting entrance requirements for selected major. **Degrees:** 354 bachelor's, 55 associate awarded. **ROTC:** Army, Air Force. **Location:** 2 miles from downtown. **Calendar:** Semester, limited summer session. **Full-time faculty:** 203 total; 67% have terminal degrees, 12% minority, 50% women. **Part-time faculty:** 99 total; 20% have terminal degrees, 3% minority, 50% women. **Class size:** 44% < 20, 45% 20-39, 5% 40-49, 6% 50-99, less than 1% >100.

Freshman class profile. 5,738 applied, 5,129 admitted, 1,379 enrolled.

Mid 50% test scores			
SAT critical reading:	440-540	GPA 3.0-3.49:	42%
SAT math:	450-550	GPA 2.0-2.99:	42%
SAT writing:	430-530	Rank in top quarter:	24%
ACT composite:	20-24	Rank in top tenth:	6%
GPA 3.75 or higher:	3%	Return as sophomores:	84%
GPA 3.50-3.74:	12%	Out-of-state:	19%
		International:	4%

Basis for selection. High school GPA as well as other factors, including standardized test scores, class rank, personal statements, activities lists. Essay considered if submitted; portfolios required for select majors. **Home schooled:** Provide complete documentation showing courses studied and all evaluations presented from home school evaluator or supervisor assigned to student in cooperation with local school district or evaluator approved through program.

High school preparation. College-preparatory program required. Required and recommended units include English 4, mathematics 3, social studies 3, science 3 and foreign language 2-3.

2015-2016 Annual costs. Tuition/fees: $14,610; $22,344 out-of-state. Room/board: $10,920. Books/supplies: $1,840. Personal expenses: $3,222.

2014-2015 Financial aid. Need-based: 1,239 full-time freshmen applied for aid; 982 deemed to have need; 939 received aid. Average need met was 56%. Average scholarship/grant was $6,573; average loan $3,469. 40% of total undergraduate aid awarded as scholarships/grants, 60% as loans/jobs. **Non-need-based:** Awarded to 1,445 full-time undergraduates, including 627 freshmen. Scholarships awarded for academics, alumni affiliation, ROTC.

Application procedures. Admission: Priority date 11/30; no deadline. $50 fee, may be waived for applicants with need. Admission notification on a rolling basis beginning on or about 10/15. Must reply by May 1 or within 2 week(s) if notified thereafter. **Financial aid:** Priority date 2/15; no closing date. FAFSA required. Applicants notified on a rolling basis.

Academics. Special study options: Accelerated study, cooperative education, cross-registration, distance learning, double major, dual enrollment of high school students, ESL, exchange student, external degree, honors, independent study, internships, liberal arts/career combination, student-designed major, study abroad, teacher certification program, weekend college. **Credit/placement by examination:** AP, CLEP, IB, SAT, ACT, institutional tests. 60 credit hours maximum toward bachelor's degree. **Support services:** Learning center, remedial instruction, study skills assistance, tutoring, writing center.

Honors college/program. Candidates will be assessed based on the academic and extracurricular documents submitted with the application, as well as responses to essay questions and letters of recommendation.

Majors. Area/ethnic studies: African-American, Asian, Latin American, women's. **Biology:** General, bacteriology, biochemistry, toxicology. **Business:** General, accounting, finance, labor relations, management information systems, marketing, organizational behavior. **Communications:** Advertising, communications/speech/rhetoric, journalism. **Computer sciences:** General, information systems, security. **Conservation:** General, environmental studies, forest sciences. **Education:** Adult ed admin, agricultural, art, early childhood, elementary, foreign languages, secondary, special ed. **Engineering:** Aerospace, agricultural, architectural, biomedical, chemical, civil, computer, electrical, engineering science, environmental, industrial, mechanical, mining, nuclear, petroleum, transportation. **English:** English lit. **Foreign languages:** Chinese, classics, comparative lit, French, German, Italian, Japanese, Russian, Spanish. **Health services:** Athletic training, communication disorders, health care admin, nursing (RN), premedicine, preveterinary. **History:** General. **Liberal arts:** Arts/sciences. **Math:** General, statistics. **Parks/recreation:** Exercise sciences, facilities management. **Philosophy/religion:** Judaic, philosophy. **Physical sciences:** Astronomy, atmospheric science, chemistry, geology, materials science, physics. **Protective services:** Criminal justice, forensics, law enforcement admin. **Psychology:** General. **Social sciences:** Anthropology, archaeology, economics, geography, international relations, political science, sociology. **Visual/performing arts:** General, acting, art, art history/conservation, film/cinema/video, graphic design, music, theater design. **Work/family studies:** Family studies, human nutrition.

Most popular majors. Business/marketing 10%, engineering/engineering technologies 18%, family/consumer sciences 8%, health sciences 18%, security/protective services 12%.

Technology on campus. 450 workstations in dormitories, library, computer center. Dormitories wired for high-speed internet access and linked to campus network. Commuter students can connect to campus network. Online course registration, online library, helpline, student web hosting, wireless network available.

Student life. Freshman orientation: Mandatory. Preregistration for classes offered. Held for two days in May, June, July and August. **Policies:** Acts of intolerance and high-risk drinking discouraged at all locations. All facilities designated as smoke-free. Students expected to abide by The Penn State Principles. **Housing:** Coed dorms, special housing for disabled, themed housing, wellness housing available. $100 nonrefundable deposit, deadline 5/1. Suites, special interest housing available. **Activities:** Bands, campus ministries, choral groups, dance, drama, film society, international student organizations, literary magazine, music ensembles, musical theater, student government, student newspaper.

Athletics. NCAA. **Intercollegiate:** Baseball M, basketball, bowling W, cross-country, diving, golf, lacrosse W, soccer, softball W, swimming, tennis, volleyball. **Intramural:** Badminton, basketball, bowling, football (non-tackle), golf, racquetball, soccer, softball, swimming, table tennis, tennis, track and field, triathlon, volleyball, weight lifting. **Team name:** Nittany Lions.

Student services. Adult student services, alcohol/substance abuse counseling, chaplain/spiritual director, career counseling, services for economically disadvantaged, student employment services, financial aid counseling, health services, minority student services, personal counseling, placement for graduates, veterans' counselor, women's services. **Physically disabled:** Services for visually, hearing impaired.

Contact. E-mail: aaadmit@psu.edu
Phone: (814) 949-5466 Toll-free number: (800) 848-9843
Fax: (814) 949-5564
Clark Brigger, Director of Undergraduate Admissions, Penn State Altoona, 3000 Ivyside Park, Altoona, PA 16801

Penn State Beaver
Monaca, Pennsylvania
www.br.psu.edu   **CB code: 2660**

- Public 4-year branch campus college
- Residential campus in small town
- 639 degree-seeking undergraduates: 5% part-time, 39% women, 9% African American, 3% Asian American, 5% Hispanic/Latino, 2% Multiracial, non-Hispanic, 3% international
- 82% of applicants admitted
- SAT or ACT (ACT writing optional) required
- 45% graduate within 6 years

General. Founded in 1964. Regionally accredited. Applicants may choose from 20 campuses. Students may transfer between campuses after meeting entrance requirements for selected major. **Degrees:** 84 bachelor's awarded. **Location:** 30 miles from Pittsburgh. **Calendar:** Semester, limited summer session. **Full-time faculty:** 32 total; 66% have terminal degrees, 22% minority, 59% women. **Part-time faculty:** 27 total; 7% have terminal degrees, 7% minority, 48% women. **Class size:** 53% < 20, 43% 20-39, 3% 40-49, 1% 50-99.

Freshman class profile. 753 applied, 620 admitted, 210 enrolled.

Mid 50% test scores			
SAT critical reading:	430-550	GPA 3.0-3.49:	41%
SAT math:	450-570	GPA 2.0-2.99:	36%
SAT writing:	410-530	Rank in top quarter:	31%
ACT composite:	18-24	Rank in top tenth:	7%
GPA 3.75 or higher:	11%	Return as sophomores:	78%
GPA 3.50-3.74:	11%	Out-of-state:	13%
		International:	4%

Basis for selection. High school GPA as well as other factors, including standardized test scores, class rank, personal statements, activities lists. Essay considered if submitted; portfolios required for select majors. **Home schooled:** Provide complete documentation showing courses studied and all evaluations presented from home school evaluator or supervisor assigned

to student in cooperation with local school district or evaluator approved through program.

High school preparation. College-preparatory program required. Required and recommended units include English 4, mathematics 3, social studies 3, science 3 and foreign language 2-3.

2015-2016 Annual costs. Tuition/fees: $13,660; $20,346 out-of-state. Room/board: $10,920. Books/supplies: $1,840. Personal expenses: $3,222.

2014-2015 Financial aid. Need-based: 198 full-time freshmen applied for aid; 168 deemed to have need; 167 received aid. Average need met was 67%. Average scholarship/grant was $7,478; average loan $3,475. 50% of total undergraduate aid awarded as scholarships/grants, 50% as loans/jobs. **Non-need-based:** Awarded to 332 full-time undergraduates, including 139 freshmen. Scholarships awarded for academics, alumni affiliation, ROTC.

Application procedures. Admission: Priority date 11/30; no deadline. $50 fee, may be waived for applicants with need. Admission notification on a rolling basis beginning on or about 10/15. Must reply by May 1 or within 2 week(s) if notified thereafter. **Financial aid:** Priority date 2/15; no closing date. FAFSA required. Applicants notified on a rolling basis.

Academics. Special study options: Cross-registration, distance learning, double major, dual enrollment of high school students, honors, independent study, internships, study abroad. **Credit/placement by examination:** AP, CLEP, IB, SAT, ACT, institutional tests. 60 credit hours maximum toward bachelor's degree. **Support services:** Learning center, pre-admission summer program, reduced course load, remedial instruction, study skills assistance, tutoring, writing center.

Honors college/program. Candidates will be assessed based on the academic and extracurricular documents submitted with the application, as well as responses to essay questions and letters of recommendation.

Majors. Area/ethnic studies: African-American, Asian, Latin American, women's. **Biology:** General, bacteriology, biochemistry, toxicology. **Business:** Accounting, business admin, finance, labor relations, management information systems, marketing, organizational behavior. **Communications:** Advertising, communications/speech/rhetoric, journalism. **Computer sciences:** General, information systems. **Conservation:** General, environmental studies, forest sciences. **Education:** Adult ed admin, agricultural, art, early childhood, elementary, foreign languages, secondary, special ed. **Engineering:** Aerospace, agricultural, architectural, biomedical, chemical, civil, computer, electrical, engineering science, environmental, industrial, mechanical, mining, nuclear, petroleum. **English:** English lit. **Foreign languages:** Chinese, classics, comparative lit, French, German, Italian, Japanese, Russian, Spanish. **Health services:** Athletic training, communication disorders, health care admin, nursing (RN), premedicine, preveterinary. **History:** General. **Liberal arts:** Arts/sciences. **Math:** General, statistics. **Parks/recreation:** Exercise sciences, facilities management. **Philosophy/religion:** Judaic, philosophy. **Physical sciences:** Astronomy, atmospheric science, chemistry, geology, materials science, physics. **Protective services:** Criminal justice, forensics, law enforcement admin. **Psychology:** General. **Social sciences:** Anthropology, archaeology, economics, geography, international relations, political science, sociology. **Visual/performing arts:** General, acting, art, art history/conservation, film/cinema/video, graphic design, music, theater design. **Work/family studies:** Family studies, human nutrition.

Most popular majors. Business/marketing 24%, communications/journalism 10%, computer/information sciences 21%, psychology 18%, security/protective services 27%.

Technology on campus. 127 workstations in library, computer center, student center. Dormitories wired for high-speed internet access and linked to campus network. Commuter students can connect to campus network. Online course registration, online library, helpline, student web hosting, wireless network available.

Student life. Freshman orientation: Mandatory. Preregistration for classes offered. Held for two days in May, June, July and August. **Policies:** Acts of intolerance and high-risk drinking discouraged at all locations. All facilities designated as smoke-free. Students expected to abide by The Penn State Principles. **Housing:** Guaranteed on-campus for freshmen. Coed dorms, special housing for disabled available. $100 nonrefundable deposit, deadline 5/1. **Activities:** Campus ministries, choral groups, drama, film society, international student organizations, radio station, student government, student newspaper.

Athletics. USCAA. **Intercollegiate:** Baseball M, basketball, bowling W, soccer, softball W, volleyball W, wrestling M. **Intramural:** Basketball, bowling M, football (non-tackle), table tennis, volleyball. **Team name:** Nittany Lions.

Student services. Adult student services, alcohol/substance abuse counseling, chaplain/spiritual director, career counseling, services for economically disadvantaged, student employment services, financial aid counseling,

Four-Year Colleges

health services, personal counseling, placement for graduates, veterans' counselor. **Physically disabled:** Services for visually, hearing impaired.

Contact. E-mail: br-admissions@psu.edu
Phone: (724) 773-3800 Toll-free number: (877) 564-6778
Fax: (724) 773-3769
Clark Brigger, Director for Undergraduate Admissions, Penn State Beaver, 100 University Drive, Monaca, PA 15061

Penn State Berks
Reading, Pennsylvania
www.bk.psu.edu   **CB code: 2660**

- Public 4-year branch campus college
- Residential campus in small city
- 2,778 degree-seeking undergraduates: 7% part-time, 43% women, 9% African American, 5% Asian American, 11% Hispanic/Latino, 2% Multiracial, non-Hispanic, 3% international
- 85% of applicants admitted
- SAT or ACT (ACT writing optional) required
- 63% graduate within 6 years

General. Founded in 1924. Regionally accredited. Applicants may choose from 20 campuses. Students may transfer between campuses after meeting entrance requirements for selected major. **Degrees:** 319 bachelor's, 24 associate awarded. **ROTC:** Army. **Location:** 5 miles from downtown. **Calendar:** Semester, limited summer session. **Full-time faculty:** 136 total; 70% have terminal degrees, 15% minority, 50% women. **Part-time faculty:** 84 total; 17% have terminal degrees, 6% minority, 51% women. **Class size:** 39% < 20, 47% 20-39, 8% 40-49, 6% 50-99.

Freshman class profile. 2,413 applied, 2,048 admitted, 793 enrolled.

Mid 50% test scores		GPA 3.0-3.49:	38%
SAT critical reading:	420-540	GPA 2.0-2.99:	41%
SAT math:	430-560	Rank in top quarter:	29%
SAT writing:	410-520	Rank in top tenth:	8%
ACT composite:	18-25	Return as sophomores:	82%
GPA 3.75 or higher:	8%	Out-of-state:	12%
GPA 3.50-3.74:	12%	International:	3%

Basis for selection. High school GPA as well as other factors, including standardized test scores, class rank, personal statements, activities lists. Essay considered if submitted; portfolios required for select majors. **Home schooled:** Provide complete documentation showing courses studied and all evaluations presented from home school evaluator or supervisor assigned to student in cooperation with local school district or evaluator approved through program.

High school preparation. College-preparatory program required. Required and recommended units include English 4, mathematics 3, social studies 3, science 3 and foreign language 2-3.

2015-2016 Annual costs. Tuition/fees: $14,610; $22,344 out-of-state. Room/board: $11,950. Books/supplies: $1,840. Personal expenses: $3,222.

2014-2015 Financial aid. **Need-based:** 745 full-time freshmen applied for aid; 612 deemed to have need; 594 received aid. Average need met was 59%. Average scholarship/grant was $6,835; average loan $3,503. 42% of total undergraduate aid awarded as scholarships/grants, 58% as loans/jobs. **Non-need-based:** Awarded to 692 full-time undergraduates, including 267 freshmen. Scholarships awarded for academics, alumni affiliation, ROTC.

Application procedures. **Admission:** Priority date 11/30; no deadline. $50 fee, may be waived for applicants with need. Admission notification on a rolling basis beginning on or about 10/15. Must reply by May 1 or within 2 week(s) if notified thereafter. **Financial aid:** Priority date 2/15; no closing date. FAFSA required. Applicants notified on a rolling basis.

Academics. **Special study options:** Accelerated study, cooperative education, cross-registration, distance learning, dual enrollment of high school students, ESL, honors, independent study, internships, study abroad, teacher certification program. **Credit/placement by examination:** AP, CLEP, IB, SAT, ACT, institutional tests. 60 credit hours maximum toward bachelor's degree. **Support services:** Learning center, pre-admission summer program, remedial instruction, study skills assistance, tutoring, writing center.

Honors college/program. Candidates will be assessed based on the academic and extracurricular documents submitted with the application, as well as responses to essay questions and letters of recommendation.

Majors. **Area/ethnic studies:** African-American, Asian, Latin American, women's. **Biology:** General, bacteriology, biochemistry, toxicology. **Business:** General, accounting, finance, labor relations, management information systems, marketing, organizational behavior. **Communications:** Advertising, communications/speech/rhetoric, journalism. **Computer sciences:** General, information systems, security. **Conservation:** General, environmental studies, forest sciences. **Education:** Adult ed admin, agricultural, art, early childhood, elementary, foreign languages, secondary, special ed. **Engineering:** Aerospace, agricultural, architectural, biomedical, chemical, civil, computer, electrical, engineering science, environmental, industrial, mechanical, mining, nuclear, petroleum. **English:** English lit, technical writing. **Foreign languages:** General, Chinese, classics, comparative lit, French, German, Italian, Japanese, Russian, Spanish. **Health services:** Athletic training, communication disorders, health care admin, nursing (RN), premedicine, preveterinary. **History:** General. **Liberal arts:** Arts/sciences. **Math:** General, statistics. **Parks/recreation:** Exercise sciences, facilities management. **Philosophy/religion:** Judaic, philosophy. **Physical sciences:** Astronomy, atmospheric science, chemistry, geology, materials science, physics. **Protective services:** Criminal justice, forensics, law enforcement admin. **Psychology:** General. **Social sciences:** Anthropology, archaeology, economics, geography, international relations, political science, sociology. **Visual/performing arts:** General, acting, art, art history/conservation, film/cinema/video, graphic design, music, theater design. **Work/family studies:** Family studies, human nutrition.

Most popular majors. Biology 11%, business/marketing 19%, computer/information sciences 10%, education 7%, engineering/engineering technologies 13%, parks/recreation 15%, psychology 13%.

Technology on campus. 311 workstations in dormitories, library, computer center, student center. Dormitories wired for high-speed internet access and linked to campus network. Commuter students can connect to campus network. Online course registration, online library, helpline, repair service, student web hosting, wireless network available.

Student life. **Freshman orientation:** Mandatory. Preregistration for classes offered. Held for two days in May, June, July and August. **Policies:** Acts of intolerance and high-risk drinking discouraged at all locations. All facilities designated as smoke-free. Students expected to abide by The Penn State Principles. **Housing:** Coed dorms, special housing for disabled available. $100 nonrefundable deposit, deadline 5/1. Honor students, suites, special interest houses available. **Activities:** Campus ministries, choral groups, dance, drama, film society, literary magazine, radio station, student government, student newspaper.

Athletics. NCAA. **Intercollegiate:** Baseball M, basketball, cross-country, golf M, soccer, softball W, tennis, volleyball W. **Intramural:** Badminton, basketball, football (non-tackle), golf, table tennis, volleyball. **Team name:** NIttany Lions.

Student services. Adult student services, alcohol/substance abuse counseling, career counseling, services for economically disadvantaged, student employment services, financial aid counseling, health services, minority student services, personal counseling, placement for graduates, veterans' counselor, women's services. **Physically disabled:** Services for visually, hearing impaired.

Contact. E-mail: admissionsbk@psu.edu
Phone: (610) 396-6060 Fax: (610) 396-6077
Clark Brigger, Director for Undergraduate Admissions, Penn State Berks, Tulpehocken Road, Reading, PA 19610

Penn State Brandywine
Media, Pennsylvania
www.brandywine.psu.edu   **CB code: 2660**

- Public 4-year branch campus college
- Commuter campus in small town
- 1,291 degree-seeking undergraduates: 9% part-time, 44% women, 15% African American, 11% Asian American, 5% Hispanic/Latino, 2% Multiracial, non-Hispanic, 1% international
- 83% of applicants admitted
- SAT or ACT (ACT writing optional) required
- 41% graduate within 6 years

General. Founded in 1966. Regionally accredited. Applicants may choose from 20 campuses. Students may transfer between campuses after meeting entrance requirements for selected major. **Degrees:** 195 bachelor's, 5 associate awarded. **ROTC:** Army, Air Force. **Location:** 20 miles from Philadelphia. **Calendar:** Semester, limited summer session. **Full-time faculty:** 68 total; 71% have terminal degrees, 15% minority, 53% women. **Part-time faculty:** 67 total; 24% have terminal degrees, 8% minority, 55% women. **Class size:** 54% < 20, 43% 20-39, 2% 40-49, less than 1% 50-99.

Freshman class profile. 1,265 applied, 1,051 admitted, 374 enrolled.

Mid 50% test scores			
SAT critical reading:	420-520	**GPA 3.0-3.49:**	28%
SAT math:	440-550	**GPA 2.0-2.99:**	54%
SAT writing:	410-510	**Rank in top quarter:**	18%
ACT composite:	18-26	**Rank in top tenth:**	4%
GPA 3.75 or higher:	6%	**Return as sophomores:**	74%
GPA 3.50-3.74:	12%	**Out-of-state:**	6%
		International:	2%

Basis for selection. High school GPA as well as other factors, including standardized test scores, class rank, personal statements, activities lists. Essay considered if submitted; portfolios required for select majors. **Home schooled:** Provide complete documentation showing courses studied and all evaluations presented from home school evaluator or supervisor assigned to student in cooperation with local school district or evaluator approved through program.

High school preparation. College-preparatory program required. Required and recommended units include English 4, mathematics 3, social studies 3, science 3 and foreign language 2-3.

2015-2016 Annual costs. Tuition/fees: $13,964; $21,158 out-of-state. Books/supplies: $1,840. Personal expenses: $1,854.

2014-2015 Financial aid. Need-based: 335 full-time freshmen applied for aid; 255 deemed to have need; 249 received aid. Average need met was 61%. Average scholarship/grant was $6,811; average loan $3,398. 49% of total undergraduate aid awarded as scholarships/grants, 51% as loans/jobs. **Non-need-based:** Awarded to 372 full-time undergraduates, including 154 freshmen. Scholarships awarded for academics, alumni affiliation, ROTC.

Application procedures. Admission: Priority date 11/30; no deadline. $50 fee, may be waived for applicants with need. Admission notification on a rolling basis beginning on or about 10/15. Must reply by May 1 or within 2 week(s) if notified thereafter. **Financial aid:** Priority date 2/15; no closing date. FAFSA required. Applicants notified on a rolling basis.

Academics. Special study options: Accelerated study, distance learning, double major, dual enrollment of high school students, ESL, honors, independent study, internships, study abroad. **Credit/placement by examination:** AP, CLEP, IB, SAT, ACT, institutional tests. 60 credit hours maximum toward bachelor's degree. **Support services:** Learning center, pre-admission summer program, reduced course load, remedial instruction, study skills assistance, tutoring, writing center.

Honors college/program. Candidates will be assessed based on the academic and extracurricular documents submitted with the application, as well as responses to essay questions and letters of recommendation.

Majors. Area/ethnic studies: African-American, American, Asian, Latin American, women's. **Biology:** General, bacteriology, biochemistry, toxicology. **Business:** Accounting, business admin, finance, labor relations, management information systems, marketing, organizational behavior. **Communications:** Advertising, communications/speech/rhetoric, journalism. **Computer sciences:** General, information systems. **Conservation:** General, environmental studies, forest sciences. **Education:** Adult ed admin, agricultural, art, early childhood, elementary, foreign languages, secondary, special ed. **Engineering:** General, aerospace, agricultural, architectural, biomedical, chemical, civil, computer, electrical, engineering science, environmental, industrial, mechanical, mining, nuclear, petroleum. **English:** English lit. **Foreign languages:** Chinese, classics, comparative lit, French, German, Italian, Japanese, Russian, Spanish. **Health services:** Athletic training, communication disorders, health care admin, nursing (RN), premedicine, preveterinary. **History:** General. **Liberal arts:** Arts/sciences. **Math:** General, statistics. **Parks/recreation:** Exercise sciences, facilities management. **Philosophy/religion:** Judaic, philosophy. **Physical sciences:** Astronomy, atmospheric science, chemistry, geology, materials science, physics. **Protective services:** Forensics, law enforcement admin. **Psychology:** General. **Social sciences:** Anthropology, archaeology, economics, geography, international relations, political science, sociology. **Visual/performing arts:** General, acting, art, art history/conservation, film/cinema/video, graphic design, music, theater design. **Work/family studies:** Family studies, human nutrition.

Most popular majors. Business/marketing 30%, communications/journalism 16%, computer/information sciences 9%, family/consumer sciences 18%, liberal arts 6%, psychology 13%.

Technology on campus. 142 workstations in library, computer center, student center. Commuter students can connect to campus network. Online course registration, online library, helpline, repair service, student web hosting, wireless network available.

Student life. Freshman orientation: Available. Preregistration for classes offered. Held for two days in May, June, July and August. **Policies:** Acts of intolerance and high-risk drinking discouraged at all locations. All facilities designated as smoke-free. Students expected to abide by The Penn State

Principles. **Activities:** Literary magazine, student government, student newspaper.

Athletics. USCAA. **Intercollegiate:** Baseball M, basketball, cheerleading, cross-country, soccer, softball W, tennis, volleyball W. **Intramural:** Basketball, soccer. **Team name:** Nittany Lions.

Student services. Adult student services, alcohol/substance abuse counseling, career counseling, services for economically disadvantaged, student employment services, financial aid counseling, minority student services, personal counseling, placement for graduates, veterans' counselor. **Physically disabled:** Services for visually, hearing impaired.

Contact. E-mail: bwadmissions@psu.edu
Phone: (610) 892-1200 Fax: (610) 892-1357
Clark Brigger, Director for Undergraduate Admissions, Penn State Brandywine, 25 Yearsley Mill Road, Media, PA 19063

Penn State DuBois
DuBois, Pennsylvania
http://dubois.psu.edu   **CB code: 2660**

- Public 4-year branch campus college
- Commuter campus in small town
- 512 degree-seeking undergraduates: 7% part-time, 44% women, 2% African American, 1% Asian American, 2% Hispanic/Latino
- 85% of applicants admitted
- SAT or ACT (ACT writing optional) required
- 41% graduate within 6 years

General. Founded in 1935. Regionally accredited. Applicants may choose from 20 campuses. Students may transfer between campuses after meeting entrance requirements for selected major. **Degrees:** 34 bachelor's, 73 associate awarded. **Location:** 120 miles from Pittsburgh. **Calendar:** Semester, limited summer session. **Full-time faculty:** 42 total; 57% have terminal degrees, 19% minority, 60% women. **Part-time faculty:** 16 total; 38% have terminal degrees, 44% women. **Class size:** 64% < 20, 32% 20-39, less than 1% 40-49, 3% 50-99.

Freshman class profile. 394 applied, 335 admitted, 163 enrolled.

Mid 50% test scores			
SAT critical reading:	420-530	**GPA 3.0-3.49:**	32%
SAT math:	420-560	**GPA 2.0-2.99:**	40%
SAT writing:	390-490	**Rank in top quarter:**	33%
ACT composite:	21-25	**Rank in top tenth:**	9%
GPA 3.75 or higher:	10%	**Return as sophomores:**	87%
GPA 3.50-3.74:	18%	**Out-of-state:**	4%
		International:	1%

Basis for selection. High school GPA as well as other factors, including standardized test scores, class rank, personal statements, activities lists. Essay considered if submitted; portfolios required for select majors. **Home schooled:** Provide complete documentation showing courses studied and all evaluations presented from home school evaluator or supervisor assigned to student in cooperation with local school district or evaluator approved through program.

High school preparation. College-preparatory program required. Required and recommended units include English 4, mathematics 3, social studies 3, science 3 and foreign language 2-3.

2015-2016 Annual costs. Tuition/fees: $13,546; $20,232 out-of-state. Books/supplies: $1,840. Personal expenses: $1,854.

2014-2015 Financial aid. Need-based: 141 full-time freshmen applied for aid; 125 deemed to have need; 124 received aid. Average need met was 63%. Average scholarship/grant was $6,813; average loan $3,220. 53% of total undergraduate aid awarded as scholarships/grants, 47% as loans/jobs. **Non-need-based:** Awarded to 157 full-time undergraduates, including 70 freshmen. Scholarships awarded for academics, alumni affiliation, ROTC.

Application procedures. Admission: Priority date 11/30; no deadline. $50 fee, may be waived for applicants with need. Admission notification on a rolling basis beginning on or about 10/15. Must reply by May 1 or within 2 week(s) if notified thereafter. **Financial aid:** Priority date 2/15; no closing date. FAFSA required. Applicants notified on a rolling basis.

Academics. Special study options: Accelerated study, cross-registration, distance learning, double major, dual enrollment of high school students, honors, independent study, internships, student-designed major, study abroad. **Credit/placement by examination:** AP, CLEP, IB, SAT, ACT, institutional tests. 60 credit hours maximum toward bachelor's degree. **Support services:**

Learning center, reduced course load, remedial instruction, study skills assistance, tutoring, writing center.

Honors college/program. Candidates will be assessed based on the academic and extracurricular documents submitted with the application, as well as responses to essay questions and letters of recommendation.

Majors. Area/ethnic studies: African-American, Asian, Latin American, women's. **Biology:** General, bacteriology, biochemistry, toxicology. **Business:** Accounting, business admin, finance, labor relations, management information systems, marketing, organizational behavior. **Communications:** Advertising, communications/speech/rhetoric, journalism. **Computer sciences:** General, information systems. **Conservation:** General, environmental studies, forest sciences. **Education:** Adult ed admin, agricultural, art, early childhood, elementary, foreign languages, secondary, special ed. **Engineering:** General, aerospace, agricultural, architectural, biomedical, chemical, civil, computer, electrical, engineering science, environmental, industrial, mechanical, mining, nuclear, petroleum. **English:** English lit. **Foreign languages:** Chinese, classics, comparative lit, French, German, Italian, Japanese, Russian, Spanish. **Health services:** Athletic training, communication disorders, health care admin, nursing (RN), premedicine, preveterinary. **History:** General. **Liberal arts:** Arts/sciences. **Math:** General, statistics. **Parks/recreation:** Exercise sciences, facilities management. **Philosophy/religion:** Judaic, philosophy. **Physical sciences:** Astronomy, atmospheric science, chemistry, geology, materials science, physics. **Protective services:** Criminal justice, forensics, law enforcement admin. **Psychology:** General. **Social sciences:** Anthropology, archaeology, economics, geography, international relations, political science, sociology. **Visual/performing arts:** General, acting, art, art history/conservation, film/cinema/video, graphic design, music, theater design. **Work/family studies:** Family studies, human nutrition.

Most popular majors. Business/marketing 41%, engineering/engineering technologies 9%, family/consumer sciences 35%, liberal arts 6%, physical sciences 9%.

Technology on campus. 212 workstations in library, computer center, student center. Online course registration, online library, helpline, repair service, student web hosting, wireless network available.

Student life. Freshman orientation: Mandatory. Preregistration for classes offered. Held for two days in May, June, July and August. **Policies:** Acts of intolerance and high-risk drinking discouraged at all locations. All facilities designated as smoke-free. Students expected to abide by The Penn State Principles. **Housing:** Independently owned housing nearby. **Activities:** Campus ministries, choral groups, film society, student government.

Athletics. USCAA. **Intercollegiate:** Basketball, cross-country, golf, volleyball W. **Intramural:** Badminton, basketball, bowling M, football (non-tackle), soccer, table tennis, volleyball. **Team name:** Nittany Lions.

Student services. Adult student services, alcohol/substance abuse counseling, chaplain/spiritual director, career counseling, services for economically disadvantaged, student employment services, financial aid counseling, health services, minority student services, personal counseling, placement for graduates, veterans' counselor, women's services. **Physically disabled:** Services for visually, hearing impaired.

Contact. E-mail: duboisinfo@psu.edu
Phone: (814) 375-4720 Toll-free number: (800) 346-7627
Fax: (814) 375-4784
Clark Brigger, Director for Undergraduate Admissions, Penn State DuBois, 1 College Place, DuBois, PA 15801

Penn State Erie, The Behrend College
Erie, Pennsylvania
http://psbehrend.psu.edu   **CB code: 2660**

◗ Public 4-year branch campus college
◗ Residential campus in small city
◗ 4,092 degree-seeking undergraduates: 4% part-time, 35% women, 4% African American, 3% Asian American, 2% Hispanic/Latino, 2% Multiracial, non-Hispanic, 9% international
◗ 151 degree-seeking graduate students
◗ 87% of applicants admitted
◗ SAT or ACT (ACT writing optional) required
◗ 69% graduate within 6 years

General. Founded in 1926. Regionally accredited. Applicants may choose from 20 campuses. Students may transfer between campuses after meeting entrance requirements for selected major. **Degrees:** 689 bachelor's, 55 associate awarded; master's offered. **ROTC:** Army. **Calendar:** Semester, limited summer session. **Full-time faculty:** 260 total; 67% have terminal degrees,

12% minority, 36% women. **Part-time faculty:** 70 total; 13% have terminal degrees, 7% minority, 51% women. **Class size:** 39% < 20, 46% 20-39, 10% 40-49, 4% 50-99, less than 1% >100.

Freshman class profile. 4,079 applied, 3,552 admitted, 1,176 enrolled.

Mid 50% test scores			
SAT critical reading:	460-560	GPA 3.0-3.49:	43%
SAT math:	480-610	GPA 2.0-2.99:	23%
SAT writing:	440-550	Rank in top quarter:	42%
ACT composite:	20-25	Rank in top tenth:	13%
GPA 3.75 or higher:	14%	Return as sophomores:	85%
GPA 3.50-3.74:	20%	Out-of-state:	13%
		International:	11%

Basis for selection. High school GPA as well as other factors, including standardized test scores, class rank, personal statements, activities lists. Essay considered if submitted; portfolios required for select majors. **Home schooled:** Provide complete documentation showing courses studied and all evaluations presented from home school evaluator or supervisor assigned to student in cooperation with local school district or evaluator approved through program.

High school preparation. College-preparatory program required. Required and recommended units include English 4, mathematics 3, social studies 3, science 3 and foreign language 2-3.

2015-2016 Annual costs. Tuition/fees: $14,610; $22,344 out-of-state. Room/board: $10,920. Books/supplies: $1,840. Personal expenses: $3,222.

2014-2015 Financial aid. Need-based: 924 full-time freshmen applied for aid; 747 deemed to have need; 731 received aid. Average need met was 58%. Average scholarship/grant was $6,901; average loan $3,512. 40% of total undergraduate aid awarded as scholarships/grants, 60% as loans/jobs. **Non-need-based:** Awarded to 1,233 full-time undergraduates, including 416 freshmen. Scholarships awarded for academics, alumni affiliation, ROTC.

Application procedures. Admission: Priority date 11/30; no deadline. $50 fee, may be waived for applicants with need. Admission notification on a rolling basis beginning on or about 10/15. Must reply by May 1 or within 2 week(s) if notified thereafter. **Financial aid:** Priority date 2/15; no closing date. FAFSA required. Applicants notified on a rolling basis.

Academics. Special study options: Accelerated study, cooperative education, distance learning, double major, dual enrollment of high school students, honors, independent study, internships, liberal arts/career combination, study abroad, teacher certification program. **Credit/placement by examination:** AP, CLEP, IB, SAT, ACT, institutional tests. 60 credit hours maximum toward bachelor's degree. **Support services:** Learning center, pre-admission summer program, remedial instruction, study skills assistance, tutoring, writing center.

Honors college/program. Candidates will be assessed based on the academic and extracurricular documents submitted with the application, as well as responses to essay questions and letters of recommendation.

Majors. Area/ethnic studies: African-American, Asian, Latin American, women's. **Biology:** General, bacteriology, biochemistry, toxicology. **Business:** Accounting, finance, international, labor relations, management information systems, managerial economics, marketing, organizational behavior. **Communications:** Advertising, communications/speech/rhetoric, journalism. **Computer sciences:** General, computer science, information systems. **Conservation:** General, environmental science, environmental studies, forest sciences. **Education:** Adult ed admin, agricultural, art, early childhood, elementary, foreign languages, secondary, special ed. **Engineering:** Aerospace, agricultural, architectural, biomedical, chemical, civil, computer, electrical, engineering science, environmental, industrial, mechanical, mining, nuclear, petroleum, polymer, software. **English:** Creative writing, English lit. **Foreign languages:** Chinese, classics, comparative lit, French, German, Italian, Japanese, Russian, Spanish. **Health services:** Athletic training, communication disorders, health care admin, nursing (RN), premedicine, preveterinary. **History:** General. **Liberal arts:** Arts/sciences. **Math:** General, statistics. **Parks/recreation:** Exercise sciences, facilities management. **Philosophy/religion:** Judaic, philosophy. **Physical sciences:** General, astronomy, atmospheric science, chemistry, geology, materials science, physics. **Protective services:** Forensics, law enforcement admin. **Psychology:** General. **Social sciences:** Anthropology, archaeology, economics, geography, international relations, political science, sociology. **Visual/performing arts:** General, acting, art, art history/conservation, film/cinema/video, graphic design, music, studio arts management, theater design. **Work/family studies:** Family studies, human nutrition.

Most popular majors. Biology 6%, business/marketing 38%, engineering/engineering technologies 30%.

Technology on campus. 778 workstations in dormitories, library, computer center, student center. Dormitories wired for high-speed internet access and linked to campus network. Commuter students can connect to campus

network. Online course registration, online library, helpline, repair service, student web hosting, wireless network available.

Student life. Freshman orientation: Mandatory. Preregistration for classes offered. Held for two days in May, June, July and August. **Policies:** Acts of intolerance and high-risk drinking discouraged at all locations. All facilities designated as smoke-free. Students expected to abide by The Penn State Principles. **Housing:** Guaranteed on-campus for freshmen. Coed dorms, single-sex dorms, special housing for disabled, apartments available. $100 nonrefundable deposit, deadline 5/1. Suites, special interest housing available. **Activities:** Bands, campus ministries, choral groups, dance, drama, film society, international student organizations, literary magazine, music ensembles, Model UN, radio station, student government, student newspaper.

Athletics. NCAA. Intercollegiate: Baseball M, basketball, cheerleading, cross-country, diving, field hockey, golf, soccer, softball W, swimming, tennis, track and field, volleyball, water polo. **Intramural:** Basketball, bowling, football (non-tackle), golf, soccer, softball, swimming, table tennis, track and field, triathlon, volleyball. **Team name:** Behrend Lions.

Student services. Adult student services, alcohol/substance abuse counseling, chaplain/spiritual director, career counseling, services for economically disadvantaged, student employment services, financial aid counseling, health services, minority student services, on-campus daycare, personal counseling, placement for graduates, veterans' counselor, women's services. **Physically disabled:** Services for visually, hearing impaired.

Contact. E-mail: behrend.admissions@psu.edu
Phone: (814) 898-6100 Toll-free number: (866) 374-3378
Fax: (814) 898-6044
Clark Brigger, Director for Undergraduate Admissions, Penn State Erie, The Behrend College, Metzgar Admissions & Alumni Center, Erie, PA 16563

Penn State Fayette, The Eberly Campus
Lemont Furnace, Pennsylvania
www.fe.psu.edu   CB code: 2660

♦ Public 4-year branch campus college
♦ Commuter campus in large town
♦ 671 degree-seeking undergraduates: 13% part-time, 59% women, 4% African American, 2% Hispanic/Latino, 3% Multi-racial, non-Hispanic, 2% international
♦ 81% of applicants admitted
♦ SAT or ACT (ACT writing optional) required
♦ 51% graduate within 6 years

General. Founded in 1934. Regionally accredited. Applicants may choose from 20 campuses. Students may transfer between campuses after meeting entrance requirements for selected major. **Degrees:** 95 bachelor's, 68 associate awarded. **Location:** 40 miles from Pittsburgh. **Calendar:** Semester, limited summer session. **Full-time faculty:** 44 total; 48% have terminal degrees, 2% minority, 46% women. **Part-time faculty:** 25 total; 12% have terminal degrees, 4% minority, 68% women. **Class size:** 59% < 20, 40% 20-39, less than 1% 50-99.

Freshman class profile. 659 applied, 533 admitted, 193 enrolled.

Mid 50% test scores		GPA 3.0-3.49:	40%
SAT critical reading:	390-510	GPA 2.0-2.99:	33%
SAT math:	410-520	Rank in top quarter:	35%
SAT writing:	370-470	Rank in top tenth:	10%
ACT composite:	17-22	Return as sophomores:	77%
GPA 3.75 or higher:	9%	Out-of-state:	8%
GPA 3.50-3.74:	18%	International:	4%

Basis for selection. High school GPA as well as other factors, including standardized test scores, class rank, personal statements, activities lists. Essay considered if submitted; portfolios required for select majors. **Home schooled:** Provide complete documentation showing courses studied and all evaluations presented from home school evaluator or supervisor assigned to student in cooperation with local school district or evaluator approved through program.

High school preparation. College-preparatory program required. Required and recommended units include English 4, mathematics 3, social studies 3, science 3 and foreign language 2-3.

2015-2016 Annual costs. Tuition/fees: $13,608; $20,294 out-of-state. Books/supplies: $1,840. Personal expenses: $1,854.

2014-2015 Financial aid. Need-based: 181 full-time freshmen applied for aid; 149 deemed to have need; 147 received aid. Average need met was

63%. Average scholarship/grant was $6,230; average loan $3,331. 49% of total undergraduate aid awarded as scholarships/grants, 51% as loans/jobs. **Non-need-based:** Awarded to 256 full-time undergraduates, including 110 freshmen. Scholarships awarded for academics, alumni affiliation, ROTC.

Application procedures. Admission: Priority date 11/30; no deadline. $50 fee, may be waived for applicants with need. Admission notification on a rolling basis beginning on or about 10/15. Must reply by May 1 or within 2 week(s) if notified thereafter. **Financial aid:** Priority date 2/15; no closing date. FAFSA required. Applicants notified on a rolling basis.

Academics. Special study options: Accelerated study, cross-registration, distance learning, double major, dual enrollment of high school students, honors, independent study, internships, student-designed major, study abroad. **Credit/placement by examination:** AP, CLEP, IB, SAT, ACT, institutional tests. 60 credit hours maximum toward bachelor's degree. **Support services:** Learning center, remedial instruction, study skills assistance, tutoring, writing center.

Honors college/program. Candidates will be assessed based on the academic and extracurricular documents submitted with the application, as well as responses to essay questions and letters of recommendation.

Majors. Area/ethnic studies: African-American, Asian, Latin American, women's. **Biology:** General, bacteriology, biochemistry, toxicology. **Business:** Accounting, business admin, communications, finance, labor relations, management information systems, marketing, organizational behavior. **Communications:** Advertising, communications/speech/rhetoric, journalism. **Computer sciences:** General, information systems. **Conservation:** General, environmental studies, forest sciences. **Education:** Adult ed admin, agricultural, art, early childhood, elementary, foreign languages, secondary, special ed. **Engineering:** Aerospace, agricultural, architectural, biomedical, chemical, civil, computer, electrical, engineering science, environmental, industrial, mechanical, mining, nuclear, petroleum. **English:** English lit. **Foreign languages:** Chinese, classics, comparative lit, French, German, Italian, Japanese, Russian, Spanish. **Health services:** Athletic training, communication disorders, health care admin, nursing (RN), premedicine, preveterinary. **History:** General. **Liberal arts:** Arts/sciences. **Math:** General, statistics. **Parks/recreation:** Exercise sciences, facilities management. **Philosophy/religion:** Judaic, philosophy. **Physical sciences:** Astronomy, atmospheric science, chemistry, geology, materials science, physics. **Protective services:** Criminal justice, forensics, law enforcement admin. **Psychology:** General. **Social sciences:** Anthropology, archaeology, economics, geography, international relations, political science, sociology. **Visual/performing arts:** General, acting, art, art history/conservation, film/cinema/video, graphic design, music, theater design. **Work/family studies:** Family studies, human nutrition.

Most popular majors. Business/marketing 11%, family/consumer sciences 12%, health sciences 58%, security/protective services 19%.

Technology on campus. 196 workstations in library, computer center, student center. Commuter students can connect to campus network. Online course registration, online library, helpline, repair service, student web hosting available.

Student life. Freshman orientation: Mandatory. Preregistration for classes offered. Held for two days in May, June, July and August. **Policies:** Acts of intolerance and high-risk drinking discouraged at all locations. All facilities designated as smoke-free. Students expected to abide by The Penn State Principles. **Housing:** Privately owned, off-campus housing available. **Activities:** Campus ministries, choral groups, drama, literary magazine, musical theater, student government, student newspaper.

Athletics. USCAA. Intercollegiate: Baseball M, basketball, cross-country, softball W, volleyball W, wrestling M. **Intramural:** Basketball, football (non-tackle), racquetball, softball, table tennis. **Team name:** Nittany Lions.

Student services. Adult student services, alcohol/substance abuse counseling, career counseling, services for economically disadvantaged, student employment services, financial aid counseling, health services, on-campus daycare, personal counseling, placement for graduates, veterans' counselor. **Physically disabled:** Services for visually, hearing impaired.

Contact. E-mail: feadm@psu.edu
Phone: (724) 430-4130 Fax: (724) 430-4184
Clark Brigger, Director for Undergraduate Admissions, Penn State Fayette, The Eberly Campus, 110 Eberly Building, Lemont Furnace, PA 15456

Penn State Greater Allegheny
McKeesport, Pennsylvania
http://ga.psu.edu

♦ Public 4-year branch campus college
♦ Residential campus in large town

- 532 degree-seeking undergraduates: 9% part-time, 41% women, 19% African American, 5% Asian American, 7% Hispanic/Latino, 3% Multiracial, non-Hispanic, 4% international
- 79% of applicants admitted
- SAT or ACT (ACT writing optional) required
- 38% graduate within 6 years

General. Founded in 1947. Regionally accredited. Applicants may choose from 20 campuses. Students may transfer between campuses after meeting entrance requirements for selected major. **Degrees:** 65 bachelor's, 1 associate awarded; master's offered. **Location:** 15 miles from Pittsburgh. **Calendar:** Semester, limited summer session. **Full-time faculty:** 34 total; 74% have terminal degrees, 29% minority, 59% women. **Part-time faculty:** 43 total; 16% have terminal degrees, 5% minority, 44% women. **Class size:** 73% < 20, 27% 20-39, less than 1% 40-49.

Freshman class profile. 594 applied, 468 admitted, 158 enrolled.

Mid 50% test scores			
SAT critical reading:	390-540	GPA 3.0-3.49:	35%
SAT math:	400-540	GPA 2.0-2.99:	45%
SAT writing:	380-510	Rank in top quarter:	22%
ACT composite:	20-25	Rank in top tenth:	6%
GPA 3.75 or higher:	6%	Return as sophomores:	80%
GPA 3.50-3.74:	14%	Out-of-state:	8%
		International:	6%

Basis for selection. High school GPA as well as other factors, including standardized test scores, class rank, personal statements, activities lists. Essay considered if submitted; portfolios required for select majors. **Home schooled:** Provide complete documentation showing courses studied and all evaluations presented from home school evaluator or supervisor assigned to student in cooperation with local school district or evaluator approved through program.

High school preparation. College-preparatory program required. Required and recommended units include English 4, mathematics 3, social studies 3, science 3 and foreign language 2-3.

2015-2016 Annual costs. Tuition/fees: $13,660; $20,346 out-of-state. Room/board: $10,920. Books/supplies: $1,840. Personal expenses: $3,222.

2014-2015 Financial aid. Need-based: 168 full-time freshmen applied for aid; 150 deemed to have need; 150 received aid. Average need met was 68%. Average scholarship/grant was $7,609; average loan $3,459. 55% of total undergraduate aid awarded as scholarships/grants, 45% as loans/jobs. **Non-need-based:** Awarded to 234 full-time undergraduates, including 116 freshmen. Scholarships awarded for academics, alumni affiliation, ROTC.

Application procedures. Admission: Priority date 11/30; no deadline. $50 fee, may be waived for applicants with need. Admission notification on a rolling basis beginning on or about 10/15. Must reply by May 1 or within 2 week(s) if notified thereafter. **Financial aid:** Priority date 2/15; no closing date. FAFSA required. Applicants notified on a rolling basis.

Academics. Special study options: Cross-registration, distance learning, double major, dual enrollment of high school students, ESL, honors, independent study, internships, liberal arts/career combination, student-designed major, study abroad. **Credit/placement by examination:** AP, CLEP, IB, SAT, ACT, institutional tests. 60 credit hours maximum toward bachelor's degree. **Support services:** Learning center, pre-admission summer program, reduced course load, remedial instruction, study skills assistance, tutoring, writing center.

Honors college/program. Candidates will be assessed based on the academic and extracurricular documents submitted with the application, as well as responses to essay questions and letters of recommendation.

Majors. Area/ethnic studies: African-American, Asian, Latin American, women's. **Biology:** General, bacteriology, biochemistry, toxicology. **Business:** Accounting, business admin, finance, labor relations, management information systems, marketing, organizational behavior. **Communications:** Advertising, communications/speech/rhetoric, journalism. **Computer sciences:** General, information systems. **Conservation:** General, environmental studies, forest sciences. **Education:** Adult ed admin, agricultural, art, early childhood, elementary, foreign languages, secondary, special ed. **Engineering:** Aerospace, agricultural, architectural, biomedical, chemical, civil, computer, electrical, engineering science, environmental, industrial, mechanical, mining, nuclear, petroleum. **English:** English lit. **Foreign languages:** Chinese, classics, comparative lit, French, German, Italian, Japanese, Russian, Spanish. **Health services:** Athletic training, communication disorders, health care admin, nursing (RN), premedicine, preveterinary. **History:** General. **Liberal arts:** Arts/sciences. **Math:** General, statistics. **Parks/recreation:** Exercise sciences, facilities management. **Philosophy/religion:** Judaic, philosophy. **Physical sciences:** Astronomy, atmospheric science, chemistry, geology, materials science, physics. **Protective services:** Criminal justice, forensics, law enforcement admin. **Psychology:** General. **Social sciences:**

Anthropology, archaeology, economics, geography, international relations, political science, sociology. **Visual/performing arts:** General, acting, art, art history/conservation, film/cinema/video, graphic design, music, theater design. **Work/family studies:** Family studies, human nutrition.

Most popular majors. Business/marketing 37%, communications/journalism 22%, English 8%, psychology 31%.

Technology on campus. 203 workstations in dormitories, library, computer center, student center. Dormitories wired for high-speed internet access and linked to campus network. Commuter students can connect to campus network. Online course registration, online library, helpline, student web hosting, wireless network available.

Student life. Freshman orientation: Mandatory. Preregistration · for classes offered. Held for two days in May, June, July and August. **Policies:** Acts of intolerance and high-risk drinking discouraged at all locations. All facilities designated as smoke-free. Students expected to abide by The Penn State Principles. **Housing:** Coed dorms, special housing for disabled, wellness housing available. $100 nonrefundable deposit, deadline 5/1. **Activities:** Campus ministries, choral groups, dance, drama, literary magazine, music ensembles, radio station, student government, student newspaper, TV station.

Athletics. USCAA. **Intercollegiate:** Baseball M, basketball, golf, soccer M, softball W, volleyball W. **Intramural:** Basketball, football (non-tackle), soccer, softball, volleyball. **Team name:** Nittany Lions.

Student services. Adult student services, alcohol/substance abuse counseling, chaplain/spiritual director, career counseling, services for economically disadvantaged, student employment services, financial aid counseling, health services, minority student services, personal counseling, placement for graduates, veterans' counselor, women's services. **Physically disabled:** Services for visually, hearing impaired.

Contact. E-mail: psuga@psu.edu
Phone: (412) 675-9010 Toll-free number: (800) 248-5466
Fax: (412) 675-9056
Clark Brigger, Director for Undergraduate Admissions, Penn State Greater Allegheny, 123 Frable Building, McKeesport, PA 15132

Penn State Harrisburg
Middletown, Pennsylvania
www.hbg.psu.edu   **CB code: 2660**

- Public 4-year branch campus college
- Residential campus in small town
- 3,740 degree-seeking undergraduates: 9% part-time, 39% women, 11% African American, 9% Asian American, 6% Hispanic/Latino, 3% Multiracial, non-Hispanic, 10% international
- 748 degree-seeking graduate students
- 85% of applicants admitted
- SAT or ACT (ACT writing optional) required
- 64% graduate within 6 years

General. Founded in 1966. Regionally accredited. Applicants may choose from 20 campuses. Students may transfer between campuses after meeting entrance requirements for selected major. **Degrees:** 739 bachelor's, 5 associate awarded; master's, doctoral offered. **ROTC:** Army. **Location:** 8 miles from Harrisburg. **Calendar:** Semester, limited summer session. **Full-time faculty:** 229 total; 85% have terminal degrees, 20% minority, 41% women. **Part-time faculty:** 142 total; 32% have terminal degrees, 10% minority, 51% women. **Class size:** 44% < 20, 47% 20-39, 6% 40-49, 3% 50-99, 1% >100.

Freshman class profile. 3,938 applied, 3,342 admitted, 858 enrolled.

Mid 50% test scores			
SAT critical reading:	440-560	GPA 3.0-3.49:	45%
SAT math:	470-610	GPA 2.0-2.99:	35%
SAT writing:	430-550	Rank in top quarter:	33%
ACT composite:	20-26	Rank in top tenth:	9%
GPA 3.75 or higher:	6%	Return as sophomores:	87%
GPA 3.50-3.74:	14%	Out-of-state:	25%
		International:	17%

Basis for selection. High school GPA as well as other factors, including standardized test scores, class rank, personal statements, activities lists. Essay considered if submitted; portfolios required for select majors. **Home schooled:** Provide complete documentation showing courses studied and all evaluations presented from home school evaluator or supervisor assigned to student in cooperation with local school district or evaluator approved through program.

High school preparation. College-preparatory program required. Required and recommended units include English 4, mathematics 3, social studies 3, science 3 and foreign language 2-3.

2015-2016 Annual costs. Tuition/fees: $14,610; $22,344 out-of-state. Room/board: $12,450. Books/supplies: $1,840. Personal expenses: $3,222.

2014-2015 Financial aid. Need-based: 575 full-time freshmen applied for aid; 464 deemed to have need; 449 received aid. Average need met was 55%. Average scholarship/grant was $7,218; average loan $3,530. 41% of total undergraduate aid awarded as scholarships/grants, 59% as loans/jobs. **Non-need-based:** Awarded to 1,253 full-time undergraduates, including 420 freshmen. Scholarships awarded for academics, alumni affiliation, ROTC.

Application procedures. Admission: Priority date 11/30; no deadline. $50 fee, may be waived for applicants with need. Admission notification on a rolling basis beginning on or about 10/15. Must reply by May 1 or within 2 week(s) if notified thereafter. **Financial aid:** Priority date 2/15; no closing date. FAFSA required. Applicants notified on a rolling basis.

Academics. Special study options: Cooperative education, cross-registration, distance learning, double major, dual enrollment of high school students, honors, independent study, internships, student-designed major, study abroad. **Credit/placement by examination:** AP, CLEP, IB, SAT, ACT, institutional tests. 60 credit hours maximum toward bachelor's degree. **Support services:** Learning center, study skills assistance, tutoring, writing center.

Honors college/program. Candidates will be assessed based on the academic and extracurricular documents submitted with the application, as well as responses to essay questions and letters of recommendation.

Majors. Area/ethnic studies: African-American, American, Asian, Latin American, women's. **Biology:** General, bacteriology, biochemistry, toxicology. **Business:** Accounting, business admin, finance, international, labor relations, management information systems, marketing, organizational behavior. **Communications:** Advertising, communications/speech/rhetoric, journalism. **Computer sciences:** General, information systems. **Conservation:** General, environmental studies, forest sciences. **Education:** Adult ed admin, agricultural, art, early childhood, elementary, foreign languages, secondary, social studies, special ed. **Engineering:** Aerospace, agricultural, architectural, biomedical, chemical, civil, computer, electrical, engineering science, environmental, industrial, mechanical, mining, nuclear, petroleum, structural. **English:** English lit. **Foreign languages:** Chinese, classics, comparative lit, French, German, Italian, Japanese, Russian, Spanish. **Health services:** Athletic training, communication disorders, health care admin, nursing (RN), premedicine, preveterinary. **History:** General. **Human services:** Public policy. **Liberal arts:** Arts/sciences, humanities. **Math:** General, applied, statistics. **Parks/recreation:** Exercise sciences, facilities management. **Philosophy/religion:** Judaic, philosophy. **Physical sciences:** Astronomy, atmospheric science, chemistry, geology, materials science, physics. **Protective services:** Criminal justice, forensics, law enforcement admin. **Psychology:** General. **Social sciences:** Anthropology, archaeology, economics, geography, international relations, political science, sociology. **Visual/performing arts:** General, acting, art, art history/conservation, film/cinema/video, graphic design, music, theater design. **Work/family studies:** Family studies, human nutrition.

Most popular majors. Business/marketing 21%, communications/journalism 6%, engineering/engineering technologies 26%, health sciences 6%, psychology 7%, security/protective services 8%.

Technology on campus. 520 workstations in dormitories, library, computer center, student center. Dormitories wired for high-speed internet access and linked to campus network. Commuter students can connect to campus network. Online course registration, online library, helpline, repair service, student web hosting, wireless network available.

Student life. Freshman orientation: Mandatory. Preregistration for classes offered. Held for two days in May, June, July and August. **Policies:** Acts of intolerance and high-risk drinking discouraged at all locations. All facilities designated as smoke-free. Students expected to abide by The Penn State Principles. **Housing:** Special housing for disabled, apartments available. $100 nonrefundable deposit, deadline 5/1. Special interest housing available. **Activities:** Choral groups, dance, drama, literary magazine, music ensembles, radio station, student government, student newspaper.

Athletics. NCAA. **Intercollegiate:** Baseball M, basketball, cross-country, golf, soccer, softball W, tennis, volleyball W. **Intramural:** Badminton, basketball, racquetball, tennis. **Team name:** Nittany Lions.

Student services. Adult student services, alcohol/substance abuse counseling, career counseling, services for economically disadvantaged, student employment services, financial aid counseling, health services, minority student services, on-campus daycare, personal counseling, placement for graduates, veterans' counselor, women's services. **Physically disabled:** Services for visually, speech, hearing impaired.

Contact. E-mail: hbgadmit@psu.edu
Phone: (717) 948-6250 Toll-free number: (800) 222-2056
Fax: (717) 948-6325
David Kuskowski, Director for Undergraduate Admissions, Penn State Harrisburg, Swatara Building, Middletown, PA 17057

Penn State Hazleton
Hazleton, Pennsylvania
http://hazleton.psu.edu/   **CB code: 2660**

▶ Public 4-year branch campus college
▶ Residential campus in large town
▶ 753 degree-seeking undergraduates: 4% part-time, 42% women, 12% African American, 3% Asian American, 19% Hispanic/Latino, 3% Multiracial, non-Hispanic, 2% international
▶ 84% of applicants admitted
▶ SAT or ACT (ACT writing optional) required
▶ 54% graduate within 6 years

General. Founded in 1934. Regionally accredited. Applicants may choose from 20 campuses. Students may transfer between campuses after meeting entrance requirements for selected major. **Degrees:** 46 bachelor's, 53 associate awarded. **ROTC:** Air Force. **Location:** 4 miles from Hazleton. **Calendar:** Semester, limited summer session. **Full-time faculty:** 50 total; 66% have terminal degrees, 12% minority, 38% women. **Part-time faculty:** 21 total; 24% have terminal degrees, 10% minority, 52% women. **Class size:** 60% < 20, 36% 20-39, 2% 40-49, 2% 50-99.

Freshman class profile. 763 applied, 640 admitted, 262 enrolled.

Mid 50% test scores			
		GPA 3.0-3.49:	43%
SAT critical reading:	410-520	GPA 2.0-2.99:	35%
SAT math:	430-540	Rank in top quarter:	36%
SAT writing:	390-500	Rank in top tenth:	11%
ACT composite:	17-25	Return as sophomores:	79%
GPA 3.75 or higher:	5%	Out-of-state:	26%
GPA 3.50-3.74:	16%	International:	1%

Basis for selection. High school GPA as well as other factors, including standardized test scores, class rank, personal statements, activities lists. Essay considered if submitted; portfolios required for select majors. **Home schooled:** Provide complete documentation showing courses studied and all evaluations presented from home school evaluator or supervisor assigned to student in cooperation with local school district or evaluator approved through program.

High school preparation. College-preparatory program required. Required and recommended units include English 4, mathematics 3, social studies 3, science 3 and foreign language 2-3.

2015-2016 Annual costs. Tuition/fees: $13,902; $21,096 out-of-state. Room/board: $10,920. Books/supplies: $1,840. Personal expenses: $3,222.

2014-2015 Financial aid. Need-based: 278 full-time freshmen applied for aid; 253 deemed to have need; 250 received aid. Average need met was 60%. Average scholarship/grant was $7,557; average loan $3,344. 49% of total undergraduate aid awarded as scholarships/grants, 51% as loans/jobs. **Non-need-based:** Awarded to 373 full-time undergraduates, including 179 freshmen. Scholarships awarded for academics, alumni affiliation, ROTC.

Application procedures. Admission: Priority date 11/30; no deadline. $50 fee, may be waived for applicants with need. Admission notification on a rolling basis beginning on or about 10/15. Must reply by May 1 or within 2 week(s) if notified thereafter. **Financial aid:** Priority date 2/15; no closing date. FAFSA required. Applicants notified on a rolling basis.

Academics. Special study options: Accelerated study, cross-registration, distance learning, double major, dual enrollment of high school students, ESL, honors, independent study, internships, student-designed major, study abroad. **Credit/placement by examination:** AP, CLEP, IB, SAT, ACT, institutional tests. 60 credit hours maximum toward bachelor's degree. **Support services:** Learning center, pre-admission summer program, remedial instruction, study skills assistance, tutoring, writing center.

Honors college/program. Candidates will be assessed based on the academic and extracurricular documents submitted with the application, as well as responses to essay questions and letters of recommendation.

Majors. Area/ethnic studies: African-American, Asian, Latin American, women's. **Biology:** General, bacteriology, biochemistry, toxicology. **Business:** Accounting, business admin, communications, finance, labor relations, management information systems, marketing, organizational behavior. **Communications:** Advertising, communications/speech/rhetoric, journalism.

Computer sciences: General, information systems. **Conservation:** General, environmental studies, forest sciences. **Education:** Adult ed admin, agricultural, art, early childhood, elementary, foreign languages, secondary, special ed. **Engineering:** General, aerospace, agricultural, architectural, biomedical, chemical, civil, computer, electrical, engineering science, environmental, industrial, mechanical, mining, nuclear, petroleum. **English:** English lit. **Foreign languages:** Chinese, classics, comparative lit, French, German, Italian, Japanese, Russian, Spanish. **Health services:** Athletic training, communication disorders, health care admin, nursing (RN), premedicine, preveterinary. **History:** General. **Liberal arts:** Arts/sciences. **Math:** General, statistics. **Parks/recreation:** Exercise sciences, facilities management. **Philosophy/religion:** Judaic, philosophy. **Physical sciences:** Astronomy, atmospheric science, chemistry, geology, materials science, physics. **Protective services:** Criminal justice, forensics, law enforcement admin. **Psychology:** General. **Social sciences:** Anthropology, archaeology, economics, geography, international relations, political science, sociology. **Visual/performing arts:** General, acting, art, art history/conservation, film/cinema/video, graphic design, music, theater design. **Work/family studies:** Family studies, human nutrition.

Most popular majors. Business/marketing 37%, computer/information sciences 17%, engineering/engineering technologies 11%, liberal arts 7%, psychology 26%.

Technology on campus. 166 workstations in library, student center. Dormitories wired for high-speed internet access and linked to campus network. Commuter students can connect to campus network. Online course registration, online library, helpline, repair service, student web hosting, wireless network available.

Student life. Freshman orientation: Mandatory. Preregistration for classes offered. Held for two days in May, June, July and August. **Policies:** Acts of intolerance and high-risk drinking discouraged at all locations. All facilities designated as smoke-free. Students expected to abide by The Penn State Principles. **Housing:** Coed dorms, themed housing available. $100 nonrefundable deposit, deadline 5/1. Townhouses and suites available. **Activities:** Choral groups, dance, drama, literary magazine, student government, student newspaper.

Athletics. USCAA. **Intercollegiate:** Baseball M, basketball, cheerleading, golf, soccer M, softball W, tennis, volleyball W. **Intramural:** Softball, table tennis, tennis, volleyball. **Team name:** Nittany Lions.

Student services. Adult student services, alcohol/substance abuse counseling, career counseling, services for economically disadvantaged, student employment services, financial aid counseling, health services, minority student services, personal counseling, placement for graduates, veterans' counselor, women's services. **Physically disabled:** Services for visually, hearing impaired.

Contact. E-mail: admissions-hn@psu.edu
Phone: (570) 450-3142 Toll-free number: (800) 279-8495
Fax: (570) 450-3182
Clark Brigger, Director for Undergraduate Admissions, Penn State Hazleton, 110 Schiavo Hall, University Park, PA 18202

Penn State Lehigh Valley
Center Valley, Pennsylvania
www.lv.psu.edu   CB code: 2660

▶ Public 4-year branch campus college

▶ Commuter campus in rural community

▶ 773 degree-seeking undergraduates: 11% part-time, 48% women, 6% African American, 10% Asian American, 16% Hispanic/Latino, 2% Multi-racial, non-Hispanic

▶ 31 graduate students

▶ 86% of applicants admitted

▶ SAT or ACT (ACT writing optional) required

▶ 51% graduate within 6 years

General. Regionally accredited. Applicants may choose from 20 campuses. Students may transfer between campuses after meeting entrance requirements for selected major. **Degrees:** 88 bachelor's, 1 associate awarded. **ROTC:** Army. **Location:** 15 miles from Allentown, 30 miles from Easton. **Calendar:** Semester, limited summer session. **Full-time faculty:** 43 total; 60% have terminal degrees, 9% minority, 65% women. **Part-time faculty:** 41 total; 27% have terminal degrees, 49% women. **Class size:** 62% < 20, 34% 20-39, 3% 40-49, less than 1% 50-99.

Freshman class profile. 843 applied, 728 admitted, 208 enrolled.

Mid 50% test scores		
SAT critical reading:	440-560	
SAT math:	450-580	
SAT writing:	420-540	
ACT composite:	19-27	
GPA 3.75 or higher:	11%	
GPA 3.50-3.74:	8%	
GPA 3.0-3.49:	36%	
GPA 2.0-2.99:	44%	
Rank in top quarter:	33%	
Rank in top tenth:	8%	
Return as sophomores:	78%	
Out-of-state:	5%	

Basis for selection. High school GPA as well as other factors, including standardized test scores, class rank, personal statements, activities lists. Essay considered if submitted; portfolios required for select majors. **Home schooled:** Provide complete documentation showing courses studied and all evaluations presented from home school evaluator or supervisor assigned to student in cooperation with local school district or evaluator approved through program.

High school preparation. College-preparatory program required. Required and recommended units include English 4, mathematics 3, social studies 3, science 3 and foreign language 2-3.

2015-2016 Annual costs. Tuition/fees: $13,964; $21,158 out-of-state. Books/supplies: $1,840. Personal expenses: $1,854.

2014-2015 Financial aid. Need-based: 191 full-time freshmen applied for aid; 144 deemed to have need; 137 received aid. Average need met was 57%. Average scholarship/grant was $7,495; average loan $3,389. 50% of total undergraduate aid awarded as scholarships/grants, 50% as loans/jobs. **Non-need-based:** Awarded to 209 full-time undergraduates, including 94 freshmen. Scholarships awarded for academics, alumni affiliation, ROTC.

Application procedures. Admission: Priority date 11/30; no deadline. $50 fee, may be waived for applicants with need. Admission notification on a rolling basis beginning on or about 10/15. Must reply by May 1 or within 2 week(s) if notified thereafter. **Financial aid:** Priority date 2/15; no closing date. FAFSA required. Applicants notified on a rolling basis.

Academics. Special study options: Cooperative education, cross-registration, distance learning, double major, dual enrollment of high school students, honors, independent study, internships, liberal arts/career combination, study abroad, teacher certification program. **Credit/placement by examination:** AP, CLEP, IB, SAT, ACT, institutional tests. 60 credit hours maximum toward bachelor's degree. **Support services:** Learning center, reduced course load, study skills assistance, tutoring, writing center.

Honors college/program. Candidates will be assessed based on the academic and extracurricular documents submitted with the application, as well as responses to essay questions and letters of recommendation.

Majors. Area/ethnic studies: African-American, Asian, Latin American, women's. **Biology:** General, bacteriology, biochemistry, toxicology. **Business:** General, accounting, business admin, communications, finance, labor relations, management information systems, marketing, organizational behavior. **Communications:** Advertising, communications/speech/rhetoric, journalism. **Computer sciences:** General, information systems. **Conservation:** General, environmental studies, forest sciences. **Education:** Adult ed admin, agricultural, art, early childhood, elementary, foreign languages, secondary, special ed. **Engineering:** Aerospace, agricultural, architectural, biomedical, chemical, civil, computer, electrical, engineering science, environmental, industrial, mechanical, mining, nuclear, petroleum. **English:** English lit, technical writing. **Foreign languages:** General, Chinese, classics, comparative lit, French, German, Italian, Japanese, Russian, Spanish. **Health services:** Athletic training, communication disorders, health care admin, nursing (RN), premedicine, preveterinary. **History:** General. **Liberal arts:** Arts/sciences. **Math:** General, statistics. **Parks/recreation:** Exercise sciences, facilities management. **Philosophy/religion:** Judaic, philosophy. **Physical sciences:** Astronomy, atmospheric science, chemistry, geology, materials science, physics. **Protective services:** Forensics, law enforcement admin. **Psychology:** General. **Social sciences:** Anthropology, archaeology, economics, geography, international relations, political science, sociology. **Visual/performing arts:** General, acting, art, art history/conservation, film/cinema/video, graphic design, music, theater design. **Work/family studies:** Family studies, human nutrition.

Most popular majors. Business/marketing 43%, health sciences 17%, psychology 31%.

Technology on campus. 155 workstations in library, computer center. Commuter students can connect to campus network. Online course registration, online library, helpline, student web hosting, wireless network available.

Student life. Freshman orientation: Mandatory. Preregistration for classes offered. Held for two days in May, June, July and August. **Policies:** Acts of intolerance and high-risk drinking discouraged at all locations. All facilities designated as smoke-free. Students expected to abide by The Penn State Principles. **Activities:** Choral groups, dance, drama, film society, literary magazine, student government, student newspaper.

Athletics. USCAA. **Intercollegiate:** Baseball M, basketball, cheerleading, cross-country, golf, soccer, softball W, volleyball W, wrestling M. **Intramural:** Badminton, basketball, racquetball, soccer, softball, volleyball W. **Team name:** Nittany Lions.

Student services. Adult student services, alcohol/substance abuse counseling, career counseling, services for economically disadvantaged, student employment services, financial aid counseling, health services, minority student services, personal counseling, placement for graduates. **Physically disabled:** Services for visually, hearing impaired.

Contact. E-mail: admissions-lv@psu.edu
Phone: (610) 285-5035 Fax: (610) 285-5220
Clark Brigger, Director for Undergraduate Admissions, Penn State Lehigh Valley, 2809 Saucon Valley Road, Center Vally, PA 18034

Penn State Mont Alto
Mont Alto, Pennsylvania
www.ma.psu.edu   CB code: 2660

▸ Public 4-year branch campus college
▸ Residential campus in rural community
▸ 809 degree-seeking undergraduates: 19% part-time, 58% women, 8% African American, 2% Asian American, 5% Hispanic/Latino, 3% Multiracial, non-Hispanic
▸ 79% of applicants admitted
▸ SAT or ACT (ACT writing optional) required
▸ 47% graduate within 6 years

General. Founded in 1929. Regionally accredited. Applicants may choose from 20 campuses. Students may transfer between campuses after meeting entrance requirements for selected major. **Degrees:** 61 bachelor's, 101 associate awarded. **ROTC:** Army. **Location:** 12 miles from Chambersburg. **Calendar:** Semester, limited summer session. **Full-time faculty:** 56 total; 46% have terminal degrees, 11% minority, 52% women. **Part-time faculty:** 36 total; 6% have terminal degrees, 58% women. **Class size:** 66% < 20, 33% 20-39, less than 1% 40-49, less than 1% 50-99.

Freshman class profile. 688 applied, 546 admitted, 246 enrolled.

Mid 50% test scores			
SAT critical reading:	420-530	GPA 3.0-3.49:	39%
SAT math:	430-540	GPA 2.0-2.99:	38%
SAT writing:	410-500	Rank in top quarter:	36%
ACT composite:	17-24	Rank in top tenth:	6%
GPA 3.75 or higher:	8%	Return as sophomores:	77%
GPA 3.50-3.74:	14%	Out-of-state:	14%
		International:	1%

Basis for selection. High school GPA as well as other factors, including standardized test scores, class rank, personal statements, activities lists. Essay considered if submitted; portfolios required for select majors. **Home schooled:** Provide complete documentation showing courses studied and all evaluations presented from home school evaluator or supervisor assigned to student in cooperation with local school district or evaluator approved through program.

High school preparation. College-preparatory program required. Required and recommended units include English 4, mathematics 3, social studies 3, science 3 and foreign language 2-3.

2015-2016 Annual costs. Tuition/fees: $13,670; $20,356 out-of-state. Room/board: $10,920. Books/supplies: $1,840. Personal expenses: $3,222.

2014-2015 Financial aid. **Need-based:** 257 full-time freshmen applied for aid; 221 deemed to have need; 219 received aid. Average need met was 62%. Average scholarship/grant was $6,387; average loan $3,578. 48% of total undergraduate aid awarded as scholarships/grants, 52% as loans/jobs. **Non-need-based:** Awarded to 304 full-time undergraduates, including 140 freshmen. Scholarships awarded for academics, alumni affiliation, ROTC.

Application procedures. **Admission:** Priority date 11/30; no deadline. $50 fee, may be waived for applicants with need. Admission notification on a rolling basis beginning on or about 10/15. Must reply by May 1 or within 2 week(s) if notified thereafter. **Financial aid:** Priority date 2/15; no closing date. FAFSA required. Applicants notified on a rolling basis starting 3/1.

Academics. **Special study options:** Accelerated study, cross-registration, distance learning, double major, dual enrollment of high school students, honors, independent study, internships, liberal arts/career combination, student-designed major, study abroad, weekend college. **Credit/placement by examination:** AP, CLEP, IB, SAT, ACT, institutional tests. 60 credit hours maximum toward bachelor's degree. **Support services:** Learning center,

pre-admission summer program, remedial instruction, study skills assistance, tutoring, writing center.

Honors college/program. Candidates will be assessed based on the academic and extracurricular documents submitted with the application, as well as responses to essay questions and letters of recommendation.

Majors. **Area/ethnic studies:** African-American, Asian, Latin American, women's. **Biology:** General, bacteriology, biochemistry, toxicology. **Business:** Accounting, business admin, finance, labor relations, management information systems, marketing, organizational behavior. **Communications:** Advertising, communications/speech/rhetoric, journalism. **Computer sciences:** General, information systems. **Conservation:** General, environmental studies, forest sciences. **Education:** Adult ed admin, agricultural, art, early childhood, elementary, foreign languages, secondary, special ed. **Engineering:** Aerospace, agricultural, architectural, biomedical, chemical, civil, computer, electrical, engineering science, environmental, industrial, mechanical, mining, nuclear, petroleum. **English:** English lit. **Foreign languages:** Chinese, classics, comparative lit, French, German, Italian, Japanese, Russian, Spanish. **Health services:** Athletic training, communication disorders, health care admin, nursing (RN), premedicine, preveterinary. **History:** General. **Liberal arts:** Arts/sciences. **Math:** General, statistics. **Parks/recreation:** Exercise sciences, facilities management. **Philosophy/religion:** Judaic, philosophy. **Physical sciences:** Astronomy, atmospheric science, chemistry, geology, materials science, physics. **Protective services:** Forensics, law enforcement admin. **Psychology:** General. **Social sciences:** Anthropology, archaeology, economics, geography, international relations, political science, sociology. **Visual/performing arts:** General, acting, art, art history/conservation, film/cinema/video, graphic design, music, theater design. **Work/family studies:** Family studies, human nutrition.

Most popular majors. Business/marketing 16%, computer/information sciences 7%, family/consumer sciences 34%, health sciences 38%.

Technology on campus. 164 workstations in dormitories, library, computer center, student center. Dormitories wired for high-speed internet access and linked to campus network. Commuter students can connect to campus network. Online course registration, online library, helpline, repair service, student web hosting, wireless network available.

Student life. **Freshman orientation:** Mandatory. Preregistration for classes offered. Held for two days in May, June, July and August. **Policies:** Acts of intolerance and high-risk drinking discouraged at all locations. All facilities designated as smoke-free. Students expected to abide by The Penn State Principles. **Housing:** Coed dorms, special housing for disabled available. $100 nonrefundable deposit, deadline 5/1. Suites, special interest housing, townhouses available. **Activities:** Jazz band, choral groups, dance, drama, student government, student newspaper.

Athletics. USCAA. **Intercollegiate:** Baseball M, basketball, cross-country, golf, soccer, softball W, volleyball W, wrestling M. **Intramural:** Badminton, basketball, table tennis, ultimate frisbee. **Team name:** Nittany Lions.

Student services. Adult student services, alcohol/substance abuse counseling, chaplain/spiritual director, career counseling, services for economically disadvantaged, student employment services, financial aid counseling, health services, minority student services, personal counseling, placement for graduates, veterans' counselor, women's services. **Physically disabled:** Services for visually, hearing impaired.

Contact. E-mail: psuma@psu.edu
Phone: (717) 749-6130 Fax: (717) 749-6132
Clark Brigger, Director for Undergraduate Admissions, Penn State Mont Alto, 1 Campus Drive, Mont Alto, PA 17237

Penn State New Kensington
New Kensington, Pennsylvania
www.nk.psu.edu   CB code: 2660

▸ Public 4-year branch campus college
▸ Commuter campus in large town
▸ 598 degree-seeking undergraduates: 17% part-time, 41% women, 5% African American, 2% Asian American, 2% Hispanic/Latino, 1% Multiracial, non-Hispanic, 2% international
▸ 79% of applicants admitted
▸ SAT or ACT (ACT writing optional) required
▸ 52% graduate within 6 years

General. Founded in 1958. Regionally accredited. Applicants may choose from 20 campuses. Students may transfer between campuses after meeting entrance requirements for selected major. **Degrees:** 88 bachelor's, 29 associate awarded. **ROTC:** Air Force. **Location:** 22 miles from Pittsburgh. **Calendar:** Semester, limited summer session. **Full-time faculty:** 35 total; 63% have terminal degrees, 20% minority, 43% women. **Part-time faculty:** 37 total; 24% have terminal degrees, 14% minority, 35% women. **Class size:** 67% < 20, 27% 20-39, 3% 40-49, 3% 50-99.

Freshman class profile. 508 applied, 402 admitted, 178 enrolled.

Mid 50% test scores		GPA 3.0-3.49:	41%
SAT critical reading:	440-530	GPA 2.0-2.99:	35%
SAT math:	440-550	Rank in top quarter:	29%
SAT writing:	410-510	Rank in top tenth:	10%
ACT composite:	19-23	Return as sophomores:	67%
GPA 3.75 or higher:	8%	Out-of-state:	1%
GPA 3.50-3.74:	16%	International:	3%

Basis for selection. High school GPA as well as other factors, including standardized test scores, class rank, personal statements, activities lists. Essay considered if submitted; portfolios required for select majors. **Home schooled:** Provide complete documentation showing courses studied and all evaluations presented from home school evaluator or supervisor assigned to student in cooperation with local school district or evaluator approved through program.

High school preparation. College-preparatory program required. Required and recommended units include English 4, mathematics 3, social studies 3, science 3 and foreign language 2-3.

2015-2016 Annual costs. Tuition/fees: $13,608; $20,294 out-of-state. Books/supplies: $1,840. Personal expenses: $1,854.

2014-2015 Financial aid. Need-based: 169 full-time freshmen applied for aid; 131 deemed to have need; 131 received aid. Average need met was 67%. Average scholarship/grant was $5,710; average loan $3,188. 47% of total undergraduate aid awarded as scholarships/grants, 53% as loans/jobs. **Non-need-based:** Awarded to 206 full-time undergraduates, including 111 freshmen. Scholarships awarded for academics, alumni affiliation, ROTC.

Application procedures. Admission: Priority date 11/30; no deadline. $50 fee, may be waived for applicants with need. Admission notification on a rolling basis beginning on or about 10/15. Must reply by May 1 or within 2 week(s) if notified thereafter. **Financial aid:** Priority date 2/15; no closing date. FAFSA required. Applicants notified on a rolling basis.

Academics. Special study options: Cross-registration, distance learning, double major, dual enrollment of high school students, external degree, honors, independent study, internships, study abroad. **Credit/placement by examination:** AP, CLEP, IB, SAT, ACT, institutional tests. 60 credit hours maximum toward bachelor's degree. **Support services:** Learning center, pre-admission summer program, remedial instruction, study skills assistance, tutoring, writing center.

Honors college/program. Candidates will be assessed based on the academic and extracurricular documents submitted with the application, as well as responses to essay questions and letters of recommendation.

Majors. Area/ethnic studies: African-American, Asian, Latin American, women's. **Biology:** General, bacteriology, biochemistry, toxicology. **Business:** Accounting, business admin, finance, labor relations, management information systems, marketing, organizational behavior. **Communications:** Advertising, communications/speech/rhetoric, journalism. **Computer sciences:** General, information systems. **Conservation:** General, environmental studies, forest sciences. **Education:** Adult ed admin, agricultural, art, early childhood, elementary, foreign languages, secondary, special ed. **Engineering:** Aerospace, agricultural, architectural, biomedical, chemical, civil, computer, electrical, engineering science, environmental, industrial, mechanical, mining, nuclear, petroleum. **English:** English lit. **Foreign languages:** Chinese, classics, comparative lit, French, German, Italian, Japanese, Russian, Spanish. **Health services:** Athletic training, communication disorders, health care admin, nursing (RN), premedicine, preveterinary. **History:** General. **Liberal arts:** Arts/sciences. **Math:** General, statistics. **Parks/recreation:** Exercise sciences, facilities management. **Philosophy/religion:** Judaic, philosophy. **Physical sciences:** Astronomy, atmospheric science, chemistry, geology, materials science, physics. **Protective services:** Criminal justice, forensics, law enforcement admin. **Psychology:** General. **Social sciences:** Anthropology, archaeology, economics, geography, international relations, political science, sociology. **Visual/performing arts:** General, acting, art, art history/conservation, film/cinema/video, graphic design, music, theater design. **Work/family studies:** Family studies, human nutrition.

Most popular majors. Business/marketing 19%, communications/journalism 10%, computer/information sciences 20%, engineering/engineering technologies 7%, health sciences 14%, psychology 14%, security/protective services 16%.

Technology on campus. 265 workstations in computer center. Commuter students can connect to campus network. Online course registration, online library, helpline, repair service, student web hosting, wireless network available.

Student life. Freshman orientation: Mandatory. Preregistration for classes offered. Held for two days in May, June, July and August. **Policies:** Acts of intolerance and high-risk drinking discouraged at all locations. All facilities designated as smoke-free. Students expected to abide by The Penn State Principles. **Housing:** Privately owned apartment complex adjacent to campus and multiple single apartments within 30 minutes available. **Activities:** Jazz band, dance, drama, literary magazine, musical theater, student government, student newspaper.

Athletics. USCAA. **Intercollegiate:** Basketball, cheerleading, golf, ice hockey, volleyball W. **Intramural:** Basketball, football (non-tackle), racquetball, soccer, softball, table tennis, volleyball. **Team name:** Nittany Lions.

Student services. Adult student services, alcohol/substance abuse counseling, chaplain/spiritual director, career counseling, services for economically disadvantaged, student employment services, financial aid counseling, health services, minority student services, placement for graduates, veterans' counselor, women's services. **Physically disabled:** Services for visually, hearing impaired.

Contact. E-mail: nkadmissions@psu.edu
Phone: (724) 334-5466 Toll-free number: (888) 968-7297
Fax: (724) 334-6111
Clark Brigger, Director for Undergraduate Admissions, Penn State New Kensington, 3550 Seventh Street Road, New Kensington, PA 15068

Penn State Schuylkill
Schuylkill Haven, Pennsylvania
www.sl.psu.edu   CB code: 2660

▸ Public 4-year branch campus college
▸ Residential campus in small town
▸ 720 degree-seeking undergraduates: 16% part-time, 60% women, 18% African American, 1% Asian American, 7% Hispanic/Latino, 1% Multiracial, non-Hispanic, 1% international
▸ 73% of applicants admitted
▸ SAT or ACT (ACT writing optional) required
▸ 45% graduate within 6 years

General. Founded in 1934. Regionally accredited. Applicants may choose from 20 campuses. Students may transfer between campuses after meeting entrance requirements for selected major. **Degrees:** 83 bachelor's, 25 associate awarded. **Location:** 4 miles from Pottsville. **Calendar:** Semester, limited summer session. **Full-time faculty:** 43 total; 77% have terminal degrees, 2% minority, 40% women. **Part-time faculty:** 28 total; 25% have terminal degrees, 54% women. **Class size:** 63% < 20, 36% 20-39, 1% 40-49.

Freshman class profile. 690 applied, 504 admitted, 220 enrolled.

Mid 50% test scores		GPA 3.0-3.49:	31%
SAT critical reading:	410-520	GPA 2.0-2.99:	53%
SAT math:	420-510	Rank in top quarter:	24%
SAT writing:	400-500	Rank in top tenth:	5%
ACT composite:	16-19	Return as sophomores:	76%
GPA 3.75 or higher:	3%	Out-of-state:	19%
GPA 3.50-3.74:	11%	International:	3%

Basis for selection. High school GPA as well as other factors, including standardized test scores, class rank, personal statements, activities lists. Essay considered if submitted; portfolios required for select majors. **Home schooled:** Provide complete documentation showing courses studied and all evaluations presented from home school evaluator or supervisor assigned to student in cooperation with local school district or evaluator approved through program.

High school preparation. College-preparatory program required. Required and recommended units include English 4, mathematics 3, social studies 3, science 3 and foreign language 2-3.

2015-2016 Annual costs. Tuition/fees: $13,902; $21,096 out-of-state. Room/board: $8,060. Books/supplies: $1,840. Personal expenses: $3,222.

2014-2015 Financial aid. Need-based: 233 full-time freshmen applied for aid; 210 deemed to have need; 208 received aid. Average need met was 63%. Average scholarship/grant was $6,779; average loan $3,339. 51% of total undergraduate aid awarded as scholarships/grants, 49% as loans/jobs. **Non-need-based:** Awarded to 346 full-time undergraduates, including 188 freshmen. Scholarships awarded for academics, alumni affiliation, ROTC.

Application procedures. Admission: Priority date 11/30; no deadline. $50 fee, may be waived for applicants with need. Admission notification on a rolling basis beginning on or about 10/15. Must reply by May 1 or within

2 week(s) if notified thereafter. **Financial aid:** Priority date 2/15; no closing date. FAFSA required. Applicants notified on a rolling basis.

Academics. Special study options: Accelerated study, distance learning, double major, dual enrollment of high school students, ESL, honors, independent study, internships, study abroad. **Credit/placement by examination:** AP, CLEP, IB, SAT, ACT, institutional tests. 60 credit hours maximum toward bachelor's degree. **Support services:** Learning center, pre-admission summer program, reduced course load, remedial instruction, study skills assistance, tutoring, writing center.

Honors college/program. Candidates will be assessed based on the academic and extracurricular documents submitted with the application, as well as responses to essay questions and letters of recommendation.

Majors. Area/ethnic studies: African-American, Asian, Latin American, women's. **Biology:** General, bacteriology, biochemistry, toxicology. **Business:** Accounting, business admin, communications, finance, labor relations, management information systems, marketing, organizational behavior. **Communications:** Advertising, communications/speech/rhetoric, journalism. **Computer sciences:** General, information systems. **Conservation:** General, environmental studies, forest sciences. **Education:** Adult ed admin, agricultural, art, early childhood, elementary, foreign languages, secondary, special ed. **Engineering:** Aerospace, agricultural, architectural, biomedical, chemical, civil, computer, electrical, engineering science, environmental, industrial, mechanical, mining, nuclear, petroleum. **English:** English lit. **Foreign languages:** Chinese, classics, comparative lit, French, German, Italian, Japanese, Russian, Spanish. **Health services:** Athletic training, clinical lab technology, communication disorders, health care admin, nursing (RN), premedicine, preveterinary. **History:** General. **Liberal arts:** Arts/sciences. **Math:** General, statistics. **Parks/recreation:** Exercise sciences, facilities management. **Philosophy/religion:** Judaic, philosophy. **Physical sciences:** Astronomy, atmospheric science, chemistry, geology, materials science, physics. **Protective services:** Criminal justice, forensics, law enforcement admin. **Psychology:** General. **Social sciences:** Anthropology, archaeology, economics, geography, international relations, political science, sociology. **Visual/performing arts:** General, acting, art, art history/conservation, film/cinema/video, graphic design, music, theater design. **Work/family studies:** Family studies, human nutrition.

Most popular majors. Business/marketing 7%, computer/information sciences 8%, health sciences 24%, psychology 28%, security/protective services 33%.

Technology on campus. 165 workstations in dormitories, library, computer center, student center. Dormitories wired for high-speed internet access and linked to campus network. Commuter students can connect to campus network. Online course registration, online library, helpline, repair service, student web hosting, wireless network available.

Student life. Freshman orientation: Mandatory. Preregistration for classes offered. Held for two days in May, June, July and August. **Policies:** Acts of intolerance and high-risk drinking discouraged at all locations. All facilities designated as smoke-free. Students expected to abide by The Penn State Principles. **Housing:** Guaranteed on-campus for freshmen. Special housing for disabled, apartments, themed housing available. $100 nonrefundable deposit, deadline 5/1. **Activities:** Campus ministries, choral groups, dance, drama, international student organizations, musical theater, radio station, student government.

Athletics. USCAA. **Intercollegiate:** Baseball M, basketball, cross-country, golf M, soccer, softball W, volleyball W, wrestling M. **Intramural:** Basketball, football (non-tackle), soccer, softball, table tennis, volleyball. **Team name:** Nittany Lions.

Student services. Adult student services, alcohol/substance abuse counseling, career counseling, services for economically disadvantaged, student employment services, financial aid counseling, health services, minority student services, personal counseling, veterans' counselor. **Physically disabled:** Services for visually, hearing impaired.

Contact. E-mail: sl-admissions@psu.edu
Phone: (570) 385-6252 Fax: (570) 385-3672
Clark Brigger, Director for Undergraduate Admissions, Penn State Schuylkill, 102 Administration Building, Schuylkill Haven, PA 17972

Penn State Shenango
Sharon, Pennsylvania
www.shenango.psu.edu   CB code: 2660

- Public 4-year branch campus college
- Commuter campus in large town

- 436 degree-seeking undergraduates: 38% part-time, 73% women, 7% African American, 1% Asian American, 2% Hispanic/Latino, 3% Multiracial, non-Hispanic
- 68% of applicants admitted
- SAT or ACT (ACT writing optional) required
- 33% graduate within 6 years

General. Founded in 1965. Regionally accredited. Applicants may choose from 20 campuses. Students may transfer between campuses after meeting entrance requirements for selected major. **Degrees:** 47 bachelor's, 57 associate awarded. **Location:** 17 miles from Youngstown, OH. **Calendar:** Semester, limited summer session. **Full-time faculty:** 28 total; 70% have terminal degrees, 7% minority, 68% women. **Part-time faculty:** 16 total; 19% have terminal degrees, 6% minority, 38% women. **Class size:** 69% < 20, 31% 20-39.

Freshman class profile. 154 applied, 105 admitted, 57 enrolled.

Mid 50% test scores			
SAT critical reading:	410-530	GPA 3.0-3.49:	30%
SAT math:	410-520	GPA 2.0-2.99:	39%
SAT writing:	400-500	Rank in top quarter:	35%
ACT composite:	19-22	Rank in top tenth:	2%
GPA 3.75 or higher:	9%	Return as sophomores:	66%
GPA 3.50-3.74:	16%	Out-of-state:	12%

Basis for selection. High school GPA as well as other factors, including standardized test scores, class rank, personal statements, activities lists. Essay considered if submitted; portfolios required for select majors. **Home schooled:** Provide complete documentation showing courses studied and all evaluations presented from home school evaluator or supervisor assigned to student in cooperation with local school district or evaluator approved through program.

High school preparation. College-preparatory program required. Required and recommended units include English 4, mathematics 3, social studies 3, science 3 and foreign language 2-3.

2015-2016 Annual costs. Tuition/fees: $13,354; $19,910 out-of-state. Books/supplies: $1,840. Personal expenses: $1,854.

2014-2015 Financial aid. Need-based: 73 full-time freshmen applied for aid; 64 deemed to have need; 64 received aid. Average need met was 62%. Average scholarship/grant was $7,526; average loan $3,333. 49% of total undergraduate aid awarded as scholarships/grants, 51% as loans/jobs. **Non-need-based:** Awarded to 160 full-time undergraduates, including 49 freshmen. Scholarships awarded for academics, alumni affiliation, ROTC.

Application procedures. Admission: Priority date 11/30; no deadline. $50 fee, may be waived for applicants with need. Admission notification on a rolling basis beginning on or about 10/15. Must reply by May 1 or within 2 week(s) if notified thereafter. **Financial aid:** Priority date 2/15; no closing date. FAFSA required. Applicants notified on a rolling basis.

Academics. Special study options: Accelerated study, cross-registration, distance learning, double major, dual enrollment of high school students, honors, independent study, internships, student-designed major, study abroad. **Credit/placement by examination:** AP, CLEP, IB, SAT, ACT, institutional tests. 60 credit hours maximum toward bachelor's degree. **Support services:** Learning center, remedial instruction, study skills assistance, tutoring, writing center.

Honors college/program. Candidates will be assessed based on the academic and extracurricular documents submitted with the application, as well as responses to essay questions and letters of recommendation.

Majors. Area/ethnic studies: African-American, Asian, Latin American, women's. **Biology:** General, bacteriology, biochemistry, toxicology. **Business:** Accounting, business admin, finance, labor relations, management information systems, marketing, organizational behavior. **Communications:** Advertising, communications/speech/rhetoric, journalism. **Computer sciences:** General, information systems. **Conservation:** General, environmental studies, forest sciences. **Education:** Adult ed admin, agricultural, art, early childhood, elementary, foreign languages, secondary, special ed. **Engineering:** Aerospace, agricultural, architectural, biomedical, chemical, civil, computer, electrical, engineering science, environmental, industrial, mechanical, mining, nuclear, petroleum. **English:** English lit. **Foreign languages:** Chinese, classics, comparative lit, French, German, Italian, Japanese, Russian, Spanish. **Health services:** Athletic training, communication disorders, health care admin, nursing (RN), premedicine, preveterinary. **History:** General. **Liberal arts:** Arts/sciences. **Math:** General, statistics. **Parks/recreation:** Exercise sciences, facilities management. **Philosophy/religion:** Judaic, philosophy. **Physical sciences:** Astronomy, atmospheric science, chemistry, geology, materials science, physics. **Protective services:** Criminal justice, forensics, law enforcement admin. **Psychology:** General. **Social sciences:** Anthropology, archaeology, economics, geography, international relations, political science, sociology. **Visual/performing arts:** General, acting, art, art history/conservation, film/cinema/video, graphic design, music, theater design. **Work/family studies:** Family studies, human nutrition.

Most popular majors. Business/marketing 17%, family/consumer sciences 23%, health sciences 36%, security/protective services 19%.

Technology on campus. 132 workstations in library, computer center, student center. Commuter students can connect to campus network. Online course registration, online library, helpline, repair service, student web hosting, wireless network available.

Student life. Freshman orientation: Mandatory. Preregistration for classes offered. Held for two days in May, June, July and August. **Policies:** Acts of intolerance and high-risk drinking discouraged at all locations. All facilities designated as smoke-free. Students expected to abide by The Penn State Principles. **Activities:** Choral groups, drama, student government.

Athletics. USCAA. **Intramural:** Basketball, football (non-tackle), golf, softball, volleyball. **Team name:** Nittany Lions.

Student services. Adult student services, alcohol/substance abuse counseling, career counseling, student employment services, financial aid counseling, minority student services, personal counseling, placement for graduates, veterans' counselor, women's services. **Physically disabled:** Services for visually, hearing impaired.

Contact. E-mail: psushenango@psu.edu
Phone: (724) 983-2803 Fax: (724) 983-2820
Clark Brigger, Director for Undergraduate Admissions, Penn State Shenango, 147 Shenango Avenue, Sharon, PA 16146

Penn State University Park
University Park, Pennsylvania

CB member

www.psu.edu

CB code: 2660

- Public 4-year university
- Residential campus in large town
- 40,179 degree-seeking undergraduates: 2% part-time, 46% women, 4% African American, 6% Asian American, 6% Hispanic/Latino, 3% Multiracial, non-Hispanic, 11% international
- 6,475 degree-seeking graduate students
- 51% of applicants admitted
- SAT or ACT (ACT writing optional) required
- 86% graduate within 6 years

General. Founded in 1855. Regionally accredited. Applicants may choose from 20 campuses. Students may transfer between campuses after meeting entrance requirements for selected major. **Degrees:** 10,876 bachelor's, 20 associate awarded; master's, professional, doctoral offered. **ROTC:** Army, Naval, Air Force. **Location:** 90 miles from Harrisburg. **Calendar:** Semester, extensive summer session. **Full-time faculty:** 2,740 total; 79% have terminal degrees, 18% minority, 39% women. **Part-time faculty:** 359 total; 33% have terminal degrees, 7% minority, 54% women. **Class size:** 39% < 20, 38% 20-39, 8% 40-49, 8% 50-99, 7% >100. **Special facilities:** Six major museums which house significant research and educational collections in the fields of agriculture, anthropology, entomology, earth and mineral sciences, the fine arts; art galleries, botanic gardens and arboretum.

Freshman class profile. 53,472 applied, 27,440 admitted, 7,626 enrolled.

Mid 50% test scores		GPA 3.0-3.49:	29%
SAT critical reading:	530-630	GPA 2.0-2.99:	4%
SAT math:	560-670	Rank in top quarter:	82%
SAT writing:	540-640	Rank in top tenth:	41%
ACT composite:	25-29	Return as sophomores:	93%
GPA 3.75 or higher:	36%	Out-of-state:	40%
GPA 3.50-3.74:	31%	International:	10%

Basis for selection. High school GPA as well as other factors, including standardized test scores, class rank, personal statements, and activities lists. Essay considered if submitted; portfolios required for select majors. **Home schooled:** Provide complete documentation showing courses studied and all evaluations presented from home school evaluator or supervisor assigned to student in cooperation with local school district or evaluator approved through program.

High school preparation. College-preparatory program required. Required and recommended units include English 4, mathematics 3, social studies 3, science 3 and foreign language 2-3. 3 units required in arts and humanities. Additional requirements for some programs.

2015-2016 Annual costs. Tuition/fees: $17,514; $31,346 out-of-state. Room/board: $10,920. Books/supplies: $1,840. Personal expenses: $3,222.

2014-2015 Financial aid. Need-based: 5,891 full-time freshmen applied for aid; 3,819 deemed to have need; 3,516 received aid. Average need met was 58%. Average scholarship/grant was $7,052; average loan $3,540. 38% of total undergraduate aid awarded as scholarships/grants, 62% as loans/jobs. **Non-need-based:** Awarded to 11,395 full-time undergraduates, including 2,584 freshmen. Scholarships awarded for academics, alumni affiliation, athletics, ROTC.

Application procedures. Admission: Priority date 11/30; no deadline. $50 fee, may be waived for applicants with need. Admission notification on a rolling basis beginning on or about 10/15. Must reply by May 1 or within 2 week(s) if notified thereafter. **Financial aid:** Priority date 2/15; no closing date. FAFSA required. Applicants notified on a rolling basis.

Academics. Special study options: Accelerated study, combined bachelor's/graduate degree, cooperative education, cross-registration, distance learning, double major, dual enrollment of high school students, ESL, exchange student, external degree, honors, independent study, internships, liberal arts/career combination, semester at sea, student-designed major, study abroad, teacher certification program, weekend college. **Credit/placement by examination:** AP, CLEP, IB, SAT, ACT, institutional tests. 60 credit hours maximum toward bachelor's degree. **Support services:** Learning center, pre-admission summer program, study skills assistance, tutoring, writing center.

Honors college/program. Candidates will be assessed based on the academic and extracurricular documents submitted with the application, as well as responses to essay questions and letters of recommendation.

Majors. Architecture: Architecture, landscape. **Area/ethnic studies:** African-American, Asian, Latin American, women's. **Biology:** General, bacteriology, biochemistry, toxicology. **Business:** Accounting, finance, labor relations, management information systems, marketing, organizational behavior. **Communications:** Advertising, communications/speech/rhetoric, journalism. **Computer sciences:** General, information systems. **Conservation:** General, environmental studies, forest sciences. **Education:** Adult ed admin, agricultural, art, early childhood, elementary, foreign languages, music, secondary, special ed. **Engineering:** Aerospace, agricultural, architectural, biomedical, chemical, civil, computer, electrical, engineering science, environmental, industrial, mechanical, mining, nuclear, petroleum. **English:** English lit. **Foreign languages:** Chinese, classics, comparative lit, French, German, Italian, Japanese, Russian, Spanish. **Health services:** Athletic training, communication disorders, health care admin, nursing (RN), premedicine, preveterinary. **History:** General. **Liberal arts:** Arts/sciences. **Math:** General, statistics. **Parks/recreation:** Exercise sciences, facilities management. **Philosophy/religion:** Judaic, philosophy. **Physical sciences:** Astronomy, atmospheric science, chemistry, geology, materials science, physics. **Protective services:** Forensics, law enforcement admin. **Psychology:** General. **Social sciences:** Anthropology, archaeology, economics, geography, international relations, political science, sociology. **Visual/performing arts:** General, acting, art, art history/conservation, film/cinema/video, graphic design, music, music performance, theater design. **Work/family studies:** Family studies, human nutrition.

Most popular majors. Biology 6%, business/marketing 15%, communications/journalism 8%, computer/information sciences 6%, engineering/engineering technologies 15%, health sciences 6%, social sciences 8%.

Technology on campus. 7,000 workstations in dormitories, library, computer center, student center. Dormitories wired for high-speed internet access and linked to campus network. Commuter students can connect to campus network. Online course registration, online library, helpline, student web hosting, wireless network available.

Student life. Freshman orientation: Mandatory. Preregistration for classes offered. Held for two days in May, June, July and August. **Policies:** Acts of intolerance and high-risk drinking discouraged at all locations. All facilities designated as smoke-free. Students expected to abide by The Penn State Principles. Freshmen not permitted cars on campus. **Housing:** Guaranteed on-campus for freshmen. Coed dorms, single-sex dorms, special housing for disabled, apartments, fraternity/sorority housing, themed housing, wellness housing available. $100 nonrefundable deposit, deadline 5/1. Suites, special interest housing available. **Activities:** Bands, campus ministries, choral groups, dance, drama, film society, international student organizations, literary magazine, music ensembles, Model UN, musical theater, opera, radio station, student government, student newspaper, symphony orchestra, TV station, Adult learners, American Indian Science and Engineering Society, Habitat for Humanity, Minorities in Agriculture and Natural Resources, National Society of Black Engineers, College Democrats, College Independents, College Republicans, Black Caucus, and Commission for Women.

Athletics. NCAA. **Intercollegiate:** Baseball M, basketball, cheerleading, cross-country, diving, fencing, field hockey W, football (tackle) M, golf, gymnastics, ice hockey, lacrosse, soccer, softball W, swimming, tennis, track and field, volleyball, wrestling M. **Intramural:** Badminton, basketball, cross-country, equestrian, football (non-tackle), football (tackle) M, golf, racquetball, soccer, softball, squash, swimming, table tennis, tennis, track and field, volleyball, wrestling. **Team name:** Nittany Lions.

Student services. Adult student services, alcohol/substance abuse counseling, chaplain/spiritual director, career counseling, services for economically disadvantaged, student employment services, financial aid counseling, health services, legal services, minority student services, on-campus daycare, personal counseling, placement for graduates, veterans' counselor, women's services. **Physically disabled:** Services for visually, hearing impaired.

Contact. E-mail: admissions@psu.edu
Phone: (814) 865-5471 Fax: (814) 863-7590
Clark Brigger, Executive Director for Undergraduate Admissions, Penn State University Park, 201 Shields Building, University Park, PA 16802

Penn State Wilkes-Barre
Lehman, Pennsylvania
www.wb.psu.edu   **CB code: 2660**

▸ Public 4-year branch campus college

▸ Commuter campus in small city

▸ 460 degree-seeking undergraduates: 6% part-time, 33% women, 3% African American, 1% Asian American, 5% Hispanic/Latino, 2% Multiracial, non-Hispanic

▸ 8 graduate students

▸ 88% of applicants admitted

▸ SAT or ACT (ACT writing optional) required

▸ 53% graduate within 6 years

General. Founded in 1916. Regionally accredited. Applicants may choose from 20 campuses. Students may transfer between campuses after meeting entrance requirements for selected major. **Degrees:** 76 bachelor's, 10 associate awarded. **ROTC:** Army, Air Force. **Location:** 10 miles from Wilkes-Barre. **Calendar:** Semester, limited summer session. **Full-time faculty:** 30 total; 63% have terminal degrees, 23% minority, 33% women. **Part-time faculty:** 19 total; 10% have terminal degrees, 47% women. **Class size:** 63% < 20, 35% 20-39, less than 1% 40-49, less than 1% 50-99.

Freshman class profile. 411 applied, 360 admitted, 143 enrolled.

Mid 50% test scores			
SAT critical reading:	430-540	GPA 3.0-3.49:	42%
SAT math:	440-550	GPA 2.0-2.99:	39%
SAT writing:	420-520	Rank in top quarter:	30%
ACT composite:	18-26	Rank in top tenth:	8%
GPA 3.75 or higher:	6%	Return as sophomores:	84%
GPA 3.50-3.74:	13%	Out-of-state:	9%
		International:	1%

Basis for selection. High school GPA as well as other factors, including standardized test scores, class rank, personal statements, activities lists. Essay considered if submitted; portfolios required for select majors. **Home schooled:** Provide complete documentation showing courses studied and all evaluations presented from home school evaluator or supervisor assigned to student in cooperation with local school district or evaluator approved through program.

High school preparation. College-preparatory program required. Required and recommended units include English 4, mathematics 3, social studies 3, science 3 and foreign language 2-3.

2015-2016 Annual costs. Tuition/fees: $13,598; $20,284 out-of-state. Books/supplies: $1,840. Personal expenses: $1,854.

2014-2015 Financial aid. Need-based: 130 full-time freshmen applied for aid; 100 deemed to have need; 98 received aid. Average need met was 64%. Average scholarship/grant was $6,485; average loan $3,241. 49% of total undergraduate aid awarded as scholarships/grants, 51% as loans/jobs. **Non-need-based:** Awarded to 188 full-time undergraduates, including 66 freshmen. Scholarships awarded for academics, alumni affiliation, ROTC.

Application procedures. Admission: Priority date 11/30; no deadline. $50 fee, may be waived for applicants with need. Admission notification on a rolling basis beginning on or about 10/15. Must reply by 5/1. Must reply by May 1 or within 2 week(s) if notified thereafter. **Financial aid:** Priority date 2/15; no closing date. FAFSA required. Applicants notified on a rolling basis.

Academics. Special study options: Accelerated study, cross-registration, distance learning, double major, dual enrollment of high school students, honors, independent study, internships, student-designed major, study abroad. **Credit/placement by examination:** AP, CLEP, IB, SAT, ACT, institutional

tests. 60 credit hours maximum toward bachelor's degree. **Support services:** Learning center, study skills assistance, tutoring, writing center.

Honors college/program. Candidates will be assessed based on the academic and extracurricular documents submitted with the application, as well as responses to essay questions and letters of recommendation.

Majors. Area/ethnic studies: African-American, Asian, Latin American, women's. **Biology:** General, bacteriology, biochemistry, toxicology. **Business:** Accounting, business admin, communications, finance, labor relations, management information systems, marketing, organizational behavior. **Communications:** Advertising, communications/speech/rhetoric, journalism. **Computer sciences:** General, information systems. **Conservation:** General, environmental studies, forest sciences. **Education:** Adult ed admin, agricultural, art, early childhood, elementary, foreign languages, secondary, special ed. **Engineering:** Aerospace, agricultural, architectural, biomedical, chemical, civil, computer, electrical, engineering science, environmental, industrial, mechanical, mining, nuclear, petroleum, surveying. **English:** English lit. **Foreign languages:** Chinese, classics, comparative lit, French, German, Italian, Japanese, Russian, Spanish. **Health services:** Athletic training, communication disorders, health care admin, nursing (RN), premedicine, preveterinary. **History:** General. **Liberal arts:** Arts/sciences. **Math:** General, statistics. **Parks/recreation:** Exercise sciences, facilities management. **Philosophy/religion:** Judaic, philosophy. **Physical sciences:** Astronomy, atmospheric science, chemistry, geology, materials science, physics. **Protective services:** Criminal justice, forensics, law enforcement admin. **Psychology:** General. **Social sciences:** Anthropology, archaeology, economics, geography, international relations, political science, sociology. **Visual/performing arts:** General, acting, art, art history/conservation, film/cinema/video, graphic design, music, theater design. **Work/family studies:** Family studies, human nutrition.

Most popular majors. Business/marketing 13%, computer/information sciences 8%, engineering/engineering technologies 25%, English 11%, security/protective services 41%.

Technology on campus. 196 workstations in library, computer center, student center. Commuter students can connect to campus network. Online course registration, online library, helpline, repair service, student web hosting, wireless network available.

Student life. Freshman orientation: Mandatory. Preregistration for classes offered. Held for two days in May, June, July and August. **Policies:** Acts of intolerance and high-risk drinking discouraged at all locations. All facilities designated as smoke-free. Students expected to abide by The Penn State Principles. **Activities:** Dance, radio station, student government, student newspaper.

Athletics. USCAA. **Intercollegiate:** Baseball M, basketball M, cross-country, golf, soccer, volleyball W. **Intramural:** Basketball, football (tackle), racquetball, softball, volleyball. **Team name:** Nittany Lions.

Student services. Adult student services, alcohol/substance abuse counseling, chaplain/spiritual director, career counseling, services for economically disadvantaged, student employment services, financial aid counseling, health services, minority student services, personal counseling, placement for graduates. **Physically disabled:** Services for visually, hearing impaired.

Contact. E-mail: wbadmissions@psu.edu
Phone: (570) 675-9238 Toll-free number: (800) 966-6613
Fax: (570) 675-9113
Clark Brigger, Director for Undergraduate Admissions, Penn State Wilkes-Barre, Hayfield House 101, Lehman, PA 18627

Penn State Worthington Scranton
Dunmore, Pennsylvania
www.sn.psu.edu   **CB code: 2660**

▸ Public 4-year branch campus college

▸ Commuter campus in large town

▸ 967 degree-seeking undergraduates: 12% part-time, 53% women, 3% African American, 5% Asian American, 6% Hispanic/Latino, 2% Multiracial, non-Hispanic

▸ 81% of applicants admitted

▸ SAT or ACT (ACT writing optional) required

▸ 43% graduate within 6 years

General. Founded in 1923. Regionally accredited. Applicants may choose from 20 campuses. Students may transfer between campuses after meeting entrance requirements for selected major. **Degrees:** 180 bachelor's, 76 associate awarded. **ROTC:** Army, Air Force. **Location:** 1 mile from Scranton. **Calendar:** Semester, limited summer session. **Full-time faculty:** 50 total; 64% have terminal degrees, 10% minority, 52% women. **Part-time faculty:**

47 total; 19% have terminal degrees, 45% women. **Class size:** 48% < 20, 48% 20-39, 2% 40-49, less than 1% 50-99.

Freshman class profile. 733 applied, 591 admitted, 230 enrolled.

Mid 50% test scores			
		GPA 3.0-3.49:	38%
SAT critical reading:	420-530	GPA 2.0-2.99:	43%
SAT math:	430-540	Rank in top quarter:	30%
SAT writing:	410-510	Rank in top tenth:	10%
ACT composite:	17-21	Return as sophomores:	75%
GPA 3.75 or higher:	5%	Out-of-state:	3%
GPA 3.50-3.74:	13%		

Basis for selection. High school GPA as well as other factors, including standardized test scores, class rank, personal statements, activities lists. Essay considered if submitted; portfolios required for select majors. **Home schooled:** Provide complete documentation showing courses studied and all evaluations presented from home school evaluator or supervisor assigned to student in cooperation with local school district or evaluator approved through program.

High school preparation. College-preparatory program required. Required and recommended units include English 4, mathematics 3, social studies 3, science 3 and foreign language 2-3.

2015-2016 Annual costs. Tuition/fees: $13,902; $21,096 out-of-state. Books/supplies: $1,840. Personal expenses: $1,854.

2014-2015 Financial aid. Need-based: 251 full-time freshmen applied for aid; 209 deemed to have need; 199 received aid. Average need met was 61%. Average scholarship/grant was $6,816; average loan $3,390. 45% of total undergraduate aid awarded as scholarships/grants, 55% as loans/jobs. **Non-need-based:** Awarded to 210 full-time undergraduates, including 88 freshmen. Scholarships awarded for academics, alumni affiliation, ROTC.

Application procedures. Admission: Priority date 11/30; no deadline. $50 fee, may be waived for applicants with need. Admission notification on a rolling basis beginning on or about 10/15. Must reply by May 1 or within 2 week(s) if notified thereafter. **Financial aid:** Priority date 2/15; no closing date. FAFSA required. Applicants notified on a rolling basis.

Academics. Special study options: Accelerated study, combined bachelor's/graduate degree, cooperative education, cross-registration, distance learning, double major, dual enrollment of high school students, honors, independent study, internships, liberal arts/career combination, study abroad. **Credit/placement by examination:** AP, CLEP, IB, SAT, ACT, institutional tests. 60 credit hours maximum toward bachelor's degree. **Support services:** Learning center, reduced course load, remedial instruction, study skills assistance, tutoring, writing center.

Honors college/program. Candidates will be assessed based on the academic and extracurricular documents submitted with the application, as well as responses to essay questions and letters of recommendation.

Majors. Area/ethnic studies: African-American, Asian, Latin American, women's. **Biology:** General, bacteriology, biochemistry, toxicology. **Business:** Accounting, business admin, communications, finance, labor relations, management information systems, marketing, organizational behavior. **Communications:** Advertising, communications/speech/rhetoric, journalism. **Computer sciences:** General, information systems. **Conservation:** General, environmental studies, forest sciences. **Education:** Adult ed admin, agricultural, art, early childhood, elementary, foreign languages, secondary, special ed. **Engineering:** Aerospace, agricultural, architectural, biomedical, chemical, civil, computer, electrical, engineering science, environmental, industrial, mechanical, mining, nuclear, petroleum. **English:** English lit. **Foreign languages:** Chinese, classics, comparative lit, French, German, Italian, Japanese, Russian, Spanish. **Health services:** Athletic training, communication disorders, health care admin, nursing (RN), premedicine, preveterinary. **History:** General. **Liberal arts:** Arts/sciences. **Math:** General, statistics. **Parks/recreation:** Exercise sciences, facilities management. **Philosophy/religion:** Judaic, philosophy. **Physical sciences:** Astronomy, atmospheric science, chemistry, geology, materials science, physics. **Protective services:** Forensics, law enforcement admin. **Psychology:** General. **Social sciences:** Anthropology, archaeology, economics, geography, international relations, political science, sociology. **Visual/performing arts:** General, acting, art, art history/conservation, film/cinema/video, graphic design, music, theater design. **Work/family studies:** Family studies, human nutrition.

Most popular majors. Business/marketing 27%, computer/information sciences 14%, English 8%, family/consumer sciences 24%, health sciences 19%.

Technology on campus. 180 workstations in library, computer center, student center. Commuter students can connect to campus network. Online course registration, online library, helpline, repair service, student web hosting, wireless network available.

Student life. Freshman orientation: Mandatory. Preregistration for classes offered. Held for two days in May, June, July and August. **Policies:** Acts of intolerance and high-risk drinking discouraged at all locations. All facilities designated as smoke-free. Students expected to abide by The Penn State Principles. **Housing:** Coed dorms, apartments available. **Activities:** Jazz band, choral groups, drama, literary magazine, music ensembles, student government, student newspaper.

Athletics. USCAA. **Intercollegiate:** Baseball M, basketball, cross-country, soccer M, softball W, volleyball W. **Intramural:** Basketball, football (tackle), soccer, softball, volleyball, weight lifting. **Team name:** Nittany Lions.

Student services. Adult student services, alcohol/substance abuse counseling, career counseling, services for economically disadvantaged, student employment services, financial aid counseling, health services, personal counseling, placement for graduates, veterans' counselor, women's services. **Physically disabled:** Services for visually, hearing impaired.

Contact. E-mail: wsadmissions@psu.edu
Phone: (570) 963-2500 Fax: (570) 963-2524
Clark Brigger, Director for Undergraduate Admissions, Penn State Worthington Scranton, Dawson Building, Room 5, 120 Ridge View Drive, Dunmore, PA 18512

Penn State York
York, Pennsylvania
www.yk.psu.edu

CB code: 2660

- Public 4-year branch campus college
- Commuter campus in large town
- 935 degree-seeking undergraduates: 14% part-time, 43% women, 6% African American, 5% Asian American, 6% Hispanic/Latino, 3% Multiracial, non-Hispanic, 15% international
- 8 degree-seeking graduate students
- 86% of applicants admitted
- SAT or ACT (ACT writing optional) required
- 50% graduate within 6 years

General. Founded in 1926. Regionally accredited. Applicants may choose from 20 campuses. Students may transfer between campuses after meeting entrance requirements for selected major. **Degrees:** 102 bachelor's, 24 associate awarded; master's offered. **Calendar:** Semester, limited summer session. **Full-time faculty:** 50 total; 72% have terminal degrees, 16% minority, 48% women. **Part-time faculty:** 43 total; 37% have terminal degrees, 9% minority, 56% women. **Class size:** 58% < 20, 40% 20-39, 2% 40-49, less than 1% 50-99.

Freshman class profile. 1,397 applied, 1,196 admitted, 320 enrolled.

Mid 50% test scores			
		GPA 3.0-3.49:	41%
SAT critical reading:	430-560	GPA 2.0-2.99:	35%
SAT math:	470-630	Rank in top quarter:	27%
SAT writing:	420-550	Rank in top tenth:	8%
ACT composite:	21-26	Return as sophomores:	80%
GPA 3.75 or higher:	6%	Out-of-state:	18%
GPA 3.50-3.74:	17%	International:	26%

Basis for selection. High school GPA as well as other factors, including standardized test scores, class rank, personal statements, activities lists. Essay considered if submitted; portfolios required for select majors. **Home schooled:** Provide complete documentation showing courses studied and all evaluations presented from home school evaluator or supervisor assigned to student in cooperation with local school district or evaluator approved through program.

High school preparation. College-preparatory program required. Required and recommended units include English 4, mathematics 3, social studies 3, science 3 and foreign language 2-3.

2015-2016 Annual costs. Tuition/fees: $13,964; $21,158 out-of-state. Books/supplies: $1,840. Personal expenses: $1,854.

2014-2015 Financial aid. Need-based: 221 full-time freshmen applied for aid; 179 deemed to have need; 177 received aid. Average need met was 62%. Average scholarship/grant was $6,499; average loan $3,349. 48% of total undergraduate aid awarded as scholarships/grants, 52% as loans/jobs. **Non-need-based:** Awarded to 334 full-time undergraduates, including 140 freshmen. Scholarships awarded for academics, alumni affiliation, ROTC.

Application procedures. Admission: Priority date 11/30; no deadline. $50 fee, may be waived for applicants with need. Admission notification on a rolling basis beginning on or about 10/15. Must reply by May 1 or within

2 week(s) if notified thereafter. **Financial aid:** Priority date 2/15; no closing date. FAFSA required. Applicants notified on a rolling basis.

Academics. Special study options: Accelerated study, cross-registration, distance learning, double major, dual enrollment of high school students, ESL, honors, independent study, internships, study abroad, weekend college. **Credit/placement by examination:** AP, CLEP, IB, SAT, ACT, institutional tests. 60 credit hours maximum toward bachelor's degree. **Support services:** Learning center, pre-admission summer program, reduced course load, remedial instruction, study skills assistance, tutoring, writing center.

Honors college/program. Candidates will be assessed based on the academic and extracurricular documents submitted with the application, as well as responses to essay questions and letters of recommendation.

Majors. Area/ethnic studies: African-American, Asian, Latin American, women's. **Biology:** General, bacteriology, biochemistry, toxicology. **Business:** Accounting, business admin, finance, labor relations, management information systems, marketing, organizational behavior. **Communications:** Advertising, communications/speech/rhetoric, journalism. **Computer sciences:** General, information systems. **Conservation:** General, environmental studies, forest sciences. **Education:** Adult ed admin, agricultural, art, early childhood, elementary, foreign languages, secondary, special ed. **Engineering:** Aerospace, agricultural, architectural, biomedical, chemical, civil, computer, electrical, engineering science, environmental, industrial, mechanical, mining, nuclear, petroleum. **English:** English lit. **Foreign languages:** Chinese, classics, comparative lit, French, German, Italian, Japanese, Russian, Spanish. **Health services:** Athletic training, communication disorders, health care admin, nursing (RN), premedicine, preveterinary. **History:** General. **Liberal arts:** Arts/sciences. **Math:** General, statistics. **Parks/recreation:** Exercise sciences, facilities management. **Philosophy/religion:** Judaic, philosophy. **Physical sciences:** Astronomy, atmospheric science, chemistry, geology, materials science, physics. **Protective services:** Forensics, law enforcement admin. **Psychology:** General. **Social sciences:** Anthropology, archaeology, economics, geography, international relations, political science, sociology. **Visual/performing arts:** General, acting, art, art history/conservation, film/cinema/video, graphic design, music, theater design. **Work/family studies:** Family studies, human nutrition.

Most popular majors. Business/marketing 35%, communications/journalism 6%, computer/information sciences 18%, engineering/engineering technologies 13%, family/consumer sciences 17%, interdisciplinary studies 8%.

Technology on campus. 169 workstations in library, computer center, student center. Commuter students can connect to campus network. Online course registration, online library, helpline, repair service, student web hosting, wireless network available.

Student life. Freshman orientation: Mandatory. Preregistration for classes offered. Held for two days in May, June, July and August. **Policies:** Acts of intolerance and high-risk drinking discouraged at all locations. All facilities designated as smoke-free. Students expected to abide by The Penn State Principles. **Housing:** Nearby room, apartment, house rentals in the local community available. **Activities:** International student organizations, literary magazine, student government.

Athletics. USCAA. **Intercollegiate:** Baseball M, basketball, soccer M, volleyball W. **Team name:** Nittany Lions.

Student services. Adult student services, alcohol/substance abuse counseling, career counseling, services for economically disadvantaged, student employment services, financial aid counseling, personal counseling, placement for graduates, veterans' counselor. **Physically disabled:** Services for visually, hearing impaired.

Contact. E-mail: ykadmissions@psu.edu
Phone: (717) 771-4040 Toll-free number: (800) 778-6227
Fax: (717) 771-4005
Clark Brigger, Director for Undergraduate Admissions, Penn State York, Room 139, Main Classroom Building, 1031 Edgecomb Avenue, York, PA 17403

Pennsylvania Academy of the Fine Arts
Philadelphia, Pennsylvania
www.pafa.edu   CB code: 3038

- Private 4-year visual arts college
- Commuter campus in very large city
- 195 degree-seeking undergraduates: 2% part-time, 64% women, 5% African American, 9% Asian American, 7% Hispanic/Latino, 6% Multiracial, non-Hispanic, 6% international
- 96 degree-seeking graduate students
- Application essay required
- 59% graduate within 6 years

General. Regionally accredited. PAFA is both a school of fine art and a museum of American art. **Degrees:** 16 bachelor's awarded; master's offered. **Calendar:** Semester, limited summer session. **Full-time faculty:** 18 total. **Part-time faculty:** 45 total. **Special facilities:** Cast Hall, museum collection, Works on Paper Gallery.

Freshman class profile.

End year in good standing:	82%	Live on campus:	43%
Return as sophomores:	82%	International:	3%

Basis for selection. Admission to all program based on committee review of all credentials: application, personal statement, recommendations, transcripts, and artistic portfolio. If considered for admission, applicants are also considered for merit-based scholarships on a competitive basis. Interviews not required but are encouraged. Portfolios are required. **Home schooled:** Transcript of courses and grades, state high school equivalency certificate, letter of recommendation (nonparent) required.

2016-2017 Annual costs. Tuition/fees: $36,058. Books/supplies: $1,511. Personal expenses: $1,444.

Financial aid. Non-need-based: Scholarships awarded for academics, alumni affiliation, art.

Application procedures. Admission: Priority date 2/15; no deadline. $60 fee, may be waived for applicants with need. Application must be submitted online. Admission notification on a rolling basis. Must reply by 5/1. **Financial aid:** Closing date 3/1. FAFSA required. Applicants notified on a rolling basis; must reply by 5/1 or within 14 week(s) of notification.

Academics. Special study options: Dual enrollment of high school students, independent study, internships. In addition to its own BFA, the Pennsylvania Academy of the Fine Arts has a Coordinated BFA with the University of Pennsylvania which dates from 1929. **Credit/placement by examination:** AP, CLEP, IB, institutional tests. **Support services:** Pre-admission summer program, study skills assistance, tutoring, writing center.

Majors. Visual/performing arts: Drawing, illustration, painting, printmaking, sculpture.

Technology on campus. 20 workstations in library, computer center. Online library, wireless network available.

Student life. Freshman orientation: Mandatory. Preregistration for classes offered. **Housing:** $500 nonrefundable deposit. Partnership with Park Towne Place apartments. PAFA has one floor dedicated to student housing and has a Resident Director and a Resident Assistant who live on this floor. **Activities:** Film society, student government.

Student services. Career counseling, financial aid counseling, health services, personal counseling.

Contact. E-mail: admissions@pafa.edu
Phone: (215) 972-7625 Fax: (215) 972-0839
André van de Putte, Dean of Enrollment, Pennsylvania Academy of the Fine Arts, 128 North Broad Street, Philadelphia, PA 19102

Pennsylvania College of Art and Design
Lancaster, Pennsylvania   CB member
www.pcad.edu   CB code: 2681

- Private 4-year visual arts college
- Commuter campus in small city
- 220 degree-seeking undergraduates: 5% part-time, 67% women, 7% African American, 4% Asian American, 4% Hispanic/Latino, 4% Multiracial, non-Hispanic
- 40% of applicants admitted
- Application essay required
- 79% graduate within 6 years

General. Regionally accredited. **Degrees:** 37 bachelor's awarded. **Location:** 80 miles from Philadelphia, 75 miles from Baltimore, 120 miles from Washington, DC. **Calendar:** Semester, limited summer session. **Full-time faculty:** 11 total; 54% have terminal degrees, 36% women. **Part-time faculty:** 34 total; 32% have terminal degrees, 3% minority, 35% women. **Class size:** 87% < 20, 13% 20-39. **Special facilities:** Visual arts gallery, design center, individual senior studios, art garden with food trucks.

Freshman class profile. 404 applied, 163 admitted, 69 enrolled.

GPA 3.75 or higher:	17%	GPA 2.0-2.99:	38%
GPA 3.50-3.74:	6%	Return as sophomores:	60%
GPA 3.0-3.49:	39%	Out-of-state:	20%

Basis for selection. Portfolio review, personal statement, and high school transcripts required. Students with GPA below 2.5 may be required to submit two letters of recommendation. Interview strongly recommended. SAT or ACT recommended. Portfolio required. **Home schooled:** Transcript of courses and grades, state high school equivalency certificate required.

High school preparation. College-preparatory program recommended.

2015-2016 Annual costs. Tuition/fees: $22,800. Books/supplies: $1,500. **Additional information:** Additional fees for required laptop, camera, software purchase: $3,400.

2014-2015 Financial aid. **Need-based:** 57 full-time freshmen applied for aid; 53 deemed to have need; 53 received aid. 34% of total undergraduate aid awarded as scholarships/grants, 66% as loans/jobs. **Non-need-based:** Awarded to 77 full-time undergraduates, including 52 freshmen. Scholarships awarded for academics, art.

Application procedures. Admission: No deadline. $40 fee, may be waived for applicants with need. Admission notification on a rolling basis. Must reply by May 1 or within 2 week(s) if notified thereafter. **Financial aid:** Priority date 3/1; no closing date. FAFSA required. Applicants notified on a rolling basis starting 4/15.

Academics. Special study options: Dual enrollment of high school students, internships. **Credit/placement by examination:** AP, CLEP, institutional tests. **Support services:** Study skills assistance.

Majors. Visual/performing arts: General, art, commercial photography, commercial/advertising art, design, digital arts, drawing, game design, graphic design, illustration, painting, photography, printmaking, sculpture, studio arts.

Technology on campus. PC or laptop required. Online library, wireless network available.

Student life. Freshman orientation: Mandatory. Preregistration for classes offered. **Housing:** Apartments available. Housing referral service available. **Activities:** Student government.

Student services. Career counseling, student employment services, financial aid counseling.

Contact. E-mail: admissions@pcad.edu
Phone: (717) 396-7833 Toll-free number: (800) 689-0379 ext. 1001
Fax: (717) 396-1339
Natalie Lascek-Speakman, Director of Admission Marketing and Recruitment, Pennsylvania College of Art and Design, PO Box 59, Lancaster, PA 17608-0059

Pennsylvania College of Health Sciences
Lancaster, Pennsylvania
www.pacollege.edu
CB code: 2374

- Private 4-year health science and nursing college
- Commuter campus in small city
- 1,342 degree-seeking undergraduates
- 53% of applicants admitted
- Application essay required

General. Regionally accredited. **Degrees:** 130 bachelor's, 321 associate awarded. **Calendar:** Semester, extensive summer session. **Full-time faculty:** 63 total. **Part-time faculty:** 105 total.

Freshman class profile. 660 applied, 347 admitted, 244 enrolled.

Basis for selection. Prior academic performance weighs heavily in admission decisions. GPA of 3.0 or above for high school graduates and 2.5 GPA or above for prior college coursework preferred. Grades in math and science courses heavily weighted. SAT or ACT scores required for applicants within two years of their high school graduation. **Home schooled:** Transcript of courses and grades required.

High school preparation. College-preparatory program recommended. Required units include English 4, mathematics 2, science 2 (laboratory 1).

2015-2016 Annual costs. Books/supplies: $2,460. **Additional information:** $512 per-credit hour charge plus flat program cost which varies by program; $300 technology fee per semester.

Financial aid. Non-need-based: Scholarships awarded for academics, leadership, state residency.

Application procedures. Admission: Closing date 2/1 (receipt date). $35 fee. Application must be submitted online. Admission notification on a rolling basis. Must reply by May 1 or within 4 week(s) if notified thereafter. **Financial aid:** Closing date 5/1. FAFSA required.

Academics. Special study options: Distance learning. **Credit/placement by examination:** AP, CLEP. **Support services:** Learning center, study skills assistance, tutoring, writing center. Smarthinking is online 24/7 tutorial, writing; clinical skills lab available some weekend hours.

Majors. Health services: Health care admin, nursing (RN).

Technology on campus. 88 workstations in library, computer center. Commuter students can connect to campus network. Online course registration, online library, wireless network available.

Student life. Freshman orientation: Mandatory. Preregistration for classes offered. New student orientation held on several different days throughout June; students are invited to specific days based on their academic program. Throughout the 4 hour program students meet with student services personnel, register for classes, and learn details essential for the start of classes. A slightly condensed program is offered in December for students starting in January. **Activities:** Literary magazine, student government.

Student services. Career counseling, financial aid counseling, health services, personal counseling.

Contact. E-mail: admission@pacollege.edu
Phone: (717) 544-4912
Michelle Meiser, Director of Admission, Pennsylvania College of Health Sciences, 410 North Lime Street, Lancaster, PA 17602

Pennsylvania College of Technology
Williamsport, Pennsylvania   **CB member**
www.pct.edu   **CB code: 2989**

- Public 4-year technical college
- Commuter campus in large town
- 5,416 degree-seeking undergraduates: 15% part-time, 36% women

General. Founded in 1965. Regionally accredited. **Degrees:** 561 bachelor's, 852 associate awarded. **ROTC:** Army. **Location:** 85 miles from Harrisburg, 70 miles from Wilkes-Barre. **Calendar:** Semester, limited summer session. **Full-time faculty:** 293 total; 5% minority, 31% women. **Part-time faculty:** 179 total; 4% minority, 65% women. **Class size:** 64% < 20, 36% 20-39. **Special facilities:** Automotive technology center, aviation center, plastics manufacturing center, community arts center, earth science center.

Freshman class profile. 3,144 applied, 2,672 admitted, 1,165 enrolled.

GPA 3.75 or higher:	13%	GPA 2.0-2.99:	38%
GPA 3.50-3.74:	12%	Rank in top quarter:	16%
GPA 3.0-3.49:	31%	Rank in top tenth:	4%

Basis for selection. Open admission, but selective for some programs. Competitive admissions to health science programs, using GPA, SAT scores, high school rank, selected course grades, completed developmental course work. Some programs have more specific requirements. SAT recommended for all bachelor's programs, dental hygiene, radiography, occupational therapy assistant, nursing applicants; college placement exams required for all applicants. **Home schooled:** Transcript of courses and grades, state high school equivalency certificate required. Must provide proof of graduation from an organization governed by the State Board of Education, such as Pennsylvania Home Schoolers Accreditation Agency. Otherwise must present GED.

2015-2016 Annual costs. Tuition/fees: $15,810; $22,470 out-of-state. Room/board: $11,108. Books/supplies: $1,400. Personal expenses: $3,162.

2014-2015 Financial aid. Need-based: 38% of total undergraduate aid awarded as scholarships/grants, 62% as loans/jobs. **Non-need-based:** Scholarships awarded for academics, alumni affiliation, leadership, ROTC.

Application procedures. Admission: Closing date 7/1 (postmark date). $50 fee, may be waived for applicants with need, free for online applicants. Admission notification on a rolling basis. **Financial aid:** Priority date 4/15; no closing date. FAFSA, institutional form required. Applicants notified on a rolling basis starting 6/1; must reply by 7/1 or within 4 week(s) of notification.

Academics. Special study options: Accelerated study, cooperative education, cross-registration, distance learning, dual enrollment of high school students, ESL, exchange student, independent study, internships, student-designed major, study abroad, weekend college. **Credit/placement by examination:** AP, CLEP, institutional tests. 30 credit hours maximum toward associate degree, 30 toward bachelor's. **Support services:** Learning center, pre-admission summer program, reduced course load, remedial instruction, study skills assistance, tutoring, writing center.

Majors. Architecture: Building sciences. **Business:** Accounting, business admin. **Computer sciences:** Database management, modeling/simulation, networking, security, web page design. **General:** Site management. **Health services:** Adult health nursing, dental hygiene, health information management, physician assistant. **Parks/recreation:** Sports admin. **Protective services:** Disaster management. **Visual/performing arts:** Commercial/advertising art, industrial design.

Most popular majors. Business/marketing 16%, computer/information sciences 10%, engineering/engineering technologies 30%, health sciences 22%, trade and industry 12%.

Technology on campus. 1,764 workstations in dormitories, library, computer center, student center. Dormitories wired for high-speed internet access and linked to campus network. Commuter students can connect to campus network. Online course registration, online library, helpline, repair service, student web hosting, wireless network available.

Student life. Freshman orientation: Available. Preregistration for classes offered. Two-day sessions offered throughout the summer. **Policies:** No alcohol or illegal drugs on campus. Smoke-free buildings and housing environments. **Housing:** Coed dorms, apartments, wellness housing available. $400 partly refundable deposit. Academic theme housing offers a living-learning atmosphere. **Activities:** Campus ministries, dance, international student organizations, student government, Alpha Omega Fellowship, Campus Crusade for Christ, Earth Smart, Human Services Club, Multicultural Society, Skills USA, Students Making a Contribution, US Green Building Council Students of Penn College.

Athletics. NCAA, USCAA. **Intercollegiate:** Archery, baseball M, basketball, bowling, cross-country, golf, soccer, softball W, tennis, volleyball, wrestling M. **Intramural:** Archery, badminton, basketball, bowling, football (non-tackle), golf, soccer, softball, table tennis, tennis, ultimate frisbee, volleyball, weight lifting. **Team name:** Wildcats.

Student services. Adult student services, alcohol/substance abuse counseling, career counseling, student employment services, financial aid counseling, health services, minority student services, on-campus daycare, personal counseling, placement for graduates, veterans' counselor. **Physically disabled:** Services for visually, speech, hearing impaired.

Contact. E-mail: admissions@pct.edu
Phone: (570) 327-4761 Toll-free number: (800) 367-9222
Fax: (570) 321-5551
Joseph Balduino, Director of Admissions, Pennsylvania College of Technology, One College Avenue, Williamsport, PA 17701-5799

Philadelphia University
Philadelphia, Pennsylvania
www.PhilaU.edu

CB member
CB code: 2666

- Private 4-year university
- Residential campus in very large city
- 2,788 degree-seeking undergraduates: 12% part-time, 67% women, 15% African American, 5% Asian American, 8% Hispanic/Latino, 2% Multiracial, non-Hispanic, 4% international
- 916 degree-seeking graduate students
- 64% of applicants admitted
- SAT or ACT (ACT writing optional) required
- 65% graduate within 6 years

General. Founded in 1884. Regionally accredited. **Degrees:** 648 bachelor's, 66 associate awarded; master's, professional, doctoral offered. **Location:** 6 miles from Center City. **Calendar:** Semester, extensive summer session. **Full-time faculty:** 123 total; 51% have terminal degrees, 13% minority, 46% women. **Part-time faculty:** 408 total; 15% minority, 47% women. **Class size:** 68% < 20, 32% 20-39, less than 1% 40-49, less than 1% 50-99. **Special facilities:** Center for sustainability, energy efficiency and design, laboratory for engineered human protection, Institute for Textile and Apparel Product Safety, Engineering and Design Institute (a partnership with Ben Franklin Technology Partners), computer aided design laboratories in architecture, graphic design and fashion design, CAD facilities, university design center, rapid prototyping.

Freshman class profile. 4,129 applied, 2,651 admitted, 527 enrolled.

Mid 50% test scores			
SAT critical reading:	490-580	Rank in top quarter:	41%
SAT math:	490-600	Rank in top tenth:	17%
SAT writing:	470-570	Return as sophomores:	83%
ACT composite:	21-26	Out-of-state:	49%
GPA 3.75 or higher:	36%	Live on campus:	87%
GPA 3.50-3.74:	19%	International:	4%
GPA 3.0-3.49:	30%	Fraternities:	1%
GPA 2.0-2.99:	15%	Sororities:	1%

Basis for selection. Academic record, GPA, and test scores most important. Extracurricular activities, counselor's recommendation and interview considered. Interview, essay recommended.

High school preparation. College-preparatory program recommended. Required and recommended units include English 3-4, mathematics 3-4, social studies 1-2, history 2, science 2 (laboratory 2) and foreign language 2-3.

2015-2016 Annual costs. Tuition/fees: $36,520. Room/board: $12,140. Books/supplies: $1,600. Personal expenses: $1,789.

2015-2016 Financial aid. Need-based: 474 full-time freshmen applied for aid; 411 deemed to have need; 411 received aid. Average need met was 79%. Average scholarship/grant was $27,568; average loan $3,741. 69% of total undergraduate aid awarded as scholarships/grants, 31% as loans/jobs. **Non-need-based:** Awarded to 688 full-time undergraduates, including 163 freshmen. Scholarships awarded for academics, athletics.

Application procedures. Admission: No deadline. $40 fee, may be waived for applicants with need. Admission notification on a rolling basis beginning on or about 11/1. Must reply by May 1 or within 1 week(s) if notified thereafter. Housing deposit not refundable after May 1st. **Financial aid:** Priority date 3/1, closing date 4/15. FAFSA required. Applicants notified on a rolling basis starting 3/1; must reply by 5/1.

Academics. Special study options: Accelerated study, combined bachelor's/graduate degree, distance learning, double major, honors, independent study, internships, liberal arts/career combination, semester at sea, study abroad. **Credit/placement by examination:** AP, CLEP, SAT, ACT, institutional tests. 60 credit hours maximum toward bachelor's degree. **Support services:** Learning center, reduced course load, remedial instruction, study skills assistance, tutoring, writing center.

Majors. Architecture: Architecture, interior, landscape. **Biology:** General, biochemistry, environmental. **Business:** Accounting, apparel, business admin, fashion, finance, international, management information systems, marketing. **Communications:** Digital media. **Communications technology:** Animation/special effects, graphics. **Conservation:** Environmental studies. **Engineering:** General, architectural, industrial, mechanical, textile. **Health services:** Health care admin, premedicine. **Physical sciences:** Chemistry. **Psychology:** General. **Visual/performing arts:** Fashion design, fiber arts, graphic design, industrial design, interior design. **Work/family studies:** Apparel marketing, clothing/textiles, textile science.

Most popular majors. Architecture 18%, business/marketing 28%, health sciences 17%, psychology 6%, visual/performing arts 16%.

Technology on campus. PC or laptop required. 600 workstations in library, computer center, student center. Dormitories wired for high-speed internet access and linked to campus network. Commuter students can connect to campus network. Online course registration, online library, helpline, student web hosting, wireless network available.

Student life. Freshman orientation: Mandatory, $100 fee. Preregistration for classes offered. 3-day residential program in summer. **Housing:** Guaranteed on-campus for freshmen. Coed dorms, single-sex dorms, special housing for disabled, apartments available. $250 fully refundable deposit. Townhouses available. **Activities:** Campus ministries, choral groups, dance, drama, international student organizations, student government, student newspaper, professional (major-related) organizations, Black awareness society, Hillel, Christian fellowship, community service corps, Minaret, Gemini Theatre, Phila Capella, Gay Lesbian Bisexual Allies Coalition.

Athletics. NCAA. **Intercollegiate:** Baseball M, basketball, cross-country, golf M, lacrosse W, rowing (crew), soccer, softball W, tennis, track and field M, volleyball W. **Intramural:** Basketball, cross-country, football (tackle) M, skiing, soccer, softball, swimming, tennis, volleyball W. **Team name:** Rams.

Student services. Adult student services, alcohol/substance abuse counseling, career counseling, student employment services, financial aid counseling, health services, personal counseling, placement for graduates. **Physically disabled:** Services for visually, hearing impaired.

Contact. E-mail: admissions@philau.edu
Phone: (215) 951-2800 Toll-free number: (800) 951-7287
Fax: (215) 951-2907
Greg Potts, Director of Admissions, Philadelphia University, 4201 Henry
Avenue, Philadelphia, PA 19144

Point Park University
Pittsburgh, Pennsylvania **CB member**
www.pointpark.edu **CB code: 2676**

▶ Private 4-year university
▶ Commuter campus in large city
▶ 3,140 degree-seeking undergraduates
▶ 71% of applicants admitted
▶ SAT or ACT (ACT writing optional), application essay, interview required

General. Founded in 1960. Regionally accredited. **Degrees:** 683 bachelor's, 4 associate awarded; master's, doctoral offered. **ROTC:** Army, Air Force. **Location:** Downtown. **Calendar:** Semester, extensive summer session. **Full-time faculty:** 141 total; 10% minority. **Part-time faculty:** 306 total. **Class size:** 73% < 20, 26% 20-39, less than 1% 40-49, less than 1% 50-99, less than 1% >100. **Special facilities:** Natural sciences labs, engineering technology labs, forensic crime scene house, computer newsrooms, MAC and PC multimedia labs, black/white and color photography darkrooms, digital photography lab, radio station, TV studio/newsroom, cinema production and editing suites, performance and dance studios, performing arts center/theaters, art galleries.

Freshman class profile. 4,021 applied, 2,836 admitted, 595 enrolled.

Mid 50% test scores			
SAT critical reading:	450-560	GPA 3.0-3.49:	35%
SAT math:	430-530	GPA 2.0-2.99:	32%
SAT writing:	430-550	Rank in top quarter:	31%
ACT composite:	19-25	Rank in top tenth:	9%
GPA 3.75 or higher:	14%	Out-of-state:	35%
GPA 3.50-3.74:	19%	Live on campus:	77%

Basis for selection. High school record, class rank, test scores most important. Recommendations, extracurricular activities, talent, character also important. Test scores must be received by the first day of class. Audition required for some majors, portfolio recommended for multimedia, technical theater, stage management programs. **Home schooled:** Transcript of courses and grades, state high school equivalency certificate required.

High school preparation. College-preparatory program recommended. Recommended units include English 4, mathematics 4, social studies 4 and science 4.

2015-2016 Annual costs. Tuition/fees: $28,250. Room/board: $10,620. Books/supplies: $1,200. Personal expenses: $1,100. **Additional information:** Students in Conservatory of Performing Arts pay full-time tuition of $34,400 per year ($976 per-credit hour). Required fees, room and board are the same for COPA and non-COPA students.

2015-2016 Financial aid. **Need-based:** 558 full-time freshmen applied for aid; 500 deemed to have need; 500 received aid. Average need met was 75%. Average scholarship/grant was $19,551; average loan $4,603. 64% of total undergraduate aid awarded as scholarships/grants, 36% as loans/jobs. **Non-need-based:** Awarded to 420 full-time undergraduates, including 144 freshmen. Scholarships awarded for academics, athletics, music/drama.

Application procedures. **Admission:** No deadline. $30 fee, may be waived for applicants with need, free for online applicants. Admission notification on a rolling basis beginning on or about 10/1. Must reply by May 1 or within 2 week(s) if notified thereafter. **Financial aid:** Priority date 3/15, closing date 12/1. FAFSA required. Applicants notified by 2/15; must reply within 2 week(s) of notification.

Academics. **Special study options:** Accelerated study, cooperative education, cross-registration, distance learning, double major, dual enrollment of high school students, ESL, exchange student, honors, independent study, internships, liberal arts/career combination, student-designed major, study abroad, teacher certification program, weekend college. Numerous off-campus programs for college credits. Several accelerated programs available. Offers professionally oriented programs in arts, business, communications, and technology. **Credit/placement by examination:** AP, CLEP, IB. 30 credit hours maximum toward associate degree, 60 toward bachelor's. **Support services:** Learning center, pre-admission summer program, reduced course load, remedial instruction, study skills assistance, tutoring.

Majors. Biology: General, biotechnology. **Business:** Accounting, business admin, human resources. **Communications:** Advertising, broadcast journalism, digital media, journalism, media studies, persuasive communications, photojournalism, radio/TV. **Communications technology:** Animation/special effects. **Computer sciences:** Information technology. **Conservation:** Environmental science. **Education:** Biology, drama/dance, early childhood, elementary, English, mathematics. **English:** English lit. **History:** General. **Human services:** General. **Liberal arts:** Arts/sciences. **Protective services:** Criminal justice, forensics. **Psychology:** General. **Social sciences:** Economics, political science. **Visual/performing arts:** Cinematography, dance, dramatic, photography, play/screenwriting.

Most popular majors. Business/marketing 22%, communications/journalism 13%, security/protective services 9%, visual/performing arts 27%.

Technology on campus. 371 workstations in dormitories, library, computer center, student center. Dormitories wired for high-speed internet access and linked to campus network. Commuter students can connect to campus network. Online course registration, online library, helpline, repair service, student web hosting, wireless network available.

Student life. Freshman orientation: Mandatory. Preregistration for classes offered. Held in summer months, includes placement testing if needed for major. **Policies:** Policies regarding student conduct, plagiarism and resident life. **Housing:** Guaranteed on-campus for all undergraduates. Coed dorms, single-sex dorms available. $400 partly refundable deposit, deadline 7/15. Living and learning communities; suite style housing available. **Activities:** Campus ministries, choral groups, dance, drama, film society, international student organizations, musical theater, radio station, student government, student newspaper, TV station.

Athletics. NAIA. **Intercollegiate:** Baseball M, basketball, cross-country, golf, soccer, softball W, volleyball W. **Intramural:** Basketball M, tennis, volleyball, weight lifting M. **Team name:** Pioneers.

Student services. Adult student services, alcohol/substance abuse counseling, career counseling, student employment services, financial aid counseling, health services, personal counseling, placement for graduates, veterans' counselor. **Physically disabled:** Services for visually, speech, hearing impaired.

Contact. E-mail: enroll@pointpark.edu
Phone: (412) 392-3430 Toll-free number: (800) 321-0129
Fax: (412) 392-3902
Joell Minford, Director of Admissions, Point Park University, 201 Wood Street, Pittsburgh, PA 15222-1984

Restaurant School at Walnut Hill College
Philadelphia, Pennsylvania
www.walnuthillcollege.edu **CB code: 4883**

▶ For-profit 4-year culinary school and business college
▶ Commuter campus in very large city
▶ 380 degree-seeking undergraduates
▶ Application essay, interview required

General. Accredited by ACCSC. Emphasis on fine dining and upscale hotels. **Degrees:** 53 bachelor's, 157 associate awarded. **Calendar:** Quarter. **Full-time faculty:** 16 total. **Part-time faculty:** 9 total. **Special facilities:** Students interact with numerous food and beverage outlets open to public. 4 uniquely themed restaurants and pastry shop/cafe.

Freshman class profile.

Out-of-state:	51%	Live on campus:	30%

Basis for selection. All students must interview with admissions representative, submit two letters of reference, 250-word essay, SAT/ACT scores and/or take a basic skills evaluation. Students who score below 900 combined on SAT/ACT Math and Critical Reading, or who did not take either test, must take in-house assessment test. Decisions are based on all information received, however the interview is the most heavily weighted. SAT or ACT recommended. **Home schooled:** Interview required.

2015-2016 Annual costs. Tuition/fees: $23,850. Personal expenses: $3,000. **Additional information:** Cost of books and supplies vary. All costs are subject to change.

Financial aid. **Non-need-based:** Scholarships awarded for leadership.

Application procedures. **Admission:** No deadline. $50 fee. Admission notification on a rolling basis. **Financial aid:** No deadline. FAFSA, institutional form required.

Academics. **Special study options:** Independent study, internships. **Credit/placement by examination:** AP, CLEP. **Support services:** Study skills assistance, tutoring.

Majors. **Business:** Hotel/motel admin, restaurant/food services.

Most popular majors. Business/marketing 15%, personal/culinary services 75%.

Technology on campus. 48 workstations in library, computer center. Dormitories wired for high-speed internet access and linked to campus network. Online library, wireless network available.

Student life. **Freshman orientation:** Mandatory. Preregistration for classes offered. 3-day program held week prior to start of classes. **Housing:** Guaranteed on-campus for all undergraduates. Coed dorms available. $850 fully refundable deposit. **Activities:** Literary magazine, music ensembles, student newspaper.

Student services. Career counseling, student employment services, financial aid counseling.

Contact. E-mail: info@walnuthillcollege.edu
Phone: (215) 222-4200 ext. 3011
Toll-free number: (877) 925-6884 ext. 3011 Fax: (215) 222-2811
Toni Morelli, Director of Admissions, Restaurant School at Walnut Hill College, 4207 Walnut Street, Philadelphia, PA 19104

Robert Morris University
Moon Township, Pennsylvania CB member
www.rmu.edu CB code: 2769

- Private 4-year university
- Residential campus in large town
- 4,485 degree-seeking undergraduates: 12% part-time, 44% women, 6% African American, 1% Asian American, 2% Hispanic/Latino, 3% Multiracial, non-Hispanic, 11% international
- 848 degree-seeking graduate students
- 78% of applicants admitted
- SAT or ACT (ACT writing optional) required
- 58% graduate within 6 years

General. Founded in 1921. Regionally accredited. **Degrees:** 930 bachelor's awarded; master's, professional, doctoral offered. **ROTC:** Army, Naval, Air Force. **Location:** 17 miles from Pittsburgh. **Calendar:** Semester, limited summer session. **Full-time faculty:** 214 total; 87% have terminal degrees, 13% minority, 43% women. **Part-time faculty:** 274 total; 32% have terminal degrees, 6% minority, 58% women. **Class size:** 51% < 20, 41% 20-39, 5% 40-49, 3% 50-99.

Freshman class profile. 6,579 applied, 5,109 admitted, 865 enrolled.

Mid 50% test scores			
SAT critical reading:	470-570	Rank in top quarter:	45%
SAT math:	470-580	Rank in top tenth:	18%
SAT writing:	450-550	Return as sophomores:	85%
ACT composite:	20-26	Out-of-state:	16%
GPA 3.75 or higher:	35%	Live on campus:	88%
GPA 3.50-3.74:	17%	International:	5%
GPA 3.0-3.49:	30%	Fraternities:	8%
GPA 2.0-2.99:	18%	Sororities:	17%

Basis for selection. Academic potential, high school GPA, class rank, test scores, and evidence of motivation important. Interview required of restricted-status applicants, recommended for all others.

High school preparation. College-preparatory program recommended. 16 units required; 19 recommended. Required and recommended units include English 4, mathematics 3-4, social studies 4, science 2, foreign language 2 and academic electives 3.

2015-2016 Annual costs. Tuition/fees: $27,194. Room/board: $12,130. Books/supplies: $1,200. Personal expenses: $1,500.

2015-2016 Financial aid. **Need-based:** 779 full-time freshmen applied for aid; 688 deemed to have need; 688 received aid. Average need met was 74%. Average scholarship/grant was $17,356; average loan $4,880. 59% of total undergraduate aid awarded as scholarships/grants, 41% as loans/jobs. **Non-need-based:** Awarded to 1,024 full-time undergraduates, including 255 freshmen. Scholarships awarded for academics, athletics, ROTC.

Application procedures. **Admission:** Priority date 4/1; no deadline. $30 fee, may be waived for applicants with need, free for online applicants.

Admission notification on a rolling basis beginning on or about 9/1. Must reply by May 1 or within 2 week(s) if notified thereafter. **Financial aid:** No deadline. FAFSA required. Applicants notified on a rolling basis starting 2/15.

Academics. **Special study options:** Combined bachelor's/graduate degree, cooperative education, cross-registration, distance learning, double major, honors, independent study, internships, study abroad, teacher certification program, weekend college. **Credit/placement by examination:** AP, CLEP, SAT, ACT, institutional tests. 30 credit hours maximum toward bachelor's degree. **Support services:** Pre-admission summer program, reduced course load, remedial instruction, study skills assistance, tutoring.

Majors. **Biology:** General. **Business:** Accounting, actuarial science, business admin, finance, hospitality admin, management information systems, marketing, organizational behavior. **Communications:** Communications/speech/rhetoric. **Computer sciences:** Information systems, modeling/simulation. **Conservation:** Environmental science. **Education:** Business, elementary. **Engineering:** Manufacturing. **English:** English lit. **Health services:** Health services admin, nuclear medical technology, nursing (RN). **History:** General. **Math:** Applied. **Parks/recreation:** Sports admin. **Protective services:** Computer forensics. **Psychology:** General. **Social sciences:** General, economics. **Visual/performing arts:** Design.

Most popular majors. Business/marketing 41%, communications/journalism 6%, engineering/engineering technologies 8%, health sciences 15%.

Technology on campus. 300 workstations in dormitories, library, computer center, student center. Dormitories wired for high-speed internet access and linked to campus network. Commuter students can connect to campus network. Online course registration, online library, helpline, wireless network available.

Student life. **Freshman orientation:** Mandatory, $200 fee. Preregistration for classes offered. 3-day program. **Housing:** Coed dorms, single-sex dorms, special housing for disabled, apartments, fraternity/sorority housing, themed housing available. $100 fully refundable deposit, deadline 5/1. **Activities:** Bands, campus ministries, choral groups, dance, drama, film society, international student organizations, literary magazine, music ensembles, musical theater, radio station, student government, student newspaper, TV station, minority student organizations, campus activities board, inter-residence hall council, inter-fraternity council/Panhellenic council, honor societies, major-related organizations, campus Republicans and Democrats, community service and volunteer organizations.

Athletics. NCAA. **Intercollegiate:** Basketball, cross-country W, field hockey W, football (tackle) M, golf M, ice hockey, lacrosse, rowing (crew) W, soccer, softball W, track and field W, volleyball W. **Intramural:** Basketball, football (non-tackle) M, handball M, softball, volleyball W. **Team name:** Colonials.

Student services. Adult student services, alcohol/substance abuse counseling, chaplain/spiritual director, career counseling, services for economically disadvantaged, student employment services, financial aid counseling, health services, minority student services, personal counseling, placement for graduates, veterans' counselor, women's services. **Physically disabled:** Services for visually, speech, hearing impaired.

Contact. E-mail: admissionsoffice@rmu.edu
Phone: (412) 397-5200 Toll-free number: (800) 762-0097
Fax: (412) 397-2425
Kellie Laurenzi, Dean of Admissions, Robert Morris University, 6001 University Boulevard, Moon Township, PA 15108-1189

Rosemont College
Rosemont, Pennsylvania CB member
www.rosemont.edu CB code: 2763

- Private 4-year liberal arts college affiliated with the Roman Catholic Church
- Residential campus in small town
- 529 degree-seeking undergraduates: 14% part-time, 65% women, 40% African American, 5% Asian American, 6% Hispanic/Latino, 4% Multiracial, non-Hispanic, 2% international
- 358 degree-seeking graduate students
- 71% of applicants admitted
- SAT or ACT required
- 46% graduate within 6 years; 15% enter graduate study

General. Founded in 1921. Regionally accredited. **Degrees:** 118 bachelor's awarded; master's offered. **ROTC:** Army, Air Force. **Location:** 11 miles from Philadelphia. **Calendar:** Semester, limited summer session. **Full-time faculty:** 25 total; 84% have terminal degrees, 4% minority, 48% women.

Part-time faculty: 121 total; 74% have terminal degrees, 15% minority, 54% women. **Class size:** 76% < 20, 24% 20-39.

Freshman class profile. 875 applied, 618 admitted, 135 enrolled.

Mid 50% test scores			
SAT critical reading:	400-520	GPA 3.0-3.49:	52%
SAT math:	380-510	GPA 2.0-2.99:	14%
SAT writing:	390-510	End year in good standing:	95%
ACT composite:	15-20	Return as sophomores:	69%
GPA 3.75 or higher:	18%	Out-of-state:	29%
GPA 3.50-3.74:	16%	Live on campus:	90%

Basis for selection. School achievement record and curriculum, recommendations, test scores, extracurricular activities strongly considered. Interview recommended. **Home schooled:** Statement describing home school structure and mission, transcript of courses and grades, letter of recommendation (nonparent) required.

High school preparation. College-preparatory program recommended. 18 units required. Required units include English 4, mathematics 2, social studies 2, history 2, science 2 (laboratory 2), foreign language 2 and academic electives 2.

2016-2017 Annual costs. Tuition/fees: $19,480. Room/board: $11,500. Books/supplies: $1,500. Personal expenses: $1,000.

Financial aid. **Non-need-based:** Scholarships awarded for academics, alumni affiliation, athletics, leadership.

Application procedures. Admission: No deadline. No application fee. Admission notification on a rolling basis. Must reply by May 1 or within 2 week(s) if notified thereafter. $350 deposit required if student plans to live on campus. $200 deposit if student plans to commute to campus. **Financial aid:** Priority date 2/15; no closing date. FAFSA required. Applicants notified on a rolling basis starting 3/5; must reply within 4 week(s) of notification.

Academics. Bridge To Success is a pre-orientation program which offers: academic support emphasizing writing and reading, college readiness, and study skills to a selected group of students. Bridge students arrive on campus in advance of all other students and attend four days of classes taught by Rosemont professors. **Special study options:** Accelerated study, combined bachelor's/graduate degree, cross-registration, distance learning, double major, ESL, exchange student, honors, independent study, internships, liberal arts/career combination, student-designed major, study abroad, teacher certification program, Washington semester. **Credit/placement by examination:** AP, CLEP, IB, SAT, ACT, institutional tests. 30 credit hours maximum toward bachelor's degree. Students may be exempted if they demonstrate mastery of subject as determined by particular department. **Support services:** Learning center, pre-admission summer program, reduced course load, remedial instruction, study skills assistance, tutoring, writing center.

Honors college/program. For new first year students, a minimum combined SAT score of 1100 (Math and Critical Reading), with no score below 500 in either Critical Reading or Math, high school GPA of 3.50 or higher. For entering transfer students, a college GPA of 3.33 or higher, with no grade below "C" and only two grades below "B" allowed.

Majors. Area/ethnic studies: Women's. **Biology:** General, biochemistry. **Business:** General, accounting, business admin, communications, management science, managerial economics, marketing, organizational behavior. **Communications:** Communications/speech/rhetoric. **Conservation:** Environmental science. **Education:** Elementary, secondary. **English:** English lit. **Foreign languages:** General, French, German, Italian, Spanish. **History:** General. **Liberal arts:** Arts/sciences, humanities. **Math:** General. **Philosophy/religion:** Philosophy, religion. **Physical sciences:** Chemistry. **Protective services:** Criminal justice. **Psychology:** General. **Social sciences:** General, economics, political science, sociology. **Visual/performing arts:** Art history/conservation, studio arts.

Most popular majors. Biology 6%, business/marketing 25%, education 14%, English 6%, psychology 8%, security/protective services 10%, social sciences 12%, visual/performing arts 6%.

Technology on campus. 100 workstations in dormitories, library, computer center, student center. Dormitories wired for high-speed internet access and linked to campus network. Commuter students can connect to campus network. Online course registration, online library, helpline, student web hosting, wireless network available.

Student life. Freshman orientation: Mandatory, $280 fee. Preregistration for classes offered. Program approximately 3 days; includes academics component. **Housing:** Guaranteed on-campus for all undergraduates. Coed dorms, wellness housing available. Honors housing available in restored architecturally significant building. **Activities:** Bands, campus ministries, choral groups, dance, drama, international student organizations, literary magazine, music ensembles, Model UN, musical theater, radio station, student government, student newspaper, premed club, politics club, Rosemont Alcohol and Drug Awareness Resource, multicultural society, Best Buddies, Triad, art society.

Athletics. NCAA. **Intercollegiate:** Basketball, cross-country, golf M, lacrosse, soccer, softball W, tennis, volleyball W. **Team name:** The Ravens.

Student services. Adult student services, alcohol/substance abuse counseling, chaplain/spiritual director, career counseling, student employment services, financial aid counseling, health services, legal services, minority student services, on-campus daycare, personal counseling, placement for graduates, veterans' counselor, women's services. **Physically disabled:** Services for visually, speech, hearing impaired.

Contact. E-mail: admissions@rosemont.edu
Phone: (610) 526-2966 Toll-free number: (800) 331-0708
Fax: (610) 520-4399
Dennis Murphy, Vice President for Enrollment Management, Rosemont College, 1400 Montgomery Avenue, Rosemont, PA 19010-1699

Saint Joseph's University
Philadelphia, Pennsylvania
www.sju.edu

CB member
CB code: 2801

- Private 4-year university affiliated with the Roman Catholic Church
- Residential campus in very large city
- 5,250 degree-seeking undergraduates: 12% part-time, 55% women, 7% African American, 2% Asian American, 6% Hispanic/Latino, 2% Multiracial, non-Hispanic, 2% international
- 3,048 degree-seeking graduate students
- 82% of applicants admitted
- Application essay required
- 79% graduate within 6 years

General. Founded in 1851. Regionally accredited. **Degrees:** 1,171 bachelor's, 3 associate awarded; master's, doctoral offered. **ROTC:** Army, Naval, Air Force. **Location:** 8 miles from downtown. **Calendar:** Semester, extensive summer session. **Full-time faculty:** 298 total; 92% have terminal degrees, 16% minority, 45% women. **Part-time faculty:** 430 total; 13% minority, 47% women. **Class size:** 31% < 20, 63% 20-39, 5% 40-49, less than 1% 50-99.

Freshman class profile. 8,325 applied, 6,814 admitted, 1,175 enrolled.

Mid 50% test scores			
SAT critical reading:	520-610	GPA 3.0-3.49:	35%
SAT math:	530-620	GPA 2.0-2.99:	13%
SAT writing:	510-620	Rank in top quarter:	48%
ACT composite:	23-28	Rank in top tenth:	19%
GPA 3.75 or higher:	32%	Return as sophomores:	88%
GPA 3.50-3.74:	20%	Out-of-state:	55%
		International:	2%

Basis for selection. Careful consideration given to applicant's academic GPA and rigor of high school record. Important factors include application essay, counselor or teacher recommendations, character and personal qualities. The continuing adult education division considers CLEP for placement. SJU is test optional beginning Fall 2014. SAT or ACT scores are considered if submitted.

High school preparation. College-preparatory program recommended. Required units include English 4, mathematics 3, social studies 3, science 3, foreign language 2 and academic electives 5.

2015-2016 Annual costs. Tuition/fees: $42,180. Room/board: $14,928. Books/supplies: $825. Personal expenses: $750. **Additional information:** Traditional undergraduate day students taking additional credits over 5 courses pay an additional per-credit-hour fee of $1,349. Part-time, adult undergraduate evening division per-credit-hour fee is $557 (non-traditional, adult continuing education). Business and Psychology majors are required to have a laptop but are not required to purchase from the University.

2015-2016 Financial aid. Need-based: 987 full-time freshmen applied for aid; 778 deemed to have need; 778 received aid. Average need met was 76%. Average scholarship/grant was $22,874; average loan $3,281. 58% of total undergraduate aid awarded as scholarships/grants, 42% as loans/jobs. **Non-need-based:** Scholarships awarded for academics, alumni affiliation, art, athletics, minority status, music/drama, ROTC.

Application procedures. Admission: Priority date 2/1; no deadline. $60 fee, may be waived for applicants with need. Admission notification by 3/15. Must reply by May 1 or within 3 week(s) if notified thereafter. **Financial aid:** Priority date 2/15; no closing date. FAFSA required. Applicants notified on a rolling basis starting 3/31; must reply by 5/1.

Academics. Special study options: Accelerated study, combined bachelor's/graduate degree, cooperative education, distance learning, double major, dual enrollment of high school students, ESL, exchange student, honors, independent study, internships, student-designed major, study abroad, teacher certification program, Washington semester, weekend college. Jesuit student exchange; Accelerated and Weekend College available through the College of Professional & Liberal Studies and the Haub Degree Completion division of adult continuing education. **Credit/placement by examination:** AP, CLEP, IB, institutional tests. **Support services:** Learning center, pre-admission summer program, reduced course load, study skills assistance, tutoring, writing center.

Majors. Area/ethnic studies: Asian, European, French. **Biology:** General, biochemistry. **Business:** Accounting, actuarial science, business admin, finance, financial planning, human resources, insurance, international, knowledge management, management information systems, marketing, organizational behavior, purchasing, small business admin, special products marketing. **Communications:** General, communications/speech/rhetoric. **Computer sciences:** General, information systems. **Conservation:** Environmental studies. **Education:** Art, elementary. **English:** English lit. **Foreign languages:** French, German, Italian, Latin, Spanish. **Health services:** Facilities admin. **History:** General. **Human services:** General. **Liberal arts:** Arts/sciences. **Math:** General. **Philosophy/religion:** Philosophy, religion. **Physical sciences:** Chemistry, physics. **Psychology:** General, industrial. **Social sciences:** Criminology, economics, international relations, political science, sociology. **Visual/performing arts:** General, music.

Most popular majors. Biology 6%, business/marketing 49%, education 7%, psychology 6%, social sciences 8%.

Technology on campus. 825 workstations in library, computer center, student center. Dormitories wired for high-speed internet access and linked to campus network. Commuter students can connect to campus network. Online course registration, online library, helpline, repair service, student web hosting, wireless network available.

Student life. Freshman orientation: Available, $250 fee. Preregistration for classes offered. **Policies:** Freshmen not permitted cars on campus. **Housing:** Guaranteed on-campus for freshmen. Coed dorms, single-sex dorms, themed housing available. $250 nonrefundable deposit, deadline 5/1. Special accommodations for students with disabilities available upon need. **Activities:** Bands, campus ministries, choral groups, dance, drama, film society, international student organizations, literary magazine, music ensembles, musical theater, radio station, student government, student newspaper, Black student union, Caribbean students association, Hand-in-Hand, College Democrats, College Republicans, Habitat for Humanity, Students for Life, community service weekly programs.

Athletics. NCAA. **Intercollegiate:** Baseball M, basketball, cross-country, field hockey W, golf M, lacrosse, rowing (crew), soccer, softball W, tennis, track and field. **Intramural:** Basketball, football (non-tackle), racquetball, rowing (crew) M, soccer, softball, tennis, ultimate frisbee, volleyball. **Team name:** Hawks.

Student services. Adult student services, alcohol/substance abuse counseling, chaplain/spiritual director, career counseling, services for economically disadvantaged, student employment services, financial aid counseling, health services, minority student services, personal counseling, veterans' counselor, women's services. **Physically disabled:** Services for visually, speech, hearing impaired.

Contact. E-mail: admit@sju.edu
Phone: (610) 660-1300 Toll-free number: (888) 232-4295
Fax: (610) 660-1314
Maureen Mathis, Assistant Provost, Office of Undergraduate Admissions, Saint Joseph's University, 5600 City Avenue, Philadelphia, PA 19131

Seton Hill University

Greensburg, Pennsylvania
www.setonhill.edu

CB member
CB code: 2812

- Private 4-year university and liberal arts college affiliated with the Roman Catholic Church
- Residential campus in large town
- 1,564 degree-seeking undergraduates: 5% part-time, 65% women
- 396 graduate students
- 76% of applicants admitted
- Application essay required
- 61% graduate within 6 years

General. Founded in 1918. Regionally accredited. **Degrees:** 341 bachelor's awarded; master's offered. **ROTC:** Army. **Location:** 35 miles from Pittsburgh. **Calendar:** Semester, limited summer session. **Full-time faculty:** 106

total; 83% have terminal degrees, 6% minority, 55% women. **Part-time faculty:** 90 total; 36% have terminal degrees, 2% minority, 52% women. **Class size:** 55% < 20, 43% 20-39, 1% 40-49, less than 1% 50-99. **Special facilities:** Performing arts center, child development center, kindergarten, women in business center, Catholic Holocaust education center.

Freshman class profile. 2,093 applied, 1,600 admitted, 392 enrolled.

Mid 50% test scores			
		GPA 3.0-3.49:	22%
SAT critical reading:	470-580	GPA 2.0-2.99:	12%
SAT math:	460-590	Rank in top quarter:	52%
SAT writing:	450-570	Rank in top tenth:	18%
ACT composite:	20-27	Out-of-state:	30%
GPA 3.75 or higher:	47%	Live on campus:	84%
GPA 3.50-3.74:	18%	International:	2%

Basis for selection. School achievement record most important, followed by test scores and recommendations. Applicants from minorities or low-income families encouraged, accepted on basis of motivation and potential. SAT or ACT recommended. Students who have not taken SAT or ACT may submit 2 graded writing samples for consideration. Interview recommended for all; audition required for music, theater programs; portfolio required for art program. Additional application required for physician assistant and BS/DO and BS/DPharm programs. **Home schooled:** Must provide SAT/ACT scores and official transcript issued by a school district or agency approving the curriculum, or GED.

High school preparation. College-preparatory program recommended. 15 units required. Required and recommended units include English 4, mathematics 2, social studies 2, science 1 (laboratory 1), foreign language 2 and academic electives 4. 4 math units recommended for science majors.

2015-2016 Annual costs. Tuition/fees: $32,420. Room/board: $10,868. Books/supplies: $1,200. Personal expenses: $2,500.

2014-2015 Financial aid. Need-based: 307 full-time freshmen applied for aid; 283 deemed to have need; 283 received aid. Average need met was 76%. Average scholarship/grant was $20,017; average loan $5,858. 70% of total undergraduate aid awarded as scholarships/grants, 30% as loans/jobs. **Non-need-based:** Awarded to 462 full-time undergraduates, including 160 freshmen. Scholarships awarded for academics, alumni affiliation, art, athletics, music/drama.

Application procedures. Admission: Priority date 5/1; deadline 8/15 (postmark date). $35 fee, may be waived for applicants with need, free for online applicants. Admission notification on a rolling basis beginning on or about 9/1. Housing deposit fully refundable until May 1. **Financial aid:** Priority date 5/1; no closing date. FAFSA, institutional form required. Applicants notified on a rolling basis starting 11/30.

Academics. Special study options: Accelerated study, combined bachelor's/graduate degree, cross-registration, distance learning, double major, dual enrollment of high school students, ESL, external degree, honors, independent study, internships, liberal arts/career combination, New York semester, semester at sea, student-designed major, study abroad, teacher certification program, United Nations semester, Washington semester, weekend college. **Credit/placement by examination:** AP, CLEP, IB, SAT, ACT. 30 credit hours maximum toward bachelor's degree. **Support services:** Learning center, pre-admission summer program, reduced course load, remedial instruction, study skills assistance, tutoring, writing center.

Majors. Biology: General, biochemistry. **Business:** Accounting, actuarial science, business admin, entrepreneurial studies, hospitality admin, human resources, international, management information systems, marketing, sales/distribution. **Communications:** Communications/speech/rhetoric, journalism. **Computer sciences:** Computer science. **Education:** Art, biology, chemistry, English, family/consumer sciences, foreign languages, mathematics, music, Spanish. **Engineering:** General. **English:** Creative writing, English lit. **Foreign languages:** Spanish. **Health services:** Art therapy, clinical lab science, dietetics, music therapy, physician assistant. **History:** General. **Human services:** Social work. **Math:** General. **Parks/recreation:** Sports admin. **Philosophy/religion:** Religion. **Physical sciences:** Chemistry. **Protective services:** Criminal justice, forensics. **Psychology:** General. **Social sciences:** Economics, international relations, political science, sociology. **Theology:** Sacred music. **Visual/performing arts:** Acting, art, art history/conservation, ceramics, commercial/advertising art, dance, dramatic, drawing, graphic design, metal/jewelry, music, music performance, musical theater, painting, printmaking, sculpture, studio arts, studio arts management, theater arts management, theater design. **Work/family studies:** General, child care management, child development.

Most popular majors. Biology 8%, business/marketing 20%, education 10%, health sciences 10%, public administration/social services 6%, visual/performing arts 11%.

Technology on campus. PC or laptop required. 153 workstations in dormitories, library, computer center, student center. Dormitories wired for high-speed internet access and linked to campus network. Online course registration, online library, helpline, repair service, student web hosting, wireless network available.

Student life. Freshman orientation: Mandatory, $25 fee. Preregistration for classes offered. One-day, on-campus family orientation in summer. 4-day orientation during weekend and weekdays prior to start of classes. **Policies:** Residence hall students involved in setting community standards. **Housing:** Guaranteed on-campus for all undergraduates. Coed dorms available. $250 deposit, deadline 7/1. Housing for honors students available. **Activities:** Bands, campus ministries, choral groups, dance, drama, international student organizations, literary magazine, music ensembles, musical theater, student government, student newspaper, symphony orchestra, social work club, liturgical groups, Respect Life, Operation Christmas Basket, Association of Black Collegians, National Coalition Building Institute, Helping Hands, Habitat for Humanity.

Athletics. NCAA. Intercollegiate: Baseball M, basketball, cross-country, equestrian W, field hockey W, football (tackle) M, golf W, lacrosse, soccer, softball W, tennis W, track and field, volleyball W, wrestling M. **Intramural:** Basketball W, equestrian W, football (non-tackle), soccer W, softball W, volleyball W. **Team name:** Griffins.

Student services. Adult student services, alcohol/substance abuse counseling, chaplain/spiritual director, career counseling, services for economically disadvantaged, student employment services, financial aid counseling, health services, minority student services, on-campus daycare, personal counseling, placement for graduates, veterans' counselor. **Physically disabled:** Services for visually, speech, hearing impaired.

Contact. E-mail: admit@setonhill.edu
Phone: (724) 838-4255 Toll-free number: (800) 826-6234
Fax: (724) 830-1294
Ashley Zullo, Director of Admissions, Seton Hill University, 1 Seton Hill Drive, Greensburg, PA 15601

Shippensburg University of Pennsylvania

Shippensburg, Pennsylvania **CB member**
www.ship.edu **CB code: 2657**

- Public 4-year university
- Residential campus in small town
- 5,963 degree-seeking undergraduates: 5% part-time, 49% women, 10% African American, 1% Asian American, 5% Hispanic/Latino, 3% Multiracial, non-Hispanic
- 938 degree-seeking graduate students
- 89% of applicants admitted
- SAT or ACT (ACT writing optional) required
- 57% graduate within 6 years

General. Founded in 1871. Regionally accredited. **Degrees:** 1,251 bachelor's awarded; master's, doctoral offered. **ROTC:** Army. **Location:** 40 miles from Harrisburg. **Calendar:** Semester, extensive summer session. **Full-time faculty:** 294 total; 93% have terminal degrees, 16% minority, 42% women. **Part-time faculty:** 71 total; 24% have terminal degrees, 6% minority, 54% women. **Class size:** 27% < 20, 51% 20-39, 16% 40-49, 6% 50-99. **Special facilities:** On-campus elementary school for student teachers, planetarium, vertebrate museum, greenhouse, herbarium, electron microscope, NMR spectrometer, fashion archives, interfaith spiritual center, women's center, performing arts center.

Freshman class profile. 6,126 applied, 5,461 admitted, 1,390 enrolled.

Mid 50% test scores			
SAT critical reading:	440-530	GPA 2.0-2.99:	30%
SAT math:	440-550	Rank in top quarter:	28%
SAT writing:	410-520	Rank in top tenth:	9%
ACT composite:	18-23	End year in good standing:	69%
GPA 3.75 or higher:	21%	Return as sophomores:	69%
GPA 3.50-3.74:	15%	Out-of-state:	7%
GPA 3.0-3.49:	33%	Live on campus:	87%

Basis for selection. Secondary school record and test scores important. Summer Bridge Program provides access and academic support to students who do not meet regular admission criteria but have demonstrated potential, desire, and motivation to succeed in college. All students are required to take SAT or ACT Tests unless out of high school for two or more years. Interviews advisable in some situations. **Home schooled:** Transcript of courses and grades, state high school equivalency certificate required. Those working with accredited agency must submit copy of both annual evaluation and homeschool diploma. All others encouraged to schedule interview and present portfolio, and must provide GED results. Grade transcripts required (if available). **Learning Disabled:** Students must register with Office of

Disability Services and provide documentation from qualified professional and must be less than 3 years old. Reasonable accommodations provided.

High school preparation. College-preparatory program required. 16 units recommended. Recommended units include English 4, mathematics 3, science 3 (laboratory 3) and foreign language 3. 3 social sciences.

2015-2016 Annual costs. Tuition/fees: $10,052; $18,878 out-of-state. Room/board: $11,428. **Additional information:** $10,590 for Dual Admit (out-of-state) students and $12,356 for STEM (Science, Technology, Engineering, or Math) and High Achieving (1200 SAT or top 10% of their class) out-of-state students.

2015-2016 Financial aid. Need-based: 1,285 full-time freshmen applied for aid; 1,005 deemed to have need; 993 received aid. Average need met was 49%. Average scholarship/grant was $6,302; average loan $3,466. 35% of total undergraduate aid awarded as scholarships/grants, 65% as loans/jobs. **Non-need-based:** Awarded to 839 full-time undergraduates, including 201 freshmen. Scholarships awarded for academics, athletics.

Application procedures. Admission: No deadline. $45 fee, may be waived for applicants with need. Admission notification on a rolling basis. Must reply by April 1 or request a May 1 extension in writing. **Financial aid:** Priority date 3/15; no closing date. FAFSA required. Applicants notified on a rolling basis; must reply within 2 week(s) of notification.

Academics. Web-based online courses and programs also available. **Special study options:** Accelerated study, combined bachelor's/graduate degree, cooperative education, distance learning, double major, dual enrollment of high school students, honors, independent study, internships, semester at sea, study abroad, teacher certification program, Washington semester. Raider Plan. **Credit/placement by examination:** AP, CLEP, IB, SAT, ACT, institutional tests. 30 credit hours maximum toward bachelor's degree. **Support services:** Learning center, pre-admission summer program, reduced course load, remedial instruction, study skills assistance, tutoring, writing center.

Majors. Biology: General. **Business:** Accounting, business admin, finance, logistics, marketing. **Communications:** Journalism. **Computer sciences:** General, systems analysis. **Conservation:** Environmental studies. **Education:** Early childhood, early childhood special, middle. **Engineering:** Electrical, software. **English:** English lit, rhetoric/composition. **Foreign languages:** French, Spanish. **Health services:** Health care admin. **History:** General. **Human services:** General, social work. **Liberal arts:** Arts/sciences. **Math:** General. **Parks/recreation:** Exercise sciences. **Physical sciences:** Chemistry, geology, physics. **Protective services:** Criminal justice. **Psychology:** General. **Social sciences:** Economics, geography, political science, sociology. **Visual/performing arts:** Art.

Most popular majors. Business/marketing 25%, education 8%, English 6%, psychology 10%, public administration/social services 6%, security/protective services 6%, social sciences 7%.

Technology on campus. 800 workstations in library, computer center, student center. Dormitories wired for high-speed internet access and linked to campus network. Commuter students can connect to campus network. Online course registration, online library, helpline, repair service, student web hosting, wireless network available.

Student life. Freshman orientation: Mandatory, $150 fee. Preregistration for classes offered. Program held in summer and prior to fall and spring semesters. **Policies:** University student code of conduct in effect. **Housing:** Guaranteed on-campus for freshmen. Coed dorms, apartments, themed housing, wellness housing available. $200 nonrefundable deposit, deadline 4/1. Suites and living-learning communities available. **Activities:** Bands, campus ministries, choral groups, dance, drama, international student organizations, literary magazine, music ensembles, musical theater, radio station, student government, student newspaper, TV station, African American Organization, Fellowship of Christian Athletes, Christian Fellowship, College Republicans, nontraditional student organization, Latino student organization, Asian-American association, College Democrats, Bridge for Kids, Multi-Ethnic Student Association.

Athletics. NCAA. Intercollegiate: Baseball M, basketball, cross-country, field hockey W, football (tackle) M, lacrosse W, soccer, softball W, swimming, tennis W, track and field, volleyball W, wrestling M. **Intramural:** Basketball, soccer, softball, volleyball. **Team name:** Raiders.

Student services. Adult student services, alcohol/substance abuse counseling, chaplain/spiritual director, career counseling, student employment services, financial aid counseling, health services, minority student services, on-campus daycare, personal counseling, placement for graduates, veterans' counselor, women's services. **Physically disabled:** Services for visually, hearing impaired.

Contact. E-mail: admiss@ship.edu
Phone: (717) 477-1231 Toll-free number: (800) 822-8028
Fax: (717) 477-4016
William Washabaugh, Acting Dean of Admissions, Shippensburg
University of Pennsylvania, 1871 Old Main Drive, Shippensburg, PA
17257-2299

Slippery Rock University of Pennsylvania
Slippery Rock, Pennsylvania   **CB member**
www.sru.edu   **CB code: 2658**

- Public 4-year university
- Residential campus in small town
- 7,471 degree-seeking undergraduates: 6% part-time, 57% women, 5% African American, 1% Asian American, 2% Hispanic/Latino, 3% Multiracial, non-Hispanic, 1% international
- 947 degree-seeking graduate students
- 68% of applicants admitted
- SAT or ACT (ACT writing optional) required
- 68% graduate within 6 years; 20% enter graduate study

General. Founded in 1889. Regionally accredited. **Degrees:** 1,750 bachelor's awarded; master's, professional, doctoral offered. **ROTC:** Army. **Location:** 50 miles from Pittsburgh. **Calendar:** Semester, extensive summer session. **Full-time faculty:** 338 total; 87% have terminal degrees, 17% minority, 51% women. **Part-time faculty:** 65 total; 14% have terminal degrees, 11% minority, 60% women. **Class size:** 16% < 20, 60% 20-39, 14% 40-49, 6% 50-99, 3% >100. **Special facilities:** Environmental education centers, crime scene investigation house, planetarium, sustainable enterprise accelerator, equestrian center, Old Stone House historic museum.

Freshman class profile. 5,781 applied, 3,952 admitted, 1,524 enrolled.

Mid 50% test scores			
SAT critical reading:	450-540	Rank in top quarter:	36%
SAT math:	460-540	Rank in top tenth:	10%
SAT writing:	420-520	End year in good standing:	85%
ACT composite:	19-24	Return as sophomores:	83%
GPA 3.75 or higher:	25%	Out-of-state:	14%
GPA 3.50-3.74:	21%	Live on campus:	94%
GPA 3.0-3.49:	38%	International:	1%
GPA 2.0-2.99:	16%	Fraternities:	7%
		Sororities:	8%

Basis for selection. Recommended minimum 3.0 GPA, or 85 percent or higher average. Minimum score of 950 SAT (exclusive of Writing) or 20 ACT recommended. Audition required for music and dance majors. **Home schooled:** Documentation of homeschool diploma or certification information regarding how homeschool material was covered.

High school preparation. College-preparatory program recommended. 16 units recommended. Recommended units include English 4, mathematics 3, social studies 3, history 3, science 3 (laboratory 1) and foreign language 2.

2015-2016 Annual costs. Tuition/fees: $9,645; $13,175 out-of-state. Room/board: $10,022. Books/supplies: $1,540. Personal expenses: $1,520. **Additional information:** Out-of-State tuition is $10,590 for freshmen or transfer students with a high school GPA of at least 3.0 out of 4.0, or returning students with a GPA of at least 2.5.

2015-2016 Financial aid. **Need-based:** 1,443 full-time freshmen applied for aid; 1,104 deemed to have need; 1,092 received aid. Average need met was 56%. Average scholarship/grant was $5,971; average loan $3,559. 47% of total undergraduate aid awarded as scholarships/grants, 53% as loans/jobs. **Non-need-based:** Awarded to 1,919 full-time undergraduates, including 633 freshmen. Scholarships awarded for academics, alumni affiliation, art, athletics, job skills, leadership, minority status, music/drama, ROTC, state residency. **Additional information:** May 1 closing date for Pennsylvania state grants.

Application procedures. **Admission:** No deadline. $30 fee, may be waived for applicants with need. Admission notification on a rolling basis beginning on or about 6/15. Must reply by May 1 or within 2 week(s) if notified thereafter. **Financial aid:** Priority date 5/1; no closing date. FAFSA required. Applicants notified on a rolling basis starting 3/15.

Academics. Exploratory Program for undecided majors, First Year Student Seminar, Living-Learning Environments in the Residence Halls, Learning Communities based on academic majors. **Special study options:** Combined bachelor's/graduate degree, distance learning, double major, dual enrollment of high school students, exchange student, honors, independent study, internships, liberal arts/career combination, student-designed major, study abroad, teacher certification program. **Credit/placement by examination:** AP, CLEP, IB, SAT, ACT, institutional tests. 45 credit hours maximum toward

bachelor's degree. **Support services:** Learning center, pre-admission summer program, reduced course load, remedial instruction, study skills assistance, tutoring, writing center.

Majors. **Biology:** General, biochemistry, biomedical sciences. **Business:** Accounting, actuarial science, business admin, finance, management science, marketing. **Communications:** General, communications/speech/rhetoric, digital media, journalism, public relations. **Computer sciences:** Computer science, information systems, information technology. **Education:** Elementary, secondary, special ed, special ed admin. **English:** Creative writing, English lit, technical writing. **Foreign languages:** French, Spanish. **Health services:** Athletic training, cytotechnology, health services admin, music therapy, nursing (RN), recreational therapy. **History:** General. **Human services:** Social work. **Math:** General, statistics. **Parks/recreation:** Exercise sciences, facilities management, health/fitness, sports admin. **Philosophy/religion:** Philosophy. **Physical sciences:** Chemistry, forensic chemistry, geology, physics. **Psychology:** General. **Social sciences:** Criminology, economics, geography, political science. **Visual/performing arts:** Acting, art, dance, music, music performance, studio arts, theater arts management, theater design.

Most popular majors. Business/marketing 11%, education 10%, health sciences 22%, parks/recreation 9%, social sciences 7%.

Technology on campus. 1,604 workstations in dormitories, library, computer center, student center. Dormitories wired for high-speed internet access and linked to campus network. Commuter students can connect to campus network. Online course registration, online library, helpline, student web hosting, wireless network available.

Student life. **Freshman orientation:** Mandatory, $90 fee. Preregistration for classes offered. Several sessions held during summer months. **Housing:** Guaranteed on-campus for freshmen. Coed dorms, special housing for disabled, apartments available. $175 partly refundable deposit. Living-learning communities available. **Activities:** Bands, campus ministries, choral groups, dance, drama, film society, international student organizations, literary magazine, music ensembles, Model UN, musical theater, radio station, student government, student newspaper, symphony orchestra, TV station, Campus Crusade for Christ, Black Action Society, Latino Student Organization, Council for Exceptional Children, American Sign Language Club, Adapted Physical Activity Council, RockOUT, Rock Catholic, Student Union for Multicultural Affairs, Fellowship of Christian Athletes.

Athletics. NCAA. **Intercollegiate:** Baseball M, basketball, cheerleading, cross-country, field hockey W, football (tackle) M, lacrosse W, soccer, softball W, tennis W, track and field, volleyball W. **Intramural:** Badminton, basketball, football (non-tackle), soccer, softball, ultimate frisbee, volleyball, water polo. **Team name:** The Rock.

Student services. Adult student services, alcohol/substance abuse counseling, chaplain/spiritual director, career counseling, services for economically disadvantaged, student employment services, financial aid counseling, health services, legal services, minority student services, on-campus daycare, personal counseling, placement for graduates, veterans' counselor, women's services. **Physically disabled:** Services for visually, speech, hearing impaired.

Contact. E-mail: asktherock@sru.edu
Phone: (724) 738-2015 Toll-free number: (800) 929-4778
Fax: (724) 738-2913
Michael May, Director of Undergraduate Recruitment & Admissions, Slippery Rock University of Pennsylvania, 1 Morrow Way, Slippery Rock, PA 16057-1383

St. Charles Borromeo Seminary - Overbrook
Wynnewood, Pennsylvania
www.scs.edu   **CB code: 2794**

- Private 4-year seminary college for men affiliated with the Roman Catholic Church
- Residential campus in large town
- 55 degree-seeking undergraduates
- Application essay, interview required

General. Founded in 1832. Regionally accredited; also accredited by ATS. College and Theology divisions enroll full-time seminary students. Graduate School of Theology division enrolls part-time undergraduate and graduate students who wish to pursue theological studies. Part-time programs open to men and women. **Degrees:** 12 bachelor's awarded; master's offered. **Location:** 4 miles from central Philadelphia. **Calendar:** Semester, limited summer session. **Full-time faculty:** 16 total; 75% have terminal degrees, 12% women. **Part-time faculty:** 17 total; 24% have terminal degrees, 47% women. **Class size:** 94% < 20, 6% 20-39. **Special facilities:** Rare book collection.

Freshman class profile.

Rank in top quarter:	33%	Live on campus:	100%
Out-of-state:	28%		

Basis for selection. Sponsorship by diocese or religious community required for admission to college and theology divisions. SAT or ACT recommended. **Home schooled:** Transcript of courses and grades, letter of recommendation (nonparent) required.

High school preparation. College-preparatory program recommended. 20 units recommended. Recommended units include English 4, mathematics 3, social studies 3, science 3 and foreign language 3. 3 to 4 units of religious education recommended. GED accepted on individual basis.

2015-2016 Annual costs. Tuition/fees: $20,050. Room/board: $12,925.

Financial aid. Non-need-based: Scholarships awarded for religious affiliation.

Application procedures. Admission: Priority date 3/1; deadline 7/15. No application fee. Application must be submitted on paper. Admission notification on a rolling basis beginning on or about 4/1. Level of admission dependent on academic background in philosophy, theology, and classical languages. **Financial aid:** Closing date 4/15. FAFSA, institutional form required. Applicants notified on a rolling basis starting 6/1; must reply by 6/1 or within 4 week(s) of notification.

Academics. Strong emphasis on philosophy, theology, classical languages, and liberal arts. **Special study options:** Accelerated study, ESL, independent study. **Credit/placement by examination:** AP, CLEP, institutional tests. 12 credit hours maximum toward bachelor's degree. **Support services:** Reduced course load, study skills assistance, tutoring.

Majors. Philosophy/religion: Philosophy.

Technology on campus. 60 workstations in library, computer center. Online library, wireless network available.

Student life. Freshman orientation: Mandatory. Preregistration for classes offered. **Policies:** Religious observance required. **Housing:** Guaranteed on-campus for all undergraduates. Wellness housing available. **Activities:** Choral groups, music ensembles, student government, student newspaper, Seminarians for Life.

Athletics. Intramural: Basketball M, football (non-tackle) M, soccer M, volleyball M.

Student services. Chaplain/spiritual director, financial aid counseling, health services, personal counseling.

Contact. E-mail: jbongard@scs.edu
Phone: (610) 785-6271 Fax: (610) 617-9267
Rev. Joseph Bongard, Vice Rector, St. Charles Borromeo Seminary - Overbrook, 100 East Wynnewood Road, Wynnewood, PA 19096

St. Francis University

Loretto, Pennsylvania   **CB member**
www.francis.edu   **CB code: 2797**

- Private 4-year university and liberal arts college affiliated with the Roman Catholic Church
- Residential campus in rural community
- 1,703 degree-seeking undergraduates: 6% part-time, 63% women, 6% African American, 1% Asian American, 2% Hispanic/Latino, 1% Multiracial, non-Hispanic, 5% international
- 590 degree-seeking graduate students
- 74% of applicants admitted
- SAT or ACT (ACT writing recommended), application essay required
- 71% graduate within 6 years; 13% enter graduate study

General. Founded in 1847. Regionally accredited. **Degrees:** 355 bachelor's, 6 associate awarded; master's, professional offered. **ROTC:** Army. **Location:** 90 miles from Pittsburgh, 20 miles from Altoona. **Calendar:** Semester, limited summer session. **Full-time faculty:** 125 total; 81% have terminal degrees, 7% minority, 56% women. **Part-time faculty:** 54 total; 2% minority, 54% women. **Class size:** 59% < 20, 39% 20-39, less than 1% 40-49, 2% 50-99. **Special facilities:** Rural health and wellness institute, small business development center, global competitiveness center, Southern Alleghenies art museum, center for remote and medically underserved areas, nature trail, field station, university owned study abroad campus in France.

Freshman class profile. 1,932 applied, 1,432 admitted, 407 enrolled.

Mid 50% test scores			
SAT critical reading:	460-570	GPA 2.0-2.99:	13%
SAT math:	470-590	Rank in top quarter:	58%
SAT writing:	450-560	Rank in top tenth:	30%
ACT composite:	21-26	End year in good standing:	96%
GPA 3.75 or higher:	46%	Return as sophomores:	86%
GPA 3.50-3.74:	16%	Out-of-state:	26%
GPA 3.0-3.49:	25%	Live on campus:	90%
		International:	5%

Basis for selection. High school record most important, followed by test scores, counselor's recommendations, major area of interest, activities, honors. Relationship to alumni also considered. Campus visit highly recommended. Admission to professional track programs places more weight on test scores. SAT Subject Tests recommended. Essay must be a minimum of 250 words; essay topics may be found on the application for admission. Physician assistant and physical therapy students must complete essay directed towards their chosen discipline. Interviews recommended. **Learning Disabled:** Send official documentation to the Office of Disability Services.

High school preparation. College-preparatory program recommended. 16 units required; 19 recommended. Required and recommended units include English 4, mathematics 2-4, social studies 2, science 1-2 (laboratory 1), foreign language 2 and academic electives 7. 1 natural science for nonscience majors, 2 for science majors also required. 1 science unit must include laboratory. Remaining units in academic electives. 4 math and 2 science required for physician assistant and occupational therapy. 4 math and 4 science required for physical therapy.

2015-2016 Annual costs. Tuition/fees: $32,128. Room/board: $11,082. Books/supplies: $2,000. Personal expenses: $2,000.

Financial aid. Non-need-based: Scholarships awarded for academics, alumni affiliation, athletics, music/drama, religious affiliation.

Application procedures. Admission: Priority date 3/1; deadline 7/30 (postmark date). $30 fee, may be waived for applicants with need. Admission notification on a rolling basis beginning on or about 9/1. Must reply by May 1 or within 2 week(s) if notified thereafter. Physician assistant students must submit a refundable tuition deposit by March 1. Application closing date for physical therapy, occupational therapy, and physician assistant programs January 15. Notification by February 1. **Financial aid:** Priority date 5/1; no closing date. FAFSA required. Applicants notified on a rolling basis starting 3/1.

Academics. Legal assistant/paralegal post-bachelor's certificate available. **Special study options:** Combined bachelor's/graduate degree, cooperative education, distance learning, double major, ESL, honors, independent study, internships, liberal arts/career combination, semester at sea, student-designed major, study abroad, teacher certification program, Washington semester. **Credit/placement by examination:** AP, CLEP, IB, SAT, ACT, institutional tests. 15 credit hours maximum toward associate degree, 30 toward bachelor's. **Support services:** Learning center, pre-admission summer program, reduced course load, remedial instruction, study skills assistance, tutoring, writing center.

Honors college/program. 3.25 GPA, 1150 SAT (580 Critical Reading, exclusive of Writing), position in top 20% of high school class required. Approximately 40 applicants admitted.

Majors. Area/ethnic studies: American. **Biology:** General, marine. **Business:** Accounting, business admin, finance, management information systems, marketing. **Communications:** Communications/speech/rhetoric, public relations. **Computer sciences:** General, computer science, information systems, programming. **Conservation:** Environmental science, environmental studies. **Education:** General, biology, chemistry, elementary, English, foreign languages, French, history, mathematics, multi-level teacher, psychology, secondary, social science, social studies, Spanish, speech. **Engineering:** General, environmental, petroleum. **English:** English lit. **Foreign languages:** General, Spanish. **Health services:** Clinical lab technology, nursing (RN), physician assistant, public health nursing. **History:** General. **Human services:** General, social work. **Math:** General. **Philosophy/religion:** Philosophy, religion. **Physical sciences:** Chemistry. **Psychology:** General. **Social sciences:** Economics, political science, sociology.

Most popular majors. Biology 7%, business/marketing 23%, communications/journalism 7%, health sciences 37%.

Technology on campus. PC or laptop required. 40 workstations in dormitories, library, computer center, student center. Dormitories wired for high-speed internet access and linked to campus network. Commuter students can connect to campus network. Online course registration, online library, helpline, repair service, wireless network available.

Student life. Freshman orientation: Mandatory. Preregistration for classes offered. Held at various times during spring and summer. **Policies:** All students required to live in campus-owned housing to receive institutional financial aid unless commuting from home (within 30 mile radius). **Housing:** Guaranteed on-campus for all undergraduates. Coed dorms, single-sex dorms, special housing for disabled, apartments, fraternity/sorority housing, wellness housing available. $100 partly refundable deposit, deadline 5/1. **Activities:** Bands, campus ministries, choral groups, dance, drama, music ensembles, radio station, student government, student newspaper, TV station, Secular Franciscan Order, student activities organization, multicultural awareness club, Historians' Round Table, Habitat for Humanity, Peace and Justice Center, current affairs club, prelaw club.

Athletics. NCAA. **Intercollegiate:** Basketball, bowling W, cross-country, field hockey W, football (tackle) M, golf, lacrosse W, soccer, softball W, swimming W, tennis, track and field, volleyball. **Intramural:** Basketball, cross-country, football (non-tackle), ice hockey, skiing, soccer, softball, swimming, table tennis, tennis, track and field, ultimate frisbee, volleyball. **Team name:** Red Flash.

Student services. Adult student services, alcohol/substance abuse counseling, chaplain/spiritual director, career counseling, student employment services, financial aid counseling, health services, minority student services, personal counseling, placement for graduates, veterans' counselor.

Contact. E-mail: admissions@francis.edu
Phone: (814) 472-3100 Toll-free number: (800) 342-5732
Fax: (814) 472-3335
Erin McCloskey, Vice President for Enrollment Management, St. Francis University, Box 600, Loretto, PA 15940

St. Vincent College
Latrobe, Pennsylvania
www.stvincent.edu

CB member
CB code: 2808

- Private 4-year liberal arts college affiliated with the Roman Catholic Church
- Residential campus in large town
- 1,596 degree-seeking undergraduates: 1% part-time, 47% women, 5% African American, 2% Asian American, 3% Hispanic/Latino, 1% Native American, 1% Multi-racial, non-Hispanic, 1% international
- 202 degree-seeking graduate students
- 70% of applicants admitted
- SAT or ACT (ACT writing optional), application essay required
- 69% graduate within 6 years

General. Founded in 1846. Regionally accredited. Affiliated with Order of Saint Benedict. **Degrees:** 342 bachelor's awarded; master's, professional offered. **ROTC:** Army, Air Force. **Location:** 35 miles from Pittsburgh. **Calendar:** Semester, extensive summer session. **Full-time faculty:** 102 total; 88% have terminal degrees, 3% minority, 31% women. **Part-time faculty:** 120 total; 46% have terminal degrees, 3% minority, 42% women. **Class size:** 49% < 20, 51% 20-39, less than 1% 40-49. **Special facilities:** Planetarium, observatory, radio telescope, wetlands program, rare book collection, spectrophotometer, spectrometer, physiograph workstations, nature reserve, digital imaging lab, Fred Rogers archives.

Freshman class profile. 1,908 applied, 1,332 admitted, 445 enrolled.

Mid 50% test scores		GPA 3.0-3.49:	26%
SAT critical reading:	470-580	GPA 2.0-2.99:	19%
SAT math:	480-580	Rank in top quarter:	44%
SAT writing:	450-560	Rank in top tenth:	17%
ACT composite:	20-26	Return as sophomores:	87%
GPA 3.75 or higher:	34%	Out-of-state:	24%
GPA 3.50-3.74:	21%	Live on campus:	90%

Basis for selection. Rigor of secondary school record, class rank, and academic GPA are very important; standardized test scores are important. Interview recommended for all; audition required for music programs; portfolio required for art programs. **Learning Disabled:** All prior test results related to learning disability should be submitted.

High school preparation. College-preparatory program recommended. 16 units required; 20 recommended. Required and recommended units include English 4, mathematics 3, social studies 3, science 1-3 (laboratory 1-3), foreign language 2 and academic electives 5. One plane geometry, 1 intermediate algebra, .5 trigonometry, and 1 physics required for 3-2 engineering program applicants.

2015-2016 Annual costs. Tuition/fees: $32,770. Room/board: $10,793. Books/supplies: $1,250. Personal expenses: $1,700.

2015-2016 Financial aid. **Need-based:** 408 full-time freshmen applied for aid; 355 deemed to have need; 355 received aid. Average need met was 84%. Average scholarship/grant was $6,153; average loan $3,341. 85% of total undergraduate aid awarded as scholarships/grants, 15% as loans/jobs. **Non-need-based:** Awarded to 1,459 full-time undergraduates, including 442 freshmen. Scholarships awarded for academics, alumni affiliation, art, leadership, minority status, music/drama, religious affiliation, state residency.

Application procedures. **Admission:** Priority date 2/1; deadline 5/1 (postmark date). $25 fee, may be waived for applicants with need, free for online applicants. Admission notification on a rolling basis beginning on or about 10/1. Must reply by May 1 or within 3 week(s) if notified thereafter. **Financial aid:** Priority date 5/1; no closing date. FAFSA required. Applicants notified on a rolling basis starting 10/1; must reply within 4 week(s) of notification.

Academics. College attempts to place career orientation in context of broader human and religious values with emphasis on liberal arts core curriculum. **Special study options:** Combined bachelor's/graduate degree, cross-registration, distance learning, double major, dual enrollment of high school students, ESL, external degree, honors, independent study, liberal arts/career combination, student-designed major, study abroad, teacher certification program. 3-2 engineering BA/BS program with University of Pittsburgh, Catholic University of America, Pennsylvania State; 4-1 BS/MBA, 3-3 BA/JD, 3-2 occupational therapy, physical therapy, and physician's assistant, 2-4 pharmacy programs with Duquesne University; 3-4 podiatry with Ohio College of Pediatric Medicine and Pennsylvania College of Pediatric Medicine. **Credit/placement by examination:** AP, CLEP, IB, institutional tests. 62 credit hours maximum toward bachelor's degree. **Support services:** Learning center, pre-admission summer program, study skills assistance, tutoring, writing center.

Majors. Biology: General, biochemistry, bioinformatics. **Business:** Accounting, business admin, finance, international, marketing. **Communications:** Communications/speech/rhetoric. **Computer sciences:** General. **Conservation:** Environmental science. **Education:** Art, business, early childhood, middle, physics, psychology. **Engineering:** General. **English:** English lit. **Foreign languages:** French, Spanish. **Health services:** Predental, premedicine, prepharmacy, preveterinary. **History:** General. **Human services:** Public policy. **Liberal arts:** Arts/sciences. **Math:** General. **Philosophy/religion:** Philosophy. **Physical sciences:** Chemistry, physics. **Psychology:** General, educational. **Social sciences:** Anthropology, criminology, economics, political science, sociology. **Theology:** Theology. **Visual/performing arts:** Graphic design, music, music performance, studio arts, studio arts management.

Most popular majors. Biology 15%, business/marketing 27%, communications/journalism 8%, education 6%, psychology 9%, social sciences 8%.

Technology on campus. 273 workstations in dormitories, library, computer center, student center. Dormitories wired for high-speed internet access and linked to campus network. Online course registration, helpline, repair service, wireless network available.

Student life. **Freshman orientation:** Mandatory, $190 fee. Preregistration for classes offered. **Housing:** Guaranteed on-campus for freshmen. Coed dorms, apartments available. $200 nonrefundable deposit, deadline 5/1. **Activities:** Bands, campus ministries, choral groups, dance, drama, literary magazine, music ensembles, musical theater, student government, student newspaper, Respect for Life club, Democrats club, College Republicans, Students for Social Justice, pre-law society, Student Council for Exceptional Children, Italian club, Habitat for Humanity.

Athletics. NCAA. **Intercollegiate:** Baseball M, basketball, cross-country, field hockey W, football (tackle) M, golf, lacrosse, soccer, softball W, swimming, tennis, track and field M, volleyball W. **Intramural:** Basketball, football (non-tackle), soccer, softball, table tennis, volleyball. **Team name:** Bearcats.

Student services. Adult student services, alcohol/substance abuse counseling, chaplain/spiritual director, career counseling, services for economically disadvantaged, student employment services, financial aid counseling, health services, minority student services, personal counseling, placement for graduates. **Physically disabled:** Services for visually, speech, hearing impaired.

Contact. E-mail: admission@stvincent.edu
Phone: (724) 805-2500 Toll-free number: (800) 782-5549
Fax: (724) 532-5069
Stephen Nietz, Assistant Vice President of Admission and Financial Aid, St. Vincent College, 300 Fraser Purchase Road, Latrobe, PA 15650-2690

Summit University
Clarks Summit, Pennsylvania
https://www.summitu.edu

CB code: 2036

- Private 4-year university and Bible college affiliated with the Baptist faith
- Residential campus in small city

♦ 553 degree-seeking undergraduates

♦ SAT or ACT (ACT writing optional), application essay required

General. Founded in 1932. Regionally accredited; also accredited by ABHE. Part of each student's curriculum includes ministry/service experiences. **Degrees:** 135 bachelor's, 37 associate awarded; master's, professional, doctoral offered. **ROTC:** Army. **Location:** 7 miles from Scranton, 20 miles from Wilkes-Barre. **Calendar:** Semester, limited summer session. **Full-time faculty:** 33 total. **Part-time faculty:** 65 total. **Class size:** 70% < 20, 20% 20-39, 4% 40-49, 6% 50-99, 1% >100.

Freshman class profile.

GPA 3.75 or higher:	24%	GPA 2.0-2.99:	22%
GPA 3.50-3.74:	24%	Out-of-state:	68%
GPA 3.0-3.49:	25%	Live on campus:	64%

Basis for selection. Academic record, test scores, personal statement, and interview most important. Audition required, interview recommended for all; portfolio required for music programs.

2015-2016 Annual costs. Tuition/fees: $23,140. Room/board: $5,800. Books/supplies: $1,000. Personal expenses: $900.

Financial aid. Non-need-based: Scholarships awarded for academics, leadership, music/drama, religious affiliation.

Application procedures. Admission: Priority date 5/1; deadline 8/15 (postmark date). $30 fee. Admission notification on a rolling basis. Must reply by May 1 or within 4 week(s) if notified thereafter. **Financial aid:** Closing date 5/1. FAFSA, institutional form required. Applicants notified on a rolling basis starting 4/1.

Academics. Special study options: Combined bachelor's/graduate degree, distance learning, double major, dual enrollment of high school students, independent study, internships, study abroad, teacher certification program. **Credit/placement by examination:** AP, CLEP, IB, SAT, ACT, institutional tests. **Support services:** Reduced course load, remedial instruction, study skills assistance, tutoring, writing center.

Majors. Business: Administrative services. **Communications:** Communications/speech/rhetoric. **Education:** Early childhood, elementary, health, mathematics, multi-level teacher, music, physical, science, secondary, social studies. **Liberal arts:** Arts/sciences. **Parks/recreation:** Health/fitness. **Philosophy/religion:** General. **Psychology:** Counseling. **Theology:** Missionary, preministerial, sacred music, youth ministry. **Visual/performing arts:** Music.

Most popular majors. Education 27%, liberal arts 21%, psychology 12%, theological studies 33%.

Technology on campus. 30 workstations in library, computer center. Dormitories wired for high-speed internet access and linked to campus network. Commuter students can connect to campus network. Online course registration, online library, helpline, wireless network available.

Student life. Freshman orientation: Mandatory. Preregistration for classes offered. Parent and student orientation weekend includes sessions on academics, student life, finances, and interaction with faculty. **Policies:** Students must abide by standard given in the student handbook. Religious observance required. **Housing:** Guaranteed on-campus for all undergraduates. Single-sex dorms, special housing for disabled, wellness housing available. $250 deposit, deadline 5/1. **Activities:** Choral groups, drama, music ensembles, student government, student newspaper, several religious and service groups.

Athletics. NCAA, NCCAA. **Intercollegiate:** Baseball M, basketball, cheerleading W, cross-country, golf M, soccer, softball W, tennis W, track and field, volleyball. **Intramural:** Basketball, soccer, softball M, volleyball. **Team name:** Defenders.

Student services. Adult student services, alcohol/substance abuse counseling, chaplain/spiritual director, career counseling, student employment services, financial aid counseling, health services, personal counseling, placement for graduates, women's services.

Contact. E-mail: admissions@summitu.edu
Phone: (570) 586-2400 ext. 9271 Toll-free number: (800) 451-7664
Fax: (570) 585-9299
Andrew Whipple, Vice President for Enrollment and Marketing Services, Summit University, 538 Venard Road, Clarks Summit, PA 18411-1297

Susquehanna University
Selinsgrove, Pennsylvania
www.susqu.edu

CB member
CB code: 2820

♦ Private 4-year university and liberal arts college affiliated with the Evangelical Lutheran Church in America

♦ Residential campus in small town

♦ 2,126 degree-seeking undergraduates: 1% part-time, 55% women, 6% African American, 2% Asian American, 6% Hispanic/Latino, 3% Multiracial, non-Hispanic, 2% international

♦ 7 graduate students

♦ 76% of applicants admitted

♦ Application essay required

♦ 71% graduate within 6 years; 16% enter graduate study

General. Founded in 1858. Regionally accredited. **Degrees:** 513 bachelor's awarded. **ROTC:** Army. **Location:** 50 miles from Harrisburg. **Calendar:** Semester, limited summer session. **Full-time faculty:** 133 total; 92% have terminal degrees, 19% minority, 45% women. **Part-time faculty:** 127 total; 31% have terminal degrees, 5% minority, 46% women. **Class size:** 57% < 20, 43% 20-39, less than 1% 40-49. **Special facilities:** Ecology field station, film library, music library, rare book room, 24-hour study center, arboretum, observatory, 450-seat teaching theater, child development center, distribution system for foreign language broadcasts, video conferencing facility, high technology center for business and communications.

Freshman class profile. 5,304 applied, 4,033 admitted, 668 enrolled.

Mid 50% test scores			
SAT critical reading:	500-610	GPA 2.0-2.99:	18%
SAT math:	510-610	Rank in top quarter:	57%
SAT writing:	480-600	Rank in top tenth:	26%
ACT composite:	23-27	End year in good standing:	94%
GPA 3.75 or higher:	30%	Return as sophomores:	86%
GPA 3.50-3.74:	18%	Out-of-state:	50%
GPA 3.0-3.49:	34%	Live on campus:	97%
		International:	1%

Basis for selection. School record and class rank most important, test scores secondary. Application essay, interview, teacher and counselor evaluations, activities, and interest in the university considered. In general, official test scores (SAT or ACT) are required; however, students have the ability to apply test score optional. Interview highly recommended for all. Audition required for music majors. Portfolio required for writing and graphic design majors. **Home schooled:** Statement describing home school structure and mission, transcript of courses and grades, letter of recommendation (nonparent) required. Student should have detailed description of course work taken.

High school preparation. College-preparatory program required. 18 units required; 25 recommended. Required and recommended units include English 4, mathematics 3-4, social studies 2-4, history 2, science 2-3 (laboratory 2-3), foreign language 2-4 and academic electives 2-3.

2016-2017 Annual costs. Tuition/fees (projected): $44,340. Room/board: $11,620. Books/supplies: $900. Personal expenses: $900.

2015-2016 Financial aid. Need-based: 603 full-time freshmen applied for aid; 537 deemed to have need; 537 received aid. Average need met was 85%. Average scholarship/grant was $30,505; average loan $2,862. 79% of total undergraduate aid awarded as scholarships/grants, 21% as loans/jobs. **Non-need-based:** Awarded to 718 full-time undergraduates, including 217 freshmen. Scholarships awarded for academics, alumni affiliation, leadership, minority status, music/drama, ROTC. **Additional information:** Graduated pay scale for federal work-study program. $1,000 Visit Grant awarded to enrolling students who make an official campus visit between March 1 of sophomore year and March 1 of senior year of high school.

Application procedures. Admission: No deadline. No application fee. Admission notification by 12/1. Admission notification on a rolling basis beginning on or about 11/1. Must reply by 5/1. **Financial aid:** Priority date 3/1, closing date 5/1. FAFSA, CSS PROFILE required. Applicants notified by 3/15; Applicants notified on a rolling basis starting 3/15; must reply by 5/1.

Academics. Special study options: Accelerated study, combined bachelor's/graduate degree, cross-registration, distance learning, double major, dual enrollment of high school students, honors, independent study, internships, semester at sea, student-designed major, study abroad, teacher certification program, United Nations semester, urban semester, Washington semester. **Credit/placement by examination:** AP, CLEP, IB, SAT, ACT, institutional tests. 65 credit hours maximum toward bachelor's degree. **Support services:** Reduced course load, study skills assistance, tutoring, writing center.

Majors. Biology: General, biochemistry, ecology, neuroscience. **Business:** Accounting, business admin, finance, international, managerial economics, marketing. **Communications:** Communications/speech/rhetoric. **Computer**

sciences: Computer science, information systems. **Conservation:** Environmental science, environmental studies. **Education:** Early childhood, elementary, music. **English:** Creative writing, English lit. **Foreign languages:** French, German, Italian, Spanish. **History:** General. **Human services:** Public policy. **Liberal arts:** Arts/sciences. **Math:** General. **Philosophy/religion:** Philosophy, religion. **Physical sciences:** Chemistry, physics. **Psychology:** General. **Social sciences:** Anthropology, economics, international relations, political science, sociology. **Visual/performing arts:** Art, art history/conservation, dramatic, graphic design, music, music performance, music theory/composition.

Most popular majors. Biology 10%, business/marketing 20%, communications/journalism 12%, education 7%, English 8%, psychology 9%, social sciences 8%, visual/performing arts 9%.

Technology on campus. 173 workstations in library, student center. Dormitories wired for high-speed internet access and linked to campus network. Online course registration, online library, helpline, repair service, wireless network available.

Student life. Freshman orientation: Mandatory. Preregistration for classes offered. 4-day program; includes community service projects. **Housing:** Guaranteed on-campus for all undergraduates. Coed dorms, special housing for disabled, apartments, fraternity/sorority housing, themed housing available. $400 nonrefundable deposit, deadline 5/1. Volunteer services living groups, scholars' house, townhouses available. **Activities:** Bands, campus ministries, choral groups, dance, drama, international student organizations, literary magazine, music ensembles, Model UN, musical theater, opera, radio station, student government, student newspaper, symphony orchestra, Habitat for Humanity, Big Brothers/Big Sisters, Lutheran Student Movement, College Democrats, College Republicans, Asian Cultural Association, Gender and Sexuality Alliance, Hispanic Organization for Latino Awareness, Student Awareness of the Value of the Environment.

Athletics. NCAA. **Intercollegiate:** Baseball M, basketball, cheerleading, cross-country, field hockey W, football (tackle) M, golf, lacrosse, soccer, softball W, swimming, tennis, track and field, volleyball W. **Intramural:** Basketball, football (non-tackle), racquetball, soccer, softball, volleyball. **Team name:** Crusaders.

Student services. Alcohol/substance abuse counseling, chaplain/spiritual director, career counseling, student employment services, financial aid counseling, health services, minority student services, on-campus daycare, personal counseling, placement for graduates, veterans' counselor, women's services. **Physically disabled:** Services for visually, speech, hearing impaired.

Contact. E-mail: suadmiss@susqu.edu
Phone: (570) 372-4260 Toll-free number: (800) 326-9672
Fax: (570) 372-2722
Philip Betz, Director of Admissions, Susquehanna University, 514 University Avenue, Selinsgrove, PA 17870-1164

Swarthmore College

Swarthmore, Pennsylvania
www.swarthmore.edu

CB member
CB code: 2821

- Private 4-year liberal arts college
- Residential campus in small town
- 1,566 degree-seeking undergraduates: 50% women, 6% African American, 17% Asian American, 13% Hispanic/Latino, 8% Multi-racial, non-Hispanic, 11% international
- 12% of applicants admitted
- SAT or ACT (ACT writing optional), application essay required
- 94% graduate within 6 years

General. Founded in 1864. Regionally accredited. **Degrees:** 397 bachelor's awarded. **ROTC:** Army, Naval, Air Force. **Location:** 11 miles from Philadelphia. **Calendar:** Semester. **Full-time faculty:** 183 total; 98% have terminal degrees, 22% minority, 45% women. **Part-time faculty:** 29 total; 76% have terminal degrees, 17% minority, 31% women. **Class size:** 76% < 20, 19% 20-39, 3% 40-49, 2% 50-99, less than 1% >100. **Special facilities:** LEED-certified science center, language resource center, observatory.

Freshman class profile. 7,818 applied, 976 admitted, 407 enrolled.

Mid 50% test scores			
SAT critical reading:	670-760	Return as sophomores:	98%
SAT math:	670-770	Out-of-state:	88%
SAT writing:	680-760	Live on campus:	100%
ACT composite:	30-34	International:	13%
Rank in top quarter:	99%	Fraternities:	13%
Rank in top tenth:	88%	Sororities:	8%

Basis for selection. High school transcripts, essays, standardized test scores, recommendations, and any supplemental materials considered. Each application is read in the context of the student's life experiences and what they have accomplished with given opportunities. The optional essay section of the SAT or the Writing section of the ACT is not required. If submitted, scores from those sections will not be considered in application review. Subject tests are not required for admission, but will be considered if submitted. Prospective engineers are encouraged to submit the Math 2 Subject Test. Scores from the old and new SAT tests will be accepted for students applying to enter in the Fall of 2017. Equal consideration will be given to scores from either version of the test. TOEFL or IELTS is strongly encouraged for non-US citizens whose native language is not English and/or who are studying in non-English language curriculums. Personal interview highly recommended; both on and off-campus interviews available. Students may submit supplemental materials for review by the creative writing, dance, music, theater, and/or visual arts faculty. **Home schooled:** Submit curricula used, including transcripts from any formal classes. Examples of research projects, papers, useful. Personal interview recommended. **Learning Disabled:** Proper documentation required.

High school preparation. College-preparatory program recommended. Recommended units include English 4, mathematics 3, social studies 3, history 3, science 3 and foreign language 3. Swarthmore does not require a specific high school curriculum. It is recommended that students pursue four years of English and at least three years each of mathematics, the sciences, history and social studies; the study of one or two foreign languages; and coursework in art and music.

2016-2017 Annual costs. Tuition/fees (projected): $47,442. Room/board: $13,958. Books/supplies: $1,290. Personal expenses: $1,270.

2015-2016 Financial aid. Need-based: 274 full-time freshmen applied for aid; 237 deemed to have need; 237 received aid. Average need met was 100%. Average scholarship/grant was $46,053. 96% of total undergraduate aid awarded as scholarships/grants, 4% as loans/jobs. **Non-need-based:** Awarded to 12 full-time undergraduates, including 1 freshmen. Scholarships awarded for academics, leadership, state residency. **Additional information:** All aid is loan-free and packaged to meet full demonstrated need. Financial aid program includes work-study opportunities.

Application procedures. Admission: Closing date 1/1 (postmark date). $60 fee, may be waived for applicants with need. Admission notification by 4/1. Must reply by 5/1. **Financial aid:** Closing date 2/15. FAFSA, CSS PROFILE required. Applicants notified by 4/1; must reply by 5/1.

Academics. Lang Center for Civic and Social Responsibility prepares students for leadership in civic engagement, public service, advocacy, and social action. **Special study options:** Accelerated study, cross-registration, double major, exchange student, honors, independent study, internships, student-designed major, study abroad, teacher certification program. The College's Honors Program features small groups of students working closely with faculty and peers; an emphasis on independent learning; and a final examination by outside scholars. Cross-registration is available at Bryn Mawr and Haverford colleges, and the University of Pennsylvania. Study abroad is encouraged and is available to students of all academic majors. **Credit/placement by examination:** AP, CLEP, IB, institutional tests. **Support services:** Reduced course load, study skills assistance, tutoring, writing center.

Majors. Area/ethnic studies: African-American, Asian, Latin American, Near/Middle Eastern, women's. **Biology:** General, biochemistry. **Computer sciences:** General. **Education:** General. **Engineering:** General. **English:** English lit. **Foreign languages:** Ancient Greek, Chinese, classics, comparative lit, French, German, Japanese, Latin, linguistics, Russian, Spanish. **History:** General. **Math:** General. **Philosophy/religion:** Islamic, philosophy, religion. **Physical sciences:** Astronomy, astrophysics, chemical physics, chemistry, physics. **Psychology:** General. **Social sciences:** Economics, political science, sociology/anthropology. **Visual/performing arts:** Art history/conservation, dance, dramatic, music, studio arts.

Most popular majors. Biology 13%, computer/information sciences 9%, foreign language 7%, psychology 7%, social sciences 24%, visual/performing arts 8%.

Technology on campus. 402 workstations in dormitories, library, computer center, student center. Dormitories wired for high-speed internet access and linked to campus network. Commuter students can connect to campus network. Online course registration, online library, helpline, repair service, student web hosting, wireless network available.

Student life. Freshman orientation: Mandatory. Preregistration for classes offered. A four-day program is held in August; optional pre-orientation programs are available. **Policies:** New students are required to live on campus. **Housing:** Guaranteed on-campus for all undergraduates. Coed dorms, single-sex dorms, special housing for disabled, gender-neutral housing, themed housing available. Special housing for disabled students available on individual basis. **Activities:** Jazz band, campus ministries, choral groups, dance, drama, film society, international student organizations, literary magazine, music ensembles, musical theater, radio station, student government, student newspaper, symphony orchestra, More than 100 student-run clubs and organizations available on campus.

Athletics. NCAA. **Intercollegiate:** Badminton W, baseball M, basketball, cross-country, field hockey W, golf M, lacrosse, soccer, softball W, swimming, tennis, track and field, volleyball W. **Intramural:** Basketball, football (non-tackle), soccer, softball, table tennis, tennis, volleyball. **Team name:** Garnet.

Student services. Alcohol/substance abuse counseling, chaplain/spiritual director, career counseling, services for economically disadvantaged, student employment services, financial aid counseling, health services, minority student services, personal counseling, placement for graduates, women's services. **Physically disabled:** Services for visually, speech, hearing impaired.

Contact. E-mail: admissions@swarthmore.edu
Phone: (610) 328-8300 Toll-free number: (800) 667-3110
Fax: (610) 328-8580
James Bock, Vice President and Dean of Admissions, Swarthmore College, 500 College Avenue, Swarthmore, PA 19081

Talmudical Yeshiva of Philadelphia
Philadelphia, Pennsylvania
CB code: 1037

- Private 4-year rabbinical college for men affiliated with the Jewish faith
- Residential campus in very large city
- 115 degree-seeking undergraduates: 5% international
- 75% of applicants admitted
- Interview required

General. Founded in 1953. Accredited by AARTS. First Talmudic degree and ordination available. **Degrees:** 24 bachelor's awarded. **Calendar:** Trimester, extensive summer session. **Full-time faculty:** 5 total. **Part-time faculty:** 1 total.

Freshman class profile. 48 applied, 36 admitted, 36 enrolled.

Live on campus:	100% **International:**	3%

Basis for selection. Institutional examinations required.

High school preparation. 20 units required. Required and recommended units include English 4, social studies 3, science 3 and foreign language 2.

2015-2016 Annual costs. Tuition/fees: $8,750. Room/board: $7,100. Books/supplies: $900.

Financial aid. All financial aid based on need.

Application procedures. Admission: Priority date 1/15; no deadline. No application fee. Application must be submitted on paper. Admission notification on a rolling basis beginning on or about 7/15. **Financial aid:** Priority date 8/1, closing date 5/1. FAFSA, institutional form required. Applicants notified on a rolling basis starting 3/15; must reply within 2 week(s) of notification.

Academics. Credit/placement by examination: AP, CLEP, IB, institutional tests. **Support services:** Tutoring.

Majors. Theology: Talmudic.

Student life. Policies: Religious observance required. Freshmen not permitted cars on campus. **Housing:** Guaranteed on-campus for all undergraduates.

Student services. Career counseling, health services, personal counseling, placement for graduates.

Contact. Phone: (215) 477-1000 Fax: (215) 477-5065
Rabbi Sholom Kamenetsky, Admissions Director, Talmudical Yeshiva of Philadelphia, 6063 Drexel Road, Philadelphia, PA 19131

Temple University
Philadelphia, Pennsylvania
www.temple.edu
CB member
CB code: 2906

- Public 4-year university
- Commuter campus in very large city

- 27,983 degree-seeking undergraduates: 10% part-time, 51% women, 13% African American, 11% Asian American, 6% Hispanic/Latino, 3% Multi-racial, non-Hispanic, 6% international
- 8,850 degree-seeking graduate students
- 56% of applicants admitted
- Application essay required
- 71% graduate within 6 years

General. Founded in 1884. Regionally accredited. Campuses in Ambler, Fort Washington, Center City Philadelphia, Harrisburg, Rome, Japan, Health Sciences Center and Podiatric Medicine. **Degrees:** 6,152 bachelor's, 6 associate awarded; master's, professional, doctoral offered. **ROTC:** Army, Naval, Air Force. **Location:** 1.5 miles from downtown. **Calendar:** Semester, extensive summer session. **Full-time faculty:** 1,440 total; 90% have terminal degrees, 20% minority, 41% women. **Part-time faculty:** 1,426 total; 18% minority, 47% women. **Class size:** 38% < 20, 45% 20-39, 8% 40-49, 6% 50-99, 2% >100. **Special facilities:** Arboretum, Charles L. Blockson Afro-American Collection, observatory, planetarium, technology center, Temple Gallery at Tyler School of Art, anthropology laboratory and museum.

Freshman class profile. 28,886 applied, 16,084 admitted, 4,906 enrolled.

Mid 50% test scores			
		GPA 2.0-2.99:	7%
SAT critical reading:	520-620	Rank in top quarter:	54%
SAT math:	530-630	Rank in top tenth:	22%
SAT writing:	500-620	Return as sophomores:	90%
ACT composite:	23-29	Out-of-state:	25%
GPA 3.75 or higher:	31%	Live on campus:	76%
GPA 3.50-3.74:	25%	International:	6%
GPA 3.0-3.49:	37%		

Basis for selection. Admissions process holistic; every aspect of student's academic history considered. Admission test optional; applicants indicate whether they want their test scores used in the consideration of their application. International applicants, home-schooled applicants and recruited student athletes must submit test scores. Audition required for dance, music programs; portfolio required for art. **Home schooled:** Statement describing home school structure and mission, transcript of courses and grades, letter of recommendation (nonparent) required.

High school preparation. College-preparatory program required. 16 units required; 22 recommended. Required and recommended units include English 4, mathematics 3-4, social studies 2, history 1, science 2-3 (laboratory 1-2), foreign language 2 and academic electives 1-3.

2016-2017 Annual costs. Tuition/fees (projected): $15,688; $25,994 out-of-state. Room/board: $11,146. Books/supplies: $1,000. Personal expenses: $4,304.

2014-2015 Financial aid. Need-based: 3,940 full-time freshmen applied for aid; 3,196 deemed to have need; 3,180 received aid. Average need met was 70%. Average scholarship/grant was $7,029; average loan $3,596. 39% of total undergraduate aid awarded as scholarships/grants, 61% as loans/jobs. **Non-need-based:** Awarded to 10,283 full-time undergraduates, including 2,686 freshmen. Scholarships awarded for academics, art, athletics, music/drama, ROTC.

Application procedures. Admission: Closing date 3/1 (postmark date). $55 fee, may be waived for applicants with need. Admission notification on a rolling basis beginning on or about 9/15. Must reply by May 1 or within 2 week(s) if notified thereafter. **Financial aid:** Closing date 3/1. FAFSA required. Applicants notified on a rolling basis starting 2/15; must reply by 5/1 or within 3 week(s) of notification.

Academics. Special study options: Accelerated study, combined bachelor's/graduate degree, cooperative education, cross-registration, distance learning, double major, dual enrollment of high school students, ESL, exchange student, external degree, honors, independent study, internships, liberal arts/career combination, study abroad, teacher certification program. **Credit/placement by examination:** AP, CLEP, IB, institutional tests. **Support services:** Learning center, pre-admission summer program, reduced course load, remedial instruction, study skills assistance, tutoring, writing center.

Majors. Architecture: Architecture, landscape, urban/community planning. **Area/ethnic studies:** African-American, American, Asian, Latin American, women's. **Biology:** General, biochemistry, biophysics, neuroscience. **Business:** General, accounting, actuarial science, entrepreneurial studies, finance, hospitality admin, human resources, insurance, international, marketing, real estate. **Communications:** Advertising, journalism, organizational, radio/TV. **Computer sciences:** General, information technology. **Conservation:** Environmental science, environmental studies. **Education:** Art, elementary, English, foreign languages, mathematics, middle, music, science, social studies, trade/industrial. **Engineering:** General, biomedical, civil, electrical, mechanical. **English:** English lit. **Foreign languages:** Classics, French, German, Italian, Japanese, linguistics, Spanish. **Health services:** Athletic training, audiology/speech pathology, music therapy, nursing (RN), public health ed, recreational therapy. **History:** General. **Human services:** Social work. **Math:** General, applied. **Parks/recreation:** General, exercise sciences, sports admin. **Philosophy/religion:** Judaic, philosophy, religion. **Physical sciences:** Chemistry, geology, physics. **Protective services:** Criminal justice. **Psychology:** General. **Social sciences:** Anthropology, economics, geography, international relations, political science, sociology. **Visual/performing arts:** General, acting, art history/conservation, ceramics, cinematography, dance, fiber arts, graphic design, jazz, metal/jewelry, music, music history, music pedagogy, music performance, music theory/composition, painting, photography, printmaking, sculpture. **Work/family studies:** Family studies.

Most popular majors. Business/marketing 21%, communications/journalism 14%, education 6%, health sciences 6%, parks/recreation 6%, psychology 6%, social sciences 6%, visual/performing arts 8%.

Technology on campus. 8,399 workstations in dormitories, library, computer center, student center. Dormitories wired for high-speed internet access and linked to campus network. Commuter students can connect to campus network. Online course registration, online library, helpline, repair service, student web hosting, wireless network available.

Student life. Freshman orientation: Mandatory. Preregistration for classes offered. Two-day program held late June through late August; includes one overnight stay on campus. Registration for orientation begins in April. **Housing:** Coed dorms, single-sex dorms, special housing for disabled, apartments, wellness housing available. $250 fully refundable deposit, deadline 5/1. Living/learning centers available. **Activities:** Bands, campus ministries, choral groups, dance, drama, film society, international student organizations, literary magazine, music ensembles, Model UN, musical theater, opera, radio station, student government, student newspaper, symphony orchestra, TV station, National Society for Leadership and Success, Asian student association, Asociacion de Estudiantes Latinos, Greek American student association, organization of African students, Progressive NAACP, American Society of Mechanical Engineers, Cherry Crusade, Habitat for Humanity, Student Peace Alliance.

Athletics. NCAA. **Intercollegiate:** Basketball, cross-country, fencing W, field hockey W, football (tackle) M, golf M, gymnastics W, lacrosse W, rowing (crew), soccer, tennis, track and field W, volleyball W. **Intramural:** Badminton, basketball, field hockey W, football (non-tackle), racquetball, soccer, softball, tennis, volleyball. **Team name:** Owls.

Student services. Adult student services, alcohol/substance abuse counseling, career counseling, services for economically disadvantaged, student employment services, financial aid counseling, health services, legal services, personal counseling, placement for graduates, veterans' counselor. **Physically disabled:** Services for visually, speech, hearing impaired.

Contact. E-mail: tuadm@temple.edu
Phone: (215) 204-7200 Toll-free number: (888) 340-2222
Fax: (215) 204-5694
Karin Mormando, Director, Undergraduate Admissions, Temple University, 103 Conwell Hall, Philadelphia, PA 19122-6096

Thiel College

Greenville, Pennsylvania   **CB member**
www.thiel.edu   **CB code: 2910**

- Private 4-year liberal arts college affiliated with the Evangelical Lutheran Church in America
- Residential campus in small town
- 903 degree-seeking undergraduates: 46% women, 9% African American, 2% Hispanic/Latino, 3% Multi-racial, non-Hispanic, 4% international
- 61% of applicants admitted
- SAT or ACT (ACT writing optional) required
- 41% graduate within 6 years

General. Founded in 1866. Regionally accredited. **Degrees:** 212 bachelor's, 4 associate awarded. **Location:** 75 miles from Pittsburgh, 75 miles from Cleveland. **Calendar:** Semester, limited summer session. **Full-time faculty:** 57 total. **Part-time faculty:** 51 total. **Class size:** 64% < 20, 34% 20-39, less than 1% 40-49, less than 1% 50-99. **Special facilities:** Wildlife sanctuary, black box theater, fitness center, TV studio, radio station.

Freshman class profile. 2,275 applied, 1,399 admitted, 206 enrolled.

Mid 50% test scores		Rank in top tenth:	9%
SAT critical reading:	410-420	End year in good standing:	90%
SAT math:	380-390	Return as sophomores:	67%
ACT composite:	17-18	Out-of-state:	38%
GPA 3.75 or higher:	13%	Live on campus:	95%
GPA 3.50-3.74:	13%	International:	2%
GPA 3.0-3.49:	29%	Fraternities:	17%
GPA 2.0-2.99:	43%	Sororities:	25%
Rank in top quarter:	13%		

Basis for selection. High school GPA, standardized test scores, class rank, curriculum, and recommendation important. SAT or ACT scores received for fall admission on rolling basis. Board scores required. **Home schooled:** Transcript of courses and grades, letter of recommendation (nonparent) required. Proof of graduation required. **Learning Disabled:** Students with disabilities must submit evidence of disability to Office of Special Needs.

High school preparation. College-preparatory program recommended. 16 units recommended. Recommended units include English 4, mathematics 2, social studies 3, science 2 (laboratory 2), foreign language 2 and academic electives 1. Engineering, math, and science majors should complete 3 years of college preparatory math and science.

2015-2016 Annual costs. Tuition/fees: $28,868. Room/board: $11,336. Books/supplies: $1,000. Personal expenses: $1,400. **Additional information:** Required fees include technology fee of $950, student services fee of $630, and health & wellness fee of $250.

2014-2015 Financial aid. Need-based: 270 full-time freshmen applied for aid; 253 deemed to have need; 253 received aid. Average need met was 69%. Average scholarship/grant was $19,115; average loan $3,851. 69% of total undergraduate aid awarded as scholarships/grants, 31% as loans/jobs. **Non-need-based:** Awarded to 136 full-time undergraduates, including 36 freshmen. Scholarships awarded for academics, alumni affiliation, leadership, music/drama, religious affiliation.

Application procedures. Admission: Priority date 4/1; no deadline. $35 fee, may be waived for applicants with need, free for online applicants. Admission notification on a rolling basis beginning on or about 8/1. Must reply by May 1 or within 2 week(s) if notified thereafter. **Financial aid:** Priority date 3/15; no closing date. FAFSA required. Applicants notified on a rolling basis starting 2/15; must reply within 2 week(s) of notification.

Academics. Special study options: Combined bachelor's/graduate degree, cooperative education, distance learning, double major, dual enrollment of high school students, ESL, honors, independent study, internships, liberal arts/career combination, semester at sea, student-designed major, study abroad, teacher certification program, United Nations semester, Washington semester. 3-2 engineering with Case Western Reserve University and University of Pittsburgh, cooperative program with the Art Institute of Pittsburgh, exchange with Duke University in forestry, cooperative program with Pittsburgh Institute of Mortuary Science. Affiliation program with Lake Erie College of Osteopathic Medicine. **Credit/placement by examination:** AP, CLEP, IB, SAT, ACT, institutional tests. 30 credit hours maximum toward bachelor's degree. **Support services:** Learning center, reduced course load, remedial instruction, study skills assistance, tutoring, writing center.

Majors. Biology: General, neuroscience. **Business:** Accounting, actuarial science, business admin, communications, e-commerce, international, management information systems. **Communications:** Communications/speech/rhetoric. **Communications technology:** Radio/TV. **Computer sciences:** General, information systems. **Conservation:** General, environmental studies. **Education:** Biology, chemistry, elementary, English, history, mathematics, physics, science, social studies. **English:** English lit, writing. **Health services:** Audiology/speech pathology, clinical lab technology, cytotechnology. **History:** General. **Math:** General. **Philosophy/religion:** Philosophy, religion. **Physical sciences:** Chemistry, physics. **Protective services:** Criminal justice. **Psychology:** General. **Social sciences:** Political science, sociology. **Theology:** Religious ed. **Visual/performing arts:** Art, commercial/advertising art.

Most popular majors. Biology 8%, business/marketing 38%, psychology 12%, security/protective services 6%, social sciences 6%.

Technology on campus. PC or laptop required. 130 workstations in library, computer center. Dormitories wired for high-speed internet access and linked to campus network. Commuter students can connect to campus network. Online course registration, online library, helpline, repair service, student web hosting, wireless network available.

Student life. Freshman orientation: Mandatory, $300 fee. Preregistration for classes offered. Weekend before classes start. **Housing:** Guaranteed on-campus for all undergraduates. Coed dorms, apartments, fraternity/sorority housing, themed housing available. $100 fully refundable deposit, deadline 7/1. **Activities:** Bands, campus ministries, choral groups, dance, drama, international student organizations, literary magazine, music ensembles, musical theater, radio station, student government, student newspaper, symphony orchestra, TV station, more than 50 student clubs and organizations.

Athletics. NCAA. Intercollegiate: Baseball M, basketball, bowling W, cheerleading, cross-country, football (tackle) M, golf, lacrosse, soccer, softball W, tennis, track and field, volleyball, wrestling M. **Intramural:** Basketball, football (non-tackle), softball, table tennis, ultimate frisbee, volleyball. **Team name:** Tomcats.

Student services. Alcohol/substance abuse counseling, chaplain/spiritual director, career counseling, financial aid counseling, health services, minority student services, personal counseling, placement for graduates. **Physically disabled:** Services for visually, speech, hearing impaired.

Contact. E-mail: admissions@thiel.edu
Phone: (724) 589-2345 Toll-free number: (800) 248-4435
Fax: (724) 589-2013
Stephen Lazowski, VP for Enrollment Management, Thiel College, 75 College Avenue, Greenville, PA 16125-2181

Thomas Jefferson University
Philadelphia, Pennsylvania
www.jefferson.edu   CB code: 2903

▶ Private 4-year university and health science college
▶ Residential campus in very large city
▶ 789 undergraduates

General. Founded in 1824. Regionally accredited. Primarily a graduate institution. **Degrees:** 427 bachelor's, 6 associate awarded; master's, professional, doctoral offered. **ROTC:** Naval, Air Force. **Calendar:** Continuous, limited summer session. **Special facilities:** Rare book collection, simulation labs, human performance lab (gait research).

Basis for selection. Admission requirements vary by program. Official transcript, recommendation letter, and personal statement required for all programs. Many programs also include an interview and may require prerequisite coursework. All international students and U.S. permanent residents must demonstrate English language proficiency as one of the conditions for admission.

2015-2016 Annual costs. Costs vary according to program. Examples of full-time (academic year) tuition rates for bachelor's degree programs in radiologic sciences: $30,223; bachelor's degree program in occupational therapy: $31,027. All full-time students pay an annual technology fee; $500, and a library fee; $350. Academic fees vary by program. On-campus room and board ranges from $708-$2335 per month depending on the facility.

Financial aid. Non-need-based: Scholarships awarded for academics, leadership, state residency. **Additional information:** Applicants must use the IRS DRT process on the FAFSA.

Application procedures. Admission: No deadline. $25 fee, may be waived for applicants with need. Application must be submitted online. Admission notification on a rolling basis. Response dates vary by program. **Financial aid:** Closing date 4/1. FAFSA, institutional form required. Applicants notified on a rolling basis starting 4/1; must reply within 2 week(s) of notification.

Academics. Special study options: Accelerated study, combined bachelor's/graduate degree, distance learning, independent study, internships, study abroad. **Credit/placement by examination:** AP, CLEP, institutional tests. **Support services:** Learning center, pre-admission summer program, study skills assistance, tutoring, writing center.

Majors. Biology: Biotechnology. **Health services:** Cardiovascular technology, clinical lab science, cytotechnology, nursing (RN), preop/surgical nursing, sonography.

Technology on campus. 100 workstations in library, computer center, student center. Dormitories wired for high-speed internet access. Commuter students can connect to campus network. Online course registration, online library, helpline, wireless network available.

Student life. Housing: Guaranteed on-campus for all undergraduates. Coed dorms, special housing for disabled, apartments available. **Activities:** Concert band, campus ministries, choral groups, dance, drama, international student organizations, literary magazine, music ensembles, student government, African American student society, Chinese students and scholars society, Hands of Hope, Jewish student association, Medical Professionals for Choice, Asian professional society, Latino health organization, occupational therapy association, physical therapy association, Student Nurses Association of Pennsylvania.

Athletics. Intramural: Badminton, basketball, football (non-tackle) M, racquetball, skiing, soccer, softball, swimming, volleyball.

Student services. Adult student services, alcohol/substance abuse counseling, career counseling, student employment services, financial aid counseling, health services, minority student services, on-campus daycare, personal counseling, placement for graduates, veterans' counselor.

Contact. E-mail: TJU.Admissions@jefferson.edu
Phone: (215) 503-8890 Toll-free number: (877) 533-3247
Fax: (215) 503-7241
Erin Finn, Director of Enrollment Services, Thomas Jefferson University, 130 South Ninth Street, Edison Building, Suite 100, Philadelphia, PA 19107

University of Pennsylvania
Philadelphia, Pennsylvania   CB member
www.upenn.edu   CB code: 2926

▶ Private 4-year university
▶ Residential campus in very large city
▶ 9,726 degree-seeking undergraduates: 3% part-time, 50% women, 7% African American, 20% Asian American, 10% Hispanic/Latino, 4% Multi-racial, non-Hispanic, 12% international
▶ 11,669 degree-seeking graduate students
▶ 10% of applicants admitted
▶ SAT or ACT (ACT writing optional), application essay required
▶ 95% graduate within 6 years; 12% enter graduate study

General. Founded in 1740. Regionally accredited. **Degrees:** 2,807 bachelor's, 1 associate awarded; master's, professional, doctoral offered. **ROTC:** Army, Naval, Air Force. **Location:** 1 mile from downtown. **Calendar:** Semester, extensive summer session. **Full-time faculty:** 1,458 total; 100% have terminal degrees, 21% minority, 38% women. **Part-time faculty:** 627 total; 100% have terminal degrees, 12% minority, 53% women. **Class size:** 68% < 20, 18% 20-39, 3% 40-49, 7% 50-99, 2% >100. **Special facilities:** Archaeology and anthropology museum, institute of contemporary art, arboretum, theater, astronomical observatory, large animal research center, equine sports medicine and imaging center, women's center, undergraduate research center, wind tunnel, cyclotron facility, dairy.

Freshman class profile. 37,268 applied, 3,787 admitted, 2,435 enrolled.

Mid 50% test scores			
SAT critical reading:	680-760	Rank in top quarter:	99%
SAT math:	700-790	Rank in top tenth:	95%
SAT writing:	690-780	Return as sophomores:	98%
ACT composite:	31-34	Out-of-state:	82%
GPA 3.75 or higher:	92%	Live on campus:	98%
GPA 3.50-3.74:	5%	International:	12%
GPA 3.0-3.49:	3%	Sororities:	27%

Basis for selection. Transcript indicating rigor of course work and achievement/evaluation most important criteria. Co-curricular involvements and testing strongly considered, as are counselor and faculty recommendations. Personal commentary (essays) and interview considered as well. Penn is interested in a diverse geographic, economic, racial, and ethnic student body. SAT Subject Tests recommended. Penn requests students submit their entire ACT and/or SAT test score history. Portfolio strongly suggested for those applying to Architecture, Digital Media Design, Music, or Fine Arts majors. **Home schooled:** Statement describing home school structure and mission, transcript of courses and grades, letter of recommendation (nonparent) required. Commentary from primary instructor most important, and at least 1 other academic reference highly recommended. SAT subject tests in major academic areas highly recommended.

High school preparation. College-preparatory program recommended. 20 units recommended. Recommended units include English 4, mathematics 4, social studies 2, history 3, science 3 (laboratory 3) and foreign language 4.

2015-2016 Annual costs. Tuition/fees: $49,536. Room/board: $13,990. Books/supplies: $1,250. Personal expenses: $2,024.

2014-2015 Financial aid. All financial aid based on need. 1,318 full-time freshmen applied for aid; 1,066 deemed to have need; 1,066 received aid. Average need met was 100%. Average scholarship/grant was $42,150; average loan $83. 91% of total undergraduate aid awarded as scholarships/grants, 9% as loans/jobs. **Additional information:** All loans have been eliminated from need-based aid packages.

Application procedures. Admission: Closing date 1/5 (postmark date). $75 fee, may be waived for applicants with need. Admission notification on a rolling basis beginning on or about 4/1. Must reply by 5/1. **Financial aid:**

Priority date 2/15; no closing date. FAFSA, institutional form, CSS PROFILE required. Applicants notified on a rolling basis starting 4/1; must reply by 5/1.

Academics. Special study options: Accelerated study, combined bachelor's/graduate degree, cross-registration, distance learning, double major, dual enrollment of high school students, ESL, exchange student, honors, independent study, internships, liberal arts/career combination, student-designed major, study abroad, teacher certification program, Washington semester. Joint degree programs among schools, accelerated degree programs, Washington Semester, pre-professional programs in: pre-dentistry, pre-law, pre-medicine, and pre-veterinary studies. **Credit/placement by examination:** AP, CLEP, IB, institutional tests. **Support services:** Learning center, pre-admission summer program, remedial instruction, study skills assistance, tutoring, writing center.

Majors. Architecture: Architecture, environmental design. **Area/ethnic studies:** African, African-American, American, East Asian, South Asian, women's. **Biology:** General, biochemistry, bioinformatics, biomedical sciences, biophysics, neuroscience. **Business:** Accounting, actuarial science, business admin, e-commerce, finance, human resources, insurance, international, management information systems, marketing, operations, real estate, sales/distribution, transportation. **Communications:** Communications/speech/rhetoric. **Computer sciences:** General, computer graphics, networking. **Conservation:** Environmental studies. **Education:** General, elementary. **Engineering:** Biomedical, chemical, computer, electrical, environmental, materials, mechanical, systems. **English:** English lit. **Foreign languages:** Classics, comparative lit, East Asian, French, German, Italian, linguistics, Russian, Semitic, Spanish. **Health services:** Community health services, health care admin, nursing (RN). **History:** General, science/technology. **Human services:** Public policy. **Liberal arts:** Arts/sciences, humanities. **Math:** General, statistics. **Philosophy/religion:** Judaic, logic, philosophy, religion. **Physical sciences:** Chemistry, geology, materials science, physics. **Psychology:** General. **Social sciences:** General, anthropology, economics, international relations, political science, sociology, urban studies. **Visual/performing arts:** General, art history/conservation, dramatic, film/cinema/video, music, studio arts.

Most popular majors. Biology 10%, business/marketing 21%, engineering/engineering technologies 10%, health sciences 9%, interdisciplinary studies 6%, social sciences 13%.

Technology on campus. Dormitories wired for high-speed internet access and linked to campus network. Commuter students can connect to campus network. Online course registration, online library, helpline, repair service, student web hosting, wireless network available.

Student life. Freshman orientation: Mandatory, $205 fee. Preregistration for classes offered. **Housing:** Guaranteed on-campus for freshmen. Coed dorms, special housing for disabled, apartments, fraternity/sorority housing, themed housing, wellness housing available. $200 nonrefundable deposit, deadline 5/1. Private off-campus housing available. **Activities:** Bands, campus ministries, choral groups, dance, drama, film society, international student organizations, literary magazine, music ensembles, Model UN, musical theater, opera, radio station, student government, student newspaper, symphony orchestra, TV station, various religious, political, ethnic, social service, performing arts, cultural, and organizations.

Athletics. NCAA. **Intercollegiate:** Baseball M, basketball, cross-country, diving, fencing, field hockey W, football (tackle) M, golf, gymnastics W, lacrosse, rowing (crew), soccer, softball W, squash, swimming, tennis, track and field, volleyball W, wrestling M. **Intramural:** Basketball, football (non-tackle), soccer, tennis, volleyball. **Team name:** Quakers.

Student services. Adult student services, alcohol/substance abuse counseling, chaplain/spiritual director, career counseling, services for economically disadvantaged, student employment services, financial aid counseling, health services, legal services, minority student services, on-campus daycare, personal counseling, placement for graduates, veterans' counselor, women's services. **Physically disabled:** Services for visually, speech, hearing impaired.

Contact. E-mail: info@admissions.upenn.edu
Phone: (215) 898-7507 Fax: (215) 898-9670
Eric Furda, Dean of Admissions, University of Pennsylvania, 1 College Hall, Philadelphia, PA 19104-6376

University of Phoenix: Harrisburg
Harrisburg, Pennsylvania
www.phoenix.edu

- For-profit 4-year university
- Commuter campus in large town
- 130 degree-seeking undergraduates
- 20 graduate students

General. Regionally accredited. **Degrees:** 2 bachelor's awarded; master's offered. **Calendar:** Differs by program. **Full-time faculty:** 6 total. **Part-time faculty:** 34 total.

Basis for selection. Open admission.

2015-2016 Annual costs. Per-credit-hour charge, $410 to $635, depending upon level and course of study. Books, material charges, and other fees vary by course and program. All fees are subject to change.

Application procedures. Admission: No deadline. No application fee. **Financial aid:** No deadline.

Academics. Credit/placement by examination: AP, CLEP.

Majors. Business: Accounting/business management, business admin, finance, marketing. **Health services:** Facilities admin, health information management, long term care admin. **Protective services:** Disaster management, law enforcement admin.

Student life. Freshman orientation: Mandatory. Preregistration for classes offered.

Contact. Toll-free number: (866) 766-0766
University of Phoenix: Harrisburg, 1625 West Fountainhead Parkway, Tempe, AZ 85282

University of Phoenix: Philadelphia
Wayne, Pennsylvania
www.phoenix.edu

- For-profit 4-year university
- Commuter campus in small city
- 639 undergraduates
- 32 graduate students

General. Regionally accredited. **Degrees:** 119 bachelor's awarded; master's offered. **Calendar:** Differs by program. **Full-time faculty:** 25 total. **Part-time faculty:** 90 total.

Basis for selection. Open admission.

2015-2016 Annual costs. Per-credit-hour charge, $410 to $635, depending upon level and course of study. Books, material charges, and other fees vary by course and program. All fees are subject to change.

Application procedures. Admission: No deadline. No application fee. **Financial aid:** No deadline.

Academics. Credit/placement by examination: AP, CLEP.

Majors. Business: Accounting/business management, business admin, finance, marketing. **Computer sciences:** General, database management, networking, programming, security, system admin, systems analysis, web page design, webmaster. **Health services:** Facilities admin, health information management, long term care admin. **Protective services:** Disaster management, law enforcement admin.

Student life. Freshman orientation: Mandatory. Preregistration for classes offered.

Contact. Toll-free number: (866) 766-0766
University of Phoenix: Philadelphia, 1625 West Fountainhead Parkway, Tempe, AZ 85282

University of Phoenix: Pittsburgh
Pittsburgh, Pennsylvania
www.phoenix.edu

- For-profit 4-year university
- Commuter campus in large city
- 110 degree-seeking undergraduates
- 20 graduate students

General. Regionally accredited. **Degrees:** 1 bachelor's awarded; master's offered. **Calendar:** Differs by program. **Full-time faculty:** 5 total. **Part-time faculty:** 45 total.

Basis for selection. Open admission.

2015-2016 Annual costs. Per-credit-hour charge, $410 to $635, depending upon level and course of study. Books, material charges, and other fees vary by course and program. All fees are subject to change.

Application procedures. Admission: No deadline. No application fee. **Financial aid:** No deadline.

Academics. Credit/placement by examination: AP, CLEP.

Majors. Business: Accounting/business management, business admin, e-commerce, entrepreneurial studies, finance, human resources, marketing, operations. **Computer sciences:** Networking, programming, security, system admin, systems analysis, web page design, webmaster. **Health services:** Facilities admin, health information management, long term care admin. **Human services:** General. **Protective services:** Disaster management, law enforcement admin.

Student life. Freshman orientation: Mandatory. Preregistration for classes offered.

Contact. Toll-free number: (866) 766-0766
University of Phoenix: Pittsburgh, 1625 West Fountainhead Parkway, Tempe, AZ 85282

University of Pittsburgh
Pittsburgh, Pennsylvania
www.pitt.edu

CB member
CB code: 2927

- Public 4-year university
- Residential campus in large city
- 18,655 degree-seeking undergraduates: 5% part-time, 51% women, 5% African American, 9% Asian American, 3% Hispanic/Latino, 3% Multiracial, non-Hispanic, 4% international
- 9,564 degree-seeking graduate students
- 54% of applicants admitted
- SAT or ACT (ACT writing optional) required
- 72% graduate within 6 years; 32% enter graduate study

General. Founded in 1787. Regionally accredited. Regional campuses in Johnstown, Bradford, Titusville, and Greensburg. **Degrees:** 4,521 bachelor's awarded; master's, professional, doctoral offered. **ROTC:** Army, Naval, Air Force. **Location:** 3 miles from downtown. **Calendar:** Semester, extensive summer session. **Full-time faculty:** 1,631 total; 95% have terminal degrees, 18% minority, 44% women. **Part-time faculty:** 547 total; 11% minority, 47% women. **Class size:** 40% < 20, 33% 20-39, 7% 40-49, 15% 50-99, 6% >100. **Special facilities:** Observatory, nationality rooms, performance hall, laboratory of ecology.

Freshman class profile. 30,626 applied, 16,503 admitted, 4,014 enrolled.

Mid 50% test scores			
SAT critical reading:	580-660	Rank in top quarter:	83%
SAT math:	600-690	Rank in top tenth:	50%
SAT writing:	570-670	Return as sophomores:	92%
ACT composite:	26-31	Out-of-state:	32%
GPA 3.75 or higher:	73%	Live on campus:	97%
GPA 3.50-3.74:	15%	International:	4%
GPA 3.0-3.49:	11%	Fraternities:	7%
GPA 2.0-2.99:	1%	Sororities:	7%

Basis for selection. GED not accepted. High school record, class rank, test scores, and activities considered. College of General Studies applicants must apply directly to that college, not through Admissions and Financial Aid. Students admitted as freshmen into the Dietrich School of Arts and Sciences, Swanson School of Engineering, School of Nursing, and College of Business Administration. Students may be conditionally accepted into the School of Pharmacy, PharmD program with the provision that they successfully complete 4 terms (2 years) of preprofessional study in Dietrich School of Arts and Sciences. Interview and essay recommended for all; audition required for music program; portfolio recommended for studio art program; essay required for pharmacy applicants. **Home schooled:** Statement describing home school structure and mission, transcript of courses and grades required.

High school preparation. College-preparatory program required. 17 units required; 23 recommended. Required and recommended units include English 4, mathematics 3-4, social studies 2-3, science 3-4 (laboratory 3-4), foreign language 2-3 and academic electives 3-5.

2015-2016 Annual costs. Tuition/fees: $18,192; $28,958 out-of-state. Room/board: $10,900. Books/supplies: $1,170. Personal expenses: $1,748.

2014-2015 Financial aid. Need-based: 3,180 full-time freshmen applied for aid; 2,160 deemed to have need; 2,089 received aid. Average need met was 61%. Average scholarship/grant was $9,239; average loan $4,747. 41% of total undergraduate aid awarded as scholarships/grants, 59% as loans/jobs. **Non-need-based:** Awarded to 1,328 full-time undergraduates, including 503 freshmen. Scholarships awarded for academics, athletics, minority status.

Application procedures. Admission: No deadline. $45 fee, may be waived for applicants with need. Admission notification on a rolling basis beginning on or about 9/1. Must reply by May 1 or within 3 week(s) if notified thereafter. **Financial aid:** Priority date 3/1; no closing date. FAFSA required. Applicants notified on a rolling basis starting 3/15.

Academics. Accelerated high school program enables students to take courses in Dietrich School of Arts and Sciences while in high school. **Special study options:** Accelerated study, combined bachelor's/graduate degree, cooperative education, cross-registration, distance learning, double major, dual enrollment of high school students, ESL, exchange student, external degree, honors, independent study, internships, liberal arts/career combination, student-designed major, study abroad, teacher certification program. Freshman seminars, early admission to some graduate programs for exceptional students. **Credit/placement by examination:** AP, CLEP, IB, SAT, ACT, institutional tests. 60 credit hours maximum toward bachelor's degree. Dietrich School of Arts and Sciences does not accept CLEP. **Support services:** Learning center, reduced course load, remedial instruction, study skills assistance, tutoring, writing center.

Honors college/program. In order to enroll in honors courses a 1400 combined SAT Math and Critical Reading scores required.

Majors. Area/ethnic studies: African-American, German, women's. **Biology:** General, bioinformatics, ecology/evolutionary, microbiology, molecular, neuroscience. **Business:** Accounting, finance, international, logistics, marketing. **Communications:** Media studies. **Computer sciences:** Computer science, information systems. **Education:** Physical. **Engineering:** Applied physics, biomedical, chemical, civil, computer, electrical, engineering science, industrial, materials, mechanical. **English:** British lit, creative writing, rhetoric/composition. **Foreign languages:** Chinese, classics, French, Italian, Japanese, linguistics, Polish, Russian, Slavic, Spanish. **Health services:** Audiology/speech pathology, dental hygiene, dietetics, health information management, nursing (RN), rehabilitation science. **History:** General, science/technology. **Human services:** General, social work. **Liberal arts:** Arts/sciences, humanities. **Math:** General, applied, statistics. **Philosophy/religion:** Philosophy, religion. **Physical sciences:** General, astronomy, chemistry, geology, physics. **Protective services:** Corrections. **Psychology:** General, educational. **Social sciences:** General, anthropology, economics, political science, sociology, urban studies. **Visual/performing arts:** Art history/conservation, dramatic, film/cinema/video, music, studio arts.

Most popular majors. Biology 8%, business/marketing 17%, engineering/engineering technologies 11%, English 7%, health sciences 13%, psychology 8%, social sciences 11%.

Technology on campus. 2,000 workstations in library, computer center, student center. Dormitories wired for high-speed internet access and linked to campus network. Commuter students can connect to campus network. Online course registration, online library, helpline, repair service, student web hosting, wireless network available.

Student life. Freshman orientation: Available. Preregistration for classes offered. Held during first week of classes; open to parents and family. **Policies:** Students must abide by the Student Code of Conduct rules provided by the school. **Housing:** Guaranteed on-campus for freshmen. Coed dorms, single-sex dorms, special housing for disabled, apartments, fraternity/sorority housing, themed housing, wellness housing available. $325 fully refundable deposit. Rooms can be adapted to meet disabled students' particular needs. **Activities:** Bands, campus ministries, choral groups, dance, drama, film society, international student organizations, literary magazine, music ensembles, Model UN, musical theater, radio station, student government, student newspaper, symphony orchestra, TV station, approximately 490 student organizations.

Athletics. NCAA. **Intercollegiate:** Baseball M, basketball, cross-country, diving, football (tackle) M, gymnastics W, soccer, softball W, swimming, tennis W, track and field, volleyball W, wrestling M. **Intramural:** Badminton, basketball, football (tackle) M, handball, racquetball, soccer, squash, table tennis, ultimate frisbee, volleyball. **Team name:** Panthers.

Student services. Adult student services, alcohol/substance abuse counseling, chaplain/spiritual director, career counseling, services for economically disadvantaged, student employment services, financial aid counseling, health services, minority student services, personal counseling, placement for graduates, veterans' counselor. **Physically disabled:** Services for visually, speech, hearing impaired.

Contact. E-mail: oafa@pitt.edu
Phone: (412) 624-7488 Fax: (412) 624-4138
Marc Harding, Chief Enrollment Officer, University of Pittsburgh, 4227 Fifth Avenue, 1st Floor, Alumni Hall, Pittsburgh, PA 15260

University of Pittsburgh at Bradford
Bradford, Pennsylvania **CB member**
www.upb.pitt.edu **CB code: 2935**

- Public 4-year university
- Residential campus in large town
- 1,435 degree-seeking undergraduates: 6% part-time, 55% women, 11% African American, 2% Asian American, 5% Hispanic/Latino, 1% Native American, 2% Multi-racial, non-Hispanic, 2% international
- 58% of applicants admitted
- SAT or ACT (ACT writing optional) required
- 54% graduate within 6 years; 22% enter graduate study

General. Founded in 1963. Regionally accredited. The region surrounding Bradford provides the setting for many types of outdoor activities, including hiking, camping, biking, skiing, four-wheeling and boating. **Degrees:** 252 bachelor's, 44 associate awarded. **ROTC:** Army. **Location:** 160 miles from Pittsburgh, 79 miles from Buffalo, New York. **Calendar:** Semester, extensive summer session. **Full-time faculty:** 71 total; 75% have terminal degrees, 17% minority, 39% women. **Part-time faculty:** 92 total; 17% have terminal degrees, 2% minority, 56% women. **Class size:** 63% < 20, 32% 20-39, 2% 40-49, 3% 50-99. **Special facilities:** Campus located in the Allegheny National Forest.

Freshman class profile. 2,121 applied, 1,228 admitted, 361 enrolled.

Mid 50% test scores			
		GPA 2.0-2.99:	33%
SAT critical reading:	440-540	Rank in top quarter:	26%
SAT math:	440-540	Rank in top tenth:	8%
SAT writing:	410-520	End year in good standing:	80%
ACT composite:	18-23	Return as sophomores:	69%
GPA 3.75 or higher:	21%	Out-of-state:	26%
GPA 3.50-3.74:	15%	Live on campus:	83%
GPA 3.0-3.49:	30%	International:	2%

Basis for selection. School achievement record, test scores, interview most important. Essay and recommendations considered. **Home schooled:** Required: Complete listing of courses taken/completed/in progress, syllabus for each course, textbook used, 1 recommendation from educator, 1 outside recommendation, personal essay, personal interview, state requirement satisfaction.

High school preparation. College-preparatory program recommended. 15 units required. Required and recommended units include English 4, mathematics 2-2.5, history 1, science 1-2 (laboratory 1-2), foreign language 2 and academic electives 5. Engineering and math students must have trigonometry and physics with a lab. Nursing majors must have 3 social science and 1 each of chemistry and biology with labs in both.

2015-2016 Annual costs. Tuition/fees: $13,372; $24,188 out-of-state. Room/board: $8,592. Books/supplies: $1,200. Personal expenses: $2,434.

2014-2015 Financial aid. Need-based: 365 full-time freshmen applied for aid; 326 deemed to have need; 324 received aid. Average need met was 75%. Average scholarship/grant was $9,669; average loan $5,616. 51% of total undergraduate aid awarded as scholarships/grants, 49% as loans/jobs. **Non-need-based:** Awarded to 143 full-time undergraduates, including 57 freshmen. Scholarships awarded for academics, alumni affiliation, ROTC, state residency.

Application procedures. Admission: Priority date 5/1; no deadline. $45 fee, may be waived for applicants with need. Admission notification on a rolling basis beginning on or about 10/16. Must reply by May 1 or within 2 week(s) if notified thereafter. **Financial aid:** Priority date 3/1; no closing date. FAFSA required. Applicants notified on a rolling basis starting 4/1; must reply within 2 week(s) of notification.

Academics. Special study options: Combined bachelor's/graduate degree, cross-registration, distance learning, double major, dual enrollment of high school students, external degree, honors, independent study, internships, semester at sea, study abroad, teacher certification program. 3-4 pre-optometry program with Pennsylvania College of Optometry, 1-4 pharmacy program with Oakland campus, 3+4 program with LECOM in Osteopathic Medicine. **Credit/placement by examination:** AP, CLEP, IB, SAT, ACT, institutional tests. 30 credit hours maximum toward associate degree, 90 toward bachelor's. **Support services:** Learning center, reduced course load, remedial instruction, study skills assistance, tutoring, writing center. Math center.

Majors. Biology: General. **Business:** General, accounting, business admin, entrepreneurial studies, hospitality admin. **Communications:** Public relations, radio/TV. **Computer sciences:** Applications programming, computer science. **Conservation:** Environmental studies. **Education:** General, elementary, physical, secondary, social science. **Engineering:** General, chemical, civil, electrical, engineering science, industrial, mechanical. **English:** Creative writing, English lit, rhetoric/composition. **Health services:** Athletic training, nursing (RN), radiologic technology/medical imaging. **Liberal arts:** Humanities. **Math:** Applied. **Parks/recreation:** General, sports admin. **Physical sciences:** General, chemistry. **Protective services:** Corrections, law enforcement admin. **Psychology:** General. **Social sciences:** General, demography, economics, political science, sociology. **Visual/performing arts:** General.

Most popular majors. Biology 6%, business/marketing 15%, communications/journalism 8%, education 7%, health sciences 18%, physical sciences 6%, security/protective services 8%, social sciences 13%.

Technology on campus. 120 workstations in library, computer center, student center. Dormitories wired for high-speed internet access and linked to campus network. Commuter students can connect to campus network. Online course registration, online library, helpline, repair service, student web hosting, wireless network available.

Student life. Freshman orientation: Mandatory, $90 fee. Preregistration for classes offered. 2-day program for students and parents in July; additional 3-day program immediately prior to start of classes. **Housing:** Guaranteed on-campus for freshmen. Coed dorms, special housing for disabled, apartments available. $125 nonrefundable deposit, deadline 5/1. Townhouse/apartment style housing available. **Activities:** Campus ministries, choral groups, dance, drama, literary magazine, music ensembles, radio station, student government, student newspaper, Black Action Committee, Christ in Action, Collegiate Liberals of America, Conservative Union, Habitat for Humanity, Ideology Expression Club.

Athletics. NCAA. Intercollegiate: Baseball M, basketball, cross-country, golf M, ice hockey M, soccer, softball W, swimming, tennis, volleyball W. **Intramural:** Basketball, football (non-tackle), golf, ice hockey, soccer, softball, swimming, table tennis, volleyball, water polo. **Team name:** Panthers.

Student services. Adult student services, alcohol/substance abuse counseling, chaplain/spiritual director, career counseling, student employment services, financial aid counseling, health services, personal counseling, placement for graduates, veterans' counselor. **Physically disabled:** Services for visually, speech, hearing impaired.

Contact. E-mail: admissions@upb.pitt.edu
Phone: (814) 362-7555 Toll-free number: (800) 872-1787
Fax: (814) 362-5150
Alexander Nazemetz, Associate Vice President, Enrollment Management, University of Pittsburgh at Bradford, 300 Campus Drive, Bradford, PA 16701

University of Pittsburgh at Greensburg
Greensburg, Pennsylvania
www.greensburg.pitt.edu **CB code: 2936**

- Public 4-year branch campus and liberal arts college
- Commuter campus in large town
- 1,559 degree-seeking undergraduates: 6% part-time, 52% women, 6% African American, 4% Asian American, 6% Hispanic/Latino, 3% Multi-racial, non-Hispanic, 1% international
- 71% of applicants admitted
- SAT or ACT with writing required
- 56% graduate within 6 years; 32% enter graduate study

General. Founded in 1963. Regionally accredited. **Degrees:** 270 bachelor's awarded. **ROTC:** Army, Air Force. **Location:** 35 miles from Pittsburgh. **Calendar:** Semester, limited summer session. **Full-time faculty:** 75 total. **Part-time faculty:** 66 total. **Class size:** 44% < 20, 49% 20-39, 6% 40-49, 1% 50-99, less than 1% >100.

Freshman class profile. 2,044 applied, 1,461 admitted, 409 enrolled.

Mid 50% test scores			
		GPA 2.0-2.99:	12%
SAT critical reading:	460-560	Rank in top quarter:	38%
SAT math:	470-560	Rank in top tenth:	11%
SAT writing:	440-530	Return as sophomores:	78%
ACT composite:	20-25	Out-of-state:	6%
GPA 3.75 or higher:	29%	Live on campus:	86%
GPA 3.50-3.74:	22%	International:	2%
GPA 3.0-3.49:	37%		

Basis for selection. High school curriculum and grades most important, followed by SAT/ACT scores and class rank. Essay is recommended, interviews and letters of recommendation are optional. **Home schooled:** Transcript of courses and grades required.

High school preparation. College-preparatory program required. 15 units required; 20 recommended. Required and recommended units include English 4, mathematics 2-4, social studies 2, history 2, science 1-2 (laboratory 1), foreign language 4, computer science 1 and academic electives 1-3.

2015-2016 Annual costs. Tuition/fees: $13,382; $24,198 out-of-state. Room/board: $9,750. Books/supplies: $1,170. Personal expenses: $1,748.

2014-2015 Financial aid. Need-based: 380 full-time freshmen applied for aid; 314 deemed to have need; 309 received aid. Average need met was 72%. Average scholarship/grant was $8,355; average loan $5,535. 46% of total undergraduate aid awarded as scholarships/grants, 54% as loans/jobs. **Non-need-based:** Awarded to 105 full-time undergraduates, including 60 freshmen. Scholarships awarded for academics, leadership, minority status, state residency.

Application procedures. Admission: No deadline. $45 fee, may be waived for applicants with need. Admission notification on a rolling basis beginning on or about 9/15. Must reply by May 1 or within 3 week(s) if notified thereafter. **Financial aid:** Priority date 2/15; no closing date. FAFSA required. Applicants notified on a rolling basis starting 3/15; must reply within 3 week(s) of notification.

Academics. Special study options: Combined bachelor's/graduate degree, cross-registration, double major, dual enrollment of high school students, ESL, exchange student, independent study, internships, liberal arts/career combination, student-designed major, study abroad. **Credit/placement by examination:** AP, CLEP, SAT, ACT, institutional tests. 30 credit hours maximum toward bachelor's degree. **Support services:** Learning center, reduced course load, remedial instruction, study skills assistance, tutoring, writing center.

Majors. Area/ethnic studies: American. **Biology:** General. **Business:** Accounting, business admin, management information systems. **Communications:** Communications/speech/rhetoric, journalism, public relations. **Computer sciences:** Information systems. **Education:** Biology, chemistry, early childhood, elementary, English, history, mathematics, multi-level teacher, science, secondary, social science, social studies. **English:** English lit, writing. **Foreign languages:** Spanish. **Health services:** Predental, premedicine, prepharmacy, preveterinary. **History:** General. **Liberal arts:** Arts/sciences. **Math:** Applied. **Physical sciences:** Chemistry. **Protective services:** Law enforcement admin. **Psychology:** General. **Social sciences:** General, anthropology, criminology, political science. **Visual/performing arts:** General.

Most popular majors. Biology 28%, business/marketing 20%, communications/journalism 11%, psychology 16%, security/protective services 7%.

Technology on campus. 400 workstations in dormitories, library, computer center. Dormitories wired for high-speed internet access and linked to campus network. Commuter students can connect to campus network. Online course registration, online library, helpline, repair service, student web hosting, wireless network available.

Student life. Freshman orientation: Mandatory, $50 fee. Preregistration for classes offered. 2-day summer orientation is held twice in the summer. Students may stay on-campus for an additional $15 fee. Incoming students register for fall classes during summer orientation. **Housing:** Coed dorms, themed housing available. $150 fully refundable deposit, deadline 5/1. **Activities:** Campus ministries, choral groups, dance, drama, international student organizations, literary magazine, musical theater, student government, student newspaper, student activities board, honor societies, academic societies, Alpha Phi Omega, Circle K, Amnesty International, Christian fellowship club, College Republicans, College Democrats.

Athletics. NCAA. **Intercollegiate:** Baseball M, basketball, cross-country, golf M, soccer, softball W, tennis, volleyball W. **Intramural:** Baseball, basketball, football (non-tackle), golf, soccer, softball, tennis, ultimate frisbee, volleyball. **Team name:** Bobcats.

Student services. Adult student services, alcohol/substance abuse counseling, career counseling, student employment services, financial aid counseling, health services, personal counseling, placement for graduates, veterans' counselor. **Physically disabled:** Services for visually, hearing impaired.

Contact. E-mail: upgadmit@pitt.edu
Phone: (724) 836-9880 Fax: (724) 836-7471
Heather Kabala, Director of Admissions, University of Pittsburgh at Greensburg, 150 Finoli Drive, Greensburg, PA 15601

University of Pittsburgh at Johnstown

Johnstown, Pennsylvania — CB member
www.upj.pitt.edu — CB code: 2934

- Public 4-year engineering and liberal arts college
- Residential campus in small city
- 2,814 degree-seeking undergraduates: 3% part-time, 45% women, 3% African American, 1% Asian American, 1% Hispanic/Latino, 2% Multiracial, non-Hispanic, 2% international
- 81% of applicants admitted
- SAT or ACT (ACT writing recommended) required
- 55% graduate within 6 years

General. Founded in 1927. Regionally accredited. **Degrees:** 247 bachelor's, 23 associate awarded. **ROTC:** Army. **Location:** 70 miles from Pittsburgh. **Calendar:** Semester, limited summer session. **Class size:** 45% < 20, 48% 20-39, 6% 40-49, 1% 50-99, less than 1% >100. **Special facilities:** 40-acre nature preserve, performing arts center, wellness center.

Freshman class profile. 3,456 applied, 2,800 admitted, 724 enrolled.

Mid 50% test scores			
SAT critical reading:	450-550	Rank in top quarter:	40%
SAT math:	460-570	Rank in top tenth:	14%
SAT writing:	420-530	Return as sophomores:	82%
ACT composite:	20-25	Out-of-state:	3%
GPA 3.75 or higher:	31%	Live on campus:	81%
GPA 3.50-3.74:	20%	International:	2%
GPA 3.0-3.49:	30%		
GPA 2.0-2.99:	18%		

Basis for selection. College preparatory curriculum, high school achievement, test scores, and class rank very important. Recommendations and essay considered. Interview recommended.

High school preparation. College-preparatory program recommended. 15 units required. Required units include English 4, mathematics 2, social studies 4, science 2 (laboratory 1) and foreign language 2. One each of trigonometry, physics, and chemistry required for engineering technology program.

2015-2016 Annual costs. Tuition/fees: $13,374; $24,190 out-of-state. Room/board: $9,200. Books/supplies: $1,152. Personal expenses: $1,722.

2014-2015 Financial aid. Need-based: 729 full-time freshmen applied for aid; 605 deemed to have need; 598 received aid. Average need met was 64%. Average scholarship/grant was $6,890; average loan $3,433. 41% of total undergraduate aid awarded as scholarships/grants, 59% as loans/jobs. **Non-need-based:** Awarded to 299 full-time undergraduates, including 125 freshmen. Scholarships awarded for academics, alumni affiliation, athletics, leadership, ROTC, state residency.

Application procedures. Admission: Closing date 5/1. No application fee. Admission notification on a rolling basis beginning on or about 8/1. Must reply by May 1 or within 2 week(s) if notified thereafter. **Financial aid:** Priority date 4/1; no closing date. FAFSA required. Applicants notified on a rolling basis starting 3/1; must reply within 2 week(s) of notification.

Academics. Special study options: Accelerated study, combined bachelor's/graduate degree, cross-registration, double major, dual enrollment of high school students, independent study, internships, liberal arts/career combination, student-designed major, study abroad, teacher certification program. **Credit/placement by examination:** AP, CLEP, IB, SAT, ACT, institutional tests. 90 credit hours maximum toward bachelor's degree. **Support services:** Learning center, reduced course load, study skills assistance, tutoring, writing center.

Majors. Biology: General. **Business:** General, accounting, finance, managerial economics, marketing. **Communications:** Communications/speech/rhetoric, journalism. **Computer sciences:** General. **Conservation:** Environmental studies. **Education:** Biology, chemistry, elementary, English, mathematics, science, secondary, social science, social studies. **English:** American lit, British lit, creative writing. **Health services:** Nursing (RN), predental, premedicine, preveterinary. **History:** General. **Liberal arts:** Arts/sciences. **Math:** General. **Physical sciences:** Chemistry, geology. **Protective services:** Law enforcement admin. **Psychology:** General. **Social sciences:** General, economics, geography, political science, sociology. **Visual/performing arts:** Dramatic.

Most popular majors. Biology 14%, business/marketing 20%, education 8%, engineering/engineering technologies 16%, English 8%, psychology 9%, social sciences 7%.

Technology on campus. 150 workstations in library, computer center. Dormitories wired for high-speed internet access and linked to campus network. Commuter students can connect to campus network. Online course registration, online library, helpline, student web hosting, wireless network available.

Student life. Freshman orientation: Mandatory, $90 fee. Preregistration for classes offered. One-day program held in June/July, followed by a four-day program at the end of August (move-in). **Policies:** To be eligible to hold office within group or organization, student must be full-time and have minimum 2.0 GPA. **Housing:** Guaranteed on-campus for all undergraduates. Coed dorms, special housing for disabled, apartments, fraternity/sorority housing, themed housing available. $150 fully refundable deposit. Townhouses, lodges, and single-sex residences available. **Activities:** Concert band, campus ministries, choral groups, dance, drama, literary magazine, music ensembles, Model UN, musical theater, radio station, student government, student newspaper, TV station, Newman Association, Black Action Society, Student Outreach Through Service, Time Out Christian Fellowship, Student Council on World Affairs, political science club, Habitat for Humanity.

Athletics. NCAA. Intercollegiate: Baseball M, basketball, cross-country W, golf, soccer, track and field W, volleyball W, wrestling M. **Intramural:** Basketball, football (non-tackle), softball, volleyball. **Team name:** Mountain Cats.

Student services. Adult student services, alcohol/substance abuse counseling, chaplain/spiritual director, career counseling, student employment services, financial aid counseling, health services, personal counseling, placement for graduates, veterans' counselor. **Physically disabled:** Services for visually, speech, hearing impaired.

Contact. E-mail: upjadmit@pitt.edu
Phone: (814) 269-7050 Toll-free number: (800) 765-4875
Fax: (814) 269-7044
Therese Grimes, Executive Director of Enrollment Services, University of Pittsburgh at Johnstown, 450 Schoolhouse Road, 157 Blackington Hall, Johnstown, PA 15904-1200

University of Scranton

Scranton, Pennsylvania
www.scranton.edu

CB member
CB code: 2929

- Private 4-year university and liberal arts college affiliated with the Roman Catholic Church
- Residential campus in small city
- 3,793 degree-seeking undergraduates: 3% part-time, 58% women, 2% African American, 2% Asian American, 9% Hispanic/Latino, 3% Multiracial, non-Hispanic, 1% international
- 1,431 degree-seeking graduate students
- 72% of applicants admitted
- SAT or ACT (ACT writing optional), application essay required
- 80% graduate within 6 years; 37% enter graduate study

General. Founded in 1888. Regionally accredited. **Degrees:** 952 bachelor's, 2 associate awarded; master's, professional offered. **ROTC:** Army, Air Force. **Location:** 125 miles from Philadelphia, 125 miles from New York City. **Calendar:** Semester, limited summer session. **Full-time faculty:** 295 total; 88% have terminal degrees, 6% minority, 40% women. **Part-time faculty:** 253 total; 16% have terminal degrees, 3% minority, 51% women. **Class size:** 51% < 20, 48% 20-39, less than 1% 40-49, less than 1% 50-99. **Special facilities:** Science center with vivarium and rooftop greenhouse and observation deck, conference and retreat center at Chapman Lake, performing arts center.

Freshman class profile. 10,049 applied, 7,256 admitted, 919 enrolled.

Mid 50% test scores		GPA 2.0-2.99:	18%
SAT critical reading:	510-610	Rank in top quarter:	62%
SAT math:	520-620	Rank in top tenth:	34%
ACT composite:	22-28	Return as sophomores:	88%
GPA 3.75 or higher:	27%	Out-of-state:	61%
GPA 3.50-3.74:	20%	Live on campus:	88%
GPA 3.0-3.49:	35%	International:	1%

Basis for selection. Courses taken, GPA, SAT/ACT scores, class rank most important. Essay, extracurricular/leadership/service activities, recommendations important. **Home schooled:** State high school equivalency certificate required.

High school preparation. College-preparatory program recommended. 16 units required. Required and recommended units include English 4, mathematics 3-4, history 2-3, science 1-2, foreign language 2 and academic electives 4. Science and business students should have 4 math; science students should have 3 or more science.

2015-2016 Annual costs. Tuition/fees: $41,044. Room/board: $13,918. Books/supplies: $1,300. Personal expenses: $1,168.

Financial aid. Non-need-based: Scholarships awarded for academics, ROTC.

Application procedures. Admission: Closing date 3/1 (receipt date). No application fee. Application must be submitted online. Admission notification on a rolling basis beginning on or about 12/15. Must reply by May 1 or within 2 week(s) if notified thereafter. **Financial aid:** Priority date 2/15; no closing date. FAFSA required. Applicants notified on a rolling basis starting 3/15; must reply by 5/1 or within 2 week(s) of notification.

Academics. Special study options: Accelerated study, combined bachelor's/graduate degree, cross-registration, distance learning, double major, dual enrollment of high school students, exchange student, honors, independent study, internships, semester at sea, student-designed major, study abroad, teacher certification program, United Nations semester, Washington semester, weekend college. Baccalaureate/Master's degree programs available. **Credit/placement by examination:** AP, CLEP, IB, institutional tests. 30 credit hours maximum toward bachelor's degree. **Support services:** Learning center, remedial instruction, study skills assistance, tutoring, writing center.

Majors. Area/ethnic studies: Chicano/Hispanic-American/Latino, French, German, Italian, women's. **Biology:** General, biochemistry, biophysics, molecular, molecular pharmacology, neuroscience. **Business:** Accounting, business admin, e-commerce, finance, human resources, international, marketing, operations, small business admin. **Communications:** Broadcast journalism, communications/speech/rhetoric, digital media, persuasive communications. **Computer sciences:** Computer science, information systems. **Conservation:** Environmental science. **Education:** Biology, chemistry, early childhood, elementary, English, foreign languages, French, German, history, Latin, mathematics, middle, physics, science, secondary, social studies, Spanish. **Engineering:** Computer, electrical, pre-engineering. **English:** English lit. **Foreign languages:** Classics, French, German, Italian, Latin, Spanish. **Health services:** Clinical lab science, health care admin, nursing (RN), public health ed. **History:** General. **Liberal arts:** Arts/sciences. **Math:** General, applied. **Parks/recreation:** Exercise sciences. **Philosophy/religion:** Philosophy, religion. **Physical sciences:** Chemistry, physics. **Protective services:** Criminal justice, forensics. **Psychology:** General. **Social sciences:** Economics, international relations, political science, sociology. **Visual/performing arts:** Dramatic.

Most popular majors. Biology 14%, business/marketing 19%, communications/journalism 6%, health sciences 18%, parks/recreation 7%.

Technology on campus. PC or laptop required. 883 workstations in dormitories, library, computer center, student center. Dormitories wired for high-speed internet access and linked to campus network. Commuter students can connect to campus network. Online course registration, online library, helpline, repair service, student web hosting, wireless network available.

Student life. Freshman orientation: Mandatory, $275 fee. Preregistration for classes offered. Overnight program for students and parents, held between end of June and mid-July. **Policies:** Freshmen not permitted cars on campus. **Housing:** Guaranteed on-campus for all undergraduates. Coed dorms, single-sex dorms, special housing for disabled, apartments, themed housing available. $150 nonrefundable deposit, deadline 5/1. **Activities:** Bands, campus ministries, choral groups, dance, drama, international student organizations, literary magazine, music ensembles, musical theater, radio station, student government, student newspaper, symphony orchestra, TV station, College Democrats, College Republicans, Colleges Against Cancer, Habitat for Humanity, International Club, Move for Those Who Can't, Scripture of Scranton, Students for Life, Sustainability Club, United Colors.

Athletics. NCAA. Intercollegiate: Baseball M, basketball, cross-country, diving, field hockey W, golf M, lacrosse, soccer, softball W, swimming, tennis, volleyball W, wrestling M. **Intramural:** Badminton, basketball, football (non-tackle), racquetball, soccer, softball, ultimate frisbee, volleyball. **Team name:** Royals.

Student services. Adult student services, alcohol/substance abuse counseling, chaplain/spiritual director, career counseling, student employment services, health services, personal counseling, placement for graduates, veterans' counselor. **Physically disabled:** Services for visually, hearing impaired.

Contact. E-mail: admissions@scranton.edu
Phone: (570) 941-7540 Toll-free number: (888) 727-2686
Fax: (570) 941-5928
Joseph Roback, Associate Vice Provost for Admissions and Enrollment, University of Scranton, 800 Linden Street, Scranton, PA 18510-4699

University of the Arts
Philadelphia, Pennsylvania
www.uarts.edu

CB member
CB code: 2664

- Private 4-year visual arts and performing arts college
- Residential campus in very large city
- 1,675 degree-seeking undergraduates: 2% part-time, 60% women, 14% African American, 3% Asian American, 10% Hispanic/Latino, 1% Native Hawaiian/Pacific islander, 5% Multi-racial, non-Hispanic, 5% international
- 164 degree-seeking graduate students
- 74% of applicants admitted
- SAT or ACT (ACT writing optional), application essay required
- 63% graduate within 6 years

General. Founded in 1870. Regionally accredited. Comprehensive arts university (home to the College of Art, Media & Design and the College of Performing Arts). **Degrees:** 385 bachelor's awarded; master's offered. **Calendar:** Semester, limited summer session. **Full-time faculty:** 99 total. **Part-time faculty:** 369 total. **Class size:** 90% < 20, 9% 20-39, less than 1% 40-49, less than 1% 50-99. **Special facilities:** 12 individual gallery spaces, including student-run art gallery, 7 performance venues including a black box theater and a 1874-seat theater, specialized music library, extensive Visual Resource Collection and digital electronic resources, multimedia laboratories, Oxberry animation stand, MIDI and recording studios, analog and digital electronic music studios, music calligraphy laboratory, center for publication arts, industrial design computer-aided product design center.

Freshman class profile. 1,608 applied, 1,185 admitted, 404 enrolled.

Mid 50% test scores			
SAT critical reading:	570-590	GPA 3.0-3.49:	26%
SAT math:	450-570	GPA 2.0-2.99:	52%
SAT writing:	450-580	Return as sophomores:	76%
ACT composite:	19-27	Out-of-state:	65%
GPA 3.75 or higher:	8%	Live on campus:	76%
GPA 3.50-3.74:	10%	International:	4%

Basis for selection. Academic records, art work portfolio, audition very important. SAT or ACT scores considered; no minimum score required. Statement of purpose and letters of recommendation also important; a minimum GPA of 2.0 or better is recommended. Class placement in English composition through SAT/ACT scores. August 15 score deadline for placement, counseling and/or credit. For international students: English proficiency demonstrated by TOEFL (80 ibt), IELTS (6.0), PTE (54), or UArts ESL Institute Completion. Interview recommended for all; audition or portfolio required for performing arts programs; portfolio required for design, visual arts, film programs; essay required for all programs. **Home schooled:** Statement describing home school structure and mission, transcript of courses and grades, state high school equivalency certificate, letter of recommendation (nonparent) required. Interview not required but recommended; GED accepted in lieu of state high school equivalency certificate.

High school preparation. College-preparatory program recommended. Required and recommended units include English 4, mathematics 3, social studies 2, history 2, science 2, foreign language 2 and visual/performing arts 2. Coursework in art, dance, music, creative writing, or theater as appropriate for specific programs recommended.

2015-2016 Annual costs. Tuition/fees: $39,908. Room/board: $14,552. Books/supplies: $1,272. Personal expenses: $1,593.

2015-2016 Financial aid. Need-based: 372 full-time freshmen applied for aid; 334 deemed to have need; 334 received aid. Average need met was 68%. Average scholarship/grant was $24,604; average loan $3,466. 68% of total undergraduate aid awarded as scholarships/grants, 32% as loans/jobs. **Non-need-based:** Awarded to 507 full-time undergraduates, including 131 freshmen. Scholarships awarded for academics, art, music/drama.

Application procedures. Admission: Priority date 3/15; no deadline. $60 fee, may be waived for applicants with need. Admission notification on a rolling basis beginning on or about 11/1. Must reply by May 1 or within 3 week(s) if notified thereafter. **Financial aid:** Priority date 3/1; no closing date. FAFSA required. Applicants notified on a rolling basis starting 2/15; must reply by 5/1 or within 2 week(s) of notification.

Academics. Special study options: Cross-registration, double major, dual enrollment of high school students, ESL, exchange student, honors, independent study, internships, liberal arts/career combination, study abroad, teacher certification program. **Credit/placement by examination:** AP, CLEP, IB, SAT, ACT, institutional tests. Credit by examination counted toward bachelor's degree varies by program. **Support services:** Learning center, pre-admission summer program, reduced course load, remedial instruction, study skills assistance, tutoring, writing center.

Majors. Computer sciences: Web page design. **Visual/performing arts:** Acting, cinematography, crafts, dance, directing/producing, drawing, fiber arts, film/cinema/video, game design, graphic design, illustration, industrial design, metal/jewelry, multimedia, music management, music performance, music theory/composition, musical theater, painting, photography, play/screenwriting, printmaking, sculpture, studio arts, theater design.

Most popular majors. Visual/performing arts 99%.

Technology on campus. PC or laptop required. 400 workstations in library, computer center, student center. Dormitories wired for high-speed internet access and linked to campus network. Commuter students can connect to campus network. Online course registration, online library, helpline, wireless network available.

Student life. Freshman orientation: Available. Preregistration for classes offered. Offers practical skills for being a successful college student-artist. Experience first-hand Philadelphia sights and sounds and get to know fellow classmates and faculty. **Policies:** Campus code of conduct. **Housing:** Coed dorms, apartments available. $200 nonrefundable deposit, deadline 5/1. **Activities:** Jazz band, choral groups, dance, drama, film society, international student organizations, literary magazine, music ensembles, musical theater, student government, student council, GLBTS student union, African Diaspora Collective, improv group, salsa club, UArts literary society, JewArts, Ladies of Service, Latino student union.

Student services. Adult student services, alcohol/substance abuse counseling, career counseling, services for economically disadvantaged, student employment services, financial aid counseling, health services, personal counseling, placement for graduates, veterans' counselor. **Physically disabled:** Services for visually, speech, hearing impaired.

Contact. E-mail: admissions@uarts.edu
Phone: (215) 717-6049 Toll-free number: (800) 616-2787
Fax: (215) 717-6045
Anthony Padilla, Dean of Admissions, University of the Arts, 320 South Broad Street, Philadelphia, PA 19102

University of the Sciences
Philadelphia, Pennsylvania
www.usciences.edu

CB member
CB code: 2663

- Private 4-year health science and pharmacy college
- Residential campus in very large city
- 2,238 degree-seeking undergraduates: 1% part-time, 61% women
- 407 degree-seeking graduate students
- 58% of applicants admitted
- SAT or ACT (ACT writing recommended) required
- 72% graduate within 6 years

General. Founded in 1821. Regionally accredited. **Degrees:** 387 bachelor's awarded; master's, professional, doctoral offered. **ROTC:** Army, Air Force. **Calendar:** Semester, limited summer session. **Full-time faculty:** 201 total; 18% minority, 55% women. **Part-time faculty:** 164 total; 23% minority, 63% women. **Class size:** 52% < 20, 28% 20-39, 3% 40-49, 10% 50-99, 6% >100. **Special facilities:** Marvin Samson Center for the History of Pharmacy; demonstration garden/outdoor classroom; BTE Technologies Advanced Evaluation and Rehabilitation Lab; cognitive neurophysiology laboratory; NMR Facility with two 400 MHz NMR spectrometers and a 90 MHz NMR spectrometer; Surface Analysis Facility with AFM/STM microscope and a spectroscopic ellipsometer; Computational Facility computer simulations and visualization of various chemical and biochemical processes and systems; Chemical Analysis Instrumentation Facility.

Freshman class profile. 3,738 applied, 2,168 admitted, 322 enrolled.

Mid 50% test scores			
SAT critical reading:	510-600	GPA 3.50-3.74:	27%
SAT math:	550-630	GPA 3.0-3.49:	22%
SAT writing:	510-610	GPA 2.0-2.99:	1%
ACT composite:	22-28	Return as sophomores:	90%
GPA 3.75 or higher:	50%	Out-of-state:	57%
		Live on campus:	79%

Basis for selection. High school curriculum, GPA, class rank (if provided by high school), and SAT or ACT test scores are the most important criteria. Essay and/or letters of recommendation not required, but reviewed if provided. **Home schooled:** Transcript of courses and grades, state high school equivalency certificate required.

High school preparation. College-preparatory program required. Required and recommended units include English 4, mathematics 3-4, science 3-4 (laboratory 3-4).

2015-2016 Annual costs. Tuition/fees: $37,466. Room/board: $14,646. Books/supplies: $1,050. Personal expenses: $2,660.

2014-2015 Financial aid. Need-based: 341 full-time freshmen applied for aid; 305 deemed to have need; 305 received aid. Average need met was 42%. Average scholarship/grant was $41,527; average loan $4,339. 79% of total undergraduate aid awarded as scholarships/grants, 21% as loans/jobs. **Non-need-based:** Awarded to 1,504 full-time undergraduates, including 328 freshmen. Scholarships awarded for academics, athletics.

Application procedures. Admission: Priority date 12/1; deadline 8/15 (receipt date). $45 fee, may be waived for applicants with need, free for online applicants. Admission notification on a rolling basis beginning on or about 10/15. Must reply by 5/1. **Financial aid:** Closing date 3/15. FAFSA required. Applicants notified on a rolling basis starting 2/15; must reply by 5/1 or within 2 week(s) of notification.

Academics. Direct-entry admission for freshman pharmacy, DPT and MPT physical therapy program, occupational therapy and physician assistant programs. Students not required to reapply to professional phase of their majors. **Special study options:** Combined bachelor's/graduate degree, cross-registration, double major, honors, independent study, internships, study abroad. **Credit/placement by examination:** AP, CLEP, IB, institutional tests. **Support services:** Learning center, pre-admission summer program, reduced course load, remedial instruction, study skills assistance, tutoring, writing center.

Majors. Biology: General, biochemistry, bioinformatics, microbiology, pharmacology/toxicology. **Business:** Marketing. **Computer sciences:** Computer science. **Conservation:** Environmental science. **Health services:** Clinical lab science, physician assistant. **Parks/recreation:** Exercise sciences, sports admin. **Physical sciences:** Chemistry, physics. **Psychology:** General, medical.

Most popular majors. Biology 14%, health sciences 82%.

Technology on campus. 190 workstations in dormitories, library, computer center, student center. Dormitories wired for high-speed internet access and linked to campus network. Commuter students can connect to campus network. Online course registration, online library, helpline, repair service, wireless network available.

Student life. Freshman orientation: Mandatory. Preregistration for classes offered. Programs for parents and students; placement testing. **Policies:** Campus is alcohol free. Freshmen not permitted cars on campus. **Housing:** Guaranteed on-campus for freshmen. Coed dorms, apartments, fraternity/sorority housing, wellness housing available. $200 nonrefundable deposit, deadline 7/1. Honor halls available. **Activities:** Concert band, choral groups, dance, drama, literary magazine, musical theater, student government, student newspaper, professional organizations, Greek letter organizations, religious groups, honor societies, student community involvement program, ethnic/diversity groups, student chapters of scientific organizations, student publications.

Athletics. NAIA, NCAA. **Intercollegiate:** Baseball M, basketball, cross-country, golf, rifle, softball W, tennis, volleyball W. **Intramural:** Archery, badminton, basketball, bowling, rifle, table tennis, volleyball. **Team name:** Devils.

Student services. Adult student services, alcohol/substance abuse counseling, career counseling, student employment services, financial aid counseling, health services, personal counseling, placement for graduates, veterans' counselor. **Physically disabled:** Services for visually, speech, hearing impaired.

Contact. E-mail: admit@usciences.edu
Phone: (215) 596-8810 Toll-free number: (888) 996-8747
Fax: (215) 596-8821
Dianna Collins, Executive Director of Admission and Enrollment Services, University of the Sciences, 600 South 43rd Street, Philadelphia, PA 19104-4495

University of Valley Forge
Phoenixville, Pennsylvania
www.valleyforge.edu   **CB code: 2579**

- Private 4-year university and liberal arts college affiliated with the Assemblies of God
- Residential campus in large town
- 770 degree-seeking undergraduates: 21% part-time, 52% women, 15% African American, 1% Asian American, 16% Hispanic/Latino, 1% Native American, 4% Multi-racial, non-Hispanic
- 70 degree-seeking graduate students

- 95% of applicants admitted
- Application essay required
- 42% graduate within 6 years

General. Founded in 1938. Regionally accredited. Daily chapel, students provided personal laptops. **Degrees:** 108 bachelor's, 11 associate awarded; master's offered. **Location:** 25 miles from Philadelphia. **Calendar:** Semester, extensive summer session. **Full-time faculty:** 32 total; 59% have terminal degrees, 16% minority, 34% women. **Part-time faculty:** 75 total; 33% have terminal degrees, 23% minority, 39% women. **Class size:** 75% < 20, 19% 20-39, 2% 40-49, 3% 50-99, less than 1% >100.

Freshman class profile. 476 applied, 450 admitted, 180 enrolled.

Mid 50% test scores			
SAT critical reading:	410-540	GPA 2.0-2.99:	35%
SAT math:	380-510	Rank in top quarter:	25%
ACT composite:	18-26	Rank in top tenth:	9%
GPA 3.75 or higher:	19%	Return as sophomores:	57%
GPA 3.50-3.74:	12%	Out-of-state:	67%
GPA 3.0-3.49:	29%	Live on campus:	67%

Basis for selection. School achievement record, written essay, test scores important, required lifestyle statement. SAT or ACT recommended. Test scores not required but strongly encouraged for academic placement and scholarship. **Home schooled:** Statement describing home school structure and mission, transcript of courses and grades required. Student must sign and date a UVF home schooled self-certification form. **Learning Disabled:** Academic recommendation from counselor, IEP, or other.

2015-2016 Annual costs. Tuition/fees: $20,424. Room/board: $8,116. **Additional information:** Cost of $700 for mandatory laptop is included in the required fees.

2015-2016 Financial aid. Need-based: Average need met was 51%. Average scholarship/grant was $10,025; average loan $3,447. 56% of total undergraduate aid awarded as scholarships/grants, 44% as loans/jobs. **Non-need-based:** Scholarships awarded for academics, leadership, music/drama, religious affiliation, state residency.

Application procedures. Admission: Closing date 8/1 (receipt date). $25 fee, may be waived for applicants with need, free for online applicants. Admission notification by 9/1. Admission notification on a rolling basis. **Financial aid:** Priority date 5/1; no closing date. FAFSA required. Applicants notified on a rolling basis starting 3/1.

Academics. Students are academically supported through the Mentored UVF Academic Success Class. **Special study options:** Accelerated study, distance learning, double major, dual enrollment of high school students, honors, independent study, internships, study abroad, teacher certification program. **Credit/placement by examination:** AP, CLEP, IB, SAT, ACT, institutional tests. 15 credit hours maximum toward associate degree, 30 toward bachelor's. **Support services:** Learning center, reduced course load, remedial instruction, study skills assistance, tutoring, writing center.

Majors. Area/ethnic studies: Deaf. **Business:** General, business admin, entrepreneurial studies. **Communications:** Digital media, intercultural. **Education:** Early childhood, elementary, middle, music, secondary. **English:** English lit. **Foreign languages:** Biblical. **Human services:** Social work. **Parks/recreation:** Sports admin. **Protective services:** Criminal justice. **Psychology:** General. **Theology:** Bible, missionary, pastoral counseling, religious ed, sacred music, theology, urban ministry, youth ministry. **Visual/performing arts:** Music performance.

Most popular majors. Business/marketing 6%, communications/journalism 18%, education 15%, psychology 10%, public administration/social services 6%, theological studies 48%.

Technology on campus. PC or laptop required. 64 workstations in library, computer center. Dormitories wired for high-speed internet access and linked to campus network. Commuter students can connect to campus network. Online course registration, online library, helpline, repair service, wireless network available.

Student life. Freshman orientation: Mandatory, $75 fee. Preregistration for classes offered. 3-day program held weekend prior to beginning of classes. **Policies:** Chapel attendance, community lifestyle statement, academic grievance, academic honesty, academic sanctions. Religious observance required. **Housing:** Guaranteed on-campus for all undergraduates. Single-sex dorms, special housing for disabled, apartments available. $100 fully refundable deposit, deadline 8/1. Rooms for the hearing impaired available. **Activities:** Bands, campus ministries, choral groups, dance, drama, international student organizations, music ensembles, radio station, student government, Chosen, Pneuma, Homeless Ministry, Light Children's Ministry, Prison Team, Social Work Club, Audience of One, The Art Of, Frontline, Dry Bones.

Athletics. NCAA, NCCAA. **Intercollegiate:** Baseball M, basketball, cross-country, golf M, soccer, softball W, volleyball W. **Intramural:** Basketball, bowling, football (non-tackle), soccer, softball, ultimate frisbee. **Team name:** Patriots.

Student services. Chaplain/spiritual director, career counseling, student employment services, financial aid counseling, health services, minority student services, personal counseling, placement for graduates. **Physically disabled:** Services for hearing impaired.

Contact. E-mail: admissions@valleyforge.edu
Phone: (610) 935-0450 Toll-free number: (800) 432-8322
Fax: (610) 917-2069
Rev. Joseph Ocasio, Director of Admissions, University of Valley Forge, 1401 Charlestown Road, Phoenixville, PA 19460-2373

Ursinus College
Collegeville, Pennsylvania
www.ursinus.edu

CB member
CB code: 2931

- Private 4-year liberal arts college
- Residential campus in small town
- 1,629 degree-seeking undergraduates: 52% women, 6% African American, 5% Asian American, 6% Hispanic/Latino, 3% Multi-racial, non-Hispanic, 2% international
- 83% of applicants admitted
- Application essay required
- 78% graduate within 6 years; 23% enter graduate study

General. Founded in 1869. Regionally accredited. **Degrees:** 364 bachelor's awarded. **Location:** 28 miles from Philadelphia. **Calendar:** Semester. **Full-time faculty:** 117 total; 91% have terminal degrees, 16% minority, 50% women. **Part-time faculty:** 62 total; 52% have terminal degrees, 10% minority, 56% women. **Class size:** 75% < 20, 24% 20-39, less than 1% 40-49, less than 1% 50-99. **Special facilities:** Performing arts center, art museum, observatory, outdoor sculpture collection.

Freshman class profile. 2,634 applied, 2,176 admitted, 429 enrolled.

Mid 50% test scores			
SAT critical reading:	520-620	GPA 2.0-2.99:	32%
SAT math:	520-630	Rank in top quarter:	53%
SAT writing:	500-610	Rank in top tenth:	25%
ACT composite:	23-30	Return as sophomores:	86%
GPA 3.75 or higher:	13%	Out-of-state:	45%
GPA 3.50-3.74:	15%	Live on campus:	97%
GPA 3.0-3.49:	39%	International:	2%

Basis for selection. Academic achievement, including course rigor and results are most important. Test scores are optional. SAT or ACT recommended. Interview recommended. **Home schooled:** Homeschooled students and students who attend schools that provide narrative comments in lieu of grades are required to submit results from one or more standardized tests (SAT Reasoning Test, SAT Subject Tests, or ACT).

High school preparation. College-preparatory program required. 15 units required; 19 recommended. Required and recommended units include English 4, mathematics 3-4, social studies 4, science 2-4 (laboratory 2) and foreign language 2-3.

2015-2016 Annual costs. Tuition/fees: $47,700. Room/board: $11,900. Books/supplies: $1,000. Personal expenses: $1,572.

2015-2016 Financial aid. Need-based: 388 full-time freshmen applied for aid; 333 deemed to have need; 333 received aid. Average need met was 88%. Average scholarship/grant was $33,250; average loan $3,370. 86% of total undergraduate aid awarded as scholarships/grants, 14% as loans/jobs. **Non-need-based:** Awarded to 610 full-time undergraduates, including 162 freshmen. Scholarships awarded for academics, alumni affiliation, leadership, minority status, music/drama, state residency.

Application procedures. Admission: Priority date 2/1; no deadline. No application fee. Admission notification on a rolling basis. Must reply by May 1 or within 2 week(s) if notified thereafter. **Financial aid:** Closing date 2/15. FAFSA, CSS PROFILE required. Applicants notified by 3/15; must reply by 5/1 or within 2 week(s) of notification.

Academics. Summer undergraduate research fellowships available. Independent Learning Experience required of all. Study abroad encouraged. All first-year students complete overview of human thought, creativity, culture, history in a 2-semester seminar called the Common Intellectual Experience (CIE). **Special study options:** Combined bachelor's/graduate degree, double major, dual enrollment of high school students, exchange student, honors,

independent study, internships, student-designed major, study abroad, teacher certification program, Washington semester. Washington Internship Program, Howard University Semester, combined plan program in engineering at Columbia University and the dual degree program in engineering at Case Western Reserve University. Students may apply for transfer to our affiliate institutions after completing three years of prescribed work toward a B.A. at Ursinus. **Credit/placement by examination:** AP, CLEP, IB, institutional tests. **Support services:** Pre-admission summer program, reduced course load, tutoring, writing center. The Center for Academic Support helps develop strategies for success in college and provides peer tutoring and study sessions.

Majors. Area/ethnic studies: American, East Asian. **Biology:** General, biochemistry, exercise physiology, neuroscience. **Communications:** Communications/speech/rhetoric. **Computer sciences:** Computer science. **Conservation:** Environmental studies. **English:** English lit. **Foreign languages:** French, German, Spanish. **History:** General. **Math:** General. **Philosophy/religion:** Philosophy. **Physical sciences:** Chemistry, physics. **Psychology:** General. **Social sciences:** Applied economics, economics, international relations, political science, sociology/anthropology. **Visual/performing arts:** Art, art history/conservation, dance, dramatic, music history.

Most popular majors. Biology 27%, communications/journalism 9%, psychology 11%, social sciences 20%.

Technology on campus. Dormitories wired for high-speed internet access and linked to campus network. Commuter students can connect to campus network. Online course registration, online library, helpline, repair service, student web hosting, wireless network available.

Student life. Freshman orientation: Mandatory. Preregistration for classes offered. Full day and/or full day with overnight held in June. A 4-day session is held in August before start of classes. **Housing:** Guaranteed on-campus for all undergraduates. Coed dorms, single-sex dorms, special housing for disabled, themed housing, wellness housing available. $500 nonrefundable deposit, deadline 5/1. SPINT, or Special Interest Housing, is an entirely student-run program; students propose and select the house themes, recruit and select future residents, and create their own events. **Activities:** Bands, campus ministries, choral groups, dance, drama, film society, international student organizations, literary magazine, music ensembles, Model UN, radio station, student government, student newspaper, TV station, Association of Latinos Motivated to Achieve, Sankofa Umoja Nia, Hillel, InterVarsity Christian Fellowship, Democrats, UC Republicans, Gender Sexuality Alliance, Best Buddies, Big Brothers Big Sisters, Environmental Action.

Athletics. NCAA. **Intercollegiate:** Baseball M, basketball, cross-country, field hockey W, football (tackle) M, golf, gymnastics W, lacrosse, soccer, softball W, swimming, tennis, track and field, volleyball W, wrestling M. **Intramural:** Badminton, basketball, field hockey, football (non-tackle), sand volleyball, soccer, softball, squash, swimming, tennis, volleyball. **Team name:** Bears.

Student services. Alcohol/substance abuse counseling, chaplain/spiritual director, career counseling, student employment services, financial aid counseling, health services, minority student services, personal counseling, placement for graduates. **Physically disabled:** Services for visually, speech, hearing impaired.

Contact. E-mail: admission@ursinus.edu
Phone: (610) 409-3200 Fax: (610) 409-3197
Dana Matassino, Director of Admission, Ursinus College, PO Box 1000, Collegeville, PA 19426-1000

Villanova University
Villanova, Pennsylvania
www.villanova.edu

CB member
CB code: 2959

- Private 4-year university affiliated with the Roman Catholic Church
- Residential campus in large town
- 7,002 degree-seeking undergraduates: 6% part-time, 53% women, 5% African American, 7% Asian American, 8% Hispanic/Latino, 2% Multi-racial, non-Hispanic, 2% international
- 3,647 degree-seeking graduate students
- 48% of applicants admitted
- SAT or ACT with writing, application essay required
- 90% graduate within 6 years; 17% enter graduate study

General. Founded in 1842. Regionally accredited. **Degrees:** 1,790 bachelor's, 1 associate awarded; master's, professional, doctoral offered. **ROTC:** Army, Naval, Air Force. **Location:** 12 miles from Philadelphia. **Calendar:** Semester, extensive summer session. **Full-time faculty:** 622 total; 88% have terminal degrees, 15% minority, 40% women. **Part-time faculty:** 410 total; 31% have terminal degrees, 7% minority, 46% women. **Class size:** 43%

< 20, 51% 20-39, 3% 40-49, 3% 50-99, less than 1% >100. **Special facilities:** Art studio and multimedia complex, astronomy and astrophysics observatories, electron microscope, structural engineering teaching and research laboratory, nursing simulation labs and applied finance lab.

Freshman class profile. 16,206 applied, 7,761 admitted, 1,700 enrolled.

Mid 50% test scores			
SAT critical reading:	590-690	Rank in top quarter:	87%
SAT math:	610-710	Rank in top tenth:	55%
SAT writing:	590-690	Return as sophomores:	96%
ACT composite:	29-32	Out-of-state:	83%
GPA 3.75 or higher:	66%	Live on campus:	99%
GPA 3.50-3.74:	21%	International:	1%
GPA 3.0-3.49:	12%	Fraternities:	14%
GPA 2.0-2.99:	1%	Sororities:	38%

Basis for selection. High school record, class rank, standardized test scores, counselor recommendation, essay, extracurricular activities considered. November 1 deadline for Honors Program consideration, Early Action and Health Affiliation Program application; December 1 deadline for Presidential Scholarship nomination and Villanova Scholarship consideration. Interview required for finalists of health affiliation programs and Presidential Scholarship consideration. **Home schooled:** Objective third-party evaluation (state high school association, for example), including syllabi, required.

High school preparation. College-preparatory program required. 22 units required; 25 recommended. Required and recommended units include English 4, mathematics 4, science 4 (laboratory 2-3), foreign language 2-4 and academic electives 2. 4 social studies and/or history required. Total units required varies by academic college. 3 laboratory science recommended.

2016-2017 Annual costs. Tuition/fees (projected): $47,766. Room/board: $12,720. Books/supplies: $1,100. Personal expenses: $1,450.

2015-2016 Financial aid. **Need-based:** 1,160 full-time freshmen applied for aid; 868 deemed to have need; 849 received aid. Average need met was 80%. Average scholarship/grant was $31,640; average loan $3,835. 71% of total undergraduate aid awarded as scholarships/grants, 29% as loans/jobs. **Non-need-based:** Awarded to 1,500 full-time undergraduates, including 345 freshmen. Scholarships awarded for academics, alumni affiliation, athletics, leadership, minority status, religious affiliation, ROTC.

Application procedures. **Admission:** Closing date 1/15 (receipt date). $80 fee, may be waived for applicants with need. Application must be submitted online. Admission notification by 4/1. Must reply by 5/1. **Financial aid:** Closing date 2/7. FAFSA, CSS PROFILE required. Applicants notified by 4/1; must reply by 5/1 or within 2 week(s) of notification.

Academics. **Special study options:** Accelerated study, combined bachelor's/graduate degree, cooperative education, cross-registration, distance learning, double major, dual enrollment of high school students, ESL, exchange student, honors, independent study, internships, liberal arts/career combination, study abroad, teacher certification program, Washington semester. **Credit/placement by examination:** AP, CLEP, IB, institutional tests. 30 credit hours maximum toward bachelor's degree. Deans make decisions regarding prior work and life experiences on individual basis. **Support services:** Reduced course load, study skills assistance, tutoring, writing center.

Majors. **Area/ethnic studies:** Latin American, women's. **Biology:** General, biochemistry, neuroscience. **Business:** Accounting, business admin, finance, international, management information systems, managerial economics, marketing, real estate. **Communications:** Media studies. **Computer sciences:** General. **Conservation:** Environmental science, environmental studies. **Education:** Secondary. **Engineering:** Chemical, civil, computer, electrical, mechanical. **English:** English lit. **Foreign languages:** Classics, French, Italian, Spanish. **Health services:** Nursing (RN), predental, premedicine. **History:** General. **Liberal arts:** Arts/sciences, humanities. **Math:** General. **Philosophy/religion:** Islamic, philosophy, religion. **Physical sciences:** General, astronomy, astrophysics, chemistry, physics. **Protective services:** Law enforcement admin. **Psychology:** General. **Social sciences:** Economics, geography, political science, sociology. **Visual/performing arts:** Art history/conservation.

Most popular majors. Business/marketing 33%, communications/journalism 7%, engineering/engineering technologies 11%, health sciences 10%, social sciences 11%.

Technology on campus. PC or laptop required. 1,200 workstations in dormitories, library, computer center, student center. Dormitories wired for high-speed internet access and linked to campus network. Commuter students can connect to campus network. Online course registration, online library, helpline, repair service, student web hosting, wireless network available.

Student life. **Freshman orientation:** Mandatory, $150 fee. Preregistration for classes offered. 4-day on-campus program prior to start of fall term. **Housing:** Guaranteed on-campus for freshmen. Coed dorms, single-sex dorms, special housing for disabled, apartments, themed housing, wellness

housing available. $700 nonrefundable deposit, deadline 5/1. On-campus housing available for transfer students on space-available basis; themed learning communities available. **Activities:** Bands, campus ministries, choral groups, dance, drama, film society, international student organizations, literary magazine, music ensembles, Model UN, musical theater, radio station, student government, student newspaper, symphony orchestra, TV station, Special Olympics, Amnesty International, Villanovans for Life, Black Cultural Society, Big Brother/Sister, Committee for the Homeless, Project Sunshine, Habitat for Humanity, Blue Key Society.

Athletics. NCAA. **Intercollegiate:** Baseball M, basketball, cross-country, diving, field hockey W, football (tackle) M, golf M, lacrosse, rowing (crew) W, soccer, softball W, swimming, tennis, track and field, volleyball W, water polo W. **Intramural:** Basketball, cross-country, football (non-tackle), soccer, softball, tennis, ultimate frisbee, volleyball. **Team name:** Wildcats.

Student services. Adult student services, alcohol/substance abuse counseling, chaplain/spiritual director, career counseling, services for economically disadvantaged, student employment services, financial aid counseling, health services, minority student services, personal counseling, placement for graduates. **Physically disabled:** Services for visually, hearing impaired.

Contact. E-mail: gotovu@villanova.edu
Phone: (610) 519-4000 Fax: (610) 519-6450
Michael Gaynor, Director of University Admission, Villanova University, Austin Hall, 800 Lancaster Avenue, Villanova, PA 19085-1672

Washington & Jefferson College
Washington, Pennsylvania   **CB member**
www.washjeff.edu   **CB code: 2967**

▸ Private 4-year liberal arts college
▸ Residential campus in large town
▸ 1,307 degree-seeking undergraduates: 48% women, 5% African American, 2% Asian American, 4% Hispanic/Latino, 3% Multi-racial, non-Hispanic, 3% international
▸ 43% of applicants admitted
▸ Application essay required
▸ 76% graduate within 6 years; 38% enter graduate study

General. Founded in 1781. Regionally accredited. **Degrees:** 296 bachelor's awarded. **ROTC:** Army, Air Force. **Location:** 27 miles from Pittsburgh. **Calendar:** 4-1-4, limited summer session. **Full-time faculty:** 110 total; 93% have terminal degrees, 16% minority, 50% women. **Part-time faculty:** 44 total; 32% have terminal degrees, 11% minority, 39% women. **Class size:** 66% < 20, 33% 20-39, less than 1% 40-49. **Special facilities:** Microplate reader, cell culture labs, isolator lab, X-ray diffraction unit, neuropsychology lab, atomic absorption unit, nuclear magnetic resonance lab, refrigerated centrifuge, global learning unit, language lab, spectrometers, laser scanning confocal microscope facility, 3-D printers, Abernathy field station, atomic force microscope, fine arts center.

Freshman class profile. 6,835 applied, 2,971 admitted, 389 enrolled.

Mid 50% test scores			
		GPA 2.0-2.99:	7%
SAT critical reading:	520-620	Rank in top quarter:	64%
SAT math:	540-630	Rank in top tenth:	34%
ACT composite:	23-28	End year in good standing:	94%
GPA 3.75 or higher:	48%	Out-of-state:	22%
GPA 3.50-3.74:	25%	Live on campus:	99%
GPA 3.0-3.49:	20%	International:	4%

Basis for selection. Entire high school record including difficulty of schedule, GPA, class rank, extracurricular activities, essay, letters of recommendation important. Interviews required of some students. **Home schooled:** Letter of recommendation (nonparent) required.

High school preparation. College-preparatory program required. 15 units required. Required and recommended units include English 3-4, mathematics 3-4, science 1-2 (laboratory 1-2), foreign language 2-3 and academic electives 6. Six or more academic elective courses from English, math, foreign language, history, and social or natural history required.

2015-2016 Annual costs. Tuition/fees: $43,226. Room/board: $11,406. Books/supplies: $800. Personal expenses: $700.

2015-2016 Financial aid. **Need-based:** 351 full-time freshmen applied for aid; 314 deemed to have need; 314 received aid. Average need met was 78%. Average scholarship/grant was $14,582; average loan $3,496. 76% of total undergraduate aid awarded as scholarships/grants, 24% as loans/jobs. **Non-need-based:** Awarded to 1,177 full-time undergraduates, including 384 freshmen. Scholarships awarded for academics, alumni affiliation, leadership. **Additional information:** Give It Forward Together is a special fund for students whose economic situations change dramatically while they are enrolled at W&J.

Application procedures. Admission: Priority date 1/15; deadline 3/1 (postmark date). $25 fee, may be waived for applicants with need, free for online applicants. Admission notification on a rolling basis beginning on or about 10/1. Must reply by 5/1. **Financial aid:** Priority date 2/15; no closing date. FAFSA required. Applicants notified on a rolling basis starting 3/1; must reply by 5/1.

Academics. The Magellan Project financially supports students who want to do independent research and study either domestically or abroad during the summer. **Special study options:** Accelerated study, combined bachelor's/ graduate degree, double major, dual enrollment of high school students, ESL, honors, independent study, internships, liberal arts/career combination, student-designed major, study abroad, teacher certification program, Washington semester. **Credit/placement by examination:** AP, CLEP, IB, SAT, ACT, institutional tests. 64 credit hours maximum toward bachelor's degree. **Support services:** Learning center, reduced course load, study skills assistance, tutoring.

Majors. Biology: General, biochemistry, biophysics, cellular/anatomical, neuroscience. **Business:** General, accounting, international. **Communications:** General. **Computer sciences:** Information technology. **Conservation:** Environmental studies. **Education:** General, art. **English:** English lit. **Foreign languages:** French, German, Spanish. **History:** General. **Math:** General. **Philosophy/religion:** Philosophy. **Physical sciences:** Chemistry, physics. **Psychology:** General. **Social sciences:** Economics, political science, sociology. **Visual/performing arts:** Art, music.

Most popular majors. Biology 13%, business/marketing 20%, English 7%, foreign language 8%, psychology 12%, social sciences 15%.

Technology on campus. 450 workstations in library, computer center, student center. Dormitories wired for high-speed internet access and linked to campus network. Commuter students can connect to campus network. Online course registration, online library, helpline, repair service, student web hosting, wireless network available.

Student life. Freshman orientation: Mandatory. Preregistration for classes offered. Planned summer events and 3-day series of sessions/activities held at beginning of fall semester. **Policies:** All students required to live in campus housing unless granted written approval or living with parents 15 miles or less from the college. Students not permitted to smoke in rooms, hallways, or lounges. A special dorm is available for students with approved pets. **Housing:** Guaranteed on-campus for all undergraduates. Coed dorms, single-sex dorms, special housing for disabled, apartments, fraternity/sorority housing, themed housing, wellness housing available. Pets allowed in dorm rooms. On-campus suites available. **Activities:** Bands, campus ministries, choral groups, dance, drama, film society, international student organizations, literary magazine, music ensembles, Model UN, musical theater, radio station, student government, student newspaper, Newman club, Hillel Society, Campus Republicans, College Democrats, Black student union, Alpha Phi Omega, Get Involved in Volunteer Experiences, Asian culture association, Gay-Straight Alliance, Indian student association.

Athletics. NCAA. **Intercollegiate:** Baseball M, basketball, cross-country, diving, field hockey W, football (tackle) M, golf, lacrosse, soccer, softball W, swimming, tennis, track and field, volleyball W, water polo, wrestling M. **Intramural:** Basketball, fencing, football (non-tackle), handball, racquetball, soccer, softball, tennis, triathlon, volleyball. **Team name:** Presidents.

Student services. Adult student services, alcohol/substance abuse counseling, chaplain/spiritual director, career counseling, student employment services, financial aid counseling, health services, minority student services, personal counseling, placement for graduates, women's services.

Contact. E-mail: admission@washjeff.edu
Phone: (724) 223-6025 Toll-free number: (888) 926-3529
Fax: (724) 223-6534
Robert Gould, Vice President for Enrollment, Washington & Jefferson College, 60 South Lincoln Street, Washington, PA 15301

Waynesburg University
Waynesburg, Pennsylvania
www.waynesburg.edu

CB member
CB code: 2969

- ◗ Private 4-year liberal arts college affiliated with the Presbyterian Church (USA)
- ◗ Residential campus in small town
- ◗ 1,422 degree-seeking undergraduates: 7% part-time, 60% women, 3% African American, 1% Asian American, 1% Hispanic/Latino, 2% Multiracial, non-Hispanic

- ◗ 439 graduate students
- ◗ 86% of applicants admitted
- ◗ SAT or ACT (ACT writing optional) required
- ◗ 62% graduate within 6 years

General. Founded in 1849. Regionally accredited. Member of the Council for Christian Colleges and Universities. **Degrees:** 382 bachelor's awarded; master's, professional, doctoral offered. **ROTC:** Army. **Location:** 50 miles from Pittsburgh. **Calendar:** Semester, limited summer session. **Full-time faculty:** 80 total; 66% have terminal degrees, 8% minority, 50% women. **Part-time faculty:** 150 total; 25% have terminal degrees, 59% women. **Class size:** 72% < 20, 26% 20-39, less than 1% 40-49, less than 1% 50-99. **Special facilities:** Geological museum, historical museum, constitutional studies and moral leadership center, research and economic development center, service leadership center.

Freshman class profile. 1,418 applied, 1,214 admitted, 356 enrolled.

Mid 50% test scores			
SAT critical reading:	450-550	GPA 3.0-3.49:	25%
SAT math:	460-550	GPA 2.0-2.99:	10%
SAT writing:	420-520	Rank in top quarter:	48%
ACT composite:	20-26	Rank in top tenth:	17%
GPA 3.75 or higher:	44%	Return as sophomores:	80%
GPA 3.50-3.74:	21%	Out-of-state:	21%
		Live on campus:	90%

Basis for selection. High school classes taken, grades, test scores, activities, community activities, interview, recommendations considered. Essay, interview recommended. **Home schooled:** Statement describing home school structure and mission, transcript of courses and grades, state high school equivalency certificate required. University should be apprised if applicant enrolled in program approved by state's department of education.

High school preparation. College-preparatory program required. 16 units required. Required and recommended units include English 4, mathematics 3, social studies 2, science 2-3 (laboratory 2), foreign language 2 and academic electives 5.

2015-2016 Annual costs. Tuition/fees: $22,030. Room/board: $9,170. Books/supplies: $1,500. Personal expenses: $400.

2015-2016 Financial aid. Need-based: Average need met was 81%. Average scholarship/grant was $14,533; average loan $3,997. 70% of total undergraduate aid awarded as scholarships/grants, 30% as loans/jobs. **Non-need-based:** Scholarships awarded for academics, alumni affiliation, job skills, state residency.

Application procedures. Admission: No deadline. $20 fee, may be waived for applicants with need. Admission notification on a rolling basis. Rolling date as specified in deposit letter. **Financial aid:** No deadline. FAFSA required. Applicants notified on a rolling basis starting 2/15; must reply within 2 week(s) of notification.

Academics. Special study options: Accelerated study, combined bachelor's/graduate degree, distance learning, double major, dual enrollment of high school students, honors, independent study, internships, liberal arts/career combination, semester at sea, student-designed major, study abroad, teacher certification program. 3-2 program in engineering with Penn State University in State College, PA and Washington University in St. Louis; 3-1 program in marine biology with Florida Institute of Technology and University of North Carolina, Wilmington. **Credit/placement by examination:** AP, CLEP, SAT, ACT, institutional tests. 15 credit hours maximum toward bachelor's degree. **Support services:** Learning center, reduced course load, study skills assistance, tutoring, writing center.

Majors. Biology: General, environmental, marine. **Business:** Accounting, business admin, finance, international. **Communications:** Advertising, broadcast journalism, communications/speech/rhetoric, digital media, journalism, public relations. **Computer sciences:** General, computer science, information technology, networking. **Education:** Biology, chemistry, elementary, English, history, mathematics, science, secondary, social studies, special ed. **Engineering:** General. **English:** British lit, creative writing, English lit. **Health services:** Athletic training, nursing (RN), predental, premedicine, preveterinary. **History:** General. **Human services:** International policy. **Math:** General. **Parks/recreation:** Exercise sciences, sports admin. **Philosophy/religion:** Religion. **Physical sciences:** Chemistry. **Protective services:** Forensics, law enforcement admin. **Psychology:** General. **Social sciences:** General, political science, sociology. **Visual/performing arts:** Art, studio arts management.

Most popular majors. Biology 7%, business/marketing 16%, communications/journalism 9%, health sciences 29%, psychology 6%, security/protective services 10%.

Technology on campus. 160 workstations in dormitories, library, computer center, student center. Dormitories wired for high-speed internet access and linked to campus network. Commuter students can connect to campus

network. Online course registration, online library, helpline, wireless network available.

Student life. Freshman orientation: Mandatory. Preregistration for classes offered. **Policies:** No alcohol or drugs permitted on campus. **Housing:** Guaranteed on-campus for all undergraduates. Single-sex dorms, special housing for disabled available. $150 partly refundable deposit. **Activities:** Bands, campus ministries, choral groups, dance, drama, literary magazine, music ensembles, musical theater, radio station, student government, student newspaper, TV station, Fellowship of Christian Athletes, Newman Club, Black student union, Waynesburg Christian Fellowship, Bonner Scholars, Alpha Phi Omega, Habitat for Humanity, leadership program.

Athletics. NCAA. Intercollegiate: Baseball M, basketball, cross-country, football (tackle) M, golf, lacrosse W, soccer, softball W, tennis, track and field, volleyball W, wrestling M. **Intramural:** Basketball, bowling, football (non-tackle), racquetball, softball, table tennis, volleyball W. **Team name:** Yellow Jackets.

Student services. Chaplain/spiritual director, career counseling, student employment services, financial aid counseling, health services, minority student services, personal counseling, placement for graduates.

Contact. E-mail: admissions@waynesburg.edu
Phone: (724) 852-3248 Toll-free number: (800) 225-7393
Fax: (724) 627-8124
Jacqueline Palko, Director of Admissions, Waynesburg University, 51 West College Street, Waynesburg, PA 15370-1222

West Chester University of Pennsylvania

West Chester, Pennsylvania	**CB member**
www.wcupa.edu	**CB code: 2659**

- Public 4-year university
- Commuter campus in large town
- 13,956 degree-seeking undergraduates: 9% part-time, 60% women, 11% African American, 2% Asian American, 5% Hispanic/Latino, 3% Multiracial, non-Hispanic
- 2,051 degree-seeking graduate students
- 59% of applicants admitted
- SAT or ACT (ACT writing optional), application essay required
- 71% graduate within 6 years

General. Founded in 1871. Regionally accredited. **Degrees:** 3,383 bachelor's awarded; master's, professional, doctoral offered. **ROTC:** Army, Air Force. **Location:** 25 miles from Philadelphia. **Calendar:** Semester, extensive summer session. **Class size:** 23% < 20, 62% 20-39, 8% 40-49, 6% 50-99, less than 1% >100. **Special facilities:** Radio station, TV station, planetarium, observatory, herbarium, speech and hearing clinic, autism clinic, center for government and community affairs, 151-acre natural area for environmental studies, mineral museum, music library, fully-equipped food preparation laboratory for nutrition and dietetics program, nursing skills laboratory, athletic training rooms, heat illness evaluation avoidance and treatment institute, dance studio, poetry center, outdoor classroom, Microsoft Demonstration and Application Center, campus forest.

Freshman class profile. 12,624 applied, 7,408 admitted, 2,395 enrolled.

Mid 50% test scores		Rank in top quarter:	40%
SAT critical reading:	490-580	Rank in top tenth:	12%
SAT math:	490-580	End year in good standing:	90%
SAT writing:	470-570	Return as sophomores:	88%
ACT composite:	21-26	Out-of-state:	16%
GPA 3.75 or higher:	33%	Live on campus:	92%
GPA 3.50-3.74:	22%	Fraternities:	20%
GPA 3.0-3.49:	34%	Sororities:	23%
GPA 2.0-2.99:	11%		

Basis for selection. College preparatory curriculum in high school, standardized test scores, and personal statement are required and evaluated. Specific course prerequisites depend on major selection. Committee review for special admissions programs and additional documentation is required of candidates for the summer academic development program. SAT or ACT scores are required for all first-time, first-year, degree-seeking applicants unless they have been out of high school for 3 years or more. Interview required for athletic training, premedical, pharmaceutical product development and respiratory care programs. Audition required for music applicants; a portfolio for art applicants. **Home schooled:** Students must submit an official transcript issued by the Pennsylvania Homeschoolers Accreditation Agency (PHAA) or official documentation that their current curriculum has been approved by their state's Board of Education.

High school preparation. College-preparatory program required. 16 units required; 21 recommended. Required and recommended units include English 4, mathematics 3-4, social studies 2, history 2, science 3 (laboratory 2), foreign language 2, computer science 1, visual/performing arts 1 and academic electives 2.

2015-2016 Annual costs. Tuition/fees: $9,462; $20,052 out-of-state. Room/board: $12,780. Books/supplies: $1,200. Personal expenses: $1,600. **Additional information:** Required fees listed are for in-state students; out-of-state students are charged $2,630.

2014-2015 Financial aid. Need-based: 2,119 full-time freshmen applied for aid; 1,530 deemed to have need; 1,530 received aid. Average need met was 40%. Average scholarship/grant was $5,574; average loan $3,450. 26% of total undergraduate aid awarded as scholarships/grants, 74% as loans/jobs. **Non-need-based:** Awarded to 1,447 full-time undergraduates, including 452 freshmen. Scholarships awarded for academics, art, athletics, leadership, music/drama.

Application procedures. Admission: Priority date 2/1; no deadline. $45 fee, may be waived for applicants with need. Admission notification on a rolling basis beginning on or about 10/1. Must reply by May 1 or within 4 week(s) if notified thereafter. **Financial aid:** Priority date 3/1; no closing date. FAFSA required. Applicants notified on a rolling basis starting 4/1; must reply within 4 week(s) of notification.

Academics. Special study options: Accelerated study, cross-registration, distance learning, double major, dual enrollment of high school students, ESL, exchange student, honors, independent study, internships, liberal arts/career combination, student-designed major, study abroad, teacher certification program, Washington semester. **Credit/placement by examination:** AP, CLEP, IB, SAT, ACT, institutional tests. 32 credit hours maximum toward bachelor's degree. **Support services:** Learning center, pre-admission summer program, reduced course load, remedial instruction, study skills assistance, tutoring, writing center. Early Alert Program: a proactive system of communication and collaboration of professors, program staff, academic advisors, and University students. The program works by identifying students, contacting them, and scheduling regular meetings to provide support and referral, as well as improve the retention.

Honors college/program. 40 seats offered each fall. Minimum SAT score of 1200 and at least 2 of the following: Minimum high school GPA of 3.5,Top 20% of graduating class, Record of high school Honors/AP courses. The Honors Seminar Program is geared toward transfer students and WCU students with a minimum of 30 earned credits. Students transferring from other institutions or native WCU students not entering Honors as incoming freshmen may apply for the Honors Seminar Program. Eligibility requires: earned minimum of 30 credits; earned minimum 3.25 cumulative GPA; record of leadership and community service while in college.

Majors. Area/ethnic studies: American, women's. **Biology:** General, biochemistry. **Business:** Accounting, business admin, finance, managerial economics, sales/distribution. **Computer sciences:** General. **Education:** Early childhood, elementary, middle, special ed. **English:** English lit, rhetoric/composition. **Foreign languages:** French, German, Latin, Russian, Spanish. **Health services:** Athletic training, audiology/speech pathology, dietetics, nursing (RN), premedicine. **History:** General. **Human services:** Social work. **Liberal arts:** Arts/sciences. **Math:** General. **Parks/recreation:** Health/fitness. **Philosophy/religion:** Philosophy. **Physical sciences:** Analytical chemistry, chemistry, geology, physics. **Protective services:** Criminal justice. **Psychology:** General. **Social sciences:** Anthropology, geography, political science, sociology. **Visual/performing arts:** Art, dance, dramatic, music, music performance, studio arts.

Most popular majors. Business/marketing 18%, education 13%, English 8%, health sciences 16%, liberal arts 8%, psychology 8%.

Technology on campus. 2,300 workstations in dormitories, library, computer center, student center. Dormitories wired for high-speed internet access and linked to campus network. Commuter students can connect to campus network. Online course registration, online library, helpline, repair service, wireless network available.

Student life. Freshman orientation: Mandatory, $155 fee. Preregistration for classes offered. One-day program in late June/early July followed by 3-day program prior to start of classes in August. Optional personal development and skill building sessions are also offered to first-year students. **Policies:** Code of conduct applicable on and off campus. Freshmen not permitted cars on campus. **Housing:** Coed dorms, special housing for disabled, apartments, gender-neutral housing, themed housing available. $200 nonrefundable deposit, deadline 5/1. **Activities:** Bands, campus ministries, choral groups, dance, drama, film society, international student organizations, literary magazine, music ensembles, Model UN, musical theater, opera, radio station, student government, student newspaper, symphony orchestra, TV station, Crusade for Christ, Hillel Jewish Student Union, College Democrats, College Republicans, Black student union, Latino American student organization, Best Buddies, Habitat for Humanity.

Athletics. NCAA. **Intercollegiate:** Baseball M, basketball, cheerleading W, cross-country, diving, field hockey W, football (tackle) M, golf, gymnastics W, lacrosse W, rugby W, soccer, softball W, swimming, tennis, track and field, volleyball W. **Intramural:** Badminton, basketball, football (non-tackle), racquetball, soccer, softball, squash, table tennis, tennis, volleyball, weight lifting. **Team name:** Golden Rams.

Student services. Adult student services, alcohol/substance abuse counseling, career counseling, services for economically disadvantaged, student employment services, financial aid counseling, health services, legal services, minority student services, personal counseling, placement for graduates, veterans' counselor, women's services. **Physically disabled:** Services for visually, speech, hearing impaired.

Contact. E-mail: ugadmiss@wcupa.edu
Phone: (610) 436-3411 Toll-free number: (877) 315-2165
Fax: (610) 436-2907
Marsha Haug, Director of Admissions, West Chester University of Pennsylvania, Emil H. Messikomer Hall, West Chester, PA 19383

Westminster College

New Wilmington, Pennsylvania	CB member
www.westminster.edu	CB code: 2975

- Private 4-year liberal arts college affiliated with the Presbyterian Church (USA)
- Residential campus in small town
- 1,103 degree-seeking undergraduates: 2% part-time, 56% women, 3% African American, 1% Asian American, 1% Hispanic/Latino, 2% Multiracial, non-Hispanic
- 188 degree-seeking graduate students
- 94% of applicants admitted
- SAT or ACT (ACT writing optional), application essay required
- 71% graduate within 6 years; 21% enter graduate study

General. Founded in 1852. Regionally accredited. **Degrees:** 283 bachelor's awarded; master's offered. **ROTC:** Army. **Location:** 60 miles from Pittsburgh, 90 miles from Cleveland. **Calendar:** Semester, limited summer session. **Full-time faculty:** 93 total; 91% have terminal degrees, 4% minority, 48% women. **Part-time faculty:** 55 total; 20% have terminal degrees, 2% minority, 47% women. **Class size:** 75% < 20, 23% 20-39, less than 1% 40-49, 1% 50-99. **Special facilities:** Observatory, environmental outdoor laboratory, planetarium, electron microscopes, radar defractor.

Freshman class profile. 1,762 applied, 1,657 admitted, 299 enrolled.

Mid 50% test scores		GPA 2.0-2.99:	15%
SAT critical reading:	470-590	Rank in top quarter:	43%
SAT math:	470-480	Rank in top tenth:	24%
SAT writing:	440-560	End year in good standing:	9%
ACT composite:	20-26	Return as sophomores:	79%
GPA 3.75 or higher:	49%	Out-of-state:	29%
GPA 3.50-3.74:	14%	Live on campus:	87%
GPA 3.0-3.49:	22%	International:	1%

Basis for selection. Class rank most important. Test scores also important. Interview recommended for all; audition recommended for music; portfolio recommended for art.

High school preparation. College-preparatory program required. 13 units required. Required units include English 4, mathematics 3, social studies 2, science 2 (laboratory 2) and foreign language 2.

2015-2016 Annual costs. Tuition/fees: $34,105. Room/board: $10,370. Books/supplies: $1,700. Personal expenses: $800.

2014-2015 Financial aid. Need-based: 273 full-time freshmen applied for aid; 255 deemed to have need; 255 received aid. Average need met was 81%. Average scholarship/grant was $24,300; average loan $3,736. 69% of total undergraduate aid awarded as scholarships/grants, 31% as loans/jobs. **Non-need-based:** Awarded to 1,089 full-time undergraduates, including 274 freshmen. Scholarships awarded for academics, alumni affiliation, leadership, minority status, music/drama, religious affiliation, state residency.

Application procedures. Admission: Closing date 5/1 (postmark date). $35 fee, may be waived for applicants with need, free for online applicants. Admission notification on a rolling basis beginning on or about 12/1. Must reply by 5/1. **Financial aid:** Priority date 5/1; no closing date. FAFSA, institutional form required. Applicants notified on a rolling basis starting 3/1; must reply by 5/1 or within 3 week(s) of notification.

Academics. General studies curriculum with a first-year common experience. Semester at London. **Special study options:** Combined bachelor's/

graduate degree, distance learning, double major, dual enrollment of high school students, exchange student, honors, independent study, internships, liberal arts/career combination, semester at sea, student-designed major, study abroad, teacher certification program, Washington semester. 3-2 engineering programs with Case Western Reserve University (OH), Penn State, Washington University (MO); 3-3 law program with Duquesne University; cooperative Master of Occupational Therapy with Duquesne University; cooperative Master of Physical Assistant with Duquesne University; 3-4 dentistry program with Case Western Reserve University (OH); cooperative Doctor of Physical Therapy with Duquesne University; 3-2 Environmental Science program with Duquesne University. **Credit/placement by examination:** AP, CLEP, IB, SAT, ACT, institutional tests. **Support services:** Learning center, reduced course load, study skills assistance, tutoring.

Majors. Biology: General, biochemistry, molecular, neuroscience. **Business:** Accounting, business admin, human resources, international, marketing. **Communications:** General, digital media, public relations. **Computer sciences:** General, computer science, information systems. **Conservation:** Environmental science. **Education:** Elementary. **Engineering:** Applied physics, electrical. **English:** English lit. **Foreign languages:** French, Latin, Spanish. **Health services:** Predental, premedicine, prepharmacy, preveterinary. **History:** General. **Math:** General. **Parks/recreation:** Sports admin. **Philosophy/religion:** Philosophy, religion. **Physical sciences:** Chemistry, physics. **Protective services:** Criminal justice. **Psychology:** General. **Social sciences:** Econometrics, political science, sociology. **Visual/performing arts:** Design, dramatic, music, music performance, studio arts. **Work/family studies:** Family studies.

Most popular majors. Biology 14%, business/marketing 17%, communications/journalism 8%, education 16%, history 6%, psychology 6%, social sciences 12%.

Technology on campus. 160 workstations in library, computer center. Dormitories linked to campus network. Commuter students can connect to campus network. Online course registration, online library, helpline, wireless network available.

Student life. Freshman orientation: Mandatory, $110 fee. Preregistration for classes offered. Three-day general social and academic orientation. **Housing:** Guaranteed on-campus for freshmen. Coed dorms, single-sex dorms, special housing for disabled, apartments, themed housing available. $200 nonrefundable deposit, deadline 5/1. **Activities:** Bands, campus ministries, choral groups, dance, drama, international student organizations, literary magazine, music ensembles, Model UN, musical theater, opera, radio station, student government, student newspaper, symphony orchestra, TV station, Fellowship of Christian Athletes, mock convention, service organizations, social awareness and action groups, Students in Action Who Value the Environment, Habitat for Humanity, Alpha Phi Omega.

Athletics. NCAA. **Intercollegiate:** Baseball M, basketball, cross-country, diving, football (tackle) M, golf, lacrosse M, skiing, soccer, softball W, swimming, tennis, track and field, volleyball W. **Intramural:** Archery, badminton, basketball, cross-country, football (tackle) M, golf, racquetball, softball M, swimming, tennis, track and field W, volleyball W, weight lifting. **Team name:** Titans.

Student services. Adult student services, alcohol/substance abuse counseling, chaplain/spiritual director, career counseling, student employment services, financial aid counseling, health services, minority student services, personal counseling, placement for graduates. **Physically disabled:** Services for visually impaired.

Contact. E-mail: admis@westminster.edu
Phone: (724) 946-7100 Toll-free number: (800) 942-8033
Fax: (724) 946-7171
Thomas Stein, Vice President for Enrollment, Westminster College, Remick Hall, Westminster College, New Wilmington, PA 16172-0001

Widener University

Chester, Pennsylvania	CB member
www.widener.edu	CB code: 2642

- Private 4-year university
- Residential campus in large town
- 3,293 degree-seeking undergraduates: 11% part-time, 55% women, 13% African American, 4% Asian American, 5% Hispanic/Latino, 2% Multiracial, non-Hispanic, 4% international
- 2,565 degree-seeking graduate students
- 68% of applicants admitted
- SAT or ACT (ACT writing optional) required
- 57% graduate within 6 years

General. Founded in 1821. Regionally accredited. **Degrees:** 682 bachelor's awarded; master's, professional, doctoral offered. **ROTC:** Army, Naval, Air Force. **Location:** 10 miles from Philadelphia. **Calendar:** Semester, limited summer session. **Full-time faculty:** 297 total; 90% have terminal degrees, 14% minority, 55% women. **Part-time faculty:** 335 total; 43% have terminal degrees, 10% minority, 50% women. **Class size:** 59% < 20, 39% 20-39, less than 1% 40-49, 1% 50-99. **Special facilities:** Astronomical observatory, restaurant lab, child development center, recording studio, education lab, commercial graphics lab, physical therapy lab, nursing simulation labs.

Freshman class profile. 5,421 applied, 3,686 admitted, 848 enrolled.

Mid 50% test scores		Rank in top quarter:	41%
SAT critical reading:	460-550	Rank in top tenth:	12%
SAT math:	470-570	Return as sophomores:	78%
ACT composite:	21-25	Out-of-state:	47%
GPA 3.75 or higher:	34%	Live on campus:	82%
GPA 3.50-3.74:	21%	International:	3%
GPA 3.0-3.49:	26%	Fraternities:	9%
GPA 2.0-2.99:	19%	Sororities:	8%

Basis for selection. Strength of curriculum, GPA, standardized test scores, class rank most important; recommendations, strength of character important. Interview recommended. **Home schooled:** Transcript of courses and grades required. Curriculum validation and interview with director of admissions required.

High school preparation. College-preparatory program required. 18 units required; 23 recommended. Required and recommended units include English 4, mathematics 3-4, social studies 3-4, science 3-4 (laboratory 2), foreign language 2 and academic electives 3.

2015-2016 Annual costs. Tuition/fees: $41,224. Room/board: $13,092. Books/supplies: $1,200. Personal expenses: $1,188.

2015-2016 Financial aid. Need-based: 829 full-time freshmen applied for aid; 731 deemed to have need; 730 received aid. Average need met was 79%. Average scholarship/grant was $29,270; average loan $3,670. 67% of total undergraduate aid awarded as scholarships/grants, 33% as loans/jobs. **Non-need-based:** Awarded to 2,331 full-time undergraduates, including 800 freshmen. Scholarships awarded for academics, leadership, music/drama, ROTC.

Application procedures. Admission: Priority date 2/15; no deadline. $35 fee, may be waived for applicants with need, free for online applicants. Admission notification on a rolling basis beginning on or about 10/1. Must reply by May 1 or within 2 week(s) if notified thereafter. **Financial aid:** Priority date 2/15; no closing date. FAFSA required. Applicants notified on a rolling basis starting 3/15; must reply within 4 week(s) of notification.

Academics. Special study options: Accelerated study, combined bachelor's/graduate degree, cooperative education, distance learning, double major, dual enrollment of high school students, ESL, honors, independent study, internships, liberal arts/career combination, student-designed major, study abroad, teacher certification program, weekend college. **Credit/placement by examination:** AP, CLEP, IB, institutional tests. Students can earn up to 2 years of credit in some fields via CLEP, challenge exams, and Advanced Placement exams. **Support services:** Learning center, pre-admission summer program, reduced course load, remedial instruction, study skills assistance, tutoring, writing center.

Majors. Area/ethnic studies: Women's. **Biology:** General, biochemistry. **Business:** Accounting, business admin, finance, financial planning, hospitality admin, human resources, international, management information systems, managerial economics, operations. **Communications:** Communications/speech/rhetoric. **Computer sciences:** General, computer science, information systems. **Conservation:** Environmental science. **Education:** Early childhood, elementary, science, special ed. **Engineering:** General, biomedical, chemical, civil, electrical, mechanical. **English:** Creative writing, English lit. **Foreign languages:** General, French, Spanish. **Health services:** Facilities admin, nursing (RN), predental, premedicine, prenursing, preveterinary. **History:** General. **Human services:** Social work. **Liberal arts:** Arts/sciences, humanities. **Math:** General. **Physical sciences:** Chemistry, physics. **Protective services:** Law enforcement admin. **Psychology:** General. **Social sciences:** Anthropology, economics, international relations, political science, sociology. **Visual/performing arts:** Studio arts.

Most popular majors. Business/marketing 19%, engineering/engineering technologies 15%, health sciences 26%, psychology 9%.

Technology on campus. 710 workstations in library, student center. Dormitories wired for high-speed internet access and linked to campus network. Commuter students can connect to campus network. Online course registration, online library, helpline, repair service, student web hosting, wireless network available.

Student life. Freshman orientation: Mandatory. Preregistration for classes offered. **Housing:** Guaranteed on-campus for freshmen. Coed dorms, single-sex dorms, apartments, cooperative housing, fraternity/sorority housing, themed housing, wellness housing available. $100 nonrefundable deposit, deadline 5/1. **Activities:** Bands, campus ministries, choral groups, dance, drama, film society, international student organizations, literary magazine, music ensembles, radio station, student government, TV station, Hillel, black student union, political affairs club, Young Republicans, Young Democrats, environmental society, Widener Big Friends, Crusade for Christ, Alpha Phi Omega, Asian student association, presidential service corps.

Athletics. NCAA. **Intercollegiate:** Baseball M, basketball, cheerleading W, cross-country, field hockey W, football (tackle) M, golf M, lacrosse, soccer, softball W, swimming, track and field, volleyball W. **Intramural:** Basketball, football (non-tackle), skiing, soccer, softball, ultimate frisbee, volleyball. **Team name:** Pride.

Student services. Adult student services, alcohol/substance abuse counseling, chaplain/spiritual director, career counseling, services for economically disadvantaged, student employment services, financial aid counseling, health services, minority student services, on-campus daycare, personal counseling, placement for graduates, veterans' counselor, women's services. **Physically disabled:** Services for visually, speech, hearing impaired.

Contact. E-mail: admissions.office@widener.edu
Phone: (610) 499-4126 Toll-free number: (888) 943-3637
Fax: (610) 499-4676
Robert Britton, Director of Admissions, Widener University, One University Place, Chester, PA 19013

Wilkes University
Wilkes-Barre, Pennsylvania   CB member
www.wilkes.edu   CB code: 2977

- Private 4-year university
- Residential campus in small city
- 2,358 degree-seeking undergraduates: 5% part-time, 47% women, 4% African American, 3% Asian American, 6% Hispanic/Latino, 4% Multiracial, non-Hispanic, 9% international
- 2,632 degree-seeking graduate students
- 82% of applicants admitted
- SAT or ACT required
- 59% graduate within 6 years

General. Founded in 1933. Regionally accredited. **Degrees:** 474 bachelor's awarded; master's, professional, doctoral offered. **ROTC:** Army, Air Force. **Location:** 100 miles from Philadelphia, 140 miles from New York City. **Calendar:** Semester, extensive summer session. **Full-time faculty:** 173 total; 90% have terminal degrees, 13% minority, 46% women. **Part-time faculty:** 170 total; 6% minority, 63% women. **Class size:** 54% < 20, 40% 20-39, less than 1% 40-49, 5% 50-99, less than 1% >100. **Special facilities:** Performing arts center, field station, telecommunications center, indoor recreation and athletic center.

Freshman class profile. 3,164 applied, 2,586 admitted, 584 enrolled.

Mid 50% test scores		Rank in top tenth:	25%
SAT critical reading:	460-580	End year in good standing:	83%
SAT math:	470-600	Return as sophomores:	77%
SAT writing:	440-550	Out-of-state:	19%
ACT composite:	21-26	Live on campus:	77%
Rank in top quarter:	50%	International:	3%

Basis for selection. 920 SAT (exclusive of Writing) and/or rank in top 50% of high school class required for unconditional admission. Conditional admission may be offered to some applicants who do not meet these standards; must attend summer program prior to first semester. Interview recommended for all; audition required for theater arts programs.

High school preparation. College-preparatory program recommended. Recommended units include English 4, mathematics 3, social studies 3, science 2 (laboratory 2) and computer science 1.

2015-2016 Annual costs. Tuition/fees: $32,356. Room/board: $13,266. Books/supplies: $1,500. Personal expenses: $2,000.

2015-2016 Financial aid. Need-based: 551 full-time freshmen applied for aid; 505 deemed to have need; 505 received aid. Average need met was 76%. Average scholarship/grant was $22,578; average loan $4,045. 62% of total undergraduate aid awarded as scholarships/grants, 38% as loans/jobs. **Non-need-based:** Awarded to 1,523 full-time undergraduates, including 453 freshmen. Scholarships awarded for academics, leadership, minority status, music/drama.

Application procedures. Admission: No deadline. $40 fee, may be waived for applicants with need. Admission notification on a rolling basis. Must reply by May 1 or within 2 week(s) if notified thereafter. **Financial aid:** Priority date 3/1; no closing date. FAFSA required. Applicants notified on a rolling basis starting 3/1.

Academics. Special study options: Accelerated study, combined bachelor's/graduate degree, cooperative education, cross-registration, distance learning, double major, dual enrollment of high school students, ESL, external degree, honors, independent study, internships, student-designed major, study abroad, teacher certification program, weekend college. **Credit/placement by examination:** AP, CLEP, institutional tests. Credit by examination may be given to within 30 credits of graduation. **Support services:** Learning center, pre-admission summer program, reduced course load, remedial instruction, study skills assistance, tutoring, writing center.

Majors. Biology: General, biochemistry, neuroscience. **Business:** Accounting, business admin, entrepreneurial studies, finance, marketing. **Communications:** Communications/speech/rhetoric, digital media. **Computer sciences:** General, information systems. **Education:** Elementary, middle, special ed. **Engineering:** Electrical, environmental, mechanical. **English:** English lit. **Foreign languages:** Spanish. **Health services:** Clinical lab science, nursing (RN). **History:** General. **Liberal arts:** Arts/sciences. **Math:** General. **Philosophy/religion:** Philosophy. **Physical sciences:** Chemistry, geology, physics. **Protective services:** Criminal justice. **Psychology:** General. **Social sciences:** International relations, political science, sociology. **Visual/performing arts:** Dramatic.

Most popular majors. Biology 6%, business/marketing 16%, communications/journalism 7%, engineering/engineering technologies 13%, health sciences 14%, liberal arts 15%, psychology 8%.

Technology on campus. 809 workstations in library, computer center, student center. Dormitories wired for high-speed internet access and linked to campus network. Commuter students can connect to campus network. Online course registration, online library, helpline, repair service, wireless network available.

Student life. Freshman orientation: Mandatory, $135 fee. Preregistration for classes offered. **Housing:** Guaranteed on-campus for all undergraduates. Coed dorms, single-sex dorms, apartments available. **Activities:** Bands, campus ministries, choral groups, dance, drama, international student organizations, literary magazine, music ensembles, musical theater, radio station, student government, student newspaper, TV station.

Athletics. NCAA. **Intercollegiate:** Baseball M, basketball, cross-country, field hockey W, football (tackle) M, golf, lacrosse, soccer, softball W, swimming, tennis, volleyball W, wrestling M. **Intramural:** Basketball, bowling, football (non-tackle) M, soccer, softball, volleyball. **Team name:** Colonels.

Student services. Adult student services, career counseling, student employment services, financial aid counseling, health services, personal counseling, placement for graduates, veterans' counselor. **Physically disabled:** Services for visually, hearing impaired.

Contact. E-mail: admissions@wilkes.edu
Phone: (570) 408-4400 Toll-free number: (800) 945-5378
Fax: (570) 408-4904
Melanie Wade, Vice President of Enrollment Services, Wilkes University, 84 West South Street, Wilkes-Barre, PA 18766

Wilson College
Chambersburg, Pennsylvania
www.wilson.edu

CB member
CB code: 2979

- Private 4-year liberal arts college affiliated with the Presbyterian Church (USA)
- Residential campus in large town
- 689 degree-seeking undergraduates
- Application essay required

General. Founded in 1869. Regionally accredited. Undergraduate residential program for single mothers and their children; childcare provided when mother is in classes. **Degrees:** 87 bachelor's, 4 associate awarded; master's offered. **ROTC:** Army. **Location:** 90 miles from Washington, DC; 145 miles from Philadelphia. **Calendar:** Semester, limited summer session. **Special facilities:** Equestrian center with two indoor and one outdoor arenas, barns for horse boarding, equestrian cross country course, center for sustainable living, classics gallery, veterinary medical technology facilities, college archives.

Freshman class profile.

GPA 3.75 or higher:	30%	GPA 2.0-2.99:	15%
GPA 3.50-3.74:	14%	Rank in top quarter:	52%
GPA 3.0-3.49:	41%	Rank in top tenth:	21%

Basis for selection. Each application considered individually for admission. Students should complete a minimum of 15 specific college prep courses in English, history, math, foreign language and natural sciences with labs. SAT/ACT optional for students with 3.0 GPA in specified college prep curriculum from a regionally accredited secondary school. Strong preference for a graded English paper written in 11th or 12th grde. **Home schooled:** Transcript of courses and grades, state high school equivalency certificate, letter of recommendation (nonparent) required. If the state of residence and/or the home school program does not issue a diploma, the student must pursue a GED.

High school preparation. College-preparatory program required. 15 units required. Required units include English 4, mathematics 3, social studies 4, science 2 (laboratory 2) and foreign language 2.

2015-2016 Annual costs. Tuition/fees: $24,392. Room/board: $10,912. Books/supplies: $1,200. Personal expenses: $2,080.

Financial aid. Non-need-based: Scholarships awarded for academics, alumni affiliation, leadership, religious affiliation, state residency.

Application procedures. Admission: Priority date 3/30; deadline 7/31 (receipt date). No application fee. Application must be submitted online. Admission notification on a rolling basis beginning on or about 9/15. Must reply by May 1 or within 2 week(s) if notified thereafter. Deferred admission granted for a maximum of two semesters. **Financial aid:** Priority date 4/30; no closing date. FAFSA, institutional form required. Applicants notified on a rolling basis starting 2/15.

Academics. Special study options: Combined bachelor's/graduate degree, cross-registration, distance learning, double major, dual enrollment of high school students, honors, independent study, internships, liberal arts/career combination, student-designed major, study abroad, teacher certification program, Washington semester. **Credit/placement by examination:** AP, CLEP, IB, SAT, ACT. 12 credit hours maximum toward associate degree, 12 toward bachelor's. **Support services:** Learning center, reduced course load, remedial instruction, study skills assistance, tutoring, writing center.

Majors. Biology: General. **Business:** Accounting, business admin. **Communications:** Media studies. **Conservation:** Environmental science, environmental studies. **Education:** Elementary. **English:** English lit. **Foreign languages:** Spanish. **Health services:** Veterinary technology/assistant. **History:** General. **Math:** General. **Parks/recreation:** Exercise sciences, sports admin. **Philosophy/religion:** Philosophy, religion. **Physical sciences:** Chemistry. **Psychology:** General. **Social sciences:** General, sociology. **Visual/performing arts:** Art.

Technology on campus. 105 workstations in dormitories, library, computer center, student center. Dormitories wired for high-speed internet access and linked to campus network. Commuter students can connect to campus network. Online library, wireless network available.

Student life. Freshman orientation: Mandatory, $285 fee. Preregistration for classes offered. Program held in August prior to arrival of upperclass students. Two days of orientation program are held off-campus. **Policies:** Honor principle, shared governance observed. **Housing:** Guaranteed on-campus for all undergraduates. Coed dorms, single-sex dorms, wellness housing available. $400 nonrefundable deposit, deadline 5/1. Pets allowed in dorm rooms. Single rooms available to all students on a space-available basis. Housing for single mothers with children available. Adult students have on-campus residency options. **Activities:** Campus ministries, choral groups, dance, drama, international student organizations, literary magazine, student government, student newspaper, religious activities committee, language clubs, interfaith support group, Black student union, Curran Scholars, Alternative Spring Break, Agape Christian Fellowship, Habitat for Humanity, Muhibbah International Club, Political Science Association.

Athletics. NCAA. **Intercollegiate:** Basketball, cross-country, field hockey W, golf M, soccer, softball W, volleyball M. **Team name:** Phoenix.

Student services. Adult student services, alcohol/substance abuse counseling, chaplain/spiritual director, career counseling, student employment services, financial aid counseling, health services, on-campus daycare, personal counseling, women's services.

Contact. E-mail: admissions@wilson.edu
Phone: (717) 262-2002 Toll-free number: (800) 421-8402
Fax: (717) 262-2546
Mary Ann Naso, Vice President for Enrollment, Wilson College, 1015 Philadelphia Avenue, Chambersburg, PA 17201-1285

Yeshivath Beth Moshe
Scranton, Pennsylvania

CB code: 1657

‣ Private 4-year rabbinical college for men affiliated with the Jewish faith
‣ Small city
‣ 52 degree-seeking undergraduates

General. Founded in 1965. Accredited by AARTS. First and second Talmudic degrees offered. Ordination available. **Degrees:** 2 bachelor's awarded; master's offered. **Calendar:** Differs by program. **Full-time faculty:** 6 total.

Basis for selection. Open admission.

2015-2016 Annual costs. Tuition/fees: $8,600. Room/board: $3,400.

Application procedures. Admission: No deadline. No application fee. Admission notification on a rolling basis. **Financial aid:** No deadline. Applicants notified on a rolling basis.

Academics. Credit/placement by examination: AP, CLEP.

Majors. Theology: Talmudic.

Student life. Activities: Choral groups, TV station.

Contact. Phone: (717) 346-1747 Fax: (717) 346-2251
Rabbi Chaim Bressler, Admissions Director, Yeshivath Beth Moshe, 930 Hickory Street, Scranton, PA 18505

York College of Pennsylvania
York, Pennsylvania
www.ycp.edu

CB member
CB code: 2991

‣ Private 4-year liberal arts college
‣ Residential campus in small city
‣ 4,421 degree-seeking undergraduates: 8% part-time, 55% women, 5% African American, 2% Asian American, 6% Hispanic/Latino, 4% Multiracial, non-Hispanic
‣ 43 degree-seeking graduate students
‣ 43% of applicants admitted
‣ SAT or ACT (ACT writing optional) required
‣ 57% graduate within 6 years

General. Founded in 1787. Regionally accredited. **Degrees:** 936 bachelor's, 24 associate awarded; master's, professional offered. **Location:** 46 miles from Baltimore, 95 miles from Philadelphia, 30 miles from Harrisburg. **Calendar:** Semester, limited summer session. **Full-time faculty:** 173 total; 89% have terminal degrees, 7% minority, 43% women. **Part-time faculty:** 296 total; 18% have terminal degrees, 2% minority, 53% women. **Class size:** 51% < 20, 47% 20-39, 2% 40-49. **Special facilities:** Engineering innovation center, telecommunications center, rare books collection, oral history room, video production studios, nursing education center, NASDAQ Financial Literacy and Training Laboratory.

Freshman class profile. 13,235 applied, 5,694 admitted, 896 enrolled.

Mid 50% test scores			
SAT critical reading:	470-570	Rank in top quarter:	30%
SAT math:	490-580	Rank in top tenth:	4%
SAT writing:	450-550	End year in good standing:	83%
ACT composite:	20-25	Return as sophomores:	78%
GPA 3.75 or higher:	37%	Out-of-state:	44%
GPA 3.50-3.74:	19%	Live on campus:	79%
GPA 3.0-3.49:	28%	International:	1%
GPA 2.0-2.99:	16%		

Basis for selection. High school record, standardized test results, personal qualities most important. Audition required for all music programs. Portfolio required for art and graphic design majors. **Home schooled:** Statement describing home school structure and mission, transcript of courses and grades, letter of recommendation (nonparent) required. Diploma required from home school association or local school district; portfolio evaluation conducted by certified teacher; syllabus for each course.

High school preparation. College-preparatory program recommended. 15 units required; 16 recommended. Required and recommended units include English 4, mathematics 3-4, social studies 3, science 3 and foreign language 2. Engineering majors require 4 units of math.

2015-2016 Annual costs. Tuition/fees: $18,240. Room/board: $10,160. Books/supplies: $1,200. Personal expenses: $1,000.

2015-2016 Financial aid. Need-based: 824 full-time freshmen applied for aid; 642 deemed to have need; 642 received aid. Average need met was 70%. Average scholarship/grant was $5,219; average loan $6,231. 67% of total undergraduate aid awarded as scholarships/grants, 33% as loans/jobs. **Non-need-based:** Awarded to 3,247 full-time undergraduates, including 883 freshmen. Scholarships awarded for academics, alumni affiliation, minority status, music/drama.

Application procedures. Admission: No deadline. No application fee. Application must be submitted online. Admission notification on a rolling basis beginning on or about 9/15. **Financial aid:** No deadline. FAFSA required. Applicants notified on a rolling basis starting 3/1; must reply within 4 week(s) of notification.

Academics. Special study options: Combined bachelor's/graduate degree, cooperative education, double major, dual enrollment of high school students, honors, independent study, internships, liberal arts/career combination, student-designed major, study abroad. **Credit/placement by examination:** AP, CLEP, IB, SAT, ACT, institutional tests. 30 credit hours maximum toward associate degree, 60 toward bachelor's. **Support services:** Learning center, pre-admission summer program, reduced course load, remedial instruction, study skills assistance, tutoring, writing center. Academic transition coaching, study groups, review sessions, writing fellows program, math mentors program, summer bridge program.

Majors. Biology: General. **Business:** Accounting, business admin, entrepreneurial studies, finance, hospitality admin, logistics, management information systems, management science, marketing. **Communications:** Communications/speech/rhetoric, media studies, public relations. **Communications technology:** Recording arts. **Computer sciences:** Computer science. **Education:** Biology, early childhood, early childhood special, English, junior high special ed, mathematics, middle, music, science, social studies, Spanish. **Engineering:** Computer, electrical, mechanical. **English:** English lit, general lit, technical writing. **Foreign languages:** Spanish. **Health services:** Clinical lab science, nuclear medical technology, nursing (RN), radiologic technology/medical imaging, respiratory therapy technology. **History:** General. **Math:** General. **Military:** "intel, generally". **Parks/recreation:** General, sports admin. **Philosophy/religion:** Philosophy. **Physical sciences:** Chemistry. **Protective services:** Forensics, law enforcement admin. **Psychology:** General. **Social sciences:** Economics, international relations, political science, sociology. **Visual/performing arts:** Commercial/advertising art, dramatic, graphic design, music, studio arts. **Work/family studies:** Family studies.

Most popular majors. Business/marketing 17%, communications/journalism 8%, education 9%, health sciences 15%, parks/recreation 8%, security/protective services 9%.

Technology on campus. 1,117 workstations in dormitories, library, computer center, student center, student center. Dormitories wired for high-speed internet access and linked to campus network. Commuter students can connect to campus network. Online course registration, online library, helpline, wireless network available.

Student life. Freshman orientation: Mandatory. Preregistration for classes offered. One-day program. **Housing:** Guaranteed on-campus for all undergraduates. Coed dorms, special housing for disabled, apartments, fraternity/sorority housing, themed housing available. $200 nonrefundable deposit. **Activities:** Bands, campus ministries, choral groups, dance, drama, international student organizations, literary magazine, music ensembles, Model UN, musical theater, radio station, student government, student newspaper, symphony orchestra, TV station, over 90 student organizations.

Athletics. NCAA. **Intercollegiate:** Baseball M, basketball, cheerleading, cross-country, field hockey W, golf M, lacrosse, soccer, softball W, swimming, tennis, track and field, volleyball W, wrestling M. **Intramural:** Badminton, basketball, football (non-tackle), racquetball, soccer, softball, table tennis, tennis, volleyball. **Team name:** Spartans.

Student services. Adult student services, alcohol/substance abuse counseling, chaplain/spiritual director, career counseling, services for economically disadvantaged, student employment services, financial aid counseling, health services, minority student services, personal counseling, placement for graduates, veterans' counselor. **Physically disabled:** Services for visually, speech, hearing impaired.

Contact. E-mail: admissions@ycp.edu
Phone: (717) 849-1600 Toll-free number: (800) 455-8018
Fax: (717) 849-1672
David Adams, Director of Admissions, York College of Pennsylvania, 441 Country Club Road, York, PA 17403-3651

Puerto Rico

American University of Puerto Rico
Bayamon, Puerto Rico
www.aupr.edu

CB member
CB code: 0961

- Private 4-year university and business college
- Commuter campus in large city
- 1,650 degree-seeking undergraduates: 17% part-time, 49% women
- 107 degree-seeking graduate students

General. Founded in 1963. Regionally accredited. Branch campus at Manati. **Degrees:** 18 bachelor's, 48 associate awarded; master's offered. **ROTC:** Army. **Location:** 12 miles from San Juan. **Calendar:** Trimester, limited summer session. **Full-time faculty:** 53 total. **Part-time faculty:** 120 total. **Special facilities:** Fully computerized classrooms.

Basis for selection. Class rank, GPA important. Interview recommended. **Home schooled:** Transcript of courses and grades, state high school equivalency certificate required.

High school preparation. 18 units recommended. Recommended units include English 3, mathematics 2, social studies 2, history 1, science 2, foreign language 3 and academic electives 5.

2016-2017 Annual costs. Tuition/fees (projected): $7,036. Books/supplies: $800.

2014-2015 Financial aid. All financial aid based on need. 85% of total undergraduate aid awarded as scholarships/grants, 15% as loans/jobs.

Application procedures. Admission: No deadline. $25 fee, may be waived for applicants with need. Admission notification on a rolling basis. **Financial aid:** Priority date 4/30, closing date 5/31. FAFSA, institutional form required. Applicants notified by 6/1; must reply within 2 week(s) of notification.

Academics. Special study options: Honors, independent study, internships, liberal arts/career combination. **Credit/placement by examination:** AP, CLEP, institutional tests. **Support services:** Learning center, reduced course load, tutoring.

Majors. Business: General, accounting, administrative services, business admin, office technology, office/clerical, purchasing. **Communications:** Communications/speech/rhetoric. **Communications technology:** General. **Computer sciences:** Programming. **Education:** General, elementary, ESL, mathematics, physical, secondary, Spanish, special ed. **Protective services:** Criminal justice.

Technology on campus. 75 workstations in computer center.

Student life. Freshman orientation: Mandatory. Preregistration for classes offered. **Activities:** Student government.

Athletics. NCAA. **Intercollegiate:** Basketball, cross-country, swimming, tennis, track and field, volleyball. **Intramural:** Basketball, cross-country, softball M, table tennis, track and field, volleyball. **Team name:** Pirates.

Student services. Career counseling, student employment services, health services, personal counseling, veterans' counselor. **Physically disabled:** Services for speech impaired.

Contact. E-mail: oficinaadmisiones@aupr.edu
Phone: (787) 620-2040 ext. 2020 Fax: (787) 785-7377
Keren Llanos, Director of Admissions, American University of Puerto Rico, PO Box 2037, Bayamon, PR 00960-2037

Atlantic University College
Guaynabo, Puerto Rico
www.atlanticu.edu

CB code: 7137

- Private 4-year liberal arts college
- Commuter campus in small city
- 1,429 undergraduates

General. Founded in 1983. Accredited by ACICS. **Degrees:** 185 bachelor's, 16 associate awarded; master's offered. **Location:** 20 miles from San Juan. **Calendar:** Quarter, extensive summer session. **Full-time faculty:** 26 total. **Special facilities:** Motion caption laboratories, audio laboratories (for study of digital graphic design, computerized animation technology).

Basis for selection. Open admission.

High school preparation. 16 units recommended. Recommended units include English 3, mathematics 2, social studies 1, history 2, science 2, foreign language 3 and academic electives 3.

2015-2016 Annual costs. Books/supplies: $800.

Financial aid. All financial aid based on need.

Application procedures. Admission: No deadline. $30 fee. Admission notification on a rolling basis. **Financial aid:** Closing date 6/30. FAFSA, institutional form required. Applicants notified on a rolling basis starting 4/1; must reply within 2 week(s) of notification.

Academics. Special study options: Combined bachelor's/graduate degree, honors, internships, liberal arts/career combination, student-designed major. **Credit/placement by examination:** AP, CLEP. **Support services:** Learning center, pre-admission summer program, remedial instruction, tutoring.

Majors. Business: Accounting, administrative services, business admin. **Computer sciences:** Security. **Education:** Early childhood special. **Visual/performing arts:** Commercial/advertising art, game design.

Most popular majors. Business/marketing 6%, computer/information sciences 12%, visual/performing arts 74%.

Technology on campus. 16 workstations in library, computer center. Online library, repair service, wireless network available.

Student life. Freshman orientation: Available. Preregistration for classes offered. **Activities:** Dance, drama, student government, student newspaper.

Athletics. Intercollegiate: Basketball. **Intramural:** Basketball, volleyball.

Student services. Alcohol/substance abuse counseling, career counseling, financial aid counseling, health services, personal counseling, placement for graduates. **Physically disabled:** Services for hearing impaired.

Contact. E-mail: contacto@atlanticu.edu
Phone: (787) 720-1022 ext. 1027 Fax: (787) 720-1092
Zaida Perez, Admissions Officer, Atlantic University College, PO Box 3918, Guaynabo, PR 00970

Bayamon Central University
Bayamon, Puerto Rico
www.ucb.edu.pr

CB member
CB code: 0840

- Private 4-year university affiliated with the Roman Catholic Church
- Commuter campus in small city
- 438 degree-seeking undergraduates: 43% part-time, 63% women
- 78 degree-seeking graduate students
- 72% of applicants admitted

General. Founded in 1970. Regionally accredited. Member of consortium of U.S. and South American universities. Virtually all students come from Spanish-speaking backgrounds. **Degrees:** 194 bachelor's, 14 associate awarded; master's, professional offered. **ROTC:** Army, Air Force. **Location:** 9 miles from San Juan. **Calendar:** Semester, limited summer session. **Full-time faculty:** 42 total. **Part-time faculty:** 120 total. **Special facilities:** Centro Estudios de los Dominicos del Caribe (CEDOC).

Freshman class profile. 519 applied, 373 admitted, 179 enrolled.

Basis for selection. School achievement record and test scores most important. Minimum 2.0 high school GPA. Fluency in Spanish, basic knowledge of English necessary. SAT is used or considered if student from another jurisdiction. SAT or ACT accepted from English-speaking students. Score report must be received by 5/15. Essay and portfolio neither required or recommended; interview recommended for those academically weak. **Home schooled:** Transcript of courses and grades required. **Learning Disabled:** Protocol for students with physical or learning disabilities available at the Admission Office and the Counseling and Orientation Office.

High school preparation. 2 units required. Required and recommended units include English 3, mathematics 3, social studies 1, history 2, science 3, computer science 1 and academic electives 6. 3 units of Spanish required.

2015-2016 Annual costs. Books/supplies: $1,504. Personal expenses: $1,350.

Financial aid. All financial aid based on need.

Application procedures. Admission: No deadline. $25 fee, may be waived for applicants with need. Application must be submitted on paper. Admission notification on a rolling basis. **Financial aid:** Priority date 5/31, closing date 7/2. FAFSA, institutional form required. Applicants notified on a rolling basis starting 5/31; must reply within 6 week(s) of notification.

Academics. All classroom instruction conducted in Spanish. Core curriculum includes courses in Spanish. Course in methodology of learning must be satisfactorily completed. **Special study options:** Double major, independent study, teacher certification program. **Credit/placement by examination:** AP, CLEP, IB. **Support services:** Learning center, reduced course load, remedial instruction, tutoring.

Majors. Biology: General. **Business:** General, accounting, administrative services, business admin, finance, human resources, management information systems, management science, marketing. **Communications:** Journalism. **Conservation:** General. **Education:** Early childhood, educational technology, elementary, English, mathematics, physical, science, secondary, Spanish, special ed. **English:** English lit. **Foreign languages:** Spanish. **Health services:** Occupational health. **Human services:** General, social work. **Philosophy/religion:** Philosophy, religion. **Physical sciences:** Chemistry. **Psychology:** General.

Most popular majors. Biology 9%, business/marketing 16%, education 11%, health sciences 35%, public administration/social services 18%.

Technology on campus. 200 workstations in library, computer center, student center. Online library, wireless network available.

Student life. Freshman orientation: Mandatory. Preregistration for classes offered. **Activities:** Drama, student government, student newspaper.

Athletics. Intercollegiate: Basketball, cross-country, swimming, table tennis, track and field, volleyball. **Intramural:** Basketball, track and field, volleyball. **Team name:** Halcones.

Student services. Alcohol/substance abuse counseling, chaplain/spiritual director, career counseling, student employment services, financial aid counseling, health services, on-campus daycare, personal counseling, placement for graduates. **Physically disabled:** Services for visually, speech, hearing impaired.

Contact. E-mail: chernandez@ucb.edu.pr
Phone: (787) 786-3030 ext. 2100 Fax: (787) 740-2200
Cristina Hernandez, Director of Admissions, Bayamon Central University, PO Box 1725, Bayamon, PR 00960-1725

Caribbean University
Bayamon, Puerto Rico
www.caribbean.edu

CB member
CB code: 0779

- Private 4-year university
- Commuter campus in small city
- 3,448 degree-seeking undergraduates: 26% part-time, 57% women, 100% Hispanic/Latino
- 727 degree-seeking graduate students

General. Founded in 1969. Regionally accredited. Additional locations in Carolina, Vega Baja, and Ponce. **Degrees:** 327 bachelor's, 159 associate awarded; master's, doctoral offered. **ROTC:** Army. **Location:** 8 miles from San Juan. **Calendar:** Continuous, limited summer session. **Full-time faculty:** 90 total; 32% have terminal degrees, 100% minority, 47% women. **Part-time faculty:** 314 total; 22% have terminal degrees, 100% minority, 56% women. **Class size:** 67% < 20, 33% 20-39. **Special facilities:** College-operated museum program at Bayamon campus.

Freshman class profile. 1,020 applied, 532 admitted, 499 enrolled.

GPA 3.75 or higher:	5%	GPA 2.0-2.99:	51%
GPA 3.50-3.74:	7%	Return as sophomores:	75%
GPA 3.0-3.49:	22%		

Basis for selection. Open admission, but selective for some programs. Most bachelor's degree programs require at least a minimum of 2.00 GPA. Entrance examination required for Engineering. The university evaluation and admission exam is required only for applicants under age 22. Interview recommended for academically weak. **Home schooled:** State high school equivalency certificate required.

High school preparation. College-preparatory program recommended. 3 units required.

2016-2017 Annual costs. Tuition/fees (projected): $6,180. Books/supplies: $1,210. Personal expenses: $1,903.

Financial aid. All financial aid based on need.

Application procedures. Admission: Closing date 8/30 (receipt date). $30 fee, may be waived for applicants with need. Application must be submitted on paper. Admission notification on a rolling basis. **Financial aid:** Priority date 5/30; no closing date. FAFSA required. Applicants notified on a rolling basis starting 7/30; must reply within 2 week(s) of notification.

Academics. Special study options: Teacher certification program. **Credit/placement by examination:** AP, CLEP. **Support services:** Learning center, remedial instruction, study skills assistance, tutoring.

Majors. Business: General, accounting, business admin, executive assistant, marketing. **Computer sciences:** Programming, systems analysis. **Education:** Elementary, physical, secondary, special ed. **Engineering:** Civil, electrical, industrial. **Health services:** Premedicine, speech-language pathology assistant. **Human services:** Social work. **Protective services:** Police science.

Most popular majors. Business/marketing 10%, education 11%, engineering/engineering technologies 14%, health sciences 39%, public administration/social services 11%, security/protective services 13%.

Technology on campus. Online library, helpline, student web hosting, wireless network available.

Student life. Freshman orientation: Mandatory. Preregistration for classes offered. **Activities:** Choral groups, dance, drama, music ensembles, student government.

Athletics. Intercollegiate: Baseball M, basketball, cheerleading, cross-country, judo, soccer, softball, table tennis M, track and field, volleyball. **Intramural:** Basketball, volleyball. **Team name:** Gryphons.

Student services. Alcohol/substance abuse counseling, career counseling, services for economically disadvantaged, student employment services, financial aid counseling, health services, personal counseling, placement for graduates, veterans' counselor. **Physically disabled:** Services for visually, speech, hearing impaired.

Contact. E-mail: rmorales@caribbean.edu
Phone: (787) 780-0070 ext. 1111 Toll-free number: (888) 780-0070
Fax: (787) 785-0101
Rosalie Morales, Admissions Director, Caribbean University, PO Box 493, Bayamon, PR 00960-0493

Carlos Albizu University: San Juan
San Juan, Puerto Rico
www.albizu.edu

CB code: 2104

- Private two-year upper-division university
- Large town
- Test scores, application essay, interview required

General. Regionally accredited. **Degrees:** 31 bachelor's awarded; master's, professional, doctoral offered. **Calendar:** Semester, limited summer session. **Full-time faculty:** 17 total. **Part-time faculty:** 6 total.

Student profile. 142 undergraduates.

Basis for selection. College transcript, application essay, interview, standardized test scores required. Transfer accepted as sophomores.

2015-2016 Annual costs. Tuition/fees: $5,596. Books/supplies: $2,606. Personal expenses: $3,681.

Application procedures. Admission: $75 fee. Application must be submitted on paper.

Academics. Special study options: Combined bachelor's/graduate degree, distance learning. **Credit/placement by examination:** AP, CLEP.

Majors. Education: Speech impaired. **Health services:** Speech pathology. **Psychology:** General.

Technology on campus. 30 workstations in computer center.

Contact. Phone: (787) 725-6500 ext. 21 Fax: (787) 721-7187
Carlos Rodriguez-Irizarry, Director of Admissions, Carlos Albizu
University: San Juan, 151 Tanca Street, San Juan, PR 00902-3711

Columbia Central University: Caguas
Caguas, Puerto Rico
www.columbiacentral.edu   CB code: 2315

- For-profit 4-year university and branch campus college
- Commuter campus in large city
- 1,535 degree-seeking undergraduates: 100% Hispanic/Latino
- 98 graduate students
- 32% graduate within 6 years

General. Founded in 1966. Regionally accredited. **Degrees:** 242 bachelor's,
297 associate awarded; master's offered. **Location:** 18 miles from San Juan.
Calendar: Continuous, extensive summer session. **Full-time faculty:** 20
total; 15% have terminal degrees, 70% women. **Part-time faculty:** 112 total;
14% have terminal degrees, 62% women.

Freshman class profile. 583 applied, 373 admitted, 372 enrolled.

Basis for selection. Open admission, but selective for some programs.
For nursing program, applicants must have 1.90 GPA. Otherwise, applicants
will be admitted under the educational opportunity program option. Parent
signature and vaccination certificate required for students under age 21.
Home schooled: State high school equivalency certificate required.

High school preparation. 15 units required. Required units include
English 3, mathematics 2, social studies 2, history 2, science 3 and academic
electives 3.

2015-2016 Annual costs. Tuition/fees: $6,290. **Additional information:**
Additional fees may apply.

Financial aid. All financial aid based on need.

Application procedures. Admission: No deadline. $50 fee. Application
must be submitted online. Admission notification on a rolling basis. **Financial
aid:** No deadline. FAFSA, institutional form required.

Academics. Credit/placement by examination: AP, CLEP. **Support services:** Tutoring.

Majors. Business: General. **Computer sciences:** System admin.

Most popular majors. Business/marketing 10%, health sciences 90%.

Technology on campus. 147 workstations in library, computer center.
Online library, wireless network available.

Student life. Freshman orientation: Mandatory. Preregistration for
classes offered.

Student services. Career counseling, student employment services, financial aid counseling, personal counseling, placement for graduates, veterans' counselor.

Contact. E-mail: info@columbiacentral.edu
Phone: (787) 743-4041 ext. 240
Toll-free number: (800) 981-4877 ext. 240 Fax: (787) 744-7031
Veronica Velazquez, Admissions Coordinator, Columbia Central
University: Caguas, PO Box 8517, Caguas, PR 00726-8517

Conservatory of Music of Puerto Rico
San Juan, Puerto Rico
www.cmpr.edu   CB code: 1115

- Public 4-year music college
- Commuter campus in large city
- 411 degree-seeking undergraduates: 32% part-time, 30% women, 96%
  Hispanic/Latino, 4% international
- 43 degree-seeking graduate students
- 75% of applicants admitted
- Interview required
- 38% graduate within 6 years

General. Founded in 1959. Regionally accredited. **Degrees:** 45 bachelor's
awarded; master's offered. **Location:** 13.1 km from Old San Juan. **Calendar:**

Semester, limited summer session. **Full-time faculty:** 53 total; 11% have
terminal degrees, 94% minority, 26% women. **Part-time faculty:** 36 total;
6% have terminal degrees, 92% minority, 25% women. **Class size:** 88%
< 20, 10% 20-39, less than 1% 40-49, 2% 50-99. **Special facilities:** Library
with more than 26,000 musical scores, technology lab (computers applied
to music), recording lab, piano lab, theater.

Freshman class profile. 99 applied, 74 admitted, 70 enrolled.

GPA 3.75 or higher:	50%	End year in good standing:	86%
GPA 3.50-3.74:	22%	Return as sophomores:	80%
GPA 3.0-3.49:	12%	Out-of-state:	1%
GPA 2.0-2.99:	16%	International:	4%

Basis for selection. Musical ability very important. School achievement
record, test scores important. Recommendations considered. Must take
entrance examination in both theory and instrument. SAT accepted from US
mainland applicants. Audition required for music performance. Essays and
interview also required for music education. **Home schooled:** State high
school equivalency certificate required.

High school preparation. College-preparatory program recommended.
Required and recommended units include English 3, mathematics 3, history
3, science 3, foreign language 3 and academic electives 3.

2015-2016 Annual costs. Books/supplies: $1,800. Personal expenses:
$1,250.

2015-2016 Financial aid. All financial aid based on need. Average need
met was 33%. Average scholarship/grant was $5,301; average loan $3,811.
65% of total undergraduate aid awarded as scholarships/grants, 35% as
loans/jobs.

Application procedures. Admission: Closing date 12/19 (receipt date).
$75 fee. Application must be submitted on paper. Admission notification by
4/30. **Financial aid:** Priority date 12/15; no closing date. FAFSA required.
Applicants notified on a rolling basis starting 4/30.

Academics. Special study options: Cross-registration, dual enrollment of
high school students, liberal arts/career combination, teacher certification
program. **Credit/placement by examination:** AP, CLEP, IB, institutional
tests. 12 credit hours maximum toward bachelor's degree. **Support services:**
Learning center, pre-admission summer program, reduced course load, remedial instruction, tutoring.

Majors. Education: Music. **Visual/performing arts:** Brass instruments,
jazz, music performance, music theory/composition, percussion instruments,
piano/keyboard, stringed instruments, voice/opera, woodwind instruments.

Most popular majors. Education 40%, visual/performing arts 60%.

Technology on campus. 17 workstations in library, computer center.
Online library, wireless network available.

Student life. Freshman orientation: Mandatory. Preregistration for
classes offered. **Activities:** Bands, choral groups, music ensembles, opera,
student government, symphony orchestra.

Student services. Career counseling, student employment services, financial aid counseling, personal counseling, placement for graduates.

Contact. E-mail: admisiones@cmpr.edu
Phone: (787) 751-0160 ext. 275 Fax: (787) 764-3581
Ana Arraiza, Admissions Coordinator, Conservatory of Music of Puerto
Rico, 951 Ave. Ponce de Leon, San Juan, PR 00907-3373

EDP University of Puerto Rico: Hato Rey
San Juan, Puerto Rico
www.edpuniversity.edu   CB code: 2243

- For-profit 4-year university
- Commuter campus in very large city
- 1,603 degree-seeking undergraduates: 100% Hispanic/Latino
- 168 graduate students
- 95% of applicants admitted
- Application essay, interview required

General. Founded in 1968. Regionally accredited. **Degrees:** 170 bachelor's,
391 associate awarded; master's offered. **ROTC:** Army. **Calendar:** Semester,
extensive summer session. **Full-time faculty:** 44 total; 7% have terminal
degrees, 100% minority, 61% women. **Part-time faculty:** 1 total; 100% have
terminal degrees, 100% minority. **Class size:** 75% < 20, 23% 20-39, 2%
40-49.

Freshman class profile. 331 applied, 316 admitted, 209 enrolled.

GPA 3.75 or higher:	8%	GPA 2.0-2.99:	52%
GPA 3.50-3.74:	9%	Return as sophomores:	71%
GPA 3.0-3.49:	29%	Out-of-state:	2%

Basis for selection. Interview and 3.0 GPA required for Nursing and Physical Therapy programs. SAT or ACT may be submitted by English-speaking applicants in place of institutional test required for admission and placement. **Home schooled:** Transcript of courses and grades required.

High school preparation. 12 units required. Required units include English 3, mathematics 3, social studies 1, science 2 and foreign language 3.

2015-2016 Annual costs. Books/supplies: $600. Personal expenses: $2,250. **Additional information:** General courses: $156 per-credit. Health courses: $160 per credit. Certificate Degree: $186 per credit. Additional fees may apply.

2014-2015 Financial aid. All financial aid based on need. 91 full-time freshmen applied for aid; 83 deemed to have need; 83 received aid. Average need met was 89%. Average scholarship/grant was $5,366; average loan $3,328. 55% of total undergraduate aid awarded as scholarships/grants, 45% as loans/jobs.

Application procedures. Admission: No deadline. $15 fee. Application must be submitted on paper. Admission notification on a rolling basis beginning on or about 8/1. **Financial aid:** No deadline. FAFSA required. Applicants notified on a rolling basis.

Academics. Special study options: Accelerated study, cooperative education, distance learning, internships, liberal arts/career combination, weekend college. **Credit/placement by examination:** AP, CLEP, institutional tests. 6 credit hours maximum toward associate degree, 90 toward bachelor's. **Support services:** Pre-admission summer program, remedial instruction, tutoring.

Majors. Business: Business admin. **Computer sciences:** Programming, web page design. **Visual/performing arts:** Fashion design, interior design.

Most popular majors. Business/marketing 21%, computer/information sciences 13%, health sciences 59%.

Technology on campus. 45 workstations in library, computer center. Online course registration, online library, helpline, repair service, wireless network available.

Student life. Freshman orientation: Available. Preregistration for classes offered. **Activities:** Literary magazine, student government.

Student services. Adult student services, alcohol/substance abuse counseling, career counseling, student employment services, financial aid counseling, on-campus daycare, personal counseling, placement for graduates, veterans' counselor. **Physically disabled:** Services for visually, hearing impaired.

Contact. Phone: (787) 765-3560 ext. 245 Fax: (787) 777-0025 Dendy Vila, Admissions Director, EDP University of Puerto Rico: Hato Rey, PO Box 192303, Hato Rey, PR 00919-2303

EDP University of Puerto Rico: San Sebastian
San Sebastian, Puerto Rico
www.edpuniverstiy.edu   CB code: 3219

- For-profit 4-year university
- Commuter campus in small city
- 1,112 degree-seeking undergraduates: 31% part-time, 66% women, 100% Hispanic/Latino
- 40 degree-seeking graduate students
- 99% of applicants admitted
- Application essay, interview required

General. Degrees: 79 bachelor's, 223 associate awarded; master's offered. **Location:** 28 miles from Mayaguez. **Calendar:** Semester, extensive summer session.

Freshman class profile. 143 applied, 141 admitted, 141 enrolled.

Basis for selection. 2.5 GPA required for Health Academic Area Programs. Interview required for Physical Therapy Technology. Candidates for admission must take either College Entrance Examination Board tests or placement test offered by institution. **Home schooled:** State high school equivalency certificate required. Seal of the Secondary School which validates

diploma required. **Learning Disabled:** Interview with student doctor, vocational rehabilitation program, or other government agencies required.

High school preparation. 18 units required. Required units include English 3, mathematics 3, history 3, science 3, foreign language 3 and academic electives 3.

2015-2016 Annual costs. Books/supplies: $600. Personal expenses: $2,250. **Additional information:** General courses: $156 per-credit. Health courses: $160 per credit. Certificate Degree: $186 per credit. Additional fees may apply.

2014-2015 Financial aid. All financial aid based on need. 160 full-time freshmen applied for aid; 154 deemed to have need; 154 received aid. Average need met was 96%. Average scholarship/grant was $5,260; average loan $3,013. 64% of total undergraduate aid awarded as scholarships/grants, 36% as loans/jobs.

Application procedures. Admission: No deadline. $15 fee. Application must be submitted on paper. Admission notification on a rolling basis. **Financial aid:** Closing date 6/30. FAFSA required. Applicants notified on a rolling basis.

Academics. Special study options: Accelerated study, cooperative education, distance learning, internships, liberal arts/career combination, weekend college. **Credit/placement by examination:** AP, CLEP, institutional tests. **Support services:** Learning center, remedial instruction, tutoring.

Majors. Business: Administrative services, business admin, office management. **Computer sciences:** General.

Most popular majors. Business/marketing 10%, computer/information sciences 7%, health sciences 79%.

Technology on campus. 176 workstations in library, computer center, student center. Online course registration, online library, helpline, wireless network available.

Student life. Freshman orientation: Available. Preregistration for classes offered.

Athletics. Intercollegiate: Volleyball W. **Team name:** ZORRO, FOX.

Student services. Adult student services, alcohol/substance abuse counseling, career counseling, services for economically disadvantaged, student employment services, financial aid counseling, on-campus daycare, personal counseling, placement for graduates, veterans' counselor.

Contact. E-mail: xrivera@edpuniversity.edu
Phone: (787) 896-2252 ext. 300 Fax: (787) 896-0066
Xiomara Rivera, Director of Admission, EDP University of Puerto Rico: San Sebastian, PO Box 1674, San Sebastian, PR 00685

Escuela de Artes Plasticas de Puerto Rico
San Juan, Puerto Rico
www.eap.edu   CB code: 7036

- Public 4-year visual arts college
- Commuter campus in large city
- 573 degree-seeking undergraduates: 27% part-time, 64% women, 100% Hispanic/Latino
- 85% of applicants admitted
- 39% graduate within 6 years

General. Founded in 1965. Regionally accredited. The EAPD is the only institution in Puerto Rico that offers Bachelor of Fine Arts (BFA) in art, design and art education. It is also accredited by National Association of Schools of Art and Design (NASAD). **Degrees:** 58 bachelor's awarded. **Location:** 12 miles from Carolina and Bayamón. **Calendar:** Semester, limited summer session. **Full-time faculty:** 15 total; 73% have terminal degrees, 100% minority, 33% women. **Part-time faculty:** 62 total; 56% have terminal degrees, 100% minority, 53% women. **Class size:** 89% < 20, 11% 20-39. **Special facilities:** Art gallery and student design center.

Freshman class profile. 123 applied, 105 admitted, 92 enrolled.

GPA 3.75 or higher:	18%	GPA 2.0-2.99:	15%
GPA 3.50-3.74:	20%	End year in good standing:	82%
GPA 3.0-3.49:	47%	Return as sophomores:	86%

Basis for selection. Applicants must satisfy two pre-admission evaluation requirements regarding to artistic skills through portfolio or seminar, and academic achievements. First evaluation consists of committee interview and review of portfolio or seminar outcomes. Second evaluation consists of high school GPA of at least 2.0 and standardized test scores. Candidates that satisfy both evaluation requirements must complete the security seminar. SAT is recommended for U.S. mainland applicants. Applicant can choose between portfolio or seminar. **Home schooled:** An attorney must certify that the student is home schooled.

High school preparation. College-preparatory program required.

2015-2016 Annual costs. Books/supplies: $3,136. Personal expenses: $524.

Financial aid. All financial aid based on need.

Application procedures. Admission: Closing date 5/4 (receipt date). $25 fee. Application must be submitted on paper. Admission notification on a rolling basis beginning on or about 6/1. Must reply by May 1 or within 4 week(s) if notified thereafter. Students must enroll during the semester they are admitted or they will have to apply again. **Financial aid:** Priority date 4/11, closing date 5/18. FAFSA required. Applicants notified by 7/11.

Academics. Special study options: Independent study, internships, liberal arts/career combination, teacher certification program. The students can complete a minor concentration of 18 hour credits in art, design, art education or art history. **Credit/placement by examination:** AP, CLEP, institutional tests. 6 credit hours maximum toward bachelor's degree. **Support services:** Learning center, reduced course load, remedial instruction, study skills assistance.

Majors. Education: Art. **Visual/performing arts:** Digital arts, fashion design, industrial design, painting, printmaking, sculpture.

Most popular majors. Education 10%, visual/performing arts 90%.

Technology on campus. 110 workstations in library, computer center. Wireless network available.

Student life. Freshman orientation: Mandatory. Preregistration for classes offered. Two-days sessions are offered twice during the academic year. **Policies:** Policies in effect regarding drugs and alcohol, academic progress, sexual harassment, security workshops, and handicap issues. **Housing:** Recommended dorms and apartments near campus available. **Activities:** Film society, student government.

Student services. Adult student services, alcohol/substance abuse counseling, career counseling, student employment services, financial aid counseling, personal counseling. **Physically disabled:** Services for visually, speech, hearing impaired.

Contact. E-mail: nmelendez@eap.edu
Phone: (787) 725-8120 ext. 333 Fax: (787) 721-3798
Nitza Meléndez, Officer of Admissions, Escuela de Artes Plasticas de Puerto Rico, PO Box 9021112, San Juan, PR 00902-1112

Inter American University of Puerto Rico: Aguadilla Campus
Aguadilla, Puerto Rico
www.aguadilla.inter.edu   CB code: 2042

- Private 4-year university and liberal arts college
- Commuter campus in small city
- 4,198 degree-seeking undergraduates: 12% part-time, 54% women, 100% Hispanic/Latino
- 289 degree-seeking graduate students
- 53% of applicants admitted
- SAT or ACT with writing required

General. Founded in 1957. Regionally accredited. **Degrees:** 419 bachelor's, 148 associate awarded; master's offered. **ROTC:** Army, Air Force. **Location:** 10 miles from Aguadilla City, 17 miles from Mayaguez. **Calendar:** Semester, extensive summer session. **Full-time faculty:** 79 total; 100% have terminal degrees, 62% women. **Part-time faculty:** 178 total; 100% have terminal degrees, 52% women. **Class size:** 52% < 20, 32% 20-39, 10% 40-49, 6% 50-99. **Special facilities:** Manuel Mendez Bellester literary collection.

Freshman class profile. 1,655 applied, 872 admitted, 855 enrolled.

GPA 3.75 or higher:	13%	GPA 2.0-2.99:	45%
GPA 3.50-3.74:	11%	End year in good standing:	80%
GPA 3.0-3.49:	24%	Return as sophomores:	75%

Basis for selection. Regular program requires 2.0 GPA from accredited secondary school and 800 SAT (exclusive of Writing) or PAA. SAT accepted for English-speaking applicants. School achievement record, test scores very

important. Pilot Program requires 1.75 GPA from accredited secondary school and College Board examination. **Home schooled:** Transcript of courses and grades, state high school equivalency certificate required. Affidavit required.

High school preparation. 18 units required. Required units include English 3, mathematics 2, history 2, science 2, foreign language 3 and academic electives 6.

2015-2016 Annual costs. Books/supplies: $845.

2015-2016 Financial aid. Need-based: 77% of total undergraduate aid awarded as scholarships/grants, 23% as loans/jobs. **Non-need-based:** Scholarships awarded for academics.

Application procedures. Admission: Priority date 5/1; deadline 5/15 (receipt date). No application fee. Admission notification on a rolling basis. **Financial aid:** Closing date 4/30. FAFSA required. Applicants notified by 6/16; must reply by 8/8.

Academics. Special study options: Accelerated study, cross-registration, distance learning, double major, ESL, honors, independent study, internships, study abroad, teacher certification program. Masters ESL. **Credit/placement by examination:** AP, CLEP, SAT, ACT. **Support services:** Learning center, remedial instruction, study skills assistance, tutoring.

Majors. Biology: General, biotechnology, microbiology. **Business:** Accounting, entrepreneurial studies, hotel/motel admin, human resources, management information systems, marketing, office management. **Computer sciences:** Computer science, networking. **Education:** Biology, early childhood special, elementary, ESL, kindergarten/preschool, physical, Spanish. **Health services:** Nursing (RN), radiologic technology/medical imaging. **Human services:** Social work. **Protective services:** Criminal justice, forensics. **Psychology:** General.

Most popular majors. Business/marketing 10%, health sciences 9%, public administration/social services 6%, security/protective services 10%.

Technology on campus. 861 workstations in library, computer center. Commuter students can connect to campus network. Online course registration, online library, wireless network available.

Student life. Freshman orientation: Mandatory. Preregistration for classes offered. One-day program in August. **Policies:** Student regulations in effect. **Activities:** Jazz band, choral groups, drama, music ensembles, student government, student newspaper, Juventud Universitaria Catolica, Asociacion Evangelica Universitaria, Future Teachers Association, criminal justice association, secretarial sciences association, hotel management association, marketing association, Honors Society, Social Work Association.

Athletics. Intercollegiate: Baseball M, basketball, cheerleading, cross-country, judo, soccer, softball, swimming, table tennis, tennis, track and field, volleyball, weight lifting, wrestling M. **Intramural:** Basketball, cross-country, soccer, softball, table tennis, tennis, track and field, volleyball, weight lifting. **Team name:** Tigers.

Student services. Adult student services, alcohol/substance abuse counseling, chaplain/spiritual director, career counseling, student employment services, financial aid counseling, health services, personal counseling, placement for graduates, veterans' counselor. **Physically disabled:** Services for visually, speech, hearing impaired.

Contact. Phone: (787) 891-0925 ext. 2101 Fax: (787) 882-3020
Doris Perez, Director of Admissions, Inter American University of Puerto Rico: Aguadilla Campus, Box 20000, Aguadilla, PR 00605

Inter American University of Puerto Rico: Arecibo Campus
Arecibo, Puerto Rico
www.arecibo.inter.edu   CB code: 1411

- Private 4-year liberal arts college
- Commuter campus in small city
- 4,303 undergraduates

General. Founded in 1957. Regionally accredited. **Degrees:** 451 bachelor's, 123 associate awarded; master's offered. **ROTC:** Army. **Location:** 45 miles from San Juan. **Calendar:** Semester, limited summer session. **Full-time faculty:** 97 total. **Part-time faculty:** 221 total.

Basis for selection. 2.0 GPA required. Test scores important; minimum admission index of 800 required. Special admissions policies apply to adults 21 years or older. SAT required of English-speaking applicants. Score reports by August 3. Interview recommended for academically weak.

High school preparation. 15 units required. Required units include English 3, mathematics 3, social studies 3, science 3 and foreign language 3.

2015-2016 Annual costs. Books/supplies: $890. Personal expenses: $880.

Financial aid. Non-need-based: Scholarships awarded for academics, athletics.

Application procedures. Admission: Priority date 5/1; no deadline. No application fee. Admission notification on a rolling basis. **Financial aid:** Closing date 5/15. FAFSA, institutional form required. Applicants notified on a rolling basis.

Academics. Special study options: Cooperative education, distance learning, honors, independent study, internships, study abroad, teacher certification program. **Credit/placement by examination:** AP, CLEP, institutional tests. 15 credit hours maximum toward associate degree, 15 toward bachelor's. **Support services:** Pre-admission summer program, remedial instruction, study skills assistance, tutoring.

Majors. Biology: General, bacteriology. **Business:** Accounting, administrative services, business admin, management science. **Computer sciences:** General, computer science. **Education:** Biology, chemistry, early childhood, elementary, health, secondary, Spanish, special ed. **Health services:** Nursing (RN). **Human services:** Social work. **Physical sciences:** Chemistry. **Protective services:** Criminal justice. **Psychology:** General.

Technology on campus. 350 workstations in library, computer center. Commuter students can connect to campus network. Helpline, wireless network available.

Student life. Freshman orientation: Mandatory. Preregistration for classes offered. **Activities:** Drama, student government, Baptist Unity, Young Catholics Association, Criminal Justice Association, Haziel Evangelical Association, Future Social Workers Association, Bahai Association, Student Counseling Association, Society for Human Resources.

Athletics. Intercollegiate: Basketball, soccer, softball, table tennis, tennis, track and field, volleyball. **Intramural:** Basketball, cheerleading, soccer, softball, table tennis, tennis, track and field, volleyball. **Team name:** Tigers.

Student services. Adult student services, alcohol/substance abuse counseling, chaplain/spiritual director, career counseling, student employment services, health services, personal counseling, veterans' counselor. **Physically disabled:** Services for visually, hearing impaired.

Contact. E-mail: pmontalvo@arecibo.inter.edu
Phone: (787) 878-5195 Fax: (787) 880-1624
Provi Montalvo, Director of Admissions, Inter American University of Puerto Rico: Arecibo Campus, PO Box 4050, Arecibo, PR 00614-4050

Inter American University of Puerto Rico: Barranquitas Campus
Barranquitas, Puerto Rico
www.br.inter.edu   **CB code: 2067**

- Private 4-year university and branch campus college
- Commuter campus in large town
- 2,073 undergraduates

General. Founded in 1957. Regionally accredited. **Degrees:** 241 bachelor's, 120 associate awarded; master's offered. **Location:** 35 miles from San Juan. **Calendar:** Semester, extensive summer session. **Full-time faculty:** 40 total. **Part-time faculty:** 120 total. **Special facilities:** Nature preserve, 35 e-classrooms.

Basis for selection. 2.0 GPA and minimum PAA or SAT score required. Interview, portfolio, essay recommended. **Home schooled:** Transcript of courses and grades, state high school equivalency certificate required.

High school preparation. 15 units required. Required units include English 3, mathematics 2, social studies 2 and science 3. 3 units of Spanish required for Puerto Rican high school graduates, 2 units liberal arts recommended.

2015-2016 Annual costs. Books/supplies: $900. Personal expenses: $2,731.

Financial aid. All financial aid based on need.

Application procedures. Admission: No deadline. No application fee. Admission notification on a rolling basis. **Financial aid:** Closing date 4/30.

FAFSA required. Applicants notified on a rolling basis; must reply within 2 week(s) of notification.

Academics. Special study options: Accelerated study, combined bachelor's/graduate degree, cross-registration, distance learning, ESL, honors, independent study, internships, liberal arts/career combination, teacher certification program, Washington semester, weekend college. **Credit/placement by examination:** AP, CLEP. **Support services:** Learning center, pre-admission summer program, remedial instruction, study skills assistance, tutoring.

Majors. Biology: General, biotechnology. **Business:** General, accounting, administrative services, business admin. **Computer sciences:** General, computer science, information systems. **Education:** General, biology, early childhood, elementary, English, mathematics, secondary, social studies, Spanish, visually handicapped. **Engineering:** General. **Health services:** Audiology/speech pathology, nursing (RN), radiologic technology/medical imaging. **Protective services:** Law enforcement admin.

Most popular majors. Business/marketing 16%, education 56%, health sciences 8%, social sciences 11%.

Technology on campus. 43 workstations in library, computer center, student center. Commuter students can connect to campus network. Online course registration, online library, helpline, wireless network available.

Student life. Freshman orientation: Mandatory. Preregistration for classes offered. **Activities:** Concert band, dance, drama, literary magazine, musical theater, student government, student newspaper.

Athletics. NAIA. **Intercollegiate:** Baseball M, basketball M, cross-country, softball, tennis, volleyball. **Team name:** Tigers.

Student services. Adult student services, career counseling, personal counseling, veterans' counselor. **Physically disabled:** Services for visually, speech, hearing impaired.

Contact. E-mail: mdiaz@br.inter.edu
Phone: (787) 857-3600 ext. 2011 Fax: (787) 857-2125
Maribel Pena, Director of Admissions, Inter American University of Puerto Rico: Barranquitas Campus, PO Box 517, Barranquitas, PR 00794

Inter American University of Puerto Rico: Bayamon Campus
Bayamon, Puerto Rico
www.bayamon.inter.edu   **CB code: 2043**

- Private 4-year university and engineering college
- Commuter campus in small city
- 4,481 degree-seeking undergraduates: 12% part-time, 43% women, 98% Hispanic/Latino, 1% Native American
- 120 degree-seeking graduate students
- 54% of applicants admitted

General. Founded in 1912. Regionally accredited. **Degrees:** 490 bachelor's, 25 associate awarded; master's offered. **ROTC:** Army, Naval, Air Force. **Location:** 15 miles from San Juan. **Calendar:** Semester, limited summer session. **Full-time faculty:** 92 total; 49% have terminal degrees, 39% women. **Part-time faculty:** 194 total; 17% have terminal degrees, 44% women. **Class size:** 36% < 20, 58% 20-39, 5% 40-49. **Special facilities:** Wetland used as a natural laboratory, mata de platano field station.

Freshman class profile. 1,865 applied, 1,002 admitted, 989 enrolled.

GPA 3.75 or higher:	12%	**GPA 2.0-2.99:**	40%
GPA 3.50-3.74:	11%	**End year in good standing:**	76%
GPA 3.0-3.49:	33%	**Return as sophomores:**	73%

Basis for selection. High school GPA and test scores most important. 2.0 GPA, 800 admission index (based on college formula) required. Achievement tests required for placement in math, English, and Spanish. Interview recommended.

High school preparation. Required units include English 3, mathematics 3, social studies 1, history 2, science 3 and foreign language 3.

2016-2017 Annual costs. Tuition/fees (projected): $6,090. Books/supplies: $845.

2015-2016 Financial aid. All financial aid based on need. Average need met was 5%. Average scholarship/grant was $701; average loan $96. 84% of total undergraduate aid awarded as scholarships/grants, 16% as loans/jobs.

Application procedures. Admission: Closing date 5/1 (receipt date). No application fee. Admission notification on a rolling basis. Must reply by 8/1. **Financial aid:** Priority date 6/30; no closing date. FAFSA required. Applicants notified on a rolling basis starting 5/10.

Academics. Special study options: Accelerated study, cooperative education, distance learning, honors, independent study, internships, study abroad. **Credit/placement by examination:** 225 credit hours maximum toward associate degree, 225 toward bachelor's. **Support services:** Learning center, pre-admission summer program, study skills assistance, tutoring.

Majors. Biology: General, bioinformatics, biotechnology, microbiology. **Business:** Accounting, auditing, entrepreneurial studies, finance, human resources, managerial economics, marketing, office management, operations. **Communications technology:** General. **Computer sciences:** Computer science, information technology, networking. **Conservation:** Environmental science. **Engineering:** Electrical, industrial, mechanical. **Health services:** Nursing (RN). **Math:** General. **Protective services:** Criminalistics, forensics. **Visual/performing arts:** Game design.

Most popular majors. Biology 9%, business/marketing 25%, communication technologies 8%, computer/information sciences 14%, engineering/engineering technologies 15%, health sciences 15%, security/protective services 8%.

Technology on campus. 610 workstations in library, computer center. Dormitories wired for high-speed internet access. Commuter students can connect to campus network. Online course registration, online library, repair service, wireless network available.

Student life. Freshman orientation: Mandatory. Preregistration for classes offered. **Housing:** Coed dorms, wellness housing available. **Activities:** Concert band, choral groups, drama, student council, business administration students association, Catholic students association, Christian University Brotherhood Association, Society of Joined Students for Science, photography club, ANCLA group, senior class association, engineering students association.

Athletics. Intercollegiate: Baseball M, basketball, cross-country, soccer M, softball, swimming, table tennis, tennis, track and field, volleyball, wrestling M. **Intramural:** Basketball, cross-country, softball, swimming, table tennis, tennis, track and field, volleyball, wrestling M. **Team name:** Tigers.

Student services. Adult student services, alcohol/substance abuse counseling, chaplain/spiritual director, career counseling, student employment services, financial aid counseling, health services, personal counseling, veterans' counselor. **Physically disabled:** Services for visually, speech, hearing impaired.

Contact. E-mail: smatos@bayamon.inter.edu
Phone: (787) 279-1912 ext. 2017 Fax: (787) 279-2205
Aurelis Baez, Director of Students Services, Inter American University of Puerto Rico: Bayamon Campus, 500 Dr. John Will Harris Road, Bayamon, PR 00957

High school preparation. 15 units required. Required units include English 3, mathematics 2, social studies 2 and science 3. 3 units Spanish required for Puerto Rican students.

2015-2016 Annual costs. Tuition/fees: $5,876. Books/supplies: $985.

2014-2015 Financial aid. All financial aid based on need. 78% of total undergraduate aid awarded as scholarships/grants, 22% as loans/jobs.

Application procedures. Admission: Closing date 5/15. No application fee. Admission notification on a rolling basis. **Financial aid:** Closing date 4/30. FAFSA required. Applicants notified by 2/1; Applicants notified on a rolling basis; must reply within 2 week(s) of notification.

Academics. Special study options: Cross-registration, distance learning, double major, dual enrollment of high school students, ESL, honors, independent study, internships, teacher certification program, Washington semester. Adult education program. **Credit/placement by examination:** AP, CLEP, institutional tests. 15 credit hours maximum toward bachelor's degree. Maximum 24 credit hours counted for adult education students. **Support services:** Tutoring.

Majors. Business: General, accounting, administrative services, business admin. **Education:** General, biology, early childhood, elementary, ESL, secondary, social studies, Spanish. **Philosophy/religion:** Religion. **Protective services:** Criminal justice.

Most popular majors. Business/marketing 38%, education 9%, legal studies 21%, science technologies 12%, social sciences 11%.

Technology on campus. 190 workstations in library, computer center. Commuter students can connect to campus network. Online course registration, online library, wireless network available.

Student life. Freshman orientation: Mandatory. Preregistration for classes offered. **Activities:** Dance, drama, student government, future teacher club, multilingual club, Christian students club, future social work club, criminal justice club, computer science club, speech and language therapy club, marketing club, accounting club, psychology club.

Athletics. Intramural: Baseball M, basketball, boxing M, cheerleading W, judo M, softball, table tennis, tennis, track and field, volleyball. **Team name:** Tigers.

Student services. Adult student services, chaplain/spiritual director, career counseling, student employment services, financial aid counseling, health services, personal counseling, placement for graduates, veterans' counselor.

Contact. E-mail: ada.caraballo@fajardo.inter.edu
Phone: (787) 860-3100 Fax: (787) 860-3470
Ada Caraballo, Admissions Director, Inter American University of Puerto Rico: Fajardo Campus, Call Box 70003, Fajardo, PR 00738-7003

Inter American University of Puerto Rico: Fajardo Campus
Fajardo, Puerto Rico
www.fajardo.inter.edu   CB code: 2065

♦ Private 4-year university and branch campus college
♦ Commuter campus in large town
♦ 2,226 degree-seeking undergraduates: 15% part-time, 60% women, 100% Hispanic/Latino
♦ 176 degree-seeking graduate students

General. Regionally accredited. **Degrees:** 211 bachelor's, 22 associate awarded; master's offered. **ROTC:** Air Force. **Location:** 34 miles from San Juan. **Calendar:** Semester, limited summer session. **Full-time faculty:** 40 total; 30% have terminal degrees, 60% women. **Part-time faculty:** 65 total; 51% women. **Class size:** 50% < 20, 44% 20-39, 5% 40-49.

Freshman class profile.

GPA 3.75 or higher:	8%	GPA 2.0-2.99:	43%
GPA 3.50-3.74:	16%	End year in good standing:	83%
GPA 3.0-3.49:	31%		

Basis for selection. High school students must have 2.0 GPA and average of 400 on first three parts of PAA. Special admissions policies apply to adults age 21 or older. PAA test required for Spanish-speaking applicants; SAT or ACT required for English-speaking applicants. **Home schooled:** Statement describing home school structure and mission required.

Inter American University of Puerto Rico: Guayama Campus
Guayama, Puerto Rico
www.guayama.inter.edu   CB code: 2077

♦ Private 4-year university
♦ Commuter campus in large town
♦ 1,898 degree-seeking undergraduates: 15% part-time, 66% women, 100% Hispanic/Latino
♦ 110 degree-seeking graduate students
♦ 48% of applicants admitted
♦ Interview required
♦ 31% graduate within 6 years

General. Founded in 1957. Regionally accredited. **Degrees:** 203 bachelor's, 94 associate awarded; master's offered. **ROTC:** Army. **Location:** 18 miles from Ponce. **Calendar:** Semester, limited summer session. **Full-time faculty:** 41 total; 27% have terminal degrees, 54% women. **Part-time faculty:** 140 total; 16% have terminal degrees, 68% women. **Class size:** 50% < 20, 46% 20-39, 3% 40-49, less than 1% 50-99. **Special facilities:** Luis Pales-Matos memorabilia.

Freshman class profile. 614 applied, 293 admitted, 266 enrolled.

GPA 3.75 or higher:	18%	GPA 3.0-3.49:	29%
GPA 3.50-3.74:	14%	GPA 2.0-2.99:	35%

Basis for selection. High school graduates must have 2.0 GPA and 800 admission index.

2015-2016 Annual costs. Tuition/fees: $6,072. Books/supplies: $1,056. Personal expenses: $3,928.

Financial aid. All financial aid based on need.

Application procedures. Admission: Priority date 2/17; no deadline. No application fee. Admission notification on a rolling basis beginning on or about 2/1. **Financial aid:** Closing date 4/29. FAFSA, institutional form required. Applicants notified by 6/15; must reply by 7/30.

Academics. Special study options: Accelerated study, distance learning, dual enrollment of high school students, ESL, exchange student, honors, internships, study abroad, teacher certification program, Washington semester, weekend college. **Credit/placement by examination:** AP, CLEP. **Support services:** Learning center, reduced course load, remedial instruction, tutoring.

Majors. Biology: General, biotechnology. **Business:** Accounting, business admin, human resources, office management. **Education:** Early childhood special, elementary, ESL, kindergarten/preschool, physical. **Health services:** Nursing (RN), respiratory therapy technology. **Protective services:** Law enforcement admin.

Most popular majors. Biology 17%, business/marketing 21%, education 13%, health sciences 33%, security/protective services 10%.

Technology on campus. 232 workstations in library, computer center, student center. Online course registration, online library, helpline, student web hosting, wireless network available.

Student life. Freshman orientation: Mandatory. Preregistration for classes offered. **Activities:** Drama, radio station, student government, CONFRA religious organization.

Athletics. Intercollegiate: Baseball M, basketball, cross-country, swimming M. **Intramural:** Baseball M, basketball, cross-country M, softball, swimming M, table tennis W, tennis W, track and field. **Team name:** Tigers.

Student services. Adult student services, chaplain/spiritual director, career counseling, student employment services, financial aid counseling, health services, personal counseling, placement for graduates, veterans' counselor. **Physically disabled:** Services for visually impaired.

Contact. E-mail: laura.ferrer@guayama.inter.edu
Phone: (787) 864-7059 Fax: (787) 864-8232
Laura Ferrer-Sanchez, Director of Admissions, Inter American University of Puerto Rico: Guayama Campus, PO Box 10004, Guayama, PR 00785

Inter American University of Puerto Rico: Metropolitan Campus

San Juan, Puerto Rico   CB member
www.metro.inter.edu/index.asp   CB code: 0873

- Private 4-year branch campus college
- Commuter campus in large city
- 6,339 degree-seeking undergraduates: 17% part-time, 55% women, 1% African American, 98% Hispanic/Latino
- 2,515 degree-seeking graduate students
- 26% of applicants admitted

General. Founded in 1962. Regionally accredited. **Degrees:** 977 bachelor's, 112 associate awarded; master's, doctoral offered. **ROTC:** Army, Air Force. **Location:** 9 miles from San Juan. **Calendar:** Trimester, limited summer session. **Full-time faculty:** 202 total; 56% have terminal degrees, 56% women. **Part-time faculty:** 380 total; 36% have terminal degrees, 55% women. **Class size:** 66% < 20, 32% 20-39, 1% 40-49, less than 1% 50-99.

Freshman class profile. 2,947 applied, 753 admitted, 717 enrolled.

GPA 3.75 or higher:	10%	GPA 2.0-2.99:	45%
GPA 3.50-3.74:	14%	End year in good standing:	90%
GPA 3.0-3.49:	30%	Return as sophomores:	73%

Basis for selection. School grade average and test scores important. 2.0 GPA plus score average of 400 in SAT. Special admissions policies apply to adults 21 years of age or older. SAT required of English-speaking applicants. **Home schooled:** Statement describing home school structure and mission, state high school equivalency certificate required. In addition to a sworn statement declaring that studies were completed by homeschooling, such students must submit satisfactory College Board test scores (English, Spanish, mathematics).

High school preparation. Required units include English 3, mathematics 3 and science 3.

2015-2016 Financial aid. Need-based: Average need met was 4%. Average scholarship/grant was $594; average loan $150. 78% of total undergraduate aid awarded as scholarships/grants, 22% as loans/jobs.

Application procedures. Admission: Closing date 5/15 (receipt date). No application fee. Admission notification on a rolling basis. Must reply by 8/15. **Financial aid:** Closing date 4/30. FAFSA required. Applicants notified on a rolling basis.

Academics. Adult education programs available. **Special study options:** Accelerated study, distance learning, ESL, honors, independent study, internships, study abroad. **Credit/placement by examination:** AP, CLEP. 12 credit hours maximum toward associate degree, 12 toward bachelor's. Departmental covalidation test. **Support services:** Learning center, pre-admission summer program, remedial instruction, study skills assistance, tutoring, writing center.

Majors. Biology: General, biomedical sciences. **Business:** Accounting, administrative services, business admin, entrepreneurial studies, finance, human resources, management information systems, managerial economics, marketing, office management, office/clerical. **Computer sciences:** General. **Education:** Bilingual, chemistry, elementary, ESL, health, history, mathematics, physical, science, Spanish, special ed. **Foreign languages:** Spanish. **Health services:** Clinical lab science, nursing (RN). **Human services:** Social work. **Math:** General. **Philosophy/religion:** Religion. **Physical sciences:** Chemistry. **Protective services:** Criminal justice, forensics. **Psychology:** General. **Social sciences:** General, political science, sociology. **Theology:** Religious ed. **Visual/performing arts:** Music performance.

Most popular majors. Biology 14%, business/marketing 17%, health sciences 27%, psychology 9%, security/protective services 10%.

Technology on campus. 623 workstations in library, computer center. Commuter students can connect to campus network. Online course registration, online library, helpline, wireless network available.

Student life. Freshman orientation: Mandatory. Preregistration for classes offered. Held 2 weeks before regular classes begin. **Activities:** Jazz band, choral groups, drama, international student organizations, music ensembles, student government, student newspaper, intercultural student association, Club ROTARACT, social work students association, criminal justice club, biological science club, biomedical students association, psychology student association, association of Latino Professional for America (ALFA), professional counseling student association, renew(ed) Christian association.

Athletics. Intercollegiate: Baseball M, basketball, judo M, softball, swimming, tennis, track and field, volleyball. **Intramural:** Basketball, softball, table tennis, tennis, volleyball. **Team name:** Tigres.

Student services. Adult student services, alcohol/substance abuse counseling, chaplain/spiritual director, career counseling, student employment services, financial aid counseling, health services, on-campus daycare, personal counseling, placement for graduates, veterans' counselor. **Physically disabled:** Services for visually, speech, hearing impaired.

Contact. E-mail: jolivieri@metro.inter.edu
Phone: (787) 250-1912 ext. 2188 Fax: (787) 763-1464
Janies Olivieri, Admissions Officer, Inter American University of Puerto Rico: Metropolitan Campus, Box 191293, San Juan, PR 00919-1293

Inter American University of Puerto Rico: Ponce Campus

Mercedita, Puerto Rico
ponce.inter.edu   CB code: 3531

- Private 4-year university
- Large town
- 5,011 degree-seeking undergraduates: 13% part-time, 59% women, 100% Hispanic/Latino
- 407 degree-seeking graduate students
- 53% of applicants admitted

General. Regionally accredited. **Degrees:** 554 bachelor's, 174 associate awarded; master's offered. **ROTC:** Naval. **Calendar:** Semester, limited summer session. **Full-time faculty:** 99 total; 50% have terminal degrees, 60% women. **Part-time faculty:** 207 total; 21% have terminal degrees, 55% women. **Class size:** 30% < 20, 58% 20-39, 10% 40-49, 2% 50-99.

Freshman class profile. 1,822 applied, 957 admitted, 916 enrolled.

GPA 3.75 or higher:	14%	GPA 2.0-2.99:	40%
GPA 3.50-3.74:	13%	End year in good standing:	87%
GPA 3.0-3.49:	30%	Return as sophomores:	76%

Basis for selection. 2.0 GPA and average of 4.0 on first three parts of PAA required. Interview is required for AVANCE program and some of the Health Sciences programs.

High school preparation. 18 units required. Required units include English 3, mathematics 3, social studies 1, history 3, science 3 (laboratory 1), foreign language 3 and academic electives 1.

2015-2016 Annual costs. Tuition/fees: $6,030. Books/supplies: $845. Personal expenses: $4,284.

2015-2016 Financial aid. All financial aid based on need. Average need met was 2%. Average scholarship/grant was $262; average loan $224. 87% of total undergraduate aid awarded as scholarships/grants, 13% as loans/jobs.

Application procedures. Admission: Closing date 5/15 (receipt date). No application fee. Admission notification on a rolling basis. **Financial aid:** No deadline. FAFSA required.

Academics. A special schedule is planned for the first year students. Registration and academic counseling is completed by the counseling center. **Special study options:** Distance learning, honors, internships, study abroad, teacher certification program. Adult programs (AVANCE), programa normativo (for first year students that do not meet admission's requirements; fast track admission for students with 3.0 or more GPA average). **Credit/placement by examination:** AP, CLEP. **Support services:** Learning center, study skills assistance, tutoring.

Majors. Biology: General, biomedical sciences, biotechnology, microbiology. **Business:** Accounting, administrative services, business admin, finance, hotel/motel admin, human resources, management science, marketing, office technology, operations. **Communications:** Public relations. **Computer sciences:** Computer science, system admin. **Conservation:** General. **Education:** Biology, early childhood, elementary, ESL, secondary, special ed. **Health services:** Nursing (RN), speech pathology. **Protective services:** Forensics, law enforcement admin. **Psychology:** General. **Social sciences:** Criminology.

Most popular majors. Biology 8%, business/marketing 31%, education 7%, health sciences 21%, security/protective services 22%.

Technology on campus. PC or laptop required. 983 workstations in library, computer center, student center. Commuter students can connect to campus network. Online course registration, online library, helpline available.

Student life. Freshman orientation: Mandatory. Preregistration for classes offered. Includes workshops, seminars, and social activities. **Activities:** Concert band, campus ministries, choral groups, dance, drama, student government, student newspaper, Juventud Cristiana Viva, Asociación Católica Estudiantil, Organización de Líderes Profesionales, Organización de Estudiantes Orientadores Universitarios, Asociación de Estudiantes Pro-agricultura Orgánica Sustentable.

Athletics. Intercollegiate: Baseball M, basketball, cross-country, judo, soccer, softball, swimming, table tennis, tennis, track and field, volleyball, weight lifting, wrestling. **Intramural:** Basketball, cross-country, soccer, softball, table tennis, tennis, track and field, volleyball, weight lifting. **Team name:** Tigers.

Student services. Adult student services, alcohol/substance abuse counseling, chaplain/spiritual director, career counseling, services for economically disadvantaged, student employment services, financial aid counseling, health services, personal counseling, placement for graduates, veterans' counselor. **Physically disabled:** Services for visually, speech, hearing impaired.

Contact. E-mail: fldiaz@poce.inter.edu
Phone: (787) 841-0110 Fax: (787) 841-0102
Franco Diaz Vega, Director of Admissions, Inter American University of Puerto Rico: Ponce Campus, 104 Turpo Industrial Park, Mercedita, PR 00715-1602

Inter American University of Puerto Rico: San German Campus
San German, Puerto Rico
www.sg.inter.edu   CB code: 0946

- Private 4-year university
- Commuter campus in large town

- 4,243 degree-seeking undergraduates: 10% part-time, 52% women, 99% Hispanic/Latino
- 707 degree-seeking graduate students
- 64% of applicants admitted
- 34% graduate within 6 years; 2% enter graduate study

General. Founded in 1912. Regionally accredited. San Germán Inter American School (PK-12) is integrated with the university. **Degrees:** 467 bachelor's, 56 associate awarded; master's, doctoral offered. **ROTC:** Army, Air Force. **Location:** 14 miles from Mayaguez, 104 miles from San Juan. **Calendar:** Semester, extensive summer session. **Full-time faculty:** 109 total; 56% have terminal degrees, 55% women. **Part-time faculty:** 182 total; 25% have terminal degrees, 61% women. **Class size:** 55% < 20, 43% 20-39, 2% 40-49. **Special facilities:** Nature preserve, museums, day care.

Freshman class profile. 1,586 applied, 1,018 admitted, 960 enrolled.

GPA 3.75 or higher:	13%	GPA 2.0-2.99:	43%
GPA 3.50-3.74:	14%	End year in good standing:	83%
GPA 3.0-3.49:	25%	Return as sophomores:	79%

Basis for selection. High school GPA and test scores important. SAT or ACT recommended. SAT required of English-speaking applicants. Essay, interview recommended for all; audition recommended for music; portfolio recommended for art programs. **Home schooled:** Statement describing home school structure and mission, transcript of courses and grades, state high school equivalency certificate required.

High school preparation. 11 units required; 18 recommended. Required and recommended units include English 3, mathematics 2-3, social studies 2-3, history 2-3, science 2-3, foreign language 3 and academic electives 3. 3 units of Spanish required of Spanish-speaking students.

2015-2016 Annual costs. Tuition/fees: $6,030. Room/board: $2,700. Books/supplies: $845. Personal expenses: $4,284.

2014-2015 Financial aid. Need-based: 1,011 full-time freshmen applied for aid; 996 deemed to have need; 627 received aid. Average need met was 3%. Average scholarship/grant was $201; average loan $245. 80% of total undergraduate aid awarded as scholarships/grants, 20% as loans/jobs. **Non-need-based:** Awarded to 119 full-time undergraduates, including 30 freshmen. Scholarships awarded for academics, athletics.

Application procedures. Admission: Closing date 5/16 (receipt date). No application fee. Admission notification on a rolling basis beginning on or about 2/15. **Financial aid:** Closing date 5/14. FAFSA, institutional form required. Applicants notified on a rolling basis; must reply by 8/1.

Academics. Bilingual program enables students to learn English or Spanish while taking courses in their native language. **Special study options:** Accelerated study, cooperative education, cross-registration, distance learning, double major, dual enrollment of high school students, ESL, honors, independent study, internships, liberal arts/career combination, study abroad, teacher certification program, weekend college. **Credit/placement by examination:** AP, CLEP, institutional tests. 12 credit hours maximum toward associate degree, 18 toward bachelor's. **Support services:** Learning center, reduced course load, remedial instruction, tutoring.

Majors. Biology: General, microbiology. **Business:** Accounting, business admin, entrepreneurial studies, finance, human resources, management information systems, marketing, office management. **Computer sciences:** Computer science. **Education:** Art, biology, chemistry, early childhood, elementary, English, ESL, health, history, kindergarten/preschool, mathematics, music, physical, science, secondary, social studies, Spanish, special ed. **Engineering:** Pre-engineering. **English:** English lit. **Health services:** Clinical lab science, nursing (RN), radiologic technology/medical imaging. **Math:** General. **Parks/recreation:** Health/fitness. **Physical sciences:** Chemistry. **Protective services:** Law enforcement admin. **Psychology:** General. **Social sciences:** Anthropology, political science, sociology. **Visual/performing arts:** General, music.

Most popular majors. Biology 25%, business/marketing 18%, engineering/engineering technologies 13%, health sciences 16%, parks/recreation 6%, psychology 8%, visual/performing arts 7%.

Technology on campus. 975 workstations in dormitories, library, computer center, student center. Dormitories wired for high-speed internet access and linked to campus network. Commuter students can connect to campus network. Online course registration, online library, wireless network available.

Student life. Freshman orientation: Mandatory. Preregistration for classes offered. General orientation program offered in spring, summer, and fall. **Housing:** Guaranteed on-campus for all undergraduates. Single-sex dorms, apartments, wellness housing available. $25 fully refundable deposit, deadline 6/30. **Activities:** Bands, choral groups, dance, drama, international student organizations, music ensembles, student government, student newspaper, Administradores Profesionales- IAAP, Beta Beta (Tri-Beta), Ciencias de Computadoras, Ciencias Políticas, Contabilidad, Doctorales de Educación, Enfermería, Estudiante Graduados en Psicología y Consejería Escolar, Estudiantes Graduados en Ciencias Bibliotecarias y de la Información, Futuros Maestros, Inter Students Paramedic Association.

Athletics. Intercollegiate: Baseball M, basketball, cross-country, soccer M, softball, swimming, table tennis, tennis, track and field, volleyball, weight lifting. **Intramural:** Basketball, cross-country, softball, table tennis, tennis, track and field, volleyball. **Team name:** Tigers.

Student services. Adult student services, alcohol/substance abuse counseling, chaplain/spiritual director, career counseling, student employment services, financial aid counseling, health services, on-campus daycare, personal counseling, placement for graduates, veterans' counselor.

Contact. E-mail: milcama@intersg.edu
Phone: (787) 892-3090 Fax: (787) 892-6350
Mildred Camacho, Director of Admissions, Inter American University of Puerto Rico: San German Campus, Box 5100, San German, PR 00683-9801

National University College: Arecibo
Arecibo, Puerto Rico
www.nuc.edu   CB code: 3222

- For-profit 3-year career college
- Commuter campus in small city
- 1,450 degree-seeking undergraduates: 34% part-time, 61% women
- 8 degree-seeking graduate students
- Interview required

General. Regionally accredited; also accredited by ACICS. Additional campuses in Bayamon, Arecibo, Rio Grande, Ponce; learning center in Caguas. **Degrees:** 142 bachelor's, 268 associate awarded. **Calendar:** Trimester. **Full-time faculty:** 21 total; 10% have terminal degrees, 81% women. **Part-time faculty:** 56 total; 4% have terminal degrees, 70% women. **Class size:** 56% <20, 44% 20-39, less than 1% 40-49.

Freshman class profile.

GPA 3.75 or higher:	3%	GPA 3.0-3.49:	20%
GPA 3.50-3.74:	5%	GPA 2.0-2.99:	65%

Basis for selection. Admissions based on high school record and institutional admissions or SAT test. College Entrance Examination Board test, institutional tests, or SAT required. **Home schooled:** State high school equivalency certificate required. **Learning Disabled:** It is in reference to the orientation and counseling office for requesting special accomodation.

High school preparation. College-preparatory program recommended. 18 units required. Required units include English 3, mathematics 3, history 3, science 3, foreign language 3 and academic electives 3.

2015-2016 Annual costs. Books/supplies: $848. Personal expenses: $2,380. **Additional information:** Tuition per-credit-hour charge $170. Registration fee $25 per term. Administrative service and technological resources fee $100 per term. Additional fees may apply.

Application procedures. Admission: Priority date 8/12; deadline 3/12. $25 fee. Application must be submitted on paper. Admission notification on a rolling basis. **Financial aid:** Priority date 12/31, closing date 4/30. FAFSA required. Applicants notified on a rolling basis starting 5/2; must reply by 5/15 or within 2 week(s) of notification.

Academics. Special study options: Distance learning, independent study, internships. **Credit/placement by examination:** AP, CLEP, institutional tests. 50 credit hours maximum toward associate degree, 50 toward bachelor's. **Support services:** Tutoring. Mentoring, counseling, workshops, service learning.

Majors. BACHELOR'S. Business: Executive assistant. **Computer sciences:** Networking. **Education:** Early childhood, health. **Protective services:** Law enforcement admin. **ASSOCIATE. Business:** Entrepreneurial studies. **Computer sciences:** Networking. **Health services:** Dental assistant, medical secretary, pharmacy assistant, physical therapy assistant. **Protective services:** Law enforcement admin.

Most popular majors. Business/marketing 9%, communications/journalism 9%, education 9%, health sciences 60%, liberal arts 14%.

Technology on campus. 230 workstations in library, computer center, student center. Online library, student web hosting, wireless network available.

Student life. Freshman orientation: Mandatory. Preregistration for classes offered. **Activities:** Choral groups, drama, student newspaper, CONFRA.

Athletics. Intramural: Basketball M, sand volleyball M, softball M, volleyball M.

Student services. Adult student services, alcohol/substance abuse counseling, career counseling, financial aid counseling, personal counseling, placement for graduates. **Physically disabled:** Services for visually impaired.

Contact. E-mail: mepagan@nuc.edu
Phone: (787) 879-5044 ext. 5203 Toll-free number: (800) 780-5134
Fax: (787) 879-5047
Jessie Candelaria, High School Coordinator, National University College: Arecibo, PO Box 4035, MSC 452, Arecibo, PR 00614

National University College: Bayamon
Bayamon, Puerto Rico   CB member
www.nuc.edu   CB code: 7135

- For-profit 3-year career college
- Commuter campus in large town
- 3,305 degree-seeking undergraduates: 40% part-time, 63% women
- 146 degree-seeking graduate students

General. Regionally accredited; also accredited by ACICS. Additional campuses in Arecibo, Rio Grande, Ponce; learning center in Caguas. **Degrees:** 405 bachelor's, 562 associate awarded; master's offered. **Location:** 25 miles from San Juan. **Calendar:** Trimester. **Full-time faculty:** 35 total; 23% have terminal degrees, 49% women. **Part-time faculty:** 107 total; 8% have terminal degrees, 75% women. **Class size:** 45% < 20, 55% 20-39.

Basis for selection. High school transcript, College Entrance Examination Board test or institutional test required for admissions.

High school preparation. 18 units required. Required units include English 3, mathematics 3, history 3, science 3, foreign language 3 and academic electives 3.

2015-2016 Annual costs. Books/supplies: $848. Personal expenses: $2,380. **Additional information:** Tuition per-credit-hour charge $170. Registration fee $25 per term. Administrative service and technological resources fee $100 per term. Additional fees may apply.

Financial aid. All financial aid based on need.

Application procedures. Admission: $25 fee. Application must be submitted on paper. Admission notification by 8/9. Admission notification on a rolling basis. **Financial aid:** Priority date 12/31, closing date 4/30. FAFSA required. Applicants notified on a rolling basis starting 5/2; must reply by 5/15 or within 2 week(s) of notification.

Academics. Special study options: Distance learning, independent study, internships. **Credit/placement by examination:** AP, CLEP, institutional tests. 50 credit hours maximum toward associate degree, 50 toward bachelor's. **Support services:** Tutoring. Mentoring, counseling, workshops, service learning.

Majors. BACHELOR'S. Business: Accounting/business management. **Education:** Early childhood. **Health services:** Nursing (RN). **Protective services:** Law enforcement admin. **ASSOCIATE. Business:** Accounting/ business management, entrepreneurial studies, office technology. **Health services:** Dental assistant, medical secretary, nursing (RN), pharmacy assistant. **Protective services:** Law enforcement admin.

Most popular majors. Business/marketing 6%, computer/information sciences 6%, education 6%, health sciences 56%, security/protective services 28%.

Technology on campus. 187 workstations in library, computer center, student center. Online library, student web hosting, wireless network available.

Student life. Freshman orientation: Available. Preregistration for classes offered. **Housing:** Wellness housing available. **Activities:** Dance, international student organizations.

Athletics. Intramural: Basketball M, sand volleyball, softball M, table tennis.

Student services. Alcohol/substance abuse counseling, career counseling, financial aid counseling, personal counseling, placement for graduates.

Contact. E-mail: emlopez@nuc.edu
Phone: (787) 780-5134 ext. 4000 Toll-free number: (800) 780-5134
Fax: (787) 779-4909
Emmeline Lopez, Admissions and Marketing Director, National University College: Bayamon, PO Box 2036, Bayamon, PR 00960

National University College: Ponce
Coto Laurel, Puerto Rico
www.nuc.edu

◆ For-profit 3-year career college
◆ Commuter campus in large city
◆ 1,229 degree-seeking undergraduates: 23% part-time, 70% women

General. Regionally accredited; also accredited by ACICS. Additional campuses in Bayamon, Arecibo, Rio Grande, Ponce; learning center in Caguas. **Degrees:** 187 bachelor's, 137 associate awarded. **Calendar:** Trimester. **Full-time faculty:** 11 total; 18% have terminal degrees, 73% women. **Part-time faculty:** 68 total; 13% have terminal degrees, 75% women. **Class size:** 55% < 20, 42% 20-39, 2% 40-49.

Basis for selection. School record, GPA, and test scores important.

High school preparation. 18 units required. Required units include English 3, mathematics 3, science 3, foreign language 3, computer science 3 and academic electives 3.

2015-2016 Annual costs. Books/supplies: $848. Personal expenses: $2,380. **Additional information:** Tuition per-credit-hour charge $170. Registration fee $25 per term. Administrative service and technological resources fee $100 per term. Additional fees may apply.

Financial aid. All financial aid based on need.

Application procedures. Admission: Closing date 9/30. $25 fee. Application must be submitted on paper. **Financial aid:** Priority date 12/31, closing date 4/30. FAFSA required. Applicants notified on a rolling basis starting 5/2; must reply by 5/15 or within 2 week(s) of notification.

Academics. Special study options: Distance learning, independent study, internships. **Credit/placement by examination:** AP, CLEP. 50 credit hours maximum toward associate degree, 50 toward bachelor's. **Support services:** Tutoring. Mentoring, counseling, workshops, service learning.

Majors. BACHELOR'S. Business: Executive assistant. **ASSOCIATE. Health services:** Pharmacy assistant, physical therapy assistant.

Most popular majors. Health sciences 96%.

Technology on campus. 63 workstations in library, computer center. Online library, student web hosting, wireless network available.

Student life. Freshman orientation: Mandatory. Preregistration for classes offered. Four-hour session held before semester begins. **Activities:** Student newspaper.

Athletics. Intramural: Basketball, softball, volleyball.

Student services. Alcohol/substance abuse counseling, career counseling, financial aid counseling, personal counseling, placement for graduates.

Contact. E-mail: mbermudez@nuc.edu
Phone: (787) 840-4474 ext. 7001 Fax: (787) 841-1360
Mayra Bermudez Sanchez, Director of Admissions, National University College: Ponce, PO Box 801243, Coto Laurel, PR 00780-1243

National University College: Rio Grande
Rio Grande, Puerto Rico
www.nuc.edu

◆ For-profit 3-year career college
◆ Commuter campus in small town
◆ 1,816 degree-seeking undergraduates: 41% part-time, 50% women
◆ 6 degree-seeking graduate students
◆ Interview required

General. Regionally accredited; also accredited by ACICS. Additional campuses in Bayamon, Arecibo, Ponce; learning center in Caguas. **Degrees:** 152 bachelor's, 258 associate awarded; master's offered. **Calendar:** Trimester. **Full-time faculty:** 14 total; 7% have terminal degrees, 71% women. **Part-time faculty:** 85 total; 7% have terminal degrees, 68% women. **Class size:** 49% < 20, 44% 20-39, 7% 40-49, less than 1% 50-99.

Basis for selection. College Entrance Examination Board test or institutional tests required for admissions.

High school preparation. 18 units required. Required units include English 3, mathematics 3, history 3, science 3, foreign language 3 and academic electives 3.

2015-2016 Annual costs. Books/supplies: $848. Personal expenses: $2,380. **Additional information:** Tuition per-credit-hour charge $170. Registration fee $25 per term. Administrative service and technological resources fee $100 per term. Additional fees may apply.

Financial aid. All financial aid based on need.

Application procedures. Admission: Priority date 8/15; deadline 3/21. $25 fee. Application must be submitted on paper. Admission notification by 8/9. Admission notification on a rolling basis. **Financial aid:** Priority date 12/31, closing date 4/30. FAFSA required. Must reply by 5/15 or within 2 week(s) of notification.

Academics. Special study options: Distance learning, independent study, internships, weekend college. **Credit/placement by examination:** AP, CLEP, institutional tests. 50 credit hours maximum toward associate degree, 50 toward bachelor's. **Support services:** Tutoring. Mentoring, counseling, workshops, service learning.

Majors. BACHELOR'S. Business: Accounting/business management, executive assistant, office technology. **Computer sciences:** Networking. **Education:** Early childhood. **Protective services:** Law enforcement admin. **ASSOCIATE. Business:** Accounting/business management. **Computer sciences:** Networking. **Health services:** Dental assistant, medical secretary, pharmacy assistant, physical therapy assistant. **Protective services:** Law enforcement admin.

Most popular majors. Business/marketing 7%, health sciences 67%, legal studies 22%.

Technology on campus. 119 workstations in library, computer center, student center. Online library, student web hosting, wireless network available.

Student life. Freshman orientation: Mandatory. Preregistration for classes offered. Three-hour sessions available. **Policies:** Reglamento Estudiantil. **Housing:** Wellness housing available. **Activities:** Choral groups, dance, student government, Consejo Universitario de Seguridad y Emergencias, Adoriman - Grupo de Apoyo Espiritual.

Athletics. Intramural: Basketball, cross-country, sand volleyball, softball, table tennis, track and field, volleyball.

Student services. Alcohol/substance abuse counseling, career counseling, financial aid counseling, personal counseling, placement for graduates, women's services.

Contact. E-mail: cramos@nuc.edu
Phone: (800) 981-0812 Fax: (787) 888-8280
Cesar Ramos, Admissions Director, National University College: Rio Grande, PO Box 3064, Rio Grande, PR 00745

Pontifical Catholic University of Puerto Rico
Ponce, Puerto Rico   CB member
www.pucpr.edu   CB code: 0910

◆ Private 4-year university affiliated with the Roman Catholic Church
◆ Commuter campus in small city
◆ 5,427 degree-seeking undergraduates
◆ SAT or ACT (ACT writing optional) required

General. Founded in 1948. Regionally accredited. Branch campuses in Arecibo and Mayaguez. **Degrees:** 774 bachelor's, 20 associate awarded; master's, professional, doctoral offered. **ROTC:** Army, Air Force. **Location:** 60 miles from San Juan. **Calendar:** Semester, limited summer session. **Full-time faculty:** 214 total; 41% have terminal degrees, 100% minority, 55% women. **Part-time faculty:** 236 total; 26% have terminal degrees, 100% minority, 44% women. **Class size:** 46% < 20, 43% 20-39, 9% 40-49, 1% 50-99.

Freshman class profile.

GPA 3.75 or higher:	24%	Live on campus:	4%
GPA 3.50-3.74:	14%	Fraternities:	1%
GPA 3.0-3.49:	28%	Sororities:	1%
GPA 2.0-2.99:	32%		

Basis for selection. School achievement record, test scores important. Admission index will be determined by GPA, math and verbal scores on aptitude test. SAT required of English-speaking applicants. Interview required for special program; essay or personal statement for some programs. **Home schooled:** Transcript of courses and grades, state high school equivalency certificate required. Home-schooled legal certification required.

High school preparation. College-preparatory program required. 15 units required. Required units include English 4, mathematics 3, history 2, science 2 and foreign language 4.

2015-2016 Annual costs. Tuition/fees: $6,270. Room only: $1,300. Books/supplies: $1,609. Personal expenses: $1,204.

Financial aid. **Non-need-based:** Scholarships awarded for academics, athletics, music/drama.

Application procedures. **Admission:** Priority date 3/15; deadline 7/15 (receipt date). $15 fee, may be waived for applicants with need. Admission notification on a rolling basis beginning on or about 2/15. **Financial aid:** Closing date 5/15. FAFSA required. Applicants notified by 6/15; must reply within 4 week(s) of notification.

Academics. **Special study options:** Accelerated study, combined bachelor's/graduate degree, double major, dual enrollment of high school students, ESL, exchange student, honors, independent study, internships, liberal arts/career combination, study abroad, teacher certification program. **Credit/placement by examination:** AP, CLEP, institutional tests. 30 credit hours maximum toward bachelor's degree. **Support services:** Learning center, preadmission summer program, reduced course load, remedial instruction, tutoring.

Majors. Architecture: Architecture. **Area/ethnic studies:** Chicano/Hispanic-American/Latino. **Biology:** General. **Business:** General, accounting, administrative services, business admin, communications, entrepreneurial studies, finance, human resources, international, management information systems, managerial economics, marketing, tourism/travel, transportation. **Communications:** Communications/speech/rhetoric. **Conservation:** General, environmental studies. **Education:** Art, biology, business, chemistry, early childhood, elementary, English, ESL, family/consumer sciences, history, mathematics, music, physical, science, secondary, social studies, Spanish, special ed. **English:** English lit. **Foreign languages:** Spanish. **Health services:** Cardiovascular technology, clinical lab science, nursing (RN), premedicine. **History:** General. **Human services:** General, social work. **Liberal arts:** Arts/sciences. **Math:** General. **Philosophy/religion:** Philosophy. **Physical sciences:** Chemistry, physics. **Psychology:** General. **Social sciences:** Criminology, political science, sociology. **Visual/performing arts:** Music, studio arts. **Work/family studies:** General.

Most popular majors. Business/marketing 17%, education 18%, health sciences 22%, liberal arts 7%, psychology 6%, public administration/social services 9%, social sciences 6%.

Technology on campus. 470 workstations in library, computer center, student center. Commuter students can connect to campus network. Online course registration, online library, wireless network available.

Student life. Freshman orientation: Mandatory. Preregistration for classes offered. **Housing:** Single-sex dorms available. $25 nonrefundable deposit. **Activities:** Choral groups, dance, drama, musical theater, radio station, student government, student newspaper, TV station, Pi Gamma Mu, Phi Alpha Theta, Beta Beta Beta, Alpha Beta Chi, Phi Delta Kappa, honor society for business students, Pioneer Students in Christ and Mary, Miles Jesu, Knights of Columbus, Phi Sigma Kappa.

Athletics. Intercollegiate: Basketball, cross-country, diving, judo, soccer, softball M, swimming, table tennis, tennis, track and field, volleyball, water polo M, wrestling M. **Intramural:** Archery, basketball, cross-country, diving, softball, swimming, table tennis, tennis, track and field, volleyball, wrestling M. **Team name:** Pioneers.

Student services. Chaplain/spiritual director, career counseling, student employment services, health services, on-campus daycare, personal counseling, placement for graduates, veterans' counselor.

Contact. E-mail: admisiones@pucpr.edu
Phone: (787) 841-2000 ext. 1000 Fax: (787) 651-2044
Ana Bonilla, Director of Admissions, Pontifical Catholic University of Puerto Rico, 2250 Las Americas Avenue, Suite 284, Ponce, PR 00717-9777

Theological University of the Caribbean
Saint Just, Puerto Rico
www.utcpr.edu

- Private 4-year Bible and seminary college affiliated with the Church of God
- Small city
- 242 degree-seeking undergraduates: 40% part-time, 40% women, 100% Hispanic/Latino
- 88% of applicants admitted
- Interview required

General. Accredited by ABHE. **Degrees:** 16 bachelor's awarded; master's offered. **Calendar:** Semester, limited summer session. **Full-time faculty:** 9 total; 33% have terminal degrees. **Part-time faculty:** 35 total; 51% have terminal degrees.

Freshman class profile. 56 applied, 49 admitted, 7 enrolled.

Basis for selection. School record, interview, and recommendations most important. **Home schooled:** Transcript of courses and grades, state high school equivalency certificate, interview, letter of recommendation (nonparent) required.

2016-2017 Annual costs. Tuition/fees (projected): $4,448. Room/board: $2,400. Books/supplies: $1,600. Personal expenses: $1,250.

2015-2016 Financial aid. All financial aid based on need. 6 full-time freshmen applied for aid; 6 deemed to have need; 6 received aid. Average need met was 60%. 79% of total undergraduate aid awarded as scholarships/grants, 21% as loans/jobs.

Application procedures. Admission: No deadline. $25 fee. **Financial aid:** No deadline. FAFSA required.

Academics. Special study options: Distance learning. **Credit/placement by examination:** AP, CLEP.

Majors. Theology: Bible, pastoral counseling, religious ed.

Technology on campus. 7 workstations in library, computer center. Dormitories wired for high-speed internet access. Online course registration, online library, wireless network available.

Student life. Freshman orientation: Mandatory. Preregistration for classes offered. **Housing:** Single-sex dorms available. **Activities:** Campus ministries, student government.

Student services. Chaplain/spiritual director, services for economically disadvantaged, personal counseling.

Contact. E-mail: admisiones@utcpr.edu
Phone: (787) 761-0808 ext. 246 Toll-free number: (787) 370-6090
Fax: (787) 748-9220
Theological University of the Caribbean, PO Box 901, Saint Just, PR 00978-0901

Turabo University
Gurabo, Puerto Rico
http://ut.suagm.edu/   CB code: 0780

- Private 4-year university and engineering college
- Commuter campus in small city
- 14,696 degree-seeking undergraduates: 27% part-time, 58% women, 100% Hispanic/Latino
- 2,813 degree-seeking graduate students
- 52% of applicants admitted

General. Founded in 1972. Regionally accredited. **Degrees:** 1,369 bachelor's, 462 associate awarded; master's, professional, doctoral offered. **ROTC:** Army, Air Force. **Location:** 17 miles from San Juan. **Calendar:** Semester, limited summer session. **Full-time faculty:** 237 total; 58% have terminal degrees, 100% minority, 49% women. **Part-time faculty:** 934 total; 24% have terminal degrees, 100% minority, 53% women. **Class size:** 56% < 20, 43% 20-39, less than 1% 40-49, less than 1% 50-99. **Special facilities:** College-operated museums.

Freshman class profile. 8,968 applied, 4,683 admitted, 2,398 enrolled.

GPA 3.75 or higher:	9%	GPA 2.0-2.99:	47%
GPA 3.50-3.74:	12%	Return as sophomores:	77%
GPA 3.0-3.49:	27%		

Basis for selection. SAT required for admission to honors and science programs. Minimum 2.0 GPA required for program in business administration; for biology, 2.5; health, 2.5; education, 2.5; engineering, 2.5. SAT or ACT recommended. Test required for English, health and honor program students. **Learning Disabled:** Interview required for international design and for some health programs.

High school preparation. 15 units required. Required units include English 3, mathematics 3, social studies 2, science 2 and foreign language 3.

2015-2016 Annual costs. Books/supplies: $1,700. Personal expenses: $2,000.

2014-2015 Financial aid. All financial aid based on need.

Application procedures. Admission: No deadline. $15 fee, may be waived for applicants with need. Admission notification on a rolling basis beginning on or about 3/1. **Financial aid:** Priority date 5/30; no closing date. FAFSA required.

Academics. Special study options: Accelerated study, distance learning, honors, independent study, internships, liberal arts/career combination, weekend college. **Credit/placement by examination:** AP, CLEP, SAT, institutional tests. **Support services:** Remedial instruction, study skills assistance, tutoring.

Majors. Architecture: Landscape. **Biology:** General, biotechnology. **Business:** Accounting, business admin, management information systems, marketing, office management. **Communications:** Communications/speech/rhetoric, journalism. **Communications technology:** Radio/TV. **Computer sciences:** General. **Education:** Biology, chemistry, early childhood, elementary, English, history, mathematics, physical, science, special ed, trade/industrial. **Engineering:** Civil, computer, electrical, mechanical. **Foreign languages:** Sign language interpretation. **Health services:** Community health services, nursing assistant, speech pathology. **Human services:** General, social work. **Liberal arts:** Humanities. **Parks/recreation:** Sports admin. **Physical sciences:** Chemistry. **Protective services:** Police science. **Psychology:** General. **Social sciences:** General, criminology, sociology. **Visual/performing arts:** Graphic design, industrial design, interior design.

Most popular majors. Business/marketing 30%, computer/information sciences 6%, education 8%, engineering/engineering technologies 6%, health sciences 13%, psychology 7%, public administration/social services 6%, social sciences 14%.

Technology on campus. Commuter students can connect to campus network. Online library, helpline available.

Student life. Freshman orientation: Available. Preregistration for classes offered. **Activities:** Choral groups, dance, drama, music ensembles, radio station, student government, student newspaper, TV station.

Athletics. NAIA. **Intercollegiate:** Baseball M, basketball, cross-country, judo, soccer M, softball, swimming, tennis, track and field, volleyball, weight lifting. **Intramural:** Basketball, softball, table tennis, tennis W, volleyball, weight lifting. **Team name:** Taínos.

Student services. Adult student services, alcohol/substance abuse counseling, career counseling, services for economically disadvantaged, student employment services, financial aid counseling, health services, on-campus daycare, personal counseling, placement for graduates, veterans' counselor. **Physically disabled:** Services for visually, speech, hearing impaired.

Contact. E-mail: admisiones_ut@suagm.edu
Phone: (787) 743-7979 Toll-free number: (800) 747-8362
Virginia Gonzalez, Associate Director of Admissions and Financial Aid, Turabo University, PO Box 3030, Gurabo, PR 00778

Universidad Adventista de las Antillas
Mayaguez, Puerto Rico   **CB member**
www.uaa.edu   **CB code: 1020**

- Private 4-year university and liberal arts college affiliated with the Seventh-day Adventists
- Commuter campus in small city
- 1,304 degree-seeking undergraduates: 6% part-time, 62% women, 1% African American, 95% Hispanic/Latino, 3% international

- 80 graduate students
- 33% graduate within 6 years

General. Founded in 1957. Regionally accredited. **Degrees:** 206 bachelor's, 5 associate awarded; master's offered. **Location:** 100 miles from San Juan. **Calendar:** Semester, limited summer session. **Full-time faculty:** 44 total; 18% have terminal degrees, 57% women. **Part-time faculty:** 51 total; 26% have terminal degrees, 43% women.

Freshman class profile. 316 applied, 306 admitted, 217 enrolled.

Return as sophomores:	73%	**International:**	2%

Basis for selection. Open admission, but selective for some programs. SAT or ACT recommended for English-speaking applicants. Interview required for admission to nursing and theology programs. **Home schooled:** Transcript of courses and grades, interview, letter of recommendation (non-parent) required. Unless homeschool program is accredited, applicant must take GED. If necessary, especially in the case of nonresident students, state high school equivalency certificate will be requested.

High school preparation. 18 units recommended. Recommended units include English 3, mathematics 3, social studies 3, science 3 and academic electives 3. 3 Spanish units recommended.

2015-2016 Annual costs. Tuition/fees: $6,850. Room/board: $5,200. Books/supplies: $1,200. Personal expenses: $3,000.

2014-2015 Financial aid. Need-based: 219 full-time freshmen applied for aid; 205 deemed to have need; 205 received aid. **Non-need-based:** Awarded to 132 full-time undergraduates, including 28 freshmen.

Application procedures. Admission: No deadline. $20 fee, may be waived for applicants with need. Admission notification on a rolling basis. **Financial aid:** No deadline. FAFSA, institutional form required. Applicants notified on a rolling basis starting 8/15; must reply within 3 week(s) of notification.

Academics. Federal programs known as TRIO SSS Regular and TRIO ESL, which provide assistance to students who are weak in Spanish, English, or mathematics. **Special study options:** Combined bachelor's/graduate degree, cooperative education, double major, ESL, internships, liberal arts/career combination, teacher certification program. **Credit/placement by examination:** AP, CLEP, institutional tests. 12 credit hours maximum toward associate degree, 12 toward bachelor's. **Support services:** Learning center, reduced course load, remedial instruction, study skills assistance, tutoring.

Majors. Biology: General. **Business:** General, administrative services. **Computer sciences:** General, computer science, information systems. **Education:** Elementary, secondary. **Health services:** Respiratory therapy technology. **History:** General. **Physical sciences:** Chemistry. **Psychology:** General. **Theology:** Theology.

Most popular majors. Biology 10%, business/marketing 9%, education 7%, health sciences 57%, psychology 7%, theological studies 9%.

Technology on campus. 50 workstations in library, computer center. Commuter students can connect to campus network. Online course registration, online library, repair service available.

Student life. Freshman orientation: Mandatory. Preregistration for classes offered. Two-day program at beginning of each semester. Counselors available to help students with enrollment. **Policies:** Religious environment designed for Seventh-day Adventist students. Religious observance required. **Housing:** Guaranteed on-campus for freshmen. Single-sex dorms, apartments available. **Activities:** Concert band, choral groups, international student organizations, music ensembles, student government, student newspaper, symphony orchestra, international club, ministerial club, office administration club, student council, green movement, 3AM, gymnastics club.

Athletics. Intramural: Basketball, gymnastics, soccer M, volleyball. **Team name:** Eagles Gym Team.

Student services. Alcohol/substance abuse counseling, chaplain/spiritual director, career counseling, services for economically disadvantaged, student employment services, financial aid counseling, health services, personal counseling, veterans' counselor.

Contact. E-mail: admissions@uaa.edu
Phone: (787) 834-9595 ext. 2208 Fax: (787) 834-9597
Yolanda Ferrer, Director of Admissions, Universidad Adventista de las Antillas, PO Box 118, Mayaguez, PR 00681-0118

Universidad Central del Caribe
Bayamon, Puerto Rico
www.uccaribe.edu   CB code: 1549

- Private 4-year university
- Small city
- 144 undergraduates

General. Regionally accredited. Many student interest groups focus on community service. **Degrees:** 151 bachelor's, 43 associate awarded; master's, professional, doctoral offered. **Calendar:** Continuous. **Full-time faculty:** 40 total. **Part-time faculty:** 2 total.

Basis for selection. GPA, school records, and recommendations most important.

2015-2016 Annual costs. Books/supplies: $600.

Application procedures. Admission: Closing date 4/1. $25 fee.

Academics. Credit/placement by examination: AP, CLEP.

Majors. Health services: Radiologic technology/medical imaging.

Student life. Freshman orientation: Mandatory. Preregistration for classes offered.

Student services. Alcohol/substance abuse counseling, career counseling, financial aid counseling, health services, minority student services.

Contact. E-mail: icordero@uccaribe.edu
Phone: (787) 740-1611 Fax: (787) 269-7550
Omar Perez, Dean for Student Affairs, Universidad Central del Caribe, Decanato de Admisiones y Asuntos Estudiantiles, Bayamon, PR 00960-6032

Universidad del Este
Carolina, Puerto Rico   CB member
www.suagm.edu/une   CB code: 0883

- Private 4-year university
- Commuter campus in small city
- 11,825 degree-seeking undergraduates: 28% part-time, 60% women, 100% Hispanic/Latino
- 1,233 degree-seeking graduate students

General. Founded in 1949. Regionally accredited. Accelerated undergraduate and graduate programs for adult students with work experience. **Degrees:** 1,133 bachelor's, 637 associate awarded; master's offered. **ROTC:** Army. **Location:** 5 miles from San Juan. **Calendar:** Semester, limited summer session. **Full-time faculty:** 177 total; 48% have terminal degrees, 87% minority, 62% women. **Part-time faculty:** 1,037 total; 16% have terminal degrees, 55% women. **Class size:** 59% < 20, 40% 20-39, 1% 40-49, less than 1% 50-99.

Freshman class profile. 10,800 applied, 4,691 admitted, 2,221 enrolled.

GPA 3.75 or higher:	7%	GPA 2.0-2.99:	50%
GPA 3.50-3.74:	9%	Return as sophomores:	77%
GPA 3.0-3.49:	25%		

Basis for selection. Open admission, but selective for some programs. Special requirements for health, hospitality, and science programs; interview recommended. SAT required for English-speaking freshman applicants. **Home schooled:** Statement describing home school structure and mission, transcript of courses and grades, letter of recommendation (nonparent) required.

2015-2016 Annual costs. Books/supplies: $1,700. Personal expenses: $2,000.

Financial aid. All financial aid based on need.

Application procedures. Admission: No deadline. $15 fee, may be waived for applicants with need. Admission notification on a rolling basis. **Financial aid:** Priority date 5/30; no closing date. FAFSA, institutional form required.

Academics. Special study options: Accelerated study, cross registration, distance learning, double major, ESL, honors, independent study, internships, liberal arts/career combination, study abroad, teacher certification program, weekend college. **Credit/placement by examination:** AP, CLEP. **Support**

services: Learning center, reduced course load, study skills assistance, tutoring.

Majors. Biology: General, biotechnology, microbiology. **Business:** Accounting, administrative services, business admin, event planning, hotel/motel admin, human resources, insurance, management information systems, marketing, office technology. **Communications:** Digital media. **Computer sciences:** System admin. **Education:** Early childhood, ESL, physical, special ed. **Health services:** Athletic training, health care admin, medical radiologic technology/radiation therapy, sonography. **Human services:** Social work. **Parks/recreation:** Physical fitness technician. **Protective services:** Criminal justice. **Psychology:** General. **Social sciences:** Political science. **Work/family studies:** Food/nutrition.

Most popular majors. Business/marketing 30%, health sciences 22%, psychology 10%, public administration/social services 12%, security/protective services 12%.

Technology on campus. Commuter students can connect to campus network. Online library, helpline, wireless network available.

Student life. Freshman orientation: Available. Preregistration for classes offered. **Activities:** Concert band, dance, international student organizations, student government, Phi Theta Kappa, Future Secretaries of America, ENACTUS, Universitarios con una misión.

Athletics. Intercollegiate: Baseball M, basketball, cheerleading, cross-country, softball W, track and field, volleyball, weight lifting M. **Intramural:** Basketball, volleyball. **Team name:** Pitirre.

Student services. Adult student services, alcohol/substance abuse counseling, career counseling, services for economically disadvantaged, student employment services, financial aid counseling, health services, personal counseling, placement for graduates, veterans' counselor. **Physically disabled:** Services for visually, speech, hearing impaired.

Contact. E-mail: admisiones_une@suagm.edu
Phone: (787) 257-8080 Toll-free number: (800) 747-8362
Fax: (787) 257-8601 ext. 3307
Ramonita Fuentes, Director of Admissions, Universidad del Este, PO Box 2010, Carolina, PR 00984-2010

Universidad Metropolitana
San Juan, Puerto Rico   CB member
www.suagm.edu/umet   CB code: 1519

- Private 4-year university and liberal arts college
- Commuter campus in large city
- 11,589 degree-seeking undergraduates: 22% part-time, 64% women
- 2,330 degree-seeking graduate students
- 65% of applicants admitted

General. Founded in 1985. Regionally accredited. **Degrees:** 1,317 bachelor's, 323 associate awarded; master's, doctoral offered. **ROTC:** Army, Naval, Air Force. **Location:** 3 miles from San Juan. **Calendar:** Semester, limited summer session. **Full-time faculty:** 179 total; 32% have terminal degrees, 100% minority, 72% women. **Part-time faculty:** 1,071 total; 27% have terminal degrees, 100% minority, 58% women. **Class size:** 51% < 20, 48% 20-39, 2% 40-49, less than 1% 50-99.

Freshman class profile. 11,494 applied, 7,455 admitted, 2,165 enrolled.

GPA 3.75 or higher:	7%	GPA 2.0-2.99:	50%
GPA 3.50-3.74:	9%	Return as sophomores:	75%
GPA 3.0-3.49:	25%		

Basis for selection. School achievement record and test scores considered. SAT required of English-speaking applicants. Interview required for academically weak. **Home schooled:** State high school equivalency certificate required.

2015-2016 Annual costs. Books/supplies: $1,700. Personal expenses: $2,000.

Financial aid. All financial aid based on need.

Application procedures. Admission: Closing date 8/15 (receipt date). $15 fee. Admission notification on a rolling basis. **Financial aid:** Priority date 5/30; no closing date. FAFSA required.

Academics. Special study options: Accelerated study, combined bachelor's/graduate degree, distance learning, honors, independent study, internships, liberal arts/career combination, teacher certification program, Washington semester, weekend college. Off-campus full-degree sites. **Credit/placement by examination:** AP, CLEP. **Support services:** Learning center, preadmission summer program, remedial instruction, tutoring.

Majors. Biology: General, molecular. **Business:** Accounting, business admin, management information systems, managerial economics, marketing, office management, project management, sales/distribution. **Communications:** Digital media. **Computer sciences:** Computer science. **Conservation:** Environmental science. **Education:** Early childhood, elementary, English, history, kindergarten/preschool, multi-level teacher, physical, secondary, Spanish, special ed. **Health services:** Cardiovascular technology, environmental health, health care admin, nursing (RN), respiratory therapy technology, speech pathology. **Human services:** Social work. **Math:** Applied. **Parks/recreation:** Health/fitness. **Physical sciences:** Chemistry. **Protective services:** Criminal justice. **Psychology:** General.

Most popular majors. Business/marketing 32%, education 7%, health sciences 33%, public administration/social services 8%, security/protective services 9%.

Technology on campus. Commuter students can connect to campus network. Online library, helpline, repair service, wireless network available.

Student life. Freshman orientation: Mandatory. Preregistration for classes offered. Held 4 weeks before the beginning of the academic year. **Activities:** Choral groups, dance, drama, radio station, student government, student newspaper, TV station, business students association, social work students association, communication students association.

Athletics. Intercollegiate: Baseball M, basketball, cheerleading, cross-country, judo, soccer, softball W, table tennis, tennis, track and field, volleyball, weight lifting. **Intramural:** Basketball, cross-country, table tennis, volleyball. **Team name:** Cocodrilos.

Student services. Adult student services, alcohol/substance abuse counseling, career counseling, services for economically disadvantaged, student employment services, financial aid counseling, health services, on-campus daycare, personal counseling, placement for graduates, veterans' counselor, women's services. **Physically disabled:** Services for visually, hearing impaired.

Contact. E-mail: admisiones-umet@suagm.edu
Phone: (787) 766-1717 ext. 6657 Toll-free number: (787) 747-8362
Fax: (787) 751-0992
Yadira Rivera Lugo, Director of Admission, Universidad Metropolitana, Apartado 21150, San Juan, PR 00928

Universidad Pentecostal Mizpa
San Juan, Puerto Rico
www.mizpa.edu

▶ Private 4-year university and Bible college affiliated with the Pentecostal Holiness Church
▶ Commuter campus in very large city
▶ 290 degree-seeking undergraduates: 50% part-time, 37% women, 100% Hispanic/Latino
▶ 26 degree-seeking graduate students
▶ Interview required

General. Accredited by ABHE. **Degrees:** 10 bachelor's, 12 associate awarded; master's offered. **Calendar:** Continuous, limited summer session. **Full-time faculty:** 12 total; 50% have terminal degrees, 92% minority, 25% women. **Part-time faculty:** 36 total; 11% have terminal degrees, 100% minority, 28% women. **Class size:** 97% < 20, 3% 20-39.

Freshman class profile.

Return as sophomores:	8%	Live on campus:	1%

Basis for selection. Religious affiliation very important; rigor of secondary school record considered. **Home schooled:** State high school equivalency certificate, interview, letter of recommendation (nonparent) required. **Learning Disabled:** Certified information concerning disability must be provided by student.

2016-2017 Annual costs. Tuition/fees (projected): $5,150. Room/board: $3,760. Books/supplies: $1,000. Personal expenses: $1,200.

2015-2016 Financial aid. All financial aid based on need. 96% of total undergraduate aid awarded as scholarships/grants, 4% as loans/jobs.

Application procedures. Admission: Priority date 4/17; deadline 8/12 (receipt date). $45 fee ($45 out-of-state). Application must be submitted on paper. Admission notification by 8/19. Admission notification on a rolling basis beginning on or about 6/17. **Financial aid:** No deadline. FAFSA required.

Academics. Special study options: External degree, weekend college. **Credit/placement by examination:** AP, CLEP, institutional tests. **Support services:** Learning center, study skills assistance, writing center.

Majors. Theology: Bible, pastoral counseling, religious ed.

Technology on campus. Dormitories linked to campus network. Commuter students can connect to campus network. Online library, wireless network available.

Student life. Freshman orientation: Mandatory. Preregistration for classes offered. **Policies:** Religious observance required. **Housing:** Single-sex dorms, wellness housing available. $150 fully refundable deposit, deadline 8/12. **Activities:** Campus ministries, radio station, student government, student newspaper, TV station.

Athletics. Intramural: Basketball M, softball, table tennis.

Student services. Adult student services, chaplain/spiritual director, career counseling, services for economically disadvantaged, student employment services, financial aid counseling, personal counseling, veterans' counselor.

Contact. E-mail: decanatoestudiante@mizpa.edu
Phone: (787) 720-4476 Fax: (787) 720-2012
Jorge Burgos, Admissions Director and Dean of Students Affairs, Universidad Pentecostal Mizpa, RR 16 Box 4800, San Juan, PR 00926

Universidad Politecnica de Puerto Rico
Hato Rey, Puerto Rico — **CB member**
www.pupr.edu — **CB code: 0614**

▶ Private 5-year university and engineering college
▶ Commuter campus in large city
▶ 3,475 degree-seeking undergraduates: 54% part-time, 20% women
▶ 798 degree-seeking graduate students
▶ 87% of applicants admitted

General. Founded in 1966. Regionally accredited. **Degrees:** 534 bachelor's awarded; master's, doctoral offered. **ROTC:** Army, Air Force. **Location:** 3 miles from San Juan. **Calendar:** Trimester, extensive summer session. **Full-time faculty:** 133 total; 35% have terminal degrees, 36% women. **Part-time faculty:** 93 total; 19% have terminal degrees, 27% women. **Class size:** 68% < 20, 31% 20-39, less than 1% 40-49, less than 1% 50-99.

Freshman class profile. 531 applied, 462 admitted, 366 enrolled.

GPA 3.75 or higher:	17%	GPA 3.0-3.49:	31%
GPA 3.50-3.74:	16%	GPA 2.0-2.99:	35%

Basis for selection. Flexible admissions policy that provides an opportunity to high school graduates or individuals who have passed a state high school equivalency examination to enroll in university credit courses and programs. SAT in English or Spanish required. **Home schooled:** Letter of recommendation (nonparent) required. College Board scores required.

High school preparation. College-preparatory program required. 15 units required. Required units include English 3, mathematics 3, social studies 3, science 3, foreign language 3 and academic electives 3.

2016-2017 Annual costs. Tuition/fees (projected): $8,040. Books/supplies: $2,342. Personal expenses: $4,224.

2015-2016 Financial aid. Need-based: Average need met was 49%. Average scholarship/grant was $4,486; average loan $2,068. 57% of total undergraduate aid awarded as scholarships/grants, 43% as loans/jobs. **Non-need-based:** Scholarships awarded for academics, music/drama.

Application procedures. Admission: No deadline. $30 fee. Admission notification on a rolling basis. **Financial aid:** Priority date 5/15, closing date 6/30. FAFSA required. Applicants notified by 7/15.

Academics. Special study options: Cooperative education, distance learning, exchange student, honors, internships. PES (Programa Especial de Escuela Superior). **Credit/placement by examination:** AP, CLEP, institutional tests. **Support services:** Learning center, pre-admission summer program, remedial instruction, tutoring.

Majors. Architecture: Architecture. **Business:** General, business admin. **Computer sciences:** Computer science. **Engineering:** Chemical, civil, computer, electrical, industrial, mechanical.

Most popular majors. Architecture 10%, business/marketing 6%, engineering/engineering technologies 81%.

Technology on campus. 700 workstations in library, computer center. Commuter students can connect to campus network. Online course registration, online library, helpline, wireless network available.

Student life. Freshman orientation: Available. Preregistration for classes offered. Week-long orientation offered each trimester. **Policies:** Student rule policy, aggression policy, security policy in effect. Drug-free campus. **Activities:** Choral groups, dance, student government, University Bible Association, drugs and alcohol committee, student association, Wellness and Health Education Peer Advisor.

Athletics. Intercollegiate: Basketball M, judo M, sand volleyball, table tennis, tennis, track and field, volleyball. **Intramural:** Basketball M, judo M. **Team name:** Beavers.

Student services. Alcohol/substance abuse counseling, career counseling, services for economically disadvantaged, student employment services, financial aid counseling, health services, personal counseling, placement for graduates, veterans' counselor. **Physically disabled:** Services for visually, speech, hearing impaired.

Contact. E-mail: admissions@pupr.edu
Phone: (787) 622-8000 ext. 310 Fax: (787) 764-8712
Teresa Cardona, Director of Admissions, Universidad Politecnica de Puerto Rico, PO Box 192017, San Juan, PR 00919-2017

University College of San Juan
San Juan, Puerto Rico
www.cunisanjuan.edu   CB code: 0391

▶ Public 4-year university and community college
▶ Commuter campus in large city
▶ 1,429 degree-seeking undergraduates: 13% part-time, 56% women, 100% Hispanic/Latino
▶ 74% of applicants admitted
▶ 61% graduate within 6 years

General. Founded in 1972. Regionally accredited. **Degrees:** 140 bachelor's, 169 associate awarded. **Calendar:** Semester, limited summer session. **Full-time faculty:** 21 total; 19% have terminal degrees, 100% minority, 48% women. **Part-time faculty:** 123 total; 100% minority, 54% women. **Class size:** 56% < 20, 44% 20-39. **Special facilities:** Language laboratory, learning resource center.

Freshman class profile. 292 applied, 216 admitted, 209 enrolled.

| GPA 3.75 or higher: | 5% | GPA 3.0-3.49: | 24% |
| GPA 3.50-3.74: | 8% | GPA 2.0-2.99: | 56% |

Basis for selection. Combined College Board PAA test scores of 2000 and 2.0 GPA required for regular students. Special consideration and priority to applicants from low-income families. SAT/ACT accepted from US applicants. Interview required for nursing program.

High school preparation. College-preparatory program required. 15 units required. Required units include English 3, mathematics 2, social studies 2, history 2, science 1, foreign language 3 and academic electives 2. 3 Spanish courses required.

2015-2016 Annual costs. Books/supplies: $1,200. Personal expenses: $920.

2014-2015 Financial aid. All financial aid based on need. 215 full-time freshmen applied for aid; 215 deemed to have need; 215 received aid. Average need met was 100%. Average scholarship/grant was $4,690. 99% of total undergraduate aid awarded as scholarships/grants, 1% as loans/jobs.

Application procedures. Admission: Closing date 5/1. $15 fee. Application must be submitted on paper. Admission notification by 6/1. Admission after July 31 on space-available basis. **Financial aid:** No deadline. FAFSA, institutional form required. Applicants notified on a rolling basis starting 8/1.

Academics. Special study options: Internships. **Credit/placement by examination:** AP, CLEP. 9 credit hours maximum toward associate degree, 4 toward bachelor's. **Support services:** Learning center, reduced course load, remedial instruction, tutoring.

Majors. Business: Accounting. **Computer sciences:** General. **Health services:** Nursing (RN). **Protective services:** Police science.

Most popular majors. Business/marketing 7%, computer/information sciences 8%, health sciences 52%, security/protective services 33%.

Technology on campus. 281 workstations in library, computer center. Commuter students can connect to campus network. Online library, wireless network available.

Student life. Freshman orientation: Mandatory. Preregistration for classes offered. One-day program in summer that offers opportunity to meet faculty and staff. **Activities:** Student government.

Athletics. Intramural: Basketball. **Team name:** Crabs.

Student services. Career counseling, services for economically disadvantaged, student employment services, financial aid counseling, health services, minority student services, personal counseling, placement for graduates, veterans' counselor. **Physically disabled:** Services for visually, speech, hearing impaired.

Contact. E-mail: admisiones@cts.sanjuancapital.com
Phone: (787) 480-2400 Fax: (787) 274-1388
Melvin Vega, Enrollment Management Director, University College of San Juan, 180 Jose R. Oliver Avenue, San Juan, PR 00918

University of Phoenix: Puerto Rico
Guaynabo, Puerto Rico
www.phoenix.edu

▶ For-profit 4-year university
▶ Small city
▶ 313 undergraduates

General. Regionally accredited. **Degrees:** 117 bachelor's awarded; master's offered. **Calendar:** Differs by program. Other Academic Calendar. **Full-time faculty:** 9 total. **Part-time faculty:** 198 total.

Basis for selection. Open admission, but selective for some programs.

2015-2016 Annual costs. Per-credit-hour charge $245; continuing education $175; electronic course materials fee $95, if applicable. Book and material charges may vary by course and program. All fees are subject to change.

Application procedures. Admission: No deadline. No application fee. **Financial aid:** No deadline.

Academics. Credit/placement by examination: AP, CLEP.

Majors. Business: Business admin, marketing. **Protective services:** Law enforcement admin.

Student life. Freshman orientation: Mandatory. Preregistration for classes offered.

Contact. Toll-free number: (866) 766-0766
University of Phoenix: Puerto Rico, 1625 W. Fountainhead Pkwy, Tempe, AZ 85282

University of Puerto Rico: Aguadilla
Aguadilla, Puerto Rico
www.uprag.edu   CB code: 0983

▶ Public 4-year liberal arts and technical college
▶ Commuter campus in small city
▶ 2,573 degree-seeking undergraduates: 7% part-time, 55% women
▶ 31% of applicants admitted
▶ 35% graduate within 6 years

General. Founded in 1972. Regionally accredited. **Degrees:** 315 bachelor's, 2 associate awarded. **ROTC:** Army. **Location:** 81 miles from San Juan. **Calendar:** Semester, limited summer session. **Full-time faculty:** 115 total; 43% have terminal degrees, 100% minority, 52% women. **Part-time faculty:** 48 total; 17% have terminal degrees, 100% minority, 40% women. **Class size:** 19% < 20, 81% 20-39.

Freshman class profile. 2,916 applied, 893 admitted, 771 enrolled.

| Mid 50% test scores | | SAT math: | 450-580 |
| SAT critical reading: | 460-560 | | |

Basis for selection. Admissions based on secondary school record and standardized test scores. Talent and ability considered. SAT and SAT Subject Tests in Spanish and math level I required of English-speaking applicants. **Home schooled:** Copy of curriculum required.

High school preparation. Recommended units include English 3, mathematics 2 and social studies 2. 3 Spanish recommended.

2015-2016 Annual costs. Tuition/fees: $2,014. Books/supplies: $1,862. Personal expenses: $1,224.

2015-2016 Financial aid. All financial aid based on need. 98% of total undergraduate aid awarded as scholarships/grants, 2% as loans/jobs.

Application procedures. Admission: Priority date 11/17; deadline 1/30 (receipt date). $20 fee, may be waived for applicants with need. Application must be submitted on paper. Admission notification by 4/2. Admission notification on a rolling basis. Must reply by 4/30. **Financial aid:** Closing date 5/6. FAFSA, institutional form required. Applicants notified on a rolling basis starting 4/1; must reply within 1 week(s) of notification.

Academics. Special study options: Combined bachelor's/graduate degree, honors, liberal arts/career combination, teacher certification program. **Credit/placement by examination:** AP, CLEP, institutional tests. **Support services:** Learning center, remedial instruction, tutoring.

Majors. Biology: General. **Business:** General, accounting, executive assistant, finance, hotel/motel admin, human resources, management information systems, marketing. **Communications technology:** Radio/TV. **Education:** Elementary, English.

Most popular majors. Biology 36%, business/marketing 50%, education 7%, engineering/engineering technologies 7%.

Technology on campus. 547 workstations in library, computer center, student center. Online library, student web hosting, wireless network available.

Student life. Freshman orientation: Available. Preregistration for classes offered. **Housing:** Family community housing and private guest house available. **Activities:** Concert band, choral groups, drama, student government, Organizacion Juventud en Cristo, Estudiantes Orientadores, Teatro Experimental 80, Bio-Study, Kayukembo Association, Companeros Alertas Ante Un Mundo Buscando Alternativas, alcohol and drug prevention organization, Centro de Reciclaje y Orientación Ambiental.

Athletics. Intercollegiate: Baseball M, basketball, cross-country, softball W, table tennis, tennis, track and field, volleyball, weight lifting. **Intramural:** Baseball M, basketball, cross-country, softball W, table tennis, tennis, track and field, volleyball, weight lifting. **Team name:** Tiburones.

Student services. Alcohol/substance abuse counseling, career counseling, student employment services, financial aid counseling, health services, personal counseling, placement for graduates. **Physically disabled:** Services for visually impaired.

Contact. E-mail: melba.serrano@upr.edu
Phone: (787) 890-2681 ext. 2280
Melba Serrano, Admissions Officer, University of Puerto Rico: Aguadilla, Box 6150, Aguadilla, PR 00604-6150

University of Puerto Rico: Arecibo
Arecibo, Puerto Rico
www.upra.edu   **CB code: 0911**

▶ Public 4-year university and liberal arts college
▶ Commuter campus in small city
▶ 3,881 degree-seeking undergraduates: 6% part-time, 58% women, 100% Hispanic/Latino
▶ 83% of applicants admitted
▶ 39% graduate within 6 years

General. Founded in 1967. Regionally accredited. **Degrees:** 527 bachelor's, 69 associate awarded. **ROTC:** Army. **Location:** 48 miles from San Juan. **Calendar:** Semester, limited summer session. **Special facilities:** Aerospace Education Lab was awarded to Integrated Science Multi-use Laboratory.

Freshman class profile. 1,208 applied, 1,006 admitted, 946 enrolled.

GPA 3.75 or higher:	47%	GPA 2.0-2.99:	4%
GPA 3.50-3.74:	23%	Return as sophomores:	83%
GPA 3.0-3.49:	26%		

Basis for selection. Admission index (defined and published for each academic program) based equally on high school GPA and PEAU and special abilities. SAT subject tests accepted. Applicants must take Academic Aptitude Test and Achievement Test offered by the College Entrance Examination Board, SAT and Subject Test. Interviews sometimes required. **Home schooled:** Statement describing home school structure and mission required. **Learning Disabled:** Integral educational services available for individuals with disabilities.

High school preparation. College-preparatory program recommended.

2015-2016 Annual costs. Tuition/fees: $2,014. Books/supplies: $1,862. Personal expenses: $1,236.

2014-2015 Financial aid. All financial aid based on need. 92% of total undergraduate aid awarded as scholarships/grants, 8% as loans/jobs.

Application procedures. Admission: Closing date 1/31 (receipt date). $30 fee, may be waived for applicants with need. Admission notification by 3/16. Admission notification on a rolling basis beginning on or about 3/16. Must reply by 4/30. Must reply by May 1 or within 4 week(s) if notified thereafter. **Financial aid:** Priority date 5/4, closing date 6/30. FAFSA, institutional form required. Applicants notified on a rolling basis starting 1/1; must reply within 4 week(s) of notification.

Academics. Special study options: Cooperative education, cross-registration, double major, ESL, exchange student, honors, internships, liberal arts/career combination, study abroad, Washington semester. Evening college, continuing education program, and professional improvement program. **Credit/placement by examination:** AP, CLEP, IB. **Support services:** Learning center, pre-admission summer program, remedial instruction, study skills assistance, tutoring, writing center.

Majors. Biology: Bacteriology. **Business:** Accounting, administrative services, business admin, finance, marketing. **Communications:** Radio/TV. **Communications technology:** Radio/TV. **Computer sciences:** Computer science. **Education:** Elementary, physical. **Health services:** Nursing (RN). **Psychology:** Industrial.

Most popular majors. Biology 19%, business/marketing 21%, communications/journalism 16%, health sciences 15%.

Technology on campus. 269 workstations in library, computer center. Commuter students can connect to campus network. Online library, student web hosting, wireless network available.

Student life. Freshman orientation: Mandatory. Preregistration for classes offered. Four-day program held (mornings) in summer. **Housing:** Authorized list provided by DACO (Departamento de Asuntos del Consumidor) for reference to accommodation off campus. **Activities:** Concert band, choral groups, dance, drama, film society, radio station, student government, student newspaper, Cheerleaders UPRA, Rhythm Busters, Federacion de Estudiantes de Iberoamericana, Asociación de Estudiantes Coro de Concierto, Asociación Nacional de Estudiantes de Educación, writers club, Capítulo de Estudiantes de Microbiología, Asociación Intercesores Cristiana, ACTRE.

Athletics. Intercollegiate: Baseball M, basketball, cross-country W, judo, sand volleyball, soccer, softball W, table tennis, track and field, volleyball, weight lifting, wrestling M. **Intramural:** Basketball M, track and field, weight lifting W. **Team name:** Los Lobos (Wolves).

Student services. Alcohol/substance abuse counseling, career counseling, services for economically disadvantaged, student employment services, financial aid counseling, health services, personal counseling, veterans' counselor. **Physically disabled:** Services for visually, speech, hearing impaired.

Contact. E-mail: admisiones.arecibo@upr.edu
Phone: (787) 815-0000 ext. 4100 Fax: (787) 817-3461
Magaly Mendez, Admissions Officer, University of Puerto Rico: Arecibo, PO Box 4010, Arecibo, PR 00614-4010

University of Puerto Rico: Bayamon University College
Bayamon, Puerto Rico
www.uprb.edu   **CB code: 0852**

▶ Public 4-year university and technical college
▶ Commuter campus in small city
▶ 5,000 degree-seeking undergraduates

General. Founded in 1971. Regionally accredited. **Degrees:** 455 bachelor's, 27 associate awarded. **ROTC:** Army. **Location:** 9 miles from San Juan. **Calendar:** Semester, limited summer session. **Full-time faculty:** 180 total;

39% have terminal degrees, 100% minority, 53% women. **Part-time faculty:** 92 total; 21% have terminal degrees, 100% minority, 61% women. **Special facilities:** Multimedia laboratory.

Basis for selection. High school GPA and test scores most important. Higher scores required of applicants to bachelor's programs. Special consideration given to applicants with special talents or handicaps. SAT and 2 SAT Subject Tests (Spanish, mathematics) accepted for English-speaking applicants from U.S. mainland. PAA required of Spanish-speaking applicants.

High school preparation. 12 units required. Required and recommended units include English 2, mathematics 2, social studies 1-2 and science 1. 3 units Spanish also required.

2015-2016 Annual costs. Tuition/fees: $2,014. Books/supplies: $1,825. Personal expenses: $1,200.

Financial aid. All financial aid based on need.

Application procedures. Admission: Priority date 12/10; deadline 1/31 (receipt date). $15 fee. Application must be submitted on paper. Admission notification on a rolling basis beginning on or about 4/25. Must reply by 5/30. **Financial aid:** Closing date 6/15. Institutional form required. Applicants notified by 7/12; must reply within 4 week(s) of notification.

Academics. Special study options: Cooperative education, cross-registration, double major, ESL, exchange student, honors, internships. **Credit/placement by examination:** AP, CLEP. **Support services:** Pre-admission summer program, reduced course load, study skills assistance, tutoring.

Majors. Biology: General. **Business:** Accounting, business admin, executive assistant, finance, logistics, marketing. **Computer sciences:** General. **Education:** Multi-level teacher, physically handicapped.

Most popular majors. Biology 14%, business/marketing 48%, computer/information sciences 10%, education 23%, engineering/engineering technologies 6%.

Technology on campus. 370 workstations in computer center. Commuter students can connect to campus network. Wireless network available.

Student life. Freshman orientation: Available. Preregistration for classes offered. **Activities:** Bands, choral groups, drama, student government, student newspaper, Confraternidad de Cristianos Unidos, Asociacion Juventud Catolica, Society for Human Resource Management, Asociacion de Estudiantes Orientadores, American Marketing Association, Asociacion de Estudiantes de Computadoras, Asociacion de Gerencia de Materiales.

Athletics. NCAA. **Intercollegiate:** Baseball M, basketball, cheerleading, cross-country, swimming, table tennis, tennis, track and field, volleyball, weight lifting, wrestling M. **Intramural:** Table tennis, tennis, volleyball. **Team name:** Vaqueros.

Student services. Adult student services, career counseling, student employment services, health services, personal counseling, placement for graduates.

Contact. E-mail: cmontes@uprb.edu
Phone: (787) 993-8952 Fax: (787) 993-8929
Carmen Montes, Director of Admissions, University of Puerto Rico: Bayamon University College, 174 Street #170 Minillas Industrial Park, Bayamon, PR 00959-1919

University of Puerto Rico: Carolina Regional College
Carolina, Puerto Rico
www.uprc.edu   **CB code: 3891**

- Public 4-year university
- Commuter campus in small city
- 3,678 degree-seeking undergraduates: 18% part-time, 61% women
- 27% of applicants admitted
- Interview required
- 36% graduate within 6 years

General. Founded in 1974. Regionally accredited. **Degrees:** 569 bachelor's, 90 associate awarded. **Location:** 10 miles from San Juan. **Calendar:** Quarter, limited summer session. **Full-time faculty:** 104 total; 96% minority, 44% women. **Part-time faculty:** 117 total; 91% minority, 37% women.

Freshman class profile. 4,237 applied, 1,124 admitted, 922 enrolled.

Mid 50% test scores			
SAT critical reading:	450-560	GPA 3.0-3.49:	33%
SAT math:	440-560	GPA 2.0-2.99:	8%
GPA 3.75 or higher:	33%	End year in good standing:	84%
GPA 3.50-3.74:	26%	Return as sophomores:	78%

Basis for selection. High school GPA and test scores important. SAT and SAT Subject Tests in Spanish, Math Level 1 required of English-speaking applicants. Interview recommended for those with exceptional ability. **Home schooled:** Transcript of courses and grades, state high school equivalency certificate required. College Entrance Examination Board admission test scores required. SAT-scores can be accepted if submitted.

High school preparation. 18 units required. Required units include English 3, mathematics 3, social studies 3, science 3, foreign language 3 and academic electives 3. 3 units of spanish language.

2015-2016 Annual costs. Tuition/fees: $2,691. Books/supplies: $2,790. Personal expenses: $1,236.

2014-2015 Financial aid. All financial aid based on need. 92% of total undergraduate aid awarded as scholarships/grants, 8% as loans/jobs.

Application procedures. Admission: Closing date 1/31 (postmark date). $20 fee. Must reply by 6/12. **Financial aid:** Closing date 4/30. FAFSA, institutional form required. Applicants notified by 6/30; Applicants notified on a rolling basis starting 6/10.

Academics. Special study options: Combined bachelor's/graduate degree, distance learning, honors, independent study, internships, study abroad. **Credit/placement by examination:** AP, CLEP, SAT. 12 credit hours maximum toward associate degree, 12 toward bachelor's. **Support services:** Learning center, pre-admission summer program, remedial instruction, tutoring.

Majors. Business: Administrative services, business admin, executive assistant, finance, hotel/motel admin, tourism promotion. **Communications:** Advertising. **Communications technology:** Graphic/printing. **Education:** Multiple handicapped, technology/industrial arts, trade/industrial. **Protective services:** Law enforcement admin. **Psychology:** Forensic.

Most popular majors. Business/marketing 39%, communications/journalism 9%, communication technologies 11%, psychology 23%, security/protective services 12%.

Technology on campus. 163 workstations in library, computer center. Online course registration, online library, wireless network available.

Student life. Freshman orientation: Mandatory. Preregistration for classes offered. **Activities:** Bands, campus ministries, choral groups, dance, drama, international student organizations, musical theater, radio station, student government, symphony orchestra, TV station, consejo de estudiantes, Asociacion Estudiantes de Sistemas de Oficina, Universitarios Cristianos en Accion, Jaguares, Asociación Estudiantil de Administración de Hoteles y Resturantes, Asociacion Estudiatil Estudios Turisticos Universitarios, Soc Nacional Honorario de Biologia Cap. Zeta Mu, Asociacion de Justicia Criminal, Organizacion Por-ambiente, Phi Beta Lambda, Enactus, Asociacion Estudiantil Departamento de diseno.

Athletics. Intercollegiate: Baseball M, basketball, cheerleading, soccer M, softball W, tennis, track and field, volleyball, weight lifting. **Intramural:** Basketball M, table tennis M. **Team name:** Jaguar.

Student services. Alcohol/substance abuse counseling, career counseling, services for economically disadvantaged, student employment services, financial aid counseling, health services, on-campus daycare, personal counseling, veterans' counselor. **Physically disabled:** Services for visually impaired.

Contact. Phone: (787) 757-1485 Fax: (787) 750-7940
Celia Méndez, Director of Admissions, University of Puerto Rico: Carolina Regional College, PO Box 4800, Carolina, PR 00984-4800

University of Puerto Rico: Cayey University College
Cayey, Puerto Rico
www.cayey.upr.edu   **CB code: 0981**

- Public 4-year university and liberal arts college
- Commuter campus in large town
- 3,737 degree-seeking undergraduates
- SAT or ACT required

General. Founded in 1967. Regionally accredited. Located on former military base. **Degrees:** 526 bachelor's awarded. **ROTC:** Army. **Location:** 30 miles from San Juan. **Calendar:** Semester, limited summer session. **Full-time faculty:** 99 total; 71% have terminal degrees, 100% minority. **Part-time faculty:** 54 total; 44% have terminal degrees, 100% minority. **Class size:** 31% < 20, 67% 20-39, less than 1% 40-49, less than 1% 50-99. **Special facilities:** Eco-park, ecological learning center, interdisciplinary research center, women's violence prevention center.

Freshman class profile.

GPA 3.75 or higher:	53%	GPA 3.0-3.49:	21%
GPA 3.50-3.74:	21%	GPA 2.0-2.99:	5%

Basis for selection. GPA and CEEB verbal and math. SAT required for English-speaking applicants. Students from Puerto Rico must submit CEEB test scores for math and verbal aptitude. SAT critical reading will be used to evaluate verbal aptitude. Audition, portfolio required for admission of candidates based on special talents such as sports; interview recommended for music, theater programs. **Home schooled:** Transcript of courses and grades, state high school equivalency certificate required.

High school preparation. College-preparatory program required. 18 units required. Required units include English 3, mathematics 3, social studies 3, history 3, science 2 and academic electives 3. 3 units of Spanish required.

2015-2016 Annual costs. Tuition/fees: $2,014. Books/supplies: $2,735. Personal expenses: $1,200.

Financial aid. All financial aid based on need.

Application procedures. Admission: Closing date 1/31 (postmark date). $20 fee. Admission notification by 4/4. Must reply by 5/4. **Financial aid:** Closing date 6/30. FAFSA required. Applicants notified by 7/30.

Academics. Special study options: Accelerated study, double major, ESL, exchange student, honors, internships, liberal arts/career combination, study abroad, teacher certification program. **Credit/placement by examination:** AP, CLEP, institutional tests. 72 credit hours maximum toward associate degree, 135 toward bachelor's. **Support services:** Learning center, pre-admission summer program, remedial instruction, tutoring, writing center.

Majors. Biology: General. **Business:** General, accounting, administrative services, business admin, office/clerical. **Education:** English, history, mathematics, physical, science, social science, social studies, Spanish, special ed. **English:** English lit. **Foreign languages:** Spanish. **History:** General. **Liberal arts:** Humanities. **Math:** General. **Physical sciences:** Chemistry. **Psychology:** General. **Social sciences:** General, economics, sociology.

Most popular majors. Biology 16%, business/marketing 26%, education 22%, physical sciences 7%, psychology 21%.

Technology on campus. 1,100 workstations in library, computer center, student center. Online course registration, online library, wireless network available.

Student life. Freshman orientation: Mandatory. Preregistration for classes offered. **Housing:** Housing available for some athletes and exchange students. **Activities:** Bands, choral groups, dance, drama, literary magazine, radio station, student government, student newspaper, student association program honors studies, psychology student association, Psy-Chi, history circle, English club, chemistry circle, American medical student association, GAIA, math circle, accounting students association, Lions Club.

Athletics. Intercollegiate: Basketball, cross-country, soccer, softball W, swimming M, table tennis, tennis, volleyball, weight lifting. **Intramural:** Basketball, cross-country, soccer, softball W, swimming M, table tennis, tennis, volleyball, weight lifting. **Team name:** Toritos.

Student services. Alcohol/substance abuse counseling, career counseling, services for economically disadvantaged, student employment services, financial aid counseling, health services, on-campus daycare, personal counseling, placement for graduates, veterans' counselor, women's services. **Physically disabled:** Services for visually impaired.

Contact. E-mail: admisiones@upr.edu
Phone: (787) 738-2161 ext. 2233
Toll-free number: (787) 738-2161 ext. 2208 Fax: (787) 738-5633
Wilfredo Lopez, Director of Admissions, University of Puerto Rico: Cayey University College, Oficina de Admisiones UPR- Cayey, Cayey, PR 00737-2230

University of Puerto Rico: Humacao
Humacao, Puerto Rico   CB member
www.uprh.edu   CB code: 0874

- Public 4-year university and liberal arts college
- Commuter campus in small city
- 3,732 degree-seeking undergraduates: 6% part-time, 64% women, 93% Hispanic/Latino, 1% Multi-racial, non-Hispanic
- 48% of applicants admitted
- 44% graduate within 6 years

General. Founded in 1962. Regionally accredited. **Degrees:** 470 bachelor's, 69 associate awarded. **Location:** 30 miles from San Juan. **Calendar:** Semester, limited summer session. **Special facilities:** Observatory, census data center, communication competencies center, Casa Roig Museum.

Freshman class profile. 2,169 applied, 1,050 admitted, 990 enrolled.

GPA 3.75 or higher:	52%	GPA 2.0-2.99:	4%
GPA 3.50-3.74:	25%	Return as sophomores:	90%
GPA 3.0-3.49:	19%		

Basis for selection. High school achievement record, test scores important. Non-native speakers of Spanish required to prove fluency through institutional examinations, interviews. SAT scores accepted from U.S. mainland students. Spanish version of Puerto Rico CEEB of the College Board required: aptitude test (verbal and mathematics) and achievement test battery (Spanish, English and mathematics). In lieu of the above, applicants may take SAT and SAT Subject Tests (Spanish Composition and Spanish Reading). SAT Subject Test (Spanish and Mathematics level) required for English speaking applicant. **Home schooled:** Sworn statement indicating that student received formal education at home. **Learning Disabled:** Director of Disabled Students Services Office (SERPI) evaluates learning disabled students to determine if they qualify for special admission.

High school preparation. 18 units recommended. Recommended units include English 3, mathematics 3, social studies 1, history 2, science 3, foreign language 3 and academic electives 3. Foreign language must be Spanish.

2015-2016 Annual costs. Tuition/fees: $2,014. Books/supplies: $1,862. Personal expenses: $1,236.

Financial aid. Non-need-based: Scholarships awarded for academics, athletics, music/drama.

Application procedures. Admission: Closing date 1/31 (receipt date). No application fee. Admission notification by 4/15. Admission notification on a rolling basis. Must reply by 5/1. **Financial aid:** Priority date 3/1, closing date 6/30. FAFSA required. Applicants notified on a rolling basis starting 4/30; must reply by 7/31.

Academics. Course work conducted in Spanish. **Special study options:** Exchange student, honors, internships, teacher certification program. **Credit/placement by examination:** AP, CLEP. **Support services:** Learning center, remedial instruction, study skills assistance, tutoring, writing center.

Majors. Biology: General, marine, microbiology. **Business:** Accounting, administrative services, business admin, human resources, international. **Communications:** Digital media. **Conservation:** Wildlife/wilderness. **Education:** Elementary, ESL. **Health services:** Nursing (RN). **Human services:** Social work. **Math:** Computational. **Physical sciences:** Chemistry, physics. **Social sciences:** General.

Most popular majors. Biology 18%, business/marketing 40%, education 9%, health sciences 9%, physical sciences 7%, public administration/social services 10%.

Technology on campus. 1,000 workstations in library, computer center. Online course registration, online library, wireless network available.

Student life. Freshman orientation: Available. Preregistration for classes offered. One-day program that describes student services and undergraduate curriculum. **Activities:** Marching band, choral groups, dance, student government, various religious and social service organizations available.

Athletics. Intercollegiate: Baseball M, basketball, cheerleading, cross-country, judo, soccer M, softball W, swimming, track and field, volleyball, weight lifting, wrestling M. **Intramural:** Basketball, softball W, volleyball. **Team name:** Buhos.

Student services. Alcohol/substance abuse counseling, career counseling, student employment services, financial aid counseling, health services, personal counseling, women's services. **Physically disabled:** Services for visually, speech, hearing impaired.

Contact. E-mail: milagros.alvarez@upr.edu
Phone: (787) 850-0000 ext. 9301
Toll-free number: (787) 850-0000 ext. 9428 Fax: (787) 850-9428
Milagros Alvarez, Director of Admissions, University of Puerto Rico:
Humacao, Call Box 860, Humacao, PR 00792

University of Puerto Rico: Mayaguez

Mayaguez, Puerto Rico   CB member
www.uprm.edu   CB code: 0912

- Public 5-year university, agricultural and engineering college
- Commuter campus in small city
- 11,518 degree-seeking undergraduates: 6% part-time, 46% women
- 1,000 degree-seeking graduate students
- 77% of applicants admitted
- SAT Subject Tests required

General. Founded in 1911. Regionally accredited. Most courses conducted in Spanish. Students must have working knowledge of Spanish and English. **Degrees:** 1,607 bachelor's awarded; master's, doctoral offered. **ROTC:** Army, Air Force. **Location:** 100 miles from San Juan. **Calendar:** Semester, limited summer session. **Class size:** 36% < 20, 57% 20-39, 2% 40-49, 5% 50-99, less than 1% >100. **Special facilities:** Planetarium, botanical garden, agricultural extension service, agricultural experimental station, natural history collection, resource center for science and engineering.

Freshman class profile. 3,318 applied, 2,566 admitted, 2,371 enrolled.

Basis for selection. Applicants must have high school diploma or its equivalent from educational institution duly accredited by Department of Education of Puerto Rico. Prospective applicants must take University Evaluation and Admissions Tests (PEAU in Spanish) administered by the College Board. First-year applicants only considered for admission in August of first semester. Applications should be submitted before November 30 of year prior to admission. SAT and SAT Subject Tests required for English-speaking applicants. Students from Puerto Rico required to submit scores from College Board Entrance Examination aptitude tests. **Home schooled:** State high school equivalency certificate required. Must supply notarized document (sworn statement) that functions as certification of student educated in home.

High school preparation. 18 units recommended. Recommended units include English 3, mathematics 2, social studies 2, history 2, science 2, foreign language 3 and academic electives 4.

2015-2016 Annual costs. Tuition/fees: $2,014. Books/supplies: $1,825. Personal expenses: $2,900.

2014-2015 Financial aid. All financial aid based on need. 1,826 full-time freshmen applied for aid; 1,688 deemed to have need; 1,482 received aid. Average need met was 44%. Average scholarship/grant was $5,577; average loan $3,382. 82% of total undergraduate aid awarded as scholarships/grants, 18% as loans/jobs.

Application procedures. Admission: Closing date 12/15 (postmark date). $20 fee. Admission notification on a rolling basis beginning on or about 4/1. Must reply by 4/15. **Financial aid:** Priority date 1/30, closing date 6/30. FAFSA, institutional form required. Applicants notified on a rolling basis starting 6/30.

Academics. Online support available. Spanish language skills (reading, writing) required to read most online course materials. **Special study options:** Cooperative education, distance learning, double major, ESL, exchange student, honors, internships, study abroad, teacher certification program. **Credit/placement by examination:** AP, CLEP, SAT, institutional tests. **Support services:** Reduced course load, remedial instruction, tutoring, writing center.

Majors. Biology: General, biotechnology, marine, microbiology. **Business:** Accounting, administrative services, business admin, finance, human resources, marketing, office management, organizational behavior, sales/distribution. **Computer sciences:** General, computer science, systems analysis. **Education:** Agricultural, mathematics, physical. **Engineering:** General, chemical, civil, computer, electrical, industrial, mechanical. **English:** English lit. **Foreign languages:** Comparative lit, French, Spanish. **Health services:** Athletic training, nursing (RN), premedicine. **History:** General. **Math:** General. **Parks/recreation:** Facilities management, health/fitness. **Philosophy/religion:** Philosophy. **Physical sciences:** General, chemistry, geology, physics. **Psychology:** General. **Social sciences:** General, economics, political science, sociology. **Visual/performing arts:** Art history/conservation, studio arts.

Most popular majors. Agriculture 7%, biology 17%, business/marketing 11%, engineering/engineering technologies 34%, health sciences 7%, psychology 6%, social sciences 7%.

Technology on campus. Commuter students can connect to campus network. Online library, wireless network available.

Student life. Freshman orientation: Mandatory. Preregistration for classes offered. Four-day session held during week preceding start of Fall classes. **Housing:** Housing available near campus. **Activities:** Bands, choral groups, dance, drama, literary magazine, radio station, student government, student newspaper, Asociación de Colegiales Evangelicos, Federación Adventista de Universitarios, Grupo de Apostolado Católico, Hermandad Colegial de Avivamiento, Jóvenes Cristianos del Parque, Asociación de Colombianos del RUM, Asociación de Estudiantes Dominicanos del RUM, Juventud Popular Universitaria, Universitarios Estadístas en Acción.

Athletics. NCAA. **Intercollegiate:** Baseball M, basketball, cross-country, gymnastics, soccer M, softball W, swimming, table tennis, tennis, track and field, volleyball, water polo M, wrestling M. **Intramural:** Archery, baseball M, basketball, cross-country, racquetball, soccer M, softball, swimming, table tennis, tennis, volleyball, water polo M, wrestling M. **Team name:** Tarzanes "Bulldogs".

Student services. Alcohol/substance abuse counseling, career counseling, student employment services, financial aid counseling, health services, personal counseling, placement for graduates, veterans' counselor, women's services. **Physically disabled:** Services for visually, speech, hearing impaired.

Contact. E-mail: admisiones@upr.edu
Phone: (787) 265-3811 Fax: (787) 834-5265
Maria Alemany, Director of Admissions, University of Puerto Rico:
Mayaguez, Admissions Office, Mayaguez, PR 00681-9000

University of Puerto Rico: Medical Sciences

San Juan, Puerto Rico
www.rcm.upr.edu   CB code: 0631

- Public 4-year university
- Commuter campus in large city
- 489 degree-seeking undergraduates
- 1,764 graduate students

General. Founded in 1950. Regionally accredited. First-time freshmen not admitted. **Degrees:** 151 bachelor's, 43 associate awarded; master's, professional, doctoral offered. **Calendar:** Continuous, limited summer session. **Full-time faculty:** 687 total. **Part-time faculty:** 188 total. **Class size:** 53% < 20, 39% 20-39, 4% 40-49, 4% 50-99.

Basis for selection. Candidates are admitted on a competitive basis. Applicants must present evidence of successful completion of all admission requirements for the program in which they are interested. In most programs, an admissions committee will also consider nonacademic factors as additional criteria in screening applicants.

2015-2016 Annual costs. Tuition/fees: $2,196. Books/supplies: $1,825. Personal expenses: $800.

Financial aid. All financial aid based on need.

Application procedures. Admission: Closing date 2/15 (receipt date). $20 fee. Application must be submitted online. **Financial aid:** Priority date 4/30, closing date 6/15. FAFSA, institutional form required. Applicants notified on a rolling basis starting 8/1; must reply within 2 week(s) of notification.

Academics. Special study options: Combined bachelor's/graduate degree, exchange student, honors, internships. **Credit/placement by examination:** AP, CLEP. **Support services:** Tutoring.

Majors. Health services: Clinical lab science, clinical lab technology, nuclear medical technology, nursing (RN), public health ed, veterinary technology/assistant.

Technology on campus. 216 workstations in library, computer center. Commuter students can connect to campus network. Helpline, repair service available.

Student life. Activities: Choral groups, dance, drama, student government.

Athletics. Intramural: Basketball M, soccer M, softball M, volleyball.

Student services. Career counseling, student employment services, financial aid counseling, health services, legal services, personal counseling, women's services. **Physically disabled:** Services for visually impaired.

Contact. E-mail: yolanda.rivera3@upr.edu
Phone: (787) 758-2525 ext. 5211 Fax: (787) 282-7117
Yolanda Rivera, Director, Central Office of Admissions, University of
Puerto Rico: Medical Sciences, PO Box 365067, San Juan, PR
00936-5067

University of Puerto Rico: Ponce
Ponce, Puerto Rico
www.uprp.edu   CB code: 0836

- Public 4-year university and branch campus college
- Commuter campus in small city
- 3,543 degree-seeking undergraduates: 7% part-time, 57% women, 100%
  Hispanic/Latino
- 51% of applicants admitted
- 38% graduate within 6 years

General. Founded in 1970. Regionally accredited. **Degrees:** 339 bachelor's,
60 associate awarded. **ROTC:** Army. **Location:** 68 miles from San Juan,
46 miles from Mayaguez. **Calendar:** Semester, limited summer session. **Full-
time faculty:** 119 total; 68% have terminal degrees, 100% minority, 56%
women. **Part-time faculty:** 84 total; 100% minority, 49% women. **Class
size:** 29% < 20, 71% 20-39.

Freshman class profile. 2,138 applied, 1,080 admitted, 927 enrolled.

GPA 3.75 or higher:	50%	GPA 2.0-2.99:	3%
GPA 3.50-3.74:	25%	Return as sophomores:	45%
GPA 3.0-3.49:	22%		

Basis for selection. Admission based on general application index, combination of high school GPA and College Board test scores (50% each). Programs have their own GAI requirements. Interview required for academically
weak and special ability. **Home schooled:** State high school equivalency
certificate required.

High school preparation. 18 units required. Required units include
English 3, mathematics 3, social studies 3, science 3 and academic electives
2. 3 units Spanish, 1 unit fine arts.

2015-2016 Annual costs. Tuition/fees: $2,019. Books/supplies: $1,682.
Personal expenses: $1,236.

2015-2016 Financial aid. All financial aid based on need. 94% of total
undergraduate aid awarded as scholarships/grants, 6% as loans/jobs.

Application procedures. Admission: Closing date 11/30. $20 fee.
Admission notification on a rolling basis beginning on or about 4/15. Must
reply by May 1 or within 3 week(s) if notified thereafter. **Financial aid:**
Closing date 5/30. FAFSA, institutional form required.

Academics. Special study options: Dual enrollment of high school students, honors, internships. **Credit/placement by examination:** AP, CLEP.
Support services: Remedial instruction, tutoring.

Majors. Biology: General. **Business:** Accounting, administrative services,
business admin, finance, marketing. **Computer sciences:** General. **Education:** Elementary. **Health services:** Athletic training. **Math:** General. **Protective services:** Forensics. **Psychology:** General.

Most popular majors. Biology 23%, business/marketing 36%, education
7%, health sciences 10%, psychology 19%.

Technology on campus. 344 workstations in library, computer center,
student center. Wireless network available.

Student life. Freshman orientation: Mandatory. Preregistration for
classes offered. **Activities:** Bands, choral groups, dance, drama, student government, Christian youth organizations.

Athletics. Intercollegiate: Basketball, cross-country, softball, table tennis,
tennis, track and field, volleyball. **Intramural:** Basketball, cross-country,
gymnastics, softball, table tennis, tennis, track and field, volleyball.

Student services. Career counseling, student employment services, health
services, on-campus daycare, personal counseling, placement for graduates,
veterans' counselor. **Physically disabled:** Services for visually impaired.

Contact. E-mail: emily.matos@upr.edu
Phone: (787) 844-8181 ext. 2531 Fax: (787) 840-8108
Emily, Director of Admissions, University of Puerto Rico: Ponce, Box
7186, Ponce, PR 00732

University of Puerto Rico: Rio Piedras
San Juan, Puerto Rico   CB member
www.uprrp.edu   CB code: 0979

- Public 4-year university
- Commuter campus in very large city
- 13,002 degree-seeking undergraduates: 11% part-time, 62% women,
  64% Hispanic/Latino
- 3,440 degree-seeking graduate students
- 30% of applicants admitted
- SAT required
- 44% graduate within 6 years

General. Founded in 1903. Regionally accredited. Most courses conducted
in Spanish. Students must have working knowledge of Spanish and English.
Degrees: 1,748 bachelor's awarded; master's, professional, doctoral offered.
ROTC: Army, Air Force. **Calendar:** Semester, limited summer session.
Full-time faculty: 798 total. **Part-time faculty:** 152 total. **Class size:** 44%
< 20, 53% 20-39, 1% 40-49, 2% 50-99, less than 1% >100. **Special facilities:**
Theater, warm-blooded animal house, herbarium, biology museum, high-
technology microscopy facility, nanotechnology lasers, virtual astronomy
lab; museum of history, anthropology and art.

Freshman class profile. 10,722 applied, 3,191 admitted, 2,769 enrolled.

Mid 50% test scores			
		GPA 3.0-3.49:	22%
SAT critical reading:	520-630	GPA 2.0-2.99:	7%
SAT math:	500-660	End year in good standing:	83%
GPA 3.75 or higher:	48%	Return as sophomores:	91%
GPA 3.50-3.74:	23%	Live on campus:	10%

Basis for selection. Admissions based on secondary school record and
standardized test scores. Talent and ability considered. Verbal and math
Academic Aptitude Test offered by the College Entrance Examination Board
required. Environmental Design requires separate application form and school
test; Fine Arts requires departmental test. **Home schooled:** Transcript of
courses and grades required. Notarized homeschooling certificate required.

High school preparation. 18 units required. Required units include
English 3, mathematics 3, social studies 3, science 3, foreign language 3,
computer science .5, visual/performing arts .5. Responsible fatherhood and
motherhood .5, health .5, physical education 1.

2015-2016 Annual costs. Tuition/fees: $2,014. Room/board: $8,280.
Books/supplies: $1,862. Personal expenses: $1,236.

2014-2015 Financial aid. All financial aid based on need. 96% of total
undergraduate aid awarded as scholarships/grants, 4% as loans/jobs. **Additional information:** Tuition waived for honor students, athletes, members
of chorus, and others with special talents.

Application procedures. Admission: Priority date 12/16; deadline 1/31
(postmark date). $20 fee. Admission notification by 4/15. Admission notifica-
tion on a rolling basis. Must reply by 3/1. **Financial aid:** Closing date 4/1.
FAFSA required.

Academics. Special study options: Combined bachelor's/graduate degree,
cooperative education, double major, exchange student, external degree, honors, internships, liberal arts/career combination, semester at sea, student-
designed major, study abroad, teacher certification program, Washington
semester. **Credit/placement by examination:** AP, CLEP, SAT, institutional
tests. 30 credit hours maximum toward bachelor's degree. **Support services:**
Remedial instruction, study skills assistance, tutoring, writing center.

Majors. Architecture: Environmental design. **Biology:** General. **Business:**
General, accounting, administrative services, finance, human resources, labor
relations, management information systems, managerial economics, marketing, operations, statistics. **Communications:** Digital media, journalism,
media studies, public relations. **Computer sciences:** Computer science. **Conservation:** Environmental science. **Education:** Elementary, family/consumer
sciences, secondary. **English:** English lit. **Foreign languages:** General, comparative lit, French, Spanish. **History:** American, European. **Human services:** Social work. **Liberal arts:** Arts/sciences. **Math:** General. **Philosophy/
religion:** Philosophy. **Physical sciences:** Chemistry, physics. **Psychology:**
General. **Social sciences:** General, anthropology, economics, geography,
political science, sociology. **Visual/performing arts:** General, art, art history/
conservation, dramatic, drawing, multimedia, music, painting, photography,
sculpture, studio arts. **Work/family studies:** General, food/nutrition.

Most popular majors. Business/marketing 22%, communications/journal-
ism 6%, family/consumer sciences 8%, foreign language 10%, social sciences
14%, visual/performing arts 8%.

Technology on campus. 154 workstations in dormitories, library, computer center, student center. Dormitories wired for high-speed internet access

and linked to campus network. Commuter students can connect to campus network. Online library, wireless network available.

Student life. **Freshman orientation:** Available. Preregistration for classes offered. Session held for 1 day in summer. **Policies:** Students represented in university administration. **Housing:** Coed dorms, wellness housing available. $35 fully refundable deposit, deadline 5/31. **Activities:** Jazz band, choral groups, dance, drama, literary magazine, musical theater, opera, radio station, student government, student newspaper, Club Avanza, Confraternidad Universitaria de Avivamiento, Jovenes Cristianos Universitarios, Juventud Universitaria Popular, Club de la Cruz Roja Americana del Recinto de Rio Piedras.

Athletics. NAIA, NCAA. **Intercollegiate:** Basketball W, cross-country, soccer M, swimming, tennis, track and field, volleyball. **Intramural:** Basketball, cross-country, gymnastics, soccer M, softball, swimming, table tennis, tennis, track and field, volleyball, water polo, wrestling M. **Team name:** Gallitos/Jerezanas.

Student services. Adult student services, alcohol/substance abuse counseling, career counseling, student employment services, health services, on-campus daycare, personal counseling, placement for graduates, veterans' counselor. **Physically disabled:** Services for visually, speech, hearing impaired.

Contact. E-mail: admisiones@uprrp.edu
Phone: (787) 764-0000 ext. 85712 Fax: (787) 764-3680
Angel Echevarría, Director of Admissions, University of Puerto Rico: Rio Piedras, Box 21907, San Juan, PR 00931-1907

University of Puerto Rico: Utuado

Utuado, Puerto Rico	**CB member**
uprutuado.edu	**CB code: 3893**

- Public 4-year agricultural college
- Commuter campus in large town
- 1,405 degree-seeking undergraduates: 4% part-time, 52% women, 100% Hispanic/Latino
- 39% of applicants admitted
- Interview required

General. Founded in 1979. Regionally accredited. **Degrees:** 36 bachelor's, 119 associate awarded. **ROTC:** Army. **Location:** 20 miles from Arecibo. **Calendar:** Semester, limited summer session. **Full-time faculty:** 66 total; 56% have terminal degrees, 100% minority, 46% women. **Part-time faculty:** 22 total; 14% have terminal degrees, 100% minority, 41% women. **Special facilities:** 118-acre farm.

Freshman class profile. 2,422 applied, 950 admitted, 564 enrolled.

Basis for selection. High school GPA, test scores important. SAT required for English-speaking students.

High school preparation. College-preparatory program required. Required units include English 3, mathematics 2, history 3, science 2 and foreign language 3. 3 fine arts required.

2015-2016 Annual costs. Tuition/fees: $2,019. Books/supplies: $1,862. Personal expenses: $1,236.

2014-2015 Financial aid. All financial aid based on need. 85% of total undergraduate aid awarded as scholarships/grants, 15% as loans/jobs.

Application procedures. **Admission:** $20 fee, may be waived for applicants with need. Must reply by May 1 or within 2 week(s) if notified thereafter. **Financial aid:** Priority date 5/31; no closing date. FAFSA required. Applicants notified on a rolling basis starting 9/30; must reply within 4 week(s) of notification.

Academics. **Special study options:** Combined bachelor's/graduate degree, cooperative education, honors, internships, teacher certification program. **Credit/placement by examination:** AP, CLEP, SAT. **Support services:** Learning center, reduced course load, remedial instruction, tutoring.

Majors. **Business:** Accounting, executive assistant. **Education:** Elementary.

Most popular majors. Business/marketing 56%, education 25%.

Technology on campus. 90 workstations in library. Online library, wireless network available.

Student life. **Freshman orientation:** Mandatory. Preregistration for classes offered. **Housing:** Wellness housing available. Private housing near college available. **Activities:** Choral groups, drama, student government.

Athletics. **Intercollegiate:** Baseball M, basketball, cross-country, judo M, soccer, softball M, table tennis, track and field, volleyball, weight lifting, wrestling M. **Intramural:** Baseball M, basketball, cross-country, soccer, softball M, table tennis, track and field, volleyball, weight lifting, wrestling M. **Team name:** Guaraguao.

Student services. Alcohol/substance abuse counseling, career counseling, financial aid counseling, health services, personal counseling, placement for graduates, veterans' counselor.

Contact. Phone: (787) 894-2828 ext. 2212 Fax: (787) 894-2891
María Robles, Admissions Officer, University of Puerto Rico: Utuado, PO Box 2500, Utuado, PR 00641

University of the Sacred Heart

San Juan, Puerto Rico	**CB member**
www.sagrado.edu	**CB code: 0913**

- Private 4-year university and liberal arts college affiliated with the Roman Catholic Church
- Commuter campus in large city
- 4,420 degree-seeking undergraduates

General. Founded in 1935. Regionally accredited. **Degrees:** 782 bachelor's, 81 associate awarded; master's offered. **Calendar:** Semester, extensive summer session. **Full-time faculty:** 126 total; 66% women. **Part-time faculty:** 296 total; 49% women. **Special facilities:** Jardin Escultorico, Museo de la Radio, Pabellon de las Artes, Patio de las Artes, Galeria Jose (Pepin) Mendez y Teatro Emilio S. Belaval.

Freshman class profile.

GPA 3.75 or higher:	16%	GPA 3.0-3.49:	34%
GPA 3.50-3.74:	14%	GPA 2.0-2.99:	35%

Basis for selection. High school GPA and highest score CEEB important. SAT scores accepted in place of CEEB. Interview required for nursing program.

High school preparation. 15 units required. Required and recommended units include English 3, mathematics 3, social studies 2, science 3, foreign language 3 and academic electives 3.

2015-2016 Annual costs. Tuition/fees: $6,950. Room only: $3,100. Books/supplies: $2,500. Personal expenses: $4,595.

Financial aid. **Non-need-based:** Scholarships awarded for academics, athletics.

Application procedures. **Admission:** Priority date 12/15; deadline 6/30. $15 fee, may be waived for applicants with need. Admission notification on a rolling basis. **Financial aid:** Priority date 4/30, closing date 5/30. FAFSA, institutional form required. Applicants notified on a rolling basis starting 6/15; must reply by 8/30.

Academics. **Special study options:** Combined bachelor's/graduate degree, cooperative education, cross-registration, double major, dual enrollment of high school students, exchange student, external degree, honors, independent study, internships, liberal arts/career combination, semester at sea, teacher certification program. International programs with universities in Mexico and Spain. **Credit/placement by examination:** AP, CLEP, institutional tests. **Support services:** Pre-admission summer program, reduced course load, remedial instruction, tutoring.

Majors. **Biology:** General. **Business:** Accounting, business admin, tourism promotion. **Communications:** Advertising, communications/speech/rhetoric, journalism. **Computer sciences:** Computer science, information systems. **Education:** General, bilingual, elementary, secondary. **Health services:** Nursing (RN). **Human services:** Social work. **Math:** General. **Parks/recreation:** Health/fitness. **Physical sciences:** Chemistry. **Psychology:** General. **Social sciences:** General. **Visual/performing arts:** General, dramatic, photography.

Most popular majors. Business/marketing 16%, communications/journalism 44%, health sciences 15%.

Technology on campus. 500 workstations in dormitories, library, computer center, student center. Commuter students can connect to campus network. Repair service available.

Student life. Freshman orientation: Available. Preregistration for classes offered. **Housing:** Single-sex dorms available. $150 deposit, deadline 6/15. **Activities:** Choral groups, drama, film society, literary magazine, radio station, student government, student newspaper, TV station, pastoral services organization, health and allied sciences organization, student council, senior class organization, judo club, soccer club, nursing club, Christian club, microbiology club, psychology club, chemistry club, justice system, telecommunication club.

Athletics. Intercollegiate: Basketball M, cross-country, swimming, tennis, track and field, volleyball, wrestling M. **Intramural:** Basketball M, swimming, volleyball. **Team name:** Dolphins.

Student services. Alcohol/substance abuse counseling, career counseling, student employment services, financial aid counseling, health services, personal counseling, placement for graduates, veterans' counselor. **Physically disabled:** Services for visually, hearing impaired.

Contact. E-mail: admision@sagrado.edu
Phone: (787) 728-1515 ext. 3236 Fax: (787) 728-2066
Lilia Planell, Institutional Statistician, University of the Sacred Heart, Universidad del Sagrado Corazon Oficina de Nuevo Ingreso, San Juan, PR 00914-0383

Rhode Island

Brown University
Providence, Rhode Island
www.brown.edu

CB member
CB code: 3094

- Private 4-year university and liberal arts college
- Residential campus in small city
- 6,320 degree-seeking undergraduates: 52% women, 7% African American, 13% Asian American, 11% Hispanic/Latino, 6% Multi-racial, non-Hispanic, 12% international
- 2,753 degree-seeking graduate students
- 9% of applicants admitted
- SAT and SAT Subject Tests or ACT (ACT writing recommended), application essay required
- 96% graduate within 6 years

General. Founded in 1764. Regionally accredited. **Degrees:** 1,641 bachelor's awarded; master's, professional, doctoral offered. **ROTC:** Army, Naval, Air Force. **Location:** 45 miles from Boston. **Calendar:** Semester, limited summer session. **Full-time faculty:** 770 total; 95% have terminal degrees, 20% minority, 35% women. **Part-time faculty:** 115 total; 78% have terminal degrees, 10% minority, 52% women. **Class size:** 70% < 20, 16% 20-39, 3% 40-49, 7% 50-99, 3% >100. **Special facilities:** Museum of anthropology, center for the creative arts, observatory, dance studio, center for computation and visualization, institute for international studies, center for the humanities, center for the study of slavery and justice.

Freshman class profile. 30,396 applied, 2,875 admitted, 1,615 enrolled.

Mid 50% test scores			
SAT critical reading:	680-780	Rank in top tenth:	91%
SAT math:	690-780	Return as sophomores:	98%
SAT writing:	690-780	Out-of-state:	95%
ACT composite:	31-34	Live on campus:	100%
Rank in top quarter:	100%	International:	11%

Basis for selection. Strength of academic course load and student's achievement in courses most important. Extracurricular activities, recommendations, personal essay important; test scores strongly considered. Portfolio recommended for art, music programs. Alumni interviews available, but not required, for all applicants. **Home schooled:** Statement describing home school structure and mission required. **Learning Disabled:** Special accommodations for standardized tests accepted.

High school preparation. College-preparatory program required. 16 units required; 20 recommended. Required and recommended units include English 4, mathematics 3-4, social studies 1, history 2, science 3-4 (laboratory 2-3), foreign language 3-4, computer science 1, visual/performing arts 1 and academic electives 1. Future science, math, engineering students will benefit from more advanced courses in those areas.

2016-2017 Annual costs. Tuition/fees: $51,366. Room/board: $13,200. Books/supplies: $1,540. Personal expenses: $2,000.

2015-2016 Financial aid. All financial aid based on need. 826 full-time freshmen applied for aid; 721 deemed to have need; 721 received aid. Average need met was 100%. Average scholarship/grant was $42,109; average loan $4,841. 89% of total undergraduate aid awarded as scholarships/grants, 11% as loans/jobs.

Application procedures. Admission: Closing date 1/1 (postmark date). $75 fee, may be waived for applicants with need. Admission notification by 3/31. Must reply by 5/1. **Financial aid:** Closing date 2/1. FAFSA, CSS PROFILE required. Applicants notified by 4/1; must reply by 5/1.

Academics. Open curriculum outside of one's major requirements. **Special study options:** Combined bachelor's/graduate degree, cross-registration, double major, exchange student, honors, independent study, internships, student-designed major, study abroad, teacher certification program. 8-year medical program (AB or ScB, plus MD); 5-year degree programs (AB & ScB); 5-year dual degree program with Rhode Island School of Design (AB or ScB, plus BFA). **Credit/placement by examination:** AP, CLEP, IB, institutional tests.

Majors. Architecture: History/criticism. **Area/ethnic studies:** African, African-American, American, Asian, Chicano/Hispanic-American/Latino, East Asian, European, French, German, Italian, Latin American, Near/Middle Eastern, Slavic, South Asian, women's. **Biology:** General, aquatic, biochemistry, biophysics, cell/histology, molecular, neuroscience. **Computer sciences:** Computer science. **Conservation:** Environmental science, environmental studies. **Education:** General. **Engineering:** Applied physics, biomedical, chemical, civil, computer, electrical, materials, mechanical. **English:** American lit, British lit, English lit. **Foreign languages:** Ancient Greek, classics, comparative lit, French, German, Italian, Latin, linguistics, Portuguese, Slavic, Spanish. **Health services:** Community health services. **History:** General. **Human services:** Public policy. **Math:** General, applied, statistics. **Philosophy/religion:** Judaic, philosophy, religion. **Physical sciences:** Chemical physics, chemistry, geochemistry, geology, geophysics, physics. **Psychology:** General. **Social sciences:** Anthropology, archaeology, economics, international economic development, international relations, political science, sociology, urban studies. **Visual/performing arts:** General, art history/conservation, dramatic, music, musicology, studio arts.

Most popular majors. Biology 13%, computer/information sciences 6%, mathematics 6%, social sciences 22%, visual/performing arts 6%.

Technology on campus. Dormitories wired for high-speed internet access and linked to campus network. Commuter students can connect to campus network. Online course registration, online library, helpline, repair service, wireless network available.

Student life. Freshman orientation: Mandatory. Preregistration for classes offered. Held over 5 days, beginning Wednesday prior to Labor Day. **Policies:** Students must live in on-campus housing for first 3 years; those entering 7th semester may request off-campus residence. Freshmen not permitted cars on campus. **Housing:** Guaranteed on-campus for all undergraduates. Coed dorms, special housing for disabled, apartments, cooperative housing, fraternity/sorority housing, themed housing, wellness housing available. **Activities:** Bands, campus ministries, choral groups, dance, drama, film society, international student organizations, literary magazine, music ensembles, Model UN, musical theater, opera, radio station, student government, student newspaper, symphony orchestra, TV station.

Athletics. NCAA. **Intercollegiate:** Baseball M, basketball, cross-country, diving, equestrian W, fencing, field hockey W, football (tackle) M, golf, gymnastics W, ice hockey, lacrosse, rowing (crew), rugby W, skiing W, soccer, softball W, squash, swimming, tennis, track and field, water polo, wrestling M. **Intramural:** Badminton, basketball, fencing, field hockey W, ice hockey, lacrosse, soccer, softball, squash, swimming, tennis. **Team name:** Bears.

Student services. Adult student services, alcohol/substance abuse counseling, chaplain/spiritual director, career counseling, student employment services, financial aid counseling, health services, legal services, minority student services, personal counseling, placement for graduates, women's services. **Physically disabled:** Services for visually, speech, hearing impaired.

Contact. E-mail: admission@brown.edu
Phone: (401) 863-2378 Fax: (401) 863-9300
James Miller, Dean of Admission, Brown University, Box 1876, Providence, RI 02912

Bryant University
Smithfield, Rhode Island
www.bryant.edu

CB member
CB code: 3095

- Private 4-year business and liberal arts college
- Residential campus in large town
- 3,430 degree-seeking undergraduates: 2% part-time, 41% women, 4% African American, 5% Asian American, 7% Hispanic/Latino, 1% Multi-racial, non-Hispanic, 8% international
- 211 degree-seeking graduate students
- 72% of applicants admitted
- Application essay required
- 80% graduate within 6 years; 15% enter graduate study

General. Founded in 1863. Regionally accredited. **Degrees:** 744 bachelor's awarded; master's offered. **ROTC:** Army. **Location:** 10 miles from Providence; 40 miles from Newport, RI. **Calendar:** Semester, extensive summer session. **Full-time faculty:** 166 total; 80% have terminal degrees, 16% minority, 43% women. **Part-time faculty:** 115 total; 11% have terminal degrees, 11% minority, 44% women. **Class size:** 24% < 20, 76% 20-39. **Special facilities:** Academic innovation center, indoor turf practice facility, financial markets center connected to worldwide financial markets, communications complex with TV studio, control room and editing suite, multimedia student exhibition space.

Freshman class profile. 6,705 applied, 4,849 admitted, 908 enrolled.

Mid 50% test scores			
SAT critical reading:	530-610	**GPA 2.0-2.99:**	18%
SAT math:	560-640	**Rank in top quarter:**	58%
SAT writing:	510-610	**Rank in top tenth:**	24%
ACT composite:	23-27	**End year in good standing:**	95%
GPA 3.75 or higher:	24%	**Return as sophomores:**	90%
GPA 3.50-3.74:	20%	**Out-of-state:**	91%
GPA 3.0-3.49:	38%	**Live on campus:**	95%
		International:	8%

Basis for selection. Very important: rigor of high school record, GPA. Important: application essay, recommendations, class rank, standardized test scores (SAT, ACT, IB). Standardized tests are optional. Applicants substitute two to three short answer questions in lieu of standardized tests. Non-resident aliens required to take TOEFL (minimum 80) or IELTS (minimum 6.5). **Home schooled:** Statement describing home school structure and mission, transcript of courses and grades required. In addition to the Common Application, applicants must submit documentation specifying the curriculum or certified program taken and a list of subjects completed; SAT or ACT scores; or official results from SAT Subject Tests, AP exams, IB exams, or CLEP exams.

High school preparation. College-preparatory program required. 16 units required; 18 recommended. Required and recommended units include English 4, mathematics 4, history 2-3, science 2-3 (laboratory 2) and foreign language 2. Mathematics must include a year beyond algebra II, with a preference for pre-calculus or calculus in senior year. History includes social sciences.

2016-2017 Annual costs. Tuition/fees (projected): $40,962. Room/board: $14,975. Books/supplies: $1,300. Personal expenses: $1,000.

2015-2016 Financial aid. Need-based: 692 full-time freshmen applied for aid; 597 deemed to have need; 595 received aid. Average need met was 48%. Average scholarship/grant was $8,993; average loan $3,813. 71% of total undergraduate aid awarded as scholarships/grants, 29% as loans/jobs. **Non-need-based:** Awarded to 2,540 full-time undergraduates, including 751 freshmen. Scholarships awarded for academics, athletics, minority status, ROTC.

Application procedures. Admission: Closing date 2/2 (postmark date). $50 fee, may be waived for applicants with need. Admission notification by 3/15. Must reply by 5/1. **Financial aid:** Priority date 2/15, closing date 2/15. FAFSA required. Applicants notified by 3/24; must reply by 5/1.

Academics. Special study options: Accelerated study, distance learning, double major, dual enrollment of high school students, ESL, honors, independent study, internships, liberal arts/career combination, study abroad, teacher certification program, Washington semester. Service learning, Practica (combines internship with research), study abroad in Dublin and the Washington Center (both combine internships with academic seminars). **Credit/placement by examination:** AP, CLEP, IB, institutional tests. 30 credit hours maximum toward bachelor's degree. Up to 12 credits available through the College Level Examination Program (CLEP) for a limited number of subject examinations. Credit may also be awarded to students who have successfully completed military service schools. Students with significant, relevant work experience and/or individual study may satisfy certain course requirements through departmental testing programs. Advanced standing possible with a score of 5, 6, or 7 on International Baccalaureate exams. **Support services:** Learning center, study skills assistance, tutoring, writing center.

Majors. Area/ethnic studies: American, gay/lesbian, women's. **Biology:** General, biochemistry. **Business:** Accounting, actuarial science, business admin, entrepreneurial studies, finance, financial planning, human resources, international, logistics, management science, marketing, nonprofit/public, statistics. **Communications:** Communications/speech/rhetoric, media studies. **Computer sciences:** General, database management, information technology. **Conservation:** Environmental science, environmental studies, management/policy. **Engineering:** Operations research. **English:** English lit, general lit. **Foreign languages:** Chinese, French, Spanish. **Health services:** Premedicine. **History:** General. **Human services:** Community org/advocacy, public policy. **Liberal arts:** Arts/sciences. **Math:** Applied, computational/applied, statistics. **Parks/recreation:** Sports studies. **Protective services:** Forensics. **Psychology:** General, applied. **Social sciences:** Applied economics, economics, international economics, international relations, political science, research methodology, sociology. **Visual/performing arts:** Design.

Most popular majors. Business/marketing 76%.

Technology on campus. PC or laptop required. 574 workstations in library, computer center, student center. Dormitories wired for high-speed internet access and linked to campus network. Commuter students can connect to campus network. Online course registration, online library, helpline, repair service, student web hosting, wireless network available.

Student life. Freshman orientation: Available, $75 fee. Preregistration for classes offered. Held over two days. **Policies:** All residence halls are smoke free. Students ages 21 and over may possess alcohol for their personal consumption in the privacy of their room. Quiet study hour policy in effect throughout the academic year. **Housing:** Guaranteed on-campus for all undergraduates. Coed dorms, special housing for disabled, apartments, gender-neutral housing, themed housing available. $400 nonrefundable deposit. Honors, Global Community and Culture housing available. **Activities:** Bands, campus ministries, choral groups, dance, drama, international student organizations, literary magazine, music ensembles, musical theater, radio station, student government, student newspaper, TV station, Intervarsity Christian Fellowship, Hillel, Bryant Liberals, Alliance for Women's Awareness, multicultural student union, Spanish cultural organization, Italian-American association, Big Brothers & Sisters of Bryant, Bulldogs Building Bridges, Oxfam Club.

Athletics. NCAA. **Intercollegiate:** Baseball M, basketball, cross-country, diving, field hockey W, football (tackle) M, golf M, lacrosse, soccer, softball W, swimming, tennis, track and field, volleyball W. **Intramural:** Basketball, football (non-tackle) M, soccer M, softball, volleyball. **Team name:** Bulldogs.

Student services. Adult student services, alcohol/substance abuse counseling, chaplain/spiritual director, career counseling, services for economically disadvantaged, student employment services, financial aid counseling, health services, minority student services, personal counseling, placement for graduates, veterans' counselor, women's services. **Physically disabled:** Services for visually, hearing impaired.

Contact. E-mail: admission@bryant.edu
Phone: (401) 232-6100 Toll-free number: (800) 622-7001
Fax: (401) 232-6741
Michelle Cloutier, Director of Admission, Bryant University, 1150 Douglas Pike, Smithfield, RI 02917-1291

Johnson & Wales University: Providence

Providence, Rhode Island — CB member
http://admissions.jwu.edu/ — CB code: 3465

- Private 4-year university
- Residential campus in small city
- 8,718 degree-seeking undergraduates: 7% part-time, 60% women, 11% African American, 1% Asian American, 11% Hispanic/Latino, 8% Multiracial, non-Hispanic, 9% international
- 736 degree-seeking graduate students
- 82% of applicants admitted
- 55% graduate within 6 years

General. Founded in 1914. Regionally accredited. **Degrees:** 1,944 bachelor's, 1,054 associate awarded; master's, doctoral offered. **ROTC:** Army. **Location:** 200 miles from New York City, 50 miles from Boston. **Calendar:** Quarter, extensive summer session. **Full-time faculty:** 294 total. **Part-time faculty:** 323 total. **Class size:** 47% < 20, 38% 20-39, 15% 40-49. **Special facilities:** University-operated hotel and restaurant, banquet facilities, information kiosk, culinary museum, equine center.

Freshman class profile. 11,971 applied, 9,807 admitted, 2,006 enrolled.

GPA 3.75 or higher:	12%	**Return as sophomores:**	78%
GPA 3.50-3.74:	17%	**Out-of-state:**	87%
GPA 3.0-3.49:	32%	**Live on campus:**	84%
GPA 2.0-2.99:	38%	**International:**	4%

Basis for selection. Academic record, secondary school curriculum, GPA, class rank, test scores important; student motivation and interest given strong consideration. SAT or ACT required for admission to honors program. Interview and letter of recommendation generally required of students in bottom quarter of class; essay and interview recommended for others. **Home schooled:** Transcript of courses and grades, state high school equivalency certificate required. SAT (exclusive of Writing) or ACT required.

High school preparation. College-preparatory program recommended. Required units include English 4, mathematics 3, social studies 2 and science 3.

2015-2016 Annual costs. Tuition/fees: $29,226. Room/board: $12,186. Books/supplies: $1,500. Personal expenses: $1,409.

2015-2016 Financial aid. Need-based: 1,944 full-time freshmen applied for aid; 1,579 deemed to have need; 1,577 received aid. Average need met was 70%. Average scholarship/grant was $6,048; average loan $3,395. 60% of total undergraduate aid awarded as scholarships/grants, 40% as loans/jobs. **Non-need-based:** Awarded to 6,736 full-time undergraduates, including 1,875 freshmen. Scholarships awarded for academics, alumni affiliation, leadership, state residency.

Application procedures. Admission: No deadline. No application fee. Admission notification on a rolling basis. **Financial aid:** No deadline. FAFSA required. Applicants notified on a rolling basis starting 3/1; must reply within 2 week(s) of notification.

Academics. Special study options: Accelerated study, cooperative education, dual enrollment of high school students, ESL, exchange student, honors, independent study, internships, study abroad. **Credit/placement by examination:** AP, CLEP, institutional tests. **Support services:** Learning center, pre-admission summer program, reduced course load, remedial instruction, study skills assistance, tutoring, writing center.

Majors. Biology: General. **Business:** General, accounting, accounting/business management, accounting/finance, apparel, auditing, banking/financial services, business admin, casino management, entrepreneurial studies, event planning, fashion, finance, financial planning, hospitality admin, hospitality/recreation, hotel/motel admin, hotel/motel/restaurant management, human resources, information resources management, international, international finance, investments/securities, logistics, marketing, merchandising, operations, personal/financial services, project management, public finance, resort management, restaurant/food services, retail management, retailing, tourism promotion, tourism/travel. **Communications:** Advertising, digital media, media studies, persuasive communications, public relations. **Communications technology:** Animation/special effects, graphics. **Computer sciences:** General, applications programming, artificial intelligence, computer graphics, information systems, information technology, IT project management, LAN/WAN management, networking, programming, security, system admin, systems analysis, web page design, webmaster. **Engineering:** Computer, computer hardware, electrical, software, systems. **English:** Canadian lit, English lit, writing. **Health services:** General, community health services, mental health counseling, premedicine, preveterinary. **Liberal arts:** Arts/sciences. **Military:** Cyber ops. **Parks/recreation:** General, facilities management, sports admin. **Protective services:** Law enforcement admin. **Psychology:** General, counseling. **Social sciences:** Political science, sociology. **Visual/performing arts:** Design, graphic design. **Work/family studies:** Apparel marketing, clothing/textiles, food/nutrition, human nutrition, institutional food production.

Most popular majors. Business/marketing 39%, family/consumer sciences 25%, parks/recreation 11%, personal/culinary services 9%.

Technology on campus. 400 workstations in library, computer center. Dormitories wired for high-speed internet access and linked to campus network. Commuter students can connect to campus network. Online library, helpline, wireless network available.

Student life. Freshman orientation: Mandatory, $300 fee. Preregistration for classes offered. **Housing:** Guaranteed on-campus for freshmen. Coed dorms, special housing for disabled, apartments, wellness housing available. $300 deposit, deadline 5/1. **Activities:** Campus ministries, dance, international student organizations, student government, student newspaper, Hillel, Christian student union, ACLU, Together Realizing Unity Can Exist, College Republicans.

Athletics. NCAA. Intercollegiate: Baseball M, basketball, cross-country, equestrian, field hockey W, golf M, ice hockey, lacrosse, rowing (crew) W, sailing, soccer, softball W, tennis, volleyball, wrestling M. **Intramural:** Basketball, soccer, softball, tennis. **Team name:** Wildcats.

Student services. Career counseling, student employment services, financial aid counseling, health services, personal counseling, placement for graduates, veterans' counselor, women's services. **Physically disabled:** Services for visually, speech, hearing impaired.

Contact. E-mail: pvd@admissions.jwu.edu
Phone: (401) 598-1000 Toll-free number: (800) 342-5598
Amy Podbelski, Director of Undergraduate Admissions, Johnson & Wales University: Providence, 8 Abbott Park Place, Providence, RI 02903

New England Institute of Technology
East Greenwich, Rhode Island
www.neit.edu   **CB code: 0339**

- Private 4-year health science and technical college
- Commuter campus in small city
- 2,813 degree-seeking undergraduates: 16% part-time, 33% women
- 106 degree-seeking graduate students
- Interview required

General. Founded in 1940. Regionally accredited. Two additional campuses located in Warwick, Rhode Island. **Degrees:** 214 bachelor's, 907 associate awarded; master's offered. **Location:** 20 miles from Providence, 50 miles

from Boston. **Calendar:** Quarter, extensive summer session. **Full-time faculty:** 133 total; 20% have terminal degrees. **Part-time faculty:** 212 total; 6% have terminal degrees.

Basis for selection. Open admission, but selective for some programs. Individual programs may have additional requirements. Basic skills testing, Ronald P. Carver reading test used for placement. Portfolios are required for advanced standing (life experience). 30 credit limit.

2016-2017 Annual costs. Tuition/fees: $24,651. Books/supplies: $1,521. Personal expenses: $1,725.

2014-2015 Financial aid. Need-based: 33% of total undergraduate aid awarded as scholarships/grants, 67% as loans/jobs. **Non-need-based:** Scholarships awarded for academics.

Application procedures. Admission: No deadline. $25 fee. Admission notification on a rolling basis. **Financial aid:** No deadline. FAFSA required.

Academics. Special study options: Accelerated study, combined bachelor's/graduate degree, distance learning, double major, dual enrollment of high school students, internships, student-designed major, weekend college. On-line/hybrid programs offered for several bachelor of science and master of science degree programs. **Credit/placement by examination:** AP, CLEP, institutional tests. 30 credit hours maximum toward associate degree, 30 toward bachelor's. **Support services:** Learning center, pre-admission summer program, reduced course load, remedial instruction, study skills assistance, tutoring, writing center.

Majors. Architecture: Technology. **Business:** General. **Communications:** Digital media. **Communications technology:** Animation/special effects, desktop publishing. **Computer sciences:** General, computer graphics, computer science, information technology, modeling/simulation, networking, programming, security, systems analysis, web page design. **General:** Building construction. **Health services:** Health care admin, nursing (RN), rehabilitation science. **Protective services:** Computer forensics, law enforcement admin. **Visual/performing arts:** Cinematography, interior design.

Technology on campus. 1,000 workstations in library, computer center. Online course registration, online library, helpline, student web hosting, wireless network available.

Student life. Freshman orientation: Mandatory. Preregistration for classes offered. Program and registration are regularly scheduled two weeks prior to the beginning of each quarter. **Activities:** Feinstein Enriching America program, Rotaract club, criminal justice club.

Student services. Adult student services, career counseling, student employment services, financial aid counseling, personal counseling, placement for graduates, veterans' counselor.

Contact. E-mail: NEITAdmissions@neit.edu
Phone: (401) 467-7744 ext. 3357
Toll-free number: (800) 736-7744 ext. 3357 Fax: (401) 886-0868
Michael Caruso, Director of Admissions, New England Institute of Technology, One New England Tech Boulevard, East Greenwich, RI 02818

Providence College
Providence, Rhode Island   **CB member**
www.providence.edu   **CB code: 3693**

- Private 4-year liberal arts college affiliated with the Roman Catholic Church .
- Residential campus in small city
- 4,119 degree-seeking undergraduates: 5% part-time, 56% women, 4% African American, 1% Asian American, 8% Hispanic/Latino, 2% Multiracial, non-Hispanic, 2% international
- 463 degree-seeking graduate students
- 57% of applicants admitted
- 85% graduate within 6 years

General. Founded in 1917. Regionally accredited. Has community-oriented evening school for part-time students, in addition to traditional undergraduate college. **Degrees:** 993 bachelor's, 1 associate awarded; master's offered. **ROTC:** Army. **Location:** 50 miles from Boston, 180 miles from New York City. **Calendar:** Semester, limited summer session. **Full-time faculty:** 297 total; 93% have terminal degrees, 14% minority, 43% women. **Part-time faculty:** 233 total; 43% have terminal degrees, 7% minority, 42% women. **Class size:** 52% < 20, 45% 20-39, less than 1% 40-49, 3% 50-99. **Special facilities:** Art galleries, radio station, television station, Blackfriars Theater, science center complex, smith hill annex.

Freshman class profile. 10,215 applied, 5,800 admitted, 1,034 enrolled.

Mid 50% test scores				
SAT critical reading:	520-620	GPA 2.0-2.99:		11%
SAT math:	530-630	Rank in top quarter:		69%
SAT writing:	520-630	Rank in top tenth:		9%
ACT composite:	23-28	Return as sophomores:		90%
GPA 3.75 or higher:	20%	Out-of-state:		87%
GPA 3.50-3.74:	22%	Live on campus:		98%
GPA 3.0-3.49:	47%	International:		2%

Basis for selection. GED not accepted. Emphasis placed on scholastic ability, motivation, character, and seriousness of purpose. Recommendations and essay considered. Strength of curriculum and grades are the most important factors. Standardized tests scores are optional. **Home schooled:** Interview required.

High school preparation. College-preparatory program required. Required and recommended units include English 4, mathematics 4, social studies 2, history 2, science 3-4 (laboratory 2) and foreign language 3-4.

2015-2016 Annual costs. Tuition/fees: $45,400. Room/board: $13,390. Books/supplies: $940. Personal expenses: $880.

2015-2016 Financial aid. Need-based: 732 full-time freshmen applied for aid; 495 deemed to have need; 495 received aid. Average need met was 84%. Average scholarship/grant was $26,300; average loan $4,855. 74% of total undergraduate aid awarded as scholarships/grants, 26% as loans/jobs. **Non-need-based:** Awarded to 1,232 full-time undergraduates, including 358 freshmen. Scholarships awarded for academics, athletics, leadership, minority status, music/drama, ROTC.

Application procedures. Admission: Closing date 1/15. $65 fee, may be waived for applicants with need. Admission notification by 4/1. Must reply by 5/1. **Financial aid:** Priority date 2/1, closing date 2/1. FAFSA, CSS PROFILE required. Applicants notified by 3/16; must reply by 5/1.

Academics. Special study options: Combined bachelor's/graduate degree, cross-registration, distance learning, double major, dual enrollment of high school students, exchange student, honors, independent study, internships, student-designed major, study abroad, teacher certification program, Washington semester. **Credit/placement by examination:** AP, CLEP, IB, SAT, ACT, institutional tests. **Support services:** Learning center, reduced course load, study skills assistance, tutoring, writing center. Disability support and student-athlete support.

Majors. Area/ethnic studies: American, women's. **Biology:** General, biochemistry, neuroscience, vision science. **Business:** Accounting, business admin, finance, marketing, organizational leadership. **Communications:** Communications/speech/rhetoric. **Computer sciences:** Computer science. **Education:** Biology, chemistry, English, foreign languages, French, history, mathematics, music, physics, secondary, Spanish, special ed. **Engineering:** Applied physics, systems. **English:** Creative writing, English lit. **Foreign languages:** French, Italian, Spanish. **Health services:** Health care admin. **History:** General. **Human services:** Community org/advocacy, social work. **Liberal arts:** Arts/sciences, humanities. **Math:** General. **Philosophy/religion:** Philosophy. **Physical sciences:** Chemistry. **Protective services:** Firefighting. **Psychology:** General. **Social sciences:** General, econometrics, economics, political science, sociology. **Theology:** Theology. **Visual/performing arts:** Art history/conservation, ceramics, dramatic, drawing, multimedia, music, painting, photography, sculpture, studio arts.

Most popular majors. Biology 9%, business/marketing 33%, education 6%, health sciences 7%, psychology 7%, social sciences 12%.

Technology on campus. 376 workstations in library, computer center, student center. Dormitories wired for high-speed internet access and linked to campus network. Online course registration, online library, helpline, wireless network available.

Student life. Freshman orientation: Mandatory. Preregistration for classes offered. Held in a two-part, multi-day fall program. **Policies:** Freshmen not permitted cars on campus. **Housing:** Guaranteed on-campus for freshmen. Coed dorms, single-sex dorms, special housing for disabled, wellness housing available. $200 nonrefundable deposit, deadline 5/1. **Activities:** Bands, campus ministries, choral groups, dance, drama, film society, international student organizations, literary magazine, music ensembles, musical theater, radio station, student government, student newspaper, TV station, Campus Ministry, College Republicans, PC Democrats, Organization of Latin American Students, Asian American Society, Board of Multicultural Student Affairs, Hellenic Student Association, International Student Organization, Students for Social Action, Motherland Dance Group.

Athletics. NCAA. **Intercollegiate:** Basketball, cross-country, diving, field hockey W, ice hockey, lacrosse M, soccer, softball W, swimming, tennis W, track and field, volleyball W. **Intramural:** Badminton, basketball, field hockey, football (non-tackle), handball, ice hockey, lacrosse, soccer, softball, table tennis, tennis, ultimate frisbee, volleyball. **Team name:** Friars.

Student services. Physically disabled: Services for visually, speech, hearing impaired.

Contact. E-mail: pcadmiss@providence.edu
Phone: (401) 865-2535 Toll-free number: (800) 721-6444
Fax: (401) 865-2826
Raul Fonts, Dean of Admissions, Providence College, Harkins Hall 103, 1 Cunningham Square, Providence, RI 02918-0001

Rhode Island College
Providence, Rhode Island
www.ric.edu

CB member
CB code: 3724

- Public 4-year liberal arts and teachers college
- Commuter campus in small city
- 7,216 degree-seeking undergraduates: 23% part-time, 68% women, 8% African American, 3% Asian American, 16% Hispanic/Latino, 2% Multiracial, non-Hispanic
- 703 degree-seeking graduate students
- 72% of applicants admitted
- SAT or ACT with writing, application essay required
- 44% graduate within 6 years

General. Founded in 1854. Regionally accredited. **Degrees:** 1,393 bachelor's awarded; master's, doctoral offered. **ROTC:** Army. **Location:** 4 miles from downtown Providence. **Calendar:** Semester, extensive summer session. **Full-time faculty:** 335 total; 89% have terminal degrees, 14% minority, 58% women. **Part-time faculty:** 437 total; 8% minority, 59% women. **Class size:** 49% < 20, 51% 20-39, less than 1% 40-49, less than 1% 50-99, less than 1% >100. **Special facilities:** Center for the performing arts, art gallery.

Freshman class profile. 4,732 applied, 3,389 admitted, 1,113 enrolled.

Mid 50% test scores			
SAT critical reading:	400-520	Rank in top quarter:	35%
SAT math:	400-510	Rank in top tenth:	11%
SAT writing:	400-500	Return as sophomores:	76%
ACT composite:	16-21	Out-of-state:	19%
		Live on campus:	41%

Basis for selection. High school academic record, GPA and class rank most important, followed by test scores, essay, and references. TOEFL required for all applicants who have been in the country for less than 5 years and are not native speakers of English. SAT scores required of non-native speakers of English who have been in the United States for more than 5 years. Interview available but not required. Audition required for music; portfolio required for bachelor of fine arts. **Home schooled:** Transcript of courses and grades, state high school equivalency certificate, interview required. Must submit GED scores unless their home school curriculum is provided by an accredited agency.

High school preparation. College-preparatory program required. 18 units required. Required units include English 4, mathematics 3, social studies 2, science 2 (laboratory 2), foreign language 2 and academic electives 5. Biology and either chemistry or physics are recommended lab sciences; 2 years of same foreign language required. Algebra I, II and geometry required. All units must be college-preparatory level.

2015-2016 Annual costs. Tuition/fees: $8,197; $19,858 out-of-state. Room/board: $10,718. Books/supplies: $1,200. Personal expenses: $1,000. **Additional information:** Connecticut and Massachusetts students whose permanent address is within a 50-mile radius of the College pay the in-state tuition rate plus 50%.

2015-2016 Financial aid. Need-based: 1,023 full-time freshmen applied for aid; 805 deemed to have need; 762 received aid. Average need met was 69%. Average scholarship/grant was $7,702; average loan $3,486. 49% of total undergraduate aid awarded as scholarships/grants, 51% as loans/jobs. **Non-need-based:** Awarded to 226 full-time undergraduates, including 62 freshmen. Scholarships awarded for academics, alumni affiliation, art, music/drama.

Application procedures. Admission: Closing date 3/15 (postmark date). $50 fee, may be waived for applicants with need. Admission notification on a rolling basis beginning on or about 12/15. Must reply by May 1 or within 2 week(s) if notified thereafter. **Financial aid:** Priority date 3/1; no closing date. FAFSA, institutional form required. Applicants notified on a rolling basis starting 3/15; must reply by 5/1 or within 3 week(s) of notification.

Academics. Special study options: Combined bachelor's/graduate degree, double major, dual enrollment of high school students, exchange student, honors, independent study, internships, student-designed major, study abroad, teacher certification program. Undergraduate research opportunities. **Credit/**

placement by examination: AP, CLEP, SAT, ACT, institutional tests. **Support services:** Learning center, pre-admission summer program, reduced course load, remedial instruction, study skills assistance, tutoring, writing center. Online tutoring offered in addition to in-person tutoring. Test preparation assistance, advising to specific groups of students, mentoring, and information about the National Student Exchange.

Majors. Area/ethnic studies: African-American, French, Latin American, women's. **Biology:** General. **Business:** Accounting, business admin, finance, human resources, international, management information systems, marketing, operations. **Communications:** Communications/speech/rhetoric, media studies, persuasive communications. **Computer sciences:** General. **Education:** Art, biology, chemistry, early childhood, elementary, elementary special ed, English, foreign languages, French, geography, health, history, mathematics, music, physical, physics, science, secondary, secondary special ed, social science, Spanish, special ed, technology/industrial arts. **English:** Creative writing, English lit. **Foreign languages:** French, Portuguese, Spanish. **Health services:** General, clinical lab technology, communication disorders, community health services, dental hygiene, health care admin, MRI technology, nuclear medical technology, nursing (RN), predental, premedicine, preoptometry, preveterinary, radiologic technology/medical imaging, respiratory therapy assistant, sonography, staff services technology. **History:** General, applied. **Human services:** General, social work, youth services. **Liberal arts:** Arts/sciences. **Math:** General. **Parks/recreation:** General, health/fitness. **Philosophy/religion:** Philosophy. **Physical sciences:** Chemistry, environmental chemistry, physics. **Protective services:** Criminal justice. **Psychology:** General. **Social sciences:** Anthropology, economics, geography, political science, sociology. **Visual/performing arts:** Acting, art history/conservation, ceramics, dance, digital arts, dramatic, film/cinema/video, graphic design, metal/jewelry, music, music performance, musical theater, painting, photography, printmaking, sculpture, theater design. **Work/family studies:** Aging.

Most popular majors. Business/marketing 16%, education 16%, health sciences 16%, psychology 12%, public administration/social services 10%, visual/performing arts 6%.

Technology on campus. 250 workstations in library, computer center, student center. Dormitories wired for high-speed internet access and linked to campus network. Commuter students can connect to campus network. Online course registration, online library, helpline, repair service, student web hosting, wireless network available.

Student life. Freshman orientation: Mandatory, $160 fee. Preregistration for classes offered. Two-day programs offered in June and/or July. **Housing:** Coed dorms, single-sex dorms, special housing for disabled available. $220 partly refundable deposit, deadline 5/15. **Activities:** Bands, choral groups, dance, drama, film society, international student organizations, literary magazine, music ensembles, musical theater, radio station, student government, student newspaper, symphony orchestra, TV station, Advocacy and Beyond, Asian student association, Feminists United, HOPE (Helping Others Promote Equality), intra-varsity student fellowship, Harambee, LIFE (Live, Inspire, Fight, Educate), Latin American student organization, VISA (Visiting International Student Association), Sojourn Collegiate Ministry.

Athletics. NCAA. **Intercollegiate:** Baseball M, basketball, cross-country, golf, gymnastics W, lacrosse W, soccer, softball W, swimming W, tennis, track and field, volleyball W, wrestling M. **Intramural:** Badminton, basketball, football (non-tackle) M, soccer, softball, swimming, tennis, volleyball, water polo. **Team name:** Anchormen, Anchorwomen.

Student services. Adult student services, alcohol/substance abuse counseling, chaplain/spiritual director, career counseling, student employment services, financial aid counseling, health services, minority student services, on-campus daycare, personal counseling, placement for graduates, veterans' counselor, women's services. **Physically disabled:** Services for visually, speech, hearing impaired.

Contact. E-mail: admissions@ric.edu
Phone: (401) 456-8234 Toll-free number: (800) 669-5760
Fax: (401) 456-8817
John McLaughlin, Director of Admissions, Rhode Island College, 600 Mount Pleasant Avenue, Providence, RI 02908

Rhode Island School of Design
Providence, Rhode Island   **CB member**
www.risd.edu   **CB code: 3726**

- Private 4-year visual arts college
- Residential campus in small city
- 2,014 degree-seeking undergraduates: 68% women, 2% African American, 26% international
- 467 degree-seeking graduate students

- 36% of applicants admitted
- SAT or ACT with writing, application essay required
- 89% graduate within 6 years

General. Founded in 1877. Regionally accredited. **Degrees:** 511 bachelor's awarded; master's offered. **ROTC:** Army. **Location:** 52 miles from Boston, 180 miles from New York City. **Calendar:** 4-1-4, limited summer session. **Full-time faculty:** 168 total; 79% have terminal degrees, 10% minority, 40% women. **Part-time faculty:** 302 total; 55% have terminal degrees, 10% minority, 45% women. **Class size:** 76% < 20, 23% 20-39, less than 1% 40-49, less than 1% 50-99. **Special facilities:** Nature lab, material resource center, museum of art, farm.

Freshman class profile. 2,516 applied, 904 admitted, 465 enrolled.

Mid 50% test scores			
		GPA 3.0-3.49:	28%
SAT critical reading:	560-680	GPA 2.0-2.99:	9%
SAT math:	580-720	End year in good standing:	97%
SAT writing:	580-690	Return as sophomores:	95%
ACT composite:	25-32	Out-of-state:	98%
GPA 3.75 or higher:	33%	Live on campus:	99%
GPA 3.50-3.74:	30%	International:	27%

Basis for selection. Academic history, visual portfolio, and 2 required drawings most important. TOEFL or IECTS required of non-native English speakers. Portfolio required for all applicants. **Home schooled:** State high school equivalency certificate required. Proof of high school equivalency/GED required.

High school preparation. College-preparatory program recommended.

2015-2016 Annual costs. Tuition/fees: $45,840. Room/board: $12,600. Books/supplies: $2,700. Personal expenses: $2,500.

2015-2016 Financial aid. Need-based: 284 full-time freshmen applied for aid; 208 deemed to have need; 208 received aid. Average need met was 67%. Average scholarship/grant was $24,005; average loan $3,500. 63% of total undergraduate aid awarded as scholarships/grants, 37% as loans/jobs. **Non-need-based:** Scholarships awarded for academics, art.

Application procedures. Admission: Closing date 2/1 (receipt date). $60 fee, may be waived for applicants with need. Admission notification by 3/22. Must reply by 5/1. **Financial aid:** Closing date 2/15. FAFSA, CSS PROFILE required. Applicants notified by 4/1; must reply by 5/1.

Academics. Special study options: Cross-registration, double major, exchange student, independent study, internships, study abroad, teacher certification program. **Credit/placement by examination:** AP, CLEP, IB, SAT, ACT, institutional tests. **Support services:** Pre-admission summer program, reduced course load, tutoring, writing center.

Majors. Architecture: Architecture, interior. **Visual/performing arts:** Ceramics, fiber arts, graphic design, illustration, industrial design, metal/jewelry, painting, photography, printmaking, sculpture. **Work/family studies:** Clothing/textiles.

Most popular majors. Architecture 15%, visual/performing arts 76%.

Technology on campus. 425 workstations in dormitories, library, computer center, student center. Dormitories wired for high-speed internet access and linked to campus network. Commuter students can connect to campus network. Online course registration, online library, helpline, repair service, student web hosting, wireless network available.

Student life. Freshman orientation: Mandatory. Preregistration for classes offered. Held in early September just before the first day of classes. **Policies:** Freshmen not permitted cars on campus. **Housing:** Guaranteed on-campus for freshmen. Coed dorms, special housing for disabled, apartments available. **Activities:** Choral groups, dance, drama, film society, international student organizations, literary magazine, musical theater, student government, BAAD (Black Artists and Designers), RISD/Brown Catholic Community, Kehillah, WON, Made in Taiwan, Queer Student Association, RISD Christian Fellowship, EPA (Espanish Association), SASA (South Asian Student Association), community service club, Alternative Spring Break, RISD Global Initiative.

Student services. Alcohol/substance abuse counseling, chaplain/spiritual director, career counseling, financial aid counseling, health services, legal services, minority student services, personal counseling, placement for graduates. **Physically disabled:** Services for hearing impaired.

Contact. E-mail: admissions@risd.edu
Phone: (401) 454-6300 Toll-free number: (800) 364-7473
Fax: (401) 454-6309
Edward Newhall, Associate V.P. Enrollment, Rhode Island School of Design, 2 College Street, Providence, RI 02903-2784

Roger Williams University
Bristol, Rhode Island
www.rwu.edu

CB member
CB code: 3729

- Private 4-year university
- Residential campus in large town
- 4,481 degree-seeking undergraduates: 12% part-time, 51% women, 2% African American, 1% Asian American, 6% Hispanic/Latino, 2% Multiracial, non-Hispanic, 5% international
- 243 degree-seeking graduate students
- 78% of applicants admitted
- Application essay required
- 64% graduate within 6 years

General. Founded in 1956. Regionally accredited. Certificate and associate programs offered only in the School of Continuing Studies in Providence and Bristol. **Degrees:** 995 bachelor's awarded; master's, professional offered. **ROTC:** Army. **Location:** 18 miles from Providence, 10 miles from Newport. **Calendar:** Semester, limited summer session. **Full-time faculty:** 206 total; 81% have terminal degrees, 13% minority, 43% women. **Part-time faculty:** 299 total; 9% minority, 44% women. **Class size:** 53% < 20, 46% 20-39, less than 1% 40-49. **Special facilities:** Marine biology wetlab, shellfish hatchery, Prudence Island field site, sailing center.

Freshman class profile. 9,597 applied, 7,532 admitted, 1,023 enrolled.

Mid 50% test scores			
SAT critical reading:	510-590	**Rank in top quarter:**	3%
SAT math:	520-610	**End year in good standing:**	79%
SAT writing:	500-590	**Return as sophomores:**	81%
ACT composite:	23-27	**Out-of-state:**	88%
GPA 3.75 or higher:	22%	**Live on campus:**	93%
GPA 3.50-3.74:	14%	**International:**	3%
GPA 3.0-3.49:	45%		

At top: **GPA 2.0-2.99:** 19%

Basis for selection. High school performance. SAT or ACT scores considered if submitted but are not required. SAT scores are required for all education majors. Programs that require portfolio reviews, auditions, or specific preparatory courses for admittance include visual arts studies, graphic design communications, architecture, creative writing, dance performance studies and theater. **Home schooled:** State high school equivalency certificate required. **Learning Disabled:** Students requesting accommodations and/or support services must provide documentation of the disability which substantially limits a major life activity.

High school preparation. College-preparatory program required. 22 units required; 26 recommended. Required and recommended units include English 4, mathematics 3-4, social studies 3, history 2-3, science 3-4 (laboratory 2-3), foreign language 2 and academic electives 2-3. Specific subject requirements vary with intended major.

2015-2016 Annual costs. Tuition/fees: $31,800. Room/board: $15,172. Books/supplies: $900. Personal expenses: $1,394.

2015-2016 Financial aid. Need-based: 922 full-time freshmen applied for aid; 714 deemed to have need; 704 received aid. Average need met was 86%. Average scholarship/grant was $14,634; average loan $3,500. 72% of total undergraduate aid awarded as scholarships/grants, 28% as loans/jobs. **Non-need-based:** Awarded to 2,514 full-time undergraduates, including 826 freshmen. Scholarships awarded for academics, leadership.

Application procedures. Admission: Closing date 2/1 (receipt date). $50 fee. Admission notification on a rolling basis beginning on or about 12/1. Must reply by 5/1. **Financial aid:** Priority date 1/1, closing date 2/1. FAFSA required. New students must complete CSS PROFILE by January 1. Applicants notified by 3/15; Applicants notified on a rolling basis starting 3/15; must reply by 5/1 or within 2 week(s) of notification.

Academics. Special study options: Accelerated study, combined bachelor's/graduate degree, cooperative education, distance learning, double major, dual enrollment of high school students, ESL, exchange student, honors, independent study, internships, liberal arts/career combination, semester at sea, student-designed major, study abroad, teacher certification program, Washington semester. **Credit/placement by examination:** AP, CLEP, IB, SAT, ACT, institutional tests. 15 credit hours maximum toward associate degree, 30 toward bachelor's. Students can test out of no more than 25% of the credits required for a degree. **Support services:** Learning center, reduced course load, study skills assistance, tutoring, writing center. Math center, science center, foreign languages tutoring center.

Honors college/program. University does not have a separate Honors College, but rather an Honors Program. It is recommended that applicants have a minimum GPA of 3.5 or SAT score of 1200. Test score submission is optional. Students complete an additional essay evaluated by a faculty committee for quality of writing, critical reflection, and fit with the Honors Program mission. Approximately 60 students admitted annually.

Majors. Architecture: Architecture, history/criticism. **Area/ethnic studies:** American. **Biology:** General, biochemistry, marine. **Business:** Accounting, business admin, construction management, finance, international, marketing, operations. **Communications:** Communications/speech/rhetoric, intercultural, journalism, media studies. **Communications technology:** Graphics. **Computer sciences:** General, computer science. **Conservation:** Environmental science. **Education:** General, elementary, English, foreign languages, history, mathematics, multi-level teacher, secondary. **Engineering:** General, civil, computer, electrical, mechanical. **English:** British lit, creative writing, English lit. **Foreign languages:** General, classics, Hispanic and Latin American. **General:** Site management. **Health services:** EMT paramedic, environmental health, health care admin, health services admin. **History:** General. **Human services:** General. **Liberal arts:** Arts/sciences, humanities. **Math:** General, applied. **Philosophy/religion:** Philosophy. **Physical sciences:** Chemistry, environmental chemistry. **Protective services:** Computer forensics, forensics, law enforcement admin, security management. **Psychology:** General, clinical. **Social sciences:** General, anthropology, economics, international relations, political science, sociology, sociology/anthropology. **Visual/performing arts:** Art, art history/conservation, dance, dramatic, graphic design, music, musicology, studio arts. **Work/family studies:** Family/community services.

Most popular majors. Architecture 8%, biology 7%, business/marketing 25%, communications/journalism 6%, psychology 7%, security/protective services 11%.

Technology on campus. 540 workstations in dormitories, library, computer center. Dormitories wired for high-speed internet access and linked to campus network. Commuter students can connect to campus network. Online course registration, online library, helpline, repair service, wireless network available.

Student life. Freshman orientation: Mandatory, $150 fee. Preregistration for classes offered. Held over two day program with overnight stay on campus during summer; separate orientations for transfer and international students. **Policies:** Freshmen not permitted cars on campus. **Housing:** Guaranteed on-campus for freshmen. Coed dorms, apartments, gender-neutral housing, themed housing, wellness housing available. $350 fully refundable deposit, deadline 5/1. Special interest academic and honors housing available; gender inclusive housing, suite-style, academic based living-learning communities, alcohol-free residence hall option available. **Activities:** Campus ministries, choral groups, dance, drama, film society, international student organizations, musical theater, radio station, student government, student newspaper, Helping Hawks, International Relations Organization, Hillel, Inter-Varsity Christian Fellowship, Multicultural Student Union, College Democrats, College Republicans, environmental and animal rights club, Habitat for Humanity and Hawks for St. Jude.

Athletics. NCAA. **Intercollegiate:** Baseball M, basketball, cross-country, diving, equestrian, field hockey W, golf M, lacrosse, sailing, soccer, softball W, swimming, tennis, track and field, volleyball, wrestling M. **Intramural:** Basketball, football (non-tackle) M, sand volleyball, soccer, softball M, volleyball. **Team name:** Hawks.

Student services. Adult student services, alcohol/substance abuse counseling, chaplain/spiritual director, career counseling, student employment services, financial aid counseling, health services, minority student services, personal counseling, placement for graduates, veterans' counselor, women's services.

Contact. E-mail: admit@rwu.edu
Phone: (401) 254-3500 Toll-free number: (800) 458-7144 ext. 3500
Fax: (401) 254-3557
Amy Tiberio, Dean of Admission, Roger Williams University, 1 Old Ferry Road, Bristol, RI 02809-2921

Salve Regina University
Newport, Rhode Island
www.salve.edu

CB member
CB code: 3759

- Private 4-year university and liberal arts college affiliated with the Roman Catholic Church
- Residential campus in large town
- 2,123 degree-seeking undergraduates: 6% part-time, 72% women, 2% African American, 1% Asian American, 6% Hispanic/Latino, 2% Multiracial, non-Hispanic, 1% international
- 489 degree-seeking graduate students
- 73% of applicants admitted

▶ Application essay required
▶ 72% graduate within 6 years

General. Founded in 1934. Regionally accredited. Affiliated with Religious Sisters of Mercy. **Degrees:** 424 bachelor's awarded; master's, professional, doctoral offered. **ROTC:** Army. **Location:** 30 miles from Providence, 60 miles from Boston. **Calendar:** Semester, limited summer session. **Full-time faculty:** 122 total; 81% have terminal degrees, 7% minority, 55% women. **Part-time faculty:** 182 total; 22% have terminal degrees, 3% minority, 53% women. **Class size:** 49% < 20, 50% 20-39, less than 1% 40-49, less than 1% 50-99. **Special facilities:** International relations and public policy center.

Freshman class profile. 4,582 applied, 3,322 admitted, 563 enrolled.

Mid 50% test scores		GPA 2.0-2.99:	25%
SAT critical reading:	510-590	Rank in top quarter:	49%
SAT math:	510-580	Rank in top tenth:	15%
SAT writing:	510-600	Return as sophomores:	86%
ACT composite:	23-26	Out-of-state:	86%
GPA 3.75 or higher:	16%	Live on campus:	97%
GPA 3.50-3.74:	18%	International:	1%
GPA 3.0-3.49:	41%		

Basis for selection. High school achievement most important, followed by rank in top half of high school class, recommendations, essay, activities, interview. Special consideration given to applicants from minority and low-income families. SAT/ACT is optional except for education or nursing programs. Students who decide not to submit scores will not be at any disadvantage during the admission process. Applicants for one of the University's studio art programs are required to submit a portfolio. **Home schooled:** Statement describing home school structure and mission, transcript of courses and grades, letter of recommendation (nonparent) required. Require two recommendations, one of which must be academic. Course syllabus required for each course; results of SAT or ACT examinations; portfolio of academic accomplishments including a reading list, course descriptions and list of extra-curricular/community involvement.

High school preparation. College-preparatory program required. 16 units required. Required units include English 4, mathematics 3, social studies 1, science 2 (laboratory 2), foreign language 2 and academic electives 4. Additional course work may be required of students who have not completed recommended units. Social studies includes history.

2015-2016 Annual costs. Tuition/fees: $36,740. Room/board: $13,250. Books/supplies: $900. Personal expenses: $1,000.

2015-2016 Financial aid. Need-based: 514 full-time freshmen applied for aid; 440 deemed to have need; 440 received aid. Average need met was 74%. Average scholarship/grant was $23,958; average loan $3,920. 70% of total undergraduate aid awarded as scholarships/grants, 30% as loans/jobs. **Non-need-based:** Awarded to 500 full-time undergraduates, including 321 freshmen. Scholarships awarded for academics, alumni affiliation, art, ROTC.

Application procedures. Admission: Priority date 2/1; no deadline. $50 fee, may be waived for applicants with need. Application must be submitted online. Admission notification on a rolling basis beginning on or about 12/25. Must reply by May 1 or within 2 week(s) if notified thereafter. **Financial aid:** Priority date 3/1; no closing date. FAFSA required. Applicants notified on a rolling basis starting 1/3; must reply by 5/1 or within 2 week(s) of notification.

Academics. Credit may be awarded for learning associated with life experience. **Special study options:** Accelerated study, combined bachelor's/graduate degree, distance learning, double major, dual enrollment of high school students, ESL, honors, independent study, internships, liberal arts/career combination, study abroad, teacher certification program, Washington semester. **Credit/placement by examination:** AP, CLEP, IB, institutional tests. **Support services:** Learning center, reduced course load, study skills assistance, tutoring, writing center.

Majors. Area/ethnic studies: American. **Biology:** General. **Business:** Accounting, business admin, finance, information resources management, management science, marketing. **Conservation:** Environmental studies. **Education:** Early childhood, elementary, music, secondary, special ed. **English:** English lit. **Foreign languages:** French, Spanish. **Health services:** Clinical lab science, nursing (RN). **History:** General. **Human services:** Social work. **Liberal arts:** Arts/sciences. **Math:** General. **Philosophy/religion:** Philosophy, religion. **Physical sciences:** Chemistry. **Protective services:** Law enforcement admin. **Psychology:** General. **Social sciences:** Economics, international economics, political science, sociology. **Visual/performing arts:** Art history/conservation, ceramics, dramatic, graphic design, music, painting, photography, studio arts.

Most popular majors. Business/marketing 27%, education 11%, health sciences 13%, psychology 10%, security/protective services 9%, social sciences 8%.

Technology on campus. PC or laptop required. 300 workstations in dormitories, library, computer center, student center. Dormitories wired for high-speed internet access and linked to campus network. Commuter students can connect to campus network. Online course registration, online library, helpline, repair service, student web hosting, wireless network available.

Student life. Freshman orientation: Mandatory, $300 fee. Preregistration for classes offered. 2-day sessions during June and July for full-time freshmen; separate sessions for international and transfer students. **Policies:** Freshmen not permitted cars on campus. **Housing:** Guaranteed on-campus for freshmen. Coed dorms, single-sex dorms, special housing for disabled, apartments, themed housing, wellness housing available. $500 nonrefundable deposit, deadline 5/1. Off-campus housing available to upperclassmen. **Activities:** Bands, campus ministries, choral groups, dance, drama, film society, international student organizations, literary magazine, music ensembles, Model UN, radio station, student government, student newspaper, Artist's Guild, Circle K, environmental club, Student Outdoor Adventures, Volunteers Interested in Researching and Guiding, Women's Issues Now, Stagefright Theater Company, College Democrats, College Republicans.

Athletics. NCAA. **Intercollegiate:** Baseball M, basketball, cross-country, field hockey W, football (tackle) M, ice hockey, lacrosse, soccer, softball W, tennis, track and field W, volleyball W. **Intramural:** Basketball, field hockey W, football (non-tackle) W, football (tackle) M, racquetball, soccer, softball, tennis, track and field W, volleyball, weight lifting. **Team name:** Seahawks.

Student services. Adult student services, alcohol/substance abuse counseling, chaplain/spiritual director, career counseling, financial aid counseling, health services, minority student services, personal counseling, veterans' counselor. **Physically disabled:** Services for visually, hearing impaired.

Contact. E-mail: sruadmis@salve.edu
Phone: (401) 341-2908 Toll-free number: (888) 467-2583
Fax: (401) 848-2823
Colleen Emerson, Dean of Undergraduate Admissions, Salve Regina University, 100 Ochre Point Avenue, Newport, RI 02840-4192

University of Rhode Island
Kingston, Rhode Island   **CB member**
www.uri.edu   **CB code: 3919**

▶ Public 4-year university
▶ Residential campus in small town
▶ 13,342 degree-seeking undergraduates: 8% part-time, 54% women, 5% African American, 3% Asian American, 9% Hispanic/Latino, 3% Multi-racial, non-Hispanic, 1% international
▶ 2,713 degree-seeking graduate students
▶ 71% of applicants admitted
▶ SAT or ACT (ACT writing optional), application essay required
▶ 63% graduate within 6 years

General. Founded in 1892. Regionally accredited. College of Continuing Education in Providence offers credit-bearing courses for degree and non-degree students. **Degrees:** 2,925 bachelor's awarded; master's, professional, doctoral offered. **ROTC:** Army. **Location:** 30 miles from Providence. **Calendar:** Semester, extensive summer session. **Full-time faculty:** 697 total; 84% have terminal degrees, 17% minority, 46% women. **Part-time faculty:** 387 total; 11% have terminal degrees, 6% minority, 58% women. **Class size:** 41% < 20, 48% 20-39, 6% 40-49, less than 1% 50-99, 5% >100. **Special facilities:** Inner space center, center for robotics research, animal science farm, planetarium, marine sciences campus, American historic textiles museum, aquaculture center, fisheries and marine technology laboratory, biotechnology center, human performance laboratory.

Freshman class profile. 21,261 applied, 15,200 admitted, 3,249 enrolled.

Mid 50% test scores		Rank in top quarter:	50%
SAT critical reading:	500-590	Rank in top tenth:	19%
SAT math:	510-600	Return as sophomores:	84%
SAT writing:	490-580	Out-of-state:	56%
ACT composite:	22-26	Live on campus:	74%
GPA 3.75 or higher:	23%	International:	2%
GPA 3.50-3.74:	22%	Fraternities:	18%
GPA 3.0-3.49:	37%	Sororities:	28%
GPA 2.0-2.99:	18%		

Basis for selection. School record primary, test scores secondary; extracurricular activities considered. Economically and socially disadvantaged students from Rhode Island admitted through special program for talent development. **Home schooled:** Statement describing home school structure and mission required. **Learning Disabled:** Foreign language admission requirement may be waived for students who were given foreign language waiver in high school because of documented learning disability. Students must substitute two college preparatory units in English, math, science, or social studies to substitute for these courses, and documentation must be received from the high school.

High school preparation. College-preparatory program required. 18 units required. Required units include English 4, mathematics 3, social studies 2, science 2 (laboratory 1), foreign language 2 and academic electives 5.

2015-2016 Annual costs. Tuition/fees: $12,862; $28,852 out-of-state. Room/board: $11,956. Books/supplies: $1,200. Personal expenses: $1,800.

2015-2016 Financial aid. Need-based: 2,362 full-time freshmen applied for aid; 1,888 deemed to have need; 1,753 received aid. Average need met was 64%. Average scholarship/grant was $10,254; average loan $5,855. 60% of total undergraduate aid awarded as scholarships/grants, 40% as loans/jobs. **Non-need-based:** Awarded to 1,966 full-time undergraduates, including 568 freshmen. Scholarships awarded for academics, alumni affiliation, art, athletics, music/drama, ROTC.

Application procedures. Admission: Closing date 2/1 (receipt date). $65 fee, may be waived for applicants with need. Application must be submitted online. Admission notification by 3/31. Admission notification on a rolling basis beginning on or about 1/31. Must reply by May 1 or within 2 week(s) if notified thereafter. **Financial aid:** Priority date 3/1; no closing date. FAFSA required. Applicants notified on a rolling basis starting 3/15; must reply by 5/1.

Academics. Special study options: Combined bachelor's/graduate degree, cross-registration, distance learning, double major, dual enrollment of high school students, exchange student, honors, independent study, internships, liberal arts/career combination, semester at sea, study abroad, teacher certification program, weekend college. **Credit/placement by examination:** AP, CLEP, IB, SAT, ACT, institutional tests. 45 credit hours maximum toward bachelor's degree. **Support services:** Learning center, pre-admission summer program, reduced course load, remedial instruction, study skills assistance, tutoring, writing center. Supplemental Instruction.

Honors college/program. To be eligible to take an Honors course in your first semester freshman year, you must meet the following criteria: cumulative high school GPA must be 3.80 or higher, or cumulative high school GPA must be 3.50 or higher and combined SAT scores must be 1200 or higher in Critical Reading and Mathematics (or must have ACT equivalent score of 27). To be eligible for continued participation in the Honors Program: Students must maintain a cumulative 3.40 or higher GPA.

Majors. Architecture: Landscape. **Area/ethnic studies:** African-American, women's. **Biology:** General, cellular/molecular, marine, microbiology. **Business:** General, accounting, apparel, business admin, finance, financial planning, international, logistics, marketing. **Communications:** Communications/speech/rhetoric, journalism, public relations. **Computer sciences:** General. **Conservation:** Economics, environmental studies, fisheries, management/policy, wildlife/wilderness. **Education:** Elementary, music, secondary. **Engineering:** Biomedical, chemical, civil, computer, electrical, industrial, mechanical, ocean. **English:** English lit, rhetoric/composition. **Foreign languages:** Chinese, classics, French, German, Italian, Spanish. **Health services:** Clinical lab science, communication disorders, dietetics, health care admin, nursing (RN). **History:** General. **Human services:** Public policy. **Liberal arts:** Humanities. **Math:** General. **Parks/recreation:** Exercise sciences. **Philosophy/religion:** Philosophy. **Physical sciences:** Chemistry, forensic chemistry, geology, physics. **Psychology:** General. **Social sciences:** Anthropology, applied economics, econometrics, economics, political science, sociology. **Visual/performing arts:** Art history/conservation, cinematography, dramatic, music, studio arts. **Work/family studies:** Clothing/textiles, family studies.

Most popular majors. Biology 6%, business/marketing 13%, communications/journalism 8%, engineering/engineering technologies 8%, family/consumer sciences 7%, health sciences 15%, psychology 6%, social sciences 8%.

Technology on campus. 2,500 workstations in dormitories, library, computer center, student center. Dormitories wired for high-speed internet access and linked to campus network. Commuter students can connect to campus network. Online course registration, online library, helpline, repair service, wireless network available.

Student life. Freshman orientation: Mandatory, $175 fee. Preregistration for classes offered. Two day programs throughout June. Family members encouraged to attend. **Housing:** Guaranteed on-campus for freshmen. Coed dorms, special housing for disabled, apartments, fraternity/sorority housing, themed housing, wellness housing available. $200 nonrefundable deposit, deadline 5/1. First-year focused residence halls; learning communities for undecided majors, honor program, health sciences, engineering, college environment and health sciences majors and nursing available. **Activities:** Bands, campus ministries, choral groups, dance, drama, film society, international student organizations, literary magazine, music ensembles, musical theater, radio station, student government, student newspaper, TV station, Hillel, Newman Club, College Democrats, College Republicans, Uhuru Sasa,

NAACP, Latin American student association, Habitat for Humanity, Asian student association, club sports council.

Athletics. NCAA. Intercollegiate: Baseball M, basketball, cheerleading W, cross-country, diving W, football (tackle) M, golf M, rowing (crew) W, soccer, softball W, swimming W, tennis W, track and field, volleyball W. **Intramural:** Football (non-tackle) M, soccer, volleyball M. **Team name:** Rams.

Student services. Adult student services, alcohol/substance abuse counseling, chaplain/spiritual director, career counseling, services for economically disadvantaged, student employment services, financial aid counseling, health services, legal services, minority student services, on-campus daycare, personal counseling, placement for graduates, veterans' counselor, women's services. **Physically disabled:** Services for visually, speech, hearing impaired.

Contact. E-mail: admission@uri.edu
Phone: (401) 874-7100 Fax: (401) 874-5523
Cynthia Bonn, Dean of Admission, University of Rhode Island, Newman Hall, Kingston, RI 02881-1322

South Carolina

Allen University
Columbia, South Carolina
www.allenuniversity.edu

CB code: 5006

◆ Private 4-year university and liberal arts college affiliated with the African Methodist Episcopal Church
◆ Residential campus in large city
◆ 670 degree-seeking undergraduates

General. Founded in 1870. Regionally accredited. **Degrees:** 77 bachelor's awarded. **ROTC:** Army, Naval. **Location:** 112 miles from Charleston; 72 miles from Charlotte, NC. **Calendar:** Semester, limited summer session. **Full-time faculty:** 44 total; 50% have terminal degrees, 86% minority. **Part-time faculty:** 19 total.

Freshman class profile.

GPA 3.75 or higher:	3%	GPA 3.0-3.49:	19%
GPA 3.50-3.74:	6%	GPA 2.0-2.99:	69%

Basis for selection. Applicants reviewed by admission committee. Decision provided to applicant in writing. SAT or ACT recommended. Interview, campus visit recommended. **Home schooled:** Statement describing home school structure and mission, transcript of courses and grades, state high school equivalency certificate, interview, letter of recommendation (nonparent) required.

High school preparation. College-preparatory program recommended. Recommended units include English 4, mathematics 4, social studies 3, history 3, science 3, foreign language 1 and computer science 1.

2015-2016 Annual costs. Tuition/fees: $12,640. Room/board: $6,660. Books/supplies: $1,000. Personal expenses: $800.

Financial aid. Non-need-based: Scholarships awarded for academics, athletics, music/drama, ROTC.

Application procedures. Admission: Priority date 6/30; deadline 7/31 (receipt date). No application fee. Admission notification on a rolling basis. Must reply by May 1 or within 2 week(s) if notified thereafter. **Financial aid:** Priority date 4/15, closing date 7/20. FAFSA required. Applicants notified on a rolling basis starting 4/1; must reply within 2 week(s) of notification.

Academics. Special study options: Cooperative education, honors, independent study, internships, teacher certification program, weekend college. Nontraditional program for returning students. **Credit/placement by examination:** AP, CLEP, SAT, ACT, institutional tests. 15 credit hours maximum toward bachelor's degree. **Support services:** Learning center, pre-admission summer program, reduced course load, study skills assistance, tutoring, writing center.

Majors. Biology: General. **Business:** Business admin. **English:** English lit. **Math:** General. **Philosophy/religion:** Religion. **Physical sciences:** Chemistry. **Social sciences:** General.

Most popular majors. Biology 11%, business/marketing 43%, English 9%, social sciences 24%, theological studies 9%.

Technology on campus. Dormitories wired for high-speed internet access and linked to campus network. Commuter students can connect to campus network. Online course registration, online library, helpline, wireless network available.

Student life. Freshman orientation: Mandatory. Preregistration for classes offered. Week-long session. Students complete financial aid forms, receive dorm assignments, and complete the registration process. **Housing:** Guaranteed on-campus for freshmen. Single-sex dorms, apartments available. $150 nonrefundable deposit, deadline 7/31. **Activities:** Campus ministries, choral groups, international student organizations, music ensembles, student government, NAACP, BASIC, chic republic, National Black MBA Association, spirit club, ICONIC Arts, Men Armed with Knowledge.

Athletics. NAIA. **Intercollegiate:** Basketball, volleyball W. **Intramural:** Basketball. **Team name:** Yellow Jackets.

Student services. Adult student services, chaplain/spiritual director, career counseling, student employment services, financial aid counseling, health services, personal counseling, placement for graduates, veterans' counselor.

Contact. E-mail: bbyrd@allenuniversity.edu
Phone: (803) 376-5735 Toll-free number: (877) 625-5368
Fax: (803) 376-5731
Nathaniel Canfall, Director of Admissions, Allen University, 1530 Harden Street, Columbia, SC 29204

Anderson University
Anderson, South Carolina
www.andersonuniversity.edu

CB member
CB code: 5008

◆ Private 4-year university affiliated with the Southern Baptist Convention
◆ Residential campus in large town
◆ 2,632 degree-seeking undergraduates: 9% part-time, 67% women
◆ 379 degree-seeking graduate students
◆ 55% of applicants admitted
◆ SAT or ACT (ACT writing optional) required
◆ 49% graduate within 6 years

General. Founded in 1911. Regionally accredited. **Degrees:** 445 bachelor's awarded; master's, professional offered. **ROTC:** Air Force. **Location:** 32 miles from Greenville, 100 miles from Atlanta. **Calendar:** Semester, limited summer session. **Full-time faculty:** 124 total; 61% have terminal degrees, 8% minority, 53% women. **Part-time faculty:** 191 total; 35% have terminal degrees, 10% minority, 53% women. **Class size:** 42% < 20, 39% 20-39, 12% 40-49, 7% 50-99, less than 1% >100. **Special facilities:** Audio recording studio.

Freshman class profile. 3,322 applied, 1,825 admitted, 663 enrolled.

Mid 50% test scores			
SAT critical reading:	480-590	GPA 2.0-2.99:	3%
SAT math:	470-590	Rank in top quarter:	62%
SAT writing:	470-590	Rank in top tenth:	37%
ACT composite:	21-26	Return as sophomores:	74%
GPA 3.75 or higher:	32%	Out-of-state:	6%
GPA 3.50-3.74:	29%	Live on campus:	92%
GPA 3.0-3.49:	36%	International:	1%

Basis for selection. Academic GPA and test scores most important. Recommendations, further grades or interview may be required for academically weak applicants. Interview recommended for some; audition required for art, music, theater programs. **Learning Disabled:** Applicants with diagnosed learning disabilities must meet regular requirements and supply summary of recent (within 1 year of enrollment) diagnostic testing.

High school preparation. College-preparatory program required. Required units include English 4, mathematics 3, science 3 (laboratory 2) and foreign language 2.

2015-2016 Annual costs. Tuition/fees: $24,860. Room/board: $8,860. Books/supplies: $2,000. Personal expenses: $2,345.

2014-2015 Financial aid. Need-based: 632 full-time freshmen applied for aid; 511 deemed to have need; 511 received aid. Average need met was 77%. Average scholarship/grant was $17,539; average loan $3,939. 70% of total undergraduate aid awarded as scholarships/grants, 30% as loans/jobs. **Non-need-based:** Awarded to 971 full-time undergraduates, including 336 freshmen. Scholarships awarded for academics, art, athletics, leadership, minority status, music/drama, religious affiliation, state residency.

Application procedures. Admission: Closing date 8/1. $25 fee, may be waived for applicants with need. Admission notification on a rolling basis beginning on or about 9/1. **Financial aid:** Priority date 3/1, closing date 6/30. FAFSA required. Applicants notified on a rolling basis starting 3/15; must reply by 5/1 or within 2 week(s) of notification.

Academics. Special study options: Accelerated study, distance learning, double major, dual enrollment of high school students, honors, independent study, internships, liberal arts/career combination, study abroad, teacher certification program, Washington semester. **Credit/placement by examination:** AP, CLEP, IB, SAT, ACT, institutional tests. 24 credit hours maximum toward bachelor's degree. **Support services:** Learning center, reduced course load, remedial instruction, study skills assistance, tutoring, writing center.

Majors. Biology: General, Biochemistry/molecular biology, exercise physiology. **Business:** General, accounting, actuarial science, business admin, human resources, international, logistics, marketing, organizational leadership. **Communications:** Digital media, media studies, persuasive communications. **Computer sciences:** General, information technology. **Education:**

Art, elementary, English, mathematics, multi-level teacher, music, physical, social studies, special ed. **Engineering:** Pre-engineering. **English:** Creative writing, English lit, writing. **Foreign languages:** Spanish. **Health services:** Athletic training, health services admin, nursing (RN), prephysical therapy. **History:** General. **Math:** General. **Parks/recreation:** Exercise sciences. **Philosophy/religion:** Christian. **Protective services:** Homeland security, infrastructure protection. **Psychology:** General. **Theology:** Bible, missionary, theology, youth ministry. **Visual/performing arts:** Acting, art, ceramics, dance, directing/producing, dramatic, graphic design, interior design, music, music management, music pedagogy, musical theater, painting, piano/keyboard, voice/opera.

Most popular majors. Business/marketing 18%, education 24%, parks/recreation 8%, security/protective services 7%.

Technology on campus. 130 workstations in library, computer center. Dormitories wired for high-speed internet access and linked to campus network. Commuter students can connect to campus network. Online course registration, online library, helpline, wireless network available.

Student life. Freshman orientation: Mandatory. Preregistration for classes offered. Two sessions held during summer. **Housing:** Guaranteed on-campus for freshmen. Single-sex dorms available. $250 fully refundable deposit, deadline 5/1. Honors and Ministry houses available. **Activities:** Bands, campus ministries, choral groups, dance, drama, international student organizations, literary magazine, music ensembles, musical theater, Gamma Beta Phi, campus activities board, Fellowship of Christian Athletes, Minorities for Change, student alumni council, Reformed University Fellowship, Young Life.

Athletics. NCAA. **Intercollegiate:** Baseball M, basketball, cheerleading W, cross-country, golf, soccer, softball W, tennis, track and field, volleyball W, wrestling M. **Intramural:** Basketball, football (non-tackle), racquetball, softball, table tennis, tennis, volleyball, weight lifting M. **Team name:** Trojans.

Student services. Adult student services, chaplain/spiritual director, career counseling, student employment services, financial aid counseling, health services, on-campus daycare, personal counseling, placement for graduates. **Physically disabled:** Services for visually impaired.

Contact. E-mail: admission@andersonuniversity.edu
Phone: (864) 231-2030 Toll-free number: (800) 542-3594
Fax: (864) 231-2033
Pam Ross, Dean of Admission, Anderson University, 316 Boulevard, Anderson, SC 29621-4002

Benedict College
Columbia, South Carolina
www.benedict.edu

CB member
CB code: 5056

- Private 4-year liberal arts college affiliated with the American Baptist Churches in the USA
- Residential campus in large city
- 2,464 degree-seeking undergraduates
- 76% of applicants admitted

General. Founded in 1870. Regionally accredited. Benedict College is a historically black institution. **Degrees:** 354 bachelor's awarded. **ROTC:** Army, Air Force. **Location:** 110 miles from Greenville, 120 miles from Charleston. **Calendar:** Semester, limited summer session. **Full-time faculty:** 139 total. **Part-time faculty:** 50 total. **Class size:** 46% < 20, 33% 20-39, 13% 40-49, 8% 50-99.

Freshman class profile. 6,780 applied, 5,183 admitted, 655 enrolled.

Mid 50% test scores			
		GPA 3.0-3.49:	19%
SAT math:	380-390	GPA 2.0-2.99:	51%
SAT writing:	370-380	Rank in top quarter:	15%
ACT composite:	15-17	Rank in top tenth:	5%
GPA 3.75 or higher:	4%	Out-of-state:	50%
GPA 3.50-3.74:	6%	Live on campus:	93%

Basis for selection. High school GPA and test scores important.

High school preparation. College-preparatory program recommended. 20 units recommended. Recommended units include English 4, mathematics 3, social studies 3 and science 2.

2015-2016 Annual costs. Tuition/fees: $18,286. Room/board: $8,104. Books/supplies: $1,000. Personal expenses: $1,400.

Application procedures. Admission: No deadline. $25 fee. Admission notification on a rolling basis. **Financial aid:** Priority date 4/15; no closing date. FAFSA required. Applicants notified on a rolling basis starting 4/15.

Academics. Special study options: Accelerated study, double major, dual enrollment of high school students, external degree, honors, internships, teacher certification program, weekend college. **Credit/placement by examination:** AP, CLEP, institutional tests. 24 credit hours maximum toward bachelor's degree. **Support services:** Learning center, pre-admission summer program, reduced course load, remedial instruction, study skills assistance, tutoring, writing center.

Majors. Biology: General. **Business:** Accounting, business admin. **Communications:** Media studies. **Computer sciences:** General, computer science. **Conservation:** Environmental science. **Education:** Early childhood, elementary. **Engineering:** Computer, electrical, environmental. **English:** English lit. **History:** General. **Human services:** Social work. **Math:** General. **Parks/recreation:** Health/fitness. **Philosophy/religion:** General. **Physical sciences:** Chemistry, physics. **Protective services:** Law enforcement admin. **Social sciences:** Economics, political science. **Visual/performing arts:** Art, multimedia. **Work/family studies:** Family studies.

Most popular majors. Biology 11%, business/marketing 21%, communications/journalism 10%, family/consumer sciences 10%, parks/recreation 7%.

Technology on campus. 385 workstations in dormitories, library, computer center, student center. Dormitories wired for high-speed internet access and linked to campus network. Commuter students can connect to campus network. Online library, helpline, repair service, wireless network available.

Student life. Freshman orientation: Mandatory. Preregistration for classes offered. **Housing:** Guaranteed on-campus for freshmen. Single-sex dorms available. **Activities:** Bands, choral groups, dance, drama, music ensembles, radio station, student government, student newspaper, Gordon-Jenkins Theological Association.

Athletics. NAIA. **Intercollegiate:** Baseball M, basketball, cross-country, football (tackle) M, golf, soccer M, softball, tennis, track and field, volleyball W, wrestling M. **Intramural:** Baseball M, basketball, softball W, volleyball W. **Team name:** Tigers.

Student services. Adult student services, chaplain/spiritual director, career counseling, student employment services, financial aid counseling, health services, minority student services, on-campus daycare, personal counseling, placement for graduates, veterans' counselor.

Contact. E-mail: admissions@benedict.edu
Phone: (803) 705-4491 Toll-free number: (800) 868-6598
Fax: (803) 253-5167
Phyllis Thompson, Director of Admissions, Benedict College, 1600 Harden Street, Columbia, SC 29204

Bob Jones University
Greenville, South Carolina
www.bju.edu

CB code: 5065

- Private 4-year Bible, liberal arts and seminary college affiliated with the nondenominational tradition
- Residential campus in small city
- 2,467 degree-seeking undergraduates: 2% part-time, 56% women
- 287 degree-seeking graduate students
- 82% of applicants admitted
- Application essay required
- 61% graduate within 6 years

General. Regionally accredited; also accredited by TRACS. **Degrees:** 51 bachelor's, 45 associate awarded; master's, doctoral offered. **Location:** 100 miles from Charlotte, NC; 128 miles from Atlanta. **Calendar:** Semester, limited summer session. **Full-time faculty:** 199 total; 62% have terminal degrees, 5% minority, 37% women. **Part-time faculty:** 28 total; 100% have terminal degrees, 4% minority, 89% women. **Special facilities:** Center for leadership development, music libraries, field house.

Freshman class profile. 1,101 applied, 903 admitted, 609 enrolled.

Mid 50% test scores			
		GPA 2.0-2.99:	21%
SAT critical reading:	450-620	Rank in top quarter:	21%
SAT math:	440-570	Rank in top tenth:	11%
SAT writing:	443-570	End year in good standing:	93%
ACT composite:	19-26	Return as sophomores:	80%
GPA 3.75 or higher:	10%	Out-of-state:	63%
GPA 3.50-3.74:	23%	International:	6%
GPA 3.0-3.49:	41%		

Basis for selection. Prospective applicants who fall outside of requirements will go to Admissions Committee for a decision. **Home schooled:** Achievement test scores.

High school preparation. College-preparatory program recommended. 16 units required. Required and recommended units include English 3, mathematics 2, social studies 2, science 1, foreign language 2 and academic electives 6.

2015-2016 Annual costs. Tuition/fees: $14,900. Room/board: $6,280. Books/supplies: $1,200. Personal expenses: $1,600.

2014-2015 Financial aid. Need-based: 530 full-time freshmen applied for aid; 442 deemed to have need; 442 received aid. Average need met was 50%. Average scholarship/grant was $12,105; average loan $12,054. 73% of total undergraduate aid awarded as scholarships/grants, 27% as loans/jobs. **Non-need-based:** Awarded to 916 full-time undergraduates, including 479 freshmen. Scholarships awarded for academics, alumni affiliation, state residency.

Application procedures. Admission: Closing date 8/1 (receipt date). No application fee. Admission notification on a rolling basis. **Financial aid:** Priority date 3/1, closing date 7/1. FAFSA required. Applicants notified on a rolling basis.

Academics. Academic Resource Center exists to support students with academic accommodations, transition advising, academic coaching, writing center, coordinates peer-led study groups, tutoring services, and technological assistance and testing services. **Special study options:** Accelerated study, distance learning, dual enrollment of high school students, ESL, independent study, internships, teacher certification program. **Credit/placement by examination:** AP, CLEP, ACT, institutional tests. **Support services:** Learning center, reduced course load, remedial instruction, study skills assistance, tutoring, writing center.

Majors. Biology: General, molecular biochemistry. **Business:** Accounting, actuarial science, business admin. **Communications:** General. **Computer sciences:** Computer science, information technology. **Education:** Early childhood, elementary, English, mathematics, middle, music, science, social studies, Spanish, special ed. **Engineering:** General. **English:** Creative writing, English lit. **Foreign languages:** Spanish. **Health services:** Communication disorders, nursing (RN), premedicine. **History:** General. **Liberal arts:** Humanities. **Math:** General. **Parks/recreation:** Health/fitness. **Physical sciences:** Chemistry, physics. **Protective services:** Criminal justice. **Psychology:** Counseling. **Social sciences:** International relations. **Theology:** Bible, missionary, sacred music. **Visual/performing arts:** Cinematography, dramatic, fashion design, graphic design, music pedagogy, music performance, piano/keyboard, studio arts, voice/opera.

Most popular majors. Business/marketing 17%, communications/journalism 6%, education 15%, health sciences 10%, theological studies 7%, visual/performing arts 14%.

Technology on campus. 420 workstations in dormitories, library, computer center. Dormitories linked to campus network. Commuter students can connect to campus network. Online course registration, online library, helpline, repair service, wireless network available.

Student life. Freshman orientation: Available. Preregistration for classes offered. Held in June. **Policies:** Religious observance required. **Housing:** Single-sex dorms, special housing for disabled available. **Activities:** Concert band, campus ministries, choral groups, drama, music ensembles, opera, radio station, student government, student newspaper, symphony orchestra, TV station.

Athletics. NCCAA. **Intercollegiate:** Basketball, cross-country, golf, soccer, track and field. **Intramural:** Baseball M, basketball, soccer, softball W, table tennis, tennis, volleyball W. **Team name:** Bruins.

Student services. Chaplain/spiritual director, career counseling, student employment services, financial aid counseling, health services, on-campus daycare, personal counseling, placement for graduates, veterans' counselor. **Physically disabled:** Services for visually, speech, hearing impaired.

Contact. E-mail: admission@bju.edu
Phone: (800) 252-6363 Toll-free number: (800) 252-6363
Fax: (800) 232-9258
Gary Deedrick, Director of Admission, Bob Jones University, 1700 Wade Hampton Boulevard, Greenville, SC 29614

Charleston Southern University
Charleston, South Carolina CB member
www.csuniv.edu CB code: 5079

- Private 4-year university and liberal arts college affiliated with the Southern Baptist Convention
- Commuter campus in large city
- 3,112 degree-seeking undergraduates
- 60% of applicants admitted
- SAT or ACT (ACT writing optional) required

General. Founded in 1964. Regionally accredited. **Degrees:** 478 bachelor's awarded; master's offered. **ROTC:** Army, Air Force. **Location:** 15 miles from downtown. **Calendar:** 4-1-4, limited summer session. **Full-time faculty:** 147 total. **Part-time faculty:** 118 total. **Special facilities:** Earthquake research center.

Freshman class profile. 4,390 applied, 2,643 admitted, 755 enrolled.

Mid 50% test scores		ACT composite:	20-25
SAT critical reading:	450-560	Out-of-state:	23%
SAT math:	460-550	Live on campus:	73%

Basis for selection. School achievement record, academic coursework, test scores, GPA most important. Interview and recommendations considered. Students may be required to take institutional math test for acceptance and/or placement. Essay, interview recommended for all; audition recommended for music programs. **Learning Disabled:** Special needs allowances require documentation and interview with Director of Special Needs.

High school preparation. College-preparatory program recommended. 23 units required. Required and recommended units include English 4, mathematics 3-4, social studies 2, history 2, science 3 (laboratory 2) and foreign language 2.

2015-2016 Annual costs. Tuition/fees: $23,400. Room/board: $9,270. Books/supplies: $1,400.

Financial aid. Non-need-based: Scholarships awarded for academics, athletics, religious affiliation, ROTC.

Application procedures. Admission: No deadline. $40 fee, may be waived for applicants with need. Admission notification on a rolling basis beginning on or about 9/1. **Financial aid:** Priority date 4/15; no closing date. FAFSA required. Applicants notified on a rolling basis starting 3/1; must reply within 2 week(s) of notification.

Academics. Special study options: Accelerated study, combined bachelor's/graduate degree, cooperative education, cross-registration, distance learning, double major, dual enrollment of high school students, honors, internships, study abroad, teacher certification program. **Credit/placement by examination:** AP, CLEP, IB, SAT, ACT, institutional tests. 30 credit hours maximum toward bachelor's degree. **Support services:** Learning center, remedial instruction, study skills assistance, tutoring, writing center.

Majors. Biology: General, biochemistry. **Business:** Accounting, business admin, finance, management information systems, marketing. **Computer sciences:** General, computer science. **Education:** Early childhood, elementary, English, mathematics, multi-level teacher, music, physical, science, social studies, Spanish. **English:** English lit. **Foreign languages:** Spanish. **Health services:** Athletic training, music therapy, nursing (RN). **History:** General, American, European. **Liberal arts:** Humanities. **Math:** General, applied. **Parks/recreation:** Health/fitness. **Philosophy/religion:** Religion. **Physical sciences:** Chemistry. **Protective services:** Criminal justice. **Psychology:** General. **Social sciences:** General, economics, political science, sociology. **Theology:** Sacred music, youth ministry. **Visual/performing arts:** Graphic design, music, music performance, voice/opera.

Most popular majors. Biology 8%, business/marketing 30%, education 9%, health sciences 10%, psychology 7%, security/protective services 9%, social sciences 9%.

Technology on campus. 150 workstations in dormitories, library, computer center, student center. Dormitories wired for high-speed internet access. Commuter students can connect to campus network. Online library, helpline, student web hosting, wireless network available.

Student life. Freshman orientation: Available. Preregistration for classes offered. **Policies:** Religious observance required. **Housing:** Guaranteed on-campus for freshmen. Single-sex dorms available. $200 fully refundable deposit, deadline 8/15. **Activities:** Bands, choral groups, dance, drama, international student organizations, literary magazine, music ensembles, musical theater, student government, student newspaper, College Republicans, Young Democrats, Afro-American society, Baptist student union, Fellowship of Christian Athletes, Campus Crusade, future teachers society.

Athletics. NCAA. **Intercollegiate:** Baseball M, basketball, cross-country, football (tackle) M, golf, soccer, softball W, tennis, track and field, volleyball W. **Intramural:** Basketball, soccer, softball, volleyball. **Team name:** Buccaneer.

Student services. Adult student services, chaplain/spiritual director, career counseling, student employment services, financial aid counseling, health services, personal counseling, placement for graduates, veterans' counselor. **Physically disabled:** Services for visually, speech, hearing impaired.

Contact. E-mail: enroll@csuniv.edu
Phone: (843) 863-7050 Toll-free number: (800) 947-7474
Fax: (843) 863-7070
Jim Rhoton, Director of Admissions, Charleston Southern University, 9200 University Boulevard, Charleston, SC 29406

The Citadel
Charleston, South Carolina CB member
www.citadel.edu CB code: 5108

- Public 4-year military college
- Residential campus in large city
- 2,616 degree-seeking undergraduates: 6% part-time, 9% women, 9% African American, 2% Asian American, 6% Hispanic/Latino, 1% Native American, 4% Multi-racial, non-Hispanic, 1% international
- 792 degree-seeking graduate students
- 77% of applicants admitted
- SAT or ACT (ACT writing optional) required
- 69% graduate within 6 years

General. Founded in 1842. Regionally accredited. Undergraduate student body make up the South Carolina Corps of Cadets. The men and women in the Corps live and study under a classical military system that makes leadership and character training an essential part of the educational experience. **Degrees:** 597 bachelor's awarded; master's offered. **ROTC:** Army, Naval, Air Force. **Location:** Downtown. **Calendar:** Semester, extensive summer session. **Full-time faculty:** 192 total; 93% have terminal degrees, 15% minority, 34% women. **Part-time faculty:** 96 total; 40% have terminal degrees, 8% minority, 44% women. **Class size:** 44% < 20, 50% 20-39, 5% 40-49, 2% 50-99. **Special facilities:** Beach house, boating center.

Freshman class profile. 2,436 applied, 1,864 admitted, 602 enrolled.

Mid 50% test scores			
SAT critical reading:	490-580	Rank in top quarter:	34%
SAT math:	490-600	Rank in top tenth:	11%
ACT composite:	21-25	Return as sophomores:	86%
GPA 3.75 or higher:	42%	Out-of-state:	45%
GPA 3.50-3.74:	16%	Live on campus:	100%
GPA 3.0-3.49:	30%	International:	2%
GPA 2.0-2.99:	12%		

Basis for selection. Admissions based on class rank, test scores, GPA, alumni recommendations, extracurricular activities. Rolling Admissions: No Deadlines. Interview recommended.

High school preparation. College-preparatory program required. 19 units required. Required units include English 4, mathematics 4, social studies 2, history 1, science 3 (laboratory 3), foreign language 2, visual/performing arts 1 and academic electives 1. 1 physical education or ROTC, 1 fine arts required. 1 of the social studies units must be U.S. history.

2015-2016 Annual costs. Tuition/fees: $13,024; $33,440 out-of-state. Room/board: $6,381.

2015-2016 Financial aid. Need-based: 499 full-time freshmen applied for aid; 373 deemed to have need; 361 received aid. Average need met was 53%. Average scholarship/grant was $14,525; average loan $3,440. 58% of total undergraduate aid awarded as scholarships/grants, 42% as loans/jobs. **Non-need-based:** Awarded to 1,039 full-time undergraduates, including 243 freshmen. Scholarships awarded for academics, alumni affiliation, athletics, leadership, minority status, music/drama, religious affiliation, ROTC, state residency.

Application procedures. Admission: No deadline. $40 fee, may be waived for applicants with need. Admission notification on a rolling basis beginning on or about 7/15. Must reply by 5/1. **Financial aid:** Priority date 3/1; no closing date. FAFSA required. Applicants notified on a rolling basis starting 4/1; must reply within 2 week(s) of notification.

Academics. 4 years of ROTC required. **Special study options:** Cooperative education, distance learning, double major, ESL, honors, independent study, internships, New York semester, study abroad, teacher certification program, Washington semester. **Credit/placement by examination:** AP, CLEP, IB, SAT, institutional tests. **Support services:** Learning center, pre-admission summer program, study skills assistance, tutoring, writing center.

Majors. Biology: General. **Business:** Business admin. **Computer sciences:** General. **Education:** Physical, secondary. **Engineering:** Civil, electrical, mechanical. **English:** English lit. **Foreign languages:** General. **History:** General. **Math:** General. **Parks/recreation:** Exercise sciences, sports admin. **Physical sciences:** Chemistry, physics. **Protective services:** Law enforcement admin. **Psychology:** General. **Social sciences:** Political science.

Most popular majors. Business/marketing 28%, education 7%, engineering/engineering technologies 13%, history 7%, security/protective services 16%, social sciences 10%.

Technology on campus. 207 workstations in dormitories, library, computer center. Dormitories wired for high-speed internet access and linked to campus network. Commuter students can connect to campus network. Online course registration, online library, helpline, repair service, wireless network available.

Student life. Freshman orientation: Mandatory. Preregistration for classes offered. **Policies:** Freshmen not permitted cars on campus. **Housing:** Guaranteed on-campus for all undergraduates. Coed dorms available. $300 fully refundable deposit, deadline 5/1. **Activities:** Bands, campus ministries, choral groups, international student organizations, literary magazine, student government, student newspaper, African American Society, American Society of Civil Engineers, Association for Computing Machinery, Alpha Phi Sigma, Summerall Guards, African Methodist Episcopal, Baptist Student Union, Campus Crusade for Christ, Knights of Columbus, Army Aviator Association of America, Women in Science & Engineering.

Athletics. NCAA. **Intercollegiate:** Baseball M, basketball M, cross-country, football (tackle) M, golf W, rifle, soccer W, tennis M, track and field, volleyball W, wrestling M. **Intramural:** Badminton, basketball, football (non-tackle), handball, racquetball, soccer, softball, swimming, table tennis, tennis, track and field, triathlon, ultimate frisbee, volleyball, weight lifting, wrestling. **Team name:** Bulldogs.

Student services. Alcohol/substance abuse counseling, chaplain/spiritual director, career counseling, student employment services, financial aid counseling, health services, minority student services, personal counseling, placement for graduates, veterans' counselor.

Contact. E-mail: admissions@citadel.edu
Phone: (843) 953-5230 Toll-free number: (800) 868-1842
Fax: (843) 953-7036
Lt. Col. John Powell, Director of Admissions, The Citadel, 171 Moultrie Street, Charleston, SC 29409

Claflin University
Orangeburg, South Carolina CB member
www.claflin.edu CB code: 5109

- Private 4-year liberal arts college affiliated with the United Methodist Church
- Residential campus in large town
- 1,809 full-time, degree-seeking undergraduates
- SAT or ACT (ACT writing optional), application essay required

General. Founded in 1869. Regionally accredited. **Degrees:** 330 bachelor's awarded; master's offered. **ROTC:** Army, Air Force. **Location:** 37 miles from Columbia. **Calendar:** Semester, limited summer session. **Full-time faculty:** 119 total; 84% have terminal degrees, 76% minority, 43% women. **Part-time faculty:** 50 total; 10% have terminal degrees, 68% minority, 44% women. **Class size:** 67% < 20, 30% 20-39, 2% 40-49, less than 1% 50-99, less than 1% >100. **Special facilities:** South Carolina Center for Biotechnology, museum, molecular science research center, chapel.

Freshman class profile.

GPA 3.75 or higher:	4%	Rank in top quarter:	26%
GPA 3.50-3.74:	6%	Rank in top tenth:	10%
GPA 3.0-3.49:	22%	Out-of-state:	23%
GPA 2.0-2.99:	59%	Live on campus:	93%

Basis for selection. Secondary school record, class rank, GPA, recommendations, test scores most important. Audition required; essay, interview, portfolio recommended for certain majors.

High school preparation. College-preparatory program recommended. 24 units required. Required units include English 4, mathematics 3, social studies 1, history 1, science 3, foreign language 2, computer science 1 and academic electives 7. 1 physical education or Junior ROTC, .5 US government, .5 economics required.

2015-2016 Annual costs. Tuition/fees: $15,520. Room/board: $8,674. Books/supplies: $1,750. Personal expenses: $2,500.

Application procedures. Admission: Priority date 1/15; deadline 8/1. $30 fee, may be waived for applicants with need. Admission notification on a rolling basis beginning on or about 10/1. **Financial aid:** Closing date 4/15. FAFSA required. Applicants notified on a rolling basis starting 5/3; must reply within 2 week(s) of notification.

Academics. Special study options: Accelerated study, cooperative education, cross-registration, double major, dual enrollment of high school students, exchange student, honors, independent study, internships, liberal arts/career combination, study abroad, teacher certification program. **Credit/placement by examination:** AP, CLEP, SAT, ACT. **Support services:** Learning center, pre-admission summer program, reduced course load, remedial instruction, tutoring, writing center.

Honors college/program. Based on achievement, leadership, 1100 SAT (exclusive of writing)/24 ACT and 3.3 GPA; 65 to 75 admitted.

Majors. Area/ethnic studies: African-American, American. **Biology:** General, biochemistry, bioinformatics, biotechnology. **Business:** Business admin, management information systems, marketing, organizational behavior. **Communications:** Media studies. **Computer sciences:** Computer science. **Conservation:** Environmental science. **Education:** Art, early childhood, elementary, English, mathematics, middle, music. **Engineering:** Software. **English:** English lit. **History:** General. **Math:** General. **Parks/recreation:** Health/fitness, sports admin. **Philosophy/religion:** Philosophy, religion. **Physical sciences:** Chemistry. **Protective services:** Law enforcement admin. **Psychology:** General. **Social sciences:** Political science, sociology. **Visual/performing arts:** Art, music, studio arts.

Most popular majors. Biology 11%, business/marketing 27%, communications/journalism 10%, parks/recreation 8%, security/protective services 10%, social sciences 18%.

Technology on campus. 540 workstations in dormitories, library, computer center, student center. Dormitories wired for high-speed internet access and linked to campus network. Commuter students can connect to campus network. Online course registration, online library, helpline, repair service, wireless network available.

Student life. Freshman orientation: Mandatory, $60 fee. Preregistration for classes offered. Early registration sessions held during summer; one-week orientation held in early fall. **Policies:** Freshmen not permitted cars on campus. **Housing:** Guaranteed on-campus for freshmen. Single-sex dorms available. $60 nonrefundable deposit, deadline 7/1. **Activities:** Bands, choral groups, dance, drama, film society, international student organizations, literary magazine, music ensembles, radio station, student government, student newspaper, TV station, Alpha Kappa Mu, literature/art/film society, Phi Beta Lambda Business Fraternity, Students in Free Enterprise, NAACP, women's group, Sigma Tau Delta English Honor Society.

Athletics. NCAA. **Intercollegiate:** Baseball M, basketball, cross-country, softball W, track and field, volleyball W. **Intramural:** Basketball, softball W, volleyball W. **Team name:** Panthers.

Student services. Adult student services, chaplain/spiritual director, career counseling, student employment services, financial aid counseling, health services, minority student services, personal counseling, placement for graduates, veterans' counselor.

Contact. E-mail: admissions@claflin.edu
Phone: (803) 535-5382 Toll-free number: (800) 922-1276
Fax: (803) 535-5385
Michael Zeigler, Director of Admissions, Claflin University, 400 Magnolia Street, Orangeburg, SC 29115

Clemson University
Clemson, South Carolina
www.clemson.edu

CB member
CB code: 5111

- Public 4-year university and engineering college
- Residential campus in large town
- 17,740 degree-seeking undergraduates: 3% part-time, 47% women, 7% African American, 2% Asian American, 3% Hispanic/Latino, 3% Multiracial, non-Hispanic, 1% international
- 4,374 degree-seeking graduate students
- 51% of applicants admitted
- SAT or ACT (ACT writing optional) required
- 81% graduate within 6 years

General. Founded in 1889. Regionally accredited. **Degrees:** 3,953 bachelor's awarded; master's, doctoral offered. **ROTC:** Army, Air Force. **Location:** 17 miles from Anderson. **Calendar:** Semester, extensive summer session. **Full-time faculty:** 1,134 total; 87% have terminal degrees, 19% minority, 36% women. **Part-time faculty:** 129 total; 62% have terminal degrees, 11% minority, 39% women. **Class size:** 49% < 20, 25% 20-39, 8% 40-49, 11% 50-99, 6% >100. **Special facilities:** Planetarium, agricultural and forestry experimental facilities, geology museum, state botanical gardens, center for sustainable living, John C. Calhoun historical site and home, performing arts center.

Freshman class profile. 22,396 applied, 11,483 admitted, 3,448 enrolled.

Mid 50% test scores			
SAT critical reading:	560-660	Rank in top quarter:	86%
SAT math:	590-690	Rank in top tenth:	56%
ACT composite:	27-31	Return as sophomores:	93%
GPA 3.75 or higher:	87%	Out-of-state:	39%
GPA 3.50-3.74:	6%	Live on campus:	98%
GPA 3.0-3.49:	6%	International:	1%
GPA 2.0-2.99:	1%	Fraternities:	18%
		Sororities:	48%

Basis for selection. Admission competitive and based largely on high school curriculum, performance in that curriculum, peer comparison, SAT/ACT, and choice of major. Campus visit recommended for all. Interview, portfolio recommended for art applicants. Audition required for performing arts program applicants. **Home schooled:** Statement describing home school structure and mission, transcript of courses and grades required. Include copies of all secondary school transcripts and course descriptions of any courses different from those traditionally offered in public school settings.

High school preparation. College-preparatory program required. Required and recommended units include English 4, mathematics 3, social studies 1, history 1, science 3 (laboratory 3), foreign language 2-3 and visual/performing arts 1. Physical education or ROTC required. Foreign language units must be in same language.

2015-2016 Annual costs. Tuition/fees: $13,882; $32,800 out-of-state. Room/board: $8,718. Books/supplies: $1,308. Personal expenses: $3,608.

2015-2016 Financial aid. Need-based: 2,765 full-time freshmen applied for aid; 1,750 deemed to have need; 1,710 received aid. Average need met was 61%. Average scholarship/grant was $10,776; average loan $3,485. 52% of total undergraduate aid awarded as scholarships/grants, 48% as loans/jobs. **Non-need-based:** Awarded to 9,346 full-time undergraduates, including 2,234 freshmen. Scholarships awarded for academics, alumni affiliation, art, athletics, leadership, minority status, music/drama, ROTC, state residency.

Application procedures. Admission: Priority date 12/1; deadline 5/1 (receipt date). $70 fee, may be waived for applicants with need. Application must be submitted online. Admission notification on a rolling basis beginning on or about 11/1. Must reply by May 1 or within 4 week(s) if notified thereafter. Scholarship candidates notified on rolling basis, beginning on or about 11/1. Preferred application date of 12/1. Those who apply by that date, and whose application file is complete, will receive admission decision on or about the week of 2/15 for fall admission. **Financial aid:** Priority date 3/1; no closing date. FAFSA required. Applicants notified by 4/1.

Academics. Special study options: Combined bachelor's/graduate degree, cooperative education, distance learning, double major, dual enrollment of high school students, ESL, exchange student, external degree, honors, independent study, internships, study abroad, teacher certification program, Washington semester. Cooperative language center. **Credit/placement by examination:** AP, CLEP, IB, institutional tests. Challenge examinations offered by each academic department. **Support services:** Learning center, pre-admission summer program, study skills assistance, tutoring, writing center.

Honors college/program. Less than 10% of freshman class invited to enroll. Minimum peer comparison must show student in top 3% of graduating secondary school class.

Majors. Architecture: Architecture, landscape. **Area/ethnic studies:** African-American, women's. **Biology:** General, animal genetics, biochemistry, biomedical sciences, microbiology. **Business:** Accounting, business admin, construction management, finance, marketing. **Communications:** Sports. **Computer sciences:** General, information systems. **Conservation:** General, forest management, forest sciences. **Education:** Agricultural, early childhood, elementary, mathematics, science, secondary, special ed. **Engineering:** Agricultural, biomedical, ceramic, chemical, civil, computer, electrical, industrial, mechanical. **English:** English lit, rhetoric/composition. **Foreign languages:** General, Spanish. **Health services:** Nursing (RN), predental, premedicine, prepharmacy, preveterinary. **History:** General. **Math:** General. **Parks/recreation:** Facilities management. **Philosophy/religion:** Philosophy. **Physical sciences:** Chemistry, geology, physics. **Psychology:** General. **Social sciences:** Anthropology, economics, political science, sociology. **Visual/performing arts:** Art, industrial design.

Most popular majors. Agriculture 7%, biology 9%, business/marketing 19%, education 6%, engineering/engineering technologies 18%, health sciences 7%, social sciences 7%.

Technology on campus. PC or laptop required. 875 workstations in library, computer center. Dormitories wired for high-speed internet access and linked to campus network. Commuter students can connect to campus network. Online course registration, online library, helpline, repair service, student web hosting, wireless network available.

Student life. Freshman orientation: Mandatory, $55 fee. Preregistration for classes offered. One and 1/2-day sessions held 8 times during June and July. Students must complete online math placement exam prior to participating in orientation. **Policies:** All students required to submit proof of legal presence in the United States. **Housing:** Guaranteed on-campus for all undergraduates. Coed dorms, single-sex dorms, special housing for disabled, apartments, fraternity/sorority housing, themed housing, wellness housing available. $150 nonrefundable deposit, deadline 5/15. Housing guaranteed so long as continuing in on-campus housing. **Activities:** Bands, campus ministries, choral groups, dance, drama, international student organizations, literary magazine, music ensembles, musical theater, radio station, student government, student newspaper, symphony orchestra, TV station, religious organizations, Young Democrats, Young Republicans, minority awareness organizations, Blue Key, Alpha Phi Omega, Mortarboard, Hillel, Fellowship of Christian Athletes.

Athletics. NCAA. **Intercollegiate:** Baseball M, basketball, cross-country, diving, football (tackle) M, golf M, rowing (crew) W, soccer, swimming, tennis, track and field, volleyball W. **Intramural:** Basketball, diving, fencing, field hockey W, football (non-tackle), golf, racquetball, soccer, softball, table tennis, tennis, track and field, volleyball. **Team name:** Tigers.

Student services. Alcohol/substance abuse counseling, chaplain/spiritual director, career counseling, student employment services, financial aid counseling, health services, minority student services, personal counseling, placement for graduates, veterans' counselor. **Physically disabled:** Services for visually, speech, hearing impaired.

Contact. E-mail: cuadmissions@clemson.edu
Phone: (864) 656-2287 Fax: (864) 656-2464
Robert Barkley, Director of Admissions, Clemson University, 105 Sikes Hall, Clemson, SC 29634-5124

Coastal Carolina University
Conway, South Carolina — **CB member**
www.coastal.edu — **CB code: 5837**

- Public 4-year university
- Commuter campus in large town
- 9,289 degree-seeking undergraduates: 6% part-time, 53% women, 20% African American, 1% Asian American, 4% Hispanic/Latino, 5% Multiracial, non-Hispanic, 1% international
- 539 degree-seeking graduate students
- 60% of applicants admitted
- SAT or ACT (ACT writing recommended) required
- 43% graduate within 6 years

General. Founded in 1954. Regionally accredited. Barrier-reef island used for marine science field studies and research. **Degrees:** 1,648 bachelor's awarded; master's, doctoral offered. **ROTC:** Army. **Location:** 9 miles from Myrtle Beach. **Calendar:** Semester, extensive summer session. **Full-time faculty:** 434 total; 78% have terminal degrees, 10% minority, 41% women. **Part-time faculty:** 210 total; 31% have terminal degrees, 7% minority, 54% women. **Class size:** 35% < 20, 56% 20-39, 7% 40-49, 2% 50-99, less than 1% >100.

Freshman class profile. 17,252 applied, 10,291 admitted, 2,368 enrolled.

Mid 50% test scores			
SAT critical reading:	450-530	Rank in top tenth:	9%
SAT math:	460-550	End year in good standing:	74%
ACT composite:	20-24	Return as sophomores:	65%
GPA 3.75 or higher:	30%	Out-of-state:	59%
GPA 3.50-3.74:	16%	Live on campus:	88%
GPA 3.0-3.49:	31%	International:	1%
GPA 2.0-2.99:	23%	Fraternities:	9%
Rank in top quarter:	31%	Sororities:	16%

Basis for selection. Secondary school record and test scores most important; class rank important if provided. Applicants whose native language is not English must take TOEFL or IELTS. Tests are not required of applicants 22 years or older. **Home schooled:** Transcript of courses and grades required. Copy of declaration of intent to home school as filed with local board of education. **Learning Disabled:** Must provide documentation of disability to Service for Students with Disabilities Office.

High school preparation. College-preparatory program required. 19 units required. Required and recommended units include English 4, mathematics 4, social studies 2, history 1, science 3 (laboratory 3), foreign language 2, computer science 1, visual/performing arts 1 and academic electives 1. 1 unit of physical education or ROTC.

2015-2016 Annual costs. Tuition/fees: $10,530; $24,320 out-of-state. Room/board: $8,690. Books/supplies: $1,150. Personal expenses: $1,660.

2014-2015 Financial aid. Need-based: 2,171 full-time freshmen applied for aid; 1,785 deemed to have need; 1,754 received aid. Average need met was 44%. Average scholarship/grant was $4,784; average loan $8,453. 44% of total undergraduate aid awarded as scholarships/grants, 56% as loans/jobs. **Non-need-based:** Awarded to 3,605 full-time undergraduates, including 1,197 freshmen. Scholarships awarded for academics, art, athletics, leadership, ROTC.

Application procedures. Admission: Priority date 12/1; deadline 8/1 (receipt date). $45 fee, may be waived for applicants with need. Admission notification on a rolling basis beginning on or about 10/1. Must reply by May 1 or within 2 week(s) if notified thereafter. **Financial aid:** Priority date 3/1; no closing date. FAFSA required. Applicants notified on a rolling basis starting 3/1; must reply by 5/15.

Academics. Professional golf management specialization in any program in the Wall College of Business, accredited by PGA. International management specialization in management program. CPA/CMA option in accounting. **Special study options:** Accelerated study, combined bachelor's/graduate degree, cooperative education, distance learning, double major, dual enrollment of high school students, honors, independent study, internships, liberal arts/career combination, student-designed major, study abroad, teacher certification program. 3-2 engineering program with Clemson University. **Credit/placement by examination:** AP, CLEP, IB, institutional tests. Credit by examination must be obtained prior to reaching senior classification (90 credit hours). Will not be awarded for courses previously audited, or courses that have been previously failed. Cannot be used to raise a grade previously earned in a college course. **Support services:** Learning center, reduced course load, tutoring, writing center.

Majors. Biology: General, biochemistry, marine. **Business:** Accounting, business admin, finance, managerial economics, marketing, resort management. **Communications:** Communications/speech/rhetoric. **Computer sciences:** General, information systems, information technology. **Education:** Early childhood, elementary, middle, physical, special ed. **English:** English lit. **Foreign languages:** Spanish. **Health services:** Health care admin, nursing (RN), public health ed. **History:** General. **Liberal arts:** Arts/sciences, humanities. **Math:** Applied. **Military:** "intel, generally". **Parks/recreation:** Exercise sciences, sports admin. **Philosophy/religion:** Philosophy. **Physical sciences:** Chemistry, physics. **Psychology:** General. **Social sciences:** Economics, political science, sociology. **Visual/performing arts:** Dramatic, graphic design, music, musical theater, studio arts.

Most popular majors. Biology 11%, business/marketing 22%, communications/journalism 8%, education 8%, liberal arts 6%, parks/recreation 11%, psychology 6%, social sciences 8%.

Technology on campus. 1,200 workstations in dormitories, library, computer center, student center. Dormitories wired for high-speed internet access and linked to campus network. Commuter students can connect to campus network. Online course registration, online library, helpline, student web hosting, wireless network available.

Student life. Freshman orientation: Mandatory, $140 fee. Preregistration for classes offered. Two day programs. **Housing:** Coed dorms, special housing for disabled, apartments, themed housing, wellness housing available. $150 nonrefundable deposit, deadline 5/1. Honors housing available. **Activities:** Bands, campus ministries, choral groups, dance, drama, international student organizations, literary magazine, music ensembles, Model UN, musical theater, radio station, student government, student newspaper, African American Association, Students Taking Active Responsibility, Baptist collegiate ministry, Campus Democrats, College Republicans, Colleges Against Cancer, Rotaract - Collegiate Rotary, NAACP, Coastal Carolina Catholics.

Athletics. NCAA. **Intercollegiate:** Baseball M, basketball, cross-country, football (tackle) M, golf, lacrosse W, sand volleyball W, soccer, softball W, tennis, track and field, volleyball W. **Intramural:** Badminton, basketball, football (non-tackle), sand volleyball, soccer, softball, table tennis, tennis, volleyball. **Team name:** Chanticleers.

Student services. Adult student services, alcohol/substance abuse counseling, career counseling, student employment services, financial aid counseling, health services, minority student services, personal counseling, placement for graduates, veterans' counselor, women's services. **Physically disabled:** Services for visually, speech, hearing impaired.

Contact. E-mail: admissions@coastal.edu
Phone: (843) 349-2170 Toll-free number: (800) 277-7000
Fax: (843) 349-2127
Amanda Craddock, Director of Admissions, Coastal Carolina University,
PO Box 261954, Conway, SC 29528-6054

Coker College
Hartsville, South Carolina CB member
www.coker.edu CB code: 5112

- Private 4-year liberal arts college
- Residential campus in large town
- 1,091 degree-seeking undergraduates: 12% part-time, 60% women, 34% African American, 3% Hispanic/Latino, 1% Native American, 5% Multiracial, non-Hispanic, 2% international
- 79 degree-seeking graduate students
- 50% of applicants admitted
- 52% graduate within 6 years

General. Founded in 1908. Regionally accredited. **Degrees:** 224 bachelor's awarded; master's offered. **Location:** 70 miles from Columbia, SC; 80 miles from Charlotte, NC. **Calendar:** Continuous, limited summer session. **Special facilities:** Botanical gardens, boathouse, clubhouse.

Freshman class profile. 1,483 applied, 737 admitted, 226 enrolled.

Mid 50% test scores			
SAT critical reading:	430-530	GPA 3.0-3.49:	34%
SAT math:	440-540	GPA 2.0-2.99:	49%
ACT composite:	18-22	Rank in top quarter:	21%
GPA 3.75 or higher:	6%	Rank in top tenth:	7%
GPA 3.50-3.74:	9%	Return as sophomores:	73%
		International:	3%

Basis for selection. Rigor of school record, academic GPA and/or standardized test scores most important. Involvement in extracurricular activities, letters of recommendation, talents and qualities also considered. Auditions or portfolios may be required for certain programs.

High school preparation. College-preparatory program recommended. 15 units required. Required units include English 4, mathematics 3, social studies 3, science 3 (laboratory 1) and foreign language 2.

2015-2016 Annual costs. Tuition/fees: $26,568. Room/board: $8,242. Books/supplies: $1,508. Personal expenses: $1,000.

2014-2015 Financial aid. Non-need-based: Scholarships awarded for academics, alumni affiliation, art, athletics, leadership, music/drama. **Additional information:** Endowed scholarship program for qualified applicants. June 1 deadline for filing South Carolina Tuition Grant forms.

Application procedures. Admission: Priority date 5/1; deadline 8/1. $25 fee, may be waived for applicants with need. Admission notification on a rolling basis beginning on or about 9/1. Must reply by May 1 or within 8 week(s) if notified thereafter. Juniors allowed to apply and make admissions decision during summer prior to senior year. **Financial aid:** Priority date 4/1, closing date 6/1. FAFSA required. Applicants notified on a rolling basis starting 3/1; must reply by 5/1 or within 3 week(s) of notification.

Academics. Special study options: Accelerated study, distance learning, double major, dual enrollment of high school students, ESL, honors, independent study, internships, student-designed major, study abroad, teacher certification program. 3-1 program with regional medical facility. **Credit/placement by examination:** AP, CLEP, IB, SAT, ACT, institutional tests. Unlimited hours of credit by examination may be counted toward degree. **Support services:** Pre-admission summer program, remedial instruction, study skills assistance, tutoring, writing center.

Honors college/program. Director of the Honors Programs reviews incoming applications and extends invitations to potential new students; 5-10 students accepted each year.

Majors. Biology: General. **Business:** General. **Communications:** Communications/speech/rhetoric. **Computer sciences:** Computer science. **Education:** General, art, biology, chemistry, early childhood, elementary, English, history, mathematics, music, physical. **English:** English lit, technical writing. **Foreign languages:** Spanish. **Health services:** Clinical lab science. **History:** General. **Human services:** Social work. **Math:** General. **Parks/recreation:** Exercise sciences, health/fitness, sports admin. **Physical sciences:** Chemistry. **Psychology:** General, counseling. **Social sciences:** Criminology, political science, sociology. **Visual/performing arts:** Acting, dance, dramatic, graphic design, music, musical theater, photography, piano/keyboard, studio arts, theater design, voice/opera.

Most popular majors. Business/marketing 27%, communications/journalism 8%, education 6%, parks/recreation 9%, psychology 13%, social sciences 16%, visual/performing arts 7%.

Technology on campus. 116 workstations in dormitories, library, computer center, student center. Dormitories wired for high-speed internet access and linked to campus network. Commuter students can connect to campus network. Online course registration, online library, helpline, wireless network available.

Student life. Freshman orientation: Available, $150 fee. Preregistration for classes offered. Three-day program held in the summer. **Housing:** Guaranteed on-campus for freshmen. Coed dorms, special housing for disabled, themed housing available. $150 partly refundable deposit, deadline 5/1. **Activities:** Campus ministries, choral groups, dance, drama, international student organizations, literary magazine, musical theater, student government, Fellowship of Christian Athletes, Pan African Sisterhood Association, Psi Chi, student government association, culture club.

Athletics. NCAA. **Intercollegiate:** Baseball M, basketball, cheerleading, cross-country, golf, lacrosse, soccer, softball W, tennis, volleyball, wrestling M. **Intramural:** Basketball, cross-country, football (non-tackle), soccer, softball, tennis, volleyball. **Team name:** Cobras.

Student services. Adult student services, career counseling, student employment services, financial aid counseling, health services, personal counseling.

Contact. E-mail: admissions@coker.edu
Phone: (843) 383-8050 Toll-free number: (800) 950-1908
Fax: (843) 383-8056
Jeremy Nere, Director of Admissions, Coker College, 300 East College Avenue, Hartsville, SC 29550

College of Charleston
Charleston, South Carolina CB member
www.cofc.edu CB code: 5113

- Public 4-year liberal arts college
- Residential campus in large city
- 10,033 degree-seeking undergraduates: 5% part-time, 63% women, 7% African American, 2% Asian American, 5% Hispanic/Latino, 4% Multiracial, non-Hispanic, 1% international
- 496 degree-seeking graduate students
- 77% of applicants admitted
- SAT or ACT (ACT writing optional), application essay required
- 68% graduate within 6 years; 38% enter graduate study

General. Founded in 1770. Regionally accredited. **Degrees:** 2,507 bachelor's awarded; master's offered. **ROTC:** Air Force. **Calendar:** Semester, limited summer session. **Full-time faculty:** 573 total; 90% have terminal degrees, 13% minority, 45% women. **Part-time faculty:** 415 total; 39% have terminal degrees, 8% minority, 55% women. **Class size:** 37% < 20, 53% 20-39, 6% 40-49, 4% 50-99, less than 1% >100. **Special facilities:** ICat program (accelerator), center for supply chain management, natural history museum, observatory, marine science laboratory, communications museum, early childhood development center, bronze sculpture foundry, sailing center, African-American history and culture research center, center for entrepreneurship, real estate center, English Language Institute, institute of contemporary art, center for livable communities, S.C. space grant consortium.

Freshman class profile. 11,722 applied, 9,043 admitted, 2,237 enrolled.

Mid 50% test scores			
SAT critical reading:	520-610	Rank in top tenth:	21%
SAT math:	510-600	End year in good standing:	93%
ACT composite:	23-28	Return as sophomores:	79%
GPA 3.75 or higher:	60%	Out-of-state:	40%
GPA 3.50-3.74:	17%	Live on campus:	90%
GPA 3.0-3.49:	20%	International:	1%
GPA 2.0-2.99:	3%	Fraternities:	21%
Rank in top quarter:	54%	Sororities:	25%

Basis for selection. Rigor of secondary school record, academic GPA, standardized test scores, and state residency are very important. Campus visits and personal meetings are encouraged. **Home schooled:** Transcript of courses and grades required. Students should indicate which school district syllabus was followed during home schooling to help understand the content of the program followed, how challenging the courses were and how grades were determined. **Learning Disabled:** Explanation of curriculum modifications are recommended. Documentation is not required in the admissions process but must be submitted to utilize disability services if enrolled.

High school preparation. College-preparatory program required. 21 units required. Required and recommended units include English 4, mathematics 4, social studies 2, history 1-2, science 3 (laboratory 3), foreign language 3, computer science 1, visual/performing arts 1 and academic electives 3. 1 physical education required.

2015-2016 Annual costs. Tuition/fees: $11,220; $28,764 out-of-state. Room/board: $11,629. **Additional information:** Room costs are the weighted average of a tiered dorm pricing system. Room costs range from $5,866 to $10,070 per academic year with the majority of available rooms at $8,758.

2014-2015 Financial aid. Need-based: 1,567 full-time freshmen applied for aid; 1,068 deemed to have need; 1,024 received aid. Average need met was 58%. Average scholarship/grant was $3,317; average loan $2,968. 53% of total undergraduate aid awarded as scholarships/grants, 47% as loans/jobs. **Non-need-based:** Awarded to 4,035 full-time undergraduates, including 1,369 freshmen. Scholarships awarded for academics, alumni affiliation, art, athletics, music/drama.

Application procedures. Admission: Priority date 2/1; deadline 4/1 (postmark date). $50 fee, may be waived for applicants with need. Notified on or before January 1 for early notification applicants, on or before April 1 for regular decision applicants. Must reply by 5/1. March 1 is the deadline for international student application submission. **Financial aid:** Priority date 3/1; no closing date. FAFSA required. Applicants notified on a rolling basis starting 4/1; must reply within 8 week(s) of notification.

Academics. Special study options: Accelerated study, combined bachelor's/graduate degree, cooperative education, cross-registration, distance learning, double major, dual enrollment of high school students, ESL, exchange student, honors, independent study, internships, liberal arts/career combination, semester at sea, study abroad, teacher certification program. Semester at Sea. **Credit/placement by examination:** AP, CLEP, IB, institutional tests. Credit is awarded for AP; Cambridge GCE; CLEP and IB. **Support services:** Learning center, pre-admission summer program, study skills assistance, tutoring, writing center. Center for Student Learning (tutoring, Supplemental Instruction, walk-in labs), summer bridge programs, and TRIO pre-college program.

Honors college/program. Admitted students are typically in the top 10% of class, have taken numerous honors and/or AP courses, and are active in extracurricular activities. Average 1340 SAT Math/Reading and 30 ACT. Approximately 200 entering freshmen enroll each year. Students encouraged to apply before 11/1.

Majors. Area/ethnic studies: African-American, Latin American/Caribbean, women's. **Biology:** General, exercise physiology, marine. **Business:** Accounting, business admin, finance, hospitality admin, international, marketing. **Communications:** General. **Computer sciences:** General, information systems. **Education:** Early childhood, elementary, middle, multi-level teacher, physical, secondary, special ed. **English:** English lit. **Foreign languages:** Classics, French, German, Spanish. **Health services:** Athletic training, public health ed. **History:** General. **Math:** General. **Philosophy/religion:** Judaic, philosophy, religion. **Physical sciences:** Astronomy, astrophysics, chemistry, geology, physics. **Psychology:** General. **Social sciences:** Anthropology, archaeology, economics, political science, sociology, urban studies. **Visual/performing arts:** Art history/conservation, dance, dramatic, music, studio arts, studio arts management.

Most popular majors. Biology 12%, business/marketing 24%, communications/journalism 8%, education 6%, psychology 7%, social sciences 9%, visual/performing arts 10%.

Technology on campus. 1,094 workstations in dormitories, library, computer center, student center. Dormitories wired for high-speed internet access and linked to campus network. Commuter students can connect to campus network. Online course registration, online library, helpline, repair service, student web hosting, wireless network available.

Student life. Freshman orientation: Mandatory, $75 fee. Preregistration for classes offered. Two-day program offered ten times during the summer. Parents attending family orientation will pay a fee of $35. **Policies:** Honor system, student code of conduct, alcohol and drug policies, students' rights and responsibilities, amnesty/good samaritan policy, student sexual misconduct policy, and other policies and guidelines such as class attendance policies set by individual instructors. Freshmen not permitted cars on campus. **Housing:** Coed dorms, single-sex dorms, special housing for disabled, apartments, fraternity/sorority housing, gender-neutral housing, themed housing available. $200 nonrefundable deposit, deadline 5/1. Restored, historic houses used as residence hall. **Activities:** Bands, campus ministries, choral groups, dance, drama, international student organizations, literary magazine, music ensembles, musical theater, radio station, student government, student newspaper, symphony orchestra, Arabic club, Asian student association, Black Student Union, Chinese club, Baptist Collegiate Ministry, Campus Outreach, Catholic Students Association, Center for Civic Engagement, Chuck De Raas (Indian dance team), Chucktown Funk (hip hop choreography), Jewish Student Union/Hillel.

Athletics. NCAA. Intercollegiate: Baseball M, basketball, cheerleading, cross-country, equestrian W, golf, sailing, sand volleyball W, soccer, softball W, tennis, volleyball W. **Intramural:** Badminton, basketball, football (non-tackle), racquetball, soccer, softball, table tennis, tennis, volleyball, weight lifting. **Team name:** Cougars.

Student services. Adult student services, alcohol/substance abuse counseling, chaplain/spiritual director, career counseling, student employment services, financial aid counseling, health services, legal services, minority student services, on-campus daycare, personal counseling, placement for graduates, veterans' counselor. **Physically disabled:** Services for visually, speech, hearing impaired.

Contact. E-mail: admissions@cofc.edu
Phone: (843) 953-5670 Fax: (843) 953-6322
Suzette Stille, Executive Director for Admissions, Information and Operations, College of Charleston, Admissions, Charleston, SC 29424-0001

Columbia College
Columbia, South Carolina
www.columbiasc.edu
CB member
CB code: 5117

- Private 4-year liberal arts college for women affiliated with the United Methodist Church
- Residential campus in large city
- 1,552 degree-seeking undergraduates: 36% part-time, 78% women
- 96 degree-seeking graduate students
- 89% of applicants admitted
- SAT or ACT with writing required
- 48% graduate within 6 years

General. Founded in 1854. Regionally accredited. **Degrees:** 252 bachelor's awarded; master's offered. **ROTC:** Army. **Location:** 70 miles from Charlotte. **Calendar:** Semester, limited summer session. **Full-time faculty:** 73 total; 84% have terminal degrees, 19% minority, 74% women. **Part-time faculty:** 96 total; 20% have terminal degrees, 18% minority, 62% women. **Class size:** 75% < 20, 25% 20-39. **Special facilities:** Institute for leadership and professional excellence.

Freshman class profile. 506 applied, 450 admitted, 185 enrolled.

Mid 50% test scores			
SAT critical reading:	430-550	GPA 3.0-3.49:	22%
SAT math:	410-520	GPA 2.0-2.99:	10%
SAT writing:	410-530	Rank in top quarter:	47%
ACT composite:	18-24	Rank in top tenth:	15%
GPA 3.75 or higher:	56%	Return as sophomores:	76%
GPA 3.50-3.74:	12%	Out-of-state:	12%
		Live on campus:	88%

Basis for selection. School record, test scores, recommendations most important. Audition recommended for dance, music programs; portfolio recommended for art programs; essay, interview recommended for borderline applicants.

High school preparation. 16 units recommended. Recommended units include English 4, mathematics 3, social studies 2, history 1, science 2 (laboratory 2), foreign language 2 and academic electives 2. 2.5 units in music, dance, art also recommended.

2015-2016 Annual costs. Tuition/fees: $28,100. Room/board: $7,400. Books/supplies: $850. Personal expenses: $3,000.

2015-2016 Financial aid. Need-based: Average need met was 79%. Average scholarship/grant was $23,134; average loan $2,862. 68% of total undergraduate aid awarded as scholarships/grants, 32% as loans/jobs. **Non-need-based:** Scholarships awarded for academics, alumni affiliation, art, athletics, leadership, music/drama.

Application procedures. Admission: No deadline. $25 fee, may be waived for applicants with need, free for online applicants. Admission notification on a rolling basis beginning on or about 10/1. Must reply by May 1 or within 4 week(s) if notified thereafter. **Financial aid:** Priority date 4/1; no closing date. FAFSA required. Applicants notified on a rolling basis starting 3/15; must reply within 4 week(s) of notification.

Academics. Special study options: Double major, dual enrollment of high school students, exchange student, honors, independent study, internships, student-designed major, study abroad, teacher certification program, Washington semester. **Credit/placement by examination:** AP, CLEP, IB, SAT, ACT, institutional tests. **Support services:** Learning center, reduced course load, remedial instruction, study skills assistance, tutoring, writing center.

Majors. Biology: General, biochemistry. **Business:** Accounting, business admin. **Communications:** Communications/speech/rhetoric, journalism. **Computer sciences:** General. **Education:** Drama/dance, early childhood, elementary, middle, music, special ed. **English:** English lit. **Foreign languages:** French, Spanish. **Health services:** Speech pathology. **History:** General. **Human services:** Social work. **Liberal arts:** Arts/sciences. **Math:** General. **Philosophy/religion:** Religion. **Physical sciences:** Chemistry. **Protective services:** Criminal justice, disaster management. **Psychology:** General. **Social sciences:** Political science. **Theology:** Religious ed. **Visual/performing arts:** Art, dance, music, music performance, piano/keyboard, studio arts, voice/opera. **Work/family studies:** Family studies.

Most popular majors. Business/marketing 10%, communications/journalism 6%, education 13%, health sciences 7%, interdisciplinary studies 8%, liberal arts 6%, psychology 12%, public administration/social services 14%.

Technology on campus. 165 workstations in dormitories, library, computer center, student center. Dormitories wired for high-speed internet access and linked to campus network. Online course registration, online library, helpline, repair service, wireless network available.

Student life. Freshman orientation: Available, $150 fee. Preregistration for classes offered. One day program in June. Four day program in August where students participate in community service project. **Policies:** All students required to live on campus during first 2 years unless living with parent or guardian. All residence halls nonsmoking. Chapel requirements in place for first-year, sophomore, and junior students. Religious observance required. **Housing:** Guaranteed on-campus for freshmen. Wellness housing available. $100 deposit, deadline 5/1. **Activities:** Concert band, choral groups, dance, drama, international student organizations, literary magazine, music ensembles, musical theater, student government, student newspaper, Young Republicans, Young Democrats, CC Serves, Sister to Sista, African-American student association, NAACP.

Athletics. NAIA. **Intercollegiate:** Basketball W, cross-country W, golf W, lacrosse W, soccer W, softball W, swimming W, tennis W, volleyball W. **Team name:** Koalas.

Student services. Adult student services, chaplain/spiritual director, career counseling, student employment services, financial aid counseling, health services, personal counseling, placement for graduates, veterans' counselor.

Contact. E-mail: admissions@columbiasc.edu
Phone: (803) 786-3871 Toll-free number: (800) 277-1301
Fax: (803) 786-3674
Ken Huus, Vice President of Enrollment Management, Columbia College, 1301 Columbia College Drive, Columbia, SC 29203

Columbia International University
Columbia, South Carolina
www.ciu.edu   **CB code: 5116**

- Private 4-year university and Bible college affiliated with the interdenominational tradition
- Residential campus in small city
- 535 degree-seeking undergraduates: 8% part-time, 50% women, 10% African American, 2% Asian American, 4% Hispanic/Latino, 2% Multiracial, non-Hispanic, 4% international
- 426 degree-seeking graduate students
- 34% of applicants admitted
- SAT or ACT (ACT writing optional), application essay required
- 54% graduate within 6 years

General. Founded in 1923. Regionally accredited; also accredited by ABHE, ATS. **Degrees:** 130 bachelor's, 30 associate awarded; master's, doctoral offered. **Location:** 75 miles from Charlotte, NC, 225 miles from Atlanta. **Calendar:** Semester, limited summer session. **Full-time faculty:** 45 total; 87% have terminal degrees, 7% minority, 24% women. **Part-time faculty:** 36 total; 56% have terminal degrees, 8% minority, 39% women. **Class size:** 72% < 20, 16% 20-39, 2% 40-49, 8% 50-99, 3% >100. **Special facilities:** Prayer towers.

Freshman class profile. 553 applied, 188 admitted, 95 enrolled.

Mid 50% test scores		GPA 2.0-2.99:	11%
SAT critical reading:	480-580	Rank in top quarter:	42%
SAT math:	450-550	Rank in top tenth:	23%
SAT writing:	640-680	Return as sophomores:	74%
ACT composite:	20-26	Out-of-state:	42%
GPA 3.75 or higher:	53%	Live on campus:	99%
GPA 3.50-3.74:	23%	International:	7%
GPA 3.0-3.49:	13%		

Basis for selection. School achievement, recommendations, test scores, essay, school and community activities, religious commitment important. **Home schooled:** Transcripts should include GPA.

High school preparation. College-preparatory program recommended. 11 units recommended. Recommended units include English 4, mathematics 2, history 2, science 1 and foreign language 2.

2016-2017 Annual costs. Tuition/fees (projected): $21,450. Room/board: $7,760. Books/supplies: $1,000. Personal expenses: $3,080.

2014-2015 Financial aid. Need-based: 92 full-time freshmen applied for aid; 81 deemed to have need; 81 received aid. Average need met was 66%. Average scholarship/grant was $14,525; average loan $3,325. 63% of total undergraduate aid awarded as scholarships/grants, 37% as loans/jobs. **Non-need-based:** Awarded to 160 full-time undergraduates, including 62 freshmen. Scholarships awarded for academics, alumni affiliation, athletics, leadership, minority status, music/drama, state residency. **Additional information:** Spouse scholarship program.

Application procedures. Admission: Closing date 8/1 (postmark date). No application fee. Admission notification on a rolling basis. **Financial aid:** Priority date 4/15; no closing date. FAFSA, institutional form required. Applicants notified on a rolling basis starting 3/1; must reply within 2 week(s) of notification.

Academics. Special study options: Combined bachelor's/graduate degree, cooperative education, cross-registration, distance learning, double major, dual enrollment of high school students, exchange student, honors, independent study, internships, liberal arts/career combination, student-designed major, study abroad, teacher certification program. **Credit/placement by examination:** AP, CLEP, IB. 15 credit hours maximum toward associate degree, 30 toward bachelor's. **Support services:** Learning center, reduced course load, study skills assistance, tutoring, writing center.

Majors. Area/ethnic studies: Near/Middle Eastern. **Business:** Nonprofit/public. **Communications:** General, digital media, media studies. **Education:** Elementary. **English:** English lit. **Foreign languages:** Biblical. **Liberal arts:** Arts/sciences, humanities. **Psychology:** General. **Theology:** Bible, preministerial, religious ed, sacred music, youth ministry.

Most popular majors. Communications/journalism 6%, interdisciplinary studies 7%, liberal arts 14%, psychology 8%, theological studies 58%.

Technology on campus. 106 workstations in dormitories, library, computer center. Dormitories wired for high-speed internet access. Commuter students can connect to campus network. Online course registration, online library, helpline, wireless network available.

Student life. Freshman orientation: Mandatory. Preregistration for classes offered. Two sessions held prior to start of fall semester. **Policies:** Standards of Christian living are outlined in the Biblical Standards Handbook. Religious observance required. **Housing:** Guaranteed on-campus for all undergraduates. Single-sex dorms, special housing for disabled, apartments available. $100 partly refundable deposit, deadline 8/1. **Activities:** Campus ministries, choral groups, drama, music ensembles, student government, student newspaper, Student Missions Connection, African American student association, student senate, student union, graduate life council, international student association, Mu Kappa.

Athletics. NCCAA. **Intercollegiate:** Basketball, cross-country, soccer M. **Intramural:** Basketball M, football (non-tackle), soccer, ultimate frisbee, volleyball. **Team name:** Rams.

Student services. Chaplain/spiritual director, career counseling, student employment services, financial aid counseling, health services, personal counseling, placement for graduates, veterans' counselor. **Physically disabled:** Services for visually, hearing impaired.

Contact. E-mail: yesciu@ciu.edu
Phone: (803) 807-5024 Toll-free number: (800) 777-2227 ext. 5024
Fax: (803) 786-4209
James McCall, Associate Director of Admissions, Columbia International University, PO Box 3122, Columbia, SC 29230-3122

Converse College
Spartanburg, South Carolina   **CB member**
www.converse.edu   **CB code: 5121**

- Private 4-year university and liberal arts college for women
- Residential campus in large town
- 796 degree-seeking undergraduates: 6% part-time, 100% women, 10% African American, 1% Asian American, 6% Hispanic/Latino, 5% Multiracial, non-Hispanic, 1% international

- 262 degree-seeking graduate students
- 56% of applicants admitted
- SAT or ACT (ACT writing optional) required
- 56% graduate within 6 years

General. Founded in 1889. Regionally accredited. **Degrees:** 150 bachelor's awarded; master's offered. **ROTC:** Army. **Location:** 70 miles from Charlotte, NC; 190 mile from of Atlanta, GA. **Calendar:** 4-1-4, limited summer session. **Full-time faculty:** 80 total; 96% have terminal degrees, 6% minority, 64% women. **Part-time faculty:** 2 total; 100% have terminal degrees, 50% women. **Class size:** 80% < 20, 20% 20-39. **Special facilities:** Science educational facility, music library, music and performing arts auditorium.

Freshman class profile. 1,360 applied, 760 admitted, 217 enrolled.

Mid 50% test scores		GPA 2.0-2.99:	3%
SAT critical reading:	480-590	Rank in top quarter:	48%
SAT math:	440-550	Rank in top tenth:	20%
ACT composite:	20-25	End year in good standing:	82%
GPA 3.75 or higher:	65%	Return as sophomores:	66%
GPA 3.50-3.74:	13%	Out-of-state:	30%
GPA 3.0-3.49:	19%	Live on campus:	76%

Basis for selection. Holistic review of a candidate's record. Greatest weight is placed on academic records including GPA and class rank and consideration of test scores (SAT or ACT, writing not required). Letters of recommendation, personal essays, and extra curricular records are not required but may be considered. Interview recommended for all; audition required for music programs. **Home schooled:** Statement describing home school structure and mission, interview, letter of recommendation (nonparent) required.

High school preparation. College-preparatory program recommended. 16 units recommended. Recommended units include English 4, mathematics 3, social studies 2, history 2, science 3 (laboratory 1), foreign language 2 and academic electives 8.

2015-2016 Annual costs. Tuition/fees: $16,850. Room/board: $9,995. Books/supplies: $1,350. Personal expenses: $2,952.

2015-2016 Financial aid. Need-based: Average need met was 65%. Average scholarship/grant was $12,531; average loan $3,701. 64% of total undergraduate aid awarded as scholarships/grants, 36% as loans/jobs. **Non-need-based:** Scholarships awarded for academics, art, athletics, music/drama, ROTC, state residency.

Application procedures. Admission: Priority date 3/1; no deadline. No application fee. Admission notification on a rolling basis. Must reply by May 1 or within 2 week(s) if notified thereafter. **Financial aid:** Priority date 3/1; no closing date. FAFSA required. Applicants notified on a rolling basis starting 3/1; must reply by 5/1 or within 2 week(s) of notification.

Academics. Special study options: Combined bachelor's/graduate degree, cross-registration, double major, honors, independent study, internships, liberal arts/career combination, student-designed major, study abroad, teacher certification program. **Credit/placement by examination:** AP, CLEP, IB, SAT, ACT, institutional tests. 30 credit hours maximum toward bachelor's degree. **Support services:** Learning center, remedial instruction, study skills assistance, tutoring, writing center.

Majors. Biology: General, biochemistry. **Business:** Accounting, finance, international, managerial economics, marketing, training/development. **Education:** General, art, Deaf/hearing impaired, early childhood, elementary, emotionally handicapped, mentally handicapped, science, secondary, social science, social studies, special ed. **English:** Creative writing, English lit. **Foreign languages:** General, Spanish. **Health services:** Art therapy, music therapy. **History:** General. **Math:** General. **Philosophy/religion:** Philosophy, religion. **Physical sciences:** Chemistry. **Psychology:** General. **Social sciences:** Economics, political science. **Visual/performing arts:** Art, art history/conservation, dramatic, interior design, music, music history, music pedagogy, music performance, music theory/composition, piano/keyboard, stringed instruments, studio arts, theater arts management, voice/opera.

Most popular majors. Biology 9%, business/marketing 8%, education 14%, English 6%, psychology 17%, visual/performing arts 19%.

Technology on campus. 75 workstations in dormitories, library, computer center, student center. Dormitories wired for high-speed internet access and linked to campus network. Commuter students can connect to campus network. Online library, helpline, repair service, wireless network available.

Student life. Freshman orientation: Mandatory, $75 fee. Preregistration for classes offered. Overnight programs held during the summer. Three day arrival orientation takes place in the fall. **Policies:** Strong honor tradition based on mutual trust and responsibility. **Housing:** Guaranteed on-campus for all undergraduates. Apartments, wellness housing available. $300 partly refundable deposit, deadline 8/1. **Activities:** Concert band, campus ministries,

choral groups, dance, drama, international student organizations, literary magazine, music ensembles, Model UN, musical theater, opera, student government, student newspaper, symphony orchestra, Student Christian Association, student activities committee, Young Republicans, community service organizations, honor organizations, student volunteer services.

Athletics. NCAA. **Intercollegiate:** Basketball W, cross-country W, equestrian W, golf W, lacrosse W, soccer W, swimming W, tennis W, track and field W, volleyball W. **Intramural:** Archery W, basketball W, soccer W, softball W, synchronized swimming W, volleyball W. **Team name:** Valkyries.

Student services. Adult student services, alcohol/substance abuse counseling, chaplain/spiritual director, career counseling, student employment services, financial aid counseling, health services, personal counseling, placement for graduates, women's services. **Physically disabled:** Services for hearing impaired.

Contact. E-mail: admissions@converse.edu
Phone: (864) 596-9040 Fax: (864) 596-9225
Converse College, 580 East Main Street, Spartanburg, SC 29302-0006

Erskine College
Due West, South Carolina — CB member
www.erskine.edu — CB code: 5188

- Private 4-year liberal arts and seminary college affiliated with the Associate Reformed Presbyterian Church
- Residential campus in rural community
- 619 degree-seeking undergraduates
- SAT or ACT (ACT writing optional), application essay required

General. Founded in 1839. Regionally accredited. Affiliated with Erskine Theological Seminary. **Degrees:** 89 bachelor's awarded; master's, doctoral offered. **Location:** 18 miles from Anderson, 45 miles from Greenville. **Calendar:** 4-1-4, limited summer session. **Full-time faculty:** 55 total. **Part-time faculty:** 26 total. **Class size:** 72% < 20, 28% 20-39. **Special facilities:** Arts center.

Freshman class profile.

GPA 3.75 or higher:	49%	Rank in top quarter:	65%
GPA 3.50-3.74:	11%	Rank in top tenth:	39%
GPA 3.0-3.49:	29%	Out-of-state:	24%
GPA 2.0-2.99:	11%	Live on campus:	96%

Basis for selection. High school transcript, testing and personal qualities considered in admissions decisions. Rigor of coursework most important. Grades, class rank, test scores, extracurricular activities, essay very important. Interview required for academically weak; audition required for music. **Home schooled:** Transcript of courses and grades, letter of recommendation (nonparent) required. High school diploma, GED, or college preparatory diploma certification required. Portfolio showing courses studied, textbooks used, course outline and extracurricular activities may be requested in some instances.

High school preparation. College-preparatory program required. 14 units required. Required units include English 4, mathematics 2, science 2 (laboratory 2). 2 social sciences and at least 4 other units from these subject areas required: history, science, Latin, modern foreign languages, advanced math and English.

2015-2016 Annual costs. Tuition/fees: $33,315. Room/board: $10,500. Books/supplies: $2,000. Personal expenses: $1,250.

Financial aid. Non-need-based: Scholarships awarded for academics, alumni affiliation, athletics, leadership, minority status, music/drama, religious affiliation, state residency. **Additional information:** Filing deadline 5/1 for institutional form, 6/30 for state form.

Application procedures. Admission: Closing date 6/30 (receipt date). No application fee. Admission notification on a rolling basis beginning on or about 11/15. **Financial aid:** Priority date 4/1; no closing date. FAFSA, institutional form required. Applicants notified on a rolling basis starting 12/15; must reply within 2 week(s) of notification.

Academics. Special study options: Double major, independent study, internships, study abroad, teacher certification program. **Credit/placement by examination:** AP, CLEP, IB, institutional tests. 18 credit hours maximum toward bachelor's degree. **Support services:** Pre-admission summer program, study skills assistance, tutoring, writing center.

Majors. Area/ethnic studies: American. **Biology:** General. **Business:** Business admin. **Education:** Early childhood, elementary, physical, secondary, social studies, special ed. **English:** English lit. **Foreign languages:** French, Spanish. **Health services:** Athletic training, clinical lab technology. **History:** General. **Math:** General. **Parks/recreation:** Sports admin. **Philosophy/religion:** Philosophy, religion. **Physical sciences:** Chemistry, physics. **Psychology:** General. **Social sciences:** Political science. **Theology:** Religious ed. **Visual/performing arts:** Art, music.

Most popular majors. Biology 24%, business/marketing 20%, education 13%, health sciences 7%, history 6%, physical sciences 9%, psychology 7%.

Technology on campus. PC or laptop required. Dormitories wired for high-speed internet access and linked to campus network. Commuter students can connect to campus network. Helpline, repair service, student web hosting, wireless network available.

Student life. Freshman orientation: Mandatory. Preregistration for classes offered. Held in August prior to first day of classes. **Policies:** Religious observance required. **Housing:** Guaranteed on-campus for all undergraduates. Single-sex dorms, wellness housing available. $300 nonrefundable deposit. **Activities:** Bands, campus ministries, choral groups, dance, drama, literary magazine, music ensembles, musical theater, radio station, student government, student newspaper, national honor societies (academics, drama, leadership), association of minority students, denominational organizations, judicial council, Fellowship of Christian Athletes, Habitat for Humanity, council for exceptional children.

Athletics. NCAA. **Intercollegiate:** Baseball M, basketball, cross-country, golf, lacrosse W, soccer, softball W, tennis, volleyball. **Intramural:** Basketball, football (non-tackle) W, football (tackle) M, racquetball, soccer, softball, tennis. **Team name:** Flying Fleet.

Student services. Alcohol/substance abuse counseling, chaplain/spiritual director, career counseling, financial aid counseling, health services, personal counseling, placement for graduates.

Contact. E-mail: admissions@erskine.edu
Phone: (864) 379-8838 Toll-free number: (800) 241-8721
Fax: (864) 379-2167
Tobe Frierson, Director of Admissions, Erskine College, PO Box 338, Due West, SC 29639-0338

Francis Marion University
Florence, South Carolina   **CB member**
www.fmarion.edu   **CB code: 5442**

- Public 4-year university and liberal arts college
- Commuter campus in small city
- 3,258 degree-seeking undergraduates: 5% part-time, 68% women, 47% African American, 1% Asian American, 2% Hispanic/Latino, 2% Multiracial, non-Hispanic, 1% international
- 258 degree-seeking graduate students
- 59% of applicants admitted
- SAT or ACT (ACT writing optional) required
- 42% graduate within 6 years

General. Founded in 1970. Regionally accredited. **Degrees:** 569 bachelor's awarded; master's offered. **ROTC:** Army. **Location:** 7 miles from downtown, 80 miles from Columbia. **Calendar:** Semester, limited summer session. **Full-time faculty:** 204 total; 86% have terminal degrees, 11% minority, 50% women. **Part-time faculty:** 88 total; 20% have terminal degrees, 16% minority, 69% women. **Special facilities:** Planetarium, observatory, arboretum, hewn timber cabins.

Freshman class profile. 3,681 applied, 2,167 admitted, 739 enrolled.

Mid 50% test scores			
SAT critical reading:	410-520	Rank in top tenth:	13%
SAT math:	410-510	End year in good standing:	71%
ACT composite:	17-22	Return as sophomores:	69%
GPA 3.75 or higher:	46%	Out-of-state:	3%
GPA 3.50-3.74:	17%	Live on campus:	64%
GPA 3.0-3.49:	28%	International:	2%
GPA 2.0-2.99:	9%	Fraternities:	1%
Rank in top quarter:	39%	Sororities:	3%

Basis for selection. Combination of standardized test scores and high school GPA are important. Proficiency in math and English required. Portfolio required for art program; audition required for music, dance and theater; R.N. required for R.N. to B.S.N. program licensure. **Learning Disabled:** Accommodations provided with documentation.

High school preparation. College-preparatory program required. 19 units required. Required units include English 4, mathematics 4, social studies 2,

history 1, science 3 (laboratory 3), foreign language 2, visual/performing arts 1 and academic electives 1. Social studies should include 1 history (U.S.). 1 unit physical education or ROTC, 2 units of same foreign language required, 1 unit of fine arts required.

2015-2016 Annual costs. Tuition/fees: $10,100; $19,668 out-of-state. Room/board: $7,472. Books/supplies: $971. Personal expenses: $586.

2015-2016 Financial aid. Need-based: 645 full-time freshmen applied for aid; 581 deemed to have need; 580 received aid. Average need met was 70%. Average scholarship/grant was $8,998; average loan $3,382. 51% of total undergraduate aid awarded as scholarships/grants, 49% as loans/jobs. **Non-need-based:** Awarded to 166 full-time undergraduates, including 52 freshmen. Scholarships awarded for academics, alumni affiliation, art, athletics, leadership, minority status, music/drama, religious affiliation, ROTC, state residency.

Application procedures. Admission: Priority date 6/1; deadline 8/1. $37 fee, may be waived for applicants with need. Admission notification on a rolling basis beginning on or about 9/1. Must reply by May 1 or within 2 week(s) if notified thereafter. **Financial aid:** Priority date 3/1; no closing date. FAFSA required. Applicants notified on a rolling basis starting 1/30.

Academics. Special study options: Accelerated study, cooperative education, distance learning, double major, dual enrollment of high school students, honors, independent study, internships, study abroad, teacher certification program, Washington semester. **Credit/placement by examination:** AP, CLEP, IB, SAT, ACT, institutional tests. 30 credit hours maximum toward bachelor's degree. **Support services:** Reduced course load, tutoring, writing center.

Majors. Biology: General. **Business:** Accounting, business admin, finance, management information systems, managerial economics, marketing. **Communications:** Media studies. **Computer sciences:** General. **Education:** Art, early childhood, elementary, English, history, mathematics, secondary, social studies. **Engineering:** Industrial. **English:** English lit. **Foreign languages:** French, German, Spanish. **Health services:** Nursing (RN), pharmaceutical sciences. **History:** General. **Liberal arts:** Arts/sciences. **Math:** General. **Physical sciences:** Chemistry, physics. **Psychology:** General. **Social sciences:** Economics, international relations, political science, sociology. **Visual/performing arts:** Art, dramatic, music.

Most popular majors. Biology 15%, business/marketing 17%, education 8%, health sciences 16%, psychology 10%, social sciences 10%.

Technology on campus. 634 workstations in dormitories, library, computer center, student center. Dormitories wired for high-speed internet access and linked to campus network. Online course registration, online library, wireless network available.

Student life. Freshman orientation: Mandatory, $118 fee. Preregistration for classes offered. Session held in summer. **Housing:** Single-sex dorms, special housing for disabled, apartments, wellness housing available. $162 nonrefundable deposit, deadline 5/1. Honors housing available. **Activities:** Jazz band, campus ministries, choral groups, dance, drama, international student organizations, literary magazine, music ensembles, Model UN, student government, student newspaper, symphony orchestra, College Democrats, College Republicans, NAACP, psychology club, education club, Catholic campus ministry, Baptist campus ministries, Young/Gifted/Blessed chorus.

Athletics. NCAA. **Intercollegiate:** Baseball M, basketball, cheerleading W, cross-country, golf M, soccer, softball W, tennis, track and field, volleyball W. **Intramural:** Basketball, football (non-tackle), racquetball, soccer, softball, table tennis, tennis, volleyball. **Team name:** Patriots.

Student services. Adult student services, chaplain/spiritual director, career counseling, student employment services, financial aid counseling, health services, minority student services, personal counseling, placement for graduates, veterans' counselor. **Physically disabled:** Services for visually, speech, hearing impaired.

Contact. E-mail: admissions@fmarion.edu
Phone: (843) 661-1231 Toll-free number: (800) 368-7551
Fax: (843) 661-4635
Perry Wilson, Director of Admissions, Francis Marion University, PO Box 100547, Florence, SC 29502-0547

Furman University
Greenville, South Carolina   **CB member**
www.furman.edu   **CB code: 5222**

- Private 4-year liberal arts college
- Residential campus in small city

- 2,713 degree-seeking undergraduates: 4% part-time, 57% women, 5% African American, 2% Asian American, 4% Hispanic/Latino, 2% Multiracial, non-Hispanic, 6% international
- 123 degree-seeking graduate students
- 65% of applicants admitted
- Application essay required
- 83% graduate within 6 years; 39% enter graduate study

General. Founded in 1826. Regionally accredited. Abundant internship and collaborative research opportunities. **Degrees:** 660 bachelor's awarded; master's offered. **ROTC:** Army. **Location:** 100 miles from Charlotte, NC; 140 miles from Atlanta. **Calendar:** Semester, extensive summer session. **Full-time faculty:** 234 total; 98% have terminal degrees, 12% minority, 35% women. **Part-time faculty:** 23 total; 39% have terminal degrees, 9% minority, 65% women. **Class size:** 57% < 20, 43% 20-39, less than 1% 50-99. **Special facilities:** Observatory, center for engaged learning, center for international education, center for collaborative learning and communication, center for sustainability.

Freshman class profile. 5,043 applied, 3,268 admitted, 672 enrolled.

Mid 50% test scores		Return as sophomores:	89%
SAT critical reading:	550-660	Out-of-state:	73%
SAT math:	550-660	Live on campus:	98%
SAT writing:	550-660	International:	7%
ACT composite:	25-30	Fraternities:	27%
Rank in top quarter:	71%	Sororities:	55%
Rank in top tenth:	39%		

Basis for selection. High school record including courses taken and grades most important, then SAT or ACT scores. Special talents such as fine arts, athletic ability, writing ability considered. Special consideration given to children of alumni and minorities. SAT or ACT recommended. Audition required for music scholarship applicants; portfolio required for art scholarship applicants. **Home schooled:** SAT Subject Tests including math, subject of student's choice recommended. Interview strongly recommended.

High school preparation. College-preparatory program recommended. 14 units required; 18 recommended. Required and recommended units include English 4, mathematics 3-4, social studies 3-4, science 2-3 (laboratory 2) and foreign language 2-3.

2015-2016 Annual costs. Tuition/fees: $46,012. Room/board: $11,522. Books/supplies: $1,200. Personal expenses: $900.

2015-2016 Financial aid. **Need-based:** 438 full-time freshmen applied for aid; 352 deemed to have need; 352 received aid. Average need met was 79%. Average scholarship/grant was $32,120; average loan $5,038. 79% of total undergraduate aid awarded as scholarships/grants, 21% as loans/jobs. **Non-need-based:** Awarded to 2,491 full-time undergraduates, including 659 freshmen. Scholarships awarded for academics, alumni affiliation, art, athletics, leadership, music/drama, religious affiliation, ROTC, state residency. **Additional information:** 5-point comprehensive education financing plan includes financial aid packaging, money management counseling, debt management counseling, outside scholarship coordination, summer job-match program.

Application procedures. **Admission:** Closing date 1/15 (postmark date). $50 fee, may be waived for applicants with need. Admission notification by 4/1. Must reply by May 1 or within 2 week(s) if notified thereafter. **Financial aid:** Closing date 1/15. FAFSA, institutional form, CSS PROFILE required. Applicants notified by 4/1; must reply by 5/1 or within 2 week(s) of notification.

Academics. Strong emphasis on research, internships and other opportunities for engaged, hands-on learning. **Special study options:** Combined bachelor's/graduate degree, double major, independent study, internships, student-designed major, study abroad, teacher certification program, United Nations semester, Washington semester. Undergraduate research program, 3-2 engineering with Auburn University, Clemson University, Georgia Institute of Technology, North Carolina State, Washington University in St. Louis, 3-2 forestry program with Duke University, 3-1 dentistry and medicine programs with any accredited medical or dental school, 3-2 nursing, pharmacy, physical therapy, and physician assistant programs with any accredited medical school. **Credit/placement by examination:** AP, CLEP, IB, institutional tests. **Support services:** Learning center, reduced course load, study skills assistance, tutoring, writing center.

Majors. **Area/ethnic studies:** Asian. **Biology:** General, neuroscience. **Business:** Accounting, business admin, management information systems. **Communications:** Communications/speech/rhetoric. **Computer sciences:** Computer science. **Education:** General, music. **English:** English lit. **Foreign languages:** Ancient Greek, French, German, Latin, Spanish. **Health services:** General, predental, premedicine, prenursing, prepharmacy, preveterinary. **History:** General. **Math:** General. **Philosophy/religion:** Philosophy, religion. **Physical sciences:** Chemistry, geology, physics. **Psychology:** General. **Social**

sciences: Anthropology, economics, political science, sociology, urban studies. **Theology:** Sacred music. **Visual/performing arts:** Art, art history/conservation, dramatic, music, music history, music performance, music theory/composition.

Most popular majors. Biology 7%, business/marketing 12%, communications/journalism 8%, foreign language 6%, health sciences 9%, philosophy/religious studies 6%, physical sciences 8%, social sciences 17%.

Technology on campus. 450 workstations in dormitories, library, computer center, student center. Dormitories wired for high-speed internet access and linked to campus network. Commuter students can connect to campus network. Online course registration, online library, helpline, student web hosting, wireless network available.

Student life. **Freshman orientation:** Mandatory. Preregistration for classes offered. Early orientation session during the summer (charge of $150) and free session at beginning of Fall semester. **Housing:** Guaranteed on-campus for freshmen. Coed dorms, single-sex dorms, apartments, themed housing, wellness housing available. $500 nonrefundable deposit, deadline 5/1. Lakeside cottages and environmentally equipped eco-cottage also available. **Activities:** Bands, campus ministries, choral groups, dance, drama, film society, international student organizations, literary magazine, music ensembles, Model UN, musical theater, opera, radio station, student government, student newspaper, symphony orchestra, TV station, Collegiate Educational Service Corps, Young Democrats, College Republicans, Student League for Black Culture, Fellowship of Christian Athletes, Council for Exceptional Children, Habitat for Humanity, arts students league.

Athletics. NCAA. **Intercollegiate:** Baseball M, basketball, cheerleading, cross-country, football (tackle) M, golf, lacrosse, soccer, softball W, tennis, track and field, volleyball W. **Intramural:** Basketball, bowling, cross-country, football (non-tackle), golf, handball, racquetball, rowing (crew), soccer, softball, swimming, tennis, track and field, ultimate frisbee, volleyball. **Team name:** Paladins.

Student services. Adult student services, alcohol/substance abuse counseling, chaplain/spiritual director, career counseling, student employment services, financial aid counseling, health services, minority student services, personal counseling, placement for graduates, veterans' counselor, women's services. **Physically disabled:** Services for visually, hearing impaired.

Contact. E-mail: admission@furman.edu
Phone: (864) 294-2034 Fax: (864) 294-2018
Brad Pochard, Associate Vice President for Admission, Furman University, 3300 Poinsett Highway, Greenville, SC 29613

ITT Technical Institute: Greenville
Greenville, South Carolina
www.itt-tech.edu   CB code: 2708

- For-profit 4-year technical college
- Commuter campus in large city
- 269 undergraduates
- Interview required

General. Accredited by ACICS. **Degrees:** 20 bachelor's, 76 associate awarded. **Calendar:** Quarter, extensive summer session. **Full-time faculty:** 9 total. **Part-time faculty:** 37 total.

Basis for selection. Satisfactory scores from on-site tests in English and mathematics required.

2015-2016 Annual costs. Per-credit-hour charge, $493; academic fee, $200. Certain programs require purchase of tools, which range from $100 to $500. All costs subject to change.

Application procedures. **Admission:** No deadline. No application fee. Admission notification on a rolling basis. **Financial aid:** No deadline. FAFSA, institutional form required. Applicants notified on a rolling basis.

Academics. **Credit/placement by examination:** AP, CLEP. **Support services:** Learning center, tutoring.

Majors. **Communications technology:** Animation/special effects. **Computer sciences:** Security. **Protective services:** Law enforcement admin.

Technology on campus. Online library available.

Student life. **Freshman orientation:** Available. Preregistration for classes offered.

Student services. Career counseling, student employment services, placement for graduates.

Contact. Phone: (864) 288-0777 Toll-free number: (800) 932-4488
Fax: (864) 297-0930
Joseph Fisher, Director of Recruitment, ITT Technical Institute:
Greenville, 6 Independence Pointe, Greenville, SC 29615

Lander University
Greenwood, South Carolina
www.lander.edu

CB member
CB code: 5363

▶ Public 4-year liberal arts and teachers college
▶ Residential campus in large town
▶ 2,670 degree-seeking undergraduates
▶ 70 graduate students
▶ SAT or ACT (ACT writing optional), interview required

General. Founded in 1872. Regionally accredited. **Degrees:** 461 bachelor's
awarded; master's offered. **ROTC:** Army. **Location:** 55 miles from Greenville, 75 miles from Columbia. **Calendar:** Semester, limited summer session.
Full-time faculty: 151 total; 10% minority, 56% women. **Part-time faculty:**
132 total; 7% minority, 54% women. **Class size:** 52% < 20, 39% 20-39, 6%
40-49, 3% 50-99. **Special facilities:** Equestrian center, sports complex/park
open to the public.

Freshman class profile.

GPA 3.75 or higher:	28%	Rank in top quarter:	40%
GPA 3.50-3.74:	22%	Rank in top tenth:	12%
GPA 3.0-3.49:	34%	Out-of-state:	7%
GPA 2.0-2.99:	16%	Live on campus:	80%

Basis for selection. Test scores, class rank, curriculum, high school GPA
important. Out-of-state students must rank in top half of high school class.
Selectivity of students may be based on transcripts and GED score. Audition
required for music programs; interview recommended for art, music programs; portfolio recommended for art programs.

High school preparation. 19 units recommended. Recommended units
include English 4, mathematics 4, social studies 2, history 1, science 3
(laboratory 3), foreign language 2, visual/performing arts 1 and academic
electives 1. One unit physical education or ROTC also recommended.

2015-2016 Annual costs. Tuition/fees: $10,752; $20,370 out-of-state.
Room/board: $8,246. Books/supplies: $1,200. Personal expenses: $1,600.

Financial aid. **Non-need-based:** Scholarships awarded for academics, art,
athletics, leadership, music/drama.

Application procedures. **Admission:** No deadline. $35 fee, may be
waived for applicants with need. Admission notification on a rolling basis.
Financial aid: Priority date 4/15; no closing date. FAFSA required. Applicants notified on a rolling basis starting 4/15; must reply within 4 week(s)
of notification.

Academics. **Special study options:** Combined bachelor's/graduate degree,
cooperative education, distance learning, double major, dual enrollment of
high school students, ESL, honors, independent study, internships, liberal arts/
career combination, study abroad, teacher certification program, Washington
semester. Interdisciplinary studies program, dual degree in engineering with
Clemson University, nursing (RN to BSN completion),criminal justice management degree, masters in clinical nurse leader, and masters in emergency
management offered online. **Credit/placement by examination:** AP, CLEP,
IB, institutional tests. 30 credit hours maximum toward bachelor's degree.
Support services: Learning center, pre-admission summer program, reduced
course load, remedial instruction, study skills assistance, tutoring, writing
center.

Honors college/program. Incoming first-year freshman who wish to
apply for admission to the Honors College should complete an application
form and have a combined Math/Critical Reading SAT score of at least 1100
or a composite ACT score of at least 25. Provide sufficient evidence of
promise of academic excellence based on any one of the following: a high
school GPA of 3.75 or above on a 4.0 scale, an academic writing sample or
creative portfolio, two letters of recommendations from mentors, including
one from a person who can address the quality of the student's academic
promise, or an interview with the Honors Committee.

Majors. **Biology:** General. **Business:** Business admin. **Computer sciences:**
General. **Conservation:** Environmental science. **Education:** Early childhood,
elementary, Montessori teacher, physical, secondary, special ed. **English:**
English lit. **Foreign languages:** Spanish. **Health services:** Nursing (RN).
History: General. **Liberal arts:** Arts/sciences, humanities. **Math:** General.
Parks/recreation: Exercise sciences. **Physical sciences:** Chemistry. **Protec-
tive services:** Law enforcement admin. **Psychology:** General. **Social sci-
ences:** Political science, sociology. **Visual/performing arts:** Art, music.

Most popular majors. Business/marketing 23%, education 12%, health
sciences 13%, liberal arts 8%, parks/recreation 10%, psychology 7%, social
sciences 7%, visual/performing arts 6%.

Technology on campus. PC or laptop required. 233 workstations in
dormitories, library, computer center. Dormitories linked to campus network.
Commuter students can connect to campus network. Online course registration, online library, helpline, repair service, wireless network available.

Student life. **Freshman orientation:** Mandatory. Preregistration for
classes offered. Held during the summer months, EXPO is a 3-day/2-night
program. **Housing:** Coed dorms, single-sex dorms available. $225 partly
refundable deposit, deadline 4/15. **Activities:** Bands, choral groups, dance,
drama, literary magazine, music ensembles, musical theater, radio station,
student government, student newspaper, TV station, Baptist Student Union,
Bible study, Young Democrats, College Republicans, Minorities on the Move,
Blue Key and Alpha Kappa Gamma (honor societies).

Athletics. NCAA. **Intercollegiate:** Baseball M, basketball, golf, soccer,
softball W, tennis, volleyball W. **Intramural:** Basketball, football (non-
tackle), golf, soccer, softball, volleyball. **Team name:** Bearcats.

Student services. Adult student services, alcohol/substance abuse counseling, career counseling, student employment services, financial aid counseling, health services, minority student services, personal counseling, placement
for graduates, veterans' counselor. **Physically disabled:** Services for visually,
speech, hearing impaired.

Contact. E-mail: admissions@lander.edu
Phone: (864) 388-8307 Toll-free number: (888) 452-6337
Fax: (864) 388-8125
Jennifer Mathis, Director of Admissions, Lander University, Stanley
Avenue, Greenwood, SC 29649-2099

Limestone College
Gaffney, South Carolina
www.limestone.edu

CB code: 5366

▶ Private 4-year liberal arts college affiliated with the nondenominational tradition
▶ Residential campus in large town
▶ 1,227 degree-seeking undergraduates: 37% women, 34% African American, 4% Hispanic/Latino, 3% Multi-racial, non-Hispanic, 9% international
▶ 53 degree-seeking graduate students
▶ 50% of applicants admitted
▶ SAT or ACT (ACT writing optional) required
▶ 39% graduate within 6 years; 19% enter graduate study

General. Founded in 1845. Regionally accredited. Evening classes available
at 8 SC sites through Limestone's Extended Campus-Classroom Program;
online classes available through Extended Campus-Internet Program.
Degrees: 154 bachelor's, 74 associate awarded; master's offered. **ROTC:**
Army. **Location:** 25 miles from Spartanburg. **Calendar:** Semester, extensive
summer session. **Full-time faculty:** 81 total; 80% have terminal degrees,
11% minority, 49% women. **Part-time faculty:** 36 total; 100% have terminal
degrees, 6% minority, 53% women. **Class size:** 62% < 20, 36% 20-39, 1%
40-49. **Special facilities:** Computer graphics art lab, museum of history.

Freshman class profile. 2,684 applied, 1,346 admitted, 402 enrolled.

Mid 50% test scores		Rank in top quarter:	19%
SAT critical reading:	400-500	Rank in top tenth:	5%
SAT math:	410-510	End year in good standing:	80%
GPA 3.75 or higher:	21%	Return as sophomores:	56%
GPA 3.50-3.74:	14%	Out-of-state:	38%
GPA 3.0-3.49:	29%	Live on campus:	87%
GPA 2.0-2.99:	35%	International:	5%

Basis for selection. SAT combined score of 910 (exclusive of Writing)
or ACT score of 19 and GPA of 2.0. Admissions committee must approve
all applicants who do not meet these standards. The SAT or ACT requirement
is waived for students admitted into the Program for Alternative Learning
Styles. Interview required for lower-ranking applicants, recommended for
all others. Audition required of first-time, first-year freshmen for music,
music education, and theater programs; portfolio required for studio art programs; essay required for Honors Program. **Learning Disabled:** Documentation required to be eligible for admission to Program for Alternative Learning Styles.

High school preparation. 12 units required. Required units include
English 4, mathematics 3, social studies 3, science 2 (laboratory 2).

2016-2017 Annual costs. Tuition/fees (projected): $23,900. Room/board: $8,550. Books/supplies: $2,304. Personal expenses: $2,432.

2015-2016 Financial aid. Need-based: 386 full-time freshmen applied for aid; 355 deemed to have need; 354 received aid. Average need met was 62%. Average scholarship/grant was $16,185; average loan $3,292. 67% of total undergraduate aid awarded as scholarships/grants, 33% as loans/jobs. **Non-need-based:** Awarded to 531 full-time undergraduates, including 147 freshmen. Scholarships awarded for academics, art, athletics, job skills, leadership, music/drama, religious affiliation, ROTC, state residency.

Application procedures. Admission: Priority date 8/1; deadline 8/26 (receipt date). $25 fee, may be waived for applicants with need, free for online applicants. Admission notification on a rolling basis beginning on or about 6/1. In cases of unusual merit and exceptional maturity and upon recommendation of a secondary school official, a student may be considered for admission into a degree program. A personal interview at the College is required. **Financial aid:** Priority date 2/1; no closing date. FAFSA required. Applicants notified on a rolling basis starting 1/15; must reply within 3 week(s) of notification.

Academics. Special study options: Accelerated study, distance learning, double major, dual enrollment of high school students, honors, independent study, internships, liberal arts/career combination, student-designed major, teacher certification program. **Credit/placement by examination:** AP, CLEP, institutional tests. 15 credit hours maximum toward associate degree, 30 toward bachelor's. **Support services:** Learning center, reduced course load, remedial instruction, study skills assistance, tutoring, writing center. Online math, writing, and tutoring services are also available.

Majors. Biology: General, cellular/molecular. **Business:** Accounting, business admin, e-commerce, finance, human resources, managerial economics, marketing, training/development. **Computer sciences:** Information technology, programming, security, webmaster. **Education:** Early childhood, elementary, English, mathematics, music, physical. **English:** English lit, writing. **Health services:** Athletic training, health care admin, predental, premedicine, prenursing, prepharmacy, preveterinary. **History:** General. **Human services:** Social work. **Liberal arts:** Arts/sciences. **Math:** General. **Parks/recreation:** Sports admin. **Physical sciences:** Chemistry. **Protective services:** Law enforcement admin. **Psychology:** General. **Visual/performing arts:** Dramatic, graphic design, jazz, music, music performance, musical theater, studio arts.

Most popular majors. Biology 8%, business/marketing 24%, education 9%, liberal arts 15%, parks/recreation 17%, public administration/social services 8%, security/protective services 8%, visual/performing arts 6%.

Technology on campus. 203 workstations in library, computer center. Dormitories wired for high-speed internet access and linked to campus network. Commuter students can connect to campus network. Online library, helpline, repair service, wireless network available.

Student life. Freshman orientation: Mandatory. Preregistration for classes offered. 5 days prior to start of semester. **Policies:** Alcohol-free campus. Students from greater than 50 miles away are required to reside in college housing. **Housing:** Guaranteed on-campus for freshmen. Single-sex dorms, apartments available. $50 fully refundable deposit. **Activities:** Bands, campus ministries, choral groups, dance, drama, international student organizations, literary magazine, music ensembles, musical theater, student government, Fellowship of Christian Athletes, Student Alumni Leadership Council, Student Organization of Social Workers, Students in Free Enterprise, Christian Education and Leadership Program, Limestone College Community Chorus, Criminal Justice Student Organization, Psychology Club.

Athletics. NCAA. **Intercollegiate:** Baseball M, basketball, cross-country, field hockey W, football (tackle) M, golf, lacrosse, soccer, softball W, swimming, tennis, track and field, volleyball, wrestling M. **Intramural:** Badminton, basketball, bowling, football (non-tackle), racquetball, softball, table tennis, ultimate frisbee, volleyball, water polo, weight lifting. **Team name:** Saints.

Student services. Adult student services, alcohol/substance abuse counseling, chaplain/spiritual director, career counseling, student employment services, financial aid counseling, health services, personal counseling, placement for graduates, veterans' counselor.

Contact. E-mail: cphenicie@limestone.edu
Phone: (864) 488-4554 Toll-free number: (800) 795-7151 ext. 4554
Fax: (864) 487-8706
Chris Phenicie, Vice President for Enrollment Services, Limestone College, 1115 College Drive, Gaffney, SC 29340-3799

Medical University of South Carolina
Charleston, South Carolina
www.musc.edu   CB code: 5407

- Public two-year upper-division university
- Commuter campus in small city

General. Founded in 1824. Regionally accredited. Upper division/graduate academic health center consisting of six colleges: dental medicine, graduate studies, health professions, medicine, nursing, and pharmacy. College offers only two undergraduate degrees. **Degrees:** 136 bachelor's awarded; master's, professional, doctoral offered. **Location:** 350 miles from Atlanta. **Calendar:** Semester, limited summer session. **Full-time faculty:** 596 total. **Part-time faculty:** 233 total. **Class size:** 47% < 20, 53% 50-99. **Special facilities:** Historical medical library, dental museum, pharmacy museum.

Student profile. 205 degree-seeking undergraduates, 2,570 graduate students. 100% entered as juniors.

Out-of-state:	12%	25 or older:	56%

2015-2016 Annual costs. Books/supplies: $6,788.

Application procedures. Admission: $95 fee. Application must be submitted online. All admission policies and dates vary by academic program and college. **Financial aid:** FAFSA required.

Academics. Special study options: Cross-registration, distance learning. **Credit/placement by examination:** AP, CLEP. Credit by exam policies vary by program.

Majors. Health services: Cardiovascular technology, nursing (RN).

Technology on campus. PC or laptop required. 300 workstations in library, student center. Commuter students can connect to campus network. Online library, helpline, student web hosting, wireless network available.

Student life. Activities: Campus ministries, choral groups, international student organizations, literary magazine, music ensembles, student government, Christian Medical Society, campus crusade, student union, community help initiative, South Carolina health initiative, minority student union, Student National Medical Association.

Athletics. Intramural: Basketball, football (non-tackle), softball, volleyball.

Student services. Alcohol/substance abuse counseling, chaplain/spiritual director, services for economically disadvantaged, financial aid counseling, health services, legal services, minority student services, personal counseling, veterans' counselor.

Contact. E-mail: oesadmis@musc.edu
Phone: (843) 792-3281 Fax: (843) 792-6615
Lyla Hudson, Director of Admissions, Medical University of South Carolina, 41 Bee Street, Charleston, SC 29425-2030

Morris College
Sumter, South Carolina   CB member
www.morris.edu   CB code: 5418

- Private 4-year liberal arts college affiliated with the Baptist faith
- Residential campus in large town
- 774 degree-seeking undergraduates: 2% part-time, 53% women, 98% African American, 1% Hispanic/Latino, 1% Multi-racial, non-Hispanic
- 78% of applicants admitted
- 34% graduate within 6 years; 16% enter graduate study

General. Founded in 1908. Regionally accredited. **Degrees:** 126 bachelor's awarded. **ROTC:** Army. **Location:** 45 miles from Columbia; 110 miles from Charlotte, NC. **Calendar:** Semester, limited summer session. **Full-time faculty:** 43 total; 67% have terminal degrees, 77% minority, 49% women. **Part-time faculty:** 18 total; 39% have terminal degrees, 83% minority, 33% women. **Class size:** 60% < 20, 39% 20-39, 1% 40-49. **Special facilities:** Radio station/training lab, electronic learning lab, television production studio, forensics labs.

Freshman class profile. 1,856 applied, 1,454 admitted, 213 enrolled.

GPA 3.50-3.74:	4%	End year in good standing:	54%
GPA 3.0-3.49:	16%	Return as sophomores:	48%
GPA 2.0-2.99:	60%	Out-of-state:	16%
Rank in top quarter:	5%	Live on campus:	94%

Basis for selection. High school record most important. Students with less than 2.0 high school GPA may be admitted on probation but limited to 13-credit-hour load during each of first 2 semesters and required to participate in tutorial and study sessions. SAT/ACT must be submitted for all degree-seeking students, except foreign students. Scores used for informational/advisement purposes only. Interview recommended, required for some students.

High school preparation. 24 units required. Required and recommended units include English 4, mathematics 4, social studies 1, history 1, science 3, foreign language 1-2, computer science 1 and academic electives 7. Government .5, economics .5, physical education or ROTC 1.

2015-2016 Annual costs. Tuition/fees: $11,454. Room/board: $5,216. Books/supplies: $2,800. Personal expenses: $75.

2015-2016 Financial aid. **Need-based:** Average need met was 67%. Average scholarship/grant was $7,455; average loan $5,446. 47% of total undergraduate aid awarded as scholarships/grants, 53% as loans/jobs. **Non-need-based:** Scholarships awarded for academics, athletics, music/drama, state residency.

Application procedures. **Admission:** Priority date 7/1; no deadline. $20 fee, may be waived for applicants with need. Admission notification on a rolling basis beginning on or about 11/1. **Financial aid:** Priority date 3/31, closing date 3/31. FAFSA, institutional form required. Applicants notified on a rolling basis starting 4/1; must reply within 2 week(s) of notification.

Academics. **Special study options:** Accelerated study, cooperative education, double major, honors, internships, liberal arts/career combination, study abroad, teacher certification program. Adult Degree Program in Organizational Management offered through evening courses; students must be at least 25 years old and have earned 60 credit hours. **Credit/placement by examination:** AP, CLEP, institutional tests. 30 credit hours maximum toward bachelor's degree. **Support services:** Learning center, reduced course load, remedial instruction, study skills assistance, tutoring, writing center.

Majors. **Biology:** General. **Business:** Business admin, operations. **Communications:** Media studies. **Education:** Biology, early childhood, elementary, English, mathematics, social studies. **English:** English lit. **Health services:** Community health services. **History:** General. **Liberal arts:** Arts/sciences. **Math:** General. **Parks/recreation:** Facilities management. **Protective services:** Law enforcement admin. **Social sciences:** Political science, sociology. **Theology:** Religious ed, theology.

Most popular majors. Biology 8%, business/marketing 25%, communications/journalism 7%, health sciences 18%, security/protective services 21%, social sciences 7%.

Technology on campus. 292 workstations in dormitories, library, computer center. Dormitories wired for high-speed internet access and linked to campus network. Commuter students can connect to campus network. Online library, wireless network available.

Student life. **Freshman orientation:** Mandatory. Preregistration for classes offered. Held during first week of semester and as needed during summer terms. **Policies:** Promotes drug-free, alcohol-free and a weapons free campus. Smoking prohibited in all buildings. **Housing:** Single-sex dorms available. $100 fully refundable deposit, deadline 8/1. **Activities:** Campus ministries, choral groups, dance, drama, radio station, student government, student newspaper, Baptist student union, NAACP, Alpha Phi Omega, Durham Ministerial Union, National Association of Blacks in Criminal Justice.

Athletics. NAIA. **Intercollegiate:** Baseball M, basketball, cheerleading, cross-country, softball W, track and field, volleyball W. **Intramural:** Basketball, football (non-tackle), table tennis. **Team name:** Hornets.

Student services. Adult student services, alcohol/substance abuse counseling, chaplain/spiritual director, career counseling, services for economically disadvantaged, student employment services, financial aid counseling, health services, personal counseling, placement for graduates, veterans' counselor.

Contact. E-mail: dcalhoun@morris.edu
Phone: (803) 934-3225 Toll-free number: (866) 853-1345
Fax: (803) 773-8241
Deborah Calhoun, Director of Admission and Records, Morris College, 100 West College Street, Sumter, SC 29150-3599

Newberry College
Newberry, South Carolina
www.newberry.edu

CB member
CB code: 5493

- Private 4-year liberal arts college affiliated with the Evangelical Lutheran Church in America
- Residential campus in large town

- 1,048 degree-seeking undergraduates: 2% part-time, 46% women, 26% African American, 4% Hispanic/Latino, 4% Multi-racial, non-Hispanic, 4% international
- 56% of applicants admitted
- SAT or ACT (ACT writing optional), application essay required
- 39% graduate within 6 years; 13% enter graduate study

General. Founded in 1856. Regionally accredited. **Degrees:** 213 bachelor's awarded. **ROTC:** Army. **Location:** 40 miles from Columbia. **Calendar:** Semester, limited summer session. **Full-time faculty:** 65 total; 78% have terminal degrees, 11% minority, 49% women. **Part-time faculty:** 66 total; 26% have terminal degrees, 6% minority, 59% women. **Class size:** 64% < 20, 36% 20-39.

Freshman class profile. 1,171 applied, 656 admitted, 267 enrolled.

Mid 50% test scores			
SAT critical reading:	420-530	Rank in top quarter:	32%
SAT math:	430-540	Rank in top tenth:	12%
SAT writing:	400-500	End year in good standing:	87%
ACT composite:	18-22	Return as sophomores:	70%
GPA 3.75 or higher:	36%	Out-of-state:	20%
GPA 3.50-3.74:	15%	Live on campus:	96%
GPA 3.0-3.49:	27%	International:	3%
GPA 2.0-2.99:	22%	Fraternities:	20%
		Sororities:	34%

Basis for selection. GPA most important, followed by rigor of secondary school record, class rank, recommendations, test scores, and essay. **Home schooled:** Students who have attended high school for any amount of time should send official transcript. GED only required if applying for Title IV federal financial aid. All home schooled students will need to provide additional information regarding curriculum, such as class summaries, papers, exams, and affiliation with home school associations, if any. Primary instructors should submit recommendations assessing student's academic competence. Bibliography of high school literature and essay are necessary to evaluate a student's exposure and thinking skills. Additional materials/evidence may be submitted. Interview may be required in some cases. **Learning Disabled:** Recommend that students provide LD evaluation to learning support staff after admission but prior to enrollment.

High school preparation. College-preparatory program recommended. 14 units required; 18 recommended. Required and recommended units include English 3-4, mathematics 2-3, social studies 2, history 1, science 2-3 (laboratory 1), foreign language 2 and academic electives 2. Elective units must be English, math or natural science.

2015-2016 Annual costs. Tuition/fees: $25,000. Room/board: $9,550. Books/supplies: $1,600. Personal expenses: $2,500.

2014-2015 Financial aid. **Need-based:** 264 full-time freshmen applied for aid; 245 deemed to have need; 245 received aid. Average need met was 69%. Average scholarship/grant was $20,370; average loan $3,488. 73% of total undergraduate aid awarded as scholarships/grants, 27% as loans/jobs. **Non-need-based:** Awarded to 319 full-time undergraduates, including 76 freshmen. Scholarships awarded for academics, alumni affiliation, athletics, music/drama, ROTC.

Application procedures. **Admission:** Priority date 3/31; no deadline. $30 fee, may be waived for applicants with need. Admission notification on a rolling basis beginning on or about 9/1. May 1 reply by date preferred. **Financial aid:** Priority date 3/15; no closing date. FAFSA required. Applicants notified on a rolling basis starting 3/15; must reply by 8/20.

Academics. **Special study options:** Double major, dual enrollment of high school students, honors, independent study, internships, student-designed major, study abroad, teacher certification program. Forest and Environmental Management Dual Degree Program with Duke University. **Credit/placement by examination:** AP, CLEP, IB, SAT, ACT, institutional tests. **Support services:** Learning center, remedial instruction, study skills assistance, tutoring, writing center.

Majors. **Biology:** General. **Business:** Accounting, business admin. **Communications:** General. **Education:** Early childhood, elementary, middle, music, physical. **English:** English lit. **Foreign languages:** Spanish. **Health services:** Nursing practice. **History:** General. **Math:** General. **Parks/recreation:** General, sports admin. **Philosophy/religion:** Philosophy, religion. **Physical sciences:** Chemistry. **Psychology:** General. **Social sciences:** Political science, sociology. **Theology:** Sacred music. **Visual/performing arts:** Art, dramatic, music, music performance, music theory/composition.

Most popular majors. Biology 9%, business/marketing 25%, education 9%, health sciences 10%, parks/recreation 14%, psychology 6%, visual/performing arts 6%.

Technology on campus. 25 workstations in library. Dormitories wired for high-speed internet access and linked to campus network. Commuter students can connect to campus network. Online course registration, online library, helpline, student web hosting, wireless network available.

Student life. Freshman orientation: Mandatory. Preregistration for classes offered. Two-day event. Students stay overnight on campus. **Policies:** Residence halls are non-smoking. **Housing:** Guaranteed on-campus for freshmen. Coed dorms, single-sex dorms, apartments available. **Activities:** Bands, campus ministries, choral groups, dance, drama, international student organizations, literary magazine, music ensembles, radio station, student government, Lutheran student movement, Christians Living Among You, Baptist collegiate ministry, Fellowship of Christian Athletes, African American student association, international student association, student government association, All Campus Events, Student Alliance for Equality, The Green Team.

Athletics. NCAA. **Intercollegiate:** Baseball M, basketball, cheerleading, cross-country, field hockey W, football (tackle) M, golf, lacrosse W, soccer, softball W, tennis, volleyball W, wrestling M. **Intramural:** Basketball, soccer, volleyball. **Team name:** Wolves.

Student services. Adult student services, alcohol/substance abuse counseling, chaplain/spiritual director, career counseling, student employment services, financial aid counseling, health services, minority student services, personal counseling, placement for graduates, veterans' counselor.

Contact. E-mail: admission@newberry.edu
Phone: (803) 321-5127 Toll-free number: (800) 845-4955 ext. 5127
Fax: (803) 321-5138
Joel Vander Horst, Director of Admissions, Newberry College, 2100 College Street, Newberry, SC 29108

North Greenville University
Tigerville, South Carolina
www.ngu.edu   CB code: 5498

- Private 4-year university and liberal arts college affiliated with the Southern Baptist Convention
- Residential campus in rural community
- 2,289 degree-seeking undergraduates: 3% part-time, 48% women, 8% African American, 3% Hispanic/Latino, 2% Multi-racial, non-Hispanic
- 210 graduate students
- 58% of applicants admitted
- SAT or ACT (ACT writing optional) required
- 55% graduate within 6 years

General. Founded in 1891. Regionally accredited. Off-site recreation and learning center for Outdoor Leadership major. **Degrees:** 378 bachelor's awarded; master's, doctoral offered. **ROTC:** Army. **Location:** 18 miles from Greenville; 54 miles from Asheville, NC. **Calendar:** Semester, limited summer session. **Full-time faculty:** 137 total; 64% have terminal degrees, 11% minority, 37% women. **Part-time faculty:** 72 total; 21% have terminal degrees, 3% minority, 53% women. **Class size:** 71% < 20, 27% 20-39, 2% 40-49, less than 1% 50-99. **Special facilities:** Bible museum.

Freshman class profile. 1,593 applied, 919 admitted, 531 enrolled.

Mid 50% test scores		GPA 3.0-3.49:	38%
SAT critical reading:	440-630	GPA 2.0-2.99:	2%
SAT math:	470-670	Rank in top quarter:	42%
SAT writing:	450-660	Rank in top tenth:	26%
ACT composite:	20-29	Return as sophomores:	73%
GPA 3.75 or higher:	26%	Out-of-state:	30%
GPA 3.50-3.74:	34%	Live on campus:	88%

Basis for selection. High school record, standardized test scores, class rank most important. Require 2 of the following: 820 SAT (exclusive of Writing); 16 ACT; 2.0 GPA; class rank top 60%. Computerized Placement Test required for those with SAT verbal and math scores below 500. Portfolio recommended for all; audition required for music, theater programs; essay required for English-deficient; interview recommended for music, theater programs. **Learning Disabled:** Meet with Director of Disability Services.

High school preparation. College-preparatory program recommended. 12 units required; 18 recommended. Required and recommended units include English 4, mathematics 3-4, social studies 1, history 1-2, science 3-4 (laboratory 3), foreign language 2, computer science 1, visual/performing arts 1 and academic electives 2.

2015-2016 Annual costs. Tuition/fees: $16,290. Room/board: $9,640. Books/supplies: $2,000. Personal expenses: $1,900.

Financial aid. Non-need-based: Scholarships awarded for academics, athletics, leadership, music/drama, religious affiliation, state residency.

Application procedures. Admission: Priority date 6/1; deadline 8/26 (postmark date). $30 fee, may be waived for applicants with need. Admission notification on a rolling basis. **Financial aid:** Priority date 6/1, closing date 6/30. FAFSA required. Applicants notified on a rolling basis starting 8/1; must reply within 2 week(s) of notification.

Academics. Special study options: Combined bachelor's/graduate degree, cross-registration, distance learning, double major, dual enrollment of high school students, ESL, honors, independent study, internships, student-designed major, study abroad, teacher certification program. **Credit/placement by examination:** AP, CLEP, IB, SAT, ACT, institutional tests. 16 credit hours maximum toward associate degree, 30 toward bachelor's. CLEP and other exam credits cannot exceed 25 percent of hours needed for degree. **Support services:** Learning center, reduced course load, remedial instruction, study skills assistance, tutoring, writing center.

Majors. Biology: General. **Business:** Accounting, business admin, international, marketing. **Communications:** Broadcast journalism, journalism, media studies. **Education:** Early childhood, elementary, English, mathematics, music, social studies. **English:** English lit. **Foreign languages:** Spanish. **Health services:** Predental, premedicine, prepharmacy. **History:** General. **Liberal arts:** Arts/sciences. **Math:** General. **Parks/recreation:** General, sports admin. **Psychology:** General. **Theology:** Bible, missionary, sacred music, youth ministry. **Visual/performing arts:** Dramatic, music, music performance, musical theater, piano/keyboard, stringed instruments, studio arts, voice/opera.

Most popular majors. Business/marketing 19%, communications/journalism 6%, education 17%, liberal arts 17%, parks/recreation 15%, psychology 6%, theological studies 10%.

Technology on campus. 97 workstations in library, computer center, student center. Dormitories wired for high-speed internet access and linked to campus network. Commuter students can connect to campus network. Online library, helpline, repair service, wireless network available.

Student life. Freshman orientation: Mandatory. Preregistration for classes offered. Five-day program held in August prior to start of fall semester. **Policies:** Drug, alcohol, smoke-free campus. Religious observance required. **Housing:** Guaranteed on-campus for all undergraduates. Single-sex dorms, special housing for disabled, apartments, wellness housing available. $100 deposit, deadline 8/26. **Activities:** Bands, campus ministries, choral groups, drama, literary magazine, music ensembles, musical theater, radio station, student government, student newspaper, symphony orchestra, TV station, Baptist student union, athletic ministries, Etude music society, Fellowship of Christians in Service, Joyful sound, business club, Teacher Education Association, Phi Beta Lambda, Dramatis Personae Society.

Athletics. NCAA, NCCAA. **Intercollegiate:** Baseball M, basketball, cheerleading, cross-country, football (tackle) M, golf, lacrosse, soccer, softball W, tennis, track and field, volleyball. **Intramural:** Basketball, football (non-tackle) M, sand volleyball, softball, table tennis, tennis, ultimate frisbee, volleyball. **Team name:** Crusaders.

Student services. Chaplain/spiritual director, career counseling, student employment services, financial aid counseling, health services, on-campus daycare, personal counseling, placement for graduates. **Physically disabled:** Services for visually impaired.

Contact. E-mail: admissions@ngu.edu
Phone: (864) 977-7001 Toll-free number: (800) 468-6642
Fax: (864) 977-7177
Keli Sewell, Vice President for Enrollment Management, North Greenville University, PO Box 1892, Tigerville, SC 29688-1892

Presbyterian College
Clinton, South Carolina   CB member
www.presby.edu   CB code: 5540

- Private 4-year pharmacy and liberal arts college affiliated with the Presbyterian Church (USA)
- Residential campus in small town
- 963 degree-seeking undergraduates: 1% part-time, 52% women, 14% African American, 1% Asian American, 3% Hispanic/Latino, 2% Multi-racial, non-Hispanic, 1% international
- 315 degree-seeking graduate students
- 62% of applicants admitted
- Application essay required
- 70% graduate within 6 years; 28% enter graduate study

General. Founded in 1880. Regionally accredited. **Degrees:** 243 bachelor's awarded; professional offered. **ROTC:** Army. **Location:** 40 miles from

Greenville, 35 miles from Spartanburg. **Calendar:** Semester, limited summer session. **Full-time faculty:** 77 total; 97% have terminal degrees, 9% minority, 39% women. **Part-time faculty:** 36 total; 39% have terminal degrees, 8% minority, 36% women. **Class size:** 66% < 20, 34% 20-39. **Special facilities:** Scanning electron and transmission microscopes, ecological research center, Confucius Institute.

Freshman class profile. 2,072 applied, 1,291 admitted, 262 enrolled.

Mid 50% test scores		Rank in top quarter:	56%
SAT critical reading:	480-590	Rank in top tenth:	27%
SAT math:	490-600	Return as sophomores:	81%
ACT composite:	20-27	Out-of-state:	32%
GPA 3.75 or higher:	32%	Live on campus:	99%
GPA 3.50-3.74:	19%	International:	1%
GPA 3.0-3.49:	29%	Fraternities:	36%
GPA 2.0-2.99:	20%	Sororities:	45%

Basis for selection. Rigor of the high school curriculum is most important, followed by high school GPA, high school recommendation, and in some cases test scores (i.e., SAT, ACT). Extracurricular activities and interviews also considered. Except for some students, standardized tests are optional for admittance. However, once admitted, all students will be required to submit either an SAT or ACT score. Interview recommended. **Home schooled:** State high school equivalency certificate required. **Learning Disabled:** Learning disabilities must be documented.

High school preparation. College-preparatory program required. 18 units required; 21 recommended. Required and recommended units include English 4, mathematics 4, social studies 2, history 2, science 2-4 (laboratory 2), foreign language 2-3 and academic electives 2. 2 or more units of laboratory science recommended for science majors.

2015-2016 Annual costs. Tuition/fees: $36,130. Room/board: $9,750. Books/supplies: $1,200. Personal expenses: $1,000.

2015-2016 Financial aid. Need-based: 257 full-time freshmen applied for aid; 214 deemed to have need; 214 received aid. Average need met was 28%. Average scholarship/grant was $28,790; average loan $3,660. 84% of total undergraduate aid awarded as scholarships/grants, 16% as loans/jobs. **Non-need-based:** Awarded to 545 full-time undergraduates, including 179 freshmen. Scholarships awarded for academics, alumni affiliation, art, athletics, job skills, leadership, minority status, music/drama, religious affiliation, ROTC, state residency.

Application procedures. Admission: Priority date 12/1; deadline 6/30 (postmark date). No application fee. Admission notification by 3/15. Must reply by 5/1. **Financial aid:** Priority date 3/15, closing date 6/30. FAFSA required. Applicants notified on a rolling basis starting 3/15; must reply by 7/1.

Academics. Special study options: Combined bachelor's/graduate degree, distance learning, double major, dual enrollment of high school students, exchange student, honors, independent study, internships, semester at sea, study abroad, teacher certification program, Washington semester. 3-2 environmental science program, 3-2 engineering program, religious educational program, dual degrees offered with Auburn University (AL), Clemson University, Vanderbilt University (TN), University of South Carolina. **Credit/placement by examination:** AP, CLEP, IB, SAT, ACT, institutional tests. 40 credit hours maximum toward bachelor's degree. **Support services:** Pre-admission summer program, study skills assistance, tutoring, writing center.

Majors. Biology: General, biochemistry. **Business:** Business admin. **Education:** Early childhood, elementary, middle, music. **English:** English lit. **Foreign languages:** General, French, Spanish. **History:** General. **Math:** General, applied. **Philosophy/religion:** Religion. **Physical sciences:** Chemistry, physics. **Psychology:** General. **Social sciences:** Political science, sociology. **Theology:** Religious ed. **Visual/performing arts:** Art, dramatic, music.

Most popular majors. Biology 17%, business/marketing 20%, education 6%, English 8%, history 7%, psychology 13%, social sciences 8%.

Technology on campus. 100 workstations in dormitories, library, computer center, student center. Dormitories wired for high-speed internet access and linked to campus network. Commuter students can connect to campus network. Online course registration, online library, student web hosting, wireless network available.

Student life. Freshman orientation: Mandatory, $100 fee. Preregistration for classes offered. Orientation includes registration, placement testing, and organization fair. **Policies:** Honor code governs conduct inside and outside classroom, on and off campus. Cultural Enrichment Program requires students to attend 40 on-campus cultural events as part of graduation requirement. All full-time students, except those commuting daily from family's residence, required to live on campus. **Housing:** Guaranteed on-campus for all undergraduates. Coed dorms, single-sex dorms, apartments, fraternity/sorority housing, themed housing, wellness housing available. $400 nonrefundable deposit, deadline 5/1. **Activities:** Bands, campus ministries, choral groups, dance, drama, international student organizations, literary magazine, music

ensembles, student government, student newspaper, symphony orchestra, Volunteer organizations, multicultural student union, Young Democrats and Republicans, interdenominational organizations, Habitat for Humanity, Amnesty International, Fellowship of Christian Athletes.

Athletics. NCAA. **Intercollegiate:** Baseball M, basketball, cheerleading, cross-country, football (tackle) M, golf, lacrosse W, soccer, softball W, tennis, volleyball W. **Intramural:** Basketball, football (non-tackle), golf, soccer, softball, table tennis, tennis, ultimate frisbee, volleyball. **Team name:** Blue Hose.

Student services. Alcohol/substance abuse counseling, chaplain/spiritual director, career counseling, student employment services, financial aid counseling, health services, minority student services, personal counseling, placement for graduates.

Contact. E-mail: admissions@presby.edu
Phone: (864) 833-8230 Toll-free number: (800) 960-7583
Fax: (864) 833-8195
Brian Fortman, Dean of Enrollment Management, Presbyterian College, 503 South Broad Street, Clinton, SC 29325-2865

South Carolina State University
Orangeburg, South Carolina
www.scsu.edu
CB member
CB code: 5618

- Public 4-year university
- Residential campus in large town
- 2,410 degree-seeking undergraduates: 8% part-time, 50% women, 96% African American, 1% Asian American
- 400 degree-seeking graduate students
- 95% of applicants admitted
- SAT or ACT (ACT writing optional) required
- 38% graduate within 6 years

General. Founded in 1896. Regionally accredited. **Degrees:** 486 bachelor's awarded; master's, doctoral offered. **ROTC:** Army. **Location:** 41 miles from Columbia, 79 miles from Charleston. **Calendar:** Semester, limited summer session. **Full-time faculty:** 136 total; 82% have terminal degrees, 76% minority, 48% women. **Part-time faculty:** 67 total; 25% have terminal degrees, 81% minority, 51% women. **Class size:** 54% < 20, 39% 20-39, 6% 40-49, less than 1% 50-99, less than 1% >100. **Special facilities:** Planetarium, charter school, child development learning center.

Freshman class profile. 2,445 applied, 2,320 admitted, 494 enrolled.

Mid 50% test scores		GPA 2.0-2.99:	59%
SAT critical reading:	340-420	Rank in top quarter:	13%
SAT math:	340-420	Rank in top tenth:	3%
ACT composite:	14-17	End year in good standing:	70%
GPA 3.75 or higher:	6%	Return as sophomores:	58%
GPA 3.50-3.74:	4%	Out-of-state:	24%
GPA 3.0-3.49:	26%	Live on campus:	96%

Basis for selection. Official high school transcript, class rank, standardized test scores and recommendation letter from a school official are used. Audition required for music education program; portfolio required for art education program. **Learning Disabled:** Documentation required.

High school preparation. College-preparatory program recommended. 22 units required. Required units include English 4, mathematics 4, social studies 3, science 3 (laboratory 3), foreign language 2 and academic electives 4. 1 fine arts and 1 PE or ROTC.

2015-2016 Annual costs. Tuition/fees: $10,088; $19,856 out-of-state. Room/board: $9,402. Books/supplies: $2,000. Personal expenses: $8,000.

2014-2015 Financial aid. Need-based: 60% of total undergraduate aid awarded as scholarships/grants, 40% as loans/jobs. **Non-need-based:** Scholarships awarded for academics, alumni affiliation, athletics.

Application procedures. Admission: Closing date 7/31 (postmark date). $25 fee, may be waived for applicants with need. Admission notification on a rolling basis. **Financial aid:** Closing date 5/1. FAFSA, institutional form required. Applicants notified on a rolling basis starting 5/15; must reply by 7/1 or within 4 week(s) of notification.

Academics. Special study options: Cooperative education, cross-registration, distance learning, double major, dual enrollment of high school students, exchange student, honors, independent study, internships, liberal arts/career combination, student-designed major, study abroad, teacher certification program, Washington semester. **Credit/placement by examination:** AP, CLEP, institutional tests. 30 credit hours maximum toward bachelor's degree. **Support services:** Learning center, pre-admission summer program, study skills assistance, tutoring, writing center.

Majors. Biology: General. **Business:** Accounting, business admin, managerial economics, marketing. **Communications:** Media studies. **Computer sciences:** General. **Education:** Art, business, early childhood, elementary, middle, music, physical, special ed, technology/industrial arts. **Engineering:** Industrial, nuclear. **English:** English lit. **Foreign languages:** General. **Health services:** Audiology/speech pathology. **History:** General. **Human services:** Social work. **Math:** General. **Parks/recreation:** Health/fitness. **Physical sciences:** Chemistry, physics. **Protective services:** Law enforcement admin. **Psychology:** General. **Social sciences:** General, political science, sociology. **Visual/performing arts:** Dramatic, music management, studio arts. **Work/family studies:** General, food/nutrition.

Most popular majors. Biology 12%, business/marketing 11%, education 11%, engineering/engineering technologies 10%, family/consumer sciences 15%, public administration/social services 6%.

Technology on campus. 300 workstations in dormitories, library, computer center, student center. Dormitories wired for high-speed internet access and linked to campus network. Commuter students can connect to campus network. Online course registration, online library, helpline, repair service, wireless network available.

Student life. Freshman orientation: Available, $100 fee. Preregistration for classes offered. **Housing:** Guaranteed on-campus for freshmen. Single-sex dorms, apartments available. $35 deposit. **Activities:** Bands, choral groups, dance, drama, international student organizations, music ensembles, radio station, student government, student newspaper.

Athletics. NCAA. **Intercollegiate:** Basketball, cheerleading, cross-country, football (tackle) M, soccer W, softball W, tennis, track and field, volleyball W. **Intramural:** Basketball, bowling, softball. **Team name:** Bulldogs.

Student services. Adult student services, alcohol/substance abuse counseling, chaplain/spiritual director, career counseling, services for economically disadvantaged, student employment services, financial aid counseling, health services, minority student services, personal counseling, placement for graduates, veterans' counselor. **Physically disabled:** Services for visually, speech, hearing impaired.

Contact. E-mail: admissions@scsu.edu
Phone: (803) 536-7185 Toll-free number: (800) 260-5956
Fax: (803) 536-8990
Anthony Wright, Director of Admissions, South Carolina State University, 300 College Street NE, Orangeburg, SC 29117

Southern Wesleyan University
Central, South Carolina
www.swu.edu   CB code: 5896

- Private 4-year university and liberal arts college affiliated with the Wesleyan Church
- Residential campus in small town
- 1,400 undergraduates
- SAT or ACT (ACT writing optional) required

General. Founded in 1906. Regionally accredited. **Degrees:** 282 bachelor's, 59 associate awarded; master's offered. **ROTC:** Army, Air Force. **Location:** 20 miles from Greenville, SC; 100 miles from Atlanta, GA. **Calendar:** Semester, limited summer session. **Full-time faculty:** 56 total. **Part-time faculty:** 53 total. **Class size:** 73% < 20, 27% 20-39, less than 1% 40-49. **Special facilities:** Collection of brass rubbings from medieval burial coverings, genealogical records from South Carolina and the south-east region of the U.S., compilation of classic theological works from the Wesleyan and Holiness denominational traditions, historical museum and archive, restored abolitionist church.

Freshman class profile.

GPA 3.75 or higher:	39%	GPA 2.0-2.99:	18%
GPA 3.50-3.74:	16%	Rank in top quarter:	34%
GPA 3.0-3.49:	25%	Rank in top tenth:	13%

Basis for selection. GPA, class rank, test scores, and religious commitment are important. Recommendations considered. Students admitted conditionally if SAT score is between 800-850 (critical reading and math) or high school GPA is less than 2.3. Students admitted conditionally take limited number of course hours and are on academic warning. SAT/ACT not required for transfer students with 2.0 college GPA. Auditions are required for acceptance into the music program. An interview is recommended for applicants

with special physical or emotional problems. **Home schooled:** Require verification of homeschooling registration with the department of education from the student's home state.

High school preparation. College-preparatory program recommended. 10 units recommended. Recommended units include English 4, mathematics 2, social studies 2 and science 2.

2015-2016 Annual costs. Tuition/fees: $23,470. Room/board: $8,020. Books/supplies: $1,020. Personal expenses: $1,050.

Financial aid. Non-need-based: Scholarships awarded for academics, athletics, music/drama.

Application procedures. Admission: Closing date 8/1 (postmark date). $25 fee, may be waived for applicants with need. Admission notification on a rolling basis beginning on or about 9/1. Must reply by 5/1. **Financial aid:** Priority date 3/31, closing date 6/30. FAFSA, institutional form required. Applicants notified on a rolling basis starting 2/1; must reply within 2 week(s) of notification.

Academics. Special study options: Distance learning, double major, dual enrollment of high school students, ESL, honors, independent study, internships, liberal arts/career combination, student-designed major, study abroad, teacher certification program, Washington semester. Students attending the traditional residential program participate in study abroad through the Council of Christian Colleges & University's Best Semester program. **Credit/placement by examination:** AP, CLEP, IB, SAT, ACT, institutional tests. 48 credit hours maximum toward associate degree, 68 toward bachelor's. International Baccalaureate (IB) Diploma Programme graduates may be awarded credit for appropriate scores on their Higher Level exams. Currently IB credit is evaluated on a case by case basis. **Support services:** Learning center, reduced course load, remedial instruction, study skills assistance, tutoring, writing center.

Majors. Biology: General. **Business:** Accounting, business admin, information resources management. **Communications:** Communications/speech/rhetoric. **Computer sciences:** General. **Education:** Biology, early childhood, elementary, English, mathematics, music, physical, special ed. **English:** English lit. **Health services:** Medical radiologic technology/radiation therapy, predental, premedicine. **History:** General. **Math:** General. **Parks/recreation:** General, sports admin. **Philosophy/religion:** Religion. **Physical sciences:** Chemistry. **Protective services:** Computer forensics, criminal justice, forensics. **Psychology:** General. **Social sciences:** General. **Visual/performing arts:** Music.

Most popular majors. Business/marketing 61%, education 11%.

Technology on campus. 256 workstations in dormitories, library, computer center, student center. Dormitories wired for high-speed internet access and linked to campus network. Commuter students can connect to campus network. Online course registration, online library, helpline, repair service, wireless network available.

Student life. Freshman orientation: Mandatory. Preregistration for classes offered. Three-day orientation held at beginning of fall semester includes information sessions for students and parents, social activities and recreation, service projects, and worship services. **Policies:** Alcohol and tobacco-free campus. As an evangelical Christian university, students are expected to follow the community lifestyle standards. Religious observance required. **Housing:** Guaranteed on-campus for all undergraduates. Coed dorms, single-sex dorms, special housing for disabled, apartments, wellness housing available. $200 fully refundable deposit, deadline 8/1. **Activities:** Bands, campus ministries, choral groups, drama, literary magazine, music ensembles, musical theater, student government, Christian athlete group, outdoors club, Student Missions Focus, women's leadership program, men's leadership program, English Majors United, science club, music club.

Athletics. NAIA, NCCAA. **Intercollegiate:** Baseball M, basketball, cross-country, golf M, soccer, softball W, volleyball W. **Intramural:** Basketball, football (non-tackle), soccer, softball, table tennis, tennis, volleyball. **Team name:** Warriors.

Student services. Adult student services, alcohol/substance abuse counseling, chaplain/spiritual director, career counseling, financial aid counseling, health services, minority student services, personal counseling. **Physically disabled:** Services for visually, hearing impaired.

Contact. E-mail: admissions@swu.edu
Phone: (864) 644-5550 Toll-free number: (800) 282-8798
Fax: (864) 644-5972
Amanda Young, Director of Admissions, Southern Wesleyan University, PO Box 1020, Central, SC 29630-1020

University of Phoenix: Columbia
Columbia, South Carolina
www.phoenix.edu

◗ For-profit 4-year university
◗ Commuter campus in small city
◗ 487 undergraduates

General. Regionally accredited. **Degrees:** 129 bachelor's awarded; master's offered. **Calendar:** Differs by program. Other academic calendar. **Full-time faculty:** 12 total. **Part-time faculty:** 121 total.

Basis for selection. Open admission.

2015-2016 Annual costs. Per-credit-hour charge, $410 to $635, depending upon level and course of study. Books, material charges, and other fees vary by course and program. All fees are subject to change.

Application procedures. Admission: No deadline. No application fee. **Financial aid:** No deadline.

Academics. Credit/placement by examination: AP, CLEP.

Majors. Business: Accounting/business management, business admin, e-commerce, entrepreneurial studies, finance, human resources, marketing, operations. **Computer sciences:** Database management, programming, security, support specialist, system admin, systems analysis, web page design, webmaster. **Health services:** Facilities admin, health information management, long term care admin. **Human services:** General. **Protective services:** Disaster management, law enforcement admin.

Student life. Freshman orientation: Mandatory. Preregistration for classes offered.

Contact. University of Phoenix: Columbia, 1001 Pinnacle Point Drive, Columbia, SC 29223-5727

University of South Carolina: Aiken
Aiken, South Carolina   **CB member**
http://web.usca.edu/   **CB code: 5840**

◗ Public 4-year university and liberal arts college
◗ Residential campus in large town
◗ 3,082 degree-seeking undergraduates: 16% part-time, 63% women, 27% African American, 1% Asian American, 4% Hispanic/Latino, 4% Multiracial, non-Hispanic, 4% international
◗ 46 degree-seeking graduate students
◗ 57% of applicants admitted
◗ SAT or ACT (ACT writing recommended) required
◗ 43% graduate within 6 years

General. Founded in 1961. Regionally accredited. **Degrees:** 483 bachelor's awarded; master's offered. **Location:** 55 miles from Columbia, SC; 15 miles from Augusta, GA. **Calendar:** Semester, limited summer session. **Full-time faculty:** 142 total; 78% have terminal degrees, 18% minority, 49% women. **Part-time faculty:** 124 total; 26% have terminal degrees, 14% minority, 52% women. **Class size:** 44% < 20, 51% 20-39, 2% 40-49, 3% 50-99, less than 1% >100. **Special facilities:** Fine arts center, science center, natatorium, planetarium, convocation center, wellness center.

Freshman class profile. 2,341 applied, 1,338 admitted, 616 enrolled.

Mid 50% test scores			
SAT critical reading:	430-540	Rank in top quarter:	43%
SAT math:	430-540	Rank in top tenth:	13%
SAT writing:	410-510	End year in good standing:	73%
ACT composite:	18-22	Return as sophomores:	72%
GPA 3.75 or higher:	51%	Out-of-state:	10%
GPA 3.50-3.74:	13%	Live on campus:	55%
GPA 3.0-3.49:	28%	International:	5%
GPA 2.0-2.99:	8%	Fraternities:	8%
		Sororities:	10%

Basis for selection. Test scores, core GPA, course selection important. Audition, essay, interview, portfolio recommended for specific majors.

High school preparation. College-preparatory program recommended. 21 units required. Required and recommended units include English 4, mathematics 4, social studies 2, history 1, science 3 (laboratory 3), foreign language 2, computer science 1, visual/performing arts 1 and academic electives 4. 1 unit physical education or ROTC required; elective college preparatory credits must come from 3 different fields.

2015-2016 Annual costs. Tuition/fees: $9,878; $19,472 out-of-state. Room/board: $7,290. Books/supplies: $1,600. Personal expenses: $2,500.

2014-2015 Financial aid. Need-based: 593 full-time freshmen applied for aid; 432 deemed to have need; 428 received aid. Average need met was 67%. Average scholarship/grant was $6,686; average loan $3,114. 48% of total undergraduate aid awarded as scholarships/grants, 52% as loans/jobs. **Non-need-based:** Awarded to 443 full-time undergraduates, including 103 freshmen. Scholarships awarded for academics, alumni affiliation, art, athletics, leadership, minority status, music/drama, state residency. **Additional information:** Students must be enrolled at least half time and be able to present documentation which verifies eligibility to work in the U.S.

Application procedures. Admission: Priority date 6/1; deadline 8/1 (postmark date). $45 fee, may be waived for applicants with need. Admission notification on a rolling basis beginning on or about 9/1. Must reply by May 1 or within 3 week(s) if notified thereafter. **Financial aid:** Priority date 3/15; no closing date. FAFSA required. Applicants notified on a rolling basis starting 4/20; must reply within 2 week(s) of notification.

Academics. Special study options: Cooperative education, distance learning, double major, dual enrollment of high school students, ESL, honors, independent study, internships, student-designed major, study abroad, teacher certification program. **Credit/placement by examination:** AP, CLEP, IB, institutional tests. 30 credit hours maximum toward bachelor's degree. **Support services:** Learning center, study skills assistance, tutoring, writing center.

Majors. Biology: General. **Business:** Business admin. **Communications:** Communications/speech/rhetoric. **Education:** Early childhood, elementary, middle, music, secondary, special ed. **Engineering:** Industrial. **English:** English lit. **Health services:** Nursing (RN). **History:** General. **Liberal arts:** Arts/sciences. **Math:** Applied. **Parks/recreation:** Exercise sciences. **Physical sciences:** Chemistry. **Psychology:** General. **Social sciences:** Political science, sociology. **Visual/performing arts:** Studio arts.

Most popular majors. Biology 7%, business/marketing 17%, communications/journalism 6%, education 11%, health sciences 21%, parks/recreation 13%, psychology 6%, social sciences 9%.

Technology on campus. 550 workstations in dormitories, library, computer center, student center. Dormitories wired for high-speed internet access and linked to campus network. Commuter students can connect to campus network. Online course registration, online library, helpline, wireless network available.

Student life. Freshman orientation: Mandatory, $85 fee. Preregistration for classes offered. Held in June, July, and August. June and July orientations offer registration. **Housing:** Coed dorms, special housing for disabled, apartments, themed housing available. $125 partly refundable deposit. **Activities:** Bands, campus ministries, choral groups, dance, drama, international student organizations, literary magazine, music ensembles, musical theater, student government, student newspaper, Campus Crusade for Christ, honor societies, Pacer Union Board, African American Students' Alliance, College Republicans, Circle K, Fellowship of Christian Athletes.

Athletics. NCAA. **Intercollegiate:** Baseball M, basketball, cross-country W, golf M, soccer, softball W, tennis, volleyball W. **Intramural:** Basketball, football (non-tackle), soccer, ultimate frisbee, volleyball. **Team name:** Pacers.

Student services. Adult student services, alcohol/substance abuse counseling, career counseling, student employment services, financial aid counseling, health services, minority student services, on-campus daycare, personal counseling, placement for graduates, veterans' counselor. **Physically disabled:** Services for visually, speech, hearing impaired.

Contact. E-mail: admit@usca.edu
Phone: (803) 641-3366 Toll-free number: (888) 969-8722
Fax: (803) 641-3727
Andrew Hendrix, Director of Admissions, University of South Carolina: Aiken, 471 University Parkway, Aiken, SC 29801-6399

University of South Carolina: Beaufort
Bluffton, South Carolina   **CB member**
www.uscb.edu   **CB code: 5845**

◗ Public 4-year university and liberal arts college
◗ Commuter campus in large town
◗ 1,966 degree-seeking undergraduates: 13% part-time, 64% women, 22% African American, 1% Asian American, 7% Hispanic/Latino, 4% Multiracial, non-Hispanic, 1% international

- 63% of applicants admitted
- SAT or ACT (ACT writing optional) required

General. Founded in 1959. Regionally accredited. Two locations: Hilton Head Gateway and Historic Beaufort. **Degrees:** 267 bachelor's awarded. **Location:** 72 miles from Charleston; 42 miles from Savannah, GA. **Calendar:** Semester, limited summer session. **Full-time faculty:** 66 total; 11% minority, 53% women. **Part-time faculty:** 48 total; 4% minority, 50% women. **Special facilities:** Performing arts center, art studios.

Freshman class profile. 1,902 applied, 1,207 admitted, 517 enrolled.

Return as sophomores:	58%	Live on campus:	40%
Out-of-state:	16%	International:	2%

Basis for selection. Test scores, rigor of secondary school record important; academic GPA considered.

High school preparation. College-preparatory program required. 19 units required. Required units include English 4, mathematics 4, social studies 2, history 1, science 3 (laboratory 3), foreign language 2, visual/performing arts 1 and academic electives 2. Electives must be from 2 areas. Computer science course recommended. 1 PE or ROTC required.

2015-2016 Annual costs. Tuition/fees: $9,848; $19,982 out-of-state. Room/board: $8,297. Books/supplies: $1,181. Personal expenses: $2,121. **Additional information:** Active duty military pay reduced tuition. Some courses require additional fees.

Financial aid. Non-need-based: Scholarships awarded for academics, art, athletics, leadership, religious affiliation, state residency.

Application procedures. Admission: Priority date 5/1; deadline 8/1 (receipt date). $40 fee, may be waived for applicants with need. Admission notification on a rolling basis beginning on or about 2/1. **Financial aid:** Priority date 3/1; no closing date. FAFSA required. Applicants notified on a rolling basis starting 5/1; must reply within 2 week(s) of notification.

Academics. Special study options: Cooperative education, distance learning, double major, dual enrollment of high school students, independent study, internships, student-designed major, study abroad, teacher certification program, weekend college. **Credit/placement by examination:** AP, CLEP, IB, institutional tests. 15 credit hours maximum toward associate degree, 30 toward bachelor's. **Support services:** Learning center, reduced course load, study skills assistance, tutoring, writing center.

Majors. Biology: General. **Business:** Business admin, hospitality admin. **Communications:** Communications/speech/rhetoric. **Education:** Early childhood, elementary. **English:** English lit. **Foreign languages:** Spanish. **Health services:** Nursing (RN), public health ed. **History:** General. **Liberal arts:** Arts/sciences. **Math:** General. **Psychology:** General. **Social sciences:** General, sociology. **Visual/performing arts:** Studio arts.

Most popular majors. Biology 6%, business/marketing 39%, health sciences 9%, psychology 12%, social sciences 9%.

Technology on campus. 114 workstations in library, computer center. Dormitories wired for high-speed internet access. Online course registration, online library, helpline, wireless network available.

Student life. Freshman orientation: Mandatory. Preregistration for classes offered. **Housing:** Special housing for disabled, apartments, wellness housing available. $250 nonrefundable deposit, deadline 5/1. **Activities:** Choral groups, drama, literary magazine, musical theater, student government, student newspaper, African American student association, Christian student fellowship, business club, veterans association, education club, Gamma Beta Phi honor society, psychology/sociology/anthropology club.

Athletics. NAIA. **Intercollegiate:** Baseball M, cross-country, golf, soccer W, softball W, track and field. **Intramural:** Football (non-tackle), soccer. **Team name:** Sand Sharks.

Student services. Alcohol/substance abuse counseling, career counseling, student employment services, financial aid counseling, personal counseling, veterans' counselor.

Contact. E-mail: admissions@uscb.edu
Phone: (843) 208-8000 Toll-free number: (877) 885-5271
Fax: (843) 208-8290
Mack Palmour, Vice Chancellor for Enrollment Management, University of South Carolina: Beaufort, One University Boulevard, Bluffton, SC 29909

University of South Carolina: Columbia

Columbia, South Carolina   **CB member**
www.sc.edu   **CB code: 5818**

- Public 4-year university
- Residential campus in small city
- 24,899 degree-seeking undergraduates
- 65% of applicants admitted
- SAT or ACT (ACT writing optional), application essay required

General. Founded in 1801. Regionally accredited. **Degrees:** 5,428 bachelor's, 4 associate awarded; master's, professional, doctoral offered. **ROTC:** Army, Naval, Air Force. **Location:** 70 miles from Charlotte, North Carolina. **Calendar:** Semester, extensive summer session. **Full-time faculty:** 1,397 total; 84% have terminal degrees, 13% minority, 42% women. **Part-time faculty:** 654 total; 36% have terminal degrees, 13% minority, 55% women. **Class size:** 36% < 20, 39% 20-39, 9% 40-49, 10% 50-99, 5% >100. **Special facilities:** Observatory, arboretum, green dorm with learning center focusing on sustainability.

Freshman class profile. 25,740 applied, 16,611 admitted, 5,156 enrolled.

Mid 50% test scores			
SAT critical reading:	550-640	GPA 2.0-2.99:	1%
SAT math:	560-650	Rank in top quarter:	66%
ACT composite:	25-30	Rank in top tenth:	30%
GPA 3.75 or higher:	79%	Out-of-state:	48%
GPA 3.50-3.74:	12%	Live on campus:	97%
GPA 3.0-3.49:	8%	Fraternities:	14%
		Sororities:	31%

Basis for selection. High school curriculum, grades in required high school courses, SAT/ACT important. **Home schooled:** Transcript of courses and grades required. If student is not member of state-recognized homeschool association, course syllabi and textbook lists may be requested.

High school preparation. College-preparatory program required. 18 units required. Required units include English 4, mathematics 4, social studies 2, history 1, science 3 (laboratory 3), foreign language 2, visual/performing arts 1 and academic electives 1. 1 unit physical education or ROTC is required.

2015-2016 Annual costs. Tuition/fees: $11,482; $30,298 out-of-state. Room/board: $9,872. Books/supplies: $994. Personal expenses: $2,420. **Additional information:** Health professions including public health, nursing and social work require additional fees.

Financial aid. Non-need-based: Scholarships awarded for academics, alumni affiliation, art, athletics, job skills, leadership, minority status, music/drama, religious affiliation, ROTC, state residency.

Application procedures. Admission: Closing date 12/1 (postmark date). $65 fee, may be waived for applicants with need. Application must be submitted online. Admission notification by 3/15. Must reply by 5/1. **Financial aid:** Priority date 4/1; no closing date. FAFSA required. Applicants notified on a rolling basis starting 4/1.

Academics. One-month May term focusing on specialized topics. **Special study options:** Accelerated study, combined bachelor's/graduate degree, cooperative education, cross-registration, distance learning, double major, dual enrollment of high school students, ESL, exchange student, external degree, honors, independent study, internships, student-designed major, study abroad, teacher certification program, Washington semester, weekend college. Alternative spring break, Dobson volunteer service program, international program for students. **Credit/placement by examination:** AP, CLEP, IB, institutional tests. Maximum number of semester hours of credit by examination allowed varies according to degree and program of study. **Support services:** Learning center, pre-admission summer program, reduced course load, study skills assistance, tutoring, writing center.

Honors college/program. Separate application. Interquartile SAT range of enrolled students is 1390-1470 (CR+M). To graduate with honors, students must have 45 honors credits drawn from the 500 honors courses taught each year.

Majors. Area/ethnic studies: African-American, European, Latin American, women's. **Biology:** General, marine. **Business:** Accounting, business admin, finance, hospitality admin, insurance, management science, managerial economics, marketing, nonprofit/public, office management, real estate, retailing, tourism/travel. **Communications:** Advertising, broadcast journalism, journalism, media studies, public relations. **Computer sciences:** General, information systems. **Conservation:** Environmental science. **Education:** Art, early childhood, elementary, physical. **Engineering:** Biomedical, chemical, civil, computer, electrical, mechanical. **English:** English lit. **Foreign languages:** Classics, comparative lit, French, German, Italian, Russian, Spanish. **Health services:** Cardiovascular technology, nursing (RN). **History:** General. **Human services:** Social work. **Liberal arts:** Arts/sciences. **Math:** General, statistics. **Parks/recreation:** Exercise sciences, sports admin. **Philosophy/religion:** Philosophy, religion. **Physical sciences:** Chemistry, geology, geophysics, physics. **Protective services:** Law enforcement admin. **Psychology:** Experimental. **Social sciences:** Anthropology, economics, geography, international relations, political science, sociology. **Visual/performing arts:** Art history/conservation, dance, dramatic, film/cinema/video, music, studio arts.

Most popular majors. Biology 10%, business/marketing 26%, communications/journalism 7%, engineering/engineering technologies 6%, health sciences 7%, psychology 6%, social sciences 7%.

Technology on campus. 2,800 workstations in dormitories, library, computer center, student center. Dormitories wired for high-speed internet access and linked to campus network. Commuter students can connect to campus network. Online course registration, online library, helpline, repair service, student web hosting, wireless network available.

Student life. Freshman orientation: Mandatory, $40 fee. Preregistration for classes offered. Parents may also attend to view campus for $40 fee. **Housing:** Guaranteed on-campus for freshmen. Coed dorms, single-sex dorms, special housing for disabled, apartments, fraternity/sorority housing, wellness housing available. $150 partly refundable deposit, deadline 5/1. Honors, wellness, residential college, pre-medical, pre-law, French, Spanish, journalism, engineering, athletic, music, global, common courses programs and environmentally friendly housing available. **Activities:** Bands, campus ministries, choral groups, dance, drama, film society, international student organizations, literary magazine, music ensembles, musical theater, opera, radio station, student government, student newspaper, symphony orchestra, TV station, Baptist Collegiate Ministry, Muslim students association, College Democrats, College Republicans, Students Associated for Latin America, Saudi students association, Association of African-American Students, Carolina service council, Dance Marathon, Habitat for Humanity.

Athletics. NCAA. **Intercollegiate:** Baseball M, basketball, cross-country W, diving, equestrian W, football (tackle) M, golf, soccer, softball W, swimming, tennis, track and field, volleyball W. **Intramural:** Basketball, bowling, football (non-tackle), golf, racquetball, soccer, softball, swimming, table tennis, tennis, ultimate frisbee, volleyball, weight lifting. **Team name:** Fighting Gamecocks.

Student services. Adult student services, alcohol/substance abuse counseling, chaplain/spiritual director, career counseling, services for economically disadvantaged, student employment services, financial aid counseling, health services, minority student services, on-campus daycare, personal counseling, placement for graduates, veterans' counselor, women's services. **Physically disabled:** Services for visually, speech, hearing impaired.

Contact. E-mail: admissions-ugrad@sc.edu
Phone: (803) 777-7700 Toll-free number: (800) 868-5872
Fax: (803) 777-0101
Mary Wagner, Director of Undergraduate Admissions, University of South Carolina: Columbia, Office of Undergraduate Admissions, Columbia, SC 29208

University of South Carolina: Upstate
Spartanburg, South Carolina
www.uscupstate.edu   CB code: 5850

▶ Public 4-year university
▶ Commuter campus in small city
▶ 5,153 degree-seeking undergraduates
▶ SAT or ACT (ACT writing optional) required

General. Founded in 1967. Regionally accredited. **Degrees:** 1,097 bachelor's awarded; master's offered. **ROTC:** Army. **Location:** 30 miles from Greenville, 70 miles from Charlotte, North Carolina. **Calendar:** Semester, extensive summer session. **Full-time faculty:** 212 total; 62% have terminal degrees, 16% minority, 58% women. **Part-time faculty:** 217 total; 28% have terminal degrees, 6% minority, 55% women. **Class size:** 50% < 20, 45% 20-39, 4% 40-49, less than 1% 50-99. **Special facilities:** Film theater, recital hall, center for international studies and language services, audiovisual production center, digital lab, centers for interdisciplinary studies, watershed ecology center.

Freshman class profile.

GPA 3.0-3.49:	11%	Rank in top tenth:	10%
GPA 2.0-2.99:	81%	Out-of-state:	8%
Rank in top quarter:	37%	Live on campus:	68%

Basis for selection. Cumulative average of C or better in preparatory courses and minimum 850 SAT (exclusive of Writing), or 18 ACT required. Higher grades may offset lower SAT/ACT scores, and higher SAT/ACT scores may offset lower grades. All applicants who are 21 years of age or younger, with the exception of transfer applicants who have completed at least 30 semester hours of college credit, must submit ACT or SAT results. Applicants who are 22 years of age or older are not required to submit SAT/ACT scores. Interviews recommended.

High school preparation. College-preparatory program required. 20 units required; 22 recommended. Required and recommended units include English 4, mathematics 3-4, social studies 2, history 1, science 3 (laboratory 3), foreign language 2-3 and academic electives 4.

2015-2016 Annual costs. Tuition/fees: $10,818; $21,468 out-of-state. Room/board: $7,848. Books/supplies: $1,600. Personal expenses: $2,810.

Financial aid. Non-need-based: Scholarships awarded for academics, athletics, minority status, ROTC, state residency. **Additional information:** Out-of-state students who are recipients of financial aid may qualify for out-of-state fee waiver. Educational benefits available to veterans and children of deceased/disabled veterans.

Application procedures. Admission: Priority date 8/15; no deadline. $40 fee, may be waived for applicants with need. Admission notification on a rolling basis beginning on or about 9/15. **Financial aid:** Priority date 3/1, closing date 7/15. FAFSA, institutional form required. Applicants notified on a rolling basis starting 5/17; must reply within 2 week(s) of notification.

Academics. Special study options: Accelerated study, cooperative education, cross-registration, distance learning, double major, dual enrollment of high school students, ESL, exchange student, honors, independent study, internships, liberal arts/career combination, student-designed major, study abroad, teacher certification program, Washington semester. **Credit/placement by examination:** AP, CLEP, IB, institutional tests. 30 credit hours maximum toward bachelor's degree. Credit also awarded for: American College Testing Program, Defense Activity for Nontraditional Education Support, Institution Credit by Examination, Military Service School Credit, Credit for Non-collegiate Programs, and Correspondence Course Credits. **Support services:** Learning center, reduced course load, remedial instruction, study skills assistance, tutoring, writing center.

Majors. Biology: General. **Business:** Business admin, nonprofit/public. **Communications:** Communications/speech/rhetoric. **Computer sciences:** General, information systems, information technology. **Education:** Art, early childhood, elementary, middle, physical, secondary, special ed. **English:** English lit. **Foreign languages:** Spanish. **Health services:** Nursing (RN). **History:** General. **Liberal arts:** Arts/sciences. **Math:** General, applied. **Physical sciences:** Chemistry. **Protective services:** Criminal justice. **Psychology:** General. **Social sciences:** Political science, sociology. **Visual/performing arts:** Commercial/advertising art, design, graphic design, music performance, theater arts management.

Most popular majors. Business/marketing 13%, computer/information sciences 6%, education 12%, health sciences 25%, interdisciplinary studies 8%, psychology 8%, security/protective services 6%.

Technology on campus. 725 workstations in dormitories, library, computer center, student center. Dormitories wired for high-speed internet access and linked to campus network. Commuter students can connect to campus network. Online course registration, online library, helpline, repair service, student web hosting, wireless network available.

Student life. Freshman orientation: Available. Preregistration for classes offered. **Housing:** Coed dorms, apartments, wellness housing available. $145 partly refundable deposit, deadline 6/1. **Activities:** Jazz band, campus ministries, choral groups, dance, drama, international student organizations, literary magazine, music ensembles, student government, student newspaper, African-American Association, Baptist student union, Campus Crusade for Christ, College Republicans, Young Democrats, student education association, campus activity board, Association for the Education of Young Children, environmental club.

Athletics. NCAA. **Intercollegiate:** Baseball M, basketball, cheerleading, cross-country, golf, soccer, softball W, tennis, track and field, volleyball W. **Intramural:** Badminton, basketball, bowling, football (non-tackle), racquetball, soccer, softball, table tennis, tennis, track and field, volleyball. **Team name:** Spartans.

Student services. Adult student services, alcohol/substance abuse counseling, chaplain/spiritual director, career counseling, services for economically disadvantaged, student employment services, financial aid counseling, health services, minority student services, on-campus daycare, personal counseling, placement for graduates, veterans' counselor, women's services. **Physically disabled:** Services for visually, speech, hearing impaired.

Contact. E-mail: dstewart@uscupstate.edu
Phone: (864) 503-5246 Toll-free number: (800) 277-8727
Fax: (864) 503-5727
Donette Stewart, Assistant Vice Chancellor for Enrollment Services, University of South Carolina: Upstate, 800 University Way, Spartanburg, SC 29303

Voorhees College
Denmark, South Carolina   **CB member**
www.voorhees.edu   **CB code: 5863**

- Private 4-year liberal arts college affiliated with the Episcopal Church
- Residential campus in small town
- 434 degree-seeking undergraduates: 3% part-time, 57% women
- 93% of applicants admitted

General. Founded in 1897. Regionally accredited. **Degrees:** 73 bachelor's awarded. **ROTC:** Army. **Location:** 50 miles from Columbia and Augusta, GA. **Calendar:** Semester, limited summer session. **Full-time faculty:** 36 total. **Part-time faculty:** 6 total.

Freshman class profile. 1,393 applied, 1,294 admitted, 105 enrolled.

Out-of-state: 15%   Live on campus: 95%

Basis for selection. Secondary school record, GPA (2.0 or above), recommendations, and standardized test scores considered in admissions decisions. **Home schooled:** Statement describing home school structure and mission, transcript of courses and grades, state high school equivalency certificate required.

High school preparation. 24 units recommended. Recommended units include English 4, mathematics 4, social studies 3, history 1, science 3, foreign language 1, computer science 1 and academic electives 7.

2015-2016 Annual costs. Tuition/fees: $12,630. Room/board: $7,346. Books/supplies: $1,500. Personal expenses: $4,860.

Application procedures. Admission: Priority date 4/15; no deadline. $25 fee, may be waived for applicants with need. Admission notification on a rolling basis beginning on or about 1/15. **Financial aid:** Priority date 4/15; no closing date. FAFSA, institutional form required. Applicants notified on a rolling basis starting 3/1; must reply within 2 week(s) of notification.

Academics. Special study options: Accelerated study, combined bachelor's/graduate degree, cooperative education, honors, independent study, internships, liberal arts/career combination, weekend college. **Credit/placement by examination:** AP, CLEP, IB, institutional tests. 15 credit hours maximum toward bachelor's degree. **Support services:** Learning center, reduced course load, remedial instruction, study skills assistance, tutoring, writing center.

Majors. Biology: General. **Business:** General, accounting, accounting/finance, business admin, management information systems, organizational behavior. **Communications:** Broadcast journalism, media studies. **Computer sciences:** General, computer science. **English:** English lit. **Health services:** Predental, premedicine, prenursing. **Math:** General. **Parks/recreation:** Health/fitness. **Protective services:** Disaster management. **Social sciences:** Sociology.

Most popular majors. Business/marketing 37%, communications/journalism 8%, education 9%, legal studies 17%, parks/recreation 8%, public administration/social services 11%.

Technology on campus. 175 workstations in dormitories, library, computer center. Dormitories wired for high-speed internet access and linked to campus network. Commuter students can connect to campus network. Online course registration, online library, helpline, repair service, wireless network available.

Student life. Freshman orientation: Mandatory. Preregistration for classes offered. One-day sessions offered in June and July. One week session offered in August. **Housing:** Guaranteed on-campus for all undergraduates. Single-sex dorms available. $75 nonrefundable deposit, deadline 7/31. Accommodations for single mothers available. **Activities:** Choral groups, radio station, student government, student newspaper.

Athletics. NAIA. **Intercollegiate:** Baseball M, basketball, cheerleading, cross-country, softball W, track and field, volleyball W. **Intramural:** Baseball M, basketball, softball W. **Team name:** Tigers.

Student services. Adult student services, chaplain/spiritual director, career counseling, student employment services, financial aid counseling, health services, personal counseling, placement for graduates, veterans' counselor.

Contact. E-mail: spellman@voorhees.edu
Phone: (803) 780-1031 Toll-free number: (866) 237-4570
Fax: (803) 780-1430
Diondra Smalls, Director of Admissions, Voorhees College, 213 Wiggins Road, Denmark, SC 29042

W.L. Bonner Bible College
Columbia, South Carolina
www.wlbc.edu

- Private 4-year Bible college
- Residential campus in small city
- 26 undergraduates

General. Accredited by ABHE. **Degrees:** 2 associate awarded. **Calendar:** Semester. **Full-time faculty:** 3 total.

Basis for selection. Satisfactory evidence of Christian commitment to the will of God, 2.0 GPA, and 700 SAT/17 ACT required.

2015-2016 Annual costs. Tuition/fees: $8,868. Room/board: $2,576.

Application procedures. Admission: No deadline. $30 fee. **Financial aid:** No deadline.

Academics. Credit/placement by examination: AP, CLEP.

Majors. Theology: Bible, pastoral counseling, women's ministry, youth ministry.

Contact. Phone: (803) 726-3496 Fax: (803) 333-9349
Sannie Wright, Director, Office of Enrollment Management/Registrar, W.L. Bonner Bible College, 4430 Argent Court, Columbia, SC 29203

Winthrop University
Rock Hill, South Carolina   **CB member**
www.winthrop.edu   **CB code: 5910**

- Public 4-year university
- Residential campus in small city
- 4,786 degree-seeking undergraduates: 5% part-time, 68% women, 30% African American, 1% Asian American, 4% Hispanic/Latino, 4% Multiracial, non-Hispanic, 2% international
- 756 degree-seeking graduate students
- 67% of applicants admitted
- SAT or ACT (ACT writing optional) required
- 56% graduate within 6 years

General. Founded in 1886. Regionally accredited. **Degrees:** 909 bachelor's awarded; master's offered. **ROTC:** Army, Air Force. **Location:** 20 miles from Charlotte, NC. **Calendar:** Semester, extensive summer session. **Full-time faculty:** 282 total; 89% have terminal degrees, 15% minority, 54% women. **Part-time faculty:** 273 total; 26% have terminal degrees, 10% minority, 66% women. **Class size:** 46% < 20, 47% 20-39, 5% 40-49, 3% 50-99. **Special facilities:** Nursery laboratory, music conservatory, art galleries, capital markets training and trading center, outdoor development center, Piedmont Wetlands research area.

Freshman class profile. 4,876 applied, 3,272 admitted, 1,090 enrolled.

Mid 50% test scores		Rank in top tenth:	22%
SAT critical reading:	460-570	Return as sophomores:	77%
SAT math:	450-560	Out-of-state:	8%
ACT composite:	20-26	Live on campus:	88%
Rank in top quarter:	51%		

Basis for selection. School achievement record, test scores, counselor recommendations important, school and community activities considered. Essay, interview recommended for all; audition recommended for dance, music, theater programs.

High school preparation. College-preparatory program recommended. 19 units required. Required units include English 4, mathematics 4, social studies 2, history 1, science 3 (laboratory 3), foreign language 2, visual/performing arts 1 and academic electives 1. 1 PE or ROTC required.

2015-2016 Annual costs. Tuition/fees: $14,456; $27,704 out-of-state. Room/board: $8,320. Books/supplies: $1,000. Personal expenses: $1,484.

2014-2015 Financial aid. Need-based: 947 full-time freshmen applied for aid; 822 deemed to have need; 821 received aid. Average need met was 63%. Average scholarship/grant was $9,441; average loan $3,382. 53% of total undergraduate aid awarded as scholarships/grants, 47% as loans/jobs. **Non-need-based:** Awarded to 1,014 full-time undergraduates, including 265 freshmen. Scholarships awarded for academics, art, athletics, leadership, music/drama.

Application procedures. Admission: No deadline. $40 fee, may be waived for applicants with need. Application must be submitted online. Admission notification on a rolling basis beginning on or about 5/1. Must reply by May 1 or within 3 week(s) if notified thereafter. Notification on the 21st of the month from October-May. **Financial aid:** Priority date 3/15; no closing date. FAFSA required. Applicants notified on a rolling basis starting 4/1; must reply within 2 week(s) of notification.

Academics. World Languages and Cultures Learning Center is available to students and instructors for teaching, learning, and practicing foreign languages. **Special study options:** Combined bachelor's/graduate degree, cross-registration, distance learning, double major, dual enrollment of high school students, exchange student, honors, independent study, internships, liberal arts/career combination, student-designed major, study abroad, teacher certification program. **Credit/placement by examination:** AP, CLEP, IB, SAT, ACT, institutional tests. 30 credit hours maximum toward bachelor's degree. **Support services:** Learning center, pre-admission summer program, study skills assistance, tutoring, writing center.

Majors. Biology: General. **Business:** Business admin, e-commerce. **Communications:** Journalism, media studies, public relations. **Computer sciences:** General. **Conservation:** Environmental science, environmental studies. **Education:** Early childhood, elementary, family/consumer sciences, middle, music, physical, special ed. **English:** English lit, technical writing. **Foreign languages:** General. **Health services:** Athletic training, clinical lab science, communication disorders. **History:** General. **Human services:** Social work. **Math:** General. **Parks/recreation:** Exercise sciences, sports admin. **Philosophy/religion:** Philosophy, religion. **Physical sciences:** Chemistry. **Psychology:** General. **Social sciences:** Economics, political science, sociology. **Visual/performing arts:** Art, art history/conservation, dance, dramatic, interior design, music, studio arts. **Work/family studies:** Human nutrition.

Most popular majors. Biology 6%, business/marketing 23%, communications/journalism 7%, education 14%, parks/recreation 7%, psychology 8%, public administration/social services 6%, visual/performing arts 9%.

Technology on campus. 620 workstations in dormitories, library, computer center, student center. Dormitories wired for high-speed internet access and linked to campus network. Commuter students can connect to campus network. Online course registration, online library, helpline, student web hosting, wireless network available.

Student life. Freshman orientation: Mandatory. Preregistration for classes offered. Two-day residential experience held in summer. **Policies:** First and second year students required to live on campus unless living with parents within 50 miles. **Housing:** Guaranteed on-campus for freshmen. Coed dorms, single-sex dorms, apartments, themed housing available. $300 nonrefundable deposit. **Activities:** Bands, campus ministries, choral groups, dance, drama, international student organizations, literary magazine, music ensembles, Model UN, musical theater, opera, radio station, student government, student newspaper, TV station, Baptist Collegiate Ministry, Catholic Campus Ministry, Reformed University Fellowship, Model United Nations, Alpha Delta Pi, Kappa Sigma, Alpha Psi Omega, African Awareness Coalition, Habitat for Humanity, Relay for Life.

Athletics. NCAA. **Intercollegiate:** Baseball M, basketball, cross-country, golf, soccer, softball W, tennis, track and field, volleyball W. **Intramural:** Badminton, basketball, cross-country, equestrian, football (non-tackle), football (tackle) M, golf, racquetball, soccer, softball, swimming, table tennis, tennis, track and field, ultimate frisbee, volleyball. **Team name:** Eagles.

Student services. Adult student services, alcohol/substance abuse counseling, career counseling, student employment services, financial aid counseling, health services, minority student services, personal counseling, placement for graduates, veterans' counselor. **Physically disabled:** Services for visually, hearing impaired.

Contact. E-mail: admissions@winthrop.edu
Phone: (803) 323-2191 Toll-free number: (800) 946-8476
Fax: (803) 323-2137
Debi Barber, Associate Vice President for Admissions, Winthrop University, 701 Oakland Avenue, Rock Hill, SC 29733

Wofford College
Spartanburg, South Carolina
www.wofford.edu

CB member
CB code: 5912

- Private 4-year liberal arts college affiliated with the United Methodist Church
- Residential campus in small city

- 1,596 degree-seeking undergraduates: 2% part-time, 50% women, 8% African American, 3% Asian American, 3% Hispanic/Latino, 3% Multiracial, non-Hispanic, 1% international
- 72% of applicants admitted
- SAT or ACT (ACT writing recommended), application essay required
- 82% graduate within 6 years

General. Founded in 1854. Regionally accredited. **Degrees:** 418 bachelor's awarded. **ROTC:** Army. **Location:** 70 miles from Charlotte, NC; 180 miles from Atlanta. **Calendar:** 4-1-4, limited summer session. **Full-time faculty:** 136 total; 92% have terminal degrees, 10% minority, 41% women. **Part-time faculty:** 19 total; 63% have terminal degrees, 16% minority, 42% women. **Class size:** 52% < 20, 47% 20-39, less than 1% 40-49, less than 1% 50-99. **Special facilities:** Arboretum, environmental studies center, South Carolina Methodist archives, center for global and community engagement.

Freshman class profile. 2,795 applied, 2,009 admitted, 442 enrolled.

Mid 50% test scores			
SAT critical reading:	520-630	GPA 2.0-2.99:	4%
SAT math:	530-630	Rank in top quarter:	72%
SAT writing:	520-620	Rank in top tenth:	42%
ACT composite:	23-29	Return as sophomores:	88%
GPA 3.75 or higher:	68%	Out-of-state:	49%
GPA 3.50-3.74:	13%	Live on campus:	96%
GPA 3.0-3.49:	15%	Fraternities:	38%
		Sororities:	45%

Basis for selection. High school record, including AP courses, most important. Test scores important. School recommendation, leadership, extracurricular activities considered. Interview recommended. **Learning Disabled:** Prospective students with learning disabilities consult with the Dean of Health Services.

High school preparation. College-preparatory program recommended. 20 units recommended. Required and recommended units include English 4, mathematics 4, social studies 3, history 2, science 3 (laboratory 3), foreign language 3, computer science 1 and visual/performing arts 1.

2015-2016 Annual costs. Tuition/fees: $38,705. Room/board: $11,180. Books/supplies: $1,200. Personal expenses: $1,280.

2015-2016 Financial aid. Need-based: 373 full-time freshmen applied for aid; 282 deemed to have need; 281 received aid. Average need met was 90%. Average scholarship/grant was $29,962; average loan $3,371. 84% of total undergraduate aid awarded as scholarships/grants, 16% as loans/jobs. **Non-need-based:** Awarded to 891 full-time undergraduates, including 265 freshmen. Scholarships awarded for academics, art, athletics, job skills, leadership, minority status, music/drama, religious affiliation, ROTC, state residency.

Application procedures. Admission: Closing date 2/1 (postmark date). $35 fee, may be waived for applicants with need. Admission notification by 3/15. Must reply by 5/1. **Financial aid:** Priority date 3/1; no closing date. FAFSA required. Applicants notified on a rolling basis starting 3/15.

Academics. January interim program devoted to internships, foreign travel, independent study, and other nontraditional academic pursuits. **Special study options:** Accelerated study, combined bachelor's/graduate degree, cross-registration, double major, dual enrollment of high school students, independent study, internships, student-designed major, study abroad, teacher certification program, Washington semester. Opportunities for studies abroad, service learning, and environmental studies. **Credit/placement by examination:** AP, CLEP, IB. 30 credit hours maximum toward bachelor's degree. **Support services:** Tutoring, writing center.

Majors. Area/ethnic studies: African-American, Latin American. **Biology:** General. **Business:** Accounting, finance, managerial economics. **Computer sciences:** Computer science. **Conservation:** Environmental studies. **Education:** General. **English:** Creative writing, English lit. **Foreign languages:** Chinese, French, German, Spanish. **History:** General. **Liberal arts:** Humanities. **Math:** General. **Philosophy/religion:** Philosophy, religion. **Physical sciences:** Chemistry, physics. **Psychology:** General. **Social sciences:** Economics, political science, sociology. **Visual/performing arts:** Dramatic, studio arts.

Most popular majors. Biology 14%, business/marketing 25%, English 7%, foreign language 13%, social sciences 12%.

Technology on campus. 156 workstations in library, computer center, student center. Dormitories wired for high-speed internet access and linked to campus network. Commuter students can connect to campus network. Online course registration, online library, helpline, student web hosting, wireless network available.

Student life. Freshman orientation: Mandatory. Preregistration for classes offered. Weekend in summer before the start of classes. **Policies:**

Honor code and honor council. Students not living with immediate family member must secure permission to live off-campus. **Housing:** Guaranteed on-campus for all undergraduates. Coed dorms, apartments, wellness housing available. $500 nonrefundable deposit, deadline 5/1. **Activities:** Bands, campus ministries, choral groups, dance, drama, international student organizations, literary magazine, music ensembles, radio station, student government, student newspaper, Fellowship of Christian Athletes, Baptist Collegiate Ministry, association of multicultural students, Catholic Newman Club, College Republicans, College Democrats, Lion's Club, Rotaract club, Spectrum, Presbyterian student association.

Athletics. NCAA. **Intercollegiate:** Baseball M, basketball, cheerleading W, cross-country, football (tackle) M, golf, rifle, soccer, tennis, track and field, volleyball W. **Intramural:** Basketball, football (non-tackle), racquetball, soccer, softball, tennis, volleyball. **Team name:** Terriers.

Student services. Alcohol/substance abuse counseling, chaplain/spiritual director, career counseling, student employment services, financial aid counseling, health services, minority student services, personal counseling, placement for graduates. **Physically disabled:** Services for visually, speech, hearing impaired.

Contact. E-mail: admission@wofford.edu
Phone: (864) 597-4130 Fax: (864) 597-4147
John Birney, Director of Admission, Wofford College, 429 North Church Street, Spartanburg, SC 29303-3663

South Dakota

Augustana University
Sioux Falls, South Dakota
www.augie.edu
CB member
CB code: 6015

- Private 4-year university affiliated with the Evangelical Lutheran Church in America
- Residential campus in small city
- 1,563 degree-seeking undergraduates: 4% part-time, 60% women, 2% African American, 1% Asian American, 2% Hispanic/Latino, 2% Multiracial, non-Hispanic, 8% international
- 224 degree-seeking graduate students
- 65% of applicants admitted
- SAT or ACT (ACT writing optional), application essay required
- 75% graduate within 6 years; 21% enter graduate study

General. Founded in 1860. Regionally accredited. **Degrees:** 382 bachelor's awarded; master's offered. **ROTC:** Army, Air Force. **Location:** 160 miles from Omaha, 230 miles from Minneapolis-St. Paul. **Calendar:** 4-1-4, limited summer session. **Full-time faculty:** 127 total; 83% have terminal degrees, 8% minority, 45% women. **Part-time faculty:** 44 total; 20% have terminal degrees, 50% women. **Class size:** 45% < 20, 51% 20-39, 3% 40-49, 2% 50-99. **Special facilities:** Western studies museum and archives, archeology lab, prairie garden, ASL laboratory.

Freshman class profile. 1,463 applied, 952 admitted, 367 enrolled.

Mid 50% test scores		Rank in top quarter:	59%
ACT composite:	23-28	Rank in top tenth:	24%
GPA 3.75 or higher:	50%	Return as sophomores:	84%
GPA 3.50-3.74:	24%	Out-of-state:	51%
GPA 3.0-3.49:	20%	Live on campus:	96%
GPA 2.0-2.99:	6%	International:	9%

Basis for selection. 20 ACT (or equivalent SAT), 2.7 GPA, rank in top half of class, high school transcript, recommendation, and writing sample required. Interview recommended for all.

High school preparation. College-preparatory program recommended. 20 units recommended. Recommended units include English 4, mathematics 4, social studies 3, science 4, foreign language 2 and visual/performing arts 3.

2015-2016 Annual costs. Tuition/fees: $29,730. Room/board: $7,404. Books/supplies: $1,000. Personal expenses: $800.

2015-2016 Financial aid. Need-based: 290 full-time freshmen applied for aid; 246 deemed to have need; 246 received aid. Average need met was 100%. Average scholarship/grant was $22,705; average loan $4,806. 74% of total undergraduate aid awarded as scholarships/grants, 26% as loans/jobs. **Non-need-based:** Awarded to 1,678 full-time undergraduates, including 404 freshmen. Scholarships awarded for academics, alumni affiliation, art, athletics, leadership, minority status, music/drama, religious affiliation, ROTC, state residency.

Application procedures. Admission: Priority date 1/15; no deadline. No application fee. Admission notification on a rolling basis beginning on or about 10/1. Must reply by May 1 or within 3 week(s) if notified thereafter. **Financial aid:** Priority date 3/1; no closing date. FAFSA required. Applicants notified on a rolling basis starting 4/1; must reply within 4 week(s) of notification.

Academics. Special study options: Accelerated study, cross-registration, distance learning, double major, dual enrollment of high school students, exchange student, external degree, honors, independent study, internships, liberal arts/career combination, student-designed major, study abroad, teacher certification program, urban semester, Washington semester. Metro-urban studies, January abroad program, Study Australia. Dual degree program in engineering. Service-learning spring break trips. Faculty-led spring break trip abroad. Honor courses in Western Civilization, Chemistry, and Religion. Civitas Honors program for students with ACT 27 and GPA 3.5. **Credit/placement by examination:** AP, CLEP, IB, SAT, ACT, institutional tests. 32 credit hours maximum toward bachelor's degree. **Support services:** Reduced course load, study skills assistance, tutoring, writing center.

Majors. Area/ethnic studies: American. **Biology:** General, biochemistry. **Business:** General, accounting, business admin, communications. **Communications:** Communications/speech/rhetoric, journalism. **Computer sciences:** Computer science. **Education:** Art, biology, elementary, emotionally handicapped, English, French, German, history, learning disabled, mathematics, mentally handicapped, multicultural, music, physical, physically handicapped, physics, psychology, secondary, social studies, Spanish, special ed, speech, speech impaired. **Engineering:** Applied physics. **English:** English lit. **Foreign languages:** General, American Sign Language, French, German, sign language interpretation, Spanish. **Health services:** Athletic training, clinical lab science, clinical lab technology, communication disorders, nursing (RN), predental, premedicine, prepharmacy, prephysical therapy, preveterinary. **History:** General. **Math:** General. **Parks/recreation:** Exercise sciences, health/fitness, sports admin. **Philosophy/religion:** Philosophy, religion. **Physical sciences:** Chemistry, physics. **Psychology:** General. **Social sciences:** Anthropology, economics, political science, sociology. **Theology:** Sacred music. **Visual/performing arts:** Art, dramatic, music.

Most popular majors. Biology 11%, business/marketing 16%, education 15%, foreign language 6%, health sciences 13%, parks/recreation 7%, psychology 6%, social sciences 6%.

Technology on campus. 255 workstations in dormitories, library, computer center. Dormitories wired for high-speed internet access and linked to campus network. Commuter students can connect to campus network. Online course registration, online library, helpline, repair service, wireless network available.

Student life. Freshman orientation: Mandatory. Preregistration for classes offered. Held 3 days before start of fall semester. **Housing:** Guaranteed on-campus for freshmen. Coed dorms, special housing for disabled, apartments, themed housing available. $200 fully refundable deposit, deadline 9/1. Housing is available for students with children. **Activities:** Bands, campus ministries, choral groups, dance, drama, international student organizations, literary magazine, music ensembles, musical theater, student government, student newspaper, symphony orchestra, Lutheran-ELCA congregation, Fellowship of Christian Athletes, Circle K, Augie Democrats, College Republicans, Augie Green, Catholics in Action, Young Life, Colleges Against Cancer.

Athletics. NCAA. **Intercollegiate:** Baseball M, basketball, cheerleading W, cross-country, football (tackle) M, golf, soccer W, softball W, swimming W, tennis, track and field, volleyball W, wrestling M. **Intramural:** Basketball, bowling, football (non-tackle), golf, racquetball, soccer, softball, tennis, triathlon, volleyball, weight lifting. **Team name:** Vikings.

Student services. Adult student services, alcohol/substance abuse counseling, chaplain/spiritual director, career counseling, student employment services, financial aid counseling, health services, minority student services, on-campus daycare, personal counseling, placement for graduates. **Physically disabled:** Services for visually, hearing impaired.

Contact. E-mail: admission@augie.edu
Phone: (605) 274-5516 Toll-free number: (800) 727-2844 ext. 1
Fax: (605) 274-5518
Adam Heinitz, Director of Admission, Augustana University, 2001 South Summit Avenue, Sioux Falls, SD 57197-9990

Black Hills State University
Spearfish, South Dakota
www.bhsu.edu
CB code: 6042

- Public 4-year university
- Commuter campus in large town
- 2,858 degree-seeking undergraduates
- SAT or ACT (ACT writing optional) required

General. Founded in 1883. Regionally accredited. Black Hills State University is the only comprehensive University in western South Dakota. **Degrees:** 487 bachelor's, 46 associate awarded; master's offered. **ROTC:** Army. **Location:** 45 miles from Rapid City. **Calendar:** Semester, extensive summer session. **Full-time faculty:** 149 total. **Part-time faculty:** 80 total. **Class size:** 51% < 20, 44% 20-39, 2% 40-49, 2% 50-99, less than 1% >100.

Basis for selection. Students must meet one of the following admissions requirements: Minimum cumulative GPA of 2.6, minimum composite ACT of 18 or 870 SAT, or class rank in the top 60% of graduating class. Portfolio recommended.

High school preparation. College-preparatory program recommended. 14 units required. Required units include English 4, mathematics 3, social studies 3, science 3 (laboratory 3) and visual/performing arts 1. Math should include algebra or advanced.

2015-2016 Annual costs. Tuition/fees: $8,004; $10,092 out-of-state. Room/board: $6,458. Books/supplies: $1,200. Personal expenses: $2,500.

Financial aid. All financial aid based on need.

Application procedures. Admission: Closing date 7/15. $20 fee. Admission notification on a rolling basis. **Financial aid:** Closing date 2/15. FAFSA required. Applicants notified on a rolling basis starting 5/15; must reply within 3 week(s) of notification.

Academics. Special study options: Distance learning, double major, dual enrollment of high school students, ESL, honors, independent study, internships, liberal arts/career combination, study abroad, teacher certification program. **Credit/placement by examination:** AP, CLEP, SAT, ACT, institutional tests. 32 credit hours maximum toward bachelor's degree. **Support services:** Learning center, remedial instruction, study skills assistance, tutoring, writing center.

Majors. Area/ethnic studies: Native American. **Biology:** General. **Business:** Accounting, business admin, human resources. **Communications:** Media studies. **Education:** Elementary, kindergarten/preschool, mathematics, music, science, special ed. **English:** English lit, rhetoric/composition. **Foreign languages:** Spanish. **History:** General. **Human services:** Community org/advocacy. **Liberal arts:** Arts/sciences. **Math:** General. **Parks/recreation:** Health/fitness, outdoor education, sports admin. **Physical sciences:** General, chemistry. **Psychology:** General. **Social sciences:** General, political science, sociology. **Visual/performing arts:** Art, commercial/advertising art, music.

Most popular majors. Biology 6%, business/marketing 17%, communications/journalism 8%, education 17%, English 6%, parks/recreation 7%, psychology 7%, public administration/social services 10%, social sciences 6%.

Technology on campus. 500 workstations in dormitories, library, student center. Dormitories wired for high-speed internet access and linked to campus network. Commuter students can connect to campus network. Online course registration, online library, helpline, wireless network available.

Student life. Freshman orientation: Available. Preregistration for classes offered. **Housing:** Guaranteed on-campus for freshmen. Coed dorms, single-sex dorms, apartments available. $100 deposit. Married student housing available. **Activities:** Concert band, campus ministries, choral groups, drama, international student organizations, literary magazine, music ensembles, musical theater, opera, radio station, student government, student newspaper, TV station, Native American special services, Inter-Greek council, United Ministry, Veterans club, Young Democrats, Young Republicans.

Athletics. NAIA. **Intercollegiate:** Basketball, cross-country, football (tackle) M, golf W, softball W, track and field, volleyball W. **Intramural:** Archery, badminton, basketball, bowling, golf, skiing, soccer, softball, swimming, table tennis, tennis, volleyball. **Team name:** Yellow Jackets.

Student services. Chaplain/spiritual director, career counseling, student employment services, financial aid counseling, health services, on-campus daycare, personal counseling, placement for graduates, veterans' counselor. **Physically disabled:** Services for visually, speech, hearing impaired.

Contact. E-mail: admissions@bhsu.edu
Phone: (605) 642-6343 Toll-free number: (800) 255-2478
Fax: (605) 642-6022
Beth Oaks, Director of Admissions, Black Hills State University, 1200 University Street, Spearfish, SD 57799

Dakota State University
Madison, South Dakota
www.dsu.edu　　　　　　　　　　　**CB code: 6247**

▶ Public 4-year university
▶ Residential campus in small town
▶ 1,896 degree-seeking undergraduates: 34% part-time, 37% women, 4% African American, 1% Asian American, 4% Hispanic/Latino, 1% Native American, 3% Multi-racial, non-Hispanic, 1% international
▶ 294 degree-seeking graduate students
▶ 81% of applicants admitted
▶ SAT or ACT (ACT writing optional) required
▶ 39% graduate within 6 years

General. Founded in 1881. Regionally accredited. **Degrees:** 242 bachelor's, 48 associate awarded; master's, doctoral offered. **ROTC:** Army, Air Force. **Location:** 45 miles from Sioux Falls. **Calendar:** Semester, limited summer session. **Full-time faculty:** 91 total; 71% have terminal degrees, 10% minority, 35% women. **Part-time faculty:** 50 total; 22% have terminal degrees,

---

36% women. **Class size:** 54% < 20, 43% 20-39, 1% 40-49, 2% 50-99. **Special facilities:** Museum.

Freshman class profile. 911 applied, 740 admitted, 346 enrolled.

Mid 50% test scores			
SAT critical reading:	440-550	Rank in top quarter:	22%
SAT math:	440-580	Rank in top tenth:	6%
ACT composite:	20-25	Return as sophomores:	74%
GPA 3.75 or higher:	15%	Out-of-state:	33%
GPA 3.50-3.74:	16%	Live on campus:	85%
GPA 3.0-3.49:	27%	International:	1%
GPA 2.0-2.99:	36%		

Basis for selection. Top 60% of class, 18 ACT, or 2.6 GPA required. Under-qualified applicants considered for probational acceptance. **Home schooled:** State high school equivalency certificate or minimum ACT required.

High school preparation. College-preparatory program recommended. Recommended units include English 4, mathematics 3, social studies 3, science 3 (laboratory 3) and visual/performing arts 1.

2015-2016 Annual costs. Tuition/fees: $8,754; $10,842 out-of-state. Room/board: $6,060. Books/supplies: $1,000. Personal expenses: $2,785.

2014-2015 Financial aid. Need-based: 247 full-time freshmen applied for aid; 197 deemed to have need; 195 received aid. Average need met was 79%. Average scholarship/grant was $4,377; average loan $3,427. 34% of total undergraduate aid awarded as scholarships/grants, 66% as loans/jobs. **Non-need-based:** Awarded to 548 full-time undergraduates, including 200 freshmen. Scholarships awarded for academics, alumni affiliation, art, athletics, leadership, minority status, music/drama, state residency. **Additional information:** Application deadline for grants and scholarships 3/1. No deadline for loan and job applications.

Application procedures. Admission: No deadline. $20 fee. Admission notification on a rolling basis. **Financial aid:** Priority date 3/1; no closing date. FAFSA required. Applicants notified on a rolling basis starting 4/1; must reply within 2 week(s) of notification.

Academics. Special study options: Cooperative education, cross-registration, distance learning, double major, dual enrollment of high school students, exchange student, honors, independent study, internships, study abroad, teacher certification program. **Credit/placement by examination:** AP, CLEP, IB, SAT, ACT, institutional tests. 16 credit hours maximum toward associate degree, 32 toward bachelor's. **Support services:** Learning center, reduced course load, remedial instruction, study skills assistance, tutoring, writing center.

Majors. Business: Accounting, business admin, finance, marketing. **Computer sciences:** General, computer graphics, information systems, LAN/WAN management, security. **Education:** Biology, business, computer, elementary, English, mathematics, physical. **English:** Technical writing. **Health services:** Health information management, respiratory therapy technology. **Liberal arts:** Arts/sciences. **Math:** Mathematics/statistics. **Parks/recreation:** Exercise sciences. **Physical sciences:** General. **Visual/performing arts:** Game design.

Most popular majors. Business/marketing 12%, computer/information sciences 39%, education 18%, health sciences 6%, liberal arts 7%, parks/recreation 6%, visual/performing arts 7%.

Technology on campus. PC or laptop required. Dormitories wired for high-speed internet access and linked to campus network. Online course registration, helpline, repair service, student web hosting, wireless network available.

Student life. Freshman orientation: Mandatory. Preregistration for classes offered. One-day session held in summer for students and parents. Additional weekend session held before start of classes. **Policies:** Alcohol/drugs/smoking prohibited. 2-year live-in and meal plan requirement, residence halls in 24/7 lockdown for student safety. **Housing:** Guaranteed on-campus for freshmen. Coed dorms, single-sex dorms, apartments available. $50 fully refundable deposit. **Activities:** Pep band, campus ministries, choral groups, drama, international student organizations, literary magazine, Model UN, radio station, student government, student newspaper, InterVarsity Christian Fellowship, Campus Crusade for Christ, Newman Club, diverse student union, international club, Colleges Against Cancer, Enactus, suicide prevention club.

Athletics. NAIA. **Intercollegiate:** Baseball M, basketball, cheerleading, cross-country, football (tackle) M, softball W, track and field, volleyball W. **Intramural:** Basketball, football (non-tackle), softball, table tennis, tennis, volleyball. **Team name:** Trojans.

Student services. Adult student services, alcohol/substance abuse counseling, chaplain/spiritual director, career counseling, student employment services, financial aid counseling, health services, minority student services, personal counseling, placement for graduates, veterans' counselor. **Physically disabled:** Services for visually, speech, hearing impaired.

Contact. E-mail: admissions@dsu.edu
Phone: (605) 256-5139 Toll-free number: (888) 378-9988
Fax: (605) 256-5020
Amy Crissinger, Associate Vice President of Enrollment Management, Dakota State University, 820 North Washington Avenue, Madison, SD 57042

Dakota Wesleyan University
Mitchell, South Dakota
www.dwu.edu   **CB code: 6155**

▸ Private 4-year university and liberal arts college affiliated with the United Methodist Church
▸ Residential campus in large town
▸ 795 degree-seeking undergraduates
▸ SAT or ACT (ACT writing optional) required

General. Founded in 1885. Regionally accredited. **Degrees:** 121 bachelor's, 45 associate awarded; master's offered. **ROTC:** Army. **Location:** 70 miles from Sioux Falls. **Calendar:** Semester, limited summer session. **Full-time faculty:** 50 total; 78% have terminal degrees, 4% minority, 58% women. **Part-time faculty:** 20 total; 70% women. **Class size:** 70% < 20, 27% 20-39, 3% 40-49. **Special facilities:** Observatory, George McGovern Legacy Museum.

Freshman class profile.

GPA 3.75 or higher:	15%	Rank in top quarter:	26%
GPA 3.50-3.74:	14%	Rank in top tenth:	9%
GPA 3.0-3.49:	34%	Out-of-state:	31%
GPA 2.0-2.99:	35%	Live on campus:	80%

Basis for selection. High school record, test scores, school activities considered. Recommendations and personal interview used for marginal students. **Home schooled:** Transcript of courses and grades required. Meeting with admissions counselor and placement testing required when appropriate. **Learning Disabled:** For special assistance, documentation of student's learning disability required.

High school preparation. College-preparatory program recommended. Recommended units include English 4, mathematics 4, social studies 4, history 3, science 3 (laboratory 1) and foreign language 2.

2015-2016 Annual costs. Tuition/fees: $24,800. Room/board: $6,800. Books/supplies: $1,200. Personal expenses: $1,500.

Financial aid. Non-need-based: Scholarships awarded for academics, alumni affiliation, art, athletics, leadership, minority status, music/drama, religious affiliation.

Application procedures. Admission: Closing date 8/25 (receipt date). $25 fee, may be waived for applicants with need. Admission notification on a rolling basis. **Financial aid:** Priority date 4/1; no closing date. FAFSA required. Applicants notified on a rolling basis starting 3/1; must reply within 2 week(s) of notification.

Academics. Special study options: Cross-registration, distance learning, double major, dual enrollment of high school students, exchange student, honors, independent study, internships, student-designed major, study abroad, teacher certification program. **Credit/placement by examination:** AP, CLEP, IB, SAT, ACT, institutional tests. 12 credit hours maximum toward associate degree, 18 toward bachelor's. **Support services:** Learning center, pre-admission summer program, reduced course load, remedial instruction, study skills assistance, tutoring, writing center.

Majors. Biology: General, biochemistry. **Business:** General, accounting. **Communications:** Communications/speech/rhetoric, journalism. **Computer sciences:** Web page design. **Conservation:** Wildlife/wilderness. **Education:** General, biology, elementary, English, history, mathematics, music, physical, special ed. **English:** Creative writing, English lit. **Health services:** Athletic training, nursing (RN). **History:** General. **Liberal arts:** Arts/sciences. **Math:** General. **Parks/recreation:** Sports admin. **Philosophy/religion:** Religion. **Protective services:** Criminal justice. **Psychology:** General. **Visual/performing arts:** Art, dramatic, music.

Most popular majors. Biology 10%, business/marketing 20%, education 13%, health sciences 10%, parks/recreation 10%.

Technology on campus. 85 workstations in dormitories, library, computer center, student center. Dormitories wired for high-speed internet access and linked to campus network. Commuter students can connect to campus

network. Online course registration, online library, helpline, repair service, student web hosting, wireless network available.

Student life. Freshman orientation: Mandatory. Preregistration for classes offered. Two-day program held the weekend before classes begin. **Housing:** Guaranteed on-campus for freshmen. Coed dorms, single-sex dorms, apartments, wellness housing available. $50 fully refundable deposit. Honor housing available for upperclassmen; ADA rooms and apartments available. **Activities:** Bands, campus ministries, choral groups, drama, literary magazine, music ensembles, student government, student newspaper, variety of organizations available.

Athletics. NAIA. **Intercollegiate:** Baseball M, basketball, cheerleading, cross-country, football (tackle) M, golf, soccer, softball W, track and field, volleyball W, wrestling M. **Intramural:** Basketball, softball, volleyball, weight lifting. **Team name:** Tigers.

Student services. Adult student services, alcohol/substance abuse counseling, chaplain/spiritual director, career counseling, services for economically disadvantaged, student employment services, financial aid counseling, health services, minority student services, on-campus daycare, personal counseling, placement for graduates. **Physically disabled:** Services for visually, hearing impaired.

Contact. E-mail: admissions@dwu.edu
Phone: (605) 995-2650 Toll-free number: (800) 333-8506
Fax: (605) 995-2699
Melissa Herr-Valburg, Director of Admissions, Dakota Wesleyan University, 1200 West University Avenue, Mitchell, SD 57301-4398

Mount Marty College
Yankton, South Dakota
www.mtmc.edu   **CB code: 6416**

▸ Private 4-year liberal arts college affiliated with the Roman Catholic Church
▸ Residential campus in large town
▸ 590 degree-seeking undergraduates: 17% part-time, 60% women, 4% African American, 1% Asian American, 8% Hispanic/Latino, 4% Native American, 1% Native Hawaiian/Pacific islander
▸ 143 degree-seeking graduate students
▸ 73% of applicants admitted
▸ SAT or ACT (ACT writing optional) required
▸ 46% graduate within 6 years

General. Founded in 1936. Regionally accredited. **Degrees:** 128 bachelor's, 38 associate awarded; master's offered. **ROTC:** Army. **Location:** 75 miles from Sioux Falls; 60 miles from Sioux City, Iowa. **Calendar:** Semester, limited summer session. **Full-time faculty:** 46 total; 61% have terminal degrees, 2% minority, 56% women. **Part-time faculty:** 11 total; 18% have terminal degrees, 64% women. **Class size:** 82% < 20, 18% 20-39. **Special facilities:** Botanical laboratory.

Freshman class profile. 408 applied, 296 admitted, 112 enrolled.

Mid 50% test scores		Rank in top quarter:	45%
ACT composite:	19-25	Rank in top tenth:	16%
GPA 3.75 or higher:	42%	Return as sophomores:	69%
GPA 3.50-3.74:	20%	Out-of-state:	41%
GPA 3.0-3.49:	19%	Live on campus:	88%
GPA 2.0-2.99:	19%		

Basis for selection. Academic record, test scores, GPA very important. 2.0 GPA and 18 ACT required for consideration. Interview recommended for all; audition required for scholarship recipients, music and theater programs. **Learning Disabled:** Students requesting disability services must submit letter and documentation to support diagnosed disability.

2015-2016 Annual costs. Tuition/fees: $24,306. Room/board: $7,326. Books/supplies: $1,000. Personal expenses: $2,066.

2015-2016 Financial aid. Need-based: 96 full-time freshmen applied for aid; 82 deemed to have need; 82 received aid. Average need met was 88%. Average scholarship/grant was $16,975; average loan $5,115. 65% of total undergraduate aid awarded as scholarships/grants, 35% as loans/jobs. **Non-need-based:** Awarded to 98 full-time undergraduates, including 19 freshmen. Scholarships awarded for academics, athletics, leadership, music/drama, religious affiliation. **Additional information:** Prestige scholarships application deadline 2/1.

Application procedures. Admission: Closing date 8/30 (receipt date). $35 fee, may be waived for applicants with need. Admission notification on a rolling basis. **Financial aid:** Priority date 3/1; no closing date. FAFSA, institutional form required. Applicants notified on a rolling basis starting 3/15; must reply within 2 week(s) of notification.

Academics. Special study options: Accelerated study, distance learning, double major, dual enrollment of high school students, honors, independent study, internships, liberal arts/career combination, student-designed major, teacher certification program. **Credit/placement by examination:** AP, CLEP, IB, SAT, ACT, institutional tests. 88 credit hours maximum toward associate degree, 24 toward bachelor's. **Support services:** Learning center, reduced course load, remedial instruction, study skills assistance, tutoring, writing center.

Majors. Biology: General. **Business:** Accounting, business admin. **Computer sciences:** General, computer science, information technology. **Education:** General, biology, chemistry, elementary, English, history, mathematics, music, physical, special ed. **English:** English lit. **Health services:** Clinical lab science, nursing (RN), radiologic technology/medical imaging. **History:** General. **Math:** General. **Parks/recreation:** Facilities management. **Philosophy/religion:** Religion. **Physical sciences:** Chemistry. **Protective services:** Criminal justice, forensics. **Psychology:** General. **Social sciences:** General. **Visual/performing arts:** Dramatic, music.

Most popular majors. Business/marketing 17%, education 15%, health sciences 38%, security/protective services 9%.

Technology on campus. 32 workstations in dormitories, library, computer center, student center. Dormitories wired for high-speed internet access and linked to campus network. Commuter students can connect to campus network. Online library, helpline, repair service, wireless network available.

Student life. Freshman orientation: Mandatory. Preregistration for classes offered. Three-day intensive program prior to beginning of fall semester. **Policies:** Alcohol, tobacco and drug-free campus. Unmarried undergraduates under 21 required to live in college housing unless living with family. **Housing:** Guaranteed on-campus for freshmen. Single-sex dorms, special housing for disabled, wellness housing available. $50 partly refundable deposit. **Activities:** Bands, campus ministries, choral groups, drama, literary magazine, music ensembles, musical theater, student government, student newspaper, Habitat for Humanity, education club, nursing club, English club, STEP club, Raising Adam.

Athletics. NAIA. **Intercollegiate:** Baseball M, basketball, cross-country, golf, soccer, softball W, tennis W, track and field, volleyball W. **Intramural:** Basketball, football (non-tackle), volleyball. **Team name:** Lancers.

Student services. Adult student services, alcohol/substance abuse counseling, chaplain/spiritual director, career counseling, student employment services, financial aid counseling, health services, on-campus daycare, personal counseling, placement for graduates, veterans' counselor.

Contact. E-mail: mmcadmit@mtmc.edu
Phone: (855) 686-2789 Toll-free number: (855) 686-2789
Fax: (605) 668-1508
Jill Paulson, Director of Admissions, Mount Marty College, 1105 West Eighth Street, Yankton, SD 57078

National American University: Rapid City
Rapid City, South Dakota
www.national.edu   CB code: 6464

- For-profit 4-year business and technical college
- Commuter campus in small city
- 1,479 undergraduates

General. Founded in 1941. Regionally accredited. **Degrees:** 96 bachelor's, 78 associate awarded; master's offered. **ROTC:** Army. **Location:** 400 miles from Denver. **Calendar:** Quarter, extensive summer session. **Full-time faculty:** 5 total. **Part-time faculty:** 225 total. **Special facilities:** Animal health laboratories, nursing facility.

Basis for selection. Open admission, but selective for some programs. All students required to complete university assessment testing prior to enrollment. Interview recommended for all. **Home schooled:** Completion of GED or accredited high school required.

2015-2016 Annual costs. Tuition/fees: $15,750. Books/supplies: $1,350. **Additional information:** Additional fees may apply.

Financial aid. All financial aid based on need.

Application procedures. Admission: No deadline. No application fee. Admission notification on a rolling basis. **Financial aid:** No deadline. FAFSA, institutional form required. Applicants notified on a rolling basis; must reply within 4 week(s) of notification.

Academics. Management program for students with associate degree in health or technical fields who desire to continue education in management. **Special study options:** Accelerated study, combined bachelor's/graduate degree, cooperative education, distance learning, independent study, internships, liberal arts/career combination. **Credit/placement by examination:** AP, CLEP, IB, institutional tests. **Support services:** Learning center, reduced course load, remedial instruction, tutoring.

Majors. Business: Accounting, accounting/business management, business admin, human resources, management information systems, marketing, personal/financial services, tourism/travel. **Computer sciences:** General, information technology, LAN/WAN management, networking, programming, security, system admin, systems analysis, web page design, webmaster. **Health services:** Facilities admin, geriatric nursing. **Protective services:** Police science.

Technology on campus. 20 workstations in library, computer center. Online library, helpline, wireless network available.

Student life. Freshman orientation: Available. Preregistration for classes offered. **Activities:** Student government, student newspaper.

Athletics. Team name: Mavericks.

Student services. Career counseling, student employment services, financial aid counseling, personal counseling, placement for graduates, veterans' counselor.

Contact. E-mail: rcadmissions@national.edu
Phone: (605) 394-4800 Toll-free number: (800) 209-0490
Fax: (605) 394-4871
Darlene Poste, Director of Admissions, National American University: Rapid City, 5301 S. Hwy 16, Rapid City, SD 57701

Northern State University
Aberdeen, South Dakota
www.northern.edu   CB code: 6487

- Public 4-year university and liberal arts college
- Residential campus in large town
- 1,693 degree-seeking undergraduates
- 530 graduate students
- SAT or ACT (ACT writing optional) required

General. Founded in 1901. Regionally accredited. Technology proficiency certification available for all degree programs. Emphasis on distance delivery technology in all degree programs, especially in teacher preparation. **Degrees:** 290 bachelor's, 21 associate awarded; master's offered. **Location:** 285 miles from Minneapolis-St. Paul. **Calendar:** Semester, limited summer session. **Full-time faculty:** 90 total; 86% have terminal degrees, 8% minority, 37% women. **Part-time faculty:** 79 total; 9% minority, 65% women. **Class size:** 54% < 20, 40% 20-39, 3% 40-49, 3% 50-99, less than 1% >100. **Special facilities:** E-learning center, center of excellence for international business.

Freshman class profile.

Rank in top quarter:	20%	Out-of-state:	35%
Rank in top tenth:	7%	Live on campus:	80%

Basis for selection. Applicants to 4-year programs should have 2.6 GPA or 18 ACT or rank in top 60% of class. C average required in core courses. Applicants not meeting requirements may apply. Applicants lacking required high school units admitted provisionally. Equivalent work must be completed within 2 years. Interview recommended for borderline applicants; portfolio recommended for art program.

High school preparation. College-preparatory program recommended. 13 units required. Required units include English 4, mathematics 3, social studies 3, science 3 (laboratory 3). Mathematics units must be algebra or above; .5 fine arts required.

2015-2016 Annual costs. Tuition/fees: $7,977; $10,065 out-of-state. Room/board: $7,088. Books/supplies: $1,200. Personal expenses: $3,800.

Financial aid. Non-need-based: Scholarships awarded for academics, art, athletics, leadership, minority status, music/drama.

Application procedures. Admission: No deadline. $20 fee. Admission notification on a rolling basis. **Financial aid:** Priority date 3/1; no closing date. FAFSA required. Applicants notified on a rolling basis starting 4/15; must reply within 2 week(s) of notification.

Academics. Special study options: Accelerated study, cooperative education, cross-registration, distance learning, double major, dual enrollment of high school students, ESL, exchange student, honors, independent study, internships, liberal arts/career combination, student-designed major, study abroad, teacher certification program. International Business; E-Learning Certification. **Credit/placement by examination:** AP, CLEP, IB, SAT, ACT, institutional tests. 32 credit hours maximum toward bachelor's degree. **Support services:** Learning center, pre-admission summer program, reduced course load, remedial instruction, study skills assistance, tutoring, writing center.

Majors. **Biology:** General, ecology. **Business:** General, accounting, banking/financial services, business admin, finance, international, management information systems, marketing, office/clerical. **Communications:** Communications/speech/rhetoric. **Computer sciences:** General. **Education:** General, art, business, early childhood, elementary, English, foreign languages, history, mathematics, multi-level teacher, music, physical, science, social science, special ed, speech. **English:** English lit, rhetoric/composition. **Foreign languages:** French, German, Spanish. **Health services:** Clinical lab science. **History:** General. **Human services:** Community org/advocacy, social work. **Math:** General. **Parks/recreation:** Health/fitness, sports admin. **Physical sciences:** Chemistry. **Psychology:** General. **Social sciences:** Criminology, economics, political science, sociology. **Visual/performing arts:** Art, music, musical theater.

Most popular majors. Biology 10%, business/marketing 33%, education 20%, social sciences 10%, visual/performing arts 8%.

Technology on campus. 135 workstations in dormitories, library, computer center, student center. Dormitories wired for high-speed internet access and linked to campus network. Commuter students can connect to campus network. Online course registration, online library, helpline, repair service, student web hosting, wireless network available.

Student life. **Freshman orientation:** Mandatory. Preregistration for classes offered. **Housing:** Coed dorms, special housing for disabled, apartments available. $50 deposit. **Activities:** Bands, campus ministries, choral groups, dance, drama, international student organizations, literary magazine, music ensembles, musical theater, student government, student newspaper, symphony orchestra, TV station, over 100 student organizations.

Athletics. NCAA. **Intercollegiate:** Baseball M, basketball, cross-country, football (tackle) M, soccer W, softball W, swimming W, track and field, volleyball W, wrestling M. **Intramural:** Basketball, football (non-tackle), racquetball, sand volleyball, soccer, softball, ultimate frisbee, volleyball. **Team name:** Wolves.

Student services. Adult student services, alcohol/substance abuse counseling, chaplain/spiritual director, career counseling, services for economically disadvantaged, student employment services, financial aid counseling, health services, legal services, minority student services, on-campus daycare, personal counseling, placement for graduates, veterans' counselor, women's services. **Physically disabled:** Services for visually, speech, hearing impaired.

Contact. E-mail: admission2@northern.edu
Phone: (605) 626-2544 Toll-free number: (800) 678-5330
Fax: (605) 626-2531
JoEllen Lindner, VP for Student Affairs and Enrollment Mgmnt, Northern State University, 1200 South Jay Street, Aberdeen, SD 57401-7198

Oglala Lakota College
Kyle, South Dakota
www.olc.edu   **CB code: 1430**

▶ Public 4-year liberal arts and teachers college
▶ Commuter campus in small town
▶ 1,319 degree-seeking undergraduates
▶ 104 graduate students

General. Founded in 1971. Regionally accredited. Tribal College and founding member of American Indian Higher Education Consortium. Located on Pine Ridge Indian Reservation. **Degrees:** 57 bachelor's, 76 associate awarded; master's offered. **Location:** 90 miles from Rapid City. **Calendar:** Semester, extensive summer session. **Full-time faculty:** 70 total. **Part-time faculty:** 1 total. **Special facilities:** Oglala Lakota College Historical Center.

Basis for selection. Open admission. Testing for placement.

2015-2016 Annual costs. Tuition/fees: $3,140. Books/supplies: $1,200. Personal expenses: $450. **Additional information:** Tuition listed is nontribal. Tribal tuition is $2,016 a year.

Financial aid. **Additional information:** Deadline for applications for Bureau of Indian Affairs Higher Education Grants is 3/15; applicants notified early summer.

Application procedures. **Admission:** No deadline. $40 fee. Application must be submitted on paper. **Financial aid:** No deadline. Applicants notified on a rolling basis.

Academics. **Special study options:** Teacher certification program. **Credit/placement by examination:** AP, CLEP, institutional tests. 13 credit hours maximum toward bachelor's degree. **Support services:** Reduced course load, remedial instruction, tutoring.

Majors. **Area/ethnic studies:** Native American. **Business:** Accounting, business admin, management information systems. **Computer sciences:** General. **Conservation:** General. **Education:** Elementary. **History:** General. **Human services:** Social work. **Liberal arts:** Arts/sciences. **Social sciences:** Sociology.

Technology on campus. 175 workstations in library, student center. Dormitories wired for high-speed internet access. Wireless network available.

Student life. **Freshman orientation:** Available. Preregistration for classes offered. **Housing:** Coed dorms available. **Activities:** Student government, student newspaper, TV station.

Athletics. **Intercollegiate:** Volleyball W. **Team name:** Brave Hearts.

Student services. Career counseling.

Contact. Phone: (605) 455-6000 Fax: (605) 455-2787
Leslie Mesteth, Registrar, Oglala Lakota College, Box 490, Kyle, SD 57752-0490

Presentation College
Aberdeen, South Dakota
www.presentation.edu   **CB code: 6582**

▶ Private 4-year business and health science college affiliated with the Roman Catholic Church
▶ Commuter campus in large town
▶ 750 undergraduates
▶ SAT or ACT (ACT writing optional) required

General. Founded in 1951. Regionally accredited. **Degrees:** 96 bachelor's, 8 associate awarded. **Location:** 200 miles from Sioux Falls, 280 miles from Minneapolis-St. Paul. **Calendar:** Semester, extensive summer session. **Full-time faculty:** 47 total. **Part-time faculty:** 27 total.

Freshman class profile.

GPA 3.75 or higher:	18%	GPA 2.0-2.99:	33%
GPA 3.50-3.74:	10%	Out-of-state:	19%
GPA 3.0-3.49:	29%	Live on campus:	90%

Basis for selection. GPA very important, followed by rigor of secondary school record and test scores. 18 ACT or 860 SAT (exclusive of Writing) required. ACT required for radiologic technology applicants. COMPASS assessment used for math placement. **Home schooled:** Official transcript from local schooling guild, detailed course descriptions, list of textbooks, and letter of academic recommendation from primary educator required.

High school preparation. 16 units recommended. Recommended units include English 4, mathematics 3, social studies 2 and science 2. CPR certificate required of nursing and allied health applicants.

2015-2016 Annual costs. Tuition/fees: $17,990. Room/board: $8,690. Books/supplies: $1,300. Personal expenses: $620.

Application procedures. **Admission:** Priority date 4/1; deadline 9/1 (receipt date). $25 fee. Admission notification on a rolling basis. **Financial aid:** Priority date 4/1; no closing date. FAFSA required. Applicants notified on a rolling basis starting 5/1; must reply within 2 week(s) of notification.

Academics. **Special study options:** Distance learning, double major, dual enrollment of high school students, external degree, internships, liberal arts/career combination. **Credit/placement by examination:** AP, CLEP, ACT, institutional tests. 15 credit hours maximum toward associate degree, 30 toward bachelor's. **Support services:** Learning center, reduced course load, remedial instruction, study skills assistance, tutoring.

Majors. **Business:** Business admin. **Communications:** Communications/speech/rhetoric. **Health services:** Health care admin, medical radiologic technology/radiation therapy, nursing (RN). **Human services:** Social work. **Parks/recreation:** General.

Technology on campus. 180 workstations in dormitories, library, computer center. Dormitories wired for high-speed internet access and linked to campus network.

Student life. Freshman orientation: Mandatory. Preregistration for classes offered. **Housing:** Coed dorms available. $250 deposit, deadline 7/15. **Activities:** Drama, student government, student newspaper, Native American club.

Athletics. NAIA. **Intercollegiate:** Baseball M, basketball, cross-country, golf, soccer, softball W, volleyball W. **Intramural:** Basketball, volleyball W. **Team name:** Saints.

Student services. Adult student services, career counseling, student employment services, health services, personal counseling, placement for graduates, veterans' counselor.

Contact. E-mail: admit@presentation.edu
Phone: (605) 229-8492 Toll-free number: (800) 437-6060
Fax: (605) 229-8425
JoEllen Lindner, Vice President for Enrollment and Student Retention Services, Presentation College, 1500 North Main Street, Aberdeen, SD 57401

Sinte Gleska University
Mission, South Dakota
www.sintegleska.edu   CB code: 7328

- Public 4-year university and liberal arts college
- Commuter campus in rural community
- 690 undergraduates

General. Founded in 1970. Regionally accredited. College tribally controlled and charted by Rosebud Sicangu Lakota Tribe (Sioux). **Degrees:** 26 bachelor's, 29 associate awarded; master's offered. **Location:** 90 miles from Pierre, 240 miles from Sioux Falls. **Calendar:** Semester, limited summer session. **Full-time faculty:** 43 total. **Part-time faculty:** 17 total.

Basis for selection. Open admission.

2015-2016 Annual costs. Tuition/fees: $3,640. Books/supplies: $500. Personal expenses: $500.

Application procedures. Admission: No deadline. $74 fee. Admission notification on a rolling basis. **Financial aid:** No deadline. FAFSA required.

Academics. One of 18 colleges with membership in American Indian Higher Education Consortium. **Special study options:** Double major, dual enrollment of high school students, independent study, internships. **Credit/placement by examination:** AP, CLEP. **Support services:** Learning center, reduced course load, remedial instruction, tutoring.

Majors. Business: Business admin, hospitality/recreation. **Computer sciences:** Computer science. **Education:** General, elementary, special ed. **Social sciences:** General.

Technology on campus. 30 workstations in library, computer center.

Student life. Activities: Student government.

Athletics. Intramural: Basketball, football (tackle) M, softball, volleyball.

Student services. Adult student services, career counseling, personal counseling, veterans' counselor.

Contact. Phone: (605) 747-2263 Fax: (605) 747-4258
Jack Herman, Registrar, Sinte Gleska University, Box 105, Mission, SD 57555

South Dakota School of Mines and Technology
Rapid City, South Dakota
www.sdsmt.edu   CB code: 6652

- Public 4-year university
- Commuter campus in small city
- 2,359 degree-seeking undergraduates: 13% part-time, 20% women, 2% African American, 1% Asian American, 4% Hispanic/Latino, 2% Native American, 4% Multi-racial, non-Hispanic, 2% international
- 343 degree-seeking graduate students
- 84% of applicants admitted

- SAT or ACT (ACT writing optional) required
- 51% graduate within 6 years; 23% enter graduate study

General. Founded in 1885. Regionally accredited. **Degrees:** 291 bachelor's, 1 associate awarded; master's, doctoral offered. **ROTC:** Army. **Location:** 222 miles from Cheyenne, WY. **Calendar:** Semester, limited summer session. **Full-time faculty:** 149 total; 91% have terminal degrees, 17% minority, 25% women. **Part-time faculty:** 26 total; 19% have terminal degrees, 4% minority, 46% women. **Class size:** 28% < 20, 56% 20-39, 8% 40-49, 6% 50-99, 1% >100. **Special facilities:** Geology/paleontology museum, engineering/mining experiment station, atmospheric science institute, CAMP-center for advanced manufacturing and production, advanced materials processing and joining lab, analytical characterization and testing laboratory, additive manufacturing laboratory, center for accelerated applications at the nanoscale, center for bioenergy, paleontology building.

Freshman class profile. 1,479 applied, 1,246 admitted, 467 enrolled.

Mid 50% test scores		Rank in top tenth:	23%
SAT critical reading:	500-630	End year in good standing:	80%
SAT math:	550-670	Return as sophomores:	75%
ACT composite:	24-29	Out-of-state:	57%
GPA 3.75 or higher:	38%	Live on campus:	90%
GPA 3.50-3.74:	22%	International:	2%
GPA 3.0-3.49:	26%	Fraternities:	38%
GPA 2.0-2.99:	14%	Sororities:	42%
Rank in top quarter:	51%		

Basis for selection. Test scores, GPA or class rank very important. ACT and/or COMPASS used for placement. **Home schooled:** 225 GED with 40 on each test (paper based) or 2250 GED with 410 on each test (computer based) may be submitted in place of SAT/ACT.

High school preparation. College-preparatory program recommended. 18.5 units required. Required units include English 4, mathematics 4, social studies 3, science 4 (laboratory 3), foreign language 2, computer science .5 and visual/performing arts 1. 1 unit of fine arts is art, theatre or music appreciation, analysis, or performance.

2015-2016 Annual costs. Tuition/fees: $8,763; $11,823 out-of-state. Room/board: $7,300. Books/supplies: $2,000. Personal expenses: $1,800.

2014-2015 Financial aid. Need-based: 570 full-time freshmen applied for aid; 340 deemed to have need; 340 received aid. Average need met was 76%. Average scholarship/grant was $4,526; average loan $3,612. 33% of total undergraduate aid awarded as scholarships/grants, 67% as loans/jobs. **Non-need-based:** Awarded to 845 full-time undergraduates, including 364 freshmen. Scholarships awarded for academics, athletics, leadership, minority status, ROTC. **Additional information:** Closing date for scholarship applications 2/1.

Application procedures. Admission: No deadline. $20 fee. Admission notification on a rolling basis beginning on or about 11/1. High school students may be enrolled fulltime but as special (non-degree seeking) students prior to high school graduation. **Financial aid:** No deadline. FAFSA required. Applicants notified on a rolling basis starting 4/15; must reply within 3 week(s) of notification.

Academics. Undergraduate teams compete in solar vehicle, ChemE Car, unmanned aero vehicle, SAE aero design, ASCE concrete canoe and bridge, SAE Formula SAE, SAE Mini Baja, ASME human-powered vehicle, SAE clean snowmobile challenge and SAMPE Composites national competitions. Site of 2 Research Experience for undergraduates programs funded by National Science Foundation. **Special study options:** Cooperative education, cross-registration, distance learning, dual enrollment of high school students, ESL, independent study, internships, study abroad. **Credit/placement by examination:** AP, CLEP, IB, SAT, ACT, institutional tests. Credits obtained through validation other than nationally recognized exams are limited to 32 credit hours for bachelor's degrees and 16 credit hours for associate degrees. No limit to credits earned through nationally recognized exams such as CLEP, AP, or DANTES. **Support services:** Learning center, reduced course load, remedial instruction, study skills assistance, tutoring.

Majors. Computer sciences: Computer science. **Engineering:** Chemical, civil, computer, electrical, environmental, geological, industrial, mechanical, metallurgical, mining. **Math:** General. **Physical sciences:** Chemistry, geology, physics.

Most popular majors. Computer/information sciences 7%, engineering/engineering technologies 78%, physical sciences 9%.

Technology on campus. PC or laptop required. 210 workstations in dormitories, student center. Dormitories wired for high-speed internet access and linked to campus network. Commuter students can connect to campus network. Online course registration, online library, helpline, repair service, student web hosting, wireless network available.

Student life. Freshman orientation: Available. Preregistration for classes offered. Held in April and May. Adventure weekends for various groups in summer. **Policies:** Dorm residents required to purchase meal plan each semester. **Housing:** Guaranteed on-campus for freshmen. Coed dorms, special housing for disabled, apartments, fraternity/sorority housing, wellness housing available. $100 fully refundable deposit, deadline 8/15. College-owned apartments can be rented by single students, groups of students and married students with families. **Activities:** Bands, campus ministries, choral groups, dance, drama, international student organizations, music ensembles, radio station, student government, student newspaper, Circle K, College Republicans, College Democrats, American Indian Science & Engineering Society, Habitat for Humanity, Muslim student association, Intervarsity Christian Fellowship.

Athletics. NCAA. **Intercollegiate:** Basketball, cross-country, football (tackle) M, golf, track and field, volleyball W. **Intramural:** Basketball, golf, racquetball, skiing, softball, swimming, track and field, volleyball. **Team name:** Hardrockers.

Student services. Adult student services, alcohol/substance abuse counseling, chaplain/spiritual director, career counseling, student employment services, financial aid counseling, health services, minority student services, on-campus daycare, personal counseling, placement for graduates, veterans' counselor, women's services. **Physically disabled:** Services for visually, speech, hearing impaired.

Contact. E-mail: admissions@sdsmt.edu
Phone: (605) 394-2414 Toll-free number: (877) 877-6044
Fax: (605) 394-1979
Molly Moore, Associate Provost of Academic Administration, South Dakota School of Mines and Technology, 501 East St. Joseph Street, Rapid City, SD 57701

South Dakota State University
Brookings, South Dakota
www.sdstate.edu   CB code: 6653

- Public 4-year university
- Residential campus in large town
- 9,835 degree-seeking undergraduates: 13% part-time, 52% women, 2% African American, 1% Asian American, 2% Hispanic/Latino, 1% Native American, 2% Multi-racial, non-Hispanic, 4% international
- 1,509 degree-seeking graduate students
- 92% of applicants admitted
- SAT or ACT (ACT writing optional) required
- 58% graduate within 6 years

General. Founded in 1881. Regionally accredited. **Degrees:** 1,910 bachelor's, 45 associate awarded; master's, professional, doctoral offered. **ROTC:** Army, Air Force. **Location:** 50 miles from Sioux Falls. **Calendar:** Semester, limited summer session. **Full-time faculty:** 546 total; 72% have terminal degrees, 13% minority, 46% women. **Part-time faculty:** 144 total; 31% have terminal degrees, 5% minority, 64% women. **Class size:** 32% < 20, 44% 20-39, 9% 40-49, 11% 50-99, 4% >100. **Special facilities:** Water resources institute, agricultural experiment station, biostress laboratory, agricultural heritage museum, animal disease research and diagnostic laboratory, geospatial sciences center of excellence, research park, performing arts center.

Freshman class profile. 5,060 applied, 4,640 admitted, 2,222 enrolled.

Mid 50% test scores			
SAT critical reading:	430-560	GPA 3.0-3.49:	30%
SAT math:	470-600	GPA 2.0-2.99:	22%
ACT composite:	20-26	Rank in top quarter:	36%
GPA 3.75 or higher:	30%	Rank in top tenth:	14%
GPA 3.50-3.74:	17%	Return as sophomores:	76%
		International:	4%

Basis for selection. School achievement record and test scores most important. **Home schooled:** Transcript of courses and grades required. Must be at least 18 years of age, or the class in which the student would have been a member must have graduated from high school. The applicant must obtain the following test scores or higher on the ACT: 18 comp, 18 English, 20 math, 17 reading and 17 science reasoning.

High school preparation. College-preparatory program required. 14 units required. Required units include English 4, mathematics 3, social studies 3, science 3 (laboratory 3) and visual/performing arts 1.

2015-2016 Annual costs. Tuition/fees: $8,172; $10,343 out-of-state. Room/board: $7,462. Books/supplies: $1,500. Personal expenses: $4,833.

2014-2015 Financial aid. Need-based: 1,806 full-time freshmen applied for aid; 1,366 deemed to have need; 1,360 received aid. Average need met

was 44%. Average scholarship/grant was $3,585; average loan $3,493. 31% of total undergraduate aid awarded as scholarships/grants, 69% as loans/jobs. **Non-need-based:** Awarded to 2,568 full-time undergraduates, including 782 freshmen. Scholarships awarded for academics, alumni affiliation, art, athletics, leadership, minority status, music/drama, state residency.

Application procedures. Admission: Closing date 9/5. $20 fee. Admission notification on a rolling basis. **Financial aid:** Priority date 3/10; no closing date. FAFSA required. Applicants notified on a rolling basis starting 4/1; must reply within 3 week(s) of notification.

Academics. Evening, weekend and other condensed degree-awarding classes available. **Special study options:** Accelerated study, combined bachelor's/graduate degree, cooperative education, cross-registration, distance learning, double major, dual enrollment of high school students, ESL, exchange student, honors, independent study, internships, study abroad, teacher certification program. **Credit/placement by examination:** AP, CLEP, IB, SAT, ACT, institutional tests. 15 credit hours maximum toward associate degree, 30 toward bachelor's. **Support services:** Pre-admission summer program, reduced course load, remedial instruction, study skills assistance, tutoring, writing center.

Majors. Architecture: Architecture. **Area/ethnic studies:** Native American. **Biology:** General, biochemistry, biotechnology, microbiology. **Business:** Entrepreneurial studies, hospitality admin, hotel/motel admin, operations. **Communications:** Advertising, communications/speech/rhetoric, journalism. **Computer sciences:** General. **Conservation:** Environmental science, management/policy, wildlife/wilderness. **Education:** Agricultural, art, early childhood, family/consumer sciences, health, music. **Engineering:** Agricultural, civil, electrical, mechanical. **English:** English lit. **Foreign languages:** French, German, Spanish. **Health services:** Athletic training, clinical lab science, dietetics, nursing (RN), pharmaceutical sciences. **History:** General. **Liberal arts:** Arts/sciences. **Math:** General. **Parks/recreation:** Facilities management, health/fitness. **Physical sciences:** Chemistry, physics. **Psychology:** General. **Social sciences:** Economics, geography, GIS/cartography, political science, sociology. **Visual/performing arts:** General, dramatic, graphic design, interior design, music, studio arts. **Work/family studies:** Apparel marketing, clothing/textiles, consumer economics, family resources, family studies, food/nutrition.

Most popular majors. Agriculture 15%, biology 6%, engineering/engineering technologies 8%, family/consumer sciences 6%, health sciences 24%, social sciences 7%.

Technology on campus. 120 workstations in dormitories, library, student center. Dormitories wired for high-speed internet access and linked to campus network. Commuter students can connect to campus network. Online course registration, online library, helpline, repair service, wireless network available.

Student life. Freshman orientation: Available, $38 fee. Preregistration for classes offered. Two-day sessions held primarily in June includes students and parents. **Policies:** Students out of high school for less than 2 years required to live in campus housing for 2 years unless living with family. **Housing:** Guaranteed on-campus for freshmen. Coed dorms, special housing for disabled, apartments, fraternity/sorority housing, themed housing, wellness housing available. $75 fully refundable deposit. Pets allowed in dorm rooms. Limited single rooms with optional meal plan available for upperclassmen. Pet permitted. **Activities:** Bands, campus ministries, choral groups, dance, drama, international student organizations, literary magazine, music ensembles, Model UN, musical theater, radio station, student government, student newspaper, symphony orchestra, university program council, residence hall association, students' association, Navigators, College Republicans, Young Democrats, Gay/Straight Alliance, Block and Bridle club, Greek Council.

Athletics. NCAA. **Intercollegiate:** Baseball M, basketball, cross-country, diving, equestrian W, football (tackle) M, golf, soccer W, softball W, swimming, tennis, track and field, volleyball W, wrestling M. **Intramural:** Badminton, basketball, cross-country, diving, football (non-tackle), golf, soccer W, softball, swimming, table tennis, tennis, track and field, ultimate frisbee, volleyball, wrestling M. **Team name:** Jackrabbits.

Student services. Alcohol/substance abuse counseling, career counseling, student employment services, financial aid counseling, health services, legal services, minority student services, personal counseling, placement for graduates, veterans' counselor, women's services. **Physically disabled:** Services for visually, hearing impaired.

Contact. E-mail: sdsu.admissions@sdstate.edu
Phone: (605) 688-4121 Toll-free number: (800) 952-3541
Fax: (605) 688-6891
Tracy Welsh, Director of Admissions and High School Relations, South Dakota State University, Box 2201 SAD 200, Brookings, SD 57007-0649

University of Sioux Falls
Sioux Falls, South Dakota
www.usiouxfalls.edu   CB code: 6651

▶ Private 4-year university and liberal arts college affiliated with the American Baptist Churches in the USA
▶ Residential campus in small city
▶ 951 degree-seeking undergraduates
▶ 311 graduate students
▶ SAT or ACT (ACT writing optional) required

General. Founded in 1883. Regionally accredited. **Degrees:** 230 bachelor's, 13 associate awarded; master's offered. **ROTC:** Air Force. **Location:** 180 miles from Omaha, 236 miles from Minneapolis. **Calendar:** 4-1-4, limited summer session. **Full-time faculty:** 63 total; 70% have terminal degrees, 2% minority, 48% women. **Part-time faculty:** 121 total; 2% minority, 64% women. **Class size:** 60% < 20, 38% 20-39, 1% 40-49, less than 1% 50-99. **Special facilities:** Rotating sculpture collection.

Freshman class profile.

Out-of-state: 35%   Live on campus: 95%

Basis for selection. ACT/SAT and GPA important. Audition required for music, theater programs; portfolio recommended for art program. **Home schooled:** Statement describing home school structure and mission, transcript of courses and grades required.

High school preparation. College-preparatory program recommended. Recommended units include English 4, mathematics 3, social studies 2, science 3 (laboratory 3) and foreign language 2.

2015-2016 Annual costs. Tuition/fees: $26,240. Room/board: $6,900. Books/supplies: $900.

Financial aid. **Non-need-based:** Scholarships awarded for academics, art, athletics, music/drama.

Application procedures. Admission: Priority date 2/1; deadline 9/1 (receipt date). $25 fee, may be waived for applicants with need, free for online applicants. Admission notification on a rolling basis. **Financial aid:** Priority date 3/1; no closing date. FAFSA required. Applicants notified on a rolling basis starting 3/1; must reply within 2 week(s) of notification.

Academics. Degree completion program offered for adults 25 and older with 64 hours previous college education. **Special study options:** Accelerated study, cross-registration, distance learning, double major, dual enrollment of high school students, honors, independent study, internships, liberal arts/career combination, student-designed major, study abroad, teacher certification program, Washington semester. **Credit/placement by examination:** AP, CLEP, IB, SAT, ACT, institutional tests. 16 credit hours maximum toward bachelor's degree. **Support services:** Learning center, reduced course load, study skills assistance, tutoring, writing center.

Majors. Biology: General. **Business:** Accounting, business admin, hospitality admin, organizational behavior. **Communications:** Journalism. **Computer sciences:** General, computer science. **Education:** Art, elementary, English, health, multi-level teacher, music. **English:** English lit, rhetoric/composition. **Foreign languages:** Spanish. **Health services:** Nursing (RN). **History:** General. **Human services:** Social work. **Liberal arts:** Arts/sciences. **Math:** General, applied. **Parks/recreation:** Exercise sciences. **Philosophy/religion:** Religion. **Physical sciences:** Chemistry. **Protective services:** Criminal justice, police science. **Psychology:** General. **Social sciences:** General, political science, sociology. **Theology:** Theology. **Visual/performing arts:** Art, dramatic, music.

Most popular majors. Business/marketing 35%, education 12%, health sciences 6%, parks/recreation 7%, psychology 9%.

Technology on campus. 175 workstations in dormitories, library, computer center, student center. Dormitories wired for high-speed internet access and linked to campus network. Commuter students can connect to campus network. Online course registration, online library, helpline, repair service, student web hosting, wireless network available.

Student life. Freshman orientation: Available. Preregistration for classes offered. Held 2 days immediately preceding fall semester. **Policies:** No alcohol at university-sponsored events. Freshmen and sophomores required to live in college housing unless over 20 years of age or given permission by director of residence life. **Housing:** Guaranteed on-campus for all undergraduates. Coed dorms, single-sex dorms, apartments available. $50 fully refundable deposit, deadline 9/1. **Activities:** Bands, campus ministries, choral groups, dance, drama, film society, international student organizations, music ensembles, Model UN, musical theater, opera, radio station, student government, student newspaper, symphony orchestra, TV station, nontraditional student

association, student volunteer groups, religious organizations, Fellowship of Christian Athletes, Campus Crusade For Christ, Young Life.

Athletics. NCAA. **Intercollegiate:** Baseball M, basketball, cross-country, football (tackle) M, golf, soccer W, softball W, tennis W, track and field, volleyball W. **Intramural:** Basketball, golf, ice hockey, soccer, softball, table tennis, tennis, ultimate frisbee, volleyball. **Team name:** Cougars.

Student services. Adult student services, alcohol/substance abuse counseling, chaplain/spiritual director, career counseling, student employment services, financial aid counseling, health services, personal counseling, placement for graduates, veterans' counselor, women's services. **Physically disabled:** Services for visually, speech, hearing impaired.

Contact. E-mail: admissions@usiouxfalls.edu
Phone: (605) 331-6600 Toll-free number: (800) 888-1047
Fax: (605) 331-6615
Aimee Vander Feen, Director of Admissions, University of Sioux Falls, 1101 West 22nd Street, Sioux Falls, SD 57105-1699

University of South Dakota
Vermillion, South Dakota
www.usd.edu   CB member   CB code: 6881

▶ Public 4-year university
▶ Residential campus in large town
▶ 6,331 degree-seeking undergraduates
▶ 2,520 graduate students
▶ SAT or ACT (ACT writing optional), interview required

General. Founded in 1862. Regionally accredited. **Degrees:** 1,202 bachelor's, 121 associate awarded; master's, professional, doctoral offered. **ROTC:** Army. **Location:** 55 miles from Sioux Falls; 35 miles from Sioux City, Iowa. **Calendar:** Semester, extensive summer session. **Full-time faculty:** 453 total; 83% have terminal degrees, 15% minority, 49% women. **Part-time faculty:** 142 total; 8% have terminal degrees, 4% minority, 55% women. **Class size:** 52% < 20, 36% 20-39, 6% 40-49, 4% 50-99, 2% >100. **Special facilities:** Center for instructional design and delivery, center for disabilities, governmental research bureau, state data center, federal technical procurement center, geological survey, archaeology lab, speech and hearing center, disaster mental health institute, national music museum.

Freshman class profile.

GPA 3.75 or higher:	27%	Rank in top tenth:	15%
GPA 3.50-3.74:	18%	Out-of-state:	38%
GPA 3.0-3.49:	31%	Live on campus:	90%
GPA 2.0-2.99:	22%	Fraternities:	32%
Rank in top quarter:	37%	Sororities:	18%

Basis for selection. Admission in good standing granted with 2.0 GPA in required courses or 2.6 overall, rank in top 60% of class, or 22 ACT. Interview recommended for dental hygiene, nursing, physician assistant programs; audition recommended for music, theater programs; portfolio recommended for art program. **Home schooled:** State high school equivalency certificate required.

High school preparation. College-preparatory program recommended. 14 units required; 18 recommended. Required and recommended units include English 4, mathematics 3-4, social studies 3, science 3-4 (laboratory 3) and foreign language 2. 1 fine arts required.

2015-2016 Annual costs. Tuition/fees: $8,457; $11,337 out-of-state. Room/board: $7,605. Books/supplies: $1,100. Personal expenses: $2,604.

Financial aid. **Non-need-based:** Scholarships awarded for academics, art, athletics, leadership, minority status, music/drama, ROTC.

Application procedures. Admission: Priority date 9/1; no deadline. $20 fee. Admission notification on a rolling basis beginning on or about 9/20. 2/15 closing date for dental hygiene and nursing programs. **Financial aid:** Priority date 3/15; no closing date. FAFSA required. Applicants notified on a rolling basis starting 5/5.

Academics. Special study options: Accelerated study, combined bachelor's/graduate degree, cross-registration, distance learning, double major, dual enrollment of high school students, ESL, exchange student, external degree, honors, independent study, internships, liberal arts/career combination, student-designed major, study abroad, teacher certification program. **Credit/placement by examination:** AP, CLEP, institutional tests. 15 credit hours maximum toward associate degree, 30 toward bachelor's. **Support services:** Learning center, pre-admission summer program, reduced course load, remedial instruction, study skills assistance, tutoring, writing center.

Honors college/program. Honors program open to students in all majors who displayed potential for honors work in high school through good grades, college preparatory curriculum, high ACT scores, and participation in school and community activities.

Majors. **Area/ethnic studies:** Native American. **Biology:** General, biomedical sciences. **Business:** Accounting, business admin, finance, managerial economics. **Communications:** Communications/speech/rhetoric, journalism, media studies. **Computer sciences:** General. **Education:** Biology, chemistry, drama/dance, early childhood, elementary, English, foreign languages, French, German, history, kindergarten/preschool, mathematics, music, physical, physics, science, social science, Spanish, special ed, speech. **English:** English lit, rhetoric/composition. **Foreign languages:** French, German, Spanish. **Health services:** Communication disorders, dental hygiene, health services admin, nursing (RN), substance abuse counseling. **History:** General. **Human services:** Social work. **Liberal arts:** Arts/sciences. **Math:** General. **Parks/recreation:** General. **Philosophy/religion:** Philosophy. **Physical sciences:** Chemistry, geology, physics. **Protective services:** Criminal justice. **Psychology:** General. **Social sciences:** Anthropology, economics, political science, sociology. **Visual/performing arts:** Art, dramatic, music, music performance, studio arts, studio arts management.

Most popular majors. Business/marketing 12%, communications/journalism 6%, education 12%, health sciences 27%, psychology 8%, social sciences 6%.

Technology on campus. 1,212 workstations in dormitories, library, computer center, student center. Dormitories wired for high-speed internet access and linked to campus network. Commuter students can connect to campus network. Online course registration, online library, helpline, repair service, student web hosting, wireless network available.

Student life. **Freshman orientation:** Mandatory. Preregistration for classes offered. **Policies:** Students required to live in residence halls for first 2 years unless living in fraternity/sorority housing or commuting from home. **Housing:** Guaranteed on-campus for freshmen. Coed dorms, special housing for disabled, apartments, fraternity/sorority housing, wellness housing available. $100 partly refundable deposit, deadline 9/1. Apartments available for students with dependent children. **Activities:** Bands, campus ministries, choral groups, dance, drama, international student organizations, literary magazine, music ensembles, musical theater, opera, radio station, student government, student newspaper, symphony orchestra, TV station, Young Democrats, College Republicans, Campus Crusade for Christ, Chinese student association, gay/lesbian/bisexual alliance, Habitat for Humanity, nontraditional student association, political science league.

Athletics. NCAA. **Intercollegiate:** Basketball, cross-country, diving, football (tackle) M, golf, soccer W, softball W, swimming, tennis W, track and field. **Intramural:** Badminton, basketball, bowling, cross-country, football (non-tackle), golf, racquetball, soccer, softball, swimming, table tennis, tennis, track and field, volleyball. **Team name:** Coyotes.

Student services. Adult student services, alcohol/substance abuse counseling, chaplain/spiritual director, career counseling, services for economically disadvantaged, student employment services, financial aid counseling, health services, legal services, minority student services, on-campus daycare, personal counseling, placement for graduates, veterans' counselor. **Physically disabled:** Services for visually, speech, hearing impaired.

Contact. E-mail: admission@usd.edu
Phone: (605) 677-5434 Toll-free number: (877) 269-6837
Fax: (605) 677-6753
Travis Vlasman, Dean of Enrollment, University of South Dakota, 414 East Clark Street, Vermillion, SD 57069-2390

Tennessee

American Baptist College
Nashville, Tennessee
www.abcnash.edu   CB code: 2401

- Private 4-year Bible and liberal arts college affiliated with the Baptist faith
- Commuter campus in large city
- 160 degree-seeking undergraduates
- Application essay required

General. Founded in 1924. Accredited by ABHE. **Degrees:** 21 bachelor's, 4 associate awarded. **Location:** Downtown. **Calendar:** Semester, limited summer session. **Full-time faculty:** 7 total. **Part-time faculty:** 8 total.

Basis for selection. Recommendations, personal essay, religious commitment important. Admissions committee selects applicants best qualified to benefit from opportunities offered by college. **Home schooled:** Transcript of courses and grades, state high school equivalency certificate required.

2015-2016 Annual costs. Tuition/fees: $11,894. Room only: $6,240. Books/supplies: $958.

Application procedures. Admission: Closing date 8/1 (receipt date). $30 fee, may be waived for applicants with need. Admission notification on a rolling basis. **Financial aid:** Priority date 5/1; no closing date. FAFSA required. Applicants notified on a rolling basis; must reply within 2 week(s) of notification.

Academics. All students major in Bible studies or theology. Additional major in business administration optional. **Special study options:** Double major, independent study. **Credit/placement by examination:** AP, CLEP, institutional tests. **Support services:** Learning center, reduced course load, remedial instruction, study skills assistance, tutoring, writing center.

Majors. Area/ethnic studies: African-American. **Business:** Business admin. **Education:** General, history, social science. **Liberal arts:** Arts/sciences. **Social sciences:** General. **Theology:** Bible, pastoral counseling, religious ed, theology.

Technology on campus. 20 workstations in library. Dormitories linked to campus network. Commuter students can connect to campus network. Online course registration, repair service, wireless network available.

Student life. Freshman orientation: Mandatory. Preregistration for classes offered. **Policies:** Religious observance required. **Housing:** Guaranteed on-campus for all undergraduates. Single-sex dorms, apartments available. $125 partly refundable deposit, deadline 8/1. **Activities:** Campus ministries, choral groups, student government, student newspaper.

Student services. Adult student services, financial aid counseling, veterans' counselor.

Contact. E-mail: admissions@abcnash.edu
Phone: (615) 256-1463 Fax: (615) 226-7855
Dee Bomer, Admissions Director, American Baptist College, 1800 Baptist World Center Drive, Nashville, TN 37207

Aquinas College
Nashville, Tennessee   CB member
www.aquinascollege.edu   CB code: 7318

- Private 4-year liberal arts college affiliated with the Roman Catholic Church
- Commuter campus in very large city
- 335 degree-seeking undergraduates
- SAT or ACT (ACT writing optional) required

General. Founded in 1961. Regionally accredited. A Catholic community of learning in the Dominican Tradition with Christ at its center. **Degrees:** 32 bachelor's, 96 associate awarded; master's offered. **Location:** 4 miles from downtown, 195 miles from Knoxville. **Calendar:** Semester, limited

summer session. **Full-time faculty:** 30 total; 47% have terminal degrees, 73% women. **Part-time faculty:** 57 total; 25% have terminal degrees, 70% women. **Class size:** 83% < 20, 9% 20-39, 2% 40-49, 6% 50-99.

Freshman class profile.

GPA 3.75 or higher:	50%	Rank in top quarter:	60%
GPA 3.50-3.74:	32%	Rank in top tenth:	30%
GPA 3.0-3.49:	4%	Out-of-state:	47%
GPA 2.0-2.99:	14%	Live on campus:	53%

Basis for selection. School achievement record, test scores important.

2015-2016 Annual costs. Tuition/fees: $20,550. Room/board: $8,900. Books/supplies: $1,200. Personal expenses: $1,748.

Financial aid. Non-need-based: Scholarships awarded for academics, alumni affiliation, leadership, religious affiliation.

Application procedures. Admission: Priority date 2/15; no deadline. $25 fee, may be waived for applicants with need. Admission notification on a rolling basis. **Financial aid:** Priority date 2/15; no closing date. FAFSA required. Applicants notified on a rolling basis starting 2/15; must reply within 2 week(s) of notification.

Academics. WriteReason Program to ensure that students communicate ideas in writing that are clear, accurate, and effective. **Special study options:** Accelerated study, double major, dual enrollment of high school students, independent study, internships, liberal arts/career combination, teacher certification program. **Credit/placement by examination:** AP, CLEP, SAT, ACT, institutional tests. 30 credit hours maximum toward associate degree, 30 toward bachelor's. **Support services:** Learning center, reduced course load, remedial instruction, study skills assistance, tutoring, writing center.

Majors. Business: Business admin, finance. **Education:** Elementary, English, history. **English:** English lit. **Health services:** Nursing (RN). **History:** General. **Liberal arts:** Humanities. **Philosophy/religion:** Philosophy. **Theology:** Theology.

Most popular majors. Business/marketing 9%, education 39%, health sciences 42%, theological studies 6%.

Technology on campus. 55 workstations in library, computer center, student center. Dormitories wired for high-speed internet access. Commuter students can connect to campus network. Online course registration, online library, helpline available.

Student life. Freshman orientation: Mandatory. Preregistration for classes offered. **Policies:** Drug-free/alcohol-free campus. **Housing:** Single-sex dorms available. $200 nonrefundable deposit, deadline 3/1. **Activities:** Campus ministries, drama, literary magazine, student government, Phi Beta Lambda, Delta Epsilon Sigma, Association of Student Nurses, Association for Supervision and Curriculum Development student chapter, Student Activities Board, Tennessee Intercollegiate State Legislature, Frassati Society, Sigma Beta Delta.

Athletics. Intramural: Sand volleyball, table tennis, tennis. **Team name:** Cavaliers.

Student services. Adult student services, alcohol/substance abuse counseling, chaplain/spiritual director, career counseling, financial aid counseling, personal counseling.

Contact. E-mail: admissions@aquinascollege.edu
Phone: (615) 297-7545 ext. 460 Toll-free number: (800) 649-9956
Fax: (615) 279-3891
Connie Hansom, Director of Admissions, Aquinas College, 4210 Harding Pike, Nashville, TN 37205-2086

Argosy University: Nashville
Nashville, Tennessee
www.argosy.edu/nashville   CB code: 5685

- For-profit 4-year university
- Very large city
- 207 degree-seeking undergraduates

General. Regionally accredited. **Degrees:** 20 bachelor's, 4 associate awarded; master's, professional, doctoral offered. **Calendar:** Differs by program. **Full-time faculty:** 13 total. **Part-time faculty:** 61 total.

Basis for selection. Open admission.

2015-2016 Annual costs. Tuition/fees: $16,842. **Additional information:** College of Health Sciences programs range $450-$575 per credit-hour-hour. Additional program fees may apply. All costs are subject to change.

Application procedures. Admission: Closing date 9/14. $50 fee. **Financial aid:** No deadline.

Academics. Credit/placement by examination: AP, CLEP.

Majors. Business: Business admin. **Liberal arts:** Arts/sciences. **Protective services:** Police science. **Psychology:** General.

Contact. Phone: (615) 525-2800
Erica Bligen, Senior Director of Admissions, Argosy University: Nashville, 100 Centerview Drive, Suite 225, Nashville, TN 37214

Austin Peay State University
Clarksville, Tennessee
CB member
www.apsu.edu
CB code: 1028

- Public 4-year university and liberal arts college
- Commuter campus in small city
- 8,915 degree-seeking undergraduates: 24% part-time, 58% women, 20% African American, 2% Asian American, 6% Hispanic/Latino, 6% Multiracial, non-Hispanic
- 893 degree-seeking graduate students
- 88% of applicants admitted
- 38% graduate within 6 years

General. Founded in 1927. Regionally accredited. **Degrees:** 1,455 bachelor's, 297 associate awarded; master's offered. **ROTC:** Army, Air Force. **Location:** 45 miles from Nashville. **Calendar:** Semester, limited summer session. **Full-time faculty:** 363 total; 12% minority, 50% women. **Part-time faculty:** 234 total; 8% minority, 62% women. **Class size:** 52% < 20, 38% 20-39, 6% 40-49, 4% 50-99, less than 1% >100. **Special facilities:** Observatory, art gallery.

Freshman class profile. 3,605 applied, 3,162 admitted, 1,554 enrolled.

Mid 50% test scores			
SAT critical reading:	490-620	Rank in top quarter:	34%
SAT math:	510-580	Rank in top tenth:	13%
ACT composite:	19-24	Return as sophomores:	71%
GPA 3.75 or higher:	16%	Out-of-state:	9%
GPA 3.50-3.74:	17%	Live on campus:	49%
GPA 3.0-3.49:	36%	Fraternities:	8%
GPA 2.0-2.99:	29%	Sororities:	12%

Basis for selection. Rigor of secondary school record, GPA, and test scores very important. ACT/SAT not required of active duty military. **Home schooled:** Transcript of courses and grades required. The transcript of a home school applicant must be an official copy from an affiliated organization as defined by state law or be accompanied by a certification of registration with the superintendent of the local education agency which the student otherwise would attend.

High school preparation. College-preparatory program required. 14 units required. Required units include English 4, mathematics 3, social studies 1, history 1, science 2 (laboratory 1), foreign language 2 and visual/performing arts 1. Mathematics units should be algebra I and II, 1 geometry or advanced mathematics. Social science units should be 1 social studies, 1 US history. Foreign language units must be in 1 language.

2015-2016 Annual costs. Tuition/fees: $7,801; $23,371 out-of-state. Room/board: $9,550. Books/supplies: $1,550. Personal expenses: $2,000.

2014-2015 Financial aid. Need-based: 1,142 full-time freshmen applied for aid; 959 deemed to have need; 949 received aid. Average scholarship/grant was $6,743; average loan $3,089. 58% of total undergraduate aid awarded as scholarships/grants, 42% as loans/jobs. **Non-need-based:** Awarded to 3,722 full-time undergraduates, including 978 freshmen. Scholarships awarded for academics, art, athletics, leadership, music/drama, ROTC, state residency.

Application procedures. Admission: Closing date 8/3. $15 fee. Admission notification on a rolling basis. **Financial aid:** Priority date 2/3; no closing date. FAFSA required. Applicants notified on a rolling basis starting 4/7.

Academics. Special study options: Accelerated study, cooperative education, distance learning, double major, dual enrollment of high school students, ESL, honors, independent study, internships, study abroad, teacher certification program. Service Members Opportunity College (associate and bachelor's degrees). **Credit/placement by examination:** AP, CLEP, IB, SAT, ACT,

institutional tests. 32 credit hours maximum toward associate degree, 60 toward bachelor's. **Support services:** Learning center, study skills assistance, tutoring, writing center.

Honors college/program. Rank in top 10% of class, 26 ACT, and commendable high school record required.

Majors. Biology: General. **Business:** General, nonprofit/public. **Communications:** Media studies. **Computer sciences:** General. **Education:** Health, special ed. **English:** English lit. **Foreign languages:** General. **Health services:** Clinical lab science, medical radiologic technology/radiation therapy, nursing (RN). **History:** General. **Human services:** Social work. **Liberal arts:** Arts/sciences. **Math:** General. **Parks/recreation:** Health/fitness. **Philosophy/religion:** Philosophy. **Physical sciences:** Chemistry, geology, physics. **Protective services:** Law enforcement admin. **Psychology:** General. **Social sciences:** Political science, sociology. **Visual/performing arts:** Art, music.

Most popular majors. Business/marketing 7%, health sciences 6%, parks/recreation 6%.

Technology on campus. 1,062 workstations in dormitories, library, computer center, student center. Dormitories wired for high-speed internet access and linked to campus network. Commuter students can connect to campus network. Online course registration, online library, helpline, wireless network available.

Student life. Freshman orientation: Mandatory, $75 fee. Preregistration for classes offered. **Policies:** Alcohol not permitted on campus. **Housing:** Coed dorms, single-sex dorms, special housing for disabled, apartments, fraternity/sorority housing, themed housing available. $200 fully refundable deposit. **Activities:** Bands, campus ministries, choral groups, dance, drama, film society, international student organizations, literary magazine, music ensembles, musical theater, opera, radio station, student government, student newspaper, symphony orchestra, TV station, Baptist Collegiate Ministry, Church of Christ Student Center, Hispanic cultural center, African American cultural center.

Athletics. NCAA. **Intercollegiate:** Baseball M, basketball, cross-country, football (tackle) M, golf, soccer W, softball W, tennis, track and field W, volleyball W. **Intramural:** Badminton, basketball, football (non-tackle), racquetball, soccer, softball, table tennis, tennis, ultimate frisbee, volleyball. **Team name:** Governors.

Student services. Adult student services, alcohol/substance abuse counseling, career counseling, student employment services, financial aid counseling, health services, on-campus daycare, personal counseling, veterans' counselor. **Physically disabled:** Services for visually, speech, hearing impaired.

Contact. E-mail: admissions@apsu.edu
Phone: (931) 221-7661 Toll-free number: (800) 844-2778
Fax: (931) 221-6168
Amy Corlew, Director of Admissions, Austin Peay State University, PO Box 4548, Clarksville, TN 37044-4548

Baptist College of Health Sciences
Memphis, Tennessee
www.bchs.edu
CB code: 6548

- Private 4-year health science and nursing college affiliated with the Baptist faith
- Commuter campus in very large city
- 1,170 degree-seeking undergraduates: 55% part-time, 91% women
- SAT or ACT (ACT writing optional) required

General. Regionally accredited. **Degrees:** 184 bachelor's, 1 associate awarded. **Calendar:** Trimester, limited summer session. **Full-time faculty:** 63 total. **Class size:** 51% < 20, 48% 20-39, less than 1% 50-99.

Freshman class profile.

GPA 3.75 or higher:	26%	GPA 3.0-3.49:	40%
GPA 3.50-3.74:	22%	GPA 2.0-2.99:	12%

Basis for selection. GED not accepted. Standardized test scores, GPA, rigor of secondary school record, math and science courses, recommendations very important; interviews may be required by some majors. **Home schooled:** Transcript of courses and grades required. Transcript must be from an accredited home school agency showing GPA, high school graduation date, and all courses and grades. **Learning Disabled:** With proper documentation, students may be allowed to take entrance exam with pencil and paper instead of on computer.

High school preparation. College-preparatory program required. 10 units required; 15 recommended. Required and recommended units include English 4, mathematics 2, social studies 1, history 1, science 2 (laboratory 2), foreign language 2 and academic electives 1.

2015-2016 Annual costs. Tuition/fees: $13,580. Room only: $2,200. Books/supplies: $1,220. Personal expenses: $2,368.

Application procedures. Admission: Priority date 3/1; deadline 5/1 (postmark date). $25 fee, may be waived for applicants with need. Admission notification on a rolling basis beginning on or about 5/1. Must reply by 6/1. **Financial aid:** No deadline.

Academics. Special study options: Accelerated study. **Credit/placement by examination:** AP, CLEP, institutional tests. 15 credit hours maximum toward bachelor's degree. **Support services:** Learning center, tutoring, writing center.

Majors. Health services: Health care admin, medical radiologic technology/ radiation therapy, nuclear medical technology, nursing (RN), radiologic technology/medical imaging, respiratory therapy technology, sonography.

Technology on campus. 57 workstations in library, computer center. Dormitories linked to campus network. Commuter students can connect to campus network. Online course registration, online library, helpline, wireless network available.

Student life. Freshman orientation: Mandatory. Preregistration for classes offered. **Housing:** Coed dorms, wellness housing available. $100 fully refundable deposit. **Activities:** Campus ministries, student government.

Student services. Chaplain/spiritual director, financial aid counseling, health services, personal counseling.

Contact. E-mail: admissions@bchs.edu
Phone: (901) 575-2247 Toll-free number: (866) 575-2247
Fax: (901) 572-2461
Lissa Morgan, Manager of Admissions, Baptist College of Health Sciences, 1003 Monroe Avenue, Memphis, TN 38104

Belmont University
Nashville, Tennessee
www.belmont.edu   **CB code: 1058**

▸ Private 4-year university affiliated with the Christian Church
▸ Residential campus in very large city
▸ 5,933 degree-seeking undergraduates: 5% part-time, 62% women, 5% African American, 2% Asian American, 5% Hispanic/Latino, 4% Multiracial, non-Hispanic, 1% international
▸ 1,364 degree-seeking graduate students
▸ 80% of applicants admitted
▸ SAT or ACT (ACT writing optional) required
▸ 69% graduate within 6 years

General. Founded in 1951. Regionally accredited. **Degrees:** 1,285 bachelor's awarded; master's, professional offered. **ROTC:** Army, Naval, Air Force. **Location:** 2 miles from downtown. **Calendar:** Semester, limited summer session. **Full-time faculty:** 342 total; 1% have terminal degrees, 12% minority, 50% women. **Part-time faculty:** 438 total; 7% minority, 52% women. **Class size:** 40% < 20, 59% 20-39, 1% 40-49, less than 1% 50-99, less than 1% >100. **Special facilities:** 22-track recording studio, Studio B on Music Row, 140-year-old antebellum mansion.

Freshman class profile. 6,145 applied, 4,934 admitted, 1,387 enrolled.

Mid 50% test scores		GPA 2.0-2.99:	9%
SAT critical reading:	530-630	Rank in top quarter:	58%
SAT math:	510-620	Rank in top tenth:	30%
ACT composite:	23-28	Return as sophomores:	83%
GPA 3.75 or higher:	33%	Out-of-state:	74%
GPA 3.50-3.74:	23%	Live on campus:	100%
GPA 3.0-3.49:	35%	International:	1%

Basis for selection. Admissions based on test scores, course selection, GPA, class rank, recommendations, leadership activity. Interview required for music business; audition required for music programs. **Home schooled:** Statement describing home school structure and mission, transcript of courses and grades, state high school equivalency certificate, interview, letter of recommendation (nonparent) required.

High school preparation. College-preparatory program required. 18 units required; 20 recommended. Required and recommended units include English

4, mathematics 3-4, social studies 3, science 3-4, foreign language 2 and academic electives 3.

2015-2016 Annual costs. Tuition/fees: $30,000. Room/board: $10,970. Books/supplies: $1,400. Personal expenses: $2,500.

2014-2015 Financial aid. Need-based: 1,138 full-time freshmen applied for aid; 802 deemed to have need; 802 received aid. Average need met was 59%. Average scholarship/grant was $15,453; average loan $3,584. 74% of total undergraduate aid awarded as scholarships/grants, 26% as loans/jobs. **Non-need-based:** Awarded to 1,550 full-time undergraduates, including 515 freshmen. Scholarships awarded for academics, art, athletics, leadership, music/drama, religious affiliation, state residency.

Application procedures. Admission: Priority date 12/1; deadline 8/1. $50 fee, may be waived for applicants with need. Admission notification on a rolling basis beginning on or about 8/1. Must reply by May 1 or within 2 week(s) if notified thereafter. **Financial aid:** Priority date 3/1; no closing date. FAFSA required. Applicants notified on a rolling basis starting 3/15; must reply by 5/1 or within 2 week(s) of notification.

Academics. Special study options: Accelerated study, combined bachelor's/graduate degree, cooperative education, cross-registration, distance learning, double major, dual enrollment of high school students, ESL, honors, independent study, internships, liberal arts/career combination, student-designed major, study abroad, teacher certification program, Washington semester. **Credit/placement by examination:** AP, CLEP, IB, SAT, ACT, institutional tests. 24 credit hours maximum toward bachelor's degree. **Support services:** Learning center, pre-admission summer program, reduced course load, tutoring, writing center.

Majors. Area/ethnic studies: Asian. **Biology:** General, Biochemistry/ molecular biology, neuroscience. **Business:** General, accounting, business admin, entrepreneurial studies, finance, international, management information systems, managerial economics, marketing. **Communications:** Broadcast journalism, communications/speech/rhetoric, journalism, media studies, persuasive communications, public relations. **Communications technology:** Recording arts. **Computer sciences:** General, web page design. **Conservation:** Environmental science. **Education:** Art, drama/dance, early childhood, elementary, middle, music, physical, secondary. **Engineering:** Applied physics. **English:** English lit. **Foreign languages:** Biblical, French, German, Spanish. **Health services:** Nursing (RN), pharmaceutical sciences, physics/ radiologic health. **History:** General. **Human services:** Social work. **Liberal arts:** Arts/sciences. **Math:** General. **Parks/recreation:** Exercise sciences. **Philosophy/religion:** Philosophy, religion. **Physical sciences:** Chemistry, physics. **Psychology:** General. **Social sciences:** International economics, international relations, political science, sociology. **Theology:** Bible. **Visual/ performing arts:** Acting, art history/conservation, arts management, cinematography, design, directing/producing, dramatic, music, music management, music pedagogy, music performance, music theory/composition, studio arts, theater design.

Most popular majors. Business/marketing 13%, communications/journalism 7%, communication technologies 6%, health sciences 11%, visual/performing arts 38%.

Technology on campus. 500 workstations in dormitories, library, computer center, student center. Dormitories wired for high-speed internet access and linked to campus network. Commuter students can connect to campus network. Online course registration, online library, helpline, wireless network available.

Student life. Freshman orientation: Mandatory, $60 fee. Preregistration for classes offered. Two day program in summer or 4-day program in fall before classes start. **Housing:** Guaranteed on-campus for freshmen. Single-sex dorms, apartments, wellness housing available. $100 nonrefundable deposit, deadline 5/1. **Activities:** Bands, campus ministries, choral groups, dance, drama, international student organizations, literary magazine, music ensembles, musical theater, opera, student government, student newspaper, symphony orchestra, TV station, Baptist student union, Christian music society, Campus Crusade for Christ, Fellowship of Christian Athletes, Black Student Alliance, Belmont Catholic Community, Belmont Students in Free Enterprise, Presbyterian Student Fellowship, Society for Political-Economic Discussion, International Business Society.

Athletics. NCAA. **Intercollegiate:** Baseball M, basketball, cross-country, golf, soccer, softball W, tennis, track and field, volleyball W. **Intramural:** Basketball, bowling, football (non-tackle), golf M, handball, racquetball, softball, table tennis, tennis, volleyball. **Team name:** Bruins.

Student services. Adult student services, alcohol/substance abuse counseling, chaplain/spiritual director, career counseling, student employment services, financial aid counseling, health services, minority student services, personal counseling, placement for graduates, veterans' counselor.

Contact. E-mail: buadmission@belmont.edu
Phone: (615) 460-6785 Fax: (615) 460-5434
David Mee, Dean of Enrollment Services, Belmont University, 1900
Belmont Boulevard, Nashville, TN 37212-3757

Bethel University
McKenzie, Tennessee
www.bethelu.edu
CB code: 1063

- Private 4-year university and liberal arts college affiliated with the Cumberland Presbyterian Church
- Residential campus in small town
- 5,236 degree-seeking undergraduates: 39% African American, 1% Hispanic/Latino, 1% Multi-racial, non-Hispanic, 1% international
- 1,434 graduate students
- 84% of applicants admitted
- SAT or ACT (ACT writing optional) required
- 30% graduate within 6 years

General. Founded in 1842. Regionally accredited. Some programs provide laptops or other technology upon full-time registration. **Degrees:** 822 bachelor's, 21 associate awarded; master's offered. **Location:** 115 miles from Nashville, 120 miles from Memphis. **Calendar:** Continuous, limited summer session. **Full-time faculty:** 152 total; 47% women. **Part-time faculty:** 268 total; 48% women. **Class size:** 72% < 20, 28% 20-39, less than 1% 40-49, less than 1% 50-99. **Special facilities:** Autism resource center.

Freshman class profile. 1,149 applied, 965 admitted, 627 enrolled.

Mid 50% test scores		End year in good standing:	76%
SAT critical reading:	400-520	Return as sophomores:	49%
SAT math:	390-500	Out-of-state:	15%
SAT writing:	400-520	Live on campus:	40%
ACT composite:	17-22	International:	2%

Basis for selection. GPA and academic units considered. Counselor recommendation and interview considered for academically marginal applicants. **Home schooled:** Transcript of courses and grades required. 19 ACT and passing score on GED required.

High school preparation. College-preparatory program recommended. Required units include English 4, mathematics 2, social studies 2 and science 2.

2015-2016 Annual costs. Tuition/fees: $15,714. Room/board: $8,782. Books/supplies: $1,200. Personal expenses: $1,500.

2014-2015 Financial aid. Non-need-based: Scholarships awarded for academics, athletics, music/drama, religious affiliation, state residency.

Application procedures. Admission: Priority date 2/3; no deadline. $30 fee. Admission notification on a rolling basis. **Financial aid:** Priority date 3/3, closing date 6/30. FAFSA, institutional form required. Applicants notified on a rolling basis starting 1/1; must reply within 2 week(s) of notification.

Academics. Special study options: Accelerated study, combined bachelor's/graduate degree, double major, dual enrollment of high school students, honors, independent study, internships, student-designed major, teacher certification program, weekend college. **Credit/placement by examination:** AP, CLEP, SAT, ACT, institutional tests. 30 credit hours maximum toward bachelor's degree. Accepts CLEP, DANTES, institutional exams for credit. **Support services:** Remedial instruction, study skills assistance, tutoring.

Majors. Biology: General. **Business:** Accounting/business management, business admin, management information systems. **Education:** Elementary, English, history, music, physical, science, secondary, special ed. **English:** English lit. **Health services:** Nursing (RN), premedicine, prepharmacy. **History:** General. **Math:** General. **Philosophy/religion:** Christian. **Physical sciences:** Chemistry. **Psychology:** General. **Social sciences:** Sociology. **Visual/performing arts:** Dramatic, music, music management.

Most popular majors. Health sciences 34%, security/protective services 38%.

Technology on campus. PC or laptop required. 650 workstations in dormitories, library. Dormitories wired for high-speed internet access and linked to campus network. Commuter students can connect to campus network. Online library, helpline, repair service, wireless network available.

Student life. Freshman orientation: Mandatory. Preregistration for classes offered. One-day Saturday program held June-August. Week-long sessions held the week prior to start of classes. **Housing:** Guaranteed on-campus for freshmen. Coed dorms, single-sex dorms, apartments available.

$175 nonrefundable deposit, deadline 8/18. **Activities:** Bands, choral groups, drama, music ensembles, musical theater, radio station, student government, student newspaper, Fellowship of Christian Athletes, honor societies, American Chemical Society, student education association, art club, Students in Free Enterprise, Arete, Campus Crusade for Christ, Relay for Life.

Athletics. NAIA. **Intercollegiate:** Baseball M, basketball, bowling, cheerleading, cross-country, football (tackle) M, golf, rifle, soccer, softball W, tennis, track and field, volleyball W. **Intramural:** Basketball, football (non-tackle), football (tackle) M, golf, soccer, softball, swimming, table tennis, volleyball W. **Team name:** Wildcats.

Student services. Adult student services, alcohol/substance abuse counseling, chaplain/spiritual director, career counseling, student employment services, financial aid counseling, personal counseling, veterans' counselor.

Contact. E-mail: admissions@bethelu.edu
Phone: (731) 352-4030 Fax: (731) 352-4069
Tina Hodges, Dean of Enrollment Services, Bethel University, 325 Cherry Avenue, McKenzie, TN 38201

Bryan College: Dayton
Dayton, Tennessee
www.bryan.edu
CB code: 1908

- Private 4-year liberal arts college affiliated with the interdenominational tradition
- Residential campus in small town
- 999 degree-seeking undergraduates: 19% part-time, 54% women
- 119 degree-seeking graduate students
- 46% of applicants admitted
- SAT or ACT (ACT writing recommended), application essay required
- 56% graduate within 6 years

General. Founded in 1930. Regionally accredited. All courses taught from Christian perspective. All faculty sign statement of faith annually. **Degrees:** 323 bachelor's, 9 associate awarded; master's offered. **Location:** 40 miles from Chattanooga. **Calendar:** Semester, limited summer session. **Full-time faculty:** 37 total; 65% have terminal degrees, 3% minority, 32% women. **Part-time faculty:** 87 total; 22% have terminal degrees, 39% women. **Class size:** 72% < 20, 24% 20-39, 2% 40-49, less than 1% 50-99, less than 1% >100. **Special facilities:** Natural history museum.

Freshman class profile. 716 applied, 326 admitted, 161 enrolled.

Mid 50% test scores		GPA 2.0-2.99:	12%
SAT critical reading:	430-560	Rank in top quarter:	51%
SAT math:	430-510	Rank in top tenth:	18%
SAT writing:	420-570	Return as sophomores:	66%
ACT composite:	19-25	Out-of-state:	65%
GPA 3.75 or higher:	45%	Live on campus:	84%
GPA 3.50-3.74:	16%	International:	6%
GPA 3.0-3.49:	26%		

Basis for selection. High school record, Christian character supported by references, and SAT or ACT scores important. 23 ACT/SAT equivalent or Pre-Professional Skills Test required of all teacher education applicants. Interview required for marginal applicants. **Home schooled:** High school transcript must specify courses and grades .

High school preparation. College-preparatory program recommended. 18 units recommended. Recommended units include English 4, mathematics 3, social studies 3, science 3, foreign language 2 and academic electives 3.

2015-2016 Annual costs. Tuition/fees: $23,300. Room/board: $6,690. Books/supplies: $1,250. Personal expenses: $1,590.

2015-2016 Financial aid. Need-based: 144 full-time freshmen applied for aid; 113 deemed to have need; 113 received aid. Average need met was 50%. Average scholarship/grant was $15,050; average loan $3,300. 67% of total undergraduate aid awarded as scholarships/grants, 33% as loans/jobs. **Non-need-based:** Scholarships awarded for academics, alumni affiliation, art, athletics, job skills, leadership, music/drama.

Application procedures. Admission: Priority date 5/1; no deadline. $35 fee, may be waived for applicants with need. Admission notification on a rolling basis. **Financial aid:** Priority date 1/31; no closing date. FAFSA required. Applicants notified on a rolling basis starting 1/1; must reply within 2 week(s) of notification.

Academics. Special study options: Accelerated study, combined bachelor's/graduate degree, distance learning, double major, dual enrollment of high school students, honors, internships, study abroad, teacher certification program, Washington semester. Adult degree completion program. **Credit/ placement by examination:** AP, CLEP, IB, SAT, ACT, institutional tests. 30 credit hours maximum toward associate degree, 31 toward bachelor's. **Support services:** Reduced course load, remedial instruction, study skills assistance, tutoring, writing center.

Majors. Biology: General. **Business:** Business admin. **Communications:** Communications/speech/rhetoric. **Computer sciences:** Computer science. **Education:** General. **English:** English lit. **Foreign languages:** Spanish. **History:** General. **Liberal arts:** Arts/sciences. **Math:** General. **Parks/recreation:** Exercise sciences. **Philosophy/religion:** Christian. **Psychology:** General. **Social sciences:** Political science. **Theology:** Bible, religious ed. **Visual/ performing arts:** Dramatic, music.

Most popular majors. Business/marketing 56%, education 8%, psychology 9%.

Technology on campus. 100 workstations in dormitories, library, computer center, student center. Dormitories wired for high-speed internet access and linked to campus network. Commuter students can connect to campus network. Online library, helpline, student web hosting, wireless network available.

Student life. Freshman orientation: Mandatory. Preregistration for classes offered. **Policies:** No alcohol, tobacco, drugs. Curfew and dress code enforced. Religious observance required. **Housing:** Guaranteed on-campus for all undergraduates. Single-sex dorms, apartments available. $100 nonrefundable deposit, deadline 8/10. **Activities:** Campus ministries, choral groups, drama, film society, international student organizations, music ensembles, musical theater, opera, student government, student newspaper, Christian service organizations, community tutoring program, Students for Life, Fellowship of Christian Athletes.

Athletics. NAIA, NCCAA. **Intercollegiate:** Baseball M, basketball, cheerleading, cross-country, golf, soccer, softball W, track and field, volleyball W. **Intramural:** Basketball, football (non-tackle) M, soccer, table tennis, tennis, volleyball. **Team name:** Lions.

Student services. Adult student services, chaplain/spiritual director, career counseling, student employment services, financial aid counseling, health services, personal counseling, placement for graduates.

Contact. E-mail: admissions@bryan.edu
Phone: (423) 775-2041 Toll-free number: (800) 277-9522
Fax: (423) 775-7199
D. Hood, Director of Admissions, Bryan College: Dayton, 721 Bryan Drive, Dayton, TN 37321-7000

Carson-Newman University
Jefferson City, Tennessee
www.cn.edu CB code: 1102

- Private 4-year liberal arts college affiliated with the Southern Baptist Convention
- Residential campus in small town
- 1,698 degree-seeking undergraduates: 2% part-time, 58% women, 8% African American, 1% Asian American, 2% Hispanic/Latino, 3% Multiracial, non-Hispanic, 3% international
- 768 degree-seeking graduate students
- 59% of applicants admitted
- SAT or ACT (ACT writing optional) required
- 45% graduate within 6 years

General. Founded in 1851. Regionally accredited. **Degrees:** 308 bachelor's awarded; master's, doctoral offered. **ROTC:** Army. **Location:** 30 miles from Knoxville. **Calendar:** Semester, extensive summer session. **Full-time faculty:** 121 total; 75% have terminal degrees, 4% minority, 54% women. **Part-time faculty:** 96 total; 30% have terminal degrees, 4% minority, 66% women. **Class size:** 55% < 20, 43% 20-39, 2% 40-49. **Special facilities:** Appalachia museum.

Freshman class profile. 5,871 applied, 3,454 admitted, 497 enrolled.

Mid 50% test scores			
SAT critical reading:	440-550	GPA 2.0-2.99:	16%
SAT math:	440-550	Rank in top quarter:	47%
ACT composite:	19-26	Rank in top tenth:	27%
GPA 3.75 or higher:	41%	Return as sophomores:	65%
GPA 3.50-3.74:	20%	Out-of-state:	27%
GPA 3.0-3.49:	23%	Live on campus:	82%
		International:	3%

Basis for selection. 2.5 GPA, 19 ACT or 920 SAT (exclusive of Writing), school and community activities, and recommendations important. Rank in

top half of class considered. Essay required for marginal students; audition required for music; portfolio required for art; interview recommended for academically weak.

High school preparation. College-preparatory program required. 20 units required. Required and recommended units include English 4, mathematics 3, social studies 2, history 1, science 3, foreign language 2 and academic electives 6.

2015-2016 Annual costs. Tuition/fees: $25,360. Room/board: $7,640. Books/supplies: $1,600. Personal expenses: $1,760.

2014-2015 Financial aid. Need-based: 420 full-time freshmen applied for aid; 420 deemed to have need; 420 received aid. Average need met was 81%. Average scholarship/grant was $19,124; average loan $2,713. 73% of total undergraduate aid awarded as scholarships/grants, 27% as loans/jobs. **Non-need-based:** Awarded to 503 full-time undergraduates, including 131 freshmen. Scholarships awarded for academics, art, athletics, leadership, music/drama, religious affiliation, ROTC, state residency.

Application procedures. Admission: No deadline. No application fee. Admission notification on a rolling basis. **Financial aid:** Priority date 2/1; no closing date. FAFSA required. Applicants notified on a rolling basis starting 2/1; must reply by 5/1.

Academics. 3-year pre-engineering programs available. **Special study options:** Accelerated study, distance learning, double major, dual enrollment of high school students, ESL, exchange student, honors, independent study, internships, liberal arts/career combination, student-designed major, study abroad, teacher certification program, Washington semester. **Credit/placement by examination:** AP, CLEP, SAT, ACT, institutional tests. 32 credit hours maximum toward associate degree, 32 toward bachelor's. **Support services:** Learning center, pre-admission summer program, reduced course load, remedial instruction, tutoring.

Majors. Biology: General, biochemistry, environmental. **Business:** General, accounting, business admin, marketing, organizational leadership, small business admin. **Communications:** Communications/speech/rhetoric, media studies. **Computer sciences:** Computer science. **Education:** Art, biology, business, chemistry, drama/dance, early childhood, elementary, English, family/consumer sciences, history, mathematics, middle, multi-level teacher, music, physical, psychology, secondary, Spanish, special ed. **Engineering:** Applied physics. **English:** Creative writing, English lit, rhetoric/composition. **Foreign languages:** French, Spanish. **Health services:** Dietetics, nursing (RN), predental, premedicine, prepharmacy. **History:** General. **Liberal arts:** Arts/sciences. **Math:** General. **Parks/recreation:** Exercise sciences, health/ fitness. **Philosophy/religion:** Philosophy, religion. **Physical sciences:** Chemistry, physics. **Psychology:** General. **Social sciences:** Economics, political science, sociology. **Theology:** Bible, sacred music, theology. **Visual/performing arts:** General, art, dramatic, film/cinema/video, graphic design, interior design, music, music performance, music theory/composition, painting, photography, piano/keyboard, voice/opera. **Work/family studies:** Advocacy, child development, clothing/textiles, family/community services, food/ nutrition, housing, merchandising.

Most popular majors. Business/marketing 34%, parks/recreation 7%, psychology 7%, visual/performing arts 8%.

Technology on campus. 100 workstations in dormitories, library, computer center. Dormitories wired for high-speed internet access and linked to campus network. Commuter students can connect to campus network. Helpline, repair service, wireless network available.

Student life. Freshman orientation: Available. Preregistration for classes offered. **Policies:** Religious observance required. **Housing:** Guaranteed on-campus for freshmen. Single-sex dorms, special housing for disabled, apartments, themed housing available. $200 fully refundable deposit. Honors house available. **Activities:** Bands, campus ministries, choral groups, dance, drama, film society, international student organizations, literary magazine, music ensembles, musical theater, student government, student newspaper, symphony orchestra, Baptist student union, Fellowship of Christian Athletes, honor societies, Appalachian Outreach, Bonners Scholars community service.

Athletics. NCAA. **Intercollegiate:** Baseball M, basketball, cross-country, football (tackle) M, golf M, soccer, softball W, tennis, track and field, volleyball W. **Intramural:** Badminton, basketball, bowling, golf, racquetball, soccer, softball, swimming, table tennis, tennis, volleyball. **Team name:** Eagles.

Student services. Adult student services, career counseling, health services, personal counseling, placement for graduates, veterans' counselor. **Physically disabled:** Services for visually, hearing impaired.

Contact. E-mail: admitme@cn.edu
Phone: (865) 471-3223 Toll-free number: (800) 678-9061
Fax: (865) 471-4817
Melanie Redding, Director of Admissions, Carson-Newman University, 1646 Russell Avenue, Jefferson City, TN 37760

Christian Brothers University
Memphis, Tennessee
www.cbu.edu

CB member
CB code: 1121

- Private 4-year university affiliated with the Roman Catholic Church
- Residential campus in very large city
- 1,408 degree-seeking undergraduates: 8% part-time, 53% women, 29% African American, 5% Asian American, 6% Hispanic/Latino, 3% Multiracial, non-Hispanic, 7% international
- 426 degree-seeking graduate students
- 46% of applicants admitted
- SAT or ACT (ACT writing optional), application essay required
- 53% graduate within 6 years; 23% enter graduate study

General. Founded in 1871. Regionally accredited. **Degrees:** 236 bachelor's awarded; master's offered. **ROTC:** Army, Naval, Air Force. **Location:** 200 miles from Nashville; 150 miles from Little Rock, AR. **Calendar:** Semester, limited summer session. **Full-time faculty:** 100 total; 87% have terminal degrees. **Part-time faculty:** 86 total; 41% have terminal degrees. **Class size:** 68% < 20, 31% 20-39, less than 1% 40-49, less than 1% 50-99.

Freshman class profile. 2,321 applied, 1,063 admitted, 312 enrolled.

Mid 50% test scores		Rank in top tenth:	18%
ACT composite:	21-27	Return as sophomores:	80%
GPA 3.75 or higher:	40%	Out-of-state:	18%
GPA 3.50-3.74:	27%	Live on campus:	67%
GPA 3.0-3.49:	24%	International:	6%
GPA 2.0-2.99:	7%	Fraternities:	12%
Rank in top quarter:	41%	Sororities:	12%

Basis for selection. Graduation from approved secondary school or GED equivalent, 2.0 GPA, rank in upper 2/3 of graduating class, and satisfactory test scores required. Audition required for some programs; interview recommended for all. **Home schooled:** Statement describing home school structure and mission, transcript of courses and grades required.

High school preparation. College-preparatory program recommended. Recommended units include English 4, mathematics 4 and science 4. College-preparatory program required for engineering applicants.

2015-2016 Annual costs. Tuition/fees: $30,186. Room/board: $6,920. Books/supplies: $1,000. Personal expenses: $1,690.

2014-2015 Financial aid. Need-based: 354 full-time freshmen applied for aid; 285 deemed to have need; 283 received aid. Average need met was 82%. Average scholarship/grant was $21,450; average loan $3,024. 74% of total undergraduate aid awarded as scholarships/grants, 26% as loans/jobs. **Non-need-based:** Awarded to 454 full-time undergraduates, including 142 freshmen. Scholarships awarded for academics, alumni affiliation, athletics, music/drama, state residency. **Additional information:** ROTC scholarships available to qualified applicants.

Application procedures. Admission: Priority date 12/1; no deadline. $25 fee, may be waived for applicants with need, free for online applicants. Admission notification on a rolling basis beginning on or about 12/1. Must reply by May 1 or within 3 week(s) if notified thereafter. **Financial aid:** Priority date 2/15; no closing date. FAFSA required. Applicants notified on a rolling basis starting 3/1; must reply within 2 week(s) of notification.

Academics. Special study options: Accelerated study, combined bachelor's/graduate degree, cooperative education, cross-registration, distance learning, double major, dual enrollment of high school students, honors, independent study, internships, liberal arts/career combination, student-designed major, study abroad, teacher certification program. **Credit/placement by examination:** AP, CLEP, IB, SAT, ACT, institutional tests. 30 credit hours maximum toward bachelor's degree. **Support services:** Pre-admission summer program, reduced course load, study skills assistance, tutoring, writing center.

Majors. Biology: General, biochemistry, biomedical sciences, ecology. **Business:** General, accounting, business admin, communications, finance, international, marketing. **Computer sciences:** Computer science. **Education:** General, early childhood, special ed. **Engineering:** Applied physics, chemical, civil, computer, electrical, mechanical. **English:** Creative writing, English lit. **Health services:** Nursing practice. **History:** General. **Liberal arts:** Arts/sciences. **Math:** General. **Philosophy/religion:** General. **Physical sciences:** Chemistry, physics. **Protective services:** Computer forensics. **Psychology:** General, applied. **Visual/performing arts:** Studio arts.

Most popular majors. Biology 7%, business/marketing 36%, engineering/engineering technologies 14%, health sciences 8%, interdisciplinary studies 7%, psychology 10%.

Technology on campus. Dormitories wired for high-speed internet access and linked to campus network. Commuter students can connect to campus network. Online course registration, online library, helpline, wireless network available.

Student life. Freshman orientation: Mandatory. Preregistration for classes offered. Held Friday-Monday before classes begin. **Policies:** Juniors and seniors may live in on-campus apartments. Freshmen and sophomores whose permanent address is beyond a 30 mile radius required to live on-campus. **Housing:** Guaranteed on-campus for freshmen. Coed dorms, single-sex dorms, apartments, themed housing available. $300 nonrefundable deposit, deadline 5/1. Apartments for married graduate students. **Activities:** Campus ministries, choral groups, drama, international student organizations, literary magazine, student government, Black Student Association, Gay-Straight Alliance, Hebrews, Hola CBU, intercultural club, National Society of Black Engineers, NAACP.

Athletics. NCAA. **Intercollegiate:** Baseball M, basketball, cross-country, golf, soccer, softball W, tennis, track and field, volleyball W. **Intramural:** Basketball, bowling, handball, soccer, softball, table tennis, volleyball. **Team name:** Buccaneers.

Student services. Adult student services, alcohol/substance abuse counseling, chaplain/spiritual director, career counseling, student employment services, financial aid counseling, health services, minority student services, personal counseling, placement for graduates, veterans' counselor.

Contact. E-mail: admissions@cbu.edu
Phone: (901) 321-3205 Toll-free number: (800) 288-7576
Fax: (901) 321-3202
Kristi Forman, Director of Admissions, Christian Brothers University, 650 East Parkway South, Memphis, TN 38104-5519

Cumberland University
Lebanon, Tennessee
www.cumberland.edu

CB code: 1146

- Private 4-year university and liberal arts college
- Commuter campus in large town
- 1,142 degree-seeking undergraduates
- SAT or ACT (ACT writing optional), application essay required

General. Founded in 1842. Regionally accredited. **Degrees:** 347 bachelor's awarded; master's offered. **ROTC:** Army. **Location:** 30 miles from Nashville. **Calendar:** Semester, limited summer session. **Full-time faculty:** 64 total; 59% have terminal degrees, 3% minority, 48% women. **Part-time faculty:** 107 total; 28% have terminal degrees, 13% minority, 62% women. **Class size:** 62% < 20, 33% 20-39, 2% 40-49, 2% 50-99, less than 1% >100.

Freshman class profile.

GPA 3.75 or higher:	28%	Rank in top tenth:	20%
GPA 3.50-3.74:	20%	Out-of-state:	12%
GPA 3.0-3.49:	33%	Live on campus:	60%
GPA 2.0-2.99:	19%	Fraternities:	19%
Rank in top quarter:	43%	Sororities:	12%

Basis for selection. High school academic record and standardized test scores most important. Audition, portfolio required for some programs; interview recommended for academically weak. **Home schooled:** Transcript of courses and grades required.

High school preparation. College-preparatory program recommended. 16 units required; 19 recommended. Required and recommended units include English 4, mathematics 3-4, social studies 2, history 2, science 3 (laboratory 1-2) and foreign language 2.

2015-2016 Annual costs. Tuition/fees: $21,210. Room/board: $8,000. Books/supplies: $1,400. Personal expenses: $3,205.

Financial aid. Non-need-based: Scholarships awarded for academics, art, athletics, music/drama.

Application procedures. Admission: Priority date 2/15; no deadline. $25 fee, may be waived for applicants with need. Admission notification on a rolling basis beginning on or about 3/1. **Financial aid:** Priority date 2/1; no closing date. FAFSA, institutional form required. Applicants notified on a rolling basis starting 5/1; must reply within 2 week(s) of notification.

Academics. Selection of major or minor not required. **Special study options:** Accelerated study, combined bachelor's/graduate degree, cooperative education, distance learning, double major, dual enrollment of high school students, independent study, internships, liberal arts/career combination, teacher certification program. **Credit/placement by examination:** AP,

CLEP, ACT, institutional tests. 30 credit hours maximum toward bachelor's degree. **Support services:** Learning center, pre-admission summer program, reduced course load, remedial instruction, study skills assistance, tutoring, writing center.

Majors. **Area/ethnic studies:** American. **Biology:** General. **Business:** General, accounting, management science. **Education:** General, biology, early childhood, elementary, English, history, mathematics, middle, multi-level teacher, music, physical, secondary, social science, special ed. **English:** English lit. **Health services:** Nursing (RN), predental, premedicine, prepharmacy, preveterinary. **History:** General. **Human services:** General. **Liberal arts:** Arts/sciences. **Math:** General. **Parks/recreation:** Health/fitness, sports admin. **Protective services:** Criminal justice. **Psychology:** General. **Social sciences:** General, political science, sociology. **Visual/performing arts:** Music, studio arts.

Most popular majors. Business/marketing 11%, education 14%, health sciences 55%.

Technology on campus. 90 workstations in library, computer center. Dormitories linked to campus network. Commuter students can connect to campus network. Online library, helpline, repair service, wireless network available.

Student life. **Freshman orientation:** Mandatory, $100 fee. Preregistration for classes offered. 1-1/2 day session held in August. **Housing:** Single-sex dorms, apartments, wellness housing available. $200 fully refundable deposit, deadline 8/1. **Activities:** Bands, campus ministries, choral groups, dance, drama, music ensembles, musical theater, radio station, student government, student newspaper, Fellowship of Christian Athletes, African American student association, Campus Crusade for Christ, Champions for Christ.

Athletics. NAIA. **Intercollegiate:** Baseball M, basketball, bowling, cheerleading, cross-country, football (tackle) M, golf, soccer, softball W, tennis, volleyball W, wrestling M. **Intramural:** Basketball, football (non-tackle) M, softball, table tennis, volleyball. **Team name:** Bulldogs.

Student services. Adult student services, chaplain/spiritual director, career counseling, student employment services, financial aid counseling, health services, personal counseling, placement for graduates. **Physically disabled:** Services for visually impaired.

Contact. E-mail: admissions@cumberland.edu
Phone: (615) 444-2562 Toll-free number: (800) 467-0562
Fax: (615) 444-2569
Beatrice LaChance, Director of Enrollment Services, Cumberland University, 1 Cumberland Square, Lebanon, TN 37087

East Tennessee State University

Johnson City, Tennessee
www.etsu.edu

CB member
CB code: 1198

- Public 4-year university
- Commuter campus in small city
- 10,960 degree-seeking undergraduates: 14% part-time, 56% women, 7% African American, 1% Asian American, 2% Hispanic/Latino, 3% Multiracial, non-Hispanic, 3% international
- 2,884 degree-seeking graduate students
- 79% of applicants admitted
- SAT or ACT (ACT writing optional) required
- 43% graduate within 6 years

General. Founded in 1911. Regionally accredited. Additional campus in Kingsport. **Degrees:** 2,229 bachelor's awarded; master's, professional, doctoral offered. **ROTC:** Army. **Location:** 90 miles from Knoxville; 60 miles from Asheville. **Calendar:** Semester, extensive summer session. **Full-time faculty:** 575 total; 11% minority, 47% women. **Part-time faculty:** 342 total; 18% minority, 58% women. **Class size:** 46% < 20, 41% 20-39, 5% 40-49, 5% 50-99, 3% >100. **Special facilities:** Appalachian archives, planetarium, observatory, arboretum, Gray Fossil Site.

Freshman class profile. 8,253 applied, 6,538 admitted, 1,999 enrolled.

Mid 50% test scores		Rank in top quarter:	47%
SAT critical reading:	420-540	Rank in top tenth:	20%
SAT math:	420-590	Return as sophomores:	71%
ACT composite:	20-26	Out-of-state:	19%
GPA 3.75 or higher:	34%	Live on campus:	55%
GPA 3.50-3.74:	19%	International:	3%
GPA 3.0-3.49:	26%	Fraternities:	5%
GPA 2.0-2.99:	21%	Sororities:	5%

Basis for selection. 2.3 High School GPA or 19 ACT (or SAT equivalent) required. Freshmen applicants age 21 or over are not required to submit ACT or SAT scores, however, these applicants must complete an assessment battery (ACT COMPASS) for placement purposes. Those with ACT Composite, Math, or English scores below 19 must complete the appropriate assessment (COMPASS). Interview recommended for dental hygiene, health-related professions, nursing, physical therapy programs; audition required for music; portfolio recommended for art. **Home schooled:** Transcript of courses and grades required.

High school preparation. College-preparatory program required. 14 units required; 16 recommended. Required and recommended units include English 4, mathematics 3-4, social studies 1, history 1, science 2-3 (laboratory 1), foreign language 2 and visual/performing arts 1.

2015-2016 Annual costs. Tuition/fees: $8,477; $26,147 out-of-state. Room/board: $9,280.

Financial aid. **Non-need-based:** Scholarships awarded for academics, alumni affiliation, art, athletics, leadership, minority status, music/drama, religious affiliation, ROTC, state residency. **Additional information:** Housing costs payable by installment.

Application procedures. **Admission:** Priority date 2/1; deadline 8/15. $25 fee, may be waived for applicants with need. Admission notification on a rolling basis beginning on or about 8/1. **Financial aid:** Priority date 4/15; no closing date. FAFSA required. Applicants notified on a rolling basis starting 4/15; must reply within 3 week(s) of notification.

Academics. **Special study options:** Combined bachelor's/graduate degree, cooperative education, distance learning, double major, dual enrollment of high school students, ESL, exchange student, external degree, honors, independent study, internships, student-designed major, study abroad, teacher certification program. **Credit/placement by examination:** AP, CLEP, IB, SAT, ACT, institutional tests. **Support services:** Learning center, reduced course load, study skills assistance, tutoring, writing center.

Majors. **Biology:** General. **Business:** Accounting, business admin, finance, managerial economics, marketing. **Communications:** Media studies. **Communications technology:** Animation/special effects. **Computer sciences:** General. **Education:** Special ed. **English:** English lit, rhetoric/composition. **Foreign languages:** General. **Health services:** Dental hygiene, environmental health, nursing (RN). **History:** General. **Human services:** Social work. **Liberal arts:** Arts/sciences. **Math:** General. **Parks/recreation:** Health/fitness, sports admin. **Philosophy/religion:** Philosophy. **Physical sciences:** Chemistry, physics. **Protective services:** Law enforcement admin. **Psychology:** General. **Social sciences:** Economics, geography, political science, sociology. **Visual/performing arts:** Art, music. **Work/family studies:** General, child development, family studies.

Most popular majors. Business/marketing 12%, health sciences 25%, liberal arts 7%, parks/recreation 7%.

Technology on campus. 1,400 workstations in dormitories, library, computer center, student center. Dormitories wired for high-speed internet access and linked to campus network. Commuter students can connect to campus network. Online course registration, online library, helpline, repair service, student web hosting, wireless network available.

Student life. **Freshman orientation:** Mandatory. Preregistration for classes offered. Five sessions during summer, each for 1-2 days. **Housing:** Coed dorms, single-sex dorms, special housing for disabled, apartments, fraternity/sorority housing, wellness housing available. $100 fully refundable deposit. **Activities:** Bands, campus ministries, choral groups, drama, international student organizations, literary magazine, music ensembles, radio station, student government, student newspaper, TV station, Baptist student union, Campus Crusade, Catholic center, Christian student fellowship, Fellowship of Christian Athletes, Real Life Fellowship, Wesley Foundation, Black Affairs Association.

Athletics. NCAA. **Intercollegiate:** Baseball M, basketball, cross-country, football (tackle) M, golf, soccer, softball W, tennis, track and field, volleyball W. **Intramural:** Basketball, cross-country, football (non-tackle), golf, handball, racquetball, softball, tennis, volleyball W, weight lifting M. **Team name:** Buccaneers.

Student services. Adult student services, alcohol/substance abuse counseling, chaplain/spiritual director, career counseling, services for economically disadvantaged, student employment services, financial aid counseling, health services, legal services, minority student services, on-campus daycare, personal counseling, placement for graduates, veterans' counselor, women's services. **Physically disabled:** Services for visually, speech, hearing impaired.

Contact. E-mail: go2etsu@etsu.edu
Phone: (423) 439-4213 Toll-free number: (800) 462-3878
Fax: (423) 439-4630
Brian Henley, Director of Admissions, East Tennessee State University, ETSU Box 70731, Johnson City, TN 37614

Fisk University
Nashville, Tennessee
www.fisk.edu

CB member
CB code: 1224

- Private 4-year liberal arts college
- Residential campus in very large city
- 805 degree-seeking undergraduates
- 81% of applicants admitted
- SAT or ACT (ACT writing optional), interview required

General. Founded in 1866. Regionally accredited. **Degrees:** 89 bachelor's awarded; master's offered. **ROTC:** Army, Naval. **Location:** 216 miles from Memphis, 225 miles from Atlanta. **Calendar:** Semester, limited summer session. **Full-time faculty:** 49 total; 84% have terminal degrees, 69% minority, 49% women. **Part-time faculty:** 26 total; 54% have terminal degrees, 81% minority, 46% women. **Class size:** 73% < 20, 25% 20-39, less than 1% 40-49, less than 1% 50-99.

Freshman class profile. 3,004 applied, 2,431 admitted, 216 enrolled.

Mid 50% test scores			
SAT critical reading:	380-480	GPA 3.0-3.49:	24%
SAT math:	410-560	GPA 2.0-2.99:	48%
SAT writing:	410-560	Rank in top quarter:	46%
ACT composite:	17-23	Rank in top tenth:	18%
GPA 3.75 or higher:	9%	Out-of-state:	64%
GPA 3.50-3.74:	16%	Live on campus:	91%

Basis for selection. School achievement record, class rank, test scores, recommendations, activities important. Essay recommended for all; audition recommended for music. Interview required for scholarship nominees and must take place prior to 2/15.

High school preparation. College-preparatory program recommended. 20 units recommended. Recommended units include English 4, mathematics 3, social studies 3, history 1, science 3, foreign language 1 and academic electives 6. 1 Algebra I, 1 Geometry, and 1 Algebra II recommended.

2015-2016 Annual costs. Tuition/fees: $21,480. Room/board: $10,276. Books/supplies: $2,100. Personal expenses: $2,100.

Financial aid: All financial aid based on need.

Application procedures. Admission: Priority date 3/1; no deadline. $50 fee, may be waived for applicants with need. Application must be submitted on paper. Admission notification on a rolling basis. **Financial aid:** Priority date 3/1, closing date 7/1. FAFSA required. Applicants notified on a rolling basis starting 4/1; must reply within 2 week(s) of notification.

Academics. Special study options: Combined bachelor's/graduate degree, cooperative education, cross-registration, double major, dual enrollment of high school students, exchange student, honors, independent study, internships, liberal arts/career combination, student-designed major, study abroad, teacher certification program. 2-2 program with Rush-Presbyterian-St. Luke's Medical Center in nursing, dual degree in science and engineering, dual degree in engineering and natural sciences in 5 years, 3-3 program with Howard University for Doctor of Pharmacy, 5-year MBA program with Vanderbilt University, 7-year MD, PhD, DDS programs with Meharry Medical College. **Credit/placement by examination:** AP, CLEP, IB, SAT, ACT, institutional tests. 30 credit hours maximum toward bachelor's degree. **Support services:** Learning center, pre-admission summer program, tutoring, writing center.

Majors. Biology: General. **Business:** Business admin. **Computer sciences:** Computer science. **Education:** Music, special ed. **English:** English lit. **Foreign languages:** Spanish. **Health services:** Nursing (RN). **History:** General. **Math:** General. **Physical sciences:** Chemistry, physics. **Psychology:** General. **Social sciences:** Political science, sociology. **Visual/performing arts:** Art, music, music performance.

Most popular majors. Biology 23%, business/marketing 18%, history 6%, psychology 26%, social sciences 12%.

Technology on campus. 100 workstations in dormitories, library, computer center. Dormitories wired for high-speed internet access and linked to campus network. Online course registration, helpline, student web hosting, wireless network available.

Student life. Freshman orientation: Mandatory, $350 fee. Preregistration for classes offered. Three to five day orientation held 1 week before classes. **Policies:** All students required to live on-campus, with few exceptions. Freshmen have 12 am curfew. **Housing:** Guaranteed on-campus for all undergraduates. Single-sex dorms, special housing for disabled available. $100 nonrefundable deposit, deadline 7/15. **Activities:** Jazz band, campus ministries, choral groups, dance, drama, literary magazine, music ensembles, radio station, student government, student newspaper, TV station, Baptist student union, Muslim student association, Nation of Islam, Caribbean student union, African student association, race relations students organization.

Athletics. NAIA. **Intercollegiate:** Basketball, cross-country, softball W, tennis, track and field, volleyball W. **Intramural:** Basketball, football (nontackle), soccer M, tennis, volleyball W, weight lifting M. **Team name:** Bulldogs.

Student services. Career counseling, student employment services, financial aid counseling, health services, personal counseling, placement for graduates.

Contact. E-mail: admit@fisk.edu
Phone: (615) 329-8665 Toll-free number: (888) 702-0022
Fax: (615) 329-8774
Anthony Jones, Director of Recruitment and Admission, Fisk University, 1000 Seventeenth Avenue North, Nashville, TN 37208-3051

Freed-Hardeman University
Henderson, Tennessee
www.fhu.edu

CB member
CB code: 1230

- Private 4-year university and liberal arts college affiliated with the Church of Christ
- Residential campus in small town
- 1,260 degree-seeking undergraduates: 3% part-time, 57% women, 5% African American, 1% Asian American, 2% Hispanic/Latino, 2% Multiracial, non-Hispanic, 2% international
- 466 graduate students
- 92% of applicants admitted
- SAT or ACT (ACT writing optional) required
- 58% graduate within 6 years

General. Founded in 1869. Regionally accredited. Campus in Verviers, Belgium. **Degrees:** 322 bachelor's awarded; master's offered. **Location:** 15 miles from Jackson, 85 miles from Memphis. **Calendar:** Semester, limited summer session. **Full-time faculty:** 94 total; 74% have terminal degrees, 6% minority, 31% women. **Part-time faculty:** 56 total; 45% have terminal degrees, 9% minority, 36% women. **Class size:** 51% < 20, 44% 20-39, 3% 40-49, 1% 50-99.

Freshman class profile. 981 applied, 901 admitted, 294 enrolled.

Mid 50% test scores			
		GPA 2.0-2.99:	9%
SAT critical reading:	500-590	Rank in top quarter:	55%
SAT math:	480-580	Rank in top tenth:	28%
ACT composite:	21-27	Return as sophomores:	74%
GPA 3.75 or higher:	52%	Out-of-state:	45%
GPA 3.50-3.74:	25%	Live on campus:	94%
GPA 3.0-3.49:	14%	International:	1%

Basis for selection. Admissions based on school achievement record, test scores, references. Applicants without minimum test score or GPA may be admitted with restrictions after further evaluation.

High school preparation. College-preparatory program recommended. 20 units recommended. Recommended units include English 4, mathematics 2, social studies 2, science 2 and academic electives 10. Additional science and math courses recommended.

2015-2016 Annual costs. Tuition/fees: $21,500. Room/board: $7,580. Books/supplies: $1,300. Personal expenses: $2,000. **Additional information:** There are NO additional fees, such as parking, lab, freshmen orientation, or graduation fees.

Financial aid. Non-need-based: Scholarships awarded for academics, art, athletics, leadership, minority status, music/drama.

Application procedures. Admission: No deadline. No application fee. Admission notification on a rolling basis. Housing deposit refundable up to 30 days prior to term. **Financial aid:** Priority date 2/1; no closing date. FAFSA, institutional form required. Applicants notified on a rolling basis starting 3/10; must reply within 4 week(s) of notification.

Academics. Students enrolled for 12 or more undergraduate hours must register for Bible class. **Special study options:** Accelerated study, combined bachelor's/graduate degree, cross-registration, distance learning, double major, dual enrollment of high school students, honors, independent study, internships, liberal arts/career combination, student-designed major, study abroad, teacher certification program. 3-2 engineering co-op. **Credit/placement by examination:** AP, CLEP, IB, SAT, ACT, institutional tests. 33

credit hours maximum toward bachelor's degree. **Support services:** Learning center, reduced course load, remedial instruction, study skills assistance, tutoring.

Honors college/program. Approximately 5% of freshmen class admitted to honors course work as result of competitive application process.

Majors. Biology: General, biochemistry. **Business:** Accounting, business admin, finance, human resources, management information systems, marketing. **Communications:** Communications/speech/rhetoric, journalism, media studies, public relations. **Computer sciences:** General. **Education:** Art, biology, curriculum, early childhood, elementary, English, history, mathematics, middle, multi-level teacher, music, physical, science, secondary, special ed. **English:** English lit. **Health services:** Health care admin. **History:** General. **Human services:** Social work. **Liberal arts:** Arts/sciences. **Math:** General. **Parks/recreation:** Exercise sciences. **Philosophy/religion:** Philosophy. **Physical sciences:** General, chemistry. **Protective services:** Criminal justice. **Psychology:** General. **Social sciences:** General. **Theology:** Bible, missionary, theology. **Visual/performing arts:** Acting, art, design, interior design, music, theater design. **Work/family studies:** Family studies.

Most popular majors. Biology 8%, business/marketing 9%, education 13%, interdisciplinary studies 11%, parks/recreation 6%, theological studies 13%.

Technology on campus. 238 workstations in dormitories, library, computer center, student center. Dormitories wired for high-speed internet access and linked to campus network. Commuter students can connect to campus network. Online course registration, online library, helpline, repair service, wireless network available.

Student life. Freshman orientation: Mandatory. Preregistration for classes offered. Held the 4 days prior to start of classes in August. **Policies:** Daily chapel is mandatory. Nightly curfew enforced. Religious observance required. **Housing:** Guaranteed on-campus for freshmen. Single-sex dorms, special housing for disabled, apartments available. $250 fully refundable deposit, deadline 5/1. Some student-teacher housing available for education majors. **Activities:** Campus ministries, choral groups, drama, international student organizations, music ensembles, musical theater, radio station, student government, student newspaper, TV station, evangelism forum, preachers club, student-alumni association, university student ambassadors, university program council, youth workers club, Impact Team, Young Republicans, Young Democrats.

Athletics. NAIA. **Intercollegiate:** Baseball M, basketball, cheerleading M, cross-country, soccer, softball W, volleyball W. **Intramural:** Badminton, basketball, football (non-tackle), racquetball, soccer, softball, table tennis, tennis, volleyball. **Team name:** Lions.

Student services. Alcohol/substance abuse counseling, chaplain/spiritual director, career counseling, student employment services, financial aid counseling, health services, on-campus daycare, personal counseling, placement for graduates, veterans' counselor. **Physically disabled:** Services for visually, hearing impaired.

Contact. E-mail: admissions@fhu.edu
Phone: (731) 989-6651 Toll-free number: (800) 348-3480
Fax: (731) 989-6047
Joseph Askew, Director of Admissions, Freed-Hardeman University, 158 East Main Street, Henderson, TN 38340

ITT Technical Institute: Knoxville
Knoxville, Tennessee
www.itt-tech.edu CB code: 7139

- For-profit 4-year technical college
- Commuter campus in small city
- 294 undergraduates
- Interview required

General. Accredited by ACICS. **Degrees:** 26 bachelor's, 57 associate awarded. **Calendar:** Quarter, extensive summer session. **Full-time faculty:** 7 total. **Part-time faculty:** 58 total.

Basis for selection. Satisfactory scores from on-site test in English and mathematics required.

2015-2016 Annual costs. Per-credit-hour charge, $493, will vary depending on program level and course of study. Academic fee, $200. Some programs require purchase of tools, which could cost an additional $100 to $500. All costs subject to change.

Application procedures. Admission: No deadline. No application fee. Admission notification on a rolling basis. **Financial aid:** No deadline. FAFSA, institutional form required. Applicants notified on a rolling basis.

Academics. Credit/placement by examination: AP, CLEP. **Support services:** Learning center, tutoring.

Majors. Business: Business admin, construction management, e-commerce. **Communications technology:** Animation/special effects. **Computer sciences:** Networking, security. **Protective services:** Criminal justice.

Technology on campus. Online library available.

Student life. Freshman orientation: Available. Preregistration for classes offered.

Student services. Career counseling, student employment services, placement for graduates.

Contact. Phone: (865) 671-2800 Toll-free number: (800) 671-2801
Fax: (865) 671-2811
Holly Winters, Director of Recruitment, ITT Technical Institute: Knoxville, 10208 Technology Drive, Knoxville, TN 37932

ITT Technical Institute: Memphis
Cordova, Tennessee
www.itt-tech.edu CB code: 2731

- For-profit 4-year technical college
- Commuter campus in very large city
- 545 undergraduates
- Interview required

General. Accredited by ACICS. **Degrees:** 22 bachelor's, 120 associate awarded. **Calendar:** Quarter, extensive summer session. **Full-time faculty:** 9 total. **Part-time faculty:** 53 total.

Basis for selection. Satisfactory scores from on-site tests in English and mathematics required.

2015-2016 Annual costs. Per-credit-hour charge, $493, will vary depending on program level and course of study. Academic fee, $200. Some programs require purchase of tools, which could cost an additional $100 to $500. All costs subject to change.

Application procedures. Admission: No application fee. Admission notification on a rolling basis. **Financial aid:** No deadline. FAFSA, institutional form required. Applicants notified on a rolling basis.

Academics. Credit/placement by examination: AP, CLEP. **Support services:** Learning center, tutoring.

Majors. Business: Accounting technology, accounting/business management, business admin, construction management, e-commerce. **Computer sciences:** Security. **Protective services:** Law enforcement admin. **Visual/performing arts:** Game design.

Technology on campus. Online library available.

Student life. Freshman orientation: Available. Preregistration for classes offered.

Student services. Career counseling, student employment services, placement for graduates.

Contact. Phone: (901) 762-0556 Toll-free number: (866) 444-5141
Fax: (901) 762-0566
James Mills, Director of Recruitment, ITT Technical Institute: Memphis, 7260 Goodlett Farms Parkway, Cordova, TN 38016

ITT Technical Institute: Nashville
Nashville, Tennessee
www.itt-tech.edu CB code: 7025

- For-profit 4-year technical college
- Commuter campus in very large city
- 552 undergraduates
- Interview required

General. Accredited by ACICS. **Degrees:** 32 bachelor's, 122 associate awarded. **Calendar:** Quarter, extensive summer session. **Full-time faculty:** 12 total. **Part-time faculty:** 86 total.

Basis for selection. Satisfactory scores from on-site English and mathematics tests required.

2015-2016 Annual costs. Per-credit-hour charge, $493, will vary depending on program level and course of study. Academic fee, $200. Some programs require purchase of tools, which could cost an additional $100 to $655. All costs subject to change.

Application procedures. Admission: No deadline. No application fee. Admission notification on a rolling basis. **Financial aid:** No deadline. FAFSA, institutional form required. Applicants notified on a rolling basis.

Academics. Credit/placement by examination: AP, CLEP. **Support services:** Learning center, tutoring.

Majors. Business: Accounting/business management, business admin, construction management, e-commerce. **Communications technology:** Animation/special effects. **Computer sciences:** Networking, security, system admin. **Protective services:** Criminal justice.

Technology on campus. Online library available.

Student life. Freshman orientation: Available. Preregistration for classes offered.

Student services. Career counseling, student employment services, placement for graduates.

Contact. Phone: (615) 889-8700 Toll-free number: (800) 331-8386 Fax: (615) 872-7209
James Royster, Director of Recruitment, ITT Technical Institute: Nashville, 2845 Elm Hill Pike, Nashville, TN 37214

Johnson University
Knoxville, Tennessee
www.johnsonu.edu   CB code: 1345

- Private 4-year university and Bible college affiliated with the Christian Church
- Residential campus in large city
- 1,099 degree-seeking undergraduates
- SAT or ACT (ACT writing recommended), application essay required

General. Founded in 1893. Regionally accredited; also accredited by ABHE. **Degrees:** 163 bachelor's, 12 associate awarded; master's, doctoral offered. **Location:** 7 miles from Knoxville. **Calendar:** Semester, limited summer session. **Full-time faculty:** 56 total; 70% have terminal degrees, 32% women. **Part-time faculty:** 104 total; 51% have terminal degrees, 30% women. **Class size:** 61% < 20, 20% 20-39, 9% 40-49, 8% 50-99, 2% >100. **Special facilities:** College-operated museum.

Basis for selection. High school transcript and 3 references, 1 from minister required. Essay, combination of high school percentile rank and ACT determines initial admission criteria. 19 ACT and 1350 SAT required for teacher education. Interview recommended.

High school preparation. 16 units required. Required units include academic electives 4. 12 of the 16 units must be content courses such as English, history, mathematics, foreign language, and science.

2015-2016 Annual costs. Tuition/fees: $12,650. Room/board: $5,750. Books/supplies: $800.

Financial aid. Non-need-based: Scholarships awarded for academics, leadership, minority status, music/drama, religious affiliation, state residency.

Application procedures. Admission: Closing date 6/1 (receipt date). $35 fee. Admission notification on a rolling basis. **Financial aid:** Closing date 3/1. FAFSA, institutional form required. Applicants notified on a rolling basis starting 4/30; must reply by 8/25 or within 2 week(s) of notification.

Academics. Special study options: Accelerated study, combined bachelor's/graduate degree, cooperative education, distance learning, double major, ESL, honors, independent study, internships, teacher certification program. **Credit/placement by examination:** AP, CLEP, SAT, ACT, institutional tests. 32 credit hours maximum toward bachelor's degree. **Support services:** Learning center, remedial instruction, study skills assistance, tutoring, writing center.

Majors. Business: Nonprofit/public. **Education:** Elementary. **Psychology:** Counseling. **Theology:** Bible, sacred music.

Technology on campus. 50 workstations in library, computer center. Dormitories linked to campus network. Commuter students can connect to campus network. Online course registration, online library, helpline, student web hosting, wireless network available.

Student life. Freshman orientation: Mandatory. Preregistration for classes offered. Held the weekend preceding first semester. **Policies:** Religious observance required. **Housing:** Guaranteed on-campus for freshmen. Single-sex dorms, apartments available. $100 fully refundable deposit, deadline 8/1. Mobile homes, duplex houses, available for family housing. **Activities:** Jazz band, campus ministries, choral groups, drama, literary magazine, music ensembles, musical theater, radio station, student government, Harvesters, Student Government Association, Campus Choir, Timothy Club, Scripture Memory Group, International Justice Mission.

Athletics. NCCAA. **Intercollegiate:** Baseball M, basketball, cross-country, soccer, tennis, volleyball W. **Intramural:** Basketball, football (non-tackle) M, racquetball, soccer, softball W, swimming, tennis, track and field, volleyball. **Team name:** Royals.

Student services. Alcohol/substance abuse counseling, chaplain/spiritual director, career counseling, student employment services, financial aid counseling, health services, on-campus daycare, personal counseling, placement for graduates. **Physically disabled:** Services for visually impaired.

Contact. E-mail: johnsonu@johnsonu.edu
Phone: (865) 251-2233 Toll-free number: (800) 827-2122
Fax: (865) 251-2336
Tim Wingfield, Director of Admissions, Johnson University, 7900 Johnson Drive, Knoxville, TN 37998-0001

King University
Bristol, Tennessee   **CB member**
www.king.edu   **CB code: 1371**

- Private 4-year nursing and liberal arts college affiliated with the Presbyterian Church (USA)
- Residential campus in large town
- 2,118 degree-seeking undergraduates
- 391 graduate students
- SAT or ACT (ACT writing optional), application essay required

General. Founded in 1867. Regionally accredited. Christian values emphasized. **Degrees:** 837 bachelor's, 13 associate awarded; master's offered. **Location:** 110 miles from Knoxville; 95 miles from Asheville, NC. **Calendar:** Semester, extensive summer session. **Full-time faculty:** 85 total; 60% have terminal degrees, 6% minority, 56% women. **Part-time faculty:** 208 total; 22% have terminal degrees, 2% minority, 63% women. **Class size:** 71% < 20, 28% 20-39, less than 1% 40-49, less than 1% 50-99. **Special facilities:** Observatory, nuclear physics laboratory.

Freshman class profile.

GPA 3.75 or higher:	32%	Rank in top quarter:	39%
GPA 3.50-3.74:	19%	Rank in top tenth:	16%
GPA 3.0-3.49:	32%	Out-of-state:	50%
GPA 2.0-2.99:	17%	Live on campus:	87%

Basis for selection. Qualified applicants have 2.4 GPA and 19 ACT/890 SAT (exclusive of Writing). Others may be conditionally accepted. SAT Writing used for financial aid eligibility purposes only. Interview recommended.

High school preparation. College-preparatory program recommended. 15 units required; 18 recommended. Required and recommended units include English 4, mathematics 3-4, social studies 1-2, history 1-2, science 1-2 (laboratory 1), foreign language 2 and academic electives 4. 2 algebra (I and II); one unit of geometry; 1 natural science required.

2015-2016 Annual costs. Tuition/fees: $26,480. Room/board: $8,180. Books/supplies: $1,340.

Financial aid. Non-need-based: Scholarships awarded for academics, art, athletics, job skills, music/drama, state residency.

Application procedures. Admission: No deadline. $25 fee, may be waived for applicants with need, free for online applicants. Admission notification on a rolling basis beginning on or about 9/1. **Financial aid:** Priority date 3/1; no closing date. FAFSA required. Applicants notified on a rolling basis starting 3/1; must reply within 2 week(s) of notification.

Academics. Special study options: Accelerated study, combined bachelor's/graduate degree, distance learning, double major, dual enrollment of high school students, honors, independent study, internships, liberal arts/career combination, student-designed major, study abroad, teacher certification program. **Credit/placement by examination:** AP, CLEP, SAT, ACT, institutional tests. 30 credit hours maximum toward bachelor's degree. **Support services:** Learning center, reduced course load, remedial instruction, study skills assistance, tutoring, writing center.

Honors college/program. Specific score on entrance exam required.

Majors. Area/ethnic studies: American. **Biology:** General, biochemistry, biophysics, neuroscience. **Business:** Accounting, business admin, management information systems. **Communications:** Digital media. **Computer sciences:** Information technology. **Education:** Music, physical. **English:** English lit. **Foreign languages:** General, French, Spanish. **Health services:** Athletic training, clinical lab science, nursing (RN). **History:** General. **Math:** General. **Philosophy/religion:** Religion. **Physical sciences:** Chemistry, physics. **Psychology:** General. **Social sciences:** Economics, political science. **Theology:** Bible, youth ministry. **Visual/performing arts:** General, photography.

Most popular majors. Business/marketing 35%, health sciences 42%.

Technology on campus. PC or laptop required. 88 workstations in library, computer center, student center. Dormitories wired for high-speed internet access and linked to campus network. Commuter students can connect to campus network. Online library, helpline, repair service, wireless network available.

Student life. Freshman orientation: Available. Preregistration for classes offered. **Policies:** Traditional undergraduates participate in Chapel and Convocation series as part of service requirements necessary to fulfill degree requirements. Religious observance required. **Housing:** Guaranteed on-campus for all undergraduates. Single-sex dorms available. $250 fully refundable deposit, deadline 8/15. **Activities:** Bands, campus ministries, choral groups, dance, drama, international student organizations, music ensembles, musical theater, student government, student newspaper, Fellowship of Christian Athletes, Young Life Leadership, student life and activities committee, Students in Free Enterprise, College Republicans, World Christian Fellowship, literary society.

Athletics. NCAA. **Intercollegiate:** Baseball M, basketball, cheerleading, cross-country, golf, soccer, softball W, swimming, tennis, track and field, volleyball, wrestling. **Intramural:** Badminton, basketball, cross-country, football (non-tackle), golf, soccer, softball W, table tennis, track and field, ultimate frisbee, volleyball. **Team name:** Tornado.

Student services. Adult student services, chaplain/spiritual director, career counseling, student employment services, financial aid counseling, health services, personal counseling, placement for graduates.

Contact. E-mail: admissions@king.edu
Phone: (423) 652-4861 Toll-free number: (800) 362-0014
Fax: (423) 652-4727
John King, VP of Development & Enrollment Management, King University, 1350 King College Road, Bristol, TN 37620-2699

Lane College
Jackson, Tennessee
www.lanecollege.edu
CB code: 1395

- Private 4-year liberal arts college affiliated with the Christian Methodist Episcopal Church
- Residential campus in small city
- 1,376 degree-seeking undergraduates: 2% part-time, 46% women, 97% African American, 2% Multi-racial, non-Hispanic
- 55% of applicants admitted
- SAT or ACT (ACT writing optional), application essay, interview required
- 32% graduate within 6 years

General. Founded in 1882. Regionally accredited. **Degrees:** 182 bachelor's awarded. **ROTC:** Army. **Location:** 80 miles from Memphis, 126 miles from Nashville. **Calendar:** Semester, limited summer session. **Full-time faculty:** 65 total; 37% women. **Part-time faculty:** 7 total; 43% women. **Class size:** 42% < 20, 51% 20-39, 6% 40-49, less than 1% 50-99.

Freshman class profile. 4,729 applied, 2,579 admitted, 444 enrolled.

Mid 50% test scores		
SAT critical reading:	320-380	
SAT math:	320-400	
ACT composite:	14-17	
GPA 3.75 or higher:	1%	
GPA 3.50-3.74:	1%	
GPA 3.0-3.49:	13%	
GPA 2.0-2.99:		65%
Rank in top quarter:		30%
Rank in top tenth:		9%
Return as sophomores:		53%
Out-of-state:		37%
Live on campus:		94%

Basis for selection. Academic record, examination scores and letters of recommendations most important. For conditional acceptance. **Learning Disabled:** Interviews and personal statements are needed when conditional acceptance or learning disabilities. Medical documents regarding disabilities are needed.

High school preparation. College-preparatory program recommended. 16 units recommended. Recommended units include English 4, mathematics 2, social studies 2, science 2 and foreign language 2.

2015-2016 Annual costs. Tuition/fees: $9,930. Room/board: $6,620. Books/supplies: $1,300. Personal expenses: $1,000.

2015-2016 Financial aid. Need-based: 444 full-time freshmen applied for aid; 444 deemed to have need; 437 received aid. Average need met was 50%. Average scholarship/grant was $7,996; average loan $3,448. 67% of total undergraduate aid awarded as scholarships/grants, 33% as loans/jobs. **Non-need-based:** Awarded to 1,270 full-time undergraduates, including 382 freshmen. Scholarships awarded for academics, athletics, religious affiliation.

Application procedures. Admission: Closing date 7/1 (postmark date). No application fee. Admission notification on a rolling basis beginning on or about 2/1. Must reply by May 1 or within 2 week(s) if notified thereafter. **Financial aid:** Priority date 3/1; no closing date. FAFSA required. Applicants notified on a rolling basis starting 3/31; must reply within 2 week(s) of notification.

Academics. Special study options: Honors, independent study, internships, study abroad. **Credit/placement by examination:** AP, CLEP, SAT, ACT. **Support services:** Study skills assistance, tutoring, writing center.

Majors. Biology: General. **Business:** Business admin. **Communications:** Media studies. **Computer sciences:** General. **Education:** Physical. **English:** English lit. **Foreign languages:** French. **History:** General. **Math:** General. **Philosophy/religion:** Religion. **Physical sciences:** Chemistry, physics. **Protective services:** Criminal justice. **Social sciences:** Sociology. **Visual/performing arts:** Music.

Most popular majors. Biology 16%, business/marketing 19%, communications/journalism 7%, computer/information sciences 7%, education 6%, security/protective services 19%, social sciences 13%.

Technology on campus. 470 workstations in library, computer center. Dormitories wired for high-speed internet access and linked to campus network. Online library, helpline, wireless network available.

Student life. Freshman orientation: Mandatory. Preregistration for classes offered. **Policies:** Religious observance required. **Housing:** Single-sex dorms available. $50 nonrefundable deposit. **Activities:** Bands, campus ministries, choral groups, dance, drama, music ensembles, radio station, student government, student newspaper, Student Ministerial Alliance, Student Christian Association, Pre-Alumni Council, mass communications club, history club, Phi Beta Lambda, Beta Kappa Chi.

Athletics. NCAA. **Intercollegiate:** Baseball M, basketball, cheerleading, cross-country, football (tackle) M, softball W, tennis, track and field, volleyball W. **Intramural:** Basketball, softball, swimming, table tennis, volleyball. **Team name:** Dragons.

Student services. Alcohol/substance abuse counseling, chaplain/spiritual director, career counseling, services for economically disadvantaged, student employment services, financial aid counseling, health services, personal counseling, placement for graduates, veterans' counselor, women's services.

Contact. E-mail: admissions@lanecollege.edu
Phone: (731) 426-7533 Toll-free number: (800) 960-7533
Fax: (731) 426-7559
Monica Scott, Director of Enrollment Management, Lane College, 545 Lane Avenue, Jackson, TN 38301-4598

Lee University
Cleveland, Tennessee
www.leeuniversity.edu
CB code: 1401

- Private 4-year university and liberal arts college affiliated with the Church of God
- Residential campus in large town

- 4,151 degree-seeking undergraduates: 9% part-time, 59% women, 6% African American, 1% Asian American, 4% Hispanic/Latino, 1% Native American, 4% international
- 454 degree-seeking graduate students
- 52% graduate within 6 years

General. Founded in 1918. Regionally accredited. **Degrees:** 784 bachelor's awarded; master's offered. **Location:** 20 miles from Chattanooga, 75 miles from Knoxville. **Calendar:** Semester, extensive summer session. **Full-time faculty:** 135 total; 96% have terminal degrees, 17% women. **Part-time faculty:** 195 total; 40% have terminal degrees, 9% minority, 20% women. **Class size:** 54% < 20, 35% 20-39, 5% 40-49, 4% 50-99, 1% >100.

Freshman class profile. 2,141 applied, 1,830 admitted, 835 enrolled.

Mid 50% test scores		GPA 2.0-2.99:	12%
SAT critical reading:	460-610	Rank in top quarter:	47%
SAT math:	440-570	Rank in top tenth:	11%
ACT composite:	21-27	Return as sophomores:	78%
GPA 3.75 or higher:	44%	Out-of-state:	51%
GPA 3.50-3.74:	20%	Live on campus:	86%
GPA 3.0-3.49:	23%	International:	3%

Basis for selection. Open admission, but selective for some programs. School achievement record and test scores considered. Students with 16 college semester hours, 24 for TN residents, are not required to provide test scores. Audition required for music program. **Home schooled:** Must have high school transcript with date of graduation and 17 ACT or 860 SAT (exclusive of Writing).

High school preparation. College-preparatory program recommended. 13 units required; 14 recommended. Required and recommended units include English 4, mathematics 3, social studies 2, history 1, science 2, foreign language 1 and computer science 1.

2015-2016 Annual costs. Tuition/fees: $15,000. Room/board: $7,045. Books/supplies: $1,200. Personal expenses: $2,610.

2015-2016 Financial aid. Need-based: 757 full-time freshmen applied for aid; 597 deemed to have need; 596 received aid. Average need met was 63%. Average scholarship/grant was $11,325; average loan $3,201. 82% of total undergraduate aid awarded as scholarships/grants, 18% as loans/jobs. **Non-need-based:** Awarded to 945 full-time undergraduates, including 285 freshmen. Scholarships awarded for academics, alumni affiliation, athletics, leadership, minority status, music/drama, religious affiliation, state residency.

Application procedures. Admission: Priority date 4/15; no deadline. $25 fee. Admission notification on a rolling basis beginning on or about 3/1. **Financial aid:** Priority date 3/15; no closing date. FAFSA required. Applicants notified on a rolling basis starting 2/1.

Academics. Special study options: Distance learning, double major, dual enrollment of high school students, ESL, external degree, honors, independent study, internships, student-designed major, study abroad, teacher certification program, Washington semester. **Credit/placement by examination:** AP, CLEP, IB, institutional tests. 32 credit hours maximum toward bachelor's degree. **Support services:** Learning center, pre-admission summer program, reduced course load, remedial instruction, tutoring, writing center.

Majors. Biology: General, biochemistry, environmental. **Business:** Accounting, business admin, management information systems. **Communications:** Advertising, communications/speech/rhetoric, digital media, journalism, public relations. **Computer sciences:** General. **Education:** General, art, biology, business, chemistry, drama/dance, early childhood, elementary, English, French, health, history, mathematics, middle, music, physical, psychology, Spanish, special ed. **English:** English lit. **Foreign languages:** French, Spanish. **Health services:** Athletic training, health care admin, prenursing. **History:** General. **Liberal arts:** Humanities. **Math:** General. **Parks/recreation:** Health/fitness. **Philosophy/religion:** Christian, philosophy. **Physical sciences:** Chemistry. **Psychology:** General. **Social sciences:** Anthropology, political science, sociology. **Theology:** Bible, missionary, pastoral counseling, preministerial, religious ed, sacred music, theology, youth ministry. **Visual/performing arts:** Dramatic, music, music performance, studio arts.

Most popular majors. Business/marketing 11%, communications/journalism 12%, education 16%, health sciences 6%, liberal arts 6%, psychology 10%, theological studies 18%.

Technology on campus. 300 workstations in dormitories, library, computer center, student center. Dormitories wired for high-speed internet access and linked to campus network. Commuter students can connect to campus network. Online library, helpline, wireless network available.

Student life. Freshman orientation: Mandatory. Preregistration for classes offered. Held weekend before classes begin. **Policies:** Religious observance required. **Housing:** Guaranteed on-campus for freshmen. Single-sex dorms, apartments available. $200 fully refundable deposit, deadline 9/1. University leases apartments and houses for students. **Activities:** Bands, campus ministries, choral groups, drama, international student organizations, literary magazine, music ensembles, Model UN, musical theater, opera, student government, student newspaper, symphony orchestra, Greek councils, student leadership council, Collegiate Sertoma, married students fellowship, Pioneers for Christ, Fellowship of Christian Athletes, Missions Alive, deaf ministry association.

Athletics. NCAA, NCCAA. **Intercollegiate:** Baseball M, basketball, cheerleading, cross-country, golf, soccer, softball W, tennis, volleyball W. **Intramural:** Basketball, bowling, football (non-tackle) M, racquetball, soccer, softball, table tennis, tennis, volleyball. **Team name:** Flames.

Student services. Alcohol/substance abuse counseling, chaplain/spiritual director, career counseling, student employment services, financial aid counseling, health services, personal counseling, placement for graduates, veterans' counselor.

Contact. E-mail: admissions@leeuniversity.edu
Phone: (423) 614-8500 Toll-free number: (800) 533-8890
Fax: (423) 614-8533
Phil Cook, Vice President for Enrollment, Lee University, 1120 North Ocoee Street, Cleveland, TN 37320-3450

LeMoyne-Owen College
Memphis, Tennessee — **CB member**
www.loc.edu — **CB code: 1403**

- Private 4-year liberal arts college affiliated with the Baptist faith
- Commuter campus in very large city
- 945 degree-seeking undergraduates: 98% African American, 1% international
- SAT or ACT (ACT writing recommended) required

General. Founded in 1862. Regionally accredited. LeMoyne-Owen College is an historically black college founded in 1862. Offering the Bachelors degree in 23 different areas, LeMoyne-Owen College is located in Memphis, Tennessee. **Degrees:** 148 bachelor's awarded. **ROTC:** Army, Air Force. **Calendar:** Semester, limited summer session. **Full-time faculty:** 51 total; 61% have terminal degrees, 55% women. **Part-time faculty:** 60 total; 18% have terminal degrees, 50% women. **Class size:** 80% < 20, 19% 20-39, 1% 40-49.

Basis for selection. High school transcript, test scores, letter of recommendation, and interview important. Special consideration given to children of alumni. Essay and interview recommended.

High school preparation. College-preparatory program recommended. 22 units required. Required units include English 4, mathematics 4, social studies 3, science 3, foreign language 2, computer science 1, visual/performing arts 1 and academic electives 4.

2015-2016 Annual costs. Tuition/fees: $10,680. Room/board: $5,910. Books/supplies: $1,600. Personal expenses: $1,800.

Financial aid. Non-need-based: Scholarships awarded for academics, athletics, music/drama.

Application procedures. Admission: Priority date 8/16; deadline 9/1 (postmark date). $25 fee. Admission notification on a rolling basis beginning on or about 6/16. Must reply by May 1 or within 2 week(s) if notified thereafter. High school students are able to admit early shortly after graduation dates. **Financial aid:** Priority date 4/15; no closing date. FAFSA required. Applicants notified on a rolling basis starting 4/1.

Academics. Special study options: Accelerated study, cooperative education, cross-registration, double major, dual enrollment of high school students, honors, independent study, internships, liberal arts/career combination, study abroad, teacher certification program, weekend college. **Credit/placement by examination:** AP, CLEP, IB, SAT, ACT, institutional tests. 24 credit hours maximum toward bachelor's degree. **Support services:** Learning center, pre-admission summer program, reduced course load, remedial instruction, study skills assistance, tutoring, writing center. Center for Active Student Education, Student Achievement Center.

Majors. Biology: General. **Business:** Business admin. **Computer sciences:** Computer science, information technology. **Education:** Early childhood, mathematics, multi-level teacher, science, social studies, special ed. **English:** English lit. **History:** General. **Human services:** Social work. **Liberal arts:** Humanities. **Math:** General. **Physical sciences:** Chemistry. **Protective services:** Police science. **Social sciences:** General, political science, sociology. **Visual/performing arts:** Art, music.

Most popular majors. Business/marketing 49%, computer/information sciences 6%, education 9%, security/protective services 9%, social sciences 11%.

Technology on campus. 237 workstations in dormitories, library, computer center, student center. Dormitories wired for high-speed internet access and linked to campus network. Commuter students can connect to campus network. Online library, wireless network available.

Student life. Freshman orientation: Mandatory. Preregistration for classes offered. **Housing:** Coed dorms, single-sex dorms, special housing for disabled available. $215 nonrefundable deposit, deadline 7/30. **Activities:** Campus ministries, choral groups, dance, drama, international student organizations, music ensembles, student government, student newspaper, NAACP, social work club, Students for Free Enterprise, pre-alumni council, National Student Business Organization, Business Students Association.

Athletics. NCAA. **Intercollegiate:** Baseball M, basketball, cheerleading, cross-country, golf, softball W, tennis, volleyball W. **Intramural:** Basketball. **Team name:** Magicians.

Student services. Adult student services, alcohol/substance abuse counseling, chaplain/spiritual director, career counseling, student employment services, financial aid counseling, health services, personal counseling, placement for graduates, veterans' counselor.

Contact. E-mail: admission@loc.edu
Phone: (901) 435-1500 Fax: (901) 435-1524
Samuel King, Director of Admissions/Recruitment, LeMoyne-Owen College, 807 Walker Avenue, Memphis, TN 38126

Lincoln Memorial University
Harrogate, Tennessee
www.lmunet.edu

CB member
CB code: 1408

- Private 4-year university and liberal arts college
- Commuter campus in small town
- 1,617 degree-seeking undergraduates
- 2,036 graduate students
- SAT or ACT (ACT writing optional) required

General. Founded in 1897. Regionally accredited. **Degrees:** 326 bachelor's, 158 associate awarded; master's, professional, doctoral offered. **ROTC:** Army. **Location:** 50 miles from Knoxville. **Calendar:** Semester, limited summer session. **Full-time faculty:** 206 total; 95% have terminal degrees, 5% minority, 54% women. **Part-time faculty:** 84 total; 14% have terminal degrees, 4% minority, 57% women. **Class size:** 82% < 20, 16% 20-39, less than 1% 40-49, 1% 50-99. **Special facilities:** Abraham Lincoln library and museum, mountain research center, driving range.

Freshman class profile.

GPA 3.75 or higher:	27%	GPA 2.0-2.99:	17%
GPA 3.50-3.74:	21%	Out-of-state:	37%
GPA 3.0-3.49:	35%	Live on campus:	70%

Basis for selection. Academic record, ACT or SAT very important.

High school preparation. College-preparatory program recommended. Required and recommended units include English 4, mathematics 3-4, social studies 1-2, history 1, science 2, foreign language 2 and visual/performing arts 1.

2015-2016 Annual costs. Tuition/fees: $20,546. Room/board: $7,300. Books/supplies: $1,400. Personal expenses: $2,000.

Financial aid. Non-need-based: Scholarships awarded for academics, alumni affiliation, athletics, music/drama, ROTC.

Application procedures. Admission: Priority date 6/1; no deadline. $25 fee, may be waived for applicants with need, free for online applicants. Admission notification on a rolling basis beginning on or about 9/1. **Financial aid:** Priority date 2/15; no closing date. FAFSA required. Applicants notified on a rolling basis starting 3/15; must reply within 3 week(s) of notification.

Academics. Special study options: Distance learning, double major, dual enrollment of high school students, ESL, honors, independent study, internships, study abroad, teacher certification program. **Credit/placement by examination:** AP, CLEP, IB, SAT, ACT, institutional tests. 16 credit hours maximum toward associate degree, 32 toward bachelor's. **Support services:** Learning center, reduced course load, remedial instruction, study skills assistance, tutoring, writing center.

Honors college/program. Complete a total of 26 credits of Honors program approved courses, especially in science and math. Maintain semester and cumulative G.P.A. of 3.00 or higher with no honors course grade less than a "C". Complete a minimum of one honors course per year. Complete one honors service-learning experience per year. Participate in one honors program social event per semester. Complete the honors thesis project and defense before a student and faculty panel.

Majors. Area/ethnic studies: American. **Biology:** General. **Business:** General, accounting, business admin, management science, managerial economics, office/clerical. **Communications:** Communications/speech/rhetoric. **Computer sciences:** General. **Conservation:** Environmental science, wildlife/wilderness. **Education:** General, art, biology, business, chemistry, early childhood, elementary, English, health, history, mathematics, middle, physical, science, secondary, social science, social studies. **English:** English lit. **Health services:** Athletic training, clinical lab science, clinical lab technology, nursing (RN), predental, premedicine, prepharmacy, preveterinary, veterinary technology/assistant. **History:** General. **Human services:** Social work. **Liberal arts:** Humanities. **Math:** General. **Parks/recreation:** Health/fitness. **Philosophy/religion:** General. **Physical sciences:** Chemistry. **Protective services:** Law enforcement admin. **Psychology:** General. **Social sciences:** General. **Visual/performing arts:** General, art.

Most popular majors. Biology 7%, business/marketing 17%, education 9%, health sciences 36%.

Technology on campus. Dormitories wired for high-speed internet access and linked to campus network. Commuter students can connect to campus network. Online library, helpline, wireless network available.

Student life. Freshman orientation: Mandatory. Preregistration for classes offered. **Housing:** Guaranteed on-campus for all undergraduates. Coed dorms, single-sex dorms, special housing for disabled, apartments available. $200 fully refundable deposit. Housing deposit refundable in full until 7/1. **Activities:** Pep band, campus ministries, choral groups, dance, drama, international student organizations, literary magazine, music ensembles, radio station, student government, TV station, Baptist collegiate ministries, Students in Free Enterprise, international student union, All Beliefs in Action.

Athletics. NCAA. **Intercollegiate:** Baseball M, basketball, cheerleading, cross-country, golf, soccer, softball W, tennis, volleyball W. **Intramural:** Basketball, football (non-tackle), soccer, softball, swimming, table tennis, tennis, ultimate frisbee, volleyball. **Team name:** Railsplitters.

Student services. Alcohol/substance abuse counseling, chaplain/spiritual director, career counseling, student employment services, financial aid counseling, health services, personal counseling, placement for graduates. **Physically disabled:** Services for visually, hearing impaired.

Contact. E-mail: admissions@lmunet.edu
Phone: (423) 869-3611 ext. 6280
Toll-free number: (800) 325-0900 ext. 6280 Fax: (423) 869-6444
Sherry McCreary, Director of Admissions, Lincoln Memorial University, 6965 Cumberland Gap Parkway, Harrogate, TN 37752-1901

Lipscomb University
Nashville, Tennessee
www.lipscomb.edu

CB code: 1161

- Private 4-year university and liberal arts college affiliated with the Church of Christ
- Residential campus in very large city
- 3,024 degree-seeking undergraduates: 10% part-time, 61% women, 7% African American, 3% Asian American, 7% Hispanic/Latino, 2% Multiracial, non-Hispanic, 2% international
- 1,649 degree-seeking graduate students
- 61% of applicants admitted
- SAT or ACT (ACT writing optional), interview required
- 55% graduate within 6 years

General. Founded in 1891. Regionally accredited. **Degrees:** 565 bachelor's awarded; master's, professional, doctoral offered. **ROTC:** Army, Air Force. **Location:** 4 miles from downtown. **Calendar:** Semester, extensive summer session. **Full-time faculty:** 206 total; 1% have terminal degrees, 6% minority, 41% women. **Part-time faculty:** 368 total; 7% minority, 46% women. **Class size:** 57% < 20, 33% 20-39, 4% 40-49, 6% 50-99.

Freshman class profile. 3,311 applied, 2,012 admitted, 669 enrolled.

Mid 50% test scores			Return as sophomores:	84%
SAT critical reading:		570-690	Out-of-state:	44%
SAT math:		560-670	Live on campus:	83%
ACT composite:		23-29	International:	2%
Rank in top quarter:		57%	Fraternities:	16%
Rank in top tenth:		29%	Sororities:	17%

Basis for selection. School achievement record, test scores, educational and personal references required. Strong moral character desired. Audition required for music; portfolio required for art; interview recommended for art, honors, music programs.

High school preparation. College-preparatory program recommended. 14 units required. Required units include English 4, mathematics 2, social studies 2, science 2, foreign language 2 and academic electives 2. Math units preferably algebra I, II. Foreign language units in the same language. 2 academic electives should be selected from natural sciences, mathematics, foreign languages, or social sciences.

2015-2016 Annual costs. Tuition/fees: $28,624. Room/board: $11,032. Books/supplies: $1,500. Personal expenses: $1,250.

2015-2016 Financial aid. **Need-based:** 662 full-time freshmen applied for aid; 430 deemed to have need; 430 received aid. Average need met was 62%. Average scholarship/grant was $3,599; average loan $3,514. 70% of total undergraduate aid awarded as scholarships/grants, 30% as loans/jobs. **Non-need-based:** Awarded to 2,443 full-time undergraduates, including 681 freshmen. Scholarships awarded for academics, art, athletics, leadership, minority status, music/drama, religious affiliation, state residency.

Application procedures. **Admission:** Priority date 10/31; no deadline. $50 fee, may be waived for applicants with need. Admission notification on a rolling basis beginning on or about 10/31. **Financial aid:** Priority date 3/31; no closing date. FAFSA required. Applicants notified on a rolling basis starting 3/1.

Academics. **Special study options:** Accelerated study, combined bachelor's/graduate degree, cross-registration, distance learning, double major, dual enrollment of high school students, ESL, honors, independent study, internships, student-designed major, study abroad, teacher certification program. **Credit/placement by examination:** AP, CLEP, IB, SAT, ACT, institutional tests. 30 credit hours maximum toward bachelor's degree. **Support services:** Learning center, pre-admission summer program, reduced course load, remedial instruction, study skills assistance, tutoring, writing center.

Majors. **Area/ethnic studies:** American. **Biology:** General, biochemistry. **Business:** Accounting, business admin, fashion, human resources, international, management information systems, managerial economics, marketing. **Communications:** Journalism, media studies, organizational, public relations. **Computer sciences:** Computer science, information technology. **Conservation:** Environmental science. **Education:** Art, biology, chemistry, drama/dance, elementary, English, ESL, French, German, history, mathematics, music, physical, physics, Spanish. **Engineering:** Computer, engineering mechanics, engineering science, mechanical. **English:** English lit, rhetoric/composition. **Foreign languages:** French, German, Spanish. **Health services:** Athletic training, dietetics, nursing (RN), predental, premedicine, prenursing, prepharmacy, preveterinary. **History:** General. **Human services:** General, social work. **Math:** General. **Parks/recreation:** Exercise sciences. **Philosophy/religion:** Philosophy. **Physical sciences:** Chemistry, physics. **Psychology:** General. **Social sciences:** Political science, urban studies. **Theology:** Bible, missionary, youth ministry. **Visual/performing arts:** Commercial/advertising art, dramatic, music performance, music theory/composition, piano/keyboard, studio arts, voice/opera. **Work/family studies:** General, clothing/textiles, family systems, institutional food production.

Most popular majors. Biology 7%, business/marketing 19%, education 9%, health sciences 14%, psychology 8%.

Technology on campus. 203 workstations in dormitories, library, computer center, student center. Dormitories wired for high-speed internet access and linked to campus network. Commuter students can connect to campus network. Online course registration, helpline, repair service, wireless network available.

Student life. **Freshman orientation:** Mandatory, $110 fee. Preregistration for classes offered. **Policies:** Daily chapel service and Bible studies required. Out-of-town undergraduates required to live on campus, except for seniors, students over age of 21, married students. Religious observance required. **Housing:** Single-sex dorms, apartments available. $150 fully refundable deposit, deadline 8/15. **Activities:** Bands, campus ministries, choral groups, dance, drama, international student organizations, music ensembles, musical theater, radio station, student government, student newspaper, College Republicans, Young Democrats, honorary societies, multicultural association, Circle K, Fellowship of Christian Athletes, Youth Encouragement Services, men and women's service clubs, homeless ministry, DAC (ministry to the hearing impaired).

Athletics. NCAA. **Intercollegiate:** Baseball M, basketball, cross-country, golf, soccer, softball W, tennis, track and field, volleyball W. **Intramural:** Badminton, basketball, football (non-tackle), racquetball, soccer, softball, tennis, volleyball. **Team name:** Bisons.

Student services. Adult student services, chaplain/spiritual director, career counseling, student employment services, financial aid counseling, health services, minority student services, personal counseling, placement for graduates. **Physically disabled:** Services for visually, speech, hearing impaired.

Contact. E-mail: admissions@lipscomb.edu
Phone: (615) 966-1776 Toll-free number: (877) 582-4766
Fax: (615) 966-1804
Ricky Holaway, Director of Admissions, Lipscomb University, One University Park Drive, Nashville, TN 37204-3951

Martin Methodist College
Pulaski, Tennessee
www.martinmethodist.edu   **CB code: 1449**

- Private 4-year liberal arts college affiliated with the United Methodist Church
- Residential campus in small town
- 1,050 degree-seeking undergraduates

General. Founded in 1870. Regionally accredited. **Degrees:** 181 bachelor's, 8 associate awarded. **Location:** 70 miles from Nashville; 40 miles from Huntsville, AL. **Calendar:** Semester, limited summer session. **Full-time faculty:** 46 total; 50% have terminal degrees. **Part-time faculty:** 40 total; 20% have terminal degrees. **Class size:** 78% < 20, 21% 20-39, less than 1% 40-49.

Freshman class profile.

GPA 3.75 or higher:	15%	GPA 2.0-2.99:	35%
GPA 3.50-3.74:	16%	Out-of-state:	13%
GPA 3.0-3.49:	31%	Live on campus:	46%

Basis for selection. High school record, interview, test scores important. Applicants must meet 2 of the following or apply for special circumstances admission status: 2.0 GPA, 18 ACT, or rank in upper 50% of class. Students conditionally admitted will be offered full enrollment after completion of a semester with 2.0 GPA. ACT recommended. Audition recommended for music; portfolio recommended for art.

High school preparation. 13 units required. Required and recommended units include English 4, mathematics 2-3, social studies 2, history 1, science 2 (laboratory 2), foreign language 2, computer science 1 and academic electives 4.

2015-2016 Annual costs. Tuition/fees: $23,100. Room/board: $8,400. Books/supplies: $1,200. Personal expenses: $7,500.

Financial aid. **Non-need-based:** Scholarships awarded for academics, art, athletics, leadership, music/drama, religious affiliation, state residency.

Application procedures. **Admission:** Priority date 5/1; deadline 8/1 (postmark date). $30 fee. Admission notification on a rolling basis. **Financial aid:** No deadline. FAFSA, institutional form required. Applicants notified on a rolling basis starting 3/1; must reply within 2 week(s) of notification.

Academics. **Special study options:** Distance learning, double major, dual enrollment of high school students, ESL, honors, independent study, internships, liberal arts/career combination, study abroad, teacher certification program. **Credit/placement by examination:** AP, CLEP, IB, ACT, institutional tests. 30 credit hours maximum toward associate degree, 30 toward bachelor's. **Support services:** Learning center, pre-admission summer program, reduced course load, remedial instruction, study skills assistance, tutoring, writing center.

Majors. **Biology:** General. **Business:** General, accounting, business admin. **Education:** Biology, business, elementary, English, history, middle, physical, secondary. **English:** English lit. **Health services:** Nursing (RN). **History:** General. **Parks/recreation:** Health/fitness, sports admin. **Philosophy/religion:** Religion. **Protective services:** Law enforcement admin. **Psychology:** General. **Theology:** Preministerial, religious ed, sacred music.

Most popular majors. Biology 10%, business/marketing 15%, education 13%, liberal arts 13%, social sciences 22%.

Technology on campus. 200 workstations in library, computer center, student center. Dormitories wired for high-speed internet access and linked to campus network. Online library, helpline, wireless network available.

Student life. Freshman orientation: Mandatory. Preregistration for classes offered. Held 3 days prior to other students' arrival. **Housing:** Guaranteed on-campus for all undergraduates. Coed dorms, single-sex dorms, apartments, themed housing available. $250 fully refundable deposit, deadline 6/1. **Activities:** Jazz band, campus ministries, choral groups, drama, international student organizations, literary magazine, music ensembles, student government, student newspaper, student Christian association, black student union, Fellowship of Christian Athletes.

Athletics. NAIA. **Intercollegiate:** Baseball M, basketball, bowling, cheerleading W, golf, soccer, softball W, tennis, volleyball W. **Intramural:** Basketball, football (non-tackle), racquetball, softball, swimming, table tennis, ultimate frisbee, volleyball, water polo. **Team name:** RedHawks.

Student services. Adult student services, chaplain/spiritual director, career counseling, student employment services, financial aid counseling, personal counseling, placement for graduates, veterans' counselor.

Contact. E-mail: lsmith2@martinmethodist.edu
Phone: (931) 363-9868 Toll-free number: (800) 467-1273
Fax: (931) 363-9803
Lisa Smith, Director of Admissions, Martin Methodist College, 433 West Madison, Pulaski, TN 38478-2799

Maryville College
Maryville, Tennessee
www.maryvillecollege.edu **CB member** **CB code: 1454**

- Private 4-year liberal arts college affiliated with the Presbyterian Church (USA)
- Residential campus in large town
- 1,170 degree-seeking undergraduates: 1% part-time, 54% women, 11% African American, 1% Asian American, 3% Hispanic/Latino, 4% Multiracial, non-Hispanic, 2% international
- 67% of applicants admitted
- SAT or ACT (ACT writing optional) required
- 53% graduate within 6 years; 30% enter graduate study

General. Founded in 1819. Regionally accredited. **Degrees:** 209 bachelor's awarded. **Location:** 15 miles from Knoxville. **Calendar:** 4-1-4, limited summer session. **Full-time faculty:** 76 total; 87% have terminal degrees, 7% minority, 51% women. **Part-time faculty:** 42 total; 50% have terminal degrees, 14% minority, 57% women. **Class size:** 54% < 20, 44% 20-39, less than 1% 40-49, less than 1% 50-99. **Special facilities:** Science center, civic arts center, college woods with ropes courses, equestrian center.

Freshman class profile. 1,701 applied, 1,136 admitted, 338 enrolled.

Mid 50% test scores			
SAT critical reading:	440-560	Rank in top quarter:	42%
SAT math:	440-540	Rank in top tenth:	20%
ACT composite:	20-26	End year in good standing:	86%
GPA 3.75 or higher:	37%	Return as sophomores:	70%
GPA 3.50-3.74:	13%	Out-of-state:	35%
GPA 3.0-3.49:	26%	Live on campus:	90%
GPA 2.0-2.99:	24%	International:	3%

Basis for selection. Admissions based on academic criteria, extracurricular involvement, and personal achievement. Successful students typically follow strong college preparatory curriculums and rank in top 25% of class. Writing samples encouraged. Essay, interview recommended for all; audition required for music; portfolio recommended for art. **Home schooled:** Transcript of courses and grades required. Pursue rigorous curriculum that includes strong emphasis on writing and reasoning. **Learning Disabled:** Students must meet the same admission criteria as other students. Accommodated test scores accepted.

High school preparation. College-preparatory program required. 15 units required; 25 recommended. Required and recommended units include English 4, mathematics 3-4, social studies 2-4, history 1-2, science 2-4 (laboratory 1-2), foreign language 2-4 and computer science 1.

2015-2016 Annual costs. Tuition/fees: $32,866. Room/board: $10,442. Books/supplies: $1,152. Personal expenses: $1,350.

2015-2016 Financial aid. Need-based: 338 full-time freshmen applied for aid; 296 deemed to have need; 296 received aid. Average need met was 90%. Average scholarship/grant was $28,621; average loan $3,492. 81% of total undergraduate aid awarded as scholarships/grants, 19% as loans/jobs. **Non-need-based:** Awarded to 327 full-time undergraduates, including 108 freshmen. Scholarships awarded for academics, alumni affiliation, art, leadership, minority status, music/drama, religious affiliation, state residency.

Application procedures. Admission: Priority date 3/1; no deadline. No application fee. Admission notification on a rolling basis beginning on or about 11/1. Must reply by May 1 or within 4 week(s) if notified thereafter. Housing deposit refundable before 5/1. **Financial aid:** Priority date 2/1; no closing date. FAFSA required. Applicants notified on a rolling basis starting 3/12; must reply by 5/1 or within 4 week(s) of notification.

Academics. All students complete 6 credit-hour research project and comprehensive examination in their major area of study. **Special study options:** Accelerated study, combined bachelor's/graduate degree, double major, dual enrollment of high school students, ESL, honors, independent study, internships, liberal arts/career combination, student-designed major, study abroad, teacher certification program, Washington semester. Undergraduate research. **Credit/placement by examination:** AP, CLEP, IB, SAT, ACT, institutional tests. 32 credit hours maximum toward bachelor's degree. Students may petition individual departments for credit by examination. **Support services:** Learning center, reduced course load, remedial instruction, study skills assistance, tutoring, writing center.

Majors. Biology: General, biochemistry, neuroscience, pharmacology. **Business:** Accounting/finance, business admin, human resources, international, marketing. **Computer sciences:** General. **Conservation:** Environmental studies. **Education:** General, biology, chemistry, drama/dance, English, ESL, health, history, mathematics, music, physical, social studies, Spanish. **Engineering:** General. **English:** English lit, technical writing. **Foreign languages:** American Sign Language, sign language interpretation, Spanish. **Health services:** Nursing (RN), predental, premedicine, prenursing, prepharmacy, preveterinary. **History:** General. **Math:** General. **Parks/recreation:** General, exercise sciences, health/fitness. **Philosophy/religion:** Philosophy, religion. **Physical sciences:** Chemistry. **Psychology:** General, counseling, developmental. **Social sciences:** Criminology, economics, international relations, political science, sociology. **Visual/performing arts:** Design, dramatic, music, music performance, music theory/composition, studio arts.

Most popular majors. Biology 7%, business/marketing 17%, education 11%, English 8%, foreign language 6%, parks/recreation 6%, psychology 16%, social sciences 10%, visual/performing arts 8%.

Technology on campus. 265 workstations in library, computer center, student center. Dormitories wired for high-speed internet access and linked to campus network. Commuter students can connect to campus network. Online course registration, online library, helpline, repair service, wireless network available.

Student life. Freshman orientation: Mandatory, $25 fee. Preregistration for classes offered. Held several days before registration; includes Mountain Challenge component. Optional 3-day wilderness experience. **Policies:** Alcohol policy prohibits consumption in company of people under legal drinking age. **Housing:** Guaranteed on-campus for all undergraduates. Coed dorms, single-sex dorms, special housing for disabled, apartments, wellness housing available. $50 fully refundable deposit, deadline 5/1. **Activities:** Bands, campus ministries, choral groups, dance, drama, international student organizations, literary magazine, music ensembles, Model UN, student government, student newspaper, symphony orchestra, Habitat for Humanity, Literary Corps, Fellowship of Christian Athletes, wellness council, student programming board, black student association.

Athletics. NCAA. **Intercollegiate:** Baseball M, basketball, cheerleading, cross-country, equestrian, football (tackle) M, golf M, soccer, softball W, tennis, volleyball W. **Intramural:** Archery, badminton, baseball M, basketball, bowling, football (non-tackle), golf, racquetball, rugby, skiing, soccer, softball, swimming, table tennis, tennis, track and field, volleyball, water polo. **Team name:** Scots.

Student services. Adult student services, alcohol/substance abuse counseling, chaplain/spiritual director, career counseling, student employment services, financial aid counseling, health services, minority student services, personal counseling, placement for graduates, veterans' counselor. **Physically disabled:** Services for visually, speech, hearing impaired.

Contact. E-mail: admissions@maryvillecollege.edu
Phone: (865) 981-8092 Toll-free number: (800) 597-2687
Fax: (865) 981-8005
Cyndi Sweet, Director of Admissions, Maryville College, 502 East Lamar Alexander Parkway, Maryville, TN 37804-5907

Memphis College of Art
Memphis, Tennessee
www.mca.edu **CB code: 1511**

- Private 4-year visual arts college
- Residential campus in very large city

- 357 degree-seeking undergraduates: 15% part-time, 65% women, 29% African American, 1% Asian American, 6% Hispanic/Latino, 3% Multi-racial, non-Hispanic
- 41 degree-seeking graduate students
- 32% of applicants admitted
- SAT or ACT (ACT writing optional) required
- 100% graduate within 6 years

General. Founded in 1936. Regionally accredited. Students have access to Memphis Brooks Museum of Art and Overton Park Zoo. Consortium with four other local colleges/universities. Mobility consortium with 30+ art colleges across the US and Canada. **Degrees:** 52 bachelor's awarded; master's offered. **Location:** 500 miles from New Orleans, 700 miles from Dallas. **Calendar:** Semester, limited summer session. **Full-time faculty:** 22 total; 86% have terminal degrees, 23% minority, 59% women. **Part-time faculty:** 32 total; 31% have terminal degrees, 16% minority, 41% women. **Class size:** 89% < 20, 11% 20-39.

Freshman class profile. 959 applied, 305 admitted, 88 enrolled.

Mid 50% test scores			
SAT critical reading:	500-620	GPA 3.0-3.49:	45%
SAT math:	410-530	GPA 2.0-2.99:	20%
ACT composite:	19-25	Return as sophomores:	72%
GPA 3.75 or higher:	22%	Out-of-state:	53%
GPA 3.50-3.74:	13%	Live on campus:	67%

Basis for selection. Art portfolio, high school transcript, test scores required; letter of recommendation from art teacher and essay considered, but not required. Portfolio required; essay, interview recommended for all. **Home schooled:** State high school equivalency certificate required.

High school preparation. College-preparatory program recommended. Recommended units include visual/performing arts 1. Portfolio should include 10 to 20 pieces of work, originals or slides, with focus on direct observational drawing.

2015-2016 Annual costs. Tuition/fees: $30,250. Room/board: $8,550. Books/supplies: $1,650. Personal expenses: $1,500. **Additional information:** Room and board are estimated amounts.

Financial aid. Non-need-based: Scholarships awarded for academics, art. **Additional information:** Students considered for institutional resources through admissions application process.

Application procedures. Admission: Priority date 3/31; no deadline. No application fee. Admission notification on a rolling basis beginning on or about 11/15. Must reply by May 1 or within 3 week(s) if notified thereafter. **Financial aid:** Priority date 2/15; no closing date. FAFSA required. Applicants notified on a rolling basis starting 3/15; must reply within 3 week(s) of notification.

Academics. Special study options: Combined bachelor's/graduate degree, cross-registration, double major, exchange student, independent study, internships, study abroad, teacher certification program. New York Studio Exchange Program. Mobility semester exchange at 30+ independent art colleges across the country (AICAD consortium). **Credit/placement by examination:** AP, CLEP, IB, SAT, ACT, institutional tests. 15 credit hours maximum toward bachelor's degree. **Support services:** Learning center, reduced course load, remedial instruction, study skills assistance, tutoring. Achievement counselor for one-on-one assistance, and group study sessions offered.

Majors. Visual/performing arts: Art, commercial/advertising art, design, digital arts, drawing, graphic design, illustration, metal/jewelry, multimedia, painting, photography, printmaking, sculpture, studio arts.

Technology on campus. 200 workstations in dormitories, library, computer center. Dormitories wired for high-speed internet access. Wireless network available.

Student life. Freshman orientation: Mandatory. Preregistration for classes offered. Four-day session includes parents. **Policies:** Considerable assistance available in matching roommates and helping students find affordable housing within walking distance. **Housing:** Coed dorms, apartments, wellness housing available. $300 partly refundable deposit. **Activities:** International student organizations, student government, student newspaper, photography club, student alliance, multicultural student association, gay-straight alliance, Give-Back Program, Clay Bodies, The Swiftness.

Student services. Adult student services, career counseling, student employment services, financial aid counseling, personal counseling, placement for graduates, veterans' counselor.

Contact. E-mail: info@mca.edu
Phone: (901) 272-5151 Toll-free number: (800) 727-1088
Fax: (901) 272-5158
Gail Massey, Director of Enrollment, Memphis College of Art, 1930 Poplar Avenue, Memphis, TN 38104-2764

Middle Tennessee State University
Murfreesboro, Tennessee CB member
www.mtsu.edu CB code: 1466

- Public 4-year university
- Commuter campus in small city
- 19,446 degree-seeking undergraduates: 17% part-time, 54% women, 22% African American, 3% Asian American, 4% Hispanic/Latino, 3% Multi-racial, non-Hispanic, 3% international
- 2,225 degree-seeking graduate students
- 73% of applicants admitted
- SAT or ACT (ACT writing optional) required
- 46% graduate within 6 years

General. Founded in 1911. Regionally accredited. **Degrees:** 4,086 bachelor's awarded; master's, doctoral offered. **ROTC:** Army, Air Force. **Location:** 32 miles from Nashville. **Calendar:** Semester, extensive summer session. **Full-time faculty:** 918 total; 81% have terminal degrees, 18% minority, 47% women. **Part-time faculty:** 329 total; 27% have terminal degrees, 10% minority, 53% women. **Class size:** 45% < 20, 45% 20-39, 3% 40-49, 6% 50-99, 1% >100. **Special facilities:** 3 recording studios, observatory, flight simulators, weather center, electronic music laboratory, digital audio edit laboratory, satellite mapping equipment, seismograph, 3 television studios, electronic newsroom, Centers for Historic Preservation and Popular Music.

Freshman class profile. 8,164 applied, 5,927 admitted, 2,839 enrolled.

Mid 50% test scores			
SAT critical reading:	480-630	Rank in top quarter:	43%
SAT math:	450-610	Rank in top tenth:	19%
ACT composite:	19-25	Out-of-state:	4%
GPA 3.75 or higher:	27%	Live on campus:	36%
GPA 3.50-3.74:	21%	International:	4%
GPA 3.0-3.49:	36%	Fraternities:	11%
GPA 2.0-2.99:	16%	Sororities:	16%

Basis for selection. 3.0 GPA or 22 ACT or combination of 19 ACT and 2.7 GPA required. Personal statement required of students who do not meet standard requirements.

High school preparation. Required units include English 4, mathematics 4, social studies 1, history 1, science 3 (laboratory 1), foreign language 2 and visual/performing arts 1. Foreign language units must be in single language. Mathematics units must include algebra I and II, geometry or other advanced mathematics. 1 US history, 1 global studies also required.

2015-2016 Annual costs. Tuition/fees: $8,404; $25,972 out-of-state. Room/board: $8,550. Books/supplies: $1,325. Personal expenses: $3,533.

2014-2015 Financial aid. Need-based: Average need met was 69%. Average scholarship/grant was $6,285; average loan $3,282. 57% of total undergraduate aid awarded as scholarships/grants, 43% as loans/jobs. **Non-need-based:** Scholarships awarded for academics, leadership. **Additional information:** Deadline for scholarships 2/15.

Application procedures. Admission: No deadline. $25 fee, may be waived for applicants with need. Admission notification on a rolling basis. **Financial aid:** Priority date 3/1; no closing date. FAFSA required. Applicants notified on a rolling basis starting 4/15; must reply within 2 week(s) of notification.

Academics. Special study options: Distance learning, double major, dual enrollment of high school students, honors, independent study, internships, student-designed major, study abroad, teacher certification program. Academic basic skills. **Credit/placement by examination:** AP, CLEP, IB, SAT, ACT, institutional tests. 66 credit hours maximum toward bachelor's degree. Up to 66 semester hours from correspondence study, credit-by-examination, credit for service-related experience, and flight training may be counted toward degree. **Support services:** Learning center, pre-admission summer program, reduced course load, remedial instruction, study skills assistance, tutoring, writing center.

Honors college/program. 26 ACT/1170 SAT and 3.0 GPA or 22 ACT/ 950 SAT and 3.5 GPA required. SAT scores exclusive of Writing.

Majors. Biology: General. **Business:** Accounting, business admin, finance, management information systems, managerial economics, marketing, office management, purchasing, sales/distribution. **Communications:** Media studies. **Computer sciences:** General, computer science. **Education:** Art, business, early childhood, health, kindergarten/preschool, sales/marketing, special ed, technology/industrial arts. **English:** English lit. **Foreign languages:** General. **Health services:** Athletic training, nursing (RN). **History:** General. **Human services:** Social work. **Liberal arts:** Arts/sciences. **Math:** General. **Parks/recreation:** Facilities management, health/fitness. **Philosophy/religion:** Philosophy. **Physical sciences:** Chemistry, geology, physics. **Protective services:** Law enforcement admin. **Psychology:** General. **Social sciences:** Anthropology, economics, international relations, political science, sociology. **Visual/performing arts:** Art, art history/conservation, dramatic, interior design, music, music management. **Work/family studies:** Clothing/textiles, family resources, food/nutrition.

Most popular majors. Business/marketing 15%, communications/journalism 6%, education 6%, interdisciplinary studies 7%, liberal arts 10%, psychology 6%, visual/performing arts 9%.

Technology on campus. 2,300 workstations in dormitories, library, computer center, student center. Dormitories wired for high-speed internet access and linked to campus network. Commuter students can connect to campus network. Online course registration, online library, helpline, wireless network available.

Student life. Freshman orientation: Mandatory, $45 fee. Preregistration for classes offered. Offered from mid-June to mid-July. **Policies:** Parents notified when student under age of 21 found responsible for use and/or possession of drugs or alcohol. **Housing:** Coed dorms, single-sex dorms, special housing for disabled, apartments, fraternity/sorority housing, themed housing available. $300 partly refundable deposit. **Activities:** Bands, campus ministries, choral groups, dance, drama, film society, international student organizations, literary magazine, music ensembles, Model UN, musical theater, radio station, student government, student newspaper, symphony orchestra, TV station, Golden Key National Honor Society, African American student association, Fellowship of Christian Athletes, Collegiate Women International, Citizens for Action, Baptist student union, aerospace maintenance club, agricultural council, Student Tennessee Education Association.

Athletics. NCAA. **Intercollegiate:** Baseball M, basketball, cross-country, football (tackle) M, golf, soccer W, softball W, tennis, track and field, volleyball W. **Intramural:** Basketball M, boxing M, equestrian, football (tackle) M, racquetball, rugby M, soccer, softball, swimming, tennis, volleyball. **Team name:** Blue Raiders.

Student services. Adult student services, chaplain/spiritual director, career counseling, student employment services, financial aid counseling, health services, minority student services, on-campus daycare, personal counseling, placement for graduates, veterans' counselor, women's services. **Physically disabled:** Services for visually, speech, hearing impaired.

Contact. E-mail: admissions@mtsu.edu
Phone: (615) 898-2111 Fax: (615) 898-5478
Melinda Thomas, Director of Admissions, Middle Tennessee State University, 1301 East Main Street, Murfreesboro, TN 37132

Milligan College
Milligan College, Tennessee
www.milligan.edu   **CB code: 1469**

▶ Private 4-year liberal arts college affiliated with the Christian Church
▶ Residential campus in small city
▶ 832 degree-seeking undergraduates: 6% part-time, 63% women, 4% African American, 2% Asian American, 6% Hispanic/Latino, 2% Multiracial, non-Hispanic, 3% international
▶ 298 degree-seeking graduate students
▶ 65% of applicants admitted
▶ SAT or ACT (ACT writing optional), application essay required
▶ 62% graduate within 6 years

General. Founded in 1866. Regionally accredited. Weekly chapels, convocation programs, vespers. **Degrees:** 252 bachelor's awarded; master's offered. **Location:** 3 miles from Johnson City. **Calendar:** Semester, limited summer session. **Full-time faculty:** 79 total; 80% have terminal degrees, 4% minority, 53% women. **Part-time faculty:** 71 total; 32% have terminal degrees, 10% minority, 42% women. **Class size:** 73% < 20, 25% 20-39, 1% 40-49, 1% 50-99, less than 1% >100.

Freshman class profile. 603 applied, 393 admitted, 187 enrolled.

Mid 50% test scores			
SAT critical reading:	470-590	Rank in top quarter:	65%
SAT math:	500-600	Rank in top tenth:	37%
SAT writing:	460-590	Return as sophomores:	78%
ACT composite:	22-28	Out-of-state:	47%
GPA 3.75 or higher:	58%	Live on campus:	91%
GPA 3.50-3.74:	14%	International:	2%
GPA 3.0-3.49:	24%		

GPA 2.0-2.99: 4%

Basis for selection. Academic work, test scores, and references from minister/church leader and high school principal/counselor required. Audition required for music; interview recommended in some instances.

High school preparation. College-preparatory program recommended. Recommended units include English 4, mathematics 4, social studies 3, science 3 (laboratory 3), foreign language 2, visual/performing arts 1 and academic electives 3.

2015-2016 Annual costs. Tuition/fees: $29,830. Room/board: $6,500. Books/supplies: $1,300. Personal expenses: $1,324.

2015-2016 Financial aid. Need-based: Average need met was 83%. Average scholarship/grant was $20,659; average loan $4,063. 74% of total undergraduate aid awarded as scholarships/grants, 26% as loans/jobs. **Non-need-based:** Scholarships awarded for academics, art, athletics, leadership, minority status, music/drama.

Application procedures. Admission: No deadline. $30 fee, may be waived for applicants with need. Admission notification on a rolling basis beginning on or about 10/1. Must reply by May 1 or within 2 week(s) if notified thereafter. Housing deposit refundable until 5/1. **Financial aid:** Closing date 3/1. FAFSA required. Applicants notified on a rolling basis starting 3/15; must reply within 2 week(s) of notification.

Academics. Special study options: Combined bachelor's/graduate degree, cooperative education, distance learning, double major, dual enrollment of high school students, honors, independent study, internships, student-designed major, study abroad, teacher certification program, Washington semester. American Studies Program in Washington, DC; Australia Studies Center; China Studies Program; Contemporary Music Center in Martha's Vineyard; Latin American Studies Program in Costa Rica; Los Angeles Film Studies Center; Middle East Studies Program in Egypt; Russian Studies Program; Scholars' Semester in Oxford; Uganda Studies Program; Summer Institute of Journalism in Washington, DC; Oxford Summer Programme. **Credit/placement by examination:** AP, CLEP, IB, SAT, ACT, institutional tests. 32 credit hours maximum toward bachelor's degree. Students may not receive credit by examination upon achieving a total of 64 credit hours. **Support services:** Reduced course load, remedial instruction, study skills assistance, tutoring, writing center.

Majors. Biology: General. **Business:** Accounting, business admin. **Communications:** Communications/speech/rhetoric. **Computer sciences:** General. **Education:** General, early childhood, music. **English:** English lit. **Health services:** Nursing (RN). **History:** General. **Liberal arts:** Humanities. **Math:** General. **Parks/recreation:** Health/fitness. **Physical sciences:** Chemistry. **Psychology:** General. **Social sciences:** Political science, sociology. **Theology:** Bible. **Visual/performing arts:** General, music.

Most popular majors. Business/marketing 22%, education 10%, health sciences 20%, parks/recreation 10%, psychology 7%.

Technology on campus. 102 workstations in library, computer center. Dormitories wired for high-speed internet access and linked to campus network. Commuter students can connect to campus network. Online library, helpline, repair service, student web hosting, wireless network available.

Student life. Freshman orientation: Available, $10 fee. Preregistration for classes offered. Weekend sessions available in April or June. Abbreviated version offered weekend prior to first day of fall classes. **Policies:** Smoking and alcoholic beverages not permitted on-campus. Students must live in college housing unless married or living with members of immediate family. Religious observance required. **Housing:** Guaranteed on-campus for all undergraduates. Single-sex dorms, special housing for disabled, apartments, themed housing available. $200 nonrefundable deposit, deadline 8/15. **Activities:** Bands, campus ministries, choral groups, dance, drama, music ensembles, Model UN, radio station, student government, student newspaper, symphony orchestra, Fellowship of Christian Athletes, missions club, service seekers, College Republicans, Habitat for Humanity, political awareness group, Roteract.

Athletics. NAIA. **Intercollegiate:** Baseball M, basketball, cross-country, golf M, soccer, softball W, swimming, tennis, track and field, volleyball W. **Intramural:** Basketball, football (non-tackle), softball, table tennis, tennis, volleyball. **Team name:** Buffaloes.

Student services. Adult student services, chaplain/spiritual director, career counseling, student employment services, financial aid counseling, health services, minority student services, personal counseling, placement for graduates.

Contact. E-mail: admissions@milligan.edu
Phone: (423) 461-8730 Toll-free number: (800) 262-8337
Fax: (423) 461-8982
Jason Makowsky, Director of Enrollment Management, Milligan College, Box 210, Milligan College, TN 37682

O'More College of Design
Franklin, Tennessee
www.omorecollege.edu
CB code: 1545

- Private 4-year visual arts college
- Commuter campus in large town
- 176 degree-seeking undergraduates: 16% part-time, 90% women
- SAT or ACT (ACT writing optional) required

General. Founded in 1970. Accredited by ACCSC. **Degrees:** 31 bachelor's awarded. **Location:** 15 miles from Nashville. **Calendar:** Semester, limited summer session. **Full-time faculty:** 14 total; 7% minority, 57% women. **Part-time faculty:** 29 total; 7% have terminal degrees, 7% minority, 45% women. **Class size:** 100% < 20. **Special facilities:** Sensory garden.

Freshman class profile.

GPA 3.75 or higher:	39%	GPA 2.0-2.99:	15%
GPA 3.50-3.74:	18%	Out-of-state:	25%
GPA 3.0-3.49:	28%		

Basis for selection. High school record most important. Test scores, grades given equal weight. Students may be required to submit a portfolio and interview with the Department Chair. **Learning Disabled:** Students are recommended to discuss with Department Chair and instructors.

High school preparation. College-preparatory program recommended. 18 units recommended. Recommended units include English 4, mathematics 3, social studies 1, history 2, science 3, foreign language 2 and academic electives 3. Art, mechanical drawing, and design courses are recommended.

2015-2016 Annual costs. Tuition/fees: $27,360. Books/supplies: $1,050.

Financial aid. All financial aid based on need.

Application procedures. Admission: Priority date 4/8; deadline 7/31 (postmark date). $50 fee, may be waived for applicants with need. **Financial aid:** Closing date 4/7. FAFSA required.

Academics. Special study options: Accelerated study, double major, dual enrollment of high school students, independent study, internships, liberal arts/career combination, study abroad. Annual study-abroad program in Ireland and annual international trip. **Credit/placement by examination:** AP, CLEP, IB, institutional tests. 9 credit hours maximum toward bachelor's degree. **Support services:** Tutoring.

Majors. Visual/performing arts: Commercial/advertising art, design, fashion design, graphic design, interior design.

Technology on campus. PC or laptop required. 35 workstations in library, computer center, student center. Repair service, student web hosting, wireless network available.

Student life. Freshman orientation: Available. Preregistration for classes offered. Held once per month during the summer months. **Activities:** Film society, student government, American Society of Interior Designers, fashion merchandisers association, American Institute of Graphic Arts, International Interior Design Association.

Student services. Career counseling, student employment services, financial aid counseling.

Contact. E-mail: admissions@omorecollege.edu
Phone: (615) 794 4254 ext. 330
Toll-free number: (888) 662-1970 ext. 330 Fax: (615) 790-1662
Lisa Smith, Director of Admission, O'More College of Design, 423 South Margin Street, Franklin, TN 37064-0908

Rhodes College
Memphis, Tennessee
www.rhodes.edu
CB member
CB code: 1730

- Private 4-year liberal arts college affiliated with the Presbyterian Church (USA)
- Residential campus in very large city
- 2,031 degree-seeking undergraduates: 56% women, 6% African American, 6% Asian American, 5% Hispanic/Latino, 4% Multi-racial, non-Hispanic, 3% international
- 17 degree-seeking graduate students
- 47% of applicants admitted
- SAT or ACT (ACT writing optional), application essay required
- 83% graduate within 6 years

General. Founded in 1848. Regionally accredited. **Degrees:** 469 bachelor's awarded; master's offered. **ROTC:** Army, Air Force. **Location:** 4 miles from downtown. **Calendar:** Semester, limited summer session. **Full-time faculty:** 183 total; 91% have terminal degrees, 13% minority, 49% women. **Part-time faculty:** 41 total; 61% have terminal degrees, 10% minority, 49% women. **Class size:** 69% < 20, 28% 20-39, 3% 40-49. **Special facilities:** Arboretum, scanning electron microscope, rooftop observatory, cell culture facility, nuclear magnetic resonance instrument.

Freshman class profile. 4,666 applied, 2,187 admitted, 562 enrolled.

Mid 50% test scores		Rank in top quarter:	83%
SAT critical reading:	600-700	Rank in top tenth:	54%
SAT math:	580-680	Return as sophomores:	91%
ACT composite:	27-32	Out-of-state:	74%
GPA 3.75 or higher:	66%	Live on campus:	97%
GPA 3.50-3.74:	18%	International:	3%
GPA 3.0-3.49:	11%	Fraternities:	31%
GPA 2.0-2.99:	5%	Sororities:	55%

Basis for selection. Academic record, standardized test scores, class rank, recommendations, essay, school and community activities important. Applications sought from international students, minorities, and children of alumni. Interview recommended. **Home schooled:** 2 SAT Subject Tests other than math or literature required.

High school preparation. College-preparatory program required. 16 units required. Required units include English 4, mathematics 3, social studies 2, science 2 (laboratory 2), foreign language 2 and academic electives 3.

2016-2017 Annual costs. Tuition/fees (projected): $43,224. Room/board: $10,746. Books/supplies: $1,125. Personal expenses: $1,490.

2015-2016 Financial aid. Need-based: 478 full-time freshmen applied for aid; 293 deemed to have need; 293 received aid. Average need met was 93%. Average scholarship/grant was $26,954; average loan $2,887. 69% of total undergraduate aid awarded as scholarships/grants, 31% as loans/jobs. **Non-need-based:** Awarded to 1,343 full-time undergraduates, including 380 freshmen. Scholarships awarded for academics, art, minority status, music/drama, religious affiliation. **Additional information:** Auditions required for theater and music achievement awards and art achievement awards. Interviews recommended for merit scholarships. Notification of admissions decision for Bellingrath Scholarship applicants by 3/15; must reply by 5/1.

Application procedures. Admission: Closing date 1/15 (postmark date). No application fee. Admission notification by 4/1. Must reply by 5/1. **Financial aid:** Priority date 3/1, closing date 3/1. FAFSA, CSS PROFILE required. Must reply by 5/1.

Academics. Expense-paid summer internships in businesses abroad. Model United Nations program, opportunities for participation in computer-simulated international negotiating, mock trial program. **Special study options:** Combined bachelor's/graduate degree, cooperative education, cross-registration, double major, dual enrollment of high school students, honors, independent study, internships, liberal arts/career combination, student-designed major, study abroad, Washington semester. **Credit/placement by examination:** AP, CLEP, IB, institutional tests. 28 credit hours maximum toward bachelor's degree. **Support services:** Tutoring, writing center.

Majors. Area/ethnic studies: African-American, Latin American, Russian/Slavic. **Biology:** General, Biochemistry/molecular biology, neuroscience. **Business:** Business admin, international. **Computer sciences:** Computer science. **Conservation:** Environmental science. **English:** English lit. **Foreign languages:** Classics, French, German, Spanish. **History:** General. **Math:** General. **Philosophy/religion:** Philosophy, religion. **Physical sciences:** Chemistry, physics. **Psychology:** General. **Social sciences:** Anthropology, economics, international economics, international relations, political economy, political science, urban studies. **Visual/performing arts:** Art, dramatic, music.

Most popular majors. Biology 19%, business/marketing 13%, English 6%, physical sciences 6%, psychology 10%, social sciences 23%, visual/performing arts 6%.

Technology on campus. 220 workstations in library, computer center, student center. Dormitories wired for high-speed internet access and linked to campus network. Commuter students can connect to campus network. Online course registration, online library, helpline, repair service, wireless network available.

Student life. Freshman orientation: Mandatory, $110 fee. Preregistration for classes offered. Two-day summer program. **Policies:** Student-run honor system central to campus life. **Housing:** Guaranteed on-campus for freshmen. Coed dorms, single-sex dorms, apartments, themed housing available. Special interest townhouses available. **Activities:** Bands, campus ministries, choral groups, dance, drama, film society, international student organizations, literary magazine, music ensembles, Model UN, musical theater, radio station, student government, student newspaper, symphony orchestra, TV station, black student association, social service club, Inter-Varsity Christian Fellowship, international house, Habitat for Humanity, interfaith circle, diversity group, College Democrats, College Republicans.

Athletics. NCAA. **Intercollegiate:** Baseball M, basketball, cross-country, field hockey W, football (tackle) M, golf, lacrosse, soccer, softball W, swimming, tennis, track and field, volleyball W. **Intramural:** Basketball, football (non-tackle), football (tackle), racquetball, soccer, squash M, table tennis, tennis, volleyball. **Team name:** Lynx.

Student services. Alcohol/substance abuse counseling, chaplain/spiritual director, career counseling, student employment services, financial aid counseling, health services, minority student services, personal counseling, placement for graduates, women's services. **Physically disabled:** Services for visually, speech, hearing impaired.

Contact. E-mail: adminfo@rhodes.edu
Phone: (901) 843-3700 Toll-free number: (800) 844-5969
Fax: (901) 843-3631
Jeff Norris, Dean of Admission and Data Services, Rhodes College, 2000 North Parkway, Memphis, TN 38112

Sewanee: The University of the South
Sewanee, Tennessee — **CB member**
www.sewanee.edu — **CB code: 1842**

- Private 4-year university and liberal arts college affiliated with the Episcopal Church
- Residential campus in small town
- 1,689 degree-seeking undergraduates: 52% women, 4% African American, 2% Asian American, 5% Hispanic/Latino, 3% Multi-racial, non-Hispanic, 3% international
- 84 degree-seeking graduate students
- 41% of applicants admitted
- Application essay required
- 78% graduate within 6 years

General. Founded in 1857. Regionally accredited; also accredited by ATS. **Degrees:** 347 bachelor's awarded; master's, professional offered. **Location:** 93 miles from Nashville; 52 miles from Chattanooga. **Calendar:** Semester, limited summer session. **Full-time faculty:** 160 total; 95% have terminal degrees, 14% minority, 41% women. **Part-time faculty:** 63 total; 71% have terminal degrees, 5% minority, 49% women. **Class size:** 63% < 20, 37% 20-39, less than 1% 40-49, less than 1% 50-99. **Special facilities:** Landscape analysis lab, observatory, materials analysis laboratory with electron microscopy, hiking and horseback riding trails, climbing.

Freshman class profile. 4,509 applied, 1,830 admitted, 469 enrolled.

Mid 50% test scores			
SAT critical reading:	580-670	Rank in top quarter:	64%
SAT math:	560-650	Rank in top tenth:	29%
SAT writing:	560-660	Return as sophomores:	89%
ACT composite:	26-30	Out-of-state:	77%
GPA 3.75 or higher:	46%	Live on campus:	100%
GPA 3.50-3.74:	18%	International:	3%
GPA 3.0-3.49:	23%	Fraternities:	57%
GPA 2.0-2.99:	13%	Sororities:	72%

Basis for selection. GED not accepted. Holistic application review process, admitting students who are prepared for its challenging academic environment and the engaging student experience. Test scores are optional for most applicants. TOEFL or IELTS required for some international students whose native language is not English. Interview recommended. **Home schooled:** Interview, letter of recommendation (nonparent) required. SAT or ACT test scores are not optional for home-schooled applicants.

High school preparation. College-preparatory program required. 13 units required; 20 recommended. Required and recommended units include English 4, mathematics 3-4, social studies 1-2, history 1-2, science 2-4 (laboratory 2-3) and foreign language 2-4.

2015-2016 Annual costs. Tuition/fees: $38,700. Room/board: $11,050.

2015-2016 Financial aid. Need-based: 323 full-time freshmen applied for aid; 235 deemed to have need; 235 received aid. Average need met was 91%. Average scholarship/grant was $24,549; average loan $3,791. 86% of total undergraduate aid awarded as scholarships/grants, 14% as loans/jobs. **Non-need-based:** Awarded to 707 full-time undergraduates, including 213 freshmen. Scholarships awarded for academics, art, religious affiliation, state residency.

Application procedures. Admission: Closing date 2/1 (postmark date). No application fee. Admission notification by 3/17. Must reply by May 1 or within 2 week(s) if notified thereafter. **Financial aid:** Priority date 2/1, closing date 2/1. FAFSA, CSS PROFILE required. Applicants notified on a rolling basis starting 3/1; must reply by 5/1 or within 2 week(s) of notification.

Academics. Special study options: Combined bachelor's/graduate degree, double major, independent study, internships, semester at sea, student-designed major, study abroad, Washington semester. **Credit/placement by examination:** AP, CLEP, IB, institutional tests. **Support services:** Study skills assistance, tutoring, writing center.

Majors. Area/ethnic studies: American, Asian, women's. **Biology:** General, biochemistry, environmental. **Computer sciences:** Computer science. **Conservation:** General, environmental studies, forest sciences. **English:** English lit. **Foreign languages:** Ancient Greek, classics, French, German, Latin, Russian, Spanish. **History:** General. **Math:** General. **Philosophy/religion:** Philosophy, religion. **Physical sciences:** Chemistry, geology, physics. **Psychology:** General. **Social sciences:** Anthropology, economics, political science. **Visual/performing arts:** Art history/conservation, dramatic, music, studio arts.

Most popular majors. Biology 10%, English 13%, foreign language 8%, history 9%, interdisciplinary studies 7%, natural resources/environmental science 7%, psychology 9%, social sciences 22%.

Technology on campus. 630 workstations in dormitories, library, computer center. Dormitories wired for high-speed internet access and linked to campus network. Commuter students can connect to campus network. Online course registration, online library, helpline, repair service, student web hosting, wireless network available.

Student life. Freshman orientation: Mandatory. Preregistration for classes offered. Four-day program held the four days before term begins. **Policies:** Student-administered honor code observed. **Housing:** Guaranteed on-campus for all undergraduates. Coed dorms, single-sex dorms, special housing for disabled, apartments, fraternity/sorority housing, themed housing, wellness housing available. $500 nonrefundable deposit, deadline 5/1. Substance-free, language, living/learning housing, first year program. **Activities:** Bands, campus ministries, choral groups, dance, drama, film society, international student organizations, literary magazine, music ensembles, Model UN, musical theater, radio station, student government, student newspaper, symphony orchestra, 95 student organizations dedicated to community engagement, outreach, political awareness, multicultural understanding, the arts, and athletics.

Athletics. NCAA. **Intercollegiate:** Baseball M, basketball, cheerleading W, cross-country, diving, equestrian, field hockey W, football (tackle) M, golf, lacrosse, soccer, softball W, swimming, tennis, track and field, volleyball W. **Intramural:** Badminton, basketball, cross-country, football (tackle) M, golf, racquetball, soccer, softball, swimming, table tennis, tennis, track and field, volleyball. **Team name:** Tigers.

Student services. Alcohol/substance abuse counseling, chaplain/spiritual director, career counseling, student employment services, financial aid counseling, health services, minority student services, personal counseling, women's services. **Physically disabled:** Services for visually, hearing impaired.

Contact. E-mail: admiss@sewanee.edu
Phone: (931) 598-1238 Toll-free number: (800) 522-2234
Fax: (931) 598-3248
LeeAnn Backlund, Dean of Admission and Financial Aid, Sewanee: The University of the South, Office of Admission, Sewanee, TN 37383-1000

South College
Knoxville, Tennessee
www.southcollegetn.edu
CB code: 0711

- For-profit 4-year career college
- Commuter campus in small city
- 1,139 degree-seeking undergraduates
- 428 graduate students
- Interview required

General. Founded in 1882. Regionally accredited. **Degrees:** 93 bachelor's, 68 associate awarded; master's, professional offered. **Location:** Downtown. **Calendar:** Quarter, extensive summer session. **Full-time faculty:** 110 total. **Part-time faculty:** 70 total.

Basis for selection. CPTS, SAT or ACT required. SAT or ACT recommended. **Home schooled:** Must provide minimum required ACT/SAT score or proof of passing GED.

2015-2016 Annual costs. Tuition/fees: $20,475. Books/supplies: $1,800. Personal expenses: $3,276.

Financial aid. All financial aid based on need.

Application procedures. Admission: No deadline. $50 fee. Admission notification on a rolling basis. **Financial aid:** No deadline. FAFSA, institutional form required. Applicants notified on a rolling basis.

Academics. Special study options: Accelerated study, double major, dual enrollment of high school students, internships, teacher certification program. **Credit/placement by examination:** AP, CLEP, institutional tests. **Support services:** Learning center, reduced course load, study skills assistance, tutoring, writing center.

Majors. Biology: General. **Business:** Business admin. **Education:** Elementary. **Health services:** Nuclear medical technology, nursing (RN), radiologic technology/medical imaging. **Protective services:** Criminal justice.

Technology on campus. 85 workstations in library, computer center. Online library, wireless network available.

Student life. Freshman orientation: Mandatory. Preregistration for classes offered. **Activities:** Literary magazine, student government, student newspaper, Collegiate Secretaries International, paralegal association, student affairs advisory council, business club, students of medical assisting, movie club, community service club.

Student services. Career counseling, student employment services, financial aid counseling, personal counseling, placement for graduates, veterans' counselor.

Contact. E-mail: admissions@southcollegetn.edu
Phone: (865) 251-1800 Fax: (865) 470-8737
Carrie Major, Admissions Director, South College, 3904 Lonas Drive, Knoxville, TN 37909

Southern Adventist University
Collegedale, Tennessee
www.southern.edu
CB code: 1727

- Private 4-year university and liberal arts college affiliated with the Seventh-day Adventists
- Residential campus in small town
- 2,697 degree-seeking undergraduates: 17% part-time, 53% women
- 452 graduate students
- 60% of applicants admitted
- SAT or ACT (ACT writing optional) required
- 48% graduate within 6 years

General. Founded in 1892. Regionally accredited. **Degrees:** 398 bachelor's, 164 associate awarded; master's, professional offered. **Location:** 18 miles from Chattanooga. **Calendar:** Semester, limited summer session. **Full-time faculty:** 172 total; 48% women. **Part-time faculty:** 3 total; 33% women. **Class size:** 61% <20, 28% 20-39, 4% 40-49, 6% 50-99, less than 1% >100. **Special facilities:** Civil War collection, Lincoln collection, Anton Memorial Organ.

Freshman class profile. 2,003 applied, 1,208 admitted, 539 enrolled.

Mid 50% test scores			
SAT critical reading:	460-580	GPA 3.50-3.74:	23%
SAT math:	450-590	GPA 3.0-3.49:	29%
SAT writing:	450-570	GPA 2.0-2.99:	15%
ACT composite:	20-26	Return as sophomores:	76%
GPA 3.75 or higher:	33%	International:	4%

Basis for selection. School achievement record and test scores important. SAT/ACT Writing component used in committee appeal. Interview recommended for all; audition required for music and gymnastics programs. **Home schooled:** Transcript of courses and grades required. Home school organization must be academically accredited or student must take GED. Portfolio required and must include copy of original research paper and written statement reflecting on value student received from home school experience.

High school preparation. College-preparatory program recommended. 18 units required; 24 recommended. Required and recommended units include English 3-4, mathematics 2-3, social studies 1, history 1-2, science 2-3, foreign language 2, computer science 1 and academic electives 9. One unit chemistry (2.0 GPA or better) required for nursing majors. 2 units foreign language required for BA program applicants. Computer competency strongly recommended.

2015-2016 Annual costs. Tuition/fees: $20,650. Room/board: $5,980. Books/supplies: $1,100. Personal expenses: $4,000.

2014-2015 Financial aid. Need-based: Average need met was 70%. Average scholarship/grant was $11,093; average loan $3,905. 50% of total undergraduate aid awarded as scholarships/grants, 50% as loans/jobs. **Non-need-based:** Scholarships awarded for academics, alumni affiliation, art, athletics, leadership, music/drama.

Application procedures. Admission: Priority date 3/1; no deadline. $25 fee, may be waived for applicants with need. Admission notification on a rolling basis. **Financial aid:** Priority date 3/1; no closing date. FAFSA required. Applicants notified on a rolling basis starting 2/15; must reply within 2 week(s) of notification.

Academics. Special study options: Accelerated study, combined bachelor's/graduate degree, cooperative education, distance learning, double major, ESL, honors, independent study, internships, student-designed major, study abroad, teacher certification program. **Credit/placement by examination:** AP, CLEP, SAT, ACT, institutional tests. 12 credit hours maximum toward associate degree, 12 toward bachelor's. **Support services:** Learning center, reduced course load, remedial instruction, study skills assistance, tutoring, writing center.

Majors. Biology: General, biochemistry, biophysics. **Business:** Accounting, business admin, finance, human resources, international, management information systems, management science, marketing, nonprofit/public. **Communications:** Advertising, broadcast journalism, intercultural, journalism, media studies, public relations. **Communications technology:** General. **Computer sciences:** Computer science, programming. **Education:** Art, biology, chemistry, elementary, English, French, history, mathematics, music, physical, physics, Spanish. **English:** English lit. **Foreign languages:** General, French, Spanish. **Health services:** Art therapy, clinical lab science, health care admin, nursing (RN). **History:** General, European. **Human services:** Social work. **Math:** General. **Parks/recreation:** Exercise sciences, sports admin. **Philosophy/religion:** Religion. **Physical sciences:** Chemistry, physics. **Psychology:** General, clinical, industrial, psychobiology. **Social sciences:** Archaeology. **Theology:** Missionary, pastoral counseling, religious ed, theology. **Visual/performing arts:** Art, cinematography, commercial/advertising art, graphic design, music, music performance, music theory/composition, photography. **Work/family studies:** Family systems.

Most popular majors. Biology 12%, business/marketing 10%, education 9%, health sciences 20%, theological studies 6%, visual/performing arts 9%.

Technology on campus. 200 workstations in dormitories, library, computer center. Dormitories wired for high-speed internet access and linked to campus network. Commuter students can connect to campus network. Online course registration, online library, helpline, repair service, student web hosting, wireless network available.

Student life. Freshman orientation: Mandatory. Preregistration for classes offered. Held prior to registration. Includes exams and instruction in course planning. **Policies:** Alcohol, tobacco, drug-free campus. Religious observance required. **Housing:** Guaranteed on-campus for all undergraduates. Single-sex dorms, apartments available. $250 fully refundable deposit, deadline 6/1. **Activities:** Concert band, campus ministries, choral groups, international student organizations, literary magazine, music ensembles, radio station, student government, student newspaper, symphony orchestra, African club, Black Christian Union, Partners at Wellness, Association of South East Asian Nation Students.

Athletics. Intramural: Badminton, basketball, football (non-tackle), soccer, softball, table tennis, tennis, triathlon, volleyball.

Student services. Chaplain/spiritual director, career counseling, student employment services, financial aid counseling, health services, personal counseling, placement for graduates, veterans' counselor.

Contact. E-mail: admissions@southern.edu
Phone: (423) 236-2835 Toll-free number: (800) 768-8437
Fax: (423) 236-1835
Adam Brown, Director of Admissions, Southern Adventist University, PO Box 370, Collegedale, TN 37315-0370

Tennessee State University
Nashville, Tennessee ·   **CB member**
www.tnstate.edu   **CB code: 1803**

- Public 4-year university
- Residential campus in very large city
- 7,176 degree-seeking undergraduates: 17% part-time, 60% women, 71% African American, 1% Asian American, 1% Hispanic/Latino, 3% Multiracial, non-Hispanic, 11% international
- 1,772 degree-seeking graduate students
- 51% of applicants admitted
- SAT or ACT with writing required
- 42% graduate within 6 years

General. Founded in 1912. Regionally accredited. **Degrees:** 872 bachelor's, 116 associate awarded; master's, doctoral offered. **ROTC:** Air Force. **Location:** 115 miles from Chattanooga, 195 miles from Memphis. **Calendar:** Semester, limited summer session. **Full-time faculty:** 407 total; 85% have terminal degrees, 62% minority, 45% women. **Part-time faculty:** 174 total; 38% have terminal degrees, 56% minority, 55% women. **Class size:** 45% < 20, 49% 20-39, 4% 40-49, 3% 50-99, less than 1% >100. **Special facilities:** Observatory, research and demonstration farm, geospatial information systems laboratory.

Freshman class profile. 9,221 applied, 4,662 admitted, 1,406 enrolled.

Mid 50% test scores		GPA 3.0-3.49:	25%
SAT critical reading:	380-440	GPA 2.0-2.99:	62%
SAT math:	390-470	Out-of-state:	28%
ACT composite:	16-20	Live on campus:	80%
GPA 3.75 or higher:	5%	International:	6%
GPA 3.50-3.74:	6%		

Basis for selection. School achievement record, test scores important. Interview required for health sciences, nursing, physical therapy programs. **Home schooled:** State high school equivalency certificate required.

High school preparation. 14 units required. Required units include English 4, mathematics 3, social studies 2, science 2 (laboratory 1) and foreign language 2. One unit visual and/or performing arts recommended.

2015-2016 Annual costs. Tuition/fees: $7,417; $20,773 out-of-state. Room/board: $7,130. Books/supplies: $1,800. Personal expenses: $1,500.

2015-2016 Financial aid. Need-based: 1,318 full-time freshmen applied for aid; 1,249 deemed to have need; 1,215 received aid. Average need met was 29%. Average scholarship/grant was $3,186; average loan $1,947. 58% of total undergraduate aid awarded as scholarships/grants, 42% as loans/jobs. **Non-need-based:** Scholarships awarded for academics.

Application procedures. Admission: Closing date 8/1. $25 fee. Application must be submitted on paper. Admission notification on a rolling basis. **Financial aid:** Priority date 4/1; no closing date. FAFSA required. Applicants notified on a rolling basis starting 4/15; must reply within 3 week(s) of notification.

Academics. Special study options: Combined bachelor's/graduate degree, cooperative education, cross-registration, distance learning, double major, ESL, exchange student, honors, independent study, internships, liberal arts/career combination, study abroad, teacher certification program. **Credit/placement by examination:** AP, CLEP, SAT, ACT, institutional tests. 33 credit hours maximum toward bachelor's degree. **Support services:** Learning center, remedial instruction, study skills assistance, tutoring, writing center.

Majors. Architecture: Architecture. **Biology:** General, biochemistry. **Business:** Accounting, administrative services, business admin, managerial economics. **Communications:** Communications/speech/rhetoric, journalism. **Computer sciences:** Computer science. **Education:** General, early childhood, physical, secondary, special ed. **Engineering:** General, architectural, civil, electrical. **English:** English lit. **Foreign languages:** French, Spanish.

Health services: Audiology/speech pathology, dental hygiene, health care admin, health information management. **History:** General. **Human services:** Social work. **Liberal arts:** Arts/sciences. **Math:** General. **Physical sciences:** Chemistry, physics. **Protective services:** Criminal justice. **Psychology:** General. **Social sciences:** General, political science, sociology, urban studies. **Visual/performing arts:** Art history/conservation, dramatic, music. **Work/family studies:** General, clothing/textiles, family studies, food/nutrition.

Most popular majors. Business/marketing 17%, health sciences 15%, liberal arts 20%, psychology 6%, visual/performing arts 7%.

Technology on campus. 450 workstations in dormitories, library, computer center, student center. Dormitories wired for high-speed internet access and linked to campus network. Commuter students can connect to campus network. Online course registration, online library, helpline, repair service, student web hosting, wireless network available.

Student life. Freshman orientation: Mandatory. Preregistration for classes offered. **Housing:** Coed dorms, single-sex dorms, apartments available. $100 fully refundable deposit, deadline 4/1. **Activities:** Bands, choral groups, dance, drama, film society, international student organizations, music ensembles, musical theater, radio station, student government, student newspaper, TV station, religious organizations, honor organization, literary organization.

Athletics. NCAA. **Intercollegiate:** Baseball M, basketball, cheerleading, cross-country, football (tackle) M, golf, softball W, tennis, track and field, volleyball W. **Intramural:** Basketball, bowling, football (non-tackle) M, racquetball, tennis, track and field, volleyball. **Team name:** Tigers.

Student services. Career counseling, student employment services, financial aid counseling, health services, minority student services, on-campus daycare, personal counseling, placement for graduates, veterans' counselor, women's services. **Physically disabled:** Services for visually, speech, hearing impaired.

Contact. E-mail: recruitment@tnstate.edu
Phone: (615) 963-5101 Fax: (615) 963-5108
John Cade, Associate Vice Provost, Tennessee State University, 3500 John A. Merritt Boulevard, Nashville, TN 37209-1561

Tennessee Technological University
Cookeville, Tennessee   **CB member**
www.tntech.edu   **CB code: 1804**

- Public 4-year university
- Residential campus in large town
- 9,475 degree-seeking undergraduates: 9% part-time, 44% women, 4% African American, 2% Asian American, 3% Hispanic/Latino, 3% Multiracial, non-Hispanic, 7% international
- 1,093 degree-seeking graduate students
- SAT or ACT (ACT writing recommended) required
- 53% graduate within 6 years

General. Founded in 1915. Regionally accredited. **Degrees:** 1,857 bachelor's awarded; master's, doctoral offered. **ROTC:** Army, Air Force. **Location:** 80 miles from Nashville, 100 miles from Knoxville. **Calendar:** Semester, extensive summer session. **Full-time faculty:** 378 total. **Part-time faculty:** 254 total. **Class size:** 34% < 20, 46% 20-39, 8% 40-49, 7% 50-99, 4% >100. **Special facilities:** Center for crafts, cooperative fishery research unit, agricultural pavilion, center for energy systems research, center for manufacturing research, center for the management, utilization and protection of water resources, childcare resource center, STEM center.

Freshman class profile.

GPA 3.75 or higher:	42%	Return as sophomores:	75%
GPA 3.50-3.74:	17%	Out-of-state:	2%
GPA 3.0-3.49:	27%	Live on campus:	66%
GPA 2.0-2.99:	14%	International:	3%
Rank in top quarter:	54%	Fraternities:	12%
Rank in top tenth:	28%	Sororities:	17%

Basis for selection. High school classes, GPA and test scores very important. Additional requirements for engineering, computer science, mathematics, nursing and pre-professional majors. Interview recommended for all; audition recommended for music; portfolio recommended for arts, crafts. **Home schooled:** 2.5 GPA and 19 ACT or GED required.

High school preparation. 14 units required. Required units include English 4, mathematics 3, social studies 1, history 1, science 2 (laboratory 1) and foreign language 2. Math units must include algebra I and II and geometry or advanced math course. Science units must be biology, chemistry, or physics with laboratories (can include physical sciences). Foreign language units must be in single language. 1 U.S. history, 1 unit visual and/or performing arts also required. Social studies must be either world, ancient, modern, or European history, or world geography.

2015-2016 Annual costs. Tuition/fees: $8,353; $24,559 out-of-state. Room/board: $9,418. Books/supplies: $780. Personal expenses: $840.

Financial aid. Non-need-based: Scholarships awarded for academics, alumni affiliation, art, athletics, leadership, minority status, music/drama, ROTC, state residency. **Additional information:** Tuition and/or fee waivers available for children of Tennessee public school teachers.

Application procedures. Admission: Priority date 5/1; deadline 8/1 (postmark date). $25 fee. Admission notification on a rolling basis. **Financial aid:** Priority date 3/15; no closing date. FAFSA required. Applicants notified on a rolling basis starting 3/15; must reply within 2 week(s) of notification.

Academics. Special study options: Accelerated study, cooperative education, distance learning, double major, dual enrollment of high school students, ESL, honors, independent study, internships, liberal arts/career combination, study abroad, teacher certification program. **Credit/placement by examination:** AP, CLEP, IB, institutional tests. 33 credit hours maximum toward bachelor's degree. **Support services:** Learning center, pre-admission summer program, reduced course load, remedial instruction, study skills assistance, tutoring, writing center.

Majors. Biology: General, biochemistry. **Business:** General, accounting, finance, labor relations, management science, managerial economics, operations. **Communications:** Communications/speech/rhetoric, journalism. **Communications technology:** General. **Computer sciences:** General, computer science, web page design. **Conservation:** General, fisheries, wildlife/wilderness. **Education:** General, agricultural, early childhood, English, health, music, physical, secondary, special ed. **Engineering:** Chemical, civil, computer, electrical, mechanical. **English:** English lit, technical writing. **Foreign languages:** French, German, Spanish. **Health services:** Nursing (RN), predental, premedicine, prepharmacy, preveterinary. **History:** General. **Math:** General. **Parks/recreation:** Health/fitness. **Physical sciences:** Chemistry, geology, physics. **Psychology:** General. **Social sciences:** Economics, political science, sociology. **Visual/performing arts:** Ceramics, drawing, fiber arts, music performance, painting, sculpture, studio arts. **Work/family studies:** General, clothing/textiles, family/community services, food/nutrition, housing.

Most popular majors. Business/marketing 16%, engineering/engineering technologies 15%, interdisciplinary studies 18%, liberal arts 6%.

Technology on campus. 600 workstations in dormitories, library, computer center. Dormitories wired for high-speed internet access and linked to campus network. Commuter students can connect to campus network. Online course registration, online library, helpline, wireless network available.

Student life. Freshman orientation: Mandatory, $45 fee. Preregistration for classes offered. **Housing:** Guaranteed on-campus for freshmen. Coed dorms, single-sex dorms, special housing for disabled, apartments, fraternity/sorority housing, themed housing available. $100 deposit. Learning Villages available. **Activities:** Bands, campus ministries, choral groups, dance, drama, international student organizations, literary magazine, music ensembles, musical theater, opera, radio station, student government, student newspaper, symphony orchestra, TV station, over 200 organizations.

Athletics. NCAA. **Intercollegiate:** Baseball M, basketball, cheerleading, cross-country, football (tackle) M, golf, soccer W, softball W, tennis M, track and field W, volleyball W. **Intramural:** Basketball, bowling, golf M, handball, racquetball, rugby M, soccer, softball, tennis, volleyball, wrestling M. **Team name:** Golden Eagles.

Student services. Alcohol/substance abuse counseling, career counseling, student employment services, financial aid counseling, health services, minority student services, on-campus daycare, personal counseling, placement for graduates, veterans' counselor, women's services. **Physically disabled:** Services for visually, speech, hearing impaired.

Contact. E-mail: admissions@tntech.edu
Phone: (931) 372-3888 Toll-free number: (800) 255-8881
Fax: (931) 372-6250
Alexis Pope, Admissions, Tennessee Technological University, Office of Admissions, Cookeville, TN 38505-0001

Tennessee Wesleyan College
Athens, Tennessee
www.twcnet.edu   CB code: 1805

♦ Private 4-year liberal arts and teachers college affiliated with the United Methodist Church
♦ Commuter campus in large town

♦ 1,014 degree-seeking undergraduates: 6% part-time, 65% women, 6% African American, 1% Asian American, 2% Hispanic/Latino, 3% Multiracial, non-Hispanic
♦ 22 degree-seeking graduate students
♦ 65% of applicants admitted
♦ SAT or ACT (ACT writing optional) required
♦ 46% graduate within 6 years

General. Founded in 1857. Regionally accredited. Baccalaureate programs in nursing and evening business school through Knoxville campus. **Degrees:** 293 bachelor's awarded; master's offered. **ROTC:** Army, Naval, Air Force. **Location:** 50 miles from Chattanooga and Knoxville. **Calendar:** Semester, extensive summer session. **Full-time faculty:** 59 total; 75% have terminal degrees, 14% minority, 44% women. **Part-time faculty:** 63 total; 35% have terminal degrees, 6% minority, 49% women. **Class size:** 69% < 20, 24% 20-39, 3% 40-49, 3% 50-99, less than 1% >100.

Freshman class profile. 1,085 applied, 703 admitted, 213 enrolled.

Mid 50% test scores			
SAT critical reading:	420-520	GPA 2.0-2.99:	22%
SAT math:	420-500	Rank in top quarter:	41%
ACT composite:	19-25	Rank in top tenth:	13%
GPA 3.75 or higher:	34%	Out-of-state:	13%
GPA 3.50-3.74:	15%	Live on campus:	67%
GPA 3.0-3.49:	28%	Fraternities:	3%
		Sororities:	10%

Basis for selection. Test scores, school records, recommendations and GPA very important. ACT/SAT not required if student has GED. Essay recommended for all; interview recommended for academically weak; audition required for music and theater.

High school preparation. College-preparatory program recommended. 10 units recommended. Recommended units include English 4, mathematics 2, social studies 1, history 1 and science 2.

2015-2016 Annual costs. Tuition/fees: $22,900. Room/board: $7,310. Books/supplies: $1,200. Personal expenses: $1,500.

2014-2015 Financial aid. Need-based: 238 full-time freshmen applied for aid; 215 deemed to have need; 204 received aid. Average need met was 67%. Average scholarship/grant was $17,001; average loan $2,995. 68% of total undergraduate aid awarded as scholarships/grants, 32% as loans/jobs. **Non-need-based:** Awarded to 281 full-time undergraduates, including 70 freshmen. Scholarships awarded for academics, alumni affiliation, athletics, minority status, music/drama, religious affiliation.

Application procedures. Admission: Closing date 8/15 (receipt date). , may be waived for applicants with need. No application fee. Admission notification on a rolling basis beginning on or about 8/1. **Financial aid:** Priority date 2/15; no closing date. FAFSA, institutional form required. Applicants notified on a rolling basis starting 2/15; must reply within 2 week(s) of notification.

Academics. Study abroad opportunities available for students wishing to extend their learning globally. **Special study options:** Accelerated study, distance learning, double major, dual enrollment of high school students, honors, independent study, internships, teacher certification program. Member of the Private College Consortium for International Studies (semester in London program). **Credit/placement by examination:** AP, CLEP, IB, SAT, ACT, institutional tests. 12 credit hours maximum toward bachelor's degree. **Support services:** Learning center, reduced course load, remedial instruction, study skills assistance, tutoring, writing center.

Majors. Area/ethnic studies: American. **Biology:** General. **Business:** Accounting, business admin, finance, human resources, marketing. **Communications:** General. **Computer sciences:** General. **Conservation:** Environmental studies. **Education:** Early childhood, elementary, multi-level teacher, secondary, special ed. **English:** English lit. **Health services:** Nursing (RN), predental, premedicine, prenursing, prepharmacy, prephysical therapy, preveterinary. **History:** General. **Liberal arts:** Arts/sciences. **Math:** General. **Parks/recreation:** Health/fitness, sports admin. **Philosophy/religion:** Christian. **Physical sciences:** Chemistry. **Protective services:** Criminal justice, forensics. **Psychology:** General. **Social sciences:** Sociology. **Theology:** Preministerial. **Visual/performing arts:** General, music.

Most popular majors. Business/marketing 36%, health sciences 27%, interdisciplinary studies 7%, parks/recreation 7%.

Technology on campus. 133 workstations in dormitories, library, computer center, student center. Dormitories wired for high-speed internet access and linked to campus network. Online library, wireless network available.

Student life. Freshman orientation: Mandatory. Preregistration for classes offered. Held in August. **Policies:** All students required to live on-campus unless residing with relative within commuting distance, married, or have children. Visitation hours in dorms by opposite sex restricted. No alcohol allowed on campus. Religious observance required. **Housing:** Guaranteed on-campus for freshmen. Coed dorms, single-sex dorms, apartments available. $100 fully refundable deposit. **Activities:** Bands, campus ministries, choral groups, drama, international student organizations, literary magazine, musical theater, student government, student newspaper, Circle K, Hackberry and Oak Society, National Student Nurses Association, student activities board, Education Angels, Fellowship of Christian Athletes, Wesleyan Christian Fellowship, College Democrats.

Athletics. NAIA. **Intercollegiate:** Baseball M, basketball, cross-country, golf, soccer, softball W, tennis, volleyball W. **Team name:** Bulldogs.

Student services. Adult student services, alcohol/substance abuse counseling, chaplain/spiritual director, career counseling, student employment services, financial aid counseling, personal counseling, placement for graduates, veterans' counselor. **Physically disabled:** Services for visually, hearing impaired.

Contact. E-mail: admissions@twcnet.edu
Phone: (423) 745-7504 Toll-free number: (800) 742-5892
Fax: (423) 745-9335
Kara Fox, Director of Enrollment Services, Tennessee Wesleyan College, 204 East College Street, Athens, TN 37303

Trevecca Nazarene University
Nashville, Tennessee
www.trevecca.edu
CB code: 1809

- Private 4-year university and liberal arts college affiliated with the Church of the Nazarene
- Residential campus in very large city
- 1,762 degree-seeking undergraduates: 29% part-time, 57% women, 11% African American, 1% Asian American, 9% Hispanic/Latino, 3% Multiracial, non-Hispanic, 1% international
- 801 degree-seeking graduate students
- 73% of applicants admitted
- SAT or ACT (ACT writing optional) required
- 51% graduate within 6 years

General. Founded in 1901. Regionally accredited. **Degrees:** 342 bachelor's, 3 associate awarded; master's, doctoral offered. **ROTC:** Army. **Location:** 200 miles from Memphis, 175 miles from Knoxville. **Calendar:** Semester, limited summer session. **Full-time faculty:** 81 total; 86% have terminal degrees, 9% minority, 35% women. **Part-time faculty:** 128 total; 41% have terminal degrees, 9% minority, 48% women. **Class size:** 71% < 20, 22% 20-39, 3% 40-49, 4% 50-99.

Freshman class profile. 1,212 applied, 879 admitted, 373 enrolled.

Mid 50% test scores		GPA 3.0-3.49:	28%
SAT critical reading:	450-560	GPA 2.0-2.99:	22%
SAT math:	440-570	Return as sophomores:	77%
ACT composite:	19-25	Out-of-state:	36%
GPA 3.75 or higher:	26%	Live on campus:	68%
GPA 3.50-3.74:	24%	International:	3%

Basis for selection. 18 ACT/860 SAT or 2.5 GPA required. Housing interview required for students 23 years of age and older. Applicants to certificate NPWI program must submit a video audition. Auditions required for various music groups/ensembles. **Home schooled:** Transcript with all subjects and grades should be provided by correspondence-school based organization or by the parent depending on method of homeschooling. **Learning Disabled:** Students should contact Disability Services for information concerning documentation of disability and services available.

High school preparation. College-preparatory program recommended. 15 units recommended. Recommended units include English 4, mathematics 2, social studies 1, history 1, science 1, foreign language 2 and academic electives 4.

2015-2016 Annual costs. Tuition/fees: $23,748. Room/board: $8,300. Books/supplies: $700. Personal expenses: $900.

2014-2015 Financial aid. **Need-based:** 44% of total undergraduate aid awarded as scholarships/grants, 56% as loans/jobs. **Non-need-based:** Scholarships awarded for academics, alumni affiliation, athletics, leadership, minority status, music/drama, religious affiliation.

Application procedures. **Admission:** Priority date 4/1; deadline 8/1. $25 fee, may be waived for applicants with need, free for online applicants. Admission notification on a rolling basis. Must reply by 5/1. Enrollment deposit of $200 due by 5/1; refundable only if notification received by 5/1.

Financial aid: Priority date 3/1; no closing date. Applicants notified on a rolling basis starting 3/1.

Academics. **Special study options:** Distance learning, double major, dual enrollment of high school students, internships, study abroad, teacher certification program. **Credit/placement by examination:** AP, CLEP, IB, SAT, ACT. 22 credit hours maximum toward associate degree, 45 toward bachelor's. Credit awarded after one semester and tuition paid. **Support services:** Learning center, remedial instruction, study skills assistance, tutoring.

Majors. **Biology:** General. **Business:** Accounting, business admin, e-commerce, international, marketing, nonprofit/public. **Communications:** Broadcast journalism, communications/speech/rhetoric, digital media, journalism, media studies, organizational. **Communications technology:** Radio/TV. **Computer sciences:** Information technology, web page design, webmaster. **Education:** Biology, business, chemistry, drama/dance, early childhood, elementary, English, history, mathematics, music, physical, physics, special ed, speech. **Engineering:** Applied physics. **English:** English lit. **Health services:** Health care admin, health information management, nursing (RN), preoccupational therapy, prephysical therapy. **History:** General. **Human services:** Public policy, social work. **Math:** General, applied. **Parks/recreation:** Physical fitness technician, sports admin, sports studies. **Philosophy/religion:** Religion. **Physical sciences:** Chemistry, physics. **Protective services:** Law enforcement admin. **Psychology:** General. **Social sciences:** Sociology. **Theology:** Lay ministry, sacred music, youth ministry. **Visual/performing arts:** Dramatic, music management, music performance, music theory/composition.

Most popular majors. Business/marketing 42%, health sciences 7%, theological studies 8%, visual/performing arts 6%.

Technology on campus. 200 workstations in dormitories, library, computer center, student center, student center. Dormitories linked to campus network. Commuter students can connect to campus network. Online course registration, online library, helpline, wireless network available.

Student life. Freshman orientation: Mandatory. Preregistration for classes offered. **Policies:** Religious observance required. **Housing:** Single-sex dorms, apartments available. **Activities:** Bands, campus ministries, choral groups, drama, international student organizations, literary magazine, music ensembles, musical theater, student government, student newspaper, symphony orchestra, mission club, ministerial association, Phi Beta Lambda.

Athletics. NCAA. **Intercollegiate:** Baseball M, basketball, cross-country, golf, soccer, softball W, track and field, volleyball W. **Intramural:** Basketball, football (non-tackle), soccer, softball, tennis, ultimate frisbee, volleyball. **Team name:** Trojans.

Student services. Chaplain/spiritual director, career counseling, student employment services, financial aid counseling, health services, personal counseling.

Contact. E-mail: admissions_und@trevecca.edu
Phone: (615) 248-1320 Toll-free number: (888) 210-4868
Fax: (615) 248-7406
Melinda Miller, Director of Admissions, Trevecca Nazarene University, 333 Murfreesboro Road, Nashville, TN 37210

Tusculum College
Greeneville, Tennessee
www.tusculum.edu
CB member
CB code: 1812

- Private 4-year liberal arts college affiliated with the Presbyterian Church (USA)
- Residential campus in large town
- 1,619 degree-seeking undergraduates: 7% part-time, 56% women, 14% African American, 3% Hispanic/Latino, 1% Native American, 1% Multiracial, non-Hispanic, 3% international
- 190 degree-seeking graduate students
- 69% of applicants admitted
- SAT or ACT (ACT writing optional), application essay required
- 36% graduate within 6 years

General. Founded in 1794. Regionally accredited. Strong civic arts focus and service-learning curriculum. **Degrees:** 384 bachelor's awarded; master's offered. **Location:** 70 miles from Knoxville, 30 miles from Johnson City. **Calendar:** Semester, limited summer session. **Full-time faculty:** 71 total; 63% have terminal degrees, 3% minority, 52% women. **Part-time faculty:** 81 total; 51% women. **Class size:** 80% < 20, 20% 20-39, less than 1% 50-99. **Special facilities:** Two museums, college archives.

Freshman class profile. 2,092 applied, 1,442 admitted, 295 enrolled.

Mid 50% test scores				
SAT critical reading:	400-490	End year in good standing:		80%
SAT math:	430-540	Return as sophomores:		59%
ACT composite:	18-23	Out-of-state:		43%
GPA 3.75 or higher:	20%	Live on campus:		84%
GPA 3.50-3.74:	10%	International:		3%
GPA 3.0-3.49:	27%			

GPA 2.0-2.99: 41%

Basis for selection. Admissions based on secondary school record and standardized test scores. Essay also important. Math and English placement tests may be required based on ACT or SAT scores. Interview recommended. **Home schooled:** Statement describing home school structure and mission, interview required. Syllabi for all courses taken and list of textbooks required.

High school preparation. 12 units required. Required units include English 4, mathematics 3, social studies 3, science 2 (laboratory 1).

2016-2017 Annual costs. Tuition/fees (projected): $23,125. Room/board: $8,500. Books/supplies: $1,471. Personal expenses: $1,798.

2015-2016 Financial aid. Need-based: 274 full-time freshmen applied for aid; 262 deemed to have need; 258 received aid. Average need met was 71%. Average scholarship/grant was $9,691; average loan $3,416. 66% of total undergraduate aid awarded as scholarships/grants, 34% as loans/jobs. **Non-need-based:** Awarded to 998 full-time undergraduates, including 267 freshmen. Scholarships awarded for academics, athletics, leadership, religious affiliation, state residency.

Application procedures. Admission: No deadline. $50 fee, may be waived for applicants with need. Admission notification on a rolling basis. **Financial aid:** Closing date 2/15. FAFSA required. Applicants notified on a rolling basis starting 3/15; must reply within 3 week(s) of notification.

Academics. Semesters comprised of 4 blocks, each 3 1/2 weeks long. Students take one course per block. Intensive 16-month professional studies program designed for non-traditional students also offered. **Special study options:** Accelerated study, combined bachelor's/graduate degree, distance learning, double major, dual enrollment of high school students, exchange student, honors, independent study, internships, student-designed major, study abroad, teacher certification program. **Credit/placement by examination:** AP, CLEP, SAT, ACT, institutional tests. 30 credit hours maximum toward bachelor's degree. **Support services:** Learning center, pre-admission summer program, remedial instruction, study skills assistance, tutoring, writing center.

Majors. Biology: General. **Business:** Business admin. **Communications:** Journalism. **Conservation:** General, environmental science. **Education:** General, special ed. **English:** English lit. **Health services:** Athletic training, nursing (RN). **History:** General. **Math:** General. **Parks/recreation:** Exercise sciences, sports admin. **Physical sciences:** Chemistry. **Protective services:** Law enforcement admin. **Psychology:** General. **Social sciences:** Political science. **Visual/performing arts:** General.

Most popular majors. Business/marketing 43%, education 14%, parks/recreation 6%, psychology 13%.

Technology on campus. 160 workstations in library, computer center, student center. Dormitories wired for high-speed internet access and linked to campus network. Commuter students can connect to campus network. Online library, helpline, repair service, wireless network available.

Student life. Freshman orientation: Mandatory. Preregistration for classes offered. Held for 4 days before classes begin.Students also take a 2-credit orientation course that meets throughout the fall semester. **Housing:** Guaranteed on-campus for freshmen. Coed dorms, single-sex dorms, apartments, themed housing available. $200 nonrefundable deposit, deadline 6/1. Pets allowed in dorm rooms. **Activities:** Bands, campus ministries, choral groups, drama, literary magazine, music ensembles, musical theater, radio station, student government, student newspaper, Black student Union, anime club, Bonner Leaders, English Students Organization, Andrew Johnson Society, business club, physical education club, campus activities board, Fellowship of Christian Athletes.

Athletics. NCAA. **Intercollegiate:** Baseball M, basketball, cheerleading W, cross-country, football (tackle) M, golf, lacrosse, soccer, softball W, tennis, volleyball W. **Intramural:** Basketball, football (tackle), soccer, softball, table tennis, tennis, volleyball. **Team name:** Pioneers.

Student services. Adult student services, alcohol/substance abuse counseling, chaplain/spiritual director, career counseling, services for economically disadvantaged, student employment services, financial aid counseling, health services, minority student services, personal counseling, placement for graduates, veterans' counselor.

Contact. E-mail: mripley@tusculum.edu
Phone: (423) 636-7300 Toll-free number: (800) 729-0256
Fax: (423) 798-1622
Melissa Ripley, Director of Admissions, Tusculum College, 60 Shiloh Road, Greeneville, TN 37743

Union University
Jackson, Tennessee
www.uu.edu　　　　　　　　　　　　　　　**CB code: 1826**

▶ Private 4-year university and liberal arts college affiliated with the Southern Baptist Convention
▶ Residential campus in small city
▶ 2,567 degree-seeking undergraduates
▶ 1,167 graduate students
▶ SAT or ACT (ACT writing optional) required

General. Founded in 1823. Regionally accredited. **Degrees:** 663 bachelor's, 8 associate awarded; master's, professional, doctoral offered. **ROTC:** Army. **Location:** 80 miles from Memphis, 120 miles from Nashville. **Calendar:** Semester, extensive summer session. **Full-time faculty:** 239 total; 80% have terminal degrees, 9% minority, 47% women. **Part-time faculty:** 5 total; 20% have terminal degrees, 20% women. **Class size:** 70% < 20, 24% 20-39, 5% 40-49, less than 1% 50-99. **Special facilities:** Aquatic center, creative communications center.

Freshman class profile.

GPA 3.75 or higher:	60%	Rank in top tenth:	33%
GPA 3.50-3.74:	16%	Out-of-state:	26%
GPA 3.0-3.49:	17%	Live on campus:	92%
GPA 2.0-2.99:	7%	Fraternities:	29%
Rank in top quarter:	62%	Sororities:	24%

Basis for selection. School achievement, recommendations, special talents, test scores important. 22 ACT or 1030 SAT (exclusive of Writing), top 50% of high school class, and 2.5 GPA required. Interview recommended for all; audition required for music; portfolio recommended for art, communications. Essay required for academic and leadership scholarships. **Home schooled:** If class rank is unavailable, students may be admitted without conditions provided they meet minimum ACT/SAT scores and GPA requirements.

High school preparation. College-preparatory program required. 15 units required; 22 recommended. Required and recommended units include English 4, mathematics 3-4, social studies 2, history 1-2, science 3-4 (laboratory 2), foreign language 1-2, computer science 1, visual/performing arts 1 and academic electives 1-4.

2015-2016 Annual costs. Tuition/fees: $29,190. Room/board: $9,090. Books/supplies: $1,250. Personal expenses: $4,834.

2015-2016 Financial aid. Need-based: 309 full-time freshmen applied for aid; 269 deemed to have need; 269 received aid. Average need met was 65%. Average scholarship/grant was $6,244; average loan $3,418. 58% of total undergraduate aid awarded as scholarships/grants, 42% as loans/jobs. **Non-need-based:** Awarded to 1,548 full-time undergraduates, including 352 freshmen. Scholarships awarded for academics, alumni affiliation, art, athletics, job skills, leadership, minority status, music/drama, religious affiliation, state residency. **Additional information:** Www.uu.edu.

Application procedures. Admission: Priority date 12/1; deadline 8/1 (postmark date). $35 fee, may be waived for applicants with need. Admission notification on a rolling basis beginning on or about 10/1. Must reply by May 1 or within 2 week(s) if notified thereafter. **Financial aid:** Priority date 2/1, closing date 2/1. FAFSA, institutional form required. Applicants notified by 12/1; Applicants notified on a rolling basis starting 3/1; must reply by 5/1 or within 2 week(s) of notification.

Academics. Special study options: Accelerated study, combined bachelor's/graduate degree, cooperative education, cross-registration, distance learning, double major, dual enrollment of high school students, ESL, exchange student, honors, independent study, internships, study abroad, teacher certification program, Washington semester. **Credit/placement by examination:** AP, CLEP, IB, SAT, ACT, institutional tests. 32 credit hours maximum toward bachelor's degree. **Support services:** Learning center, pre-admission summer program, reduced course load, remedial instruction, study skills assistance, tutoring, writing center.

Majors. Biology: General, cellular/molecular, conservation, zoology. **Business:** Accounting, business admin, international, managerial economics, marketing. **Communications:** Advertising, broadcast journalism, communications/speech/rhetoric, digital media, journalism, public relations. **Computer sciences:** Computer science, web page design. **Education:** General, art, biology, business, chemistry, early childhood special, elementary, English, ESL, foreign languages, French, history, kindergarten/preschool, mathematics, middle, music, physical, science, secondary, Spanish, special ed. **Engineering:** Applied physics, electrical, mechanical. **English:** English lit, rhetoric/composition. **Foreign languages:** French, Spanish. **Health services:** Athletic training, clinical lab science, nursing (RN). **History:** General. **Human services:** Social work. **Math:** General. **Parks/recreation:** Exercise sciences, sports admin. **Philosophy/religion:** Christian, ethics, philosophy, religion. **Physical sciences:** General, chemical physics, chemistry, physics. **Psychology:** General. **Social sciences:** Economics, political science, sociology. **Theology:** Sacred music, theology, youth ministry. **Visual/performing arts:** Dramatic, music, music performance, music theory/composition, studio arts. **Work/family studies:** Family systems.

Most popular majors. Education 8%, health sciences 26%, interdisciplinary studies 18%, psychology 6%, public administration/social services 7%.

Technology on campus. 300 workstations in dormitories, library, computer center, student center. Dormitories wired for high-speed internet access and linked to campus network. Commuter students can connect to campus network. Online course registration, online library, helpline, repair service, wireless network available.

Student life. Freshman orientation: Available, $70 fee. Preregistration for classes offered. Held 4 days before classes begin. **Policies:** Full-time resident students required to attend 14 chapel services per semester. Smoke and alcohol-free campus. Religious observance required. **Housing:** Guaranteed on-campus for all undergraduates. Single-sex dorms, special housing for disabled, apartments available. $100 nonrefundable deposit, deadline 5/1. **Activities:** Bands, campus ministries, choral groups, drama, film society, international student organizations, literary magazine, music ensembles, student government, student newspaper, Fellowship of Christian Athletes, ministerial association, student activity council, Mu Kappa, honors student association, Tennessee Intercollegiate State Legislature, LIFE Groups, Klemata.

Athletics. NCAA, NCCAA. Intercollegiate: Baseball M, basketball, cheerleading W, cross-country, golf, soccer, softball W, volleyball W. **Intramural:** Basketball, cheerleading W, cross-country, football (non-tackle), golf, racquetball, softball, swimming, table tennis, tennis, volleyball, weight lifting. **Team name:** Bulldogs.

Student services. Adult student services, alcohol/substance abuse counseling, chaplain/spiritual director, career counseling, student employment services, financial aid counseling, health services, personal counseling, placement for graduates, veterans' counselor. **Physically disabled:** Services for visually, speech, hearing impaired.

Contact. E-mail: info@uu.edu
Phone: (731) 661-5000 Toll-free number: (800) 338-6466
Fax: (731) 661-5017
Rich Grimm, Senior Vice President for Enrollment Services, Union University, 1050 Union University Drive, Jackson, TN 38305-3697

University of Memphis
Memphis, Tennessee   CB member
www.memphis.edu   CB code: 1459

- Public 4-year university
- Commuter campus in very large city
- 15,548 degree-seeking undergraduates: 23% part-time, 59% women, 37% African American, 3% Asian American, 4% Hispanic/Latino, 4% Multi-racial, non-Hispanic, 1% international
- 3,814 degree-seeking graduate students
- 92% of applicants admitted
- SAT or ACT (ACT writing optional) required
- 45% graduate within 6 years

General. Founded in 1912. Regionally accredited. **Degrees:** 2,899 bachelor's awarded; master's, professional, doctoral offered. **ROTC:** Army, Naval, Air Force. **Location:** 10 miles from downtown. **Calendar:** Semester, extensive summer session. **Full-time faculty:** 881 total; 76% have terminal degrees, 25% minority, 43% women. **Part-time faculty:** 554 total; 22% have terminal degrees, 26% minority, 58% women. **Class size:** 48% < 20, 36% 20-39, 6% 40-49, 8% 50-99, 2% >100. **Special facilities:** FedEx Institute of Technology, Crews Center for Entrepreneurship, Institute of Egyptian Art and Archaeology, Center for Earthquake Research and Information, museum, Confucius Institute.

Freshman class profile. 7,556 applied, 6,955 admitted, 2,105 enrolled.

Mid 50% test scores			
SAT critical reading:	430-580	Rank in top quarter:	41%
SAT math:	460-570	Rank in top tenth:	15%
SAT writing:	410-550	Return as sophomores:	78%
ACT composite:	20-26	Out-of-state:	13%
GPA 3.75 or higher:	32%	Live on campus:	51%
GPA 3.50-3.74:	15%	International:	1%
GPA 3.0-3.49:	30%	Fraternities:	6%
GPA 2.0-2.99:	23%	Sororities:	10%

Basis for selection. GPA and test scores important. Admissions Index calculated by multiplying GPA by 30 and adding ACT score. Admissions competitive based on calculated index, and includes evaluation of high school curriculum. Interview required for university college; audition required for music; portfolio required for fine arts. **Home schooled:** Transcript of courses and grades required. Applicants must comply with state law by submitting proof of registration with local education agency.

High school preparation. College-preparatory program required. Required units include English 4, mathematics 3, social studies 1, history 1, science 2 (laboratory 1), foreign language 2 and visual/performing arts 1.

2015-2016 Annual costs. Tuition/fees: $9,269; $20,981 out-of-state. Room/board: $9,061. Books/supplies: $1,415. **Additional information:** Reduced out of state tuition rate possible for students who graduated from a high school within 250-mile radius of University of Memphis.

2015-2016 Financial aid. Need-based: 1,902 full-time freshmen applied for aid; 1,494 deemed to have need; 1,293 received aid. Average need met was 82%. Average scholarship/grant was $6,820; average loan $3,283. 56% of total undergraduate aid awarded as scholarships/grants, 44% as loans/jobs. **Non-need-based:** Awarded to 6,906 full-time undergraduates, including 1,314 freshmen. Scholarships awarded for academics, alumni affiliation, art, athletics, leadership, music/drama, ROTC, state residency.

Application procedures. Admission: Closing date 7/1 (postmark date). $25 fee, may be waived for applicants with need. Admission notification on a rolling basis. Must meet registration deadline. **Financial aid:** Priority date 3/1, closing date 5/1. Applicants notified on a rolling basis starting 3/15; must reply by 8/1.

Academics. University enables students to create non-traditional degrees. **Special study options:** Accelerated study, cooperative education, cross-registration, distance learning, double major, dual enrollment of high school students, ESL, exchange student, external degree, honors, independent study, internships, liberal arts/career combination, student-designed major, study abroad, teacher certification program. **Credit/placement by examination:** AP, CLEP, IB, SAT, ACT, institutional tests. 45 credit hours maximum toward bachelor's degree. **Support services:** Learning center, pre-admission summer program, reduced course load, remedial instruction, study skills assistance, tutoring, writing center.

Honors college/program. 27 ACT or 1200 SAT (exclusive of Writing), 3.5 GPA required.

Majors. Architecture: Environmental design. **Area/ethnic studies:** African-American. **Biology:** General. **Business:** Accounting, business admin, finance, hotel/motel admin, international, logistics, management information systems, managerial economics, marketing, selling. **Communications:** Journalism, media studies. **Computer sciences:** Computer science. **Education:** Multi-level teacher, physical, special ed. **Engineering:** Biomedical, civil, computer, electrical, mechanical. **English:** English lit. **Foreign languages:** General. **History:** General. **Human services:** Social work. **Liberal arts:** Arts/sciences. **Math:** General. **Parks/recreation:** Exercise sciences, sports admin. **Philosophy/religion:** Philosophy. **Physical sciences:** Chemistry, geology, physics. **Protective services:** Law enforcement admin. **Psychology:** General. **Social sciences:** Anthropology, economics, geography, international relations, political science, sociology. **Visual/performing arts:** Art, art history/conservation, dramatic, interior design, music.

Most popular majors. Business/marketing 18%, education 8%, health sciences 8%, interdisciplinary studies 12%, liberal arts 6%, psychology 6%.

Technology on campus. 1,255 workstations in dormitories, library, computer center, student center. Dormitories wired for high-speed internet access and linked to campus network. Commuter students can connect to campus network. Online course registration, online library, helpline, repair service, wireless network available.

Student life. Freshman orientation: Mandatory, $100 fee. Preregistration for classes offered. One- or 2-day sessions, evening program for adult students. Fees vary by program. **Housing:** Coed dorms, single-sex dorms, special housing for disabled, apartments, cooperative housing, fraternity/sorority housing available. **Activities:** Bands, campus ministries, choral groups, dance, drama, international student organizations, literary magazine, music ensembles, Model UN, musical theater, opera, radio station, student government, student newspaper, symphony orchestra, All Greek programming board, Asian American Association, Black Student Association, Blue Crew, campus outreach, Hispanic Student Association, student activities council, Students Advocating Service.

Athletics. NCAA. **Intercollegiate:** Baseball M, basketball, cross-country, football (tackle) M, golf, rifle, soccer, softball W, tennis, track and field, volleyball W. **Intramural:** Basketball, bowling, football (non-tackle), golf, racquetball, soccer, softball, table tennis, tennis, track and field, ultimate frisbee, volleyball, water polo. **Team name:** Tigers.

Student services. Adult student services, alcohol/substance abuse counseling, career counseling, student employment services, financial aid counseling, health services, legal services, minority student services, on-campus daycare, personal counseling, placement for graduates, veterans' counselor, women's services. **Physically disabled:** Services for visually, speech, hearing impaired.

Contact. E-mail: recruitment@memphis.edu
Phone: (901) 678-2111 Toll-free number: (800) 669-2678
Fax: (901) 678-3053
Gloria Moore, Associate Director of Admissions, University of Memphis, 101 Wilder Tower, Memphis, TN 38152

University of Phoenix: Chattanooga
Chattanooga, Tennessee
www.phoenix.edu

- For-profit 4-year university
- Small city

General. Regionally accredited. **Calendar:** Differs by program.

Annual costs/financial aid. Per-credit-hour charge, $410 to $635, depending upon level and course of study. Books, material charges, and other fees vary by course and program. All fees are subject to change.

Contact. 1208 Pointe Centre Drive, Chattanooga, TN 37421-3983

University of Phoenix: Knoxville
Knoxville, Tennessee
www.phoenix.edu

- For-profit 4-year branch campus college
- Small city
- 170 degree-seeking undergraduates

General. Regionally accredited. **Degrees:** 5 bachelor's awarded; master's offered. **Calendar:** Differs by program. **Full-time faculty:** 3 total. **Part-time faculty:** 14 total.

Basis for selection. Open admission.

2015-2016 Annual costs. Per-credit-hour charge, $410 to $635, depending upon level and course of study. Books, material charges, and other fees vary by course and program. All fees are subject to change.

Application procedures. Admission: No deadline. No application fee.

Academics. Credit/placement by examination: AP, CLEP.

Majors. Business: Accounting/business management, business admin, finance, human resources, marketing. **Computer sciences:** Database management, networking, programming, security, systems analysis, web page design, webmaster. **Health services:** Facilities admin, health information management, long term care admin. **Human services:** General. **Protective services:** Disaster management, law enforcement admin, security management.

Student life. Freshman orientation: Mandatory. Preregistration for classes offered.

Contact. University of Phoenix: Knoxville, 10133 Sherrill Boulevard, Knoxville, TN 37932-3347

University of Phoenix: Memphis
Cordova, Tennessee
www.phoenix.edu

- For-profit 4-year university
- Very large city
- 1,280 degree-seeking undergraduates

General. Regionally accredited. **Degrees:** 112 bachelor's awarded; master's offered. **Calendar:** Differs by program. **Full-time faculty:** 18 total. **Part-time faculty:** 130 total.

Basis for selection. Open admission, but selective for some programs.

2015-2016 Annual costs. Per-credit-hour charge, $410 to $635, depending upon level and course of study. Books, material charges, and other fees vary by course and program. All fees are subject to change.

Application procedures. Admission: No deadline. No application fee. **Financial aid:** No deadline.

Academics. Credit/placement by examination: AP, CLEP.

Majors. Business: Accounting/business management, business admin, e-commerce, entrepreneurial studies, finance, human resources, marketing, operations. **Computer sciences:** Database management, networking, programming, security, support specialist, system admin, systems analysis, web page design, webmaster. **Education:** Elementary. **Health services:** Facilities admin, health information management, long term care admin. **Human services:** General. **Protective services:** Disaster management, law enforcement admin.

Student life. Freshman orientation: Mandatory. Preregistration for classes offered.

Contact. Toll-free number: (877) 766-0766
University of Phoenix: Memphis, 65 Germantown Court, Cordova, TN 38018-7290

University of Phoenix: Nashville
Nashville, Tennessee
www.phoenix.edu

- For-profit 4-year university
- Very large city
- 1,830 degree-seeking undergraduates

General. Regionally accredited. **Degrees:** 504 bachelor's awarded; master's offered. **Calendar:** Differs by program. **Full-time faculty:** 13 total. **Part-time faculty:** 208 total.

Basis for selection. Open admission, but selective for some programs.

2015-2016 Annual costs. Per-credit-hour charge, $410 to $635, depending upon level and course of study. Books, material charges, and other fees vary by course and program. All fees are subject to change.

Application procedures. Admission: No deadline. No application fee. **Financial aid:** No deadline.

Academics. Credit/placement by examination: AP, CLEP.

Majors. Business: Accounting, accounting/business management, business admin, e-commerce, entrepreneurial studies, finance, human resources, marketing, operations. **Computer sciences:** Database management, networking, programming, security, support specialist, system admin, systems analysis, web page design, webmaster. **Education:** Elementary. **Health services:** Facilities admin, nursing (RN). **Human services:** General. **Protective services:** Law enforcement admin.

Student life. Freshman orientation: Mandatory. Preregistration for classes offered.

Contact. Toll-free number: (866) 766-0766
University of Phoenix: Nashville, 616 Marriott Drive, Nashville, TN 37214-5048

University of Tennessee: Chattanooga
Chattanooga, Tennessee
www.utc.edu   CB code: 1831

- Public 4-year university
- Commuter campus in small city
- 9,977 degree-seeking undergraduates: 12% part-time, 56% women, 11% African American, 2% Asian American, 3% Hispanic/Latino, 7% Multiracial, non-Hispanic, 1% international
- 1,268 degree-seeking graduate students
- 79% of applicants admitted
- SAT or ACT (ACT writing optional) required
- 44% graduate within 6 years

General. Founded in 1886. Regionally accredited. **Degrees:** 1,825 bachelor's awarded; master's, professional, doctoral offered. **ROTC:** Army. **Location:** 130 miles from Nashville, 118 miles from Atlanta. **Calendar:** Semester, extensive summer session. **Full-time faculty:** 469 total; 2% have terminal degrees, 16% minority, 45% women. **Part-time faculty:** 291 total; 1% have terminal degrees, 8% minority, 53% women. **Class size:** 38% < 20, 41% 20-39, 11% 40-49, 9% 50-99, 2% >100. **Special facilities:** Art galleries, theater, observatory, arboretum, river walk.

Freshman class profile. 6,752 applied, 5,349 admitted, 1,865 enrolled.

Mid 50% test scores			
SAT critical reading:	460-570	GPA 3.0-3.49:	32%
SAT math:	450-580	GPA 2.0-2.99:	15%
ACT composite:	21-26	Return as sophomores:	71%
GPA 3.75 or higher:	34%	Out-of-state:	5%
GPA 3.50-3.74:	19%	Live on campus:	81%

Basis for selection. High school curriculum and GPA very important. 2.85 GPA with 18 ACT (870 SAT) or 2.5 GPA with 21 ACT (990 SAT) required. Special talents, recommendations, essay or personal statement considered. Essay recommended. **Home schooled:** Transcript of courses and grades required. 2.85 GPA, 21 ACT/ 990 SAT and completion of all 16 high school units. **Learning Disabled:** Students may register for services through the Disability Resource Center after admission.

High school preparation. College-preparatory program recommended. 16 units required. Required units include English 4, mathematics 4, history 2, science 3 (laboratory 3), foreign language 2 and visual/performing arts 1. History consists of one unit of European or world history, or world geography. The second unit is U.S. History.

2015-2016 Annual costs. Tuition/fees: $8,356; $24,474 out-of-state. Room/board: $8,388. Books/supplies: $1,400. Personal expenses: $1,700.

2015-2016 Financial aid. **Need-based:** 1,751 full-time freshmen applied for aid; 1,127 deemed to have need; 1,112 received aid. Average need met was 68%. Average scholarship/grant was $8,140; average loan $3,324. 51% of total undergraduate aid awarded as scholarships/grants, 49% as loans/jobs. **Non-need-based:** Awarded to 1,089 full-time undergraduates, including 285 freshmen. Scholarships awarded for academics, alumni affiliation, art, athletics, leadership, music/drama, ROTC, state residency.

Application procedures. **Admission:** Closing date 5/1. $30 fee, may be waived for applicants with need. Admission notification on a rolling basis. May defer admission for one semester. **Financial aid:** Priority date 5/1; no closing date. FAFSA required. Applicants notified on a rolling basis starting 3/1; must reply within 4 week(s) of notification.

Academics. **Special study options:** Accelerated study, cooperative education, cross-registration, distance learning, double major, dual enrollment of high school students, ESL, exchange student, honors, independent study, internships, student-designed major, study abroad, teacher certification program. Washington Center Internship, Southeastern Command and Leadership Academy, Senator Tommy Burks Victim Assistance Academy. **Credit/placement by examination:** AP, CLEP, IB, SAT, ACT. 24 credit hours maximum toward bachelor's degree. May only be used for elective credit hours. **Support services:** Learning center, pre-admission summer program, reduced course load, remedial instruction, study skills assistance, tutoring, writing center.

Honors college/program. Based on application, teacher evaluations, essay, official high school transcript, and ACT or SAT; about 45 applicants admitted each year.

Majors. Architecture: Interior. **Biology:** General. **Business:** Business admin. **Communications:** General. **Computer sciences:** Computer science. **Conservation:** Environmental science. **Education:** Art, early childhood, middle, secondary, special ed. **Engineering:** General, chemical, civil, electrical, mechanical. **English:** English lit. **Foreign languages:** General. **Health services:** Nursing (RN). **History:** General. **Human services:** Community org/advocacy, social work. **Liberal arts:** Humanities. **Math:** General, applied. **Parks/recreation:** Exercise sciences. **Physical sciences:** Chemistry, geology, physics. **Protective services:** Law enforcement admin. **Psychology:** General. **Social sciences:** Economics, political science. **Visual/performing arts:** Art, dramatic, interior design, music.

Most popular majors. Biology 7%, business/marketing 18%, education 10%, engineering/engineering technologies 7%, health sciences 7%, parks/recreation 9%, psychology 6%, social sciences 6%.

Technology on campus. 965 workstations in library, computer center, student center. Dormitories wired for high-speed internet access and linked to campus network. Commuter students can connect to campus network. Online course registration, online library, helpline, repair service, wireless network available.

Student life. Freshman orientation: Mandatory, $65 fee. Preregistration for classes offered. Two-day sessions held in summer. **Housing:** Guaranteed on-campus for freshmen. Coed dorms, special housing for disabled, apartments, themed housing available. $225 fully refundable deposit, deadline 8/1. **Activities:** Bands, campus ministries, choral groups, dance, drama, film society, international student organizations, literary magazine, music ensembles, Model UN, musical theater, opera, radio station, student government, student newspaper, symphony orchestra, TV station, Bahai club, Baptist collegiate ministry, Campus Crusade for Christ, Fellowship of Christian Athletes, Omega Phi Alpha, Sigma Alpha Iota, Habitat for Humanity, College Democrats, College Republicans, National Society of Black Engineers.

Athletics. NCAA. **Intercollegiate:** Basketball, cross-country, football (tackle) M, golf, soccer W, softball W, tennis, track and field, volleyball W, wrestling M. **Intramural:** Badminton, basketball, cross-country, football (non-tackle), racquetball, soccer, softball W, swimming, table tennis, tennis, volleyball, wrestling M. **Team name:** Mocs.

Student services. Adult student services, alcohol/substance abuse counseling, chaplain/spiritual director, career counseling, student employment services, financial aid counseling, health services, minority student services, on-campus daycare, personal counseling, placement for graduates, veterans' counselor, women's services. **Physically disabled:** Services for visually, speech, hearing impaired.

Contact. E-mail: utcmocs@utc.edu
Phone: (423) 425-4662 Toll-free number: (800) 882-6627
Fax: (423) 425-4157
Lee Pierce, Director of Admissions, University of Tennessee: Chattanooga, 615 McCallie Avenue, Chattanooga, TN 37403

University of Tennessee: Knoxville
Knoxville, Tennessee   CB member
www.utk.edu   CB code: 1843

- Public 4-year university
- Commuter campus in large city
- 21,661 degree-seeking undergraduates: 6% part-time, 49% women, 7% African American, 3% Asian American, 3% Hispanic/Latino, 3% Multiracial, non-Hispanic, 1% international
- 5,819 degree-seeking graduate students
- 76% of applicants admitted
- SAT or ACT (ACT writing optional), application essay required
- 70% graduate within 6 years

General. Founded in 1794. Regionally accredited. **Degrees:** 4,634 bachelor's awarded; master's, professional, doctoral offered. **ROTC:** Army, Air Force. **Location:** 224 miles from Atlanta, 178 miles from Nashville. **Calendar:** Semester, extensive summer session. **Full-time faculty:** 1,526 total; 87% have terminal degrees, 19% minority, 42% women. **Part-time faculty:** 205 total; 56% have terminal degrees, 11% minority, 57% women. **Class size:** 28% < 20, 52% 20-39, 6% 40-49, 8% 50-99, 6% >100. **Special facilities:** Museum of natural history and culture, art galleries, music center, international house, center for public policy.

Freshman class profile. 17,081 applied, 13,032 admitted, 4,719 enrolled.

Mid 50% test scores			
SAT critical reading:	520-630	Rank in top quarter:	90%
SAT math:	530-630	Rank in top tenth:	54%
ACT composite:	24-30	Return as sophomores:	85%
GPA 3.75 or higher:	64%	Out-of-state:	16%
GPA 3.50-3.74:	13%	Live on campus:	90%
GPA 3.0-3.49:	17%	International:	2%
GPA 2.0-2.99:	6%	Fraternities:	22%
		Sororities:	29%

Basis for selection. Holistic review of grades in core academic subjects, SAT/ACT, extracurricular school and community activities, awards, essays, personal statement, and recommendations that address the applicant's potential for success in college. Audition required for music. Essay required for nursing, pre-pharmacy.

High school preparation. College-preparatory program required. 16 units required. Required units include English 4, mathematics 4, social studies 1, history 1, science 3 (laboratory 3), foreign language 2 and visual/performing arts 1.

2015-2016 Annual costs. Tuition/fees: $12,436; $30,626 out-of-state. Room/board: $9,926. Books/supplies: $1,598. Personal expenses: $4,002. **Additional information:** Out-of-state students pay additional required fees of $230.

2015-2016 Financial aid. All financial aid based on need. 4,429 full-time freshmen applied for aid; 2,804 deemed to have need; 2,804 received aid. Average need met was 62%. Average scholarship/grant was $11,049; average loan $5,234. 68% of total undergraduate aid awarded as scholarships/grants, 32% as loans/jobs. **Additional information:** Application priority date for scholarships 2/1.

Application procedures. Admission: Priority date 11/1; deadline 12/1 (postmark date). $50 fee, may be waived for applicants with need. Admission notification by 3/31. Admission notification on a rolling basis beginning on or about 10/15. Must reply by May 1 or within 2 week(s) if notified thereafter. **Financial aid:** Priority date 2/15; no closing date. FAFSA required. Applicants notified on a rolling basis starting 3/15; must reply within 3 week(s) of notification.

Academics. Expanded academic support offerings available in three locations on campus including the Hodges Commons in the Library, Greve Hall, and North and South Carrick Residence Hall. **Special study options:** Accelerated study, combined bachelor's/graduate degree, cooperative education, distance learning, double major, dual enrollment of high school students, ESL, exchange student, external degree, honors, independent study, internships, liberal arts/career combination, student-designed major, study abroad, teacher certification program. **Credit/placement by examination:** AP, CLEP, IB, SAT, ACT, institutional tests. **Support services:** Study skills assistance, tutoring.

Majors. Architecture: Architecture. **Biology:** General. **Business:** Accounting, business admin, finance, hotel/motel admin, human resources, logistics, managerial economics, marketing, statistics. **Communications:** Advertising, communications/speech/rhetoric, journalism, public relations. **Computer sciences:** Computer science. **Conservation:** Economics, forestry, wildlife/wilderness. **Education:** Special ed. **Engineering:** Aerospace, agricultural, biomedical, chemical, civil, computer, electrical, industrial, materials, mechanical, nuclear. **English:** English lit. **Foreign languages:** Classics, French, German, Italian, Russian, Spanish. **Health services:** Nursing (RN). **History:** General. **Human services:** General, social work. **Math:** General, statistics. **Parks/recreation:** Exercise sciences, sports admin. **Philosophy/religion:** Philosophy, religion. **Physical sciences:** Chemistry, geology, physics. **Psychology:** General. **Social sciences:** Anthropology, economics, geography, political science, sociology. **Visual/performing arts:** Art history/conservation, commercial/advertising art, dramatic, interior design, music, studio arts. **Work/family studies:** Consumer economics, family studies, food/nutrition.

Most popular majors. Business/marketing 21%, communications/journalism 7%, engineering/engineering technologies 10%, parks/recreation 6%, psychology 8%, social sciences 8%.

Technology on campus. 1,200 workstations in dormitories, library, student center. Dormitories wired for high-speed internet access and linked to campus network. Commuter students can connect to campus network. Online course registration, online library, helpline, repair service, student web hosting, wireless network available.

Student life. Freshman orientation: Mandatory, $150 fee. Preregistration for classes offered. Two-day session; parents may attend for $50 per parent which does not include housing. **Policies:** Freshmen must live on-campus unless residing with parent or legal guardian. **Housing:** Guaranteed on-campus for freshmen. Coed dorms, single-sex dorms, special housing for disabled, apartments, fraternity/sorority housing, themed housing available. **Activities:** Bands, campus ministries, choral groups, dance, drama, film society, international student organizations, literary magazine, music ensembles, Model UN, musical theater, opera, radio station, student government, student newspaper, symphony orchestra, TV station, UT hosts more than 400 student organizations for undergraduate and graduate students.

Athletics. NCAA. **Intercollegiate:** Baseball M, basketball, cross-country, diving, football (tackle) M, golf, rowing (crew) W, soccer W, softball W, swimming, tennis, track and field, volleyball W. **Intramural:** Badminton, basketball, bowling, field hockey, football (non-tackle), racquetball, sand

volleyball, soccer, softball, table tennis, tennis, ultimate frisbee, volleyball, water polo, weight lifting. **Team name:** Volunteers.

Student services. Alcohol/substance abuse counseling, career counseling, student employment services, financial aid counseling, health services, minority student services, personal counseling, placement for graduates, veterans' counselor, women's services. **Physically disabled:** Services for visually, speech, hearing impaired.

Contact. E-mail: admissions@utk.edu
Phone: (865) 974-2184
Kari Alldredge, Assistant Dean and Director of Undergraduate Admissions, University of Tennessee: Knoxville, 320 Student Services Building, Circle Park, Knoxville, TN 37996-0230

University of Tennessee: Martin
Martin, Tennessee
www.utm.edu   **CB code: 1844**

- Public 4-year university
- Residential campus in small town
- 5,988 degree-seeking undergraduates: 10% part-time, 58% women
- 327 degree-seeking graduate students
- 70% of applicants admitted
- SAT or ACT (ACT writing optional) required
- 46% graduate within 6 years

General. Founded in 1927. Regionally accredited. Coordinates online education for UT system. **Degrees:** 1,199 bachelor's awarded; master's offered. **ROTC:** Army. **Location:** 125 miles from Memphis, 150 miles from Nashville. **Calendar:** Semester, extensive summer session. **Full-time faculty:** 289 total; 4% have terminal degrees, 13% minority, 46% women. **Part-time faculty:** 221 total; 4% minority, 53% women. **Class size:** 60% < 20, 31% 20-39, 5% 40-49, 4% 50-99. **Special facilities:** Teacher resource center, 680-acre agriculture, natural resources teaching, demonstration complex, teaching/research facility resort, international education center.

Freshman class profile. 3,400 applied, 2,368 admitted, 1,024 enrolled.

Mid 50% test scores			
ACT composite:		20-25	
GPA 3.75 or higher:		35%	
GPA 3.50-3.74:		22%	
GPA 3.0-3.49:		28%	
GPA 2.0-2.99:		15%	
Rank in top quarter:		46%	

Rank in top tenth:	17%
Return as sophomores:	75%
Out-of-state:	6%
Live on campus:	60%
International:	4%
Fraternities:	19%
Sororities:	21%

Basis for selection. 2.85 GPA with 18 ACT or 2.5 GPA with 21 ACT required. Students not meeting regular admission requirements may be considered for conditional admission. Auditions required in fine and performing arts. **Home schooled:** 21 ACT and 2.85 GPA required.

High school preparation. College-preparatory program required. 16 units required. Required units include English 4, mathematics 4, social studies 1, history 1, science 3 (laboratory 1), foreign language 2 and visual/performing arts 1.

2015-2016 Annual costs. Tuition/fees: $8,326; $22,270 out-of-state. Room/board: $5,896. Books/supplies: $1,400. Personal expenses: $2,592.

2015-2016 Financial aid. All financial aid based on need. 981 full-time freshmen applied for aid; 739 deemed to have need; 730 received aid. Average need met was 79%. Average scholarship/grant was $6,735; average loan $3,314. 59% of total undergraduate aid awarded as scholarships/grants, 41% as loans/jobs.

Application procedures. Admission: Priority date 8/1; no deadline. $30 fee. Admission notification on a rolling basis beginning on or about 4/1. **Financial aid:** Priority date 2/15; no closing date. FAFSA required. Applicants notified by 3/15; must reply within 2 week(s) of notification.

Academics. Special study options: Accelerated study, cooperative education, cross-registration, distance learning, double major, dual enrollment of high school students, ESL, exchange student, honors, independent study, internships, student-designed major, study abroad, teacher certification program. 3-1 pharmacy program, 3-1 veterinary medicine program, 3-1 dentistry program, 3-1 medicine program, 3-1 optometry program, 3-1 podiatry program, 3-1 chiropractory program. **Credit/placement by examination:** AP, CLEP, SAT, ACT, institutional tests. 30 credit hours maximum toward bachelor's degree. **Support services:** Study skills assistance, tutoring, writing center.

Majors. Biology: General. **Business:** Accounting, business admin, finance, management information systems, managerial economics, marketing. **Communications:** Communications/speech/rhetoric. **Computer sciences:** Computer science. **Conservation:** Management/policy. **Education:** Secondary, special ed. **Engineering:** General. **English:** English lit. **Foreign languages:** French, Spanish. **Health services:** Nursing (RN). **History:** General. **Human services:** Social work. **Math:** General. **Parks/recreation:** Health/fitness. **Philosophy/religion:** Philosophy. **Physical sciences:** Chemistry, geology. **Protective services:** Law enforcement admin. **Psychology:** General. **Social sciences:** International relations, political science, sociology. **Visual/performing arts:** General, music. **Work/family studies:** General.

Most popular majors. Agriculture 10%, business/marketing 16%, education 10%, interdisciplinary studies 13%, parks/recreation 11%.

Technology on campus. 308 workstations in dormitories, library, student center. Dormitories wired for high-speed internet access and linked to campus network. Commuter students can connect to campus network. Online course registration, online library, helpline, repair service, student web hosting, wireless network available.

Student life. Freshman orientation: Available, $165 fee. Preregistration for classes offered. 4-day program held in August. **Policies:** Freshmen must live on-campus. **Housing:** Guaranteed on-campus for freshmen. Coed dorms, single-sex dorms, special housing for disabled, apartments available. $100 fully refundable deposit, deadline 8/1. Honors Housing available. **Activities:** Bands, campus ministries, choral groups, dance, drama, film society, international student organizations, literary magazine, music ensembles, Model UN, musical theater, radio station, student government, student newspaper, TV station, Chi Alpha Christian Fellowship, Interfaith student center, Rotaract, Free Thinkers club, Fellowship of Christian Athletes, College Democrats, College Republicans, Reformed University Fellowship, Japanese animation research society.

Athletics. NCAA. **Intercollegiate:** Baseball M, basketball, cheerleading W, cross-country, equestrian W, football (tackle) M, golf M, rifle, rodeo, soccer W, softball W, tennis W, volleyball W. **Intramural:** Basketball, football (non-tackle), golf, racquetball, soccer, softball, table tennis, tennis, ultimate frisbee, volleyball, water polo. **Team name:** Skyhawks.

Student services. Adult student services, alcohol/substance abuse counseling, chaplain/spiritual director, career counseling, services for economically disadvantaged, student employment services, financial aid counseling, health services, minority student services, on-campus daycare, personal counseling, placement for graduates, veterans' counselor, women's services. **Physically disabled:** Services for visually, speech, hearing impaired.

Contact. E-mail: admitme@utm.edu
Phone: (731) 881-7020 Toll-free number: (800) 829-8861
Fax: (731) 881-7029
Judy Rayburn, Director of Admissions, University of Tennessee: Martin, 201 Administration Building, Martin, TN 38238

Vanderbilt University
Nashville, Tennessee **CB member**
www.vanderbilt.edu **CB code: 1871**

- Private 4-year university
- Residential campus in very large city
- 6,857 degree-seeking undergraduates: 1% part-time, 50% women, 8% African American, 12% Asian American, 8% Hispanic/Latino, 5% Multiracial, non-Hispanic, 7% international
- 5,617 degree-seeking graduate students
- 12% of applicants admitted
- SAT or ACT (ACT writing optional), application essay required
- 92% graduate within 6 years; 39% enter graduate study

General. Founded in 1873. Regionally accredited. **Degrees:** 1,644 bachelor's awarded; master's, professional, doctoral offered. **ROTC:** Army, Naval, Air Force. **Location:** 240 miles from Atlanta, 300 miles from St. Louis. **Calendar:** Semester, limited summer session. **Full-time faculty:** 920 total; 96% have terminal degrees, 15% minority, 37% women. **Part-time faculty:** 259 total. **Class size:** 66% < 20, 23% 20-39, 3% 40-49, 7% 50-99, 2% >100. **Special facilities:** Observatory, electron microscopes, television news archive, national arboretum, video productions, black cultural center, women's center, cinema and art museum, art gallery, recreation and wellness center, outdoor recreation center.

Freshman class profile. 31,464 applied, 3,674 admitted, 1,607 enrolled.

Mid 50% test scores			
SAT critical reading:	710-790	Rank in top quarter:	97%
SAT math:	720-800	Rank in top tenth:	91%
SAT writing:	690-770	Return as sophomores:	97%
ACT composite:	32-35	Out-of-state:	90%
GPA 3.75 or higher:	67%	Live on campus:	100%
GPA 3.50-3.74:	20%	International:	7%
GPA 3.0-3.49:	12%	Fraternities:	30%
GPA 2.0-2.99:	1%	Sororities:	47%

Basis for selection. Academic achievement, recommendation, essay, test scores, activities important. Audition required for music program. **Home schooled:** Statement describing home school structure and mission required.

High school preparation. College-preparatory program required. 18 units required; 21 recommended. Required and recommended units include English 4, mathematics 3-4, social studies 2-3, history 1, science 3-4 (laboratory 2-3), foreign language 2 and academic electives 3. Additional unit in math and 2 in science recommended for engineering applicants. Music applicants do not require 2 units of science. Engineering program recommends 2 years of language. Education & Human Development program does not require language.

2015-2016 Annual costs. Tuition/fees: $44,712. Room/board: $14,670. Books/supplies: $1,370. Personal expenses: $2,780.

2015-2016 Financial aid. Need-based: 1,027 full-time freshmen applied for aid; 854 deemed to have need; 839 received aid. Average need met was 100%. Average scholarship/grant was $41,718; average loan $2,781. 96% of total undergraduate aid awarded as scholarships/grants, 4% as loans/jobs. **Non-need-based:** Awarded to 2,360 full-time undergraduates, including 671 freshmen. Scholarships awarded for academics, athletics, leadership, music/drama, ROTC, state residency. **Additional information:** Financial aid packages awarded to incoming and returning undergraduate students are need-based loan-free.

Application procedures. Admission: Closing date 1/1 (postmark date). $50 fee, may be waived for applicants with need. Admission notification by 4/1. Must reply by May 1 or within 2 week(s) if notified thereafter. **Financial aid:** Priority date 2/1; no closing date. FAFSA, CSS PROFILE required. Applicants notified by 4/1; must reply by 5/1.

Academics. Special study options: Accelerated study, combined bachelor's/graduate degree, double major, dual enrollment of high school students, ESL, honors, independent study, internships, liberal arts/career combination, student-designed major, study abroad, teacher certification program, Washington semester. **Credit/placement by examination:** AP, CLEP, IB, institutional tests. 30 credit hours maximum toward bachelor's degree. **Support services:** Learning center, study skills assistance, tutoring, writing center.

Majors. Area/ethnic studies: African-American, American, Asian, European, Latin American, women's. **Biology:** General, ecology/evolutionary, molecular, neuroscience. **Communications:** Communications/speech/rhetoric. **Computer sciences:** Computer science. **Education:** General, early childhood, elementary, foreign languages, music, secondary, special ed. **Engineering:** Biomedical, chemical, civil, computer, electrical, engineering science, mechanical. **English:** English lit. **Foreign languages:** Classics, French, German, Portuguese, Russian, Spanish. **History:** General. **Human services:** Public policy. **Math:** General. **Philosophy/religion:** Judaic, philosophy, religion. **Physical sciences:** Chemistry, geology, physics. **Psychology:** General, developmental. **Social sciences:** General, anthropology, economics, political science, sociology. **Visual/performing arts:** Art history/conservation, brass instruments, dramatic, film/cinema/video, music, music theory/composition, percussion instruments, piano/keyboard, stringed instruments, studio arts, voice/opera, woodwind instruments. **Work/family studies:** Child development.

Most popular majors. Biology 8%, engineering/engineering technologies 13%, interdisciplinary studies 10%, psychology 6%, social sciences 28%.

Technology on campus. 400 workstations in library, computer center, student center. Dormitories wired for high-speed internet access and linked to campus network. Commuter students can connect to campus network. Online course registration, online library, helpline, repair service, student web hosting, wireless network available.

Student life. Freshman orientation: Mandatory, $718 fee. Preregistration for classes offered. **Policies:** Freshmen not permitted cars on campus. **Housing:** Guaranteed on-campus for freshmen. Coed dorms, single-sex dorms, special housing for disabled, apartments, fraternity/sorority housing, themed housing available. **Activities:** Bands, campus ministries, choral groups, dance, drama, film society, international student organizations, literary magazine, music ensembles, Model UN, musical theater, opera, student government, student newspaper, symphony orchestra, TV station, Over 300 clubs and organizations.

Athletics. NCAA. **Intercollegiate:** Baseball M, basketball, bowling W, cheerleading, cross-country, football (tackle) M, golf, lacrosse W, soccer W, swimming W, tennis, track and field W. **Intramural:** Badminton, basketball, bowling, football (non-tackle), golf, racquetball, soccer, softball, squash, swimming, table tennis, tennis, track and field, volleyball, water polo, wrestling. **Team name:** Commodores.

Student services. Alcohol/substance abuse counseling, chaplain/spiritual director, career counseling, student employment services, financial aid counseling, health services, minority student services, on-campus daycare, personal counseling, placement for graduates, women's services. **Physically disabled:** Services for visually, speech, hearing impaired.

Contact. E-mail: admissions@vanderbilt.edu
Phone: (615) 322-2561 Toll-free number: (800) 288-0432
Fax: (615) 343-7765
John Gaines, Director, Admissions, Vanderbilt University, 2305 West End Avenue, Nashville, TN 37203-1727

Virginia College School of Business and Health in Knoxville
Knoxville, Tennessee
www.vc.edu/knoxville

- For-profit 4-year career college
- Small city
- 330 undergraduates

General. Regionally accredited; also accredited by ACICS. **Degrees:** 47 associate awarded. **Calendar:** Quarter. **Full-time faculty:** 5 total. **Part-time faculty:** 34 total.

Basis for selection. Open admission.

2015-2016 Annual costs. Diploma programs: $14,652-$23,220. Associate programs: $37,152-$40,700. Clock hour diploma program: Cosmetology $21,225.

Academics. Credit/placement by examination: AP.

Majors. **Business:** Business admin, human resources. **Protective services:** Law enforcement admin.

Contact. E-mail: knoxville.info@vc.edu
Phone: (865) 745-4500
Sergio Takahashi, Director of Admissions, Virginia College School of Business and Health in Knoxville, 5003 North Broadway Street, Knoxville, TN 37918

Visible Music College
Memphis, Tennessee
www.visible.edu
CB code: 5450

- Private 3-year music and performing arts college affiliated with the Christian Church
- Very large city
- 111 degree-seeking undergraduates
- SAT or ACT (ACT writing optional), application essay, interview required

General. Regionally accredited; also accredited by TRACS. Provides practical ministry training and discipleship in addition to modern music education. **Degrees:** 3 bachelor's awarded. **Calendar:** Semester, limited summer session. **Full-time faculty:** 20 total. **Part-time faculty:** 9 total. **Special facilities:** Recording studios.

Basis for selection. Personal relationship with Jesus Christ required, having had a salvation experience. 18 ACT or 750 SAT (exclusive of Writing) or 1500 SAT (including Writing) required. Audition is required. Audition required for Modern Music Ministry program.

2015-2016 Annual costs. Tuition/fees: $19,500. Room/board: $5,000. Books/supplies: $800.

Application procedures. Admission: Closing date 6/30. $40 fee, may be waived for applicants with need. Admission notification on a rolling basis. **Financial aid:** No deadline.

Academics. Credit/placement by examination: AP, CLEP.

Majors. Communications: Digital media. **Theology:** Theology. **Visual/performing arts:** Music management, music performance.

Contact. E-mail: seeyourself@visible.edu
Phone: (901) 377-2991 Toll-free number: (877) 558-4742
Fax: (901) 377-0544
Geordy Wells, Admissions Coordinator, Visible Music College, 200 Madison Ave, Memphis, TN 38103

Watkins College of Art, Design & Film
Nashville, Tennessee
www.watkins.edu
CB code: 4927

- Private 4-year visual arts college
- Commuter campus in very large city
- 305 degree-seeking undergraduates
- 39% of applicants admitted
- SAT or ACT (ACT writing optional), application essay required

General. Regionally accredited. **Degrees:** 40 bachelor's awarded. **Calendar:** Semester, limited summer session. **Full-time faculty:** 18 total. **Part-time faculty:** 38 total. **Class size:** 88% < 20, 11% 20-39, less than 1% 40-49, less than 1% 50-99.

Freshman class profile. 342 applied, 135 admitted, 77 enrolled.

Mid 50% test scores		GPA 3.75 or higher:	16%
SAT critical reading:	380-600	GPA 3.50-3.74:	23%
SAT math:	510-690	GPA 3.0-3.49:	35%
SAT writing:	480-660	GPA 2.0-2.99:	24%
ACT composite:	18-24		

Basis for selection. Artistic exercises and academic essays, test scores, prior academic record and letter of recommendation. Portfolio or specific artistic exercises required for BFA degree application. **Home schooled:** Transcript of courses and grades, state high school equivalency certificate, letter of recommendation (nonparent) required. **Learning Disabled:** Doctor's report required.

High school preparation. Recommended units include English 4, mathematics 2, social studies 2, history 2, science 1, computer science 2 and visual/performing arts 4.

2015-2016 Annual costs. Tuition/fees: $23,100. Room only: $6,380. Books/supplies: $1,500. Personal expenses: $2,500.

Financial aid. Non-need-based: Scholarships awarded for academics, art, minority status.

Application procedures. Admission: Priority date 3/1; deadline 7/15 (postmark date). $50 fee, may be waived for applicants with need. Admission notification on a rolling basis. Must reply by May 1 or within 2 week(s) if notified thereafter. **Financial aid:** Priority date 4/1, closing date 8/1. FAFSA, institutional form required. Applicants notified on a rolling basis starting 5/1; must reply within 2 week(s) of notification.

Academics. Special study options: Cooperative education, cross-registration, dual enrollment of high school students, exchange student, independent study, internships, study abroad. Cooperative agreement with all AICAD colleges; cooperative agreement with Belmont University. **Credit/placement by examination:** AP, CLEP, IB, institutional tests. **Support services:** Study skills assistance, tutoring, writing center.

Majors. Visual/performing arts: Art, film/cinema/video, graphic design, interior design, photography, studio arts.

Technology on campus. 200 workstations in library, computer center, student center. Dormitories wired for high-speed internet access and linked to campus network. Commuter students can connect to campus network. Online course registration, online library, helpline, wireless network available.

Student life. Freshman orientation: Mandatory. Preregistration for classes offered. Two-day program held one week prior to beginning of classes. **Housing:** Guaranteed on-campus for freshmen. Coed dorms, apartments available. $300 partly refundable deposit, deadline 7/15. **Activities:** Film society, student government.

Student services. Alcohol/substance abuse counseling, career counseling, services for economically disadvantaged, financial aid counseling, personal counseling. **Physically disabled:** Services for visually, speech, hearing impaired.

Contact. E-mail: admissions@watkins.edu
Phone: (615) 383-4848 ext. 7418 Toll-free number: (866) 887-6395
Fax: (615) 383-4849
Jenna Maurice, Director of Admissions, Watkins College of Art,
Design & Film, 2298 Rosa L. Parks Boulevard, Nashville, TN 37228

Welch College
Nashville, Tennessee
www.welch.edu

CB code: 1232

- Private 4-year Bible and teachers college affiliated with the Free Will Baptists
- Residential campus in very large city
- 243 degree-seeking undergraduates: 9% part-time, 48% women, 9% African American, 1% Asian American, 3% Hispanic/Latino, 2% Multiracial, non-Hispanic
- Application essay required
- 33% graduate within 6 years; 21% enter graduate study

General. Founded in 1942. Regionally accredited; also accredited by ABHE. **Degrees:** 38 bachelor's, 11 associate awarded. **ROTC:** Army, Air Force. **Location:** 3 miles from downtown. **Calendar:** Semester, limited summer session. **Full-time faculty:** 16 total; 62% have terminal degrees, 25% women. **Part-time faculty:** 28 total; 54% have terminal degrees, 4% minority, 50% women. **Class size:** 92% < 20, 4% 20-39, 2% 40-49, 2% 50-99.

Freshman class profile. 115 applied, 79 admitted, 45 enrolled.

Mid 50% test scores			
SAT critical reading:	450-550	**GPA 2.0-2.99:**	15%
SAT math:	500-580	**Rank in top quarter:**	52%
SAT writing:	460-600	**Rank in top tenth:**	39%
ACT composite:	17-25	**End year in good standing:**	95%
GPA 3.75 or higher:	44%	**Return as sophomores:**	66%
GPA 3.50-3.74:	9%	**Out-of-state:**	62%
GPA 3.0-3.49:	32%	**Live on campus:**	87%

Basis for selection. Open admission. Applicants without high school diploma or GED must pass GED prior to receiving degree.

High school preparation. 22 units recommended. Recommended units include English 4, mathematics 4, social studies 3, history 2, science 4, foreign language 3 and academic electives 2.

2015-2016 Annual costs. Tuition/fees: $17,398. Room/board: $7,048. Books/supplies: $876. Personal expenses: $1,700.

2014-2015 Financial aid. Need-based: 46 full-time freshmen applied for aid; 45 deemed to have need; 45 received aid. Average need met was 41%. Average scholarship/grant was $5,944; average loan $3,500. 73% of total undergraduate aid awarded as scholarships/grants, 27% as loans/jobs. **Non-need-based:** Awarded to 189 full-time undergraduates, including 41 freshmen. Scholarships awarded for academics, alumni affiliation, art, music/drama.

Application procedures. Admission: Priority date 4/15; no deadline. $35 fee, may be waived for applicants with need. Admission notification on a rolling basis. **Financial aid:** Priority date 4/15; no closing date. FAFSA, institutional form required. Applicants notified on a rolling basis starting 3/15; must reply within 2 week(s) of notification.

Academics. Special study options: Distance learning, double major, dual enrollment of high school students, independent study, internships, teacher certification program. **Credit/placement by examination:** AP, CLEP, IB, institutional tests. 16 credit hours maximum toward bachelor's degree. **Support services:** Reduced course load, remedial instruction, tutoring.

Majors. Biology: General. **Business:** Business admin. **Education:** Early childhood, elementary, music, physical, secondary. **English:** English lit. **History:** General. **Parks/recreation:** Exercise sciences. **Psychology:** General. **Theology:** Bible, missionary, pastoral counseling, religious ed, theology. **Visual/performing arts:** Music.

Most popular majors. Business/marketing 10%, education 24%, psychology 8%, theological studies 37%.

Technology on campus. 34 workstations in library, computer center, student center. Commuter students can connect to campus network. Online library, repair service, wireless network available.

Student life. Freshman orientation: Mandatory. Preregistration for classes offered. Held the week-end prior to the beginning of classes each semester. **Policies:** Single students under the age of 25 required to live on campus unless living with parents or close relatives. Religious observance required. **Housing:** Guaranteed on-campus for all undergraduates. Single-sex dorms available. $100 fully refundable deposit, deadline 8/1. **Activities:** Campus ministries, choral groups, drama, music ensembles, musical theater, student government, ministerial and missionary organizations, Christian service assignments, organization for business students, literary societies.

Athletics. NCCAA. **Intercollegiate:** Basketball, cross-country, golf, volleyball W. **Intramural:** Basketball, table tennis, tennis, ultimate frisbee, volleyball. **Team name:** Flames.

Student services. Chaplain/spiritual director, career counseling, student employment services, financial aid counseling, personal counseling, placement for graduates, veterans' counselor.

Contact. E-mail: recruit@welch.edu
Phone: (615) 844-5000 Toll-free number: (888) 979-3524
Fax: (615) 269-6028
Debbie Mouser, Director of Enrollment Services, Welch College, 3606 West End Avenue, Nashville, TN 37205-2403

Williamson College
Franklin, Tennessee
www.williamsoncc.edu

CB code: 7388

- Private 4-year liberal arts college affiliated with the interdenominational tradition
- Commuter campus in small city
- 69 degree-seeking undergraduates
- Application essay required

General. Accredited by ABHE. Accelerated degree completion programs available for working adults. **Degrees:** 15 bachelor's awarded. **Location:** 15 miles from downtown. **Calendar:** Semester, limited summer session. **Full-time faculty:** 5 total; 100% have terminal degrees, 40% women. **Part-time faculty:** 20 total. **Class size:** 100% < 20.

Freshman class profile.

GPA 3.75 or higher:	62%	**GPA 2.0-2.99:**	13%
GPA 3.0-3.49:	25%		

Basis for selection. Open admission, but selective for some programs. Test scores, essay, GPA required for some programs. **Home schooled:** Transcript of courses and grades required.

2015-2016 Annual costs. Tuition/fees: $11,550. Books/supplies: $1,000. Personal expenses: $1,400.

Financial aid. Non-need-based: Scholarships awarded for academics, state residency.

Application procedures. Admission: No deadline. $25 fee. Admission notification on a rolling basis. **Financial aid:** Priority date 5/1; no closing date. FAFSA required. Applicants notified on a rolling basis starting 5/1; must reply within 2 week(s) of notification.

Academics. Special study options: Accelerated study, distance learning, dual enrollment of high school students, independent study, internships, liberal arts/career combination. **Credit/placement by examination:** AP, CLEP. 15 credit hours maximum toward associate degree, 32 toward bachelor's. **Support services:** Study skills assistance, tutoring, writing center.

Majors. Business: Nonprofit/public. **Philosophy/religion:** Religion.

Most popular majors. Business/marketing 21%, theological studies 77%.

Technology on campus. PC or laptop required. 3 workstations in library, computer center. Online library, wireless network available.

Student life. Freshman orientation: Mandatory, $350 fee. Preregistration for classes offered. **Activities:** Campus ministries, music ensembles, student government.

Student services. Adult student services, chaplain/spiritual director, financial aid counseling, personal counseling.

Contact. E-mail: info@williamsoncc.edu
Phone: (615) 771-7821 Fax: (615) 771-7810
Susan Mays, Director of Admissions, Williamson College, 274 Mallory Station Road, Franklin, TN 37067

Texas

Abilene Christian University

Abilene, Texas — **CB member**
www.acu.edu — **CB code: 6001**

- Private 4-year university affiliated with the Church of Christ
- Residential campus in small city
- 3,695 degree-seeking undergraduates: 3% part-time, 59% women, 9% African American, 1% Asian American, 16% Hispanic/Latino, 5% Multiracial, non-Hispanic, 4% international
- 767 degree-seeking graduate students
- 50% of applicants admitted
- SAT or ACT (ACT writing recommended), application essay required
- 61% graduate within 6 years; 28% enter graduate study

General. Founded in 1906. Regionally accredited. **Degrees:** 732 bachelor's, 3 associate awarded; master's, doctoral offered. **Location:** 150 miles from Dallas, Fort Worth. **Calendar:** Semester, limited summer session. **Full-time faculty:** 253 total; 77% have terminal degrees, 9% minority, 36% women. **Part-time faculty:** 151 total; 32% have terminal degrees, 3% minority, 50% women. **Class size:** 45% < 20, 40% 20-39, 7% 40-49, 8% 50-99, less than 1% >100. **Special facilities:** Maker lab, AT&T Learning Studio, converged media newsroom, writing center, speaking center, learning commons, center for christian service and leadership, center for speech & language disorders, demonstration farm and ranch, observatory, center for restoration studies.

Freshman class profile. 10,804 applied, 5,393 admitted, 1,072 enrolled.

Mid 50% test scores			
SAT critical reading:	470-590	Rank in top quarter:	58%
SAT math:	480-590	Rank in top tenth:	22%
SAT writing:	450-570	End year in good standing:	95%
ACT composite:	22-27	Return as sophomores:	79%
GPA 3.75 or higher:	38%	Out-of-state:	11%
GPA 3.50-3.74:	27%	Live on campus:	96%
GPA 3.0-3.49:	28%	International:	3%
		GPA 2.0-2.99:	7%

Basis for selection. High school records (including courses taken, grade trends and rank in class), score on SAT or ACT, essay responses, extracurricular activities and honors. Admission or denial of admission not based on any single factor. In lieu of writing essay, ACT or SAT writing score may be submitted. Audition required for music and theater programs. **Home schooled:** Transcript of courses and grades required.

High school preparation. College-preparatory program required. 14 units recommended. Recommended units include English 4, mathematics 3, history 1, science 3 (laboratory 2) and foreign language 2. 1 social science.

2015-2016 Annual costs. Tuition/fees: $30,830. Room/board: $9,310. Books/supplies: $1,250. Personal expenses: $1,900.

2014-2015 Financial aid. **Need-based:** 847 full-time freshmen applied for aid; 700 deemed to have need; 700 received aid. Average need met was 73%. Average scholarship/grant was $20,695; average loan $3,577. 84% of total undergraduate aid awarded as scholarships/grants, 16% as loans/jobs. **Non-need-based:** Awarded to 3,552 full-time undergraduates, including 1,055 freshmen. Scholarships awarded for academics, art, athletics, leadership, minority status, music/drama, religious affiliation, state residency. **Additional information:** Early estimate service available.

Application procedures. **Admission:** Closing date 2/15 (postmark date). $50 fee, may be waived for applicants with need. Admission notification on a rolling basis beginning on or about 2/15. Must reply by 5/1. Admitted students planning to enroll should confirm the offer by submitting a $250 enrollment deposit (non-refundable after May 1), along with letter of intent to the Admissions Office. Enrollment deposit is a pre-payment toward total bill. **Financial aid:** Priority date 3/1; no closing date. FAFSA required. Applicants notified on a rolling basis starting 4/1.

Academics. **Special study options:** Combined bachelor's/graduate degree, cross-registration, distance learning, double major, dual enrollment of high school students, ESL, honors, independent study, internships, student-designed major, study abroad, teacher certification program. **Credit/placement by examination:** AP, CLEP, IB, SAT, ACT, institutional tests. 15 credit hours maximum toward associate degree, 30 toward bachelor's. **Support services:** Pre-admission summer program, reduced course load, remedial instruction, study skills assistance, tutoring, writing center.

Honors college/program. Must have high school GPA of 3.75 or rank in top 10 percent of high school class; SAT of 1210 (exclusive of Writing) or ACT of 27; submit satisfactory resume (achievements, awards, offices, etc.) and honors college application essay. 150 freshmen admitted. Students take 18 hours of Honors courses in their first 2 years, all general education requirements; 2 special topic 1-hour colloquia, and 3-5 Upper division units, optional Honors Project Thesis for Honors Scholar.

Majors. **Biology:** General, biochemistry. **Business:** Accounting, business admin, finance, information resources management, marketing. **Communications:** Communications/speech/rhetoric, digital media, journalism. **Computer sciences:** Computer science, information technology. **Conservation:** Environmental science. **Education:** Art, biology, computer, elementary, elementary special ed, English, history, mathematics, music, physics, science, secondary, secondary special ed, social studies, Spanish. **Engineering:** General. **English:** English lit. **Foreign languages:** Spanish. **Health services:** Dietetics, nursing (RN), predental, premedicine, preoptometry, prepharmacy, preveterinary, speech pathology. **History:** General. **Human services:** Social work. **Math:** General. **Parks/recreation:** Sports admin. **Physical sciences:** Chemistry, physics. **Protective services:** Law enforcement admin. **Psychology:** General. **Social sciences:** Political science, sociology. **Theology:** Bible. **Visual/performing arts:** Dramatic, game design, graphic design, interior design, music, piano/keyboard, studio arts, voice/opera. **Work/family studies:** Family studies.

Most popular majors. Biology 6%, business/marketing 19%, communications/journalism 7%, education 9%, health sciences 14%, interdisciplinary studies 6%, psychology 6%, visual/performing arts 7%.

Technology on campus. 466 workstations in dormitories, library, computer center, student center. Dormitories wired for high-speed internet access and linked to campus network. Commuter students can connect to campus network. Online course registration, online library, helpline, repair service, student web hosting, wireless network available.

Student life. **Freshman orientation:** Mandatory, $200 fee. Preregistration for classes offered. Held multiple times in June and August. Overnight, two-day event open to parents. **Policies:** Religious observance required. **Housing:** Guaranteed on-campus for freshmen. Single-sex dorms, special housing for disabled, apartments available. **Activities:** Bands, campus ministries, choral groups, dance, drama, international student organizations, literary magazine, music ensembles, Model UN, musical theater, opera, radio station, student government, student newspaper, symphony orchestra, TV station, Seekers of the Word, Hispanos Unidos, College Democrats, ACU College Republicans, Lighthouse (Catholic student organization), Fellowship of Christian Athletes, Jeremiah's Project, Treadaway Kids, Wishing Well, Black Students Association.

Athletics. NCAA. **Intercollegiate:** Baseball M, basketball, cross-country, football (tackle) M, golf M, soccer W, softball W, tennis, track and field, volleyball W. **Intramural:** Basketball, bowling, football (non-tackle), golf, racquetball, soccer, softball, tennis, volleyball, water polo. **Team name:** Wildcats.

Student services. Alcohol/substance abuse counseling, chaplain/spiritual director, career counseling, student employment services, financial aid counseling, health services, minority student services, personal counseling, placement for graduates, veterans' counselor. **Physically disabled:** Services for visually, speech, hearing impaired.

Contact. E-mail: info@admissions.acu.edu
Phone: (325) 674-2650 Toll-free number: (800) 460-6228
Fax: (325) 674-2130
Tamara Long, Director of Admissions, Abilene Christian University, ACU Box 29000, Abilene, TX 79699

Amberton University

Garland, Texas
www.amberton.edu — **CB code: 6140**

- Private 4-year university affiliated with the nondenominational tradition
- Commuter campus in small city
- 231 degree-seeking undergraduates: 42% part-time, 59% women, 26% African American, 11% Asian American, 11% Hispanic/Latino, 1% Native American
- 1,148 degree-seeking graduate students

General. Founded in 1971. Regionally accredited. Upper level and graduate institution designed for adult students. Must have previous college and be over 21 years old to attend. **Degrees:** 78 bachelor's awarded; master's offered.

Location: 12 miles from downtown Dallas. **Calendar:** Four 10-week sessions. Extensive summer session. **Full-time faculty:** 15 total. **Part-time faculty:** 50 total.

Basis for selection. Applicants must be at least 21 years of age, have completed college work in a U.S. institution, and be a U.S. citizen.

2016-2017 Annual costs. Tuition/fees (projected): $7,500. Books/supplies: $500.

Financial aid. Additional information: Amberton University is eligible to participate in federal aid programs but chooses not to. There is no federal aid available at Amberton.

Application procedures. Admission: No deadline. No application fee. Application must be submitted on paper. Admission notification on a rolling basis. **Financial aid:** No deadline.

Academics. Special study options: Distance learning, independent study, weekend college. **Credit/placement by examination:** AP, CLEP. 30 credit hours maximum toward bachelor's degree.

Majors. Business: General, accounting, business admin. **Liberal arts:** Arts/sciences.

Most popular majors. Business/marketing 90%, liberal arts 10%.

Technology on campus. 25 workstations in library, computer center. Online library available.

Student services. Adult student services, career counseling, personal counseling, placement for graduates, veterans' counselor.

Contact. E-mail: advisor@amberton.edu
Phone: (972) 279-6511 ext. 180 Fax: (972) 279-9773
Jonathan Schultz, Academic Dean, Amberton University, 1700 Eastgate Drive, Garland, TX 75041-5595

Angelo State University
San Angelo, Texas   **CB member**
www.angelo.edu   **CB code: 6644**

▸ Public 4-year university
▸ Residential campus in small city
▸ 5,403 degree-seeking undergraduates: 12% part-time, 55% women, 8% African American, 1% Asian American, 32% Hispanic/Latino, 3% Multiracial, non-Hispanic, 4% international
▸ 1,084 degree-seeking graduate students
▸ 77% of applicants admitted
▸ SAT or ACT (ACT writing optional) required
▸ 37% graduate within 6 years

General. Founded in 1928. Regionally accredited. ASU is a Hispanic-serving institution. **Degrees:** 1,026 bachelor's awarded; master's, professional offered. **ROTC:** Air Force. **Location:** 200 miles from Austin, 210 miles from San Antonio, 220 miles from Fort Worth, 250 miles from Dallas. **Calendar:** Semester, extensive summer session. **Full-time faculty:** 263 total; 81% have terminal degrees, 18% minority, 44% women. **Part-time faculty:** 62 total; 40% have terminal degrees, 21% minority, 52% women. **Class size:** 23% < 20, 62% 20-39, 6% 40-49, 9% 50-99, 1% >100. **Special facilities:** Agricultural research center, food safety and product development lab, 6,000-acre farm/ranch, natural history collections, global immersion center/planetarium, West Texas Collection regional historical archive.

Freshman class profile. 3,822 applied, 2,934 admitted, 1,351 enrolled.

Mid 50% test scores			
SAT critical reading:	420-520	Return as sophomores:	63%
SAT math:	430-530	Out-of-state:	1%
SAT writing:	400-490	Live on campus:	68%
ACT composite:	18-23	International:	3%
Rank in top quarter:	31%	Fraternities:	5%
Rank in top tenth:	14%	Sororities:	3%

Basis for selection. Should rank in the top half of high school class, have minimum 16 ACT or 760 SAT (exclusive of Writing). If ranked in third quartile, must have 23 ACT or 1030 SAT. If ranked in fourth quartile, must have 30 ACT or 1270 SAT. **Home schooled:** Transcript of courses and grades, state high school equivalency certificate required.

High school preparation. College-preparatory program recommended. 26 units recommended. Recommended units include English 4, mathematics 4, social studies 3.5, science 4, foreign language 2, visual/performing arts 1, academic electives 5.5. Economics 0.5, speech 0.5, physical education 1; or be on track to complete the recommended units or an advanced curriculum.

2015-2016 Annual costs. Tuition/fees: $7,864; $19,564 out-of-state. Room/board: $7,702. Books/supplies: $1,200. Personal expenses: $1,580. **Additional information:** Angelo State University also offers a guaranteed tuition program that locks in tuition price for four years.

2014-2015 Financial aid. Need-based: 1,125 full-time freshmen applied for aid; 855 deemed to have need; 854 received aid. Average need met was 83%. Average scholarship/grant was $3,598; average loan $3,203. 11% of total undergraduate aid awarded as scholarships/grants, 89% as loans/jobs. **Non-need-based:** Awarded to 2,144 full-time undergraduates, including 902 freshmen. Scholarships awarded for academics, art, athletics, leadership, music/drama, ROTC, state residency.

Application procedures. Admission: Closing date 8/23 (receipt date). $35 fee, may be waived for applicants with need. Admission notification on a rolling basis beginning on or about 9/1. **Financial aid:** Priority date 4/1; no closing date. FAFSA required. Applicants notified on a rolling basis starting 4/1; must reply within 4 week(s) of notification.

Academics. Special study options: Combined bachelor's/graduate degree, distance learning, double major, dual enrollment of high school students, ESL, honors, independent study, internships, study abroad, teacher certification program. 4+1 programs in various fields with Texas Tech University. **Credit/placement by examination:** AP, CLEP, SAT, ACT. Unlimited credits by examination provided student meets hours required in residence. **Support services:** Learning center, reduced course load, remedial instruction, study skills assistance, tutoring, writing center.

Honors college/program. Students must have 3.25 GPA in coursework done at ASU. If enrolling from high school, must be in the top 10% of graduating class and have 27 ACT or 1200 (exclusive of Writing) SAT. Some classes are strictly honors only, but normal classes can be given honors credit by contract: student meets with professor before semester and discusses additional work necessary to qualify for honors credit.

Majors. Biology: General, biochemistry, ecology, evolutionary. **Business:** Accounting, business admin, finance, international, management information systems, marketing, real estate. **Communications:** Communications/speech/rhetoric, journalism. **Computer sciences:** General. **Conservation:** Management/policy. **Engineering:** Applied physics. **English:** English lit. **Foreign languages:** French, German, Spanish. **Health services:** Athletic training, clinical lab science, nursing (RN). **History:** General. **Math:** General. **Parks/recreation:** Health/fitness. **Physical sciences:** Chemistry, physics. **Protective services:** Criminal justice. **Psychology:** General. **Social sciences:** Political science, sociology. **Visual/performing arts:** Art, dramatic, music, studio arts. **Work/family studies:** Child development.

Most popular majors. Agriculture 8%, business/marketing 12%, communications/journalism 6%, health sciences 13%, interdisciplinary studies 10%, parks/recreation 8%, psychology 8%.

Technology on campus. 600 workstations in dormitories, library, computer center, student center. Dormitories wired for high-speed internet access and linked to campus network. Commuter students can connect to campus network. Online course registration, online library, helpline, repair service, student web hosting, wireless network available.

Student life. Freshman orientation: Available, $25 fee. Preregistration for classes offered. Sessions offered several times during the summer. **Policies:** Single undergraduates with 12-60 semester credit hours of college-level work who do not live with parents are required to reside in University-owned housing. **Housing:** Coed dorms, special housing for disabled, apartments, themed housing available. $200 nonrefundable deposit, deadline 7/15. **Activities:** Bands, campus ministries, choral groups, dance, drama, international student organizations, literary magazine, music ensembles, musical theater, radio station, student government, student newspaper, symphony orchestra, TV station, African student association, Association of Mexican-American Students, Baptist student ministry, Block and Bridle, Korean student organization, Newman center, nontraditional student organization, student veterans organization, Young Americans for Liberty.

Athletics. NCAA. **Intercollegiate:** Baseball M, basketball, cross-country, football (tackle) M, golf W, soccer W, softball W, track and field, volleyball W. **Intramural:** Badminton, basketball, football (non-tackle), golf, racquetball, soccer, softball, table tennis, tennis, ultimate frisbee, volleyball. **Team name:** Rams and Rambelles.

Student services. Adult student services, alcohol/substance abuse counseling, chaplain/spiritual director, career counseling, services for economically disadvantaged, student employment services, financial aid counseling, health services, minority student services, personal counseling, placement for graduates, veterans' counselor. **Physically disabled:** Services for visually, hearing impaired.

Contact. E-mail: admissions@angelo.edu
Phone: (325) 942-2041 Toll-free number: (800) 946-8627
Fax: (325) 942-2078
Sharla Adam, Director of Admissions, Angelo State University, ASU
Station #11014, San Angelo, TX 76909-1014

Argosy University: Dallas
Farmers Branch, Texas
www.argosy.edu/dallas

- For-profit 4-year university
- Very large city
- 271 degree-seeking undergraduates: 88% part-time, 72% women
- 225 graduate students

General. Regionally accredited. **Degrees:** 14 bachelor's, 2 associate
awarded; master's, professional, doctoral offered. **Calendar:** Differs by program. **Full-time faculty:** 10 total. **Part-time faculty:** 48 total.

Basis for selection. Open admission.

2015-2016 Annual costs. Tuition/fees: $16,842. **Additional informa-
tion:** Tuition indicated is for programs in the College of Arts and Sciences.
College of Health Sciences programs are $450 per credit-hour.

Application procedures. Admission: Closing date 9/13. $50 fee. **Finan-
cial aid:** No deadline.

Academics. Credit/placement by examination: AP, CLEP.

Majors. Business: Business admin. **Liberal arts:** Arts/sciences. **Protective
services:** Law enforcement admin. **Psychology:** General.

Contact. E-mail: audadmis@argosy.edu
Phone: (214) 459-2237
Casey McMullen, Senior Director of Admissions, Argosy University:
Dallas, 5001 Lyndon B. Johnson Freeway, Heritage Square, Farmers
Branch, TX 75244

Arlington Baptist College
Arlington, Texas
www.arlingtonbaptistcollege.edu | **CB code: 6039**

- Private 4-year Bible and teachers college affiliated with the Baptist faith
- Commuter campus in very large city
- 212 degree-seeking undergraduates: 15% part-time, 37% women
- 19 degree-seeking graduate students
- Application essay required
- 48% graduate within 6 years; 15% enter graduate study

General. Founded in 1939. Accredited by ABHE. Institution is a historical
site and historical tours are available upon request. **Degrees:** 30 bachelor's
awarded; master's offered. **Location:** 10 miles from Fort Worth, 25 miles
from Dallas. **Calendar:** Semester, limited summer session. **Full-time faculty:**
10 total; 40% have terminal degrees, 30% women. **Part-time faculty:** 23
total; 17% have terminal degrees, 9% minority, 26% women. **Class size:**
81% < 20, 15% 20-39, 1% 40-49, 2% 50-99.

Freshman class profile. 96 applied, 91 admitted, 34 enrolled.

GPA 3.75 or higher:	13%	Rank in top tenth:	2%
GPA 3.50-3.74:	9%	End year in good standing:	60%
GPA 3.0-3.49:	35%	Return as sophomores:	45%
GPA 2.0-2.99:	37%	Out-of-state:	3%
Rank in top quarter:	14%	Live on campus:	60%

Basis for selection. Open admission. Interview recommended for all;
audition required for music. **Home schooled:** Transcript of courses and
grades, interview required. Advised to obtain GED. **Learning Disabled:**
Students should submit information on disability for the purpose of accommodations.

High school preparation. 16 units recommended. Recommended units
include English 3, mathematics 2, social studies 3, history 3 and science 1.

2015-2016 Annual costs. Tuition/fees: $11,010. Room/board: $5,800.
Books/supplies: $800. Personal expenses: $720.

2014-2015 Financial aid. All financial aid based on need. 40 full-time
freshmen applied for aid; 38 deemed to have need; 38 received aid. Average

scholarship/grant was $22,378. 28% of total undergraduate aid awarded as
scholarships/grants, 72% as loans/jobs.

Application procedures. Admission: Priority date 8/1; no deadline. $25
fee, may be waived for applicants with need. Admission notification on a
rolling basis. **Financial aid:** Closing date 8/15. FAFSA, institutional form
required. Applicants notified on a rolling basis starting 12/1; must reply
by 8/15.

Academics. Special study options: Distance learning, double major, dual
enrollment of high school students, external degree, teacher certification
program. **Credit/placement by examination:** AP, CLEP, institutional tests.
30 credit hours maximum toward bachelor's degree. **Support services:**
Reduced course load, remedial instruction, tutoring.

Majors. Business: Business admin. **Education:** General, elementary,
English, kindergarten/preschool, middle, multi-level teacher, music, science,
secondary, social studies. **Philosophy/religion:** Religion. **Psychology:** Counseling. **Theology:** Bible, missionary, pastoral counseling, religious ed, sacred
music, youth ministry. **Visual/performing arts:** Music.

Most popular majors. Education 25%, theological studies 50%.

Technology on campus. 25 workstations in library, computer center.
Online course registration, wireless network available.

Student life. Freshman orientation: Mandatory. Preregistration for
classes offered. Orientation includes placement testing. **Policies:** Religious
observance required. **Housing:** Guaranteed on-campus for freshmen. Single-
sex dorms, wellness housing available. $25 nonrefundable deposit. **Activities:**
Campus ministries, music ensembles, ministry teams.

Athletics. NCCAA. **Intercollegiate:** Baseball M, basketball, cross-country,
volleyball W. **Team name:** Patriots.

Student services. Chaplain/spiritual director, career counseling, student
employment services, financial aid counseling, personal counseling, placement for graduates, veterans' counselor.

Contact. E-mail: kmarvin@arlingtonbaptistcollege.edu
Phone: (817) 461-8741 Fax: (817) 274-1138
Kim Marvin, Director of Admissions, Arlington Baptist College, 3001
West Division Street, Arlington, TX 76012

Art Institute of Dallas
Dallas, Texas
www.aid.edu | **CB code: 2680**

- For-profit 4-year visual arts college
- Very large city
- 1,155 undergraduates

General. Regionally accredited. **Degrees:** 152 bachelor's, 98 associate
awarded; master's offered. **Calendar:** Quarter. **Full-time faculty:** 43 total.
Part-time faculty: 71 total.

Basis for selection. Open admission, but selective for some programs.
Some animation, art and design associate degree programs may require portfolio evaluation.

2015-2016 Annual costs. Personal expenses: $2,880.

Application procedures. Admission: No deadline. $50 fee. Admission
notification on a rolling basis. **Financial aid:** No deadline. FAFSA required.
Applicants notified on a rolling basis.

Academics. Credit/placement by examination: AP, CLEP.

Majors. Visual/performing arts: Cinematography, commercial photography, graphic design, interior design, studio arts.

Student life. Freshman orientation: Available. Preregistration for
classes offered.

Contact. E-mail: cwilliams@aii.edu
Phone: (214) 692-8080 Toll-free number: (800) 275-4243
Dawn Polk-Bridges, Director of Admissions, Art Institute of Dallas, Two
North Park, 8080 Park Lane, Dallas, TX 75231

Art Institute of Houston
Houston, Texas
www.artinstitutes.edu/houston   CB code: 8271

- For-profit 4-year culinary school and visual arts college
- Commuter campus in very large city
- 1,600 undergraduates
- Application essay required

General. Regionally accredited. **Degrees:** 250 bachelor's, 150 associate awarded. **Calendar:** Quarter, extensive summer session. **Full-time faculty:** 52 total. **Part-time faculty:** 110 total. **Special facilities:** Photography studio, audio studio, video lab, 5 multi-purpose culinary lab kitchens.

Basis for selection. Proof of graduation from accredited high school, GED, or foreign equivalent required for admissions. SAT or ACT recommended. Observes TASP guidelines. ASSET or COMPASS testing may be required. Remediation may be required if test scores fall below required ranges; some remediation available on campus. **Home schooled:** Transcript of courses and grades required.

2015-2016 Annual costs. Tuition/fees: $23,574. Room only: $6,228. Books/supplies: $150.

Application procedures. Admission: No deadline. , may be waived for applicants with need. No application fee. Application must be submitted online. Admission notification on a rolling basis. **Financial aid:** Priority date 3/1; no closing date. FAFSA, institutional form required.

Academics. Special study options: Distance learning, honors, internships. **Credit/placement by examination:** AP, CLEP, SAT, ACT, institutional tests. **Support services:** Learning center, remedial instruction, study skills assistance, tutoring, writing center.

Majors. Visual/performing arts: Graphic design, interior design.

Technology on campus. 300 workstations in library, computer center. Online library, helpline, wireless network available.

Student life. Freshman orientation: Mandatory. Preregistration for classes offered. **Housing:** Apartments available. $250 fully refundable deposit. **Activities:** International student organizations.

Student services. Career counseling, student employment services, financial aid counseling. **Physically disabled:** Services for hearing impaired.

Contact. E-mail: aihadm@aii.edu
Phone: (713) 623-2040 Toll-free number: (800) 275-4244
Fax: (713) 966-2797
Jane Chastant, Senior Director of Admissions, Art Institute of Houston, 4140 Southwest Freeway, Houston, TX 77027

Austin College
Sherman, Texas   CB member
www.austincollege.edu   CB code: 6016

- Private 4-year liberal arts and teachers college affiliated with the Presbyterian Church (USA)
- Residential campus in small city
- 1,250 degree-seeking undergraduates: 1% part-time, 52% women, 7% African American, 13% Asian American, 19% Hispanic/Latino, 1% Native American, 1% Multi-racial, non-Hispanic, 3% international
- 17 degree-seeking graduate students
- 54% of applicants admitted
- SAT or ACT (ACT writing recommended), application essay required
- 73% graduate within 6 years; 35% enter graduate study

General. Founded in 1849. Regionally accredited. **Degrees:** 272 bachelor's awarded; master's offered. **Location:** 60 miles from Dallas. **Calendar:** 4-1-4, limited summer session. **Full-time faculty:** 91 total; 98% have terminal degrees, 11% minority, 29% women. **Part-time faculty:** 29 total; 38% have terminal degrees, 17% minority, 62% women. **Class size:** 67% < 20, 30% 20-39, 2% 40-49, less than 1% 50-99. **Special facilities:** Environmental research center and prairie restoration project (174 acres), tissue culture facility for study of cellular molecular interactions of eukaryotic cells, high performance numeric and graphics computing facility for advanced scientific computing and 3-D graphics, observatory with 24-inch telescope.

Freshman class profile. 3,357 applied, 1,816 admitted, 355 enrolled.

Mid 50% test scores			
SAT critical reading:	540-650	Rank in top quarter:	71%
SAT math:	540-640	Rank in top tenth:	36%
SAT writing:	500-630	Return as sophomores:	83%
ACT composite:	22-28	Out-of-state:	7%
GPA 3.75 or higher:	34%	Live on campus:	95%
GPA 3.50-3.74:	28%	International:	3%
GPA 3.0-3.49:	30%	Fraternities:	32%
GPA 2.0-2.99:	8%	Sororities:	36%

Basis for selection. Academic transcript record, test scores, recommendations, extracurricular involvement, essay important. Interview considered. Interview recommended for all; audition recommended for music, theater (required for scholarship consideration); portfolio recommended for art (required for scholarship consideration). **Home schooled:** Transcript of courses and grades required.

High school preparation. College-preparatory program recommended. Required and recommended units include English 4, mathematics 3-4, social studies 2-4, science 3-4 (laboratory 1-2), foreign language 2-4 and visual/performing arts 1.

2015-2016 Annual costs. Tuition/fees: $36,230. Room/board: $11,793. Books/supplies: $1,250. Personal expenses: $850.

2015-2016 Financial aid. Need-based: 306 full-time freshmen applied for aid; 257 deemed to have need; 257 received aid. Average need met was 95%. Average scholarship/grant was $28,997; average loan $5,531. 83% of total undergraduate aid awarded as scholarships/grants, 17% as loans/jobs. **Non-need-based:** Awarded to 330 full-time undergraduates, including 227 freshmen. Scholarships awarded for academics; alumni affiliation, art, leadership, music/drama, religious affiliation.

Application procedures. Admission: Priority date 12/1; deadline 3/1 (postmark date). No application fee. Admission notification by 4/1. Must reply by 5/1. **Financial aid:** Priority date 4/1; no closing date. FAFSA required. Applicants notified on a rolling basis starting 2/15; must reply by 5/1.

Academics. Special study options: Combined bachelor's/graduate degree, double major, exchange student, honors, independent study, internships, student-designed major, study abroad, teacher certification program, Washington semester. Phi Beta Kappa. **Credit/placement by examination:** AP, CLEP, IB, institutional tests. **Support services:** Learning center, study skills assistance, tutoring.

Majors. Area/ethnic studies: American, Asian, Latin American. **Biology:** General, biochemistry. **Business:** General, business admin, finance, nonprofit/public. **Communications:** General, communications/speech/rhetoric, media studies. **Computer sciences:** Computer science. **Conservation:** Environmental studies. **Education:** Elementary. **English:** Creative writing, English lit. **Foreign languages:** Classics, East Asian, French, German, Latin, Spanish. **History:** General. **Math:** General. **Philosophy/religion:** Philosophy, religion. **Physical sciences:** Chemistry, physics. **Psychology:** General. **Social sciences:** Anthropology, economics, international relations, political science, sociology. **Visual/performing arts:** Art, dramatic, music, theater arts management.

Most popular majors. Biology 12%, business/marketing 16%, foreign language 8%, history 7%, psychology 9%, social sciences 17%.

Technology on campus. 286 workstations in dormitories, library, computer center, student center. Dormitories wired for high-speed internet access and linked to campus network. Commuter students can connect to campus network. Online course registration, online library, helpline, student web hosting, wireless network available.

Student life. Freshman orientation: Mandatory. Preregistration for classes offered. Held in May and June, new student orientation in August prior to start of classes. **Housing:** Guaranteed on-campus for freshmen. Coed dorms, single-sex dorms, special housing for disabled, apartments, themed housing available. Language emphasis residence, suite-style housing available for upper-level students with private bedroom, common area, and kitchenette. **Activities:** Bands, campus ministries, choral groups, dance, drama, international student organizations, literary magazine, music ensembles, Model UN, musical theater, student government, student newspaper, symphony orchestra, Alpha Phi Omega, Intervarsity Christian Fellowship, Black Expressions, Young Democrats, Service Station, Los Amigos, Habitat for Humanity, Activators, Amnesty International, Indian Cultural Association.

Athletics. NCAA. **Intercollegiate:** Baseball M, basketball, cross-country, diving, football (tackle) M, soccer, softball W, swimming, tennis, volleyball W. **Intramural:** Basketball, football (non-tackle), soccer, softball, volleyball. **Team name:** Kangaroos.

Student services. Chaplain/spiritual director, career counseling, financial aid counseling, health services, personal counseling. **Physically disabled:** Services for visually, speech, hearing impaired.

Contact. E-mail: admission@austincollege.edu
Phone: (903) 813-3000 Toll-free number: (800) 526-4276
Fax: (903) 813-3198
Nan Davis, Vice President for Institutional Enrollment, Austin College, 900 North Grand Avenue, Suite 6N, Sherman, TX 75090-4400

Austin Graduate School of Theology
Austin, Texas
www.austingrad.edu   CB code: 4969

- Private two-year upper-division Bible and seminary college affiliated with the Church of Christ
- Commuter campus in very large city
- Application essay required

General. Founded in 1917. Regionally accredited. Highly diverse ethnic and socioeconomic student body grounded in Christian faith traditions. **Degrees:** 6 bachelor's awarded; master's offered. **Location:** 80 miles from San Antonio, 150 miles from Houston. **Calendar:** Semester, limited summer session. **Full-time faculty:** 4 total; 100% have terminal degrees. **Part-time faculty:** 7 total; 57% have terminal degrees, 14% minority. **Class size:** 90% < 20, 10% 20-39.

Student profile. 20 degree-seeking undergraduates.

Basis for selection. Open admission. College transcript, application essay required. Transcript, GPA, recommendations required. High school transcript, test scores required for applicants with fewer than 35 hours. Transfer accepted as sophomores, juniors, seniors.

2015-2016 Annual costs. Tuition/fees: $10,850. Books/supplies: $600. Personal expenses: $1,998.

Financial aid. Non-need-based: Scholarships awarded for academics, leadership. **Additional information:** Generous scholarships for students taking at least 12 hours. Federal work study program available. Institutional work study program (need-based) available.

Application procedures. Admission: Priority date 6/1. No application fee. Application must be submitted on paper. **Financial aid:** No deadline. FAFSA, institutional form required.

Academics. Special study options: Dual enrollment of high school students, liberal arts/career combination. Liberal arts/career combination program in religion; combined bachelor's/graduate program in ministry. **Credit/placement by examination:** AP, CLEP. 18 credit hours maximum toward bachelor's degree.

Majors. Theology: Bible, theology.

Technology on campus. 4 workstations in library, computer center, student center. Online library, wireless network available.

Student life. Policies: Religious observance required. **Activities:** Student government.

Student services. Financial aid counseling, personal counseling.

Contact. E-mail: admissions@austingrad.edu
Phone: (512) 476-2772 ext. 103 Toll-free number: (866) 287-4723
Fax: (512) 476-3919
Lauren Porter, Registrar, Austin Graduate School of Theology, 7640 Guadalupe Street, Austin, TX 78752-1333

Baptist Missionary Association Theological Seminary
Jacksonville, Texas
www.bmats.edu   CB code: 7042

- Private 4-year Bible and seminary college affiliated with the Baptist faith
- Commuter campus in large town
- 63 degree-seeking undergraduates

General. Founded in 1955. Regionally accredited. **Degrees:** 5 bachelor's awarded; master's offered. **Location:** 120 miles from Dallas. **Calendar:** Semester, limited summer session. **Full-time faculty:** 5 total. **Part-time faculty:** 7 total.

Basis for selection. Open admission, but selective for some programs. Essay or personal statement very important. Religious commitment, interview, recommendations, school and community activities important.

2015-2016 Annual costs. Tuition/fees: $5,550. **Additional information:** $100 distance learning fee added per course.

2014-2015 Financial aid. Need-based: 790 full-time freshmen applied for aid; 577 deemed to have need; 550 received aid. Average need met was 58%. Average scholarship/grant was $6,233; average loan $5,766. 41% of total undergraduate aid awarded as scholarships/grants, 59% as loans/jobs. **Non-need-based:** Awarded to 831 full-time undergraduates, including 232 freshmen. Scholarships awarded for academics, state residency.

Application procedures. Admission: Closing date 7/1. $35 fee. **Financial aid:** Priority date 3/1; no closing date. FAFSA required. Applicants notified on a rolling basis starting 3/1; must reply by 3/1.

Academics. Special study options: Internships. **Credit/placement by examination:** AP, CLEP.

Majors. Philosophy/religion: Religion. **Theology:** Theology.

Technology on campus. 2 workstations in library.

Student life. Activities: Student government.

Student services. Career counseling, personal counseling.

Contact. E-mail: bmatsem@bmats.edu
Phone: (903) 586-2501 Fax: (903) 586-0378
Philip Attebery, Dean/Registrar, Baptist Missionary Association Theological Seminary, 1530 East Pine Street, Jacksonville, TX 75766

Baptist University of the Americas
San Antonio, Texas
www.bua.edu   CB code: 7685

- Private 4-year university and Bible college affiliated with the Baptist faith
- Commuter campus in very large city
- 194 degree-seeking undergraduates

General. Accredited by ABHE. Baptist University of the Americas trains cross-culturally students in Biblical/Theological Studies and Ministry Studies, at a higher education academic level, from a Hispanic context. **Degrees:** 29 bachelor's, 3 associate awarded. **Calendar:** Semester, limited summer session. **Full-time faculty:** 9 total. **Part-time faculty:** 24 total.

Basis for selection. Open admission. Observes THEA requirements.

2015-2016 Annual costs. Tuition/fees: $7,320. Room only: $2,500. Books/supplies: $500. Personal expenses: $1,925.

Application procedures. Admission: No deadline. $25 fee. **Financial aid:** No deadline.

Academics. Special study options: ESL, independent study. **Credit/placement by examination:** AP, CLEP. **Support services:** Learning center, remedial instruction, study skills assistance, tutoring, writing center.

Majors. Business: Business admin. **Foreign languages:** Spanish. **Theology:** Bible, theology.

Technology on campus. Dormitories wired for high-speed internet access and linked to campus network. Online library, repair service available.

Student life. Freshman orientation: Available, $25 fee. Preregistration for classes offered. **Housing:** $200 deposit. **Activities:** Campus ministries, drama, international student organizations.

Contact. E-mail: mary.ranjel@bua.edu
Phone: (210) 924-4338
Mary Ranjel, Director of Admissions, Baptist University of the Americas, 8019 South Pan Am Expressway, San Antonio, TX 78224

Baylor University

Waco, Texas

www.baylor.edu

CB member

CB code: 6032

▶ Private 4-year university affiliated with the Baptist faith

▶ Residential campus in small city

▶ 14,139 degree-seeking undergraduates: 2% part-time, 58% women, 7% African American, 6% Asian American, 14% Hispanic/Latino, 5% Multi-racial, non-Hispanic, 3% international

▶ 2,596 degree-seeking graduate students

▶ 44% of applicants admitted

▶ SAT or ACT (ACT writing recommended), application essay required

▶ 70% graduate within 6 years

General. Founded in 1845. Regionally accredited. **Degrees:** 2,931 bachelor's awarded; master's, professional, doctoral offered. **ROTC:** Army, Air Force. **Location:** 100 miles from Dallas-Fort Worth, 100 miles from Austin. **Calendar:** Semester, extensive summer session. **Full-time faculty:** 957 total; 82% have terminal degrees, 13% minority, 39% women. **Part-time faculty:** 228 total; 12% minority, 56% women. **Class size:** 54% < 20, 28% 20-39, 9% 40-49, 7% 50-99, 3% >100. **Special facilities:** Museum of natural science, Texas collection library, Armstrong Browning library.

Freshman class profile. 32,136 applied, 14,033 admitted, 3,394 enrolled.

Mid 50% test scores		Rank in top tenth:	42%
SAT critical reading:	560-650	End year in good standing:	94%
SAT math:	580-670	Return as sophomores:	89%
SAT writing:	530-640	Out-of-state:	31%
ACT composite:	25-30	Live on campus:	99%
Rank in top quarter:	75%	International:	2%

Basis for selection. Competitive high school performance and competitive scores on ACT or SAT most important; above-average achievement and potential expected. Audition required for music and theater programs; interview recommended for marginal achievers; portfolio recommended for art. **Home schooled:** Transcript of courses and grades required. If applicant graduated from home school not officially recognized by state in which school is located, applicant must be 17 years old before first day of class unless GED certificate submitted prior to registration.

High school preparation. College-preparatory program required. Required units include English 4, mathematics 4, social studies 2, history 1, science 4 (laboratory 2) and foreign language 2.

2016-2017 Annual costs. Tuition/fees (projected): $42,096. Room/board: $11,654. Books/supplies: $1,442. Personal expenses: $2,554.

2015-2016 Financial aid. **Need-based:** 2,559 full-time freshmen applied for aid; 1,939 deemed to have need; 1,939 received aid. Average need met was 70%. Average scholarship/grant was $22,926; average loan $2,602. 67% of total undergraduate aid awarded as scholarships/grants, 33% as loans/jobs. **Non-need-based:** Awarded to 12,425 full-time undergraduates, including 3,344 freshmen. Scholarships awarded for academics, art, athletics, job skills, leadership, music/drama, religious affiliation, ROTC.

Application procedures. **Admission:** Priority date 11/1; deadline 2/1 (postmark date). , may be waived for applicants with need. No application fee. Application must be submitted online. Notified by 1/15 for 11/1 applications and by 4/10 for 2/1 applications; applications after 2/1 on space available basis. Must reply by May 1 or within 2 week(s) if notified thereafter. $500 enrollment deposit required by May 1. This is a non-refundable, non-transferable deposit paid to assure enrollment place and will be applied to first semester charges. **Financial aid:** FAFSA required. CSS PROFILE accepted but not required for international applicants. Applicants notified by 3/1; Applicants notified on a rolling basis starting 3/1; must reply by 5/1 or within 2 week(s) of notification.

Academics. Online support (website advising resources and tutoring) available. Tutoring available evenings and weekends. **Special study options:** Accelerated study, combined bachelor's/graduate degree, double major, honors, internships, student-designed major, study abroad, teacher certification program. **Credit/placement by examination:** AP, CLEP, IB, institutional tests. 60 credit hours maximum toward bachelor's degree. **Support services:** Learning center, reduced course load, study skills assistance, tutoring, writing center.

Honors college/program. Baylor Interdisciplinary Core: all regularly admitted students may apply, phone interview may be required; Honors Program/College: has a separate application form.

Majors. **Area/ethnic studies:** American, Asian, Latin American, Slavic. **Biology:** General, biochemistry, bioinformatics, exercise physiology, neuroscience. **Business:** General, accounting, business admin, entrepreneurial studies, fashion, finance, financial planning, human resources, insurance, international, logistics, management information systems, managerial economics, marketing, real estate, sales/distribution. **Communications:** Communications/speech/rhetoric, digital media, journalism. **Computer sciences:** Computer science, information technology. **Conservation:** Environmental science, environmental studies. **Education:** Biology, chemistry, elementary, English, health occupations, mathematics, music, physical, science, social studies, special ed. **Engineering:** General, electrical, mechanical. **English:** English lit, technical writing. **Foreign languages:** Ancient Greek, Arabic, Biblical, classics, French, German, Latin, linguistics, Russian, Spanish. **Health services:** Athletic training, clinical lab science, communication disorders, environmental health, nursing (RN), prenursing. **History:** General. **Human services:** General, social work. **Liberal arts:** Humanities. **Math:** General, applied, statistics. **Parks/recreation:** Exercise sciences, health/fitness. **Philosophy/religion:** Philosophy, religion. **Physical sciences:** Astronomy, astrophysics, chemistry, geology, geophysics, physics. **Psychology:** General. **Social sciences:** Anthropology, geography, international relations, political science, sociology. **Theology:** Sacred music. **Visual/performing arts:** Acting, art history/conservation, dramatic, fashion design, interior design, music, music history, music pedagogy, music performance, music theory/composition, studio arts, theater design. **Work/family studies:** General, family studies, human nutrition.

Most popular majors. Biology 12%, business/marketing 26%, communications/journalism 8%, health sciences 15%, social sciences 6%.

Technology on campus. 1,676 workstations in dormitories, library, computer center, student center. Dormitories wired for high-speed internet access and linked to campus network. Commuter students can connect to campus network. Online course registration, online library, helpline, repair service, student web hosting, wireless network available.

Student life. **Freshman orientation:** Mandatory. Preregistration for classes offered. Ten 2-day sessions primarily in June. **Policies:** All students required to participate in chapel-forum for 2 semesters. **Housing:** Guaranteed on-campus for freshmen. Coed dorms, single-sex dorms, special housing for disabled, apartments, themed housing, wellness housing available. Living-learning centers available. **Activities:** Bands, campus ministries, choral groups, dance, drama, international student organizations, literary magazine, music ensembles, Model UN, musical theater, opera, radio station, student government, student newspaper, symphony orchestra, TV station, Baylor Democrats, College Republicans, Young Conservatives of Texas, Association of Black Students, Hispanic student association, Asians for Christ, Alpha Phi Omega (coed service), Baylor Chamber of Commerce, Habitat for Humanity, Uproar/The Industry.

Athletics. NCAA. **Intercollegiate:** Baseball M, basketball, cheerleading W, cross-country, equestrian W, football (tackle) M, golf, soccer W, softball W, tennis, track and field, volleyball W. **Intramural:** Basketball, bowling, football (non-tackle), racquetball, sand volleyball, soccer, softball, swimming, table tennis, tennis, ultimate frisbee, volleyball. **Team name:** Bears.

Student services. Alcohol/substance abuse counseling, chaplain/spiritual director, career counseling, student employment services, financial aid counseling, health services, legal services, on-campus daycare, personal counseling, placement for graduates, veterans' counselor. **Physically disabled:** Services for visually, speech, hearing impaired.

Contact. E-mail: admissions@baylor.edu
Phone: (254) 710-3435 Toll-free number: (800) 229-5678
Fax: (254) 710-3436
Jennifer Carron, Assistant Vice President of Admissions Services, Baylor University, One Bear Place #97056, Waco, TX 76798-7056

Chamberlain College of Nursing: Houston

Houston, Texas

www.chamberlain.edu

CB code: 6586

▶ For-profit 4-year nursing college

▶ Commuter campus in very large city

▶ 361 degree-seeking undergraduates

▶ SAT or ACT required

General. **Degrees:** 107 bachelor's awarded. **Calendar:** Semester. **Full-time faculty:** 9 total; 56% minority, 100% women. **Part-time faculty:** 25 total; 56% minority, 96% women.

Basis for selection. Admission decisions based on interview, proof of high school diploma/GED, and satisfactory test scores. For more information about such tests and scores, contact admissions office.

2015-2016 Annual costs. Tuition/fees: $18,160. Books/supplies: $1,400. Personal expenses: $2,452.

Application procedures. **Admission:** No deadline. $95 fee. Admission notification on a rolling basis. **Financial aid:** No deadline.

Academics. **Credit/placement by examination:** AP, CLEP.

Majors. **Health services:** Nursing (RN).

Student life. **Housing:** Private apartments, student housing, private rooms available.

Contact. Phone: (713) 277-9800
Chamberlain College of Nursing: Houston, 11025 Equity Drive, Houston, TX 77041

College of Biblical Studies-Houston
Houston, Texas
www.cbshouston.edu
CB code: 3946

♦ Private 4-year Bible college
♦ Commuter campus in very large city
♦ 401 degree-seeking undergraduates: 83% part-time, 49% women, 51% African American, 1% Asian American, 27% Hispanic/Latino, 3% Multi-racial, non-Hispanic
♦ Application essay required

General. Accredited by ABHE. Multi-denominational and multi-ethnic Christian Bible college. **Degrees:** 54 bachelor's, 41 associate awarded. **Calendar:** Semester, extensive summer session. **Full-time faculty:** 17 total; 71% have terminal degrees, 47% minority, 12% women. **Part-time faculty:** 10 total; 10% have terminal degrees, 60% minority, 10% women. **Class size:** 86% < 20, 12% 20-39, 1% 40-49.

Freshman class profile. 90 applied, 55 admitted, 15 enrolled.

Basis for selection. Open admission, but selective for some programs. Must have high diploma or equivalent, generally be 18 years or older, and have the ability to benefit in the educational program pursued. ASSET testing may be required for associate or baccalaureate level programs. **Home schooled:** State high school equivalency certificate required.

2015-2016 Annual costs. Tuition/fees: $8,343. Books/supplies: $975. Personal expenses: $2,916.

Application procedures. **Admission:** No deadline. $40 fee. Admission notification on a rolling basis. **Financial aid:** No deadline.

Academics. **Special study options:** Accelerated study, dual enrollment of high school students, independent study. Associate degree in biblical studies taught in Spanish. **Credit/placement by examination:** AP, CLEP, institutional tests. **Support services:** Remedial instruction, tutoring.

Majors. **Theology:** Bible, preministerial.

Technology on campus. 57 workstations in library, computer center. Commuter students can connect to campus network. Online course registration, online library, wireless network available.

Student life. **Freshman orientation:** Mandatory. Preregistration for classes offered. **Policies:** Students are expected to be Christians. Religious observance required. **Activities:** Campus ministries, student government.

Student services. Adult student services, career counseling, financial aid counseling. **Physically disabled:** Services for visually impaired.

Contact. E-mail: cbs@cbshouston.edu
Phone: (713) 785-5995 Fax: (713) 785-5998
Maggie Rodriguez, Director of Admission, College of Biblical Studies-Houston, 7000 Regency Square Boulevard, #110, Houston, TX 77036-3211

Concordia University Texas
Austin, Texas
www.concordia.edu
CB code: 6127

♦ Private 4-year university and liberal arts college affiliated with the Lutheran Church - Missouri Synod
♦ Commuter campus in very large city
♦ 1,525 degree-seeking undergraduates
♦ 937 graduate students
♦ SAT or ACT (ACT writing optional) required

General. Founded in 1926. Regionally accredited. **Degrees:** 290 bachelor's, 1 associate awarded; master's offered. **ROTC:** Army, Air Force. **Calendar:** Semester, extensive summer session. **Full-time faculty:** 71 total; 68% have terminal degrees, 11% minority, 37% women. **Part-time faculty:** 271 total; 58% have terminal degrees, 24% minority, 49% women. **Class size:** 66% < 20, 34% 20-39. **Special facilities:** 250 acres of dedicated nature and wildlife preserve.

Freshman class profile.

GPA 3.75 or higher:	17%	Rank in top quarter:	38%
GPA 3.50-3.74:	23%	Rank in top tenth:	14%
GPA 3.0-3.49:	34%	Out-of-state:	6%
GPA 2.0-2.99:	25%	Live on campus:	70%

Basis for selection. School achievement record, test scores, and 2.5 GPA important. Interview recommended for academically weak. **Home schooled:** Transcript of courses and grades required.

2015-2016 Annual costs. Tuition/fees: $28,160. Room/board: $9,284. Books/supplies: $1,274.

2014-2015 Financial aid. **Need-based:** 215 full-time freshmen applied for aid; 181 deemed to have need; 179 received aid. Average need met was 77%. Average scholarship/grant was $17,243; average loan $7,179. 72% of total undergraduate aid awarded as scholarships/grants, 28% as loans/jobs. **Non-need-based:** Awarded to 317 full-time undergraduates, including 84 freshmen. Scholarships awarded for academics, leadership, music/drama, religious affiliation.

Application procedures. **Admission:** Closing date 8/1. $25 fee, may be waived for applicants with need. Admission notification on a rolling basis beginning on or about 8/15. Must reply by 8/1. Reply by August 15 if residence hall applicant. **Financial aid:** Priority date 5/1; no closing date. FAFSA required. Applicants notified on a rolling basis starting 2/15; must reply within 3 week(s) of notification.

Academics. **Special study options:** Accelerated study, cross-registration, distance learning, double major, dual enrollment of high school students, honors, independent study, internships, liberal arts/career combination, student-designed major, study abroad, teacher certification program. **Credit/placement by examination:** AP, CLEP, IB, SAT, ACT, institutional tests. 15 credit hours maximum toward associate degree, 30 toward bachelor's. **Support services:** Learning center, reduced course load, remedial instruction, study skills assistance, tutoring, writing center.

Majors. **Biology:** General. **Business:** General, business admin, training/development. **Communications:** Communications/speech/rhetoric. **Computer sciences:** Computer science. **Conservation:** Environmental studies. **Education:** Elementary, middle, secondary, special ed. **English:** English lit. **Health services:** Health care admin, nursing (RN). **History:** General. **Liberal arts:** Arts/sciences. **Math:** General. **Parks/recreation:** Health/fitness. **Protective services:** Law enforcement admin. **Social sciences:** General. **Theology:** Religious ed. **Visual/performing arts:** Music.

Most popular majors. Business/marketing 31%, education 9%, health sciences 24%, parks/recreation 8%, social sciences 6%.

Technology on campus. 45 workstations in library, computer center, student center. Dormitories wired for high-speed internet access and linked to campus network. Commuter students can connect to campus network. Online library, helpline, wireless network available.

Student life. **Freshman orientation:** Available. Preregistration for classes offered. **Housing:** Guaranteed on-campus for freshmen. Coed dorms, special housing for disabled available. $275 deposit, deadline 5/1. **Activities:** Bands, campus ministries, choral groups, drama, literary magazine, music ensembles, Model UN, musical theater, opera, radio station, student government, student newspaper, Sisters in Christ, Lutheran Student Fellowship, Lutheran Women's Missionary League, Pro Life, College Republicans, Pre-Sem Club (pre-seminary students), Fellowship of Christian Athletes, students active for the environment, writer's guild.

Athletics. NCAA. **Intercollegiate:** Baseball M, basketball, cross-country, golf, soccer, softball W, tennis W, volleyball W. **Intramural:** Badminton, basketball, bowling, handball, racquetball, softball, table tennis, tennis, volleyball. **Team name:** Tornados.

Student services. Adult student services, alcohol/substance abuse counseling, chaplain/spiritual director, career counseling, student employment services, financial aid counseling, personal counseling, placement for graduates, veterans' counselor. **Physically disabled:** Services for visually, speech, hearing impaired.

Contact. E-mail: admissions@concordia.edu
Phone: (512) 313-4600 Toll-free number: (800) 865-4282
Fax: (512) 313-4269
Kristin Coulter, Director of Admissions, Concordia University Texas, 11400 Concordia University Drive, Austin, TX 78726

Criswell College
Dallas, Texas
www.criswell.edu

CB code: 0794

- Private 4-year Bible and seminary college affiliated with the Southern Baptist Convention
- Commuter campus in very large city
- 262 undergraduates
- 88 graduate students
- Application essay required

General. Founded in 1970. Regionally accredited. **Degrees:** 37 bachelor's, 5 associate awarded; master's offered. **Location:** Near downtown Dallas. **Calendar:** Semester, limited summer session.

Basis for selection. Rigor of courses taken, character, religious commitment very important. SAT or ACT recommended. Interview recommended.

High school preparation. Recommended units include English 4, mathematics 2, social studies 2, science 3 and foreign language 2.

2015-2016 Annual costs. Tuition/fees: $10,120. Books/supplies: $855. Personal expenses: $935.

Application procedures. Admission: Priority date 5/1; no deadline. $35 fee, may be waived for applicants with need. Admission notification on a rolling basis. **Financial aid:** Closing date 4/15. FAFSA, institutional form required. Applicants notified on a rolling basis.

Academics. Special study options: Distance learning, double major, dual enrollment of high school students, independent study, internships. **Credit/placement by examination:** AP, CLEP, SAT, ACT. **Support services:** Reduced course load, study skills assistance, tutoring, writing center.

Majors. Psychology: General. **Theology:** Bible.

Technology on campus. 25 workstations in library, computer center. Online library, wireless network available.

Student life. Freshman orientation: Mandatory. Preregistration for classes offered. **Policies:** Religious observance required. **Housing:** Apartments available. **Activities:** Campus ministries, student government.

Student services. Chaplain/spiritual director, career counseling, student employment services, financial aid counseling, personal counseling, veterans' counselor.

Contact. E-mail: admission@criswell.edu
Phone: (214) 818-1305 Toll-free number: (800) 899-0012
Fax: (214) 818-1310
Russell Marriott, Director of Admissions, Criswell College, 4010 Gaston Avenue, Dallas, TX 75246-1537

Dallas Baptist University
Dallas, Texas
www.dbu.edu

CB member
CB code: 6159

- Private 4-year university affiliated with the Baptist faith
- Residential campus in very large city
- 3,220 degree-seeking undergraduates: 26% part-time, 60% women, 15% African American, 2% Asian American, 15% Hispanic/Latino, 1% Native American, 7% international
- 2,004 degree-seeking graduate students
- 42% of applicants admitted
- SAT or ACT (ACT writing optional), application essay required
- 58% graduate within 6 years

General. Founded in 1898. Regionally accredited. Dallas Baptist University offers a Christ-centered education that fully integrates Biblical faith and academic learning. **Degrees:** 785 bachelor's, 7 associate awarded; master's, doctoral offered. **ROTC:** Army, Air Force. **Location:** 13 miles from downtown Dallas, 29 miles from Fort Worth. **Calendar:** 4-1-4, extensive summer session. **Full-time faculty:** 126 total; 82% have terminal degrees, 10% minority, 40% women. **Part-time faculty:** 503 total; 43% have terminal degrees, 9% minority, 43% women. **Class size:** 69% < 20, 28% 20-39, 1% 40-49, 2% 50-99, less than 1% >100. **Special facilities:** Music business recording studio, prayer and botanical gardens, gazebos, arboretum, fitness trail, nature trail.

Freshman class profile. 2,949 applied, 1,236 admitted, 499 enrolled.

Mid 50% test scores			
SAT critical reading:	520-610	Rank in top quarter:	46%
SAT math:	510-600	Rank in top tenth:	19%
ACT composite:	19-24	Return as sophomores:	71%
GPA 3.75 or higher:	36%	Out-of-state:	7%
GPA 3.50-3.74:	21%	Live on campus:	97%
GPA 3.0-3.49:	29%	Fraternities:	42%
GPA 2.0-2.99:	13%	Sororities:	56%

Basis for selection. All factors are considered for admission, including test scores, class rank, essay and GPA. Interview recommended. **Learning Disabled:** Submit all documentation to the Undergraduate Admissions Office.

High school preparation. College-preparatory program recommended. 18 units recommended. Recommended units include English 4, mathematics 3, social studies 3, history 4, science 2 (laboratory 1) and foreign language 2.

2015-2016 Annual costs. Tuition/fees: $24,890. Room/board: $7,326. Books/supplies: $1,260. Personal expenses: $1,998.

2015-2016 Financial aid. Need-based: 429 full-time freshmen applied for aid; 307 deemed to have need; 303 received aid. Average need met was 63%. Average scholarship/grant was $4,032; average loan $3,377. 55% of total undergraduate aid awarded as scholarships/grants, 45% as loans/jobs. **Non-need-based:** Awarded to 1,823 full-time undergraduates, including 435 freshmen. Scholarships awarded for academics, athletics, job skills, leadership, music/drama, religious affiliation.

Application procedures. Admission: Priority date 11/1; no deadline. $25 fee, may be waived for applicants with need, free for online applicants. Admission notification on a rolling basis. **Financial aid:** No deadline. FAFSA, institutional form required. Applicants notified on a rolling basis starting 2/1.

Academics. Special study options: Accelerated study, combined bachelor's/graduate degree, cross-registration, distance learning, double major, dual enrollment of high school students, ESL, exchange student, honors, independent study, internships, study abroad, teacher certification program, Washington semester, weekend college. **Credit/placement by examination:** AP, CLEP, IB, SAT, ACT, institutional tests. 30 credit hours maximum toward bachelor's degree. Credit by examination not counted toward residency hours. Credits recorded on permanent record after student has completed minimum of 12 hours in residence. CLEP hours limited to 15. **Support services:** Learning center, pre-admission summer program, remedial instruction, study skills assistance, tutoring, writing center.

Majors. Biology: General, cellular/anatomical. **Business:** Accounting, business admin, entrepreneurial studies, finance, hospitality admin, management information systems, marketing. **Communications:** General, communications/speech/rhetoric, digital media, persuasive communications. **Computer sciences:** General, computer science. **Conservation:** Environmental science. **Education:** Biology, computer, elementary, English, history, mathematics, music, physical, science, speech. **English:** English lit. **Health services:** Health care admin. **History:** General. **Math:** General. **Parks/recreation:** Health/fitness, sports admin. **Philosophy/religion:** Philosophy. **Protective services:** Criminal justice. **Psychology:** General. **Social sciences:** Political science, sociology. **Theology:** Bible, missionary, religious ed, sacred music. **Visual/performing arts:** Art, music, music management, music performance, music theory/composition, piano/keyboard, voice/opera.

Most popular majors. Business/marketing 29%, communications/journalism 7%, interdisciplinary studies 11%, psychology 11%, theological studies 10%, visual/performing arts 6%.

Technology on campus. 214 workstations in dormitories, library, computer center, student center. Dormitories wired for high-speed internet access and linked to campus network. Commuter students can connect to campus network. Online library, helpline, wireless network available.

Student life. Freshman orientation: Available. Preregistration for classes offered. **Policies:** Religious observance required. **Housing:** Single-sex dorms, special housing for disabled, apartments, wellness housing available. $175 nonrefundable deposit. **Activities:** Pep band, campus ministries, choral groups, dance, drama, international student organizations, music ensembles, musical theater, opera, student government, College Republicans, Organization of Latin American Students, International Chinese Fellowship, Korean Student Association, Japanese Student Society, Black Student Union, Baptist Student Ministries, Our Calling, African Students Union, South Asian Student Association.

Athletics. NCAA, NCCAA. **Intercollegiate:** Baseball M, basketball M, cross-country, golf, sand volleyball W, soccer, tennis, track and field, volleyball W. **Intramural:** Badminton, basketball, football (non-tackle), golf, sand volleyball, soccer, softball, table tennis, tennis, ultimate frisbee, volleyball. **Team name:** Patriots.

Student services. Adult student services, alcohol/substance abuse counseling, chaplain/spiritual director, career counseling, services for economically disadvantaged, student employment services, financial aid counseling, health services, personal counseling, placement for graduates, veterans' counselor. **Physically disabled:** Services for visually, speech, hearing impaired.

Contact. E-mail: admiss@dbu.edu
Phone: (214) 333-5360 Toll-free number: (800) 460-1328
Fax: (214) 333-5447
Bobby Soto, Director of Undergraduate Admissions, Dallas Baptist University, 3000 Mountain Creek Parkway, Dallas, TX 75211-9299

Dallas Christian College
Dallas, Texas
www.dallas.edu
CB code: 0792

- Private 4-year Bible college affiliated with the nondenominational tradition
- Commuter campus in very large city
- 315 degree-seeking undergraduates: 23% part-time, 44% women, 30% African American, 16% Hispanic/Latino, 2% Native American, 5% Multi-racial, non-Hispanic
- SAT or ACT (ACT writing recommended), application essay, interview required

General. Founded in 1950. Accredited by ABHE. **Degrees:** 49 bachelor's, 1 associate awarded. **Location:** 10 miles from downtown. **Calendar:** 4-1-4, limited summer session. **Full-time faculty:** 14 total; 57% have terminal degrees, 14% minority, 43% women. **Part-time faculty:** 31 total; 23% have terminal degrees, 16% minority, 23% women. **Class size:** 70% < 20, 26% 20-39, 3% 40-49.

Freshman class profile. 60 enrolled.

GPA 3.75 or higher:	15%	Rank in top tenth:	8%
GPA 3.50-3.74:	14%	Return as sophomores:	41%
GPA 3.0-3.49:	46%	Out-of-state:	12%
GPA 2.0-2.99:	23%	Live on campus:	99%
Rank in top quarter:	29%	International:	2%

Basis for selection. School record and recommendations, followed by test scores. Class rank also important.

High school preparation. College-preparatory program recommended. Recommended units include English 4, mathematics 3, social studies 3, history 3, science 2 and foreign language 2.

2015-2016 Annual costs. Tuition/fees: $15,500. Room/board: $7,920. Books/supplies: $1,000.

Financial aid. All financial aid based on need.

Application procedures. Admission: Priority date 7/1; deadline 7/15 (postmark date). $30 fee. Admission notification on a rolling basis. Must reply by 8/15. **Financial aid:** Priority date 5/15; no closing date. FAFSA, institutional form required. Applicants notified on a rolling basis; must reply within 2 week(s) of notification.

Academics. Special study options: Accelerated study, distance learning, double major, dual enrollment of high school students, independent study, internships, liberal arts/career combination, teacher certification program. Online degree options, and FLEXCampus courses allowing online students to sit in "live" via webcam. Degree completion programs are also available. **Credit/placement by examination:** AP, CLEP, IB, SAT, ACT, institutional tests. 12 credit hours maximum toward associate degree, 30 toward bachelor's. **Support services:** Reduced course load, remedial instruction, study skills assistance, tutoring.

Majors. Business: Business admin. **Education:** General, early childhood, elementary, English, history, multi-level teacher, music, secondary. **Liberal arts:** Arts/sciences. **Psychology:** General. **Theology:** Bible, religious ed, sacred music, theology.

Most popular majors. Business/marketing 20%, interdisciplinary studies 18%, theological studies 58%.

Technology on campus. 16 workstations in library, student center. Dormitories wired for high-speed internet access. Commuter students can connect to campus network. Online course registration, online library, helpline, wireless network available.

Student life. Freshman orientation: Mandatory, $150 fee. Preregistration for classes offered. Held 3 days prior to semester start. **Policies:** All resident

students and those taking 6 hours or more required to attend campus chapel services up to 2 times per week. **Housing:** Guaranteed on-campus for all undergraduates. Single-sex dorms, wellness housing available. $150 deposit, deadline 8/10. **Activities:** Pep band, campus ministries, choral groups, drama, music ensembles, student government, student newspaper.

Athletics. NCCAA. **Intercollegiate:** Baseball M, basketball, soccer, volleyball W. **Intramural:** Football (non-tackle), sand volleyball, soccer, table tennis, volleyball. **Team name:** Crusaders.

Student services. Adult student services, chaplain/spiritual director, student employment services, financial aid counseling, personal counseling, placement for graduates.

Contact. E-mail: dcc@dallas.edu
Phone: (972) 241-3371 ext. 155 Toll-free number: (800) 688-1029
Fax: (972) 241-8021
Matthew Meeks, Vice President for Enrollment Management, Dallas Christian College, 2700 Christian Parkway, Dallas, TX 75234-7299

DeVry University: Houston
Houston, Texas
www.devry.edu
CB code: 4132

- For-profit 4-year university
- Commuter campus in very large city
- 640 degree-seeking undergraduates

General. Additional locations: Houston Galleria, Austin, San Antonio. **Degrees:** 164 bachelor's, 48 associate awarded; master's offered. **Calendar:** Semester. **Full-time faculty:** 25 total; 32% minority, 36% women. **Part-time faculty:** 140 total; 44% minority, 47% women.

Basis for selection. Interview, high school GPA, and test scores most important.

High school preparation. College-preparatory program recommended.

2015-2016 Annual costs. Tuition/fees: $18,959. Books/supplies: $1,320. Personal expenses: $2,376. **Additional information:** Annual tuition: $10,810-$21,163; fees $50-$90.

Application procedures. Admission: No deadline. $40 fee. Admission notification on a rolling basis. **Financial aid:** No deadline.

Academics. Special study options: Accelerated study, distance learning. **Credit/placement by examination:** AP, CLEP.

Majors. Business: General, business admin. **Computer sciences:** Networking, systems analysis. **Health services:** Health care admin.

Most popular majors. Business/marketing 83%, computer/information sciences 10%, engineering/engineering technologies 7%.

Contact. Phone: (713) 973-3000 Toll-free number: (866) 338-7941
Fax: (713) 896-7650
DeVry University: Houston, 11125 Equity Drive, Houston, TX 77041-8217

DeVry University: Irving
Dallas, Texas
www.devry.edu
CB code: 6180

- For-profit 4-year university
- Commuter campus in small city
- 578 degree-seeking undergraduates
- Interview required

General. Founded in 1969. Regionally accredited. Additional locations: Fort Worth, Richardson; Oklahoma City (OK). **Degrees:** 399 bachelor's, 72 associate awarded; master's offered. **Location:** 12 miles from Dallas. **Calendar:** Semester, extensive summer session. **Full-time faculty:** 38 total; 24% minority, 34% women. **Part-time faculty:** 64 total; 28% minority, 52% women.

Basis for selection. Applicants must have a high school diploma or equivalent or a degree from an accredited postsecondary institution, demonstrating proficiency in basic college-level skills through SAT or ACT scores or institution-administered placement examinations, and be at least 17 years of age on the first day of classes. New students may enter at beginning of any semester.

High school preparation. College-preparatory program recommended.

2015-2016 Annual costs. Tuition/fees: $17,132. Books/supplies: $1,320. Personal expenses: $2,376.

Financial aid. All financial aid based on need.

Application procedures. Admission: No deadline. $40 fee. Admission notification on a rolling basis. **Financial aid:** No deadline.

Academics. Special study options: Accelerated study, distance learning. **Credit/placement by examination:** AP, CLEP, institutional tests. No more than 35% of credit toward graduation requirement accepted. **Support services:** Learning center, remedial instruction, tutoring.

Majors. Business: General, business admin. **Communications:** General. **Computer sciences:** Networking, systems analysis, web page design. **Engineering:** Software.

Most popular majors. Business/marketing 55%, computer/information sciences 29%, engineering/engineering technologies 16%.

Technology on campus. 450 workstations in library, computer center. Online course registration, online library, helpline available.

Student life. Freshman orientation: Mandatory. Preregistration for classes offered. **Housing:** Off-campus housing available. **Activities:** Association of Information Technology Professionals, campus Bible study, Christian Students Fellowship, Habitat for Humanity, Institute of Electrical and Electronics Engineers, Institute of Management Accountants, minority student union, National Society of Black Engineers, Society of Women Engineers, Telecommunications Management and Associations, Society of Hispanic Professional Engineers, gamers club.

Athletics. Intramural: Basketball, football (tackle) M, volleyball.

Student services. Career counseling, student employment services, financial aid counseling, placement for graduates, veterans' counselor. **Physically disabled:** Services for visually, hearing impaired.

Contact. Phone: (972) 929-5777 Toll-free number: (800) 633-3879 Fax: (972) 929-2860
DeVry University: Irving, 4800 Regent Boulevard, Suite 200, Dallas, TX 75063-2439

East Texas Baptist University
Marshall, Texas
www.etbu.edu   **CB code: 6187**

- Private 4-year university and liberal arts college affiliated with the Baptist faith
- Residential campus in large town
- 1,139 degree-seeking undergraduates: 4% part-time, 53% women, 20% African American, 10% Hispanic/Latino, 1% Native American, 3% Multi-racial, non-Hispanic, 1% international
- 75 degree-seeking graduate students
- 55% of applicants admitted
- SAT or ACT (ACT writing optional) required
- 46% graduate within 6 years; 36% enter graduate study

General. Founded in 1912. Regionally accredited. **Degrees:** 174 bachelor's awarded; master's offered. **Location:** 23 miles from Longview, 40 miles from Shreveport, LA. **Calendar:** Semester, limited summer session. **Full-time faculty:** 73 total; 84% have terminal degrees, 11% minority, 37% women. **Part-time faculty:** 46 total; 22% have terminal degrees, 13% minority, 54% women. **Class size:** 64% < 20, 32% 20-39, 4% 40-49. **Special facilities:** Environmental studies area.

Freshman class profile. 1,456 applied, 805 admitted, 342 enrolled.

Mid 50% test scores		Rank in top quarter:	42%
SAT critical reading:	440-530	Rank in top tenth:	14%
SAT math:	470-570	End year in good standing:	86%
ACT composite:	18-23	Return as sophomores:	52%
GPA 3.75 or higher:	20%	Out-of-state:	12%
GPA 3.50-3.74:	25%	Live on campus:	94%
GPA 3.0-3.49:	36%	Fraternities:	1%
GPA 2.0-2.99:	19%	Sororities:	1%

Basis for selection. A minimum score of 18 ACT/860 SAT required. Admission may also be granted to those ranked in upper 30% of their class from an accredited high school. Evidence of good character also required. Audition recommended for music program. **Learning Disabled:** Student should provide documentation of learning disability to the Office of Academic Success and Graduate Services, which verifies documentation and assists in acquiring reasonable accommodations.

2015-2016 Annual costs. Tuition/fees: $24,218. Room/board: $8,629.

2014-2015 Financial aid. Need-based: 346 full-time freshmen applied for aid; 323 deemed to have need; 323 received aid. Average need met was 31%. Average scholarship/grant was $6,312; average loan $3,091. 56% of total undergraduate aid awarded as scholarships/grants, 44% as loans/jobs. **Non-need-based:** Awarded to 1,086 full-time undergraduates, including 359 freshmen. Scholarships awarded for academics, alumni affiliation, leadership, religious affiliation, state residency.

Application procedures. Admission: Closing date 9/1 (receipt date). $25 fee, may be waived for applicants with need. Admission notification on a rolling basis beginning on or about 9/1. **Financial aid:** Priority date 6/1; no closing date. FAFSA, institutional form required. Applicants notified on a rolling basis starting 1/1.

Academics. Special study options: Accelerated study, distance learning, double major, dual enrollment of high school students, ESL, exchange student, honors, independent study, internships, student-designed major, study abroad, teacher certification program, Washington semester. **Credit/placement by examination:** AP, CLEP, IB, SAT, ACT, institutional tests. **Support services:** Learning center, reduced course load, remedial instruction, study skills assistance, tutoring, writing center.

Majors. Biology: General. **Business:** General. **Communications:** Media studies. **Education:** General, biology, drama/dance, elementary, English, history, mathematics, music, physical, social studies, Spanish, speech. **English:** English lit, rhetoric/composition. **Foreign languages:** Spanish. **Health services:** Athletic training, nursing (RN). **History:** General. **Math:** General. **Parks/recreation:** Exercise sciences, health/fitness. **Philosophy/religion:** Religion. **Physical sciences:** Chemistry. **Protective services:** Law enforcement admin. **Psychology:** General, developmental. **Social sciences:** Political science, sociology. **Theology:** Bible, missionary, pastoral counseling, sacred music, youth ministry. **Visual/performing arts:** Dramatic, music, piano/keyboard, voice/opera.

Most popular majors. Biology 6%, business/marketing 15%, education 18%, health sciences 11%, interdisciplinary studies 19%, theological studies 6%.

Technology on campus. 200 workstations in dormitories, library, computer center, student center. Dormitories wired for high-speed internet access and linked to campus network. Commuter students can connect to campus network. Online course registration, online library, helpline, repair service, wireless network available.

Student life. Freshman orientation: Available. Preregistration for classes offered. Four days of activities, lectures, seminar sessions, community service activities. Held the week before classes begin in the fall term. **Policies:** Required chapel attendance, health and wellness checks in residence halls, visitation hours for residence halls. Religious observance required. **Housing:** Guaranteed on-campus for all undergraduates. Single-sex dorms, special housing for disabled, apartments, wellness housing available. Pets allowed in dorm rooms. **Activities:** Bands, campus ministries, choral groups, dance, drama, international student organizations, literary magazine, music ensembles, Model UN, musical theater, opera, radio station, student government, student newspaper, symphony orchestra, Delta Pi Theta, Fellowship of Christian Athletes, Political Awareness Society, Speak, Baptist Student Ministry, Cultural Outreach Ministries, Pi Sigma, Sisters United.

Athletics. NCAA. **Intercollegiate:** Baseball M, basketball, cross-country, football (tackle) M, soccer, softball W, tennis, track and field, volleyball W. **Intramural:** Basketball, football (non-tackle), sand volleyball, soccer, softball, table tennis, ultimate frisbee, volleyball. **Team name:** Tigers.

Student services. Adult student services, chaplain/spiritual director, career counseling, student employment services, financial aid counseling, personal counseling, placement for graduates, veterans' counselor.

Contact. E-mail: admissions@etbu.edu
Phone: (903) 923-2000 Toll-free number: (800) 804-3828
Fax: (903) 923-2001
Vince Blankenship, Vice President for Enrollment Management and Marketing, East Texas Baptist University, One Tiger Drive, Marshall, TX 75670-1498

Hardin-Simmons University

Abilene, Texas

CB member

www.hsutx.edu

CB code: 6268

- Private 4-year university affiliated with the Baptist faith
- Residential campus in small city
- 1,599 degree-seeking undergraduates: 8% part-time, 54% women, 7% African American, 1% Asian American, 15% Hispanic/Latino, 4% Multiracial, non-Hispanic, 1% international
- 474 degree-seeking graduate students
- 60% of applicants admitted
- SAT or ACT (ACT writing optional) required
- 53% graduate within 6 years

General. Founded in 1891. Regionally accredited. Part of 2-member consortium (with McMurry University) comprising Abilene Intercollegiate School of Nursing. **Degrees:** 338 bachelor's awarded; master's, professional, doctoral offered. **Location:** 152 miles from Fort Worth. **Calendar:** Semester, extensive summer session. **Full-time faculty:** 134 total; 92% have terminal degrees, 4% minority, 38% women. **Part-time faculty:** 70 total; 56% have terminal degrees, 11% minority, 44% women. **Class size:** 68% < 20, 30% 20-39, less than 1% 40-49, 1% 50-99. **Special facilities:** Rare and fine book room, observatory.

Freshman class profile. 1,595 applied, 957 admitted, 413 enrolled.

Mid 50% test scores			
SAT critical reading:	450-570	GPA 3.0-3.49:	22%
SAT math:	470-570	GPA 2.0-2.99:	10%
SAT writing:	430-540	Rank in top quarter:	49%
ACT composite:	19-25	Rank in top tenth:	20%
GPA 3.75 or higher:	51%	Return as sophomores:	68%
GPA 3.50-3.74:	17%	Out-of-state:	4%
		Live on campus:	88%

Basis for selection. Applicants admitted on basis of acceptable combination of test scores and prior academic record. Special cases considered individually. Non-native speakers of English require score of 550 on TOEFL (75 iBT), unless transferring 24 or more credits. Audition required for music program; interview recommended for special cases. Written essay, interview, and separate application required for honors program. **Home schooled:** GED scores required only if applicant plans to apply for federal need-based financial aid. **Learning Disabled:** No special admission requirements for students with disabilities; accepted students apply to Office for Students with Disabilities.

High school preparation. College-preparatory program recommended. 26 units required. Required units include English 4, mathematics 4, social studies 4, science 4, foreign language 2, visual/performing arts 1, academic electives 5.5. 1 physical education, 0.5 speech communication.

2015-2016 Annual costs. Tuition/fees: $24,500. Room/board: $7,740. Books/supplies: $800. Personal expenses: $1,976. **Additional information:** Tuition is a Block Tuition, which covers 34 hours for fall, spring, May term and two summer sessions.

2015-2016 Financial aid. Need-based: 412 full-time freshmen applied for aid; 325 deemed to have need; 325 received aid. Average need met was 90%. Average scholarship/grant was $8,245; average loan $3,080. 61% of total undergraduate aid awarded as scholarships/grants, 39% as loans/jobs. **Non-need-based:** Awarded to 1,394 full-time undergraduates, including 412 freshmen. Scholarships awarded for academics, alumni affiliation, art, leadership, minority status, music/drama, religious affiliation.

Application procedures. Admission: No deadline. No application fee. Admission notification on a rolling basis beginning on or about 9/1. **Financial aid:** Priority date 3/1; no closing date. FAFSA required. Applicants notified on a rolling basis starting 3/1; must reply by 6/1.

Academics. Special study options: Accelerated study, cross-registration, distance learning, double major, dual enrollment of high school students, honors, independent study, internships, study abroad, teacher certification program. **Credit/placement by examination:** AP, CLEP, SAT, ACT, institutional tests. 42 credit hours maximum toward bachelor's degree. Maximum 14 credits in any one major. **Support services:** Pre-admission summer program, reduced course load, remedial instruction, study skills assistance, tutoring, writing center.

Majors. Biology: General, Biochemistry/molecular biology. **Business:** Accounting, business admin, finance, management information systems, management science, marketing, nonprofit/public. **Communications:** General. **Computer sciences:** Programming. **Conservation:** Environmental science. **Education:** Art, business, computer, drama/dance, early childhood, English, history, mathematics, music, physical, science, social studies, Spanish, speech. **English:** English lit. **Foreign languages:** Spanish. **Health services:**

Athletic training, audiology/speech pathology, nursing (RN), prenursing. **History:** General. **Human services:** Social work. **Math:** General. **Parks/recreation:** Exercise sciences. **Philosophy/religion:** Christian, philosophy. **Physical sciences:** Chemistry, geology, physics. **Protective services:** Criminal justice. **Psychology:** General. **Social sciences:** Economics, political science, sociology. **Theology:** Bible, missionary, preministerial, sacred music, theology, youth ministry. **Visual/performing arts:** Dramatic, graphic design, music, music management, music performance, music theory/composition, piano/keyboard, stringed instruments, studio arts, voice/opera.

Most popular majors. Biology 9%, business/marketing 12%, education 7%, health sciences 12%, parks/recreation 12%, psychology 8%, security/protective services 7%, theological studies 6%, visual/performing arts 9%.

Technology on campus. 258 workstations in dormitories, library, computer center, student center. Dormitories wired for high-speed internet access and linked to campus network. Online course registration, online library, helpline, repair service, wireless network available.

Student life. Freshman orientation: Available, $10 fee. Preregistration for classes offered. Held Wednesday through Sunday the week before classes begin. **Policies:** Single, undergraduate students under 21 who have not completed 60 credit hours and are not living at home required to live in residence halls. All housing is alcohol, drug and smoke-free. Religious observance required. **Housing:** Guaranteed on-campus for freshmen. Single-sex dorms, special housing for disabled, apartments available. $100 fully refundable deposit. Single, duplex housing available with priority given to families. **Activities:** Bands, campus ministries, choral groups, drama, international student organizations, literary magazine, music ensembles, Model UN, musical theater, opera, student government, student newspaper, symphony orchestra, Alpha Phi Omega, Baptist student ministries, Epsilon Pi Alpha, HSU Green, Phi Mu Alpha, Theta Alpha Zeta, Tri Phi, Zeta Chi, Sigma Alpha.

Athletics. NCAA. **Intercollegiate:** Baseball M, basketball, cheerleading, cross-country, football (tackle) M, golf, soccer, softball W, tennis, track and field, volleyball W. **Intramural:** Basketball, football (non-tackle), golf, handball, racquetball, soccer, softball, tennis. **Team name:** Cowboys/Cowgirls.

Student services. Chaplain/spiritual director, career counseling, student employment services, financial aid counseling, health services, personal counseling, placement for graduates, veterans' counselor. **Physically disabled:** Services for visually, speech, hearing impaired.

Contact. E-mail: enroll@hsutx.edu
Phone: (325) 670-1206 Toll-free number: (877) 464-7889
Fax: (325) 671-2115
Jim Jones, Associate VP for Enrollment Services, Hardin-Simmons University, PO Box 16050, Abilene, TX 79698-0001

Houston Baptist University

Houston, Texas

CB member

www.hbu.edu

CB code: 6282

- Private 4-year university and liberal arts college affiliated with the Baptist faith
- Commuter campus in very large city
- 2,240 degree-seeking undergraduates: 6% part-time, 61% women, 19% African American, 10% Asian American, 30% Hispanic/Latino, 5% Multi-racial, non-Hispanic, 4% international
- 857 degree-seeking graduate students
- 33% of applicants admitted
- SAT or ACT (ACT writing optional) required
- 33% graduate within 6 years

General. Founded in 1960. Regionally accredited. Christian liberal arts university. **Degrees:** 387 bachelor's awarded; master's offered. **ROTC:** Army, Naval, Air Force. **Location:** 10 miles from downtown Houston. **Calendar:** Semester, extensive summer session. **Full-time faculty:** 131 total; 80% have terminal degrees, 20% minority, 47% women. **Part-time faculty:** 113 total; 50% have terminal degrees, 18% minority, 51% women. **Class size:** 58% < 20, 39% 20-39, 2% 40-49, 2% 50-99. **Special facilities:** Cultural arts center, American architecture and decorative arts museum, Bible in America museum, Southern history museum.

Freshman class profile. 14,519 applied, 4,825 admitted, 545 enrolled.

Mid 50% test scores			
SAT critical reading:	470-580	Rank in top quarter:	56%
SAT math:	490-570	Rank in top tenth:	25%
SAT writing:	440-550	Return as sophomores:	70%
ACT composite:	21-26	Out-of-state:	3%
GPA 3.75 or higher:	27%	Live on campus:	54%
GPA 3.50-3.74:	22%	International:	2%
GPA 3.0-3.49:	32%	Fraternities:	12%
GPA 2.0-2.99:	17%	Sororities:	14%

Basis for selection. School achievement record, test scores, recommendations, class rank, special talents, and skills most important.

High school preparation. 25 units recommended. Recommended units include English 4, mathematics 4, social studies 2, history 2, science 4, foreign language 2, computer science .5, visual/performing arts .5 and academic electives 5.

2015-2016 Annual costs. Tuition/fees: $29,800. Room/board: $7,715. Books/supplies: $1,000. Personal expenses: $2,448.

2015-2016 Financial aid. Need-based: 472 full-time freshmen applied for aid; 430 deemed to have need; 426 received aid. Average need met was 71%. Average scholarship/grant was $19,007; average loan $4,109. 63% of total undergraduate aid awarded as scholarships/grants, 37% as loans/jobs. **Non-need-based:** Awarded to 2,225 full-time undergraduates, including 591 freshmen. Scholarships awarded for academics, alumni affiliation, art, athletics, music/drama.

Application procedures. Admission: No deadline. $25 fee, may be waived for applicants with need, free for online applicants. Admission notification on a rolling basis beginning on or about 10/1. **Financial aid:** No deadline. FAFSA required. Applicants notified on a rolling basis starting 3/15; must reply within 4 week(s) of notification.

Academics. Special study options: Combined bachelor's/graduate degree, cooperative education, distance learning, double major, dual enrollment of high school students, honors, independent study, internships, liberal arts/career combination, study abroad, teacher certification program. **Credit/placement by examination:** AP, CLEP, IB, SAT, ACT, institutional tests. CLEP credit limited to students with 63 or fewer credit hours. **Support services:** Reduced course load, remedial instruction, tutoring, writing center.

Honors college/program. Admission is a competitive process by application only. Students should have at least a 1250 SAT or 27 ACT, 3.2 GPA, two letters of recommendation (one academic, one character), leadership experience and service to the church and community. Finalists will be invited for a personal interview as part of the Honors College selection process.

Majors. Biology: General, molecular. **Business:** General, accounting, business admin, entrepreneurial studies, finance, international, managerial economics, marketing. **Communications:** Communications/speech/rhetoric, media studies. **Education:** Art, early childhood, elementary, English, mathematics, middle, music, physical, science, secondary, social studies, Spanish, speech. **English:** English lit, writing. **Foreign languages:** Biblical, French, Spanish. **Health services:** Athletic training, nursing (RN). **History:** General. **Human services:** Public policy. **Math:** General. **Parks/recreation:** Exercise sciences, health/fitness. **Philosophy/religion:** Christian, philosophy. **Physical sciences:** Chemistry, physics. **Psychology:** General. **Social sciences:** Economics, political science, sociology. **Theology:** Pastoral counseling, sacred music. **Visual/performing arts:** Film/cinema/video, music, music performance, music theory/composition, piano/keyboard, studio arts, voice/opera. **Work/family studies:** Child development.

Most popular majors. Biology 17%, business/marketing 18%, health sciences 17%, parks/recreation 7%, psychology 7%.

Technology on campus. 95 workstations in dormitories, library, computer center. Dormitories wired for high-speed internet access and linked to campus network. Commuter students can connect to campus network. Online course registration, online library, helpline, repair service, wireless network available.

Student life. Freshman orientation: Available. Preregistration for classes offered. 2-day overnight summer orientation and registration. 2-1/2 day camp held off campus prior to start of classes. **Policies:** Spiritual Life Program graduation requirement for all undergraduate students. **Housing:** Guaranteed on-campus for freshmen. Coed dorms, single-sex dorms, special housing for disabled, apartments, fraternity/sorority housing, themed housing available. $200 partly refundable deposit. **Activities:** Bands, campus ministries, choral groups, dance, drama, international student organizations, music ensembles, student government, student newspaper, Christian Life on Campus, Psi Chi, Nursing Association, Black Student Fellowship, Toastmasters, Digital Eon, Vietnamese student association, Indian student association, Sisters for the Lord, Brothers Under Christ.

Athletics. NCAA. Intercollegiate: Baseball M, basketball, cheerleading, cross-country, football (tackle) M, golf, sand volleyball W, soccer, softball W, track and field, volleyball W. **Intramural:** Badminton, basketball, bowling, football (non-tackle), softball, table tennis, volleyball. **Team name:** Huskies.

Student services. Adult student services, alcohol/substance abuse counseling, chaplain/spiritual director, career counseling, student employment services, financial aid counseling, health services, placement for graduates, women's services. **Physically disabled:** Services for visually, speech, hearing impaired.

Contact. E-mail: admissions@hbu.edu
Phone: (281) 649-3211 Toll-free number: (800) 969-3210
Ed Borges, Director of Admissions, Houston Baptist University, 7502 Fondren Road, Houston, TX 77074-3298

Howard Payne University
Brownwood, Texas
www.hputx.edu   CB code: 6278

- Private 4-year university and liberal arts college affiliated with the Baptist faith
- Residential campus in large town
- 951 degree-seeking undergraduates
- 86% of applicants admitted
- SAT or ACT (ACT writing optional) required

General. Founded in 1889. Regionally accredited. **Degrees:** 194 bachelor's awarded; master's offered. **Location:** 150 miles from Dallas, 77 miles from Abilene. **Calendar:** Semester, limited summer session. **Full-time faculty:** 84 total; 67% have terminal degrees, 6% minority, 39% women. **Part-time faculty:** 77 total; 30% have terminal degrees, 12% minority, 38% women. **Class size:** 73% < 20, 25% 20-39, 1% 40-49, less than 1% 50-99. **Special facilities:** General Douglas MacArthur Academy of Freedom, Faith and Life Leadership Center, art center, Center for Social Justice.

Freshman class profile. 935 applied, 802 admitted, 275 enrolled.

Mid 50% test scores			
SAT critical reading:	420-530	GPA 3.0-3.49:	36%
SAT math:	430-530	GPA 2.0-2.99:	27%
ACT composite:	18-23	Rank in top quarter:	33%
GPA 3.75 or higher:	17%	Rank in top tenth:	17%
GPA 3.50-3.74:	19%	Out-of-state:	1%
		Live on campus:	84%

Basis for selection. Average GPA of 3.0 on 4.0 scale, ACT composite score of 19, or SAT score of 910 (exclusive of Writing). ACT/SAT scores used to exempt students from placement tests in English, math, or reading. Interview may be required by admissions committee for select applicants. Audition required for music program. **Home schooled:** Transcript of courses and grades required. **Learning Disabled:** If a student meets requirements for admission, accommodations may be initiated by Student Success Services.

High school preparation. College-preparatory program recommended. Recommended units include English 4, mathematics 4, social studies 3, history 2, science 4 (laboratory 3), foreign language 2, computer science .5, visual/performing arts 1, academic electives 4.5.

2015-2016 Annual costs. Tuition/fees: $25,600. Room/board: $7,489.

2014-2015 Financial aid. Need-based: 288 full-time freshmen applied for aid; 270 deemed to have need; 269 received aid. Average need met was 78%. Average scholarship/grant was $17,215; average loan $3,412. 72% of total undergraduate aid awarded as scholarships/grants, 28% as loans/jobs. **Non-need-based:** Awarded to 297 full-time undergraduates, including 80 freshmen. Scholarships awarded for academics, alumni affiliation, art, leadership, music/drama, religious affiliation, state residency.

Application procedures. Admission: Priority date 3/15; no deadline. No application fee. Application must be submitted online. Admission notification on a rolling basis beginning on or about 10/15. Must reply by May 1 or within 2 week(s) if notified thereafter. **Financial aid:** No deadline. FAFSA, institutional form required. Applicants notified on a rolling basis starting 2/15; must reply within 2 week(s) of notification.

Academics. Special study options: Accelerated study, distance learning, double major, dual enrollment of high school students, honors, independent study, internships, liberal arts/career combination, study abroad, teacher certification program. Extension classes in El Paso and New Braunfels. **Credit/placement by examination:** AP, CLEP, IB, SAT, ACT, institutional tests. 15 credit hours maximum toward associate degree, 30 toward bachelor's. **Support services:** Reduced course load, remedial instruction, study skills assistance, tutoring, writing center.

Honors college/program. Academy of Freedom, minimum 24 composite ACT, 1100 SAT combined Math and Critical Reading, priority application deadline 2/1, 25 students maximum at freshman level.

Majors. Biology: General. **Business:** General, accounting, business admin, finance, management information systems, marketing. **Communications:** Communications/speech/rhetoric, digital media, media studies, organizational, persuasive communications, radio/TV. **Computer sciences:** General, computer science. **Education:** Art, biology, business, computer, drama/dance, elementary, English, ESL, history, mathematics, middle, music, physical, secondary, social studies, Spanish, speech. **Engineering:** Engineering mechanics. **English:** English lit. **Foreign languages:** Ancient Greek, Biblical, Spanish. **Health services:** Athletic training, health care admin. **History:** General, American, European. **Human services:** Public policy, social work. **Liberal arts:** Arts/sciences, humanities. **Math:** General. **Parks/recreation:** Health/fitness, sports admin. **Philosophy/religion:** Christian, philosophy. **Physical sciences:** Chemistry. **Protective services:** Criminal justice. **Psychology:** General. **Social sciences:** General, anthropology, criminology, international relations, political science, sociology. **Theology:** Bible, missionary, religious ed, sacred music, theology, youth ministry. **Visual/performing arts:** Art, dramatic, music performance, piano/keyboard, studio arts, voice/opera. **Work/family studies:** Family studies.

Most popular majors. Business/marketing 20%, education 19%, parks/recreation 6%, psychology 7%, social sciences 8%, theological studies 9%.

Technology on campus. 260 workstations in dormitories, library, computer center, student center. Dormitories wired for high-speed internet access and linked to campus network. Commuter students can connect to campus network. Online library, helpline, repair service, wireless network available.

Student life. Freshman orientation: Mandatory. Preregistration for classes offered. Orientation is held 5 days before the fall semester classes begin. Also offered one afternoon in January prior to the beginning of the spring semester. **Policies:** Chapel is an important part of student life at HPU and is a required element for graduation. Four (4) semesters of Chapel credits are required to graduate. A team of University administrators, under the auspices of the Office of Student Life, direct Chapel. The mission of Chapel is to promote a vibrant relationship with Jesus Christ in a praise and worship format. Occasionally, a Student Assembly will be held for the purpose of promoting cultural awareness, academic life, student activities, and world events in a student-friendly setting that integrates faith and life. Religious observance required. **Housing:** Guaranteed on-campus for freshmen. Single-sex dorms, apartments available. $100 nonrefundable deposit, deadline 6/1. **Activities:** Bands, campus ministries, choral groups, drama, music ensembles, Model UN, musical theater, student government, student newspaper, Baptist Student Ministry, Fellowship of Christian Athletes, student activities council, Student Government Association, AGT, Kappa Kappa Psi, Tau Beta Sigma, Alpha Psi Omega.

Athletics. NCAA. **Intercollegiate:** Baseball M, basketball, cheerleading, football (tackle) M, golf, soccer, softball W, tennis, volleyball W. **Intramural:** Basketball, football (non-tackle), softball, table tennis, tennis, ultimate frisbee, volleyball. **Team name:** Yellow Jackets.

Student services. Adult student services, chaplain/spiritual director, career counseling, student employment services, financial aid counseling, health services, personal counseling, placement for graduates.

Contact. E-mail: enroll@hputx.edu
Phone: (325) 649-8020 Toll-free number: (800) 880-4478
Fax: (325) 649-8901
PJ Gramling, Director of Admission, Howard Payne University, 1000 Fisk Street, Brownwood, TX 76801-2794

Huston-Tillotson University
Austin, Texas
www.htu.edu

CB member
CB code: 6280

- Private 4-year business and liberal arts college affiliated with the United Methodist Church
- Residential campus in very large city
- 968 degree-seeking undergraduates: 5% part-time, 56% women, 67% African American, 23% Hispanic/Latino, 4% international
- 6 degree-seeking graduate students
- 47% of applicants admitted
- SAT or ACT (ACT writing optional) required

General. Founded in 1876. Regionally accredited. **Degrees:** 17 bachelor's awarded; master's offered. **ROTC:** Army, Naval, Air Force. **Location:** 80 miles from San Antonio. **Calendar:** Semester, extensive summer session. **Full-time faculty:** 50 total; 76% have terminal degrees, 58% minority, 54% women. **Part-time faculty:** 46 total; 41% have terminal degrees, 37% minority, 67% women. **Class size:** 75% < 20, 25% 20-39.

Freshman class profile. 2,210 applied, 1,048 admitted, 146 enrolled.

Mid 50% test scores			
SAT critical reading:	330-440	GPA 3.0-3.49:	35%
SAT math:	350-460	GPA 2.0-2.99:	50%
ACT composite:	14-18	Return as sophomores:	54%
GPA 3.75 or higher:	5%	Out-of-state:	7%
GPA 3.50-3.74:	8%	Live on campus:	77%
		International:	1%

Basis for selection. School achievement record important. Test scores and interview considered.

High school preparation. College-preparatory program recommended. Required units include English 3, mathematics 3 and science 3. Health, physical education recommended.

2015-2016 Annual costs. Tuition/fees: $14,346. Room/board: $7,568. Books/supplies: $1,040. Personal expenses: $2,780.

2014-2015 Financial aid. Need-based: Average scholarship/grant was $6,089; average loan $4,068. 47% of total undergraduate aid awarded as scholarships/grants, 53% as loans/jobs. **Non-need-based:** Scholarships awarded for academics, athletics, leadership, minority status, music/drama, religious affiliation, state residency.

Application procedures. Admission: Priority date 3/15; deadline 5/1 (postmark date). $25 fee, may be waived for applicants with need. Admission notification by 5/1. Admission notification on a rolling basis beginning on or about 1/1. Must reply by May 1 or within 1 week(s) if notified thereafter. **Financial aid:** Priority date 3/15; no closing date. FAFSA, institutional form required. Applicants notified on a rolling basis starting 4/8; must reply within 2 week(s) of notification.

Academics. Special study options: Cooperative education, cross-registration, distance learning, double major, dual enrollment of high school students, ESL, external degree, honors, independent study, internships, liberal arts/career combination, study abroad, teacher certification program. **Credit/placement by examination:** AP, CLEP, SAT, ACT, institutional tests. 15 credit hours maximum toward bachelor's degree. **Support services:** Learning center, pre-admission summer program, remedial instruction, tutoring, writing center.

Majors. Biology: General. **Business:** Accounting, business admin, international, marketing. **Computer sciences:** General, computer science. **Education:** General, physical. **English:** Writing. **History:** General. **Math:** General. **Physical sciences:** Chemistry. **Protective services:** Criminal justice. **Psychology:** General. **Social sciences:** General, political science, sociology. **Visual/performing arts:** Music.

Most popular majors. Business/marketing 26%, education 9%, parks/recreation 21%, psychology 6%, security/protective services 12%, social sciences 6%.

Technology on campus. 400 workstations in dormitories, library, computer center, student center. Dormitories wired for high-speed internet access and linked to campus network. Commuter students can connect to campus network. Online library, helpline, wireless network available.

Student life. Freshman orientation: Mandatory. Preregistration for classes offered. **Housing:** Guaranteed on-campus for all undergraduates. Single-sex dorms, wellness housing available. $150 fully refundable deposit, deadline 5/1. **Activities:** Bands, campus ministries, choral groups, dance, international student organizations, literary magazine, student government, NAACP student chapter, Toastmasters.

Athletics. NAIA. **Intercollegiate:** Baseball M, basketball, soccer, track and field, volleyball W. **Intramural:** Basketball, cheerleading W, soccer, softball, table tennis, volleyball. **Team name:** Rams.

Student services. Adult student services, career counseling, student employment services, financial aid counseling, health services, personal counseling, placement for graduates, veterans' counselor. **Physically disabled:** Services for visually, hearing impaired.

Contact. E-mail: admission@htu.edu
Phone: (512) 505-3028 Toll-free number: (877) 505-3028
Fax: (512) 505-3192
Dwayne Shorter, Director of Admission, Huston-Tillotson University, 900 Chicon Street, Austin, TX 78702-2795

Jarvis Christian College
Hawkins, Texas
www.jarvis.edu

CB code: 6319

- Private 4-year liberal arts college affiliated with the Christian Church (Disciples of Christ)
- Residential campus in rural community
- 863 degree-seeking undergraduates: 2% part-time, 52% women, 83% African American, 11% Hispanic/Latino

General. Founded in 1912. Regionally accredited. **Degrees:** 65 bachelor's awarded. **Location:** 100 miles from Dallas; 100 miles from Shreveport,

Louisiana. **Calendar:** Semester, limited summer session. **Full-time faculty:** 32 total; 75% have terminal degrees, 69% minority, 28% women. **Part-time faculty:** 5 total; 40% have terminal degrees, 80% minority, 40% women. **Class size:** 48% < 20, 40% 20-39, 7% 40-49, 4% 50-99, less than 1% >100. **Special facilities:** Observatory, natatorium, archives of black Christian church (Disciples of Christ), East Texas Natural History Museum.

Freshman class profile. 983 applied, 535 admitted, 251 enrolled.

Mid 50% test scores		GPA 2.0-2.99:	53%
SAT critical reading:	300-400	Rank in top quarter:	16%
SAT math:	320-400	Rank in top tenth:	1%
SAT writing:	310-390	End year in good standing:	46%
ACT composite:	13-17	Return as sophomores:	53%
GPA 3.75 or higher:	5%	Out-of-state:	17%
GPA 3.50-3.74:	8%	Live on campus:	88%
GPA 3.0-3.49:	25%		

Basis for selection. Open admission, but selective for some programs. To be admitted to the Teacher Education Program, all students must have A degree plan signed by the student's adviser and Declaration of Major Form, a copy of an official transcript, which reflects completion of 60 semester hours of general education coursework with a 2.50 cumulative grade point average, a record of the Texas Higher Education Assessment (THEA) examination, which reflects achievement of a minimum score of 255 in the reading section and a minimum score of 230 on the mathematics and writing, respectively. (This requirement can be met by other tests accepted for the Texas Success Initiative), a philosophy of education paper, three (3) recommendations from content and professional education faculty with whom the student has taken classes. **Home schooled:** State high school equivalency certificate required.

High school preparation. 21 units required. Required units include English 4, mathematics 3, social studies 1, history 1.5, science 2, visual/performing arts 1, academic electives 8.5.

2015-2016 Annual costs. Tuition/fees: $11,369. Room/board: $8,183. Books/supplies: $1,000.

2014-2015 Financial aid. Need-based: 181 full-time freshmen applied for aid; 181 deemed to have need; 175 received aid. Average need met was 96%. Average scholarship/grant was $9,387; average loan $9,923. 46% of total undergraduate aid awarded as scholarships/grants, 54% as loans/jobs. **Non-need-based:** Awarded to 133 full-time undergraduates, including 43 freshmen. Scholarships awarded for academics, athletics, religious affiliation. **Additional information:** High school transcript required for scholarship consideration.

Application procedures. Admission: No deadline. $50 fee. Admission notification on a rolling basis beginning on or about 4/1. **Financial aid:** No deadline. FAFSA required. Applicants notified on a rolling basis starting 5/1; must reply by 5/30 or within 2 week(s) of notification.

Academics. Special study options: Cross-registration, double major, dual enrollment of high school students, honors, study abroad, teacher certification program. **Credit/placement by examination:** AP, CLEP, IB, institutional tests. 18 credit hours maximum toward bachelor's degree. **Support services:** Learning center, pre-admission summer program, remedial instruction, study skills assistance, tutoring, writing center.

Majors. Biology: General. **Business:** Business admin. **Education:** General, biology, business, elementary, English, history, mathematics, middle, physical, reading, secondary, special ed. **English:** English lit. **History:** General. **Human services:** Social work. **Math:** General. **Philosophy/religion:** Religion. **Physical sciences:** Chemistry. **Protective services:** Criminal justice. **Social sciences:** Sociology.

Most popular majors. Biology 9%, business/marketing 21%, education 37%, security/protective services 17%.

Technology on campus. 359 workstations in dormitories, library, computer center. Dormitories wired for high-speed internet access and linked to campus network. Helpline, wireless network available.

Student life. Freshman orientation: Mandatory. Preregistration for classes offered. Orientation takes place immediately after registration and lasts for about three days. **Policies:** Religious services available, regardless of denomination. Religious observance required. **Housing:** Guaranteed on-campus for all undergraduates. Coed dorms, single-sex dorms, special housing for disabled, apartments, wellness housing available. $200 nonrefundable deposit, deadline 8/1. Single parents housing available on limited basis. **Activities:** Marching band, campus ministries, music ensembles, student government, Men on the Frontline, Beta Beta Beta Biology Honor Society, Pre-Alumni, National Institute of Science, Beta Kappa Chi National Scientific Honor Society, minority student leadership organization, student activity counsel board, Enactus, Sisters of Strength, National Association of Blacks in Criminal Justice.

Athletics. NAIA. **Intercollegiate:** Baseball M, basketball, bowling, cheerleading, cross-country, golf M, soccer, softball W, volleyball. **Intramural:** Baseball M, basketball, volleyball. **Team name:** Bulldogs.

Student services. Alcohol/substance abuse counseling, chaplain/spiritual director, career counseling, services for economically disadvantaged, student employment services, financial aid counseling, health services, minority student services, personal counseling, placement for graduates, women's services. **Physically disabled:** Services for visually, speech, hearing impaired.

Contact. E-mail: recruitment@jarvis.edu
Phone: (903) 730-4890 ext. 2201 Fax: (903) 769-1282
Brandon Byrd, Director of Recruitment and Enrollment Management, Jarvis Christian College, PO Box 1470, Hawkins, TX 75765-1470

The King's University
Southlake, Texas
www.tku.edu
CB code: 3896

▶ Private 4-year Bible and seminary college affiliated with the nondenominational tradition
▶ Commuter campus in very large city
▶ 473 degree-seeking undergraduates
▶ Application essay required

General. Regionally accredited; also accredited by ABHE, TRACS. Evangelical Charismatic institution. **Degrees:** 18 bachelor's, 4 associate awarded; master's, professional offered. **Location:** 20 miles from downtown Los Angeles. **Calendar:** Quarter, extensive summer session. **Full-time faculty:** 9 total. **Part-time faculty:** 49 total.

Basis for selection. Demonstration of commitment to Christian faith required, essays, references important. SAT or ACT recommended. **Home schooled:** Statement describing home school structure and mission, transcript of courses and grades required.

2015-2016 Annual costs. Tuition/fees: $12,690. Books/supplies: $1,000. Personal expenses: $2,114.

Financial aid. Additional information: Specific scholarships may require specific essays.

Application procedures. Admission: No deadline. $75 fee. Admission notification on a rolling basis. Must reply by May 1 or within 4 week(s) if notified thereafter. Must reply within 30 days. **Financial aid:** No deadline. FAFSA required. Applicants notified on a rolling basis; must reply within 4 week(s) of notification.

Academics. Special study options: Accelerated study, distance learning, external degree, independent study, internships, study abroad. **Credit/placement by examination:** AP, CLEP, IB, institutional tests. 45 credit hours maximum toward associate degree, 45 toward bachelor's. **Support services:** Pre-admission summer program, reduced course load, remedial instruction, study skills assistance.

Majors. Theology: Bible.

Technology on campus. Commuter students can connect to campus network. Online course registration, online library, helpline, wireless network available.

Student life. Freshman orientation: Mandatory. Preregistration for classes offered. Held the first week of the Fall Quarter. **Policies:** Drug-and alcohol-free campus. Religious observance required. **Activities:** Campus ministries, music ensembles, student government, student newspaper, C.S. Lewis club, women in ministry group, Delta Epsilon, National Association of Evangelicals.

Student services. Adult student services, alcohol/substance abuse counseling, chaplain/spiritual director, career counseling, student employment services, financial aid counseling, personal counseling, placement for graduates, veterans' counselor, women's services.

Contact. E-mail: admissions@tku.edu
Phone: (817) 552-7376
Marilyn Chappell, Director of Admissions, The King's University, 2121 E Southlake Blvd, Southlake, TX 76092

Lamar University
Beaumont, Texas
www.lamar.edu

CB member
CB code: 6360

- Public 4-year university
- Commuter campus in small city
- 9,009 degree-seeking undergraduates: 30% part-time, 58% women, 27% African American, 5% Asian American, 15% Hispanic/Latino, 2% Multiracial, non-Hispanic, 2% international
- 5,175 degree-seeking graduate students
- 79% of applicants admitted
- SAT or ACT (ACT writing optional) required
- 32% graduate within 6 years

General. Founded in 1923. Regionally accredited. **Degrees:** 1,711 bachelor's, 7 associate awarded; master's, professional, doctoral offered. **ROTC:** Air Force. **Location:** 75 miles from Houston. **Calendar:** Semester, limited summer session. **Full-time faculty:** 414 total; 54% have terminal degrees, 28% minority, 43% women. **Part-time faculty:** 103 total; 12% have terminal degrees, 21% minority, 59% women. **Class size:** 32% < 20, 48% 20-39, 9% 40-49, 9% 50-99, 2% >100. **Special facilities:** Hazardous waste research center, city museum.

Freshman class profile. 4,529 applied, 3,583 admitted, 1,474 enrolled.

Mid 50% test scores			
SAT critical reading:	420-530	Rank in top tenth:	16%
SAT math:	440-540	Return as sophomores:	58%
SAT writing:	400-500	Out-of-state:	2%
ACT composite:	18-23	Live on campus:	57%
Rank in top quarter:	25%	International:	1%

Basis for selection. High school class rank, SAT scores, and completion of 14 high school units of college preparatory courses. SAT Subject Tests recommended for students with strong academic background. Interview required for early entry and of students accepted with GED tests. **Home schooled:** Transcript of courses and grades required. Must submit SAT or ACT.

High school preparation. College-preparatory program required. 14 units required. Required units include English 4, mathematics 3, social studies 2.5, science 2, academic electives 2.5.

2016-2017 Annual costs. Tuition/fees (projected): $9,362; $21,062 out-of-state. Room/board: $7,870. Books/supplies: $1,000. Personal expenses: $1,800.

2014-2015 Financial aid. All financial aid based on need. 1,098 full-time freshmen applied for aid; 858 deemed to have need; 843 received aid. Average need met was 50%. Average scholarship/grant was $6,750; average loan $2,758. 62% of total undergraduate aid awarded as scholarships/grants, 38% as loans/jobs.

Application procedures. Admission: Closing date 8/11. $25 fee, may be waived for applicants with need. Application must be submitted online. Admission notification on a rolling basis. **Financial aid:** Priority date 4/1; no closing date. FAFSA, institutional form required. Applicants notified on a rolling basis starting 4/1; must reply within 2 week(s) of notification.

Academics. Special study options: Accelerated study, cooperative education, distance learning, double major, dual enrollment of high school students, ESL, honors, independent study, internships, study abroad, teacher certification program. **Credit/placement by examination:** AP, CLEP, IB, institutional tests. 15 credit hours maximum toward associate degree, 30 toward bachelor's. **Support services:** Learning center, pre-admission summer program, reduced course load, remedial instruction, study skills assistance, tutoring, writing center. Student Support Services, STARS.

Honors college/program. SAT of at least 1200 (Reading and Math) or ACT 27, top 10% of graduating class, record of academic achievement and community involvement, two letters of recommendation from teachers, counselors, administrators, or supervisors, transfers must have 3.5 GPA, International students TOEFL score 525.

Majors. Biology: General, biochemistry. **Business:** General, accounting, business admin, entrepreneurial studies, finance, human resources, management information systems, managerial economics, marketing, operations, retailing. **Communications:** General, advertising. **Computer sciences:** General. **Conservation:** Environmental science. **Engineering:** Chemical, civil, construction, electrical, industrial, mechanical. **English:** English lit. **Foreign languages:** General, American Sign Language. **Health services:** General, communication disorders, nursing (RN). **History:** General. **Human services:** Social work. **Math:** General. **Parks/recreation:** Exercise sciences, sports admin. **Physical sciences:** Chemistry, forensic chemistry, geology, physics.

Protective services: Criminal justice. **Psychology:** General. **Social sciences:** Political science, sociology. **Visual/performing arts:** Dramatic, graphic design, music, music management, studio arts. **Work/family studies:** Clothing/textiles, family studies, institutional food production.

Most popular majors. Business/marketing 15%, engineering/engineering technologies 11%, health sciences 16%, interdisciplinary studies 16%, liberal arts 6%, security/protective services 6%.

Technology on campus. 644 workstations in dormitories, library, computer center, student center. Dormitories wired for high-speed internet access and linked to campus network. Commuter students can connect to campus network. Online course registration, online library, helpline, repair service, student web hosting, wireless network available.

Student life. Freshman orientation: Available, $50 fee. Preregistration for classes offered. One-day program available June-August. **Housing:** Guaranteed on-campus for freshmen. Coed dorms, single-sex dorms, special housing for disabled, wellness housing available. $150 deposit, deadline 8/1. **Activities:** Bands, campus ministries, choral groups, dance, drama, film society, international student organizations, literary magazine, music ensembles, musical theater, opera, radio station, student government, student newspaper, symphony orchestra, TV station, Catholic Student Union, Church of Latter-Day Saints, Episcopal Center, Church of Christ Student Center, Wesley Foundation, International Student Advisory Council.

Athletics. NCAA. **Intercollegiate:** Baseball M, basketball, cross-country, football (tackle) M, golf, soccer W, softball W, tennis, track and field, volleyball W. **Intramural:** Badminton, basketball, cricket, cross-country, football (non-tackle) M, racquetball, soccer, softball, swimming, table tennis, tennis, track and field, volleyball, weight lifting. **Team name:** Cardinals.

Student services. Adult student services, alcohol/substance abuse counseling, career counseling, student employment services, health services, personal counseling, placement for graduates, veterans' counselor. **Physically disabled:** Services for visually, speech, hearing impaired.

Contact. E-mail: admissions@lamar.edu
Phone: (409) 880-8888 Fax: (409) 880-8463
Melissa Gallien, Director of Admissions, Lamar University, Box 10009, Beaumont, TX 77710

LeTourneau University
Longview, Texas
www.letu.edu

CB code: 6365

- Private 4-year university affiliated with the nondenominational tradition
- Residential campus in small city
- 1,933 degree-seeking undergraduates: 36% part-time, 47% women, 10% African American, 1% Asian American, 10% Hispanic/Latino, 4% Multiracial, non-Hispanic, 3% international
- 509 degree-seeking graduate students
- 45% of applicants admitted
- 51% graduate within 6 years

General. Founded in 1946. Regionally accredited. **Degrees:** 452 bachelor's, 11 associate awarded; master's offered. **Location:** 120 miles from Dallas, 60 miles from Shreveport, Louisiana. **Calendar:** Semester, extensive summer session. **Full-time faculty:** 90 total; 87% have terminal degrees, 13% minority, 20% women. **Part-time faculty:** 126 total; 52% have terminal degrees, 8% minority, 40% women. **Class size:** 68% < 20, 28% 20-39, 2% 40-49, 2% 50-99, less than 1% >100.

Freshman class profile. 2,203 applied, 1,002 admitted, 301 enrolled.

Mid 50% test scores			
SAT critical reading:	500-630	GPA 2.0-2.99:	8%
SAT math:	520-650	Rank in top quarter:	53%
SAT writing:	460-600	Rank in top tenth:	32%
ACT composite:	22-29	Return as sophomores:	69%
GPA 3.75 or higher:	42%	Out-of-state:	33%
GPA 3.50-3.74:	21%	Live on campus:	90%
GPA 3.0-3.49:	29%	International:	3%

Basis for selection. Applicants should rank in top half of high school graduating class, have minimum ACT of 20 or minimum SAT of 950 (exclusive of Writing), and GPA of 2.5.

High school preparation. College-preparatory program recommended.

2015-2016 Annual costs. Tuition/fees: $27,900. Room/board: $9,580.

2015-2016 Financial aid. Need-based: 247 full-time freshmen applied for aid; 211 deemed to have need; 211 received aid. Average need met was 78%. Average scholarship/grant was $18,937; average loan $4,214. 56% of total undergraduate aid awarded as scholarships/grants, 44% as loans/jobs. **Non-need-based:** Awarded to 134 full-time undergraduates, including 44 freshmen. Scholarships awarded for academics, leadership, minority status, religious affiliation, state residency.

Application procedures. Admission: No deadline. No application fee. Admission notification on a rolling basis beginning on or about 9/15. **Financial aid:** Priority date 2/15; no closing date. FAFSA required. Applicants notified on a rolling basis starting 3/15; must reply within 2 week(s) of notification.

Academics. Special study options: Accelerated study, combined bachelor's/graduate degree, cooperative education, cross-registration, distance learning, double major, dual enrollment of high school students, ESL, exchange student, honors, independent study, internships, study abroad, teacher certification program. **Credit/placement by examination:** AP, CLEP, IB, SAT, ACT, institutional tests. Credit must be established by end of student's first year at school. **Support services:** Reduced course load, remedial instruction, study skills assistance, tutoring, writing center. Math lab, online tutoring, peer advisers, supplemental instruction.

Honors college/program. Honors College participants must complete at least 16 credit hours of honors courses. This includes 12 hours of Honors general education requirements (such as Honors Bible, history, and English courses that count toward the student's degree program), as well as four one-hour Honors seminars. In general, admission to the Honors College requires a minimum ACT score of 27 or SAT score of 1220 and a high school GPA of 3.65. However, the admission committee will review all applications to the Honors College. Criteria for admission are as follows: a history of academic engagement; a history of community engagement; and potential for academic, campus, community, and global engagement.

Majors. Biology: General. **Business:** Accounting, business admin, management information systems, marketing. **Communications:** Media studies. **Computer sciences:** General, computer science. **Education:** Biology, business, chemistry, computer, elementary, English, history, mathematics, middle, multi-level teacher, physical, science, secondary. **Engineering:** General, computer, electrical, mechanical. **English:** English lit. **Health services:** Clinical nurse specialist. **History:** General. **Math:** General. **Parks/recreation:** Exercise sciences, health/fitness, sports admin. **Physical sciences:** Chemistry, physical chemistry. **Psychology:** General. **Social sciences:** Criminology. **Theology:** Bible.

Most popular majors. Business/marketing 30%, education 10%, engineering/engineering technologies 24%, psychology 6%, trade and industry 7%.

Technology on campus. Dormitories wired for high-speed internet access and linked to campus network. Commuter students can connect to campus network. Online course registration, online library, helpline, wireless network available.

Student life. Freshman orientation: Mandatory. Preregistration for classes offered. **Policies:** Religious observance required. **Housing:** Guaranteed on-campus for all undergraduates. Single-sex dorms, special housing for disabled, apartments, fraternity/sorority housing, themed housing available. $150 fully refundable deposit. **Activities:** Jazz band, campus ministries, choral groups, drama, international student organizations, student government, student newspaper.

Athletics. NCAA. **Intercollegiate:** Baseball M, basketball, cross-country, golf, soccer, softball W, tennis, volleyball W. **Intramural:** Badminton, basketball, cross-country, football (non-tackle), golf, racquetball, sand volleyball, soccer, softball, swimming, table tennis, tennis, volleyball. **Team name:** YellowJackets.

Student services. Chaplain/spiritual director, career counseling, student employment services, financial aid counseling, health services, personal counseling, placement for graduates, veterans' counselor. **Physically disabled:** Services for visually, speech, hearing impaired.

Contact. E-mail: admissions@letu.edu
Phone: (903) 233-4300 Toll-free number: (800) 759-8811
Fax: (903) 233-4301
LeTourneau University, PO Box 7001, Longview, TX 75607-7001

Lubbock Christian University
Lubbock, Texas
www.lcu.edu   CB code: 6378

- Private 4-year university and liberal arts college affiliated with the Church of Christ
- Commuter campus in small city

- 1,496 degree-seeking undergraduates: 15% part-time, 59% women, 5% African American, 1% Asian American, 25% Hispanic/Latino, 1% Native American, 2% international
- 462 degree-seeking graduate students
- 96% of applicants admitted
- SAT or ACT (ACT writing optional) required
- 42% graduate within 6 years; 23% enter graduate study

General. Founded in 1957. Regionally accredited. **Degrees:** 375 bachelor's awarded; master's offered. **ROTC:** Army, Air Force. **Location:** 300 miles from Dallas; 325 miles from Albuquerque, NM. **Calendar:** Semester, limited summer session. **Full-time faculty:** 99 total; 73% have terminal degrees, 4% minority, 43% women. **Part-time faculty:** 80 total; 26% have terminal degrees, 11% minority, 44% women. **Class size:** 62% < 20, 33% 20-39, 2% 40-49, 3% 50-99.

Freshman class profile. 867 applied, 833 admitted, 275 enrolled.

Mid 50% test scores			
SAT critical reading:	440-550	Rank in top quarter:	43%
SAT math:	430-560	Rank in top tenth:	19%
SAT writing:	420-550	End year in good standing:	88%
ACT composite:	19-25	Return as sophomores:	73%
GPA 3.75 or higher:	31%	Out-of-state:	12%
GPA 3.50-3.74:	31%	Live on campus:	77%
GPA 3.0-3.49:	28%	International:	1%
GPA 2.0-2.99:	10%	Fraternities:	33%
		Sororities:	29%

Basis for selection. ACT or SAT required and minimum scores are established; evidence of secondary completion required. For applicants applying after June 1 that have ACT of 15-17 or SAT (Critical Reading and Math) of 710-850, written appeal and essay required for consideration. **Home schooled:** Transcript of courses and grades required.

High school preparation. College-preparatory program recommended. 21 units recommended. Recommended units include English 4, mathematics 3, social studies 1, history 2, science 3 (laboratory 2), foreign language 2, computer science 1, visual/performing arts 1 and academic electives 2.

2015-2016 Annual costs. Tuition/fees: $20,360. Room/board: $6,070. Books/supplies: $1,100. Personal expenses: $2,388.

2014-2015 Financial aid. Need-based: 176 full-time freshmen applied for aid; 143 deemed to have need; 143 received aid. Average need met was 69%. Average scholarship/grant was $10,419; average loan $4,216. 36% of total undergraduate aid awarded as scholarships/grants, 64% as loans/jobs. **Non-need-based:** Awarded to 323 full-time undergraduates, including 73 freshmen. Scholarships awarded for academics, athletics, leadership, music/drama, religious affiliation.

Application procedures. Admission: Closing date 6/1 (receipt date). $25 fee, may be waived for applicants with need. Admission notification on a rolling basis beginning on or about 11/1. Must reply by 6/1. $200 non-refundable tuition advance due by 6/1 or, if accepted after 6/1, within two weeks of acceptance, to register for classes. **Financial aid:** Priority date 6/1; no closing date. FAFSA, institutional form required. Applicants notified on a rolling basis starting 3/1.

Academics. Special study options: Distance learning, double major, dual enrollment of high school students, honors, internships, liberal arts/career combination, study abroad, teacher certification program. Biblical studies. **Credit/placement by examination:** AP, CLEP, IB, SAT, ACT, institutional tests. 45 credit hours maximum toward bachelor's degree. **Support services:** Learning center, reduced course load, remedial instruction, study skills assistance, tutoring, writing center.

Honors college/program. Minimum of 27 composite on ACT or 1210 on SAT (Critical Reading, Math); 61 honors students admitted in Fall 2015; honors designation can be obtained with any degree by completing 15 hours of honors-specific coursework.

Majors. Biology: General, biochemistry, biomedical sciences. **Business:** Accounting, business admin, finance, financial planning, information resources management, marketing, organizational leadership. **Communications:** Digital media, media studies, organizational. **Computer sciences:** General. **Conservation:** General. **Education:** Agricultural, art, drama/dance, early childhood, elementary, middle, music, physical, secondary, Spanish, special ed. **Engineering:** General. **English:** Creative writing, general lit, technical writing, writing. **Health services:** Athletic training, clinical lab science, nursing (RN), predental, premedicine, prenursing, preoccupational therapy, prepharmacy, prephysical therapy, preveterinary. **History:** General. **Human services:** Social work. **Liberal arts:** Humanities. **Math:** General. **Parks/recreation:** Health/fitness, sports admin, sports studies. **Physical sciences:** Chemistry. **Protective services:** Law enforcement admin. **Psychology:** General. **Social sciences:** Economics. **Theology:** Bible, missionary, theology, youth ministry. **Visual/performing arts:** Design, music, music management. **Work/family studies:** Family systems.

Most popular majors. Business/marketing 15%, education 13%, health sciences 27%, parks/recreation 9%.

Technology on campus. 235 workstations in dormitories, library, computer center, student center. Dormitories wired for high-speed internet access and linked to campus network. Commuter students can connect to campus network. Online course registration, online library, helpline, repair service, wireless network available.

Student life. Freshman orientation: Mandatory, $110 fee. Preregistration for classes offered. Week-long orientation held the week before fall semester begins. **Policies:** Chapel attendance required for full-time in-residence students age 24 or under. Religious observance required. **Housing:** Guaranteed on-campus for freshmen. Single-sex dorms, apartments, wellness housing available. **Activities:** Bands, campus ministries, choral groups, drama, international student organizations, music ensembles, musical theater, radio station, student government, student newspaper, Minority Student Alliance, Paisano, College Republicans, Aggie club, International justice mission, Enactus, pre-health professionals club, Student Senate, pre-vet club.

Athletics. NCAA. **Intercollegiate:** Baseball M, basketball, cheerleading, cross-country, golf, soccer, softball W, volleyball W. **Intramural:** Badminton, basketball, football (non-tackle), golf, handball, sand volleyball, softball, ultimate frisbee, volleyball. **Team name:** Chaparrals.

Student services. Adult student services, alcohol/substance abuse counseling, chaplain/spiritual director, career counseling, student employment services, financial aid counseling, health services, personal counseling, placement for graduates, veterans' counselor. **Physically disabled:** Services for visually, speech, hearing impaired.

Contact. E-mail: admissions@lcu.edu
Phone: (806) 720-7151 Toll-free number: (800) 933-7601 ext. 7151
Fax: (806) 720-7162
Chris Hayes, Director of Recruiting, Lubbock Christian University, 5601 19th Street, Lubbock, TX 79407-2099

McMurry University
Abilene, Texas
www.mcm.edu   **CB code: 6402**

▶ Private 4-year university and liberal arts college affiliated with the United Methodist Church

▶ Residential campus in small city

▶ 1,002 degree-seeking undergraduates: 9% part-time, 45% women, 18% African American, 1% Asian American, 25% Hispanic/Latino, 1% Native American, 1% Multi-racial, non-Hispanic, 1% international

▶ 2 degree-seeking graduate students

▶ 53% of applicants admitted

▶ SAT or ACT (ACT writing recommended) required

▶ 35% graduate within 6 years; 15% enter graduate study

General. Founded in 1923. Regionally accredited. Three-week May term available; additional off-campus extension at Dyess Air Force Base; part of two-member consortium providing collegiate nursing education in Texas. **Degrees:** 195 bachelor's awarded; master's offered. **Location:** 155 miles from Fort Worth, 220 miles from Austin. **Calendar:** Semester, extensive summer session. **Full-time faculty:** 80 total; 78% have terminal degrees, 45% women. **Part-time faculty:** 32 total; 16% have terminal degrees, 41% women. **Class size:** 73% < 20, 25% 20-39, 1% 40-49, less than 1% 50-99. **Special facilities:** Buffalo Gap historical village.

Freshman class profile. 1,378 applied, 735 admitted, 297 enrolled.

Mid 50% test scores			
SAT critical reading:	380-470	GPA 2.0-2.99:	27%
SAT math:	410-510	Rank in top quarter:	28%
SAT writing:	370-450	Rank in top tenth:	10%
ACT composite:	16-21	End year in good standing:	82%
GPA 3.75 or higher:	26%	Return as sophomores:	63%
GPA 3.50-3.74:	12%	Out-of-state:	3%
GPA 3.0-3.49:	35%	Live on campus:	84%
		International:	3%

Basis for selection. Evaluated based on overall academic preparation including high school rank and GPA, ACT or SAT scores, and leadership and extracurricular activities. Interview recommended for all; audition required for music and theater; portfolio required for art; interview required for admission to Honors Program. **Learning Disabled:** Appropriate documentation required for students seeking special accommodations.

High school preparation. College-preparatory program recommended. 18 units required. Required units include English 4, mathematics 4, social studies 4, science 4 and foreign language 2.

2015-2016 Annual costs. Tuition/fees: $25,588. Room/board: $8,162. Books/supplies: $1,200. Personal expenses: $2,028. **Additional information:** Students pay a block tuition rate for 12 or more hours per semester for fall and spring semesters. Required fees (other than the $175 freshmen orientation fee) are included in tuition cost. The use of a tablet PC and school-related software is also included in tuition cost.

2014-2015 Financial aid. Need-based: 145 full-time freshmen applied for aid; 141 deemed to have need; 141 received aid. Average need met was 71%. Average scholarship/grant was $16,862; average loan $4,318. 61% of total undergraduate aid awarded as scholarships/grants, 39% as loans/jobs. **Non-need-based:** Awarded to 238 full-time undergraduates, including 18 freshmen. Scholarships awarded for academics, art, athletics, job skills, leadership, music/drama, religious affiliation.

Application procedures. Admission: Priority date 3/15; deadline 8/15 (receipt date). $25 fee, may be waived for applicants with need. Admission notification on a rolling basis beginning on or about 9/1. Must reply by May 1 or within 2 week(s) if notified thereafter. **Financial aid:** Priority date 3/15; no closing date. FAFSA, institutional form required. Applicants notified on a rolling basis starting 2/15; must reply within 3 week(s) of notification.

Academics. Students receive credit for both nontraditional and traditional courses during 3-week May term. Opportunities for bachelor's degree after early admission to dental school or pharmacy school. **Special study options:** Accelerated study, combined bachelor's/graduate degree, cross-registration, double major, dual enrollment of high school students, honors, independent study, internships, liberal arts/career combination, student-designed major, teacher certification program. **Credit/placement by examination:** AP, CLEP, IB, SAT, ACT, institutional tests. 45 credit hours maximum toward bachelor's degree. With departmental approval, examinations may be given for credit in areas not covered by AP or CLEP. **Support services:** Learning center, reduced course load, remedial instruction, study skills assistance, tutoring, writing center.

Majors. Biology: General, biochemistry, biomedical sciences. **Business:** General, accounting, business admin, finance, management information systems, marketing. **Computer sciences:** General, information technology. **Education:** Art, biology, chemistry, computer, early childhood, elementary, English, history, mathematics, middle, physical, secondary, Spanish. **English:** Creative writing, English lit. **Foreign languages:** Spanish. **Health services:** Athletic training, nursing (RN). **History:** General, applied. **Math:** General. **Parks/recreation:** Exercise sciences. **Philosophy/religion:** Christian. **Physical sciences:** Chemistry, physics. **Psychology:** General. **Social sciences:** Political science, sociology. **Visual/performing arts:** Conducting, dramatic, music, studio arts.

Most popular majors. Biology 6%, business/marketing 26%, education 16%, health sciences 7%, parks/recreation 8%, psychology 8%, social sciences 8%, visual/performing arts 7%.

Technology on campus. PC or laptop required. 50 workstations in library, computer center, student center. Dormitories wired for high-speed internet access and linked to campus network. Commuter students can connect to campus network. Online library, helpline, student web hosting, wireless network available.

Student life. Freshman orientation: Available, $175 fee. Preregistration for classes offered. Summer weekend orientation plus 4-day orientation before first week of classes. **Housing:** Guaranteed on-campus for all undergraduates. Coed dorms, single-sex dorms, special housing for disabled, apartments, wellness housing available. $150 nonrefundable deposit, deadline 5/1. **Activities:** Bands, campus ministries, choral groups, drama, literary magazine, music ensembles, Model UN, musical theater, student government, student newspaper, Alpha Phi Omega, Fellowship of Christian Athletes, Religious Life, Servant Leadership, Kappa Delta Sigma, student ambassador board, Zeta Phi Beta, campus activities board.

Athletics. NCAA, NCCAA. **Intercollegiate:** Baseball M, basketball, cross-country, diving, football (tackle) M, golf, soccer, swimming, tennis, track and field, volleyball W. **Intramural:** Basketball, cheerleading, football (non-tackle), soccer, softball, ultimate frisbee, volleyball. **Team name:** War Hawks.

Student services. Alcohol/substance abuse counseling, chaplain/spiritual director, career counseling, student employment services, financial aid counseling, health services, personal counseling, placement for graduates, veterans' counselor.

Contact. E-mail: admissions@mcm.edu
Phone: (325) 793-4700 Toll-free number: (800) 460-2392
Fax: (325) 793-4701
David Heringer, Vice President for Enrollment Management, McMurry University, South 14th and Sayles Boulevard, Abilene, TX 79697-0001

Midwestern State University

Wichita Falls, Texas

CB member

www.mwsu.edu

CB code: 6408

- Public 4-year university and liberal arts college
- Commuter campus in small city
- 5,277 degree-seeking undergraduates: 23% part-time, 57% women, 14% African American, 3% Asian American, 17% Hispanic/Latino, 1% Native American, 4% Multi-racial, non-Hispanic, 9% international
- 736 degree-seeking graduate students
- 76% of applicants admitted
- SAT or ACT (ACT writing optional) required
- 44% graduate within 6 years

General. Founded in 1922. Regionally accredited. **Degrees:** 993 bachelor's, 38 associate awarded; master's offered. **ROTC:** Air Force. **Location:** 130 miles from Dallas-Fort Worth. **Calendar:** Semester, extensive summer session. **Full-time faculty:** 236 total; 80% have terminal degrees, 16% minority, 51% women. **Part-time faculty:** 109 total; 31% have terminal degrees, 17% minority, 49% women. **Class size:** 39% < 20, 43% 20-39, 6% 40-49, 12% 50-99, less than 1% >100. **Special facilities:** Kurzweil reading machine for the blind, greenhouse, 2 biologic study properties, North Texas Regional simulation center, Wichita Falls Museum of Art.

Freshman class profile. 2,854 applied, 2,169 admitted, 826 enrolled.

Mid 50% test scores		Rank in top quarter:	39%
SAT critical reading:	450-540	Rank in top tenth:	14%
SAT math:	450-550	Return as sophomores:	70%
SAT writing:	420-510	Out-of-state:	5%
ACT composite:	19-24	Live on campus:	66%
GPA 3.75 or higher:	36%	International:	3%
GPA 3.50-3.74:	17%	Fraternities:	10%
GPA 3.0-3.49:	27%	Sororities:	19%
GPA 2.0-2.99:	20%		

Basis for selection. For unconditional admission, students must graduate from accredited high school, meet requirements, submit official transcripts and ACT/SAT scores. Entrance exams determined by class rank. Texas public universities require THEA test score on file prior to enrollment unless student exempt. Audition required for applied music program. **Home schooled:** Home-schooled applicants go through individual review.

High school preparation. College-preparatory program recommended. 26 units required. Required units include English 4, mathematics 4, social studies 4, science 4, foreign language 2, visual/performing arts 1, academic electives 5.5. Speech .5, physical education 1.

2015-2016 Annual costs. Tuition/fees: $8,005; $9,955 out-of-state. Room/board: $7,070. Books/supplies: $1,350. Personal expenses: $1,818.

2015-2016 Financial aid. Need-based: 741 full-time freshmen applied for aid; 539 deemed to have need; 536 received aid. Average need met was 70%. Average scholarship/grant was $8,369; average loan $5,177. 46% of total undergraduate aid awarded as scholarships/grants, 54% as loans/jobs. **Non-need-based:** Awarded to 1,739 full-time undergraduates, including 401 freshmen. Scholarships awarded for academics, alumni affiliation, art, athletics, leadership, music/drama.

Application procedures. Admission: Priority date 3/1; deadline 8/1 (receipt date). $25 fee, may be waived for applicants with need. Admission notification on a rolling basis beginning on or about 9/1. **Financial aid:** Priority date 3/1; no closing date. FAFSA, institutional form required. Applicants notified on a rolling basis starting 4/15; must reply within 4 week(s) of notification.

Academics. Special study options: Combined bachelor's/graduate degree, distance learning, double major, dual enrollment of high school students, ESL, honors, independent study, internships, liberal arts/career combination, study abroad, teacher certification program. **Credit/placement by examination:** AP, CLEP, IB, SAT, ACT, institutional tests. 26 credit hours maximum toward associate degree, 60 toward bachelor's. **Support services:** Learning center, reduced course load, remedial instruction, study skills assistance, tutoring, writing center.

Majors. Biology: General, exercise physiology. **Business:** General, accounting, business admin, finance, management information systems, managerial economics, marketing. **Communications:** Media studies. **Computer sciences:** General. **Conservation:** Environmental science. **Education:** Bilingual, early childhood, English, mathematics, science, social studies. **Engineering:** General, mechanical. **English:** English lit. **Foreign languages:** Spanish. **Health services:** Athletic training, clinical lab science, dental hygiene, nursing (RN), predental, premedicine, prepharmacy, preveterinary, radiologic technology/medical imaging, respiratory therapy technology. **History:** General. **Human services:** Social work. **Liberal arts:** Humanities. **Math:** General. **Parks/recreation:** General, exercise sciences. **Physical sciences:** Chemistry, geology. **Protective services:** Criminal justice. **Psychology:** General. **Social sciences:** Political science, sociology. **Visual/performing arts:** Art, dramatic, music, studio arts.

Most popular majors. Business/marketing 17%, health sciences 33%, interdisciplinary studies 13%.

Technology on campus. 429 workstations in dormitories, library, computer center, student center. Dormitories wired for high-speed internet access and linked to campus network. Commuter students can connect to campus network. Online course registration, online library, wireless network available.

Student life. Freshman orientation: Mandatory. Preregistration for classes offered. **Housing:** Guaranteed on-campus for freshmen. Coed dorms, single-sex dorms, special housing for disabled, apartments, wellness housing available. $100 fully refundable deposit. Cooperative housing units for honors students and biology students available. **Activities:** Bands, campus ministries, choral groups, dance, drama, film society, international student organizations, literary magazine, music ensembles, student government, student newspaper, TV station, Methodist student foundation, Baptist student center, Student Ambassadors, black student union, organization of Hispanic students, University Democrats, College Republicans, Amnesty International.

Athletics. NCAA. **Intercollegiate:** Basketball, cross-country W, football (tackle) M, golf, soccer, softball W, tennis, volleyball W. **Intramural:** Archery, badminton, basketball, bowling, football (non-tackle), golf, soccer, softball, table tennis, tennis, ultimate frisbee, volleyball. **Team name:** Mustangs.

Student services. Alcohol/substance abuse counseling, career counseling, student employment services, financial aid counseling, health services, personal counseling, placement for graduates, veterans' counselor. **Physically disabled:** Services for visually, speech, hearing impaired.

Contact. E-mail: admissions@mwsu.edu
Phone: (940) 397-4334 Toll-free number: (800) 842-1922
Fax: (940) 397-4672
Leah Vineyard, Director of Admissions, Midwestern State University, 3410 Taft Boulevard, Wichita Falls, TX 76308-2099

National American University: Austin

Austin, Texas

www.national.edu

- For-profit 4-year university
- Very large city
- 207 undergraduates

General. Regionally accredited. **Degrees:** 9 bachelor's, 15 associate awarded. **Calendar:** Quarter. **Full-time faculty:** 3 total. **Part-time faculty:** 9 total.

Basis for selection. Open admission, but selective for some programs.

2015-2016 Annual costs. Tuition/fees: $16,470. Books/supplies: $1,350. **Additional information:** Additional fees may apply.

Application procedures. Admission: No deadline. **Financial aid:** No deadline.

Academics. Credit/placement by examination: AP, CLEP.

Majors. Business: Accounting, business admin, organizational leadership. **Computer sciences:** Information technology. **Health services:** Health care admin. **Protective services:** Law enforcement admin.

Contact. E-mail: sljones@national.edu
Phone: (512) 651-4700
Shalonda Jones, Director of Admissions, National American University: Austin, 13801 Burnet Road, Suite 300, Austin, TX 78727

Northwood University: Texas

Cedar Hill, Texas

www.northwood.edu

CB code: 6499

- Private 4-year university and business college
- Commuter campus in large town

◗ 208 degree-seeking undergraduates
◗ SAT or ACT (ACT writing optional), application essay required

General. Founded in 1966. Regionally accredited. Specialty university offering only business degrees in professional management; 3 residential campuses in Michigan, Florida, and Texas; program centers in 8 states. **Degrees:** 125 bachelor's awarded; master's offered. **Location:** 18 miles from Dallas, 28 miles from Fort Worth. **Calendar:** Semester, limited summer session. **Full-time faculty:** 5 total; 40% have terminal degrees, 40% minority, 40% women. **Part-time faculty:** 24 total; 88% have terminal degrees, 29% minority, 42% women. **Class size:** 81% < 20, 19% 20-39.

Freshman class profile.

GPA 3.75 or higher:	15%	GPA 2.0-2.99:	9%
GPA 3.50-3.74:	17%	Rank in top quarter:	27%
GPA 3.0-3.49:	59%	Rank in top tenth:	10%

Basis for selection. Minimum GPA of 2.0 and strong interest in business or related field. Test scores considered. Students with lower GPA possibly admitted on probation. Interview recommended. **Home schooled:** Transcript of courses and grades, state high school equivalency certificate required.

High school preparation. College-preparatory program recommended. 17 units recommended. Recommended units include English 4, mathematics 3, social studies 3, science 3 (laboratory 2), foreign language 1 and computer science 1.

2015-2016 Annual costs. Tuition/fees: $24,170. Room/board: $9,590.

Financial aid. **Non-need-based:** Scholarships awarded for academics, athletics, leadership.

Application procedures. **Admission:** Closing date 8/1. $25 fee, may be waived for applicants with need, free for online applicants. Admission notification on a rolling basis beginning on or about 9/1. **Financial aid:** Priority date 3/1; no closing date. FAFSA required. Applicants notified on a rolling basis starting 3/1.

Academics. **Special study options:** Accelerated study, distance learning, weekend college. **Credit/placement by examination:** AP, CLEP, IB, SAT, ACT, institutional tests. 12 credit hours maximum toward bachelor's degree. **Support services:** Learning center, reduced course load, remedial instruction, study skills assistance, tutoring, writing center.

Majors. **Business:** Accounting, business admin, marketing.

Most popular majors. Business/marketing 98%.

Technology on campus. 50 workstations in library, computer center. Dormitories wired for high-speed internet access and linked to campus network. Commuter students can connect to campus network. Online course registration, online library, helpline, student web hosting, wireless network available.

Student life. **Freshman orientation:** Mandatory, $125 fee. Preregistration for classes offered. Multiple sessions throughout the summer. **Housing:** $250 fully refundable deposit, deadline 5/1. **Activities:** Christian Fellowship.

Athletics. NAIA. **Team name:** Knights.

Student services. Adult student services, career counseling, student employment services, financial aid counseling, personal counseling, placement for graduates.

Contact. E-mail: txadmit@northwood.edu
Toll-free number: (800) 622-9000
Darien Moore, Director of Admissions, Northwood University: Texas, 1114 West FM 1382, Cedar Hill, TX 75104-1204

Our Lady of the Lake University of San Antonio
San Antonio, Texas   CB member
www.ollusa.edu   CB code: 6550

◗ Private 4-year university affiliated with the Roman Catholic Church
◗ Commuter campus in very large city
◗ 1,498 degree-seeking undergraduates: 11% part-time, 69% women, 9% African American, 1% Asian American, 70% Hispanic/Latino, 1% Native American, 2% Multi-racial, non-Hispanic, 1% international
◗ 1,805 degree-seeking graduate students
◗ 68% of applicants admitted
◗ SAT or ACT (ACT writing optional) required
◗ 38% graduate within 6 years

General. Founded in 1895. Regionally accredited. **Degrees:** 317 bachelor's awarded; master's, professional, doctoral offered. **ROTC:** Army. **Location:** 4 miles from downtown, 80 miles from Austin. **Calendar:** Semester, limited summer session. **Full-time faculty:** 101 total; 92% have terminal degrees, 45% minority, 65% women. **Part-time faculty:** 234 total; 57% have terminal degrees, 46% minority, 59% women. **Class size:** 64% < 20, 36% 20-39. **Special facilities:** International folk culture center, speech and hearing clinic, community counseling center, elementary school, child development center, center for social work research, center for women in church and society.

Freshman class profile. 3,113 applied, 2,120 admitted, 308 enrolled.

Mid 50% test scores			
SAT critical reading:	420-510	GPA 2.0-2.99:	30%
SAT math:	420-510	Rank in top quarter:	25%
ACT composite:	18-21	Rank in top tenth:	9%
GPA 3.75 or higher:	21%	Return as sophomores:	59%
GPA 3.50-3.74:	15%	Out-of-state:	1%
GPA 3.0-3.49:	34%	Live on campus:	69%
		International:	1%

Basis for selection. High school academic record and test scores important. ACT/SAT scores are not required for non-traditional students with a GED or the students who have graduated but never tested. Those students are required to take a placement test (Accuplacer) upon entry. **Home schooled:** Transcript of courses and grades required.

High school preparation. College-preparatory program recommended. 14 units required. Required units include English 4, mathematics 3, science 2 (laboratory 2) and foreign language 2. 2 additional credits in English, math, social sciences, or nature sciences.

2015-2016 Annual costs. Tuition/fees: $26,148. Room/board: $7,556. Books/supplies: $1,200. Personal expenses: $1,850.

2014-2015 Financial aid. **Need-based:** 347 full-time freshmen applied for aid; 324 deemed to have need; 324 received aid. Average need met was 89%. Average scholarship/grant was $9,545; average loan $3,516. 65% of total undergraduate aid awarded as scholarships/grants, 35% as loans/jobs. **Non-need-based:** Awarded to 1,133 full-time undergraduates, including 349 freshmen. Scholarships awarded for academics, alumni affiliation, art, athletics, music/drama, religious affiliation.

Application procedures. **Admission:** Priority date 11/14; deadline 8/1 (receipt date). $35 fee, may be waived for applicants with need. Admission notification on a rolling basis beginning on or about 11/14. May 1st highly recommended. **Financial aid:** Priority date 5/1; no closing date. FAFSA, institutional form required. Applicants notified on a rolling basis starting 3/1; must reply within 2 week(s) of notification.

Academics. **Special study options:** Accelerated study, combined bachelor's/graduate degree, cross-registration, distance learning, double major, dual enrollment of high school students, honors, independent study, internships, study abroad, teacher certification program, weekend college. **Credit/placement by examination:** AP, CLEP, IB, SAT, ACT, institutional tests. No limit to number of credit hours that may be awarded through Dual, AP, CLEP or that may be counted towards bachelor's degree. **Support services:** Learning center, reduced course load, study skills assistance, tutoring, writing center.

Majors. **Area/ethnic studies:** Chicano/Hispanic-American/Latino. **Biology:** General, biochemistry. **Business:** Accounting, business admin, human resources, international, marketing, organizational leadership, training/development. **Communications:** Broadcast journalism, communications/speech/rhetoric, journalism, public relations. **Computer sciences:** General. **Education:** General, bilingual, biology, English, history, kindergarten/preschool, mathematics, multi-level teacher, music, science, social studies, Spanish, special ed, speech impaired, technology/industrial arts. **English:** English lit. **Foreign languages:** Spanish. **Health services:** Communication disorders, speech pathology. **History:** General. **Human services:** Social work. **Liberal arts:** Arts/sciences. **Math:** General. **Parks/recreation:** Exercise sciences. **Philosophy/religion:** Philosophy, religion. **Physical sciences:** Chemistry. **Protective services:** Criminal justice. **Psychology:** General. **Social sciences:** Political science, sociology. **Visual/performing arts:** Art, dramatic, music. **Work/family studies:** Business.

Most popular majors. Business/marketing 20%, health sciences 16%, psychology 10%, public administration/social services 13%, security/protective services 7%.

Technology on campus. 208 workstations in dormitories, library, computer center; student center. Dormitories wired for high-speed internet access and linked to campus network. Commuter students can connect to campus network. Online course registration, online library, helpline, repair service, wireless network available.

Student life. Freshman orientation: Mandatory, $100 fee. Preregistration for classes offered. Held 5-6 times during summer. **Housing:** Guaranteed on-campus for freshmen. Coed dorms, single-sex dorms, special housing for disabled available. $100 fully refundable deposit. **Activities:** Bands, campus ministries, choral groups, dance, drama, international student organizations, literary magazine, music ensembles, musical theater, student government, student newspaper, religious organizations, black and Hispanic clubs, service clubs.

Athletics. NAIA. **Intercollegiate:** Basketball, cross-country, golf M, soccer, softball W, tennis, volleyball W. **Intramural:** Basketball, football (non-tackle), golf, racquetball, soccer W, softball, swimming, tennis, volleyball. **Team name:** Saints.

Student services. Adult student services, alcohol/substance abuse counseling, chaplain/spiritual director, career counseling, student employment services, financial aid counseling, health services, personal counseling, placement for graduates, veterans' counselor, women's services. **Physically disabled:** Services for visually, speech, hearing impaired.

Contact. E-mail: admission@ollusa.edu
Phone: (210) 431-3961 Toll-free number: (800) 436-6558
Fax: (210) 431-4036
Mary Scotka, Vice President, Enrollment Management, Our Lady of the Lake University of San Antonio, 411 Southwest 24th Street, San Antonio, TX 78207-4689

Paul Quinn College
Dallas, Texas
www.pqc.edu
CB member
CB code: 6577

- Private 4-year liberal arts college affiliated with the African Methodist Episcopal Church
- Residential campus in very large city
- 420 degree-seeking undergraduates
- SAT or ACT with writing, application essay, interview required

General. Founded in 1872. Regionally accredited. Historically Black College. **Degrees:** 27 bachelor's awarded. **Location:** 12 miles from Dallas. **Calendar:** Semester, limited summer session. **Full-time faculty:** 9 total; 67% have terminal degrees, 89% minority, 44% women. **Part-time faculty:** 19 total; 53% have terminal degrees, 37% women. **Class size:** 84% < 20, 11% 20-39, 3% 40-49, 2% >100. **Special facilities:** 2-acre organic farm.

Freshman class profile.

GPA 3.75 or higher:	9%	GPA 2.0-2.99:	52%
GPA 3.50-3.74:	3%	Out-of-state:	10%
GPA 3.0-3.49:	18%	Live on campus:	80%

Basis for selection. Minimum 2.5 GPA on a 4.0 scale. ACT or SAT scores, grades, letter of recommendation and admissions essay reviewed.

High school preparation. Required and recommended units include English 4, mathematics 3, social studies 2, science 3 and foreign language 2.

2015-2016 Annual costs. Tuition/fees: $8,275. Room/board: $6,000. Personal expenses: $600.

Financial aid. All financial aid based on need.

Application procedures. Admission: No deadline. No application fee. Admission notification on a rolling basis. **Financial aid:** Priority date 7/1; no closing date. FAFSA, institutional form required. Applicants notified on a rolling basis starting 7/15; must reply within 2 week(s) of notification.

Academics. Special study options: Combined bachelor's/graduate degree, cooperative education, distance learning, honors, independent study, internships, liberal arts/career combination, teacher certification program. **Credit/placement by examination:** AP, CLEP. 12 credit hours maximum toward bachelor's degree. **Support services:** Learning center, pre-admission summer program, reduced course load, remedial instruction, study skills assistance, tutoring, writing center.

Majors. Biology: General. **Business:** Accounting, business admin. **Education:** Elementary, secondary. **Health services:** General. **Liberal arts:** Arts/sciences. **Philosophy/religion:** Religion.

Most popular majors. Biology 6%, business/marketing 50%, education 13%, health sciences 6%, legal studies 25%.

Technology on campus. 88 workstations in dormitories, library, computer center. Dormitories wired for high-speed internet access and linked to campus network. Online course registration, helpline, wireless network available.

Student life. Freshman orientation: Mandatory. Preregistration for classes offered. **Policies:** Students must wear business casual clothing between 8:30 AM and 5:30 PM Monday through Friday, or whenever they are in class. Students may wear PQC apparel with jeans or a PQC purple wristband with jeans on Friday's after Chapel/College assembly. Religious observance required. **Housing:** Guaranteed on-campus for all undergraduates. Coed dorms available. $175 nonrefundable deposit. **Activities:** Choral groups, dance, drama, student government, Latino Student Association.

Athletics. NAIA. **Intercollegiate:** Basketball, track and field. **Team name:** Tigers.

Student services. Career counseling, student employment services, financial aid counseling, health services, personal counseling, placement for graduates.

Contact. E-mail: admissions@pqc.edu
Phone: (214) 379-5449 Toll-free number: (877) 346-1063
Fax: (214) 379-5448
Jessika Lara, Director of Recruiting, Paul Quinn College, 3837 Simpson Stuart Road, Dallas, TX 75241

Prairie View A&M University
Prairie View, Texas
www.pvamu.edu
CB member
CB code: 6580

- Public 4-year university
- Commuter campus in small town
- 6,923 degree-seeking undergraduates: 9% part-time, 60% women, 86% African American, 3% Asian American, 6% Hispanic/Latino, 1% Multiracial, non-Hispanic, 2% international
- 1,309 degree-seeking graduate students
- 86% of applicants admitted
- SAT or ACT (ACT writing optional) required
- 34% graduate within 6 years

General. Founded in 1876. Regionally accredited. Historically Black College. **Degrees:** 1,159 bachelor's awarded; master's, doctoral offered. **ROTC:** Army, Naval, Air Force. **Location:** 47 miles from Houston. **Calendar:** Semester, extensive summer session. **Full-time faculty:** 379 total; 60% have terminal degrees, 79% minority, 42% women. **Part-time faculty:** 82 total; 37% have terminal degrees, 72% minority, 60% women. **Class size:** 22% < 20, 58% 20-39, 10% 40-49, 9% 50-99, less than 1% >100. **Special facilities:** Nuclear magnetic resonance spectrometric differentiator, scanning calorimeter, high pressure liquid chromatograph, solid state engineering laboratory, computer-aided design and drafting laboratory, center for learning and teaching effectiveness, international dairy goat research center, cooperative agricultural research center, solar observatory.

Freshman class profile. 5,075 applied, 4,364 admitted, 1,645 enrolled.

Mid 50% test scores			
		GPA 2.0-2.99:	49%
SAT critical reading:	380-460	Rank in top quarter:	19%
SAT math:	390-470	Rank in top tenth:	5%
SAT writing:	360-440	End year in good standing:	99%
ACT composite:	16-20	Return as sophomores:	66%
GPA 3.75 or higher:	5%	Out-of-state:	7%
GPA 3.50-3.74:	10%	Live on campus:	80%
GPA 3.0-3.49:	36%	International:	1%

Basis for selection. Score on institution's entrance examination, personal qualities, high school GPA important. Students may be admitted conditionally if grades or test scores are below minimum requirement. **Home schooled:** Transcript of courses and grades, state high school equivalency certificate required.

High school preparation. 26 units required. Required units include English 4, mathematics 4, social studies 4, science 4, foreign language 2, visual/performing arts 1, academic electives 5.5. 1 physical education, .5 speech.

2015-2016 Annual costs. Tuition/fees: $9,745; $22,272 out-of-state. Room/board: $7,849. Books/supplies: $1,300. Personal expenses: $2,552.

2014-2015 Financial aid. Need-based: 1,475 full-time freshmen applied for aid; 1,199 deemed to have need; 992 received aid. Average need met was 87%. Average scholarship/grant was $4,120; average loan $3,875. 55% of total undergraduate aid awarded as scholarships/grants, 45% as loans/jobs. **Non-need-based:** Awarded to 1,427 full-time undergraduates, including 396 freshmen. Scholarships awarded for academics, athletics, ROTC.

Application procedures. Admission: Closing date 6/1 (receipt date). $25 fee, may be waived for applicants with need. Application must be submitted online. Admission notification by 8/15. Admission notification on a rolling basis. **Financial aid:** Closing date 3/15. FAFSA required. Applicants notified by 6/1; must reply by 8/1.

Academics. Special study options: Accelerated study, cooperative education, cross-registration, distance learning, double major, dual enrollment of high school students, exchange student, honors, independent study, internships, semester at sea, student-designed major, study abroad, teacher certification program, weekend college. **Credit/placement by examination:** AP, CLEP, SAT, ACT, institutional tests. 30 credit hours maximum toward bachelor's degree. **Support services:** Learning center, pre-admission summer program, reduced course load, remedial instruction, study skills assistance, tutoring, writing center.

Majors. Architecture: Architecture. **Biology:** General. **Business:** Accounting, business admin, finance, management information systems. **Communications:** Communications/speech/rhetoric. **Computer sciences:** General. **Engineering:** Chemical, civil, computer, electrical, mechanical. **English:** English lit. **Foreign languages:** Spanish. **Health services:** Nursing (RN). **History:** General. **Human services:** Social work. **Math:** General. **Parks/recreation:** Health/fitness. **Physical sciences:** Chemistry, physics. **Protective services:** Criminal justice, juvenile corrections. **Psychology:** General. **Social sciences:** Political science, sociology. **Visual/performing arts:** Dramatic, graphic design, music, music performance. **Work/family studies:** Human nutrition.

Most popular majors. Biology 6%, business/marketing 11%, engineering/engineering technologies 17%, health sciences 16%, psychology 6%, security/protective services 12%.

Technology on campus. 500 workstations in dormitories, library, computer center, student center. Dormitories wired for high-speed internet access and linked to campus network. Commuter students can connect to campus network. Online course registration, online library, helpline, wireless network available.

Student life. Freshman orientation: Mandatory, $60 fee. Preregistration for classes offered. 1 day for Phase 1; 3 days for Phase 2. **Housing:** Guaranteed on-campus for freshmen. Single-sex dorms, special housing for disabled, apartments available. $150 fully refundable deposit, deadline 7/1. **Activities:** Bands, campus ministries, choral groups, dance, drama, international student organizations, literary magazine, music ensembles, musical theater, radio station, student government, student newspaper, symphony orchestra, TV station, Prairie View Mime Ministry, Fellowship of College Christian Students, African Student Association, Asian Immersion Club, Brothers Leading and Cultivating Knowledge, Helpers Advancing the Lives of Others, Model United Nations; Panther Ambassadors, National Society of Collegiate Scholars, Classic Dance Ensemble.

Athletics. NAIA, NCAA. **Intercollegiate:** Baseball M, basketball, bowling W, cross-country, football (tackle) M, golf, soccer W, softball W, tennis, track and field, volleyball. **Intramural:** Baseball M, basketball, bowling W, cross-country, golf, soccer W, softball W, tennis, track and field, volleyball. **Team name:** Panthers.

Student services. Adult student services, alcohol/substance abuse counseling, chaplain/spiritual director, career counseling, student employment services, financial aid counseling, health services, minority student services, personal counseling, placement for graduates, veterans' counselor. **Physically disabled:** Services for hearing impaired.

Contact. E-mail: admissions@pvamu.edu
Phone: (936) 261-1000
Lenice Brown, Director of Admissions, Prairie View A&M University, PO Box 519, MS 1009, Prairie View, TX 77446

Rice University
Houston, Texas
www.rice.edu

CB member
CB code: 6609

- Private 4-year university
- Residential campus in very large city
- 3,879 degree-seeking undergraduates: 1% part-time, 47% women, 7% African American, 24% Asian American, 14% Hispanic/Latino, 4% Multi-racial, non-Hispanic, 12% international
- 2,744 degree-seeking graduate students
- 16% of applicants admitted
- SAT and SAT Subject Tests or ACT with writing, application essay required
- 86% graduate within 6 years

General. Founded in 1891. Regionally accredited. **Degrees:** 1,033 bachelor's awarded; master's, doctoral offered. **ROTC:** Army, Naval, Air Force. **Location:** 3 miles from downtown Houston. **Calendar:** Semester, limited summer session. **Full-time faculty:** 665 total; 98% have terminal degrees, 18% minority, 31% women. **Part-time faculty:** 197 total; 68% have terminal degrees, 15% minority, 34% women. **Class size:** 69% < 20, 18% 20-39, 6% 40-49, 5% 50-99, 2% >100. **Special facilities:** Wetland center for biochemical research, arboretum, nanotechnology lab, center for study of languages and culture, civil engineering lab, concert hall with grand organ, institute for public policy, observatory, digital media center, Oshman engineering design kitchen, biosciences research collaborative.

Freshman class profile. 17,951 applied, 2,865 admitted, 969 enrolled.

Mid 50% test scores			
SAT critical reading:	680-760	Rank in top tenth:	89%
SAT math:	710-800	Return as sophomores:	97%
SAT writing:	680-770	Out-of-state:	53%
ACT composite:	32-35	Live on campus:	99%
Rank in top quarter:	96%	International:	12%

Basis for selection. High school course selection and performance, test scores, teacher and counselor recommendations, extracurricular activity, and application answers/essay most important. Demonstrated interest is also considered as is an (optional) interview. If student submits SAT, two SAT Subject Tests are also required (recommend subject tests be in subjects related to student's area of interest). If student submits ACT Plus Writing, then no SAT Subject Tests are required. Audition required for music; portfolio required for architecture. Interview recommended for all freshman applicants. **Home schooled:** Statement describing home school structure and mission, letter of recommendation (nonparent) required.

High school preparation. College-preparatory program required. 16 units required; 20 recommended. Required and recommended units include English 4, mathematics 3-4, social studies 2-4, science 2-4 (laboratory 2-4), foreign language 2-4 and academic electives 3. Minimum of pre-calculus, physics, and chemistry required to be considered for engineering and natural science majors, although 2nd year of chemistry or biology may replace physics requirement.

2015-2016 Annual costs. Tuition/fees: $42,253. Room/board: $13,650. Books/supplies: $800. Personal expenses: $1,550.

2015-2016 Financial aid. Need-based: 745 full-time freshmen applied for aid; 380 deemed to have need; 377 received aid. Average need met was 100%. Average scholarship/grant was $36,568; average loan $2,675. 92% of total undergraduate aid awarded as scholarships/grants, 8% as loans/jobs. **Non-need-based:** Awarded to 746 full-time undergraduates, including 158 freshmen. Scholarships awarded for academics, art, athletics, leadership, minority status, music/drama, ROTC, state residency.

Application procedures. Admission: Closing date 1/1 (postmark date). $75 fee, may be waived for applicants with need. Admission notification by 4/1. Must reply by 5/1. **Financial aid:** Closing date 3/1. FAFSA, CSS PROFILE required. Applicants notified by 4/1; must reply by 5/1.

Academics. Special study options: Combined bachelor's/graduate degree, cross-registration, double major, dual enrollment of high school students, ESL, exchange student, independent study, internships, liberal arts/career combination, student-designed major, study abroad, teacher certification program. 8-year guaranteed medical school program with Baylor College of Medicine for up to 6 entering freshmen. **Credit/placement by examination:** AP, CLEP, IB, institutional tests. **Support services:** Study skills assistance, tutoring, writing center.

Majors. Architecture: Architecture. **Area/ethnic studies:** Asian, Chicano/Hispanic-American/Latino, German, Latin American, Slavic, women's. **Biology:** General, biochemistry, ecology, evolutionary. **Business:** Business admin. **Computer sciences:** Computer science. **Engineering:** Biomedical, chemical, civil, computer, electrical, environmental, materials, mechanical. **English:** English lit. **Foreign languages:** Ancient Greek, classics, French, German, Latin, linguistics, Slavic, Spanish. **History:** General. **Human services:** Public policy. **Math:** General, applied, statistics. **Parks/recreation:** Exercise sciences, sports admin. **Philosophy/religion:** Philosophy, religion. **Physical sciences:** Astronomy, astrophysics, chemical physics, chemistry, geology, geophysics, physical chemistry, physics. **Psychology:** General. **Social sciences:** General, anthropology, economics, political science, sociology. **Visual/performing arts:** General, art, art history/conservation, music, music history, music performance, music theory/composition, studio arts.

Most popular majors. Biology 8%, engineering/engineering technologies 19%, parks/recreation 7%, psychology 7%, social sciences 15%.

Technology on campus. Dormitories wired for high-speed internet access and linked to campus network. Commuter students can connect to campus network. Online course registration, online library, helpline, student web hosting, wireless network available.

Student life. Freshman orientation: Mandatory. Preregistration for classes offered. Held the week before start of classes. **Policies:** Academic honor code. All undergraduates are granted membership in one of 11 residential college communities and maintain that affiliation for their entire college career. Each college is self governing and designed to facilitate student and faculty networking, leadership development, pre-major advising, and social interaction. **Housing:** Guaranteed on-campus for freshmen. Coed dorms, special housing for disabled available. $100 nonrefundable deposit, deadline 5/1. **Activities:** Bands, campus ministries, choral groups, dance, drama, film society, international student organizations, literary magazine, music ensembles, Model UN, musical theater, opera, radio station, student government, student newspaper, symphony orchestra, TV station, Hispanic student association, Hillel, Black student association, Young Democrats, Young Republicans, Chinese student association, Baptist student union, Catholic student center, student volunteer program.

Athletics. NCAA. **Intercollegiate:** Baseball M, basketball, cheerleading, cross-country, football (non-tackle) W, football (tackle) M, golf M, soccer W, swimming W, tennis, track and field, volleyball W. **Intramural:** Badminton, basketball, racquetball, soccer, softball, swimming, table tennis, tennis, track and field, volleyball. **Team name:** Owls.

Student services. Alcohol/substance abuse counseling, chaplain/spiritual director, career counseling, student employment services, financial aid counseling, health services, minority student services, personal counseling, placement for graduates, women's services. **Physically disabled:** Services for visually, speech, hearing impaired.

Contact. E-mail: admi@rice.edu
Phone: (713) 348-7423 Fax: (713) 348-5323
Dan Warner, Director of Admission, Rice University, 6100 Main Street, Houston, TX 77251-1892

Sam Houston State University

Huntsville, Texas   CB member
www.shsu.edu   CB code: 6643

▸ Public 4-year university

▸ Residential campus in large town

▸ 17,401 degree-seeking undergraduates: 19% part-time, 61% women, 19% African American, 1% Asian American, 20% Hispanic/Latino, 1% Native American, 3% Multi-racial, non-Hispanic, 1% international

▸ 854 degree-seeking graduate students

▸ 73% of applicants admitted

▸ SAT or ACT (ACT writing optional) required

▸ 50% graduate within 6 years

General. Founded in 1879. Regionally accredited. **Degrees:** 3,438 bachelor's awarded; master's, doctoral offered. **ROTC:** Army. **Location:** 69 miles from Houston, 170 miles from Dallas. **Calendar:** Semester, extensive summer session. **Full-time faculty:** 531 total; 95% have terminal degrees, 14% minority, 40% women. **Part-time faculty:** 374 total; 36% have terminal degrees, 60% women. **Class size:** 28% < 20, 50% 20-39, 9% 40-49, 10% 50-99, 3% >100. **Special facilities:** Sam Houston Memorial Museum, Huntsville State Park, observatory, Texas Prison Museum.

Freshman class profile. 9,290 applied, 6,762 admitted, 2,637 enrolled.

Mid 50% test scores		Return as sophomores:	80%
SAT critical reading:	450-550	Out-of-state:	2%
SAT math:	430-540	Live on campus:	86%
ACT composite:	18-23	International:	1%
Rank in top quarter:	41%	Fraternities:	12%
Rank in top tenth:	15%	Sororities:	8%

Basis for selection. Students' test scores and school achievement records are very important. Students graduating in the top 25% of their class from an accredited high school are exempt from test requirements. Special admission requirements for certain programs.

High school preparation. College-preparatory program recommended. 23 units required. Required units include English 4, mathematics 3, social studies 1, history 2, science 3 (laboratory 1), foreign language 2, visual/performing arts 1 and academic electives 5.

2015-2016 Annual costs. Tuition/fees: $9,337; $21,037 out-of-state. Room/board: $8,676. Books/supplies: $1,124. Personal expenses: $1,790.

2014-2015 Financial aid. Need-based: 2,017 full-time freshmen applied for aid; 1,575 deemed to have need; 1,574 received aid. Average need met was 63%. Average scholarship/grant was $9,054; average loan $3,000. 34% of total undergraduate aid awarded as scholarships/grants, 66% as loans/jobs. **Non-need-based:** Awarded to 1,754 full-time undergraduates, including 373

freshmen. Scholarships awarded for academics, alumni affiliation, art, athletics, leadership, music/drama, religious affiliation, ROTC, state residency.

Application procedures. Admission: Priority date 6/15; deadline 8/1 (postmark date). $45 fee, may be waived for applicants with need. **Financial aid:** Priority date 3/15; no closing date. FAFSA required. Applicants notified on a rolling basis starting 4/1; must reply within 4 week(s) of notification.

Academics. Special study options: Accelerated study, distance learning, double major, dual enrollment of high school students, ESL, honors, independent study, internships, study abroad, teacher certification program, weekend college. **Credit/placement by examination:** AP, CLEP, IB, SAT, ACT, institutional tests. 30 credit hours maximum toward bachelor's degree. **Support services:** Learning center, pre-admission summer program, reduced course load, remedial instruction, study skills assistance, tutoring, writing center.

Majors. Architecture: Interior. **Biology:** General, biomedical sciences. **Business:** General, accounting, banking/financial services, business admin, entrepreneurial studies, fashion, finance, human resources, international, management information systems, managerial economics, marketing. **Communications:** Communications/speech/rhetoric, media studies. **Communications technology:** Animation/special effects. **Computer sciences:** General. **English:** English lit. **Foreign languages:** Spanish. **Health services:** General, athletic training, health care admin, music therapy, nursing (RN). **History:** General. **Math:** General. **Parks/recreation:** Exercise sciences. **Philosophy/religion:** Philosophy. **Physical sciences:** Chemistry, forensic chemistry, geology, physics. **Protective services:** Criminal justice. **Psychology:** General. **Social sciences:** Geography, political science, sociology. **Visual/performing arts:** Commercial/advertising art, dance, dramatic, music, musical theater, photography, studio arts. **Work/family studies:** General, food/nutrition, institutional food production.

Most popular majors. Business/marketing 24%, interdisciplinary studies 11%, security/protective services 20%.

Technology on campus. 1,600 workstations in dormitories, library, computer center, student center. Dormitories wired for high-speed internet access and linked to campus network. Commuter students can connect to campus network. Online course registration, online library, helpline, student web hosting, wireless network available.

Student life. Freshman orientation: Mandatory, $120 fee. Preregistration for classes offered. Held overnight throughout summer and before classes commence. Parent participation. **Housing:** Guaranteed on-campus for freshmen. Coed dorms, single-sex dorms, special housing for disabled, apartments, fraternity/sorority housing, themed housing available. $200 partly refundable deposit. **Activities:** Bands, campus ministries, choral groups, dance, drama, film society, international student organizations, literary magazine, music ensembles, musical theater, opera, radio station, student government, student newspaper, symphony orchestra, Democratic and Republican student associations, Baptist student ministry, Church of Christ student center, Lutheran student center, Hillel, Muslim students association, student Pagan association, ROTARACT, Habitat for Humanity, Wesley Foundation.

Athletics. NCAA. **Intercollegiate:** Baseball M, basketball, bowling W, cheerleading, cross-country, equestrian, football (tackle) M, golf, rodeo, soccer W, softball W, tennis W, track and field, volleyball W. **Intramural:** Basketball, football (non-tackle), handball, racquetball, sand volleyball, soccer, softball, tennis, ultimate frisbee, volleyball. **Team name:** Bearkats.

Student services. Alcohol/substance abuse counseling, career counseling, student employment services, financial aid counseling, health services, legal services, minority student services, personal counseling, placement for graduates, veterans' counselor. **Physically disabled:** Services for visually, speech, hearing impaired.

Contact. E-mail: admissions@shsu.edu
Phone: (936) 294-1828 Toll-free number: (866) 232-7528
Trevor Thorn, Director of Admissions, Sam Houston State University, Box 2418, Huntsville, TX 77341-2418

Schreiner University

Kerrville, Texas   CB member
www.schreiner.edu   CB code: 6647

▸ Private 4-year liberal arts college affiliated with the Presbyterian Church (USA)

▸ Residential campus in large town

▸ 1,126 degree-seeking undergraduates: 7% part-time, 59% women, 4% African American, 1% Asian American, 35% Hispanic/Latino, 3% Multi-racial, non-Hispanic, 1% international

▸ 48 degree-seeking graduate students

- 90% of applicants admitted
- SAT or ACT with writing required
- 40% graduate within 6 years

General. Founded in 1923. Regionally accredited. **Degrees:** 180 bachelor's, 2 associate awarded; master's offered. **Location:** 60 miles from San Antonio, 80 miles from Austin. **Calendar:** Semester, limited summer session. **Full-time faculty:** 60 total; 77% have terminal degrees, 12% minority, 48% women. **Part-time faculty:** 49 total; 6% minority, 59% women. **Class size:** 67% < 20, 32% 20-39, less than 1% 40-49. **Special facilities:** Observatory.

Freshman class profile. 943 applied, 850 admitted, 289 enrolled.

Mid 50% test scores			
SAT critical reading:	440-540	GPA 3.0-3.49:	31%
SAT math:	450-550	GPA 2.0-2.99:	1%
SAT writing:	420-520	Rank in top quarter:	36%
ACT composite:	19-24	Rank in top tenth:	11%
GPA 3.75 or higher:	25%	Return as sophomores:	70%
GPA 3.50-3.74:	43%	Out-of-state:	1%
		Live on campus:	89%

Basis for selection. High school courses taken, grades, class rank, extracurricular activities, test scores, recommendations, interviews considered. Interview recommended for all; essay required for applicants not meeting certain admissions standards; portfolio recommended for fine arts.

High school preparation. College-preparatory program recommended. 24 units recommended. Recommended units include English 4, mathematics 3, social studies 2, history 2, science 3 (laboratory 2), foreign language 2, computer science 1, visual/performing arts 1, academic electives 3.5.

2015-2016 Annual costs. Tuition/fees: $25,086. Room/board: $9,540. Books/supplies: $100. Personal expenses: $1,000.

2014-2015 Financial aid. Need-based: 277 full-time freshmen applied for aid; 230 deemed to have need; 230 received aid. Average need met was 70%. Average scholarship/grant was $15,429; average loan $3,061. 70% of total undergraduate aid awarded as scholarships/grants, 30% as loans/jobs. **Non-need-based:** Awarded to 199 full-time undergraduates, including 79 freshmen. Scholarships awarded for academics, art, leadership, music/drama, religious affiliation.

Application procedures. Admission: Priority date 5/1; deadline 8/1. $25 fee, may be waived for applicants with need. Admission notification on a rolling basis. Must reply by 5/1. August 1 application deadline is on a space-available basis. **Financial aid:** Priority date 5/1; no closing date. FAFSA required. Applicants notified on a rolling basis starting 2/15; must reply within 2 week(s) of notification.

Academics. Special study options: Accelerated study, combined bachelor's/graduate degree, cooperative education, distance learning, double major, dual enrollment of high school students, exchange student, honors, independent study, internships, liberal arts/career combination, student-designed major, study abroad, teacher certification program. **Credit/placement by examination:** AP, CLEP, IB, SAT, ACT, institutional tests. **Support services:** Learning center, reduced course load, remedial instruction, study skills assistance, tutoring, writing center.

Majors. Biology: General, biochemistry. **Business:** Accounting, business admin, finance, management information systems, marketing. **Communications:** Communications/speech/rhetoric. **Education:** Biology, chemistry, early childhood, English, history, mathematics, middle, music, physical. **Engineering:** General. **English:** English lit. **Health services:** Nursing (RN). **History:** General. **Liberal arts:** Arts/sciences. **Math:** General. **Parks/recreation:** Exercise sciences, sports admin. **Philosophy/religion:** Religion. **Physical sciences:** Chemistry. **Psychology:** General. **Social sciences:** Political science. **Visual/performing arts:** Commercial/advertising art, design, dramatic, graphic design, music.

Most popular majors. Biology 12%, business/marketing 22%, education 8%, English 6%, health sciences 12%, parks/recreation 7%, psychology 11%, visual/performing arts 7%.

Technology on campus. 123 workstations in library, computer center, student center. Dormitories wired for high-speed internet access and linked to campus network. Commuter students can connect to campus network. Online library, helpline, repair service, student web hosting, wireless network available.

Student life. Freshman orientation: Mandatory. Preregistration for classes offered. Overnight program prior to start of classes. **Housing:** Guaranteed on-campus for all undergraduates. Coed dorms, special housing for disabled, apartments, gender-neutral housing, themed housing, wellness housing available. $200 nonrefundable deposit, deadline 5/1. Learning communities available, military housing. **Activities:** Pep band, campus ministries, choral groups, dance, drama, literary magazine, music ensembles, musical

theater, student government, student newspaper, symphony orchestra, community outreach program, pre-law society, Celtic Cross, Episcopal-Lutheran association, Fellowship of Christian Athletes, Young Catholic Adults, Young Republicans, Green society, Hispanic culture club, Asian culture club, Schreiner Democrats, Shades United.

Athletics. NCAA. **Intercollegiate:** Baseball M, basketball, cheerleading W, golf, soccer, softball W, tennis, volleyball W. **Intramural:** Basketball, football (non-tackle), football (tackle), golf, racquetball, soccer, swimming, table tennis, tennis, volleyball. **Team name:** Mountaineers.

Student services. Adult student services, chaplain/spiritual director, career counseling, student employment services, financial aid counseling, health services, minority student services, personal counseling, placement for graduates. **Physically disabled:** Services for visually, speech, hearing impaired.

Contact. E-mail: admissions@schreiner.edu
Phone: (830) 792-7217 Toll-free number: (800) 343-4919
Fax: (830) 792-7226
Caroline Randall, Associate Dean for Enrollment Services, Schreiner University, 2100 Memorial Boulevard, Kerrville, TX 78028-5697

Southern Methodist University
Dallas, Texas **CB member**
www.smu.edu **CB code: 6660**

- Private 4-year university affiliated with the United Methodist Church
- Residential campus in very large city
- 6,348 degree-seeking undergraduates: 3% part-time, 50% women, 5% African American, 7% Asian American, 11% Hispanic/Latino, 4% Multiracial, non-Hispanic, 8% international
- 4,918 degree-seeking graduate students
- 49% of applicants admitted
- SAT or ACT (ACT writing optional), application essay required
- 79% graduate within 6 years

General. Founded in 1911. Regionally accredited. Courses also offered at SMU-in-Plano and SMU-in-Taos in New Mexico. **Degrees:** 1,785 bachelor's awarded; master's, professional, doctoral offered. **ROTC:** Army, Air Force. **Location:** 5 miles from downtown Dallas. **Calendar:** Semester, extensive summer session. **Full-time faculty:** 740 total; 82% have terminal degrees, 19% minority, 39% women. **Part-time faculty:** 376 total; 30% have terminal degrees, 10% minority, 42% women. **Class size:** 58% < 20, 29% 20-39, 6% 40-49, 6% 50-99, 2% >100. **Special facilities:** Museum of art, film/video archives, seismological observatory, electron microscopy laboratory, paleontology museum, engineering innovation laboratory.

Freshman class profile. 12,992 applied, 6,360 admitted, 1,374 enrolled.

Mid 50% test scores			
SAT critical reading:	600-690	GPA 2.0-2.99:	5%
SAT math:	620-720	Rank in top quarter:	75%
SAT writing:	600-690	Rank in top tenth:	44%
ACT composite:	28-32	Return as sophomores:	90%
GPA 3.75 or higher:	46%	Out-of-state:	60%
GPA 3.50-3.74:	23%	Live on campus:	98%
GPA 3.0-3.49:	26%	International:	7%

Basis for selection. GED not accepted. Students evaluated comprehensively. High school curriculum, GPA, test scores, class/community activities, recommendations, and essay important. Special talents considered. Audition required for performing arts; portfolio required for studio art. **Home schooled:** Statement describing home school structure and mission, transcript of courses and grades required. Complete home school supplement. SAT Subject Tests recommended.

High school preparation. College-preparatory program required. 15 units required; 20 recommended. Required and recommended units include English 4, mathematics 3-4, social studies 3, history 3, science 3 (laboratory 2), foreign language 2-3 and academic electives 3.

2015-2016 Annual costs. Tuition/fees: $48,190. Room/board: $15,575. Books/supplies: $1,000. Personal expenses: $1,800.

2015-2016 Financial aid. Need-based: 669 full-time freshmen applied for aid; 438 deemed to have need; 435 received aid. Average need met was 88%. Average scholarship/grant was $20,909; average loan $3,358. 77% of total undergraduate aid awarded as scholarships/grants, 23% as loans/jobs. **Non-need-based:** Awarded to 3,720 full-time undergraduates, including 943 freshmen. Scholarships awarded for academics, alumni affiliation, art, athletics, leadership, music/drama.

Application procedures. Admission: Closing date 1/15 (postmark date). $60 fee, may be waived for applicants with need. Admission notification by 4/1. Must reply by May 1 or within 2 week(s) if notified thereafter. **Financial aid:** Priority date 2/15; no closing date. FAFSA, CSS PROFILE required. Applicants notified on a rolling basis starting 4/1; must reply within 3 week(s) of notification.

Academics. Special study options: Accelerated study, combined bachelor's/graduate degree, cooperative education, distance learning, double major, dual enrollment of high school students, ESL, exchange student, honors, independent study, internships, liberal arts/career combination, student-designed major, study abroad, teacher certification program, Washington semester, weekend college. **Credit/placement by examination:** AP, CLEP, IB, SAT, ACT, institutional tests. No limit on number of AP credits that may be counted toward bachelor's degree. Maximum of 8 hours of International Baccalaureate credits may be counted toward bachelor's degree. **Support services:** Learning center, pre-admission summer program, remedial instruction, study skills assistance, tutoring, writing center.

Majors. Area/ethnic studies: African-American, Chicano/Hispanic-American/Latino, Italian, Latin American. **Biology:** General, biochemistry. **Business:** Accounting, business admin, finance, financial planning, insurance, marketing, real estate. **Communications:** Advertising, journalism, public relations. **Computer sciences:** Computer science. **Conservation:** Environmental science, environmental studies. **Education:** Music. **Engineering:** Civil, computer, electrical, environmental, mechanical, operations research. **English:** Creative writing, English lit. **Foreign languages:** French, German, Spanish. **Health services:** Music therapy. **History:** General. **Human services:** International policy, public policy. **Math:** General, statistics. **Parks/recreation:** Sports admin. **Philosophy/religion:** Philosophy, religion. **Physical sciences:** Chemistry, geology, geophysics, physics. **Psychology:** General. **Social sciences:** Anthropology, econometrics, economics, political science, sociology. **Visual/performing arts:** Art history/conservation, cinematography, dance, dramatic, music, music performance, music theory/composition, piano/keyboard, studio arts, voice/opera.

Most popular majors. Business/marketing 22%, communications/journalism 11%, engineering/engineering technologies 10%, social sciences 14%, visual/performing arts 7%.

Technology on campus. 758 workstations in dormitories, library, computer center, student center. Dormitories wired for high-speed internet access and linked to campus network. Commuter students can connect to campus network. Online course registration, online library, helpline, repair service, student web hosting, wireless network available.

Student life. Freshman orientation: Mandatory. Preregistration for classes offered. **Housing:** Guaranteed on-campus for freshmen. Coed dorms, apartments, cooperative housing, fraternity/sorority housing, themed housing available. $100 nonrefundable deposit, deadline 5/1. **Activities:** Bands, campus ministries, choral groups, dance, drama, film society, international student organizations, literary magazine, music ensembles, Model UN, musical theater, opera, radio station, student government, student newspaper, symphony orchestra, TV station, over 180 student organizations available.

Athletics. NCAA. **Intercollegiate:** Basketball, cross-country W, diving, equestrian W, football (tackle) M, golf, rowing (crew) W, soccer, swimming, tennis, track and field W, volleyball W. **Intramural:** Basketball, bowling, golf, racquetball, soccer, softball, swimming, table tennis, tennis, volleyball. **Team name:** Mustangs.

Student services. Adult student services, alcohol/substance abuse counseling, chaplain/spiritual director, career counseling, student employment services, financial aid counseling, health services, minority student services, on-campus daycare, personal counseling, placement for graduates, veterans' counselor, women's services. **Physically disabled:** Services for visually, speech, hearing impaired.

Contact. E-mail: ugadmission@smu.edu
Phone: (214) 768-2058 Toll-free number: (800) 323-0672
Fax: (214) 768-0103
Wes Waggoner, Dean of Admission and Executive Director of Enrollment Services, Southern Methodist University, PO Box 750181, Dallas, TX 75275-0181

Southwestern Adventist University
Keene, Texas
www.swau.edu   CB code: 6671

- Private 4-year university and liberal arts college affiliated with the Seventh-day Adventists
- Residential campus in small town

- 724 degree-seeking undergraduates: 9% part-time, 57% women, 13% African American, 3% Asian American, 42% Hispanic/Latino, 2% Native Hawaiian/Pacific islander, 4% Multi-racial, non-Hispanic, 15% international
- 11 graduate students
- 49% of applicants admitted
- SAT or ACT (ACT writing optional) required
- 50% graduate within 6 years; 29% enter graduate study

General. Founded in 1893. Regionally accredited. **Degrees:** 142 bachelor's, 5 associate awarded; master's offered. **Location:** 55 miles from Dallas, 25 miles from Fort Worth. **Calendar:** Semester, limited summer session. **Full-time faculty:** 47 total; 64% have terminal degrees, 23% minority, 32% women. **Part-time faculty:** 51 total; 22% have terminal degrees, 29% minority, 43% women. **Class size:** 77% < 20, 18% 20-39, 3% 40-49, 2% 50-99. **Special facilities:** Observatory, museum of student life, paleontology museum, simulation laboratory for nursing.

Freshman class profile. 1,476 applied, 716 admitted, 147 enrolled.

Mid 50% test scores			
SAT critical reading:	400-560	GPA 2.0-2.99:	38%
SAT math:	380-500	Rank in top quarter:	26%
SAT writing:	200-360	Rank in top tenth:	8%
ACT composite:	17-22	End year in good standing:	85%
GPA 3.75 or higher:	16%	Return as sophomores:	73%
GPA 3.50-3.74:	13%	Out-of-state:	13%
GPA 3.0-3.49:	33%	Live on campus:	65%
		International:	14%

Basis for selection. H.S. GPA minimum 2.5 and ACT minimum composite 17 or SAT minimum of 830 combined math and critical reading. **Home schooled:** A state high school equivalency certificate is accepted instead of a high school diploma or GED. **Learning Disabled:** Prospective students must submit a letter with documentation of their learning disability.

High school preparation. College-preparatory program recommended. 26 units required. Required and recommended units include English 4, mathematics 3-4, social studies 4, science 4, foreign language 2, visual/performing arts 1 and academic electives 6. 1 physical education required.

2015-2016 Annual costs. Tuition/fees: $19,916. Room/board: $7,400. Books/supplies: $1,400. Personal expenses: $1,356.

2014-2015 Financial aid. Need-based: 147 full-time freshmen applied for aid; 137 deemed to have need; 136 received aid. Average need met was 63%. Average scholarship/grant was $11,624; average loan $2,976. 57% of total undergraduate aid awarded as scholarships/grants, 43% as loans/jobs. **Non-need-based:** Awarded to 109 full-time undergraduates, including 28 freshmen. Scholarships awarded for academics, leadership, music/drama.

Application procedures. Admission: Priority date 3/15; deadline 6/1 (postmark date). $25 fee. Admission notification on a rolling basis beginning on or about 11/15. **Financial aid:** Priority date 3/15; no closing date. FAFSA, institutional form required. Applicants notified on a rolling basis starting 3/15.

Academics. Special study options: Accelerated study, cross-registration, distance learning, double major, ESL, external degree, honors, independent study, internships, liberal arts/career combination, student-designed major, study abroad, teacher certification program. **Credit/placement by examination:** AP, CLEP, IB, SAT, ACT, institutional tests. 16 credit hours maximum toward associate degree, 16 toward bachelor's. **Support services:** Learning center, pre-admission summer program, reduced course load, remedial instruction, study skills assistance, tutoring, writing center.

Majors. Biology: General. **Business:** Accounting, business admin, communications, finance, international, management science. **Communications:** Broadcast journalism, communications/speech/rhetoric, journalism. **Computer sciences:** Computer science. **Education:** Elementary, physical. **English:** English lit. **Health services:** Clinical lab technology, nursing (RN). **History:** General. **Math:** General, applied. **Parks/recreation:** Health/fitness. **Philosophy/religion:** Religion. **Physical sciences:** Chemistry, theoretical physics. **Psychology:** General, school. **Social sciences:** General, international relations. **Theology:** Theology. **Visual/performing arts:** Music.

Most popular majors. Business/marketing 11%, education 8%, health sciences 34%, liberal arts 9%, parks/recreation 6%, psychology 9%, theological studies 8%.

Technology on campus. 200 workstations in library, computer center. Dormitories wired for high-speed internet access and linked to campus network. Commuter students can connect to campus network. Online course registration, online library, helpline, repair service, student web hosting, wireless network available.

Student life. Freshman orientation: Mandatory, $200 fee. Preregistration for classes offered. Held the week prior to fall registration starting Wednesday evening through Monday noon. **Policies:** We promote a healthy, active lifestyle which includes refraining from the use of alcohol, tobacco and illegal drugs. **Housing:** Guaranteed on-campus for all undergraduates. Single-sex dorms, apartments available. $100 fully refundable deposit, deadline 6/1. **Activities:** Concert band, campus ministries, choral groups, drama, international student organizations, music ensembles, musical theater, radio station, student government, student newspaper, symphony orchestra, TV station.

Athletics. USCAA. **Intercollegiate:** Basketball, soccer. **Intramural:** Badminton, basketball, football (non-tackle), gymnastics, racquetball, soccer, table tennis, tennis W, volleyball. **Team name:** Knights.

Student services. Adult student services, alcohol/substance abuse counseling, chaplain/spiritual director, career counseling, student employment services, financial aid counseling, health services, personal counseling, placement for graduates, veterans' counselor.

Contact. E-mail: admissions@swau.edu
Phone: (817) 202-6749 Toll-free number: (800) 433-2240
Fax: (817) 202-6753
Rahneeka Hazelton, Director of Admissions, Southwestern Adventist University, Box 567, Keene, TX 76059

Southwestern Assemblies of God University
Waxahachie, Texas
www.sagu.edu   CB code: 6669

- Private 4-year university and Bible college affiliated with the Assemblies of God
- Residential campus in large town
- 1,639 degree-seeking undergraduates: 13% part-time, 52% women, 11% African American, 1% Asian American, 21% Hispanic/Latino, 2% Native American, 2% Multi-racial, non-Hispanic
- 313 graduate students
- SAT or ACT (ACT writing optional), application essay required
- 41% graduate within 6 years

General. Founded in 1927. Regionally accredited. **Degrees:** 275 bachelor's, 205 associate awarded; master's, professional offered. **ROTC:** Army. **Location:** 20 miles from Dallas. **Calendar:** Semester, limited summer session. **Full-time faculty:** 74 total. **Part-time faculty:** 80 total.

Freshman class profile.

GPA 3.75 or higher:	23%	Return as sophomores:	74%
GPA 3.50-3.74:	20%	Out-of-state:	35%
GPA 3.0-3.49:	31%	Live on campus:	81%
GPA 2.0-2.99:	25%		

Basis for selection. Minister's reference and 1 personal reference required. Interview recommended. **Learning Disabled:** Enrollment with the Achievement Center indicated.

2015-2016 Annual costs. Tuition/fees: $20,530. Room/board: $6,660. Books/supplies: $1,298.

Application procedures. Admission: Priority date 7/1; no deadline. $35 fee, may be waived for applicants with need. Admission notification on a rolling basis beginning on or about 3/1. **Financial aid:** Priority date 3/1; no closing date. FAFSA required. Applicants notified on a rolling basis starting 6/1; must reply within 2 week(s) of notification.

Academics. Special study options: Distance learning, double major, dual enrollment of high school students, external degree, independent study, internships, teacher certification program. **Credit/placement by examination:** AP, CLEP, SAT, ACT, institutional tests. 15 credit hours maximum toward associate degree, 30 toward bachelor's. **Support services:** Learning center, reduced course load, remedial instruction, tutoring.

Majors. Business: General, accounting, business admin, marketing. **Education:** Early childhood, elementary, English, mathematics, music, reading, secondary, social studies. **English:** English lit. **Health services:** Clinical pastoral counseling. **History:** General. **Math:** General. **Philosophy/religion:** Christian. **Psychology:** General. **Theology:** Bible, missionary, pastoral counseling, religious ed, sacred music, youth ministry. **Visual/performing arts:** Music performance, piano/keyboard, voice/opera.

Technology on campus. 45 workstations in dormitories, library, computer center, student center. Dormitories wired for high-speed internet access and linked to campus network. Online library, repair service, wireless network available.

Student life. Freshman orientation: Mandatory. Preregistration for classes offered. **Policies:** Dress code observed. Unmarried students 23 and under required to live in college housing unless alternative arrangements agreed to upon enrollment. Religious observance required. **Housing:** Guaranteed on-campus for freshmen. Coed dorms, single-sex dorms, apartments available. $150 partly refundable deposit. **Activities:** Bands, campus ministries, choral groups, drama, music ensembles, musical theater, student government, student newspaper, prayer groups, ministry labs.

Athletics. NAIA, NCCAA. **Intercollegiate:** Baseball M, basketball, cheerleading, cross-country, football (tackle) M, soccer, softball W, volleyball W. **Intramural:** Basketball, football (non-tackle) W, racquetball, table tennis, volleyball. **Team name:** Lions.

Student services. Adult student services, chaplain/spiritual director, career counseling, student employment services, financial aid counseling, health services, personal counseling, placement for graduates, veterans' counselor.

Contact. E-mail: admissions@sagu.edu
Phone: (972) 937-7248 Toll-free number: (888) 937-7248
Fax: (972) 923-0006
Joshua Martin, Assistant Director of Admissions, Southwestern Assemblies of God University, 1200 Sycamore Street, Waxahachie, TX 75165

Southwestern Baptist Theological Seminary
Fort Worth, Texas
www.swbts.edu   CB code: 4546

- Private 4-year Bible and seminary college affiliated with the Christian Church
- Residential campus in very large city
- 580 degree-seeking undergraduates
- 3,200 graduate students
- Application essay required

General. Regionally accredited. **Degrees:** 40 bachelor's awarded; master's, professional, doctoral offered. **Location:** 40 miles from Dallas. **Calendar:** Semester, limited summer session. **Full-time faculty:** 117 total. **Special facilities:** Archaeology museum, dead sea scrolls museum, music library, music performance labs, theological library.

Basis for selection. Commitment to Christian ministry is important. Neither the ACT nor SAT is required of undergraduate students seeking admission, but an English writing course will be required of students who report a low score or do not report a score.

2016-2017 Annual costs. Tuition/fees (projected): $14,640. Room only: $1,890. Books/supplies: $400.

Application procedures. Admission: No deadline. $35 fee, may be waived for applicants with need. Application must be submitted online. Admission notification on a rolling basis. **Financial aid:** No deadline.

Academics. Special study options: Accelerated study, distance learning, dual enrollment of high school students, independent study, internships. **Credit/placement by examination:** AP, CLEP, SAT, ACT. **Support services:** Tutoring, writing center.

Majors. Liberal arts: Humanities. **Theology:** Sacred music. **Visual/performing arts:** Music, music history, music performance.

Student life. Freshman orientation: Mandatory. Preregistration for classes offered. One day program held the Tuesday before classes begin. **Housing:** Single-sex dorms, special housing for disabled, apartments available. **Activities:** Concert band, campus ministries, choral groups, music ensembles, student newspaper.

Athletics. Intramural: Basketball, football (non-tackle), racquetball, soccer, swimming, table tennis, tennis, volleyball, weight lifting.

Student services. Chaplain/spiritual director, student employment services, financial aid counseling, health services, on-campus daycare, personal counseling, women's services. **Physically disabled:** Services for visually, speech, hearing impaired.

Contact. E-mail: admissions@swbts.edu
Phone: (800) 792-8701
Kyle Walker, Director of Admissions, Southwestern Baptist Theological Seminary, PO Box 22000, Fort Worth, TX 76122

Southwestern Christian College
Terrell, Texas
www.swcc.edu   CB code: 6705

▶ Private 4-year Bible and liberal arts college affiliated with the Church of Christ
▶ Residential campus in large town
▶ 149 degree-seeking undergraduates: 10% part-time, 46% women
▶ Application essay required
▶ 44% graduate within 6 years

General. Founded in 1949. Regionally accredited. **Degrees:** 33 associate awarded. **Location:** 30 miles from Dallas. **Calendar:** Semester. **Full-time faculty:** 12 total.

Freshman class profile. 121 applied, 97 admitted, 60 enrolled.

End year in good standing:	56%	Live on campus:	94%
Return as sophomores:	55%	International:	17%
Out-of-state:	85%		

Basis for selection. Open admission. Interview recommended. **Home schooled:** Transcript of courses and grades required.

2015-2016 Annual costs. Tuition/fees: $8,042. Room/board: $5,334. Books/supplies: $1,016. Personal expenses: $400.

Financial aid. **Non-need-based:** Scholarships awarded for academics, athletics, music/drama.

Application procedures. Admission: Closing date 7/31 (receipt date). $20 fee, may be waived for applicants with need. Admission notification on a rolling basis. **Financial aid:** Closing date 6/1. FAFSA required. Applicants notified on a rolling basis starting 7/15; must reply within 2 week(s) of notification.

Academics. Special study options: Independent study, internships. **Credit/placement by examination:** AP, CLEP, institutional tests. 8 credit hours maximum toward associate degree, 12 toward bachelor's. **Support services:** Learning center, reduced course load, remedial instruction.

Majors. Theology: Bible.

Student life. Freshman orientation: Mandatory, $10 fee. Preregistration for classes offered. **Policies:** High moral standards required. Profanity, vulgarity, gambling, drinking alcoholic beverages, attending dances or places of questionable amusement are against college's ideals and rules. **Housing:** Guaranteed on-campus for all undergraduates. Single-sex dorms available. $50 nonrefundable deposit, deadline 7/31. **Activities:** Jazz band, choral groups, drama, music ensembles, student government, student newspaper.

Athletics. NJCAA. **Intercollegiate:** Basketball, track and field. **Team name:** Rams.

Student services. Career counseling, personal counseling.

Contact. E-mail: swccadmissions@yahoo.com
Phone: (972) 524-3341 Toll-free number: (800) 925-9357
Fax: (972) 563-7133
Warren Roberts, Director of Admissions and Retention, Southwestern Christian College, Box 10, Terrell, TX 75160

Southwestern University
Georgetown, Texas   CB member
www.southwestern.edu   CB code: 6674

▶ Private 4-year liberal arts and performing arts college affiliated with the United Methodist Church
▶ Residential campus in large town
▶ 1,514 degree-seeking undergraduates: 1% part-time, 57% women, 5% African American, 4% Asian American, 22% Hispanic/Latino, 4% Multiracial, non-Hispanic, 2% international
▶ 44% of applicants admitted
▶ SAT or ACT (ACT writing optional), application essay required
▶ 75% graduate within 6 years

General. Founded in 1840. Regionally accredited. **Degrees:** 299 bachelor's awarded. **Location:** 28 miles from Austin. **Calendar:** Semester, limited summer session. **Full-time faculty:** 112 total; 98% have terminal degrees, 19% minority, 49% women. **Part-time faculty:** 52 total; 62% have terminal

degrees, 21% minority, 50% women. **Class size:** 76% < 20, 22% 20-39, less than 1% 40-49, 1% 50-99. **Special facilities:** Observatory.

Freshman class profile. 3,736 applied, 1,652 admitted, 359 enrolled.

Mid 50% test scores		Rank in top tenth:	32%
SAT critical reading:	520-640	Return as sophomores:	86%
SAT math:	520-630	Out-of-state:	14%
ACT composite:	23-29	Live on campus:	100%
Rank in top quarter:	68%	International:	2%

Basis for selection. Holistic admission review with academic performance, recommendations, test scores, essay, extracurriculars and interview considered. Greatest emphasis is on academic performance. Audition required for music, theater programs; portfolio required for art program. **Home schooled:** Interview required.

High school preparation. College-preparatory program required. 17 units required; 20 recommended. Required and recommended units include English 4, mathematics 4, social studies 2-3, history 1-2, science 3-4 (laboratory 2-3), foreign language 2-3 and academic electives 1.

2015-2016 Annual costs. Tuition/fees: $37,560. Room/board: $11,498. Books/supplies: $1,200. Personal expenses: $900.

2015-2016 Financial aid. Need-based: 316 full-time freshmen applied for aid; 245 deemed to have need; 245 received aid. Average need met was 92%. Average scholarship/grant was $30,100; average loan $4,106. 75% of total undergraduate aid awarded as scholarships/grants, 25% as loans/jobs. **Non-need-based:** Awarded to 1,445 full-time undergraduates, including 354 freshmen. Scholarships awarded for academics, alumni affiliation, art, leadership, minority status, music/drama, religious affiliation.

Application procedures. Admission: Priority date 2/1; no deadline. No application fee. Admission notification on a rolling basis beginning on or about 10/15. Must reply by May 1 or within 2 week(s) if notified thereafter. **Financial aid:** Priority date 3/1; no closing date. FAFSA required. Applicants notified on a rolling basis starting 3/1; must reply by 5/1 or within 2 week(s) of notification.

Academics. Special study options: Combined bachelor's/graduate degree, double major, honors, independent study, internships, liberal arts/career combination, New York semester, student-designed major, study abroad, teacher certification program, Washington semester. **Credit/placement by examination:** AP, CLEP, IB, SAT, ACT, institutional tests. **Support services:** Reduced course load, study skills assistance, tutoring, writing center.

Majors. Area/ethnic studies: Latin American, women's. **Biology:** General, biochemistry. **Business:** General. **Communications:** Communications/speech/rhetoric. **Computer sciences:** General. **Conservation:** Environmental studies. **Education:** General. **English:** English lit. **Foreign languages:** Ancient Greek, classics, French, German, Latin, Spanish. **History:** General. **Math:** General, computational. **Parks/recreation:** Exercise sciences. **Philosophy/religion:** Philosophy, religion. **Physical sciences:** General, chemistry, physics. **Psychology:** General. **Social sciences:** Anthropology, economics, international relations, political science, sociology. **Visual/performing arts:** Art, art history/conservation, dramatic, music.

Most popular majors. Biology 13%, business/marketing 14%, communications/journalism 7%, English 7%, psychology 7%, social sciences 12%, visual/performing arts 10%.

Technology on campus. 410 workstations in dormitories, library, computer center, student center. Dormitories wired for high-speed internet access and linked to campus network. Commuter students can connect to campus network. Online course registration, online library, helpline, repair service, student web hosting, wireless network available.

Student life. Freshman orientation: Mandatory. Preregistration for classes offered. 2-day advising and registration sessions May-July, full week orientation prior to start of regular classes, with First Year and Transfer seminars starting then. **Housing:** Guaranteed on-campus for freshmen. Coed dorms, single-sex dorms, special housing for disabled, apartments, fraternity/sorority housing available. $250 nonrefundable deposit, deadline 5/1. **Activities:** Bands, campus ministries, choral groups, dance, drama, international student organizations, literary magazine, music ensembles, Model UN, musical theater, opera, radio station, student government, student newspaper, symphony orchestra, Alpha Phi Omega, Ebony, Mexican American student association, political science society, international club, Equal Voice For Women's Perspective.

Athletics. NCAA. **Intercollegiate:** Baseball M, basketball, cross-country, diving, football (tackle) M, golf, lacrosse, soccer, softball W, swimming, tennis, track and field, volleyball W. **Intramural:** Basketball, football (non-tackle), racquetball, soccer, table tennis, tennis, ultimate frisbee, volleyball. **Team name:** Bucs/Pirates.

Student services. Alcohol/substance abuse counseling, chaplain/spiritual director, career counseling, student employment services, financial aid counseling, health services, minority student services, personal counseling, placement for graduates, veterans' counselor, women's services. **Physically disabled:** Services for visually, speech, hearing impaired.

Contact. E-mail: admission@southwestern.edu
Phone: (512) 863-1200 Toll-free number: (800) 252-3166
Fax: (512) 863-9601
Christine Bowman, Director of Admissions, Southwestern University, PO Box 770, Georgetown, TX 78627-0770

St. Edward's University
Austin, Texas
www.stedwards.edu

CB member
CB code: 6619

- Private 4-year university and liberal arts college affiliated with the Roman Catholic Church
- Residential campus in very large city
- 4,020 degree-seeking undergraduates: 12% part-time, 61% women, 4% African American, 3% Asian American, 40% Hispanic/Latino, 4% Multiracial, non-Hispanic, 9% international
- 597 degree-seeking graduate students
- 77% of applicants admitted
- SAT or ACT (ACT writing recommended), application essay required
- 63% graduate within 6 years

General. Founded in 1885. Regionally accredited. Partner campus in Angers, France at Universite Catholique de l'Ouest. **Degrees:** 845 bachelor's awarded; master's offered. **ROTC:** Army, Air Force. **Location:** 80 miles from San Antonio, 180 miles from Dallas. **Calendar:** Semester, limited summer session. **Full-time faculty:** 191 total; 90% have terminal degrees, 14% minority, 53% women. **Part-time faculty:** 277 total; 47% have terminal degrees, 16% minority, 50% women. **Class size:** 56% < 20, 43% 20-39, less than 1% 40-49, less than 1% 50-99, less than 1% >100. **Special facilities:** Fine arts facility with photography laboratory; Global Digital Classroom; theater; chapel; interdisciplinary research laboratory at Wild Basin Wilderness Preserve; partner campus in Angers, France at Universite Catholique de l'Ouest.

Freshman class profile. 5,034 applied, 3,899 admitted, 873 enrolled.

Mid 50% test scores			
SAT critical reading:	530-620	Rank in top tenth:	24%
SAT math:	510-600	End year in good standing:	91%
SAT writing:	500-600	Return as sophomores:	85%
ACT composite:	23-27	Out-of-state:	19%
Rank in top quarter:	58%	Live on campus:	90%
		International:	7%

Basis for selection. Holistic review process, with grades and curriculum, class rank and test scores (both preferably in top 50th percentile) most important components. Extracurricular activities, leadership and service, application essay, letters of recommendation reviewed as complement to student's academic record. Test scores must be received by 2/1 for scholarship consideration. Interviews recommended. **Learning Disabled:** Students are welcome to submit learning disability documentation with admission application.

High school preparation. College-preparatory program recommended. 14 units required; 20 recommended. Required and recommended units include English 4, mathematics 3-4, social studies 1, history 2-3, science 2-3 (laboratory 2-3), foreign language 2-3, computer science 1 and academic electives 1.

2016-2017 Annual costs. Tuition/fees: $40,828. Room/board: $12,172. Books/supplies: $1,050. Personal expenses: $1,900.

2015-2016 Financial aid. Need-based: 716 full-time freshmen applied for aid; 613 deemed to have need; 606 received aid. Average need met was 75%. Average scholarship/grant was $20,893; average loan $3,486. 82% of total undergraduate aid awarded as scholarships/grants, 18% as loans/jobs. **Non-need-based:** Awarded to 1,896 full-time undergraduates, including 559 freshmen. Scholarships awarded for academics, athletics, music/drama, state residency.

Application procedures. Admission: Priority date 2/1; deadline 5/1 (postmark date). $50 fee, may be waived for applicants with need. Admission notification on a rolling basis beginning on or about 11/1. Must reply by May 1 or within 2 week(s) if notified thereafter. For merit scholarship consideration, students must apply by the February 1 priority deadline. **Financial aid:** Priority date 2/1; no closing date. FAFSA required. Applicants notified on a rolling basis starting 2/1; must reply by 5/1 or within 2 week(s) of notification.

Academics. Special study options: Combined bachelor's/graduate degree, double major, honors, internships, study abroad, teacher certification program, Washington semester. **Credit/placement by examination:** AP, CLEP, IB, SAT, ACT, institutional tests. **Support services:** Reduced course load, study skills assistance, tutoring, writing center. Math lab, Mission Resource Center, Supplemental Instruction, Peer Coaching.

Majors. Biology: General, biochemistry, bioinformatics. **Business:** Accounting, accounting technology, business admin, entrepreneurial studies, finance, international, marketing. **Communications:** General, digital media. **Computer sciences:** General, computer science. **Conservation:** Environmental studies. **Education:** Art, biology, chemistry, drama/dance, English, history, mathematics, multi-level teacher, physical, social studies, Spanish, special ed. **English:** English lit, writing. **Foreign languages:** French, Spanish. **Health services:** Clinical lab science. **History:** General. **Human services:** Social work. **Liberal arts:** Arts/sciences. **Math:** General. **Parks/recreation:** Exercise sciences. **Philosophy/religion:** Christian, philosophy. **Physical sciences:** Chemistry, environmental chemistry, forensic chemistry. **Protective services:** Criminal justice, forensics. **Psychology:** General. **Social sciences:** Criminology, economics, political science, sociology. **Theology:** Theology. **Visual/performing arts:** Acting, art, arts management, dramatic, game design, graphic design, photography.

Most popular majors. Biology 6%, business/marketing 26%, communications/journalism 11%, English 6%, psychology 11%, visual/performing arts 8%.

Technology on campus. 967 workstations in dormitories, library, computer center, student center. Dormitories wired for high-speed internet access and linked to campus network. Commuter students can connect to campus network. Online course registration, online library, helpline, repair service, student web hosting, wireless network available.

Student life. Freshman orientation: Mandatory, $250 fee. Preregistration for classes offered. Two day sessions held 6 times during summer. **Policies:** Student organizations must receive annual university recognition through Office of Student Life, and must also go through annual risk management training. **Housing:** Guaranteed on-campus for freshmen. Coed dorms, special housing for disabled, apartments, themed housing available. $150 nonrefundable deposit, deadline 5/1. Community style living (casas/casitas) and 6 living-learning communities (business, global understanding, honors (by invitation), natural sciences, social justice, active living, and leadership). **Activities:** Bands, campus ministries, choral groups, dance, drama, film society, international student organizations, literary magazine, music ensembles, Model UN, musical theater, radio station, student government, student newspaper, TV station, Fellowship of Christian Athletes, Hillel Toppers, Muslim Student Association, Saudi Arabian Student Association, Rotaract club, Asian Students Association, Ballet Folklorico, Latino Student Leaders Organization, Circle K International, Alpha Phi Omega.

Athletics. NCAA. **Intercollegiate:** Baseball M, basketball, cheerleading, cross-country, golf, soccer, softball W, tennis, volleyball W. **Intramural:** Basketball, bowling, football (non-tackle), golf, racquetball, sand volleyball, soccer, tennis, volleyball. **Team name:** Hilltoppers.

Student services. Adult student services, alcohol/substance abuse counseling, chaplain/spiritual director, career counseling, services for economically disadvantaged, student employment services, financial aid counseling, health services, minority student services, personal counseling, placement for graduates, veterans' counselor. **Physically disabled:** Services for visually, speech, hearing impaired.

Contact. E-mail: seu.admit@stedwards.edu
Phone: (512) 448-8500 Toll-free number: (800) 555-0164
Fax: (512) 464-8877
Tracy Manier, Associate VP and Dean of Undergraduate Admission, St. Edward's University, 3001 South Congress Avenue, Austin, TX 78704-6489

St. Mary's University
San Antonio, Texas
www.stmarytx.edu

CB member
CB code: 6637

- Private 4-year university and liberal arts college affiliated with the Roman Catholic Church
- Residential campus in very large city
- 2,305 degree-seeking undergraduates: 5% part-time, 54% women, 3% African American, 2% Asian American, 70% Hispanic/Latino, 8% international
- 1,316 degree-seeking graduate students
- 55% of applicants admitted

♦ SAT or ACT (ACT writing optional) required
♦ 63% graduate within 6 years

General. Founded in 1852. Regionally accredited. **Degrees:** 519 bachelor's awarded; master's, professional, doctoral offered. **ROTC:** Army, Air Force. **Location:** 5 miles from downtown. **Calendar:** Semester, limited summer session. **Full-time faculty:** 204 total; 94% have terminal degrees, 28% minority, 36% women. **Part-time faculty:** 163 total; 55% have terminal degrees, 32% minority, 41% women. **Class size:** 60% < 20, 40% 20-39. **Special facilities:** Learning commons, earth science museum, music and drama theater, amphitheater, trading room.

Freshman class profile. 5,832 applied, 3,219 admitted, 593 enrolled.

Mid 50% test scores			
SAT critical reading:	460-560	GPA 3.0-3.49:	33%
		GPA 2.0-2.99:	13%
SAT math:	470-570	End year in good standing:	76%
SAT writing:	440-540	Return as sophomores:	76%
ACT composite:	20-25	Out-of-state:	2%
GPA 3.75 or higher:	25%	Live on campus:	75%
GPA 3.50-3.74:	29%	International:	7%

Basis for selection. Balanced consideration given to all aspects of high school performance, including selection of college-preparatory courses, GPA and grade pattern throughout high school, class rank, standardized test scores, and record of service and leadership. **Home schooled:** Transcript of courses and grades required.

High school preparation. College-preparatory program recommended. 16 units required; 19 recommended. Required and recommended units include English 4, mathematics 3-4, social studies 3-4, science 3-4, foreign language 2-3 and academic electives 1. Applicants to science and engineering program should complete 4 units of math and 3 units of lab science.

2015-2016 Annual costs. Tuition/fees: $27,160. Room/board: $8,908. Books/supplies: $1,300. Personal expenses: $2,000.

2014-2015 Financial aid. Need-based: 399 full-time freshmen applied for aid; 368 deemed to have need; 368 received aid. Average need met was 73%. Average scholarship/grant was $19,362; average loan $4,116. 67% of total undergraduate aid awarded as scholarships/grants, 33% as loans/jobs. **Non-need-based:** Awarded to 576 full-time undergraduates, including 130 freshmen. Scholarships awarded for academics, alumni affiliation, athletics, music/drama, religious affiliation, ROTC, state residency.

Application procedures. Admission: Priority date 1/15; no deadline. No application fee. Admission notification on a rolling basis beginning on or about 10/20. Must reply by May 1 or within 2 week(s) if notified thereafter. **Financial aid:** Priority date 3/31; no closing date. Applicants notified on a rolling basis starting 3/1; must reply by 5/1 or within 2 week(s) of notification.

Academics. Writing across the curriculum program requires students in all undergraduate programs to take writing-intensive courses. **Special study options:** Accelerated study, combined bachelor's/graduate degree, cross-registration, distance learning, double major, dual enrollment of high school students, exchange student, honors, independent study, internships, study abroad, teacher certification program, Washington semester. **Credit/placement by examination:** AP, CLEP, SAT, ACT, institutional tests. 30 credit hours maximum toward bachelor's degree. **Support services:** Learning center, pre-admission summer program, reduced course load, remedial instruction, study skills assistance, tutoring, writing center.

Majors. Biology: General, biochemistry. **Business:** Accounting, business admin, entrepreneurial studies, finance, financial planning, international, marketing. **Communications:** Communications/speech/rhetoric. **Computer sciences:** General, computer science. **Conservation:** Environmental science. **Education:** Art, curriculum. **Engineering:** Computer, electrical, engineering science, industrial, mechanical, software. **English:** English lit. **Foreign languages:** Spanish. **History:** General. **Human services:** General. **Math:** General. **Parks/recreation:** Exercise sciences. **Philosophy/religion:** Philosophy. **Physical sciences:** Chemistry, physics. **Protective services:** Forensics, law enforcement admin. **Psychology:** General. **Social sciences:** Criminology, economics, international relations, political science, sociology. **Theology:** Theology. **Visual/performing arts:** Music.

Most popular majors. Biology 12%, business/marketing 24%, parks/recreation 10%, psychology 6%, security/protective services 9%, social sciences 15%.

Technology on campus. PC or laptop required. 100 workstations in dormitories, library, computer center, student center. Dormitories wired for high-speed internet access and linked to campus network. Commuter students can connect to campus network. Online course registration, online library, helpline, repair service, wireless network available.

Student life. Freshman orientation: Mandatory, $160 fee. Preregistration for classes offered. Two-part program. Part one is offered twice in June and once in August. Parallel program offered for parents. June sessions offer campus accommodations for students and parents. The second part occurs in August during the four days before classes start. Transfer student orientation is a one-day program, offered twice in June and once in August. **Housing:** Guaranteed on-campus for freshmen. Coed dorms, themed housing available. $200 nonrefundable deposit, deadline 5/1. Nontraditional residence halls available for students 21 years old or above. **Activities:** Bands, campus ministries, choral groups, dance, drama, international student organizations, literary magazine, music ensembles, musical theater, opera, student government, student newspaper, Catholic Student Group, Belles of St. Mary's, St. Mary's University Students for Liberty, St. Mary's University College Democrats, Alpha Phi Omega, Red Cross club, Habitat for Humanity, Native American Students' Association, Association for Latino Professionals in For America.

Athletics. NCAA. **Intercollegiate:** Baseball M, basketball, cheerleading, golf, soccer, softball W, tennis, volleyball W. **Intramural:** Badminton, basketball, football (non-tackle), racquetball, sand volleyball, soccer, softball, swimming, table tennis, tennis, volleyball. **Team name:** Rattlers.

Student services. Adult student services, alcohol/substance abuse counseling, chaplain/spiritual director, career counseling, student employment services, financial aid counseling, health services, personal counseling, placement for graduates. **Physically disabled:** Services for visually, speech, hearing impaired.

Contact. E-mail: uadm@stmarytx.edu
Phone: (210) 436-3126 Toll-free number: (800) 367-7868
Fax: (210) 431-6742
Nelson Delgado, Director of Admission, St. Mary's University, One Camino Santa Maria, San Antonio, TX 78228-8504

Stephen F. Austin State University
Nacogdoches, Texas   **CB member**
www.sfasu.edu   **CB code: 6682**

♦ Public 4-year university
♦ Residential campus in large town
♦ 10,562 degree-seeking undergraduates: 11% part-time, 63% women
♦ 1,677 degree-seeking graduate students
♦ 62% of applicants admitted
♦ SAT or ACT (ACT writing recommended) required
♦ 41% graduate within 6 years

General. Founded in 1923. Regionally accredited. **Degrees:** 2,158 bachelor's awarded; master's, doctoral offered. **ROTC:** Army. **Location:** 140 miles from Houston, 70 miles from Longview. **Calendar:** Semester, extensive summer session. **Full-time faculty:** 517 total; 72% have terminal degrees, 7% minority, 48% women. **Part-time faculty:** 187 total; 44% have terminal degrees, 9% minority, 59% women. **Class size:** 29% < 20, 49% 20-39, 11% 40-49, 11% 50-99, less than 1% >100. **Special facilities:** Computerized observatory; experimental forest; arboretum; beef, poultry and swine research facilities; equine, goat and sheep centers; soil, plant and water analysis labs; biotechnology/environmental science research center; Stone Fort museum; agricultural pond; forest resources institute; geographic information systems lab; regional geospatial service center; early childhood research center.

Freshman class profile. 11,382 applied, 7,008 admitted, 2,282 enrolled.

Mid 50% test scores			
SAT critical reading:	440-550	Rank in top tenth:	12%
SAT math:	450-550	Return as sophomores:	71%
SAT writing:	420-530	Out-of-state:	1%
ACT composite:	19-24	Live on campus:	90%
Rank in top quarter:	40%	Fraternities:	22%
		Sororities:	20%

Basis for selection. Applicants must complete prescribed high school preparation and submit official transcript and SAT or ACT scores. No minimum score required for those ranking in top 10% of graduating class; others in the first quartile must have composite score of 850 SAT, 17 ACT; second quartile 950 SAT, 20 ACT; third quartile 1100 SAT, 24 ACT. All SAT scores exclusive of Writing. Applicants not meeting rank-in-class and test requirements reviewed on individual basis. All first-time incoming freshmen must submit an SAT or ACT score. Those with GED are also required to submit an SAT or ACT score. **Home schooled:** Applicants individually assessed based on probability of success.

High school preparation. 26 units required. Required units include English 4, mathematics 4, social studies 3.5, science 4 (laboratory 4), foreign language 2, visual/performing arts 1 and academic electives 6. 1 physical education, .5 economics, and .5 speech units required.

2015-2016 Annual costs. Tuition/fees: $9,342; $21,042 out-of-state. Room/board: $8,868. Books/supplies: $1,192. Personal expenses: $1,854.

2014-2015 Financial aid. Need-based: 1,732 full-time freshmen applied for aid; 1,361 deemed to have need; 1,361 received aid. Average need met was 56%. Average scholarship/grant was $9,101; average loan $3,626. 58% of total undergraduate aid awarded as scholarships/grants, 42% as loans/jobs. **Non-need-based:** Awarded to 3,265 full-time undergraduates, including 890 freshmen. Scholarships awarded for academics, alumni affiliation, art, leadership, music/drama, state residency. **Additional information:** For students who qualify, Purple Promise tuition guarantee program covers the remaining balance of any tuition and mandatory fees not covered by other gift aid, for 15 hours per regular semester for up to 4 years.

Application procedures. Admission: No deadline. $45 fee, may be waived for applicants with need. Application must be submitted online. Admission notification on a rolling basis beginning on or about 9/1. **Financial aid:** Priority date 4/1; no closing date. FAFSA required. Applicants notified on a rolling basis starting 4/1.

Academics. Special study options: Accelerated study, combined bachelor's/graduate degree, distance learning, double major, dual enrollment of high school students, independent study, internships, liberal arts/career combination, student-designed major, study abroad, teacher certification program. **Credit/placement by examination:** AP, CLEP, IB, SAT, ACT, institutional tests. 32 credit hours maximum toward bachelor's degree. **Support services:** Learning center, pre-admission summer program, reduced course load, remedial instruction, study skills assistance, tutoring, writing center.

Majors. Architecture: Interior. **Biology:** General, biochemistry. **Business:** General, accounting, business admin, fashion, finance, hospitality admin, international, managerial economics, marketing, special products marketing. **Communications:** Media studies. **Computer sciences:** General, information technology. **Conservation:** Environmental science, forest management, forestry, wildlife/wilderness. **English:** Creative writing, English lit, rhetoric/composition. **Foreign languages:** General, Hispanic and Latin American. **Health services:** Audiology/hearing, communication disorders, nursing (RN), rehabilitation science. **History:** General. **Human services:** General, social work. **Liberal arts:** Arts/sciences. **Math:** General. **Parks/recreation:** Exercise sciences. **Philosophy/religion:** Philosophy. **Physical sciences:** Chemistry, geology, physics. **Protective services:** Corrections, police science. **Psychology:** General. **Social sciences:** Economics, geography, GIS/cartography, political science, sociology. **Visual/performing arts:** Art, art history/conservation, dance, dramatic, music. **Work/family studies:** General, food/nutrition.

Most popular majors. Business/marketing 20%, health sciences 15%, interdisciplinary studies 13%, parks/recreation 7%, visual/performing arts 7%.

Technology on campus. 1,000 workstations in dormitories, library, computer center, student center. Dormitories wired for high-speed internet access and linked to campus network. Commuter students can connect to campus network. Online course registration, online library, helpline, repair service, student web hosting, wireless network available.

Student life. Freshman orientation: Available, $140 fee. Preregistration for classes offered. Five 2-day sessions held each summer for students and parents. **Policies:** Students must live in college housing until 60 semester hours completed. Off-campus housing permitted if student is 21 or older, married, commutes from permanent address of parent or relative, or enrolls for 8 hours or less. **Housing:** Guaranteed on-campus for freshmen. Coed dorms, single-sex dorms, wellness housing available. $100 fully refundable deposit. **Activities:** Bands, campus ministries, choral groups, dance, drama, film society, international student organizations, literary magazine, music ensembles, musical theater, opera, radio station, student government, student newspaper, symphony orchestra, TV station, African American student association, Canterbury Episcopal student association, Campus Crusade for Christ, Jewish student fellowship, Habitat for Humanity, SFA Democrats, Young Republicans, social services.

Athletics. NCAA. **Intercollegiate:** Baseball M, basketball, bowling W, cross-country, football (tackle) M, golf, soccer W, softball W, tennis W, track and field, volleyball W. **Intramural:** Badminton, baseball M, basketball, cross-country, football (non-tackle), lacrosse M, racquetball, rodeo, rugby, soccer M, softball, table tennis, tennis, volleyball, water polo, wrestling M. **Team name:** Lumberjacks/Ladyjacks.

Student services. Adult student services, alcohol/substance abuse counseling, career counseling, student employment services, financial aid counseling, health services, legal services, minority student services, on-campus daycare, personal counseling, placement for graduates, veterans' counselor. **Physically disabled:** Services for visually, speech, hearing impaired.

Contact. E-mail: admissions@sfasu.edu
Phone: (936) 468-2504 Fax: (936) 468-3849
Monique Cossich, Executive Director of Enrollment Management, Stephen F. Austin State University, Box 13051, SFA Station, Nacogdoches, TX 75962-3051

Sul Ross State University

Alpine, Texas
www.sulross.edu

CB member
CB code: 6685

- Public 4-year university
- Residential campus in small town
- 1,354 degree-seeking undergraduates: 20% part-time, 47% women
- 528 degree-seeking graduate students
- 80% of applicants admitted
- SAT or ACT (ACT writing recommended) required

General. Founded in 1917. Regionally accredited. Off-campus upper-level and graduate programs also available at Rio Grande College in Del Rio, Eagle Pass, Uvalde and Castroville. **Degrees:** 173 bachelor's awarded; master's offered. **Location:** 140 miles from Odessa, 220 miles from El Paso. **Calendar:** Semester, limited summer session. **Full-time faculty:** 93 total; 2% have terminal degrees, 26% minority, 44% women. **Part-time faculty:** 55 total; 14% minority, 47% women. **Class size:** 62% < 20, 32% 20-39, 3% 40-49, 3% 50-99. **Special facilities:** Center for big bend studies, materials characterization laboratory, museum of the big bend.

Freshman class profile. 1,143 applied, 914 admitted, 351 enrolled.

Mid 50% test scores		GPA 3.0-3.49:	43%
SAT critical reading:	350-460	GPA 2.0-2.99:	24%
SAT math:	390-480	Rank in top quarter:	20%
SAT writing:	360-430	Rank in top tenth:	3%
ACT composite:	15-20	Return as sophomores:	60%
GPA 3.75 or higher:	12%	Out-of-state:	2%
GPA 3.50-3.74:	17%	Live on campus:	86%

Basis for selection. Students must meet one of following criteria: ACT score of 20, SAT score of 800 (exclusive of Writing), or rank in top half of graduating class. Probational admission for all other applicants.

High school preparation. 15 units required; 31 recommended. Required and recommended units include English 4, mathematics 3-4, history 1-2, science 2-4 (laboratory 2), foreign language 3, computer science 1 and visual/performing arts 1. 1 U.S. government, 1 world history/geography, 1 economics, 1.5 physical education, 0.5 health education required; 1 health education, 4 technical area recommended.

2015-2016 Annual costs. Tuition/fees: $7,211; $18,911 out-of-state. Room/board: $7,810. Books/supplies: $1,366. Personal expenses: $1,552.

2014-2015 Financial aid. Need-based: Average scholarship/grant was $7,426; average loan $2,645. 63% of total undergraduate aid awarded as scholarships/grants, 37% as loans/jobs. **Non-need-based:** Scholarships awarded for academics, alumni affiliation, art, leadership, music/drama, state residency.

Application procedures. Admission: No deadline. $25 fee, may be waived for applicants with need. Admission notification on a rolling basis. **Financial aid:** Priority date 3/1; no closing date. FAFSA required. Applicants notified by 3/3.

Academics. Special study options: Combined bachelor's/graduate degree, distance learning, double major, dual enrollment of high school students, ESL, honors, independent study, internships, study abroad, teacher certification program. **Credit/placement by examination:** AP, CLEP, institutional tests. 30 credit hours maximum toward bachelor's degree. **Support services:** Learning center, pre-admission summer program, reduced course load, remedial instruction, study skills assistance, tutoring, writing center.

Majors. Biology: General. **Business:** Business admin, office management. **Communications:** Communications/speech/rhetoric. **Computer sciences:** General. **Conservation:** General. **Education:** Elementary. **English:** English lit, rhetoric/composition. **Foreign languages:** Spanish. **History:** General. **Math:** General. **Parks/recreation:** Health/fitness. **Physical sciences:** Chemistry, geology. **Protective services:** Criminal justice. **Psychology:** General. **Social sciences:** General, political science. **Visual/performing arts:** Art, dramatic.

Most popular majors. Agriculture 7%, biology 14%, business/marketing 8%, English 6%, interdisciplinary studies 6%, liberal arts 8%, natural resources/environmental science 8%, parks/recreation 11%, physical sciences 7%.

Technology on campus. 200 workstations in library, computer center. Dormitories wired for high-speed internet access and linked to campus network. Commuter students can connect to campus network. Online library, helpline, repair service, wireless network available.

Student life. Freshman orientation: Available, $100 fee. Preregistration for classes offered. **Housing:** Guaranteed on-campus for freshmen. Coed dorms, apartments available. **Activities:** Marching band, campus ministries, choral groups, music ensembles, musical theater, student government, student newspaper, Wesley Foundation, Newman club, Baptist student union, Fellowship of Christian Athletes, Spanish club, rodeo club, black student association, international student association, nontraditional student association.

Athletics. NCAA. **Intercollegiate:** Baseball M, basketball, cross-country, football (tackle) M, softball W, tennis, track and field, volleyball W. **Intramural:** Basketball, football (non-tackle), racquetball, soccer, softball, tennis, volleyball, water polo, weight lifting. **Team name:** Lobos.

Student services. Alcohol/substance abuse counseling, chaplain/spiritual director, career counseling, student employment services, financial aid counseling, health services, on-campus daycare, personal counseling, placement for graduates, veterans' counselor. **Physically disabled:** Services for visually, hearing impaired.

Contact. E-mail: admissions@sulross.edu
Phone: (432) 837-8050 Toll-free number: (888) 722-7778
Fax: (432) 837-8431
MaryBeth Marks, Director of Admissions, Sul Ross State University, PO Box C-2, Alpine, TX 79832

Tarleton State University
Stephenville, Texas — CB member
www.tarleton.edu — CB code: 6817

- Public 4-year university
- Residential campus in large town
- 10,749 degree-seeking undergraduates: 23% part-time, 61% women, 8% African American, 1% Asian American, 18% Hispanic/Latino, 1% Native American, 3% Multi-racial, non-Hispanic
- 1,580 degree-seeking graduate students
- 71% of applicants admitted
- SAT or ACT (ACT writing recommended) required
- 44% graduate within 6 years

General. Founded in 1899. Regionally accredited. Courses available at several off-campus locations within 150-mile radius. **Degrees:** 2,098 bachelor's, 48 associate awarded; master's, doctoral offered. **ROTC:** Army. **Location:** 65 miles from Fort Worth. **Calendar:** Semester, extensive summer session. **Full-time faculty:** 350 total; 5% minority, 54% women. **Part-time faculty:** 337 total; 14% minority, 58% women. **Class size:** 33% < 20, 54% 20-39, 3% 40-49, 8% 50-99, 1% >100. **Special facilities:** University farm and equine center, dairy center, planetarium, center for industrial history of Texas, cultural and educational center.

Freshman class profile. 6,288 applied, 4,482 admitted, 1,955 enrolled.

Mid 50% test scores		Rank in top quarter:	37%
SAT critical reading:	420-520	Rank in top tenth:	9%
SAT math:	430-530	Out-of-state:	1%
SAT writing:	400-500	Live on campus:	90%
ACT composite:	18-23		

Basis for selection. Quarter rank (percentile) in class, graduation program, and test scores. If a student is in the top quarter of their graduating class and completing the recommended or distinguished program, only test scores required. Remainder of students must meet score requirements. **Home schooled:** Must provide proof of curriculum completed from an agency or teacher. **Learning Disabled:** Contact Director of Disability Services for appropriate accommodation.

High school preparation. College-preparatory program recommended. 19 units required. Required and recommended units include English 4, mathematics 3, social studies 2, history 1, science 2-3, foreign language 2 and academic electives 2-4.

2015-2016 Annual costs. Tuition/fees: $7,705; $19,713.5 out-of-state. Room/board: $8,832. Books/supplies: $1,207. Personal expenses: $1,836.

2014-2015 Financial aid. Need-based: 1,774 full-time freshmen applied for aid; 1,340 deemed to have need; 1,322 received aid. Average need met was 58%. Average scholarship/grant was $7,284; average loan $3,089. 62% of total undergraduate aid awarded as scholarships/grants, 38% as loans/jobs. **Non-need-based:** Awarded to 112 full-time undergraduates, including 83 freshmen. Scholarships awarded for academics, alumni affiliation, athletics, leadership, music/drama, ROTC. **Additional information:** Tuition guarantee program covers tuition and fees for qualified freshman.

Application procedures. Admission: Priority date 3/1; deadline 8/21 (receipt date). $45 fee, may be waived for applicants with need. Admission notification on a rolling basis beginning on or about 9/1. **Financial aid:**

Priority date 3/15; no closing date. FAFSA required. Applicants notified on a rolling basis starting 5/1; must reply within 2 week(s) of notification.

Academics. Special study options: Accelerated study, combined bachelor's/graduate degree, distance learning, double major, dual enrollment of high school students, honors, internships, study abroad, teacher certification program. Specialized bachelor of applied arts and science degree for students with practical work experience in field of study; cooperative doctoral program in educational administration offered in partnership with Texas A&M University-Commerce; 2-2 engineering with Texas A&M University and University of Texas Arlington. **Credit/placement by examination:** AP, CLEP, SAT, ACT, institutional tests. Students can earn the majority of credits toward their degree by examination. **Support services:** Learning center, preadmission summer program, reduced course load, remedial instruction, study skills assistance, tutoring, writing center.

Majors. Biology: General, biomedical sciences, zoology. **Business:** General, accounting, business admin, finance, human resources, international, management information systems, managerial economics, marketing, office management. **Communications:** Communications/speech/rhetoric. **Computer sciences:** General. **Conservation:** Wildlife/wilderness. **Engineering:** Applied physics, environmental. **English:** English lit. **Foreign languages:** Spanish. **Health services:** Clinical lab science, nursing (RN). **History:** General. **Human services:** Social work. **Liberal arts:** Arts/sciences. **Math:** General. **Parks/recreation:** Exercise sciences, health/fitness. **Physical sciences:** Chemistry, geology, hydrology, physics. **Protective services:** Criminal justice, law enforcement admin. **Psychology:** General. **Social sciences:** Economics, political science, sociology. **Visual/performing arts:** Dramatic, music, studio arts. **Work/family studies:** General.

Most popular majors. Agriculture 10%, business/marketing 20%, health sciences 7%, interdisciplinary studies 14%, parks/recreation 7%, psychology 6%, security/protective services 8%.

Technology on campus. 1,200 workstations in dormitories, library, computer center, student center, student center. Dormitories wired for high-speed internet access and linked to campus network. Commuter students can connect to campus network. Online course registration, online library, helpline, repair service, student web hosting, wireless network available.

Student life. Freshman orientation: Mandatory. Preregistration for classes offered. Held multiple times during the summer. **Housing:** Guaranteed on-campus for freshmen. Coed dorms, single-sex dorms, apartments available. $100 fully refundable deposit, deadline 3/1. **Activities:** Bands, campus ministries, choral groups, dance, drama, international student organizations, literary magazine, music ensembles, musical theater, radio station, student government, student newspaper, symphony orchestra, Los Tejanos, Chinese student association, progressive united Black student organization, student social work association, Alpha Phi Omega, Circle K, Fellowship of Christian Athletes, Fellowship of Christian Cowboys, College Republicans, Young Democrats.

Athletics. NCAA. **Intercollegiate:** Baseball M, basketball, cheerleading, cross-country, football (tackle) M, golf W, rodeo, softball W, tennis W, track and field, volleyball W. **Intramural:** Archery, basketball, football (non-tackle) M, football (tackle), golf, racquetball, rodeo, soccer, softball, table tennis, tennis, volleyball. **Team name:** Texans.

Student services. Adult student services, alcohol/substance abuse counseling, chaplain/spiritual director, career counseling, services for economically disadvantaged, student employment services, financial aid counseling, health services, legal services, minority student services, on-campus daycare, personal counseling, placement for graduates, veterans' counselor. **Physically disabled:** Services for visually, speech, hearing impaired.

Contact. E-mail: uadm@tarleton.edu
Phone: (254) 968-9125 Toll-free number: (800) 687-8236
Fax: (254) 968-9951
Cindy Hess, Director of Admissions, Tarleton State University, Box T-0030, Stephenville, TX 76402

Texas A&M International University
Laredo, Texas — CB member
www.tamiu.edu — CB code: 0359

- Public 4-year university
- Commuter campus in small city
- 6,349 degree-seeking undergraduates: 28% part-time, 60% women, 95% Hispanic/Latino, 2% international
- 789 degree-seeking graduate students
- 49% of applicants admitted
- SAT or ACT (ACT writing recommended) required
- 41% graduate within 6 years

General. Founded in 1969. Regionally accredited. **Degrees:** 996 bachelor's awarded; master's, doctoral offered. **ROTC:** Army. **Location:** 150 miles from San Antonio. **Calendar:** Semester, extensive summer session. **Full-time faculty:** 225 total; 49% have terminal degrees, 43% minority, 48% women. **Part-time faculty:** 132 total; 17% have terminal degrees, 64% minority, 54% women. **Class size:** 33% < 20, 44% 20-39, 8% 40-49, 11% 50-99, 4% >100. **Special facilities:** Planetarium.

Freshman class profile. 6,547 applied, 3,185 admitted, 1,082 enrolled.

Mid 50% test scores		GPA 2.0-2.99:	7%
SAT critical reading:	390-500	Rank in top quarter:	50%
SAT math:	420-510	Rank in top tenth:	18%
ACT composite:	16-20	End year in good standing:	80%
GPA 3.75 or higher:	33%	Return as sophomores:	76%
GPA 3.50-3.74:	30%	Out-of-state:	1%
GPA 3.0-3.49:	28%	International:	2%

Basis for selection. Students in top 40% of graduating class admitted with no minimum ACT or SAT score (must submit either SAT or ACT test score). Students in bottom 60% need minimum score of 900 on SAT (exclusive of Writing), or 19 on ACT.

High school preparation. Required and recommended units include English 4, mathematics 3, social studies 3, history 3, science 2, foreign language 2 and academic electives 2. 1 computer technology, 1 fine arts required; three years of foreign language recommended.

2015-2016 Annual costs. Tuition/fees: $7,990; $19,894 out-of-state. Room/board: $8,259. Books/supplies: $1,820. Personal expenses: $1,635.

Financial aid. Non-need-based: Scholarships awarded for academics, art, athletics, leadership, music/drama.

Application procedures. Admission: Closing date 8/1 (postmark date). No application fee. Admission notification on a rolling basis beginning on or about 11/1. **Financial aid:** Priority date 3/15; no closing date. FAFSA, institutional form required. Applicants notified on a rolling basis starting 4/15; must reply within 2 week(s) of notification.

Academics. Special study options: Distance learning, double major, dual enrollment of high school students, honors, internships, study abroad, teacher certification program. **Credit/placement by examination:** AP, CLEP, IB, SAT, ACT. 33 credit hours maximum toward bachelor's degree. **Support services:** Learning center, pre-admission summer program, reduced course load, remedial instruction, study skills assistance, tutoring, writing center.

Majors. Biology: General. **Business:** Accounting, business admin, finance, management information systems, managerial economics, marketing. **Communications:** Communications/speech/rhetoric. **Conservation:** General. **Education:** Bilingual, biology, early childhood, elementary, English, history, mathematics, reading, social studies, Spanish, special ed. **Engineering:** Systems. **English:** English lit. **Foreign languages:** Spanish. **Health services:** Nursing (RN), preop/surgical nursing. **History:** General. **Math:** General. **Parks/recreation:** Health/fitness. **Physical sciences:** Chemistry. **Protective services:** Criminal justice. **Psychology:** General. **Social sciences:** General, political science, sociology, urban studies.

Technology on campus. 200 workstations in dormitories, library, computer center, student center. Dormitories wired for high-speed internet access and linked to campus network. Commuter students can connect to campus network. Online library, helpline, wireless network available.

Student life. Freshman orientation: Mandatory, $125 fee. Preregistration for classes offered. Four overnight sessions held June-August and 1 one-day session in August for late registrants. **Housing:** Coed dorms, apartments available. $300 partly refundable deposit. On-campus housing, not owned by college (private contractor) available. **Activities:** Bands, campus ministries, choral groups, dance, drama, international student organizations, literary magazine, music ensembles, Model UN, student government, student newspaper, student ambassadors, Association of International Students, Tau Sigma Chi (criminal justice), High Twisters, Ballet Folklorico, student system group, student finance society, student government association.

Athletics. NCAA. **Intercollegiate:** Baseball M, basketball, cross-country, golf, soccer, softball W, volleyball W. **Intramural:** Baseball, basketball, soccer, table tennis, volleyball, weight lifting. **Team name:** Dust Devils.

Student services. Alcohol/substance abuse counseling, career counseling, services for economically disadvantaged, student employment services, financial aid counseling, health services, personal counseling, placement for graduates, veterans' counselor, women's services. **Physically disabled:** Services for visually, speech, hearing impaired.

Contact. E-mail: adms@tamiu.edu
Phone: (956) 326-2200 Fax: (956) 326-2199
Rosie Dickinson, Director of Admissions, Texas A&M International University, 5201 University Boulevard, Laredo, TX 78041-1900

Texas A&M University
College Station, Texas — CB member
www.tamu.edu — CB code: 6003

- Public 4-year university
- Residential campus in small city
- 48,708 degree-seeking undergraduates: 11% part-time, 49% women, 3% African American, 6% Asian American, 22% Hispanic/Latino, 3% Multiracial, non-Hispanic, 1% international
- 14,333 degree-seeking graduate students
- 66% of applicants admitted
- SAT or ACT with writing, application essay required
- 79% graduate within 6 years

General. Founded in 1876. Regionally accredited. **Degrees:** 10,164 bachelor's awarded; master's, professional, doctoral offered. **ROTC:** Army, Naval, Air Force. **Location:** 90 miles from Houston, 100 miles from Austin. **Calendar:** Semester, extensive summer session. **Full-time faculty:** 2,834 total; 90% have terminal degrees, 27% minority, 34% women. **Part-time faculty:** 765 total; 72% have terminal degrees, 17% minority, 36% women. **Class size:** 21% < 20, 43% 20-39, 9% 40-49, 17% 50-99, 10% >100. **Special facilities:** Reactor, cyclotron, observatory, agriculture research property, 18-hole golf course, supercomputer center, oceanographic research vessel, Italian study center, George H. W. Bush Presidential Library and Museum.

Freshman class profile. 33,970 applied, 22,371 admitted, 10,318 enrolled.

Mid 50% test scores		Rank in top quarter:	91%
SAT critical reading:	520-640	Rank in top tenth:	66%
SAT math:	550-670	Return as sophomores:	90%
SAT writing:	490-610	Out-of-state:	5%
ACT composite:	25-30	Live on campus:	70%

Basis for selection. Automatic admission to applicants in top 10% of Texas high school class (with completed application), as specified by state law. Strong senior year course schedule recommended. Test scores required of all applicants but not used for admission of applicants from top 10% of any Texas high school class. **Learning Disabled:** Must provide documentation from qualified professional licensed or certified to diagnose disability.

High school preparation. College-preparatory program required. 22 units required; 26 recommended. Required and recommended units include English 4, mathematics 3-4, social studies 3-4, science 3-4 (laboratory 1-2), foreign language 2, visual/performing arts 1 and academic electives 5.

2015-2016 Annual costs. Tuition/fees: $9,428; $28,021 out-of-state. Room/board: $10,338. Books/supplies: $1,194. Personal expenses: $2,378.

2014-2015 Financial aid. Need-based: 7,375 full-time freshmen applied for aid; 4,582 deemed to have need; 4,463 received aid. Average need met was 73%. Average scholarship/grant was $11,610; average loan $5,900. 67% of total undergraduate aid awarded as scholarships/grants, 33% as loans/jobs. **Non-need-based:** Awarded to 3,982 full-time undergraduates, including 1,633 freshmen. Scholarships awarded for academics, alumni affiliation, art, athletics, job skills, leadership, music/drama, religious affiliation, ROTC, state residency. **Additional information:** Short-term loans available.

Application procedures. Admission: Closing date 12/1 (receipt date). $75 fee, may be waived for applicants with need. Admission notification on a rolling basis beginning on or about 12/15. Must reply by 5/1. Housing deposit due at time of application. **Financial aid:** Priority date 3/15; no closing date. FAFSA required. Applicants notified on a rolling basis starting 4/1.

Academics. Core curriculum requirements in foreign language and computer science may be satisfied by selected high school courses. **Special study options:** Accelerated study, combined bachelor's/graduate degree, cooperative education, cross-registration, distance learning, double major, dual enrollment of high school students, ESL, exchange student, honors, independent study, internships, liberal arts/career combination, study abroad, teacher certification program. **Credit/placement by examination:** AP, CLEP, IB, institutional tests. **Support services:** Learning center, pre-admission summer program, remedial instruction, tutoring, writing center.

Majors. Architecture: Architecture, landscape, urban/community planning. **Area/ethnic studies:** Women's. **Biology:** General, biochemistry, biomedical sciences, cellular/molecular, entomology, environmental, marine, microbiology, molecular genetics, zoology. **Business:** Accounting, business admin, finance, logistics, management information systems, management science, marketing, sales/distribution, tourism/travel, training/development, transportation. **Communications:** General, digital media. **Computer sciences:** Computer graphics, computer science, LAN/WAN management. **Conservation:** General, environmental science, environmental studies, fisheries, forestry, water/wetlands/marine, wildlife/wilderness. **Engineering:** Aerospace, agricultural, biomedical, chemical, civil, computer, electrical, industrial, marine, mechanical, nuclear, ocean, petroleum. **English:** English lit. **Foreign languages:** General, classics, French, German, Russian, Spanish. **Health services:** General, community health services, dental hygiene, nursing (RN). **History:** General. **Math:** General, applied. **Parks/recreation:** General, exercise sciences, facilities management, sports admin. **Philosophy/religion:** Philosophy. **Physical sciences:** Atmospheric science, chemistry, geology, geophysics, physics. **Protective services:** Forensics. **Psychology:** General. **Social sciences:** Anthropology, economics, geography, GIS/cartography, political science, sociology. **Visual/performing arts:** General, dramatic, music. **Work/family studies:** Food/nutrition.

Most popular majors. Agriculture 10%, biology 8%, business/marketing 17%, engineering/engineering technologies 17%, interdisciplinary studies 9%, social sciences 6%.

Technology on campus. 1,979 workstations in dormitories, library, computer center, student center. Dormitories wired for high-speed internet access and linked to campus network. Commuter students can connect to campus network. Online course registration, online library, helpline, repair service, student web hosting, wireless network available.

Student life. Freshman orientation: Mandatory, $25 fee. Preregistration for classes offered. Held during numerous 2 day programs offered throughout before each term. **Housing:** Coed dorms, single-sex dorms, apartments, cooperative housing, fraternity/sorority housing, themed housing available. $300 fully refundable deposit. Campus housing guaranteed to members of Corps of Cadets and recipients of major 4-year endowed academic scholarships. Freshman honors dorm available. **Activities:** Bands, campus ministries, choral groups, dance, drama, film society, international student organizations, literary magazine, music ensembles, musical theater, radio station, student government, student newspaper, symphony orchestra, TV station, Black awareness committee, committee for the awareness of Mexican American culture, student Y association, student conference on national affairs, social service organizations, College Republicans, Aggie Democrats, political forum, Aggies for Christ, Corps of Cadets.

Athletics. NCAA. **Intercollegiate:** Baseball M, basketball, cross-country, diving, equestrian W, football (tackle) M, golf, soccer W, softball W, swimming, tennis, track and field, volleyball W. **Intramural:** Basketball, football (tackle), golf, soccer, softball, table tennis, tennis, volleyball. **Team name:** Aggies.

Student services. Alcohol/substance abuse counseling, career counseling, student employment services, financial aid counseling, health services, legal services, minority student services, on-campus daycare, personal counseling, placement for graduates, veterans' counselor, women's services. **Physically disabled:** Services for visually, speech, hearing impaired.

Contact. E-mail: admissions@tamu.edu
Phone: (979) 845-1060 Fax: (979) 845-8737
Lynn Barnes, Director of Admissions, Texas A&M University, 750 Agronomy Road, Suite 1601, College Station, TX 77843-0200

Texas A&M University-Baylor College of Dentistry
Dallas, Texas
www.bcd.tamhsc.edu   CB code: 6059

▸ Public two-year upper-division health science college
▸ Commuter campus in very large city
▸ Application essay, interview required

General. Founded in 1905. Regionally accredited. **Articulation:** Agreement with Collin County Community College District. **Calendar:** Semester. **Full-time faculty:** 114 total; 100% have terminal degrees, 28% minority, 36% women. **Part-time faculty:** 131 total; 100% have terminal degrees, 22% minority, 41% women.

Student profile. 59 degree-seeking undergraduates, 515 graduate students. 60% transferred from two-year, 40% transferred from four-year institutions.

Out-of-state:	4%	25 or older:	25%

Basis for selection. High school transcript, college transcript, application essay, interview required. School achievement most important. Essay, interview, and recommendations highly considered. Transfer accepted as juniors.

2015-2016 Annual costs. Personal expenses: $2,850.

Financial aid. Non-need-based: Scholarships awarded for academics.

Application procedures. Admission: Priority date 12/31. $35 fee. **Financial aid:** FAFSA, institutional form required.

Academics. Participation in research activities under faculty sponsorship and annual research fellowships awarded by college offered. **Special study options:** Combined bachelor's/graduate degree, internships. **Credit/placement by examination:** AP, CLEP.

Majors. Health services: Dental hygiene.

Technology on campus. 25 workstations in library, computer center. Commuter students can connect to campus network. Online library, helpline, wireless network available.

Student life. Housing: Baylor Medical Center nursing dormitory housing available. **Activities:** Student government.

Student services. Student employment services, financial aid counseling, health services, personal counseling.

Contact. Phone: (214) 828-8230 Fax: (214) 828-8346
Barbara Miller, Director, Texas A&M University-Baylor College of Dentistry, PO Box 660677, Dallas, TX 75266-0677

Texas A&M University-Commerce
Commerce, Texas   CB member
www.tamuc.edu   CB code: 6188

▸ Public 4-year university
▸ Commuter campus in small town
▸ 7,642 degree-seeking undergraduates: 29% part-time, 59% women
▸ 4,660 degree-seeking graduate students
▸ 47% of applicants admitted
▸ SAT or ACT (ACT writing optional) required
▸ 52% graduate within 6 years

General. Founded in 1889. Regionally accredited. Six off-site locations. **Degrees:** 1,476 bachelor's awarded; master's, doctoral offered. **ROTC:** Air Force. **Location:** 60 miles from Dallas. **Calendar:** Semester, extensive summer session. **Full-time faculty:** 356 total; 74% have terminal degrees, 37% minority, 48% women. **Part-time faculty:** 349 total; 39% have terminal degrees, 20% minority, 59% women. **Class size:** 39% < 20, 50% 20-39, 6% 40-49, 4% 50-99, less than 1% >100. **Special facilities:** Instructional university farm, planetarium, equine pavilion.

Freshman class profile. 7,195 applied, 3,413 admitted, 1,080 enrolled.

Mid 50% test scores		Rank in top quarter:	35%
SAT critical reading:	420-540	Rank in top tenth:	11%
SAT math:	440-540	Return as sophomores:	72%
ACT composite:	18-24	Out-of-state:	2%
GPA 3.75 or higher:	32%	Live on campus:	80%
GPA 3.50-3.74:	15%	Fraternities:	12%
GPA 3.0-3.49:	31%	Sororities:	13%
GPA 2.0-2.99:	22%		

Basis for selection. ACT or SAT scores most important, followed by high school grades and class rank. Students admitted with 20 ACT or 920 SAT (exclusive of Writing). Portfolio required for art program, audition recommended for music program.

High school preparation. College-preparatory program required. 14 units required. Required units include English 4, mathematics 3, social studies 4 and science 3.

2016-2017 Annual costs. Tuition/fees (projected): $7,432; $19,132 out-of-state. Room/board: $8,326. Books/supplies: $1,400. Personal expenses: $1,868.

2014-2015 Financial aid. Need-based: 894 full-time freshmen applied for aid; 755 deemed to have need; 742 received aid. Average need met was 72%. Average scholarship/grant was $10,903; average loan $3,459. 47% of total undergraduate aid awarded as scholarships/grants, 53% as loans/jobs. **Non-need-based:** Awarded to 276 full-time undergraduates, including 90 freshmen. Scholarships awarded for academics, alumni affiliation, art, athletics, job skills, leadership, music/drama, ROTC, state residency. **Additional information:** Work-study also available for full-time students.

Application procedures. Admission: Priority date 6/1; deadline 8/15. No application fee. Admission notification on a rolling basis beginning on or about 10/1. **Financial aid:** Priority date 4/1; no closing date. FAFSA required. Applicants notified on a rolling basis starting 5/1; must reply within 4 week(s) of notification.

Academics. **Special study options:** Accelerated study, combined bachelor's/graduate degree, cooperative education, cross-registration, distance learning, double major, dual enrollment of high school students, ESL, honors, independent study, internships, liberal arts/career combination, student-designed major, study abroad, teacher certification program. **Credit/placement by examination:** AP, CLEP, IB, SAT, ACT, institutional tests. **Support services:** Learning center, pre-admission summer program, remedial instruction, study skills assistance, tutoring, writing center.

Honors college/program. Membership in the Honors College requires completion of an application for the Honors College, interview with the Honors College advisor, and commitment to the four-year Honors College program. Must be an entering freshman with benchmark scores of 27 or higher on the ACT or an SAT score (Critical Reading and Math) of 1200; and graduate in the top 10% of the high school graduation class.

Majors. Biology: General. **Business:** General, accounting, business admin, finance, management information systems, marketing. **Communications:** Journalism, radio/TV. **Computer sciences:** General, information systems. **Conservation:** Environmental science, wildlife/wilderness. **Engineering:** Construction, industrial. **English:** English lit, rhetoric/composition. **Foreign languages:** Spanish. **Health services:** General, athletic training, nursing (RN). **History:** General. **Human services:** Social work. **Liberal arts:** Arts/sciences. **Math:** General. **Parks/recreation:** Exercise sciences, sports admin. **Physical sciences:** Chemistry, physics. **Protective services:** Criminal justice. **Psychology:** General. **Social sciences:** Economics, political science, sociology. **Visual/performing arts:** Dramatic, graphic design, music, studio arts.

Most popular majors. Business/marketing 16%, interdisciplinary studies 32%, liberal arts 7%, parks/recreation 6%.

Technology on campus. 405 workstations in library. Dormitories wired for high-speed internet access and linked to campus network. Commuter students can connect to campus network. Online course registration, online library, helpline, repair service, wireless network available.

Student life. Freshman orientation: Mandatory, $100 fee. Preregistration for classes offered. Held throughout summer; includes advising, assessment testing, and parental involvement. **Housing:** Guaranteed on-campus for freshmen. Coed dorms, single-sex dorms, special housing for disabled, apartments, fraternity/sorority housing, themed housing, wellness housing available. **Activities:** Bands, campus ministries, choral groups, dance, drama, film society, international student organizations, literary magazine, music ensembles, Model UN, musical theater, opera, radio station, student government, student newspaper, TV station.

Athletics. NCAA. **Intercollegiate:** Basketball, cross-country, football (tackle) M, golf, soccer W, track and field, volleyball W. **Intramural:** Archery, badminton, baseball M, basketball, bowling, cross-country, golf, racquetball, softball, swimming, table tennis, tennis, track and field, volleyball. **Team name:** Lions.

Student services. Adult student services, alcohol/substance abuse counseling, career counseling, services for economically disadvantaged, student employment services, financial aid counseling, health services, legal services, minority student services, on-campus daycare, personal counseling, placement for graduates, veterans' counselor. **Physically disabled:** Services for visually, speech, hearing impaired.

Contact. E-mail: jody.todhunter@tamuc.edu
Phone: (903) 886-5000 Toll-free number: (888) 868-2682
Fax: (903) 468-8698
Jody Todhunter, Director of Undergraduate Admissions, Texas A&M University-Commerce, Box 3011, Commerce, TX 75429-3011

Texas A&M University-Corpus Christi

Corpus Christi, Texas
www.tamucc.edu
CB member
CB code: 0366

- Public 4-year university
- Commuter campus in large city
- 9,801 degree-seeking undergraduates: 25% part-time, 59% women, 7% African American, 2% Asian American, 48% Hispanic/Latino, 1% Multiracial, non-Hispanic, 3% international
- 1,804 degree-seeking graduate students
- 84% of applicants admitted
- SAT or ACT (ACT writing optional) required
- 37% graduate within 6 years

General. Founded in 1947. Regionally accredited. **Degrees:** 1,486 bachelor's awarded; master's, doctoral offered. **ROTC:** Army. **Location:** 150 miles from San Antonio, 200 miles from Houston. **Calendar:** Semester, extensive

summer session. **Full-time faculty:** 417 total; 74% have terminal degrees, 19% minority, 49% women. **Part-time faculty:** 177 total; 34% have terminal degrees, 27% minority, 63% women. **Class size:** 18% < 20, 54% 20-39, 7% 40-49, 16% 50-99, 4% >100. **Special facilities:** National spill control school, institute for surveying and science, center for coastal studies, center for environmental studies and services, early childhood development center, South Texas Institute for the Arts.

Freshman class profile. 8,829 applied, 7,393 admitted, 2,228 enrolled.

Mid 50% test scores			
SAT critical reading:	430-530	Rank in top quarter:	38%
SAT math:	440-540	Rank in top tenth:	10%
SAT writing:	410-510	End year in good standing:	79%
ACT composite:	17-23	Return as sophomores:	59%
GPA 3.75 or higher:	16%	Out-of-state:	2%
GPA 3.50-3.74:	18%	Live on campus:	61%
GPA 3.0-3.49:	37%	International:	2%
GPA 2.0-2.99:	28%	Fraternities:	5%
		Sororities:	5%

Basis for selection. High school GPA, class rank, and course work most important. Test scores, school and community leadership activities, special talents also considered. Minimum 900 SAT (exclusive of Writing), required. Applicants not meeting minimum requirements may apply to admission committee for special consideration. Local placement exams in reading, writing and math required of all first-time freshmen.

High school preparation. 15 units required. Required units include English 4, mathematics 4, social studies 4, science 4 and foreign language 2.

2015-2016 Annual costs. Tuition/fees: $8,620; $20,208 out-of-state. Room/board: $9,874. Books/supplies: $868. Personal expenses: $1,527.

2015-2016 Financial aid. Need-based: 1,785 full-time freshmen applied for aid; 1,363 deemed to have need; 1,315 received aid. Average need met was 52%. Average scholarship/grant was $6,812; average loan $3,375. 60% of total undergraduate aid awarded as scholarships/grants, 40% as loans/jobs. **Non-need-based:** Awarded to 1,278 full-time undergraduates, including 312 freshmen. Scholarships awarded for academics, art, athletics, leadership, music/drama, ROTC.

Application procedures. Admission: Closing date 7/1 (receipt date). $50 fee, may be waived for applicants with need. Admission notification on a rolling basis beginning on or about 12/1. **Financial aid:** Priority date 3/31, closing date 6/30. FAFSA required. Applicants notified on a rolling basis starting 4/1; must reply within 2 week(s) of notification.

Academics. Special study options: Accelerated study, combined bachelor's/graduate degree, cooperative education, distance learning, double major, dual enrollment of high school students, ESL, honors, independent study, internships, study abroad, teacher certification program. **Credit/placement by examination:** AP, CLEP, IB, SAT, ACT, institutional tests. 45 credit hours maximum toward bachelor's degree. DANTES, ACT, PEP accepted. **Support services:** Learning center, remedial instruction, study skills assistance, tutoring, writing center.

Majors. Biology: General, biomedical sciences. **Business:** General, accounting, business admin, finance, management information systems, managerial economics, marketing. **Communications:** Communications/speech/rhetoric. **Computer sciences:** General. **Conservation:** General. **Engineering:** Mechanical. **English:** English lit. **Foreign languages:** Spanish. **Health services:** Athletic training, clinical lab science, clinical nurse specialist, nurse practitioner, nursing (RN). **History:** General. **Math:** General. **Parks/recreation:** Health/fitness. **Physical sciences:** Chemistry, geology. **Protective services:** Criminal justice. **Psychology:** General. **Social sciences:** Economics, political science, sociology. **Visual/performing arts:** General, music, studio arts.

Most popular majors. Biology 9%, business/marketing 18%, health sciences 18%, interdisciplinary studies 12%, parks/recreation 6%, psychology 6%.

Technology on campus. 500 workstations in library, computer center. Dormitories wired for high-speed internet access and linked to campus network. Commuter students can connect to campus network. Online course registration, online library, helpline, repair service, student web hosting, wireless network available.

Student life. Freshman orientation: Available. Preregistration for classes offered. Held various times in summer before fall entry. **Policies:** No alcohol on campus except by adult students in their own apartments. **Housing:** Guaranteed on-campus for freshmen. Coed dorms, apartments available. $200 nonrefundable deposit, deadline 7/18. **Activities:** Bands, campus ministries, choral groups, dance, drama, international student organizations, music ensembles, musical theater, student government, student newspaper, Baptist student union, Newman Club, Friends Meeting, LDS students association, Amigos, computer science club, African-American cultural society.

Athletics. NCAA. **Intercollegiate:** Baseball, basketball, cross-country, golf W, softball W, tennis, track and field, volleyball W. **Intramural:** Badminton, baseball M, basketball, cross-country, golf, racquetball, soccer, softball, swimming, table tennis, tennis, track and field, volleyball. **Team name:** Islanders.

Student services. Alcohol/substance abuse counseling, chaplain/spiritual director, career counseling, student employment services, financial aid counseling, health services, personal counseling, placement for graduates, veterans' counselor. **Physically disabled:** Services for visually, speech, hearing impaired.

Contact. E-mail: admiss@tamucc.edu
Phone: (361) 825-2624 Toll-free number: (800) 482-6822
Fax: (361) 825-5887
Oscar Reyna, Executive Director, Admissions, Texas A&M University-Corpus Christi, 6300 Ocean Drive, Unit 5774, Corpus Christi, TX 78412-5774

Texas A&M University-Galveston

Galveston, Texas — CB member
www.tamug.edu — CB code: 6835

- Public 4-year university and maritime college
- Residential campus in small city
- 2,168 degree-seeking undergraduates
- 136 graduate students
- SAT or ACT with writing, application essay required

General. Founded in 1962. Regionally accredited. Institution houses Texas Maritime Academy, 1 of 5 seacoast maritime academies in the U.S. preparing graduates for licensing as officers in the Merchant Marine. **Degrees:** 322 bachelor's awarded; master's, doctoral offered. **ROTC:** Naval. **Location:** 50 miles from Houston. **Calendar:** Semester, limited summer session. **Full-time faculty:** 102 total; 70% have terminal degrees, 24% minority, 28% women. **Part-time faculty:** 50 total; 46% have terminal degrees, 20% minority, 32% women. **Class size:** 51% < 20, 30% 20-39, 7% 40-49, 10% 50-99, 2% >100. **Special facilities:** Fleet of research and training boats, 300-acre wetlands on west Galveston Bay, wetlands research center, ship bridge simulator.

Freshman class profile.

Rank in top quarter:	44%	Out-of-state:	9%
Rank in top tenth:	11%	Live on campus:	87%

Basis for selection. School achievement record and test scores most important. Adverse circumstances, leadership, exceptional talents, course selections, and references reviewed on individual basis. **Home schooled:** Transcript of courses and grades, letter of recommendation (nonparent) required.

High school preparation. College-preparatory program recommended. 15 units required; 19 recommended. Required and recommended units include English 4, mathematics 4, social studies 4, science 4 (laboratory 2), foreign language 2 and computer science 1. 1 unit computer literacy required. Science courses must be selected from biology, chemistry or physics.

2015-2016 Annual costs. Tuition/fees: $9,988; $22,260 out-of-state. Room/board: $10,026. Books/supplies: $1,600. Personal expenses: $300.

Financial aid. Non-need-based: Scholarships awarded for academics, state residency.

Application procedures. Admission: Closing date 8/1 (postmark date). $75 fee, may be waived for applicants with need. Admission notification on a rolling basis. **Financial aid:** Priority date 4/1; no closing date. FAFSA required. Applicants notified on a rolling basis starting 3/15; must reply within 3 week(s) of notification.

Academics. All academic programs are ocean-related. USCG ship officer's license may be earned through license option program. **Special study options:** Accelerated study, combined bachelor's/graduate degree, cooperative education, double major, dual enrollment of high school students, honors, independent study, internships, semester at sea, study abroad. Merchant marine licensing program available with marine biology, marine science, marine transportation, and marine engineering technology degrees. **Credit/placement by examination:** AP, CLEP, IB, institutional tests. Credit hours awarded depends on program the student is pursuing. **Support services:** Learning center, preadmission summer program, remedial instruction, study skills assistance, tutoring, writing center.

Majors. Biology: Marine. **Business:** Business admin, international, international finance, tourism/travel, transportation. **Conservation:** General, fisheries. **Engineering:** Marine, ocean, systems. **Liberal arts:** Arts/sciences. **Physical sciences:** Oceanography.

Most popular majors. Biology 26%, business/marketing 24%, engineering/engineering technologies 15%, interdisciplinary studies 9%, natural resources/environmental science 8%, trade and industry 18%.

Technology on campus. 215 workstations in library, computer center. Dormitories wired for high-speed internet access and linked to campus network. Commuter students can connect to campus network. Online course registration, online library, helpline, repair service, wireless network available.

Student life. Freshman orientation: Mandatory, $100 fee. Preregistration for classes offered. 2 days at a time offered several times during the summer. **Housing:** Coed dorms, single-sex dorms, special housing for disabled, apartments, wellness housing available. $300 fully refundable deposit. **Activities:** Campus ministries, dance, drama, literary magazine, student government, student newspaper, Circle K, Campus Crusade for Christ, emergency care team, outdoor and environmental conservation, Catholic student association, SEED (Students Encouraging Ethnic Diversity), Wesley Foundation, Sisterhood of University Leaders, Student Veterans Association, Black Student Alliance, Gay Straight Alliance.

Athletics. Intercollegiate: Rowing (crew), sailing. **Intramural:** Basketball, football (non-tackle), racquetball, sand volleyball, soccer, softball, tennis, volleyball. **Team name:** Aggies.

Student services. Alcohol/substance abuse counseling, chaplain/spiritual director, career counseling, student employment services, financial aid counseling, health services, minority student services, personal counseling, placement for graduates, veterans' counselor. **Physically disabled:** Services for hearing impaired.

Contact. E-mail: seaaggie@tamug.edu
Phone: (409) 740-4414 Toll-free number: (877) 322-4443
Fax: (409) 740-4731
Cheryl Moon, Executive Director of Enrollment Services, Texas A&M University-Galveston, PO Box 1675, Galveston, TX 77553-1675

Texas A&M University-Kingsville

Kingsville, Texas — CB member
www.tamuk.edu — CB code: 6822

- Public 4-year university
- Commuter campus in large town
- 5,630 degree-seeking undergraduates: 10% part-time, 45% women, 7% African American, 1% Asian American, 70% Hispanic/Latino, 1% Multiracial, non-Hispanic, 3% international
- 2,559 degree-seeking graduate students
- 82% of applicants admitted
- SAT or ACT (ACT writing optional) required
- 33% graduate within 6 years

General. Founded in 1925. Regionally accredited. **Degrees:** 985 bachelor's awarded; master's, doctoral offered. **ROTC:** Army. **Location:** 40 miles from Corpus Christi, 240 miles from Houston. **Calendar:** Semester, extensive summer session. **Full-time faculty:** 320 total; 82% have terminal degrees, 33% minority, 36% women. **Part-time faculty:** 140 total; 34% have terminal degrees, 41% minority, 49% women. **Class size:** 38% < 20, 51% 20-39, 5% 40-49, 5% 50-99, less than 1% >100. **Special facilities:** Observatory, museum, 3-D printer.

Freshman class profile. 7,344 applied, 6,049 admitted, 1,278 enrolled.

Mid 50% test scores			
		GPA 2.0-2.99:	20%
SAT critical reading:	400-510	Rank in top quarter:	43%
SAT math:	440-540	Rank in top tenth:	16%
SAT writing:	380-480	Return as sophomores:	69%
ACT composite:	17-22	Out-of-state:	1%
GPA 3.75 or higher:	25%	Live on campus:	71%
GPA 3.50-3.74:	21%	International:	2%
GPA 3.0-3.49:	33%		

Basis for selection. Applicants who do not meet the regular admission requirements will automatically be reviewed by the Undergraduate Admissions Committee using a holistic review that includes the applicant's rank in class, standardized entrance test scores, performance in specific high school courses, extracurricular activities, community service, talents and awards, leadership skills, employment, and other factors that support a student's ability to succeed at the university. A Texas Success Initiative (TSI) assessment may be required prior to enrollment. Application to the Music department is in addition to regular application to TAMUK and may require an audition, exam, and recommendation from applicant's music director/teacher. **Home schooled:** Transcript of courses and grades required.

High school preparation. College-preparatory program recommended. 26 units recommended. Recommended units include English 4, mathematics 4, social studies 4, science 4 (laboratory 1), foreign language 2, academic electives 5.5. 1 physical education, .5 speech.

2015-2016 Annual costs. Tuition/fees: $7,700; $20,190 out-of-state. Room/board: $7,344. Books/supplies: $1,344. Personal expenses: $2,472.

2014-2015 Financial aid. Need-based: 1,019 full-time freshmen applied for aid; 900 deemed to have need; 886 received aid. Average need met was 71%. Average scholarship/grant was $1,922; average loan $2,261. 52% of total undergraduate aid awarded as scholarships/grants, 48% as loans/jobs. **Non-need-based:** Awarded to 479 full-time undergraduates, including 72 freshmen. Scholarships awarded for academics, athletics, leadership, minority status, state residency.

Application procedures. Admission: Priority date 12/15; deadline 8/1. $25 fee. Admission notification on a rolling basis. **Financial aid:** Priority date 3/15; no closing date. FAFSA required. Applicants notified by 4/15; Applicants notified on a rolling basis starting 4/15; must reply within 12 week(s) of notification.

Academics. Special study options: Distance learning, double major, dual enrollment of high school students, ESL, honors, independent study, internships, study abroad, teacher certification program. **Credit/placement by examination:** AP, CLEP, IB, SAT, ACT, institutional tests. For some courses not designated for credit by the CLEP, departmental exams may also be an option. **Support services:** Tutoring, writing center.

Honors college/program. Students, including transfer students and non-freshmen, can apply to the honors college after they have been accepted. Application documents that may be required include an application form, essay, two recommendation forms/letters, a current resume, head-shot, and transcript(s).

Majors. Biology: General, biomedical sciences. **Business:** General, accounting, business admin, finance, international, management information systems, marketing. **Communications:** General. **Computer sciences:** General. **Conservation:** Wildlife/wilderness. **Engineering:** General, architectural, chemical, civil, electrical, environmental, mechanical, petroleum. **English:** English lit. **Foreign languages:** Spanish. **Health services:** Communication disorders, dietetics, veterinary technology/assistant. **History:** General. **Human services:** Social work. **Math:** General. **Parks/recreation:** Exercise sciences. **Physical sciences:** Chemistry, geology, physics. **Protective services:** Criminal justice. **Psychology:** General. **Social sciences:** Criminology, political science, sociology. **Visual/performing arts:** Dramatic, music, music performance, studio arts. **Work/family studies:** General, clothing/textiles, family studies.

Most popular majors. Agriculture 7%, biology 6%, business/marketing 7%, engineering/engineering technologies 18%, health sciences 14%, interdisciplinary studies 12%, social sciences 8%.

Technology on campus. 400 workstations in library, student center. Dormitories wired for high-speed internet access and linked to campus network. Online course registration, online library, helpline, wireless network available.

Student life. Freshman orientation: Mandatory, $75 fee. Preregistration for classes offered. **Housing:** Guaranteed on-campus for freshmen. Coed dorms, single-sex dorms, special housing for disabled, themed housing available. $150 partly refundable deposit. **Activities:** Bands, campus ministries, choral groups, dance, drama, international student organizations, music ensembles, musical theater, radio station, student government, student newspaper, symphony orchestra, TV station, Baptist Student Ministry, Hispanic Student Association, Indian Students Association.

Athletics. NCAA. **Intercollegiate:** Baseball M, basketball, cross-country, football (tackle) M, golf W, softball W, tennis W, track and field, volleyball W. **Intramural:** Badminton, basketball, cricket, football (non-tackle), racquetball, soccer, softball, tennis, ultimate frisbee, volleyball W. **Team name:** Javelinas.

Student services. Career counseling, student employment services, financial aid counseling, health services, on-campus daycare, personal counseling, placement for graduates, women's services.

Contact. E-mail: admissions@tamuk.edu
Phone: (361) 593-4885 Toll-free number: (800) 687-6000
Fax: (361) 593-5509
Shelly Key, Executive Director of Admissions, Texas A&M University-Kingsville, MSC 128, Kingsville, TX 78363-8202

Texas A&M University-Texarkana
Texarkana, Texas
www.tamut.edu   CB code: 6206

- Public two-year upper-division university
- Commuter campus in small city
- 69% of applicants admitted
- Test scores required

General. Founded in 1971. Regionally accredited. **Degrees:** 360 bachelor's awarded; master's offered. **Articulation:** Agreements with Texarkana College, Northeast Texas Community College, Panola College, Paris Junior College, Cossatot College; Rich Mountain College, University of Arkansas Community College at Hope. **Location:** 180 miles from Dallas, 145 miles from Little Rock, Arkansas. **Calendar:** Semester; limited summer session. **Full-time faculty:** 72 total; 85% have terminal degrees, 38% minority, 44% women. **Part-time faculty:** 63 total; 30% have terminal degrees, 44% minority, 81% women. **Class size:** 55% < 20, 42% 20-39, 2% 40-49, 1% 50-99.

Student profile. 1,415 degree-seeking undergraduates, 406 degree-seeking graduate students. 537 applied as first time-transfer students, 369 admitted, 292 enrolled.

Women:	60%	Part-time:	34%

Basis for selection. College transcript, standardized test scores required. Minimum 2.0 GPA; must satisfy Texas Success Initiative. Transfer accepted as sophomores, juniors, seniors.

2015-2016 Annual costs. Tuition/fees: $7,036; $19,568 out-of-state. Room/board: $7,872. Books/supplies: $1,160.

Financial aid. Need-based: 784 applied for aid; 678 deemed to have need; 677 received aid. Average need met was 77%. 40% of total undergraduate aid awarded as scholarships/grants, 60% as loans/jobs. **Non-need-based:** Awarded to 204 undergraduates. Scholarships awarded for academics, alumni affiliation, art, athletics, job skills, leadership, music/drama, state residency.

Application procedures. Admission: Rolling admission. $30 fee, may be waived for applicants with need. **Financial aid:** Priority date 3/15, closing date 9/30. Applicants notified on a rolling basis; must reply within 10 weeks of notification. Transfer students must have completed minimum of 54 semester hours of transferable college credit to apply for financial aid and notified applicants must reply within 45 days from date of award letter. Exceptions made on individual basis. April 1 financial aid deadline for scholarships. FAFSA required.

Academics. Special study options: Cross-registration, distance learning, double major, dual enrollment of high school students, ESL, honors, independent study, internships, liberal arts/career combination, study abroad, teacher certification program. **Credit/placement by examination:** AP, CLEP, IB, institutional tests. 30 credit hours maximum toward bachelor's degree. BAAS degree limits credit by exam to 18 semester credit hours.

Majors. Biology: General. **Business:** Accounting, business admin. **Communications:** Media studies. **Computer sciences:** General. **Engineering:** Electrical. **English:** English lit. **Health services:** Nursing (RN). **History:** General. **Math:** General. **Protective services:** Criminal justice. **Psychology:** General. **Social sciences:** Political science.

Most popular majors. Biology 6%, business/marketing 23%, health sciences 8%, history 6%, interdisciplinary studies 29%, psychology 8%.

Technology on campus. 119 workstations in dormitories, library, computer center, student center. Dormitories wired for high-speed internet access and linked to campus network. Commuter students can connect to campus network. Online course registration, online library, helpline, wireless network available.

Student life. Housing: Guaranteed on-campus for freshmen. Coed dorms available. $100 partly refundable deposit. **Activities:** Dance, drama, student government, student newspaper, multicultural association.

Athletics. NAIA. **Intercollegiate:** Baseball M, soccer W, tennis. **Team name:** Eagles.

Student services. Career counseling, student employment services, financial aid counseling, personal counseling, placement for graduates, veterans' counselor.

Contact. E-mail: admissions@tamut.edu
Phone: (903) 223-3069 Fax: (903) 223-3140
Toney Favors, Director of Admissions, Texas A&M University-Texarkana, 7101 University Avenue, Texarkana, TX 75503

Texas Christian University

Fort Worth, Texas

CB member

www.tcu.edu

CB code: 6820

- Private 4-year university affiliated with the Christian Church (Disciples of Christ)
- Residential campus in very large city
- 8,851 degree-seeking undergraduates: 3% part-time, 60% women, 5% African American, 3% Asian American, 11% Hispanic/Latino, 1% Native American, 5% international
- 1,406 degree-seeking graduate students
- 43% of applicants admitted
- SAT or ACT (ACT writing optional), application essay required
- .76% graduate within 6 years; 21% enter graduate study

General. Founded in 1873. Regionally accredited. **Degrees:** 2,088 bachelor's awarded; master's, professional, doctoral offered. **ROTC:** Army, Air Force. **Location:** 5 miles from downtown Fort Worth, 35 miles from Dallas. **Calendar:** Semester, limited summer session. **Special facilities:** Geological center for remote sensing, nuclear magnetic resonance facility, observatory, film library, performance complex, behavioral research institute, meteorite collection, two lab schools, speech and hearing clinic, transmission electron microscope, Beowulf computing cluster, optical spectroscopy and microscopy laboratory, health professions learning center, new media writing center, multimedia editing suites, high-end computing lab, 3-D printing lab, institute providing instruction for care and treatment of vulnerable children.

Freshman class profile. 18,423 applied, 7,974 admitted, 2,073 enrolled.

Mid 50% test scores		End year in good standing:	93%
SAT critical reading:	530-630	Return as sophomores:	90%
SAT math:	550-650	Out-of-state:	53%
SAT writing:	530-640	Live on campus:	97%
ACT composite:	25-30	International:	4%
Rank in top quarter:	76%	Fraternities:	45%
Rank in top tenth:	44%	Sororities:	55%

Basis for selection. GED not accepted. Class rank, rigor of curriculum, test scores, essays, resumes and letters of recommendation are reviewed. The January SAT and February ACT in an applicant's senior year are the latest exams accepted. Auditions required for music and theater; portfolio required for art. Interview recommended for all. **Home schooled:** Statement describing home school structure and mission, transcript of courses and grades, letter of recommendation (nonparent) required. Interview with admissions officer recommended, additional weight may be placed on SAT/ACT scores in admissions process.

High school preparation. College-preparatory program required. 17 units required; 20 recommended. Required and recommended units include English 4, mathematics 3-4, social studies 3-4, science 3-4 (laboratory 1), foreign language 2-4 and academic electives 2.

2015-2016 Annual costs. Tuition/fees: $40,720. Room/board: $11,800.

2015-2016 Financial aid. Need-based: 1,299 full-time freshmen applied for aid; 866 deemed to have need; 860 received aid. Average need met was 70%. Average scholarship/grant was $25,971; average loan $2,734. 74% of total undergraduate aid awarded as scholarships/grants, 26% as loans/jobs. **Non-need-based:** Awarded to 4,670 full-time undergraduates, including 1,268 freshmen. Scholarships awarded for academics, alumni affiliation, art, minority status, music/drama, religious affiliation, ROTC, state residency.

Application procedures. Admission: Closing date 2/15 (postmark date). $40 fee, may be waived for applicants with need. Admission notification by 4/1. Admission notification on a rolling basis. Must reply by May 1 or within 2 week(s) if notified thereafter. An enrollment fee of $900 that includes the non-refundable housing and tuition deposits are due 5/1. These fees are applied to tuition and housing costs at time of payment. **Financial aid:** Priority date 5/1, closing date 5/1. FAFSA, CSS PROFILE required. Applicants notified on a rolling basis starting 3/15; must reply by 5/1.

Academics. Special study options: Accelerated study, combined bachelor's/graduate degree, distance learning, double major, ESL, honors, independent study, internships, liberal arts/career combination, study abroad, teacher certification program, Washington semester. **Credit/placement by examination:** AP, CLEP, IB, institutional tests. Credit by examination may be awarded only in the first 66 semester hours of college credit. Amount of credit varies by type of exam. **Support services:** Study skills assistance, writing center.

Honors college/program. Admission to the Honors College is by invitation only. Students do not need to submit a separate Honors College application. Various quantitative and qualitative factors are considered, such as strength of the high school curriculum, rank in class, high school grade point average, SAT and/or ACT scores, and involvement in community service, extracurricular activities, and leadership. Students who are not invited to join the John V. Roach Honors College as incoming first-year students may join upon earning at least a 3.50 cumulative GPA in at least 12 graded hours at TCU.

Majors. Biology: General, biochemistry, neuroscience. **Business:** Accounting, actuarial science, entrepreneurial studies, fashion, finance, international, international finance, international marketing, logistics, marketing, real estate. **Communications:** Advertising, communications/speech/rhetoric, journalism, persuasive communications, public relations. **Computer sciences:** General, information technology, systems analysis. **Conservation:** Environmental science. **Education:** Art, bilingual, Deaf/hearing impaired, early childhood, elementary, English, mathematics, middle, music, physical, science, secondary, social studies. **Engineering:** General. **English:** Creative writing, English lit. **Foreign languages:** French, German, Spanish. **Health services:** Athletic training, dietetics, movement therapy, nursing (RN), speech pathology. **History:** General. **Human services:** Social work. **Math:** General. **Parks/recreation:** Health/fitness, sports studies. **Philosophy/religion:** Philosophy, religion. **Physical sciences:** Chemistry, geology, physics. **Protective services:** Criminal justice. **Psychology:** General, developmental. **Social sciences:** Anthropology, economics, geography, international economics, international relations, political science, sociology. **Theology:** Sacred music. **Visual/performing arts:** Acting, art history/conservation, ballet, ceramics, dance, design, directing/producing, dramatic, graphic design, interior design, music, music performance, music theory/composition, musical theater, painting, photography, piano/keyboard, printmaking, sculpture, stringed instruments, studio arts, theater design, voice/opera.

Most popular majors. Business/marketing 24%, communications/journalism 15%, health sciences 14%, social sciences 10%, visual/performing arts 6%.

Technology on campus. 1,400 workstations in dormitories, library, computer center, student center. Dormitories wired for high-speed internet access and linked to campus network. Commuter students can connect to campus network. Online course registration, online library, helpline, repair service, student web hosting, wireless network available.

Student life. Freshman orientation: Mandatory. Preregistration for classes offered. Held at approximately 10 sessions in June and August, parents encouraged to attend. **Housing:** Guaranteed on-campus for freshmen. Coed dorms, single-sex dorms, special housing for disabled, apartments, fraternity/sorority housing, themed housing available. **Activities:** Bands, campus ministries, choral groups, dance, drama, international student organizations, literary magazine, music ensembles, Model UN, musical theater, opera, radio station, student government, student newspaper, symphony orchestra, 256 social, religious, service, academic, and pre-professional organizations.

Athletics. NCAA. **Intercollegiate:** Baseball M, basketball, cross-country, diving, equestrian W, football (tackle) M, golf, rifle W, sand volleyball W, soccer W, swimming, tennis, track and field, volleyball W. **Intramural:** Basketball, bowling, football (non-tackle), golf, racquetball, sand volleyball, soccer, table tennis, tennis, ultimate frisbee. **Team name:** Horned Frogs.

Student services. Alcohol/substance abuse counseling, chaplain/spiritual director, career counseling, student employment services, financial aid counseling, health services, minority student services, personal counseling, placement for graduates, veterans' counselor, women's services. **Physically disabled:** Services for visually, speech, hearing impaired.

Contact. E-mail: frogmail@tcu.edu
Phone: (817) 257-7490 Toll-free number: (800) 828-3764
Fax: (817) 257-7268
Raymond Brown, Dean of Admissions, Texas Christian University, TCU Box 297013, Fort Worth, TX 76129

Texas College

Tyler, Texas

www.texascollege.edu

CB code: 6821

- Private 4-year liberal arts college affiliated with the Christian Methodist Episcopal Church
- Residential campus in small city
- 813 degree-seeking undergraduates

General. Founded in 1894. Regionally accredited. Charter member college of the United Negro College Fund. **Degrees:** 87 bachelor's, 33 associate awarded. **Location:** 90 miles from Dallas, 100 miles from Shreveport, Louisiana. **Calendar:** Semester, limited summer session. **Full-time faculty:** 35 total. **Part-time faculty:** 7 total. **Class size:** 60% < 20, 17% 20-39, 6% 40-49, 15% 50-99, 1% >100.

Basis for selection. Open admission. **Home schooled:** Transcript of courses and grades required. Must submit notarized copy of home school transcript showing date of graduation and course requirements that meet state graduation requirements as approved by the Texas Board of Education. **Learning Disabled:** Students requiring special assistance should provide documentation of disability to the Records/Registrar's Office and the need for assistance to the Office of Academic Affairs.

High school preparation. 22 units required. Required units include English 4, mathematics 3, social studies 3, science 3, visual/performing arts 1 and academic electives 6. Economics .5, physical education 1, speech .5.

2015-2016 Annual costs. Tuition/fees: $10,008. Room/board: $8,000. Books/supplies: $2,400. Personal expenses: $1,700.

Financial aid. Non-need-based: Scholarships awarded for academics, athletics, leadership, music/drama.

Application procedures. Admission: No deadline. $20 fee, may be waived for applicants with need. Admission notification on a rolling basis. **Financial aid:** Priority date 6/1; no closing date. FAFSA, institutional form required. Applicants notified on a rolling basis starting 4/15.

Academics. Special study options: Distance learning, double major, dual enrollment of high school students, independent study, internships, teacher certification program. **Credit/placement by examination:** AP, CLEP, institutional tests. 32 credit hours maximum toward bachelor's degree. **Support services:** Learning center, reduced course load, remedial instruction, study skills assistance, tutoring, writing center.

Majors. Biology: General. **Business:** Business admin. **Computer sciences:** General. **Education:** Elementary, mathematics, middle, physical. **English:** English lit. **History:** General. **Human services:** Social work. **Liberal arts:** Arts/sciences. **Math:** General. **Philosophy/religion:** Religion. **Protective services:** Law enforcement admin. **Social sciences:** Political science, sociology. **Visual/performing arts:** Music, studio arts.

Most popular majors. Biology 6%, business/marketing 28%, education 15%, public administration/social services 8%, social sciences 33%.

Technology on campus. 200 workstations in dormitories, library, computer center. Dormitories wired for high-speed internet access and linked to campus network. Commuter students can connect to campus network. Online library, helpline, student web hosting, wireless network available.

Student life. Freshman orientation: Mandatory. Preregistration for classes offered. Held 2-3 days prior to first day of classes each semester. **Policies:** Students required to attend chapel weekly. Religious observance required. **Housing:** Guaranteed on-campus for freshmen. Single-sex dorms, wellness housing available. $150 nonrefundable deposit, deadline 8/1. **Activities:** Bands, choral groups, dance, international student organizations, music ensembles, student government, Young Adults for Christ, Fellowship of Christian Athletes, pre-alumni council, Omega Psi Phi, Delta Sigma Theta, Alpha Kappa Alpha.

Athletics. NAIA. **Intercollegiate:** Baseball M, basketball, cheerleading, football (tackle) M, soccer, softball W, track and field, volleyball W. **Intramural:** Basketball, football (non-tackle), soccer. **Team name:** Steers.

Student services. Adult student services, chaplain/spiritual director, career counseling, student employment services, financial aid counseling, health services, personal counseling.

Contact. E-mail: iwilliams@texascollege.edu
Phone: (903) 593-8311 ext. 2297 Toll-free number: (800) 306-6299
Fax: (903) 593-6551
Isaac Williams, Dean of Admissions, Texas College, 2404 North Grand Avenue, Tyler, TX 75712-4500

Texas Lutheran University
Seguin, Texas
www.tlu.edu

CB member
CB code: 6823

- Private 4-year university and liberal arts college affiliated with the Evangelical Lutheran Church in America
- Residential campus in large town
- 1,319 degree-seeking undergraduates: 3% part-time, 50% women, 9% African American, 1% Asian American, 32% Hispanic/Latino
- 9 degree-seeking graduate students
- 51% of applicants admitted
- SAT or ACT (ACT writing optional), application essay required
- 47% graduate within 6 years

General. Founded in 1891. Regionally accredited. **Degrees:** 300 bachelor's awarded; master's offered. **ROTC:** Army, Air Force. **Location:** 30 miles

from San Antonio, 55 miles from Austin. **Calendar:** Semester, limited summer session. **Full-time faculty:** 81 total; 82% have terminal degrees, 11% minority, 52% women. **Part-time faculty:** 45 total; 27% have terminal degrees, 18% minority, 60% women. **Class size:** 60% < 20, 40% 20-39, less than 1% 40-49. **Special facilities:** Biology field station, Mexican-American study center, life enrichment center, geological museum, center for servant leadership.

Freshman class profile. 1,863 applied, 945 admitted, 395 enrolled.

Mid 50% test scores			
SAT critical reading:	450-550	GPA 2.0-2.99:	12%
SAT math:	470-570	Rank in top quarter:	49%
SAT writing:	430-520	Rank in top tenth:	20%
ACT composite:	19-23	End year in good standing:	89%
GPA 3.75 or higher:	39%	Return as sophomores:	73%
GPA 3.50-3.74:	22%	Out-of-state:	1%
GPA 3.0-3.49:	27%	Live on campus:	84%
		International:	1%

Basis for selection. Quality of academic curriculum pursued and class rank most important. Academic record and test scores also important. Interview recommended. **Home schooled:** Transcript of courses and grades, letter of recommendation (nonparent) required. Greater emphasis placed on SAT or ACT scores.

High school preparation. College-preparatory program recommended. 17 units required; 23 recommended. Required and recommended units include English 4, mathematics 3-4, social studies 3-4, history 2, science 3-4 (laboratory 2), foreign language 2-3, computer science 1 and academic electives 1.

2015-2016 Annual costs. Tuition/fees: $27,900. Room/board: $9,390. Books/supplies: $950. Personal expenses: $1,100.

2015-2016 Financial aid. Need-based: 74% of total undergraduate aid awarded as scholarships/grants, 26% as loans/jobs. **Non-need-based:** Scholarships awarded for academics, alumni affiliation, leadership, music/drama, religious affiliation.

Application procedures. Admission: Priority date 12/15; deadline 2/1 (postmark date). $300 fee, may be waived for applicants with need. Admission notification on a rolling basis beginning on or about 10/1. **Financial aid:** Priority date 4/1; no closing date. FAFSA required. Applicants notified on a rolling basis starting 3/1; must reply within 4 week(s) of notification.

Academics. Special study options: Combined bachelor's/graduate degree, double major, dual enrollment of high school students, exchange student, external degree, honors, independent study, internships, study abroad, teacher certification program, Washington semester. International studies curriculum, dual BS program in applied science and engineering in conjunction with Texas state institutions. **Credit/placement by examination:** AP, CLEP, IB, institutional tests. 30 credit hours maximum toward bachelor's degree. **Support services:** Study skills assistance, tutoring, writing center.

Majors. Biology: General, molecular. **Business:** General, accounting, business admin. **Communications:** Communications/speech/rhetoric. **Computer sciences:** General, computer science, information systems. **Education:** Elementary, English, history, mathematics, middle, multi-level teacher, music, physical, reading, social studies. **English:** English lit. **Foreign languages:** Spanish. **Health services:** Athletic training. **History:** General, applied. **Math:** General. **Parks/recreation:** Exercise sciences, health/fitness, sports admin. **Philosophy/religion:** Philosophy. **Physical sciences:** Chemistry, physics. **Psychology:** General. **Social sciences:** Economics, political science, sociology. **Theology:** Preministerial, youth ministry. **Visual/performing arts:** General, art, dramatic, music, music history, music performance.

Most popular majors. Biology 8%, business/marketing 21%, education 12%, parks/recreation 16%, psychology 11%, social sciences 6%, visual/performing arts 8%.

Technology on campus. 243 workstations in dormitories, library, computer center, student center. Dormitories wired for high-speed internet access and linked to campus network. Commuter students can connect to campus network. Online course registration, online library, helpline, wireless network available.

Student life. Freshman orientation: Mandatory. Preregistration for classes offered. Held 2 days prior to start of fall semester. **Housing:** Guaranteed on-campus for freshmen. Coed dorms, single-sex dorms, apartments available. $200 fully refundable deposit, deadline 8/1. **Activities:** Bands, campus ministries, choral groups, dance, drama, international student organizations, literary magazine, music ensembles, musical theater, student government, student newspaper, symphony orchestra, black student union, Mexican American student association, Young Democrats, College Republicans, Fellowship of Christian Athletes, Students Make a Difference, Lutheran student movement, Canterbury, Catholic student organization.

Athletics. NCAA. **Intercollegiate:** Baseball M, basketball, cross-country, football (tackle) M, golf, soccer, softball W, tennis, track and field, volleyball

W. **Intramural:** Basketball, bowling, football (non-tackle), handball, racquetball, softball, swimming, tennis, volleyball. **Team name:** Bulldogs.

Student services. Alcohol/substance abuse counseling, chaplain/spiritual director, career counseling, student employment services, financial aid counseling, health services, personal counseling, placement for graduates, veterans' counselor.

Contact. E-mail: admissions@tlu.edu
Phone: (830) 372-8050 Toll-free number: (800) 771-8521
Fax: (830) 372-8096
Adam Navarro-Jusino, Director of Admissions, Texas Lutheran University, 1000 West Court Street, Seguin, TX 78155-5999

Texas Southern University
Houston, Texas — **CB member**
www.tsu.edu — **CB code: 6824**

- Public 4-year university
- Commuter campus in very large city
- 6,696 degree-seeking undergraduates: 12% part-time, 57% women, 80% African American, 2% Asian American, 6% Hispanic/Latino, 1% Native American, 8% international
- 2,269 degree-seeking graduate students
- 51% of applicants admitted

General. Founded in 1947. Regionally accredited. **Degrees:** 927 bachelor's awarded; master's, professional, doctoral offered. **ROTC:** Army. **Location:** 2 miles from downtown. **Calendar:** Semester, extensive summer session. **Full-time faculty:** 331 total; 87% minority, 47% women. **Part-time faculty:** 268 total; 88% minority, 48% women. **Class size:** 40% < 20, 34% 20-39, 10% 40-49, 13% 50-99, 2% >100. **Special facilities:** University museum, aviation simulation equipment.

Freshman class profile. 10,487 applied, 5,338 admitted, 1,457 enrolled.

Mid 50% test scores		Rank in top quarter:	19%
SAT critical reading:	360-440	Rank in top tenth:	5%
SAT math:	370-460	End year in good standing:	50%
SAT writing:	350-430	Return as sophomores:	46%
ACT composite:	15-19	Out-of-state:	11%
GPA 3.75 or higher:	2%	Live on campus:	53%
GPA 3.50-3.74:	5%	International:	2%
GPA 3.0-3.49:	25%	Fraternities:	3%
GPA 2.0-2.99:	68%	Sororities:	1%

Basis for selection. Special requirements for pharmacy, law, accounting, marketing, and computer science programs. For selective programs high school achievement, interview, essay important; test scores, individual abilities, high school activities considered. For special academic programs like Honors College and the Urban Academic Village, personal statements and/or interviews are more heavily weighted. **Home schooled:** Transcript of courses and grades, state high school equivalency certificate required. Submit directly from the parent school district, an official assessment of course mastery for use in grade placement and/or awarding of credit. All Texas residents must also submit the Texas Private High School Certification completed by the high school counselor or school official.

High school preparation. College-preparatory program recommended. Recommended units include English 4, mathematics 3, social studies 4, science 2, foreign language 2 and academic electives 6.

2015-2016 Annual costs. Tuition/fees: $8,726; $20,426 out-of-state. Room/board: $10,566. Books/supplies: $1,450. Personal expenses: $2,374.

Financial aid. All financial aid based on need.

Application procedures. Admission: Priority date 7/31; deadline 8/15 (postmark date). $42 fee, may be waived for applicants with need. Admission notification on a rolling basis. Must reply by 7/31. **Financial aid:** Priority date 5/15; no closing date. FAFSA required. Applicants notified on a rolling basis starting 6/1.

Academics. Special study options: Cooperative education, distance learning, double major, ESL, honors, independent study, internships, study abroad, teacher certification program, weekend college. **Credit/placement by examination:** AP, CLEP, IB, SAT, ACT, institutional tests. **Support services:** Learning center, pre-admission summer program, remedial instruction, study skills assistance, tutoring, writing center.

Honors college/program. For regular admission, GPA of 3.5 or higher, ACT composite score of at least 23 (preferably 24), with at least 19 each in Verbal and Math from the same test date; or SAT combined score of at least

1070 (preferably 1200) in Math and Critical Reading, with at least 500 in each section from the same test date. Conditional admission possible with GPA of 3.5 or higher; and ACT composite score of less than 23; or SAT combined score of less than 1070 (Math and Critical Reading, on the same test date).

Majors. Biology: General. **Business:** Accounting, banking/financial services, business admin, management information systems, marketing, operations. **Communications:** Communications/speech/rhetoric, journalism, media studies, radio/TV. **Computer sciences:** General. **Engineering:** Civil, electrical. **English:** English lit. **Foreign languages:** Spanish. **Health services:** Clinical lab science, dietetics, environmental health, health care admin, health information management, respiratory therapy technology. **History:** General. **Human services:** General, social work. **Math:** General. **Parks/recreation:** Exercise sciences, sports admin. **Physical sciences:** Chemistry, physics. **Protective services:** Disaster management, law enforcement admin. **Psychology:** General. **Social sciences:** Political science, sociology. **Visual/performing arts:** General, dramatic, music, studio arts. **Work/family studies:** General.

Most popular majors. Biology 7%, business/marketing 23%, communications/journalism 8%, engineering/engineering technologies 7%, health sciences 13%, liberal arts 9%, security/protective services 6%.

Technology on campus. 500 workstations in library, computer center, student center. Dormitories wired for high-speed internet access and linked to campus network. Online course registration, online library, helpline, wireless network available.

Student life. Freshman orientation: Mandatory. Preregistration for classes offered. Two-day orientation held every semester during registration week. Includes participation in seminars, advising, placement test. **Housing:** Guaranteed on-campus for freshmen. Single-sex dorms, apartments available. $350 partly refundable deposit, deadline 6/1. **Activities:** Bands, choral groups, drama, film society, music ensembles, musical theater, opera, radio station, student government, student newspaper, symphony orchestra, TV station, Alpha Phi Omega, Gamma Phi Delta Christian Fraternity, Tigers for Christ, Alpha Eta Rho international aviation fraternity, sociology club, political science club, student psychological club, NAACP, association of black journalists, bilingual education association, environmental health club.

Athletics. NCAA. **Intercollegiate:** Baseball M, basketball, bowling W, cross-country, football (tackle) M, golf, soccer W, softball W, tennis, track and field, volleyball W. **Intramural:** Basketball, bowling W, cheerleading, softball W, tennis, track and field, volleyball W. **Team name:** Tigers.

Student services. Alcohol/substance abuse counseling, chaplain/spiritual director, career counseling, student employment services, financial aid counseling, health services, on-campus daycare, personal counseling, placement for graduates, veterans' counselor. **Physically disabled:** Services for speech impaired.

Contact. E-mail: admissions@tsu.edu
Phone: (713) 313-7849 Toll-free number: (866) 878-4968
Fax: (713) 313-7851
Brian Armstrong, Executive Director of Recruitment, Texas Southern University, 3100 Cleburne Street, Houston, TX 77004

Texas State University
San Marcos, Texas — **CB member**
www.txstate.edu — **CB code: 6667**

- Public 4-year university
- Commuter campus in large town
- 33,480 degree-seeking undergraduates: 18% part-time, 57% women, 9% African American, 2% Asian American, 35% Hispanic/Latino, 3% Multiracial, non-Hispanic
- 3,928 degree-seeking graduate students
- 71% of applicants admitted
- SAT or ACT with writing, application essay required
- 53% graduate within 6 years; 21% enter graduate study

General. Founded in 1899. Regionally accredited. **Degrees:** 6,148 bachelor's awarded; master's, professional, doctoral offered. **ROTC:** Army, Air Force. **Location:** 30 miles from Austin, 49 miles from San Antonio. **Calendar:** Semester, extensive summer session. **Full-time faculty:** 1,294 total; 78% have terminal degrees, 19% minority, 49% women. **Part-time faculty:** 566 total; 31% have terminal degrees, 20% minority, 53% women. **Class size:** 29% < 20, 45% 20-39, 10% 40-49, 8% 50-99, 8% >100. **Special facilities:** Southwestern writers collection (original manuscripts), observatory, archaeological forensic lab, clean room for microchip production, sound recording studio, ranch, aquatic research center.

Freshman class profile. 20,711 applied, 14,672 admitted, 5,724 enrolled.

Mid 50% test scores		Rank in top tenth:	12%
SAT critical reading:	460-560	End year in good standing:	75%
SAT math:	470-560	Return as sophomores:	78%
SAT writing:	440-530	Out-of-state:	2%
ACT composite:	21-25	Live on campus:	92%
Rank in top quarter:	48%		

Basis for selection. Applicants who rank in top 10% of high school class have no minimum test score requirements. Otherwise score requirements are as follows: rank in next 15%, 920 SAT verbal /20 ACT; rank in second quarter, 1010 SAT/22 ACT; rank in third quarter, 1180 SAT/26 ACT; rank in bottom quarter, 1270 SAT /29 ACT. All SAT scores are for combined Critical Reading and Math. Writing sections on the SAT or ACT will be used as validity checks on the essay requirements to the admissions application process. Audition required for music program. **Home schooled:** Transcript of courses and grades required. General admission requirements include test scores required for student graduating in the bottom quarter of an accredited high school, (i.e., 26 ACT/1180 SAT (Critical Reading + Math)). **Learning Disabled:** Students with learning disabilities must meet general admission standards. Students may qualify for assistance programs by providing documented diagnostic test results, but these assistance programs are reserved for admitted students.

High school preparation. College-preparatory program required. 26 units required. Required and recommended units include English 4, mathematics 4, social studies 2, history 1-2, science 4 (laboratory 2), foreign language 2, visual/performing arts 1 and academic electives 7. Social studies may consist of geography, government, or economics. Students must complete 3 credits of either history or social studies combined. Physical education also required.

2015-2016 Annual costs. Tuition/fees: $9,944; $21,644 out-of-state. Room/board: $7,840. Books/supplies: $820. Personal expenses: $1,730.

2015-2016 Financial aid. **Need-based:** 5,476 full-time freshmen applied for aid; 3,503 deemed to have need; 3,342 received aid. Average need met was 85%. Average scholarship/grant was $8,779; average loan $4,983. 52% of total undergraduate aid awarded as scholarships/grants, 48% as loans/jobs. **Non-need-based:** Awarded to 2,418 full-time undergraduates, including 915 freshmen. Scholarships awarded for academics, art, athletics, leadership, minority status, music/drama, ROTC, state residency. **Additional information:** Federal and state work study programs are available for those that qualify. Employment time varies by hiring departments.

Application procedures. **Admission:** Priority date 3/1; deadline 5/1 (receipt date). $75 fee, may be waived for applicants with need. Admission notification on a rolling basis beginning on or about 9/1. Deadline for McCoy College of Business and the Department of Communication Design, March 15 for fall, October 15 for spring. **Financial aid:** Priority date 4/1; no closing date. FAFSA required. Applicants notified on a rolling basis starting 5/1; must reply within 3 week(s) of notification.

Academics. **Special study options:** Accelerated study, combined bachelor's/graduate degree, distance learning, double major, dual enrollment of high school students, ESL, exchange student, honors, independent study, internships, study abroad, teacher certification program, Washington semester, weekend college. **Credit/placement by examination:** AP, CLEP, IB, institutional tests. Credit hours earned by exam do not count as credit earned in residence, and 25% of course work must be completed in residency. **Support services:** Learning center, reduced course load, remedial instruction, study skills assistance, tutoring, writing center. The Student Learning Assistance Center (SLAC) offers a variety of academic support programs including a walk-in tutoring lab, supplemental instruction, and online resources at no additional cost.

Honors college/program. Graduating from High School in the top 10% of class, or scoring a 27 ACT/1180 SAT (combined Math and Critical Reading) are required for admissions to the Honors College. In fall 2015 approximately 345 freshmen were admitted to the Honors College. To graduate in the Honors College a student must complete 5 honors courses with one being a thesis, maintain a minimum GPA of 3.25, and complete all other degree requirements for their major.

Majors. **Architecture:** Urban/community planning. **Area/ethnic studies:** American, Asian, European, Near/Middle Eastern. **Biology:** General, aquatic, biochemistry, microbiology, wildlife. **Business:** Accounting, business admin, fashion, finance, managerial economics, marketing. **Communications:** Advertising, journalism, media studies, public relations, radio/TV. **Communications technology:** Recording arts. **Computer sciences:** General, computer science. **Conservation:** Environmental science, water/wetlands/marine. **Engineering:** Electrical, industrial, manufacturing. **English:** English lit. **Foreign languages:** French, German, Spanish. **Health services:** Athletic training, clinical lab science, communication disorders, health care admin, health information management, medical radiologic technology/radiation therapy, nursing (RN), public health ed, respiratory therapy technology. **History:** General. **Human services:** General, social work. **Math:** General, applied. **Parks/recreation:** Exercise sciences, facilities management, sports admin. **Philosophy/religion:** Philosophy. **Physical sciences:** Chemistry, physics. **Protective services:** Corrections, criminal justice, police science. **Psychology:** General. **Social sciences:** Anthropology, economics, geography, GIS/cartography, international relations, political science, sociology. **Visual/performing arts:** Art, art history/conservation, dance, design, dramatic, interior design, jazz, music, music performance, musical theater, photography, studio arts. **Work/family studies:** Advocacy, family studies, food/nutrition.

Most popular majors. Business/marketing 18%, communications/journalism 7%, interdisciplinary studies 9%, parks/recreation 7%, psychology 7%, security/protective services 6%, social sciences 6%, visual/performing arts 8%.

Technology on campus. 1,843 workstations in dormitories, library, computer center, student center. Dormitories wired for high-speed internet access and linked to campus network. Commuter students can connect to campus network. Online course registration, online library, helpline, repair service, student web hosting, wireless network available.

Student life. **Freshman orientation:** Mandatory, $175 fee. Preregistration for classes offered. Two day program combined with welcome week prior to start of semester. **Policies:** New freshmen under the age of 20 with fewer than 30 credit hours are required to live in on-campus university housing. All students who graduated from high school within the preceding 12 months of the semester of their admission are also required to live on campus. **Housing:** Guaranteed on-campus for freshmen. Coed dorms, single-sex dorms, special housing for disabled, apartments, fraternity/sorority housing, themed housing available. $100 fully refundable deposit. **Activities:** Bands, campus ministries, choral groups, dance, drama, film society, international student organizations, literary magazine, music ensembles, Model UN, musical theater, opera, radio station, student government, student newspaper, symphony orchestra, more than 350 social, service, religious, political, professional (student) organizations.

Athletics. NCAA. **Intercollegiate:** Baseball M, basketball, cheerleading, cross-country, football (tackle) M, golf, soccer W, softball W, tennis W, track and field, volleyball W. **Intramural:** Basketball, bowling, football (non-tackle), golf, handball, racquetball, sand volleyball, soccer, softball, table tennis, tennis, ultimate frisbee, volleyball. **Team name:** Bobcats.

Student services. Adult student services, alcohol/substance abuse counseling, chaplain/spiritual director, career counseling, student employment services, financial aid counseling, health services, legal services, minority student services, personal counseling, placement for graduates, veterans' counselor. **Physically disabled:** Services for visually, speech, hearing impaired.

Contact. E-mail: admissions@txstate.edu
Phone: (512) 245-2364 Fax: (512) 245-8044
Stephanie Anderson, Assistant VP for Enrollment Management, Texas State University, 429 North Guadalupe Street, San Marcos, TX 78666-5709

Texas Tech University

Lubbock, Texas — CB member
www.ttu.edu — CB code: 6827

- Public 4-year university
- Commuter campus in small city
- 28,868 degree-seeking undergraduates: 10% part-time, 45% women, 6% African American, 3% Asian American, 23% Hispanic/Latino, 3% Multiracial, non-Hispanic, 5% international
- 6,305 degree-seeking graduate students
- 63% of applicants admitted
- SAT or ACT (ACT writing optional) required
- 60% graduate within 6 years

General. Founded in 1923. Regionally accredited. **Degrees:** 5,332 bachelor's awarded; master's, professional, doctoral offered. **ROTC:** Army, Air Force. **Location:** 348 miles from Dallas, 321 miles from Albuquerque, New Mexico. **Calendar:** Semester, extensive summer session. **Full-time faculty:** 1,383 total; 14% minority, 39% women. **Part-time faculty:** 248 total; 12% minority, 53% women. **Class size:** 28% < 20, 33% 20-39, 18% 40-49, 12% 50-99, 8% >100. **Special facilities:** Museum, observatory, national ranching heritage center, special collections library, archaeological dig/state park, international cultural center, fiber and biopolymer research institute, arid and semi-arid land studies center, child development research center, institutes for environmental and human health, Vietnam center, planetarium, national wind institute, center for autism education and research.

Freshman class profile. 23,010 applied, 14,510 admitted, 5,160 enrolled.

Mid 50% test scores		End year in good standing:	83%
SAT critical reading:	510-600	Return as sophomores:	83%
SAT math:	520-620	Out-of-state:	6%
SAT writing:	470-570	Live on campus:	93%
ACT composite:	23-27	International:	4%
Rank in top quarter:	55%	Fraternities:	17%
Rank in top tenth:	20%	Sororities:	30%

Basis for selection. Class rank and test scores considered first, and students meeting the following score requirements (exclusive of Writing) eligible for unconditional admission: class rank in top 10%, no minimum test scores; rank in next 15%, with 1140 SAT or 25 ACT; rank in second quarter, with 1230 SAT or 28 ACT; rank in third quarter, with 1270 SAT or 29 ACT. Applicants who do not meet assured admission criteria will have records reviewed in holistic manner. Either ACT or SAT required of all students. International students are not required to provide SAT, but are encouraged to take the test for scholarship application. If the international student graduated from a U.S. high school, then SAT is required. Auditions, portfolios and essays are required for admission to some programs. **Learning Disabled:** Admission based upon applicant meeting the published admission criteria of the university with no preference provided on the basis of disability.

High school preparation. College-preparatory program required. 22 units required; 26 recommended. Required and recommended units include English 4, mathematics 3-4, social studies 3-3.5, history 3-3.5, science 3-4 (laboratory 3-4), foreign language 2 and visual/performing arts 1. .5 speech and .5 economics recommended. 1 physical education required.

2015-2016 Annual costs. Tuition/fees: $9,567; $21,267 out-of-state. Room/board: $8,405. Books/supplies: $1,200. Personal expenses: $2,120.

2014-2015 Financial aid. Need-based: 3,610 full-time freshmen applied for aid; 2,651 deemed to have need; 2,651 received aid. Average need met was 73%. Average scholarship/grant was $8,247; average loan $5,002. 45% of total undergraduate aid awarded as scholarships/grants, 55% as loans/jobs. **Non-need-based:** Awarded to 6,867 full-time undergraduates, including 2,114 freshmen. Scholarships awarded for academics, art, athletics, job skills, leadership, music/drama, ROTC. **Additional information:** Red Raider Guarantee program provides free tuition and mandatory fees for up to 15 credit hours per semester to new entering freshman who are Texas residents, enrolled full-time with family adjusted gross incomes that do not exceed $40,000. Eligible students who complete and submit the Free Application for Federal Student Aid (FAFSA) by required deadline are guaranteed to receive funds based on available state and federal allocations. Applications received after the deadline will be awarded based on available funding. Students may qualify for the program for up to eight (8) semesters of full-time enrollment.

Application procedures. Admission: Priority date 2/1; deadline 8/1 (receipt date). $60 fee, may be waived for applicants with need. Admission notification on a rolling basis beginning on or about 10/1. **Financial aid:** Priority date 3/15; no closing date. FAFSA required. Applicants notified on a rolling basis; must reply within 2 week(s) of notification.

Academics. For some programs, incoming freshmen and transfer students must own a computer that meets or exceeds the set of specifications. **Special study options:** Accelerated study, combined bachelor's/graduate degree, cooperative education, distance learning, double major, dual enrollment of high school students, ESL, external degree, honors, independent study, internships, student-designed major, study abroad, teacher certification program, weekend college. **Credit/placement by examination:** AP, CLEP, IB, SAT, ACT, institutional tests. Course credit by examination may not be used to satisfy the 30-hour minimum residence credit requirement for graduation. Students may not use credit-by-exam options to attempt to remove or replace a grade that has already been earned in a Texas Tech course. **Support services:** Learning center, pre-admission summer program, remedial instruction, study skills assistance, tutoring, writing center.

Honors college/program. Requires separate application. Recommend 1260 SAT, or 27 ACT, or top 10% class rank; 2 teacher recommendations via an on-line recommendation form.

Majors. Architecture: Architecture, interior, landscape. **Area/ethnic studies:** Latin American, Russian/Slavic. **Biology:** General, biochemistry, cellular/molecular, microbiology, zoology. **Business:** General, accounting, business admin, fashion, finance, hotel/motel admin, international, marketing. **Communications:** Advertising, journalism, media studies, public relations, radio/TV. **Computer sciences:** General, information systems. **Conservation:** General, enforcement. **Engineering:** Chemical, civil, computer, construction, electrical, environmental, industrial, mechanical, petroleum. **English:** English lit, rhetoric/composition, technical writing. **Foreign languages:** General, classics, French, German, Spanish. **Health services:** Dietetics. **History:** General. **Human services:** Social work. **Liberal arts:** Arts/sciences. **Math:** General. **Parks/recreation:** Exercise sciences, sports admin. **Philosophy/religion:** Philosophy. **Physical sciences:** Chemistry, geology, physics. **Psychology:** General. **Social sciences:** Anthropology, economics, geography, international economics, political science, sociology. **Visual/performing arts:** Art, dance, dramatic, fashion design, music. **Work/family studies:** General, child care management, child development, family resources, family studies, family/community services, food/nutrition.

Most popular majors. Agriculture 6%, business/marketing 21%, communications/journalism 6%, engineering/engineering technologies 12%, family/consumer sciences 8%, interdisciplinary studies 8%.

Technology on campus. 1,830 workstations in dormitories, library, computer center, student center. Dormitories wired for high-speed internet access and linked to campus network. Commuter students can connect to campus network. Online course registration, online library, helpline, repair service, student web hosting, wireless network available.

Student life. Freshman orientation: Mandatory. Preregistration for classes offered. Two-day sessions held in June, July. One-day sessions only for transfer students held in May, June and July. Transfer students with more than 30 transferring hours have the choice to attend a two-day or one-day session. If transferring less than 30 hours, students are required to attend a two-day session. **Policies:** Freshmen required to live on campus. **Housing:** Guaranteed on-campus for freshmen. Coed dorms, single-sex dorms, special housing for disabled, apartments available. $400 partly refundable deposit. Honors, learning communities, international communities available. **Activities:** Bands, campus ministries, choral groups, dance, drama, film society, international student organizations, literary magazine, music ensembles, musical theater, opera, radio station, student government, student newspaper, symphony orchestra, TV station, Alpha Phi Omega, American Society for Engineering, Campus Crusade for Christ, Chi Alpha Christian Fellowship, India student association, Knights Raiders chess club, Meat Judging Team, Student Agricultural Council, Tech Habitat for Humanity Campus Chapter, Visions of Light Gospel Choir.

Athletics. NCAA. **Intercollegiate:** Baseball M, basketball, cross-country, football (tackle) M, golf, soccer W, softball W, tennis, track and field, volleyball W. **Intramural:** Baseball, basketball, bowling, football (non-tackle), golf, racquetball, sand volleyball, soccer, softball, table tennis, tennis, volleyball, weight lifting M. **Team name:** Red Raiders/ Lady Raiders.

Student services. Alcohol/substance abuse counseling, career counseling, student employment services, financial aid counseling, health services, legal services, personal counseling, placement for graduates, veterans' counselor. **Physically disabled:** Services for visually, speech, hearing impaired.

Contact. E-mail: admissions@ttu.edu
Phone: (806) 742-1480 Fax: (806) 742-0062
Ethan Logan, Executive Director of Undergraduate Recruitment and Admissions, Texas Tech University, Box 45005, Lubbock, TX 79409-5005

Texas Tech University Health Sciences Center
Lubbock, Texas
www.ttuhsc.edu   CB code: 3423

- Public two-year upper-division university
- Commuter campus in small city
- Application essay required

General. Founded in 1969. Regionally accredited. **Degrees:** 1,126 bachelor's awarded; master's, professional, doctoral offered. **Calendar:** Semester, limited summer session. **Full-time faculty:** 862 total. **Part-time faculty:** 62 total. **Class size:** 58% < 20, 30% 20-39, 4% 40-49, 6% 50-99, 2% >100.

Student profile. 1,221 degree-seeking undergraduates, 2,738 graduate students.

Out-of-state:	5%	25 or older:	53%

Basis for selection. College transcript, application essay required. Transfer accepted as juniors.

2015-2016 Annual costs. Tuition/fees: $9,312; $21,012 out-of-state. Room/board: $9,964. Books/supplies: $2,070. **Additional information:** Figures shown are for traditional BSN in the School of Nursing.

Financial aid. Non-need-based: Scholarships awarded for academics.

Application procedures. Admission: $40 fee. **Financial aid:** No deadline. Applicants notified on a rolling basis.

Academics. Special study options: Combined bachelor's/graduate degree, distance learning. **Credit/placement by examination:** AP, CLEP.

Majors. Health services: Clinical lab science, communication disorders, health care admin, nursing (RN).

Technology on campus. PC or laptop required. 160 workstations in library. Commuter students can connect to campus network. Online library, wireless network available.

Student services. Physically disabled: Services for visually, speech, hearing impaired.

Contact. Phone: (806) 743-2300
Texas Tech University Health Sciences Center, 3601 Fourth Street, Lubbock, TX 79430

Texas Wesleyan University
Fort Worth, Texas — CB member
www.txwes.edu — CB code: 6828

- Private 4-year university affiliated with the United Methodist Church
- Commuter campus in very large city
- 1,780 degree-seeking undergraduates: 13% part-time, 53% women, 13% African American, 1% Asian American, 25% Hispanic/Latino, 1% Native American, 4% Multi-racial, non-Hispanic, 26% international
- 659 degree-seeking graduate students
- 46% of applicants admitted
- SAT or ACT (ACT writing optional) required
- 36% graduate within 6 years

General. Founded in 1890. Regionally accredited. **Degrees:** 263 bachelor's awarded; master's, professional, doctoral offered. **ROTC:** Army, Air Force. **Location:** 2 miles from downtown. **Calendar:** Semester, limited summer session. **Full-time faculty:** 136 total; 88% have terminal degrees, 15% minority, 51% women. **Part-time faculty:** 97 total; 18% minority, 52% women. **Class size:** 63% < 20, 36% 20-39, less than 1% 40-49.

Freshman class profile. 3,062 applied, 1,407 admitted, 369 enrolled.

Mid 50% test scores			
SAT critical reading:	470-550	Rank in top quarter:	42%
SAT math:	460-540	Rank in top tenth:	16%
SAT writing:	420-510	End year in good standing:	86%
ACT composite:	19-23	Return as sophomores:	57%
GPA 3.75 or higher:	26%	Out-of-state:	2%
GPA 3.50-3.74:	22%	Live on campus:	38%
GPA 3.0-3.49:	37%	International:	40%
GPA 2.0-2.99:	15%	Fraternities:	5%
		Sororities:	9%

Basis for selection. Regular freshmen admission requires minimum 2.5 high school GPA, 19 ACT or 920 SAT combined score (exclusive of Writing), top 50% ranking in senior class. **Home schooled:** Transcript of courses and grades required.

High school preparation. College-preparatory program recommended. 24 units recommended. Recommended units include English 4, mathematics 4, history 8, science 3 (laboratory 2) and foreign language 3.

2015-2016 Annual costs. Tuition/fees: $24,454. Room/board: $8,651. Books/supplies: $1,600. Personal expenses: $2,800.

2014-2015 Financial aid. All financial aid based on need. 190 full-time freshmen applied for aid; 172 deemed to have need; 170 received aid. Average need met was 79%. Average scholarship/grant was $19,605; average loan $3,026. 55% of total undergraduate aid awarded as scholarships/grants, 45% as loans/jobs.

Application procedures. Admission: Priority date 1/15; no deadline. No application fee. Admission notification on a rolling basis. **Financial aid:** Priority date 3/1; no closing date. FAFSA required. Applicants notified on a rolling basis.

Academics. Special study options: Accelerated study, combined bachelor's/graduate degree, double major, dual enrollment of high school students, ESL, exchange student, honors, independent study, internships, liberal arts/career combination, study abroad, teacher certification program, weekend college. **Credit/placement by examination:** AP, CLEP, IB, SAT, ACT, institutional tests. 30 credit hours maximum toward bachelor's degree. **Support services:** Learning center, pre-admission summer program, reduced course load, remedial instruction, study skills assistance, tutoring, writing center.

Majors. Biology: General, biochemistry. **Business:** Accounting, business admin, finance, management science, marketing. **Communications:** Journalism, public relations, radio/TV. **Computer sciences:** Computer science. **Education:** General, bilingual, biology, English, history, mathematics, music, Spanish. **English:** Creative writing, English lit. **Foreign languages:** Spanish. **Health services:** Athletic training, predental. **History:** General. **Liberal arts:**

Arts/sciences. Math: General. **Parks/recreation:** Exercise sciences. **Philosophy/religion:** Christian, religion. **Physical sciences:** Chemistry. **Protective services:** Criminal justice. **Psychology:** General. **Social sciences:** Political science, sociology. **Visual/performing arts:** Music, theater arts management.

Most popular majors. Business/marketing 19%, education 8%, interdisciplinary studies 16%, psychology 9%, security/protective services 6%.

Technology on campus. 418 workstations in library, computer center. Dormitories wired for high-speed internet access and linked to campus network. Commuter students can connect to campus network. Online library, helpline, repair service, wireless network available.

Student life. Freshman orientation: Mandatory. Preregistration for classes offered. **Housing:** Guaranteed on-campus for freshmen. Coed dorms, special housing for disabled, apartments available. $225 partly refundable deposit. **Activities:** Bands, campus ministries, choral groups, dance, drama, international student organizations, music ensembles, Model UN, musical theater, opera, radio station, student government, student newspaper, TV station, College Republicans, black student association, Saudi Arabia student association, Alpha Phi Omega, Wesleyan Justice Project, veteran's association.

Athletics. NAIA. **Intercollegiate:** Baseball M, basketball, cheerleading, cross-country, golf, soccer, softball W, table tennis, tennis W, track and field, volleyball W. **Team name:** Rams.

Student services. Adult student services, alcohol/substance abuse counseling, chaplain/spiritual director, career counseling, student employment services, financial aid counseling, health services, personal counseling, placement for graduates, veterans' counselor.

Contact. E-mail: admissions@txwes.edu
Phone: (817) 531-4422 Toll-free number: (800) 580-8980
Fax: (817) 531-7515
Chadd Bridwell, Enrollment Services Assistant Vice President, Texas Wesleyan University, 1201 Wesleyan Street, Fort Worth, TX 76105-1536

Texas Woman's University
Denton, Texas — CB member
www.twu.edu — CB code: 6826

- Public 4-year university
- Residential campus in small city
- 8,803 degree-seeking undergraduates: 25% part-time, 90% women
- 5,093 degree-seeking graduate students
- 75% of applicants admitted
- 41% graduate within 6 years

General. Founded in 1901. Regionally accredited. **Degrees:** 2,062 bachelor's awarded; master's, professional, doctoral offered. **ROTC:** Army, Air Force. **Location:** 35 miles from Dallas and Fort Worth. **Calendar:** Semester, extensive summer session. **Full-time faculty:** 483 total; 76% have terminal degrees, 16% minority, 76% women. **Part-time faculty:** 398 total; 33% have terminal degrees, 22% minority, 78% women. **Class size:** 45% < 20, 39% 20-39, 6% 40-49, 7% 50-99, 3% >100. **Special facilities:** Art collection, Little Chapel-in-the-Woods, Texas Women's Hall of Fame, Texas First Ladies historic costume collection, woman's collection, Women Airforce Service Pilots memorabilia, botanical gardens, Gertrude Gibson Guest House, collection of children's book art, cookbook collection.

Freshman class profile. 4,772 applied, 3,558 admitted, 1,158 enrolled.

Mid 50% test scores			
SAT critical reading:	410-520	Rank in top quarter:	45%
SAT math:	420-530	Rank in top tenth:	18%
ACT composite:	17-23	Return as sophomores:	65%
GPA 3.75 or higher:	11%	Out-of-state:	2%
GPA 3.50-3.74:	12%	Live on campus:	83%
GPA 3.0-3.49:	32%	International:	1%
GPA 2.0-2.99:	45%	Fraternities:	1%
		Sororities:	5%

Basis for selection. School achievement record and test scores most important: Texas Academic Skills Program, 1000 SAT score or ACT of 21. Texas Education Code and the Texas Success Initiative (TSI) requires new students, unless exempt, to be tested to assess readiness in reading, writing, and math prior to enrolling. Interview and audition required for drama and music programs; interview required and portfolio recommended for art program. **Home schooled:** Transcript of courses and grades required. Must submit official transcript showing completion of secondary school education and date of completion; SAT or ACT test score results. Applications missing these items will be reviewed by an admission officer and applicants given the opportunity to provide additional information to support their request for individual consideration.

High school preparation. College-preparatory program recommended. 14 units required; 26 recommended. Required and recommended units include English 4, mathematics 3-4, social studies 3-3.5, science 3-4, foreign language 2, computer science 1, visual/performing arts 1, academic electives 1-5.5.

2015-2016 Annual costs. Tuition/fees: $8,522; $20,222 out-of-state. Room/board: $7,443. Books/supplies: $1,050. Personal expenses: $2,088.

Financial aid. Non-need-based: Scholarships awarded for academics, art, athletics, music/drama, ROTC.

Application procedures. Admission: Priority date 3/1; deadline 7/15 (receipt date). $50 fee, may be waived for applicants with need. Admission notification on a rolling basis beginning on or about 3/1. **Financial aid:** Priority date 4/1; no closing date. FAFSA required.

Academics. Special study options: Accelerated study, combined bachelor's/graduate degree, cooperative education, cross-registration, distance learning, double major, dual enrollment of high school students, external degree, honors, independent study, internships, study abroad, teacher certification program, weekend college. **Credit/placement by examination:** AP, CLEP, SAT, ACT, institutional tests. 30 credit hours maximum toward bachelor's degree. **Support services:** Learning center, pre-admission summer program, reduced course load, remedial instruction, study skills assistance, tutoring, writing center.

Majors. Biology: General, biochemistry, zoology. **Business:** Accounting, administrative services, business admin, fashion, finance, marketing. **Computer sciences:** General. **English:** English lit. **Health services:** Clinical lab science, dental hygiene, dietetics, music therapy, nursing (RN). **History:** General. **Human services:** Social work. **Math:** General. **Parks/recreation:** Health/fitness. **Physical sciences:** Chemistry. **Protective services:** Criminal justice. **Psychology:** General. **Social sciences:** Political science, sociology. **Visual/performing arts:** Art, dance, dramatic, fashion design, music. **Work/family studies:** General, child development, family studies, food/nutrition.

Most popular majors. Business/marketing 9%, family/consumer sciences 6%, health sciences 28%, interdisciplinary studies 11%, liberal arts 14%, parks/recreation 6%.

Technology on campus. 1,000 workstations in dormitories, library, computer center, student center. Dormitories linked to campus network. Commuter students can connect to campus network. Online course registration, helpline, wireless network available.

Student life. Freshman orientation: Mandatory, $100 fee. Preregistration for classes offered. Held over a two day event. **Housing:** Guaranteed on-campus for freshmen. Coed dorms, single-sex dorms, special housing for disabled, apartments, fraternity/sorority housing, themed housing available. $150 partly refundable deposit, deadline 8/4. Living-learning communities available. **Activities:** Bands, campus ministries, choral groups, dance, drama, international student organizations, music ensembles, opera, student government, student newspaper, Alpha Theta Omega, LULAC, multicultural African organization, NAACP, Alpha Kappa Alpha Sorority, Delta Sigma Theta Sorority, Zeta Phi Beta Sorority, Golden Key international honor society.

Athletics. NCAA. **Intercollegiate:** Basketball W, gymnastics W, soccer W, softball W, volleyball W. **Intramural:** Basketball, football (non-tackle), golf, racquetball, soccer, softball, swimming, table tennis M, tennis, volleyball, weight lifting. **Team name:** Pioneers.

Student services. Adult student services, alcohol/substance abuse counseling, career counseling, student employment services, financial aid counseling, health services, minority student services, personal counseling, placement for graduates, veterans' counselor, women's services. **Physically disabled:** Services for visually, speech, hearing impaired.

Contact. E-mail: admissions@twu.edu
Phone: (940) 898-3188 Toll-free number: (866) 809-6130
Fax: (940) 898-3081
Erma Nieto-Brecht, Director of Admissions, Texas Woman's University, Box 425589, Denton, TX 76204-5589

Trinity University
San Antonio, Texas

CB member

www.trinity.edu

CB code: 6831

▶ Private 4-year university affiliated with the Presbyterian Church (USA)
▶ Residential campus in very large city
▶ 2,253 degree-seeking undergraduates: 3% part-time, 52% women, 4% African American, 6% Asian American, 20% Hispanic/Latino, 5% Multiracial, non-Hispanic, 7% international
▶ 206 degree-seeking graduate students

▶ 48% of applicants admitted
▶ SAT or ACT (ACT writing optional), application essay required
▶ 83% graduate within 6 years

General. Founded in 1869. Regionally accredited. **Degrees:** 523 bachelor's awarded; master's offered. **ROTC:** Army, Air Force. **Location:** 3 miles from downtown. **Calendar:** Semester, limited summer session. **Full-time faculty:** 231 total; 99% have terminal degrees, 20% minority, 43% women. **Part-time faculty:** 78 total; 35% have terminal degrees, 8% minority, 32% women. **Class size:** 63% < 20, 33% 20-39, 2% 40-49, 2% 50-99.

Freshman class profile. 5,563 applied, 2,672 admitted, 602 enrolled.

Mid 50% test scores			
SAT critical reading:	580-690	GPA 2.0-2.99:	10%
SAT math:	580-680	Rank in top quarter:	75%
SAT writing:	560-660	Rank in top tenth:	47%
ACT composite:	27-32	Return as sophomores:	90%
GPA 3.75 or higher:	33%	Out-of-state:	20%
GPA 3.50-3.74:	27%	Live on campus:	100%
GPA 3.0-3.49:	30%	International:	6%

Basis for selection. GPA, high school rank, test scores, essay, interview, recommendations, extracurricular involvement, and achievement important. **Home schooled:** At least 3 SAT Subject Tests recommended, including natural science and foreign language.

High school preparation. College-preparatory program required. 15 units required. Required units include English 4, mathematics 3, social studies 3, science 3 (laboratory 2) and foreign language 2.

2015-2016 Annual costs. Tuition/fees: $37,856. Room/board: $12,362. Books/supplies: $1,000. Personal expenses: $900.

2015-2016 Financial aid. Need-based: 421 full-time freshmen applied for aid; 269 deemed to have need; 269 received aid. Average need met was 98%. Average scholarship/grant was $29,089; average loan $4,468. 83% of total undergraduate aid awarded as scholarships/grants, 17% as loans/jobs. **Non-need-based:** Awarded to 1,317 full-time undergraduates, including 410 freshmen. Scholarships awarded for academics, art, leadership, music/drama.

Application procedures. Admission: Closing date 2/1 (postmark date). No application fee. Admission notification by 4/1. Must reply by 5/1. **Financial aid:** Priority date 2/15; no closing date. FAFSA, CSS PROFILE required. Applicants notified by 3/15; must reply by 5/1.

Academics. Special study options: Accelerated study, combined bachelor's/graduate degree, double major, honors, independent study, internships, liberal arts/career combination, New York semester, semester at sea, student-designed major, study abroad, teacher certification program, United Nations semester, urban semester, Washington semester. **Credit/placement by examination:** AP, CLEP, IB, institutional tests. 36 credit hours maximum toward bachelor's degree. **Support services:** Writing center.

Majors. Area/ethnic studies: Asian, European, Latin American. **Biology:** General, biochemistry. **Business:** Accounting, business admin, finance, international, management science, marketing. **Communications:** Communications/speech/rhetoric. **Computer sciences:** General. **Education:** Elementary. **Engineering:** Engineering science. **English:** English lit, rhetoric/composition. **Foreign languages:** Chinese, classics, French, German, Russian, Spanish. **History:** General. **Math:** General. **Philosophy/religion:** Philosophy, religion. **Physical sciences:** Chemistry, geology, physics. **Psychology:** General. **Social sciences:** Anthropology, economics, political science, sociology, urban studies. **Visual/performing arts:** Art, art history/conservation, dramatic, music, music performance, music theory/composition, theater design, voice/opera.

Most popular majors. Biology 12%, business/marketing 24%, communications/journalism 7%, foreign language 7%, social sciences 15%.

Technology on campus. 400 workstations in library, computer center, student center. Dormitories wired for high-speed internet access and linked to campus network. Commuter students can connect to campus network. Online course registration, online library, helpline, student web hosting, wireless network available.

Student life. Freshman orientation: Available. Preregistration for classes offered. **Housing:** Guaranteed on-campus for freshmen. Coed dorms, special housing for disabled, themed housing, wellness housing available. $500 nonrefundable deposit, deadline 5/1. **Activities:** Bands, campus ministries, choral groups, dance, drama, film society, international student organizations, literary magazine, music ensembles, Model UN, musical theater, opera, radio station, student government, student newspaper, symphony orchestra, TV station, Phi Beta Kappa, academic honor societies, activities council, Young Democrats, Young Republicans, association of student representatives, Alpha Phi Omega, religious organizations, minority student organizations, Trinity Multicultural Network.

Athletics. NCAA. **Intercollegiate:** Baseball M, basketball, cross-country, diving, football (tackle) M, golf, soccer, softball W, swimming, tennis, track and field, volleyball W. **Intramural:** Basketball, cross-country, football (non-tackle), racquetball, soccer, softball, swimming, table tennis, tennis, volleyball, wrestling. **Team name:** Tigers.

Student services. Chaplain/spiritual director, career counseling, student employment services, financial aid counseling, health services, personal counseling, placement for graduates, veterans' counselor. **Physically disabled:** Services for visually, hearing impaired.

Contact. E-mail: admissions@trinity.edu
Phone: (210) 999-7207 Toll-free number: (800) 874-6489
Fax: (210) 999-8164
Christopher Ellertson, Dean of Admissions and Financial Aid, Trinity University, One Trinity Place, San Antonio, TX 78212-7200

University of Dallas
Irving, Texas
www.udallas.edu

CB member
CB code: 6868

- Private 4-year university and liberal arts college affiliated with the Roman Catholic Church
- Residential campus in small city
- 1,336 degree-seeking undergraduates: 2% part-time, 56% women, 2% African American, 5% Asian American, 21% Hispanic/Latino, 3% Multiracial, non-Hispanic, 2% international
- 1,043 degree-seeking graduate students
- 83% of applicants admitted
- SAT or ACT (ACT writing optional), application essay required
- 70% graduate within 6 years

General. Founded in 1956. Regionally accredited. 12-acre campus located just outside of Rome, Italy. **Degrees:** 299 bachelor's awarded; master's, doctoral offered. **ROTC:** Army, Air Force. **Location:** 5 miles from Dallas. **Calendar:** Semester, limited summer session. **Full-time faculty:** 148 total; 9% minority, 37% women. **Part-time faculty:** 84 total; 13% minority, 32% women. **Class size:** 66% < 20, 30% 20-39, 3% 40-49, 2% 50-99.

Freshman class profile. 2,001 applied, 1,653 admitted, 393 enrolled.

Mid 50% test scores			
		GPA 2.0-2.99:	4%
SAT critical reading:	540-690	Rank in top quarter:	67%
SAT math:	540-650	Rank in top tenth:	39%
SAT writing:	530-650	Return as sophomores:	81%
ACT composite:	24-30	Out-of-state:	54%
GPA 3.75 or higher:	60%	Live on campus:	90%
GPA 3.50-3.74:	20%	International:	2%
GPA 3.0-3.49:	16%		

Basis for selection. Sufficient academic preparation and ability required along with evidence of good character. Critical writing and composition skills important. Holistic review of all elements submitted, including standardized test scores, transcript, writing samples, and letters of recommendation. **Home schooled:** Statement describing home school structure and mission, transcript of courses and grades required. Transcript must be from a recognized, accredited consortium or association; or a comprehensive course description (including list of books used, laboratory work done, and narrative description or experiential learning) is required. Homeschool supplement and self-certification forms also required.

High school preparation. College-preparatory program recommended. Required and recommended units include English 4, mathematics 3-4, social studies 3-4, history 3-4, science 3-4 (laboratory 3), foreign language 2-3 and visual/performing arts 1-2.

2016-2017 Annual costs. Tuition/fees: $37,230. Room/board: $11,540. Books/supplies: $1,200. Personal expenses: $1,400.

2015-2016 Financial aid. **Need-based:** 316 full-time freshmen applied for aid; 268 deemed to have need; 268 received aid. Average need met was 83%. Average scholarship/grant was $28,287; average loan $4,386. 89% of total undergraduate aid awarded as scholarships/grants, 11% as loans/jobs. **Non-need-based:** Awarded to 467 full-time undergraduates, including 117 freshmen. Scholarships awarded for academics, alumni affiliation, art, minority status, music/drama, religious affiliation, ROTC, state residency.

Application procedures. **Admission:** Priority date 1/15; deadline 8/1 (postmark date). $50 fee, may be waived for applicants with need. Application must be submitted online. Admission notification on a rolling basis. Must reply by May 1 or within 4 week(s) if notified thereafter. Two early action deadlines: November 1 and December 1. Notification is 3-4 weeks later. **Financial aid:** Priority date 3/1, closing date 8/1. FAFSA required. Applicants

notified on a rolling basis starting 3/1; must reply by 5/1 or within 4 week(s) of notification.

Academics. **Special study options:** Combined bachelor's/graduate degree, cooperative education, double major, dual enrollment of high school students, independent study, internships, liberal arts/career combination, student-designed major, study abroad, teacher certification program. **Credit/placement by examination:** AP, CLEP, IB, institutional tests. 32 credit hours maximum toward bachelor's degree. **Support services:** Reduced course load, study skills assistance, tutoring, writing center.

Majors. **Biology:** General, biochemistry. **Business:** Business admin. **Computer sciences:** General. **Education:** General, elementary. **English:** English lit. **Foreign languages:** Classics, French, German, Spanish. **History:** General. **Math:** General. **Philosophy/religion:** Philosophy. **Physical sciences:** Chemistry, physics. **Psychology:** General. **Social sciences:** Economics, political science. **Theology:** Preministerial, theology. **Visual/performing arts:** Art history/conservation, ceramics, dramatic, painting, printmaking, sculpture.

Most popular majors. Biology 12%, business/marketing 14%, English 9%, history 10%, social sciences 17%, theological studies 9%.

Technology on campus. 125 workstations in library, computer center, student center. Dormitories wired for high-speed internet access and linked to campus network. Commuter students can connect to campus network. Online course registration, online library, helpline, repair service, wireless network available.

Student life. **Freshman orientation:** Mandatory. Preregistration for classes offered. **Housing:** Guaranteed on-campus for freshmen. Single-sex dorms, apartments available. $200 nonrefundable deposit. **Activities:** Campus ministries, choral groups, dance, drama, film society, international student organizations, literary magazine, music ensembles, student government, student newspaper, Best Buddies, Crusaders for Kids, Alpha Phi Omega, Crusaders for Life, Latino Association of Students, Rotaract Club, Alexander Hamilton Society, Asian-American Student Association, International Student Association.

Athletics. NCAA. **Intercollegiate:** Baseball M, basketball, cross-country, golf, lacrosse, soccer, softball W, track and field, volleyball W. **Intramural:** Basketball, football (non-tackle), sand volleyball, soccer, softball, volleyball. **Team name:** Crusaders.

Student services. Alcohol/substance abuse counseling, chaplain/spiritual director, career counseling, student employment services, financial aid counseling, health services, personal counseling, placement for graduates, veterans' counselor. **Physically disabled:** Services for visually impaired.

Contact. E-mail: crusader@udallas.edu
Phone: (972) 721-5266 Toll-free number: (800) 628-6999
Fax: (972) 721-5017
Elizabeth Griffin Smith, Director of Admission, University of Dallas, 1845 East Northgate Drive, Irving, TX 75062-4736

University of Houston
Houston, Texas
www.uh.edu

CB member
CB code: 6870

- Public 4-year university
- Commuter campus in very large city
- 33,404 degree-seeking undergraduates: 27% part-time, 49% women, 10% African American, 22% Asian American, 32% Hispanic/Latino, 3% Multi-racial, non-Hispanic, 5% international
- 7,874 degree-seeking graduate students
- 60% of applicants admitted
- SAT or ACT (ACT writing optional) required
- 51% graduate within 6 years

General. Founded in 1927. Regionally accredited. **Degrees:** 6,425 bachelor's awarded; master's, professional, doctoral offered. **ROTC:** Army, Naval, Air Force. **Location:** 3 miles from downtown. **Calendar:** Semester, extensive summer session. **Full-time faculty:** 1,501 total; 85% have terminal degrees, 27% minority, 39% women. **Part-time faculty:** 765 total; 54% have terminal degrees, 20% minority, 36% women. **Class size:** 28% < 20, 41% 20-39, 7% 40-49, 14% 50-99, 10% >100. **Special facilities:** Theater complex, observatory, opera house, art museum.

Freshman class profile. 17,971 applied, 10,732 admitted, 4,187 enrolled.

Mid 50% test scores			
		End year in good standing:	87%
SAT critical reading:	510-610	Return as sophomores:	86%
SAT math:	540-640	Out-of-state:	3%
ACT composite:	23-28	Live on campus:	50%
Rank in top quarter:	64%	International:	5%
Rank in top tenth:	30%		

Basis for selection. Those ranked in top 10% of high school class are automatically accepted provided they apply by June 1. Before December 1, applicants in top 25% with minimum combined score of 1000 SAT or 21 ACT composite are admitted, and applicants in the top 26%-50% with minimum combined score of 1100 SAT or 24 ACT composite are admitted. Students submitting after December 1 or applicants attending a school that doesn't rank are considered for admission under the school's individual/holistic review process, which examines rigor of high school curriculum, first-generation college attendance, socioeconomic background, special talents, abilities or awards, family responsibilities, leadership, public service and extracurricular activities. Audition and application required for music, theater, and dance programs; essay recommended for honors college and individual review. Portfolio suggested for architecture program. **Home schooled:** Transcript of courses and grades, state high school equivalency certificate required. Must submit minimum SAT score of 1180 or a 26 composite score on the ACT and transcript (can be created by parent). In order to qualify for financial aid, must pass GED exam. **Learning Disabled:** Intake appointment with counselor scheduled upon receipt of required documentation of limitations due to disability.

High school preparation. College-preparatory program required. Required and recommended units include English 4, mathematics 4, social studies 4, science 4 (laboratory 2), foreign language 2, computer science 1 and visual/performing arts 1.

2015-2016 Annual costs. Tuition/fees: $10,664; $25,364 out-of-state. Books/supplies: $1,300. Personal expenses: $2,700.

2015-2016 Financial aid. Need-based: 3,093 full-time freshmen applied for aid; 2,484 deemed to have need; 2,412 received aid. Average need met was 66%. Average scholarship/grant was $9,671; average loan $5,270. 54% of total undergraduate aid awarded as scholarships/grants, 46% as loans/jobs. **Non-need-based:** Awarded to 1,648 full-time undergraduates, including 663 freshmen. Scholarships awarded for academics, alumni affiliation, art, athletics, job skills, leadership, music/drama, ROTC, state residency. **Additional information:** The Cougar Promise guarantees free tuition and mandatory fees to new in-state freshmen with family incomes at or below $45,000. Qualifying students will have tuition and fees guaranteed for up to four years as long as students continue to meet eligibility criteria and maintain at least a 2.5 GPA. Covers tuition and fees during the fall and spring semesters only. Eligibility is determined when a student fills out the FAFSA. Those who miss the April 1 deadline will be awarded based on the availability of funds.

Application procedures. Admission: Priority date 12/1; deadline 7/1 (receipt date). $50 fee, may be waived for applicants with need. Admission notification by 4/15. Admission notification on a rolling basis beginning on or about 9/15. Must reply by 6/1. **Financial aid:** Priority date 4/1; no closing date. FAFSA required. Applicants notified on a rolling basis starting 5/1.

Academics. Special study options: Accelerated study, combined bachelor's/graduate degree, cooperative education, cross-registration, distance learning, double major, dual enrollment of high school students, ESL, exchange student, honors, independent study, internships, student-designed major, study abroad, teacher certification program, weekend college. Academic enrichment programs, certification programs and affiliated studies. **Credit/placement by examination:** AP, CLEP, IB, institutional tests. **Support services:** Learning center, reduced course load, remedial instruction, study skills assistance, tutoring, writing center.

Honors college/program. All students encouraged to apply. High school and/or academic record, extracurricular activities, test scores, and essay considered. No specific requirements for admission, however the average honors student is in the top 10 percent of their high school class with SAT score of 1300 or above.

Majors. Architecture: Architecture, environmental design, interior. **Biology:** General, biochemistry, biomedical sciences, biotechnology. **Business:** Accounting, business admin, communications, entrepreneurial studies, finance, hotel/motel admin, management information systems, marketing, operations, organizational leadership, sales/distribution, training/development. **Communications:** General, advertising, communications/speech/rhetoric, health, journalism, media studies, public relations, radio/TV. **Computer sciences:** General, computer graphics, information systems, systems analysis. **Conservation:** Environmental science. **Engineering:** Biomedical, chemical, civil, computer, electrical, industrial, mechanical, petroleum. **English:** Creative writing, English lit. **Foreign languages:** General, American Sign Language, Chinese, French, Italian, linguistics, Spanish. **Health services:** General, communication disorders, nursing (RN), pharmaceutical sciences. **History:** General. **Liberal arts:** Arts/sciences. **Math:** General, biological. **Parks/recreation:** Exercise sciences, sports admin. **Philosophy/religion:** Philosophy, religion. **Physical sciences:** Chemistry, geology, geophysics, physics. **Psychology:** General. **Social sciences:** Anthropology, economics, political science, sociology. **Visual/performing arts:** Art, art history/conservation, dance, dramatic, graphic design, industrial design, music, music performance, painting, photography, sculpture. **Work/family studies:** Business, family studies, human nutrition.

Most popular majors. Biology 6%, business/marketing 30%, communications/journalism 7%, engineering/engineering technologies 9%, psychology 7%, social sciences 7%.

Technology on campus. 1,006 workstations in dormitories, library, computer center, student center. Dormitories wired for high-speed internet access and linked to campus network. Commuter students can connect to campus network. Online course registration, online library, helpline, repair service, student web hosting, wireless network available.

Student life. Freshman orientation: Mandatory, $120 fee. Preregistration for classes offered. Overnight two-day program required prior to academic advising and course registration. **Housing:** Coed dorms, single-sex dorms, special housing for disabled, apartments, fraternity/sorority housing, themed housing, wellness housing available. **Activities:** Bands, campus ministries, choral groups, dance, drama, film society, international student organizations, literary magazine, music ensembles, musical theater, opera, radio station, student government, student newspaper, symphony orchestra, TV station, African Student Organization, Council of Ethnic Organizations, Indian Student Association, Bhakti Yoga Society, Asian Campus Fellowship, Catholic Student Organization, Student Government Association, Skeptics Society, National Society of Collegiate Scholars, Phi Alpha Theta-Zeta Kappa, Hispanic Business Student Association, Gamma Iota Sigma.

Athletics. NCAA. **Intercollegiate:** Baseball M, basketball, cross-country, diving W, football (tackle) M, golf, soccer W, softball W, swimming W, tennis W, track and field, volleyball W. **Intramural:** Badminton, basketball, bowling, football (non-tackle), golf, racquetball, soccer, softball, swimming, table tennis, tennis, track and field, volleyball, weight lifting. **Team name:** Cougars.

Student services. Adult student services, alcohol/substance abuse counseling, chaplain/spiritual director, career counseling, student employment services, financial aid counseling, health services, minority student services, on-campus daycare, personal counseling, placement for graduates, veterans' counselor, women's services. **Physically disabled:** Services for visually, speech, hearing impaired.

Contact. E-mail: admissions@uh.edu
Phone: (713) 743-1010 Fax: (713) 743-7542
Djuana Young, Executive Director of Admissions, University of Houston, Office of Admission, Houston, TX 77004

University of Houston-Clear Lake
Houston, Texas   CB member
www.uhcl.edu   CB code: 6916

- Public 4-year university
- Commuter campus in very large city
- 5,403 degree-seeking undergraduates: 51% part-time, 65% women, 36% African American, 9% Asian American, 1% Hispanic/Latino, 6% Native American, 43% Multi-racial, non-Hispanic, 2% international
- 3,319 degree-seeking graduate students
- 66% of applicants admitted
- SAT or ACT (ACT writing optional) required

General. Founded in 1971. Regionally accredited. **Degrees:** 1,297 bachelor's awarded; master's, doctoral offered. **Location:** 21 miles from downtown. **Calendar:** Semester, limited summer session. **Full-time faculty:** 308 total; 27% minority, 44% women. **Part-time faculty:** 253 total; 25% minority, 59% women. **Class size:** 27% < 20, 59% 20-39, 8% 40-49, 6% 50-99, less than 1% >100. **Special facilities:** Environmental institute of Houston, nature preserves.

Freshman class profile. 1,010 applied, 663 admitted, 200 enrolled.

Mid 50% test scores			
SAT critical reading:	460-560	GPA 3.50-3.74:	31%
SAT math:	480-560	GPA 3.0-3.49:	21%
SAT writing:	430-520	GPA 2.0-2.99:	22%
ACT composite:	20-24	Rank in top quarter:	44%
GPA 3.75 or higher:	26%	Rank in top tenth:	16%
		Return as sophomores:	71%

Basis for selection. Those ranked in top 10% of high school class are automatically accepted. Applicants in top 25% with minimum combined score of 950 SAT (exclusive of Writing) or 20 ACT composite are admitted, and applicants in the top 26%-50% with minimum combined score of 1050 SAT (exclusive of Writing) or 23 ACT composite are admitted. All other applicants, including those attending a school that doesn't rank, are considered for admission under the school's individual review process, which examines rigor of high school curriculum, first-generation college attendance, socioeconomic background, special talents, abilities or awards, family responsibilities, leadership, public service and extracurricular activities. Essays or personal statements required of people/applicants undergoing individual review. **Home schooled:** State high school equivalency certificate, letter of recommendation (nonparent) required. Essays or personal statement regarding education and career goals.

High school preparation. 26 units required. Required units include English 4, mathematics 4, social studies 4, science 4, foreign language 2, visual/performing arts 1, academic electives 1.5. Speech .5, physical education 1.

2015-2016 Annual costs. Tuition/fees: $6,639; $21,099 out-of-state. Books/supplies: $1,050. Personal expenses: $3,138.

2014-2015 Financial aid. Need-based: 152 full-time freshmen applied for aid; 122 deemed to have need; 105 received aid. Average need met was 65%. Average scholarship/grant was $10,871; average loan $2,744. 62% of total undergraduate aid awarded as scholarships/grants, 38% as loans/jobs. **Non-need-based:** Awarded to 894 full-time undergraduates, including 82 freshmen. Scholarships awarded for academics, art, leadership, state residency. **Additional information:** UHCL offers the automatic transfer scholarship to any first-time transfer student if their transfer GPA is 2.75 or above upon receiving all transcripts. No application necessary for the scholarship.

Application procedures. Admission: Priority date 2/1; deadline 6/1 (postmark date). $45 fee, may be waived for applicants with need. Application must be submitted online. Admission notification on a rolling basis beginning on or about 9/15. **Financial aid:** Priority date 3/15; no closing date. FAFSA required. Applicants notified on a rolling basis starting 5/1; must reply within 2 week(s) of notification.

Academics. Special study options: Combined bachelor's/graduate degree, distance learning, double major, ESL, independent study, internships, study abroad, teacher certification program. **Credit/placement by examination:** AP, CLEP, IB, SAT, ACT. 30 credit hours maximum toward bachelor's degree. **Support services:** Writing center.

Majors. Area/ethnic studies: Women's. **Biology:** General. **Business:** General, accounting, business admin, finance, management information systems, marketing. **Communications:** General. **Computer sciences:** General, computer science. **Conservation:** Environmental science. **Engineering:** Computer. **English:** English lit. **Health services:** Health care admin, nursing (RN). **History:** General. **Human services:** General, social work. **Liberal arts:** Humanities. **Math:** General. **Parks/recreation:** Exercise sciences. **Physical sciences:** General, chemistry, physics. **Psychology:** General. **Social sciences:** Anthropology, criminology, geography, political science, sociology. **Visual/performing arts:** Studio arts.

Most popular majors. Business/marketing 26%, interdisciplinary studies 28%, science technologies 8%.

Technology on campus. 800 workstations in library, computer center, student center. Commuter students can connect to campus network. Online course registration, online library, helpline, wireless network available.

Student life. Freshman orientation: Mandatory. Preregistration for classes offered. **Housing:** Special housing for disabled, apartments, themed housing available. Limited apartments on campus. **Activities:** Campus ministries, drama, international student organizations, student government, student newspaper, black student association, Chinese student association, Latino and Hispanic Heritage student association, Indian student association, Muslim student association, Baptist student ministry, Soka Peace Group, Student Veterans of America.

Athletics. Team name: Hawks.

Student services. Alcohol/substance abuse counseling, career counseling, student employment services, financial aid counseling, health services, minority student services, personal counseling, placement for graduates, veterans' counselor, women's services. **Physically disabled:** Services for visually, speech, hearing impaired.

Contact. E-mail: admissions@uhcl.edu
Phone: (281) 283-2500 Fax: (281) 283-2522
Rauchelle Jones, Executive Director of Admissions, University of Houston-Clear Lake, 2700 Bay Area Boulevard, Houston, TX 77058-1098

University of Houston-Downtown

Houston, Texas　　　　　　　　　　**CB member**
www.uhd.edu　　　　　　　　　　　**CB code: 6922**

- Public 4-year university
- Commuter campus in very large city

- 13,101 degree-seeking undergraduates: 49% part-time, 60% women, 23% African American, 9% Asian American, 43% Hispanic/Latino, 1% Multi-racial, non-Hispanic, 5% international
- 1,017 degree-seeking graduate students
- 78% of applicants admitted
- SAT or ACT (ACT writing optional) required

General. Founded in 1974. Regionally accredited. Campus at Lone Star College University Center. Classes also offered at these Lone Star College (LSC) sites: Kingwood, CyFair, and Atascocita Center. **Degrees:** 2,338 bachelor's awarded; master's offered. **ROTC:** Army, Air Force. **Calendar:** Semester, extensive summer session. **Full-time faculty:** 352 total; 84% have terminal degrees, 35% minority, 49% women. **Part-time faculty:** 365 total; 43% have terminal degrees, 48% minority, 52% women. **Class size:** 27% < 20, 58% 20-39, 11% 40-49, 4% 50-99.

Freshman class profile. 3,460 applied, 2,686 admitted, 877 enrolled.

Mid 50% test scores		Rank in top quarter:	29%
SAT critical reading:	390-480	Rank in top tenth:	6%
SAT math:	420-510	Return as sophomores:	66%
SAT writing:	390-470	Out-of-state:	1%
ACT composite:	16-20	International:	6%

Basis for selection. Students who do not meet regular admissions criteria may be considered for admission by way of individual review. Each applicant's file will be reviewed by a committee and a student may be admitted to UHD or considered for an alternative option. **Home schooled:** Transcript of courses and grades required.

High school preparation. College-preparatory program required. 26 units required. Required units include English 4, mathematics 4, social studies 2, history 2, science 4, foreign language 2, visual/performing arts 1, academic electives 5.5. 1 unit required in physical education, 0.5 in speech.

2015-2016 Annual costs. Tuition/fees: $6,938; $18,638 out-of-state. Books/supplies: $1,167. Personal expenses: $3,962. **Additional information:** College of Business tuition rates are an additional $2 per credit hour. College of Science and Technology tuition rates are an additional $3 per credit hour.

2014-2015 Financial aid. Need-based: 813 full-time freshmen applied for aid; 731 deemed to have need; 654 received aid. Average need met was 62%. Average scholarship/grant was $8,903; average loan $4,560. 44% of total undergraduate aid awarded as scholarships/grants, 56% as loans/jobs. **Non-need-based:** Awarded to 372 full-time undergraduates, including 1 freshmen.

Application procedures. Admission: Closing date 7/1 (postmark date). $35 fee, may be waived for applicants with need. Application must be submitted online. Admission notification on a rolling basis. **Financial aid:** Priority date 4/1; no closing date. FAFSA required. Applicants notified on a rolling basis starting 2/1; must reply within 4 week(s) of notification.

Academics. 13 undergraduate degrees available for online completion. **Special study options:** Distance learning, double major, dual enrollment of high school students, ESL, honors, independent study, internships, study abroad, teacher certification program, weekend college. Service learning, learning communities. **Credit/placement by examination:** AP, CLEP, IB, SAT, ACT, institutional tests. 24 credit hours maximum toward bachelor's degree. **Support services:** Learning center, reduced course load, remedial instruction, study skills assistance, tutoring, writing center.

Majors. Biology: General, biotechnology. **Business:** General, accounting, business admin, finance, insurance, international, management information systems, marketing, purchasing. **Communications:** General. **Computer sciences:** General. **English:** English lit, technical writing. **Foreign languages:** Spanish. **History:** General. **Human services:** Social work. **Liberal arts:** Arts/sciences, humanities. **Math:** General, applied. **Philosophy/religion:** Philosophy. **Physical sciences:** Chemistry. **Protective services:** Criminal justice. **Psychology:** General. **Social sciences:** General, political science, sociology. **Visual/performing arts:** General.

Most popular majors. Business/marketing 34%, interdisciplinary studies 25%, psychology 8%, security/protective services 9%.

Technology on campus. 583 workstations in library, computer center, student center. Online course registration, online library, helpline, student web hosting, wireless network available.

Student life. Freshman orientation: Mandatory, $80 fee. Preregistration for classes offered. Held over one day for students and parents from May to July. **Policies:** Students must have at least a 2.5 GPA to be an officer in student organizations and at least 2.0 GPA to be a member. **Activities:** Jazz band, campus ministries, drama, international student organizations, literary magazine, Model UN, student government, student newspaper, black student alliance, bilingual education student organization, Revolution, Muslim student association, environmental club, international business association, student veterans organization, Texas Freedom Network Student Chapter.

Athletics. Intramural: Badminton, basketball, bowling, soccer, softball, tennis, volleyball. **Team name:** Gators.

Student services. Alcohol/substance abuse counseling, career counseling, student employment services, financial aid counseling, health services, legal services, personal counseling, placement for graduates, veterans' counselor. **Physically disabled:** Services for visually, hearing impaired.

Contact. E-mail: uhdadmit@uhd.edu
Phone: (713) 221-8522 Fax: (713) 221-8157
Spencer Lightsy, Director of Admissions, University of Houston-Downtown, One Main Street, Suite S350, Houston, TX 77002

University of Houston-Victoria
Victoria, Texas
www.uhv.edu   CB code: 6917

◗ Public 4-year university
◗ Commuter campus in small city
◗ 2,991 degree-seeking undergraduates
◗ 1,395 graduate students

General. Founded in 1973. Regionally accredited. **Degrees:** 645 bachelor's awarded; master's offered. **ROTC:** Air Force. **Location:** 100 miles from Houston and San Antonio. **Calendar:** Semester, limited summer session. **Full-time faculty:** 136 total; 87% have terminal degrees, 32% minority, 49% women. **Part-time faculty:** 103 total; 42% have terminal degrees, 25% minority, 60% women. **Class size:** 31% < 20, 49% 20-39, 14% 40-49, 6% 50-99.

Basis for selection. College transcript, SAT, ACT, high school ranking.

High school preparation. College-preparatory program recommended.

2015-2016 Annual costs. Tuition/fees: $7,086; $18,786 out-of-state. Room/board: $7,664. Books/supplies: $1,200. Personal expenses: $2,076.

Financial aid. Non-need-based: Scholarships awarded for academics, athletics, leadership, state residency. **Additional information:** Short-term loans available at registration.

Application procedures. Admission: Closing date 8/25. No application fee. Application must be submitted online. Admission notification by 4/15. Admission notification on a rolling basis. **Financial aid:** Priority date 3/15; no closing date. FAFSA, institutional form required. Applicants notified by 3/30; Applicants notified on a rolling basis starting 3/30; must reply within 3 week(s) of notification.

Academics. Online course support. **Special study options:** Accelerated study, distance learning, double major, dual enrollment of high school students, independent study, internships, study abroad, teacher certification program. **Credit/placement by examination:** AP, CLEP, SAT, ACT.

Majors. Biology: General. **Business:** General, accounting, business admin, marketing. **Communications:** Communications/speech/rhetoric. **Computer sciences:** General, information systems. **Education:** General. **English:** English lit, rhetoric/composition. **Health services:** Nursing (RN). **History:** General. **Math:** General. **Protective services:** Law enforcement admin. **Psychology:** General.

Most popular majors. Biology 6%, business/marketing 29%, health sciences 19%, interdisciplinary studies 20%, psychology 9%.

Technology on campus. 250 workstations in library, computer center, student center. Commuter students can connect to campus network. Online course registration, online library, helpline, repair service, wireless network available.

Student life. Housing: Coed dorms available. $150 fully refundable deposit, deadline 8/22. **Activities:** Student government.

Athletics. NAIA. **Intercollegiate:** Baseball M, softball W. **Team name:** Jaguar.

Student services. Career counseling, student employment services, financial aid counseling, placement for graduates, veterans' counselor. **Physically disabled:** Services for visually, hearing impaired.

Contact. E-mail: admission@uhv.edu
Phone: (361) 570-4110 Toll-free number: (877) 970-4848
Fax: (361) 580-5500
Denee Thomas, Admission Officer, University of Houston-Victoria, 3007 North Ben Wilson, Victoria, TX 77901-4450

University of Mary Hardin-Baylor
Belton, Texas   CB member
www.umhb.edu   CB code: 6396

◗ Private 4-year university affiliated with the Baptist faith
◗ Residential campus in large town
◗ 3,173 degree-seeking undergraduates: 8% part-time, 63% women, 15% African American, 2% Asian American, 20% Hispanic/Latino, 1% Native American, 3% Multi-racial, non-Hispanic, 2% international
◗ 674 degree-seeking graduate students
◗ 80% of applicants admitted
◗ SAT or ACT (ACT writing recommended) required
◗ 43% graduate within 6 years

General. Founded in 1845. Regionally accredited. **Degrees:** 553 bachelor's awarded; master's, professional, doctoral offered. **ROTC:** Army, Air Force. **Location:** 60 miles from Austin. **Calendar:** Semester, limited summer session. **Full-time faculty:** 167 total; 74% have terminal degrees, 14% minority, 55% women. **Part-time faculty:** 111 total; 47% have terminal degrees, 9% minority, 52% women. **Class size:** 51% < 20, 39% 20-39, 6% 40-49, 3% 50-99, less than 1% >100.

Freshman class profile. 7,504 applied, 6,033 admitted, 726 enrolled.

Mid 50% test scores			
SAT critical reading:	460-560	Rank in top quarter:	50%
SAT math:	470-570	Rank in top tenth:	20%
SAT writing:	430-530	End year in good standing:	76%
ACT composite:	20-26	Return as sophomores:	69%
GPA 3.75 or higher:	35%	Out-of-state:	3%
GPA 3.50-3.74:	28%	Live on campus:	94%
GPA 3.0-3.49:	27%	International:	1%
GPA 2.0-2.99:	10%		

Basis for selection. School achievement record and test scores important. Must either rank in top 10% of graduating class; rank in the top half of class and score 950 SAT or 20 ACT; or rank in lower half of class and score 990 SAT or 21 ACT (all SAT scores exclusive of Writing). Academically deficient students may be accepted on individual basis by approval of admissions committee. Interview recommended for academically marginal; audition recommended for music. **Home schooled:** Transcript of courses and grades required. Admission based on ACT or SAT test scores.

High school preparation. College-preparatory program recommended. 24 units required. Required units include English 4, mathematics 3, social studies 3.5, science 3 and foreign language 2.

2015-2016 Annual costs. Tuition/fees: $26,200. Room/board: $7,300.

2015-2016 Financial aid. Need-based: 603 full-time freshmen applied for aid; 526 deemed to have need; 526 received aid. Average need met was 63%. Average scholarship/grant was $15,392; average loan $3,240. 64% of total undergraduate aid awarded as scholarships/grants, 36% as loans/jobs. **Non-need-based:** Awarded to 457 full-time undergraduates, including 125 freshmen. Scholarships awarded for academics, alumni affiliation, art, leadership, music/drama, religious affiliation.

Application procedures. Admission: No deadline. $35 fee, may be waived for applicants with need. Admission notification on a rolling basis. Notified as soon as we receive required documents to grant an admissions decision. (ie. High school transcript with class rank and receipt of qualifying test scores). Must reply by May 1 or within 2 week(s) if notified thereafter. **Financial aid:** Priority date 2/15; no closing date. FAFSA required. Applicants notified on a rolling basis starting 2/15; must reply within 2 week(s) of notification.

Academics. Special study options: Combined bachelor's/graduate degree, distance learning, double major, dual enrollment of high school students, ESL, honors, independent study, internships, study abroad, teacher certification program. **Credit/placement by examination:** AP, CLEP, IB, SAT, ACT, institutional tests. 31 credit hours maximum toward bachelor's degree. No more than one-fourth of total credit hours required for degree may be earned through credit by examination. **Support services:** Learning center, remedial instruction, study skills assistance, tutoring, writing center.

Majors. Biology: General, biochemistry. **Business:** Accounting, business admin, entrepreneurial studies, finance, international, management information systems, managerial economics, marketing. **Communications:** General, communications/speech/rhetoric, media studies. **Computer sciences:** General, computer graphics, computer science, information systems. **Education:** Art, biology, chemistry, elementary, English, history, mathematics, multi-level teacher, music, physical, science, social studies, Spanish, speech. **Engineering:** Pre-engineering. **English:** English lit. **Foreign languages:** Spanish. **Health services:** Clinical lab science, nursing (RN), prephysical therapy. **History:** General. **Human services:** Social work. **Math:** General. **Parks/recreation:** Exercise sciences, sports admin. **Philosophy/religion:** Christian. **Physical sciences:** Chemistry. **Protective services:** Law enforcement admin. **Psychology:** General, clinical, experimental, medical. **Social sciences:** Political science, sociology. **Theology:** Bible, pastoral counseling, sacred music. **Visual/performing arts:** Design, film/cinema/video, graphic design, music, music performance, studio arts.

Most popular majors. Business/marketing 12%, education 13%, health sciences 27%, psychology 8%.

Technology on campus. 275 workstations in dormitories, library, computer center, student center. Dormitories wired for high-speed internet access and linked to campus network. Commuter students can connect to campus network. Online course registration, online library, helpline, wireless network available.

Student life. Freshman orientation: Available, $30 fee. Preregistration for classes offered. One-day orientation in summer for students and parents. Full-week orientation for students only before start of classes. **Policies:** Religious observance required. **Housing:** Guaranteed on-campus for freshmen. Single-sex dorms, special housing for disabled, apartments available. $150 partly refundable deposit, deadline 5/1. **Activities:** Bands, campus ministries, choral groups, drama, film society, international student organizations, literary magazine, music ensembles, Model UN, musical theater, opera, student government, student newspaper, Baptist Student Ministry, Catholic student organization, College Democrats, College Republicans, Crusaders for Christ, Fellowship of Christian Athletes, Focus (community-wide worship), Habitat for Humanity.

Athletics. NCAA. **Intercollegiate:** Baseball M, basketball, football (tackle) M, golf, soccer, softball W, tennis, volleyball W. **Intramural:** Basketball, football (non-tackle), golf, soccer, softball, table tennis, volleyball, weight lifting. **Team name:** Crusaders.

Student services. Alcohol/substance abuse counseling, chaplain/spiritual director, career counseling, student employment services, financial aid counseling, health services, personal counseling, placement for graduates, veterans' counselor. **Physically disabled:** Services for visually, speech, hearing impaired.

Contact. E-mail: admissions@umhb.edu
Phone: (254) 295-4520 Toll-free number: (800) 727-8642 ext. 4520
Fax: (254) 295-5049
Brent Burks, Director of Admissions and Recruiting, University of Mary Hardin-Baylor, 900 College Street, Belton, TX 76513

University of North Texas

Denton, Texas

www.unt.edu

CB member

CB code: 6481

- Public 4-year university
- Residential campus in small city
- 30,503 degree-seeking undergraduates: 18% part-time, 52% women, 13% African American, 6% Asian American, 23% Hispanic/Latino, 4% Multi-racial, non-Hispanic, 3% international
- 6,672 degree-seeking graduate students
- 70% of applicants admitted
- SAT or ACT with writing required
- 52% graduate within 6 years

General. Founded in 1890. Regionally accredited. **Degrees:** 6,519 bachelor's awarded; master's, professional, doctoral offered. **ROTC:** Army, Air Force. **Location:** 35 miles from Dallas and Fort Worth. **Calendar:** Semester, extensive summer session. **Full-time faculty:** 1,006 total; 77% have terminal degrees, 28% minority, 43% women. **Part-time faculty:** 430 total; 3% have terminal degrees, 24% minority, 60% women. **Class size:** 24% < 20, 45% 20-39, 8% 40-49, 13% 50-99, 11% >100. **Special facilities:** Laser, observatory, accelerators, environmental science facility, planetarium.

Freshman class profile. 16,254 applied, 11,394 admitted, 4,661 enrolled.

Mid 50% test scores			
SAT critical reading:	490-600	Return as sophomores:	79%
SAT math:	500-600	Out-of-state:	4%
SAT writing:	460-570	Live on campus:	86%
ACT composite:	20-26	International:	2%
Rank in top quarter:	55%	Fraternities:	5%
Rank in top tenth:	21%	Sororities:	8%

Basis for selection. It is recommended that students apply well in advance of stated application deadlines. School achievement record most important. Test score minimums vary with class rank: top 10% no minimum. High school students may be admitted on an individual basis after completion of the junior year of high school. Must rank in the top quarter of their class, have strong B average, 3 units of English and 2 units each of solid mathematics, social sciences and natural sciences, minimum SAT score of 1180 (exclusive of Writing) or ACT composite of 26, letters from high school counselor or principal recommending early admission, letter from parents or guardians stating approval, and interview with Office of Admissions. Audition required for music program. **Home schooled:** Statement describing home school structure and mission, transcript of courses and grades required. An interview, essay and letters of recommendation may be required after a review of the application.

High school preparation. College-preparatory program required. 26 units required. Required units include English 4, mathematics 4, social studies 2, history 2, science 4 (laboratory 4), foreign language 2, computer science 1, visual/performing arts 1, academic electives 3.5. 0.5 health, 1.5 physical education, 0.5 speech.

2015-2016 Annual costs. Tuition/fees: $10,091; $21,791 out-of-state. Room/board: $8,199. Books/supplies: $1,000. Personal expenses: $1,366.

2015-2016 Financial aid. Need-based: 3,752 full-time freshmen applied for aid; 2,852 deemed to have need; 2,754 received aid. Average need met was 69%. Average scholarship/grant was $10,846; average loan $3,134. 50% of total undergraduate aid awarded as scholarships/grants, 50% as loans/jobs. **Non-need-based:** Awarded to 6,631 full-time undergraduates, including 1,736 freshmen.

Application procedures. Admission: Priority date 3/1; deadline 8/1 (postmark date). $75 fee, may be waived for applicants with need. Application must be submitted online. Admission notification on a rolling basis beginning on or about 8/1. **Financial aid:** Priority date 3/15; no closing date. FAFSA required. Applicants notified on a rolling basis starting 4/1.

Academics. Special study options: Combined bachelor's/graduate degree, distance learning, double major, dual enrollment of high school students, ESL, exchange student, honors, independent study, internships, student-designed major, study abroad, teacher certification program. **Credit/placement by examination:** AP, CLEP, IB, institutional tests. 90 credit hours maximum toward bachelor's degree. **Support services:** Learning center, pre-admission summer program, remedial instruction, study skills assistance, tutoring, writing center.

Honors college/program. 1200 or above on the SAT or 27 on ACT. GPA, class rank, advanced courses important.

Majors. Architecture: Interior. **Biology:** General, biochemistry. **Business:** General, accounting, banking/financial services, e-commerce, fashion, financial planning, hospitality admin, insurance, logistics, management information systems, managerial economics, marketing, operations, organizational behavior, real estate, sales/distribution, special products marketing. **Communications:** Broadcast journalism, journalism, radio/TV. **Computer sciences:** General, information systems, information technology. **Engineering:** Computer, electrical, materials, mechanical. **English:** English lit, rhetoric/composition. **Foreign languages:** French, German, Spanish. **Health services:** Audiology/speech pathology, clinical lab science, cytotechnology, vocational rehab counseling. **History:** General. **Human services:** General, social work. **Math:** General. **Parks/recreation:** Exercise sciences, facilities management, health/fitness. **Philosophy/religion:** Philosophy. **Physical sciences:** Chemistry, materials science, physics. **Protective services:** Criminal justice, disaster management. **Psychology:** General, behavior analysis. **Social sciences:** General, anthropology, economics, geography, political science, sociology. **Visual/performing arts:** Art, art history/conservation, commercial/advertising art, dance, dramatic, fashion design, jazz, music, music history, music performance, music theory/composition, studio arts. **Work/family studies:** Family studies.

Most popular majors. Business/marketing 20%, communications/journalism 6%, interdisciplinary studies 13%, liberal arts 6%, psychology 6%, visual/performing arts 9%.

Technology on campus. 735 workstations in dormitories, library, computer center, student center. Dormitories wired for high-speed internet access and linked to campus network. Commuter students can connect to campus network. Online course registration, online library, helpline, student web hosting, wireless network available.

Student life. Freshman orientation: Mandatory, $180 fee. Preregistration for classes offered. Seven sessions during June and July; one in August. Orientation includes overnight stay in one of the resident halls. **Housing:** Guaranteed on-campus for freshmen. Coed dorms, single-sex dorms, special housing for disabled, apartments, fraternity/sorority housing, themed housing, wellness housing available. $400 partly refundable deposit, deadline 8/24. Learning communities available. **Activities:** Bands, campus ministries, choral groups, dance, drama, film society, international student organizations, literary magazine, music ensembles, Model UN, musical theater, opera, radio station, student government, student newspaper, symphony orchestra, TV station, honorary societies; religious, ethnic, and social service organizations.

Athletics. NCAA. **Intercollegiate:** Basketball, cross-country, diving W, football (tackle) M, golf, soccer W, softball W, swimming W, tennis W, track and field, volleyball W. **Intramural:** Basketball, football (non-tackle), racquetball, sand volleyball, soccer, softball, table tennis, tennis, ultimate frisbee, volleyball. **Team name:** Mean Green.

Student services. Adult student services, alcohol/substance abuse counseling, career counseling, student employment services, financial aid counseling, health services, legal services, minority student services, personal counseling, placement for graduates, veterans' counselor, women's services. **Physically disabled:** Services for visually, speech, hearing impaired.

Contact. E-mail: undergrad@unt.edu
Phone: (940) 565-2681 Toll-free number: (800) 868-8211
Fax: (940) 565-2408
Rebecca Lothringer, Director of Admissions, University of North Texas, 1401 West Prairie Suite 309, Denton, TX 76203-5017

University of Phoenix: Austin
Austin, Texas
www.phoenix.edu

- For-profit 4-year university
- Commuter campus in very large city
- 660 degree-seeking undergraduates
- 46 graduate students

General. Regionally accredited. **Degrees:** 42 bachelor's awarded; master's offered. **Calendar:** Differs by program. **Full-time faculty:** 7 total. **Part-time faculty:** 95 total.

Basis for selection. Open admission.

2015-2016 Annual costs. Per-credit-hour charge, $410 to $635, depending upon level and course of study; electronic course materials fee, $95, if applicable. Book and material charges may vary by course and program. All fees are subject to change.

Application procedures. Admission: No deadline. No application fee. **Financial aid:** No deadline.

Academics. Credit/placement by examination: AP, CLEP.

Majors. Business: Accounting, accounting/business management, business admin, e-commerce, entrepreneurial studies, finance, human resources, marketing, operations. **Communications:** General. **Conservation:** Environmental studies. **English:** English lit. **Health services:** Facilities admin, health information management, long term care admin, nursing (RN). **Human services:** General. **Protective services:** Disaster management, law enforcement admin, security management.

Student life. Freshman orientation: Mandatory. Preregistration for classes offered.

Contact. Toll-free number: (866) 766-0766
University of Phoenix: Austin, 10801 North MoPac, Austin, TX 78759-5459

University of Phoenix: Dallas Fort Worth
Dallas, Texas
www.phoenix.edu

- For-profit 4-year university
- Commuter campus in very large city
- 1,240 degree-seeking undergraduates
- 167 graduate students

General. Regionally accredited. **Degrees:** 111 bachelor's awarded; master's offered. **Calendar:** Differs by program. **Full-time faculty:** 11 total. **Part-time faculty:** 115 total.

Basis for selection. Open admission.

2015-2016 Annual costs. Per-credit-hour charge, $410 to $635, depending upon level and course of study; electronic course materials fee, $95, if

applicable. Book and material charges may vary by course and program. All fees are subject to change.

Application procedures. Admission: No deadline. No application fee. **Financial aid:** No deadline.

Academics. Credit/placement by examination: AP, CLEP.

Majors. Business: Accounting, accounting/business management, business admin, e-commerce, entrepreneurial studies, finance, human resources, marketing, operations. **Communications:** General. **Computer sciences:** Database management, networking, programming, security, systems analysis, web page design, webmaster. **Conservation:** Environmental studies. **English:** English lit. **Health services:** Facilities admin, health information management, long term care admin, nursing (RN). **Human services:** General. **Protective services:** Disaster management, law enforcement admin, security management.

Student life. Freshman orientation: Mandatory. Preregistration for classes offered.

Contact. Toll-free number: (866) 766-0766
University of Phoenix: Dallas Fort Worth, 12400 Coit Road, Dallas, TX 75251-2004

University of Phoenix: Houston Westside
Houston, Texas
www.phoenix.edu

- For-profit 4-year university
- Very large city
- 2,000 degree-seeking undergraduates
- 276 graduate students

General. Regionally accredited. **Degrees:** 974 bachelor's awarded; master's offered. **Calendar:** Differs by program. **Full-time faculty:** 14 total. **Part-time faculty:** 254 total.

Basis for selection. Open admission.

2015-2016 Annual costs. Per-credit-hour charge, $410 to $635, depending upon level and course of study; electronic course materials fee, $95, if applicable. Book and material charges may vary by course and program. All fees are subject to change.

Application procedures. Admission: No deadline. No application fee. **Financial aid:** No deadline.

Academics. Credit/placement by examination: AP, CLEP.

Majors. Business: Accounting, accounting/business management, business admin, e-commerce, entrepreneurial studies, finance, human resources, marketing, operations. **Communications:** General. **Computer sciences:** Database management, networking, security, systems analysis. **Conservation:** Environmental studies. **English:** English lit. **Health services:** Facilities admin, health information management, long term care admin, nursing (RN). **Human services:** General. **Protective services:** Disaster management, law enforcement admin, security management.

Student life. Freshman orientation: Mandatory. Preregistration for classes offered.

Contact. Toll-free number: (866) 766-0766
University of Phoenix: Houston Westside, 11451 Katy Freeway, Houston, TX 77079-2004

University of Phoenix: San Antonio
San Antonio, Texas
www.phoenix.edu

- For-profit 4-year university
- Commuter campus in very large city
- 930 degree-seeking undergraduates
- 240 graduate students

General. Regionally accredited. **Degrees:** 115 bachelor's awarded; master's offered. **Calendar:** Differs by program. **Full-time faculty:** 12 total. **Part-time faculty:** 142 total.

Basis for selection. Open admission.

2015-2016 Annual costs. Per-credit-hour charge, $410 to $635, depending upon level and course of study; electronic course materials fee, $95, if applicable. Book and material charges may vary by course and program. All fees are subject to change.

Application procedures. Admission: No deadline. No application fee. **Financial aid:** No deadline.

Academics. Credit/placement by examination: AP, CLEP.

Majors. Business: Accounting, accounting/business management, business admin, e-commerce, entrepreneurial studies, finance, human resources, marketing, operations. **Communications:** General. **Computer sciences:** Database management, networking, programming, security, systems analysis, web page design, webmaster. **Conservation:** Environmental studies. **English:** English lit. **Health services:** Facilities admin, health information management, long term care admin, nursing (RN). **Human services:** General. **Protective services:** Disaster management, law enforcement admin, security management.

Student life. Freshman orientation: Mandatory. Preregistration for classes offered.

Contact. Toll-free number: (866) 766-0766
University of Phoenix: San Antonio, 8200 IH010 West, San Antonio, TX 78230-3876

University of St. Thomas
Houston, Texas

www.stthom.edu

CB member
CB code: 6880

- Private 4-year university and liberal arts college affiliated with the Roman Catholic Church
- Commuter campus in very large city
- 1,729 degree-seeking undergraduates: 22% part-time, 59% women, 7% African American, 12% Asian American, 40% Hispanic/Latino, 2% Multi-racial, non-Hispanic, 10% international
- 1,548 degree-seeking graduate students
- 79% of applicants admitted
- SAT or ACT with writing required
- 57% graduate within 6 years

General. Founded in 1947. Regionally accredited. **Degrees:** 301 bachelor's awarded; master's, doctoral offered. **ROTC:** Army, Air Force. **Location:** 3 miles from downtown. **Calendar:** Semester, limited summer session. **Full-time faculty:** 192 total; 93% have terminal degrees, 31% minority, 47% women. **Part-time faculty:** 164 total; 43% have terminal degrees, 29% minority, 49% women. **Class size:** 65% < 20, 35% 20-39. **Special facilities:** Meditation garden.

Freshman class profile. 866 applied, 682 admitted, 243 enrolled.

Mid 50% test scores			
SAT critical reading:	480-600	GPA 2.0-2.99:	10%
SAT math:	500-610	Rank in top quarter:	53%
SAT writing:	470-580	Rank in top tenth:	29%
ACT composite:	22-27	End year in good standing:	87%
GPA 3.75 or higher:	35%	Return as sophomores:	83%
GPA 3.50-3.74:	21%	Out-of-state:	4%
GPA 3.0-3.49:	34%	Live on campus:	29%
		International:	7%

Basis for selection. School achievement record, test scores, graded essay most important. Cumulative high school GPA of 2.8 required, as well as minimum 1070 SAT (exclusive of Writing) or 23 ACT. High school class rank in upper 50%, if ranking available. Essay or personal statement may be required of some applicants. Audition required for applied music, drama, voice programs; portfolio required for art program.

High school preparation. College-preparatory program recommended. 18 units required. Required units include English 4, mathematics 3, social studies 2, history 1, science 3 (laboratory 2) and foreign language 2. Three units of electives in college preparatory classes.

2016-2017 Annual costs. Tuition/fees (projected): $30,310. Room/board: $8,500. Books/supplies: $1,094. Personal expenses: $2,068.

2015-2016 Financial aid. Need-based: 191 full-time freshmen applied for aid; 166 deemed to have need; 161 received aid. Average need met was 75%. Average scholarship/grant was $22,566; average loan $3,281. 78% of total undergraduate aid awarded as scholarships/grants, 22% as loans/jobs. **Non-need-based:** Awarded to 514 full-time undergraduates, including 95 freshmen. Scholarships awarded for academics, athletics, music/drama, religious affiliation, ROTC.

Application procedures. Admission: Priority date 2/1; deadline 5/1. No application fee. Admission notification on a rolling basis beginning on or about 11/1. Must reply by May 1 or within 2 week(s) if notified thereafter. **Financial aid:** Priority date 4/15; no closing date. FAFSA required. Applicants notified on a rolling basis starting 2/15; must reply within 2 week(s) of notification.

Academics. Special study options: Accelerated study, combined bachelor's/graduate degree, distance learning, double major, dual enrollment of high school students, honors, independent study, internships, liberal arts/career combination, student-designed major, study abroad, teacher certification program, weekend college. **Credit/placement by examination:** AP, CLEP, IB, SAT, ACT, institutional tests. 30 credit hours maximum toward bachelor's degree. Validation of credit by examination contingent upon completion of at least 24 semester hours in residence at institution. **Support services:** Learning center, reduced course load, remedial instruction, study skills assistance, tutoring, writing center.

Majors. Biology: General, biochemistry, bioinformatics. **Business:** Accounting, business admin, finance, international, marketing. **Communications:** Communications/speech/rhetoric. **Computer sciences:** Computer science. **Conservation:** Environmental science, environmental studies. **Education:** General, elementary, music, secondary. **English:** English lit. **Foreign languages:** French, Spanish. **Health services:** Nursing (RN). **History:** General. **Liberal arts:** Arts/sciences. **Math:** General, applied. **Philosophy/religion:** Philosophy. **Physical sciences:** Chemistry. **Psychology:** General. **Social sciences:** Economics, international economic development, international relations, political science. **Theology:** Pastoral counseling, theology. **Visual/performing arts:** Dramatic, music, studio arts.

Most popular majors. Biology 13%, business/marketing 24%, communications/journalism 6%, health sciences 8%, liberal arts 7%, psychology 7%, social sciences 12%.

Technology on campus. 348 workstations in dormitories, library, computer center. Dormitories wired for high-speed internet access and linked to campus network. Online course registration, online library, helpline, wireless network available.

Student life. Freshman orientation: Available. Preregistration for classes offered. Held in August and January. **Policies:** Annual Risk Management Training reviews school's policies on alcohol, travel, speakers, and other student life issues. **Housing:** Coed dorms, special housing for disabled, apartments available. $300 fully refundable deposit. Pets allowed in dorm rooms. **Activities:** Bands, campus ministries, choral groups, dance, drama, international student organizations, literary magazine, music ensembles, Model UN, musical theater, opera, student government, student newspaper, symphony orchestra, Al-Nadi cultural society, black student union, Vietnamese student association, Bilingual Education Organization, Celts for Life, Pi Sigma Alpha, ECOS, French club, Irish club, Chi Rho.

Athletics. NAIA. **Intercollegiate:** Basketball, golf, soccer, volleyball W. **Intramural:** Basketball, bowling, football (non-tackle), racquetball, tennis, ultimate frisbee, volleyball. **Team name:** Celts.

Student services. Adult student services, chaplain/spiritual director, career counseling, student employment services, financial aid counseling, health services, personal counseling, placement for graduates, veterans' counselor. **Physically disabled:** Services for visually, speech, hearing impaired.

Contact. E-mail: admissions@stthom.edu
Phone: (713) 525-3500 Toll-free number: (800) 856-8565
Fax: (713) 525-3558
Arthur Ortiz, Assistant Vice President for Enrollment, University of St. Thomas, 3800 Montrose Boulevard, Houston, TX 77006-4626

University of Texas at Arlington
Arlington, Texas

www.uta.edu

CB member
CB code: 6013

- Public 4-year university
- Commuter campus in large city
- 30,358 degree-seeking undergraduates
- SAT or ACT with writing required

General. Founded in 1895. Regionally accredited. **Degrees:** 7,020 bachelor's awarded; master's, professional, doctoral offered. **ROTC:** Army, Naval, Air Force. **Location:** 15 miles from Dallas and Fort Worth. **Calendar:** 4-1-4-1 January and May terms. Extensive summer session. **Class size:** 31% < 20, 36% 20-39, 10% 40-49, 16% 50-99, 7% >100. **Special facilities:** College of Nursing Smart Hospital, planetarium, research institute, Amphibian and Reptile Diversity Research Center, Urban Design Center (partnership with the city of Arlington), Shimadzu Institute for Research Technologies,

Nanotechnology Research and Education Center, studio arts center, glass-blowing studio, UT Arlington Libraries Multicultural Collection, transonic wind tunnel.

Freshman class profile.

Rank in top quarter:	72%	Out-of-state:	1%
Rank in top tenth:	27%		

Basis for selection. Admission based on test scores and high school rank. Fourth quarter of high school class must be approved by director of admissions or associate director. SAT or ACT math scores are used for placement of students majoring in architecture, engineering, biology, biochemistry, chemistry, math, physics, and for students in the bachelor's geology or bachelor's psychology program. Interview recommended for academically weak; audition recommended for music; portfolio recommended for art, architecture programs. **Home schooled:** Transcript of courses and grades, letter of recommendation (nonparent) required.

High school preparation. College-preparatory program required. 20 units required. Required and recommended units include English 4, mathematics 3-4, social studies 3-4, science 3, foreign language 2-3 and academic electives 5. 1 computing proficiency, 1 fine arts, 1 music/theater art, 1.5 physical education, .5 health recommended.

2015-2016 Annual costs. Tuition/fees: $8,878; $21,114 out-of-state. Room/board: $8,398. Books/supplies: $1,206. Personal expenses: $1,660.

Financial aid. Non-need-based: Scholarships awarded for academics, art, athletics, leadership, music/drama, ROTC. **Additional information:** Free tuition to eligible students whose household income is $65,000 or less through the Maverick Promise program.

Application procedures. Admission: Priority date 6/1; no deadline. $60 fee, may be waived for applicants with need. Notified 3-7 days after application completed. **Financial aid:** Priority date 4/15; no closing date. FAFSA required. Applicants notified on a rolling basis starting 4/1; must reply within 3 week(s) of notification.

Academics. Special study options: Combined bachelor's/graduate degree, cross-registration, distance learning, double major, dual enrollment of high school students, ESL, honors, independent study, internships, student-designed major, study abroad, teacher certification program. **Credit/placement by examination:** AP, CLEP, IB, institutional tests. Credit by exam does not count as credit earned in residence. Credit by examination cannot be used to satisfy the general degree requirement for (a) 30 semester hours in residence and (b) at least 18 semester hours in residence of advanced coursework (courses numbered 3000 and 4000), to include 12 hours of advanced coursework in the major field. **Support services:** Learning center, reduced course load, remedial instruction, study skills assistance, tutoring, writing center.

Majors. Architecture: Architecture, interior. **Biology:** General, biochemistry, microbiology. **Business:** Accounting, banking/financial services, business admin, international, management information systems, managerial economics, marketing, real estate. **Communications:** Advertising, digital media, journalism, public relations, radio/TV. **Computer sciences:** Computer science, information systems. **Engineering:** Aerospace, biomedical, civil, computer, electrical, industrial, mechanical, software. **English:** English lit, rhetoric/composition. **Foreign languages:** General, French, German, linguistics, Russian, Spanish, translation. **Health services:** Athletic training, clinical lab science, nursing (RN). **History:** General. **Human services:** Social work. **Math:** General. **Parks/recreation:** Exercise sciences. **Philosophy/religion:** Philosophy. **Physical sciences:** Chemistry, geology, physics. **Protective services:** Criminal justice. **Psychology:** General. **Social sciences:** Anthropology, economics, political science, sociology. **Visual/performing arts:** Art, art history/conservation, dramatic, music, music performance, studio arts. **Work/family studies:** Child development.

Most popular majors. Biology 6%, business/marketing 12%, engineering/engineering technologies 6%, health sciences 36%, interdisciplinary studies 6%, liberal arts 6%.

Technology on campus. 500 workstations in dormitories, library. Dormitories wired for high-speed internet access and linked to campus network. Commuter students can connect to campus network. Online course registration, online library, helpline, student web hosting, wireless network available.

Student life. Freshman orientation: Mandatory. Preregistration for classes offered. One-and-a-half-day sessions held in June, July, August. Students stay in residence halls. **Housing:** Coed dorms, single-sex dorms, apartments, fraternity/sorority housing available. $150 partly refundable deposit. Priority given to students with dependent children. **Activities:** Bands, campus ministries, choral groups, dance, drama, film society, international student

organizations, literary magazine, music ensembles, opera, radio station, student government, student newspaper, symphony orchestra, University Democrats, association of Mexican American students, Vietnamese student association, Wesley Foundation, Mavericks for Christ, Business Beta Gamma Sigma, College Republicans, Business Delta Sigma Pi.

Athletics. NCAA. **Intercollegiate:** Baseball M, basketball, golf M, softball W, tennis, track and field, volleyball W. **Intramural:** Badminton, basketball, bowling, golf M, racquetball, soccer, softball, table tennis, tennis, track and field, volleyball. **Team name:** Mavericks.

Student services. Alcohol/substance abuse counseling, chaplain/spiritual director, career counseling, services for economically disadvantaged, student employment services, financial aid counseling, health services, legal services, minority student services, on-campus daycare, personal counseling, placement for graduates, veterans' counselor. **Physically disabled:** Services for visually, hearing impaired.

Contact. Phone: (817) 272-6287 Fax: (817) 272-5114
Hans Gatterdam, Executive Director of Admissions, Records and Registration, University of Texas at Arlington, UTA Box 19088, Arlington, TX 76019

University of Texas at Austin
Austin, Texas
www.utexas.edu

CB member
CB code: 6882

- Public 4-year university
- Residential campus in very large city
- 39,057 degree-seeking undergraduates: 7% part-time, 52% women, 4% African American, 20% Asian American, 22% Hispanic/Latino, 4% Multi-racial, non-Hispanic, 5% international
- 11,331 degree-seeking graduate students
- 39% of applicants admitted
- SAT or ACT with writing, application essay required
- 80% graduate within 6 years

General. Founded in 1883. Regionally accredited. **Degrees:** 9,503 bachelor's awarded; master's, professional, doctoral offered. **ROTC:** Army, Naval, Air Force. **Location:** 80 miles from San Antonio, 167 miles from Houston. **Calendar:** Semester, extensive summer session. **Full-time faculty:** 2,729 total; 89% have terminal degrees, 21% minority, 39% women. **Part-time faculty:** 315 total; 64% have terminal degrees, 18% minority, 42% women. **Class size:** 35% < 20, 33% 20-39, 6% 40-49, 16% 50-99, 10% ≥100. **Special facilities:** LBJ Presidential Library and Museum, center for American history, arts and humanities center, observatory, concert hall, natural science center, courtyard gallery, visual arts center, museum of art.

Freshman class profile. 43,592 applied, 17,006 admitted, 7,743 enrolled.

Mid 50% test scores			
		Rank in top tenth:	72%
SAT critical reading:	570-680	Out-of-state:	9%
SAT math:	600-710	Live on campus:	66%
SAT writing:	560-680	International:	5%
ACT composite:	26-31	Fraternities:	13%
Rank in top quarter:	92%	Sororities:	14%

Basis for selection. In accordance with Texas Education Code, students are admissible automatically to the University as first-time freshmen if they (1) graduate within the top percentages of their class from an accredited Texas high school and (2) submit all required credentials by the appropriate deadlines, but available seats are limited to 75% of first-time in college cohort. Some Texas freshman applicants not admitted to UT Austin are offered participation in the Coordinated Admission Program, which offers students the opportunity to begin undergraduate studies at a participating UT System university and earn the right to complete their undergraduate coursework at the University of Texas at Austin. Portfolio required for art program. Audition required for music and dance program. Approval of review committee required of theater, dance, art, art history, and design program applicants. University-administered calculus readiness test required of engineering program applicants. **Home schooled:** Transcript of courses and grades required. Must submit a transcript of the high-school work completed. Some indicators of academic competitiveness include SAT or ACT scores and SAT Subject Test scores, the curriculum used in the home-school environment, awards and honors won in competition with traditionally schooled students, grades earned in college courses taken in conjunction with home schooling.

High school preparation. College-preparatory program required. 26 units required. Required units include English 4, mathematics 4, social studies 4, science 4, foreign language 2 and academic electives 6. 1 fine arts required.

2015-2016 Annual costs. Tuition/fees: $9,830; $34,836 out-of-state. Room/board: $11,456. Books/supplies: $750. Personal expenses: $2,820.

2015-2016 Financial aid. **Need-based:** 5,879 full-time freshmen applied for aid; 3,314 deemed to have need; 3,308 received aid. Average need met was 68%. Average scholarship/grant was $9,229; average loan $3,306. 64% of total undergraduate aid awarded as scholarships/grants, 36% as loans/jobs. **Non-need-based:** Awarded to 4,851 full-time undergraduates, including 1,730 freshmen. Scholarships awarded for academics, art, athletics, leadership, music/drama, ROTC, state residency.

Application procedures. **Admission:** Closing date 12/1 (receipt date). $75 fee, may be waived for applicants with need. Admission notification by 3/1. Admission notification on a rolling basis. Must reply by May 1 or within 2 week(s) if notified thereafter. Housing deposit fully refundable before 5/1, not refundable after 5/1. **Financial aid:** Priority date 3/15; no closing date. FAFSA, institutional form required. Applicants notified on a rolling basis starting 3/15; must reply by 5/1 or within 3 week(s) of notification.

Academics. **Special study options:** Accelerated study, combined bachelor's/graduate degree, cooperative education, cross-registration, distance learning, double major, dual enrollment of high school students, ESL, exchange student, honors, independent study, internships, liberal arts/career combination, student-designed major, study abroad, teacher certification program, Washington semester. **Credit/placement by examination:** AP, CLEP, IB, SAT, ACT, institutional tests. Credit by examination is accepted as credit only; it will not affect a student's cumulative grade point average. Students assessed a fee of $6 per credit hour for the credit by examination requested. After credit has been reported to the Registrar, it cannot be changed. Undergraduates may be eligible for a tuition rebate of up to $1,000 if, at graduation, they have attempted no more than three semester hours beyond the minimum number of hours required for the degree. Credit-by-exam hours could make a student ineligible, but the first nine (9) hours earned by examination (that is, credit earned on the basis of AP courses, CLEP or credit granted for high SAT or ACT scores) shall not be counted in the rebate calculation. **Support services:** Learning center, reduced course load, remedial instruction, study skills assistance, tutoring, writing center.

Majors. **Architecture:** Architecture. **Area/ethnic studies:** General, African-American, American, Asian, European, Latin American, Near/Middle Eastern, Russian/Slavic, women's. **Biology:** General, biochemistry, neuroscience. **Business:** General, accounting, business admin, finance, logistics, management information systems, marketing. **Communications:** Advertising, communications/speech/rhetoric, journalism, public relations, radio/TV. **Computer sciences:** General. **Engineering:** Aerospace, architectural, biomedical, chemical, civil, electrical, mechanical, petroleum. **English:** English lit, writing. **Foreign languages:** Ancient Greek, Arabic, classics, East Asian, French, German, Hebrew, Iranian, Italian, Latin, linguistics, Portuguese, Russian, Scandinavian, Semitic, Spanish, Turkish. **Health services:** Athletic training, clinical lab science, communication disorders, nursing (RN), public health ed. **History:** General. **Human services:** Social work. **Liberal arts:** Arts/sciences, humanities. **Math:** General. **Parks/recreation:** Exercise sciences, health/fitness, sports admin. **Philosophy/religion:** Islamic, Judaic, philosophy, religion. **Physical sciences:** Astronomy, chemistry, geology, geophysics, hydrology, physics. **Psychology:** General. **Social sciences:** Anthropology, archaeology, economics, geography, political science, sociology, urban studies. **Visual/performing arts:** General, art, art history/conservation, dance, design, dramatic, interior design, jazz, music, music management, music performance, music technology, music theory/composition, studio arts. **Work/family studies:** General, clothing/textiles, family studies, food/nutrition.

Most popular majors. Biology 9%, business/marketing 11%, communications/journalism 12%, engineering/engineering technologies 12%, social sciences 12%.

Technology on campus. 3,150 workstations in dormitories, library, computer center, student center. Dormitories wired for high-speed internet access and linked to campus network. Commuter students can connect to campus network. Online course registration, online library, helpline, repair service, student web hosting, wireless network available.

Student life. **Freshman orientation:** Mandatory. Preregistration for classes offered. **Housing:** Coed dorms, single-sex dorms, special housing for disabled, apartments available. $300 deposit. Honors residence, living-learning halls available. **Activities:** Bands, campus ministries, choral groups, dance, drama, film society, international student organizations, literary magazine, music ensembles, Model UN, musical theater, radio station, student government, student newspaper, symphony orchestra, TV station.

Athletics. NCAA. **Intercollegiate:** Baseball M, basketball, cross-country, diving, football (tackle) M, golf, rowing (crew) W, soccer W, softball W, swimming, tennis, track and field, volleyball W. **Intramural:** Badminton, basketball, football (non-tackle), golf, handball, racquetball, soccer, softball, swimming, table tennis, tennis, track and field, ultimate frisbee, volleyball. **Team name:** Longhorns.

Student services. Adult student services, alcohol/substance abuse counseling, career counseling, services for economically disadvantaged, student employment services, financial aid counseling, health services, legal services,

minority student services, on-campus daycare, personal counseling, placement for graduates, veterans' counselor, women's services. **Physically disabled:** Services for visually, speech, hearing impaired.

Contact. Phone: (512) 475-7399 Fax: (512) 475-7478
Susan Kearns, Director of Admissions, University of Texas at Austin, PO Box 8058, Austin, TX 78713-8058

University of Texas at Brownsville
Brownsville, Texas **CB member**
www.utb.edu **CB code: 6825**

- Public 4-year university
- Commuter campus in small city
- 6,798 degree-seeking undergraduates
- 1,005 graduate students
- SAT or ACT (ACT writing optional) required

General. Founded in 1977. Regionally accredited. **Degrees:** 1,139 bachelor's, 398 associate awarded; master's, doctoral offered. **ROTC:** Army. **Location:** 150 miles from Corpus Christi. **Calendar:** Semester, extensive summer session.

Freshman class profile.

GPA 3.75 or higher:	16%	Rank in top tenth:	18%
GPA 3.50-3.74:	16%	Out-of-state:	4%
GPA 3.0-3.49:	50%	Live on campus:	14%
GPA 2.0-2.99:	17%	Fraternities:	1%
Rank in top quarter:	45%		

Basis for selection. Admission standards vary by student type. **Home schooled:** Statement describing home school structure and mission, transcript of courses and grades, state high school equivalency certificate, interview, letter of recommendation (nonparent) required.

High school preparation. 26 units recommended. Recommended units include English 4, mathematics 4, social studies 4, science 3 (laboratory 1), foreign language 2 and visual/performing arts 1.

2015-2016 Annual costs. Books/supplies: $1,196. Personal expenses: $1,917.

Financial aid. **Non-need-based:** Scholarships awarded for academics, alumni affiliation, art, athletics, minority status, music/drama, state residency.

Application procedures. **Admission:** Priority date 4/1; deadline 8/1 (receipt date). No application fee. Admission notification on a rolling basis. **Financial aid:** Priority date 3/1, closing date 8/15. FAFSA required. Must reply by 7/1 or within 12 week(s) of notification.

Academics. **Special study options:** Accelerated study, combined bachelor's/graduate degree, cross-registration, distance learning, double major, ESL, independent study, internships, student-designed major, study abroad, teacher certification program. **Credit/placement by examination:** AP, CLEP, IB, SAT, ACT, institutional tests. 96 credit hours maximum toward bachelor's degree. **Support services:** Learning center, pre-admission summer program, reduced course load, remedial instruction, study skills assistance, tutoring, writing center.

Majors. **Biology:** General. **Business:** General, accounting, business admin, entrepreneurial studies, finance, international, marketing. **Communications:** Communications/speech/rhetoric. **Computer sciences:** General, information systems. **Conservation:** Environmental science. **Engineering:** Applied physics. **English:** English lit. **Foreign languages:** Spanish, translation. **Health services:** Nursing (RN). **History:** General. **Human services:** General. **Math:** General. **Parks/recreation:** Health/fitness. **Physical sciences:** Chemistry, physics. **Protective services:** Corrections, criminal justice, law enforcement admin. **Psychology:** General. **Social sciences:** Political science, sociology. **Visual/performing arts:** Art, music.

Most popular majors. Biology 8%, business/marketing 14%, health sciences 7%, interdisciplinary studies 20%, parks/recreation 7%, psychology 9%, security/protective services 9%.

Technology on campus. 650 workstations in dormitories, library, computer center, student center. Dormitories wired for high-speed internet access and linked to campus network. Commuter students can connect to campus network. Online course registration, online library, helpline, repair service, student web hosting, wireless network available.

Student life. **Freshman orientation:** Mandatory, $50 fee. Preregistration for classes offered. **Housing:** Coed dorms, single-sex dorms, special housing for disabled, apartments, themed housing available. $200 fully refundable deposit. Pets allowed in dorm rooms. **Activities:** Bands, campus ministries, choral groups, dance, drama, film society, international student organizations, music ensembles, opera, radio station, student government, student newspaper, symphony orchestra.

Athletics. NAIA. **Intercollegiate:** Cross-country, golf, soccer, volleyball W. **Team name:** Ocelots.

Student services. Adult student services, alcohol/substance abuse counseling, chaplain/spiritual director, career counseling, services for economically disadvantaged, student employment services, financial aid counseling, health services, minority student services, on-campus daycare, personal counseling, placement for graduates, veterans' counselor. **Physically disabled:** Services for visually, speech, hearing impaired.

Contact. E-mail: admissions@utb.edu
Phone: (956) 882-8295 Toll-free number: (877) 882-8721
Fax: (956) 882-7810
Carlo Tamayo, Director of Admissions and Recruitment, University of Texas at Brownsville, One West University Blvd., Brownsville, TX 78520

University of Texas at Dallas
Richardson, Texas   **CB member**
www.utdallas.edu   **CB code: 6897**

▶ Public 4-year university
▶ Residential campus in very large city
▶ 15,283 degree-seeking undergraduates: 18% part-time, 43% women, 6% African American, 29% Asian American, 18% Hispanic/Latino, 4% Multi-racial, non-Hispanic, 3% international
▶ 8,681 degree-seeking graduate students
▶ 61% of applicants admitted
▶ SAT or ACT (ACT writing optional) required
▶ 67% graduate within 6 years

General. Founded in 1969. Regionally accredited. **Degrees:** 3,127 bachelor's awarded; master's, professional, doctoral offered. **ROTC:** Army, Air Force. **Location:** 18 miles from downtown Dallas. **Calendar:** Semester, extensive summer session. **Full-time faculty:** 854 total; 93% have terminal degrees, 26% minority, 31% women. **Part-time faculty:** 344 total; 62% have terminal degrees, 18% minority, 46% women. **Class size:** 26% < 20, 32% 20-39, 20% 40-49, 17% 50-99, 5% >100. **Special facilities:** Geological information library, history of aviation library, motion capture lab, rare book library, philatelic research library, center for communications disorders, Holocaust collection, translation library, performance hall.

Freshman class profile. 11,237 applied, 6,909 admitted, 2,733 enrolled.

Mid 50% test scores		End year in good standing:	86%
SAT critical reading:	560-670	Return as sophomores:	84%
SAT math:	600-700	Out-of-state:	4%
SAT writing:	520-650	Live on campus:	60%
ACT composite:	25-31	International:	3%
Rank in top quarter:	64%	Fraternities:	8%
Rank in top tenth:	33%	Sororities:	8%

Basis for selection. In-state high school students in top 10% of class automatically admitted to state public universities. Assured admission at UTD for applicants who score 1200 SAT (Critical Reading and Math) or 26 ACT, OR who rank in top 15% of class. Completion of required high school course work required. All others reviewed for admission. Texas Higher Education Assessment test required for some based on high school performance. International students must take TOEFL (minimum score 550 on paper-based or 80 on Internet-based), IELTS Academic (minimum score 6.5) or PTE Academic (minimum score 67).

High school preparation. College-preparatory program required. 18 units required; 24 recommended. Required and recommended units include English 4, mathematics 4, social studies 3-4, science 3 (laboratory 3), foreign language 2-3, computer science 1, visual/performing arts .5-1, academic electives 1.5-2.5. 0.5 health and 1.5 physical education recommended.

2015-2016 Annual costs. Tuition/fees: $11,806; $31,328 out-of-state. Room/board: $9,944. Books/supplies: $1,200. Personal expenses: $2,040.

2014-2015 Financial aid. **Need-based:** 1,794 full-time freshmen applied for aid; 1,329 deemed to have need; 1,298 received aid. Average need met was 76%. Average scholarship/grant was $11,085; average loan $3,318. 68% of total undergraduate aid awarded as scholarships/grants, 32% as loans/jobs. **Non-need-based:** Awarded to 2,961 full-time undergraduates, including 857 freshmen. Scholarships awarded for academics.

Application procedures. Admission: Closing date 7/1 (postmark date). $50 fee, may be waived for applicants with need. Admission notification on a rolling basis. **Financial aid:** Priority date 3/31, closing date 4/12. FAFSA required. Applicants notified on a rolling basis starting 3/1; must reply within 2 week(s) of notification.

Academics. **Special study options:** Accelerated study, combined bachelor's/graduate degree, cooperative education, cross-registration, distance learning, double major, dual enrollment of high school students, ESL, honors, independent study, internships, liberal arts/career combination, student-designed major, study abroad, teacher certification program, Washington semester, weekend college. 3-2 engineering and 2-2 transfer programs. **Credit/placement by examination:** AP, CLEP, IB, institutional tests. 30 credit hours maximum toward bachelor's degree. No limit on lower-level courses, 6 hours limit on upper-level courses. SAT Subject Tests in Math Levels I and II accepted for advanced placement. **Support services:** Learning center, pre-admission summer program, reduced course load, remedial instruction, study skills assistance, tutoring, writing center. Student success center.

Honors college/program. Incoming freshman with minimum SAT score of (reading/math) or ACT composite 31 and a high school GPA of 3.6 or class rank in the top 10% encouraged to apply to Collegium V. Students must be accepted to UTD before their applications will be considered. To earn CV Honors, students are required to graduate with a 3.5 GPA and earn 24 credit hours in honors related work. Approximately 390 students enrolled.

Majors. **Area/ethnic studies:** American. **Biology:** General, biochemistry, molecular, neuroscience. **Business:** General, accounting, actuarial science, finance, international, management science, marketing. **Communications:** Digital media. **Computer sciences:** General, information technology. **Engineering:** Biomedical, computer, electrical, mechanical, software, telecommunications. **Foreign languages:** Comparative lit. **Health services:** Audiology/speech pathology, health care admin. **History:** General. **Human services:** General, public policy. **Math:** General. **Physical sciences:** Chemistry, geology, physics. **Psychology:** General, developmental. **Social sciences:** Criminology, economics, GIS/cartography, political science, sociology. **Visual/performing arts:** General, game design.

Most popular majors. Biology 15%, business/marketing 28%, computer/information sciences 8%, engineering/engineering technologies 10%, health sciences 6%, psychology 7%, social sciences 7%.

Technology on campus. 650 workstations in library, computer center, student center. Dormitories wired for high-speed internet access and linked to campus network. Commuter students can connect to campus network. Online course registration, online library, helpline, student web hosting, wireless network available.

Student life. **Freshman orientation:** Mandatory, $100 fee. Preregistration for classes offered. Family 1-day sessions and student 2-day sessions held in April, July and August. **Housing:** Coed dorms, apartments available. $100 partly refundable deposit, deadline 6/30. Pets allowed in dorm rooms. Living-learning communities for freshmen available. **Activities:** Bands, choral groups, dance, drama, film society, international student organizations, literary magazine, music ensembles, Model UN, musical theater, radio station, student government, student newspaper, symphony orchestra, TV station, College Republicans, University Democrats, black student alliance, Friendship Association of Chinese Students and Scholars, LULAC, Christians on Campus, Muslim student association, Habitat for Humanity, world aid organization, Alpha Phi Omega (service fraternity).

Athletics. NCAA. **Intercollegiate:** Baseball M, basketball, cross-country, golf, soccer, softball W, tennis, volleyball W. **Intramural:** Basketball, cheerleading, football (tackle), swimming, tennis, ultimate frisbee, volleyball, water polo. **Team name:** Comets.

Student services. Alcohol/substance abuse counseling, career counseling, student employment services, financial aid counseling, health services, legal services, minority student services, on-campus daycare, personal counseling, placement for graduates, veterans' counselor, women's services. **Physically disabled:** Services for visually, speech, hearing impaired.

Contact. E-mail: interest@utdallas.edu
Phone: (972) 883-2270 Toll-free number: (800) 889-2443
Fax: (972) 883-2599
Wray Weldon, Assistant Provost, Enrollment Services, University of Texas at Dallas, Admission and Enrollment Services, Richardson, TX 75080-3021

University of Texas at El Paso
El Paso, Texas   **CB member**
www.utep.edu   **CB code: 6829**

▶ Public 4-year university
▶ Commuter campus in very large city
▶ 20,004 degree-seeking undergraduates

General. Founded in 1913. Regionally accredited. Bilingual community, programs, and student body; located within 100 yards of Mexico. **Degrees:** 3,262 bachelor's awarded; master's, professional, doctoral offered. **Calendar:** Semester, extensive summer session. **Full-time faculty:** 710 total; 42% minority, 41% women. **Part-time faculty:** 479 total; 55% minority, 47% women. **Class size:** 33% < 20, 44% 20-39, 10% 40-49, 8% 50-99, 5% >100. **Special facilities:** Solar energy facility.

Freshman class profile.

GPA 3.75 or higher:	10%	Rank in top quarter:	39%
GPA 3.50-3.74:	19%	Rank in top tenth:	18%
GPA 3.0-3.49:	47%	Out-of-state:	2%
GPA 2.0-2.99:	22%		

Basis for selection. Minimum GED score of 45, or top half of high school class with 20 ACT or 920 SAT (exclusive of Writing). Provisional admission for in-state residents not meeting these criteria. For students in top quarter of high school class, any score acceptable.

High school preparation. College-preparatory program required. 26 units required. Required units include English 4, mathematics 4, social studies 2, history 2, science 4, foreign language 2, visual/performing arts 1 and academic electives 6.

2015-2016 Annual costs. Tuition/fees: $7,059; $18,169 out-of-state. Room only: $4,806. Books/supplies: $1,188. Personal expenses: $1,782.

2014-2015 Financial aid. **Need-based:** 2,757 full-time freshmen applied for aid; 2,328 deemed to have need; 2,266 received aid. Average need met was 68%. Average scholarship/grant was $9,916; average loan $4,265. **Non-need-based:** Awarded to 2,342 full-time undergraduates, including 841 freshmen. Scholarships awarded for academics, alumni affiliation, art, athletics, job skills, leadership, minority status, music/drama, religious affiliation, ROTC, state residency. **Additional information:** Emergency loans available.

Application procedures. **Admission:** Priority date 5/1; deadline 7/31 (postmark date). No application fee. Admission notification on a rolling basis. Notification of early action applicants when admission file is complete. **Financial aid:** Priority date 3/15; no closing date. FAFSA, institutional form required. Must reply within 2 week(s) of notification.

Academics. **Special study options:** Accelerated study, combined bachelor's/graduate degree, cooperative education, distance learning, double major, ESL, exchange student, honors, independent study, internships, student-designed major, study abroad, teacher certification program. **Credit/placement by examination:** AP, CLEP, IB, SAT, ACT, institutional tests. **Support services:** Learning center, pre-admission summer program, reduced course load, remedial instruction, study skills assistance, tutoring, writing center.

Majors. **Area/ethnic studies:** Chicano/Hispanic-American/Latino, Latin American. **Biology:** General, microbiology, molecular biochemistry. **Business:** General, accounting, business admin, finance, management information systems, managerial economics, marketing, operations. **Communications:** General, advertising, communications/speech/rhetoric, digital media, organizational. **Computer sciences:** General. **Conservation:** Environmental science. **Engineering:** Civil, electrical, industrial, mechanical, metallurgical. **English:** Creative writing, English lit. **Foreign languages:** French, linguistics, Spanish. **Health services:** Clinical lab science, nursing (RN), public health ed. **History:** General. **Human services:** Social work. **Math:** General, applied. **Parks/recreation:** Health/fitness. **Philosophy/religion:** Philosophy. **Physical sciences:** Chemistry, geology, geophysics, physics. **Protective services:** Criminal justice. **Psychology:** General. **Social sciences:** Anthropology, political science, sociology. **Visual/performing arts:** Art, art history/conservation, ceramics, dance, dramatic, drawing, graphic design, metal/jewelry, music, music management, music performance, music theory/composition, musical theater, painting, piano/keyboard, printmaking, sculpture, studio arts, theater arts management, voice/opera.

Most popular majors. Biology 8%, business/marketing 16%, education 8%, engineering/engineering technologies 9%, health sciences 12%, interdisciplinary studies 8%, psychology 7%, security/protective services 6%.

Technology on campus. 2,500 workstations in library, computer center, student center. Dormitories wired for high-speed internet access. Commuter students can connect to campus network. Online course registration, online library, helpline, repair service, student web hosting, wireless network available.

Student life. **Freshman orientation:** Available. Preregistration for classes offered. Three to five day program. **Housing:** Special housing for disabled, apartments available. $200 fully refundable deposit. **Activities:** Bands, choral groups, dance, drama, international student organizations, music ensembles, musical theater, radio station, student government, student newspaper, black student coalition, Mexican student organizations, Society of Hispanic Professional Engineers.

Athletics. NCAA. **Intercollegiate:** Basketball, cross-country, football (tackle) M, golf, rifle, soccer W, softball W, tennis, track and field, volleyball W. **Intramural:** Badminton, baseball M, basketball, bowling, fencing, football (tackle) M, golf, gymnastics, handball, racquetball, skiing, soccer, softball, squash, swimming, table tennis, tennis, track and field, volleyball, water polo, wrestling M. **Team name:** Miners.

Student services. Alcohol/substance abuse counseling, chaplain/spiritual director, career counseling, student employment services, financial aid counseling, health services, on-campus daycare, personal counseling, placement for graduates, veterans' counselor, women's services. **Physically disabled:** Services for visually, speech, hearing impaired.

Contact. E-mail: futureminer@utep.edu
Phone: (915) 747-5890 Fax: (915) 747-8893
Amanda Vasquez, Director, Enrollment Management, University of Texas at El Paso, 500 West University Avenue, El Paso, TX 79968

University of Texas at San Antonio

San Antonio, Texas — **CB member**
www.utsa.edu — **CB code: 6919**

- Public 4-year university
- Commuter campus in very large city
- 23,921 degree-seeking undergraduates: 16% part-time, 49% women, 9% African American, 6% Asian American, 53% Hispanic/Latino, 3% Multiracial, non-Hispanic, 3% international
- 4,066 degree-seeking graduate students
- 78% of applicants admitted
- SAT or ACT (ACT writing recommended) required
- 31% graduate within 6 years

General. Founded in 1969. Regionally accredited. Additional downtown and Institute of Texan Cultures campuses. **Degrees:** 4,685 bachelor's awarded; master's, doctoral offered. **ROTC:** Army, Air Force. **Location:** 15 miles from downtown. **Calendar:** Semester, limited summer session. **Full-time faculty:** 908 total; 83% have terminal degrees, 35% minority, 39% women. **Part-time faculty:** 447 total; 47% have terminal degrees, 32% minority, 49% women. **Class size:** 17% < 20, 40% 20-39, 11% 40-49, 21% 50-99, 11% >100. **Special facilities:** Institute of Texan cultures, center for archaeological research, neuroscience research center, center for water research, center for lasers and materials science, center for economic development, culture and policy institute, institute for music research, center for professional excellence.

Freshman class profile. 15,577 applied, 12,145 admitted, 4,920 enrolled.

Mid 50% test scores			
		Rank in top tenth:	19%
SAT critical reading:	460-570	Return as sophomores:	68%
SAT math:	470-580	Out-of-state:	2%
SAT writing:	430-540	Live on campus:	49%
ACT composite:	20-25	International:	1%
Rank in top quarter:	62%		

Basis for selection. Texas residents who graduate in top 10% of high school graduating class admitted, regardless of ACT or SAT scores. Those not in top 10% must meet appropriate ACT or SAT scores based on class rank. If test score/rank criteria not met, additional factors may be taken into consideration. Out-of-state applicants must graduate in top half of graduating class in addition to meeting corresponding ACT or SAT score requirements. Auditions are required for Music majors. Acceptance to the University does not guarantee acceptance to selective academic programs such as Engineering, Business, Architecture, and Biology, which may require pre-requisite coursework and individual review by the related academic department.Other applicants not meeting guaranteed admission criteria, may be considered by way of individual review that includes additional factors beyond high school class rank and SAT/ACT test scores. Essay and letters of recommendation are recommended, but not required. **Home schooled:** Applicants are considered by way of individual review that includes SAT/ACT test scores and additional factors such as academic accomplishment, honors and awards, community service, evidence of leadership, special talent development, evidence of having overcome challenges, and special or unique experiences. **Learning Disabled:** While admissions requirements are identical, students with disabilities may apply for accommodations via the Office for Students with Disabilities. Note, a thorough documentation process is required to qualify for accommodations.

High school preparation. College-preparatory program recommended. 23 units required. Required units include English 4, mathematics 3, social studies 3, history 1, science 3, foreign language 2, visual/performing arts 1 and academic electives 5. 1 speech required.

2015-2016 Annual costs. Tuition/fees: $8,737; $20,890 out-of-state. Room/board: $7,564. Books/supplies: $1,000. Personal expenses: $1,836.

2014-2015 Financial aid. Need-based: 4,245 full-time freshmen applied for aid; 3,410 deemed to have need; 3,283 received aid. Average need met was 61%. Average scholarship/grant was $8,071; average loan $3,266. 59% of total undergraduate aid awarded as scholarships/grants, 41% as loans/jobs. **Non-need-based:** Awarded to 4,089 full-time undergraduates, including 1,606 freshmen. Scholarships awarded for academics, alumni affiliation, art, athletics, job skills, leadership, music/drama, ROTC, state residency.

Application procedures. Admission: Priority date 3/1; deadline 6/1 (receipt date). $60 fee, may be waived for applicants with need. Admission notification by 9/1. Admission notification on a rolling basis. **Financial aid:** Priority date 3/15; no closing date. FAFSA required. Applicants notified on a rolling basis starting 4/1.

Academics. Special study options: Combined bachelor's/graduate degree, distance learning, double major, ESL, exchange student, honors, independent study, internships, student-designed major, study abroad, teacher certification program. **Credit/placement by examination:** AP, CLEP, IB, institutional tests. In order to be eligible to receive credit for American Government through AP or CLEP with appropriate cut-off score achieved, the Texas Politics and Society requirement must be satisfied. **Support services:** Learning center, pre-admission summer program, remedial instruction, study skills assistance, tutoring, writing center. Supplemental instruction and academic coaching.

Honors college/program. First-time freshman should be in the to 10% of their graduating class or have a composite SAT score of 1200 or higher or a composite ACT score of 27 or higher. The Honors Program also accepts transfer students and students who wish to enroll after a semester or more at UTSA. Such students are eligible to apply if they have a GPA of 3.4 or better.

Majors. Architecture: Architecture, interior. **Area/ethnic studies:** American, Chicano/Hispanic-American/Latino, women's. **Biology:** General, biochemistry, microbiology/immunology. **Business:** General, accounting, actuarial science, business admin, entrepreneurial studies, finance, human resources, international, management information systems, management science, managerial economics, marketing, real estate, tourism/travel. **Communications:** Communications/speech/rhetoric. **Computer sciences:** General, security. **Conservation:** Environmental science. **Education:** General, bilingual, elementary, ESL, middle. **Engineering:** Biomedical, civil, computer, electrical, mechanical. **English:** English lit, technical writing. **Foreign languages:** General, classics, Spanish. **General:** Site management. **Health services:** General, clinical lab science, dietetics. **History:** General. **Human services:** General. **Liberal arts:** Humanities. **Math:** General, statistics. **Parks/recreation:** Exercise sciences. **Philosophy/religion:** Philosophy. **Physical sciences:** Chemistry, geology, physics. **Protective services:** Criminal justice. **Psychology:** General. **Social sciences:** Anthropology, geography, international relations, political science, sociology. **Visual/performing arts:** Art, art history/conservation, music, music management, music performance, music theory/composition, studio arts.

Most popular majors. Biology 7%, business/marketing 25%, education 7%, engineering/engineering technologies 7%, parks/recreation 6%, psychology 8%.

Technology on campus. 400 workstations in dormitories, library, computer center, student center. Dormitories wired for high-speed internet access and linked to campus network. Commuter students can connect to campus network. Online course registration, online library, helpline, repair service, student web hosting, wireless network available.

Student life. Freshman orientation: Mandatory, $150 fee. Preregistration for classes offered. Held three days/two nights in June, July or August with optional housing available. **Housing:** Coed dorms, special housing for disabled, apartments, themed housing available. $300 partly refundable deposit. ADA rooms and strobe lights available. **Activities:** Bands, campus ministries, choral groups, dance, film society, international student organizations, literary magazine, music ensembles, Model UN, opera, radio station, student government, student newspaper, symphony orchestra, Baptist Student Ministry, Campus Crusade for Christ, Catholic Student Association, College Republicans,Chi Alpha Christian Fellowship, Hillel, Intervarsity Christian Fellowship, United Methodist Student Movement, Young Life College, Young Democrats,Young Americans for Civil Liberties.

Athletics. NCAA. **Intercollegiate:** Baseball M, basketball, cross-country, football (tackle) M, golf, soccer W, softball W, tennis, track and field, volleyball W. **Intramural:** Badminton, basketball, football (non-tackle), golf, racquetball, soccer, softball, table tennis, tennis, ultimate frisbee, volleyball. **Team name:** Roadrunners.

Student services. Alcohol/substance abuse counseling, career counseling, student employment services, financial aid counseling, health services, on-campus daycare, personal counseling, placement for graduates, veterans' counselor, women's services. **Physically disabled:** Services for visually, speech, hearing impaired.

Contact. E-mail: prospects@utsa.edu
Phone: (210) 458-8000 Toll-free number: (800) 669-0919
Fax: (210) 458-7857
Beverly Woodson Day, Director of Admissions, University of Texas at San Antonio, One UTSA Circle, San Antonio, TX 78249-0617

University of Texas at Tyler
Tyler, Texas — CB member
www.uttyler.edu — CB code: 6850

- Public 4-year university
- Commuter campus in small city
- 6,059 degree-seeking undergraduates: 25% part-time, 57% women, 9% African American, 3% Asian American, 16% Hispanic/Latino, 8% Multi-racial, non-Hispanic, 2% international
- 2,286 degree-seeking graduate students
- 64% of applicants admitted
- SAT or ACT (ACT writing optional) required
- 41% graduate within 6 years

General. Founded in 1971. Regionally accredited. Off-campus sites at Palestine and Longview. Internet courses available. **Degrees:** 1,226 bachelor's awarded; master's, doctoral offered. **Location:** 80 miles from Dallas. **Calendar:** Semester, limited summer session. **Full-time faculty:** 280 total; 69% have terminal degrees, 17% minority, 54% women. **Part-time faculty:** 173 total; 10% have terminal degrees, 10% minority, 57% women. **Class size:** 34% < 20, 47% 20-39, 9% 40-49, 8% 50-99, 2% >100. **Special facilities:** Desktop manufacturing lab, computer-based virtual lab instruments.

Freshman class profile. 2,468 applied, 1,591 admitted, 778 enrolled.

Mid 50% test scores			
SAT critical reading:	480-570	Rank in top quarter:	35%
SAT math:	490-590	Rank in top tenth:	10%
SAT writing:	450-560	Return as sophomores:	62%
ACT composite:	20-25	Out-of-state:	2%
GPA 3.75 or higher:	27%	Live on campus:	14%
GPA 3.50-3.74:	21%	International:	1%
GPA 3.0-3.49:	33%	Fraternities:	8%
GPA 2.0-2.99:	17%	Sororities:	10%

Basis for selection. Top 10% accepted automatically, others admitted based on ACT/SAT scores and high school preparation. **Home schooled:** Transcript of courses and grades required.

High school preparation. College-preparatory program required. Required and recommended units include English 4, mathematics 3-4, social studies 3-4, history 4, science 3-4 (laboratory 3) and foreign language 2.

2015-2016 Annual costs. Tuition/fees: $7,312; $19,236 out-of-state. Room/board: $7,775. Books/supplies: $1,580. Personal expenses: $1,460.

Financial aid. Non-need-based: Scholarships awarded for academics, art, music/drama. **Additional information:** Apply early for all programs.

Application procedures. Admission: Closing date 8/24. $40 fee, may be waived for applicants with need. Application must be submitted online. Admission notification on a rolling basis. **Financial aid:** Priority date 4/1; no closing date. FAFSA required. Applicants notified on a rolling basis starting 4/15; must reply within 2 week(s) of notification.

Academics. Special study options: Cooperative education, distance learning, double major, dual enrollment of high school students, honors, independent study, internships, student-designed major, study abroad, teacher certification program. **Credit/placement by examination:** AP, CLEP, IB, SAT, ACT. AP, CLEP and International Baccalaureate awarded transfer credit with no maximum limit. **Support services:** Learning center, remedial instruction, study skills assistance, tutoring, writing center.

Honors college/program. Admission Committee typically looks at students with minimum 28 ACT composite score or minimum 1860 SAT combined score, and 3.5 or higher high school GPA.

Majors. Biology: General. **Business:** Accounting, business admin, construction management, finance, managerial economics, marketing, training/development. **Communications:** Media studies. **Computer sciences:** General. **Engineering:** Civil, electrical, mechanical. **English:** English lit, rhetoric/composition. **Foreign languages:** General, Spanish. **Health services:** General, nursing (RN). **History:** General. **Math:** General. **Parks/recreation:**

Exercise sciences. **Philosophy/religion:** Religion. **Physical sciences:** Chemistry. **Protective services:** Criminal justice. **Psychology:** General. **Social sciences:** General, political science. **Visual/performing arts:** Art, music.

Most popular majors. Business/marketing 21%, engineering/engineering technologies 10%, health sciences 21%, interdisciplinary studies 10%, parks/recreation 8%, psychology 6%.

Technology on campus. Dormitories wired for high-speed internet access and linked to campus network. Commuter students can connect to campus network. Online course registration, online library, wireless network available.

Student life. Freshman orientation: Mandatory, $75 fee. Preregistration for classes offered. Held in summer for students and parents. **Housing:** Coed dorms available. **Activities:** Bands, choral groups, international student organizations, music ensembles, Model UN, student government, student newspaper, Bible study fellowship, University Democrats, Nurses Christian Fellowship, Wesley Foundation Student Fellowship, Baptist student ministry, Patriots Special Olympics Texas Volunteers (Patriots SOTX), University Mothers Against Drunk Driving (UMADD), Indian student association.

Athletics. NCAA. **Intercollegiate:** Baseball M, basketball, cheerleading, cross-country, golf, soccer, softball W, tennis, track and field, volleyball W. **Intramural:** Baseball M, basketball, bowling, football (non-tackle), football (tackle), golf, racquetball, soccer, softball, table tennis, tennis, volleyball. **Team name:** Patriots.

Student services. Adult student services, alcohol/substance abuse counseling, career counseling, student employment services, financial aid counseling, health services, personal counseling, veterans' counselor. **Physically disabled:** Services for visually, speech, hearing impaired.

Contact. E-mail: admrequest@uttyler.edu
Phone: (903) 566-7203 Toll-free number: (800) 888-9537
Fax: (903) 566-7068
Sarah Bowdin, Director of Admissions, University of Texas at Tyler, 3900 University Boulevard, Tyler, TX 75799

University of Texas Health Science Center at Houston
Houston, Texas
www.uth.tmc.edu   **CB code: 6906**

▶ Public two-year upper-division university and health science college
▶ Commuter campus in very large city
▶ Interview required

General. Founded in 1972. Regionally accredited. Located in the Texas Medical Center. **Degrees:** 421 bachelor's awarded; master's, professional, doctoral offered. **Location:** 5 miles from downtown. **Calendar:** Semester, limited summer session. **Full-time faculty:** 1,329 total. **Part-time faculty:** 296 total.

Student profile. 657 degree-seeking undergraduates, 3,491 degree-seeking graduate students. 70% entered as juniors.

Women:	85%	Part-time:	18%

Basis for selection. College transcript, interview required. Applicants must submit official transcript from all previous institutions. Application closing dates, admissions policies vary by program. Dental hygiene application closing date: December 31. Minimum number of credits: 28. Nursing application closing date: January 1. Minimum number of credits: 60. Transfer accepted as sophomores, juniors.

2015-2016 Annual costs. Books/supplies: $1,348.

Application procedures. Admission: Deadline 12/31. $60 fee. **Financial aid:** FAFSA, institutional form required.

Academics. Upper division bachelor's program for nursing, with accelerated RN-master's program. **Special study options:** Accelerated study, combined bachelor's/graduate degree, distance learning. **Credit/placement by examination:** AP, CLEP. All CLEP must appear on college transcript with credit hours and grade.

Majors. Health services: Dental hygiene, nursing (RN).

Technology on campus. PC or laptop required. Helpline available.

Student life. Housing: Apartments available. University operates apartment complex as only student housing available. Complex located approximately 1 mile from campus. **Activities:** Student government.

Student services. Adult student services, alcohol/substance abuse counseling, financial aid counseling, health services, on-campus daycare, personal counseling. **Physically disabled:** Services for visually, hearing impaired.

Contact. E-mail: admissions@uth.tmc.edu
Phone: (713) 500-3361 Fax: (713) 500-3356
Robert Jenkins, Registrar, University of Texas Health Science Center at Houston, Box 20036, Houston, TX 77225

University of Texas Medical Branch at Galveston
Galveston, Texas
www.utmb.edu   **CB code: 6887**

▶ Public two-year upper-division health science and nursing college
▶ Commuter campus in large town

General. Founded in 1881. Regionally accredited. The 84-acre campus includes four schools, three institutes for advanced study, a major medical library, a network of hospitals and clinics that provide a full range of primary and specialized medical care, an affiliated Shriners Burns Hospital, and numerous research facilities. UTMB is a component of the University of Texas System. **Degrees:** 419 bachelor's awarded; master's, professional, doctoral offered. **Location:** 50 miles from Houston. **Calendar:** Continuous, limited summer session.

Student profile. 745 degree-seeking undergraduates, 2,424 degree-seeking graduate students.

Women:	83%	International:	2%
African American:	10%	Part-time:	17%
Asian American:	19%	Out-of-state:	1%
Hispanic/Latino:	21%	25 or older:	37%
Multi-racial, non-Hispanic:	3%		

Basis for selection. College transcript required. Students with 60 hours from accredited college or university considered. Nonresident enrollment limited by legislature to not more than 10% of any class. Transfer decisions based on competitive comparison of transcripts, allied health experience, departmental testing, and personal interviews. Specific prerequisites and application closing dates vary by program. Transfer accepted as juniors, seniors.

Financial aid. Non-need-based: Scholarships awarded for academics, minority status, state residency.

Application procedures. Admission: $50 fee. Application must be submitted online. **Financial aid:** FAFSA required.

Academics. Special study options: Distance learning, independent study, internships. **Credit/placement by examination:** AP, CLEP, IB. 30 credit hours maximum toward bachelor's degree.

Majors. Health services: Clinical lab science, nursing (RN), respiratory therapy technology.

Technology on campus. Dormitories wired for high-speed internet access and linked to campus network. Commuter students can connect to campus network. Online library, helpline, repair service, wireless network available.

Student life. Housing: Coed dorms, apartments, fraternity/sorority housing available. $200 fully refundable deposit. **Activities:** Campus ministries, international student organizations, student government, Wesley Foundation, Newman Center, sports clubs, Christian Medical and Dental Society, Jewish student and faculty organization, multicultural awareness council, student national medical association, Texas Association of Latin American Medical Students.

Athletics. Intramural: Basketball, football (non-tackle), soccer, softball, volleyball.

Student services. Alcohol/substance abuse counseling, chaplain/spiritual director, career counseling, student employment services, financial aid counseling, health services, legal services, personal counseling, veterans' counselor, women's services. **Physically disabled:** Services for visually, speech, hearing impaired.

Contact. E-mail: enrollment.services@utmb.edu
Phone: (409) 772-1215 Fax: (409) 772-4466
University of Texas Medical Branch at Galveston, 301 University Boulevard, Galveston, TX 77555-1305

University of Texas of the Permian Basin

Odessa, Texas   **CB member**
www.utpb.edu   **CB code: 0448**

- Public 4-year university
- Commuter campus in small city
- 3,436 degree-seeking undergraduates: 40% part-time, 55% women, 7% African American, 2% Asian American, 47% Hispanic/Latino, 1% Native American, 1% Multi-racial, non-Hispanic, 1% international
- 722 degree-seeking graduate students
- 84% of applicants admitted
- SAT or ACT (ACT writing optional) required
- 40% graduate within 6 years

General. Founded in 1969. Regionally accredited. **Degrees:** 696 bachelor's awarded; master's offered. **Location:** 150 miles from Lubbock, 350 miles from Dallas. **Calendar:** Semester, extensive summer session. **Full-time faculty:** 134 total; 78% have terminal degrees, 18% minority, 49% women. **Part-time faculty:** 117 total; 28% have terminal degrees, 23% minority, 58% women. **Class size:** 28% < 20, 49% 20-39, 9% 40-49, 12% 50-99, less than 1% >100. **Special facilities:** Presidential archives and library.

Freshman class profile. 1,154 applied, 975 admitted, 504 enrolled.

Mid 50% test scores		Return as sophomores:	71%
SAT critical reading:	420-530	Out-of-state:	5%
SAT math:	460-540	Live on campus:	49%
ACT composite:	18-22	International:	1%
Rank in top quarter:	54%	Fraternities:	1%
Rank in top tenth:	24%	Sororities:	3%

Basis for selection. Secondary school record, class rank, test scores important. Students not meeting the requirements may be admitted on a case by case basis. Foreign students whose native language is not English must take TOEFL. Requirement may be waived for non-English speakers transferring from a U.S. college or high school. Essay not required but considered if provided. **Home schooled:** Transcript of courses and grades, state high school equivalency certificate required. SAT minimum of 1150 (CR+M) or ACT minimum of 24. **Learning Disabled:** No special requirements but must meet minimum admission standards.

High school preparation. College-preparatory program required. 26 units required. Required units include English 4, mathematics 4, social studies 4, science 4 (laboratory 3), foreign language 2, computer science 1, visual/performing arts 1 and academic electives 6.

2015-2016 Annual costs. Tuition/fees: $6,458; $7,508 out-of-district; $7,508 out-of-state. Room/board: $8,904. Books/supplies: $1,000. Personal expenses: $1,817.

2014-2015 Financial aid. Need-based: 330 full-time freshmen applied for aid; 254 deemed to have need; 254 received aid. Average need met was 75%. Average scholarship/grant was $8,360; average loan $2,713. 71% of total undergraduate aid awarded as scholarships/grants, 29% as loans/jobs. **Non-need-based:** Awarded to 1,337 full-time undergraduates, including 324 freshmen. Scholarships awarded for academics, art, athletics, leadership, music/drama, state residency.

Application procedures. Admission: Priority date 7/15; deadline 8/22 (receipt date). No application fee. Application must be submitted online. Admission notification on a rolling basis beginning on or about 9/1. Must reply by May 1 or within 2 week(s) if notified thereafter. **Financial aid:** Priority date 7/15; no closing date. FAFSA required. Applicants notified on a rolling basis starting 3/15.

Academics. Special study options: Accelerated study, combined bachelor's/graduate degree, cross-registration, distance learning, double major, dual enrollment of high school students, ESL, external degree, honors, independent study, internships, study abroad, teacher certification program. **Credit/placement by examination:** AP, CLEP, IB, SAT, ACT, institutional tests. 28 credit hours maximum toward bachelor's degree. Credit/placement awarded for AP or CLEP exams. **Support services:** Learning center, reduced course load, remedial instruction, study skills assistance, tutoring, writing center. AVID Learning Techniques.

Majors. Biology: General. **Business:** Accounting, business admin, finance, managerial economics, marketing. **Communications:** General. **Computer sciences:** General, information systems. **Engineering:** Mechanical, petroleum. **English:** English lit. **Foreign languages:** Spanish. **Health services:** Athletic training, nursing (RN). **History:** General. **Human services:** Social work. **Liberal arts:** Humanities. **Math:** General. **Parks/recreation:** Exercise sciences. **Physical sciences:** Chemistry, geology. **Protective services:** Criminal justice. **Psychology:** General. **Social sciences:** Criminology, political science, sociology. **Visual/performing arts:** Art, music. **Work/family studies:** Family studies.

Most popular majors. Business/marketing 24%, engineering/engineering technologies 7%, interdisciplinary studies 10%, parks/recreation 7%, psychology 11%, social sciences 8%.

Technology on campus. 170 workstations in dormitories, library, computer center. Dormitories wired for high-speed internet access and linked to campus network. Commuter students can connect to campus network. Online course registration, online library, helpline, wireless network available.

Student life. Freshman orientation: Mandatory, $75 fee. Preregistration for classes offered. Held during summer for freshmen and right before start of the semester for transfers/graduates entering in the fall semester. **Housing:** Coed dorms, apartments available. $200 fully refundable deposit, deadline 7/15. Family housing units available. **Activities:** Bands, campus ministries, choral groups, dance, drama, film society, international student organizations, literary magazine, music ensembles, musical theater, student government, symphony orchestra, (re)Act, Baptist Student Ministries, Black Leadership Council, Catholic Student Association, Christians United for Israel, Christians on Campus, Environmental Justice Club, Falcon Veteran Assoc., Student Cooperative Club, Students for Sensible Drug Policy, Students in Philanthropy.

Athletics. NCAA. **Intercollegiate:** Baseball M, basketball, cross-country, soccer, softball W, swimming, tennis, volleyball W. **Intramural:** Basketball, bowling, cross-country, football (non-tackle) W, golf, soccer, softball W, swimming, table tennis, tennis, volleyball. **Team name:** Falcons.

Student services. Alcohol/substance abuse counseling, career counseling, services for economically disadvantaged, student employment services, financial aid counseling, health services, minority student services, on-campus daycare, personal counseling, placement for graduates, veterans' counselor. **Physically disabled:** Services for visually, speech, hearing impaired.

Contact. E-mail: admissions@utpb.edu
Phone: (432) 552-2605 Toll-free number: (866) 552-8872
Fax: (432) 552-3605
Scott Smiley, Director of Admissions, University of Texas of the Permian Basin, 4901 East University, Odessa, TX 79762

University Of Texas Rio Grande Valley

Edinburg, Texas
www.utrgv.edu   **CB code: 6568**

- Public 4-year university
- Small city
- 24,677 degree-seeking undergraduates: 29% part-time, 56% women, 1% African American, 1% Asian American, 91% Hispanic/Latino, 3% international
- 3,610 degree-seeking graduate students
- 82% of applicants admitted
- SAT or ACT (ACT writing optional) required

General. Regionally accredited. **ROTC:** Army. **Calendar:** Semester. **Full-time faculty:** 1,041 total; 54% minority, 42% women. **Part-time faculty:** 217 total; 53% minority, 45% women. **Class size:** 15% < 20, 58% 20-39, 9% 40-49, 16% 50-99, 2% >100.

Freshman class profile. 9,055 applied, 7,447 admitted, 4,202 enrolled.

Mid 50% test scores		Rank in top quarter:	47%
SAT critical reading:	410-520	Rank in top tenth:	17%
SAT math:	430-530	Out-of-state:	2%
SAT writing:	400-500	Live on campus:	8%
ACT composite:	17-21	International:	3%

Basis for selection. Class rank and standardized test score most important. Rigor of secondary school record, essay, and GPA also considered.

High school preparation. 22 units required; 26 recommended. Required and recommended units include English 4, mathematics 3-4, social studies 3-4, science 2-4, foreign language 2, visual/performing arts 1, academic electives 7.5. Units required: .5 Speech, 1 Physical Education.

2015-2016 Annual costs. Books/supplies: $1,194. Personal expenses: $1,858.

2015-2016 Financial aid. Need-based: 3,574 full-time freshmen applied for aid; 3,366 deemed to have need; 3,366 received aid. Average need met was 68%. Average scholarship/grant was $10,191; average loan $3,252. 73% of total undergraduate aid awarded as scholarships/grants, 27% as loans/jobs.

Non-need-based: Awarded to 2,007 full-time undergraduates, including 208 freshmen. Scholarships awarded for academics, alumni affiliation, art, athletics, leadership, music/drama.

Application procedures. Admission: Priority date 2/1; deadline 7/1. No application fee. Admission notification on a rolling basis beginning on or about 12/1. **Financial aid:** Priority date 3/15; no closing date. FAFSA required. Applicants notified on a rolling basis.

Academics. Special study options: Accelerated study, distance learning, double major, dual enrollment of high school students, ESL, exchange student, honors, independent study, internships, study abroad, teacher certification program. **Credit/placement by examination:** AP, CLEP.

Majors. Area/ethnic studies: American, Chicano/Hispanic-American/Latino. **Biology:** General. **Business:** General, accounting, business admin, finance, international, management information systems, marketing. **Communications:** General, communications/speech/rhetoric, journalism, media studies. **Computer sciences:** General, computer science. **Conservation:** Environmental science. **Engineering:** Civil, computer, electrical, industrial, mechanical. **English:** English lit. **Foreign languages:** French, Spanish. **Health services:** General, audiology/speech pathology, clinical lab science, communication disorders, dietetics, nursing (RN), physician assistant, rehabilitation science, substance abuse counseling. **History:** General. **Human services:** Social work. **Math:** General. **Parks/recreation:** Exercise sciences, health/fitness. **Philosophy/religion:** Philosophy. **Physical sciences:** General, chemistry, physics. **Protective services:** Law enforcement admin. **Psychology:** General. **Social sciences:** General, anthropology, economics, political science, sociology. **Visual/performing arts:** Dance, dramatic, music, music performance, studio arts. **Work/family studies:** Child care management.

Student life. Housing: Single-sex dorms, special housing for disabled, apartments available. **Activities:** Bands, campus ministries, choral groups, dance, drama, film society, international student organizations, literary magazine, music ensembles, musical theater, opera, radio station, student government, student newspaper, symphony orchestra, TV station.

Contact. E-mail: admissions@utrgv.edu
Phone: (956) 665-2999 Toll-free number: (888) 802-4026
Fax: (856) 665-2687
University Of Texas Rio Grande Valley, 1201 West University Drive, Edinburg, TX 78539

University of Texas-Pan American
Edinburg, Texas — **CB member**
www.utpa.edu — **CB code: 6570**

▶ Public 4-year university
▶ Commuter campus in small city
▶ 17,994 degree-seeking undergraduates
▶ 2,815 graduate students
▶ SAT or ACT (ACT writing optional) required

General. Founded in 1927. Regionally accredited. Hispanic-serving institution. **Degrees:** 2,759 bachelor's awarded; master's, doctoral offered. **ROTC:** Army. **Location:** 250 miles from San Antonio, 300 miles from Austin. **Calendar:** Semester, extensive summer session. **Special facilities:** Coastal studies laboratory at South Padre Island, planetarium.

Freshman class profile.

Rank in top quarter: 53% Rank in top tenth: 22%

Basis for selection. For regular admission, rank in top quartile of class or acceptable ACT/SAT scores required. Students who do not meet criteria for admission placed in Provisional Enrollment Program. **Home schooled:** Students graduating from a private or home school required to file completed Texas Private High School Certification with transcript.

High school preparation. 24 units required. Required units include English 4, mathematics 4, social studies 3.5, science 4, foreign language 2, academic electives 3.5. Economics .5, fine arts 1, physical education 1, speech .5, Algebra 2 required of business and engineering majors. Geometry, trigonometry, chemistry, and physics required of engineering majors.

2015-2016 Annual costs. Tuition/fees: $7,292; $18,992 out-of-state. Room/board: $6,592. Books/supplies: $1,150. Personal expenses: $2,014.

Financial aid. Non-need-based: Scholarships awarded for academics, alumni affiliation, art, athletics, ROTC.

Application procedures. Admission: Priority date 2/1; deadline 7/31 (receipt date). No application fee. Admission notification on a rolling basis.

Financial aid: Priority date 3/15; no closing date. FAFSA required. Applicants notified on a rolling basis starting 3/15.

Academics. Special study options: Accelerated study, combined bachelor's/graduate degree, cooperative education, distance learning, double major, dual enrollment of high school students, ESL, exchange student, honors, independent study, internships, study abroad, teacher certification program, weekend college. **Credit/placement by examination:** AP, CLEP, IB, institutional tests. 45 credit hours maximum toward bachelor's degree. **Support services:** Learning center, pre-admission summer program, remedial instruction, study skills assistance, tutoring, writing center.

Majors. Area/ethnic studies: Chicano/Hispanic-American/Latino. **Biology:** General. **Business:** Accounting, business admin, finance, international, management information systems, marketing. **Communications:** General, communications/speech/rhetoric, media studies. **Computer sciences:** Computer science. **Conservation:** Environmental science. **Engineering:** Civil, computer, electrical, industrial, manufacturing, mechanical. **English:** English lit. **Foreign languages:** French, Spanish. **Health services:** General, clinical lab science, communication disorders, dietetics, nursing (RN). **History:** General. **Human services:** Social work. **Math:** General. **Parks/recreation:** Exercise sciences. **Philosophy/religion:** Philosophy. **Physical sciences:** General, chemistry, physics. **Protective services:** Law enforcement admin. **Psychology:** General. **Social sciences:** General, anthropology, economics, political science, sociology. **Visual/performing arts:** Dance, dramatic, music, music performance, studio arts. **Work/family studies:** Child care management.

Most popular majors. Biology 8%, business/marketing 14%, health sciences 15%, interdisciplinary studies 7%, psychology 7%, security/protective services 9%.

Technology on campus. 900 workstations in dormitories, library, computer center. Dormitories wired for high-speed internet access and linked to campus network. Commuter students can connect to campus network. Online course registration, online library, helpline, student web hosting, wireless network available.

Student life. Freshman orientation: Mandatory, $75 fee. Preregistration for classes offered. Several 1-day sessions held prior to beginning of semester. **Housing:** Coed dorms, single-sex dorms, apartments available. $150 fully refundable deposit, deadline 7/1. **Activities:** Bands, campus ministries, choral groups, dance, drama, international student organizations, music ensembles, musical theater, student government, student newspaper, symphony orchestra, Episcopal Canterbury Association, Latter-day Saints student association, Baha'i association, Baptist student union, Campus Crusade for Christ, Fellowship of Christian Athletes, Asian American students association, Society of Hispanic Professional Engineers.

Athletics. NCAA. **Intercollegiate:** Baseball M, basketball, cheerleading, cross-country, golf, soccer, tennis, track and field, volleyball W. **Intramural:** Basketball, cheerleading, football (non-tackle), golf, racquetball, soccer, softball, table tennis, tennis, ultimate frisbee, volleyball. **Team name:** Broncs/Lady Broncs.

Student services. Alcohol/substance abuse counseling, career counseling, services for economically disadvantaged, student employment services, financial aid counseling, health services, on-campus daycare, personal counseling, placement for graduates, veterans' counselor, women's services. **Physically disabled:** Services for visually, speech, hearing impaired.

Contact. E-mail: admissions@utpa.edu
Phone: (956) 665-2999 Toll-free number: (866) 441-8872
Fax: (956) 665-2687
Magdalena Hinojosa, Senior Associate Vice President for Enrollment Services, University of Texas-Pan American, 1201 West University Drive, Edinburg, TX 78539-2999

University of the Incarnate Word
San Antonio, Texas — **CB member**
www.uiw.edu — **CB code: 6303**

▶ Private 4-year university affiliated with the Roman Catholic Church
▶ Commuter campus in very large city
▶ 6,249 degree-seeking undergraduates: 32% part-time, 60% women, 7% African American, 2% Asian American, 59% Hispanic/Latino, 1% Multiracial, non-Hispanic, 5% international
▶ 2,206 degree-seeking graduate students
▶ 92% of applicants admitted
▶ SAT or ACT (ACT writing optional) required
▶ 51% graduate within 6 years

General. Founded in 1881. Regionally accredited. Virtual campus offers online courses. International campuses in Mexico City and in Heidelberg,

Germany. **Degrees:** 1,332 bachelor's, 20 associate awarded; master's, professional, doctoral offered. **ROTC:** Army, Air Force. **Location:** 5 miles from San Antonio. **Calendar:** Semester, extensive summer session. **Full-time faculty:** 286 total; 62% have terminal degrees, 30% minority, 55% women. **Part-time faculty:** 314 total; 20% have terminal degrees, 37% minority, 48% women. **Class size:** 54% < 20, 43% 20-39, less than 1% 40-49, 2% 50-99. **Special facilities:** LEED platinum solar house, Holy Land garden, San Antonio River Headwaters, art center.

Freshman class profile. 4,050 applied, 3,735 admitted, 906 enrolled.

Mid 50% test scores			
SAT critical reading:	430-530	GPA 3.0-3.49:	35%
SAT math:	430-530	GPA 2.0-2.99:	9%
SAT writing:	410-510	Return as sophomores:	76%
ACT composite:	18-23	Out-of-state:	3%
GPA 3.75 or higher:	25%	Live on campus:	42%
GPA 3.50-3.74:	30%	International:	5%

Basis for selection. Test scores and school achievement record most important. Extracurricular activities and positions of leadership held by the student also taken into consideration. Letters of recommendation from people familiar with the student's character and student essays explaining extenuating circumstances not required but are encouraged and will be reviewed if submitted. Rolling policy for submission of test scores. Personal statement and interview with the Dean of Admissions recommended for students whose academic record is considered to be below average. **Home schooled:** Statement describing home school structure and mission, transcript of courses and grades required. Required to submit official copy of SAT or ACT exam scores. Interview, letters of recommendation, assessment testing may be required.

High school preparation. College-preparatory program required. 16 units required; 18 recommended. Required and recommended units include English 4, mathematics 3-4, social studies 3-4, science 3, foreign language 2 and visual/performing arts 1.

2015-2016 Annual costs. Tuition/fees: $27,798. Room/board: $11,364. Books/supplies: $1,200. Personal expenses: $1,788.

2014-2015 Financial aid. Need-based: 803 full-time freshmen applied for aid; 734 deemed to have need; 733 received aid. Average need met was 63%. Average scholarship/grant was $17,375; average loan $3,544. 63% of total undergraduate aid awarded as scholarships/grants, 37% as loans/jobs. **Non-need-based:** Awarded to 1,018 full-time undergraduates, including 195 freshmen. Scholarships awarded for academics, alumni affiliation, art, athletics, leadership, minority status, music/drama, religious affiliation, ROTC. **Additional information:** Students encouraged to pursue outside scholarship programs.

Application procedures. Admission: Priority date 2/1; no deadline. $20 fee, may be waived for applicants with need. Admission notification on a rolling basis. Must reply by May 1 or within 4 week(s) if notified thereafter. Notification approximately 2 weeks following submission. **Financial aid:** Priority date 4/1; no closing date. FAFSA required. Applicants notified on a rolling basis starting 2/15; must reply within 2 week(s) of notification.

Academics. Special study options: Accelerated study, combined bachelor's/graduate degree, cross-registration, distance learning, double major, dual enrollment of high school students, ESL, exchange student, honors, independent study, internships, study abroad, teacher certification program. **Credit/placement by examination:** AP, CLEP, IB, SAT, ACT, institutional tests. 30 credit hours maximum toward bachelor's degree. **Support services:** Learning center, reduced course load, remedial instruction, study skills assistance, tutoring, writing center.

Honors college/program. Incoming freshmen should submit an application, have a minimum high school GPA of 3.5, and combined SAT score (Verbal, Math and Writing) of 1800 and/or a 27 composite ACT score. Applicants also need an essay, teacher recommendation, and interview. Students enroll in advanced courses, participate in one mission trip, a travel or study abroad experience, additional professional development experiences, and complete a senior project.

Majors. Biology: General, biochemistry, vision science. **Business:** Accounting, banking/financial services, business admin, human resources, international, management information systems, managerial economics, marketing, organizational behavior, sales/distribution. **Communications:** Communications/speech/rhetoric, digital media, journalism, media studies, radio/TV. **Communications technology:** Animation/special effects. **Computer sciences:** General. **Conservation:** Environmental science. **Education:** Art, elementary, music, physical. **English:** English lit. **Foreign languages:** Spanish. **Health services:** Athletic training, music therapy, nuclear medical technology, nursing (RN), prepharmacy, rehabilitation science. **History:** General. **Liberal arts:** Arts/sciences. **Math:** General. **Parks/recreation:** Exercise sciences, sports admin. **Philosophy/religion:** Philosophy, religion. **Physical sciences:** Chemistry, meteorology. **Psychology:** General. **Social sciences:** International relations, political science, sociology. **Visual/performing arts:**

Art, art history/conservation, dramatic, fashion design, graphic design, interior design, music, music management, music performance, studio arts. **Work/family studies:** Apparel marketing, child care management, child development.

Most popular majors. Biology 10%, business/marketing 41%, health sciences 11%.

Technology on campus. PC or laptop required. 360 workstations in library, computer center. Dormitories wired for high-speed internet access and linked to campus network. Commuter students can connect to campus network. Online course registration, online library, helpline, repair service, wireless network available.

Student life. Freshman orientation: Mandatory. Preregistration for classes offered. 1-day sessions offered for freshmen and transfer students, usually beginning in mid-May for the Fall semesters and mid-November for Spring semesters. Parents encouraged to participate. **Housing:** Coed dorms, single-sex dorms, special housing for disabled, apartments available. $225 fully refundable deposit, deadline 5/1. **Activities:** Bands, campus ministries, choral groups, dance, drama, international student organizations, literary magazine, music ensembles, musical theater, radio station, student government, student newspaper, symphony orchestra, TV station, Alpha Phi Omega, Knights of Columbus, St. Vincent de Paul Society, Catholic Daughters of America, black student association, Hispanic Latino association, international student association, Multicultural Greek Alliance, Project Africa, StandOut Alliance.

Athletics. NCAA. **Intercollegiate:** Baseball M, basketball, cross-country, diving, football (tackle) M, golf, soccer, softball W, swimming, synchronized swimming W, tennis, track and field, volleyball W. **Intramural:** Basketball, football (non-tackle), racquetball, soccer, softball, tennis, ultimate frisbee, volleyball, water polo. **Team name:** Cardinals.

Student services. Adult student services, alcohol/substance abuse counseling, chaplain/spiritual director, career counseling, services for economically disadvantaged, student employment services, financial aid counseling, health services, personal counseling, veterans' counselor. **Physically disabled:** Services for visually, speech, hearing impaired.

Contact. E-mail: admis@uiwtx.edu
Phone: (210) 829-6005 Toll-free number: (800) 749-9673
Fax: (210) 829-3921
Jennielle Strother, Dean of Enrollment, University of the Incarnate Word, 4301 Broadway, San Antonio, TX 78209-6397

Wayland Baptist University
Plainview, Texas
www.wbu.edu

CB member
CB code: 6930

- Private 4-year university and liberal arts college affiliated with the Southern Baptist Convention
- Residential campus in large town
- 3,583 degree-seeking undergraduates: 71% part-time, 48% women, 17% African American, 2% Asian American, 28% Hispanic/Latino, 1% Native American, 1% Native Hawaiian/Pacific islander, 4% Multi-racial, non-Hispanic, 1% international
- 1,375 degree-seeking graduate students
- 99% of applicants admitted
- SAT or ACT (ACT writing optional) required
- 33% graduate within 6 years

General. Founded in 1908. Regionally accredited. Off-campus sites in Amarillo, Lubbock, San Antonio, Wichita Falls, Alaska, Arizona, Hawaii, Oklahoma, New Mexico. **Degrees:** 1,156 bachelor's, 185 associate awarded; master's offered. **ROTC:** Army, Air Force. **Location:** 50 miles from Lubbock, 70 miles from Amarillo. **Calendar:** Semester, limited summer session. **Full-time faculty:** 154 total; 79% have terminal degrees, 15% minority, 36% women. **Part-time faculty:** 423 total; 36% have terminal degrees, 11% minority, 40% women. **Class size:** 86% < 20, 13% 20-39, less than 1% 40-49, less than 1% 50-99. **Special facilities:** Museum of the Llano Estacado.

Freshman class profile. 550 applied, 544 admitted, 314 enrolled.

Mid 50% test scores			
SAT critical reading:	390-490	GPA 2.0-2.99:	30%
SAT math:	400-520	Rank in top quarter:	26%
SAT writing:	370-470	Rank in top tenth:	10%
ACT composite:	16-23	Out-of-state:	12%
GPA 3.75 or higher:	23%	Live on campus:	71%
GPA 3.50-3.74:	15%	International:	3%
GPA 3.0-3.49:	30%	Fraternities:	2%
		Sororities:	1%

Basis for selection. Regular freshman admission based on combination of class rank and on either the ACT composite or SAT score. Interview, audition recommended for music and theater. **Learning Disabled:** Students must provide documentation of their particular disability.

High school preparation. 9 units required. Required and recommended units include English 3, mathematics 2-3, social studies 2 and science 2-3.

2015-2016 Annual costs. Tuition/fees: $16,830. Room/board: $5,952. Books/supplies: $1,650. Personal expenses: $2,190.

2015-2016 Financial aid. Need-based: 228 full-time freshmen applied for aid; 207 deemed to have need; 188 received aid. Average need met was 56%. Average scholarship/grant was $10,962; average loan $3,487. 42% of total undergraduate aid awarded as scholarships/grants, 58% as loans/jobs. **Non-need-based:** Awarded to 335 full-time undergraduates, including 67 freshmen. Scholarships awarded for academics, art, athletics, leadership, music/drama, religious affiliation, state residency.

Application procedures. Admission: Priority date 8/1; no deadline. $35 fee. Admission notification on a rolling basis beginning on or about 3/1. **Financial aid:** No deadline. FAFSA, institutional form required. Applicants notified on a rolling basis starting 2/1; must reply within 2 week(s) of notification.

Academics. Special study options: Accelerated study, combined bachelor's/graduate degree, distance learning, double major, dual enrollment of high school students, external degree, honors, internships, study abroad, teacher certification program. **Credit/placement by examination:** AP, CLEP, IB, SAT, ACT, institutional tests. 30 credit hours maximum toward bachelor's degree. **Support services:** Learning center, reduced course load, remedial instruction, study skills assistance, tutoring, writing center.

Majors. Biology: General, molecular. **Business:** Business admin. **Communications:** Communications/speech/rhetoric, media studies. **Computer sciences:** Computer science. **Conservation:** Environmental science, environmental studies. **Education:** Business, early childhood, elementary, English, middle, multi-level teacher, music, physical, science, social studies, technology/industrial arts, trade/industrial. **English:** English lit. **Foreign languages:** Spanish. **Health services:** Nursing (RN). **History:** General. **Math:** General. **Parks/recreation:** Facilities management, health/fitness, sports admin. **Philosophy/religion:** Christian. **Physical sciences:** Chemistry, geology. **Protective services:** Law enforcement admin. **Psychology:** General. **Social sciences:** Sociology, U.S. government. **Theology:** Missionary, religious ed, sacred music. **Visual/performing arts:** Art, dramatic, graphic design, music, music performance, musical theater, studio arts.

Most popular majors. Business/marketing 38%, health sciences 8%, liberal arts 27%, public administration/social services 6%, security/protective services 8%.

Technology on campus. 272 workstations in library, computer center. Dormitories wired for high-speed internet access and linked to campus network. Commuter students can connect to campus network. Online library, helpline, wireless network available.

Student life. Freshman orientation: Mandatory, $15 fee. Preregistration for classes offered. Entry seminar course designed to help students succeed academically, socially, and spiritually. Taken during initial term of enrollment. **Policies:** Religious observance required. **Housing:** Guaranteed on-campus for freshmen. Single-sex dorms, apartments available. $100 fully refundable deposit, deadline 4/9. **Activities:** Bands, campus ministries, choral groups, dance, drama, music ensembles, musical theater, radio station, student government, student newspaper, TV station, Over 20 religious, service, and special interest organizations available.

Athletics. NAIA. **Intercollegiate:** Baseball M, basketball, cheerleading, cross-country, football (tackle) M, golf, soccer, swimming, track and field, volleyball, wrestling. **Intramural:** Basketball, football (non-tackle), softball, volleyball W. **Team name:** Pioneers, Flying Queens.

Student services. Chaplain/spiritual director, career counseling, student employment services, financial aid counseling, health services, personal counseling, placement for graduates.

Contact. E-mail: admityou@wbu.edu
Phone: (806) 291-3500 Toll-free number: (800) 588-1928
Fax: (806) 291-1960
Debbie Stennett, Director of Admissions, Wayland Baptist University, 1900 West Seventh Street, CMB #1294, Plainview, TX 79072

West Coast University: Dallas
Dallas, Texas
www.westcoastuniversity.edu   **CB code: 7979**

- For-profit 4-year branch campus and nursing college
- Commuter campus in very large city
- 428 undergraduates
- Interview required

General. Regionally accredited. **Degrees:** 137 bachelor's awarded. **Calendar:** Semester. **Full-time faculty:** 7 total. **Part-time faculty:** 19 total. **Class size:** 81% < 20, 19% 20-39. **Special facilities:** Simulation labs.

Basis for selection. Open admission, but selective for some programs. **Home schooled:** Evidence that the home school meets state requirements.

Financial aid. Non-need-based: Scholarships awarded for academics.

Application procedures. Admission: No deadline. No application fee. Application must be submitted on paper. **Financial aid:** Closing date 6/30. FAFSA, institutional form required. Applicants notified on a rolling basis.

Academics. Special study options: Accelerated study, distance learning, internships, study abroad, weekend college. **Credit/placement by examination:** AP, CLEP, institutional tests. May challenge test-out of 12 semester credits, maximum. Must achieve score of 75% or higher, one attempt only. Must be taken before enrolling in the course in which equivalency is sought. **Support services:** Study skills assistance, tutoring.

Majors. Health services: Nursing (RN).

Technology on campus. 129 workstations in library, computer center. Commuter students can connect to campus network. Online library, helpline, wireless network available.

Student life. Freshman orientation: Mandatory. Preregistration for classes offered. **Activities:** Student government.

Student services. Adult student services, career counseling, services for economically disadvantaged, student employment services, financial aid counseling, placement for graduates.

Contact. Phone: (214) 453-4207 ext. 46207 Fax: (214) 453-4534
Shamir Patel, Director of Admissions, West Coast University: Dallas, 8435 North Stemmons Freeway, Dallas, TX 75247

West Texas A&M University
Canyon, Texas   **CB member**
www.wtamu.edu   **CB code: 6938**

- Public 4-year university
- Commuter campus in large town
- 7,253 degree-seeking undergraduates: 22% part-time, 55% women, 6% African American, 1% Asian American, 27% Hispanic/Latino, 1% Native American, 2% Multi-racial, non-Hispanic, 2% international
- 2,153 degree-seeking graduate students
- 67% of applicants admitted
- SAT or ACT (ACT writing optional) required
- 43% graduate within 6 years

General. Founded in 1909. Regionally accredited. **Degrees:** 1,423 bachelor's awarded; master's, doctoral offered. **Location:** 17 miles from Amarillo. **Calendar:** Semester, limited summer session. **Full-time faculty:** 317 total; 72% have terminal degrees, 15% minority, 45% women. **Part-time faculty:** 107 total; 10% have terminal degrees, 8% minority, 50% women. **Class size:** 30% < 20, 50% 20-39, 9% 40-49, 10% 50-99, less than 1% >100. **Special facilities:** 24,000-acre farm and ranch, alternative energy institute, historical museum, event center.

Freshman class profile. 5,557 applied, 3,717 admitted, 1,425 enrolled.

Mid 50% test scores			
SAT critical reading:	420-540	Rank in top tenth:	14%
SAT math:	440-540	End year in good standing:	67%
ACT composite:	18-23	Return as sophomores:	64%
GPA 3.75 or higher:	27%	Out-of-state:	10%
GPA 3.50-3.74:	21%	Live on campus:	83%
GPA 3.0-3.49:	36%	International:	1%
GPA 2.0-2.99:	16%	Fraternities:	7%
Rank in top quarter:	39%	Sororities:	12%

Basis for selection. Freshman applicants must be in top half of graduating class, have minimum 950 SAT (exclusive of Writing) or 20 ACT, or attend a summer provisional term. Texas Success Initiative Testing required of all incoming students before entrance. Audition required for music program; portfolio recommended for art, theater programs.

High school preparation. College-preparatory program required. 26 units required. Required units include English 4, mathematics 4, social studies 4, science 4, foreign language 2, visual/performing arts 1 and academic electives 6. Physical education 1, speech .5.

2016-2017 Annual costs. Tuition/fees (projected): $7,936; $8,959 out-of-state. Books/supplies: $1,000. Personal expenses: $2,150.

2014-2015 Financial aid. **Need-based:** 1,101 full-time freshmen applied for aid; 906 deemed to have need; 906 received aid. Average need met was 61%. Average scholarship/grant was $6,584; average loan $3,209. 45% of total undergraduate aid awarded as scholarships/grants, 55% as loans/jobs. **Non-need-based:** Awarded to 2,298 full-time undergraduates, including 673 freshmen. Scholarships awarded for academics, art, athletics, leadership, music/drama. **Additional information:** Scholarship deadline February 1.

Application procedures. **Admission:** Priority date 8/1; no deadline. $40 fee, may be waived for applicants with need. Admission notification on a rolling basis beginning on or about 9/1. No reply required. **Financial aid:** Priority date 4/15; no closing date. FAFSA required. Applicants notified on a rolling basis starting 3/1; must reply within 2 week(s) of notification.

Academics. **Special study options:** Accelerated study, combined bachelor's/graduate degree, cooperative education, distance learning, double major, ESL, honors, independent study, internships, liberal arts/career combination, study abroad, teacher certification program, Washington semester. **Credit/placement by examination:** AP, CLEP, IB, institutional tests. Only 6 of a student's last 30 hours can come from CLEP. **Support services:** Learning center, remedial instruction, study skills assistance, tutoring, writing center.

Honors college/program. High school graduates must have minimum 26 ACT Composite score, or minimum 1200 SAT score (Math and Critical Reading). Current WTAMU students or community college transfers must have cumulative GPA of 3.5 or greater on 18 or more college/university hours (excluding dual credit hours).

Majors. Biology: General, biotechnology, wildlife. **Business:** General, accounting, business admin, finance, management information systems, managerial economics, marketing. **Communications:** Advertising, broadcast journalism, communications/speech/rhetoric, journalism. **Computer sciences:** Computer science. **Conservation:** Environmental science. **Engineering:** Civil, environmental, mechanical. **English:** English lit. **Foreign languages:** Spanish. **Health services:** Athletic training, communication disorders, music therapy, nursing (RN). **History:** General. **Human services:** General, social work. **Math:** General. **Parks/recreation:** Exercise sciences. **Physical sciences:** Chemistry, geology, physics. **Protective services:** Criminal justice. **Psychology:** General. **Social sciences:** General, political science, sociology. **Visual/performing arts:** Art, dance, dramatic, graphic design, music, music performance, music theory/composition, musical theater, studio arts.

Most popular majors. Agriculture 9%, business/marketing 15%, health sciences 11%, interdisciplinary studies 12%, liberal arts 10%, public administration/social services 6%.

Technology on campus. 1,800 workstations in dormitories, library, computer center, student center. Dormitories wired for high-speed internet access and linked to campus network. Commuter students can connect to campus network. Online course registration, online library, helpline, student web hosting, wireless network available.

Student life. Freshman orientation: Available, $50 fee. Preregistration for classes offered. Two day summer orientation and preregistration and 3-day orientation before school starts. **Policies:** Students with fewer than 60 semester hours accumulated, enrolled in 9 or more semester hours, and under 21 on first day of class each semester required to live in university residence halls. **Housing:** Guaranteed on-campus for all undergraduates. Coed dorms, single-sex dorms, special housing for disabled, fraternity/sorority housing available. $150 fully refundable deposit, deadline 6/1. Honors hall available. **Activities:** Bands, campus ministries, choral groups, dance, drama, international student organizations, literary magazine, music ensembles, musical theater, opera, radio station, student government, student newspaper, symphony orchestra, TV station, Chinese student association, Hispanic association, agriculture organizations, Students in Free Enterprise, pre-professional organizations, Black students association, College Republicans, Catholic student association.

Athletics. NCAA. **Intercollegiate:** Baseball M, basketball, cross-country, equestrian W, football (tackle) M, golf, soccer, softball W, volleyball W. **Intramural:** Archery, badminton, basketball, bowling, football (non-tackle),

golf, racquetball, rodeo, soccer, softball, swimming, table tennis, tennis, volleyball. **Team name:** Buffaloes.

Student services. Alcohol/substance abuse counseling, career counseling, services for economically disadvantaged, student employment services, financial aid counseling, health services, on-campus daycare, personal counseling, placement for graduates, veterans' counselor. **Physically disabled:** Services for visually, speech, hearing impaired.

Contact. E-mail: admissions@wtamu.edu
Phone: (806) 651-2020 Toll-free number: (800) 999-8268
Fax: (806) 651-5268
Kyle Moore, Director of Admissions, West Texas A&M University, WTAMU Box 60907, Canyon, TX 79016-0001

Wiley College
Marshall, Texas
www.wileyc.edu

CB member
CB code: 6940

- Private 4-year liberal arts college affiliated with the United Methodist Church
- Residential campus in large town
- 1,172 degree-seeking undergraduates: 6% part-time, 59% women, 83% African American, 1% Native American, 10% international

General. Founded in 1873. Regionally accredited. **Degrees:** 186 bachelor's awarded. **Location:** 40 miles from Shreveport, Louisiana, 150 miles from Dallas. **Calendar:** Semester, extensive summer session. **Full-time faculty:** 52 total; 62% have terminal degrees, 46% minority, 46% women. **Part-time faculty:** 29 total; 14% have terminal degrees, 69% minority, 34% women. **Class size:** 60% < 20, 35% 20-39, 3% 40-49, 2% 50-99. **Special facilities:** Nature trail.

Freshman class profile. 1,777 applied, 793 admitted, 153 enrolled.

GPA 3.75 or higher:	2%	Rank in top tenth:	3%
GPA 3.50-3.74:	2%	Return as sophomores:	54%
GPA 3.0-3.49:	36%	Out-of-state:	36%
GPA 2.0-2.99:	52%	Live on campus:	90%
Rank in top quarter:	15%	International:	5%

Basis for selection. Open admission, but selective for some programs.

High school preparation. 16 units recommended. Recommended units include English 4, mathematics 2, social studies 2, science 2 and academic electives 6.

2016-2017 Annual costs. Tuition/fees (projected): $11,828. Room/board: $7,052. Books/supplies: $1,500. Personal expenses: $1,012.

2014-2015 Financial aid. **Need-based:** 204 full-time freshmen applied for aid; 198 deemed to have need; 194 received aid. Average need met was 57%. Average scholarship/grant was $8,970; average loan $3,090. 58% of total undergraduate aid awarded as scholarships/grants, 42% as loans/jobs. **Non-need-based:** Awarded to 169 full-time undergraduates, including 51 freshmen.

Application procedures. **Admission:** No deadline. $25 fee, may be waived for applicants with need. Application must be submitted on paper. Admission notification on a rolling basis. $50 application fee for non-traditional students. **Financial aid:** Priority date 4/15, closing date 4/15. FAFSA, institutional form required. Applicants notified on a rolling basis.

Academics. **Special study options:** Accelerated study, cross-registration, distance learning, double major, dual enrollment of high school students, honors, independent study, internships, liberal arts/career combination, study abroad, teacher certification program. **Credit/placement by examination:** AP, CLEP, institutional tests. **Support services:** Learning center, reduced course load, remedial instruction, study skills assistance, tutoring.

Majors. Biology: General. **Business:** Accounting, business admin, hospitality admin, nonprofit/public, operations. **Communications:** Journalism. **Computer sciences:** Computer science. **Education:** Elementary, physical, secondary. **English:** English lit. **History:** General. **Math:** General. **Philosophy/religion:** Religion. **Physical sciences:** Chemistry. **Protective services:** Law enforcement admin. **Social sciences:** Sociology. **Visual/performing arts:** Music.

Most popular majors. Business/marketing 27%, communications/journalism 6%, interdisciplinary studies 25%, security/protective services 21%.

Technology on campus. 177 workstations in dormitories, library, computer center. Dormitories wired for high-speed internet access and linked to campus network. Commuter students can connect to campus network. Online course registration, online library, helpline, wireless network available.

Student life. **Freshman orientation:** Mandatory, $30 fee. Preregistration for classes offered. **Policies:** Student residential halls are smoke-free, drug-free, and weapon-free. Religious observance required. **Housing:** Coed dorms, single-sex dorms available. $50 deposit. **Activities:** Jazz band, campus ministries, choral groups, international student organizations, music ensembles, radio station, student government, student newspaper, national service fraternity, interdenominational student movement, religion majors club.

Athletics. NAIA. **Intercollegiate:** Baseball M, basketball, cross-country, soccer, softball W, track and field, volleyball W. **Intramural:** Baseball M, basketball, cheerleading, softball, table tennis, tennis, track and field, volleyball, weight lifting M. **Team name:** Wildcats.

Student services. Adult student services, chaplain/spiritual director, career counseling, services for economically disadvantaged, student employment services, financial aid counseling, health services, personal counseling, placement for graduates, veterans' counselor.

Contact. E-mail: admissions@wileyc.edu
Phone: (903) 927-3311 Toll-free number: (800) 658-6889
Fax: (903) 927-3366
Jamecia Murray, Director of Admissions, Wiley College, 711 Wiley Avenue, Marshall, TX 75670

Utah

Argosy University: Salt Lake City
Draper, Utah
www.argosy.edu
CB code: 6238

- For-profit 4-year university
- Commuter campus in small city
- 97 degree-seeking undergraduates: 71% part-time, 71% women
- 137 graduate students

General. Degrees: 22 bachelor's, 9 associate awarded; master's, doctoral offered. **Calendar:** Differs by program. **Full-time faculty:** 3 total. **Part-time faculty:** 58 total.

Basis for selection. Open admission.

2015-2016 Annual costs. Tuition/fees: $16,842. **Additional information:** Tuition indicated is for programs in the College of Arts and Sciences. College of Health Sciences programs are $575 per-credit-hour.

Application procedures. Admission: Closing date 9/12. $50 fee. **Financial aid:** No deadline.

Academics. Credit/placement by examination: AP, CLEP.

Majors. Business: Business admin. **Liberal arts:** Arts/sciences. **Protective services:** Law enforcement admin. **Psychology:** General.

Contact. Phone: (601) 601-5000 Toll-free number: (888) 639-4756 Todd Harrison, Senior Director of Admissions, Argosy University: Salt Lake City, 121 Election Road, Suite 300, Draper, UT 84020

Brigham Young University
Provo, Utah
CB member
www.byu.edu
CB code: 4019

- Private 4-year university affiliated with the Church of Jesus Christ of Latter-day Saints
- Residential campus in small city
- 30,221 degree-seeking undergraduates: 10% part-time, 48% women, 2% Asian American, 6% Hispanic/Latino, 1% Native Hawaiian/Pacific islander, 4% Multi-racial, non-Hispanic, 3% international
- 3,248 degree-seeking graduate students
- SAT or ACT (ACT writing recommended); application essay, interview required
- 80% graduate within 6 years

General. Founded in 1875. Regionally accredited. Additional educational center in Salt Lake City. **Degrees:** 6,653 bachelor's awarded; master's, professional, doctoral offered. **ROTC:** Army, Air Force. **Location:** 45 miles from Salt Lake City. **Calendar:** Semester, limited summer session. **Full-time faculty:** 1,252 total; 92% have terminal degrees, 5% minority, 21% women. **Part-time faculty:** 514 total; 31% have terminal degrees, 8% minority, 62% women. **Class size:** 56% < 20, 26% 20-39, 4% 40-49, 6% 50-99, 9% >100. **Special facilities:** Aquatic ecology laboratory, science and anthropological museums, veterinary pathology laboratory, fine arts museum, reading and writing laboratories, math and language computer laboratories, supercomputer.

Freshman class profile.

GPA 3.75 or higher:	73%	Return as sophomores:	86%
GPA 3.50-3.74:	18%	Out-of-state:	65%
GPA 3.0-3.49:	9%	Live on campus:	79%
Rank in top quarter:	87%	International:	2%
Rank in top tenth:	55%		

Basis for selection. GED not accepted. School achievement record, test scores, endorsements and recommendations important. Students must maintain ideals and standards in harmony with The Church of Jesus Christ of Latter-Day Saints. Interview is ecclesiastical. **Learning Disabled:** Untimed ACT accepted.

High school preparation. College-preparatory program recommended. Recommended units include English 4, mathematics 4, history 2, science 3 and foreign language 2. 2 units of literature/writing required.

2015-2016 Annual costs. Tuition/fees: $5,150. Room/board: $7,330. Books/supplies: $992. Personal expenses: $1,924.

2014-2015 Financial aid. Need-based: 1,993 full-time freshmen applied for aid; 1,268 deemed to have need; 1,152 received aid. Average need met was 30%. Average scholarship/grant was $4,908; average loan $3,241. 76% of total undergraduate aid awarded as scholarships/grants, 24% as loans/jobs. **Non-need-based:** Awarded to 11,566 full-time undergraduates, including 2,420 freshmen. Scholarships awarded for academics, art, athletics, leadership, minority status, music/drama, religious affiliation, ROTC, state residency. **Additional information:** Students notified of scholarships on or about 4/20.

Application procedures. Admission: Priority date 12/1; deadline 2/1 (receipt date). $35 fee. Admission notification by 2/28. Admission notification on a rolling basis. Must reply by 5/1. **Financial aid:** Priority date 4/15; no closing date. FAFSA required. Applicants notified on a rolling basis starting 4/1.

Academics. Special study options: Accelerated study, combined bachelor's/graduate degree, cooperative education, cross-registration, distance learning, double major, ESL, external degree, honors, independent study, internships, liberal arts/career combination, study abroad, teacher certification program, Washington semester. **Credit/placement by examination:** AP, CLEP, IB, SAT, ACT, institutional tests. **Support services:** Learning center, pre-admission summer program, reduced course load, remedial instruction, study skills assistance, tutoring, writing center.

Majors. Area/ethnic studies: American, Asian, European, French, German, Latin American, Russian/Eastern European/Eurasian. **Biology:** Biochemistry, bioinformatics, biophysics, biostatistics, biotechnology, conservation, exercise physiology, microbiology, molecular, neuroscience, physiology, wildlife. **Business:** General, accounting, actuarial science, business admin, construction management, entrepreneurial studies, finance, information resources management, logistics, management information systems, managerial economics, marketing, organizational behavior, statistics. **Communications:** Advertising, journalism, public relations. **Communications technology:** Animation/special effects, recording arts. **Computer sciences:** Computer graphics, computer science, information technology. **Conservation:** Environmental science. **Education:** Biology, chemistry, drama/dance, early childhood, elementary, English, family/consumer sciences, French, German, health, history, Latin, mathematics, music, physical, physics, science, social science, Spanish, special ed. **Engineering:** Chemical, civil, computer, electrical, manufacturing, mechanical. **English:** English lit. **Foreign languages:** General, ancient Greek, Arabic, Biblical, Chinese, classics, comparative lit, French, German, Germanic, Japanese, Korean, Latin, linguistics, Portuguese, Russian, Spanish, translation. **Health services:** Athletic training, audiology/speech pathology, clinical lab science, dietetics, nursing (RN), recreational therapy. **History:** General. **Liberal arts:** Humanities. **Math:** General, statistics. **Parks/recreation:** General, health/fitness. **Philosophy/religion:** Philosophy. **Physical sciences:** Astronomy, chemistry, geology, hydrology, physics. **Psychology:** General. **Social sciences:** Anthropology, archaeology, economics, geography, GIS/cartography, international relations, political science, sociology. **Visual/performing arts:** Acting, art, art history/conservation, ballet, dance, design, dramatic, film/cinema/video, graphic design, illustration, industrial design, jazz, music, music history, music performance, music theory/composition, musical theater, photography, piano/keyboard, stringed instruments, studio arts, theater history, voice/opera. **Work/family studies:** General, facilities/event planning, family studies, family systems.

Most popular majors. Biology 12%, business/marketing 12%, education 8%, engineering/engineering technologies 7%, foreign language 6%, health sciences 9%, social sciences 8%, visual/performing arts 6%.

Technology on campus. 2,000 workstations in dormitories, library, computer center, student center. Dormitories wired for high-speed internet access and linked to campus network. Commuter students can connect to campus network. Online course registration, online library, helpline, repair service, student web hosting, wireless network available.

Student life. Freshman orientation: Available. Preregistration for classes offered. **Policies:** Honor code enforced. Religious observance required. **Housing:** Single-sex dorms, special housing for disabled, apartments available. $150 partly refundable deposit. Foreign language houses available. **Activities:** Bands, choral groups, dance, drama, film society, literary magazine, music ensembles, musical theater, opera, radio station, student government, student newspaper, symphony orchestra, TV station, College Republicans, College Democrats, African American club, black student union, Latin American student association, Intercollegiate Knights, Circle-K International, Southeast Asian club, Baptist student union.

Athletics. NCAA. **Intercollegiate:** Baseball M, basketball, cheerleading, cross-country, diving, football (tackle) M, golf, gymnastics W, soccer W, softball W, swimming, tennis, track and field, volleyball. **Intramural:** Badminton, basketball, football (non-tackle), football (tackle), golf, racquetball, soccer, softball, tennis, volleyball, water polo, wrestling M. **Team name:** Cougars.

Student services. Chaplain/spiritual director, career counseling, services for economically disadvantaged, student employment services, financial aid counseling, health services, minority student services, personal counseling, placement for graduates, veterans' counselor, women's services. **Physically disabled:** Services for visually, speech, hearing impaired.

Contact. E-mail: admissions@byu.edu
Phone: (801) 422-2507 Fax: (801) 422-0005
Tom Gourley, Director of Admissions, Brigham Young University, A-153 ASB, Provo, UT 84602

Broadview University: Orem
Orem, Utah
www.broadviewuniversity.edu

▶ For-profit 4-year university and career college
▶ Commuter campus in small city
▶ 124 undergraduates
▶ Interview required

General. Regionally accredited; also accredited by ACICS. **Degrees:** 5 bachelor's, 34 associate awarded. **Calendar:** Quarter, extensive summer session.

Basis for selection. Open admission.

2015-2016 Annual costs. Tuition/fees: $18,027. Books/supplies: $1,260. **Additional information:** Per-credit-hour charge for 1-11 hours, $435; for 12-16 hours, $375. Course fees: $100 to $650 per course.

Application procedures. Admission: No deadline. $50 fee. Admission notification on a rolling basis. **Financial aid:** No deadline. FAFSA, institutional form required. Applicants notified on a rolling basis starting 7/1; must reply within 2 week(s) of notification.

Academics. Special study options: Distance learning, independent study, internships, liberal arts/career combination. **Credit/placement by examination:** AP, CLEP. **Support services:** Remedial instruction, study skills assistance, tutoring, writing center.

Majors. Business: Business admin. **Computer sciences:** Information technology. **Health services:** Health care admin. **Protective services:** Law enforcement admin.

Technology on campus. 60 workstations in library, computer center, student center. Commuter students can connect to campus network. Online library, helpline, student web hosting, wireless network available.

Student life. Freshman orientation: Mandatory. Preregistration for classes offered. Day and evening sessions available the week prior to classes starting. **Activities:** Literary magazine.

Student services. Career counseling, student employment services, financial aid counseling, placement for graduates.

Contact. Phone: (801) 822-5800 Toll-free number: (877) 822-5838
Rachel Chapman, Associate Director of Admissions, Broadview University: Orem, 898 North 1200 West, Orem, UT 84057

Dixie State University
St George, Utah
www.dixie.edu   CB code: 4283

▶ Public 4-year university
▶ Commuter campus in small city
▶ 7,208 degree-seeking undergraduates: 27% part-time, 53% women, 3% African American, 1% Asian American, 11% Hispanic/Latino, 1% Native American, 1% Native Hawaiian/Pacific islander, 3% Multi-racial, non-Hispanic, 3% international

General. Founded in 1911. Regionally accredited. **Degrees:** 612 bachelor's, 1,013 associate awarded. **ROTC:** Army. **Location:** 305 miles from Salt Lake City, 121 miles from Las Vegas. **Calendar:** Semester, limited summer session. **Full-time faculty:** 211 total; 69% have terminal degrees, 10% minority, 42% women. **Part-time faculty:** 371 total; 17% have terminal degrees,

3% minority, 50% women. **Class size:** 45% < 20, 45% 20-39, 8% 40-49, 2% 50-99. **Special facilities:** Beach volleyball field.

Freshman class profile. 4,041 applied, 4,041 admitted, 1,700 enrolled.

Mid 50% test scores			
SAT critical reading:	410-500	GPA 3.0-3.49:	28%
SAT math:	410-510	GPA 2.0-2.99:	27%
SAT writing:	390-480	Rank in top quarter:	28%
ACT composite:	17-23	Rank in top tenth:	10%
GPA 3.75 or higher:	26%	Return as sophomores:	58%
GPA 3.50-3.74:	17%	Out-of-state:	25%
		International:	2%

Basis for selection. Open admission, but selective for some programs. Some health occupation programs have prerequisites. Applicants for bachelor's degrees in elementary education, business administration, and nursing must have associate degree or advance standing. **Home schooled:** Letter of recommendation (nonparent) required. Copy of formal letter of release from high school counselor or secondary school district that states student is no longer required to attend secondary school required. Statement from student certifying that they have completed the equivalent of a high school diploma required.

High school preparation. College-preparatory program recommended. 16 units recommended. Recommended units include English 4, mathematics 4, history 3, science 2 (laboratory 1) and foreign language 2. One computer literacy unit recommended.

2015-2016 Annual costs. Tuition/fees: $4,620; $13,206 out-of-state. Room/board: $6,098. Books/supplies: $900. Personal expenses: $5,048.

2015-2016 Financial aid. Need-based: 1,009 full-time freshmen applied for aid; 862 deemed to have need; 862 received aid. Average need met was 38%. Average scholarship/grant was $6,195; average loan $3,408. 37% of total undergraduate aid awarded as scholarships/grants, 63% as loans/jobs. **Non-need-based:** Awarded to 397 full-time undergraduates, including 152 freshmen. Scholarships awarded for academics, alumni affiliation, art, athletics, job skills, leadership, minority status, music/drama, state residency.

Application procedures. Admission: Closing date 8/15 (receipt date). $35 fee. Admission notification on a rolling basis. Students who have received approval for early release from high school must provide copy of formal letter or release from high school counselor, as well as written authorization from parent or legal guardian and demonstrate college readiness by submitting ACT, SAT, or Accuplacer equivalent to the following ACT minimums for early enrollment students: Reading 17, English 19, Math 18. **Financial aid:** Priority date 5/1, closing date 6/30. FAFSA required. Applicants notified on a rolling basis starting 3/1.

Academics. Bachelor's and master's degree course work from Utah's 4-year universities presented over distance-learning media and on-campus instruction. Four-year programs in accounting, biology, business administration, computer technology, communication, elementary education, English, nursing, dental hygiene, integrated studies, mathematics, music, psychology, and theater offered on campus. **Special study options:** Accelerated study, cooperative education, distance learning, double major, dual enrollment of high school students, ESL, honors, independent study, internships, student-designed major, study abroad, teacher certification program, weekend college. **Credit/placement by examination:** AP, CLEP, SAT, ACT. 30 credit hours maximum toward associate degree, 30 toward bachelor's. **Support services:** Learning center, remedial instruction, study skills assistance, tutoring, writing center.

Majors. Biology: General. **Business:** General, accounting, finance, management information systems, marketing, operations. **Communications:** Digital media, media studies, organizational. **Computer sciences:** Computer graphics, computer science, information technology. **Education:** Art, biology, elementary, English, mathematics, music, science. **English:** General lit, technical writing. **Foreign languages:** Spanish. **Health services:** Dental hygiene, nursing (RN). **History:** General. **Math:** General. **Psychology:** General. **Social sciences:** Criminology. **Visual/performing arts:** Ceramics, cinematography, drawing, graphic design, interior design, music, painting, photography, sculpture, theater design.

Most popular majors. Biology 7%, business/marketing 20%, communications/journalism 16%, computer/information sciences 6%, education 9%, health sciences 10%, interdisciplinary studies 8%, psychology 7%, visual/performing arts 6%.

Technology on campus. 400 workstations in dormitories, library, computer center, student center. Dormitories wired for high-speed internet access and linked to campus network. Commuter students can connect to campus network. Online course registration, online library, helpline, repair service, wireless network available.

Student life. Freshman orientation: Mandatory. Preregistration for classes offered. All-day sessions offered on Mondays and Tuesdays June-August. **Policies:** Stringent drug and alcohol policies. **Housing:** Coed dorms, single-sex dorms, apartments, wellness housing available. $75 fully refundable deposit. **Activities:** Bands, campus ministries, choral groups, dance, drama, international student organizations, literary magazine, music ensembles, Model UN, musical theater, radio station, student government, student newspaper, symphony orchestra, TV station, Native American student association, Polynesian cultural club, black student association, Hispanic student association, diversity club, Latter-Day Saints student association, campus Christian connection, Phi Beta Lambda, College Democrats, College Republicans.

Athletics. NCAA. **Intercollegiate:** Baseball M, basketball, cross-country, football (tackle) M, golf, soccer, softball W, tennis W, volleyball W. **Intramural:** Basketball, football (non-tackle), table tennis, tennis. **Team name:** Red Storm.

Student services. Adult student services, alcohol/substance abuse counseling, career counseling, services for economically disadvantaged, student employment services, financial aid counseling, health services, minority student services, personal counseling, placement for graduates, veterans' counselor. **Physically disabled:** Services for visually, speech, hearing impaired.

Contact. E-mail: admissions@dixie.edu
Phone: (435) 652-7777 Fax: (435) 656-4015
Laralee Davenport, Assistant Director of Admissions, Dixie State University, 225 South 700 East, St. George, UT 84770-3876

Independence University
Murray, Utah
www.independence.edu

- For-profit 4-year business and health science college
- Commuter campus in very large city
- 1,280 undergraduates

General. Founded in 1975. Regionally accredited; also accredited by ACCSC. Primarily serves home-study students. **Degrees:** 105 bachelor's, 199 associate awarded; master's offered. **Calendar:** Differs by program. **Full-time faculty:** 10 total. **Part-time faculty:** 100 total.

Basis for selection. Open admission.

2015-2016 Annual costs. Diploma programs: $15,042-$19,447. Associate programs: $34,390-$51,188. Bachelor's programs: $55,800-$81,719. Additional $4,000 fee for Workshop courses and any pre-requisites.

Financial aid. All financial aid based on need. **Additional information:** Financial aid available for resident students only, not correspondence students.

Application procedures. Admission: No deadline. No application fee. Admission notification on a rolling basis. **Financial aid:** Closing date 7/23. FAFSA required. Applicants notified on a rolling basis.

Academics. Special study options: Distance learning, liberal arts/career combination. **Credit/placement by examination:** AP, CLEP. 30 credit hours maximum toward associate degree, 30 toward bachelor's. **Support services:** Tutoring.

Majors. Business: General. **Health services:** Health care admin.

Most popular majors. Business/marketing 11%, health sciences 89%.

Student life. Freshman orientation: Available. Preregistration for classes offered. **Activities:** Student newspaper.

Contact. E-mail: admissions@independence.edu
Toll-free number: (800) 972-5149
Jeannie Carr, Director of Admissions, Independence University, 4021 South 700 East, Suite 400, Murray, UT 84107

ITT Technical Institute: Murray
Murray, Utah
www.itt-tech.edu   CB code: 3601

- For-profit 4-year technical college
- Commuter campus in small city
- 471 undergraduates
- Interview required

General. Founded in 1984. Accredited by ACICS. **Degrees:** 64 bachelor's, 138 associate awarded. **Location:** 10 miles from Salt Lake City. **Calendar:**

Quarter, extensive summer session. **Full-time faculty:** 8 total. **Part-time faculty:** 55 total.

Basis for selection. Satisfactory scores from on-site tests in English and math required.

2015-2016 Annual costs. Per-credit-hour charge, $493, will vary depending on program level and course of study. Academic fee, $200. Some programs require purchase of tools, which could cost an additional $100 to $500. All costs subject to change.

Application procedures. Admission: No deadline. No application fee. Admission notification on a rolling basis. **Financial aid:** No deadline. FAFSA, institutional form required. Applicants notified on a rolling basis.

Academics. Credit/placement by examination: AP, CLEP. **Support services:** Learning center, tutoring.

Majors. Business: Business admin, construction management, project management. **Communications technology:** Animation/special effects. **Computer sciences:** Security. **Protective services:** Law enforcement admin. **Visual/performing arts:** Graphic design.

Most popular majors. Business/marketing 21%, computer/information sciences 44%, engineering/engineering technologies 14%, security/protective services 17%.

Technology on campus. Online library available.

Student life. Freshman orientation: Available. Preregistration for classes offered.

Student services. Career counseling, student employment services, placement for graduates.

Contact. Phone: (801) 263-3313 Toll-free number: (800) 365-2136 Fax: (801) 263-3497
Gary Wood, Director of Recruitment, ITT Technical Institute: Murray, 920 West LeVoy Drive, Murray, UT 84123

Neumont University
Salt Lake City, Utah
www.neumont.edu   CB code: 4516

- For-profit 4-year engineering and technical college
- Residential campus in very large city
- 429 degree-seeking undergraduates: 10% women
- 83% of applicants admitted
- Application essay required

General. Regionally accredited; also accredited by ACICS. **Degrees:** 86 bachelor's awarded. **Location:** Downtown. **Calendar:** Quarter, extensive summer session. **Full-time faculty:** 15 total; 13% have terminal degrees, 7% minority. **Part-time faculty:** 27 total; 7% have terminal degrees, 7% minority, 18% women. **Special facilities:** 3D printing lab, game lab, IS server lab, gaming bunker.

Freshman class profile. 727 applied, 603 admitted, 169 enrolled.

Mid 50% test scores		GPA 3.50-3.74:	15%
SAT critical reading:	450-620	GPA 3.0-3.49:	36%
SAT math:	460-640	GPA 2.0-2.99:	30%
SAT writing:	400-570	Return as sophomores:	85%
ACT composite:	20-29	Out-of-state:	87%
GPA 3.75 or higher:	17%	Live on campus:	90%

Basis for selection. GPA, standardized test scores, type of high school curriculum, number and type of higher-level courses in math and science, academic potential, involvement in extra-curricular or community activities, work ethic, and interest in the field of computer science important. SAT or ACT recommended. Application review session with Admissions Officer is highly recommended; may be conducted by phone or in-person. **Home schooled:** Transcript of courses and grades, state high school equivalency certificate required.

High school preparation. College-preparatory program recommended.

2016-2017 Annual costs. Tuition/fees: $24,450. Room only: $5,670. Books/supplies: $1,200.

2014-2015 Financial aid. Need-based: 75 full-time freshmen applied for aid; 75 deemed to have need; 75 received aid. Average need met was 14%. Average scholarship/grant was $2,719. 44% of total undergraduate aid awarded as scholarships/grants, 56% as loans/jobs. **Non-need-based:**

Awarded to 338 full-time undergraduates, including 120 freshmen. Scholarships awarded for academics, job skills, leadership, state residency.

Application procedures. Admission: No deadline. $35 fee, may be waived for applicants with need. Application must be submitted online. Admission notification on a rolling basis. **Financial aid:** Closing date 8/1. FAFSA, institutional form required. Applicants notified on a rolling basis.

Academics. Full bachelor's degree programs can be completed in 3 years through intense, year-round academic model. **Special study options:** Accelerated study, cooperative education, internships. **Credit/placement by examination:** AP, CLEP, IB, institutional tests. **Support services:** Remedial instruction, study skills assistance, tutoring, writing center.

Majors. Business: Management information systems. **Computer sciences:** Computer science, information technology, web page design, webmaster. **Visual/performing arts:** Game design.

Technology on campus. PC or laptop required. Dormitories wired for high-speed internet access and linked to campus network. Commuter students can connect to campus network. Online course registration, online library, helpline, repair service, student web hosting, wireless network available.

Student life. Freshman orientation: Mandatory. Preregistration for classes offered. **Housing:** Guaranteed on-campus for all undergraduates. Single-sex dorms, apartments available. $500 partly refundable deposit, deadline 8/1. **Activities:** Choral groups, student government.

Student services. Career counseling, financial aid counseling, personal counseling, placement for graduates.

Contact. E-mail: admissions@neumont.edu
Phone: (801) 302-2800 Toll-free number: (888) 638-6668
Fax: (801) 302-2880
Karick Heaton, Director of Enrollment, Neumont University, 143 South Main Street, Salt Lake City, UT 84111

Southern Utah University
Cedar City, Utah   **CB member**
www.suu.edu   **CB code: 4092**

♦ Public 4-year university
♦ Residential campus in large town
♦ 5,977 degree-seeking undergraduates: 10% part-time, 53% women, 2% African American, 1% Asian American, 6% Hispanic/Latino, 1% Native American, 1% Native Hawaiian/Pacific islander, 1% Multi-racial, non-Hispanic, 6% international
♦ 776 degree-seeking graduate students
♦ 72% of applicants admitted
♦ SAT or ACT (ACT writing optional) required
♦ 39% graduate within 6 years

General. Founded in 1897. Regionally accredited. **Degrees:** 928 bachelor's, 294 associate awarded; master's offered. **ROTC:** Army. **Location:** 265 miles from Salt Lake City, 160 miles from Las Vegas. **Calendar:** Semester, limited summer session. **Full-time faculty:** 308 total; 63% have terminal degrees, 6% minority, 33% women. **Part-time faculty:** 194 total; 25% have terminal degrees, 6% minority, 45% women. **Class size:** 42% < 20, 43% 20-39, 8% 40-49, 6% 50-99, 1% >100. **Special facilities:** Natural life museum, observatory, Shakespearean theater, fine arts gallery.

Freshman class profile. 8,387 applied, 6,050 admitted, 1,427 enrolled.

Mid 50% test scores			
SAT critical reading:	450-590	**GPA 2.0-2.99:**	12%
SAT math:	450-570	**Rank in top quarter:**	47%
SAT writing:	440-570	**Rank in top tenth:**	18%
ACT composite:	20-27	**Return as sophomores:**	64%
GPA 3.75 or higher:	41%	**Out-of-state:**	21%
GPA 3.50-3.74:	21%	**Live on campus:**	30%
GPA 3.0-3.49:	26%	**International:**	5%

Basis for selection. High school GPA, test scores most important. **Home schooled:** Transcript of courses and grades required.

High school preparation. College-preparatory program recommended. Recommended units include English 4, mathematics 4, social studies 3, science 3 (laboratory 1) and foreign language 2. 1 unit of social studies should be U.S. history and government; 2 math units should be elementary algebra or above; English units should have a composition and literature emphasis.

2015-2016 Annual costs. Tuition/fees: $6,300; $19,132 out-of-state. Room/board: $6,957.

2014-2015 Financial aid. Need-based: 889 full-time freshmen applied for aid; 730 deemed to have need; 728 received aid. Average need met was 61%. Average scholarship/grant was $4,310; average loan $3,111. 57% of total undergraduate aid awarded as scholarships/grants, 43% as loans/jobs. **Non-need-based:** Awarded to 1,810 full-time undergraduates, including 664 freshmen. Scholarships awarded for academics, alumni affiliation, art, athletics, job skills, leadership, minority status, music/drama, ROTC, state residency.

Application procedures. Admission: Priority date 12/1; deadline 5/1. $50 fee. Decision is sent immediately. Commitment fee requested by May 1st. **Financial aid:** Priority date 12/1; no closing date. FAFSA required. Applicants notified on a rolling basis starting 11/1; must reply by 5/1.

Academics. Special study options: Combined bachelor's/graduate degree, cooperative education, distance learning, double major, dual enrollment of high school students, ESL, exchange student, honors, independent study, internships, liberal arts/career combination, student-designed major, study abroad, teacher certification program, weekend college. **Credit/placement by examination:** AP, CLEP, SAT, ACT, institutional tests. **Support services:** Learning center, pre-admission summer program, reduced course load, remedial instruction, study skills assistance, tutoring, writing center.

Majors. Biology: General. **Business:** Accounting, business admin, finance, hospitality admin, marketing. **Communications:** Communications/speech/rhetoric. **Computer sciences:** General, computer science. **Education:** Art, biology, business, chemistry, drama/dance, elementary, English, family/consumer sciences, French, history, mathematics, music, physical, science, social science, Spanish, technology/industrial arts. **Engineering:** Engineering science. **English:** English lit. **Foreign languages:** French, Spanish. **General:** Site management. **Health services:** Athletic training, nursing (RN). **History:** General. **Math:** General. **Parks/recreation:** General, exercise sciences. **Philosophy/religion:** Philosophy. **Physical sciences:** Chemistry, geology. **Protective services:** Police science. **Psychology:** General. **Social sciences:** Anthropology, economics, political science, sociology. **Visual/performing arts:** Art, art history/conservation, dance, dramatic, graphic design, music, studio arts. **Work/family studies:** General, human nutrition.

Most popular majors. Business/marketing 13%, education 20%, health sciences 7%, psychology 6%, social sciences 6%, visual/performing arts 7%.

Technology on campus. Dormitories wired for high-speed internet access and linked to campus network. Commuter students can connect to campus network. Online course registration, online library, helpline, student web hosting, wireless network available.

Student life. Freshman orientation: Mandatory. Preregistration for classes offered. One-day program held throughout summer. Parents welcome and encouraged to attend. **Housing:** Coed dorms, special housing for disabled, apartments, themed housing available. **Activities:** Bands, choral groups, dance, drama, international student organizations, literary magazine, music ensembles, musical theater, opera, radio station, student government, student newspaper, symphony orchestra, TV station, Latter-day Saint student association, Newman Club, Campus Christian Fellowship, Arabic club, multicultural club, Queer Straight Alliance, Young Democrats of Utah, College Republicans, Student Alliance of Interfaith Leaders.

Athletics. NCAA. **Intercollegiate:** Basketball, cross-country, football (tackle) M, golf, gymnastics W, soccer W, softball W, tennis, track and field, volleyball W. **Intramural:** Basketball, golf, soccer, tennis, volleyball. **Team name:** Thunderbirds.

Student services. Career counseling, services for economically disadvantaged, student employment services, financial aid counseling, minority student services, personal counseling, placement for graduates, veterans' counselor, women's services. **Physically disabled:** Services for visually, speech, hearing impaired.

Contact. E-mail: adminfo@suu.edu
Phone: (435) 586-7740 Fax: (435) 865-8223
Brandon Wright, Executive Director of Admissions & Recruitment, Southern Utah University, 351 West University Boulevard, Cedar City, UT 84720

Stevens-Henager College: Logan
Logan, Utah
www.stevenshenager.edu

♦ For-profit 4-year health science and technical college
♦ Large town
♦ 140 undergraduates

General. Accredited by ACCSC. **Degrees:** 13 bachelor's, 40 associate awarded. **Calendar:** Differs by program. **Full-time faculty:** 3 total; 33% have terminal degrees. **Part-time faculty:** 14 total; 43% women.

Basis for selection. Open admission. **Home schooled:** State high school equivalency certificate required.

2015-2016 Annual costs. Associate programs: $42,387-$58,692. Bachelor's programs: $31,620-$74,778. Amounts are for the entire program and include books and supplies.

Application procedures. Admission: No deadline. Admission notification on a rolling basis.

Academics. Special study options: Accelerated study, distance learning, internships. **Credit/placement by examination:** AP, CLEP.

Majors. Business: Accounting, business admin. **Computer sciences:** Computer science. **Health services:** Health care admin.

Most popular majors. Business/marketing 46%, computer/information sciences 36%, health sciences 18%.

Student life. Freshman orientation: Mandatory. Preregistration for classes offered.

Student services. Career counseling, student employment services, financial aid counseling, personal counseling, placement for graduates, veterans' counselor.

Contact. E-mail: clay.buttars@stevenshenager.edu
Phone: (435) 792-6970 ext. 5002 Fax: (435) 755-7611
Clay Buttars, Director of Admissions, Stevens-Henager College: Logan, 755 South Main, Logan, UT 84321

Stevens-Henager College: Murray
Salt Lake City, Utah
www.stevenshenager.edu

- For-profit 4-year business and health science college
- Commuter campus in large town
- 2,541 undergraduates
- Interview required

General. Accredited by ACCSC. **Degrees:** 316 bachelor's, 344 associate awarded; master's offered. **Location:** 5 Miles from Salt Lake City. **Calendar:** Differs by program. **Full-time faculty:** 9 total. **Part-time faculty:** 20 total.

Basis for selection. Open admission, but selective for some programs. Consideration given to secondary school record, GPA, recommendations, test scores, interview, residency and level of interest. **Home schooled:** State high school equivalency certificate required.

2015-2016 Annual costs. Associate programs: $42,387-$58,692. Bachelor's programs: $31,620-$74,778. Amounts are for the entire program and include books and supplies.

Financial aid. Additional information: Financial aid application must be completed prior to enrollment.

Application procedures. Admission: No deadline. No application fee. Admission notification on a rolling basis. **Financial aid:** No deadline.

Academics. Credit/placement by examination: AP, CLEP.

Majors. Business: Accounting technology, business admin. **Computer sciences:** General. **Health services:** Health care admin.

Technology on campus. Commuter students can connect to campus network. Online library available.

Student life. Freshman orientation: Mandatory. Preregistration for classes offered.

Student services. Adult student services, career counseling, financial aid counseling, placement for graduates.

Contact. Phone: (800) 622-2640 Fax: (801) 262-7660
Ken Reynolds, Admissions Director, Stevens-Henager College: Murray, 383 West Vine Street, Salt Lake City, UT 84123

Stevens-Henager College: Ogden
Ogden, Utah
www.stevenshenager.edu   CB code: 4751

- For-profit 4-year liberal arts college
- Commuter campus in small city
- 320 undergraduates
- Interview required

General. Accredited by ACCSC. **Degrees:** 24 bachelor's, 86 associate awarded. **Location:** 35 miles from Salt Lake City. **Calendar:** Differs by program. **Full-time faculty:** 15 total. **Part-time faculty:** 15 total.

Basis for selection. Open admission, but selective for some programs. Special requirements for surgical technology program.

High school preparation. Recommended units include history 4.

2015-2016 Annual costs. Personal expenses: $4,000. **Additional information:** Associate programs: $42,387-$58,692. Bachelor's programs: $31,620-$74,778. Amounts are for the entire program and include books and supplies.

Application procedures. Admission: No deadline. No application fee. Application must be submitted on paper. Admission notification on a rolling basis.

Academics. Special study options: Accelerated study, cooperative education, distance learning, liberal arts/career combination. **Credit/placement by examination:** AP, CLEP. **Support services:** Tutoring.

Majors. Business: Accounting, business admin. **Computer sciences:** General. **Health services:** Health care admin.

Technology on campus. 15 workstations in library, computer center. Commuter students can connect to campus network. Online library available.

Student life. Freshman orientation: Mandatory. Preregistration for classes offered. **Housing:** $100 deposit.

Student services. Financial aid counseling, placement for graduates.

Contact. Phone: (801) 394-7791 Toll-free number: (800) 622-2640
Fax: (801) 621-0853
Cynthia Williams, Director of Admissions, Stevens-Henager College: Ogden, 1890 South 1350 West, Ogden, UT 84401

Stevens-Henager College: Orem
Orem, Utah
www.stevenshenager.edu

- For-profit 4-year health science and career college
- Large city
- 351 undergraduates
- Application essay, interview required

General. Founded in 1891. Accredited by ACCSC. **Degrees:** 45 bachelor's, 41 associate awarded; master's offered. **Location:** 35 miles from Salt Lake City. **Calendar:** Differs by program, extensive summer session. **Full-time faculty:** 20 total; 45% have terminal degrees, 20% minority, 50% women. **Part-time faculty:** 15 total.

Freshman class profile.

Out-of-state: 10% **Live on campus:**   16%

Basis for selection. Open admission. **Home schooled:** Transcript of courses and grades, state high school equivalency certificate required. **Learning Disabled:** Written notice of prospective student's disability from medical care provider required.

2015-2016 Annual costs. Personal expenses: $2,123. **Additional information:** Associate programs: $42,387-$58,692. Bachelor's programs: $31,620-$74,778. Amounts are for the entire program and include books and supplies.

Application procedures. Admission: No deadline. No application fee. Admission notification on a rolling basis. **Financial aid:** No deadline. FAFSA required. Applicants notified on a rolling basis; must reply within 3 week(s) of notification.

Academics. Special study options: Accelerated study, combined bachelor's/graduate degree, distance learning, dual enrollment of high school students, external degree, independent study, internships. **Credit/placement by examination:** AP, CLEP, IB, institutional tests. **Support services:** Learning center, reduced course load, remedial instruction, study skills assistance, tutoring, writing center.

Majors. Business: Accounting, business admin. **Computer sciences:** General, computer graphics, computer science. **Health services:** Health care admin.

Technology on campus. 26 workstations in library, computer center, student center. Commuter students can connect to campus network. Online library, helpline, repair service, wireless network available.

Student life. Freshman orientation: Mandatory. Preregistration for classes offered. **Activities:** Student government, Future Business Leaders Association, Latter-day Saints student association.

Student services. Career counseling, student employment services, personal counseling, placement for graduates.

Contact. E-mail: jesse.hafen@stevenshenager.edu
Phone: (801) 418-6636 Fax: (801) 375-9836
Jesse Hafen, Director of Admissions, Stevens-Henager College: Orem, 1476 South Sand Hill Road, Orem, UT 84058

University of Phoenix: Utah
Salt Lake City, Utah
www.phoenix.edu

- For-profit 4-year university
- Small city
- 919 undergraduates

General. Regionally accredited. **Degrees:** 321 bachelor's awarded; master's offered. **Calendar:** Differs by program. Other Academic Calendar. **Full-time faculty:** 42 total. **Part-time faculty:** 213 total.

Basis for selection. Open admission.

2015-2016 Annual costs. Per-credit-hour charge $410 to $635, depending upon level and course of study; electronic course materials fee $95-$200, if applicable. Book and material charges may vary by course and program. All fees are subject to change.

Application procedures. Admission: No deadline. No application fee. **Financial aid:** No deadline.

Academics. Credit/placement by examination: AP, CLEP.

Majors. Business: Accounting, accounting/business management, business admin, e-commerce, entrepreneurial studies, finance, human resources, marketing, operations. **Communications:** General. **Computer sciences:** Database management, networking, programming, security, system admin, systems analysis, web page design, webmaster. **Conservation:** Environmental studies. **Education:** Elementary. **English:** English lit. **Health services:** Facilities admin, health information management, long term care admin, nursing (RN). **Human services:** General. **Protective services:** Disaster management, law enforcement admin, security management.

Student life. Freshman orientation: Mandatory. Preregistration for classes offered.

Contact. Toll-free number: (866) 766-0766
University of Phoenix: Utah, 5373 South Green Street, Salt Lake City, UT 84123-4642

University of Utah
Salt Lake City, Utah
www.utah.edu

CB member
CB code: 4853

- Public 4-year university
- Commuter campus in very large city
- 22,761 degree-seeking undergraduates: 26% part-time, 43% women, 1% African American, 6% Asian American, 11% Hispanic/Latino, 1% Native Hawaiian/Pacific islander, 4% Multi-racial, non-Hispanic, 6% international
- 7,757 degree-seeking graduate students

- 81% of applicants admitted
- 64% graduate within 6 years; 27% enter graduate study

General. Founded in 1850. Regionally accredited. **Degrees:** 5,240 bachelor's awarded; master's, professional, doctoral offered. **ROTC:** Army, Naval, Air Force. **Location:** 2 miles from downtown. **Calendar:** Semester, limited summer session. **Full-time faculty:** 1,449 total; 3% have terminal degrees, 15% minority, 39% women. **Part-time faculty:** 662 total; less than 1% have terminal degrees, 11% minority, 46% women. **Class size:** 41% < 20, 35% 20-39, 6% 40-49, 12% 50-99, 5% >100. **Special facilities:** Olympic Cauldron Park, arboretum, natural history museum, fine arts museum, architecture exhibition hall, cancer research institute, observatory.

Freshman class profile. 12,174 applied, 9,913 admitted, 3,410 enrolled.

Mid 50% test scores			
SAT critical reading:	500-640	Rank in top quarter:	53%
SAT math:	510-660	Rank in top tenth:	25%
SAT writing:	490-620	End year in good standing:	88%
ACT composite:	21-28	Return as sophomores:	89%
GPA 3.75 or higher:	42%	Out-of-state:	25%
GPA 3.50-3.74:	22%	Live on campus:	45%
GPA 3.0-3.49:	30%	International:	2%
GPA 2.0-2.99:	6%	Fraternities:	6%
		Sororities:	13%

Basis for selection. Academic preparation and performance as well as personal achievements and characteristics. ACT/SAT required for domestic freshmen applicants, ACT/SAT are not required for transfer applicants who have more than 30 semester hours of transfer credit or for any international applicant. Audition required for dance, drama, music programs; portfolio required for art program. **Home schooled:** Transcript of courses and grades, state high school equivalency certificate required. Applicant's high school class has graduated, ACT composite score is at least 23 (SAT 1050), GED composite of 550 or higher and all sub-scores are 500 or higher. Students with a 25 ACT (1130 SAT) are not required to take the GED. **Learning Disabled:** Disclosure of learning disabilities not required; Center for Disability Services assists students with disabilities in the admission process.

High school preparation. College-preparatory program recommended. 16 units required; 20 recommended. Required and recommended units include English 4, mathematics 2-4, social studies 1, history 1-2, science 3 (laboratory 1-2), foreign language 2-3 and academic electives 4. 4 units from at least 2 of the following: history, english, math beyond algebra, laboratory science, foreign language, social science, fine arts.

2015-2016 Annual costs. Tuition/fees: $8,197; $26,022 out-of-state. Room/board: $9,000. Books/supplies: $1,006. Personal expenses: $2,448.

2015-2016 Financial aid. Need-based: 2,057 full-time freshmen applied for aid; 1,456 deemed to have need; 1,442 received aid. Average need met was 66%. Average scholarship/grant was $7,988; average loan $3,286. 34% of total undergraduate aid awarded as scholarships/grants, 66% as loans/jobs. **Non-need-based:** Awarded to 4,896 full-time undergraduates, including 1,729 freshmen. Scholarships awarded for academics, alumni affiliation, art, athletics, leadership, minority status, music/drama, ROTC, state residency.

Application procedures. Admission: Priority date 12/1; deadline 4/1 (receipt date). $45 fee, may be waived for applicants with need. Admission notification on a rolling basis beginning on or about 1/15. Must reply by May 1 or within 2 week(s) if notified thereafter. **Financial aid:** Priority date 3/15; no closing date. FAFSA required. Applicants notified on a rolling basis starting 4/1; must reply within 6 week(s) of notification.

Academics. Special study options: Accelerated study, combined bachelor's/graduate degree, distance learning, double major, dual enrollment of high school students, ESL, exchange student, honors, independent study, internships, student-designed major, study abroad, teacher certification program, Washington semester. **Credit/placement by examination:** AP, CLEP, IB, SAT, ACT. **Support services:** Learning center, pre-admission summer program, reduced course load, remedial instruction, study skills assistance, tutoring, writing center.

Honors college/program. All application elements considered, including GPA and test scores. Most important element is the response to the essay question. No minimum GPA or test score requirements for admission. Average admission profile for incoming Honors freshman for Fall 2015: 3.87 unweighted GPA, and 30 ACT (1356 SAT).

Majors. Architecture: Architecture. **Area/ethnic studies:** Asian, Latin American, women's. **Biology:** General. **Business:** General, accounting, business admin, entrepreneurial studies, finance, marketing, operations. **Communications:** General. **Computer sciences:** Computer science, information systems. **Conservation:** Environmental studies. **Education:** General, elementary, social science, special ed. **Engineering:** General, biomedical, chemical, civil, computer, electrical, geological, materials, mechanical, metallurgical, mining. **English:** English lit, rhetoric/composition. **Foreign languages:** Arabic, Chinese, classics, comparative lit, French, German, Hebrew, Iranian,

Japanese, linguistics, Russian, Spanish, Turkish. **Health services:** Athletic training, audiology/speech pathology, clinical lab science, nursing (RN), public health ed. **History:** General. **Human services:** Social work. **Liberal arts:** Humanities. **Math:** General, applied. **Parks/recreation:** General, exercise sciences, health/fitness. **Philosophy/religion:** Logic, philosophy. **Physical sciences:** General, atmospheric science, chemistry, geology, geophysics, physics. **Psychology:** General. **Social sciences:** General, anthropology, economics, GIS/cartography, political science, sociology, urban studies. **Visual/performing arts:** General, art, art history/conservation, ballet, dance, dramatic, film/cinema/video, industrial design, music. **Work/family studies:** Consumer economics, family studies.

Most popular majors. Business/marketing 13%, communications/journalism 8%, engineering/engineering technologies 8%, health sciences 8%, parks/recreation 6%, psychology 7%, social sciences 14%.

Technology on campus. 1,099 workstations in dormitories, library, computer center, student center. Dormitories wired for high-speed internet access and linked to campus network. Commuter students can connect to campus network. Online course registration, online library, helpline, repair service, student web hosting, wireless network available.

Student life. Freshman orientation: Mandatory, $50 fee. Preregistration for classes offered. **Housing:** Coed dorms, single-sex dorms, special housing for disabled, apartments, gender-neutral housing, themed housing available. $200 fully refundable deposit. Limited visitation, 24-hour quiet housing available. **Activities:** Bands, campus ministries, choral groups, dance, drama, film society, international student organizations, literary magazine, music ensembles, musical theater, opera, radio station, student government, student newspaper, symphony orchestra, TV station, InterVarsity Christian Fellowship, Latter-Day Saint Student Association, Muslim Student Association, College Democrats, College Republicans, The Andrew Goodman Foundation at the University of Utah, Cross Culture club, International Student Council, Black Student Union, Freshmen Service Corps.

Athletics. NCAA. **Intercollegiate:** Baseball M, basketball, cheerleading, cross-country W, diving, football (tackle) M, golf M, gymnastics W, skiing, soccer W, softball W, swimming, tennis, track and field W, volleyball W. **Intramural:** Basketball, football (non-tackle), racquetball, rifle, skiing, soccer, softball, tennis, ultimate frisbee, volleyball, water polo. **Team name:** Utes.

Student services. Adult student services, career counseling, student employment services, financial aid counseling, health services, minority student services, on-campus daycare, personal counseling, placement for graduates, veterans' counselor, women's services. **Physically disabled:** Services for visually, speech, hearing impaired.

Contact. E-mail: admissions@utah.edu
Phone: (801) 581-8761 Toll-free number: (800) 685-8856
Fax: (801) 585-7864
Matthew Lopez, Director of Admissions, University of Utah, 201 South 1460 East, Room 250 S, Salt Lake City, UT 84112-9057

Utah State University
Logan, Utah — CB member
www.usu.edu — CB code: 4857

- Public 4-year university
- Residential campus in small city
- 22,265 degree-seeking undergraduates: 24% part-time, 52% women, 1% African American, 1% Asian American, 6% Hispanic/Latino, 2% Native American, 2% Multi-racial, non-Hispanic, 2% international
- 2,587 degree-seeking graduate students
- SAT or ACT (ACT writing optional) required
- 49% graduate within 6 years

General. Founded in 1888. Regionally accredited. **Degrees:** 3,551 bachelor's, 1,272 associate awarded; master's, professional, doctoral offered. **ROTC:** Army, Air Force. **Location:** 80 miles from Salt Lake City. **Calendar:** Semester, extensive summer session. **Full-time faculty:** 878 total; 81% have terminal degrees, 10% minority, 36% women. **Part-time faculty:** 229 total; 30% have terminal degrees, 5% minority, 49% women. **Class size:** 42% < 20, 37% 20-39, 6% 40-49, 8% 50-99, 6% >100. **Special facilities:** Agricultural experiment stations, water research laboratory, space shuttle experiments, forestry research facility, botanical gardens, teaching greenhouse, research park, laboratory school, off-campus theater performance lab, anthropology museum.

Freshman class profile. 4,751 enrolled.

Mid 50% test scores		Out-of-state:	29%
SAT critical reading:	480-600	International:	1%
SAT math:	470-610	Fraternities:	2%
ACT composite:	20-27	Sororities:	2%

Basis for selection. High school record, test scores most important. Audition required for music; portfolio required for art. **Home schooled:** Early entry policy applies: junior equivalent, letters of approval. **Learning Disabled:** Recent documentation/diagnosis required for special consideration.

High school preparation. College-preparatory program required. Required and recommended units include English 4, mathematics 3, history 1, science 3 (laboratory 1), foreign language 2 and academic electives 4. Some social studies electives required.

2015-2016 Annual costs. Tuition/fees: $6,663; $19,133 out-of-state. Room/board: $5,790.

2015-2016 Financial aid. Need-based: 2,658 full-time freshmen applied for aid; 2,094 deemed to have need; 2,036 received aid. Average need met was 61%. Average scholarship/grant was $4,399; average loan $3,319. 59% of total undergraduate aid awarded as scholarships/grants, 41% as loans/jobs. **Non-need-based:** Awarded to 4,747 full-time undergraduates, including 1,702 freshmen. Scholarships awarded for academics, alumni affiliation, art, athletics, leadership, minority status, music/drama, religious affiliation, ROTC, state residency.

Application procedures. Admission: No deadline. $50 fee. Admission notification on a rolling basis. **Financial aid:** No deadline. FAFSA required. Applicants notified on a rolling basis starting 4/1; must reply within 4 week(s) of notification.

Academics. Special study options: Accelerated study, cooperative education, cross-registration, distance learning, double major, dual enrollment of high school students, ESL, exchange student, honors, independent study, internships, liberal arts/career combination, student-designed major, study abroad, teacher certification program, weekend college. **Credit/placement by examination:** AP, CLEP, IB, SAT, ACT, institutional tests. 30 credit hours maximum toward bachelor's degree. 16 credits of lower division course work per language. **Support services:** Learning center, pre-admission summer program, reduced course load, remedial instruction, study skills assistance, tutoring, writing center.

Majors. Architecture: Environmental design, landscape. **Area/ethnic studies:** American, Asian. **Biology:** General, biochemistry, conservation, wildlife. **Business:** Accounting, business admin, entrepreneurial studies, finance, human resources, international, marketing, operations. **Communications:** Intercultural, journalism. **Computer sciences:** General, information systems. **Conservation:** Environmental studies, fisheries, forestry, wildlife/wilderness. **Education:** Agricultural, biology, chemistry, early childhood, early childhood special, elementary, English, family/consumer sciences, French, geography, German, health, mathematics, physical, physics, psychology, science, secondary, social studies, Spanish, special ed, technology/industrial arts. **Engineering:** Agricultural, civil, computer, electrical, environmental, mechanical. **English:** English lit, rhetoric/composition. **Foreign languages:** French, German, Spanish. **Health services:** Clinical lab science, communication disorders, music therapy. **History:** General. **Human services:** Social work. **Liberal arts:** Arts/sciences. **Math:** General, statistics. **Parks/recreation:** General. **Philosophy/religion:** Philosophy, religion. **Physical sciences:** Chemistry, geology, physics. **Psychology:** General. **Social sciences:** Anthropology, economics, geography, political science, sociology. **Visual/performing arts:** Art, dramatic, interior design, music. **Work/family studies:** General, clothing/textiles, family studies, food/nutrition.

Most popular majors. Business/marketing 13%, education 15%, engineering/engineering technologies 7%, family/consumer sciences 6%, health sciences 10%, social sciences 11%.

Technology on campus. 925 workstations in dormitories, library, computer center, student center. Dormitories wired for high-speed internet access and linked to campus network. Commuter students can connect to campus network. Online course registration, helpline, repair service, student web hosting, wireless network available.

Student life. Freshman orientation: Mandatory, $25 fee. Preregistration for classes offered. Sessions ranging from half-day to 4-days available in June and July. **Housing:** Coed dorms, single-sex dorms, special housing for disabled, apartments, fraternity/sorority housing, themed housing available. $250 partly refundable deposit. **Activities:** Bands, campus ministries, choral groups, dance, drama, film society, international student organizations, music ensembles, musical theater, opera, radio station, student government, student newspaper, symphony orchestra, TV station, Latter-Day Saints student organization, Catholic student organization, Lutheran student organization, Baptist student organization, Christian Fellowship, Black student union, Hispanic student union, Native American student union, Polynesian student union, Asian American student union.

Athletics. NCAA. **Intercollegiate:** Basketball, cross-country, football (tackle) M, golf M, gymnastics W, soccer W, softball W, tennis, track and field, volleyball W. **Intramural:** Badminton, basketball, football (non-tackle), racquetball, soccer, softball, table tennis, tennis, ultimate frisbee, volleyball. **Team name:** Aggies.

Student services. Adult student services, alcohol/substance abuse counseling, career counseling, student employment services, financial aid counseling, health services, minority student services, on-campus daycare, personal counseling, placement for graduates, veterans' counselor, women's services. **Physically disabled:** Services for visually, speech, hearing impaired.

Contact. E-mail: admit@usu.edu
Phone: (435) 797-1079 Toll-free number: (800) 488-8108
Fax: (435) 797-3708
Jeff Sorensen, Associate Director of Admissions, Utah State University, 0160 Old Main Hill, Logan, UT 84322-0160

Utah Valley University
Orem, Utah
www.uvu.edu

CB member
CB code: 4870

- Public 4-year university and technical college
- Commuter campus in small city
- 25,751 degree-seeking undergraduates: 36% part-time, 44% women, 1% African American, 1% Asian American, 10% Hispanic/Latino, 1% Native American, 1% Native Hawaiian/Pacific islander, 3% Multi-racial, non-Hispanic, 2% international
- 185 degree-seeking graduate students
- 30% graduate within 6 years

General. Founded in 1941. Regionally accredited. **Degrees:** 2,915 bachelor's, 1,996 associate awarded; master's offered. **ROTC:** Army, Air Force. **Location:** 45 miles from Salt Lake City. **Calendar:** Semester, extensive summer session. **Full-time faculty:** 642 total; 68% have terminal degrees, 14% minority, 34% women. **Part-time faculty:** 1,204 total; 7% have terminal degrees, 8% minority, 37% women. **Class size:** 46% < 20, 44% 20-39, 5% 40-49, 4% 50-99, 1% >100. **Special facilities:** Provo airport campus, art museum.

Freshman class profile. 9,183 applied, 9,178 admitted, 4,245 enrolled.

Mid 50% test scores		Rank in top quarter:	25%
ACT composite:	18-25	Rank in top tenth:	8%
GPA 3.75 or higher:	26%	Return as sophomores:	61%
GPA 3.50-3.74:	18%	Out-of-state:	22%
GPA 3.0-3.49:	29%	International:	1%
GPA 2.0-2.99:	25%		

Basis for selection. Open admission. Students under 21 years of age must complete ACT/SAT prior to registration for placement purposes only. New Student Assessment may be required for some. **Home schooled:** State high school equivalency certificate required. **Learning Disabled:** Students with learning disabilities may apply for reasonable accommodations and assistance through the Accessibility Services Department.

2015-2016 Annual costs. Tuition/fees: $5,386; $15,202 out-of-state.

2015-2016 Financial aid. Need-based: 1,874 full-time freshmen applied for aid; 1,453 deemed to have need; 1,392 received aid. Average need met was 68%. Average scholarship/grant was $4,701; average loan $2,315. 47% of total undergraduate aid awarded as scholarships/grants, 53% as loans/jobs. **Non-need-based:** Awarded to 2,432 full-time undergraduates, including 560 freshmen. Scholarships awarded for academics, alumni affiliation, art, athletics, ROTC.

Application procedures. Admission: Closing date 8/1 (postmark date). $35 fee, may be waived for applicants with need. Admission notification on a rolling basis beginning on or about 1/1. **Financial aid:** No deadline. FAFSA required. Applicants notified on a rolling basis.

Academics. Special study options: Cooperative education, cross-registration, distance learning, double major, dual enrollment of high school students, ESL, honors, independent study, internships, student-designed major, study abroad, teacher certification program, weekend college. Evening school, alternative delivery courses, weekend courses. **Credit/placement by examination:** AP, CLEP, IB, institutional tests. 16 credit hours maximum toward associate degree, 16 toward bachelor's. No more than 25% of credits applied toward associate degree, diploma, or certificate may be awarded through challenge credit. **Support services:** Learning center, reduced course load, remedial instruction, study skills assistance, tutoring, writing center.

Majors. Biology: General, biotechnology, botany. **Business:** Accounting, business admin, construction management, finance, financial planning, hospitality admin, marketing, operations. **Communications:** Communications/speech/rhetoric. **Computer sciences:** Computer science, information systems, networking, web page design. **Conservation:** Environmental science. **Education:** Art, biology, business, chemistry, Deaf/hearing impaired, drama/dance, elementary, English, health, history, mathematics, music, physical,

science, Spanish. **Engineering:** Computer hardware, software. **English:** English lit. **Foreign languages:** American Sign Language, Spanish. **Health services:** Community health, dental hygiene, nursing (RN). **History:** General. **Human services:** Social work. **Math:** General. **Parks/recreation:** Health/fitness. **Philosophy/religion:** Philosophy. **Physical sciences:** Chemistry, geology, physics. **Protective services:** Firefighting, forensics, law enforcement admin. **Psychology:** General. **Social sciences:** Economics, political science. **Visual/performing arts:** Dance, design, dramatic, music, music performance, music technology.

Most popular majors. Business/marketing 20%, computer/information sciences 7%, education 12%, health sciences 7%, psychology 10%, security/protective services 6%, trade and industry 9%.

Technology on campus. 1,000 workstations in library, computer center, student center. Commuter students can connect to campus network. Online course registration, online library, helpline, repair service, wireless network available.

Student life. Freshman orientation: Mandatory. Preregistration for classes offered. **Housing:** Only off-campus non college-owned housing is available. **Activities:** Bands, choral groups, dance, drama, film society, international student organizations, literary magazine, music ensembles, musical theater, student government, student newspaper, symphony orchestra, TV station, Baptist student union, Black student union, German club, Japan club, Latin American club, Latter-Day Saint student association, multi-cultural voices, Native Sun, Russian club.

Athletics. NCAA. **Intercollegiate:** Baseball M, basketball, cross-country, golf, soccer W, softball W, track and field, volleyball W, wrestling M. **Intramural:** Football (tackle). **Team name:** Wolverines.

Student services. Adult student services, alcohol/substance abuse counseling, career counseling, services for economically disadvantaged, student employment services, financial aid counseling, health services, legal services, minority student services, on-campus daycare, personal counseling, placement for graduates, veterans' counselor, women's services. **Physically disabled:** Services for visually, speech, hearing impaired.

Contact. E-mail: admissions@uvu.edu
Phone: (801) 863-8466 Fax: (801) 225-4677
Andrew Stone, Director of Admissions, Utah Valley University, 800 West University Parkway, Orem, UT 84058-5999

Weber State University
Ogden, Utah
https://www.weber.edu

CB member
CB code: 4941

- Public 4-year university
- Commuter campus in small city
- 17,795 degree-seeking undergraduates: 39% part-time, 53% women
- 619 degree-seeking graduate students

General. Founded in 1889. Regionally accredited. **Degrees:** 2,505 bachelor's, 2,216 associate awarded; master's offered. **ROTC:** Army, Naval, Air Force. **Location:** Approximately 35.8 miles from Salt Lake City. **Calendar:** Semester, extensive summer session. **Full-time faculty:** 487 total; 84% have terminal degrees, 13% minority, 47% women. **Part-time faculty:** 778 total; 11% have terminal degrees, 14% minority, 49% women. **Class size:** 47% < 20, 41% 20-39, 6% 40-49, 5% 50-99, less than 1% >100. **Special facilities:** Planetarium, natural science museum, visual arts center, performing arts center.

Freshman class profile.

GPA 3.75 or higher:	20%	Out-of-state:	10%
GPA 3.50-3.74:	18%	Live on campus:	13%
GPA 3.0-3.49:	27%	Fraternities:	1%
GPA 2.0-2.99:	30%	Sororities:	1%

Basis for selection. Open admission, but selective for some programs. Special requirements for nursing, dental hygiene, and health professions programs. **Home schooled:** Applicants without GED must have 25 ACT.

High school preparation. 15 units recommended. Recommended units include English 4, mathematics 2, history 1, science 2 and academic electives 4. 4 additional courses recommended with at least 2 from history, English, math beyond algebra, laboratory science, fine arts, and computer science.

2015-2016 Annual costs. Tuition/fees: $5,339; $14,252 out-of-state. Room/board: $4,596. Books/supplies: $1,200. Personal expenses: $3,000.

Financial aid. All financial aid based on need. **Additional information:** Dream Weber program provides free tuition and general student fees to students whose annual household income is $40,000 or less.

Application procedures. Admission: Closing date 8/21 (postmark date). $30 fee. Admission notification on a rolling basis. **Financial aid:** Priority date 3/1; no closing date. FAFSA, institutional form required. Applicants notified on a rolling basis starting 3/15; must reply within 2 week(s) of notification.

Academics. Special study options: Accelerated study, cooperative education, distance learning, double major, dual enrollment of high school students, ESL, exchange student, external degree, honors, independent study, internships, student-designed major, study abroad, teacher certification program. First Year Experience. **Credit/placement by examination:** AP, CLEP, IB, institutional tests. 15 credit hours maximum toward associate degree, 30 toward bachelor's. **Support services:** Learning center, pre-admission summer program, reduced course load, remedial instruction, study skills assistance, tutoring, writing center.

Majors. Biology: Botany, microbiology, zoology. **Business:** Accounting, administrative services, business admin, finance, human resources, logistics, management information systems, managerial economics, marketing, selling. **Communications:** Communications/speech/rhetoric, journalism, organizational, persuasive communications, political, public relations, radio/TV. **Computer sciences:** General, computer science, information systems, networking, security. **Education:** Art, biology, business, chemistry, drama/dance, early childhood, elementary, English, French, German, history, mathematics, music, physical, physics, science, social science, social studies, Spanish, special ed. **Engineering:** General. **English:** Creative writing, English lit, technical writing. **Foreign languages:** French, German, Spanish. **Health services:** Athletic training, clinical lab science, clinical lab technology, dental hygiene, health care admin, health information management, long term care admin, medical radiologic technology/radiation therapy, nuclear medical technology, nursing (RN), physician assistant, prechiropractic, predental, premedicine, prepharmacy, prephysical therapy, preveterinary, respiratory therapy technology, sonography. **History:** General. **Human services:** Social work. **Liberal arts:** Arts/sciences. **Math:** General, applied. **Parks/recreation:** Health/fitness. **Philosophy/religion:** Philosophy. **Physical sciences:** Chemistry, geology, physics. **Protective services:** Corrections, criminal justice, forensics, police science. **Psychology:** General. **Social sciences:** Anthropology, econometrics, economics, geography, international economics, political science, sociology. **Visual/performing arts:** Art, commercial/advertising art, dance, design, dramatic, multimedia, music, music pedagogy, music performance, photography, piano/keyboard, voice/opera. **Work/family studies:** Child development, family systems.

Most popular majors. Business/marketing 15%, computer/information sciences 6%, education 9%, health sciences 30%, security/protective services 7%.

Technology on campus. 1,000 workstations in dormitories, library, computer center, student center. Dormitories wired for high-speed internet access. Online course registration, online library, helpline, repair service, wireless network available.

Student life. Freshman orientation: Available. Preregistration for classes offered. Student and parent orientations offered by appointment. **Housing:** Single-sex dorms, special housing for disabled, apartments, wellness housing available. $200 partly refundable deposit, deadline 8/1. **Activities:** Bands, campus ministries, choral groups, dance, drama, film society, international student organizations, literary magazine, music ensembles, Model UN, musical theater, opera, radio station, student government, student newspaper, symphony orchestra, TV station, American Red Cross, Amnesty International, Black Scholars United, College Democrats, Golden Key Honour Society, international club, Intervarsity Christian Fellowship, Latinos In Action, Latter-day Saint student association, College Republicans.

Athletics. NCAA. **Intercollegiate:** Basketball, cheerleading, football (tackle) M, golf, soccer W, softball W, tennis, track and field, volleyball W. **Intramural:** Badminton, baseball, basketball, fencing, football (non-tackle), golf, soccer, softball, swimming, table tennis, tennis, ultimate frisbee, volleyball. **Team name:** Wildcats.

Student services. Adult student services, alcohol/substance abuse counseling, chaplain/spiritual director, career counseling, services for economically disadvantaged, student employment services, financial aid counseling, health services, legal services, minority student services, on-campus daycare, personal counseling, placement for graduates, veterans' counselor, women's services. **Physically disabled:** Services for visually, speech, hearing impaired.

Contact. E-mail: admissions@weber.edu
Phone: (801) 626-6743 Toll-free number: (800) 848-7770
Fax: (801) 626-6747
Scott Teichert, Director of Admissions, Weber State University, 1137 University Circle, Ogden, UT 84408-1137

Western Governors University
Salt Lake City, Utah
www.wgu.edu   CB code: 3949

- Private 4-year virtual university
- Very large city
- 61,027 degree-seeking undergraduates: 61% women, 9% African American, 4% Asian American, 8% Hispanic/Latino, 1% Native American, 1% Native Hawaiian/Pacific islander, 3% Multi-racial, non-Hispanic
- 16,205 degree-seeking graduate students
- Interview required

General. Regionally accredited. **Degrees:** 8,207 bachelor's awarded; master's offered. **Calendar:** Differs by program, extensive summer session. **Full-time faculty:** 1,093 total; 76% women. **Part-time faculty:** 602 total; 58% women.

Basis for selection. Open admission, but selective for some programs. Interview with an Enrollment Counselor, prior college and work experience, results from the mandatory WGU Collegiate Readiness Assessment, and time commitment to studies are considered for all admission decisions. Other specific admission requirements may also apply for certain degree programs.

2015-2016 Annual costs. Tuition/fees: $6,070. Books/supplies: $200. Personal expenses: $500.

2014-2015 Financial aid. All financial aid based on need. 123 full-time freshmen applied for aid; 87 deemed to have need; 87 received aid. Average need met was 100%. Average scholarship/grant was $4,483; average loan $1,436. 54% of total undergraduate aid awarded as scholarships/grants, 46% as loans/jobs.

Application procedures. Admission: No deadline. $65 fee, may be waived for applicants with need. Application must be submitted online. Admission notification on a rolling basis. **Financial aid:** No deadline. FAFSA required. Applicants notified on a rolling basis.

Academics. All students are provided mentoring support through their degree program. Students have access to online communities, textbooks, interactive learning resources, webinars, and academic mentors in their field of study. Students with prior education and experience in their field of study can often accelerate degree completion. **Special study options:** Accelerated study, distance learning, independent study, teacher certification program. **Credit/placement by examination:** AP, CLEP. **Support services:** Learning center, study skills assistance, tutoring, writing center.

Majors. Business: Accounting, business admin, finance, human resources, information resources management, management information systems, marketing, sales/distribution. **Computer sciences:** Applications programming, database management, information technology, networking, security, system admin. **Education:** General, biology, chemistry, early childhood, earth science, elementary, mathematics, physics, science, special ed. **Health services:** Medical informatics, nursing (RN).

Most popular majors. Business/marketing 31%, computer/information sciences 12%, education 28%, health sciences 29%.

Technology on campus. PC or laptop required. Online library, helpline available.

Student life. Freshman orientation: Mandatory. Preregistration for classes offered. Students have access to the orientation course prior to their enrollment start date.

Student services. Adult student services, career counseling, student employment services, financial aid counseling, personal counseling, veterans' counselor.

Contact. E-mail: info@wgu.edu
Phone: (801) 274-3280 Toll-free number: (866) 225-5948
Fax: (801) 274-3305
Daren Upham, VP of Enrollment, Western Governors University, 4001 South 700 East, Salt Lake City, UT 84107

Westminster College
Salt Lake City, Utah
www.westminstercollege.edu   CB code: 4948

- Private 4-year liberal arts college
- Commuter campus in very large city

◆ 2,135 degree-seeking undergraduates: 5% part-time, 56% women, 2% African American, 2% Asian American, 10% Hispanic/Latino, 4% Multiracial, non-Hispanic, 5% international
◆ 659 degree-seeking graduate students
◆ 96% of applicants admitted
◆ SAT or ACT (ACT writing recommended) required
◆ 62% graduate within 6 years

General. Founded in 1875. Regionally accredited. **Degrees:** 571 bachelor's awarded; master's offered. **ROTC:** Army, Naval, Air Force. **Location:** 6 miles from downtown. **Calendar:** 4-1-4, extensive summer session. **Full-time faculty:** 151 total; 82% have terminal degrees, 12% minority, 49% women. **Part-time faculty:** 237 total; 79% have terminal degrees, 9% minority, 56% women. **Class size:** 72% < 20, 27% 20-39, less than 1% 40-49. **Special facilities:** Mass spectrometers, high performance liquid chromatography systems, nuclear magnetic resonance instrumentation, polymerase chain reaction machines, advanced optic lab, food science brewery, Meade Lx200 telescope.

Freshman class profile. 2,001 applied, 1,920 admitted, 468 enrolled.

Mid 50% test scores		Rank in top quarter:	53%
SAT critical reading:	500-620	Rank in top tenth:	20%
SAT math:	500-620	End year in good standing:	82%
ACT composite:	22-27	Return as sophomores:	82%
GPA 3.75 or higher:	36%	Out-of-state:	44%
GPA 3.50-3.74:	28%	Live on campus:	68%
GPA 3.0-3.49:	28%	International:	3%
GPA 2.0-2.99:	8%		

Basis for selection. Quality of academic preparation (which includes both rigor of course work and grades), extracurricular activities, individual talents and character, recommendations, and ACT or SAT scores considered. Campus visit to meet with admissions counselor recommended. Conditional admission for students who have scored 45 or higher on internet-based TOEFL. Interviews and application essay is important.

High school preparation. College-preparatory program recommended. Required and recommended units include English 4, mathematics 2-3, social studies 2, history 1, science 3, foreign language 2-3 and academic electives 2-3.

2015-2016 Annual costs. Tuition/fees: $31,228. Room/board: $8,712. Books/supplies: $1,000. Personal expenses: $2,300.

2015-2016 Financial aid. Need-based: 385 full-time freshmen applied for aid; 310 deemed to have need; 310 received aid. Average need met was 81%. Average scholarship/grant was $21,011; average loan $3,018. 65% of total undergraduate aid awarded as scholarships/grants, 35% as loans/jobs. **Non-need-based:** Awarded to 851 full-time undergraduates, including 185 freshmen. Scholarships awarded for academics, alumni affiliation, art, athletics, leadership, minority status, music/drama, ROTC.

Application procedures. Admission: Priority date 12/15; deadline 8/15. $50 fee, may be waived for applicants with need. Admission notification on a rolling basis beginning on or about 9/1. Must reply by May 1 or within 3 week(s) if notified thereafter. **Financial aid:** Priority date 4/15; no closing date. FAFSA required. Applicants notified on a rolling basis starting 3/1; must reply within 3 week(s) of notification.

Academics. Curriculum combines professional and liberal arts study. **Special study options:** Accelerated study, combined bachelor's/graduate degree, cooperative education, cross-registration, distance learning, double major, dual enrollment of high school students, ESL, honors, independent study, internships, liberal arts/career combination, semester at sea, student-designed major, study abroad, teacher certification program, weekend college. **Credit/placement by examination:** AP, CLEP, IB, SAT, ACT, institutional tests. 40 credit hours maximum toward bachelor's degree. **Support services:** Pre-admission summer program, reduced course load, remedial instruction, study skills assistance, tutoring, writing center.

Honors college/program. 26 ACT (1760 SAT), strong academic preparation required. Campus visit strongly recommended.

Majors. Biology: General, neuroscience. **Business:** Accounting, business admin, finance, international, management science, managerial economics, marketing. **Communications:** Communications/speech/rhetoric. **Computer sciences:** Computer science. **Conservation:** Environmental studies. **Education:** General, early childhood, elementary, secondary, special ed. **English:** English lit. **Health services:** Nursing (RN). **History:** General. **Math:** General. **Philosophy/religion:** Philosophy. **Physical sciences:** Chemistry, physics. **Protective services:** Criminal justice. **Psychology:** General. **Social sciences:** Economics, political science, sociology. **Visual/performing arts:** Art, dramatic, music, studio arts management.

Most popular majors. Biology 6%, business/marketing 24%, health sciences 21%, psychology 7%, social sciences 8%.

Technology on campus. PC or laptop required. 405 workstations in dormitories, library, computer center, student center. Dormitories wired for high-speed internet access. Commuter students can connect to campus network. Online course registration, online library, helpline, student web hosting, wireless network available.

Student life. Freshman orientation: Mandatory, $300 fee. Preregistration for classes offered. **Housing:** Guaranteed on-campus for freshmen. Coed dorms, special housing for disabled, apartments available. $200 nonrefundable deposit, deadline 6/1. Off-campus school owned house and apartments available. **Activities:** Jazz band, campus ministries, choral groups, dance, drama, film society, international student organizations, literary magazine, music ensembles, musical theater, student government, student newspaper, symphony orchestra, Reel Griffins, LDSSA, Hillel, Root Newspaper, residence hall association, The Tipping Point, V Day, Alphabet Soup, trail running club, Tri Beta.

Athletics. NCAA. **Intercollegiate:** Basketball, cross-country, golf, lacrosse, skiing, soccer, track and field, volleyball W. **Intramural:** Basketball, football (non-tackle), racquetball, soccer, volleyball. **Team name:** Griffins.

Student services. Alcohol/substance abuse counseling, chaplain/spiritual director, career counseling, student employment services, financial aid counseling, health services, minority student services, personal counseling, placement for graduates, veterans' counselor, women's services. **Physically disabled:** Services for visually, speech, hearing impaired.

Contact. E-mail: admission@westminstercollege.edu
Phone: (801) 832-2200 Toll-free number: (800) 748-4753
Fax: (801) 832-3101
Darlene Dilley, Director of Admissions, Westminster College, 1840 South 1300 East, Salt Lake City, UT 84105

Vermont

Bennington College
Bennington, Vermont
www.bennington.edu

CB member
CB code: 3080

- Private 4-year liberal arts college
- Residential campus in large town
- 683 degree-seeking undergraduates: 65% women, 2% African American, 2% Asian American, 6% Hispanic/Latino, 1% Native American, 5% Multi-racial, non-Hispanic, 13% international
- 98 degree-seeking graduate students
- 63% of applicants admitted
- Application essay required
- 68% graduate within 6 years; 14% enter graduate study

General. Founded in 1932. Regionally accredited. **Degrees:** 143 bachelor's awarded; master's offered. **Location:** 40 miles from Albany, New York; 150 miles from Boston. **Calendar:** Semester. **Full-time faculty:** 60 total; 72% have terminal degrees, 10% minority, 53% women. **Part-time faculty:** 51 total; 57% have terminal degrees, 18% minority, 43% women. **Class size:** 89% < 20, 10% 20-39, less than 1% >100. **Special facilities:** Observatory, greenhouse, nature preserves, visual and performance arts center with three theaters, Center for the Advancement of Public Action with United Nations-inspired meeting room.

Freshman class profile. 1,106 applied, 692 admitted, 206 enrolled.

Mid 50% test scores		End year in good standing:	94%
SAT critical reading:	590-730	Return as sophomores:	82%
SAT math:	550-670	Out-of-state:	98%
SAT writing:	580-700	Live on campus:	99%
ACT composite:	26-32	International:	10%

Basis for selection. Intellectual curiosity, a creative spark, and a capacity for self-direction are most important; evidence of these characteristics are welcome in any part of the application. While not required, an interview is strongly recommended. **Home schooled:** Statement describing home school structure and mission, state high school equivalency certificate, letter of recommendation (nonparent) required.

High school preparation. College-preparatory program recommended.

2015-2016 Annual costs. Tuition/fees: $48,220. Room/board: $14,200.

2014-2015 Financial aid. Need-based: 155 full-time freshmen applied for aid; 155 deemed to have need; 155 received aid. Average need met was 77%. Average scholarship/grant was $25,079; average loan $3,116. 82% of total undergraduate aid awarded as scholarships/grants, 18% as loans/jobs. **Non-need-based:** Awarded to 550 full-time undergraduates, including 184 freshmen. Scholarships awarded for academics, alumni affiliation, art, leadership, minority status, music/drama. **Additional information:** All applicants for undergraduate admission considered for scholarships based on quality of overall application.

Application procedures. Admission: Closing date 1/3 (postmark date). No application fee. Admission notification by 4/1. Must reply by May 1 or within 2 week(s) if notified thereafter. **Financial aid:** Priority date 1/15, closing date 2/15. FAFSA, institutional form required. CSS PROFILE required of early decision applicants only. Applicants notified by 3/26; must reply by 5/1.

Academics. Special study options: Independent study, internships, student-designed major, study abroad. Annual 7-week winter internship/field work period; Postbaccalaureate program in preparation for medical or allied health school graduate programs. **Credit/placement by examination:** AP, CLEP, IB. **Support services:** Study skills assistance, tutoring.

Majors. Architecture: Architecture, environmental design. **Area/ethnic studies:** American, Asian, European, gay/lesbian, Latin American, women's. **Biology:** General, botany, cellular/molecular, ecology, environmental, evolutionary, zoology. **Communications:** General, digital media, journalism. **Communications technology:** Animation/special effects. **Computer sciences:** General, computer science. **Conservation:** Environmental science, environmental studies. **Education:** General. **English:** American lit, British lit, creative writing, English lit, writing. **Foreign languages:** General, Chinese, French, Germanic, Italian, Japanese, Spanish. **Health services:** Premedicine.

History: General. **Human services:** Public policy. **Liberal arts:** Arts/sciences, humanities. **Math:** General. **Philosophy/religion:** Judaic, philosophy, religion. **Physical sciences:** General, astronomy, chemistry, geology, physics. **Psychology:** General, social. **Social sciences:** General, anthropology, international relations, political science. **Visual/performing arts:** General, acting, art history/conservation, ceramics, cinematography, dance, design, directing/producing, dramatic, drawing, fashion design, film/cinema/video, jazz, multimedia, music, music history, music performance, music theory/composition, musicology, painting, photography, piano/keyboard, play/screenwriting, printmaking, sculpture, stringed instruments, studio arts, theater design, theater history, voice/opera. **Work/family studies:** Child development.

Most popular majors. English 20%, foreign language 8%, psychology 6%, social sciences 10%, visual/performing arts 30%.

Technology on campus. 40 workstations in library, computer center, student center. Dormitories wired for high-speed internet access and linked to campus network. Commuter students can connect to campus network. Online library, helpline, repair service, student web hosting, wireless network available.

Student life. Freshman orientation: Mandatory. Preregistration for classes offered. Session begins 4 days before start of classes; includes faculty workshops, student and faculty performances, and campus-wide Convocation. Students may opt to participate in pre-orientation backpacking, biking, or service trip. **Housing:** Guaranteed on-campus for all undergraduates. Coed dorms, themed housing available. **Activities:** Jazz band, dance, drama, film society, international student organizations, literary magazine, music ensembles, student newspaper, Bennington Connects, Democracy Matters, Interfaith Community, Kulanu.

Student services. Alcohol/substance abuse counseling, career counseling, student employment services, financial aid counseling, health services, minority student services, personal counseling, women's services.

Contact. E-mail: admissions@bennington.edu
Phone: (802) 440-4312 Toll-free number: (800) 833-6845
Fax: (802) 440-4320
Hung Bui, VP and Dean of Admissions and Financial Aid, Bennington College, One College Drive, Bennington, VT 05201-6003

Burlington College
Burlington, Vermont
www.burlington.edu

CB code: 1119

- Private 4-year liberal arts college
- Commuter campus in small city
- 177 degree-seeking undergraduates
- 26 graduate students
- Application essay required

General. Founded in 1972. Regionally accredited. Space leased at Vermont Woodworking School, Fairfax, Vermont for those pursuing certificate or degree in Craftsmanship and Design. **Degrees:** 23 bachelor's, 4 associate awarded; master's offered. **Calendar:** Semester, limited summer session. **Full-time faculty:** 9 total. **Part-time faculty:** 56 total. **Class size:** 97% < 20, 3% 20-39.

Freshman class profile.

GPA 3.50-3.74:	20%	Rank in top tenth:	8%
GPA 3.0-3.49:	12%	Out-of-state:	65%
GPA 2.0-2.99:	56%	Live on campus:	59%
Rank in top quarter:	15%		

Basis for selection. Attention given to transcript, GPA, and letters of recommendation; application essay most important. Test-optional. Portfolio required for BFA degree programs. **Home schooled:** Statement describing home school structure and mission, state high school equivalency certificate, letter of recommendation (nonparent) required. One of the following required: self-certification statement or copy of secondary school completion credential. Portfolio style transcripts accepted. **Learning Disabled:** Students diagnosed with disability as defined under federal or state law may request academic adjustments and/or auxiliary aid by notifying Dean of Student Affairs in writing.

High school preparation. College-preparatory program recommended. 24 units recommended. Recommended units include English 4, mathematics 3, social studies 4, history 3, science 2 (laboratory 2), foreign language 2 and academic electives 4.

2015-2016 Annual costs. Tuition/fees: $23,656. Room only: $7,200. Books/supplies: $1,064. Personal expenses: $900.

Financial aid. Non-need-based: Scholarships awarded for academics, leadership.

Application procedures. Admission: Closing date 8/1 (postmark date). $50 fee, may be waived for applicants with need. Admission notification on a rolling basis beginning on or about 11/1. Must reply by May 1 or within 2 week(s) if notified thereafter. Typically receive admissions decision 2-3 weeks after complete application is received. **Financial aid:** No deadline. FAFSA required. Applicants notified on a rolling basis starting 2/15.

Academics. Special study options: Cross-registration, distance learning, double major, dual enrollment of high school students, exchange student, external degree, independent study, internships, liberal arts/career combination, student-designed major, study abroad. Self-designed degree programs, independent study option. **Credit/placement by examination:** AP, CLEP, IB, institutional tests. 45 credit hours maximum toward associate degree, 90 toward bachelor's. **Support services:** Reduced course load, study skills assistance, tutoring, writing center.

Majors. Area/ethnic studies: Latin American/Caribbean. **Business:** Hospitality admin. **Social sciences:** International relations. **Visual/performing arts:** Documentaries, film/cinema/video, graphic design, photography, studio arts.

Most popular majors. Interdisciplinary studies 10%, legal studies 10%, psychology 16%, public administration/social services 6%, trade and industry 58%.

Technology on campus. 21 workstations in library, computer center. Dormitories wired for high-speed internet access. Commuter students can connect to campus network. Online library, wireless network available.

Student life. Freshman orientation: Mandatory, $150 fee. Preregistration for classes offered. Two to three - day program at beginning of term. **Policies:** On-campus student housing is required for any full-time, first-year college students from outside the greater Burlington area. Waivers are granted by petition in certain circumstances. Assistance procuring off-campus housing is offered through the Director of Student Life. **Housing:** Guaranteed on-campus for freshmen. Coed dorms, single-sex dorms, special housing for disabled, apartments available. $350 nonrefundable deposit. **Activities:** Film society, literary magazine, radio station, student government, student newspaper, Institute for Civic Engagement, Institute for Contemplative Studies.

Student services. Career counseling, student employment services, financial aid counseling, legal services.

Contact. E-mail: admissions@burlington.edu
Phone: (802) 862-9616 ext. 104
Toll-free number: (800) 862-9616 ext. 104 Fax: (802) 660-4331
Galen Hench, Director of Admissions, Burlington College, 351 North Avenue, Burlington, VT 05401

Castleton State College
Castleton, Vermont
www.castleton.edu

CB member
CB code: 3765

- Public 4-year liberal arts college
- Residential campus in small town
- 1,890 degree-seeking undergraduates: 9% part-time, 52% women
- 58 degree-seeking graduate students
- SAT or ACT (ACT writing optional), application essay required

General. Founded in 1787. Regionally accredited. **Degrees:** 352 bachelor's, 80 associate awarded; master's offered. **ROTC:** Army. **Location:** 12 miles from Rutland. **Calendar:** Semester, limited summer session. **Full-time faculty:** 102 total; 98% have terminal degrees, 5% minority, 53% women. **Part-time faculty:** 126 total; 25% have terminal degrees, 2% minority, 48% women. **Class size:** 70% < 20, 27% 20-39, less than 1% 40-49, 1% 50-99, less than 1% >100. **Special facilities:** Medical college museum, outdoor classroom, observatory.

Freshman class profile.

GPA 3.75 or higher:	11%	Rank in top quarter:	29%
GPA 3.50-3.74:	10%	Rank in top tenth:	6%
GPA 3.0-3.49:	26%	Out-of-state:	36%
GPA 2.0-2.99:	51%	Live on campus:	84%

Basis for selection. School achievement record, test scores, essay, recommendations, class rank very important. Interview recommended for all; audition recommended for music.

High school preparation. College-preparatory program required. 16 units required; 18 recommended. Required and recommended units include English 4, mathematics 3, social studies 3, history 3, science 3 (laboratory 2) and foreign language 2.

2015-2016 Annual costs. Tuition/fees: $11,282; $26,690 out-of-state. Room/board: $9,696. Books/supplies: $1,200. Personal expenses: $825. **Additional information:** Nursing students pay $13,320 in-state, $28,728 out-of-state. Qualified international students and New England Board of Higher Education rate for students from other New England states: 150% of Vermont resident tuition [$15,408]. International rate for qualified nursing students $20,016. International students pay a $100 international fee per semester.

Financial aid. Non-need-based: Scholarships awarded for academics, alumni affiliation, music/drama, state residency.

Application procedures. Admission: Priority date 5/1; no deadline. $40 fee, may be waived for applicants with need. Admission notification on a rolling basis beginning on or about 11/1. Must reply by May 1 or within 2 week(s) if notified thereafter. **Financial aid:** Priority date 4/1; no closing date. FAFSA required. Applicants notified by 2/21; must reply within 2 week(s) of notification.

Academics. Special study options: Combined bachelor's/graduate degree, cooperative education, cross-registration, double major, dual enrollment of high school students, ESL, honors, independent study, internships, liberal arts/career combination, student-designed major, study abroad, teacher certification program. 5-year Master's in Accounting through Castleton; 5-year MBA with Clarkson University; 7-year physical therapy with Sage Graduate School; 6-year occupational therapy with Sage Graduate School. **Credit/placement by examination:** AP, CLEP, SAT, ACT, institutional tests. 30 credit hours maximum toward associate degree, 60 toward bachelor's. **Support services:** Learning center, pre-admission summer program, reduced course load, remedial instruction, study skills assistance, tutoring, writing center.

Majors. Biology: General. **Business:** General, accounting, business admin, management science, marketing. **Communications:** Digital media, journalism, media studies. **Computer sciences:** General. **Conservation:** Environmental science. **Education:** Art, biology, chemistry, drama/dance, elementary, English, foreign languages, history, mathematics, middle, music, physical, physics, science, secondary, social science, social studies, Spanish. **English:** American lit, English lit. **Foreign languages:** Spanish. **Health services:** Athletic training, nursing (RN). **History:** General. **Human services:** Social work. **Math:** General, statistics. **Parks/recreation:** Exercise sciences, health/fitness, sports admin. **Philosophy/religion:** Philosophy. **Physical sciences:** Geology. **Protective services:** Criminal justice. **Psychology:** General. **Social sciences:** General, criminology, sociology. **Visual/performing arts:** General, art, dramatic, music.

Most popular majors. Business/marketing 13%, communications/journalism 10%, health sciences 20%, parks/recreation 9%, psychology 6%, visual/performing arts 6%.

Technology on campus. 225 workstations in dormitories, library, computer center. Dormitories wired for high-speed internet access and linked to campus network. Commuter students can connect to campus network. Repair service, wireless network available.

Student life. Freshman orientation: Mandatory. Preregistration for classes offered. Two-and-a-half day program. **Housing:** Guaranteed on-campus for freshmen. Coed dorms available. $200 nonrefundable deposit, deadline 5/1. **Activities:** Bands, choral groups, dance, drama, film society, international student organizations, literary magazine, music ensembles, Model UN, musical theater, radio station, student government, student newspaper, TV station, Christian fellowships, political discussion group, Spanish club, social issues club, community service club, women's issues group.

Athletics. NCAA. **Intercollegiate:** Baseball M, basketball, cross-country, field hockey W, football (tackle) M, golf M, ice hockey, lacrosse, skiing, soccer, softball W, tennis, volleyball W. **Intramural:** Basketball, football (non-tackle), racquetball, soccer M, softball, swimming, table tennis, tennis, volleyball, water polo. **Team name:** Spartans.

Student services. Adult student services, alcohol/substance abuse counseling, career counseling, services for economically disadvantaged, student employment services, financial aid counseling, health services, personal counseling, placement for graduates, women's services.

Contact. E-mail: info@castleton.edu
Phone: (802) 468-1213 Toll-free number: (800) 639-8521
Fax: (802) 468-1476
Maurice Ouimet, Dean of Enrollment, Castleton State College, Seminary Street, Castleton, VT 05735

Champlain College
Burlington, Vermont
www.champlain.edu

CB member
CB code: 3291

▶ Private 4-year liberal arts and career college
▶ Residential campus in small city
▶ 3,249 degree-seeking undergraduates: 27% part-time, 42% women, 5% African American, 2% Asian American, 5% Hispanic/Latino, 3% Multiracial, non-Hispanic, 1% international
▶ 604 degree-seeking graduate students
▶ 66% of applicants admitted
▶ SAT or ACT (ACT writing optional), application essay required
▶ 58% graduate within 6 years

General. Founded in 1878. Regionally accredited. **Degrees:** 516 bachelor's, 28 associate awarded; master's offered. **ROTC:** Army. **Location:** 200 miles from Boston, 90 miles from Montreal. **Calendar:** Semester, extensive summer session. **Full-time faculty:** 113 total; 68% have terminal degrees, 38% women. **Part-time faculty:** 370 total; 14% have terminal degrees, 45% women. **Class size:** 68% < 20, 32% 20-39. **Special facilities:** Emergent media center, center for digital investigation, game studio.

Freshman class profile. 5,587 applied, 3,697 admitted, 554 enrolled.

Mid 50% test scores		GPA 2.0-2.99:	31%
SAT critical reading:	520-630	Rank in top quarter:	34%
SAT math:	510-630	Rank in top tenth:	10%
SAT writing:	490-600	End year in good standing:	90%
ACT composite:	23-29	Return as sophomores:	79%
GPA 3.75 or higher:	16%	Out-of-state:	83%
GPA 3.50-3.74:	16%	Live on campus:	97%
GPA 3.0-3.49:	37%		

Basis for selection. GPA, level of difficulty of high school curriculum, essay, SAT/ACT and counselor recommendations most important. Waiting list for radiography program. Portfolios required for certain majors. Interviews may be requested by applicant once full application is submitted, but not required. **Home schooled:** Transcript of courses and grades, state high school equivalency certificate, letter of recommendation (nonparent) required. GED or 2 SAT Subject Tests required. **Learning Disabled:** Interview.

High school preparation. College-preparatory program recommended. 20 units required. Required and recommended units include English 4, mathematics 3-4, social studies 2, history 4, science 3-4 (laboratory 3), foreign language 2-4 and academic electives 4.

2015-2016 Annual costs. Tuition/fees: $37,536. Room/board: $14,050. Books/supplies: $1,000. Personal expenses: $1,000.

2015-2016 Financial aid. Need-based: 473 full-time freshmen applied for aid; 405 deemed to have need; 404 received aid. Average need met was 70%. Average scholarship/grant was $19,068; average loan $3,969. 65% of total undergraduate aid awarded as scholarships/grants, 35% as loans/jobs. **Non-need-based:** Awarded to 775 full-time undergraduates, including 170 freshmen. Scholarships awarded for academics, leadership, minority status.

Application procedures. Admission: Closing date 2/1 (postmark date). No application fee. Admission notification by 3/25. Must reply by May 1 or within 2 week(s) if notified thereafter. Students eligible to defer admission once tuition deposit and housing deposit (if required) are received. **Financial aid:** Priority date 2/15; no closing date. FAFSA required. Applicants notified on a rolling basis starting 3/1; must reply by 5/1 or within 2 week(s) of notification.

Academics. Special study options: Accelerated study, combined bachelor's/graduate degree, cross-registration, distance learning, double major, independent study, internships, liberal arts/career combination, study abroad, teacher certification program. Clinical internships at Fletcher Allen Medical Center. **Credit/placement by examination:** AP, CLEP, IB, institutional tests. 75 credit hours maximum toward bachelor's degree. **Support services:** Reduced course load, study skills assistance, tutoring, writing center.

Majors. Business: General, accounting, business admin, hospitality admin, international, management information systems, marketing. **Communications:** Broadcast journalism, communications/speech/rhetoric, media studies, public relations. **Computer sciences:** Applications programming, computer graphics, computer science, information technology, networking, programming, security, system admin, web page design, webmaster. **Conservation:** Environmental studies. **Education:** Early childhood, elementary, middle, secondary. **English:** Writing. **Health services:** Facilities admin, medical informatics. **Human services:** Social work. **Liberal arts:** Arts/sciences. **Protective services:** Computer forensics, criminal justice, financial forensics. **Psychology:** General. **Visual/performing arts:** General, arts management, digital arts, film/cinema/video, game design, graphic design, multimedia.

Most popular majors. Business/marketing 26%, communications/journalism 10%, computer/information sciences 13%, education 6%, security/protective services 10%, visual/performing arts 17%.

Technology on campus. 260 workstations in library, computer center, student center. Dormitories wired for high-speed internet access and linked to campus network. Commuter students can connect to campus network. Online course registration, online library, helpline, wireless network available.

Student life. Freshman orientation: Available, $60 fee. Preregistration for classes offered. Three-day program. **Policies:** No alcohol permitted on campus. Freshmen not permitted cars on campus. **Housing:** Guaranteed on-campus for freshmen. Coed dorms, single-sex dorms, special housing for disabled, apartments, wellness housing available. $400 nonrefundable deposit, deadline 5/1. **Activities:** Choral groups, drama, international student organizations, literary magazine, musical theater, radio station, student government, student newspaper, cultural diversity committee, community service, wilderness club, heritage society, reader's exchange, flash animation club, intercollegiate writers exchange, anime club.

Athletics. Intramural: Basketball, field hockey W, football (non-tackle), ice hockey M, lacrosse M, skiing, soccer, table tennis, tennis, ultimate frisbee, volleyball. **Team name:** Beavers.

Student services. Adult student services, alcohol/substance abuse counseling, career counseling, student employment services, financial aid counseling, health services, minority student services, personal counseling, placement for graduates, veterans' counselor. **Physically disabled:** Services for visually, hearing impaired.

Contact. E-mail: admission@champlain.edu
Phone: (802) 860-2727 Toll-free number: (800) 570-5858
Fax: (802) 860-2767
Chris Perlong, Director, Undergraduate Admission, Champlain College, PO Box 670, Burlington, VT 05402-0670

College of St. Joseph in Vermont
Rutland, Vermont
www.csj.edu

CB member
CB code: 3297

▶ Private 4-year liberal arts and teachers college affiliated with the Roman Catholic Church
▶ Residential campus in large town
▶ 230 degree-seeking undergraduates
▶ Application essay required

General. Founded in 1950. Regionally accredited. **Degrees:** 30 bachelor's, 10 associate awarded; master's offered. **Location:** 70 miles from Burlington; 100 miles from Albany, NY. **Calendar:** Semester, extensive summer session. **Full-time faculty:** 12 total; 75% have terminal degrees, 8% minority, 33% women. **Part-time faculty:** 47 total; 17% have terminal degrees, 4% minority, 49% women. **Class size:** 97% < 20, 3% 20-39.

Freshman class profile.

GPA 3.75 or higher:	5%	Rank in top quarter:	20%
GPA 3.50-3.74:	4%	Out-of-state:	36%
GPA 3.0-3.49:	36%	Live on campus:	70%
GPA 2.0-2.99:	54%		

Basis for selection. Course selection, GPA in college preparatory courses, 2 academic letters of recommendation, personal statement/essay, ACT or SAT scores most important. Extracurricular activities and evidence of leadership skills considered. SAT or ACT recommended. Although not required, interviews are available. **Home schooled:** Statement describing home school structure and mission, transcript of courses and grades, interview, letter of recommendation (nonparent) required. Successful completion of GED.

High school preparation. College-preparatory program recommended. 16 units recommended. Recommended units include English 4, mathematics 3, social studies 2, science 2 (laboratory 2) and academic electives 5.

2015-2016 Annual costs. Tuition/fees: $21,900. Room/board: $10,500. Books/supplies: $1,300. Personal expenses: $1,350.

Financial aid. Non-need-based: Scholarships awarded for academics, alumni affiliation.

Application procedures. Admission: Priority date 5/1; no deadline. $25 fee, may be waived for applicants with need. Admission notification on a rolling basis beginning on or about 11/15. Must reply by May 1 or within 2 week(s) if notified thereafter. **Financial aid:** Priority date 3/1; no closing date. FAFSA, institutional form required. Applicants notified on a rolling basis starting 3/1.

Academics. Experiential educational options including internships available. **Special study options:** Accelerated study, double major, dual enrollment of high school students, independent study, internships, liberal arts/career combination, teacher certification program. **Credit/placement by examination:** AP, CLEP, IB, SAT, ACT, institutional tests. 12 credit hours maximum toward associate degree, 12 toward bachelor's. **Support services:** Learning center, reduced course load, remedial instruction, study skills assistance, tutoring, writing center.

Majors. Business: Accounting, business admin, operations. **Education:** English, history, multi-level teacher, secondary, social studies. **English:** English lit. **Health services:** Radiologic technology/medical imaging, substance abuse counseling. **History:** General. **Liberal arts:** Arts/sciences. **Parks/recreation:** Sports admin. **Protective services:** Law enforcement admin. **Psychology:** General.

Most popular majors. Business/marketing 29%, English 8%, history 8%, interdisciplinary studies 11%, liberal arts 11%, psychology 11%, public administration/social services 13%.

Technology on campus. 33 workstations in library, computer center, student center. Dormitories wired for high-speed internet access and linked to campus network. Online library, wireless network available.

Student life. Freshman orientation: Mandatory, $150 fee. Preregistration for classes offered. Four day orientation before upperclassmen move into dorms. **Housing:** Guaranteed on-campus for all undergraduates. Single-sex dorms available. $200 nonrefundable deposit, deadline 5/1. Some single rooms available and graduate housing available. **Activities:** Campus ministries, student government, student newspaper, human services club, business club, honor societies, farming club.

Athletics. USCAA. **Intercollegiate:** Baseball M, basketball, bowling, soccer, softball W. **Intramural:** Soccer. **Team name:** Fighting Saints.

Student services. Adult student services, alcohol/substance abuse counseling, chaplain/spiritual director, career counseling, services for economically disadvantaged, student employment services, financial aid counseling, personal counseling, placement for graduates, veterans' counselor. **Physically disabled:** Services for visually, speech, hearing impaired.

Contact. E-mail: admissions@csj.edu
Phone: (802) 773-5900 ext. 3286 Toll-free number: (877) 270-9998
Fax: (802) 776-5310
Judy Morgan, Director of Admissions, College of St. Joseph in Vermont, 71 Clement Road, Rutland, VT 05701-3899

Goddard College
Plainfield, Vermont
www.goddard.edu CB code: 3416

- Private 4-year liberal arts college
- Commuter campus in rural community
- 181 degree-seeking undergraduates: 4% part-time, 64% women
- 328 degree-seeking graduate students
- Application essay, interview required

General. Founded in 1938. Regionally accredited. All programs operate exclusively on a low-residency model entailing 8 days on campus at the beginning of each semester. Students study from home or elsewhere the rest of the term. This is neither a residential model nor an online approach, but blends aspects of both to provide maximum operational flexibility for students with other commitments while maintaining academic rigor. **Degrees:** 83 bachelor's awarded; master's offered. **Location:** 10 miles from Montpelier, 45 miles from Burlington. **Calendar:** Semester. **Full-time faculty:** 15 total; 67% have terminal degrees, 73% women. **Part-time faculty:** 79 total; 85% have terminal degrees, 78% women. **Special facilities:** Radio broadcast and internet station.

Basis for selection. Academic performance and potential, maturity, ability to work independently, personal statement, interview most important; creative portfolio, additional writing sample, and/or TOEFL score may be requested. Portfolio required for creative writing program. **Home schooled:** State high school equivalency certificate required. GED recommended. Students can self-certify.

High school preparation. College-preparatory program recommended. Recommended units include English 4, mathematics 4, social studies 4, science 4 (laboratory 3) and foreign language 2.

2015-2016 Annual costs. Tuition/fees: $15,476. Room/board: $1,564. Books/supplies: $600.

2014-2015 Financial aid. Need-based: 4 full-time freshmen applied for aid; 4 deemed to have need; 3 received aid. Average need met was 30%. Average scholarship/grant was $11,630; average loan $4,216. 32% of total undergraduate aid awarded as scholarships/grants, 68% as loans/jobs. **Non-need-based:** Awarded to 12 full-time undergraduates, including 1 freshmen. Scholarships awarded for academics, art, job skills, leadership, music/drama, state residency.

Application procedures. Admission: $65 fee, may be waived for applicants with need. Admission notification on a rolling basis. Application closing dates and reply dates vary by program. **Financial aid:** No deadline. FAFSA required. Applicants notified on a rolling basis starting 4/15; must reply within 4 week(s) of notification.

Academics. Special study options: Combined bachelor's/graduate degree, distance learning, external degree, independent study, internships, student-designed major, study abroad, teacher certification program. Guided independent study programs convenient for working adults. MFA in Creative Writing and MFA in Interdisciplinary Arts also offered in Port Townsend, WA. Non-licensure BA and MA Education programs also offered in Seattle, WA. **Credit/placement by examination:** AP, CLEP, IB. 30 credit hours maximum toward bachelor's degree. **Support services:** Study skills assistance, writing center.

Majors. Area/ethnic studies: General, African-American, American, European, gay/lesbian, Latin American, Native American, Near/Middle Eastern, women's. **Business:** Business admin. **Conservation:** Environmental studies. **Education:** General, art, curriculum, early childhood, elementary, English, foundations, history, middle, multi-level teacher, secondary, social studies. **English:** Creative writing, English lit. **Health services:** Aromatherapy, community health, community health services, environmental health, herbalism, movement therapy, polarity therapy, public health ed, Reiki, somatic bodywork. **History:** General. **Liberal arts:** Arts/sciences, humanities. **Psychology:** General, clinical. **Social sciences:** General, cultural anthropology.

Most popular majors. Education 14%, health sciences 17%, interdisciplinary studies 62%.

Technology on campus. PC or laptop required. 100 workstations in library, computer center, student center. Dormitories wired for high-speed internet access and linked to campus network. Commuter students can connect to campus network. Online library, helpline, wireless network available.

Student life. Freshman orientation: Mandatory. Preregistration for classes offered. Full-day, conducted the day before registration. **Policies:** Dogs not allowed on campus, with the exception of service dogs. **Housing:** Coed dorms, single-sex dorms, apartments, themed housing, wellness housing available. $250 nonrefundable deposit. Housing available 8 days per semester, for the duration of the on-campus residencies. **Activities:** Literary magazine, radio station, student government.

Student services. Financial aid counseling. **Physically disabled:** Services for hearing impaired.

Contact. E-mail: admissions@goddard.edu
Phone: (802) 454-8311 ext. 243 Toll-free number: (800) 906-8312
Fax: (802) 454-1029
Gariot Louima, Dean of Enrollment, Goddard College, 123 Pitkin Road, Plainfield, VT 05667

Green Mountain College
Poultney, Vermont CB member
www.greenmtn.edu CB code: 3418

- Private 4-year liberal arts college affiliated with the United Methodist Church
- Residential campus in small town
- 582 degree-seeking undergraduates: 3% part-time, 51% women, 4% African American, 1% Asian American, 3% Hispanic/Latino, 1% Native American, 1% Multi-racial, non-Hispanic, 3% international
- 267 degree-seeking graduate students
- 66% of applicants admitted
- Application essay required
- 38% graduate within 6 years

General. Founded in 1834. Regionally accredited. **Degrees:** 113 bachelor's awarded; master's offered. **Location:** 20 miles from Rutland, 35 miles from Killington. **Calendar:** Continuous, limited summer session. **Full-time faculty:** 40 total; 92% have terminal degrees, 5% minority, 35% women. **Part-time faculty:** 39 total; 20% have terminal degrees, 3% minority, 41% women. **Class size:** 55% < 20, 45% 20-39. **Special facilities:** Student-operated organically managed farm, ropes course, 80-acre nature preserve, collection of

Welsh artifacts and literature, collection of early American decoration, art collection.

Freshman class profile. 825 applied, 544 admitted, 132 enrolled.

Mid 50% test scores		End year in good standing:	89%
SAT critical reading:	480-590	Return as sophomores:	66%
SAT math:	460-530	Out-of-state:	90%
SAT writing:	430-580	Live on campus:	98%
ACT composite:	18-24	International:	7%

Basis for selection. Academic achievement, recommendations, interview, essay, test scores or Insight portfolio submission, personal statement, school and community activities important. SAT/ACT required for students with GED and students attending high schools outside of the US. Interview recommended; audition recommended for theater or music; portfolio recommended for art. **Home schooled:** Statement describing home school structure and mission, transcript of courses and grades, state high school equivalency certificate, letter of recommendation (nonparent) required. Applicants advised to develop thorough portfolio of all work completed; on-campus interview highly encouraged. SAT/ACT required.

High school preparation. College-preparatory program recommended. 21 units required. Required and recommended units include English 4, mathematics 3-4, social studies 3, history 1-2, science 3-4 (laboratory 2), foreign language 1-2 and academic electives 5.

2015-2016 Annual costs. Tuition/fees: $35,340. Room/board: $11,492. Personal expenses: $590.

2015-2016 Financial aid. Need-based: 118 full-time freshmen applied for aid; 111 deemed to have need; 111 received aid. Average need met was 83%. Average scholarship/grant was $29,878; average loan $3,480. 79% of total undergraduate aid awarded as scholarships/grants, 21% as loans/jobs. **Non-need-based:** Awarded to 134 full-time undergraduates, including 39 freshmen. Scholarships awarded for academics, alumni affiliation, religious affiliation, state residency. **Additional information:** Service/recognition awards available to all students, determined by admission application and supplemental documentation. VT resident grant matching UVM tuition, to help meet on average 90% of a student's demonstrated need.

Application procedures. Admission: Priority date 3/1; no deadline. $30 fee, may be waived for applicants with need, free for online applicants. Admission notification on a rolling basis beginning on or about 9/1. Must reply by May 1 or within 2 week(s) if notified thereafter. **Financial aid:** Priority date 3/1; no closing date. FAFSA required. Applicants notified on a rolling basis starting 11/1; must reply by 5/1 or within 3 week(s) of notification.

Academics. Special study options: Accelerated study, combined bachelor's/graduate degree, distance learning, double major, dual enrollment of high school students, ESL, exchange student, honors, independent study, internships, liberal arts/career combination, student-designed major, study abroad, teacher certification program. Exchange programs at Aberystwyth University (Wales), Hannam University (Korea), Nogoya University (Japan). Credit granted for programs of National Outdoor Leadership School. Member of Eco-League Consortium: students can spend up to 2 semesters at one of 5 other schools: Alaska Pacific University, College of the Atlantic, Dickinson College, Northland College, Prescott College. **Credit/placement by examination:** AP, CLEP, IB, SAT, ACT, institutional tests. **Support services:** Learning center, reduced course load, remedial instruction, study skills assistance, tutoring, writing center.

Majors. Biology: General. **Business:** Hospitality/recreation, managerial economics, resort management. **Communications:** Media studies. **Conservation:** General, environmental studies. **Education:** Art, elementary, English, secondary, social studies. **English:** Creative writing, English lit. **History:** General. **Liberal arts:** Arts/sciences. **Parks/recreation:** General. **Philosophy/religion:** Philosophy. **Psychology:** General. **Social sciences:** Sociology. **Visual/performing arts:** Art, studio arts.

Most popular majors. Agriculture 6%, architecture 7%, business/marketing 18%, English 7%, liberal arts 6%, natural resources/environmental science 15%, parks/recreation 11%, psychology 8%, visual/performing arts 7%.

Technology on campus. 104 workstations in library, computer center, student center. Dormitories wired for high-speed internet access and linked to campus network. Commuter students can connect to campus network. Online course registration, online library, helpline, wireless network available.

Student life. Freshman orientation: Mandatory, $250 fee. Preregistration for classes offered. Held week before classes begin in August and January. Students may opt to come to campus earlier in the summer for wilderness trips. **Housing:** Guaranteed on-campus for all undergraduates. Coed dorms, themed housing, wellness housing available. $400 nonrefundable deposit. **Activities:** Bands, choral groups, drama, film society, international student organizations, literary magazine, music ensembles, Model UN, student government, student newspaper, outdoor adventure programs, environmental

volunteer and research groups, UNICEF, Club Activism, DREAM Mentoring Club, Intercultural Club, and Rotaract Club.

Athletics. NCAA. **Intercollegiate:** Basketball, cross-country, golf, lacrosse, soccer, tennis, track and field, volleyball W. **Team name:** Eagles.

Student services. Chaplain/spiritual director, career counseling, student employment services, financial aid counseling, health services, personal counseling, placement for graduates.

Contact. E-mail: admiss@greenmtn.edu
Phone: (802) 287-8207 Toll-free number: (800) 776-6675
Fax: (802) 287-8099
Jeffrey Mon, Dean of Enrollment Management and Marketing, Green Mountain College, One Brennan Circle, Poultney, VT 05764

Johnson State College

Johnson, Vermont
www.jsc.edu

CB member
CB code: 3766

- Public 4-year liberal arts college
- Residential campus in small town
- 1,320 degree-seeking undergraduates: 28% part-time, 67% women, 3% African American, 1% Asian American, 3% Hispanic/Latino, 1% Native American, 3% Multi-racial, non-Hispanic, 1% international
- 146 degree-seeking graduate students
- Application essay required
- 35% graduate within 6 years

General. Founded in 1828. Regionally accredited. **Degrees:** 313 bachelor's, 6 associate awarded; master's offered. **ROTC:** Army. **Location:** 50 miles from Burlington, 90 miles from Montreal. **Calendar:** Semester, limited summer session. **Full-time faculty:** 42 total; 5% minority, 38% women. **Part-time faculty:** 145 total; 62% women. **Class size:** 79% < 20, 21% 20-39. **Special facilities:** 1,000-acre nature preserve, visual arts center, human performance laboratory, interactive multimedia, math/science laboratory, recording studio, community service learning center, Vermont interactive television site, snowboard park.

Freshman class profile.

Return as sophomores:	68%	Live on campus:	88%
Out-of-state:	34%		

Basis for selection. High school transcript, GPA, SAT/ACT (Test Optional), class rank, recommendations, and essay important. SAT or ACT recommended. Tests not required with GED. Interview recommended. Music Performance requires audition CD or DVD. **Home schooled:** Transcript of courses and grades, state high school equivalency certificate, letter of recommendation (nonparent) required. Applicants encouraged to complete GED or other state certified achievement test to demonstrate aptitude.

High school preparation. 9 units required; 15 recommended. Required and recommended units include English 4, mathematics 3-4, social studies 2, history 2, science 2-3 (laboratory 1-2) and foreign language 1. Math units must include algebra I, geometry and algebra II.

2015-2016 Annual costs. Tuition/fees: $11,018; $23,714 out-of-state. Room/board: $9,696. Books/supplies: $1,200. Personal expenses: $700. **Additional information:** New England Board of Higher Education rate for students from other New England states: 150% of Vermont resident tuition. Available to degree candidates in academic areas not offered by educational institutions in their home states.

2015-2016 Financial aid. Non-need-based: Scholarships awarded for academics, alumni affiliation, art, leadership, music/drama, state residency.

Application procedures. Admission: Priority date 3/1; no deadline. $40 fee, may be waived for applicants with need. Admission notification on a rolling basis. Must reply by May 1 or within 2 week(s) if notified thereafter. **Financial aid:** Priority date 3/1; no closing date. FAFSA required. Applicants notified on a rolling basis starting 2/15; must reply within 3 week(s) of notification.

Academics. Special study options: Distance learning, double major, dual enrollment of high school students, exchange student, external degree, independent study, internships, study abroad, teacher certification program. **Credit/placement by examination:** AP, CLEP, IB, institutional tests. **Support services:** Learning center, pre-admission summer program, reduced course load, remedial instruction, study skills assistance, tutoring, writing center.

Majors. Biology: General, cell/histology, molecular. **Business:** General, accounting, business admin, hospitality admin. **Communications:** General, digital media, journalism, persuasive communications, photojournalism. **Conservation:** General, environmental studies. **Education:** General, art, biology, drama/dance, elementary, English, history, mathematics, middle, multi-level teacher, music, physical, science, secondary, social science, social studies. **English:** English lit. **Foreign languages:** Comparative lit. **Health services:** Premedicine. **History:** General. **Liberal arts:** Arts/sciences. **Math:** General. **Parks/recreation:** General, exercise sciences, health/fitness, outdoor education, sports admin. **Protective services:** Police science. **Psychology:** General, medical. **Social sciences:** Anthropology, political science, sociology. **Visual/performing arts:** General, art, dramatic, jazz, music, musical theater, studio arts, theater design, voice/opera.

Most popular majors. Business/marketing 13%, health sciences 6%, liberal arts 26%, psychology 20%, visual/performing arts 9%.

Technology on campus. 131 workstations in library, computer center, student center. Dormitories wired for high-speed internet access and linked to campus network. Commuter students can connect to campus network. Online course registration, online library, helpline, wireless network available.

Student life. Freshman orientation: Mandatory, $245 fee. Preregistration for classes offered. One-day program held weekend prior to beginning of classes. **Policies:** Campus housing required for first four semesters of college. **Housing:** Guaranteed on-campus for all undergraduates. Coed dorms, apartments, gender-neutral housing, wellness housing available. $100 nonrefundable deposit, deadline 5/1. **Activities:** Bands, campus ministries, choral groups, dance, drama, film society, international student organizations, literary magazine, music ensembles, musical theater, radio station, student government, student newspaper, behavioral science club, Christian fellowship club, diversity committee, political awareness club, Habitat for Humanity, Native American club, Students Enriching and Responding Through Volunteer Efforts, Earth awareness club.

Athletics. NCAA. Intercollegiate: Basketball, cross-country, golf M, lacrosse M, soccer, softball W, tennis, track and field, volleyball W. **Intramural:** Badminton, basketball, golf, lacrosse, racquetball, rugby, soccer, softball, swimming, table tennis, tennis, ultimate frisbee, volleyball, water polo, weight lifting. **Team name:** Badgers.

Student services. Adult student services, alcohol/substance abuse counseling, career counseling, services for economically disadvantaged, student employment services, financial aid counseling, health services, personal counseling, placement for graduates, veterans' counselor, women's services. **Physically disabled:** Services for visually, hearing impaired.

Contact. E-mail: jscadmissions@jsc.edu
Phone: (802) 635-1219 Toll-free number: (800) 635-2356
Fax: (802) 635-1230
Penny Howrigan, Associate Dean of Enrollment Services, Johnson State College, 337 College Hill, Johnson, VT 05656

Lyndon State College
Lyndonville, Vermont
www.lyndonstate.edu   **CB code: 3767**

- Public 4-year liberal arts and teachers college
- Residential campus in small town
- 1,447 undergraduates
- SAT or ACT (ACT writing recommended), application essay required

General. Founded in 1911. Regionally accredited. **Degrees:** 247 bachelor's, 31 associate awarded; master's offered. **ROTC:** Army, Air Force. **Location:** 10 miles from St. Johnsbury, 75 miles from Burlington. **Calendar:** Semester, limited summer session. **Full-time faculty:** 54 total. **Part-time faculty:** 85 total. **Special facilities:** Meteorology laboratory and observation deck, ropes course, rock climbing wall, ski resorts, force plate, music production studio, television studio.

Freshman class profile.

Out-of-state: 43%   **Live on campus:**   50%

Basis for selection. School record, GPA, recommendations, test scores, and personal essay most important. **Home schooled:** Statement describing home school structure and mission, transcript of courses and grades, state high school equivalency certificate, letter of recommendation (nonparent) required. **Learning Disabled:** Students must meet with learning specialist and provide documentation of disability.

High school preparation. College-preparatory program recommended. Required and recommended units include English 4, mathematics 3-4, social studies 2, history 1, science 2-4 (laboratory 2) and foreign language 2. Physics and pre-calc for meteorology and computer science recommended.

2015-2016 Annual costs. Tuition/fees: $11,018; $22,418 out-of-state. Room/board: $9,696. Books/supplies: $1,000. Personal expenses: $600. **Additional information:** New England Board of Higher Education rate for students from other New England states: 150% of Vermont resident tuition. Available to degree candidates in academic areas not offered by educational institutions in their home states.

Financial aid. Non-need-based: Scholarships awarded for academics, leadership.

Application procedures. Admission: Priority date 5/1; no deadline. $46 fee, may be waived for applicants with need. Admission notification on a rolling basis beginning on or about 11/1. Must reply by May 1 or within 2 week(s) if notified thereafter. **Financial aid:** Priority date 2/1; no closing date. FAFSA required. Applicants notified on a rolling basis starting 4/1; must reply within 2 week(s) of notification.

Academics. Special study options: Combined bachelor's/graduate degree, cooperative education, distance learning, double major, dual enrollment of high school students, ESL, independent study, internships, liberal arts/career combination, student-designed major, study abroad, teacher certification program. **Credit/placement by examination:** AP, CLEP, IB, SAT, ACT, institutional tests. 60 credit hours maximum toward bachelor's degree. **Support services:** Learning center, pre-admission summer program, reduced course load, remedial instruction, study skills assistance, tutoring, writing center.

Majors. Business: Accounting, accounting/business management, accounting/finance, business admin, entrepreneurial studies, finance, marketing, resort management, small business admin. **Communications:** Broadcast journalism, communications/speech/rhetoric, journalism, media studies, photojournalism, radio/TV. **Communications technology:** General. **Computer sciences:** General, computer graphics, information technology. **Conservation:** Environmental science. **Education:** General, early childhood, elementary, English, physical, science, social science, special ed. **English:** English lit. **Health services:** Athletic training, physical therapy assistant, physician assistant, prenursing. **Liberal arts:** Arts/sciences. **Math:** General. **Parks/recreation:** Exercise sciences, facilities management, health/fitness, sports admin. **Philosophy/religion:** Philosophy. **Physical sciences:** Atmospheric science, climatology, meteorology. **Protective services:** Criminal justice. **Psychology:** General. **Social sciences:** General. **Visual/performing arts:** General, commercial/advertising art, design, digital arts, graphic design, illustration, music management, music performance.

Technology on campus. 310 workstations in dormitories, library, computer center, student center. Dormitories wired for high-speed internet access and linked to campus network. Commuter students can connect to campus network. Online course registration, online library, helpline, repair service, wireless network available.

Student life. Freshman orientation: Mandatory, $25 fee. Preregistration for classes offered. **Policies:** Unmarried students under 23 must live on-campus for 2 consecutive years (1 year requirement for sophomore-level transfers) unless residing with parents within 45-mile commuting distance. Exceptions made on case-by-case basis. **Housing:** Guaranteed on-campus for all undergraduates. Coed dorms, single-sex dorms, special housing for disabled, apartments, wellness housing available. $100 partly refundable deposit, deadline 5/1. **Activities:** Concert band, choral groups, dance, drama, international student organizations, literary magazine, music ensembles, Model UN, musical theater, radio station, student government, student newspaper, TV station, American Meteorological Society (student chapter), community service learning group, alternative spring break.

Athletics. NCAA. Intercollegiate: Baseball M, basketball, cross-country, ice hockey, lacrosse M, soccer, softball W, tennis. **Intramural:** Baseball M, basketball, cross-country, handball, ice hockey, lacrosse M, racquetball, rugby, soccer, softball, squash, swimming, table tennis, tennis, track and field, volleyball, water polo M, weight lifting. **Team name:** Hornets.

Student services. Adult student services, alcohol/substance abuse counseling, career counseling, student employment services, financial aid counseling, health services, personal counseling, placement for graduates, veterans' counselor. **Physically disabled:** Services for visually, hearing impaired.

Contact. E-mail: admissions@lyndonstate.edu
Phone: (802) 626-6413 Toll-free number: (800) 225-1998
Fax: (802) 626-6335
Vincent Maloney, Director of Admissions, Lyndon State College, 1001 College Road, Lyndonville, VT 05851

Marlboro College

Marlboro, Vermont
www.marlboro.edu

CB member
CB code: 3509

- Private 4-year liberal arts college
- Residential campus in rural community
- 182 degree-seeking undergraduates: 2% part-time, 48% women
- 87 graduate students
- Application essay required

General. Founded in 1946. Regionally accredited. **Degrees:** 49 bachelor's awarded; master's offered. **Location:** 12 miles from Brattleboro; 70 miles from Albany, NY. **Calendar:** Semester. **Full-time faculty:** 38 total; 87% have terminal degrees, 3% minority, 45% women. **Part-time faculty:** 13 total; 46% have terminal degrees, 77% women. **Class size:** 98% < 20, 2% 20-39. **Special facilities:** Aviary, observatory, darkroom, theater 3/4 round, robotics lab, DNA lab, nature preserve, organic campus farm.

Freshman class profile.

GPA 3.75 or higher:	24%	Rank in top quarter:	31%
GPA 3.50-3.74:	12%	Rank in top tenth:	8%
GPA 3.0-3.49:	43%	Out-of-state:	84%
GPA 2.0-2.99:	15%	Live on campus:	94%

Basis for selection. Academic ability, intellectual potential, writing skills, demonstrated leadership qualities, and potential to offer contribution to college community most important. Interview strongly advised. **Home schooled:** Statement describing home school structure and mission, letter of recommendation (nonparent) required. Provide documentation of home school curriculum and projects. List of textbooks preferred. Writing sample required. **Learning Disabled:** Additional documentation may be required.

High school preparation. 14 units recommended. Recommended units include English 4, mathematics 3, social studies 2, history 2, science 3 and foreign language 2.

2015-2016 Annual costs. Tuition/fees: $39,250. Room/board: $10,590. Books/supplies: $1,200.

2015-2016 Financial aid. Need-based: 34 full-time freshmen applied for aid; 31 deemed to have need; 31 received aid. Average need met was 78%. Average scholarship/grant was $29,231; average loan $3,451. 74% of total undergraduate aid awarded as scholarships/grants, 26% as loans/jobs. **Non-need-based:** Awarded to 27 full-time undergraduates, including 3 freshmen. Scholarships awarded for academics, leadership.

Application procedures. Admission: Priority date 3/1; no deadline. $50 fee, may be waived for applicants with need. Admission notification on a rolling basis. Must reply by May 1 or within 2 week(s) if notified thereafter. **Financial aid:** Closing date 3/1. FAFSA required. Applicants notified on a rolling basis starting 3/1; must reply within 2 week(s) of notification.

Academics. Students self-design field of study, often interdisciplinary in nature. They work closely with faculty to determine concentration and have formal review in senior year by internal and external faculty. **Special study options:** Combined bachelor's/graduate degree, cross-registration, double major, exchange student, independent study, internships, student-designed major, study abroad. World Studies Program: opportunity to integrate study-abroad experience and/or internship in undergraduate course of study. **Credit/ placement by examination:** AP, CLEP, IB, institutional tests. **Support services:** Learning center, reduced course load, study skills assistance, tutoring, writing center.

Majors. Area/ethnic studies: American, Asian, East Asian, European, Latin American, Near/Middle Eastern, Russian/Eastern European/Eurasian, Russian/Slavic, South Asian, Southeast Asian, Western European. **Biology:** General, biochemistry, botany, cell/histology, ecology, genetics, molecular, plant physiology. **Computer sciences:** General, computer science. **Conservation:** General, environmental studies. **English:** American lit, British lit, creative writing, English lit, writing. **Foreign languages:** General, comparative lit, linguistics, Spanish, translation. **History:** General. **Liberal arts:** Arts/sciences. **Math:** General. **Philosophy/religion:** Philosophy, religion. **Physical sciences:** Astronomy, chemistry, organic chemistry, physics, theoretical physics. **Psychology:** General. **Social sciences:** General, anthropology, economics, political science, sociology. **Visual/performing arts:** General, art, art history/conservation, ceramics, cinematography, dance, dramatic, drawing, film/cinema/video, music, music history, painting, photography, play/screenwriting, sculpture, studio arts, theater design, theater history.

Most popular majors. Area/ethnic studies 13%, biology 7%, English 13%, philosophy/religious studies 9%, social sciences 14%, visual/performing arts 27%.

Technology on campus. 45 workstations in dormitories, library, computer center. Dormitories wired for high-speed internet access and linked to campus network. Commuter students can connect to campus network. Online course registration, online library, helpline, student web hosting, wireless network available.

Student life. Freshman orientation: Mandatory. Preregistration for classes offered. Five-day program in late August; pre-orientation outdoor trips held the week prior to on-campus orientation and student enrollment. **Policies:** Self-governing community based on old-fashioned, historical New England-style town meeting. Students, faculty, and staff have equal vote. Elected community court enforces bylaws. **Housing:** Guaranteed on-campus for freshmen. Coed dorms, single-sex dorms, special housing for disabled, apartments, cooperative housing, wellness housing available. $400 nonrefundable deposit, deadline 5/1. **Activities:** Dance, drama, film society, literary magazine, music ensembles, musical theater, radio station, student government, student newspaper, Amnesty International, animal rights, gay/lesbian and bisexual group, committee on environmental quality, fire and safety commission.

Athletics. Intercollegiate: Soccer. **Intramural:** Basketball, fencing, soccer, volleyball.

Student services. Alcohol/substance abuse counseling, career counseling, student employment services, financial aid counseling, health services, personal counseling, placement for graduates. **Physically disabled:** Services for visually, speech, hearing impaired.

Contact. E-mail: admissions@marlboro.edu
Phone: (802) 258-9236 Toll-free number: (800) 343-0049
Fax: (802) 451-7555
Brigid Lawler, Dean of Admissions, Marlboro College, PO Box A, Marlboro, VT 05344-0300

Middlebury College

Middlebury, Vermont
www.middlebury.edu

CB member
CB code: 3526

- Private 4-year liberal arts college
- Residential campus in small town
- 2,516 degree-seeking undergraduates: 1% part-time, 53% women, 3% African American, 6% Asian American, 9% Hispanic/Latino, 5% Multiracial, non-Hispanic, 11% international
- 16 degree-seeking graduate students
- 17% of applicants admitted
- SAT and SAT Subject Tests or ACT (ACT writing optional), application essay required
- 94% graduate within 6 years; 12% enter graduate study

General. Founded in 1800. Regionally accredited. **Degrees:** 685 bachelor's awarded; master's, doctoral offered. **ROTC:** Army. **Location:** 200 miles from Boston, 250 miles from New York City. **Calendar:** 4-1-4, limited summer session. **Full-time faculty:** 283 total; 94% have terminal degrees, 18% minority, 45% women. **Part-time faculty:** 63 total; 87% have terminal degrees, 22% minority, 43% women. **Class size:** 67% < 20, 28% 20-39, 4% 40-49, 1% 50-99. **Special facilities:** Observatory, fine arts center, downhill and cross country ski areas, interactive language laboratories, 18-hole golf course.

Freshman class profile. 8,891 applied, 1,551 admitted, 589 enrolled.

Mid 50% test scores			
SAT critical reading:	630-750	Return as sophomores:	97%
SAT math:	640-750	Out-of-state:	94%
SAT writing:	650-760	Live on campus:	100%
ACT composite:	29-33	International:	10%

Basis for selection. School record most important (including course selection and course load), followed by class rank, extracurricular activities, letters of recommendation, and test scores. ACT/SAT or 3 SAT Subject Tests required.

High school preparation. College-preparatory program recommended. Recommended units include English 4, mathematics 4, social studies 3, science 3 (laboratory 3) and foreign language 4.

2015-2016 Annual costs. Tuition/fees: $47,828. Room/board: $13,628. Books/supplies: $1,000. Personal expenses: $1,000.

2015-2016 Financial aid. All financial aid based on need. 339 full-time freshmen applied for aid; 287 deemed to have need; 287 received aid. Average need met was 100%. Average scholarship/grant was $42,741; average loan $3,766. 93% of total undergraduate aid awarded as scholarships/grants, 7%

as loans/jobs. **Additional information:** Need-blind admissions policy; meets full demonstrated financial need of students who qualify for admission, to extent resources permit.

Application procedures. Admission: Closing date 1/1 (postmark date). $65 fee, may be waived for applicants with need. Admission notification by 4/1. Must reply by 5/1. **Financial aid:** Priority date 11/15, closing date 2/1. FAFSA, institutional form, CSS PROFILE required. Applicants notified by 4/1; must reply by 5/1.

Academics. Special study options: Accelerated study, double major, exchange student, honors, independent study, internships, student-designed major, study abroad, teacher certification program, Washington semester. Pre-professional combined programs, Washington Semester, semester at Woods Hole Marine Biological Laboratory, Maritime Studies, dual degree engineering programs with Dartmouth and Columbia, exchange programs with Spelman and Swarthmore Colleges and the Association of Vermont Independent Colleges. **Credit/placement by examination:** AP, CLEP, IB, institutional tests. Maximum of five courses with non-standard grading may be counted toward graduation. AP credits applied toward graduation will be counted toward the 16-course limit in the department granting the credit unless the department specifically states that the credits do not count toward the major. AP credits do not fulfill distribution requirements. **Support services:** Learning center, reduced course load, study skills assistance, tutoring, writing center.

Majors. Architecture: Architecture. **Area/ethnic studies:** African, American, East Asian, European, Latin American, Near/Middle Eastern, Russian/Slavic, South Asian, women's. **Biology:** General, biochemistry, Biochemistry/molecular biology, neuroscience. **Computer sciences:** Computer science. **Conservation:** Environmental studies. **Foreign languages:** Arabic, Chinese, classics, comparative lit, French, German, Italian, Japanese, Russian, Spanish. **History:** General. **Liberal arts:** Arts/sciences. **Math:** General. **Philosophy/religion:** Philosophy, religion. **Physical sciences:** Chemistry, geology, physics. **Psychology:** General. **Social sciences:** Economics, geography, international relations, political science, sociology. **Visual/performing arts:** Art history/conservation, dance, dramatic, film/cinema/video, music, studio arts.

Most popular majors. Area/ethnic studies 8%, biology 12%, English 6%, foreign language 7%, natural resources/environmental science 7%, social sciences 31%, visual/performing arts 7%.

Technology on campus. 250 workstations in dormitories, library, computer center, student center. Dormitories wired for high-speed internet access and linked to campus network. Commuter students can connect to campus network. Online course registration, online library, helpline, repair service, student web hosting, wireless network available.

Student life. Freshman orientation: Mandatory. Preregistration for classes offered. **Housing:** Guaranteed on-campus for all undergraduates. Coed dorms, special housing for disabled, apartments, themed housing available. $300 nonrefundable deposit, deadline 5/1. Pets allowed in dorm rooms. **Activities:** Bands, campus ministries, choral groups, dance, drama, film society, international student organizations, literary magazine, music ensembles, Model UN, musical theater, radio station, student government, student newspaper, symphony orchestra, African American Alliance, Alianza, Islamic Society, Sunday Night Group, Hillel, Queers and Allies, Amnesty International, Alternative Breaks, Socially Responsible investment club, Community Friends.

Athletics. NCAA. **Intercollegiate:** Baseball M, basketball, cross-country, diving, field hockey W, football (tackle) M, golf, ice hockey, lacrosse, skiing, soccer, softball W, squash, swimming, tennis, track and field, volleyball W. **Intramural:** Badminton, basketball, football (non-tackle), golf, ice hockey, soccer, softball, squash, table tennis, tennis, volleyball. **Team name:** Panthers.

Student services. Alcohol/substance abuse counseling, chaplain/spiritual director, career counseling, student employment services, financial aid counseling, health services, minority student services, personal counseling, placement for graduates, women's services. **Physically disabled:** Services for visually, speech, hearing impaired.

Contact. E-mail: admissions@middlebury.edu
Phone: (802) 443-3000 Fax: (802) 443-0258
Greg Buckles, Dean of Admissions, Middlebury College, The Emma Willard House, Middlebury, VT 05753-6002

Norwich University
Northfield, Vermont
www.norwich.edu

CB member
CB code: 3669

- Private 4-year university and military college
- Residential campus in small town

- 2,806 degree-seeking undergraduates: 19% part-time, 22% women, 3% African American, 3% Asian American, 8% Hispanic/Latino, 5% Multiracial, non-Hispanic, 1% international
- 552 degree-seeking graduate students
- 57% of applicants admitted
- 56% graduate within 6 years

General. Founded in 1819. Regionally accredited. **Degrees:** 579 bachelor's awarded; master's offered. **ROTC:** Army, Naval, Air Force. **Location:** 50 miles from Burlington, 180 miles from Boston. **Calendar:** Semester, limited summer session. **Full-time faculty:** 157 total; 74% have terminal degrees, 10% minority, 39% women. **Part-time faculty:** 206 total; 58% have terminal degrees, 7% minority, 32% women. **Class size:** 54% < 20, 41% 20-39, 3% 40-49, 1% 50-99, less than 1% >100. **Special facilities:** University-operated museum.

Freshman class profile. 3,530 applied, 2,016 admitted, 627 enrolled.

Mid 50% test scores			
SAT critical reading:	470-580	Rank in top quarter:	38%
SAT math:	470-580	Rank in top tenth:	12%
SAT writing:	450-540	Return as sophomores:	79%
ACT composite:	20-26	Out-of-state:	86%
GPA 3.75 or higher:	7%	Live on campus:	87%
GPA 3.50-3.74:	14%	International:	1%
GPA 3.0-3.49:	40%		
GPA 2.0-2.99:	39%		

Basis for selection. High school record, recommendations, activities, honors, awards, test scores important. Class rank considered and is criterion for financial aid.

High school preparation. College-preparatory program recommended. 17 units recommended. Recommended units include English 4, mathematics 3, social studies 2, science 3 (laboratory 3) and foreign language 2.

2016-2017 Annual costs. Tuition/fees (projected): $37,354. Room/board: $12,920. Books/supplies: $1,500. Personal expenses: $1,500.

2015-2016 Financial aid. Need-based: Average need met was 79%. Average scholarship/grant was $27,184; average loan $4,849. 78% of total undergraduate aid awarded as scholarships/grants, 22% as loans/jobs. **Non-need-based:** Scholarships awarded for academics, ROTC, state residency. **Additional information:** Winners of ROTC scholarships receive full room and board; must maintain 2.75 GPA. Renewable up to 4 years.

Application procedures. Admission: Priority date 2/1; no deadline. $35 fee, may be waived for applicants with need. Admission notification on a rolling basis beginning on or about 9/1. Must reply by May 1 or within 2 week(s) if notified thereafter. **Financial aid:** Priority date 3/1; no closing date. FAFSA required. Applicants notified on a rolling basis starting 2/15; must reply by 8/1.

Academics. Special study options: Combined bachelor's/graduate degree, distance learning, double major, dual enrollment of high school students, exchange student, honors, independent study, internships, liberal arts/career combination, study abroad, teacher certification program. **Credit/placement by examination:** AP, CLEP, IB, SAT, ACT, institutional tests. 12 credit hours maximum toward bachelor's degree. **Support services:** Learning center, pre-admission summer program, reduced course load, remedial instruction, tutoring.

Majors. Architecture: Architecture. **Biology:** General, biochemistry. **Business:** Accounting, business admin, construction management. **Communications:** Media studies. **Computer sciences:** Computer science, security. **Conservation:** Environmental science. **Education:** Physical. **Engineering:** Civil, electrical, environmental, mechanical. **English:** English lit. **Foreign languages:** Chinese, Spanish. **Health services:** Athletic training. **History:** General. **Math:** General. **Military:** "intel, generally". **Physical sciences:** Chemistry, geology, physics. **Protective services:** Law enforcement admin. **Psychology:** General. **Social sciences:** Economics, international relations, national security policy, political science.

Most popular majors. Business/marketing 11%, engineering/engineering technologies 10%, health sciences 10%, history 6%, military 14%, security/protective services 18%, social sciences 10%.

Technology on campus. 150 workstations in library, computer center. Dormitories linked to campus network. Commuter students can connect to campus network. Online course registration, online library, helpline, repair service, wireless network available.

Student life. Freshman orientation: Available, $10 fee. Preregistration for classes offered. Held Wednesday-Sunday; includes 1-day cruise dinner. **Policies:** ROTC participants must live in dormitories. **Housing:** Guaranteed on-campus for freshmen. Coed dorms available. $250 fully refundable deposit, deadline 7/18. Cadet and Civilian housing. **Activities:** Bands, campus ministries, choral groups, dance, drama, film society, international student organizations, literary magazine, music ensembles, Model UN, radio station, student government, student newspaper, Arnold Air Society, Special Operations Company Association of the United States Army, volunteer organization, Christian Fellowship, ambulance rescue squad, Young Republicans, Square and Compass.

Athletics. NCAA. **Intercollegiate:** Baseball M, basketball, cross-country, diving, football (tackle) M, golf, ice hockey, lacrosse, rifle, rugby, soccer, softball W, swimming, wrestling M. **Intramural:** Basketball, cross-country, fencing, football (tackle) M, ice hockey, lacrosse M, racquetball, skiing, soccer, softball, tennis, track and field, volleyball. **Team name:** Cadets.

Student services. Adult student services, chaplain/spiritual director, career counseling, student employment services, financial aid counseling, health services, personal counseling, placement for graduates, veterans' counselor.

Contact. E-mail: nuadm@norwich.edu
Phone: (802) 485-2001 Toll-free number: (800) 468-6679
Fax: (802) 485-2032
Sherri Gilmore, Director of Admissions, Norwich University, 158 Harmon Drive, Northfield, VT 05663

Saint Michael's College
Colchester, Vermont
www.smcvt.edu

CB member
CB code: 3757

▶ Private 4-year liberal arts college affiliated with the Roman Catholic Church
▶ Residential campus in small city
▶ 1,941 degree-seeking undergraduates: 1% part-time, 55% women, 3% African American, 2% Asian American, 4% Hispanic/Latino, 2% Multiracial, non-Hispanic, 3% international
▶ 168 degree-seeking graduate students
▶ 76% of applicants admitted
▶ Application essay required
▶ 76% graduate within 6 years; 16% enter graduate study

General. Founded in 1904. Regionally accredited. **Degrees:** 469 bachelor's awarded; master's offered. **ROTC:** Army, Air Force. **Location:** 3 miles from Burlington. **Calendar:** Semester, limited summer session. **Full-time faculty:** 148 total; 91% have terminal degrees, 7% minority, 43% women. **Part-time faculty:** 102 total; 37% have terminal degrees, 9% minority, 60% women. **Class size:** 59% < 20, 39% 20-39, less than 1% 40-49, 1% 50-99. **Special facilities:** Observatory, art gallery, maker space, arts center.

Freshman class profile. 4,767 applied, 3,621 admitted, 478 enrolled.

Mid 50% test scores			
SAT critical reading:	540-630	GPA 2.0-2.99:	13%
SAT math:	530-630	Rank in top quarter:	56%
SAT writing:	530-630	Rank in top tenth:	26%
ACT composite:	24-28	End year in good standing:	60%
GPA 3.75 or higher:	38%	Return as sophomores:	87%
GPA 3.50-3.74:	20%	Out-of-state:	88%
GPA 3.0-3.49:	29%	Live on campus:	98%
		International:	3%

Basis for selection. Overall high school record and strength of college preparatory curriculum, high school rank in class, standardized test scores (optional), application essay, letters of recommendation, extracurricular interests, campus visit considered. SAT/ACT optional; if students choose to submit SAT/ACT, it will be used as an important academic factor. SAT Subject Tests may be used for language placement. Campus visit strongly encouraged. **Home schooled:** Statement describing home school structure and mission, transcript of courses and grades, state high school equivalency certificate required. SAT/ACT take on additional emphasis.

High school preparation. College-preparatory program required. 16 units required; 20 recommended. Required and recommended units include English 4, mathematics 4, social studies 3-4, science 3-4 (laboratory 2-3) and foreign language 2-4. Physics, math, chemistry, biology emphasized for science applicants. History courses fulfill social studies requirement.

2015-2016 Annual costs. Tuition/fees: $40,750. Room/board: $10,975. Books/supplies: $1,280. Personal expenses: $450.

2015-2016 Financial aid. **Need-based:** 378 full-time freshmen applied for aid; 297 deemed to have need; 297 received aid. Average need met was 81%. Average scholarship/grant was $22,338; average loan $5,070. 81% of total undergraduate aid awarded as scholarships/grants, 19% as loans/jobs. **Non-need-based:** Awarded to 935 full-time undergraduates, including 257

freshmen. Scholarships awarded for academics, art, athletics, music/drama, ROTC.

Application procedures. Admission: Priority date 11/1; deadline 2/1 (postmark date). $50 fee, may be waived for applicants with need. Admission notification by 4/1. Must reply by May 1 or within 2 week(s) if notified thereafter. Second early action closing date 12/1, notification date 2/1. **Financial aid:** Priority date 2/1; no closing date. FAFSA required. Applicants notified on a rolling basis starting 3/21; must reply by 5/1 or within 2 week(s) of notification.

Academics. All students required to achieve low-intermediate level of a second language. **Special study options:** Combined bachelor's/graduate degree, cross-registration, distance learning, double major, dual enrollment of high school students, ESL, exchange student, honors, independent study, internships, liberal arts/career combination, semester at sea, student-designed major, study abroad, teacher certification program, Washington semester. 3-2 engineering with University of Vermont and Clarkson University, 4-1 MBA with Clarkson University, International exchange student program (Thailand, Japan, Korea), Pre-Pharmacy Duel Degree (BS, D.Pharm.) with Albany College of Pharmacy and Health Sciences, Burlington, Vermont Area Independent College Consortium. **Credit/placement by examination:** AP, CLEP, IB, institutional tests. 30 credit hours maximum toward bachelor's degree. **Support services:** Learning center, reduced course load, study skills assistance, tutoring, writing center.

Majors. Area/ethnic studies: American. **Biology:** General, biochemistry, neuroscience. **Business:** Accounting, business admin. **Communications:** Journalism, media studies. **Computer sciences:** Computer science, information systems. **Conservation:** Environmental science, environmental studies. **Education:** Art, elementary, secondary. **Engineering:** General. **English:** English lit. **Foreign languages:** Classics, French, Latin, Spanish. **Health services:** Prepharmacy. **History:** General. **Math:** General. **Philosophy/religion:** Philosophy, religion. **Physical sciences:** Chemistry, physics. **Psychology:** General. **Social sciences:** Anthropology, economics, international relations, political science, sociology. **Visual/performing arts:** Art, art history/conservation, dramatic, music, studio arts.

Most popular majors. Biology 11%, business/marketing 20%, communications/journalism 6%, natural resources/environmental science 7%, psychology 9%, social sciences 14%.

Technology on campus. 490 workstations in dormitories, library, computer center, student center. Dormitories wired for high-speed internet access and linked to campus network. Commuter students can connect to campus network. Online course registration, online library, helpline, repair service, student web hosting, wireless network available.

Student life. Freshman orientation: Mandatory. Preregistration for classes offered. Four-days in August that leads up to the first week of classes. **Policies:** Limited number of parking permits available for first-time, first-year students during spring semester. **Housing:** Guaranteed on-campus for all undergraduates. Coed dorms, single-sex dorms, special housing for disabled, apartments, themed housing, wellness housing available. $500 nonrefundable deposit, deadline 5/1. Ambassador housing program allows American students to live with international students. Honors housing available. **Activities:** Bands, campus ministries, choral groups, dance, drama, literary magazine, music ensembles, musical theater, radio station, student government, student newspaper, Fire and rescue squad, Mobilization of Volunteer Efforts, Martin Luther King society, Diversity Coalition, environmental club, Alianza Society, Student Global AIDS Campaign, Peace and Justice club, Common Ground, Founders Society.

Athletics. NCAA. **Intercollegiate:** Baseball M, basketball, cross-country, diving, field hockey W, golf M, ice hockey, lacrosse, skiing, soccer, softball W, swimming, tennis, volleyball W. **Intramural:** Basketball, football (non-tackle), ice hockey, racquetball, soccer, softball, squash, table tennis, volleyball. **Team name:** Purple Knights.

Student services. Alcohol/substance abuse counseling, chaplain/spiritual director, career counseling, student employment services, financial aid counseling, health services, minority student services, on-campus daycare, personal counseling, placement for graduates, veterans' counselor, women's services. **Physically disabled:** Services for visually, speech, hearing impaired.

Contact. E-mail: admission@smcvt.edu
Phone: (802) 654-3000 Toll-free number: (800) 762-8000
Fax: (802) 654-2906
Jacqueline Murphy, Director of Admissions, Saint Michael's College, One Winooski Park, Colchester, VT 05439

Southern Vermont College
Bennington, Vermont
www.svc.edu

CB member
CB code: 3796

- Private 4-year liberal arts college
- Residential campus in large town
- 431 degree-seeking undergraduates: 3% part-time, 61% women, 11% African American, 9% Hispanic/Latino, 1% Native American, 1% Multiracial, non-Hispanic, 1% international
- 63% of applicants admitted
- SAT or ACT (ACT writing optional), application essay required
- 33% graduate within 6 years

General. Founded in 1926. Regionally accredited. **Degrees:** 91 bachelor's awarded. **Location:** 40 miles from Albany, NY; 90 miles from Springfield, MA. **Calendar:** Semester, limited summer session. **Full-time faculty:** 24 total; 62% have terminal degrees, 4% minority, 79% women. **Part-time faculty:** 22 total; 27% have terminal degrees, 64% women. **Class size:** 77% < 20, 22% 20-39, less than 1% 40-49. **Special facilities:** Healthcare education center, radiology and nursing labs.

Freshman class profile. 497 applied, 312 admitted, 103 enrolled.

Mid 50% test scores			
SAT critical reading:	400-490	**GPA 2.0-2.99:**	58%
SAT math:	400-500	**Rank in top quarter:**	14%
SAT writing:	380-470	**Rank in top tenth:**	2%
ACT composite:	17-20	**Return as sophomores:**	70%
GPA 3.75 or higher:	4%	**Out-of-state:**	73%
GPA 3.50-3.74:	10%	**Live on campus:**	85%
GPA 3.0-3.49:	25%	**International:**	2%

Basis for selection. Potential for academic achievement most important. Test scores, interview, 300 word personal essay and personal references also important. Admissions criteria not intended as absolute cut-offs, but students failing to meet these standards must demonstrate potential for academic success in other ways. Campus visit and interview recommended. **Home schooled:** Statement describing home school structure and mission, transcript of courses and grades, letter of recommendation (nonparent) required. **Learning Disabled:** Documentation of learning disabilities required.

High school preparation. College-preparatory program recommended. Required and recommended units include English 4, mathematics 3-4, social studies 2-4, history 4, science 3-4 and foreign language 2.

2015-2016 Annual costs. Tuition/fees: $23,260. Room/board: $10,700.

2014-2015 Financial aid. Need-based: 85 full-time freshmen applied for aid; 85 deemed to have need; 85 received aid. Average need met was 47%. Average loan was $4,500. 67% of total undergraduate aid awarded as scholarships/grants, 33% as loans/jobs. **Non-need-based:** Awarded to 73 full-time undergraduates, including 10 freshmen. Scholarships awarded for academics, leadership.

Application procedures. Admission: Priority date 5/1; no deadline. $30 fee, may be waived for applicants with need, free for online applicants. Admission notification on a rolling basis beginning on or about 9/1. Must reply by May 1 or within 2 week(s) if notified thereafter. **Financial aid:** Priority date 3/1; no closing date. FAFSA required. Applicants notified on a rolling basis starting 3/1; must reply by 5/1 or within 2 week(s) of notification.

Academics. Special study options: Combined bachelor's/graduate degree, cross-registration, double major, dual enrollment of high school students, independent study, internships, liberal arts/career combination, student-designed major, study abroad. **Credit/placement by examination:** AP, CLEP, institutional tests. **Support services:** Learning center, reduced course load, remedial instruction, study skills assistance, tutoring, writing center. Students receive free walk-in tutoring, individualized tutoring, study group sessions, workshops for skill review, proofreading, and note-taking. Learning Differences Support Program available.

Majors. Biology: General, cellular/molecular, ecology, environmental. **Business:** Business admin, entrepreneurial studies. **Communications:** General. **English:** Creative writing, English lit. **Health services:** Health care admin, nursing (RN), radiologic technology/medical imaging. **History:** General. **Liberal arts:** Arts/sciences. **Parks/recreation:** Sports admin. **Protective services:** Police science. **Psychology:** General. **Social sciences:** Political science.

Most popular majors. Business/marketing 25%, health sciences 30%, psychology 15%, security/protective services 12%.

Technology on campus. 50 workstations in dormitories, library, computer center. Dormitories wired for high-speed internet access and linked to campus network. Commuter students can connect to campus network. Online course registration, online library, repair service, student web hosting, wireless network available.

Student life. Freshman orientation: Mandatory. Preregistration for classes offered. Overnight summer program. **Policies:** Freshmen not permitted cars on campus. **Housing:** Guaranteed on-campus for freshmen. Coed dorms, wellness housing available. $200 nonrefundable deposit. **Activities:** Dance, drama, music ensembles, student government, Diversity Advisory Committee, Gay-Straight Alliance, drama club, mountaineer events board, community service club.

Athletics. NCAA. **Intercollegiate:** Baseball M, basketball, cross-country, lacrosse W, soccer, softball W, volleyball. **Intramural:** Basketball, soccer, volleyball. **Team name:** Mountaineers.

Student services. Adult student services, alcohol/substance abuse counseling, career counseling, student employment services, financial aid counseling, health services, personal counseling, placement for graduates, veterans' counselor. **Physically disabled:** Services for visually, speech, hearing impaired.

Contact. E-mail: admissions@svc.edu
Phone: (802) 447-6300 Fax: (802) 681-2868
Daniel Summers, Dean of Admissions, Southern Vermont College, 982 Mansion Drive, Bennington, VT 05201-6002

Sterling College
Craftsbury Common, Vermont
www.sterlingcollege.edu

CB member
CB code: 3752

- Private 4-year liberal arts college
- Residential campus in rural community
- 119 degree-seeking undergraduates: 49% women
- 72% of applicants admitted
- Application essay, interview required
- 52% graduate within 6 years

General. Founded in 1958. Regionally accredited. **Degrees:** 18 bachelor's awarded. **Location:** 50 miles from Burlington. **Calendar:** Differs by program, extensive summer session. **Full-time faculty:** 10 total; 20% have terminal degrees, 50% women. **Part-time faculty:** 7 total; 14% have terminal degrees, 43% women. **Class size:** 100% < 20. **Special facilities:** Nature trails, woodlots, farm, edible forest garden, cross-country ski trails, back-country recreation, solar and wind powered barns, organic gardens, greenhouse, low and high ropes challenge course, sugar house, 300-acre educational swamp (boreal forest and muskeg).

Freshman class profile. 101 applied, 73 admitted, 24 enrolled.

Return as sophomores:	52%	**Live on campus:**	94%
Out-of-state:	93%		

Basis for selection. Demonstrated interest in programs via activities and essay, motivation, interview/campus visit, academic record, letters of recommendation. **Home schooled:** Transcript of courses and grades required. Portfolio of educational and life experience may be submitted in lieu of diploma or equivalency. Students must meet homeschool requirements for their particular state of residence.

High school preparation. College-preparatory program recommended. Recommended units include English 4, mathematics 3, social studies 2, history 3, science 3 (laboratory 3) and foreign language 2.

2016-2017 Annual costs. Tuition/fees (projected): $36,577. Room/board: $4,780. Books/supplies: $1,500. Personal expenses: $1,000.

Financial aid. Non-need-based: Scholarships awarded for academics, leadership, state residency.

Application procedures. Admission: Closing date 4/1. $35 fee, may be waived for applicants with need. Admission notification on a rolling basis. Must reply by May 1 or within 3 week(s) if notified thereafter. Exceptions made to early admission of high school students, on a case by case basis. **Financial aid:** Priority date 3/15; no closing date. FAFSA, institutional form required. Applicants notified on a rolling basis starting 2/1; must reply by 5/1 or within 3 week(s) of notification.

Academics. Special study options: Cross-registration, double major, dual enrollment of high school students, independent study, internships, student-designed major, study abroad. 2-week and 5-week Global Field Studies. **Credit/placement by examination:** AP, CLEP, IB, institutional tests. Credit for life experience and credit by exam evaluated on a case-by-case basis. **Support services:** Learning center, reduced course load, remedial instruction, study skills assistance, tutoring, writing center.

Majors. Biology: Conservation, ecology, environmental, wildlife. **Conservation:** General, environmental studies, water/wetlands/marine, wildlife/wilderness. **Education:** Curriculum. **Liberal arts:** Arts/sciences. **Parks/recreation:** General.

Most popular majors. Agriculture 17%, biology 31%, liberal arts 35%, parks/recreation 14%.

Technology on campus. 21 workstations in library, computer center. Dormitories wired for high-speed internet access and linked to campus network. Commuter students can connect to campus network. Online library, helpline, repair service, wireless network available.

Student life. Freshman orientation: Mandatory. Preregistration for classes offered. **Policies:** Community governance. **Housing:** Guaranteed on-campus for all undergraduates. Coed dorms, wellness housing available. $20 deposit. **Activities:** Film society, literary magazine, music ensembles, student government, Service learning, all-college work days, Equity group, Alliance group.

Athletics. Intramural: Table tennis.

Student services. Adult student services, alcohol/substance abuse counseling, career counseling, financial aid counseling, health services, personal counseling, veterans' counselor.

Contact. E-mail: admission@sterlingcollege.edu
Phone: (802) 586-7711 ext. 100
Toll-free number: (800) 648-3591 ext. 100 Fax: (802) 586-2596
Tim Patterson, Director of Admission, Sterling College, PO Box 72, Craftsbury Common, VT 05827-0072

University of Vermont
Burlington, Vermont

www.uvm.edu

CB member
CB code: 3920

- Public 4-year university
- Residential campus in large town
- 10,081 degree-seeking undergraduates: 4% part-time, 56% women, 1% African American, 3% Asian American, 4% Hispanic/Latino, 3% Multiracial, non-Hispanic, 4% international
- 1,817 degree-seeking graduate students
- 71% of applicants admitted
- SAT or ACT (ACT writing optional), application essay required
- 77% graduate within 6 years

General. Founded in 1791. Regionally accredited. **Degrees:** 2,340 bachelor's awarded; master's, professional, doctoral offered. **ROTC:** Army. **Location:** 225 miles from Boston; 100 miles from Montreal. **Calendar:** Semester, extensive summer session. **Full-time faculty:** 609 total; 86% have terminal degrees, 15% minority, 47% women. **Part-time faculty:** 188 total; 27% have terminal degrees, 7% minority, 60% women. **Class size:** 50% < 20, 29% 20-39, 6% 40-49, 10% 50-99, 5% >100. **Special facilities:** Horse farm, dairy farm, geology museum, natural areas, science center, research vessel on Lake Champlain, ecosystem science laboratory on Lake Champlain, art and anthropology museum, maple research facility.

Freshman class profile. 25,274 applied, 17,907 admitted, 2,400 enrolled.

Mid 50% test scores			
		GPA 2.0-2.99:	11%
SAT critical reading:	550-650	Rank in top quarter:	74%
SAT math:	550-640	Rank in top tenth:	32%
SAT writing:	540-650	End year in good standing:	88%
ACT composite:	25-30	Return as sophomores:	86%
GPA 3.75 or higher:	39%	Out-of-state:	80%
GPA 3.50-3.74:	21%	Live on campus:	98%
GPA 3.0-3.49:	29%	International:	1%

Basis for selection. School achievement record of primary importance; test scores also important. Essay, extracurricular activities considered. Letter of recommendation required. Special consideration to Vermont residents, children of alumni, minority students, and foreign students. Informational interview recommended. Music applicants must present audition tape or CD. **Home schooled:** Transcript of courses and grades, state high school equivalency certificate, letter of recommendation (nonparent) required. Applicants must provide proof of completion of minimum entrance requirements and completion of GED.

High school preparation. College-preparatory program required. 16 units required. Required units include English 4, mathematics 3, social studies 3, science 2 (laboratory 1) and foreign language 2. Additional mathematics and/or science units required in engineering, business, health science programs.

2015-2016 Annual costs. Tuition/fees: $16,738; $39,130 out-of-state. Room/board: $11,180. Books/supplies: $1,200. Personal expenses: $1,682.

2014-2015 Financial aid. Need-based: 1,777 full-time freshmen applied for aid; 1,347 deemed to have need; 1,347 received aid. Average need met was 70%. Average scholarship/grant was $16,660; average loan $3,655. 81% of total undergraduate aid awarded as scholarships/grants, 19% as loans/jobs. **Non-need-based:** Awarded to 3,320 full-time undergraduates, including 975 freshmen. Scholarships awarded for academics, alumni affiliation, athletics, leadership, minority status, music/drama, ROTC, state residency.

Application procedures. Admission: Closing date 1/15 (postmark date). $55 fee, may be waived for applicants with need. Application must be submitted online. Admission notification by 3/31. Must reply by May 1 or within 3 week(s) if notified thereafter. Waitlist admits have 2 days to reply. Early action candidates may have final decision deferred until completion of fall semester review. **Financial aid:** Priority date 2/10; no closing date. FAFSA required. Applicants notified on a rolling basis starting 3/31; must reply within 4 week(s) of notification.

Academics. Special study options: Combined bachelor's/graduate degree, cooperative education, cross-registration, distance learning, double major, dual enrollment of high school students, ESL, exchange student, honors, independent study, internships, liberal arts/career combination, student-designed major, study abroad, teacher certification program, Washington semester. Evening university option available in several programs, limited ESL available. **Credit/placement by examination:** AP, CLEP, IB, institutional tests. Half of major and half of minor requirements must be completed in residence. **Support services:** Learning center, pre-admission summer program, reduced course load, study skills assistance, tutoring, writing center.

Honors college/program. Admissions based on excellent SAT and/or ACT scores, class rank, challenging course work, and ability to overcome obstacles; about 100 admitted each year.

Majors. Area/ethnic studies: Asian, European, Italian, Latin American/Caribbean, Russian/Slavic, women's. **Biology:** General, biochemistry, botany, microbiology, molecular, neuroscience, wildlife, zoology. **Business:** Business admin, entrepreneurial studies. **Communications:** Public relations. **Computer sciences:** Computer science, systems analysis. **Conservation:** General, environmental science, environmental studies, forestry, nature tourism. **Education:** General, art, early childhood, early childhood special, elementary, English, foreign languages, mathematics, middle, music, physical, science, secondary, social studies. **Engineering:** General, civil, electrical, environmental, industrial, mechanical. **English:** English lit. **Foreign languages:** Ancient Greek, Chinese, classics, French, German, Japanese, Latin, linguistics, Russian, Spanish. **Health services:** General, athletic training, clinical lab science, communication disorders, dietetics, medical radiologic technology/radiation therapy, nuclear medical technology, nursing (RN). **History:** General. **Human services:** Social work. **Liberal arts:** Arts/sciences. **Math:** General, statistics. **Parks/recreation:** Exercise sciences. **Philosophy/religion:** Philosophy, religion. **Physical sciences:** Chemistry, geology, physics. **Psychology:** General. **Social sciences:** Anthropology, economics, geography, international economic development, political science, sociology. **Visual/performing arts:** Art history/conservation, dramatic, film/cinema/video, music, music performance, studio arts. **Work/family studies:** Family studies.

Most popular majors. Biology 10%, business/marketing 10%, education 6%, engineering/engineering technologies 8%, health sciences 9%, natural resources/environmental science 9%, social sciences 12%.

Technology on campus. 600 workstations in dormitories, library, computer center, student center. Dormitories wired for high-speed internet access and linked to campus network. Commuter students can connect to campus network. Online course registration, online library, helpline, repair service, student web hosting, wireless network available.

Student life. Freshman orientation: Mandatory. Preregistration for classes offered. 2-day sessions held at various times in June; additional session held prior to start of term in August. **Policies:** Student code of conduct. Freshmen not permitted cars on campus. **Housing:** Guaranteed on-campus for freshmen. Coed dorms, apartments, fraternity/sorority housing, themed housing, wellness housing available. **Activities:** Bands, campus ministries, choral groups, dance, drama, film society, international student organizations, literary magazine, music ensembles, musical theater, radio station, student government, student newspaper, symphony orchestra, TV station, Hillel, black student union, Asian American student union, gay/lesbian/bisexual/transgender alliance, Alianza Latina, Catholic center, Volunteers in Action, Vermont student environmental program, ALANA Coalition.

Athletics. NCAA. Intercollegiate: Basketball, cross-country, diving W, field hockey W, ice hockey, lacrosse, skiing, soccer, swimming W, track and field. **Intramural:** Badminton, basketball, football (non-tackle), ice hockey, racquetball, soccer, squash, table tennis, tennis, ultimate frisbee, volleyball. **Team name:** Catamounts.

Student services. Alcohol/substance abuse counseling, chaplain/spiritual director, career counseling, services for economically disadvantaged, student employment services, financial aid counseling, health services, minority student services, on-campus daycare, personal counseling, placement for graduates, veterans' counselor, women's services. **Physically disabled:** Services for visually, speech, hearing impaired.

Contact. E-mail: admissions@uvm.edu
Phone: (802) 656-3370 Fax: (802) 656-8611
Beth Wiser, Director of Admissions, University of Vermont, 194 South Prospect Street, Burlington, VT 05401-3596

Vermont Technical College
Randolph Center, Vermont

CB member

www.vtc.edu

CB code: 3941

- Public 4-year nursing and technical college
- Residential campus in small town
- 1,372 degree-seeking undergraduates: 22% part-time, 48% women, 1% African American, 1% Asian American, 2% Hispanic/Latino, 1% Native American, 3% Multi-racial, non-Hispanic, 2% international
- 67% of applicants admitted
- 51% graduate within 6 years

General. Founded in 1866. Regionally accredited. **Degrees:** 117 bachelor's, 313 associate awarded. **ROTC:** Army. **Location:** 25 miles from Montpelier, 60 miles from Burlington. **Calendar:** Semester, limited summer session. **Full-time faculty:** 76 total; 78% have terminal degrees, 4% minority, 47% women. **Part-time faculty:** 82 total; 49% have terminal degrees, 1% minority, 45% women. **Class size:** 70% < 20, 29% 20-39, less than 1% 40-49, less than 1% 50-99. **Special facilities:** 500-acre farmstead and orchard, lighted ski hill.

Freshman class profile. 564 applied, 376 admitted, 201 enrolled.

Mid 50% test scores			
SAT critical reading:	400-520	GPA 2.0-2.99:	50%
SAT math:	430-540	Rank in top quarter:	14%
SAT writing:	400-490	Rank in top tenth:	2%
ACT composite:	17-22	End year in good standing:	83%
GPA 3.75 or higher:	4%	Return as sophomores:	70%
GPA 3.50-3.74:	12%	Out-of-state:	21%
GPA 3.0-3.49:	27%	Live on campus:	78%
		International:	2%

Basis for selection. School achievement record most important, followed by test scores, recommendations, and recommended interview. Veterinary technology, dental hygiene, and nursing programs highly selective. Entrance exam required for nursing applicants. SAT/ACT not required of nursing applicants or non-traditional students. ACCUPLACER may be used in place of SAT/ACT. Interview and essay required for VAST applicants. **Home schooled:** Statement describing home school structure and mission required. Students may attend Vermont Academy of Science and Technology to obtain diploma and first year of college simultaneously.

High school preparation. College-preparatory program required. 16 units required. Required and recommended units include English 4, mathematics 3-4, social studies 2, history 2, science 2-3 (laboratory 1-2), foreign language 2 and academic electives 2.

2015-2016 Annual costs. Tuition/fees: $13,490; $24,866 out-of-state. Room/board: $9,696. Books/supplies: $1,200. Personal expenses: $650.

2014-2015 Financial aid. **Need-based:** 440 full-time freshmen applied for aid; 402 deemed to have need; 398 received aid. Average need met was 44%. Average scholarship/grant was $6,028; average loan $3,528. 36% of total undergraduate aid awarded as scholarships/grants, 64% as loans/jobs. **Non-need-based:** Awarded to 93 full-time undergraduates, including 72 freshmen. Scholarships awarded for academics.

Application procedures. **Admission:** Priority date 12/1; no deadline. $47 fee, may be waived for applicants with need. Admission notification on a rolling basis beginning on or about 12/15. Must reply by May 1 or within 2 week(s) if notified thereafter. Nursing, dental hygiene, respiratory therapy and veterinary technology applicants may not defer acceptance. **Financial aid:** Priority date 3/1; no closing date. FAFSA required. Applicants notified on a rolling basis starting 1/31; must reply within 2 week(s) of notification.

Academics. 3-year preparatory program options for students planning engineering programs. **Special study options:** Distance learning, double major, dual enrollment of high school students, ESL, honors, independent study, internships. Vermont Academy of Science and Technology program combines senior year of high school and first year of college. **Credit/placement by examination:** AP, CLEP, institutional tests. 30 credit hours maximum toward

associate degree, 60 toward bachelor's. No more than 50% of the degree requirements may be counted toward any degree. **Support services:** Learning center, pre-admission summer program, reduced course load, remedial instruction, study skills assistance, tutoring, writing center.

Majors. **Business:** General, business admin. **Computer sciences:** General, information technology, programming. **General:** Maintenance. **Health services:** Dental hygiene.

Most popular majors. Agriculture 11%, business/marketing 23%, computer/information sciences 13%, engineering/engineering technologies 35%, health sciences 8%, trade and industry 10%.

Technology on campus. 250 workstations in dormitories, library, computer center. Dormitories wired for high-speed internet access and linked to campus network. Commuter students can connect to campus network. Online library, helpline, repair service, student web hosting, wireless network available.

Student life. **Freshman orientation:** Mandatory, $100 fee. Preregistration for classes offered. Held 2 days prior to start of classes. **Housing:** Coed dorms, special housing for disabled, themed housing, wellness housing available. $100 partly refundable deposit, deadline 6/1. Williston Campus has townhouse style residence halls. **Activities:** Campus ministries, international student organizations, radio station, student government, American Institute of Architects, American Society of Civil Engineers, Institute of Electrical and Electronic Engineers, Society of Manufacturing Engineers, Society of Women Engineers, National Association of Veterinary Technicians, Women Issues Christian Fellowship, Phi Theta Kappa, Tau Alpha Pi.

Athletics. NAIA, USCAA. **Intercollegiate:** Baseball M, basketball, cross-country, soccer, softball W. **Intramural:** Basketball, football (non-tackle), golf, skiing, soccer, softball, swimming, table tennis, tennis, volleyball, water polo. **Team name:** Knights.

Student services. Alcohol/substance abuse counseling, career counseling, services for economically disadvantaged, student employment services, financial aid counseling, health services, minority student services, personal counseling, placement for graduates, veterans' counselor, women's services. **Physically disabled:** Services for visually, hearing impaired.

Contact. E-mail: admissions@vtc.edu
Phone: (802) 728-1244 Toll-free number: (800) 442-8821
Fax: (802) 728-1390
Jessica Van Deren, Assistant Dean of Enrollment, Vermont Technical College, PO Box 500, Randolph Center, VT 05061-0500

Virginia

American National University: Salem
Roanoke, Virginia
www.an.edu   CB code: 5502

- For-profit 4-year business college
- Commuter campus in large city
- 145 degree-seeking undergraduates
- Interview required

General. Founded in 1886. Accredited by ACICS. **Degrees:** 35 bachelor's, 54 associate awarded; master's offered. **Calendar:** Quarter, limited summer session. **Full-time faculty:** 6 total. **Part-time faculty:** 29 total.

Basis for selection. Open admission.

2016-2017 Annual costs. Tuition/fees: $14,460.

Financial aid. All financial aid based on need.

Application procedures. Admission: Closing date 9/1 (receipt date). $50 fee, may be waived for applicants with need. Admission notification on a rolling basis. **Financial aid:** No deadline. FAFSA required. Applicants notified on a rolling basis.

Academics. Special study options: Double major, internships. **Credit/placement by examination:** AP, CLEP, institutional tests. **Support services:** Tutoring.

Majors. Business: Accounting, business admin.

Technology on campus. 35 workstations in library, computer center.

Student life. Freshman orientation: Mandatory. Preregistration for classes offered. **Housing:** Coed dorms available. Hotel accommodations available. **Activities:** Student government.

Student services. Career counseling, financial aid counseling, placement for graduates.

Contact. Phone: (540) 986-1800 Fax: (540) 444-4198
Larry Steele, Director of Admissions, American National University: Salem, 1813 East Main Street, Salem, VA 24153

Argosy University: Washington D.C.
Arlington, Virginia
www.argosy.edu/washingtondc

- For-profit 4-year university
- Commuter campus in very large city
- 121 degree-seeking undergraduates: 87% part-time, 57% women
- 672 graduate students

General. Regionally accredited. **Degrees:** 16 bachelor's awarded; master's, professional, doctoral offered. **Calendar:** Differs by program. **Full-time faculty:** 28 total. **Part-time faculty:** 114 total.

Basis for selection. Open admission.

2015-2016 Annual costs. Tuition/fees: $16,842. **Additional information:** Tuition indicated is for programs in the College of Arts and Sciences. College of Health Sciences programs are $575 per credit-hour.

Application procedures. Admission: Closing date 9/13. $50 fee. **Financial aid:** No deadline.

Academics. Credit/placement by examination: AP, CLEP.

Majors. Business: Business admin. **Liberal arts:** Arts/sciences. **Protective services:** Police science. **Psychology:** General.

Contact. E-mail: auwadmissions@argosy.edu
Phone: (703) 526-5800 Toll-free number: (866) 703-2777
Frank Marranzini, Senior Director of Admissions, Argosy University: Washington D.C., 1550 Wilson Boulevard, Suite 600, Arlington, VA 22209

Art Institute of Washington
Arlington, Virginia
www.aiw.artinstitutes.edu   CB code: 3836

- For-profit 4-year culinary school and visual arts college
- Commuter campus in small city
- 878 degree-seeking undergraduates
- Application essay, interview required

General. Regionally accredited. **Degrees:** 105 bachelor's, 101 associate awarded. **Location:** One mile from Washington, DC. **Calendar:** Quarter, extensive summer session. **Full-time faculty:** 56 total. **Part-time faculty:** 52 total.

Basis for selection. Secondary school record, essay, placement test scores, interview most important; portfolio also considered. SAT or ACT recommended. Students may take math and English placement test at the college, free of charge, in lieu of SAT/ACT. **Home schooled:** Transcript of courses and grades required.

2015-2016 Annual costs. Tuition/fees: $21,970. Room only: $10,398.

Application procedures. Admission: No deadline. $50 fee. Admission notification on a rolling basis. **Financial aid:** No deadline. FAFSA, institutional form required.

Academics. Special study options: Accelerated study, independent study, internships, study abroad. **Credit/placement by examination:** AP, CLEP, IB, SAT, ACT. **Support services:** Learning center, pre-admission summer program, reduced course load, remedial instruction, study skills assistance, tutoring, writing center.

Majors. Communications: Advertising, digital media. **Communications technology:** Animation/special effects, graphics, recording arts. **Computer sciences:** Web page design. **Visual/performing arts:** Game design, graphic design, interior design.

Technology on campus. Online course registration, online library, student web hosting, wireless network available.

Student life. Freshman orientation: Mandatory. Preregistration for classes offered. **Housing:** Coed dorms available. $250 partly refundable deposit. **Activities:** Radio station.

Student services. Adult student services, alcohol/substance abuse counseling, career counseling, student employment services, financial aid counseling. **Physically disabled:** Services for visually, speech, hearing impaired.

Contact. E-mail: aiwadm@aii.edu
Phone: (703) 358-9550 Fax: (703) 358-9759
Keith VonSchultz, Registrar, Art Institute of Washington, 1820 North Fort Myer Drive, Arlington, VA 22209-1802

Averett University
Danville, Virginia
www.averett.edu   CB code: 5017

- Private 4-year university and liberal arts college affiliated with the Baptist faith
- Residential campus in large town
- 873 degree-seeking undergraduates: 2% part-time, 50% women, 33% African American, 1% Asian American, 4% Hispanic/Latino, 1% Native American, 4% international
- 3 degree-seeking graduate students
- 61% of applicants admitted
- SAT or ACT (ACT writing optional) required
- 35% graduate within 6 years

General. Founded in 1859. Regionally accredited. **Degrees:** 173 bachelor's awarded; master's offered. **Location:** 145 miles from Richmond, 45 miles from Greensboro, NC. **Calendar:** Semester, limited summer session. **Full-time faculty:** 60 total; 70% have terminal degrees, 10% minority, 55% women. **Part-time faculty:** 57 total; 5% have terminal degrees, 14% minority,

58% women. **Class size:** 80% < 20, 19% 20-39, less than 1% 40-49. **Special facilities:** 121-acre equestrian center, flight center.

Freshman class profile. 2,250 applied, 1,378 admitted, 267 enrolled.

Mid 50% test scores			
		GPA 2.0-2.99:	40%
SAT critical reading:	400-500	Rank in top quarter:	30%
SAT math:	400-500	Rank in top tenth:	11%
SAT writing:	380-490	Return as sophomores:	71%
ACT composite:	17-22	Out-of-state:	43%
GPA 3.75 or higher:	19%	Live on campus:	88%
GPA 3.50-3.74:	12%	International:	4%
GPA 3.0-3.49:	28%		

Basis for selection. Rigor of secondary school record and GPA very important; standardized test scores important. Recommendations, essay, interview, extracurricular activities, talent/ability/alumni/ae relation, volunteer work, work experience and level of interest all considered. Auditions and interviews required for music program. **Home schooled:** Transcript of courses and grades, state high school equivalency certificate required. Provide proof that student applicant completed home school evaluation in accordance to the law. **Learning Disabled:** Documentation of neuropsychological or comprehensive psychoeducational evaluation required for access to learning disabled services. Minimum SAT requirements may be waived.

High school preparation. College-preparatory program required. 19 units required. Required and recommended units include English 4, mathematics 3, social studies 3, history 3, science 3 (laboratory 2) and foreign language 2.

2015-2016 Annual costs. Tuition/fees: $30,900. Room/board: $8,700. Books/supplies: $1,000. Personal expenses: $1,600.

2015-2016 Financial aid. **Need-based:** 244 full-time freshmen applied for aid; 225 deemed to have need; 225 received aid. Average need met was 68%. Average scholarship/grant was $18,693; average loan $3,745. 73% of total undergraduate aid awarded as scholarships/grants, 27% as loans/jobs. **Non-need-based:** Awarded to 175 full-time undergraduates, including 62 freshmen. Scholarships awarded for academics, alumni affiliation, art, job skills, leadership, minority status, music/drama, religious affiliation, state residency.

Application procedures. **Admission:** No deadline. No application fee. Admission notification on a rolling basis beginning on or about 9/1. Deferred admission is up to 1 year. **Financial aid:** No deadline. FAFSA required. Applicants notified on a rolling basis starting 2/15; must reply within 2 week(s) of notification.

Academics. **Special study options:** Combined bachelor's/graduate degree, distance learning, double major, honors, independent study, internships, student-designed major, study abroad, teacher certification program. Undergraduates may take graduate level classes. **Credit/placement by examination:** AP, CLEP, IB, SAT, ACT, institutional tests. 45 credit hours maximum toward associate degree, 90 toward bachelor's. **Support services:** Reduced course load, remedial instruction, study skills assistance, tutoring, writing center.

Majors. **Biology:** General, ecology. **Business:** Accounting, business admin, finance, management science, marketing. **Communications:** Journalism. **Computer sciences:** Computer science, information systems. **Conservation:** Environmental science. **Education:** Art, biology, chemistry, English, health, mathematics, multi-level teacher, social studies. **English:** English lit. **Foreign languages:** General. **Health services:** Athletic training, medical radiologic technology/radiation therapy, nursing (RN), premedicine. **History:** General. **Liberal arts:** Arts/sciences. **Math:** General. **Parks/recreation:** Health/fitness, sports admin. **Philosophy/religion:** Religion. **Protective services:** Law enforcement admin. **Psychology:** General. **Social sciences:** Political science, sociology. **Visual/performing arts:** Art, dramatic, music, theater history.

Most popular majors. Business/marketing 15%, education 8%, health sciences 15%, parks/recreation 11%, security/protective services 14%, social sciences 7%.

Technology on campus. 150 workstations in library, computer center, student center. Dormitories wired for high-speed internet access. Online course registration, online library, wireless network available.

Student life. **Freshman orientation:** Mandatory. Preregistration for classes offered. Held in June and July. **Policies:** Students expected to live on campus until senior status. Exceptions made for students living within 30 mile radius of campus with parent or guardian. Alcohol not permitted in living areas regardless of age. **Housing:** Guaranteed on-campus for all undergraduates. Coed dorms, single-sex dorms, apartments available. Coed housing by floor or suite available. **Activities:** Pep band, campus ministries, choral groups, dance, drama, literary magazine, musical theater, student government, student newspaper, Cougar activity board, student athlete advising committee, Christian Student Union, Catholic Campus Ministry, Royal Delights dance team.

Athletics. NCAA. **Intercollegiate:** Baseball M, basketball, cross-country, equestrian, football (tackle) M, golf M, soccer, softball W, tennis, volleyball W. **Intramural:** Basketball, football (non-tackle), soccer, softball, volleyball. **Team name:** Cougars.

Student services. Adult student services, alcohol/substance abuse counseling, chaplain/spiritual director, career counseling, student employment services, financial aid counseling, personal counseling, placement for graduates, veterans' counselor.

Contact. Phone: (434) 791-5600 Toll-free number: (800) 283-7388 Fax: (434) 797-2784
Joel Nester, Director of Admissions, Averett University, Office of Admissions, Danville, VA 24541

Bluefield College
Bluefield, Virginia
www.bluefield.edu   **CB code: 5063**

◆ Private 4-year liberal arts and teachers college affiliated with the Baptist faith
◆ Residential campus in small town
◆ 914 degree-seeking undergraduates: 15% part-time, 57% women, 22% African American, 1% Asian American, 4% Hispanic/Latino, 2% Multiracial, non-Hispanic, 4% international
◆ 17 degree-seeking graduate students
◆ 93% of applicants admitted
◆ SAT or ACT (ACT writing optional) required
◆ 37% graduate within 6 years

General. Founded in 1920. Regionally accredited. **Degrees:** 221 bachelor's awarded; master's offered. **Location:** 90 miles from Roanoke. **Calendar:** Semester, limited summer session. **Full-time faculty:** 38 total; 74% have terminal degrees, 3% minority, 45% women. **Part-time faculty:** 54 total; 28% have terminal degrees, 4% minority, 57% women. **Class size:** 71% < 20, 27% 20-39, 1% 40-49.

Freshman class profile. 624 applied, 579 admitted, 150 enrolled.

Mid 50% test scores			
		Rank in top tenth:	7%
SAT critical reading:	400-520	End year in good standing:	71%
SAT math:	400-520	Return as sophomores:	53%
ACT composite:	17-22	Out-of-state:	34%
GPA 3.75 or higher:	21%	Live on campus:	73%
GPA 3.50-3.74:	17%	International:	7%
GPA 3.0-3.49:	24%	Fraternities:	2%
GPA 2.0-2.99:	37%	Sororities:	3%
Rank in top quarter:	25%		

Basis for selection. Students must have 2 of the following: 2.0 GPA; 18 ACT/860 SAT (exclusive of writing); rank in top half of class. **Home schooled:** Must supply written description and transcript of curriculum.

High school preparation. College-preparatory program recommended. 22 units recommended. Recommended units include English 4, mathematics 3, social studies 3, science 3, visual/performing arts 1 and academic electives 6. 2 units of health and physical education.

2015-2016 Annual costs. Tuition/fees: $23,295. Room/board: $8,185. Books/supplies: $1,800. Personal expenses: $1,800.

2014-2015 Financial aid. **Need-based:** 137 full-time freshmen applied for aid; 124 deemed to have need; 124 received aid. Average need met was 64%. Average scholarship/grant was $14,671; average loan $3,700. 53% of total undergraduate aid awarded as scholarships/grants, 47% as loans/jobs. **Non-need-based:** Awarded to 238 full-time undergraduates, including 66 freshmen. Scholarships awarded for academics, art, athletics, music/drama.

Application procedures. **Admission:** Closing date 8/31 (receipt date). $30 fee, may be waived for applicants with need, free for online applicants. Admission notification by 8/31. Admission notification on a rolling basis beginning on or about 10/15. **Financial aid:** Priority date 6/1; no closing date. FAFSA required. Applicants notified on a rolling basis starting 3/1; must reply within 3 week(s) of notification.

Academics. **Special study options:** Combined bachelor's/graduate degree, distance learning, double major, dual enrollment of high school students, honors, independent study, internships, study abroad, teacher certification program. **Credit/placement by examination:** AP, CLEP, IB, SAT, ACT, institutional tests. 15 credit hours maximum toward associate degree, 30 toward bachelor's. **Support services:** Learning center, reduced course load, remedial instruction, study skills assistance, tutoring, writing center.

Majors. Biology: General, exercise physiology. **Business:** Accounting, business admin, e-commerce, marketing. **Communications:** General, journalism. **Communications technology:** Graphics. **Computer sciences:** Information technology. **Education:** General, art, biology, business, chemistry, early childhood, elementary, English, health, history, mathematics, middle, multilevel teacher, music, physical, secondary, social studies. **English:** English lit, general lit, writing. **Health services:** Predental, premedicine, prepharmacy, prephysical therapy, preveterinary. **History:** General. **Math:** General. **Parks/recreation:** Facilities management, health/fitness, sports admin. **Philosophy/religion:** Christian. **Physical sciences:** Chemistry. **Protective services:** Forensics, law enforcement admin, police science. **Psychology:** General. **Theology:** Bible, preministerial, sacred music, theology, youth ministry. **Visual/performing arts:** Art, dramatic, graphic design, music, music performance, music theory/composition.

Most popular majors. Business/marketing 25%, health sciences 11%, parks/recreation 8%, public administration/social services 22%, security/protective services 13%.

Technology on campus. 105 workstations in dormitories, library, computer center. Dormitories wired for high-speed internet access and linked to campus network. Commuter students can connect to campus network. Online library, wireless network available.

Student life. Freshman orientation: Mandatory. Preregistration for classes offered. **Policies:** Weekly convocation attendance required. Limited visitation hours in dormitories. Religious observance required. **Housing:** Single-sex dorms, special housing for disabled, apartments, wellness housing available. $150 fully refundable deposit. **Activities:** Bands, campus ministries, choral groups, drama, international student organizations, literary magazine, music ensembles, musical theater, student government, student newspaper, Fellowship of Christian Athletes, Alpha Delta, Phi Mu Delta, Kappa Psi Omicron, Sigma Alpha Alpha, Bonner Leaders, Baptist collegiate ministry, Elevate, residence halls Bible studies, student union board.

Athletics. NAIA, NCCAA. **Intercollegiate:** Baseball M, basketball, cross-country, football (tackle) M, golf M, soccer, softball W, tennis, volleyball. **Intramural:** Basketball, bowling, football (non-tackle), golf, softball, swimming, table tennis, tennis, ultimate frisbee, volleyball. **Team name:** Rams.

Student services. Chaplain/spiritual director, career counseling, financial aid counseling, health services, personal counseling, veterans' counselor.

Contact. E-mail: admissions@bluefield.edu
Phone: (276) 326-4231 Toll-free number: (800) 872-0175
Fax: (276) 326-4395
Evan Sherman, Director of Traditional Admissions, Bluefield College, 3000 College Avenue, Bluefield, VA 24605

Bridgewater College
Bridgewater, Virginia
www.bridgewater.edu

CB member
CB code: 5069

- Private 4-year liberal arts college affiliated with the Church of the Brethren
- Residential campus in small town
- 1,823 degree-seeking undergraduates: 53% women, 11% African American, 1% Asian American, 5% Hispanic/Latino, 5% Multi-racial, non-Hispanic, 1% international
- 49% of applicants admitted
- SAT or ACT (ACT writing optional) required
- 53% graduate within 6 years

General. Founded in 1880. Regionally accredited. **Degrees:** 347 bachelor's awarded. **Location:** 8 miles from Harrisonburg, 130 miles from Washington, DC. **Calendar:** 4-1-4, limited summer session. **Full-time faculty:** 117 total; 79% have terminal degrees, 5% minority, 47% women. **Part-time faculty:** 37 total; 46% have terminal degrees, 5% minority, 57% women. **Class size:** 47% < 20, 50% 20-39, 2% 40-49. **Special facilities:** Museum of the Shenandoah Valley and Church of the Brethren; 75-acre equestrian center for equestrian competitions and boarding of college- and student-owned horses.

Freshman class profile. 7,187 applied, 3,541 admitted, 542 enrolled.

Mid 50% test scores			
SAT critical reading:	460-570	**Rank in top quarter:**	45%
SAT math:	460-560	**Rank in top tenth:**	15%
SAT writing:	440-540	**Return as sophomores:**	78%
ACT composite:	20-27	**Out-of-state:**	29%
GPA 3.75 or higher:	34%	**Live on campus:**	93%
GPA 3.50-3.74:	17%	**International:**	1%
GPA 3.0-3.49:	35%		
GPA 2.0-2.99:	14%		

Basis for selection. High school GPA most important, followed by the strength of curriculum and test scores. Prefer applicants in top half of high school graduating class. Consider those in bottom half with strong compensating qualities. Interview required for some, recommended for all. **Home schooled:** GED required for students applying for Title IV financial aid.

High school preparation. College-preparatory program recommended. 17 units required; 19 recommended. Required and recommended units include English 4, mathematics 3, science 3 (laboratory 3), foreign language 2 and academic electives 4. 3 units in History or Social Studies.

2016-2017 Annual costs. Tuition/fees (projected): $32,590. Room/board: $11,920. Books/supplies: $1,150. Personal expenses: $1,080.

2015-2016 Financial aid. Need-based: 520 full-time freshmen applied for aid; 469 deemed to have need; 469 received aid. Average need met was 86%. Average scholarship/grant was $26,134; average loan $4,283. 80% of total undergraduate aid awarded as scholarships/grants, 20% as loans/jobs. **Non-need-based:** Awarded to 1,810 full-time undergraduates, including 544 freshmen. Scholarships awarded for academics, minority status, music/drama, religious affiliation, state residency.

Application procedures. Admission: Closing date 5/1 (postmark date). No application fee. Application must be submitted online. Admission notification on a rolling basis beginning on or about 9/1. Must reply by May 1 or within 2 week(s) if notified thereafter. **Financial aid:** Priority date 3/1; no closing date. FAFSA required. Applicants notified on a rolling basis starting 3/15; must reply by 5/1 or within 2 week(s) of notification.

Academics. Special study options: Combined bachelor's/graduate degree, distance learning, double major, honors, independent study, internships, liberal arts/career combination, study abroad, teacher certification program. 3-2 engineering with George Washington University (BA/BA) and 3-2 engineering with Virginia Tech (BA/BA), 3-2 nursing with Vanderbilt University (BA/MN), 3-4 physical therapy with Shenandoah University (BA/DPT);3-4 veterinary science with Virginia Tech (BA/DVM). **Credit/placement by examination:** AP, CLEP, IB, institutional tests. **Support services:** Learning center, reduced course load, study skills assistance, tutoring, writing center.

Majors. Biology: General, biochemistry. **Business:** Business admin, management information systems. **Communications:** Media studies. **Computer sciences:** Computer science. **Conservation:** Environmental science. **English:** English lit. **Foreign languages:** French, Spanish. **Health services:** Athletic training. **History:** General. **Liberal arts:** Arts/sciences. **Math:** General. **Parks/recreation:** Health/fitness. **Physical sciences:** Chemistry, physics. **Psychology:** General. **Social sciences:** Economics, international relations, political science, sociology. **Visual/performing arts:** Music history, studio arts. **Work/family studies:** General, human nutrition.

Most popular majors. Biology 14%, business/marketing 19%, family/consumer sciences 6%, parks/recreation 13%, physical sciences 6%, psychology 6%, social sciences 6%.

Technology on campus. PC or laptop required. 158 workstations in library, student center. Dormitories wired for high-speed internet access and linked to campus network. Commuter students can connect to campus network. Online course registration, online library, helpline, repair service, student web hosting, wireless network available.

Student life. Freshman orientation: Mandatory. Preregistration for classes offered. Two spring 2-day sessions. One-day, summer program offered for students unable to attend a spring session. Further orientation activities 2 days preceding classes. Parents included in spring and summer orientations. **Policies:** Alcoholic beverages not permitted on campus. Smoking and other tobacco products permitted only in designated areas. All full time students are required to live in College housing except: (1) students living at home with their parents or legal guardians if the principal residence is in one of the following counties: Augusta, Highland, Page, Rockingham or Shenandoah; (2) transfer students who have earned a minimum of 12 college credits at the time of matriculation; (3) students who are married or are custodial parents; (4) students 23 years of age or older; (5) current or former members of the armed forces; (6) part-time students (taking fewer than 12 credit hours per semester); (7) students who are fifth-year seniors.; and (8) students who have a physical or mental health need that cannot reasonably be addressed through resources and special arrangements available on campus. Students are not required to live on campus during the summer sessions. **Housing:** Guaranteed on-campus for all undergraduates. Coed dorms, single-sex dorms, special housing for disabled, apartments available. Honor housing available. **Activities:** Bands, campus ministries, choral groups, dance, drama, international student organizations, literary magazine, music ensembles, radio station, student government, student newspaper, BC Allies, BC Interfaith Board, Black Student Association, Brethren Student Movement, Campus Crusade for Christ, Catholic Campus Ministry, Eco-Action Club, Fellowship of Christian Athletes, Habitat for Humanity, New Community Project.

Athletics. NCAA. **Intercollegiate:** Baseball M, basketball, cross-country, field hockey W, football (tackle) M, golf, lacrosse, soccer, softball W, swimming W, tennis, track and field, volleyball W. **Intramural:** Badminton, basketball, bowling, football (non-tackle), golf, racquetball, sand volleyball, soccer, softball, table tennis, tennis, ultimate frisbee, volleyball. **Team name:** Eagles.

Student services. Alcohol/substance abuse counseling, chaplain/spiritual director, career counseling, student employment services, financial aid counseling, health services, minority student services, personal counseling, placement for graduates. **Physically disabled:** Services for visually impaired.

Contact. E-mail: admissions@bridgewater.edu
Phone: (540) 828-5375 Toll-free number: (800) 759-8328
Fax: (540) 828-5481
Jarret Smith, Director of Admissions, Bridgewater College, 402 East College Street, Bridgewater, VA 22812-1599

Catholic Distance University
Hamilton, Virginia
www.cdu.edu

- Private two-year upper-division virtual university affiliated with the Roman Catholic Church
- Commuter campus in rural community

General. Accredited by DETC. Catholic school of theology. **Degrees:** 17 bachelor's, 6 associate awarded; master's offered. **Calendar:** Continuous, limited summer session. **Part-time faculty:** 42 total; 71% have terminal degrees, 19% women.

Student profile. 153 degree-seeking undergraduates.

Basis for selection. Open admission.

2015-2016 Annual costs. Books/supplies: $300.

Application procedures. Admission: $50 fee.

Academics. Online student center available for academic support and technical support. **Special study options:** Distance learning. **Credit/placement by examination:** AP, CLEP.

Majors. Theology: Religious ed, theology.

Contact. E-mail: admissions@cdu.edu
Phone: (540) 338-2700 ext. 710
Toll-free number: (888) 254-4238 ext. 710 Fax: (540) 338-4788
Carol Ciullo, Director of Admissions, Catholic Distance University, 120 East Colonial Highway, Hamilton, VA 20158-9012

Chamberlain College of Nursing: Arlington
Arlington, Virginia
www.chamberlain.edu   CB code: 6522

- For-profit 4-year nursing college
- Commuter campus in small city
- 394 degree-seeking undergraduates

General. Degrees: 114 bachelor's awarded. **Calendar:** Semester. **Full-time faculty:** 10 total; 40% minority, 90% women. **Part-time faculty:** 11 total; 27% minority, 100% women.

Basis for selection. Admission decisions based on interview, proof of high school diploma/GED, and satisfactory test scores. For more information about such tests and scores, contact admissions office.

2015-2016 Annual costs. Tuition/fees: $18,160. Books/supplies: $1,400. Personal expenses: $2,452.

Application procedures. Admission: No deadline. $95 fee. Admission notification on a rolling basis. **Financial aid:** No deadline.

Academics. Credit/placement by examination: AP, CLEP.

Majors. Health services: Nursing (RN).

Contact. Chamberlain College of Nursing: Arlington, 2450 Crystal Drive, Arlington, VA 22202

Christendom College
Front Royal, Virginia
www.christendom.edu   CB code: 5691

- Private 4-year liberal arts college affiliated with the Roman Catholic Church
- Residential campus in large town
- 469 degree-seeking undergraduates
- 92% of applicants admitted
- SAT or ACT (ACT writing optional), application essay required

General. Founded in 1977. Regionally accredited. **Degrees:** 102 bachelor's awarded; master's offered. **Location:** 70 miles from Washington, DC. **Calendar:** Semester, limited summer session. **Full-time faculty:** 23 total; 65% have terminal degrees, 9% women. **Part-time faculty:** 21 total; 67% have terminal degrees, 38% women. **Class size:** 56% < 20, 40% 20-39, 4% 40-49.

Freshman class profile. 281 applied, 259 admitted, 149 enrolled.

Mid 50% test scores			
SAT critical reading:	640-680	GPA 3.0-3.49:	12%
SAT math:	500-630	GPA 2.0-2.99:	6%
SAT writing:	530-660	Rank in top quarter:	75%
ACT composite:	23-28	Rank in top tenth:	50%
GPA 3.75 or higher:	59%	Out-of-state:	75%
GPA 3.50-3.74:	23%	Live on campus:	98%

Basis for selection. Secondary school record, essay, test scores, class rank, GPA, recommendations important. Applicants can present additional material and explain scores, evaluations, etc. which they believe do not adequately reflect their abilities. Interview recommended. **Home schooled:** Transcript forms required (available from college).

High school preparation. 14 units recommended. Recommended units include English 4, mathematics 2, social studies 1, history 2, science 2, foreign language 2 and academic electives 1.

2015-2016 Annual costs. Tuition/fees: $24,780. Room/board: $8,980. Books/supplies: $500. Personal expenses: $300.

Financial aid. Non-need-based: Scholarships awarded for academics, alumni affiliation. **Additional information:** Institution does not accept direct federal aid, nor does it participate in indirect programs of federal aid.

Application procedures. Admission: Priority date 3/1; no deadline. $25 fee. Admission notification on a rolling basis. **Financial aid:** Priority date 4/1, closing date 6/1. Institutional form required. Applicants notified on a rolling basis starting 2/1; must reply within 4 week(s) of notification.

Academics. Special study options: Double major, honors, independent study, internships, liberal arts/career combination, study abroad. Junior semester in Rome and Summer Institute in Ireland. **Credit/placement by examination:** AP, CLEP, institutional tests. **Support services:** Pre-admission summer program, reduced course load, study skills assistance, writing center. Academic success coach available to work with all students help develop strong study skills.

Majors. English: English lit. **Foreign languages:** Classics. **History:** General. **Math:** General. **Philosophy/religion:** Philosophy. **Social sciences:** Political science. **Theology:** Theology.

Most popular majors. English 16%, history 24%, philosophy/religious studies 32%, social sciences 17%, theological studies 8%.

Technology on campus. 70 workstations in library, computer center. Commuter students can connect to campus network. Online course registration, online library, wireless network available.

Student life. Freshman orientation: Mandatory. Preregistration for classes offered. Held weekend before school starts. **Policies:** Although no student is required to participate, college encourages religious activities. **Housing:** Guaranteed on-campus for all undergraduates. Single-sex dorms, wellness housing available. $250 deposit, deadline 3/15. **Activities:** Campus ministries, choral groups, dance, drama, film society, music ensembles, musical theater, radio station, student government, student newspaper, Legion of Mary, Shield of Roses, St. Genesius Society, Holy Rood Guild, College Republicans, Mission Trips club, works of mercy group.

Athletics. USCAA. **Intercollegiate:** Baseball M, basketball, rugby M, soccer, softball W, volleyball W. **Intramural:** Basketball, boxing M, cross-country, fencing, football (non-tackle), handball, racquetball, skiing, soccer, softball, table tennis, tennis, ultimate frisbee, volleyball. **Team name:** Crusaders.

Student services. Chaplain/spiritual director, career counseling, student employment services, financial aid counseling, health services, personal counseling, placement for graduates.

Contact. E-mail: admissions@christendom.edu
Phone: (540) 636-2900 Toll-free number: (800) 877-5456
Fax: (540) 636-1655
Samuel Phillips, Director of Admissions, Christendom College, 134 Christendom Drive, Front Royal, VA 22630

Christopher Newport University
Newport News, Virginia   **CB member**
www.cnu.edu   **CB code: 5128**

◆ Public 4-year university and liberal arts college

◆ Residential campus in small city

◆ 5,040 degree-seeking undergraduates: 2% part-time, 57% women, 8% African American, 3% Asian American, 5% Hispanic/Latino, 5% Multiracial, non-Hispanic

◆ 113 degree-seeking graduate students

◆ 60% of applicants admitted

◆ Application essay required

◆ 70% graduate within 6 years; 25% enter graduate study

General. Founded in 1960. Regionally accredited. **Degrees:** 1,137 bachelor's awarded; master's offered. **ROTC:** Army. **Location:** 20 miles from Norfolk, 70 miles from Richmond, 170 miles from Washington, DC. **Calendar:** Semester, limited summer session. **Full-time faculty:** 275 total; 87% have terminal degrees, 14% minority, 48% women. **Part-time faculty:** 180 total; 29% have terminal degrees, 14% minority, 45% women. **Class size:** 59% < 20, 30% 20-39, 8% 40-49, 3% 50-99. **Special facilities:** Center for the arts, mariners' museum library collection.

Freshman class profile. 7,366 applied, 4,427 admitted, 1,224 enrolled.

Mid 50% test scores		GPA 2.0-2.99:	2%
SAT critical reading:	540-630	Rank in top quarter:	53%
SAT math:	530-620	Rank in top tenth:	17%
ACT composite:	23-27	End year in good standing:	95%
GPA 3.75 or higher:	53%	Return as sophomores:	87%
GPA 3.50-3.74:	22%	Out-of-state:	9%
GPA 3.0-3.49:	23%	Live on campus:	97%

Basis for selection. GED not accepted. Holistic review allows all aspects of an applicant's background to be considered: varying immediate academic environments and curriculum availability, GPA and recent performance trends, standardized test scores, extracurricular activities, demonstrated leadership, written essays and letters of recommendation, interview ratings, and diversity of experiences all influence admission decisions. Freshman applicants who have achieved a cumulative 3.50 GPA (on a 4.00 scale), or rank in the upper 10% of their high school graduation classes, and have pursued a rigorous curriculum, may apply to the University without submitting a standardized test score (ACT or SAT). Test optional applicants will be reviewed for the strength of their core academic curriculum, extra-curricular activites, recommendations, and interview rating. Interview recommended for all students, required for scholarship applicants. Audition required for music. Audition recommended for theater and Dance majors. Portfolio recommended for art. **Home schooled:** Statement describing home school structure and mission required. Submit copy of high school transcript and course descriptions, along with ACT or SAT score. Homeschool Supplement Form is required at time of application submission.

High school preparation. College-preparatory program required. 26 units required. Required and recommended units include English 4, mathematics 4, social studies 4, science 4 (laboratory 3), foreign language 3, visual/performing arts 1 and academic electives 2. 4 units to complete Virginia's ASD or equivalent.

2015-2016 Annual costs. Tuition/fees: $12,526; $23,428 out-of-state. Room/board: $10,614. **Additional information:** Out-of-state students pay annual $396 capital fee.

2015-2016 Financial aid. Need-based: 989 full-time freshmen applied for aid; 590 deemed to have need; 563 received aid. Average need met was 68%. Average scholarship/grant was $6,535; average loan $3,387. 11% of total undergraduate aid awarded as scholarships/grants, 89% as loans/jobs. **Non-need-based:** Awarded to 1,142 full-time undergraduates, including 455 freshmen. Scholarships awarded for academics, alumni affiliation, art, leadership, music/drama, state residency.

Application procedures. Admission: Closing date 2/1 (receipt date). $50 fee, may be waived for applicants with need. Application must be submitted online. Must reply by 5/1. **Financial aid:** Priority date 3/1; no closing date.

FAFSA required. Applicants notified on a rolling basis starting 3/1; must reply by 5/1.

Academics. Special programs for leadership, honors and service learning. **Special study options:** Cross-registration, double major, dual enrollment of high school students, honors, independent study, internships, student-designed major, study abroad, teacher certification program. **Credit/placement by examination:** AP, CLEP, IB, SAT, ACT, institutional tests. 60 credit hours maximum toward bachelor's degree. **Support services:** Study skills assistance, tutoring, writing center.

Majors. Area/ethnic studies: American. **Biology:** General, biochemistry, cellular/molecular, environmental, neuroscience. **Business:** Accounting, business admin, finance, marketing. **Communications:** Communications/speech/rhetoric. **Computer sciences:** Computer science, information systems, information technology. **Conservation:** Environmental studies. **Engineering:** Computer, electrical. **English:** English lit. **Foreign languages:** Classics, French, German, Spanish. **History:** General, **Human services:** Social work. **Math:** General, applied, computational. **Philosophy/religion:** Philosophy. **Physical sciences:** Chemistry. **Psychology:** General. **Social sciences:** Economics, political science, sociology. **Visual/performing arts:** Dramatic, music performance, studio arts.

Most popular majors. Biology 14%, business/marketing 11%, communications/journalism 11%, computer/information sciences 6%, psychology 15%, social sciences 14%.

Technology on campus. 540 workstations in dormitories, library, computer center, student center. Dormitories wired for high-speed internet access and linked to campus network. Commuter students can connect to campus network. Online course registration, online library, helpline, student web hosting, wireless network available.

Student life. Freshman orientation: Mandatory, $250 fee. Preregistration for classes offered. Two programs required: 1.5-day program with overnight stay in residence halls, offered June-July, and welcome week program prior to start of classes in fall. **Policies:** All unmarried 1st, 2nd, and 3rd year students are required to live on campus unless they reside with their parents or legal guardians in Newport News, Hampton, Poquoson, Yorktown, Seaford, Grafton, or Tabb. **Housing:** Guaranteed on-campus for freshmen. Coed dorms, apartments, fraternity/sorority housing, themed housing available. $250 nonrefundable deposit, deadline 5/1. Learning communities available. **Activities:** Bands, campus ministries, choral groups, dance, drama, film society, literary magazine, music ensembles, Model UN, musical theater, opera, radio station, student government, student newspaper, symphony orchestra, TV station, Intervarsity Christian Fellowship, United Campus Ministries, Young Life Christian Fellowship, College Republicans, Young Democrats, Colleges Against Cancer, Operation Smile, TOMS Christopher Newport Campus Club, Multicultural Student Association.

Athletics. NCAA. **Intercollegiate:** Baseball M, basketball, cross-country, field hockey W, football (tackle) M, golf M, lacrosse, soccer, softball W, tennis, track and field, volleyball W. **Intramural:** Basketball, football (nontackle), football (tackle), sand volleyball, soccer, softball, tennis, ultimate frisbee, volleyball. **Team name:** Captains.

Student services. Alcohol/substance abuse counseling, chaplain/spiritual director, career counseling, student employment services, financial aid counseling, health services, personal counseling, placement for graduates. **Physically disabled:** Services for visually, speech, hearing impaired.

Contact. E-mail: admit@cnu.edu
Phone: (757) 594-7015 Toll-free number: (800) 333-4268
Fax: (757) 594-7333
Robert Lange, Dean of Admission, Christopher Newport University, 1 Avenue of the Arts, Newport News, VA 23606-3072

College of William and Mary
Williamsburg, Virginia   **CB member**
www.wm.edu   **CB code: 5115**

◆ Public 4-year university

◆ Residential campus in large town

◆ 6,260 degree-seeking undergraduates: 1% part-time, 57% women, 7% African American, 8% Asian American, 9% Hispanic/Latino, 4% Multiracial, non-Hispanic, 6% international

◆ 2,075 degree-seeking graduate students

◆ 34% of applicants admitted

◆ SAT or ACT (ACT writing optional), application essay required

◆ 90% graduate within 6 years; 19% enter graduate study

General. Founded in 1693. Regionally accredited. **Degrees:** 1,629 bachelor's awarded; master's, professional, doctoral offered. **ROTC:** Army. **Location:** 50 miles from Richmond, 50 miles from Norfolk. **Calendar:** Semester, limited summer session. **Special facilities:** Observatory, continuous beam accelerator, 3 interdisciplinary centers (humanities, international studies, writing resources), marine science institute, materials processes research center, public policy research center, health policy research center, center for geospatial analysis, center for archaeological research, institute for the theory and practice of international relations, environmental field laboratory, center for international studies, special collections research center, media center, museum of art, college woods, Lake Matoaka and Matoaka Trails.

Freshman class profile. 14,952 applied, 5,153 admitted, 1,518 enrolled.

Mid 50% test scores			
SAT critical reading:	630-730	Rank in top quarter:	96%
SAT math:	630-730	Rank in top tenth:	81%
SAT writing:	620-720	Return as sophomores:	96%
ACT composite:	28-32	Out-of-state:	33%
GPA 3.75 or higher:	92%	Live on campus:	100%
GPA 3.50-3.74:	6%	International:	7%
GPA 3.0-3.49:	2%	Fraternities:	15%
		Sororities:	24%

Basis for selection. Primary importance is placed on the academic record, including in-class achievement, rigor of curriculum and standardized testing. Extracurricular involvements, writing samples, recommendations, talents and abilities also receive consideration. Preference given to Virginia residents. Children of alumni receive special consideration. On campus interviews are offered as an optional component. We do not have other interview options. **Home schooled:** Homeschooled students are strongly encouraged to submit scores from three SAT Subject tests.

High school preparation. College-preparatory program recommended. Recommended units include English 4, mathematics 4, social studies 4, science 4 (laboratory 3) and foreign language 4.

2015-2016 Annual costs. Tuition/fees: $19,372; $40,516 out-of-state. Room/board: $10,978.

Financial aid. **Non-need-based:** Scholarships awarded for academics, art, athletics, music/drama, ROTC.

Application procedures. **Admission:** Closing date 1/1 (postmark date). $70 fee, may be waived for applicants with need. Admission notification by 4/1. Must reply by 5/1. **Financial aid:** Priority date 3/1; no closing date. FAFSA, CSS PROFILE required. Applicants notified on a rolling basis starting 3/15; must reply by 5/1.

Academics. **Special study options:** Accelerated study, combined bachelor's/graduate degree, distance learning, double major, dual enrollment of high school students, honors, independent study, internships, student-designed major, study abroad, teacher certification program, Washington semester. Joint degree program with University of St Andrews. **Credit/placement by examination:** AP, CLEP, IB, institutional tests. **Support services:** Pre-admission summer program, study skills assistance, tutoring, writing center.

Majors. **Area/ethnic studies:** General, African-American, American, Chinese, Latin American, women's. **Biology:** General, neuroscience. **Business:** Banking/financial services, business admin, marketing. **Computer sciences:** General. **Conservation:** Environmental studies. **English:** English lit. **Foreign languages:** Chinese, classics, French, German, linguistics, Spanish. **History:** General. **Human services:** Public policy. **Math:** General. **Parks/recreation:** Health/fitness. **Philosophy/religion:** Philosophy, religion. **Physical sciences:** Chemistry, geology, physics. **Psychology:** General. **Social sciences:** Anthropology, economics, international relations, political science, sociology. **Visual/performing arts:** Art, dramatic, music.

Most popular majors. Biology 10%, business/marketing 11%, English 6%, history 6%, interdisciplinary studies 7%, psychology 7%, social sciences 24%.

Technology on campus. PC or laptop required. 275 workstations in library, computer center, student center. Dormitories wired for high-speed internet access and linked to campus network. Commuter students can connect to campus network. Online course registration, online library, helpline, repair service, student web hosting, wireless network available.

Student life. **Freshman orientation:** Mandatory, $258 fee. Preregistration for classes offered. Five-day program immediately preceding fall semester. **Policies:** All students pledge to uphold the Honor Code. Freshman students are required to live on campus. Students negotiate some residential policies, such as quiet hours and visitation, through self-determination. Freshmen not permitted cars on campus. **Housing:** Guaranteed on-campus for freshmen. Coed dorms, special housing for disabled, apartments, fraternity/sorority housing, themed housing available. $350 nonrefundable deposit, deadline 5/1. International Studies Hall, Eco-House, Community Scholars Center, Africana House, Multicultural Unit, 8 Language Houses (Arabic, Chinese, French, German, Italian, Japanese, Russian, Spanish) available. **Activities:**

Bands, campus ministries, choral groups, dance, drama, film society, international student organizations, literary magazine, music ensembles, Model UN, musical theater, opera, radio station, student government, student newspaper, symphony orchestra, TV station, AIDS Tanzania, Pan Asian Culture Council, Black Student Organization, College Partnership for Kids, College Republicans, Branch Out Alternative Breaks, Latin American Student Union, Student Environmental Action Coalition, I-Faith, Young Democrats.

Athletics. NCAA. **Intercollegiate:** Baseball M, basketball, cross-country, field hockey W, football (tackle) M, golf, gymnastics, lacrosse W, soccer, swimming, tennis, track and field, volleyball W. **Intramural:** Basketball, bowling, football (non-tackle), golf, racquetball, soccer, softball, table tennis, tennis, volleyball, weight lifting. **Team name:** Tribe.

Student services. Adult student services, alcohol/substance abuse counseling, chaplain/spiritual director, career counseling, services for economically disadvantaged, student employment services, financial aid counseling, health services, legal services, minority student services, on-campus daycare, personal counseling, placement for graduates, veterans' counselor, women's services. **Physically disabled:** Services for visually, hearing impaired.

Contact. E-mail: admission@wm.edu
Phone: (757) 221-4223 Fax: (757) 221-1242
Tim Wolfe, Dean of Admission, College of William and Mary, PO Box 8795, Williamsburg, VA 23187-8795

DeVry University: Arlington
Arlington, Virginia
www.devry.edu
CB code: 3813

- For-profit 4-year university
- Commuter campus in very large city
- 424 degree-seeking undergraduates
- Interview required

General. Additional locations: Manassas, Norfolk; Bethesda (MD); Charlotte, Raleigh-Durham (NC). **Degrees:** 165 bachelor's, 15 associate awarded; master's offered. **Calendar:** Semester, extensive summer session. **Full-time faculty:** 15 total; 53% minority, 40% women. **Part-time faculty:** 166 total; 40% minority, 42% women.

Basis for selection. Applicant must have high school diploma or equivalent, degree from an accredited postsecondary institution, or submit acceptable test scores and be at least 17 years of age. CPT also accepted.

High school preparation. Required units include mathematics 1. Math unit must be algebra or higher.

2015-2016 Annual costs. Tuition/fees: $17,132. Books/supplies: $1,300. Personal expenses: $3,152.

Financial aid. All financial aid based on need.

Application procedures. **Admission:** No deadline. $40 fee. Admission notification on a rolling basis. **Financial aid:** No deadline. FAFSA required. Applicants notified on a rolling basis.

Academics. **Special study options:** Accelerated study, cooperative education, distance learning. **Credit/placement by examination:** AP, CLEP. **Support services:** Learning center, remedial instruction, tutoring.

Majors. **Business:** Business admin. **Computer sciences:** Networking, systems analysis, web page design. **Engineering:** Software.

Most popular majors. Business/marketing 63%, computer/information sciences 16%, engineering/engineering technologies 21%.

Technology on campus. Online course registration, online library, helpline available.

Student life. **Freshman orientation:** Mandatory. Preregistration for classes offered. **Activities:** Linux users' group.

Athletics. **Intramural:** Basketball, volleyball.

Student services. Career counseling, student employment services, financial aid counseling, placement for graduates, veterans' counselor. **Physically disabled:** Services for visually, hearing impaired.

Contact. E-mail: admissions@crys.devry.edu
Phone: (703) 414-4100 Toll-free number: (866) 338-7932
Fax: (703) 414-4040
Director of Admissions, DeVry University: Arlington, 2450 Crystal Drive, Arlington, VA 22202

Eastern Mennonite University

Harrisonburg, Virginia
CB member
www.emu.edu
CB code: 5181

▶ Private 4-year university and liberal arts college affiliated with the Mennonite Church

▶ Residential campus in small city

▶ 1,214 degree-seeking undergraduates: 10% part-time, 65% women, 10% African American, 3% Asian American, 8% Hispanic/Latino, 2% Multiracial, non-Hispanic, 3% international

▶ 337 degree-seeking graduate students

▶ 62% of applicants admitted

▶ SAT or ACT with writing required

▶ 61% graduate within 6 years

General. Founded in 1917. Regionally accredited. Cross-cultural study (usually a semester in another country) and community service required of all students. **Degrees:** 340 bachelor's, 3 associate awarded; master's offered. **Location:** 110 miles from Richmond, 110 miles from Washington, DC. **Calendar:** Semester, limited summer session. **Special facilities:** Museum of natural history, arboretum, campus garden, student-run coffee shop.

Freshman class profile. 1,656 applied, 1,022 admitted, 254 enrolled.

Mid 50% test scores		GPA 2.0-2.99:	19%
SAT critical reading:	430-570	End year in good standing:	73%
SAT math:	440-560	Return as sophomores:	73%
ACT composite:	18-26	Out-of-state:	34%
GPA 3.75 or higher:	31%	Live on campus:	84%
GPA 3.50-3.74:	16%	International:	2%
GPA 3.0-3.49:	34%		

Basis for selection. 2.6 GPA required. 900 SAT (exclusive of Writing) or 19 ACT required. Conditional admission possible for motivated applicants who fail to reach minimum admissions requirements. Interviews recommended. **Home schooled:** Detailed record of coursework completed for grades 9-12 required. **Learning Disabled:** Interview recommended for learning disabled; meet with academic support center personnel.

High school preparation. College-preparatory program recommended. 21 units recommended. Recommended units include English 4, mathematics 3, social studies 3, science 3 (laboratory 3), foreign language 2 and academic electives 6.

2015-2016 Annual costs. Tuition/fees: $32,300. Room/board: $10,250.

Financial aid. Non-need-based: Scholarships awarded for academics, alumni affiliation, art, leadership, religious affiliation, state residency.

Application procedures. Admission: No deadline. $25 fee, may be waived for applicants with need. Admission notification on a rolling basis. **Financial aid:** Priority date 3/1; no closing date. FAFSA required. Applicants notified on a rolling basis starting 3/1; must reply within 4 week(s) of notification.

Academics. Cross-cultural education component required in 3-week or 3-month program to locations around the world. **Special study options:** Combined bachelor's/graduate degree, distance learning, double major, dual enrollment of high school students, ESL, honors, independent study, internships, liberal arts/career combination, study abroad, teacher certification program, Washington semester. Adult degree completion programs in nursing and management. **Credit/placement by examination:** AP, CLEP, IB, SAT, ACT, institutional tests. 30 credit hours maximum toward bachelor's degree. **Support services:** Learning center, reduced course load, study skills assistance, tutoring, writing center.

Majors. Biology: General, biochemistry. **Business:** Accounting, business admin, international, organizational behavior. **Communications:** General, digital media. **Computer sciences:** Computer science. **Conservation:** Environmental studies. **Education:** Physical. **English:** English lit, writing. **Foreign languages:** Spanish. **Health services:** Clinical lab science, nursing (RN). **History:** General. **Human services:** Social work. **Liberal arts:** Arts/sciences. **Math:** General. **Parks/recreation:** Exercise sciences, sports admin. **Physical sciences:** Chemistry. **Psychology:** General. **Social sciences:** General, economics. **Theology:** Bible, preministerial. **Visual/performing arts:** Art, dramatic, music, photography.

Most popular majors. Business/marketing 15%, health sciences 35%, liberal arts 8%.

Technology on campus. 100 workstations in library, computer center, student center. Dormitories wired for high-speed internet access and linked to campus network. Commuter students can connect to campus network. Online library, helpline, student web hosting, wireless network available.

Student life. Freshman orientation: Mandatory. Preregistration for classes offered. Held over a five day program before the start of the semester. **Policies:** Alcohol and drug use by students prohibited. Chapel attendance expected. Students must sign and adhere to Community Lifestyle Commitment. Emphasis on justice and peacebuilding. **Housing:** Guaranteed on-campus for freshmen. Coed dorms, single-sex dorms, special housing for disabled, apartments, themed housing, wellness housing available. $200 fully refundable deposit, deadline 5/1. International communities available. **Activities:** Jazz band, campus ministries, choral groups, dance, drama, film society, international student organizations, literary magazine, music ensembles, musical theater, student government, student newspaper, symphony orchestra, Young People's Christian Association, Peace Fellowship, Black student union, Latino Student Alliance, Earth Keepers, Social Work is People, Safe Space, Alpha Omega Dancers for Christ, Fellowship of Christian Athletes, Sustainable Food Initiative.

Athletics. NCAA. **Intercollegiate:** Baseball M, basketball, cross-country, field hockey W, golf, soccer, softball W, track and field, volleyball. **Intramural:** Basketball, football (non-tackle), golf, soccer, softball, table tennis, tennis, volleyball. **Team name:** Royals.

Student services. Adult student services, alcohol/substance abuse counseling, chaplain/spiritual director, career counseling, student employment services, financial aid counseling, health services, minority student services, personal counseling, placement for graduates. **Physically disabled:** Services for visually, speech, hearing impaired.

Contact. E-mail: admiss@emu.edu
Phone: (540) 432-4118 Toll-free number: (800) 368-2665
Fax: (540) 432-4444
Matthew Ruth, Director of Admissions, Eastern Mennonite University, 1200 Park Road, Harrisonburg, VA 22802-2462

ECPI University

Virginia Beach, Virginia
www.ecpi.edu
CB code: 7140

▶ For-profit 4-year university and health science college

▶ Commuter campus in very large city

▶ 10,242 degree-seeking undergraduates

▶ 42 graduate students

▶ Interview required

General. Founded in 1966. Regionally accredited. Campuses in Virginia, North Carolina, and South Carolina. **Degrees:** 1,072 bachelor's, 1,905 associate awarded; master's offered. **Calendar:** Semester, extensive summer session. **Full-time faculty:** 410 total; 18% have terminal degrees, 30% minority, 57% women. **Part-time faculty:** 395 total; 15% have terminal degrees, 43% minority, 59% women. **Class size:** 84% < 20, 15% 20-39, less than 1% 40-49.

Basis for selection. Interview, previous academic performance, and admissions assessment scores important. **Learning Disabled:** Consideration may be given on case-by-case basis.

2015-2016 Annual costs. Tuition/fees: $15,420. Books/supplies: $720. Personal expenses: $1,950.

Financial aid. Non-need-based: Scholarships awarded for academics.

Application procedures. Admission: No deadline. $45 fee. Admission notification on a rolling basis. **Financial aid:** No deadline. FAFSA required. Applicants notified on a rolling basis.

Academics. Special study options: Accelerated study, distance learning, internships, study abroad, weekend college. **Credit/placement by examination:** AP, CLEP, institutional tests. 15 credit hours maximum toward associate degree, 30 toward bachelor's. **Support services:** Learning center, remedial instruction, study skills assistance, tutoring, writing center.

Majors. Business: Accounting, business admin, restaurant/food services. **Computer sciences:** General, modeling/simulation, programming, security, webmaster. **Health services:** Health care admin, nursing (RN). **Protective services:** Criminal justice.

Most popular majors. Business/marketing 18%, computer/information sciences 45%, engineering/engineering technologies 17%, security/protective services 16%.

Technology on campus. 6,000 workstations in library, computer center, student center. Commuter students can connect to campus network. Online library, helpline, wireless network available.

Student life. Freshman orientation: Mandatory. Preregistration for classes offered. Half-day orientation held day prior to start of term. **Activities:**

Student Veterans Association, honor societies, community outreach organizations, program specific student clubs and organizations (information systems, network security, electronics engineering, health/medical, business, criminal justice, culinary).

Student services. Adult student services, alcohol/substance abuse counseling, career counseling, services for economically disadvantaged, student employment services, financial aid counseling, legal services, personal counseling, placement for graduates, veterans' counselor.

Contact. Phone: (757) 490-9090 Toll-free number: (800) 986-1200
Fax: (757) 671-8661
David Preece, Director of Admissions, ECPI University, 5555 Greenwich Road, Suite 300, Virginia Beach, VA 23462-6542

Emory & Henry College
Emory, Virginia   **CB member**
www.ehc.edu   **CB code: 5185**

- Private 4-year liberal arts college affiliated with the United Methodist Church
- Residential campus in rural community
- 1,010 degree-seeking undergraduates: 1% part-time, 48% women, 11% African American, 1% Asian American, 4% Hispanic/Latino, 1% Native American, 2% Multi-racial, non-Hispanic
- 56 degree-seeking graduate students
- 76% of applicants admitted
- SAT or ACT (ACT writing optional) required
- 54% graduate within 6 years

General. Founded in 1836. Regionally accredited. **Degrees:** 244 bachelor's awarded; master's offered. **Location:** 25 miles from Bristol, VA. **Calendar:** Semester, limited summer session. **Full-time faculty:** 85 total; 81% have terminal degrees, 47% women. **Part-time faculty:** 51 total; 16% have terminal degrees, 39% women. **Class size:** 74% < 20, 26% 20-39. **Special facilities:** Observatory, 1912 art depot, outdoor leadership center, disc golf course, golf course.

Freshman class profile. 1,456 applied, 1,112 admitted, 304 enrolled.

Mid 50% test scores			
		GPA 3.0-3.49:	25%
SAT critical reading:	430-550	**GPA 2.0-2.99:**	24%
SAT math:	430-540	**Rank in top quarter:**	26%
SAT writing:	400-520	**Rank in top tenth:**	10%
ACT composite:	18-24	**Return as sophomores:**	70%
GPA 3.75 or higher:	35%	**Out-of-state:**	32%
GPA 3.50-3.74:	16%	**Live on campus:**	90%

Basis for selection. School achievement record, test scores, involvement in extracurricular and community activities, class rank, recommendations used. Audition required for preprofessional degrees in acting, directing, musical theater, and design/production. Auditions required for performance and teacher preparation tracks within music program. Portfolio recommended for art program.

High school preparation. College-preparatory program required. 15 units required. Required and recommended units include English 4, mathematics 3, history 3, science 3 (laboratory 2) and foreign language 2. 1 fine arts recommended.

2015-2016 Annual costs. Tuition/fees: $30,900. Room/board: $10,510. Books/supplies: $1,000. Personal expenses: $1,200.

2015-2016 Financial aid. Need-based: 289 full-time freshmen applied for aid; 265 deemed to have need; 265 received aid. Average need met was 91%. Average scholarship/grant was $25,667; average loan $3,262. 80% of total undergraduate aid awarded as scholarships/grants, 20% as loans/jobs. Non-need-based: Awarded to 100 full-time undergraduates, including 16 freshmen. Scholarships awarded for academics, alumni affiliation, art, music/drama, state residency. **Additional information:** Virginia residents eligible for additional in-state tuition grants.

Application procedures. Admission: Priority date 3/15; no deadline. No application fee. Admission notification on a rolling basis beginning on or about 1/1. Must reply by May 1 or within 4 week(s) if notified thereafter. **Financial aid:** Priority date 4/1; no closing date. FAFSA required. Applicants notified on a rolling basis starting 2/1; must reply within 3 week(s) of notification.

Academics. Special study options: Distance learning, double major, dual enrollment of high school students, honors, independent study, internships, liberal arts/career combination, student-designed major, study abroad, teacher certification program. **Credit/placement by examination:** AP, CLEP, IB,

SAT, ACT, institutional tests. **Support services:** Learning center, pre-admission summer program, reduced course load, study skills assistance, tutoring, writing center.

Majors. Area/ethnic studies: East Asian, European, French, Near/Middle Eastern, Spanish/Iberian. **Biology:** General. **Business:** Accounting, business admin, international. **Communications:** Media studies. **Conservation:** Environmental science, environmental studies. **Education:** Art, biology, business, chemistry, English, French, mathematics, music, physical, Spanish. **English:** Creative writing, English lit. **Foreign languages:** French, Spanish. **Health services:** Athletic training, prepharmacy, preveterinary. **History:** General, applied. **Human services:** Community org/advocacy. **Math:** General. **Parks/recreation:** Health/fitness, sports admin. **Philosophy/religion:** Philosophy, religion. **Physical sciences:** Chemistry, physics. **Psychology:** General. **Social sciences:** Anthropology, economics, geography, political science, sociology, U.S. government. **Visual/performing arts:** Acting, art, directing/producing, dramatic, graphic design, music, music performance, musical theater.

Most popular majors. Biology 8%, business/marketing 10%, education 13%, parks/recreation 8%, psychology 9%, social sciences 14%, visual/performing arts 10%.

Technology on campus. 250 workstations in library, computer center, student center. Dormitories wired for high-speed internet access and linked to campus network. Commuter students can connect to campus network. Online course registration, online library, helpline, wireless network available.

Student life. Freshman orientation: Mandatory. Preregistration for classes offered. Orientation occurs before registration. Students participate in community service activity and attend fine arts event following weekend as part of extended orientation. **Housing:** Guaranteed on-campus for all undergraduates. Coed dorms, single-sex dorms, special housing for disabled, themed housing, wellness housing available. $400 fully refundable deposit, deadline 8/1. Small houses available. **Activities:** Pep band, campus ministries, choral groups, dance, drama, international student organizations, literary magazine, music ensembles, musical theater, radio station, student government, student newspaper, TV station, literary debate society, College Democrats, College Republicans, Alpha Phi Omega, outdoor leadership program, Habitat for Humanity, Campus Christian Fellowship, Association for Religious Diversity, Gay-Straight Alliance, multicultural student associations.

Athletics. NCAA. **Intercollegiate:** Baseball M, basketball, cheerleading, cross-country, equestrian, football (tackle) M, soccer, softball W, swimming W, tennis, volleyball W. **Intramural:** Badminton, basketball, bowling, football (non-tackle), golf, racquetball, soccer, softball, table tennis, tennis, ultimate frisbee, volleyball. **Team name:** Wasps.

Student services. Alcohol/substance abuse counseling, chaplain/spiritual director, career counseling, student employment services, financial aid counseling, health services, on-campus daycare, personal counseling, placement for graduates, veterans' counselor. **Physically disabled:** Services for visually, hearing impaired.

Contact. E-mail: ehadmiss@ehc.edu
Phone: (276) 944-6133 Toll-free number: (800) 848-5493
Anthony Graham, Associate Director of Admissions, Emory & Henry College, PO Box 10, Emory, VA 24327

Ferrum College
Ferrum, Virginia   **CB member**
www.ferrum.edu   **CB code: 5213**

- Private 4-year liberal arts college affiliated with the United Methodist Church
- Residential campus in rural community
- 1,451 degree-seeking undergraduates
- SAT or ACT (ACT writing optional) required

General. Founded in 1913. Regionally accredited. **Degrees:** 248 bachelor's awarded. **Location:** 35 miles from Roanoke; 65 miles from Greensboro, NC. **Calendar:** Semester, limited summer session. **Full-time faculty:** 79 total; 80% have terminal degrees, 6% minority, 46% women. **Part-time faculty:** 35 total; 26% have terminal degrees, 40% women. **Class size:** 56% < 20, 44% 20-39. **Special facilities:** Farm museum, state center for Blue Ridge folklore, forest and agricultural acreage used as outdoor labs in science, high and low ropes courses, dinner theater.

Freshman class profile.

GPA 3.75 or higher:	7%	**Rank in top tenth:**	2%
GPA 3.50-3.74:	6%	**Out-of-state:**	21%
GPA 3.0-3.49:	24%	**Live on campus:**	93%
GPA 2.0-2.99:	59%	**Fraternities:**	2%
Rank in top quarter:	15%	**Sororities:**	4%

Basis for selection. High school record most important, followed by test scores, counselor recommendations, areas of intended college study, and extracurricular activities. **Home schooled:** Transcript of courses and grades required.

High school preparation. College-preparatory program required. Required and recommended units include English 4, mathematics 3, social studies 1, history 3, science 2 (laboratory 1) and foreign language 2.

2015-2016 Annual costs. Tuition/fees: $30,835. Room/board: $10,320. Books/supplies: $800. Personal expenses: $1,200.

Financial aid. Non-need-based: Scholarships awarded for academics, leadership, religious affiliation, state residency.

Application procedures. Admission: Priority date 3/1; no deadline. $25 fee, may be waived for applicants with need, free for online applicants. Admission notification on a rolling basis beginning on or about 9/15. **Financial aid:** No deadline. FAFSA required. Applicants notified on a rolling basis.

Academics. Field experiences and internships emphasized. Academic services/support available fall and spring academic semesters. **Special study options:** Double major, dual enrollment of high school students, exchange student, honors, independent study, internships, liberal arts/career combination, student-designed major, study abroad, teacher certification program. **Credit/placement by examination:** AP, CLEP, IB, institutional tests. **Support services:** Learning center, pre-admission summer program, reduced course load, remedial instruction, study skills assistance, tutoring, writing center.

Majors. Biology: General. **Business:** Accounting, business admin, finance, management information systems, marketing. **Communications:** Media studies. **Computer sciences:** Information systems. **Conservation:** Environmental science. **Education:** General. **English:** English lit. **Foreign languages:** Russian, Spanish. **Health services:** Clinical lab science. **History:** General. **Human services:** Social work. **Liberal arts:** Arts/sciences. **Math:** General. **Parks/recreation:** General, health/fitness, sports admin. **Philosophy/religion:** Philosophy, religion. **Physical sciences:** Chemistry. **Protective services:** Criminal justice. **Psychology:** General. **Social sciences:** General, international relations, political science. **Visual/performing arts:** General, art, dramatic.

Most popular majors. Business/marketing 11%, computer/information sciences 7%, education 8%, health sciences 11%, liberal arts 10%, natural resources/environmental science 8%, security/protective services 7%, visual/performing arts 6%.

Technology on campus. PC or laptop required. 600 workstations in dormitories, library, computer center, student center. Dormitories wired for high-speed internet access and linked to campus network. Commuter students can connect to campus network. Online course registration, online library, helpline, repair service, student web hosting, wireless network available.

Student life. Freshman orientation: Mandatory. Preregistration for classes offered. Two-day program held immediately prior to fall semester. **Policies:** All housing substance-free; no alcohol or tobacco products allowed. **Housing:** Guaranteed on-campus for all undergraduates. Coed dorms, single-sex dorms, special housing for disabled, apartments, themed housing, wellness housing available. **Activities:** Bands, campus ministries, choral groups, dance, drama, international student organizations, literary magazine, music ensembles, Model UN, musical theater, radio station, student government, student newspaper, environmental action coalition, Big Buddy/Little Buddy, African American student association, Bonner Scholars, Student Christian Fellowship, Kappa Delta Chi, Habitat for Humanity, Colleges Against Cancer, Alpha Phi Omega.

Athletics. NCAA. **Intercollegiate:** Baseball M, basketball, cheerleading, cross-country, football (tackle) M, golf M, lacrosse W, soccer, softball W, tennis, volleyball W. **Intramural:** Basketball, bowling, football (non-tackle), racquetball, soccer, softball, swimming, table tennis, tennis, volleyball. **Team name:** Panthers.

Student services. Adult student services, alcohol/substance abuse counseling, chaplain/spiritual director, career counseling, student employment services, financial aid counseling, health services, minority student services, personal counseling, placement for graduates, veterans' counselor.

Contact. E-mail: admissions@ferrum.edu
Phone: (540) 365-4290 Toll-free number: (800) 868-9797
Fax: (540) 365-4266
Gilda Woods, Associate Vice President and Dean of Admissions, Ferrum College, Spilman-Daniel House, 40 Stratton Lane, Ferrum, VA 24088

George Mason University
Fairfax, Virginia **CB member**
www2.gmu.edu **CB code: 5827**

- Public 4-year university
- Residential campus in large town
- 22,304 degree-seeking undergraduates: 18% part-time, 51% women, 11% African American, 19% Asian American, 13% Hispanic/Latino, 5% Multi-racial, non-Hispanic, 5% international
- 9,997 degree-seeking graduate students
- 69% of applicants admitted
- 69% graduate within 6 years

General. Founded in 1972. Regionally accredited. **Degrees:** 4,996 bachelor's awarded; master's, professional, doctoral offered. **ROTC:** Army, Air Force. **Location:** 21 miles from Washington, DC. **Calendar:** Semester, extensive summer session. **Full-time faculty:** 1,243 total; 91% have terminal degrees, 15% minority, 43% women. **Part-time faculty:** 1,314 total; 16% minority, 49% women. **Class size:** 30% < 20, 46% 20-39, 11% 40-49, 11% 50-99, 3% >100. **Special facilities:** Center for the Arts, Hylton Performing Arts Center, astronomy observatory, Smithsonian Conservation and Research Center, Library of Congress Federal Theater Project Collection.

Freshman class profile. 21,981 applied, 15,138 admitted, 3,181 enrolled.

Mid 50% test scores			
SAT critical reading:	520-620	Rank in top tenth:	21%
SAT math:	520-630	End year in good standing:	88%
ACT composite:	23-29	Return as sophomores:	87%
GPA 3.75 or higher:	40%	Out-of-state:	21%
GPA 3.50-3.74:	28%	Live on campus:	69%
GPA 3.0-3.49:	30%	International:	3%
GPA 2.0-2.99:	2%	Fraternities:	6%
Rank in top quarter:	56%	Sororities:	11%

Basis for selection. Academic record with emphasis on courses taken, GPA and test scores rank as the most important aspects. Special talents, abilities and character/personal qualities also considered. Essay or personal statement not required, but strongly preferred. Audition required for dance and music. Portfolio required for art and visual technology and computer game design. Interview and audition or portfolio required for theater. **Home schooled:** Transcript of courses and grades, letter of recommendation (non-parent) required. Students who are home-schooled do not qualify for our score optional consideration. Test scores must be provided.

High school preparation. College-preparatory program required. 17 units required; 23 recommended. Required and recommended units include English 4, mathematics 3-4, social studies 3-4, science 2-3 (laboratory 2-3), foreign language 2-3 and academic electives 3-5.

2015-2016 Annual costs. Tuition/fees: $10,952; $31,598 out-of-state. Room/board: $10,510. Books/supplies: $1,150. Personal expenses: $2,336.

2014-2015 Financial aid. Need-based: 2,480 full-time freshmen applied for aid; 1,755 deemed to have need; 1,667 received aid. Average need met was 64%. Average scholarship/grant was $6,540; average loan $3,415. 41% of total undergraduate aid awarded as scholarships/grants, 59% as loans/jobs. **Non-need-based:** Awarded to 2,684 full-time undergraduates, including 926 freshmen. Scholarships awarded for academics, athletics, minority status, music/drama, ROTC.

Application procedures. Admission: Priority date 11/1; deadline 1/15. $60 fee, may be waived for applicants with need. Admission notification by 3/31. Must reply by 5/1. **Financial aid:** Closing date 3/1. FAFSA required. Applicants notified by 4/1; Applicants notified on a rolling basis starting 4/1; must reply within 3 week(s) of notification.

Academics. Special study options: Accelerated study, combined bachelor's/graduate degree, cooperative education, cross-registration, distance learning, double major, dual enrollment of high school students, ESL, exchange student, honors, independent study, internships, liberal arts/career combination, semester at sea, student-designed major, study abroad, teacher certification program. **Credit/placement by examination:** AP, CLEP, IB, institutional tests. **Support services:** Learning center, pre-admission summer program, reduced course load, study skills assistance, tutoring, writing center.

Honors college/program. Students must apply by our early action deadline (November 1) for priority consideration and complete the Honors College essay.

Majors. Area/ethnic studies: Latin American, Russian/Slavic. **Biology:** General, neuroscience. **Business:** Accounting, business admin, finance, marketing, tourism/travel. **Communications technology:** Animation/special effects. **Computer sciences:** General, computer science, information technology. **Conservation:** Environmental science. **Education:** Health, physical. **Engineering:** Biomedical, civil, computer, electrical, mechanical, systems. **English:** Creative writing, English lit, rhetoric/composition. **Foreign languages:** General. **Health services:** Athletic training, clinical lab science, community health, nursing (RN). **History:** General. **Human services:** General, social work. **Liberal arts:** Arts/sciences. **Math:** General. **Parks/recreation:** Exercise sciences. **Philosophy/religion:** Philosophy, religion. **Physical sciences:** Astronomy, atmospheric science, chemistry, geology, physics. **Protective services:** Forensics, infrastructure protection, police science. **Psychology:** General. **Social sciences:** Anthropology, economics, geography, international relations, sociology. **Visual/performing arts:** General, art history/conservation, cinematography, dance, dramatic, music performance. **Work/family studies:** Family studies.

Most popular majors. Biology 7%, business/marketing 17%, computer/information sciences 7%, English 8%, health sciences 9%, psychology 7%, security/protective services 6%, social sciences 13%.

Technology on campus. 622 workstations in library, computer center. Dormitories wired for high-speed internet access and linked to campus network. Commuter students can connect to campus network. Online course registration, online library, helpline, repair service, student web hosting, wireless network available.

Student life. **Freshman orientation:** Mandatory, $300 fee. Preregistration for classes offered. Two-day overnight program held in June and July. **Housing:** Guaranteed on-campus for freshmen. Coed dorms, special housing for disabled, apartments, themed housing available. $300 nonrefundable deposit, deadline 5/1. **Activities:** Bands, campus ministries, choral groups, dance, drama, film society, international student organizations, literary magazine, music ensembles, Model UN, musical theater, opera, radio station, student government, student newspaper, symphony orchestra, TV station, Campus Crusade for Christ, Catholic Campus Ministry, Muslim Student Association, Pakistani Student Association, Alpha Phi Omega, Circle K International, Hispanic Student Association, Filipino Cultural Association, Environmental Action Group, Colleges Against Cancer.

Athletics. NCAA. **Intercollegiate:** Baseball M, basketball, cross-country, diving, golf M, lacrosse W, rowing (crew) W, soccer, softball W, swimming, tennis, track and field, volleyball, wrestling M. **Intramural:** Basketball, golf, handball, racquetball, soccer, softball, swimming, ultimate frisbee, water polo. **Team name:** Patriots.

Student services. Adult student services, alcohol/substance abuse counseling, chaplain/spiritual director, career counseling, services for economically disadvantaged, student employment services, financial aid counseling, health services, minority student services, on-campus daycare, personal counseling, placement for graduates, veterans' counselor, women's services. **Physically disabled:** Services for visually, speech, hearing impaired.

Contact. E-mail: admissions@gmu.edu
Phone: (703) 993-2400 Toll-free number: (888) 627-6612
Fax: (703) 993-2392
Matthew Boyce, Director of Undergraduate Admissions, George Mason University, 4400 University Drive, MSN 3A4, Fairfax, VA 22030-4444

Hampden-Sydney College

Hampden-Sydney, Virginia

CB member
CB code: 5291

www.hsc.edu

- Private 4-year liberal arts college for men affiliated with the Presbyterian Church (USA)
- Residential campus in small town
- 1,087 degree-seeking undergraduates: 6% African American, 1% Asian American, 2% Hispanic/Latino, 6% Multi-racial, non-Hispanic
- 55% of applicants admitted
- SAT or ACT (ACT writing optional), application essay required
- 63% graduate within 6 years; 21% enter graduate study

General. Founded in 1776. Regionally accredited. **Degrees:** 213 bachelor's awarded. **ROTC:** Army. **Location:** 60 miles from Richmond. **Calendar:** Semester, limited summer session. **Full-time faculty:** 87 total; 94% have terminal degrees, 6% minority, 29% women. **Part-time faculty:** 22 total; 68% have terminal degrees, 4% minority, 23% women. **Class size:** 73% < 20, 27% 20-39, less than 1% 40-49. **Special facilities:** International communications center, observatory, college operated museum, athlete hall of fame museum, hiking trails, center for leadership, men's studies center, energy research lab.

Freshman class profile. 3,683 applied, 2,018 admitted, 305 enrolled.

Mid 50% test scores			
SAT critical reading:	500-620	GPA 2.0-2.99:	19%
SAT math:	500-610	Rank in top quarter:	37%
SAT writing:	460-580	Rank in top tenth:	12%
ACT composite:	21-27	End year in good standing:	96%
GPA 3.75 or higher:	30%	Return as sophomores:	83%
GPA 3.50-3.74:	19%	Out-of-state:	26%
GPA 3.0-3.49:	32%	Live on campus:	100%
		Fraternities:	34%

Basis for selection. High school academic record, recommendations, test scores, extracurricular activities, essay most important. SAT Subject Tests recommended. SAT Subject Test in Math Level 1 recommended. Interview recommended. **Home schooled:** Letter of recommendation (nonparent) required. Curriculum statement required.

High school preparation. College-preparatory program recommended. 16 units required. Required and recommended units include English 4, mathematics 3-4, social studies 1, history 1, science 2-3 (laboratory 1), foreign language 2-3 and academic electives 3.

2015-2016 Annual costs. Tuition/fees: $41,310. Room/board: $13,060. Books/supplies: $1,000. Personal expenses: $1,810.

2015-2016 Financial aid. Need-based: 251 full-time freshmen applied for aid; 200 deemed to have need; 200 received aid. Average need met was 77%. Average scholarship/grant was $28,626; average loan $3,810. 81% of total undergraduate aid awarded as scholarships/grants, 19% as loans/jobs. **Non-need-based:** Awarded to 476 full-time undergraduates, including 137 freshmen. Scholarships awarded for academics, leadership, minority status, music/drama, ROTC, state residency.

Application procedures. Admission: Closing date 3/1 (postmark date). $30 fee, may be waived for applicants with need, free for online applicants. Admission notification by 4/15. Admission notification on a rolling basis. Must reply by 5/1. **Financial aid:** Priority date 3/1, closing date 5/1. FAFSA required. Applicants notified by 3/15; must reply by 5/1 or within 2 week(s) of notification.

Academics. Public service concentration for men interested in government involves classwork and internship followed by paper presented and defended publicly. **Special study options:** Combined bachelor's/graduate degree, cooperative education, cross-registration, double major, dual enrollment of high school students, exchange student, honors, independent study, internships, semester at sea, study abroad, Washington semester, Appalachian semester, junior year exchange program with members of Virginia consortium. **Credit/placement by examination:** AP, CLEP, IB, institutional tests. **Support services:** Reduced course load, study skills assistance, tutoring, writing center.

Majors. Biology: General. **Business:** Managerial economics. **Computer sciences:** Computer science. **English:** English lit. **Foreign languages:** Ancient Greek, classics, French, German, Latin, Spanish. **History:** General. **Math:** General, applied. **Philosophy/religion:** Philosophy, religion. **Physical sciences:** Chemistry, physics. **Psychology:** General. **Social sciences:** Econometrics, economics, international relations, political science. **Visual/performing arts:** Dramatic, studio arts.

Most popular majors. Biology 11%, business/marketing 15%, history 12%, physical sciences 6%, psychology 6%, social sciences 32%.

Technology on campus. 200 workstations in dormitories, library, computer center. Dormitories wired for high-speed internet access and linked to campus network. Commuter students can connect to campus network. Online course registration, online library, helpline, repair service, wireless network available.

Student life. Freshman orientation: Mandatory, $325 fee. Preregistration for classes offered. Held four days before the start of classes. **Policies:** All entering freshman participate in a presentation and discussion regarding the college's Honor Code. **Housing:** Guaranteed on-campus for all undergraduates. Apartments, fraternity/sorority housing, themed housing available. Language housing available. **Activities:** Pep band, campus ministries, choral groups, drama, international student organizations, literary magazine, music ensembles, radio station, student government, student newspaper, Inter-Varsity Christian Fellowship, Republican Society, H-SC Volunteer Fire Department, Good Men and Good Citizens, Student Environmental Action Coalition, museum board, Fellowship of Christian Athletes, Minority Student Union, President's Men, Society of '91.

Athletics. NCAA. **Intercollegiate:** Baseball M, basketball M, cross-country M, football (tackle) M, golf M, lacrosse M, soccer M, swimming M, tennis M, wrestling M. **Intramural:** Basketball M, racquetball M, rugby M, soccer M, softball M, volleyball M. **Team name:** Tigers.

Student services. Alcohol/substance abuse counseling, chaplain/spiritual director, career counseling, student employment services, financial aid counseling, health services, minority student services, personal counseling, placement for graduates, veterans' counselor.

Contact. E-mail: hsapp@hsc.edu
Phone: (434) 223-6120 Toll-free number: (800) 755-0753
Fax: (434) 223-6346
Anita Garland, Dean of Admissions, Hampden-Sydney College, PO Box 667, Hampden-Sydney, VA 23943

Hampton University
Hampton, Virginia CB member
www.hamptonu.edu CB code: 5292

▸ Private 4-year university
▸ Residential campus in small city
▸ 3,419 degree-seeking undergraduates: 5% part-time, 66% women
▸ 850 degree-seeking graduate students
▸ 69% of applicants admitted
▸ Application essay required
▸ 61% graduate within 6 years; 26% enter graduate study

General. Founded in 1868. Regionally accredited. **Degrees:** 667 bachelor's awarded; master's, professional, doctoral offered. **ROTC:** Army, Naval. **Location:** 6 miles from Norfolk. **Calendar:** Semester, extensive summer session. **Full-time faculty:** 317 total; 86% have terminal degrees, 74% minority, 52% women. **Part-time faculty:** 82 total; 26% have terminal degrees, 82% minority, 61% women. **Class size:** 61% < 20, 31% 20-39, 4% 40-49, 3% 50-99, less than 1% >100. **Special facilities:** African American literature and history collection, university archives, North American Indian/African/Oceanic/Black American art collections, proton therapy institute, medical research, atmospheric sciences with satellites in earth's orbit.

Freshman class profile. 10,258 applied, 7,083 admitted, 930 enrolled.

Mid 50% test scores			
SAT critical reading:	470-540	GPA 3.0-3.49:	36%
SAT math:	470-550	GPA 2.0-2.99:	33%
ACT composite:	19-24	End year in good standing:	77%
GPA 3.75 or higher:	15%	Return as sophomores:	77%
GPA 3.50-3.74:	16%	Out-of-state:	80%
		Live on campus:	98%

Basis for selection. Academic record, rank in top half of graduating class, personal references, intended major, and personal statement important. Extracurricular activities, essay, school recommendation considered. Test optional policy: Students with a cumulative GPA of at least 3.3 or rank in the top 10 percent of their class, choose whether or not to submit SAT or ACT. Applicants choosing not to submit standardized test scores are strongly encouraged to submit at least one recommendation from a teacher in a core subject area. Students attending schools outside the United States and students wishing to be considered for merit based scholarships must submit scores. Audition required for music. **Home schooled:** Transcript of courses and grades required. Must present secondary school record if it exists, GED test scores, verification by state/regional official. SAT or ACT required.

High school preparation. College-preparatory program recommended. 17 units required. Required and recommended units include English 4, mathematics 3, social studies 2, science 2 (laboratory 2), foreign language 2 and academic electives 6. One Chemistry, Biology with lab, Algebra I and II, Geometry required.

2015-2016 Annual costs. Tuition/fees: $22,850. Room/board: $10,176. Books/supplies: $1,100. Personal expenses: $1,000.

2014-2015 Financial aid. Need-based: 632 full-time freshmen applied for aid; 507 deemed to have need; 484 received aid. Average need met was 39%. Average scholarship/grant was $5,138; average loan $5,396. 29% of total undergraduate aid awarded as scholarships/grants, 71% as loans/jobs. **Non-need-based:** Awarded to 671 full-time undergraduates, including 486 freshmen. Scholarships awarded for academics, athletics, job skills, leadership, music/drama, ROTC.

Application procedures. Admission: Priority date 11/1; deadline 3/1 (postmark date). $35 fee. Admission notification on a rolling basis beginning on or about 12/15. Must reply by 6/1. **Financial aid:** Priority date 2/15, closing date 4/15. FAFSA required. Applicants notified on a rolling basis starting 3/1; must reply within 2 week(s) of notification.

Academics. Students may take courses at other Tidewater consortium schools. **Special study options:** Accelerated study, combined bachelor's/graduate degree, cooperative education, cross-registration, distance learning,

double major, dual enrollment of high school students, ESL, honors, independent study, internships, study abroad, teacher certification program. Graduate-level programs for undergraduates, co-op programs in arts, business, education, engineering, social/behavioral science. **Credit/placement by examination:** AP, CLEP, IB, SAT, ACT, institutional tests. 30 credit hours maximum toward bachelor's degree. **Support services:** Learning center, pre-admission summer program, reduced course load, remedial instruction, study skills assistance, tutoring, writing center. Academic skills workshops held throughout year.

Honors college/program. Students who complete one semester with 3.2 GPA may apply.

Majors. Biology: General, marine, molecular. **Business:** Accounting, banking/financial services, business admin, finance, management information systems, managerial economics, marketing. **Communications:** Advertising, broadcast journalism, journalism, media studies, public relations. **Computer sciences:** General, computer science, networking. **Conservation:** Environmental science. **Education:** General, health, physical, special ed. **Engineering:** General, chemical, computer, electrical. **English:** English lit, rhetoric/composition. **Foreign languages:** Spanish. **Health services:** Audiology/speech pathology, communication disorders, nursing (RN). **History:** General. **Liberal arts:** Arts/sciences. **Math:** General. **Parks/recreation:** General, facilities management, sports admin. **Physical sciences:** Chemistry, physics. **Protective services:** Fire services admin, law enforcement admin. **Psychology:** General. **Social sciences:** Political science, sociology. **Theology:** Theology. **Visual/performing arts:** Art, commercial/advertising art, dramatic, music, music performance.

Most popular majors. Biology 9%, business/marketing 23%, communications/journalism 14%, health sciences 9%, psychology 11%.

Technology on campus. 1,500 workstations in dormitories, library, computer center, student center. Dormitories wired for high-speed internet access and linked to campus network. Commuter students can connect to campus network. Online course registration, online library, helpline, repair service, student web hosting, wireless network available.

Student life. Freshman orientation: Mandatory. Preregistration for classes offered. One-week orientation held in August. **Policies:** Code of conduct policy, zero tolerance policy for drugs and weapons of any kind. Freshmen not permitted cars on campus. **Housing:** Guaranteed on-campus for freshmen. Coed dorms, single-sex dorms, special housing for disabled, apartments, wellness housing available. $500 fully refundable deposit, deadline 5/1. **Activities:** Bands, campus ministries, choral groups, dance, drama, international student organizations, literary magazine, music ensembles, musical theater, opera, radio station, student government, student newspaper, symphony orchestra, TV station, Christian student association, Big Brothers/Big Sisters, political science/pre-law club, Women in Communications, Muslim Student Fellowship, service learning and leadership organizations, National Leadership of Black Journalists.

Athletics. NCAA. **Intercollegiate:** Basketball, bowling W, cheerleading W, cross-country, football (tackle) M, golf, sailing, softball W, tennis, track and field, volleyball W. **Intramural:** Badminton, basketball, bowling W, football (non-tackle) M, lacrosse, soccer M, softball W, swimming, table tennis, volleyball. **Team name:** Pirates.

Student services. Adult student services, alcohol/substance abuse counseling, chaplain/spiritual director, career counseling, services for economically disadvantaged, student employment services, financial aid counseling, health services, minority student services, on-campus daycare, personal counseling, placement for graduates, veterans' counselor, women's services. **Physically disabled:** Services for visually, speech, hearing impaired.

Contact. E-mail: admit@hamptonu.edu
Phone: (757) 727-5328 Toll-free number: (800) 624-3328
Fax: (757) 727-5095
Angela Boyd, Dean of Admission, Hampton University, Office of Admission, Hampton, VA 23668

Hollins University
Roanoke, Virginia CB member
www.hollins.edu CB code: 5294

▸ Private 4-year university and liberal arts college for women
▸ Residential campus in small city
▸ 630 degree-seeking undergraduates: 2% part-time, 100% women, 12% African American, 3% Asian American, 7% Hispanic/Latino, 1% Native American, 4% Multi-racial, non-Hispanic, 5% international
▸ 147 degree-seeking graduate students
▸ 61% of applicants admitted

◆ SAT or ACT (ACT writing optional), application essay required
◆ 57% graduate within 6 years; 30% enter graduate study

General. Founded in 1842. Regionally accredited. **Degrees:** 143 bachelor's awarded; master's offered. **Location:** 175 miles from Richmond, 250 miles from Washington, DC. **Calendar:** 4-1-4, limited summer session. **Full-time faculty:** 68 total; 96% have terminal degrees, 13% minority, 59% women. **Part-time faculty:** 29 total; 38% have terminal degrees, 21% minority, 59% women. **Class size:** 89% < 20, 11% 20-39, less than 1% 40-49. **Special facilities:** EEG and biofeedback equipment, chromatography research facility, spectrophotometry research facility, electrochemistry research facility, Eleanor D. Wilson museum.

Freshman class profile. 2,233 applied, 1,362 admitted, 196 enrolled.

Mid 50% test scores		GPA 2.0-2.99:	7%
SAT critical reading:	520-630	Rank in top quarter:	36%
SAT math:	470-580	Rank in top tenth:	23%
SAT writing:	480-630	End year in good standing:	82%
ACT composite:	21-30	Return as sophomores:	81%
GPA 3.75 or higher:	45%	Out-of-state:	57%
GPA 3.50-3.74:	21%	Live on campus:	98%
GPA 3.0-3.49:	27%	International:	5%

Basis for selection. School achievement record, school recommendation, and test scores very important. Essay, talent/ability important. Interview, class rank, character, alumnae relation, extracurricular activities, volunteer work, work experience considered. Interview recommended. **Home schooled:** Applicants encouraged to interview with admission officer and provide detailed summary of text books used in their studies.

High school preparation. College-preparatory program recommended. 16 units required. Required units include English 4, mathematics 3, social studies 3, science 3 (laboratory 2) and foreign language 2.

2015-2016 Annual costs. Tuition/fees: $35,635. Room/board: $12,300. Books/supplies: $600. Personal expenses: $1,200.

2015-2016 Financial aid. Need-based: 182 full-time freshmen applied for aid; 164 deemed to have need; 164 received aid. Average need met was 84%. Average scholarship/grant was $30,113; average loan $3,725. 80% of total undergraduate aid awarded as scholarships/grants, 20% as loans/jobs. **Non-need-based:** Awarded to 614 full-time undergraduates, including 196 freshmen. Scholarships awarded for academics, alumni affiliation, art, leadership, music/drama, state residency.

Application procedures. Admission: Priority date 2/1; no deadline. No application fee. Admission notification on a rolling basis beginning on or about 11/1. Must reply by May 1 or within 2 week(s) if notified thereafter. **Financial aid:** Priority date 2/15; no closing date. FAFSA required. Applicants notified on a rolling basis starting 3/1; must reply by 5/1.

Academics. Special study options: Accelerated study, combined bachelor's/graduate degree, cross-registration, double major, dual enrollment of high school students, exchange student, independent study, internships, student-designed major, study abroad, teacher certification program, Washington semester. **Credit/placement by examination:** AP, CLEP, IB, institutional tests. 32 credit hours maximum toward bachelor's degree. **Support services:** Tutoring, writing center.

Majors. Area/ethnic studies: Women's. **Biology:** General. **Business:** General. **Communications:** Communications/speech/rhetoric. **Conservation:** Environmental science, environmental studies. **English:** Creative writing, English lit. **Foreign languages:** Classics, French, Spanish. **History:** General. **Math:** General. **Philosophy/religion:** Philosophy, religion. **Physical sciences:** Chemistry. **Psychology:** General. **Social sciences:** Economics, international relations, political science, sociology. **Visual/performing arts:** Art history/conservation, dance, dramatic, film/cinema/video, music, studio arts.

Most popular majors. Biology 13%, business/marketing 10%, English 17%, psychology 9%, social sciences 14%, visual/performing arts 14%.

Technology on campus. 98 workstations in dormitories, library, computer center, student center. Dormitories wired for high-speed internet access and linked to campus network. Commuter students can connect to campus network. Online course registration, online library, helpline, repair service, student web hosting, wireless network available.

Student life. Freshman orientation: Mandatory, $225 fee. Preregistration for classes offered. Four-day program the week before the start of the fall term. **Housing:** Guaranteed on-campus for all undergraduates. Special housing for disabled, apartments, themed housing, wellness housing available. $400 nonrefundable deposit. **Activities:** Concert band, campus ministries, choral groups, dance, drama, international student organizations, literary magazine, music ensembles, Model UN, musical theater, radio station, student government, TV station, black student alliance, community garden, Global Interest Association, OUTloud, Spiritual and Religious Life Association, Students

Helping Achieve Rewarding Experiences, College Republicans, Students for Environmental Action, Feminist Majority Leadership Association, Student Anti-Genocide Coalition.

Athletics. NCAA. **Intercollegiate:** Basketball W, equestrian W, golf W, lacrosse W, soccer W, swimming W, tennis W, volleyball W.

Student services. Adult student services, alcohol/substance abuse counseling, chaplain/spiritual director, career counseling, student employment services, financial aid counseling, health services, minority student services, personal counseling, placement for graduates, women's services. **Physically disabled:** Services for visually, hearing impaired.

Contact. E-mail: huadm@hollins.edu
Phone: (540) 362-6401 Toll-free number: (800) 456-9595
Fax: (540) 362-6218
Ashley Browning, Director of Admission, Hollins University, PO Box 9707, Roanoke, VA 24020-1707

ITT Technical Institute: Chantilly
Chantilly, Virginia
www.itt-tech.edu
CB code: 4086

◆ For-profit 4-year technical college
◆ Commuter campus in large town
◆ 546 undergraduates

General. Accredited by ACICS. **Degrees:** 85 bachelor's, 158 associate awarded. **Calendar:** Quarter. **Full-time faculty:** 9 total. **Part-time faculty:** 40 total.

Basis for selection. Additional requirements for some programs.

2015-2016 Annual costs. Per-credit-hour charge, $493; academic fee, $200. Certain programs require purchase of tools, which range from $150 to $655. All costs subject to change.

Application procedures. Admission: No deadline.

Academics. Credit/placement by examination: AP, CLEP.

Majors. Business: Business admin, construction management. **Computer sciences:** Security. **Protective services:** Law enforcement admin.

Contact. Phone: (703) 263-2541 Toll-free number: (888) 895-8324
Fax: (703) 263-0846
Steve Anderson, Director of Recruitment, ITT Technical Institute: Chantilly, 14420 Albemarle Point Place, Chantilly, VA 20151

ITT Technical Institute: Norfolk
Norfolk, Virginia
www.itt-tech.edu
CB code: 2737

◆ For-profit 4-year technical college
◆ Commuter campus in large city
◆ 698 undergraduates
◆ Interview required

General. Accredited by ACICS. **Degrees:** 64 bachelor's, 154 associate awarded. **Location:** 81 miles from Richmond, 145 miles from Washington, DC. **Calendar:** Quarter, extensive summer session. **Full-time faculty:** 18 total. **Part-time faculty:** 75 total.

Basis for selection. Satisfactory scores from on-site tests in English and mathematics required.

2015-2016 Annual costs. Per-credit-hour charge, $493; academic fee, $200. Certain programs require purchase of tools, which range from $150 to $655. All costs subject to change.

Application procedures. Admission: No deadline. No application fee. Admission notification on a rolling basis. **Financial aid:** No deadline. FAFSA, institutional form required. Applicants notified on a rolling basis.

Academics. Credit/placement by examination: AP, CLEP. **Support services:** Learning center, tutoring.

Majors. Business: Business admin, construction management, e-commerce. **Communications technology:** Animation/special effects. **Computer sciences:** Programming, security. **Protective services:** Law enforcement admin.

Technology on campus. Online library available.

Student life. Freshman orientation: Available. Preregistration for classes offered.

Student services. Career counseling, student employment services, placement for graduates.

Contact. Phone: (757) 466-1260 Toll-free number: (888) 253-8324 Fax: (757) 466-7630
Jack Keesee, Director of Recruitment, ITT Technical Institute: Norfolk, 863 Glenrock Road, Suite 100, Norfolk, VA 23502

ITT Technical Institute: Richmond
Richmond, Virginia
www.itt-tech.edu   CB code: 2748

- For-profit 4-year technical college
- Commuter campus in small city
- 569 undergraduates
- Interview required

General. Accredited by ACICS. **Degrees:** 33 bachelor's, 158 associate awarded. **Location:** 98 miles from Washington, DC. **Calendar:** Quarter, extensive summer session. **Full-time faculty:** 8 total. **Part-time faculty:** 56 total.

Basis for selection. Satisfactory scores from on-site tests in English and mathematics required.

2015-2016 Annual costs. Per-credit-hour charge, $493; academic fee, $200. Certain programs require purchase of tools, which range from $100 to $655. All costs subject to change.

Application procedures. Admission: No deadline. No application fee. Admission notification on a rolling basis. **Financial aid:** No deadline. FAFSA, institutional form required. Applicants notified on a rolling basis.

Academics. Credit/placement by examination: AP, CLEP. **Support services:** Learning center, tutoring.

Majors. Business: Business admin, construction management. **Communications technology:** Animation/special effects. **Computer sciences:** Programming, security. **Protective services:** Law enforcement admin.

Technology on campus. Online library available.

Student life. Freshman orientation: Available. Preregistration for classes offered.

Student services. Career counseling, student employment services, placement for graduates.

Contact. Phone: (804) 330-4992 Toll-free number: (888) 330-4888 Fax: (804) 330-4993
Elaine Bartoli, Director of Recruitment, ITT Technical Institute: Richmond, 300 Gateway Centre Parkway, Richmond, VA 23235

ITT Technical Institute: Springfield
Springfield, Virginia
www.itt-tech.edu   CB code: 5149

- For-profit 4-year technical college
- Commuter campus in large town
- 757 undergraduates

General. Accredited by ACICS. **Degrees:** 57 bachelor's, 160 associate awarded. **Calendar:** Quarter. **Full-time faculty:** 11 total. **Part-time faculty:** 39 total.

Basis for selection. Additional requirements for some programs.

2015-2016 Annual costs. Per-credit-hour charge, $493; academic fee, $200. Certain programs require purchase of tools, which range from $150 to $655. All fees are subject to change.

Academics. Credit/placement by examination: AP, CLEP.

Majors. Business: Business admin, construction management. **Computer sciences:** Programming, security. **Protective services:** Law enforcement admin.

Contact. Phone: (703) 440-9535 Toll-free number: (866) 817-8324 Fax: (703) 440-9561
Paul Ochoa, Director of Recruitment, ITT Technical Institute: Springfield, 7300 Boston Boulevard, Springfield, VA 22153

James Madison University
Harrisonburg, Virginia   CB member
www.jmu.edu   CB code: 5392

- Public 4-year university
- Residential campus in large town
- 19,019 degree-seeking undergraduates: 4% part-time, 59% women, 4% African American, 4% Asian American, 6% Hispanic/Latino, 4% Multiracial, non-Hispanic, 2% international
- 1,668 degree-seeking graduate students
- 73% of applicants admitted
- SAT or ACT (ACT writing optional) required
- 83% graduate within 6 years

General. Founded in 1908. Regionally accredited. **Degrees:** 4,165 bachelor's awarded; master's, professional, doctoral offered. **ROTC:** Army, Air Force. **Location:** 123 miles from Washington, DC. **Calendar:** Semester, extensive summer session. **Full-time faculty:** 1,002 total; 75% have terminal degrees, 11% minority, 47% women. **Part-time faculty:** 457 total; 26% have terminal degrees, 13% minority, 57% women. **Class size:** 34% < 20, 46% 20-39, 8% 40-49, 8% 50-99, 4% >100. **Special facilities:** Arboretum, observatory, planetarium, mineral museum, science on a sphere, performing arts center.

Freshman class profile. 21,439 applied, 15,559 admitted, 4,408 enrolled.

Mid 50% test scores		Return as sophomores:	91%
SAT critical reading:	520-610	Out-of-state:	28%
SAT math:	520-610	Live on campus:	91%
ACT composite:	23-27	International:	2%
Rank in top quarter:	41%	Fraternities:	3%
Rank in top tenth:	23%	Sororities:	14%

Basis for selection. Rigor of high school curriculum, as shown by the quantity and quality of courses, most important. Class rank or GPA, test scores, extracurricular activities, special skills or talents important. Counselor recommendation considered. Applicants with solid achievement in 5 or more academic courses in each of 4 years of high school have decided advantage in admissions process. Audition required for dance, music, theater programs; portfolio and interview required for art. Nursing, justice studies, media arts and design, political science, psychology, and social work students must apply to their applicable departments in addition to applying for undergraduate admission. **Home schooled:** Statement describing home school structure and mission required. **Learning Disabled:** Admission decisions are made without regard to disabilities.

High school preparation. College-preparatory program required. Required and recommended units include English 4, mathematics 4, social studies 2, history 2, science 3-4 and foreign language 3-5. 3 of same foreign language recommended, or 2 of one language and 2 of another. Social studies may include units in history. History and social studies "units required" and "units recommended" are combined for the two subjects.

2015-2016 Annual costs. Tuition/fees: $10,018; $25,142 out-of-state. Room/board: $9,396. Books/supplies: $876. Personal expenses: $1,854.

2015-2016 Financial aid. Need-based: 3,685 full-time freshmen applied for aid; 1,952 deemed to have need; 1,713 received aid. Average need met was 40%. Average scholarship/grant was $7,861; average loan $3,474. 57% of total undergraduate aid awarded as scholarships/grants, 43% as loans/jobs. **Non-need-based:** Awarded to 1,201 full-time undergraduates, including 320 freshmen. Scholarships awarded for academics, alumni affiliation, art, athletics, leadership, minority status, music/drama, state residency.

Application procedures. Admission: Priority date 11/1; deadline 1/15 (postmark date). $70 fee, may be waived for applicants with need. Admission notification by 4/1. Must reply by May 1 or within 2 week(s) if notified thereafter. **Financial aid:** Priority date 3/1; no closing date. FAFSA required. Applicants notified on a rolling basis starting 4/1; must reply within 4 week(s) of notification.

Academics. Special study options: Accelerated study, combined bachelor's/graduate degree, distance learning, double major, dual enrollment of high school students, honors, independent study, internships, study abroad, teacher certification program, Washington semester. Continuing education programs offered on campus. **Credit/placement by examination:** AP, CLEP, IB, institutional tests. Students enrolled in the BIS program earn up to 30 credits toward their bachelor's degrees through non-traditional means, such as prior learning experience and CLEP exams. Eight non-traditional credits, considered earned credits, the remainder treated as transfer credits when calculating the minimum credits earned at the university in order to obtain a degree from JMU. **Support services:** Learning center, study skills assistance, tutoring, writing center.

Majors. Biology: General, biotechnology. **Business:** Accounting, business admin, finance, hospitality admin, international, managerial economics, marketing. **Communications:** Communications/speech/rhetoric. **Computer sciences:** General, information systems. **Engineering:** General. **English:** English lit, technical writing. **Foreign languages:** General. **Health services:** Athletic training, community health services, health care admin, nursing (RN), speech pathology. **History:** General. **Human services:** General, social work. **Liberal arts:** Arts/sciences. **Math:** General. **Parks/recreation:** Health/fitness. **Physical sciences:** Chemistry, geology, physics. **Psychology:** General. **Social sciences:** General, anthropology, economics, geography, international relations, political science, sociology. **Visual/performing arts:** Art, art history/conservation, dramatic, music performance. **Work/family studies:** Food/nutrition.

Most popular majors. Business/marketing 15%, communications/journalism 7%, education 8%, health sciences 16%, parks/recreation 6%, social sciences 7%.

Technology on campus. 1,583 workstations in dormitories, library, computer center, student center. Dormitories wired for high-speed internet access and linked to campus network. Commuter students can connect to campus network. Online course registration, online library, helpline, repair service, student web hosting, wireless network available.

Student life. Freshman orientation: Mandatory, $180 fee. Preregistration for classes offered. Held for one day in June or July, plus 5-day program in August prior to the beginning of classes. **Policies:** Freshmen not permitted cars on campus. **Housing:** Guaranteed on-campus for freshmen. Coed dorms, special housing for disabled, apartments, fraternity/sorority housing, themed housing, wellness housing available. $250 nonrefundable deposit, deadline 5/1. Fraternities located off campus. **Activities:** Bands, campus ministries, choral groups, dance, drama, film society, international student organizations, literary magazine, music ensembles, musical theater, opera, radio station, student government, student newspaper, symphony orchestra, 353 student organizations and clubs.

Athletics. NCAA. **Intercollegiate:** Baseball M, basketball, cross-country W, diving W, field hockey W, football (tackle) M, golf, lacrosse W, soccer, softball W, swimming W, tennis, track and field W, volleyball W. **Intramural:** Basketball, bowling, football (non-tackle), racquetball, sand volleyball, soccer, softball, tennis, volleyball. **Team name:** Dukes.

Student services. Adult student services, alcohol/substance abuse counseling, chaplain/spiritual director, career counseling, student employment services, financial aid counseling, health services, minority student services, personal counseling, placement for graduates. **Physically disabled:** Services for visually, speech, hearing impaired.

Contact. E-mail: admissions@jmu.edu
Phone: (540) 568-5681 Fax: (540) 568-3332
Michael Walsh, Director of Admissions, James Madison University, Sonner Hall, MSC 0101, Harrisonburg, VA 22807

Jefferson College of Health Sciences
Roanoke, Virginia
www.jchs.edu
CB code: 5099

- Private 4-year health science and nursing college
- Commuter campus in small city
- 787 degree-seeking undergraduates: 17% part-time, 81% women
- 262 degree-seeking graduate students
- SAT or ACT (ACT writing optional) required

General. Founded in 1982. Regionally accredited. Part of academic medical center including Carilion Clinic and Virginia Tech Carilion School of Medicine. **Degrees:** 174 bachelor's, 74 associate awarded; master's offered. **Location:** 164 miles from Richmond; 100 miles from Greensboro, NC. **Calendar:** Semester, limited summer session. **Full-time faculty:** 75 total; 3% minority, 64% women. **Part-time faculty:** 95 total; 12% minority, 61% women. **Class size:** 68% < 20, 30% 20-39, less than 1% 40-49, less than 1% 50-99, less than 1% >100. **Special facilities:** Virginia intercollegiate anatomy lab.

Freshman class profile.

GPA 3.75 or higher:	37%	GPA 2.0-2.99:	18%
GPA 3.50-3.74:	14%	Live on campus:	45%
GPA 3.0-3.49:	31%		

Basis for selection. Competitive admission for most programs. **Home schooled:** State high school equivalency certificate required. Must meet criteria in curriculum, covering 4 years of English, 3 years of math, and 3 years of science instruction.

High school preparation. College-preparatory program recommended. 16 units required. Required and recommended units include English 4, mathematics 2-3 and science 2-4.

2015-2016 Annual costs. Tuition/fees: $24,400. Room only: $5,870. Books/supplies: $1,200. Personal expenses: $4,208.

Financial aid. Non-need-based: Scholarships awarded for academics.

Application procedures. Admission: No deadline. $35 fee, may be waived for applicants with need, free for online applicants. Admission notification on a rolling basis. Must reply by May 1 or within 2 week(s) if notified thereafter. **Financial aid:** No deadline. FAFSA, institutional form required. Applicants notified on a rolling basis; must reply within 2 week(s) of notification.

Academics. Special study options: Accelerated study, cross-registration, distance learning, double major, independent study, internships, liberal arts/career combination. **Credit/placement by examination:** AP, CLEP, IB, SAT, ACT, institutional tests. Maximum of 18 credit hours may be satisfied by CLEP/DANTES examinations. **Support services:** Learning center, pre-admission summer program, reduced course load, study skills assistance, tutoring, writing center.

Majors. Biology: Biomedical sciences. **Health services:** EMT paramedic, health care admin, nursing (RN), premedicine, respiratory therapy technology. **Parks/recreation:** Exercise sciences. **Psychology:** Medical.

Most popular majors. Biology 8%, health sciences 85%, parks/recreation 6%.

Technology on campus. 60 workstations in library, computer center. Dormitories wired for high-speed internet access and linked to campus network. Online course registration, online library, helpline, wireless network available.

Student life. Freshman orientation: Mandatory. Preregistration for classes offered. One-day orientation held multiple times during summer. **Housing:** Coed dorms available. $250 nonrefundable deposit. On-campus housing is on a first come, first serve basis, irrespective of class status. **Activities:** Student government, student newspaper, student nurse association, student occupational therapy association, student physical therapy assistant assembly, AMSA, PA Society, Hands of Healing.

Athletics. Team name: Blue Healers.

Student services. Adult student services, career counseling, student employment services, financial aid counseling, personal counseling, veterans' counselor. **Physically disabled:** Services for visually impaired.

Contact. E-mail: admissions@jchs.edu
Phone: (540) 985-8483 Toll-free number: (888) 985-8483
Fax: (540) 985-9773
Judith McKeon, Director of Admissions, Jefferson College of Health Sciences, 101 Elm Avenue, SE, Roanoke, VA 24013-2222

Liberty University
Lynchburg, Virginia
www.liberty.edu
CB member
CB code: 5385

- Private 4-year university affiliated with the Christian Church
- Residential campus in small city
- 12,999 degree-seeking undergraduates: 3% part-time, 52% women, 6% African American, 2% Asian American, 5% Hispanic/Latino, 1% Native American, 2% Multi-racial, non-Hispanic, 5% international
- 1,346 degree-seeking graduate students
- 21% of applicants admitted
- SAT or ACT (ACT writing optional), application essay required
- 54% graduate within 6 years

General. Founded in 1971. Regionally accredited. **Degrees:** 2,124 bachelor's, 11 associate awarded; master's, professional, doctoral offered. **ROTC:** Army, Air Force. **Location:** 120 miles from Richmond; 150 miles from Raleigh, NC. **Calendar:** Semester, limited summer session. **Class size:** 32% < 20, 62% 20-39, 2% 40-49, 2% 50-99, 2% >100. **Special facilities:** Snowflex ski slope, ice rink, running and hiking trails, paintball fields, indoor soccer complex.

Freshman class profile. 31,089 applied, 6,452 admitted, 2,972 enrolled.

Mid 50% test scores			
SAT critical reading:	480-600	GPA 2.0-2.99:	14%
SAT math:	470-590	Rank in top quarter:	47%
SAT writing:	460-580	Rank in top tenth:	23%
ACT composite:	20-27	Return as sophomores:	83%
GPA 3.75 or higher:	36%	Out-of-state:	66%
GPA 3.50-3.74:	19%	Live on campus:	91%
GPA 3.0-3.49:	31%	International:	5%

Basis for selection. Secondary school record, standardized test scores, and essays most important. Applicants who fail to meet minimum required GPA may be admitted on academic warning status and will be limited to 13 semester hours of coursework. **Home schooled:** Transcript of courses and grades required.

High school preparation. College-preparatory program recommended. 17 units recommended. Recommended units include English 4, mathematics 3, social studies 2, science 2 (laboratory 2), foreign language 2 and academic electives 4.

2015-2016 Annual costs. Tuition/fees: $22,000. Room/board: $8,786.

2015-2016 Financial aid. Need-based: 2,750 full-time freshmen applied for aid; 2,484 deemed to have need; 2,484 received aid. Average need met was 28%. Average scholarship/grant was $11,807; average loan $3,434. 63% of total undergraduate aid awarded as scholarships/grants, 37% as loans/jobs. **Non-need-based:** Awarded to 1,281 full-time undergraduates, including 343 freshmen. Scholarships awarded for academics, alumni affiliation, athletics, leadership, music/drama, religious affiliation, ROTC, state residency.

Application procedures. Admission: Priority date 1/31; no deadline. $40 fee, may be waived for applicants with need. Admission notification on a rolling basis. Must reply by May 1 or within 2 week(s) if notified thereafter. **Financial aid:** Priority date 1/15; no closing date. FAFSA required. Applicants notified on a rolling basis starting 3/15; must reply within 3 week(s) of notification.

Academics. Special study options: Accelerated study, cooperative education, distance learning, double major, dual enrollment of high school students, ESL, external degree, honors, independent study, internships, student-designed major, study abroad, teacher certification program, Washington semester, weekend college. Associate school of the Institute of Holy Land Studies in Jerusalem. **Credit/placement by examination:** AP, CLEP, IB, SAT, ACT, institutional tests. 30 credit hours maximum toward bachelor's degree. **Support services:** Learning center, reduced course load, remedial instruction, study skills assistance, tutoring, writing center.

Honors college/program. 3.5 unweighted high school GPA, 1270 SAT/ 29 ACT, application, essay, 3 letters of recommendation required; deadline 4/1.

Majors. Biology: General, biochemistry, biomedical sciences, cellular/ molecular, environmental, wildlife, zoology. **Business:** General, accounting, business admin, management information systems. **Communications:** General, communications/speech/rhetoric, digital media, journalism. **Computer sciences:** General, information technology, webmaster. **Education:** ESL. **Engineering:** Computer, electrical, industrial, mechanical, software. **English:** English lit. **Foreign languages:** American Sign Language, Spanish. **Health services:** Athletic training, nursing (RN), public health ed. **History:** General. **Human services:** Social work. **Liberal arts:** Arts/sciences. **Math:** General. **Parks/recreation:** Exercise sciences, health/fitness, sports admin. **Philosophy/religion:** Christian, philosophy, religion. **Physical sciences:** Chemistry. **Protective services:** Criminal justice, forensics. **Psychology:** General. **Social sciences:** General, international relations, political science. **Theology:** Bible, missionary, pastoral counseling, sacred music, youth ministry. **Visual/performing arts:** Brass instruments, cinematography, dramatic, graphic design, jazz, music, music history, music management, music pedagogy, music performance, music theory/composition, musicology, piano/keyboard, stringed instruments, studio arts, voice/opera. **Work/family studies:** General, clothing/textiles, family studies.

Most popular majors. Business/marketing 14%, communications/journalism 7%, health sciences 11%, parks/recreation 7%, philosophy/religious studies 6%, psychology 8%, visual/performing arts 6%.

Technology on campus. 800 workstations in library, computer center, student center. Dormitories wired for high-speed internet access and linked to campus network. Commuter students can connect to campus network. Online course registration, online library, helpline, repair service, wireless network available.

Student life. Freshman orientation: Available. Preregistration for classes offered. Four 1-day events in June/July. **Policies:** All students involved in Christian or community service. Students required to live on campus unless living with parents, over age 21, or married. **Housing:** Guaranteed on-campus for freshmen. Single-sex dorms, special housing for disabled, apartments,

wellness housing available. $250 nonrefundable deposit. **Activities:** Bands, campus ministries, choral groups, drama, international student organizations, literary magazine, music ensembles, musical theater, radio station, student government, student newspaper, symphony orchestra, TV station, Circle K, Youthquest, Light Ministries, Fellowship of Christian Athletes, Students Teaching Elementary School, College Republicans, Campus SERVE.

Athletics. NCAA. Intercollegiate: Baseball M, basketball, cheerleading, cross-country, diving W, field hockey W, football (tackle) M, golf M, lacrosse W, soccer, softball W, swimming W, tennis, track and field, volleyball W. **Intramural:** Basketball, football (non-tackle), racquetball, soccer, softball, table tennis, tennis, ultimate frisbee, volleyball. **Team name:** Flames.

Student services. Alcohol/substance abuse counseling, chaplain/spiritual director, career counseling, student employment services, financial aid counseling, health services, minority student services, personal counseling, placement for graduates, veterans' counselor, women's services. **Physically disabled:** Services for visually, hearing impaired.

Contact. E-mail: admissions@liberty.edu
Phone: (434) 582-5985 Toll-free number: (800) 543-5317
Fax: (800) 542-2311
Terrell Elam, Director of Residential Admissions, Liberty University, 1971 University Boulevard, Lynchburg, VA 24515

Longwood University
Farmville, Virginia
www.longwood.edu

CB member
CB code: 5368

- Public 4-year university
- Residential campus in small town
- 4,399 degree-seeking undergraduates: 6% part-time, 67% women, 9% African American, 1% Asian American, 5% Hispanic/Latino, 4% Multiracial, non-Hispanic, 1% international
- 401 degree-seeking graduate students
- 79% of applicants admitted
- SAT or ACT (ACT writing optional), application essay required
- 66% graduate within 6 years

General. Founded in 1839. Regionally accredited. **Degrees:** 909 bachelor's awarded; master's offered. **ROTC:** Army. **Location:** 65 miles from Richmond, 60 miles from Charlottesville. **Calendar:** Semester, limited summer session. **Full-time faculty:** 251 total; 81% have terminal degrees, 8% minority, 52% women. **Part-time faculty:** 78 total; 36% have terminal degrees, 14% minority, 68% women. **Class size:** 53% < 20, 43% 20-39, 2% 40-49, less than 1% 50-99. **Special facilities:** Golf course, flora collection, greenhouse, Hull Springs Farm, center for cyber security, center for the visual arts.

Freshman class profile. 4,716 applied, 3,721 admitted, 1,053 enrolled.

Mid 50% test scores			
SAT critical reading:	450-550	Rank in top quarter:	34%
SAT math:	440-540	Rank in top tenth:	10%
ACT composite:	18-23	End year in good standing:	80%
GPA 3.75 or higher:	24%	Return as sophomores:	80%
GPA 3.50-3.74:	20%	Out-of-state:	6%
GPA 3.0-3.49:	43%	Live on campus:	97%
GPA 2.0-2.99:	13%	International:	1%

Basis for selection. Rank in top half of class, 1000 SAT and 2.7 GPA in college preparatory courses required. Extracurricular activities and recommendations also considered. Early Action applicants must have 3.0 GPA and 1000 SAT. Audition is required for music. **Home schooled:** Statement describing home school structure and mission, letter of recommendation (nonparent) required. Applications reviewed on case-by-case basis.

High school preparation. College-preparatory program required. 24 units required. Required and recommended units include English 4, mathematics 3-4, social studies 1, history 2, science 3-4 (laboratory 2-3), foreign language 2-4 and visual/performing arts 1. 2 physical education.

2015-2016 Annual costs. Tuition/fees: $11,910; $26,070 out-of-state. Room/board: $10,272.

2014-2015 Financial aid. Need-based: 861 full-time freshmen applied for aid; 613 deemed to have need; 574 received aid. Average need met was 80%. Average scholarship/grant was $7,443; average loan $4,407. 47% of total undergraduate aid awarded as scholarships/grants, 53% as loans/jobs. **Non-need-based:** Awarded to 436 full-time undergraduates, including 103 freshmen. Scholarships awarded for academics, alumni affiliation, art, athletics, leadership, music/drama, ROTC, state residency.

Application procedures. Admission: Priority date 3/1; no deadline. $50 fee, may be waived for applicants with need. Admission notification on a rolling basis beginning on or about 1/15. Must reply by May 1 or within 1 week(s) if notified thereafter. **Financial aid:** Priority date 3/1; no closing date. FAFSA required. Applicants notified on a rolling basis starting 4/1; must reply within 4 week(s) of notification.

Academics. Special study options: Accelerated study, combined bachelor's/graduate degree, cross-registration, distance learning, double major, dual enrollment of high school students, ESL, honors, independent study, internships, study abroad, teacher certification program. Summer field programs in Archaeology and Botany. **Credit/placement by examination:** AP, CLEP, IB, institutional tests. **Support services:** Learning center, reduced course load, study skills assistance, tutoring, writing center.

Honors college/program. 1200 SAT and 3.5 GPA required; about 40-50 freshman admitted each year.

Majors. Biology: General. **Business:** Business admin. **Communications:** Communications/speech/rhetoric. **Computer sciences:** Computer science. **Conservation:** Environmental science. **English:** English lit. **Foreign languages:** General. **Health services:** Athletic training, audiology/speech pathology, nursing (RN), recreational therapy. **History:** General. **Human services:** Social work. **Liberal arts:** Arts/sciences. **Math:** General. **Parks/recreation:** Exercise sciences. **Physical sciences:** Chemistry, physics. **Protective services:** Criminal justice. **Psychology:** General. **Social sciences:** Anthropology, economics, political science, sociology. **Visual/performing arts:** General, graphic design.

Most popular majors. Business/marketing 11%, communications/journalism 6%, health sciences 9%, liberal arts 19%, parks/recreation 7%, psychology 7%, security/protective services 6%, social sciences 7%, visual/performing arts 6%.

Technology on campus. PC or laptop required. 325 workstations in dormitories, library, computer center, student center. Dormitories wired for high-speed internet access and linked to campus network. Commuter students can connect to campus network. Online course registration, online library, helpline, repair service, student web hosting, wireless network available.

Student life. Freshman orientation: Mandatory, $165 fee. Preregistration for classes offered. One-day orientation held during spring and summer. **Policies:** Freshmen not permitted cars on campus. **Housing:** Guaranteed on-campus for freshmen. Coed dorms, single-sex dorms, special housing for disabled, apartments, fraternity/sorority housing, themed housing, wellness housing available. $400 nonrefundable deposit, deadline 5/1. **Activities:** Bands, campus ministries, choral groups, dance, drama, music ensembles, radio station, student government, student newspaper, TV station, College Democrats, Unity Alliance, Interfraternity Council, Habitat for Humanity, Alpha Phi Omega, Students Educating for Active Leadership, College Republicans, Peer Helpers, Big Sibling Program.

Athletics. NCAA. Intercollegiate: Baseball M, basketball, cheerleading, cross-country, field hockey W, football (tackle) M, golf, lacrosse W, soccer, softball W, tennis. **Intramural:** Bowling, football (non-tackle), football (tackle) W, golf, racquetball, sand volleyball, softball M, table tennis, tennis, ultimate frisbee, volleyball, weight lifting. **Team name:** Lancers.

Student services. Alcohol/substance abuse counseling, career counseling, student employment services, financial aid counseling, health services, minority student services, personal counseling, placement for graduates, women's services. **Physically disabled:** Services for visually, speech, hearing impaired.

Contact. E-mail: admissions@longwood.edu
Phone: (434) 395-2060 Toll-free number: (800) 281-4677 ext. 2
Fax: (434) 395-2332
Jennifer Green, Asso. VP for Enrollment Management & Student Success, Longwood University, 201 High Street, Farmville, VA 23909-1898

Lynchburg College

Lynchburg, Virginia
www.lynchburg.edu

CB member
CB code: 5372

- Private 4-year liberal arts college affiliated with the Christian Church (Disciples of Christ)
- Residential campus in small city
- 2,064 degree-seeking undergraduates: 4% part-time, 59% women, 11% African American, 1% Asian American, 5% Hispanic/Latino, 4% Multiracial, non-Hispanic, 3% international
- 525 degree-seeking graduate students
- 69% of applicants admitted
- SAT or ACT (ACT writing optional) required
- 56% graduate within 6 years

General. Founded in 1903. Regionally accredited. **Degrees:** 509 bachelor's awarded; master's, professional, doctoral offered. **Location:** 120 miles from Richmond, 60 miles from Roanoke. **Calendar:** Semester, limited summer session. **Full-time faculty:** 169 total; 82% have terminal degrees, 8% minority, 52% women. **Part-time faculty:** 113 total; 31% have terminal degrees, less than 1% minority, 52% women. **Class size:** 58% < 20, 40% 20-39, 2% 40-49, less than 1% 50-99. **Special facilities:** 470-acre nature study center, center for media development, forensic cadaver lab, astronomical observatory, fine arts gallery.

Freshman class profile. 4,916 applied, 3,412 admitted, 527 enrolled.

Mid 50% test scores			
		GPA 3.50-3.74:	15%
SAT critical reading:	460-570	GPA 3.0-3.49:	29%
SAT math:	450-550	GPA 2.0-2.99:	26%
SAT writing:	430-540	Return as sophomores:	75%
ACT composite:	19-24	Out-of-state:	34%
GPA 3.75 or higher:	30%	Live on campus:	89%

Basis for selection. School record, test scores, school and community involvement, recommendation, academic quality of secondary school attended, essay, and interview all considered. Audition recommended for music, theater arts programs; portfolio recommended for studio art. Essay or personal statement strongly encouraged. **Learning Disabled:** Documentation must be received no later than 45 days prior to the first day of class.

High school preparation. College-preparatory program required. 16 units required; 20 recommended. Required and recommended units include English 4, mathematics 3-4, social studies 2, history 2, science 3-4 (laboratory 2), foreign language 2-3 and academic electives 1.

2015-2016 Annual costs. Tuition/fees: $35,555. Room/board: $9,590. Books/supplies: $1,000. Personal expenses: $1,350.

2015-2016 Financial aid. Need-based: 476 full-time freshmen applied for aid; 423 deemed to have need; 423 received aid. Average need met was 78%. Average scholarship/grant was $23,854; average loan $2,239. 80% of total undergraduate aid awarded as scholarships/grants, 20% as loans/jobs. **Non-need-based:** Awarded to 580 full-time undergraduates, including 193 freshmen. Scholarships awarded for academics, art, leadership, music/drama, state residency.

Application procedures. Admission: No deadline. $30 fee, may be waived for applicants with need, free for online applicants. Admission notification on a rolling basis beginning on or about 9/1. Must reply by May 1 or within 2 week(s) if notified thereafter. **Financial aid:** Priority date 3/1; no closing date. FAFSA required. Applicants notified on a rolling basis starting 3/5; must reply within 2 week(s) of notification.

Academics. Special study options: Combined bachelor's/graduate degree, cross-registration, distance learning, double major, honors, independent study, internships, study abroad, teacher certification program. **Credit/placement by examination:** AP, CLEP, IB, institutional tests. **Support services:** Study skills assistance, tutoring, writing center.

Majors. Biology: General, biomedical sciences, exercise physiology. **Business:** Accounting, business admin, human resources, management science, marketing. **Communications:** General. **Computer sciences:** General. **Conservation:** Environmental science, environmental studies. **Education:** Elementary, secondary. **English:** English lit. **Foreign languages:** French, Spanish. **Health services:** Athletic training, nursing (RN), public health ed. **History:** General. **Math:** General. **Parks/recreation:** Health/fitness, sports admin. **Philosophy/religion:** Philosophy, religion. **Physical sciences:** Chemistry, physics. **Psychology:** General. **Social sciences:** Criminology, economics, international relations, political science, sociology. **Visual/performing arts:** Art, dramatic, music.

Most popular majors. Biology 11%, business/marketing 13%, communications/journalism 6%, education 6%, health sciences 17%, psychology 6%, social sciences 14%.

Technology on campus. Dormitories wired for high-speed internet access and linked to campus network. Commuter students can connect to campus network. Online library, repair service, wireless network available.

Student life. Freshman orientation: Mandatory. Preregistration for classes offered. Held during summer for fall semester students and in January for spring semester students. Separate but concurrent orientation programs available to parents and other guests of new students. **Policies:** Honor system in effect. Freshmen not permitted cars on campus. **Housing:** Guaranteed on-campus for all undergraduates. Coed dorms, single-sex dorms, special housing for disabled, apartments, fraternity/sorority housing, themed housing, wellness housing available. $200 nonrefundable deposit, deadline 5/1. College-owned townhomes, houses, and special interest houses available. **Activities:**

Bands, campus ministries, choral groups, dance, drama, film society, international student organizations, literary magazine, music ensembles, Model UN, musical theater, student government, student newspaper, symphony orchestra, over 80 clubs and organizations.

Athletics. NCAA. **Intercollegiate:** Baseball M, basketball, cheerleading W, cross-country, equestrian, field hockey W, golf M, lacrosse, soccer, softball W, tennis, track and field, volleyball W. **Intramural:** Basketball, football (non-tackle), sand volleyball, soccer, tennis, ultimate frisbee, volleyball. **Team name:** Hornets.

Student services. Adult student services, chaplain/spiritual director, career counseling, student employment services, financial aid counseling, health services, minority student services, personal counseling, veterans' counselor. **Physically disabled:** Services for visually, hearing impaired.

Contact. E-mail: admissions@lynchburg.edu
Phone: (434) 544-8300 Toll-free number: (800) 426-8101 ext. 8300
Fax: (434) 544-8653
Sharon Walters-Bower, Director of Admissions, Lynchburg College, 1501 Lakeside Drive, Lynchburg, VA 24501-3199

Mary Baldwin College
Staunton, Virginia   CB member
www.mbc.edu   CB code: 5397

- Private 4-year liberal arts college for women affiliated with the Presbyterian Church (USA)
- Residential campus in large town
- 1,265 degree-seeking undergraduates
- 97% of applicants admitted
- SAT or ACT (ACT writing optional), interview required

General. Founded in 1842. Regionally accredited. Bachelor's degree available for younger women (13-15) in program for exceptionally gifted. Adult degree program available on main campus and at several satellite campuses throughout Virginia. Men admitted to adult program. **Degrees:** 252 bachelor's awarded; master's, professional offered. **ROTC:** Army, Naval, Air Force. **Location:** 100 miles from Richmond, 150 miles from Washington, DC. **Calendar:** 4-1-4, limited summer session. **Full-time faculty:** 86 total; 84% have terminal degrees, 63% women. **Part-time faculty:** 133 total; 84% have terminal degrees, 60% women. **Class size:** 59% < 20, 41% 20-39. **Special facilities:** Electron microscope, gas chromatoscope.

Freshman class profile. 2,774 applied, 2,693 admitted, 177 enrolled.

Mid 50% test scores		GPA 3.0-3.49:	36%
SAT critical reading:	440-600	GPA 2.0-2.99:	21%
SAT math:	420-540	Rank in top quarter:	42%
SAT writing:	420-570	Rank in top tenth:	14%
ACT composite:	17-24	Out-of-state:	45%
GPA 3.75 or higher:	23%	Live on campus:	63%
GPA 3.50-3.74:	20%		

Basis for selection. School achievement record most important; test scores, involvement in school or civic groups also important; recommendations considered; 3.0 GPA recommended. Portfolio recommended for art majors.

High school preparation. Required and recommended units include English 4, mathematics 3, social studies 3, science 2 (laboratory 1), foreign language 2-3 and academic electives 2. Higher requirements for Virginia Women's Institute for Leadership.

2015-2016 Annual costs. Tuition/fees: $30,331. Room/board: $9,000. Books/supplies: $900. Personal expenses: $2,000.

Financial aid. Non-need-based: Scholarships awarded for academics, leadership, state residency.

Application procedures. Admission: No deadline. No application fee. Admission notification on a rolling basis beginning on or about 9/1. Regular admission notification within 48 hours of receipt of all necessary materials. International students should submit application by 6/1 to allow time to get a visa. **Financial aid:** Priority date 3/1; no closing date. FAFSA required. Applicants notified on a rolling basis starting 2/27; must reply by 5/1 or within 2 week(s) of notification.

Academics. Students complete requirements in experiential education, international education, women's studies. May term offers opportunity for individualized programming, externships, study abroad. Institute combines academics, physical training and leadership development in rigorous 4-year bachelor's program. **Special study options:** Combined bachelor's/graduate degree, semester at sea. Summer exchange program with Doshisha Women's

College in Kyoto, Japan. **Credit/placement by examination:** AP, CLEP, IB, institutional tests. 25% of required credits may be counted toward bachelor's degree. **Support services:** Learning center, reduced course load, study skills assistance, tutoring, writing center.

Honors college/program. 1150 SAT (exclusive of Writing)/25 ACT, 3.5 high school GPA, essay, interview required for admission. About 36 freshmen admitted.

Majors. Area/ethnic studies: Asian. **Biology:** General. **Business:** Business admin. **Communications:** Communications/speech/rhetoric. **Computer sciences:** General. **English:** English lit. **Foreign languages:** French, Spanish. **Health services:** Clinical lab science, health care admin. **History:** General. **Math:** General, applied. **Philosophy/religion:** Philosophy, religion. **Physical sciences:** Chemistry, physics. **Psychology:** General. **Social sciences:** Anthropology, economics, international relations, political science, sociology. **Visual/performing arts:** Art, dramatic, music, studio arts management.

Most popular majors. Area/ethnic studies 8%, English 6%, history 10%, interdisciplinary studies 6%, psychology 16%, social sciences 17%, visual/performing arts 9%.

Technology on campus. 244 workstations in dormitories, library, computer center. Dormitories wired for high-speed internet access and linked to campus network. Commuter students can connect to campus network. Online course registration, online library, helpline, repair service, wireless network available.

Student life. Freshman orientation: Mandatory. Preregistration for classes offered. **Policies:** College prohibits drinking under age 21. Honor code observed. Working dogs (to aid the handicapped) allowed in dorm rooms. **Housing:** Guaranteed on-campus for all undergraduates. **Activities:** Bands, choral groups, dance, drama, international student organizations, music ensembles, student government, student newspaper, Circle K, Habitat for Humanity, College Republicans, College Democrats, black student alliance, Latinas Unidas, Christian student union, Campus Crusade for Christ, Anointed Voices of Praise Gospel Choir.

Athletics. NCAA. **Intercollegiate:** Basketball W, cross-country W, field hockey W, soccer W, softball W, swimming W, tennis W, volleyball W. **Team name:** Squirrels.

Student services. Adult student services, chaplain/spiritual director, career counseling, student employment services, health services, minority student services, personal counseling, placement for graduates, women's services. **Physically disabled:** Services for visually, hearing impaired.

Contact. E-mail: admit@mbc.edu
Phone: (540) 887-7019 Toll-free number: (800) 468-2262
Fax: (540) 887-7279
Mary Baldwin College, Office of Admissions, Staunton, VA 24401

Marymount University
Arlington, Virginia   CB member
www.marymount.edu   CB code: 5405

- Private 4-year university affiliated with the Roman Catholic Church
- Commuter campus in small city
- 2,305 degree-seeking undergraduates: 9% part-time, 66% women, 15% African American, 8% Asian American, 17% Hispanic/Latino, 1% Native Hawaiian/Pacific islander, 3% Multi-racial, non-Hispanic, 12% international
- 1,019 degree-seeking graduate students
- 86% of applicants admitted
- Application essay required
- 50% graduate within 6 years; 32% enter graduate study

General. Founded in 1950. Regionally accredited. Courses taught in three sites in Northern Virginia: Main Campus, Arlington, and Reston. **Degrees:** 606 bachelor's awarded; master's, doctoral offered. **ROTC:** Army. **Location:** 7 miles from Washington, DC. **Calendar:** Semester, extensive summer session. **Full-time faculty:** 159 total; 89% have terminal degrees, 11% minority, 70% women. **Part-time faculty:** 195 total; 42% have terminal degrees, 20% minority, 65% women. **Class size:** 51% < 20, 49% 20-39, less than 1% 40-49, less than 1% 50-99.

Freshman class profile. 2,143 applied, 1,838 admitted, 393 enrolled.

Mid 50% test scores			
SAT critical reading:	450-560	**GPA 2.0-2.99:**	29%
SAT math:	430-550	**Rank in top quarter:**	37%
SAT writing:	430-540	**Rank in top tenth:**	12%
ACT composite:	19-24	**End year in good standing:**	92%
GPA 3.75 or higher:	17%	**Return as sophomores:**	73%
GPA 3.50-3.74:	19%	**Out-of-state:**	55%
GPA 3.0-3.49:	35%	**Live on campus:**	71%
		International:	9%

Basis for selection. GPA in academic courses and rigor of secondary school record are most important. Recommendations from guidance counselors/teachers and admissions interview are also important. Test scores submitted are considered though not required of all applicants. If both SAT and ACT are submitted, the highest equivalent score will be used. For students with a high school GPA of 3.0 or higher, SAT/ACT is optional. For students with below a 3.0, SAT/ACT is required. Interview generally recommended but requested of some applicants, including for honors program. **Home schooled:** Statement describing home school structure and mission required. Standardized test scores required.

High school preparation. College-preparatory program required. 15 units required. Required and recommended units include English 4, mathematics 3, social studies 3, science 2 and foreign language 3.

2015-2016 Annual costs. Tuition/fees: $28,310. Room/board: $12,220. Books/supplies: $1,000. Personal expenses: $1,680.

Financial aid. Non-need-based: Scholarships awarded for academics, alumni affiliation, leadership, music/drama, ROTC, state residency.

Application procedures. Admission: Priority date 4/1; no deadline. $40 fee, may be waived for applicants with need. Notified within 3-4 weeks after application received. Must reply by May 1 or within 3 week(s) if notified thereafter. **Financial aid:** Priority date 3/1; no closing date. FAFSA required. Applicants notified by 3/15; must reply within 2 week(s) of notification.

Academics. All undergraduates complete an internship before graduation. **Special study options:** Accelerated study, combined bachelor's/graduate degree, cross-registration, distance learning, double major, dual enrollment of high school students, honors, independent study, internships, student-designed major, study abroad, teacher certification program. Member of the Consortium of Universities of the Washington Metropolitan Area. **Credit/placement by examination:** AP, CLEP, IB, institutional tests. 30 credit hours maximum toward bachelor's degree. Credit for prior work/life experience available through Portfolio Assessment and College-Level Examination Program. As a member of Servicemembers Opportunity Colleges (SOC), Marymount also accepts Defense Activity for Non-Traditional Education Support (DANTES) credits. **Support services:** Learning center, reduced course load, remedial instruction, study skills assistance, tutoring, writing center. Advising walk-in support; workshops on academic support topics; pre-law advising; and student success courses for students experiencing academic difficulty.

Honors college/program. Admission is competitive and limited to 20 new students each year. 3.5 GPA and 1200 SAT/26 ACT required. 617 (paper) or 105 (Internet) TOEFL required for international students. A strong background in English composition and literature is necessary. Program encourages academic independence and celebrates an interdisciplinary approach to learning through academic (tutorials, seminars) and extracurricular programs with a focus on stewardship and service to the community.

Majors. Biology: General, biochemistry, cellular/molecular. **Business:** Business admin, fashion. **Communications:** General. **Computer sciences:** Information technology. **Education:** Elementary, special ed. **English:** English lit. **Health services:** Nursing (RN), public health ed. **History:** General. **Liberal arts:** Arts/sciences. **Math:** General. **Philosophy/religion:** Philosophy, religion. **Protective services:** Forensics, law enforcement admin. **Psychology:** General. **Social sciences:** Economics, political science, sociology. **Visual/performing arts:** Design, fashion design, interior design, studio arts.

Most popular majors. Business/marketing 21%, health sciences 31%, psychology 7%, visual/performing arts 9%.

Technology on campus. 250 workstations in dormitories, library, computer center. Dormitories wired for high-speed internet access and linked to campus network. Commuter students can connect to campus network. Online course registration, online library, helpline, wireless network available.

Student life. Freshman orientation: Mandatory. Preregistration for classes offered. Weekend sessions held in summer. **Policies:** Freshmen not permitted cars on campus. **Housing:** Guaranteed on-campus for freshmen. Coed dorms, single-sex dorms, themed housing available. $300 nonrefundable deposit, deadline 5/1. **Activities:** Campus ministries, choral groups, dance, drama, international student organizations, literary magazine, student government, student newspaper, African Caribbean Student Association, Black Student Alliance, Campus Crusade for Christ, Campus Ministry Association, International Affairs Society, Ladies Inspiring Strength for Tomorrow, Latino

Student Association, Muslim Student Association, South Asian Society, Saudi Student Association.

Athletics. NCAA. **Intercollegiate:** Baseball M, basketball, cross-country, golf, lacrosse, soccer, swimming, triathlon, volleyball. **Intramural:** Basketball, cheerleading W, football (non-tackle), soccer, ultimate frisbee, volleyball, water polo. **Team name:** Saints.

Student services. Alcohol/substance abuse counseling, chaplain/spiritual director, career counseling, student employment services, financial aid counseling, health services, minority student services, personal counseling, veterans' counselor. **Physically disabled:** Services for visually, speech, hearing impaired.

Contact. E-mail: admissions@marymount.edu
Phone: (703) 284-1500 Toll-free number: (800) 548-7638
Fax: (703) 522-0349
Heather Renault, Director, Undergraduate Admissions, Marymount University, 2807 North Glebe Road, Arlington, VA 22207-4224

Norfolk State University
Norfolk, Virginia **CB member**
www.nsu.edu **CB code: 5864**

- Public 4-year university
- Commuter campus in small city
- 5,284 degree-seeking undergraduates: 17% part-time, 64% women
- 631 degree-seeking graduate students
- SAT or ACT (ACT writing optional) required

General. Founded in 1935. Regionally accredited. **Degrees:** 992 bachelor's, 15 associate awarded; master's, professional, doctoral offered. **ROTC:** Army, Naval. **Location:** 5 miles from downtown. **Calendar:** Semester, extensive summer session. **Full-time faculty:** 278 total; 36% have terminal degrees, 77% minority, 50% women. **Part-time faculty:** 139 total; 76% minority, 59% women. **Special facilities:** Planetarium, crystal laboratory, laser laboratory, nuclear magnetic resonance laboratory, institute for service learning, literacy center for entrepreneurial studies, center for materials research, institute for minorities in applied sciences, assistive technology laboratory.

Freshman class profile.

GPA 3.75 or higher:	5%	**Rank in top quarter:**	26%
GPA 3.50-3.74:	6%	**Rank in top tenth:**	13%
GPA 3.0-3.49:	27%	**Out-of-state:**	23%
GPA 2.0-2.99:	62%	**Live on campus:**	82%

Basis for selection. Combination of academic preparation, aptitude, achievements, and motivation predict a reasonable probability of success are most important. Interview recommended for electronics, engineering, nursing programs; audition recommended for music; portfolio recommended for art. **Home schooled:** Transcript of courses and grades required.

High school preparation. 22 units required. Required units include English 4, mathematics 3, history 3, science 3 and academic electives 9. 2 science required for nursing applicants: 1 chemistry, 1 biology, 2 high school math (1 algebra), 2 science required for business applicants. 1 geometry, 2 algebra recommended for mathematics applicants. 2 mathematics must include algebra for computer science applicants.

2015-2016 Annual costs. Tuition/fees: $8,366; $20,884 out-of-state. Room/board: $8,668. Books/supplies: $1,814. Personal expenses: $1,827.

Financial aid. Non-need-based: Scholarships awarded for academics, alumni affiliation, athletics, leadership, music/drama, ROTC, state residency.

Application procedures. Admission: Closing date 5/31 (postmark date). $45 fee, may be waived for applicants with need. Admission notification on a rolling basis. Must reply by May 1 or within 2 week(s) if notified thereafter. **Financial aid:** Priority date 5/31; no closing date. FAFSA required. Applicants notified on a rolling basis starting 4/1; must reply within 2 week(s) of notification.

Academics. Special study options: Combined bachelor's/graduate degree, cooperative education, cross-registration, distance learning, double major, dual enrollment of high school students, ESL, honors, independent study, internships, liberal arts/career combination, teacher certification program. **Credit/placement by examination:** AP, CLEP, SAT, ACT, institutional tests. No limit on number of credits university will accept, as long as student passes exam and has departmental approval. **Support services:** Learning center, reduced course load, study skills assistance, tutoring, writing center.

Majors. Biology: General. **Business:** General, accounting, hospitality admin. **Communications:** Journalism, media studies. **Computer sciences:**

General. **Education:** Business, kindergarten/preschool, special ed, trade/industrial. **Engineering:** Electrical. **English:** English lit. **Health services:** Clinical lab science, health care admin, health information management, nursing (RN). **History:** General. **Human services:** Social work. **Math:** General. **Parks/recreation:** Exercise sciences. **Physical sciences:** Chemistry, optics, physics. **Psychology:** General. **Social sciences:** Political science, sociology. **Visual/performing arts:** Art, music.

Most popular majors. Business/marketing 12%, communications/journalism 6%, health sciences 11%, interdisciplinary studies 11%, psychology 8%, public administration/social services 9%, social sciences 12%, trade and industry 20%.

Technology on campus. 1,010 workstations in dormitories, library, computer center. Dormitories linked to campus network. Online library, helpline available.

Student life. Freshman orientation: Mandatory. Preregistration for classes offered. Held during June, July and August. **Housing:** Single-sex dorms available. $300 nonrefundable deposit, deadline 5/31. **Activities:** Bands, dance, drama, music ensembles, opera, radio station, student government, student newspaper, symphony orchestra, TV station, Beta Psi Club, Omega Psi Phi, Alpha Kappa Alpha, Delta Sigma Theta, Alpha Delta Mu, Young Democrats, Young Republicans, Alpha Phi Alpha, Kappa Alpha Psi.

Athletics. NCAA. **Intercollegiate:** Baseball M, basketball, bowling W, cross-country, football (tackle) M, softball W, tennis, track and field, volleyball W. **Intramural:** Basketball, bowling, cheerleading, football (non-tackle) M, soccer M, softball, swimming, table tennis, tennis, volleyball. **Team name:** Spartans.

Student services. Adult student services, alcohol/substance abuse counseling, chaplain/spiritual director, career counseling, student employment services, financial aid counseling, health services, on-campus daycare, personal counseling, placement for graduates, veterans' counselor, women's services. **Physically disabled:** Services for visually, speech, hearing impaired.

Contact. E-mail: admissions@nsu.edu
Phone: (757) 823-8396 Fax: (757) 823-2078
Lakeisha Mayes, Director of Admissions, Norfolk State University, 700 Park Avenue, Norfolk, VA 23504

Old Dominion University
Norfolk, Virginia
www.odu.edu

CB member
CB code: 5126

- Public 4-year university
- Residential campus in large city
- 19,870 degree-seeking undergraduates: 23% part-time, 54% women, 27% African American, 4% Asian American, 7% Hispanic/Latino, 6% Multi-racial, non-Hispanic, 1% international
- 3,640 degree-seeking graduate students
- 83% of applicants admitted
- SAT or ACT (ACT writing optional) required
- 53% graduate within 6 years

General. Founded in 1930. Regionally accredited. Classes are available on the main campus in Norfolk, VA, at three regional Higher Ed Centers, and via technology, wherever a student has access to a high-speed internet connection and a computer/device. Courses are offered either synchronously or asynchronously. **Degrees:** 3,858 bachelor's awarded; master's, professional, doctoral offered. **ROTC:** Army, Naval. **Location:** 2 miles from downtown Norfolk; 200 miles from Washington, DC. **Calendar:** Semester, extensive summer session. **Full-time faculty:** 828 total; 82% have terminal degrees, 19% minority, 44% women. **Part-time faculty:** 527 total; 32% have terminal degrees, 17% minority, 56% women. **Class size:** 36% < 20, 45% 20-39, 9% 40-49, 7% 50-99, 3% >100. **Special facilities:** Student art gallery, centers for urban research/service, economic education and child study centers, laser optics lab, planetarium, robotics lab, sub-/super-sonic wind tunnels, marine science research vessel, random wave pool.

Freshman class profile. 9,510 applied, 7,904 admitted, 2,956 enrolled.

Mid 50% test scores			
SAT critical reading:	460-570	Rank in top tenth:	8%
SAT math:	460-570	End year in good standing:	79%
ACT composite:	18-24	Return as sophomores:	82%
GPA 3.75 or higher:	18%	Out-of-state:	9%
GPA 3.50-3.74:	15%	Live on campus:	76%
GPA 3.0-3.49:	37%	International:	2%
GPA 2.0-2.99:	30%	Fraternities:	11%
Rank in top quarter:	32%	Sororities:	12%

Basis for selection. Students who submit acceptable GPA and SAT/ACT scores are admitted. Those who do not meet acceptable GPA or SAT scores are reviewed by an admissions committee. Factors include grades in core curriculum courses, student essay, student activity, resume/letters of recommendation, high school attended, IB and AP courses taken. Audition required for music. **Home schooled:** Transcript of courses and grades required. Scores from SAT or ACT must be submitted. GED not required. Students not attending program that requires regular curriculum review and submission of test scores to local school board must submit Stanford 9 results. **Learning Disabled:** Documentation of disabilities must be submitted before receiving services from Office of Educational Accessibility.

High school preparation. College-preparatory program recommended. 16 units required; 17 recommended. Required and recommended units include English 4, mathematics 3-4, social studies 3, science 3 and foreign language 3.

2015-2016 Annual costs. Tuition/fees: $9,768; $26,508 out-of-state. Room/board: $10,404. Books/supplies: $1,000. Personal expenses: $1,975.

2015-2016 Financial aid. Need-based: 2,624 full-time freshmen applied for aid; 2,086 deemed to have need; 2,012 received aid. Average need met was 49%. Average scholarship/grant was $7,330; average loan $3,512. 56% of total undergraduate aid awarded as scholarships/grants, 44% as loans/jobs. **Non-need-based:** Awarded to 3,379 full-time undergraduates, including 1,184 freshmen. Scholarships awarded for academics, alumni affiliation, art, athletics, leadership, music/drama, ROTC, state residency.

Application procedures. Admission: Priority date 12/1; deadline 2/1 (receipt date). $50 fee, may be waived for applicants with need. Admission notification on a rolling basis beginning on or about 10/15. Must reply by May 1 or within 4 week(s) if notified thereafter. Students are required to submit following: $50 application fee, high school transcripts, application, SAT or ACT scores. **Financial aid:** Priority date 2/15, closing date 3/15. FAFSA required. Applicants notified on a rolling basis starting 3/15; must reply within 2 week(s) of notification.

Academics. Guaranteed work or internship experience for credit in all fields of study. **Special study options:** Accelerated study, combined bachelor's/graduate degree, cooperative education, cross-registration, distance learning, double major, dual enrollment of high school students, ESL, exchange student, honors, independent study, internships, liberal arts/career combination, student-designed major, study abroad, teacher certification program. Experiential learning. **Credit/placement by examination:** AP, CLEP, IB, institutional tests. 60 credit hours maximum toward bachelor's degree. Credit hours earned for assessment of prior learning outside of the college classroom not to exceed 60. Work life credits awarded through certification or department evaluations. Essay required to receive CLEP credit in Analysis and Interpretation of Literature. **Support services:** Learning center, reduced course load, study skills assistance, tutoring, writing center.

Honors college/program. Must have minimum GPA of 3.40; minimum total SAT 1200. Honor students are free to pursue any major. College offers specially-designed low-enrollment courses and senior honors seminar. Several out-of-class, off-campus experiences are available. All honor students receive an annual stipend. Honors College requires a separate application to apply.

Majors. Area/ethnic studies: African-American, Asian, women's. **Biology:** General, biochemistry. **Business:** Accounting, business admin, finance, management information systems, managerial economics, marketing. **Computer sciences:** General. **Education:** Physical. **Engineering:** General, civil, computer, electrical, mechanical. **English:** English lit, rhetoric/composition. **Foreign languages:** General. **Health services:** Audiology/speech pathology, clinical lab science, dental hygiene, nuclear medical technology, nursing (RN). **History:** General. **Math:** General. **Parks/recreation:** Facilities management. **Philosophy/religion:** Philosophy. **Physical sciences:** Chemistry, physics. **Psychology:** General. **Social sciences:** Criminology, economics, geography, international relations, political science, sociology. **Visual/performing arts:** Art, art history/conservation, dramatic, music performance.

Most popular majors. Biology 6%, business/marketing 15%, education 7%, engineering/engineering technologies 10%, English 7%, health sciences 17%, interdisciplinary studies 6%, psychology 7%, social sciences 13%.

Technology on campus. 2,005 workstations in dormitories, library, computer center, student center. Dormitories wired for high-speed internet access and linked to campus network. Commuter students can connect to campus network. Online course registration, online library, helpline, repair service, wireless network available.

Student life. Freshman orientation: Mandatory, $75 fee. Preregistration for classes offered. One-day event held on various days throughout the summer. Students will meet with advisor in their academic area and select their class schedule. **Policies:** All student sponsored dances are restricted to ODU students only. Students must agree to hazing policy and can agree to FERPA (Family Educational Rights and Privacy Act) when they sign up on-line for their organizations. Freshmen not permitted cars on campus. **Housing:**

Guaranteed on-campus for freshmen. Coed dorms, single-sex dorms, special housing for disabled, apartments, themed housing available. $250 partly refundable deposit, deadline 5/15. Learning communities available. **Activities:** Bands, campus ministries, choral groups, dance, drama, international student organizations, music ensembles, Model UN, musical theater, radio station, student government, student newspaper, College Democrats, College Republicans, Black Student Alliance, Caribbean Student Association, Latino Student Alliance, Colleges Against Cancer, ODU Out, Alpha Phi Omega, Baptist Collegiate Ministries, Catholic Campus Ministry.

Athletics. NCAA. **Intercollegiate:** Baseball M, basketball, diving, field hockey W, football (tackle) M, golf, lacrosse W, rowing (crew) W, sailing, soccer, tennis, wrestling M. **Intramural:** Badminton, basketball, football (non-tackle), golf, handball, racquetball, soccer, softball, table tennis, tennis, ultimate frisbee, volleyball. **Team name:** Monarchs.

Student services. Adult student services, alcohol/substance abuse counseling, chaplain/spiritual director, career counseling, services for economically disadvantaged, student employment services, financial aid counseling, health services, minority student services, on-campus daycare, personal counseling, placement for graduates, veterans' counselor, women's services. **Physically disabled:** Services for visually, speech, hearing impaired.

Contact. E-mail: admissions@odu.edu
Phone: (757) 683-3685 Toll-free number: (800) 348-7926
Fax: (757) 683-3255
Jeremy Dickerson, Director of Undergraduate Admissions, Old Dominion University, 108 Rollins Hall, Norfolk, VA 23529

Patrick Henry College
Purcellville, Virginia
www.phc.edu   CB code: 2804

- Private 4-year liberal arts college affiliated with the nondenominational tradition
- Residential campus in small town
- 294 degree-seeking undergraduates: 5% part-time, 46% women
- 95% of applicants admitted
- SAT or ACT (ACT writing optional), application essay, interview required
- 69% graduate within 6 years; 35% enter graduate study

General. Regionally accredited; also accredited by TRACS. **Degrees:** 88 bachelor's awarded. **Location:** 50 miles from Washington, DC. **Calendar:** Semester, limited summer session. **Full-time faculty:** 19 total; 95% have terminal degrees, 5% women. **Part-time faculty:** 23 total; 61% have terminal degrees, 35% women. **Class size:** 59% < 20, 37% 20-39, 3% 40-49, 1% 50-99.

Freshman class profile. 227 applied, 216 admitted, 76 enrolled.

Mid 50% test scores			
SAT critical reading:	620-740	GPA 3.50-3.74:	12%
SAT math:	520-670	GPA 3.0-3.49:	10%
SAT writing:	580-710	GPA 2.0-2.99:	1%
ACT composite:	28-31	Return as sophomores:	78%
GPA 3.75 or higher:	77%	Out-of-state:	85%
		Live on campus:	99%

Basis for selection. Academic history, recommendations, test scores, essay, interview, character, and religious commitment very important. Reading list of books read in history, literature, theology, and philosophy required.

High school preparation. College-preparatory program required. 18 units required; 21 recommended. Required and recommended units include English 4, mathematics 3, history 2, science 2-3 (laboratory 2-3), foreign language 1-2 and academic electives 3.

2015-2016 Annual costs. Tuition/fees: $27,922. Room/board: $10,727. Books/supplies: $1,000. Personal expenses: $1,000.

2014-2015 Financial aid. **Need-based:** 58 full-time freshmen applied for aid; 38 deemed to have need; 38 received aid. Average need met was 35%. Average scholarship/grant was $5,200; average loan $11,600. 24% of total undergraduate aid awarded as scholarships/grants, 76% as loans/jobs. **Non-need-based:** Awarded to 255 full-time undergraduates, including 71 freshmen. Scholarships awarded for academics, leadership, music/drama.

Application procedures. Admission: Priority date 2/1; deadline 6/15 (postmark date). $20 fee, may be waived for applicants with need. Admission notification on a rolling basis beginning on or about 10/1. **Financial aid:** Priority date 3/15, closing date 6/15. CSS PROFILE required. Applicants notified on a rolling basis starting 3/1; must reply within 4 week(s) of notification.

Academics. **Special study options:** Cooperative education, cross-registration, double major, dual enrollment of high school students, independent study, internships, liberal arts/career combination. **Credit/placement by examination:** AP, CLEP, IB, institutional tests. Credits from Program on Non-Collegiate Sponsored Instruction, Dantes Subject Standardized Tests, and IB evaluated on case by case basis. **Support services:** Learning center, reduced course load, study skills assistance, tutoring, writing center.

Majors. **Business:** Managerial economics. **Communications:** Journalism. **English:** English lit. **History:** General. **Liberal arts:** Arts/sciences. **Military:** Strategic intel. **Social sciences:** Political science.

Most popular majors. Communications/journalism 12%, history 7%, liberal arts 12%, social sciences 67%.

Technology on campus. PC or laptop required. 6 workstations in library. Dormitories wired for high-speed internet access and linked to campus network. Commuter students can connect to campus network. Online course registration, online library, helpline, repair service, student web hosting, wireless network available.

Student life. **Freshman orientation:** Mandatory. Preregistration for classes offered. Held for 4 days prior to beginning of fall classes. **Policies:** Students are accountable to the College's community standards. Religious observance required. **Housing:** Guaranteed on-campus for freshmen. Single-sex dorms available. $275 fully refundable deposit, deadline 7/1. **Activities:** Choral groups, drama, film society, literary magazine, music ensembles, Model UN, radio station, student government, student newspaper, symphony orchestra, Streaming Media Film, College Republicans, College Democrats, Alexis de Tocqueville Society, Sans Frontieres, Libertas Society, Titan Society.

Athletics. USCAA. **Intercollegiate:** Basketball, soccer. **Intramural:** Football (non-tackle) M, softball M, tennis, volleyball. **Team name:** The Sentinels.

Student services. Chaplain/spiritual director, career counseling, student employment services, financial aid counseling, health services, personal counseling. **Physically disabled:** Services for visually, hearing impaired.

Contact. E-mail: admissions@phc.edu
Phone: (540) 441-8110 Toll-free number: (888) 338-1776 ext. 8881
Fax: (540) 441-8119
Stephen Allen, Director of Admissions & Communications, Patrick Henry College, 10 Patrick Henry Circle, Purcellville, VA 20132-3197

Radford University
Radford, Virginia   CB member
www.radford.edu   CB code: 5565

- Public 4-year university
- Residential campus in large town
- 8,839 degree-seeking undergraduates: 4% part-time, 56% women, 13% African American, 1% Asian American, 7% Hispanic/Latino, 5% Multiracial, non-Hispanic, 1% international
- 845 degree-seeking graduate students
- 83% of applicants admitted
- 59% graduate within 6 years; 18% enter graduate study

General. Founded in 1910. Regionally accredited. **Degrees:** 1,847 bachelor's awarded; master's, doctoral offered. **ROTC:** Army. **Location:** 45 miles from Roanoke. **Calendar:** Semester, extensive summer session. **Full-time faculty:** 455 total; 82% have terminal degrees, 12% minority, 52% women. **Part-time faculty:** 273 total; 16% have terminal degrees, 6% minority, 60% women. **Class size:** 31% < 20, 49% 20-39, 9% 40-49, 9% 50-99, less than 1% >100. **Special facilities:** Trading room, center for visual and performing arts, observatory, planetarium, nature conservancy, motion analysis lab, clinical simulation center, cadaver lab, speech-language-hearing center, earth sciences museum, GIS center; games, animation, modeling and simulation lab.

Freshman class profile. 7,617 applied, 6,328 admitted, 1,962 enrolled.

Mid 50% test scores			
SAT critical reading:	450-530	Rank in top quarter:	18%
SAT math:	440-520	Rank in top tenth:	6%
SAT writing:	420-510	End year in good standing:	80%
ACT composite:	18-22	Return as sophomores:	75%
GPA 3.75 or higher:	13%	Out-of-state:	7%
GPA 3.50-3.74:	12%	Live on campus:	96%
GPA 3.0-3.49:	36%	International:	1%
GPA 2.0-2.99:	39%	Fraternities:	10%
		Sororities:	9%

Basis for selection. High school records, including grades, strength of academic program, and performance trend: standardized test scores, optional student essay, and evidence of interest and motivation as indicated in supplied materials. SAT or ACT recommended. Radford University will offer high school students with a 3.50 GPA (on a 4.00 scale) and a rigorous program of study to be considered for admission without submitting SAT or ACT test results. Applicants who wish to be considered for merit-based scholarships will be required to submit an official SAT or ACT score report. Informal interviews available and written statements will be considered if submitted. **Home schooled:** SAT subject tests in Math and English recommended. If curriculum is not supported by a recognized home school organization, the student may need to supply course descriptions (including text book information, where appropriate.).

High school preparation. College-preparatory program recommended. 20 units recommended. Recommended units include English 4, mathematics 4, social studies 2, history 2, science 4 (laboratory 4) and foreign language 4. Pre-nursing students should complete units in both biology and chemistry.

2015-2016 Annual costs. Tuition/fees: $9,809; $21,647 out-of-state. Room/board: $8,677. Books/supplies: $1,100. Personal expenses: $1,900. **Additional information:** Room rate reflects weighted average room rate. Board rate reflects 19 meal plan.

2015-2016 Financial aid. Need-based: 1,678 full-time freshmen applied for aid; 1,219 deemed to have need; 1,151 received aid. Average need met was 74%. Average scholarship/grant was $7,750; average loan $3,344. 39% of total undergraduate aid awarded as scholarships/grants, 61% as loans/jobs. **Non-need-based:** Awarded to 1,375 full-time undergraduates, including 384 freshmen. Scholarships awarded for academics, alumni affiliation, art, athletics, leadership, music/drama, ROTC, state residency. **Additional information:** Student's need and grades considered. Top consideration given to those with greatest need and who apply by deadline.

Application procedures. Admission: Priority date 2/1; no deadline. $50 fee, may be waived for applicants with need. Admission notification by 4/1. Must reply by 5/1. **Financial aid:** Priority date 2/15; no closing date. FAFSA required. Applicants notified on a rolling basis starting 4/15; must reply within 2 week(s) of notification.

Academics. Students have opportunity to participate in research collaboration with faculty. **Special study options:** Accelerated study, cross-registration, distance learning, double major, dual enrollment of high school students, ESL, honors, independent study, internships, student-designed major, study abroad, teacher certification program. **Credit/placement by examination:** AP, CLEP, IB, SAT. **Support services:** Learning center, study skills assistance, tutoring, writing center.

Honors college/program. If students meet two of the following criteria, they are invited to apply: 1100 SAT/24 ACT, 3.5 GPA, top 20% of high school class. Application requires submission of an essay (addressing a prompt), and academic credentials. Only 80 students admitted each fall. Any new freshman who earns at least a 3.5 GPA in the Fall semester of their Freshman year will also be invited to apply. At the end of the Fall semester, 20 additional students are admitted.

Majors. Biology: General. **Business:** Accounting, business admin, finance, marketing. **Communications:** Communications/speech/rhetoric, journalism. **Computer sciences:** Computer science, information systems. **Education:** Physical. **English:** English lit. **Foreign languages:** General. **Health services:** Athletic training, communication disorders, nursing (RN). **History:** General. **Human services:** Social work. **Math:** General. **Parks/recreation:** General. **Physical sciences:** Chemistry, geology, physics. **Protective services:** Criminal justice. **Psychology:** General. **Social sciences:** General, anthropology, economics, GIS/cartography, political science, sociology. **Visual/performing arts:** Art, dance, design, dramatic, music. **Work/family studies:** Food/nutrition.

Most popular majors. Business/marketing 18%, communications/journalism 9%, education 8%, health sciences 7%, interdisciplinary studies 8%, psychology 7%, security/protective services 9%, social sciences 6%, visual/performing arts 7%.

Technology on campus. 850 workstations in dormitories, library, computer center, student center. Dormitories wired for high-speed internet access and linked to campus network. Commuter students can connect to campus network. Online course registration, online library, helpline, repair service, student web hosting, wireless network available.

Student life. Freshman orientation: Available, $275 fee. Preregistration for classes offered. Four 2-day and three one-day sessions in June for new freshmen, one-day session in January and late August for new freshmen and transfers. **Policies:** In accepting admission, each student makes a commitment to support and uphold the Honor Code without compromise or exception. **Housing:** Guaranteed on-campus for freshmen. Coed dorms, special housing for disabled, apartments, themed housing, wellness housing available. $200 nonrefundable deposit, deadline 5/1. **Activities:** Bands, campus ministries,

choral groups, dance, drama, film society, international student organizations, literary magazine, music ensembles, Model UN, musical theater, opera, radio station, student government, student newspaper, Crossroads Presbyterian Fellowship, Baptist Collegiate Ministry, Deliverance Gospel Choir, Young Democrats, College Republicans, Gay-Straight Alliance, La Sociedad Hispancia, Students Helping Honduras, Alpha Phi Omega Co-Ed Service Fraternity, Highlander Helpers Backpack Program.

Athletics. NCAA. **Intercollegiate:** Baseball M, basketball, cross-country, golf, lacrosse W, soccer, softball W, tennis, track and field W, volleyball W. **Intramural:** Basketball, cross-country, football (non-tackle), football (tackle), soccer, softball, table tennis, tennis, ultimate frisbee, volleyball. **Team name:** Highlanders.

Student services. Adult student services, alcohol/substance abuse counseling, chaplain/spiritual director, career counseling, services for economically disadvantaged, student employment services, financial aid counseling, health services, minority student services, personal counseling, placement for graduates, veterans' counselor, women's services. **Physically disabled:** Services for visually, speech, hearing impaired.

Contact. E-mail: admissions@radford.edu
Phone: (540) 831-5371 Fax: (540) 831-5038
James Pennix, Dean of Admissions and Enrollment Management, Radford University, PO Box 6903, Radford, VA 24142

Randolph College
Lynchburg, Virginia   CB member
www.randolphcollege.edu   CB code: 5567

- Private 4-year liberal arts college affiliated with the United Methodist Church
- Residential campus in small city
- 665 degree-seeking undergraduates: 1% part-time, 66% women, 12% African American, 2% Asian American, 5% Hispanic/Latino, 1% Native American, 5% Multi-racial, non-Hispanic, 8% international
- 15 degree-seeking graduate students
- 81% of applicants admitted
- SAT or ACT (ACT writing optional), application essay required
- 69% graduate within 6 years

General. Founded in 1891. Regionally accredited. **Degrees:** 128 bachelor's awarded; master's offered. **Location:** 60 miles from Roanoke and Charlottesville. **Calendar:** Semester, limited summer session. **Full-time faculty:** 68 total; 94% have terminal degrees, 16% minority, 57% women. **Part-time faculty:** 4 total; 50% have terminal degrees, 75% women. **Class size:** 85% < 20, 14% 20-39, less than 1% 40-49, less than 1% 50-99. **Special facilities:** Observatory, 3 nature preserves, botanical garden, 100-acre equestrian center, museum of American art, science and mathematics resource center, learning resources center, writing lab, artificial turf field and track facility, organic garden.

Freshman class profile. 1,207 applied, 972 admitted, 184 enrolled.

Mid 50% test scores			
SAT critical reading:	460-570	GPA 2.0-2.99:	14%
SAT math:	450-550	Rank in top quarter:	35%
SAT writing:	440-550	Rank in top tenth:	13%
ACT composite:	19-24	Return as sophomores:	78%
GPA 3.75 or higher:	30%	Out-of-state:	30%
GPA 3.50-3.74:	16%	Live on campus:	90%
GPA 3.0-3.49:	40%	International:	3%

Basis for selection. Rigor of high school curriculum and achievement most important, followed by teacher and counselor recommendations, test scores, activities, personal achievement. Interview recommended. Essay submission may be essay written on topic of applicant's choice, copy of graded essay written by applicant in 11th or 12th grade, or SAT/ACT writing component. **Learning Disabled:** Submit documentation to Director of the Learning Resources Center, who will work in consultation with Office of the Dean of the College and faculty to determine reasonable and appropriate accommodations.

High school preparation. College-preparatory program required. 16 units required. Required and recommended units include English 4, mathematics 3-4, history 2, science 3 (laboratory 2), foreign language 3 and academic electives 1-3.

2015-2016 Annual costs. Tuition/fees: $35,410. Room/board: $12,106. Books/supplies: $1,000. Personal expenses: $700.

2015-2016 Financial aid. Need-based: 155 full-time freshmen applied for aid; 144 deemed to have need; 144 received aid. Average need met was

76%. Average scholarship/grant was $25,373; average loan $3,707. 77% of total undergraduate aid awarded as scholarships/grants, 23% as loans/jobs. **Non-need-based:** Awarded to 248 full-time undergraduates, including 85 freshmen. Scholarships awarded for academics, alumni affiliation, art, music/drama, religious affiliation, state residency.

Application procedures. Admission: Priority date 11/15; deadline 2/15 (postmark date). No application fee. Admission notification by 4/1. Admission notification on a rolling basis beginning on or about 12/15. Must reply by May 1 or within 2 week(s) if notified thereafter. **Financial aid:** Priority date 4/1; no closing date. FAFSA required. Applicants notified on a rolling basis starting 10/1; must reply by 5/1 or within 2 week(s) of notification.

Academics. Honor system includes self-scheduled examinations. **Special study options:** Accelerated study, combined bachelor's/graduate degree, cross-registration, double major, dual enrollment of high school students, exchange student, honors, independent study, internships, liberal arts/career combination, student-designed major, study abroad, teacher certification program, Washington semester. **Credit/placement by examination:** AP, CLEP, IB, SAT, ACT, institutional tests. Applicants with scores at or above 50th percentile awarded credit for CLEP subject examinations in subject areas offered by college. However, subject tests in foreign languages granted credit only if they represent achievement beyond that of previous high school or college preparation. **Support services:** Learning center, reduced course load, study skills assistance, tutoring, writing center.

Majors. Biology: General. **Business:** General. **Communications:** Communications/speech/rhetoric. **Conservation:** Environmental studies. **Engineering:** Applied physics. **English:** British lit, creative writing, English lit. **Foreign languages:** Ancient Greek, classics, French, Latin, Spanish. **History:** General. **Math:** General. **Philosophy/religion:** Philosophy, religion. **Physical sciences:** Chemistry, physics. **Psychology:** General. **Social sciences:** Economics, political science, sociology. **Visual/performing arts:** Art history/conservation, dance, dramatic, music history, music performance, music theory/composition, studio arts.

Most popular majors. Biology 15%, business/marketing 10%, English 9%, mathematics 6%, physical sciences 9%, psychology 6%, social sciences 13%, visual/performing arts 12%.

Technology on campus. 155 workstations in dormitories, library, computer center, student center. Dormitories wired for high-speed internet access and linked to campus network. Commuter students can connect to campus network. Online course registration, online library, helpline, student web hosting, wireless network available.

Student life. Freshman orientation: Mandatory, $150 fee. Preregistration for classes offered. Held over two Two-day summer sessions. **Policies:** Honor code is fundamental to the conduct and governance of the College. **Housing:** Guaranteed on-campus for all undergraduates. Coed dorms, themed housing available. $300 fully refundable deposit, deadline 5/1. **Activities:** Pep band, campus ministries, choral groups, dance, drama, international student organizations, literary magazine, music ensembles, Model UN, radio station, student government, student newspaper, Young Democrats, College Republicans, Amnesty International, Club Asia, Catholic students association, Black Student Alliance, Circle K, Pan World club.

Athletics. NCAA. **Intercollegiate:** Basketball, cross-country, equestrian, lacrosse, soccer, softball W, tennis, volleyball W. **Intramural:** Basketball, softball, table tennis, tennis, volleyball. **Team name:** Wildcats.

Student services. Adult student services, alcohol/substance abuse counseling, chaplain/spiritual director, career counseling, student employment services, financial aid counseling, health services, minority student services, personal counseling, placement for graduates, women's services. **Physically disabled:** Services for visually, hearing impaired.

Contact. E-mail: admissions@randolphcollege.edu
Phone: (434) 947-8100 Toll-free number: (800) 745-7692
Fax: (434) 947-8996
Margaret Blount, Director of Admissions, Randolph College, 2500 Rivermont Avenue, Lynchburg, VA 24503-1555

Randolph-Macon College
Ashland, Virginia
www.rmc.edu

CB member
CB code: 5566

- Private 4-year liberal arts college affiliated with the United Methodist Church
- Residential campus in small town
- 1,405 degree-seeking undergraduates: 2% part-time, 54% women, 8% African American, 2% Asian American, 5% Hispanic/Latino, 4% Multiracial, non-Hispanic, 2% international

- 60% of applicants admitted
- SAT or ACT (ACT writing recommended), application essay required
- 58% graduate within 6 years

General. Founded in 1830. Regionally accredited. **Degrees:** 299 bachelor's awarded. **ROTC:** Army. **Location:** 15 miles from Richmond, 90 miles from Washington, DC. **Calendar:** 4-1-4, limited summer session. **Full-time faculty:** 101 total; 96% have terminal degrees, 8% minority, 46% women. **Part-time faculty:** 59 total; 48% have terminal degrees, 7% minority, 46% women. **Class size:** 63% < 20, 37% 20-39. **Special facilities:** Observatory with 12-inch reflecting telescope and 3-meter radio telescope, greenhouse, new field laboratory at the DuMond Conservancy for Primates and Tropical Forests in Miami, Florida.

Freshman class profile. 2,968 applied, 1,790 admitted, 405 enrolled.

Mid 50% test scores			
SAT critical reading:	500-600	Rank in top quarter:	56%
SAT math:	500-580	Rank in top tenth:	21%
SAT writing:	480-580	Return as sophomores:	78%
ACT composite:	22-27	Out-of-state:	26%
GPA 3.75 or higher:	45%	Live on campus:	96%
GPA 3.50-3.74:	19%	International:	1%
GPA 3.0-3.49:	25%	Fraternities:	21%
GPA 2.0-2.99:	11%	Sororities:	25%

Basis for selection. High school academic record and course schedule is most important, meeting with an admissions counselor recommended but not required. Interview recommended. **Home schooled:** Statement describing home school structure and mission, transcript of courses and grades, letter of recommendation (nonparent) required. **Learning Disabled:** Students with learning disabilities encouraged to meet with director of disability support services.

High school preparation. College-preparatory program required. 16 units required; 22 recommended. Required and recommended units include English 4, mathematics 3-4, social studies 2-3, history 1-3, science 3-4 (laboratory 2-4), foreign language 4 and academic electives 1-2.

2015-2016 Annual costs. Tuition/fees: $37,600. Room/board: $10,880. Books/supplies: $1,100. Personal expenses: $740.

2015-2016 Financial aid. Need-based: 381 full-time freshmen applied for aid; 307 deemed to have need; 307 received aid. Average need met was 83%. Average scholarship/grant was $24,571; average loan $5,015. 79% of total undergraduate aid awarded as scholarships/grants, 21% as loans/jobs. **Non-need-based:** Awarded to 582 full-time undergraduates, including 182 freshmen. Scholarships awarded for academics, alumni affiliation, minority status, religious affiliation, ROTC, state residency.

Application procedures. Admission: Priority date 2/1; deadline 3/1 (postmark date). $30 fee, may be waived for applicants with need, free for online applicants. Admission notification by 4/1. Must reply by May 1 or within 2 week(s) if notified thereafter. Applications accepted after March 1 on space-available basis. **Financial aid:** Priority date 2/15, closing date 3/1. FAFSA required. Applicants notified on a rolling basis starting 3/1; must reply by 5/1 or within 2 week(s) of notification.

Academics. Comprehensive liberal arts core curriculum. All students must complete an internship, study abroad, or original research project for graduation. Interdisciplinary First-Year Experience for all freshmen. **Special study options:** Accelerated study, combined bachelor's/graduate degree, cross-registration, double major, dual enrollment of high school students, exchange student, honors, independent study, internships, liberal arts/career combination, study abroad, teacher certification program, United Nations semester, Washington semester. Priority acceptance agreement for medical, nursing, or physician assistant school with VCU (medical and nursing), George Washington University (medical and nursing), and Eastern Virginia Medical School (medical and PA). Member of Seven College consortium. Dual degree programs: 3-2 in engineering with Columbia University and University of Virginia, 3-2 in forestry with Duke University, 4-1 in accounting with Virginia Commonwealth University. **Credit/placement by examination:** AP, CLEP, IB, institutional tests. 75 credit hours maximum toward bachelor's degree. At least one-half major course of study must be completed at Randolph-Macon College. **Support services:** Learning center, pre-admission summer program, reduced course load, study skills assistance, tutoring, writing center.

Majors. Area/ethnic studies: Asian, women's. **Biology:** General. **Business:** Accounting, managerial economics. **Communications:** General. **Computer sciences:** General. **Conservation:** Environmental studies. **Engineering:** Applied physics. **English:** English lit. **Foreign languages:** Ancient Greek, classics, French, German, Latin, Spanish. **History:** General. **Math:** General. **Philosophy/religion:** Philosophy, religion. **Physical sciences:** Chemistry, physics. **Psychology:** General. **Social sciences:** Economics, political science, sociology. **Visual/performing arts:** Art history/conservation, dramatic, music, studio arts, studio arts management.

Most popular majors. Biology 10%, business/marketing 15%, communications/journalism 8%, English 6%, psychology 14%, social sciences 16%, visual/performing arts 9%.

Technology on campus. 350 workstations in library, computer center, student center. Dormitories wired for high-speed internet access and linked to campus network. Commuter students can connect to campus network. Online course registration, online library, helpline, repair service, student web hosting, wireless network available.

Student life. Freshman orientation: Mandatory, $100 fee. Preregistration for classes offered. 4-day program held for students and parents prior to start of fall classes. **Housing:** Guaranteed on-campus for all undergraduates. Coed dorms, single-sex dorms, special housing for disabled, apartments, fraternity/sorority housing, themed housing, wellness housing available. Honors house, special interest housing available. **Activities:** Bands, campus ministries, choral groups, dance, drama, film society, international student organizations, literary magazine, music ensembles, musical theater, opera, radio station, student government, student newspaper, TV station, Leadership Fellows, Service Fellows, Diversity Council, Nourish International, Habitat for Humanity, over 80 other clubs and organizations.

Athletics. NCAA. **Intercollegiate:** Baseball M, basketball, field hockey W, football (tackle) M, golf, lacrosse, soccer, softball W, swimming, tennis, volleyball W. **Intramural:** Badminton, basketball, football (non-tackle), lacrosse, racquetball, rugby, soccer, softball, table tennis, tennis, ultimate frisbee, volleyball, water polo. **Team name:** Yellow Jackets.

Student services. Alcohol/substance abuse counseling, chaplain/spiritual director, career counseling, student employment services, financial aid counseling, health services, minority student services, personal counseling, placement for graduates, women's services. **Physically disabled:** Services for visually, speech, hearing impaired.

Contact. E-mail: admissions@rmc.edu
Phone: (804) 752-7305 Toll-free number: (800) 888-1762
Fax: (804) 752-4707
David Lesesne, Dean of Admissions and Financial Aid, Randolph-Macon College, PO Box 5005, Ashland, VA 23005-5505

Regent University
Virginia Beach, Virginia
www.regent.edu

CB code: 4452

- Private 4-year university affiliated with the interdenominational tradition
- Residential campus in large city
- 2,867 degree-seeking undergraduates: 38% part-time, 62% women, 25% African American, 2% Asian American, 7% Hispanic/Latino, 1% Native American, 5% Multi-racial, non-Hispanic, 1% international
- 4,051 degree-seeking graduate students
- 86% of applicants admitted
- SAT or ACT (ACT writing optional), application essay required
- 48% graduate within 6 years; 33% enter graduate study

General. Founded in 1977. Regionally accredited. **Degrees:** 473 bachelor's, 18 associate awarded; master's, professional, doctoral offered. **ROTC:** Army, Naval. **Location:** 8 miles from Norfolk. **Calendar:** Semester, extensive summer session. **Full-time faculty:** 145 total; 94% have terminal degrees, 17% minority, 33% women. **Part-time faculty:** 507 total; 66% have terminal degrees, 20% minority, 41% women. **Class size:** 61% < 20, 39% 20-39. **Special facilities:** Moot court/city council chamber, communication and performing arts center, theater, experimental theater, cinema-television production studio, film sound stage, screening theaters, technical studios, teaching labs, science labs, and chapel.

Freshman class profile. 1,665 applied, 1,426 admitted, 355 enrolled.

Mid 50% test scores			
		GPA 2.0-2.99:	16%
SAT critical reading:	470-600	Rank in top quarter:	34%
SAT math:	430-550	Rank in top tenth:	14%
SAT writing:	440-580	End year in good standing:	87%
ACT composite:	19-27	Return as sophomores:	79%
GPA 3.75 or higher:	37%	Out-of-state:	52%
GPA 3.50-3.74:	19%	Live on campus:	53%
GPA 3.0-3.49:	28%	International:	2%

Basis for selection. GPA, test scores, essay all required along with application. **Home schooled:** Transcript of courses and grades required.

High school preparation. College-preparatory program recommended. 16 units recommended. Recommended units include English 4, mathematics 3, social studies 3, science 3 and foreign language 3.

2015-2016 Annual costs. Tuition/fees: $16,700. Room/board: $8,480. Books/supplies: $1,000. Personal expenses: $1,950.

2015-2016 Financial aid. Need-based: 267 full-time freshmen applied for aid; 233 deemed to have need; 232 received aid. Average need met was 53%. Average scholarship/grant was $9,395; average loan $3,424. 61% of total undergraduate aid awarded as scholarships/grants, 39% as loans/jobs. **Non-need-based:** Awarded to 340 full-time undergraduates, including 95 freshmen. Scholarships awarded for academics, alumni affiliation, leadership, ROTC.

Application procedures. Admission: Priority date 5/1; deadline 8/1 (receipt date). $50 fee. Admission notification on a rolling basis. Must reply by 5/1. **Financial aid:** Priority date 3/15; no closing date. FAFSA, institutional form required. Applicants notified on a rolling basis starting 12/1; must reply within 2 week(s) of notification.

Academics. Special study options: Combined bachelor's/graduate degree, distance learning, double major, dual enrollment of high school students, internships, liberal arts/career combination, study abroad, teacher certification program, Washington semester. **Credit/placement by examination:** AP, CLEP, IB. 15 credit hours maximum toward associate degree, 30 toward bachelor's. **Support services:** Remedial instruction, study skills assistance, tutoring, writing center.

Majors. Biology: Biophysics. **Business:** Accounting, business admin, international, organizational behavior. **Communications:** Communications/speech/rhetoric. **Communications technology:** Animation/special effects. **Computer sciences:** Information technology. **Education:** General. **English:** English lit. **History:** General. **Human services:** Public policy. **Math:** General. **Philosophy/religion:** Religion. **Protective services:** Law enforcement admin. **Psychology:** General. **Social sciences:** Political science. **Theology:** Bible, theology. **Visual/performing arts:** Cinematography, theater arts management.

Most popular majors. Business/marketing 18%, communications/journalism 21%, English 10%, psychology 15%, theological studies 16%.

Technology on campus. 130 workstations in library, computer center, student center. Dormitories wired for high-speed internet access and linked to campus network. Commuter students can connect to campus network. Online course registration, online library, helpline, wireless network available.

Student life. Freshman orientation: Mandatory. Preregistration for classes offered. **Housing:** Guaranteed on-campus for freshmen. Apartments available. $350 nonrefundable deposit, deadline 5/1. **Activities:** Concert band, campus ministries, choral groups, dance, drama, international student organizations, musical theater, student government, student newspaper, Animation & special effects club, Christian Association of Psychological Studies, dance club, Newman Society, psychology club, Regent Association of Volleyball Enthusiasts, Regent Outdoor Adventure Group, Regent Undergraduate Debate Association, Student Alumni Ambassadors, Regent University Conservative Union.

Athletics. Intramural: Basketball, football (non-tackle), sand volleyball, soccer, softball, ultimate frisbee, volleyball.

Student services. Chaplain/spiritual director, career counseling, student employment services, financial aid counseling, health services, legal services, personal counseling, placement for graduates, veterans' counselor.

Contact. E-mail: admissions@regent.edu
Phone: (757) 352-4127 Toll-free number: (800) 373-5504
Fax: (757) 352-4381
Heidi Cece, Executive Director of University Admissions, Regent University, 1000 Regent University Drive, Virginia Beach, VA 23464-9800

Roanoke College
Salem, Virginia
www.roanoke.edu

CB member
CB code: 5571

- Private 4-year liberal arts college affiliated with the Evangelical Lutheran Church in America
- Residential campus in large town
- 1,961 degree-seeking undergraduates: 2% part-time, 59% women, 6% African American, 1% Asian American, 4% Hispanic/Latino, 4% Multi-racial, non-Hispanic, 2% international
- 72% of applicants admitted
- SAT or ACT (ACT writing optional) required
- 66% graduate within 6 years; 31% enter graduate study

General. Founded in 1842. Regionally accredited. **Degrees:** 435 bachelor's awarded. **Location:** 7 miles from Roanoke. **Calendar:** Semester, extensive summer session. **Full-time faculty:** 164 total; 87% have terminal degrees, 10% minority, 49% women. **Part-time faculty:** 55 total; 36% have terminal degrees, 9% minority, 53% women. **Class size:** 53% < 20, 47% 20-39, less than 1% 40-49. **Special facilities:** Nuclear magnetic resonance equipment, center for community research, center for church and society, center for learning and teaching, writing center.

Freshman class profile. 4,325 applied, 3,134 admitted, 508 enrolled.

Mid 50% test scores			
SAT critical reading:	490-610	Rank in top quarter:	45%
SAT math:	480-590	Rank in top tenth:	15%
SAT writing:	480-600	End year in good standing:	85%
ACT composite:	21-27	Return as sophomores:	80%
GPA 3.75 or higher:	35%	Out-of-state:	51%
GPA 3.50-3.74:	18%	Live on campus:	92%
GPA 3.0-3.49:	29%	International:	2%
GPA 2.0-2.99:	18%	Sororities:	4%

Basis for selection. Rigor of secondary school record, academic GPA, and character/personal qualities are most important. IB exams are also used for placement. Students who have at least a 3.25 academic GPA may submit two graded writing samples in lieu of SAT or ACT test scores. Essay, interview recommended for all; audition recommended for music; portfolio recommended for graphic/visual arts. **Home schooled:** Transcript of courses and grades required. **Learning Disabled:** Documentation of learning disability needed for special services after enrollment.

High school preparation. College-preparatory program recommended. 16 units required. Required and recommended units include English 4, mathematics 3, social studies 2, science 2 (laboratory 2), foreign language 4 and academic electives 5. Mathematics must include Algebra II.

2016-2017 Annual costs. Tuition/fees (projected): $41,304. Room/board: $12,810. Books/supplies: $1,000. Personal expenses: $1,000. **Additional information:** Freshmen commuter students pay a lower total of required fees, $1334. Freshmen also pay a $125 fee for the on-campus orientation program.

2015-2016 Financial aid. Need-based: 454 full-time freshmen applied for aid; 387 deemed to have need; 387 received aid. Average need met was 81%. Average scholarship/grant was $27,462; average loan $4,270. 73% of total undergraduate aid awarded as scholarships/grants, 27% as loans/jobs. **Non-need-based:** Awarded to 1,864 full-time undergraduates, including 493 freshmen. Scholarships awarded for academics, art, minority status, music/drama, religious affiliation.

Application procedures. Admission: Closing date 3/15 (postmark date). $30 fee, may be waived for applicants with need, free for online applicants. Admission notification by 4/1. Admission notification on a rolling basis beginning on or about 10/1. Must reply by May 1 or within 2 week(s) if notified thereafter. All students must submit a registration deposit of $500. **Financial aid:** Priority date 3/1; no closing date. FAFSA required. Applicants notified on a rolling basis starting 10/15; must reply within 2 week(s) of notification.

Academics. Special study options: Accelerated study, combined bachelor's/graduate degree, cross-registration, double major, dual enrollment of high school students, ESL, honors, independent study, internships, liberal arts/career combination, study abroad, teacher certification program, Washington semester. **Credit/placement by examination:** AP, CLEP, IB, institutional tests. 32 credit hours maximum toward bachelor's degree. Maximum 32 hours of credit examination represent a maximum of 8 courses by credit by examination, AP tests, IB tests, or CLEP tests. **Support services:** Learning center, reduced course load, study skills assistance, tutoring, writing center. Writing Center and Subject Tutoring services available on the weekend. Other academic support services primarily available Monday to Friday.

Majors. Biology: General, biochemistry. **Business:** Business admin. **Communications:** General. **Computer sciences:** General, computer science. **Conservation:** Environmental studies. **Education:** Physical. **English:** Creative writing, English lit. **Foreign languages:** French, Spanish. **Health services:** Athletic training. **History:** General. **Math:** General. **Parks/recreation:** Exercise sciences, sports admin. **Philosophy/religion:** Christian, philosophy, religion. **Physical sciences:** Chemistry, physics. **Protective services:** Criminal justice. **Psychology:** General. **Social sciences:** Economics, international relations, political science, sociology. **Visual/performing arts:** Art, art history/conservation, dramatic, music.

Most popular majors. Biology 10%, business/marketing 14%, communications/journalism 8%, history 8%, parks/recreation 8%, psychology 12%, social sciences 12%.

Technology on campus. 270 workstations in library, computer center, student center. Dormitories wired for high-speed internet access and linked to campus network. Commuter students can connect to campus network. Online course registration, online library, helpline, repair service, wireless network available.

Student life. Freshman orientation: Mandatory, $125 fee. Preregistration for classes offered. One full day on campus in June. **Housing:** Guaranteed on-campus for freshmen. Coed dorms, single-sex dorms, special housing for disabled, apartments, fraternity/sorority housing, themed housing available. $300 fully refundable deposit, deadline 5/1. **Activities:** Bands, campus ministries, choral groups, dance, drama, film society, international student organizations, literary magazine, music ensembles, Model UN, radio station, student government, student newspaper, Alpha Phi Omega Service Fraternity, Catholic Campus Ministry, College Republicans, Earthbound, Fellowship of Christian Athletes, Habitat for Humanity, Hillel, Hispanic Organization for Leadership & Achievement, InterVarsity Christian Fellowship, RC Lutherans.

Athletics. NCAA. **Intercollegiate:** Baseball M, basketball, cross-country, field hockey W, golf M, lacrosse, soccer, softball W, tennis, track and field, volleyball W. **Intramural:** Basketball, football (non-tackle), handball, racquetball, soccer, softball, volleyball. **Team name:** Maroons.

Student services. Adult student services, alcohol/substance abuse counseling, chaplain/spiritual director, career counseling, student employment services, financial aid counseling, health services, minority student services, personal counseling, placement for graduates.

Contact. E-mail: admissions@roanoke.edu
Phone: (540) 375-2270 Toll-free number: (800) 388-2276
Fax: (540) 375-2267
Brenda Poggendorf, Vice President of Enrollment & Dean of Admissions and Financial Aid, Roanoke College, 221 College Lane, Salem, VA 24153-3794

Shenandoah University
Winchester, Virginia **CB member**
www.su.edu **CB code: 5613**

- Private 4-year university affiliated with the United Methodist Church
- Residential campus in large town
- 1,991 degree-seeking undergraduates: 3% part-time, 59% women, 11% African American, 3% Asian American, 6% Hispanic/Latino, 1% Native American, 4% Multi-racial, non-Hispanic, 4% international
- 1,687 degree-seeking graduate students
- 82% of applicants admitted
- SAT or ACT (ACT writing optional) required
- 55% graduate within 6 years

General. Founded in 1875. Regionally accredited. Incoming students receive university-owned MacBook Pro laptop and Apple iPad. **Degrees:** 433 bachelor's awarded; master's, professional, doctoral offered. **Location:** 98 miles from Baltimore, 76 miles from Washington, DC. **Calendar:** Semester, limited summer session. **Full-time faculty:** 250 total; 82% have terminal degrees, 11% minority, 57% women. **Part-time faculty:** 189 total; 38% have terminal degrees, 10% minority, 60% women. **Class size:** 61% < 20, 35% 20-39, 2% 40-49, 1% 50-99, less than 1% >100. **Special facilities:** Outdoor learning laboratory, green rooftop, Feltner Museum.

Freshman class profile. 2,044 applied, 1,677 admitted, 446 enrolled.

Mid 50% test scores			
SAT critical reading:	430-560	GPA 3.0-3.49:	31%
SAT math:	440-560	GPA 2.0-2.99:	25%
SAT writing:	410-540	End year in good standing:	88%
ACT composite:	19-25	Return as sophomores:	77%
GPA 3.75 or higher:	29%	Out-of-state:	46%
GPA 3.50-3.74:	15%	Live on campus:	92%
		International:	1%

Basis for selection. GPA and standardized test scores, along with recommendation. Nursing applicants must pass Test of Essential Academic Skills V - (TEASV). All incoming ESL students take an institutional TOEFL. This is not an in-house test, but it will be administered in house. Essays are encouraged. Audition, portfolio review or interview is required for ALL conservatory programs in the admissions process. **Home schooled:** State high school equivalency certificate required. May request GED score. Applicants must submit written documentation of local school district approval of the home school arrangement if available. **Learning Disabled:** If a student needs special accommodations, IEP documentation should be provided, so desired outcome will be achieved.

High school preparation. College-preparatory program recommended. 10 units required. Required and recommended units include English 4, mathematics 3, science 2 (laboratory 1) and foreign language 2.

2016-2017 Annual costs. Tuition/fees: $31,322. Room/board: $9,990. Books/supplies: $1,500. Personal expenses: $2,000.

2015-2016 Financial aid. Need-based: 398 full-time freshmen applied for aid; 343 deemed to have need; 343 received aid. Average need met was 32%. Average scholarship/grant was $5,150; average loan $2,841. 37% of total undergraduate aid awarded as scholarships/grants, 63% as loans/jobs. **Non-need-based:** Awarded to 576 full-time undergraduates, including 248 freshmen. Scholarships awarded for academics, music/drama, religious affiliation.

Application procedures. Admission: Priority date 2/1; no deadline. $30 fee, may be waived for applicants with need. Admission notification on a rolling basis. Must reply by May 1 or within 2 week(s) if notified thereafter. New students can apply for housing until 8/1. **Financial aid:** No deadline. FAFSA required. Applicants notified on a rolling basis starting 3/15; must reply within 4 week(s) of notification.

Academics. Special study options: Accelerated study, combined bachelor's/graduate degree, distance learning, double major, dual enrollment of high school students, ESL, independent study, internships, student-designed major, study abroad, teacher certification program. **Credit/placement by examination:** AP, CLEP, IB, SAT, ACT, institutional tests. 90 credit hours maximum toward bachelor's degree. AP placement grade may be higher for exams taken in student's major. CEEB, CLEP, academic department exams used. Challenge exams allow students to earn credit by passing a comprehensive exam on the content of the course. **Support services:** Learning center, reduced course load, study skills assistance, tutoring, writing center. One-on-one academic counseling and coaching, disability services, exam proctoring/testing center, study skills workshop.

Majors. Biology: General, exercise physiology. **Business:** Business admin, entrepreneurial studies, managerial economics. **Communications:** Communications/speech/rhetoric. **Conservation:** Environmental studies. **Education:** Music, physical. **English:** English lit. **Foreign languages:** Spanish. **Health services:** Music therapy, nursing (RN), respiratory therapy technology. **History:** General. **Liberal arts:** Arts/sciences. **Math:** General. **Parks/recreation:** Sports admin. **Philosophy/religion:** Religion. **Physical sciences:** Chemistry. **Protective services:** Law enforcement admin. **Psychology:** General. **Social sciences:** Political science, sociology. **Theology:** Sacred music. **Visual/performing arts:** Acting, dance, jazz, music performance, music technology, music theory/composition, musical theater, piano/keyboard, theater design.

Most popular majors. Biology 9%, business/marketing 8%, education 7%, health sciences 31%, psychology 7%, visual/performing arts 20%.

Technology on campus. PC or laptop required. 20 workstations in library. Dormitories wired for high-speed internet access and linked to campus network. Commuter students can connect to campus network. Online course registration, online library, helpline, repair service, wireless network available.

Student life. Freshman orientation: Available. Preregistration for classes offered. Welcome week is the week prior to the fall semester. An additional one-day student/family session offered June-July for meeting the dean of your academic program. **Policies:** All first- and second-year undergraduates must live on-campus. Exceptions are for students who are married, living with parents, and/or over age of 22. Fish kept in 10-gallon-or-less tank and properly attended assistance animals for individuals with disabilities allowed in dorm rooms. **Housing:** Guaranteed on-campus for all undergraduates. Coed dorms, special housing for disabled, apartments available. $100 nonrefundable deposit, deadline 4/5. Honors, freshmen-only and upperclassmen-only housing available. **Activities:** Bands, campus ministries, choral groups, dance, drama, international student organizations, literary magazine, music ensembles, musical theater, radio station, student government, student newspaper, symphony orchestra, Circle K International, The Boat Village Health Effort, Christian Pharmacists Fellowship International, Catholic Campus Ministry, Muslim Student Association, Estudiantes Unidos, Fellowship of Christian Athletes, Black Student Union, Jewish Student Union, Harambee Gospel Choir.

Athletics. NCAA. **Intercollegiate:** Baseball M, basketball, cross-country, field hockey W, football (tackle) M, golf, lacrosse, soccer, softball W, tennis, track and field, volleyball W. **Intramural:** Basketball, football (non-tackle), soccer, softball, ultimate frisbee, volleyball. **Team name:** Hornets.

Student services. Adult student services, alcohol/substance abuse counseling, chaplain/spiritual director, career counseling, student employment services, financial aid counseling, health services, minority student services, personal counseling, veterans' counselor, women's services. **Physically disabled:** Services for visually, speech, hearing impaired.

Contact. E-mail: admit@su.edu
Phone: (540) 665-4581 Toll-free number: (800) 432-2266
Fax: (540) 665-4627
Andrew Woodall, Executive Director of Recruitment and Admissions, Shenandoah University, Office of Admissions, Winchester, VA 22601-5195

Southern Virginia University
Buena Vista, Virginia
www.svu.edu

CB member
CB code: 5625

- Private 4-year liberal arts college affiliated with the Church of Jesus Christ of Latter-day Saints
- Residential campus in small town
- 703 degree-seeking undergraduates
- SAT or ACT (ACT writing recommended) required

General. Degrees: 118 bachelor's awarded. **ROTC:** Army. **Location:** 60 miles from Roanoke, 60 miles from Charlottesville. **Calendar:** Semester, extensive summer session. **Full-time faculty:** 38 total; 84% have terminal degrees, 8% minority, 42% women. **Part-time faculty:** 26 total; 38% have terminal degrees, 42% women. **Class size:** 66% < 20, 33% 20-39, less than 1% 40-49, less than 1% 50-99.

Freshman class profile.

GPA 3.75 or higher:	35%	Rank in top quarter:	45%
GPA 3.50-3.74:	16%	Rank in top tenth:	18%
GPA 3.0-3.49:	27%	Out-of-state:	86%
GPA 2.0-2.99:	21%	Live on campus:	99%

Basis for selection. GPA, test scores, interview, religious affiliation or commitment all important. **Home schooled:** Transcript of courses and grades required.

High school preparation. College-preparatory program recommended. Recommended units include English 4, mathematics 3, social studies 2, history 2, science 3 (laboratory 2), foreign language 2, computer science 1, visual/performing arts 1 and academic electives 1.

2015-2016 Annual costs. Tuition/fees: $14,900. Room/board: $7,600. Books/supplies: $1,200. Personal expenses: $1,500.

Financial aid. Non-need-based: Scholarships awarded for academics, art, athletics, leadership, music/drama, ROTC.

Application procedures. Admission: Closing date 9/12. $35 fee, may be waived for applicants with need. Admission notification on a rolling basis beginning on or about 10/15. **Financial aid:** Priority date 5/1; no closing date. FAFSA required. Applicants notified on a rolling basis starting 2/15.

Academics. Special study options: Cross-registration, double major, independent study, internships, study abroad, teacher certification program. **Credit/placement by examination:** AP, CLEP, IB, SAT, ACT, institutional tests. **Support services:** Learning center, remedial instruction, study skills assistance, tutoring, writing center.

Majors. Biology: General. **Business:** Business admin. **Computer sciences:** General. **English:** English lit. **Foreign languages:** Spanish. **History:** General. **Liberal arts:** Arts/sciences. **Philosophy/religion:** Philosophy. **Visual/performing arts:** Art, dramatic, music. **Work/family studies:** Family systems.

Most popular majors. Biology 6%, business/marketing 20%, English 13%, family/consumer sciences 6%, history 7%, liberal arts 22%, visual/performing arts 20%.

Technology on campus. 48 workstations in library, computer center. Dormitories wired for high-speed internet access and linked to campus network. Commuter students can connect to campus network. Online course registration, online library, helpline, repair service, wireless network available.

Student life. Freshman orientation: Mandatory. Preregistration for classes offered. **Policies:** Must abide by the honor code, the dress and grooming standards, and the residential living policies. Most housing is wheelchair accessible. **Housing:** Guaranteed on-campus for freshmen. Single-sex dorms, special housing for disabled, apartments available. $250 fully refundable deposit, deadline 9/2. **Activities:** Bands, campus ministries, choral groups, dance, drama, international student organizations, literary magazine, music ensembles, musical theater, opera, student government, student newspaper, symphony orchestra.

Athletics. NAIA, USCAA. **Intercollegiate:** Baseball M, basketball, cheerleading, cross-country, football (tackle) M, soccer, softball W, tennis, volleyball W, wrestling M. **Team name:** Knights.

Student services. Chaplain/spiritual director, career counseling, financial aid counseling, health services, personal counseling.

Contact. E-mail: admissions@svu.edu
Phone: (540) 261-2756 Toll-free number: (800) 229-8420
Fax: (540) 264-8559
Brett Garcia, Dean of Admissions, Southern Virginia University, One
University Hill Drive, Buena Vista, VA 24416-3097

Stratford University: Falls Church
Falls Church, Virginia
www.stratford.edu   CB code: 3778

- For-profit 4-year health science and career college
- Commuter campus in large city
- 625 degree-seeking undergraduates: 49% African American, 10% Asian American, 8% Hispanic/Latino, 1% Native American
- 735 graduate students
- Interview required

General. Accredited by ACICS. **Degrees:** 166 bachelor's, 379 associate awarded; master's, doctoral offered. **Location:** 12 miles from Washington, DC. **Calendar:** Quarter, extensive summer session. **Full-time faculty:** 29 total; 45% women. **Part-time faculty:** 135 total. **Special facilities:** Commercial kitchen facilities, nursing labs, student success center.

Basis for selection. Open admission. **Home schooled:** Transcript of courses and grades, state high school equivalency certificate, interview required.

2015-2016 Annual costs. Tuition/fees: $16,750. **Additional information:** NSG course tuition is $410 per credit.

2015-2016 Financial aid. All financial aid based on need.

Application procedures. Admission: No deadline. $50 fee, may be waived for applicants with need. Admission notification on a rolling basis. **Financial aid:** No deadline. FAFSA required. Applicants notified on a rolling basis starting 1/1.

Academics. Special study options: Accelerated study, distance learning, ESL, independent study, internships, weekend college. **Credit/placement by examination:** AP, CLEP. **Support services:** Learning center, remedial instruction, study skills assistance, tutoring. Student success center.

Majors. Business: General, accounting technology, business admin, hospitality admin, restaurant/food services. **Computer sciences:** General, information technology, networking.

Most popular majors. Business/marketing 17%, computer/information sciences 83%.

Technology on campus. Commuter students can connect to campus network. Online course registration, online library available.

Student life. Freshman orientation: Mandatory. Preregistration for classes offered. **Activities:** Student newspaper.

Student services. Adult student services, career counseling, financial aid counseling, placement for graduates, veterans' counselor.

Contact. E-mail: fallschurchadmissions@stratford.edu
Phone: (703) 821-8570 Toll-free number: (800) 444-0804
Akeem Brown, Director of Admissions, Stratford University: Falls Church, 7777 Leesburg Pike Suite 1LN, Falls Church, VA 22043

Stratford University: Woodbridge
Woodbridge, Virginia
www.stratford.edu

- For-profit 4-year university and branch campus college
- Commuter campus in large town
- 450 degree-seeking undergraduates: 41% African American, 4% Asian American, 13% Hispanic/Latino, 4% Native American
- 47 graduate students
- Interview required

General. Accredited by ACICS. **Degrees:** 59 bachelor's, 88 associate awarded; master's offered. **Location:** 27 miles from Washington, DC; 13 miles from Quantico Marine Base. **Calendar:** Quarter, extensive summer session. **Full-time faculty:** 17 total. **Part-time faculty:** 52 total.

Basis for selection. Open admission. **Home schooled:** Transcript of courses and grades, state high school equivalency certificate, interview required.

2015-2016 Annual costs. Tuition/fees: $11,100. Personal expenses: $2,058. **Additional information:** Classes with lab components or additional instructional materials will require extra fees. Books are included in tuition.

2014-2015 Financial aid. Need-based: 43% of total undergraduate aid awarded as scholarships/grants, 57% as loans/jobs.

Application procedures. Admission: No deadline. $50 fee, may be waived for applicants with need. Admission notification on a rolling basis. **Financial aid:** FAFSA required.

Academics. Special study options: Accelerated study, combined bachelor's/graduate degree, cooperative education, distance learning, independent study, internships. **Credit/placement by examination:** AP, CLEP, institutional tests. **Support services:** Remedial instruction, study skills assistance, tutoring, writing center. Free tutoring and student success center.

Majors. Business: Accounting, business admin, hospitality admin. **Computer sciences:** Information systems.

Technology on campus. Commuter students can connect to campus network. Online course registration, online library, wireless network available.

Student life. Freshman orientation: Mandatory. Preregistration for classes offered.

Student services. Adult student services, career counseling, financial aid counseling, veterans' counselor.

Contact. E-mail: admissions@stratford.edu
Phone: (703) 897-1982 Toll-free number: (888) 546-1250
Ashley Collins, Director of Admissions, Stratford University: Woodbridge, 14349 Gideon Drive, Woodbridge, VA 22192

Sweet Briar College
Sweet Briar, Virginia   CB member
www.sbc.edu   CB code: 5634

- Private 4-year liberal arts college for women
- Residential campus in rural community
- 236 degree-seeking undergraduates: 2% part-time, 100% women, 9% African American, 3% Asian American, 9% Hispanic/Latino, 2% Native American, 5% Multi-racial, non-Hispanic
- 3 degree-seeking graduate students
- 95% of applicants admitted
- SAT or ACT (ACT writing optional), application essay required
- 64% graduate within 6 years

General. Founded in 1901. Regionally accredited. **Degrees:** 130 bachelor's awarded; master's offered. **Location:** 12 miles from Lynchburg; 166 miles from Washington, DC. **Calendar:** Semester, limited summer session. **Full-time faculty:** 49 total; 84% have terminal degrees, 14% minority, 47% women. **Part-time faculty:** 22 total; 50% have terminal degrees, 9% minority, 59% women. **Class size:** 98% < 20, 2% 20-39. **Special facilities:** Indoor and outdoor riding facilities, three nature sanctuaries, art barn, college-run nursery school and kindergarten for student teaching, observatory, environmental education and nature center.

Freshman class profile. 99 applied, 94 admitted, 24 enrolled.

Mid 50% test scores			
SAT critical reading:	500-660	GPA 3.0-3.49:	20%
SAT math:	440-580	GPA 2.0-2.99:	25%
SAT writing:	450-640	Rank in top quarter:	50%
ACT composite:	22-27	Rank in top tenth:	25%
GPA 3.75 or higher:	35%	Out-of-state:	58%
GPA 3.50-3.74:	10%	Live on campus:	83%

Basis for selection. High school curriculum and grades are of primary importance, followed by school and teacher recommendations, test scores, and writing ability as demonstrated by essay or personal statement. Interview, extracurricular activities, and personal characteristics are also considered. **Learning Disabled:** Applicant must submit written request for accommodated admissions review to Office of Admissions and enclose appropriate documentation with request.

High school preparation. College-preparatory program required. 16 units required; 20 recommended. Required and recommended units include English

4, mathematics 3-4, social studies 3-4, science 3-4 (laboratory 2-3) and foreign language 2-4. Math prep must be at least through Algebra II; Foreign language must be two consecutive years of the same language.

2016-2017 Annual costs. Tuition/fees: $36,425. Room/board: $12,635. Books/supplies: $1,250. Personal expenses: $1,300.

2014-2015 Financial aid. Need-based: 145 full-time freshmen applied for aid; 127 deemed to have need; 127 received aid. Average need met was 73%. Average scholarship/grant was $25,651; average loan $5,631. 80% of total undergraduate aid awarded as scholarships/grants, 20% as loans/jobs. **Non-need-based:** Awarded to 186 full-time undergraduates, including 41 freshmen. Scholarships awarded for academics, art, leadership, music/drama, state residency.

Application procedures. Admission: Closing date 2/1 (postmark date). $40 fee, may be waived for applicants with need. Admission notification on a rolling basis beginning on or about 9/1. Must reply by 5/1. **Financial aid:** Priority date 2/15; no closing date. FAFSA required. Applicants notified on a rolling basis starting 3/1; must reply by 5/1.

Academics. General Education Program: students complete requirements that involve communication and quantitative reasoning skills; rationale for broad liberal arts background; emphasis on internships; regular progress self-assessments. Summer research program provides opportunities for high-level work with faculty. **Special study options:** Accelerated study, combined bachelor's/graduate degree, cross-registration, double major, dual enrollment of high school students, exchange student, honors, independent study, internships, liberal arts/career combination, student-designed major, study abroad, teacher certification program, Washington semester. **Credit/placement by examination:** AP, CLEP, IB, institutional tests. Exemption from 1 or more of degree requirements and/or admission to advanced courses may be granted on basis of Advanced Placement Exams, International Baccalaureate Program, transfer credit, or, in some cases, placement tests taken at college. **Support services:** Learning center, study skills assistance, tutoring, writing center.

Majors. Area/ethnic studies: German. **Biology:** General, Biochemistry/molecular biology. **Business:** General. **Conservation:** Environmental science, environmental studies. **Engineering:** Engineering science. **English:** Creative writing, English lit. **Foreign languages:** General, classics, French, German, Spanish. **History:** General. **Liberal arts:** Arts/sciences. **Math:** General. **Philosophy/religion:** Philosophy, religion. **Physical sciences:** Chemistry, physics, theoretical physics. **Psychology:** General. **Social sciences:** Anthropology, archaeology, economics, international relations, political science, sociology. **Visual/performing arts:** Art history/conservation, dance, dramatic, music, studio arts.

Most popular majors. Biology 7%, business/marketing 16%, engineering/engineering technologies 8%, English 7%, foreign language 8%, liberal arts 8%, social sciences 15%, visual/performing arts 10%.

Technology on campus. 117 workstations in library, computer center. Dormitories wired for high-speed internet access and linked to campus network. Commuter students can connect to campus network. Online course registration, online library, helpline, repair service, student web hosting, wireless network available.

Student life. Freshman orientation: Mandatory. Preregistration for classes offered. Held Saturday-Tuesday in August leading up to beginning of classes. **Policies:** Self-governing student body; honor system observed. **Housing:** Guaranteed on-campus for all undergraduates. Special housing for disabled, apartments, themed housing available. **Activities:** Campus ministries, choral groups, dance, drama, international student organizations, literary magazine, music ensembles, musical theater, student government, student newspaper, Campus Christian Fellowship, campus spirituality coalition, College Republicans, Young Democrats, Spanish club, Habitat for Humanity, student environmental organization, Campus Events Organization, business club.

Athletics. NCAA. **Intercollegiate:** Field hockey W, lacrosse W, soccer W, softball W, swimming W, tennis W. **Team name:** Vixens.

Student services. Alcohol/substance abuse counseling, chaplain/spiritual director, career counseling, student employment services, financial aid counseling, health services, personal counseling, placement for graduates, women's services. **Physically disabled:** Services for hearing impaired.

Contact. E-mail: admissions@sbc.edu
Phone: (434) 381-6142 Toll-free number: (800) 381-6142
Fax: (434) 381-6152
Steven Nape, Dean of Enrollment Management, Sweet Briar College, PO Box 1052, Sweet Briar, VA 24595-1502

University of Management and Technology
Arlington, Virginia
www.umtweb.edu

- For-profit 4-year university
- Very large city
- 896 degree-seeking undergraduates
- 303 graduate students

General. Accredited by DETC. **Degrees:** 598 bachelor's, 139 associate awarded; master's, doctoral offered. **Location:** 0.1 miles from the District of Columbia. **Calendar:** Semester, extensive summer session. **Full-time faculty:** 44 total.

Basis for selection. Open admission, but selective for some programs.

2016-2017 Annual costs. Tuition/fees (projected): $9,450. Books/supplies: $675. Personal expenses: $450.

Application procedures. Admission: No deadline. $30 fee, may be waived for applicants with need. Application must be submitted online. Admission notification on a rolling basis. **Financial aid:** No deadline.

Academics. Special study options: Accelerated study, combined bachelor's/graduate degree, distance learning, independent study. **Credit/placement by examination:** AP, CLEP. 45 credit hours maximum toward associate degree, 90 toward bachelor's.

Majors. Business: Business admin, international, market research, marketing. **Computer sciences:** General, computer science, information systems, information technology, LAN/WAN management, networking, security, systems analysis, web page design, webmaster. **Engineering:** Software. **Health services:** Health care admin. **Protective services:** Homeland security, law enforcement admin.

Technology on campus. PC or laptop required.

Contact. E-mail: admissions@umtweb.edu
Phone: (703) 516-0035 Toll-free number: (800) 924-4883
Fax: (703) 516-0985
University of Management and Technology, 1901 Fort Myer Drive, Suite 700, Arlington, VA 22209-1609

University of Mary Washington
Fredericksburg, Virginia
www.umw.edu

CB member
CB code: 5398

- Public 4-year university
- Residential campus in small city
- 4,262 degree-seeking undergraduates: 11% part-time, 64% women, 6% African American, 4% Asian American, 8% Hispanic/Latino, 5% Multiracial, non-Hispanic, 1% international
- 291 degree-seeking graduate students
- 83% of applicants admitted
- Application essay required
- 70% graduate within 6 years; 17% enter graduate study

General. Founded in 1908. Regionally accredited. **Degrees:** 990 bachelor's awarded; master's offered. **ROTC:** Army. **Location:** 50 miles from Richmond, 50 miles from Washington, DC. **Calendar:** Continuous, limited summer session. **Full-time faculty:** 245 total; 88% have terminal degrees, 18% minority, 46% women. **Part-time faculty:** 138 total; 46% have terminal degrees, 16% minority, 49% women. **Class size:** 53% < 20, 41% 20-39, 2% 40-49, 3% 50-99, less than 1% >100. **Special facilities:** Historic preservation center, center for leadership and media studies, center for honor leadership and service, James Monroe museum and memorial library, center for Asian studies, multicultural center, Gari Melcher's home and studio at Belmont.

Freshman class profile. 5,549 applied, 4,588 admitted, 972 enrolled.

Mid 50% test scores			
SAT critical reading:	510-550	GPA 2.0-2.99:	7%
SAT math:	490-590	Rank in top quarter:	41%
SAT writing:	490-590	Rank in top tenth:	14%
ACT composite:	22-27	End year in good standing:	84%
GPA 3.75 or higher:	34%	Return as sophomores:	82%
GPA 3.50-3.74:	20%	Out-of-state:	14%
GPA 3.0-3.49:	39%	Live on campus:	89%
		International:	1%

Basis for selection. Rigor of high school program most important, followed by GPA, standardized test scores, activities, essays, recommendations.

Test optional admission consideration available to students with a 3.5 cumulative GPA on a 4.0 scale. Audition recommended for music. **Home schooled:** Transcript of courses and grades required. 3 SAT Subject Tests to demonstrate abilities in core curriculum recommended.

High school preparation. College-preparatory program required. 15 units required; 20 recommended. Required and recommended units include English 4, mathematics 3-4, social studies 2, history 1-2, science 3-4 (laboratory 3-4) and foreign language 2-4.

2015-2016 Annual costs. Tuition/fees: $10,974; $24,814 out-of-state. Room/board: $10,202. Books/supplies: $1,200. Personal expenses: $1,500.

2014-2015 Financial aid. Need-based: 665 full-time freshmen applied for aid; 367 deemed to have need; 349 received aid. Average need met was 50%. Average scholarship/grant was $2,851; average loan $3,502. 52% of total undergraduate aid awarded as scholarships/grants, 48% as loans/jobs. **Non-need-based:** Awarded to 798 full-time undergraduates, including 396 freshmen. Scholarships awarded for academics, alumni affiliation, art, leadership, music/drama, state residency.

Application procedures. Admission: Priority date 2/1; no deadline. $50 fee, may be waived for applicants with need. Admission notification by 4/1. Must reply by May 1 or within 2 week(s) if notified thereafter. **Financial aid:** Priority date 3/15, closing date 6/1. FAFSA required. Applicants notified on a rolling basis starting 3/15; must reply by 5/1 or within 2 week(s) of notification.

Academics. UMW provides grants for undergraduate research program enabling students to work individually with faculty members. **Special study options:** Accelerated study, combined bachelor's/graduate degree, distance learning, double major, honors, independent study, internships, semester at sea, student-designed major, study abroad, teacher certification program, Washington semester. **Credit/placement by examination:** AP, CLEP, IB, institutional tests. Credit from CLEP scores applicable to adult degree; limited to BA/BS degree program. **Support services:** Pre-admission summer program, study skills assistance, tutoring, writing center. Digital Knowledge Center.

Majors. Area/ethnic studies: American. **Biology:** General. **Business:** Business admin. **Computer sciences:** General. **English:** English lit. **Foreign languages:** General, classics. **Health services:** Nursing (RN). **History:** General. **Liberal arts:** Arts/sciences. **Math:** General. **Physical sciences:** Chemistry, physics. **Psychology:** General. **Social sciences:** Anthropology, economics, geography, international relations, political science, sociology. **Visual/performing arts:** General, art history/conservation, music.

Most popular majors. Biology 8%, business/marketing 15%, English 12%, liberal arts 6%, psychology 11%, social sciences 17%.

Technology on campus. 371 workstations in library, computer center, student center. Dormitories wired for high-speed internet access and linked to campus network. Commuter students can connect to campus network. Online course registration, online library, helpline, repair service, student web hosting, wireless network available.

Student life. Freshman orientation: Mandatory, $275 fee. Preregistration for classes offered. Session held in June; additional session held the 3 days before classes. **Policies:** Honor system in effect. Freshmen not permitted cars on campus. **Housing:** Guaranteed on-campus for freshmen. Coed dorms, single-sex dorms, special housing for disabled, apartments, gender-neutral housing, themed housing, wellness housing available. $250 nonrefundable deposit, deadline 5/1. Year-round housing available. **Activities:** Bands, campus ministries, choral groups, dance, drama, film society, international student organizations, literary magazine, music ensembles, Model UN, musical theater, radio station, student government, student newspaper, symphony orchestra, Baptist student union, Catholic student union, Hispanic student association, Asian student association, Young Democrats, Campus Christian Community, College Republicans, PRISM, BOND, Young Life.

Athletics. NCAA. **Intercollegiate:** Baseball M, basketball, cross-country, equestrian, field hockey W, golf, lacrosse, soccer, softball W, swimming, tennis, track and field, volleyball W. **Intramural:** Badminton, basketball, soccer. **Team name:** Eagles.

Student services. Adult student services, alcohol/substance abuse counseling, chaplain/spiritual director, career counseling, services for economically disadvantaged, student employment services, financial aid counseling, health services, minority student services, personal counseling, placement for graduates, veterans' counselor, women's services. **Physically disabled:** Services for visually, speech, hearing impaired.

Contact. E-mail: admit@umw.edu
Phone: (540) 654-2000 Toll-free number: (800) 468-5614
Fax: (540) 654-1857
Melissa Yakabouski, Director of Admissions, University of Mary Washington, 1301 College Avenue, Fredericksburg, VA 22401-5300

University of Phoenix: Northern Virginia
Reston, Virginia
www.phoenix.edu

- For-profit 4-year university
- Small city
- 790 degree-seeking undergraduates

General. Regionally accredited. **Degrees:** 92 bachelor's awarded; master's offered. **Calendar:** Differs by program. **Full-time faculty:** 15 total. **Part-time faculty:** 110 total.

Basis for selection. Open admission, but selective for some programs.

2015-2016 Annual costs. Per-credit-hour charge, $410 to $635, depending upon level and course of study. Books, material charges, and other fees vary by course and program. All fees are subject to change.

Application procedures. Admission: No deadline. No application fee. **Financial aid:** No deadline.

Academics. Credit/placement by examination: AP, CLEP.

Majors. Business: Accounting/business management, business admin, e-commerce, entrepreneurial studies, finance, human resources, marketing, operations. **Communications:** General. **Computer sciences:** General, database management, networking, programming, security, system admin, systems analysis, web page design, webmaster. **Conservation:** Environmental studies. **English:** English lit. **Health services:** Facilities admin, health information management, long term care admin, nursing (RN). **Human services:** General. **Protective services:** Disaster management, law enforcement admin, security management.

Student life. Freshman orientation: Mandatory. Preregistration for classes offered.

Contact. Toll-free number: (866) 766-0766
University of Phoenix: Northern Virginia, 11730 Plaza America Drive, Reston, VA 20190-4750

University of Phoenix: Richmond
Glen Allen, Virginia
www.phoenix.edu

- For-profit 4-year university
- Large town
- 680 degree-seeking undergraduates

General. Regionally accredited. **Degrees:** 252 bachelor's awarded; master's offered. **Calendar:** Differs by program. **Full-time faculty:** 19 total. **Part-time faculty:** 96 total.

Basis for selection. Open admission, but selective for some programs.

2015-2016 Annual costs. Per-credit-hour charge, $410 to $635, depending upon level and course of study. Books, material charges, and other fees vary by course and program. All fees are subject to change.

Application procedures. Admission: No deadline. No application fee. **Financial aid:** No deadline.

Academics. Credit/placement by examination: AP, CLEP.

Majors. Business: Accounting, accounting/business management, business admin, finance, human resources, marketing. **Computer sciences:** Database management, networking, programming, security, system admin, systems analysis, web page design, webmaster. **Health services:** Facilities admin, health information management, long term care admin. **Human services:** General. **Protective services:** Disaster management, law enforcement admin, security management.

Student life. Freshman orientation: Mandatory. Preregistration for classes offered.

Contact. Toll-free number: (866) 766-0766
University of Phoenix: Richmond, 9750 West Broad Street, Glen Allen, VA 23060-4169

University of Richmond

Richmond, Virginia   **CB member**
www.richmond.edu   **CB code: 5569**

▶ Private 4-year university and liberal arts college

▶ Residential campus in small city

▶ 2,889 degree-seeking undergraduates: 1% part-time, 52% women, 6% African American, 7% Asian American, 8% Hispanic/Latino, 4% Multiracial, non-Hispanic, 9% international

▶ 554 degree-seeking graduate students

▶ 31% of applicants admitted

▶ SAT or ACT (ACT writing optional), application essay required

▶ 88% graduate within 6 years; 19% enter graduate study

General. Founded in 1830. Regionally accredited. **Degrees:** 777 bachelor's awarded; master's, professional offered. **ROTC:** Army. **Location:** 6 miles from downtown; 90 miles from Washington, DC. **Calendar:** Semester, limited summer session. **Class size:** 69% < 20, 31% 20-39, less than 1% 50-99. **Special facilities:** Museum of art and print study center, greenhouse, electron microscope, radionuclide complex, neuroscience research laboratory, music technology laboratory, art technology laboratory, spatial analysis lab, herbarium, high field nuclear magnetic resonance spectrometer, gallery of design from nature, ancient world gallery, Virginia Baptist Historical Society museum, real-time stock trading floor, digital scholarship laboratory, culinary arts center, center for pro bono law clinic and civic engagement programs.

Freshman class profile. 9,977 applied, 3,104 admitted, 807 enrolled.

Mid 50% test scores			
SAT critical reading:	600-700	Rank in top tenth:	61%
SAT math:	620-720	Return as sophomores:	93%
SAT writing:	610-700	Out-of-state:	85%
ACT composite:	29-32	Live on campus:	99%
Rank in top quarter:	89%	International:	10%

Basis for selection. Holistic review evaluates character, service, special talents, creativity, independence, and life experience alongside traditional measures of academic success like grades, rigor of curriculum, test scores, essays and recommendations. Campus visits highly recommended. **Home schooled:** Statement describing home school structure and mission, transcript of courses and grades, interview, letter of recommendation (nonparent) required. Must submit narrative description of home schooling environment and provide results of AP tests or SAT Subject Tests in history, foreign language and natural science.

High school preparation. College-preparatory program recommended. 13 units required; 20 recommended. Required and recommended units include English 4, mathematics 3-4, history 2-4, science 2-4 (laboratory 2-4) and foreign language 2-4.

2015-2016 Annual costs. Tuition/fees: $48,090. Room/board: $11,120. Books/supplies: $1,100. Personal expenses: $1,060.

2015-2016 Financial aid. Need-based: 487 full-time freshmen applied for aid; 342 deemed to have need; 342 received aid. Average need met was 100%. Average scholarship/grant was $39,666; average loan $3,065. 90% of total undergraduate aid awarded as scholarships/grants, 10% as loans/jobs. **Non-need-based:** Awarded to 972 full-time undergraduates, including 196 freshmen. Scholarships awarded for academics, art, athletics, leadership, music/drama, ROTC.

Application procedures. Admission: Closing date 1/15 (postmark date). $50 fee, may be waived for applicants with need. Admission notification by 4/1. Must reply by May 1 or within 2 week(s) if notified thereafter. **Financial aid:** Closing date 2/15. FAFSA, CSS PROFILE required. Applicants notified by 4/1; must reply within 4 week(s) of notification.

Academics. The Richmond Guarantee: all traditional undergraduate students will receive up to $4,000 from the University for one summer research or internship experience before they graduate. **Special study options:** Combined bachelor's/graduate degree, cross-registration, double major, ESL, exchange student, honors, independent study, internships, student-designed major, study abroad, teacher certification program, Washington semester. **Credit/placement by examination:** AP, CLEP, IB, institutional tests. 7 credit hours maximum toward bachelor's degree. Maximum of 7 units of credit, including credit by examination and transfer credit, allowed toward units required for degree. **Support services:** Learning center, study skills assistance, tutoring, writing center.

Majors. Area/ethnic studies: African, American, Asian, Chinese, European, German, Italian, Latin American, Near/Middle Eastern, Russian/Slavic, women's. **Biology:** General. **Business:** Accounting, business admin. **Communications:** Journalism. **Computer sciences:** General. **Conservation:** Environmental studies. **English:** English lit, rhetoric/composition. **Foreign languages:** Ancient Greek, French, Latin, Spanish. **Health services:** Ethics. **History:** General. **Liberal arts:** Humanities. **Math:** General. **Philosophy/religion:** Philosophy, religion. **Physical sciences:** Chemistry, physics. **Protective services:** Criminal justice. **Psychology:** General. **Social sciences:** Anthropology, economics, geography, international economic development, international economics, international relations, political science, sociology. **Visual/performing arts:** Art history/conservation, dance, dramatic, film/cinema/video, music, studio arts.

Most popular majors. Biology 9%, business/marketing 36%, social sciences 14%.

Technology on campus. 1,109 workstations in dormitories, library, computer center, student center. Dormitories wired for high-speed internet access and linked to campus network. Commuter students can connect to campus network. Online course registration, online library, helpline, repair service, student web hosting, wireless network available.

Student life. Freshman orientation: Mandatory. Preregistration for classes offered. Held Wednesday-Sunday the week before classes begin. **Housing:** Guaranteed on-campus for freshmen. Coed dorms, single-sex dorms, special housing for disabled, apartments, themed housing available. $300 nonrefundable deposit, deadline 5/1. **Activities:** Bands, campus ministries, choral groups, dance, drama, film society, international student organizations, literary magazine, music ensembles, Model UN, musical theater, radio station, student government, student newspaper, symphony orchestra, Alpha Phi Omega, Amnesty International, black student alliance, global health and human rights club, Habitat for Humanity, multicultural student union, Omicron Delta Kappa, Common Ground, alliance for sexual diversity.

Athletics. NCAA. **Intercollegiate:** Baseball M, basketball, cross-country, diving W, field hockey W, football (tackle) M, golf, lacrosse, soccer W, swimming W, tennis, track and field W. **Team name:** Spiders.

Student services. Alcohol/substance abuse counseling, chaplain/spiritual director, career counseling, student employment services, financial aid counseling, health services, minority student services, personal counseling, placement for graduates, veterans' counselor, women's services. **Physically disabled:** Services for visually, speech, hearing impaired.

Contact. E-mail: admission@richmond.edu
Phone: (804) 289-8640 Toll-free number: (800) 700-1662
Fax: (804) 287-6003
Gil Villanueva, Dean of Admissions, University of Richmond, Brunet Hall: 28 Westhampton Way, Richmond, VA 23173

University of the Potomac

Herndon, Virginia
www.potomac.edu   **CB code: 2604**

▶ For-profit 4-year business college

▶ Commuter campus in large town

▶ 15 degree-seeking undergraduates

▶ Interview required

General. Degrees: 21 bachelor's, 1 associate awarded; master's offered. **Location:** 30 miles from Washington, DC. **Calendar:** Differs by program, extensive summer session. **Full-time faculty:** 4 total. **Part-time faculty:** 62 total.

Basis for selection. Open admission.

2015-2016 Annual costs. Books/supplies: $630. **Additional information:** Bachelor degree programs: $541; Associate degree programs: $541; certificates: $250. Books and supplies range depending on program level and course of study. All costs are subject to change.

Application procedures. Admission: No deadline. No application fee. Admission notification on a rolling basis. **Financial aid:** No deadline. FAFSA, institutional form required. Applicants notified on a rolling basis.

Academics. Credit earned for work related research projects. **Special study options:** Accelerated study, distance learning, independent study, internships, weekend college. **Credit/placement by examination:** AP, CLEP, institutional tests. 15 credit hours maximum toward associate degree, 30 toward bachelor's. **Support services:** Learning center, remedial instruction, tutoring.

Majors. Business: Accounting, business admin, international, management information systems, purchasing. **Computer sciences:** General, LAN/WAN management, security. **Protective services:** Computer forensics.

Most popular majors. Business/marketing 78%, computer/information sciences 22%.

Technology on campus. 16 workstations in library, computer center, student center. Online library, wireless network available.

Student life. Freshman orientation: Mandatory. Preregistration for classes offered. **Activities:** Student government.

Student services. Adult student services, financial aid counseling.

Contact. E-mail: admissions@potomac.edu
Phone: (703) 709-5875 Fax: (703) 709-8972
Niambi Green, Admissions Director, University of the Potomac, 2070 Chain Bridge Road, Vienna, VA 20170

University of Virginia
Charlottesville, Virginia
www.virginia.edu

CB member
CB code: 5820

- Public 4-year university
- Residential campus in small city
- 15,690 degree-seeking undergraduates: 3% part-time, 55% women, 6% African American, 13% Asian American, 6% Hispanic/Latino, 5% Multi-racial, non-Hispanic, 5% international
- 6,398 degree-seeking graduate students
- 30% of applicants admitted
- SAT or ACT with writing, application essay required
- 93% graduate within 6 years

General. Founded in 1819. Regionally accredited. **Degrees:** 3,836 bachelor's awarded; master's, professional, doctoral offered. **ROTC:** Army, Naval, Air Force. **Location:** 70 miles from Richmond, 120 miles from Washington, DC. **Calendar:** Semester, extensive summer session. **Full-time faculty:** 1,365 total; 91% have terminal degrees, 16% minority, 37% women. **Part-time faculty:** 100 total; 67% have terminal degrees, 8% minority, 63% women. **Class size:** 56% < 20, 24% 20-39, 6% 40-49, 8% 50-99, 6% >100. **Special facilities:** Observatory, center for biological timing, experimental farm, art museum.

Freshman class profile. 30,840 applied, 9,186 admitted, 3,685 enrolled.

Mid 50% test scores			
SAT critical reading:	620-720	**Rank in top quarter:**	97%
SAT math:	630-740	**Rank in top tenth:**	89%
SAT writing:	620-720	**End year in good standing:**	97%
ACT composite:	29-33	**Return as sophomores:**	97%
GPA 3.75 or higher:	94%	**Out-of-state:**	30%
GPA 3.50-3.74:	3%	**Live on campus:**	100%
GPA 3.0-3.49:	2%	**International:**	5%
GPA 2.0-2.99:	1%		

Basis for selection. School achievement record, class rank, test scores most important. Extracurricular activities and interests, quality of writing, recommendation also important. Special consideration for minorities, children of alumni, and in-state students. School diploma may be waived for especially qualified applicants. Following international tests accepted: International Baccalaureate, German Abitur, British AICE, French Baccalaureate, Swiss Federal Maturity Certificate. SAT Subject Tests recommended. Two SAT subject tests of the student's choosing are strongly recommended.

High school preparation. College-preparatory program required. 16 units required. Required and recommended units include English 4, mathematics 4-5, social studies 1-4, science 2-4 and foreign language 2-5. 3 units of science (1 chemistry, 1 physics) required if applying to the School of Engineering and Applied Science.

2015-2016 Annual costs. Tuition/fees: $14,468; $43,082 out-of-state. Room/board: $10,400. Books/supplies: $1,270. Personal expenses: $2,416. **Additional information:** All Commerce students both in-state and out-of-state pay an additional $5,000 Tuition Differential in 2014-15 and beyond. 1st-year Engineering students both in-state and out-of-state pay an additional $4,000 Tuition Differential in 2015-16. 2nd and 3rd year Engineering students both in-state and out-of-state pay an additional $2,000 Tuition Differential in 2015-16. 3rd and 4th year Batten school students both in-state and out-of-state pay an additional $2,500 Tuition Differential in 2015-16.

2015-2016 Financial aid. Need-based: 2,638 full-time freshmen applied for aid; 1,275 deemed to have need; 1,275 received aid. Average need met was 100%. Average scholarship/grant was $19,470; average loan $5,208. 79% of total undergraduate aid awarded as scholarships/grants, 21% as loans/jobs. **Non-need-based:** Awarded to 1,273 full-time undergraduates, including 320 freshmen. Scholarships awarded for academics, athletics, leadership, minority status, music/drama, state residency.

Application procedures. Admission: Closing date 1/1 (receipt date). $60 fee, may be waived for applicants with need. Application must be submitted online. Admission notification by 4/1. Must reply by May 1 or within 2 week(s) if notified thereafter. Deferred admission maximum postponement is one year. **Financial aid:** Priority date 3/1; no closing date. FAFSA, CSS PROFILE required. Must reply by 5/1.

Academics. Special study options: Accelerated study, combined bachelor's/graduate degree, cooperative education, double major, ESL, exchange student, honors, independent study, internships, liberal arts/career combination, student-designed major, study abroad, teacher certification program. Special January terms (during Winter Break) where students can take one course. **Credit/placement by examination:** AP, CLEP, IB, institutional tests. 60 credit hours maximum toward bachelor's degree. **Support services:** Learning center, pre-admission summer program, reduced course load, study skills assistance, tutoring, writing center.

Majors. Architecture: Architecture, history/criticism, urban/community planning. **Area/ethnic studies:** African-American, Latin American. **Biology:** General. **Business:** General. **Computer sciences:** General. **Conservation:** Environmental science. **Engineering:** General, aerospace, biomedical, chemical, civil, computer, electrical, mechanical, systems. **English:** English lit. **Foreign languages:** Classics, comparative lit, French, German, Italian, Slavic, Spanish. **Health services:** Audiology/speech pathology, health care admin, nursing (RN). **History:** General. **Human services:** Public policy. **Liberal arts:** Arts/sciences. **Math:** General. **Parks/recreation:** Exercise sciences. **Philosophy/religion:** Philosophy, religion. **Physical sciences:** Astronomy, chemistry, physics. **Psychology:** General. **Social sciences:** Anthropology, economics, international relations, political science, sociology. **Visual/performing arts:** Art, dramatic, music. **Work/family studies:** Child development.

Most popular majors. Biology 6%, business/marketing 9%, engineering/engineering technologies 14%, liberal arts 12%, psychology 6%, social sciences 17%.

Technology on campus. Dormitories wired for high-speed internet access and linked to campus network. Commuter students can connect to campus network. Online course registration, online library, helpline, repair service, student web hosting, wireless network available.

Student life. Freshman orientation: Mandatory, $210 fee. Preregistration for classes offered. Two-day program held in July; August session held for international students. **Housing:** Guaranteed on-campus for freshmen. Coed dorms, apartments, fraternity/sorority housing, themed housing available. French, German, Spanish, and Russian houses, a multi-lingual house, and three residential colleges available. **Activities:** Bands, campus ministries, choral groups, dance, drama, film society, international student organizations, literary magazine, music ensembles, Model UN, musical theater, opera, radio station, student government, student newspaper, symphony orchestra, TV station, Alpha Phi Omega (coed community service fraternity), Black Student Alliance, general clubs and religious organizations, political organizations, service fraternities and sororities, debating union.

Athletics. NCAA. **Intercollegiate:** Baseball M, basketball, cross-country, diving, field hockey W, football (tackle) M, golf, lacrosse, rowing (crew) W, soccer, softball W, swimming, tennis, track and field, volleyball W, wrestling M. **Intramural:** Badminton, basketball, football (non-tackle), golf, racquetball, soccer, softball, table tennis, tennis, ultimate frisbee, volleyball, water polo, wrestling. **Team name:** Cavaliers.

Student services. Alcohol/substance abuse counseling, career counseling, services for economically disadvantaged, student employment services, financial aid counseling, health services, legal services, minority student services, on-campus daycare, personal counseling, placement for graduates, veterans' counselor, women's services. **Physically disabled:** Services for visually, speech, hearing impaired.

Contact. E-mail: undergradadmission@virginia.edu
Phone: (434) 982-3200 Fax: (434) 924-3587
Gregory Roberts, Dean of Undergraduate Admissions, University of Virginia, Box 400160, Charlottesville, VA 22904-4160

University of Virginia's College at Wise
Wise, Virginia
www.uvawise.edu

CB member
CB code: 5124

- Public 4-year liberal arts college
- Commuter campus in small town
- 1,396 degree-seeking undergraduates: 5% part-time, 50% women, 12% African American, 1% Asian American, 2% Hispanic/Latino
- 77% of applicants admitted

◗ SAT or ACT (ACT writing recommended) required

◗ 41% graduate within 6 years

General. Founded in 1954. Regionally accredited. **Degrees:** 290 bachelor's awarded. **ROTC:** Army. **Location:** 60 miles from Bristol. **Calendar:** Semester, limited summer session. **Full-time faculty:** 103 total; 74% have terminal degrees, 13% minority, 43% women. **Part-time faculty:** 89 total; 12% have terminal degrees, 2% minority, 62% women. **Class size:** 69% < 20, 28% 20-39, 3% 40-49, less than 1% 50-99. **Special facilities:** Observatory, scanning electron microscope, oral communication center, nursing assessment stations.

Freshman class profile. 1,042 applied, 801 admitted, 295 enrolled.

Mid 50% test scores			
		Rank in top quarter:	42%
SAT critical reading:	420-530	Rank in top tenth:	31%
SAT math:	430-510	End year in good standing:	74%
SAT writing:	410-510	Return as sophomores:	72%
ACT composite:	17-22	Out-of-state:	7%
GPA 3.75 or higher:	30%	Live on campus:	72%
GPA 3.50-3.74:	15%	Fraternities:	4%
GPA 3.0-3.49:	31%	Sororities:	2%
GPA 2.0-2.99:	24%		

Basis for selection. Applications reviewed on rolling basis. Emphasis given to academic courses and grades earned in those courses. Interview required for marginal applicants.

High school preparation. 18 units required. Required units include English 4, mathematics 3, social studies 1, history 1, science 2 (laboratory 2), foreign language 2 and academic electives 5. 1 American history, 1 world history required.

2015-2016 Annual costs. Tuition/fees: $9,355; $24,957 out-of-state. Room/board: $10,256. Books/supplies: $1,300. Personal expenses: $1,410.

2014-2015 Financial aid. Need-based: 275 full-time freshmen applied for aid; 232 deemed to have need; 232 received aid. Average need met was 75%. Average scholarship/grant was $8,889; average loan $2,907. 73% of total undergraduate aid awarded as scholarships/grants, 27% as loans/jobs. **Non-need-based:** Awarded to 771 full-time undergraduates, including 187 freshmen. Scholarships awarded for academics, alumni affiliation, art, athletics, job skills, leadership, music/drama, religious affiliation, state residency.

Application procedures. Admission: Priority date 12/1; deadline 8/15 (postmark date). $25 fee, may be waived for applicants with need. Admission notification by 8/20. Admission notification on a rolling basis. Must reply by May 1 or within 2 week(s) if notified thereafter. Early action notification on a rolling basis. **Financial aid:** Closing date 4/1. FAFSA required. Applicants notified on a rolling basis starting 2/16; must reply within 4 week(s) of notification.

Academics. Special study options: Accelerated study, cooperative education, distance learning, double major, dual enrollment of high school students, honors, independent study, internships, liberal arts/career combination, student-designed major, study abroad, teacher certification program. **Credit/placement by examination:** AP, CLEP, IB, institutional tests. **Support services:** Learning center, pre-admission summer program, reduced course load, remedial instruction, study skills assistance, tutoring, writing center.

Majors. Biology: General. **Business:** Accounting, business admin, management information systems. **Communications:** Communications/speech/rhetoric. **Computer sciences:** Computer science. **Conservation:** Environmental studies. **English:** English lit. **Foreign languages:** General, French, Spanish. **Health services:** Clinical lab science, nursing (RN). **History:** General. **Human services:** General. **Liberal arts:** Arts/sciences. **Math:** General. **Physical sciences:** Chemistry. **Protective services:** Criminal justice. **Psychology:** General. **Social sciences:** Economics, political science, sociology. **Visual/performing arts:** Art, dramatic.

Most popular majors. Biology 8%, business/marketing 17%, education 16%, health sciences 6%, history 9%, psychology 11%, social sciences 12%, visual/performing arts 6%.

Technology on campus. 300 workstations in dormitories, library, computer center, student center. Dormitories wired for high-speed internet access and linked to campus network. Commuter students can connect to campus network. Online library, helpline, repair service, student web hosting, wireless network available.

Student life. Freshman orientation: Mandatory, $45 fee. Preregistration for classes offered. Held over two days for students and parents. Dormitory space available (free for students, $35 per night for parents). **Housing:** Coed dorms, single-sex dorms, special housing for disabled, apartments available. $150 deposit, deadline 5/1. **Activities:** Concert band, choral groups, dance, drama, international student organizations, literary magazine, music ensembles, musical theater, radio station, student government, student newspaper, TV station, Young Republicans, Young Democrats, multicultural alliance,

honors societies, professional organizations, student activities board, Baptist student union, Wesley Foundation.

Athletics. NCAA. **Intercollegiate:** Baseball M, basketball, cross-country, football (tackle) M, golf M, softball W, tennis, track and field, volleyball W. **Intramural:** Badminton, basketball, football (non-tackle), racquetball, soccer, softball, table tennis, tennis, volleyball, water polo. **Team name:** Cavaliers.

Student services. Alcohol/substance abuse counseling, chaplain/spiritual director, career counseling, services for economically disadvantaged, student employment services, financial aid counseling, health services, minority student services, personal counseling, placement for graduates. **Physically disabled:** Services for visually, speech, hearing impaired.

Contact. E-mail: admissions@uvawise.edu
Phone: (276) 328-0102 Toll-free number: (888) 282-9324
Fax: (276) 328-0251
Russell Necessary, Vice Chancellor of Enrollment Management,
University of Virginia's College at Wise, 1 College Avenue, Wise, VA 24293-4412

Virginia Baptist College
Fredericksburg, Virginia
www.vbc.edu   **CB code: 4230**

◗ Private 4-year Bible college affiliated with the Baptist faith

◗ Commuter campus in large city

◗ 72 degree-seeking undergraduates: 40% part-time, 36% women, 19% African American, 1% Asian American, 6% Hispanic/Latino, 1% Multi-racial, non-Hispanic, 3% international

◗ 23 degree-seeking graduate students

◗ Interview required

◗ 100% graduate within 6 years

General. Regionally accredited; also accredited by TRACS. **Degrees:** 2 bachelor's, 1 associate awarded; master's offered. **Location:** 50 miles from Washington, DC. **Calendar:** Semester, limited summer session. **Full-time faculty:** 5 total; 40% have terminal degrees, 20% women. **Part-time faculty:** 14 total; 14% have terminal degrees, 21% women. **Class size:** 98% < 20, 2% 20-39.

Freshman class profile. 11 applied, 10 admitted, 10 enrolled.

End year in good standing:	74%	Out-of-state:	38%
Return as sophomores:	50%	Live on campus:	23%

Basis for selection. Open admission. The student must agree to respect and adhere to the doctrinal statement and standard of conduct of Virginia Baptist College.

2015-2016 Annual costs. Tuition/fees: $5,540. Room only: $3,200. Books/supplies: $600. Personal expenses: $4,131.

2015-2016 Financial aid. Need-based: 5 full-time freshmen applied for aid; 5 deemed to have need; 5 received aid. Average need met was 100%. Average scholarship/grant was $3,663. **Non-need-based:** Awarded to 7 full-time undergraduates, including 3 freshmen. Scholarships awarded for academics, alumni affiliation, leadership, religious affiliation.

Application procedures. Admission: No deadline. $25 fee, may be waived for applicants with need. Application must be submitted online. **Financial aid:** No deadline. FAFSA, institutional form required. Applicants notified on a rolling basis.

Academics. Special study options: Combined bachelor's/graduate degree, distance learning, dual enrollment of high school students, internships. **Credit/placement by examination:** AP, CLEP, IB, institutional tests. Credit by examination that has been accepted or completed at another accredited institution will be accepted in most cases. **Support services:** Reduced course load, remedial instruction, study skills assistance, tutoring.

Majors. Education: Elementary, secondary.

Most popular majors. Education 33%, theological studies 67%.

Technology on campus. PC or laptop required. 2 workstations in library. Dormitories wired for high-speed internet access. Online course registration, online library, wireless network available.

Student life. Freshman orientation: Mandatory. Preregistration for classes offered. Orientation is online. Student must pass a quiz with a 70% before their orientation is considered complete. **Policies:** Students are required to sign a doctrinal statement and standard of conduct agreement each school year. Religious observance required. **Housing:** Single-sex dorms available. **Activities:** Campus ministries, choral groups, music ensembles, student government.

Student services. Adult student services, chaplain/spiritual director, career counseling, services for economically disadvantaged, financial aid counseling, personal counseling, placement for graduates.

Contact. E-mail: office@vbc.edu
Phone: (540) 785-5440
Anthony Retterer, Director of Admissions, Virginia Baptist College, 4105 Plank Road, Fredericksburg, VA 22407

Virginia Commonwealth University
Richmond, Virginia — CB member
www.vcu.edu — CB code: 5570

- Public 4-year university
- Residential campus in small city
- 22,516 degree-seeking undergraduates: 11% part-time, 58% women, 18% African American, 13% Asian American, 8% Hispanic/Latino, 5% Multi-racial, non-Hispanic, 3% international
- 6,516 degree-seeking graduate students
- 72% of applicants admitted
- 62% graduate within 6 years; 24% enter graduate study

General. Founded in 1838. Regionally accredited. **Degrees:** 5,043 bachelor's awarded; master's, professional, doctoral offered. **ROTC:** Army. **Location:** 100 miles from Washington, DC. **Calendar:** Semester, extensive summer session. **Full-time faculty:** 2,264 total; 22% minority, 44% women. **Part-time faculty:** 1,015 total; 16% minority, 51% women. **Class size:** 34% < 20, 45% 20-39, 5% 40-49, 7% 50-99, 8% >100.

Freshman class profile. 16,293 applied, 11,798 admitted, 4,090 enrolled.

Mid 50% test scores		GPA 2.0-2.99:	7%
SAT critical reading:	500-610	Rank in top quarter:	49%
SAT math:	490-590	Rank in top tenth:	19%
SAT writing:	480-590	End year in good standing:	81%
ACT composite:	21-27	Return as sophomores:	86%
GPA 3.75 or higher:	39%	Out-of-state:	11%
GPA 3.50-3.74:	20%	Live on campus:	82%
GPA 3.0-3.49:	34%	International:	3%

Basis for selection. Strength of high school transcripts, grades and test scores important. Art portfolios or auditions required for some programs. Latest date by which SAT or ACT scores must be received for fall-term admission varies. Test scores required of freshman applicants over 22. Test score optional for all freshman who meet specifc criteria.

High school preparation. College-preparatory program recommended. 20 units required; 24 recommended. Required and recommended units include English 4, mathematics 3-4, social studies 1, history 2-3, science 3-4 (laboratory 1), foreign language 2-3 and visual/performing arts 1.

2015-2016 Annual costs. Tuition/fees: $12,772; $30,838 out-of-state. Room/board: $9,586.

2014-2015 Financial aid. Need-based: 3,111 full-time freshmen applied for aid; 2,459 deemed to have need; 2,220 received aid. Average need met was 52%. Average scholarship/grant was $7,771; average loan $3,351. 42% of total undergraduate aid awarded as scholarships/grants, 58% as loans/jobs. **Non-need-based:** Awarded to 4,132 full-time undergraduates, including 1,003 freshmen. Scholarships awarded for academics, alumni affiliation, art, athletics, leadership, music/drama.

Application procedures. Admission: $50 fee, may be waived for applicants with need. Admission notification on a rolling basis beginning on or about 11/15. Must reply by May 1 or within 2 week(s) if notified thereafter. **Financial aid:** Priority date 3/1; no closing date. FAFSA required. Applicants notified on a rolling basis starting 4/1; must reply within 2 week(s) of notification.

Academics. Special study options: Accelerated study, cooperative education, distance learning, double major, dual enrollment of high school students, ESL, honors, independent study, internships, student-designed major, study abroad, teacher certification program. **Credit/placement by examination:** AP, CLEP, IB, institutional tests. **Support services:** Learning center, reduced course load, study skills assistance, tutoring, writing center.

Majors. Area/ethnic studies: African-American, women's. **Biology:** General, bioinformatics. **Business:** General, accounting, managerial economics,

marketing, real estate. **Communications:** Media studies. **Computer sciences:** General, information systems. **Conservation:** Environmental studies. **Education:** Art, health. **Engineering:** Biomedical, chemical, computer, electrical, mechanical. **English:** English lit. **Foreign languages:** General. **Health services:** Clinical lab science, dental hygiene, nursing (RN), radiologic technology/medical imaging. **History:** General. **Human services:** Social work. **Math:** General. **Parks/recreation:** General. **Philosophy/religion:** Philosophy, religion. **Physical sciences:** Chemistry, physics. **Protective services:** Forensics, homeland security, law enforcement admin. **Psychology:** General. **Social sciences:** Anthropology, political science, sociology, urban studies. **Visual/performing arts:** Art history/conservation, cinematography, crafts, dance, dramatic, fashion design, graphic design, illustration, interior design, music performance, painting, photography, sculpture.

Most popular majors. Biology 8%, business/marketing 13%, health sciences 7%, psychology 10%, security/protective services 7%, visual/performing arts 13%.

Technology on campus. PC or laptop required. 1,500 workstations in dormitories, library, computer center, student center. Dormitories wired for high-speed internet access and linked to campus network. Commuter students can connect to campus network. Online course registration, online library, helpline, repair service, student web hosting, wireless network available.

Student life. Freshman orientation: Mandatory, $45 fee. Preregistration for classes offered. Two-day program. **Housing:** Guaranteed on-campus for freshmen. Coed dorms, special housing for disabled, apartments, themed housing, wellness housing available. $250 nonrefundable deposit, deadline 6/30. **Activities:** Bands, campus ministries, choral groups, dance, drama, film society, international student organizations, literary magazine, music ensembles, Model UN, musical theater, opera, radio station, student government, student newspaper, symphony orchestra, Christian Student Fellowship, Nation to Nation, Virginia 21, African student union, Japanese club, Latino student association, Baking a Cure, camping club, Music Alliance, Green Unity.

Athletics. NCAA. **Intercollegiate:** Baseball M, basketball, cross-country, field hockey W, golf M, lacrosse W, soccer, tennis, track and field, volleyball W. **Intramural:** Badminton, basketball, football (non-tackle), handball, ice hockey, lacrosse, racquetball, soccer, softball, table tennis, tennis, ultimate frisbee, volleyball, water polo. **Team name:** Rams.

Student services. Adult student services, alcohol/substance abuse counseling, career counseling, student employment services, financial aid counseling, health services, minority student services, on-campus daycare, personal counseling, placement for graduates, veterans' counselor, women's services. **Physically disabled:** Services for visually, speech, hearing impaired.

Contact. E-mail: ugrad@vcu.edu
Phone: (804) 828-1222 Toll-free number: (800) 841-3638
Fax: (804) 828-1899
Sybil Halloran, Assistant Vice Provost Student Recruitment and Admissions, Virginia Commonwealth University, Box 842526, Richmond, VA 23284-2526

Virginia Military Institute
Lexington, Virginia — CB member
www.vmi.edu — CB code: 5858

- Public 4-year liberal arts and military college
- Residential campus in small town
- 1,717 degree-seeking undergraduates: 11% women, 6% African American, 4% Asian American, 5% Hispanic/Latino, 1% Native American, 1% Native Hawaiian/Pacific islander, 2% Multi-racial, non-Hispanic, 2% international
- 53% of applicants admitted
- SAT or ACT (ACT writing optional) required
- 74% graduate within 6 years

General. Founded in 1839. Regionally accredited. Mandatory ROTC classes and optional commissioning in the Army, Air Force, Navy, or Marines. **Degrees:** 375 bachelor's awarded. **ROTC:** Army, Naval, Air Force. **Location:** 55 miles from Roanoke, 140 miles from Richmond. **Calendar:** Semester, limited summer session. **Full-time faculty:** 133 total; 98% have terminal degrees, 13% minority, 30% women. **Part-time faculty:** 64 total; 42% have terminal degrees, 6% minority, 30% women. **Class size:** 66% < 20, 34% 20-39, less than 1% 50-99. **Special facilities:** Historical museums, research library, observatory, particle accelerator.

Freshman class profile. 1,779 applied, 940 admitted, 453 enrolled.

Mid 50% test scores			
		GPA 2.0-2.99:	7%
SAT critical reading:	520-620	Rank in top quarter:	46%
SAT math:	520-610	Rank in top tenth:	17%
ACT composite:	23-27	Return as sophomores:	92%
GPA 3.75 or higher:	38%	Out-of-state:	38%
GPA 3.50-3.74:	23%	Live on campus:	100%
GPA 3.0-3.49:	32%	International:	1%

Basis for selection. GED not accepted. Admissions based on secondary school record, class rank, standardized test scores, character, and personal qualities. Interview, extracurricular activities, state residency, minority status, and volunteer work also important. **Home schooled:** Require transcript with list of texts used or group affiliation.

High school preparation. College-preparatory program required. 16 units required; 19 recommended. Required and recommended units include English 4, mathematics 3-4, social studies 2, history 1, science 3-4 (laboratory 3-4) and foreign language 3-4.

2015-2016 Annual costs. Tuition/fees: $16,536; $39,550 out-of-state. Room/board: $8,666. Books/supplies: $1,000. Personal expenses: $1,750.

2014-2015 Financial aid. **Need-based:** 372 full-time freshmen applied for aid; 265 deemed to have need; 260 received aid. Average need met was 85%. Average scholarship/grant was $15,054; average loan $3,672. 78% of total undergraduate aid awarded as scholarships/grants, 22% as loans/jobs. **Non-need-based:** Awarded to 768 full-time undergraduates, including 177 freshmen. Scholarships awarded for academics, alumni affiliation, athletics, leadership, music/drama, ROTC, state residency.

Application procedures. Admission: Closing date 2/1 (postmark date). $40 fee, may be waived for applicants with need. Admission notification on a rolling basis beginning on or about 1/1. Must reply by May 1 or within 2 week(s) if notified thereafter. **Financial aid:** Priority date 3/1, closing date 3/1. FAFSA, institutional form required. Applicants notified on a rolling basis starting 4/1; must reply by 5/1.

Academics. Special study options: Cross-registration, double major, honors, independent study, internships, study abroad, teacher certification program. Summer Transition program: Optional for incoming freshmen. **Credit/placement by examination:** AP, CLEP, IB, institutional tests. No policy, but it is unlikely any student would receive more than 36 hours credit. **Support services:** Learning center, pre-admission summer program, study skills assistance, tutoring, writing center.

Majors. Biology: General. **Computer sciences:** Computer science. **Engineering:** Civil, electrical, mechanical. **English:** English lit. **Foreign languages:** General. **History:** General. **Math:** General. **Physical sciences:** Chemistry, physics. **Psychology:** General. **Social sciences:** Economics, international relations, political science.

Most popular majors. Biology 11%, engineering/engineering technologies 24%, history 11%, psychology 12%, social sciences 27%.

Technology on campus. PC or laptop required. 200 workstations in dormitories, library, computer center. Dormitories wired for high-speed internet access and linked to campus network. Online course registration, online library, helpline, repair service, wireless network available.

Student life. Freshman orientation: Mandatory. Preregistration for classes offered. Held 8 days before beginning of fall classes. Optional month-long summer orientation program coincides with summer academic session, and participants can complete 1 freshman course. **Policies:** Student-run honor system integral part of institution. Freshmen not permitted cars on campus. **Housing:** Guaranteed on-campus for all undergraduates. Barracks houses 3-5 students per room. **Activities:** Bands, campus ministries, choral groups, dance, drama, international student organizations, literary magazine, music ensembles, musical theater, student government, student newspaper, more than 50 clubs and student organizations available.

Athletics. NCAA. **Intercollegiate:** Baseball M, basketball M, cross-country, diving M, football (tackle) M, lacrosse M, rifle, soccer, swimming, tennis M, track and field, wrestling M. **Intramural:** Basketball, football (non-tackle), soccer, softball. **Team name:** Keydets.

Student services. Alcohol/substance abuse counseling, chaplain/spiritual director, career counseling, student employment services, financial aid counseling, health services, personal counseling, placement for graduates.

Contact. E-mail: admissions@vmi.edu
Phone: (540) 464-7211 Toll-free number: (800) 767-4207
Fax: (540) 464-7746
Col. Vernon Beitzel, Director of Admissions, Virginia Military Institute, VMI Office of Admissions, Lexington, VA 24450-9967

Virginia Polytechnic Institute and State University

Blacksburg, Virginia CB member
www.vt.edu CB code: 5859

◗ Public 4-year university
◗ Residential campus in large town
◗ 25,327 degree-seeking undergraduates: 2% part-time, 43% women, 4% African American, 9% Asian American, 5% Hispanic/Latino, 4% Multiracial, non-Hispanic, 6% international
◗ 7,279 degree-seeking graduate students
◗ 73% of applicants admitted
◗ SAT or ACT (ACT writing optional) required
◗ 83% graduate within 6 years

General. Founded in 1872. Regionally accredited. Option of enrolling as member of cadet corps with either a civilian track or an ROTC track. **Degrees:** 5,890 bachelor's, 49 associate awarded; master's, professional, doctoral offered. **ROTC:** Army, Naval, Air Force. **Location:** 38 miles from Roanoke. **Calendar:** Semester, limited summer session. **Full-time faculty:** 1,731 total; 90% have terminal degrees, 18% minority, 33% women. **Part-time faculty:** 235 total; 47% have terminal degrees, 12% minority, 42% women. **Class size:** 28% < 20, 43% 20-39, 9% 40-49, 13% 50-99, 7% >100. **Special facilities:** Natural history, geology and art museums, observatory, wind tunnel, black cultural center, digital music center, robotics laboratory, multimedia laboratory, media center, women's center, math emporium, experimental theater, advanced communications/information technology center, teaching forest.

Freshman class profile. 22,280 applied, 16,355 admitted, 6,324 enrolled.

Mid 50% test scores			
		GPA 2.0-2.99:	1%
SAT critical reading:	540-640	Rank in top quarter:	80%
SAT math:	560-680	Rank in top tenth:	39%
SAT writing:	530-630	Return as sophomores:	94%
GPA 3.75 or higher:	77%	Out-of-state:	28%
GPA 3.50-3.74:	15%	Live on campus:	99%
GPA 3.0-3.49:	7%	International:	7%

Basis for selection. High school course work, grades, and test scores are considered most important. Prospective students encouraged to pursue rigorous preparatory course of study through senior year. Audition required for music. **Home schooled:** Transcript of courses and grades required. Must submit standardized test scores.

High school preparation. 18 units required. Required and recommended units include English 4, mathematics 3-4, social studies 1, history 1, science 2-3 (laboratory 2), foreign language 3 and academic electives 4. Preference given to applicants with math beyond algebra II. 4 math units required for general engineering, biochemistry, chemistry, computer science, math, physics and statistics. 3 units of science including physics required for engineering and recommended for all science-related majors.

2015-2016 Annual costs. Tuition/fees: $12,485; $28,525 out-of-state. Room/board: $8,266. Books/supplies: $1,130. Personal expenses: $1,310. **Additional information:** Out-of-state students pay an additional $604 for Capital & Equipment Fee (o-o-s student fees $2593).

2014-2015 Financial aid. **Need-based:** 4,232 full-time freshmen applied for aid; 2,418 deemed to have need; 2,121 received aid. Average need met was 64%. Average scholarship/grant was $7,469; average loan $4,078. 50% of total undergraduate aid awarded as scholarships/grants, 50% as loans/jobs. **Non-need-based:** Awarded to 6,589 full-time undergraduates, including 1,721 freshmen. Scholarships awarded for academics, art, athletics, leadership, minority status, music/drama, ROTC, state residency.

Application procedures. Admission: Closing date 1/15 (postmark date). $60 fee, may be waived for applicants with need. Admission notification by 4/1. Must reply by 5/1. $400 deposit required at time of admissions acceptance; refund request must be mailed to Office of Undergraduate Admissions, postmarked by 5/1. **Financial aid:** Closing date 3/1. FAFSA required. Applicants notified by 4/1; must reply by 5/1 or within 4 week(s) of notification.

Academics. Special study options: Accelerated study, combined bachelor's/graduate degree, cooperative education, distance learning, double major, ESL, honors, independent study, internships, liberal arts/career combination, semester at sea, study abroad, teacher certification program, Washington semester. **Credit/placement by examination:** AP, CLEP, IB, institutional tests. 12 credit hours maximum toward bachelor's degree. **Support services:** Learning center, study skills assistance, tutoring, writing center. Extensive array of services and programs designed to facilitate the academic achievement of all undergraduate students through The Student Success Center and other academic support unites on campus. Additional learning assistance and academic enrichment initiatives are implemented through the colleges and various academic departments.

Honors college/program. 1350 SAT math and critical reading, 3.7 unweighted GPA, application, letters of recommendation, and personal statement required.

Majors. Architecture: Architecture, landscape. **Biology:** General, biochemistry, computational, microbiology, neuroscience. **Business:** Accounting, business admin, construction management, finance, hospitality admin, management science, managerial economics, marketing, real estate. **Communications:** Communications/speech/rhetoric. **Computer sciences:** General. **Conservation:** Environmental science, environmental studies, forestry. **Engineering:** Aerospace, agricultural, chemical, civil, computer, construction, electrical, engineering mechanics, industrial, materials, mechanical, mining. **English:** English lit. **Foreign languages:** General. **History:** General. **Human services:** Public policy. **Math:** General, computational/applied, statistics. **Philosophy/religion:** Philosophy. **Physical sciences:** Chemistry, geology, meteorology, physics. **Psychology:** General. **Social sciences:** Applied economics, economics, geography, international relations, political science, sociology. **Visual/performing arts:** Art, dramatic, industrial design, interior design, music. **Work/family studies:** Business, family studies, food/nutrition.

Most popular majors. Biology 8%, business/marketing 19%, engineering/ engineering technologies 25%, family/consumer sciences 9%, social sciences 8%.

Technology on campus. PC or laptop required. 947 workstations in dormitories, library. Dormitories wired for high-speed internet access and linked to campus network. Commuter students can connect to campus network. Online course registration, online library, helpline, repair service, student web hosting, wireless network available.

Student life. Freshman orientation: Available, $175 fee. Preregistration for classes offered. Held over three days. **Policies:** Freshmen required to live on campus, unless living with parents or close relatives, married, veteran, or at least 21 years old. Honor system enforced. **Housing:** Guaranteed on-campus for freshmen. Coed dorms, single-sex dorms, special housing for disabled, fraternity/sorority housing, themed housing, wellness housing available. Cadets live in cadet residence halls. **Activities:** Bands, campus ministries, choral groups, dance, drama, international student organizations, literary magazine, music ensembles, musical theater, radio station, student government, student newspaper, over 600 clubs and organizations available.

Athletics. NCAA. **Intercollegiate:** Baseball M, basketball, cheerleading, cross-country, diving, football (tackle) M, golf, lacrosse W, soccer, softball W, swimming, tennis, track and field, volleyball W, wrestling M. **Intramural:** Basketball, bowling, football (non-tackle), racquetball, soccer, softball, swimming, table tennis, tennis, ultimate frisbee, volleyball. **Team name:** Hokies.

Student services. Alcohol/substance abuse counseling, chaplain/spiritual director, career counseling, student employment services, financial aid counseling, health services, legal services, minority student services, personal counseling, placement for graduates, veterans' counselor, women's services. **Physically disabled:** Services for visually, hearing impaired.

Contact. E-mail: admissions@vt.edu
Phone: (540) 231-6267 Fax: (540) 231-3242
Mildred Johnson, Associate Vice Provost for Enrollment Management and Director of Undergraduate Admissions, Virginia Polytechnic Institute and State University, 925 Prices Fork Road, Blacksburg, VA 24061-0202

Virginia State University
Petersburg, Virginia — CB member
www.vsu.edu — CB code: 5860

- Public 4-year university
- Residential campus in large town
- 4,176 degree-seeking undergraduates
- 77% of applicants admitted
- SAT or ACT (ACT writing optional) required

General. Founded in 1882. Regionally accredited. **Degrees:** 817 bachelor's, 3 associate awarded; master's, doctoral offered. **ROTC:** Army. **Location:** 25 miles from Richmond. **Calendar:** Semester, limited summer session. **Full-time faculty:** 296 total; 42% women. **Part-time faculty:** 150 total; 54% women.

Freshman class profile. 6,650 applied, 5,119 admitted, 790 enrolled.

Mid 50% test scores			
SAT critical reading:	390-480	GPA 3.0-3.49:	26%
SAT math:	380-460	GPA 2.0-2.99:	64%
SAT writing:	370-450	Rank in top quarter:	17%
ACT composite:	15-21	Rank in top tenth:	3%
GPA 3.75 or higher:	4%	Out-of-state:	38%
GPA 3.50-3.74:	6%	Live on campus:	94%

Basis for selection. School achievement record most important; recommendation required. Essay recommended for all; audition required for music; portfolio recommended for art.

High school preparation. College-preparatory program recommended. 11 units required. Required and recommended units include English 4, mathematics 3, history 2, science 2 (laboratory 1) and foreign language 2. Math requirement must include algebra I.

2015-2016 Annual costs. Tuition/fees: $8,226; $17,760 out-of-state. Room/board: $10,252. Books/supplies: $1,300. Personal expenses: $825.

Financial aid. Non-need-based: Scholarships awarded for academics, alumni affiliation, art, athletics, job skills, leadership, minority status, music/ drama, religious affiliation, ROTC. **Additional information:** Strongly recommend that students apply for scholarship assistance through federal, state, local and private agencies.

Application procedures. Admission: Priority date 3/31; deadline 5/1 (postmark date). $25 fee, may be waived for applicants with need. Admission notification on a rolling basis. Must reply by May 1 or within 2 week(s) if notified thereafter. **Financial aid:** Priority date 3/31, closing date 5/1. FAFSA, institutional form required. Applicants notified on a rolling basis starting 3/1; must reply within 2 week(s) of notification.

Academics. Special study options: Cooperative education, double major, dual enrollment of high school students, honors, independent study, internships, study abroad, teacher certification program. **Credit/placement by examination:** AP, CLEP, institutional tests. 12 credit hours maximum toward bachelor's degree. **Support services:** Study skills assistance, tutoring, writing center.

Majors. Biology: General. **Business:** Accounting, business admin, hospitality admin, management information systems, managerial economics, marketing. **Communications:** Media studies. **Computer sciences:** Computer science. **Education:** Business, physical. **Engineering:** Computer, manufacturing. **English:** English lit. **History:** General. **Human services:** General, social work. **Liberal arts:** Arts/sciences. **Math:** General. **Physical sciences:** Chemistry, physics. **Protective services:** Criminal justice. **Psychology:** General. **Social sciences:** Political science, sociology. **Visual/performing arts:** General, music performance. **Work/family studies:** Communication.

Most popular majors. Business/marketing 16%, communications/journalism 11%, education 12%, engineering/engineering technologies 7%, psychology 8%, security/protective services 11%.

Technology on campus. 1,600 workstations in dormitories, library, student center. Dormitories wired for high-speed internet access and linked to campus network. Commuter students can connect to campus network. Online course registration, online library, helpline, repair service, wireless network available.

Student life. Freshman orientation: Mandatory, $75 fee. Preregistration for classes offered. Two-day program held various times in summer. **Housing:** Guaranteed on-campus for freshmen. Coed dorms, single-sex dorms, apartments available. $300 fully refundable deposit. **Activities:** Bands, campus ministries, choral groups, dance, drama, music ensembles, radio station, student government, student newspaper, TV station, NAACP, Black Students Against Drugs, Muslim student organization, peer mediators, Betterment of Brothers and Sisters, Caribbean students association, Institute for Leadership Development.

Athletics. NCAA. **Intercollegiate:** Baseball M, basketball, bowling W, cheerleading, cross-country, football (tackle) M, golf, softball W, tennis, track and field, volleyball W. **Intramural:** Basketball, football (tackle) M, swimming, table tennis, tennis, track and field, volleyball W. **Team name:** Trojans.

Student services. Alcohol/substance abuse counseling, chaplain/spiritual director, career counseling, services for economically disadvantaged, student employment services, financial aid counseling, health services, personal counseling, placement for graduates, veterans' counselor. **Physically disabled:** Services for visually, speech, hearing impaired.

Contact. E-mail: admiss@vsu.edu
Phone: (804) 524-5902 Toll-free number: (800) 871-7611
Fax: (804) 524-5055
Irene Logan, Director of Admissions, Virginia State University, 1 Hayden Drive, Petersburg, VA 23806

Virginia Union University
Richmond, Virginia
www.vuu.edu

CB member
CB code: 5862

- Private 4-year university and liberal arts college affiliated with the Baptist faith
- Residential campus in small city
- 1,441 degree-seeking undergraduates: 2% part-time, 57% women
- 427 degree-seeking graduate students
- 49% of applicants admitted
- SAT or ACT (ACT writing recommended) required

General. Founded in 1865. Regionally accredited. **Degrees:** 207 bachelor's awarded; master's, professional offered. **ROTC:** Army. **Location:** 90 miles from Norfolk, 100 miles from Washington, DC. **Calendar:** Semester, limited summer session. **Full-time faculty:** 75 total; 65% have terminal degrees, 72% minority, 61% women. **Part-time faculty:** 63 total; 70% minority, 46% women. **Class size:** 23% < 20, 27% 20-39, less than 1% 50-99, 50% >100. **Special facilities:** Police academy, learning resource center.

Freshman class profile. 7,337 applied, 3,598 admitted, 456 enrolled.

Mid 50% test scores		GPA 2.0-2.99:	73%
SAT critical reading:	340-430	Rank in top quarter:	15%
SAT math:	340-430	Rank in top tenth:	7%
ACT composite:	14-18	End year in good standing:	72%
GPA 3.75 or higher:	3%	Return as sophomores:	60%
GPA 3.50-3.74:	3%	Out-of-state:	44%
GPA 3.0-3.49:	20%	Live on campus:	90%

Basis for selection. Secondary school record, test scores, extracurricular activities most important. Essay, interview, and talent or ability also important. Essay recommended for all. Interview recommended for academically weak. Audition required for band, choir, music, university players. **Home schooled:** Transcript of courses and grades, state high school equivalency certificate required.

High school preparation. College-preparatory program recommended. 16 units required. Required units include English 4, mathematics 3, social studies 2, science 2, foreign language 2 and academic electives 3.

2015-2016 Annual costs. Tuition/fees: $15,746. Room/board: $8,074. Books/supplies: $1,500. Personal expenses: $1,865.

2015-2016 Financial aid. Need-based: 447 full-time freshmen applied for aid; 430 deemed to have need; 430 received aid. Average need met was 51%. Average scholarship/grant was $10,168; average loan $3,219. 54% of total undergraduate aid awarded as scholarships/grants, 46% as loans/jobs. **Non-need-based:** Awarded to 103 full-time undergraduates, including 37 freshmen. Scholarships awarded for academics, athletics, ROTC, state residency.

Application procedures. Admission: Priority date 6/1; deadline 6/30 (receipt date). $25 fee, may be waived for applicants with need. Admission notification on a rolling basis beginning on or about 9/1. **Financial aid:** Priority date 4/27; no closing date. FAFSA required. Applicants notified on a rolling basis starting 5/1; must reply within 2 week(s) of notification.

Academics. Special study options: Cooperative education, double major, dual enrollment of high school students, honors, independent study, internships, liberal arts/career combination, study abroad, teacher certification program, weekend college. **Credit/placement by examination:** AP, CLEP, IB, institutional tests. 18 credit hours maximum toward bachelor's degree. **Support services:** Learning center, reduced course load, remedial instruction, tutoring, writing center.

Majors. Biology: General. **Business:** Accounting, business admin, finance, human resources, management information systems, sales/distribution. **Communications:** Journalism, media studies. **Computer sciences:** General. **Education:** Biology, business, chemistry, English, history, mathematics, multilevel teacher, music, special ed. **English:** English lit. **History:** General. **Human services:** General, social work. **Math:** General. **Philosophy/religion:** Religion. **Physical sciences:** Chemistry. **Psychology:** General. **Social sciences:** Criminology, political science. **Visual/performing arts:** Art, dramatic, music performance, music theory/composition, studio arts.

Most popular majors. Biology 12%, business/marketing 20%, communications/journalism 6%, computer/information sciences 8%, psychology 11%, public administration/social services 6%, social sciences 22%.

Technology on campus. PC or laptop required. 300 workstations in library, computer center. Dormitories linked to campus network. Online course registration, wireless network available.

Student life. Freshman orientation: Mandatory, $200 fee. Preregistration for classes offered. **Housing:** Coed dorms, single-sex dorms available. $250 deposit, deadline 7/1. **Activities:** Bands, campus ministries, choral groups, dance, drama, music ensembles, musical theater, opera, student government, student newspaper, Honda Campus All-Star Challenge Team, psychology club, pre-alumni council, NAACP, pre-law society, Alpha Kappa Mu honor society, Psi Chi National Honor Society, Alpha Omega Christian Society, Panthers Claw pep club.

Athletics. NCAA. **Intercollegiate:** Basketball, bowling W, cheerleading, cross-country, football (tackle) M, golf, softball W, tennis, track and field, volleyball W. **Intramural:** Basketball, football (non-tackle) M, softball. **Team name:** Panthers.

Student services. Career counseling, student employment services, health services, personal counseling, placement for graduates.

Contact. E-mail: enrollmentmanagement@vuu.edu
Phone: (804) 342-3571 Toll-free number: (800) 368-3227
Fax: (804) 342-3511
Kristie White, Director of Enrollment Management, Virginia Union University, 1500 North Lombardy Street, Richmond, VA 23220

Virginia University of Lynchburg
Lynchburg, Virginia
www.vul.edu

- Private 4-year liberal arts and seminary college
- Commuter campus in small city
- 470 undergraduates

General. Regionally accredited; also accredited by TRACS. **Degrees:** 26 bachelor's, 45 associate awarded; master's, doctoral offered. **Location:** 63 miles from Charlottesville. **Calendar:** Semester, limited summer session. **Full-time faculty:** 14 total.

Basis for selection. Open admission. **Home schooled:** Transcript of courses and grades, state high school equivalency certificate required.

2015-2016 Annual costs. Tuition/fees: $7,880. Room/board: $8,520. Books/supplies: $700.

Application procedures. Admission: No deadline. $25 fee, may be waived for applicants with need. Application must be submitted on paper. Admission notification on a rolling basis. **Financial aid:** No deadline.

Academics. Special study options: Distance learning, external degree. **Credit/placement by examination:** AP, CLEP, IB, institutional tests. **Support services:** Learning center, reduced course load, remedial instruction, study skills assistance, tutoring, writing center.

Majors. Business: Business admin, management science. **Philosophy/religion:** Religion. **Social sciences:** Sociology.

Technology on campus. 10 workstations in library, computer center. Dormitories wired for high-speed internet access and linked to campus network. Commuter students can connect to campus network. Online course registration, online library, helpline, wireless network available.

Student life. Freshman orientation: Mandatory. Preregistration for classes offered. **Housing:** Coed dorms available. $100 partly refundable deposit. **Activities:** Campus ministries, choral groups, student government.

Athletics. USCAA. **Intramural:** Basketball, football (tackle), track and field. **Team name:** Dragons.

Student services. Adult student services, chaplain/spiritual director, career counseling, financial aid counseling, health services, personal counseling, veterans' counselor.

Contact. E-mail: yburns@vul.edu
Phone: (434) 528-5276 ext. 1150 Fax: (434) 528-4257
Yolanda Burns, Director of Admissions, Virginia University of Lynchburg, 2058 Garfield Avenue, Lynchburg, VA 24501-6417

Virginia Wesleyan College
Norfolk, Virginia
www.vwc.edu

CB member
CB code: 5867

- Private 4-year liberal arts college affiliated with the United Methodist Church
- Residential campus in large city

◗ 1,410 degree-seeking undergraduates: 6% part-time, 64% women, 24% African American, 1% Asian American, 8% Hispanic/Latino, 1% Native American, 5% Multi-racial, non-Hispanic, 1% international

◗ 93% of applicants admitted

◗ Application essay required

◗ 47% graduate within 6 years

General. Founded in 1961. Regionally accredited. **Degrees:** 314 bachelor's awarded. **ROTC:** Army. **Location:** 8 miles from downtown Norfolk. **Calendar:** 4-1-4, limited summer session. **Full-time faculty:** 92 total; 92% have terminal degrees, 11% minority, 47% women. **Part-time faculty:** 37 total; 22% have terminal degrees, 16% minority, 43% women. **Class size:** 82% < 20, 18% 20-39. **Special facilities:** Research vessel, Center for Sacred Music, greenhouse, Center for the Study of Religious Freedom.

Freshman class profile. 1,850 applied, 1,712 admitted, 349 enrolled.

Mid 50% test scores		GPA 2.0-2.99:	29%
SAT critical reading:	430-550	Rank in top quarter:	33%
SAT math:	430-540	Rank in top tenth:	13%
SAT writing:	410-540	Return as sophomores:	65%
GPA 3.75 or higher:	21%	Out-of-state:	27%
GPA 3.50-3.74:	16%	International:	1%
GPA 3.0-3.49:	34%		

Basis for selection. Above average grades in solid college-preparatory curriculum, SAT scores, campus interview, personal statement, extracurricular activities important. Test optional admission to prospective freshmen who present a 3.25 GPA on a 4.0 scale and who have taken a strong, college preparatory curriculum in high school. **Home schooled:** Transcript of courses and grades required. **Learning Disabled:** Interview with student disabilities coordinator, appropriate documentation dated within past 3-5 years.

High school preparation. College-preparatory program recommended. 12 units required; 16 recommended. Required and recommended units include English 4, mathematics 3, history 1, science 2 (laboratory 2), foreign language 2, computer science 1 and academic electives 4.

2015-2016 Annual costs. Tuition/fees: $34,428. Room/board: $8,680. Books/supplies: $1,000. Personal expenses: $1,500.

2014-2015 Financial aid. Need-based: 406 full-time freshmen applied for aid; 368 deemed to have need; 368 received aid. Average need met was 71%. Average scholarship/grant was $21,369; average loan $6,356. 76% of total undergraduate aid awarded as scholarships/grants, 24% as loans/jobs. **Non-need-based:** Awarded to 465 full-time undergraduates, including 81 freshmen. Scholarships awarded for academics, alumni affiliation, leadership, religious affiliation, ROTC, state residency.

Application procedures. Admission: Priority date 3/1; no deadline., may be waived for applicants with need. No application fee. Admission notification on a rolling basis beginning on or about 9/15. Must reply by May 1 or within 2 week(s) if notified thereafter. **Financial aid:** Priority date 3/1; no closing date. FAFSA required. Applicants notified on a rolling basis starting 2/15; must reply by 5/1 or within 2 week(s) of notification.

Academics. Special study options: Combined bachelor's/graduate degree, cross-registration, double major, honors, independent study, internships, liberal arts/career combination, student-designed major, study abroad, teacher certification program. Alternative teacher certification program; living and learning communities; distance learning/hybrid courses offerings. **Credit/placement by examination:** AP, CLEP, IB, institutional tests. 32 credit hours maximum toward bachelor's degree. **Support services:** Learning center, reduced course load, remedial instruction, study skills assistance, tutoring, writing center.

Majors. Area/ethnic studies: Women's. **Biology:** General. **Business:** Business admin. **Communications:** Communications/speech/rhetoric. **Computer sciences:** Computer science. **Conservation:** Environmental studies. **Education:** General, art, elementary, learning disabled, middle, secondary. **English:** English lit. **Foreign languages:** General, French, German, Spanish. **Health services:** Predental, premedicine, prepharmacy, preveterinary. **History:** General. **Human services:** Social work. **Math:** General. **Parks/recreation:** General. **Philosophy/religion:** Philosophy, religion. **Physical sciences:** Chemistry. **Protective services:** Criminal justice. **Psychology:** General. **Social sciences:** General, international relations, political science, sociology. **Visual/performing arts:** Art, dramatic, music, theater history.

Most popular majors. Biology 8%, business/marketing 15%, communications/journalism 6%, education 6%, interdisciplinary studies 8%, parks/recreation 6%, psychology 8%, security/protective services 12%, social sciences 9%.

Technology on campus. 150 workstations in library, computer center, student center. Dormitories wired for high-speed internet access and linked to campus network. Online course registration, online library, helpline, repair service, student web hosting, wireless network available.

Student life. Freshman orientation: Mandatory. Preregistration for classes offered. One-day event scheduled twice during the months of June and July; multi-day academic-related orientation in August. **Policies:** Virginia State Alcohol and Drug Laws enforced. **Housing:** Guaranteed on-campus for freshmen. Coed dorms, single-sex dorms, special housing for disabled, apartments, fraternity/sorority housing, themed housing, wellness housing available. **Activities:** Campus ministries, choral groups, dance, drama, international student organizations, literary magazine, music ensembles, Model UN, musical theater, radio station, student government, student newspaper, political science association, Habitat for Humanity, black student union, Holy Fire, Honors & Scholars, Campus Kaleidoscope, SALSA, activities council.

Athletics. NCAA. **Intercollegiate:** Baseball M, basketball, cheerleading, cross-country, field hockey W, golf M, lacrosse, soccer, softball W, tennis, track and field, volleyball W. **Intramural:** Basketball, field hockey W, football (non-tackle), racquetball, soccer, swimming, table tennis, ultimate frisbee, volleyball, weight lifting. **Team name:** Marlins.

Student services. Adult student services, alcohol/substance abuse counseling, chaplain/spiritual director, career counseling, student employment services, financial aid counseling, health services, minority student services, personal counseling, veterans' counselor, women's services. **Physically disabled:** Services for visually, hearing impaired.

Contact. E-mail: admissions@vwc.edu
Phone: (757) 455-3208 Toll-free number: (800) 737-8684
Fax: (757) 461-5238
David Waggoner, Dean of Admissions, Virginia Wesleyan College, 1584 Wesleyan Drive, Norfolk, VA 23502-5599

Washington and Lee University
Lexington, Virginia **CB member**
www.wlu.edu **CB code: 5887**

◗ Private 4-year university and liberal arts college

◗ Residential campus in small town

◗ 1,844 degree-seeking undergraduates: 49% women, 2% African American, 3% Asian American, 3% Hispanic/Latino, 3% Multi-racial, non-Hispanic, 4% international

◗ 314 degree-seeking graduate students

◗ 24% of applicants admitted

◗ SAT or ACT with writing, application essay required

◗ 91% graduate within 6 years; 26% enter graduate study

General. Founded in 1749. Regionally accredited. **Degrees:** 467 bachelor's awarded; master's, professional offered. **ROTC:** Army. **Location:** 50 miles from Roanoke, 190 miles from Washington, DC. **Calendar:** 4-4-1. **Full-time faculty:** 249 total; 96% have terminal degrees, 12% minority, 38% women. **Part-time faculty:** 82 total; 84% have terminal degrees, 7% minority, 30% women. **Class size:** 74% < 20, 25% 20-39, less than 1% 40-49. **Special facilities:** Center for global learning, multimedia center, Japanese tea room, museum of archaeology and anthropology, IQ Center (integrative and qualitative lab).

Freshman class profile. 5,377 applied, 1,284 admitted, 454 enrolled.

Mid 50% test scores		Rank in top tenth:	85%
SAT critical reading:	650-730	End year in good standing:	99%
SAT math:	660-740	Return as sophomores:	96%
SAT writing:	650-730	Out-of-state:	88%
ACT composite:	30-33	Live on campus:	100%
Rank in top quarter:	99%	International:	6%

Basis for selection. School achievement record most important, followed closely by test scores, school and community activities, recommendations and personal qualities. Special consideration given to children of alumni and applicants from minorities and low-income families. SAT Subject Tests recommended. 2 unrelated SAT Subject Tests recommended. Interview recommended. **Home schooled:** Transcript of courses and grades, letter of recommendation (nonparent) required. 2 SAT Subject Tests in unrelated fields, interview with admissions officer recommended; documentation of reading lists and syllabi required. **Learning Disabled:** Students requesting accommodation must provide appropriate documentation of disability and need for accommodation, by virtue of the specific functional limitations of the disability.

High school preparation. College-preparatory program recommended. 17 units required; 24 recommended. Required and recommended units include English 4, mathematics 3-4, social studies 1-2, history 1-2, science 1-4 (laboratory 1), foreign language 3-4 and academic electives 4.

2015-2016 Annual costs. Tuition/fees: $46,417. Room/board: $10,985. Books/supplies: $1,800. Personal expenses: $2,033.

2015-2016 Financial aid. Need-based: 233 full-time freshmen applied for aid; 201 deemed to have need; 201 received aid. Average need met was 100%. Average scholarship/grant was $40,857; average loan $816. 95% of total undergraduate aid awarded as scholarships/grants, 5% as loans/jobs. **Non-need-based:** Awarded to 334 full-time undergraduates, including 78 freshmen. Scholarships awarded for academics. **Additional information:** W&L Promise guarantees free tuition to any undergraduate student with family income below $75,000. All students meeting the relevant Early Decision I, Early Decision II, or Regular Decision need-based financial aid deadline will receive aid package that covers their family's institutionally determined need. Loan assistance offered only to offset any additional educational expenses.

Application procedures. Admission: Closing date 1/1 (postmark date). $50 fee, may be waived for applicants with need. Admission notification by 4/1. Must reply by 5/1. **Financial aid:** Priority date 2/15, closing date 2/15. FAFSA, CSS PROFILE required. Applicants notified by 4/1; must reply by 5/1.

Academics. Special study options: Cross-registration, double major, exchange student, honors, independent study, internships, liberal arts/career combination, New York semester, student-designed major, study abroad, teacher certification program, Washington semester. Member Seven College Consortium, professional ethics seminars in business, law, medicine, journalism. **Credit/placement by examination:** AP, CLEP, IB, institutional tests. **Support services:** Study skills assistance, tutoring, writing center. Math center, multimedia center, school communication center.

Majors. Area/ethnic studies: East Asian, Russian/Slavic. **Biology:** General, biochemistry, neuroscience. **Business:** Accounting/business management, business admin. **Communications:** Journalism, persuasive communications. **Computer sciences:** Computer science. **Conservation:** Environmental studies. **Engineering:** Applied physics, engineering chemistry. **English:** English lit. **Foreign languages:** Classics, East Asian, French, German, Romance, Spanish. **History:** General. **Liberal arts:** Arts/sciences. **Math:** General. **Philosophy/religion:** Philosophy, religion. **Physical sciences:** Chemistry, geology, physics. **Psychology:** General. **Social sciences:** Economics, political science, sociology, sociology/anthropology. **Visual/performing arts:** Art history/conservation, dramatic, music, studio arts.

Most popular majors. Biology 10%, business/marketing 26%, English 6%, foreign language 6%, social sciences 19%.

Technology on campus. 176 workstations in dormitories, library, computer center, student center. Dormitories wired for high-speed internet access and linked to campus network. Commuter students can connect to campus network. Online course registration, online library, helpline, repair service, student web hosting, wireless network available.

Student life. Freshman orientation: Mandatory. Preregistration for classes offered. Held 4 days prior to beginning of fall term. **Policies:** Student-run honor system observed with single sanction. **Housing:** Guaranteed on-campus for freshmen. Coed dorms, special housing for disabled, apartments, fraternity/sorority housing, themed housing, wellness housing available. $150 nonrefundable deposit, deadline 5/1. Arts, recreation and culture; Casa Hispanica; global service; John Chavis; leadership and engagement; Outing Club; sustainability houses available. **Activities:** Bands, campus ministries, choral groups, dance, drama, film society, international student organizations, literary magazine, music ensembles, Model UN, musical theater, radio station, student government, student newspaper, symphony orchestra, TV station, Multicultural Student Association, Hillel, Habitat for Humanity, Model UN, Run for America, Nabors Service League, Pan-Asian Association for Cultural Exchange, Campus Kitchen, Women in Technology and Science, Community Financial Freedom.

Athletics. NCAA. **Intercollegiate:** Baseball M, basketball, cross-country, equestrian, field hockey W, football (tackle) M, golf, lacrosse, soccer, swimming, tennis, track and field, volleyball W, wrestling M. **Intramural:** Badminton, basketball, football (non-tackle), handball, ultimate frisbee, volleyball. **Team name:** Generals.

Student services. Alcohol/substance abuse counseling, chaplain/spiritual director, career counseling, student employment services, financial aid counseling, health services, minority student services, personal counseling, placement for graduates. **Physically disabled:** Services for visually, hearing impaired.

Contact. E-mail: admissions@wlu.edu
Phone: (540) 458-8710 Fax: (540) 458-8062
Sally Richmond, Vice President for Admissions and Financial Aid, Washington and Lee University, 204 West Washington Street, Lexington, VA 24450-2116

Westwood College: Annandale
Annandale, Virginia
www.westwood.edu/locations/virginia/annandale-satellite-campus

- For-profit 3-year career college
- Very large city
- 812 degree-seeking undergraduates
- SAT or ACT required

General. Regionally accredited; also accredited by ACICS. This Westwood College campus offers a unique hands-on, career-focused curriculum providing associate degrees that can be earned in as little as three months and bachelor's degrees that can be earned in as little as three years. Degree programs are available in the fields of technology, healthcare, business, design and justice. **Degrees:** 47 bachelor's, 74 associate awarded. **Calendar:** Differs by program. **Full-time faculty:** 4 total. **Part-time faculty:** 29 total.

Basis for selection. Open admission. Admissions policy does require consideration of test scores and an interview.

2015-2016 Annual costs. Books/supplies: $1,106. **Additional information:** Business Administration: AAS $36,428. Construction Management: AAS $36,428. Criminal Justice: AAS $38,717. Graphic Design: AAS $40,278. Healthcare Office Administration: AAS $35,259. Medical Assisting: AAS $35,259. Information Technology: AOS $34,825. Business Administration: Major in Management: BS $72,856. Construction Management: BS $72,856. Criminal Justice: Major in Administration: BS $77,434. Medical Assisting: DP $25,185. Additional costs and fees such as books, tool kits, lab fee and online fees may apply.

Application procedures. Admission: No deadline. No application fee. **Financial aid:** No deadline.

Academics. Credit/placement by examination: AP, CLEP.

Majors. BACHELOR'S. Business: Accounting/business management, business admin, construction management. **Computer sciences:** LAN/WAN management. **Health services:** Health care admin. **Protective services:** Law enforcement admin. **Visual/performing arts:** Design. **ASSOCIATE. Business:** Business admin, construction management. **Computer sciences:** Networking. **Health services:** Health information technology, medical assistant, office admin. **Protective services:** Law enforcement admin. **Visual/performing arts:** Graphic design.

Contact. E-mail: AdmissionsRepresentativesWW-Campus@westwood.edu
Phone: (703) 642-3770 Toll-free number: (877) 305-0049
Nadia Oukheira, Admissions Support, Westwood College: Annandale, 7619 Little River Turnpike, Suite 500, Annandale, VA 22003

Westwood College: Arlington Ballston
Arlington, Virginia
www.westwood.edu/locations/virginia/arlington-ballston-campus

- For-profit 3-year career college
- Very large city
- 812 degree-seeking undergraduates

General. Regionally accredited; also accredited by ACICS. This Westwood College campus offers a unique hands-on, career-focused curriculum providing associate degrees that can be earned in as little as three months and bachelor's degrees that can be earned in as little as three years. Degree programs are available in the fields of technology, healthcare, business, design and justice. **Degrees:** 55 bachelor's, 85 associate awarded. **Calendar:** Differs by program. **Full-time faculty:** 7 total. **Part-time faculty:** 30 total.

Basis for selection. Open admission.

2015-2016 Annual costs. Business Administration: AAS $36,428. Construction Management: AAS $36,428. Criminal Justice: AAS $38,717. Dental Assisting: AAS $29,897. Graphic Design: AAS $40,278. Health Information Technology: AAS $40,296. Medical Assisting: AAS $35,259. Information Technology: AOS $34,825. Business Administration: Major in Management: BS $72,856. Criminal Justice: Major in Administration: BS $77,434. Graphic Design: Major in Visual Communications: BS $76,720. Medical Assisting: DP $25,185. Additional costs and fees such as books, tool kits, lab fee and online fees may apply.

Application procedures. Admission: No deadline. No application fee. **Financial aid:** No deadline.

Academics. Credit/placement by examination: AP, CLEP.

Majors. BACHELOR'S. Business: Accounting/business management, business admin, construction management. **Communications technology:** Graphics. **Computer sciences:** LAN/WAN management. **Health services:** Health care admin. **Protective services:** Law enforcement admin. **Visual/performing arts:** Design. **ASSOCIATE. Business:** Business admin, construction management. **Communications technology:** Graphics. **Computer sciences:** Networking. **Health services:** Dental assistant, health information technology, medical assistant. **Protective services:** Law enforcement admin. **Visual/performing arts:** Graphic design.

Contact. E-mail: AdmissionsRepresentativesWW-Campus@westwood.edu
Phone: (703) 243-3900 Toll-free number: (877) 268-5278
Isiah Brooms, Director of Admissions, Westwood College: Arlington Ballston, 4420 North Fairfax Drive, Arlington, VA 22203

Washington

Antioch University Seattle
Seattle, Washington
www.antiochseattle.edu
CB code: 3070

▶ Private two-year upper-division university and liberal arts college
▶ Commuter campus in very large city
▶ Application essay, interview required

General. Founded in 1976. Regionally accredited. Individualized degree programs offered on both graduate and undergraduate levels. **Degrees:** 52 bachelor's awarded; master's, professional offered. **Location:** 1 mile from downtown. **Calendar:** Quarter, extensive summer session. **Full-time faculty:** 39 total. **Part-time faculty:** 96 total.

Student profile. 230 undergraduates, 40 graduate students.

Basis for selection. High school transcript, college transcript, application essay, interview required. Transfer accepted as juniors, seniors.

2015-2016 Annual costs. Tuition/fees: $27,435. Books/supplies: $1,020. Personal expenses: $555.

Application procedures. Admission: Rolling admission. $25 fee, may be waived for applicants with need. **Financial aid:** Applicants notified on a rolling basis starting 3/15; must reply within 2 weeks of notification. FAFSA required.

Academics. Bachelor's program is a completion program only. Students generally transfer in with at least 90 credits. **Special study options:** Accelerated study, cross-registration, dual enrollment of high school students, independent study, student-designed major, study abroad, teacher certification program, weekend college. **Credit/placement by examination:** AP, CLEP.

Majors. Liberal arts: Arts/sciences.

Technology on campus. 16 workstations in library, computer center. Commuter students can connect to campus network. Online library, helpline, wireless network available.

Student life. Activities: Literary magazine, student government, student newspaper.

Student services. Career counseling, financial aid counseling, personal counseling, veterans' counselor. **Physically disabled:** Services for visually impaired.

Contact. E-mail: admissions.aus@antioch.edu
Phone: (206) 268-4202 Toll-free number: (888) 268-4477
Fax: (206) 268-4242
Antioch University Seattle, 2326 Sixth Avenue, Seattle, WA 98121-1814

Argosy University: Seattle
Seattle, Washington
www.argosy.edu/seattle

▶ For-profit 4-year university
▶ Commuter campus in very large city
▶ 153 degree-seeking undergraduates: 61% part-time, 60% women
▶ 125 graduate students

General. Regionally accredited. **Degrees:** 20 bachelor's, 6 associate awarded; master's, professional, doctoral offered. **Calendar:** Differs by program. **Full-time faculty:** 9 total. **Part-time faculty:** 59 total.

Basis for selection. Open admission.

2015-2016 Annual costs. Tuition/fees: $16,842. **Additional information:** Tuition indicated is for programs in the College of Arts and Sciences. College of Health Sciences programs range $450-$575 per credit-hour-hour. Additional program fees may apply. All costs are subject to change.

Application procedures. Admission: Closing date 9/14. $50 fee. **Financial aid:** No deadline.

Academics. Credit/placement by examination: AP, CLEP.

Majors. Business: Business admin. **Liberal arts:** Arts/sciences. **Protective services:** Police science. **Psychology:** General.

Contact. E-mail: ausadmissions@argosy.edu
Phone: (206) 393-3516 Toll-free number: (888) 283-2777
Tina Jacobs, Senior Director of Admissions, Argosy University: Seattle, 2601-A Elliott Avenue, Seattle, WA 98121

Art Institute of Seattle
Seattle, Washington
www.ais.edu
CB code: 4805

▶ For-profit 4-year culinary school and visual arts college
▶ Commuter campus in very large city
▶ 1,703 degree-seeking undergraduates
▶ Application essay, interview required

General. Founded in 1982. Regionally accredited. **Degrees:** 147 bachelor's, 117 associate awarded. **Calendar:** Quarter, extensive summer session. **Full-time faculty:** 44 total; 9% minority, 36% women. **Part-time faculty:** 62 total; 18% minority, 31% women. **Class size:** 70% < 20, 30% 20-39. **Special facilities:** Gallery with rotating art/design shows.

Basis for selection. Open admission, but selective for some programs. Secondary school record, essay, interview most important; recommendations, academic records, test scores required. Some programs require a portfolio. **Learning Disabled:** Admissions notifies counselors of students who disclose learning disabilities and special needs. Counselor determines eligibility.

2015-2016 Annual costs. Books/supplies: $1,215. Personal expenses: $1,850. **Additional information:** Diploma programs range from $20,520-$22,669; Associates programs: $44,110-$46,264; Bachelors programs: $87,450-$89,914. Books, supplies, fees range depending on program level and course of study. All costs are subject to change.

Financial aid. Non-need-based: Scholarships awarded for academics, art.

Application procedures. Admission: No deadline. $50 fee. Admission notification on a rolling basis. **Financial aid:** No deadline. FAFSA required. Applicants notified on a rolling basis.

Academics. We also offer diplomas in the following areas: Baking and Pastry, Art of Cooking, Digital Design, Residential Design, Web Design and Development, and Web Design and Interactive Communications. **Special study options:** Distance learning, independent study, internships. **Credit/placement by examination:** AP, CLEP, IB, institutional tests. **Support services:** Learning center, reduced course load, remedial instruction, study skills assistance, tutoring.

Majors. Business: Apparel. **Communications technology:** Recording arts. **Computer sciences:** Computer graphics, web page design. **Visual/performing arts:** Cinematography, commercial photography, fashion design, game design, graphic design, industrial design, interior design.

Most popular majors. Business/marketing 10%, communication technologies 8%, computer/information sciences 20%, personal/culinary services 10%, visual/performing arts 53%.

Technology on campus. 480 workstations in library, computer center, student center. Dormitories wired for high-speed internet access. Online course registration, online library, helpline, student web hosting, wireless network available.

Student life. Freshman orientation: Available. Preregistration for classes offered. One day program held 1 week before start of the quarter. **Housing:** Guaranteed on-campus for all undergraduates. Coed dorms available. $250 deposit. AIS housing located 1 mile from campus. Students share 1 bedroom and studio apartments in secured apartment complexes. **Activities:** Student government.

Student services. Adult student services, career counseling, student employment services, financial aid counseling, personal counseling, placement for graduates, veterans' counselor. **Physically disabled:** Services for visually, speech, hearing impaired.

Contact. E-mail: aisadm@edmc.edu
Phone: (206) 448-6600 Toll-free number: (800) 275-2471
Fax: (206) 269-0275
Liane Soohoo, Senior Director of Admissions, Art Institute of Seattle, 2323 Elliott Avenue, Seattle, WA 98121-1622

Bastyr University
Kenmore, Washington
www.bastyr.edu
CB code: 0181

- Private two-year upper-division university and health science college
- Commuter campus in small city
- Application essay required

General. Founded in 1978. Regionally accredited. **Degrees:** 93 bachelor's awarded; master's, professional offered. **Location:** 6 miles from Seattle. **Calendar:** Quarter, limited summer session. **Full-time faculty:** 43 total; 21% minority, 60% women. **Part-time faculty:** 163 total; 21% minority, 66% women. **Special facilities:** Whole-food dining commons, research institute and laboratory, natural health sciences library and bookstore, medicinal herb and culinary garden, reflexology path, LEED-platinum student village.

Student profile. 287 degree-seeking undergraduates, 977 degree-seeking graduate students. 100% entered as juniors. 75% transferred from two-year, 25% transferred from four-year institutions.

Women:	87%	Live on campus:	10%
Part-time:	24%	25 or older:	78%
Out-of-state:	4%		

Basis for selection. High school transcript, college transcript, application essay required. Transfer accepted as juniors, seniors.

2015-2016 Annual costs. Tuition/fees: $24,273. Room/board: $15,550. Books/supplies: $2,250. Personal expenses: $3,050.

Financial aid. Need-based: 191 applied for aid; 189 deemed to have need; 188 received aid. Average need met was 43%. 31% of total undergraduate aid awarded as scholarships/grants, 69% as loans/jobs. **Non-need-based:** Awarded to 183 undergraduates. Scholarships awarded for academics, alumni affiliation, job skills, leadership.

Application procedures. Admission: Priority date 3/15. $75 fee. **Financial aid:** No deadline. Applicants notified on a rolling basis; must reply within 3 weeks of notification. FAFSA, institutional form required.

Academics. Special study options: Double major, independent study, internships, study abroad, weekend college. Combined BS/MS programs. **Credit/placement by examination:** AP, CLEP.

Majors. Health services: Acupuncture, Chinese medicine/herbology, herbalism, midwifery. **Parks/recreation:** Exercise sciences. **Psychology:** General. **Work/family studies:** Food/nutrition.

Most popular majors. Health sciences 90%, psychology 10%.

Technology on campus. 72 workstations in library, computer center. Dormitories wired for high-speed internet access and linked to campus network. Online library, helpline, wireless network available.

Student life. Housing: Coed dorms, special housing for disabled, apartments available. Eco-friendly LEED-platinum-certified Student Village on campus. **Activities:** Campus ministries, choral groups, dance, international student organizations, music ensembles, student government, Student Physicians for Social Responsibility, Herbal Ways club, intuition club, nature cure club, Ayurvedic club, karate club, Bastyr Supernaturals soccer club, Bach Flower Remedies club, Christian Fellowship, pediatrics club, student nutrition association, sports medicine club.

Athletics. Intramural: Basketball.

Student services. Career counseling, financial aid counseling, health services, personal counseling. **Physically disabled:** Services for visually impaired.

Contact. E-mail: admissions@bastyr.edu
Phone: (425) 602-3330 Fax: (425) 602-3090
Chris Masterson, Assistant Vice President for Recruitment and Retention, Bastyr University, 14500 Juanita Drive, NE, Kenmore, WA 98028

Central Washington University
Ellensburg, Washington
www.cwu.edu
CB member
CB code: 4044

- Public 4-year university
- Residential campus in large town
- 10,102 degree-seeking undergraduates: 11% part-time, 51% women, 4% African American, 4% Asian American, 14% Hispanic/Latino, 1% Native American, 1% Native Hawaiian/Pacific islander, 7% Multi-racial, non-Hispanic, 3% international
- 881 degree-seeking graduate students
- 81% of applicants admitted
- SAT or ACT (ACT writing optional) required
- 51% graduate within 6 years

General. Founded in 1890. Regionally accredited. **Degrees:** 2,671 bachelor's awarded; master's offered. **ROTC:** Army, Air Force. **Location:** 105 miles from Seattle. **Calendar:** Quarter, limited summer session. **Full-time faculty:** 502 total; 12% minority, 43% women. **Part-time faculty:** 223 total; 5% minority, 58% women. **Class size:** 46% < 20, 43% 20-39, 6% 40-49, 5% 50-99. **Special facilities:** Geodesy lab, data analysis center, education technology center, Northwest Native American and Circum-Pacific artifacts museum.

Freshman class profile. 4,959 applied, 4,039 admitted, 1,661 enrolled.

Mid 50% test scores			
SAT critical reading:	430-540	GPA 3.50-3.74:	15%
SAT math:	440-540	GPA 3.0-3.49:	37%
SAT writing:	420-520	GPA 2.0-2.99:	37%
ACT composite:	18-24	Return as sophomores:	79%
GPA 3.75 or higher:	11%	Out-of-state:	6%
		Live on campus:	89%

Basis for selection. Admission generally based on weighted combination of test scores and GPA. Interview, essay, and recommendations required for students whose grades or test scores do not reflect their potential for success. Additional academic support provided within alternate admission program. Test scores not required for admission if high school cumulative GPA is 3.4 or higher. **Home schooled:** Must submit transcripts for any periods enrolled in secondary school, submit ACT or SAT scores, write substantial essay about applicant's preparation for college and how schooling meets or parallels core requirements.

High school preparation. College-preparatory program required. 15 units required; 17 recommended. Required and recommended units include English 4, mathematics 3-4, social studies 3, science 2-3 (laboratory 1-2) and foreign language 2. One year of a performing or fine art or additional year of study in any main subject area is also required. Coursework in U.S. history and U.S. government recommended and will count toward social studies requirements.

2015-2016 Annual costs. Tuition/fees: $8,688; $21,501 out-of-state. Room/board: $9,780. Books/supplies: $1,002. Personal expenses: $1,752.

2014-2015 Financial aid. Need-based: 1,163 full-time freshmen applied for aid; 855 deemed to have need; 855 received aid. Average need met was 84%. Average scholarship/grant was $8,869; average loan $3,812. 51% of total undergraduate aid awarded as scholarships/grants, 49% as loans/jobs. **Non-need-based:** Awarded to 137 full-time undergraduates, including 62 freshmen. Scholarships awarded for academics, alumni affiliation, art, athletics, job skills, leadership, minority status, music/drama, religious affiliation, ROTC, state residency.

Application procedures. Admission: Priority date 3/1; no deadline. $50 fee, may be waived for applicants with need. Admission notification on a rolling basis beginning on or about 11/1. Priority deadline May 1. Partial housing deposit refundable if requested prior to July 31. **Financial aid:** Priority date 3/1, closing date 5/1. FAFSA required. Applicants notified on a rolling basis starting 5/15; must reply within 4 week(s) of notification.

Academics. Extended degree programs at locations in Yakima, Wenatchee, and greater Seattle area. **Special study options:** Cooperative education, distance learning, double major, dual enrollment of high school students, ESL, exchange student, honors, independent study, internships, liberal arts/career combination, student-designed major, study abroad, teacher certification program. **Credit/placement by examination:** AP, CLEP, IB, SAT, ACT, institutional tests. 45 credit hours maximum toward bachelor's degree. **Support services:** Learning center, reduced course load, remedial instruction, study skills assistance, tutoring, writing center.

Honors college/program. General education program emphasizes history, philosophy, literature. Applicants should score in upper 10 percent on SAT and ACT Verbal Composite and Quantitative Composite. 3.0 GPA required. 25 freshmen generally admitted.

Majors. Area/ethnic studies: Pacific. **Biology:** General, exercise physiology. **Business:** Accounting, actuarial science, business admin, construction management, marketing, special products marketing. **Communications:** General, journalism, public relations. **Computer sciences:** Computer science, information technology. **Conservation:** Environmental studies. **Education:** Art, biology, chemistry, drama/dance, early childhood, elementary, English, ESL, family/consumer sciences, foreign languages, French, German, health, history, mathematics, middle, music, physical, physics, reading, sales/marketing, science, social science, Spanish, special ed, technology/industrial arts, trade/industrial. **English:** Creative writing, English lit. **Foreign languages:** French, Japanese, Russian, Spanish. **Health services:** EMT paramedic. **History:** General. **Human services:** Public policy. **Math:** General. **Parks/recreation:** General, exercise sciences, facilities management. **Philosophy/religion:** General, philosophy. **Physical sciences:** Chemistry, geology, physics. **Protective services:** Criminal justice. **Psychology:** General. **Social sciences:** General, anthropology, economics, geography, political science, sociology. **Visual/performing arts:** Art, commercial/advertising art, dramatic, film/cinema/video, music, music management, music performance, music theory/composition, percussion instruments, piano/keyboard, stringed instruments, studio arts, voice/opera. **Work/family studies:** General, apparel marketing, family systems, institutional food production.

Most popular majors. Biology 7%, business/marketing 23%, education 12%, psychology 6%, security/protective services 7%, social sciences 12%.

Technology on campus. 700 workstations in dormitories, library, computer center, student center. Dormitories wired for high-speed internet access and linked to campus network. Commuter students can connect to campus network. Online course registration, online library, helpline, student web hosting, wireless network available.

Student life. Freshman orientation: Mandatory, $50 fee. Preregistration for classes offered. Two day introduction to campus held for students and parents. **Policies:** All first year students are required to live on campus. **Housing:** Guaranteed on-campus for freshmen. Coed dorms, special housing for disabled, apartments, gender-neutral housing, themed housing, wellness housing available. $200 partly refundable deposit, deadline 6/1. Academic interests, upperclassmen, over 21 housing available. **Activities:** Bands, campus ministries, choral groups, dance, drama, film society, international student organizations, literary magazine, music ensembles, musical theater, opera, radio station, student government, student newspaper, symphony orchestra, TV station, religious, political, ethnic, minority student organizations, professional societies, major field clubs available.

Athletics. NCAA. **Intercollegiate:** Baseball M, basketball, cheerleading, cross-country, football (tackle) M, rugby, soccer W, softball W, track and field, volleyball W. **Intramural:** Badminton, basketball, football (nontackle), soccer, softball, table tennis, tennis, volleyball. **Team name:** Wildcats.

Student services. Adult student services, alcohol/substance abuse counseling, career counseling, services for economically disadvantaged, student employment services, financial aid counseling, health services, minority student services, on-campus daycare, personal counseling, placement for graduates, veterans' counselor, women's services. **Physically disabled:** Services for visually, speech, hearing impaired.

Contact. E-mail: admissions@cwu.edu
Phone: (509) 963-1211 Fax: (509) 963-3022
Kathy Gaer-Carlton, Director of Admissions, Central Washington University, 400 East University Way, Ellensburg, WA 98926-7463

City University of Seattle
Seattle, Washington
www.cityu.edu   CB code: 4042

- Private 4-year university
- Commuter campus in very large city
- 905 degree-seeking undergraduates: 5% African American, 4% Asian American, 3% Hispanic/Latino, 1% Native American, 1% Native Hawaiian/Pacific islander, 1% Multi-racial, non-Hispanic, 7% international
- 1,061 graduate students

General. Founded in 1973. Regionally accredited. University maintains satellite sites in Renton, Everett, North Seattle, Tacoma, and Vancouver, Washington; Victoria, Vancouver, Edmonton, and Calgary, Canada; Trencin and Bratislava, Slovakia; Prague, Czech Republic; Sofia and Pratvetz, Bulgaria; Athens, Greece; Zurich, Switzerland; and Beijing, China; partnership in Queensland, Australia. **Degrees:** 199 bachelor's, 5 associate awarded; master's, doctoral offered. **Calendar:** Quarter, extensive summer session. **Full-time faculty:** 49 total. **Part-time faculty:** 536 total. **Class size:** 94% < 20, 6% 20-39, less than 1% 50-99.

Freshman class profile. 26 enrolled.

Basis for selection. Open admission, but selective for some programs. Programs in education and counseling require additional admissions materials and interviews with faculty.

2015-2016 Annual costs. Tuition/fees: $16,020. Books/supplies: $1,026. Personal expenses: $1,932.

2014-2015 Financial aid. Non-need-based: Scholarships awarded for academics, alumni affiliation, leadership, minority status, state residency. **Additional information:** All degree programs approved for veteran's administration education benefits.

Application procedures. Admission: No deadline. $50 fee. Admission notification on a rolling basis. **Financial aid:** No deadline. FAFSA required. Applicants notified on a rolling basis starting 5/1.

Academics. Online tutoring service available to all registered students at all times. **Special study options:** Accelerated study, cooperative education, distance learning, double major, dual enrollment of high school students, ESL, exchange student, independent study, internships, study abroad, teacher certification program, weekend college. **Credit/placement by examination:** AP, CLEP, IB. 45 credit hours maximum toward associate degree, 90 toward bachelor's. **Support services:** Reduced course load, tutoring, writing center.

Majors. Business: Accounting, business admin, international, management information systems, marketing. **Communications:** Communications/speech/rhetoric. **Computer sciences:** Programming. **Education:** Elementary, middle, special ed. **Liberal arts:** Arts/sciences. **Protective services:** Police science. **Psychology:** General.

Most popular majors. Business/marketing 62%, education 20%, psychology 8%.

Technology on campus. PC or laptop required. 150 workstations in library, computer center. Commuter students can connect to campus network. Online course registration, online library, helpline, wireless network available.

Student life. Housing: Guaranteed on-campus for all undergraduates. Coed dorms available. Homestay available. **Activities:** International student organizations.

Student services. Adult student services, career counseling, financial aid counseling, personal counseling, veterans' counselor. **Physically disabled:** Services for visually, hearing impaired.

Contact. E-mail: info@cityu.edu
Phone: (425) 709-5315 Toll-free number: (888) 422-4898
Fax: (425) 709-5319
Amy Portwood, Director of Admissions/Student Affairs, City University of Seattle, 521 Wall Street, Seattle, WA 98121

Cornish College of the Arts
Seattle, Washington
www.cornish.edu   CB code: 0058

- Private 4-year visual arts and performing arts college
- Commuter campus in very large city
- 720 degree-seeking undergraduates: 1% part-time, 64% women
- 4 graduate students
- 66% of applicants admitted
- Application essay required
- 55% graduate within 6 years

General. Founded in 1914. Regionally accredited. **Degrees:** 194 bachelor's awarded. **Calendar:** Semester, limited summer session. **Full-time faculty:** 58 total; 36% have terminal degrees, 10% minority, 60% women. **Part-time faculty:** 131 total; 9% minority, 51% women. **Class size:** 90% < 20, 10% 20-39.

Freshman class profile. 1,139 applied, 752 admitted, 291 enrolled.

GPA 3.75 or higher:	18%	GPA 2.0-2.99:	30%
GPA 3.50-3.74:	15%	Live on campus:	72%
GPA 3.0-3.49:	35%	International:	1%

Basis for selection. Portfolio (for visual artists) or audition (for performing artists), academic achievement history, creative ability, and artistic goals considered. SAT or ACT recommended. Interview recommended for all; audition required for dance, music, theater; portfolio required for art, design, performance production. Alternative audition and portfolio arrangements for long-distance applicants. **Home schooled:** Transcript of courses and grades, state high school equivalency certificate required.

High school preparation. College-preparatory program recommended. Recommended units include English 4, mathematics 2, science 2, foreign language 2 and visual/performing arts 4.

2015-2016 Annual costs. Tuition/fees: $37,240. Room/board: $10,680. Books/supplies: $1,800. Personal expenses: $2,000.

2014-2015 Financial aid. **Need-based:** 123 full-time freshmen applied for aid; 116 deemed to have need; 116 received aid. Average need met was 54%. Average scholarship/grant was $17,190; average loan $3,171. 77% of total undergraduate aid awarded as scholarships/grants, 23% as loans/jobs. **Non-need-based:** Awarded to 161 full-time undergraduates, including 32 freshmen. Scholarships awarded for academics, art, music/drama.

Application procedures. **Admission:** Priority date 2/1; no deadline. $40 fee, may be waived for applicants with need. Admission notification on a rolling basis. Must reply by May 1 or within 2 week(s) if notified thereafter. **Financial aid:** Priority date 2/15; no closing date. FAFSA required. Applicants notified on a rolling basis starting 3/15; must reply by 5/1 or within 2 week(s) of notification.

Academics. **Special study options:** Exchange student, independent study, internships, study abroad. **Credit/placement by examination:** AP, CLEP, IB, institutional tests. 30 credit hours maximum toward bachelor's degree. A total of 30 credits through a combination of prior work experience and credit by exam allowed. **Support services:** Remedial instruction, study skills assistance, tutoring, writing center.

Majors. **Visual/performing arts:** General, acting, art, brass instruments, cinematography, commercial/advertising art, dance, design, directing/producing, dramatic, drawing, film/cinema/video, graphic design, illustration, interior design, jazz, music performance, music theory/composition, musical theater, painting, percussion instruments, photography, piano/keyboard, play/screenwriting, printmaking, sculpture, stringed instruments, studio arts, theater design, voice/opera, woodwind instruments.

Technology on campus. 91 workstations in library, computer center, student center. Dormitories wired for high-speed internet access and linked to campus network. Online course registration, online library, helpline, wireless network available.

Student life. **Freshman orientation:** Mandatory, $175 fee. Preregistration for classes offered. Begins the summer before class starts each fall. Students will meet the Chair of their department for advising and register for classes. **Housing:** Guaranteed on-campus for freshmen. Coed dorms available. $300 deposit, deadline 5/1. **Activities:** Bands, choral groups, dance, drama, film society, international student organizations, literary magazine, music ensembles, musical theater, opera, radio station, student government, art history club, Birds and Whistles, Black student alliance, bowling club, digital illustration club, Inform the Misinformed Campaign/Corporate Watchdogs, movie club, Salt and Light (Bible study), sports/intramural club, Quidditch Team.

Student services. Adult student services, alcohol/substance abuse counseling, career counseling, student employment services, financial aid counseling, personal counseling, placement for graduates. **Physically disabled:** Services for visually impaired.

Contact. E-mail: admission@cornish.edu
Phone: (206) 726-5016 Toll-free number: (800) 726-2787
Fax: (206) 726-5019
Sharron Starling, Director of Admission, Cornish College of the Arts, 1000 Lenora Street, Seattle, WA 98121

DeVry University: Federal Way
Federal Way, Washington
www.devry.edu   **CB code: 3696**

- For-profit 4-year university
- Commuter campus in large city
- 311 degree-seeking undergraduates
- Interview required

General. Additional locations: Seattle Bellevue; Portland (OR). **Degrees:** 79 bachelor's, 6 associate awarded; master's offered. **ROTC:** Army. **Calendar:** Semester, extensive summer session. **Full-time faculty:** 14 total; 21% minority, 7% women. **Part-time faculty:** 75 total; 3% minority, 40% women.

Basis for selection. Applicants must have high school diploma or equivalent, or a degree from an accredited postsecondary institution. Must demonstrate proficiency in basic college level skills through test scores and/or institutionally-administered placement exams, and be at least 17 years of age

on the first day of classes. New students may enter at the beginning of any semester. CPT also accepted.

High school preparation. College-preparatory program recommended. Required units include mathematics 1. Math unit must be algebra or higher.

2015-2016 Annual costs. Tuition/fees: $18,959. Books/supplies: $1,320. Personal expenses: $2,376. **Additional information:** Annual tuition: $10,810-$21,163; fees $50-$90.

Financial aid. All financial aid based on need.

Application procedures. **Admission:** No deadline. $40 fee. Admission notification on a rolling basis. **Financial aid:** No deadline. FAFSA required. Applicants notified on a rolling basis.

Academics. **Special study options:** Accelerated study, distance learning, study abroad. **Credit/placement by examination:** AP, CLEP. **Support services:** Learning center, remedial instruction, tutoring.

Majors. **Business:** General, accounting, business admin. **Communications:** General. **Computer sciences:** Networking, systems analysis, web page design. **Engineering:** Software.

Most popular majors. Business/marketing 44%, computer/information sciences 31%, engineering/engineering technologies 24%.

Technology on campus. 335 workstations in library, computer center. Online course registration, online library, helpline available.

Student life. **Freshman orientation:** Mandatory. Preregistration for classes offered. **Housing:** Private apartments, student-plan housing, private rooms available. **Activities:** Student government, student newspaper, alternative sports, business & technology club, gaming, robotics, Institution of Electrical and Electronic Engineers, network gaming.

Student services. Career counseling, student employment services, financial aid counseling, placement for graduates, veterans' counselor. **Physically disabled:** Services for visually, hearing impaired.

Contact. E-mail: admissions@sea.devry.edu
Phone: (253) 943-2810 Toll-free number: (877) 923-3879
Fax: (253) 943-3291
DeVry University: Federal Way, 3600 South 344th Way, Federal Way, WA 98001-9558

DigiPen Institute of Technology
Redmond, Washington
www.digipen.edu   **CB code: 4138**

- For-profit 4-year visual arts and engineering college
- Residential campus in large town
- 978 full-time, degree-seeking undergraduates
- 84 graduate students
- 47% of applicants admitted
- Application essay required

General. Accredited by ACCSC. **Degrees:** 106 bachelor's awarded; master's offered. **Location:** 20 miles from downtown Seattle. **Calendar:** Semester, limited summer session. **Full-time faculty:** 64 total; 41% have terminal degrees, 25% women. **Part-time faculty:** 54 total; 20% have terminal degrees, 22% women. **Class size:** 56% < 20, 29% 20-39, 3% 40-49, 9% 50-99, 2% >100. **Special facilities:** Computer labs, sound labs, team space labs.

Freshman class profile. 773 applied, 360 admitted, 199 enrolled.

Mid 50% test scores		ACT composite:	26-30
SAT critical reading:	540-660	Return as sophomores:	72%
SAT math:	560-670	Out-of-state:	50%
SAT writing:	520-610		

Basis for selection. Selective admissions for all programs. Applicants apply to their program of choice and submit additional materials depending on program selection. Non-native English speakers must provide a minimum TOEFL ibt score of 80 or provide other proof of proficiency in the English language. Other acceptable tests can be found on institution's website. Test scores are waived for international students or students who have completed one year of full-time, college-level coursework post high school. Portfolios of 15-20 pieces of artwork required from Bachelor of Fine Arts in Digital Art and Animation applicants. Portfolio of 2 unedited videos of live, musical performance required from Bachelor of Arts in Music and Sound Design applicants. Portfolio requirements can be found on institution's website. **Home schooled:** Transcript of courses and grades, state high school equivalency certificate required. In addition to standard application materials, in-state applicants should submit detailed transcripts that provides course titles, brief description of each course's content, grade or performance assessment for each course, details concerning duration of study, and expected graduation date. Out-of-state applicants should submit transcript from nationally recognized home school program or detailed transcript (as described for Washington residents) and passing GED scores. Other proof of high school equivalence will be considered on a case-by-case basis by the admissions office. **Learning Disabled:** Students experiencing disabilities may contact the Disability Support Services Office to self-identify and arrange for appropriate accommodations.

High school preparation. College-preparatory program recommended. Recommended units include English 4, mathematics 4, science 4, computer science 1 and visual/performing arts 1. Applicants for all Bachelor of Science programs are required to have taken through pre-calculus and are recommended to take classes in computer science and physics; Bachelor of Fine Arts in Digital Art and Animation program applicants are recommended to take as many art classes as possible; Bachelor of Arts in Music and Sound Design applicants are required to have musical training on an instrument or voice.

2016-2017 Annual costs. Tuition/fees (projected): $28,100. Books/supplies: $1,050. Personal expenses: $2,000. **Additional information:** Flat-rate fee structure; students typically take 18-20 credits each semester which equates to 36-40 credits per year. Tuition for this credit amount is $28,800 and $31,600 for nonresident aliens.

2014-2015 Financial aid. Need-based: 116 full-time freshmen applied for aid; 94 deemed to have need; 94 received aid. Average need met was 79%. Average scholarship/grant was $8,097; average loan $3,361. **Non-need-based:** Awarded to 58 full-time undergraduates, including 20 freshmen. Scholarships awarded for academics, art, leadership. **Additional information:** Federal Work Study available. Many aid programs are on a first-come, first-served basis.

Application procedures. Admission: Priority date 2/1; no deadline. $35 fee, may be waived for applicants with need. Admission notification on a rolling basis beginning on or about 11/1. Applicants are asked to reply within four weeks of notification. Date provided on Student Action List in the acceptance packet. Extension requests will be considered on a case-by-case basis. Students are enrolled each fall on a rolling admissions basis. Qualified students are accepted and enrolled into programs beginning the September prior to the next fall intake. Students will continue to be accepted until all spaces are filled. **Financial aid:** Priority date 2/1, closing date 4/15. FAFSA required. Applicants notified on a rolling basis starting 2/15; must reply within 2 week(s) of notification.

Academics. Special study options: Accelerated study, combined bachelor's/graduate degree, ESL, independent study, internships, study abroad. Branch campuses in Singapore and Spain; students in some programs may take advantage of study abroad opportunities at either of those campuses. 4+1 Option: BS in Computer Science in Real-Time Interactive Simulation; students have the opportunity to complete both the BS and Master of Science in Computer Science program through an accelerated schedule. **Credit/placement by examination:** AP, CLEP, IB, institutional tests. **Support services:** Learning center, pre-admission summer program, reduced course load, study skills assistance, tutoring. Student Success Advisor and Faculty Mentor work with their advisees to address any and all issues. Freshmen are also assigned a Peer Advising Leader.

Majors. Communications technology: Animation/special effects. **Computer sciences:** Applications programming, modeling/simulation. **Engineering:** Computer. **Visual/performing arts:** Music theory/composition.

Most popular majors. Communication technologies 27%, computer/information sciences 57%, interdisciplinary studies 12%.

Technology on campus. 794 workstations in computer center, student center. Dormitories wired for high-speed internet access. Online course registration, online library, helpline, student web hosting, wireless network available.

Student life. Freshman orientation: Mandatory. Preregistration for classes offered. Three to four day orientation held the week before classes begin. **Policies:** Students are required to follow all policies and procedures listed in the Student Handbook, Course Catalog, and Student Enrollment Agreement. **Housing:** Single-sex dorms, special housing for disabled available. $300 partly refundable deposit, deadline 6/1. Apartment-style housing available to a limited number of students. The units are furnished and the costs includes all utilities and high-speed internet. **Activities:** Jazz band, choral groups, international student organizations, music ensembles, student government.

Student services. Alcohol/substance abuse counseling, career counseling, student employment services, financial aid counseling, personal counseling, placement for graduates, veterans' counselor. **Physically disabled:** Services for hearing impaired.

Contact. E-mail: admissions@digipen.edu
Phone: (425) 629-5001 Toll-free number: (866) 478-5236
Fax: (425) 558-0378
Danial Powers, Director of Admissions, DigiPen Institute of Technology, 9931 Willows Road NE, Redmond, WA 98052

Eastern Washington University
Cheney, Washington
www.ewu.edu
CB code: 4301

- Public 4-year university
- Commuter campus in large town
- 10,761 degree-seeking undergraduates: 9% part-time, 54% women, 4% African American, 3% Asian American, 14% Hispanic/Latino, 1% Native American, 6% Multi-racial, non-Hispanic, 4% international
- 1,061 degree-seeking graduate students
- 82% of applicants admitted
- SAT or ACT (ACT writing optional) required
- 46% graduate within 6 years

General. Founded in 1882. Regionally accredited. The College of Business and Public Administration and the College of Health Science and Public Health are located at the Spokane campus. **Degrees:** 2,369 bachelor's awarded; master's, professional offered. **ROTC:** Army. **Location:** 17 miles from Spokane, 266 miles from Seattle. **Calendar:** Quarter, extensive summer session. **Full-time faculty:** 450 total; 100% have terminal degrees, 17% minority, 45% women. **Part-time faculty:** 216 total; 12% minority, 62% women. **Class size:** 34% < 20, 43% 20-39, 10% 40-49, 13% 50-99, less than 1% >100. **Special facilities:** Planetarium, national wildlife refuge, anthropology museum, laboratory for ecological studies, art, photography and print gallery, children's center, English Language Institute, state crime lab, Washington State digital archives building, GIS and computer-mapping laboratory and map library, Spokane Intercollegiate Research and Technology Institute, health sciences building in Spokane.

Freshman class profile. 5,168 applied, 4,243 admitted, 1,724 enrolled.

Mid 50% test scores			
SAT critical reading:	420-540	GPA 3.0-3.49:	35%
SAT math:	430-550	GPA 2.0-2.99:	33%
SAT writing:	410-520	Return as sophomores:	78%
ACT composite:	18-23	Out-of-state:	7%
GPA 3.75 or higher:	15%	Live on campus:	76%
GPA 3.50-3.74:	17%	International:	2%

Basis for selection. Admission based on index combining GPA, test scores and requisite high school core curriculum. Essay and special review considered for applicants who do not meet these standards. Limited number enrolled below index and core requirements. Letters of recommendation from teachers and/or counselors encouraged. Interview or essay required for returning adult applicants and high school students below admission index. **Home schooled:** Must show evidence of completing required core courses.

High school preparation. College-preparatory program required. 15 units required. Required units include English 4, mathematics 3, social studies 3, science 2 (laboratory 2), foreign language 2 and visual/performing arts 1. Math requirement includes algebra, geometry, and trigonometry or advanced algebra. Quantitative Reasoning required in the Senior year. One year fine arts or core elective required. Foreign language requirement includes 2 years in one foreign language (American Sign Language accepted).

2015-2016 Annual costs. Tuition/fees: $7,866; $22,272 out-of-state. Room/board: $10,263.

2014-2015 Financial aid. Need-based: 1,450 full-time freshmen applied for aid; 1,112 deemed to have need; 1,077 received aid. Average need met was 57%. Average scholarship/grant was $8,521; average loan $3,068. 54% of total undergraduate aid awarded as scholarships/grants, 46% as loans/jobs. **Non-need-based:** Awarded to 2,334 full-time undergraduates, including 772 freshmen. Scholarships awarded for academics, alumni affiliation, art, athletics, job skills, music/drama, state residency. **Additional information:** The High Demand Scholarship program helps low income students pursue "high demand" careers.

Application procedures. Admission: Priority date 2/15; deadline 5/15. $50 fee, may be waived for applicants with need. Admission notification on a rolling basis beginning on or about 9/1. Must reply by May 1 or within 4 week(s) if notified thereafter. **Financial aid:** Priority date 2/15; no closing date. FAFSA required. Applicants notified on a rolling basis starting 4/1; must reply within 4 week(s) of notification.

Academics. Extensive internship opportunities available. The Communication Disorders program operates on a semester schedule. Programs available in the following Washington locations: Riverpoint/Spokane, Clark College, Lake Washington, North Seattle Community College, South Seattle Community College, Pierce College, Yakima MSW Program, Bellevue Community College and Everett Community College. **Special study options:** Combined bachelor's/graduate degree, distance learning, double major, dual enrollment of high school students, ESL, honors, independent study, internships, student-designed major, study abroad, teacher certification program. Nursing consortium with Washington State University, Whitworth College, Gonzaga University. Dual degree program: Master's of Social Work (EWU) and Law (Gonzaga). **Credit/placement by examination:** AP, CLEP, IB, institutional tests. 45 credit hours maximum toward bachelor's degree. **Support services:** Learning center, pre-admission.summer program, remedial instruction, study skills assistance, tutoring, writing center. Veterans resource center, transfer center.

Majors. Architecture: Urban/community planning. **Area/ethnic studies:** Women's. **Biology:** General. **Business:** Accounting, business admin, finance, human resources, management information systems, managerial economics, marketing. **Communications:** Communications/speech/rhetoric, journalism. **Communications technology:** Graphics. **Computer sciences:** General. **Conservation:** Environmental science. **Education:** Art, biology, business, chemistry, early childhood, early childhood special, English, French, health, mathematics, music, physics, reading, science, social studies, Spanish, special ed. **Engineering:** Electrical, mechanical. **English:** English lit, technical writing. **Foreign languages:** French, Spanish. **Health services:** Athletic training, community health services, dental hygiene, health care admin, nursing (RN), recreational therapy, speech pathology. **History:** General. **Human services:** Social work. **Liberal arts:** Humanities. **Math:** General. **Parks/recreation:** General, exercise sciences, facilities management. **Philosophy/religion:** Philosophy. **Physical sciences:** Chemistry, geology, physics. **Psychology:** General, developmental. **Social sciences:** Anthropology, criminology, economics, geography, international relations, political science, sociology. **Visual/performing arts:** Art history/conservation, dramatic, film/cinema/video, music, studio arts. **Work/family studies:** Child development.

Most popular majors. Biology 10%, business/marketing 18%, education 6%, engineering/engineering technologies 7%, health sciences 10%, interdisciplinary studies 7%, psychology 8%, social sciences 8%.

Technology on campus. 1,000 workstations in dormitories, library, computer center, student center. Dormitories wired for high-speed internet access and linked to campus network. Commuter students can connect to campus network. Online course registration, online library, helpline, student web hosting, wireless network available.

Student life. Freshman orientation: Mandatory. Preregistration for classes offered. One-day sessions held in summer, plus a week-long program prior to start of classes. **Policies:** Student conduct code, academic integrity policy, alcohol/substance use and abuse policy. **Housing:** Guaranteed on-campus for freshmen. Coed dorms, special housing for disabled, apartments, fraternity/sorority housing, themed housing, wellness housing available. $250 nonrefundable deposit, deadline 5/15. Living and learning communities. **Activities:** Bands, campus ministries, choral groups, dance, drama, film society, international student organizations, literary magazine, music ensembles, Model UN, musical theater, radio station, student government, student newspaper, symphony orchestra, Black Student Union, M.E.Ch.A, Saudi Club, Compassionate Interfaith Society, CRU (Campus Crusade for Christ), Eagles Volunteering Around the Community, Sustainable Food Project, ROTC Fighting Eagles, TRiO club.

Athletics. NCAA. **Intercollegiate:** Basketball, cross-country, football (tackle) M, golf W, soccer W, tennis, track and field, volleyball W. **Intramural:** Baseball, basketball, bowling, cross-country, football (tackle), golf W, racquetball, soccer, softball, tennis, track and field, volleyball. **Team name:** Eagles.

Student services. Adult student services, alcohol/substance abuse counseling, career counseling, services for economically disadvantaged, student employment services, financial aid counseling, health services, minority student services, on-campus daycare, personal counseling, placement for graduates, veterans' counselor, women's services. **Physically disabled:** Services for visually, speech, hearing impaired.

Contact. E-mail: admissions@ewu.edu
Phone: (509) 359-2397 Fax: (509) 359-6692
Boubacar Bouaré, Assistant Director, Records Management, Eastern Washington University, 304 Sutton Hall, Cheney, WA 99004

Evergreen State College
Olympia, Washington | **CB member**
www.evergreen.edu | **CB code: 4292**

- Public 4-year liberal arts college
- Commuter campus in small city

- 3,821 degree-seeking undergraduates: 6% part-time, 55% women, 5% African American, 3% Asian American, 10% Hispanic/Latino, 2% Native American, 8% Multi-racial, non-Hispanic
- 311 degree-seeking graduate students
- 98% of applicants admitted
- SAT or ACT (ACT writing optional) required
- 54% graduate within 6 years; 21% enter graduate study

General. Founded in 1967. Regionally accredited. **Degrees:** 1,058 bachelor's awarded; master's offered. **Location:** 6 miles from downtown, 60 miles from Seattle. **Calendar:** Quarter, limited summer session. **Full-time faculty:** 157 total; 96% have terminal degrees, 24% minority; 55% women. **Part-time faculty:** 67 total; 45% have terminal degrees, 25% minority, 58% women. **Class size:** 36% < 20, 40% 20-39, 13% 40-49, 11% 50-99, less than 1% >100. **Special facilities:** Center for Creative and Applied Media, sustainable agriculture lab building, organic farm and community gardens, Longhouse Education and Cultural Center, animation and design studio, ceramics studio, metal shop, wood shop, photography studios and darkrooms, 3,000 feet of waterfront property on Puget Sound.

Freshman class profile. 1,744 applied, 1,707 admitted, 595 enrolled.

Mid 50% test scores			
		GPA 3.0-3.49:	33%
SAT critical reading:	490-630	GPA 2.0-2.99:	46%
SAT math:	450-560	Rank in top quarter:	25%
SAT writing:	460-590	Rank in top tenth:	9%
ACT composite:	20-26	Return as sophomores:	66%
GPA 3.75 or higher:	7%	Out-of-state:	38%
GPA 3.50-3.74:	13%	Live on campus:	74%

Basis for selection. School achievement record, test scores, strength of curriculum taken in high school, personal statement, and understanding of interdisciplinary study. Official TOEFL test scores are required for most students whose native language is not English. Essay or personal statement required for international and home-schooled applicants, recommended for all other applicants. Interviews optional (by appointment for non-residents). **Home schooled:** Transcript of courses and grades required. Personal statement required.

High school preparation. College-preparatory program recommended. 15 units required. Required units include English 4, mathematics 3, social studies 3, science 2 (laboratory 2), foreign language 2 and academic electives 1. One fine, visual, or performing arts elective or college prep elective from the areas above required.

2015-2016 Annual costs. Tuition/fees: $8,380; $22,795 out-of-state. Room/board: $9,492. Books/supplies: $1,050. Personal expenses: $2,076.

2014-2015 Financial aid. Need-based: 425 full-time freshmen applied for aid; 341 deemed to have need; 324 received aid. Average need met was 56%. Average scholarship/grant was $8,832; average loan $3,362. 53% of total undergraduate aid awarded as scholarships/grants, 47% as loans/jobs. **Non-need-based:** Awarded to 58 full-time undergraduates, including 19 freshmen. Scholarships awarded for academics, art, athletics, leadership, state residency. **Additional information:** Application packets for all scholarships and tuition awards EXCEPT the Merit Award (due by May 2) must be received by February 1. To meet the financial aid priority deadline, the Federal Processor must process the official results of the FAFSA by March 1. FAFSA applications that are rejected or incomplete cannot be considered for priority awarding.

Application procedures. Admission: Priority date 2/1; no deadline. $50 fee, may be waived for applicants with need. Admission notification on a rolling basis beginning on or about 11/1. Must reply by May 1 or within 4 week(s) if notified thereafter. **Financial aid:** Priority date 3/1; no closing date. FAFSA required. Applicants notified on a rolling basis starting 4/1; must reply within 6 week(s) of notification.

Academics. Special study options: Accelerated study, double major, exchange student, independent study, internships, semester at sea, student-designed major, study abroad, teacher certification program, weekend college. **Credit/placement by examination:** AP, CLEP, IB. 135 credit hours maximum toward bachelor's degree. **Support services:** Learning center, reduced course load, study skills assistance, tutoring, writing center.

Majors. Area/ethnic studies: Native American. **Biology:** General, Biochemistry/molecular biology, ecology, zoology. **Business:** Business admin. **Communications:** Digital media, media studies. **Computer sciences:** General. **Conservation:** General, environmental science, environmental studies. **Education:** General. **English:** English lit. **Foreign languages:** General, classics. **Liberal arts:** Arts/sciences, humanities. **Math:** Mathematics/statistics. **Philosophy/religion:** Philosophy, religion. **Physical sciences:** General. **Psychology:** General. **Social sciences:** General, political economy, political science, sociology. **Visual/performing arts:** General, art, cinematography, dramatic, film/cinema/video, multimedia, studio arts.

Most popular majors. Interdisciplinary studies 18%, liberal arts 82%.

Technology on campus. 556 workstations in dormitories, library, computer center, student center. Dormitories wired for high-speed internet access and linked to campus network. Commuter students can connect to campus network. Online course registration, online library, helpline, student web hosting, wireless network available.

Student life. **Freshman orientation:** Mandatory, $175 fee. Preregistration for classes offered. New matriculated students entering in the Fall quarter are assessed a one-time $175 fee to fund an enhanced student transition program designed to increase student academic success. New students entering Winter or Spring quarter are charged $45. The week-long fall orientation offers academic and social events to familiarize students with teaching, learning, and resources at campus. **Housing:** Guaranteed on-campus for freshmen. Coed dorms, special housing for disabled, apartments, gender-neutral housing, themed housing, wellness housing available. $250 nonrefundable deposit, deadline 7/14. Freshman halls, freshman quiet, apartment-style (quiet, allergen free, substance free, sustainability, rainbow fort, no theme) available. **Activities:** Bands, campus ministries, choral groups, dance, drama, film society, literary magazine, music ensembles, radio station, student government, student newspaper, TV station, Common Bread, Geoduck Student Union, Native Student Alliance, Movimento Estudiantil Xicano de Aztlan (MEXA), Black Student Union, Asian Pacific Islander Coalition (APIC), Womyn's Resource Center, Coalition Against Sexual Violence (CASV), Evergreen Queer Alliance (EQA), Transgender Resources and Education Xtravaganza (T-REX), Campus Food Coalition, Evergreen Students for Sustainable Animal Agriculture (ESSAA).

Athletics. NAIA. **Intercollegiate:** Basketball, soccer, track and field, volleyball W. **Intramural:** Basketball, soccer, volleyball, wrestling. **Team name:** Geoducks.

Student services. Adult student services, alcohol/substance abuse counseling, career counseling, services for economically disadvantaged, student employment services, financial aid counseling, health services, minority student services, on-campus daycare, personal counseling, placement for graduates, veterans' counselor, women's services. **Physically disabled:** Services for visually, speech, hearing impaired.

Contact. E-mail: admissions@evergreen.edu
Phone: (360) 867-6170 Fax: (360) 867-5114
Steve Hunter, Director of Admissions, Evergreen State College, 2700 Evergreen Parkway NW, Olympia, WA 98505

Faith Evangelical College & Seminary
Tacoma, Washington
www.faithseminary.edu

- Private 4-year Bible and seminary college affiliated with the interdenominational tradition
- Large city
- 239 undergraduates
- 250 graduate students
- Application essay required

General. Regionally accredited; also accredited by TRACS. **Degrees:** 47 bachelor's awarded; master's, professional offered. **Location:** 30 Miles from Seattle, WA. **Calendar:** Quarter, extensive summer session. **Full-time faculty:** 9 total. **Part-time faculty:** 1 total.

Basis for selection. Open admission, but selective for some programs. Undergraduate program applicants must possess a high school diploma or equivalent with a minimum GPA of 2.3 on a 4.0 scale. Equivalency is defined as a state approved Equivalency Diploma or Entrance Examination, a GED, or an approved home-school certificate. The aforementioned is not required if the applicant has completed an associate degree from a recognized institution. Low requisite cumulative GPA mandates probational enrollment. Personal recommendation and Clergy recommendation. **Home schooled:** Transcript of courses and grades, state high school equivalency certificate, letter of recommendation (nonparent) required. **Learning Disabled:** A Statement of Disabilities may be necessary to determine if reasonable accommodations can be made to allow for an ability to benefit.

2015-2016 Annual costs. Tuition/fees: $7,890. Books/supplies: $350. Personal expenses: $2,052.

Application procedures. **Admission:** No deadline. $40 fee. Admission notification on a rolling basis. **Financial aid:** Closing date 8/15.

Academics. **Special study options:** Distance learning. Evening classes, online Classes, DVD distance education. **Credit/placement by examination:** AP, CLEP.

Majors. **Business:** Organizational leadership. **Philosophy/religion:** Religion. **Theology:** Theology.

Contact. E-mail: admissions@faithseminary.edu
Phone: (253) 752-2020 ext. 121
Toll-free number: (888) 777-7675 ext. 121 Fax: (253) 759-1790
Mark Wagner, Dean of Students, Faith Evangelical College & Seminary, Faith Evangelical College & Seminary, Tacoma, WA 98407

Gonzaga University
Spokane, Washington
www.gonzaga.edu
CB member
CB code: 4330

- Private 4-year university and liberal arts college affiliated with the Roman Catholic Church
- Residential campus in large city
- 4,960 degree-seeking undergraduates: 1% part-time, 53% women, 1% African American, 5% Asian American, 10% Hispanic/Latino, 1% Native American, 6% Multi-racial, non-Hispanic, 2% international
- 2,373 degree-seeking graduate students
- 73% of applicants admitted
- SAT or ACT (ACT writing optional), application essay required
- 83% graduate within 6 years

General. Founded in 1887. Regionally accredited. **Degrees:** 1,324 bachelor's awarded; master's, professional, doctoral offered. **ROTC:** Army. **Location:** 300 miles from Seattle. **Calendar:** Semester, extensive summer session. **Full-time faculty:** 422 total; 83% have terminal degrees, 10% minority, 45% women. **Part-time faculty:** 291 total; 5% have terminal degrees, 8% minority, 49% women. **Class size:** 35% < 20, 58% 20-39, 5% 40-49, 2% 50-99, less than 1% >100. **Special facilities:** 2 electron microscopes, art museum.

Freshman class profile. 6,729 applied, 4,945 admitted, 1,337 enrolled.

Mid 50% test scores			
SAT critical reading:	540-640	GPA 2.0-2.99:	1%
SAT math:	550-650	Rank in top quarter:	71%
ACT composite:	25-29	Rank in top tenth:	39%
GPA 3.75 or higher:	50%	Return as sophomores:	95%
GPA 3.50-3.74:	25%	Out-of-state:	56%
GPA 3.0-3.49:	24%	Live on campus:	98%
		International:	1%

Basis for selection. GED not accepted. Academic achievement, scholastic aptitude, personal characteristics important. GPA below 3.0 reevaluated to include only grades in academic subjects. Course content and test scores important. Gonzaga recommends interviews for borderline applicants, but they are not required. **Home schooled:** Letter of recommendation (nonparent) required. Students must complete the Common Application and the Common Application Home School Supplement. One letter of recommendation, by someone other than a parent, addressing academic accomplishments. The Common Application School Report, which can be filled out by a parent/guardian.

High school preparation. College-preparatory program required. Required and recommended units include English 4, mathematics 3-4, social studies 2-3, history 2-3, science 3-4 (laboratory 3-4), foreign language 2-3 and academic electives 2-3. Algebra, geometry, trigonometry required of engineering applicants. Of 6 additional electives 4 must be from subjects mentioned and the arts.

2015-2016 Annual costs. Tuition/fees: $37,990. Room/board: $10,440. Books/supplies: $1,092. Personal expenses: $1,860.

2014-2015 Financial aid. **Need-based:** 877 full-time freshmen applied for aid; 638 deemed to have need; 638 received aid. Average need met was 79%. Average scholarship/grant was $20,411; average loan $4,714. 57% of total undergraduate aid awarded as scholarships/grants, 43% as loans/jobs. **Non-need-based:** Awarded to 2,555 full-time undergraduates, including 561 freshmen. Scholarships awarded for academics, alumni affiliation, athletics, leadership, minority status, music/drama, ROTC.

Application procedures. **Admission:** Priority date 11/15; deadline 2/1 (postmark date). $50 fee, may be waived for applicants with need. Admission notification by 3/15. Must reply by May 1 or within 2 week(s) if notified thereafter. **Financial aid:** Priority date 2/1, closing date 6/30. FAFSA required. Applicants notified by 3/1; Applicants notified on a rolling basis starting 3/1; must reply by 5/1.

Academics. **Special study options:** Combined bachelor's/graduate degree, cross-registration, distance learning, double major, dual enrollment of high school students, ESL, exchange student, honors, independent study, internships, liberal arts/career combination, semester at sea, study abroad, teacher certification program, Washington semester. **Credit/placement by examination:** AP, CLEP, IB, SAT, ACT. 32 credit hours maximum toward bachelor's degree. **Support services:** Pre-admission summer program, study skills assistance, writing center.

Majors. Area/ethnic studies: Asian, European, Latin American, women's. **Biology:** General, biochemistry. **Business:** Accounting, banking/financial services, business admin, international, management information systems, managerial economics. **Communications:** Broadcast journalism, journalism, public relations. **Computer sciences:** Computer science. **Conservation:** Environmental studies. **Education:** Music, physical, special ed. **Engineering:** General, civil, computer, electrical, mechanical. **English:** English lit, rhetoric/composition. **Foreign languages:** Comparative lit, French, Italian, Spanish. **Health services:** Preop/surgical nursing. **History:** General. **Liberal arts:** Arts/sciences. **Math:** General. **Parks/recreation:** Sports admin. **Philosophy/religion:** Philosophy, religion. **Physical sciences:** Chemistry, physics. **Protective services:** Criminal justice. **Psychology:** General. **Social sciences:** Economics, international relations, political science, sociology. **Visual/performing arts:** Dramatic, music performance, studio arts.

Most popular majors. Biology 10%, business/marketing 24%, communications/journalism 7%, engineering/engineering technologies 12%, psychology 6%, social sciences 14%.

Technology on campus. 900 workstations in library, computer center. Dormitories wired for high-speed internet access and linked to campus network. Commuter students can connect to campus network. Online course registration, online library, helpline, repair service, student web hosting, wireless network available.

Student life. Freshman orientation: Mandatory, $60 fee. Preregistration for classes offered. **Policies:** International students, freshmen and sophomores under 21 must live on campus, unless living at home. **Housing:** Guaranteed on-campus for freshmen. Coed dorms, single-sex dorms, special housing for disabled, apartments, themed housing available. $200 fully refundable deposit, deadline 5/1. Rental houses available. **Activities:** Bands, campus ministries, choral groups, dance, drama, international student organizations, literary magazine, music ensembles, Model UN, musical theater, radio station, student government, student newspaper, symphony orchestra, TV station, 108 student clubs and service organizations.

Athletics. NCAA. **Intercollegiate:** Baseball M, basketball, cross-country, golf, rowing (crew), soccer, tennis, track and field, volleyball W. **Intramural:** Badminton, basketball, racquetball, soccer, softball, tennis, volleyball, weight lifting, wrestling M. **Team name:** Bulldogs.

Student services. Adult student services, alcohol/substance abuse counseling, chaplain/spiritual director, career counseling, student employment services, financial aid counseling, health services, minority student services, personal counseling, veterans' counselor. **Physically disabled:** Services for visually, speech, hearing impaired.

Contact. E-mail: mcculloh@gu.gonzaga.edu
Phone: (509) 323-6572 Toll-free number: (800) 322-2584
Fax: (509) 323-5780
Julie McCulloh, Dean of Admissions, Gonzaga University, 502 East Boone Avenue, Spokane, WA 99258-0001

Heritage University
Toppenish, Washington
www.heritage.edu

CB code: 4344

- Private 4-year liberal arts and teachers college affiliated with the interdenominational tradition
- Commuter campus in small town
- 819 degree-seeking undergraduates: 10% part-time, 73% women, 1% African American, 1% Asian American, 63% Hispanic/Latino, 7% Native American, 5% Multi-racial, non-Hispanic, 2% international
- 344 degree-seeking graduate students

General. Founded in 1982. Regionally accredited. **Degrees:** 161 bachelor's, 15 associate awarded; master's offered. **Location:** 165 miles from Seattle, 20 miles from Yakima. **Calendar:** Semester, limited summer session. **Full-time faculty:** 74 total; 31% minority, 61% women. **Part-time faculty:** 92 total; 27% minority, 61% women. **Class size:** 77% < 20, 23% 20-39. **Special facilities:** Solar telescope, portable planetarium.

Freshman class profile.

GPA 3.75 or higher:	11%	GPA 2.0-2.99:	45%
GPA 3.50-3.74:	17%	Return as sophomores:	74%
GPA 3.0-3.49:	24%	International:	7%

Basis for selection. Open admission. All students take institutional placement test. **Home schooled:** State high school equivalency certificate required.

High school preparation. College-preparatory program recommended. Recommended units include English 3, mathematics 2, history 3, science 1 (laboratory 1) and academic electives 4.

2015-2016 Annual costs. Tuition/fees: $19,242. Books/supplies: $1,030. Personal expenses: $1,960.

Financial aid. Non-need-based: Scholarships awarded for academics, leadership, minority status. **Additional information:** Undergraduates eligible for and receiving Federal Pell Grant and/or State Need Grant can receive institutional grant aid necessary to reduce their gap with tuition to no more than their eligibility for subsidized Stafford loans.

Application procedures. Admission: Priority date 4/15; no deadline. No application fee. Admission notification on a rolling basis. **Financial aid:** Priority date 2/10; no closing date. FAFSA, institutional form required. Applicants notified on a rolling basis starting 3/1; must reply within 2 week(s) of notification.

Academics. Special study options: Cooperative education, distance learning, double major, dual enrollment of high school students, ESL, honors, independent study, internships, liberal arts/career combination, student-designed major, teacher certification program. **Credit/placement by examination:** AP, CLEP, institutional tests. 14 credit hours maximum toward associate degree, 30 toward bachelor's. **Support services:** Learning center, pre-admission summer program, reduced course load, remedial instruction, study skills assistance, tutoring, writing center.

Majors. Area/ethnic studies: Native American. **Biology:** General, biomedical sciences. **Business:** Accounting, business admin, entrepreneurial studies. **Computer sciences:** Computer science. **Conservation:** General, environmental science. **Education:** Art, bilingual, biology, chemistry, early childhood, elementary, English, ESL, mathematics, middle, multi-level teacher, science, secondary, special ed. **English:** English lit. **Health services:** Clinical lab science. **Human services:** Social work. **Math:** General. **Physical sciences:** General, astronomy, chemistry. **Protective services:** Criminal justice. **Psychology:** General.

Most popular majors. Business/marketing 11%, education 45%, public administration/social services 22%.

Technology on campus. 160 workstations in library, computer center. Commuter students can connect to campus network. Online course registration, online library, helpline, repair service, wireless network available.

Student life. Freshman orientation: Mandatory, $25 fee. Preregistration for classes offered. Typically held one day during the week before classes start for the fall and spring semesters. Also available on-line and evening. **Activities:** Student government, Native American, Heritage Community Volunteers in Action, Heritage Educators Association, social work club, Nursing students club.

Athletics. Team name: Eagles.

Student services. Adult student services, career counseling, services for economically disadvantaged, student employment services, financial aid counseling, minority student services, on-campus daycare, personal counseling, placement for graduates.

Contact. E-mail: admissions@heritage.edu
Phone: (509) 865-8508 Toll-free number: (888) 272-6190
Fax: (509) 865-8659
Magnus Altmayer, Assistant Director of Admissions, Heritage University, 3240 Fort Road, Toppenish, WA 98948-9599

International Academy of Design and Technology: Seattle
Seattle, Washington
www.iadt.edu/seattle

- For-profit 4-year career college
- Commuter campus in very large city
- 340 undergraduates

General. Accredited by ACICS. **Degrees:** 76 bachelor's, 11 associate awarded. **Calendar:** Quarter. **Full-time faculty:** 3 total. **Part-time faculty:** 41 total.

Basis for selection. SAT or ACT, and Wonderlic entrance assessment required; specific scores determine eligibility to specific programs. Applicants for certain programs are required to submit to a background check. Portfolio required for Fashion Design program.

2015-2016 Annual costs. Books/supplies: $1,400. **Additional information:** Tuition for associate degree program: $32,800; bachelor degree program: $64,800; certificate for Web Design and Development: $15,050. Program cost varies depending on number of credits taken. Estimated cost of books and supplies included in tuition. Credit-hour charges vary from $300-$500. All costs are subject to change.

Application procedures. Admission: No deadline. $50 fee. **Financial aid:** No deadline.

Academics. Special study options: Study abroad, weekend college. **Credit/placement by examination:** AP, CLEP.

Majors. Business: Fashion, merchandising. **Communications technology:** Animation/special effects. **Computer sciences:** Information technology, web page design. **Visual/performing arts:** Digital arts, fashion design, game design, graphic design, interior design.

Most popular majors. Business/marketing 6%, visual/performing arts 94%.

Contact. Phone: (206) 575-1865 Toll-free number: (866) 903-4238 Fax: (206) 575-1724
Melissa Maxwell, Director of Admissions, International Academy of Design and Technology: Seattle, 645 Andover Park West, Seattle, WA 98188

ITT Technical Institute: Everett
Everett, Washington
www.itt-tech.edu   CB code: 2697

- For-profit 4-year technical college
- Commuter campus in large town
- 279 undergraduates
- Interview required

General. Accredited by ACICS. **Degrees:** 34 bachelor's, 71 associate awarded. **Calendar:** Quarter, extensive summer session. **Full-time faculty:** 7 total. **Part-time faculty:** 25 total.

Basis for selection. Satisfactory scores from on-site tests in English and mathematics required.

2015-2016 Annual costs. Per-credit-hour charge, $493; academic fee, $200. Some programs require purchase of tools, which could cost an additional $500. All costs subject to change.

Application procedures. Admission: No application fee. Admission notification on a rolling basis. **Financial aid:** No deadline. FAFSA, institutional form required. Applicants notified on a rolling basis.

Academics. Credit/placement by examination: AP, CLEP. **Support services:** Learning center, tutoring.

Majors. Business: Business admin, construction management, e-commerce, project management. **Communications technology:** Animation/special effects. **Computer sciences:** Programming, security. **Protective services:** Law enforcement admin.

Most popular majors. Business/marketing 29%, communication technologies 27%, computer/information sciences 24%, security/protective services 20%.

Technology on campus. Online library available.

Student life. Freshman orientation: Available. Preregistration for classes offered.

Student services. Career counseling, student employment services, placement for graduates.

Contact. Phone: (425) 485-0303 Toll-free number: (800) 272-3791 Fax: (425) 485-3438
Jon Scherrer, Director of Recruitment, ITT Technical Institute: Everett, 1615 75th Street S.W., Suite 220, Everett, WA 98203

ITT Technical Institute: Seattle
Seattle, Washington
www.itt-tech.edu   CB code: 3599

- For-profit 4-year technical college
- Commuter campus in very large city
- 414 undergraduates
- Interview required

General. Founded in 1932. Accredited by ACICS. **Degrees:** 51 bachelor's, 101 associate awarded. **Location:** 12 miles from downtown. **Calendar:** Quarter, extensive summer session. **Full-time faculty:** 9 total. **Part-time faculty:** 63 total.

Basis for selection. Satisfactory scores from on-site tests in English and mathematics required.

2015-2016 Annual costs. Per-credit-hour charge, $493; academic fee, $200. Some programs require purchase of tools, which could cost an additional $100 to $500. All costs subject to change.

Application procedures. Admission: No deadline. No application fee. Admission notification on a rolling basis. **Financial aid:** No deadline. FAFSA, institutional form required. Applicants notified on a rolling basis.

Academics. Credit/placement by examination: AP, CLEP. **Support services:** Learning center, tutoring.

Majors. Business: Business admin, construction management, project management. **Communications technology:** Animation/special effects. **Computer sciences:** Programming, security. **Protective services:** Law enforcement admin.

Most popular majors. Business/marketing 12%, communication technologies 20%, computer/information sciences 32%, engineering/engineering technologies 34%.

Technology on campus. Online library available.

Student life. Freshman orientation: Available. Preregistration for classes offered.

Student services. Career counseling, student employment services, placement for graduates.

Contact. Phone: (206) 244-3300 Toll-free number: (800) 422-2029 Fax: (206) 246-7635
Jose Luis Saez, Director of Recruitment, ITT Technical Institute: Seattle, 12720 Gateway Drive, Suite 100, Seattle, WA 98168

ITT Technical Institute: Spokane
Spokane Valley, Washington
www.itt-tech.edu   CB code: 7027

- For-profit 4-year technical college
- Commuter campus in large town
- 295 undergraduates
- Interview required

General. Accredited by ACICS. **Degrees:** 9 bachelor's, 81 associate awarded. **Location:** 5 miles from downtown. **Calendar:** Quarter, extensive summer session. **Full-time faculty:** 5 total. **Part-time faculty:** 47 total.

Basis for selection. Satisfactory scores from on-site test in English and mathematics required.

2015-2016 Annual costs. Per-credit-hour charge, $493; academic fee, $200. Some programs require purchase of tools, which could cost an additional $500. All costs subject to change.

Application procedures. Admission: No deadline. No application fee. Admission notification on a rolling basis. **Financial aid:** No deadline. FAFSA, institutional form required. Applicants notified on a rolling basis.

Academics. Credit/placement by examination: AP, CLEP. **Support services:** Learning center, tutoring.

Majors. Business: Business admin, construction management, project management. **Communications technology:** Animation/special effects. **Computer sciences:** Networking, security. **Protective services:** Law enforcement admin.

Most popular majors. Business/marketing 26%, communication technologies 8%, computer/information sciences 34%, engineering/engineering technologies 13%, security/protective services 18%.

Technology on campus. 50 workstations in computer center. Online library available.

Student life. Freshman orientation: Available. Preregistration for classes offered.

Student services. Career counseling, student employment services, placement for graduates.

Contact. Phone: (509) 926-2900 Toll-free number: (800) 777-8324 Fax: (509) 926-2908
Gregory Alexander, Director of Recruitment, ITT Technical Institute: Spokane, 13518 East Indiana Avenue, Spokane Valley, WA 99216

Northwest College of Art & Design
Poulsbo, Washington
www.ncad.edu
CB code: 2432

- For-profit 4-year visual arts college
- Commuter campus in small town
- 99 undergraduates
- Application essay, interview required

General. Founded in 1982. Accredited by ACCSC. **Degrees:** 18 bachelor's awarded. **Location:** 30 miles from Seattle, 60 miles from Tacoma. **Calendar:** Semester, extensive summer session. **Part-time faculty:** 16 total.

Basis for selection. Requirements include admissions interview, essay, portfolio, high school diploma or GED. TOEFL test required for international students from non-English speaking countries. SAT required for students with a GED. **Home schooled:** GED required except when home school programs show proof of school or program accreditation.

2015-2016 Annual costs. Tuition/fees: $19,050. Books/supplies: $3,120. Personal expenses: $1,640.

Financial aid. Non-need-based: Scholarships awarded for academics, art, state residency.

Application procedures. Admission: No deadline. $50 fee. Admission notification on a rolling basis. **Financial aid:** Priority date 3/1, closing date 6/1. FAFSA required. Applicants notified on a rolling basis.

Academics. Special study options: Accelerated study, double major, internships. **Credit/placement by examination:** AP, CLEP.

Majors. Visual/performing arts: Design.

Technology on campus. PC or laptop required. Wireless network available.

Student life. Freshman orientation: Mandatory, $15 fee. Preregistration for classes offered.

Student services. Adult student services, career counseling, student employment services, financial aid counseling, placement for graduates.

Contact. E-mail: admissions@ncad.edu
Phone: (360) 779-9993 Toll-free number: (800) 769-2787
Fax: (360) 779-9933
Kim Perigard, Admissions, Northwest College of Art & Design, 16301 Creative Drive NE, Poulsbo, WA 98370-8651

Northwest University
Kirkland, Washington
CB member
www.northwestu.edu
CB code: 4541

- Private 4-year university and liberal arts college affiliated with the Assemblies of God
- Residential campus in small city
- 1,619 degree-seeking undergraduates: 22% part-time, 58% women
- 681 degree-seeking graduate students
- 94% of applicants admitted
- SAT or ACT (ACT writing optional), application essay required
- 50% graduate within 6 years

General. Founded in 1934. Regionally accredited. **Degrees:** 247 bachelor's, 15 associate awarded; master's, professional offered. **ROTC:** Army. **Location:** 10 miles from Seattle. **Calendar:** Semester, limited summer session. **Full-time faculty:** 63 total; 86% have terminal degrees, 11% minority, 41% women. **Part-time faculty:** 308 total; 11% minority, 54% women. **Class size:** 62% < 20, 28% 20-39, 7% 40-49, 3% 50-99, less than 1% >100.

Freshman class profile. 569 applied, 535 admitted, 196 enrolled.

Mid 50% test scores			
SAT critical reading:	430-540	GPA 3.0-3.49:	30%
SAT math:	420-540	GPA 2.0-2.99:	40%
SAT writing:	400-520	Return as sophomores:	71%
ACT composite:	18-24	Out-of-state:	3.6%
GPA 3.75 or higher:	16%	Live on campus:	57%
GPA 3.50-3.74:	12%	International:	1%

Basis for selection. Essay, references, transcript, SAT or ACT. GPA of 2.3 required: those with GPA below 2.3 but greater than 2.0 admitted with an academic success plan if space is available. TOEFL (minimum score 70) required for non-native speakers of English. Audition recommended for music and drama scholarships. **Home schooled:** Transcript of courses and grades, letter of recommendation (nonparent) required.

High school preparation. College-preparatory program recommended. 16 units recommended. Recommended units include English 4, mathematics 3, social studies 2, history 2, science 2, foreign language 2 and academic electives 3.

2015-2016 Annual costs. Tuition/fees: $28,086. Room/board: $7,790. Books/supplies: $1,000. Personal expenses: $1,650.

2014-2015 Financial aid. Need-based: 851 full-time freshmen applied for aid; 529 deemed to have need; 479 received aid. Average need met was 70%. Average scholarship/grant was $8,691; average loan $3,297. 66% of total undergraduate aid awarded as scholarships/grants, 34% as loans/jobs. **Non-need-based:** Awarded to 792 full-time undergraduates, including 288 freshmen. Scholarships awarded for academics, art, athletics, leadership, music/drama, religious affiliation.

Application procedures. Admission: Priority date 3/1; deadline 8/1 (postmark date). $30 fee, may be waived for applicants with need. Admission notification on a rolling basis beginning on or about 10/1. **Financial aid:** Priority date 2/15, closing date 8/1. FAFSA, institutional form required. Applicants notified on a rolling basis starting 3/3; must reply within 4 week(s) of notification.

Academics. Special study options: Accelerated study, combined bachelor's/graduate degree, distance learning, double major, dual enrollment of high school students, ESL, independent study, internships, student-designed major, study abroad, teacher certification program. **Credit/placement by examination:** AP, CLEP, IB, SAT, ACT, institutional tests. 30 credit hours maximum toward associate degree, 30 toward bachelor's. **Support services:** Learning center, reduced course load, remedial instruction, study skills assistance, tutoring, writing center.

Majors. Biology: General. **Business:** Business admin. **Communications:** Communications/speech/rhetoric, media studies, organizational. **Conservation:** Environmental science. **Education:** Elementary, middle, secondary. **English:** English lit. **Health services:** Nursing (RN), premedicine. **History:** General. **Math:** General. **Philosophy/religion:** Philosophy. **Psychology:** General. **Social sciences:** Political science. **Theology:** Bible, missionary, pastoral counseling, sacred music, theology, youth ministry. **Visual/performing arts:** Music.

Most popular majors. Business/marketing 15%, communications/journalism 13%, education 7%, health sciences 14%, liberal arts 6%, psychology 10%, theological studies 18%, visual/performing arts 8%.

Technology on campus. 135 workstations in dormitories, library, computer center, student center. Dormitories wired for high-speed internet access and linked to campus network. Commuter students can connect to campus network. Online course registration, online library, helpline, repair service, student web hosting, wireless network available.

Student life. Freshman orientation: Mandatory. Preregistration for classes offered. Held in August the week before classes begin. **Policies:** Religious observance required. **Housing:** Guaranteed on-campus for all undergraduates. Single-sex dorms, apartments available. $300 fully refundable deposit, deadline 5/1. **Activities:** Bands, campus ministries, choral groups, drama, international student organizations, music ensembles, musical theater, radio station, student government, student newspaper, community outreach groups, Psi Chi Honor Society (psychology), Association of International Students, Environmental Stewardship Club, Students in Free Enterprise.

Athletics. NAIA, NCCAA. **Intercollegiate:** Basketball, cross-country, soccer, softball W, track and field, volleyball W. **Intramural:** Football (non-tackle). **Team name:** Eagles.

Student services. Adult student services, alcohol/substance abuse counseling, chaplain/spiritual director, career counseling, student employment services, financial aid counseling, health services, personal counseling, veterans' counselor. **Physically disabled:** Services for visually impaired.

Contact. E-mail: admissions@northwestu.edu
Phone: (425) 889-5231 Toll-free number: (800) 669-3781
Fax: (425) 889-5224
Andy Hall, Director of Admissions, Northwest University, 5520 108th
Avenue, NE, Kirkland, WA 98083-0579

Pacific Lutheran University
Tacoma, Washington
www.plu.edu

CB member
CB code: 4597

- Private 4-year university affiliated with the Evangelical Lutheran Church in America
- Residential campus in small city
- 2,809 degree-seeking undergraduates: 2% part-time, 62% women, 3% African American, 8% Asian American, 8% Hispanic/Latino, 1% Native American, 1% Native Hawaiian/Pacific islander, 7% Multi-racial, non-Hispanic, 4% international
- 310 degree-seeking graduate students
- 76% of applicants admitted
- SAT or ACT (ACT writing optional), application essay required
- 68% graduate within 6 years; 24% enter graduate study

General. Founded in 1890. Regionally accredited. **Degrees:** 771 bachelor's awarded; master's, professional offered. **ROTC:** Army. **Location:** 7 miles from downtown Tacoma, 30 miles from Seattle. **Calendar:** 4-1-4, extensive summer session. **Full-time faculty:** 223 total; 91% have terminal degrees, 16% minority, 52% women. **Part-time faculty:** 116 total; 17% have terminal degrees, 14% minority, 63% women. **Class size:** 53% < 20, 41% 20-39, 3% 40-49, 3% 50-99. **Special facilities:** Herbarium, invertebrate and vertebrate museums, greenhouse, field station and boat equipped for studies of Puget Sound, Scandinavian cultural center, observatory, performing arts center, bicycle co-op, science center with a 500 MHz NMR spectrometer, music center with concert hall, black box theater.

Freshman class profile. 3,623 applied, 2,737 admitted, 643 enrolled.

Mid 50% test scores			
SAT critical reading:	480-620	Rank in top quarter:	85%
SAT math:	500-610	Rank in top tenth:	50%
SAT writing:	470-600	End year in good standing:	88%
ACT composite:	22-28	Return as sophomores:	83%
GPA 3.75 or higher:	55%	Out-of-state:	28%
GPA 3.50-3.74:	19%	Live on campus:	83%
GPA 3.0-3.49:	20%	International:	2%
		GPA 2.0-2.99:	6%

Basis for selection. Grades, test scores, essay, recommendations, service, leadership. Admission on rolling basis until class is full. Interview recommended for borderline, exceptional; audition required for music, forensics, theater; portfolio recommended for art. **Home schooled:** Must provide proof of high-school equivalency.

High school preparation. College-preparatory program required. 17 units recommended. Required and recommended units include English 4, mathematics 2-3, social studies 2, science 2 (laboratory 2), foreign language 2, visual/performing arts 1 and academic electives 3. Computer science, speech, debate, music also recommended. 2 years visual or performing arts recommended.

2015-2016 Annual costs. Tuition/fees: $37,950. Room/board: $10,330. Books/supplies: $1,050. Personal expenses: $1,860.

2015-2016 Financial aid. Need-based: 583 full-time freshmen applied for aid; 511 deemed to have need; 509 received aid. Average need met was 89%. Average scholarship/grant was $26,137; average loan $6,776. 74% of total undergraduate aid awarded as scholarships/grants, 26% as loans/jobs. **Non-need-based:** Awarded to 2,422 full-time undergraduates, including 558 freshmen. Scholarships awarded for academics, alumni affiliation, art, leadership, music/drama, religious affiliation, ROTC.

Application procedures. Admission: Priority date 2/1; no deadline. $40 fee, may be waived for applicants with need, free for online applicants. Admission notification on a rolling basis beginning on or about 10/1. Must reply by May 1 or within 2 week(s) if notified thereafter. Housing deposit is refundable only through May 1. **Financial aid:** Priority date 1/15; no closing date. FAFSA required. Applicants notified on a rolling basis starting 3/1; must reply by 5/1 or within 3 week(s) of notification.

Academics. Freshman year program includes topic-oriented writing and critical conversation classes. **Special study options:** Combined bachelor's/graduate degree, cooperative education, cross-registration, double major, dual enrollment of high school students, exchange student, honors, independent study, internships, liberal arts/career combination, student-designed major, study abroad, teacher certification program. **Credit/placement by examination:** AP, CLEP, IB, institutional tests. 30 credit hours maximum toward bachelor's degree. **Support services:** Pre-admission summer program, reduced course load, study skills assistance, tutoring, writing center. Drop in labs, language resource center and conversation tables, group review sessions, free flashcards.

Majors. Area/ethnic studies: Chinese, Scandinavian, women's. **Biology:** General. **Business:** Business admin. **Communications:** Communications/speech/rhetoric. **Computer sciences:** Computer science. **Education:** Elementary, secondary. **Engineering:** Computer, engineering science. **English:** English lit. **Foreign languages:** Chinese, classics, French, German, Hispanic and Latin American, Scandinavian. **Health services:** Nursing (RN). **History:** General. **Human services:** Social work. **Math:** General. **Parks/recreation:** General, health/fitness. **Philosophy/religion:** Philosophy, religion. **Physical sciences:** Chemistry, geology, physics. **Psychology:** General. **Social sciences:** Anthropology, economics, political science, sociology. **Visual/performing arts:** Art, music, studio arts, theater arts management.

Most popular majors. Biology 7%, business/marketing 13%, education 8%, health sciences 9%, parks/recreation 6%, psychology 6%, social sciences 12%, visual/performing arts 6%.

Technology on campus. 250 workstations in library, student center. Dormitories wired for high-speed internet access and linked to campus network. Commuter students can connect to campus network. Online library, helpline, student web hosting, wireless network available.

Student life. Freshman orientation: Available. Preregistration for classes offered. Four-day experience held right before school begins in the fall. **Policies:** All single, full-time students must live in university housing, unless student lives at home with parent or legal guardian, is 20 years of age or older on or before a specific college-designated date, or has achieved junior status. **Housing:** Guaranteed on-campus for all undergraduates. Coed dorms, single-sex dorms, special housing for disabled, apartments, gender-neutral housing, themed housing, wellness housing available. $200 nonrefundable deposit, deadline 5/1. First in the Family Community, Community for Creative Expression, Social Action and Leadership Community. **Activities:** Bands, campus ministries, choral groups, dance, drama, film society, international student organizations, literary magazine, music ensembles, Model UN, musical theater, opera, radio station, student government, student newspaper, symphony orchestra, TV station, Intervarsity Christian Fellowship, Advocates for Social Justice, Asian & Pacific Islanders club, B.L.A.C.K. at PLU, environmental action, Puentes, social work organization, Amnesty International, Habitat for Humanity, Young Life.

Athletics. NCAA. **Intercollegiate:** Baseball M, basketball, football (tackle) M, golf, rowing (crew) W, soccer, softball W, swimming, tennis, track and field, volleyball W. **Intramural:** Badminton, basketball, bowling, cross-country, football (non-tackle), soccer, softball, tennis, volleyball, water polo. **Team name:** Lutes.

Student services. Adult student services, chaplain/spiritual director, career counseling, student employment services, financial aid counseling, health services, minority student services, personal counseling, placement for graduates, veterans' counselor, women's services. **Physically disabled:** Services for visually, speech, hearing impaired.

Contact. E-mail: admission@plu.edu
Phone: (253) 535-7151 Toll-free number: (800) 274-6758
Fax: (253) 536-5136
David Gunovich, Dean of Enrollment Services, Pacific Lutheran University, 12180 Park Ave South, Tacoma, WA 98447-0003

Saint Martin's University
Lacey, Washington
www.stmartin.edu

CB member
CB code: 4674

- Private 4-year university affiliated with the Roman Catholic Church
- Residential campus in large town
- 1,177 degree-seeking undergraduates: 16% part-time, 52% women, 7% African American, 5% Asian American, 14% Hispanic/Latino, 1% Native American, 2% Native Hawaiian/Pacific islander, 6% Multi-racial, non-Hispanic, 5% international
- 337 degree-seeking graduate students
- 93% of applicants admitted

- SAT or ACT (ACT writing recommended), application essay required
- 49% graduate within 6 years

General. Founded in 1895. Regionally accredited. Saint Martin's Abbey, located on campus, is the home of the Benedictine monks. **Degrees:** 438 bachelor's awarded; master's offered. **ROTC:** Army, Air Force. **Location:** 3 miles from Olympia, 60 miles from Seattle. **Calendar:** Semester, limited summer session. **Full-time faculty:** 76 total; 88% have terminal degrees, 14% minority, 42% women. **Part-time faculty:** 141 total; 22% have terminal degrees, 52% women. **Class size:** 66% < 20, 24% 20-39, 5% 40-49, 3% 50-99, less than 1% >100. **Special facilities:** Engineering facility.

Freshman class profile. 945 applied, 880 admitted, 179 enrolled.

Mid 50% test scores		GPA 2.0-2.99:	18%
SAT critical reading:	460-580	Rank in top quarter:	55%
SAT math:	460-570	Rank in top tenth:	18%
SAT writing:	440-550	Return as sophomores:	77%
ACT composite:	21-26	Out-of-state:	25%
GPA 3.75 or higher:	20%	Live on campus:	75%
GPA 3.50-3.74:	26%	International:	1%
GPA 3.0-3.49:	36%		

Basis for selection. Applications for admission are reviewed holistically. Official transcripts, SAT/ACT scores, school report form, letter of recommendation and essay are required for all first-year applicants. Interview recommended. **Home schooled:** Statement describing home school structure and mission, transcript of courses and grades, letter of recommendation (nonparent) required. **Learning Disabled:** Students with disabilities should initiate contact with the Office of Disability Support Services.

High school preparation. College-preparatory program recommended. 17 units recommended. Recommended units include English 4, mathematics 3, social studies 2, science 3 (laboratory 1), foreign language 2 and academic electives 3.

2015-2016 Annual costs. Tuition/fees: $33,194. Room/board: $10,340. Books/supplies: $1,000. Personal expenses: $1,000. **Additional information:** Students in Accounting, Business, Computer Science, Engineering, and Nursing classes pay additional $60 per semester credit hour fee.

2014-2015 Financial aid. **Need-based:** 99 full-time freshmen applied for aid; 91 deemed to have need; 90 received aid. Average need met was 82%. Average scholarship/grant was $23,250; average loan $2,823. 73% of total undergraduate aid awarded as scholarships/grants, 27% as loans/jobs. **Non-need-based:** Awarded to 338 full-time undergraduates, including 52 freshmen. Scholarships awarded for academics, alumni affiliation, art, athletics, leadership, minority status, music/drama, religious affiliation, ROTC, state residency.

Application procedures. **Admission:** Priority date 11/1; deadline 7/31 (receipt date). No application fee. Application must be submitted online. Admission notification on a rolling basis beginning on or about 10/15. Must reply by 8/7. **Financial aid:** Priority date 3/1; no closing date. FAFSA required. Applicants notified on a rolling basis starting 2/15; must reply within 3 week(s) of notification.

Academics. **Special study options:** Combined bachelor's/graduate degree, distance learning, double major, ESL, exchange student, independent study, internships, study abroad, teacher certification program, Washington semester. **Credit/placement by examination:** AP, CLEP, IB, institutional tests. 30 credit hours maximum toward bachelor's degree. **Support services:** Learning center, pre-admission summer program, reduced course load, remedial instruction, study skills assistance, tutoring, writing center.

Majors. Biology: General. **Business:** Accounting, business admin. **Communications:** General. **Computer sciences:** Computer science. **Education:** General, elementary, special ed. **Engineering:** Civil, mechanical. **English:** English lit. **Health services:** Nursing (RN). **History:** General. **Human services:** Community org/advocacy, social work. **Math:** General. **Philosophy/religion:** Religion. **Physical sciences:** Chemistry. **Protective services:** Criminal justice. **Psychology:** General. **Social sciences:** Anthropology, political science. **Visual/performing arts:** Dramatic, music.

Most popular majors. Biology 8%, business/marketing 26%, education 10%, engineering/engineering technologies 13%, psychology 11%, security/protective services 6%.

Technology on campus. 80 workstations in library, computer center. Dormitories wired for high-speed internet access and linked to campus network. Commuter students can connect to campus network. Online library, helpline, repair service, wireless network available.

Student life. Freshman orientation: Mandatory. Preregistration for classes offered. Freshmen orientation program begins on the Thursday before school starts in the fall. **Housing:** Guaranteed on-campus for freshmen. Coed dorms, special housing for disabled, apartments, themed housing available.

$200 fully refundable deposit, deadline 7/1. Norcia and Oikos learning communities offer students a themed living experience that goes beyond traditional residence hall living. **Activities:** Bands, campus ministries, choral groups, dance, drama, international student organizations, Model UN, musical theater, student government, student newspaper, Circle K, Hawaiian club, international club, non-traditional students group, social action club, College Republicans, Gay/Straight Alliance, Young Democrats, Saint for Life.

Athletics. NCAA. **Intercollegiate:** Baseball M, basketball, cross-country, golf, soccer, softball W, track and field, volleyball W. **Intramural:** Basketball, football (non-tackle), soccer, softball, volleyball. **Team name:** Saints.

Student services. Adult student services, alcohol/substance abuse counseling, chaplain/spiritual director, career counseling, student employment services, financial aid counseling, health services, personal counseling, veterans' counselor. **Physically disabled:** Services for visually, hearing impaired.

Contact. E-mail: admissions@stmartin.edu
Phone: (360) 438-4596 Toll-free number: (800) 368-8803
Fax: (360) 412-6189
Emilie Schnabel, Admissions, Assistant Director, Saint Martin's University, 5000 Abbey Way SE, Lacey, WA 98503-7500

Seattle Pacific University
Seattle, Washington — **CB member**
www.spu.edu — **CB code: 4694**

- Private 4-year university affiliated with the Free Methodist Church of North America
- Residential campus in very large city
- 3,187 degree-seeking undergraduates: 3% part-time, 68% women, 4% African American, 11% Asian American, 10% Hispanic/Latino, 8% Multi-racial, non-Hispanic, 4% international
- 947 degree-seeking graduate students
- 82% of applicants admitted
- SAT or ACT (ACT writing optional), application essay required
- 75% graduate within 6 years

General. Founded in 1891. Regionally accredited. **Degrees:** 759 bachelor's awarded; master's, doctoral offered. **ROTC:** Army, Naval, Air Force. **Location:** 3 miles from downtown. **Calendar:** Quarter, limited summer session. **Full-time faculty:** 205 total; 90% have terminal degrees, 14% minority, 45% women. **Part-time faculty:** 180 total; 10% have terminal degrees, 6% minority, 63% women. **Class size:** 48% < 20, 42% 20-39, 7% 40-49, 3% 50-99, less than 1% >100. **Special facilities:** 2 island campuses used for biological studies.

Freshman class profile. 5,227 applied, 4,266 admitted, 688 enrolled.

Mid 50% test scores		GPA 2.0-2.99:	7%
SAT critical reading:	510-620	Rank in top quarter:	3%
SAT math:	490-610	Rank in top tenth:	1%
ACT composite:	22-27	Return as sophomores:	87%
GPA 3.75 or higher:	36%	Out-of-state:	42%
GPA 3.50-3.74:	24%	Live on campus:	94%
GPA 3.0-3.49:	33%	International:	2%

Basis for selection. Admission decisions based primarily based on grades, grade trend, test scores, essays, letters of recommendation and extracurricular activities. Audition required for music, performing art workshop; portfolio required for fine art scholarship. **Home schooled:** Copy of reading list and information regarding the curriculum used in homeschool program. **Learning Disabled:** Contact Disability Support Services in the Center for Learning to make arrangements for an interview to determine the level of assistance needed. Students required to provide documentation of the nature of the disability.

High school preparation. College-preparatory program recommended. Recommended units include English 4, mathematics 3, history 2, science 3 and foreign language 3.

2015-2016 Annual costs. Tuition/fees: $37,086. Room/board: $10,353. Books/supplies: $1,041. Personal expenses: $1,938.

2015-2016 Financial aid. **Need-based:** 611 full-time freshmen applied for aid; 519 deemed to have need; 518 received aid. Average need met was 81%. Average scholarship/grant was $27,581; average loan $3,773. 68% of total undergraduate aid awarded as scholarships/grants, 32% as loans/jobs. **Non-need-based:** Awarded to 816 full-time undergraduates, including 157 freshmen. Scholarships awarded for academics, alumni affiliation, art, athletics, leadership, minority status, music/drama, religious affiliation, ROTC.

Application procedures. Admission: Closing date 2/1 (postmark date). $50 fee, may be waived for applicants with need. Admission notification on a rolling basis beginning on or about 3/1. Must reply by May 1 or within 2 week(s) if notified thereafter. **Financial aid:** Priority date 2/1; no closing date. FAFSA required. Applicants notified on a rolling basis starting 3/15; must reply by 5/1 or within 3 week(s) of notification.

Academics. Special study options: Distance learning, double major, ESL, exchange student, external degree, honors, independent study, internships, liberal arts/career combination, student-designed major, study abroad, teacher certification program, Washington semester. **Credit/placement by examination:** AP, CLEP, IB, SAT, ACT, institutional tests. 45 credit hours maximum toward bachelor's degree. **Support services:** Learning center, reduced course load, remedial instruction, study skills assistance, tutoring, writing center.

Majors. Area/ethnic studies: European, Latin American. **Biology:** General, biochemistry. **Business:** Accounting. **Communications:** Communications/ speech/rhetoric. **Computer sciences:** Computer science. **Education:** Art, English, mathematics, music, science, social science, special ed. **Engineering:** Computer, electrical, engineering science. **English:** English lit. **Foreign languages:** Classics, French, German, Latin, Russian, Spanish. **Health services:** Nursing (RN). **History:** General. **Liberal arts:** Arts/sciences. **Math:** General, computational. **Parks/recreation:** Exercise sciences. **Philosophy/ religion:** Philosophy. **Physical sciences:** Chemistry, physics. **Psychology:** General. **Social sciences:** Economics, political science, sociology. **Theology:** Religious ed. **Visual/performing arts:** General, art, dramatic, interior design, music. **Work/family studies:** Clothing/textiles, food/nutrition.

Most popular majors. Biology 9%, business/marketing 10%, family/consumer sciences 6%, health sciences 11%, psychology 10%, social sciences 10%, visual/performing arts 9%.

Technology on campus. 475 workstations in dormitories, library, computer center, student center. Dormitories wired for high-speed internet access and linked to campus network. Commuter students can connect to campus network. Online course registration, online library, helpline, repair service, wireless network available.

Student life. Freshman orientation: Mandatory. Preregistration for classes offered. **Policies:** Religious observance required. **Housing:** Coed dorms, special housing for disabled, apartments available. $300 fully refundable deposit, deadline 6/1. **Activities:** Bands, campus ministries, choral groups, dance, drama, international student organizations, literary magazine, music ensembles, musical theater, radio station, student government, student newspaper, symphony orchestra, more than 25 clubs and organizations.

Athletics. NCAA. **Intercollegiate:** Basketball, cross-country, gymnastics W, rowing (crew), soccer, track and field, volleyball W. **Intramural:** Archery, basketball, bowling, cross-country, football (non-tackle), softball, tennis, volleyball, weight lifting. **Team name:** Falcons.

Student services. Adult student services, chaplain/spiritual director, career counseling, student employment services, financial aid counseling, health services, minority student services, personal counseling, placement for graduates, veterans' counselor. **Physically disabled:** Services for visually, hearing impaired.

Contact. E-mail: admissions@spu.edu
Phone: (206) 281-2021 Toll-free number: (800) 366-3344
Fax: (206) 281-2544
Ineliz Soto-Fuller, Director of Undergraduate Admissions, Seattle Pacific University, 3307 Third Avenue West, Suite 115, Seattle, WA 98119-1997

Seattle University

Seattle, Washington
www.seattleu.edu

CB member
CB code: 4695

- Private 4-year university affiliated with the Roman Catholic Church
- Residential campus in very large city
- 4,670 degree-seeking undergraduates: 5% part-time, 60% women, 3% African American, 16% Asian American, 9% Hispanic/Latino, 1% Native Hawaiian/Pacific islander, 7% Multi-racial, non-Hispanic, 11% international
- 2,676 degree-seeking graduate students
- 73% of applicants admitted
- SAT or ACT (ACT writing optional) required
- 79% graduate within 6 years

General. Founded in 1891. Regionally accredited. Courses also offered at Bellevue Campus. **Degrees:** 1,181 bachelor's awarded; master's, professional, doctoral offered. **ROTC:** Army, Naval, Air Force. **Location:** One mile from downtown. **Calendar:** Quarter, extensive summer session. **Full-time faculty:**

512 total; 85% have terminal degrees, 19% minority, 51% women. **Part-time faculty:** 246 total; 48% have terminal degrees, 18% minority, 51% women. **Class size:** 57% < 20, 40% 20-39, 3% 40-49, less than 1% 50-99. **Special facilities:** Design center (where engineering students work with major companies in the area), observatory.

Freshman class profile. 7,806 applied, 5,700 admitted, 1,002 enrolled.

Mid 50% test scores			
SAT critical reading:	530-650	GPA 3.0-3.49:	29%
SAT math:	530-630	GPA 2.0-2.99:	2%
SAT writing:	530-630	Return as sophomores:	85%
ACT composite:	25-29	Out-of-state:	67%
GPA 3.75 or higher:	40%	Live on campus:	93%
GPA 3.50-3.74:	29%	International:	4%

Basis for selection. 2.75 GPA minimum, higher for some programs. Secondary school record, recommendations, test scores most important. Essay, school, community activities also important. Applicants must submit one test with writing component. ACT writing component is required if applicant does not submit SAT Reasoning scores. **Home schooled:** Transcript of courses and grades, letter of recommendation (nonparent) required. SAT II, ACT subject tests, AP tests, IB tests and/or transcript(s) of courses taken at college(s).

High school preparation. College-preparatory program required. 17 units required. Required units include English 4, mathematics 3, social studies 3, history 1, science 2 (laboratory 2), foreign language 2 and academic electives 2.

2015-2016 Annual costs. Tuition/fees: $39,690. Room/board: $11,121. Books/supplies: $1,500. Personal expenses: $2,436.

2015-2016 Financial aid. Need-based: 846 full-time freshmen applied for aid; 665 deemed to have need; 665 received aid. Average need met was 69%. Average scholarship/grant was $22,736; average loan $3,521. 78% of total undergraduate aid awarded as scholarships/grants, 22% as loans/jobs. **Non-need-based:** Awarded to 1,496 full-time undergraduates, including 530 freshmen. Scholarships awarded for academics, alumni affiliation, athletics, leadership, minority status, music/drama, ROTC, state residency.

Application procedures. Admission: Priority date 1/15; no deadline. $55 fee, may be waived for applicants with need. Admission notification on a rolling basis beginning on or about 3/1. Must reply by May 1 or within 4 week(s) if notified thereafter. **Financial aid:** Priority date 2/1; no closing date. FAFSA required. Applicants notified on a rolling basis; must reply by 5/1 or within 2 week(s) of notification.

Academics. Special study options: Cross-registration, double major, honors, independent study, internships, liberal arts/career combination, student-designed major, study abroad, teacher certification program. **Credit/placement by examination:** AP, CLEP, IB, institutional tests. 45 credit hours maximum toward bachelor's degree. Special arrangements for nursing majors who take NLN exams. 50 credits maximum. **Support services:** Learning center, pre-admission summer program, reduced course load, study skills assistance, tutoring, writing center.

Majors. Area/ethnic studies: Asian, women's. **Biology:** General, biochemistry. **Business:** General, accounting, business admin, finance, international, management information systems, managerial economics, marketing. **Communications:** Journalism, media studies, public relations. **Computer sciences:** Computer science. **Conservation:** Environmental science, environmental studies. **Engineering:** Civil, computer hardware, electrical, mechanical. **English:** Creative writing, English lit. **Foreign languages:** General, French, Spanish. **Health services:** Clinical lab science, nursing (RN), sonography. **History:** General. **Human services:** General, social work. **Liberal arts:** Arts/sciences, humanities. **Math:** General. **Parks/recreation:** Exercise sciences. **Philosophy/religion:** Philosophy, religion. **Physical sciences:** General, chemistry, physics. **Protective services:** Criminal justice, criminalistics, forensics, law enforcement admin. **Psychology:** General. **Social sciences:** Economics, political science, sociology. **Visual/performing arts:** General, art history/conservation, digital arts, dramatic, film/cinema/video, music, photography, stringed instruments, studio arts.

Most popular majors. Business/marketing 24%, engineering/engineering technologies 7%, health sciences 14%, social sciences 7%, visual/performing arts 6%.

Technology on campus. 467 workstations in dormitories, library, computer center, student center. Dormitories wired for high-speed internet access and linked to campus network. Commuter students can connect to campus network. Online course registration, online library, helpline, student web hosting, wireless network available.

Student life. Freshman orientation: Mandatory. Preregistration for classes offered. Three days prior to start of classes. **Housing:** Guaranteed on-campus for freshmen. Coed dorms, special housing for disabled, apartments, themed housing, wellness housing available. $300 nonrefundable deposit, deadline 5/1. Single-gender floors available. **Activities:** Bands, campus ministries, choral groups, dance, drama, international student organizations, literary magazine, music ensembles, Model UN, radio station, student government, student newspaper, 65 clubs available.

Athletics. NCAA. **Intercollegiate:** Baseball M, basketball, cross-country, golf, soccer, softball W, swimming, tennis, track and field, volleyball W. **Intramural:** Basketball, football (non-tackle), soccer, softball, tennis, volleyball. **Team name:** Redhawks.

Student services. Adult student services, alcohol/substance abuse counseling, chaplain/spiritual director, career counseling, student employment services, financial aid counseling, health services, minority student services, personal counseling, placement for graduates, veterans' counselor, women's services. **Physically disabled:** Services for visually, speech, hearing impaired.

Contact. E-mail: admissions@seattleu.edu
Phone: (206) 296-2000 Toll-free number: (800) 426-7123
Fax: (206) 296-5656
Melore Nielsen, Dean of Admissions, Seattle University, 901 12th Avenue, Seattle, WA 98122-4340

Trinity Lutheran College
Everett, Washington
www.tlc.edu
CB code: 4408

- Private 4-year liberal arts college affiliated with the Lutheran Church
- Residential campus in small city
- 195 degree-seeking undergraduates
- SAT or ACT (ACT writing optional), application essay required

General. Founded in 1944. Regionally accredited. All students participate in off-campus service learning practicums. **Degrees:** 41 bachelor's awarded. **Location:** 30 miles from Seattle. **Calendar:** 4-1-4, limited summer session. **Full-time faculty:** 16 total; 44% have terminal degrees, 6% minority, 31% women. **Part-time faculty:** 26 total; 31% have terminal degrees, 8% minority, 50% women. **Class size:** 91% < 20, 7% 20-39, 1% 40-49, 1% 50-99. **Special facilities:** Children, youth and family resource center; preschool and Christian school.

Freshman class profile.

GPA 3.75 or higher:	16%	GPA 2.0-2.99:	46%
GPA 3.50-3.74:	6%	Out-of-state:	12%
GPA 3.0-3.49:	28%	Live on campus:	90%

Basis for selection. High school GPA, test scores, one recommendation. Interview considered. Interviews may be required upon request after application review, possibly due to not meeting particular requirements. **Home schooled:** Statement describing home school structure and mission, transcript of courses and grades, letter of recommendation (nonparent) required.

High school preparation. Recommended units include English 4, mathematics 3, history 2, science 2 and foreign language 1.

2015-2016 Annual costs. Tuition/fees: $29,650. Room only: $5,800. Books/supplies: $500. Personal expenses: $1,200.

Financial aid. **Non-need-based:** Scholarships awarded for academics, alumni affiliation, art, athletics, leadership, music/drama, religious affiliation.

Application procedures. **Admission:** Priority date 12/1; no deadline. No application fee. Application must be submitted online. Admission notification on a rolling basis. **Financial aid:** Closing date 3/1. FAFSA, institutional form required. Applicants notified on a rolling basis starting 3/15; must reply within 2 week(s) of notification.

Academics. **Special study options:** Combined bachelor's/graduate degree, cooperative education, distance learning, double major, dual enrollment of high school students, independent study, internships, liberal arts/career combination, student-designed major, study abroad, urban semester. Study trips to Holy Lands, Italy, Greece, Africa, India, South America. **Credit/placement by examination:** AP, CLEP, IB, institutional tests. 8 credit hours maximum toward associate degree, 8 toward bachelor's. **Support services:** Reduced course load, remedial instruction, study skills assistance, tutoring, writing center.

Majors. **Business:** Business admin, nonprofit/public. **Communications:** Media studies. **Education:** Early childhood. **Philosophy/religion:** Christian, religion. **Psychology:** General. **Theology:** Bible, missionary, sacred music, theology, youth ministry.

Most popular majors. Business/marketing 36%, communications/journalism 16%, psychology 26%, public administration/social services 14%.

Technology on campus. 15 workstations in dormitories, library, computer center, student center. Dormitories wired for high-speed internet access and linked to campus network. Commuter students can connect to campus network. Online library, helpline, wireless network available.

Student life. Freshman orientation: Mandatory. Preregistration for classes offered. Three day session held before classes begin. **Policies:** Dry campus. Residency requirement for those under 21. **Housing:** Guaranteed on-campus for freshmen. Apartments, wellness housing available. $300 fully refundable deposit. **Activities:** Choral groups, drama, music ensembles, musical theater, student government, student newspaper, Student prayer team, chapel planning team, Eagle Outreach, Women of Color club, diversity center, Athletes in Action.

Athletics. NAIA, NCCAA. **Intercollegiate:** Cross-country, golf, soccer, swimming, tennis, track and field. **Intramural:** Basketball, cross-country, football (non-tackle), soccer, ultimate frisbee, volleyball, weight lifting. **Team name:** Eagles.

Student services. Adult student services, chaplain/spiritual director, career counseling, student employment services, financial aid counseling, minority student services, on-campus daycare, personal counseling. **Physically disabled:** Services for visually impaired.

Contact. E-mail: admissions@tlc.edu
Phone: (425) 249-4800 Toll-free number: (800) 843-5659
Fax: (425) 249-4801
Mia Kosinski, Director of Admissions, Trinity Lutheran College, 2802 Wetmore Avenue, Everett, WA 98201

University of Phoenix: Western Washington
Tukwila, Washington
www.phoenix.edu

- For-profit 4-year university
- Large town
- 607 undergraduates
- 90 graduate students

General. Regionally accredited. **Degrees:** 160 bachelor's awarded; master's offered. **Calendar:** Differs by program. **Full-time faculty:** 12 total. **Part-time faculty:** 103 total.

Basis for selection. Open admission.

2015-2016 Annual costs. Per-credit-hour charge, $410 to $635, depending upon level and course of study. Books, material charges, and other fees vary by course and program. All fees are subject to change.

Application procedures. Admission: No deadline. No application fee. **Financial aid:** No deadline.

Academics. Credit/placement by examination: AP, CLEP.

Majors. Business: Accounting/business management, business admin, e-commerce, entrepreneurial studies, finance, human resources, marketing, operations. **Computer sciences:** Database management, networking, programming, security, system admin, systems analysis, web page design, webmaster. **Health services:** Facilities admin, health information management, long term care admin. **Human services:** General. **Protective services:** Disaster management, law enforcement admin.

Student life. Freshman orientation: Mandatory. Preregistration for classes offered.

Contact. Toll-free number: (866) 766-0766
University of Phoenix: Western Washington, 1625 West Fountainhead Parkway, Tempe, AZ 85282

University of Puget Sound
Tacoma, Washington
www.pugetsound.edu
CB member
CB code: 4067

- Private 4-year university and liberal arts college
- Residential campus in small city
- 2,476 degree-seeking undergraduates: 1% part-time, 59% women, 1% African American, 6% Asian American, 7% Hispanic/Latino, 8% Multiracial, non-Hispanic
- 292 degree-seeking graduate students

- 79% of applicants admitted
- Application essay required
- 78% graduate within 6 years

General. Founded in 1888. Regionally accredited. **Degrees:** 616 bachelor's awarded; master's, professional offered. **ROTC:** Army. **Location:** 35 miles from Seattle, 28 miles from Olympia. **Calendar:** Semester, limited summer session. **Full-time faculty:** 237 total; 92% have terminal degrees, 9% minority, 49% women. **Part-time faculty:** 44 total; 9% minority, 59% women. **Class size:** 61% < 20, 37% 20-39, 1% 40-49, less than 1% 50-99. **Special facilities:** Museum of natural history, concert hall, observatory, arboretum, sculpture building, theaters, greenhouse, science laboratories (including electron microscopes, confocal microscope, DNA sequencer, NMR, X-ray diffractometer, microcomputer labs, sedimentology lab, stereoscopic and petrographic microscopes, computerized plotting/digitizing board and image analysis system, portable seismograph, gravimeter, proton precession magnetometer, ICP, GPS and GIS lab), occupational and physical therapy outpatient clinics and laboratories, electronic music composition lab, electronic music keyboard lab with MIDI workstations, three electronic music classrooms, and one music v-room.

Freshman class profile. 5,827 applied, 4,616 admitted, 652 enrolled.

Mid 50% test scores			
SAT critical reading:	560-680	GPA 2.0-2.99:	8%
SAT math:	540-660	Rank in top quarter:	68%
SAT writing:	550-660	Rank in top tenth:	37%
ACT composite:	25-30	Return as sophomores:	86%
GPA 3.75 or higher:	32%	Out-of-state:	84%
GPA 3.50-3.74:	27%	Live on campus:	100%
GPA 3.0-3.49:	33%	Fraternities:	26%
		Sororities:	31%

Basis for selection. All applications evaluated through a holistic process. High school record most important followed by academic GPA. Writing ability as demonstrated through the essay and short answer questions. Recommendations and activities important. SAT or ACT recommended. If applicants have taken both SAT and ACT, they should submit all scores. Audition required for music. **Home schooled:** Statement describing home school structure and mission, transcript of courses and grades, state high school equivalency certificate, letter of recommendation (nonparent) required.

High school preparation. College-preparatory program recommended. 19 units recommended. Recommended units include English 4, mathematics 4, social studies 3, history 3, science 4 (laboratory 4), foreign language 3 and visual/performing arts 1. One fine, visual, or performing art recommended.

2015-2016 Annual costs. Tuition/fees: $44,976. Room/board: $11,480. Books/supplies: $1,000. Personal expenses: $1,800.

2015-2016 Financial aid. **Need-based:** 490 full-time freshmen applied for aid; 354 deemed to have need; 354 received aid. Average need met was 76%. Average scholarship/grant was $24,324; average loan $5,018. 68% of total undergraduate aid awarded as scholarships/grants, 32% as loans/jobs. **Non-need-based:** Awarded to 1,340 full-time undergraduates, including 352 freshmen. Scholarships awarded for academics, alumni affiliation, art, leadership, music/drama, religious affiliation.

Application procedures. **Admission:** Closing date 1/15 (postmark date). $50 fee, may be waived for applicants with need. Admission notification by 4/1. Must reply by May 1 or within 2 week(s) if notified thereafter. **Financial aid:** Priority date 2/1; no closing date. FAFSA required. Students applying for Early Decision must complete the CSS PROFILE for notification of need-based financial aid eligibility. Applicants notified by 3/15; Applicants notified on a rolling basis; must reply by 5/1 or within 2 week(s) of notification.

Academics. All students complete core curriculum, including courses in scholarly inquiry, fine arts, humanistic, mathematical, natural scientific and social scientific approaches, and a connections course intended to develop an understanding of the interrelationship of fields of knowledge. **Special study options:** Cooperative education, double major, honors, independent study, internships, liberal arts/career combination, student-designed major, study abroad, teacher certification program. Institution offers year of study in Asia, 3-2 engineering program, business leadership program. **Credit/placement by examination:** AP, CLEP, IB, institutional tests. **Support services:** Learning center, reduced course load, study skills assistance, tutoring, writing center.

Honors college/program. Undergraduates apply to the Honors program when they apply for admission, and are selected on the basis of academic performance. The 30 or so students in each cohort pursue an intensive program in Puget Sound's core curriculum.

Majors. **Area/ethnic studies:** Asian. **Biology:** General, biochemistry, cellular/molecular. **Business:** Business admin, management information systems. **Communications:** Communications/speech/rhetoric. **Computer sciences:** Computer science. **Education:** Music. **English:** English lit, rhetoric/composition. **Foreign languages:** General, Chinese, classics, East Asian, French,

German, Japanese, Spanish. **History:** General. **Math:** General. **Parks/recreation:** Exercise sciences. **Philosophy/religion:** Philosophy, religion. **Physical sciences:** Chemistry, geology, physics. **Psychology:** General. **Social sciences:** Economics, international economics, political economy, political science, sociology. **Visual/performing arts:** Art, dramatic, music, music management, music performance.

Most popular majors. Biology 11%, business/marketing 12%, English 6%, foreign language 10%, parks/recreation 6%, psychology 8%, social sciences 17%, visual/performing arts 7%.

Technology on campus. Dormitories wired for high-speed internet access and linked to campus network. Commuter students can connect to campus network. Online course registration, online library, helpline, repair service, student web hosting, wireless network available.

Student life. **Freshman orientation:** Mandatory. Preregistration for classes offered. Freshman orientation is a ten day period just prior to the start of classes, and includes Prelude (academic orientation), Passages (off-campus team building) and Perspectives (on-campus orientation to life at Puget Sound). **Policies:** All students required to live on-campus for their first two academic years with the university. **Housing:** Guaranteed on-campus for freshmen. Coed dorms, special housing for disabled, apartments, fraternity/sorority housing, themed housing, wellness housing available. $200 non-refundable deposit, deadline 5/1. Coed by floor, coed by door, academically-themed programs, campus houses, suite style available. **Activities:** Bands, campus ministries, choral groups, dance, drama, film society, international student organizations, literary magazine, music ensembles, Model UN, musical theater, opera, radio station, student government, student newspaper, symphony orchestra, Asian Pacific American Student Union, B-GLAD (Sexual Orientation), Black Student Union, Catholic Campus Fellowship, Community for Hispanic Awareness, Jewish Student Organization, Muslim Student Alliance, Relay for Life, VAVA (Anti-sexual violence), Students for a Sustainable Campus.

Athletics. NCAA. **Intercollegiate:** Baseball M, basketball, cross-country, football (tackle) M, golf, lacrosse W, rowing (crew), soccer, softball W, swimming, track and field, volleyball W. **Intramural:** Basketball, football (non-tackle), racquetball, soccer, softball, tennis, volleyball. **Team name:** Loggers.

Student services. Alcohol/substance abuse counseling, chaplain/spiritual director, career counseling, student employment services, financial aid counseling, health services, legal services, minority student services, personal counseling, placement for graduates. **Physically disabled:** Services for visually, speech, hearing impaired.

Contact. E-mail: admission@pugetsound.edu
Phone: (253) 879-3211 Toll-free number: (800) 396-7191
Fax: (253) 879-3993
James Miller, Senior Associate Director of Admission, University of Puget Sound, 1500 North Warner Street, Tacoma, WA 98416-1062

University of Washington
Seattle, Washington   CB member
www.washington.edu   CB code: 4854

- Public 4-year university
- Residential campus in very large city
- 30,022 degree-seeking undergraduates: 6% part-time, 52% women, 3% African American, 24% Asian American, 7% Hispanic/Latino, 7% Multiracial, non-Hispanic, 15% international
- 14,085 degree-seeking graduate students
- 53% of applicants admitted
- SAT or ACT with writing, application essay required
- 84% graduate within 6 years

General. Founded in 1861. Regionally accredited. **Degrees:** 7,491 bachelor's awarded; master's, professional, doctoral offered. **ROTC:** Army, Naval, Air Force. **Location:** 5 miles from downtown Seattle. **Calendar:** Quarter, extensive summer session. **Full-time faculty:** 1,643 total; 90% have terminal degrees, 23% minority, 43% women. **Part-time faculty:** 1,021 total; 41% have terminal degrees, 12% minority, 49% women. **Class size:** 38% < 20, 33% 20-39, 8% 40-49, 12% 50-99, 9% >100. **Special facilities:** Arboretum, observatory, anthropological museum, applied physics laboratory, planetarium.

Freshman class profile. 36,840 applied, 19,646 admitted, 6,789 enrolled.

Mid 50% test scores			
SAT critical reading:	540-660	GPA 3.0-3.49:	9%
SAT math:	580-710	End year in good standing:	96%
SAT writing:	530-650	Return as sophomores:	94%
ACT composite:	26-31	Out-of-state:	24%
GPA 3.75 or higher:	64%	Live on campus:	65%
GPA 3.50-3.74:	27%	International:	16%

Basis for selection. Applicants holistically reviewed on the basis of completion of core subject requirements, grades and test scores and supplemental factors including personal statement, completion of substantial number of courses beyond minimum, grades in college-preparatory courses, enrollment in AP or honors courses, cultural diversity and documented evidence of exceptional artistic talent. Auditions required for admission to performing arts programs. Application interviews not available, only informational appointments. **Home schooled:** Transcript of courses and grades required. Each applicant is reviewed case-by-case. To confirm successful completion of certain core subject requirements or levels, applicants may be asked to provide additional documentation or placement testing information. **Learning Disabled:** Applicants with documented disabilities not expected to disclose them at time of application, but welcome do so in the applicant's own written materials, or via relevant documentation or letters. Students encouraged to first speak with an admissions counselor.

High school preparation. College-preparatory program required. 15 units required; 20 recommended. Required and recommended units include English 4, mathematics 3-4, social studies 3-4, history 1, science 2-4 (laboratory 2-3), foreign language 2-3, computer science 1, visual/performing arts .5-1, academic electives 0.5. One semester (.5) elective from required subjects list and .5 fine arts course.

2015-2016 Annual costs. Tuition/fees: $11,839; $34,143 out-of-state. Room/board: $11,310. Books/supplies: $1,206. Personal expenses: $2,265.

2015-2016 Financial aid. **Need-based:** 4,573 full-time freshmen applied for aid; 2,755 deemed to have need; 2,572 received aid. Average need met was 82%. Average scholarship/grant was $15,000; average loan $5,500. 77% of total undergraduate aid awarded as scholarships/grants, 23% as loans/jobs. **Non-need-based:** Awarded to 1,950 full-time undergraduates, including 680 freshmen. Scholarships awarded for academics, alumni affiliation, art, athletics, leadership, music/drama, ROTC, state residency. **Additional information:** Tuition not due until third week of term.

Application procedures. **Admission:** Closing date 12/1 (postmark date). $60 fee, may be waived for applicants with need. Admission notification by 3/31. Admission notification on a rolling basis beginning on or about 3/15. Must reply by 5/1. **Financial aid:** Priority date 2/28; no closing date. FAFSA required. Applicants notified by 4/1; Applicants notified on a rolling basis starting 4/1; must reply by 5/1 or within 3 week(s) of notification.

Academics. **Special study options:** Combined bachelor's/graduate degree, cooperative education, cross-registration, distance learning, double major, dual enrollment of high school students, ESL, exchange student, honors, independent study, internships, student-designed major, study abroad, teacher certification program. Quarter at Friday Harbor Laboratories, San Juan Islands. **Credit/placement by examination:** AP, CLEP, IB, institutional tests. 90 credit hours maximum toward bachelor's degree. **Support services:** Learning center, pre-admission summer program, reduced course load, remedial instruction, study skills assistance, tutoring, writing center.

Majors. **Architecture:** Architecture, building sciences, landscape, urban/community planning. **Area/ethnic studies:** Asian, Canadian, Chinese, European, Japanese, Korean, Latin American, Native American, Scandinavian, South Asian, Southeast Asian, women's. **Biology:** General, bacteriology, biochemistry, botany, cellular/molecular, conservation, ecology, marine, microbiology, neurobiology/behavior, physiology. **Business:** Accounting, business admin, entrepreneurial studies, finance, human resources, management information systems, management science, marketing. **Communications:** Communications/speech/rhetoric, journalism, political. **Computer sciences:** General, computer science, informatics, information technology. **Conservation:** Environmental science, fisheries, forest management, forest resources, forestry, wildlife/wilderness. **Education:** Early childhood, mathematics, music. **Engineering:** General, aerospace, biomedical, biomolecular, chemical, civil, computer, electrical, industrial, materials, mechanical, robotics. **English:** English lit, rhetoric/composition, technical writing. **Foreign languages:** Ancient Greek, Biblical, Chinese, classics, comparative lit, Danish, French, Germanic, Italian, Japanese, Korean, Latin, linguistics, Norwegian, Romance, Russian, Slavic, South Asian, Spanish, Swedish, Uralic. **Health services:** Clinical lab science, communication disorders, dental hygiene, EMT paramedic, environmental health, health information management, nursing (RN), orthotics/prosthetics, physician assistant. **History:** General. **Human services:** Social work. **Liberal arts:** Arts/sciences. **Math:** General, applied, computational/applied, statistics. **Philosophy/religion:** Islamic, Judaic, philosophy, religion. **Physical sciences:** Astronomy, atmospheric science, chemistry, climatology, geology, meteorology, oceanography, physics, planetary. **Psychology:** General. **Social sciences:** General,

anthropology, economics, geography, national security policy, physical anthropology, political economy, political science, sociology. **Visual/performing arts:** Acting, art, art history/conservation, ceramics, dance, design, directing/producing, dramatic, industrial design, jazz, multimedia, music, music history, music performance, music theory/composition, musicology, painting, percussion instruments, photography, piano/keyboard, sculpture, stringed instruments, studio arts, voice/opera.

Most popular majors. Biology 11%, business/marketing 10%, communications/journalism 10%, engineering/engineering technologies 8%, social sciences 13%.

Technology on campus. 2,000 workstations in dormitories, library, computer center, student center. Dormitories wired for high-speed internet access and linked to campus network. Commuter students can connect to campus network. Online course registration, online library, helpline, repair service, student web hosting, wireless network available.

Student life. **Freshman orientation:** Mandatory, $272 fee. Preregistration for classes offered. Advising and registration throughout the summer. **Housing:** Coed dorms, special housing for disabled, apartments, fraternity/sorority housing, themed housing available. $500 nonrefundable deposit, deadline 6/1. Special interest houses available. **Activities:** Bands, choral groups, dance, drama, film society, international student organizations, literary magazine, music ensembles, Model UN, musical theater, opera, radio station, student government, student newspaper, symphony orchestra, TV station, Approximately 800 student organizations.

Athletics. NCAA. **Intercollegiate:** Baseball M, basketball, cheerleading, cross-country, football (tackle) M, golf, gymnastics W, rowing (crew), sand volleyball W, soccer, softball W, tennis, track and field, volleyball W. **Intramural:** Badminton, basketball, bowling, football (non-tackle), racquetball, rowing (crew), soccer, softball, swimming, tennis, ultimate frisbee, volleyball. **Team name:** Huskies.

Student services. Alcohol/substance abuse counseling, career counseling, services for economically disadvantaged, student employment services, financial aid counseling, health services, legal services, minority student services, on-campus daycare, personal counseling, placement for graduates, veterans' counselor, women's services. **Physically disabled:** Services for visually, speech, hearing impaired.

Contact. Phone: (206) 543-9686 Fax: (206) 685-3655
Paul Seegert, Director of Admissions, University of Washington, 1410 Northeast Campus Parkway, Box 355852, Seattle, WA 98195-5852

University of Washington Bothell
Bothell, Washington   **CB member**
www.uwb.edu   **CB code: 4467**

- Public 4-year branch campus college
- Residential campus in large town
- 4,660 degree-seeking undergraduates: 13% part-time, 50% women, 6% African American, 26% Asian American, 9% Hispanic/Latino, 1% Native Hawaiian/Pacific islander, 6% Multi-racial, non-Hispanic, 8% international
- 525 degree-seeking graduate students
- 79% of applicants admitted
- SAT or ACT (ACT writing recommended), application essay required
- 70% graduate within 6 years

General. **Degrees:** 1,376 bachelor's awarded; master's offered. **ROTC:** Army, Naval, Air Force. **Location:** 20 miles from Seattle. **Calendar:** Quarter, limited summer session. **Full-time faculty:** 182 total; 93% have terminal degrees, 33% minority, 52% women. **Part-time faculty:** 112 total; 51% have terminal degrees, 21% minority, 49% women. **Class size:** 25% < 20, 49% 20-39, 22% 40-49, 4% 50-99, less than 1% >100. **Special facilities:** 58 acres of wetlands.

Freshman class profile. 2,840 applied, 2,236 admitted, 694 enrolled.

Mid 50% test scores			
SAT critical reading:	450-570	GPA 3.0-3.49:	46%
SAT math:	470-590	GPA 2.0-2.99:	23%
SAT writing:	430-550	End year in good standing:	87%
ACT composite:	19-25	Return as sophomores:	84%
GPA 3.75 or higher:	10%	Out-of-state:	2%
GPA 3.50-3.74:	21%	Live on campus:	24%
		International:	2%

Basis for selection. GPA, test scores, academic rigor, and essays/personal statement are very important. Non-resident alien applicants must report scores from TOEFL or the International English Language Testing System (IELTS).

SAT essay component used for admission for the Business program only. **Home schooled:** Transcript of courses and grades required.

High school preparation. College-preparatory program required. 15 units required; 21 recommended. Required and recommended units include English 4, mathematics 4, social studies 3-4, science 2-4 (laboratory 2-3), foreign language 2, visual/performing arts .5-1, academic electives 0.5. One semester (.5) elective from required subject lists and .5 fine arts course.

2015-2016 Annual costs. Tuition/fees: $11,758; $34,062 out-of-state. Room/board: $10,833. Books/supplies: $1,206. Personal expenses: $2,265.

2015-2016 Financial aid. Need-based: 397 full-time freshmen applied for aid; 342 deemed to have need; 321 received aid. Average need met was 82%. Average scholarship/grant was $15,000; average loan $5,500. 75% of total undergraduate aid awarded as scholarships/grants, 25% as loans/jobs. **Non-need-based:** Awarded to 180 full-time undergraduates, including 35 freshmen. Scholarships awarded for academics, alumni affiliation, art, athletics, leadership, music/drama, ROTC, state residency.

Application procedures. Admission: Priority date 1/15; no deadline. $60 fee, may be waived for applicants with need. Application must be submitted online. Admission notification on a rolling basis beginning on or about 9/1. Must reply by May 1 or within 3 week(s) if notified thereafter. **Financial aid:** Priority date 2/28; no closing date. FAFSA required. Applicants notified by 4/1; must reply by 5/1 or within 3 week(s) of notification.

Academics. Special study options: Combined bachelor's/graduate degree, cross-registration, double major, ESL, independent study, internships, student-designed major, study abroad, teacher certification program. **Credit/placement by examination:** AP, CLEP, IB, institutional tests. 90 credit hours maximum toward bachelor's degree. **Support services:** Learning center, pre-admission summer program, reduced course load, study skills assistance, tutoring, writing center.

Majors. Area/ethnic studies: American, women's. **Biology:** General, biochemistry. **Business:** Accounting, business admin. **Communications:** Digital media, media studies. **Computer sciences:** General, applications programming, computer science, information systems, programming, systems analysis, web page design. **Conservation:** Environmental science, environmental studies. **Education:** General, elementary. **Engineering:** Computer, electrical, mechanical. **Health services:** Nursing (RN). **Liberal arts:** Humanities. **Math:** General. **Philosophy/religion:** Ethics. **Physical sciences:** Chemistry, physics. **Psychology:** Community. **Social sciences:** Political economy.

Most popular majors. Biology 10%, business/marketing 19%, communications/journalism 6%, computer/information sciences 16%, engineering/engineering technologies 7%, health sciences 16%, psychology 7%.

Technology on campus. 498 workstations in library, computer center, student center. Dormitories wired for high-speed internet access. Commuter students can connect to campus network. Online course registration, online library, helpline, student web hosting, wireless network available.

Student life. Freshman orientation: Mandatory, $250 fee. Preregistration for classes offered. **Housing:** Coed dorms, single-sex dorms, special housing for disabled, apartments, themed housing available. $50 nonrefundable deposit, deadline 5/1. Living-learning communities available. **Activities:** Campus ministries, dance, film society, international student organizations, literary magazine, radio station, student government, student newspaper, African Student Association, Black Student Union, Chinese Student Association, Japanese Student Association, Korean Student Association, Latinx Student Union, Mexican Student Union, Taiwanese Student Association, Vietnamese Student Association, Gender Equity club.

Athletics. Intramural: Basketball, football (non-tackle), soccer, softball, tennis, volleyball. **Team name:** Huskies.

Student services. Career counseling, student employment services, financial aid counseling, personal counseling, veterans' counselor. **Physically disabled:** Services for visually, speech, hearing impaired.

Contact. E-mail: info@uwb.edu
Phone: (425) 352-5000 Toll-free number: (800) 736-6650
Fax: (425) 352-5455
Director of Admission, University of Washington Bothell, Box 358500, Enrollment Management, Bothell, WA 98011

University of Washington Tacoma

Tacoma, Washington   **CB member**
www.tacoma.uw.edu   **CB code: 4445**

- Public 4-year university
- Commuter campus in small city

- 3,884 degree-seeking undergraduates: 11% part-time, 52% women, 7% African American, 18% Asian American, 12% Hispanic/Latino, 1% Native American, 2% Native Hawaiian/Pacific islander, 8% Multi-racial, non-Hispanic, 5% international
- 673 degree-seeking graduate students
- 83% of applicants admitted
- SAT or ACT (ACT writing optional), application essay required
- 63% graduate within 6 years

General. Regionally accredited. Campus set in the historic Warehouse District of downtown Tacoma. The university has earned architectural awards for transforming the buildings into modern classrooms. **Degrees:** 1,294 bachelor's awarded; master's offered. **ROTC:** Army, Naval, Air Force. **Location:** 30 miles from Seattle. **Calendar:** Quarter, limited summer session. **Full-time faculty:** 222 total; 84% have terminal degrees, 28% minority, 54% women. **Part-time faculty:** 68 total; 40% have terminal degrees, 13% minority, 43% women. **Class size:** 36% < 20, 54% 20-39, 11% 40-49, less than 1% 50-99. **Special facilities:** Center for Urban Waters: a collective for scientists, analysts, engineers and policy makers seeking creative and sustainable solutions to the restoration and protection of urban waterways; access to the environmental and oceanic labs at Friday Harbor; experimental forest lands and gardens; museums.

Freshman class profile. 1,577 applied, 1,302 admitted, 461 enrolled.

Mid 50% test scores			
SAT critical reading:	410-550	GPA 3.0-3.49:	42%
SAT math:	440-550	GPA 2.0-2.99:	30%
SAT writing:	400-520	End year in good standing:	81%
ACT composite:	16-22	Return as sophomores:	78%
GPA 3.75 or higher:	12%	Out-of-state:	3%
GPA 3.50-3.74:	16%	Live on campus:	13%
		International:	1%

Basis for selection. Admissions based on school achievement record, including quality of test scores, fullness of application including essay and involvement. **Home schooled:** Transcript of courses and grades required.

High school preparation. College-preparatory program required. 15 units required. Required units include English 4, mathematics 3, social studies 3, science 2 (laboratory 2), foreign language 2, visual/performing arts .5, academic electives 0.5. 1 Quantitative course senior year.

2015-2016 Annual costs. Tuition/fees: $11,905; $34,209 out-of-state. Room/board: $10,833. Books/supplies: $1,206. Personal expenses: $2,265.

2015-2016 Financial aid. Need-based: 397 full-time freshmen applied for aid; 342 deemed to have need; 321 received aid. Average need met was 82%. Average scholarship/grant was $15,000; average loan $5,500. 69% of total undergraduate aid awarded as scholarships/grants, 31% as loans/jobs. **Non-need-based:** Awarded to 180 full-time undergraduates, including 35 freshmen. Scholarships awarded for academics, alumni affiliation, art, athletics, leadership, music/drama, ROTC, state residency.

Application procedures. Admission: Priority date 1/15; deadline 6/30 (receipt date). $60 fee, may be waived for applicants with need. Application must be submitted online. Admission notification on a rolling basis beginning on or about 11/1. Must reply by May 1 or within 2 week(s) if notified thereafter. **Financial aid:** Priority date 2/28; no closing date. FAFSA required. Applicants notified by 4/1; must reply by 5/1.

Academics. Special study options: Cross-registration, distance learning, double major, dual enrollment of high school students, honors, independent study, internships, student-designed major, study abroad, teacher certification program. **Credit/placement by examination:** AP, CLEP, IB, SAT, ACT, institutional tests. 90 credit hours maximum toward bachelor's degree. **Support services:** Learning center, pre-admission summer program, remedial instruction, study skills assistance, tutoring, writing center.

Majors. Area/ethnic studies: General, American. **Biology:** Biomedical sciences. **Business:** Accounting, business admin, finance, management science, marketing. **Communications:** Media studies. **Computer sciences:** General, information technology, systems analysis. **Conservation:** Environmental science, environmental studies. **English:** Writing. **Foreign languages:** Hispanic and Latin American. **Health services:** Nursing (RN). **History:** General, American, Asian, European. **Human services:** Social work. **Liberal arts:** Arts/sciences. **Math:** Mathematics/statistics. **Protective services:** Police science. **Psychology:** General. **Social sciences:** International relations, political economy, political science, urban studies.

Most popular majors. Business/marketing 10%, communications/journalism 13%, computer/information sciences 15%, natural resources/environmental science 6%, psychology 18%, social sciences 12%.

Technology on campus. 166 workstations in library, computer center, student center. Commuter students can connect to campus network. Online course registration, online library, helpline, student web hosting, wireless network available.

Student life. Freshman orientation: Mandatory. Preregistration for classes offered. **Housing:** Apartments available. $250 partly refundable deposit, deadline 6/1. On-campus housing program houses a small number of students in apartments. Off-campus housing listings as well as resources to obtain off-campus living options available. **Activities:** Campus ministries, drama, international student organizations, literary magazine, student government, student newspaper, Accounting Student Association, Asian Pacific Islander Student Union, Black Student Union, CIVITAS, game developer's club, Global Business Society, Grey Hat Group, International Student Association, Korean American International Student Team, Latinos Embracing Education.

Athletics. Team name: Huskies.

Student services. Alcohol/substance abuse counseling, career counseling, student employment services, financial aid counseling, health services, minority student services, personal counseling, veterans' counselor, women's services. **Physically disabled:** Services for visually, speech, hearing impaired.

Contact. E-mail: uwtinfo@u.washington.edu
Phone: (253) 692-4742 Toll-free number: (800) 736-7750
Fax: (253) 692-4414
Karl Smith, Associate Vice Chancellor & Chief Admissions Officer, University of Washington Tacoma, Campus Box 358430, Tacoma, WA 98402-3100

Walla Walla University
College Place, Washington
www.wallawalla.edu
CB code: 4940

- Private 4-year university and liberal arts college affiliated with the Seventh-day Adventists
- Residential campus in large town
- 1,622 degree-seeking undergraduates: 4% part-time, 50% women, 3% African American, 7% Asian American, 14% Hispanic/Latino, 1% Native American, 1% Native Hawaiian/Pacific islander
- 178 degree-seeking graduate students
- SAT or ACT (ACT writing optional) required
- 50% graduate within 6 years

General. Founded in 1892. Regionally accredited. Branch campus in Portland, Oregon for students in the final two years of the nursing program. Summer biology courses offered at school's marine research facility near Anacortes, Washington. Graduate social work program with course offerings also in Billings and Missoula, Montana. **Degrees:** 296 bachelor's, 19 associate awarded; master's offered. **ROTC:** Army. **Location:** 270 miles from Seattle, 250 miles from Portland, OR. **Calendar:** Quarter, extensive summer session. **Full-time faculty:** 108 total; 10% have terminal degrees, 5% minority, 42% women. **Part-time faculty:** 64 total; 8% have terminal degrees, 3% minority, 58% women. **Class size:** 55% < 20, 32% 20-39, 6% 40-49, 7% 50-99. **Special facilities:** Marine biological research facility near Puget Sound, observatory on engineering/mathematics building.

Freshman class profile. 1,816 applied, 1,025 admitted, 362 enrolled.

Mid 50% test scores			
SAT critical reading:	460-590	GPA 3.0-3.49:	29%
SAT math:	460-570	GPA 2.0-2.99:	9%
SAT writing:	450-570	Rank in top quarter:	40%
ACT composite:	20-27	Rank in top tenth:	15%
GPA 3.75 or higher:	43%	Out-of-state:	67%
GPA 3.50-3.74:	19%	International:	1%

Basis for selection. Open admission, but selective for some programs. Must have combined 2.5 high school GPA. If entering with GED, must have average score of 50 or higher and each test must be 45 or higher. Official TOEFL scores required for prospective students whose first language is not English. Audition recommended. **Home schooled:** May be admitted by acceptable score on ACT test, GED test, or transcript from accredited home school organization.

High school preparation. College-preparatory program recommended. 11 units required. Required units include English 4, mathematics 3, history 2, science 1 (laboratory 1). Mathematics units must be algebra and geometry. 2 laboratory units recommended.

2016-2017 Annual costs. Tuition/fees: $26,982. Room/board: $6,990. Books/supplies: $1,050. Personal expenses: $1,845.

2014-2015 Financial aid. Need-based: 274 full-time freshmen applied for aid; 234 deemed to have need; 234 received aid. Average need met was 93%. Average scholarship/grant was $5,433; average loan $3,127. 65% of total undergraduate aid awarded as scholarships/grants, 35% as loans/jobs. **Non-need-based:** Awarded to 1,298 full-time undergraduates, including 338 freshmen. Scholarships awarded for academics, leadership, music/drama, state residency.

Application procedures. Admission: No deadline. $40 fee, may be waived for applicants with need. Admission notification on a rolling basis beginning on or about 6/1. **Financial aid:** Priority date 4/30; no closing date. FAFSA, institutional form required. Applicants notified on a rolling basis starting 2/15.

Academics. Special study options: Combined bachelor's/graduate degree, cooperative education, distance learning, double major, dual enrollment of high school students, honors, independent study, internships, liberal arts/career combination, study abroad, teacher certification program. **Credit/placement by examination:** AP, CLEP, IB, SAT, ACT, institutional tests. 12 credit hours maximum toward associate degree, 24 toward bachelor's. **Support services:** Learning center, pre-admission summer program, reduced course load, remedial instruction, study skills assistance, tutoring, writing center.

Majors. Biology: General, biochemistry, biophysics. **Business:** Accounting, business admin, finance, human resources, international, management science. **Communications:** Communications/speech/rhetoric, journalism, media studies. **Communications technology:** Graphic/printing. **Computer sciences:** General, computer graphics, computer science, data processing, information systems. **Education:** General, business, elementary, music, physical, special ed, voc/tech. **Engineering:** General, biomedical, civil, computer, electrical, mechanical. **English:** English lit. **Foreign languages:** French, Spanish. **Health services:** Nursing (RN). **History:** General. **Human services:** Social work. **Liberal arts:** Arts/sciences. **Math:** General. **Philosophy/religion:** Religion. **Physical sciences:** Chemistry, physics. **Psychology:** General. **Social sciences:** Sociology. **Theology:** Theology. **Visual/performing arts:** Art, music, music performance.

Most popular majors. Biology 7%, business/marketing 10%, education 6%, engineering/engineering technologies 14%, health sciences 24%.

Technology on campus. 105 workstations in dormitories, library, computer center. Dormitories wired for high-speed internet access and linked to campus network. Commuter students can connect to campus network. Online course registration, online library, helpline, repair service, student web hosting, wireless network available.

Student life. Freshman orientation: Mandatory. Preregistration for classes offered. Held during week before classes begin. **Policies:** Chapel requirement once a week; worship policy for resident students. Religious observance required. **Housing:** Guaranteed on-campus for all undergraduates. Single-sex dorms, special housing for disabled, apartments available. $200 nonrefundable deposit. **Activities:** Bands, campus ministries, choral groups, dance, drama, film society, international student organizations, literary magazine, music ensembles, musical theater, radio station, student government, student newspaper, symphony orchestra, TV station, student entrepreneur group, student missionary groups, drama, ethnic student organizations, academic department clubs, service clubs, music groups.

Athletics. NCCAA. **Intercollegiate:** Basketball, soccer M, softball W, volleyball W. **Intramural:** Badminton, basketball, football (non-tackle), racquetball, soccer, softball, table tennis, tennis, volleyball. **Team name:** Wolves.

Student services. Chaplain/spiritual director, career counseling, student employment services, financial aid counseling, health services, minority student services, on-campus daycare, personal counseling, placement for graduates, veterans' counselor. **Physically disabled:** Services for visually, speech, hearing impaired.

Contact. E-mail: dallas@wallawalla.edu
Phone: (509) 527-2608 Toll-free number: (800) 541-8900
Fax: (509) 527-2397
Dallas Weis, Director for Admissions/International Student Advisor, Walla Walla University, 204 South College Avenue, College Place, WA 99324-3000

Washington State University
Pullman, Washington
www.wsu.edu
CB member
CB code: 4705

- Public 4-year university
- Residential campus in large town

♦ 24,100 degree-seeking undergraduates: 12% part-time, 52% women, 3% African American, 5% Asian American, 13% Hispanic/Latino, 1% Native American, 8% Multi-racial, non-Hispanic, 5% international

♦ 4,940 degree-seeking graduate students

♦ 80% of applicants admitted

♦ SAT or ACT (ACT writing optional) required

♦ 64% graduate within 6 years

General. Founded in 1890. Regionally accredited. Regional campuses in Spokane, Tri-Cities, Vancouver, Everett, and Global Campus (online degree programs). **Degrees:** 5,513 bachelor's awarded; master's, professional, doctoral offered. **ROTC:** Army, Naval, Air Force. **Location:** 75 miles from Spokane. **Calendar:** Semester, extensive summer session. **Full-time faculty:** 1,356 total; 87% have terminal degrees, 14% minority, 41% women. **Part-time faculty:** 530 total; 49% have terminal degrees, 9% minority, 51% women. **Class size:** 31% < 20, 36% 20-39, 8% 40-49, 16% 50-99, 9% >100. **Special facilities:** Multiple museums, entomological collection, livestock centers, labs, and barns, radio and TV stations, digital recording studio, music listening library, fine arts studio facilities, child development lab, financial markets lab (trading room), food sensory evaluation lab, culinary lab and teaching kitchen, social and economic sciences research center, planetarium and astronomical observatory, specialized teaching and research labs for science and engineering, including a bio-molecular x-ray crystallography center, genomics and gene sequencing lab, virtual reality computer-integrated manufacturing lab, hydraulics lab, laboratory for atmospheric research, wildlife center, ecological reserves, greenhouses, agronomic research farms, horticultural orchard, organic teaching farm and market, veterinary teaching hospital, human anatomy lab, water research center, nuclear radiation center.

Freshman class profile. 19,766 applied, 15,742 admitted, 4,727 enrolled.

Mid 50% test scores		Rank in top quarter:	54%
SAT critical reading:	450-570	Rank in top tenth:	35%
SAT math:	460-580	Return as sophomores:	78%
SAT writing:	430-550	Out-of-state:	17%
ACT composite:	20-26	Live on campus:	86%
GPA 3.75 or higher:	19%	International:	3%
GPA 3.50-3.74:	18%	Fraternities:	15%
GPA 3.0-3.49:	39%	Sororities:	27%
GPA 2.0-2.99:	24%		

Basis for selection. Combination of high school GPA and SAT or ACT scores, completion of required course work, and personal statement. Special circumstances and recommendations considered in some cases. Assured admission for U.S. high school students ranked in top 10% of high school class or with minimum 3.5 GPA. Updated admission requirements for English proficiency for nonnative speakers: MELAB minimum score of 77, IELTS minimum score of 6.5. Minimum scores for TOEFL: 550 paper-based, 79 internet-based, 213 computer based, and SAT 500 critical reading sub score. An appeal process is available for those denied admission. **Home schooled:** Transcript of courses and grades required. An academic resume (homeschool transcript) should provide documentation of all subjects studied, text books used, and detailed proof that home-based instruction fulfills core requirements. Resume must include signature of parent or guardian responsible for the student's curriculum. **Learning Disabled:** Upon acceptance a student can opt to notify Access Center of desire to have assistance with disability.

High school preparation. College-preparatory program required. 16 units required; 17 recommended. Required and recommended units include English 4, mathematics 3-4, social studies 3, science 2, foreign language 2, visual/performing arts 1 and academic electives 1. 4 English, 3 math (1 credit each of algebra, geometry, and algebra II) and social science, 2 of the same world language (includes Native American languages and American Sign Language), and lab science (including 1 that is algebra-based), and 1 of fine, visual, or performing arts, or 1 elective from any of the other required subjects.

2015-2016 Annual costs. Tuition/fees: $10,916; $24,516 out-of-state. Room/board: $11,356. **Additional information:** Note that fees vary by campus.

2014-2015 Financial aid. **Need-based:** 3,699 full-time freshmen applied for aid; 2,823 deemed to have need; 2,659 received aid. Average need met was 63%. Average scholarship/grant was $11,772; average loan $3,516. 70% of total undergraduate aid awarded as scholarships/grants, 30% as loans/jobs. **Non-need-based:** Awarded to 7,144 full-time undergraduates, including 2,368 freshmen. Scholarships awarded for academics, alumni affiliation, art, athletics, job skills, leadership, minority status, music/drama, religious affiliation, ROTC, state residency.

Application procedures. Admission: Priority date 1/31; no deadline. $50 fee, may be waived for applicants with need. Admission notification on a rolling basis beginning on or about 11/1. Must reply by May 1 or within 2 week(s) if notified thereafter. **Financial aid:** Closing date 1/31. FAFSA required. Applicants notified on a rolling basis starting 4/15; must reply within 2 week(s) of notification.

Academics. Special study options: Accelerated study, combined bachelor's/graduate degree, cooperative education, cross-registration, distance learning, double major, dual enrollment of high school students, ESL, exchange student, external degree, honors, independent study, internships, liberal arts/career combination, semester at sea, student-designed major, study abroad, teacher certification program. **Credit/placement by examination:** AP, CLEP, IB, SAT, ACT, institutional tests. **Support services:** Learning center, pre-admission summer program, reduced course load, study skills assistance, tutoring, writing center.

Honors college/program. Acceptance is competitive. In addition to a completed WSU application, all Honors applicants are required to submit an essay. Selection based on GPA, SAT/ACT scores, essay responses, strength of high school or college coursework, Running Start credits, AP/IB programs, honors courses, and evidence of overall motivation, organizational skills, and a desire for challenge. Honors students complete a curriculum that replaces the University Common requirements. Approximately 200 students admitted each year.

Majors. Architecture: Architecture, interior, landscape. **Area/ethnic studies:** Asian, women's. **Biology:** General, biochemistry, biomedical sciences, genetics, microbiology, molecular genetics, neuroscience, zoology. **Business:** General, accounting, business admin, construction management, entrepreneurial studies, finance, hospitality admin, international, management information systems, marketing, operations, real estate. **Communications:** Digital media, media studies. **Computer sciences:** General, computer science. **Conservation:** General, environmental science, forestry, wildlife/wilderness. **Education:** Bilingual, elementary, ESL, kindergarten/preschool, multi-level teacher, physical, reading, science, secondary, special ed. **Engineering:** Biomedical, chemical, civil, computer, electrical, manufacturing, materials, mechanical. **English:** English lit. **Foreign languages:** General, Chinese, French, linguistics, Spanish. **Health services:** Athletic training, audiology/speech pathology, nursing (RN), premedicine. **History:** General. **Human services:** Public policy. **Liberal arts:** Arts/sciences, humanities. **Math:** General, applied. **Parks/recreation:** Exercise sciences, sports admin. **Philosophy/religion:** Philosophy, religion. **Physical sciences:** General, chemistry, geology, physics. **Protective services:** Law enforcement admin. **Psychology:** General. **Social sciences:** General, anthropology, economics, political science, sociology. **Visual/performing arts:** Interior design, music, music performance, music theory/composition, studio arts. **Work/family studies:** General, clothing/textiles, family studies, food/nutrition, human nutrition.

Most popular majors. Biology 6%, business/marketing 20%, communications/journalism 8%, engineering/engineering technologies 11%, health sciences 7%, psychology 6%, social sciences 12%.

Technology on campus. 2,500 workstations in dormitories, library, computer center, student center. Dormitories wired for high-speed internet access and linked to campus network. Commuter students can connect to campus network. Online course registration, online library, helpline, student web hosting, wireless network available.

Student life. Freshman orientation: Mandatory, $230 fee. Preregistration for classes offered. Two and a half and three day programs offered during the summer months. Available to new students (freshmen and transfer) and parents. **Policies:** Washington State Law requires single undergraduate freshmen under 20 years of age to live in organized living groups officially recognized by the university (residence halls, fraternities and sororities), for one academic year. Running Start students are considered freshmen with college credits, not regularly enrolled students, and are subject to the live-in requirements. **Housing:** Guaranteed on-campus for freshmen. Coed dorms, single-sex dorms, special housing for disabled, apartments, cooperative housing, fraternity/sorority housing, themed housing, wellness housing available. $150 nonrefundable deposit, deadline 6/1. Freshman Focus living/learning communities available. **Activities:** Bands, campus ministries, choral groups, dance, drama, film society, international student organizations, literary magazine, music ensembles, Model UN, musical theater, opera, radio station, student government, student newspaper, symphony orchestra, TV station, over 350 clubs and special interest groups.

Athletics. NCAA. **Intercollegiate:** Baseball M, basketball, cheerleading, cross-country, football (tackle) M, golf, rowing (crew) W, soccer W, swimming W, tennis W, track and field, volleyball W. **Intramural:** Badminton, basketball, football (non-tackle), golf, racquetball, soccer, softball, table tennis, tennis, triathlon, ultimate frisbee, volleyball. **Team name:** Cougars.

Student services. Adult student services, alcohol/substance abuse counseling, career counseling, services for economically disadvantaged, student employment services, financial aid counseling, health services, legal services, minority student services, on-campus daycare, personal counseling, placement for graduates, veterans' counselor, women's services. **Physically disabled:** Services for visually, speech, hearing impaired.

Contact. E-mail: admissions@wsu.edu
Phone: (509) 335-5586 Toll-free number: (888) 468-6978
Fax: (509) 335-4902
Wendy Peterson, Director of Admissions, Washington State University, 370 Lighty Student Services Bldg, Pullman, WA 99164-1067

Western Washington University
Bellingham, Washington
www.wwu.edu

CB member
CB code: 4947

- Public 4-year university
- Residential campus in small city
- 14,336 degree-seeking undergraduates: 8% part-time, 55% women, 2% African American, 7% Asian American, 8% Hispanic/Latino, 9% Multiracial, non-Hispanic, 1% international
- 930 graduate students
- 82% of applicants admitted
- SAT or ACT (ACT writing optional), application essay required
- 72% graduate within 6 years

General. Founded in 1893. Regionally accredited. **Degrees:** 3,210 bachelor's awarded; master's offered. **Location:** 90 miles from Seattle. **Calendar:** Quarter, extensive summer session. **Full-time faculty:** 598 total; 87% have terminal degrees, 14% minority, 46% women. **Part-time faculty:** 330 total; 36% have terminal degrees, 11% minority, 57% women. **Class size:** 37% < 20, 41% 20-39, 6% 40-49, 12% 50-99, 4% >100. **Special facilities:** Wind tunnel, electron microscope, neutron generator laboratory, planetarium, air pollution laboratory, motor vehicle research laboratory, electronic music studio, 11-acre recreational park on lake, marine laboratory, integrated laboratory network.

Freshman class profile. 9,933 applied, 8,183 admitted, 2,809 enrolled.

Mid 50% test scores			
SAT critical reading:	500-620	GPA 2.0-2.99:	9%
SAT math:	500-600	Rank in top quarter:	54%
SAT writing:	470-580	Rank in top tenth:	23%
ACT composite:	22-27	End year in good standing:	86%
GPA 3.75 or higher:	23%	Return as sophomores:	83%
GPA 3.50-3.74:	24%	Out-of-state:	14%
GPA 3.0-3.49:	44%	Live on campus:	90%

Basis for selection. Academic achievement most significant factor. Curriculum rigor (level and difficulty of courses), grade trends, school, community activities, special talent, multicultural experience, personal circumstances considered. All students encouraged to take courses beyond minimums. Consideration given to motivation, achievements outside of classroom, multicultural experience, and attributes that will enhance institution's learning community. Audition recommended for music; portfolio required for art.

High school preparation. College-preparatory program required. 16 units required. Required units include English 4, mathematics 3, social studies 3, science 2 (laboratory 1), foreign language 2, visual/performing arts .5, academic electives 0.5. Mathematics requirement includes 1 geometry and 2 algebra. Sciences include 1 algebra-based chemistry or physics. Foreign language should be in 1 language. Fine arts .5, academic elective .5 required.

2015-2016 Annual costs. Tuition/fees: $8,611; $20,963 out-of-state. Room/board: $10,342. Books/supplies: $1,098. Personal expenses: $1,833.

2015-2016 Financial aid. **Need-based:** 2,298 full-time freshmen applied for aid; 1,522 deemed to have need; 1,484 received aid. Average need met was 87%. Average scholarship/grant was $9,297; average loan $3,804. 52% of total undergraduate aid awarded as scholarships/grants, 48% as loans/jobs. **Non-need-based:** Awarded to 605 full-time undergraduates, including 215 freshmen. Scholarships awarded for academics, alumni affiliation, art, athletics, job skills, leadership, minority status, music/drama, state residency. **Additional information:** Short-term student loans ranging from $100 to $1,000 available on a quarterly basis.

Application procedures. **Admission:** Closing date 1/31 (postmark date). $55 fee, may be waived for applicants with need. Admission notification on a rolling basis beginning on or about 11/1. Must reply by May 1 or within 2 week(s) if notified thereafter. **Financial aid:** Priority date 2/15; no closing date. FAFSA required. Applicants notified on a rolling basis starting 3/20; must reply by 5/11 or within 3 week(s) of notification.

Academics. **Special study options:** Combined bachelor's/graduate degree, distance learning, double major, ESL, exchange student, honors, independent study, internships, student-designed major, study abroad, teacher certification program. **Credit/placement by examination:** AP, CLEP, IB, institutional tests. 135 credit hours maximum toward bachelor's degree. **Support services:** Learning center, study skills assistance, tutoring, writing center.

Majors. **Area/ethnic studies:** American, Canadian, East Asian. **Biology:** General, biochemistry, botany, cell/histology, cellular/molecular, ecology, evolutionary, marine, zoology. **Business:** Accounting, business admin, finance, human resources, international, management information systems, marketing, operations. **Communications:** Communications/speech/rhetoric,

journalism. **Computer sciences:** General. **Conservation:** Environmental science, environmental studies. **Education:** Art, biology, chemistry, drama/dance, elementary, English, German, history, mathematics, music, physical, science, social science, social studies, Spanish, special ed, speech, technology/industrial arts. **Engineering:** Electrical, manufacturing, polymer. **English:** Creative writing, English lit. **Foreign languages:** General, French, German, Japanese, linguistics, Spanish. **Health services:** Audiology/speech pathology, community health services. **History:** General. **Liberal arts:** Humanities. **Math:** General, applied. **Parks/recreation:** General, health/fitness. **Philosophy/religion:** Philosophy. **Physical sciences:** Chemistry, geology, geophysics, physics. **Psychology:** General, developmental. **Social sciences:** Anthropology, archaeology, economics, geography, political science, sociology. **Visual/performing arts:** General, art, art history/conservation, ceramics, commercial/advertising art, dance, design, dramatic, drawing, fiber arts, graphic design, industrial design, multimedia, music, music history, music performance, music theory/composition, painting, photography, printmaking, sculpture. **Work/family studies:** Child development.

Most popular majors. Business/marketing 14%, education 6%, English 6%, health sciences 7%, interdisciplinary studies 6%, social sciences 12%, visual/performing arts 6%.

Technology on campus. 2,153 workstations in dormitories, library, computer center, student center. Dormitories wired for high-speed internet access and linked to campus network. Commuter students can connect to campus network. Online course registration, online library, helpline, repair service, student web hosting, wireless network available.

Student life. **Freshman orientation:** Available. Preregistration for classes offered. 6 programs offered for students and family members, early-mid August. Program 1-2 days, based on housing needs. **Housing:** Coed dorms, special housing for disabled, apartments, themed housing, wellness housing available. $200 partly refundable deposit, deadline 6/15. Multicultural floors, honors, quiet floors, freshman interest groups available. **Activities:** Bands, campus ministries, choral groups, dance, drama, film society, international student organizations, literary magazine, music ensembles, musical theater, opera, radio station, student government, student newspaper, symphony orchestra, TV station, Campus Christian Fellowship, veteran's outreach center, volunteer services and resources, international student club, The Inn (nondenominational), ethnic student center, Mecha, Circle K, American Red Cross chapter.

Athletics. NCAA. **Intercollegiate:** Basketball, cross-country, golf, rowing (crew), soccer, softball W, track and field, volleyball W. **Intramural:** Basketball, football (non-tackle), golf, racquetball, soccer, softball, table tennis, tennis, volleyball. **Team name:** Vikings.

Student services. Adult student services, alcohol/substance abuse counseling, chaplain/spiritual director, career counseling, student employment services, financial aid counseling, health services, minority student services, on-campus daycare, personal counseling, placement for graduates, veterans' counselor. **Physically disabled:** Services for visually, speech, hearing impaired.

Contact. E-mail: admit@wwu.edu
Phone: (360) 650-3440 Fax: (360) 650-7369
Jeanne Gaffney, Associate Dir of Admissions, Western Washington University, 516 High Street, Bellingham, WA 98225-9009

Whitman College
Walla Walla, Washington
www.whitman.edu

CB member
CB code: 4951

- Private 4-year liberal arts college
- Residential campus in large town
- 1,444 degree-seeking undergraduates: 1% part-time, 58% women, 1% African American, 5% Asian American, 7% Hispanic/Latino, 7% Multiracial, non-Hispanic, 5% international
- 43% of applicants admitted
- SAT or ACT with writing, application essay required
- 87% graduate within 6 years

General. Founded in 1883. Regionally accredited. **Degrees:** 374 bachelor's awarded. **Location:** 160 miles from Spokane, 235 miles from Portland, Oregon; 260 miles from Seattle. **Calendar:** Semester. **Full-time faculty:** 170 total; 95% have terminal degrees, 7% minority, 50% women. **Part-time faculty:** 64 total; 55% have terminal degrees, 5% minority, 45% women. **Class size:** 70% < 20, 30% 20-39, less than 1% 40-49. **Special facilities:** Asian art collection, natural history museum, planetarium, two electron microscopes, outdoor observatory, outdoor sculpture walk, organic garden.

Freshman class profile. 3,790 applied, 1,619 admitted, 364 enrolled.

Mid 50% test scores		Rank in top quarter:	88%
SAT critical reading:	600-720	Rank in top tenth:	54%
SAT math:	610-700	End year in good standing:	99%
SAT writing:	600-700	Return as sophomores:	93%
ACT composite:	27-32	Out-of-state:	66%
GPA 3.75 or higher:	55%	Live on campus:	100%
GPA 3.50-3.74:	27%	International:	7%
GPA 3.0-3.49:	17%	Fraternities:	38%
GPA 2.0-2.99:	1%	Sororities:	41%

Basis for selection. Scholastic record, quality of written expression, level of motivation very important. Evidence of talent, imagination, creativity, leadership, responsibility, maturity also considered. Writing for all students. TOEFL, ELPT, or APIEL accepted as language proficiency exams. Interview recommended.

High school preparation. College-preparatory program recommended. 15 units recommended. Recommended units include English 4, mathematics 4, social studies 2, history 2, science 3 (laboratory 3) and foreign language 2.

2015-2016 Annual costs. Tuition/fees: $46,138. Room/board: $11,564. Books/supplies: $1,400.

2015-2016 Financial aid. Need-based: 237 full-time freshmen applied for aid; 183 deemed to have need; 183 received aid. Average need met was 96%. Average scholarship/grant was $33,224; average loan $4,453. 85% of total undergraduate aid awarded as scholarships/grants, 15% as loans/jobs. **Non-need-based:** Awarded to 700 full-time undergraduates, including 157 freshmen. Scholarships awarded for academics, art, minority status, music/drama.

Application procedures. Admission: Priority date 11/15; deadline 1/15 (postmark date). $50 fee, may be waived for applicants with need. Admission notification on a rolling basis beginning on or about 4/1. Must reply by 5/1. **Financial aid:** Priority date 11/15, closing date 2/1. FAFSA, CSS PROFILE required. Applicants notified by 4/1; must reply by 5/1.

Academics. Special study options: Accelerated study, combined bachelor's/graduate degree, cooperative education, cross-registration, double major, dual enrollment of high school students, exchange student, honors, independent study, internships, liberal arts/career combination, student-designed major, study abroad, urban semester, Washington semester. Study abroad opportunities in over 20 countries; Summer program in China interdisciplinary field program that focuses on public land conservation in the American West; Summer program that provides an opportunity to do fieldwork centered on the natural and human ecologies of Wallowa County, OR. 3-2 engineering and computer science programs with California Institute of Technology, Columbia University (NY), Duke University (NC), Washington University (MO) and University of Washington; 3-2 forestry and environmental management programs with Duke University; 3-2 oceanography and biology or geology program with University of Washington; 3-3 law program with Columbia University; 3-2 program with Monterey Institute of International Studies; undergraduate research conference. **Credit/placement by examination:** AP, CLEP, IB, institutional tests. 30 credit hours maximum toward bachelor's degree. **Support services:** Learning center, pre-admission summer program, reduced course load, study skills assistance, tutoring, writing center.

Majors. Area/ethnic studies: General, Asian, German. **Biology:** General, Biochemistry/molecular biology, environmental. **Communications:** Communications/speech/rhetoric. **Conservation:** Environmental studies, forest management. **Engineering:** Pre-engineering. **English:** English lit. **Foreign languages:** Ancient Greek, classics, French, Latin, Spanish. **History:** General. **Math:** General. **Philosophy/religion:** Philosophy, religion. **Physical sciences:** Astronomy, astrophysics, chemistry, geology, oceanography, physics. **Psychology:** General. **Social sciences:** Anthropology, economics, political science, sociology. **Visual/performing arts:** Art history/conservation, dramatic, film/cinema/video, jazz, music, music history, music performance, music theory/composition, studio arts.

Most popular majors. Biology 19%, mathematics 6%, physical sciences 11%, psychology 9%, social sciences 20%, visual/performing arts 11%.

Technology on campus. 410 workstations in library, computer center, student center. Dormitories wired for high-speed internet access and linked to campus network. Commuter students can connect to campus network. Online course registration, online library, helpline, repair service, student web hosting, wireless network available.

Student life. Freshman orientation: Available. Preregistration for classes offered. **Housing:** Guaranteed on-campus for freshmen. Coed dorms, single-sex dorms, fraternity/sorority housing, themed housing available. $300 nonrefundable deposit, deadline 5/1. German, French, Spanish, Japanese language houses. Asian Studies, multi-ethnic, environmental, fine arts, community service, writing, global awareness houses available, college-owned rentals. **Activities:** Bands, campus ministries, choral groups, dance, drama, film

society, international student organizations, literary magazine, music ensembles, Model UN, musical theater, radio station, student government, student newspaper, symphony orchestra, Multi-ethnic cultural association, many religious groups, community service, political organizations, environmental groups.

Athletics. NCAA. **Intercollegiate:** Baseball M, basketball, cross-country, golf, lacrosse W, soccer, swimming, tennis, volleyball W. **Intramural:** Basketball, football (non-tackle), soccer, softball, table tennis, tennis, triathlon, ultimate frisbee, volleyball. **Team name:** Missionaries.

Student services. Alcohol/substance abuse counseling, chaplain/spiritual director, career counseling, services for economically disadvantaged, student employment services, financial aid counseling, health services, minority student services, on-campus daycare, personal counseling, placement for graduates, veterans' counselor, women's services. **Physically disabled:** Services for visually, speech, hearing impaired.

Contact. E-mail: admission@whitman.edu
Phone: (509) 527-5176 Toll-free number: (877) 462-9448
Fax: (509) 527-4967
Tony Cabasco, Dean of Admission and Financial Aid, Whitman College, 345 Boyer Avenue, Walla Walla, WA 99362-2046

Whitworth University
Spokane, Washington   **CB member**
www.whitworth.edu   **CB code: 4953**

▸ Private 4-year university and liberal arts college affiliated with the Presbyterian Church (USA)

▸ Residential campus in large city

▸ 2,320 degree-seeking undergraduates: 1% part-time, 62% women, 2% African American, 5% Asian American, 8% Hispanic/Latino, 1% Native American, 6% Multi-racial, non-Hispanic, 2% international

▸ 276 degree-seeking graduate students

▸ 62% of applicants admitted

▸ Application essay required

▸ 75% graduate within 6 years

General. Founded in 1890. Regionally accredited. **Degrees:** 544 bachelor's awarded; master's offered. **ROTC:** Army. **Location:** 6 miles from downtown, 280 miles from Seattle. **Calendar:** 4-1-4, limited summer session. **Full-time faculty:** 187 total; 72% have terminal degrees, 9% minority, 46% women. **Part-time faculty:** 142 total; 4% have terminal degrees, 11% minority, 51% women. **Class size:** 59% < 20, 38% 20-39, 2% 40-49, less than 1% 50-99, less than 1% >100. **Special facilities:** Rec center with indoor track, climbing wall, courts and fitness center, science building has labs and cadaver lab, radio station.

Freshman class profile. 4,545 applied, 2,837 admitted, 584 enrolled.

Mid 50% test scores		GPA 3.0-3.49:	20%
SAT critical reading:	530-630	GPA 2.0-2.99:	3%
SAT math:	530-640	Return as sophomores:	86%
SAT writing:	510-630	Out-of-state:	32%
ACT composite:	23-29	Live on campus:	93%
GPA 3.75 or higher:	57%	International:	2%
GPA 3.50-3.74:	20%		

Basis for selection. School achievement, extracurricular activities, recommendations most important. SAT or ACT recommended. Test Score Optional. Interview recommended.

High school preparation. College-preparatory program recommended. 18 units recommended. Recommended units include English 4, mathematics 3, social studies 3, history 3, science 3 (laboratory 2) and foreign language 2.

2015-2016 Annual costs. Tuition/fees: $39,096. Room/board: $10,714. Books/supplies: $888. Personal expenses: $972.

2015-2016 Financial aid. Need-based: 513 full-time freshmen applied for aid; 443 deemed to have need; 441 received aid. Average need met was 81%. Average scholarship/grant was $26,608; average loan $4,249. 76% of total undergraduate aid awarded as scholarships/grants, 24% as loans/jobs. **Non-need-based:** Awarded to 818 full-time undergraduates, including 180 freshmen. Scholarships awarded for academics, alumni affiliation, art, minority status, music/drama, ROTC.

Application procedures. Admission: Priority date 3/1; deadline 8/1 (postmark date). No application fee. Admission notification on a rolling basis beginning on or about 10/1. Must reply by 5/1. Housing deposit is refundable up until May 1. Postponed admission is allowed for up to one year. **Financial**

aid: Priority date 3/1; no closing date. FAFSA required. Applicants notified on a rolling basis starting 3/15.

Academics. Special study options: Combined bachelor's/graduate degree, cross-registration, double major, dual enrollment of high school students, ESL, honors, independent study, internships, student-designed major, study abroad, teacher certification program, Washington semester. 3-2 engineering programs. **Credit/placement by examination:** AP, CLEP, IB, SAT, ACT, institutional tests. 32 credit hours maximum toward bachelor's degree. **Support services:** Learning center, reduced course load, study skills assistance, tutoring, writing center.

Majors. Area/ethnic studies: American. **Biology:** General, biophysics. **Business:** Accounting, business admin, international, marketing. **Communications:** Communications/speech/rhetoric, journalism. **Computer sciences:** General, computer science. **Education:** General, biology, chemistry, elementary, ESL, French, history, mathematics, middle, multi-level teacher, music, physical, physics, secondary, Spanish, special ed, speech. **Engineering:** Applied physics. **English:** English lit. **Foreign languages:** French, Spanish. **Health services:** Athletic training, nursing (RN). **History:** General. **Liberal arts:** Arts/sciences. **Math:** General, applied. **Parks/recreation:** Health/fitness. **Philosophy/religion:** Philosophy, religion. **Physical sciences:** Chemistry, physics. **Psychology:** General. **Social sciences:** General, economics, international relations, political science, sociology. **Visual/performing arts:** General, art, jazz, music, music performance, piano/keyboard, voice/opera.

Most popular majors. Biology 7%, business/marketing 15%, education 7%, interdisciplinary studies 6%, physical sciences 8%, psychology 8%, social sciences 11%.

Technology on campus. 175 workstations in library, computer center, student center. Dormitories wired for high-speed internet access and linked to campus network. Commuter students can connect to campus network. Online course registration, online library, helpline, repair service, wireless network available.

Student life. Freshman orientation: Mandatory. Preregistration for classes offered. Held Saturday morning of Labor Day weekend. **Housing:** Guaranteed on-campus for freshmen. Coed dorms, single-sex dorms, special housing for disabled, themed housing available. $100 fully refundable deposit, deadline 5/1. **Activities:** Bands, campus ministries, choral groups, dance, drama, international student organizations, literary magazine, music ensembles, musical theater, radio station, student government, student newspaper, symphony orchestra, Black Student Union, Fellowship of Christian Athletes, international club, Hawaiian club, political activist club, Native American club, Amnesty International, Habitat for Humanity, Asian American club, Circle-K International.

Athletics. NCAA. **Intercollegiate:** Baseball M, basketball, cross-country, football (tackle) M, golf, soccer, softball W, swimming, tennis, track and field, volleyball W. **Intramural:** Basketball, soccer, softball, table tennis, tennis, ultimate frisbee, volleyball. **Team name:** Pirates.

Student services. Adult student services, chaplain/spiritual director, career counseling, student employment services, financial aid counseling, health services, minority student services, personal counseling, placement for graduates, veterans' counselor. **Physically disabled:** Services for visually, speech, hearing impaired.

Contact. E-mail: admissions@whitworth.edu
Phone: (509) 777-4786 Toll-free number: (800) 533-4668
Fax: (509) 777-3758
Greg Orwig, Vice President, Admissions and Financial Aid, Whitworth University, 300 West Hawthorne Road, Spokane, WA 99251-0002

West Virginia

Alderson-Broaddus University
Philippi, West Virginia

www.ab.edu

CB member

CB code: 5005

- Private 4-year liberal arts college affiliated with the American Baptist Churches in the USA
- Residential campus in small town
- 1,066 degree-seeking undergraduates: 2% part-time, 46% women, 16% African American, 1% Asian American, 4% Hispanic/Latino, 1% Multiracial, non-Hispanic, 5% international
- 69 degree-seeking graduate students
- 54% of applicants admitted
- SAT and SAT Subject Tests or ACT (ACT writing optional) required
- 36% graduate within 6 years; 7% enter graduate study

General. Founded in 1871. Regionally accredited. **Degrees:** 111 bachelor's, 7 associate awarded; master's offered. **Location:** 100 miles from Charleston, 125 miles from Pittsburgh. **Calendar:** Semester, limited summer session. **Full-time faculty:** 62 total; 47% have terminal degrees, 6% minority, 55% women. **Part-time faculty:** 35 total; 20% have terminal degrees, 9% minority, 54% women. **Class size:** 62% < 20, 28% 20-39, 6% 40-49, 4% 50-99, less than 1% >100. **Special facilities:** Gross anatomy laboratory, hydro-therapy pool, simulation lab, recording studio.

Freshman class profile. 4,206 applied, 2,258 admitted, 333 enrolled.

Mid 50% test scores			
SAT critical reading:	440-510	GPA 2.0-2.99:	32%
SAT math:	450-530	Rank in top quarter:	31%
SAT writing:	410-490	Rank in top tenth:	11%
ACT composite:	19-23	End year in good standing:	80%
GPA 3.75 or higher:	23%	Return as sophomores:	55%
GPA 3.50-3.74:	14%	Out-of-state:	67%
GPA 3.0-3.49:	30%	Live on campus:	96%
		International:	4%

Basis for selection. High school record, rank in top half of class, test scores, interview very important. Physician's assistant and nursing applicants should have strong background in science. Interview required for physician's assistant applicants, recommended for all others. Audition required for music. **Home schooled:** Transcript of courses and grades required.

High school preparation. College-preparatory program recommended. 11 units required; 14 recommended. Required and recommended units include English 4, mathematics 3, social studies 1-3, science 3 (laboratory 1-3) and foreign language 1.

2015-2016 Annual costs. Tuition/fees: $24,140. Room/board: $7,606. Books/supplies: $800. Personal expenses: $1,620.

2015-2016 Financial aid. Need-based: 317 full-time freshmen applied for aid; 289 deemed to have need; 289 received aid. Average need met was 91%. Average scholarship/grant was $18,841; average loan $3,526. 68% of total undergraduate aid awarded as scholarships/grants, 32% as loans/jobs. **Non-need-based:** Awarded to 246 full-time undergraduates, including 78 freshmen. Scholarships awarded for academics, athletics, music/drama, state residency.

Application procedures. Admission: No deadline. No application fee. Admission notification on a rolling basis. **Financial aid:** Priority date 3/1; no closing date. FAFSA required. Applicants notified on a rolling basis starting 3/1; must reply within 2 week(s) of notification.

Academics. Special study options: Accelerated study, double major, honors, independent study, internships, liberal arts/career combination, study abroad, teacher certification program. Business department offers on-line certificate program. **Credit/placement by examination:** AP, CLEP, SAT, ACT, institutional tests. 40 credit hours maximum toward associate degree, 60 toward bachelor's. **Support services:** Learning center, reduced course load, remedial instruction, study skills assistance, tutoring.

Majors. Biology: General. **Business:** Accounting, business admin, marketing. **Communications:** Journalism, media studies, public relations. **Computer sciences:** Computer science. **Conservation:** Environmental science, management/policy. **Education:** Elementary, music, physical, secondary.

English: English lit. **Health services:** Athletic training, medical radiologic technology/radiation therapy, nursing (RN). **Math:** Applied. **Parks/recreation:** Exercise sciences, sports admin. **Philosophy/religion:** Christian. **Physical sciences:** Chemistry. **Psychology:** General. **Social sciences:** Criminology, political science. **Theology:** Preministerial. **Visual/performing arts:** Graphic design, music, music performance, studio arts. **Work/family studies:** Family systems.

Most popular majors. Biology 12%, business/marketing 10%, education 16%, health sciences 31%, parks/recreation 6%, visual/performing arts 6%.

Technology on campus. 100 workstations in dormitories, library, student center. Dormitories wired for high-speed internet access and linked to campus network. Commuter students can connect to campus network. Online course registration, online library, helpline, student web hosting, wireless network available.

Student life. Freshman orientation: Available. Preregistration for classes offered. Held Saturday prior to start of fall classes. **Policies:** Participation in campus activities stressed. Voluntary weekly chapel service offered. **Housing:** Coed dorms, special housing for disabled, wellness housing available. $100 fully refundable deposit. **Activities:** Bands, campus ministries, choral groups, dance, drama, literary magazine, music ensembles, musical theater, radio station, student government, student newspaper, TV station, College Players, Baptist Campus Ministries, Mission Team, outdoor club, forensics team, Battler Columns, campus activities board, Enactus, Hu C. Myers Society, Alpha Beta Nu.

Athletics. NCAA. **Intercollegiate:** Baseball M, basketball, cheerleading, cross-country, football (tackle) M, golf, gymnastics W, lacrosse, soccer, softball W, swimming, tennis W, track and field, volleyball, wrestling M. **Intramural:** Badminton, basketball, bowling, football (non-tackle), golf, racquetball, soccer, softball W, table tennis, tennis, triathlon, ultimate frisbee, volleyball. **Team name:** Battlers.

Student services. Adult student services, alcohol/substance abuse counseling, chaplain/spiritual director, career counseling, financial aid counseling, health services, personal counseling, placement for graduates, veterans' counselor. **Physically disabled:** Services for visually, hearing impaired.

Contact. E-mail: admissions@ab.edu
Phone: (304) 457-6256 Toll-free number: (800) 263-1549
Fax: (304) 457-6239
Erika Thon, Director of Admissions, Alderson-Broaddus University, 101 College Hill Drive, Philippi, WV 26416

American Public University System
Charles Town, West Virginia

www.apus.edu

- For-profit 4-year virtual university
- Small town
- 40,833 degree-seeking undergraduates: 91% part-time, 37% women, 19% African American, 2% Asian American, 11% Hispanic/Latino, 1% Native American, 1% Native Hawaiian/Pacific islander, 4% Multi-racial, non-Hispanic, 1% international
- 9,473 degree-seeking graduate students

General. Regionally and nationally accredited online institution serving military and public service communities through American Military University and American Public University. **Degrees:** 5,258 bachelor's, 2,051 associate awarded; master's offered. **Location:** Online university. **Calendar:** Differs by program, extensive summer session. **Full-time faculty:** 431 total; 61% have terminal degrees, 15% minority, 56% women. **Part-time faculty:** 1,839 total; 61% have terminal degrees, 22% minority, 47% women.

Freshman class profile. 1,953 enrolled.

Basis for selection. Open admission.

2015-2016 Annual costs. Tuition/fees: $8,100. Personal expenses: $1,920. **Additional information:** Required technology fee of $50 per course.

2014-2015 Financial aid. Need-based: 286 full-time freshmen applied for aid; 285 deemed to have need; 284 received aid. Average need met was 53%. Average scholarship/grant was $2,502; average loan $1,732. 51% of total undergraduate aid awarded as scholarships/grants, 49% as loans/jobs. **Non-need-based:** Awarded to 218 full-time undergraduates, including 29 freshmen. **Additional information:** Students should complete a Federal Student Aid Intent Form and register for classes at least 37 days prior to start to allow sufficient time for financial aid process.

Application procedures. Admission: No deadline. No application fee. Application must be submitted online. Admission notification on a rolling basis. **Financial aid:** No deadline. FAFSA, institutional form required. Applicants notified on a rolling basis starting 3/1.

Academics. Special study options: Distance learning. **Credit/placement by examination:** AP, CLEP, IB, institutional tests. 15 credit hours maximum toward associate degree, 30 toward bachelor's. **Support services:** Learning center, remedial instruction, study skills assistance, tutoring, writing center.

Majors. Business: Accounting, business admin, entrepreneurial studies, hospitality admin, logistics, marketing, retailing. **Computer sciences:** Information technology, IT project management, security, webmaster. **Conservation:** Environmental science. **Engineering:** Electrical. **English:** English lit. **Health services:** Nursing (RN). **History:** General, military. **Math:** Computational/applied. **Parks/recreation:** Exercise sciences. **Philosophy/religion:** Philosophy, religion. **Protective services:** Criminal justice, disaster management, fire services admin, forensics, homeland security, security management. **Psychology:** General. **Social sciences:** International relations, political science, sociology. **Work/family studies:** Child care management.

Most popular majors. Business/marketing 23%, computer/information sciences 10%, interdisciplinary studies 9%, parks/recreation 6%, security/protective services 23%.

Technology on campus. PC or laptop required. Online course registration, online library available.

Student life. Freshman orientation: Mandatory. Preregistration for classes offered.

Student services. Career counseling, student employment services.

Contact. E-mail: info@apus.edu
Toll-free number: (877) 777-9081
Terry Grant, Vice President, Enrollment Management and Student Support, American Public University System, 111 West Congress Street, Charles Town, WV 25414

Appalachian Bible College
Mount Hope, West Virginia
https://abc.edu   **CB code: 7305**

▶ Private 4-year Bible college affiliated with the nondenominational tradition
▶ Residential campus in large town
▶ 173 degree-seeking undergraduates: 3% part-time, 49% women
▶ SAT or ACT (ACT writing optional), application essay required

General. Founded in 1950. Regionally accredited; also accredited by ABHE. Accreditation by both the Higher Learning Commission and The Association for Biblical Higher Education. **Degrees:** 33 bachelor's, 4 associate awarded; master's offered. **Location:** One mile from Beckley. **Calendar:** Semester, limited summer session. **Full-time faculty:** 14 total. **Part-time faculty:** 20 total.

Freshman class profile.

Out-of-state:	64%	**Live on campus:**	89%

Basis for selection. Profession of Jesus Christ as Savior, essential agreement with doctrinal statement of college, Christ-like character very important. Minimum 2.0 GPA, test scores, achievement and potential in English also considered. Interview recommended. **Home schooled:** Must provide accurate record of curriculum used, subjects studied, grades earned for grade levels 9-12.

High school preparation. College-preparatory program recommended. Recommended units include English 4, mathematics 3, social studies 3, history 3, science 3, foreign language 1 and academic electives 4.

2015-2016 Annual costs. Tuition/fees: $13,590. Room/board: $7,350. Books/supplies: $900. Personal expenses: $1,208.

Financial aid. Non-need-based: Scholarships awarded for leadership.

Application procedures. Admission: Priority date 4/1; no deadline. $35 fee, may be waived for applicants with need. Admission notification on a rolling basis. **Financial aid:** Priority date 6/15, closing date 9/15. FAFSA, institutional form required. Applicants notified on a rolling basis starting 1/15.

Academics. Special study options: Combined bachelor's/graduate degree, cooperative education, double major, dual enrollment of high school students,

---

independent study, internships, teacher certification program. **Credit/placement by examination:** AP, CLEP, SAT, ACT, institutional tests. 29 credit hours maximum toward bachelor's degree. **Support services:** Reduced course load, remedial instruction, study skills assistance, tutoring.

Majors. Education: Elementary. **Theology:** Bible.

Technology on campus. 30 workstations in dormitories, library, computer center, student center. Dormitories wired for high-speed internet access and linked to campus network. Commuter students can connect to campus network. Online library, helpline, repair service, student web hosting, wireless network available.

Student life. Freshman orientation: Mandatory. Preregistration for classes offered. Held for 3 days immediately prior to beginning of semester. **Policies:** Required attendance at chapel three times a week as well as annual lecture series, Bible conference, and missions conference. Religious observance required. **Housing:** Single-sex dorms, apartments, wellness housing available. $25 nonrefundable deposit. Townhouses for married students. **Activities:** Campus ministries, choral groups, drama, music ensembles, student government.

Athletics. NCCAA. **Intercollegiate:** Basketball, soccer M, volleyball W. **Intramural:** Basketball, soccer M, ultimate frisbee, volleyball. **Team name:** Warriors.

Student services. Chaplain/spiritual director, career counseling, financial aid counseling, health services, personal counseling, placement for graduates, veterans' counselor.

Contact. E-mail: admissions@abc.edu
Phone: (304) 877-6428 ext. 313
Toll-free number: (800) 678-9222 ext. 313 Fax: (304) 877-5082
Benjamin Cale, Director of Admissions, Appalachian Bible College, Director of Admissions, Mount Hope, WV 25880

Bethany College
Bethany, West Virginia   **CB member**
www.bethanywv.edu   **CB code: 5060**

▶ Private 4-year liberal arts college affiliated with the Christian Church (Disciples of Christ)
▶ Residential campus in rural community
▶ 700 degree-seeking undergraduates: 1% part-time, 40% women, 18% African American, 5% Hispanic/Latino, 1% Native American, 2% Multiracial, non-Hispanic, 2% international
▶ 27 degree-seeking graduate students
▶ 70% of applicants admitted
▶ SAT or ACT (ACT writing optional), application essay required
▶ 47% graduate within 6 years

General. Founded in 1840. Regionally accredited. **Degrees:** 124 bachelor's awarded; master's offered. **Location:** 14 miles from Wheeling, 40 miles from Pittsburgh. **Calendar:** Semester. **Full-time faculty:** 51 total; 80% have terminal degrees, 6% minority, 35% women. **Part-time faculty:** 32 total; 28% have terminal degrees, 62% women. **Class size:** 79% < 20, 17% 20-39, 2% 40-49, 1% 50-99, less than 1% >100. **Special facilities:** Alexander Campbell mansion and museum, partner in the Bowen Central Library of Appalachia, 1300 acres of forest in the foothills of the Allegheny Mountains, farm, outdoor classroom.

Freshman class profile. 1,168 applied, 820 admitted, 208 enrolled.

Mid 50% test scores			
SAT critical reading:	380-490	**GPA 2.0-2.99:**	53%
SAT math:	400-510	Rank in top quarter:	20%
SAT writing:	370-470	Rank in top tenth:	5%
ACT composite:	17-22	Return as sophomores:	63%
GPA 3.75 or higher:	9%	Out-of-state:	88%
GPA 3.50-3.74:	11%	Live on campus:	96%
GPA 3.0-3.49:	21%	International:	3%

Basis for selection. Rank in top half of graduating class, test scores, interview, activities, and recommendations are important. Interviews strongly recommended. **Home schooled:** Statement describing home school structure and mission required. **Learning Disabled:** Students with learning disabilities must apply by 2/15 for priority consideration in limited-enrollment learning disabled program. Students should submit official diagnosis of learning disability after acceptance.

High school preparation. College-preparatory program recommended. 15 units recommended. Recommended units include English 4, mathematics 3, social studies 3, science 3 and foreign language 2.

2015-2016 Annual costs. Tuition/fees: $26,500. Room/board: $9,800. Books/supplies: $1,300. Personal expenses: $1,300.

2015-2016 Financial aid. Need-based: 208 full-time freshmen applied for aid; 191 deemed to have need; 191 received aid. Average need met was 81%. Average scholarship/grant was $9,532; average loan $4,753. 65% of total undergraduate aid awarded as scholarships/grants, 35% as loans/jobs. **Non-need-based:** Awarded to 570 full-time undergraduates, including 189 freshmen. Scholarships awarded for academics, alumni affiliation, leadership, music/drama, religious affiliation, state residency. **Additional information:** Scholarships available for travel program.

Application procedures. Admission: Priority date 3/1; no deadline. No application fee. Admission notification on a rolling basis beginning on or about 10/1. Must reply by May 1 or within 3 week(s) if notified thereafter. Maximum postponement for deferred admission is one year. **Financial aid:** Priority date 3/1; no closing date. FAFSA required. Applicants notified on a rolling basis starting 2/15; must reply within 2 week(s) of notification.

Academics. Special study options: Accelerated study, combined bachelor's/graduate degree, distance learning, double major, dual enrollment of high school students, ESL, independent study, internships, liberal arts/career combination, student-designed major, study abroad, teacher certification program, urban semester, Washington semester. **Credit/placement by examination:** AP, CLEP, IB, SAT, ACT, institutional tests. 80 credit hours maximum toward bachelor's degree. **Support services:** Learning center, pre-admission summer program, reduced course load, remedial instruction, study skills assistance, tutoring, writing center.

Majors. Biology: General, biochemistry. **Business:** General, accounting, finance, international, international finance. **Communications:** Advertising, broadcast journalism, communications/speech/rhetoric, journalism, public relations, radio/TV. **Communications technology:** Graphics. **Computer sciences:** General, computer science. **Conservation:** Environmental studies. **Education:** General, art, biology, chemistry, elementary, English, foreign languages, French, German, history, learning disabled, mathematics, multilevel teacher, multiple handicapped, physical, secondary, social studies, Spanish, special ed. **English:** English lit. **Foreign languages:** Spanish. **History:** General. **Human services:** Social work. **Math:** General. **Parks/recreation:** Health/fitness, sports admin. **Philosophy/religion:** Religion. **Physical sciences:** Chemistry. **Psychology:** General. **Social sciences:** Economics, international relations, political science. **Visual/performing arts:** General, art, design, dramatic, music, studio arts.

Most popular majors. Biology 9%, business/marketing 6%, communications/journalism 18%, education 15%, history 6%, psychology 16%, public administration/social services 7%.

Technology on campus. 145 workstations in dormitories, library, computer center, student center. Dormitories wired for high-speed internet access and linked to campus network. Commuter students can connect to campus network. Online library, helpline, repair service, student web hosting, wireless network available.

Student life. Freshman orientation: Mandatory, $125 fee. Preregistration for classes offered. Held prior to start of fall classes. **Housing:** Guaranteed on-campus for all undergraduates. Coed dorms, single-sex dorms, special housing for disabled, apartments, fraternity/sorority housing available. $150 fully refundable deposit, deadline 8/20. **Activities:** Bands, campus ministries, choral groups, dance, drama, international student organizations, literary magazine, music ensembles, musical theater, radio station, student government, student newspaper, TV station, equestrian club, new media club, multicultural clubs (German, Spanish, Japanese), social awareness club, Student National Education Association, multiple honor societies.

Athletics. NCAA. **Intercollegiate:** Baseball M, basketball, cross-country, diving, football (tackle) M, golf, lacrosse M, soccer, softball W, swimming, tennis, track and field, volleyball W. **Intramural:** Basketball, football (non-tackle), racquetball, soccer, softball, tennis, volleyball. **Team name:** Bison.

Student services. Alcohol/substance abuse counseling, chaplain/spiritual director, career counseling, student employment services, financial aid counseling, health services, minority student services, personal counseling, placement for graduates, veterans' counselor, women's services. **Physically disabled:** Services for visually, speech, hearing impaired.

Contact. E-mail: enrollment@bethanywv.edu
Phone: (304) 829-7611 Toll-free number: (800) 922-7611
Fax: (304) 829-7142
Mollie Cecere, Director of Enrollment Management, Bethany College, Office of Enrollment, Bethany, WV 26032-0428

Bluefield State College
Bluefield, West Virginia
www.bluefieldstate.edu

CB code: 5064

- Public 4-year liberal arts and technical college
- Commuter campus in large town
- 1,486 degree-seeking undergraduates: 18% part-time, 60% women, 9% African American, 1% Asian American, 1% Hispanic/Latino, 2% Multiracial, non-Hispanic, 3% international
- 77% of applicants admitted
- SAT or ACT (ACT writing optional) required

General. Founded in 1895. Regionally accredited. Off-campus locations in Lewisburg, Welch, and Beckley. **Degrees:** 170 bachelor's, 87 associate awarded. **Location:** 100 miles from Charleston; 100 miles from Roanoke, Virginia. **Calendar:** Semester, limited summer session. **Full-time faculty:** 77 total; 40% have terminal degrees, 18% minority, 47% women. **Part-time faculty:** 52 total; 12% have terminal degrees, 6% minority, 46% women. **Class size:** 77% < 20, 19% 20-39, 3% 40-49, less than 1% 50-99. **Special facilities:** Instructional technology center.

Freshman class profile. 618 applied, 475 admitted, 267 enrolled.

Mid 50% test scores		GPA 2.0-2.99:	32%
SAT critical reading:	440-520	Rank in top quarter:	56%
SAT math:	450-520	Rank in top tenth:	31%
ACT composite:	17-22	Return as sophomores:	58%
GPA 3.75 or higher:	23%	Out-of-state:	3%
GPA 3.50-3.74:	14%	Fraternities:	1%
GPA 3.0-3.49:	31%	Sororities:	1%

Basis for selection. 2.5 GPA, college preparatory program, test scores required for applicants to health, teacher education, humanities, social science and business administration programs. High school requirements not necessary for associate's program.

High school preparation. College-preparatory program recommended. 17 units required. Required units include English 4, mathematics 4, social studies 3, (laboratory 3), foreign language 2 and visual/performing arts 1.

2015-2016 Annual costs. Tuition/fees: $6,120; $11,280 out-of-state. Books/supplies: $1,600. Personal expenses: $1,100. **Additional information:** Tuition for students residing in bordering counties is $8,700.

2015-2016 Financial aid. Need-based: 255 full-time freshmen applied for aid; 223 deemed to have need; 223 received aid. Average need met was 59%. Average scholarship/grant was $3,507; average loan $3,424. 66% of total undergraduate aid awarded as scholarships/grants, 34% as loans/jobs. **Non-need-based:** Awarded to 406 full-time undergraduates, including 105 freshmen. Scholarships awarded for academics, athletics.

Application procedures. Admission: No application fee. Admission notification on a rolling basis beginning on or about 8/1. **Financial aid:** Priority date 3/1; no closing date. FAFSA, institutional form required. Applicants notified on a rolling basis starting 6/1.

Academics. Special study options: Distance learning, double major, dual enrollment of high school students, honors, independent study, internships, teacher certification program. **Credit/placement by examination:** AP, CLEP, IB, ACT, institutional tests. **Support services:** Learning center, pre-admission summer program, reduced course load, remedial instruction, study skills assistance, tutoring, writing center.

Majors. Business: Accounting, business admin. **Computer sciences:** General. **Education:** Elementary. **Health services:** Nursing (RN), radiologic technology/medical imaging. **Liberal arts:** Arts/sciences, humanities. **Protective services:** Criminal justice. **Social sciences:** General.

Most popular majors. Business/marketing 10%, education 9%, engineering/engineering technologies 19%, health sciences 16%, history 8%, liberal arts 22%, security/protective services 6%, social sciences 11%.

Technology on campus. 370 workstations in library, computer center. Online library, helpline, student web hosting, wireless network available.

Student life. Freshman orientation: Available. Preregistration for classes offered. One day in July or August. **Activities:** Choral groups, drama, international student organizations, Model UN, radio station, student government, student newspaper, Minorities on the Move, student nurses association.

Athletics. NCAA. **Intercollegiate:** Baseball M, basketball, cheerleading, cross-country, golf M, softball W, tennis, volleyball W. **Intramural:** Badminton, basketball, bowling, football (non-tackle) M, golf, racquetball, softball, swimming, table tennis, tennis, volleyball. **Team name:** Big Blues.

Student services. Career counseling, student employment services, financial aid counseling, health services, minority student services, personal counseling, placement for graduates, veterans' counselor. **Physically disabled:** Services for visually, speech, hearing impaired.

Contact. E-mail: bscadmit@bluefieldstate.edu
Phone: (304) 327-4065 Toll-free number: (800) 654-7798
Fax: (304) 325-7747
Kenny Mandeville, Director of Admissions, Bluefield State College, 219 Rock Street, Bluefield, WV 24701

Concord University
Athens, West Virginia
www.concord.edu

CB member
CB code: 5120

- Public 4-year university and liberal arts college
- Residential campus in small town
- 2,250 degree-seeking undergraduates
- 304 graduate students
- SAT or ACT (ACT writing optional) required

General. Founded in 1872. Regionally accredited. **Degrees:** 438 bachelor's awarded; master's offered. **Location:** 5 miles from Princeton, 80 miles from Charleston. **Calendar:** Semester, extensive summer session. **Full-time faculty:** 119 total; 74% have terminal degrees, 4% minority, 47% women. **Part-time faculty:** 93 total; 24% have terminal degrees, 2% minority, 53% women. **Class size:** 64% < 20, 31% 20-39, 4% 40-49, 1% 50-99. **Special facilities:** Southern West Virginia Technology Center, observatory.

Freshman class profile.

GPA 3.75 or higher:	27%	Rank in top quarter:	48%
GPA 3.50-3.74:	17%	Rank in top tenth:	18%
GPA 3.0-3.49:	27%	Out-of-state:	13%
GPA 2.0-2.99:	28%	Live on campus:	52%

Basis for selection. 2.0 GPA and 870 SAT (exclusive of Writing) or 18 ACT required. **Home schooled:** Statement describing home school structure and mission, transcript of courses and grades required.

High school preparation. College-preparatory program recommended. 17 units required. Required units include English 4, mathematics 4, social studies 3, science 3 (laboratory 3), foreign language 2 and visual/performing arts 1. Math courses must include algebra I and another higher level course. Social science requirement includes 1 US history.

2015-2016 Annual costs. Tuition/fees: $6,744; $14,824 out-of-state. Room/board: $8,668. Books/supplies: $1,100. Personal expenses: $2,169.

2015-2016 Financial aid. **Need-based:** Average need met was 90%. Average scholarship/grant was $4,781; average loan $2,596. 62% of total undergraduate aid awarded as scholarships/grants, 38% as loans/jobs. **Non-need-based:** Scholarships awarded for academics, alumni affiliation, leadership. **Additional information:** March 1 priority deadline for state forms. April 15 priority deadline for FAFSA.

Application procedures. **Admission:** No deadline. $25 fee, may be waived for applicants with need, free for online applicants. Admission notification on a rolling basis beginning on or about 9/1. **Financial aid:** Priority date 3/1; no closing date. FAFSA required. Applicants notified on a rolling basis starting 5/1; must reply within 2 week(s) of notification.

Academics. **Special study options:** Accelerated study, cooperative education, distance learning, double major, dual enrollment of high school students, ESL, honors, independent study, internships, student-designed major, study abroad. **Credit/placement by examination:** AP, CLEP, SAT, ACT, institutional tests. **Support services:** Learning center, reduced course load, remedial instruction, study skills assistance, tutoring, writing center. English as a second language program for foreign students, mentoring programs for pre-law and pre-med students.

Majors. **Biology:** General, genetics. **Business:** General, accounting, business admin, finance, hospitality admin, hospitality/recreation, hotel/motel admin, human resources, managerial economics, marketing, resort management, restaurant/food services, tourism promotion, tourism/travel. **Communications:** Advertising, broadcast journalism, communications/speech/rhetoric, journalism, public relations. **Computer sciences:** General, computer science. **Education:** General, art, biology, business, chemistry, early childhood, elementary, English, health, learning disabled, mathematics, mentally handicapped, music, physical, science, social studies, speech. **English:** British lit, English lit, writing. **Health services:** Athletic training, clinical lab science, predental, premedicine, prepharmacy, preveterinary. **History:** General. **Human services:** General, social work. **Liberal arts:** Arts/sciences, library science. **Math:** General. **Parks/recreation:** General, facilities management,

health/fitness, sports admin. **Physical sciences:** Chemistry, geology. **Psychology:** General. **Social sciences:** Geography, political science, sociology. **Visual/performing arts:** Art, commercial/advertising art, dramatic, graphic design, music, studio arts.

Most popular majors. Business/marketing 18%, education 18%, liberal arts 21%, physical sciences 7%, public administration/social services 7%, social sciences 6%.

Technology on campus. 250 workstations in dormitories, library, computer center, student center. Dormitories wired for high-speed internet access and linked to campus network. Commuter students can connect to campus network. Online course registration, online library, helpline, wireless network available.

Student life. **Freshman orientation:** Mandatory, $85 fee. Preregistration for classes offered. **Housing:** Guaranteed on-campus for freshmen. Coed dorms, single-sex dorms available. $50 deposit. **Activities:** Bands, campus ministries, choral groups, drama, film society, international student organizations, radio station, student government, student newspaper, TV station, over 50 clubs and organizations.

Athletics. NCAA. **Intercollegiate:** Baseball M, basketball, cross-country, football (tackle) M, golf, soccer, softball W, tennis, track and field, volleyball W. **Intramural:** Archery, badminton, basketball, bowling, football (tackle) M, golf, handball, racquetball, soccer W, softball, swimming, tennis, track and field, volleyball, water polo. **Team name:** Mountain Lions.

Student services. Career counseling, student employment services, financial aid counseling, health services, on-campus daycare, personal counseling, placement for graduates, veterans' counselor.

Contact. E-mail: admissions@concord.edu
Phone: (888) 384-5249 Toll-free number: (800) 344-6679
Fax: (304) 384-3218
Kent Gamble, Director of Enrollment, Concord University, PO Box 1000, Athens, WV 24712-1000

Davis and Elkins College
Elkins, West Virginia
www.dewv.edu

CB member
CB code: 5151

- Private 4-year liberal arts college affiliated with the Presbyterian Church (USA)
- Residential campus in small town
- 874 undergraduates
- SAT or ACT (ACT writing optional) required

General. Founded in 1904. Regionally accredited. **Degrees:** 115 bachelor's, 44 associate awarded. **Location:** 130 miles from Pittsburgh; 200 miles from Washington, DC. **Calendar:** 4-1-4, extensive summer session. **Full-time faculty:** 53 total; 66% have terminal degrees, 8% minority, 53% women. **Class size:** 64% < 20, 33% 20-39, 1% 40-49, 1% 50-99. **Special facilities:** Pearl S. Buck collection, 8 buildings on the national historic registry.

Freshman class profile.

GPA 3.75 or higher:	19%	GPA 2.0-2.99:	40%
GPA 3.50-3.74:	18%	Live on campus:	63%
GPA 3.0-3.49:	23%		

Basis for selection. Admission based on school achievement record, 2.0 GPA, test scores, and extracurricular activities. Recommended interview also important. Interviews encouraged. **Home schooled:** Transcript of courses and grades required. **Learning Disabled:** Must complete a separate application for the Supported Learning Program.

High school preparation. College-preparatory program recommended. 15 units required. Required and recommended units include English 4, mathematics 3-4, social studies 3-4, science 3-4 (laboratory 1-2), foreign language 1-2 and academic electives 4.

2015-2016 Annual costs. Tuition/fees: $27,842. Room/board: $9,250. Books/supplies: $1,200. Personal expenses: $1,500.

Financial aid. **Non-need-based:** Scholarships awarded for academics, alumni affiliation, art, athletics, leadership, music/drama, religious affiliation, state residency.

Application procedures. **Admission:** No deadline. No application fee. Admission notification on a rolling basis beginning on or about 6/13. **Financial aid:** Priority date 3/1, closing date 8/1. FAFSA required. Applicants notified on a rolling basis; must reply by 8/30.

Academics. Special study options: Cross-registration, double major, dual enrollment of high school students, external degree, honors, independent study, internships, liberal arts/career combination, student-designed major, study abroad, teacher certification program. **Credit/placement by examination:** AP, CLEP, IB, SAT, ACT, institutional tests. **Support services:** Learning center, reduced course load, remedial instruction, study skills assistance, tutoring, writing center.

Majors. Biology: General. **Business:** Accounting, business admin, finance, hospitality admin, international, international marketing, management information systems, marketing. **Computer sciences:** Computer science. **Conservation:** Environmental science. **Education:** Business, drama/dance, elementary, mathematics, physical. **English:** English lit. **History:** General. **Math:** General. **Parks/recreation:** General, exercise sciences, sports admin. **Philosophy/religion:** Religion. **Physical sciences:** Chemistry. **Psychology:** General. **Social sciences:** Criminology, economics, political science, sociology. **Theology:** Religious ed. **Visual/performing arts:** Dramatic, painting, theater design.

Technology on campus. 80 workstations in library. Dormitories wired for high-speed internet access and linked to campus network. Helpline, repair service, wireless network available.

Student life. Freshman orientation: Mandatory. Preregistration for classes offered. **Housing:** Guaranteed on-campus for all undergraduates. Coed dorms, single-sex dorms, fraternity/sorority housing, themed housing, wellness housing available. $200 fully refundable deposit. **Activities:** Bands, campus ministries, choral groups, dance, drama, international student organizations, literary magazine, music ensembles, musical theater, radio station, student government, student newspaper, Alpha Phi Omega, Appalachian music and dance, Green Works.

Athletics. NCAA. **Intercollegiate:** Baseball M, basketball, cross-country, golf M, soccer, softball W, swimming, tennis, volleyball W. **Intramural:** Basketball, football (non-tackle), soccer, softball M, ultimate frisbee, volleyball, water polo. **Team name:** Senators.

Student services. Chaplain/spiritual director, career counseling, student employment services, financial aid counseling, health services, personal counseling, placement for graduates, veterans' counselor, women's services.

Contact. E-mail: admissions@dewv.edu
Phone: (304) 637-1230 Toll-free number: (800) 624-3157 ext. 1230
Fax: (304) 637-1800
Sandy Neel, Director of Admission and Counsel to the President, Davis and Elkins College, 100 Campus Drive, Elkins, WV 26241-3996

Fairmont State University
Fairmont, West Virginia
www.fairmontstate.edu   CB code: 5211

‣ Public 4-year university
‣ Commuter campus in large town
‣ 3,707 degree-seeking undergraduates: 13% part-time, 55% women, 5% African American, 2% Hispanic/Latino, 3% Multi-racial, non-Hispanic, 2% international
‣ 228 degree-seeking graduate students
‣ 66% of applicants admitted
‣ SAT or ACT (ACT writing recommended) required

General. Founded in 1865. Regionally accredited. **Degrees:** 602 bachelor's, 90 associate awarded; master's offered. **ROTC:** Army, Air Force. **Location:** 90 miles from Pittsburgh. **Calendar:** Semester, limited summer session. **Full-time faculty:** 173 total; 62% have terminal degrees, 5% minority, 50% women. **Part-time faculty:** 152 total; 20% have terminal degrees, 7% minority, 51% women. **Class size:** 54% < 20, 36% 20-39, 5% 40-49, 5% 50-99. **Special facilities:** West Virginia folk life center.

Freshman class profile. 2,943 applied, 1,930 admitted, 826 enrolled.

Mid 50% test scores		Rank in top quarter:	33%
SAT critical reading:	410-530	Rank in top tenth:	10%
SAT math:	420-510	End year in good standing:	76%
ACT composite:	18-23	Return as sophomores:	64%
GPA 3.75 or higher:	24%	Out-of-state:	12%
GPA 3.50-3.74:	19%	Live on campus:	54%
GPA 3.0-3.49:	29%	International:	1%
GPA 2.0-2.99:	27%		

Basis for selection. 2.0 GPA (or GED) and 18 ACT/870 SAT (exclusive of Writing) required for bachelor's programs. 3.0 GPA required with scores below 18 ACT or 870 SAT. **Home schooled:** GED required.

High school preparation. College-preparatory program recommended. 26 units required. Required units include English 4, mathematics 4, social studies 2, history 1, science 3 (laboratory 2), foreign language 2 and academic electives 8. 1 unit U.S. history required. Math must include algebra and at least 1 higher unit. 2 units lab science required for biology, chemistry, and physics majors.

2015-2016 Annual costs. Tuition/fees: $6,620; $13,970 out-of-state. Room/board: $8,766. Books/supplies: $1,000. Personal expenses: $1,500.

2014-2015 Financial aid. All financial aid based on need. 661 full-time freshmen applied for aid; 510 deemed to have need; 499 received aid. Average need met was 72%. Average scholarship/grant was $6,596; average loan $3,015. 67% of total undergraduate aid awarded as scholarships/grants, 33% as loans/jobs.

Application procedures. Admission: Priority date 3/1; deadline 8/15 (postmark date). No application fee. Admission notification on a rolling basis beginning on or about 10/1. **Financial aid:** Closing date 3/1. FAFSA required. Applicants notified on a rolling basis starting 4/1; must reply within 2 week(s) of notification.

Academics. Special study options: Accelerated study, cooperative education, cross-registration, distance learning, double major, dual enrollment of high school students, ESL, honors, independent study, internships, liberal arts/career combination, study abroad, teacher certification program, Washington semester, weekend college. **Credit/placement by examination:** AP, CLEP, IB, SAT, ACT, institutional tests. 28 credit hours maximum toward bachelor's degree. **Support services:** Learning center, reduced course load, remedial instruction, study skills assistance, tutoring.

Majors. Biology: General. **Business:** Accounting, business admin. **Communications:** Communications/speech/rhetoric. **Communications technology:** Printing press operator. **Computer sciences:** General, information systems. **Education:** General. **English:** English lit. **Foreign languages:** French, Spanish. **Health services:** Health care admin, nursing (RN). **History:** General. **Math:** General. **Parks/recreation:** Exercise sciences. **Physical sciences:** Chemistry. **Protective services:** Criminal justice, forensics. **Psychology:** General. **Social sciences:** National security policy, political science, sociology. **Visual/performing arts:** Commercial/advertising art, dramatic, music, studio arts. **Work/family studies:** General.

Most popular majors. Business/marketing 15%, education 10%, engineering/engineering technologies 12%, health sciences 10%, liberal arts 8%, psychology 7%, security/protective services 11%.

Technology on campus. 950 workstations in dormitories, library, computer center, student center. Dormitories wired for high-speed internet access and linked to campus network. Commuter students can connect to campus network. Online library, helpline, student web hosting, wireless network available.

Student life. Freshman orientation: Available. Preregistration for classes offered. Various weeknights and Saturdays throughout spring and summer. **Policies:** Alcohol not allowed. **Housing:** Guaranteed on-campus for freshmen. Coed dorms, single-sex dorms, apartments available. $200 fully refundable deposit, deadline 7/18. **Activities:** Bands, campus ministries, choral groups, dance, drama, international student organizations, literary magazine, music ensembles, musical theater, student government, student newspaper, symphony orchestra, black student union, Circle K, disabled students society, society of non-traditional students.

Athletics. NCAA. **Intercollegiate:** Baseball M, basketball, cheerleading W, cross-country, football (tackle) M, golf, softball W, swimming, tennis, volleyball W. **Intramural:** Badminton, basketball, bowling, football (non-tackle) M, golf, handball, softball, table tennis, tennis, volleyball. **Team name:** Falcons.

Student services. Adult student services, career counseling, student employment services, financial aid counseling, health services, on-campus daycare, personal counseling, placement for graduates, veterans' counselor. **Physically disabled:** Services for visually, hearing impaired.

Contact. E-mail: admit@fairmontstate.edu
Phone: (304) 367-4892 Toll-free number: (800) 641-5678
Fax: (304) 367-4789
Amie Fazalare, Director of Recruiting, Fairmont State University, Office of Admissions, Fairmont, WV 26554-2470

Glenville State College
Glenville, West Virginia   CB member
www.glenville.edu   CB code: 5254

‣ Public 4-year liberal arts and teachers college
‣ Commuter campus in small town

- 1,243 degree-seeking undergraduates: 16% part-time, 41% women, 19% African American, 1% Asian American, 2% Hispanic/Latino, 1% Multiracial, non-Hispanic
- 72% of applicants admitted
- SAT or ACT (ACT writing optional) required

General. Founded in 1872. Regionally accredited. **Degrees:** 136 bachelor's, 55 associate awarded. **ROTC:** Army. **Location:** 87 miles from Charleston, 86 miles from Morgantown. **Calendar:** Semester, limited summer session. **Full-time faculty:** 63 total; 57% have terminal degrees, 6% minority, 32% women. **Part-time faculty:** 67 total; 2% have terminal degrees, 3% minority, 51% women. **Class size:** 68% < 20, 29% 20-39, 2% 40-49, less than 1% 50-99, less than 1% >100.

Freshman class profile. 1,430 applied, 1,036 admitted, 341 enrolled.

Mid 50% test scores			
		Rank in top quarter:	26%
SAT critical reading:	370-470	Rank in top tenth:	8%
SAT math:	380-480	End year in good standing:	86%
ACT composite:	17-22	Return as sophomores:	62%
GPA 3.75 or higher:	16%	Out-of-state:	23%
GPA 3.50-3.74:	12%	Live on campus:	70%
GPA 3.0-3.49:	28%	Fraternities:	5%
GPA 2.0-2.99:	39%	Sororities:	13%

Basis for selection. Students must have graduated from accredited high school with 2.0 GPA or 18 ACT/860 SAT (exclusive of Writing). Associate degree programs open to all students who have graduated from high school or hold a GED. Students who want to pursue bachelor's degree, but do not meet the requirements may enter 2-year program and later transfer into bachelor's degree program. Audition required for music. **Home schooled:** GED required. Case by case evaluation. **Learning Disabled:** Students must provide documentation of their disability to the disabilities coordinator to receive services.

High school preparation. College-preparatory program recommended. 28 units required. Required units include English 4, mathematics 4, social studies 3, science 3 (laboratory 3), foreign language 2, visual/performing arts 1 and academic electives 15. 3 math units must be algebra I or higher. Social studies should include US history. English should include courses in grammar, composition, and literature.

2015-2016 Annual costs. Tuition/fees: $7,032; $15,888 out-of-state. Books/supplies: $1,200. Personal expenses: $2,124. **Additional information:** Tuition for students in residing in border counties is $11,472.

Financial aid. **Non-need-based:** Scholarships awarded for academics, athletics, music/drama, state residency.

Application procedures. Admission: No deadline. $20 fee, may be waived for applicants with need. Admission notification on a rolling basis. **Financial aid:** Priority date 2/1; no closing date. FAFSA required. Applicants notified on a rolling basis starting 3/1; must reply within 3 week(s) of notification.

Academics. Students can receive credit for employment, military, and/or life experience in Regents Bachelor of Arts program (designed for nontraditional students). **Special study options:** Combined bachelor's/graduate degree, distance learning, double major, dual enrollment of high school students, internships, student-designed major, study abroad, teacher certification program, Washington semester. **Credit/placement by examination:** AP, CLEP, SAT, ACT, institutional tests. Unlimited number of hours of credit may be counted for degree. **Support services:** Remedial instruction, study skills assistance, tutoring, writing center.

Majors. Biology: General. **Business:** General, business admin. **Conservation:** Management/policy. **Education:** Elementary, kindergarten/preschool, secondary, special ed. **English:** English lit. **History:** General. **Parks/recreation:** Exercise sciences, sports admin. **Physical sciences:** Chemistry. **Protective services:** Criminalistics. **Social sciences:** General. **Visual/performing arts:** Art, music performance.

Most popular majors. Business/marketing 17%, education 21%, liberal arts 10%, natural resources/environmental science 16%, security/protective services 12%, social sciences 13%.

Technology on campus. 194 workstations in library, computer center, student center. Dormitories wired for high-speed internet access and linked to campus network. Commuter students can connect to campus network. Online course registration, online library, wireless network available.

Student life. Freshman orientation: Mandatory, $100 fee. Preregistration for classes offered. **Policies:** All unmarried students who have earned less than 58 credit hours required to reside on campus. Alcoholic beverages and controlled substances not permitted on campus. All students required to adhere to Student Code of Conduct. Community service required of student

organizations. **Housing:** Guaranteed on-campus for freshmen. Single-sex dorms, special housing for disabled, apartments, wellness housing available. $100 partly refundable deposit, deadline 4/1. **Activities:** Bands, campus ministries, choral groups, drama, literary magazine, music ensembles, radio station, student government, student newspaper, TV station, Fellowship of Christian Athletes, environmental organization, students in free enterprise, Student National Education Association, student athlete advisory committee, student awareness organization, Music Educators National Conference, Kappa Delta Pi.

Athletics. NCAA. **Intercollegiate:** Baseball M, basketball, cross-country, football (tackle) M, golf, softball W, track and field, volleyball W. **Intramural:** Badminton, basketball, football (non-tackle), soccer, softball, table tennis, volleyball. **Team name:** Pioneers.

Student services. Adult student services, alcohol/substance abuse counseling, chaplain/spiritual director, career counseling, services for economically disadvantaged, student employment services, financial aid counseling, health services, minority student services, personal counseling, placement for graduates, veterans' counselor. **Physically disabled:** Services for visually, speech, hearing impaired.

Contact. E-mail: admissions@glenville.edu
Phone: (304) 462-4128 Toll-free number: (800) 924-2010
Fax: (304) 462-8619
Ashley Weir, Vice President of Enrollment, Glenville State College, 200 High Street, Glenville, WV 26351-1292

Marshall University
Huntington, West Virginia
www.marshall.edu

CB member
CB code: 5396

- Public 4-year university
- Commuter campus in small city
- 8,780 degree-seeking undergraduates: 10% part-time, 57% women, 7% African American, 1% Asian American, 2% Hispanic/Latino, 3% Multiracial, non-Hispanic, 1% international
- 3,152 degree-seeking graduate students
- 79% of applicants admitted
- SAT or ACT (ACT writing optional) required
- 45% graduate within 6 years

General. Founded in 1837. Regionally accredited. **Degrees:** 1,590 bachelor's, 115 associate awarded; master's, professional, doctoral offered. **ROTC:** Army. **Location:** 126 miles from Lexington, KY; 160 miles from Columbus, OH. **Calendar:** Semester, limited summer session. **Full-time faculty:** 500 total; 74% have terminal degrees, 17% minority, 47% women. **Part-time faculty:** 216 total; 14% have terminal degrees, 7% minority, 50% women. **Class size:** 45% < 20, 47% 20-39, 4% 40-49, 4% 50-99, less than 1% >100. **Special facilities:** Confederate history collection, superconducting nuclear magnetic resonance spectrometer.

Freshman class profile. 2,856 applied, 2,261 admitted, 1,913 enrolled.

Mid 50% test scores			
		GPA 3.0-3.49:	25%
SAT critical reading:	440-490	GPA 2.0-2.99:	18%
SAT math:	430-480	Return as sophomores:	73%
ACT composite:	20-25	Out-of-state:	20%
GPA 3.75 or higher:	39%	International:	1%
GPA 3.50-3.74:	17%		

Basis for selection. Full admission requires 2.0 GPA and 19 ACT/910 SAT (exclusive of Writing). Conditional admission granted with below 2.0 GPA or the above scores, on a limited, first-come, first-served basis. Programs and colleges may have different requirements for admissions. Audition required for music majors; interview recommended for academically weak, learning disabled; portfolio recommended. **Home schooled:** Applicants should apply early and have home schooling well documented.

High school preparation. College-preparatory program recommended. 20 units required. Required units include English 4, mathematics 4, social studies 3, science 3 (laboratory 3), foreign language 2 and visual/performing arts 1.

2015-2016 Annual costs. Tuition/fees: $6,814; $15,602 out-of-state. Room/board: $9,832. Books/supplies: $1,100. Personal expenses: $1,148.

2015-2016 Financial aid. Need-based: 1,831 full-time freshmen applied for aid; 1,383 deemed to have need; 1,371 received aid. Average need met was 49%. Average scholarship/grant was $6,685; average loan $5,416. 43% of total undergraduate aid awarded as scholarships/grants, 57% as loans/jobs. **Non-need-based:** Awarded to 3,804 full-time undergraduates, including

1,299 freshmen. Scholarships awarded for academics, alumni affiliation, art, athletics, minority status, music/drama, ROTC, state residency.

Application procedures. Admission: No deadline. $30 fee, may be waived for applicants with need. Admission notification on a rolling basis beginning on or about 9/1. **Financial aid:** Priority date 3/1; no closing date. FAFSA required. Applicants notified on a rolling basis starting 4/1.

Academics. Special study options: Accelerated study, combined bachelor's/graduate degree, cooperative education, cross-registration, distance learning, double major, dual enrollment of high school students, ESL, exchange student, honors, independent study, internships, study abroad, teacher certification program, Washington semester. **Credit/placement by examination:** AP, CLEP, IB, SAT, ACT, institutional tests. **Support services:** Learning center, pre-admission summer program, reduced course load, remedial instruction, study skills assistance, tutoring, writing center.

Honors college/program. 26 ACT/1170 SAT (exclusive of writing) and 3.5 GPA required.

Majors. Biology: General. **Business:** Accounting, business admin, finance, international, management information systems, managerial economics, marketing. **Communications:** Journalism. **Computer sciences:** General. **Conservation:** Environmental science. **Education:** Elementary, kindergarten/preschool, physical, school counseling, secondary. **Engineering:** General. **English:** Creative writing, English lit, general lit, rhetoric/composition. **Foreign languages:** General. **Health services:** Athletic training, clinical lab science, cytotechnology, dietetics, nursing (RN), radiologic technology/medical imaging, respiratory therapy technology, speech pathology. **History:** General. **Human services:** Social work. **Liberal arts:** Humanities. **Math:** General. **Parks/recreation:** Exercise sciences, facilities management. **Physical sciences:** Chemistry, geology, physics. **Protective services:** Criminal justice. **Psychology:** General. **Social sciences:** Economics, geography, international relations, political science, sociology. **Visual/performing arts:** Art. **Work/family studies:** General.

Most popular majors. Business/marketing 18%, education 11%, health sciences 16%, liberal arts 12%, psychology 6%.

Technology on campus. 1,461 workstations in dormitories, library, computer center, student center. Dormitories wired for high-speed internet access and linked to campus network. Commuter students can connect to campus network. Online course registration, online library, helpline, student web hosting, wireless network available.

Student life. Freshman orientation: Available. Preregistration for classes offered. One-day programs in June, July, August. **Housing:** Guaranteed on-campus for freshmen. Coed dorms, single-sex dorms, special housing for disabled, themed housing available. $200 deposit, deadline 5/15. **Activities:** Bands, campus ministries, choral groups, dance, drama, international student organizations, literary magazine, music ensembles, Model UN, musical theater, opera, radio station, student government, student newspaper, symphony orchestra, TV station, Black United Students, College Republicans, Lambda Society, Habitat for Humanity, student organization for alumni relations.

Athletics. NCAA. **Intercollegiate:** Baseball M, basketball, cross-country, football (tackle) M, golf, soccer, softball W, swimming W, tennis W, track and field W, volleyball W. **Intramural:** Basketball, bowling, football (tackle), golf, racquetball, soccer, softball, swimming, tennis, track and field, volleyball. **Team name:** Thundering Herd.

Student services. Adult student services, alcohol/substance abuse counseling, chaplain/spiritual director, career counseling, student employment services, health services, minority student services, on-campus daycare, personal counseling, placement for graduates, veterans' counselor, women's services. **Physically disabled:** Services for visually, speech, hearing impaired.

Contact. E-mail: admissions@marshall.edu
Phone: (304) 696-3160 Toll-free number: (800) 642-3499
Fax: (304) 696-3135
Tammy Johnson, Director of Admissions, Marshall University, One John Marshall Drive, Huntington, WV 25755

Ohio Valley University
Vienna, West Virginia
www.ovu.edu   CB code: 5519

- Private 4-year university and liberal arts college affiliated with the Church of Christ
- Residential campus in small city
- 411 degree-seeking undergraduates: 5% part-time, 48% women, 12% African American, 5% Hispanic/Latino, 3% Multi-racial, non-Hispanic, 9% international

- 33 degree-seeking graduate students
- 47% of applicants admitted
- 30% graduate within 6 years

General. Founded in 1960. Regionally accredited. **Degrees:** 73 bachelor's, 18 associate awarded; master's offered. **Location:** 95 miles from Columbus, OH; 120 miles from Pittsburgh, PA. **Calendar:** Semester, limited summer session. **Full-time faculty:** 20 total; 65% have terminal degrees, 5% minority, 40% women. **Part-time faculty:** 68 total; 18% have terminal degrees, 3% minority, 48% women. **Class size:** 88% < 20, 12% 20-39.

Freshman class profile. 882 applied, 415 admitted, 121 enrolled.

Mid 50% test scores		Rank in top quarter:	10%
SAT critical reading:	380-500	Rank in top tenth:	8%
SAT math:	400-530	Return as sophomores:	56%
SAT writing:	370-480	Out-of-state:	66%
ACT composite:	17-22	Live on campus:	80%
GPA 3.75 or higher:	12%	International:	5%
GPA 3.50-3.74:	14%	Fraternities:	50%
GPA 3.0-3.49:	26%	Sororities:	50%
GPA 2.0-2.99:	44%		

Basis for selection. School achievement record, test scores and reference considered. Essay, interview recommended.

High school preparation. 12 units required. Required units include English 3, mathematics 3, social studies 2, history 1, science 3 (laboratory 1).

2015-2016 Annual costs. Tuition/fees: $19,840. Room/board: $7,220. Books/supplies: $1,000. Personal expenses: $800.

2014-2015 Financial aid. Need-based: 93 full-time freshmen applied for aid; 88 deemed to have need; 86 received aid. Average need met was 70%. Average scholarship/grant was $11,523; average loan $3,320. 59% of total undergraduate aid awarded as scholarships/grants, 41% as loans/jobs. **Non-need-based:** Awarded to 203 full-time undergraduates, including 40 freshmen. Scholarships awarded for academics, athletics, leadership, music/drama, state residency.

Application procedures. Admission: Closing date 8/15 (postmark date). No application fee. Admission notification on a rolling basis. Must reply by May 1 or within 2 week(s) if notified thereafter. **Financial aid:** Priority date 2/15; no closing date. FAFSA required. Applicants notified on a rolling basis starting 3/1; must reply within 4 week(s) of notification.

Academics. Bible course required of full-time students each semester. **Special study options:** Distance learning, double major, dual enrollment of high school students, ESL, honors, independent study, internships, student-designed major, study abroad, teacher certification program, Washington semester. Degree completion programs and special certifications. **Credit/placement by examination:** AP, CLEP, IB, SAT, ACT, institutional tests. 30 credit hours maximum toward associate degree, 30 toward bachelor's. Challenge course testing. **Support services:** Learning center, pre-admission summer program, reduced course load, remedial instruction, study skills assistance, tutoring.

Majors. Biology: General, biochemistry. **Business:** Accounting, business admin, nonprofit/public. **Computer sciences:** Information technology. **Education:** General, elementary, English, mathematics, multi-level teacher, physical, science, secondary, social studies. **English:** English lit. **Health services:** General. **History:** General. **Liberal arts:** Arts/sciences, humanities. **Math:** General. **Philosophy/religion:** Religion. **Psychology:** General. **Social sciences:** Criminology, sociology. **Theology:** Bible.

Most popular majors. Biology 8%, business/marketing 23%, education 29%, psychology 8%, security/protective services 7%, theological studies 7%.

Technology on campus. 44 workstations in dormitories, library, computer center. Dormitories wired for high-speed internet access and linked to campus network. Commuter students can connect to campus network. Online library, repair service, wireless network available.

Student life. Freshman orientation: Mandatory. Preregistration for classes offered. One-week session held in late August. **Policies:** Chapel/assembly attendance required 3 times a week. Religious observance required. **Housing:** Guaranteed on-campus for all undergraduates. Single-sex dorms, special housing for disabled, apartments available. $150 partly refundable deposit, deadline 8/1. **Activities:** Jazz band, campus ministries, choral groups, drama, literary magazine, music ensembles, musical theater, student government, student newspaper, prospective ministers and prospective missionaries clubs, women's club, Diversity at the University club, ACEPP.

Athletics. NCAA. **Intercollegiate:** Baseball M, basketball, cross-country, golf, lacrosse M, soccer, softball W, volleyball W, wrestling M. **Intramural:** Basketball, bowling, cross-country, football (non-tackle), soccer, softball, table tennis, track and field, volleyball. **Team name:** Fighting Scots.

Student services. Adult student services, alcohol/substance abuse counseling, chaplain/spiritual director, career counseling, student employment services, financial aid counseling, health services, minority student services, personal counseling, placement for graduates.

Contact. E-mail: contact@ovu.edu
Phone: (304) 865-6200 Toll-free number: (877) 446-8669
Fax: (304) 865-6175
Lisa West, Director of Admissions, Ohio Valley University, One Campus View Drive, Vienna, WV 26105

Salem International University
Salem, West Virginia
www.salemu.edu
CB code: 5608

▶ For-profit 4-year university and liberal arts college
▶ Residential campus in rural community
▶ 402 undergraduates
▶ Interview required

General. Founded in 1888. Regionally accredited. Established in 1888 as Salem College, Salem International University has a strong tradition of academic excellence and innovation. Our beautiful 100-acre campus is nestled in the Appalachian mountains of West Virginia. **Degrees:** 65 bachelor's, 89 associate awarded; master's offered. **Location:** 12 miles from Clarksburg, 125 miles from Pittsburgh. **Calendar:** Semester, limited summer session. **Full-time faculty:** 27 total; 44% have terminal degrees, 48% women. **Part-time faculty:** 35 total; 3% have terminal degrees, 54% women. **Class size:** 77% < 20, 17% 20-39, 6% 40-49.

Freshman class profile.

Out-of-state:	46%	Fraternities:	5%
Live on campus:	90%	Sororities:	8%

Basis for selection. School achievement record, test scores, counselor recommendations most important. ACT or SAT is required for athletes. Enrolled students must take ACCUPLACER, which assists in advising. Essay required for Nursing applicants. **Home schooled:** State high school equivalency certificate required.

High school preparation. 16 units recommended. Recommended units include English 4, mathematics 2, social studies 3, science 2 and foreign language 2.

2015-2016 Annual costs. Books/supplies: $660. Personal expenses: $320. **Additional information:** Certificate programs: $20,925-$25,740, room and board $7,000. Associate programs: $35,400-$47,190, room and board $14,000. Bachelor's programs: $35,400-$70,800, room and board $14,000-$28,000.

Financial aid. **Non-need-based:** Scholarships awarded for academics.

Application procedures. **Admission:** No deadline. $20 fee. Admission notification on a rolling basis. Notified within five days. **Financial aid:** Priority date 4/15; no closing date. FAFSA required. Applicants notified on a rolling basis starting 2/15; must reply within 4 week(s) of notification.

Academics. In keeping with college's mission to foster global awareness, all students required to complete international core curriculum. **Special study options:** Accelerated study, distance learning, double major, independent study, internships, student-designed major, study abroad, teacher certification program. **Credit/placement by examination:** AP, CLEP, IB, institutional tests. 24 credit hours maximum toward bachelor's degree. **Support services:** Learning center, remedial instruction, study skills assistance, tutoring, writing center.

Majors. **Biology:** General. **Business:** Business admin. **Computer sciences:** General, computer science. **Education:** General, multi-level teacher, secondary. **Health services:** Nursing (RN). **Liberal arts:** Arts/sciences. **Protective services:** Criminal justice.

Most popular majors. Business/marketing 68%, computer/information sciences 6%, education 6%, health sciences 9%, security/protective services 12%.

Technology on campus. 50 workstations in library, computer center. Dormitories wired for high-speed internet access and linked to campus network. Commuter students can connect to campus network. Online library, helpline, repair service, wireless network available.

Student life. **Freshman orientation:** Available, $30 fee. Preregistration for classes offered. Program includes introduction to international aspects of college. Special orientation for international students with U.S. life-skills training. **Policies:** Unless local resident, freshmen and sophomores required to live on-campus. **Housing:** Guaranteed on-campus for all undergraduates. Coed dorms, single-sex dorms, wellness housing available. Private rooms subject to availability. **Activities:** Choral groups, international student organizations, student government, student newspaper, Gamma Beta Phi honor society, Alpha Phi Omega fraternity service organization, Campus Crusade for Christ, Rainbow Alliance, international woman's alliance, Christian Student Fellowship, Indian student association, Chinese student association.

Athletics. NCAA. **Intercollegiate:** Baseball M, basketball, golf, soccer, softball W, tennis M, volleyball W, water polo. **Intramural:** Basketball, football (non-tackle), racquetball, skiing M, soccer, swimming, table tennis, tennis, volleyball. **Team name:** Tigers.

Student services. Career counseling, services for economically disadvantaged, financial aid counseling.

Contact. E-mail: admissions@salemu.edu
Phone: (888) 283-4562 Toll-free number: (888) 283-4562 Fax: (304)
Dennis McNaboe, Director of Admissions, Salem International University, 223 West Main Street, Salem, WV 26426

Shepherd University
Shepherdstown, West Virginia
www.shepherd.edu
CB code: 5615

▶ Public 4-year university
▶ Commuter campus in small town
▶ 3,320 degree-seeking undergraduates: 12% part-time, 59% women, 10% African American, 2% Asian American, 3% Hispanic/Latino, 2% Multiracial, non-Hispanic
▶ 159 degree-seeking graduate students
▶ 90% of applicants admitted
▶ SAT or ACT (ACT writing optional) required
▶ 48% graduate within 6 years

General. Founded in 1871. Regionally accredited. **Degrees:** 775 bachelor's awarded; master's offered. **ROTC:** Air Force. **Location:** 8 miles from Martinsburg; 70 miles from Washington, DC. **Calendar:** Semester, extensive summer session. **Full-time faculty:** 139 total; 88% have terminal degrees, 12% minority, 47% women. **Part-time faculty:** 228 total; 23% have terminal degrees, 7% minority, 51% women. **Class size:** 56% < 20, 42% 20-39, less than 1% 40-49, 1% 50-99. **Special facilities:** Computer-controlled theater, recital hall with concert grand piano, recording studio, nursery school, 3 theaters, Civil War center, observatory, legislative studies center, nursing building, center for contemporary arts.

Freshman class profile. 1,648 applied, 1,481 admitted, 638 enrolled.

Mid 50% test scores			
SAT critical reading:	440-550	GPA 3.0-3.49:	28%
SAT math:	430-540	GPA 2.0-2.99:	29%
ACT composite:	19-24	End year in good standing:	71%
GPA 3.75 or higher:	27%	Return as sophomores:	66%
GPA 3.50-3.74:	16%	Out-of-state:	39%
		Live on campus:	45%

Basis for selection. 2.0 GPA and 17 ACT/820 SAT (exclusive of Writing) required. Essays and recommendations optional but important. Interview required for honors program and nursing applicants; recommended for others. Audition required for music program applicants. **Home schooled:** Transcript of courses and grades required. Portfolio of completed work required.

High school preparation. College-preparatory program recommended. 21 units required. Required units include English 4, mathematics 4, social studies 2, history 1, science 3 (laboratory 3), foreign language 2, visual/performing arts 1 and academic electives 6. History unit must include US history; science unit must include biology. All science courses must be college preparatory laboratory sciences.

2015-2016 Annual costs. Tuition/fees: $6,830; $16,628 out-of-state. Room/board: $9,682. Books/supplies: $1,000. Personal expenses: $1,200.

2015-2016 Financial aid. **Need-based:** 616 full-time freshmen applied for aid; 430 deemed to have need; 421 received aid. Average need met was 78%. Average scholarship/grant was $5,559; average loan $3,299. 54% of total undergraduate aid awarded as scholarships/grants, 46% as loans/jobs. **Non-need-based:** Awarded to 1,519 full-time undergraduates, including 431 freshmen. Scholarships awarded for academics, art, athletics, job skills, leadership, minority status, music/drama, state residency.

Application procedures. **Admission:** No deadline. $45 fee, may be waived for applicants with need. Admission notification on a rolling basis beginning on or about 9/1. Must reply by May 1 or within 3 week(s) if notified thereafter. **Financial aid:** Priority date 3/1; no closing date. FAFSA required. Applicants notified on a rolling basis starting 3/15; must reply within 3 week(s) of notification.

Academics. Special study options: Combined bachelor's/graduate degree, cooperative education, double major, honors, independent study, internships, liberal arts/career combination, study abroad, teacher certification program, Washington semester. **Credit/placement by examination:** AP, CLEP, IB, SAT, ACT, institutional tests. 32 credit hours maximum toward bachelor's degree. No limit for students pursuing Regents' Bachelor of Arts degree. **Support services:** Learning center, remedial instruction, study skills assistance, tutoring, writing center.

Majors. Biology: General. **Business:** Accounting, business admin. **Communications:** Communications/speech/rhetoric. **Computer sciences:** General, applications programming. **Conservation:** General, environmental studies. **Education:** Early childhood, elementary, secondary. **English:** English lit. **Foreign languages:** Spanish. **Health services:** Nursing (RN). **History:** General. **Human services:** Social work. **Math:** General. **Parks/recreation:** General. **Physical sciences:** Chemistry. **Psychology:** General. **Social sciences:** Economics, political science, sociology. **Visual/performing arts:** Art, music. **Work/family studies:** General.

Most popular majors. Business/marketing 11%, education 15%, health sciences 9%, liberal arts 14%, parks/recreation 9%, social sciences 8%.

Technology on campus. 603 workstations in library, computer center, student center. Dormitories wired for high-speed internet access and linked to campus network. Commuter students can connect to campus network. Online course registration, online library, helpline, student web hosting, wireless network available.

Student life. Freshman orientation: Mandatory, $140 fee. Preregistration for classes offered. Two day sessions held in June and July. August held on Friday and Saturday prior to first day of classes. **Housing:** Guaranteed on-campus for all undergraduates. Coed dorms, special housing for disabled, apartments, themed housing, wellness housing available. $200 partly refundable deposit, deadline 6/1. Honors housing available. **Activities:** Bands, choral groups, dance, drama, international student organizations, literary magazine, music ensembles, Model UN, musical theater, radio station, student government, student newspaper, symphony orchestra, College Republicans, University Democrats, Allies Gay-Straight Alliance, Sistaz, Rotoract, Young Life, Black Student Union, Connections Interfaith Group, Catholic Campus Ministries, Fellowship of Christian Athletes, International Student Union.

Athletics. NCAA. **Intercollegiate:** Baseball M, basketball, football (tackle) M, golf M, lacrosse W, soccer, softball W, tennis, volleyball W. **Intramural:** Basketball, football (non-tackle), racquetball, sand volleyball, soccer, softball, ultimate frisbee, volleyball. **Team name:** Rams.

Student services. Adult student services, alcohol/substance abuse counseling, career counseling, services for economically disadvantaged, student employment services, financial aid counseling, health services, minority student services, personal counseling, placement for graduates, veterans' counselor. **Physically disabled:** Services for visually, speech, hearing impaired.

Contact. E-mail: admission@shepherd.edu
Phone: (304) 876-5212 Toll-free number: (800) 344-5231 ext. 5212
Fax: (304) 876-5165
Kristen Lorenz, Director of Admissions, Shepherd University, PO Box 5000, Shepherdstown, WV 25443-5000

University of Charleston
Charleston, West Virginia
www.ucwv.edu

CB member
CB code: 5419

- Private 4-year university
- Residential campus in small city
- 1,706 degree-seeking undergraduates: 24% part-time, 48% women, 9% African American, 1% Asian American, 2% Hispanic/Latino, 1% Native American, 7% international
- 600 degree-seeking graduate students
- 52% of applicants admitted
- SAT or ACT (ACT writing optional) required
- 47% graduate within 6 years

General. Founded in 1888. Regionally accredited. Locations in Charleston, Beckley, Martinsburg, and online. **Degrees:** 209 bachelor's, 38 associate awarded; master's, professional offered. **Location:** 200 miles from Pittsburgh; 200 miles from Charlotte, NC. **Calendar:** Semester, limited summer session. **Full-time faculty:** 116 total; 10% minority, 67% women. **Part-time faculty:**

87 total; 7% minority, 42% women. **Class size:** 65% < 20, 33% 20-39, less than 1% 40-49, less than 1% 50-99.

Freshman class profile. 1,949 applied, 1,022 admitted, 319 enrolled.

Mid 50% test scores			
SAT critical reading:	430-520	GPA 2.0-2.99:	27%
SAT math:	440-530	Return as sophomores:	66%
ACT composite:	19-24	Out-of-state:	39%
GPA 3.75 or higher:	34%	Live on campus:	76%
GPA 3.50-3.74:	15%	International:	10%
GPA 3.0-3.49:	23%	Fraternities:	5%
		Sororities:	20%

Basis for selection. School achievement record and courses taken most important. Test scores, school recommendation, school and community activities, class rank, and interview also considered. GPA recomputed to reflect performance in academic subjects only. Essay, interview, portfolio recommended for all; audition required for music. **Home schooled:** Interview, letter of recommendation (nonparent) required. Students in diploma-granting organization must submit evidence of coursework completed and level of performance. In absence of such a document, students must submit detailed portfolio which will be used to evaluate level of preparation for college-level work. **Learning Disabled:** Students requesting accommodations must submit documentation of their disabilities from an appropriate, licensed professional qualified in the appropriate specialty area.

High school preparation. College-preparatory program recommended. Required and recommended units include English 4, mathematics 4, social studies 1, history 1, science 2 (laboratory 2), foreign language 1, computer science 1 and visual/performing arts 1. Algebra required for 4-year nursing program.

2015-2016 Annual costs. Tuition/fees: $27,100. Room/board: $9,100. Books/supplies: $1,500. Personal expenses: $250.

Financial aid. Non-need-based: Scholarships awarded for academics, alumni affiliation, art, athletics, leadership, music/drama, ROTC. **Additional information:** All university tuition discounts (scholarships) based on family or student need and talent. Higher need awards given to middle and lower income students.

Application procedures. Admission: No deadline. $25 fee, may be waived for applicants with need. Admission notification on a rolling basis beginning on or about 10/1. For most health science programs, application deadline is January 15, early decision recommended. **Financial aid:** Priority date 3/1, closing date 8/15. FAFSA, institutional form required. Applicants notified on a rolling basis starting 3/1; must reply by 5/1 or within 4 week(s) of notification.

Academics. Special study options: Combined bachelor's/graduate degree, double major, dual enrollment of high school students, ESL, independent study, internships, liberal arts/career combination, student-designed major, study abroad, teacher certification program. **Credit/placement by examination:** AP, CLEP, IB, SAT, ACT, institutional tests. Veteran students may apply for credit by alternative means such as transfer credit from previous college work, and nationally standardized tests including College Level Examination Program (CLEP) and Defense Activity for Non-Traditional Education Support (DANTES), or through Prior Learning Assessment (PLA) portfolio assessment. Maximum combined credits granted is 30 credit hours. **Support services:** Learning center, reduced course load, remedial instruction, study skills assistance, tutoring, writing center. Online tutoring through Smarthinking, standardized testing and services available for students with disabilities.

Majors. Biology: General, biochemistry. **Business:** Accounting, business admin, finance. **Communications:** Media studies. **Education:** General, biology, elementary, English, health, physical, science, secondary, social studies, special ed. **Health services:** Athletic training, medical radiologic technology/radiation therapy, nursing (RN), predental, premedicine, prepharmacy, preveterinary, sonography. **History:** General. **Human services:** Social work. **Parks/recreation:** Sports admin. **Physical sciences:** Chemistry. **Protective services:** Law enforcement admin. **Psychology:** General. **Social sciences:** Political science. **Visual/performing arts:** Art, interior design.

Most popular majors. Biology 12%, business/marketing 26%, education 8%, health sciences 19%, psychology 7%.

Technology on campus. Dormitories wired for high-speed internet access and linked to campus network. Commuter students can connect to campus network. Online library, helpline, student web hosting, wireless network available.

Student life. Freshman orientation: Mandatory. Preregistration for classes offered. New student orientation held during summer before start of fall classes. Day-long orientations and an optional overnight stay are available. **Policies:** All fulltime freshmen and sophomores under 21 years of age (as of the first day of classes of the academic year) must reside on campus, unless he/she is commuting from his/her parent's home within a sixty-mile radius of the University, the student is married, or the student cares for a dependent child or children. **Housing:** Guaranteed on-campus for freshmen. Coed dorms, special housing for disabled, apartments available. $100 fully refundable deposit, deadline 5/1. Single rooms and suites available. **Activities:** Pep band, campus ministries, choral groups, international student organizations, student government, student newspaper, honorary societies, Fellowship Christian Athletes, Young Republicans, College Democrats.

Athletics. NCAA. **Intercollegiate:** Baseball M, basketball, cheerleading, cross-country, football (tackle) M, golf, rowing (crew) W, soccer, softball W, tennis, track and field, volleyball. **Intramural:** Basketball, bowling, football (non-tackle) M, tennis, volleyball. **Team name:** Golden Eagles.

Student services. Alcohol/substance abuse counseling, career counseling, student employment services, financial aid counseling, health services, legal services, personal counseling, placement for graduates, veterans' counselor. **Physically disabled:** Services for visually, speech, hearing impaired.

Contact. E-mail: admissions@ucwv.edu
Phone: (304) 357-4750 Toll-free number: (800) 995-4682
Fax: (304) 357-4781
Joan Clark, Vice President for Admissions, University of Charleston, 2300 MacCorkle Avenue, SE, Charleston, WV 25304

West Liberty University
West Liberty, West Virginia
www.westliberty.edu CB code: 5901

- Public 4-year university
- Residential campus in rural community
- 2,013 degree-seeking undergraduates: 8% part-time, 60% women, 4% African American, 1% Asian American, 1% Hispanic/Latino, 1% Multiracial, non-Hispanic, 2% international
- 168 degree-seeking graduate students
- 72% of applicants admitted
- SAT or ACT with writing required
- 48% graduate within 6 years

General. Founded in 1837. Regionally accredited. **Degrees:** 511 bachelor's, 34 associate awarded; master's offered. **Location:** 10 miles from Wheeling, 50 miles from Pittsburgh. **Calendar:** Semester, limited summer session. **Full-time faculty:** 129 total; 62% have terminal degrees, 46% women. **Part-time faculty:** 80 total; 5% have terminal degrees, 55% women. **Class size:** 68% < 20, 29% 20-39, 3% 40-49, less than 1% 50-99. **Special facilities:** Media arts center, rare book room, rare sheet music collection.

Freshman class profile. 1,692 applied, 1,220 admitted, 409 enrolled.

Mid 50% test scores			
		GPA 2.0-2.99:	25%
SAT critical reading:	380-510	Rank in top quarter:	43%
SAT math:	400-540	Rank in top tenth:	15%
SAT writing:	330-520	Return as sophomores:	70%
ACT composite:	18-24	Out-of-state:	42%
GPA 3.75 or higher:	33%	Live on campus:	81%
GPA 3.50-3.74:	13%	Fraternities:	2%
GPA 3.0-3.49:	29%	Sororities:	2%

Basis for selection. 2.0 GPA or 17 ACT or 810 SAT (exclusive of Writing) required. Audition required for music education; portfolio recommended for art.

High school preparation. College-preparatory program required. 17 units required. Required units include English 4, mathematics 4, social studies 2, history 1, science 3 (laboratory 3), foreign language 2 and academic electives 1. Math must be algebra I and higher. Social science must include American history.

2015-2016 Annual costs. Tuition/fees: $6,702; $14,112 out-of-state. Room/board: $8,810. Books/supplies: $1,420. Personal expenses: $1,682.

Financial aid. Non-need-based: Scholarships awarded for academics, alumni affiliation, art, athletics, music/drama, state residency. **Additional information:** Non-need based student employment available at food service, college union, bookstore, and tutoring office. Resident assistant and campus security jobs also available.

Application procedures. Admission: No deadline. No application fee. Admission notification on a rolling basis beginning on or about 9/1. **Financial aid:** Priority date 3/1; no closing date. FAFSA required. Applicants notified on a rolling basis starting 3/1; must reply within 2 week(s) of notification.

Academics. Freshman experience course available. **Special study options:** Accelerated study, distance learning, double major, dual enrollment of high

school students, external degree, independent study, internships, liberal arts/career combination, student-designed major, study abroad, teacher certification program, Washington semester. **Credit/placement by examination:** AP, CLEP, SAT, ACT, institutional tests. **Support services:** Reduced course load, remedial instruction, tutoring.

Majors. Biology: General, bacteriology, biotechnology. **Business:** General, accounting, banking/financial services, business admin, managerial economics, tourism promotion, tourism/travel. **Communications:** Communications/speech/rhetoric. **Computer sciences:** Information systems. **Education:** Art, biology, chemistry, early childhood, elementary, English, health, mathematics, mentally handicapped, music, physical, science, secondary, social science, special ed. **English:** English lit. **Health services:** Clinical lab science, dental hygiene. **History:** General. **Liberal arts:** Arts/sciences. **Math:** General. **Parks/recreation:** Exercise sciences. **Physical sciences:** Chemistry. **Protective services:** Criminal justice. **Psychology:** General. **Social sciences:** General, political science, sociology. **Visual/performing arts:** Commercial/advertising art.

Most popular majors. Business/marketing 15%, education 16%, health sciences 7%, liberal arts 13%, parks/recreation 9%, security/protective services 8%.

Technology on campus. 300 workstations in dormitories, library, computer center, student center. Dormitories wired for high-speed internet access and linked to campus network. Commuter students can connect to campus network. Online course registration, helpline, repair service available.

Student life. Freshman orientation: Mandatory, $30 fee. Preregistration for classes offered. Held Friday through Sunday before first day of classes. **Housing:** Guaranteed on-campus for all undergraduates. Coed dorms, single-sex dorms, special housing for disabled, apartments, fraternity/sorority housing available. $100 fully refundable deposit, deadline 6/1. Honors residence available for students who meet criteria. **Activities:** Bands, campus ministries, choral groups, dance, drama, international student organizations, literary magazine, music ensembles, musical theater, radio station, student government, student newspaper, TV station, Amnesty International, Students for Life, B-Pride, Electric Square, non-traditional student support group, Students in Free Enterprise, Students for Unity and Understanding.

Athletics. NCAA. **Intercollegiate:** Baseball M, basketball, cross-country, football (tackle) M, golf, softball W, tennis, track and field, volleyball W, wrestling M. **Intramural:** Basketball, golf, handball M, racquetball, softball, table tennis, tennis, volleyball. **Team name:** Hilltoppers.

Student services. Alcohol/substance abuse counseling, chaplain/spiritual director, career counseling, student employment services, financial aid counseling, health services, minority student services, personal counseling, placement for graduates, veterans' counselor. **Physically disabled:** Services for visually, hearing impaired.

Contact. E-mail: admissions@westliberty.edu
Phone: (304) 336-8076 Toll-free number: (800) 732-6204
Fax: (304) 336-8403
Brenda King, Director of Admissions and Recruitment, West Liberty University, 208 University Drive, West Liberty, WV 26074

West Virginia State University
Institute, West Virginia
www.wvstateu.edu CB member CB code: 5903

- Public 4-year liberal arts and teachers college
- Commuter campus in small town
- 2,033 degree-seeking undergraduates: 11% part-time, 54% women
- 59 degree-seeking graduate students
- 94% of applicants admitted
- SAT or ACT (ACT writing optional) required

General. Founded in 1891. Regionally accredited. **Degrees:** 432 bachelor's awarded; master's offered. **ROTC:** Army. **Location:** 8 miles from Charleston. **Calendar:** Semester, limited summer session. **Full-time faculty:** 109 total. **Part-time faculty:** 86 total. **Class size:** 53% < 20, 43% 20-39, 2% 40-49, 1% 50-99, less than 1% >100.

Freshman class profile. 1,439 applied, 1,354 admitted, 365 enrolled.

Mid 50% test scores			
		GPA 3.0-3.49:	31%
SAT critical reading:	390-510	GPA 2.0-2.99:	43%
SAT math:	400-500	End year in good standing:	70%
SAT writing:	370-480	Out-of-state:	18%
ACT composite:	16-23	Live on campus:	29%
GPA 3.75 or higher:	14%	International:	2%
GPA 3.50-3.74:	10%		

Basis for selection. School achievement record and test scores considered. **Home schooled:** Applicants must provide detailed description of home school curriculum.

High school preparation. College-preparatory program recommended. Required and recommended units include English 4, mathematics 2, social studies 3, science 2, foreign language 1 and academic electives 1.

2015-2016 Annual costs. Tuition/fees: $6,662; $15,572 out-of-state. Room/board: $10,806. Books/supplies: $1,402. **Additional information:** Tuition for students residing in bordering counties is $12,156.

Financial aid. Non-need-based: Scholarships awarded for academics, athletics, ROTC, state residency.

Application procedures. Admission: Closing date 8/18 (receipt date). $20 fee, may be waived for applicants with need. Admission notification on a rolling basis. **Financial aid:** No deadline. Applicants notified on a rolling basis.

Academics. Special study options: Cooperative education, distance learning, double major, dual enrollment of high school students, honors, internships, study abroad, teacher certification program. Visiting scholars. **Credit/placement by examination:** AP, CLEP, IB, SAT, ACT, institutional tests. **Support services:** Learning center, reduced course load, remedial instruction, study skills assistance, tutoring, writing center.

Majors. Biology: General. **Business:** General, accounting, banking/financial services, business admin. **Communications:** Communications/speech/rhetoric. **Computer sciences:** Computer science. **Education:** General, art, early childhood, elementary, English, gifted/talented, health, mathematics, mentally handicapped, middle, music, physical, science, secondary, social studies, special ed. **English:** English lit, technical writing. **Health services:** Recreational therapy. **History:** General. **Human services:** Social work. **Liberal arts:** Arts/sciences. **Math:** General, applied. **Parks/recreation:** Facilities management. **Physical sciences:** Chemistry, physics. **Protective services:** Criminal justice, police science. **Psychology:** General. **Social sciences:** Economics, political science, sociology. **Visual/performing arts:** Ceramics, commercial/advertising art, drawing, fiber arts, music, painting, photography, printmaking, sculpture, studio arts.

Most popular majors. Business/marketing 13%, education 14%, liberal arts 22%, psychology 6%, security/protective services 9%.

Technology on campus. 200 workstations in dormitories, library, computer center, student center. Dormitories linked to campus network. Commuter students can connect to campus network. Helpline available.

Student life. Freshman orientation: Mandatory, $40 fee. Preregistration for classes offered. **Policies:** Two-year on-campus residency requirement for all freshmen. Students wishing to live on-campus for more than two years are welcome and encouraged to do so. **Housing:** Guaranteed on-campus for freshmen. Coed dorms, apartments, cooperative housing available. **Activities:** Bands, campus ministries, choral groups, drama, international student organizations, literary magazine, music ensembles, musical theater, radio station, student government, student newspaper, symphony orchestra, TV station, DNA science club, pre-alumni club, College Students for Christ, NAACP, access awareness council, Fellowship for Christian Athletes, poetry workshop.

Athletics. NCAA. **Intercollegiate:** Baseball M, basketball, cheerleading W, cross-country W, football (tackle) M, golf M, softball W, tennis, volleyball W. **Intramural:** Baseball M, basketball, cheerleading W, cross-country W, football (tackle) M, golf M, softball W, tennis, volleyball W. **Team name:** Yellow Jackets.

Student services. Adult student services, alcohol/substance abuse counseling, career counseling, services for economically disadvantaged, student employment services, financial aid counseling, health services, personal counseling, placement for graduates, veterans' counselor. **Physically disabled:** Services for visually, speech, hearing impaired.

Contact. E-mail: admissions@wvstateu.edu
Phone: (304) 204-4345 Toll-free number: (800) 987-2112
Fax: (304) 766-5182
Amanda Anderson, Director of Admissions, West Virginia State University, 124 Ferrell Hall, Institute, WV 25112-1000

West Virginia University
Morgantown, West Virginia
www.wvu.edu

CB member
CB code: 5904

- Public 4-year university
- Residential campus in small city

- 21,580 degree-seeking undergraduates: 5% part-time, 46% women, 5% African American, 1% Asian American, 4% Hispanic/Latino, 3% Multi-racial, non-Hispanic, 6% international
- 1,387 degree-seeking graduate students
- 86% of applicants admitted
- SAT or ACT with writing required
- 57% graduate within 6 years

General. Founded in 1867. Regionally accredited. Regional centers at Charleston, Clarksburg, Potomac State College in Keyser, Shepherdstown, WVU Institute of Technology, and West Liberty. Health Sciences Center operates division in Charleston and Martinsburg. **Degrees:** 4,437 bachelor's awarded; master's, professional, doctoral offered. **ROTC:** Army, Air Force. **Location:** 70 miles from Pittsburgh, 200 miles from Baltimore. **Calendar:** Semester, extensive summer session. **Full-time faculty:** 1,132 total; 80% have terminal degrees, 14% minority, 43% women. **Part-time faculty:** 346 total; 31% have terminal degrees, 5% minority, 51% women. **Class size:** 50% < 20, 30% 20-39, 7% 40-49, 8% 50-99, 5% >100. **Special facilities:** Personal rapid transit system (PRT), arboretum, planetarium, herbarium, pharmacy museum, 2 art galleries, art museum, 5 experimental farms, 3 forests, software development center, mineral and energy resources museum, black culture and research center, health sciences center.

Freshman class profile. 15,353 applied, 13,174 admitted, 4,782 enrolled.

Mid 50% test scores			
SAT critical reading:	460-560	Rank in top quarter:	46%
SAT math:	470-580	Rank in top tenth:	20%
ACT composite:	21-27	Return as sophomores:	79%
GPA 3.75 or higher:	36%	Out-of-state:	53%
GPA 3.50-3.74:	17%	Live on campus:	85%
GPA 3.0-3.49:	28%	International:	4%
GPA 2.0-2.99:	19%	Fraternities:	6%
		Sororities:	5%

Basis for selection. GPA and SAT/ACT most important. 2.0 GPA and 910 SAT (exclusive of Writing)/19 ACT required of state residents. 2.5 GPA and 990 SAT/21 ACT required of nonresidents. Applicants with high GPA, high test scores, or special talents (athletics or the arts) who do not meet all admissions criteria may be considered on individual basis. Up to 5% of each incoming class may be admitted under this special policy. Interview required for dental hygiene; audition required for drama, music; portfolio required for art. Essay required for some programs. **Home schooled:** State high school equivalency certificate required. Typed manuscript of completed courses required, including content of courses, measurement of student assessment, grades, and number of credits earned for each course. Description should be separated by year of study and be signed by the person who administrated the curriculum. West Virginia homeschooled students who are applying for West Virginia PROMISE Scholarship or West Virginia Higher Education Grant must take GED.

High school preparation. College-preparatory program recommended. 17 units required. Required units include English 4, mathematics 4, social studies 3, science 3 (laboratory 3), foreign language 2 and visual/performing arts 1.

2015-2016 Annual costs. Tuition/fees: $7,632; $7,632 out-of-district; $21,432 out-of-state. Room/board: $9,872. Books/supplies: $900. Personal expenses: $900.

2014-2015 Financial aid. Need-based: 4,305 full-time freshmen applied for aid; 2,939 deemed to have need; 2,883 received aid. Average need met was 72%. Average scholarship/grant was $4,814; average loan $2,826. 49% of total undergraduate aid awarded as scholarships/grants, 51% as loans/jobs. **Non-need-based:** Awarded to 12,927 full-time undergraduates, including 3,681 freshmen. Scholarships awarded for academics, alumni affiliation, art, athletics, job skills, leadership, minority status, music/drama, religious affiliation, ROTC, state residency.

Application procedures. Admission: Priority date 3/1; deadline 8/1. $45 fee ($60 out-of-state), may be waived for applicants with need. Admission notification on a rolling basis beginning on or about 9/15. **Financial aid:** Closing date 3/1. FAFSA required. Applicants notified on a rolling basis starting 3/15; must reply within 2 week(s) of notification.

Academics. Special study options: Accelerated study, combined bachelor's/graduate degree, cooperative education, distance learning, double major, ESL, exchange student, external degree, honors, independent study, internships, semester at sea, student-designed major, study abroad, teacher certification program, United Nations semester, Washington semester. **Credit/placement by examination:** AP, CLEP, IB, SAT, ACT, institutional tests. 38 credit hours maximum toward bachelor's degree. **Support services:** Learning center, pre-admission summer program, reduced course load, remedial instruction, study skills assistance, tutoring, writing center.

Honors college/program. Admission based on GPA, ACT/SAT, community service, and extracurricular experience. No application deadline, but students wanting placement in honors housing should apply early.

Majors. Architecture: Landscape. **Biology:** General, biochemistry, exercise physiology, microbiology/immunology. **Business:** General, accounting, business admin, finance, hospitality admin, management information systems, managerial economics, marketing. **Communications:** General, advertising, broadcast journalism, communications/speech/rhetoric, journalism, media studies, public relations. **Computer sciences:** Computer science. **Conservation:** Forest management, wildlife/wilderness, wood science. **Education:** Agricultural, elementary, physical. **Engineering:** Aerospace, biomedical, chemical, civil, computer, electrical, industrial, mechanical, mining, petroleum. **English:** English lit. **Foreign languages:** General. **Health services:** Athletic training, audiology/speech pathology, clinical lab science, dental hygiene, nursing (RN), prenursing, prepharmacy. **History:** General. **Human services:** Social work. **Liberal arts:** Arts/sciences. **Math:** General. **Parks/recreation:** Exercise sciences, facilities management, health/fitness. **Philosophy/religion:** Philosophy. **Physical sciences:** Chemistry, geology, physics. **Protective services:** Forensics. **Psychology:** General. **Social sciences:** Economics, geography, political science, sociology. **Visual/performing arts:** Art, art history/conservation, design, dramatic, music, theater history. **Work/family studies:** Child development, food/nutrition.

Most popular majors. Biology 6%, business/marketing 12%, communications/journalism 8%, engineering/engineering technologies 13%, health sciences 7%, interdisciplinary studies 9%, liberal arts 6%, social sciences 8%.

Technology on campus. 3,000 workstations in dormitories, library, computer center, student center. Dormitories wired for high-speed internet access and linked to campus network. Commuter students can connect to campus network. Online course registration, online library, helpline, repair service, student web hosting, wireless network available.

Student life. Freshman orientation: Available, $45 fee. Preregistration for classes offered. Held during summer; several options ranging in length and fees. **Policies:** Anti-hazing, affirmative action and nondiscrimination policies. Mandatory freshmen housing program places faculty residence hall leaders adjacent to residence halls. Freshmen not permitted cars on campus. **Housing:** Guaranteed on-campus for freshmen. Coed dorms, single-sex dorms, special housing for disabled, apartments, fraternity/sorority housing, themed housing, wellness housing available. $225 partly refundable deposit, deadline 5/1. Special interest floors available. **Activities:** Bands, campus ministries, choral groups, dance, drama, international student organizations, literary magazine, music ensembles, Model UN, musical theater, opera, radio station, student government, student newspaper, symphony orchestra, TV station, Habitat for Humanity, Sierra Student Coalition, Hillel House, Circle K, College Republicans, Muslim student association, First Baptist Church College Ministry, Gender equality movement, Food recovery network.

Athletics. NCAA. **Intercollegiate:** Baseball M, basketball, cross-country W, diving, football (tackle) M, golf M, gymnastics W, rifle, rowing (crew) W, soccer, swimming, tennis W, track and field W, volleyball W, wrestling M. **Intramural:** Basketball, golf M, soccer, tennis W. **Team name:** Mountaineers.

Student services. Adult student services, alcohol/substance abuse counseling, chaplain/spiritual director, career counseling, services for economically disadvantaged, student employment services, financial aid counseling, health services, legal services, minority student services, on-campus daycare, personal counseling, placement for graduates, veterans' counselor, women's services. **Physically disabled:** Services for visually, speech, hearing impaired.

Contact. E-mail: go2wvu@mail.wvu.edu
Phone: (304) 293-2121 Toll-free number: (800) 344-9881
Fax: (304) 293-8832
Stephen Lee, Executive Director of Admissions and Recruitment, West Virginia University, Office of Admissions, Morgantown, WV 26506-6009

West Virginia University Institute of Technology
Montgomery, West Virginia
www.wvutech.edu   **CB code: 5902**

- Public 4-year engineering and liberal arts college
- Commuter campus in small town
- 1,116 degree-seeking undergraduates: 12% part-time, 35% women, 8% African American, 1% Asian American, 4% Hispanic/Latino, 1% Native American, 3% Multi-racial, non-Hispanic, 9% international
- 61% of applicants admitted
- SAT or ACT with writing required

General. Founded in 1895. Regionally accredited. **Degrees:** 152 bachelor's awarded. **ROTC:** Army. **Location:** 30 miles from Charleston. **Calendar:** Semester, limited summer session. **Full-time faculty:** 83 total; 71% have terminal degrees, 10% minority, 37% women. **Part-time faculty:** 31 total; 19% have terminal degrees, 58% women. **Class size:** 63% < 20, 32% 20-39, 3% 40-49, 2% 50-99. **Special facilities:** Hiking trail.

Freshman class profile. 929 applied, 571 admitted, 268 enrolled.

Mid 50% test scores			
SAT critical reading:	410-530	**GPA 2.0-2.99:**	26%
SAT math:	420-560	**Rank in top quarter:**	45%
ACT composite:	18-24	**Rank in top tenth:**	17%
GPA 3.75 or higher:	28%	**Return as sophomores:**	53%
GPA 3.50-3.74:	16%	**Out-of-state:**	37%
GPA 3.0-3.49:	30%	**Live on campus:**	69%
		International:	11%

Basis for selection. 20 GPA and 18 ACT/870 SAT (exclusive of Writing) required. Engineering applicants must have 19 ACT math. Interview recommended for engineering. **Home schooled:** Students may be required to take GED exam.

High school preparation. College-preparatory program required. 17 units required. Required units include English 4, mathematics 4, social studies 3, science 3 (laboratory 3), foreign language 2 and visual/performing arts 1. 2 algebra, 1 plane geometry, 1 advanced math required of engineering majors. 1 algebra, 1 chemistry, 1 biology required of dental hygiene majors. 2 laboratory sciences, including chemistry, 2 higher mathematics required for nursing program.

2015-2016 Annual costs. Tuition/fees: $7,632; $21,432 out-of-state. Room/board: $9,872. Books/supplies: $1,050. Personal expenses: $945.

2014-2015 Financial aid. Need-based: 258 full-time freshmen applied for aid; 204 deemed to have need; 204 received aid. Average need met was 7%. Average scholarship/grant was $5,394; average loan $2,532. 60% of total undergraduate aid awarded as scholarships/grants, 40% as loans/jobs. **Non-need-based:** Awarded to 404 full-time undergraduates, including 131 freshmen. Scholarships awarded for academics, alumni affiliation, art, athletics, job skills, leadership, minority status, music/drama, ROTC, state residency.

Application procedures. Admission: Priority date 5/1; no deadline. No application fee. Admission notification on a rolling basis beginning on or about 8/1. **Financial aid:** Closing date 3/1. FAFSA required. Applicants notified by 3/15; Applicants notified on a rolling basis starting 3/15; must reply within 2 week(s) of notification.

Academics. Special study options: Combined bachelor's/graduate degree, cooperative education, distance learning, double major, dual enrollment of high school students, internships, study abroad. Cooperative programs in engineering and business. **Credit/placement by examination:** AP, CLEP, SAT, ACT, institutional tests. 90 credit hours maximum toward bachelor's degree. **Support services:** Learning center, pre-admission summer program, reduced course load, remedial instruction, study skills assistance, tutoring.

Majors. Biology: General. **Business:** General, accounting, business admin. **Computer sciences:** General, computer science, programming, systems analysis. **Education:** Physical, voc/tech. **Engineering:** Aerospace, chemical, civil, computer, electrical, mechanical. **Health services:** Health care admin, nursing (RN). **History:** General. **Human services:** Community org/advocacy. **Math:** General. **Physical sciences:** Chemistry. **Protective services:** Forensics, law enforcement admin. **Psychology:** General. **Social sciences:** Political science.

Most popular majors. Business/marketing 11%, computer/information sciences 7%, engineering/engineering technologies 38%, liberal arts 19%, security/protective services 9%.

Technology on campus. 100 workstations in library, computer center, student center. Dormitories wired for high-speed internet access and linked to campus network. Online course registration, online library, helpline, wireless network available.

Student life. Freshman orientation: Available. Preregistration for classes offered. **Housing:** Guaranteed on-campus for all undergraduates. Coed dorms, single-sex dorms, fraternity/sorority housing available. $200 fully refundable deposit, deadline 7/1. **Activities:** Marching band, campus ministries, drama, international student organizations, musical theater, student government, student newspaper, Christian student union, Alpha Phi Omega service fraternity.

Athletics. NAIA, USCAA. **Intercollegiate:** Baseball M, basketball, cross-country, golf M, soccer, softball W, swimming, track and field, volleyball W, wrestling M. **Intramural:** Basketball, cross-country, softball, swimming, volleyball. **Team name:** Golden Bears.

Student services. Career counseling, student employment services, financial aid counseling, health services, personal counseling, placement for graduates. **Physically disabled:** Services for speech impaired.

Contact. E-mail: tech-admissions@mail.wvu.edu
Phone: (304) 442-3167 Toll-free number: (888) 554-8324
Fax: (304) 442-3067
William Allen, Director of Admissions, West Virginia University Institute of Technology, 405 Fayette Pike, Montgomery, WV 25136-2436

West Virginia Wesleyan College
Buckhannon, West Virginia
www.wvwc.edu   CB code: 5905

- Private 4-year liberal arts college affiliated with the United Methodist Church
- Residential campus in small town
- 1,371 degree-seeking undergraduates: 1% part-time, 55% women, 9% African American, 2% Hispanic/Latino, 3% Multi-racial, non-Hispanic, 5% international
- 129 degree-seeking graduate students
- 77% of applicants admitted
- SAT or ACT (ACT writing optional) required
- 50% graduate within 6 years; 33% enter graduate study

General. Founded in 1890. Regionally accredited. **Degrees:** 238 bachelor's awarded; master's offered. **Location:** 115 miles from Charleston, 135 miles from Pittsburgh. **Calendar:** Semester, limited summer session. **Full-time faculty:** 91 total; 74% have terminal degrees, 8% minority, 57% women. **Part-time faculty:** 61 total; 21% have terminal degrees, 2% minority, 51% women. **Class size:** 58% < 20, 39% 20-39, 3% 40-49, less than 1% 50-99. **Special facilities:** Planetarium, botany museum, herbarium, greenhouse, performing arts center, research center.

Freshman class profile. 1,782 applied, 1,376 admitted, 392 enrolled.

Mid 50% test scores			
SAT critical reading:	420-540	**GPA 2.0-2.99:**	17%
SAT math:	420-550	**Rank in top quarter:**	53%
SAT writing:	400-530	**Rank in top tenth:**	25%
ACT composite:	20-25	**Return as sophomores:**	72%
GPA 3.75 or higher:	41%	**Out-of-state:**	43%
GPA 3.50-3.74:	12%	**Live on campus:**	93%
GPA 3.0-3.49:	30%	**International:**	5%

Basis for selection. School achievement record and test scores required. Essay, interview recommended for all; audition recommended for drama, music; portfolio recommended for art. **Home schooled:** Transcript of courses and grades, state high school equivalency certificate required.

High school preparation. College-preparatory program recommended. Required and recommended units include English 4, mathematics 3, social studies 3, science 3 (laboratory 1) and foreign language 2.

2015-2016 Annual costs. Tuition/fees: $28,992. Room/board: $8,066. Books/supplies: $2,500. Personal expenses: $2,500.

2015-2016 Financial aid. Need-based: 77% of total undergraduate aid awarded as scholarships/grants, 23% as loans/jobs. **Non-need-based:** Scholarships awarded for academics, alumni affiliation, art, athletics, leadership, music/drama, religious affiliation.

Application procedures. Admission: Priority date 5/1; deadline 8/15. $35 fee, may be waived for applicants with need. Admission notification on a rolling basis beginning on or about 10/1. Must reply by May 1 or within 3 week(s) if notified thereafter. **Financial aid:** Priority date 2/15; no closing date. FAFSA required. Applicants notified on a rolling basis starting 3/1; must reply within 4 week(s) of notification.

Academics. Special study options: Combined bachelor's/graduate degree, distance learning, double major, ESL, exchange student, honors, independent study, internships, liberal arts/career combination, New York semester, student-designed major, study abroad, teacher certification program, Washington semester. **Credit/placement by examination:** AP, CLEP, IB, SAT, ACT, institutional tests. 30 credit hours maximum toward bachelor's degree. **Support services:** Learning center, reduced course load, remedial instruction, study skills assistance, tutoring, writing center.

Majors. Biology: General. **Business:** Accounting, business admin, managerial economics, marketing. **Communications:** General, public relations. **Computer sciences:** General, computer science, information systems. **Conservation:** Environmental studies. **Education:** General, art, biology, chemistry, elementary, English, health, history, kindergarten/preschool, learning disabled, mathematics, music, physical, science, secondary, social studies, special ed. **Engineering:** Pre-engineering. **English:** Creative writing, English lit. **Health services:** Art therapy, athletic training, nursing (RN), predental, premedicine, prepharmacy, preveterinary. **History:** General. **Math:** General.

Parks/recreation: Exercise sciences, health/fitness, sports admin. **Philosophy/religion:** Philosophy, religion. **Physical sciences:** Chemistry, materials chemistry, physics. **Protective services:** Law enforcement admin. **Psychology:** General. **Social sciences:** Economics, international relations, political science, sociology. **Visual/performing arts:** Art, ceramics, dramatic, drawing, graphic design, music, painting, photography, studio arts, studio arts management, theater arts management.

Most popular majors. Business/marketing 10%, education 10%, health sciences 7%, parks/recreation 11%, physical sciences 9%, psychology 10%, social sciences 7%, visual/performing arts 8%.

Technology on campus. PC or laptop required. Dormitories wired for high-speed internet access and linked to campus network. Commuter students can connect to campus network. Online library, helpline, repair service, wireless network available.

Student life. Freshman orientation: Mandatory, $200 fee. Preregistration for classes offered. Held weekend before fall class registration; provides programs for new students and parents. **Policies:** Full-time students required to live on campus unless married, living with parents, or have received written permission from the Housing Committee to live off campus. **Housing:** Guaranteed on-campus for all undergraduates. Coed dorms, single-sex dorms, special housing for disabled, apartments, fraternity/sorority housing available. $200 nonrefundable deposit, deadline 5/1. **Activities:** Bands, campus ministries, choral groups, dance, drama, international student organizations, literary magazine, music ensembles, musical theater, opera, radio station, student government, student newspaper, Christian life council, Fellowship of Christian Athletes, Alpha Phi Omega service fraternity, black student union, College Republicans, Young Democrats, green club, Wesleyan service corps.

Athletics. NCAA. **Intercollegiate:** Baseball M, basketball, cross-country, football (tackle) M, golf, lacrosse W, soccer, softball W, swimming, tennis, track and field, volleyball W. **Intramural:** Basketball, football (non-tackle), racquetball, softball, table tennis, volleyball, water polo M. **Team name:** Bobcats.

Student services. Alcohol/substance abuse counseling, chaplain/spiritual director, career counseling, financial aid counseling, health services, minority student services, personal counseling, placement for graduates. **Physically disabled:** Services for visually, speech, hearing impaired.

Contact. E-mail: admission@wvwc.edu
Phone: (304) 473-8510 Toll-free number: (800) 722-9933
Fax: (304) 473-8108
John Waltz, Director of Admission, West Virginia Wesleyan College, 59 College Avenue, Buckhannon, WV 26201-2998

Wheeling Jesuit University
Wheeling, West Virginia   CB member
www.wju.edu   CB code: 5906

- Private 4-year university and liberal arts college affiliated with the Roman Catholic Church
- Residential campus in small city
- 1,131 degree-seeking undergraduates
- 388 graduate students
- SAT or ACT (ACT writing optional) required

General. Founded in 1954. Regionally accredited. **Degrees:** 248 bachelor's awarded; master's, professional offered. **Location:** 55 miles from Pittsburgh; 125 miles from Columbus, OH. **Calendar:** Semester, limited summer session. **Full-time faculty:** 81 total; 59% have terminal degrees, 5% minority, 53% women. **Part-time faculty:** 99 total; 22% have terminal degrees, 3% minority, 42% women. **Class size:** 69% < 20, 31% 20-39, less than 1% 50-99.

Freshman class profile.

GPA 3.75 or higher:	31%	**Rank in top quarter:**	38%
GPA 3.50-3.74:	14%	**Rank in top tenth:**	16%
GPA 3.0-3.49:	32%	**Out-of-state:**	74%
GPA 2.0-2.99:	23%	**Live on campus:**	90%

Basis for selection. High school GPA, quality of courses taken, and test scores most important. Some exception made to minimum when warranted by high school record. Personal recommendations and extracurricular activities important. In-state and out-of-state applicants treated equally. Interview, essay recommended. **Learning Disabled:** Students need to submit written documentation of disability.

High school preparation. College-preparatory program recommended. 15 units required; 17 recommended. Required and recommended units include English 4, mathematics 2, social studies 1, history 1, science 1-2 (laboratory 1-2), foreign language 2 and academic electives 6. Applicants for programs in natural sciences should have 1 biology and 1 chemistry. Applicants preparing for future study in physical therapy doctorate program should have 3 years of college preparatory math and 3 years of lab science, including physics.

2015-2016 Annual costs. Tuition/fees: $28,030. Room/board: $7,070. Books/supplies: $1,300. Personal expenses: $800.

2015-2016 Financial aid. Need-based: Average need met was 93%. Average scholarship/grant was $9,997; average loan $4,457. 43% of total undergraduate aid awarded as scholarships/grants, 57% as loans/jobs. **Non-need-based:** Scholarships awarded for academics, alumni affiliation, athletics, music/drama, religious affiliation.

Application procedures. Admission: No deadline. $25 fee, may be waived for applicants with need, free for online applicants. Admission notification on a rolling basis beginning on or about 9/15. **Financial aid:** Priority date 3/1, closing date 8/1. FAFSA required. Applicants notified on a rolling basis starting 3/10; must reply within 2 week(s) of notification.

Academics. Special study options: Combined bachelor's/graduate degree, distance learning, double major, dual enrollment of high school students, ESL, exchange student, honors, independent study, internships, liberal arts/career combination, semester at sea, student-designed major, study abroad, teacher certification program, United Nations semester, Washington semester. Off-campus study. **Credit/placement by examination:** AP, CLEP, IB, SAT, ACT, institutional tests. 30 credit hours maximum toward bachelor's degree. **Support services:** Learning center, remedial instruction, study skills assistance, tutoring, writing center.

Majors. Biology: General. **Business:** Accounting, business admin, organizational leadership. **Communications:** Organizational. **Computer sciences:** General. **Education:** General. **Engineering:** Engineering science. **English:** English lit. **Foreign languages:** French, Spanish. **Health services:** Athletic training, health care admin, nuclear medical technology, nursing (RN), respiratory therapy technology. **History:** General. **Liberal arts:** Arts/sciences. **Math:** General. **Philosophy/religion:** Philosophy. **Physical sciences:** General, chemistry, physics. **Protective services:** Criminal justice. **Psychology:** General. **Social sciences:** International relations, political science. **Theology:** Theology.

Most popular majors. Business/marketing 21%, health sciences 32%, psychology 8%.

Technology on campus. 215 workstations in dormitories, library, computer center, student center. Dormitories wired for high-speed internet access and linked to campus network. Commuter students can connect to campus network. Online course registration, online library, helpline, wireless network available.

Student life. Freshman orientation: Mandatory, $250 fee. Preregistration for classes offered. One and a half day session held in summer; 3-day session held prior to beginning of fall semester. **Housing:** Guaranteed on-campus for all undergraduates. Coed dorms, single-sex dorms, special housing for disabled, apartments, themed housing available. **Activities:** Bands, campus ministries, choral groups, drama, international student organizations, literary magazine, music ensembles, musical theater, student government, student newspaper, symphony orchestra, Appalachian Experience Club, Circle K International, Justice and Peace in Our Times, political science club, Students for Life, Mother Jones House, music ministry, liturgical ministry, praise and worship, small prayer groups.

Athletics. NCAA. **Intercollegiate:** Baseball M, basketball, cross-country, golf, lacrosse, soccer, softball W, swimming, track and field, volleyball W. **Intramural:** Basketball, soccer, softball, tennis, volleyball. **Team name:** Cardinals.

Student services. Adult student services, alcohol/substance abuse counseling, chaplain/spiritual director, career counseling, student employment services, financial aid counseling, health services, personal counseling, placement for graduates. **Physically disabled:** Services for visually, hearing impaired.

Contact. E-mail: admiss@wju.edu
Phone: (304) 243-2359 Toll-free number: (800) 624-6992
Fax: (304) 243-2397
Kimberly Klaus, Director of Undergraduate Enrollment, Wheeling Jesuit University, 316 Washington Avenue, Wheeling, WV 26003-6295

Wisconsin

Alverno College
Milwaukee, Wisconsin
CB member
www.alverno.edu
CB code: 1012

◆ Private 4-year liberal arts college for women affiliated with the Roman Catholic Church

◆ Commuter campus in very large city

◆ 1,528 degree-seeking undergraduates: 23% part-time, 100% women, 15% African American, 5% Asian American, 23% Hispanic/Latino, 1% Native American, 4% Multi-racial, non-Hispanic

◆ 648 degree-seeking graduate students

◆ 63% of applicants admitted

◆ SAT or ACT (ACT writing optional), application essay required

◆ 42% graduate within 6 years; 16% enter graduate study

General. Founded in 1887. Regionally accredited. **Degrees:** 392 bachelor's, 10 associate awarded; master's offered. **ROTC:** Army, Air Force. **Location:** 5 miles from downtown. **Calendar:** Semester, limited summer session. **Full-time faculty:** 98 total; 91% have terminal degrees, 7% minority, 78% women. **Part-time faculty:** 140 total; 49% have terminal degrees, 11% minority, 81% women. **Class size:** 76% < 20, 24% 20-39. **Special facilities:** Multimedia productions facility, independent science research areas, native prairie, clinical nursing resource center.

Freshman class profile. 740 applied, 465 admitted, 231 enrolled.

Mid 50% test scores		GPA 2.0-2.99:	50%
ACT composite:	16-22	Return as sophomores:	69%
GPA 3.75 or higher:	10%	Out-of-state:	10%
GPA 3.50-3.74:	11%	Live on campus:	39%
GPA 3.0-3.49:	29%	Sororities:	1%

Basis for selection. Admissions based on review of transcripts, GPA, academic units, standardized tests, essay, and Communication Placement Assessment results. Audition required for music therapy; portfolio required for studio art. **Home schooled:** Letter of recommendation (nonparent) required. Portfolio of work required.

High school preparation. College-preparatory program required. 17 units required. Required and recommended units include English 4, mathematics 3, social studies 3, science 3, foreign language 2 and academic electives 4.

2015-2016 Annual costs. Tuition/fees: $25,660. Room/board: $7,634. Books/supplies: $625. Personal expenses: $2,300.

2015-2016 Financial aid. Need-based: 214 full-time freshmen applied for aid; 203 deemed to have need; 203 received aid. Average scholarship/grant was $17,376; average loan $3,006. 62% of total undergraduate aid awarded as scholarships/grants, 38% as loans/jobs. **Non-need-based:** Awarded to 979 full-time undergraduates, including 206 freshmen. Scholarships awarded for academics, alumni affiliation.

Application procedures. Admission: No deadline. No application fee. Admission notification on a rolling basis beginning on or about 9/1. Must reply by May 1 or within 2 week(s) if notified thereafter. **Financial aid:** Priority date 3/1; no closing date. FAFSA required. Applicants notified on a rolling basis starting 3/1; must reply within 2 week(s) of notification.

Academics. Required internships in all majors provide research opportunities through federal government, local organizations and businesses. Students in every major area spend from 8 to 12 hours per week for one semester in field internship. Students also have opportunities to do service learning through individual courses. Degrees with honor awarded based on outstanding achievement and application of learning in service to others. **Special study options:** Accelerated study, double major, honors, independent study, internships, semester at sea, student-designed major, study abroad, teacher certification program, Washington semester, weekend college. **Credit/placement by examination:** AP, CLEP, IB, institutional tests. Each student's background and experience are looked at on an individual basis by the department faculty. **Support services:** Learning center, pre-admission summer program, reduced course load, remedial instruction, study skills assistance, tutoring, writing center.

Majors. Area/ethnic studies: Women's. **Biology:** General, molecular. **Business:** General, business admin, international. **Communications:** Communications/speech/rhetoric. **Computer sciences:** General. **Conservation:** Environmental science. **Education:** General, art, elementary, English, middle, music, science, social studies. **English:** English lit. **Health services:** Art therapy, music therapy. **History:** General. **Human services:** Community org/advocacy. **Liberal arts:** Arts/sciences. **Math:** General. **Philosophy/religion:** Philosophy, religion. **Physical sciences:** Chemistry. **Psychology:** General. **Social sciences:** General, international relations, political science, sociology. **Visual/performing arts:** Art, music.

Most popular majors. Biology 6%, business/marketing 11%, health sciences 38%, liberal arts 15%, psychology 6%.

Technology on campus. 737 workstations in dormitories, library, computer center. Dormitories wired for high-speed internet access and linked to campus network. Commuter students can connect to campus network. Online course registration, online library, student web hosting, wireless network available.

Student life. Freshman orientation: Mandatory. Preregistration for classes offered. Overnight program held during the summer. **Housing:** Themed housing available. $100 partly refundable deposit, deadline 7/1. All housing smoke-free. Semi-apartment living within residence halls available to older students. **Activities:** Campus ministries, choral groups, dance, drama, international student organizations, literary magazine, music ensembles, Model UN, radio station, student government, student newspaper, Circle K, Co-Exist, Black Students United, Muslim student association, Women of Asian Ethnicity, student nurses association, global studies club, Alverno College Republicans.

Athletics. NCAA. **Intercollegiate:** Basketball W, cross-country W, golf W, soccer W, softball W, tennis W, volleyball W. **Intramural:** Basketball W, volleyball W. **Team name:** Alverno Inferno.

Student services. Adult student services, chaplain/spiritual director, career counseling, financial aid counseling, health services, on-campus daycare, personal counseling. **Physically disabled:** Services for visually, speech, hearing impaired.

Contact. E-mail: admissions@alverno.edu
Phone: (414) 382-6101 Toll-free number: (800) 933-3401
Fax: (414) 382-6055
Kate Lundeen, Vice President for Enrollment Services, Alverno College, 3400 South 43rd Street, Milwaukee, WI 53234-3922

Bellin College
Green Bay, Wisconsin
www.bellincollege.edu
CB code: 1046

◆ Private 4-year Nursing + Health Sciences

◆ Commuter campus in small city

◆ 315 degree-seeking undergraduates: 36% part-time, 91% women, 1% African American, 1% Asian American, 3% Hispanic/Latino, 1% Native American, 1% Multi-racial, non-Hispanic

◆ 46 degree-seeking graduate students

◆ 88% of applicants admitted

◆ SAT or ACT (ACT writing optional), application essay, interview required

◆ 64% graduate within 6 years

General. Founded in 1909. Regionally accredited. Associated with a health system and hospital. **Degrees:** 97 bachelor's awarded; master's offered. **ROTC:** Army. **Location:** 120 miles of Milwaukee. **Calendar:** Semester, limited summer session. **Full-time faculty:** 21 total. **Part-time faculty:** 11 total. **Class size:** 47% < 20, 37% 20-39, 16% 40-49.

Freshman class profile. 33 applied, 29 admitted, 29 enrolled.

Mid 50% test scores		GPA 3.0-3.49:	39%
ACT composite:	21-25	End year in good standing:	68%
GPA 3.75 or higher:	40%	Return as sophomores:	68%
GPA 3.50-3.74:	21%		

Basis for selection. 23 ACT and 3.25 GPA required, although students with 21-22 ACT will be reviewed for admission. Personal interview very important. Three references required, including 1 academic and 1 from employer if working. BSRS 20 ACT and 3.0 GPA.

High school preparation. College-preparatory program required. 13 units required. Required units include English 4, mathematics 3, social studies 3 and science 3. Math must include 1 algebra and 2 advanced math. Sciences must include 1 chemistry, 1 biology, and 1 advanced science.

2016-2017 Annual costs. Tuition/fees (projected): $21,140. Books/supplies: $1,650. Personal expenses: $665.

2014-2015 Financial aid. Need-based: 36% of total undergraduate aid awarded as scholarships/grants, 64% as loans/jobs. **Non-need-based:** Scholarships awarded for academics. **Additional information:** Freshmen and sophomores receive aid through University of Wisconsin-Green Bay. Juniors and seniors receive aid through Bellin College. All aid stats reflect only those enrolled students receiving aid through Bellin College. Bellin College does not award federal and state aid to first-time full time freshman. Those students receive aid through UWGB.

Application procedures. Admission: Priority date 5/1; no deadline. No application fee. Admission notification on a rolling basis beginning on or about 9/1. Must reply by May 1 or within 3 week(s) if notified thereafter. We accept applications for fall term beginning one year prior to entry. **Financial aid:** Priority date 3/1; no closing date. FAFSA required. Applicants notified on a rolling basis starting 4/1; must reply within 2 week(s) of notification.

Academics. Students fulfill general education requirements at University of Wisconsin-Green Bay, University of Wisconsin Colleges, St Norbert College or another accredited college or university of their choice. **Special study options:** Accelerated study, combined bachelor's/graduate degree, dual enrollment of high school students, independent study, study abroad. **Credit/placement by examination:** AP, CLEP, ACT. **Support services:** Remedial instruction, study skills assistance, tutoring. Writing tutor.

Majors. Health services: Nursing (RN), radiologist assistant.

Technology on campus. 30 workstations in library, computer center. Commuter students can connect to campus network. Online library, helpline, wireless network available.

Student life. Freshman orientation: Mandatory. Preregistration for classes offered. One-day session in early summer and half-day session within a week prior to fall semester. **Housing:** Students may live in dorms at institutions in which they are dually enrolled, such as University of Wisconsin-Green Bay or St. Norbert College. **Activities:** Student government, student nurses association, ambassadors club, honor society, student senate, IHI Open School, Men in Nursing.

Student services. Career counseling, student employment services, financial aid counseling, health services, personal counseling.

Contact. E-mail: admissions@bellincollege.edu
Phone: (920) 433-6650 Toll-free number: (800) 236-8707
Fax: (920) 469-1735
Katie Klaus, Director of Admissions, Bellin College, 3201 Eaton Road, Green Bay, WI 54311

Beloit College
Beloit, Wisconsin
www.beloit.edu

CB member
CB code: 1059

- Private 4-year liberal arts college
- Residential campus in large town
- 1,271 degree-seeking undergraduates: 55% women, 5% African American, 3% Asian American, 9% Hispanic/Latino, 3% Multi-racial, non-Hispanic, 9% international
- 69% of applicants admitted
- Application essay required
- 81% graduate within 6 years

General. Founded in 1846. Regionally accredited. **Degrees:** 310 bachelor's awarded. **Location:** 60 miles from Madison, 90 miles from Chicago. **Calendar:** Semester, limited summer session. **Full-time faculty:** 107 total; 98% have terminal degrees, 17% minority, 58% women. **Part-time faculty:** 41 total; 49% have terminal degrees, 7% minority, 51% women. **Class size:** 69% < 20, 30% 20-39, less than 1% 40-49. **Special facilities:** LEED-certified science center, anthropology museum, art museum, observatory, 2 nature preserves, social science research laboratory, immunology laboratory, 2 electron microscopes, superconducting NMR, ICAP spectrometer, marketing research center, center for entrepreneurial leadership.

Freshman class profile. 3,552 applied, 2,443 admitted, 392 enrolled.

Mid 50% test scores			
SAT critical reading:	540-670	GPA 2.0-2.99:	21%
SAT math:	540-650	Rank in top quarter:	64%
ACT composite:	24-30	Rank in top tenth:	29%
GPA 3.75 or higher:	19%	Return as sophomores:	88%
GPA 3.50-3.74:	22%	Out-of-state:	85%
GPA 3.0-3.49:	38%	Live on campus:	98%
		International:	9%

Basis for selection. Rigor of high school curriculum and high school record most important. Test scores, recommendations, essays, interviews, and extracurricular activities also very important. Interview recommended. **Home schooled:** Letter of recommendation (nonparent) required. Submit evidence of coursework completed and level of performance.

High school preparation. College-preparatory program required. Recommended units include English 4, mathematics 3, social studies 4, science 3 (laboratory 3) and foreign language 3.

2015-2016 Annual costs. Tuition/fees: $45,050. Room/board: $7,890. Books/supplies: $1,000. Personal expenses: $1,300.

2015-2016 Financial aid. Need-based: 316 full-time freshmen applied for aid; 274 deemed to have need; 274 received aid. Average need met was 95%. Average scholarship/grant was $31,060; average loan $5,354. 79% of total undergraduate aid awarded as scholarships/grants, 21% as loans/jobs. **Non-need-based:** Awarded to 806 full-time undergraduates, including 255 freshmen. Scholarships awarded for academics, leadership, minority status, music/drama.

Application procedures. Admission: Priority date 1/15; no deadline. No application fee. Admission notification on a rolling basis beginning on or about 1/16. Must reply by May 1 or within 2 week(s) if notified thereafter. Official transcript indicating all junior year courses, including those anticipated to be taken through the year's end. In most cases, interview with Office of Admissions will be required. **Financial aid:** Priority date 3/1, closing date 3/1. FAFSA required. PROFILE required for early decision/early action applicants only. Applicants notified on a rolling basis starting 3/1; must reply by 5/1.

Academics. Heavy emphasis placed on international education, interdisciplinary study, and experiential learning. **Special study options:** Combined bachelor's/graduate degree, double major, ESL, exchange student, independent study, internships, liberal arts/career combination, student-designed major, study abroad, teacher certification program, urban semester, Washington semester. Field schools in archeology and geology, Center for Language Studies, intensive summer foreign language program, 3-2 programs in engineering and forestry. **Credit/placement by examination:** AP, CLEP, IB. 32 credit hours maximum toward bachelor's degree. **Support services:** Learning center, study skills assistance, tutoring, writing center.

Majors. Area/ethnic studies: Women's. **Biology:** General, biochemistry, ecology, environmental, molecular. **Business:** Managerial economics. **Computer sciences:** Computer science. **Conservation:** Environmental studies, forestry. **Education:** General, art, science. **Engineering:** General. **English:** Creative writing, English lit. **Foreign languages:** General, Chinese, classics, comparative lit, French, German, Japanese, Russian, Spanish. **Health services:** Nursing (RN). **History:** General. **Liberal arts:** Arts/sciences. **Math:** General. **Philosophy/religion:** Philosophy, religion. **Physical sciences:** Chemistry, environmental chemistry, geology, physics. **Psychology:** General. **Social sciences:** Anthropology, economics, international relations, political science, sociology. **Visual/performing arts:** Art history/conservation, dance, dramatic, music.

Most popular majors. Biology 6%, education 6%, English 9%, foreign language 11%, physical sciences 10%, psychology 6%, social sciences 21%, visual/performing arts 8%.

Technology on campus. 300 workstations in library, student center. Dormitories wired for high-speed internet access and linked to campus network. Commuter students can connect to campus network. Online course registration, online library, helpline, student web hosting, wireless network available.

Student life. Freshman orientation: Mandatory. Preregistration for classes offered. Held 10 days prior to fall semester. **Policies:** Residence hall system is student managed. **Housing:** Guaranteed on-campus for all undergraduates. Coed dorms, single-sex dorms, apartments, cooperative housing, fraternity/sorority housing, themed housing available. Special-interest housing available to students that have completed at least one semester. **Activities:** Campus ministries, choral groups, dance, drama, international student organizations, literary magazine, music ensembles, Model UN, musical theater, radio station, student government, student newspaper, TV station, volunteer community, tutoring service, Voces Latinas, Black Students United, peace and justice club, outdoor environmental club, Sexuality and Gender Alliance, Slow Food, College Democrats/Republicans, Ultimate Frisbee Family.

Athletics. NCAA. **Intercollegiate:** Baseball M, basketball, cross-country, diving, football (tackle) M, lacrosse, soccer, softball W, swimming, tennis W, track and field, volleyball W. **Intramural:** Badminton, basketball, bowling, football (non-tackle), racquetball, soccer, swimming, table tennis, ultimate frisbee, volleyball. **Team name:** Bucs.

Student services. Alcohol/substance abuse counseling, chaplain/spiritual director, career counseling, services for economically disadvantaged, student employment services, financial aid counseling, health services, minority student services, on-campus daycare, personal counseling, placement for graduates, women's services. **Physically disabled:** Services for visually, hearing impaired.

Contact. E-mail: admiss@beloit.edu
Phone: (608) 363-2500 Toll-free number: (800) 923-5648
Fax: (608) 363-2075
Jim Zielinski, Director of Admissions, Beloit College, 700 College Street, Beloit, WI 53511-5595

Cardinal Stritch University
Milwaukee, Wisconsin
www.stritch.edu   CB code: 1100

- Private 4-year university affiliated with the Roman Catholic Church
- Commuter campus in very large city
- 1,971 degree-seeking undergraduates: 11% part-time, 66% women, 21% African American, 2% Asian American, 11% Hispanic/Latino, 1% Native American, 3% Multi-racial, non-Hispanic, 6% international
- 1,167 degree-seeking graduate students
- 77% of applicants admitted
- SAT or ACT (ACT writing optional), application essay required
- 44% graduate within 6 years

General. Founded in 1937. Regionally accredited. **Degrees:** 453 bachelor's, 142 associate awarded; master's, doctoral offered. **Location:** 7 miles from downtown, 85 miles from Chicago. **Calendar:** Semester, limited summer session. **Class size:** 78% < 20, 21% 20-39, less than 1% 40-49, less than 1% 50-99.

Freshman class profile. 783 applied, 602 admitted, 171 enrolled.

Mid 50% test scores			
SAT critical reading:	440-540	Rank in top quarter:	46%
SAT math:	480-570	Rank in top tenth:	20%
ACT composite:	20-24	Return as sophomores:	70%
GPA 3.75 or higher:	20%	Out-of-state:	24%
GPA 3.50-3.74:	14%	Live on campus:	63%
GPA 3.0-3.49:	33%	International:	19%
GPA 2.0-2.99:	32%	Fraternities:	18%

Basis for selection. Admissions based on GPA and test scores. Conditional admission available to applicants not meeting all admissions criteria. Institutional tests used for admission of academically weak students. Interview recommended for all; portfolio recommended for art; audition recommended for music and theatre.

High school preparation. College-preparatory program recommended. 16 units required. Required units include English 4, mathematics 2, social studies 2, history 2, science 3 and academic electives 6.

2015-2016 Annual costs. Tuition/fees: $27,540. Room/board: $7,700. Books/supplies: $700. Personal expenses: $3,318.

2015-2016 Financial aid. Need-based: 130 full-time freshmen applied for aid; 117 deemed to have need; 117 received aid. Average need met was 83%. Average scholarship/grant was $22,011; average loan $3,328. 60% of total undergraduate aid awarded as scholarships/grants, 40% as loans/jobs. **Non-need-based:** Scholarships awarded for academics, alumni affiliation, art, athletics, music/drama, religious affiliation.

Application procedures. Admission: No deadline. No application fee. Admission notification on a rolling basis beginning on or about 9/15. **Financial aid:** Priority date 3/15; no closing date. FAFSA required. Applicants notified on a rolling basis starting 2/19; must reply within 2 week(s) of notification.

Academics. Special study options: Accelerated study, distance learning, double major, independent study, internships, study abroad, teacher certification program. **Credit/placement by examination:** AP, CLEP, IB, SAT, ACT, institutional tests. 30 credit hours maximum toward associate degree, 60 toward bachelor's. **Support services:** Learning center, reduced course load, remedial instruction, study skills assistance, tutoring, writing center.

Majors. Biology: General. **Business:** General, accounting, business admin, human resources, international, management information systems, organizational leadership. **Communications:** General. **Computer sciences:** Computer science. **Education:** General, early childhood, elementary, secondary, special ed. **English:** English lit, writing. **Foreign languages:** Spanish. **Health services:** Nursing (RN), respiratory therapy technology. **History:** General. **Math:** General. **Parks/recreation:** Sports admin. **Philosophy/religion:** Religion. **Physical sciences:** Chemistry. **Protective services:** Criminal justice.

Psychology: General. **Social sciences:** Political science, sociology. **Visual/performing arts:** General, art, dramatic, game design, graphic design, music performance, photography, studio arts.

Most popular majors. Business/marketing 57%, education 8%, health sciences 6%.

Technology on campus. 441 workstations in dormitories, library, computer center, student center. Dormitories wired for high-speed internet access and linked to campus network. Commuter students can connect to campus network. Online course registration, online library, helpline, wireless network available.

Student life. Freshman orientation: Mandatory. Preregistration for classes offered. Week-long program held prior to start of classes. **Housing:** Coed dorms, apartments available. $50 fully refundable deposit. **Activities:** Campus ministries, choral groups, drama, international student organizations, literary magazine, music ensembles, Model UN, musical theater, radio station, student government, symphony orchestra, Asian Student Association, Black Student Union, Care for Creation Small Faith Sharing Group, Franciscan Servant Scholars, Hispanic club, Hispanic Professionals of Greater Milwaukee, Ignite Group, Interfaith Gathering Group, Students for Justice in Palestine, Urban Fellows FWS program.

Athletics. NAIA. **Intercollegiate:** Basketball, cross-country, soccer, softball W, volleyball. **Intramural:** Golf, tennis, track and field. **Team name:** Wolves.

Student services. Adult student services, alcohol/substance abuse counseling, chaplain/spiritual director, career counseling, student employment services, financial aid counseling, health services, personal counseling, placement for graduates, veterans' counselor. **Physically disabled:** Services for hearing impaired.

Contact. E-mail: admityou@stritch.edu
Phone: (414) 410-4040 Toll-free number: (800) 347-8822 ext. 4040
Fax: (414) 410-4092
Emmy Stoecklein, Director of Admission, Cardinal Stritch University, 6801 North Yates Road, Box 516, Milwaukee, WI 53217-7516

Carroll University
Waukesha, Wisconsin
www.carrollu.edu   CB code: 1101

- Private 4-year university and liberal arts college affiliated with the Presbyterian Church (USA)
- Residential campus in small city
- 3,021 degree-seeking undergraduates
- SAT or ACT (ACT writing optional) required

General. Founded in 1846. Regionally accredited. **Degrees:** 643 bachelor's awarded; master's, professional offered. **ROTC:** Army, Air Force. **Location:** 15 miles from Milwaukee. **Calendar:** Semester, extensive summer session. **Full-time faculty:** 127 total; 68% have terminal degrees, 4% minority, 51% women. **Part-time faculty:** 203 total; 14% have terminal degrees, 65% women. **Class size:** 57% < 20, 39% 20-39, 1% 40-49, 3% 50-99, less than 1% >100. **Special facilities:** Scientific study and conservancy, class 1 trout stream, wetland and upland habitats.

Freshman class profile.

GPA 3.75 or higher:	27%	Rank in top tenth:	25%
GPA 3.50-3.74:	25%	Out-of-state:	28%
GPA 3.0-3.49:	31%	Live on campus:	86%
GPA 2.0-2.99:	17%	Fraternities:	4%
Rank in top quarter:	53%	Sororities:	9%

Basis for selection. School achievement record most important, followed by test scores. Recommendations, essay, interview considered. Essay, interview recommended for all; audition recommended for music, theater; portfolio recommended for art. **Home schooled:** Transcript of courses and grades required.

High school preparation. College-preparatory program recommended. 17 units recommended. Recommended units include English 4, mathematics 4, social studies 3, history 3, science 3 (laboratory 2).

2015-2016 Annual costs. Tuition/fees: $29,535. Room/board: $9,032. Books/supplies: $1,236. Personal expenses: $1,564.

Financial aid. Non-need-based: Scholarships awarded for academics, alumni affiliation, art, leadership, music/drama, ROTC.

Application procedures. Admission: Priority date 3/15; no deadline. No application fee. Admission notification on a rolling basis beginning on or about 8/1. **Financial aid:** No deadline. FAFSA required. Applicants notified on a rolling basis starting 2/15; must reply by 5/1 or within 2 week(s) of notification.

Academics. Education majors must maintain 2.75 GPA in major and teaching minors. Nursing students must maintain 2.75 GPA. Six majors available for pre-physical therapy programs. **Special study options:** Combined bachelor's/graduate degree, distance learning, double major, dual enrollment of high school students, ESL, exchange student, honors, independent study, internships, liberal arts/career combination, semester at sea, student-designed major, study abroad, teacher certification program, United Nations semester, Washington semester. **Credit/placement by examination:** AP, CLEP, IB, institutional tests. 24 credit hours maximum toward bachelor's degree. **Support services:** Learning center, pre-admission summer program, reduced course load, remedial instruction, study skills assistance, tutoring, writing center.

Majors. Area/ethnic studies: European. **Biology:** General, animal behavior, biochemistry. **Business:** Accounting, actuarial science, business admin, finance, human resources, management information systems, marketing, organizational behavior, small business admin. **Communications:** Communications/speech/rhetoric, journalism, organizational, public relations. **Communications technology:** Graphics, printing management. **Computer sciences:** General, information systems. **Conservation:** General, environmental science. **Education:** General, art, biology, chemistry, early childhood, elementary, English, foreign languages, geography, health, history, mathematics, middle, music, physical, psychology, science, social science, social studies, Spanish. **Engineering:** Applied physics, software. **English:** Creative writing, English lit. **Foreign languages:** Spanish. **Health services:** Athletic training, clinical lab science, nursing (RN), predental, premedicine, prepharmacy, preveterinary, public health ed, radiologic technology/medical imaging. **History:** General, European. **Math:** General, applied. **Parks/recreation:** Exercise sciences, facilities management, health/fitness. **Philosophy/religion:** Religion. **Physical sciences:** Chemistry. **Protective services:** Criminal justice, forensics. **Psychology:** General. **Social sciences:** Political science, sociology. **Visual/performing arts:** Art, commercial/advertising art, dramatic, music, photography, studio arts.

Most popular majors. Biology 6%, business/marketing 15%, education 13%, health sciences 10%, parks/recreation 13%, psychology 10%.

Technology on campus. 250 workstations in dormitories, library, computer center, student center. Dormitories wired for high-speed internet access and linked to campus network. Commuter students can connect to campus network. Online course registration, online library, helpline, student web hosting, wireless network available.

Student life. Freshman orientation: Mandatory, $250 fee. Preregistration for classes offered. **Policies:** Freshmen not permitted cars on campus. **Housing:** Guaranteed on-campus for freshmen. Coed dorms, single-sex dorms, apartments, themed housing available. $100 nonrefundable deposit. **Activities:** Bands, campus ministries, choral groups, dance, drama, international student organizations, literary magazine, music ensembles, radio station, student government, student newspaper, Bible study group, Intervarsity Christian Fellowship, Fellowship of Christian Athletes, black student union, Queers & Allies, Questions & Answers, international experience club, Latin American student organization, University Republicans, College Democrats.

Athletics. NCAA. **Intercollegiate:** Baseball M, basketball, cross-country, football (tackle) M, golf, lacrosse, soccer, softball W, swimming, tennis, track and field, volleyball W. **Intramural:** Basketball, bowling, cheerleading, football (non-tackle), soccer, tennis, volleyball. **Team name:** Pioneers.

Student services. Adult student services, alcohol/substance abuse counseling, chaplain/spiritual director, career counseling, student employment services, financial aid counseling, health services, minority student services, personal counseling, placement for graduates. **Physically disabled:** Services for visually, hearing impaired.

Contact. E-mail: info@carrollu.edu
Phone: (262) 524-7220 Toll-free number: (800) 227-7655
Fax: (262) 951-3037
Jim Wiseman, Vice President for Enrollment, Carroll University, 100 North East Avenue, Waukesha, WI 53186-9988

Carthage College
Kenosha, Wisconsin
www.carthage.edu

CB member
CB code: 1103

- Private 4-year liberal arts college affiliated with the Evangelical Lutheran Church in America
- Residential campus in small city

- 2,863 degree-seeking undergraduates: 8% part-time, 54% women, 4% African American, 1% Asian American, 4% Hispanic/Latino, 3% Multiracial, non-Hispanic, 1% international
- 91 degree-seeking graduate students
- 70% of applicants admitted
- SAT or ACT (ACT writing optional) required
- 59% graduate within 6 years

General. Founded in 1847. Regionally accredited. **Degrees:** 561 bachelor's awarded; master's offered. **ROTC:** Air Force. **Location:** 60 miles from Chicago, 30 miles from Milwaukee. **Calendar:** 4-1-4, limited summer session. **Full-time faculty:** 150 total. **Part-time faculty:** 98 total. **Class size:** 54% < 20, 45% 20-39, 1% 40-49. **Special facilities:** Planetarium, paleontology institute, center for children's literature, undergraduate science research laboratory, computer/mathematics research laboratory, greenhouse, arboretum, Audubon sanctuary, geographic information systems (GIS) lab, 24-hour cyber-cafe.

Freshman class profile. 7,165 applied, 5,028 admitted, 752 enrolled.

Mid 50% test scores			
SAT critical reading:	500-620	GPA 2.0-2.99:	24%
SAT math:	500-620	Rank in top quarter:	58%
ACT composite:	22-28	Rank in top tenth:	33%
GPA 3.75 or higher:	24%	Return as sophomores:	77%
GPA 3.50-3.74:	21%	Out-of-state:	70%
GPA 3.0-3.49:	31%	International:	1%

Basis for selection. High school GPA (calculated based on academic courses) and test scores most important. Interview and essay required for nursing majors. **Home schooled:** Transcript of courses and grades required.

High school preparation. College-preparatory program recommended. 18 units recommended. Recommended units include English 4, mathematics 3, social studies 3, science 3 (laboratory 2), foreign language 2 and academic electives 3.

2015-2016 Annual costs. Tuition/fees: $38,375. Room/board: $10,460.

Financial aid. Non-need-based: Scholarships awarded for academics, alumni affiliation, art, leadership, minority status, music/drama, religious affiliation.

Application procedures. Admission: Priority date 12/3; no deadline. $35 fee, may be waived for applicants with need. Admission notification on a rolling basis. Offers of admission guaranteed through May 1, accepted after May 1 on a space-available basis. **Financial aid:** Priority date 2/15; no closing date. FAFSA required. Applicants notified on a rolling basis starting 3/1.

Academics. All students take 2-course combination of oral and written communication skills and cross-cultural studies. Students must also complete symposium and senior thesis. **Special study options:** Accelerated study, combined bachelor's/graduate degree, cross-registration, double major, dual enrollment of high school students, honors, independent study, internships, liberal arts/career combination, student-designed major, study abroad, teacher certification program, Washington semester. **Credit/placement by examination:** AP, CLEP, IB, institutional tests. 32 credit hours maximum toward bachelor's degree. **Support services:** Learning center, reduced course load, study skills assistance, tutoring, writing center.

Majors. Area/ethnic studies: Asian. **Biology:** General, neuroscience. **Business:** Accounting, business admin, entrepreneurial studies, finance, marketing. **Communications:** General, persuasive communications. **Communications technology:** Graphics. **Computer sciences:** Computer science. **Conservation:** Environmental science. **Education:** Art, elementary, music, special ed. **English:** English lit. **Foreign languages:** Ancient Greek, Chinese, classics, French, German, Japanese, Latin, Spanish. **Health services:** Athletic training, nursing (RN). **History:** General. **Human services:** Social work. **Math:** General. **Parks/recreation:** Exercise sciences. **Philosophy/religion:** Philosophy, religion. **Physical sciences:** Chemistry, physics. **Protective services:** Police science. **Psychology:** General. **Social sciences:** General, economics, geography, GIS/cartography, international economics, political science, sociology. **Visual/performing arts:** Art history/conservation, directing/producing, dramatic, graphic design, music, musical theater, studio arts, theater design.

Most popular majors. Biology 6%, business/marketing 28%, communications/journalism 7%, education 10%, social sciences 8%, visual/performing arts 7%.

Technology on campus. 275 workstations in dormitories, library, computer center, student center. Dormitories wired for high-speed internet access and linked to campus network. Commuter students can connect to campus network. Online library, helpline, repair service, student web hosting, wireless network available.

Student life. Freshman orientation: Mandatory. Preregistration for classes offered. Held a few days immediately prior to start of classes. **Housing:** Guaranteed on-campus for all undergraduates. Coed dorms, single-sex dorms, apartments, fraternity/sorority housing, themed housing, wellness housing available. $300 deposit, deadline 5/1. **Activities:** Bands, campus ministries, choral groups, dance, drama, film society, international student organizations, literary magazine, music ensembles, Model UN, musical theater, opera, radio station, student government, student newspaper, symphony orchestra, Black Student Union, International Friendship Society, United Women of Color, Christian Fellowship, Latinos Unidos, Circle K International, College Republicans, Young Democrats.

Athletics. NCAA. **Intercollegiate:** Baseball M, basketball, cross-country, diving, football (tackle) M, golf, lacrosse, soccer, softball W, swimming, tennis, track and field, volleyball, water polo W. **Intramural:** Basketball, football (non-tackle), racquetball, sand volleyball, soccer, softball, volleyball, water polo M. **Team name:** Red Men, Lady Reds.

Student services. Adult student services, alcohol/substance abuse counseling, chaplain/spiritual director, career counseling, student employment services, financial aid counseling, health services, personal counseling, placement for graduates, veterans' counselor.

Contact. E-mail: admissions@carthage.edu
Phone: (262) 551-6000 Toll-free number: (800) 351-4058
Fax: (262) 551-5762
Nick Mulvey, Vice President for Enrollment, Carthage College, 2001 Alford Park Drive, Kenosha, WI 53140-1994

Columbia College of Nursing
Glendale, Wisconsin
www.ccon.edu
CB code: 3409

▶ Private 4-year nursing college
▶ Commuter campus in very large city
▶ 150 degree-seeking undergraduates: 13% part-time, 90% women, 5% African American, 4% Asian American, 5% Hispanic/Latino, 2% Native Hawaiian/Pacific islander, 3% international
▶ 4 degree-seeking graduate students

General. Founded in 1901. Regionally accredited. Affiliated with Columbia St. Mary's Hospital system. **Degrees:** 81 bachelor's awarded. **Location:** 90 miles from Chicago, 70 miles from Madison. **Calendar:** Semester, limited summer session. **Full-time faculty:** 21 total; 33% have terminal degrees, 90% women. **Part-time faculty:** 3 total; 100% women. **Class size:** 70% < 20, 11% 20-39, 9% 40-49, 9% 50-99.

Basis for selection. Students are admitted as first semester juniors. They transfer 62 credits from another accredited institution of higher learning. Admission to nursing major requires 2.8 GPA and all prerequisites successfully completed with grade of C or better. A score of 80% or higher on the HEST A2 nursing entrance exam is required.

High school preparation. Required and recommended units include English 4, mathematics 1-2, science 2-3 and foreign language 2. Algebra required. Chemistry, biology required as science units.

2015-2016 Annual costs. Tuition/fees: $27,330. Books/supplies: $1,400. Personal expenses: $2,650.

2015-2016 Financial aid. Need-based: 34% of total undergraduate aid awarded as scholarships/grants, 66% as loans/jobs. **Non-need-based:** Scholarships awarded for academics.

Application procedures. Admission: Closing date 3/1 (receipt date). $50 fee. Application must be submitted online. Admission notification on a rolling basis beginning on or about 4/1. **Financial aid:** Priority date 4/15; no closing date. FAFSA required. CCON is an upper division school and all students are junior or senior level students and 100% of student body transfers in. Applicants notified on a rolling basis starting 4/15; must reply by 6/1.

Academics. Students complete their first 62 credits at another institution of higher learning and their last 62 credits at institution. **Special study options:** Independent study, study abroad. Cultural immersion options. **Credit/placement by examination:** AP, CLEP. **Support services:** Learning center, remedial instruction, study skills assistance, tutoring, writing center.

Majors. Health services: Nursing (RN).

Technology on campus. 45 workstations in library, computer center. Online library, wireless network available.

Student life. Activities: Student government, student newspaper, student nursing organization, nursing honor society.

Student services. Career counseling, financial aid counseling, health services, personal counseling.

Contact. E-mail: tyler.lorenz@ccon.edu
Phone: (414) 326-2334 Toll-free number: (800) Fax: (414) 326-2331
Kelsey Benna, Academic Advisor, Columbia College of Nursing, 4425 North Port Washington Road, Glendale, WI 53212-1099

Concordia University Wisconsin
Mequon, Wisconsin
www.cuw.edu
CB code: 1139

▶ Private 4-year university and liberal arts college affiliated with the Lutheran Church - Missouri Synod
▶ Residential campus in large town
▶ 4,057 degree-seeking undergraduates: 26% part-time, 65% women, 15% African American, 2% Asian American, 2% Hispanic/Latino, 1% Native American, 3% Multi-racial, non-Hispanic, 2% international
▶ 3,499 degree-seeking graduate students
▶ 69% of applicants admitted
▶ SAT or ACT (ACT writing optional) required
▶ 58% graduate within 6 years

General. Founded in 1881. Regionally accredited. **Degrees:** 726 bachelor's, 45 associate awarded; master's, professional offered. **Location:** 15 miles from Milwaukee. **Calendar:** 4-1-4, limited summer session. **Full-time faculty:** 197 total; 75% have terminal degrees, 5% minority, 51% women. **Part-time faculty:** 385 total; 26% have terminal degrees, 10% minority, 67% women. **Class size:** 51% < 20, 45% 20-39, 1% 40-49, 2% 50-99. **Special facilities:** Access to Lake Michigan, Center for Environmental Studies.

Freshman class profile. 2,837 applied, 1,959 admitted, 627 enrolled.

Mid 50% test scores			
SAT critical reading:	450-570	GPA 2.0-2.99:	23%
SAT math:	450-590	Rank in top quarter:	45%
SAT writing:	420-540	Rank in top tenth:	20%
ACT composite:	20-26	Return as sophomores:	76%
GPA 3.75 or higher:	25%	Out-of-state:	33%
GPA 3.50-3.74:	21%	Live on campus:	92%
GPA 3.0-3.49:	31%	International:	2%

Basis for selection. School achievement record and test scores important. Essay, interview recommended; audition recommended for music.

High school preparation. College-preparatory program recommended. 16 units required. Required and recommended units include English 3-4, mathematics 2-3, social studies 2, science 2, foreign language 2 and academic electives 5. Two liberal arts required.

2015-2016 Annual costs. Tuition/fees: $26,900. Room/board: $9,980. Books/supplies: $1,500.

2015-2016 Financial aid. Need-based: 589 full-time freshmen applied for aid; 505 deemed to have need; 505 received aid. Average need met was 80%. Average scholarship/grant was $15,624; average loan $7,191. 64% of total undergraduate aid awarded as scholarships/grants, 36% as loans/jobs. **Non-need-based:** Scholarships awarded for academics, art, minority status, music/drama.

Application procedures. Admission: Priority date 5/1; deadline 8/15. $35 fee, may be waived for applicants with need, free for online applicants. Admission notification on a rolling basis beginning on or about 10/15. **Financial aid:** Priority date 3/15, closing date 4/15. FAFSA required. Applicants notified on a rolling basis starting 2/15; must reply within 3 week(s) of notification.

Academics. Special study options: Accelerated study, combined bachelor's/graduate degree, cross-registration, distance learning, double major, dual enrollment of high school students, ESL, exchange student, independent study, internships, liberal arts/career combination, student-designed major, study abroad, teacher certification program. Cooperative programs with Cardinal Stritch University, Marquette University, and Milwaukee Institute of Art and Design. **Credit/placement by examination:** AP, CLEP, IB, ACT, institutional tests. 15 credit hours maximum toward associate degree, 30 toward bachelor's. **Support services:** Learning center, reduced course load, remedial instruction, tutoring, writing center.

Majors. Biology: General, exercise physiology. **Business:** General, accounting, actuarial science, business admin, finance, international finance, marketing. **Communications:** Broadcast journalism, communications/speech/rhetoric, digital media, media studies. **Computer sciences:** General. **Conservation:** Environmental studies. **Education:** General, art, biology, business, early childhood, elementary, English, health, history, kindergarten/preschool, mathematics, middle, multi-level teacher, music, physical, science, secondary, social science, social studies, Spanish. **English:** English lit. **Foreign languages:** Biblical, German, Spanish. **Health services:** Athletic training, clinical/medical social work, medical radiologic technology/radiation therapy, nursing (RN). **History:** General. **Human services:** Social work. **Liberal arts:** Arts/sciences, humanities. **Math:** General. **Philosophy/religion:** Religion. **Protective services:** Criminal justice. **Psychology:** General. **Social sciences:** Economics. **Theology:** Bible, missionary, pastoral counseling, preministerial, religious ed, sacred music, theology, youth ministry. **Visual/performing arts:** Art, commercial/advertising art, graphic design, illustration, interior design, music performance, photography, piano/keyboard.

Most popular majors. Business/marketing 27%, education 7%, health sciences 32%, security/protective services 9%.

Technology on campus. 200 workstations in dormitories, library, computer center, student center. Dormitories wired for high-speed internet access and linked to campus network. Commuter students can connect to campus network. Online library, helpline, repair service available.

Student life. Freshman orientation: Available. Preregistration for classes offered. Held before start of fall semester, includes sessions for parents. **Policies:** Lutheran church services available every Sunday. Chapel services held daily. **Housing:** Single-sex dorms available. $160 deposit, deadline 4/15. **Activities:** Bands, campus ministries, choral groups, dance, drama, international student organizations, music ensembles, musical theater, radio station, student government, student newspaper, Jeremiah Project, Servant Events.

Athletics. NCAA. **Intercollegiate:** Baseball M, basketball, cross-country, football (tackle) M, golf, lacrosse M, soccer, softball W, tennis, track and field, volleyball, wrestling M. **Intramural:** Basketball, soccer, softball, table tennis, tennis, volleyball. **Team name:** Falcons.

Student services. Adult student services, alcohol/substance abuse counseling, chaplain/spiritual director, career counseling, student employment services, financial aid counseling, health services, minority student services, personal counseling, placement for graduates, veterans' counselor. **Physically disabled:** Services for hearing impaired.

Contact. E-mail: admission@cuw.edu
Phone: (262) 243-5700 Toll-free number: (888) 628-9472
Fax: (262) 243-4545
Kenneth Gaschk, Vice President of Enrollment Services, Concordia University Wisconsin, 12800 North Lake Shore Drive, Mequon, WI 53097

Edgewood College

Madison, Wisconsin

www.edgewood.edu

CB member

CB code: 1202

◗ Private 4-year liberal arts college affiliated with the Roman Catholic Church
◗ Commuter campus in small city
◗ 1,758 degree-seeking undergraduates: 12% part-time, 71% women, 3% African American, 3% Asian American, 6% Hispanic/Latino, 3% Multiracial, non-Hispanic, 3% international
◗ 605 degree-seeking graduate students
◗ 77% of applicants admitted
◗ SAT or ACT (ACT writing optional) required
◗ 60% graduate within 6 years

General. Founded in 1927. Regionally accredited. **Degrees:** 459 bachelor's awarded; master's, professional, doctoral offered. **ROTC:** Army, Naval, Air Force. **Location:** 82 miles from Milwaukee, 140 miles from Chicago. **Calendar:** Semester, limited summer session. **Full-time faculty:** 159 total; 74% have terminal degrees, 10% minority, 58% women. **Part-time faculty:** 150 total; 33% have terminal degrees, 12% minority, 66% women. **Class size:** 80% < 20, 19% 20-39, 1% 40-49. **Special facilities:** Boardwalk and pier, zoo.

Freshman class profile. 1,160 applied, 891 admitted, 298 enrolled.

Mid 50% test scores		GPA 2.0-2.99:	21%
SAT critical reading:	450-600	Rank in top quarter:	45%
SAT math:	480-560	Rank in top tenth:	13%
ACT composite:	20-25	Return as sophomores:	81%
GPA 3.75 or higher:	22%	Out-of-state:	11%
GPA 3.50-3.74:	23%	Live on campus:	84%
GPA 3.0-3.49:	33%	International:	3%

Basis for selection. Students must meet 2 of the following: 2.5 GPA, rank in top 50% of graduating class, 18 ACT (or equivalent SAT). **Home schooled:** Statement describing home school structure and mission, transcript of courses and grades required.

High school preparation. College-preparatory program recommended. Required units include English 4, mathematics 2, social studies 2, history 1, science 2 (laboratory 1) and foreign language 2.

2015-2016 Annual costs. Tuition/fees: $26,550. Room/board: $9,400. Books/supplies: $800. Personal expenses: $2,350.

2014-2015 Financial aid. Need-based: 276 full-time freshmen applied for aid; 239 deemed to have need; 239 received aid. Average need met was 78%. Average scholarship/grant was $16,868; average loan $4,421. 58% of total undergraduate aid awarded as scholarships/grants, 42% as loans/jobs. **Non-need-based:** Awarded to 382 full-time undergraduates, including 75 freshmen. Scholarships awarded for academics, alumni affiliation, art, leadership, music/drama, religious affiliation.

Application procedures. Admission: Priority date 3/1; deadline 8/15 (receipt date). $30 fee, may be waived for applicants with need. Admission notification on a rolling basis beginning on or about 9/15. **Financial aid:** Priority date 3/1; no closing date. FAFSA required. Applicants notified on a rolling basis starting 3/15; must reply by 5/1.

Academics. Special study options: Accelerated study, cooperative education, cross-registration, distance learning, double major, dual enrollment of high school students, honors, independent study, internships, liberal arts/career combination, student-designed major, study abroad, teacher certification program. **Credit/placement by examination:** AP, CLEP, IB, ACT, institutional tests. **Support services:** Learning center, reduced course load, remedial instruction, study skills assistance, tutoring, writing center.

Majors. Area/ethnic studies: General. **Biology:** General, biomedical sciences. **Business:** General, accounting, business admin, management information systems, organizational behavior. **Communications:** General. **Computer sciences:** General. **Conservation:** Environmental science. **Education:** Art, biology, business, chemistry, computer, drama/dance, early childhood, early childhood special, elementary, English, French, mathematics, music, science, Spanish. **English:** English lit. **Foreign languages:** French, Spanish. **Health services:** Art therapy, cytotechnology, music therapy, nursing (RN). **History:** General. **Math:** General. **Philosophy/religion:** Religion. **Physical sciences:** Chemistry, physics. **Protective services:** Criminal justice. **Psychology:** General. **Social sciences:** General, economics, international relations, political science, sociology. **Theology:** Religious ed. **Visual/performing arts:** Art, dramatic, graphic design, music, music management, music technology.

Most popular majors. Business/marketing 22%, education 12%, health sciences 25%, psychology 8%, social sciences 6%.

Technology on campus. 100 workstations in dormitories, library, computer center, student center. Dormitories wired for high-speed internet access and linked to campus network. Commuter students can connect to campus network. Online course registration, online library, helpline, wireless network available.

Student life. Freshman orientation: Mandatory. Preregistration for classes offered. Held 4 days before the start of classes. **Policies:** Freshmen not permitted cars on campus. **Housing:** Guaranteed on-campus for freshmen. Coed dorms, special housing for disabled, apartments, cooperative housing available. $150 fully refundable deposit. **Activities:** Bands, campus ministries, choral groups, dance, drama, international student organizations, literary magazine, music ensembles, Model UN, musical theater, student government, student newspaper, symphony orchestra, Young Life, Association of Latino(a) Students (ALAS), Black Student Union (BSU), international club, SAFE, ethnic studies club, Asian Pacific American Network, Edgewood Vets, Peace Group.

Athletics. NCAA. **Intercollegiate:** Baseball M, basketball, cross-country, golf, soccer, softball W, tennis, track and field, volleyball W. **Intramural:** Basketball, soccer, swimming, volleyball. **Team name:** Eagles.

Student services. Adult student services, alcohol/substance abuse counseling, chaplain/spiritual director, career counseling, student employment services, financial aid counseling, health services, minority student services, personal counseling, placement for graduates, veterans' counselor. **Physically disabled:** Services for visually, speech, hearing impaired.

Contact. E-mail: admissions@edgewood.edu
Phone: (608) 663-2294 Toll-free number: (800) 444-4861 ext. 2294
Fax: (608) 663-2214
Christine Benedict, VP for Enrollment Management, Edgewood College, 1000 Edgewood College Drive, Madison, WI 53711-1997

Globe University: Green Bay
Green Bay, Wisconsin
www.globeuniversity.edu

- For-profit 4-year university and career college
- Commuter campus in small city
- 185 undergraduates
- Interview required

General. Regionally accredited; also accredited by ACICS. **Degrees:** 10 bachelor's, 58 associate awarded. **Calendar:** Quarter, extensive summer session.

Basis for selection. Open admission.

2015-2016 Annual costs. Tuition/fees: $18,702. Books/supplies: $1,260.

Application procedures. Admission: No deadline. $50 fee. Admission notification on a rolling basis. **Financial aid:** No deadline. FAFSA, institutional form required. Applicants notified on a rolling basis starting 7/1; must reply within 2 week(s) of notification.

Academics. Special study options: Distance learning, independent study, internships, liberal arts/career combination. **Credit/placement by examination:** AP, CLEP. **Support services:** Remedial instruction, study skills assistance, tutoring, writing center.

Majors. Business: Accounting, business admin. **Computer sciences:** Information technology. **Protective services:** Law enforcement admin.

Technology on campus. 60 workstations in library, computer center, student center. Commuter students can connect to campus network. Online library, helpline, student web hosting, wireless network available.

Student life. Freshman orientation: Mandatory. Preregistration for classes offered. Day and evening sessions held the week prior to classes starting. **Activities:** Literary magazine.

Student services. Career counseling, student employment services, financial aid counseling, placement for graduates.

Contact. E-mail: josieyoung@globeuniversity.edu
Phone: (920) 264-1600 Toll-free number: (877) 626-1616
Josie Young, Director of Admissions, Globe University: Green Bay, 2620 Development Drive, Green Bay, WI 54311

Herzing University: Brookfield
Brookfield, Wisconsin
www.herzing.edu

- For-profit 4-year business and technical college
- Large town
- 290 degree-seeking undergraduates

General. Regionally accredited. **Degrees:** 43 bachelor's, 30 associate awarded; master's offered. **Calendar:** Semester. **Full-time faculty:** 17 total. **Part-time faculty:** 16 total.

Basis for selection. Wonderlic exam required for some programs.

2015-2016 Annual costs. Certificate programs: $13,670 to $26,820. Associate programs: $26,180 to $53,640. Bachelor's programs: $61,515 to $88,065.

Academics. Credit/placement by examination: AP, CLEP.

Majors. Business: Business admin, entrepreneurial studies, human resources, international. **Computer sciences:** Networking. **Health services:** Health care admin, health information management. **Protective services:** Criminal justice. **Visual/performing arts:** Graphic design.

Contact. E-mail: info@brk.herzing.edu
Monica Beere, Director of Admissions, Herzing University: Brookfield, 555 South Executive Drive, Brookfield, WI 53005

Herzing University: Kenosha
Kenosha, Wisconsin
www.herzing.edu

- For-profit 4-year business and technical college
- Small city
- 371 degree-seeking undergraduates

General. Regionally accredited. **Degrees:** 50 bachelor's, 49 associate awarded; master's offered. **Calendar:** Semester. **Full-time faculty:** 13 total. **Part-time faculty:** 6 total.

Basis for selection. Wonderlic exam required for some programs.

2015-2016 Annual costs. Certificate programs: $13,670 to $26,820. Associate programs: $26,180 to $53,640. Bachelor's programs: $61,515 to $88,065.

Academics. Credit/placement by examination: AP, CLEP.

Majors. Business: Accounting, business admin, entrepreneurial studies, human resources, international, marketing. **Computer sciences:** Networking. **Health services:** Nursing (RN). **Protective services:** Criminal justice. **Visual/performing arts:** Graphic design.

Contact. E-mail: info@ken.herzing.edu
Monica Beere, Director of Admissions, Herzing University: Kenosha, 4006 Washington Road, Kenosha, WI 53144

Herzing University: Madison
Madison, Wisconsin
www.herzing.edu/madison   **CB code: 0388**

- For-profit 3-year business and career college
- Commuter campus in small city
- 2,369 undergraduates
- Interview required

General. Founded in 1948. Regionally accredited. **Degrees:** 276 bachelor's, 332 associate awarded; master's offered. **Location:** 90 miles from Milwaukee, 150 miles from Chicago. **Calendar:** Differs by program, extensive summer session. **Full-time faculty:** 29 total. **Part-time faculty:** 22 total.

Basis for selection. Open admission, but selective for some programs. Interview and placement test required prior to acceptance. Application process varies by program. **Home schooled:** State high school equivalency certificate required. **Learning Disabled:** Must provide documentation to admissions advisor prior to starting classes.

2015-2016 Annual costs. Personal expenses: $3,213. **Additional information:** Certificate programs: $13,670 to $26,820. Associate programs: $26,180 to $53,640. Bachelor's programs: $61,515 to $88,065.

Application procedures. Admission: No deadline. No application fee. Application must be submitted on paper. Admission notification on a rolling basis. **Financial aid:** No deadline. FAFSA, institutional form required. Applicants notified on a rolling basis.

Academics. Bachelors degree may be acquired in 3 years, associate degree in 1 year, 8 months. **Special study options:** Combined bachelor's/graduate degree, cooperative education, distance learning, honors, independent study, internships, liberal arts/career combination, study abroad, weekend college. **Credit/placement by examination:** AP, CLEP, institutional tests. **Support services:** Learning center, reduced course load, remedial instruction, study skills assistance, tutoring, writing center.

Majors. BACHELOR'S. Business: Accounting, accounting/business management, accounting/finance, business admin, entrepreneurial studies, human resources, international, marketing, office management, office technology, office/clerical. **Communications technology:** Animation/special effects. **Computer sciences:** General, applications programming, computer graphics, computer science, information systems, information technology, LAN/WAN management, networking, programming. **Engineering:** Software. **Health services:** Facilities admin, health care admin, health information management, health information technology, office admin, ward supervisor. **Protective services:** Criminal justice, homeland security. **Visual/performing arts:** Game design, graphic design. **ASSOCIATE. Business:** Accounting, business admin, office management, office technology, office/clerical. **Communications technology:** Animation/special effects. **Computer sciences:** General, applications programming, computer graphics, computer science, information systems, information technology, LAN/WAN management, networking, programming. **Engineering:** Software. **Health services:** Dental hygiene, health information management, insurance coding, medical assistant, nursing (RN), office admin, office assistant, office computer specialist, radiologic technology/medical imaging, receptionist, surgical technology. **Visual/performing arts:** Graphic design.

Technology on campus. 450 workstations in library, computer center, student center. Commuter students can connect to campus network. Online library, helpline, repair service, wireless network available.

Student life. Freshman orientation: Mandatory. Preregistration for classes offered. **Activities:** Student government, student newspaper.

Student services. Adult student services, career counseling, student employment services, financial aid counseling, personal counseling, placement for graduates. **Physically disabled:** Services for visually, speech, hearing impaired.

Contact. E-mail: info@msn.herzing.edu
Phone: (608) 249-6611 Toll-free number: (800) 582-1227
Fax: (608) 249-8593
Matthew Schneider, Director of Admissions, Herzing University: Madison, 5218 East Terrace Drive, Madison, WI 53718

ITT Technical Institute: Green Bay
Green Bay, Wisconsin
www.itt-tech.edu

- For-profit 4-year technical college
- Small city
- 109 undergraduates

General. Accredited by ACICS. **Degrees:** 18 bachelor's, 27 associate awarded. **Calendar:** Trimester. **Full-time faculty:** 7 total. **Part-time faculty:** 39 total.

Basis for selection. Satisfactory scores from on-site tests in English and mathematics required.

2015-2016 Annual costs. Per-credit-hour charge, $493, will vary depending on program level and course of study. Academic fee, $200. Some programs require purchase of tools, which could cost an additional $100 to $500. All costs subject to change.

Academics. Credit/placement by examination: AP, CLEP.

Majors. Business: Accounting/business management, business admin, construction management, e-commerce. **Communications technology:** Animation/special effects. **Computer sciences:** Security. **Protective services:** Criminal justice.

Technology on campus. Online library available.

Student life. Freshman orientation: Available. Preregistration for classes offered.

Contact. Phone: (920) 662-9000 Toll-free number: (888) 884-3626
Fax: (920) 662-9384
Raymond Sweetman, Director of Recruitment, ITT Technical Institute: Green Bay, 470 Security Boulevard, Green Bay, WI 54313

ITT Technical Institute: Greenfield
Greenfield, Wisconsin
www.itt-tech.edu   CB code: 2706

- For-profit 4-year technical college
- Commuter campus in large town
- 422 undergraduates
- Interview required

General. Accredited by ACICS. **Degrees:** 49 bachelor's, 99 associate awarded. **Calendar:** Quarter, extensive summer session. **Full-time faculty:** 9 total. **Part-time faculty:** 60 total.

Basis for selection. Satisfactory scores from on-site tests in English and mathematics required.

2015-2016 Annual costs. Per-credit-hour charge, $493, will vary depending on program level and course of study. Academic fee, $200. Some programs require purchase of tools, which could cost an additional $100 to $500. All costs subject to change.

Application procedures. Admission: No application fee. Admission notification on a rolling basis. **Financial aid:** No deadline. FAFSA, institutional form required. Applicants notified on a rolling basis.

Academics. Credit/placement by examination: AP, CLEP. **Support services:** Learning center, tutoring.

Majors. Business: Accounting/business management, business admin, construction management, e-commerce. **Communications technology:** Animation/special effects. **Computer sciences:** Networking, security. **Protective services:** Law enforcement admin. **Visual/performing arts:** Game design.

Technology on campus. Online library available.

Student life. Freshman orientation: Available. Preregistration for classes offered.

Student services. Career counseling, student employment services, placement for graduates.

Contact. Phone: (414) 282-9494 Fax: (414) 282-9698
Brian Guenther, Director of Recruitment, ITT Technical Institute: Greenfield, 6300 West Layton Avenue, Greenfield, WI 53220-4612

Lakeland College
Sheboygan, Wisconsin
www.lakeland.edu   CB code: 1393

- Private 4-year liberal arts college affiliated with the United Church of Christ
- Residential campus in small city
- 2,196 degree-seeking undergraduates: 58% part-time, 57% women
- 811 graduate students
- SAT or ACT (ACT writing recommended) required

General. Founded in 1862. Regionally accredited. Evening, online, and graduate classes offered for nontraditional students at 7 in-state sites. Associate of Arts degree program and study abroad opportunities available at our Tokyo, Japan campus. **Degrees:** 576 bachelor's awarded; master's offered. **Location:** 60 miles from Milwaukee, 60 miles from Green Bay. **Calendar:** 4-4-1. Limited summer session. **Full-time faculty:** 58 total. **Part-time faculty:** 266 total. **Class size:** 69% < 20, 30% 20-39, 1% 40-49.

Freshman class profile.

GPA 3.75 or higher:	10%	Rank in top tenth:	8%
GPA 3.50-3.74:	9%	Out-of-state:	15%
GPA 3.0-3.49:	29%	Live on campus:	90%
GPA 2.0-2.99:	49%	Fraternities:	3%
Rank in top quarter:	24%	Sororities:	3%

Basis for selection. Applicants with 19 ACT, 2.0 GPA and rank in the top half of class admitted. Essays are recommended. **Home schooled:** Transcript of courses and grades, state high school equivalency certificate required.

High school preparation. Recommended units include English 4, mathematics 2, social studies 2, history 2, science 2, foreign language 2 and academic electives 2.

2015-2016 Annual costs. Tuition/fees: $25,050. Room/board: $8,620. Books/supplies: $950. Personal expenses: $1,500. **Additional information:** There are flight fees on a per courses basis for the Aviation Minor.

Financial aid. Non-need-based: Scholarships awarded for academics, alumni affiliation, art, religious affiliation.

Application procedures. Admission: No deadline. $20 fee, may be waived for applicants with need. Admission notification on a rolling basis. **Financial aid:** Priority date 3/15; no closing date. FAFSA, institutional form required. Applicants notified on a rolling basis starting 2/15; must reply within 2 week(s) of notification.

Academics. Applicants whose test scores reflect weakness in basic skills must take basic skills courses in freshman year. **Special study options:** Combined bachelor's/graduate degree, cooperative education, distance learning, double major, dual enrollment of high school students, ESL, honors, independent study, internships, liberal arts/career combination, study abroad, teacher certification program. Engineering program with University of Wisconsin-Madison, nursing program with Bellin College of Nursing. **Credit/placement by examination:** AP, CLEP, IB, institutional tests. 30 credit hours maximum toward bachelor's degree. **Support services:** Learning center, reduced course load, remedial instruction, study skills assistance, tutoring, writing center.

Majors. Biology: General, biochemistry. **Business:** Accounting, business admin, international, marketing, nonprofit/public, resort management. **Computer sciences:** Computer science. **Education:** Elementary, kindergarten/preschool, middle, secondary. **English:** English lit, writing. **Foreign languages:** German, Spanish. **History:** General. **Math:** General. **Philosophy/religion:** Religion. **Physical sciences:** Chemistry. **Protective services:** Law enforcement admin. **Psychology:** General. **Visual/performing arts:** Art, music.

Most popular majors. Business/marketing 68%, computer/information sciences 19%, education 11%.

Technology on campus. 218 workstations in dormitories, library, computer center, student center. Dormitories wired for high-speed internet access and linked to campus network. Commuter students can connect to campus network. Online course registration, online library, helpline, wireless network available.

Student life. Freshman orientation: Mandatory. Preregistration for classes offered. **Housing:** Guaranteed on-campus for freshmen. Coed dorms, single-sex dorms, special housing for disabled, apartments available. $50 deposit. Honor apartments and apartments for students with senior standing available. **Activities:** Concert band, choral groups, drama, international student organizations, music ensembles, student government, student newspaper, campus activities board, black student union, Mortar Board, global students association, business fraternity, Inter-Greek Council.

Athletics. NCAA. **Intercollegiate:** Baseball M, basketball, cross-country, football (tackle) M, golf, soccer, softball W, tennis, track and field, volleyball W, wrestling M. **Team name:** Muskies.

Student services. Alcohol/substance abuse counseling, chaplain/spiritual director, career counseling, services for economically disadvantaged, student employment services, financial aid counseling, health services, on-campus daycare, personal counseling, placement for graduates, veterans' counselor. **Physically disabled:** Services for visually impaired.

Contact. E-mail: admissions@lakeland.edu
Phone: (920) 565-1022 Toll-free number: (800) 242-3347
Fax: (920) 565-1062
Zachary Voelz, Vice President for Enrollment Management, Lakeland College, Box 359, Sheboygan, WI 53082-0359

Lawrence University
Appleton, Wisconsin **CB member**
www.lawrence.edu **CB code: 1398**

▸ Private 4-year music and liberal arts college
▸ Residential campus in small city
▸ 1,527 degree-seeking undergraduates: 2% part-time, 55% women, 3% African American, 5% Asian American, 7% Hispanic/Latino, 4% Multiracial, non-Hispanic, 10% international
▸ 68% of applicants admitted
▸ Application essay required
▸ 76% graduate within 6 years

General. Founded in 1847. Regionally accredited. **Degrees:** 326 bachelor's awarded. **Location:** 100 miles from Milwaukee, 30 miles from Green Bay. **Calendar:** Trimester. **Full-time faculty:** 166 total; 91% have terminal degrees, 11% minority, 40% women. **Part-time faculty:** 31 total; 45% have terminal degrees, 13% minority, 52% women. **Class size:** 80% < 20, 16% 20-39, 3% 40-49, 2% 50-99. **Special facilities:** Laser physics laboratory, nuclear magnetic resonance spectrometer, physics/computational graphics laboratory, Lake Michigan shoreline retreat center.

Freshman class profile. 3,014 applied, 2,057 admitted, 400 enrolled.

Mid 50% test scores		GPA 2.0-2.99:	7%
SAT critical reading:	560-690	Rank in top quarter:	77%
SAT math:	610-730	Rank in top tenth:	42%
SAT writing:	580-690	Return as sophomores:	89%
ACT composite:	26-32	Out-of-state:	74%
GPA 3.75 or higher:	46%	Live on campus:	99%
GPA 3.50-3.74:	26%	International:	14%
GPA 3.0-3.49:	21%		

Basis for selection. Strength of curriculum, school achievement record most important. Recommendations, out-of-class activities, test scores considered. Music applicants judged on musicianship, teacher's recommendations and academic ability. Testing optional, with this exception: An official TOEFL, IELTS, SAT or ACT report is required for all international students whose native language is not English, or whose previous instruction was not in English for a substantial portion of their education. Interview recommended

for all; portfolio recommended for studio art; audition required for conservatory of music study. **Home schooled:** Require evidence of coursework completed and level of performance, letters of recommendation and GED if applicable. Recommend standardized test results.

High school preparation. College-preparatory program recommended. 16 units recommended. Recommended units include English 4, mathematics 3, social studies 2, history 2, science 3 and foreign language 2. Strong musical preparation required of music applicants.

2015-2016 Annual costs. Tuition/fees: $43,740. Room/board: $9,210. Books/supplies: $900. Personal expenses: $975.

2015-2016 Financial aid. Need-based: 311 full-time freshmen applied for aid; 234 deemed to have need; 234 received aid. Average need met was 97%. Average scholarship/grant was $31,540; average loan $4,771. 84% of total undergraduate aid awarded as scholarships/grants, 16% as loans/jobs. **Non-need-based:** Awarded to 534 full-time undergraduates, including 157 freshmen. Scholarships awarded for academics, alumni affiliation, leadership, minority status, music/drama.

Application procedures. Admission: Closing date 1/15 (postmark date). No application fee. Admission notification by 4/1. Must reply by May 1 or within 2 week(s) if notified thereafter. **Financial aid:** Priority date 3/1; no closing date. FAFSA required. CSS PROFILE required for applicants seeking institutionally-funded need-based aid. Applicants notified on a rolling basis starting 3/1; must reply by 5/1 or within 2 week(s) of notification.

Academics. As an adjunct to a major, students may pursue 1 interdisciplinary area of study such as biomedical ethics, innovation & entrepreneurship, international studies, or cognitive science. **Special study options:** Combined bachelor's/graduate degree, double major, independent study, internships, semester at sea, student-designed major, study abroad, teacher certification program, urban semester, Washington semester. Study abroad programs in 27 countries; marine biology term, Oak Ridge science semester; urban semester in Chicago; Newberry Library Program in humanities; environmental studies and forestry programs with Duke University; occupational therapy program with Washington University, St. Louis. **Credit/placement by examination:** AP, CLEP, IB, institutional tests. 30 credit hours maximum toward bachelor's degree. Course credit awarded for scores of at least 5 on International Baccalaureate examinations. **Support services:** Learning center, reduced course load, study skills assistance, tutoring, writing center.

Majors. Area/ethnic studies: Chinese, East Asian, Japanese, Russian/Slavic. **Biology:** General, biochemistry, neuroscience. **Computer sciences:** General. **Conservation:** Environmental studies. **Education:** Music. **English:** English lit. **Foreign languages:** Ancient Greek, Chinese, classics, East Asian, French, German, Japanese, Latin, linguistics, Russian, Spanish. **History:** General. **Math:** General. **Philosophy/religion:** Philosophy, religion. **Physical sciences:** Chemistry, geology, physics. **Psychology:** General. **Social sciences:** Anthropology, economics, political science. **Visual/performing arts:** Art, art history/conservation, dramatic, music, music performance, music theory/composition, studio arts.

Most popular majors. Biology 15%, English 6%, foreign language 6%, history 6%, psychology 9%, social sciences 13%, visual/performing arts 22%.

Technology on campus. 354 workstations in dormitories, library, computer center, student center. Dormitories wired for high-speed internet access and linked to campus network. Commuter students can connect to campus network. Online course registration, online library, helpline, repair service, wireless network available.

Student life. Freshman orientation: Mandatory. Preregistration for classes offered. Held 5 days prior to start of fall classes. **Policies:** Honor code in effect. **Housing:** Guaranteed on-campus for all undergraduates. Coed dorms, single-sex dorms, special housing for disabled, apartments, cooperative housing, fraternity/sorority housing, gender-neutral housing, themed housing available. $400 nonrefundable deposit, deadline 5/1. Apartment-style units available to upperclass students. All single students required to live on-campus for 4 years. **Activities:** Bands, choral groups, dance, drama, film society, international student organizations, literary magazine, music ensembles, Model UN, musical theater, opera, radio station, student government, student newspaper, symphony orchestra, Christian fellowship, Hillel, black organization of students, Latin American student organization, social service groups, political and academic clubs, professional sororities and fraternities.

Athletics. NCAA. **Intercollegiate:** Baseball M, basketball, cross-country, diving, fencing, football (tackle) M, golf M, ice hockey M, soccer, softball W, swimming, tennis, track and field, volleyball W. **Intramural:** Badminton, basketball, bowling, fencing, football (non-tackle), golf, handball, racquetball, soccer, softball, squash, table tennis, tennis, volleyball, water polo. **Team name:** Vikings.

Student services. Alcohol/substance abuse counseling, chaplain/spiritual director, career counseling, student employment services, financial aid counseling, health services, minority student services, personal counseling, placement for graduates. **Physically disabled:** Services for visually, speech, hearing impaired.

Contact. E-mail: admissions@lawrence.edu
Phone: (920) 832-6500 Toll-free number: (800) 227-0982
Fax: (920) 832-6782
Mary Beth Petrie, Director of Admissions, Lawrence University, 711 East Boldt Way SPC 29, Appleton, WI 54911-5699

Maranatha Baptist University
Watertown, Wisconsin
www.mbu.edu   CB code: 2732

- Private 4-year Bible and liberal arts college affiliated with the Baptist faith
- Residential campus in large town
- 730 degree-seeking undergraduates: 14% part-time, 54% women, 1% African American, 1% Asian American, 3% Hispanic/Latino, 4% Multiracial, non-Hispanic, 1% international
- 99 degree-seeking graduate students
- 69% of applicants admitted
- SAT or ACT (ACT writing optional), application essay required
- 60% graduate within 6 years

General. Founded in 1968. Regionally accredited. **Degrees:** 132 bachelor's, 10 associate awarded; master's, professional offered. **ROTC:** Army, Air Force. **Location:** 45 miles from Milwaukee, 38 miles from Madison. **Calendar:** Semester, limited summer session. **Full-time faculty:** 39 total; 41% have terminal degrees, 10% minority, 38% women. **Part-time faculty:** 71 total; 30% have terminal degrees, 27% minority, 35% women. **Class size:** 65% < 20, 26% 20-39, 6% 40-49, 3% 50-99.

Freshman class profile. 338 applied, 232 admitted, 187 enrolled.

Mid 50% test scores		Return as sophomores:	66%
SAT critical reading:	450-600	Out-of-state:	77%
SAT math:	450-530	Live on campus:	81%
SAT writing:	410-550	International:	1%
ACT composite:	20-26		

Basis for selection. Recommendations, religious commitment most important. Secondary school record, test scores, character also important. Class rank, essay considered. At-risk students placed on admissions probation. Audition required for fine arts.

High school preparation. College-preparatory program recommended. 18 units required. Required and recommended units include English 4, mathematics 3, social studies 3, history 3, science 3, foreign language 2, computer science 1 and academic electives 2. Two units of physical education and one unit of word processing recommended.

2015-2016 Annual costs. Tuition/fees: $13,940. Room/board: $6,550. Books/supplies: $1,072.

2014-2015 Financial aid. Need-based: 150 full-time freshmen applied for aid; 132 deemed to have need; 132 received aid. Average need met was 55%. Average scholarship/grant was $7,389; average loan $3,266. 43% of total undergraduate aid awarded as scholarships/grants, 57% as loans/jobs. **Non-need-based:** Awarded to 70 full-time undergraduates, including 21 freshmen. Scholarships awarded for academics, alumni affiliation.

Application procedures. Admission: No deadline. $50 fee. Admission notification on a rolling basis. **Financial aid:** Priority date 3/1; no closing date. FAFSA required. Applicants notified on a rolling basis starting 2/1; must reply within 2 week(s) of notification.

Academics. Hands-on ministerial work available. **Special study options:** Distance learning, double major, independent study, internships, liberal arts/career combination, study abroad, teacher certification program. **Credit/placement by examination:** AP, CLEP, SAT, ACT, institutional tests. 30 credit hours maximum toward associate degree, 30 toward bachelor's. Only 12 credits may be counted in any one field of study. **Support services:** Reduced course load, remedial instruction, study skills assistance, tutoring, writing center.

Majors. Biology: General. **Business:** Accounting, accounting/business management, business admin, marketing, office management. **Education:** Biology, business, early childhood, elementary, English, history, mathematics, music, physical, science, social studies. **English:** English lit. **Foreign**

languages: Biblical. **Health services:** Nursing (RN). **Liberal arts:** Humanities. **Parks/recreation:** Sports admin. **Theology:** Bible, missionary, pastoral counseling, sacred music, youth ministry. **Visual/performing arts:** Music pedagogy, music performance.

Most popular majors. Business/marketing 18%, education 23%, interdisciplinary studies 19%, liberal arts 14%, theological studies 12%.

Technology on campus. 120 workstations in dormitories, library, computer center. Dormitories wired for high-speed internet access and linked to campus network. Commuter students can connect to campus network. Online library, repair service, student web hosting, wireless network available.

Student life. Freshman orientation: Mandatory. Preregistration for classes offered. Held Saturday through Monday before classes begin. **Policies:** Religious observance required. **Housing:** Guaranteed on-campus for all undergraduates. Single-sex dorms, apartments available. $175 nonrefundable deposit. **Activities:** Concert band, campus ministries, choral groups, drama, music ensembles, musical theater, student government, symphony orchestra.

Athletics. NCAA, NCCAA. **Intercollegiate:** Baseball M, basketball, cross-country, football (tackle) M, soccer, softball W, volleyball W, wrestling M. **Intramural:** Basketball, soccer W, volleyball. **Team name:** Crusaders.

Student services. Chaplain/spiritual director, career counseling, financial aid counseling, health services, on-campus daycare, personal counseling, placement for graduates, veterans' counselor.

Contact. E-mail: admissions@mbu.edu
Phone: (920) 206-2327 Toll-free number: (800) 622-2947
Fax: (920) 261-9109
James Harrison, Director of Admissions, Maranatha Baptist University, 745 West Main Street, Watertown, WI 53094

Marian University
Fond du Lac, Wisconsin   CB member
www.marianuniversity.edu   CB code: 1443

- Private 4-year university and liberal arts college affiliated with the Roman Catholic Church
- Residential campus in large town
- 1,538 degree-seeking undergraduates: 16% part-time, 71% women, 6% African American, 1% Asian American, 6% Hispanic/Latino, 1% Multiracial, non-Hispanic, 2% international
- 493 degree-seeking graduate students
- 84% of applicants admitted
- SAT or ACT (ACT writing optional) required
- 41% graduate within 6 years

General. Founded in 1936. Regionally accredited. **Degrees:** 336 bachelor's awarded; master's, doctoral offered. **ROTC:** Army. **Location:** 60 miles from Milwaukee, 65 miles from Green Bay. **Calendar:** Semester, extensive summer session. **Full-time faculty:** 86 total; 59% have terminal degrees, 7% minority, 62% women. **Part-time faculty:** 140 total; 20% have terminal degrees, 5% minority, 52% women. **Class size:** 78% < 20, 21% 20-39, less than 1% 40-49, less than 1% 50-99.

Freshman class profile. 1,162 applied, 974 admitted, 282 enrolled.

Mid 50% test scores		Rank in top quarter:	27%
ACT composite:	17-23	Rank in top tenth:	11%
GPA 3.75 or higher:	14%	Return as sophomores:	66%
GPA 3.50-3.74:	15%	Out-of-state:	18%
GPA 3.0-3.49:	28%	Live on campus:	81%
GPA 2.0-2.99:	38%	Sororities:	5%

Basis for selection. School achievement record most important, followed by test scores. Applicants must meet 2 of following 3 criteria: 2.0 GPA, top half of class, 18 ACT. Special admissions procedures required for nursing and education divisions. If admission criteria not met, students may be admitted on provisional basis. ACT recommended. Interview, audition recommended. **Home schooled:** Transcript of courses and grades required. **Learning Disabled:** Copies of paperwork needed to qualify for supportive services.

High school preparation. College-preparatory program required. 20 units required. Required and recommended units include English 4, mathematics 2-3, social studies 2, history 1, science 2 (laboratory 1), foreign language 2, computer science 1, visual/performing arts 1 and academic electives 2. Biology and chemistry prerequisite for nursing program.

2015-2016 Annual costs. Tuition/fees: $27,310. Room/board: $6,750. Books/supplies: $700. Personal expenses: $1,520.

2014-2015 Financial aid. Need-based: 249 full-time freshmen applied for aid; 233 deemed to have need; 233 received aid. Average need met was 55%. Average scholarship/grant was $7,647; average loan $6,720. 67% of total undergraduate aid awarded as scholarships/grants, 33% as loans/jobs. **Non-need-based:** Awarded to 159 full-time undergraduates, including 31 freshmen. Scholarships awarded for academics, state residency.

Application procedures. Admission: Priority date 4/1; no deadline. $20 fee, may be waived for applicants with need. Admission notification on a rolling basis. Must reply by May 1 or within 4 week(s) if notified thereafter. **Financial aid:** Priority date 3/1; no closing date. FAFSA, institutional form required. Applicants notified on a rolling basis starting 3/1; must reply within 4 week(s) of notification.

Academics. Special study options: Accelerated study, combined bachelor's/graduate degree, cooperative education, distance learning, double major, dual enrollment of high school students, honors, independent study, internships, liberal arts/career combination, student-designed major, study abroad, teacher certification program. Accelerated programs for adults in business, nursing, operation management, radiologic technology, organizational communication, administration of justice. **Credit/placement by examination:** AP, CLEP, IB, institutional tests. 30 credit hours maximum toward bachelor's degree. Writing sample required for placement and counseling. **Support services:** Learning center, pre-admission summer program, reduced course load, remedial instruction, study skills assistance, tutoring, writing center.

Honors college/program. Unrestricted admissions with 25 ACT, 3.5 GPA, positive recommendation, application essay.

Majors. Biology: General. **Business:** Accounting, business admin, finance, human resources, management information systems, marketing, operations. **Communications:** Communications/speech/rhetoric, organizational. **Computer sciences:** Information technology. **Education:** Art, early childhood, elementary, English, music, science, secondary, social studies, Spanish. **English:** British lit, English lit, writing. **Foreign languages:** Spanish. **Health services:** Cytotechnology, health care admin, nursing (RN), radiologic technology/medical imaging. **History:** General. **Human services:** Social work. **Liberal arts:** Arts/sciences. **Math:** General. **Parks/recreation:** Sports admin. **Philosophy/religion:** Religion. **Physical sciences:** Chemistry. **Protective services:** Forensics, homeland security, police science. **Psychology:** General. **Visual/performing arts:** Graphic design, music, music management, studio arts.

Most popular majors. Business/marketing 9%, health sciences 18%, security/protective services 7%.

Technology on campus. 500 workstations in library, computer center, student center. Dormitories wired for high-speed internet access and linked to campus network. Commuter students can connect to campus network. Online course registration, online library, helpline, repair service, wireless network available.

Student life. Freshman orientation: Mandatory. Preregistration for classes offered. **Policies:** Emphasis on community volunteer activity. Service transcript available for graduates. **Housing:** Guaranteed on-campus for all undergraduates. Coed dorms, single-sex dorms, special housing for disabled, apartments, themed housing available. $100 nonrefundable deposit. Townhouses, penthouses, residential suites and learning communities available. **Activities:** Bands, campus ministries, choral groups, international student organizations, literary magazine, music ensembles, Model UN, student government, student newspaper, symphony orchestra, environmental club, social justice committee, African American student union, Association Latina, math and science association.

Athletics. NCAA. **Intercollegiate:** Baseball M, basketball, cross-country, golf, ice hockey, soccer, softball W, tennis, track and field, volleyball W. **Intramural:** Badminton, basketball, bowling, football (non-tackle) M, skiing, softball M, tennis, volleyball. **Team name:** Sabres.

Student services. Adult student services, alcohol/substance abuse counseling, chaplain/spiritual director, career counseling, services for economically disadvantaged, student employment services, financial aid counseling, health services, minority student services, on-campus daycare, personal counseling, placement for graduates, women's services. **Physically disabled:** Services for visually, speech, hearing impaired.

Contact. E-mail: admissions@marianuniversity.edu
Phone: (920) 923-7650 Toll-free number: (800) 262-7426
Fax: (920) 923-8755
Shannon LaLuzerne, Senior Director of Admissions, Marian University, 45 South National Avenue, Fond du Lac, WI 54935-4699

Marquette University
Milwaukee, Wisconsin — CB member
www.marquette.edu — CB code: 1448

- Private 4-year university affiliated with the Roman Catholic Church
- Residential campus in very large city
- 8,143 degree-seeking undergraduates: 2% part-time, 53% women, 4% African American, 6% Asian American, 10% Hispanic/Latino, 4% Multiracial, non-Hispanic, 4% international
- 3,075 degree-seeking graduate students
- 74% of applicants admitted
- SAT or ACT (ACT writing optional), application essay required
- 80% graduate within 6 years

General. Founded in 1881. Regionally accredited. **Degrees:** 1,822 bachelor's awarded; master's, professional, doctoral offered. **ROTC:** Army, Naval, Air Force. **Location:** Downtown. **Calendar:** Semester, extensive summer session. **Full-time faculty:** 630 total; 90% have terminal degrees, 14% minority, 41% women. **Part-time faculty:** 522 total; 52% have terminal degrees, 8% minority, 44% women. **Class size:** 40% < 20, 39% 20-39, 8% 40-49, 9% 50-99, 4% >100. **Special facilities:** 15th century St. Joan of Arc chapel.

Freshman class profile. 20,486 applied, 15,202 admitted, 1,876 enrolled.

Mid 50% test scores			
SAT critical reading:	530-640	Rank in top tenth:	34%
SAT math:	540-660	Return as sophomores:	90%
SAT writing:	510-640	Out-of-state:	69%
ACT composite:	24-30	Live on campus:	94%
Rank in top quarter:	68%	International:	3%

Basis for selection. High school course selection, trend of performance, test scores and class rank most important. Essay, leadership, community service and extracurricular activities considered. **Home schooled:** Provide detailed list of curriculum and bibliography. Personal interview may be required.

High school preparation. College-preparatory program required. 16 units required; 20 recommended. Required and recommended units include English 4, mathematics 2-4, social studies 2-3, history 2, science 2-4 (laboratory 2-3), foreign language 2 and academic electives 2-5. Algebra, geometry, and intermediate algebra required for arts & sciences, business administration and health sciences. Algebra and geometry required for nursing. 3 years of science recommended for premedical, predental and science majors. Students interested in international business strongly urged to complete 4 units of single foreign language.

2015-2016 Annual costs. Tuition/fees: $37,170. Room/board: $11,220. Books/supplies: $1,008. Personal expenses: $1,800.

2015-2016 Financial aid. Need-based: 1,520 full-time freshmen applied for aid; 1,162 deemed to have need; 1,162 received aid. Average need met was 77%. Average scholarship/grant was $21,049; average loan $3,655. 71% of total undergraduate aid awarded as scholarships/grants, 29% as loans/jobs. **Non-need-based:** Awarded to 3,866 full-time undergraduates, including 871 freshmen. Scholarships awarded for academics, athletics, leadership, music/drama, ROTC.

Application procedures. Admission: Closing date 12/1 (postmark date). No application fee. Application must be submitted online. Admission notification by 1/31. Admission notification on a rolling basis. Must reply by May 1 or within 2 week(s) if notified thereafter. **Financial aid:** Priority date 2/1; no closing date. FAFSA required. Applicants notified on a rolling basis starting 3/5; must reply by 5/1 or within 3 week(s) of notification.

Academics. Special study options: Accelerated study, combined bachelor's/graduate degree, cooperative education, cross-registration, distance learning, double major, ESL, honors, independent study, internships, student-designed major, study abroad, teacher certification program, Washington semester, weekend college. **Credit/placement by examination:** AP, CLEP, IB, institutional tests. 30 credit hours maximum toward bachelor's degree. **Support services:** Learning center, pre-admission summer program, reduced course load, study skills assistance, tutoring, writing center.

Majors. Biology: General, Biochemistry/molecular biology, biomedical sciences, physiology. **Business:** Accounting, business admin, entrepreneurial studies, finance, human resources, managerial economics, marketing, organizational leadership, real estate. **Communications:** Advertising, digital media, journalism, media studies, public relations. **Computer sciences:** General, information technology. **Education:** Biology, chemistry, elementary, mathematics, secondary. **Engineering:** Biomedical, civil, computer, construction, electrical, environmental, mechanical. **English:** English lit, writing. **Foreign languages:** Classics, French, German, Spanish. **Health services:** Athletic training, audiology/speech pathology, clinical lab science, nursing (RN).

History: General. **Math:** General, computational. **Philosophy/religion:** Philosophy. **Physical sciences:** Chemistry, physics. **Psychology:** General. **Social sciences:** Anthropology, criminology, economics, political science, sociology. **Theology:** Theology. **Visual/performing arts:** Dramatic.

Most popular majors. Biology 10%, business/marketing 28%, communications/journalism 11%, engineering/engineering technologies 10%, health sciences 7%, psychology 6%, social sciences 9%.

Technology on campus. 1,132 workstations in dormitories, library, computer center, student center. Dormitories wired for high-speed internet access and linked to campus network. Commuter students can connect to campus network. Online course registration, online library, helpline, student web hosting, wireless network available.

Student life. Freshman orientation: Available. Preregistration for classes offered. Four day session held week before classes begin; June program also available. **Policies:** Written policies in effect concerning racial and sexual harassment, alcohol, drugs and safety. **Housing:** Guaranteed on-campus for freshmen. Coed dorms, single-sex dorms, special housing for disabled, apartments, cooperative housing, fraternity/sorority housing, themed housing, wellness housing available. $300 nonrefundable deposit, deadline 5/1. Special housing for engineering, nursing, and honor students available. **Activities:** Bands, campus ministries, choral groups, dance, drama, international student organizations, literary magazine, music ensembles, Model UN, musical theater, radio station, student government, student newspaper, symphony orchestra, TV station, JUSTICE, College Republicans, College Democrats, Campus Crusade for Christ, Intervarsity, Latin American student organization.

Athletics. NCAA. **Intercollegiate:** Basketball, cheerleading, cross-country, golf M, lacrosse, soccer, tennis, track and field, volleyball W. **Intramural:** Badminton, basketball, football (non-tackle), racquetball, softball, tennis, ultimate frisbee, volleyball, water polo, weight lifting. **Team name:** Golden Eagles.

Student services. Adult student services, alcohol/substance abuse counseling, chaplain/spiritual director, career counseling, services for economically disadvantaged, student employment services, financial aid counseling, health services, minority student services, on-campus daycare, personal counseling, placement for graduates. **Physically disabled:** Services for visually, speech, hearing impaired.

Contact. E-mail: admissions@marquette.edu
Phone: (414) 288-7302 Toll-free number: (800) 222-6544
Fax: (414) 288-3764
Robert Blust, Dean of Undergraduate Admissions, Marquette University, PO Box 1881, Milwaukee, WI 53201-1881

Milwaukee Institute of Art & Design
Milwaukee, Wisconsin
www.miad.edu　　　　　　　　　　　**CB code: 1506**

▶ Private 4-year visual arts college
▶ Commuter campus in very large city
▶ 621 degree-seeking undergraduates: 3% part-time, 65% women, 7% African American, 4% Asian American, 13% Hispanic/Latino, 5% Multiracial, non-Hispanic, 1% international
▶ 62% of applicants admitted
▶ Interview required
▶ 55% graduate within 6 years

General. Founded in 1974. Regionally accredited. **Degrees:** 165 bachelor's awarded. **Location:** 90 miles from Chicago. **Calendar:** Semester, limited summer session. **Full-time faculty:** 37 total; 89% have terminal degrees, 8% minority, 38% women. **Part-time faculty:** 71 total; 42% have terminal degrees, 1% minority, 37% women. **Class size:** 88% < 20, 12% 20-39, less than 1% 40-49. **Special facilities:** Gallery of industrial design, public art project, 6 art galleries, foundry, 3-D lab.

Freshman class profile. 678 applied, 419 admitted, 181 enrolled.

GPA 3.75 or higher:	12%	Rank in top tenth:	10%
GPA 3.50-3.74:	13%	Return as sophomores:	72%
GPA 3.0-3.49:	30%	Out-of-state:	36%
GPA 2.0-2.99:	43%	Live on campus:	72%
Rank in top quarter:	30%	International:	1%

Basis for selection. Portfolio and interview most important. 3.0 GPA in art curriculum recommended. Portfolio of 15-20 pieces of artwork required. SAT or ACT recommended. **Home schooled:** Transcript of courses and grades required.

High school preparation. Recommended units include visual/performing arts 4. 4 years high school visual art study highly recommended.

2015-2016 Annual costs. Tuition/fees: $33,560. Room/board: $9,050. Books/supplies: $1,400. Personal expenses: $1,110.

2014-2015 Financial aid. Need-based: 137 full-time freshmen applied for aid; 125 deemed to have need; 125 received aid. Average need met was 65%. Average scholarship/grant was $19,094; average loan $4,691. 68% of total undergraduate aid awarded as scholarships/grants, 32% as loans/jobs. **Non-need-based:** Awarded to 144 full-time undergraduates, including 31 freshmen. Scholarships awarded for academics, art.

Application procedures. Admission: Priority date 2/15; deadline 8/1 (postmark date). $25 fee. Admission notification on a rolling basis beginning on or about 12/1. Must reply by May 1 or within 2 week(s) if notified thereafter. **Financial aid:** Priority date 2/15; no closing date. FAFSA required. Applicants notified on a rolling basis starting 3/1; must reply by 5/1 or within 4 week(s) of notification.

Academics. Special study options: Cross-registration, double major, exchange student, independent study, internships, New York semester, semester at sea, study abroad. **Credit/placement by examination:** AP, CLEP. **Support services:** Learning center, reduced course load, remedial instruction, study skills assistance, tutoring, writing center.

Majors. Visual/performing arts: Drawing, graphic design, illustration, industrial design, interior design, painting, photography, printmaking, sculpture, studio arts.

Technology on campus. PC or laptop required. 90 workstations in library, computer center. Dormitories wired for high-speed internet access. Commuter students can connect to campus network. Online course registration, helpline, wireless network available.

Student life. Freshman orientation: Mandatory. Preregistration for classes offered. Four-day program held prior to fall semester. **Housing:** Coed dorms available. $175 nonrefundable deposit, deadline 5/1. **Activities:** Student government, Interior Design Society of America, National Industrial Design Society, student activities committee, AIGA Student Chapter.

Student services. Alcohol/substance abuse counseling, career counseling, student employment services, financial aid counseling, health services, minority student services, personal counseling, placement for graduates, veterans' counselor.

Contact. E-mail: admissions@miad.edu
Phone: (414) 291-8070 Toll-free number: (888) 749-6423
Fax: (414) 291-8077
David Sigman, Director of Admissions, Milwaukee Institute of Art & Design, 273 East Erie Street, Milwaukee, WI 53202

Milwaukee School of Engineering
Milwaukee, Wisconsin　　　　　　　**CB member**
www.msoe.edu　　　　　　　　　　**CB code: 1476**

▶ Private 4-year university
▶ Residential campus in very large city
▶ 2,712 degree-seeking undergraduates: 6% part-time, 25% women, 2% African American, 3% Asian American, 5% Hispanic/Latino, 2% Multiracial, non-Hispanic, 13% international
▶ 227 degree-seeking graduate students
▶ 65% of applicants admitted
▶ SAT or ACT (ACT writing optional) required
▶ 64% graduate within 6 years; 8% enter graduate study

General. Founded in 1903. Regionally accredited. **Degrees:** 438 bachelor's awarded; master's offered. **ROTC:** Army, Naval, Air Force. **Location:** 90 miles from Chicago. **Calendar:** Quarter, limited summer session. **Full-time faculty:** 134 total; 78% have terminal degrees, 10% minority, 31% women. **Part-time faculty:** 131 total; 34% have terminal degrees, 15% minority, 44% women. **Class size:** 42% < 20, 58% 20-39, less than 1% 40-49. **Special facilities:** Museum, teaching and research laboratories for fluid power motion control, construction management, energy systems, renewable energy, rapid prototyping, software development, health and wellness fitness facility, indoor ice hockey arena.

Freshman class profile. 2,326 applied, 1,511 admitted, 518 enrolled.

Mid 50% test scores		End year in good standing:	87%
SAT critical reading:	580-670	Return as sophomores:	87%
SAT math:	610-730	Out-of-state:	33%
ACT composite:	25-30	Live on campus:	76%
GPA 3.75 or higher:	43%	International:	6%
GPA 3.50-3.74:	24%	Fraternities:	4%
GPA 3.0-3.49:	27%	Sororities:	9%
GPA 2.0-2.99:	6%		

Basis for selection. Admissions based on secondary school record and standardized test scores. **Home schooled:** Transcript of courses and grades required. **Learning Disabled:** Untimed standardized tests required.

High school preparation. College-preparatory program recommended. 12 units required. Required and recommended units include English 4, mathematics 4, science 4 (laboratory 3). For business and technical communication, math units should include 1 algebra. For biomedical engineering, science units should include 1 biological science.

2016-2017 Annual costs. Tuition/fees: $37,980. Room/board: $8,835. Books/supplies: $1,200. Personal expenses: $1,500.

2014-2015 Financial aid. Need-based: 524 full-time freshmen applied for aid; 452 deemed to have need; 452 received aid. Average need met was 83%. Average scholarship/grant was $24,676; average loan $3,552. 75% of total undergraduate aid awarded as scholarships/grants, 25% as loans/jobs. **Non-need-based:** Awarded to 653 full-time undergraduates, including 176 freshmen. Scholarships awarded for academics, ROTC.

Application procedures. Admission: Priority date 1/1; no deadline. No application fee. Admission notification on a rolling basis beginning on or about 10/1. **Financial aid:** Priority date 3/15; no closing date. FAFSA required. Applicants notified on a rolling basis starting 3/1; must reply within 2 week(s) of notification.

Academics. Students receive an average of 600 hours of laboratory experience. **Special study options:** Accelerated study, combined bachelor's/graduate degree, double major, dual enrollment of high school students, ESL, honors, independent study, internships, study abroad. Bachelor of Science in business, mechanical engineering, and in electrical engineering with Lubeck University of Applied Sciences, Germany; exchange program with Czech Technical University, bachelor's or master's option in an engineering discipline. **Credit/placement by examination:** AP, CLEP, IB, SAT, ACT. **Support services:** Learning center, pre-admission summer program, reduced course load, study skills assistance, tutoring, writing center.

Majors. Business: General, actuarial science, business admin, construction management, international, management information systems. **Communications:** Communications/speech/rhetoric. **Engineering:** General, architectural, biomedical, biomolecular, civil, computer, electrical, industrial, mechanical, software. **Health services:** Nursing (RN).

Most popular majors. Business/marketing 14%, engineering/engineering technologies 73%, health sciences 12%.

Technology on campus. PC or laptop required. 150 workstations in dormitories, library, computer center, student center. Dormitories wired for high-speed internet access and linked to campus network. Commuter students can connect to campus network. Online course registration, online library, helpline, repair service, student web hosting, wireless network available.

Student life. Freshman orientation: Mandatory. Preregistration for classes offered. Held the whole week before classes begin. **Policies:** Smoke-free campus and residential facilities. **Housing:** Guaranteed on-campus for all undergraduates. Coed dorms, special housing for disabled, apartments, fraternity/sorority housing, wellness housing available. $175 nonrefundable deposit, deadline 6/1. **Activities:** Bands, campus ministries, choral groups, dance, drama, international student organizations, literary magazine, music ensembles, radio station, student government, student newspaper, symphony orchestra, Residence Hall Association, Circle-K, Society of Hispanic Professional Engineers, National Society of Black Engineers, Student Nurses Association, Campus Volunteer Services, Habitat for Humanity, Engineers Without Borders, College Republicans.

Athletics. NCAA. **Intercollegiate:** Baseball M, basketball, cheerleading, cross-country, golf M, ice hockey M, lacrosse M, rowing (crew) M, soccer, softball W, tennis, track and field, volleyball, wrestling M. **Intramural:** Basketball, football (non-tackle), ice hockey, soccer, softball, volleyball. **Team name:** Raiders.

Student services. Adult student services, alcohol/substance abuse counseling, career counseling, services for economically disadvantaged, student employment services, financial aid counseling, health services, minority student services, personal counseling, placement for graduates, veterans' counselor, women's services. **Physically disabled:** Services for visually, speech, hearing impaired.

Contact. E-mail: explore@msoe.edu
Phone: (414) 277-6763 Toll-free number: (800) 332-6763
Fax: (414) 277-7475
Seandra Mitchell, Director, Undergraduate Admission, Milwaukee School of Engineering, 1025 North Broadway, Milwaukee, WI 53202-3109

Mount Mary University
Milwaukee, Wisconsin
www.mtmary.edu   **CB code: 1490**

- Private 4-year university and liberal arts college for women affiliated with the Roman Catholic Church
- Commuter campus in very large city
- 804 degree-seeking undergraduates: 11% part-time, 100% women, 19% African American, 8% Asian American, 14% Hispanic/Latino, 4% Multiracial, non-Hispanic, 2% international
- 441 degree-seeking graduate students
- 53% of applicants admitted
- SAT or ACT (ACT writing optional), application essay required
- 42% graduate within 6 years

General. Founded in 1913. Regionally accredited. **Degrees:** 136 bachelor's awarded; master's, professional offered. **Location:** Seven miles from downtown. **Calendar:** Semester, limited summer session. **Full-time faculty:** 67 total; 78% have terminal degrees, 88% women. **Part-time faculty:** 127 total; 28% have terminal degrees, 73% women. **Class size:** 88% < 20, 11% 20-39, less than 1% 40-49. **Special facilities:** A historic costume collection, labyrinth, art gallery, and archives.

Freshman class profile. 764 applied, 402 admitted, 148 enrolled.

Mid 50% test scores		Rank in top quarter:	50%
ACT composite:	17-21	Rank in top tenth:	26%
GPA 3.75 or higher:	12%	Return as sophomores:	68%
GPA 3.50-3.74:	13%	Out-of-state:	11%
GPA 3.0-3.49:	38%	Live on campus:	61%
GPA 2.0-2.99:	36%	International:	3%

Basis for selection. Evaluation of application, high school record and ACT/SAT scores. Essay or personal statement required for students who do not meet direct admission requirements. **Home schooled:** ACT or Mount Mary Assessment Testing. **Learning Disabled:** Students are encouraged to talk with Accessibility Services Coordinator at least one semester prior to enrollment to determine if reasonable accommodations can be made.

High school preparation. College-preparatory program recommended. 16 units required; 20 recommended. Required and recommended units include English 4, mathematics 2-3, social studies 2, history 2, science 4-5 (laboratory 2), foreign language 2 and academic electives 2.

2015-2016 Annual costs. Tuition/fees: $26,760. Room/board: $7,890. Books/supplies: $1,200.

2014-2015 Financial aid. Need-based: Average need met was 77%. Average scholarship/grant was $21,603; average loan $3,292. 69% of total undergraduate aid awarded as scholarships/grants, 31% as loans/jobs. **Non-need-based:** Scholarships awarded for academics, alumni affiliation, art, leadership, music/drama.

Application procedures. Admission: No deadline. No application fee. Admission notification on a rolling basis beginning on or about 9/15. **Financial aid:** Priority date 3/1; no closing date. FAFSA required. Applicants notified on a rolling basis starting 3/1; must reply within 2 week(s) of notification.

Academics. Special study options: Accelerated study, combined bachelor's/graduate degree, double major, honors, independent study, internships, liberal arts/career combination, student-designed major, study abroad, teacher certification program. **Credit/placement by examination:** AP, CLEP, IB, SAT, ACT, institutional tests. Maximum of 24 credits earned through a combination of credit exams, credit from life experience, directed and independent study. **Support services:** Learning center, reduced course load, remedial instruction, study skills assistance, tutoring, writing center. Counseling, Accessibility Accommodations, Academic Counseling, & Testing Services.

Majors. Biology: General. **Business:** Accounting, business admin, communications, fashion, marketing. **Communications:** Communications/speech/rhetoric. **Education:** General, art, biology, business, chemistry, English, foreign languages, history, mathematics, middle, multi-level teacher, science, social studies, Spanish. **English:** English lit. **Foreign languages:** Spanish. **Health services:** Art therapy, dietetics, occupational therapy, radiologic technology/medical imaging. **History:** General. **Human services:** Social work.

Liberal arts: Arts/sciences. **Math:** General. **Philosophy/religion:** Philosophy. **Physical sciences:** Chemistry. **Protective services:** Law enforcement admin. **Psychology:** General. **Social sciences:** General, sociology. **Theology:** Religious ed, theology. **Visual/performing arts:** Art, fashion design, graphic design, interior design.

Most popular majors. Business/marketing 17%, communications/journalism 7%, health sciences 21%, psychology 12%, public administration/social services 7%, visual/performing arts 20%.

Technology on campus. 226 workstations in dormitories, library, computer center, student center. Dormitories wired for high-speed internet access and linked to campus network. Commuter students can connect to campus network. Online course registration, online library, helpline, wireless network available.

Student life. Freshman orientation: Mandatory. Preregistration for classes offered. A two day program, held in the fall. **Housing:** Guaranteed on-campus for freshmen. $100 fully refundable deposit, deadline 5/1. **Activities:** Campus ministries, choral groups, dance, international student organizations, literary magazine, music ensembles, Model UN, student government, student newspaper, commuter council, hall council, gospel choir, programming and activities council and department-affiliated clubs.

Athletics. NCAA. **Intercollegiate:** Basketball W, cross-country W, golf W, soccer W, softball W, tennis W, volleyball W. **Team name:** Blue Angels.

Student services. Adult student services, chaplain/spiritual director, career counseling, services for economically disadvantaged, student employment services, financial aid counseling, minority student services, on-campus daycare, personal counseling, veterans' counselor, women's services. **Physically disabled:** Services for visually, speech, hearing impaired.

Contact. E-mail: mmu-admiss@mtmary.edu
Phone: (414) 930-3024 Toll-free number: (800) 321-6265
Fax: (414) 930-3708
Rebecca Surges, Director of Undergraduate Admissions, Mount Mary University, 2900 North Menomonee River Parkway, Milwaukee, WI 53222-4597

Northland College
Ashland, Wisconsin
www.northland.edu

CB member
CB code: 1561

- Private 4-year liberal arts college affiliated with the United Church of Christ
- Residential campus in small town
- 518 degree-seeking undergraduates: 1% part-time, 48% women
- 12 graduate students
- 57% of applicants admitted
- SAT or ACT (ACT writing optional) required
- 58% graduate within 6 years

General. Founded in 1892. Regionally accredited. **Degrees:** 124 bachelor's awarded. **Location:** 65 miles from Duluth, MN. **Calendar:** 4-1-4, limited summer session. **Full-time faculty:** 52 total; 85% have terminal degrees, 6% minority, 44% women. **Part-time faculty:** 12 total; 25% have terminal degrees, 17% minority, 42% women. **Class size:** 66% < 20, 34% 20-39. **Special facilities:** Field stations for natural science courses, atmospheric and environmental satellite links, Indigenous Cultures Center/Native American Museum.

Freshman class profile. 852 applied, 487 admitted, 128 enrolled.

Mid 50% test scores		Rank in top quarter:	46%
ACT composite:	21-28	Rank in top tenth:	22%
GPA 3.75 or higher:	26%	Return as sophomores:	70%
GPA 3.50-3.74:	22%	Out-of-state:	53%
GPA 3.0-3.49:	30%	Live on campus:	95%
GPA 2.0-2.99:	21%		

Basis for selection. High school curriculum evaluation, class rank, guidance counselor recommendation, GPA, and test scores considered. **Learning Disabled:** Strongly recommend students contact disabilities coordinator.

High school preparation. College-preparatory program recommended. 18 units required; 21 recommended. Required and recommended units include English 4, mathematics 3, social studies 3, science 3 (laboratory 2), foreign language 2 and academic electives 3-4.

2015-2016 Annual costs. Tuition/fees: $32,754. Room/board: $8,349. Books/supplies: $800. Personal expenses: $1,650.

2015-2016 Financial aid. Need-based: 122 full-time freshmen applied for aid; 108 deemed to have need; 108 received aid. Average need met was 87%. Average scholarship/grant was $24,770; average loan $4,407. 83% of total undergraduate aid awarded as scholarships/grants, 17% as loans/jobs. **Non-need-based:** Awarded to 146 full-time undergraduates, including 47 freshmen. Scholarships awarded for academics, alumni affiliation, art, job skills, leadership, minority status, music/drama, religious affiliation, state residency.

Application procedures. Admission: Priority date 12/1; no deadline. No application fee. Admission notification on a rolling basis beginning on or about 9/1. Must reply by May 1 or within 2 week(s) if notified thereafter. **Financial aid:** Priority date 3/15; no closing date. FAFSA required. Applicants notified on a rolling basis starting 3/1; must reply by 5/1 or within 4 week(s) of notification.

Academics. Special study options: Cross-registration, double major, dual enrollment of high school students, exchange student, independent study, internships, student-designed major, study abroad, teacher certification program. 3-2 cooperative degree programs in engineering with Michigan Technological University and Washington University. Member of the Ecoleague exchange consortium with Alaska Pacific University, Green Mountain College, Prescott College, and College of the Atlantic. **Credit/placement by examination:** AP, CLEP, IB, SAT, ACT, institutional tests. 30 credit hours maximum toward bachelor's degree. **Support services:** Remedial instruction, tutoring.

Majors. Area/ethnic studies: Native American, women's. **Biology:** General. **Business:** Business admin, entrepreneurial studies. **Conservation:** Environmental studies. **Education:** Multi-level teacher, science, secondary, social studies. **Engineering:** General. **English:** Creative writing, English lit. **History:** General. **Human services:** Community org/advocacy. **Liberal arts:** Humanities. **Math:** General. **Parks/recreation:** Outdoor education. **Philosophy/religion:** Religion. **Physical sciences:** Chemistry, geology, hydrology, meteorology. **Psychology:** General. **Social sciences:** Sociology. **Visual/performing arts:** Graphic design, studio arts.

Most popular majors. Biology 17%, business/marketing 7%, education 7%, natural resources/environmental science 24%, physical sciences 10%, public administration/social services 7%.

Technology on campus. 125 workstations in dormitories, library, computer center, student center. Dormitories wired for high-speed internet access and linked to campus network. Commuter students can connect to campus network. Online course registration, online library, repair service, wireless network available.

Student life. Freshman orientation: Mandatory. Preregistration for classes offered. **Housing:** Guaranteed on-campus for freshmen. Coed dorms, single-sex dorms, special housing for disabled, apartments, cooperative housing, themed housing, wellness housing available. $100 nonrefundable deposit, deadline 5/1. **Activities:** Bands, campus ministries, choral groups, dance, drama, international student organizations, literary magazine, music ensembles, radio station, student government, student newspaper, symphony orchestra.

Athletics. NCAA. **Intercollegiate:** Baseball M, basketball, cross-country, golf, ice hockey M, lacrosse, soccer, softball W, volleyball W. **Team name:** Lumberjacks, Lumberjills.

Student services. Alcohol/substance abuse counseling, chaplain/spiritual director, career counseling, services for economically disadvantaged, student employment services, financial aid counseling, health services, minority student services, personal counseling, placement for graduates, women's services. **Physically disabled:** Services for visually, hearing impaired.

Contact. E-mail: admit@northland.edu
Phone: (715) 682-1224 Toll-free number: (800) 753-1840
Fax: (715) 682-1258
Teege Mettille, Director of Admissions, Northland College, 1411 Ellis Avenue, Ashland, WI 54806-3999

Rasmussen College: Appleton
Appleton, Wisconsin
www.rasmussen.edu

- For-profit 4-year branch campus and career college
- Small city
- 374 degree-seeking undergraduates

General. Regionally accredited. **Degrees:** 26 bachelor's, 67 associate awarded. **Calendar:** Quarter. **Full-time faculty:** 3 total. **Part-time faculty:** 35 total.

Freshman class profile. 121 applied, 96 admitted, 96 enrolled.

Basis for selection. Open admission, but selective for some programs.

2016-2017 Annual costs. Tuition/fees (projected): $13,455.

Application procedures. Admission: No deadline. No application fee. **Financial aid:** No deadline. FAFSA, institutional form required. Applicants notified on a rolling basis.

Academics. Credit/placement by examination: AP, CLEP.

Majors. Business: Accounting, accounting/business management, business admin, entrepreneurial studies, finance, human resources, information resources management, marketing. **Computer sciences:** Computer science, security, system admin, web page design. **Health services:** Health care admin, health information management, nursing (RN). **Protective services:** Criminal justice, special ops. **Visual/performing arts:** Digital arts, game design.

Contact. Phone: (920) 750-5900
Susan Hammerstrom, Director of Admissions, Rasmussen College: Appleton, 3500 East Destination Drive, Appleton, WI 54915

Ripon College

Ripon, Wisconsin	
	CB member
www.ripon.edu	**CB code: 1664**

- Private 4-year liberal arts college
- Residential campus in small town
- 781 degree-seeking undergraduates: 50% women, 3% African American, 1% Asian American, 6% Hispanic/Latino, 2% Multi-racial, non-Hispanic, 4% international
- 66% of applicants admitted
- SAT or ACT (ACT writing optional) required
- 69% graduate within 6 years; 29% enter graduate study

General. Founded in 1851. Regionally accredited. **Degrees:** 196 bachelor's awarded. **ROTC:** Army. **Location:** 80 miles from Milwaukee, 80 miles from Madison. **Calendar:** Semester. **Full-time faculty:** 64 total; 97% have terminal degrees, 11% minority, 42% women. **Part-time faculty:** 19 total; 53% have terminal degrees, 32% women. **Class size:** 75% < 20, 23% 20-39, 1% 40-49, 1% 50-99. **Special facilities:** Woodland preservation area with outdoor classroom.

Freshman class profile. 1,874 applied, 1,239 admitted, 216 enrolled.

Mid 50% test scores		Rank in top tenth:	21%
SAT critical reading:	450-640	End year in good standing:	91%
SAT math:	500-620	Return as sophomores:	83%
ACT composite:	21-27	Out-of-state:	30%
GPA 3.75 or higher:	27%	Live on campus:	98%
GPA 3.50-3.74:	19%	International:	5%
GPA 3.0-3.49:	33%	Fraternities:	11%
GPA 2.0-2.99:	21%	Sororities:	8%
Rank in top quarter:	51%		

Basis for selection. School achievement record, interview, class rank, test scores, recommendations, extracurricular or community activities important. **Home schooled:** Transcript of courses and grades, interview required.

High school preparation. College-preparatory program recommended. 17 units required. Required and recommended units include English 4, mathematics 2-4, social studies 2-4, science 2-4 and foreign language 2. Math must include 1 algebra and geometry. 7 units chosen from additional units in math, science, social science, foreign language.

2016-2017 Annual costs. Tuition/fees (projected): $38,325. Room/board: $8,177. Books/supplies: $750. Personal expenses: $500.

2015-2016 Financial aid. Need-based: 208 full-time freshmen applied for aid; 188 deemed to have need; 188 received aid. Average need met was 87%. Average scholarship/grant was $27,230; average loan $4,325. 77% of total undergraduate aid awarded as scholarships/grants, 23% as loans/jobs. **Non-need-based:** Awarded to 216 full-time undergraduates, including 61 freshmen. Scholarships awarded for academics, alumni affiliation, art, leadership, minority status, music/drama, religious affiliation, ROTC, state residency.

Application procedures. Admission: Priority date 3/15; no deadline. $30 fee, may be waived for applicants with need. Admission notification on a rolling basis beginning on or about 9/15. Must reply by May 1 or within 2 week(s) if notified thereafter. **Financial aid:** Priority date 3/1, closing date

6/15. FAFSA required. Applicants notified on a rolling basis starting 3/1; must reply within 2 week(s) of notification.

Academics. Special study options: Accelerated study, combined bachelor's/graduate degree, double major, exchange student, internships, student-designed major, study abroad, teacher certification program, urban semester, Washington semester. Domestic and international off-campus study programs. **Credit/placement by examination:** AP, CLEP, IB. Amount of credit and placement for AP exams subject to departmental approval. **Support services:** Learning center, study skills assistance, tutoring.

Majors. Area/ethnic studies: Latin American, women's. **Biology:** General, biochemistry. **Business:** Business admin. **Communications:** Communications/speech/rhetoric. **Computer sciences:** Computer science. **Conservation:** Environmental studies. **Education:** General. **Engineering:** Pre-engineering. **English:** English lit. **Foreign languages:** General, Spanish. **Health services:** Predental, premedicine, prenursing, prepharmacy, preveterinary. **History:** General. **Math:** General. **Parks/recreation:** Exercise sciences. **Philosophy/religion:** Philosophy, religion. **Physical sciences:** Chemistry, physics. **Psychology:** General. **Social sciences:** Economics, political science, sociology. **Visual/performing arts:** Art history/conservation, dramatic, music, studio arts.

Most popular majors. Biology 9%, business/marketing 10%, English 9%, history 7%, interdisciplinary studies 6%, parks/recreation 9%, physical sciences 6%, psychology 8%, social sciences 19%.

Technology on campus. 150 workstations in dormitories, library, computer center. Dormitories wired for high-speed internet access and linked to campus network. Commuter students can connect to campus network. Helpline, student web hosting, wireless network available.

Student life. Freshman orientation: Available, $65 fee. Preregistration for classes offered. Two day overnight orientation held in late June. **Housing:** Guaranteed on-campus for all undergraduates. Coed dorms, single-sex dorms, fraternity/sorority housing, themed housing, wellness housing available. $200 nonrefundable deposit, deadline 8/15. **Activities:** Bands, campus ministries, choral groups, dance, drama, film society, international student organizations, literary magazine, music ensembles, musical theater, radio station, student government, student newspaper, symphony orchestra, Campus Christian Fellowship, Black Student Union, equestrian club, outdoor club; music appreciation society, College Democrats, College Republicans.

Athletics. NCAA. **Intercollegiate:** Baseball M, basketball, cross-country, diving, football (tackle) M, soccer, softball W, swimming, tennis, track and field, volleyball W. **Intramural:** Basketball, bowling, football (non-tackle), racquetball, soccer, volleyball. **Team name:** Red Hawks.

Student services. Career counseling, student employment services, financial aid counseling, health services, personal counseling, placement for graduates.

Contact. E-mail: adminfo@ripon.edu
Phone: (920) 748-8337 Toll-free number: (800) 947-4766
Fax: (920) 748-8335
Leigh Mlodzik, Dean of Admission, Ripon College, 300 West Seward Street, Ripon, WI 54971-0248

Silver Lake College of the Holy Family

Manitowoc, Wisconsin	
www.sl.edu	**CB code: 1300**

- Private 4-year liberal arts college affiliated with the Roman Catholic Church
- Large town
- 296 degree-seeking undergraduates
- 193 graduate students
- SAT or ACT (ACT writing recommended) required

General. Founded in 1935. Regionally accredited. **Degrees:** 66 bachelor's awarded; master's offered. **Location:** 80 miles from Milwaukee, 30 miles from Green Bay. **Calendar:** Semester, limited summer session. **Full-time faculty:** 42 total; 69% women. **Part-time faculty:** 46 total. **Class size:** 95% < 20, 5% 20-39. **Special facilities:** Nature preserve.

Freshman class profile.

GPA 3.75 or higher:	11%	GPA 2.0-2.99:	54%
GPA 3.50-3.74:	7%	Out-of-state:	4%
GPA 3.0-3.49:	15%	Live on campus:	87%

Basis for selection. Admission based on formula of GPA x ACT x 10. Those below 300 will be denied admission, 301-449 granted provisional admission, and 450 and above accepted. Audition and interview recommended for music; portfolio and interview recommended for art. **Home schooled:** Transcript of courses and grades required. **Learning Disabled:** IEP should be submitted to Director of Learning Resources.

High school preparation. College-preparatory program recommended. 16 units required. Required units include English 4, mathematics 3, social studies 2, history 1, science 3 (laboratory 1) and foreign language 1. 1 unit of fine arts may be substituted for foreign language requirement.

2015-2016 Annual costs. Tuition/fees: $14,650. Room/board: $12,760. Books/supplies: $1,066. Personal expenses: $2,322.

Financial aid. **Non-need-based:** Scholarships awarded for academics, art, athletics, leadership, music/drama, state residency.

Application procedures. **Admission:** Priority date 8/1; no deadline. $50 fee, may be waived for applicants with need. Admission notification on a rolling basis beginning on or about 9/1. **Financial aid:** Priority date 5/1; no closing date. FAFSA required. Applicants notified on a rolling basis starting 3/15.

Academics. **Special study options:** Accelerated study, distance learning, double major, dual enrollment of high school students, independent study, internships, liberal arts/career combination, student-designed major, teacher certification program. **Credit/placement by examination:** AP, CLEP, IB, SAT, ACT, institutional tests. 60 credit hours maximum toward bachelor's degree. **Support services:** Learning center, reduced course load, remedial instruction, study skills assistance, tutoring.

Majors. **Biology:** General. **Business:** Accounting, business admin, human resources. **Computer sciences:** Computer science, information systems. **Education:** Art, early childhood, early childhood special, elementary, learning disabled, mentally handicapped, music. **English:** English lit. **Health services:** Nursing (RN). **History:** General. **Math:** General. **Psychology:** General. **Theology:** Theology. **Visual/performing arts:** Art, music, music pedagogy.

Most popular majors. Business/marketing 38%, education 19%, psychology 16%, theological studies 6%.

Technology on campus. 78 workstations in dormitories, library, computer center, student center. Dormitories wired for high-speed internet access and linked to campus network. Commuter students can connect to campus network. Online course registration, online library, wireless network available.

Student life. **Freshman orientation:** Mandatory. Preregistration for classes offered. **Housing:** Guaranteed on-campus for all undergraduates. Coed dorms, special housing for disabled, wellness housing available. $100 nonrefundable deposit, deadline 8/1. **Activities:** Jazz band, campus ministries, choral groups, literary magazine, music ensembles, student government, student newspaper, Wisconsin Art Education Association, National Art Education Association Student Chapter, Student Education Association, Student Council for Exceptional Children, Early Childhood Association, Human Resource Management Association, Psychology Student Organization, Young Democrats and Republicans.

Athletics. USCAA. **Intercollegiate:** Basketball, cross-country, golf, soccer. **Team name:** Lakers.

Student services. Adult student services, alcohol/substance abuse counseling, chaplain/spiritual director, career counseling, student employment services, financial aid counseling, health services, personal counseling, placement for graduates.

Contact. E-mail: admslc@sl.edu
Phone: (920) 686-6175 Toll-free number: (800) 236-4752 ext. 175
Fax: (920) 686-6322
Jamie Grant, Executive Director of Enrollment Management, Silver Lake College of the Holy Family, 2406 South Alverno Road, Manitowoc, WI 54220-9319

St. Norbert College

De Pere, Wisconsin **CB member**
www.snc.edu **CB code: 1706**

- Private 4-year liberal arts college affiliated with the Roman Catholic Church
- Residential campus in large town
- 2,052 degree-seeking undergraduates: 1% part-time, 57% women, 1% African American, 1% Asian American, 4% Hispanic/Latino, 1% Native American, 2% Multi-racial, non-Hispanic, 2% international
- 77 degree-seeking graduate students
- 78% of applicants admitted
- SAT or ACT (ACT writing recommended) required
- 73% graduate within 6 years; 17% enter graduate study

General. Founded in 1898. Regionally accredited. **Degrees:** 487 bachelor's awarded; master's offered. **ROTC:** Army. **Location:** 5 miles from Green Bay. **Calendar:** Semester, limited summer session. **Full-time faculty:** 136 total; 90% have terminal degrees, 8% minority, 48% women. **Part-time faculty:** 63 total; 36% have terminal degrees, 8% minority, 44% women. **Class size:** 48% < 20, 51% 20-39, 1% 40-49, less than 1% 50-99. **Special facilities:** Marina, on-campus hotel and conference center, fine and performing arts centers, center for international education, center for peace, justice and public understanding, center for leadership and service, children's center, center for women's and gender studies, innovation studio, Strategic Research Institute, center for Norbertine studies.

Freshman class profile. 3,814 applied, 2,963 admitted, 601 enrolled.

Mid 50% test scores		Rank in top tenth:	26%
ACT composite:	22-27	Return as sophomores:	82%
GPA 3.75 or higher:	41%	Out-of-state:	24%
GPA 3.50-3.74:	18%	Live on campus:	97%
GPA 3.0-3.49:	27%	International:	1%
GPA 2.0-2.99:	14%	Fraternities:	12%
Rank in top quarter:	54%	Sororities:	13%

Basis for selection. High school record, rigor of courses, and grades earned important. Preference given to students successfully completing challenging courses. Counselor and teacher recommendations, community service considered. Students not in college preparatory programs may be offered admission if test results, class rank, and grades demonstrate aptitude for college work. Essay, interview recommended for all; audition recommended for music. **Learning Disabled:** Students should submit documentation of specific disability to receive proper level of support from institution.

High school preparation. College-preparatory program recommended. 16 units recommended. Recommended units include English 4, mathematics 3, social studies 2, history 2, science 3 (laboratory 3) and foreign language 2. As many college-prep elective units as possible.

2015-2016 Annual costs. Tuition/fees: $34,237. Room/board: $8,794. Books/supplies: $950. Personal expenses: $750.

2014-2015 Financial aid. **Need-based:** 490 full-time freshmen applied for aid; 428 deemed to have need; 428 received aid. Average need met was 84%. Average scholarship/grant was $20,551; average loan $3,701. 65% of total undergraduate aid awarded as scholarships/grants, 35% as loans/jobs. **Non-need-based:** Awarded to 550 full-time undergraduates, including 115 freshmen. Scholarships awarded for academics, art, leadership, minority status, music/drama, ROTC, state residency.

Application procedures. **Admission:** Priority date 4/1; no deadline. $10 fee, may be waived for applicants with need. Admission notification on a rolling basis beginning on or about 10/1. Must reply by May 1 or within 3 week(s) if notified thereafter. **Financial aid:** Priority date 3/1; no closing date. FAFSA required. Applicants notified by 3/15; must reply within 2 week(s) of notification.

Academics. Study abroad strongly supported, and students are allowed to apply all of their financial aid to their study abroad program costs; student/faculty collaborative research. **Special study options:** Distance learning, double major, ESL, honors, independent study, internships, student-designed major, study abroad, teacher certification program, Washington semester. Foundation for International Education (London) Internship. **Credit/placement by examination:** AP, CLEP, IB, institutional tests. **Support services:** Learning center, reduced course load, remedial instruction, study skills assistance, tutoring, writing center.

Majors. **Biology:** General, biochemistry. **Business:** General, accounting, business admin, finance, human resources, international, management information systems, marketing. **Communications:** Communications/speech/rhetoric, media studies. **Computer sciences:** Computer graphics, computer science. **Conservation:** Environmental science. **Education:** Early childhood, elementary, music. **English:** Creative writing, English lit. **Foreign languages:** French, German, Spanish. **Health services:** Predental, premedicine, prenursing, prepharmacy, preveterinary. **History:** General. **Liberal arts:** Humanities. **Math:** General. **Philosophy/religion:** Philosophy, religion. **Physical sciences:** Chemistry, geology, physics. **Psychology:** General. **Social sciences:** Anthropology, economics, international relations, political science, sociology. **Theology:** Religious ed. **Visual/performing arts:** Art, commercial/advertising art, dramatic, graphic design, music.

Most popular majors. Biology 6%, business/marketing 25%, communications/journalism 12%, education 14%, psychology 6%, social sciences 10%.

Technology on campus. PC or laptop required. 214 workstations in dormitories, library, computer center, student center. Dormitories wired for high-speed internet access and linked to campus network. Commuter students can connect to campus network. Online course registration, online library, helpline, repair service, wireless network available.

Student life. Freshman orientation: Mandatory. Preregistration for classes offered. Two day summer program for students and parents. **Housing:** Guaranteed on-campus for all undergraduates. Coed dorms, single-sex dorms, special housing for disabled, apartments, wellness housing available. Townhouses and college-owned houses near campus available. **Activities:** Bands, campus ministries, choral groups, dance, drama, film society, international student organizations, literary magazine, music ensembles, musical theater, opera, radio station, student government, student newspaper, TV station, College Republicans, College Democrats, Japan club, Spanish club, Beyond Borders, Discoveries International, Rainbow Alliance, Black Student Union, La Alianza,.

Athletics. NCAA. **Intercollegiate:** Baseball M, basketball, cross-country, football (tackle) M, golf, ice hockey, soccer, softball W, tennis, track and field, volleyball W. **Intramural:** Basketball, football (non-tackle), sand volleyball, soccer, volleyball. **Team name:** Green Knights.

Student services. Alcohol/substance abuse counseling, chaplain/spiritual director, career counseling, student employment services, financial aid counseling, health services, minority student services, on-campus daycare, personal counseling, placement for graduates, veterans' counselor, women's services. **Physically disabled:** Services for visually, speech, hearing impaired.

Contact. E-mail: admit@snc.edu
Phone: (920) 403-3005 Toll-free number: (800) 236-4878
Fax: (920) 403-4072
Ed Lamm, V.P. of Enrollment Management and Communications, St. Norbert College, 100 Grant Street, De Pere, WI 54115-2099

University of Phoenix: Milwaukee
Milwaukee, Wisconsin
www.phoenix.edu

- For-profit 4-year university
- Very large city
- 284 undergraduates

General. Regionally accredited. **Degrees:** 88 bachelor's awarded; master's offered. **Calendar:** Differs by program. **Full-time faculty:** 8 total. **Part-time faculty:** 116 total.

Basis for selection. Open admission, but selective for some programs.

2015-2016 Annual costs. Per-credit-hour charge, $410 to $635, depending upon level and course of study. Books, material charges, and other fees vary by course and program. All fees are subject to change.

Application procedures. Admission: No deadline. No application fee. **Financial aid:** No deadline.

Academics. Credit/placement by examination: AP, CLEP.

Majors. Business: Accounting, accounting/business management, business admin, e-commerce, entrepreneurial studies, finance, human resources, marketing, operations. **Communications:** General. **Computer sciences:** Database management, networking, programming, security, systems analysis, web page design, webmaster. **Conservation:** Environmental studies. **Health services:** Facilities admin, health information management, long term care admin, nursing (RN). **Human services:** General. **Protective services:** Disaster management, law enforcement admin, security management.

Student life. Freshman orientation: Mandatory. Preregistration for classes offered.

Contact. Toll-free number: (866) 766-0766
University of Phoenix: Milwaukee, 10850 West Park Place, Milwaukee, WI 53224-3606

University of Wisconsin-Eau Claire
Eau Claire, Wisconsin
www.uwec.edu   CB code: 1913

- Public 4-year university
- Residential campus in small city
- 9,697 degree-seeking undergraduates: 6% part-time, 60% women
- 498 degree-seeking graduate students
- 85% of applicants admitted

- SAT or ACT (ACT writing optional) required
- 67% graduate within 6 years; 14% enter graduate study

General. Founded in 1916. Regionally accredited. **Degrees:** 2,120 bachelor's, 28 associate awarded; master's, professional offered. **ROTC:** Army. **Location:** 90 miles from Minneapolis-St. Paul. **Calendar:** Semester, extensive summer session. **Full-time faculty:** 437 total; 82% have terminal degrees, 15% minority, 51% women. **Part-time faculty:** 85 total; 27% have terminal degrees, 9% minority, 60% women. **Class size:** 23% < 20, 54% 20-39, 10% 40-49, 10% 50-99, 3% >100. **Special facilities:** Art gallery, bird museum, human development center, planetarium, natural preserve, ropes course, material sciences center, clinical simulation skills lab, 200 kev transmission electron microscope, x-ray photoelectron spectroscopy system, scanning tunneling microscope, scanning electron microscope with energy dispersive x-ray microanalysis, x-ray fluorescence spectrometer, x-ray diffractometer, high resolution inductively coupled plasma mass spectrometer.

Freshman class profile. 5,810 applied, 4,950 admitted, 2,230 enrolled.

Mid 50% test scores		Rank in top tenth:	18%
SAT critical reading:	500-640	End year in good standing:	79%
SAT math:	510-670	Return as sophomores:	83%
ACT composite:	22-26	Out-of-state:	33%
Rank in top quarter:	49%	Live on campus:	95%

Basis for selection. Test scores, class rank/GPA, rigor of courses, 4 year grade trend, essays, involvement, and special talent. Some applicants not admitted to fall semester may be considered for following spring semester. Audition required for music programs. **Learning Disabled:** Appropriate documentation must be sent to our Services for Students with Disabilities to consider any exceptions to admission policy/guidelines.

High school preparation. College-preparatory program required. 17 units required. Required units include English 4, mathematics 3, social studies 3, science 3 and academic electives 4.

2015-2016 Annual costs. Tuition/fees: $8,822; $16,395 out-of-state. Room/board: $7,322. Books/supplies: $400. Personal expenses: $2,120. **Additional information:** Fees include mandatory textbook rental fees.

2014-2015 Financial aid. Need-based: 1,732 full-time freshmen applied for aid; 1,107 deemed to have need; 1,094 received aid. Average need met was 87%. Average scholarship/grant was $5,932; average loan $3,994. 43% of total undergraduate aid awarded as scholarships/grants, 57% as loans/jobs. **Non-need-based:** Awarded to 565 full-time undergraduates, including 156 freshmen. Scholarships awarded for academics, art, leadership, minority status, music/drama, state residency.

Application procedures. Admission: Priority date 12/1; deadline 8/25. $44 fee, may be waived for applicants with need. Admission notification on a rolling basis beginning on or about 9/15. Must reply by May 1 or within 3 week(s) if notified thereafter. Closing and priority dates may vary by program. **Financial aid:** Priority date 4/15; no closing date. FAFSA required. Applicants notified on a rolling basis starting 4/15.

Academics. Baccalaureate degree includes service-learning requirement, freshman seminars, capstone courses, internships in most majors, and opportunities for students to collaborate with faculty on research and scholarly projects. **Special study options:** Accelerated study, combined bachelor's/ graduate degree, distance learning, double major, dual enrollment of high school students, ESL, exchange student, external degree, honors, independent study, internships, student-designed major, study abroad, teacher certification program. Collaborative programs in Early Childhood Education. **Credit/ placement by examination:** AP, CLEP, IB, institutional tests. 15 credit hours maximum toward associate degree, 30 toward bachelor's. **Support services:** Learning center, pre-admission summer program, reduced course load, remedial instruction, study skills assistance, tutoring, writing center.

Majors. Area/ethnic studies: Latin American, Native American, women's. **Biology:** General, molecular. **Business:** Accounting, business admin, finance, information resources management, international, marketing, organizational leadership. **Communications:** Communications/speech/rhetoric, journalism, media studies. **Computer sciences:** General. **Education:** Elementary, science, social studies, special ed. **English:** English lit. **Foreign languages:** French, Germanic, Spanish. **Health services:** Athletic training, communication disorders, environmental health, health care admin, nursing (RN). **History:** General. **Human services:** Social work. **Liberal arts:** Arts/sciences. **Math:** General. **Parks/recreation:** Exercise sciences. **Philosophy/religion:** Philosophy, religion. **Physical sciences:** Chemistry, geology, physics. **Protective services:** Criminal justice. **Psychology:** General. **Social sciences:** Economics, geography, political science, sociology. **Visual/performing arts:** Art, dramatic, music.

Most popular majors. Biology 6%, business/marketing 20%, communications/journalism 6%, education 7%, health sciences 14%, parks/recreation 6%, psychology 6%, visual/performing arts 6%.

Technology on campus. 900 workstations in dormitories, library, computer center, student center. Dormitories wired for high-speed internet access and linked to campus network. Commuter students can connect to campus network. Online course registration, online library, helpline, wireless network available.

Student life. Freshman orientation: Mandatory, $175 fee. Preregistration for classes offered. One-day session, 20 dates to choose from in June. **Housing:** Guaranteed on-campus for freshmen. Coed dorms, single-sex dorms, apartments, themed housing, wellness housing available. $75 fully refundable deposit. **Activities:** Bands, campus ministries, choral groups, dance, drama, film society, international student organizations, literary magazine, music ensembles, Model UN, musical theater, opera, radio station, student government, student newspaper, symphony orchestra, TV station, College Republicans, College Democrats, Newman Student Association, Ecumenical Religious Center Student Association, Alpha Phi Omega Service Fraternity, Mortar Board, Black Student Organization, Native American Student Organization, Hmong Student Organization.

Athletics. NCAA. **Intercollegiate:** Basketball, cross-country, diving, football (tackle) M, golf, gymnastics W, ice hockey, soccer W, softball W, swimming, tennis, track and field, volleyball W, wrestling M. **Intramural:** Basketball, football (non-tackle), soccer, softball, tennis, ultimate frisbee, volleyball. **Team name:** Blugolds.

Student services. Adult student services, alcohol/substance abuse counseling, career counseling, services for economically disadvantaged, student employment services, financial aid counseling, health services, legal services, minority student services, on-campus daycare, personal counseling, placement for graduates, veterans' counselor, women's services. **Physically disabled:** Services for visually, speech, hearing impaired.

Contact. E-mail: admissions@uwec.edu
Phone: (715) 836-5415 Fax: (715) 836-2409
Heather Kretz, Admissions Director, University of Wisconsin-Eau Claire, 111 Schofield Hall, Eau Claire, WI 54701

University of Wisconsin-Green Bay

Green Bay, Wisconsin
www.uwgb.edu

CB member
CB code: 1859

- Public 4-year university and liberal arts college
- Residential campus in small city
- 5,487 degree-seeking undergraduates: 28% part-time, 67% women, 2% African American, 3% Asian American, 4% Hispanic/Latino, 1% Native American, 2% Multi-racial, non-Hispanic, 1% international
- 218 degree-seeking graduate students
- 85% of applicants admitted
- SAT or ACT (ACT writing optional) required
- 47% graduate within 6 years; 25% enter graduate study

General. Founded in 1965. Regionally accredited. **Degrees:** 1,283 bachelor's, 20 associate awarded; master's offered. **ROTC:** Army. **Location:** 80 miles from Milwaukee. **Calendar:** Semester, limited summer session. **Full-time faculty:** 187 total; 88% have terminal degrees, 22% minority, 48% women. **Part-time faculty:** 134 total; 60% women. **Class size:** 32% < 20, 50% 20-39, 8% 40-49, 8% 50-99, 1% >100. **Special facilities:** Natural history museum, herbarium, 290-acre arboretum, performing arts center.

Freshman class profile. 2,138 applied, 1,811 admitted, 789 enrolled.

Mid 50% test scores		Return as sophomores:	75%
ACT composite:	21-25	Out-of-state:	6%
GPA 3.75 or higher:	25%	Live on campus:	80%
GPA 3.50-3.74:	21%	International:	2%
GPA 3.0-3.49:	38%	Fraternities:	1%
GPA 2.0-2.99:	16%	Sororities:	1%
End year in good standing:	85%		

Basis for selection. 17 ACT, 2.25 GPA and extracurricular or community involvement important. Priority given to students with 23 ACT or 3.25 GPA. Students not meeting standard admission requirements may be considered on individual basis. Interview may be requested of borderline applicants; audition required for music. **Home schooled:** Transcript of courses and grades required.

High school preparation. College-preparatory program required. 17 units required; 19 recommended. Required and recommended units include English 4, mathematics 3, social studies 3, science 3 (laboratory 1), foreign language 2 and academic electives 4. Math must include algebra or more advanced course. 2 of the 4 required academic electives must be from English, math, science, social studies, or foreign language.

2015-2016 Annual costs. Tuition/fees: $7,824; $15,397 out-of-state. Room/board: $7,270. Books/supplies: $800. Personal expenses: $2,100.

2015-2016 Financial aid. Need-based: 702 full-time freshmen applied for aid; 471 deemed to have need; 456 received aid. Average need met was 70%. Average scholarship/grant was $6,244; average loan $3,161. 53% of total undergraduate aid awarded as scholarships/grants, 47% as loans/jobs. **Non-need-based:** Awarded to 484 full-time undergraduates, including 156 freshmen. Scholarships awarded for academics, art, athletics, leadership, minority status, music/drama. **Additional information:** Auditions required for music and theater scholarships. Tuition is waived for eligible Wisconsin veterans and their family members under the Wisconsin GI Bill. Veterans from outside of Wisconsin are charged the in-state tuition rate regardless of residency. Waivers for children of Wisconsin police/firemen who were slain in the line of duty.

Application procedures. Admission: Priority date 4/15; no deadline. $44 fee, may be waived for applicants with need. Admission notification on a rolling basis beginning on or about 9/15. **Financial aid:** Priority date 4/1; no closing date. FAFSA required. Applicants notified on a rolling basis starting 1/1; must reply within 3 week(s) of notification.

Academics. Teacher certification available in conjunction with bachelor's degree. **Special study options:** Combined bachelor's/graduate degree, distance learning, double major, dual enrollment of high school students, exchange student, external degree, independent study, internships, liberal arts/career combination, student-designed major, study abroad, teacher certification program. **Credit/placement by examination:** AP, CLEP, IB, ACT, institutional tests. 47 credit hours maximum toward associate degree, 93 toward bachelor's. **Support services:** Pre-admission summer program, reduced course load, remedial instruction, study skills assistance, tutoring, writing center.

Majors. Area/ethnic studies: Native American. **Biology:** General. **Business:** Accounting, business admin. **Communications:** Communications/speech/rhetoric. **Computer sciences:** Computer science, information systems. **Conservation:** Environmental science, environmental studies. **Education:** Elementary, music. **English:** English lit. **Foreign languages:** French, German, Spanish. **Health services:** Health information management, nursing (RN). **History:** General. **Human services:** General, social work. **Liberal arts:** Arts/sciences, humanities. **Math:** General. **Philosophy/religion:** Philosophy. **Physical sciences:** Chemistry, physics. **Psychology:** General. **Social sciences:** Economics, political science, urban studies. **Visual/performing arts:** Art, arts management, design, dramatic, music, music performance.

Most popular majors. Business/marketing 15%, health sciences 8%, interdisciplinary studies 17%, liberal arts 11%, psychology 8%, social sciences 6%.

Technology on campus. 600 workstations in dormitories, library, computer center, student center. Dormitories wired for high-speed internet access and linked to campus network. Commuter students can connect to campus network. Online course registration, online library, helpline, repair service, wireless network available.

Student life. Freshman orientation: Available, $212 fee. Preregistration for classes offered. Held for 2-3 days during the week before fall classes begin. **Housing:** Coed dorms, apartments, wellness housing available. $225 fully refundable deposit. Suite-style apartments with private bathrooms available. **Activities:** Bands, choral groups, dance, drama, film society, international student organizations, literary magazine, music ensembles, Model UN, musical theater, radio station, student government, student newspaper, TV station, College Republicans, College Democrats, Habitat for Humanity, Circle K, Ten Percent Society, Athletes in Action, American Marketing Association, psychology and human development club, Wisconsin Education Association Council.

Athletics. NCAA. **Intercollegiate:** Basketball, cheerleading, cross-country, diving, golf, skiing, soccer, softball W, swimming, tennis, volleyball W. **Intramural:** Basketball, football (non-tackle), golf, racquetball, soccer, softball, tennis, volleyball. **Team name:** Phoenix.

Student services. Adult student services, alcohol/substance abuse counseling, career counseling, student employment services, financial aid counseling, health services, minority student services, personal counseling, placement for graduates, veterans' counselor. **Physically disabled:** Services for visually, hearing impaired.

Contact. E-mail: admissions@uwgb.edu
Phone: (920) 465-2111 Toll-free number: (800) 621-2313
Fax: (920) 465-5754
Jen Jones, Director of Admissions, University of Wisconsin-Green Bay, 2420 Nicolet Drive, Green Bay, WI 54311-7001

University of Wisconsin-La Crosse
La Crosse, Wisconsin   **CB member**
www.uwlax.edu   **CB code: 1914**

- Public 4-year university
- Residential campus in small city
- 9,424 degree-seeking undergraduates: 4% part-time, 56% women, 1% African American, 2% Asian American, 3% Hispanic/Latino, 3% Multi-racial, non-Hispanic, 1% international
- 745 degree-seeking graduate students
- 80% of applicants admitted
- SAT or ACT (ACT writing optional) required
- 69% graduate within 6 years

General. Founded in 1909. Regionally accredited. **Degrees:** 1,933 bachelor's, 27 associate awarded; master's, doctoral offered. **ROTC:** Army. **Location:** 140 miles from Madison, 160 miles from Minneapolis-St. Paul. **Calendar:** Semester, limited summer session. **Full-time faculty:** 522 total; 84% have terminal degrees, 12% minority, 51% women. **Part-time faculty:** 94 total; 36% have terminal degrees, 8% minority, 58% women. **Class size:** 29% < 20, 57% 20-39, 3% 40-49, 10% 50-99, 1% >100. **Special facilities:** Greenhouse, planetarium, nuclear radiation laboratory, river studies center, archaeology center.

Freshman class profile. 5,975 applied, 4,765 admitted, 2,054 enrolled.

Mid 50% test scores		Rank in top tenth:	23%
SAT critical reading:	520-580	Return as sophomores:	85%
SAT math:	520-590	Out-of-state:	17%
SAT writing:	510-580	Live on campus:	95%
ACT composite:	23-26	Fraternities:	1%
Rank in top quarter:	61%	Sororities:	1%

Basis for selection. Academic preparation (rigor of courses, class rank, GPA, test scores) very important. Demonstrated leadership, extracurricular involvement, special talent, personal statement, recommendations, and ability to add diversity to campus community considered. Interviews optional but may be considered. Auditions may be required for some scholarships. Portfolios and essays optional but will be considered. **Home schooled:** Interview may be required. **Learning Disabled:** Information regarding learning disability may be considered in admission decision.

High school preparation. College-preparatory program required. 17 units required; 23 recommended. Required and recommended units include English 4, mathematics 3-4, social studies 3-4, science 3-4 (laboratory 2-3), foreign language 3 and academic electives 4.

2015-2016 Annual costs. Tuition/fees: $8,832; $16,783 out-of-state. Room/board: $5,850. Books/supplies: $300. Personal expenses: $2,000.

2014-2015 Financial aid. **Need-based:** 1,710 full-time freshmen applied for aid; 1,035 deemed to have need; 1,026 received aid. Average need met was 68%. Average scholarship/grant was $5,493; average loan $3,375. 44% of total undergraduate aid awarded as scholarships/grants, 56% as loans/jobs. **Non-need-based:** Awarded to 2,162 full-time undergraduates, including 785 freshmen. Scholarships awarded for academics, alumni affiliation, art, leadership, minority status, music/drama.

Application procedures. **Admission:** Priority date 2/1; no deadline. $44 fee, may be waived for applicants with need. Admission notification on a rolling basis beginning on or about 9/15. **Financial aid:** Priority date 3/15; no closing date. FAFSA required. Applicants notified on a rolling basis starting 4/1.

Academics. **Special study options:** Combined bachelor's/graduate degree, cooperative education, cross-registration, distance learning, double major, dual enrollment of high school students, ESL, exchange student, independent study, internships, liberal arts/career combination, study abroad, teacher certification program. **Credit/placement by examination:** AP, CLEP, IB, SAT, ACT, institutional tests. 16 credit hours maximum toward associate degree, 32 toward bachelor's. **Support services:** Learning center, pre-admission summer program, reduced course load, remedial instruction, study skills assistance, tutoring, writing center.

Majors. **Biology:** General, biochemistry, microbiology. **Business:** Accounting, business admin, finance, international, management information systems, marketing. **Communications:** Communications/speech/rhetoric. **Computer sciences:** General. **Education:** Elementary, health, science, social studies. **English:** English lit. **Foreign languages:** French, German, Spanish. **Health services:** General, athletic training, clinical lab science, community health, medical radiologic technology/radiation therapy, nuclear medical technology, recreational therapy. **History:** General. **Math:** General, statistics. **Parks/recreation:** Exercise sciences, facilities management. **Philosophy/religion:** Philosophy. **Physical sciences:** Chemistry, physics. **Psychology:** General.

Social sciences: Archaeology, economics, geography, political science, sociology. **Visual/performing arts:** Art, dramatic, music.

Most popular majors. Biology 15%, business/marketing 21%, education 8%, health sciences 9%, parks/recreation 8%, psychology 10%, social sciences 9%.

Technology on campus. 200 workstations in dormitories, library, computer center, student center. Dormitories wired for high-speed internet access and linked to campus network. Commuter students can connect to campus network. Online course registration, online library, helpline, wireless network available.

Student life. **Freshman orientation:** Available, $140 fee. Preregistration for classes offered. One-day program held in June and prior to start of fall term. **Housing:** Coed dorms, special housing for disabled, apartments, themed housing available. $75 fully refundable deposit, deadline 5/1. First Year Experience housing available. **Activities:** Bands, campus ministries, choral groups, dance, drama, international student organizations, literary magazine, music ensembles, musical theater, radio station, student government, student newspaper, symphony orchestra, TV station, Black Students Unity, Native American Council, Hispanic student organization, Asian association, Amnesty International, Newman Club, hall councils, Intervarsity Christian Fellowship, Cru.

Athletics. NAIA, NCAA. **Intercollegiate:** Baseball M, basketball, cross-country, diving, football (tackle) M, gymnastics W, soccer W, softball W, swimming, tennis, track and field, volleyball W, wrestling M. **Intramural:** Badminton, basketball, cheerleading, football (non-tackle), golf, racquetball, soccer, softball, table tennis, tennis, ultimate frisbee, volleyball, weight lifting. **Team name:** Eagles.

Student services. Adult student services, alcohol/substance abuse counseling, chaplain/spiritual director, career counseling, services for economically disadvantaged, student employment services, financial aid counseling, health services, legal services, minority student services, on-campus daycare, personal counseling, placement for graduates, veterans' counselor, women's services. **Physically disabled:** Services for visually, speech, hearing impaired.

Contact. E-mail: admissions@uwlax.edu
Phone: (608) 785-8939 Fax: (608) 785-8940
Corey Sjoquist, Director of Admissions, University of Wisconsin-La Crosse, 1725 State Street, Cleary Center, La Crosse, WI 54601

University of Wisconsin-Madison
Madison, Wisconsin   **CB member**
www.wisc.edu   **CB code: 1846**

- Public 4-year university
- Residential campus in small city
- 29,580 degree-seeking undergraduates: 5% part-time, 51% women
- 11,727 degree-seeking graduate students
- 49% of applicants admitted
- SAT or ACT with writing, application essay required

General. Founded in 1849. Regionally accredited. **Degrees:** 6,854 bachelor's awarded; master's, professional, doctoral offered. **ROTC:** Army, Naval, Air Force. **Location:** 90 miles from Milwaukee, 150 miles from Chicago. **Calendar:** Semester, extensive summer session. **Full-time faculty:** 2,443 total; 92% have terminal degrees, 18% minority, 38% women. **Part-time faculty:** 453 total; 65% have terminal degrees, 9% minority, 49% women. **Class size:** 46% < 20, 29% 20-39, 6% 40-49, 10% 50-99, 9% >100. **Special facilities:** Teaching nuclear reactor, observatory, botanical gardens, arboretum, museums.

Freshman class profile. 32,780 applied, 16,121 admitted, 6,270 enrolled.

GPA 3.75 or higher:	76%	Rank in top tenth:	56%
GPA 3.50-3.74:	18%	Out-of-state:	37%
GPA 3.0-3.49:	5%	Live on campus:	92%
GPA 2.0-2.99:	1%	Fraternities:	9%
Rank in top quarter:	94%	Sororities:	8%

Basis for selection. Secondary school record including level of challenge relative to high school offerings, evidence of either increasing or consistent level of academic challenge and performance, course grades, class rank, ACT or SAT test scores important. Application statement/essay, recommendations, extracurricular activities and personal characteristics also considered. Audition required for music; portfolio recommended for fine arts.

High school preparation. College-preparatory program required. 19 units required; 22 recommended. Required and recommended units include English 4, mathematics 4, social studies 3-4, science 3-4, foreign language 3-4 and academic electives 2. Math units must include 1 each algebra and geometry, plus 1 year advanced math. Statistics, business math, and/or computer courses will not fulfill math requirement. Applicants strongly advised to present academic credentials well in excess of minimum units.

2015-2016 Annual costs. Tuition/fees: $10,415; $29,665 out-of-state. Room/board: $8,804. Books/supplies: $1,200. Personal expenses: $3,286. **Additional information:** Wisconsin has a tuition reciprocity agreement with Minnesota. Minnesota students pay $12,240 plus required fees ($1142).

2015-2016 Financial aid. Need-based: 56% of total undergraduate aid awarded as scholarships/grants, 44% as loans/jobs. **Non-need-based:** Scholarships awarded for academics, alumni affiliation, art, athletics, job skills, leadership, minority status, music/drama, ROTC, state residency.

Application procedures. Admission: Closing date 2/1 (receipt date). $44 fee, may be waived for applicants with need. Admission notification on a rolling basis beginning on or about 11/1. Must reply by 5/1. **Financial aid:** No deadline. FAFSA required. Applicants notified on a rolling basis starting 4/1; must reply within 3 week(s) of notification.

Academics. Special study options: Accelerated study, combined bachelor's/graduate degree, cooperative education, distance learning, double major, dual enrollment of high school students, ESL, exchange student, honors, independent study, internships, liberal arts/career combination, student-designed major, study abroad, teacher certification program. **Credit/placement by examination:** AP, CLEP, IB, institutional tests. **Support services:** Learning center, pre-admission summer program, reduced course load, remedial instruction, study skills assistance, tutoring, writing center.

Majors. Architecture: Landscape. **Area/ethnic studies:** African-American, Asian, Latin American/Caribbean, Scandinavian, women's. **Biology:** General, biochemistry, botany, conservation, entomology, genetics, microbiology, molecular, pharmacology/toxicology, plant pathology, zoology. **Business:** General, accounting, actuarial science, business admin, finance, financial planning, insurance, international, management information systems, marketing, operations, real estate, retailing. **Communications:** Communications/speech/rhetoric, journalism. **Computer sciences:** General. **Conservation:** Environmental science, environmental studies, forest sciences, wildlife/wilderness. **Education:** Art, elementary, music, physical, special ed. **Engineering:** Agricultural, applied physics, biomedical, chemical, civil, computer, electrical, engineering mechanics, geological, industrial, materials, mechanical, nuclear. **English:** English lit. **Foreign languages:** African, Chinese, classics, comparative lit, French, Germanic, Italian, Japanese, Latin, linguistics, Polish, Portuguese, Russian, Spanish. **Health services:** Athletic training, audiology/speech pathology, nursing (RN), premedicine, vocational rehab counseling. **History:** General, science/technology. **Human services:** Social work. **Math:** General, applied, statistics. **Parks/recreation:** Exercise sciences. **Philosophy/religion:** Judaic, philosophy, religion. **Physical sciences:** Astrophysics, atmospheric science, chemistry, geology, physics. **Psychology:** General. **Social sciences:** Anthropology, economics, geography, GIS/cartography, political science, rural sociology, sociology. **Visual/performing arts:** Art, art history/conservation, dance, dramatic, interior design, music, music performance. **Work/family studies:** Clothing/textiles, family studies, family/community services.

Most popular majors. Biology 12%, business/marketing 12%, communications/journalism 6%, engineering/engineering technologies 10%, social sciences 14%.

Technology on campus. 3,350 workstations in dormitories, library, computer center, student center. Dormitories wired for high-speed internet access and linked to campus network. Commuter students can connect to campus network. Online course registration, online library, helpline, repair service, student web hosting, wireless network available.

Student life. Freshman orientation: Mandatory, $200 fee. Preregistration for classes offered. Held in the summer. **Policies:** Freshmen not permitted cars on campus. **Housing:** Coed dorms, single-sex dorms, cooperative housing, fraternity/sorority housing, themed housing, wellness housing available. $300 partly refundable deposit, deadline 5/1. Residential learning communities, apartments for student families available. **Activities:** Bands, choral groups, dance, drama, film society, international student organizations, literary magazine, music ensembles, musical theater, opera, radio station, student government, student newspaper, symphony orchestra, TV station.

Athletics. NCAA. **Intercollegiate:** Basketball, cheerleading, cross-country, football (tackle) M, golf, ice hockey, rowing (crew), soccer, softball W, swimming, tennis, track and field, volleyball W, wrestling M. **Intramural:** Basketball, field hockey, football (non-tackle), ice hockey, soccer, tennis, ultimate frisbee, volleyball. **Team name:** Badgers.

Student services. Adult student services, alcohol/substance abuse counseling, career counseling, services for economically disadvantaged, student employment services, financial aid counseling, health services, minority student services, personal counseling, placement for graduates, veterans' counselor, women's services. **Physically disabled:** Services for visually, speech, hearing impaired.

Contact. E-mail: onwisconsin@admissions.wisc.edu
Phone: (608) 262-3961 Fax: (608) 262-7706
Adele Brumfield, Director of Undergraduate Admissions and Recruitment, University of Wisconsin-Madison, 702 West Johnson Street, Suite 1101, Madison, WI 53715-1007

University of Wisconsin-Milwaukee
Milwaukee, Wisconsin **CB member**
www.uwm.edu **CB code: 1473**

- Public 4-year university
- Residential campus in very large city
- 20,886 degree-seeking undergraduates
- 73% of applicants admitted

General. Founded in 1956. Regionally accredited. **Degrees:** 3,688 bachelor's awarded; master's, professional, doctoral offered. **ROTC:** Army, Naval, Air Force. **Location:** 90 miles from Chicago. **Calendar:** Semester, extensive summer session. **Full-time faculty:** 1,114 total; 76% have terminal degrees, 23% minority, 48% women. **Part-time faculty:** 620 total; 27% have terminal degrees, 11% minority, 48% women. **Class size:** 43% < 20, 41% 20-39, 6% 40-49, 6% 50-99, 4% >100. **Special facilities:** Planetarium, geological museum, American Geological Society Collection.

Freshman class profile. 10,321 applied, 7,499 admitted, 3,316 enrolled.

Mid 50% test scores			
ACT composite:	20-25	GPA 2.0-2.99:	43%
GPA 3.75 or higher:	9%	Rank in top quarter:	27%
GPA 3.50-3.74:	12%	Rank in top tenth:	9%
GPA 3.0-3.49:	33%	Out-of-state:	12%
		Live on campus:	71%

Basis for selection. Academic record and class rank in top half important. If applicant ranks in lower half of class, 21 ACT required. Additional requirements for architecture. Students who do not meet standard admission requirements may apply through Academic Opportunity Program Office. UW System placement exams in Math and English are required for all freshmen. Freshmen may also be placed using UW System exams for Chemistry and Foreign Languages. Audition required for dance, music, theater.

High school preparation. College-preparatory program required. 17 units required; 20 recommended. Required and recommended units include English 4, mathematics 3-4, social studies 3, science 3 (laboratory 1), foreign language 2 and academic electives 2. Math includes algebra, geometry, and beyond. 3 social studies or history required.

2015-2016 Annual costs. Tuition/fees: $9,429; $19,602 out-of-state. Room/board: $10,030. Books/supplies: $800. Personal expenses: $2,000.

2014-2015 Financial aid. Need-based: 2,944 full-time freshmen applied for aid; 2,417 deemed to have need; 2,351 received aid. Average need met was 39%. Average scholarship/grant was $6,340; average loan $3,508. 54% of total undergraduate aid awarded as scholarships/grants, 46% as loans/jobs. **Non-need-based:** Awarded to 2,902 full-time undergraduates, including 719 freshmen. Scholarships awarded for academics, art, athletics, leadership, music/drama.

Application procedures. Admission: Priority date 3/1; no deadline. $44 fee, may be waived for applicants with need. Admission notification on a rolling basis beginning on or about 9/15. **Financial aid:** Priority date 3/1; no closing date. FAFSA required. Applicants notified on a rolling basis starting 3/15.

Academics. Special study options: Accelerated study, combined bachelor's/graduate degree, cooperative education, cross-registration, distance learning, double major, dual enrollment of high school students, ESL, external degree, honors, independent study, internships, liberal arts/career combination, student-designed major, study abroad, teacher certification program, weekend college. **Credit/placement by examination:** AP, CLEP, IB, institutional tests. 52 credit hours maximum toward bachelor's degree. **Support services:** Learning center, pre-admission summer program, reduced course load, remedial instruction, study skills assistance, tutoring, writing center.

Majors. Architecture: Architecture. **Area/ethnic studies:** African-American, Latin American/Caribbean, women's. **Biology:** General, biochemistry, microbiology. **Business:** General, accounting, actuarial science, finance, management information systems, marketing, operations, real estate, training/development. **Communications:** Communications/speech/rhetoric. **Computer sciences:** Computer science, information systems. **Conservation:** Environmental science. **Education:** General, art, music, special ed. **Engineering:** General, civil, computer, electrical, industrial, materials, mechanical. **English:** English lit. **Foreign languages:** Classics, comparative lit, French, Germanic, Italian, linguistics, Russian, Spanish. **Health services:** Athletic training, audiology/speech pathology, clinical lab science, facilities admin, nursing (RN), occupational therapy, premedicine, recreational therapy. **History:** General. **Human services:** Social work. **Math:** General, applied. **Parks/recreation:** Exercise sciences. **Philosophy/religion:** Philosophy, religion. **Physical sciences:** Chemistry, geology, meteorology, physics. **Protective services:** Criminal justice. **Psychology:** General. **Social sciences:** Anthropology, economics, geography, sociology. **Visual/performing arts:** Art, art history/conservation, dance, dramatic, film/cinema/video, music.

Most popular majors. Business/marketing 22%, communications/journalism 6%, education 8%, engineering/engineering technologies 6%, health sciences 9%, social sciences 7%, visual/performing arts 7%.

Technology on campus. 500 workstations in dormitories, library, computer center, student center. Dormitories wired for high-speed internet access and linked to campus network. Commuter students can connect to campus network. Online course registration, online library, helpline, repair service, student web hosting, wireless network available.

Student life. Freshman orientation: Available. Preregistration for classes offered. **Housing:** Coed dorms, special housing for disabled, apartments available. $100 partly refundable deposit. Living Learning communities available. **Activities:** Bands, campus ministries, choral groups, dance, drama, film society, international student organizations, literary magazine, music ensembles, Model UN, musical theater, radio station, student government, student newspaper, symphony orchestra.

Athletics. NCAA. **Intercollegiate:** Baseball M, basketball, cross-country, diving, soccer, swimming, tennis W, track and field, volleyball W. **Intramural:** Badminton, basketball, football (non-tackle), racquetball, soccer, volleyball. **Team name:** Panthers.

Student services. Adult student services, alcohol/substance abuse counseling, career counseling, student employment services, financial aid counseling, health services, legal services, minority student services, on-campus daycare, personal counseling, placement for graduates, veterans' counselor, women's services. **Physically disabled:** Services for visually, speech, hearing impaired.

Contact. E-mail: uwmlook@uwm.edu
Phone: (414) 229-2222 Fax: (414) 229-6940
Brian Troyer, Director of Admissions and Recruitment, University of Wisconsin-Milwaukee, P.O. Box 413, Milwaukee, WI 53201

University of Wisconsin-Oshkosh
Oshkosh, Wisconsin   **CB member**
www.uwosh.edu   **CB code: 1916**

- Public 4-year university
- Residential campus in small city
- 9,935 degree-seeking undergraduates: 14% part-time, 57% women, 2% African American, 4% Asian American, 4% Hispanic/Latino, 1% Native American, 2% Multi-racial, non-Hispanic, 1% international
- 933 degree-seeking graduate students
- 68% of applicants admitted
- ACT (writing optional) required
- 51% graduate within 6 years

General. Founded in 1871. Regionally accredited. **Degrees:** 2,045 bachelor's, 24 associate awarded; master's, professional offered. **ROTC:** Army. **Location:** 90 miles from Milwaukee. **Calendar:** Semester, limited summer session. **Full-time faculty:** 427 total; 79% have terminal degrees, 10% minority, 47% women. **Part-time faculty:** 183 total; 27% have terminal degrees, 7% minority, 74% women. **Class size:** 41% < 20, 47% 20-39, 3% 40-49, 7% 50-99, 3% >100. **Special facilities:** Planetarium.

Freshman class profile. 5,660 applied, 3,870 admitted, 1,567 enrolled.

Mid 50% test scores		End year in good standing:	85%
ACT composite:	20-24	Return as sophomores:	78%
GPA 3.75 or higher:	12%	Out-of-state:	6%
GPA 3.50-3.74:	16%	Live on campus:	91%
GPA 3.0-3.49:	46%	International:	1%
GPA 2.0-2.99:	26%	Fraternities:	4%
Rank in top quarter:	31%	Sororities:	3%
Rank in top tenth:	8%		

Basis for selection. Students must rank in top half of high school class or have 22 ACT if rank is in third quartile. Out-of-state applicants may submit SAT scores. Interview recommended for all; audition required for music. **Home schooled:** State high school equivalency certificate required.

High school preparation. College-preparatory program required. 17 units required. Required and recommended units include English 4, mathematics

3-4, social studies 3-4, history 1, science 3-4 (laboratory 3), foreign language 2, visual/performing arts 1 and academic electives 4. Social studies must include 1 history.

2015-2016 Annual costs. Books/supplies: $1,000. Personal expenses: $500.

Financial aid. Non-need-based: Scholarships awarded for academics, art, job skills, leadership, minority status, music/drama, ROTC, state residency.

Application procedures. Admission: No deadline. $44 fee, may be waived for applicants with need. Admission notification on a rolling basis beginning on or about 9/15. **Financial aid:** Priority date 3/15; no closing date. FAFSA required. Applicants notified on a rolling basis starting 4/15; must reply within 2 week(s) of notification.

Academics. Special study options: Accelerated study, combined bachelor's/graduate degree, cooperative education, distance learning, double major, dual enrollment of high school students, ESL, exchange student, honors, independent study, internships, liberal arts/career combination, student-designed major, study abroad, teacher certification program, weekend college. **Credit/placement by examination:** AP, CLEP, IB, institutional tests. 32 credit hours maximum toward bachelor's degree. **Support services:** Learning center, pre-admission summer program, reduced course load, study skills assistance, tutoring, writing center.

Majors. Biology: General, bacteriology. **Business:** Accounting, finance, human resources, management information systems, operations. **Communications:** Broadcast journalism, communications/speech/rhetoric, journalism, persuasive communications. **Computer sciences:** Computer science. **Education:** Elementary, emotionally handicapped, learning disabled, mentally handicapped, music, physical, science, secondary, social science, special ed. **English:** English lit. **Foreign languages:** French, German, Spanish. **Health services:** Clinical lab technology, nursing (RN), predental, premedicine, prepharmacy, preveterinary. **History:** General. **Human services:** Social work. **Liberal arts:** Arts/sciences. **Math:** General. **Philosophy/religion:** Philosophy, religion. **Physical sciences:** Chemistry, geology, physics. **Psychology:** General. **Social sciences:** Anthropology, economics, geography, political science, sociology, urban studies. **Visual/performing arts:** Art, cinematography, dramatic, music, studio arts.

Most popular majors. Business/marketing 18%, communications/journalism 8%, education 14%, health sciences 13%, public administration/social services 7%.

Technology on campus. 475 workstations in dormitories, library, computer center, student center. Dormitories wired for high-speed internet access and linked to campus network. Commuter students can connect to campus network. Online course registration, online library, helpline, wireless network available.

Student life. Freshman orientation: Available. Preregistration for classes offered. **Policies:** Select group of freshmen take part in residential college experience with more individualized instruction. **Housing:** Guaranteed on-campus for freshmen. Coed dorms, fraternity/sorority housing, themed housing available. $150 partly refundable deposit, deadline 5/1. **Activities:** Pep band, campus ministries, choral groups, dance, drama, film society, international student organizations, music ensembles, Model UN, radio station, student government, student newspaper, TV station, black student union, Asian student association, American Indian student association, Hispanic Cultures United, InterVarsity Christian Fellowship, Athletes in Action, community involvement program, Habitat for Humanity.

Athletics. NCAA. **Intercollegiate:** Baseball M, basketball, cross-country, diving, football (tackle) M, golf W, gymnastics W, rifle, soccer W, softball W, swimming, track and field, volleyball W, wrestling M. **Intramural:** Basketball, racquetball, skiing, soccer, softball, volleyball. **Team name:** Titans.

Student services. Adult student services, alcohol/substance abuse counseling, career counseling, services for economically disadvantaged, student employment services, financial aid counseling, health services, legal services, minority student services, on-campus daycare, personal counseling, placement for graduates, veterans' counselor, women's services. **Physically disabled:** Services for visually, speech, hearing impaired.

Contact. E-mail: admissions@uwosh.edu
Phone: (920) 424-3164 Fax: (920) 424-1207
Jill Endries, Director of Admissions, University of Wisconsin-Oshkosh, 800 Algoma Boulevard, Oshkosh, WI 54901-8602

University of Wisconsin-Parkside
Kenosha, Wisconsin

CB member
www.uwp.edu
CB code: 1860

- Public 4-year university
- Commuter campus in small city
- 4,168 degree-seeking undergraduates: 22% part-time, 52% women, 9% African American, 3% Asian American, 13% Hispanic/Latino, 4% Multiracial, non-Hispanic, 2% international
- 118 degree-seeking graduate students
- 82% of applicants admitted
- 33% graduate within 6 years

General. Founded in 1968. Regionally accredited. **Degrees:** 690 bachelor's awarded; master's offered. **ROTC:** Army. **Location:** 30 miles from Milwaukee, 60 miles from Chicago. **Calendar:** Semester, extensive summer session. **Full-time faculty:** 160 total; 76% have terminal degrees, 24% minority, 50% women. **Part-time faculty:** 71 total; 24% have terminal degrees, 8% minority, 45% women. **Class size:** 47% < 20, 37% 20-39, 9% 40-49, 7% 50-99, less than 1% >100.

Freshman class profile. 1,662 applied, 1,356 admitted, 620 enrolled.

Mid 50% test scores		Rank in top quarter:	37%
ACT composite:	18-23	Rank in top tenth:	12%
GPA 3.75 or higher:	9%	Return as sophomores:	74%
GPA 3.50-3.74:	13%	Out-of-state:	15%
GPA 3.0-3.49:	29%	Live on campus:	34%
GPA 2.0-2.99:	47%	International:	1%

Basis for selection. Rank in top half of class with specified distribution of high school units required for standard admission. Conditional admissions may be granted to applicants in top 65% of class or with 18 ACT. Students age 21 or older are not required to submit ACT or SAT scores. Test scores also used for placement in English and math courses. Audition required for theater, recommended for music; portfolio recommended for art.

High school preparation. College-preparatory program required. 17 units required; 20 recommended. Required and recommended units include English 4, mathematics 3-4, social studies 3-4, science 3-4 (laboratory 1-2), foreign language 2 and academic electives 4-7.

2015-2016 Annual costs. Tuition/fees: $7,481; $15,470 out-of-state. Room/board: $7,712. Books/supplies: $752. Personal expenses: $1,812. **Additional information:** Minnesota reciprocity tuition: $293.15 per-credit-hour. Midwest Student Exchange Program tuition: $393.65 per-credit-hour.

2014-2015 Financial aid. Need-based: 470 full-time freshmen applied for aid; 363 deemed to have need; 363 received aid. Average need met was 66%. Average scholarship/grant was $6,574; average loan $3,471. 59% of total undergraduate aid awarded as scholarships/grants, 41% as loans/jobs. **Non-need-based:** Awarded to 964 full-time undergraduates, including 209 freshmen. Scholarships awarded for academics, art, athletics, leadership, music/drama, state residency.

Application procedures. Admission: Priority date 3/1; deadline 7/15 (postmark date). $44 fee, may be waived for applicants with need. Admission notification on a rolling basis beginning on or about 9/15. **Financial aid:** Priority date 3/15; no closing date. FAFSA required. Applicants notified on a rolling basis starting 4/1; must reply within 2 week(s) of notification.

Academics. Special study options: Combined bachelor's/graduate degree, distance learning, double major, dual enrollment of high school students, exchange student, honors, independent study, internships, liberal arts/career combination, study abroad, teacher certification program, weekend college. Cooperative nursing program with University of Wisconsin-Milwaukee. **Credit/placement by examination:** AP, CLEP, IB, SAT, ACT, institutional tests. 30 credit hours maximum toward bachelor's degree. Retroactive credit policy for foreign language study. **Support services:** Learning center, reduced course load, remedial instruction, study skills assistance, tutoring, writing center.

Majors. Area/ethnic studies: French, German. **Biology:** General, molecular. **Business:** General, accounting, business admin, finance, human resources, management information systems. **Communications:** Communications/speech/rhetoric. **Computer sciences:** Computer science. **English:** English lit. **Foreign languages:** French, German, Spanish. **Health services:** Predental, premedicine, preveterinary. **History:** General. **Liberal arts:** Arts/sciences. **Math:** General. **Parks/recreation:** Sports admin. **Philosophy/religion:** Philosophy. **Physical sciences:** Chemistry, geology, physics. **Protective services:** Criminal justice. **Psychology:** General. **Social sciences:** Economics, geography, political science, sociology. **Visual/performing arts:** Art, dramatic, music.

Most popular majors. Biology 6%, business/marketing 24%, parks/recreation 8%, psychology 10%, security/protective services 12%, social sciences 10%, visual/performing arts 6%.

Technology on campus. 225 workstations in dormitories, library, computer center, student center. Dormitories wired for high-speed internet access and linked to campus network. Commuter students can connect to campus network. Online course registration, online library, helpline, student web hosting, wireless network available.

Student life. Freshman orientation: Mandatory, $52 fee. Preregistration for classes offered. Day-long session offered several times throughout summer. **Housing:** Coed dorms, special housing for disabled, apartments, themed housing available. **Activities:** Bands, choral groups, dance, drama, international student organizations, literary magazine, music ensembles, musical theater, radio station, student government, student newspaper, symphony orchestra, Campus Crusade for Christ, Intervarsity Christian Fellowship, ethnic organization, Amnesty International, black student union, activities board.

Athletics. NCAA. **Intercollegiate:** Baseball M, basketball, cross-country, golf M, soccer, softball W, track and field, volleyball W, wrestling M. **Intramural:** Basketball, racquetball, soccer, softball, table tennis, tennis, volleyball. **Team name:** Rangers.

Student services. Adult student services, alcohol/substance abuse counseling, career counseling, services for economically disadvantaged, student employment services, financial aid counseling, health services, minority student services, on-campus daycare, personal counseling, placement for graduates, veterans' counselor, women's services. **Physically disabled:** Services for visually, speech, hearing impaired.

Contact. E-mail: admissions@uwp.edu
Phone: (262) 595-2355 Fax: (262) 595-2008
Troy Moldenhauer, Director of Admissions and Recruitment, University of Wisconsin-Parkside, PO Box 2000, Kenosha, WI 53141-2000

University of Wisconsin-Platteville
Platteville, Wisconsin

CB member
www.uwplatt.edu
CB code: 1917

- Public 4-year university
- Residential campus in large town
- 7,785 degree-seeking undergraduates: 9% part-time, 34% women, 1% African American, 1% Asian American, 3% Hispanic/Latino, 2% Multiracial, non-Hispanic, 1% international
- 843 degree-seeking graduate students
- 77% of applicants admitted
- SAT or ACT (ACT writing optional) required
- 53% graduate within 6 years

General. Founded in 1866. Regionally accredited. **Degrees:** 1,468 bachelor's, 1 associate awarded; master's offered. **ROTC:** Army. **Location:** 25 miles from Dubuque, IA; 75 miles from Madison. **Calendar:** Semester, limited summer session. **Full-time faculty:** 347 total; 23% minority, 38% women. **Part-time faculty:** 79 total; 11% minority, 46% women. **Class size:** 20% < 20, 68% 20-39, 8% 40-49, 3% 50-99, 1% >100. **Special facilities:** Pioneer farm, nature trail, disc golf course, cadaver lab, forensic crime scene house, radio station.

Freshman class profile. 4,401 applied, 3,393 admitted, 1,621 enrolled.

Mid 50% test scores		Return as sophomores:	74%
ACT composite:	21-26	Out-of-state:	20%
Rank in top quarter:	35%	Live on campus:	99%
Rank in top tenth:	11%	International:	1%

Basis for selection. Class rank, test scores, and high school transcripts are most important. Audition required for music scholarships. **Home schooled:** Transcript of courses and grades required.

High school preparation. College-preparatory program recommended. 17 units required. Required units include English 4, mathematics 3, science 3 (laboratory 3) and academic electives 4.

2015-2016 Annual costs. Tuition/fees: $7,488; $15,339 out-of-state. Room/board: $7,160. Books/supplies: $400. Personal expenses: $2,000.

2015-2016 Financial aid. All financial aid based on need. 1,364 full-time freshmen applied for aid; 1,203 deemed to have need; 1,203 received aid. Average need met was 64%. Average scholarship/grant was $4,093; average loan $2,830. 32% of total undergraduate aid awarded as scholarships/grants, 68% as loans/jobs.

Application procedures. Admission: No deadline. $44 fee, may be waived for applicants with need. Admission notification on a rolling basis beginning on or about 9/15. Must reply by 6/1. **Financial aid:** Priority date 3/15; no closing date. FAFSA required. Applicants notified on a rolling basis starting 6/1; must reply within 2 week(s) of notification.

Academics. Special study options: Combined bachelor's/graduate degree, cooperative education, distance learning, double major, dual enrollment of high school students, ESL, exchange student, external degree, honors, independent study, internships, student-designed major, study abroad, teacher certification program. **Credit/placement by examination:** AP, CLEP, institutional tests. 30 credit hours maximum toward bachelor's degree. **Support services:** Learning center, study skills assistance, tutoring, writing center.

Majors. Biology: General. **Business:** General, accounting, business admin, entrepreneurial studies, finance, human resources, investments/securities, organizational behavior. **Communications:** Communications/speech/rhetoric. **Computer sciences:** Computer science. **Conservation:** General. **Education:** Agricultural, art, biology, chemistry, early childhood, elementary, English, German, history, mathematics, science, social science, social studies, Spanish, speech, technology/industrial arts, voc/tech. **Engineering:** General, applied physics, civil, electrical, environmental, industrial, mechanical, software. **English:** English lit. **Foreign languages:** German, Spanish. **General:** Maintenance. **History:** General. **Liberal arts:** Arts/sciences. **Math:** General. **Parks/recreation:** Health/fitness. **Philosophy/religion:** Philosophy. **Physical sciences:** Chemistry, physics. **Protective services:** Law enforcement admin. **Psychology:** General. **Social sciences:** General, economics, geography, political science, sociology. **Visual/performing arts:** Art, commercial/advertising art, dramatic, music.

Most popular majors. Agriculture 12%, biology 6%, business/marketing 15%, education 11%, engineering/engineering technologies 30%, security/protective services 10%.

Technology on campus. Dormitories wired for high-speed internet access and linked to campus network. Commuter students can connect to campus network. Online course registration, online library, helpline, repair service, student web hosting available.

Student life. Freshman orientation: Available. Preregistration for classes offered. **Policies:** Student governance is given authority under Wisconsin state statute. **Housing:** Guaranteed on-campus for freshmen. Coed dorms, single-sex dorms, special housing for disabled, apartments, themed housing, wellness housing available. $150 partly refundable deposit. **Activities:** Bands, campus ministries, choral groups, dance, drama, international student organizations, literary magazine, music ensembles, musical theater, opera, radio station, student government, student newspaper, symphony orchestra, TV station, black student union, ASIA student group, Hmong club, inter-tribal council, Young Democrats, College Republicans, Circle K, InterVarsity, Campus Crusade.

Athletics. NCAA. **Intercollegiate:** Baseball M, basketball, cross-country, football (tackle) M, golf W, soccer, softball W, track and field, volleyball W, wrestling M. **Intramural:** Badminton, basketball, bowling, football (non-tackle), racquetball, soccer, softball, tennis, ultimate frisbee, volleyball, water polo. **Team name:** Pioneers.

Student services. Adult student services, alcohol/substance abuse counseling, career counseling, services for economically disadvantaged, student employment services, financial aid counseling, health services, minority student services, on-campus daycare, personal counseling, placement for graduates, veterans' counselor, women's services. **Physically disabled:** Services for visually, speech, hearing impaired.

Contact. E-mail: admit@uwplatt.edu
Phone: (608) 342-1125 Toll-free number: (800) 362-5515
Fax: (608) 342-1122
Heidi Tuescher-Gille, Director of Admissions and Enrollment Services, University of Wisconsin-Platteville, One University Plaza, Platteville, WI 53818

University of Wisconsin-River Falls
River Falls, Wisconsin
www.uwrf.edu   **CB code: 1918**

- Public 4-year university and liberal arts college
- Residential campus in large town
- 5,278 degree-seeking undergraduates: 9% part-time, 61% women, 2% African American, 3% Asian American, 3% Hispanic/Latino, 2% Multiracial, non-Hispanic, 1% international
- 431 degree-seeking graduate students
- 90% of applicants admitted

- SAT or ACT (ACT writing optional), application essay required
- 55% graduate within 6 years; 24% enter graduate study

General. Founded in 1874. Regionally accredited. **Degrees:** 1,182 bachelor's awarded; master's offered. **ROTC:** Army. **Location:** 30 miles from Minneapolis-St. Paul. **Calendar:** Semester, limited summer session. **Full-time faculty:** 171 total; 6% minority, 39% women. **Part-time faculty:** 72 total; 1% minority, 49% women. **Class size:** 43% < 20, 40% 20-39, 9% 40-49, 6% 50-99, 1% >100. **Special facilities:** 2 laboratory farms, 20-inch reflecting telescope, USDA-approved food science laboratory, computerized greenhouse, 42-foot rappelling and climbing wall, indoor track and field house, ice arena, electron microscope, observatory, education regional archive collection.

Freshman class profile. 2,467 applied, 2,215 admitted, 1,066 enrolled.

Mid 50% test scores		GPA 2.0-2.99:	25%
SAT critical reading:	430-540	Rank in top quarter:	33%
SAT math:	410-540	Rank in top tenth:	10%
SAT writing:	390-490	End year in good standing:	78%
ACT composite:	20-25	Return as sophomores:	74%
GPA 3.75 or higher:	20%	Out-of-state:	49%
GPA 3.50-3.74:	20%	Live on campus:	89%
GPA 3.0-3.49:	35%	International:	1%

Basis for selection. Rank in top 40% of class with 18 ACT, or rank in top 60% with 22 ACT required. Minority student applications given special consideration. Elementary Education and Animal Science applicants must rank in the top 40% of class with 24 ACT. ACT recommended.

High school preparation. College-preparatory program required. 17 units required; 22 recommended. Required and recommended units include English 4, mathematics 3-4, social studies 3-4, science 3-4 (laboratory 1), foreign language 2 and academic electives 4. Vocational agriculture units also recommended for applicants to College of Agriculture. Wisconsin residents who receive GED must also complete Wisconsin high school equivalency diploma.

2015-2016 Annual costs. Tuition/fees: $7,937; $15,510 out-of-state. Room/board: $6,475. Books/supplies: $360. Personal expenses: $2,440.

2014-2015 Financial aid. All financial aid based on need. 792 full-time freshmen applied for aid; 565 deemed to have need; 521 received aid. Average need met was 52%. Average scholarship/grant was $4,608; average loan $3,953. 29% of total undergraduate aid awarded as scholarships/grants, 71% as loans/jobs.

Application procedures. Admission: Priority date 2/1; no deadline. $44 fee, may be waived for applicants with need. Admission notification on a rolling basis beginning on or about 9/15. **Financial aid:** Priority date 3/15; no closing date. FAFSA required. Applicants notified on a rolling basis starting 4/15.

Academics. Special study options: Combined bachelor's/graduate degree, cross-registration, distance learning, double major, dual enrollment of high school students, ESL, exchange student, external degree, honors, independent study, internships, liberal arts/career combination, study abroad, teacher certification program. **Credit/placement by examination:** AP, CLEP, IB, institutional tests. 27 credit hours maximum toward bachelor's degree. Placement in English, foreign languages, and math based on university system placement exams. **Support services:** Learning center, reduced course load, remedial instruction, study skills assistance, tutoring, writing center.

Majors. Biology: General, biochemistry, biotechnology. **Business:** Accounting, business admin, marketing. **Communications:** Communications/speech/rhetoric, journalism. **Computer sciences:** General. **Conservation:** General, environmental science. **Education:** Agricultural, art, elementary, ESL, music, physical, speech impaired. **English:** Creative writing, English lit, general lit, rhetoric/composition. **Foreign languages:** French, German, Spanish. **Health services:** General, communication disorders. **History:** General. **Human services:** Social work. **Math:** General. **Physical sciences:** Chemistry, geology, organic chemistry, physics, planetary, polymer chemistry. **Psychology:** General. **Social sciences:** General, criminology, economics, geography, political science, sociology. **Visual/performing arts:** General, art, music, studio arts.

Most popular majors. Agriculture 18%, biology 8%, business/marketing 16%, communications/journalism 10%, education 10%, social sciences 7%.

Technology on campus. 700 workstations in dormitories, library, computer center, student center. Dormitories wired for high-speed internet access and linked to campus network. Commuter students can connect to campus network. Online course registration, online library, helpline, repair service, student web hosting, wireless network available.

Student life. Freshman orientation: Mandatory. Preregistration for classes offered. Held weekend prior to classes starting. **Policies:** Freshmen and sophomores must live in residence halls unless they reside with parents.

Housing: Guaranteed on-campus for freshmen. Coed dorms, single-sex dorms, special housing for disabled, themed housing available. $175 partly refundable deposit, deadline 6/1. **Activities:** Bands, campus ministries, choral groups, dance, drama, international student organizations, literary magazine, music ensembles, Model UN, musical theater, radio station, student government, student newspaper, symphony orchestra, TV station, African American Alliance, Hispanic Student Coalition, Native American Council, Hmong student association, Habitat for Humanity, Fellowship of Christian Athletes, Young Democrats, Young Republicans, Young Life, Intervarsity Christian Fellowship.

Athletics. NCAA. **Intercollegiate:** Basketball, cross-country, football (tackle) M, golf W, ice hockey, soccer W, softball W, tennis W, track and field, volleyball W. **Intramural:** Badminton, basketball, football (non-tackle), sand volleyball, soccer, softball, ultimate frisbee, volleyball. **Team name:** Falcons.

Student services. Adult student services, alcohol/substance abuse counseling, chaplain/spiritual director, career counseling, services for economically disadvantaged, student employment services, financial aid counseling, health services, minority student services, on-campus daycare, personal counseling, placement for graduates, veterans' counselor, women's services. **Physically disabled:** Services for visually, speech, hearing impaired.

Contact. E-mail: admit@uwrf.edu
Phone: (715) 425-3500 Fax: (715) 425-0676
Sarah Egerstrom, Director of Admission, University of Wisconsin-River Falls, 410 South 3rd Street, River Falls, WI 54022-5001

University of Wisconsin-Stevens Point
Stevens Point, Wisconsin
www.uwsp.edu   CB code: 1919

- Public 4-year university
- Residential campus in large town
- 8,684 degree-seeking undergraduates

General. Founded in 1894. Regionally accredited. **Degrees:** 1,866 bachelor's, 28 associate awarded; master's, professional offered. **ROTC:** Army. **Location:** 110 miles from Madison, 240 miles from Chicago. **Calendar:** Semester, extensive summer session. **Full-time faculty:** 401 total; 89% have terminal degrees, 12% minority, 44% women. **Part-time faculty:** 131 total; 37% have terminal degrees, 3% minority, 52% women. **Class size:** 32% < 20, 60% 20-39, 4% 40-49, 3% 50-99, 1% >100. **Special facilities:** Natural history museum, planetarium and observatory, nature preserve, Foucault pendulum, electron microscope, 1,000-acre natural resources summer camp, fire science center, multicultural center.

Freshman class profile.

GPA 3.75 or higher:	21%	Rank in top quarter:	40%
GPA 3.50-3.74:	19%	Rank in top tenth:	14%
GPA 3.0-3.49:	38%	Out-of-state:	12%
GPA 2.0-2.99:	22%	Live on campus:	91%

Basis for selection. Applicants must rank in top 25% of class, or have 21 ACT/990 SAT (exclusive of Writing) and rank in top 50% of class, or have 3.25 GPA. Campus visit recommended. Students interested in dance, drama, music, and musical theater required to complete on-campus performance audition and/or interview.

High school preparation. College-preparatory program required. 17 units required; 22 recommended. Required and recommended units include English 4, mathematics 3-4, social studies 3-4, science 3-4 and academic electives 4. Additional 2 units from English, math, social sciences, sciences, or foreign language and 2 units from above areas or fine arts, computer science, or other academic areas.

2015-2016 Annual costs. Tuition/fees: $7,491; $15,758 out-of-state. Room/board: $7,012. Books/supplies: $500. Personal expenses: $1,916.

2014-2015 Financial aid. Need-based: 1,461 full-time freshmen applied for aid; 932 deemed to have need; 932 received aid. Average need met was 65%. Average scholarship/grant was $5,371; average loan $4,253. 43% of total undergraduate aid awarded as scholarships/grants, 57% as loans/jobs. **Non-need-based:** Awarded to 3,702 full-time undergraduates, including 654 freshmen. Scholarships awarded for academics, alumni affiliation, art, music/drama, ROTC. **Additional information:** Tuition discounts offered to qualified residents from other states. Tuition waiver for state veterans.

Application procedures. Admission: No deadline. $44 fee, may be waived for applicants with need. Admission notification on a rolling basis beginning on or about 9/15. **Financial aid:** Priority date 3/15, closing date 5/1. FAFSA required. Applicants notified on a rolling basis starting 3/1; must reply within 4 week(s) of notification.

Academics. Special study options: Accelerated study, distance learning, double major, dual enrollment of high school students, ESL, honors, independent study, internships, student-designed major, study abroad, teacher certification program. Cooperative program with University of Wisconsin: Eau Claire and St. Joseph's Hospital; collaborative degree program with University of Wisconsin-Marshfield, University of Wisconsin-Marathon and University of Wisconsin-Marinette. **Credit/placement by examination:** AP, CLEP, IB, institutional tests. 16 credit hours maximum toward associate degree, 32 toward bachelor's. **Support services:** Learning center, pre-admission summer program, reduced course load, remedial instruction, study skills assistance, tutoring, writing center.

Majors. Architecture: Interior. **Biology:** General, biochemistry. **Business:** Accounting, business admin. **Communications:** Communications/speech/rhetoric. **Computer sciences:** General, web page design. **Conservation:** General, fisheries, forestry, water/wetlands/marine, wildlife/wilderness, wood science. **Education:** Early childhood, elementary, family/consumer sciences, music, physical, secondary. **English:** English lit. **Foreign languages:** French, German, Spanish. **Health services:** General, athletic training, audiology/speech pathology, clinical lab science. **History:** General. **Human services:** General, social work. **Liberal arts:** Arts/sciences. **Math:** General. **Parks/recreation:** Health/fitness. **Philosophy/religion:** Philosophy. **Physical sciences:** Chemistry, geology, physics. **Psychology:** General. **Social sciences:** General, economics, geography, political science, sociology. **Visual/performing arts:** General, art, dance, dramatic, interior design, music, music history, music performance, studio arts management.

Most popular majors. Biology 9%, business/marketing 10%, education 10%, health sciences 7%, natural resources/environmental science 14%, social sciences 9%, visual/performing arts 9%.

Technology on campus. 634 workstations in dormitories, library, computer center, student center. Dormitories wired for high-speed internet access and linked to campus network. Commuter students can connect to campus network. Online course registration, online library, helpline, repair service, student web hosting, wireless network available.

Student life. Freshman orientation: Mandatory, $45 fee. Preregistration for classes offered. **Policies:** Non-smoking policy for all campus buildings. **Housing:** Coed dorms, single-sex dorms, themed housing, wellness housing available. $125 partly refundable deposit. Freshman interest-group housing available. **Activities:** Bands, campus ministries, choral groups, dance, drama, film society, international student organizations, music ensembles, Model UN, musical theater, opera, radio station, student government, student newspaper, symphony orchestra, TV station, American Indians Reaching for Opportunities, black student union, College Republicans, College Democrats, Lutheran Collegians, Association for Community Tasks, Newman Catholic student association, Habitat for Humanity, Gay-Straight Alliance, Hmong and Southeast Asian American Club.

Athletics. NCAA. **Intercollegiate:** Baseball M, basketball, cross-country, diving, football (tackle) M, golf W, ice hockey, soccer W, softball W, swimming, tennis W, track and field, volleyball W, wrestling M. **Intramural:** Badminton, basketball, football (non-tackle), football (tackle) M, golf, ice hockey, racquetball, soccer, softball, table tennis, tennis, ultimate frisbee, volleyball. **Team name:** Pointers.

Student services. Adult student services, alcohol/substance abuse counseling, career counseling, services for economically disadvantaged, student employment services, financial aid counseling, health services, minority student services, on-campus daycare, personal counseling, placement for graduates, veterans' counselor, women's services. **Physically disabled:** Services for visually, speech, hearing impaired.

Contact. E-mail: admiss@uwsp.edu
Phone: (715) 346-2441 Fax: (715) 346-3296
Bill Jordan, Director of Admissions, University of Wisconsin-Stevens Point, Student Services Center, Stevens Point, WI 54481

University of Wisconsin-Stout
Menomonie, Wisconsin
www.uwstout.edu   CB code: 1740

- Public 4-year university
- Residential campus in large town
- 8,194 degree-seeking undergraduates: 17% part-time, 45% women, 2% African American, 1% Hispanic/Latino, 4% Native American, 87% Native Hawaiian/Pacific islander, 4% Multi-racial, non-Hispanic, 3% international
- 812 degree-seeking graduate students
- 84% of applicants admitted

▶ SAT or ACT (ACT writing optional) required
▶ 53% graduate within 6 years

General. Founded in 1891. Regionally accredited. **Degrees:** 1,697 bachelor's awarded; master's offered. **ROTC:** Army, Air Force. **Location:** 60 miles from Minneapolis-St. Paul. **Calendar:** 4-1-4, limited summer session. **Full-time faculty:** 392 total; 75% have terminal degrees, 13% minority, 44% women. **Part-time faculty:** 93 total; 30% have terminal degrees, 3% minority, 56% women. **Class size:** 33% < 20, 63% 20-39, 2% 40-49, 1% 50-99, less than 1% >100. **Special facilities:** Teleproduction center, technology transfer institute, vocational rehabilitation institute.

Freshman class profile. 3,535 applied, 2,964 admitted, 1,540 enrolled.

Mid 50% test scores			
ACT composite:	20-24	Rank in top tenth:	8%
GPA 3.75 or higher:	16%	Return as sophomores:	76%
GPA 3.50-3.74:	22%	Out-of-state:	38%
GPA 3.0-3.49:	33%	Live on campus:	95%
GPA 2.0-2.99:	28%	International:	1%
Rank in top quarter:	28%	Fraternities:	5%
		Sororities:	12%

Basis for selection. Rank in top half of class or 22 ACT required. Limited enrollment in all programs. Applied science and manufacturing engineering require upper 40% of class or 22 ACT along with 22 ACT math. **Learning Disabled:** Current IEP may be submitted with application.

High school preparation. Required and recommended units include English 4, mathematics 3, social studies 3, science 3, foreign language 2 and academic electives 4. Electives in English, math, social sciences, and sciences, technology business, fine art, family & consumer education, sciences.

2015-2016 Annual costs. Tuition/fees: $9,203; $16,949 out-of-state. Room/board: $6,504. Books/supplies: $396. Personal expenses: $2,070. **Additional information:** Laptop is included with payment of fees.

2015-2016 Financial aid. **Need-based:** 1,326 full-time freshmen applied for aid; 916 deemed to have need; 886 received aid. Average need met was 80%. Average scholarship/grant was $5,795; average loan $3,748. 41% of total undergraduate aid awarded as scholarships/grants, 59% as loans/jobs. **Non-need-based:** Awarded to 1,199 full-time undergraduates, including 426 freshmen. Scholarships awarded for academics.

Application procedures. **Admission:** Priority date 1/1; no deadline. $44 fee, may be waived for applicants with need. Admission notification on a rolling basis beginning on or about 9/1. Must reply by 5/1. Early application recommended. Art-graphic design deadline of 11/1; not all qualified applicants will be admitted. **Financial aid:** Priority date 3/15; no closing date. FAFSA required. Applicants notified on a rolling basis starting 3/21; must reply within 4 week(s) of notification.

Academics. **Special study options:** Accelerated study, cooperative education, cross-registration, distance learning, double major, dual enrollment of high school students, ESL, exchange student, external degree, honors, independent study, internships, study abroad, teacher certification program. **Credit/placement by examination:** AP, CLEP, IB, institutional tests. **Support services:** Learning center, pre-admission summer program, reduced course load, remedial instruction, study skills assistance, tutoring, writing center.

Majors. **Business:** Business admin, construction management, hospitality admin, logistics, operations, real estate, sales/distribution. **Computer sciences:** Information technology, networking. **Education:** Art, early childhood, family/consumer sciences, sales/marketing, science, special ed, technology/industrial arts, voc/tech. **Engineering:** Computer, manufacturing, polymer. **English:** Technical writing. **Health services:** Dietetics, vocational rehab counseling. **Math:** Applied. **Parks/recreation:** Golf management. **Psychology:** General. **Social sciences:** General. **Work/family studies:** Clothing/textiles, family studies, institutional food production.

Most popular majors. Business/marketing 34%, computer/information sciences 6%, education 9%, engineering/engineering technologies 12%, family/consumer sciences 8%, health sciences 8%, visual/performing arts 8%.

Technology on campus. PC or laptop required. 590 workstations in dormitories, library, computer center, student center. Dormitories wired for high-speed internet access and linked to campus network. Commuter students can connect to campus network. Online course registration, online library, helpline, repair service, student web hosting, wireless network available.

Student life. **Freshman orientation:** Available. Preregistration for classes offered. 1-day program with additional activities held the week before classes begin. **Housing:** Guaranteed on-campus for freshmen. Coed dorms, special housing for disabled, apartments, wellness housing available. $125 partly refundable deposit. **Activities:** Bands, campus ministries, choral groups, dance, drama, film society, international student organizations, literary magazine, music ensembles, Model UN, musical theater, radio station, student government, student newspaper, black student union, Hmong student organization, Lutheran student fellowship, College Democrats, College Republicans, Chi Alpha Christians in Action, single parent association, Club Los Hispanos.

Athletics. NCAA. **Intercollegiate:** Baseball M, basketball, cross-country, football (tackle) M, gymnastics W, ice hockey M, soccer W, softball W, tennis W, track and field, volleyball W. **Intramural:** Baseball M, basketball, golf, ice hockey, racquetball, soccer, softball, volleyball. **Team name:** Blue Devils.

Student services. Chaplain/spiritual director, career counseling, student employment services, health services, on-campus daycare, personal counseling, placement for graduates, veterans' counselor. **Physically disabled:** Services for visually, speech, hearing impaired.

Contact. E-mail: admissions@uwstout.edu
Phone: (715) 232-1411 Toll-free number: (800) 447-8688
Fax: (715) 232-1667
Pam Holsinger-Fuchs, Executive Director of Enrollment Services, University of Wisconsin-Stout, 1 Clocktower Plaza, Menomonie, WI 54751

University of Wisconsin-Superior
Superior, Wisconsin
www.uwsuper.edu   **CB code: 1920**

▶ Public 4-year university and liberal arts college
▶ Residential campus in small city
▶ 2,254 degree-seeking undergraduates: 17% part-time, 61% women, 2% African American, 1% Asian American, 2% Hispanic/Latino, 2% Native American, 3% Multi-racial, non-Hispanic, 8% international
▶ 121 degree-seeking graduate students
▶ 72% of applicants admitted
▶ SAT or ACT (ACT writing optional) required
▶ 40% graduate within 6 years

General. Founded in 1893. Regionally accredited. **Degrees:** 469 bachelor's, 20 associate awarded; master's offered. **ROTC:** Air Force. **Location:** 2 miles from Duluth, Minnesota; 150 miles from Minneapolis-St. Paul. **Calendar:** Semester, limited summer session. **Full-time faculty:** 131 total; 71% have terminal degrees, 9% minority, 53% women. **Part-time faculty:** 78 total; 15% have terminal degrees, 4% minority, 54% women. **Class size:** 60% < 20, 36% 20-39, 3% 40-49, 1% 50-99, less than 1% >100. **Special facilities:** Observatory, Lake Superior national estuarine research reserve, research vessel, Lake Superior Research Institute, transportation and logistics research center, gender equity resource center, writing center, first nations center, Superior challenge ropes course, recital hall, veteran and non-traditional student center, northern center for community and economic development.

Freshman class profile. 996 applied, 713 admitted, 367 enrolled.

Mid 50% test scores			
ACT composite:	19-23	Rank in top tenth:	10%
GPA 3.75 or higher:	12%	End year in good standing:	86%
GPA 3.50-3.74:	15%	Return as sophomores:	67%
GPA 3.0-3.49:	34%	Out-of-state:	45%
GPA 2.0-2.99:	37%	Live on campus:	72%
Rank in top quarter:	21%	International:	18%

Basis for selection. Must rank in at least the upper 50% of graduating class or achieve a minimum composite score of 21 on the ACT. Essay, audition/portfolio (if applicable), interview recommended. **Home schooled:** Statement describing home school structure and mission, transcript of courses and grades required.

High school preparation. College-preparatory program required. 17 units required. Required and recommended units include English 4, mathematics 3-4, social studies 3-4, science 3-4, foreign language 2 and academic electives 4.

2015-2016 Annual costs. Tuition/fees: $8,036; $15,609 out-of-state. Room/board: $6,410. Books/supplies: $900. Personal expenses: $2,220.

2015-2016 Financial aid. **Need-based:** 267 full-time freshmen applied for aid; 201 deemed to have need; 193 received aid. Average need met was 82%. Average scholarship/grant was $5,225; average loan $3,592. 53% of total undergraduate aid awarded as scholarships/grants, 47% as loans/jobs. **Non-need-based:** Awarded to 388 full-time undergraduates, including 120 freshmen. Scholarships awarded for academics, alumni affiliation, art, leadership, minority status, music/drama, state residency. **Additional information:** Non resident Tuition Waiver (NTW) available to non-resident students on limited basis.

Application procedures. Admission: Priority date 4/1; deadline 8/1 (postmark date). $44 fee, may be waived for applicants with need. Admission notification on a rolling basis beginning on or about 9/16. Must reply by May 1 or within 4 week(s) if notified thereafter. **Financial aid:** Priority date 3/15; no closing date. FAFSA required. Applicants notified on a rolling basis starting 4/1; must reply by 5/1 or within 4 week(s) of notification.

Academics. Special study options: Accelerated study, combined bachelor's/graduate degree, cooperative education, cross-registration, distance learning, double major, dual enrollment of high school students, ESL, exchange student, external degree, independent study, internships, liberal arts/career combination, student-designed major, study abroad, teacher certification program. Engineering with University of Wisconsin-Madison and Michigan Technological University, Forestry with Michigan Technological University. **Credit/placement by examination:** AP, CLEP, IB, SAT, ACT, institutional tests. 32 credit hours maximum toward associate degree, 32 toward bachelor's. **Support services:** Learning center, pre-admission summer program, reduced course load, remedial instruction, study skills assistance, tutoring, writing center.

Majors. Biology: General, aquatic, botany, cell/histology, ecology, environmental, molecular. **Business:** General, accounting, business admin, finance, international, management information systems, marketing. **Communications:** Broadcast journalism, communications/speech/rhetoric, journalism, media studies. **Computer sciences:** Computer science. **Education:** Biology, chemistry, elementary, English, history, mathematics, multi-level teacher, music, physical, science, social science, social studies. **English:** English lit, rhetoric/composition, writing. **Health services:** General, art therapy. **History:** General. **Human services:** General, public policy, social work. **Liberal arts:** Arts/sciences. **Math:** General. **Physical sciences:** Chemistry. **Protective services:** Criminal justice, police science. **Psychology:** General. **Social sciences:** General, economics, political science, sociology. **Visual/performing arts:** General, art, art history/conservation, dramatic, music, music performance, studio arts.

Most popular majors. Biology 12%, business/marketing 11%, communications/journalism 9%, education 11%, interdisciplinary studies 13%, public administration/social services 7%, social sciences 9%.

Technology on campus. 370 workstations in dormitories, library, computer center, student center. Dormitories wired for high-speed internet access and linked to campus network. Commuter students can connect to campus network. Online course registration, online library, helpline, repair service, student web hosting, wireless network available.

Student life. Freshman orientation: Mandatory, $150 fee. Preregistration for classes offered. Sessions held in spring and summer; 2 1/2 day program just prior to classes beginning. **Housing:** Guaranteed on-campus for freshmen. Coed dorms, special housing for disabled, apartments available. Suites available in nontraditional residence halls for married students. Single parents have access to student residences. **Activities:** Bands, campus ministries, choral groups, dance, drama, international student organizations, literary magazine, music ensembles, musical theater, opera, radio station, student government, student newspaper, symphony orchestra, Amnesty International, International Peace Studies Association, Criminal Justice Association, Black Student Union, Circle of Native Nations, Social Work Student Association, Chinese Students and Scholars Association, Stimulus Club, Political Science Association.

Athletics. NCAA. **Intercollegiate:** Baseball M, basketball, cross-country, ice hockey, soccer, softball W, track and field, volleyball W. **Intramural:** Badminton, basketball, bowling, cheerleading, football (non-tackle), racquetball, rifle, soccer, softball, swimming, table tennis, tennis, ultimate frisbee, volleyball. **Team name:** Yellowjackets.

Student services. Adult student services, alcohol/substance abuse counseling, chaplain/spiritual director, career counseling, services for economically disadvantaged, student employment services, financial aid counseling, health services, minority student services, personal counseling, placement for graduates, veterans' counselor, women's services. **Physically disabled:** Services for visually, hearing impaired.

Contact. E-mail: admissions@uwsuper.edu
Phone: (715) 394-8230 Fax: (715) 394-8407
Robert Strand, Director of Admissions, University of Wisconsin-Superior, Belknap and Catlin, Superior, WI 54880

University of Wisconsin-Whitewater
Whitewater, Wisconsin
www.uww.edu
CB code: 1921

- Public 4-year university
- Residential campus in large town

- 10,584 degree-seeking undergraduates: 7% part-time, 49% women, 4% African American, 2% Asian American, 6% Hispanic/Latino, 5% Multiracial, non-Hispanic, 1% international
- 1,122 degree-seeking graduate students
- 68% of applicants admitted
- SAT or ACT (ACT writing optional) required
- 60% graduate within 6 years

General. Founded in 1868. Regionally accredited. **Degrees:** 2,124 bachelor's, 108 associate awarded; master's, professional offered. **ROTC:** Army, Air Force. **Location:** 40 miles from Madison, 50 miles from Milwaukee. **Calendar:** Semester, extensive summer session. **Class size:** 36% < 20, 48% 20-39, 9% 40-49, 5% 50-99, 1% >100. **Special facilities:** Observatory, nature preserve and recreation area, weather station.

Freshman class profile. 7,286 applied, 4,931 admitted, 2,189 enrolled.

Mid 50% test scores		Rank in top quarter:	32%
ACT composite:	20-26	Rank in top tenth:	11%
GPA 3.75 or higher:	15%	Return as sophomores:	81%
GPA 3.50-3.74:	17%	Out-of-state:	18%
GPA 3.0-3.49:	44%	Live on campus:	95%
GPA 2.0-2.99:	24%	International:	1%

Basis for selection. College prep curriculum and rank in top 40% of high school class important. Audition required for music; portfolio recommended for art. **Home schooled:** Transcript of courses and grades required. **Learning Disabled:** Disability should be referenced in essay and include review by Center for Students with Disabilities. Medical documentation may be requested.

High school preparation. College-preparatory program required. 17 units required; 18 recommended. Required and recommended units include English 4, mathematics 3-4, social studies 3-4, science 3-4, foreign language 2 and academic electives 4.

2015-2016 Annual costs. Tuition/fees: $7,600; $15,173 out-of-state. Room/board: $6,144. Books/supplies: $600. Personal expenses: $2,000.

2015-2016 Financial aid. Need-based: Average need met was 58%. Average scholarship/grant was $5,320; average loan $3,397. 47% of total undergraduate aid awarded as scholarships/grants, 53% as loans/jobs. **Non-need-based:** Scholarships awarded for academics, art, leadership, minority status, music/drama, state residency.

Application procedures. Admission: Priority date 1/1; deadline 5/1 (postmark date). $44 fee, may be waived for applicants with need. Admission notification by 5/1. Admission notification on a rolling basis beginning on or about 9/15. **Financial aid:** Priority date 3/1; no closing date. FAFSA required. Applicants notified on a rolling basis starting 4/1; must reply within 3 week(s) of notification.

Academics. Special study options: Accelerated study, combined bachelor's/graduate degree, cooperative education, cross-registration, distance learning, double major, dual enrollment of high school students, ESL, exchange student, external degree, honors, independent study, internships, liberal arts/career combination, student-designed major, study abroad, teacher certification program, weekend college. **Credit/placement by examination:** AP, CLEP, IB, SAT, ACT, institutional tests. 30 credit hours maximum toward associate degree, 60 toward bachelor's. **Support services:** Learning center, pre-admission summer program, reduced course load, remedial instruction, study skills assistance, tutoring, writing center.

Majors. Area/ethnic studies: Japanese, women's. **Biology:** General. **Business:** General, accounting, business admin, entrepreneurial studies, finance, human resources, international, managerial economics, marketing, office management, operations. **Communications:** General, broadcast journalism, communications/speech/rhetoric, journalism. **Computer sciences:** General, computer science, information technology, systems analysis, web page design. **Conservation:** Environmental science. **Education:** General, art, biology, business, chemistry, computer, drama/dance, driver/safety, early childhood, elementary, English, French, German, history, learning disabled, mathematics, music, physical, sales/marketing, science, secondary, social science, social studies, Spanish, special ed, speech. **English:** English lit. **Foreign languages:** French, German, Spanish. **Health services:** Speech pathology. **History:** General. **Human services:** General, public policy, social work. **Liberal arts:** Arts/sciences. **Math:** General. **Physical sciences:** Chemistry, physics. **Psychology:** General. **Social sciences:** General, economics, geography, political science, sociology. **Visual/performing arts:** Art, art history/conservation, dance, digital arts, dramatic, music, music theory/composition, theater arts management, theater history.

Most popular majors. Business/marketing 35%, communications/journalism 6%, education 16%, public administration/social services 6%, social sciences 7%.

Technology on campus. 1,373 workstations in dormitories, library, computer center, student center. Dormitories wired for high-speed internet access and linked to campus network. Commuter students can connect to campus network. Online course registration, online library, helpline, repair service, student web hosting, wireless network available.

Student life. Freshman orientation: Mandatory, $75 fee. Preregistration for classes offered. Full-day program held in summer. **Housing:** Guaranteed on-campus for freshmen. Coed dorms, single-sex dorms, special housing for disabled, themed housing available. $125 fully refundable deposit, deadline 5/1. **Activities:** Bands, campus ministries, choral groups, dance, drama, international student organizations, literary magazine, music ensembles, musical theater, opera, radio station, student government, student newspaper, symphony orchestra, TV station, Campus Crusade for Christ, Diamond Way Buddhist, College Democrats, College Republicans, Arabic club, black student union, Adopt-A-School Program, America Reads.

Athletics. NCAA. **Intercollegiate:** Baseball M, basketball, bowling W, cross-country, diving, football (tackle) M, golf W, gymnastics W, soccer, softball W, swimming, tennis, track and field, volleyball W, wrestling M. **Intramural:** Badminton, basketball, bowling, football (non-tackle), golf, racquetball, soccer, softball, table tennis, tennis, volleyball. **Team name:** Warhawks.

Student services. Adult student services, alcohol/substance abuse counseling, chaplain/spiritual director, career counseling, services for economically disadvantaged, student employment services, financial aid counseling, health services, legal services, minority student services, on-campus daycare, personal counseling, placement for graduates, veterans' counselor, women's services. **Physically disabled:** Services for visually, speech, hearing impaired.

Contact. E-mail: uwwadmit@uww.edu
Phone: (262) 472-1440 Fax: (262) 472-1515
Jeff Blahnik, Director of Admissions, University of Wisconsin-Whitewater, 800 West Main Street, Whitewater, WI 53190-1790

Viterbo University
La Crosse, Wisconsin
www.viterbo.edu

CB member
CB code: 1878

- ▸ Private 4-year university affiliated with the Roman Catholic Church
- ▸ Residential campus in small city
- ▸ 1,983 degree-seeking undergraduates
- ▸ 683 graduate students
- ▸ SAT or ACT (ACT writing optional) required

General. Founded in 1890. Regionally accredited. **Degrees:** 475 bachelor's, 12 associate awarded; master's offered. **ROTC:** Army. **Location:** 150 miles from Minneapolis-St. Paul, 150 miles from Madison. **Calendar:** Semester, limited summer session. **Full-time faculty:** 122 total; 56% have terminal degrees, 5% minority, 57% women. **Part-time faculty:** 214 total; 21% have terminal degrees, less than 1% minority, 65% women. **Class size:** 70% < 20, 27% 20-39, 1% 40-49, 2% 50-99. **Special facilities:** Center for ethics, science and technology; fine arts center; center for recreation and education in conjunction with Boys and Girls Club of America.

Freshman class profile.

GPA 3.75 or higher:	35%	Rank in top quarter:	48%
GPA 3.50-3.74:	19%	Rank in top tenth:	19%
GPA 3.0-3.49:	30%	Out-of-state:	34%
GPA 2.0-2.99:	16%	Live on campus:	94%

Basis for selection. High school GPA and ACT score most important, then placement testing. Auditions and portfolio reviews required for students applying to School of Fine Arts (music, theater, art, dance). Interview required for students not meeting admission requirements. **Home schooled:** Transcript of courses and grades required. **Learning Disabled:** All students encouraged to file ADA petition for reasonable accommodations, preferably 8 weeks prior to start of classes.

High school preparation. College-preparatory program recommended. 16 units required; 19 recommended. Required and recommended units include English 3, mathematics 2-3, social studies 2, history 2, science 2 and academic electives 5. Chemistry required for nursing, dietetics, natural sciences, allied health preprofessional students. Portfolios or auditions required for fine arts students.

2015-2016 Annual costs. Tuition/fees: $25,050. Room/board: $8,260. Books/supplies: $1,000. Personal expenses: $2,000.

Financial aid. Non-need-based: Scholarships awarded for academics, alumni affiliation, art, athletics, leadership, minority status, music/drama, ROTC.

Application procedures. Admission: Closing date 8/15 (receipt date). $25 fee, may be waived for applicants with need, free for online applicants. Admission notification on a rolling basis. Must reply by May 1 or within 2 week(s) if notified thereafter. **Financial aid:** Priority date 3/15; no closing date. FAFSA, institutional form required. Applicants notified on a rolling basis starting 4/1; must reply within 3 week(s) of notification.

Academics. Learning Center offers individual and small group tutoring in all subject areas daily. Library services available daily, on weekends and evenings. **Special study options:** Accelerated study, combined bachelor's/graduate degree, cross-registration, distance learning, double major, dual enrollment of high school students, honors, independent study, internships, liberal arts/career combination, student-designed major, study abroad, teacher certification program, urban semester, Washington semester, weekend college. Weekend college is primarily for students at master's level. **Credit/placement by examination:** AP, CLEP, IB, SAT, ACT, institutional tests. 30 credit hours maximum toward bachelor's degree. 16 hours awarded for military services. **Support services:** Learning center, reduced course load, remedial instruction, study skills assistance, tutoring, writing center.

Majors. Biology: General, biochemistry. **Business:** Accounting, business admin, entrepreneurial studies, management information systems, marketing. **Communications:** Organizational. **Computer sciences:** General. **Education:** Art, biology, business, chemistry, drama/dance, elementary, English, mathematics, music, science, secondary, social studies, Spanish, technology/industrial arts. **English:** English lit. **Foreign languages:** Spanish. **Health services:** General, clinical lab technology, dietetics, nursing (RN). **Human services:** Social work. **Liberal arts:** Arts/sciences. **Math:** General. **Parks/recreation:** Exercise sciences, sports admin. **Philosophy/religion:** Philosophy, religion. **Physical sciences:** Chemistry, theoretical physics. **Protective services:** Criminal justice. **Psychology:** General. **Social sciences:** General, sociology. **Visual/performing arts:** General, art, design, dramatic, graphic design, music, music pedagogy, music performance, studio arts, studio arts management.

Most popular majors. Business/marketing 14%, education 7%, health sciences 41%, visual/performing arts 8%.

Technology on campus. 396 workstations in dormitories, library, computer center, student center. Dormitories wired for high-speed internet access and linked to campus network. Commuter students can connect to campus network. Online course registration, online library, helpline, wireless network available.

Student life. Freshman orientation: Mandatory. Preregistration for classes offered. One-day program offered 4 times in the summer for incoming freshmen and parents. **Policies:** Standards of conduct, sexual harassment code, anti-hazing initiation policy, academic honesty policy, academic due process, campus security policy, residence hall terms and conditions, alcohol and drug policy, student event policies. **Housing:** Guaranteed on-campus for freshmen. Coed dorms, single-sex dorms, apartments, themed housing available. $100 fully refundable deposit, deadline 5/1. **Activities:** Pep band, campus ministries, choral groups, dance, drama, international student organizations, literary magazine, music ensembles, musical theater, student government, student newspaper, Connect, Students in Free Enterprise, Circle K, student nurses association, education club, Sigma Pi Delta, CREW, Global Rhythms, psychology club.

Athletics. NAIA. **Intercollegiate:** Baseball M, basketball, bowling, cross-country, golf, soccer, softball W, volleyball W. **Intramural:** Badminton, basketball, bowling, cross-country, football (non-tackle), golf, handball, racquetball, rugby M, skiing, soccer, softball, table tennis, tennis, volleyball. **Team name:** V-Hawks.

Student services. Adult student services, alcohol/substance abuse counseling, chaplain/spiritual director, career counseling, services for economically disadvantaged, student employment services, financial aid counseling, health services, personal counseling, placement for graduates, veterans' counselor, women's services. **Physically disabled:** Services for visually, hearing impaired.

Contact. E-mail: admission@viterbo.edu
Phone: (608) 796-3010 Toll-free number: (800) 848-3726
Fax: (608) 796-3020
Robert Forget, Dean of Admission, Viterbo University, 900 Viterbo Drive, La Crosse, WI 54601-8804

Wisconsin Lutheran College
Milwaukee, Wisconsin
www.wlc.edu/

CB code: 1513

- ▸ Private 4-year liberal arts college affiliated with the Wisconsin Evangelical Lutheran Synod
- ▸ Residential campus in very large city

♦ 1,060 degree-seeking undergraduates
♦ 105 graduate students
♦ SAT or ACT (ACT writing optional) required

Contact. E-mail: admissions@wlc.edu
Phone: (414) 443-8811 Fax: (414) 443-8547
Lucas Faust, Executive Director of Enrollment, Wisconsin Lutheran
College, 8800 West Bluemound Road, Milwaukee, WI 53226-4699

General. Founded in 1973. Regionally accredited. **Degrees:** 237 bachelor's
awarded; master's offered. **ROTC:** Air Force. **Calendar:** Semester, limited
summer session.

Freshman class profile.

GPA 3.75 or higher:	28%	**GPA 2.0-2.99:**	20%
GPA 3.50-3.74:	17%	**Rank in top quarter:**	41%
GPA 3.0-3.49:	34%	**Rank in top tenth:**	13%

Basis for selection. ACT, GPA considered. Interview recommended for
some; audition required for music scholarships. **Home schooled:** Transcript
of courses and grades, letter of recommendation (nonparent) required.

High school preparation. College-preparatory program recommended.
17 units recommended. Recommended units include English 4, mathematics
4, social studies 3, science 3 and foreign language 3.

2015-2016 Annual costs. Tuition/fees: $27,040. Room/board: $9,250.
Books/supplies: $700. Personal expenses: $1,646.

Financial aid. Non-need-based: Scholarships awarded for academics, art,
leadership, music/drama, ROTC.

Application procedures. Admission: Priority date 3/1; no deadline. $20
fee, may be waived for applicants with need, free for online applicants.
Admission notification on a rolling basis beginning on or about 9/1. Must
reply by May 1 or within 2 week(s) if notified thereafter. **Financial aid:**
Priority date 3/1; no closing date. FAFSA, institutional form required. Applicants notified on a rolling basis starting 3/15; must reply within 2 week(s)
of notification.

Academics. Special study options: Distance learning, double major, dual
enrollment of high school students, ESL, honors, independent study, internships, student-designed major, study abroad, teacher certification program.
Credit/placement by examination: AP, CLEP, IB, SAT, ACT, institutional
tests. **Support services:** Learning center, reduced course load, study skills
assistance, tutoring, writing center.

Majors. Biology: General, biochemistry, marine. **Business:** Business admin.
Communications: Communications/speech/rhetoric. **Computer sciences:**
Computer science. **Conservation:** Environmental science, environmental
studies. **Education:** General, art, biology, chemistry, drama/dance, early
childhood, elementary, English, German, mathematics, multi-level teacher,
psychology, science, secondary, Spanish, special ed. **English:** English lit.
Foreign languages: Chinese, German, Spanish. **Health services:** Nursing
(RN). **History:** General. **Math:** General. **Parks/recreation:** Exercise sciences. **Philosophy/religion:** Philosophy, religion. **Physical sciences:** Chemistry, physics. **Psychology:** General. **Social sciences:** General, physical
anthropology. **Visual/performing arts:** Art, cinematography, design, dramatic, music.

Most popular majors. Biology 8%, business/marketing 28%, communica-
tions/journalism 10%, education 9%, health sciences 8%, psychology 6%,
visual/performing arts 7%.

Technology on campus. 100 workstations in dormitories, library, computer center, student center. Dormitories wired for high-speed internet access
and linked to campus network. Commuter students can connect to campus
network. Online course registration, online library, helpline, repair service,
wireless network available.

Student life. Freshman orientation: Mandatory. Preregistration for
classes offered. Two day program held over the weekend before start of fall
semester. **Policies:** All traditional age, unmarried students less than 5 years
out of high school must live in college housing. Upperclassmen eligible
for college apartments. Drug-free, alcohol-free campus. Smoking permitted
outside only. **Housing:** Guaranteed on-campus for all undergraduates. Single-
sex dorms, apartments available. $100 fully refundable deposit, deadline 5/1.
Activities: Bands, campus ministries, choral groups, dance, drama, international student organizations, music ensembles, student government, student newspaper.

Athletics. NCAA. **Intercollegiate:** Baseball M, basketball, cross-country,
football (tackle) M, golf, soccer, softball W, tennis, track and field, volleyball
W. **Team name:** Warriors.

Student services. Adult student services, chaplain/spiritual director,
career counseling, student employment services, financial aid counseling,
health services, minority student services, personal counseling, placement
for graduates. **Physically disabled:** Services for visually, hearing impaired.

Wyoming

University of Wyoming
Laramie, Wyoming
www.uwyo.edu

CB member
CB code: 4855

- Public 4-year university
- Residential campus in large town
- 9,842 degree-seeking undergraduates: 15% part-time, 51% women, 1% African American, 1% Asian American, 7% Hispanic/Latino, 1% Native American, 3% Multi-racial, non-Hispanic, 4% international
- 2,438 degree-seeking graduate students
- 96% of applicants admitted
- SAT or ACT (ACT writing optional) required
- 55% graduate within 6 years

General. Founded in 1886. Regionally accredited. Undergraduate and graduate degree programs offered in Casper. Extension classes available in off-campus locations throughout the state. Online classes offered nationally. **Degrees:** 2,022 bachelor's awarded; master's, professional, doctoral offered. **ROTC:** Army, Air Force. **Location:** 45 miles from Cheyenne, 130 miles from Denver. **Calendar:** Semester, extensive summer session. **Full-time faculty:** 754 total; 81% have terminal degrees, 10% minority, 41% women. **Part-time faculty:** 65 total; 15% have terminal degrees, 8% minority, 52% women. **Class size:** 38% < 20, 44% 20-39, 8% 40-49, 6% 50-99, 4% >100. **Special facilities:** Museums (art, geological, anthropology, entomology, law), herbariums, spatial data and visualization center, botany conservatory, zoological center, learning resource center, meteorological station, Grand Teton National Park research center, planetarium, veterinary laboratory, materials characterization laboratory, biological research facility, on-site elementary school, infrared telescope observatory, institute of environment/natural resources, fishery and wildlife research unit, American heritage center, insect galleries.

Freshman class profile. 4,654 applied, 4,453 admitted, 1,692 enrolled.

Mid 50% test scores			
SAT critical reading:	480-620	Rank in top quarter:	50%
SAT math:	490-620	Rank in top tenth:	22%
ACT composite:	22-27	Return as sophomores:	76%
GPA 3.75 or higher:	36%	Out-of-state:	46%
GPA 3.50-3.74:	19%	Live on campus:	88%
GPA 3.0-3.49:	29%	International:	2%
GPA 2.0-2.99:	16%	Fraternities:	8%
		Sororities:	9%

Basis for selection. For assured admission, required to submit high school GPA, ACT/SAT, and complete 19 required units in a pre-college curriculum. Test scores are not required for students over the age of 21 or for non-degree-seeking students. **Home schooled:** Home school credit evaluation form required. **Learning Disabled:** Must formally apply to University Disability Support Services for accommodations and provide documentation of disability.

High school preparation. College-preparatory program required. 19 units required. Required units include English 4, mathematics 4, social studies 3, science 4 (laboratory 3), foreign language 2 and academic electives 2. 2 academic electives must be chosen from fine and performing arts, social and behavioral studies, humanities, additional foreign language, or career-technical courses.

2015-2016 Annual costs. Tuition/fees: $4,891; $15,631 out-of-state. Room/board: $10,037. Books/supplies: $1,200. Personal expenses: $2,200.

2014-2015 Financial aid. Need-based: 1,207 full-time freshmen applied for aid; 761 deemed to have need; 753 received aid. Average need met was 65%. Average scholarship/grant was $5,255; average loan $3,163. 60% of total undergraduate aid awarded as scholarships/grants, 40% as loans/jobs. **Non-need-based:** Awarded to 4,565 full-time undergraduates, including 1,137 freshmen. Scholarships awarded for academics, alumni affiliation, art, athletics, leadership, minority status, music/drama, ROTC, state residency.

Application procedures. Admission: Priority date 3/1; deadline 8/10 (postmark date). $40 fee, may be waived for applicants with need. Application must be submitted online. Within 2 weeks of receipt of required materials. Must reply by May 1 or within 3 week(s) if notified thereafter. **Financial aid:** Priority date 3/1; no closing date. FAFSA required. Applicants notified on a rolling basis starting 4/3; must reply within 3 week(s) of notification.

Academics. Remedial instruction offered on campus through Laramie County Community College. **Special study options:** Accelerated study, distance learning, double major, exchange student, external degree, honors, independent study, internships, student-designed major, study abroad, Washington semester. **Credit/placement by examination:** AP, CLEP, IB, SAT, ACT, institutional tests. Unlimited hours of credit by examination counted toward bachelor's degree, as long as course requirements are still met. Individual departments may allow additional tests on a case-by-case basis. **Support services:** Learning center, pre-admission summer program, reduced course load, study skills assistance, tutoring, writing center.

Majors. Area/ethnic studies: American, Native American, women's. **Biology:** General, botany, microbiology, molecular, physiology, wildlife, zoology. **Business:** Accounting, business admin, finance, management science, managerial economics, marketing. **Communications:** Communications/speech/rhetoric, journalism. **Computer sciences:** Computer science. **Conservation:** Environmental studies. **Education:** Agricultural, elementary, elementary special ed, music, physical, secondary, special ed, technology/industrial arts, trade/industrial. **Engineering:** Architectural, chemical, civil, computer, electrical, mechanical, petroleum, systems. **English:** English lit. **Foreign languages:** French, German, Russian, Spanish. **Health services:** Audiology/speech pathology, dental hygiene, nursing (RN). **History:** General. **Human services:** Social work. **Liberal arts:** Humanities. **Math:** General, statistics. **Parks/recreation:** Exercise sciences. **Philosophy/religion:** Philosophy, religion. **Physical sciences:** General, astronomy, astrophysics, chemistry, geology, physics. **Protective services:** Criminal justice. **Psychology:** General. **Social sciences:** General, anthropology, geography, political science, sociology. **Visual/performing arts:** Art, dramatic, music, music performance. **Work/family studies:** General.

Most popular majors. Biology 8%, business/marketing 13%, education 10%, engineering/engineering technologies 10%, health sciences 12%, social sciences 6%.

Technology on campus. 1,536 workstations in dormitories, library, computer center, student center. Dormitories wired for high-speed internet access and linked to campus network. Commuter students can connect to campus network. Online course registration, online library, helpline, student web hosting, wireless network available.

Student life. Freshman orientation: Available, $60 fee. Preregistration for classes offered. Held over nine 2-day sessions offered in May and June. **Policies:** New freshmen subject to live-in policy. **Housing:** Guaranteed on-campus for freshmen. Coed dorms, single-sex dorms, special housing for disabled, apartments, fraternity/sorority housing, themed housing available. $100 nonrefundable deposit, deadline 5/1. **Activities:** Bands, campus ministries, choral groups, dance, drama, film society, international student organizations, literary magazine, music ensembles, Model UN, musical theater, opera, student government, student newspaper, symphony orchestra, TV station, black student leaders, local church organizations, College Republicans, Rocky Mountain Democrats, Fellowship of Christian Athletes, Amnesty International, lesbian/gay/bisexual/transgendered association, Movimiento Estudantil Chicano de Atzlan, student health advisory council.

Athletics. NCAA. **Intercollegiate:** Basketball, cross-country, diving, football (tackle) M, golf, soccer W, swimming, tennis W, track and field, volleyball W, wrestling M. **Intramural:** Badminton, basketball, bowling, cross-country, football (non-tackle), golf, racquetball, soccer, softball, swimming, table tennis, tennis, track and field, ultimate frisbee, volleyball, water polo, wrestling M. **Team name:** Cowboys, Cowgirls.

Student services. Adult student services, alcohol/substance abuse counseling, career counseling, services for economically disadvantaged, student employment services, financial aid counseling, health services, legal services, minority student services, on-campus daycare, personal counseling, placement for graduates, veterans' counselor, women's services. **Physically disabled:** Services for visually, speech, hearing impaired.

Contact. E-mail: admissions@uwyo.edu
Phone: (307) 766-5160 Toll-free number: (800) 342-5996
Fax: (307) 766-4042
Shelley Dodd, Director of Admissions, University of Wyoming, Dept 3435, Laramie, WY 82071

Virgin Islands

University of the Virgin Islands
St. Thomas, Virgin Islands
www.uvi.edu

CB member
CB code: 0879

- Public 4-year university
- Commuter campus in small city
- 1,989 degree-seeking undergraduates: 27% part-time, 67% women, 73% African American, 1% Asian American, 8% Hispanic/Latino, 1% Multiracial, non-Hispanic, 6% international
- 172 degree-seeking graduate students
- 95% of applicants admitted

General. Founded in 1962. Regionally accredited. Two campuses, on two islands. Academic center on St. John. **Degrees:** 185 bachelor's, 55 associate awarded; master's offered. **ROTC:** Army. **Location:** 45 miles from San Juan, Puerto Rico. **Calendar:** Semester, limited summer session. **Full-time faculty:** 109 total; 80% have terminal degrees, 49% minority, 48% women. **Part-time faculty:** 148 total; 82% minority, 56% women. **Class size:** 75% < 20, 24% 20-39, less than 1% 40-49, less than 1% 50-99. **Special facilities:** Amphitheater, Caribbean collection, African art collection.

Freshman class profile. 1,094 applied, 1,039 admitted, 390 enrolled.

Mid 50% test scores			
SAT critical reading:	350-470	**GPA 2.0-2.99:**	59%
SAT math:	330-440	**Rank in top quarter:**	29%
SAT writing:	370-450	**Rank in top tenth:**	14%
ACT composite:	16-21	**Return as sophomores:**	73%
GPA 3.75 or higher:	7%	**Out-of-state:**	4%
GPA 3.50-3.74:	6%	**Live on campus:**	29%
GPA 3.0-3.49:	23%	**International:**	2%

Basis for selection. Secondary school record important in admission decisions. Students must have a minimum 2.0 GPA. **Home schooled:** Statement describing home school structure and mission, transcript of courses and grades, state high school equivalency certificate required.

High school preparation. College-preparatory program recommended. 15 units required. Required units include English 4, mathematics 3, social studies 3, science 3 and foreign language 2.

2016-2017 Annual costs. Tuition/fees: $5,014; $13,834 out-of-state. Room/board: $10,280. Books/supplies: $1,750. Personal expenses: $2,040.

Financial aid. Non-need-based: Scholarships awarded for academics, athletics.

Application procedures. Admission: Closing date 4/30 (postmark date). $25 fee, may be waived for applicants with need. Admission notification on a rolling basis beginning on or about 10/1. Must reply by 6/15. **Financial aid:** Priority date 3/1; no closing date. FAFSA required. Applicants notified on a rolling basis starting 4/1; must reply within 2 week(s) of notification.

Academics. Special study options: Distance learning, double major, exchange student, external degree, honors, independent study, internships, study abroad. **Credit/placement by examination:** AP, CLEP, IB, SAT, ACT, institutional tests. **Support services:** Learning center, pre-admission summer program, reduced course load, remedial instruction, study skills assistance, tutoring, writing center.

Majors. Biology: General, marine. **Business:** Accounting, business admin, hotel/motel admin, management information systems. **Communications:** Communications/speech/rhetoric. **Computer sciences:** Computer science. **Education:** Early childhood, elementary, music. **English:** English lit. **Health services:** Nursing (RN). **Liberal arts:** Arts/sciences. **Math:** General. **Physical sciences:** Chemistry. **Protective services:** Police science. **Psychology:** General. **Social sciences:** General.

Most popular majors. Biology 12%, business/marketing 35%, education 13%, health sciences 6%, psychology 13%.

Technology on campus. 300 workstations in library, computer center, student center. Dormitories wired for high-speed internet access and linked to campus network. Commuter students can connect to campus network. Online course registration, online library, helpline, wireless network available.

Student life. Freshman orientation: Mandatory, $90 fee. Preregistration for classes offered. One-week orientation activities held on both campuses. **Housing:** Coed dorms, single-sex dorms available. $100 partly refundable deposit, deadline 4/1. **Activities:** Bands, choral groups, dance, drama, international student organizations, literary magazine, music ensembles, Model UN, radio station, student government, student newspaper, political clubs, Future Business Leaders of America, Virgin Islands student association, British Virgin Islands student association, environment association, health educators, Golden Key International honor society, accounting association, ROTARACT, St. Kitts/Nevis association, Delta Sigma and AKA Sororities.

Athletics. Intercollegiate: Basketball, cheerleading W, cross-country, soccer M, track and field. **Intramural:** Archery, badminton, basketball, bowling, fencing, football (non-tackle), golf, gymnastics, racquetball, softball, table tennis, tennis, track and field, volleyball. **Team name:** Buccaneers.

Student services. Career counseling, student employment services, financial aid counseling, health services, personal counseling, placement for graduates. **Physically disabled:** Services for visually, speech, hearing impaired.

Contact. E-mail: admissions@uvi.edu
Phone: (340) 693-1160 Fax: (340) 693-1155
Xuri Allen, Director of Admissions and Recruitment, University of the Virgin Islands, #2 John Brewers Bay, St. Thomas, VI 00802-9990

Austria

MODUL University Vienna
Vienna, Austria
www.modul.ac.at

CB member

- Private 4-year university
- Very large city
- 136 degree-seeking undergraduates
- 16 graduate students
- Application essay, interview required

General. Degrees: 89 bachelor's awarded; master's, doctoral offered. **Calendar:** Semester. **Full-time faculty:** 30 total. **Part-time faculty:** 20 total.

Freshman class profile. 136 enrolled.

Basis for selection. Bachelor's program requires minimum 76 TOEFL iBT score, or minimum 5.5 IELTS. Requirement waived for native English speakers and graduates of schools conducted in English. CV and two recommendation letters. **Home schooled:** Transcript of courses and grades, state high school equivalency certificate, interview, letter of recommendation (nonparent) required. For students whose mother tongue is not English or who have not completed education in English, a proof of proficiency of English language is needed (on a B2 level, i.e. IELTS 6.0, no sub- score lower than 5.5, TOEFL 76 Internet- Based).

2015-2016 Annual costs. Tuition fees for 3- year Bachelor study programs (for all 3 years) for those students starting in spring or fall 2016 is $34,000. *Tuition fee for the 4- year Bachelor program (for all 4 years) for those students starting in spring or fall 2016 is $47,000. *Tuition fees for the MSc programs (for all 2 years) are $24,000. The tuition for the MBA program is $25,000 for the whole program. * Tuition fee for the PhD program (for all 4 years) is $45,000. These amounts are divided in installments that are paid at the beginning of every semester.

Application procedures. Admission: No application fee. Admission application closing dates: 8/1 for EU citizens, 5/1 for international students.

Academics. Credit/placement by examination: AP. **Support services:** Tutoring.

Majors. Business: Hospitality admin, international marketing, travel services.

Technology on campus. Dormitories wired for high-speed internet access. Online course registration, online library, wireless network available.

Student life. Freshman orientation: Mandatory. Preregistration for classes offered. **Housing:** Cooperative housing available. **Activities:** Choral groups, music ensembles, student government.

Student services. Career counseling, student employment services.

Contact. E-mail: admissions@modul.ac.at
Phone: (43) 132-03555 ext. 200
Markus Bernhard, Director of Admissions, MODUL University Vienna, AT

Webster Vienna Private University
Vienna, Austria
www.webster.ac.at   CB code: 9131

◗ Private 4-year business and liberal arts college
◗ Very large city

General. Calendar: Semester.

Contact. Phone: (43) 126-99293
Director of Admissions, Palais Wenkheim, Vienna, AT

Belgium

Vesalius College
Brussels, Belgium   CB member
www.vesalius.edu   CB code: 3574

◗ Private 3-year university and liberal arts college
◗ Very large city
◗ 300 degree-seeking undergraduates
◗ 73% of applicants admitted
◗ SAT or ACT (ACT writing recommended), application essay required

General. Calendar: Semester, limited summer session. **Full-time faculty:** 30 total.

Freshman class profile. 107 applied, 78 admitted, 61 enrolled.

Basis for selection. GED not accepted. Holistic application approach; academic results, extra curricular activities, strong references and well-written essay important. Application fee is 50 Euros. SAT/ACT not required of students with full IB Diploma. **Home schooled:** Statement describing home school structure and mission, transcript of courses and grades, letter of recommendation (nonparent) required.

2015-2016 Annual costs. Books/supplies: $2,200. **Additional information:** Tuition: 11,800 euros; estimated cost of housing, books and supplies and other expenses: 8,460-11,580 euros per year.

Financial aid. Non-need-based: Scholarships awarded for academics, leadership.

Application procedures. Admission: Priority date 4/15; no deadline.

Academics. Special study options: Internships, study abroad. **Credit/placement by examination:** AP, CLEP. **Support services:** Study skills assistance, tutoring, writing center.

Majors. Business: General. **Communications:** General. **Social sciences:** Economics, international economics, international relations, political science.

Technology on campus. Commuter students can connect to campus network. Helpline, wireless network available.

Student life. Freshman orientation: Mandatory. Preregistration for classes offered. Held one week before start of semester. **Housing:** Home stay program available where students live with a local family, immerse in the culture and learn one of the local languages. **Activities:** International student organizations, Model UN, student government.

Student services. Career counseling, personal counseling.

Contact. E-mail: vesalius@vub.ac.be
Willemijn Nieuwenhuys, Director Student Recruitment & External Relations, Vesalius College, Pleinlaan 2, Brussels, BE

Bulgaria

American University in Bulgaria
Blagoevgrad, Bulgaria   CB member
www.aubg.edu   CB code: 2451

◗ Private 4-year university
◗ Residential campus in small city
◗ 894 degree-seeking undergraduates: 49% women
◗ 19 degree-seeking graduate students
◗ 58% of applicants admitted
◗ Application essay required
◗ 89% graduate within 6 years

General. AUBG is accredited in both the EU and the US. Credits are fully transferable to and from the United States. **Degrees:** 237 bachelor's awarded; master's offered. **Location:** 50 miles from Sofia and Greece. **Calendar:** Semester. **Full-time faculty:** 51 total; 74% have terminal degrees, 37% women. **Part-time faculty:** 24 total; 71% have terminal degrees, 21% women. **Class size:** 28% < 20, 72% 20-39.

Freshman class profile. 637 applied, 368 admitted, 200 enrolled.

Mid 50% test scores			
SAT critical reading:	490-610	GPA 3.0-3.49:	19%
SAT math:	590-710	GPA 2.0-2.99:	2%
GPA 3.75 or higher:	60%	Return as sophomores:	93%
GPA 3.50-3.74:	19%	Live on campus:	93%

Basis for selection. Within four weeks after all required documents are received at the AUBG Admissions Office, admissions committee's decision is sent in an official letter to the prospective student at the mailing address given in the application form.

2015-2016 Annual costs. Tuition/fees: $11,850. Room/board: $1,590. Books/supplies: $300.

2015-2016 Financial aid. Need-based: 78% of total undergraduate aid awarded as scholarships/grants, 22% as loans/jobs. **Non-need-based:** Scholarships awarded for academics.

Application procedures. Admission: Priority date 3/1; deadline 6/1. $25 fee. Admission notification on a rolling basis beginning on or about 3/1. Must reply within a month after admission decision is sent. **Financial aid:** No deadline. Institutional form required. Applicants notified on a rolling basis.

Academics. Special study options: Double major, exchange student, honors, independent study, internships, student-designed major, study abroad. **Credit/placement by examination:** AP, IB, SAT, ACT, institutional tests. **Support services:** Learning center, study skills assistance, tutoring, writing center.

Majors. Area/ethnic studies: American. **Business:** Business admin. **Communications:** Journalism, media studies. **Computer sciences:** General, computer science. **History:** General. **Math:** General. **Social sciences:** Economics, international relations, political science.

Most popular majors. Business/marketing 38%, communications/journalism 11%, computer/information sciences 11%, social sciences 17%.

Technology on campus. 270 workstations in dormitories, library. Dormitories wired for high-speed internet access and linked to campus network. Online course registration, online library, helpline, repair service, wireless network available.

Student life. Freshman orientation: Mandatory. Preregistration for classes offered. Held during the last week of August. **Housing:** Guaranteed on-campus for all undergraduates. Coed dorms, special housing for disabled available. **Activities:** Concert band, choral groups, drama, international student organizations, Model UN, musical theater, radio station, student government, student newspaper, Better Community club, Rotaract club, AIESEC Blagoevgrad, Youth Empowerment Initiative club, Women in Business, political science club, Logos club, chess club.

Athletics. Team name: Griffins.

Student services. Career counseling, student employment services, financial aid counseling, health services, personal counseling. **Physically disabled:** Services for visually impaired.

Contact. E-mail: admissions@aubg.edu
Phone: (73) 888-111
Boriana Shalyavska, Director of Admissions, American University in Bulgaria, 12 Svoboda Bachvarova Street ABF, Blagoevgrad, BG

Canada

McGill University	
Montreal, Canada	CB member
www.mcgill.ca	CB code: 0935

▶ Public 4-year university
▶ Commuter campus in very large city
▶ 23,770 degree-seeking undergraduates
▶ 56% of applicants admitted

General. Founded in 1821. Additional campus 20 miles west of downtown Montreal campus. **Degrees:** 5,359 bachelor's awarded; master's, doctoral offered. **Location:** Downtown. **Calendar:** Semester, limited summer session. **Full-time faculty:** 2,329 total. **Part-time faculty:** 3,365 total. **Class size:** 35% < 20, 27% 20-39, 7% 40-49, 20% 50-99, 11% >100. **Special facilities:** Museum of Canadian history, museum of natural history, entomological museum and research laboratory, ecomuseum, Canadian architecture collection, arboretum, nature reserve, herbarium, Canadian history archives, arctic research station, subarctic research station, sound recording studio.

Freshman class profile. 24,772 applied, 13,868 admitted, 5,515 enrolled.

Mid 50% test scores		GPA 3.50-3.74:	38%
SAT critical reading:	650-730	GPA 3.0-3.49:	49%
SAT math:	640-730	GPA 2.0-2.99:	1%
SAT writing:	650-730	Out-of-state:	43%
ACT composite:	29-32	Live on campus:	51%
GPA 3.75 or higher:	12%		

Basis for selection. GED not accepted. School achievement record, grades in prerequisite courses, test scores most important. Advanced Placement (AP) results, class rank, recommendations also considered. Generally, 3.3 high school GPA required. For demonstration of English proficiency, TOEFL, Michigan, IELTS or APIEL acceptable. SAT (including Subject Tests) or ACT required for U.S. students, optional for Canadian students. Audition required of music majors. Portfolio required of architecture majors. Language tests required for TESL education programs. **Home schooled:** Statement describing home school structure and mission, transcript of courses and grades, letter of recommendation (nonparent) required. Description should include comprehensive list of all texts (and editions) studied, personal statement from applicant and separate statement from home educator. Further information and/or interview(s) with admissions officer, associate dean, or program director may be required. **Learning Disabled:** No special admission requirements, no specific allowances. Students free to add extenuating circumstances information with application.

High school preparation. College-preparatory program required. 15 units recommended. Recommended units include English 4, mathematics 4, social studies 1, history 1, science 3 (laboratory 3) and foreign language 3. 15-20 total recommended academic units; 3 or more combined recommended units for social studies and history. High school requirements vary according to program.

2015-2016 Annual costs. Annual cost of bachelor's degree programs ranges from $4,894-$5,289 for Quebec residents, $9,679-$10,074 for non-Quebec Canadians, and $19,266-$43,135 for international students.

Financial aid. All financial aid based on need. **Additional information:** McGill offers awards ranging in value from $3,000 renewable to $10,000 renewable and based on outstanding academic achievement or combination of outstanding academic achievement and leadership qualities. Finalists for scholarships valued at over $5,000 may be interviewed. Students who meet following eligibility conditions may apply for entrance awards: must be entering a university for the first time to undertake full-time undergraduate degree program; must be in top 5% of class based on last 2 years of full-time studies.

Application procedures. **Admission:** Closing date 1/15 (postmark date). $100 fee. Admission notification on a rolling basis beginning on or about 1/30. Must reply by May 1 or within 3 week(s) if notified thereafter. Reply by dates are later for CEGEP and Canadian high schools. Closing dates for transfer students are 1/15 for international students, 5/1 for Canadian students, and 6/15 for Quebec students. **Financial aid:** Closing date 6/30. Institutional form required. Applicants notified on a rolling basis starting 3/1; must reply within 4 week(s) of notification.

Academics. Students permitted to submit papers and exams in French. **Special study options:** Accelerated study, combined bachelor's/graduate degree, cooperative education, cross-registration, distance learning, double major, ESL, exchange student, honors, independent study, internships, study abroad, teacher certification program, Washington semester. **Credit/placement by examination:** AP, CLEP, IB, institutional tests. 30 credit hours maximum toward bachelor's degree. Maximum 30 AP credits on 120-credit program. **Support services:** Pre-admission summer program, reduced course load, remedial instruction, study skills assistance, tutoring.

Majors. Architecture: Architecture. **Area/ethnic studies:** African, Canadian, Caribbean, Chicano/Hispanic-American/Latino, East Asian, German, Italian, Latin American, Near/Middle Eastern, regional, Russian/Slavic, Spanish/Iberian, women's. **Biology:** General, anatomy, animal behavior, aquatic, bacteriology, biochemistry, biomedical sciences, botany, cell/histology, cellular/anatomical, ecology, environmental, genetics, marine, microbiology, molecular, neuroanatomy, physiology, wildlife, zoology. **Business:** General, accounting, accounting/finance, entrepreneurial studies, finance, human resources, international, international finance, labor relations, management science, managerial economics, marketing, operations, organizational behavior. **Computer sciences:** General, computer science. **Conservation:** General, economics, environmental science, environmental studies, wildlife/wilderness. **Education:** General, bilingual, biology, chemistry, early childhood, elementary, English, ESL, French, geography, health, history, mathematics, music, physical, physics, science, secondary, social science, social studies. **Engineering:** Agricultural, chemical, civil, computer, electrical, materials, mechanical, metallurgical, mining, software. **English:** English lit. **Foreign languages:** Classics, East Asian, French, German, Italian, linguistics, Russian, Spanish, translation. **Health services:** Nursing (RN). **History:** General, Asian, Canadian history, European. **Human services:** Social work. **Liberal arts:** Humanities. **Math:** General, applied, probability, statistics. **Parks/recreation:** Exercise sciences, health/fitness. **Philosophy/religion:** Judaic, philosophy, religion. **Physical sciences:** Analytical chemistry, atmospheric physics, atmospheric science, chemistry, geology, geophysics, hydrology, inorganic chemistry, organic chemistry, physics, planetary. **Psychology:** General. **Social sciences:** Anthropology, economics, geography, international economic development, political science, sociology, urban studies. **Theology:** Religious ed, sacred music, theology. **Visual/performing arts:** Art history/conservation, dramatic, jazz, music, music history, music pedagogy, music performance, music theory/composition, piano/keyboard, stringed instruments, voice/opera. **Work/family studies:** Food/nutrition, human nutrition.

Most popular majors. Biology 11%, business/marketing 13%, education 7%, engineering/engineering technologies 8%, health sciences 8%, psychology 6%, social sciences 17%.

Technology on campus. 3,730 workstations in dormitories, library, computer center, student center. Dormitories wired for high-speed internet access and linked to campus network. Commuter students can connect to campus network. Online course registration, online library, helpline, repair service, wireless network available.

Student life. Freshman orientation: Available. Preregistration for classes offered. One-day campus-wide orientation session held at end of August; new students meet administrators, senior students from their programs. **Housing:** Guaranteed on-campus for freshmen. Coed dorms, single-sex dorms, special housing for disabled, apartments, wellness housing available. $1,500 partly refundable deposit, deadline 6/15. Shared facilities housing, which is similar to cooperative housing available; however, chores and costs not shared among the students. **Activities:** Bands, choral groups, dance, drama, film society, international student organizations, literary magazine, music ensembles, musical theater, opera, radio station, student government, student newspaper, symphony orchestra, TV station, over 100 clubs/service groups/independent student organizations available.

Athletics. Intercollegiate: Badminton, baseball M, basketball, cheerleading, cross-country, fencing, field hockey W, football (tackle) M, golf, ice hockey, lacrosse, rowing (crew), rugby, sailing, skiing, soccer, squash, swimming, synchronized swimming W, tennis, track and field, volleyball, wrestling. **Intramural:** Badminton, basketball, football (non-tackle), ice hockey, soccer, squash, table tennis, tennis, volleyball. **Team name:** Redmen, Martlets.

Student services. Adult student services, alcohol/substance abuse counseling, chaplain/spiritual director, career counseling, services for economically disadvantaged, student employment services, financial aid counseling, health services, legal services, minority student services, on-campus daycare, personal counseling, placement for graduates, women's services. **Physically disabled:** Services for visually, speech, hearing impaired.

Contact. E-mail: admissions@mcgill.ca
Phone: (514) 398-3910 Fax: (514) 398-4193
Kim Bartlett, Director, Admissions and Recruitment, McGill University, 845 Sherbrooke Street West, Montreal, CC H3A-2T5

Memorial University of Newfoundland
St. John's, Canada **CB member**
www.mun.ca **CB code: 0885**

▶ Public 4-year university
▶ Commuter campus in small city
▶ 15,113 undergraduates

General. Founded in 1925. Additional campus (Sir Wilfred Grenfell College) in Corner Brook, Newfoundland; campus in Harlow, England. **Location:** Located in St. John's. **Calendar:** Trimester, limited summer session. **Full-time faculty:** 1,151 total. **Part-time faculty:** 45 total. **Special facilities:** Center for cold ocean resources engineering, botanical gardens, archaeology unit, ocean sciences center, flume tank, center for fisheries innovation, marine simulator.

Basis for selection. Open admission, but selective for some programs. GED not accepted. School achievement in a university preparatory high school program most important. Non-native speakers of English must submit TOEFL, Michigan Test of English Proficiency (minimum score of 85), or other acceptable test, unless graduating from English-language high school. Interviews, auditions, and essay required of music, theater, and visual arts majors. Portfolio required of visual arts majors.

High school preparation. 16 units required. Required units include English 3, mathematics 3, social studies 1, science 2, foreign language 1 and academic electives 6.

2015-2016 Annual costs. Tuition/fees: $2,550. Books/supplies: $1,000. **Additional information:** Annual tuition fees for medical students: Canadian citizens $6,250, international students $30,000.

Application procedures. Admission: Closing date 3/1 (receipt date). $40 fee. Admission notification on a rolling basis beginning on or about 4/30. Application fee $40 for in-province residents, $80 for out-of-province and international students. Housing deposit $500. Costs in Canadian dollars. **Financial aid:** Priority date 3/15; no closing date.

Academics. 3-year diplomas in fisheries and nautical science available from Marine Institute. **Special study options:** Accelerated study, cooperative education, distance learning, double major, ESL, exchange student, honors, internships, liberal arts/career combination, study abroad, teacher certification program. **Credit/placement by examination:** AP, CLEP, IB. **Support services:** Learning center, reduced course load, remedial instruction, study skills assistance, tutoring, writing center.

Majors. Area/ethnic studies: Canadian, regional, Russian/Slavic, women's. **Biology:** General, bacteriology, biochemistry, cell/histology, ecology, entomology, marine, neuroscience, parasitology. **Business:** Business admin, marketing. **Computer sciences:** General, computer science. **Conservation:** General, environmental studies, forestry. **Education:** General, adult/continuing, bilingual, biology, chemistry, curriculum, early childhood, elementary, French, history, music, physical, physics, reading, science, secondary, social science, social studies, special ed. **Engineering:** General, civil, electrical, marine, mechanical, ocean. **English:** English lit, writing. **Foreign languages:** Classics, French, German, linguistics, Spanish. **Health services:** Preop/surgical nursing. **History:** General. **Liberal arts:** Arts/sciences, humanities. **Math:** General, applied, statistics. **Parks/recreation:** General, facilities management. **Philosophy/religion:** Philosophy, religion. **Physical sciences:** Chemistry, geology, oceanography, physics. **Psychology:** General. **Social sciences:** Anthropology, archaeology, demography, economics, geography, political science, sociology. **Visual/performing arts:** General, dramatic, music, music history, music performance, music theory/composition, studio arts, theater design.

Most popular majors. Biology 6%, business/marketing 12%, education 21%, engineering/engineering technologies 6%, health sciences 11%, science technologies 7%.

Technology on campus. 850 workstations in dormitories, library, computer center. Dormitories wired for high-speed internet access and linked to campus network. Commuter students can connect to campus network. Online course registration, online library, helpline, repair service, student web hosting, wireless network available.

Student life. Freshman orientation: Mandatory. Preregistration for classes offered. Held a few days prior to start of classes. **Housing:** Coed dorms, single-sex dorms, special housing for disabled, apartments available. $500 nonrefundable deposit, deadline 5/31. **Activities:** Bands, choral groups, dance, drama, international student organizations, literary magazine, music ensembles, musical theater, radio station, student government, student newspaper, symphony orchestra.

Athletics. Intercollegiate: Basketball, cross-country, diving, fencing, field hockey W, soccer, swimming, volleyball. **Intramural:** Badminton, basketball, boxing, cheerleading, cross-country, diving, fencing, field hockey W, ice hockey M, judo, racquetball, rifle, soccer, softball, squash, swimming, table tennis, tennis, volleyball, water polo, weight lifting M, wrestling. **Team name:** Seahawks.

Student services. Chaplain/spiritual director, career counseling, student employment services, health services, on-campus daycare, personal counseling, placement for graduates, women's services. **Physically disabled:** Services for visually, speech, hearing impaired.

Contact. E-mail: admissions@mun.ca
Phone: (709) 737-4431 Fax: (709) 737-4893
Sheila Singleton, Registrar, Memorial University of Newfoundland, Memorial University of Newfoundland, Admissions Office-Arts and Admin. Bldg, St. John's, Newfoundland, Canada, CC A1C-S7

Queen's University
Kingston, Canada **CB member**
www.queensu.ca **CB code: 0949**

▶ Public 4-year university
▶ Residential campus in small city
▶ 17,833 degree-seeking undergraduates
▶ Application essay required

General. Degrees: 4,000 bachelor's awarded; master's, professional, doctoral offered. **Calendar:** Semester, limited summer session. **Full-time faculty:** 838 total; 98% have terminal degrees, 36% women.

Freshman class profile.

Return as sophomores: 95% **Live on campus:** 90%

Basis for selection. GED not accepted. GPA, SAT/ACT (if applicable), mandatory application essay very important. **Home schooled:** Statement describing home school structure and mission, transcript of courses and grades, state high school equivalency certificate required.

2015-2016 Annual costs. Domestic annual tuition fees: Engineering and Applied Science $12,993.97, Arts and Science $12,770.77, Commerce $17,414.31, Law $18,693.32, Medicine $25,555.06, Nursing $7,352.86. International annual tuition and fee: Engineering and Applied Science $36,395.17, Arts and Science $32,137.05, Commerce $39,285.58, Law $42,230.06, Medicine $87,257.66, Nursing $32,188.66, School of Religion $15,858.91.

Application procedures. Admission: Closing date 2/15 (receipt date). Application must be submitted online. Admission notification on a rolling basis beginning on or about 12/1. Must reply by 5/1. Separate application for a place in residence is due by June 8.

Academics. Special study options: Combined bachelor's/graduate degree, distance learning, double major, ESL, exchange student, honors, internships, study abroad, teacher certification program. **Credit/placement by examination:** AP, CLEP, IB, SAT, ACT. **Support services:** Learning center, preadmission summer program, reduced course load, remedial instruction, study skills assistance, tutoring, writing center.

Majors. Area/ethnic studies: French, German, Italian, Latin American/Caribbean, Spanish/Iberian. **Biology:** General, biochemistry. **Business:** General, business admin. **Computer sciences:** General, computer science. **Conservation:** Environmental science, environmental studies. **Education:** General. **Engineering:** General, applied physics, chemical, civil, computer, electrical, engineering chemistry, geological, mechanical, mining, software. **English:** English lit. **Foreign languages:** Classics, French, German, Hebrew, Hispanic and Latin American, Italian, linguistics, Spanish. **History:** General. **Liberal arts:** Humanities. **Math:** General, mathematics/statistics, statistics. **Parks/recreation:** Exercise sciences, health/fitness. **Philosophy/religion:** General, Judaic, philosophy, religion. **Physical sciences:** General, astronomy, astrophysics, chemistry, geology, physics. **Psychology:** General. **Social sciences:** General, applied economics, economics, geography, political science, sociology. **Visual/performing arts:** General, art, art history/conservation, dramatic, film/cinema/video, music, studio arts.

Technology on campus. Dormitories wired for high-speed internet access and linked to campus network. Online course registration, online library, helpline, repair service, wireless network available.

Student life. Freshman orientation: Available. Preregistration for classes offered. Held the week before classes begin in September; covers residence events and information on academic endeavors, student life. **Housing:** Guaranteed on-campus for freshmen. Coed dorms, single-sex dorms, cooperative housing, themed housing, wellness housing available. $525 partly refundable deposit, deadline 6/8. **Activities:** Bands, choral groups, dance, drama, film society, international student organizations, literary magazine, music ensembles, Model UN, musical theater, radio station, student government, student newspaper, TV station, Asian cooking club, Campus for Christ, Indian students association, Israel on Campus, Journalists for Human Rights, Japanese Relations at Queen's, New Democrat Party, Interfaith Council, Project on International Development, African Caribbean students association.

Athletics. Intercollegiate: Basketball, cross-country, football (tackle) M, ice hockey, rowing (crew), rugby, soccer, volleyball. **Intramural:** Basketball, football (non-tackle) M, ice hockey, soccer, ultimate frisbee, volleyball, water polo. **Team name:** Gaels.

Student services. Adult student services, alcohol/substance abuse counseling, chaplain/spiritual director, career counseling, services for economically disadvantaged, student employment services, financial aid counseling, health services, legal services, on-campus daycare, personal counseling, women's services. **Physically disabled:** Services for visually, speech, hearing impaired.

Contact. E-mail: admission@queensu.ca
Phone: (613) 533-2218 Fax: (613) 533-6810
Stuart Pinchin, Associate Registrar, Undergraduate Admission, Queen's University, 74 Union Street, Kingston, CC

Simon Fraser University
Burnaby, Canada
www.sfu.ca

CB member
CB code: 0999

- Public 4-year university
- Commuter campus in very large city
- 24,355 degree-seeking undergraduates: 48% part-time, 53% women
- 3,766 degree-seeking graduate students
- 63% of applicants admitted
- 66% graduate within 6 years

General. Founded in 1965. Regionally accredited. Harbour Centre campus in downtown Vancouver; Surrey campus in Surrey, British Columbia. **Degrees:** 5,223 bachelor's awarded; master's, doctoral offered. **Location:** 9 miles from Vancouver, British Columbia; 130 miles from Seattle, Washington. **Calendar:** Trimester, extensive summer session. **Full-time faculty:** 961 total; 89% have terminal degrees, 35% women. **Part-time faculty:** 8 total; 62% have terminal degrees, 62% women. **Class size:** 28% < 20, 33% 20-39, 6% 40-49, 17% 50-99, 15% >100. **Special facilities:** Art gallery, child care facility, hyperbaric chamber, underwater laboratory, combative room, apiary, archaeology museum.

Freshman class profile. 15,368 applied, 9,738 admitted, 3,431 enrolled.

GPA 3.75 or higher:	9%	Return as sophomores:	85%
GPA 3.50-3.74:	42%	Out-of-state:	7%
GPA 3.0-3.49:	49%		

Basis for selection. GED not accepted. Senior academic courses, test scores, and advanced academic course work (IB, AP, honors, etc.). Successful applicants normally have 2.8 GPA (3.0 for programs in Business Administration) and 1550 SAT (22 ACT). Academic background, GPA, and test scores most important. Canadian residents not required to submit SAT/ACT. Audition/interview may be required for school of contemporary arts. Applicants may submit personal information profile and at least 1 letter of reference. The Beedie School of Business also has a supplementary application process. **Home schooled:** Transcript of courses and grades required. Applicants must meet state high school graduation requirements.

High school preparation. 13 units required. Required units include English 4, mathematics 3, social studies 1, history 1, science 2 (laboratory 1), foreign language 1 and academic electives 3.

2015-2016 Annual costs. Tuition/fees: $6,031. Room/board: $9,336. Books/supplies: $2,040.

2014-2015 Financial aid. Need-based: 25% of total undergraduate aid awarded as scholarships/grants, 75% as loans/jobs. **Non-need-based:** Scholarships awarded for academics, alumni affiliation, art, athletics, leadership, music/drama, state residency.

Application procedures. Admission: Closing date 2/28 (receipt date). $75 fee. Application must be submitted online. Admission notification by 6/30. Admission notification on a rolling basis beginning on or about 1/15. **Financial aid:** Priority date 6/1, closing date 11/15. FAFSA, institutional form required. Applicants notified on a rolling basis.

Academics. Special study options: Cooperative education, cross-registration, distance learning, double major, exchange student, honors, independent study, internships, study abroad, teacher certification program. Dual degree program with Zhejiang University in China. **Credit/placement by examination:** AP, CLEP, IB, SAT, ACT. 60 credit hours maximum toward bachelor's degree. **Support services:** Learning center, study skills assistance, writing center.

Majors. Area/ethnic studies: Women's. **Biology:** General, biochemistry, molecular. **Business:** Accounting/business management, actuarial science, business admin, entrepreneurial studies, finance, management information systems, management science, marketing. **Communications:** Communications/speech/rhetoric, digital media. **Computer sciences:** General, information systems, programming. **Conservation:** General, environmental science, environmental studies. **Education:** General. **Engineering:** Engineering science. **English:** English lit. **Foreign languages:** French, linguistics. **Health services:** International public health. **History:** General. **Liberal arts:** Arts/sciences. **Math:** General, applied, statistics. **Parks/recreation:** Exercise sciences. **Philosophy/religion:** Philosophy. **Physical sciences:** Chemical physics, chemistry, geology, physics, theoretical physics. **Protective services:** Police science. **Psychology:** General. **Social sciences:** Anthropology, archaeology, criminology, economics, geography, political science, sociology. **Visual/performing arts:** General, cinematography, dance, design, dramatic, music.

Most popular majors. Business/marketing 7%, social sciences 10%.

Technology on campus. 900 workstations in library, computer center, student center. Dormitories wired for high-speed internet access. Commuter students can connect to campus network. Online course registration, online library, helpline, repair service, student web hosting, wireless network available.

Student life. Freshman orientation: Available, $30 fee. Preregistration for classes offered. Depending on type of program, 1 or 2 days immediately preceding the start of classes for a particular term. **Housing:** Coed dorms, single-sex dorms, special housing for disabled, apartments available. $450 nonrefundable deposit. **Activities:** Campus ministries, dance, drama, film society, international student organizations, radio station, student government, student newspaper, First Nations student center, center for students with disabilities, crisis line, public interest research group, women's center, interfaith center, harassment resolution office, student society.

Athletics. NCAA. Intercollegiate: Basketball, cross-country, diving, football (tackle) M, golf M, soccer, softball W, swimming, track and field, volleyball W, wrestling. **Intramural:** Badminton, basketball, football (non-tackle), soccer, softball, tennis, volleyball. **Team name:** The Clan.

Student services. Alcohol/substance abuse counseling, chaplain/spiritual director, career counseling, financial aid counseling, health services, legal services, minority student services, on-campus daycare, personal counseling, women's services. **Physically disabled:** Services for visually, speech, hearing impaired.

Contact. E-mail: undergraduate-admissions@sfu.ca
Phone: (778) 782-3397 Fax: (778) 782-4969
Louise Legris, Director of Admission, Simon Fraser University, 8888 University Drive, Burnaby, CC

University of Alberta
Edmonton, Canada
www.ualberta.ca

CB member
CB code: 0963

- Public 4-year university
- Commuter campus in very large city
- 30,626 degree-seeking undergraduates
- 7,204 graduate students

General. Founded in 1906. Regionally accredited. French-speaking element within university. **Degrees:** 6,552 bachelor's awarded; master's, professional, doctoral offered. **Location:** 180 miles from Calgary. **Calendar:** Semester, extensive summer session. **Full-time faculty:** 3,787 total. **Special facilities:** Center for the arts, museums, research library system, botanical gardens, research farm, agricultural research stations, professional development center, nanotechnology institute, heart institute, diabetes institute.

Basis for selection. Most undergraduate admission is based on completion of 5 appropriate Grade 12 subjects (program specific), including English.

Must present at least 70% to apply and must present a competitive average for admission, with minimum grade of 50% in each subject (based on 50% passing grade). Competitive averages range from 70-85%. SAT Subject Tests recommended. Auditions, portfolios, letters of intent/essays, or interviews required for several programs.

High school preparation. Required and recommended units include English 3, mathematics 3, social studies 3, history 3, science 3 (laboratory 3), foreign language 3 and academic electives 3. Specific course requirements vary by program.

2016-2017 Annual costs. Books/supplies: $1,600. **Additional information:** Full-time undergraduate tuition and required fees (most degree programs): Canadian citizens and permanent residents, $8,434; non-Canadian citizens, $23,189.98. standard double-occupancy on-campus room, $3,310; board, $3,227. Figures are in Canadian dollars.

Application procedures. Admission: Closing date 5/1 (postmark date). $125 fee. Admission notification on a rolling basis beginning on or about 12/1. Early Admission contingent upon completion of admission criteria and maintaining competitive average. **Financial aid:** Closing date 5/1. FAFSA, institutional form required. Applicants notified on a rolling basis.

Academics. Special study options: Accelerated study, combined bachelor's/graduate degree, cooperative education, distance learning, double major, dual enrollment of high school students, ESL, exchange student, honors, independent study, internships, student-designed major, study abroad, teacher certification program. **Credit/placement by examination:** AP, CLEP, IB. **Support services:** Learning center, pre-admission summer program, reduced course load, remedial instruction, study skills assistance, tutoring, writing center.

Majors. Area/ethnic studies: African, East Asian, Latin American, Near/ Middle Eastern, Russian/Eastern European/Eurasian, Scandinavian, Southeast Asian, women's. **Biology:** General, animal physiology, biochemistry, bioinformatics, botany, cell/histology, conservation, environmental, exercise physiology, immunology, microbiology, molecular genetics, neurobiology/ anatomy, neuroscience, pharmacology, pharmacology/toxicology, physiology, plant molecular, zoology. **Business:** General, accounting, actuarial science, business admin, communications, entrepreneurial studies, finance, human resources, international, international finance, management information systems, marketing, operations, organizational behavior, retailing, sales/ distribution. **Computer sciences:** General, computer science, programming. **Conservation:** General, environmental studies, forest management, forestry, management/policy, wildlife/wilderness. **Education:** General, art, bilingual, biology, chemistry, comparative, computer, drama/dance, early childhood, elementary, English, ESL, foreign languages, French, history, mathematics, middle, music, physical, physics, science, secondary, social studies, special ed, trade/industrial. **Engineering:** General, applied physics, chemical, civil, computer, electrical, engineering mechanics, materials, mechanical, mining, petroleum, software. **English:** Creative writing, English lit. **Foreign languages:** General, Chinese, classics, comparative lit, French, German, Italian, Japanese, Latin, linguistics, modern Greek, Romance, Scandinavian, Spanish. **Health services:** Athletic training, clinical lab technology, dental hygiene, dietician assistant, kinesiotherapy, nursing (RN), occupational therapy assistant, predental, premedicine, preop/surgical nursing, prepharmacy, preveterinary. **History:** General. **Math:** General, applied, computational, computational/applied, financial, mathematics/statistics, probability, statistics. **Parks/ recreation:** General, exercise sciences, sports admin. **Philosophy/religion:** Philosophy, religion. **Physical sciences:** Atmospheric science, chemistry, physics. **Protective services:** Criminal justice. **Psychology:** General. **Social sciences:** Anthropology, criminology, economics, geography, international relations, political science, sociology. **Visual/performing arts:** Dramatic, film/cinema/video, metal/jewelry, music, music history, music theory/composition, printmaking, studio arts, theater design. **Work/family studies:** Clothing/textiles, family resources, family studies, family/community services, food/nutrition, human nutrition.

Technology on campus. 1,300 workstations in dormitories, library, computer center, student center. Dormitories wired for high-speed internet access and linked to campus network. Commuter students can connect to campus network. Online course registration, online library, helpline, student web hosting, wireless network available.

Student life. Freshman orientation: Available. Preregistration for classes offered. **Housing:** Guaranteed on-campus for freshmen. Coed dorms, singlesex dorms, special housing for disabled, apartments, fraternity/sorority housing available. **Activities:** Bands, campus ministries, choral groups, dance, drama, film society, international student organizations, literary magazine, music ensembles, Model UN, musical theater, opera, radio station, student government, student newspaper, symphony orchestra, more than 400 clubs available.

Athletics. Intercollegiate: Basketball, cross-country, field hockey W, football (tackle) M, golf, ice hockey, rugby W, soccer, swimming, tennis, track and field, volleyball, wrestling. **Intramural:** Archery, badminton, baseball, basketball, bowling, cross-country, diving, football (non-tackle) M, football (tackle) M, golf, gymnastics, ice hockey, judo, racquetball, rugby, skiing, soccer, softball, squash, swimming, table tennis, tennis, track and field, triathlon, ultimate frisbee, volleyball, water polo, wrestling. **Team name:** Golden Bears, Pandas, Vikings.

Student services. Adult student services, alcohol/substance abuse counseling, chaplain/spiritual director, career counseling, services for economically disadvantaged, student employment services, financial aid counseling, health services, legal services, minority student services, on-campus daycare, personal counseling, placement for graduates, women's services. **Physically disabled:** Services for visually, speech, hearing impaired.

Contact. Phone: (780) 492-3113 Fax: (780) 492-7172
Christina Caputo, Admissions Team Lead, University of Alberta, Administration Building, Edmonton, CC

University of British Columbia
Vancouver, Canada — CB member
www.ubc.ca — CB code: 0965

- Public 4-year university
- Commuter campus in very large city
- 32,547 degree-seeking undergraduates: 26% part-time, 54% women
- 16,229 degree-seeking graduate students
- 70% of applicants admitted
- Application essay required
- 76% graduate within 6 years

General. Founded in 1915. 17 faculties, 15 schools and 3 colleges across two major campuses (Vancouver and Okanagan) and two satellite campuses. **Degrees:** 7,668 bachelor's awarded; master's, professional, doctoral offered. **Location:** 6 miles from downtown Vancouver (Vancouver campus), 5 miles from downtown Kelowna (Okanagan campus). **Calendar:** Semester, extensive summer session. **Full-time faculty:** 3,119 total. **Part-time faculty:** 642 total. **Class size:** 26% < 20, 32% 20-39, 10% 40-49, 16% 50-99, 16% >100. **Special facilities:** Museum of anthropology, museum of biodiversity, museum of geological sciences, botany collection and herbarium, botanical garden, Japanese garden, astronomical observatories, performing arts center, opera theater, drama theater, global issues center, winter sports center, particle accelerator, forests, model farm.

Freshman class profile. 20,733 applied, 14,491 admitted, 6,838 enrolled.

Basis for selection. GED not accepted. Academic averages most important. Minimum requirement is strong B+ average; for science and engineering-based programs, A average likely to be required. Evaluation of those from US curriculum made on best 8 academic courses from junior and senior years. Most applicants must submit personal statement including short essay responses and extra-curricular achievements and interests. US curriculum students must submit SAT/ACT (including Writing component). Exceptions may be granted for countries where tests are not available. Minimum competitive score for SAT is 1500. Minimum competitive score for ACT is 24 + 8 writing. All applicants must meet English language admission standard. Applicants must also meet specific program requirements. Applications encouraged from students completing enriched secondary school programs such as International Baccalaureate (IB), Advanced Placement (AP), General Certificate of Education (GCE), and French Baccalaureate. Generous first-year credit offered to students with high academic achievement in these programs. School of Music (Vancouver) requires interview, audition, and/ or portfolio. Fine Arts programs (Okanagan) require portfolio and letter of intent.

High school preparation. College-preparatory program required. 19 units required. Required units include English 4, mathematics 3 and academic electives 12.

2015-2016 Annual costs. Tuition/fees: $5,923; $5,923 out-of-district. Room/board: $9,762. Books/supplies: $2,200. Personal expenses: $3,500. **Additional information:** Tuition for international students (those who are not Canadian citizens or permanent residents) entering first-year in 2015-16 is projected to be $880 per credit for most undergraduate programs; examples of full-time tuition costs include 30-credit Arts program, $26,399, and 35-credit Engineering program $31,678. Tuition for Canadian citizens is projected to be $166 per credit for most programs. Although student fees vary according to program, they are generally $935 to $1,689; fees cover extended health and dental insurance, as well as a local public-transit pass so that all students enjoy low-cost local transit without additional charge. Basic on-campus room and board expenses are projected to be $9,800. Books and supplies cost an average of $2,020. Amounts shown are in Canadian dollars and are for the 8-month academic year.

Financial aid. Non-need-based: Scholarships awarded for academics, athletics, leadership. **Additional information:** Need-based financial aid from public funds is available to Canadian citizens and permanent residents. In addition, some merit and/or need-based financial aid is available for international students. International students may also be offered merit awards, based on the strength of their application including personal profile questions.

Application procedures. Admission: Priority date 12/10; deadline 1/31 (receipt date). $64 fee ($108 out-of-state). Application must be submitted online. Admission notification on a rolling basis beginning on or about 1/30. Must reply by 6/1. Deposit of $250 for Canadian students or $500 for international students required. Students applying for on-campus student housing must reply by 6/1. Housing deposit ($700 Canadian) due at time of accepting housing offer. Students must normally accept admission offers by 6/1. **Financial aid:** Closing date 12/10. Institutional form required. Applicants notified by 4/1; must reply by 4/30.

Academics. Several cross-disciplinary options available in first-year study. Undergraduate students encouraged to engage in research projects, and findings can be presented at the annual Undergraduate Research Conference. **Special study options:** Combined bachelor's/graduate degree, cooperative education, cross-registration, distance learning, double major, dual enrollment of high school students, ESL, exchange student, honors, internships, student-designed major, study abroad, teacher certification program. Study abroad available at 175 partner institutions in 42 countries. Joint Bachelor degree option with l'Institut d'études politiques de Paris (Sciences Po), France. **Credit/placement by examination:** AP, CLEP, IB. UBC offers credits to students entering from enriched programs, including Advanced Placement, International Baccalaureate, British patterned Advanced Levels, or French Baccalaureate. Exact credits offered depend on degree program and will be determined at time of entry. **Support services:** Learning center, pre-admission summer program, reduced course load, study skills assistance, tutoring, writing center.

Majors. Architecture: Environmental design. **Area/ethnic studies:** Asian, Canadian, Chicano/Hispanic-American/Latino, East Asian, European, German, Italian, Latin American, Russian/Eastern European/Eurasian, Russian/Slavic, Slavic, South Asian, Southeast Asian, Western European, women's. **Biology:** General, anatomy, animal physiology, bacteriology, biochemistry, biophysics, biotechnology, cell/histology, conservation, ecology, environmental, epidemiology, evolutionary, genetics, molecular, molecular biochemistry, neuroscience, pathology, pharmacology/toxicology, physiology, reproductive, zoology. **Business:** General, accounting, business admin, finance, human resources, international, international finance, international marketing, investments/securities, labor relations, management information systems, management science, managerial economics, marketing, operations, real estate, transportation. **Computer sciences:** General, artificial intelligence, computer science. **Conservation:** General, economics, environmental science, environmental studies, forest management, forest resources, forest sciences, forestry, wood science. **Education:** General, elementary, middle, multi-level teacher, Native American, physical, secondary. **Engineering:** General, applied physics, biomedical, chemical, civil, computer, electrical, engineering mechanics, environmental, forest, geological, materials, mechanical, metallurgical, mining, operations research, software. **English:** British lit, Canadian lit, creative writing, English lit. **Foreign languages:** Chinese, classics, French, German, Germanic, Italian, Japanese, Korean, Latin, linguistics, Native American, Portuguese, Romance, Slavic, South Asian, Spanish, Urdu. **Health services:** Clinical lab assistant, dental hygiene, nurse midwife, nursing (RN), preveterinary. **History:** General. **Human services:** Social work. **Math:** General, applied, statistics. **Parks/recreation:** Exercise sciences, health/fitness, sports admin. **Philosophy/religion:** Philosophy, religion. **Physical sciences:** Astronomy, atmospheric science, chemistry, geology, geophysics, materials science, oceanography, physics, planetary, theoretical physics. **Psychology:** General. **Social sciences:** Anthropology, archaeology, Canadian government, economics, geography, international relations, political science, sociology. **Visual/performing arts:** General, art, art history/conservation, cinematography, conducting, dramatic, film/cinema/video, music, music history, music performance, music theory/composition, musicology, piano/keyboard, stringed instruments, theater arts management, theater design, voice/opera. **Work/family studies:** General, family/community services, food/nutrition, human nutrition.

Technology on campus. Dormitories wired for high-speed internet access and linked to campus network. Commuter students can connect to campus network. Online course registration, online library, helpline, repair service, student web hosting, wireless network available.

Student life. Freshman orientation: Available. Preregistration for classes offered. Full-week program before school start, 1-day parents orientation available. **Housing:** Guaranteed on-campus for freshmen. Coed dorms, single-sex dorms, apartments, fraternity/sorority housing, themed housing available. $700 partly refundable deposit. Cultural houses in partnership with universities in Japan, Korea, and Mexico available. **Activities:** Bands, choral groups, dance, drama, film society, international student organizations, literary magazine, music ensembles, Model UN, musical theater, opera, radio station, student government, student newspaper, symphony orchestra, TV station, over 350 clubs, societies, and other groups.

Athletics. NAIA. **Intercollegiate:** Baseball M, basketball, cross-country, equestrian, field hockey, football (tackle) M, golf, ice hockey, rowing (crew), rugby, skiing, soccer, softball W, swimming, track and field, volleyball. **Intramural:** Badminton, basketball, cheerleading, cross-country, football (non-tackle), ice hockey, judo, racquetball, skiing, soccer, softball W, squash, swimming, tennis, triathlon, ultimate frisbee, volleyball, water polo, wrestling M. **Team name:** Thunderbirds.

Student services. Alcohol/substance abuse counseling, career counseling, student employment services, financial aid counseling, health services, minority student services, on-campus daycare, personal counseling, placement for graduates, women's services. **Physically disabled:** Services for visually, speech, hearing impaired.

Contact. Phone: (604) 822-8999 Toll-free number: (877) 272-1422 Fax: (604) 822-9858
Andrew Arida, Director, Undergraduate Admissions, University of British Columbia, 2016 - 1874 East Mall, Vancouver, CC

University of Manitoba
Winnipeg, Canada
www.umanitoba.ca   **CB code: 0973**

- Public 4-year university
- Commuter campus in very large city
- 25,298 undergraduates

General. Founded in 1877. **Location:** 10 miles from downtown Winnipeg. **Calendar:** Semester, limited summer session. **Full-time faculty:** 1,700 total. **Part-time faculty:** 1,600 total. **Special facilities:** Planetarium, astronomical observatory, farm education center.

Basis for selection. Open admission, but selective for some programs. **Home schooled:** State high school equivalency certificate required.

High school preparation. 30 units required.

2015-2016 Annual costs. Annual tuition fees for Canadian/permanent residents $3,700-$20,500, for international students $12,900-$23,800. Books and supplies $500-$16,500.

Application procedures. Admission: $90 fee.

Academics. Special study options: Combined bachelor's/graduate degree, cooperative education, distance learning, double major, ESL, honors, independent study, internships, liberal arts/career combination, study abroad, teacher certification program, weekend college. **Credit/placement by examination:** AP, CLEP, IB. 30 credit hours maximum toward bachelor's degree. **Support services:** Learning center, reduced course load, study skills assistance, tutoring.

Majors. Architecture: Environmental design. **Area/ethnic studies:** Asian, Canadian, Latin American, Near/Middle Eastern, Russian/Eastern European/Eurasian, Russian/Slavic, women's. **Biology:** Bacteriology, biochemistry, botany, cell/histology, ecology, entomology, genetics, molecular, pathology, pharmacology, plant pathology, plant physiology, zoology. **Business:** Accounting, actuarial science, business admin, finance, international, labor relations, market research. **Computer sciences:** General, computer science, data processing, information systems, programming, systems analysis. **Conservation:** General, environmental studies. **Education:** General, adult ed admin, business, curriculum, early childhood, educational technology, elementary, ESL, family/consumer sciences, foundations, leadership, middle, multi-level teacher, music, physical, secondary, special ed, technology/industrial arts. **Engineering:** General, agricultural, civil, computer, electrical, mechanical. **English:** American lit, British lit, creative writing, English lit, writing. **Foreign languages:** Biblical, classics, comparative lit, French, German, Hebrew, Italian, linguistics, modern Greek, Russian, Spanish. **Health services:** Athletic training, dental hygiene, nursing (RN), occupational therapy, physical therapy. **History:** General. **Human services:** General, social work. **Math:** General, applied, statistics. **Parks/recreation:** General, exercise sciences, health/fitness, sports admin. **Philosophy/religion:** Judaic, philosophy, religion. **Physical sciences:** Astronomy, chemistry, geology, materials science, physics. **Psychology:** General, clinical, counseling, educational. **Social sciences:** Anthropology, criminology, economics, geography, political science, sociology. **Visual/performing arts:** Art, art history/conservation, commercial/advertising art, dramatic, film/cinema/video, interior design, music, music history, music performance, music theory/composition, piano/keyboard, studio arts, theater history, voice/opera. **Work/family studies:** General, clothing/textiles, family/community services, food/nutrition.

Technology on campus. 392 workstations in library, computer center. Commuter students can connect to campus network. Online course registration, online library, helpline, repair service, student web hosting, wireless network available.

Student life. Freshman orientation: Mandatory. Preregistration for classes offered. **Housing:** Coed dorms available. **Activities:** Bands, choral groups, dance, drama, music ensembles, musical theater, radio station, student government, student newspaper, symphony orchestra.

Athletics. Intercollegiate: Basketball, cheerleading, cross-country, diving, field hockey W, football (tackle) M, ice hockey, skiing, soccer, swimming, synchronized swimming W, tennis, track and field, volleyball, weight lifting M, wrestling. **Intramural:** Archery, basketball, cross-country, diving, field hockey W, football (non-tackle) M, handball, ice hockey, judo M, racquetball, soccer, squash, swimming, tennis, volleyball. **Team name:** Bisons.

Student services. Adult student services, alcohol/substance abuse counseling, chaplain/spiritual director, career counseling, student employment services, financial aid counseling, health services, legal services, on-campus daycare, personal counseling, placement for graduates. **Physically disabled:** Services for visually, speech, hearing impaired.

Contact. E-mail: admissions@umanitoba.ca
Phone: (204) 474-8808 Fax: (204) 474-7554
Iris Reece-Tougas, Director of Admissions, University of Manitoba, 424 University Centre, Winnipeg, CC R3T 2-N2

University of Toronto

Toronto, Canada	**CB member**
www.utoronto.ca	**CB code: 0982**

▶ Public 4-year university
▶ Commuter campus in very large city
▶ 70,454 degree-seeking undergraduates: 9% part-time, 55% women
▶ 17,270 degree-seeking graduate students
▶ 82% of applicants admitted
▶ SAT or ACT with writing, SAT Subject Tests, application essay required

General. Degrees: 12,064 bachelor's awarded; master's, professional, doctoral offered. **Location:** 95 miles from Buffalo, NY. **Calendar:** Semester, extensive summer session. **Full-time faculty:** 5,779 total. **Part-time faculty:** 7,460 total. **Special facilities:** Greenhouses, observatory, university-operated art galleries and theaters, teaching hospitals, 150-acre farm, 44 libraries.

Freshman class profile. 75,784 applied, 62,148 admitted, 16,017 enrolled.

Basis for selection. Typically, applicants who are competitive for admission to the University of Toronto are in the top third of their class. Only those applicants who have attained a high level of academic achievement and who present credits to satisfy any prerequisites of specific courses or programs in which they intend to enroll will be admitted. The Faculty of Arts and Science St. George campus, University of Toronto Mississauga, University of Toronto Scarborough, the Faculty of Music, and the Faculty of Physical Education and Health/Kinesiology will consider applications from students in the USA and other countries who have completed or who are completing 12th grade in an accredited high school; such applicants must present high scores in SAT Reasoning or ACT examinations including the Writing Test component and at least three SAT Subject Tests or AP/IB subjects appropriate to their proposed area of study. Scores below 500 in any part of the SAT Reasoning or SAT Subject Tests are not acceptable. Many programs require higher scores. Students seeking admission to science or business/commerce programs are strongly advised to complete AP Calculus (AB or BC) or IB Mathematics (HL or SL or Math Methods with Calculus option). Student profiles required for some programs. **Home schooled:** Statement describing home school structure and mission, transcript of courses and grades required. Application should include course outlines, textbooks and method of evaluation used, samples of written work, relevant details of any independent evaluations or assessments; results of standardized tests may also be considered. **Learning Disabled:** Students can send a letter with supporting documentation.

2015-2016 Annual costs. Books/supplies: $1,000. **Additional information:** Full-time undergraduate tuition, with costs varying according to program of study: Canadian citizens and permanent residents, $6,220 to $13,620; non-Canadian citizens, $38,460 to $43,540. Required fees: $1,265 to $2,459. Standard double-occupancy on-campus room and board: $10,484 to $14,895. Figures, which cover the academic year, are in Canadian dollars.

Financial aid. All financial aid based on need.

Application procedures. Admission: Closing date 2/1 (receipt date). $255 fee. Admission notification on a rolling basis. Application deadlines vary by program. **Financial aid:** No deadline.

Academics. Special study options: Combined bachelor's/graduate degree, cooperative education, double major, ESL, exchange student, honors, independent study, internships, student-designed major, study abroad, teacher certification program. **Credit/placement by examination:** AP, CLEP, SAT, ACT. **Support services:** Learning center, reduced course load, study skills assistance, tutoring, writing center. Each college and academic division offers academic support through their registrar's offices.

Majors. Architecture: Architecture, environmental design, history/criticism, urban/community planning. **Area/ethnic studies:** African, African-American, American, Asian, Canadian, Caribbean, Chinese, East Asian, European, French, gay/lesbian, German, Italian, Latin American, Native American, Near/Middle Eastern, Polish, Russian/Eastern European/Eurasian, Russian/Slavic, Slavic, Spanish/Iberian, Ukraine, women's. **Biology:** General, animal physiology, biochemistry, Biochemistry/molecular biology, bioinformatics, biophysics, biotechnology, botany, cellular/anatomical, conservation, ecology, environmental, genetics, molecular, molecular biochemistry, molecular biophysics, molecular pharmacology, neuroscience, pharmacology, pharmacology/toxicology, toxicology, zoology. **Business:** General. **Communications:** Communications/speech/rhetoric, digital media, health, journalism, media studies. **Communications technology:** General. **Computer sciences:** General, artificial intelligence, computer science, information systems, information technology, programming, systems analysis. **Conservation:** General, environmental science, environmental studies, forestry. **Education:** General, elementary, middle, multi-level teacher, secondary. **Engineering:** General, aerospace, agricultural, applied physics, biomedical, chemical, civil, computer, engineering science, environmental, industrial, materials, mechanical. **English:** Creative writing, English lit. **Foreign languages:** Ancient Greek, Biblical, Bosnian/Serbo/Croatian, Celtic, classics, Czech, French, German, Germanic, Hebrew, Italian, Latin, linguistics, Polish, Portuguese, Russian, Slavic, Slovak, South Asian, Southeast Asian, Spanish, Ukrainian. **Health services:** EMT paramedic, ethics, pharmaceutical sciences, predental, premedicine, prepharmacy. **History:** General, European, science/technology. **Liberal arts:** Arts/sciences, humanities. **Math:** General, probability, statistics. **Parks/recreation:** Exercise sciences, health/fitness. **Philosophy/religion:** Buddhist, Christian, ethics, Judaic, logic, philosophy, religion. **Physical sciences:** General, astronomy, astrophysics, chemistry, forensic chemistry, paleontology, physics, planetary. **Psychology:** General, forensic. **Social sciences:** Anthropology, archaeology, Canadian government, criminology, economics, geography, international economic development, international economics, international relations, physical anthropology, political science, sociology, U.S. government, urban studies. **Theology:** Religious ed, theology. **Visual/performing arts:** General, art, art history/conservation, dramatic, film/cinema/video, jazz, music, music history, music performance, music theory/composition, stringed instruments, studio arts, voice/opera.

Technology on campus. Dormitories wired for high-speed internet access and linked to campus network. Commuter students can connect to campus network. Online course registration, online library, helpline, repair service, student web hosting, wireless network available.

Student life. Freshman orientation: Available. Preregistration for classes offered. Usually held the week before classes begin. **Policies:** Code of Student Conduct. **Housing:** Guaranteed on-campus for freshmen. Coed dorms, single-sex dorms, special housing for disabled, apartments, cooperative housing available. $600 nonrefundable deposit. **Activities:** Bands, campus ministries, choral groups, dance, drama, film society, international student organizations, literary magazine, music ensembles, Model UN, musical theater, opera, radio station, student government, student newspaper, symphony orchestra, TV station, Black Students' Association, Because I am a Girl, Canadian Asian Student Society, Engineers Without Borders, Greenpeace Student Network, Habitat for Humanity, Operation Smile, Science for Peace, Swing Dance Club, United Nations Society.

Athletics. Intercollegiate: Badminton, baseball M, basketball, cross-country, fencing, field hockey W, football (non-tackle) M, football (tackle) M, golf, ice hockey, lacrosse, rowing (crew), rugby M, skiing, soccer, softball W, swimming, synchronized swimming W, tennis, track and field, volleyball, water polo, wrestling M. **Intramural:** Badminton, baseball M, basketball, cross-country, fencing, field hockey W, football (non-tackle) M, football (tackle) M, golf, ice hockey, lacrosse, rowing (crew) M, rugby M, skiing, soccer, softball W, swimming, tennis, track and field, volleyball, water polo, wrestling M. **Team name:** Varsity Blues.

Student services. Adult student services, alcohol/substance abuse counseling, chaplain/spiritual director, career counseling, services for economically disadvantaged, student employment services, financial aid counseling, health services, legal services, minority student services, on-campus daycare, personal counseling, placement for graduates, women's services. **Physically disabled:** Services for visually, speech, hearing impaired.

Contact. Phone: (416) 978-2190 Fax: (416) 978-7022
Merike Remmel, Director of Admissions, University of Toronto, 172 St. George Street, Toronto, CC

University of Waterloo
Waterloo, Canada
www.uwaterloo.ca

CB code: 0996

- Public 4-year university
- Residential campus in large city
- 28,716 degree-seeking undergraduates
- 4,181 graduate students
- SAT or ACT (ACT writing optional), application essay, interview required

General. Regionally accredited. Four affiliated university colleges: Conrad Grebel College, St. Jerome's University, St. Paul's University, and Renison University College. **Degrees:** 5,778 bachelor's awarded; master's, doctoral offered. **Location:** 62 miles from Toronto. **Calendar:** Trimester, extensive summer session. **Full-time faculty:** 1,141 total; 89% have terminal degrees, 26% women. **Special facilities:** Museum of earth sciences, observatory, greenhouses, optometry clinic, museum of vision science, real-time programming lab, centre for education in mathematics and computing, ecology lab, living wetland lab, student design centre, quantum nano centre, velocity residence, velocity garage and velocity foundry.

Basis for selection. GED not accepted. Applicants must meet minimum admission averages which are determined annually based on the number of applicants and the number of spaces available. Other factors, such as extracurricular activities and contest scores, as well as grades are considered. All applicants are encouraged to complete Admission Information Form (AIF) to augment their application and to explain any extenuating circumstances that may have affected past academic performance. 1100 SAT normally required (exclusive of Writing). SAT Writing evaluated on individual basis. Faculty of Arts and Faculty of Environment require 600 SAT Critical Reading. 26 ACT normally required. Faculty of Arts and Faculty of Environment require 26 ACT English. Selected accounting and financial management applicants will be invited to write the Accounting and Financial Management Admission Assessment. Selected architecture applicants will be invited for interview, writing exercise, and discussion of their portfolios. Social work applicants will need letter of reference and personal statement that confirm sufficient practical experience and personal suitability. **Home schooled:** Transcript of courses and grades, state high school equivalency certificate required. Admissions office prefers that applicants complete final year of pre-university studies at traditional (accredited) high school. **Learning Disabled:** Contact AccessAbility (Office for Persons with Disabilities).

2015-2016 Annual costs. Books/supplies: $2,000. Personal expenses: $2,900. **Additional information:** Full-time undergraduate tuition, with costs varying according to program of study: Canadian citizens and permanent residents, $6,100 to $12,800; international students, $21,000 to $31,000. Books and supplies $2,000-$4,300. Additional fees may apply. Figures, which cover the academic year, are in Canadian dollars and are estimated averages based on 2015 figures. Exact amounts for 2016-17 will be available in July 2016.

Financial aid. All financial aid based on need. **Additional information:** Students who are not residents of the Province of Ontario (Canada) as defined by the Ontario Student Assistance Program (OSAP) should apply for financial aid in home states/countries.

Application procedures. Admission: Closing date 3/28 (postmark date). $165 fee. Application must be submitted online. Admission notification by 5/28. Admission notification on a rolling basis beginning on or about 12/15. Must reply by 6/1. **Financial aid:** No deadline. Institutional form required.

Academics. Special study options: Combined bachelor's/graduate degree, cooperative education, cross-registration, distance learning, double major, ESL, exchange student, honors, independent study, liberal arts/career combination, student-designed major, study abroad. **Credit/placement by examination:** AP, CLEP, IB, SAT, ACT. **Support services:** Learning center, pre-admission summer program, reduced course load, remedial instruction, study skills assistance, tutoring, writing center.

Majors. Architecture: Architecture, urban/community planning. **Area/ethnic studies:** East Asian, French, Italian, Latin American, Russian/Eastern European/Eurasian, Russian/Slavic, women's. **Biology:** General, biochemistry, bioinformatics, biomedical sciences, biotechnology. **Business:** General, accounting, actuarial science, business admin, finance, human resources, information resources management, international, investments/securities, tourism/travel. **Communications:** Communications/speech/rhetoric, digital media. **Computer sciences:** Computer science. **Conservation:** Environmental science, environmental studies, management/policy. **Education:** French, mathematics. **Engineering:** General, chemical, civil, computer, electrical, environmental, geological, mechanical, operations research, robotics, software, systems. **English:** English lit, rhetoric/composition. **Foreign languages:** German. **Health services:** Premedicine, prepharmacy, recreational therapy. **History:** General. **Human services:** Social work. **Liberal arts:**

Arts/sciences. **Math:** General, applied, computational, statistics. **Parks/recreation:** General, exercise sciences. **Philosophy/religion:** Islamic, Judaic, philosophy, religion. **Physical sciences:** General, chemistry, geology, physics, theoretical physics. **Psychology:** General. **Social sciences:** Anthropology, criminology, economics, geography, international economic development, political science, sociology. **Theology:** Sacred music. **Visual/performing arts:** General, dramatic, music, studio arts.

Technology on campus. Dormitories wired for high-speed internet access and linked to campus network. Commuter students can connect to campus network. Online course registration, online library, helpline, repair service, wireless network available.

Student life. Freshman orientation: Available, $100 fee. Preregistration for classes offered. Three to five day academic and social program. **Housing:** Guaranteed on-campus for freshmen. Coed dorms, special housing for disabled, apartments, themed housing available. $500 nonrefundable deposit, deadline 6/1. Living-learning communities allow students to live in small groups, with all students in a given community enrolled in the same academic program. **Activities:** Bands, campus ministries, choral groups, dance, drama, film society, international student organizations, literary magazine, music ensembles, Model UN, musical theater, opera, student government, student newspaper, symphony orchestra, Aboriginal students association, Caribbean students association, University Association of New Democrats, Chinese drama club, Hindu students association, Konnichiwa Japan, Latin American student association, Polish students association, World Vision club, International Health Development Association.

Athletics. Intercollegiate: Badminton, baseball M, basketball, cheerleading, cross-country, field hockey W, football (tackle) M, golf, ice hockey, rugby, skiing, soccer, squash M, swimming, tennis, track and field, volleyball. **Intramural:** Badminton, baseball, basketball, cricket, football (non-tackle), ice hockey, soccer, softball, squash, ultimate frisbee, volleyball. **Team name:** Warriors.

Student services. Alcohol/substance abuse counseling, chaplain/spiritual director, career counseling, student employment services, financial aid counseling, health services, legal services, on-campus daycare, personal counseling. **Physically disabled:** Services for visually, speech, hearing impaired.

Contact. E-mail: myapplication@uwaterloo.ca
Phone: (519) 888-4567 ext. 33106 Fax: (519) 746-2882
Andre Jardin, Associate Registrar, Admissions, University of Waterloo, Ontario Universities Application Centre, Guelph, CC

Egypt

American University in Cairo
New Cairo, Egypt
www.aucegypt.edu

CB member
CB code: 0903

- Private 4-year university
- Commuter campus in very large city
- 5,561 degree-seeking undergraduates: 8% part-time, 53% women
- 1,178 degree-seeking graduate students
- 37% of applicants admitted
- Application essay required
- 79% graduate within 6 years

General. Founded in 1919. Regionally accredited. Language of instruction is English; 75% of degree-seeking students must be of Egyptian nationality. **Degrees:** 949 bachelor's awarded; master's, doctoral offered. **Location:** 40 kilometers from downtown. **Calendar:** Semester, extensive summer session. **Full-time faculty:** 406 total; 74% have terminal degrees, 50% women. **Part-time faculty:** 311 total; 67% have terminal degrees, 47% women. **Class size:** 41% < 20, 56% 20-39, 2% 40-49, less than 1% 50-99, less than 1% >100.

Freshman class profile. 3,150 applied, 1,161 admitted, 897 enrolled.

Mid 50% test scores			
SAT critical reading:	450-530	GPA 3.50-3.74:	14%
SAT math:	560-670	GPA 3.0-3.49:	32%
SAT writing:	510-630	GPA 2.0-2.99:	43%
GPA 3.75 or higher:	11%	Return as sophomores:	93%

Basis for selection. Applicants from the United States expected to have completed college preparatory (academic) high school program and submit

1350 SAT. Arab students must take Thanawiya 'Amma, with minimum score of 75% required. CE/GCSE/IGCSE certificates will also be considered for admission. TOEFL/IELTS tests are required for all students for placement. **Home schooled:** Transcript of courses and grades, state high school equivalency certificate required.

High school preparation. 22 units recommended. Recommended units include English 3, mathematics 3, social studies 3, science 2 and foreign language 2. One unit fine arts recommended.

2015-2016 Annual costs. Tuition/fees: $9,216.

2014-2015 Financial aid. Need-based: 791 full-time freshmen applied for aid; 791 deemed to have need; 495 received aid. Average scholarship/grant was $2,666. 99% of total undergraduate aid awarded as scholarships/grants, 1% as loans/jobs. **Non-need-based:** Awarded to 1,724 full-time undergraduates, including 301 freshmen. Scholarships awarded for art, athletics.

Application procedures. Admission: Priority date 3/2; deadline 5/15 (receipt date). $50 fee. Admission notification on a rolling basis beginning on or about 7/20. **Financial aid:** Priority date 6/15, closing date 9/15. Institutional form required.

Academics. Special study options: Double major, ESL, independent study, internships, liberal arts/career combination, study abroad. **Credit/placement by examination:** AP, CLEP, IB, SAT, institutional tests. **Support services:** Learning center, reduced course load, remedial instruction, study skills assistance, tutoring, writing center.

Majors. Area/ethnic studies: Near/Middle Eastern. **Biology:** General. **Business:** Accounting, actuarial science, business admin. **Communications:** Journalism, media studies. **Computer sciences:** General. **Engineering:** Architectural, computer, construction, electrical, mechanical, petroleum. **English:** English lit. **Foreign languages:** Arabic, comparative lit. **History:** General, Asian. **Math:** General. **Philosophy/religion:** Philosophy. **Physical sciences:** Chemistry, physics. **Psychology:** General. **Social sciences:** Anthropology, archaeology, economics, political science, sociology. **Visual/performing arts:** Art, dramatic.

Most popular majors. Business/marketing 35%, communications/journalism 11%, engineering/engineering technologies 27%, social sciences 14%.

Technology on campus. 935 workstations in dormitories, library, computer center. Dormitories wired for high-speed internet access and linked to campus network. Commuter students can connect to campus network. Online course registration, online library, helpline, repair service, wireless network available.

Student life. Freshman orientation: Available. Preregistration for classes offered. Held in August for 3 days. **Policies:** Non-smoking campus. **Housing:** Single-sex dorms, special housing for disabled, apartments, themed housing available. $300 nonrefundable deposit. **Activities:** Concert band, choral groups, dance, drama, film society, international student organizations, music ensembles, Model UN, student government, student newspaper, African students association, community service society, Model Arab League.

Athletics. Intercollegiate: Basketball, boxing M, fencing, football (tackle), gymnastics, handball, judo, rowing (crew), rugby M, soccer, squash, swimming, table tennis, tennis, track and field, volleyball, water polo M, wrestling M. **Intramural:** Basketball, football (tackle), soccer, squash, swimming, table tennis, tennis, track and field, volleyball, weight lifting M.

Student services. Adult student services, career counseling, student employment services, financial aid counseling, health services, on-campus daycare, personal counseling, placement for graduates. **Physically disabled:** Services for visually, hearing impaired.

Contact. E-mail: enrolauc@aucegypt.edu
Phone: (202) 261-5 ext. 1459 Fax: (212) 730-1600
Ghada Hazem, Director of Admissions, American University in Cairo,
420 Fifth Avenue, Third Floor, New York, NY 10018-2729

France

American University of Paris
Paris, France
www.aup.edu

CB member
CB code: 0866

- Private 4-year university and liberal arts college
- Commuter campus in very large city

- 738 degree-seeking undergraduates: 6% part-time, 70% women
- 163 degree-seeking graduate students
- 77% of applicants admitted
- Application essay required
- 60% graduate within 6 years

General. Founded in 1962. Regionally accredited. **Degrees:** 147 bachelor's awarded; master's offered. **Location:** Downtown. **Calendar:** Semester, extensive summer session. **Full-time faculty:** 67 total; 82% have terminal degrees, 43% women. **Part-time faculty:** 62 total; 42% have terminal degrees, 44% women. **Class size:** 77% < 20, 23% 20-39, less than 1% 40-49.

Freshman class profile. 1,366 applied, 1,055 admitted, 196 enrolled.

Return as sophomores: 69% **Out-of-state:** 100%

Basis for selection. Most important sources include academic transcripts of all secondary and/or university-level coursework, as well as applicable test scores such as SAT, ACT, and national exams. SAT or ACT recommended. Non-English speakers required to take TOEFL, TOEIC, or IELTS. Interviews recommended. **Home schooled:** Statement describing home school structure and mission, transcript of courses and grades, state high school equivalency certificate, interview, letter of recommendation (nonparent) required.

High school preparation. 18 units recommended. Recommended units include English 4, mathematics 3, social studies 3, history 2, science 2 (laboratory 1) and foreign language 3.

2016-2017 Annual costs. Tuition/fees (projected): $31,550. Books/supplies: $1,100.

2014-2015 Financial aid. Need-based: 67 full-time freshmen applied for aid; 61 deemed to have need; 56 received aid. Average need met was 26%. Average scholarship/grant was $11,858; average loan $3,500. 85% of total undergraduate aid awarded as scholarships/grants, 15% as loans/jobs. **Non-need-based:** Awarded to 84 full-time undergraduates, including 43 freshmen. Scholarships awarded for academics, alumni affiliation, leadership.

Application procedures. Admission: No deadline. $70 fee, may be waived for applicants with need. Admission notification on a rolling basis. Must reply by May 1 or within 2 week(s) if notified thereafter. **Financial aid:** Priority date 3/15; no closing date. FAFSA, institutional form required. Applicants notified on a rolling basis.

Academics. Special study options: Cooperative education, cross-registration, double major, dual enrollment of high school students, exchange student, honors, independent study, internships, student-designed major, study abroad. **Credit/placement by examination:** AP, CLEP, IB, institutional tests. **Support services:** Learning center, pre-admission summer program, reduced course load, study skills assistance, tutoring, writing center.

Majors. Area/ethnic studies: European, Near/Middle Eastern. **Business:** Entrepreneurial studies, international, international finance, management information systems, marketing. **Communications:** Intercultural, journalism. **Computer sciences:** Computer science. **Conservation:** Environmental science. **Foreign languages:** Comparative lit. **History:** General. **Philosophy/religion:** Philosophy. **Psychology:** General. **Social sciences:** International economics, political science. **Visual/performing arts:** Art history/conservation, film/cinema/video, studio arts.

Most popular majors. Business/marketing 34%, communications/journalism 14%, foreign language 7%, social sciences 24%, visual/performing arts 9%.

Technology on campus. 135 workstations in library, computer center, student center. Commuter students can connect to campus network. Online course registration, online library, helpline, student web hosting, wireless network available.

Student life. Freshman orientation: Mandatory, $460 fee. Preregistration for classes offered. Held throughout the week before classes begin. Consists of assistance with academic advising and course registration, housing, immigration, as well as workshops devoted to life in Paris and academic life in a multicultural environment. **Policies:** Freshmen not permitted cars on campus. **Housing:** The Housing Office assists students in finding affordable accommodations within easy commuting distance from school. Most students are housed before they arrive. Students live in a variety of neighborhoods in Paris, in shared apartments, independent rooms or with French families and landlords. **Activities:** Choral groups, dance, drama, film society, international student organizations, literary magazine, music ensembles, Model UN, student government, student newspaper.

Athletics. Intercollegiate: Basketball M, equestrian, soccer M. **Intramural:** Equestrian, soccer M.

Student services. Career counseling, student employment services, financial aid counseling, health services, personal counseling.

Contact. E-mail: admissions@aup.edu
Phone: (331) 406-20720 Fax: (331) 470-53532
Tim Rogers, Vice President, Enrollment Management, American University of Paris, 5 boulevard de la Tour Maubourg, Paris, FR

Institut d'Etudes Politiques de Paris
Paris, France   **CB member**
www.sciencespo.fr

- Public 3-year university
- Commuter campus in very large city
- 4,408 degree-seeking undergraduates: 57% women
- 5,539 graduate students
- SAT or ACT with writing, application essay, interview required

General. **Degrees:** 1 bachelor's awarded; master's, doctoral offered. **Location:** Downtown. **Calendar:** Semester, limited summer session. **Full-time faculty:** 60 total. **Part-time faculty:** 2,700 total.

Basis for selection. Comprehensive application form and an oral interview in which applicants present their international background, knowledge of foreign languages, extracurricular activities as well as future career plans. All of the above considered in addition to candidates' academic qualities, allowing selection of candidates with different backgrounds and experiences. Interviews held in 70 cities across the world. Applicants must have completed and submitted their application, including all the required documents, at least four weeks prior the proposed interview date. SAT and SAT Subject Tests or ACT, SAT Subject Tests recommended. SAT Subject test optional; if candidates have taken Advanced Placement exam(s), they must include the results in their application, along with school profile and reference letter from school counselor.

2015-2016 Annual costs. Tuition/fees: $13,250. Books/supplies: $1,100. **Additional information:** Full-time tuition for students whose tax residence is not in European Union: 9,940 euros; housing rates vary, and all accommodations are off-campus. Typically, students should expect to spend 4,500-9,000 euros for living expenses. Costs cover academic year. Students whose tax residence is in the European Union pay fees according to a sliding scale, the amount depends on income and household size.

Financial aid. **Non-need-based:** Scholarships awarded for academics.

Application procedures. **Admission:** Closing date 5/2. $120 fee. Application must be submitted online. Admission notification on a rolling basis. Reply policy dependent on program. **Financial aid:** Closing date 5/2. Institutional form required. Applicants notified on a rolling basis.

Academics. Most undergraduates complete bachelor's degree programs in 3 academic years. Students come from 130 countries, and 40% are non-French citizens. All undergraduates take core curriculum featuring political science, economics, history, international relations, law, and sociology. Joint programs with other schools and colleges available. **Special study options:** Combined bachelor's/graduate degree, double major, dual enrollment of high school students, ESL, internships, study abroad. Dual degree conventions with several major universities; dual BA, MA, PhD with Columbia University; dual MA with Georgetown University; dual MA with University of Pennsylvania. **Credit/placement by examination:** AP, CLEP. **Support services:** Pre-admission summer program, reduced course load, study skills assistance, tutoring.

Majors. **Social sciences:** General.

Technology on campus. Online course registration, online library, helpline, wireless network available.

Student life. **Freshman orientation:** Mandatory. Preregistration for classes offered. Held one or two weeks before classes start. **Activities:** Concert band, choral groups, dance, drama, film society, international student organizations, literary magazine, music ensembles, Model UN, radio station, student newspaper, symphony orchestra.

Student services. Career counseling, financial aid counseling, health services, personal counseling, placement for graduates. **Physically disabled:** Services for visually, speech, hearing impaired.

Contact. E-mail: admissions@sciencespo.fr
Phone: (33) 014-5495082 Fax: (33) 014-5484749
Anne Lesegretain, Director, Admissions Office, Institut d'Etudes Politiques de Paris, Service des Admissions, Paris, FR

Paris College of Art
Paris, France   **CB member**
www.paris.edu   **CB code: 4627**

- Private 4-year university and visual arts college
- Commuter campus in very large city
- 148 degree-seeking undergraduates: 84% women
- Application essay, interview required

General. Fully international student body. Small classes. One on one internship placement. One on one service with Careers and Student Life offices. International faculty. Partnerships with Parisian art and design institutions. Focus on company projects within the classroom. Annual end of the year show and fashion show. Workshop week. PCA artist talks. **Degrees:** 26 bachelor's awarded; master's offered. **Location:** Downtown. **Calendar:** Semester, limited summer session. **Full-time faculty:** 1 total. **Part-time faculty:** 94 total.

Freshman class profile.

Out-of-state:	100% **Live on campus:**	6%

Basis for selection. A large part of the Admissions Committee's decision is based upon evaluation of the portfolio and home exam. A prospective student's potential for artistic achievement is one of the most important criteria in evaluating candidates for admission. Portfolio of art work and home assignment.

2015-2016 Annual costs. Tuition/fees: $29,820. Books/supplies: $780.

Financial aid. **Non-need-based:** Scholarships awarded for academics, art, job skills, leadership. **Additional information:** All students accepted to Undergraduate, Graduate, Certificate and Visiting programs of study are eligible to apply for and receive financial assistance.

Application procedures. **Admission:** Priority date 3/1; deadline 7/1. $68 fee. Application must be submitted online. Admission notification on a rolling basis. Must reply by May 1 or within 2 week(s) if notified thereafter. **Financial aid:** Priority date 2/1; no closing date. Institutional form required. Applicants notified on a rolling basis starting 2/2.

Academics. **Special study options:** Accelerated study, ESL, independent study, internships, study abroad. **Credit/placement by examination:** AP, CLEP, IB. 18 credit hours maximum toward bachelor's degree. **Support services:** Pre-admission summer program, writing center.

Majors. **Visual/performing arts:** Art history/conservation, fashion design, illustration, interior design, photography, studio arts.

Technology on campus. PC or laptop required. 40 workstations in computer center. Wireless network available.

Student life. **Freshman orientation:** Mandatory. Preregistration for classes offered. Held during the 5 days before the first day of classes. **Housing:** Coed dorms available.

Student services. Career counseling, personal counseling.

Contact. E-mail: admissions@paris.edu
Phone: (33) 145-771999
Krauskopf Sara, Director of Admissions, Paris College of Art, 15 rue Fenelon, Paris, FR

Germany

University of Karlsruhe
Karlsruhe, Germany   **CB member**
www.carlbenzschool.de   **CB code: 3592**

- Public 3-year university
- Commuter campus in small city
- 120 degree-seeking undergraduates: 17% women
- 34% of applicants admitted
- Application essay, interview required

General. Partnerships with industry; special internship arrangement and placement for graduates. **Degrees:** 20 bachelor's awarded; master's offered. **Calendar:** Semester, limited summer session. **Full-time faculty:** 300 total. **Class size:** 100% 20-39. **Special facilities:** Accelerator ANKA, BioLiq, prototype for energy from chemical fuel plant.

Freshman class profile. 117 applied, 40 admitted, 31 enrolled.

End year in good standing:	70%	Live on campus:	90%
Return as sophomores:	95%		

Basis for selection. GED not accepted. Admission is based on class rank, high school transcripts, statement of purpose. SAT or ACT recommended. **Home schooled:** Statement describing home school structure and mission, transcript of courses and grades, state high school equivalency certificate, interview, letter of recommendation (nonparent) required. SAT is not mandatory, yet applicants might enhance their chances by adding this element to their application package. **Learning Disabled:** Successful completion of entrance examination prior to official enrollment.

High school preparation. College-preparatory program required. Required and recommended units include mathematics 4, science 4 and computer science 4.

2015-2016 Annual costs. Annual tuition and fees for the Bachelor program in Mechanical Engineering: 14,000 EUR.

Application procedures. Admission: Priority date 4/15; deadline 7/15 (receipt date). No application fee. Admission notification by 1/1. Admission notification on a rolling basis. Must reply by 7/31. Complete application file should be submitted by June 1st. After review of file, candidate is invited for interview; letters of admission are usually sent within four weeks following interview. The final enrollment decision is based on entrance examination. A preparatory course is offered starting mid-August of each year.

Academics. Special study options: Double major, dual enrollment of high school students, exchange student, internships, study abroad. **Credit/placement by examination:** AP, CLEP, institutional tests. **Support services:** Pre-admission summer program, study skills assistance, tutoring, writing center.

Majors. Architecture: Architecture. **Biology:** General. **Communications:** Journalism. **Computer sciences:** General, information technology. **Engineering:** Electrical, mechanical. **Physical sciences:** Chemistry, geology, physics. **Social sciences:** Economics.

Technology on campus. PC or laptop required. 20 workstations in computer center. Dormitories wired for high-speed internet access and linked to campus network. Online course registration, online library, student web hosting, wireless network available.

Student life. Freshman orientation: Available. Preregistration for classes offered. **Policies:** Freshmen not permitted cars on campus. **Housing:** Guaranteed on-campus for freshmen. Coed dorms available. $400 partly refundable deposit, deadline 8/15. **Activities:** International student organizations, music ensembles.

Contact. E-mail: birgitta.kappes@kit.edu
Phone: (721) 608-47880
Birgitta Kappes, Head of Student Office, University of Karlsruhe, Schlossplatz 19, Karlsruhe, GE

Greece

Deree College, The American College of Greece
Athens, Greece   **CB member**
www.acg.edu   **CB code: 0925**

- Private 4-year business and liberal arts college
- Commuter campus in very large city
- 2,511 degree-seeking undergraduates
- 168 graduate students
- 74% of applicants admitted
- Application essay, interview required
- 36% graduate within 6 years

General. Regionally accredited. **Degrees:** 276 bachelor's awarded; master's offered. **Calendar:** Semester, extensive summer session. **Full-time faculty:** 137 total. **Part-time faculty:** 52 total.

Freshman class profile. 1,120 applied, 832 admitted, 726 enrolled.

Basis for selection. Rigor of secondary school record, academic GPA, and interview very important. Recommendations and application essay important. Standardized test scores considered if submitted. Applicants must provide evidence of proficiency in English. Applicants must provide certified copy of national identity card (Greek citizens) or a valid passport (non-Greek citizens). **Home schooled:** Transcript of courses and grades, state high school equivalency certificate, interview, letter of recommendation (nonparent) required. **Learning Disabled:** Applicants must submit a medical verification from an expert.

2015-2016 Annual costs. Comprehensive fee: $13,360. **Additional information:** The comprehensive fee includes 30 credits (semester hours) tuition and room Only.

Application procedures. Admission: Priority date 6/15; no deadline. No application fee. **Financial aid:** Closing date 9/1.

Academics. Special study options: Double major, honors, independent study, internships, study abroad. **Credit/placement by examination:** AP, IB. **Support services:** Tutoring, writing center.

Majors. Business: General, accounting/finance, entrepreneurial studies, finance, hospitality admin, human resources, international, logistics, management information systems, marketing, operations, tourism/travel. **Communications:** General. **Computer sciences:** General, information technology. **Conservation:** Environmental studies. **English:** English lit. **History:** General. **Philosophy/religion:** Philosophy. **Psychology:** General. **Social sciences:** Economics, sociology. **Visual/performing arts:** General, art history/conservation, graphic design, music performance, theater arts management.

Technology on campus. 306 workstations in dormitories, library, computer center. Dormitories wired for high-speed internet access and linked to campus network. Commuter students can connect to campus network. Online course registration, online library, helpline, repair service, wireless network available.

Student life. Freshman orientation: Mandatory. Preregistration for classes offered. **Policies:** Freshmen not permitted cars on campus. **Housing:** Guaranteed on-campus for freshmen. Coed dorms, single-sex dorms, apartments available. **Activities:** Dance, drama, music ensembles, student government, student newspaper.

Athletics. Intercollegiate: Basketball, rugby, soccer, swimming, volleyball M, water polo M. **Intramural:** Archery, basketball, soccer, table tennis, tennis.

Student services. Career counseling, student employment services.

Contact. E-mail: admissions@acg.edu
Phone: (210) 600-9800 ext. 1410 Fax: (210) 608-2344
Loukia Kanatsouli, Dean of Enrollment and International Students, Deree College, The American College of Greece, 6 Gravias Street, Athens, GR

Guatemala

Universidad del Valle de Guatemala
Guatemala City, Guatemala   **CB member**
www.uvg.edu.gt   **CB code: 3875**

- Private 5-year university and technical college
- Commuter campus in very large city
- Interview required

General. Calendar: Semester. **Full-time faculty:** 54 total. **Part-time faculty:** 426 total.

Basis for selection. Open admission, but selective for some programs and for out-of-state students.

2015-2016 Annual costs. Books/supplies: $250.

2015-2016 Financial aid. All financial aid based on need.

Application procedures. Admission: Closing date 1/16. $40 fee. Application must be submitted on paper. Admission notification on a rolling basis. **Financial aid:** Institutional form required.

Academics. Special study options: Combined bachelor's/graduate degree, exchange student, study abroad, teacher certification program, weekend college. **Credit/placement by examination:** AP, CLEP, IB. **Support services:** Reduced course load, tutoring.

Majors. Computer sciences: General. **Education:** General. **Engineering:** Agricultural, chemical, civil, computer, electrical, engineering mechanics, forest, industrial, mechanical. **History:** General. **Math:** General. **Psychology:** General. **Social sciences:** Anthropology, archaeology, sociology.

Technology on campus. 100 workstations in library, computer center. Commuter students can connect to campus network. Online library, student web hosting, wireless network available.

Student life. Freshman orientation: Available. Preregistration for classes offered. **Activities:** Concert band, choral groups, dance, drama, music ensembles, student government, student newspaper.

Student services. Career counseling, services for economically disadvantaged, financial aid counseling, personal counseling.

Contact. E-mail: info@uvg.edu.gt
Phone: (2) 364-0336 ext. 451
Eugenia Rosales, Secretaria General, Universidad del Valle de Guatemala, 18 Avenida 11-95 zona 15, Vista Hermosa III, Guatemala City, GT

Italy

American University of Rome

Rome, Italy
www.aur.edu/american-university-rome

CB member
CB code: 0262

- Private 4-year university and liberal arts college
- Residential campus in very large city
- 223 degree-seeking undergraduates
- 23 graduate students
- Application essay, interview required

General. Degrees: 69 bachelor's awarded; master's offered. **Location:** In the heart of Rome, Italy. **Calendar:** Semester, limited summer session. **Full-time faculty:** 9 total. **Part-time faculty:** 63 total.

Basis for selection. Minimum 2.5 GPA. Leadership, motivation, academic improvement, level of high school program's difficulty, activities and potential for growth important considerations. Candidates for admission are reviewed by the Admissions Committee. Students are selected without regard to age, race, sex, creed, national or ethnic origin or handicap. Applicants whose native language is not English (unless they have been attending an English speaking school/university for at least 3 years) must submit official TOEFL score or IELTS English language proficiency exam, or take the English Language placement exam offered at AUR. Personal statement 250-500 words, 2 short answer essay questions 150-250 words each required. **Home schooled:** Transcript of courses and grades, interview, letter of recommendation (nonparent) required.

2015-2016 Annual costs. Tuition/fees: $23,870. **Room/board:** $12,800. **Books/supplies:** $622. **Additional information:** Health insurance coverage (if not covered by another policy): $260. Permit to stay fee $264. Costs are for academic year.

Application procedures. Admission: Priority date 1/1; no deadline. $53 fee. Application must be submitted online. Admission notification on a rolling basis. Application fee of $50 (Us and Canadian Citizens) $50 (All other nationalities). Personal statement 250-500 words, 2 short answer essay questions 150-250 words required. A 3-minute personal video may take the place of one of the 2 short answer essay questions. Official high school transcripts, one academic recommendation from the principal, a guidance counselor, teacher or professor, official results of the SAT or ACT for high school students graduating from a U.S. high school system in the US (optional), copy of a valid passport, interview required. **Financial aid:** Closing date 5/1.

Academics. General Education program is designed to prepare students to live and work across cultures. The gateway course is the First Year Seminar, which guides students in their first semester and helps them settle in to studying in Rome, followed by five sections: Foundational Skills, The Individual in a Multicultural Society, US Government and Society, Roma Caput Mundi, and Rome is Our Classroom. **Special study options:** Double major, ESL, internships, student-designed major, study abroad. **Credit/placement by examination:** AP, CLEP, institutional tests. **Support services:** Learning center, study skills assistance, tutoring, writing center. Math center, Italian help desk, library research skills workshops, career development and placement workshops, writing center.

Majors. Area/ethnic studies: Italian. **Business:** Business admin. **Communications:** General. **English:** English lit. **Social sciences:** Archaeology, international relations. **Visual/performing arts:** Art history/conservation, digital arts, studio arts.

Technology on campus. 63 workstations in dormitories, library, computer center. Dormitories wired for high-speed internet access. Commuter students can connect to campus network. Online course registration, online library, repair service, student web hosting, wireless network available.

Student life. Freshman orientation: Mandatory. Preregistration for classes offered. One-week program held on campus. Rome walking tour, mathematics and English entry exams for first year students, Italian placement tests, advising and registration. **Housing:** Single-sex dorms available. **Activities:** Dance, drama, international student organizations, literary magazine, Model UN, musical theater, student government, volunteer club, sustainable gardening club.

Athletics. Team name: Wolves.

Student services. Chaplain/spiritual director, career counseling, financial aid counseling, health services, personal counseling.

Contact. E-mail: admissions@aur.edu
Phone: (888) 791-8327 Toll-free number: (877) 592-1287
Arianna D'Amico, Director of Admissions and Financial Aid, American University of Rome, Via Pietro Roselli, 2, Rome, IT

John Cabot University

Rome, Italy
www.johncabot.edu

CB member
CB code: 2795

- Private 4-year university and liberal arts college
- Residential campus in very large city
- 643 degree-seeking undergraduates
- 58% of applicants admitted
- Application essay, interview required
- 59% graduate within 6 years; 40% enter graduate study

General. Regionally accredited. **Degrees:** 138 bachelor's, 8 associate awarded. **Location:** Historic center of Rome. **Calendar:** Semester, extensive summer session. **Full-time faculty:** 100 total. **Part-time faculty:** 30 total. **Special facilities:** Studio art facility, multimedia lab.

Freshman class profile. 815 applied, 474 admitted, 178 enrolled.

Mid 50% test scores			
SAT critical reading:	490-585	GPA 3.0-3.49:	25%
SAT math:	480-605	GPA 2.0-2.99:	34%
GPA 3.75 or higher:	15%	Return as sophomores:	84%
GPA 3.50-3.74:	17%	Live on campus:	47%

Basis for selection. A personal essay, SAT/ACT scores, high school transcript, 2 letters of recommendation, and interview required. SAT or ACT requirement is for Freshman applicants only. **Home schooled:** Statement describing home school structure and mission, transcript of courses and grades, state high school equivalency certificate, interview, letter of recommendation (nonparent) required. **Learning Disabled:** Students with disabilities should identify themselves so they can be put in touch with the Coordinator of Learning Disability Accommodations.

2015-2016 Annual costs. Tuition/fees: $23,900. **Room/board:** $10,790. **Books/supplies:** $1,000. **Personal expenses:** $4,000.

Financial aid. Non-need-based: Scholarships awarded for academics, leadership. **Additional information:** At John Cabot University we are committed to making our American-style liberal arts education as accessible as possible. Our generous scholarship program provides numerous awards based on merit, financial need and your geographic origin. We also participate in the U.S. Title IV Program for Stafford Loans and PLUS.

Application procedures. **Admission:** Priority date 11/15; deadline 6/1. $50 fee, may be waived for applicants with need. Admission notification by 4/1. Admission notification on a rolling basis beginning on or about 12/15. Must reply by May 1 or within 2 week(s) if notified thereafter. **Financial aid:** Closing date 6/1.

Academics. **Special study options:** Double major, dual enrollment of high school students, ESL, exchange student, honors, independent study, internships, study abroad. **Credit/placement by examination:** AP, CLEP, IB, institutional tests. **Support services:** Study skills assistance, tutoring, writing center.

Majors. **Area/ethnic studies:** Italian. **Business:** Business admin, finance, international, marketing. **Communications:** General, communications/ speech/rhetoric. **English:** English lit. **History:** General. **Liberal arts:** Humanities. **Social sciences:** Economics, international relations, political science. **Visual/performing arts:** Art history/conservation.

Most popular majors. Business/marketing 31%, communications/journalism 18%, social sciences 40%.

Technology on campus. 150 workstations in dormitories, library, computer center, student center. Dormitories wired for high-speed internet access and linked to campus network. Commuter students can connect to campus network. Online course registration, online library, helpline, repair service, wireless network available.

Student life. **Freshman orientation:** Mandatory. Preregistration for classes offered. Held the week before classes start. Activities span 5 full days and continue through the first two weeks of classes. **Policies:** Freshmen not permitted cars on campus. **Housing:** Guaranteed on-campus for all undergraduates. Coed dorms, apartments available. $1,000 nonrefundable deposit, deadline 6/1. **Activities:** Dance, drama, film society, international student organizations, literary magazine, Model UN, musical theater, student government, student newspaper, Multicultural club, University Interfaith Initiative, International Relations Society, Model UN, Universities Fighting World Hunger, LGBT-Straight Alliance club, Stand, Ipazia club, community service program.

Athletics. **Intercollegiate:** Basketball, soccer, volleyball. **Intramural:** Basketball, cheerleading, cricket, lacrosse, sailing, skiing, soccer, swimming, tennis, track and field, volleyball, weight lifting. **Team name:** Gladiators.

Student services. Alcohol/substance abuse counseling, career counseling, student employment services, financial aid counseling, health services, personal counseling, placement for graduates.

Contact. E-mail: admissions@johncabot.edu
Toll-free number: (855) 528-7662
Danette Anderson, Director of Marketing and Enrollment, John Cabot University, Via della Lungara, 233, Rome, IT

Korea

Yonsei University
Seoul, Korea
www.yonsei.ac.kr/eng/

CB member
CB code: 9893

◗ Private 4-year university
◗ Commuter campus in very large city
◗ Application essay, interview required

General. **ROTC:** Army. **Calendar:** Semester, limited summer session. **Full-time faculty:** 1,725 total. **Part-time faculty:** 2,137 total.

Basis for selection. Admission based on two stages: (1) high school and junior high school academic performance, foreign language proficiency certification, teachers' recommendations, personal statement, and other application information; (2) candidates selected from 1st stage in admission process will proceed to interview, and each candidate will be scored for interview evaluation. Final admission granted to top scoring candidates based on combined scores from 1st and 2nd rounds of selection process. **Home schooled:** State high school equivalency certificate required.

2015-2016 Annual costs. Annual costs for international students: admission fee 1,034,000 won, tuition 7,212,000 won, miscellaneous fees 48,000 won.

Application procedures. **Admission:** Closing date 5/15 (postmark date). $200 fee.

Academics. **Special study options:** Accelerated study, combined bachelor's/graduate degree, cooperative education, cross-registration, double major, dual enrollment of high school students, study abroad, teacher certification program. **Credit/placement by examination:** AP, CLEP, institutional tests. **Support services:** Learning center, pre-admission summer program, study skills assistance, tutoring, writing center.

Majors. **Architecture:** Architecture, urban/community planning. **Biology:** General, biochemistry. **Business:** General. **Communications:** Media studies. **Computer sciences:** General, information technology. **Education:** General. **Engineering:** Ceramic, chemical, civil, computer, electrical, metallurgical. **English:** English lit. **Foreign languages:** Chinese, French, German, Korean, Russian. **Health services:** Nursing (RN), predental, premedicine. **History:** General. **Human services:** General. **Liberal arts:** Library science. **Math:** General, statistics. **Philosophy/religion:** Philosophy. **Physical sciences:** Chemistry. **Psychology:** General. **Social sciences:** Economics. **Theology:** Theology.

Technology on campus. 1,050 workstations in dormitories, library, computer center, student center. Dormitories wired for high-speed internet access. Commuter students can connect to campus network. Online course registration, online library, helpline, repair service, student web hosting, wireless network available.

Student life. **Freshman orientation:** Available. Preregistration for classes offered. **Housing:** Coed dorms available. **Activities:** Bands, campus ministries, choral groups, dance, drama, film society, international student organizations, literary magazine, music ensembles, Model UN, musical theater, opera, radio station, student government, student newspaper, symphony orchestra, TV station.

Student services. Chaplain/spiritual director, career counseling, services for economically disadvantaged, student employment services, financial aid counseling, health services, minority student services, personal counseling, placement for graduates, women's services. **Physically disabled:** Services for visually, speech, hearing impaired.

Contact. E-mail: ysadms@yonsei.ac.kr
Phone: (822) 212-34131 Fax: (822) 212-38614
Eun-kyung Kim, Admissions Officer, Yonsei University, 50 Yonsei-ro, Seodaemun-gu, Seoul, KR

Kuwait

American University of Kuwait
Safat, Kuwait
www.auk.edu.kw

CB member
CB code: 4185

◗ For-profit 4-year university and liberal arts college
◗ Commuter campus in very large city
◗ 2,309 degree-seeking undergraduates: 12% part-time, 57% women
◗ 99% of applicants admitted
◗ 75% graduate within 6 years

General. **Degrees:** 321 bachelor's awarded. **Calendar:** Semester, limited summer session. **Full-time faculty:** 90 total; 77% have terminal degrees, 39% women. **Part-time faculty:** 28 total; 29% have terminal degrees, 61% women. **Class size:** 22% < 20, 76% 20-39, 2% 40-49.

Freshman class profile. 322 applied, 320 admitted, 311 enrolled.

GPA 3.75 or higher:	6%	GPA 2.0-2.99:	56%
GPA 3.50-3.74:	7%	Return as sophomores:	93%
GPA 3.0-3.49:	26%		

Basis for selection. GED not accepted. Admission open to those who meet minimum standards. Secondary school record and GPA most important. **Learning Disabled:** Evaluation conducted to determine if student is capable of success at AUK and if university has resources to assist in special needs based on evaluation and academic history.

2016-2017 Annual costs. Tuition/fees: $21,476. **Additional information:** Tuition: KWD 6300. Required fees: KWD 230. Per-credit-hour charge: KWD 210 (per-credit-hour charge for Engineering Programs KWD 230).

Application procedures. Admission: Priority date 2/21; deadline 9/6. $115 fee. Notified 3 days after receiving a complete application. **Financial aid:** No deadline.

Academics. Special study options: Accelerated study, double major, ESL, exchange student, independent study, internships, study abroad. **Credit/placement by examination:** AP, CLEP, IB, institutional tests. **Support services:** Pre-admission summer program, remedial instruction, study skills assistance, tutoring, writing center.

Majors. Business: Accounting, business admin, finance, marketing. **Communications:** Advertising, journalism, public relations. **Computer sciences:** General, computer science. **Engineering:** Computer. **English:** English lit. **Social sciences:** General, anthropology, economics, international relations. **Visual/performing arts:** Graphic design.

Most popular majors. Business/marketing 23%, communications/journalism 17%, engineering/engineering technologies 18%, English 9%, social sciences 13%, visual/performing arts 18%.

Technology on campus. 122 workstations in library, computer center. Commuter students can connect to campus network. Online course registration, online library, helpline, repair service, wireless network available.

Student life. Freshman orientation: Mandatory. Preregistration for classes offered. **Policies:** Religious observance required. **Activities:** Drama, international student organizations, literary magazine, Model UN, student government, student newspaper, community service club, human rights club, Al-Akhdar environmental club, Hope club, Arabic literature club, cooperation club, international club, Armenian club, Lebanese culture club, patriots club.

Athletics. Intercollegiate: Badminton, basketball, soccer, table tennis, tennis, volleyball. **Intramural:** Badminton, basketball, soccer, volleyball. **Team name:** Wolfpack.

Student services. Career counseling, student employment services, health services, personal counseling, placement for graduates.

Contact. E-mail: admissions@auk.edu.kw
Phone: (965) 222-48399 ext. 3148
Maher Dabbouseh, Director of Admissions, American University of Kuwait, P.O. Box 3323, Safat, KW

Lebanon

American University of Beirut

Beirut, Lebanon — CB member
www.aub.edu.lb — CB code: 0902

- Private 4-year university
- Commuter campus in very large city
- 6,805 degree-seeking undergraduates: 4% part-time, 50% women
- 1,604 degree-seeking graduate students
- 71% of applicants admitted
- SAT required
- 83% graduate within 6 years; 22% enter graduate study

General. Regionally accredited. Most students are from the Arab world. **Degrees:** 1,479 bachelor's awarded; master's, professional, doctoral offered. **Location:** In Beirut City. **Calendar:** Semester, extensive summer session. **Full-time faculty:** 797 total; 83% have terminal degrees, 34% women. **Part-time faculty:** 316 total; 36% have terminal degrees, 54% women. **Class size:** 36% < 20, 49% 20-39, 7% 40-49, 6% 50-99, 2% >100. **Special facilities:** Archaeological museum, geological museum, rare biological collection.

Freshman class profile. 4,667 applied, 3,314 admitted, 1,768 enrolled.

Mid 50% test scores			
SAT critical reading:	440-540	Rank in top quarter:	56%
SAT math:	580-690	Rank in top tenth:	30%
SAT writing:	460-550	End year in good standing:	93%
GPA 3.75 or higher:	5%	Return as sophomores:	92%
GPA 3.50-3.74:	12%	Live on campus:	20%
GPA 3.0-3.49:	32%		
GPA 2.0-2.99:	41%		

Basis for selection. Admission based on composite scores: 50% SAT (25% verbal, 25% math) and 50% standardized school grades. Holders of Lebanese, French, and International Baccalaureate, among other regional governmental secondary diplomas, will be admitted directly into the sophomore class. SAT must be taken before January of the year preceding admissions. Essay or personal statement required from freshmen applicants. **Home schooled:** State high school equivalency certificate required. Most applicants must take 3 SAT Subject Tests. **Learning Disabled:** Considered on a case by case basis.

2015-2016 Annual costs. Tuition/fees: $21,247. Room only: $2,758. Books/supplies: $300. Personal expenses: $300.

2014-2015 Financial aid. Need-based: 137 full-time freshmen applied for aid; 54 deemed to have need; 51 received aid. Average scholarship/grant was $5,387; average loan $2,227. 92% of total undergraduate aid awarded as scholarships/grants, 8% as loans/jobs. **Non-need-based:** Awarded to 66 full-time undergraduates, including 6 freshmen. Scholarships awarded for academics.

Application procedures. Admission: Priority date 11/30; deadline 12/20 (receipt date). $80 fee. Admission notification by 4/28. Must reply by 6/30. Early action applicants must have a minimum SAT and must have been in top 25th percentile of their class for the past two years. **Financial aid:** Priority date 9/21, closing date 12/18. FAFSA, institutional form required. Applicants notified by 6/15; must reply by 6/30.

Academics. Special study options: Cross-registration, double major, ESL, exchange student, honors, independent study, internships, liberal arts/career combination, study abroad, teacher certification program. **Credit/placement by examination:** AP, CLEP, IB, SAT, institutional tests. **Support services:** Learning center, remedial instruction, study skills assistance, tutoring, writing center.

Majors. Architecture: Architecture. **Business:** Business admin. **Computer sciences:** Computer science. **Education:** Elementary. **Engineering:** Chemical, civil, construction, electrical, mechanical. **Foreign languages:** Arabic. **Health services:** Environmental health, nursing (RN). **History:** General. **Human services:** General. **Philosophy/religion:** Philosophy. **Physical sciences:** Chemistry, physics. **Psychology:** General. **Social sciences:** Archaeology, sociology/anthropology.

Most popular majors. Biology 9%, business/marketing 21%, engineering/engineering technologies 16%, history 9%.

Technology on campus. 1,863 workstations in dormitories, library, computer center, student center. Dormitories wired for high-speed internet access and linked to campus network. Commuter students can connect to campus network. Online course registration, online library, helpline, repair service, student web hosting, wireless network available.

Student life. Freshman orientation: Mandatory. Preregistration for classes offered. Week-long program held in late August, one week before classes begin. **Policies:** Student code of conduct; violations may be of an academic or non-academic nature. Designated smoking areas. **Housing:** Guaranteed on-campus for freshmen. Single-sex dorms, wellness housing available. **Activities:** Choral groups, dance, drama, film society, international student organizations, music ensembles, Model UN, student government, student newspaper, Palestinian cultural club, Syrian cultural club, Jordanian cultural club, Lebanese Armenian heritage club, Lebanese Red Cross club, unicef club, drama club, secular club, women's rights club, Junior Chamber International.

Athletics. Intercollegiate: Basketball, cheerleading W, cross-country, football (tackle) M, gymnastics M, handball M, rugby, sand volleyball, skiing, soccer, squash, swimming, table tennis, tennis, track and field, triathlon, volleyball, water polo M. **Intramural:** Basketball, cross-country, diving, fencing, gymnastics M, handball, racquetball, soccer, squash, swimming, table tennis, tennis, volleyball, weight lifting.

Student services. Alcohol/substance abuse counseling, career counseling, student employment services, financial aid counseling, health services, personal counseling, placement for graduates. **Physically disabled:** Services for visually, hearing impaired.

Contact. E-mail: admissions@aub.edu.lb
Phone: (961) 137-4374 ext. 2590 Fax: (961) 175-0775
Salim Kanaan, Director of Admissions and Financial Aid, American University of Beirut, PO Box 11-0236, Beirut, LB

Lebanese American University

Chouran-Beirut, Lebanon — CB member
www.lau.edu.lb — CB code: 2595

- Private 4-year university
- Commuter campus in very large city

- 7,536 degree-seeking undergraduates: 6% part-time, 50% women
- 762 degree-seeking graduate students
- 89% of applicants admitted
- SAT or ACT (ACT writing recommended) required
- 76% graduate within 6 years; 71% enter graduate study

General. Regionally accredited. **Degrees:** 1,691 bachelor's, 12 associate awarded; master's, professional offered. **Location:** Downtown. **Calendar:** Semester, limited summer session. **Full-time faculty:** 293 total; 75% have terminal degrees, 43% women. **Part-time faculty:** 487 total; 24% have terminal degrees, 55% women. **Class size:** 40% < 20, 47% 20-39, 13% 40-49, less than 1% 50-99.

Freshman class profile. 4,236 applied, 3,765 admitted, 1,808 enrolled.

Mid 50% test scores		GPA 3.0-3.49:	28%
SAT critical reading:	380-470	GPA 2.0-2.99:	54%
SAT math:	510-620	End year in good standing:	82%
SAT writing:	410-510	Return as sophomores:	89%
GPA 3.75 or higher:	8%	Out-of-state:	17%
GPA 3.50-3.74:	6%	Live on campus:	8%

Basis for selection. Rigor of secondary school record, academic GPA and standardized test scores most important. Class rank, recommendations, and other factors considered. Transfer applicants applying to the School of Architecture and Design must submit a portfolio. **Learning Disabled:** Students with learning disabilities should submit medical report explaining their case so university can decide if accommodations can be provided. Students should meet all general admissions requirements.

2015-2016 Annual costs. Tuition/fees: $15,393. Room only: $6,114. Books/supplies: $426. Personal expenses: $6,446.

2014-2015 Financial aid. **Need-based:** 1,193 full-time freshmen applied for aid; 579 deemed to have need; 579 received aid. Average scholarship/grant was $3,000; average loan $1,342. 51% of total undergraduate aid awarded as scholarships/grants, 49% as loans/jobs. **Non-need-based:** Awarded to 1,464 full-time undergraduates, including 479 freshmen. Scholarships awarded for academics, athletics, job skills, leadership.

Application procedures. **Admission:** Priority date 1/31; deadline 7/15 (receipt date). $65 fee. Admission notification on a rolling basis beginning on or about 3/1. **Financial aid:** Closing date 5/31. Institutional form required. Applicants notified on a rolling basis starting 1/1.

Academics. **Special study options:** Combined bachelor's/graduate degree, cross-registration, double major, ESL, honors, internships, liberal arts/career combination, New York semester, study abroad, teacher certification program. **Credit/placement by examination:** AP, CLEP, IB, SAT, ACT, institutional tests. 24 credit hours maximum toward bachelor's degree. Any degree equivalent to the Lebanese Baccalaureate. **Support services:** Learning center, reduced course load, tutoring, writing center.

Majors. **Architecture:** Architecture, interior. **Biology:** General, bioinformatics. **Business:** Business admin, hospitality admin. **Communications:** Journalism, radio/TV. **Computer sciences:** Computer science. **Education:** General. **Engineering:** Civil, computer, electrical, industrial, mechanical, petroleum, robotics. **English:** English lit. **Foreign languages:** Arabic, translation. **Health services:** Dietetics, nursing practice, pharmaceutical sciences. **History:** General. **Human services:** Social work. **Math:** General. **Philosophy/religion:** Philosophy. **Physical sciences:** Chemistry. **Psychology:** General. **Social sciences:** Economics, international relations, political science. **Visual/performing arts:** General, fashion design, graphic design, interior design, studio arts.

Most popular majors. Architecture 8%, biology 8%, business/marketing 41%, engineering/engineering technologies 11%, health sciences 6%, visual/performing arts 6%.

Technology on campus. 1,231 workstations in dormitories, library, computer center, student center. Dormitories wired for high-speed internet access and linked to campus network. Commuter students can connect to campus network. Online course registration, online library, helpline, repair service, wireless network available.

Student life. **Freshman orientation:** Mandatory. Preregistration for classes offered. Held before classes begin. **Policies:** To be a member in a club, the student should be a current student with good academic standing and enrolled in at least 6 credits per semester. **Housing:** Single-sex dorms, special housing for disabled, apartments available. **Activities:** Choral groups, dance, drama, film society, international student organizations, literary magazine, Model UN, musical theater, student government, student newspaper, Red Cross, UNESCO, Armenian Club, Syrian Cultural Club, Palestinian Club, Saudi Arabian Club, Jordanian Club and USA Club.

Athletics. **Intercollegiate:** Badminton, basketball, handball M, rugby M, skiing, soccer, swimming, table tennis, tennis, track and field, volleyball, water polo M. **Intramural:** Basketball, soccer, swimming, table tennis, tennis, volleyball.

Student services. Alcohol/substance abuse counseling, career counseling, student employment services, financial aid counseling, health services, on-campus daycare, personal counseling, placement for graduates.

Contact. E-mail: admissions@lau.edu.lb
Phone: (961) 178-6456 ext. 1111 Fax: (961) 178-6454
Nada Hajj, University Director of Admissions, Lebanese American University, PO Box 13-5053/S-14, Chouran-Beirut, LB

Notre Dame University: Louaize	
Zouk Mosbeh, Lebanon	CB member
www.ndu.edu.lb	CB code: 7696

- Private 4-year university and liberal arts college affiliated with the Roman Catholic Church
- Commuter campus in small town
- 7,152 degree-seeking undergraduates
- 81 degree-seeking graduate students
- Application essay required

General. **Degrees:** 1,017 bachelor's awarded; master's offered. **Location:** 20 km from Beirut. **Calendar:** Semester, limited summer session. **Full-time faculty:** 242 total. **Part-time faculty:** 468 total. **Class size:** 100% 20-39. **Special facilities:** Museum, engineering and science laboratories, hotel management laboratories, science labs, observatory, arts labs, radio/TV studios, trading room (facility for Banking and Finance students interested in learning to use tools specifically designed for work in a trading environment).

Freshman class profile. 141 applied, 117 admitted, 109 enrolled.

Basis for selection. Open admission, but selective for some programs. SAT or NDU entrance exams required for the Aptitude (Math evaluation). SAT/TOEFL/IELTS for English Proficiency and High School Grades (1st, 2nd and 3rd Secondary or Grades 10/11/12) required. **Home schooled:** Transcript of courses and grades, state high school equivalency certificate, letter of recommendation (nonparent) required. **Learning Disabled:** Special exams required based on recommendations from University student counselor and abiding by Admissions Procedures for Students with Special Needs.

2015-2016 Annual costs. Tuition/fees: $11,000. Books/supplies: $750. **Additional information:** Room and board costs vary depending on single to shared accommodation from $1,500 to $2,400 per semester.

Financial aid. All financial aid based on need.

Application procedures. **Admission:** Priority date 3/31; deadline 7/31 (receipt date). $70 fee. Application must be submitted on paper. Admission notification on a rolling basis beginning on or about 4/30. Must reply by 8/31. **Financial aid:** Priority date 4/26, closing date 6/10.

Academics. **Special study options:** Cross-registration, exchange student, internships, study abroad, teacher certification program. **Credit/placement by examination:** AP, CLEP, IB. 106 credit hours maximum toward bachelor's degree. **Support services:** Learning center, reduced course load, remedial instruction, tutoring, writing center.

Majors. **Architecture:** Architecture. **Biology:** General. **Business:** Accounting, actuarial science, business admin, event planning, hospitality admin, human resources, international, logistics, management information systems, marketing, restaurant/food services, tourism/travel. **Communications:** Advertising, journalism, media studies, radio/TV. **Computer sciences:** General, computer graphics, computer science, information technology. **Conservation:** Environmental science. **Education:** General. **Engineering:** Civil, computer, electrical, mechanical. **English:** English lit. **Foreign languages:** General, translation. **Health services:** Clinical lab science, facilities admin, nursing (RN). **Human services:** General. **Math:** General, statistics. **Physical sciences:** Chemistry, physics. **Psychology:** General. **Social sciences:** GIS/cartography, international relations, political science. **Visual/performing arts:** General, design, fashion design, graphic design, interior design, music, photography, studio arts.

Technology on campus. 400 workstations in dormitories, library, computer center, student center. Dormitories wired for high-speed internet access and linked to campus network. Commuter students can connect to campus network. Online course registration, online library, helpline, repair service, wireless network available.

Student life. **Freshman orientation:** Mandatory. Preregistration for classes offered. Held few days before registration. Preregistration is available for students after completing their first semester at NDU. **Housing:** Guaranteed on-campus for all undergraduates. Coed dorms, single-sex dorms available. $1,700 partly refundable deposit, deadline 8/31. **Activities:** Choral groups, drama, international student organizations, musical theater.

Student services. Alcohol/substance abuse counseling, chaplain/spiritual director, career counseling, student employment services, financial aid counseling, health services, personal counseling, placement for graduates. **Physically disabled:** Services for visually, hearing impaired.

Contact. E-mail: admission@ndu.edu.lb
Phone: (961) 922-5164 ext. 2156 Fax: (961) 922-5164
Viviane Nakhle, Director of Admissions, Notre Dame University: Louaize, PO Box 72 Zouk Mikael, Zouk Mosbeh, LB

Mexico

Instituto Tecnologico Autonomo de Mexico
Mexico City, Mexico
www.itam.mx
CB member
CB code: 7144

◆ Private 4-year business and engineering college
◆ Residential campus in very large city
◆ SAT or ACT required

General. **Calendar:** Semester, limited summer session. **Full-time faculty:** 476 total. **Part-time faculty:** 454 total.

Basis for selection. High school records and admission test mandatory. **Home schooled:** Complete high school diploma, minimum GPA, and admission test.

Application procedures. **Admission:** No deadline. $54 fee, may be waived for applicants with need. Application must be submitted on paper. Admission notification on a rolling basis.

Academics. **Special study options:** Combined bachelor's/graduate degree, double major, ESL, exchange student, liberal arts/career combination, study abroad. **Credit/placement by examination:** AP, CLEP, IB, institutional tests. **Support services:** Study skills assistance, tutoring, writing center.

Majors. **Business:** Accounting, accounting/business management, actuarial science, business admin. **Communications:** Digital media. **Communications technology:** Computer typography. **Computer sciences:** General. **Engineering:** Computer. **Math:** Applied. **Social sciences:** Economics, international relations, political science.

Technology on campus. 140 workstations in library, computer center. Commuter students can connect to campus network. Online library, wireless network available.

Student life. **Freshman orientation:** Available. Preregistration for classes offered. **Activities:** Concert band, choral groups, dance, drama, international student organizations, literary magazine, music ensembles, Model UN, radio station, student government, student newspaper.

Athletics. **Intercollegiate:** Baseball M, basketball, cheerleading, rugby M, soccer, softball, volleyball. **Team name:** Dragones.

Student services. Student employment services, health services, legal services.

Contact. E-mail: admisiones@itam.mx
Phone: (5) 556-284156 Toll-free number: (55) 018-00000 ext. 4826
Fax: (5) 554-904655
Gisela Carmona, Director of Admissions, Instituto Tecnologico Autonomo de Mexico, Rio Hondo 1, Colonia Progreso Tizapan, Mexico City, MX

Instituto Tecnologico y de Estudios Superiores de Occidente
Tlaquepaque, Mexico
www.iteso.mx
CB member
CB code: 7145

◆ Private 4-year business and engineering college affiliated with the Roman Catholic Church
◆ Commuter campus in very large city
◆ 9,469 full-time, degree-seeking undergraduates

General. **Degrees:** 1,453 bachelor's awarded; master's, doctoral offered. **Location:** In metropolitan Guadalajara. **Calendar:** Semester, extensive summer session.

Freshman class profile. 3,203 applied, 2,476 admitted, 2,156 enrolled.

Basis for selection. Open admission, but selective for some programs.

2015-2016 Annual costs. Books/supplies: $753. **Additional information:** Cash cost per credit: 1,497.82 MXN. Cost per funded loan is 1,522.78 MXN. Cost per semester carrying a course load of 46 credits is 70,049.72 MXN, which includes life insurance parent or guardian (1,150 MXN).

Academics. **Special study options:** Combined bachelor's/graduate degree, ESL, exchange student, internships, liberal arts/career combination, study abroad. **Credit/placement by examination:** AP, CLEP.

Majors. **Architecture:** Architecture. **Business:** Accounting, business admin, international, labor relations, marketing. **Communications:** Digital media, media studies, organizational, radio/TV. **Computer sciences:** Information technology. **Education:** General, multicultural, statistics. **Human services:** General. **Philosophy/religion:** Philosophy. **Psychology:** General. **Visual/performing arts:** Design, fashion design, graphic design, industrial design, interior design.

Technology on campus. Online library, repair service, wireless network available.

Student life. **Activities:** Choral groups, dance, drama, literary magazine, music ensembles, musical theater, radio station, student newspaper.

Student services. Career counseling, health services.

Contact. E-mail: admision@iteso.mx
Phone: (52) 333-6693535 Toll-free number: (01) 800-7149092
Fax: (52) 333-1342956
Alfonso Saldívar, Chief of the Admissions Office, Instituto Tecnologico y de Estudios Superiores de Occidente, AP 31-175, Tlaquepaque, MX 45090

Universidad Anahuac
Huixquilucan, Mexico
www.anahuac.mx
CB member
CB code: 7146

◆ Private 6-year university and business college affiliated with the Roman Catholic Church
◆ Commuter campus in small city
◆ SAT, application essay, interview required

General. Founded in 1964. **Location:** 4 miles from Mexico City. **Calendar:** Semester, limited summer session. **Full-time faculty:** 1,131 total; 13% have terminal degrees, 37% women. **Part-time faculty:** 1,087 total; 20% have terminal degrees, 41% women.

Basis for selection. GED not accepted. Admission decisions based on careful consideration of all factors, not on numerical factors alone. The exam used is de PAA, not the SAT.

2015-2016 Annual costs. Books/supplies: $700. Personal expenses: $600.

Financial aid. All financial aid based on need.

Application procedures. **Admission:** Closing date 7/31 (receipt date). $100 fee. Application must be submitted on paper. **Financial aid:** Closing date 3/14. Institutional form required. Applicants notified on a rolling basis starting 8/13; must reply within 2 week(s) of notification.

Academics. **Special study options:** Combined bachelor's/graduate degree, cooperative education, double major, dual enrollment of high school students, ESL, exchange student, teacher certification program. **Credit/placement by**

examination: AP, CLEP, institutional tests. **Support services:** Learning center, pre-admission summer program, reduced course load, remedial instruction, study skills assistance, tutoring.

Majors. Architecture: Architecture. **Biology:** Biomedical sciences. **Business:** General, accounting, actuarial science, business admin, international, management information systems, market research, tourism/travel. **Communications:** Advertising, communications/speech/rhetoric, public relations. **Communications technology:** General. **Computer sciences:** Data processing, information systems. **Education:** General. **Engineering:** Biomedical, civil, electrical, engineering mechanics, systems. **Health services:** Medical secretary. **Human services:** General. **Math:** Applied. **Psychology:** General, school. **Social sciences:** Economics, international relations, political science. **Visual/performing arts:** General, design, digital arts, dramatic, graphic design, industrial design. **Work/family studies:** General.

Most popular majors. Business/marketing 15%, engineering/engineering technologies 8%, health sciences 15%, legal studies 6%, mathematics 8%, psychology 12%, public administration/social services 13%.

Technology on campus. 500 workstations in library, computer center, student center. Online course registration, online library, helpline, wireless network available.

Student life. Freshman orientation: Mandatory. Preregistration for classes offered. Orientation mandatory for some students. **Housing:** Host families provide housing for international and out-of-state students. **Activities:** Bands, campus ministries, choral groups, dance, drama, music ensembles, musical theater, opera, radio station, student government, Anahuac Challenge, Anahuac for Mexico, Anahuac Social Action, Anahuac Social Foundation, Center for Integral Community Development, Perpetual Adoration Society, Red Cross, Youth Weekend Mission Program.

Athletics. Intercollegiate: Baseball M, basketball M, cheerleading W, diving, football (tackle), golf, judo, soccer, swimming, tennis, volleyball. **Intramural:** Cheerleading W, diving, judo, soccer, swimming, tennis, volleyball. **Team name:** Leones.

Student services. Chaplain/spiritual director, career counseling, student employment services, financial aid counseling, health services, personal counseling, placement for graduates.

Contact. E-mail: pbertha@anahuac.mx
Phone: (555) 627-0210 ext. 8458 Toll-free number: (800) 508-9800
Fax: (555) 596-1938
Bertha Pérez Vera, Chief of Admissions, Universidad Anahuac, Av. Lomas Anahuac #46., Huixquilucan, MX

Universidad Autonoma de Coahuila
Saltillo, Mexico   **CB member**
www.uadec.mx   **CB code: 7148**

- Public 4-year university
- Commuter campus in very large city
- 26,397 degree-seeking undergraduates
- 47% of applicants admitted

General. Degrees: 2,630 bachelor's awarded; master's, doctoral offered. **Location:** 55 miles from Monterrey. **Calendar:** Semester, limited summer session. **Special facilities:** Museum, observatory.

Freshman class profile. 19,757 applied, 9,192 admitted, 8,387 enrolled.

Basis for selection. Scores from PAA and PIENSE II most important. **Home schooled:** Statement describing home school structure and mission, transcript of courses and grades, state high school equivalency certificate required.

High school preparation. College-preparatory program required.

2015-2016 Annual costs. Books/supplies: $80.

Financial aid. All financial aid based on need.

Application procedures. Admission: Closing date 5/8 (postmark date). $30 fee. Admission notification by 8/1. Admission notification on a rolling basis beginning on or about 6/13. **Financial aid:** No deadline. Institutional form required.

Academics. Special study options: Accelerated study, combined bachelor's/graduate degree, cooperative education, cross-registration, distance learning, double major, ESL, exchange student, independent study, internships, study abroad, urban semester. **Credit/placement by examination:** AP, CLEP. **Support services:** Learning center, pre-admission summer program,

---

reduced course load, remedial instruction, study skills assistance, tutoring, writing center.

Majors. Architecture: Architecture. **Business:** Accounting, business admin, human resources. **Communications technology:** General. **Computer sciences:** Systems analysis. **Education:** General. **Engineering:** Engineering mechanics, mechanical, metallurgical, mining. **Health services:** Nursing (RN). **Human services:** General. **Math:** Applied. **Physical sciences:** Chemistry. **Psychology:** General. **Social sciences:** Economics, political science, sociology. **Visual/performing arts:** Commercial/advertising art, music, music theory/composition, piano/keyboard, voice/opera.

Technology on campus. 120 workstations in library, computer center. Commuter students can connect to campus network. Online library, helpline, student web hosting, wireless network available.

Student life. Freshman orientation: Mandatory. Preregistration for classes offered. **Housing:** Cooperative housing available. $30 fully refundable deposit, deadline 7/25. **Activities:** Bands, choral groups, dance, drama, literary magazine, music ensembles, musical theater, opera, radio station, student newspaper.

Athletics. Intercollegiate: Baseball, basketball, boxing, cheerleading, football (tackle), gymnastics, judo, soccer, softball, tennis, triathlon, volleyball, weight lifting, wrestling. **Intramural:** Baseball, basketball, boxing, cheerleading, football (tackle), gymnastics, judo, soccer, softball, tennis, triathlon, volleyball, weight lifting, wrestling. **Team name:** Wolves (Lobos).

Student services. Alcohol/substance abuse counseling, career counseling, services for economically disadvantaged, student employment services, financial aid counseling, health services, legal services, minority student services, personal counseling, placement for graduates, women's services. **Physically disabled:** Services for visually, speech, hearing impaired.

Contact. E-mail: armandoesparza@uadec.edu.mx
Phone: (844) 438-1648 ext. 1655 Fax: (844) 438-1651
Lic. Armando Zatarayn, Director of Admissions, Universidad Autonoma de Coahuila, Blvd. V. Carranza y Gonzalez Lobo, Saltillo, MX

Morocco

Al Akhawayn University
Ifrane, Morocco   **CB member**
www.aui.ma   **CB code: 6596**

- Public 4-year university and liberal arts college
- Residential campus in small town
- 1,883 undergraduates

General. Location: 40 miles from Fez. **Calendar:** Semester, extensive summer session. **Full-time faculty:** 131 total; 63% have terminal degrees, 25% women. **Part-time faculty:** 13 total; 77% have terminal degrees, 8% women. **Class size:** 58% < 20, 41% 20-39, less than 1% 40-49, less than 1% 50-99.

Freshman class profile.

GPA 3.75 or higher:	2%	Rank in top quarter:	77%
GPA 3.50-3.74:	5%	Rank in top tenth:	58%
GPA 3.0-3.49:	30%	Live on campus:	79%
GPA 2.0-2.99:	63%		

Basis for selection. GED not accepted. Due to competitive nature of selection process, only candidates with promising academic backgrounds are admitted. SAT quantitative, 500 minimum; Verbal and Writing average should be 500 minimum. An 80 point allowance is made for non-native speakers of English, who must take TOEFL for English placement. SAT required of US high school graduates. Other high school graduates take General Admission Test, an institutional test devoted to three areas: general knowledge, verbal skills (sentence completion, critical reading, writing) and quantitative skills (both numerical and spatial). Most domestic applicants are invited to an interview, which allows for evaluation of personality, motivation, communicative force, and general cognitive ability.

2015-2016 Annual costs. Books/supplies: $847. **Additional information:** Annual tuition 28,500, registration fee 5,100, housing 5,000, cash wallet/restaurant 8,500, semester insurance 660, book estimates 3,000. Additional fees may apply. All costs are in Moroccan Dirhams (MAD).

Financial aid. Non-need-based: Scholarships awarded for academics, athletics.

Application procedures. Admission: Priority date 3/31; deadline 5/31 (postmark date). $35 fee. Application must be submitted online. Admission notification by 7/15. **Financial aid:** Closing date 10/31. Institutional form required. Applicants notified by 7/15.

Academics. Special study options: Combined bachelor's/graduate degree, ESL, external degree, honors, independent study, internships, study abroad. **Credit/placement by examination:** AP, CLEP, institutional tests. 6 credit hours maximum toward bachelor's degree. **Support services:** Reduced course load, study skills assistance, tutoring, writing center.

Majors. Business: Business admin, training/development. **Communications:** Communications/speech/rhetoric. **Engineering:** General.

Most popular majors. Business/marketing 59%, computer/information sciences 12%, engineering/engineering technologies 21%.

Technology on campus. 150 workstations in dormitories, library, computer center. Dormitories wired for high-speed internet access and linked to campus network. Commuter students can connect to campus network. Online library, helpline, repair service, student web hosting, wireless network available.

Student life. Freshman orientation: Mandatory. Preregistration for classes offered. Orientation held during registration, which takes place immediately prior to first day of classes. **Housing:** Single-sex dorms available. **Activities:** Concert band, choral groups, dance, drama, film society, international student organizations, Model UN, radio station, student government, student newspaper, TV station.

Athletics. Intercollegiate: Basketball, soccer, tennis, volleyball. **Intramural:** Basketball, soccer, volleyball. **Team name:** AUI Lions.

Student services. Chaplain/spiritual director, financial aid counseling, health services, personal counseling.

Contact. E-mail: admissions@aui.ma
Phone: (535) 862-086 Fax: (535) 862-177
Latifa Ouanaim, Director of Admissions, Al Akhawayn University, PO Box 104, Ifrane, MK

Netherlands

Webster University the Netherlands
Leiden, Netherlands
CB member
www.webster.nl
CB code: 7953

- Private 4-year university and liberal arts college
- Small city
- 184 degree-seeking undergraduates
- Application essay, interview required

General. Degrees: 42 bachelor's awarded; master's offered. **Location:** 30 minutes from Amsterdam, 10 minutes from The Hague, 30 minutes from Rotterdam. **Calendar:** Semester, limited summer session. **Part-time faculty:** 65 total.

Basis for selection. Grades from 10th, 11th, and 12th, minimum 2.5 GPA average, 2 recommendation letters, and 1 motivation statement required.

2016-2017 Annual costs. Tuition/fees (projected): $17,500. Room only: $5,900.

Application procedures. Admission: Priority date 3/1; deadline 8/1. $35 fee. Admission notification on a rolling basis.

Academics. Special study options: Combined bachelor's/graduate degree, double major, honors, internships, study abroad. **Credit/placement by examination:** AP, CLEP, IB. **Support services:** Learning center, writing center.

Majors. Business: Business admin. **Communications:** Media studies. **Psychology:** General. **Social sciences:** International relations.

Technology on campus. Dormitories wired for high-speed internet access. Commuter students can connect to campus network. Online library, wireless network available.

Student life. Freshman orientation: Mandatory. Preregistration for classes offered. **Housing:** $500 partly refundable deposit.

Student services. Career counseling, personal counseling.

Contact. E-mail: admissions@webster.nl
Phone: (071) 516-8000
Jean van Marissing, Admissions Director, Webster University the Netherlands, Boommarkt 1, Leiden, NL

New Zealand

University of Auckland
Auckland, New Zealand
CB member
www.auckland.ac.nz
CB code: 7207

- Public 4-year university
- Very large city
- 40,000 undergraduates

General. Location: Downtown. **Calendar:** Semester, extensive summer session.

Basis for selection. In addition to the minimum admission requirements, international students must satisfy additional criteria to gain entry to certain degree programs at the university. These additional requirements vary, depending on the program of study. US applicants must satisfy one of the following requirements: 1) successful completion of high school diploma from accredited high school, plus ACT composite score of 24 or equivalent SAT result; OR successful completion of General Education Development (GED) Certificate from acceptable GED body, plus ACT composite score of 24 or equivalent SAT result; OR one year's successful bachelor degree-level study at accredited institution or university with good passing grades; OR successful completion of associate degree from accredited community college. SAT and ACT minimum scores vary by program of study.

2015-2016 Annual costs. International tuition fees vary depending on program, ranging from $26,840 NZ for Bachelor of Arts (except performance and science-based courses) to $70,910 NZ for Bachelor of Medicine and Surgery.

Application procedures. Admission: No deadline. No application fee. Application must be submitted online.

Academics. Credit/placement by examination: AP, CLEP.

Majors. Architecture: Architecture, urban/community planning. **Biology:** Biomedical sciences. **Business:** General. **Education:** General. **Human services:** Social work. **Theology:** Theology. **Visual/performing arts:** General, dance.

Contact. University of Auckland, Private Bag 92019, Auckland, NZ

University of Canterbury
Christchurch, New Zealand
CB member
www.canterbury.ac.nz
CB code: 7225

- Public 4-year university
- Large city
- 12,000 undergraduates
- SAT or ACT (ACT writing optional) required

General. Calendar: Semester. **Full-time faculty:** 735 total.

Basis for selection. Applicants educated in the United States must have score of 1600 on SAT or average score of 24 on ACT.

2015-2016 Annual costs. Tuition fees vary depending on program and are banded by subject area. Estimated total annual tuition fees for international students in 2016 range from $NZ 23,300 to $NZ 38,900. For study abroad students, there is a flat fee for one semester of undergraduate courses. This is $NZ 12,250 in 2016. Student Services levy was $NZ 745 in 2015, or $NZ 372.50 per semester.

Application procedures. Admission: Closing date 7/1. No application fee.

Academics. Credit/placement by examination: AP, CLEP.

Majors. Biology: General. **Conservation:** Forestry. **Education:** Early childhood. **Engineering:** Civil. **English:** English lit. **Visual/performing arts:** Studio arts.

Contact. E-mail: admission@canterbury.ac.nz
Phone: (643) 364-2555
Lynn McClelland, Director, Student Services and Communications, University of Canterbury, Private Bag 4800, Christchurch, NZ

Pakistan

Forman Christian College
Lahore, Pakistan   CB member
www.fccollege.edu.pk

- Private 4-year university and liberal arts college affiliated with the Presbyterian Church (USA)
- Commuter campus in very large city
- 3,387 degree-seeking undergraduates: 34% women
- 314 degree-seeking graduate students
- 48% of applicants admitted

General. Multi-religious, emphasizes tolerance. **Degrees:** 579 bachelor's awarded; master's, doctoral offered. **Calendar:** Semester, limited summer session. **Full-time faculty:** 196 total; 50% have terminal degrees, 16% minority, 43% women. **Part-time faculty:** 36 total; 31% have terminal degrees, 22% minority, 58% women. **Class size:** 37% < 20, 56% 20-39, 6% 40-49, 1% 50-99.

Freshman class profile. 2,615 applied, 1,253 admitted, 817 enrolled.

Basis for selection. Students admitted based on scores earned on annual exams (O-level or 10th Grade, A-level or Intermediate) and scores on ACCUPLACER (ESL Language Use, ESL Reading Skills, Arithmetic). ACCUPLACER used to determine admission and course placements. **Learning Disabled:** Special requirements or procedures for students with learning disabilities are considered on case by case basis.

2015-2016 Annual costs. Tuition/fees: $1,974. Room/board: $980. Books/supplies: $650. Personal expenses: $55.

2014-2015 Financial aid. All financial aid based on need. 91% of total undergraduate aid awarded as scholarships/grants, 9% as loans/jobs.

Application procedures. Admission: Closing date 9/1 (receipt date). $20 fee. Application must be submitted online. Admission notification on a rolling basis beginning on or about 3/2. **Financial aid:** No deadline. Institutional form required. Applicants notified on a rolling basis.

Academics. Special study options: Double major, ESL, independent study, internships. **Credit/placement by examination:** AP, CLEP, institutional tests. 15 credit hours maximum toward bachelor's degree. **Support services:** Reduced course load, remedial instruction.

Majors. Biology: General. **Business:** Business admin. **Communications:** Media studies. **Computer sciences:** General, information technology. **Conservation:** Environmental science. **Education:** General. **Engineering:** Software. **English:** English lit. **Foreign languages:** Urdu. **History:** General. **Math:** General, statistics. **Philosophy/religion:** Christian, Islamic, philosophy. **Physical sciences:** Chemistry, physics. **Psychology:** General. **Social sciences:** Economics, geography, political science, sociology.

Most popular majors. Business/marketing 13%, communications/journalism 14%, computer/information sciences 9%, science technologies 11%, social sciences 27%.

Technology on campus. 111 workstations in library, computer center. Dormitories wired for high-speed internet access and linked to campus network. Commuter students can connect to campus network. Online course registration, online library, helpline, wireless network available.

Student life. Freshman orientation: Mandatory. Preregistration for classes offered. Variety of times during the three weeks prior to start of classes. **Policies:** Freshmen not permitted cars on campus. **Housing:** Single-sex dorms available. **Activities:** Campus ministries, drama, international student organizations, music ensembles, Model UN, Islamic Society, Christian Life Program, Political Science Society, Red Crescent Society, Forman Sociological Association, Earth Watch, International Student Affairs, Rotoract, Formanite Educational Society.

Athletics. Intercollegiate: Badminton, basketball, boxing M, cricket M, field hockey M, handball M, rugby M, soccer M, squash W, swimming, table tennis, tennis, track and field, volleyball, weight lifting M. **Intramural:** Badminton, basketball, boxing M, cricket M, field hockey M, rugby M, soccer M, swimming, table tennis, tennis, track and field, volleyball M, weight lifting M. **Team name:** Formanites.

Student services. Chaplain/spiritual director, career counseling, student employment services, financial aid counseling, health services, minority student services, personal counseling, placement for graduates, women's services. **Physically disabled:** Services for visually impaired.

Contact. E-mail: admissions@fccollege.edu.pk
Phone: (42) 992-31584 ext. 377
Amber Mall, Director of Admissions, Forman Christian College, Ferozepur Road, Lahore, PK

Poland

Warsaw University of Technology
Warsaw, Poland
https://www.pw.edu.pl/engpw

- Public 3-year engineering and technical college
- Residential campus in very large city

General. Location: Downtown. **Calendar:** Semester. **Special facilities:** Museum, youth hostel in mountains, two sea yachts.

Basis for selection. Open admission, but selective for some programs. GED not accepted. **Home schooled:** Transcript of courses and grades required.

Application procedures. Admission: Closing date 6/20 (receipt date). $30 fee ($70 out-of-state). Application must be submitted online. Admission notification on a rolling basis.

Academics. Special study options: Combined bachelor's/graduate degree, distance learning, double major, exchange student, internships, study abroad, weekend college. **Credit/placement by examination:** AP, CLEP.

Majors. Computer sciences: Computer science. **Engineering:** Aerospace, civil, computer, electrical, environmental.

Technology on campus. Student web hosting, wireless network available.

Student life. Freshman orientation: Available. Preregistration for classes offered. **Housing:** Guaranteed on-campus for all undergraduates. Coed dorms available. **Activities:** Bands, choral groups, dance, drama, international student organizations, literary magazine, music ensembles, radio station, student government, student newspaper, symphony orchestra.

Student services. Career counseling. **Physically disabled:** Services for visually, speech, hearing impaired.

Contact. E-mail: students@cwm.pw.edu.pl
Phone: (48) 222-34 ext. 5091
Zdzisław Mączeński, Admissions Director, Warsaw University of Technology, Plac Politechniki 1, Warsaw, PL

Singapore

Singapore Management University
Singapore, Singapore   **CB member**
www.smu.edu.sg   **CB code: 2861**

- Private 4-year university
- Commuter campus in small city
- 7,110 full-time, degree-seeking undergraduates

General. **Degrees:** 1,600 bachelor's awarded; master's, doctoral offered. **Calendar:** Semester, limited summer session. **Full-time faculty:** 233 total. **Part-time faculty:** 262 total.

Basis for selection. GED not accepted. Holistic selection approach based on academic records, co-curricular activities, SAT scores if applicable, and admissions interview for shortlisted applicants; application fee is $15 (Singapore dollars). **Home schooled:** Statement describing home school structure and mission, transcript of courses and grades, state high school equivalency certificate, interview required.

2015-2016 Annual costs. Tuition/fees: $11,200. **Additional information:** Annual tuition fees for most degree programs quoted is for Singapore citizens. Permanent residents pay $15,700. Foreign Students pay $22,400. Bachelor of Law: Singapore citizens pay $12,400; permanent residents pay $17,350; foreign students pay $24,800.

Application procedures. **Admission:** Closing date 4/1. $15 fee. Admission notification by 7/15. Admission notification on a rolling basis beginning on or about 4/1. **Financial aid:** No deadline.

Academics. **Special study options:** Combined bachelor's/graduate degree, double major, exchange student, honors, internships, study abroad. **Credit/placement by examination:** AP, CLEP, SAT, ACT.

Majors. **Business:** Accounting, business admin, communications, finance, marketing, operations, organizational behavior. **Computer sciences:** Information systems. **Psychology:** General. **Social sciences:** General, economics, political science, sociology.

Technology on campus. PC or laptop required.

Student life. **Freshman orientation:** Mandatory. Preregistration for classes offered. **Activities:** Bands, campus ministries, choral groups, dance, drama, international student organizations, literary magazine, music ensembles, musical theater, radio station, student newspaper, symphony orchestra.

Athletics. **Intramural:** Archery, badminton, basketball, bowling, cricket, cross-country, fencing, football (non-tackle), football (tackle) M, golf, handball, judo, rifle, rugby, sailing, soccer M, squash, swimming, table tennis, tennis, track and field, volleyball, water polo.

Student services. Career counseling, student employment services, financial aid counseling, health services, personal counseling. **Physically disabled:** Services for visually, speech, hearing impaired.

Contact. E-mail: admissions@smu.edu.sg
Phone: (65) 682-80305 Fax: (65) 682-80303
Christina Leong, Director, Office of Undergraduate Admissions, Singapore Management University, 81 Victoria Street, Singapore, SG 25975

Spain

Les Roches International School of Hotel Management Marbella
Marbella, Spain   **CB member**
www.lesroches.es

- Private 3-year university and branch campus college
- Small city

General. **Calendar:** Continuous. **Full-time faculty:** 29 total. **Part-time faculty:** 11 total.

Basis for selection. English language requirements for non-native speakers of English or students who have not studied English in the 3 years prior to admission: TOEFL 500/IELTS 5.0 overall, or "C" minimum on Cambridge First Certificate in English.

2015-2016 Annual costs. Annual cost for BBA in International Hotel Management: tuition 26,500, room and board 12,260, internship program 480, books and materials 645, uniform 580, kitchen tool kit 155, private health insurance 1,110. BBA in International Hotel Management with Intensive English and Service Program: tuition 15,930, room and board 12,260, books and materials 550, uniform 300, private health insurance 740.

Academics. **Credit/placement by examination:** AP.

Majors. **Business:** Hospitality admin.

Contact. E-mail: info@lesroches.es
Phone: (34) 952-764437
Mariana Macri, Admissions Coordinator, Les Roches International School of Hotel Management Marbella, Urb. Lomas de Rio Verde, Crta. Istan Km 1, Marbella, ES

Saint Louis University: Madrid
Madrid, Spain   **CB member**
www.slu.edu/madrid   **CB code: 2586**

- Private 4-year university affiliated with the Roman Catholic Church
- Very large city
- 346 degree-seeking undergraduates: 41% women
- 16 graduate students
- 22% of applicants admitted
- Application essay required

General. Regionally accredited. Students, faculty, and staff representing more than 65 nationalities. **Degrees:** 55 bachelor's awarded; master's offered. **Calendar:** Semester, limited summer session. **Full-time faculty:** 38 total; 87% have terminal degrees, 55% women. **Part-time faculty:** 56 total; 38% have terminal degrees, 62% women.

Freshman class profile. 570 applied, 125 admitted, 101 enrolled.

Basis for selection. Because student applications are received from all over the world, SLU-Madrid's admission requirements are flexible enough to account for differences in secondary school educational systems. All students required to complete the university entry requirements of the country where they completed their secondary education.

2016-2017 Annual costs. Tuition/fees (projected): $20,460. Room/board: $7,700. **Additional information:** Rates calculated at a 1.1 exchange rate. Room and board (on campus): host family half room & board through the University. Room only ($5,667): host family kitchen privileges through the University.

Application procedures. **Admission:** No deadline. No application fee. Application must be submitted online. Admission notification on a rolling basis. **Financial aid:** Priority date 3/1; no closing date.

Academics. **Special study options:** Distance learning, double major, ESL, honors, independent study, internships, liberal arts/career combination, study abroad. **Credit/placement by examination:** AP, CLEP, IB. **Support services:** Tutoring, writing center.

Majors. **Business:** International. **Communications:** Communications/speech/rhetoric. **English:** English lit. **Foreign languages:** Spanish. **History:** General. **Psychology:** General. **Social sciences:** Economics, international relations. **Visual/performing arts:** Art history/conservation.

Most popular majors. Business/marketing 29%, communications/journalism 20%, foreign language 12%, interdisciplinary studies 9%, social sciences 27%.

Technology on campus. Online course registration, helpline, wireless network available.

Student life. **Freshman orientation:** Mandatory. Preregistration for classes offered. **Housing:** "Host family" housing available. **Activities:** Campus ministries, choral groups, dance, drama, literary magazine, student government, student newspaper.

Athletics. **Intramural:** Soccer. **Team name:** Billikens.

Student services. Chaplain/spiritual director, career counseling, financial aid counseling, personal counseling.

Contact. E-mail: admissions-madrid@slu.edu
Phone: (34) 915-545858 Fax: (91) 554-6202
Heidi Buffington, Director of Admissions, Saint Louis University: Madrid, Avenida del Valle, 34, Madrid, ES

Switzerland

Ecole Hoteliere de Lausanne
Lausanne, Switzerland
www.ehl.edu
CB member
CB code: 4102

- Private 4-year university and business college
- Residential campus in small city
- Application essay, interview required

General. EHL is both a school (fully equipped to provide the best possible learning experience for its students) and a hotel (complete with restaurants, accommodations, conference and banqueting facilities); students, employees, and visitors benefit from the full range of hospitality experiences. **Location:** 4 miles from Lausanne, 35 miles from Geneva. **Calendar:** Continuous. **Full-time faculty:** 52 total; 21% have terminal degrees, 36% women. **Part-time faculty:** 54 total; 22% have terminal degrees, 37% women. **Class size:** 33% < 20, 46% 20-39, 9% 40-49, 5% 50-99, 6% >100. **Special facilities:** Onsite restaurants and bars that function as classrooms include a fine-dining training restaurant, "Le Berceau des Sens" (The Cradle of the Senses).

Freshman class profile.

GPA 3.75 or higher:	37%	GPA 2.0-2.99:	5%
GPA 3.50-3.74:	26%	Live on campus:	99%
GPA 3.0-3.49:	32%		

Basis for selection. GED not accepted. Candidates who meet minimum requirements invited for Selection Day at EHL or abroad, which includes quantitative and analytical aptitude test (computer-based), hospitality aptitude test (computer-based), role play exercise, and interview. Students selected on basis of overall quality of application and Selection Day scores. SAT only required for students enrolled in American high school curriculum; evidence of higher achievement (3 AP exams, SAT Subject Tests or IB Higher Level certificates) also required. **Home schooled:** Transcript of courses and grades, state high school equivalency certificate required.

High school preparation. College-preparatory program required.

2015-2016 Annual costs. Tuition/fees: $31,560. Room only: $3,900. Books/supplies: $900. Personal expenses: $5,400. **Additional information:** Cost for food and beverage is a compulory fee on campus. On campus accomodations are available but not mandatory.

Financial aid. All financial aid based on need. **Additional information:** EHL is eligible to participate in Title IV financial aid programs (Direct Loans).

Application procedures. Admission: Priority date 12/1; deadline 2/1 (receipt date). $300 fee. Application must be submitted online. Admission notification by 4/19. Admission notification on a rolling basis beginning on or about 2/15. Must reply by May 1 or within 2 week(s) if notified thereafter. **Financial aid:** Closing date 2/1. FAFSA, institutional form required. Applicants notified by 6/15; must reply within 2 week(s) of notification.

Academics. Special study options: Internships, study abroad. **Credit/placement by examination:** AP, CLEP, institutional tests. **Support services:** Study skills assistance, tutoring, writing center.

Majors. Business: Hospitality admin.

Technology on campus. PC or laptop required. Dormitories wired for high-speed internet access and linked to campus network. Commuter students can connect to campus network. Online course registration, online library, repair service, student web hosting, wireless network available.

Student life. Freshman orientation: Mandatory. Preregistration for classes offered. Held 2 weeks before classes begin. **Housing:** Guaranteed on-campus for freshmen. Single-sex dorms, apartments available. **Activities:** Concert band, dance, drama, international student organizations, student government, student newspaper.

Athletics. Intramural: Badminton, basketball, cricket, equestrian, field hockey, golf, ice hockey, rugby, sailing, soccer, squash, tennis, volleyball.

Student services. Alcohol/substance abuse counseling, chaplain/spiritual director, career counseling, student employment services, financial aid counseling, health services, personal counseling, placement for graduates.

Contact. E-mail: admissions@ehl.ch
Phone: (41) 217-851121 Fax: (41) 217-8511121
Sandra Labrecque, Admissions Officer, Ecole Hoteliere de Lausanne, Route de Cojonnex 18, Lausanne, CH

Franklin University Switzerland
Sorengo (Lugano), Switzerland
www.fus.edu
CB member
CB code: 0922

- Private 4-year liberal arts college
- Residential campus in small city
- 394 undergraduates
- SAT or ACT with writing, application essay required

General. Founded in 1969. Regionally accredited. Undergraduate degree programs are accredited in United States and Switzerland. Classes taught in English. Students from 60 nations. **Location:** 60 miles from Milan, Italy; 80 miles from Zurich. **Calendar:** Semester, extensive summer session. **Full-time faculty:** 26 total; 92% have terminal degrees, 46% women. **Part-time faculty:** 28 total; 61% have terminal degrees, 54% women. **Class size:** 68% < 20, 32% 20-39.

Freshman class profile.

GPA 3.75 or higher:	21%	GPA 2.0-2.99:	24%
GPA 3.50-3.74:	16%	Live on campus:	98%
GPA 3.0-3.49:	39%		

Basis for selection. High school academic record, recommendations, extracurricular participation most important. Essay, test scores, interview also important. TOEFL or IELTS required for students whose first language is not English. SAT Subject Tests recommended. Essay and personal statement required. Interview recommended for all. **Home schooled:** Statement describing home school structure and mission, transcript of courses and grades, letter of recommendation (nonparent) required.

High school preparation. College-preparatory program required. 17 units required; 19 recommended. Required and recommended units include English 4, mathematics 3, social studies 1, history 3, science 2-3, foreign language 2-3 and academic electives 2. Electives include computer science, art, music.

2015-2016 Annual costs. Tuition/fees: $40,420. Room/board: $14,570. Books/supplies: $1,600. Personal expenses: $1,600.

Financial aid. All financial aid based on need.

Application procedures. Admission: Priority date 3/15; no deadline. $90 fee. Admission notification on a rolling basis beginning on or about 12/15. Must reply by May 1 or within 2 week(s) if notified thereafter. **Financial aid:** Priority date 2/15, closing date 4/15. FAFSA, institutional form required. Applicants notified on a rolling basis starting 3/10; must reply by 5/1 or within 3 week(s) of notification.

Academics. 2-week credit-bearing academic travel program required each semester. **Special study options:** Double major, ESL, honors, independent study, internships, semester at sea, study abroad, Washington semester. Sophomore and junior year abroad programs with cooperating colleges/universities. **Credit/placement by examination:** AP, CLEP, IB, institutional tests. 15 credit hours maximum toward associate degree, 27 toward bachelor's. **Support services:** Learning center, reduced course load, study skills assistance, tutoring, writing center.

Majors. Business: International finance, international marketing. **Communications:** Media studies. **Conservation:** Environmental studies. **Foreign languages:** General, French, Italian. **History:** General. **Social sciences:** International economics, international relations. **Visual/performing arts:** Art history/conservation, design.

Most popular majors. Business/marketing 38%, communications/journalism 8%, liberal arts 11%, social sciences 20%, visual/performing arts 9%.

Technology on campus. 140 workstations in library, computer center, student center. Dormitories wired for high-speed internet access and linked to campus network. Commuter students can connect to campus network. Online library, helpline, repair service, student web hosting, wireless network available.

Student life. Freshman orientation: Mandatory, $400 fee. Preregistration for classes offered. **Policies:** All students required to live in on-campus housing their first year. **Housing:** Guaranteed on-campus for all undergraduates. Coed dorms, single-sex dorms, apartments, themed housing, wellness housing available. $400 partly refundable deposit, deadline 6/15. College-owned and leased apartments on and adjacent to campus and in Lugano; freshmen and sophomores must live in college housing. **Activities:** Dance, drama, literary magazine, Model UN, student government, student newspaper, Baobab Initiative (student-run enterprise formed to help a small village in Zambia), language clubs, cultural and ethnic clubs, literary society, honor society, drama society, creative arts club, Christian Fellowship, Environmental Action Alliance.

Athletics. Intramural: Basketball, soccer, volleyball. **Team name:** Falcons.

Student services. Alcohol/substance abuse counseling, career counseling, student employment services, financial aid counseling, health services, personal counseling, placement for graduates, women's services.

Contact. E-mail: info@fc.edu
Phone: (212) 922-9650 Fax: (212) 922-9870
Karen Ballard, Dean of Admissions, Franklin University Switzerland, U.S. Admissions: The Graybar Building, Suite 2746, New York, NY 10170

Les Roches International School of Hotel Management
Bluche, Switzerland   **CB member**
www.lesroches.edu/les_roches_bluche   **CB code: 5875**

- Private 4-year university and career college
- Residential campus in rural community
- 1,123 degree-seeking undergraduates
- 201 graduate students
- Application essay required

General. Regionally accredited. **Degrees:** 210 bachelor's, 143 associate awarded; master's offered. **Location:** 7 miles from Sierre, 114 miles from Geneva. **Calendar:** Semester. **Full-time faculty:** 63 total. **Part-time faculty:** 13 total. **Special facilities:** Craft-based learning facilities for hotel operations including demonstration kitchen and bar, 4 kitchens and restaurants (buffet-style, fine dining, sports bar and bistro), model hotel room, cleaning science area, full-sized practice reception.

Basis for selection. English language requirements: TOEFL 500/IELTS 5.0 or equivalent, proof required for non-native English speakers or students who do not have 3 years' worth of 100% English-taught education. **Home schooled:** State high school equivalency certificate required. **Learning Disabled:** Students with learning disabilities must provide official report from licensed physician detailing prognosis, treatment and learning assistance requirements, if applicable.

2015-2016 Annual costs. Books/supplies: $750. **Additional information:** Annual cost for BBA in International Hotel Management: tuition 44,000, room and board 20,400, estimated books and materials 1,300, health insurance 2,250, uniform 780, kitchen tool kit 230. BBA in Global Hospitality Management: tuition 48,500, room and board 14,050, health insurance 1,165, additional fees 3,200.

Application procedures. Admission: Priority date 5/15; deadline 8/1. $100 fee. Admission notification on a rolling basis. Must reply by May 1 or within 2 week(s) if notified thereafter. **Financial aid:** No deadline.

Academics. Special study options: ESL, honors, internships, study abroad. 10-week hospitality management taster course, January - March. Undergraduate curriculum combines hands-on courses in hotel operation (18 weeks) with theoretical management courses, two internship semesters, and final year of business administration courses. **Credit/placement by examination:** AP, CLEP. **Support services:** Tutoring. Extra support available to students with dyslexia.

Majors. Business: Hotel/motel admin.

Technology on campus. PC or laptop required. 10 workstations in library, computer center. Dormitories wired for high-speed internet access and linked to campus network. Online library, helpline, repair service, wireless network available.

Student life. Freshman orientation: Mandatory. Preregistration for classes offered. **Housing:** Guaranteed on-campus for all undergraduates. Coed dorms, single-sex dorms, apartments available. $3,000 nonrefundable deposit, deadline 5/15. **Activities:** Dance, film society, student government.

Athletics. Intramural: Badminton, basketball, rugby M, skiing, soccer, squash, swimming, tennis, volleyball.

Student services. Career counseling, financial aid counseling, health services, personal counseling, placement for graduates.

Contact. E-mail: admissions@lesroches.edu
Phone: (21) 989-2644
Liza Humphrey, Director of Enrollment, Les Roches International School of Hotel Management, Rue du Lac 118, Clarens, CH

Turkey

Koc University
Istanbul, Turkey   **CB member**
www.ku.edu.tr/en   **CB code: 1931**

- Private 4-year university
- Residential campus in very large city
- 4,642 degree-seeking undergraduates
- 1,035 graduate students
- 8% of applicants admitted

General. Degrees: 649 bachelor's awarded; master's, doctoral offered. **Location:** 10 miles from Istanbul. **Calendar:** Semester, limited summer session. **Full-time faculty:** 422 total; 63% have terminal degrees, 50% women. **Part-time faculty:** 69 total; 9% have terminal degrees, 51% women. **Class size:** 51% < 20, 29% 20-39, 6% 40-49, 13% 50-99, less than 1% >100. **Special facilities:** College-operated laboratories, ice rink.

Freshman class profile. 12,752 applied, 962 admitted, 920 enrolled.

Mid 50% test scores			
		SAT writing:	460-520
SAT critical reading:	420-510	**ACT composite:**	24-31
SAT math:	600-700		

Basis for selection. GED not accepted. Most Turkish undergraduates admitted based on scores of the national university entrance exams conducted in Turkey every year. For international students, applications evaluated first by the admissions committee and then by respective faculty deans. If necessary, interviews may be arranged with candidates via e-mail or phone. 13 types of exams and diplomas are accepted from prospective international students, depending on educational system in which they received secondary education. Such applicants must provide minimum acceptable score/grade in at least one of the 13 exams/diplomas. SAT/ACT is not required for all prospective international students; however, either of these two tests is required for students who cannot submit other types of exams/diplomas. Examples of other exams: ABITUR (students coming from German educational system) and French baccalaureate.

2016-2017 Annual costs. Books/supplies: $200. **Additional information:** Tuition and fees for the School of Medicine is 76.600 TL, for the School of Nursing is 13.000 TL, and for all other departments, including ELC (English Language Center), is 55.000 TL. This fee covers tuition and registration and also allows full use of the library, computer laboratories, and infirmary services.

Application procedures. Admission: Priority date 3/1; deadline 7/1. $70 fee. Admission notification on a rolling basis. **Financial aid:** Priority date 3/1, closing date 7/1.

Academics. Special study options: Double major, ESL, independent study, internships, study abroad. **Credit/placement by examination:** AP, CLEP, IB. **Support services:** Learning center, pre-admission summer program, reduced course load, study skills assistance, writing center.

Majors. Biology: Molecular. **Business:** Business admin. **Engineering:** Computer, electrical, industrial, mechanical. **History:** General. **Math:** General. **Philosophy/religion:** Philosophy. **Physical sciences:** Physics. **Psychology:** General. **Social sciences:** Archaeology, economics, international relations, sociology.

Most popular majors. Business/marketing 16%, engineering/engineering technologies 29%, legal studies 8%, social sciences 23%.

Technology on campus. Dormitories wired for high-speed internet access and linked to campus network. Commuter students can connect to campus network. Online course registration, online library, helpline, repair service, wireless network available.

Student life. Freshman orientation: Mandatory. Preregistration for classes offered. **Housing:** Coed dorms, single-sex dorms, special housing for disabled available. $135 deposit. **Activities:** Concert band, choral groups, dance, drama, film society, radio station, student government, student newspaper.

Athletics. Intercollegiate: Basketball, football (tackle) M, rowing (crew), soccer M, swimming, tennis, volleyball W. **Intramural:** Badminton, basketball, football (tackle) M, ice hockey, rowing (crew), soccer, squash, swimming, table tennis, tennis, volleyball, weight lifting. **Team name:** Rams.

Student services. Career counseling, student employment services, financial aid counseling, health services, personal counseling. **Physically disabled:** Services for visually, hearing impaired.

Contact. E-mail: registrar@ku.edu.tr
Phone: (212) 338-1602
Zafer Gurelli, Registrar, Koc University, Rumelifeneri Yolu, Istanbul, TR

United Arab Emirates

American University in Dubai
Dubai, United Arab Emirates   **CB member**
www.aud.edu   **CB code: 2688**

▶ Private 4-year university
▶ Commuter campus in very large city
▶ 2,347 degree-seeking undergraduates: 12% part-time, 50% women
▶ 125 degree-seeking graduate students
▶ 68% of applicants admitted
▶ Application essay required

General. Regionally accredited. **Degrees:** 446 bachelor's awarded; master's offered. **Calendar:** Semester, extensive summer session. **Full-time faculty:** 135 total; 36% women. **Part-time faculty:** 57 total; 74% women.

Freshman class profile. 1,413 applied, 960 admitted, 627 enrolled.

Basis for selection. GED not accepted. Well-rounded students who demonstrate a probability for success in the institution's programs of study sought. Such factors as high school completion, recommendations from school personnel familiar with the potential of applicants, leadership and student activity records, scholastic achievement test scores, evidence of school and community service, student work or employment records, and distinctive talents or abilities considered. Students can take math placement test or submit acceptable SAT score. All engineering applicants must take SAT and Math Placement; combined score of 1000 (exclusive of Writing) required for admission to the program. **Home schooled:** Not accepted unless they receive equivalency from the UAE Ministry of Education upon their registration. **Learning Disabled:** Student should declare disability upon applying. Student services provides support on a case by case basis.

2015-2016 Annual costs. Books/supplies: $800. **Additional information:** Annual tuition: AED39,000. Part-time tuition: AED3,400 per credit. Lab and activity fees: AED600.

Financial aid. Non-need-based: Scholarships awarded for academics, athletics.

Application procedures. Admission: Priority date 5/30; no deadline. $55 fee. Admission notification on a rolling basis. Students will be notified of their admissions status within 10 days after applying. **Financial aid:** No deadline.

Academics. Special study options: Combined bachelor's/graduate degree, double major, ESL, internships, study abroad. **Credit/placement by examination:** AP, CLEP, IB, SAT, institutional tests. **Support services:** Preadmission summer program, reduced course load, remedial instruction, study skills assistance, tutoring, writing center.

Majors. Architecture: Architecture. **Business:** General, accounting, business admin, e-commerce, finance, management science, marketing. **Communications:** Journalism, media studies. **Communications technology:** Graphics. **Engineering:** Civil, computer, electrical, mechanical. **Visual/performing arts:** General, commercial/advertising art, graphic design, illustration, interior design, photography.

Technology on campus. 936 workstations in library, computer center. Dormitories wired for high-speed internet access. Commuter students can connect to campus network. Online course registration, online library, helpline, repair service, wireless network available.

Student life. Freshman orientation: Mandatory. Preregistration for classes offered. **Policies:** Dress code; no alcohol and no drugs on campus. **Housing:** Single-sex dorms, special housing for disabled, wellness housing available. $685 nonrefundable deposit, deadline 7/2. **Activities:** Dance, drama, international student organizations, Model UN, student government, student newspaper, African Union club, Egyptian cultural club, Indian cultural club, Khaleej student association, Lebanese Live 'n Give, Palestinian student association, Pakistani student association, Yemeni cultural club, Islamic awareness club.

Athletics. Intercollegiate: Basketball, cricket M, soccer, tennis, volleyball. **Intramural:** Basketball, football (tackle), soccer, swimming, table tennis, tennis, track and field, volleyball. **Team name:** Knights.

Student services. Alcohol/substance abuse counseling, career counseling, student employment services, health services, on-campus daycare, personal counseling, placement for graduates. **Physically disabled:** Services for visually, speech, hearing impaired.

Contact. E-mail: admissions@aud.edu
Phone: (4) 399-9000 ext. 171 Fax: (4) 399-8899
Carol Maalouf, Director of Admissions, American University in Dubai, PO Box 28282, Dubai, AE

United Kingdom

King's College London
London, United Kingdom   **CB member**
www.kcl.ac.uk   **CB code: 7884**

▶ Public 3-year university
▶ Residential campus in very large city
▶ 10,000 undergraduates
▶ 15,000 graduate students
▶ 38% of applicants admitted
▶ SAT or ACT, SAT Subject Tests, application essay required

General. Location: Downtown. **Calendar:** Semester, limited summer session. **Full-time faculty:** 1,060 total. **Part-time faculty:** 130 total. **Special facilities:** Museum of pathology.

Freshman class profile. 900 applied, 341 admitted, 67 enrolled.

Basis for selection. Entry requirements vary according to program of study. Prospective students are encouraged to refer to online descriptions of undergraduate programs and corresponding minimum entry requirements before submitting application for admission. 1900 SAT (minimum of 600 in each of the three sections) or 27 ACT required, in addition to three subject tests at AP/SAT level in any combination (minimum score of 5/600 on each). Interviews are required for Medicine, Dentistry, and Physiotherapy but are not required for all other programs. **Home schooled:** State high school equivalency certificate, letter of recommendation (nonparent) required.

2016-2017 Annual costs. Room only: $8,590. Books/supplies: $300. **Additional information:** All students who need a visa to study in the UK are required to have a minimum amount of funding of $10,765 per nine month program to cover the cost of housing, food, and incidentals.

Financial aid. Non-need-based: Scholarships awarded for academics, alumni affiliation.

Application procedures. Admission: Closing date 1/15 (receipt date). $35 fee. Admission notification by 3/15. Admission notification on a rolling basis beginning on or about 10/1. **Financial aid:** No deadline. FAFSA required.

Academics. Special study options: Combined bachelor's/graduate degree, double major, ESL, exchange student, internships, New York semester, study abroad, Washington semester. **Credit/placement by examination:** AP, CLEP, SAT, ACT. **Support services:** Learning center, study skills assistance, tutoring, writing center.

Majors. Area/ethnic studies: European, French, German, Spanish/Iberian, Western European. **Business:** Business admin. **Communications:** Advertising. **Computer sciences:** Computer science, programming, security. **English:** English lit. **Foreign languages:** French, German, Spanish. **History:** General, European. **Math:** General. **Philosophy/religion:** Philosophy. **Physical sciences:** Physics. **Theology:** Theology. **Visual/performing arts:** Music.

Technology on campus. Dormitories wired for high-speed internet access and linked to campus network. Online library, helpline, repair service, wireless network available.

Student life. Freshman orientation: Available. Preregistration for classes offered. **Policies:** Freshmen not permitted cars on campus. **Housing:** Coed dorms, apartments available. **Activities:** Bands, campus ministries, choral groups, dance, drama, film society, international student organizations, music ensembles, radio station, student government, student newspaper, symphony orchestra.

Athletics. Team name: King's.

Student services. Alcohol/substance abuse counseling, chaplain/spiritual director, career counseling, student employment services, financial aid counseling, health services, personal counseling, placement for graduates. **Physically disabled:** Services for visually, speech, hearing impaired.

Contact. E-mail: paul.teulon@kcl.ac.uk
Phone: (020) 783-65454
Paul Teulon, Director of Admissions, King's College London, Capital House (1st Floor), London, GB

Richmond, The American International University in London
Richmond-upon-Thames, United Kingdom   CB member
www.richmond.ac.uk   CB code: 0823

- Private 4-year university and liberal arts college
- Residential campus in very large city
- 776 degree-seeking undergraduates
- 37 graduate students
- Application essay required

General. Founded in 1972. Regionally accredited. Students spend first two years on Richmond Hill campus and second two on Kensington campus in London. Study centers in Florence and Rome. Degrees are accredited in both the US and the UK. **Degrees:** 135 bachelor's awarded; master's offered. **Location:** Richmond upon Thames campus on the outskirts of London; Kensington campus in central London. **Calendar:** Semester, limited summer session. **Full-time faculty:** 50 total. **Part-time faculty:** 113 total.

Basis for selection. School achievement record most important. Letters of recommendation and personal statement considered. SAT/ACT considered but not required.

High school preparation. 19 units required. Required and recommended units include English 4, mathematics 3-4, social studies 1, history 1, science 3-4 (laboratory 1), foreign language 2-3, computer science 1, visual/performing arts 1 and academic electives 2-4.

2015-2016 Annual costs. Tuition/fees: $36,000. Room/board: $14,116. Books/supplies: $700. Personal expenses: $8,787.

Financial aid. Non-need-based: Scholarships awarded for academics, alumni affiliation. **Additional information:** U.S. government loan programs available for eligible U.S. citizens/students.

Application procedures. Admission: Priority date 3/1; no deadline. $50 fee, may be waived for applicants with need. Admission notification on a rolling basis. **Financial aid:** Priority date 3/15, closing date 8/1. FAFSA required. Applicants notified on a rolling basis starting 3/1; must reply by 5/1 or within 4 week(s) of notification.

Academics. English language development programs for non-native English speakers. **Special study options:** Combined bachelor's/graduate

---

degree, cross-registration, double major, independent study, internships, liberal arts/career combination, study abroad. **Credit/placement by examination:** AP, CLEP, IB, institutional tests. **Support services:** Pre-admission summer program, reduced course load, remedial instruction, study skills assistance, tutoring, writing center.

Majors. Business: Entrepreneurial studies, fashion, finance, international, marketing. **Communications:** General, digital media, journalism, media studies, persuasive communications. **History:** General. **Psychology:** General. **Social sciences:** Economics, international economic development, international relations, political science, U.S. government. **Visual/performing arts:** Design, dramatic, film/cinema/video, studio arts.

Most popular majors. Business/marketing 43%, communications/journalism 14%, psychology 13%, social sciences 18%, visual/performing arts 10%.

Technology on campus. 140 workstations in library, computer center. Helpline, student web hosting, wireless network available.

Student life. Freshman orientation: Mandatory. Preregistration for classes offered. Session held Monday-Sunday prior to beginning of classes. **Housing:** Guaranteed on-campus for freshmen. Coed dorms, single-sex dorms, apartments, wellness housing available. $500 nonrefundable deposit, deadline 5/1. **Activities:** Bands, campus ministries, dance, drama, film society, international student organizations, music ensembles, Model UN, musical theater, student government, Amnesty International, Christian fellowship, community service club, The Green Project, Christian union.

Athletics. Intramural: Table tennis. **Team name:** Roebucks.

Student services. Alcohol/substance abuse counseling, career counseling, student employment services, financial aid counseling, health services, minority student services, personal counseling, placement for graduates.

Contact. E-mail: usadmissions@richmond.ac.uk
Phone: (617) 450-5617 Fax: (617) 450-5601
Nicholas Atkinson, Director of U.S. Admissions, Richmond, The American International University in London, 343 Congress Street, Suite 3100, Boston, MA 02210-1214

University of Chichester
Chichester, United Kingdom   CB member
www.chi.ac.uk/   CB code: 7869

- Public 6-year university
- Residential campus in large town
- 5,793 degree-seeking undergraduates
- 551 graduate students
- 67% of applicants admitted
- SAT or ACT (ACT writing recommended) required

General. Degrees: 1,390 bachelor's awarded; master's, doctoral offered. **Location:** We are 70 miles from London, on the South Coast, inbetween Portsmouth and Brighton. **Calendar:** Semester. **Full-time faculty:** 500 total. **Part-time faculty:** 250 total.

Basis for selection. Decisions are made largely on an academic basis. We look for, roughly, 550 in two subjects in SATs, 26 in the ACT, or 3 APs at Level 3, or further equivalent, with a 3.0 high school GPA. Portfolio based courses may require an interview or remote audition. Most course applications are assessed predominantly on grades, as is common in the UK. A short personal statement is also required.

High school preparation. 3.0 in High School Diploma plus ACT / SAT / AP or equivalent.

2015-2016 Annual costs. Tuition/fees: $13,685.

Application procedures. Admission: No deadline. No application fee. **Financial aid:** No deadline.

Academics. Special study options: Honors, liberal arts/career combination, study abroad, teacher certification program. **Credit/placement by examination:** AP. **Support services:** Learning center, pre-admission summer program, study skills assistance, tutoring, writing center.

Majors. Business: General. **Communications:** General. **Education:** General. **Engineering:** General. **English:** Creative writing, English lit, general lit, writing. **Liberal arts:** Humanities. **Psychology:** General. **Social sciences:** General, political science. **Theology:** Theology. **Visual/performing arts:** Dance, music.

Four-Year Colleges

Technology on campus. Dormitories wired for high-speed internet access and linked to campus network. Commuter students can connect to campus network. Online course registration, online library, helpline, student web hosting, wireless network available.

Student life. Freshman orientation: Available. Preregistration for classes offered. **Housing:** Coed dorms available. Accommodation in University Halls of Residence is provided for international students who book before August. **Activities:** Bands, choral groups, dance, drama, film society, international student organizations, literary magazine, musical theater, student government, student newspaper, symphony orchestra.

Contact. E-mail: Admissions@chi.ac.uk
Phone: (124) 381-6002
Bob Savill, Admissions Director, University of Chichester, College Lane, Chichester, GB

University of Greenwich
Greenwich, United Kingdom   **CB member**
www.gre.ac.uk

- Public 3-year university and business college
- Very large city
- 25,000 undergraduates
- 4,000 graduate students
- SAT or ACT (ACT writing optional) required

General. In addition to the main campus in Greenwich (London), there is the Avery Hill campus in Eltham (London) and the Medway campus in Chatham Maritime (Kent). All degrees may be awarded with or without honors. Students wishing to receive degrees with honors must take additional courses that amount to at least 60 credits beyond regular degree programs. **Calendar:** Semester.

Basis for selection. Applicant's entire academic profile, including personal statement and extracurricular activities (as well as employment history), considered; admission decisions made in conjunction with international office and academic departments. SAT Subject Tests required only for students applying for admission to science and engineering programs, which require physics/chemistry or biology-based tests.

2015-2016 Annual costs. $17,900 out-of-state.

Application procedures. Admission: Closing date 7/31. No application fee. **Financial aid:** No deadline.

Academics. Credit/placement by examination: AP.

Majors. Business: Business admin, finance, international. **Communications:** Media studies. **English:** Creative writing, English lit. **History:** General. **Psychology:** General. **Social sciences:** Economics. **Visual/performing arts:** Film/cinema/video.

Contact. E-mail: international@gre.ac.uk
Phone: (020) 833-18136
Mark Blakemore, Director of Admissions, University of Greenwich, International Office, Eltham, GB

University of Sussex
Brighton, United Kingdom
www.sussex.ac.uk   **CB code: 9166**

- Public 3-year university
- Residential campus in small city
- 10,089 undergraduates
- 3,545 graduate students

General. Calendar: Semester. **Full-time faculty:** 1,000 total.

Academics. Special study options: Honors, internships, study abroad. **Credit/placement by examination:** AP, CLEP.

Majors. Business: Business admin. **English:** English lit. **History:** General. **Psychology:** General. **Social sciences:** Anthropology, international relations. **Visual/performing arts:** Art history/conservation.

Technology on campus. Dormitories linked to campus network. Helpline, wireless network available.

Student life. Freshman orientation: Available. Preregistration for classes offered. **Housing:** Guaranteed on-campus for freshmen. Coed dorms available. **Activities:** Concert band, campus ministries, dance, drama, film society, international student organizations, music ensembles, student government, student newspaper.

Student services. Chaplain/spiritual director, career counseling, financial aid counseling, health services, on-campus daycare.

Contact. E-mail: Ug.enquiries@sussex.ac.uk
Phone: (44) 127-3876677
Rob Evans, Director of Admissions, University of Sussex, Sussex House, Brighton, GB

Two-year colleges

Alabama

Alabama Southern Community College
Monroeville, Alabama
www.ascc.edu CB code: 1644

▶ Public 2-year community and junior college
▶ Commuter campus in small town

General. Founded in 1965. Regionally accredited. Institution has 3 campuses and 2 centers. **Enrollment:** 1,151 degree-seeking undergraduates. **Degrees:** 190 associate awarded. **Location:** 85 miles from Mobile. **Calendar:** Semester, extensive summer session. **Full-time faculty:** 58 total. **Part-time faculty:** 75 total. **Special facilities:** Nature trail.

Transfer out. Colleges most students transferred to 2015: University of Alabama, Auburn University, Troy University, University of West Alabama, University of South Alabama.

Basis for selection. Open admission.

2015-2016 Annual costs. Tuition/fees: $4,320; $7,770 out-of-state. Per-credit charge: $115 in-state; $230 out-of-state. Books/supplies: $1,500. Personal expenses: $1,500.

Financial aid. Need-based: Work-study available nights, weekends and for part-time students.

Application procedures. Admission: No deadline. No application fee. Admission notification on a rolling basis. **Financial aid:** Priority date 7/15; no closing date. FAFSA required. Applicants notified on a rolling basis; must reply within 4 week(s) of notification.

Academics. Special study options: Accelerated study, dual enrollment of high school students. Degrees in allied health available through University of Alabama at Birmingham, registered nurse program through Jefferson Davis State Junior College. **Credit/placement by examination:** AP, CLEP. **Support services:** GED preparation and test center, learning center, reduced course load, remedial instruction, tutoring.

Majors. Business: General, administrative services. **Engineering:** Electrical. **Health services:** Licensed practical nurse, nursing (RN), nursing assistant. **Liberal arts:** Arts/sciences. **Protective services:** Firefighting.

Most popular majors. Business/marketing 18%, engineering/engineering technologies 16%, health sciences 15%, liberal arts 51%.

Technology on campus. 40 workstations in library, computer center, student center. Online course registration, wireless network available.

Student life. Freshman orientation: Mandatory. Preregistration for classes offered. **Activities:** Concert band, campus ministries, choral groups,

student government, Circle K, Phi Theta Kappa, Rotaract, Student Government Association.

Athletics. NJCAA. **Intercollegiate:** Baseball M, basketball, cheerleading, softball W. **Team name:** Eagles.

Student services. Adult student services, career counseling, financial aid counseling, personal counseling, veterans' counselor. **Transfer:** Transfer adviser, college fairs on campus for students transferring to 4-year colleges.

Contact. E-mail: admissions@ascc.edu
Phone: (251) 575-3156 Fax: (251) 575-5238
Jana Horton, Director of Admissions, Alabama Southern Community College, PO Box 2000, Monroeville, AL 36461

Bevill State Community College
Jasper, Alabama
www.bscc.edu CB code: 0723

▶ Public 2-year community college
▶ Commuter campus in small town

General. Founded in 1969. Regionally accredited. Additional campuses in Fayette, Hamilton, and Sumiton. Learning site in Carrollton. **Enrollment:** 3,210 degree-seeking undergraduates; 399 non-degree-seeking students. **Degrees:** 495 associate awarded. **Location:** 25 miles from Birmingham. **Calendar:** Semester, limited summer session. **Full-time faculty:** 117 total; 15% have terminal degrees, 6% minority, 57% women. **Part-time faculty:** 169 total; 9% have terminal degrees, 11% minority, 62% women. **Special facilities:** Observatory, simulated underground mine, mining museum, small business incubator. **Partnerships:** Formal partnerships with 3M, Alabama Power, McWane Cast Iron Pipe Co.

Student profile. Among degree-seeking undergraduates, 937 enrolled as first-time, first-year students.

Part-time:	43%	25 or older:	27%
Women:	63%	Live on campus:	1%

Transfer out. Colleges most students transferred to 2015: University of Alabama, Auburn University, University of North Alabama, University of Alabama Birmingham, University of Montevallo.

Basis for selection. Open admission, but selective for some programs. Admission to nursing programs competitive and limited. High school diploma not required in some technical programs. COMPASS required for placement unless applicant has 470 or above in SAT Writing, Reading, & Math, or 20 in comparable sections of the ACT. **Adult students:** COMPASS placement testing required unless student is senior citizen or non-award seeking major taking classes for vocational reasons. **Home schooled:** Transcript of courses and grades required. 16 ACT required.

2015-2016 Annual costs. Tuition/fees: $4,678; $8,358 out-of-state. Per-credit charge: $115 in-state; $230 out-of-state. Room/board: $1,850. Books/supplies: $1,200. Personal expenses: $4,050.

Financial aid. Need-based: Need-based aid available for part-time students. Work-study available nights, weekends and for part-time students. **Non-need-based:** Scholarships awarded for academics, leadership, music/drama.

Application procedures. Admission: No deadline. No application fee. Admission notification on a rolling basis beginning on or about 7/1. **Financial aid:** Priority date 5/1; no closing date. FAFSA required. Applicants notified on a rolling basis starting 7/1.

Academics. Special study options: Accelerated study, cooperative education, distance learning, dual enrollment of high school students, ESL, honors, weekend college. License preparation in nursing, paramedic, physical therapy. **Credit/placement by examination:** AP, CLEP. Only 25% of program credits can be awarded through nontraditional means. **Support services:** GED preparation and test center, learning center, reduced course load, remedial instruction, tutoring, writing center.

Majors. Business: Administrative services. **Computer sciences:** General, computer science. **General:** Electrician. **Health services:** EMT paramedic, nursing (RN). **Liberal arts:** Arts/sciences. **Work/family studies:** Child care management.

Technology on campus. 1,200 workstations in library, computer center, student center. Commuter students can connect to campus network. Online course registration, online library, helpline, wireless network available.

Student life. Freshman orientation: Mandatory, $30 fee. Preregistration for classes offered. **Housing:** Coed dorms, wellness housing available. **Activities:** Bands, campus ministries, choral groups, dance, music ensembles, student government, Cross Seekers, Circle K, College Democrats, College Republicans, Phi Theta Kappa.

Athletics. Intramural: Basketball, bowling, boxing, football (non-tackle), softball, table tennis.

Student services. Career counseling, services for economically disadvantaged, student employment services, financial aid counseling, placement for graduates. **Physically disabled:** Services for visually, speech, hearing impaired. **Transfer:** Transfer adviser, college fairs on campus for students transferring to 4-year colleges.

Contact. Phone: (205) 387-0511 ext. 5726
Toll-free number: (800) 648-3271 ext. 5400 Fax: (205) 648-3311
Melissa Stowe, Assistant Dean for Admissions, Financial Aid, & Student Records, Bevill State Community College, 1411 Indiana Avenue, Jasper, AL 35501

Bishop State Community College
Mobile, Alabama
www.bishop.edu   CB code: 1517

- Public 2-year community college
- Commuter campus in small city

General. Founded in 1963. Regionally accredited. **Enrollment:** 2,930 degree-seeking undergraduates. **Degrees:** 245 associate awarded. **ROTC:** Army, Air Force. **Calendar:** Semester, limited summer session. **Full-time faculty:** 87 total. **Part-time faculty:** 73 total.

Basis for selection. Open admission. **Home schooled:** GED or 16 ACT required.

2015-2016 Annual costs. Tuition/fees: $4,320; $7,770 out-of-state. Per-credit charge: $115 in-state; $230 out-of-state. Books/supplies: $700. Personal expenses: $1,033.

Financial aid. Need-based: Work-study available nights, weekends and for part-time students. **Non-need-based:** Scholarships awarded for academics, athletics.

Application procedures. Admission: No deadline. No application fee. Admission notification on a rolling basis. **Financial aid:** Priority date 4/1; no closing date. FAFSA, institutional form required. Applicants notified on a rolling basis; must reply within 2 week(s) of notification.

Academics. Special study options: Accelerated study, cooperative education, distance learning, dual enrollment of high school students, weekend college. Degree programs available in allied health through University of Alabama at Birmingham. License preparation in nursing. **Credit/placement by examination:** AP, CLEP. **Support services:** GED preparation and test center, learning center, reduced course load, remedial instruction, tutoring.

Majors. Business: Accounting, administrative services. **Communications technology:** Graphic/printing. **Computer sciences:** General. **Education:** General, early childhood. **Health services:** EMT paramedic, health information technology, nursing (RN), physical therapy assistant. **Liberal arts:** Arts/sciences. **Protective services:** Law enforcement admin. **Work/family studies:** Child care management, institutional food production.

Most popular majors. Family/consumer sciences 6%, health sciences 40%, interdisciplinary studies 13%, liberal arts 30%.

Technology on campus. 71 workstations in library, computer center. Commuter students can connect to campus network. Online course registration, helpline, wireless network available.

Student life. Freshman orientation: Available. Preregistration for classes offered. **Activities:** Bands, campus ministries, choral groups, dance, international student organizations, music ensembles, student government.

Athletics. NJCAA. **Intercollegiate:** Baseball M, basketball, cheerleading W, softball W. **Team name:** Wildcats.

Student services. Career counseling, services for economically disadvantaged, student employment services, financial aid counseling, on-campus daycare, personal counseling, placement for graduates, veterans' counselor. **Physically disabled:** Services for visually, speech, hearing impaired. **Transfer:** Transfer adviser for students transferring to 4-year colleges.

Contact. E-mail: admiss@bishop.edu
Phone: (251) 405-7005 Fax: (251) 690-6998
Terry Hazzard, Dean of Students, Bishop State Community College, 351 North Broad Street, Mobile, AL 36603-5898

Calhoun Community College
Decatur, Alabama   CB member
www.calhoun.edu   CB code: 1356

- Public 2-year community and junior college
- Commuter campus in small city

General. Founded in 1963. Regionally accredited. Satellite campus at Research Park in Huntsville. **Enrollment:** 9,380 degree-seeking undergraduates. **Degrees:** 1,136 associate awarded. **Location:** 20 miles from Huntsville. **Calendar:** Semester, limited summer session. **Full-time faculty:** 137 total. **Part-time faculty:** 333 total. **Partnerships:** Formal partnership with Boeing.

Transfer out. Colleges most students transferred to 2015: Athens State University, University of North Alabama, Auburn University, University of Alabama, University of Alabama at Huntsville.

Basis for selection. Open admission, but selective for some programs. SAT/ACT used for placement. Students from unaccredited high schools required to have 16 ACT or 790 SAT (exclusive of Writing). Selective admission to nursing program. Portfolio recommended for art majors. **Home schooled:** Transcript of courses and grades required. 16 ACT/790 SAT (exclusive of Writing), successful completion of GED or high school graduation examination required.

High school preparation. 26 units recommended. Recommended units include English 4, mathematics 4, social studies 4, science 4, foreign language 2 and academic electives 10. In-state high school graduates must pass state high school competency examination.

2015-2016 Annual costs. Tuition/fees: $4,320; $7,770 out-of-state. Per-credit charge: $115 in-state; $230 out-of-state. Books/supplies: $1,500. Personal expenses: $1,000.

Financial aid. Need-based: Work-study available nights, weekends and for part-time students. **Non-need-based:** Scholarships awarded for academics.

Application procedures. Admission: No deadline. No application fee. Admission notification on a rolling basis. **Financial aid:** Priority date 5/1; no closing date. FAFSA, institutional form required. Applicants notified on a rolling basis starting 7/1; must reply within 2 week(s) of notification.

Academics. Numerous courses available online. **Special study options:** Accelerated study, distance learning, dual enrollment of high school students, liberal arts/career combination, weekend college. License preparation in dental hygiene, nursing, paramedic, real estate. **Credit/placement by examination:** AP, CLEP, IB, institutional tests. 30 credit hours maximum toward associate degree. AP Exam credit limited to 18 semester hours. **Support services:** GED preparation and test center, reduced course load, remedial instruction, tutoring, writing center.

Majors. Biology: General. **Business:** Accounting, business admin, real estate. **Communications technology:** Photo/film/video. **Computer sciences:** General, applications programming, computer graphics, programming. **Education:** General, secondary. **English:** English lit. **General:** Electrician. **Health services:** Cytogenetics, dental assistant, EMT paramedic, nursing (RN), predental, premedicine, prenursing, prepharmacy, preveterinary. **History:** General. **Liberal arts:** Arts/sciences. **Math:** General. **Military:** Munitions. **Parks/recreation:** Health/fitness. **Physical sciences:** Chemistry. **Protective services:** Fire safety technology. **Social sciences:** General. **Visual/performing arts:** Commercial/advertising art, music, photography, theater arts management. **Work/family studies:** Child care management, child development.

Most popular majors. Engineering/engineering technologies 7%, health sciences 29%, liberal arts 55%.

Technology on campus. 166 workstations in library, student center. Commuter students can connect to campus network. Online course registration, online library, helpline, wireless network available.

Student life. Freshman orientation: Mandatory. Preregistration for classes offered. **Activities:** Jazz band, campus ministries, choral groups, drama, music ensembles, student government, student newspaper, TV station, BACCHUS/SADD, black students alliance, criminal justice club, Native American club, Phi Theta Kappa, allied health students association, The Centurians.

Athletics. NJCAA. **Intercollegiate:** Baseball M, softball W. **Team name:** Warhawks.

Student services. Career counseling, financial aid counseling, minority student services, on-campus daycare, veterans' counselor. **Transfer:** Transfer adviser, college fairs on campus for students transferring to 4-year colleges.

Contact. E-mail: admissions@calhoun.edu
Phone: (256) 306-2593 Toll-free number: (855) 501-0860
Fax: (256) 306-2941
Pauletta Burns, Director of Admissions and College Registrar, Calhoun Community College, PO Box 2216, Decatur, AL 35609-2216

Central Alabama Community College
Alexander City, Alabama
www.cacc.edu   CB code: 0715

- Public 2-year community college
- Commuter campus in large town

General. Founded in 1965. Regionally accredited. Two campuses: Childersburg, predominantly for technical courses, and Alexander City, predominantly for transfer courses. Instructional site in Talladega. **Enrollment:** 1,594 degree-seeking undergraduates; 189 non-degree-seeking students. **Degrees:** 244 associate awarded. **Calendar:** Semester, extensive summer session. **Full-time faculty:** 57 total; 16% have terminal degrees, 7% minority, 47% women. **Part-time faculty:** 108 total; 12% minority, 70% women. **Class size:** 58% < 20, 38% 20-39, 2% 40-49, 1% 50-99. **Special facilities:** Wildlife museum, wellness center, pioneer village.

Student profile. Among degree-seeking undergraduates, 58% enrolled in a transfer program, 42% enrolled in a vocational program, 439 enrolled as first-time, first-year students.

Part-time:	40%	African American:	25%
Out-of-state:	1%	Hispanic/Latino:	1%
Women:	59%	25 or older:	39%

Basis for selection. Open admission, but selective for some programs. Graduates of non-accredited high schools and certain nursing applicants may be required to take SAT or ACT. Admission to nursing program based on a point system. **Home schooled:** Transcript of courses and grades required. A score of 16 or above on the ACT test or a score of 790 on the SAT.

High school preparation. 24 units required. Required units include English 4, mathematics 4, social studies 1, history 2, science 4, computer science .5, visual/performing arts .5, academic electives 5.5.

2015-2016 Annual costs. Tuition/fees: $4,320; $7,770 out-of-state. Per-credit charge: $115 in-state; $230 out-of-state. Books/supplies: $1,400. Personal expenses: $1,950.

2014-2015 Financial aid. Need-based: 70% of total undergraduate aid awarded as scholarships/grants, 30% as loans/jobs. Need-based aid available for part-time students. Work-study available nights, weekends and for part-time students. **Non-need-based:** Scholarships awarded for academics, athletics, music/drama, state residency.

Application procedures. Admission: No deadline. No application fee. Admission notification on a rolling basis. **Financial aid:** Priority date 7/15; no closing date. FAFSA required. Applicants notified on a rolling basis.

Academics. Special study options: Accelerated study, cooperative education, dual enrollment of high school students, independent study. License preparation in nursing. **Credit/placement by examination:** AP, CLEP, institutional tests. Students must complete a minimum of 25% of credit hours with Central Alabama Community College. **Support services:** GED preparation and test center, learning center, remedial instruction, study skills assistance, tutoring.

Majors. Business: Administrative services, business admin. **Computer sciences:** General. **Health services:** Nursing (RN).

Most popular majors. Business/marketing 9%, health sciences 26%, liberal arts 50%.

Technology on campus. 170 workstations in library, computer center, student center. Online course registration, online library, helpline, wireless network available.

Student life. Freshman orientation: Mandatory. Preregistration for classes offered. **Activities:** Jazz band, choral groups, dance, drama, radio station, student government.

Athletics. NJCAA. **Intercollegiate:** Baseball M, golf M, softball W, tennis W. **Team name:** Trojans.

Student services. Career counseling, financial aid counseling, personal counseling, veterans' counselor. **Transfer:** Pre-admission transcript evaluation for new students. Transfer adviser, college fairs on campus for students transferring to 4-year colleges.

Contact. Phone: (256) 215-4255 Toll-free number: (800) 643-2657
Hester Hamby, Admissions Specialist, Central Alabama Community College, 1675 Cherokee Road, Alexander City, AL 35010

Chattahoochee Valley Community College
Phenix City, Alabama
www.cv.edu   CB code: 1187

- Public 2-year community college
- Commuter campus in small city

General. Founded in 1974. Regionally accredited. **Enrollment:** 1,806 undergraduates. **Degrees:** 198 associate awarded. **Location:** 5 miles from Columbus, GA. **Calendar:** Semester, extensive summer session. **Full-time faculty:** 39 total. **Part-time faculty:** 81 total.

Transfer out. Colleges most students transferred to 2015: Columbus State University, Auburn University, Columbus Technical College, Southern Union State Community College, Troy State University.

Basis for selection. Open admission, but selective for some programs. COMPASS placement exam waived for students submitting appropriate ACT/SAT scores. Additional requirements for health occupation programs. **Home schooled:** State high school equivalency certificate required. Program must be accredited by state or federal department of education.

2015-2016 Annual costs. Tuition/fees: $4,380; $7,830 out-of-state. Per-credit charge: $115 in-state; $230 out-of-state. Books/supplies: $1,200. Personal expenses: $750.

Financial aid. Need-based: Need-based aid available for part-time students. Work-study available nights, weekends and for part-time students. **Non-need-based:** Scholarships awarded for academics, art, athletics, leadership, music/drama.

Application procedures. Admission: Priority date 7/1; no deadline. No application fee. Application must be submitted on paper. Admission notification on a rolling basis. **Financial aid:** Priority date 7/1; no closing date. FAFSA required. Applicants notified on a rolling basis; must reply within 1 week(s) of notification.

Academics. Special study options: Accelerated study, distance learning, dual enrollment of high school students, ESL, liberal arts/career combination. License preparation in nursing, paramedic. **Credit/placement by examination:** AP, CLEP, institutional tests. 18 credit hours maximum toward associate degree. **Support services:** GED preparation and test center, learning center, reduced course load, remedial instruction, tutoring, writing center.

Majors. Business: Accounting, administrative services, business admin. **Computer sciences:** General. **Health services:** Nursing (RN). **Liberal arts:** Arts/sciences. **Protective services:** Fire services admin, police science. **Visual/performing arts:** Design, music history.

Technology on campus. 150 workstations in library, computer center. Online library, wireless network available.

Student life. Freshman orientation: Available. Preregistration for classes offered. **Activities:** Choral groups, music ensembles.

Athletics. NJCAA. **Intercollegiate:** Baseball M, basketball, softball W. **Team name:** Pirates.

Student services. Adult student services, financial aid counseling. **Physically disabled:** Services for visually, hearing impaired.

Contact. E-mail: admissions@cv.edu
Phone: (334) 291-4929 Fax: (334) 291-4994
Sanquita Alexander, Director of Admissions/Registrar, Chattahoochee Valley Community College, 2602 College Drive, Phenix City, AL 36869

Community College of the Air Force
Maxwell-Gunter AFB, Alabama
www.au.af.mil/au/barnes/ccaf/
CB code: 1175

- Public 2-year community and technical college
- Commuter campus in small city
- Interview required

General. Founded in 1972. Regionally accredited. Multi-campus, world-wide, for United States Air Force enlisted personnel. Administrative offices at Maxwell Air Force Base, Gunter Annex. Primary campuses are technical training centers located at Air Force bases in several states. Other campuses include USAF PME Centers, USAF Command Sponsored Schools, and Field Training Detachments. **Enrollment:** 274,094 undergraduates. **Degrees:** 20,957 associate awarded. **Location:** 160 miles from Atlanta, 90 miles from Birmingham. **Calendar:** Differs by program, extensive summer session. **Full-time faculty:** 6,093 total.

Basis for selection. Admission is restricted to enlisted members of the U.S. Air Force, Air National Guard, Air Force Reserve Command, and other-service instructors serving as CCAS affiliated school faculty. All eligible students automatically enrolled into degree program for their occupational specialty upon completion of Basic Military Training. Armed Services Vocational Aptitude Battery required.

2015-2016 Annual costs. Students pay no tuition or fees.

Financial aid. **Need-based:** Work-study available nights, weekends and for part-time students. **Additional information:** Air Force Tuition Assistance program available for general and technical education courses taken at civilian colleges and universities. Pays 75% of tuition costs.

Application procedures. **Admission:** No deadline. No application fee. Admission notification on a rolling basis. **Financial aid:** No deadline.

Academics. **Special study options:** Accelerated study, distance learning, independent study, internships, liberal arts/career combination. License preparation in aviation, physical therapy, radiology. **Credit/placement by examination:** AP, CLEP, institutional tests. 30 credit hours maximum toward associate degree. **Support services:** Reduced course load, remedial instruction, tutoring.

Majors. **Business:** Human resources, management information systems, office management, operations, purchasing. **Communications:** Public relations. **Communications technology:** General. **Computer sciences:** General, networking. **Education:** Technology/industrial arts. **Health services:** Cardiovascular technology, dental assistant, dental lab technology, health care admin, histologic assistant, medical assistant, nuclear medical technology, ophthalmic lab technology, pharmacy assistant, physical therapy assistant, radiologic technology/medical imaging, sonography, surgical technology. **History:** General. **Human services:** Social work. **Parks/recreation:** General. **Physical sciences:** Atmospheric science. **Protective services:** Criminal justice, fire safety technology. **Visual/performing arts:** Music.

Student life. **Policies:** Air Force bases provide housing, student services, activities, and athletics.

Athletics. **Intramural:** Badminton, baseball M, basketball, bowling, boxing M, cross-country, football (non-tackle) M, golf, handball, racquetball, rifle, soccer M, softball, squash, swimming, table tennis, tennis, track and field, volleyball, weight lifting.

Student services. Adult student services, alcohol/substance abuse counseling, chaplain/spiritual director, career counseling, financial aid counseling, health services, legal services, on-campus daycare, personal counseling, veterans' counselor. **Transfer:** Transfer adviser, college fairs on campus for students transferring to 4-year colleges.

Contact. E-mail: registrar.ccaf@us.af.mil
Phone: (334) 649-5000 Fax: (334) 649-5106
David Turner, Director of Enrollment Management, Community College of the Air Force, 100 South Turner Boulevard, Maxwell-Gunter AFB, AL 36114-3011

Enterprise State Community College
Enterprise, Alabama
www.escc.edu
CB code: 1213

- Public 2-year community college
- Commuter campus in large town

General. Founded in 1963. Regionally accredited. Courses offered at Enterprise, Ozark, Fort Rucker, Mobile, Andalusia, Albertville and Decatur.

Enrollment: 1,529 degree-seeking undergraduates. **Degrees:** 240 associate awarded. **Location:** 25 miles from Dothan, 85 miles from Montgomery. **Calendar:** Semester, limited summer session. **Full-time faculty:** 53 total; 38% women. **Part-time faculty:** 46 total; 54% women.

Student profile. Among degree-seeking undergraduates, 396 enrolled as first-time, first-year students, 392 transferred in from other institutions.

Part-time: 41% **Women:** 48%

Transfer out. **Colleges most students transferred to 2015:** Troy University, Auburn University, University of Alabama.

Basis for selection. Open admission. **Home schooled:** If sponsoring organization is not accredited, the student must either take Alabama High School Exit Exam and pass all five parts or submit 16 ACT.

High school preparation. 28 units recommended. Recommended units include English 4, mathematics 4, social studies 4 and science 4.

2015-2016 Annual costs. Tuition/fees: $4,320; $7,770 out-of-state. Per-credit charge: $115 in-state; $230 out-of-state. Books/supplies: $1,000. Personal expenses: $1,000.

2014-2015 Financial aid. **Need-based:** 77% of total undergraduate aid awarded as scholarships/grants, 23% as loans/jobs. Work-study available nights, weekends and for part-time students. **Non-need-based:** Scholarships awarded for academics, art, athletics, leadership, music/drama, state residency.

Application procedures. **Admission:** No deadline. No application fee. Admission notification on a rolling basis. **Financial aid:** Priority date 6/15; no closing date. FAFSA required. Applicants notified on a rolling basis starting 6/1; must reply within 2 week(s) of notification.

Academics. Federal Aviation Administration certified Aviation Maintenance Technology program. **Special study options:** Distance learning, dual enrollment of high school students, ESL, honors, internships, weekend college. Bachelor's degree programs available on campus, License preparation in aviation, paramedic. **Credit/placement by examination:** AP, CLEP, institutional tests. 30 credit hours maximum toward associate degree. **Support services:** GED preparation and test center, learning center, remedial instruction, tutoring.

Majors. **Business:** Administrative services, business admin, management information systems, office management. **Computer sciences:** General. **Health services:** EMT paramedic, health information technology, medical assistant. **Liberal arts:** Arts/sciences.

Technology on campus. Commuter students can connect to campus network. Online course registration, helpline, wireless network available.

Student life. **Freshman orientation:** Mandatory. Preregistration for classes offered. **Activities:** Concert band, campus ministries, choral groups, dance, drama, music ensembles, student government, student newspaper, community band, concert choir.

Athletics. NJCAA. **Intercollegiate:** Baseball M, basketball, softball W. **Team name:** Boll Weevils.

Student services. Adult student services, career counseling, services for economically disadvantaged, student employment services, financial aid counseling, personal counseling, placement for graduates, veterans' counselor, women's services. **Physically disabled:** Services for visually, speech, hearing impaired. **Transfer:** Transfer adviser, college fairs on campus for students transferring to 4-year colleges.

Contact. E-mail: jholley@escc.edu
Phone: (334) 347-2623 ext. 2234 Fax: (334) 347-5569
Joey Holley, Director of Admissions, Enterprise State Community College, Box 1300, Enterprise, AL 36331

Faulkner State Community College
Bay Minette, Alabama
www.faulknerstate.edu
CB code: 1939

- Public 2-year community college
- Commuter campus in large town

General. Founded in 1965. Regionally accredited. Branch campuses in Fairhope and Gulf Shores. **Enrollment:** 4,372 degree-seeking undergraduates; 208 non-degree-seeking students. **Degrees:** 324 associate awarded. **Location:** 35 miles from Mobile. **Calendar:** Semester, extensive summer session. **Full-time faculty:** 91 total; 8% have terminal degrees, 12% minority,

54% women. **Part-time faculty:** 123 total; 2% have terminal degrees, 11% minority, 50% women.

Student profile. Among degree-seeking undergraduates, 1,300 enrolled as first-time, first-year students, 4,580 transferred in from other institutions.

Part-time:	41%	**25 or older:**	27%
Out-of-state:	1%	**Live on campus:**	10%
Women:	62%		

Transfer out. Colleges most students transferred to 2015: University of South Alabama, Auburn University, University of Alabama, Troy University, University of Alabama at Birmingham, University of West Florida.

Basis for selection. Open admission, but selective for some programs. Special requirements for nursing and surgical technology programs. Audition recommended for music majors, portfolio for art majors. **Home schooled:** If school is non-accredited, 16 ACT or GED required.

2015-2016 Annual costs. Tuition/fees: $4,320; $7,770 out-of-state. Per-credit charge: $115 in-state; $230 out-of-state. Room/board: $5,800. Books/supplies: $1,450. Personal expenses: $886.

2014-2015 Financial aid. Need-based: 53% of total undergraduate aid awarded as scholarships/grants, 47% as loans/jobs. Work-study available nights, weekends and for part-time students. **Non-need-based:** Scholarships awarded for academics, art, athletics, leadership, music/drama.

Application procedures. Admission: No deadline. No application fee. Application must be submitted on paper. Admission notification on a rolling basis. **Financial aid:** Priority date 7/1; no closing date. FAFSA, institutional form required. Applicants notified on a rolling basis starting 7/1; must reply within 2 week(s) of notification.

Academics. Special study options: Accelerated study, cooperative education, distance learning, double major, dual enrollment of high school students, honors, independent study, internships. License preparation in nursing, paramedic. **Credit/placement by examination:** AP, CLEP. 20 credit hours maximum toward associate degree. **Support services:** GED preparation and test center, learning center, remedial instruction, study skills assistance, tutoring, writing center.

Majors. Biology: General. **Business:** Administrative services, business admin, finance, hospitality admin, office technology. **Communications:** Journalism. **Computer sciences:** General, computer graphics, systems analysis. **Conservation:** Forestry. **Education:** Business, early childhood, elementary, physical. **English:** English lit. **Health services:** Clinical lab science, clinical lab technology, dental assistant, EMT paramedic, medical secretary, predental, premedicine, prenursing, prepharmacy, preveterinary. **Liberal arts:** Arts/sciences. **Math:** General. **Parks/recreation:** Facilities management. **Physical sciences:** Chemistry. **Social sciences:** General. **Visual/performing arts:** General, art, commercial/advertising art, music, studio arts. **Work/family studies:** General.

Technology on campus. 100 workstations in dormitories, library, computer center, student center. Dormitories wired for high-speed internet access and linked to campus network. Commuter students can connect to campus network. Online course registration, online library, helpline, wireless network available.

Student life. Freshman orientation: Mandatory. Preregistration for classes offered. **Housing:** Coed dorms, single-sex dorms available. $50 nonrefundable deposit. **Activities:** Bands, campus ministries, choral groups, drama, music ensembles, student government, student newspaper, Pow-wow Leadership, Phi Beta Lambda, Baptist campus ministries, Phi Theta Kappa, Psi Beta, Association of Computational Machinery, Engineering club, Fusion, National Student Nurses' Association, scholars' bowl.

Athletics. NJCAA. **Intercollegiate:** Baseball M, basketball, cheerleading, golf, softball W, tennis, volleyball W. **Intramural:** Basketball M, bowling, racquetball, softball, volleyball W. **Team name:** Sun Chiefs.

Student services. Career counseling, student employment services, financial aid counseling, personal counseling, placement for graduates, veterans' counselor. **Physically disabled:** Services for visually impaired. **Transfer:** Transfer adviser, college fairs on campus for students transferring to 4-year colleges.

Contact. E-mail: admissions@faulknerstate.edu
Phone: (251) 580-2111 Toll-free number: (800) 381-3722
Fax: (251) 580-2285
Michael Nikolakis, Dean of Student Services, Faulkner State Community College, 1900 Highway 31 South, Bay Minette, AL 36507

Gadsden State Community College
Gadsden, Alabama
www.gadsdenstate.edu   CB code: 1262

▸ Public 2-year community and technical college
▸ Commuter campus in small city

General. Founded in 1985. Regionally accredited. Off-campus sites include Ayers Campus, McClellan Campus, Gadsden State Cherokee and Valley Street Campus (HBCU). **Enrollment:** 4,613 degree-seeking undergraduates. **Degrees:** 634 associate awarded. **ROTC:** Army. **Location:** 60 miles from Birmingham. **Calendar:** Semester, extensive summer session. **Full-time faculty:** 149 total. **Part-time faculty:** 153 total. **Special facilities:** Advanced technology center, language institute, aquaculture education, cadaver lab.

Student profile. Among degree-seeking undergraduates, 53% enrolled in a transfer program, 47% enrolled in a vocational program.

Out-of-state:	3%	**Live on campus:**	2%
25 or older:	33%		

Transfer out. 14% of students enrolled in the transfer program go on to 4-year colleges. **Colleges most students transferred to 2015:** Jacksonville State University, Auburn University, University of Alabama, University of Alabama at Birmingham, University of Alabama at Huntsville.

Basis for selection. Open admission, but selective for some programs. Special requirements for health-related programs. Career Program Assessment Test required for some programs. Interview recommended for computer technology, court reporting, and most health science majors. **Home schooled:** Transcript of courses and grades required. 16 ACT or 790 SAT required. **Learning Disabled:** Accommodations must be requested for each school term. Students are responsible for providing adequate documentation of disability, requesting accommodation through appropriate campus officer, maintaining contact with that person, and notifying the officer of any changes in accommodations needed and of new courses for which accommodations are required each semester.

High school preparation. 27 units recommended. Recommended units include English 4, mathematics 4, social studies 4, science 4 (laboratory 2) and academic electives 9. Electives must include .5 unit computer, .5 unit of fine arts.

2015-2016 Annual costs. Tuition/fees: $4,020; $7,470 out-of-state. Per-credit charge: $115 in-state; $230 out-of-state. Room/board: $3,600. Books/supplies: $1,500. Personal expenses: $825.

Financial aid. Need-based: Need-based aid available for part-time students. Work-study available nights, weekends and for part-time students. **Non-need-based:** Scholarships awarded for academics, alumni affiliation, art, athletics, job skills, leadership, minority status, music/drama, state residency.

Application procedures. Admission: No deadline. No application fee. Admission notification on a rolling basis. **Financial aid:** Priority date 4/15; no closing date. FAFSA, institutional form required. Applicants notified on a rolling basis starting 6/10.

Academics. Special study options: Accelerated study, cooperative education, cross-registration, distance learning, dual enrollment of high school students, ESL, honors, independent study, internships, weekend college. License preparation in nursing, paramedic, radiology. **Credit/placement by examination:** AP, CLEP, institutional tests. 20 credit hours maximum toward associate degree. **Support services:** GED preparation and test center, remedial instruction, study skills assistance, tutoring, writing center.

Majors. Business: Accounting technology, administrative services, sales/distribution. **Computer sciences:** General. **Health services:** Clinical lab technology, EMT paramedic, nursing (RN), radiologic technology/medical imaging, substance abuse counseling. **Liberal arts:** Arts/sciences. **Work/family studies:** Child care management.

Most popular majors. Business/marketing 8%, engineering/engineering technologies 12%, health sciences 29%, liberal arts 35%, trade and industry 10%.

Technology on campus. 250 workstations in dormitories, library, computer center, student center. Dormitories wired for high-speed internet access. Online course registration, online library, wireless network available.

Student life. Freshman orientation: Mandatory, $132 fee. Preregistration for classes offered. Required one credit hour class completed during first semester. **Housing:** Coed dorms available. $200 fully refundable deposit. **Activities:** Bands, campus ministries, choral groups, dance, drama, international student organizations, music ensembles, student government, Circle-K, international club, Baptist student union, Phi Beta Lambda.

Two-Year Colleges

Athletics. NJCAA. **Intercollegiate:** Basketball, softball W, tennis M, volleyball W. **Team name:** Cardinals.

Student services. Adult student services, career counseling, services for economically disadvantaged, student employment services, financial aid counseling, personal counseling, placement for graduates, veterans' counselor. **Physically disabled:** Services for visually, speech, hearing impaired. **Transfer:** Pre-admission transcript evaluation for new students. Transfer adviser, college fairs on campus for students transferring to 4-year colleges.

Contact. Phone: (256) 549-8210 Toll-free number: (800) 226-5563 Fax: (256) 549-8205
Jennie Dobson, Assistant to the President/Registrar, Gadsden State Community College, 1001 George Wallace Drive, Gadsden, AL 35902-0227

George C. Wallace Community College at Dothan
Dothan, Alabama
www.wallace.edu   **CB code: 1264**

- Public 2-year community college
- Commuter campus in small city

General. Founded in 1949. Regionally accredited. Additional campus in Eufaula. **Enrollment:** 4,173 degree-seeking undergraduates; 596 non-degree-seeking students. **Degrees:** 609 associate awarded. **Location:** 100 miles from Montgomery; 98 miles from Columbus, GA. **Calendar:** Semester, extensive summer session. **Full-time faculty:** 130 total. **Part-time faculty:** 99 total.

Student profile. Among degree-seeking undergraduates, 973 enrolled as first-time, first-year students.

Part-time:	49%	**Women:**	66%
Out-of-state:	4%		

Transfer out. Colleges most students transferred to 2015: University of Alabama, Auburn University, University of Alabama at Birmingham, Troy University.

Basis for selection. Certain allied health and nursing programs have additional requirements. Most require a minimum grade point average and rank based on grades earned in certain courses and scores made on specific assessment tests. **Home schooled:** Transcript of courses and grades required.

2015-2016 Annual costs. Tuition/fees: $4,260; $7,710 out-of-state. Per-credit charge: $115 in-state; $230 out-of-state. Books/supplies: $1,900. Personal expenses: $666.

2014-2015 Financial aid. Need-based: 99% of total undergraduate aid awarded as scholarships/grants, 1% as loans/jobs. Work-study available nights, weekends and for part-time students. **Non-need-based:** Scholarships awarded for academics, athletics, leadership.

Application procedures. Admission: No deadline. No application fee. Admission notification on a rolling basis. **Financial aid:** Priority date 5/1; no closing date. FAFSA required. Applicants notified on a rolling basis.

Academics. Special study options: Accelerated study, cooperative education, cross-registration, distance learning, dual enrollment of high school students, ESL. License preparation in nursing, paramedic, physical therapy, radiology. **Credit/placement by examination:** AP, CLEP, institutional tests. Credit awarded for challenge and validation examinations; experiential, specialized, or occupational training; military training; and professional certification, licensure, or registry. No more than 25% of total credit required for any program may be awarded through nontraditional means. **Support services:** GED preparation and test center, learning center, pre-admission summer program, remedial instruction, study skills assistance, tutoring.

Majors. Business: Administrative services. **Computer sciences:** General. **General:** Electrician. **Health services:** EMT paramedic, medical assistant, medical radiologic technology/radiation therapy, nursing (RN), physical therapy assistant, radiologic technology/medical imaging, respiratory therapy assistant, respiratory therapy technology. **Liberal arts:** Arts/sciences. **Protective services:** Police science. **Work/family studies:** Child care management.

Most popular majors. Health sciences 39%, liberal arts 38%.

Technology on campus. Online library, wireless network available.

Student life. Freshman orientation: Available. Preregistration for classes offered. Held during the summer semester. **Policies:** Tobacco-free campus. **Activities:** Bands, campus ministries, choral groups, drama, music ensembles, musical theater, student government, Association of Student Practical Nursing, Baptist Campus Ministries, College Bible Study, leadership development program, Phi Theta Kappa, Respiratory Therapy Association for Better Breathing, Roteract, Association of Nursing Students, philosophy club.

Athletics. NJCAA. **Intercollegiate:** Baseball M, softball W. **Team name:** Govs (M), Lady Govs (W).

Student services. Adult student services, career counseling, services for economically disadvantaged, student employment services, financial aid counseling, personal counseling, placement for graduates, veterans' counselor. **Physically disabled:** Services for visually, speech, hearing impaired. **Transfer:** Transfer adviser, college fairs on campus for students transferring to 4-year colleges.

Contact. E-mail: admissions@wallace.edu
Phone: (334) 983-3521 Toll-free number: (800) 543-2426
Fax: (334) 983-6066
Keith Saulsberry, Director of Enrollment Services/Registrar, George C. Wallace Community College at Dothan, 1141 Wallace Drive, Dothan, AL 36303-0943

George C. Wallace State Community College at Selma
Selma, Alabama
www.wccs.edu   **CB code: 3146**

- Public 2-year community and technical college
- Commuter campus in large town

General. Founded in 1963. Regionally accredited. **Enrollment:** 1,498 degree-seeking undergraduates. **Degrees:** 222 associate awarded. **Location:** 50 miles from Montgomery, 90 miles from Birmingham. **Calendar:** Semester, extensive summer session. **Full-time faculty:** 53 total. **Part-time faculty:** 54 total.

Basis for selection. Open admission, but selective for some programs. Generic/mobility (RN) nursing candidates need 20 ACT. Practical (LPN) nursing candidates need 18 ACT, or 41 on the Nursing Entrance Test.

2015-2016 Annual costs. Tuition/fees: $4,020; $8,040 out-of-state. Per-credit charge: $134 in-state; $268 out-of-state. Books/supplies: $825. Personal expenses: $1,000.

Financial aid. Need-based: Work-study available nights, weekends and for part-time students. **Non-need-based:** Scholarships awarded for academics, athletics.

Application procedures. Admission: Priority date 8/21; no deadline. No application fee. Application must be submitted online. Admission notification on a rolling basis. **Financial aid:** Priority date 6/1; no closing date. FAFSA required. Applicants notified on a rolling basis starting 6/15.

Academics. Special study options: Accelerated study, double major, dual enrollment of high school students. **Credit/placement by examination:** AP, CLEP, institutional tests. 30 credit hours maximum toward associate degree. **Support services:** GED preparation and test center, learning center, reduced course load, remedial instruction, study skills assistance, tutoring.

Majors. Business: Administrative services, business admin. **Computer sciences:** General. **General:** Electrician. **Health services:** Nursing (RN). **Liberal arts:** Arts/sciences.

Student life. Freshman orientation: Available. Preregistration for classes offered. **Activities:** Student government, Baptist student union, Phi Theta Kappa, Fellowship of Christian Athletes.

Athletics. NJCAA. **Intercollegiate:** Baseball M, basketball, softball W. **Intramural:** Baseball M, basketball, softball. **Team name:** Patriots.

Student services. Career counseling, student employment services, personal counseling, placement for graduates, veterans' counselor. **Physically disabled:** Services for visually, speech, hearing impaired. **Transfer:** Transfer adviser, college fairs on campus for students transferring to 4-year colleges.

Contact. E-mail: info@wccs.edu
Phone: (334) 876-9295 Fax: (334) 876-9300
Lonzy Clifton, Director of Admissions and Records, George C. Wallace State Community College at Selma, PO Box 2530, Selma, AL 36702-2530

Jefferson Davis Community College
Brewton, Alabama
www.jdcc.edu   CB code: 1355

◗ Public 2-year nursing and community college
◗ Commuter campus in small town

General. Founded in 1965. Regionally accredited. **Enrollment:** 1,033 degree-seeking undergraduates; 53 non-degree-seeking students. **Degrees:** 148 associate awarded. **Location:** 60 miles from Pensacola, FL. **Calendar:** Semester, limited summer session. **Full-time faculty:** 35 total. **Part-time faculty:** 37 total. **Class size:** 72% < 20, 28% 20-39. **Special facilities:** Museum, golf course, telecommunications center.

Student profile. Among degree-seeking undergraduates, 310 enrolled as first-time, first-year students.

Part-time:	44%	25 or older:	48%
Out-of-state:	8%	Live on campus:	6%
Women:	57%		

Basis for selection. Open admission, but selective for some programs. Special admissions requirements for nursing program. **Home schooled:** 16 ACT required.

High school preparation. 24 units recommended. Recommended units include English 4, mathematics 4, social studies 4, science 4 and academic electives 8.

2015-2016 Annual costs. Tuition/fees: $4,020; $7,470 out-of-state. Per-credit charge: $115 in-state; $230 out-of-state. Room only: $3,000. Books/supplies: $1,600. Personal expenses: $600.

Financial aid. Need-based: Need-based aid available for part-time students. Work-study available nights, weekends and for part-time students. **Non-need-based:** Scholarships awarded for academics, athletics, leadership.

Application procedures. Admission: No deadline. No application fee. Admission notification on a rolling basis. **Financial aid:** No deadline. FAFSA required. Applicants notified on a rolling basis; must reply within 2 week(s) of notification.

Academics. Special study options: Cooperative education, distance learning, dual enrollment of high school students, ESL, honors, independent study. Bachelor's degree programs available on campus. License preparation in nursing, paramedic. **Credit/placement by examination:** AP, CLEP. **Support services:** GED preparation and test center, learning center, remedial instruction, study skills assistance, tutoring.

Majors. Business: Administrative services. **Health services:** Nursing (RN). **Liberal arts:** Arts/sciences.

Most popular majors. Business/marketing 7%, health sciences 36%, liberal arts 55%.

Technology on campus. 420 workstations in library, computer center. Dormitories wired for high-speed internet access. Online course registration, helpline, wireless network available.

Student life. Freshman orientation: Mandatory. Preregistration for classes offered. **Housing:** Coed dorms, wellness housing available. $150 partly refundable deposit. **Activities:** Campus ministries, student government, student newspaper, Baptist student union, Phi Theta Kappa, Phi Beta Lambda, Psi Beta.

Athletics. NJCAA. **Intercollegiate:** Baseball M, basketball M, softball W, volleyball W. **Team name:** Warhawks.

Student services. Adult student services, chaplain/spiritual director, career counseling, services for economically disadvantaged, financial aid counseling, personal counseling, veterans' counselor. **Physically disabled:** Services for visually impaired. **Transfer:** Pre-admission transcript evaluation for new students. Transfer adviser, college fairs on campus for students transferring to 4-year colleges.

Contact. Phone: (251) 809-1594 Fax: (251) 809-1593 Robin Sessions, Registrar, Jefferson Davis Community College, PO Box 958, Brewton, AL 36427

General. Founded in 1963. Regionally accredited. **Enrollment:** 7,381 degree-seeking undergraduates. **Degrees:** 886 associate awarded. **ROTC:** Army, Air Force. **Location:** 12 miles from downtown. **Calendar:** Semester, extensive summer session. **Full-time faculty:** 145 total; 63% women. **Part-time faculty:** 297 total; 62% women.

Student profile.

Out-of-state:	2%	25 or older:	35%

Transfer out. Colleges most students transferred to 2015: University of Alabama at Birmingham, University of Alabama, Auburn University.

Basis for selection. Open admission, but selective for some programs. Students registering for 5 or more hours of credit must take ACT ASSET or ACT COMPASS for placement. Exemptions given for students who have completed college level math or English courses, or students who have equivalent ACT scores. Applicants from non-accredited high schools admitted with high school diploma and 16 ACT or equivalent SAT. **Home schooled:** Must have 16 ACT or pass Alabama Public High School Graduation Exam.

High school preparation. 24 units recommended. Recommended units include English 4, mathematics 4, social studies 4, science 4, foreign language 2, computer science .5, visual/performing arts .5, academic electives 3.5. Health education .5, physical education 1.

2015-2016 Annual costs. Tuition/fees: $4,380; $7,830 out-of-state. Per-credit charge: $115 in-state; $230 out-of-state. Books/supplies: $1,982. Personal expenses: $2,250.

Financial aid. Need-based: Need-based aid available for part-time students. Work-study available nights, weekends and for part-time students. **Non-need-based:** Scholarships awarded for academics, art, leadership, music/drama. **Additional information:** Any Alabama resident over age 60 may attend classes tuition free, on a space available basis.

Application procedures. Admission: No deadline. No application fee. Admission notification on a rolling basis. **Financial aid:** Closing date 5/1. FAFSA, institutional form required. Applicants notified on a rolling basis starting 6/1.

Academics. Special study options: Accelerated study, distance learning, dual enrollment of high school students, ESL, honors, independent study, internships. Bachelor's degree programs available on campus. License preparation in nursing, paramedic, radiology, real estate. **Credit/placement by examination:** AP, CLEP, IB, institutional tests. 20 credit hours maximum toward associate degree. **Support services:** GED preparation and test center, learning center, reduced course load, remedial instruction, study skills assistance.

Majors. Business: Accounting technology, administrative services, hospitality admin, office management. **Computer sciences:** General. **Health services:** Clinical lab technology, EMT paramedic, nursing (RN), physical therapy assistant, radiologic technology/medical imaging, veterinary technology/assistant. **Liberal arts:** Arts/sciences. **Protective services:** Fire services admin, police science. **Work/family studies:** Child care management.

Most popular majors. Business/marketing 15%, health sciences 43%, liberal arts 29%.

Technology on campus. 278 workstations in library, computer center, student center. Commuter students can connect to campus network. Online course registration, online library, helpline, wireless network available.

Student life. Freshman orientation: Available. Preregistration for classes offered. **Activities:** Bands, choral groups, music ensembles, student government, BACCHUS, Students in Free Enterprise, Ambassadors, speech team, PTK, nursing club, SKD.

Student services. Adult student services, career counseling, student employment services, financial aid counseling, placement for graduates, veterans' counselor, women's services. **Physically disabled:** Services for visually, speech, hearing impaired. **Transfer:** Transfer adviser, college fairs on campus for students transferring to 4-year colleges.

Contact. E-mail: help@jeffstateonline.com Phone: (205) 856-7704 Toll-free number: (800) 239-5900 ext. 7704 Fax: (205) 856-6070 Lillian Owens, Director, Admissions & Retention, Jefferson State Community College, 2601 Carson Road, Birmingham, AL 35215-3098

Jefferson State Community College
Birmingham, Alabama
www.jeffstateonline.com   CB code: 1352

◗ Public 2-year community college
◗ Commuter campus in large city

Lawson State Community College
Birmingham, Alabama
www.lawsonstate.edu   CB code: 1933

◗ Public 2-year community college
◗ Commuter campus in small city

General. Founded in 1949. Regionally accredited. **Enrollment:** 3,090 undergraduates. **Degrees:** 239 associate awarded. **Calendar:** Semester, limited summer session. **Full-time faculty:** 95 total. **Part-time faculty:** 118 total. **Class size:** 100% >100.

Student profile.

Out-of-state: 1% Live on campus: 2%

Transfer out. Colleges most students transferred to 2015: Miles College, University of Alabama at Birmingham, Alabama A&M University, Alabama State University, Jefferson State Community College.

Basis for selection. Open admission, but selective for some programs. Advanced placement option for licensed practical nurses (LPN) and nursing education. Nursing students must pass nursing entrance exam or have 20 ACT or comparable SAT.

2015-2016 Annual costs. Tuition/fees: $4,320; $7,800 out-of-state. Per-credit charge: $116 in-state; $232 out-of-state. Room/board: $4,760. Books/supplies: $1,500. Personal expenses: $500.

Financial aid. All financial aid based on need. Need-based aid available for part-time students. Work-study available nights, weekends and for part-time students.

Application procedures. Admission: No deadline. No application fee. Admission notification on a rolling basis. **Financial aid:** Closing date 6/1. FAFSA required. Applicants notified on a rolling basis starting 8/1; must reply within 2 week(s) of notification.

Academics. Special study options: Accelerated study, double major, dual enrollment of high school students, internships, liberal arts/career combination, student-designed major. License preparation in dental hygiene, nursing, real estate. **Credit/placement by examination:** AP, CLEP, institutional tests. **Support services:** GED preparation and test center, learning center, reduced course load, remedial instruction, tutoring, writing center.

Majors. Business: Accounting, administrative services, business admin, office management, office technology, operations. **Computer sciences:** Computer science. **Health services:** Medical secretary, nursing (RN). **Human services:** Social work. **Liberal arts:** Arts/sciences. **Protective services:** Police science.

Most popular majors. Business/marketing 20%, computer/information sciences 9%, engineering/engineering technologies 10%, health sciences 18%, liberal arts 34%.

Technology on campus. 512 workstations in dormitories, library, computer center, student center. Dormitories linked to campus network. Online course registration, online library, wireless network available.

Student life. Freshman orientation: Mandatory. Preregistration for classes offered. **Housing:** Coed dorms available. **Activities:** Jazz band, choral groups, dance, drama, music ensembles, student government, scholars bowl team, Sophist club.

Athletics. NJCAA. **Intercollegiate:** Baseball M, basketball, volleyball W. **Intramural:** Baseball M, basketball. **Team name:** Cougars.

Student services. Adult student services, career counseling, services for economically disadvantaged, student employment services, financial aid counseling, health services, on-campus daycare, personal counseling, placement for graduates, veterans' counselor. **Physically disabled:** Services for hearing impaired. **Transfer:** College fairs on campus for students transferring to 4-year colleges.

Contact. E-mail: jshelley@lawsonstate.edu
Phone: (205) 929-6309 Fax: (205) 923-7106
Jeff Shelley, Director of Admissions, Lawson State Community College, 3060 Wilson Road SW, Birmingham, AL 35221-1717

Lurleen B. Wallace Community College
Andalusia, Alabama
www.lbwcc.edu   **CB code: 1429**

▸ Public 2-year community college
▸ Commuter campus in small town

General. Founded in 1969. Regionally accredited. Additional campuses in Opp, Greenville, Luverne. **Enrollment:** 1,412 degree-seeking undergraduates; 320 non-degree-seeking students. **Degrees:** 206 associate awarded. **Location:** 90 miles from Montgomery. **Calendar:** Semester, limited summer session. **Full-time faculty:** 55 total; 7% have terminal degrees, 9% minority, 64% women. **Part-time faculty:** 50 total; 2% have terminal degrees, 10%

---

minority, 54% women. **Special facilities:** Nature trail, tennis courts, 9-hole golf course, children's playground.

Student profile. Among degree-seeking undergraduates, 57% enrolled in a transfer program, 43% enrolled in a vocational program, 492 enrolled as first-time, first-year students, 313 transferred in from other institutions.

Part-time:	27%	Hispanic/Latino:	1%
Out-of-state:	3%	Native American:	1%
Women:	59%	Multi-racial, non-Hispanic:	1%
African American:	27%	25 or older:	19%

Transfer out. Colleges most students transferred to 2015: Troy University, Auburn University, Auburn University at Montgomery, University of Alabama.

Basis for selection. Open admission. ACCUPLACER required for placement unless student scores 20 ACT math and English. **Learning Disabled:** Students with disabilities encouraged to meet with ADA coordinator.

High school preparation. College-preparatory program recommended.

2015-2016 Annual costs. Tuition/fees: $4,320; $7,770 out-of-state. Per-credit charge: $115 in-state; $230 out-of-state. Books/supplies: $1,192. Personal expenses: $1,000.

2014-2015 Financial aid. Need-based: Need-based aid available for part-time students. Work-study available nights, weekends and for part-time students. **Non-need-based:** Scholarships awarded for academics, art, athletics, leadership, music/drama.

Application procedures. Admission: No deadline. No application fee. Admission notification on a rolling basis. **Financial aid:** Closing date 8/1. FAFSA required. Applicants notified on a rolling basis.

Academics. Special study options: Accelerated study, cooperative education, distance learning, dual enrollment of high school students, honors, independent study. License preparation in nursing, paramedic. **Credit/placement by examination:** AP, CLEP, institutional tests. **Support services:** GED preparation and test center, reduced course load, remedial instruction, study skills assistance, tutoring. Math Booster Camp.

Majors. Business: Administrative services. **Computer sciences:** General. **Conservation:** Forest technology. **Health services:** EMT paramedic, nursing (RN), sonography. **Liberal arts:** Arts/sciences. **Work/family studies:** Child care management.

Technology on campus. Online library, wireless network available.

Student life. Freshman orientation: Available. Preregistration for classes offered. Held during summer at the Greenville, MacArthur, Andalusia campuses. **Activities:** Jazz band, campus ministries, dance, drama, music ensembles, musical theater, student government, Non-Traditional Student Association, Student Ambassadors, Christian Student Ministries, Campus Civitan, Mu Alpha Theta, Phi Theta Kappa, Saints Angels, Student Government Association, Student Veterans' Association.

Athletics. NJCAA. **Intercollegiate:** Baseball M, basketball, softball W. **Team name:** Saints.

Student services. Career counseling, services for economically disadvantaged, financial aid counseling, personal counseling, veterans' counselor. **Transfer:** Transfer adviser, college fairs on campus for students transferring to 4-year colleges.

Contact. E-mail: jriley@lbwcc.edu
Phone: (334) 881-2281 Fax: (334) 881-2201
Jan Riley, Director of Admissions & Records, Lurleen B. Wallace Community College, Box 1418, Andalusia, AL 36420

Marion Military Institute
Marion, Alabama
www.marionmilitary.edu   **CB code: 1447**

▸ Public 2-year junior and military college
▸ Residential campus in small town
▸ SAT or ACT (ACT writing optional) required

General. Founded in 1842. Regionally accredited. One of 5 military junior colleges that provides academic prep for the U.S. Service Academies and one of 5 military junior colleges that provides an Early Commissioning Program for U.S. Army. **Enrollment:** 450 degree-seeking undergraduates. **Degrees:** 100 associate awarded. **ROTC:** Army, Air Force. **Location:** 70 miles from Birmingham, 52 miles from Tuscaloosa. **Calendar:** Semester.

Full-time faculty: 20 total. **Part-time faculty:** 19 total. **Special facilities:** Alabama Military Hall of Honor, golf course. **Partnerships:** Formal partnership with Sanders Flight Training Center, Inc.

Student profile. Among degree-seeking undergraduates, 100% enrolled in a transfer program, 275 enrolled as first-time, first-year students.

Out-of-state:	53%	Hispanic/Latino:	9%
Women:	20%	Native American:	1%
African American:	21%	Multi-racial, non-Hispanic:	5%
Asian American:	2%	Live on campus:	100%

Transfer out. Colleges most students transferred to 2015: US Coast Guard Academy, US Military Academy, US Air Force Academy, University of Alabama, Auburn University Montgomery.

Basis for selection. 16 ACT (or SAT equivalent) required for general admissions. Additional criteria for applicants to the Early Commissioning Program or Service Academy Preparatory Program. Interview recommended. **Home schooled:** Applicants must have been enrolled in approved programs.

High school preparation. College-preparatory program required. 25 units required. Required and recommended units include English 4, mathematics 4, social studies 1, history 3, science 4, foreign language 2 and academic electives 8.

2015-2016 Annual costs. Tuition/fees: $8,550; $14,550 out-of-state. Per-credit charge: $200 in-state; $400 out-of-state. Room/board: $4,450.

Financial aid. Need-based: Work-study available nights, weekends and for part-time students.

Academics. Special study options: ESL, independent study. **Credit/placement by examination:** AP, CLEP, SAT, ACT, institutional tests. **Support services:** Remedial instruction, study skills assistance, tutoring.

Majors. Liberal arts: Arts/sciences.

Technology on campus. 90 workstations in library, computer center. Dormitories wired for high-speed internet access and linked to campus network. Commuter students can connect to campus network. Online course registration, online library, helpline, wireless network available.

Student life. Freshman orientation: Mandatory. Preregistration for classes offered. Occurs approximately one week before start of academic period. **Policies:** Structured military school environment. Students must live on campus. **Housing:** Guaranteed on-campus for all undergraduates. Coed dorms, wellness housing available. **Activities:** Bands, campus ministries, choral groups, drama, music ensembles, musical theater, student government, Scabbard & Blade, Normandy Society, Christian Ministries, Swamp Fox, Honor Guard, White Knights, Young Libertarians, Young Republicans, Black Student Union, Flying Tigers.

Athletics. NJCAA. **Intercollegiate:** Baseball M, basketball M, softball W, tennis. **Intramural:** Basketball, cross-country, football (non-tackle), golf, rifle, swimming, track and field, volleyball, weight lifting. **Team name:** Tigers.

Student services. Chaplain/spiritual director, financial aid counseling, health services, personal counseling, veterans' counselor. **Transfer:** Transfer adviser, college fairs on campus for students transferring to 4-year colleges.

Contact. E-mail: admissions@marionmilitary.edu
Phone: (334) 683-2305 Toll-free number: (800) 664-1842
Fax: (334) 683-2383
Brittany Crawford, Director of Admissions, Marion Military Institute, 1101 Washington Street, Marion, AL 36756-0420

Northeast Alabama Community College
Rainsville, Alabama
www.nacc.edu   **CB code: 1576**

- Public 2-year community college
- Commuter campus in rural community

General. Founded in 1963. Regionally accredited. **Enrollment:** 2,051 degree-seeking undergraduates; 654 non-degree-seeking students. **Degrees:** 391 associate awarded. **Location:** 55 miles from Huntsville, and 110 miles from Birmingham. **Calendar:** Semester, extensive summer session. **Full-time faculty:** 53 total. **Part-time faculty:** 98 total. **Special facilities:** Community theater, walking/nature trail.

Student profile. Among degree-seeking undergraduates, 63% enrolled in a transfer program, 37% enrolled in a vocational program, 599 enrolled as first-time, first-year students.

Part-time:	43%	Asian American:	1%
Women:	63%	Hispanic/Latino:	9%
African American:	2%	Native American:	3%

Transfer out. Colleges most students transferred to 2015: Jacksonville State University, University of Alabama at Huntsville, Athens State University, University of Alabama, Auburn University.

Basis for selection. Open admission. **Home schooled:** Transcript of courses and grades required. 16 ACT required. **Learning Disabled:** Students who may require accommodations are encouraged to communicate with Disability Services.

High school preparation. 24 units recommended. Recommended units include English 4, mathematics 4, social studies 2, history 2, science 4 (laboratory 2), foreign language 2, computer science .5, academic electives 3.5.

2015-2016 Annual costs. Tuition/fees: $4,320; $7,770 out-of-state. Per-credit charge: $115 in-state; $230 out-of-state. Personal expenses: $1,500.

Financial aid. Need-based: Need-based aid available for part-time students. Work-study available nights, weekends and for part-time students. **Non-need-based:** Scholarships awarded for academics, art, leadership, minority status, music/drama.

Application procedures. Admission: No deadline. No application fee. Admission notification on a rolling basis. **Financial aid:** No deadline. FAFSA required. Applicants notified on a rolling basis.

Academics. Special study options: Accelerated study, cooperative education, distance learning, dual enrollment of high school students, ESL, internships. License preparation in nursing, paramedic. **Credit/placement by examination:** AP, CLEP, institutional tests. 16 credit hours maximum toward associate degree. **Support services:** GED preparation and test center, learning center, remedial instruction, study skills assistance, tutoring, writing center.

Majors. Business: Administrative services, business admin. **Computer sciences:** General. **Health services:** EMT paramedic, medical assistant, nursing (RN). **Liberal arts:** Arts/sciences. **Protective services:** Police science. **Work/family studies:** Child care management.

Most popular majors. Business/marketing 13%, health sciences 19%, liberal arts 40%, trade and industry 12%.

Technology on campus. 550 workstations in library, computer center. Commuter students can connect to campus network. Online course registration, online library, helpline, wireless network available.

Student life. Freshman orientation: Mandatory. Preregistration for classes offered. **Activities:** Bands, campus ministries, choral groups, dance, drama, literary magazine, music ensembles, musical theater, student government.

Athletics. Intramural: Basketball. **Team name:** Mustangs.

Student services. Career counseling, student employment services, financial aid counseling, personal counseling, placement for graduates, veterans' counselor. **Physically disabled:** Services for visually, speech, hearing impaired. **Transfer:** Pre-admission transcript evaluation for new students. Transfer adviser, college fairs on campus for students transferring to 4-year colleges.

Contact. E-mail: harveya@nacc.edu
Phone: (256) 228-6001 ext. 2222 Fax: (256) 638-6043
Sherie Grace, Dean of Student Services, Northeast Alabama Community College, Admissions Office, NACC, Rainsville, AL 35986-0159

Northwest-Shoals Community College
Muscle Shoals, Alabama
www.nwscc.edu   **CB code: 0188**

- Public 2-year community and technical college
- Commuter campus in large town

General. Founded in 1966. Regionally accredited. Two campuses: Phil Campbell Campus located in Franklin County and Muscle Shoals Campus located in Colbert County. **Enrollment:** 3,022 degree-seeking undergraduates; 645 non-degree-seeking students. **Degrees:** 363 associate awarded. **Location:** 60 miles from Huntsville, AL; 120 miles from Birmingham; 134 miles from Memphis, TN. **Calendar:** Semester, extensive summer session.

Full-time faculty: 77 total; 10% have terminal degrees, 10% minority, 54% women. **Part-time faculty:** 75 total; 8% minority, 51% women.

Student profile. Among degree-seeking undergraduates, 701 enrolled as first-time, first-year students, 155 transferred in from other institutions.

Part-time:	46%	25 or older:	26%
Women:	59%		

Transfer out. Colleges most students transferred to 2015: University of North Alabama, University of Alabama, Athens State University, University of Alabama at Huntsville.

Basis for selection. Open admission, but selective for some programs. Additional requirements for health occupation programs. **Home schooled:** Equivalent number of required units for graduation and 16 ACT or 790 SAT (exclusive of Writing) required.

High school preparation. 24 units recommended. Required and recommended units include English 4, mathematics 4, social studies 4 and science 4. Any combination of courses in the disciplines of physical education, health education, and/or fine arts, computer applications; electives 5.5 credits.

2015-2016 Annual costs. Tuition/fees: $4,291; $7,741 out-of-state. Per-credit charge: $115 in-state; $230 out-of-state. Books/supplies: $1,750. Personal expenses: $1,000.

2014-2015 Financial aid. Need-based: 59% of total undergraduate aid awarded as scholarships/grants, 41% as loans/jobs. Need-based aid available for part-time students. Work-study available nights, weekends and for part-time students. **Non-need-based:** Scholarships awarded for academics, art, leadership, minority status, music/drama.

Application procedures. Admission: No deadline. No application fee. Admission notification on a rolling basis. **Financial aid:** Priority date 4/1, closing date 8/1. FAFSA required. Applicants notified on a rolling basis starting 6/1; must reply within 2 week(s) of notification.

Academics. Special study options: Accelerated study, cooperative education, cross-registration, distance learning, double major, dual enrollment of high school students, honors, independent study, internships, liberal arts/career combination. License preparation in nursing, paramedic. **Credit/placement by examination:** AP, CLEP, institutional tests. 30 credit hours maximum toward associate degree. **Support services:** GED preparation and test center, learning center, study skills assistance, tutoring.

Majors. Business: Administrative services. **Computer sciences:** General, applications programming, information systems, information technology, programming. **Health services:** EMT paramedic, medical assistant, nursing (RN). **Liberal arts:** Arts/sciences. **Protective services:** Police science. **Work/family studies:** Child care management.

Most popular majors. Business/marketing 6%, health sciences 31%, interdisciplinary studies 14%, liberal arts 34%.

Technology on campus. 1,000 workstations in library, computer center, student center. Online course registration, online library, wireless network available.

Student life. Freshman orientation: Mandatory. Preregistration for classes offered. Held in two formats. A general 1-credit hour course is conducted to orient new students to institution, develop good study habits, and explore college major/career options. A 3-credit hour course is conducted for students who are placed in three transitional studies courses. **Activities:** Jazz band, campus ministries, choral groups, music ensembles, student government, Phi Theta Kappa, Ambassadors, Circle K, College Bowl Team, Science Club, American Society of Heating, Refrigerating and Air Conditioning Engineers, Patriots for Christ, NW-SCC fishing club, Skills USA.

Athletics. Intramural: Basketball, football (non-tackle), table tennis. **Team name:** Patriots.

Student services. Career counseling, financial aid counseling, on-campus daycare, veterans' counselor. **Physically disabled:** Services for visually, speech, hearing impaired. **Transfer:** Pre-admission transcript evaluation for new students. Transfer adviser, college fairs on campus for students transferring to 4-year colleges.

Contact. E-mail: motown@nwscc.edu
Phone: (256) 331-5363 Fax: (256) 331-5366
Tom Carter, Assistant Dean of Recruitment, Admissions and Financial Aid, Northwest-Shoals Community College, PO Box 2545, Muscle Shoals, AL 35662-2545

Prince Institute of Professional Studies
Montgomery, Alabama
www.princeinstitute.edu
CB code: 3450

- For-profit 2-year technical and career college
- Commuter campus in large city

General. Accredited by ACICS. **Calendar:** Quarter.

Annual costs/financial aid. Tuition/fees (2015-2016): $10,510. Books/supplies: $1,200. Personal expenses: $2,187. Need-based financial aid available to full-time and part-time students.

Contact. Phone: (334) 271-1670 ext. 209
Admissions Director, 7735 Atlanta Highway, Montgomery, AL 36117-4231

Remington College: Mobile
Mobile, Alabama
http://mobile.remingtoncollege.edu
CB code: 3157

- Private 2-year career college
- Commuter campus in large city

General. Accredited by ACCSC. **Enrollment:** 881 undergraduates. **Degrees:** 34 associate awarded. **Calendar:** Quarter, extensive summer session. **Full-time faculty:** 16 total. **Part-time faculty:** 32 total.

Basis for selection. Open admission. **Home schooled:** Transcript of courses and grades, state high school equivalency certificate required.

2015-2016 Annual costs. Tuition for associate degree programs, $33,900; tuition for diploma programs vary and range from $15,995 to $20,995.

Financial aid. All financial aid based on need. Work-study available nights, weekends and for part-time students.

Application procedures. Admission: No deadline. $50 fee. **Financial aid:** FAFSA required.

Academics. Special study options: Cooperative education, distance learning, honors, liberal arts/career combination. **Credit/placement by examination:** AP, CLEP. **Support services:** Tutoring.

Majors. Computer sciences: System admin. **Protective services:** Law enforcement admin.

Technology on campus. PC or laptop required. Online library, helpline, repair service, wireless network available.

Student life. Freshman orientation: Mandatory. Preregistration for classes offered. Held the week before class for 2 1/2 hours.

Student services. Career counseling, financial aid counseling, placement for graduates. **Transfer:** Pre-admission transcript evaluation for new students.

Contact. E-mail: admissions@remingtoncollege.edu
Phone: (251) 243-0639 Toll-free number: (800) 866-0850
Brent Malveaux, Director of Admissions, Remington College: Mobile, 828 Downtowner Loop West, Mobile, AL 36609-5404

Shelton State Community College
Tuscaloosa, Alabama
www.sheltonstate.edu
CB code: 3338

- Public 2-year community and technical college
- Commuter campus in small city

General. Founded in 1963. Regionally accredited. Designated as Alabama's Community College of the Fine Arts; includes C.A. Fredd campus, a Historically Black College. **Enrollment:** 4,477 degree-seeking undergraduates; 356 non-degree-seeking students. **Degrees:** 426 associate awarded. **ROTC:** Army, Air Force. **Location:** 60 miles from Birmingham. **Calendar:** Semester, extensive summer session. **Full-time faculty:** 93 total; 6% have terminal degrees, 18% minority, 55% women. **Part-time faculty:** 213 total. **Class size:** 39% < 20, 57% 20-39, 4% 40-49. **Special facilities:** Observatories, community theater. **Partnerships:** Shelton State has a partnership with Mercedes-Benz International USA; students are enrolled in the Industrial Electronics program at Shelton while having the opportunity to work at

Mercedes-Benz. When they complete their AAS, the top 75% are guaranteed jobs at the Mercedes plant.

Student profile. Among degree-seeking undergraduates, 1,144 enrolled as first-time, first-year students.

Part-time:	51%	**Asian American:**	1%
Out-of-state:	5%	**Multi-racial, non-Hispanic:**	2%
Women:	55%	**25 or older:**	32%
African American:	35%		

Transfer out. Colleges most students transferred to 2015: University of Alabama, Auburn University, Stillman College, University of Alabama at Birmingham, University of Montevallo.

Basis for selection. Open admission. Any individual with a high school diploma or GED is able to apply. COMPASS test required of all students for placement unless the student submits an ACT or SAT score that meets placement requirements. Visit the college website for necessary scores.

2015-2016 Annual costs. Tuition/fees: $4,020; $7,470 out-of-state. Per-credit charge: $115 in-state; $230 out-of-state. Books/supplies: $1,200. Personal expenses: $500.

Financial aid. All financial aid based on need. Need-based aid available for part-time students. Work-study available nights, weekends and for part-time students.

Application procedures. Admission: Priority date 8/10; no deadline. No application fee. Application must be submitted online. Admission notification on a rolling basis. **Financial aid:** Priority date 6/30; no closing date. FAFSA required. Applicants notified on a rolling basis starting 7/30.

Academics. Special study options: Accelerated study, distance learning, dual enrollment of high school students, liberal arts/career combination. License preparation in nursing, real estate. **Credit/placement by examination:** AP, CLEP, IB, institutional tests. 20 credit hours maximum toward associate degree. **Support services:** GED preparation and test center, learning center, reduced course load, remedial instruction, study skills assistance, tutoring.

Majors. Architecture: Technology. **Business:** Administrative services. **General:** Electrician. **Health services:** Nursing (RN), respiratory therapy technology. **Liberal arts:** Arts/sciences.

Most popular majors. Business/marketing 20%, engineering/engineering technologies 7%, health sciences 24%, liberal arts 36%, trade and industry 12%.

Technology on campus. 450 workstations in library, computer center, student center. Commuter students can connect to campus network. Online course registration, wireless network available.

Student life. Freshman orientation: Mandatory. Preregistration for classes offered. **Activities:** Jazz band, choral groups, dance, drama, music ensembles, musical theater, student government, Phi Theta Kappa, Circle K.

Athletics. NJCAA. **Intercollegiate:** Baseball M, basketball, cheerleading, softball W. **Team name:** Buccaneers.

Student services. Career counseling, student employment services, financial aid counseling, personal counseling, veterans' counselor. **Physically disabled:** Services for visually, speech, hearing impaired. **Transfer:** College fairs on campus for students transferring to 4-year colleges.

Contact. E-mail: admissions@sheltonstate.edu
Phone: (205) 391-2214 Fax: (205) 391-3910
Amanda Harbison, Associate Dean of Enrollment Services, Shelton State Community College, 9500 Old Greensboro Road, Tuscaloosa, AL 35405-8522

Snead State Community College
Boaz, Alabama
www.snead.edu

CB code: 1721

- Public 2-year community college
- Commuter campus in small town

General. Founded in 1898. Regionally accredited. **Enrollment:** 2,179 degree-seeking undergraduates. **Degrees:** 457 associate awarded. **Location:** 65 miles from Birmingham. **Calendar:** Semester, extensive summer session. **Full-time faculty:** 34 total. **Part-time faculty:** 96 total. **Partnerships:** Formal partnership with Marshall County Tech Prep Consortium (grant writer and fiscal agent for eight secondary schools).

Student profile.

Out-of-state:	1%	**Live on campus:**	5%
25 or older:	29%		

Transfer out. Colleges most students transferred to 2015: Jacksonville State University, Auburn University, University of Alabama, University of Alabama at Birmingham, University of Alabama in Huntsville.

Basis for selection. Open admission. 16 ACT or equivalent SAT required for high school graduates from non-accredited schools and for those receiving occupational diplomas.

High school preparation. 24 units recommended. Recommended units include English 4, mathematics 4, social studies 4, science 4, foreign language 3, academic electives 2.5. 1 unit physical education, .5 unit health education, 1 unit career preparedness.

2015-2016 Annual costs. Tuition/fees: $4,380; $7,830 out-of-state. Per-credit charge: $115 in-state; $230 out-of-state. Room/board: $3,110. Books/supplies: $1,050. Personal expenses: $1,200.

Financial aid. Need-based: Need-based aid available for part-time students. Work-study available nights, weekends and for part-time students. **Non-need-based:** Scholarships awarded for academics, alumni affiliation, art, athletics, leadership, music/drama.

Application procedures. Admission: Closing date 8/14 (postmark date). No application fee. Application must be submitted online. Admission notification on a rolling basis. **Financial aid:** No deadline. FAFSA required. Applicants notified on a rolling basis starting 4/15.

Academics. Special study options: Accelerated study, distance learning, dual enrollment of high school students, independent study, internships, student-designed major. **Credit/placement by examination:** AP, CLEP, institutional tests. 20 credit hours maximum toward associate degree. **Support services:** GED preparation and test center, remedial instruction, study skills assistance, tutoring.

Majors. Business: Administrative services. **Computer sciences:** General. **Engineering:** General. **Health services:** Nursing (RN). **Liberal arts:** Arts/sciences. **Work/family studies:** Child care management.

Technology on campus. 350 workstations in library, computer center, student center. Dormitories wired for high-speed internet access. Online course registration, online library available.

Student life. Freshman orientation: Available. Preregistration for classes offered. Typically offered for 2 weeks during July. Day, evening, and Saturday sessions held. **Housing:** Coed dorms available. $200 deposit. **Activities:** Jazz band, campus ministries, choral groups, dance, drama, music ensembles, student government, Ambassadors, agricultural organization, Phi Beta Lambda, Phi Theta Kappa, College Republicans, Civitans.

Athletics. NJCAA. **Intercollegiate:** Baseball M, basketball, softball W, tennis W. **Intramural:** Basketball, softball, table tennis, volleyball. **Team name:** Parsons.

Student services. Career counseling, student employment services, financial aid counseling, veterans' counselor. **Physically disabled:** Services for visually, speech, hearing impaired. **Transfer:** Pre-admission transcript evaluation for new students. Transfer adviser, college fairs on campus for students transferring to 4-year colleges.

Contact. E-mail: studentservices@snead.edu
Phone: (256) 593-5120 ext. 207 Fax: (256) 593-7180
Lesley Kubik, Admissions and Records Director, Snead State Community College, PO Box 734, Boaz, AL 35957-0734

Southern Union State Community College
Wadley, Alabama
www.suscc.edu

CB code: 1728

- Public 2-year community and technical college
- Commuter campus in small city

General. Founded in 1963. Regionally accredited. Additional campuses in Opelika and Valley. **Enrollment:** 4,734 undergraduates. **Degrees:** 652 associate awarded. **ROTC:** Army. **Location:** 90 miles from Atlanta, 90 miles from Birmingham. **Calendar:** Semester, extensive summer session. **Full-time faculty:** 88 total. **Part-time faculty:** 189 total.

Student profile.

Out-of-state:	20%	Live on campus:	4%
25 or older:	25%		

Basis for selection. Open admission, but selective for some programs. Criteria for some health sciences programs include test scores. **Home schooled:** Transcript of courses and grades required.

2015-2016 Annual costs. Tuition/fees: $4,020; $7,470 out-of-state. Per-credit charge: $115 in-state; $230 out-of-state. Room/board: $3,200. Books/supplies: $400. Personal expenses: $1,100.

Financial aid. Need-based: Need-based aid available for part-time students. Work-study available nights, weekends and for part-time students. **Non-need-based:** Scholarships awarded for alumni affiliation, art, athletics.

Application procedures. Admission: No deadline. No application fee. Admission notification on a rolling basis. **Financial aid:** Priority date 4/1; no closing date. FAFSA required. Applicants notified on a rolling basis.

Academics. Special study options: Accelerated study, distance learning, dual enrollment of high school students. License preparation in nursing, paramedic, radiology. **Credit/placement by examination:** AP, CLEP, institutional tests. **Support services:** GED preparation and test center, pre-admission summer program, remedial instruction, study skills assistance, tutoring.

Majors. Business: General, administrative services. **Computer sciences:** General. **Health services:** EMT paramedic, health information technology, insurance coding, medical radiologic technology/radiation therapy, nursing (RN), radiologic technology/medical imaging. **Liberal arts:** Arts/sciences. **Work/family studies:** Child care management.

Most popular majors. Business/marketing 6%, health sciences 31%, liberal arts 50%.

Technology on campus. Commuter students can connect to campus network. Online library, wireless network available.

Student life. Freshman orientation: Available. Preregistration for classes offered. Held during June and July. **Housing:** Single-sex dorms, wellness housing available. $200 fully refundable deposit. **Activities:** Campus ministries, choral groups, dance, drama, musical theater, student government, student newspaper, association of radiologic students, global environmental organization of students, music club, letterman's club, National Student Nurses' Association, Phi Beta Lambda, Phi Theta Kappa, Southern Union Players.

Athletics. NJCAA. **Intercollegiate:** Baseball M, basketball, cheerleading, softball W, volleyball W. **Team name:** Bison.

Student services. Adult student services, career counseling, financial aid counseling.

Contact. E-mail: cstringfellow@suscc.edu
Phone: (256) 395-2211 Fax: (256) 395-2215
Catherine Stringfellow, Registrar, Southern Union State Community College, 750 Roberts Street, Wadley, AL 36276

Virginia College in Mobile
Mobile, Alabama
www.vc.edu

▶ For-profit 2-year technical and career college
▶ Commuter campus in large city

General. Accredited by ACICS. Mobile campus includes Culinard: The Culinary Institute of Virginia College, which offers 36-week programs in pastry and culinary arts. **Enrollment:** 575 undergraduates. **Degrees:** 78 associate awarded. **Calendar:** Differs by program. **Full-time faculty:** 23 total. **Part-time faculty:** 50 total.

Basis for selection. Open admission, but selective for some programs.

2015-2016 Annual costs. Certificate/diploma programs: $13,932-$23,220; Associate degree programs: $37,152-$49,059.

Financial aid. Need-based: Work-study available nights, weekends and for part-time students.

Application procedures. Admission: No deadline. Admission notification on a rolling basis.

Academics. Special study options: Accelerated study, independent study. **Credit/placement by examination:** AP, CLEP.

Majors. Business: Administrative services, business admin, executive assistant. **Health services:** Health care admin, insurance coding, licensed practical nurse, medical assistant, office assistant, surgical technology.

Contact. Phone: (251) 343-7227 Toll-free number: (888) 208-6932
Fax: (251) 343-7287
April Martin, Director of Admissions, Virginia College in Mobile, 3725 Airport Boulevard, Suite 165, Mobile, AL 36608

Virginia College in Montgomery
Montgomery, Alabama
www.vc.edu

▶ For-profit 2-year health science and career college
▶ Commuter campus in large city

General. Regionally accredited; also accredited by ACICS. **Enrollment:** 622 undergraduates. **Degrees:** 87 associate awarded. **Calendar:** Quarter. **Full-time faculty:** 17 total. **Part-time faculty:** 80 total.

Basis for selection. Selective admissions to certain programs.

2015-2016 Annual costs. Diploma programs $13,932-$23,220; Associate degree programs $37,152-$49,059.

Financial aid. Need-based: Work-study available nights, weekends and for part-time students.

Application procedures. Financial aid: Closing date 9/30.

Academics. Credit/placement by examination: AP, CLEP.

Majors. Business: Administrative services, business admin. **Health services:** Massage therapy, nursing (RN), office admin, surgical technology.

Contact. Phone: (334) 277-3390
Lawrence Brown, Director of Admissions, Virginia College in Montgomery, 6200 Atlanta Highway, Montgomery, AL 36117

Wallace State Community College at Hanceville
Hanceville, Alabama
www.wallacestate.edu   CB code: 0528

▶ Public 2-year health science and community college
▶ Commuter campus in small town

General. Founded in 1966. Regionally accredited. **Enrollment:** 4,822 degree-seeking undergraduates; 598 non-degree-seeking students. **Degrees:** 819 associate awarded. **Location:** 35 miles from Birmingham, 50 miles from Huntsville. **Calendar:** Semester, extensive summer session. **Full-time faculty:** 131 total; 66% women. **Part-time faculty:** 312 total; 69% women. **Special facilities:** Genealogy collection, recording studio, nature trail, college-operated museum, advanced visualization center (3-D).

Student profile. Among degree-seeking undergraduates, 1,113 enrolled as first-time, first-year students.

Part-time:	46%	Native American:	1%
Women:	63%	International:	1%
African American:	6%	25 or older:	26%
Asian American:	1%	Live on campus:	2%
Hispanic/Latino:	4%		

Transfer out. Colleges most students transferred to 2015: Athens State College, University of Alabama, University of Alabama in Huntsville, University of Alabama at Birmingham, Auburn University.

Basis for selection. Open admission, but selective for some programs. ACT required of applicants to certain allied health programs. National League for Nursing, Pre-Nursing and Guidance Examination required for nursing applicants. Interview recommended for health program applicants; auditions recommended for music education majors.

2015-2016 Annual costs. Tuition/fees: $4,320; $7,770 out-of-state. Per-credit charge: $115 in-state; $230 out-of-state. Room only: $1,800. Books/supplies: $1,400. Personal expenses: $900.

Financial aid. All financial aid based on need. Need-based aid available for part-time students. Work-study available nights, weekends and for part-time students.

Application procedures. Admission: No deadline. No application fee. Admission notification on a rolling basis. **Financial aid:** Priority date 5/1; no closing date. FAFSA required. Applicants notified on a rolling basis starting 7/15; must reply within 2 week(s) of notification.

Academics. Special study options: Accelerated study, cooperative education, distance learning, double major, dual enrollment of high school students, external degree, honors, internships, liberal arts/career combination. License preparation in aviation, dental hygiene, nursing, occupational therapy, paramedic, physical therapy, radiology, real estate. **Credit/placement by examination:** AP, CLEP, institutional tests. The PLA credit may not count toward the 25% of institution coursework necessary for graduation. **Support services:** GED preparation and test center, learning center, reduced course load, remedial instruction, study skills assistance, tutoring.

Majors. Business: General, administrative services, business admin, office management. **Computer sciences:** General. **Education:** General. **Engineering:** General, electrical. **Health services:** Clinical lab technology, dental assistant, dental hygiene, EMT paramedic, health information technology, medical assistant, nursing (RN), occupational therapy assistant, physical therapy assistant, radiologic technology/medical imaging, respiratory therapy technology, sonography, substance abuse counseling. **Liberal arts:** Arts/sciences. **Protective services:** Police science. **Visual/performing arts:** Design. **Work/family studies:** Child care management.

Most popular majors. Health sciences 50%, liberal arts 31%.

Technology on campus. 237 workstations in library, computer center. Commuter students can connect to campus network. Online course registration, online library, helpline, wireless network available.

Student life. Freshman orientation: Mandatory. Preregistration for classes offered. One hour session aids in the transition to the Institution; 2 hour session, required for all developmental students, develops knowledge and skills toward a successful college experience. **Housing:** Single-sex dorms, wellness housing available. $200 fully refundable deposit. **Activities:** Bands, choral groups, drama, music ensembles, student government, Baptist campus ministry.

Athletics. NJCAA. **Intercollegiate:** Baseball M, basketball, cheerleading, golf, softball W, volleyball W. **Intramural:** Basketball, football (tackle), softball. **Team name:** Lions.

Student services. Chaplain/spiritual director, career counseling, student employment services, financial aid counseling, placement for graduates, veterans' counselor. **Physically disabled:** Services for visually, speech, hearing impaired. **Transfer:** Transfer adviser, college fairs on campus for students transferring to 4-year colleges.

Contact. E-mail: admissions@wallacestate.edu
Phone: (256) 352-8238 Toll-free number: (866) 350-9722
Fax: (256) 352-8129
Jennifer Hill, Assistant Dean of Student Affairs, Wallace State Community College at Hanceville, 801 Main Street NW/PO Box 2000, Hanceville, AL 35077-2000

Alaska

Ilisagvik College
Barrow, Alaska
www.ilisagvik.edu

CB code: 0469

◗ Public 2-year community college
◗ Commuter campus in rural community

General. Tribal college. **Enrollment:** 77 degree-seeking undergraduates; 116 non-degree-seeking students. **Degrees:** 14 associate awarded. **Location:** 500 miles from Fairbanks. **Calendar:** Semester, limited summer session. **Full-time faculty:** 10 total; 50% have terminal degrees, 50% women. **Part-time faculty:** 17 total; 47% women.

Student profile. Among degree-seeking undergraduates, 8% enrolled in a transfer program, 30% enrolled in a vocational program, 37 enrolled as first-time, first-year students, 3 transferred in from other institutions.

Part-time:	62%	Native American:	62%
Women:	66%	International:	4%
African American:	4%		

Basis for selection. Open admission.

2015-2016 Annual costs. Tuition/fees: $3,340; $3,340 out-of-state. Per-credit charge: $125 in-state; $125 out-of-state. Room/board: $15,000. Books/supplies: $800. Personal expenses: $2,730.

2014-2015 Financial aid. All financial aid based on need. 88% of total undergraduate aid awarded as scholarships/grants, 12% as loans/jobs. Need-based aid available for part-time students. Work-study available nights, weekends and for part-time students.

Application procedures. Admission: No application fee. Application must be submitted on paper. Admission notification on a rolling basis. **Financial aid:** Closing date 4/15. FAFSA required. Applicants notified by 4/15.

Academics. Many Inupiat Eskimo traditional courses offered. **Special study options:** Double major, dual enrollment of high school students, ESL, independent study. **Credit/placement by examination:** AP, CLEP. 12 credit hours maximum toward associate degree. **Support services:** GED preparation and test center, remedial instruction, tutoring.

Majors. Area/ethnic studies: Native American. **Business:** Accounting technology, business admin, office management. **Education:** Native American. **General:** Building construction. **Protective services:** Firefighting.

Most popular majors. Business/marketing 14%, health sciences 43%, liberal arts 29%, trade and industry 14%.

Technology on campus. Dormitories linked to campus network. Commuter students can connect to campus network. Helpline, wireless network available.

Student life. Freshman orientation: Available. Preregistration for classes offered. **Housing:** Coed dorms, apartments available. **Activities:** Student government.

Student services. Career counseling, financial aid counseling, personal counseling. **Transfer:** Pre-admission transcript evaluation for new students.

Contact. E-mail: registration@ilisagvik.edu
Phone: (907) 852-1763 Toll-free number: (800) 478-7337 ext. 1763
Fax: (907) 852-1784
Dararath Charoonsophonsak, Registrar, Ilisagvik College, 100 Stevenson Road, Barrow, AK 99723

Arizona

Arizona Western College
Yuma, Arizona
www.azwestern.edu

CB member
CB code: 4013

- ◆ Public 2-year community college
- ◆ Commuter campus in small city

General. Founded in 1963. Regionally accredited. Satellite sites in Parker, San Luis-Somerton, Wellton. Campus shared with Northern Arizona University, which offers completion of bachelor's, master's and doctoral programs. **Enrollment:** 6,120 degree-seeking undergraduates; 1,394 non-degree-seeking students. **Degrees:** 885 associate awarded. **Location:** 7 miles from Yuma. **Calendar:** Semester, limited summer session. **Full-time faculty:** 126 total; 17% have terminal degrees, 20% minority, 49% women. **Part-time faculty:** 348 total; 5% have terminal degrees, 29% minority, 51% women. **Class size:** 53% < 20, 23% 20-39, 6% 40-49, 9% 50-99, 9% >100. **Partnerships:** Formal partnerships with Yuma Educational Consortium, Yuma Regional Medical Center.

Student profile. Among degree-seeking undergraduates, 61% enrolled in a transfer program, 41% enrolled in a vocational program, 1,640 enrolled as first-time, first-year students.

Part-time:	62%	Hispanic/Latino:	72%
Out-of-state:	3%	Native American:	1%
Women:	58%	Multi-racial, non-Hispanic:	1%
African American:	2%	International:	3%
Asian American:	1%	25 or older:	31%

Transfer out. Colleges most students transferred to 2015: Northern Arizona University at Yuma, Arizona State University, University of Arizona, University of Phoenix.

Basis for selection. Open admission, but selective for some programs. Special requirements for students under age 18, international students, undergraduate exchange program, Colorado River Consortium, nursing program, massage therapy program, radiologic technology program. **Home schooled:** Admissions decision dependent upon one or more of the following: placement test scores, academic history, current course enrollment, instructor approval. **Learning Disabled:** Proof of disability written by specialist must be submitted to Coordinator of Services for Students with Disabilities at least 8 weeks before start of classes to ensure accommodations by the first day of class.

High school preparation. College-preparatory program recommended.

2016-2017 Annual costs. Tuition/fees (projected): $2,655; $8,650 out-of-state. Per-credit charge: $80 in-state; $278 out-of-state. Room/board: $6,559. Books/supplies: $1,631. Personal expenses: $3,804.

2014-2015 Financial aid. Need-based: 92% of total undergraduate aid awarded as scholarships/grants, 8% as loans/jobs. Need-based aid available for part-time students. Work-study available nights, weekends and for part-time students. **Non-need-based:** Scholarships awarded for academics, art, athletics, leadership, minority status, music/drama.

Application procedures. Admission: No deadline. No application fee. Admission notification on a rolling basis. **Financial aid:** Priority date 4/1; no closing date. FAFSA, institutional form required. Applicants notified on a rolling basis starting 5/1.

Academics. Special study options: Accelerated study, cooperative education, distance learning, dual enrollment of high school students, ESL, honors, independent study, internships, study abroad, teacher certification program, weekend college. License preparation in nursing, occupational therapy, paramedic, physical therapy, radiology. **Credit/placement by examination:** AP, CLEP, IB, institutional tests. 24 credit hours maximum toward associate degree. **Support services:** GED preparation and test center, learning center, reduced course load, remedial instruction, study skills assistance, tutoring, writing center.

Majors. Architecture: Technology. **Area/ethnic studies:** Native American. **Biology:** General. **Business:** General, accounting, business admin, construction management, hospitality admin, logistics, office management. **Communications:** General. **Communications technology:** Radio/TV. **Computer sciences:** General, computer graphics. **Conservation:** Environmental science. **Education:** Early childhood, elementary, secondary. **Engineering:** General.

English: English lit. **Foreign languages:** Spanish. **General:** Carpentry, plumbing, site management. **Health services:** Community health, EMT paramedic, massage therapy, nursing (RN), prenursing, radiologic technology/medical imaging. **History:** General. **Math:** General. **Parks/recreation:** Facilities management, health/fitness. **Philosophy/religion:** Philosophy. **Physical sciences:** Chemistry, geology, physics. **Protective services:** Firefighting, homeland security, investigation and interviewing, law enforcement admin. **Social sciences:** General, political science, sociology. **Visual/performing arts:** Dramatic, music, studio arts. **Work/family studies:** General.

Most popular majors. Business/marketing 11%, health sciences 10%, liberal arts 39%, security/protective services 11%.

Technology on campus. 500 workstations in dormitories, library, computer center, student center. Dormitories wired for high-speed internet access and linked to campus network. Commuter students can connect to campus network. Online course registration, online library, helpline, repair service, student web hosting, wireless network available.

Student life. Freshman orientation: Available. Preregistration for classes offered. **Housing:** Coed dorms, single-sex dorms, special housing for disabled, wellness housing available. $100 fully refundable deposit. **Activities:** Bands, choral groups, dance, drama, international student organizations, literary magazine, music ensembles, musical theater, radio station, student government, student newspaper, TV station, AACHE, Phi Theta Kappa, Native American club, Hispanic students club.

Athletics. NJCAA. **Intercollegiate:** Baseball M, basketball, football (tackle) M, soccer, softball W, volleyball W. **Team name:** Matadors.

Student services. Adult student services, alcohol/substance abuse counseling, career counseling, services for economically disadvantaged, student employment services, financial aid counseling, health services, minority student services, on-campus daycare, personal counseling, placement for graduates, veterans' counselor, women's services. **Physically disabled:** Services for visually, speech, hearing impaired. **Transfer:** Pre-admission transcript evaluation for new students. Transfer center, transfer adviser, college fairs on campus for students transferring to 4-year colleges.

Contact. E-mail: nicole.harral@azwestern.edu
Phone: (928) 344-7550 Toll-free number: (888) 293-0392
Fax: (928) 344-7543
Nicole Harral, Director of Admissions/Registrar, Arizona Western College, PO Box 929, Yuma, AZ 85366-0929

Brookline College: Phoenix
Phoenix, Arizona
www.brooklinecollege.edu

CB code: 2188

- ◆ For-profit 2-year nursing and career college
- ◆ Commuter campus in very large city
- ◆ Interview required

General. Accredited by ACICS. Additional campuses in Tempe, Tucson, and Albuquerque. **Enrollment:** 1,429 undergraduates. **Degrees:** 103 bachelor's, 128 associate awarded; master's offered. **Calendar:** Differs by program, extensive summer session. **Full-time faculty:** 19 total. **Part-time faculty:** 17 total.

Basis for selection. Open admission. Must be 18 years of age or 17 years 6 months with parent or legal guardian consent. Must be citizen of the US or eligible non-citizen as classified by Department of Homeland Security. **Home schooled:** Letter of Attestation required.

2015-2016 Annual costs. Personal expenses: $5,880. **Additional information:** Diploma programs: $15,225-$20,000;Associate degree programs:$30,000-$31,800; Bachelor's degree programs:$15,500-$85,000. Fees vary by course and program. All fees are subject to change.

Financial aid. All financial aid based on need. Work-study available nights, weekends and for part-time students.

Application procedures. Admission: No deadline. No application fee. Admission notification on a rolling basis. **Financial aid:** No deadline. FAFSA, institutional form required.

Academics. Special study options: Accelerated study, distance learning. Bachelor's degree programs available on campus. License preparation in nursing. **Credit/placement by examination:** AP, CLEP, institutional tests. **Support services:** GED preparation and test center, learning center, tutoring.

Majors. Business: Accounting, business admin. **Health services:** Clinical lab technology, health care admin, health information technology. **Protective services:** Law enforcement admin.

Most popular majors. Business/marketing 16%, health sciences 63%, legal studies 21%.

Technology on campus. 240 workstations in library, computer center. Commuter students can connect to campus network. Online library available.

Student life. Freshman orientation: Mandatory. Preregistration for classes offered.

Student services. Career counseling, services for economically disadvantaged, financial aid counseling, placement for graduates. **Transfer:** Pre-admission transcript evaluation for new students.

Contact. E-mail: phnx-admissions@brooklinecollege.edu
Phone: (602) 242-6265 Toll-free number: (800) 793-2428
Fax: (602) 973-2572
Donna Green, Admissions Director, Brookline College: Phoenix, 2445 West Dunlap Avenue, Suite 100, Phoenix, AZ 85021-5820

Brookline College: Tempe
Tempe, Arizona
www.brooklinecollege.edu   CB code: 3455

- For-profit 2-year branch campus and career college
- Commuter campus in very large city
- Interview required

General. Accredited by ACICS. Additional campuses in Phoenix, Tucson, Oklahoma City, and Albuquerque. **Enrollment:** 418 undergraduates. **Degrees:** 10 associate awarded. **Calendar:** Differs by program, extensive summer session. **Full-time faculty:** 9 total. **Part-time faculty:** 2 total.

Basis for selection. Open admission, but selective for some programs. Must be 18 years of age or 17 years 6 months with parent or legal guardian consent. Must be US citizen or eligible non-citizen as classified by Department of Homeland Security. **Home schooled:** Letter of Attestation required.

2015-2016 Annual costs. Personal expenses: $5,880. **Additional information:** Diploma programs: $15,225-$28,500; Associate degree programs: $30,000. Fees vary by course and program. All fees are subject to change.

Financial aid. All financial aid based on need. Work-study available nights, weekends and for part-time students.

Application procedures. Admission: No deadline. No application fee. Admission notification on a rolling basis. **Financial aid:** No deadline. FAFSA, institutional form required.

Academics. Special study options: Accelerated study. **Credit/placement by examination:** AP, CLEP. **Support services:** GED preparation and test center, learning center, tutoring.

Majors. Business: Business admin. **Health services:** Clinical lab technology. **Protective services:** Law enforcement admin.

Most popular majors. Business/marketing 55%, health sciences 6%, legal studies 39%.

Technology on campus. 240 workstations in library. Commuter students can connect to campus network. Online library available.

Student life. Freshman orientation: Mandatory. Preregistration for classes offered.

Student services. Career counseling, services for economically disadvantaged, financial aid counseling, placement for graduates. **Transfer:** Pre-admission transcript evaluation for new students.

Contact. E-mail: ckindred@brooklinecollege.edu
Phone: (480) 545-8755 Toll-free number: (888) 886-2428
Fax: (480) 926-1371
Cheryl Kindred, Campus Director, Brookline College: Tempe, 1140-1150 South Priest Drive, Tempe, AZ 85281-5240

Brookline College: Tucson
Tucson, Arizona
www.brooklinecollege.edu   CB code: 3454

- For-profit 2-year branch campus and career college
- Commuter campus in very large city
- Interview required

General. Accredited by ACICS. Additional campuses in Phoenix, Tempe, Albuquerque, and Oklahoma City. **Enrollment:** 507 undergraduates. **Degrees:** 13 bachelor's, 47 associate awarded. **Calendar:** Differs by program, extensive summer session. **Full-time faculty:** 9 total. **Part-time faculty:** 6 total.

Basis for selection. Open admission. Must be 18 years of age or 17 years 6 months with parent or legal guardian consent. Must be US citizen or eligible non-citizen as classified by Department of Homeland Security. **Home schooled:** Letter of Attestation required.

2015-2016 Annual costs. Personal expenses: $5,880. **Additional information:** Diploma programs: $12,750-$15,225;Associate degree programs:$30,000; Bachelor's degree programs:Criminal Justice:$60,00. Fees vary by course and program. All fees are subject to change.

Financial aid. All financial aid based on need. Need-based aid available for part-time students. Work-study available nights, weekends and for part-time students.

Application procedures. Admission: No deadline. No application fee. Admission notification on a rolling basis. **Financial aid:** No deadline. FAFSA, institutional form required.

Academics. Special study options: Accelerated study. **Credit/placement by examination:** AP, CLEP, institutional tests. **Support services:** GED preparation and test center, learning center, tutoring.

Majors. Business: Business admin. **Health services:** Clinical lab technology. **Protective services:** Law enforcement admin.

Most popular majors. Business/marketing 34%, health sciences 6%, legal studies 60%.

Technology on campus. 240 workstations in library, computer center. Commuter students can connect to campus network. Online library available.

Student life. Freshman orientation: Mandatory. Preregistration for classes offered.

Student services. Career counseling, services for economically disadvantaged, financial aid counseling, placement for graduates. **Transfer:** Pre-admission transcript evaluation for new students.

Contact. E-mail: lpechota@brooklinecollege.edu
Phone: (520) 748-9799 Toll-free number: (888) 292-2428
Fax: (520) 748-9355
Leigh Pechota, Campus Director, Brookline College: Tucson, 5441 East 22nd Street, Suite 125, Tucson, AZ 85711-5444

Bryan University
Tempe, Arizona
www.bryanuniversity.edu

- For-profit 2-year virtual career college
- Commuter campus in very large city

General. Regionally accredited; also accredited by ACICS. **Enrollment:** 928 degree-seeking undergraduates. **Degrees:** 161 associate awarded; master's offered. **Location:** Downtown. **Calendar:** Continuous, limited summer session.

Basis for selection. Open admission, but selective for some programs. Admissions decisions are based on review of the application and supporting documents. **Home schooled:** State high school equivalency certificate required.

High school preparation. College-preparatory program required.

2015-2016 Annual costs. Associate programs: $27,425-$32,865. Bachelor's programs: $43,925.

Financial aid. Need-based: Work-study available nights, weekends and for part-time students.

Application procedures. Admission: No deadline. $50 fee. Admission notification on a rolling basis. **Financial aid:** No deadline.

Academics. Special study options: Accelerated study, distance learning, internships. **Credit/placement by examination:** AP, CLEP. **Support services:** Learning center, remedial instruction, study skills assistance, tutoring, writing center.

Technology on campus. PC or laptop required. Commuter students can connect to campus network. Online course registration, online library, helpline, repair service, wireless network available.

Student life. Freshman orientation: Mandatory. Preregistration for classes offered. **Activities:** Student newspaper.

Student services. Adult student services, alcohol/substance abuse counseling, career counseling, student employment services, financial aid counseling, health services, legal services, personal counseling, placement for graduates. **Transfer:** Re-entry adviser, pre-admission transcript evaluation for new students.

Contact. E-mail: info@bryanuniversity.edu
Phone: (888) 768-6861 Fax: (602) 759-8743
John Ledesma, Director of Admissions, Bryan University, 350 W Washington St #100, Tempe, AZ 85281

Carrington College: Mesa
Mesa, Arizona
www.carrington.edu

- For-profit 2-year career college
- Very large city

General. Regionally accredited; also accredited by ACICS. **Enrollment:** 718 degree-seeking undergraduates. **Degrees:** 73 associate awarded. **Calendar:** Differs by program. **Full-time faculty:** 23 total. **Part-time faculty:** 32 total.

Basis for selection. Open admission.

2015-2016 Annual costs. Tuition costs vary by program. Total program cost for the largest program (Medical Assisting-Cert.) is $14,944.

Financial aid. Need-based: Work-study available nights, weekends and for part-time students.

Application procedures. Admission: No deadline. No application fee. Admission notification on a rolling basis. **Financial aid:** No deadline.

Academics. Credit/placement by examination: AP, CLEP.

Majors. Health services: Dental hygiene, office admin, physical therapy assistant, respiratory therapy technology.

Contact. Phone: (888) 720-5014
Director of Enrollment Services, Carrington College: Mesa, 1001 Southern Avenue, Suite 130, Mesa, AZ 85210

Carrington College: Phoenix
Phoenix, Arizona
www.carrington.edu

- For-profit 2-year career college
- Very large city

General. Regionally accredited; also accredited by ACICS. **Enrollment:** 617 degree-seeking undergraduates. **Degrees:** 1 associate awarded. **Calendar:** Differs by program. **Full-time faculty:** 16 total. **Part-time faculty:** 14 total.

Basis for selection. Open admission.

2015-2016 Annual costs. Tuition costs vary by program. Total program cost for the largest program (Medical Assisting-Cert.) is $14,944.

Financial aid. Need-based: Work-study available nights, weekends and for part-time students.

Application procedures. Admission: No deadline. No application fee. Admission notification on a rolling basis. **Financial aid:** No deadline.

Academics. Special study options: Bachelor's degree programs available on campus. **Credit/placement by examination:** AP, CLEP.

Majors. Health services: Office admin.

Contact. Phone: (888) 720-5014
Director of Enrollment Services, Carrington College: Phoenix, 8503 North 27th Avenue, Phoenix, AZ 85051-4063

Carrington College: Phoenix Westside
Phoenix, Arizona
www.carrington.edu

- For-profit 2-year career college
- Very large city

General. Regionally accredited; also accredited by ACICS. **Enrollment:** 503 degree-seeking undergraduates. **Degrees:** 167 associate awarded. **Calendar:** Differs by program. **Full-time faculty:** 20 total. **Part-time faculty:** 27 total.

Basis for selection. Open admission.

2015-2016 Annual costs. Tuition costs vary by program. Total program cost for the largest program (Registered Nursing-Assoc.) is $52,594.

Financial aid. Need-based: Work-study available nights, weekends and for part-time students.

Application procedures. Admission: No deadline. No application fee. Admission notification on a rolling basis. **Financial aid:** No deadline.

Academics. Credit/placement by examination: AP, CLEP.

Majors. Health services: Clinical lab technology, medical radiologic technology/radiation therapy, nursing (RN), respiratory therapy technology.

Contact. Phone: (602) 433-1333 Toll-free number: (888) 720-5014
Carrington College: Phoenix Westside, 2701 West Bethany Home Road, Phoenix, AZ 85017-5885

Carrington College: Tucson
Tucson, Arizona
www.carrington.edu

- For-profit 2-year career college
- Very large city

General. Regionally accredited; also accredited by ACICS. **Enrollment:** 424 degree-seeking undergraduates. **Calendar:** Differs by program. **Full-time faculty:** 11 total. **Part-time faculty:** 13 total.

Basis for selection. Open admission.

2015-2016 Annual costs. Tuition costs vary by program. Total program cost for the largest program (Medical Assisting-Cert.) is $14,944.

Financial aid. Need-based: Work-study available nights, weekends and for part-time students.

Application procedures. Admission: No deadline. No application fee. Admission notification on a rolling basis. **Financial aid:** No deadline.

Academics. Credit/placement by examination: AP, CLEP.

Majors. Health services: Clinical lab technology, office admin.

Contact. Phone: (888) 720-5014
Carrington College: Tucson, 201 North Bonita Avenue, Tucson, AZ 85745

Central Arizona College
Coolidge, Arizona
www.centralaz.edu   CB code: 4122

- Public 2-year community college
- Commuter campus in small city

General. Founded in 1962. Regionally accredited. **Enrollment:** 5,462 degree-seeking undergraduates. **Degrees:** 569 associate awarded. **Location:** 45 miles from Phoenix, 60 miles from Tucson. **Calendar:** Semester, limited summer session. **Full-time faculty:** 90 total. **Part-time faculty:** 383 total. **Class size:** 56% < 20, 44% 20-39, less than 1% 40-49, less than 1% 50-99. **Special facilities:** Observatory, 2 recording studios, digital audio Mac labs, burn training facility, safety vehicle training track and firing range for law enforcement training, theater. **Partnerships:** Formal partnership with CAVIT.

Student profile.

Out-of-state: 4%   25 or older: 14%

Transfer out. Colleges most students transferred to 2015: Arizona State University, Northern Arizona University, University of Arizona.

Basis for selection. Open admission, but selective for some programs. Special requirement for nursing and radiology technology programs. **Learning Disabled:** Student must register disability and present appropriate documentation.

High school preparation. College-preparatory program recommended.

2015-2016 Annual costs. Tuition/fees: $2,460; $10,740 out-of-state. Per-credit charge: $82 in-state; $164 out-of-state. Room/board: $6,800. Books/supplies: $1,350. Personal expenses: $750.

Financial aid. Need-based: Need-based aid available for part-time students. Work-study available nights, weekends and for part-time students.

Application procedures. Admission: No deadline. No application fee. Admission notification on a rolling basis. **Financial aid:** Priority date 5/1, closing date 7/15. FAFSA required. Must reply within 3 week(s) of notification.

Academics. Special study options: Distance learning, dual enrollment of high school students, ESL, honors, independent study, internships, liberal arts/career combination, teacher certification program, weekend college. Bachelor's degree programs available on campus. License preparation in nursing, paramedic, radiology, real estate. **Credit/placement by examination:** AP, CLEP, institutional tests. 30 credit hours maximum toward associate degree. **Support services:** GED preparation and test center, learning center, pre-admission summer program, reduced course load, remedial instruction, study skills assistance, tutoring, writing center.

Majors. Biology: General. **Business:** General, accounting, accounting technology, administrative services, business admin, hospitality/recreation, hotel/motel/restaurant management, marketing, office technology. **Communications:** Journalism, sports. **Communications technology:** Desktop publishing. **Computer sciences:** General, applications programming, data processing, programming. **Education:** General, early childhood, elementary, special ed. **English:** English lit, writing. **Health services:** Clinical nutrition, dietetic technician, EMT paramedic, health care admin, health information management, massage therapy, medical assistant, medical secretary, medical transcription, nursing (RN), nursing assistant, pharmacy assistant, preveterinary, radiologic technology/medical imaging. **Human services:** General, social work. **Liberal arts:** Arts/sciences, humanities. **Math:** General. **Parks/recreation:** Exercise sciences. **Physical sciences:** Chemistry. **Protective services:** Corrections, criminal justice, fire safety technology, firefighting, police science. **Psychology:** General. **Social sciences:** General, criminology. **Visual/performing arts:** General, art, dramatic, music. **Work/family studies:** Child care service, child development, family studies.

Most popular majors. Health sciences 26%, liberal arts 52%.

Technology on campus. 500 workstations in dormitories, library, computer center, student center. Dormitories wired for high-speed internet access and linked to campus network. Commuter students can connect to campus network. Online course registration, online library, helpline, wireless network available.

Student life. Freshman orientation: Available. Preregistration for classes offered. **Policies:** Student code of conduct must be followed. **Housing:** Coed dorms, special housing for disabled, wellness housing available. $100 fully refundable deposit. **Activities:** Bands, choral groups, drama, international student organizations, music ensembles, student government, student newspaper, Phi Theta, Kappa/Lamba, art club, Playmasters, Campus Crusade For Christ, Native American club, rodeo club, Student Nurses Association of Arizona.

Athletics. NJCAA. **Intercollegiate:** Baseball M, basketball, cross-country, rodeo, softball W, track and field, volleyball W. **Team name:** Vaqueros.

Student services. Adult student services, career counseling, student employment services, financial aid counseling, on-campus daycare. **Physically disabled:** Services for visually, hearing impaired. **Transfer:** Re-entry adviser, pre-admission transcript evaluation for new students. Transfer center, transfer adviser, college fairs on campus for students transferring to 4-year colleges.

Contact. E-mail: Admissions@centralaz.edu
Phone: (520) 494-5260 Toll-free number: (800) 237-9814
Fax: (520) 494-5083
Luis Sanchez, Director of Admission and Records, Central Arizona College, Admissions Office, Coolidge, AZ 85128-9030

Chandler-Gilbert Community College
Chandler, Arizona
www.cgc.maricopa.edu   CB code: 0535

- Public 2-year community college
- Commuter campus in small city

General. Regionally accredited. Additional campuses in Sun Lakes, Queen Creek and Williams. **Enrollment:** 9,234 degree-seeking undergraduates; 5,420 non-degree-seeking students. **Degrees:** 1,171 associate awarded. **Location:** 20 miles from Phoenix. **Calendar:** Semester, limited summer session. **Full-time faculty:** 134 total. **Part-time faculty:** 499 total. **Class size:** 31% < 20, 63% 20-39, 3% 40-49, 2% 50-99, 1% >100.

Student profile. Among degree-seeking undergraduates, 4% already have a bachelor's degree or higher, 1,188 enrolled as first-time, first-year students.

Part-time:	61%	Hispanic/Latino:	24%
Out-of-state:	2%	Native American:	2%
Women:	51%	Multi-racial, non-Hispanic:	2%
African American:	5%	25 or older:	21%
Asian American:	5%		

Transfer out. Colleges most students transferred to 2015: Arizona State University, Northern Arizona University, University of Arizona.

Basis for selection. Open admission, but selective for some programs. Special requirements for nursing and aviation.

2015-2016 Annual costs. Tuition/fees: $2,550; $9,780 out-of-state. Per-credit charge: $84 in-state; $325 out-of-state. Books/supplies: $1,264. Personal expenses: $6,542.

Financial aid. Need-based: Work-study available nights, weekends and for part-time students.

Application procedures. Admission: No deadline. No application fee. **Financial aid:** No deadline.

Academics. Special study options: Distance learning, dual enrollment of high school students, ESL, honors, independent study, teacher certification program, weekend college. License preparation in aviation, nursing. **Credit/placement by examination:** AP, CLEP, IB, institutional tests. 30 credit hours maximum toward associate degree. **Support services:** Learning center, reduced course load, remedial instruction, study skills assistance, tutoring, writing center.

Majors. Business: General, accounting, nonprofit/public, office technology, retailing. **Computer sciences:** General, computer science, data entry, information technology, networking, system admin, vendor certification. **Education:** Elementary. **Health services:** Clinical nutrition, dietetic technician, massage therapy, nursing assistant. **Visual/performing arts:** Music management.

Technology on campus. 171 workstations in library, computer center. Commuter students can connect to campus network. Online course registration, online library, wireless network available.

Student life. Freshman orientation: Mandatory. Preregistration for classes offered. One-day sessions held at beginning of term. **Housing:** Student housing available on-campus only at Williams campus in cooperation with Arizona State University Polytechnic; students attending any campus can apply for housing at Williams campus. **Activities:** Bands, choral groups, dance, drama, music ensembles, musical theater, radio station, student government, political science organization, Christians in Action, Latter Day Saints student association, intercultural exchange club, Wall Street club, Phi Theta Kappa, black student union, Hispanic student organization.

Athletics. NJCAA. **Intercollegiate:** Baseball M, basketball, golf, soccer, softball W, volleyball W. **Team name:** Coyotes.

Student services. Adult student services, alcohol/substance abuse counseling, career counseling, services for economically disadvantaged, student employment services, financial aid counseling, personal counseling, placement for graduates, veterans' counselor. **Physically disabled:** Services for visually, speech, hearing impaired. **Transfer:** Pre-admission transcript evaluation for new students. Transfer center, transfer adviser, college fairs on campus for students transferring to 4-year colleges.

Contact. Phone: (480) 732-7320
Linda Shaw, Director of Admissions, Chandler-Gilbert Community College, 2626 East Pecos Road, Chandler, AZ 85225-2499

Two-Year Colleges

Cochise College
Douglas, Arizona
www.cochise.edu
CB member
CB code: 4097

- Public 2-year community college
- Commuter campus in large town

General. Founded in 1962. Regionally accredited. Courses offered at 2 campuses; 4 extended learning centers located in 2 counties, automotive complex, and online. **Enrollment:** 3,949 degree-seeking undergraduates; 560 non-degree-seeking students. **Degrees:** 691 associate awarded. **Location:** 120 miles from Tucson. **Calendar:** Semester, limited summer session. **Full-time faculty:** 86 total; 26% minority, 54% women. **Part-time faculty:** 239 total; 31% minority, 46% women. **Class size:** 87% < 20, 13% 20-39. **Special facilities:** Asian art collection, college airport. **Partnerships:** Formal partnerships with City of Sierra Vista, AEPCO, SSVEC, SW Gas, Sierra Vista Herald, Mantech, JITC, General Dynamics, STG, Fort Huachuca Public Affairs, Fort Huachuca Biometrics/Forensic Unit, Fort Huachuca Accommodation Schools, Fort Huachuca STEP Program, Desert Automotive, Sierra Vista Fire Department, Douglas Fire Department, Fry Fire Department, Child and Family Resources, NAMI, Cochise County Workforce Development, Cochise County Court System, City of Douglas, Bisbee Fire Department, Sierra Vista Chamber of Commerce, Cochise County, Bayada Nurse, Legacy Home Support, Visiting Angels, Copper Queen Hospital, Castle and Cooke, Data Systems Technology, Lockheed Martin, Cherokee Technologies Inc., Life Care Center, Hacienda-Kindred Health Care, Chiricahua Community Health Centers, Gila Health Resources, Tucson Medical Center, University of Arizona Medical Center, Sierra Vista Regional Hospital, Community Montessori School of Bisbee, Cochise County Juvenile Courts/Detention, DEA-Sierra Vista, Bisbee Public Schools, Sierra Vista Public Schools, Benson Public Schools, KE & G, SSVEC, Bisbee Hospitality Group, Sierra Vista Fire Department for Paramedic and EMT programs, Southeast Arizona Area Health Education Center, Hacienda and Cochise County Health department, Hospitals at Benson, Douglas, Nogales, Sierra Vista and Willcox, Arizona Health Facility Authority.

Student profile. Among degree-seeking undergraduates, 61% enrolled in a transfer program, 39% enrolled in a vocational program, 3% already have a bachelor's degree or higher, 798 enrolled as first-time, first-year students, 832 transferred in from other institutions.

Part-time:	57%	Native American:	1%
Out-of-state:	7%	Native Hawaiian/Pacific islander:	1%
Women:	52%	Multi-racial, non-Hispanic:	3%
African American:	6%	International:	1%
Asian American:	2%	25 or older:	13%
Hispanic/Latino:	48%	Live on campus:	2%

Transfer out. 39% of students enrolled in the transfer program go on to 4-year colleges. **Colleges most students transferred to 2015:** Pima Community College, University of Arizona, Rio Salado College, Mesa Community College, New Mexico Military Institute.

Basis for selection. Open admission, but selective for some programs. Nursing program requires additional application and satisfactory score on HESI Entrance Exam. Aviation students must be TSA approved and must have airman medical exam class 2 or 3 to start training. **Learning Disabled:** Students with learning disabilities need to provide documentation regarding their disability.

2016-2017 Annual costs. Tuition/fees (projected): $2,370; $7,500 out-of-state. Per-credit charge: $79 in-state; $250 out-of-state. Room/board: $6,564. Books/supplies: $1,800. Personal expenses: $1,550.

2014-2015 Financial aid. Need-based: 466 full-time freshmen applied for aid; 386 deemed to have need; 379 received aid. Average scholarship/grant was $3,873; average loan $3,303. 86% of total undergraduate aid awarded as scholarships/grants, 14% as loans/jobs. Need-based aid available for part-time students. Work-study available nights, weekends and for part-time students. **Non-need-based:** Awarded to 346 full-time undergraduates, including 162 freshmen.

Application procedures. Admission: No deadline. No application fee. Admission notification on a rolling basis. **Financial aid:** Priority date 5/1, closing date 6/15. FAFSA required. Applicants notified on a rolling basis starting 6/1.

Academics. Special study options: Distance learning, dual enrollment of high school students, ESL, honors, independent study, internships. License preparation in aviation, nursing, paramedic. **Credit/placement by examination:** AP, CLEP, IB, institutional tests. 30 credit hours maximum toward associate degree. **Support services:** GED preparation and test center, learning center, pre-admission summer program, reduced course load, remedial instruction, study skills assistance, tutoring, writing center.

Majors. Biology: General. **Business:** Administrative services, business admin, logistics. **Communications:** Communications/speech/rhetoric, digital media, journalism. **Computer sciences:** Computer science, information systems, networking, programming, security. **Education:** Adult/continuing, early childhood, elementary. **Engineering:** General, robotics. **English:** English lit. **General:** Building construction. **Health services:** EMT paramedic, nursing (RN), respiratory therapy technology. **Human services:** Social work. **Liberal arts:** Humanities. **Math:** General. **Military:** "intel, generally", air and space ops. **Parks/recreation:** Health/fitness. **Philosophy/religion:** Philosophy. **Physical sciences:** Chemistry, physics. **Protective services:** Firefighting, police science. **Psychology:** General. **Social sciences:** General, economics. **Visual/performing arts:** Art, dramatic, music.

Most popular majors. Liberal arts 13%, military 61%.

Technology on campus. 706 workstations in dormitories, library, computer center, student center. Dormitories wired for high-speed internet access and linked to campus network. Commuter students can connect to campus network. Online course registration, online library, helpline, repair service, wireless network available.

Student life. Freshman orientation: Available. Preregistration for classes offered. 30-minute program available on-line at all times. **Housing:** Coed dorms, special housing for disabled, apartments available. $150 partly refundable deposit. **Activities:** Dance, drama, literary magazine, music ensembles, student government, student newspaper, American Sign Language club, Catholic Collegians, COMMUNITIE club, Latter-day Saint Student Association, Literary Guild, Phi Theta Kappa International Honor Society, pre-pharmacy club, ROTARACT, Skills USA BCT, technology club.

Athletics. NJCAA. **Intercollegiate:** Baseball M, basketball, rodeo, soccer W. **Team name:** Apaches.

Student services. Career counseling, services for economically disadvantaged, student employment services, financial aid counseling, personal counseling, placement for graduates, veterans' counselor. **Physically disabled:** Services for visually, speech, hearing impaired. **Transfer:** Pre-admission transcript evaluation for new students. Transfer adviser, college fairs on campus for students transferring to 4-year colleges.

Contact. E-mail: admissions@cochise.edu
Phone: (520) 515-5336 Toll-free number: (800) 593-9567
Fax: (520) 515-5452
Martha Skinner, Division Assistant Student Services, Cochise College, 901 North Colombo Avenue, Sierra Vista, AZ 85635-2317

Coconino County Community College
Flagstaff, Arizona
www.coconino.edu
CB code: 1712

- Public 2-year community college
- Commuter campus in small city

General. Regionally accredited. **Enrollment:** 2,837 degree-seeking undergraduates. **Degrees:** 332 associate awarded. **ROTC:** Army, Air Force. **Location:** 140 miles from Phoenix. **Calendar:** Semester, limited summer session. **Full-time faculty:** 38 total. **Part-time faculty:** 163 total. **Special facilities:** Community garden, wind turbine, green building, telescope.

Student profile.

Out-of-state:	7%	25 or older:	42%

Transfer out. Colleges most students transferred to 2015: Northern Arizona University, Arizona State University, University of Arizona.

Basis for selection. Open admission, but selective for some programs. Special requirements for nursing program.

2015-2016 Annual costs. Tuition/fees: $2,910; $9,810 out-of-state. Per-credit charge: $92 in-state; $322 out-of-state. Books/supplies: $1,210. Personal expenses: $1,308.

Financial aid. Need-based: Work-study available nights, weekends and for part-time students.

Application procedures. Admission: No deadline. No application fee. Application must be submitted on paper. Admission notification on a rolling basis. **Financial aid:** Priority date 4/15, closing date 6/30.

Academics. Writing center, learning center and tutoring available. **Special study options:** Distance learning, dual enrollment of high school students, honors, internships. License preparation in nursing, paramedic, real estate. **Credit/placement by examination:** AP, CLEP. **Support services:** GED preparation and test center, learning center, remedial instruction, study skills assistance, tutoring, writing center.

Majors. Architecture: Technology. **Business:** General, accounting, business admin, construction management, finance, hospitality admin, marketing. **Computer sciences:** System admin. **Conservation:** Environmental science. **Education:** General, early childhood, elementary. **Engineering:** General. **General:** Carpentry. **Health services:** Medical secretary, nursing assistant. **Human services:** Social work. **Protective services:** Criminal justice, firefighting. **Psychology:** General. **Social sciences:** Anthropology, sociology. **Visual/performing arts:** Art.

Most popular majors. Education 6%, liberal arts 60%, security/protective services 8%.

Technology on campus. 100 workstations in library, computer center, student center. Online course registration, online library, helpline available.

Student life. Freshman orientation: Available. Preregistration for classes offered. **Activities:** Dance, literary magazine, music ensembles, symphony orchestra.

Athletics. Team name: Comets.

Student services. Adult student services, career counseling, financial aid counseling, on-campus daycare, veterans' counselor. **Physically disabled:** Services for visually, speech, hearing impaired. **Transfer:** Pre-admission transcript evaluation for new students. Transfer adviser, college fairs on campus for students transferring to 4-year colleges.

Contact. E-mail: admissions&registration@coconino.edu
Phone: (928) 527-1222 ext. 4299
Toll-free number: (800) 350-7122 ext. 4299 Fax: (928) 226-4110
Kimmi Grulke, Registrar/Director for Admissions, Coconino County Community College, 2800 South Lone Tree Road, Flagstaff, AZ 86001

Dine College
Tsaile, Arizona   **CB member**
www.dinecollege.edu   **CB code: 4550**

▶ Public 2-year community college
▶ Residential campus in rural community

General. Founded in 1968. Regionally accredited. Tribally controlled community college, chartered by the Navajo Nation. **Enrollment:** 1,369 degree-seeking undergraduates. **Degrees:** 5 bachelor's, 151 associate awarded. **Location:** 55 miles from Window Rock. **Calendar:** Semester, limited summer session. **Full-time faculty:** 63 total; 44% women. **Part-time faculty:** 33 total; 58% women. **Special facilities:** Learning center, museums.

Student profile.

Out-of-state:	17%	Live on campus:	20%
25 or older:	49%		

Transfer out. Colleges most students transferred to 2015: Northern Arizona University, Arizona State University, Fort Lewis College, University of Arizona, University of New Mexico.

Basis for selection. Open admission. **Home schooled:** Statement describing home school structure and mission, transcript of courses and grades, state high school equivalency certificate required. **Learning Disabled:** Must submit a doctor statement on learning disabilities.

2015-2016 Annual costs. Tuition/fees: $1,730; $1,730 out-of-state. Books/supplies: $1,400. Personal expenses: $2,500.

2014-2015 Financial aid. All financial aid based on need. 99% of total undergraduate aid awarded as scholarships/grants, 1% as loans/jobs. Need-based aid available for part-time students. Work-study available nights, weekends and for part-time students.

Application procedures. Admission: No deadline. $20 fee. Application must be submitted on paper. Admission notification on a rolling basis. **Financial aid:** Priority date 4/15, closing date 10/31. FAFSA, institutional form required. Applicants notified on a rolling basis starting 3/1; must reply within 4 week(s) of notification.

Academics. Special study options: Distance learning, double major, dual enrollment of high school students, independent study. Bachelor's degree programs available on campus. **Credit/placement by examination:** AP, CLEP, institutional tests. 12 credit hours maximum toward associate degree. **Support services:** Learning center, pre-admission summer program, remedial instruction, tutoring.

Majors. Area/ethnic studies: Native American. **Biology:** General. **Business:** Administrative services, business admin, office/clerical. **Computer sciences:** General, computer science. **Conservation:** Environmental science. **Education:** General, early childhood, elementary. **Engineering:** Pre-engineering. **Foreign languages:** Native American. **Health services:** Public health ed. **Liberal arts:** Arts/sciences. **Psychology:** General. **Social sciences:** General. **Visual/performing arts:** Studio arts.

Most popular majors. Biological/life sciences 23%, business/marketing 18%, education 16%, liberal arts 15%, social sciences 25%.

Technology on campus. 104 workstations in dormitories, library, computer center, student center. Dormitories wired for high-speed internet access and linked to campus network. Commuter students can connect to campus network. Online library, helpline, repair service, wireless network available.

Student life. Freshman orientation: Available. Preregistration for classes offered. Held the day before final registration. **Housing:** Coed dorms, single-sex dorms, wellness housing available. Family housing available. **Activities:** Radio station, student government, Red Dawn Indian club.

Athletics. NJCAA. **Intercollegiate:** Archery, cross-country, rodeo. **Intramural:** Archery, cross-country, rodeo. **Team name:** Warrior.

Student services. Alcohol/substance abuse counseling, career counseling, financial aid counseling, personal counseling, veterans' counselor. **Transfer:** Pre-admission transcript evaluation for new students. Transfer adviser, college fairs on campus for students transferring to 4-year colleges.

Contact. Phone: (928) 724-6631 Fax: (928) 724-3349
Louise Litzin, Registrar, Dine College, PO Box C 04, Tsaile, AZ 86556

Eastern Arizona College
Thatcher, Arizona
www.eac.edu   **CB code: 4297**

▶ Public 2-year community college
▶ Commuter campus in large town

General. Founded in 1888. Regionally accredited. Near archaeological sites. Several continuing education centers within 165 miles of campus. **Enrollment:** 4,524 degree-seeking undergraduates; 1,796 non-degree-seeking students. **Degrees:** 440 associate awarded. **Location:** 160 miles from Phoenix, 130 miles from Tucson. **Calendar:** Semester, limited summer session. **Full-time faculty:** 93 total; 14% have terminal degrees, 12% minority, 37% women. **Part-time faculty:** 253 total; 6% have terminal degrees, 17% minority, 64% women. **Class size:** 76% < 20, 19% 20-39, 2% 40-49, 2% 50-99, less than 1% >100. **Special facilities:** Observatory, golf course, wilderness area. **Partnerships:** Formal partnerships with local high schools allow high school students to obtain degrees in areas such as office technology and drafting.

Student profile. Among degree-seeking undergraduates, 2,263 enrolled as first-time, first-year students, 636 transferred in from other institutions.

Part-time:	61%	Hispanic/Latino:	21%
Out-of-state:	4%	Native American:	8%
Women:	55%	Multi-racial, non-Hispanic:	1%
African American:	4%	International:	2%
Asian American:	1%	Live on campus:	6%

Basis for selection. Open admission, but selective for some programs. Special requirements for nursing and several paramedical programs.

High school preparation. 15 units recommended. Recommended units include English 4, mathematics 4, social studies 1, history 1, science 3 (laboratory 3) and foreign language 2.

2015-2016 Annual costs. Tuition/fees: $2,080; $9,580 out-of-state. Per-credit charge: $100 in-state; $235 out-of-state. Room/board: $5,980. Books/supplies: $1,100. Personal expenses: $2,104.

2014-2015 Financial aid. Need-based: 665 full-time freshmen applied for aid; 562 deemed to have need; 314 received aid. Average need met was 27%. Average scholarship/grant was $6,560. 95% of total undergraduate aid awarded as scholarships/grants, 5% as loans/jobs. Need-based aid available for part-time students. Work-study available nights, weekends and for part-time students. **Non-need-based:** Awarded to 194 full-time undergraduates, including 74 freshmen. Scholarships awarded for academics, art, athletics, leadership, music/drama, state residency. **Additional information:** Limited number of tuition waivers for New Mexico residents. Unlimited number of waivers for those meeting WUE requirements.

Application procedures. Admission: No deadline. No application fee. Admission notification on a rolling basis. **Financial aid:** Priority date 3/1;

no closing date. FAFSA, institutional form required. Applicants notified on a rolling basis starting 3/15.

Academics. **Special study options:** Cooperative education, distance learning, double major, dual enrollment of high school students, independent study. Bachelor's degree programs available on campus. License preparation in nursing, paramedic. **Credit/placement by examination:** AP, CLEP, IB, institutional tests. 48 credit hours maximum toward associate degree. **Support services:** GED preparation and test center, learning center, reduced course load, remedial instruction, study skills assistance, tutoring, writing center.

Majors. **Biology:** General, environmental, wildlife. **Business:** Administrative services, business admin, entrepreneurial studies, office technology. **Computer sciences:** Information systems, system admin. **Conservation:** Forestry. **Education:** Art, business, elementary, secondary, technology/industrial arts. **English:** English lit. **Foreign languages:** General. **Health services:** EMT paramedic, nursing (RN), pharmacy assistant, premedicine, prepharmacy. **History:** General. **Liberal arts:** Arts/sciences. **Math:** General. **Parks/recreation:** Health/fitness. **Physical sciences:** Chemistry, geology, physics. **Protective services:** Law enforcement admin, police science. **Psychology:** General. **Social sciences:** Anthropology, political science, sociology. **Visual/performing arts:** Art, commercial/advertising art, dramatic, music, studio arts.

Most popular majors. Business/marketing 11%, health sciences 14%, interdisciplinary studies 11%, liberal arts 39%.

Technology on campus. 564 workstations in library, computer center. Dormitories wired for high-speed internet access and linked to campus network. Online course registration, online library, wireless network available.

Student life. **Freshman orientation:** Available. Preregistration for classes offered. Half-day session given the week prior to beginning of classes each semester and weekly during summer months. **Housing:** Single-sex dorms, wellness housing available. $150 fully refundable deposit. **Activities:** Bands, choral groups, dance, drama, literary magazine, music ensembles, musical theater, student government, symphony orchestra, Latter Day Saints student association, Newman club, drama club, Hispanic leaders, intertribal club, Phi Theta Kappa, Spanish club, Gila Force, Rowdy Reptiles.

Athletics. NJCAA. **Intercollegiate:** Baseball M, basketball, football (tackle) M, golf M, softball W, tennis W, volleyball W. **Intramural:** Basketball, soccer, swimming, tennis, volleyball. **Team name:** Gila Monsters.

Student services. Adult student services, alcohol/substance abuse counseling, career counseling, services for economically disadvantaged, student employment services, financial aid counseling, minority student services, personal counseling, placement for graduates, veterans' counselor, women's services. **Physically disabled:** Services for visually, speech, hearing impaired. **Transfer:** Re-entry adviser, pre-admission transcript evaluation for new students. Transfer adviser, college fairs on campus for students transferring to 4-year colleges.

Contact. E-mail: admissions@eac.edu
Phone: (928) 428-8272 Toll-free number: (800) 678-3808 ext. 8272
Fax: (928) 428-2578
Erik Lehmann, Admissions Counselor, Eastern Arizona College, 615 North Stadium Avenue, Thatcher, AZ 85552-0769

Estrella Mountain Community College
Avondale, Arizona
www.estrellamountain.edu   **CB code: 3810**

- Public 2-year community college
- Commuter campus in small city

General. Regionally accredited. **Enrollment:** 7,735 degree-seeking undergraduates; 1,429 non-degree-seeking students. **Degrees:** 895 associate awarded. **ROTC:** Air Force. **Location:** 15 miles from Phoenix. **Calendar:** Semester, limited summer session. **Full-time faculty:** 78 total. **Part-time faculty:** 438 total.

Student profile. Among degree-seeking undergraduates, 1,656 enrolled as first-time, first-year students.

Part-time:	63%	Women:	59%

Transfer out. **Colleges most students transferred to 2015:** Arizona State University.

Basis for selection. Open admission.

2015-2016 Annual costs. Tuition/fees: $2,550; $9,780 out-of-state. Books/supplies: $1,240. Personal expenses: $3,780.

Financial aid. **Need-based:** Need-based aid available for part-time students. Work-study available nights, weekends and for part-time students. **Non-need-based:** Scholarships awarded for leadership.

Application procedures. **Admission:** No deadline. No application fee. **Financial aid:** Priority date 4/1; no closing date. Applicants notified on a rolling basis starting 4/15.

Academics. **Special study options:** Accelerated study, distance learning, dual enrollment of high school students, ESL, honors, independent study, internships, teacher certification program, weekend college. License preparation in nursing, paramedic. **Credit/placement by examination:** AP, CLEP, IB. 30 credit hours maximum toward associate degree. **Support services:** GED test center, learning center, pre-admission summer program, reduced course load, remedial instruction, study skills assistance, tutoring, writing center.

Majors. **Business:** Accounting, banking/financial services, business admin, marketing, office technology, organizational behavior. **Computer sciences:** Networking, programming, security, support specialist, systems analysis, web page design. **Education:** Elementary, teacher assistance. **Health services:** EMT paramedic, nursing (RN), speech pathology. **Liberal arts:** Arts/sciences. **Physical sciences:** General. **Protective services:** Criminal justice. **Psychology:** General. **Visual/performing arts:** General, dramatic, studio arts.

Most popular majors. Business/marketing 15%, health sciences 8%, liberal arts 53%, physical sciences 11%.

Technology on campus. 198 workstations in library, computer center, student center. Commuter students can connect to campus network. Online course registration, online library, helpline, wireless network available.

Student life. **Freshman orientation:** Mandatory. Preregistration for classes offered. **Activities:** Student government.

Athletics. **Intercollegiate:** Cross-country, golf. **Team name:** Mountain Lions.

Student services. Adult student services, alcohol/substance abuse counseling, career counseling, financial aid counseling, personal counseling, veterans' counselor. **Physically disabled:** Services for visually, speech, hearing impaired. **Transfer:** Pre-admission transcript evaluation for new students. College fairs on campus for students transferring to 4-year colleges.

Contact. E-mail: frank.amparo@estrellamountain.edu
Phone: (623) 935-8888 Fax: (623) 935-8870
Frank Amparo, Director of Admission and Records, Estrella Mountain Community College, 3000 North Dysart Road, Avondale, AZ 85392

GateWay Community College
Phoenix, Arizona
www.gatewaycc.edu   **CB code: 0455**

- Public 2-year community and technical college
- Commuter campus in very large city

General. Founded in 1968. Regionally accredited. **Enrollment:** 5,653 degree-seeking undergraduates. **Degrees:** 520 associate awarded. **ROTC:** Army, Naval, Air Force. **Calendar:** Semester, limited summer session. **Full-time faculty:** 98 total. **Part-time faculty:** 321 total. **Partnerships:** Formal partnerships with Johnson Control, Toyota, Honda, Nissan, Banner Health.

Student profile.

Out-of-state:	5%	25 or older:	62%

Transfer out. **Colleges most students transferred to 2015:** Arizona State University, Northern Arizona University, University of Arizona Grand Canyon University.

Basis for selection. Open admission, but selective for some programs. Special requirements for nursing and some allied health programs. General Aptitude Test Battery required of health science applicants.

2015-2016 Annual costs. Tuition/fees: $2,550; $9,780 out-of-state. Books/supplies: $1,200. Personal expenses: $484.

Financial aid. **Need-based:** Need-based aid available for part-time students. Work-study available nights, weekends and for part-time students. **Non-need-based:** Scholarships awarded for athletics.

Application procedures. **Admission:** No deadline. No application fee. Admission notification on a rolling basis. **Financial aid:** Priority date 7/1, closing date 4/15. FAFSA, institutional form required. Applicants notified on a rolling basis; must reply within 4 week(s) of notification.

Academics. Special study options: Accelerated study, cooperative education, cross-registration, distance learning, double major, dual enrollment of high school students, ESL, external degree, honors, independent study, internships, liberal arts/career combination, study abroad. License preparation in nursing, physical therapy, radiology. **Credit/placement by examination:** AP, CLEP, IB, institutional tests. 30 credit hours maximum toward associate degree. **Support services:** Learning center, reduced course load, remedial instruction, study skills assistance, tutoring, writing center.

Majors. Business: General, accounting, administrative services, banking/financial services, international, office management. **Computer sciences:** General, information systems, LAN/WAN management, networking, system admin, systems analysis. **Engineering:** General. **General:** Carpentry, electrician, maintenance, masonry, pipefitting, power transmission. **Health services:** Clinical lab science, electroencephalograph technology, health care admin, medical radiologic technology/radiation therapy, medical transcription, nuclear medical technology, nursing (RN), physical therapy assistant, polysomnography, radiologic technology/medical imaging, respiratory therapy technology, sonography, surgical technology. **Liberal arts:** Arts/sciences. **Social sciences:** Sociology.

Most popular majors. Health sciences 67%, liberal arts 23%, trade and industry 6%.

Technology on campus. 100 workstations in library, computer center, student center. Commuter students can connect to campus network. Online course registration, online library, helpline, wireless network available.

Student life. Freshman orientation: Mandatory. Preregistration for classes offered. **Activities:** Film society, student government, student newspaper, MEHCA, Indian Tribal club, single parents association, women's club, health sciences club, business club.

Athletics. NJCAA. **Intercollegiate:** Cross-country, golf, soccer M, softball W, tennis. **Team name:** Geckos.

Student services. Adult student services, alcohol/substance abuse counseling, career counseling, services for economically disadvantaged, student employment services, financial aid counseling, minority student services, on-campus daycare, personal counseling, placement for graduates, veterans' counselor, women's services. **Physically disabled:** Services for visually, speech, hearing impaired. **Transfer:** Re-entry adviser, pre-admission transcript evaluation for new students. Transfer center, transfer adviser, college fairs on campus for students transferring to 4-year colleges.

Contact. E-mail: enroll@gatewaycc.edu
Phone: (602) 286-8200 Fax: (602) 286-8072
Kristie Fok, Director of Enrollment Services, GateWay Community College, 108 North 40th Street, Phoenix, AZ 85034

Glendale Community College
Glendale, Arizona
www.gccaz.edu   CB code: 4338

- Public 2-year community college
- Commuter campus in small city

General. Founded in 1965. Regionally accredited. **Location:** 17 miles from Phoenix. **Calendar:** Semester.

Annual costs/financial aid. Tuition/fees (2015-2016): $2,550; $9,780 out-of-state. Books/supplies: $1,200. Personal expenses: $3,852. Need-based financial aid available to full-time and part-time students.

Contact. Phone: (623) 845-3333
Dean, Enrollment Services, 6000 West Olive Avenue, Glendale, AZ 85302

Golf Academy of America: Phoenix
Chandler, Arizona
www.golfacademy.edu   CB code: 3460

- For-profit 2-year college of golf course management
- Small city

General. Accredited by ACICS. **Enrollment:** 154 undergraduates. **Degrees:** 104 associate awarded. **Calendar:** Semester. **Full-time faculty:** 4 total. **Part-time faculty:** 16 total.

Basis for selection. Golf Program requires playing ability experience.

2015-2016 Annual costs. Tuition/fees: $17,150. Books/supplies: $700. Personal expenses: $2,862. **Additional information:** International tuition: $17,840. Tuition includes activity fees.

Financial aid. Need-based: Work-study available nights, weekends and for part-time students.

Application procedures. Admission: $50 fee.

Academics. Credit/placement by examination: AP, CLEP.

Majors. Business: Business admin. **Parks/recreation:** Facilities management.

Student life. Freshman orientation: Mandatory. Preregistration for classes offered.

Contact. E-mail: phoenix.info@golfacademy.edu
Phone: (480) 857-1574 Toll-free number: (800) 342-7342
Fax: (480) 905-8705
Mark Shabaker, Director of Admissions, Golf Academy of America: Phoenix, 2031 North Arizona Avenue, Suite 2, Chandler, AZ 85225

Le Cordon Bleu College of Culinary Arts: Scottsdale
Scottsdale, Arizona
www.chefs.edu/Scottsdale   CB code: 3028

- For-profit 2-year culinary school and technical college
- Commuter campus in large city
- Application essay, interview required

General. Regionally accredited; also accredited by ACCSC. **Enrollment:** 1,190 degree-seeking undergraduates. **Degrees:** 127 bachelor's, 350 associate awarded. **Location:** 2 miles from downtown. **Calendar:** Differs by program. **Full-time faculty:** 17 total. **Part-time faculty:** 34 total.

Student profile.

Out-of-state:	55%	25 or older: 60%

Basis for selection. Open admission.

2015-2016 Annual costs. Personal expenses: $2,275. **Additional information:** Certificate programs: $19,500. Associate programs: $40,000. Books and supplies are included.

Financial aid. Need-based: Work-study available nights, weekends and for part-time students.

Application procedures. Admission: No deadline. $50 fee. Admission notification on a rolling basis. **Financial aid:** No deadline.

Academics. Special study options: Distance learning, internships. **Credit/placement by examination:** AP, CLEP. **Support services:** Learning center, remedial instruction, tutoring.

Student life. Freshman orientation: Mandatory. Preregistration for classes offered.

Student services. Alcohol/substance abuse counseling, career counseling, financial aid counseling, placement for graduates.

Contact. E-mail: sciadmissions@scichefs.com
Phone: (480) 990-3773 Toll-free number: (800) 848-2433
Fax: (480) 990-0351
Shannon Ferrer, Director of Admissions, Le Cordon Bleu College of Culinary Arts: Scottsdale, 8100 East Camelback Road, Suite 1001, Scottsdale, AZ 85251

Mesa Community College
Mesa, Arizona   CB member
www.mesacc.edu   CB code: 4513

- Public 2-year community college
- Commuter campus in very large city

General. Founded in 1965. Regionally accredited. **Enrollment:** 21,491 undergraduates. **Degrees:** 2,102 associate awarded. **ROTC:** Army, Naval,

Air Force. **Location:** 12 miles from Phoenix. **Calendar:** Semester, extensive summer session. **Full-time faculty:** 341 total. **Part-time faculty:** 812 total. **Class size:** 44% < 20, 52% 20-39, 3% 40-49, less than 1% 50-99, less than 1% >100.

Student profile.

Out-of-state: 2%   **25 or older:**   37%

Transfer out. Colleges most students transferred to 2015: Arizona State University, Northern Arizona University, University of Arizona.

Basis for selection. Open admission, but selective for some programs. General education requirements and 2.5 GPA required for nursing, mortuary science, and fire academy programs.

2015-2016 Annual costs. Tuition/fees: $2,535; $9,765 out-of-state. Per-credit charge: $84 in-state; $325 out-of-state. Books/supplies: $1,280. Personal expenses: $3,780.

Financial aid. Need-based: Need-based aid available for part-time students. Work-study available nights, weekends and for part-time students. **Non-need-based:** Scholarships awarded for academics, athletics. **Additional information:** Awards available for Maricopa County residents.

Application procedures. Admission: No deadline. No application fee. Admission notification on a rolling basis. **Financial aid:** Priority date 5/1; no closing date. FAFSA, institutional form required. Applicants notified on a rolling basis starting 7/1.

Academics. Associate of General Studies degree allows students to take half of credits in required courses, and dictate own program of electives. **Special study options:** Cooperative education, cross-registration, distance learning, dual enrollment of high school students, ESL, exchange student, honors, independent study, internships, liberal arts/career combination, student-designed major, study abroad, teacher certification program, weekend college. License preparation in dental hygiene, nursing, real estate. **Credit/placement by examination:** AP, CLEP, IB, institutional tests. 30 credit hours maximum toward associate degree. **Support services:** GED preparation and test center, learning center, remedial instruction, study skills assistance, tutoring, writing center.

Honors college/program. 3.5 GPA required.

Majors. Biology: Biotechnology. **Business:** General, fashion, marketing, organizational behavior, real estate. **Communications:** Journalism, public relations. **Communications technology:** Recording arts. **Computer sciences:** General, networking, systems analysis, web page design. **Engineering:** Manufacturing. **Health services:** Dental hygiene, EMT paramedic, nursing (RN), veterinary technology/assistant. **Liberal arts:** Library assistant. **Parks/recreation:** General, exercise sciences. **Physical sciences:** General. **Protective services:** Criminal justice, police science. **Social sciences:** Geography. **Visual/performing arts:** Design, interior design, music management. **Work/family studies:** Child development, institutional food production.

Most popular majors. Business/marketing 8%, health sciences 12%, liberal arts 55%, physical sciences 8%.

Technology on campus. 1,000 workstations in library, computer center, student center. Commuter students can connect to campus network. Online course registration, online library, helpline, repair service, student web hosting, wireless network available.

Student life. Freshman orientation: Available. Preregistration for classes offered. Students may attend orientation at either campus location. **Activities:** Jazz band, choral groups, dance, drama, international student organizations, music ensembles, Model UN, musical theater, opera, student government, student newspaper.

Athletics. NJCAA. **Intercollegiate:** Baseball M, basketball, cheerleading, cross-country, football (tackle) M, golf, soccer, softball W, tennis, track and field, volleyball W, wrestling M. **Team name:** Thunderbirds.

Student services. Adult student services, alcohol/substance abuse counseling, career counseling, services for economically disadvantaged, student employment services, financial aid counseling, legal services, minority student services, on-campus daycare, personal counseling, placement for graduates, veterans' counselor. **Physically disabled:** Services for visually, speech, hearing impaired. **Transfer:** Re-entry adviser, pre-admission transcript evaluation for new students. Transfer adviser, college fairs on campus for students transferring to 4-year colleges.

Contact. E-mail: admissions@mesacc.edu
Phone: (480) 461-7000 Fax: (480) 461-7805
Gerri Silva, Coordinator of Student Services, Mesa Community College, 1833 West Southern Avenue, Mesa, AZ 85202

Two-Year Colleges

Mohave Community College
Kingman, Arizona
www.mohave.edu   **CB code: 0443**

- Public 2-year community college
- Commuter campus in small city

General. Founded in 1971. Regionally accredited. **Enrollment:** 3,199 degree-seeking undergraduates. **Degrees:** 396 associate awarded. **Location:** 200 miles from Phoenix, 100 miles from Las Vegas. **Calendar:** Semester, limited summer session.

Transfer out. Colleges most students transferred to 2015: Northern Arizona University, University of Arizona, Arizona State University.

Basis for selection. Open admission, but selective for some programs. Special requirements for nursing, dental hygiene and EMT/paramedic programs.

2015-2016 Annual costs. Tuition/fees: $2,640; $8,715 out-of-state. Per-credit charge: $81 in-state; $284 out-of-state. Books/supplies: $1,000.

Financial aid. All financial aid based on need. Need-based aid available for part-time students. Work-study available nights, weekends and for part-time students.

Application procedures. Admission: No deadline. No application fee. **Financial aid:** Priority date 4/15, closing date 7/15. FAFSA, institutional form required. Applicants notified on a rolling basis starting 5/1; must reply within 2 week(s) of notification.

Academics. Special study options: Distance learning, dual enrollment of high school students, ESL, independent study, internships, liberal arts/career combination, student-designed major. License preparation in dental hygiene, nursing, paramedic, physical therapy. **Credit/placement by examination:** AP, CLEP, IB, institutional tests. 20 credit hours maximum toward associate degree. **Support services:** GED preparation, learning center, reduced course load, remedial instruction, study skills assistance, tutoring.

Majors. Business: Accounting, administrative services, business admin, finance. **Computer sciences:** General. **Education:** General. **English:** English lit. **Health services:** Dental hygiene, nursing (RN), pharmacy assistant, physical therapy assistant, surgical technology. **Liberal arts:** Arts/sciences. **Protective services:** Firefighting, police science.

Technology on campus. 300 workstations in library, computer center. Commuter students can connect to campus network. Online course registration, online library, helpline, wireless network available.

Student life. Freshman orientation: Mandatory. Preregistration for classes offered. **Activities:** Student government.

Student services. Adult student services, career counseling, student employment services, financial aid counseling, veterans' counselor. **Physically disabled:** Services for visually, speech, hearing impaired.

Contact. E-mail: bzoll@mohave.edu
Phone: (928) 757-0847 Toll-free number: (866) 664-2832
Fax: (928) 757-0808
Brian Zoll, Registrar, Mohave Community College, 1971 Jagerson Avenue, Kingman, AZ 86409

Northland Pioneer College
Holbrook, Arizona
www.npc.edu   **CB code: 0325**

- Public 2-year community and technical college
- Commuter campus in small town

General. Founded in 1973. Regionally accredited. 10 locations in Navajo and Apache Counties. **Enrollment:** 3,233 undergraduates. **Degrees:** 194 associate awarded. **Location:** 200 miles from Phoenix, 90 miles from Flagstaff. **Calendar:** Semester, limited summer session. **Full-time faculty:** 76 total. **Part-time faculty:** 134 total.

Student profile.

Out-of-state: 1%   **25 or older:**   69%

Transfer out. Colleges most students transferred to 2015: Northern Arizona University, University of Arizona, Arizona State University, Western New Mexico University, Brigham Young University.

Basis for selection. Open admission, but selective for some programs. Students under 18 must have satisfactory placement test score. Special requirements for nursing and cosmetology.

2015-2016 Annual costs. Tuition/fees: $2,110; $10,270 out-of-state. Per-credit charge: $68 in-state; $325 out-of-state. Books/supplies: $1,400. Personal expenses: $3,292.

Financial aid. Need-based: Need-based aid available for part-time students. Work-study available nights, weekends and for part-time students. **Non-need-based:** Scholarships awarded for academics, art, job skills, leadership, minority status, music/drama, state residency.

Application procedures. Admission: No deadline. No application fee. Admission notification on a rolling basis. **Financial aid:** Priority date 6/1; no closing date. FAFSA, institutional form required. Applicants notified on a rolling basis starting 5/15; must reply within 2 week(s) of notification.

Academics. Special study options: Cooperative education, distance learning, dual enrollment of high school students, honors, independent study, internships, liberal arts/career combination. License preparation in nursing, paramedic, real estate. **Credit/placement by examination:** AP, CLEP, IB, institutional tests. 52 credit hours maximum toward associate degree. **Support services:** GED preparation and test center, learning center, remedial instruction, study skills assistance, tutoring, writing center.

Majors. Business: General, accounting, administrative services, business admin. **Communications technology:** General. **Computer sciences:** General, computer graphics, data processing, networking. **Education:** General, early childhood, elementary. **General:** Carpentry, electrician, plumbing. **Health services:** EMT paramedic, medical assistant, medical transcription, nursing (RN). **Liberal arts:** Arts/sciences, library assistant. **Parks/recreation:** General. **Protective services:** Criminal justice, firefighting. **Work/family studies:** Child care management.

Most popular majors. Business/marketing 13%, education 9%, health sciences 22%.

Technology on campus. 140 workstations in library, computer center. Commuter students can connect to campus network. Online course registration, online library, helpline, wireless network available.

Student life. Freshman orientation: Available. Preregistration for classes offered. **Activities:** Jazz band, choral groups, dance, drama, literary magazine, music ensembles, musical theater, student government, symphony orchestra, National Honor Society, Phi Theta Kappa.

Student services. Adult student services, career counseling, services for economically disadvantaged, student employment services, financial aid counseling, placement for graduates, veterans' counselor. **Physically disabled:** Services for visually, hearing impaired. **Transfer:** Pre-admission transcript evaluation for new students. Transfer adviser, college fairs on campus for students transferring to 4-year colleges.

Contact. E-mail: admissions@npc.edu
Phone: (928) 536-6257 Toll-free number: (800) 266-7845
Fax: (928) 524-7612
Jake Hinton-Rivera, Director of Enrollment Services, Northland Pioneer College, PO Box 610, Holbrook, AZ 86025-0610

Paradise Valley Community College

Phoenix, Arizona — CB member
www.pvc.maricopa.edu — CB code: 2179

- Public 2-year community college
- Commuter campus in very large city

General. Founded in 1985. Regionally accredited. **Enrollment:** 2,867 full-time, degree-seeking students. **Degrees:** 774 associate awarded. **ROTC:** Army. **Calendar:** Semester, limited summer session. **Full-time faculty:** 113 total. **Part-time faculty:** 444 total. **Special facilities:** Studio theater, performing arts center.

Student profile.

Out-of-state:	3%	**25 or older:** 50%

Transfer out. Colleges most students transferred to 2015: Arizona State University, Arizona State University West, Northern Arizona University, University of Arizona.

Basis for selection. Open admission.

2015-2016 Annual costs. Tuition/fees: $2,550; $9,780 out-of-state. Books/supplies: $1,264. Personal expenses: $2,805.

Financial aid. Need-based: Need-based aid available for part-time students. Work-study available nights, weekends and for part-time students.

Application procedures. Admission: No deadline. No application fee. Admission notification on a rolling basis. **Financial aid:** No deadline. FAFSA required. Applicants notified on a rolling basis starting 6/1.

Academics. Special study options: Accelerated study, cooperative education, cross-registration, distance learning, dual enrollment of high school students, ESL, honors, independent study, internships, teacher certification program, weekend college. License preparation in nursing, paramedic. **Credit/placement by examination:** AP, CLEP, institutional tests. 30 credit hours maximum toward associate degree. **Support services:** Learning center, remedial instruction, study skills assistance, tutoring, writing center.

Majors. Business: General, accounting, accounting technology, administrative services, business admin, customer service support, international, marketing, office technology, office/clerical, organizational behavior. **Communications technology:** Recording arts. **Computer sciences:** General, networking, word processing. **Education:** Early childhood, educational technology, elementary. **Health services:** Dietetic technician, EMT paramedic, nursing (RN). **Liberal arts:** Arts/sciences. **Physical sciences:** General. **Protective services:** Criminal justice, firefighting. **Visual/performing arts:** General, dramatic, music management.

Technology on campus. 600 workstations in library, computer center, student center. Commuter students can connect to campus network. Online course registration, helpline, wireless network available.

Student life. Freshman orientation: Mandatory. Preregistration for classes offered. **Activities:** Jazz band, choral groups, dance, drama, international student organizations, literary magazine, music ensembles, musical theater, opera, student government, student newspaper, Phi Theta Kappa, student Christian association, human service club, Returning Adults to Education, environmental club, Latter Day Saints student association, recreational outdoor club.

Athletics. NJCAA. **Intercollegiate:** Baseball M, cross-country, golf, soccer, softball W, tennis, track and field. **Team name:** Pumas.

Student services. Adult student services, alcohol/substance abuse counseling, career counseling, student employment services, financial aid counseling, minority student services, on-campus daycare, personal counseling, placement for graduates, veterans' counselor, women's services. **Physically disabled:** Services for visually, speech, hearing impaired. **Transfer:** Transfer adviser, college fairs on campus for students transferring to 4-year colleges.

Contact. Phone: (602) 787-7020 Fax: (602) 787-6625
Shirley Green, Associate Dean Student Services, Paradise Valley Community College, 18401 North 32nd Street, Phoenix, AZ 85032

Paralegal Institute

Scottsdale, Arizona
www.theparalegalinstitute.edu — CB code: 3888

- For-profit 2-year virtual career college
- Very large city

General. Accredited by DETC. **Calendar:** Differs by program.

Annual costs/financial aid. Associate degree programs: $3,900- $5,700. Books, supplies, fees range depending on program level and course of study. All costs are subject to change.

Contact. Phone: (602) 212-0501
Director of Admissions, 7332 East Butherus Drive, Suite 102, Scottsdale, AZ 85260

Penn Foster College

Scottsdale, Arizona
www.pennfostercollege.edu

- For-profit 2-year virtual college
- Commuter campus in small city

General. Founded in 1975. Accredited by DETC. All courses offered via distance learning. **Enrollment:** 21,888 undergraduates. **Calendar:** Differs by program. **Full-time faculty:** 43 total. **Part-time faculty:** 111 total.

Basis for selection. Open admission. **Home schooled:** High School graduation (school and date) required to be verified by sworn attestation. **Learning**

Disabled: Evidence of disability recommended so that accommodations can be made.

Financial aid. Need-based: Work-study available nights, weekends and for part-time students.

Application procedures. Admission: No deadline. No application fee. Admission notification on a rolling basis.

Academics. Students allowed 12 months to complete semester (15-20 credit hours). **Special study options:** Distance learning, external degree, independent study. Bachelor's degree programs available on campus. **Credit/ placement by examination:** AP, CLEP. 9 credit hours maximum toward associate degree, 9 toward bachelor's. **Support services:** Remedial instruction, tutoring.

Majors. Business: General, accounting, finance, hospitality admin, marketing, retail management. **Computer sciences:** General. **Education:** Early childhood. **Health services:** Health information technology. **Protective services:** Firefighting, police science.

Most popular majors. Health sciences 85%.

Technology on campus. PC or laptop required. Online library available.

Student life. Freshman orientation: Mandatory. Preregistration for classes offered. **Policies:** Active student online Community for social and academic sharing.

Student services. Veterans' counselor. **Transfer:** Pre-admission transcript evaluation for new students.

Contact. E-mail: info@pennfoster.edu
Phone: (800) 800-3232 Toll-free number: (800) 275-4410
Grace Sakovich, Admissions Director, Penn Foster College, 14300 North Northsight Boulevard, Suite 120, Scottsdale, AZ 85260

Phoenix College
Phoenix, Arizona
www.phoenixcollege.edu   **CB code: 4606**

- Public 2-year community college
- Commuter campus in very large city

General. Founded in 1920. Regionally accredited. **Enrollment:** 9,921 degree-seeking undergraduates; 2,186 non-degree-seeking students. **Degrees:** 1,057 associate awarded. **ROTC:** Army, Air Force. **Calendar:** Semester, limited summer session. **Full-time faculty:** 136 total; 59% women. **Part-time faculty:** 619 total; 58% women. **Class size:** 62% < 20, 37% 20-39, less than 1% 40-49, less than 1% 50-99.

Student profile. Among degree-seeking undergraduates, 32% enrolled in a transfer program, 34% enrolled in a vocational program, 7% already have a bachelor's degree or higher, 1,504 enrolled as first-time, first-year students, 1,407 transferred in from other institutions.

Part-time:	69%	25 or older:	45%
Women:	63%		

Basis for selection. Open admission, but selective for some programs. ASSET, COMPASS, Accuplacer and CELSA test scores used for placement.

2016-2017 Annual costs. Tuition/fees (projected): $2,550; $9,780 out-of-state. Books/supplies: $1,264. Personal expenses: $5,724.

2015-2016 Financial aid. Need-based: 65% of total undergraduate aid awarded as scholarships/grants, 35% as loans/jobs. Work-study available nights, weekends and for part-time students.

Application procedures. Admission: No deadline. No application fee. Admission notification on a rolling basis. **Financial aid:** Priority date 6/30; no closing date. FAFSA required. Applicants notified on a rolling basis.

Academics. Special study options: Cooperative education, cross-registration, distance learning, dual enrollment of high school students, ESL, honors, independent study, internships, liberal arts/career combination, study abroad. License preparation in nursing. **Credit/placement by examination:** AP, CLEP, IB, institutional tests. 30 credit hours maximum toward associate degree. **Support services:** GED test center, learning center, reduced course load, remedial instruction, study skills assistance, tutoring, writing center.

Honors college/program. Requires 3.0 GPA.

Majors. Architecture: Architecture. **Business:** General, accounting, administrative services, banking/financial services, business admin, construction

management, fashion, marketing. **Communications technology:** Recording arts. **Computer sciences:** General, computer graphics, systems analysis, web page design. **Education:** General, elementary. **Foreign languages:** Sign language interpretation. **General:** Building inspection. **Health services:** Clinical lab technology, dental assistant, dental hygiene, EMT paramedic, health information technology, histologic technology, massage therapy, medical assistant, medical transcription, nursing (RN), office admin, premedicine. **Liberal arts:** Arts/sciences. **Physical sciences:** General. **Protective services:** Criminal justice, firefighting, forensics. **Visual/performing arts:** General, art, commercial photography, commercial/advertising art, dramatic, fashion design, graphic design, interior design, music management, studio arts. **Work/family studies:** General, child care management, family/community services, institutional food production.

Technology on campus. 243 workstations in library, computer center, student center. Online course registration, online library, helpline, wireless network available.

Student life. Freshman orientation: Available. Preregistration for classes offered. **Activities:** Bands, choral groups, dance, drama, international student organizations, music ensembles, Model UN, musical theater, opera, student government, symphony orchestra, TV station.

Athletics. NJCAA. **Intercollegiate:** Baseball M, basketball, football (tackle) M, soccer, softball W, volleyball W. **Team name:** PC Bears.

Student services. Adult student services, career counseling, services for economically disadvantaged, student employment services, financial aid counseling, minority student services, on-campus daycare, personal counseling, placement for graduates, veterans' counselor. **Physically disabled:** Services for visually, speech, hearing impaired. **Transfer:** Re-entry adviser, pre-admission transcript evaluation for new students. Transfer adviser, college fairs on campus for students transferring to 4-year colleges.

Contact. E-mail: info@pcmail.maricopa.edu
Phone: (602) 285-7502 Fax: (602) 285-7813
Brenda Starck, Dean, Phoenix College, 1202 West Thomas Road, Phoenix, AZ 85013

Pima Community College
Tucson, Arizona   **CB member**
www.pima.edu   **CB code: 4623**

- Public 2-year community and technical college
- Commuter campus in very large city

General. Founded in 1966. Regionally accredited. 6 campuses, distance education/online courses available. **Enrollment:** 33,082 undergraduates. **Degrees:** 2,848 associate awarded. **ROTC:** Army, Naval, Air Force. **Location:** 116 miles from Phoenix. **Calendar:** Semester, extensive summer session. **Full-time faculty:** 373 total. **Part-time faculty:** 993 total. **Special facilities:** Performing arts center, arts center, public safety institute.

Transfer out. Colleges most students transferred to 2015: University of Arizona, Arizona State University, Northern Arizona University, University of Phoenix, Eastern New Mexico University.

Basis for selection. Open admission, but selective for some programs. Special requirements for programs in the health related professions, such as nursing.

2015-2016 Annual costs. Tuition/fees: $2,450; $10,745 out-of-state. Per-credit charge: $76 in-state; $352 out-of-state. Books/supplies: $1,600. Personal expenses: $1,300.

Financial aid. Need-based: Need-based aid available for part-time students. Work-study available nights, weekends and for part-time students. **Non-need-based:** Scholarships awarded for academics, alumni affiliation, art, athletics, minority status, music/drama.

Application procedures. Admission: No deadline. No application fee. Admission notification on a rolling basis. **Financial aid:** Priority date 4/4; no closing date. FAFSA required. Applicants notified on a rolling basis starting 5/1; must reply within 2 week(s) of notification.

Academics. Upward Bound and Talent Search programs available. **Special study options:** Accelerated study, distance learning, dual enrollment of high school students, ESL, honors, independent study, internships, student-designed major, teacher certification program, weekend college. Bachelor's degree programs available on campus. License preparation in aviation, nursing, radiology, real estate. **Credit/placement by examination:** AP, CLEP, IB, institutional tests. 45 credit hours maximum toward associate degree.

Support services: GED preparation and test center, learning center, pre-admission summer program, reduced course load, remedial instruction, study skills assistance, tutoring, writing center.

Majors. Area/ethnic studies: Native American. **Business:** General, accounting, administrative services, fashion, hospitality admin, logistics. **Communications:** Digital media. **Computer sciences:** General, networking, systems analysis. **Education:** General, early childhood. **Foreign languages:** Sign language interpretation, translation. **General:** Maintenance. **Health services:** Clinical lab assistant, clinical lab technology, dental hygiene, dental lab technology, EMT paramedic, health information technology, histologic assistant, massage therapy, nursing (RN), pharmacy assistant, radiologic technology/medical imaging, respiratory therapy technology, veterinary technology/assistant. **Liberal arts:** Arts/sciences. **Protective services:** Criminal justice, firefighting, police science. **Social sciences:** Anthropology, political science, sociology. **Visual/performing arts:** General, cinematography, design, game design. **Work/family studies:** Child development.

Most popular majors. Business/marketing 16%, health sciences 16%, liberal arts 48%.

Technology on campus. 686 workstations in library, computer center, student center. Commuter students can connect to campus network. Online course registration, online library, helpline, wireless network available.

Student life. Freshman orientation: Available. Preregistration for classes offered. Orientation programs based on majors. **Activities:** Bands, choral groups, dance, drama, international student organizations, literary magazine, music ensembles, musical theater, student government, student newspaper, symphony orchestra, TV station.

Athletics. NJCAA. **Intercollegiate:** Baseball M, basketball, cross-country, football (tackle) M, golf, soccer, softball W, tennis, track and field, volleyball W. **Team name:** Aztecs.

Student services. Alcohol/substance abuse counseling, career counseling, services for economically disadvantaged, financial aid counseling, health services, minority student services, personal counseling, veterans' counselor, women's services. **Physically disabled:** Services for visually, speech, hearing impaired. **Transfer:** Pre-admission transcript evaluation for new students. Transfer adviser, college fairs on campus for students transferring to 4-year colleges.

Contact. E-mail: coadmissions@pima.edu
Phone: (520) 206-4640 Toll-free number: (800) 860-7462
Fax: (520) 206-4790
Terra Benson, Director and Registrar, Pima Community College, 4905B East Broadway, Tucson, AZ 85709-1120

Refrigeration School
Phoenix, Arizona
www.refrigerationschool.com   **CB code: 2888**

- For-profit 2-year technical college
- Commuter campus in very large city
- Interview required

General. Accredited by ACCSC. **Enrollment:** 1,185 degree-seeking undergraduates. **Degrees:** 64 associate awarded. **Calendar:** Differs by program. **Full-time faculty:** 20 total. **Part-time faculty:** 4 total.

Basis for selection. Open admission, but selective for some programs. **Home schooled:** State high school equivalency certificate required.

2015-2016 Annual costs. Tuition/fees: $20,325. Personal expenses: $2,093.

2014-2015 Financial aid. Need-based: 44% of total undergraduate aid awarded as scholarships/grants, 56% as loans/jobs. Work-study available nights, weekends and for part-time students.

Application procedures. Admission: No deadline. No application fee. Admission notification on a rolling basis.

Academics. Credit/placement by examination: AP, CLEP. **Support services:** GED preparation, tutoring.

Technology on campus. 4 workstations in library, computer center.

Student life. Freshman orientation: Mandatory. Preregistration for classes offered.

Student services. Student employment services, financial aid counseling.

Contact. Phone: (602) 275-7133 Toll-free number: (877) 477-4669
Fax: (602) 267-4805
John Palumbo, Regional Director of Admissions, Refrigeration School, 4210 East Washington Street, Phoenix, AZ 85034-1816

Rio Salado College
Tempe, Arizona   **CB member**
www.riosalado.edu   **CB code: 0997**

- Public 2-year community college
- Commuter campus in very large city

General. Founded in 1978. Regionally accredited. Access to libraries at Arizona State University and 10 Maricopa County community colleges. **Enrollment:** 58,980 undergraduates. **Degrees:** 681 associate awarded. **Location:** 120 miles from Tucson, 10 miles from Phoenix. **Calendar:** Semester, extensive summer session. **Full-time faculty:** 22 total. **Part-time faculty:** 874 total. **Class size:** 83% < 20, 14% 20-39, 3% 40-49. **Special facilities:** Public radio stations.

Transfer out. Colleges most students transferred to 2015: Arizona State University, University of Arizona, Northern Arizona University.

Basis for selection. Open admission, but selective for some programs. Dental hygiene program has GPA requirements.

2015-2016 Annual costs. Tuition/fees: $2,560; $9,790 out-of-state. Per-credit charge: $84 in-state; $325 out-of-state. Books/supplies: $1,000. Personal expenses: $2,988.

Financial aid. All financial aid based on need. Need-based aid available for part-time students. Work-study available nights, weekends and for part-time students.

Application procedures. Admission: No deadline. No application fee. Admission notification on a rolling basis. **Financial aid:** Priority date 6/30; no closing date. FAFSA, institutional form required. Applicants notified on a rolling basis starting 6/30.

Academics. Agreement with Army allows military personnel to take Internet courses. Online clinical dental assisting program offered. **Special study options:** Accelerated study, cooperative education, cross-registration, distance learning, double major, dual enrollment of high school students, ESL, honors, independent study, internships, liberal arts/career combination, teacher certification program, weekend college. License preparation in dental hygiene, nursing. **Credit/placement by examination:** AP, CLEP, institutional tests. 30 credit hours maximum toward associate degree. **Support services:** GED preparation and test center, learning center, remedial instruction, study skills assistance, tutoring, writing center.

Majors. Business: General, accounting, banking/financial services, business admin, international, office management. **Computer sciences:** General. **Health services:** Dental hygiene, nursing assistant, substance abuse counseling. **Human services:** General. **Protective services:** Law enforcement admin.

Technology on campus. 500 workstations in library, computer center. Commuter students can connect to campus network. Online course registration, online library, helpline, wireless network available.

Student life. Freshman orientation: Mandatory. Preregistration for classes offered. Online orientation materials available. **Activities:** Radio station, TV station, Phi Theta Kappa.

Student services. Adult student services, career counseling, student employment services, financial aid counseling, personal counseling, veterans' counselor. **Physically disabled:** Services for visually, speech, hearing impaired. **Transfer:** Re-entry adviser, pre-admission transcript evaluation for new students. Transfer adviser for students transferring to 4-year colleges.

Contact. E-mail: admissions.standards@riosalado.edu
Phone: (480) 517-8150 Toll-free number: (800) 729-1197
Fax: (480) 517-8199
Laurel Redman, Associate Dean, Student Enrollment Services, Rio Salado College, 2323 West 14th Street, Tempe, AZ 85281

Scottsdale Community College
Scottsdale, Arizona
www.scottsdalecc.edu   **CB code: 4755**

- Public 2-year community college
- Commuter campus in small city

General. Founded in 1969. Regionally accredited. **Enrollment:** 3,445 degree-seeking undergraduates; 9,977 non-degree-seeking students. **Degrees:** 939 associate awarded. **Location:** 10 miles from Tempe. **Calendar:** Semester, limited summer session. **Full-time faculty:** 177 total; 28% have terminal degrees, 14% minority, 49% women. **Part-time faculty:** 434 total; 9% have terminal degrees, 14% minority, 57% women. **Class size:** 52% < 20, 47% 20-39, less than 1% 40-49, less than 1% 50-99. **Special facilities:** Student-operated restaurant associated with school of culinary arts.

Student profile. Among degree-seeking undergraduates, 51% enrolled in a transfer program, 21% enrolled in a vocational program, 10% already have a bachelor's degree or higher.

Out-of-state:	5%	25 or older:	35%

Basis for selection. Open admission.

High school preparation. 16 units recommended. Recommended units include English 4, mathematics 4, social studies 2, history 1, science 3 and foreign language 2.

2015-2016 Annual costs. Tuition/fees: $2,550; $9,780 out-of-state. Per-credit charge: $84 in-state; $325 out-of-state. Books/supplies: $1,264. Personal expenses: $6,542.

Financial aid. Need-based: Need-based aid available for part-time students. Work-study available nights, weekends and for part-time students. **Non-need-based:** Scholarships awarded for academics, athletics.

Application procedures. Admission: No deadline. No application fee. Admission notification on a rolling basis. **Financial aid:** Priority date 6/1; no closing date. FAFSA required. Applicants notified on a rolling basis starting 7/1; must reply by 7/15 or within 3 week(s) of notification.

Academics. Special study options: Cooperative education, cross-registration, distance learning, dual enrollment of high school students, ESL, honors, internships, study abroad, teacher certification program. **Credit/placement by examination:** AP, CLEP, institutional tests. 52 credit hours maximum toward associate degree. **Support services:** Learning center, remedial instruction, tutoring, writing center.

Majors. Architecture: Environmental design. **Area/ethnic studies:** Native American. **Business:** General, accounting, administrative services, fashion, hospitality admin, international, management information systems, retailing. **Communications:** Public relations. **Communications technology:** Radio/TV. **Computer sciences:** General, information systems. **Education:** Early childhood. **General:** Building inspection. **Health services:** EMT paramedic, nursing (RN). **Liberal arts:** Arts/sciences. **Parks/recreation:** General. **Physical sciences:** General. **Protective services:** Criminal justice, firefighting, law enforcement admin. **Visual/performing arts:** General, cinematography, dance, dramatic, interior design, music, studio arts. **Work/family studies:** Child care management.

Most popular majors. Business/marketing 13%, health sciences 13%, liberal arts 45%, physical sciences 6%, visual/performing arts 11%.

Technology on campus. 998 workstations in library, computer center, student center. Commuter students can connect to campus network. Online course registration, online library, helpline, wireless network available.

Student life. Freshman orientation: Mandatory. Preregistration for classes offered. **Activities:** Bands, choral groups, dance, drama, international student organizations, music ensembles, student government, student newspaper, symphony orchestra, TV station, American Indian honor society, black student union, Latino student association, green club, GLBT-straight alliance, Rotoract, advocacy group, student leadership club.

Athletics. NAIA, NJCAA. **Intercollegiate:** Baseball M, basketball, football (tackle) M, golf M, soccer, softball W, volleyball W. **Team name:** Artichokes.

Student services. Alcohol/substance abuse counseling, career counseling, student employment services, financial aid counseling, personal counseling, veterans' counselor. **Physically disabled:** Services for visually, speech, hearing impaired. **Transfer:** Transfer adviser, college fairs on campus for students transferring to 4-year colleges.

Contact. E-mail: admissions@scottsdalecc.edu
Phone: (480) 423-6100 Fax: (480) 423-6200
Fran Vitale, Director of Admissions and Records, Scottsdale Community College, 9000 East Chaparral Road, Scottsdale, AZ 85256-2626

Sessions College for Professional Design
Tempe, Arizona
www.sessions.edu   CB code: 6356

- Private 2-year virtual visual arts college
- Very large city
- Application essay required

General. Regionally accredited; also accredited by DETC. Fully online degree and certificate programs in the visual arts and design. **Enrollment:** 124 degree-seeking undergraduates. **Degrees:** 22 associate awarded. **Calendar:** Semester, extensive summer session. **Part-time faculty:** 26 total; 27% have terminal degrees, 8% minority, 50% women.

Student profile. Among degree-seeking undergraduates, 22 enrolled as first-time, first-year students.

Part-time:	34%	Hispanic/Latino:	14%
Women:	65%	Native American:	1%
African American:	13%	Multi-racial, non-Hispanic:	6%
Asian American:	2%		

Basis for selection. Open admission, but selective for some programs. Open admissions to certificate programs with high school diploma/GED. Admission process for degree programs requires review of art/design portfolio, essay, and prior transcripts. Degree program applicants must provide a portfolio of 5-10 art/design samples. **Home schooled:** Transcript of courses and grades, state high school equivalency certificate required.

2016-2017 Annual costs. Tuition/fees (projected): $11,950.

Financial aid. Need-based: Work-study available nights, weekends and for part-time students.

Application procedures. Admission: Priority date 6/15; deadline 7/15 (receipt date). $50 fee. Application must be submitted online. Admission notification on a rolling basis. **Financial aid:** No deadline.

Academics. Special study options: Distance learning. **Credit/placement by examination:** AP, CLEP.

Majors. Communications technology: Animation/special effects. **Computer sciences:** Web page design. **Visual/performing arts:** Commercial photography, commercial/advertising art, graphic design, illustration.

Technology on campus. PC or laptop required. Online course registration, online library available.

Student life. Freshman orientation: Mandatory. Preregistration for classes offered.

Contact. E-mail: admissions@sessions.edu
Phone: (480) 212-1704 Toll-free number: (800) 258-4115
Mhelanie Hernandez, Director of Admissions and Marketing, Sessions College for Professional Design, 51 West Third St, Suite E-301, Tempe, AZ 85281

South Mountain Community College
Phoenix, Arizona   CB member
www.southmountaincc.edu   CB code: 4734

- Public 2-year community college
- Commuter campus in very large city

General. Founded in 1979. Regionally accredited. Learning Center in Guadalupe. Arizona Agribusiness Equine Charter school located on campus. **Enrollment:** 1,340 degree-seeking undergraduates. **Degrees:** 442 associate awarded. **Location:** 8 miles from downtown. **Calendar:** Semester, limited summer session. **Full-time faculty:** 58 total. **Part-time faculty:** 212 total. **Partnerships:** Formal partnership with Arizona Agribusiness Equine Charter School.

Student profile. Among degree-seeking undergraduates, 3,410 transferred in from other institutions.

Out-of-state:	1%	25 or older:	40%

Basis for selection. Open admission.

2016-2017 Annual costs. Tuition/fees (projected): $2,550; $9,780 out-of-state. Per-credit charge: $84 in-state; $325 out-of-state. Books/supplies: $1,280. Personal expenses: $3,744.

Financial aid. Need-based: Need-based aid available for part-time students. Work-study available nights, weekends and for part-time students. **Non-need-based:** Scholarships awarded for academics, athletics, minority status, music/drama.

Application procedures. Admission: No deadline. $15 fee. Admission notification on a rolling basis. **Financial aid:** Priority date 5/1; no closing date. FAFSA required. Applicants notified on a rolling basis starting 5/15; must reply within 3 week(s) of notification.

Academics. Special study options: Cooperative education, cross-registration, dual enrollment of high school students, ESL, honors, independent study. **Credit/placement by examination:** AP, CLEP, IB, institutional tests. 30 credit hours maximum toward associate degree. **Support services:** GED preparation and test center, learning center, remedial instruction, tutoring, writing center.

Majors. Biology: General. **Business:** Administrative services, business admin, customer service support, international, logistics, office technology. **Computer sciences:** General, information systems, security, system admin, systems analysis. **Education:** General, early childhood, music, physical. **English:** English lit. **History:** General. **Liberal arts:** Arts/sciences. **Math:** General. **Physical sciences:** General, chemistry, physics. **Psychology:** General. **Social sciences:** Political science, sociology. **Visual/performing arts:** Art, music. **Work/family studies:** General.

Most popular majors. Computer/information sciences 27%, liberal arts 62%.

Technology on campus. 125 workstations in library, computer center.

Student life. Freshman orientation: Available. Preregistration for classes offered. **Activities:** Concert band, choral groups, dance, drama, music ensembles, student government, student newspaper, African-American unity coalition, Society of Hispanic Engineers and Scientists, Christian student club, Native American club, forensic club, music club, volunteers program, Phi Theta Kappa.

Athletics. NJCAA. **Intercollegiate:** Baseball M, basketball, golf, soccer M, softball W, tennis, volleyball W. **Team name:** Cougars.

Student services. Career counseling, student employment services, on-campus daycare, personal counseling, veterans' counselor. **Transfer:** Re-entry adviser, pre-admission transcript evaluation for new students. Transfer adviser, college fairs on campus for students transferring to 4-year colleges.

Contact. Phone: (602) 243-8124 Fax: (602) 243-8199
Corina Canchola, Supervisor of Admissions, Registration & Records, South Mountain Community College, 7050 South 24th Street, Phoenix, AZ 85042

Tohono O'odham Community College
Sells, Arizona
www.tocc.edu

- Public 2-year community college
- Commuter campus in rural community

General. Enrollment: 192 degree-seeking undergraduates; 19 non-degree-seeking students. **Degrees:** 13 associate awarded. **Location:** 60 miles from Tucson. **Calendar:** Semester, limited summer session. **Full-time faculty:** 17 total; 29% have terminal degrees, 29% minority, 41% women. **Part-time faculty:** 31 total; 13% have terminal degrees, 23% minority, 58% women. **Class size:** 86% < 20, 14% 20-39.

Student profile. Among degree-seeking undergraduates, 60% enrolled in a transfer program, 5% enrolled in a vocational program, 2% already have a bachelor's degree or higher, 38 enrolled as first-time, first-year students, 17 transferred in from other institutions.

Part-time:	58%	25 or older:	65%
Women:	56%	Live on campus:	10%

Basis for selection. Open admission. Open enrollment. **Home schooled:** Transcript of courses and grades, state high school equivalency certificate required.

2015-2016 Annual costs. Tuition/fees: $2,055; $4,620 out-of-state. Room only: $2,400. Books/supplies: $750. Personal expenses: $1,750.

2014-2015 Financial aid. All financial aid based on need. 99% of total undergraduate aid awarded as scholarships/grants, 1% as loans/jobs. Need-based aid available for part-time students. Work-study available nights, weekends and for part-time students.

Application procedures. Admission: No deadline. No application fee. Application must be submitted on paper. Admission notification on a rolling basis. **Financial aid:** No deadline. FAFSA, institutional form required. Applicants notified on a rolling basis.

Academics. Special study options: Dual enrollment of high school students, independent study. **Credit/placement by examination:** AP, CLEP. **Support services:** GED preparation, learning center, remedial instruction, study skills assistance, tutoring, writing center.

Majors. Business: Business admin. **Education:** Early childhood special, elementary. **General:** Carpentry, electrician, painting, plumbing, site management. **Liberal arts:** Arts/sciences. **Social sciences:** General.

Technology on campus. Dormitories wired for high-speed internet access and linked to campus network. Online library, helpline, repair service, wireless network available.

Student life. Freshman orientation: Mandatory. Preregistration for classes offered. Orientation class offers information on student services and academic support services. **Housing:** Coed dorms, single-sex dorms available. **Activities:** Student government.

Athletics. NJCAA. **Intercollegiate:** Basketball. **Team name:** Jegos.

Student services. Adult student services, career counseling, student employment services, financial aid counseling, personal counseling, placement for graduates. **Transfer:** Re-entry adviser, pre-admission transcript evaluation for new students. College fairs on campus for students transferring to 4-year colleges.

Contact. E-mail: lluna@tocc.edu
Phone: (520) 383-8401 ext. 35 Fax: (520) 383-0029
Leslie Luna, Registrar, Tohono O'odham Community College, PO Box 3129, Sells, AZ 85634-3129

Universal Technical Institute
Avondale, Arizona
www.uti.edu/Phoenix   CB code: 2504

- For-profit 2-year technical and career college
- Commuter campus in small city

General. Founded in 1965. Accredited by ACCSC. Electives available: Ford FACT, BMW FastTrack, GM Technician Career Training, Cummins Diesel Engines, Cummins Power Generation, Daimler Truck Finish First. **Enrollment:** 2,000 undergraduates. **Degrees:** 1,065 associate awarded. **Location:** 17 miles from Phoenix, 11 miles from Glendale. **Calendar:** Differs by program, extensive summer session. **Full-time faculty:** 90 total. **Partnerships:** Formal partnerships with Ford, General Motors, BMW, Cummins, Daimler.

Basis for selection. Open admission. **Home schooled:** Must pass Wonderlic Scholastic Level Exam. **Learning Disabled:** Students seeking accommodations must provide copy of IEP from high school and/or medical documentation. They must also complete paperwork requesting accommodation and meet with School Counselor or Student Services Director prior to starting school.

Financial aid. Need-based: Work-study available nights, weekends and for part-time students.

Application procedures. Admission: No deadline. $50 fee. Admission notification on a rolling basis. **Financial aid:** No deadline. FAFSA required.

Academics. Special study options: Accelerated study. **Credit/placement by examination:** AP, CLEP. **Support services:** Learning center, tutoring.

Technology on campus. 78 workstations in computer center.

Student life. Freshman orientation: Mandatory. Preregistration for classes offered. **Housing:** Housing partnership with Collegiate Housing Services. Shared housing options and individual housing options available. **Activities:** Student government.

Student services. Career counseling, services for economically disadvantaged, student employment services, financial aid counseling, veterans' counselor. **Physically disabled:** Services for hearing impaired.

Contact. E-mail: info@uticorp.com
Phone: (623) 245-4600 Toll-free number: (800) 859-1202
Fax: (623) 245-4605
Admissions Director, Universal Technical Institute, 10695 West Pierce Street, Avondale, AZ 85323

Yavapai College
Prescott, Arizona
www.yc.edu   CB code: 4996

▸ Public 2-year community college
▸ Commuter campus in large town

Contact. E-mail: registration@yc.edu
Phone: (928) 445-7300 ext. 2148 Toll-free number: (800) 922-6787
Fax: (928) 776-2151
Terri Eckel, Director of Admissions, Yavapai College, 1100 East Sheldon Street, Prescott, AZ 86301

General. Founded in 1966. Regionally accredited. Classes offered at branch campus in Clarkdale and several locations in Yavapai County. **Enrollment:** 8,273 undergraduates. **Degrees:** 543 associate awarded. **ROTC:** Army, Air Force. **Location:** 100 miles from Phoenix. **Calendar:** Semester, limited summer session. **Full-time faculty:** 114 total. **Part-time faculty:** 115 total. **Special facilities:** Solar laboratory, solar greenhouse, performance hall, career technical educational center.

Student profile.

Out-of-state:	6%	Live on campus:	10%
25 or older:	24%		

Transfer out. Colleges most students transferred to 2015: Arizona State University, Northern Arizona University, University of Arizona, Old Dominion University.

Basis for selection. Open admission, but selective for some programs. Limited admission for registered nursing, gunsmithing, and independent filmmaking. Interview required of nursing majors. Essay for independent filmmaking.

2015-2016 Annual costs. Tuition/fees: $2,250; $10,560 out-of-state. Per-credit charge: $75 in-state; $353 out-of-state. Room/board: $8,858. Books/supplies: $1,000. Personal expenses: $1,900.

Financial aid. Need-based: Need-based aid available for part-time students. Work-study available nights, weekends and for part-time students. **Non-need-based:** Scholarships awarded for academics, athletics.

Application procedures. Admission: No deadline. No application fee. Admission notification on a rolling basis. **Financial aid:** Priority date 4/1; no closing date. FAFSA required. Applicants notified on a rolling basis.

Academics. Special study options: Accelerated study, distance learning, dual enrollment of high school students, ESL, honors, independent study, internships, liberal arts/career combination, teacher certification program, weekend college. 2-2 program with Northern Arizona University for bachelor degree in education and business, program with Old Dominion University offering bachelor degree completion. Bachelor's degree programs available on campus. License preparation in nursing, paramedic, real estate. **Credit/placement by examination:** AP, CLEP, IB, institutional tests. 30 credit hours maximum toward associate degree. **Support services:** GED preparation and test center, learning center, pre-admission summer program, reduced course load, remedial instruction, study skills assistance, tutoring, writing center.

Majors. Architecture: Environmental design. **Business:** Accounting, administrative services, business admin, office management, office technology. **Computer sciences:** General. **Education:** Early childhood. **General:** Maintenance. **Health services:** Medical secretary, nursing (RN). **Liberal arts:** Arts/sciences. **Protective services:** Firefighting, law enforcement admin. **Visual/performing arts:** Commercial/advertising art, industrial design.

Technology on campus. 1,609 workstations in dormitories, library, computer center. Dormitories wired for high-speed internet access and linked to campus network. Commuter students can connect to campus network. Online course registration, online library, wireless network available.

Student life. Freshman orientation: Available. Preregistration for classes offered. **Housing:** Coed dorms, special housing for disabled, wellness housing available. $150 deposit. **Activities:** Bands, choral groups, dance, drama, literary magazine, music ensembles, musical theater, student government, student newspaper, nursing association, Native American club, international student club, Hispanic club, Campus Crusade for Christ, Bahai club, PTK, Veterans' club.

Athletics. NJCAA. **Intercollegiate:** Baseball M, basketball, soccer M, volleyball W. **Team name:** Roughriders.

Student services. Adult student services, career counseling, student employment services, financial aid counseling, health services, personal counseling, placement for graduates, veterans' counselor. **Physically disabled:** Services for visually, hearing impaired. **Transfer:** College fairs on campus for students transferring to 4-year colleges.

Arkansas

Arkansas Northeastern College
Blytheville, Arkansas
www.anc.edu   CB code: 1267

- Public 2-year community college
- Commuter campus in large town

General. Founded in 1974. Regionally accredited. **Enrollment:** 1,361 degree-seeking undergraduates. **Degrees:** 126 associate awarded. **Location:** 50 miles from Jonesboro. 65 miles from Memphis, TN. **Calendar:** Semester, limited summer session. **Full-time faculty:** 76 total. **Part-time faculty:** 60 total. **Class size:** 66% < 20, 32% 20-39, less than 1% 40-49, 1% 50-99.

Student profile.

Out-of-state: 18% **25 or older:**   50%

Transfer out. Colleges most students transferred to 2015: Arkansas State University, Southeast Missouri State University.

Basis for selection. Open admission, but selective for some programs. Structured admissions criteria for enrollment into certificate and degree programs. In addition, entrance exams are required for both the LPN and RN programs.

2015-2016 Annual costs. Tuition/fees: $2,180; $2,480 out-of-district; $3,980 out-of-state. Per-credit charge: $65 in-district; $75 out-of-district; $125 out-of-state. Books/supplies: $1,335. Personal expenses: $6,460.

2014-2015 Financial aid. Need-based: 97% of total undergraduate aid awarded as scholarships/grants, 3% as loans/jobs. Need-based aid available for part-time students. Work-study available nights, weekends and for part-time students. **Non-need-based:** Scholarships awarded for academics, art, minority status, music/drama, state residency.

Application procedures. Admission: No deadline. No application fee. Admission notification on a rolling basis. **Financial aid:** Priority date 4/15; no closing date. FAFSA, institutional form required. Applicants notified on a rolling basis starting 3/1; must reply within 2 week(s) of notification.

Academics. Special study options: Accelerated study, distance learning, double major, dual enrollment of high school students. Bachelor's degree programs available on campus. License preparation in aviation, nursing, paramedic. **Credit/placement by examination:** AP, CLEP, institutional tests. 15 credit hours maximum toward associate degree. Placement tests required for algebra and English composition. **Support services:** GED preparation and test center, learning center, reduced course load, remedial instruction, study skills assistance, tutoring, writing center.

Majors. Business: General, administrative services, management information systems. **Education:** Early childhood, middle. **Health services:** Nursing (RN). **Liberal arts:** Arts/sciences. **Protective services:** Police science. **Social sciences:** Criminology. **Work/family studies:** Child care service.

Most popular majors. Business/marketing 13%, education 11%, engineering/engineering technologies 10%, health sciences 24%, liberal arts 36%.

Technology on campus. 400 workstations in library, computer center. Commuter students can connect to campus network. Online course registration, online library, wireless network available.

Student life. Freshman orientation: Available. Preregistration for classes offered. **Activities:** Choral groups, drama, music ensembles, cultural diversity association, Baptist college ministry, adult student association.

Student services. Adult student services, career counseling, services for economically disadvantaged, student employment services, financial aid counseling, on-campus daycare, personal counseling, placement for graduates, veterans' counselor. **Physically disabled:** Services for visually, speech, hearing impaired. **Transfer:** Pre-admission transcript evaluation for new students. Transfer adviser, college fairs on campus for students transferring to 4-year colleges.

Contact. E-mail: advising@smail.anc.edu
Phone: (870) 762-1020 ext. 1103 Fax: (870) 763-1654
Courtney Fisher, Director of Admission, Arkansas Northeastern College, PO Box 1109, Blytheville, AR 72316-1109

Arkansas State University Mid-South
West Memphis, Arkansas
www.asumidsouth.edu   CB code: 3880

- Public 2-year community and junior college
- Commuter campus in large town

General. Regionally accredited. **Enrollment:** 1,896 undergraduates. **Degrees:** 160 associate awarded. **Location:** 8 miles from Memphis, TN. **Calendar:** Semester, limited summer session. **Full-time faculty:** 46 total. **Part-time faculty:** 81 total. **Class size:** 77% < 20, 23% 20-39.

Student profile. 79 transferred in from other institutions.

Out-of-state: 10% **25 or older:**   53%

Transfer out. Colleges most students transferred to 2015: Arkansas State University, University of Memphis.

Basis for selection. Open admission. **Home schooled:** Transcript of courses and grades required.

2015-2016 Annual costs. Tuition/fees: $3,190; $3,790 out-of-district; $4,990 out-of-state. Per-credit charge: $90 in-district; $110 out-of-district; $150 out-of-state. Books/supplies: $2,000. Personal expenses: $1,000.

2014-2015 Financial aid. Need-based: 174 full-time freshmen applied for aid; 173 deemed to have need; 173 received aid. Average need met was 29%. 99% of total undergraduate aid awarded as scholarships/grants, 1% as loans/jobs. Need-based aid available for part-time students. Work-study available nights, weekends and for part-time students. **Non-need-based:** Scholarships awarded for academics, state residency.

Application procedures. Admission: No deadline. No application fee. Admission notification on a rolling basis. **Financial aid:** Priority date 4/30; no closing date. FAFSA, institutional form required. Applicants notified on a rolling basis starting 6/1; must reply within 2 week(s) of notification.

Academics. Special study options: Cooperative education, distance learning, dual enrollment of high school students, liberal arts/career combination. Bachelor's degree programs available on campus. **Credit/placement by examination:** AP, CLEP, institutional tests. 30 credit hours maximum toward associate degree. **Support services:** GED preparation and test center, learning center, reduced course load, remedial instruction, study skills assistance, tutoring, writing center.

Majors. Business: Office technology. **Computer sciences:** General. **Education:** Middle. **Liberal arts:** Arts/sciences. **Protective services:** Forensics, law enforcement admin.

Technology on campus. 250 workstations in library, computer center, student center. Commuter students can connect to campus network. Online course registration, online library available.

Student life. Freshman orientation: Available. Preregistration for classes offered.

Athletics. NJCAA. **Team name:** Groundhounds.

Student services. Adult student services, career counseling, services for economically disadvantaged, student employment services, financial aid counseling, minority student services, veterans' counselor. **Physically disabled:** Services for visually, speech, hearing impaired. **Transfer:** Transfer adviser, college fairs on campus for students transferring to 4-year colleges.

Contact. E-mail: admission@midsouthcc.edu
Phone: (870) 733-6728 Toll-free number: (866) 733-6722
Fax: (870) 733-6719
John Easley, Associate Vice Chancellor for Enrollment Management, Arkansas State University Mid-South, 2000 West Broadway, West Memphis, AR 72301

Arkansas State University: Beebe
Beebe, Arkansas
www.asub.edu   CB code: 0782

- Public 2-year community college
- Commuter campus in small town

General. Founded in 1927. Regionally accredited. Approved as Serviceman's Opportunity College. **Enrollment:** 2,889 degree-seeking undergraduates; 1,046 non-degree-seeking students. **Degrees:** 672 associate awarded.

ROTC: Army. **Location:** 35 miles from Little Rock. **Calendar:** Semester, extensive summer session.

Student profile. Among degree-seeking undergraduates, 52% enrolled in a transfer program, 48% enrolled in a vocational program, 759 enrolled as first-time, first-year students.

Part-time:	30%	Asian American:	1%
Women:	57%	Hispanic/Latino:	6%
African American:	6%	Multi-racial, non-Hispanic:	4%

Basis for selection. Open admission, but selective for some programs.

High school preparation. College-preparatory program recommended. 15 units recommended. Recommended units include English 3, mathematics 1, social studies 2 and science 2.

2015-2016 Annual costs. Tuition/fees: $3,330; $5,430 out-of-state. Per-credit charge: $96 in-state; $166 out-of-state. Room/board: $4,842. Books/supplies: $1,256. Personal expenses: $2,005.

Financial aid. Need-based: Need-based aid available for part-time students. Work-study available nights, weekends and for part-time students. **Non-need-based:** Scholarships awarded for academics, leadership, music/drama.

Application procedures. Admission: No deadline. No application fee. Admission notification on a rolling basis. **Financial aid:** Priority date 6/1; no closing date. FAFSA, institutional form required. Applicants notified on a rolling basis starting 6/1; must reply within 2 week(s) of notification.

Academics. Special study options: Accelerated study, distance learning, double major, dual enrollment of high school students, external degree, honors, independent study, internships. Bachelor's degree programs available on campus. License preparation in nursing, paramedic. **Credit/placement by examination:** AP, CLEP, institutional tests. 30 credit hours maximum toward associate degree. **Support services:** Learning center, reduced course load, remedial instruction, tutoring.

Majors. Business: General, hospitality admin, management information systems. **Conservation:** Environmental science. **Education:** Early childhood, middle. **Health services:** Clinical lab technology, EMT paramedic, pharmacy assistant, veterinary technology/assistant. **Liberal arts:** Arts/sciences. **Protective services:** Criminal justice, forensics, law enforcement admin, police science. **Visual/performing arts:** Music.

Most popular majors. Business/marketing 12%, education 6%, health sciences 19%, liberal arts 42%, trade and industry 9%.

Technology on campus. Dormitories linked to campus network. Online course registration, online library, repair service, wireless network available.

Student life. Freshman orientation: Mandatory. Preregistration for classes offered. **Housing:** Coed dorms available. $150 partly refundable deposit. **Activities:** Bands, campus ministries, choral groups, drama, international student organizations, music ensembles, student government, Gamma Beta Phi, Phi Beta Lambda, student advisory board, leadership council, Tau Alpha Pi, National Technical Honor Society.

Athletics. Intramural: Archery, badminton, basketball, bowling, football (non-tackle), golf, racquetball, softball, table tennis, tennis, track and field, volleyball.

Student services. Career counseling, services for economically disadvantaged, financial aid counseling, personal counseling, placement for graduates, veterans' counselor. **Transfer:** Transfer adviser, college fairs on campus for students transferring to 4-year colleges.

Contact. E-mail: rahayes@asub.edu
Phone: (501) 882-8860 Toll-free number: (800) 632-9985
Fax: (501) 882-8895
Robin Hayes, Director of Admissions, Arkansas State University: Beebe, PO Box 1000, Beebe, AR 72012-1000

Arkansas State University: Mountain Home
Mountain Home, Arkansas
www.asumh.edu
CB code: 6057

- Public 2-year community and technical college
- Commuter campus in large town

General. Enrollment: 1,224 degree-seeking undergraduates. **Degrees:** 272 associate awarded. **Location:** 130 miles from Little Rock. **Calendar:** Semester, limited summer session. **Full-time faculty:** 48 total. **Part-time faculty:** 31 total. **Class size:** 63% < 20, 37% 20-39.

Student profile.

Out-of-state:	1%	25 or older:	36%

Transfer out. Colleges most students transferred to 2015: Arkansas State University-Jonesboro, University of Central Arkansas-Conway, University of Arkansas-Fayetteville.

Basis for selection. Open admission, but selective for some programs. Additional requirements for practical nursing, respiratory care, funeral science, and phlebotomy programs. **Home schooled:** Statement describing home school structure and mission, transcript of courses and grades, state high school equivalency certificate required. **Learning Disabled:** Students with learning disabilities must document them with disability coordinator.

High school preparation. College-preparatory program recommended. Recommended units include English 4, mathematics 4, social studies 3 and science 4.

2015-2016 Annual costs. Tuition/fees: $3,420; $5,400 out-of-state. Per-credit charge: $92 in-state; $158 out-of-state. Books/supplies: $1,400. Personal expenses: $1,584.

Financial aid. Need-based: Need-based aid available for part-time students. Work-study available nights, weekends and for part-time students. **Non-need-based:** Scholarships awarded for academics, alumni affiliation, leadership, state residency. **Additional information:** Satisfactory academic progress policy for Title IV aid.

Application procedures. Admission: Closing date 8/15 (receipt date). No application fee. Admission notification on a rolling basis. **Financial aid:** Priority date 6/1; no closing date. FAFSA, institutional form required. Applicants notified on a rolling basis starting 5/1; must reply within 2 week(s) of notification.

Academics. Special study options: Cooperative education, distance learning, dual enrollment of high school students, ESL, honors, independent study, liberal arts/career combination. License preparation in funeral sciences, practical nursing, respiratory care, and paramedic tech. Bachelor's degree programs available on campus. License preparation in nursing, paramedic. **Credit/placement by examination:** AP, CLEP, institutional tests. 15 credit hours maximum toward associate degree, 15 toward bachelor's. **Support services:** GED preparation and test center, learning center, remedial instruction, study skills assistance, tutoring, writing center.

Majors. Business: General, administrative services. **Computer sciences:** Information systems. **Education:** Early childhood, multi-level teacher. **Health services:** EMT paramedic, respiratory therapy technology. **Liberal arts:** Arts/sciences. **Protective services:** Law enforcement admin.

Most popular majors. Business/marketing 17%, education 15%, liberal arts 52%.

Technology on campus. 100 workstations in library, computer center, student center. Commuter students can connect to campus network. Online course registration, online library, helpline, wireless network available.

Student life. Freshman orientation: Available. Preregistration for classes offered. **Activities:** Campus ministries, drama, literary magazine, student government, Circle K, criminal justice club, mortuary science club, student ambassadors, student practical nurses association, Phi Beta Lambda, Phi Delta Kappa, Phi Theta Kappa, Rotaract.

Student services. Adult student services, career counseling, student employment services, financial aid counseling, placement for graduates, veterans' counselor. **Physically disabled:** Services for visually, hearing impaired. **Transfer:** Pre-admission transcript evaluation for new students. College fairs on campus for students transferring to 4-year colleges.

Contact. E-mail: rblagg@asumh.edu
Phone: (870) 508-6100 ext. 104 Fax: (870) 508-6287
Rosalyn Blagg, Assistant Vice Chancellor for Enrollment, Arkansas State University: Mountain Home, 1600 South College Street, Mountain Home, AR 72653

Arkansas State University: Newport
Newport, Arkansas
www.asun.edu
CB code: 6631

- Public 2-year community and liberal arts college
- Commuter campus in small town

General. Enrollment: 1,455 degree-seeking undergraduates. **Degrees:** 199 associate awarded. **Location:** 100 miles from Little Rock, 45 miles from Jonesboro. **Calendar:** Semester, limited summer session. **Full-time faculty:**

77 total. **Part-time faculty:** 34 total. **Special facilities:** Commercial Truck Driving Program/Ranges.

Transfer out. Colleges most students transferred to 2015: University of Central Arkansas, Arkansas State University: Jonesboro, University of Arkansas, Arkansas Tech University.

Basis for selection. Students may be required to remove deficiencies before entering certain programs or courses. **Home schooled:** Transcript of courses and grades, state high school equivalency certificate required. Conditional enrollment; must provide placement scores. **Learning Disabled:** Coordinated by Vice Chancellor for Student Services.

2015-2016 Annual costs. Tuition/fees: $3,270; $5,010 out-of-state. Per-credit charge: $91 in-state; $149 out-of-state. Books/supplies: $1,200.

Financial aid. Need-based: Work-study available nights, weekends and for part-time students.

Application procedures. Admission: No deadline. No application fee. Admission notification on a rolling basis. **Financial aid:** Priority date 5/1; no closing date.

Academics. Special study options: Cooperative education, distance learning, dual enrollment of high school students, independent study, internships, liberal arts/career combination, study abroad, teacher certification program. License preparation in nursing. **Credit/placement by examination:** AP, CLEP, institutional tests. 30 credit hours maximum toward associate degree. **Support services:** GED preparation and test center, learning center, remedial instruction, study skills assistance, tutoring.

Majors. Business: General, management information systems. **Education:** Middle. **Health services:** EMT paramedic. **Liberal arts:** Arts/sciences.

Technology on campus. Commuter students can connect to campus network. Online course registration, online library, helpline, repair service, wireless network available.

Student life. Freshman orientation: Mandatory. Preregistration for classes offered. **Activities:** Drama, student government.

Student services. Career counseling, services for economically disadvantaged, financial aid counseling, personal counseling, veterans' counselor. **Physically disabled:** Services for visually, speech, hearing impaired. **Transfer:** College fairs on campus for students transferring to 4-year colleges.

Contact. E-mail: rsummers@asun.edu
Phone: (870) 512-7800 Toll-free number: (800) 976-1676
Fax: (870) 512-7825
Candace Gross, Registrar/Director of Admissions, Arkansas State University: Newport, 7648 Victory Boulevard, Newport, AR 72112

Black River Technical College
Pocahontas, Arkansas
www.blackrivertech.edu　　　　　**CB code: 3879**

▶ Public 2-year technical college
▶ Commuter campus in small town

General. Regionally accredited. **Enrollment:** 1,745 undergraduates. **Degrees:** 273 associate awarded. **Location:** 35 miles from Jonesboro. **Calendar:** Semester, extensive summer session.

Transfer out. Colleges most students transferred to 2015: Williams Baptist College, Arkansas State University.

Basis for selection. Open admission, but selective for some programs. High school transcript and standardized test scores most important. **Home schooled:** Transcript of courses and grades required.

2015-2016 Annual costs. Tuition/fees: $3,240; $6,330 out-of-state. Per-credit charge: $86 in-state; $189 out-of-state. Books/supplies: $2,328.

Financial aid. Need-based: Need-based aid available for part-time students. Work-study available nights, weekends and for part-time students. **Non-need-based:** Scholarships awarded for academics, leadership, minority status, music/drama, state residency.

Application procedures. Admission: No deadline. No application fee. **Financial aid:** Priority date 4/1, closing date 6/30. FAFSA, institutional form required. Applicants notified on a rolling basis starting 4/1.

Academics. Special study options: Accelerated study, distance learning, dual enrollment of high school students, independent study, internships,

weekend college. License preparation in nursing, paramedic. **Credit/placement by examination:** AP, CLEP, institutional tests. **Support services:** GED preparation and test center, learning center, remedial instruction, study skills assistance, tutoring.

Majors. Business: Accounting, business admin, management information systems. **Protective services:** Police science. **Social sciences:** Economics. **Visual/performing arts:** Art.

Technology on campus. Commuter students can connect to campus network. Online course registration, online library, helpline, wireless network available.

Student life. Freshman orientation: Mandatory. Preregistration for classes offered. **Activities:** Choral groups, music ensembles, student government.

Student services. Career counseling, student employment services, financial aid counseling, health services, placement for graduates, veterans' counselor. **Physically disabled:** Services for visually, speech, hearing impaired. **Transfer:** Pre-admission transcript evaluation for new students. College fairs on campus for students transferring to 4-year colleges.

Contact. E-mail: marya@blackrivertech.edu
Phone: (870) 248-4000 Fax: (870) 248-4100
Mary Anderson, Academic Advisor, Black River Technical College, Highway 304 East, Pocahontas, AR 72455

Bryan University: Rogers
Rogers, Arkansas
www.bryanu.edu

▶ For-profit 2-year career college
▶ Small city
▶ Interview required

General. Regionally accredited; also accredited by ACICS. **Enrollment:** 61 undergraduates. **Degrees:** 59 associate awarded. **Calendar:** Quarter. **Full-time faculty:** 1 total. **Part-time faculty:** 15 total.

Basis for selection. Open admission. All applicants seeking to matriculate into an Associate degree program must also provide evidence to the University of one of the following by the end of the add/drop period of the student's first quarter: Completion and successful achievement of the required threshold score or higher on the Wonderlic Scholastic Level Examination (SLE) test administered by the University, a minimum of 13.5 quarter credit hours (9 semester credit hours) earned academic credit from an accredited institution recognized by the United States Department of Education, official ACT college entrance test scores revealing a composite score of at least 17 on both the English and Mathematics sections of the exam or Official SAT college entrance test scores revealing a score of at least 460 on both the Mathematics and Critical Reading sections of the exam. For graduates of an accredited institution recognized by the United States Department of Education, evidence is considered an official transcript revealing earned academic credit totaling the required amount. For international students, an official transcript translation and evaluation from a member of the Association of International Credentials Evaluators (AICE) or the National Association of Credential Evaluation Services (NACES) must be provided directly to the university by the end of the add/drop period of the student's first quarter. Prospective students must wait a minimum of 24 hours before attempting to achieve the required SLE score for their program through retesting. If the required SLE score is not achieved by the second attempt, the student must wait 6 months to retest. The SLE is designed to help ensure that the applicant has the skills necessary to successfully pursue a college-level academic associate degree program. Threshold values that must be met for each program are available in the current catalog supplement. **Home schooled:** Transcript of courses and grades required.

2015-2016 Annual costs. Tuition and fees very by program and level. Diploma programs: $19,312-$28,770; Associate degree programs: $31,968-$34,097; Bachelor degree programs: $52,610. Books and supplies vary depending on program. All costs are subject to change.

Financial aid. Need-based: Work-study available nights, weekends and for part-time students.

Application procedures. Admission: No deadline. $50 fee. Admission notification on a rolling basis.

Academics. Credit/placement by examination: AP, CLEP.

Majors. Business: General. **Computer sciences:** Networking. **Health services:** Clinical lab science, medical assistant. **Parks/recreation:** Health/fitness. **Protective services:** Law enforcement admin.

Most popular majors. Business/marketing 17%, health sciences 58%, parks/recreation 12%, security/protective services 11%.

Contact. Phone: (479) 899-6644 Toll-free number: (855) 566-0650 Fax: (479) 899-6535
Bene Perez, Admissions Manager, Bryan University: Rogers, 3704 West Walnut Street, Rogers, AR 72756

College of the Ouachitas
Malvern, Arkansas
www.coto.edu   CB code: 3619

▸ Public 2-year community and technical college
▸ Commuter campus in small town

General. Regionally accredited. **Enrollment:** 764 degree-seeking undergraduates; 582 non-degree-seeking students. **Degrees:** 152 associate awarded. **ROTC:** Army. **Location:** 45 miles from Little Rock. **Calendar:** Semester, limited summer session. **Full-time faculty:** 31 total. **Part-time faculty:** 60 total. **Partnerships:** Formal partnership with National Apprenticeship Training Foundation.

Student profile. Among degree-seeking undergraduates, 145 enrolled as first-time, first-year students.

Part-time: 35%   Women: 70%
Out-of-state: 1%   25 or older: 56%

Transfer out. Colleges most students transferred to 2015: Henderson State University, University of Central Arkansas.

Basis for selection. Open admission, but selective for some programs. Admission to practical nursing, registered nursing, and cosmetology programs based on test scores.

High school preparation. College-preparatory program recommended.

2015-2016 Annual costs. Tuition/fees: $3,620; $6,410 out-of-state. Per-credit charge: $93 in-state; $186 out-of-state. Books/supplies: $1,000. Personal expenses: $1,382.

2014-2015 Financial aid. Need-based: Need-based aid available for part-time students. Work-study available nights, weekends and for part-time students. **Non-need-based:** Scholarships awarded for academics.

Application procedures. Admission: No deadline. No application fee. **Financial aid:** No deadline. FAFSA required. Applicants notified on a rolling basis starting 7/1; must reply within 6 week(s) of notification.

Academics. Associate of Arts in General Education and Associate of Applied Science in Criminal Justice offered online. **Special study options:** Accelerated study, distance learning, dual enrollment of high school students, honors, independent study, internships, liberal arts/career combination. License preparation in nursing. **Credit/placement by examination:** AP, CLEP, institutional tests. **Support services:** GED preparation and test center, learning center, pre-admission summer program, remedial instruction, study skills assistance, tutoring.

Majors. Business: General, accounting, business admin, office/clerical. **Computer sciences:** General. **Education:** Early childhood. **Health services:** Health information technology, nursing (RN), office admin. **Liberal arts:** Arts/sciences. **Protective services:** Criminal justice, forensics. **Work/family studies:** Child care management.

Most popular majors. Business/marketing 9%, health sciences 56%, liberal arts 22%.

Technology on campus. 150 workstations in library, computer center, student center. Online course registration, online library, helpline, wireless network available.

Student life. Freshman orientation: Mandatory. Preregistration for classes offered. Orientation offered on-campus and online. **Activities:** Student government.

Student services. Adult student services, alcohol/substance abuse counseling, chaplain/spiritual director, career counseling, services for economically disadvantaged, student employment services, financial aid counseling, personal counseling, placement for graduates, veterans' counselor. **Physically disabled:** Services for visually, speech, hearing impaired. **Transfer:** Pre-admission transcript evaluation for new students. College fairs on campus for students transferring to 4-year colleges.

Contact. E-mail: info@coto.edu
Phone: (501) 337-5000 ext. 1118 Fax: (501) 337-9382
Keesha Johnson, Registrar, College of the Ouachitas, One College Circle, Malvern, AR 72104

Cossatot Community College of the University of Arkansas
De Queen, Arkansas
www.cccua.edu   CB code: 3613

▸ Public 2-year community college
▸ Commuter campus in small town

General. Regionally accredited. Off-campus sites located in Nashville and Ashdown. **Enrollment:** 969 degree-seeking undergraduates. **Degrees:** 188 associate awarded. **Location:** 60 miles from Texarkana. **Calendar:** Semester, limited summer session. **Full-time faculty:** 37 total. **Part-time faculty:** 46 total. **Class size:** 69% < 20, 31% 20-39.

Student profile.

Out-of-state: 2%   25 or older: 38%

Transfer out. Colleges most students transferred to 2015: Henderson State University, Texas A&M - Texarkana, Arkansas Tech University, University of Central Arkansas, Southern Arkansas University.

Basis for selection. Open admission, but selective for some programs. Admission to nursing programs based upon test scores and previous course grades. **Home schooled:** Transcript of courses and grades required.

High school preparation. 22 units required. Required units include English 4, mathematics 4, social studies 2, history 1, science 3 (laboratory 2), foreign language 1 and academic electives 5.

2015-2016 Annual costs. Tuition/fees: $2,670; $3,030 out-of-district; $5,820 out-of-state. Per-credit charge: $65 in-district; $77 out-of-district; $170 out-of-state. Books/supplies: $1,492. Personal expenses: $2,699.

Financial aid. Need-based: Need-based aid available for part-time students. Work-study available nights, weekends and for part-time students. **Additional information:** Active or honorably discharged military and their dependents receive tuition discounts.

Application procedures. Admission: No deadline. No application fee. Admission notification on a rolling basis. **Financial aid:** Priority date 5/1; no closing date. FAFSA, institutional form required. Applicants notified on a rolling basis starting 3/1.

Academics. Special study options: Accelerated study, cooperative education, distance learning, double major, dual enrollment of high school students, ESL, exchange student, independent study, internships, liberal arts/career combination, student-designed major. Bachelor's degree programs available on campus. License preparation in nursing. **Credit/placement by examination:** AP, CLEP, institutional tests. 15 credit hours maximum toward associate degree. **Support services:** GED preparation and test center, learning center, remedial instruction, study skills assistance, tutoring.

Majors. Business: General, management information systems. **Communications technology:** Radio/TV. **Education:** Elementary, middle. **General:** Carpentry. **Health services:** Medical assistant, nursing (RN). **Liberal arts:** Arts/sciences. **Protective services:** Forensics, law enforcement admin. **Work/family studies:** Child care management.

Most popular majors. Business/marketing 13%, education 9%, health sciences 16%, liberal arts 55%.

Technology on campus. 95 workstations in library, computer center. Commuter students can connect to campus network. Online course registration, online library, helpline, wireless network available.

Student life. Freshman orientation: Available. Preregistration for classes offered. Course offered each semester. **Activities:** Student government, student newspaper, Baptist Collegiate Ministry, Phi Theta Kappa, journalism club, Arkansas Licensed Practical Nursing Association, Amnesty International, SkillsUSA.

Athletics. NAIA. **Intercollegiate:** Rodeo. **Team name:** Colts.

Student services. Adult student services, alcohol/substance abuse counseling, career counseling, services for economically disadvantaged, student employment services, financial aid counseling, minority student services, on-campus daycare, personal counseling, placement for graduates, veterans' counselor. **Physically disabled:** Services for visually, speech, hearing impaired. **Transfer:** Pre-admission transcript evaluation for new students. Transfer adviser, college fairs on campus for students transferring to 4-year colleges.

Contact. E-mail: ncowling@cccua.edu
Phone: (870) 584-4471 Toll-free number: (800) 844-4471
Fax: (870) 642-8766
Justin White, Director of Admissions, Cossatot Community College of the University of Arkansas, 183 College Drive, De Queen, AR 71832

Crowley's Ridge College
Paragould, Arkansas
www.crc.edu
CB code: 6131

♦ Private 2-year liberal arts college affiliated with the Church of Christ
♦ Residential campus in large town

General. Regionally accredited. **Enrollment:** 176 degree-seeking undergraduates. **Degrees:** 10 bachelor's, 15 associate awarded. **Location:** 23 miles from Jonesboro. **Calendar:** Semester, limited summer session. **Full-time faculty:** 12 total; 58% women. **Part-time faculty:** 7 total; 43% have terminal degrees, 43% women.

Transfer out. Colleges most students transferred to 2015: Arkansas State University, Williams Baptist College, Harding University, Freed-Hardeman University.

Basis for selection. Open admission. Placement in freshman composition and algebra determined by ACT and ASSET scores. Development courses required for students with ACT score under 19. ACT scores of under 16 require meeting with Director of Admissions. Interview required for applicants with less than 2.0 GPA and 15 ACT. **Home schooled:** Transcript of courses and grades required. **Learning Disabled:** Contact Dean of Students to determine what help is available.

2015-2016 Annual costs. Tuition/fees: $11,300. Room/board: $6,100. Books/supplies: $600.

Financial aid. Need-based: Work-study available nights, weekends and for part-time students. **Non-need-based:** Scholarships awarded for academics, athletics, leadership, music/drama.

Application procedures. Admission: Closing date 8/10. No application fee. Admission notification on a rolling basis. **Financial aid:** No deadline. FAFSA required. Applicants notified on a rolling basis starting 5/30.

Academics. Special study options: Dual enrollment of high school students, independent study. Bachelor's degree programs available on campus. **Credit/placement by examination:** AP, CLEP. 34 credit hours maximum toward associate degree. **Support services:** Remedial instruction, study skills assistance, tutoring.

Majors. Education: General. **Liberal arts:** Arts/sciences. **Philosophy/religion:** Religion.

Most popular majors. Liberal arts 88%, philosophy/religious studies 12%.

Technology on campus. 15 workstations in dormitories, library, computer center. Dormitories linked to campus network.

Student life. Freshman orientation: Available. Preregistration for classes offered. Takes place third week of August immediately before start of fall semester. **Policies:** Chapel attendance required. **Housing:** Guaranteed on-campus for all undergraduates. Single-sex dorms, apartments available. $100 nonrefundable deposit. **Activities:** Choral groups, drama, student government.

Athletics. NCCAA. **Intercollegiate:** Baseball M, basketball, softball W, volleyball W. **Intramural:** Basketball, football (non-tackle), softball, table tennis, tennis, volleyball. **Team name:** Pioneers.

Student services. Chaplain/spiritual director, financial aid counseling. **Transfer:** Pre-admission transcript evaluation for new students. College fairs on campus for students transferring to 4-year colleges.

Contact. E-mail: njoneshill@crc.edu
Phone: (870) 236-6901 ext. 14 Toll-free number: (800) 264-1096
Fax: (870) 236-7748
Nancy Joneshill, Admissions Director, Crowley's Ridge College, 100 College Drive, Paragould, AR 72450

East Arkansas Community College
Forrest City, Arkansas
www.eacc.edu
CB code: 0847

♦ Public 2-year community college
♦ Commuter campus in large town

General. Founded in 1973. Regionally accredited. **Enrollment:** 1,268 undergraduates. **Degrees:** 95 associate awarded. **Location:** 40 miles from Memphis, TN. **Calendar:** Semester, limited summer session. **Full-time faculty:** 33 total. **Part-time faculty:** 62 total. **Special facilities:** Fine arts center.

Student profile.

Out-of-state:	1%	25 or older:	47%

Transfer out. Colleges most students transferred to 2015: Arkansas State University.

Basis for selection. Open admission, but selective for some programs. COMPASS and ACT used in admissions process. Interview required for allied health. **Home schooled:** Transcript of courses and grades, state high school equivalency certificate required.

2015-2016 Annual costs. Tuition/fees: $2,790; $3,090 out-of-district; $3,600 out-of-state. Per-credit charge: $82 in-district; $92 out-of-district; $109 out-of-state. Books/supplies: $1,200. Personal expenses: $900.

Financial aid. All financial aid based on need. Need-based aid available for part-time students. Work-study available nights, weekends and for part-time students.

Application procedures. Admission: No deadline. No application fee. Admission notification on a rolling basis. **Financial aid:** Priority date 3/1, closing date 7/1. FAFSA required. Applicants notified on a rolling basis starting 5/15; must reply within 2 week(s) of notification.

Academics. Special study options: Cooperative education, distance learning, dual enrollment of high school students, honors, internships, liberal arts/career combination. Bachelor's degree programs available on campus. License preparation in nursing, paramedic, radiology. **Credit/placement by examination:** AP, CLEP, institutional tests. 12 credit hours maximum toward associate degree. **Support services:** Learning center, remedial instruction, tutoring.

Majors. Business: Administrative services, business admin, finance, management information systems. **Computer sciences:** Web page design. **Education:** Middle, multi-level teacher. **Health services:** EMT paramedic, medical assistant, medical radiologic technology/radiation therapy, nursing (RN), occupational therapy assistant. **Protective services:** Police science. **Work/family studies:** Child care management.

Technology on campus. 35 workstations in library, computer center. Commuter students can connect to campus network.

Student life. Freshman orientation: Available. Preregistration for classes offered. **Activities:** Choral groups, student government, student newspaper.

Athletics. Intramural: Basketball, softball, tennis, volleyball.

Student services. Career counseling, student employment services, health services, personal counseling, placement for graduates, veterans' counselor. **Physically disabled:** Services for visually, hearing impaired. **Transfer:** Transfer adviser, college fairs on campus for students transferring to 4-year colleges.

Contact. E-mail: admissions@eacc.edu
Phone: (870) 633-4480 ext. 300 Toll-free number: (877) 797-3222
Fax: (870) 633-3840
Sharon Collier, Director of Enrollment Management/IR/Admissions, East Arkansas Community College, 1700 Newcastle Road, Forrest City, AR 72335-2204

National Park College
Hot Springs, Arkansas
www.npcc.edu
CB code: 6243

♦ Public 2-year liberal arts and technical college
♦ Commuter campus in large town

General. Founded in 1973. Regionally accredited. Located in the Hot Springs National Park. **Enrollment:** 3,244 undergraduates. **Degrees:** 441 associate awarded. **Location:** 53 miles from Little Rock. **Calendar:** Semester, extensive summer session. **Full-time faculty:** 98 total. **Part-time faculty:**

119 total. **Class size:** 63% < 20, 37% 20-39, less than 1% 40-49, less than 1% 50-99.

Student profile.

Out-of-state: 1% **25 or older:** 56%

Transfer out. Colleges most students transferred to 2015: Henderson State University, Arkadelphia-University of Arkansas, University of Arkansas-Little Rock, University of Arkansas-Fayetteville.

Basis for selection. Open admission, but selective for some programs. Limited admission to allied health programs and nursing. Interview required for some health-related majors. **Home schooled:** State Mandated Notification to High School to be Home-Schooled.

High school preparation. College-preparatory program recommended. 18 units recommended. Recommended units include English 4, mathematics 4, social studies 3, history 2, science 3 (laboratory 3) and foreign language 2.

2015-2016 Annual costs. Tuition/fees: $3,160; $3,460 out-of-district; $4,540 out-of-state. Per-credit charge: $88 in-district; $98 out-of-district; $134 out-of-state. Books/supplies: $1,200. Personal expenses: $2,716.

Financial aid. Need-based: Need-based aid available for part-time students. Work-study available nights, weekends and for part-time students. **Non-need-based:** Scholarships awarded for academics, minority status, music/drama, state residency.

Application procedures. Admission: No deadline. No application fee. Application must be submitted online. Admission notification on a rolling basis beginning on or about 3/1. **Financial aid:** Priority date 7/1; no closing date. FAFSA, institutional form required. Applicants notified on a rolling basis.

Academics. Special study options: Cooperative education, cross-registration, distance learning, double major, dual enrollment of high school students, honors, independent study, internships, liberal arts/career combination, student-designed major. Bachelor's degree programs available on campus. License preparation in aviation, nursing, paramedic, radiology, real estate. **Credit/placement by examination:** AP, CLEP, institutional tests. 18 credit hours maximum toward associate degree. **Support services:** Learning center, reduced course load, remedial instruction, study skills assistance, tutoring, writing center.

Majors. Business: General, accounting technology, administrative services, hospitality admin, management information systems. **Education:** Multi-level teacher. **Health services:** Clinical lab technology, EMT paramedic, health information technology, medical assistant, medical radiologic technology/radiation therapy, medical secretary, nursing (RN), pharmacy assistant, respiratory therapy technology. **Liberal arts:** Arts/sciences. **Parks/recreation:** General. **Protective services:** Police science. **Visual/performing arts:** Commercial/advertising art. **Work/family studies:** Child care management.

Most popular majors. Business/marketing 9%, education 8%, health sciences 23%, liberal arts 49%.

Technology on campus. 470 workstations in library, computer center, student center. Online library available.

Student life. Freshman orientation: Mandatory. Preregistration for classes offered. 2 day orientation, held one week prior to beginning of classes. **Activities:** Choral groups, dance, literary magazine, music ensembles, student government, student newspaper, Baptist student union, Black Awareness, Association for Barrier Awareness.

Athletics. Intramural: Baseball, basketball, bowling, skin diving, softball, table tennis, tennis, volleyball.

Student services. Adult student services, career counseling, services for economically disadvantaged, student employment services, financial aid counseling, health services, personal counseling, placement for graduates, veterans' counselor. **Physically disabled:** Services for visually, speech, hearing impaired. **Transfer:** Pre-admission transcript evaluation for new students. Transfer adviser, college fairs on campus for students transferring to 4-year colleges.

Contact. E-mail: admissions@npcc.edu
Phone: (501) 760-4363 Toll-free number: (800) 761-1825
Fax: (501) 760-4100
Holly Garrett, Director of Student Affairs, National Park College, 101 College Drive, Hot Springs, AR 71913

North Arkansas College
Harrison, Arkansas
www.northark.edu

CB code: 1423

▸ Public 2-year community and technical college
▸ Commuter campus in large town

General. Founded in 1974. Regionally accredited. **Enrollment:** 2,157 undergraduates. **Degrees:** 351 associate awarded. **Location:** 75 miles from Fayetteville. **Calendar:** Semester, limited summer session. **Full-time faculty:** 65 total. **Part-time faculty:** 79 total. **Class size:** 59% < 20, 39% 20-39, 1% 40-49, 1% 50-99. **Special facilities:** Community health resource center, lyric theater.

Student profile.

Out-of-state: 2% **25 or older:** 44%

Transfer out. Colleges most students transferred to 2015: Arkansas Tech University, University of Arkansas, University of Central Arkansas, Franklin University, Ozark Technical Community College.

Basis for selection. Open admission, but selective for some programs. Allied health programs require separate application. To receive college credit for CLEP exams, student must score at 50th percentile or higher, based on national norms, and may not have earned college credit nor have ever been enrolled in course for which he/she is writing the test.

High school preparation. College-preparatory program required.

2015-2016 Annual costs. Tuition/fees: $2,550; $3,270 out-of-district; $5,400 out-of-state. Books/supplies: $1,088. Personal expenses: $2,337.

Financial aid. Need-based: Need-based aid available for part-time students. Work-study available nights, weekends and for part-time students. **Non-need-based:** Scholarships awarded for academics, athletics, state residency.

Application procedures. Admission: No deadline. No application fee. Application must be submitted on paper. Admission notification on a rolling basis. **Financial aid:** Priority date 5/1; no closing date. FAFSA, institutional form required. Applicants notified on a rolling basis starting 5/1.

Academics. Special study options: Distance learning, dual enrollment of high school students, ESL, honors, independent study, internships, student-designed major. Bachelor's degree programs available on campus. License preparation in nursing, paramedic, radiology, real estate. **Credit/placement by examination:** AP, CLEP, institutional tests. 20 credit hours maximum toward associate degree. Only one-third of the credit hours for a degree can be from Advanced Placement, CLEP, the College Now Program, Challenge Test, various other examinations, or independent studies. Credit for Advanced Placement, CLEP, or Professional Certification Examinations will not be posted to an academic record until the student has successfully completed at least 12 semester credit hours of work. **Support services:** GED preparation and test center, learning center, pre-admission summer program, remedial instruction, study skills assistance, tutoring, writing center.

Majors. Business: General. **Computer sciences:** General. **Education:** Multi-level teacher. **Health services:** Clinical lab technology, EMT paramedic, medical radiologic technology/radiation therapy, nursing (RN), surgical technology. **Liberal arts:** Arts/sciences. **Protective services:** Forensics, law enforcement admin.

Most popular majors. Business/marketing 16%, computer/information sciences 8%, health sciences 30%, liberal arts 37%.

Technology on campus. 250 workstations in library, computer center. Online course registration, online library, wireless network available.

Student life. Freshman orientation: Available. Preregistration for classes offered. **Activities:** Drama, literary magazine, student government, Baptist student union, Future Farmers of America, Health Occupations Students of America, Phi Beta Lambda, Phi Theta Kappa, Pioneer Hands club, Rad Tech club, Skills USA, student nurses association.

Athletics. NJCAA. **Intercollegiate:** Baseball M, basketball, cheerleading W, rodeo, softball W. **Intramural:** Archery, badminton, basketball, football (non-tackle) M, golf, racquetball, softball, table tennis, tennis, volleyball, weight lifting. **Team name:** Pioneers.

Student services. Adult student services, alcohol/substance abuse counseling, career counseling, services for economically disadvantaged, student employment services, financial aid counseling, placement for graduates, veterans' counselor. **Physically disabled:** Services for visually, speech, hearing impaired. **Transfer:** Pre-admission transcript evaluation for new students.

Transfer adviser, college fairs on campus for students transferring to 4-year colleges.

Contact. E-mail: admissions@northark.edu
Phone: (870) 391-3505 Toll-free number: (800) 679-6622
Fax: (870) 391-3339
Charla Jennings, Director of Enrollment Services, North Arkansas College, 1515 Pioneer Drive, Harrison, AR 72601

Northwest Arkansas Community College
Bentonville, Arkansas
www.nwacc.edu   CB code: 7101

- Public 2-year community college
- Commuter campus in small city

General. Regionally accredited. **Enrollment:** 5,205 degree-seeking undergraduates. **Degrees:** 780 associate awarded. **ROTC:** Army, Air Force. **Location:** 30 miles from Fayetteville. **Calendar:** Semester, extensive summer session. **Class size:** 51% < 20, 49% 20-39.

Student profile.

Out-of-state:	3%	25 or older:	38%

Transfer out. Colleges most students transferred to 2015: University of Arkansas, John Brown University.

Basis for selection. Open admission, but selective for some programs. Additional requirements for nursing, physical therapy, respiratory therapy, emergency medical technician/paramedic programs.

High school preparation. College-preparatory program recommended. 22 units recommended. Recommended units include English 4, mathematics 4, social studies 3, science 3 (laboratory 2), foreign language 2 and academic electives 4.

2015-2016 Annual costs. Tuition/fees: $3,208; $4,633 out-of-district; $4,708 out-of-state. Per-credit charge: $75 in-district; $122.5 out-of-district; $125 out-of-state. Books/supplies: $1,200. Personal expenses: $900.

Financial aid. Need-based: Need-based aid available for part-time students. Work-study available nights, weekends and for part-time students. **Non-need-based:** Scholarships awarded for academics, leadership, music/drama, state residency.

Application procedures. Admission: No deadline. $10 fee. Admission notification on a rolling basis. **Financial aid:** Priority date 4/1; no closing date. FAFSA, institutional form required. Applicants notified on a rolling basis starting 4/1; must reply within 2 week(s) of notification.

Academics. Special study options: Distance learning, double major, dual enrollment of high school students, ESL, honors, independent study, internships, liberal arts/career combination, teacher certification program, weekend college. License preparation in nursing, paramedic, physical therapy. **Credit/placement by examination:** AP, CLEP. 15 credit hours maximum toward associate degree. **Support services:** GED preparation and test center, learning center, remedial instruction, study skills assistance, tutoring, writing center.

Majors. Business: Accounting, administrative services, banking/financial services, business admin. **Computer sciences:** General, LAN/WAN management, programming, webmaster. **Education:** Early childhood, middle. **Engineering:** Environmental. **Health services:** EMT paramedic, nursing (RN), physical therapy assistant, respiratory therapy technology. **Liberal arts:** Arts/sciences. **Protective services:** Criminal justice, firefighting, forensics, homeland security, law enforcement admin. **Visual/performing arts:** Commercial/advertising art. **Work/family studies:** Child care management.

Technology on campus. 300 workstations in library, computer center, student center. Commuter students can connect to campus network. Online course registration, online library, helpline, wireless network available.

Student life. Freshman orientation: Mandatory. Preregistration for classes offered. **Activities:** Jazz band, campus ministries, choral groups, drama, international student organizations, literary magazine, music ensembles, musical theater, student government, student newspaper, symphony orchestra.

Athletics. Intramural: Basketball, bowling, golf, soccer, softball, table tennis, volleyball.

Student services. Adult student services, alcohol/substance abuse counseling, career counseling, financial aid counseling, personal counseling, placement for graduates, veterans' counselor. **Transfer:** Transfer center, transfer adviser, college fairs on campus for students transferring to 4-year colleges.

Contact. E-mail: admissions@nwacc.edu
Phone: (479) 619-4324 Toll-free number: (800) 995-6922
Fax: (479) 619-2229
Zac Pharr, Director of Advising and Admissions, Northwest Arkansas Community College, One College Drive, Bentonville, AR 72712

Ozarka College
Melbourne, Arkansas
www.ozarka.edu   CB code: 3621

- Public 2-year community and technical college
- Commuter campus in rural community

General. Regionally accredited. **Enrollment:** 1,326 degree-seeking undergraduates. **Degrees:** 229 associate awarded. **Location:** 125 miles from Little Rock; 160 miles from Memphis, TN. **Calendar:** Semester, limited summer session. **Full-time faculty:** 38 total. **Part-time faculty:** 60 total.

Transfer out. Colleges most students transferred to 2015: Arkansas State University, Lyon College, University of Arkansas, University of Central Arkansas, Williams Baptist College.

Basis for selection. Open admission, but selective for some programs. Admission to licensed practical nursing, Registered Nursing, automotive technology and culinary arts programs based on test scores, and/or essay, interview. **Adult students:** ACT/ASSET/COMPASS/SAT accepted for placement in math and English. **Home schooled:** Transcript of courses and grades required.

2015-2016 Annual costs. Tuition/fees: $3,445; $6,385 out-of-state. Per-credit charge: $88 in-state; $186 out-of-state. Books/supplies: $800.

Financial aid. Need-based: Need-based aid available for part-time students. Work-study available nights, weekends and for part-time students.

Application procedures. Admission: No deadline. No application fee. Admission notification on a rolling basis. **Financial aid:** No deadline. FAFSA required. Applicants notified on a rolling basis; must reply within 2 week(s) of notification.

Academics. Special study options: Cooperative education, distance learning, dual enrollment of high school students, liberal arts/career combination. Bachelor's degree programs available on campus. License preparation in aviation, nursing. **Credit/placement by examination:** AP, CLEP, institutional tests. 36 credit hours maximum toward associate degree. **Support services:** GED preparation and test center, learning center, remedial instruction, study skills assistance, tutoring.

Majors. Business: Business admin, information resources management. **Education:** General, elementary, middle. **Health services:** Licensed practical nurse, medical transcription. **Liberal arts:** Arts/sciences. **Protective services:** Law enforcement admin.

Technology on campus. 175 workstations in library, computer center. Commuter students can connect to campus network. Online course registration, helpline, wireless network available.

Student life. Freshman orientation: Mandatory. Preregistration for classes offered. **Activities:** Student government.

Student services. Chaplain/spiritual director, career counseling, services for economically disadvantaged, financial aid counseling, on-campus daycare, veterans' counselor, women's services. **Transfer:** Pre-admission transcript evaluation for new students. College fairs on campus for students transferring to 4-year colleges.

Contact. E-mail: admissions@ozarka.edu
Phone: (870) 368-2024 Toll-free number: (800) 821-4335 ext. 2024
Fax: (870) 368-2091
Dylan Mowery, Director of Admissions, Ozarka College, 218 College Drive, Melbourne, AR 72556-0010

Phillips Community College of the University of Arkansas
Helena, Arkansas
www.pccua.edu   CB code: 6583

- Public 2-year community college
- Commuter campus in large town

General. Founded in 1965. Regionally accredited. Campuses in Helena, Phillips County, Stuttgart, DeWitt. **Enrollment:** 708 degree-seeking undergraduates. **Degrees:** 167 associate awarded. **Location:** 117 miles from Little Rock. **Calendar:** Semester, limited summer session. **Full-time faculty:** 78 total; 4% have terminal degrees, 17% minority, 73% women. **Part-time faculty:** 54 total; 28% minority, 70% women. **Class size:** 90% < 20, 9% 20-39, less than 1% 40-49, less than 1% 50-99. **Special facilities:** Performing arts center, Grand Prairie Center.

Student profile.

Out-of-state: 3% 25 or older: 49%

Basis for selection. Open admission, but selective for some programs. Additional requirements for nursing program. Interview required of applicants with no high school transcript or test scores. **Adult students:** ASSET or COMPASS test required for students taking English or math. **Home schooled:** Transcript of courses and grades, state high school equivalency certificate required.

2015-2016 Annual costs. Tuition/fees: $2,593; $2,968 out-of-district; $4,325 out-of-state. Per-credit charge: $67 in-district; $80 out-of-district; $125 out-of-state. Books/supplies: $1,100. Personal expenses: $2,250.

Financial aid. All financial aid based on need. Need-based aid available for part-time students. Work-study available nights, weekends and for part-time students. **Additional information:** Tuition waivers given to firefighters and law enforcement officers.

Application procedures. Admission: No deadline. No application fee. Admission notification on a rolling basis. **Financial aid:** Priority date 4/12, closing date 6/12. FAFSA required. Applicants notified on a rolling basis starting 4/12; must reply within 2 week(s) of notification.

Academics. Special study options: Distance learning, dual enrollment of high school students, honors, independent study, internships, weekend college. Bachelor's degree programs available on campus. License preparation in nursing. **Credit/placement by examination:** AP, CLEP, institutional tests. 30 credit hours maximum toward associate degree. **Support services:** GED preparation and test center, learning center, remedial instruction, study skills assistance, tutoring.

Majors. Biology: General. **Business:** General, business admin, office technology. **Communications technology:** Graphic/printing. **Computer sciences:** Computer science, information technology, LAN/WAN management. **Education:** General, early childhood, elementary. **Engineering:** General. **English:** English lit, rhetoric/composition. **Health services:** Nursing (RN), phlebotomy. **Liberal arts:** Arts/sciences. **Math:** General. **Physical sciences:** Chemistry, physics. **Protective services:** Forensics, law enforcement admin. **Psychology:** General. **Social sciences:** General. **Visual/performing arts:** Printmaking.

Most popular majors. Business/marketing 12%, computer/information sciences 9%, education 20%, health sciences 13%, liberal arts 36%.

Technology on campus. 275 workstations in library, computer center, student center. Commuter students can connect to campus network. Online course registration, wireless network available.

Student life. Freshman orientation: Mandatory. Preregistration for classes offered. **Activities:** Choral groups, dance, drama, musical theater, Baptist Collegiate Ministries, Phi Theta Kappa, Arkansas Licensed Practical Nurses Association, National Student Nurses Association, Young Democrats, book club.

Athletics. Intramural: Archery, badminton, basketball, football (non-tackle) M, golf, soccer, softball, table tennis, tennis, volleyball.

Student services. Adult student services, career counseling, services for economically disadvantaged, student employment services, financial aid counseling, personal counseling, placement for graduates, veterans' counselor. **Physically disabled:** Services for visually, hearing impaired. **Transfer:** Transfer adviser, college fairs on campus for students transferring to 4-year colleges.

Contact. E-mail: lboone@pccua.edu
Phone: (870) 338-6474 ext. 1336 Fax: (870) 338-7542
Scott Post, Vice Chancellor for Student Services/Registrar, Phillips Community College of the University of Arkansas, 1000 Campus Drive, Helena, AR 72342

Pulaski Technical College
North Little Rock, Arkansas
www.pulaskitech.edu   CB code: 3622

- Public 2-year community and technical college
- Commuter campus in small city

General. Regionally accredited. **Enrollment:** 6,844 degree-seeking undergraduates. **Degrees:** 1,197 associate awarded. **Location:** 4 miles from Little Rock. **Calendar:** Semester, extensive summer session. **Full-time faculty:** 179 total; 10% minority, 55% women. **Part-time faculty:** 344 total; 3% have terminal degrees, 21% minority, 57% women. **Class size:** 55% < 20, 45% 20-39.

Student profile.

Out-of-state: 1% 25 or older: 60%

Transfer out. Colleges most students transferred to 2015: University of Arkansas at Little Rock, University of Central Arkansas.

Basis for selection. Open admission, but selective for some programs. Additional requirements for dental assisting, practical nursing, respiratory therapy, occupational therapy assistant and military technology programs. **Adult students:** COMPASS or ACT scores may be used for placement.

2015-2016 Annual costs. Tuition/fees: $4,590; $6,330 out-of-state. Per-credit charge: $110 in-state; $168 out-of-state. Books/supplies: $1,225. Personal expenses: $2,790.

Financial aid. Need-based: Need-based aid available for part-time students. Work-study available nights, weekends and for part-time students.

Application procedures. Admission: No deadline. No application fee. Admission notification on a rolling basis. **Financial aid:** Closing date 5/15. FAFSA, institutional form required. Applicants notified on a rolling basis starting 5/1; must reply within 2 week(s) of notification.

Academics. Special study options: Cooperative education, distance learning, double major, dual enrollment of high school students, external degree, internships, liberal arts/career combination, weekend college. License preparation in aviation, dental hygiene, nursing, occupational therapy. **Credit/placement by examination:** AP, CLEP, institutional tests. **Support services:** Learning center, pre-admission summer program, remedial instruction, study skills assistance, tutoring.

Majors. Business: General, hospitality admin, management information systems. **Education:** Early childhood. **Health services:** Occupational therapy assistant, respiratory therapy technology. **Liberal arts:** Arts/sciences. **Protective services:** Forensics, law enforcement admin. **Work/family studies:** Child care management.

Most popular majors. Business/marketing 19%, engineering/engineering technologies 17%, health sciences 8%, liberal arts 11%, personal/culinary services 6%, security/protective services 6%, trade and industry 20%.

Technology on campus. 281 workstations in library, computer center, student center. Commuter students can connect to campus network. Online course registration, online library, helpline, wireless network available.

Student life. Freshman orientation: Available. Preregistration for classes offered. Online orientation is ongoing. **Activities:** Campus ministries, choral groups, literary magazine, student government, Metro student ministries, Culture Shock, philosophy club, student ambassadors, Phi Theta Kappa, College Democrats, Fusion, Phi Beta Lambda.

Student services. Adult student services, career counseling, services for economically disadvantaged, student employment services, financial aid counseling, minority student services, personal counseling, veterans' counselor. **Physically disabled:** Services for visually, hearing impaired. **Transfer:** Transfer adviser, college fairs on campus for students transferring to 4-year colleges.

Contact. E-mail: admissions@pulaskitech.edu
Phone: (501) 812-2231 Fax: (501) 812-2316
Clark Atkins, Director of Admissions, Pulaski Technical College, 3000 West Scenic Drive, North Little Rock, AR 72118-3347

Remington College: Little Rock
Little Rock, Arkansas
http://little-rock.remingtoncollege.edu

- Private 2-year technical college
- Commuter campus in very large city

General. Accredited by ACCSC. **Enrollment:** 383 undergraduates. **Degrees:** 8 associate awarded. **Calendar:** Quarter. **Full-time faculty:** 8 total. **Part-time faculty:** 6 total.

Basis for selection. Open admission, but selective for some programs. Wonderlic Exam required for admission.

2015-2016 Annual costs. Associate of Applied Science in Business Administration: $33,900; Associate of Applied Science in Criminal Justice: $33,900. All costs are subject to change.

Financial aid. Need-based: Work-study available nights, weekends and for part-time students.

Application procedures. Admission: No deadline. $50 fee. Admission notification on a rolling basis. **Financial aid:** No deadline. FAFSA required.

Academics. Credit/placement by examination: AP, CLEP.

Majors. Protective services: Law enforcement admin.

Student life. Activities: American Association of Medical Assistants, National Technical Honor Society, Professional Business Leaders of America.

Student services. Career counseling, financial aid counseling.

Contact. E-mail: admissions@remingtoncollege.edu
Phone: (501) 303-4385
Jonathan Porter, Director of Admissions, Remington College: Little Rock, 19 Remington Drive, Little Rock, AR 72204

Rich Mountain Community College
Mena, Arkansas
www.rmcc.edu   **CB code: 0226**

▶ Public 2-year community college
▶ Commuter campus in small town

General. Founded in 1983. Regionally accredited. **Enrollment:** 500 degree-seeking undergraduates; 429 non-degree-seeking students. **Degrees:** 88 associate awarded. **Location:** 85 miles from Fort Smith, 80 miles from Hot Springs. **Calendar:** Semester, limited summer session. **Full-time faculty:** 33 total; 12% have terminal degrees, 64% women. **Part-time faculty:** 35 total; 9% have terminal degrees, 63% women. **Class size:** 84% < 20, 16% 20-39.

Student profile. Among degree-seeking undergraduates, 147 enrolled as first-time, first-year students, 31 transferred in from other institutions.

Part-time:	33%	Native American:	3%
Out-of-state:	10%	Multi-racial, non-Hispanic:	3%
Women:	70%	International:	1%
Asian American:	1%	25 or older:	60%
Hispanic/Latino:	6%		

Basis for selection. Open admission, but selective for some programs. Limited admission to licensed practical nurse and registered nurse programs.

2015-2016 Annual costs. Tuition/fees: $3,060; $3,480 out-of-district; $6,750 out-of-state. Per-credit charge: $72 in-district; $86 out-of-district; $195 out-of-state.

2014-2015 Financial aid. Need-based: 99% of total undergraduate aid awarded as scholarships/grants, 1% as loans/jobs. Need-based aid available for part-time students. Work-study available nights, weekends and for part-time students. **Non-need-based:** Scholarships awarded for academics.

Application procedures. Admission: No deadline. No application fee. Admission notification on a rolling basis. **Financial aid:** Priority date 7/1; no closing date. FAFSA, institutional form required. Applicants notified on a rolling basis starting 6/1; must reply within 2 week(s) of notification.

Academics. Special study options: Cooperative education, distance learning, dual enrollment of high school students, external degree, internships. License preparation in nursing. **Credit/placement by examination:** AP, CLEP, institutional tests. 30 credit hours maximum toward associate degree. **Support services:** GED preparation and test center, remedial instruction, study skills assistance, tutoring.

Majors. Business: General, information resources management. **Health services:** Nursing (RN). **Liberal arts:** Arts/sciences.

Most popular majors. Health sciences 15%, interdisciplinary studies 23%, liberal arts 51%.

Technology on campus. 73 workstations in library, computer center. Commuter students can connect to campus network. Wireless network available.

Student life. Freshman orientation: Mandatory. Preregistration for classes offered. **Activities:** Drama, radio station, student government, TV station, Baptist student union.

Student services. Adult student services, career counseling, services for economically disadvantaged, financial aid counseling, personal counseling, veterans' counselor. **Physically disabled:** Services for visually, hearing impaired. **Transfer:** Pre-admission transcript evaluation for new students. Transfer adviser, college fairs on campus for students transferring to 4-year colleges.

Contact. E-mail: wmcdaniel@rmcc.edu
Phone: (479) 394-7622 ext. 1440 Fax: (479) 394-2760
Wendy McDaniel, Director of Admissions, Rich Mountain Community College, 1100 College Drive, Mena, AR 71953

South Arkansas Community College
El Dorado, Arkansas
www.southark.edu   **CB code: 1550**

▶ Public 2-year community and junior college
▶ Commuter campus in large town

General. Founded in 1975. Regionally accredited. **Enrollment:** 1,183 degree-seeking undergraduates; 354 non-degree-seeking students. **Degrees:** 164 associate awarded. **Location:** 115 miles from Little Rock. **Calendar:** Semester, limited summer session. **Full-time faculty:** 58 total. **Part-time faculty:** 48 total.

Student profile. Among degree-seeking undergraduates, 18% enrolled in a transfer program, 54% enrolled in a vocational program, 258 enrolled as first-time, first-year students.

Part-time:	49%	African American:	39%
Out-of-state:	9%	Hispanic/Latino:	6%
Women:	76%	25 or older:	40%

Transfer out. 69% of students enrolled in the transfer program go on to 4-year colleges. **Colleges most students transferred to 2015:** Southern Arkansas University, Louisiana Tech, University of Arkansas at Monticello.

Basis for selection. Open admission, but selective for some programs. **Home schooled:** Transcript of courses and grades, state high school equivalency certificate required.

High school preparation. College-preparatory program recommended.

2015-2016 Annual costs. Tuition/fees: $2,990; $3,380 out-of-district; $5,660 out-of-state. Per-credit charge: $83 in-district; $96 out-of-district; $172 out-of-state. Books/supplies: $1,000. Personal expenses: $643.

Financial aid. Need-based: Need-based aid available for part-time students. Work-study available nights, weekends and for part-time students.

Application procedures. Admission: Priority date 7/31; no deadline. No application fee. Admission notification on a rolling basis. **Financial aid:** Closing date 7/1. FAFSA, institutional form required. Applicants notified on a rolling basis starting 7/1; must reply within 2 week(s) of notification.

Academics. Special study options: Distance learning, dual enrollment of high school students, liberal arts/career combination. License preparation in nursing, occupational therapy, paramedic, physical therapy, radiology. **Credit/placement by examination:** AP, CLEP, IB, institutional tests. 30 credit hours maximum toward associate degree. **Support services:** GED preparation and test center, learning center, reduced course load, remedial instruction, study skills assistance, tutoring.

Majors. Business: General, administrative services, business admin. **Education:** General, secondary. **Health services:** Clinical lab technology, EMT paramedic, medical radiologic technology/radiation therapy, nursing (RN), occupational therapy assistant, physical therapy assistant, radiologic technology/medical imaging, radiologist assistant, respiratory therapy assistant, surgical technology. **Liberal arts:** Arts/sciences. **Protective services:** Police science.

Most popular majors. Liberal arts 26%, security/protective services 8%, trade and industry 47%.

Technology on campus. Online course registration, student web hosting, wireless network available.

Student life. Freshman orientation: Available. Preregistration for classes offered. **Activities:** Choral groups, literary magazine, Phi Beta Lambda, Phi Theta Kappa, student leadership group.

Student services. Adult student services, career counseling, services for economically disadvantaged, student employment services, financial aid counseling, personal counseling, veterans' counselor. **Physically disabled:**

Services for visually, speech, hearing impaired. **Transfer:** Transfer adviser, college fairs on campus for students transferring to 4-year colleges.

Contact. E-mail: registrar@southark.edu
Phone: (870) 862-8131 Toll-free number: (800) 955-2289
Fax: (870) 864-7137
Dean Inman, Dean of Enrollment Services, South Arkansas Community College, Box 7010, El Dorado, AR 71731-7010

Southeast Arkansas College
Pine Bluff, Arkansas
www.seark.edu   CB code: 3624

▶ Public 2-year community college
▶ Commuter campus in small city

General. Regionally accredited. **Enrollment:** 1,291 degree-seeking undergraduates. **Degrees:** 128 associate awarded. **Location:** 42 miles from Little Rock. **Calendar:** Semester, limited summer session. **Full-time faculty:** 42 total. **Part-time faculty:** 101 total. **Class size:** 73% < 20, 27% 20-39, less than 1% 40-49, less than 1% 50-99.

Transfer out. Colleges most students transferred to 2015: University of Arkansas at Pine Bluff, University of Arkansas at Monticello, University of Arkansas at Little Rock.

Basis for selection. Open admission, but selective for some programs. Additional requirements for some health programs. ACT, ASSET or COMPASS required for placement. **Learning Disabled:** Learning disability must be officially documented.

High school preparation. Recommended units include English 4, mathematics 2, social studies 2, history 2, science 2 and foreign language 1.

2015-2016 Annual costs. Tuition/fees: $3,070; $5,590 out-of-state. Personal expenses: $4,200.

Financial aid. Need-based: Need-based aid available for part-time students. Work-study available nights, weekends and for part-time students. **Non-need-based:** Scholarships awarded for academics, leadership, state residency.

Application procedures. Admission: No deadline. No application fee in-state; $164 out-of-state. Application must be submitted on paper. **Financial aid:** Priority date 6/1; no closing date. FAFSA required. Applicants notified on a rolling basis starting 5/1; must reply within 2 week(s) of notification.

Academics. Special study options: Distance learning, dual enrollment of high school students, independent study, internships. License preparation in nursing, paramedic, radiology. **Credit/placement by examination:** AP, CLEP, institutional tests. 15 credit hours maximum toward associate degree. Credit awarded through challenge exams. **Support services:** Learning center, remedial instruction, study skills assistance, tutoring.

Majors. Business: General, management information systems. **Computer sciences:** General, networking. **Education:** Multi-level teacher. **Health services:** EMT paramedic, medical radiologic technology/radiation therapy, nursing (RN), respiratory therapy technology, surgical technology. **Liberal arts:** Arts/sciences. **Protective services:** Criminal justice, forensics, law enforcement admin. **Work/family studies:** Child care service.

Most popular majors. Business/marketing 12%, health sciences 21%, liberal arts 41%, security/protective services 12%.

Technology on campus. 400 workstations in library, computer center. Commuter students can connect to campus network. Wireless network available.

Student life. Freshman orientation: Available. Preregistration for classes offered. One-hour program held one weekday morning and one weekday evening before start of classes. **Activities:** Campus ministries, student government.

Student services. Adult student services, alcohol/substance abuse counseling, career counseling, services for economically disadvantaged, student employment services, financial aid counseling, personal counseling, placement for graduates, veterans' counselor. **Physically disabled:** Services for visually, speech, hearing impaired. **Transfer:** Pre-admission transcript evaluation for new students. College fairs on campus for students transferring to 4-year colleges.

Contact. E-mail: bdunn@seark.edu
Phone: (870) 850-8605
Barbara Dunn, Admissions and Enrollment Management Coordinator, Southeast Arkansas College, 1900 Hazel Street, Pine Bluff, AR 71603

Southern Arkansas University Tech
Camden, Arkansas
www.sautech.edu   CB code: 6704

▶ Public 2-year community and technical college
▶ Commuter campus in large town

General. Founded in 1967. Regionally accredited. **Enrollment:** 697 degree-seeking undergraduates; 953 non-degree-seeking students. **Degrees:** 147 associate awarded. **Location:** 90 miles from Little Rock. **Calendar:** Semester, limited summer session. **Full-time faculty:** 37 total. **Part-time faculty:** 74 total. **Class size:** 81% < 20, 18% 20-39, less than 1% 40-49. **Special facilities:** Fire training academy, environmental academy, law enforcement academy, career technical academy, business and industry center, welding academy. **Partnerships:** Formal partnerships with area businesses/industries and high schools.

Student profile. Among degree-seeking undergraduates, 27% enrolled in a transfer program, 73% enrolled in a vocational program, 1% already have a bachelor's degree or higher, 174 enrolled as first-time, first-year students, 115 transferred in from other institutions.

Part-time:	29%	Hispanic/Latino:	2%
Out-of-state:	2%	Multi-racial, non-Hispanic:	4%
Women:	48%	25 or older:	28%
African American:	34%	Live on campus:	2%

Transfer out. Colleges most students transferred to 2015: Southern Arkansas University, Henderson State University, University of Arkansas at Monticello, University of Central Arkansas, South Arkansas Community College.

Basis for selection. Open admission, but selective for some programs. Additional application and testing for Practical Nursing program; additional testing for Welding Academy. This institution is an open-admissions institution. **Home schooled:** State high school equivalency certificate required. Applicants must take the GED test.

High school preparation. College-preparatory program recommended. 23 units recommended. Recommended units include English 4, mathematics 4, social studies 2, history 2, science 3, foreign language 2 and academic electives 6.

2015-2016 Annual costs. Tuition/fees: $3,240; $4,680 out-of-state. Room only: $1,300. Books/supplies: $1,600. Personal expenses: $4,433.

Financial aid. Need-based: Need-based aid available for part-time students. Work-study available nights, weekends and for part-time students. **Non-need-based:** Scholarships awarded for academics, state residency.

Application procedures. Admission: Priority date 4/15; deadline 6/1 (postmark date). No application fee. Admission notification on a rolling basis. **Financial aid:** Priority date 6/1; no closing date. FAFSA required. Applicants notified on a rolling basis starting 5/1.

Academics. Special study options: Distance learning, double major, dual enrollment of high school students, honors, independent study, internships. Articulation agreements for Nursing Assistant and Practical Nursing programs. Bachelor's degree programs available on campus. License preparation in aviation, nursing. **Credit/placement by examination:** AP, CLEP, institutional tests. 15 credit hours maximum toward associate degree. **Support services:** GED preparation and test center, learning center, pre-admission summer program, remedial instruction, study skills assistance, tutoring, writing center.

Majors. Business: Business admin, office management. **Computer sciences:** General. **Education:** Multi-level teacher. **Protective services:** Fire services admin, firefighting. **Work/family studies:** Child care service.

Most popular majors. Business/marketing 15%, computer/information sciences 12%, interdisciplinary studies 37%, liberal arts 15%, trade and industry 11%.

Technology on campus. 250 workstations in library, computer center. Dormitories wired for high-speed internet access and linked to campus network. Commuter students can connect to campus network. Online course registration, online library, helpline, repair service, wireless network available.

Student life. Freshman orientation: Mandatory. Preregistration for classes offered. 8 half-day programs in July or early August. **Housing:** Apartments available. $100 partly refundable deposit, deadline 7/15. Off-campus housing is available. **Activities:** Campus ministries, drama, radio station, student government, TV station, Phi Beta Lambda, Phi Theta Kappa, aviation club, multimedia graphics club, multimedia film/video club, computer club, electronics club, multi-cultural club, Student Ambassadors, Student Leadership Team.

Athletics. Intramural: Basketball, football (non-tackle), soccer, softball, tennis, volleyball, weight lifting. **Team name:** Varmits.

Student services. Adult student services, alcohol/substance abuse counseling, chaplain/spiritual director, career counseling, services for economically disadvantaged, student employment services, financial aid counseling, health services, minority student services, on-campus daycare, personal counseling, placement for graduates, veterans' counselor. **Physically disabled:** Services for visually, speech, hearing impaired. **Transfer:** Re-entry adviser, pre-admission transcript evaluation for new students. Transfer center, transfer adviser, college fairs on campus for students transferring to 4-year colleges.

Contact. E-mail: lsmith@sautech.edu
Phone: (870) 574-4558 Fax: (870) 574-4478
Patricia Sindle, Director, Enrollment Services, Southern Arkansas University Tech, PO Box 3499, Camden, AR 71711-1599

University of Arkansas: Community College at Batesville

Batesville, Arkansas
www.uaccb.edu   CB code: 3628

▶ Public 2-year community college
▶ Commuter campus in small town

General. Regionally accredited. **Enrollment:** 1,090 degree-seeking undergraduates. **Degrees:** 209 associate awarded. **Location:** 90 miles from Little Rock. **Calendar:** Semester, limited summer session. **Full-time faculty:** 43 total. **Part-time faculty:** 79 total.

Transfer out. Colleges most students transferred to 2015: Lyon College, Arkansas State University, University of Arkansas, University of Central Arkansas, Arkansas Tech University.

Basis for selection. Open admission, but selective for some programs. In accordance with Arkansas state law, students in technical certificate and associate degree programs must have 15 ACT, or 63 COMPASS Reading, or 36 ASSET Reading. Admission to nursing program based on GPA in prerequisite courses and nursing entrance exam. **Home schooled:** Transcript of courses and grades required.

High school preparation. College-preparatory program recommended.

2015-2016 Annual costs. Tuition/fees: $2,850; $3,240 out-of-district; $5,220 out-of-state. Per-credit charge: $70 in-district; $83 out-of-district; $149 out-of-state. Books/supplies: $1,200. Personal expenses: $2,100.

Financial aid. All financial aid based on need. Work-study available nights, weekends and for part-time students.

Application procedures. Admission: No deadline. No application fee. Admission notification on a rolling basis. **Financial aid:** No deadline. FAFSA required. Applicants notified on a rolling basis starting 3/1; must reply within 2 week(s) of notification.

Academics. Special study options: Cooperative education, distance learning, double major, dual enrollment of high school students, ESL, independent study, internships, liberal arts/career combination, weekend college. Bachelor's degree programs available on campus. License preparation in paramedic. **Credit/placement by examination:** AP, CLEP, institutional tests. 30 credit hours maximum toward associate degree. **Support services:** GED preparation and test center, remedial instruction, study skills assistance, tutoring.

Majors. Business: General, accounting, administrative services, business admin. **Computer sciences:** General. **Education:** Early childhood. **Health services:** EMT paramedic, nursing (RN). **Liberal arts:** Arts/sciences. **Protective services:** Criminal justice.

Most popular majors. Business/marketing 14%, health sciences 37%, liberal arts 38%.

Technology on campus. 25 workstations in library, computer center. Online course registration available.

Student life. Freshman orientation: Available. Preregistration for classes offered. **Activities:** Student government, Baptist Collegiate Ministry, Young Democrats, College Republicans.

Student services. Adult student services, career counseling, services for economically disadvantaged, student employment services, financial aid counseling, personal counseling, veterans' counselor. **Physically disabled:** Services for visually, speech, hearing impaired. **Transfer:** College fairs on campus for students transferring to 4-year colleges.

Contact. E-mail: casey.bromley@uaccb.edu
Phone: (870) 612-2000 Toll-free number: (800) 508-7878
Fax: (870) 793-4988
Christopher Dickie, Director of Enrollment Services, University of Arkansas: Community College at Batesville, Box 3350, Batesville, AR 72503

University of Arkansas: Community College at Hope

Hope, Arkansas
www.uacch.edu   CB code: 3629

▶ Public 2-year community and technical college
▶ Commuter campus in small town

General. Regionally accredited. **Enrollment:** 1,045 degree-seeking undergraduates; 361 non-degree-seeking students. **Degrees:** 204 associate awarded. **Location:** 30 miles from Texarkana. **Calendar:** Semester, limited summer session. **Full-time faculty:** 42 total; 5% have terminal degrees, 7% minority, 67% women. **Part-time faculty:** 82 total; 15% have terminal degrees, 5% minority, 66% women. **Class size:** 74% < 20, 23% 20-39, 3% 40-49.

Student profile. Among degree-seeking undergraduates, 27% enrolled in a transfer program, 46% enrolled in a vocational program, 236 enrolled as first-time, first-year students.

Part-time:	37%	Asian American:	1%
Women:	71%	Hispanic/Latino:	6%
African American:	42%	25 or older:	31%

Basis for selection. Open admission, but selective for some programs. Additional requirements for nursing and funeral services.

High school preparation. College-preparatory program recommended.

2015-2016 Annual costs. Tuition/fees: $2,480; $2,660 out-of-district; $4,790 out-of-state. Per-credit charge: $63 in-district; $69 out-of-district; $140 out-of-state. Books/supplies: $1,000. Personal expenses: $2,761.

2014-2015 Financial aid. Need-based: 97% of total undergraduate aid awarded as scholarships/grants, 3% as loans/jobs. Need-based aid available for part-time students. Work-study available nights, weekends and for part-time students. **Non-need-based:** Scholarships awarded for academics.

Application procedures. Admission: No deadline. No application fee. Admission notification on a rolling basis. **Financial aid:** Closing date 7/6. FAFSA, institutional form required. Applicants notified on a rolling basis starting 1/1; must reply within 4 week(s) of notification.

Academics. Special study options: Distance learning, double major, dual enrollment of high school students, independent study, liberal arts/career combination. Bachelor's degree programs available on campus. License preparation in nursing, paramedic. **Credit/placement by examination:** AP, CLEP, institutional tests. **Support services:** GED test center, remedial instruction, study skills assistance, tutoring.

Majors. Business: General. **Computer sciences:** General. **Education:** Multi-level teacher. **Health services:** EMT paramedic, nursing (RN), office admin, respiratory therapy technology. **Liberal arts:** Arts/sciences. **Protective services:** Forensics, law enforcement admin, police science. **Work/family studies:** Child care management.

Most popular majors. Business/marketing 9%, engineering/engineering technologies 9%, family/consumer sciences 6%, health sciences 16%, interdisciplinary studies 8%, liberal arts 41%, personal/culinary services 8%.

Technology on campus. 20 workstations in library. Commuter students can connect to campus network. Online course registration, online library, helpline, wireless network available.

Student life. Freshman orientation: Available. Preregistration for classes offered. **Activities:** Music ensembles, student government, student newspaper.

Athletics. Intercollegiate: Rifle.

Student services. Adult student services, career counseling, services for economically disadvantaged, student employment services, financial aid counseling, placement for graduates, veterans' counselor. **Physically disabled:** Services for visually, speech, hearing impaired. **Transfer:** Pre-admission transcript evaluation for new students. College fairs on campus for students transferring to 4-year colleges.

Contact. E-mail: judy.anderson@uacch.edu
Phone: (870) 777-5722 Fax: (870) 722-6630
Judy Anderson, Dean of Enrollment Services, University of Arkansas: Community College at Hope, 2500 South Main, Hope, AR 71802-0140

University of Arkansas: Community College at Morrilton
Morrilton, Arkansas
www.uaccm.edu   CB code: 3881

◗ Public 2-year community college
◗ Commuter campus in small town

General. Regionally accredited. **Enrollment:** 1,970 degree-seeking undergraduates; 72 non-degree-seeking students. **Degrees:** 426 associate awarded. **Location:** 26 miles from Russellville, 15 miles from Conway. **Calendar:** Semester, limited summer session. **Full-time faculty:** 62 total; 6% have terminal degrees, 2% minority, 55% women. **Part-time faculty:** 13 total; 38% have terminal degrees, 8% minority, 54% women. **Class size:** 40% < 20, 59% 20-39, less than 1% 40-49.

Student profile. Among degree-seeking undergraduates, 70% enrolled in a transfer program, 30% enrolled in a vocational program, 1% already have a bachelor's degree or higher, 574 enrolled as first-time, first-year students, 240 transferred in from other institutions.

Part-time:	31%	Native American:	1%
Women:	59%	Multi-racial, non-Hispanic:	5%
African American:	10%	International:	2%
Asian American:	1%	25 or older:	31%
Hispanic/Latino:	6%		

Transfer out. Colleges most students transferred to 2015: University of Central Arkansas, Arkansas Tech University, University of Arkansas at Fayetteville, University of Arkansas at Little Rock.

Basis for selection. Students must have at least an ACT composite score of 15 or a COMPASS reading score of 63 in order to enroll. SAT or ACT recommended. Unconditional admission for public high school graduates who successfully completed the high school core curriculum OR home school, private school, or GED graduates who have at least an ACT composite score of 19, SAT score of 910, COMPASS reading score of 83, or ASSET reading score of 43. **Home schooled:** Transcript of courses and grades required. **Learning Disabled:** Students with documented disability must submit a written request for academic accommodations though the College Counseling Services Office at the beginning of each semester or term.

2015-2016 Annual costs. Tuition/fees: $3,575; $3,785 out-of-district; $4,880 out-of-state. Per-credit charge: $85 in-district; $92 out-of-district; $128 out-of-state. Books/supplies: $1,264. Personal expenses: $3,609.

2015-2016 Financial aid. Need-based: 469 full-time freshmen applied for aid; 395 deemed to have need; 374 received aid. Average need met was 49%. Average scholarship/grant was $2,710; average loan $1,571. 79% of total undergraduate aid awarded as scholarships/grants, 21% as loans/jobs. Need-based aid available for part-time students. Work-study available nights, weekends and for part-time students. **Non-need-based:** Awarded to 483 full-time undergraduates, including 261 freshmen. Scholarships awarded for academics, leadership, state residency.

Application procedures. Admission: No deadline. No application fee. Admission notification on a rolling basis. **Financial aid:** Priority date 7/1; no closing date. FAFSA, institutional form required.

Academics. Special study options: Cooperative education, distance learning, dual enrollment of high school students, independent study, internships, liberal arts/career combination. License preparation in nursing, paramedic. **Credit/placement by examination:** AP, CLEP, SAT, ACT, institutional tests. 30 credit hours maximum toward associate degree. **Support services:** GED preparation and test center, learning center, reduced course load, remedial instruction, study skills assistance, tutoring, writing center.

Majors. Business: General. **Education:** Multi-level teacher. **Health services:** Nursing (RN). **Liberal arts:** Arts/sciences. **Protective services:** Forensics, law enforcement admin. **Visual/performing arts:** Commercial/advertising art. **Work/family studies:** Child development.

Most popular majors. Business/marketing 19%, engineering/engineering technologies 13%, health sciences 11%, liberal arts 55%, trade and industry 6%.

Technology on campus. 500 workstations in library, computer center, student center. Commuter students can connect to campus network. Online library, wireless network available.

Student life. Freshman orientation: Mandatory. Preregistration for classes offered. One-day program, held 2 days before classes start for fall and spring semesters. **Policies:** Alcohol-, tobacco-, and drug-free campus. All students, employees, and visitors are expected to comply with policies and procedures. **Activities:** Campus ministries, drama, student government, student newspaper, Baptist collegiate ministry, Catholic campus ministry, Church of Christ student organization, Phi Beta Lambda, Phi Theta Kappa, art alliance club, automotive collision repair technology club, computer information systems club, early childhood student organization, petroleum technology student organization.

Athletics. Intramural: Basketball, football (non-tackle), table tennis, ultimate frisbee, volleyball. **Team name:** Timberwolves.

Student services. Alcohol/substance abuse counseling, career counseling, student employment services, financial aid counseling, on-campus daycare, personal counseling, placement for graduates, veterans' counselor. **Physically disabled:** Services for visually, speech, hearing impaired. **Transfer:** College fairs on campus for students transferring to 4-year colleges.

Contact. E-mail: adm@uaccm.edu
Phone: (501) 977-2053 Toll-free number: (800) 264-1094
Fax: (501) 977-2123
Rachel Mullins, Director of Admissions, University of Arkansas: Community College at Morrilton, 1537 University Boulevard, Morrilton, AR 72110

California

Allan Hancock College
Santa Maria, California
www.hancockcollege.edu

CB code: 4002

▶ Public 2-year community college
▶ Commuter campus in small city

General. Founded in 1920. Regionally accredited. **Enrollment:** 8,716 degree-seeking undergraduates. **Degrees:** 1,237 associate awarded. **Location:** 70 miles from Santa Barbara, 175 miles from Los Angeles. **Calendar:** Semester, extensive summer session. **Full-time faculty:** 155 total. **Part-time faculty:** 448 total.

Transfer out. Colleges most students transferred to 2015: California Polytechnic State University, San Luis Obispo; UC Santa Barbara, CSU, San Diego; CSU, Northridge; CSU, Fresno.

Basis for selection. Open admission, but selective for some programs. Special requirements for allied health and drama programs. Students required to make separate application for admission to nursing, drama, police academy programs. Interviews required for allied health applicants. Auditions required for drama applicants. **Adult students:** SAT/ACT scores not required.

2015-2016 Annual costs. Tuition/fees: $1,418; $6,968 out-of-state. Per-credit charge: $46 in-state; $231 out-of-state. Books/supplies: $1,656. Personal expenses: $3,114.

Financial aid. All financial aid based on need. Need-based aid available for part-time students. Work-study available nights, weekends and for part-time students.

Application procedures. Admission: No deadline. No application fee. Admission notification on a rolling basis. **Financial aid:** Priority date 5/1; no closing date. FAFSA required. Applicants notified on a rolling basis starting 6/1.

Academics. Special study options: Accelerated study, cooperative education, distance learning, double major, dual enrollment of high school students, ESL, honors, independent study, internships, liberal arts/career combination, study abroad, weekend college. Bachelor's degree programs available on campus. License preparation in dental hygiene, nursing, paramedic, real estate. **Credit/placement by examination:** AP, CLEP, institutional tests. 30 credit hours maximum toward associate degree. **Support services:** GED preparation and test center, learning center, reduced course load, remedial instruction, study skills assistance, tutoring, writing center.

Majors. Architecture: Technology. **Biology:** General. **Business:** General, accounting, administrative services, business admin, international marketing, management information systems, management science, office technology, office/clerical. **Communications technology:** Animation/special effects, graphic/printing, graphics, photo/film/video. **Computer sciences:** General, computer science, information technology. **Conservation:** Environmental studies. **Education:** Early childhood, elementary, physical. **Engineering:** General. **English:** English lit. **Foreign languages:** Spanish. **Health services:** Dental assistant, health information management, health information technology, licensed practical nurse, medical assistant, nursing (RN), physical therapy assistant. **Liberal arts:** Arts/sciences. **Math:** General, computational. **Parks/recreation:** General. **Physical sciences:** Chemistry, physics. **Protective services:** Fire safety technology. **Psychology:** General. **Social sciences:** General, international relations. **Visual/performing arts:** Art, commercial photography, commercial/advertising art, dance, design, fashion design, film/cinema/video, interior design, music, photography. **Work/family studies:** General, fashion consultant, housing.

Most popular majors. Health sciences 10%, liberal arts 61%, security/protective services 11%.

Technology on campus. 180 workstations in library, computer center. Online library, wireless network available.

Student life. Freshman orientation: Available. Preregistration for classes offered. **Activities:** Bands, choral groups, dance, drama, film society, literary magazine, music ensembles, musical theater, student government, student newspaper.

Athletics. Intercollegiate: Baseball M, basketball, cross-country, football (tackle) M, golf, soccer, softball W, tennis, track and field, volleyball W. **Team name:** Bulldogs.

Student services. Adult student services, career counseling, services for economically disadvantaged, student employment services, health services, on-campus daycare, personal counseling, placement for graduates, veterans' counselor. **Physically disabled:** Services for visually, hearing impaired. **Transfer:** Pre-admission transcript evaluation for new students. Transfer center, transfer adviser, college fairs on campus for students transferring to 4-year colleges.

Contact. Phone: (805) 922-6966 ext. 3248 Fax: (805) 922-3477 Marian Quaid-Maltagliati, Director, Admissions and Records, Allan Hancock College, 800 South College Drive, Santa Maria, CA 93454-6399

American Academy of Dramatic Arts: West
Los Angeles, California
www.aada.edu

CB code: 7024

▶ Private 2-year performing arts college
▶ Commuter campus in very large city
▶ Application essay, interview required

General. Founded in 1974. Regionally accredited. **Enrollment:** 275 degree-seeking undergraduates. **Degrees:** 107 associate awarded. **Calendar:** Semester, limited summer session. **Full-time faculty:** 9 total; 11% have terminal degrees, 11% minority, 78% women. **Part-time faculty:** 41 total; 17% minority, 54% women. **Class size:** 100% < 20. **Special facilities:** Performance theater.

Student profile.

Out-of-state:	54%	25 or older:	11%

Basis for selection. Each candidate evaluated individually; consideration based on dramatic ability and potential, academic qualifications and readiness, in terms of maturity and motivation. Auditions required. **Adult students:** SAT/ACT scores not required. **Home schooled:** Statement describing home school structure and mission, transcript of courses and grades, state high school equivalency certificate, interview, letter of recommendation (nonparent) required.

2015-2016 Annual costs. Tuition/fees: $30,650. Books/supplies: $570. Personal expenses: $1,500.

Financial aid. All financial aid based on need. Work-study available nights, weekends and for part-time students. **Additional information:** The Academy participates in various federal and state financial aid programs and offers a choice of payment plans. The Academy offers a variety of scholarships and assistance opportunities and a choice of payment plans for International Students. The Academy also participates with foreign government aid programs, if available.

Application procedures. Admission: Priority date 3/1; deadline 7/25 (receipt date). $50 fee. Admission notification on a rolling basis. **Financial aid:** Priority date 7/1; no closing date. Institutional form required. Applicants notified on a rolling basis starting 6/1; must reply within 3 week(s) of notification.

Academics. Select group of students invited to return for additional year of study and performance after graduation in repertory situation. **Special study options:** Internships. Students may study 1 year in each of 2 campuses (NY and CA). **Credit/placement by examination:** AP, CLEP, institutional tests. 9 credit hours maximum toward associate degree. **Support services:** Study skills assistance, tutoring.

Majors. Visual/performing arts: Acting.

Technology on campus. 8 workstations in library, computer center, student center. Wireless network available.

Student life. Freshman orientation: Mandatory. Preregistration for classes offered. Held the Thursday prior to a class start. **Activities:** Choral groups, dance, drama, student government.

Student services. Alcohol/substance abuse counseling, career counseling, student employment services, financial aid counseling, personal counseling, veterans' counselor.

Contact. E-mail: shong@aada.edu
Phone: (323) 464-2777 ext. 103 Toll-free number: (800) 222-2867
Fax: (323) 464-1250
Steven Hong, Director of Admissions, American Academy of Dramatic Arts: West, 1336 N. La Brea Avenue, Los Angeles, CA 90028

American River College
Sacramento, California
www.arc.losrios.edu   CB code: 4004

▶ Public 2-year community college
▶ Commuter campus in large city

General. Founded in 1955. Regionally accredited. **Enrollment:** 19,923 degree-seeking undergraduates. **Degrees:** 2,312 associate awarded. **Location:** 10 miles from downtown. **Calendar:** Semester, limited summer session. **Full-time faculty:** 350 total. **Part-time faculty:** 463 total.

Basis for selection. Open admission, but selective for some programs. Limited admission to nursing program. **Home schooled:** Transcript of courses and grades, interview, letter of recommendation (nonparent) required.

2015-2016 Annual costs. Tuition/fees: $1,416; $7,956 out-of-state. Per-credit charge: $46 in-state; $264 out-of-state. Books/supplies: $1,746. Personal expenses: $3,132.

Financial aid. All financial aid based on need. Need-based aid available for part-time students. Work-study available nights, weekends and for part-time students.

Application procedures. Admission: No deadline. No application fee. Application must be submitted online. Admission notification on a rolling basis beginning on or about 7/1. **Financial aid:** Priority date 3/2, closing date 6/30. FAFSA required. Applicants notified on a rolling basis starting 7/1; must reply within 2 week(s) of notification.

Academics. Special study options: Accelerated study, cooperative education, cross-registration, distance learning, ESL, honors, independent study, internships, liberal arts/career combination, study abroad, weekend college. **Credit/placement by examination:** AP, CLEP, IB. 15 credit hours maximum toward associate degree. **Support services:** Learning center, pre-admission summer program, reduced course load, remedial instruction, study skills assistance, tutoring, writing center.

Majors. Architecture: Landscape. **Business:** Accounting, administrative services, fashion, hospitality/recreation, management information systems, office/clerical, real estate. **Communications:** Journalism. **Communications technology:** Graphic/printing. **Computer sciences:** General, database management, networking, programming. **Conservation:** General. **Education:** Teacher assistance. **Health services:** Nursing (RN), respiratory therapy technology. **Liberal arts:** Arts/sciences. **Parks/recreation:** General. **Protective services:** Fire safety technology, police science. **Social sciences:** GIS/cartography. **Visual/performing arts:** Dramatic, interior design. **Work/family studies:** General, child care management, institutional food production.

Technology on campus. Online course registration, helpline available.

Student life. Freshman orientation: Available. Preregistration for classes offered. **Activities:** Bands, choral groups, dance, drama, international student organizations, literary magazine, music ensembles, Model UN, musical theater, student government, student newspaper, symphony orchestra.

Athletics. Intercollegiate: Baseball M, basketball, cross-country, football (tackle) M, golf, soccer, softball W, swimming, tennis, track and field, volleyball W, water polo M. **Team name:** Beavers.

Student services. Adult student services, career counseling, services for economically disadvantaged, student employment services, financial aid counseling, health services, minority student services, on-campus daycare, personal counseling, placement for graduates, veterans' counselor. **Physically disabled:** Services for visually, speech, hearing impaired. **Transfer:** Transfer center, transfer adviser for students transferring to 4-year colleges.

Contact. E-mail: recadmis@arc.losrios.edu
Phone: (916) 484-8261 Fax: (916) 484-8864
Robin Neal, Dean of Enrollment Services, American River College, 4700 College Oak Drive, Sacramento, CA 95841

Antelope Valley College
Lancaster, California
www.avc.edu   CB code: 4005

▶ Public 2-year liberal arts and technical college
▶ Commuter campus in large city

General. Founded in 1929. Regionally accredited. CSU Bakersfield extension office on campus. **Enrollment:** 10,056 degree-seeking undergraduates. **Degrees:** 1,468 associate awarded. **Location:** 50 miles from Los Angeles. **Calendar:** Semester, extensive summer session. **Full-time faculty:** 171 total.

Part-time faculty: 378 total. **Class size:** 22% < 20, 67% 20-39, 7% 40-49, 3% 50-99, less than 1% >100.

Transfer out. Colleges most students transferred to 2015: California State University: Northridge, California State University: Bakersfield, University of California: Los Angeles.

Basis for selection. Open admission, but selective for some programs. Limited enrollment for nursing programs. Selective enrollment for R.N., radiologic technology, and respiratory therapy programs.

2015-2016 Annual costs. Tuition/fees: $1,420; $7,420 out-of-state. Per-credit charge: $46 in-state; $246 out-of-state. Books/supplies: $1,764. Personal expenses: $3,149.

Financial aid. Need-based: Need-based aid available for part-time students. Work-study available nights, weekends and for part-time students.

Application procedures. Admission: No deadline. No application fee in-state; $186 out-of-state. Admission notification on a rolling basis. **Financial aid:** No deadline. FAFSA, institutional form required. Applicants notified on a rolling basis starting 7/15; must reply within 2 week(s) of notification.

Academics. Special study options: Accelerated study, cooperative education, distance learning, dual enrollment of high school students, ESL, honors, independent study, internships, study abroad, teacher certification program, weekend college. Bachelor's degree programs available on campus. License preparation in aviation, nursing, radiology, real estate. **Credit/placement by examination:** AP, CLEP, institutional tests. Maximum of 4 courses allowed. **Support services:** Learning center, reduced course load, remedial instruction, study skills assistance, tutoring, writing center.

Majors. Biology: General. **Business:** General, administrative services, business admin, real estate. **Communications technology:** Graphic/printing. **Computer sciences:** General, computer graphics, computer science, data processing, information systems, programming. **Education:** Teacher assistance. **Engineering:** General. **Foreign languages:** American Sign Language. **Health services:** Medical assistant, medical secretary, nursing (RN), office assistant. **Liberal arts:** Arts/sciences. **Math:** General. **Parks/recreation:** Health/fitness. **Protective services:** Fire safety technology. **Visual/performing arts:** General, cinematography, interior design, multimedia, music, photography. **Work/family studies:** General, child care management, child care service, child development, clothing/textiles, communication, family resources, food/nutrition, home furnishings.

Technology on campus. 300 workstations in library, computer center, student center. Online course registration, online library available.

Student life. Freshman orientation: Available. Preregistration for classes offered. Online orientation available. **Activities:** Bands, choral groups, dance, drama, music ensembles, Model UN, musical theater, student government, student newspaper, symphony orchestra.

Athletics. NAIA. Intercollegiate: Baseball M, basketball, cheerleading, cross-country, football (tackle) M, golf, soccer W, softball W, track and field, volleyball W. **Team name:** Marauders.

Student services. Adult student services, career counseling, services for economically disadvantaged, student employment services, financial aid counseling, health services, minority student services, on-campus daycare, personal counseling, veterans' counselor. **Physically disabled:** Services for visually, speech, hearing impaired. **Transfer:** Re-entry adviser for new students. Transfer center, transfer adviser, college fairs on campus for students transferring to 4-year colleges.

Contact. E-mail: registration@avc.edu
Phone: (661) 722-6300 ext. 6504 Fax: (661) 722-6531
LaDonna Trimble, Dean of Enrollment Services, Antelope Valley College, 3041 West Avenue K, Lancaster, CA 93536-5426

Art Institute of California: Los Angeles
Santa Monica, California
www.artinstitutes.edu/losangeles   CB code: 2490

▶ For-profit 2-year visual arts and career college
▶ Commuter campus in large city
▶ Application essay, interview required

General. Accredited by ACICS. **Enrollment:** 1,436 degree-seeking undergraduates. **Degrees:** 214 bachelor's, 128 associate awarded. **Calendar:** Quarter, extensive summer session. **Full-time faculty:** 68 total. **Part-time faculty:** 68 total. **Class size:** 57% < 20, 43% 20-39.

Basis for selection. High school record and general appropriateness of educational background to specific program applied for most important. Portfolio, interview, standardized test scores also important. SAT or ACT recommended.

2015-2016 Annual costs. Books/supplies: $2,199. Personal expenses: $3,096. **Additional information:** Diploma programs range from $24,496-$30,789, books and supplies range from $600-$800, room and board ranges from $15,576-$19,470. Associates programs range from $47,055-$49,444, books and supplies range from $1,050-$1,400, room and board range from $23,382-31,176. Bachelors programs range from from $93,678-$95,854, books and supplies range from $2,450-$2,800, room and board $58,410.

Financial aid. Need-based: Need-based aid available for part-time students. Work-study available nights, weekends and for part-time students. **Non-need-based:** Scholarships awarded for academics.

Application procedures. Admission: No deadline. No application fee. Admission notification on a rolling basis. **Financial aid:** No deadline. FAFSA required. Applicants notified on a rolling basis.

Academics. Special study options: Independent study, internships, study abroad. Bachelor's degree programs available on campus. **Credit/placement by examination:** AP, CLEP, SAT, ACT, institutional tests. **Support services:** Reduced course load, tutoring, writing center.

Majors. Computer sciences: Computer graphics, web page design. **Visual/performing arts:** Cinematography, commercial/advertising art, design, graphic design.

Technology on campus. 250 workstations in library, computer center. Student web hosting available.

Student life. Freshman orientation: Mandatory. Preregistration for classes offered. One day program before start of quarter. **Housing:** Guaranteed on-campus for all undergraduates. Apartments available. $250 deposit. **Activities:** Literary magazine, gay, lesbian, straight alliance.

Student services. Alcohol/substance abuse counseling, career counseling, student employment services, financial aid counseling, personal counseling, placement for graduates.

Contact. E-mail: ailaadm@aii.edu
Phone: (310) 752-4700 Toll-free number: (888) 646-4610
Fax: (310) 752-4708
Jesus Moreno, Director of Admissions, Art Institute of California: Los Angeles, 2900 31st Street, Santa Monica, CA 90405-3035

Bakersfield College
Bakersfield, California
www.bakersfieldcollege.edu   CB code: 4015

- Public 2-year community college
- Commuter campus in large city

General. Founded in 1913. Regionally accredited. **Enrollment:** 19,472 degree-seeking undergraduates. **Degrees:** 946 associate awarded. **Location:** 114 miles from Los Angeles. **Calendar:** Semester, limited summer session. **Full-time faculty:** 249 total; 20% minority, 49% women. **Part-time faculty:** 215 total; 25% minority, 52% women. **Special facilities:** Planetarium.

Transfer out. Colleges most students transferred to 2015: California State University: Bakersfield, Northridge, Fresno, Humboldt, Long Beach.

Basis for selection. Open admission, but selective for some programs. Nursing and other allied health programs have additional admission requirements including required coursework.

2015-2016 Annual costs. Tuition/fees: $1,418; $7,418 out-of-state. Per-credit charge: $46 in-state; $246 out-of-state. Books/supplies: $1,710. Personal expenses: $2,150.

Financial aid. Need-based: Work-study available nights, weekends and for part-time students.

Application procedures. Admission: No deadline. No application fee. **Financial aid:** Priority date 3/2, closing date 6/30. FAFSA required. Applicants notified on a rolling basis starting 6/1; must reply within 2 week(s) of notification.

Academics. Special study options: Cooperative education, distance learning, double major, dual enrollment of high school students, ESL. **Credit/placement by examination:** AP, CLEP, institutional tests. 12 credit hours maximum toward associate degree. **Support services:** Learning center,

---

reduced course load, remedial instruction, study skills assistance, tutoring, writing center.

Majors. Architecture: Technology. **Biology:** General. **Business:** General, accounting technology, administrative services, sales/distribution. **Communications:** Communications/speech/rhetoric, journalism. **Computer sciences:** General. **Conservation:** Forestry. **Engineering:** Pre-engineering. **English:** English lit. **Foreign languages:** American Sign Language, Spanish. **General:** Building construction, carpentry, electrician, plumbing. **Health services:** Nursing (RN), radiologic technology/medical imaging. **History:** General. **Liberal arts:** Arts/sciences. **Math:** General. **Parks/recreation:** Exercise sciences, health/fitness. **Philosophy/religion:** Philosophy. **Physical sciences:** Chemistry, geology, physics. **Protective services:** Corrections, fire safety technology, forest/wildland firefighting, police science. **Psychology:** General. **Social sciences:** Anthropology, economics, political science, sociology. **Visual/performing arts:** Art, dramatic, music. **Work/family studies:** Child care service, food/nutrition.

Student life. Freshman orientation: Available. Preregistration for classes offered. **Activities:** Bands, campus ministries, choral groups, dance, drama, literary magazine, music ensembles, student government, student newspaper.

Athletics. Intercollegiate: Baseball M, basketball, cheerleading, cross-country, football (tackle) M, golf, soccer W, softball W, swimming, tennis, track and field, volleyball W, wrestling M. **Team name:** Renegades.

Student services. Career counseling, services for economically disadvantaged, student employment services, financial aid counseling, health services, on-campus daycare, personal counseling. **Physically disabled:** Services for visually, speech, hearing impaired. **Transfer:** Transfer center, transfer adviser, college fairs on campus for students transferring to 4-year colleges.

Contact. Phone: (661) 395-4301
Sue Vaughn, Director of Enrollment Services, Bakersfield College, 1801 Panorama Drive, Bakersfield, CA 93305

Barstow Community College
Barstow, California
www.barstow.edu   CB code: 4020

- Public 2-year community college
- Commuter campus in large town

General. Founded in 1959. Regionally accredited. **Enrollment:** 1,178 degree-seeking undergraduates. **Degrees:** 273 associate awarded. **Location:** 70 miles from San Bernardino. **Calendar:** Semester, limited summer session. **Full-time faculty:** 35 total. **Part-time faculty:** 70 total.

Student profile.

Out-of-state:	10%	25 or older: 43%

Basis for selection. Open admission.

2015-2016 Annual costs. Tuition/fees: $1,388; $7,388 out-of-state. Per-credit charge: $46 in-state; $246 out-of-state. Books/supplies: $1,656. Personal expenses: $2,595.

Financial aid. All financial aid based on need. Need-based aid available for part-time students. Work-study available nights, weekends and for part-time students.

Application procedures. Admission: No deadline. No application fee. Admission notification on a rolling basis. **Financial aid:** Closing date 6/17. FAFSA required. Applicants notified on a rolling basis starting 7/1.

Academics. Special study options: Accelerated study, cooperative education, distance learning, double major, dual enrollment of high school students, ESL, independent study, liberal arts/career combination. **Credit/placement by examination:** AP, CLEP, institutional tests. 30 credit hours maximum toward associate degree. **Support services:** Learning center, reduced course load, remedial instruction, study skills assistance, tutoring.

Majors. Business: General, accounting, office management, office/clerical. **Computer sciences:** Computer science. **General:** Electrician. **Liberal arts:** Humanities. **Math:** General. **Protective services:** Police science. **Psychology:** General. **Social sciences:** General, sociology. **Work/family studies:** Child development.

Technology on campus. 40 workstations in library, computer center. Online course registration, online library, wireless network available.

Student life. Freshman orientation: Available. Preregistration for classes offered. **Activities:** Bands, choral groups, dance, drama, music ensembles, musical theater, student government, Christian Club, Alpha Gamma Sigma, Phi Theta Kappa.

Athletics. NJCAA. **Intercollegiate:** Baseball M, basketball M, cross-country, softball W. **Intramural:** Badminton, baseball M, basketball, bowling, soccer, softball, swimming, tennis, volleyball. **Team name:** Vikings.

Student services. Adult student services, career counseling, services for economically disadvantaged, student employment services, financial aid counseling, personal counseling, placement for graduates, veterans' counselor. **Physically disabled:** Services for visually, speech, hearing impaired. **Transfer:** Pre-admission transcript evaluation for new students. Transfer center, transfer adviser, college fairs on campus for students transferring to 4-year colleges.

Contact. E-mail: admit@barstow.edu
Phone: (760) 252-2411 ext. 7236 Fax: (760) 252-6754
Heather Caldon, Director of Enrollment Services, Barstow Community College, 2700 Barstow Road, Barstow, CA 92311-9984

Berkeley City College
Berkeley, California
www.berkeleycitycollege.edu　　　　CB code: 7711

▶ Public 2-year community college
▶ Commuter campus in small city

General. Founded in 1974. Regionally accredited. **Enrollment:** 3,840 degree-seeking undergraduates. **Degrees:** 235 associate awarded. **Location:** 15 miles from San Francisco. **Calendar:** Semester, limited summer session. **Full-time faculty:** 66 total. **Part-time faculty:** 137 total.

Transfer out. Colleges most students transferred to 2015: University of California system, California State University system, private colleges.

Basis for selection. Open admission. No interviews or essays required. **Adult students:** Students who plan to earn an associate degree or certificate, and/or who plan to transfer must take an Assessment Test in Mathematics and English. **Learning Disabled:** Students must coordinate their schedules and programs with the college's Programs and Services for Students with Disabilities Office.

2015-2016 Annual costs. Tuition/fees: $1,420; $7,810 out-of-state. Per-credit charge: $46 in-state; $259 out-of-state. Books/supplies: $1,710. Personal expenses: $3,096.

Financial aid. All financial aid based on need. Need-based aid available for part-time students. Work-study available nights, weekends and for part-time students.

Application procedures. Admission: No deadline. No application fee. Admission notification on a rolling basis. **Financial aid:** No deadline. Applicants notified on a rolling basis.

Academics. Special study options: Accelerated study, cooperative education, cross-registration, distance learning, dual enrollment of high school students, ESL, honors, independent study, liberal arts/career combination, study abroad, weekend college. **Credit/placement by examination:** AP, CLEP, institutional tests. 6 credit hours maximum toward associate degree. **Support services:** Learning center, reduced course load, remedial instruction, study skills assistance, tutoring, writing center. First year experience, learning communities.

Majors. Biology: Biotechnology. **Business:** Business admin, office/clerical, small business admin. **Communications:** Digital media. **Communications technology:** General. **Computer sciences:** General. **English:** English lit. **Foreign languages:** Sign language interpretation, Spanish. **Health services:** Community health services. **Human services:** Social work. **Liberal arts:** Arts/sciences, humanities. **Math:** General. **Philosophy/religion:** Philosophy. **Psychology:** General. **Social sciences:** General, political science, sociology. **Visual/performing arts:** Art, art history/conservation, digital arts.

Technology on campus. Commuter students can connect to campus network. Online course registration, online library, wireless network available.

Student life. Freshman orientation: Mandatory. Preregistration for classes offered. **Housing:** Students can apply for UC Berkeley off-campus co-ops if they intend to transfer. **Activities:** Choral groups, dance, film society, international student organizations, literary magazine, music ensembles, student government, Phi Theta Kappa, Spanish club, X club, Bahai club, black students union, global studies club, associated students club, digital arts club, Milvia Street literary magazine, film club.

Student services. Adult student services, career counseling, services for economically disadvantaged, student employment services, financial aid counseling, health services, minority student services, personal counseling, veterans' counselor. **Physically disabled:** Services for visually, speech, hearing impaired. **Transfer:** Pre-admission transcript evaluation for new students. Transfer center, transfer adviser, college fairs on campus for students transferring to 4-year colleges.

Contact. E-mail: lnewsom@peralta.edu
Phone: (510) 981-2805 Fax: (510) 841-7333
Loretta Newsom, Admissions and Records Specialist, Berkeley City College, 2050 Center Street, Berkeley, CA 94704

Bryan College: Sacramento
Gold River, California
www.bryancollege.edu

▶ For-profit 2-year career college
▶ Very large city
▶ Interview required

General. Accredited by ACCSC. **Enrollment:** 544 undergraduates. **Degrees:** 135 associate awarded. **Location:** 10 miles from downtown Sacramento. **Calendar:** Differs by program, limited summer session. **Full-time faculty:** 39 total. **Part-time faculty:** 12 total.

Basis for selection. Open admission. Admission process includes on campus interview, application/meet with director of admissions for recommendation, assessment.

2015-2016 Annual costs. Associate programs: $25,222-$51,778, books and supplies $750-$1,532.

Financial aid. Need-based: Work-study available nights, weekends and for part-time students.

Application procedures. Admission: No deadline. $20 fee. **Financial aid:** No deadline.

Academics. Special study options: Massage therapy students get hands-on experience in public massage clinic. Personal training students work with fitness professionals to gain field experience. **Credit/placement by examination:** AP, CLEP. **Support services:** Learning center.

Majors. Biology: Exercise physiology. **Health services:** Massage therapy.

Contact. E-mail: admissions@bryancollege.com
Phone: (916) 649-2400 Toll-free number: (866) 649-2400
Fax: (916) 641-8649
Orquedia Chavez, Director of Admissions, Bryan College: Sacramento, 2317 Gold Meadow Way, Gold River, CA 95670

Butte College
Oroville, California
www.butte.edu　　　　CB code: 4226

▶ Public 2-year community college
▶ Commuter campus in small city

General. Founded in 1966. Regionally accredited. **Enrollment:** 11,164 degree-seeking undergraduates; 997 non-degree-seeking students. **Degrees:** 1,406 associate awarded. **Location:** 100 miles from Sacramento. **Calendar:** Semester, extensive summer session. **Full-time faculty:** 165 total. **Part-time faculty:** 541 total. **Special facilities:** Wild game refuge, nature trails, black box theater.

Student profile. Among degree-seeking undergraduates, 1,973 enrolled as first-time, first-year students, 984 transferred in from other institutions.

Part-time:	49%	**Women:**	52%
Out-of-state:	1%	**25 or older:**	33%

Transfer out. Colleges most students transferred to 2015: CSU Chico.

Basis for selection. Open admission, but selective for some programs. Health Occupations, Welding, Auto, Cosmetology programs have special requirements.

2015-2016 Annual costs. Tuition/fees: $1,496; $7,796 out-of-state. Per-credit charge: $46 in-state; $256 out-of-state. Books/supplies: $1,660. Personal expenses: $2,522.

2014-2015 Financial aid. All financial aid based on need. 76% of total undergraduate aid awarded as scholarships/grants, 24% as loans/jobs. Need-based aid available for part-time students. Work-study available nights, weekends and for part-time students.

Application procedures. Admission: No deadline. No application fee. Admission notification on a rolling basis. **Financial aid:** Priority date 5/1; no closing date. FAFSA required. Applicants notified on a rolling basis starting 7/9.

Academics. Special study options: Cooperative education, cross-registration, distance learning, double major, dual enrollment of high school students, ESL, honors, independent study, internships, liberal arts/career combination, study abroad. License preparation in nursing, paramedic, real estate. **Credit/placement by examination:** AP, CLEP, institutional tests. 9 credit hours maximum toward associate degree. **Support services:** GED preparation and test center, learning center, remedial instruction, study skills assistance, tutoring.

Majors. Biology: General. **Business:** Accounting, accounting technology, administrative services, business admin, real estate, retail management, sales/distribution, small business admin. **Communications:** Communications/speech/rhetoric, radio/TV. **Communications technology:** Animation/special effects, recording arts. **Computer sciences:** Computer science, data entry, information technology. **Conservation:** General, environmental science. **Engineering:** Pre-engineering. **English:** English lit. **Health services:** EMT paramedic, licensed practical nurse, medical secretary, nursing (RN), respiratory therapy technology. **History:** General. **Liberal arts:** Arts/sciences, humanities. **Math:** General. **Parks/recreation:** Exercise sciences, health/fitness. **Physical sciences:** General, chemistry, geology, physics. **Protective services:** Fire safety technology, police science. **Psychology:** General. **Social sciences:** General, anthropology, geography, political science, sociology. **Visual/performing arts:** General, art, ceramics, dramatic, graphic design, interior design, music, photography. **Work/family studies:** Apparel marketing, child care service, food/nutrition.

Most popular majors. Business/marketing 10%, health sciences 9%, liberal arts 7%, parks/recreation 16%, social sciences 38%.

Technology on campus. 200 workstations in library, computer center. Commuter students can connect to campus network. Online course registration, online library, helpline, wireless network available.

Student life. Freshman orientation: Mandatory. Preregistration for classes offered. **Activities:** Bands, choral groups, dance, drama, film society, international student organizations, music ensembles, musical theater, radio station, student government, student newspaper, symphony orchestra, TV station, African Student Association, Asian Student Association, Chinese student club, Gender Sexuality Alliance, international club, Latter Day Saints club, marxist club.

Athletics. NJCAA. **Intercollegiate:** Baseball M, basketball, cross-country, football (tackle) M, golf W, soccer, softball W, track and field, volleyball W. **Team name:** Roadrunners.

Student services. Adult student services, alcohol/substance abuse counseling, career counseling, services for economically disadvantaged, student employment services, financial aid counseling, health services, minority student services, on-campus daycare, personal counseling, placement for graduates, veterans' counselor, women's services. **Physically disabled:** Services for visually, speech, hearing impaired. **Transfer:** Re-entry adviser, pre-admission transcript evaluation for new students. Transfer center, transfer adviser, college fairs on campus for students transferring to 4-year colleges.

Contact. E-mail: admissions@butte.edu
Phone: (530) 895-2361 Fax: (530) 879-4313
Monica Boyes, Director, Admissions and Records, Butte College, 3536 Butte Campus Drive, Oroville, CA 95965

Cabrillo College
Aptos, California
www.cabrillo.edu
CB code: 4084

◗ Public 2-year community college
◗ Commuter campus in large town

General. Founded in 1959. Regionally accredited. **Enrollment:** 7,785 degree-seeking undergraduates. **Degrees:** 1,338 associate awarded. **Location:** 25 miles from San Jose, 35 miles from Monterey. **Calendar:** Semester, extensive summer session. **Full-time faculty:** 184 total; 21% have terminal degrees, 21% minority, 53% women. **Part-time faculty:** 375 total; 10% have terminal degrees, 21% minority, 60% women. **Special facilities:** Observatory, planetarium, horticulture organic gardens, LEED platinum green technology center.

Student profile.

Out-of-state: 2% 25 or older: 43%

Transfer out. Colleges most students transferred to 2015: University of California, Santa Cruz, San Jose State University, California State University, Monterey Bay, San Francisco State University,.

Basis for selection. Open admission, but selective for some programs. Special prerequisite requirements for nursing, dental hygiene, and radiologic technology. International applicants have special admission requirements. **Learning Disabled:** The Accessibility Support Center offers a variety of services and accommodations to enable students with disabilities to function independently in the educational environment.

High school preparation. College-preparatory program recommended.

2015-2016 Annual costs. Tuition/fees: $1,411; $7,411 out-of-state. Per-credit charge: $46 in-state; $246 out-of-state. Books/supplies: $1,746. Personal expenses: $2,871.

Financial aid. Need-based: Need-based aid available for part-time students. Work-study available nights, weekends and for part-time students.

Application procedures. Admission: No deadline. No application fee. Admission notification on a rolling basis beginning on or about 6/1. **Financial aid:** No deadline. FAFSA, institutional form required. Applicants notified on a rolling basis starting 7/31; must reply within 3 week(s) of notification.

Academics. Special study options: Cooperative education, distance learning, dual enrollment of high school students, ESL, honors, independent study, internships, liberal arts/career combination, study abroad. License preparation in dental hygiene, nursing, radiology. **Credit/placement by examination:** AP, CLEP, institutional tests. **Support services:** Learning center, pre-admission summer program, reduced course load, remedial instruction, study skills assistance, tutoring, writing center. Learning communities.

Majors. Area/ethnic studies: Asian. **Biology:** General. **Business:** General, accounting, banking/financial services, business admin, construction management, entrepreneurial studies, office technology, real estate. **Communications:** Journalism. **Computer sciences:** General, data processing. **English:** English lit, rhetoric/composition. **Foreign languages:** General, French, German, Italian, Japanese, Spanish. **Health services:** Dental hygiene, licensed practical nurse, medical assistant, medical radiologic technology/radiation therapy, nursing (RN). **History:** General. **Liberal arts:** Arts/sciences, library assistant. **Math:** General. **Physical sciences:** Chemistry, physics. **Protective services:** Firefighting, police science. **Psychology:** General. **Social sciences:** General, anthropology, economics, geography, political science, sociology. **Visual/performing arts:** General, art, dance, music, studio arts. **Work/family studies:** General, child care management.

Technology on campus. 350 workstations in library, computer center, student center. Online course registration, wireless network available.

Student life. Freshman orientation: Available. Preregistration for classes offered. Online program available. **Activities:** Bands, choral groups, dance, drama, music ensembles, musical theater, student government, student newspaper, Various literacy, recreational, cultural, environmental, political clubs, and/or ethnic organizations.

Athletics. Intercollegiate: Baseball M, basketball, cross-country, diving, football (tackle) M, golf M, soccer M, softball W, swimming, tennis, track and field, volleyball W, water polo. **Team name:** Seahawks.

Student services. Adult student services, career counseling, services for economically disadvantaged, student employment services, financial aid counseling, health services, personal counseling, placement for graduates, veterans' counselor. **Physically disabled:** Services for visually, speech, hearing impaired. **Transfer:** Transfer center, transfer adviser, college fairs on campus for students transferring to 4-year colleges.

Contact. Phone: (831) 479-6201 Fax: (831) 479-5782
Tama Bolton, Director of Admissions and Records, Cabrillo College, 6500 Soquel Drive, Aptos, CA 95003

Canada College
Redwood City, California
www.canadacollege.edu
CB code: 4109

◗ Public 2-year community college
◗ Commuter campus in small city

General. Founded in 1968. Regionally accredited. **Enrollment:** 3,844 degree-seeking undergraduates; 1,589 non-degree-seeking students. **Degrees:**

Two-Year Colleges

350 associate awarded. **ROTC:** Army, Air Force. **Calendar:** Semester, limited summer session. **Full-time faculty:** 81 total; 38% minority, 67% women. **Part-time faculty:** 160 total; 29% minority, 60% women. **Class size:** 30% < 20, 59% 20-39, 11% 40-49.

Student profile. Among degree-seeking undergraduates, 59% enrolled in a transfer program, 40% enrolled in a vocational program, 13% already have a bachelor's degree or higher, 470 enrolled as first-time, first-year students.

Part-time:	90%	Hispanic/Latino:	35%
Out-of-state:	2%	Native Hawaiian/Pacific islander:	2%
Women:	62%	Multi-racial, non-Hispanic:	17%
African American:	3%	International:	5%
Asian American:	11%		

Transfer out. 95% of students enrolled in the transfer program go on to 4-year colleges. **Colleges most students transferred to 2015:** San Francisco State University, San Jose State University, Notre Dame de Namur University, California State University: East Bay, University of California: Davis.

Basis for selection. Open admission, but selective for some programs. Special admission requirements for radiologic technology programs, middle college and college for working adults. **Adult students:** SAT/ACT scores not required. **Home schooled:** "R4" form from State of California.

2015-2016 Annual costs. Tuition/fees: $1,436; $8,006 out-of-state. Per-credit charge: $46 in-state; $265 out-of-state. Books/supplies: $1,746. Personal expenses: $3,132.

2014-2015 Financial aid. Need-based: 92% of total undergraduate aid awarded as scholarships/grants, 8% as loans/jobs. Need-based aid available for part-time students. Work-study available nights, weekends and for part-time students.

Application procedures. Admission: No deadline. No application fee in-state; $213 out-of-state. Admission notification on a rolling basis. **Financial aid:** Priority date 3/2; no closing date. FAFSA required. Applicants notified on a rolling basis starting 5/1; must reply within 2 week(s) of notification.

Academics. Special study options: Cooperative education, cross-registration, distance learning, double major, dual enrollment of high school students, ESL, honors, independent study, internships, study abroad, weekend college. Bachelor's degree programs available on campus. License preparation in radiology. **Credit/placement by examination:** AP, CLEP, IB, institutional tests. 12 credit hours maximum toward associate degree. **Support services:** Learning center, pre-admission summer program, reduced course load, remedial instruction, study skills assistance, tutoring, writing center. Significant Supplemental Instruction is available to students in STEM, ESL and basic skills classes.

Honors college/program. Interdisciplinary Honors Program offered to students in all majors who have a minimum transfer gpa of 3.3 and college-level preparations in English and Math.

Majors. Biology: General. **Business:** Accounting, administrative services, business admin, fashion, small business admin. **Communications:** Communications/speech/rhetoric. **Communications technology:** Animation/special effects. **Computer sciences:** Computer science. **Education:** Early childhood. **Engineering:** General. **English:** English lit. **Foreign languages:** Spanish. **Health services:** Medical assistant, medical transcription, radiologic technology/medical imaging. **History:** General. **Liberal arts:** Arts/sciences, humanities. **Math:** General. **Parks/recreation:** Exercise sciences, physical fitness technician. **Philosophy/religion:** Philosophy. **Physical sciences:** Chemistry, geology, physics. **Psychology:** General. **Social sciences:** General, anthropology, economics, geography, political science, sociology. **Visual/performing arts:** General, art, dance, dramatic, fashion design, interior design, music. **Work/family studies:** Apparel marketing, child care service, textile manufacture.

Most popular majors. Business/marketing 10%, family/consumer sciences 11%, health sciences 8%, interdisciplinary studies 6%, liberal arts 19%, psychology 7%, social sciences 14%.

Technology on campus. 700 workstations in library, computer center. Commuter students can connect to campus network. Online course registration, repair service, wireless network available.

Student life. Freshman orientation: Mandatory. Preregistration for classes offered. Orientation sessions are held multiple times per week during entire registration periods. **Policies:** Free speech areas have been designated on campus to maximize the opportunity for free discussion and expression, while minimizing the potential for disruption of classroom and college activities. All free speech organizations, vendors, and any on campus posting must first go through the Center for Student Life and Leadership Development. In order to promote a healthy learning environment, there are designated smoking areas on campus. **Activities:** Concert band, campus ministries, choral groups, dance, drama, film society, international student organizations, music ensembles, musical theater, student government, symphony orchestra, Associated Students of Canada College, Beating the Odds Community, Bridging Hispanic Minds to Success, Equal Opportunities club, International Culture Exchange, Phi Theta Kappa, Spectrum Alliance, Woman/Hispanic science and engineering, Christian Fellowship, Civil Liberties.

Athletics. Intercollegiate: Baseball M, basketball M, golf W, soccer, tennis W, volleyball W. **Team name:** Colts.

Student services. Adult student services, career counseling, services for economically disadvantaged, student employment services, financial aid counseling, health services, personal counseling, veterans' counselor. **Physically disabled:** Services for visually, hearing impaired. **Transfer:** Re-entry adviser for new students. Transfer center, transfer adviser, college fairs on campus for students transferring to 4-year colleges.

Contact. E-mail: canadaadmissions@smccd.edu
Phone: (650) 306-3226 Fax: (650) 306-3113
Ruth Miller, Registrar, Canada College, 4200 Farm Hill Boulevard, Redwood City, CA 94061

Carrington College: Citrus Heights
Citrus Heights, California
www.carrington.edu

▸ For-profit 2-year health science and technical college
▸ Very large city

General. Regionally accredited. **Enrollment:** 517 degree-seeking undergraduates. **Degrees:** 74 associate awarded. **Calendar:** Differs by program. **Full-time faculty:** 13 total. **Part-time faculty:** 11 total.

Basis for selection. Admission requirements vary by program.

2015-2016 Annual costs. Tuition costs vary by program. Total program cost for the largest program (Veterinary Technology-Assoc.) is $34,166.

Financial aid. Need-based: Work-study available nights, weekends and for part-time students.

Application procedures. Admission: No deadline.

Academics. Credit/placement by examination: AP, CLEP.

Majors. Business: General, accounting. **Health services:** Dental assistant, health care admin, insurance specialist, massage therapy, medical assistant, pharmacy assistant, surgical technology, veterinary technology/assistant. **Protective services:** Criminal justice.

Contact. Toll-free number: (888) 720-5014
Carrington College: Citrus Heights, 7301 Greenback Lane, Suite A, Citrus Heights, CA 95621

Carrington College: Pleasant Hill
Pleasant Hill, California
www.carrington.edu   CB code: 2922

▸ For-profit 2-year health science and technical college
▸ Commuter campus in small city

General. Regionally accredited. **Enrollment:** 599 degree-seeking undergraduates. **Degrees:** 137 associate awarded. **Calendar:** Differs by program. **Full-time faculty:** 9 total. **Part-time faculty:** 9 total.

Basis for selection. CPAt examination important.

2015-2016 Annual costs. Tuition costs vary by program. Total program cost for the largest program (Veterinary Technology-Assoc.) is $34,166.

Financial aid. Need-based: Work-study available nights, weekends and for part-time students.

Application procedures. Admission: No deadline. No application fee. Admission notification on a rolling basis. **Financial aid:** No deadline. Applicants notified on a rolling basis.

Academics. Credit/placement by examination: AP, CLEP.

Majors. Business: General, accounting. **Health services:** Massage therapy, medical assistant, pharmacy assistant, physical therapy assistant, respiratory therapy assistant, veterinary technology/assistant. **Protective services:** Criminal justice.

Contact. Phone: (925) 609-6650 Toll-free number: (888) 720-5014 Fax: (925) 609-6666
Carrington College: Pleasant Hill, 380 Civic Drive, Suite 300, Pleasant Hill, CA 94523

Carrington College: Sacramento
Sacramento, California
www.carrington.edu
CB code: 2917

- For-profit 2-year health science and technical college
- Commuter campus in large city

General. Regionally accredited. **Enrollment:** 1,385 degree-seeking undergraduates. **Degrees:** 496 associate awarded. **Calendar:** Differs by program. **Full-time faculty:** 34 total. **Part-time faculty:** 65 total.

Basis for selection. Admission requirements vary by programs.

2015-2016 Annual costs. Books/supplies: $448. Personal expenses: $1,686. **Additional information:** Tuition costs vary by program. Total program cost for the largest program (Health Studies-Assoc (offered online)) is $14,416.

Financial aid. **Need-based:** Work-study available nights, weekends and for part-time students.

Application procedures. **Admission:** No deadline.

Academics. **Credit/placement by examination:** AP, CLEP.

Majors. **Health services:** Dental hygiene, health information technology, licensed practical nurse, medical assistant, nursing (RN), pharmacy assistant, veterinary technology/assistant.

Contact. Toll-free number: (888) 720-5014
Carrington College: Sacramento, 8909 Folsom Boulevard, Sacramento, CA 95826

Carrington College: San Jose
San Jose, California
www.carrington.edu

- For-profit 2-year technical college
- Commuter campus in very large city

General. Regionally accredited. **Enrollment:** 805 degree-seeking undergraduates. **Degrees:** 181 associate awarded. **Calendar:** Differs by program. **Full-time faculty:** 22 total. **Part-time faculty:** 38 total.

Basis for selection. Limited admission to dental programs.

2015-2016 Annual costs. Tuition costs vary by program. Total program cost for the largest program (Medical Assisting-Cert.) is $18,363.

Financial aid. **Need-based:** Work-study available nights, weekends and for part-time students.

Application procedures. **Admission:** No deadline. No application fee. Admission notification on a rolling basis.

Academics. **Credit/placement by examination:** AP, CLEP.

Majors. **Business:** General, accounting. **Computer sciences:** Computer graphics. **Health services:** Dental assistant, dental hygiene, health information technology, insurance specialist, massage therapy, medical assistant, pharmacy assistant, surgical technology, veterinary technology/assistant. **Protective services:** Criminal justice.

Contact. Phone: (408) 960-0161 Toll-free number: (888) 720-5014 Fax: (408) 360-0848
Carrington College: San Jose, 6201 San Ignacio Avenue, San Jose, CA 95119

Carrington College: San Leandro
San Leandro, California
www.carrington.edu
CB code: 2918

- For-profit 2-year health science and technical college
- Commuter campus in small city
- Interview required

General. Regionally accredited. **Enrollment:** 509 degree-seeking undergraduates. **Degrees:** 85 associate awarded. **Location:** 10 miles from Oakland. **Calendar:** Differs by program. **Full-time faculty:** 20 total. **Part-time faculty:** 15 total. **Special facilities:** Labs.

Basis for selection. CPAT score, interest important. CPAT required.

2015-2016 Annual costs. Tuition costs vary by program. Total program cost for the largest program (Medical Assisting-Cert.) is $18,363.

Financial aid. **Need-based:** Work-study available nights, weekends and for part-time students.

Application procedures. **Admission:** No deadline. No application fee. Admission notification on a rolling basis. **Financial aid:** No deadline. Applicants notified on a rolling basis.

Academics. **Special study options:** Distance learning. **Credit/placement by examination:** AP, CLEP. **Support services:** Study skills assistance, tutoring.

Majors. **Business:** General, accounting. **Health services:** Insurance specialist, licensed practical nurse, medical secretary, pharmacy assistant, veterinary technology/assistant.

Technology on campus. 55 workstations in library, computer center. Online library available.

Student life. **Activities:** Student newspaper.

Contact. Phone: (510) 276-3888 Toll-free number: (888) 720-5014 Fax: (510) 276-3653
Carrington College: San Leandro, 1555 East 14th Street, Suite 500, San Leandro, CA 94578

Carrington College: Stockton
Stockton, California
www.carrington.edu
CB code: 4886

- For-profit 2-year technical and career college
- Small city
- Application essay, interview required

General. Regionally accredited. **Enrollment:** 549 degree-seeking undergraduates. **Degrees:** 112 associate awarded. **Location:** 40 miles from Sacramento. **Calendar:** Differs by program. **Full-time faculty:** 7 total. **Part-time faculty:** 11 total.

Basis for selection. Admissions decisions are based upon high school diploma (GED or ATB) formal interview with applicant, a completed application and a passing score on an entrance exam.

2015-2016 Annual costs. Tuition costs vary by program. Total program cost for the largest program (Veterinary Technology-Assoc.) is $34,166.

Financial aid. **Need-based:** Work-study available nights, weekends and for part-time students.

Application procedures. **Admission:** No deadline. No application fee.

Academics. **Special study options:** Accelerated study. **Credit/placement by examination:** AP, CLEP. **Support services:** Learning center, tutoring.

Majors. **Health services:** Dental assistant, health care admin, massage therapy, medical assistant, pharmacy assistant, veterinary technology/assistant. **Protective services:** Police science.

Technology on campus. 25 workstations in library, computer center. Online library available.

Student life. **Freshman orientation:** Mandatory. Preregistration for classes offered. **Activities:** Student newspaper.

Contact. Toll-free number: (888) 720-5014
Carrington College: Stockton, 1313 West Robinhood Drive, Suite B,
Stockton, CA 95207

Cerritos College
Norwalk, California
www.cerritos.edu   CB code: 4083

♦ Public 2-year community college
♦ Commuter campus in large city

General. Founded in 1955. Regionally accredited. **Enrollment:** 17,603
degree-seeking undergraduates. **Degrees:** 1,340 associate awarded. **Location:**
15 miles from Los Angeles. **Calendar:** Semester, limited summer session.
Full-time faculty: 284 total. **Part-time faculty:** 456 total. **Special facilities:**
Health occupations lab, green energy auto lab.

Basis for selection. Open admission, but selective for some programs.
Limited admissions to nursing program, PTA, Pharm, Dental Hygiene.

2015-2016 Annual costs. Tuition/fees: $1,418; $8,018 out-of-state. Per-
credit charge: $46 in-state; $266 out-of-state. Books/supplies: $1,710. Per-
sonal expenses: $3,096.

Financial aid. Need-based: Work-study available nights, weekends and
for part-time students.

Application procedures. Admission: No deadline. No application fee.
Admission notification on a rolling basis. **Financial aid:** Priority date 5/8;
no closing date. FAFSA required. Applicants notified on a rolling basis; must
reply within 2 week(s) of notification.

Academics. Special study options: Cooperative education, distance learning, dual enrollment of high school students, honors. License preparation in
dental hygiene, nursing, physical therapy. **Credit/placement by examination:** AP, CLEP, institutional tests. 12 credit hours maximum toward associate
degree. **Support services:** Learning center, remedial instruction, tutoring.

Majors. Architecture: Architecture. **Area/ethnic studies:** Chicano/
Hispanic-American/Latino, women's. **Biology:** General, bacteriology,
biomedical sciences, botany, zoology. **Business:** General, accounting, administrative services, banking/financial services, business admin, human
resources, logistics, office management, office/clerical, real estate. **Communications:** Journalism. **Communications technology:** Desktop publishing,
graphics, radio/TV. **Computer sciences:** General, applications programming,
data processing, programming, systems analysis. **Conservation:** Wildlife/
wilderness. **Education:** Bilingual, early childhood, special ed, teacher assistance. **English:** English lit, rhetoric/composition. **Foreign languages:** French,
German, Spanish. **Health services:** Dental assistant, dental hygiene, health
information technology, licensed practical nurse, medical assistant, nursing
(RN), physical therapy assistant. **History:** General. **Math:** General. **Parks/
recreation:** General, exercise sciences. **Philosophy/religion:** Philosophy.
Physical sciences: Chemistry, geology, physics, planetary. **Protective services:** Police science. **Psychology:** General. **Social sciences:** Anthropology,
criminology, economics, geography, international relations, political science,
sociology. **Visual/performing arts:** Art, dramatic, interior design, music,
photography. **Work/family studies:** General, clothing/textiles, institutional
food production.

Technology on campus. 100 workstations in computer center.

Student life. Activities: Bands, choral groups, dance, drama, film society,
literary magazine, music ensembles, musical theater, radio station, student
government, student newspaper, symphony orchestra, Ahora, Indian club,
Vietnamese club, Black Student Union.

Athletics. NJCAA. **Intercollegiate:** Baseball M, basketball, cross-country,
diving, football (tackle) M, golf M, soccer M, softball W, swimming, tennis,
track and field, volleyball W, water polo M, wrestling M. **Team name:** Falcons.

Student services. Adult student services, career counseling, financial aid
counseling, health services, on-campus daycare, personal counseling, veterans' counselor, women's services. **Physically disabled:** Services for visually,
speech, hearing impaired. **Transfer:** Transfer adviser, college fairs on campus
for students transferring to 4-year colleges.

Contact. Phone: (562) 860-2451 ext. 2211 Fax: (562) 467-5068
Stephanie Murguia, Dean, Admissions and Records, Cerritos College,
11110 Alondra Boulevard, Norwalk, CA 90650

Cerro Coso Community College
Ridgecrest, California
www.cerrocoso.edu   CB code: 4027

♦ Public 2-year community college
♦ Commuter campus in large town

General. Founded in 1973. Regionally accredited. Multiple site locations:
Bishop, Mammoth Lake, Ridgecrest, Lake Isabella, East Kern and online.
Enrollment: 2,580 degree-seeking undergraduates. **Degrees:** 337 associate
awarded. **Location:** 120 miles from Bakersfield. **Calendar:** Semester, limited
summer session. **Full-time faculty:** 57 total; 26% have terminal degrees.
Part-time faculty: 124 total. **Class size:** 44% < 20, 52% 20-39, 3% 40-49, 1%
50-99. **Special facilities:** Nature preserve, sculpture garden, comprehensive
learning resource center.

Student profile.

Out-of-state: 2% **25 or older:**   63%

Basis for selection. Open admission. Interview required of nursing
majors.

2015-2016 Annual costs. Tuition/fees: $1,382; $8,642 out-of-state. Per-
credit charge: $46 in-state; $288 out-of-state. Books/supplies: $1,710. Per-
sonal expenses: $3,096.

Financial aid. Need-based: Need-based aid available for part-time students. Work-study available nights, weekends and for part-time students.

Application procedures. Admission: No deadline. No application fee.
Admission notification on a rolling basis. **Financial aid:** Priority date 5/15;
no closing date. FAFSA required. Applicants notified on a rolling basis
starting 6/1; must reply within 2 week(s) of notification.

Academics. Special study options: Cooperative education, distance learning, double major, dual enrollment of high school students, ESL, honors,
independent study, internships, study abroad. License preparation in nursing.
Credit/placement by examination: AP, CLEP. 30 credit hours maximum
toward associate degree. **Support services:** GED preparation and test center,
learning center, remedial instruction, study skills assistance, tutoring.

Majors. Business: General, administrative services, business admin, office
management, office technology, office/clerical. **Computer sciences:** General.
Education: Early childhood. **Health services:** Licensed practical nurse. **Liberal arts:** Arts/sciences. **Parks/recreation:** Facilities management. **Physical
sciences:** General. **Protective services:** Fire safety technology, police science. **Social sciences:** General. **Visual/performing arts:** Art. **Work/family
studies:** Child care management.

Most popular majors. Business/marketing 18%, computer/information
sciences 6%, health sciences 6%, liberal arts 52%, social sciences 13%.

Technology on campus. Online course registration, online library available.

Student life. Freshman orientation: Available. Preregistration for classes
offered. One week before class starts. **Activities:** Bands, choral groups,
drama, literary magazine, student government, student newspaper, symphony orchestra.

Athletics. Intercollegiate: Baseball M, basketball W. **Team name:** Coyotes.

Student services. Career counseling, student employment services, financial aid counseling, on-campus daycare, personal counseling, placement for
graduates, veterans' counselor. **Physically disabled:** Services for visually,
speech, hearing impaired. **Transfer:** Transfer adviser, college fairs on campus
for students transferring to 4-year colleges.

Contact. E-mail: admissions@cerrocoso.edu
Phone: (760) 384-6357 Fax: (760) 384-6377
Dave Cornell, Director of Admission and Records, Cerro Coso
Community College, 3000 College Heights Boulevard, Ridgecrest, CA
93555-7777

Chabot College
Hayward, California
www.chabotcollege.edu   CB code: 4725

♦ Public 2-year community college
♦ Commuter campus in large city

General. Founded in 1961. Regionally accredited. **Enrollment:** 8,998 degree-seeking undergraduates. **Degrees:** 841 associate awarded. **ROTC:** Army, Air Force. **Location:** 30 miles from San Francisco, 14 miles from Oakland, 20 miles from Berkeley. **Calendar:** Semester, extensive summer session. **Full-time faculty:** 165 total; 32% minority, 53% women. **Part-time faculty:** 285 total; 32% minority, 50% women. **Special facilities:** On-campus planetarium.

Student profile.

Out-of-state: 1% **25 or older:**   45%

Transfer out. Colleges most students transferred to 2015: CSU: East Bay, San Jose State University, UC: Berkeley, San Francisco State University, UC: Davis.

Basis for selection. Open admission, but selective for some programs. Special requirements for nursing, dental hygiene, and paramedic programs.

2015-2016 Annual costs. Tuition/fees: $1,414; $8,704 out-of-state. Per-credit charge: $46 in-state; $289 out-of-state. Books/supplies: $1,710. Personal expenses: $3,096.

Financial aid. Need-based: Work-study available nights, weekends and for part-time students. **Additional information:** Tuition and/or fee waivers for low-income students.

Application procedures. Admission: Closing date 8/30. No application fee. Admission notification on a rolling basis. Early action available for local high school students only. **Financial aid:** Priority date 8/1; no closing date. FAFSA, institutional form required. Applicants notified on a rolling basis.

Academics. Special study options: Cooperative education, cross-registration, distance learning, double major, dual enrollment of high school students, ESL, independent study, internships, liberal arts/career combination, student-designed major, study abroad, weekend college. License preparation in dental hygiene, nursing, real estate. **Credit/placement by examination:** AP, CLEP, institutional tests. 15 credit hours maximum toward associate degree. English and math tests required for placement. **Support services:** Learning center, pre-admission summer program, reduced course load, remedial instruction, study skills assistance, tutoring, writing center.

Majors. Biology: General. **Business:** General, accounting, administrative services, banking/financial services, logistics, management information systems, management science, office management, office technology, office/clerical, real estate, sales/distribution, tourism/travel. **Communications:** Broadcast journalism, journalism. **Communications technology:** General, radio/TV. **Computer sciences:** General, applications programming, computer science, data processing, information systems, programming. **Education:** Early childhood, teacher assistance. **Engineering:** General. **English:** English lit, rhetoric/composition. **Foreign languages:** French, German, Italian, Portuguese, Spanish. **General:** Maintenance, power transmission. **Health services:** Clinical lab technology, dental hygiene, health information management, health information technology, medical assistant, nursing (RN), predental, premedicine, prepharmacy, preveterinary. **History:** General. **Liberal arts:** Arts/sciences, library assistant. **Math:** General. **Parks/recreation:** General. **Philosophy/religion:** Philosophy. **Physical sciences:** Physics. **Protective services:** Firefighting, police science. **Psychology:** General. **Social sciences:** General, criminology, geography, political science, sociology. **Visual/performing arts:** Art, ceramics, commercial/advertising art, dance, dramatic, drawing, music, music performance, painting, photography, sculpture, studio arts. **Work/family studies:** Child care management, clothing/textiles.

Most popular majors. Business/marketing 10%, health sciences 15%, liberal arts 50%.

Technology on campus. Online course registration, wireless network available.

Student life. Freshman orientation: Available. Preregistration for classes offered. Introduction to college experience, programs, services, assessment tests, and registration process. **Activities:** Bands, choral groups, drama, film society, literary magazine, musical theater, radio station, student government, student newspaper, TV station, various religious, political, ethnic, and social service organizations.

Athletics. NJCAA. **Intercollegiate:** Baseball M, basketball, cross-country, football (tackle) M, golf M, soccer, softball W, swimming, tennis, track and field, volleyball W, water polo W, wrestling M. **Intramural:** Archery, badminton, basketball, bowling, handball, racquetball, soccer, softball, table tennis, tennis, volleyball. **Team name:** Gladiators.

Student services. Adult student services, career counseling, services for economically disadvantaged, student employment services, health services, minority student services, on-campus daycare, personal counseling, placement for graduates, veterans' counselor. **Physically disabled:** Services for visually, speech, hearing impaired. **Transfer:** Re-entry adviser for new students. Transfer center, college fairs on campus for students transferring to 4-year colleges.

Contact. E-mail: ccarcom@chabotcollege.edu
Phone: (510) 723-6700 Fax: (510) 723-7510
Paulette Lino, Director of Admissions & Records, Chabot College, 25555 Hesperian Boulevard, Hayward, CA 94545

Chaffey College
Rancho Cucamonga, California
www.chaffey.edu   **CB code: 4046**

- Public 2-year community college
- Commuter campus in small city

General. Founded in 1883. Regionally accredited. **Enrollment:** 14,699 degree-seeking undergraduates. **Degrees:** 2,042 associate awarded. **Location:** 50 miles from Los Angeles. **Calendar:** Semester, limited summer session. **Full-time faculty:** 202 total. **Part-time faculty:** 625 total. **Special facilities:** Nature preserve, natural history collection, planetarium, 2 swimming pools, children's center.

Transfer out. Colleges most students transferred to 2015: CSU San Bernardino, California State Polytechnic University: Pomona, CSU Fullerton, University of LaVerne, Loma Linda University.

Basis for selection. Open admission. Assessment testing is recommended.

2015-2016 Annual costs. Tuition/fees: $1,414; $7,744 out-of-state. Per-credit charge: $46 in-state; $257 out-of-state. Books/supplies: $1,710. Personal expenses: $3,096.

Financial aid. Need-based: Need-based aid available for part-time students. Work-study available nights, weekends and for part-time students. **Non-need-based:** Scholarships awarded for academics. **Additional information:** State of California Board of Governors fee waivers to qualified state residents. Criteria for eligibility: households which receive public assistance, meet state's low income guidelines, and demonstrate need as defined by Title IV programs.

Application procedures. Admission: No deadline. No application fee. Admission notification on a rolling basis. **Financial aid:** No deadline. FAFSA required. Applicants notified on a rolling basis starting 7/15; must reply within 2 week(s) of notification.

Academics. Special study options: Accelerated study, cooperative education, dual enrollment of high school students, ESL, honors, independent study, internships, liberal arts/career combination, study abroad, weekend college. License preparation in aviation, nursing. **Credit/placement by examination:** AP, CLEP, institutional tests. **Support services:** GED preparation, learning center, remedial instruction, tutoring, writing center.

Majors. Biology: General. **Business:** Accounting, administrative services, business admin, fashion, office management, sales/distribution. **Communications:** Broadcast journalism, communications/speech/rhetoric. **Computer sciences:** General, applications programming. **Conservation:** Environmental studies. **Education:** General, early childhood, physical. **Engineering:** General. **English:** English lit. **Foreign languages:** French, German, Spanish. **Health services:** Dental assistant, medical radiologic technology/radiation therapy, nursing (RN). **History:** General. **Liberal arts:** Arts/sciences. **Math:** General. **Philosophy/religion:** Philosophy, religion. **Physical sciences:** Chemistry, geology, physics, planetary. **Psychology:** General. **Social sciences:** General, anthropology, economics, geography, political science, sociology. **Visual/performing arts:** Art, commercial/advertising art, dance, design, dramatic, fashion design, graphic design, interior design, multimedia, music, photography, studio arts. **Work/family studies:** General, child care management.

Technology on campus. 950 workstations in library, computer center. Repair service available.

Student life. Freshman orientation: Mandatory. Preregistration for classes offered. 3-hour session covers registration procedures, fees, financial aid, programs and services, counseling, course descriptions. **Activities:** Bands, choral groups, dance, drama, film society, music ensembles, Model UN, musical theater, student government, student newspaper, multicultural organizations, Vietnamese club, MECHA, Alpha Gamma Sigma, Black Student Union, ski club, religious organizations, French club, German club, Spanish club, Lambda.

Athletics. Intercollegiate: Baseball M, basketball, diving, football (tackle) M, softball W, swimming, volleyball W, water polo M. **Team name:** Panthers.

Student services. Alcohol/substance abuse counseling, career counseling, services for economically disadvantaged, student employment services, financial aid counseling, health services, on-campus daycare, personal counseling, veterans' counselor. **Physically disabled:** Services for visually, speech, hearing impaired. **Transfer:** Pre-admission transcript evaluation for new students. Transfer center, transfer adviser, college fairs on campus for students transferring to 4-year colleges.

Contact. Phone: (909) 652-6600 Fax: (909) 652-6006
Cecilia Carrera, Director of Admissions, Chaffey College, 5885 Haven Avenue, Rancho Cucamonga, CA 91737-3002

Citrus College
Glendora, California
www.citruscollege.edu   CB code: 4051

▶ Public 2-year community college
▶ Commuter campus in small city

General. Founded in 1915. Regionally accredited. **Enrollment:** 9,475 degree-seeking undergraduates. **Degrees:** 2,383 associate awarded. **Location:** 25 miles from Los Angeles. **Calendar:** Semester, extensive summer session. **Full-time faculty:** 153 total; 19% have terminal degrees. **Part-time faculty:** 355 total.

Basis for selection. Open admission. **Adult students:** SAT/ACT scores not required.

2015-2016 Annual costs. Tuition/fees: $1,450; $8,170 out-of-state. Per-credit charge: $46 in-state; $270 out-of-state. Books/supplies: $1,665. Personal expenses: $3,105.

2014-2015 Financial aid. Need-based: 90% of total undergraduate aid awarded as scholarships/grants, 10% as loans/jobs. Need-based aid available for part-time students. Work-study available nights, weekends and for part-time students.

Application procedures. Admission: No deadline. No application fee. Application must be submitted online. Admission notification on a rolling basis. **Financial aid:** Closing date 3/1. FAFSA required. Applicants notified on a rolling basis; must reply within 2 week(s) of notification.

Academics. Special study options: Cooperative education, distance learning, double major, dual enrollment of high school students, ESL, honors, study abroad. License preparation in nursing. **Credit/placement by examination:** AP, CLEP, IB. 12 credit hours maximum toward associate degree. **Support services:** Learning center, pre-admission summer program, remedial instruction, study skills assistance, tutoring, writing center.

Majors. Biology: Botany, zoology. **Business:** General, management information systems, office management, office/clerical. **Computer sciences:** General, data processing. **Engineering:** General. **English:** English lit. **Health services:** Dental assistant, licensed practical nurse, medical assistant, nursing (RN). **Liberal arts:** Arts/sciences, library assistant. **Math:** General. **Parks/recreation:** Health/fitness. **Physical sciences:** Chemistry, physics. **Psychology:** General. **Social sciences:** General. **Visual/performing arts:** Art, dance, music, photography, studio arts.

Technology on campus. 1,100 workstations in library, computer center. Online course registration, online library, wireless network available.

Student life. Freshman orientation: Mandatory. Preregistration for classes offered. **Activities:** Jazz band, dance, drama, international student organizations, literary magazine, music ensembles, musical theater, student government, student newspaper, Native American student association, Latinos Unidos student Association.

Athletics. Intercollegiate: Baseball M, basketball, cross-country, football (tackle) M, golf, soccer, softball W, swimming W, volleyball W, water polo. **Team name:** Owls.

Student services. Career counseling, services for economically disadvantaged, student employment services, financial aid counseling, health services, legal services, minority student services, personal counseling, placement for graduates, veterans' counselor. **Physically disabled:** Services for visually, speech, hearing impaired. **Transfer:** Transfer center, transfer adviser, college fairs on campus for students transferring to 4-year colleges.

Contact. E-mail: admissions@citruscollege.edu
Phone: (626) 914-8511 Fax: (626) 914-8613
Gerald Sequeira, Dean of Admissions, Citrus College, 1000 West Foothill Boulevard, Glendora, CA 91741-1899

City College of San Francisco
San Francisco, California
www.ccsf.edu   CB code: 4052

▶ Public 2-year community college
▶ Commuter campus in very large city

General. Founded in 1935. Regionally accredited. **Enrollment:** 13,638 degree-seeking undergraduates. **Degrees:** 1,695 associate awarded. **ROTC:** Army. **Location:** Downtown. **Calendar:** Semester, extensive summer session. **Full-time faculty:** 808 total; 36% minority. **Part-time faculty:** 1,012 total; 40% minority. **Special facilities:** Observatory, Diego Rivera Pan-American Mural.

Student profile.

Out-of-state:	5%	25 or older: 65%

Transfer out. Colleges most students transferred to 2015: San Francisco State University, California State University: East Bay, San Jose State University, University of California: Berkeley, University of California: Davis.

Basis for selection. Open admission, but selective for some programs. If applicant lacks high school diploma or equivalent, must be 18 or older and demonstrate ability to benefit. Program for registered nursing and a few other programs have a competitive/ special admissions process. All students entering the credit program are tested for placement into English or ESL and mathematics courses. **Adult students:** SAT/ACT scores not required. Credit programs require placement tests in English or ESL and mathematics. Free noncredit classes require placement tests depending on intended course of study.

2015-2016 Annual costs. Tuition/fees: $1,414; $7,954 out-of-state. Per-credit charge: $46 in-state; $264 out-of-state. Books/supplies: $1,710. Personal expenses: $3,096.

Financial aid. Need-based: Work-study available nights, weekends and for part-time students. **Additional information:** Board of Governor fee waiver for low income students.

Application procedures. Admission: No deadline. No application fee. Admission notification on a rolling basis. **Financial aid:** Priority date 3/1; no closing date. FAFSA required. Applicants notified on a rolling basis starting 7/1.

Academics. Free, noncredit classes offered in some subjects. Working Adults Degree Program. Bookloan program for low-income students. Intercollegiate Speech and Debate. Learning assistance, diversity, and student success programs. **Special study options:** Accelerated study, distance learning, dual enrollment of high school students, ESL, honors, independent study, internships, liberal arts/career combination, study abroad, weekend college. Credit is available for service-learning. License preparation in dental hygiene, nursing, paramedic, radiology. **Credit/placement by examination:** AP, CLEP, institutional tests. 45 credit hours maximum toward associate degree. Various limitations and stipulations on credit by examination. **Support services:** GED preparation and test center, learning center, pre-admission summer program, remedial instruction, study skills assistance, tutoring, writing center.

Majors. Architecture: Environmental design, interior. **Biology:** General. **Business:** Accounting, administrative services, business admin, fashion, hospitality/recreation, human resources, management information systems, marketing, office technology, office/clerical, operations, real estate, tourism promotion, tourism/travel. **Communications:** Journalism. **Communications technology:** General, graphic/printing. **Computer sciences:** General, computer science. **Education:** Teacher assistance. **Engineering:** General, mechanical. **General:** Site management. **Health services:** Clinical lab science, dental assistant, EMT paramedic, health information management, health information technology, medical assistant, medical radiologic technology/radiation therapy, medical secretary, nursing (RN), office admin, office assistant, physician assistant, ward clerk. **Liberal arts:** Library assistant. **Physical sciences:** Chemistry. **Protective services:** Fire safety technology, police science. **Visual/performing arts:** Cinematography, graphic design, interior design, photography, printmaking. **Work/family studies:** Child development, human nutrition.

Technology on campus. 750 workstations in library, computer center, student center. Commuter students can connect to campus network. Online course registration, online library, helpline, wireless network available.

Student life. Freshman orientation: Mandatory. Preregistration for classes offered. **Activities:** Jazz band, choral groups, dance, drama, film society, literary magazine, music ensembles, musical theater, opera, radio station, student government, student newspaper, symphony orchestra, TV station, City College Press Club, Cartoon Illustration and Art, La Raza Unida, Chinese Culture Club, Christian Fellowship Club, Le Cercle Francais, African

American Changing Times, LBGTstr8 Alliance, Students Linking Education and Activism, Women of Color Organization.

Athletics. NJCAA. **Intercollegiate:** Badminton W, baseball M, basketball, cheerleading, cross-country, football (tackle) M, judo W, soccer, softball W, tennis, track and field, volleyball W. **Intramural:** Archery, badminton, baseball, basketball, cheerleading, fencing, football (non-tackle), golf, gymnastics, judo, racquetball, soccer, swimming, tennis, volleyball, weight lifting. **Team name:** Rams.

Student services. Adult student services, alcohol/substance abuse counseling, career counseling, services for economically disadvantaged, student employment services, financial aid counseling, health services, minority student services, on-campus daycare, personal counseling, placement for graduates, veterans' counselor, women's services. **Physically disabled:** Services for visually, speech, hearing impaired. **Transfer:** Transfer center, transfer adviser, college fairs on campus for students transferring to 4-year colleges.

Contact. E-mail: admits@ccsf.edu
Phone: (415) 239-3285 Fax: (415) 239-3936
MaryLou Leyba-Frank, Dean of Admissions and Records, City College of San Francisco, Office of Admissions and Records E-107, San Francisco, CA 94112

Coastline Community College
Fountain Valley, California · **CB member**
www.coastline.edu **CB code: 0933**

- Public 2-year community college
- Commuter campus in small city

General. Founded in 1976. Regionally accredited. Classes held at community-based sites during the daytime, evenings, weekends, and through extensive distance learning education. **Enrollment:** 7,361 degree-seeking undergraduates. **Degrees:** 1,875 associate awarded. **Location:** 30 miles from Los Angeles. **Calendar:** Semester, limited summer session. **Full-time faculty:** 45 total. **Part-time faculty:** 265 total. **Class size:** 45% < 20, 40% 20-39, 6% 40-49, 6% 50-99, 2% >100. **Special facilities:** Workplace preparation center.

Student profile.

Out-of-state: 1% 25 or older: 73%

Transfer out. Colleges most students transferred to 2015: CSU Fullerton, CSU Long Beach, UC Irvine.

Basis for selection. Open admission. If submitted, SAT/ACT used for placement and counseling, in lieu of college administered English and math tests.

2015-2016 Annual costs. Tuition/fees: $1,400; $8,330 out-of-state. Per-credit charge: $46 in-state; $277 out-of-state. Books/supplies: $1,656. Personal expenses: $3,114.

Financial aid. All financial aid based on need. Need-based aid available for part-time students. Work-study available nights, weekends and for part-time students. **Additional information:** Board of Governor's Grant: statewide fee waiver program for students or dependents receiving HFOL/TANF, SSI, General Relief, or whose income meets set standards or who are considered eligible through Federal needs analysis.

Application procedures. Admission: No deadline. No application fee. Admission notification on a rolling basis. **Financial aid:** Priority date 3/2; no closing date. FAFSA, institutional form required. Applicants notified on a rolling basis starting 8/1; must reply within 2 week(s) of notification.

Academics. Special study options: Accelerated study, cooperative education, distance learning, dual enrollment of high school students, ESL, independent study, liberal arts/career combination, study abroad, weekend college. Midnight college via telecourse delivery. License preparation in physical therapy, real estate. **Credit/placement by examination:** AP, CLEP. 30 credit hours maximum toward associate degree. **Support services:** GED preparation, reduced course load, remedial instruction, tutoring.

Majors. Business: General, accounting, business admin, entrepreneurial studies, management science, office technology, real estate. **Computer sciences:** General. **Liberal arts:** Arts/sciences.

Technology on campus. 100 workstations in computer center.

Student life. Freshman orientation: Available. Preregistration for classes offered. **Activities:** Choral groups, dance, student government.

Student services. Career counseling, services for economically disadvantaged, student employment services, financial aid counseling, health services, personal counseling, veterans' counselor. **Physically disabled:** Services for hearing impaired. **Transfer:** Transfer center, transfer adviser, college fairs on campus for students transferring to 4-year colleges.

Contact. E-mail: jmcdonald@cccd,edu
Phone: (714) 241-6176 Fax: (714) 241-6288
Jennifer McDonald, Director of Admissions and Records, Coastline Community College, 11460 Warner Avenue, Fountain Valley, CA 92708

College of Alameda
Alameda, California
www.alameda.peralta.edu **CB code: 4118**

- Public 2-year community college
- Commuter campus in small city

General. Founded in 1970. Regionally accredited. **Enrollment:** 3,035 degree-seeking undergraduates. **Degrees:** 230 associate awarded. **Calendar:** Semester, limited summer session. **Full-time faculty:** 72 total; 17% have terminal degrees, 42% minority. **Part-time faculty:** 117 total.

Student profile.

Out-of-state: 2% 25 or older: 44%

Basis for selection. Open admission.

High school preparation. College-preparatory program recommended.

2015-2016 Annual costs. Tuition/fees: $1,416; $8,016 out-of-state. Per-credit charge: $46 in-state; $266 out-of-state. Books/supplies: $1,710. Personal expenses: $3,096.

Financial aid. Need-based: Work-study available nights, weekends and for part-time students.

Application procedures. Admission: No deadline. No application fee. Admission notification on a rolling basis. **Financial aid:** Priority date 3/2; no closing date. FAFSA required. Applicants notified on a rolling basis starting 7/1; must reply within 2 week(s) of notification.

Academics. Special study options: Cooperative education, cross-registration, dual enrollment of high school students, honors, independent study, liberal arts/career combination. License preparation in aviation. **Credit/placement by examination:** AP, CLEP, institutional tests. **Support services:** Learning center, remedial instruction, tutoring.

Majors. Area/ethnic studies: African-American. **Biology:** General. **Business:** General, accounting, administrative services, business admin, entrepreneurial studies, fashion, marketing, office/clerical. **Education:** Teacher assistance. **English:** English lit. **Foreign languages:** Spanish. **Health services:** Dental assistant, health aide. **History:** General. **Liberal arts:** Arts/sciences. **Math:** General. **Philosophy/religion:** Philosophy. **Psychology:** General. **Social sciences:** General, anthropology, economics, geography, political science, sociology. **Visual/performing arts:** General, music, studio arts.

Technology on campus. Online course registration available.

Student life. Freshman orientation: Available. Preregistration for classes offered. **Activities:** Jazz band, choral groups, dance, drama, student government, student newspaper.

Athletics. Intercollegiate: Basketball, bowling, cross-country M, fencing, golf, soccer M, tennis, track and field, volleyball. **Intramural:** Golf, sailing, softball W. **Team name:** COUGARS.

Student services. Adult student services, career counseling, services for economically disadvantaged, student employment services, health services, on-campus daycare, personal counseling, placement for graduates, veterans' counselor. **Physically disabled:** Services for visually, speech, hearing impaired. **Transfer:** Transfer adviser, college fairs on campus for students transferring to 4-year colleges.

Contact. E-mail: admissions@peralta.edu
Phone: (510) 748-2228 Fax: (510) 748-5227
Kelly Compton, Vice President of Student Services, College of Alameda, 555 Ralph Appezzato Memorial Parkway, Alameda, CA 94501

College of Marin
Kentfield, California
www.marin.edu CB code: 4061

- Public 2-year community college
- Commuter campus in small town

General. Founded in 1926. Regionally accredited. Additional campus at Indian Valley - Novato, CA. **Enrollment:** 2,672 degree-seeking undergraduates. **Degrees:** 299 associate awarded. **Location:** 15 miles from San Francisco. **Calendar:** Semester, limited summer session. **Full-time faculty:** 90 total. **Part-time faculty:** 249 total.

Transfer out. Colleges most students transferred to 2015: University of California: Berkeley, San Francisco State, University of California: Davis.

Basis for selection. Open admission, but selective for some programs. Limited admissions to registered nursing program. **Adult students:** SAT/ACT scores not required.

2015-2016 Annual costs. Tuition/fees: $1,418; $8,888 out-of-state. Per-credit charge: $46 in-state; $295 out-of-state. Books/supplies: $1,620. Personal expenses: $3,078.

Financial aid. All financial aid based on need. Need-based aid available for part-time students. Work-study available nights, weekends and for part-time students.

Application procedures. Admission: No deadline. No application fee. Admission notification on a rolling basis. **Financial aid:** Priority date 3/2; no closing date. FAFSA required. Applicants notified on a rolling basis starting 5/15.

Academics. Special study options: Distance learning, ESL. **Credit/placement by examination:** AP, CLEP, institutional tests. **Support services:** GED preparation, remedial instruction, study skills assistance, tutoring, writing center.

Majors. Architecture: Environmental design. **Area/ethnic studies:** General. **Biology:** General, environmental. **Business:** General, accounting, business admin, real estate. **Communications:** Media studies. **Computer sciences:** General, computer science, web page design. **English:** English lit, rhetoric/composition. **Foreign languages:** General, French, Spanish. **Health services:** Dental assistant, medical assistant, nursing (RN). **History:** General. **Liberal arts:** Arts/sciences. **Math:** General. **Physical sciences:** General, chemistry, physics. **Psychology:** General. **Social sciences:** General, geography. **Visual/performing arts:** Dance, dramatic, music, studio arts. **Work/family studies:** Child care service.

Technology on campus. Online course registration available.

Student life. Activities: Concert band, choral groups, dance, drama, student government, student newspaper.

Athletics. Intercollegiate: Baseball M, basketball, cross-country, diving, soccer, softball, squash, tennis, track and field.

Student services. Career counseling, services for economically disadvantaged, on-campus daycare, personal counseling. **Transfer:** Transfer center, transfer adviser, college fairs on campus for students transferring to 4-year colleges.

Contact. Phone: (415) 485-9412
Robert Balestreri, Dean of Enrollment Services, College of Marin, 835 College Avenue, Kentfield, CA 94904

College of San Mateo
San Mateo, California
www.collegeofsanmateo.edu CB code: 4070

- Public 2-year community college
- Commuter campus in small city

General. Founded in 1922. Regionally accredited. **Enrollment:** 5,263 degree-seeking undergraduates. **Degrees:** 635 associate awarded. **Location:** 15 miles from San Francisco. **Calendar:** Semester, limited summer session. **Full-time faculty:** 141 total. **Part-time faculty:** 208 total. **Special facilities:** Planetarium.

Student profile.

Out-of-state:	2%	25 or older:	51%

Basis for selection. Open admission, but selective for some programs. Nursing program has separate requirements. Completion of CSM Placement tests for English, reading and mathematics recommended prior to orientation and counseling session.

2015-2016 Annual costs. Tuition/fees: $1,418; $8,288 out-of-state. Per-credit charge: $46 in-state; $275 out-of-state. Books/supplies: $1,638. Personal expenses: $2,772.

Financial aid. All financial aid based on need. Need-based aid available for part-time students. Work-study available nights, weekends and for part-time students.

Application procedures. Admission: No deadline. No application fee. Admission notification on a rolling basis. **Financial aid:** No deadline. FAFSA required. Applicants notified on a rolling basis starting 6/15.

Academics. Special study options: Cross-registration, distance learning, double major, dual enrollment of high school students, ESL, honors, independent study, internships, liberal arts/career combination, study abroad, weekend college. Summer bridge. License preparation in nursing, real estate. **Credit/placement by examination:** AP, CLEP, IB, institutional tests. 12 credit hours maximum toward associate degree. **Support services:** Learning center, pre-admission summer program, reduced course load, remedial instruction, study skills assistance, tutoring, writing center. Peer mentoring, operation homecoming (veteran program), writing in the End Zone (college prep and athletics).

Majors. Architecture: Architecture. **Area/ethnic studies:** General. **Biology:** General, biomedical sciences, biotechnology. **Business:** General, accounting, business admin, marketing, office/clerical, real estate, retail management. **Communications:** General, broadcast journalism, digital media, journalism, radio/TV. **Communications technology:** General, graphics, radio/TV. **Computer sciences:** General, applications programming, web page design. **Engineering:** General. **English:** English lit. **Foreign languages:** Spanish. **General:** Building inspection, pipefitting. **Health services:** Dental assistant, nursing (RN), substance abuse counseling. **Math:** General. **Physical sciences:** Chemistry, geology, physics. **Protective services:** Fire safety technology. **Psychology:** General. **Social sciences:** General. **Visual/performing arts:** Art history/conservation, dance, digital arts, graphic design, multimedia, music, photography, studio arts.

Technology on campus. 150 workstations in library, computer center, student center. Commuter students can connect to campus network. Online course registration, online library, wireless network available.

Student life. Freshman orientation: Mandatory. Preregistration for classes offered. Students must complete orientation prior to meeting with a counselor. **Housing:** Center for Student Life maintains up to date listings of housing available in the community. **Activities:** Bands, choral groups, dance, international student organizations, music ensembles, radio station, student government, student newspaper, symphony orchestra, TV station, Asian student union, Christian Fellowship/Intervarsity, CSM Democrats, International Club, Latinos Unidos Club, Puente project, veterans alliance club.

Athletics. Intercollegiate: Baseball M, basketball W, cheerleading, cross-country, football (tackle) M, softball W, swimming, track and field, water polo W. **Team name:** Bulldogs.

Student services. Adult student services, alcohol/substance abuse counseling, career counseling, services for economically disadvantaged, student employment services, financial aid counseling, health services, minority student services, on-campus daycare, personal counseling, veterans' counselor. **Physically disabled:** Services for visually, speech, hearing impaired. **Transfer:** Pre-admission transcript evaluation for new students. Transfer center, transfer adviser, college fairs on campus for students transferring to 4-year colleges.

Contact. E-mail: villarealh@smccd.edu
Phone: (650) 574-6165 Fax: (650) 574-6506
Henry Villareal, Dean of Admissions and Records, College of San Mateo, 1700 West Hillsdale Boulevard, San Mateo, CA 94402-3784

College of the Canyons
Santa Clarita, California
www.canyons.edu CB code: 4117

- Public 2-year community college
- Commuter campus in large city

General. Founded in 1967. Regionally accredited. **Enrollment:** 14,279 degree-seeking undergraduates; 2,653 non-degree-seeking students. **Degrees:** 1,359 associate awarded. **Location:** 36 miles from Los Angeles. **Calendar:** Semester, extensive summer session. **Full-time faculty:** 175 total; 57%

women. **Part-time faculty:** 549 total. **Special facilities:** Performing arts center, proscenium performing arts stage, experimental "black box" theater, university center for access to upper-division and graduate programs.

Student profile. Among degree-seeking undergraduates, 2,390 enrolled as first-time, first-year students.

Part-time:	57%	Hispanic/Latino:	48%
Out-of-state:	3%	Multi-racial, non-Hispanic:	4%
Women:	52%	International:	1%
African American:	4%	25 or older:	26%
Asian American:	9%		

Transfer out. Colleges most students transferred to 2015: California State University: Northridge, University of California: Los Angeles, University of California: Santa Barbara. University of California: San Diego.

Basis for selection. Open admission, but selective for some programs. Limited admission to nursing program. Nursing applicant selections are made using both multi-criteria screening and random screening. Applicants must take institutional English, ESL, chemistry, and mathematics placement tests. **Home schooled:** Transcript of courses and grades required. Per state guidelines, students must be associated with program approved through Los Angeles County, or must be taught by person holding California teaching credential, or must hold a current private school affidavit filed with the State Superintendent of Public Instruction.

2015-2016 Annual costs. Books/supplies: $1,791. Personal expenses: $3,177.

2015-2016 Financial aid. Need-based: 80% of total undergraduate aid awarded as scholarships/grants, 20% as loans/jobs. Need-based aid available for part-time students. Work-study available nights, weekends and for part-time students. **Non-need-based:** Scholarships awarded for academics, alumni affiliation, art, athletics, job skills, leadership, minority status, music/drama, religious affiliation, ROTC, state residency.

Application procedures. Admission: No deadline. No application fee. Admission notification on a rolling basis. **Financial aid:** Closing date 3/2. FAFSA, institutional form required. Applicants notified on a rolling basis starting 6/1; must reply within 4 week(s) of notification.

Academics. Special study options: Accelerated study, cooperative education, cross-registration, distance learning, double major, dual enrollment of high school students, ESL, honors, internships, liberal arts/career combination, study abroad, weekend college. Bachelor's degree programs available on campus. License preparation in nursing, real estate. **Credit/placement by examination:** AP, CLEP, institutional tests. 18 credit hours maximum toward associate degree. Students must be enrolled half-time and be in good academic standing to qualify. **Support services:** GED preparation, learning center, remedial instruction, study skills assistance, tutoring, writing center.

Majors. Business: Accounting technology, administrative services, business admin, hospitality admin, hotel/motel admin, real estate, sales/distribution, small business admin. **Communications:** Communications/speech/rhetoric, journalism. **Communications technology:** Animation/special effects. **Computer sciences:** Computer science, networking. **Engineering:** Pre-engineering. **English:** English lit. **Foreign languages:** French, sign language interpretation, Spanish. **General:** Site management. **Health services:** Athletic training, clinical lab technology, nursing (RN). **History:** General. **Liberal arts:** Arts/sciences, humanities. **Math:** General. **Parks/recreation:** General, health/fitness. **Philosophy/religion:** Philosophy. **Physical sciences:** Geology, physics. **Protective services:** Fire safety technology, police science. **Psychology:** General. **Social sciences:** General, geography, political science, sociology. **Visual/performing arts:** Art, cinematography, dramatic, graphic design, interior design, music, musical theater, photography. **Work/family studies:** Child care service.

Most popular majors. Business/marketing 15%, health sciences 10%, psychology 10%, security/protective services 7%, social sciences 17%, visual/performing arts 6%.

Technology on campus. 2,078 workstations in library, computer center, student center. Online course registration, online library, helpline, wireless network available.

Student life. Freshman orientation: Mandatory. Preregistration for classes offered. Online. **Activities:** Jazz band, choral groups, dance, drama, international student organizations, literary magazine, music ensembles, Model UN, musical theater, student government, symphony orchestra, Political science club, Grace on Campus, Latter-day Saints Student Association, Gamma Beta Phi, Model UN club, honors club, Phi Theta Kappa, Alpha Omega, Association of Latino American students, Society of Hispanic Professional Engineers.

Athletics. Intercollegiate: Baseball M, basketball, cross-country, football (tackle) M, golf, soccer, softball W, swimming, track and field, volleyball W. **Team name:** Cougars.

Student services. Adult student services, career counseling, services for economically disadvantaged, student employment services, financial aid counseling, health services, minority student services, on-campus daycare, personal counseling, placement for graduates, veterans' counselor, women's services. **Physically disabled:** Services for visually, speech, hearing impaired. **Transfer:** Re-entry adviser, pre-admission transcript evaluation for new students. Transfer center, transfer adviser, college fairs on campus for students transferring to 4-year colleges.

Contact. E-mail: admissions@canyons.edu
Phone: (661) 362-3280 Fax: (661) 259-8302
Jasmine Ruys, Director, Admissions, Records and Online Services, College of the Canyons, 26455 Rockwell Canyon Road, Santa Clarita, CA 91355

College of the Desert
Palm Desert, California
www.collegeofthedesert.edu   CB code: 4085

▸ Public 2-year community college
▸ Commuter campus in small city

General. Founded in 1958. Regionally accredited. **Enrollment:** 7,179 degree-seeking undergraduates. **Degrees:** 786 associate awarded. **Location:** 20 miles from Palm Springs, 120 miles from Los Angeles. **Calendar:** Semester, limited summer session. **Full-time faculty:** 106 total; 23% have terminal degrees, 17% minority, 47% women. **Part-time faculty:** 307 total; 16% have terminal degrees, 22% minority, 47% women. **Special facilities:** Performing arts center, golf institute, public safety academy.

Student profile.

Out-of-state:	3%	25 or older:	13%

Basis for selection. Open admission, but selective for some programs. Separate application requirements for nursing, golf management and public safety academy. Interviews required for nursing/allied health majors. **Adult students:** SAT/ACT scores not required.

2015-2016 Annual costs. Tuition/fees: $1,380; $7,380 out-of-state. Per-credit charge: $46 in-district; $246 out-of-district. Books/supplies: $1,746. Personal expenses: $3,132.

Financial aid. Need-based: Need-based aid available for part-time students. Work-study available nights, weekends and for part-time students. **Non-need-based:** Scholarships awarded for academics, art, minority status, music/drama.

Application procedures. Admission: No application fee. Application must be submitted online. Admission notification on a rolling basis. **Financial aid:** Priority date 3/2; no closing date. FAFSA required. Applicants notified on a rolling basis starting 7/1.

Academics. Special study options: Cooperative education, distance learning, double major, dual enrollment of high school students, ESL, honors, independent study, liberal arts/career combination. License preparation in nursing, real estate. **Credit/placement by examination:** AP, CLEP, institutional tests. **Support services:** GED preparation and test center, learning center, remedial instruction, study skills assistance, tutoring, writing center.

Majors. Architecture: Technology. **Biology:** General. **Business:** Business admin, construction management, hotel/motel admin, managerial economics, office management, restaurant/food services. **Communications:** Communications/speech/rhetoric, journalism, media studies, organizational. **Computer sciences:** General, computer science. **Conservation:** General, environmental science, environmental studies. **Education:** Early childhood. **English:** American lit, English lit, rhetoric/composition, writing. **Foreign languages:** French, German, Italian, Spanish. **Health services:** Dietetic technician, licensed practical nurse, nursing (RN). **History:** General. **Liberal arts:** Arts/sciences. **Math:** General. **Parks/recreation:** General, facilities management, golf management. **Philosophy/religion:** Philosophy. **Physical sciences:** Chemistry, geology, physics. **Protective services:** Fire safety technology, law enforcement admin. **Psychology:** General. **Social sciences:** General, anthropology, economics, geography, political science, sociology. **Visual/performing arts:** Acting, art, art history/conservation, dance, dramatic, drawing, graphic design, music, painting, photography, printmaking, studio arts, theater history. **Work/family studies:** Child care management, food/nutrition, human nutrition.

Most popular majors. Business/marketing 15%, health sciences 32%, psychology 7%, security/protective services 7%, social sciences 12%.

Technology on campus. 125 workstations in library, computer center, student center. Online course registration, online library, wireless network available.

Student life. Freshman orientation: Mandatory. Preregistration for classes offered. **Activities:** Choral groups, dance, drama, international student organizations, music ensembles, musical theater, opera, radio station, student government, student newspaper.

Athletics. Intercollegiate: Baseball M, basketball, cheerleading, cross-country, fencing, football (tackle) M, golf, soccer, softball W, tennis, volleyball W. **Team name:** Roadrunners.

Student services. Adult student services, career counseling, services for economically disadvantaged, financial aid counseling, health services, minority student services, on-campus daycare, personal counseling, placement for graduates, veterans' counselor. **Physically disabled:** Services for visually, speech, hearing impaired. **Transfer:** Re-entry adviser, pre-admission transcript evaluation for new students. Transfer center, transfer adviser, college fairs on campus for students transferring to 4-year colleges.

Contact. Phone: (760) 773-2516 Fax: (760) 862-1379
Sally Rodriguez, Admissions & Records Director, College of the Desert, 43500 Monterey Avenue, Palm Desert, CA 92260

College of the Redwoods
Eureka, California
www.redwoods.edu CB code: 4100

- Public 2-year community college
- Commuter campus in large town

General. Founded in 1964. Regionally accredited. Centers at Crescent City; instructional sites in Hoopa, Klamath, downtown Eureka. **Enrollment:** 2,635 degree-seeking undergraduates. **Degrees:** 497 associate awarded. **Location:** 275 miles from San Francisco. **Calendar:** Semester, limited summer session. **Full-time faculty:** 87 total; 13% minority. **Part-time faculty:** 218 total; 10% minority. **Class size:** 42% < 20, 52% 20-39, 4% 40-49, 2% 50-99, less than 1% >100. **Special facilities:** Observatory, fish hatchery, organic farm, fine woodworking shop.

Student profile.

Out-of-state:	4%	Live on campus:	1%
25 or older:	43%		

Transfer out. Colleges most students transferred to 2015: Humboldt State University, California State University: Chico.

Basis for selection. Open admission, but selective for some programs. Admission for nursing applicants based on school record and test scores. **Home schooled:** Must submit a copy of affidavit filed with County Office of Education.

2015-2016 Annual costs. Tuition/fees: $1,418; $7,598 out-of-state. Per-credit charge: $46 in-state; $252 out-of-state. Room/board: $7,560. Books/supplies: $1,746. Personal expenses: $1,638. **Additional information:** Optional $10 student fee and $10 technology fee.

Financial aid. Need-based: Need-based aid available for part-time students. Work-study available nights, weekends and for part-time students.

Application procedures. Admission: Priority date 8/14; no deadline. No application fee. Admission notification on a rolling basis. **Financial aid:** Priority date 4/15; no closing date. FAFSA, institutional form required. Applicants notified on a rolling basis starting 5/1; must reply within 6 week(s) of notification.

Academics. Special study options: Cooperative education, cross-registration, distance learning, double major, dual enrollment of high school students, ESL, honors, independent study, teacher certification program. License preparation in nursing. **Credit/placement by examination:** AP, CLEP, institutional tests. **Support services:** GED preparation and test center, learning center, pre-admission summer program, remedial instruction, tutoring, writing center.

Majors. Business: General, administrative services, hospitality admin, managerial economics, office technology, real estate. **Communications:** Journalism. **Computer sciences:** General. **Conservation:** Fisheries, forestry. **Education:** Early childhood. **Engineering:** Electrical. **English:** English lit. **General:** Maintenance. **Liberal arts:** Arts/sciences. **Math:** General. **Physical sciences:** Planetary. **Protective services:** Law enforcement admin. **Psychology:** General. **Social sciences:** General. **Visual/performing arts:** Commercial/advertising art.

Most popular majors. Business/marketing 7%, health sciences 19%, liberal arts 35%, physical sciences 21%.

Technology on campus. 578 workstations in dormitories, library, computer center, student center. Dormitories wired for high-speed internet access. Online course registration, online library available.

Student life. Freshman orientation: Available. Preregistration for classes offered. **Housing:** Coed dorms available. Limited housing also available for police academy students. **Activities:** Jazz band, choral groups, dance, student government, student newspaper, Native American club, international students club, apologetics club, Bible study, Latter-day Saints club, veterans club, EOPS club.

Athletics. Intercollegiate: Baseball M, basketball, cross-country, football (tackle) M, golf M, soccer W, track and field, volleyball W. **Intramural:** Badminton, bowling, diving, golf, gymnastics, soccer, volleyball, water polo. **Team name:** Corsairs.

Student services. Career counseling, services for economically disadvantaged, student employment services, financial aid counseling, health services, on-campus daycare, personal counseling, placement for graduates, veterans' counselor. **Physically disabled:** Services for visually, speech, hearing impaired. **Transfer:** Transfer center, transfer adviser, college fairs on campus for students transferring to 4-year colleges.

Contact. E-mail: admissions@redwoods.edu
Phone: (707) 476-4200 Toll-free number: (800) 641-0400
Fax: (707) 476-4406
Rianne Connor, Manager, Admissions and Records, College of the Redwoods, 7351 Tompkins Hill Road, Eureka, CA 95501-9300

College of the Sequoias
Visalia, California
www.cos.edu CB code: 4071

- Public 2-year community college
- Commuter campus in small city

General. Founded in 1925. Regionally accredited. Broad range of two year transfer, vocational, and basic skill programs offered. **Enrollment:** 7,755 degree-seeking undergraduates. **Degrees:** 1,122 associate awarded. **ROTC:** Air Force. **Location:** 45 miles from Fresno. **Calendar:** Semester, limited summer session. **Full-time faculty:** 174 total. **Part-time faculty:** 315 total. **Class size:** 33% < 20, 54% 20-39, 5% 40-49, 3% 50-99, 5% >100. **Special facilities:** Self-sufficient farm.

Student profile.

Out-of-state:	3%	25 or older:	39%

Transfer out. Colleges most students transferred to 2015: California State University: Fresno, California State University: Bakersfield, California Polytechnic State University: San Luis Obispo, California State University: Long Beach, California State University: Davis.

Basis for selection. Open admission, but selective for some programs. Limited admission to nursing program. Interviews required for work program, nursing majors. Auditions required for music majors.

High school preparation. College-preparatory program recommended.

2015-2016 Annual costs. Tuition/fees: $1,450; $7,450 out-of-state. Per-credit charge: $46 in-state; $246 out-of-state. Books/supplies: $1,600. Personal expenses: $2,500.

Financial aid. Need-based: Work-study available nights, weekends and for part-time students.

Application procedures. Admission: No deadline. No application fee. Admission notification on a rolling basis. **Financial aid:** Priority date 3/2; no closing date. FAFSA, institutional form required. Applicants notified on a rolling basis starting 6/1; must reply within 2 week(s) of notification.

Academics. Special study options: Distance learning, dual enrollment of high school students, ESL, honors, independent study, internships, student-designed major, study abroad, weekend college. License preparation in nursing, paramedic, physical therapy. **Credit/placement by examination:** AP, CLEP, institutional tests. 12 credit hours maximum toward associate degree. **Support services:** Learning center, pre-admission summer program, reduced course load, remedial instruction, study skills assistance, tutoring, writing center.

Majors. Business: General, accounting, administrative services, management information systems, office/clerical, real estate, sales/distribution. **Communications:** Communications/speech/rhetoric, journalism. **Computer sciences:** Computer science. **Education:** Physical. **Engineering:** General. **English:** English lit, rhetoric/composition. **Foreign languages:** General.

Two-Year Colleges

French. **General:** Carpentry, maintenance. **Health services:** Nursing (RN). **Liberal arts:** Arts/sciences. **Math:** General. **Parks/recreation:** Facilities management. **Protective services:** Fire safety technology, law enforcement admin. **Social sciences:** General. **Visual/performing arts:** Art, commercial/advertising art, dramatic, multimedia, music, studio arts, theater design. **Work/family studies:** General, child care management.

Most popular majors. Business/marketing 6%, health sciences 22%, liberal arts 49%.

Technology on campus. 325 workstations in library, computer center. Online course registration, helpline, wireless network available.

Student life. Freshman orientation: Available. Preregistration for classes offered. Both online and in person. In person classes are held just before the beginning of each semester. **Activities:** Bands, choral groups, dance, drama, music ensembles, musical theater, student government, student newspaper, symphony orchestra.

Athletics. Intercollegiate: Baseball M, basketball, cross-country, diving, football (tackle) M, golf, soccer W, softball W, swimming, tennis, track and field, volleyball W. **Team name:** Giants.

Student services. Adult student services, alcohol/substance abuse counseling, career counseling, services for economically disadvantaged, student employment services, financial aid counseling, health services, minority student services, personal counseling, placement for graduates, veterans' counselor. **Physically disabled:** Services for visually, speech, hearing impaired. **Transfer:** Transfer adviser, college fairs on campus for students transferring to 4-year colleges.

Contact. Phone: (559) 730-3727 Fax: (559) 737-4883
College of the Sequoias, 915 South Mooney Boulevard, Visalia, CA 93277

College of the Siskiyous
Weed, California
www.siskiyous.edu   CB code: 4087

▸ Public 2-year community and junior college
▸ Commuter campus in small town

General. Founded in 1957. Regionally accredited. **Enrollment:** 788 degree-seeking undergraduates. **Degrees:** 174 associate awarded. **Location:** 285 miles from San Francisco, 80 miles from Medford, Oregon. **Calendar:** Semester, limited summer session. **Full-time faculty:** 36 total; 11% have terminal degrees, 11% minority, 33% women. **Part-time faculty:** 150 total. **Class size:** 57% < 20, 35% 20-39, 3% 40-49, 4% 50-99, less than 1% >100.

Transfer out. Colleges most students transferred to 2015: California State University: Chico, Southern Oregon University, University of California: Davis, Simpson University, Humboldt State University.

Basis for selection. Open admission, but selective for some programs. **Adult students:** SAT/ACT scores not required.

2015-2016 Annual costs. Tuition/fees: $1,430; $8,060 out-of-state. Per-credit charge: $46 in-state; $267 out-of-state. Room/board: $8,925. Books/supplies: $1,746. Personal expenses: $3,159.

2014-2015 Financial aid. All financial aid based on need. 63% of total undergraduate aid awarded as scholarships/grants, 37% as loans/jobs. Need-based aid available for part-time students. Work-study available nights, weekends and for part-time students.

Application procedures. Admission: No deadline. No application fee. Admission notification on a rolling basis. **Financial aid:** Priority date 4/30; no closing date. FAFSA required. Applicants notified on a rolling basis starting 6/1; must reply within 2 week(s) of notification.

Academics. Special study options: Cooperative education, distance learning, dual enrollment of high school students, ESL, exchange student, independent study, liberal arts/career combination. License preparation in nursing, paramedic. **Credit/placement by examination:** AP, CLEP, institutional tests. 15 credit hours maximum toward associate degree. **Support services:** Learning center, pre-admission summer program, reduced course load, remedial instruction, study skills assistance, tutoring, writing center.

Majors. Biology: General. **Business:** General, accounting, accounting technology, administrative services, business admin, office management. **Communications:** Broadcast journalism, communications/speech/rhetoric, digital media, media studies, radio/TV. **Computer sciences:** General, computer science, programming. **Education:** General, early childhood, early childhood

special. **Engineering:** General. **English:** English lit, writing. **Foreign languages:** Spanish. **Health services:** EMT paramedic, licensed practical nurse, nursing (RN), predental, premedicine, prenursing, prepharmacy, preveterinary, substance abuse counseling. **History:** General. **Liberal arts:** Arts/sciences, humanities. **Math:** General. **Parks/recreation:** Health/fitness. **Philosophy/religion:** Philosophy. **Physical sciences:** General, chemistry, physics. **Protective services:** Criminal justice, fire safety technology, fire services admin, firefighting, law enforcement admin, police science. **Psychology:** General. **Social sciences:** General, anthropology. **Visual/performing arts:** General, dramatic, music, music performance, voice/opera. **Work/family studies:** Child care management, child care service, family studies, family/community services.

Most popular majors. Biological/life sciences 29%, health sciences 36%, liberal arts 8%, security/protective services 8%.

Technology on campus. 260 workstations in dormitories, library, computer center, student center. Dormitories wired for high-speed internet access and linked to campus network. Commuter students can connect to campus network. Online course registration, online library, helpline, repair service, wireless network available.

Student life. Freshman orientation: Mandatory. Preregistration for classes offered. Multiple sessions offered during three months prior to the start of the semester. Online orientation available. **Housing:** Guaranteed on-campus for all undergraduates. Coed dorms, wellness housing available. $125 fully refundable deposit. **Activities:** Bands, choral groups, dance, drama, international student organizations, music ensembles, musical theater, student government, symphony orchestra, TV station, Latino Student Union, Black Student Union, Phi Theta Kappa Honor Society, International Affairs Organization, Intervarsity Christian club, Disabled Student Alliance, speech and forensics club, Associated Student Board, Gay and Lesbian Alliance, Native American Alliance.

Athletics. Intercollegiate: Baseball M, basketball, cross-country, football (tackle) M, softball W, track and field, volleyball W. **Intramural:** Basketball. **Team name:** Eagles.

Student services. Adult student services, alcohol/substance abuse counseling, career counseling, services for economically disadvantaged, student employment services, financial aid counseling, health services, legal services, on-campus daycare, personal counseling, veterans' counselor. **Physically disabled:** Services for visually, speech, hearing impaired. **Transfer:** Pre-admission transcript evaluation for new students. Transfer center, transfer adviser, college fairs on campus for students transferring to 4-year colleges.

Contact. E-mail: registration@siskiyous.edu
Phone: (530) 938-5500 Toll-free number: (888) 397-4339
Fax: (530) 938-5367
Meghan Witherell, Director of Enrollment Services, College of the Siskiyous, 800 College Avenue, Weed, CA 96094-2899

Columbia College
Sonora, California
www.gocolumbia.edu   CB code: 4108

▸ Public 2-year community college
▸ Commuter campus in small town

General. Founded in 1968. Regionally accredited. **Enrollment:** 1,595 degree-seeking undergraduates. **Degrees:** 250 associate awarded. **Location:** 100 miles from Sacramento. **Calendar:** Semester, limited summer session. **Full-time faculty:** 49 total; 22% minority. **Part-time faculty:** 58 total. **Class size:** 100% < 20. **Special facilities:** Jogging/fitness trail, arboretum, astronomy dome, seismograph, on-campus fire house.

Transfer out. Colleges most students transferred to 2015: CSU Stanislaus.

Basis for selection. Open admission.

2015-2016 Annual costs. Tuition/fees: $1,418; $7,988 out-of-state. Per-credit charge: $46 in-state; $265 out-of-state. Books/supplies: $1,666. Personal expenses: $3,104.

Financial aid. Need-based: Need-based aid available for part-time students. Work-study available nights, weekends and for part-time students. **Non-need-based:** Scholarships awarded for academics.

Application procedures. Admission: No deadline. No application fee. Admission notification on a rolling basis. Matriculation procedures required before new or returning students may register. Early application assures accommodation to new student priority registration periods. **Financial aid:**

Priority date 3/2, closing date 6/1. FAFSA, institutional form required. Applicants notified on a rolling basis starting 6/15; must reply within 2 week(s) of notification.

Academics. Special study options: Cooperative education, distance learning, double major, ESL, independent study, internships, liberal arts/career combination. License preparation in paramedic. **Credit/placement by examination:** AP, CLEP, IB, institutional tests. 12 credit hours maximum toward associate degree. **Support services:** GED preparation and test center, learning center, remedial instruction, study skills assistance, tutoring, writing center.

Majors. Biology: General. **Business:** General, accounting technology, administrative services, business admin, hospitality admin. **Communications:** General. **Computer sciences:** General, information technology, programming. **Conservation:** General, environmental science, forest technology, forestry. **English:** English lit, rhetoric/composition. **Liberal arts:** Arts/sciences. **Math:** General. **Parks/recreation:** Health/fitness. **Physical sciences:** Chemistry, physics, planetary. **Protective services:** Fire safety technology. **Social sciences:** General. **Visual/performing arts:** Art, music, photography. **Work/family studies:** Child development.

Most popular majors. Biological/life sciences 7%, business/marketing 8%, education 31%, English 6%, health sciences 10%, natural resources/environmental science 8%, security/protective services 7%, social sciences 7%.

Technology on campus. 120 workstations in library, computer center, student center. Online course registration, online library, wireless network available.

Student life. Freshman orientation: Mandatory. Preregistration for classes offered. One hour session prior to registration. **Housing:** Coed dorms, special housing for disabled, apartments available. **Activities:** Bands, choral groups, dance, drama, music ensembles, student government, symphony orchestra.

Athletics. Intercollegiate: Basketball M, volleyball W. **Team name:** Claim Jumpers.

Student services. Adult student services, alcohol/substance abuse counseling, career counseling, services for economically disadvantaged, student employment services, financial aid counseling, health services, on-campus daycare, personal counseling, placement for graduates, veterans' counselor. **Physically disabled:** Services for visually, speech, hearing impaired. **Transfer:** Re-entry adviser for new students. Transfer center, transfer adviser, college fairs on campus for students transferring to 4-year colleges.

Contact. Phone: (209) 588-5231 Fax: (209) 588-5337
Melissa Raby, Dean of Student Services, Columbia College, 11600 Columbia College Drive, Sonora, CA 95370

Concorde Career College: Garden Grove
Garden Grove, California
www.concorde.edu   CB code: 2238

- For-profit 2-year health science and technical college
- Small city

General. Regionally accredited; also accredited by ACCSC. **Enrollment:** 974 undergraduates. **Degrees:** 148 associate awarded. **Calendar:** Differs by program. **Full-time faculty:** 40 total.

Basis for selection. Open admission, but selective for some programs.

2015-2016 Annual costs. Diploma programs: medical assistant $15,025; vocational nurse $27,245; dental assistant $13,826; medical office administration $14,655. Associate programs: medical assistant $15,025; dental assistant $13,826; dental hygiene $56,284; physical therapy assistant $38,161; respiratory therapy $39,284. Books and supplies vary by program ranging from $1,123-$2,490.

Financial aid. Need-based: Work-study available nights, weekends and for part-time students.

Application procedures. Admission: No deadline. $100 fee.

Academics. Credit/placement by examination: AP, CLEP.

Majors. Health services: Respiratory therapy technology.

Contact. E-mail: agueco@concorde.edu
Phone: (714) 703-1900
Vincent David, Director of Admissions, Concorde Career College: Garden Grove, 12951 Euclid Street, #101, Garden Grove, CA 92840

Concorde Career College: North Hollywood
North Hollywood, California
www.concorde.edu

- For-profit 2-year health science college
- Large city

General. Accredited by ACCSC. **Enrollment:** 620 undergraduates. **Degrees:** 109 associate awarded. **Calendar:** Differs by program. **Full-time faculty:** 24 total. **Part-time faculty:** 20 total.

Basis for selection. Entrance assessment for all programs. High school graduate or GED for all programs. Institutional exam scores important. CPAT, Wonderlic used.

2015-2016 Annual costs. Diploma programs: medical assistant $15,083; vocational nurse $27,222; dental assistant $13,262; surgical technology $26,422; medical office administration $14,197. Associate programs: medical assistant $15,083; dental assistant $13,262; physical therapy assistant $39,551; respiratory therapy $39,321; surgical technology $26,422. Books and supplies vary by program ranging from $1,207-$4,512.

Financial aid. Need-based: Work-study available nights, weekends and for part-time students.

Application procedures. Admission: No deadline. No application fee. Admission notification on a rolling basis. **Financial aid:** No deadline.

Academics. Credit/placement by examination: AP, CLEP.

Majors. Health services: Respiratory therapy technology.

Contact. Phone: (818) 766-8151 Toll-free number: (800) 464-1212
Fax: (818) 766-1587
Allan Gueco, Director of Admissions, Concorde Career College: North Hollywood, 12412 Victory Boulevard, North Hollywood, CA 91606

Concorde Career College: San Bernardino
San Bernardino, California
www.concorde.edu

- For-profit 2-year technical college
- Small city

General. Regionally accredited; also accredited by ACCSC. **Enrollment:** 668 undergraduates. **Degrees:** 148 associate awarded. **Calendar:** Differs by program. **Full-time faculty:** 52 total. **Part-time faculty:** 15 total.

Basis for selection. High school diploma required and GED accepted.

2015-2016 Annual costs. Diploma programs: medical assistant $15,083; vocational nurse $27,352; dental assistant $13,041; surgical technology $25,403; medical administrative assistant $14,330. Associate programs: medical assistant $15,083; dental hygiene $54,273; dental assistant $13,041; respiratory therapy $39,284; surgical technology $25,403. Books and supplies vary by program ranging from $1,207-$3,872.

Financial aid. Need-based: Work-study available nights, weekends and for part-time students.

Application procedures. Financial aid: Closing date 3/2.

Academics. Credit/placement by examination: AP, CLEP.

Majors. Health services: Respiratory therapy technology.

Contact. Concorde Career College: San Bernardino, 201 East Airport Dr., San Bernardino, CA 92408

Concorde Career College: San Diego
San Diego, California
www.concorde.edu

- For-profit 2-year health science and nursing college
- Very large city

General. Regionally accredited; also accredited by ACCSC. **Enrollment:** 967 undergraduates. **Degrees:** 120 associate awarded. **Calendar:** Continuous. **Full-time faculty:** 83 total. **Part-time faculty:** 3 total.

Basis for selection. Open admission. **Home schooled:** Transcript of courses and grades required.

2015-2016 Annual costs. Diploma programs: medical assistant $15,512; vocational nurse $30,656; dental assistant $13,887; surgical technology $27,192; medical office administration $15,171. Associate programs: dental hygiene $55,162; physical therapy assistant $39,457; respiratory therapy $36,288; surgical technology $27,192. Books and supplies vary by program ranging from $1,087-$10,069.

Financial aid. Need-based: Work-study available nights, weekends and for part-time students.

Application procedures. Admission: No deadline. $100 fee.

Academics. Credit/placement by examination: AP, CLEP.

Majors. Health services: Respiratory therapy assistant.

Contact. E-mail: creese@concorde.edu
Joe Long, Director of Admissions, Concorde Career College: San Diego, 4393 Imperial Avenue, San Diego, CA 92113

Contra Costa College
San Pablo, California
www.contracosta.edu
CB code: 4943

- Public 2-year community college
- Commuter campus in large town

General. Founded in 1948. Regionally accredited. Middle College High School on-campus. 100% pass rate on NCLEX for nursing program graduates. **Enrollment:** 2,883 degree-seeking undergraduates. **Degrees:** 555 associate awarded. **ROTC:** Naval. **Location:** 20 miles from San Francisco. **Calendar:** Semester, limited summer session. **Full-time faculty:** 78 total; 58% women. **Part-time faculty:** 211 total; 54% women. **Class size:** 22% < 20, 58% 20-39, 13% 40-49, 6% 50-99, 1% >100. **Special facilities:** Center for scientific excellence.

Basis for selection. Open admission.

High school preparation. College-preparatory program recommended.

2015-2016 Annual costs. Tuition/fees: $1,390; $8,680 out-of-state. Per-credit charge: $46 in-state; $289 out-of-state.

Financial aid. Need-based: Work-study available nights, weekends and for part-time students.

Application procedures. Admission: No deadline. No application fee. Admission notification on a rolling basis. **Financial aid:** Priority date 3/2; no closing date. FAFSA required. Applicants notified on a rolling basis; must reply within 2 week(s) of notification.

Academics. Special study options: Accelerated study, cross-registration, distance learning, double major, dual enrollment of high school students, ESL, honors, independent study, study abroad. License preparation in dental hygiene, nursing, paramedic, radiology, real estate. **Credit/placement by examination:** AP, CLEP, institutional tests. **Support services:** Learning center, remedial instruction, tutoring, writing center.

Majors. Area/ethnic studies: African-American, Chicano/Hispanic-American/Latino. **Biology:** General, biotechnology. **Business:** Administrative services, business admin, office/clerical, real estate. **Communications:** Communications/speech/rhetoric, journalism. **Computer sciences:** General, applications programming, computer science, networking, support specialist. **Education:** Early childhood, kindergarten/preschool, Montessori teacher. **Engineering:** General. **English:** English lit. **Foreign languages:** Spanish. **Health services:** Nursing (RN), office assistant. **History:** General. **Liberal arts:** Arts/sciences, humanities. **Math:** General. **Parks/recreation:** Exercise sciences. **Physical sciences:** Chemistry, geology, physics. **Protective services:** Corrections, law enforcement admin. **Psychology:** General. **Social sciences:** General, anthropology, economics, geography, sociology. **Visual/performing arts:** General, music.

Most popular majors. Liberal arts 59%, psychology 7%, social sciences 9%.

Technology on campus. Commuter students can connect to campus network. Online course registration, online library, helpline, wireless network available.

Student life. Freshman orientation: Available. Preregistration for classes offered. **Activities:** Jazz band, choral groups, dance, drama, international student organizations, literary magazine, music ensembles, musical theater, student government, student newspaper, TV station.

Athletics. Intercollegiate: Baseball M, basketball, football (tackle) M, soccer, softball W, volleyball W. **Team name:** Comets.

Student services. Adult student services, alcohol/substance abuse counseling, career counseling, services for economically disadvantaged, student employment services, financial aid counseling, health services, minority student services, on-campus daycare, personal counseling, veterans' counselor, women's services. **Physically disabled:** Services for visually, speech, hearing impaired. **Transfer:** Transfer center, college fairs on campus for students transferring to 4-year colleges.

Contact. Phone: (510) 235-7800 ext. 7500
Mikeal Aldaco, Director of Admissions and Records, Contra Costa College, 2600 Mission Bell Drive, San Pablo, CA 94806

Copper Mountain College
Joshua Tree, California
www.cmccd.edu
CB code: 3889

- Public 2-year community college
- Commuter campus in small town

General. Regionally accredited. **Enrollment:** 1,375 degree-seeking undergraduates. **Degrees:** 182 associate awarded. **Location:** 120 miles from Los Angeles, 45 miles from Palm Springs. **Calendar:** Semester, limited summer session. **Full-time faculty:** 42 total. **Part-time faculty:** 95 total.

Transfer out. Colleges most students transferred to 2015: California State University: San Bernardino.

Basis for selection. Open admission, but selective for some programs. Limited admission to some allied health programs. **Adult students:** Accuplacer assessment tests required.

2015-2016 Annual costs. Tuition/fees: $1,380; $7,110 out-of-state. Per-credit charge: $46 in-state; $237 out-of-state. Books/supplies: $1,710. Personal expenses: $3,096.

Financial aid. Need-based: Need-based aid available for part-time students. Work-study available nights, weekends and for part-time students.

Application procedures. Admission: No deadline. No application fee. Application must be submitted online. Admission notification on a rolling basis. **Financial aid:** Priority date 3/2; no closing date. FAFSA required.

Academics. Special study options: Distance learning, dual enrollment of high school students, ESL, independent study, internships, study abroad. License preparation in nursing, paramedic. **Credit/placement by examination:** AP, CLEP, institutional tests. **Support services:** GED preparation, remedial instruction, study skills assistance, tutoring.

Majors. Business: Business admin. **Communications:** Communications/speech/rhetoric. **Computer sciences:** General, computer science. **Conservation:** Environmental studies. **English:** English lit. **Foreign languages:** Spanish. **Health services:** Licensed practical nurse. **History:** General. **Liberal arts:** Arts/sciences. **Math:** General. **Philosophy/religion:** Philosophy. **Protective services:** Fire safety technology, law enforcement admin. **Psychology:** General. **Social sciences:** General, anthropology, economics, political science. **Visual/performing arts:** Art.

Technology on campus. 40 workstations in library, computer center. Online course registration, online library, helpline, wireless network available.

Student life. Freshman orientation: Mandatory. Preregistration for classes offered. Two hour group orientation offered about 16 times prior to each semester. Online orientation available. **Activities:** Literary magazine, student government, student newspaper.

Student services. Adult student services, career counseling, services for economically disadvantaged, student employment services, financial aid counseling, veterans' counselor. **Physically disabled:** Services for visually, speech, hearing impaired. **Transfer:** Pre-admission transcript evaluation for new students. Transfer center, transfer adviser, college fairs on campus for students transferring to 4-year colleges.

Contact. E-mail: lburns@cmccd.edu
Phone: (760) 366-3791 ext. 4232
Toll-free number: (866) 366-3791 ext. 4232 Fax: (760) 366-5257
Gregory Brown, Vice President of Student Services, Copper Mountain College, 6162 Rotary Way, Joshua Tree, CA 92252

Cosumnes River College
Sacramento, California
www.crc.losrios.edu   CB code: 4121

♦ Public 2-year junior college
♦ Commuter campus in large city

General. Founded in 1970. Regionally accredited. Classes offered at Folsom Lake Center, El Dorado Center and Folsom Prison. **Enrollment:** 10,629 degree-seeking undergraduates. **Degrees:** 838 associate awarded. **Location:** 12 miles from downtown. **Calendar:** Semester, limited summer session. **Full-time faculty:** 182 total. **Part-time faculty:** 236 total.

Basis for selection. Open admission.

2015-2016 Annual costs. Tuition/fees: $1,416; $7,956 out-of-state. Per-credit charge: $46 in-state; $264 out-of-state. Books/supplies: $1,656. Personal expenses: $3,114.

Financial aid. Need-based: Work-study available nights, weekends and for part-time students.

Application procedures. Admission: No deadline. No application fee. Admission notification on a rolling basis beginning on or about 3/1. First-time students encouraged to participate in orientation and matriculation sessions. English and mathematics tests for placement recommended. **Financial aid:** Priority date 5/1; no closing date. FAFSA required. Applicants notified on a rolling basis starting 7/20; must reply within 4 week(s) of notification.

Academics. Special study options: Cooperative education, distance learning, double major, dual enrollment of high school students, ESL, honors, independent study, internships, study abroad. **Credit/placement by examination:** AP, CLEP. 15 credit hours maximum toward associate degree. **Support services:** Learning center, reduced course load, remedial instruction, tutoring.

Majors. Architecture: Environmental design, interior, landscape. **Area/ethnic studies:** American, women's. **Business:** General, accounting, business admin, entrepreneurial studies, finance, real estate. **Communications:** Advertising, broadcast journalism, journalism, public relations. **Communications technology:** General. **Computer sciences:** Information systems, programming. **Education:** Early childhood. **General:** Maintenance. **Health services:** Health information technology, medical assistant. **Liberal arts:** Arts/sciences. **Protective services:** Fire safety technology, law enforcement admin. **Social sciences:** Sociology. **Visual/performing arts:** Art, art history/conservation, cinematography, commercial photography, dramatic, interior design, music, photography, studio arts.

Most popular majors. Business/marketing 8%, health sciences 6%, liberal arts 52%, trade and industry 6%.

Student life. Activities: Bands, choral groups, drama, radio station, student government, student newspaper, TV station, African-American Students Association, Hispanic/Latino Scholars, Asian American Club, Christian Club, earth club.

Athletics. Intercollegiate: Baseball M, basketball, soccer, softball W, tennis, track and field, volleyball W. **Intramural:** Badminton, bowling, fencing, golf, racquetball, skiing, swimming, tennis, track and field, volleyball.

Student services. Adult student services, career counseling, student employment services, health services, on-campus daycare, personal counseling, placement for graduates, veterans' counselor. **Physically disabled:** Services for hearing impaired. **Transfer:** Transfer adviser for students transferring to 4-year colleges.

Contact. Phone: (916) 691-7410 Fax: (916) 691-7467
Celia Esposito-Noy, Vice President, Student Services and Enrollment Management, Cosumnes River College, 8401 Center Parkway, Sacramento, CA 95823

Crafton Hills College
Yucaipa, California
www.craftonhills.edu   CB code: 4126

♦ Public 2-year community college
♦ Commuter campus in small city

General. Founded in 1972. Regionally accredited. Located in southern California; offers majors in the liberal arts and sciences, career and technical studies. **Enrollment:** 3,422 degree-seeking undergraduates. **Degrees:** 620 associate awarded. **Location:** 17 miles from San Bernardino, 69 miles from Los Angeles. **Calendar:** Semester, limited summer session. **Full-time faculty:** 70 total; 20% minority. **Part-time faculty:** 155 total; 29% minority.

Special facilities: Walking trails, child care services for preschool-aged children.

Basis for selection. Open admission.

High school preparation. College-preparatory program recommended.

2015-2016 Annual costs. Tuition/fees: $1,425; $7,425 out-of-state. Per-credit charge: $46 in-state; $246 out-of-state. Books/supplies: $1,746. Personal expenses: $3,132.

Financial aid. All financial aid based on need. Need-based aid available for part-time students. Work-study available nights, weekends and for part-time students.

Application procedures. Admission: No deadline. No application fee. Application must be submitted online. Admission notification on a rolling basis. Students under 18 admitted with special permission. **Financial aid:** Priority date 4/15, closing date 6/2. FAFSA, institutional form required. Applicants notified on a rolling basis starting 7/31; must reply within 2 week(s) of notification.

Academics. Special study options: Cooperative education, cross-registration, distance learning, double major, dual enrollment of high school students, honors, study abroad. License preparation in paramedic, radiology. **Credit/placement by examination:** AP, CLEP, institutional tests. 36 credit hours maximum toward associate degree. Currently enrolled students who feel that their knowledge is equivalent to the course content of a currently approved course may apply for credit by examination. **Support services:** Learning center, remedial instruction, study skills assistance, tutoring, writing center.

Majors. Biology: General, bacteriology. **Business:** Administrative services, business admin, marketing, office/clerical. **Computer sciences:** General, programming. **Education:** Early childhood, health occupations. **English:** English lit. **Foreign languages:** General, French, Spanish. **Health services:** EMT paramedic, medical radiologic technology/radiation therapy, respiratory therapy technology. **History:** General. **Liberal arts:** Arts/sciences. **Math:** General. **Physical sciences:** Chemistry, geology, physics. **Protective services:** Firefighting, law enforcement admin. **Psychology:** General. **Social sciences:** General, anthropology, economics, geography, political science, sociology. **Visual/performing arts:** Art, dramatic, music.

Most popular majors. Health sciences 16%, interdisciplinary studies 48%, public administration/social services 7%, social sciences 6%.

Technology on campus. 172 workstations in library, computer center. Online course registration, helpline, wireless network available.

Student life. Freshman orientation: Available. Preregistration for classes offered. **Activities:** Jazz band, drama, music ensembles, musical theater, student government, student newspaper.

Student services. Career counseling, student employment services, health services, on-campus daycare, personal counseling, placement for graduates, veterans' counselor. **Physically disabled:** Services for visually, speech, hearing impaired. **Transfer:** Pre-admission transcript evaluation for new students. Transfer center, transfer adviser, college fairs on campus for students transferring to 4-year colleges.

Contact. E-mail: admissions@craftonhills.edu
Phone: (909) 389-3372 Fax: (909) 389-9141
Dean, Student Services, Crafton Hills College, 11711 Sand Canyon Road, Yucaipa, CA 92399-1799

Cuesta College
San Luis Obispo, California
www.cuesta.org   CB code: 4101

♦ Public 2-year community college
♦ Commuter campus in large town

General. Founded in 1964. Regionally accredited. Additional North County Campus in Paso Robles and South County Center(s) in Arroyo Grande and Nipomo. **Enrollment:** 5,739 degree-seeking undergraduates. **Degrees:** 961 associate awarded. **Location:** 200 miles from Los Angeles, 6 miles from San Luis Obispo. **Calendar:** Semester, extensive summer session. **Full-time faculty:** 185 total. **Part-time faculty:** 368 total. **Special facilities:** Adobe museum (Chumash Indian).

Student profile.

Out-of-state:	3%	25 or older:	33%

Transfer out. Colleges most students transferred to 2015: California Polytechnic State University: San Luis Obispo, CSU: Chico, San Francisco State University, California State Polytechnic University: Pomona.

Basis for selection. Open admission, but selective for some programs. Nursing program requires critical thinking and math assessments. Prerequisite courses evaluated. **Learning Disabled:** No special admission but must be assessed and qualified to receive services.

2015-2016 Annual costs. Tuition/fees: $1,418; $7,418 out-of-state. Per-credit charge: $46 in-state; $246 out-of-state. Books/supplies: $1,710. Personal expenses: $3,096.

Financial aid. Need-based: Work-study available nights, weekends and for part-time students.

Application procedures. Admission: No deadline. No application fee. Admission notification on a rolling basis. **Financial aid:** Priority date 3/2; no closing date. FAFSA required. Applicants notified on a rolling basis starting 4/15.

Academics. Special study options: Cooperative education, distance learning, double major, ESL, honors, independent study, student-designed major, study abroad, weekend college. Bachelor's degree programs available on campus. **Credit/placement by examination:** AP, CLEP, institutional tests. 12 credit hours maximum toward associate degree. **Support services:** Learning center, remedial instruction, study skills assistance, tutoring, writing center.

Majors. Biology: General. **Business:** General, real estate. **Communications:** Broadcast journalism, communications/speech/rhetoric, journalism. **Computer sciences:** Computer science. **Education:** Art, early childhood, mathematics, physical, special ed. **Engineering:** Electrical. **Health services:** Nursing (RN). **Liberal arts:** Arts/sciences, library assistant. **Math:** General. **Physical sciences:** Chemistry, physics. **Protective services:** Law enforcement admin. **Visual/performing arts:** Interior design.

Technology on campus. 300 workstations in library, computer center, student center. Online course registration, online library available.

Student life. Freshman orientation: Available. Preregistration for classes offered. **Activities:** Jazz band, choral groups, dance, drama, music ensembles, musical theater, radio station, student government, student newspaper, TV station, Alpha Gamma Sigma (honor society).

Athletics. Intercollegiate: Baseball M, basketball, cross-country, diving, soccer W, softball W, swimming, tennis W, track and field, volleyball W, water polo, wrestling M.

Student services. Adult student services, career counseling, student employment services, financial aid counseling, health services, legal services, on-campus daycare, personal counseling, veterans' counselor. **Physically disabled:** Services for visually, speech, hearing impaired. **Transfer:** Re-entry adviser for new students. Transfer center, transfer adviser, college fairs on campus for students transferring to 4-year colleges.

Contact. E-mail: admit@bass.cuesta.cc.ca.us
Phone: (805) 546-3140 Fax: (805) 546-3975
Joy Chambers, Director of Admissions and Records, Cuesta College, Box 8106, San Luis Obispo, CA 93403

Cuyamaca College
El Cajon, California
www.cuyamaca.edu   CB code: 4252

- Public 2-year community college
- Commuter campus in small city

General. Founded in 1978. Regionally accredited. **Enrollment:** 5,814 degree-seeking undergraduates. **Degrees:** 701 associate awarded. **ROTC:** Air Force. **Location:** 18 miles from San Diego. **Calendar:** Semester, limited summer session. **Full-time faculty:** 80 total; 12% have terminal degrees, 20% minority. **Part-time faculty:** 250 total; 10% have terminal degrees, 27% minority. **Special facilities:** Automotive technology facility, water gardens, child care facility, museum.

Transfer out. Colleges most students transferred to 2015: San Diego State University, National University.

Basis for selection. Open admission.

2015-2016 Annual costs. Tuition/fees: $1,428; $7,428 out-of-state. Per-credit charge: $46 in-state; $246 out-of-state. Books/supplies: $1,600. Personal expenses: $2,500.

Financial aid. Need-based: Work-study available nights, weekends and for part-time students.

Application procedures. Admission: No deadline. No application fee in-state; $163 out-of-state. Admission notification on a rolling basis. **Financial aid:** Priority date 3/2; no closing date. FAFSA required. Applicants notified on a rolling basis; must reply within 2 week(s) of notification.

Academics. Special study options: Cooperative education, cross-registration, distance learning, double major, dual enrollment of high school students, ESL, honors, independent study, internships, study abroad. License preparation in real estate. **Credit/placement by examination:** AP, CLEP, institutional tests. **Support services:** Remedial instruction, tutoring.

Majors. Business: Accounting, business admin, real estate. **Communications technology:** General. **Engineering:** General, computer, electrical, surveying. **Foreign languages:** Spanish. **Liberal arts:** Arts/sciences. **Physical sciences:** General. **Work/family studies:** Child care management.

Most popular majors. Business/marketing 19%, legal studies 9%, liberal arts 30%, mathematics 6%.

Technology on campus. Online course registration available.

Student life. Freshman orientation: Available. Preregistration for classes offered. **Activities:** Concert band, dance, drama, international student organizations, music ensembles, student government, Christian club, Latter-Day Saint student association, MECHA, Multi Culture Union, Sudanese cultural club.

Athletics. Intercollegiate: Basketball, cross-country, golf M, soccer, tennis W, track and field, volleyball W. **Team name:** Coyotes.

Student services. Adult student services, career counseling, financial aid counseling, health services, on-campus daycare, personal counseling, veterans' counselor. **Physically disabled:** Services for visually, speech, hearing impaired. **Transfer:** Pre-admission transcript evaluation for new students: Transfer center, transfer adviser, college fairs on campus for students transferring to 4-year colleges.

Contact. Phone: (619) 660-4275 Fax: (619) 660-4575
Cuyamaca College, 900 Rancho San Diego Parkway, El Cajon, CA 92019-4304

Cypress College
Cypress, California
www.cypresscollege.edu   CB code: 4104

- Public 2-year community college
- Commuter campus in small city

General. Founded in 1966. Regionally accredited. **Enrollment:** 9,348 degree-seeking undergraduates; 6,947 non-degree-seeking students. **Degrees:** 942 associate awarded. **Location:** 30 miles from Los Angeles. **Calendar:** Semester, limited summer session. **Full-time faculty:** 205 total; 32% minority, 57% women. **Part-time faculty:** 478 total; 38% minority, 53% women. **Class size:** 22% < 20, 55% 20-39, 16% 40-49, 6% 50-99, less than 1% >100.

Student profile. Among degree-seeking undergraduates, 1,388 enrolled as first-time, first-year students, 745 transferred in from other institutions.

Part-time:	65%	Women:	56%
Out-of-state:	1%	25 or older:	30%

Transfer out. Colleges most students transferred to 2015: CSU Fullerton, CSU Long Beach.

Basis for selection. Open admission. College administered English and math placement exams.

High school preparation. College-preparatory program required.

2015-2016 Annual costs. Tuition/fees: $1,414; $7,684 out-of-state. Per-credit charge: $46 in-state; $255 out-of-state. Books/supplies: $1,764. Personal expenses: $3,159.

Financial aid. Need-based: Need-based aid available for part-time students. Work-study available nights, weekends and for part-time students.

Application procedures. Admission: No deadline. No application fee. Admission notification on a rolling basis. **Financial aid:** FAFSA required.

Academics. Special study options: Distance learning, dual enrollment of high school students, ESL, honors, independent study, internships, liberal arts/career combination, study abroad. License preparation in aviation, dental hygiene, nursing, radiology, real estate. **Credit/placement by examination:** AP, CLEP, IB, institutional tests. 12 credit hours maximum toward associate degree. **Support services:** Learning center, reduced course load, remedial instruction, study skills assistance, tutoring, writing center.

Majors. **Area/ethnic studies:** Asian, Latin American. **Business:** General, accounting, administrative services, business admin, hospitality/recreation, management information systems, management science, office technology, office/clerical, tourism promotion. **Communications:** Journalism. **Computer sciences:** General, data processing, information systems. **Education:** General, elementary, physical, secondary, technology/industrial arts. **Engineering:** General. **English:** English lit, rhetoric/composition. **Foreign languages:** French, German, Spanish. **Health services:** Dental assistant, dental hygiene, dental lab technology, health information management, health information technology, medical assistant, medical radiologic technology/radiation therapy, nursing (RN), predental, premedicine, prepharmacy, preveterinary. **History:** General. **Liberal arts:** Arts/sciences. **Math:** General. **Philosophy/religion:** Philosophy. **Physical sciences:** Chemistry, geology, physics. **Psychology:** General. **Social sciences:** Anthropology, economics, geography, political science, sociology. **Visual/performing arts:** General, art, commercial/advertising art, dance, dramatic, music, music performance, theater design. **Work/family studies:** Institutional food production.

Most popular majors. Business/marketing 16%, health sciences 16%, interdisciplinary studies 11%, liberal arts 24%, personal/culinary services 6%, psychology 7%.

Technology on campus. 200 workstations in library, computer center, student center. Online course registration, helpline, wireless network available.

Student life. **Freshman orientation:** Available. Preregistration for classes offered. **Activities:** Bands, choral groups, dance, drama, international student organizations, literary magazine, music ensembles, musical theater, student government, student newspaper.

Athletics. NJCAA. **Intercollegiate:** Baseball M, basketball, diving, golf, soccer, softball W, swimming, tennis, volleyball W, water polo, wrestling M. **Intramural:** Badminton, baseball M, basketball, softball, volleyball. **Team name:** Chargers.

Student services. Adult student services, career counseling, services for economically disadvantaged, student employment services, financial aid counseling, health services, on-campus daycare, personal counseling, veterans' counselor. **Physically disabled:** Services for visually, speech, hearing impaired. **Transfer:** Re-entry adviser, pre-admission transcript evaluation for new students. Transfer center, transfer adviser, college fairs on campus for students transferring to 4-year colleges.

Contact. Phone: (714) 484-7346 Fax: (714) 484-7446
Paul de Dios, Dean of Admissions and Records, Cypress College, 9200 Valley View Street, Cypress, CA 90630

De Anza College
Cupertino, California
www.deanza.edu   CB code: 4286

- Public 2-year community college
- Commuter campus in large town

General. Founded in 1967. Regionally accredited. **Enrollment:** 22,620 undergraduates. **Degrees:** 1,703 associate awarded. **ROTC:** Army, Air Force. **Location:** 5 miles from San Jose, 40 miles from San Francisco. **Calendar:** Quarter, extensive summer session. **Full-time faculty:** 282 total; 38% minority, 55% women. **Part-time faculty:** 477 total; 29% minority, 56% women. **Special facilities:** Planetarium, California history center, environmental studies area, advanced technology center, art museum, performing arts facility, 2 LEED Platinum buildings.

Student profile.

Out-of-state: 1%   25 or older: 37%

Transfer out. **Colleges most students transferred to 2015:** University of California: Davis, San Jose State, San Francisco State, University of California: Berkeley, University of California: Santa Cruz.

Basis for selection. Open admission, but selective for some programs. Limited admission for nursing and physical therapist assistant applicants.

2015-2016 Annual costs. Tuition/fees: $1,427; $8,267 out-of-state. Per-credit charge: $31 in-state; $183 out-of-state. Books/supplies: $1,710. Personal expenses: $3,096.

Financial aid. All financial aid based on need. Need-based aid available for part-time students. Work-study available nights, weekends and for part-time students.

Application procedures. **Admission:** No deadline. No application fee. Admission notification on a rolling basis. **Financial aid:** No deadline. FAFSA required. Applicants notified on a rolling basis starting 5/15; must reply within 2 week(s) of notification.

Academics. **Special study options:** Cross-registration, distance learning, dual enrollment of high school students, ESL, honors, independent study, internships, study abroad, weekend college. License preparation in nursing, physical therapy, real estate. **Credit/placement by examination:** AP, CLEP, institutional tests. 45 credit hours maximum toward associate degree. **Support services:** Learning center, pre-admission summer program, remedial instruction, study skills assistance, tutoring, writing center.

Majors. **Area/ethnic studies:** African-American, Asian-American, Chicano/Hispanic-American/Latino, Latin American, Native American. **Biology:** General. **Business:** Accounting, administrative services, business admin, marketing, purchasing, real estate, taxation. **Communications:** Communications/speech/rhetoric. **Computer sciences:** General, applications programming, computer science, programming, systems analysis. **Education:** Early childhood. **Engineering:** General, computer, electrical, mechanical. **English:** English lit, technical writing. **Foreign languages:** French, German, Spanish. **Health services:** Medical assistant, nursing (RN). **History:** General. **Liberal arts:** Arts/sciences. **Math:** General. **Philosophy/religion:** Philosophy. **Physical sciences:** Astronomy, chemistry, geology, physics. **Protective services:** Law enforcement admin, security services. **Psychology:** General. **Social sciences:** Anthropology, economics, geography, political science, sociology. **Visual/performing arts:** Art, art history/conservation, ceramics, cinematography, commercial/advertising art, music, painting, photography, printmaking, sculpture.

Technology on campus. 300 workstations in library, computer center, student center. Online course registration, online library, repair service, wireless network available.

Student life. **Freshman orientation:** Available. Preregistration for classes offered. Two day counseling course for new, incoming students. **Activities:** Bands, choral groups, dance, drama, international student organizations, literary magazine, music ensembles, student government, student newspaper, symphony orchestra, TV station.

Athletics. **Intercollegiate:** Badminton, baseball M, basketball, cross-country, diving, football (tackle) M, golf, soccer, softball W, swimming, tennis, track and field, volleyball W, water polo. **Intramural:** Badminton, baseball M, basketball, bowling, fencing, gymnastics, racquetball, soccer W, swimming, tennis, volleyball. **Team name:** Dons.

Student services. Adult student services, alcohol/substance abuse counseling, career counseling, services for economically disadvantaged, student employment services, financial aid counseling, health services, legal services, minority student services, on-campus daycare, personal counseling, placement for graduates, veterans' counselor, women's services. **Physically disabled:** Services for visually, speech, hearing impaired. **Transfer:** Re-entry adviser for new students. Transfer center, transfer adviser, college fairs on campus for students transferring to 4-year colleges.

Contact. E-mail: webreg@fhda.edu
Phone: (408) 864-5300 Fax: (408) 864-8329
Kathleen Moberg, Dean of Admissions and Records, De Anza College, 21250 Stevens Creek Boulevard, Cupertino, CA 95014

Deep Springs College
Dyer, Nevada
www.deepsprings.edu   CB code: 4281

- Private 2-year liberal arts college for men
- Residential campus in rural community
- Application essay, interview required

General. Founded in 1917. Regionally accredited. Located in California's High Desert; requires students to work on ranch and farm, cook, clean, and do routine maintenance, as well as hire faculty, admit students and self-govern. **Enrollment:** 28 degree-seeking undergraduates. **Degrees:** 11 associate awarded. **Location:** 45 miles from Bishop, CA, 27 miles from Big Pine, CA. **Calendar:** Differs by program, limited summer session. **Full-time faculty:** 3 total; 100% have terminal degrees, 67% women. **Part-time faculty:** 13 total; 77% have terminal degrees, 23% women. **Class size:** 100% < 20. **Special facilities:** Student-operated 2,600-acre cattle ranch, alfalfa farm, dairy, organic garden, uninhabited desert.

Student profile.

Out-of-state: 82% Live on campus: 100%

Transfer out. Colleges most students transferred to 2015: Yale University, Brown University, Shimer College, Northwestern University.

Basis for selection. Essays and interview most important. School achievement record, extracurricular activities, and recommendations strongly considered. Admissions process created and run by student committee. International applicants SAT/ACT are optional.

2015-2016 Annual costs. Books/supplies: $1,000. **Additional information:** All students receive a full scholarship covering tuition, room and board. Students buy their own books and necessary supplies.

Financial aid. Need-based: Work-study available nights, weekends and for part-time students. **Non-need-based:** Scholarships awarded for academics, job skills, leadership. **Additional information:** Every admitted student is awarded a scholarship for the full cost of tuition and room and board. For students in need, additional funds are available for books, travel, and incidental expenses.

Application procedures. Admission: Closing date 11/7 (postmark date). No application fee. Admission notification by 4/15. Must reply by 5/1. 40 to 50 applicants are invited to complete the second round of the application process between January and March. The second round includes a three to four day campus visit, an interview, and three additional essays. Alternatively, foreign students and those with economic hardship may schedule a phone interview. Financial aid is available for students with economic hardship to visit the college for second round interviews. **Financial aid:** No deadline. Institutional form required.

Academics. Before graduating, students are required to take three classes: Composition, Public Speaking, and Summer Seminar (interdisciplinary course broadly oriented around questions of political theory). Though not a graduation requirement, all students take Horsemanship during their first year. Students also enroll in two to three full classes during each semester. Regular curriculum includes courses in humanities, social sciences and natural sciences. **Special study options:** Independent study. **Credit/placement by examination:** AP, CLEP.

Majors. Liberal arts: Arts/sciences.

Technology on campus. 7 workstations in library, computer center. Wireless network available.

Student life. Freshman orientation: Mandatory. Preregistration for classes offered. **Policies:** All students work at least 20 hours a week in the labor program, serving in various positions around the ranch, farm, and college throughout their career. Students self-govern, managing community issues and serving on student committees which handle day-to-day operations of the college, including but not limited to community events, admissions, faculty hiring, public relations, and review/reinvitation. Drugs and alcohol are prohibited, and students do not leave valley during academic term; family and friends may only visit during academic breaks. **Housing:** Guaranteed on-campus for all undergraduates. Special housing for disabled, cooperative housing, themed housing, wellness housing available. Pets allowed in dorm rooms. **Activities:** Concert band, campus ministries, choral groups, dance, drama, film society, international student organizations, literary magazine, music ensembles, musical theater, radio station, student government, student newspaper.

Athletics. Intercollegiate: Rodeo M. **Intramural:** Basketball M, boxing M, cross-country M, equestrian M, football (non-tackle) M, rifle M, rodeo M, rugby M, skiing M, soccer M, swimming M, table tennis M, ultimate frisbee M, volleyball M, weight lifting M, wrestling M.

Student services. Career counseling, financial aid counseling, health services, personal counseling, placement for graduates. **Transfer:** Transfer adviser for students transferring to 4-year colleges.

Contact. E-mail: apcom@deepsprings.edu
Phone: (760) 872-2000 ext. 33 Fax: (760) 874-7077
Jack Davis, Chair, Applications Committee, Deep Springs College, Applications Committee, Dyer, NV 89010-9803

Diablo Valley College
Pleasant Hill, California
www.dvc.edu CB code: 4295

- Public 2-year community college
- Commuter campus in large town

General. Founded in 1948. Regionally accredited. College for Kids available on-campus which provides enrichment activities for fourth through ninth graders. **Enrollment:** 9,588 degree-seeking undergraduates. **Degrees:** 1,302 associate awarded. **ROTC:** Army, Naval. **Location:** 25 miles from San Francisco. **Calendar:** Semester, extensive summer session. **Full-time faculty:** 215 total; 50% women. **Part-time faculty:** 490 total; 53% women. **Class size:** 19% < 20, 63% 20-39, 13% 40-49, 4% 50-99, less than 1% >100. **Partnerships:** Formal partnerships with Wells Fargo, Chevron, Pacific Bell, City of San Ramon, Contra Costa/Tri-Valley Telecommunication Incubator.

Student profile.

Out-of-state: 1% 25 or older: 32%

Basis for selection. Open admission. **Adult students:** SAT/ACT scores not required. **Home schooled:** Applicants must supply a copy of their private school affidavit.

2015-2016 Annual costs. Tuition/fees: $1,390; $8,080 out-of-state. Per-credit charge: $46 in-state; $269 out-of-state. Books/supplies: $1,710. Personal expenses: $3,096.

Financial aid. Need-based: Need-based aid available for part-time students. Work-study available nights, weekends and for part-time students.

Application procedures. Admission: Priority date 4/1; no deadline. No application fee. Admission notification on a rolling basis beginning on or about 4/1. **Financial aid:** Priority date 3/2, closing date 5/1. FAFSA, institutional form required. Applicants notified on a rolling basis starting 6/1; must reply within 2 week(s) of notification.

Academics. The college offers a comprehensive educational program that includes courses in general education, transfer, vocational, basic skills, and life-long learning. These courses are offered in flexible formats that include different hours, days, term length, and a variety of instructional delivery methods (classroom and on-line). **Special study options:** Accelerated study, cooperative education, cross-registration, distance learning, dual enrollment of high school students, ESL, honors, independent study, internships, liberal arts/career combination, study abroad, weekend college. Study abroad programs in Florence, Italy; Salamanca, Spain; Capetown, South Africa; Ghana; and London, England. License preparation in dental hygiene. **Credit/placement by examination:** AP, CLEP, institutional tests. **Support services:** Learning center, pre-admission summer program, reduced course load, remedial instruction, study skills assistance, tutoring, writing center.

Majors. Architecture: Technology. **Biology:** General. **Business:** General, accounting, accounting technology, business admin, entrepreneurial studies, marketing, office management, operations, real estate, restaurant/food services, small business admin. **Communications:** Communications/speech/rhetoric, digital media. **Communications technology:** Radio/TV. **Computer sciences:** General, computer science, networking, support specialist, system admin. **Education:** Early childhood, physical, special ed. **English:** English lit. **General:** Building inspection, plumbing, site management. **Health services:** Athletic training, clinical lab assistant, dental assistant, dental hygiene, dental lab technology, respiratory therapy assistant. **Liberal arts:** Archival admin, arts/sciences, humanities. **Math:** General. **Protective services:** Law enforcement admin. **Psychology:** General. **Social sciences:** Geography, political science, sociology. **Visual/performing arts:** Digital arts, music, studio arts, theater design.

Most popular majors. Biological/life sciences 16%, business/marketing 17%, interdisciplinary studies 22%, liberal arts 9%, psychology 6%, social sciences 9%.

Technology on campus. Commuter students can connect to campus network. Online course registration, online library, helpline, repair service, wireless network available.

Student life. Freshman orientation: Mandatory. Preregistration for classes offered. **Policies:** No smoking except in the quad. **Activities:** Bands, choral groups, dance, drama, film society, international student organizations, literary magazine, music ensembles, musical theater, student government, student newspaper, symphony orchestra, TV station, Alpha Gamma Sigma, Asian student union, DVC Republicans, DVC Democrats, Black student union, Latino students' alliance, Muslim student association, Christians on Campus, Greater China Cultural Association, Taiwan Discovery Club.

Athletics. NJCAA. **Intercollegiate:** Baseball M, basketball, cross-country, football (tackle) M, soccer W, softball W, swimming, tennis, track and field, volleyball W, water polo. **Team name:** Vikings.

Student services. Adult student services, career counseling, services for economically disadvantaged, student employment services, financial aid counseling, on-campus daycare, personal counseling, placement for graduates, veterans' counselor, women's services. **Physically disabled:** Services for visually, speech, hearing impaired. **Transfer:** Re-entry adviser, pre-admission transcript evaluation for new students. Transfer center, transfer adviser, college fairs on campus for students transferring to 4-year colleges.

Contact. Phone: (925) 685-1310 Fax: (925) 609-8085
Elizabeth Hauscarriague, Dean of Outreach, Enrollment & Matriculation,
Diablo Valley College, 321 Golf Club Road, Pleasant Hill, CA
94523-1529

East Los Angeles College
Monterey Park, California
www.elac.edu

CB member
CB code: 4296

- Public 2-year community college
- Commuter campus in very large city

General. Founded in 1945. Regionally accredited. **Enrollment:** 17,536
degree-seeking undergraduates. **Degrees:** 1,813 associate awarded. **Location:**
7 miles from Los Angeles. **Calendar:** Semester, limited summer session.
Full-time faculty: 288 total; 18% have terminal degrees, 41% minority.
Part-time faculty: 709 total; 10% have terminal degrees, 40% minority.
Class size: 21% < 20, 51% 20-39, 18% 40-49, 10% 50-99. **Special facilities:**
Vincent Price art museum.

Transfer out. Colleges most students transferred to 2015: California
State University: Los Angeles, California State University: Dominguez Hills,
University of California: Los Angeles, California State Polytechnic Univer-
sity: Pomona, University of California: San Diego.

Basis for selection. Open admission, but selective for some programs.
Limited admission to nursing and allied health associate programs. Institution
uses Assessment Placement Test for English and mathematics placement.
Interview required for some nursing, respiratory technology majors. **Adult
students:** SAT/ACT scores not required.

2015-2016 Annual costs. Tuition/fees: $1,402; $7,312 out-of-state. Per-
credit charge: $46 in-state; $243 out-of-state. Books/supplies: $1,710. Per-
sonal expenses: $3,096.

Financial aid. All financial aid based on need. Need-based aid available
for part-time students. Work-study available nights, weekends and for part-
time students. **Additional information:** Need-based enrollment fee waivers
available through a state aid program.

Application procedures. Admission: No deadline. No application fee.
Financial aid: Priority date 4/30; no closing date. FAFSA, institutional form
required. Applicants notified on a rolling basis; must reply within 4 week(s)
of notification.

Academics. Special study options: Accelerated study, cooperative education, cross-registration, distance learning, double major, dual enrollment of
high school students, ESL, honors, independent study, internships, study
abroad, weekend college. ITV (Instructional Television) and Saturday classes.
License preparation in nursing, paramedic, real estate. **Credit/placement by
examination:** AP, CLEP. 15 credit hours maximum toward associate degree.
Support services: GED preparation, learning center, reduced course load,
remedial instruction, study skills assistance, tutoring, writing center.

Majors. Architecture: Technology. **Business:** Accounting technology,
administrative services, business admin, insurance, real estate, sales/distribu-
tion. **Communications:** Journalism. **Communications technology:** Anima-
tion/special effects, desktop publishing, photo/film/video. **Computer sciences:** Information technology. **Health services:** Community health, health
information technology, medical assistant, medical secretary, nursing (RN),
respiratory therapy technology. **Liberal arts:** Arts/sciences, humanities.
Math: General. **Parks/recreation:** Health/fitness. **Protective services:** Firefighting, police science. **Social sciences:** General, anthropology. **Visual/
performing arts:** Dramatic, graphic design, music, photography. **Work/
family studies:** Child development.

Most popular majors. Health sciences 6%, liberal arts 50%, security/
protective services 10%, social sciences 14%.

Technology on campus. 1,895 workstations in library, computer center,
student center. Online course registration, online library, helpline, wireless
network available.

Student life. Freshman orientation: Available. Preregistration for classes
offered. **Policies:** All Student Life activities conform to Title V, LACCD
regulations, LACCD Board Rules, Roberts rules of order, and CA Brown
Act. **Activities:** Bands, campus ministries, choral groups, dance, drama, film
society, international student organizations, radio station, student government,
student newspaper, Associated Students Union, Christians on Campus, Asia
club, International Students Club, MEChA, Circle K International, Vietnamese Student Association, Students for Equal Rights, Students for Political
Awareness, Students Against Substance Abuse.

Athletics. NJCAA. **Intercollegiate:** Badminton W, baseball M, basketball,
cross-country, football (tackle) M, soccer, softball W, track and field, volleyball W, wrestling M. **Intramural:** Cheerleading W. **Team name:** Huskies.

Student services. Adult student services, alcohol/substance abuse counseling, career counseling, services for economically disadvantaged, student
employment services, financial aid counseling, health services, minority student services, on-campus daycare, personal counseling, placement for graduates, veterans' counselor, women's services. **Physically disabled:** Services
for visually, speech, hearing impaired. **Transfer:** Pre-admission transcript
evaluation for new students. Transfer center, transfer adviser, college fairs
on campus for students transferring to 4-year colleges.

Contact. E-mail: admissions2@elac.edu
Phone: (323) 265-8712 Fax: (323) 265-8688
Jeremy Allred, Dean of Admissions, East Los Angeles College, 1301
Avenida Cesar Chavez, Monterey Park, CA 91754-6099

El Camino College
Torrance, California
www.elcamino.edu

CB code: 4302

- Public 2-year community and junior college
- Commuter campus in very large city

General. Founded in 1947. Regionally accredited. **Enrollment:** 32,699 full-
time, degree-seeking students. **Degrees:** 1,977 associate awarded. **Location:**
15 miles from Los Angeles. **Calendar:** Semester, limited summer session.
Full-time faculty: 336 total; 53% women. **Part-time faculty:** 673 total; 51%
women. **Special facilities:** Anthropology museum, planetarium, conference
center, computer/media center, child development center.

Student profile. Among full-time, degree-seeking students, 32,696
enrolled as first-time, first-year students.

Out-of-state: 5% **25 or older:** 31%

Transfer out. Colleges most students transferred to 2015: California
State University: Long Beach, California State University: Dominguez Hills,
California State University: Fullerton, University of California: Los Angeles.

Basis for selection. Open admission, but selective for some programs.
Allied health programs require completion of preparatory courses (anatomy,
microbiology, college-level English and mathematics). Interview required
for nursing, honors program, x-ray technician, respiratory care majors. **Adult
students:** SAT/ACT scores not required. **Home schooled:** Statement describing home school structure and mission, transcript of courses and grades, state
high school equivalency certificate, letter of recommendation (nonparent)
required. Home school must be registered with state of California. **Learning
Disabled:** Contact Special Resources Center and provide evidence of learning disability.

2015-2016 Annual costs. Tuition/fees: $1,419; $8,469 out-of-state. Per-
credit charge: $46 in-state; $281 out-of-state. Books/supplies: $1,200. Per-
sonal expenses: $2,844.

Financial aid. Need-based: Need-based aid available for part-time students. Work-study available nights, weekends and for part-time students.
Non-need-based: Scholarships awarded for academics, art, athletics, leadership, music/drama. **Additional information:** Students may apply for Pell
grants until June 30.

Application procedures. Admission: No deadline. No application fee.
Application must be submitted online. Admission notification on a rolling
basis beginning on or about 8/20. **Financial aid:** Priority date 3/2, closing
date 6/30. FAFSA, institutional form required. Applicants notified on a rolling
basis starting 7/15.

Academics. Special study options: Cooperative education, cross-
registration, distance learning, double major, dual enrollment of high school
students, ESL, honors, independent study, liberal arts/career combination,
study abroad, weekend college. License preparation in nursing, paramedic,
radiology, real estate. **Credit/placement by examination:** AP, CLEP, IB,
institutional tests. 15 credit hours maximum toward associate degree. **Support
services:** Learning center, remedial instruction, study skills assistance, tutoring, writing center.

Majors. Area/ethnic studies: African-American, American, Asian-
American, Chicano/Hispanic-American/Latino, Native American. **Biology:**
General, botany, zoology. **Business:** General, administrative services, business admin, office management, real estate, sales/distribution. **Communications:** Journalism. **Communications technology:** General. **Computer sciences:** General, computer science. **Education:** Early childhood. **Engineering:** General. **English:** English lit, rhetoric/composition. **Foreign languages:**
French, German, Japanese, Spanish. **General:** Maintenance. **Health services:**

Licensed practical nurse, medical radiologic technology/radiation therapy, nursing (RN), predental, premedicine, prepharmacy, respiratory therapy technology. **History:** General. **Math:** General. **Parks/recreation:** Health/fitness. **Philosophy/religion:** Philosophy. **Physical sciences:** Astronomy, chemistry, geology, physics. **Protective services:** Fire safety technology, law enforcement admin, police science. **Psychology:** General. **Social sciences:** Anthropology, economics, geography, political science, sociology. **Visual/performing arts:** Art, dance, dramatic, music, photography, studio arts. **Work/family studies:** General.

Most popular majors. English 34%, visual/performing arts 66%.

Technology on campus. 500 workstations in library, computer center, student center. Online course registration, wireless network available.

Student life. Freshman orientation: Available. Preregistration for classes offered. **Activities:** Bands, choral groups, dance, drama, literary magazine, music ensembles, musical theater, student government, student newspaper, symphony orchestra, Alpha Gamma Sigma, anthropology club, Gay-Straight Alliance, Iota Kappa Chi (nursing), Puente club, veterans club, Muslim students association, Native American club, fashion design club.

Athletics. NJCAA. **Intercollegiate:** Badminton W, baseball M, basketball, cross-country, football (tackle) M, golf M, soccer, softball W, swimming, tennis, track and field, volleyball, water polo. **Team name:** Warriors.

Student services. Adult student services, career counseling, services for economically disadvantaged, student employment services, financial aid counseling, health services, on-campus daycare, personal counseling, placement for graduates, veterans' counselor. **Physically disabled:** Services for visually, speech, hearing impaired. **Transfer:** Re-entry adviser, pre-admission transcript evaluation for new students. Transfer center, transfer adviser, college fairs on campus for students transferring to 4-year colleges.

Contact. E-mail: admissionshelp@elcamino.edu
Phone: (310) 660-3414 Fax: (310) 660-3818
Bill Mulrooney, Director of Admissions and Records, El Camino College, 16007 Crenshaw Boulevard, Torrance, CA 90506

Empire College
Santa Rosa, California
www.empcol.edu   CB code: 4275

- For-profit 2-year business college
- Commuter campus in large city
- Interview required

General. Accredited by ACICS. **Enrollment:** 232 degree-seeking undergraduates. **Degrees:** 103 associate awarded. **Location:** 55 miles from San Francisco. **Calendar:** Differs by program. **Full-time faculty:** 25 total. **Part-time faculty:** 18 total. **Special facilities:** Law library.

Transfer out. Colleges most students transferred to 2015: Santa Rosa Junior College.

Basis for selection. Open admission, but selective for some programs. Official copy of high school or college transcript, or GED or high school proficiency certificate required. All applicants, except 2-year and 4-year college graduates required to take the Wonderlic Scholastic Level Exam (SLE). Students scoring below 16 will not be admitted into a full program at the college. The Director of Education has the final authority to accept or reject applicants.

High school preparation. College-preparatory program required.

2015-2016 Annual costs. Associates degree programs range from $25,585-$27,680, Books range from $4,000-$5,400. Undergraduate Certificates Health Administration - range from $9,905-$19,350, Books and supplies range from $1,600-$4,600.

Financial aid. All financial aid based on need. Work-study available nights, weekends and for part-time students.

Application procedures. Admission: No deadline. $150 fee. Admission notification on a rolling basis. No fall term, ongoing 5-week application/entry. **Financial aid:** No deadline. FAFSA required. Applicants notified on a rolling basis.

Academics. Special study options: Accelerated study, double major, internships. **Credit/placement by examination:** AP, CLEP. **Support services:** Tutoring.

Majors. Business: Accounting, administrative services. **Computer sciences:** Information systems. **Health services:** Medical secretary.

Technology on campus. 600 workstations in library, computer center. Online library, student web hosting, wireless network available.

Student life. Freshman orientation: Mandatory. Preregistration for classes offered. **Activities:** Student newspaper.

Student services. Career counseling, student employment services, financial aid counseling, placement for graduates. **Transfer:** Re-entry adviser, pre-admission transcript evaluation for new students.

Contact. E-mail: dstraub@empirecollege.com
Phone: (707) 546-4000 ext. 238 Fax: (707) 546-4058
Dahnja Straub, Director of Admissions, Empire College, 3035 Cleveland Avenue, Santa Rosa, CA 95403-2100

Epic Bible College
Sacramento, California
https://epic.edu/

- Private 2-year Bible college
- Very large city

General. Regionally accredited; also accredited by TRACS. **Enrollment:** 271 undergraduates. **Degrees:** 17 bachelor's, 14 associate awarded; master's offered. **Calendar:** Quarter. **Full-time faculty:** 5 total. **Part-time faculty:** 15 total.

Basis for selection. Must have expressed personal experience of Christian conversion.

2015-2016 Annual costs. Books/supplies: $900.

Financial aid. Need-based: Work-study available nights, weekends and for part-time students.

Application procedures. Admission: Closing date 8/15.

Academics. Special study options: Bachelor's degree programs available on campus. **Credit/placement by examination:** AP, CLEP.

Majors. Philosophy/religion: Christian. **Theology:** Preministerial.

Contact. Phone: (916) 348-4689
Kathy Clarke, Director of Records, Epic Bible College, 4330 Auburn Boulevard, Sacramento, CA 95841

Evergreen Valley College
San Jose, California
www.evc.edu   CB code: 4273

- Public 2-year community and junior college
- Commuter campus in very large city

General. Founded in 1975. Regionally accredited. **Enrollment:** 4,760 degree-seeking undergraduates. **Degrees:** 533 associate awarded. **Location:** 7 miles from downtown. **Calendar:** Semester, extensive summer session. **Full-time faculty:** 122 total; 33% have terminal degrees. **Part-time faculty:** 204 total. **Special facilities:** Hiking trails, parks, observatory, natural habitat, cross-country course.

Transfer out. Colleges most students transferred to 2015: San Jose State.

Basis for selection. Open admission, but selective for some programs. Limited admission for nursing and criminal justice programs. **Home schooled:** Interview required. Must complete form R-42 and state affidavit.

2015-2016 Annual costs. Tuition/fees: $1,416; $7,386 out-of-state. Per-credit charge: $46 in-state; $245 out-of-state. Books/supplies: $1,746. Personal expenses: $3,132.

Financial aid. Need-based: Work-study available nights, weekends and for part-time students.

Application procedures. Admission: No deadline. No application fee. Admission notification on a rolling basis. **Financial aid:** Priority date 5/31; no closing date. FAFSA required. Applicants notified on a rolling basis.

Academics. Special study options: Accelerated study, cooperative education, cross-registration, distance learning, double major, dual enrollment of high school students, ESL, honors, independent study, internships, liberal arts/career combination, weekend college. License preparation in nursing, paramedic. **Credit/placement by examination:** AP, CLEP, institutional tests. 12 credit hours maximum toward associate degree. Assessment testing as prescribed by California law required for placement in English and mathematics. **Support services:** Learning center, reduced course load, remedial instruction, study skills assistance, tutoring, writing center.

Majors. Business: Administrative services, fashion, management information systems, office technology, office/clerical. **Computer sciences:** General, applications programming. **Health services:** Nursing (RN). **Liberal arts:** Arts/sciences. **Protective services:** Police science. **Visual/performing arts:** Commercial/advertising art.

Technology on campus. 800 workstations in library, computer center, student center.

Student life. Freshman orientation: Mandatory. Preregistration for classes offered. **Activities:** Choral groups, dance, drama, literary magazine, music ensembles, musical theater, student government, student newspaper, Black Students Union, ASPIRE, Enlace, AFFIRM.

Athletics. NJCAA. **Intercollegiate:** Soccer, track and field, volleyball W, wrestling M. **Intramural:** Basketball, football (non-tackle) M. **Team name:** Hawks.

Student services. Alcohol/substance abuse counseling, career counseling, services for economically disadvantaged, student employment services, financial aid counseling, health services, minority student services, on-campus daycare, personal counseling, veterans' counselor. **Physically disabled:** Services for visually, speech, hearing impaired. **Transfer:** Transfer center, transfer adviser, college fairs on campus for students transferring to 4-year colleges.

Contact. E-mail: lynn.gulkin@evc.edu
Phone: (408) 270-6441 Fax: (408) 223-9351
Octavio Cruz, Dean of Enrollment Services, Evergreen Valley College, 3095 Yerba Buena Road, San Jose, CA 95135

Fashion Institute of Design and Merchandising: Los Angeles

Los Angeles, California — **CB member**
www.fidm.edu — **CB code: 4457**

- For-profit 2-year visual arts and business college
- Commuter campus in very large city
- Application essay, interview required

General. Founded in 1969. Regionally accredited. Branch campuses in Orange County, San Francisco and San Diego. **Enrollment:** 2,814 degree-seeking undergraduates. **Degrees:** 207 bachelor's, 1,519 associate awarded. **Calendar:** Quarter, extensive summer session. **Full-time faculty:** 73 total; 26% minority, 63% women. **Part-time faculty:** 179 total; 14% minority, 64% women. **Class size:** 70% < 20, 30% 20-39. **Special facilities:** Hollywood costume collection, costume study collection and museum, textile museum, fragrance bottle collection, fashion library.

Student profile. Among degree-seeking undergraduates, 471 enrolled as first-time, first-year students.

Part-time:	10%	Native American:	1%
Out-of-state:	34.1%	Native Hawaiian/Pacific islander:	1%
Women:	88%	Multi-racial, non-Hispanic:	3%
African American:	5%	International:	17%
Asian American:	11%	25 or older:	16%
Hispanic/Latino:	22%		

Basis for selection. High school transcripts, standardized test scores, references, portfolio or admissions project, essays, and evidence of interest in major area through work experience, high school preparation, or extracurricular activities considered. In addition to transcript evaluation, SAT and/or ACT scores considered to determine if additional testing is required. SAT or ACT recommended. Portfolio or admissions project required of all candidates. Telephone interview required of out-of-state applicants. Interview not required for international students. **Home schooled:** Statement describing home school structure and mission, transcript of courses and grades, interview, letter of recommendation (nonparent) required. Admissions or standardized testing required. **Learning Disabled:** Interview with Education Specialist to discuss reasonable accommodation.

High school preparation. College-preparatory program recommended.

2015-2016 Annual costs. Tuition/fees: $32,790. Per-credit charge: $355. Books/supplies: $2,640. Personal expenses: $4,185.

2014-2015 Financial aid. Need-based: Average scholarship/grant was $7,875; average loan $4,096. 34% of total undergraduate aid awarded as

scholarships/grants, 66% as loans/jobs. Work-study available nights, weekends and for part-time students. **Non-need-based:** Scholarships awarded for academics. **Additional information:** Tuition/fee expenses may be reduced by applying for admission by December 31 of year before student plans to attend.

Application procedures. Admission: No deadline. $225 fee ($375 out-of-state). Admission notification on a rolling basis. **Financial aid:** Priority date 3/1; no closing date. FAFSA, institutional form required. Applicants notified on a rolling basis starting 3/15; must reply within 3 week(s) of notification.

Academics. Faculty and staff come from related industries. Project-oriented courses give students hands-on experience. **Special study options:** Accelerated study, cooperative education, distance learning, ESL, exchange student, independent study, internships, study abroad, weekend college. Bachelor's degree programs available on campus. **Credit/placement by examination:** AP, CLEP, IB, institutional tests. 45 credit hours maximum toward associate degree, 45 toward bachelor's. **Support services:** Learning center, reduced course load, remedial instruction, study skills assistance, tutoring, writing center.

Majors. Business: Fashion, logistics, marketing. **Visual/performing arts:** Cinematography, costume design, design, fashion design, graphic design, interior design, metal/jewelry. **Work/family studies:** Apparel marketing.

Most popular majors. Business/marketing 45%, family/consumer sciences 6%, visual/performing arts 49%.

Technology on campus. 433 workstations in library, computer center, student center. Commuter students can connect to campus network. Online course registration, online library, helpline, wireless network available.

Student life. Freshman orientation: Mandatory. Preregistration for classes offered. **Housing:** Apartments available. **Activities:** International student organizations, student government, honor society, design council, ASID, Phi Theta Kappa.

Student services. Adult student services, alcohol/substance abuse counseling, career counseling, student employment services, financial aid counseling, personal counseling, placement for graduates, women's services. **Physically disabled:** Services for visually, hearing impaired. **Transfer:** Pre-admission transcript evaluation for new students. Transfer center, transfer adviser for students transferring to 4-year colleges.

Contact. E-mail: admissionsdirector@fidm.edu
Phone: (213) 624-1200 Toll-free number: (800) 624-1200
Fax: (213) 624-4799
Susan Aronson, Executive Director of Admissions, Fashion Institute of Design and Merchandising: Los Angeles, 919 South Grand Avenue, Los Angeles, CA 90015-1421

Fashion Institute of Design and Merchandising: San Diego

San Diego, California
www.fidm.edu — **CB code: 2949**

- For-profit 2-year visual arts and business college
- Commuter campus in very large city
- Application essay, interview required

General. Regionally accredited. Other campuses in Los Angeles, Orange County, and San Francisco. **Enrollment:** 119 degree-seeking undergraduates. **Degrees:** 18 associate awarded. **Calendar:** Quarter, extensive summer session. **Full-time faculty:** 2 total; 50% women. **Part-time faculty:** 18 total; 17% minority, 83% women. **Class size:** 68% < 20, 32% 20-39. **Special facilities:** Hollywood costume study collection and museum, textile museum, historical Annette Green fragrance bottle collection, fashion library.

Student profile. Among degree-seeking undergraduates, 61 enrolled as first-time, first-year students.

Part-time:	5%	Native American:	3%
Out-of-state:	21%	Native Hawaiian/Pacific islander:	1%
Women:	94%	Multi-racial, non-Hispanic:	6%
African American:	4%	International:	3%
Asian American:	5%	25 or older:	11%
Hispanic/Latino:	29%		

Basis for selection. High school transcripts, standardized test scores, references, portfolio or admissions project, essays and evidence of interest in major through work experience, high school preparation, or extracurricular activities considered. In addition to transcript evaluation, SAT and/or ACT scores are considered to determine if additional testing is required. SAT or

ACT recommended. Portfolio or admissions project required of all applicants. Out-of-state applicants are interviewed by telephone. International students are not required to interview. **Home schooled:** Statement describing home school structure and mission, transcript of courses and grades, interview, letter of recommendation (nonparent) required. Admissions or standardized testing required. **Learning Disabled:** Interview with Education Specialist to discuss reasonable accommodation.

High school preparation. College-preparatory program recommended.

2015-2016 Annual costs. Tuition/fees: $32,790. Per-credit charge: $355. Books/supplies: $2,640. Personal expenses: $4,185.

2014-2015 Financial aid. Need-based: Average scholarship/grant was $7,793; average loan $2,780. 61% of total undergraduate aid awarded as scholarships/grants, 39% as loans/jobs. Work-study available nights, weekends and for part-time students. **Non-need-based:** Scholarships awarded for academics. **Additional information:** Tuition/fee expenses may be reduced by applying for admission by December 31 of year before student plans to attend.

Application procedures. Admission: No deadline. $225 fee ($375 out-of-state). Admission notification on a rolling basis. **Financial aid:** No deadline. FAFSA, institutional form required. Applicants notified on a rolling basis starting 3/15; must reply within 3 week(s) of notification.

Academics. Special study options: Accelerated study, cooperative education, distance learning, ESL, exchange student, independent study, internships, study abroad, weekend college. **Credit/placement by examination:** AP, CLEP, IB, institutional tests. 15 credit hours maximum toward associate degree. **Support services:** Learning center, reduced course load, remedial instruction, study skills assistance, tutoring, writing center.

Majors. Business: Fashion. **Visual/performing arts:** Design, fashion design.

Technology on campus. 36 workstations in library, computer center, student center. Commuter students can connect to campus network. Online course registration, online library, helpline, wireless network available.

Student life. Freshman orientation: Mandatory. Preregistration for classes offered. **Activities:** Student government, honor students society, alumni association, ASID student chapter, Design Council, Phi Theta Kappa, student activities committee.

Student services. Adult student services, alcohol/substance abuse counseling, career counseling, student employment services, financial aid counseling, personal counseling, placement for graduates, women's services. **Physically disabled:** Services for visually, hearing impaired. **Transfer:** Pre-admission transcript evaluation for new students. Transfer center, transfer adviser for students transferring to 4-year colleges.

Contact. E-mail: admissionsdirector@fidm.edu
Phone: (619) 235-2049 Toll-free number: (800) 243-3436
Fax: (619) 232-4322
Denise Baca, Campus & Admissions Director, Fashion Institute of Design and Merchandising: San Diego, 350 Tenth Avenue, Third Floor, San Diego, CA 92101

Fashion Institute of Design and Merchandising: San Francisco
San Francisco, California
www.fidm.edu   **CB code: 4988**

◗ For-profit 2-year visual arts and business college
◗ Commuter campus in very large city
◗ Application essay, interview required

General. Founded in 1969. Regionally accredited. Other campuses in Los Angeles, Orange County, and San Diego. **Enrollment:** 395 degree-seeking undergraduates. **Degrees:** 35 bachelor's, 218 associate awarded. **Calendar:** Quarter, extensive summer session. **Full-time faculty:** 12 total; 8% minority, 67% women. **Part-time faculty:** 37 total; 11% minority, 68% women. **Class size:** 91% < 20, 9% 20-39. **Special facilities:** Access to Hollywood costume collection, costume study collection and museum, textiles museum, Annette Green fragrance bottle collection, fashion library.

Student profile. Among degree-seeking undergraduates, 68 enrolled as first-time, first-year students.

Part-time:	15%	Native American:	1%
Out-of-state:	6%	Native Hawaiian/Pacific islander:	3%
Women:	91%	Multi-racial, non-Hispanic:	5%
African American:	4%	International:	5%
Asian American:	19%	25 or older:	18%
Hispanic/Latino:	22%		

Basis for selection. Recommendations and application essay very important. Rigor of secondary school record and academic GPA important. In addition to transcript evaluation, SAT and/or ACT scores are considered to determine if additional testing is required. SAT or ACT recommended. Portfolio or admissions project is required of all candidates. Telephone interview required of out-of-state applicants. Interview not required for international students. **Home schooled:** Statement describing home school structure and mission, transcript of courses and grades, interview, letter of recommendation (nonparent) required. Admissions or standardized testing required.

High school preparation. College-preparatory program recommended. High school transcripts, standardized test scores, references, portfolio or admissions project, essays, and evidence of interest in major through work experience, high school preparation, or extracurricular activities accepted.

2015-2016 Annual costs. Tuition/fees: $32,790. Per-credit charge: $355. Books/supplies: $2,640. Personal expenses: $4,185.

2014-2015 Financial aid. Need-based: Average scholarship/grant was $10,004; average loan $4,196. 44% of total undergraduate aid awarded as scholarships/grants, 56% as loans/jobs. Work-study available nights, weekends and for part-time students. **Non-need-based:** Scholarships awarded for academics. **Additional information:** Tuition/fee expenses may be reduced by applying for admission by December 31 of year before student plans to attend.

Application procedures. Admission: No deadline. $225 fee ($375 out-of-state). Admission notification on a rolling basis. **Financial aid:** Priority date 3/1; no closing date. FAFSA, institutional form required. Applicants notified on a rolling basis starting 3/15; must reply within 3 week(s) of notification.

Academics. Special study options: Accelerated study, cooperative education, distance learning, ESL, exchange student, independent study, internships, study abroad, weekend college. Bachelor's degree programs available on campus. **Credit/placement by examination:** AP, CLEP, IB, institutional tests. 45 credit hours maximum toward associate degree, 45 toward bachelor's. **Support services:** Learning center, reduced course load, remedial instruction, study skills assistance, tutoring, writing center.

Majors. Business: Fashion. **Visual/performing arts:** Design, fashion design, graphic design, interior design. **Work/family studies:** Apparel marketing.

Most popular majors. Business/marketing 52%, visual/performing arts 48%.

Technology on campus. 135 workstations in library, computer center, student center. Commuter students can connect to campus network. Online course registration, online library, helpline, wireless network available.

Student life. Freshman orientation: Mandatory. Preregistration for classes offered. **Activities:** Student government, honor society, design council, ASID student chapter, Phi Theta Kappa.

Student services. Adult student services, alcohol/substance abuse counseling, career counseling, student employment services, financial aid counseling, personal counseling, placement for graduates, women's services. **Physically disabled:** Services for visually, hearing impaired. **Transfer:** Pre-admission transcript evaluation for new students. Transfer center, transfer adviser for students transferring to 4-year colleges.

Contact. E-mail: admissionsdirector@fidm.edu
Phone: (415) 675-5200 Toll-free number: (800) 422-3436
Fax: (415) 296-7299
Sheryl Badalamenti, Director of Admissions, Fashion Institute of Design and Merchandising: San Francisco, 55 Stockton Street, San Francisco, CA 94108-5805

Feather River College
Quincy, California
www.frc.edu   **CB code: 4318**

◗ Public 2-year community and liberal arts college
◗ Commuter campus in small town

General. Founded in 1968. Regionally accredited. **Enrollment:** 1,646 degree-seeking undergraduates; 102 non-degree-seeking students. **Degrees:** 178 associate awarded. **Location:** 150 miles from Sacramento, 80 miles from Reno, Nevada. **Calendar:** Semester, limited summer session. **Full-time faculty:** 26 total; 42% women. **Part-time faculty:** 80 total; 6% minority, 49% women. **Class size:** 56% < 20, 38% 20-39, 4% 40-49, 2% 50-99. **Special facilities:** Fish hatchery, horse boarding and training facility, state wildlife preserve.

Two-Year Colleges

Student profile. Among degree-seeking undergraduates, 633 enrolled as first-time, first-year students, 372 transferred in from other institutions.

Part-time: 54% **Women:** 47%

Transfer out. Colleges most students transferred to 2015: CSU: Chico, Humboldt State University, University of Nevada: Reno, California Polytechnic State University: San Luis Obispo.

Basis for selection. Open admission.

2015-2016 Annual costs. Tuition/fees: $1,461; $7,491 out-of-state. Per-credit charge: $46 in-state; $247 out-of-state. Room only: $5,350. Books/supplies: $1,746. Personal expenses: $2,322.

2014-2015 Financial aid. All financial aid based on need. 72% of total undergraduate aid awarded as scholarships/grants, 28% as loans/jobs. Need-based aid available for part-time students. Work-study available nights, weekends and for part-time students.

Application procedures. Admission: No deadline. No application fee. **Financial aid:** Priority date 3/2; no closing date. FAFSA required. Applicants notified on a rolling basis starting 4/1; must reply within 3 week(s) of notification.

Academics. General education/core courses are offered that satisfy all lower division requirements of California State University, University of California, and University of Nevada system. **Special study options:** Cooperative education, cross-registration, distance learning, double major, dual enrollment of high school students, ESL, honors, independent study, internships, liberal arts/career combination. License preparation in nursing, paramedic. **Credit/placement by examination:** AP, CLEP, institutional tests. 12 credit hours maximum toward associate degree. **Support services:** GED preparation and test center, learning center, reduced course load, remedial instruction, study skills assistance, tutoring.

Majors. Biology: General. **Business:** General, administrative services. **Conservation:** General, environmental studies, forestry, wildlife/wilderness. **English:** English lit. **Health services:** Licensed practical nurse. **History:** General. **Liberal arts:** Arts/sciences, humanities. **Math:** General. **Parks/recreation:** General, health/fitness. **Physical sciences:** General. **Protective services:** Police science. **Social sciences:** General. **Visual/performing arts:** General. **Work/family studies:** Child care service, food/nutrition.

Most popular majors. Agriculture 10%, liberal arts 63%, parks/recreation 8%.

Technology on campus. 120 workstations in dormitories, library, computer center, student center. Dormitories wired for high-speed internet access. Online course registration, online library, wireless network available.

Student life. Freshman orientation: Mandatory. Preregistration for classes offered. Online orientation available. **Housing:** Coed dorms, apartments available. **Activities:** Student government, Phi Theta Kappa.

Athletics. NJCAA. **Intercollegiate:** Baseball M, basketball, cross-country, football (tackle) M, rodeo, soccer, softball W, track and field W, volleyball W. **Intramural:** Cheerleading W, volleyball W. **Team name:** Golden Eagles.

Student services. Adult student services, career counseling, services for economically disadvantaged, student employment services, financial aid counseling, health services, on-campus daycare, personal counseling, placement for graduates, veterans' counselor. **Physically disabled:** Services for visually, speech, hearing impaired. **Transfer:** Re-entry adviser, pre-admission transcript evaluation for new students. Transfer center, transfer adviser, college fairs on campus for students transferring to 4-year colleges.

Contact. Phone: (530) 283-0202 ext. 600
Toll-free number: (800) 442-9799 ext. 600 Fax: (530) 283-9961
Leslie Mikesell, Registrar, Feather River College, 570 Golden Eagle Avenue, Quincy, CA 95971

Folsom Lake College
Folsom, California
www.flc.losrios.edu CB code: 4462

- Public 2-year community college
- Commuter campus in small city

General. Regionally accredited. **Enrollment:** 5,835 degree-seeking undergraduates. **Degrees:** 706 associate awarded. **Location:** 25 miles from Sacramento. **Calendar:** Semester, limited summer session. **Full-time faculty:** 117 total. **Part-time faculty:** 196 total. **Special facilities:** Regional visual and performing arts center, observatory.

Transfer out. Colleges most students transferred to 2015: California State University: Sacramento, University of California: Davis, California State University: Chico, California State University: San Diego, University of California: Berkeley.

Basis for selection. Open admission. **Adult students:** SAT/ACT scores not required.

2015-2016 Annual costs. Tuition/fees: $1,416; $7,956 out-of-state. Per-credit charge: $46 in-state; $264 out-of-state. Books/supplies: $1,764. Personal expenses: $3,158.

Financial aid. Need-based: Work-study available nights, weekends and for part-time students.

Application procedures. Admission: No deadline. No application fee. **Financial aid:** Closing date 6/30. FAFSA required.

Academics. Special study options: Cooperative education, cross-registration, distance learning, ESL, internships, study abroad. **Credit/placement by examination:** AP, CLEP, institutional tests. **Support services:** Learning center, remedial instruction, study skills assistance, tutoring, writing center.

Majors. Area/ethnic studies: American, women's. **Biology:** General. **Business:** General, accounting, administrative services, management science, marketing, real estate, small business admin. **Communications:** Organizational. **Computer sciences:** General. **Education:** Early childhood. **English:** English lit. **Health services:** Clinical lab technology. **Liberal arts:** Arts/sciences. **Math:** General. **Parks/recreation:** Exercise sciences. **Physical sciences:** Geology. **Protective services:** Firefighting, law enforcement admin. **Psychology:** General. **Visual/performing arts:** Art, art history/conservation. **Work/family studies:** Aging, family studies.

Technology on campus. 1,300 workstations in library, computer center. Online course registration, online library, wireless network available.

Student life. Freshman orientation: Mandatory. Preregistration for classes offered. **Activities:** Bands, choral groups, dance, drama, international student organizations, literary magazine, music ensembles, student government, student newspaper.

Athletics. Intercollegiate: Baseball M, golf M, soccer, softball W, tennis. **Team name:** Falcons.

Student services. Career counseling, services for economically disadvantaged, student employment services, financial aid counseling, health services, veterans' counselor. **Physically disabled:** Services for visually, speech, hearing impaired. **Transfer:** Transfer center, transfer adviser, college fairs on campus for students transferring to 4-year colleges.

Contact. Phone: (916) 608-6500 Fax: (916) 608-6569
Christine Wurzer, Admissions and Records Supervisor, Folsom Lake College, 10 College Parkway, Folsom, CA 95630

Foothill College
Los Altos Hills, California
www.foothill.edu CB code: 4315

- Public 2-year community college
- Commuter campus in large town

General. Founded in 1958. Regionally accredited. **Enrollment:** 6,740 degree-seeking undergraduates. **Degrees:** 837 associate awarded. **ROTC:** Army, Naval, Air Force. **Location:** 40 miles from San Francisco. **Calendar:** Quarter, limited summer session. **Full-time faculty:** 193 total; 35% minority, 61% women. **Special facilities:** Center for innovation, Japanese cultural center, observatory, bamboo garden, dental health clinic, travel careers computer lab, math center.

Transfer out. Colleges most students transferred to 2015: San Jose State, University of California: Berkeley, University of California: Santa Cruz, University of California: Los Angeles, University of California: Davis.

Basis for selection. Open admission, but selective for some programs. Allied health programs have special prerequisites: point system used to rank required college-level and general education classes, top 20-40 students selected for admission. Must be 2-year transfer.

2015-2016 Annual costs. Tuition/fees: $1,503; $8,343 out-of-state. Per-credit charge: $31 in-state; $183 out-of-state. Books/supplies: $1,710. Personal expenses: $3,096.

Two-Year Colleges

2015-2016 Financial aid. Need-based: Need-based aid available for part-time students. Work-study available nights, weekends and for part-time students.

Application procedures. Admission: No deadline. No application fee. Admission notification on a rolling basis. **Financial aid:** Priority date 3/30; no closing date. FAFSA, institutional form required. Applicants notified on a rolling basis starting 5/1; must reply within 3 week(s) of notification.

Academics. NASA Ames Research Center internships available. **Special study options:** Cooperative education, cross-registration, distance learning, ESL, exchange student, honors, independent study, internships, liberal arts/career combination, study abroad, weekend college. Bachelor's degree programs available on campus. License preparation in dental hygiene, paramedic, radiology. **Credit/placement by examination:** AP, CLEP, institutional tests. 20 credit hours maximum toward associate degree. **Support services:** Learning center, remedial instruction, study skills assistance, tutoring, writing center.

Honors college/program. Must have minimum 3.5 cumulative high school GPA or SAT total of at least 2100 or Enhanced ACT Composite of 26 or minimum 3.3 cumulative GPA in 10 or more units completed at another accredited college or university. Minimum AP English score of 3 or 2, minimum score on assessment test of ENGL Reading 93 and ENGL Writing 111 or completion of English 1A with a grade of B or better. Letter of recommendation and personal statement required.

Majors. Area/ethnic studies: American, women's. **Biology:** General, bioinformatics, biotechnology. **Business:** Accounting, business admin, international, office technology, real estate, tourism promotion. **Communications:** Broadcast journalism, communications/speech/rhetoric, media studies, radio/TV. **Computer sciences:** General, computer graphics, computer science, database management, information technology, LAN/WAN management, programming. **Education:** Early childhood. **Engineering:** General, software. **English:** Creative writing, English lit, rhetoric/composition. **Foreign languages:** Chinese, French, Japanese, linguistics, Spanish. **General:** Electrician. **Health services:** Athletic training, dental assistant, dental hygiene, medical radiologic technology/radiation therapy, pharmacy assistant, physician assistant, predental, premedicine, prepharmacy, preveterinary, radiologic technology/medical imaging, respiratory therapy assistant, respiratory therapy technology, sonography, veterinary technology/assistant. **History:** General. **Liberal arts:** Arts/sciences, library assistant. **Math:** General. **Philosophy/religion:** Philosophy. **Physical sciences:** Chemistry, geology, physics. **Psychology:** General. **Social sciences:** General, anthropology, economics, geography, political science, sociology. **Visual/performing arts:** Art, art history/conservation, commercial/advertising art, dramatic, music, photography, studio arts, theater design. **Work/family studies:** Child development.

Technology on campus. 200 workstations in library, computer center, student center. Commuter students can connect to campus network. Online course registration, online library, wireless network available.

Student life. Freshman orientation: Available. Preregistration for classes offered. **Activities:** Bands, choral groups, dance, drama, film society, music ensembles, musical theater, radio station, student government, student newspaper, symphony orchestra, TV station, 32 different multicultural/ethnic campus clubs.

Athletics. Intercollegiate: Basketball, diving, football (tackle) M, golf, soccer, softball W, swimming, tennis, volleyball W, water polo W. **Intramural:** Basketball, cheerleading, football (non-tackle), soccer, softball, volleyball. **Team name:** Owls.

Student services. Adult student services, alcohol/substance abuse counseling, career counseling, services for economically disadvantaged, student employment services, financial aid counseling, health services, legal services, minority student services, personal counseling, placement for graduates, veterans' counselor. **Physically disabled:** Services for visually, speech, hearing impaired. **Transfer:** Transfer adviser, college fairs on campus for students transferring to 4-year colleges.

Contact. E-mail: galoyannazy@foothill.edu
Phone: (650) 949-7325 Fax: (650) 949-7048
Nazy Galoyan, Dean, Admissions and Records, Foothill College, 12345 El Monte Road, Los Altos Hills, CA 94022

Fremont College
Cerritos, California
www.fremont.edu   CB code: 3007

- For-profit 2-year branch campus and career college
- Commuter campus in very large city
- Application essay, interview required

General. Regionally accredited; also accredited by ACCSC. Year-round program with starts every 10 weeks. Main campus: Cerritos. Branch campus: Los Angeles. **Enrollment:** 276 degree-seeking undergraduates. **Degrees:** 18 bachelor's, 174 associate awarded. **Location:** Downtown. **Calendar:** Quarter, limited summer session. **Full-time faculty:** 8 total; 25% have terminal degrees, 25% minority. **Part-time faculty:** 23 total; 56% have terminal degrees, 30% minority, 65% women. **Class size:** 58% < 20, 42% 20-39.

Basis for selection. Open admission, but selective for some programs and for out-of-state students. High school diploma or GED and successful completion of entrance exam required. **Home schooled:** State high school equivalency certificate required.

2015-2016 Annual costs. Personal expenses: $2,190. **Additional information:** Bachelor's in Business Leadership, Healthcare Mgmt - $35,495, Associate's in Healthcare Information Technology - $35,685, Sports & Rehabilitation Therapy - $34,085, Multimedia Design, Digital Marketing, Paralegal - $35,495, Undergraduate Certificates Health Administration - $17,435, Massage Therapy - $22,885, Web & Mobile Marketing - $17,840. Books and supplies included in tuition cost.

Financial aid. All financial aid based on need. Work-study available nights, weekends and for part-time students.

Application procedures. Admission: No deadline. $10 fee. **Financial aid:** No deadline. FAFSA, institutional form required.

Academics. Special study options: Accelerated study, distance learning. **Credit/placement by examination:** AP, CLEP, IB. **Support services:** Learning center, tutoring.

Majors. Business: General. **Parks/recreation:** Exercise sciences.

Technology on campus. PC or laptop required. 30 workstations in library, computer center. Online library, wireless network available.

Student life. Freshman orientation: Mandatory. Preregistration for classes offered.

Student services. Financial aid counseling, placement for graduates. **Transfer:** Pre-admission transcript evaluation for new students.

Contact. E-mail: info@fremont.edu
Phone: (213) 355-8000 Toll-free number: (800) 373-6668
Fax: (213) 355-8088
Natasha Dawson, Director of Admissions, Fremont College, 18000 Studebaker Road, Cerritos, CA 90703

Fresno City College
Fresno, California   CB member
www.fresnocitycollege.edu   CB code: 4311

- Public 2-year community and liberal arts college
- Commuter campus in very large city

General. Founded in 1910. Regionally accredited. **Enrollment:** 16,384 degree-seeking undergraduates. **Degrees:** 1,244 associate awarded. **ROTC:** Army, Air Force. **Location:** 185 miles from San Francisco. **Calendar:** Semester, extensive summer session. **Full-time faculty:** 332 total; 27% minority. **Part-time faculty:** 632 total; 26% minority. **Class size:** 28% < 20, 59% 20-39, 7% 40-49, 4% 50-99, 3% >100. **Special facilities:** Anthropology museum, greenhouse and koi pond, high-tech laboratory for disabled students.

Student profile.

Out-of-state:	2%	25 or older:	39%

Transfer out. Colleges most students transferred to 2015: California State University: Fresno, University of Phoenix, National University, Fresno Pacific University.

Basis for selection. Open admission, but selective for some programs. Limited admission to allied health programs, police academy, and apprenticeship programs.

2015-2016 Annual costs. Tuition/fees: $1,420; $8,470 out-of-state. Per-credit charge: $46 in-state; $281 out-of-state. Books/supplies: $1,262. Personal expenses: $2,236.

Financial aid. All financial aid based on need. Need-based aid available for part-time students. Work-study available nights, weekends and for part-time students. **Additional information:** Board of Governors Grant Program to offset enrollment fees based on untaxed income, low income, or calculated need. Students qualifying for program also automatically exempt from health fees. March 2 application deadline for California grants.

Application procedures. Admission: No deadline. No application fee. Application must be submitted online. Admission notification on a rolling basis. **Financial aid:** Priority date 4/15, closing date 6/30. FAFSA required. Applicants notified on a rolling basis starting 4/1.

Academics. Special study options: Accelerated study, cross-registration, distance learning, double major, dual enrollment of high school students, ESL, honors, independent study, internships, study abroad, weekend college. License preparation in dental hygiene, nursing, radiology, real estate. **Credit/placement by examination:** AP, CLEP, institutional tests. 48 credit hours maximum toward associate degree. **Support services:** Learning center, pre-admission summer program, reduced course load, remedial instruction, study skills assistance, tutoring, writing center.

Majors. Area/ethnic studies: African-American, Chicano/Hispanic-American/Latino, Native American, women's. **Business:** General, accounting, administrative services, banking/financial services, business admin, fashion, insurance, office/clerical, purchasing, real estate. **Communications:** Communications/speech/rhetoric, journalism. **Communications technology:** Graphic/printing. **Computer sciences:** General, computer science, data processing, information systems, programming. **Conservation:** General. **Education:** Bilingual, early childhood, multi-level teacher. **Engineering:** General. **English:** English lit, rhetoric/composition. **Foreign languages:** General, Spanish. **General:** Carpentry, electrician, maintenance, pipefitting, power transmission. **Health services:** Clinical lab technology, dental hygiene, health information technology, medical assistant, medical radiologic technology/radiation therapy, medical secretary, medical transcription, nursing (RN), radiologic technology/medical imaging, respiratory therapy technology, substance abuse counseling. **History:** General. **Human services:** General, social work. **Liberal arts:** Arts/sciences, library assistant. **Math:** General. **Parks/recreation:** General, facilities management. **Physical sciences:** Chemistry. **Protective services:** Corrections, firefighting, law enforcement admin, police science. **Psychology:** General. **Social sciences:** General, anthropology, criminology, geography, sociology. **Visual/performing arts:** General, art, crafts, dance, dramatic, music, music management, photography, piano/keyboard, printmaking, theater design, voice/opera. **Work/family studies:** General, child care management, clothing/textiles, food/nutrition, institutional food production.

Most popular majors. Health sciences 30%, liberal arts 55%.

Technology on campus. 400 workstations in library, computer center. Commuter students can connect to campus network. Online course registration, online library, wireless network available.

Student life. Freshman orientation: Available. Preregistration for classes offered. **Activities:** Bands, choral groups, dance, drama, film society, international student organizations, literary magazine, music ensembles, musical theater, student government, student newspaper, symphony orchestra, TV station, Christian Athletes in Acting, MECHA, Pan American Association, Alpha Gamma Sigma, Phi Theta Kappa.

Athletics. NJCAA. Intercollegiate: Badminton, baseball M, basketball, cheerleading, cross-country, football (tackle) M, golf, soccer, softball W, tennis, track and field, volleyball W, wrestling M. **Intramural:** Basketball, football (non-tackle), soccer, softball, table tennis, volleyball, weight lifting. **Team name:** Rams.

Student services. Adult student services, career counseling, services for economically disadvantaged, student employment services, financial aid counseling, health services, minority student services, on-campus daycare, personal counseling, placement for graduates, veterans' counselor. **Physically disabled:** Services for visually, speech, hearing impaired. **Transfer:** Transfer center, transfer adviser, college fairs on campus for students transferring to 4-year colleges.

Contact. E-mail: info@scccd.com
Phone: (559) 442-4600 Toll-free number: (866) 245-3276
Fax: (559) 237-4232
John Cummings, District Dean of Admissions, Records and Institutional Research, Fresno City College, 1101 East University Avenue, Fresno, CA 93741

Fullerton College
Fullerton, California
www.fullcoll.edu
CB code: 4314

- Public 2-year community and technical college
- Commuter campus in small city

General. Founded in 1913. Regionally accredited. **Enrollment:** 13,268 degree-seeking undergraduates; 7,904 non-degree-seeking students. **Degrees:** 1,817 associate awarded. **Location:** 35 miles from Los Angeles. **Calendar:** Semester, extensive summer session. **Full-time faculty:** 281 total. **Part-time faculty:** 685 total.

Student profile. Among degree-seeking undergraduates, 2,089 enrolled as first-time, first-year students.

Part-time:	57%	Women:	52%
Out-of-state:	5%		

Basis for selection. Open admission. College-administered English, reading, and math exams used for placement. **Home schooled:** Signatures from the principal and counseling department's host high school, and from the college president are required.

2015-2016 Annual costs. Tuition/fees: $1,443; $7,713 out-of-state. Per-credit charge: $46 in-state; $255 out-of-state. Books/supplies: $1,764. Personal expenses: $3,159.

2015-2016 Financial aid. Need-based: 93% of total undergraduate aid awarded as scholarships/grants, 7% as loans/jobs. Need-based aid available for part-time students. Work-study available nights, weekends and for part-time students.

Application procedures. Admission: No deadline. No application fee. Admission notification on a rolling basis. **Financial aid:** No deadline. FAFSA required. Applicants notified on a rolling basis.

Academics. Special study options: Cross-registration, distance learning, double major, dual enrollment of high school students, ESL, honors, independent study, internships, study abroad. License preparation in real estate. **Credit/placement by examination:** AP, CLEP, IB, institutional tests. 15 credit hours maximum toward associate degree. **Support services:** Learning center, pre-admission summer program, remedial instruction, study skills assistance, tutoring, writing center.

Majors. Architecture: Landscape. **Area/ethnic studies:** Latin American. **Biology:** General, bacteriology, zoology. **Business:** Accounting, administrative services, business admin, fashion, international, management information systems, purchasing, real estate, tourism promotion. **Communications:** Broadcast journalism, communications/speech/rhetoric, journalism. **Communications technology:** Graphic/printing. **Computer sciences:** General, applications programming, data processing. **Conservation:** General, fisheries, forestry. **Education:** Business, trade/industrial. **Engineering:** General. **English:** English lit, rhetoric/composition. **Foreign languages:** General. **General:** Carpentry, maintenance. **Health services:** Clinical lab science, prenursing. **History:** General. **Liberal arts:** Arts/sciences, library assistant. **Math:** General. **Parks/recreation:** General. **Philosophy/religion:** Philosophy. **Physical sciences:** Astronomy, chemistry, geology, physics. **Protective services:** Police science. **Psychology:** General. **Social sciences:** Anthropology, economics, geography, political science, sociology. **Visual/performing arts:** General, art, commercial/advertising art, dance, design, dramatic, fashion design, music. **Work/family studies:** General, child care management, family studies.

Technology on campus. 500 workstations in library, computer center. Commuter students can connect to campus network. Online course registration, online library, helpline, wireless network available.

Student life. Freshman orientation: Available. Preregistration for classes offered. **Activities:** Bands, choral groups, dance, drama, film society, literary magazine, music ensembles, musical theater, radio station, student government, student newspaper, symphony orchestra, TV station, volunteer bureau, Movimiento Estudiantil Chicano de Aztlan.

Athletics. Intercollegiate: Badminton, baseball M, basketball, cross-country, diving, football (tackle) M, golf M, gymnastics, soccer, softball W, swimming, tennis, track and field, volleyball, water polo M. **Team name:** Hornets.

Student services. Adult student services, career counseling, services for economically disadvantaged, student employment services, financial aid counseling, health services, minority student services, on-campus daycare, personal counseling, placement for graduates, veterans' counselor. **Physically disabled:** Services for visually, speech, hearing impaired. **Transfer:** Transfer center, transfer adviser, college fairs on campus for students transferring to 4-year colleges.

Contact. E-mail: admissions@fullcoll.edu
Phone: (714) 992-7075 Fax: (714) 992-9903
Albert Abutin, Dean, Admissions and Records, Fullerton College, 321 East Chapman Avenue, Fullerton, CA 92832-2095

Gavilan College
Gilroy, California
www.gavilan.edu

CB code: 4678

- Public 2-year community college
- Large town

General. Founded in 1919. Regionally accredited. **Enrollment:** 7,215 undergraduates. **Degrees:** 443 associate awarded. **Location:** 35 miles from San Jose. **Calendar:** Semester, limited summer session. **Full-time faculty:** 78 total; 10% have terminal degrees. **Part-time faculty:** 215 total; 2% have terminal degrees. **Special facilities:** Golf course, hiking trails.

Transfer out. Colleges most students transferred to 2015: San Jose State, California State University: Monterey Bay, University of California: Santa Cruz.

Basis for selection. Open admission.

2015-2016 Annual costs. Tuition/fees: $1,418; $7,838 out-of-state. Per-credit charge: $46 in-state; $260 out-of-state. Room/board: $11,493. Books/supplies: $1,746.

Financial aid. Need-based: Work-study available nights, weekends and for part-time students.

Application procedures. Admission: No deadline. No application fee. Application must be submitted on paper. Admission notification on a rolling basis. **Financial aid:** Priority date 6/30; no closing date. FAFSA required. Applicants notified on a rolling basis starting 7/15; must reply within 2 week(s) of notification.

Academics. Special study options: Distance learning, dual enrollment of high school students, ESL, honors, independent study, internships, liberal arts/career combination, study abroad. License preparation in aviation, nursing. **Credit/placement by examination:** AP, CLEP, institutional tests. **Support services:** Learning center, reduced course load, remedial instruction, study skills assistance, tutoring, writing center.

Majors. Biology: General, ecology. **Business:** General. **Communications:** Communications/speech/rhetoric, journalism. **Computer sciences:** General, computer graphics. **English:** English lit. **Foreign languages:** Spanish. **Health services:** Nursing (RN). **History:** General. **Liberal arts:** Arts/sciences. **Math:** General. **Philosophy/religion:** Philosophy. **Physical sciences:** Astronomy, chemistry, geology. **Protective services:** Corrections. **Psychology:** General. **Social sciences:** General, anthropology, economics, geography, political science, sociology. **Visual/performing arts:** Art, art history/conservation, dramatic, music, music performance, studio arts, theater design.

Most popular majors. Education 6%, health sciences 18%, liberal arts 61%, security/protective services 6%.

Technology on campus. 600 workstations in library, computer center. Wireless network available.

Student life. Freshman orientation: Mandatory. Preregistration for classes offered. **Activities:** Choral groups, drama, literary magazine, music ensembles, musical theater, student government, student newspaper, symphony orchestra, TV station.

Athletics. Intercollegiate: Baseball M, basketball, football (tackle) M, golf, soccer W, softball W, tennis, volleyball W. **Team name:** Rams.

Student services. Adult student services, career counseling, services for economically disadvantaged, financial aid counseling, health services, on-campus daycare, personal counseling, veterans' counselor. **Physically disabled:** Services for visually, speech, hearing impaired. **Transfer:** Transfer center, transfer adviser, college fairs on campus for students transferring to 4-year colleges.

Contact. Phone: (408) 848-4735 Fax: (408) 848-4940
Candice Whitney, Director of Admissions and Records, Gavilan College, 5055 Santa Teresa Boulevard, Gilroy, CA 95020

Glendale Community College
Glendale, California
www.glendale.edu

CB code: 4327

- Public 2-year community college
- Commuter campus in small city

General. Founded in 1927. Regionally accredited. **Enrollment:** 8,156 degree-seeking undergraduates. **Degrees:** 604 associate awarded. **Location:**

10 miles from Los Angeles. **Calendar:** Semester, extensive summer session. **Full-time faculty:** 247 total; 27% minority. **Part-time faculty:** 516 total; 22% minority. **Class size:** 24% < 20, 57% 20-39, 13% 40-49, 5% 50-99, less than 1% >100. **Special facilities:** Science center with planetarium, Baja California (Mexico) field station.

Transfer out. Colleges most students transferred to 2015: California State University: Northridge, University of California: Los Angeles, California State University: Los Angeles, University of Southern California.

Basis for selection. Open admission, but selective for some programs. Nursing program has special requirements.

2015-2016 Annual costs. Tuition/fees: $1,416; $7,566 out-of-state. Per-credit charge: $46 in-state; $251 out-of-state. Books/supplies: $1,746. Personal expenses: $3,132.

Financial aid. All financial aid based on need. Need-based aid available for part-time students. Work-study available nights, weekends and for part-time students.

Application procedures. Admission: Priority date 4/15; no deadline. No application fee. Admission notification on a rolling basis. **Financial aid:** Priority date 4/15; no closing date. FAFSA, institutional form required. Applicants notified on a rolling basis starting 6/15; must reply within 2 week(s) of notification.

Academics. Special study options: Cooperative education, distance learning, dual enrollment of high school students, ESL, honors, independent study, internships, study abroad. License preparation in aviation, nursing, real estate. **Credit/placement by examination:** AP, CLEP, institutional tests. 12 credit hours maximum toward associate degree. **Support services:** GED preparation and test center, learning center, remedial instruction, study skills assistance, tutoring, writing center.

Honors college/program. Scholars program admits academically accomplished students and offers priority transfer opportunities at UCLA, USC, Pepperdine, and others.

Majors. Biology: General. **Business:** General, accounting, administrative services, hospitality/recreation, office management, real estate. **Communications:** Broadcast journalism, journalism. **Computer sciences:** General. **Education:** Early childhood, multi-level teacher. **English:** English lit, writing. **Foreign languages:** General, French, Spanish. **Health services:** Licensed practical nurse, medical assistant, medical secretary, nursing (RN). **History:** General. **Liberal arts:** Arts/sciences, humanities. **Math:** General. **Parks/recreation:** General. **Philosophy/religion:** Philosophy. **Physical sciences:** Chemistry, physics. **Protective services:** Fire safety technology, law enforcement admin, police science. **Psychology:** General. **Social sciences:** General, anthropology, economics, sociology. **Visual/performing arts:** General, commercial/advertising art, dance, theater design. **Work/family studies:** General, child care management, clothing/textiles, food/nutrition.

Most popular majors. Business/marketing 11%, health sciences 20%, liberal arts 49%.

Technology on campus. 1,000 workstations in library, computer center. Online course registration, helpline, repair service, wireless network available.

Student life. Freshman orientation: Available. Preregistration for classes offered. **Activities:** Bands, choral groups, dance, drama, international student organizations, literary magazine, music ensembles, Model UN, musical theater, radio station, student government, student newspaper, TV station, International Student Association, Armenian Student Association, Korean Christian Club, Organization of Latin for Higher Education, Association of Latin American Students.

Athletics. Intercollegiate: Baseball M, basketball, cross-country, football (tackle) M, soccer M, tennis, track and field, volleyball W. **Team name:** Vaqueros.

Student services. Adult student services, career counseling, services for economically disadvantaged, student employment services, financial aid counseling, health services, on-campus daycare, personal counseling, placement for graduates, veterans' counselor. **Physically disabled:** Services for visually, speech, hearing impaired. **Transfer:** Re-entry adviser for new students. Transfer center, transfer adviser, college fairs on campus for students transferring to 4-year colleges.

Contact. E-mail: info@glendale.edu
Phone: (818) 240-1000 ext. 5910
Michelle Mora, Director of Admissions and Records, Glendale Community College, 1500 North Verdugo Road, Glendale, CA 91208-2809

Golden West College
Huntington Beach, California
www.goldenwestcollege.edu

CB code: 4339

◆ Public 2-year community college
◆ Commuter campus in small city

General. Founded in 1966. Regionally accredited. **Enrollment:** 8,990 degree-seeking undergraduates. **Degrees:** 1,133 associate awarded. **Location:** 40 miles from Los Angeles. **Calendar:** Semester, limited summer session. **Full-time faculty:** 125 total. **Part-time faculty:** 294 total. **Class size:** 16% < 20, 58% 20-39, 9% 40-49, 13% 50-99, 3% >100. **Special facilities:** Outdoor amphitheatre, California native garden.

Transfer out. Colleges most students transferred to 2015: California State University: Long Beach, California State University: Dominguez Hills, California State University: Fullerton, University of California: Irvine, University of California: Los Angeles.

Basis for selection. Open admission, but selective for some programs. Any student at least 18 years of age eligible for admission. Limited admission to police academy and nursing program. Nursing applicants accepted on basis of prerequisite courses completed and GPA. SAT or ACT scores can be used for counseling and placement in lieu of institutional placement exams.

2015-2016 Annual costs. Tuition/fees: $1,452; $8,382 out-of-state. Per-credit charge: $46 in-state; $277 out-of-state. Books/supplies: $1,664. Personal expenses: $3,104.

Financial aid. Need-based: Work-study available nights, weekends and for part-time students. **Non-need-based:** Scholarships awarded for academics.

Application procedures. Admission: Priority date 4/1; no deadline. No application fee. Admission notification on a rolling basis. **Financial aid:** Closing date 6/30. FAFSA, institutional form required. Applicants notified on a rolling basis starting 7/1; must reply within 3 week(s) of notification.

Academics. Special study options: Accelerated study, cooperative education, cross-registration, distance learning, double major, dual enrollment of high school students, ESL, honors, independent study, study abroad, weekend college. License preparation in nursing, real estate. **Credit/placement by examination:** AP, CLEP, institutional tests. 6 credit hours maximum toward associate degree. **Support services:** Learning center, pre-admission summer program, reduced course load, remedial instruction, study skills assistance, tutoring, writing center.

Majors. Biology: General. **Business:** General, accounting, administrative services, business admin, office management, office technology, office/clerical, real estate, sales/distribution. **Communications:** Broadcast journalism, journalism, public relations. **Computer sciences:** General. **Education:** Physical. **English:** English lit, rhetoric/composition. **Foreign languages:** General, French, German, sign language interpretation, Spanish. **Health services:** Nursing (RN), predental, premedicine, prepharmacy, preveterinary. **History:** General. **Liberal arts:** Arts/sciences. **Math:** General. **Philosophy/religion:** Philosophy. **Physical sciences:** Astronomy, chemistry, geology. **Protective services:** Criminal justice, law enforcement admin. **Psychology:** General. **Social sciences:** General, anthropology, economics, political science, sociology. **Visual/performing arts:** Art, commercial/advertising art, dance, dramatic, music, music performance, music theory/composition, photography, studio arts.

Technology on campus. Online course registration, online library, wireless network available.

Student life. Freshman orientation: Mandatory. Preregistration for classes offered. Program held prior to enrollment. **Activities:** Bands, choral groups, dance, drama, film society, international student organizations, literary magazine, music ensembles, musical theater, student government, student newspaper.

Athletics. NJCAA. **Intercollegiate:** Baseball M, cross-country, football (tackle) M, soccer, softball W, swimming, track and field, volleyball, water polo. **Team name:** Rustlers.

Student services. Adult student services, career counseling, services for economically disadvantaged, student employment services, health services, on-campus daycare, personal counseling, placement for graduates, veterans' counselor. **Physically disabled:** Services for visually, speech, hearing impaired. **Transfer:** Transfer center, transfer adviser, college fairs on campus for students transferring to 4-year colleges.

Contact. Phone: (714) 895-8306 Fax: (714) 895-8960
Jennifer Ortberg, Director, Admissions & Records, Golden West College, 15744 Golden West Street, Box 2748, Huntington Beach, CA 92647-2748

Golf Academy of America: San Diego
Carlsbad, California
www.golfacademy.edu

CB code: 3495

◆ For-profit 2-year college of golf course management
◆ Small city

General. Accredited by ACICS. **Enrollment:** 168 undergraduates. **Degrees:** 146 associate awarded. **Location:** San Diego, CA - 34 Miles. **Calendar:** Semester, limited summer session. **Full-time faculty:** 6 total. **Part-time faculty:** 13 total. **Special facilities:** Golf Ranges, Updated Golf Technology, Golf Club Repair Lab.

Basis for selection. Open admission. High school diploma or GED required. Application required, reviewed by the Director of Admissions. Serious medical conditions which may prevent a person from swinging a golf club may disqualify a prospective student.

2015-2016 Annual costs. Tuition/fees: $17,250. **Additional information:** International tuition: $18,040. Tuition includes all fees and textbooks.

Financial aid. Need-based: Work-study available nights, weekends and for part-time students.

Application procedures. Admission: No deadline. $100 fee. **Financial aid:** No deadline.

Academics. Credit/placement by examination: AP, CLEP.

Majors. Parks/recreation: Facilities management.

Student life. Freshman orientation: Available. Preregistration for classes offered.

Contact. E-mail: henry.salgado@golfacademy.edu
Phone: (760) 734-1208 Toll-free number: (800) 342-7342
Henry Salgado, Director of Admissions, Golf Academy of America: San Diego, 1950 Camino Vida Roble, Suite 125, Carlsbad, CA 92008

Grossmont College
El Cajon, California
www.grossmont.edu

CB code: 4334

◆ Public 2-year nursing and community college
◆ Commuter campus in small city

General. Founded in 1961. Regionally accredited. **Enrollment:** 13,253 degree-seeking undergraduates. **Degrees:** 1,857 associate awarded. **Location:** 25 miles from San Diego. **Calendar:** Semester, extensive summer session. **Full-time faculty:** 224 total; 28% minority, 54% women. **Part-time faculty:** 547 total; 24% minority. **Class size:** 19% < 20, 60% 20-39, 16% 40-49, 4% 50-99, less than 1% >100. **Special facilities:** Observatory.

Student profile.

Out-of-state:	2%	25 or older:	30%

Transfer out. Colleges most students transferred to 2015: San Diego State University, University of California San Diego, National University.

Basis for selection. Open admission, but selective for some programs. Limited admission to health professions programs.

2015-2016 Annual costs. Tuition/fees: $1,418; $7,418 out-of-state. Per-credit charge: $46 in-state; $246 out-of-state. Books/supplies: $1,600. Personal expenses: $2,500.

Financial aid. All financial aid based on need. Need-based aid available for part-time students. Work-study available nights, weekends and for part-time students.

Application procedures. Admission: No deadline. No application fee in-state; $163 out-of-state. Admission notification on a rolling basis. **Financial aid:** Priority date 3/2, closing date 6/30. FAFSA required. Applicants notified on a rolling basis starting 7/15; must reply within 2 week(s) of notification.

Academics. Special study options: Accelerated study, cross-registration, distance learning, double major, dual enrollment of high school students, ESL, honors, independent study, internships, student-designed major, study abroad. License preparation in nursing, occupational therapy, physical therapy. **Credit/placement by examination:** AP, CLEP, institutional tests. Students may earn a maximum of 18 units on the CLEP general examinations.

Support services: Learning center, reduced course load, remedial instruction, study skills assistance, tutoring, writing center.

Majors. Area/ethnic studies: Native American. **Biology:** General. **Business:** General, administrative services, business admin, executive assistant, hospitality admin, international, management science, marketing, sales/distribution, tourism promotion, tourism/travel. **Communications:** Broadcast journalism, communications/speech/rhetoric, digital media, journalism. **Computer sciences:** General, applications programming, computer science, LAN/WAN management, programming, webmaster. **English:** Creative writing, English lit, rhetoric/composition. **Foreign languages:** American Sign Language, Arabic, French, German, Japanese, Russian, Spanish. **Health services:** Athletic training, cardiovascular technology, nursing (RN), occupational therapy assistant, respiratory therapy technology, speech-language pathology assistant. **History:** General. **Liberal arts:** Arts/sciences. **Math:** General. **Parks/recreation:** Exercise sciences. **Philosophy/religion:** Philosophy. **Physical sciences:** Chemistry, geology, physics. **Protective services:** Corrections, forensics, police science, security services. **Social sciences:** Economics, geography, political science. **Visual/performing arts:** Acting, art history/conservation, ceramics, cinematography, dance, digital arts, drawing, jazz, music, musical theater, painting, photography, sculpture, theater design. **Work/family studies:** Child care management, child development.

Most popular majors. Business/marketing 11%, health sciences 14%, liberal arts 45%.

Technology on campus. 500 workstations in library, computer center. Commuter students can connect to campus network. Online course registration, online library, wireless network available.

Student life. Freshman orientation: Available. Preregistration for classes offered. **Activities:** Bands, choral groups, dance, drama, music ensembles, musical theater, radio station, student government, student newspaper, symphony orchestra.

Athletics. Intercollegiate: Baseball M, basketball, football (tackle) M, soccer W, softball W, swimming, tennis, volleyball, water polo. **Team name:** Griffins.

Student services. Adult student services, alcohol/substance abuse counseling, career counseling, services for economically disadvantaged, student employment services, financial aid counseling, health services, on-campus daycare, personal counseling, placement for graduates. **Physically disabled:** Services for visually, speech, hearing impaired. **Transfer:** Re-entry adviser, pre-admission transcript evaluation for new students. Transfer center, transfer adviser, college fairs on campus for students transferring to 4-year colleges.

Contact. Phone: (619) 644-7186 Fax: (619) 644-7933
Wendy Stewart, Dean Counseling and Enrollment Services, Grossmont College, 8800 Grossmont College Drive, El Cajon, CA 92020

Hartnell College
Salinas, California
www.hartnell.edu   **CB code: 4340**

▶ Public 2-year community college
▶ Commuter campus in small city

General. Founded in 1920. Regionally accredited. **Enrollment:** 10,226 degree-seeking undergraduates; 364 non-degree-seeking students. **Degrees:** 784 associate awarded. **Location:** 110 miles from San Francisco, 65 miles from San Jose. **Calendar:** Semester, limited summer session. **Full-time faculty:** 100 total; 25% have terminal degrees, 43% minority, 56% women. **Part-time faculty:** 235 total; 12% have terminal degrees, 41% minority, 51% women.

Student profile. Among degree-seeking undergraduates, 3,076 enrolled as first-time, first-year students.

Part-time: 74% **Women:**   46%

Basis for selection. Open admission, but selective for some programs. Limited admission to both LVN and RN nursing and Respiratory Care programs. Interview required for nursing, physician's assistant, animal health technician majors.

2015-2016 Annual costs. Tuition/fees: $1,400; $7,040 out-of-state. Per-credit charge: $46 in-state; $234 out-of-state. Books/supplies: $1,764. Personal expenses: $3,159.

2014-2015 Financial aid. Need-based: 98% of total undergraduate aid awarded as scholarships/grants, 2% as loans/jobs. Work-study available nights, weekends and for part-time students.

Application procedures. Admission: No deadline. No application fee. Admission notification on a rolling basis. **Financial aid:** Priority date 8/1; no closing date. FAFSA required. Applicants notified on a rolling basis.

Academics. Special study options: Cooperative education. **Credit/placement by examination:** AP, CLEP, institutional tests. 12 credit hours maximum toward associate degree. **Support services:** GED preparation, learning center, remedial instruction, tutoring.

Majors. Area/ethnic studies: General. **Biology:** General. **Business:** Administrative services, banking/financial services, business admin, real estate. **Communications:** Communications/speech/rhetoric. **Communications technology:** Animation/special effects. **Computer sciences:** General, support specialist, web page design. **Education:** Teacher assistance. **Engineering:** Pre-engineering. **English:** English lit. **Foreign languages:** Spanish. **General:** Site management. **Health services:** Nursing (RN), respiratory therapy technology, substance abuse counseling. **History:** General. **Liberal arts:** Arts/sciences. **Math:** General. **Parks/recreation:** Exercise sciences. **Physical sciences:** Astronomy, chemistry, geology, physics. **Protective services:** Police science. **Psychology:** General. **Social sciences:** General, political science, sociology. **Visual/performing arts:** Art, dramatic, music, photography. **Work/family studies:** Child care service.

Most popular majors. Business/marketing 7%, health sciences 6%, liberal arts 42%, psychology 11%, security/protective services 10%.

Technology on campus. 500 workstations in library, student center.

Student life. Freshman orientation: Mandatory. Preregistration for classes offered. **Activities:** Bands, choral groups, drama, music ensembles, musical theater, student government.

Athletics. Intercollegiate: Baseball M, basketball, cross-country, football (tackle) M, soccer M, softball W, track and field. **Team name:** Panthers.

Student services. Career counseling, services for economically disadvantaged, student employment services, personal counseling, placement for graduates, veterans' counselor. **Physically disabled:** Services for visually, hearing impaired. **Transfer:** Transfer center, college fairs on campus for students transferring to 4-year colleges.

Contact. Phone: (831) 755-6711 Fax: (831) 759-6014
Mary Dominguez, Dean of Student Affairs-Enrollment Services, Hartnell College, 411 Central Avenue, Salinas, CA 93901

Imperial Valley College
Imperial, California   **CB member**
www.imperial.edu   **CB code: 4358**

▶ Public 2-year nursing and community college
▶ Commuter campus in large town

General. Founded in 1922. Regionally accredited. **Enrollment:** 8,043 undergraduates. **Degrees:** 1,129 associate awarded. **Location:** 6 miles from El Centro. **Calendar:** Semester, limited summer session. **Full-time faculty:** 115 total; 20% have terminal degrees, 30% minority, 44% women. **Part-time faculty:** 199 total; 4% have terminal degrees, 66% minority, 44% women. **Class size:** 17% < 20, 72% 20-39, 9% 40-49, 2% 50-99, less than 1% >100. **Special facilities:** Planetarium. **Partnerships:** Formal partnership with Cisco.

Student profile.

Out-of-state: 2% **25 or older:**   32%

Transfer out. Colleges most students transferred to 2015: San Diego State University, California State Polytechnic University: Pomona, California State University: San Marcos, California State University: San Bernadino, California State University: Long Beach.

Basis for selection. Open admission, but selective for some programs. Limited admission for registered nursing program. **Adult students:** SAT/ACT scores not required.

High school preparation. College-preparatory program recommended.

2015-2016 Annual costs. Tuition/fees: $1,414; $8,014 out-of-state. Per-credit charge: $46 in-state; $266 out-of-state. Books/supplies: $1,746. Personal expenses: $3,132.

Financial aid. All financial aid based on need. Need-based aid available for part-time students. Work-study available nights, weekends and for part-time students.

Application procedures. **Admission:** No deadline. No application fee. Application must be submitted online. Admission notification on a rolling basis. **Financial aid:** Priority date 3/2, closing date 6/30. FAFSA required. Applicants notified on a rolling basis starting 5/1.

Academics. **Special study options:** Accelerated study, distance learning, double major, dual enrollment of high school students, ESL, honors, liberal arts/career combination. License preparation in nursing, paramedic. **Credit/placement by examination:** AP, CLEP, institutional tests. 15 credit hours maximum toward associate degree. **Support services:** GED test center, learning center, reduced course load, remedial instruction, study skills assistance, tutoring, writing center.

Majors. **Biology:** General. **Business:** Accounting technology, administrative services, banking/financial services, business admin, marketing, office technology, office/clerical. **Communications:** Communications/speech/rhetoric, journalism. **Computer sciences:** General, computer science, web page design. **Education:** Early childhood. **Engineering:** General. **English:** English lit. **Foreign languages:** General, American Sign Language, Arabic, French, Spanish. **Health services:** EMT paramedic, licensed practical nurse, nursing (RN), substance abuse counseling. **History:** General. **Liberal arts:** Arts/sciences, humanities. **Math:** General. **Parks/recreation:** Health/fitness. **Physical sciences:** General. **Protective services:** Corrections, firefighting, law enforcement admin. **Psychology:** General. **Social sciences:** General, anthropology. **Visual/performing arts:** Art, music. **Work/family studies:** Child development.

Most popular majors. Business/marketing 8%, health sciences 9%, legal studies 10%, psychology 7%, social sciences 10%.

Technology on campus. 125 workstations in library, computer center. Commuter students can connect to campus network. Online course registration, online library, helpline, wireless network available.

Student life. **Freshman orientation:** Mandatory. Preregistration for classes offered. One day program. **Policies:** Smoke free campus. **Activities:** Jazz band, choral groups, music ensembles, student government, Christian club, Movimiento Estudiantil Chicano de Aztlan, Upward Bound club, French club, Spirit club, agriculture club, business club, Educational Talent Search club, Lamplighter's club.

Athletics. NJCAA. **Intercollegiate:** Baseball M, basketball, soccer, tennis, volleyball W. **Team name:** Arabs.

Student services. Adult student services, alcohol/substance abuse counseling, career counseling, services for economically disadvantaged, student employment services, financial aid counseling, health services, on-campus daycare, personal counseling, veterans' counselor. **Physically disabled:** Services for visually, speech, hearing impaired. **Transfer:** Pre-admission transcript evaluation for new students. Transfer center, transfer adviser, college fairs on campus for students transferring to 4-year colleges.

Contact. E-mail: gloria.carmona@imperial.edu
Phone: (760) 352-8320 Fax: (760) 355-2663
Gloria Hoisington, Director of Admissions & Records, Imperial Valley College, Box 158, Imperial, CA 92251-0158

Institute of Technology: Clovis
Clovis, California
www.it-colleges.edu

▶ For-profit 2-year culinary school and career college
▶ Small city

General. Regionally accredited; also accredited by ACCSC. **Enrollment:** 1,509 undergraduates. **Degrees:** 350 associate awarded. **Calendar:** Differs by program. **Full-time faculty:** 131 total. **Part-time faculty:** 63 total.

Basis for selection. Admission requirements vary by programs.

2015-2016 Annual costs. Books/supplies: $1,746. Personal expenses: $3,132. **Additional information:** Accounting (AAS): $27,825. Administrative Office Professional: $15,825. Baking and Pastry Specialist: $18,025. Computerized Accounting (Diploma): $15,833. Criminology/Emergency Response (AAS): $25,025. Culinary Arts Professional (AOS): $31,025.. Culinary Arts Specialist: $20,025. Heating, Ventilation and Air Conditioning: $18,074. Human Resource Administrator (AAS): $26,825. Professional Medical Assistant: $17,634.

Financial aid. **Need-based:** Work-study available nights, weekends and for part-time students.

Application procedures. **Admission:** $75 fee.

Academics. **Credit/placement by examination:** AP, CLEP.

Majors. **Business:** Accounting, human resources. **Social sciences:** Criminology.

Contact. E-mail: rgardner@it-email.com
Phone: (559) 297-4500
Ron Gardner, Director of Admissions, Institute of Technology: Clovis, 564 West Herndon Avenue, Clovis, CA 93612

Irvine Valley College
Irvine, California
www.ivc.edu   **CB code: 3356**

▶ Public 2-year community college
▶ Commuter campus in small city

General. Regionally accredited. **Enrollment:** 9,957 degree-seeking undergraduates. **Degrees:** 973 associate awarded. **ROTC:** Air Force. **Location:** 50 miles from Los Angeles. **Calendar:** Semester, extensive summer session. **Full-time faculty:** 125 total. **Part-time faculty:** 356 total. **Special facilities:** Dance studio, Microsoft Office user specialist testing site, telescope, performing arts center.

Transfer out. **Colleges most students transferred to 2015:** University of California: Irvine, California State University: Fullerton.

Basis for selection. Open admission.

2015-2016 Annual costs. Tuition/fees: $1,418; $8,048 out-of-state. Per-credit charge: $46 in-state; $267 out-of-state. Books/supplies: $1,638. Personal expenses: $2,826.

Financial aid. All financial aid based on need. Need-based aid available for part-time students. Work-study available nights, weekends and for part-time students.

Application procedures. **Admission:** No deadline. No application fee. Admission notification on a rolling basis. **Financial aid:** No deadline. FAFSA, institutional form required. Applicants notified on a rolling basis starting 4/30.

Academics. **Special study options:** Accelerated study, cooperative education, cross-registration, distance learning, double major, dual enrollment of high school students, ESL, honors, independent study, internships, study abroad, weekend college. **Credit/placement by examination:** AP, CLEP, institutional tests. 12 credit hours maximum toward associate degree. Minimum 2.0 GPA in at least 12 units completed at IVC required to enroll in credit by examination. **Support services:** Learning center, remedial instruction, study skills assistance, tutoring, writing center.

Majors. **Area/ethnic studies:** Women's. **Biology:** General, ecology. **Business:** General, accounting, business admin, office management, office technology, real estate. **Communications:** Advertising. **Computer sciences:** General, applications programming, networking, programming, systems analysis. **Conservation:** General. **Education:** Early childhood, physical. **English:** British lit, rhetoric/composition, writing. **Foreign languages:** French, Spanish. **History:** General. **Liberal arts:** Arts/sciences. **Math:** General. **Parks/recreation:** Health/fitness. **Philosophy/religion:** Philosophy. **Physical sciences:** Chemistry, geology. **Protective services:** Law enforcement admin, police science. **Psychology:** General. **Social sciences:** Anthropology, economics, geography, political science, sociology. **Visual/performing arts:** General, art, dance, dramatic, music, photography, studio arts, theater design.

Most popular majors. Business/marketing 9%, liberal arts 77%.

Technology on campus. 250 workstations in library, computer center. Commuter students can connect to campus network. Online course registration, online library, helpline available.

Student life. **Freshman orientation:** Mandatory. Preregistration for classes offered. **Housing:** Homestay referral for international students available. **Activities:** Bands, choral groups, dance, drama, literary magazine, music ensembles, musical theater, student government, student newspaper, symphony orchestra, administration of justice club, Phi Theta Kappa honor society, Muslim Student Association, biology society, dance club, geology club, health sciences society, journalism club, Phi Theta Kappa, Psi Beta.

Athletics. **Intercollegiate:** Badminton W, baseball M, basketball, cross-country, golf, soccer, softball W, tennis, volleyball. **Intramural:** Basketball, soccer, tennis, volleyball. **Team name:** Lasers.

Student services. Adult student services, career counseling, services for economically disadvantaged, student employment services, financial aid counseling, health services, on-campus daycare, personal counseling, placement for graduates, veterans' counselor, women's services. **Physically disabled:** Services for visually, speech, hearing impaired. **Transfer:** Re-entry adviser for new students. Transfer center, transfer adviser, college fairs on campus for students transferring to 4-year colleges.

Contact. E-mail: admissions@ivc.edu
Phone: (949) 451-5461 Fax: (949) 451-5443
Arleen Elseroad, Director of Admissions, Records & Enrollment Services, Irvine Valley College, 5500 Irvine Center Drive, Irvine, CA 92618-4399

Kaplan College: Palm Springs
Palm Springs, California
www.kc-palmsprings.com

- For-profit 2-year health science and technical college
- Commuter campus in large town

General. Accredited by ACCSC. **Enrollment:** 379 undergraduates. **Degrees:** 28 associate awarded. **Calendar:** Differs by program. **Full-time faculty:** 11 total. **Part-time faculty:** 21 total.

Basis for selection. Open admission, but selective for some programs. Prospective student must meet with an Admissions Representative, provide a high school diploma or GED, pass an entrance assessment and pay the applicable enrollment fee. Students must also complete the Financial Aid process or make payment arrangements with the college. **Home schooled:** State high school equivalency certificate required.

2015-2016 Annual costs. Associate degree program: Criminal Justice $30,356. Diploma programs: Dental Assistant $16,640; Massage Therapy $14,970; Medical Assistant $15,615; Medical Office Specialist $15,615.

Financial aid. Need-based: Work-study available nights, weekends and for part-time students.

Application procedures. Admission: $10 fee.

Academics. Special study options: Accelerated study, internships. **Credit/placement by examination:** AP, CLEP. **Support services:** Study skills assistance, tutoring.

Student life. Freshman orientation: Mandatory. Preregistration for classes offered.

Student services. Financial aid counseling.

Contact. Phone: (760) 327-4562
Leslie Rowden, Director of Admissions, Kaplan College: Palm Springs, 2475 East Tahquitz Canyon Way, Palm Springs, CA 92262

Kaplan College: Riverside
Riverside, California
www.riverside.kaplancollege.com   CB code: 3541

- For-profit 2-year junior and technical college
- Commuter campus in very large city
- Interview required

General. Regionally accredited; also accredited by ACCSC. **Enrollment:** 167 undergraduates. **Degrees:** 24 associate awarded. **Location:** 15 miles from Los Angeles. **Calendar:** Differs by program. **Full-time faculty:** 6 total. **Part-time faculty:** 8 total. **Class size:** 86% < 20, 14% 20-39.

Basis for selection. Open admission. **Home schooled:** Interview required.

2015-2016 Annual costs. Associate programs: Criminal Justice $29,292. Diploma programs: Dental Assistant $17,120; Massage Therapy ; Medical Assistant, Medical Billing and Coding Specialist $15,304.

Financial aid. All financial aid based on need. Work-study available nights, weekends and for part-time students.

Application procedures. Admission: No deadline. $10 fee. Application must be submitted on paper. **Financial aid:** No deadline. FAFSA, institutional form required.

Academics. Special study options: Internships, liberal arts/career combination. **Credit/placement by examination:** AP, CLEP. **Support services:** Learning center, study skills assistance, tutoring.

Majors. Business: Accounting, accounting technology, accounting/business management, business admin, office management. **Computer sciences:** Information technology, LAN/WAN management, system admin.

Most popular majors. Business/marketing 17%, computer/information sciences 35%, legal studies 46%.

Technology on campus. 20 workstations in library, computer center. Online library available.

Student life. Freshman orientation: Mandatory. Preregistration for classes offered. **Activities:** Student newspaper.

Student services. Career counseling, student employment services, financial aid counseling, placement for graduates.

Contact. Phone: (951) 276-1704 Toll-free number: (800) 935-1857
Enrique Alvarez, Director of Admissions, Kaplan College: Riverside, 4040 Vine Street, Riverside, CA 92507

Kaplan College: Sacramento
Sacramento, California
https://www.kaplancollege.com/sacramento-ca

- For-profit 2-year technical college
- Commuter campus in large city

General. Accredited by ACICS. **Enrollment:** 429 undergraduates. **Degrees:** 23 associate awarded. **Location:** Downtown. **Calendar:** Differs by program. **Full-time faculty:** 9 total. **Part-time faculty:** 31 total.

Basis for selection. Open admission, but selective for some programs. Specific assessment requirements for all programs. **Adult students:** SAT/ACT scores not required. All students are required to pass an assessment at the level their specific program requires.

2015-2016 Annual costs. Associate degree program: Criminal Justice $29,292. Diploma programs: Vocational Nursing $31,685; Dental Assistant $17,122; Medical Assistant, Medical Office Specialist $15,727.

Financial aid. All financial aid based on need. Work-study available nights, weekends and for part-time students.

Application procedures. Admission: No deadline. $20 fee.

Academics. Special study options: License preparation in nursing. **Credit/placement by examination:** AP, CLEP. **Support services:** Study skills assistance, tutoring.

Technology on campus. 50 workstations in student center. Online library, helpline available.

Student life. Freshman orientation: Available. Preregistration for classes offered. **Activities:** Student newspaper.

Student services. Career counseling, financial aid counseling, placement for graduates. **Transfer:** Pre-admission transcript evaluation for new students.

Contact. Phone: (916) 649-8168 Toll-free number: (800) 935-1857
Fax: (916) 649-8344
Heidi Wingo, Director of Admissions, Kaplan College: Sacramento, 4330 Watt Avenue, Suite 400, Sacramento, CA 95821

Kaplan College: Salida
Salida, California
www.modesto.kaplancollege.com

- For-profit 2-year health science and technical college
- Commuter campus in small city
- Interview required

General. Accredited by ACCSC. **Enrollment:** 429 undergraduates. **Degrees:** 87 associate awarded. **Calendar:** Differs by program. **Full-time faculty:** 25 total. **Part-time faculty:** 21 total.

Basis for selection. Open admission. **Home schooled:** Transcript of courses and grades required.

2015-2016 Annual costs. Associate degree programs: Criminal Justice $29,292; Respiratory Care $48,445. Diploma programs: Dental Assistant

$17,144; Medical Assistant, Medical Office Specialist $15,841; Therapeutic Health Technician $14,923; Vocational Nursing $31,709.

Financial aid. Need-based: Work-study available nights, weekends and for part-time students.

Application procedures. Admission: No deadline. $10 fee. Application must be submitted on paper.

Academics. Special study options: Accelerated study. **Credit/placement by examination:** AP, CLEP. **Support services:** Learning center, tutoring.

Majors. Health services: Respiratory therapy assistant, surgical technology. **Protective services:** Criminal justice.

Technology on campus. 90 workstations in library, computer center. Online library, wireless network available.

Student life. Freshman orientation: Mandatory. Preregistration for classes offered.

Student services. Adult student services, career counseling, student employment services, financial aid counseling, placement for graduates, veterans' counselor.

Contact. Phone: (209) 543-7000 Fax: (888) 280-9565
Doug Stucker, Director of Admissions, Kaplan College: Salida, 5172 Kiernan Court, Salida, CA 95368

Kaplan College: San Diego
San Diego, California
www.kaplancollege.com CB code: 3064

- For-profit 2-year business and health science college
- Commuter campus in very large city

General. Accredited by ACCSC. **Enrollment:** 1,297 undergraduates. **Degrees:** 193 associate awarded. **Calendar:** Differs by program. **Full-time faculty:** 48 total. **Part-time faculty:** 46 total.

Basis for selection. Open admission, but selective for some programs.

2015-2016 Annual costs. Personal expenses: $2,925. **Additional information:** Associate programs: Criminal Justice $30,335; Health Information Technology $29,165; Nursing $57,550.50; Vocational Nursing $34,487. Diploma programs: Dental Assistant $16,647; Medical Assistant $15,707.60; Medical Billing & Coding Specialist $16,017.6; Nurse Assistant $4,819.20; Patient Care Technician $17,276.20; Phlebotomy $3,270.

Financial aid. Need-based: Work-study available nights, weekends and for part-time students.

Application procedures. Admission: $10 fee.

Academics. Credit/placement by examination: AP, CLEP.

Majors. Business: Business admin.

Student life. Freshman orientation: Available. Preregistration for classes offered.

Contact. Phone: (858) 279-4500 Toll-free number: (800) 400-8232 Fax: (858) 279-4885
Serica Martinez, Director of Admissions, Kaplan College: San Diego, 9055 Balboa Avenue, San Diego, CA 92123

Kaplan College: Vista
Vista, California
www.mariccollege.edu

- For-profit 2-year technical college
- Commuter campus in small city

General. Accredited by ACCSC. **Enrollment:** 812 undergraduates. **Degrees:** 20 associate awarded. **Calendar:** Differs by program. **Full-time faculty:** 12 total. **Part-time faculty:** 39 total.

Basis for selection. Open admission, but selective for some programs. Institutional entrance exam important. High school diploma/GED required for some programs. Timed institutional examination administered onsite.

2015-2016 Annual costs. Associate degree program: Criminal Justice $30,335. Diploma programs: Dental Assistant $16,647; Healthcare Assistant $15,707; Holistic Health Practitioner $20,625; Massage Therapy $14,970; Medical Assistant $15,708; Medical Billing and Coding Specialist $16,018; Nursing Assistant $4,819; Pharmacy Technician $15,482; Phlebotomy Technician $3,270; Vocational Nursing $32,941; X-Ray Technician/Back Office Medical Assistant $27,873.

Financial aid. Need-based: Work-study available nights, weekends and for part-time students.

Application procedures. Admission: No deadline. $10 fee.

Academics. Credit/placement by examination: AP, CLEP.

Majors. Computer sciences: LAN/WAN management. **Protective services:** Criminal justice.

Student life. Freshman orientation: Available. Preregistration for classes offered.

Contact. Phone: (760) 630-1555 Fax: (760) 630-1656
Renee Codner, Director of Admissions, Kaplan College: Vista, 2022 University Drive, Vista, CA 92083

Lake Tahoe Community College
South Lake Tahoe, California
www.ltcc.edu CB code: 4420

- Public 2-year community college
- Commuter campus in large town

General. Founded in 1975. Regionally accredited. **Enrollment:** 1,457 degree-seeking undergraduates. **Degrees:** 168 associate awarded. **Location:** 55 miles from Reno, Nevada, 110 miles from Sacramento. **Calendar:** Quarter, limited summer session. **Full-time faculty:** 41 total; 51% women. **Part-time faculty:** 175 total. **Special facilities:** Demonstration garden, art galleries, amphitheater, fitness center, culinary facility, theater.

Transfer out. Colleges most students transferred to 2015: California State University, University of California, and University of Nevada: Reno.

Basis for selection. Open admission. Open admission policy for students who are at least 18 or have graduated from high school. Special admission criteria apply to international students. **Learning Disabled:** Assistance is available through the Disability Resource Center.

2015-2016 Annual costs. Tuition/fees: $1,415; $7,670 out-of-state. Per-credit charge: $31 in-state; $170 out-of-state. Books/supplies: $1,656. Personal expenses: $3,114.

Financial aid. Need-based: Need-based aid available for part-time students. Work-study available nights, weekends and for part-time students.

Application procedures. Admission: No deadline. No application fee. Application must be submitted online. Admission notification on a rolling basis. **Financial aid:** Closing date 6/30. FAFSA required. Applicants notified on a rolling basis starting 7/1; must reply within 2 week(s) of notification.

Academics. Special study options: Cooperative education, distance learning, double major, ESL, internships, study abroad. License preparation in dental hygiene, real estate. **Credit/placement by examination:** AP, CLEP, IB, institutional tests. **Support services:** GED preparation, learning center, reduced course load, remedial instruction, study skills assistance, tutoring, writing center.

Majors. Business: General, accounting, entrepreneurial studies, finance, marketing. **Computer sciences:** General. **Education:** Early childhood. **English:** English lit. **Foreign languages:** Spanish. **Health services:** Health information management, medical assistant, substance abuse counseling. **Liberal arts:** Arts/sciences, humanities. **Math:** General. **Parks/recreation:** Health/fitness. **Physical sciences:** Geology. **Protective services:** Firefighting, law enforcement admin. **Psychology:** General. **Social sciences:** General, anthropology, sociology. **Visual/performing arts:** Art, dance, dramatic, music, studio arts.

Technology on campus. 200 workstations in library, computer center, student center. Online course registration, online library, wireless network available.

Student life. Freshman orientation: Mandatory. Preregistration for classes offered. Held during the registration period for each quarter. Orientation, assessment, and advising services provided. **Activities:** Choral groups, dance, drama, music ensembles, musical theater, student government, Alpha

Gamma Sigma, art club, international club, math club, Performing Arts League, Rotoract.

Athletics. Intercollegiate: Soccer. **Team name:** Coyotes.

Student services. Adult student services, career counseling, services for economically disadvantaged, student employment services, financial aid counseling, minority student services, on-campus daycare, personal counseling, placement for graduates, veterans' counselor. **Physically disabled:** Services for visually, speech, hearing impaired. **Transfer:** Transfer center, transfer adviser, college fairs on campus for students transferring to 4-year colleges.

Contact. E-mail: enrollmentservices@ltcc.edu
Phone: (530) 541-4660 ext. 211 Fax: (530) 542-1781
Alysa Borelli, Director of Enrollment Services, Lake Tahoe Community College, One College Drive, South Lake Tahoe, CA 96150-4524

Laney College
Oakland, California
www.laney.peralta.edu   CB code: 4406

- Public 2-year community college
- Commuter campus in large city

General. Founded in 1953. Regionally accredited. Vocational programs include programs with PGE and a solar program with UC Lawrence Laboratories. **Enrollment:** 12,154 undergraduates. **Degrees:** 512 associate awarded. **Location:** 10 miles from San Francisco. **Calendar:** Semester, extensive summer session. **Full-time faculty:** 124 total. **Part-time faculty:** 300 total. **Special facilities:** CAD laboratory.

Student profile. 61% enrolled in a transfer program, 27% enrolled in a vocational program, 11% already have a bachelor's degree or higher.

Out-of-state: 2% 25 or older: 61%

Transfer out. Colleges most students transferred to 2015: California State University: East Bay, San Francisco State, University of California: Berkeley.

Basis for selection. Open admission.

2015-2016 Annual costs. Tuition/fees: $1,420; $7,870 out-of-state. Per-credit charge: $46 in-state; $261 out-of-state. Books/supplies: $1,764. Personal expenses: $3,160.

Financial aid. Need-based: Work-study available nights, weekends and for part-time students.

Application procedures. Admission: No deadline. No application fee. Admission notification on a rolling basis. **Financial aid:** Priority date 4/1, closing date 6/30. FAFSA, institutional form required. Applicants notified on a rolling basis; must reply within 2 week(s) of notification.

Academics. Special study options: Cooperative education, distance learning, dual enrollment of high school students, ESL, honors, independent study, liberal arts/career combination, study abroad, weekend college. **Credit/placement by examination:** AP, CLEP, institutional tests. **Support services:** Learning center, pre-admission summer program, remedial instruction, study skills assistance, tutoring.

Majors. Area/ethnic studies: African-American, Asian, Latin American. **Business:** General, accounting, administrative services, banking/financial services, management information systems, office technology, office/clerical, operations, sales/distribution. **Communications:** Broadcast journalism, journalism. **Communications technology:** General, graphic/printing. **Computer sciences:** General, information systems. **Education:** General. **English:** English lit. **General:** Carpentry, maintenance. **Liberal arts:** Arts/sciences. **Math:** General. **Social sciences:** General. **Visual/performing arts:** Art, ceramics, commercial/advertising art, dance, design, dramatic, music.

Technology on campus. 400 workstations in library, computer center, student center. Online course registration, online library available.

Student life. Freshman orientation: Mandatory. Preregistration for classes offered. **Activities:** Pep band, dance, drama, literary magazine, musical theater, student government, student newspaper, TV station.

Athletics. Intercollegiate: Badminton W, baseball M, basketball M, football (tackle) M, softball W, swimming, track and field W, volleyball W, water polo W. **Team name:** Eagles.

Student services. Adult student services, career counseling, services for economically disadvantaged, student employment services, financial aid counseling, health services, minority student services, on-campus daycare,

---

personal counseling, placement for graduates, veterans' counselor. **Physically disabled:** Services for visually, speech, hearing impaired. **Transfer:** Re-entry adviser for new students. Transfer center, transfer adviser, college fairs on campus for students transferring to 4-year colleges.

Contact. E-mail: admissions@peralta.edu
Phone: (510) 464-3121 Fax: (510) 464-3240
Ron Gerhard, Director of Admissions and Records, Laney College, 900 Fallon Street, Oakland, CA 94607

Las Positas College
Livermore, California
www.laspositascollege.edu   CB code: 6507

- Public 2-year community college
- Commuter campus in small city

General. Founded in 1991. Regionally accredited. **Enrollment:** 6,162 degree-seeking undergraduates. **Degrees:** 576 associate awarded. **Location:** 43 miles from San Francisco, 39 miles from San Jose. **Calendar:** Semester, limited summer session. **Full-time faculty:** 107 total. **Part-time faculty:** 260 total.

Transfer out. Colleges most students transferred to 2015: California State University: East Bay.

Basis for selection. Open admission. High school diploma or GED required for student under 18 years.

2015-2016 Annual costs. Tuition/fees: $1,436; $8,726 out-of-state. Per-credit charge: $46 in-district; $289 out-of-district; $289 out-of-state. Books/supplies: $1,710. Personal expenses: $3,096.

Financial aid. Need-based: Work-study available nights, weekends and for part-time students.

Application procedures. Admission: No deadline. No application fee. Admission notification on a rolling basis. **Financial aid:** Priority date 5/1; no closing date. Institutional form required. Applicants notified on a rolling basis starting 7/1; must reply within 2 week(s) of notification.

Academics. Special study options: Accelerated study, distance learning, dual enrollment of high school students, ESL, honors, independent study, internships, student-designed major. **Credit/placement by examination:** AP, CLEP. **Support services:** Learning center, remedial instruction, tutoring.

Majors. Biology: General. **Business:** Business admin.

Technology on campus. 285 workstations in library, computer center.

Student life. Freshman orientation: Available. Preregistration for classes offered. **Activities:** Jazz band, choral groups, dance, drama, international student organizations, literary magazine, music ensembles, musical theater, student government, student newspaper.

Athletics. Intercollegiate: Basketball, cross-country, soccer. **Intramural:** Basketball, bowling, fencing, handball M, racquetball, skin diving, soccer, swimming, volleyball. **Team name:** Hawks.

Student services. Adult student services, career counseling, student employment services, financial aid counseling, health services, personal counseling, veterans' counselor. **Physically disabled:** Services for visually, speech, hearing impaired. **Transfer:** Transfer center, transfer adviser, college fairs on campus for students transferring to 4-year colleges.

Contact. Phone: (925) 424-1000 Fax: (925) 443-0742
Sylvia Rodriguez, Registrar, Las Positas College, 3033 Collier Canyon Road, Livermore, CA 94551

Lassen Community College
Susanville, California
www.lassencollege.edu   CB code: 4383

- Public 2-year community college
- Residential campus in large town

General. Founded in 1925. Regionally accredited. **Enrollment:** 2,183 degree-seeking undergraduates; 200 non-degree-seeking students. **Degrees:** 240 associate awarded. **Location:** 100 miles from Chico, 84 miles from Reno. **Calendar:** Semester, limited summer session. **Full-time faculty:** 29

total; 3% have terminal degrees, 41% women. **Part-time faculty:** 63 total; 46% women. **Special facilities:** Coppervale ski area.

Student profile. Among degree-seeking undergraduates, 414 enrolled as first-time, first-year students.

Part-time:	69%	Women:	32%
Out-of-state:	4%	25 or older:	46%

Transfer out. Colleges most students transferred to 2015: California State University: Chico, University of Nevada: Reno, California State University: Sacramento, Humboldt State University, University of California: Davis.

Basis for selection. Open admission, but selective for some programs. Limited admission to nursing program and gunsmithing program.

2015-2016 Annual costs. Tuition/fees: $1,407; $7,392 out-of-state. Per-credit charge: $46 in-state; $249 out-of-state. Room only: $2,800. Books/supplies: $1,710. Personal expenses: $2,278.

2014-2015 Financial aid. All financial aid based on need. 79% of total undergraduate aid awarded as scholarships/grants, 21% as loans/jobs. Work-study available nights, weekends and for part-time students. **Additional information:** Board of Governors Grant: low-income California residents can have registration fees waived.

Application procedures. Admission: No deadline. No application fee. Admission notification on a rolling basis. Institutional placement tests recommended. **Financial aid:** Priority date 7/1; no closing date. FAFSA required. Applicants notified on a rolling basis starting 7/1; must reply within 2 week(s) of notification.

Academics. Gunsmithing and summer NRA programs offered. **Special study options:** Cooperative education, distance learning, dual enrollment of high school students, honors, independent study, internships. License preparation in nursing. **Credit/placement by examination:** AP, CLEP, institutional tests. 15 credit hours maximum toward associate degree. **Support services:** Learning center, pre-admission summer program, reduced course load, remedial instruction, study skills assistance, tutoring, writing center.

Majors. Biology: General. **Business:** Accounting, administrative services, business admin. **Education:** General, early childhood, physical. **English:** English lit. **Health services:** Licensed practical nurse. **History:** General. **Liberal arts:** Arts/sciences. **Math:** General. **Physical sciences:** General. **Protective services:** Corrections, law enforcement admin, police science. **Psychology:** General. **Social sciences:** General. **Visual/performing arts:** Art history/conservation, digital arts, studio arts.

Most popular majors. Security/protective services 6%, social sciences 65%.

Technology on campus. 40 workstations in library, computer center. Dormitories wired for high-speed internet access. Online course registration, online library, helpline, wireless network available.

Student life. Freshman orientation: Mandatory. Preregistration for classes offered. **Housing:** Coed dorms available. **Activities:** Student government, over 20 student organizations and clubs.

Athletics. NJCAA. **Intercollegiate:** Baseball M, basketball, rodeo, soccer, softball W, volleyball W, wrestling M. **Intramural:** Basketball, skiing, table tennis, ultimate frisbee, volleyball. **Team name:** Cougars.

Student services. Career counseling, services for economically disadvantaged, financial aid counseling, health services, on-campus daycare, personal counseling, veterans' counselor. **Physically disabled:** Services for visually, speech, hearing impaired. **Transfer:** Transfer center, transfer adviser, college fairs on campus for students transferring to 4-year colleges.

Contact. E-mail: lccadmissions@lassencollege.edu
Phone: (530) 251-8808 Fax: (530) 257-8802
Patrick Walton, Dean of Student Services, Lassen Community College, PO Box 3000, Susanville, CA 96130

Le Cordon Bleu College of Culinary Arts: Los Angeles
Pasadena, California
www.chefs.edu/los-angeles   CB code: 7422

- For-profit 2-year culinary school
- Commuter campus in very large city
- Interview required

General. Regionally accredited; also accredited by ACICS. **Enrollment:** 1,350 degree-seeking undergraduates. **Degrees:** 136 associate awarded. **Location:** 15 miles from downtown Los Angeles. **Calendar:** Differs by program, extensive summer session. **Full-time faculty:** 79 total; 1% have terminal degrees, 30% minority. **Part-time faculty:** 5 total; 80% minority. **Special facilities:** Fine-dining restaurant and casual cafe where students gain practical work experience.

Basis for selection. Open admission. Students whose first language is not English are required to submit evidence of English Proficiency. This may be done by submitting a TOEFL test score of 500 or higher (for the CPT version, a score of 150 or higher). Entrance Test is required by state agency for diploma programs. Wonderlic SLE Exam used to comply with these regulations. **Learning Disabled:** Students requesting special needs and services required to submit Application for Auxiliary Aid request. Application must include supporting documentation as evidence of disability.

2015-2016 Annual costs. Certificate programs: $19,500. Associate programs: $40,000. Books and supplies are included.

Financial aid. Need-based: Need-based aid available for part-time students. Work-study available nights, weekends and for part-time students.

Application procedures. Admission: No deadline. $50 fee. Admission notification on a rolling basis. **Financial aid:** No deadline. FAFSA required. Applicants notified on a rolling basis.

Academics. Credit/placement by examination: AP, CLEP. **Support services:** Learning center, study skills assistance, tutoring.

Technology on campus. 40 workstations in library, computer center, student center. Commuter students can connect to campus network. Online library available.

Student life. Freshman orientation: Mandatory. Preregistration for classes offered. **Activities:** International student organizations, student newspaper.

Student services. Adult student services, career counseling, financial aid counseling, placement for graduates. **Transfer:** Re-entry adviser, pre-admission transcript evaluation for new students.

Contact. E-mail: admissionsinfo@la.chefs.edu
Phone: (626) 229-1300 Toll-free number: (888) 900-2433
Fax: (626) 585-0486
Glenn Reible, Vice President of Admissions, Le Cordon Bleu College of Culinary Arts: Los Angeles, 530 East Colorado Boulevard, Pasadena, CA 91101

Le Cordon Bleu College of Culinary Arts: San Francisco
San Francisco, California
www.chefs.edu/San-Francisco   CB code: 2209

- For-profit 2-year culinary school and career college
- Commuter campus in very large city
- Interview required

General. Founded in 1977. Accredited by ACCSC. All programs offered sanctioned by Le Cordon Bleu. **Enrollment:** 442 undergraduates. **Degrees:** 77 associate awarded. **Location:** Downtown. **Calendar:** Differs by program. **Full-time faculty:** 28 total. **Part-time faculty:** 23 total. **Special facilities:** Student-staffed public restaurant, mixology lab, gaming room, professional production kitchens, demonstration kitchens, pastry kitchens, confiseries, butchery lab, culinary library.

Basis for selection. The school has an open enrollment policy but the student needs to complete an interview with an admissions representative, pass a short entrance exam, have a High School diploma or equivalent before starting school. Wonderlic testing required for all programs.

2015-2016 Annual costs. Certificate programs: $19,500. Associate programs: $40,000. Books and supplies are included.

Financial aid. Need-based: Work-study available nights, weekends and for part-time students.

Application procedures. Admission: No deadline. $50 fee. Admission notification on a rolling basis. **Financial aid:** No deadline. FAFSA required. Applicants notified on a rolling basis; must reply within 1 week(s) of notification.

Academics. Special study options: Internships. **Credit/placement by examination:** AP, CLEP. **Support services:** Study skills assistance, tutoring.

Technology on campus. Student web hosting, wireless network available.

Student life. Freshman orientation: Mandatory. Preregistration for classes offered. **Housing:** $600 fully refundable deposit. **Activities:** Brewing arts association, Cuisine Des Femmes, Asian food club, baking and pastry arts club, dinner club, wine club.

Student services. Career counseling, student employment services, financial aid counseling, placement for graduates. **Transfer:** Re-entry adviser, pre-admission transcript evaluation for new students.

Contact. E-mail: admissions@caculinary.edu
Phone: (415) 771-3500 Toll-free number: (800) 229-2433
Fax: (415) 621-5625
Donna Ingenito, Director of Admissions, Le Cordon Bleu College of Culinary Arts: San Francisco, 350 Rhode Island Street, San Francisco, CA 94103

Long Beach City College
Long Beach, California
www.lbcc.edu   CB code: 4388

▶ Public 2-year community college
▶ Commuter campus in large city

General. Founded in 1927. Regionally accredited. **Enrollment:** 16,317 degree-seeking undergraduates. **Degrees:** 1,110 associate awarded. **Location:** 20 miles from downtown Los Angeles. **Calendar:** Semester, limited summer session. **Full-time faculty:** 270 total. **Part-time faculty:** 643 total. **Class size:** 35% < 20, 47% 20-39, 10% 40-49, 7% 50-99, 1% >100.

Student profile.

Out-of-state: 1%   25 or older: 51%

Transfer out. Colleges most students transferred to 2015: California State University: Long Beach, California State University: Dominguez Hills, California State University: Los Angeles, California State University: Fullerton, University of California: Los Angeles.

Basis for selection. Open admission.

2015-2016 Annual costs. Tuition/fees: $1,418; $9,188 out-of-state. Per-credit charge: $46 in-state; $305 out-of-state. Books/supplies: $1,710. Personal expenses: $3,096.

Financial aid. All financial aid based on need. Need-based aid available for part-time students. Work-study available nights, weekends and for part-time students.

Application procedures. Admission: No deadline. No application fee. Admission notification on a rolling basis. **Financial aid:** Priority date 5/29; no closing date. FAFSA, institutional form required. Applicants notified on a rolling basis starting 7/6; must reply within 2 week(s) of notification.

Academics. Special study options: Accelerated study, cooperative education, cross-registration, distance learning, dual enrollment of high school students, ESL, honors, independent study, internships, liberal arts/career combination, study abroad, weekend college. License preparation in aviation, nursing, radiology, real estate. **Credit/placement by examination:** AP, CLEP, IB, institutional tests. 40 credit hours maximum toward associate degree. Students must first complete 12 units in residence. **Support services:** GED preparation, learning center, pre-admission summer program, remedial instruction, study skills assistance, tutoring, writing center.

Majors. Biology: General. **Business:** General, accounting, administrative services, business admin, fashion, hotel/motel admin, office technology, office/clerical, real estate, restaurant/food services, sales/distribution, tourism promotion, tourism/travel. **Communications:** Advertising, broadcast journalism, journalism, public relations, publishing. **Communications technology:** General, desktop publishing, graphic/printing. **Computer sciences:** Applications programming, data processing, word processing. **Education:** Teacher assistance. **Engineering:** General. **English:** English lit, rhetoric/composition. **Foreign languages:** General, Spanish. **General:** Carpentry. **Health services:** Dietetic technician, licensed practical nurse, medical assistant, medical radiologic technology/radiation therapy, nursing (RN). **Human services:** General. **Liberal arts:** Arts/sciences. **Math:** General. **Parks/recreation:** Health/fitness. **Physical sciences:** General. **Protective services:** Fire safety technology, law enforcement admin. **Social sciences:** General. **Visual/performing arts:** Art, commercial photography, commercial/advertising art, dance, design, dramatic, drawing, fashion design, film/cinema/video, interior design, multimedia, music, printmaking, sculpture, theater design. **Work/family studies:** General, child care management, child development, consumer economics, family resources, institutional food production.

Most popular majors. Business/marketing 7%, health sciences 19%, liberal arts 44%, security/protective services 7%.

Technology on campus. 500 workstations in library, computer center, student center. Online course registration, online library, helpline, wireless network available.

Student life. Freshman orientation: Available. Preregistration for classes offered. **Activities:** Bands, campus ministries, choral groups, dance, drama, international student organizations, literary magazine, music ensembles, musical theater, radio station, student government, student newspaper, symphony orchestra, TV station, College Republicans, Students for a Democratic Society.

Athletics. NJCAA. **Intercollegiate:** Baseball M, basketball, cross-country, football (tackle) M, golf, soccer, softball W, swimming, tennis, track and field, volleyball, water polo. **Intramural:** Archery, badminton, basketball, bowling, golf, racquetball, soccer, softball, swimming, table tennis, tennis, track and field, volleyball, wrestling M. **Team name:** Vikings.

Student services. Career counseling, student employment services, health services, on-campus daycare, personal counseling, veterans' counselor. **Physically disabled:** Services for visually, speech, hearing impaired. **Transfer:** Re-entry adviser for new students. Transfer center, transfer adviser, college fairs on campus for students transferring to 4-year colleges.

Contact. E-mail: rmiyashiro@lbcc.edu
Phone: (562) 938-4485 Fax: (562) 938-4858
Ross Miyashiro, Dean of Admissions and Records, Long Beach City College, 4901 East Carson Street, Long Beach, CA 90808

Los Angeles City College
Los Angeles, California
www.lacitycollege.edu   CB code: 4391

▶ Public 2-year community college
▶ Commuter campus in very large city

General. Founded in 1929. Regionally accredited. **Enrollment:** 9,959 degree-seeking undergraduates. **Degrees:** 568 associate awarded. **Location:** 5 miles from downtown. **Calendar:** Semester, limited summer session.

Basis for selection. Open admission. Auditions required of theater academy, music majors.

2015-2016 Annual costs. Tuition/fees: $1,402; $8,062 out-of-state. Per-credit charge: $46 in-state; $268 out-of-state. Books/supplies: $1,746. Personal expenses: $3,132.

Financial aid. All financial aid based on need. Need-based aid available for part-time students. Work-study available nights, weekends and for part-time students. **Additional information:** Fee waivers available for public assistance and Social Security insurance recipients; fee credits available for low income families.

Application procedures. Admission: Closing date 9/1. No application fee. Admission notification on a rolling basis beginning on or about 4/30. **Financial aid:** Priority date 3/2; no closing date. FAFSA required. Applicants notified by 7/6; Applicants notified on a rolling basis starting 7/6; must reply within 2 week(s) of notification.

Academics. Special study options: Accelerated study, cooperative education, cross-registration, distance learning, dual enrollment of high school students, ESL, honors, independent study. License preparation in dental hygiene, nursing, radiology. **Credit/placement by examination:** AP, CLEP, institutional tests. 15 credit hours maximum toward associate degree. **Support services:** Learning center, remedial instruction, tutoring.

Majors. Area/ethnic studies: African-American, Asian-American. **Biology:** General. **Business:** Accounting, administrative services, banking/financial services, business admin, entrepreneurial studies, management information systems, office technology, office/clerical, real estate, tourism promotion, tourism/travel. **Communications:** Advertising, broadcast journalism, journalism, public relations. **Communications technology:** General. **Computer sciences:** General, applications programming. **Engineering:** General, software. **English:** English lit. **Foreign languages:** Chinese, French, German, Italian, Japanese, Spanish. **Health services:** Dental lab technology, health information technology, medical radiologic technology/radiation therapy, medical secretary. **Liberal arts:** Arts/sciences. **Math:** General. **Physical sciences:** Chemistry, physics. **Protective services:** Police science. **Psychology:** General. **Visual/performing arts:** Art, cinematography, commercial/advertising art, dramatic, film/cinema/video, music, photography. **Work/family studies:** General, child care management.

Technology on campus. 200 workstations in library, computer center. Wireless network available.

Student life. Activities: Bands, choral groups, dance, drama, music ensembles, musical theater, radio station, student government, student newspaper.

Athletics. NJCAA. **Team name:** CUBS.

Student services. Career counseling, services for economically disadvantaged, student employment services, financial aid counseling, health services, on-campus daycare, personal counseling, veterans' counselor. **Physically disabled:** Services for visually, speech, hearing impaired. **Transfer:** Transfer adviser, college fairs on campus for students transferring to 4-year colleges.

Contact. Phone: (323) 953-4381 Fax: (323) 953-4013
William Marmolejo, Dean of Admissions, Los Angeles City College, 855 North Vermont Avenue, Los Angeles, CA 90029-3589

Los Angeles County College of Nursing and Allied Health
Los Angeles, California
http://dhs.lacounty.gov/wps/portal/dhs/conah CB code: 4405

- Public 2-year nursing and community college
- Commuter campus in very large city

General. Clinical component of studies undertaken in cooperation with Los Angeles County Department of Health Services medical centers. Applicant must be resident of the County of Los Angeles. **Enrollment:** 196 degree-seeking undergraduates. **Degrees:** 87 associate awarded. **Location:** 2 miles from downtown. **Calendar:** Semester, limited summer session. **Full-time faculty:** 43 total.

Basis for selection. Admissions criteria include high school diploma or equivalency, prior college experience, minimum cumulative 2.0 GPA in college work, satisfactory score on Test of Essential Academic Skills. Residency in Los Angeles County required. Point system applied when there are more qualified applicants than openings. **Learning Disabled:** Must submit documentation to obtain accommodations.

High school preparation. College-preparatory program recommended. Recommended units include English 3, mathematics 3, social studies 2, history 1, science 3 (laboratory 2), foreign language 2, computer science 1 and academic electives 2.

2015-2016 Annual costs. Tuition/fees: $4,925. Per-credit charge: $240. Books/supplies: $2,123. Personal expenses: $1,746. **Additional information:** Books/supplies/uniforms $600-900 Only accept Los Angeles County residents.

Financial aid. Need-based: Work-study available nights, weekends and for part-time students.

Application procedures. Admission: Closing date 2/15 (receipt date). $5 fee. Application must be submitted on paper. Admission notification by 6/1. Must reply by May 1 or within 2 week(s) if notified thereafter.

Academics. Special study options: License preparation in nursing. **Credit/placement by examination:** AP, CLEP, institutional tests. **Support services:** Reduced course load, tutoring.

Majors. Health services: Nursing (RN).

Technology on campus. 25 workstations in library, computer center. Online library, wireless network available.

Student life. Freshman orientation: Mandatory. Preregistration for classes offered. **Activities:** Student government.

Student services. Financial aid counseling. **Transfer:** Pre-admission transcript evaluation for new students.

Contact. E-mail: collegeofnursing@dhs.lacounty.gov
Phone: (323) 226-4911 Fax: (323) 226-6343
Maria Caballero, Dean, Administrative and Student Services, Los Angeles County College of Nursing and Allied Health, 1237 North Mission Road, Los Angeles, CA 90033-1084

Los Angeles Harbor College
Wilmington, California
www.lahc.edu   **CB code: 4395**

- Public 2-year community college
- Commuter campus in small city

General. Founded in 1949. Regionally accredited. **Enrollment:** 6,636 degree-seeking undergraduates. **Degrees:** 680 associate awarded. **Location:** 15 miles from downtown. **Calendar:** Semester, limited summer session. **Full-time faculty:** 113 total; 19% have terminal degrees, 50% minority, 58% women. **Part-time faculty:** 309 total; 46% minority, 46% women. **Special facilities:** Observatory, nature museum.

Transfer out. Colleges most students transferred to 2015: California State University: Long Beach, California State University: Dominguez Hills.

Basis for selection. Open admission.

High school preparation. 10 units recommended. Recommended units include English 4, mathematics 3, science 2 (laboratory 1). Nursing program requires high school diploma with chemistry and algebra, or college equivalent.

2015-2016 Annual costs. Tuition/fees: $1,404; $7,194 out-of-state. Per-credit charge: $46 in-state; $239 out-of-state. Books/supplies: $1,710. Personal expenses: $3,096.

Financial aid. All financial aid based on need. Need-based aid available for part-time students. Work-study available nights, weekends and for part-time students.

Application procedures. Admission: Closing date 9/10. No application fee. Admission notification on a rolling basis. High school students accepted on part-time basis. **Financial aid:** Priority date 3/2; no closing date. FAFSA, institutional form required. Applicants notified on a rolling basis; must reply within 2 week(s) of notification.

Academics. Special study options: Accelerated study, cooperative education, cross-registration, distance learning, double major, dual enrollment of high school students, ESL, honors, independent study, liberal arts/career combination, study abroad, weekend college. License preparation in nursing, paramedic, physical therapy, real estate. **Credit/placement by examination:** AP, CLEP, IB, institutional tests. **Support services:** GED preparation, learning center, remedial instruction, study skills assistance, tutoring, writing center.

Majors. Architecture: Technology. **Business:** General, accounting, administrative services, business admin, management information systems, office management, office technology, office/clerical, real estate. **Computer sciences:** General, applications programming, data entry, information systems. **Engineering:** Electrical. **Health services:** Medical secretary, nursing (RN). **Liberal arts:** Arts/sciences, library assistant. **Protective services:** Firefighting, police science. **Psychology:** General. **Visual/performing arts:** Art, interior design. **Work/family studies:** Child care management.

Most popular majors. Health sciences 17%, interdisciplinary studies 12%, liberal arts 57%, security/protective services 12%.

Technology on campus. 660 workstations in library, computer center, student center. Commuter students can connect to campus network. Online course registration, online library, wireless network available.

Student life. Freshman orientation: Available. Preregistration for classes offered. **Activities:** Bands, choral groups, dance, drama, literary magazine, music ensembles, musical theater, student government, student newspaper, TV station, Equal Opportunity Program Student Association.

Athletics. NJCAA. **Intercollegiate:** Baseball M, basketball, football (tackle) M, soccer, volleyball W. **Team name:** Seahawks.

Student services. Adult student services, career counseling, student employment services, health services, legal services, on-campus daycare, personal counseling, placement for graduates, veterans' counselor. **Physically disabled:** Services for visually, speech, hearing impaired. **Transfer:** Transfer center, transfer adviser, college fairs on campus for students transferring to 4-year colleges.

Contact. E-mail: arhelp@lahc.edu
Phone: (310) 233-4090 Fax: (310) 233-4662
David Ching, Dean of Admissions and Records, Los Angeles Harbor College, 1111 Figueroa Place, Wilmington, CA 90744-2397

Two-Year Colleges

Los Angeles Mission College
Sylmar, California
www.lamission.edu   CB code: 4404

◗ Public 2-year community college
◗ Commuter campus in large town

General. Founded in 1974. Regionally accredited. College serves nontraditional student body. **Enrollment:** 7,295 degree-seeking undergraduates. **Degrees:** 717 associate awarded. **ROTC:** Army, Air Force. **Location:** 20 miles from Los Angeles city center. **Calendar:** Semester, limited summer session. **Full-time faculty:** 83 total. **Part-time faculty:** 246 total.

Basis for selection. Open admission.

2015-2016 Annual costs. Tuition/fees: $1,404; $7,854 out-of-state. Per-credit charge: $46 in-state; $261 out-of-state. Books/supplies: $1,764. Personal expenses: $3,159.

2014-2015 Financial aid. Need-based: 94% of total undergraduate aid awarded as scholarships/grants, 6% as loans/jobs. Need-based aid available for part-time students. Work-study available nights, weekends and for part-time students. **Additional information:** Board of Governors Fee Waiver available to those in receipt of TANF (CalWORKS), Social Security Insurance, or General Relief. Students may also qualify based on family income.

Application procedures. Admission: Priority date 4/20; no deadline. No application fee. Admission notification on a rolling basis. **Financial aid:** Priority date 5/1; no closing date. FAFSA required. Applicants notified on a rolling basis starting 5/1.

Academics. Bilingual instruction. **Special study options:** Accelerated study, distance learning, double major, dual enrollment of high school students, ESL, honors, independent study, internships, study abroad, weekend college. **Credit/placement by examination:** AP, CLEP, IB, institutional tests. 15 credit hours maximum toward associate degree. **Support services:** GED preparation, learning center, pre-admission summer program, reduced course load, remedial instruction, study skills assistance, tutoring, writing center.

Majors. Business: Accounting, administrative services, business admin, management science, market research, office management, office/clerical, real estate. **Computer sciences:** General. **Education:** Teacher assistance. **English:** English lit. **Foreign languages:** Spanish. **Liberal arts:** Arts/sciences. **Math:** General. **Philosophy/religion:** Philosophy. **Protective services:** Criminal justice. **Psychology:** General. **Visual/performing arts:** Art, interior design. **Work/family studies:** Clothing/textiles, food/nutrition, institutional food production.

Technology on campus. 220 workstations in library, computer center, student center. Online course registration, online library, repair service, wireless network available.

Student life. Freshman orientation: Mandatory. Preregistration for classes offered. **Activities:** Choral groups, dance, drama, literary magazine, student government.

Athletics. Intercollegiate: Badminton, basketball, bowling, soccer, volleyball. **Team name:** Eagles.

Student services. Adult student services, career counseling, services for economically disadvantaged, financial aid counseling, health services, on-campus daycare, personal counseling, veterans' counselor, women's services. **Physically disabled:** Services for visually, speech, hearing impaired.

Contact. Phone: (818) 364-7661
Rosalie Torres, Senior Supervisor, Admissions and Records, Los Angeles Mission College, 13356 Eldridge Avenue, Sylmar, CA 91342-3245

Los Angeles Pierce College
Woodland Hills, California
www.piercecollege.edu   CB code: 4398

◗ Public 2-year community college
◗ Commuter campus in very large city

General. Founded in 1947. Regionally accredited. **Enrollment:** 14,714 degree-seeking undergraduates. **Degrees:** 1,280 associate awarded. **Location:** 27 miles from downtown. **Calendar:** Semester, extensive summer session. **Full-time faculty:** 220 total. **Part-time faculty:** 511 total. **Special facilities:** Braille nature trail, life science museum, nature center, weather station, working farm, botanical garden.

Transfer out. Colleges most students transferred to 2015: California State University: Northridge, University of California: Los Angeles.

Basis for selection. Open admission, but selective for some programs. Limited admission to nursing and animal health technology programs. All students required to take English and math placement tests prior to course registration.

2015-2016 Annual costs. Tuition/fees: $1,404; $7,854 out-of-state. Per-credit charge: $46 in-state; $261 out-of-state. Books/supplies: $1,710. Personal expenses: $3,132.

Financial aid. All financial aid based on need. Need-based aid available for part-time students. Work-study available nights, weekends and for part-time students.

Application procedures. Admission: Closing date 9/10 (receipt date). No application fee. Admission notification on a rolling basis. **Financial aid:** Priority date 3/2; no closing date. FAFSA, institutional form required. Applicants notified on a rolling basis starting 8/1.

Academics. Special study options: Accelerated study, cooperative education, distance learning, dual enrollment of high school students, ESL, honors, student-designed major, study abroad. **Credit/placement by examination:** AP, CLEP, institutional tests. 15 credit hours maximum toward associate degree. **Support services:** GED preparation, learning center, pre-admission summer program, remedial instruction, study skills assistance, tutoring, writing center.

Majors. Architecture: Technology. **Area/ethnic studies:** Latin American. **Business:** General, accounting, business admin, management science, marketing. **Communications:** Journalism, photojournalism. **Computer sciences:** General, applications programming, computer science, data processing, programming. **Conservation:** Management/policy. **Education:** Early childhood, kindergarten/preschool. **Engineering:** General. **Foreign languages:** French, Italian, sign language interpretation, Spanish. **Health services:** Nursing (RN), preveterinary, substance abuse counseling, veterinary technology/assistant. **Liberal arts:** Arts/sciences. **Social sciences:** Criminology. **Visual/performing arts:** Commercial/advertising art, dramatic, industrial design, music, studio arts, theater design.

Technology on campus. Commuter students can connect to campus network. Online course registration, online library, repair service available.

Student life. Freshman orientation: Available. Preregistration for classes offered. **Activities:** Bands, choral groups, dance, drama, international student organizations, literary magazine, music ensembles, musical theater, student government, student newspaper, symphony orchestra, Bible Fellowship, Alpha Gamma Sigma honor society, Phi Theta Kappa honor society, Phi Beta Lambda business association, Hillel, Union of African American Students, Muslim students association.

Athletics. Intercollegiate: Baseball M, basketball, cheerleading, diving, football (tackle) M, soccer W, softball W, swimming, tennis M, volleyball. **Team name:** Brahmas.

Student services. Adult student services, career counseling, services for economically disadvantaged, student employment services, financial aid counseling, health services, on-campus daycare, personal counseling, placement for graduates, veterans' counselor. **Physically disabled:** Services for visually, speech, hearing impaired. **Transfer:** Transfer center, transfer adviser, college fairs on campus for students transferring to 4-year colleges.

Contact. E-mail: pierceinfo@piercecollege.edu
Phone: (818) 719-6404 Fax: (818) 716-1087
Marco De La Garza, Dean of Admissions and Records, Los Angeles Pierce College, 6201 Winnetka Avenue, Woodland Hills, CA 91371

Los Angeles Southwest College
Los Angeles, California
www.lasc.edu   CB code: 4409

◗ Public 2-year community college
◗ Commuter campus in very large city

General. Founded in 1967. Regionally accredited. **Enrollment:** 4,578 degree-seeking undergraduates. **Degrees:** 544 associate awarded. **Calendar:** Semester, limited summer session. **Full-time faculty:** 78 total. **Part-time faculty:** 203 total. **Special facilities:** Career services center.

Transfer out. Colleges most students transferred to 2015: Cal State University: Dominguez Hills, Los Angeles, Long Beach, Northridge, UCLA.

Basis for selection. Open admission, but selective for some programs. Limited admission to nursing and allied health programs.

2015-2016 Annual costs. Tuition/fees: $1,402; $8,062 out-of-state. Per-credit charge: $46 in-state; $268 out-of-state. Books/supplies: $1,638. Personal expenses: $3,096.

Financial aid. Need-based: Need-based aid available for part-time students. Work-study available nights, weekends and for part-time students. **Additional information:** Board of Governors Enrollment Fee Waiver available to students receiving AFDC, SSI/SSP, or General Assistance. May also qualify on basis of income.

Application procedures. Admission: No deadline. No application fee. Late registration allowed through third week of classes, if permitted by instructor. **Financial aid:** No deadline. FAFSA required. Applicants notified on a rolling basis; must reply within 2 week(s) of notification.

Academics. Special study options: Accelerated study, cooperative education, cross-registration, double major, dual enrollment of high school students, ESL, honors, independent study, liberal arts/career combination, study abroad, weekend college. **Credit/placement by examination:** AP, CLEP, institutional tests. 15 credit hours maximum toward associate degree. **Support services:** Learning center, reduced course load, remedial instruction, tutoring.

Majors. Area/ethnic studies: African-American. **Biology:** General, molecular. **Business:** General, accounting, administrative services, banking/financial services, business admin, insurance, management information systems, office technology, office/clerical, real estate. **Communications:** Advertising, journalism. **Communications technology:** General. **Computer sciences:** General, applications programming, computer graphics, computer science, programming. **Education:** General, early childhood, foreign languages, mathematics, music, teacher assistance. **Engineering:** General, electrical. **English:** English lit. **Foreign languages:** General, French, Spanish. **Health services:** Clinical lab technology, nursing (RN), respiratory therapy technology. **History:** General. **Liberal arts:** Arts/sciences. **Math:** General. **Parks/recreation:** General. **Philosophy/religion:** Philosophy. **Physical sciences:** Chemistry, geology, physics. **Psychology:** General. **Social sciences:** Geography, political science, sociology. **Visual/performing arts:** Art, art history/conservation, commercial/advertising art, dramatic, fashion design, music, photography. **Work/family studies:** Child care management.

Technology on campus. Helpline, repair service available.

Student life. Freshman orientation: Available. Preregistration for classes offered. **Activities:** Bands, choral groups, dance, drama, literary magazine, musical theater, student government, student newspaper.

Athletics. NJCAA. **Intercollegiate:** Basketball M, cross-country, football (tackle) M, tennis W, track and field. **Intramural:** Baseball M, basketball, bowling, golf, softball, tennis, track and field, volleyball. **Team name:** Cougars.

Student services. Career counseling, student employment services, on-campus daycare, personal counseling, placement for graduates. **Transfer:** Transfer adviser for students transferring to 4-year colleges.

Contact. Phone: (323) 241-5321
Kim Carpenter, Admissions and Records Supervisor, Los Angeles Southwest College, 1600 West Imperial Highway, Los Angeles, CA 90047-4899

Los Angeles Trade and Technical College
Los Angeles, California
www.lattc.edu   CB code: 4400

- Public 2-year community and technical college
- Commuter campus in very large city

General. Founded in 1925. Regionally accredited. Specialized culinary arts program; fashion, cosmetology, nursing programs. **Enrollment:** 8,610 degree-seeking undergraduates. **Degrees:** 397 associate awarded. **Calendar:** Semester, extensive summer session. **Full-time faculty:** 191 total. **Part-time faculty:** 293 total. **Class size:** 46% < 20, 38% 20-39, 9% 40-49, 4% 50-99, 4% >100.

Student profile.

Out-of-state: 8%   **25 or older:**   60%

Transfer out. Colleges most students transferred to 2015: University of California: Los Angeles, California State University: Los Angeles, California State University: Dominguez Hills, University of Southern California.

Basis for selection. Open admission, but selective for some programs. Limited admission to nursing program. Portfolio recommended of commercial art majors.

2015-2016 Annual costs. Tuition/fees: $1,418; $7,868 out-of-state. Per-credit charge: $46 in-state; $261 out-of-state. Books/supplies: $1,710. Personal expenses: $3,096.

Financial aid. All financial aid based on need. Need-based aid available for part-time students. Work-study available nights, weekends and for part-time students.

Application procedures. Admission: Closing date 8/31 (receipt date). No application fee. **Financial aid:** Priority date 5/1, closing date 6/30. FAFSA required. Applicants notified on a rolling basis.

Academics. Special study options: Accelerated study, cooperative education, cross-registration, distance learning, double major, dual enrollment of high school students, ESL, honors, independent study, liberal arts/career combination, study abroad, weekend college. License preparation in nursing. **Credit/placement by examination:** AP, CLEP, institutional tests. 15 credit hours maximum toward associate degree. **Support services:** GED preparation, learning center, pre-admission summer program, reduced course load, remedial instruction, study skills assistance, tutoring, writing center.

Majors. Business: General, accounting, administrative services, business admin, entrepreneurial studies, fashion, hospitality/recreation, labor relations, office/clerical, real estate. **Communications:** Journalism. **Communications technology:** General, graphic/printing. **Computer sciences:** General, computer science. **Engineering:** General. **General:** Carpentry, electrician, maintenance, pipefitting, power transmission. **Health services:** Licensed practical nurse. **Human services:** Community org/advocacy. **Liberal arts:** Arts/sciences. **Visual/performing arts:** Commercial/advertising art, fashion design, photography. **Work/family studies:** Clothing/textiles, institutional food production.

Most popular majors. Computer/information sciences 11%, health sciences 11%, liberal arts 34%, trade and industry 30%, visual/performing arts 8%.

Technology on campus. 550 workstations in library, computer center. Commuter students can connect to campus network. Online course registration, wireless network available.

Student life. Freshman orientation: Mandatory. Preregistration for classes offered. **Activities:** Dance, student government, student newspaper, political organizations.

Athletics. NJCAA. **Intercollegiate:** Basketball, cross-country, tennis, track and field. **Intramural:** Golf, swimming. **Team name:** Beaver.

Student services. Adult student services, career counseling, services for economically disadvantaged, student employment services, financial aid counseling, health services, minority student services, on-campus daycare, personal counseling, placement for graduates, veterans' counselor. **Physically disabled:** Services for visually, speech, hearing impaired. **Transfer:** Pre-admission transcript evaluation for new students. Transfer center, transfer adviser, college fairs on campus for students transferring to 4-year colleges.

Contact. Phone: (213) 763-7000 Fax: (213) 286-5386
Carolyn Clark, Registrar, Los Angeles Trade and Technical College, 400 West Washington Boulevard, Los Angeles, CA 90015-4181

Los Angeles Valley College
Valley Glen, California
www.lavc.edu   CB code: 5546

- Public 2-year community college
- Commuter campus in very large city

General. Founded in 1949. Regionally accredited. **Enrollment:** 11,870 degree-seeking undergraduates. **Degrees:** 886 associate awarded. **Location:** 15 miles from downtown. **Calendar:** Semester, limited summer session. **Full-time faculty:** 214 total. **Part-time faculty:** 402 total. **Special facilities:** Planetarium.

Student profile.

Out-of-state: 2%   **25 or older:**   69%

Basis for selection. Open admission, but selective for some programs. Registered nursing program has competitive admission based on points accumulated for prerequisite courses, grades, and placement test scores. Institutional placement tests required of all students.

2015-2016 Annual costs. Tuition/fees: $1,404; $7,854 out-of-state. Per-credit charge: $46 in-state; $261 out-of-state. Books/supplies: $1,638. Personal expenses: $3,096.

Financial aid. All financial aid based on need. Need-based aid available for part-time students. Work-study available nights, weekends and for part-time students.

Application procedures. **Admission:** No deadline. No application fee. Admission notification on a rolling basis. **Financial aid:** Priority date 5/1; no closing date. FAFSA required. Applicants notified on a rolling basis.

Academics. **Special study options:** Cooperative education, dual enrollment of high school students, honors, independent study. License preparation in nursing, paramedic. **Credit/placement by examination:** AP, CLEP, IB, institutional tests. 15 credit hours maximum toward associate degree. **Support services:** Learning center, remedial instruction, study skills assistance, tutoring, writing center.

Majors. **Area/ethnic studies:** American. **Biology:** General. **Business:** General, administrative services, fashion, hospitality/recreation, management information systems, office technology, office/clerical. **Communications:** Broadcast journalism, journalism. **Computer sciences:** Applications programming, data processing. **English:** English lit. **Foreign languages:** French, German, Italian, Spanish. **Health services:** Nursing (RN), respiratory therapy technology. **History:** General. **Liberal arts:** Arts/sciences. **Math:** General. **Parks/recreation:** General. **Philosophy/religion:** Philosophy. **Physical sciences:** Chemistry, geology, physics, planetary. **Protective services:** Police science. **Psychology:** General. **Social sciences:** Economics, geography, political science, sociology. **Visual/performing arts:** Art, art history/conservation, commercial/advertising art, music. **Work/family studies:** General.

Technology on campus. 300 workstations in library, computer center, student center. Online course registration, wireless network available.

Student life. **Freshman orientation:** Available. Preregistration for classes offered. **Activities:** Bands, choral groups, dance, drama, film society, literary magazine, music ensembles, musical theater, radio station, student government, student newspaper, symphony orchestra.

Athletics. NJCAA. **Intercollegiate:** Baseball M, basketball, cross-country, diving, football (tackle) M, soccer W, softball W, swimming, track and field, water polo M. **Team name:** Monarchs.

Student services. Career counseling, student employment services, health services, on-campus daycare, personal counseling, placement for graduates, veterans' counselor. **Physically disabled:** Services for visually, speech, hearing impaired. **Transfer:** Transfer adviser, college fairs on campus for students transferring to 4-year colleges.

Contact. E-mail: trudgej@lavc.edu
Phone: (818) 947-2553 Fax: (818) 947-2501
Ashley Dunn, Registrar, Admissions and Records, Los Angeles Valley College, 5800 Fulton Avenue, Valley Glen, CA 91401-4096

Los Medanos College
Pittsburg, California
www.losmedanos.edu   **CB code: 4396**

- Public 2-year community college
- Commuter campus in small city

General. Founded in 1973. Regionally accredited. **Enrollment:** 3,924 degree-seeking undergraduates. **Degrees:** 1,148 associate awarded. **Location:** 45 miles from San Francisco. **Calendar:** Semester, limited summer session. **Full-time faculty:** 98 total; 53% women. **Part-time faculty:** 235 total; 47% women. **Class size:** 17% < 20, 64% 20-39, 15% 40-49, 4% 50-99, less than 1% >100.

Student profile.

Out-of-state: 9%   **25 or older:**   33%

Basis for selection. Open admission.

2015-2016 Annual costs. Tuition/fees: $1,390; $7,540 out-of-state. Per-credit charge: $46 in-state; $251 out-of-state. Books/supplies: $1,566. Personal expenses: $2,664.

Financial aid. All financial aid based on need. Need-based aid available for part-time students. Work-study available nights, weekends and for part-time students.

Application procedures. **Admission:** No deadline. Admission notification on a rolling basis. **Financial aid:** Priority date 3/2; no closing date.

FAFSA required. Applicants notified on a rolling basis starting 6/1; must reply within 2 week(s) of notification.

Academics. **Special study options:** Accelerated study, cooperative education, cross-registration, double major, ESL, honors, independent study, study abroad. License preparation in nursing, real estate. **Credit/placement by examination:** AP, CLEP, institutional tests. 20 credit hours maximum toward associate degree. **Support services:** Learning center, remedial instruction, tutoring, writing center.

Majors. **Biology:** General. **Business:** Accounting, entrepreneurial studies, labor relations, office management, real estate, tourism promotion, travel services. **Communications:** Journalism. **Communications technology:** Graphics, recording arts. **Computer sciences:** Networking, support specialist. **Conservation:** Environmental science. **Engineering:** General. **Health services:** Nursing (RN). **Liberal arts:** Arts/sciences. **Math:** General. **Physical sciences:** Chemistry. **Protective services:** Firefighting. **Psychology:** General. **Social sciences:** Anthropology, sociology. **Visual/performing arts:** Commercial/advertising art, music, music performance, studio arts. **Work/family studies:** Child development.

Most popular majors. Family/consumer sciences 7%, interdisciplinary studies 15%, liberal arts 55%.

Technology on campus. Online course registration, online library, wireless network available.

Student life. **Freshman orientation:** Mandatory. Preregistration for classes offered. **Activities:** Bands, choral groups, drama, music ensembles, student government, student newspaper.

Athletics. **Intercollegiate:** Baseball M, basketball, football (tackle) M, soccer M, softball W, volleyball W. **Intramural:** Basketball, softball, tennis. **Team name:** Mustang.

Student services. Career counseling, student employment services, financial aid counseling, on-campus daycare, personal counseling, placement for graduates. **Physically disabled:** Services for visually, speech, hearing impaired. **Transfer:** Transfer adviser, college fairs on campus for students transferring to 4-year colleges.

Contact. Phone: (925) 439-2181 ext. 7500
Robin Armour, Director of Admissions and Records, Los Medanos College, 2700 East Leland Road, Pittsburg, CA 94565

Mendocino College
Ukiah, California
www.mendocino.edu   **CB code: 4517**

- Public 2-year community college
- Commuter campus in large town

General. Founded in 1973. Regionally accredited. **Enrollment:** 1,439 degree-seeking undergraduates. **Degrees:** 317 associate awarded. **Location:** 60 miles from Santa Rosa, 110 miles from San Francisco. **Calendar:** Semester, limited summer session. **Full-time faculty:** 49 total; 18% have terminal degrees, 4% minority. **Part-time faculty:** 228 total; 8% minority. **Class size:** 45% < 20, 54% 20-39, less than 1% 40-49. **Special facilities:** Gallery and theater complex, point arena field station.

Student profile.

Out-of-state: 3%   **25 or older:**   38%

Transfer out. **Colleges most students transferred to 2015:** Sonoma State University, Humboldt State University, University of California.

Basis for selection. Open admission.

2015-2016 Annual costs. Tuition/fees: $1,420; $7,420 out-of-state. Per-credit charge: $46 in-state; $246 out-of-state. Books/supplies: $1,746. Personal expenses: $3,132.

Financial aid. **Need-based:** Need-based aid available for part-time students. Work-study available nights, weekends and for part-time students. **Non-need-based:** Scholarships awarded for academics, leadership, music/drama, state residency.

Application procedures. **Admission:** Priority date 5/1; no deadline. No application fee. Admission notification on a rolling basis beginning on or about 7/1. **Financial aid:** Priority date 5/31; no closing date. FAFSA required. Applicants notified on a rolling basis starting 7/1; must reply within 2 week(s) of notification.

Academics. Special study options: Distance learning, double major, dual enrollment of high school students, ESL, independent study, internships, student-designed major. License preparation in nursing, paramedic, real estate. **Credit/placement by examination:** AP, CLEP, institutional tests. 12 credit hours maximum toward associate degree. **Support services:** GED test center, learning center, pre-admission summer program, remedial instruction, study skills assistance, tutoring.

Majors. Biology: General. **Business:** General, accounting, administrative services, business admin, entrepreneurial studies. **Communications:** Communications/speech/rhetoric. **Computer sciences:** General. **Conservation:** General. **English:** English lit, rhetoric/composition. **Foreign languages:** French, Spanish. **Health services:** Substance abuse counseling. **Liberal arts:** Arts/sciences. **Math:** General. **Parks/recreation:** Sports admin. **Protective services:** Law enforcement admin. **Psychology:** General. **Social sciences:** General. **Visual/performing arts:** Art, dramatic, music.

Most popular majors. Business/marketing 17%, family/consumer sciences 6%, health sciences 8%, liberal arts 9%, physical sciences 11%, psychology 8%, security/protective services 7%, social sciences 11%.

Technology on campus. 144 workstations in library, student center. Commuter students can connect to campus network. Online course registration, online library, wireless network available.

Student life. Freshman orientation: Available. Preregistration for classes offered. Orientation held before and during first week of class. **Policies:** Smoking restricted to two remote areas. **Activities:** Bands, choral groups, dance, drama, film society, music ensembles, musical theater, radio station, student government.

Athletics. NJCAA. **Intercollegiate:** Baseball M, basketball, cheerleading W, football (tackle) M, soccer W, softball W, volleyball W. **Team name:** Eagles.

Student services. Adult student services, career counseling, services for economically disadvantaged, financial aid counseling, on-campus daycare, personal counseling, veterans' counselor, women's services. **Physically disabled:** Services for visually, speech, hearing impaired. **Transfer:** Transfer center, transfer adviser, college fairs on campus for students transferring to 4-year colleges.

Contact. E-mail: webaccess@mendocino.edu
Phone: (707) 468-3101 Fax: (707) 468-3430
Anastasia Simpson-Logg, Director of Admissions and Records, Mendocino College, 1000 Hensley Creek/Box 3000, Ukiah, CA 95482

Merced College
Merced, California
www.mccd.edu
CB code: 4500

- Public 2-year community college
- Commuter campus in small city

General. Founded in 1962. Regionally accredited. Off-campus centers at Los Banos. **Enrollment:** 7,322 degree-seeking undergraduates. **Degrees:** 818 associate awarded. **Location:** 50 miles from Fresno. **Calendar:** Semester, limited summer session. **Full-time faculty:** 170 total. **Part-time faculty:** 335 total.

Transfer out. Colleges most students transferred to 2015: CSU Stanislaus, CSU Fresno, UC Davis.

Basis for selection. Open admission.

2015-2016 Annual costs. Tuition/fees: $1,436; $7,676 out-of-state. Per-credit charge: $46 in-state; $254 out-of-state. Books/supplies: $1,638. Personal expenses: $3,096.

Financial aid. Need-based: Work-study available nights, weekends and for part-time students. **Non-need-based:** Scholarships awarded for academics.

Application procedures. Admission: No deadline. No application fee. Application must be submitted on paper. Admission notification on a rolling basis. Must reply by May 1 or within 4 week(s) if notified thereafter. **Financial aid:** Priority date 6/1; no closing date. FAFSA required. Applicants notified on a rolling basis starting 1/2; must reply within 3 week(s) of notification.

Academics. Special study options: Cooperative education, distance learning, dual enrollment of high school students, honors, internships, study abroad. License preparation in nursing, paramedic, radiology, real estate. **Credit/placement by examination:** AP, CLEP, institutional tests. 12 credit hours maximum toward associate degree. **Support services:** Learning center, pre-admission summer program, remedial instruction, tutoring.

Majors. Biology: General. **Business:** General, accounting, administrative services, business admin, merchandising, real estate. **Communications:** Communications/speech/rhetoric, journalism. **Computer sciences:** General, information systems. **Education:** Early childhood. **Engineering:** General. **English:** English lit. **Foreign languages:** French, German, Spanish. **Health services:** Licensed practical nurse, medical radiologic technology/radiation therapy, medical secretary, nursing (RN), office admin, substance abuse counseling. **History:** General. **Human services:** Social work. **Liberal arts:** Arts/sciences. **Parks/recreation:** Health/fitness. **Philosophy/religion:** Philosophy. **Physical sciences:** General, chemistry, geology, physics. **Protective services:** Firefighting, police science. **Psychology:** General. **Social sciences:** General, anthropology, archaeology, physical anthropology. **Visual/performing arts:** General, art history/conservation, dramatic, music, photography. **Work/family studies:** General, child development, family studies.

Technology on campus. 400 workstations in library, computer center. Commuter students can connect to campus network. Online library, helpline available.

Student life. Freshman orientation: Available. Preregistration for classes offered. **Activities:** Bands, choral groups, dance, drama, international student organizations, music ensembles, musical theater, student government, student newspaper, symphony orchestra, Black student union, Movimiento Estudiantil Chicano de Aztlan, intervarsity Christian group, Rotaract.

Athletics. NJCAA. **Intercollegiate:** Baseball M, basketball, cheerleading W, cross-country, diving, football (tackle) M, golf, softball W, swimming, track and field, volleyball W, water polo. **Team name:** Blue Devils.

Student services. Alcohol/substance abuse counseling, career counseling, services for economically disadvantaged, student employment services, financial aid counseling, health services, on-campus daycare, personal counseling, placement for graduates, veterans' counselor. **Physically disabled:** Services for visually, speech, hearing impaired. **Transfer:** Transfer center, transfer adviser, college fairs on campus for students transferring to 4-year colleges.

Contact. Phone: (209) 384-6187 Fax: (209) 384-6339
Everett Lovelace, Dean of Student Services, Merced College, Lesher Student Services Building, floor 2, Merced, CA 95348

Merritt College
Oakland, California
www.merritt.edu
CB code: 4502

- Public 2-year community college
- Large city

General. Founded in 1953. Regionally accredited. **Enrollment:** 3,155 degree-seeking undergraduates. **Degrees:** 295 associate awarded. **Location:** 15 miles from San Francisco. **Calendar:** Semester, extensive summer session. **Full-time faculty:** 77 total. **Part-time faculty:** 147 total. **Special facilities:** Anthropology museum, landscape/horticulture complex.

Student profile.

Out-of-state:	5%	
25 or older:		60%

Basis for selection. Open admission.

2015-2016 Annual costs. Tuition/fees: $1,420; $8,020 out-of-state. Per-credit charge: $46 in-state; $266 out-of-state. Books/supplies: $1,710. Personal expenses: $3,096.

Financial aid. Need-based: Need-based aid available for part-time students. Work-study available nights, weekends and for part-time students.

Application procedures. Admission: No deadline. No application fee. Admission notification on a rolling basis. **Financial aid:** Priority date 4/1, closing date 6/30. FAFSA, institutional form required. Applicants notified on a rolling basis starting 6/1.

Academics. Special study options: Cooperative education, cross-registration, distance learning, dual enrollment of high school students, honors, independent study. **Credit/placement by examination:** AP, CLEP, institutional tests. 15 credit hours maximum toward associate degree. **Support services:** Learning center, pre-admission summer program, reduced course load, remedial instruction, tutoring.

Majors. Area/ethnic studies: African-American. **Business:** General, real estate. **Computer sciences:** General. **Education:** General, business, early childhood. **Engineering:** Electrical. **English:** English lit. **Foreign languages:**

French, Spanish. **Health services:** Licensed practical nurse, medical radiologic technology/radiation therapy, nursing (RN). **Human services:** Community org/advocacy. **Liberal arts:** Arts/sciences. **Math:** General. **Parks/recreation:** General. **Social sciences:** General. **Work/family studies:** Child care management, family/community services.

Technology on campus. 200 workstations in library, computer center, student center.

Student life. Activities: Choral groups, dance, student government, student newspaper, Merritt Christian Fellowship, LaRaza Student Union, Native American Association, Black Student Union, Asian Student Union, Ecology Action Club, Disabled Students Coalition.

Athletics. Intercollegiate: Basketball, cross-country, track and field. **Intramural:** Badminton, golf, tennis, volleyball.

Student services. Adult student services, career counseling, student employment services, health services, on-campus daycare, personal counseling, placement for graduates, veterans' counselor. **Physically disabled:** Services for visually, speech, hearing impaired. **Transfer:** Transfer adviser, college fairs on campus for students transferring to 4-year colleges.

Contact. E-mail: admissions@peralta.edu
Phone: (510) 436-2487
Howard Perdue, Dean of Admissions and Records, Merritt College, 12500 Campus Drive, Oakland, CA 94619

MiraCosta College
Oceanside, California
www.miracosta.edu   **CB code: 4582**

- Public 2-year community and junior college
- Commuter campus in large city

General. Founded in 1934. Regionally accredited. **Enrollment:** 12,320 degree-seeking undergraduates; 2,742 non-degree-seeking students. **Degrees:** 1,387 associate awarded. **Location:** 35 miles from San Diego. **Calendar:** Semester, limited summer session. **Full-time faculty:** 190 total; 34% minority, 52% women. **Part-time faculty:** 573 total; 28% minority, 65% women. **Class size:** 16% < 20, 73% 20-39, 11% 40-49, less than 1% 50-99. **Special facilities:** Bioprocessing training facility, music recording studios. **Partnerships:** Formal partnerships with Cisco Academy.

Student profile. Among degree-seeking undergraduates, 69% enrolled in a transfer program, 5% enrolled in a vocational program, 3,414 enrolled as first-time, first-year students.

Part-time:	69%	Hispanic/Latino:	38%
Out-of-state:	1%	Multi-racial, non-Hispanic:	7%
Women:	56%	International:	2%
African American:	4%	25 or older:	36%
Asian American:	6%		

Transfer out. Colleges most students transferred to 2015: San Diego State University, Cal State: San Marcos, University of California: San Diego,.

Basis for selection. Open admission, but selective for some programs. Must be either 18 years of age or high school graduate. Concurrently enrolled high school students require principal and parental permission with grade level limitations. Nursing programs require special application with course and GPA requirements. Locally administered tests may be used for placement and counseling. **Home schooled:** Must complete both Math and English placement exams and meet with the Dean of Counseling.

2015-2016 Annual costs. Tuition/fees: $1,428; $7,428 out-of-state. Per-credit charge: $46 in-state; $246 out-of-state. Books/supplies: $1,764. Personal expenses: $3,159.

Financial aid. Need-based: Need-based aid available for part-time students. Work-study available nights, weekends and for part-time students. **Additional information:** Waiver of in-state fees for eligible low-income students.

Application procedures. Admission: No deadline. No application fee. Admission notification on a rolling basis. **Financial aid:** Priority date 4/12; no closing date. FAFSA, institutional form required. Applicants notified on a rolling basis; must reply within 1 week(s) of notification.

Academics. Special study options: Accelerated study, cooperative education, distance learning, double major, dual enrollment of high school students, ESL, honors, independent study, internships, liberal arts/career combination, study abroad, teacher certification program. Study abroad programs in Japan, Mexico, Costa Rica and several countries in Europe. License preparation in nursing, real estate. **Credit/placement by examination:** AP, CLEP, IB,

institutional tests. 15 credit hours maximum toward associate degree. **Support services:** GED preparation and test center, learning center, pre-admission summer program, reduced course load, remedial instruction, study skills assistance, tutoring, writing center.

Honors college/program. Minimum 3.25 cumulative Degree Applicable GPA for students who have completed 12 units or more of college credit courses. High School Students or college students who have completed less than 12 units of college credit courses must have a minimum 3.50 Weighted Cumulative high school GPA. Eligibility for ENGL 100 (as established by English assessment test or equivalent). Complete application includes: complete online application, submit two letters of recommendation (at least one from an instructor), submit unofficial transcripts, and sign Statement of Academic Integrity (included in the online application).

Majors. Architecture: Landscape, technology. **Biology:** Biotechnology. **Business:** Accounting, accounting technology, administrative services, business admin, entrepreneurial studies, hospitality admin, management science, marketing, office management, real estate, restaurant/food services, retail management. **Computer sciences:** General, computer science, programming, system admin, web page design. **Health services:** Clinical nutrition, licensed practical nurse, medical secretary, nursing (RN), surgical technology. **History:** General. **Liberal arts:** Arts/sciences, humanities. **Math:** General. **Protective services:** Police science. **Social sciences:** General, sociology. **Visual/performing arts:** General, dance, digital arts, music performance. **Work/family studies:** Child care management, child care service, child development, family studies.

Most popular majors. Business/marketing 13%, health sciences 7%, interdisciplinary studies 14%, liberal arts 42%.

Technology on campus. 1,000 workstations in library, computer center, student center. Commuter students can connect to campus network. Online course registration, online library, helpline, wireless network available.

Student life. Freshman orientation: Available. Preregistration for classes offered. One-hour session offered 14 times prior to classes each semester. Online orientations and online advising offered 24/7. **Activities:** Bands, choral groups, dance, drama, international student organizations, literary magazine, music ensembles, musical theater, student government, student newspaper, symphony orchestra, Veterans club, MECHA/Latina organization, black student union, Chinese club, Phi Theta Kappa, Single Parents on Campus, Japanese club, Allied Health club, Amnesty International, Gay Straight Alliance.

Athletics. Intercollegiate: Basketball, sand volleyball W, soccer. **Intramural:** Basketball, cross-country, football (non-tackle), soccer, softball, table tennis, tennis, ultimate frisbee, volleyball. **Team name:** Spartans.

Student services. Alcohol/substance abuse counseling, career counseling, services for economically disadvantaged, student employment services, financial aid counseling, health services, on-campus daycare, personal counseling, veterans' counselor. **Physically disabled:** Services for visually, speech, hearing impaired. **Transfer:** Transfer center, transfer adviser, college fairs on campus for students transferring to 4-year colleges.

Contact. E-mail: admissions@miracosta.edu
Phone: (760) 795-6620 Toll-free number: (888) 201-8480
Fax: (760) 795-6626
Jane Sparks, Director of Admissions and Records, MiraCosta College, One Barnard Drive, Oceanside, CA 92056-3899

Mission College
Santa Clara, California
www.missioncollege.edu   **CB code: 7587**

- Public 2-year community college
- Small city

General. Founded in 1975. Regionally accredited. **Enrollment:** 3,175 degree-seeking undergraduates. **Degrees:** 621 associate awarded. **ROTC:** Naval, Air Force. **Location:** 8 miles from San Jose. **Calendar:** Semester, limited summer session. **Full-time faculty:** 146 total. **Part-time faculty:** 189 total.

Transfer out. Colleges most students transferred to 2015: San Jose State.

Basis for selection. Open admission, but selective for some programs. Limited admission to vocational nursing and allied health programs. Interviews required of nursing, psychiatric technician majors.

2015-2016 Annual costs. Tuition/fees: $1,454; $7,574 out-of-state. Per-credit charge: $46 in-state; $250 out-of-state. Books/supplies: $2,460. Personal expenses: $3,105.

Two-Year Colleges

Financial aid. Need-based: Work-study available nights, weekends and for part-time students.

Application procedures. Admission: No deadline. No application fee. Admission notification on a rolling basis. **Financial aid:** Priority date 5/1; no closing date. Applicants notified on a rolling basis starting 8/1; must reply within 2 week(s) of notification.

Academics. Special study options: Cooperative education, dual enrollment of high school students, honors, independent study, weekend college. Bachelor's degree programs available on campus. **Credit/placement by examination:** AP, CLEP, institutional tests. 12 credit hours maximum toward associate degree. **Support services:** GED preparation, learning center, remedial instruction, tutoring.

Majors. Biology: General. **Business:** General, accounting, administrative services, banking/financial services, business admin, management information systems, management science, office management, office/clerical, real estate. **Communications technology:** Graphic/printing. **Computer sciences:** Applications programming, computer science, information systems. **Engineering:** General. **Health services:** Licensed practical nurse, nursing (RN). **Liberal arts:** Arts/sciences. **Math:** General. **Physical sciences:** Chemistry, physics. **Protective services:** Fire safety technology. **Social sciences:** General. **Visual/performing arts:** Art, commercial/advertising art.

Student life. Freshman orientation: Available. Preregistration for classes offered. **Activities:** Jazz band, dance, music ensembles, musical theater, student government.

Athletics. NCAA. **Intercollegiate:** Baseball M, basketball W, soccer M, softball W, tennis. **Team name:** Saints.

Student services. Adult student services, career counseling, student employment services, health services, on-campus daycare, personal counseling, placement for graduates, veterans' counselor. **Transfer:** Transfer center, transfer adviser, college fairs on campus for students transferring to 4-year colleges.

Contact. E-mail: askmc@wvm.edu
Phone: (408) 988-2200 Fax: (408) 980-8980
Asmare Tadesse, Assistant Director of Admissions & Records, Mission College, 3000 Mission College Boulevard, Santa Clara, CA 95054-1897

Modesto Junior College
Modesto, California
www.mjc.edu   CB code: 4486

▸ Public 2-year community and junior college
▸ Commuter campus in large city

General. Founded in 1921. Regionally accredited. **Enrollment:** 16,253 degree-seeking undergraduates; 1,325 non-degree-seeking students. **Degrees:** 500 associate awarded. **Location:** 73 miles from Sacramento. **Calendar:** Semester, limited summer session. **Full-time faculty:** 243 total. **Part-time faculty:** 354 total. **Special facilities:** Performing arts and media center, agricultural center for education, planetarium, observatory, great valley museum.

Student profile. Among degree-seeking undergraduates, 3,076 enrolled as first-time, first-year students.

Part-time: 62% **Women:**   58%

Transfer out. Colleges most students transferred to 2015: California State University: Stanislaus, California State University: Fresno, California State University: Sacramento, University of California: Davis, University of California: San Diego.

Basis for selection. Open admission, but selective for some programs. Limited admission offered to nursing (RN), medical assisting, and related majors. Selective admission to fire academy.

High school preparation. Certain programs require specific courses.

2015-2016 Annual costs. Tuition/fees: $1,416; $7,926 out-of-state. Per-credit charge: $46 in-state; $263 out-of-state. Books/supplies: $1,710. Personal expenses: $3,096.

Financial aid. All financial aid based on need. Need-based aid available for part-time students. Work-study available nights, weekends and for part-time students. **Additional information:** Modesto Junior College scholarship priority deadline 12/15.

Application procedures. Admission: No deadline. No application fee. Admission notification on a rolling basis. **Financial aid:** Priority date 3/2;

no closing date. FAFSA, institutional form required. Applicants notified on a rolling basis starting 5/1; must reply within 2 week(s) of notification.

Academics. Special study options: Cooperative education, distance learning, double major, dual enrollment of high school students, ESL, honors, independent study, internships, liberal arts/career combination, study abroad, weekend college. License preparation in nursing, real estate. **Credit/placement by examination:** AP, CLEP, institutional tests. 30 credit hours maximum toward associate degree. **Support services:** GED preparation, learning center, pre-admission summer program, remedial instruction, study skills assistance, tutoring, writing center.

Majors. Architecture: Landscape, urban/community planning. **Business:** General, accounting, administrative services, business admin, fashion, finance, management information systems, marketing, real estate. **Communications:** Broadcast journalism, communications/speech/rhetoric, journalism. **Communications technology:** Graphic/printing. **Computer sciences:** General, computer graphics, computer science, programming. **Conservation:** General, forestry, wildlife/wilderness. **Engineering:** General, electrical. **English:** English lit, rhetoric/composition. **Foreign languages:** General, Spanish. **General:** Electrician, maintenance, pipefitting. **Health services:** Dental assistant, medical assistant, nursing (RN), respiratory therapy technology. **Parks/recreation:** General, health/fitness. **Protective services:** Firefighting, law enforcement admin. **Social sciences:** General. **Visual/performing arts:** General, art, cinematography, commercial photography, commercial/advertising art, dramatic, fashion design, interior design, music, photography, studio arts. **Work/family studies:** General, child care management, clothing/textiles, family/community services, food/nutrition.

Technology on campus. 137 workstations in library, computer center, student center. Commuter students can connect to campus network. Online course registration available.

Student life. Freshman orientation: Available. Preregistration for classes offered. Held for one hour during registration. **Activities:** Bands, choral groups, dance, drama, film society, international student organizations, music ensembles, musical theater, opera, radio station, student government, student newspaper, symphony orchestra, TV station, Christian Collegiate Fellowship, Able-Disabled Association, foreign, ethnic, minority student and women re-entry clubs, Young Farmers.

Athletics. Intercollegiate: Baseball M, basketball, cross-country, diving, football (tackle) M, golf, soccer, softball W, swimming, tennis, track and field, volleyball W, water polo, wrestling M. **Team name:** Pirates.

Student services. Adult student services, career counseling, services for economically disadvantaged, student employment services, financial aid counseling, health services, minority student services, on-campus daycare, personal counseling, placement for graduates, veterans' counselor. **Physically disabled:** Services for visually, speech, hearing impaired. **Transfer:** Reentry adviser for new students. Transfer center, transfer adviser, college fairs on campus for students transferring to 4-year colleges.

Contact. Phone: (209) 575-6013 Fax: (209) 575-6859
Laura Yager, Director, Admissions, and Records, Modesto Junior College, 435 College Avenue, Modesto, CA 95350-5800

Monterey Peninsula College
Monterey, California
www.mpc.edu   CB code: 4490

▸ Public 2-year community college
▸ Commuter campus in large town

General. Founded in 1947. Regionally accredited. **Enrollment:** 4,256 degree-seeking undergraduates. **Degrees:** 479 associate awarded. **Location:** 120 miles from San Francisco. **Calendar:** Semester, limited summer session. **Full-time faculty:** 114 total. **Part-time faculty:** 274 total.

Basis for selection. Open admission, but selective for some programs. Additional requirements, including interview, for dental assistant, nursing, administrative justice and police academy programs.

2015-2016 Annual costs. Tuition/fees: $1,450; $7,450 out-of-state. Per-credit charge: $46 in-state; $246 out-of-state. Books/supplies: $1,710. Personal expenses: $3,105.

Financial aid. Need-based: Need-based aid available for part-time students. Work-study available nights, weekends and for part-time students.

Application procedures. Admission: No deadline. No application fee. Admission notification on a rolling basis. **Financial aid:** Closing date 6/30. FAFSA, institutional form required. Applicants notified on a rolling basis starting 6/1.

Academics. Special study options: Cooperative education, cross-registration, distance learning, double major, dual enrollment of high school students, ESL, independent study, weekend college. **Credit/placement by examination:** AP, CLEP, institutional tests. 30 credit hours maximum toward associate degree. **Support services:** Learning center, remedial instruction, tutoring.

Majors. Area/ethnic studies: Women's. **Biology:** General. **Business:** General, accounting, business admin, hospitality admin, hospitality/recreation, international, office/clerical, real estate. **Communications:** Communications/speech/rhetoric. **Computer sciences:** General, data processing, LAN/WAN management, programming, web page design, word processing. **English:** English lit. **Foreign languages:** General. **Health services:** Dental assistant, medical assistant, nursing (RN), predental, premedicine, prepharmacy, preveterinary. **History:** General. **Liberal arts:** Arts/sciences. **Math:** General. **Philosophy/religion:** Philosophy. **Physical sciences:** Chemistry, physics. **Protective services:** Fire safety technology, law enforcement admin. **Psychology:** General. **Social sciences:** Anthropology, economics, political science, sociology. **Visual/performing arts:** Acting, art, art history/conservation, ceramics, dance, directing/producing, dramatic, drawing, graphic design, interior design, metal/jewelry, music, painting, photography, printmaking, sculpture, studio arts. **Work/family studies:** General, child care service, child development, clothing/textiles, family/community services, fashion consultant, institutional food production.

Student life. Activities: Bands, choral groups, dance, drama, music ensembles, musical theater, opera, student government.

Athletics. NJCAA. **Intercollegiate:** Baseball M, basketball, cross-country, football (tackle) M, golf, softball W, swimming, tennis W, track and field, volleyball W. **Team name:** Lobos.

Student services. Career counseling, student employment services, health services, on-campus daycare, personal counseling. **Physically disabled:** Services for visually, speech, hearing impaired. **Transfer:** Transfer center, transfer adviser, college fairs on campus for students transferring to 4-year colleges.

Contact. Phone: (831) 646-4002 Fax: (831) 646-4015
Vera Coleman, Director of Admissions and Records, Monterey Peninsula College, 980 Fremont Street, Monterey, CA 93940-4799

Moorpark College
Moorpark, California
www.moorparkcollege.edu   **CB code: 4512**

‣ Public 2-year community college
‣ Commuter campus in small city

General. Founded in 1963. Regionally accredited. **Enrollment:** 10,232 degree-seeking undergraduates. **Degrees:** 1,497 associate awarded. **Location:** 50 miles from Los Angeles. **Calendar:** Semester, limited summer session. **Full-time faculty:** 160 total. **Part-time faculty:** 326 total. **Special facilities:** Exotic animal compound and teaching zoo, observatory.

Student profile.

Out-of-state:	78%	25 or older:	60%

Transfer out. Colleges most students transferred to 2015: California State University, University of Southern California, University of California: Los Angeles, UC Santa Barbara.

Basis for selection. Open admission, but selective for some programs. Limited admission to nursing program, exotic animal training management program, radiologic technology.

2015-2016 Annual costs. Tuition/fees: $1,448; $8,348 out-of-state. Per-credit charge: $46 in-state; $276 out-of-state. Books/supplies: $1,710. Personal expenses: $3,096.

Financial aid. All financial aid based on need. Need-based aid available for part-time students. Work-study available nights, weekends and for part-time students.

Application procedures. Admission: Priority date 7/30; no deadline. No application fee. Admission notification on a rolling basis. **Financial aid:** Priority date 5/14; no closing date. FAFSA required. Applicants notified on a rolling basis starting 6/15.

Academics. Special study options: Accelerated study, cooperative education, distance learning, dual enrollment of high school students, ESL, honors, independent study, internships, study abroad. License preparation in nursing, radiology. **Credit/placement by examination:** AP, CLEP. 12 credit hours maximum toward associate degree. **Support services:** Learning center, remedial instruction, study skills assistance, tutoring, writing center.

Majors. Biology: General, biotechnology. **Business:** General, business admin. **Communications:** Communications/speech/rhetoric, digital media, journalism, radio/TV. **Communications technology:** General, graphic/printing, graphics. **Computer sciences:** General, applications programming, information systems. **Conservation:** Environmental science. **Education:** Early childhood. **Engineering:** General. **English:** English lit. **Foreign languages:** Spanish. **Health services:** Medical radiologic technology/radiation therapy, nursing (RN). **History:** General. **Liberal arts:** Arts/sciences. **Math:** General. **Parks/recreation:** Exercise sciences, physical fitness technician. **Philosophy/religion:** Philosophy. **Physical sciences:** Astrophysics, chemistry, geology, physics. **Protective services:** Police science. **Psychology:** General. **Social sciences:** General. **Visual/performing arts:** General, acting, cinematography, commercial/advertising art, directing/producing, dramatic, music, photography, studio arts, theater design. **Work/family studies:** General, child care management, family studies.

Most popular majors. Agriculture 34%, biological/life sciences 7%, business/marketing 98%, communications/journalism 53%, computer/information sciences 14%, engineering/engineering technologies 7%, family/consumer sciences 21%, health sciences 82%, history 18%, mathematics 17%, natural resources/environmental science 6%, parks/recreation 35%, physical sciences 16%, psychology 84%, security/protective services 27%, social sciences 63%, visual/performing arts 29%.

Technology on campus. 400 workstations in library, computer center. Online course registration, online library, helpline, wireless network available.

Student life. Freshman orientation: Mandatory. Preregistration for classes offered. Online orientation. **Activities:** Bands, choral groups, dance, drama, international student organizations, literary magazine, music ensembles, musical theater, opera, student government, student newspaper, symphony orchestra, TV station, Alpha Gamma Sigma, Muslim Student Association.

Athletics. Intercollegiate: Baseball M, basketball, cross-country, football (tackle) M, soccer, softball W, track and field W, volleyball. **Team name:** Raiders.

Student services. Alcohol/substance abuse counseling, career counseling, services for economically disadvantaged, student employment services, financial aid counseling, health services, on-campus daycare, personal counseling, veterans' counselor. **Physically disabled:** Services for visually, speech, hearing impaired. **Transfer:** Transfer center, transfer adviser, college fairs on campus for students transferring to 4-year colleges.

Contact. E-mail: mcadmissions@vcccd.net
Phone: (805) 378-1429 Fax: (805) 378-1499
Registrar, Moorpark College, 7075 Campus Road, Moorpark, CA 93021

Moreno Valley College
Moreno Valley, California
www.rcc.edu/morenovalley   **CB code: 6512**

‣ Public 2-year community college
‣ Commuter campus in small city

General. Regionally accredited. **Enrollment:** 6,095 degree-seeking undergraduates. **Degrees:** 524 associate awarded. **Calendar:** Semester, limited summer session. **Full-time faculty:** 76 total; 30% have terminal degrees, 45% minority, 58% women. **Part-time faculty:** 322 total; 32% minority, 40% women.

Basis for selection. Open admission.

2015-2016 Annual costs. Tuition/fees: $1,416; $7,416 out-of-state. Per-credit charge: $46 in-state; $246 out-of-state. Books/supplies: $1,666. Personal expenses: $3,106.

Financial aid. Need-based: Work-study available nights, weekends and for part-time students.

Application procedures. Admission: No deadline. No application fee. **Financial aid:** Closing date 3/1.

Academics. Special study options: Distance learning, ESL, honors, weekend college. License preparation in dental hygiene. **Credit/placement by examination:** AP, CLEP. **Support services:** Remedial instruction, tutoring, writing center.

Majors. Business: General, accounting, real estate. **Computer sciences:** Programming. **Education:** Early childhood. **Health services:** Dental hygiene, medical assistant, physician assistant. **Parks/recreation:** Health/fitness. **Protective services:** Firefighting.

Student life. Activities: Student newspaper.

Athletics. Team name: Lions.

Student services. Transfer: Transfer center, transfer adviser, college fairs on campus for students transferring to 4-year colleges.

Contact. Phone: (951) 571-6101
Jamie Clifton, Director, Enrollment Services, Moreno Valley College, 16130 Lasselle Street, Moreno Valley, CA 92551

Mount San Antonio College
Walnut, California
www.mtsac.edu   CB code: 4494

- Public 2-year community college
- Commuter campus in small city

General. Founded in 1946. Regionally accredited. **Enrollment:** 26,441 degree-seeking undergraduates. **Degrees:** 2,081 associate awarded. **ROTC:** Air Force. **Location:** 30 miles from Los Angeles. **Calendar:** Semester, extensive summer session. **Full-time faculty:** 419 total. **Part-time faculty:** 860 total. **Special facilities:** Planetarium, wildlife sanctuary.

Transfer out. Colleges most students transferred to 2015: California State Polytechnic University: Pomona, California State University: Los Angeles, California State University: Fullerton.

Basis for selection. Open admission.

2015-2016 Annual costs. Tuition/fees: $1,418; $8,228 out-of-state. Per-credit charge: $46 in-state; $273 out-of-state. Books/supplies: $1,764. Personal expenses: $3,159.

Financial aid. All financial aid based on need. Need-based aid available for part-time students. Work-study available nights, weekends and for part-time students.

Application procedures. Admission: No deadline. No application fee. Admission notification on a rolling basis. **Financial aid:** Priority date 4/15; no closing date. FAFSA required. Applicants notified on a rolling basis starting 7/1.

Academics. Special study options: Cooperative education, cross-registration, distance learning, dual enrollment of high school students, ESL, honors, internships, study abroad, teacher certification program, weekend college. License preparation in aviation, nursing, paramedic, radiology, real estate. **Credit/placement by examination:** AP, CLEP. 12 credit hours maximum toward associate degree. **Support services:** GED preparation, learning center, pre-admission summer program, remedial instruction, study skills assistance, tutoring, writing center.

Majors. Biology: General, marine. **Business:** General, accounting, administrative services, banking/financial services, business admin, entrepreneurial studies, fashion, office/clerical, real estate. **Communications:** Advertising, broadcast journalism, journalism. **Communications technology:** General. **Computer sciences:** Data processing. **Conservation:** General, forestry. **Engineering:** General. **Foreign languages:** Sign language interpretation. **Health services:** EMT paramedic, medical radiologic technology/radiation therapy, medical secretary, nursing (RN), respiratory therapy technology. **Liberal arts:** Arts/sciences. **Parks/recreation:** General, facilities management. **Protective services:** Firefighting, police science. **Visual/performing arts:** Design, interior design, photography. **Work/family studies:** General, clothing/textiles.

Most popular majors. English 14%, health sciences 14%, interdisciplinary studies 19%, liberal arts 12%, social sciences 18%.

Technology on campus. 600 workstations in library, computer center, student center. Commuter students can connect to campus network. Online course registration, online library, helpline, wireless network available.

Student life. Freshman orientation: Mandatory. Preregistration for classes offered. **Activities:** Bands, choral groups, dance, drama, film society, literary magazine, music ensembles, musical theater, radio station, student government, student newspaper, symphony orchestra, TV station, Asian student association, Chinese club, Black student alliance, Indo-Pak club, Democratic club, Republican club, sign language club, MECHA, Muslim student association.

Athletics. Intercollegiate: Baseball M, basketball, cheerleading, cross-country, football (tackle) M, golf W, soccer, softball W, swimming, tennis, track and field, volleyball, water polo, wrestling M. **Team name:** Mounties.

Student services. Adult student services, alcohol/substance abuse counseling, career counseling, services for economically disadvantaged, student employment services, financial aid counseling, health services, minority student services, on-campus daycare, personal counseling, placement for graduates, veterans' counselor. **Physically disabled:** Services for visually, speech, hearing impaired. **Transfer:** Re-entry adviser, pre-admission transcript evaluation for new students. Transfer center, transfer adviser, college fairs on campus for students transferring to 4-year colleges.

Contact. Phone: (909) 274-4415
George Bradshaw, Director of Admissions and Records, Mount San Antonio College, 1100 North Grand Avenue, Walnut, CA 91789

Mount San Jacinto College
San Jacinto, California
www.msjc.edu   CB code: 4501

- Public 2-year community college
- Commuter campus in small city

General. Founded in 1962. Regionally accredited. **Enrollment:** 8,336 degree-seeking undergraduates. **Degrees:** 1,702 associate awarded. **Location:** 35 miles from Riverside, 45 miles from Palm Springs. **Calendar:** Semester, limited summer session. **Full-time faculty:** 127 total. **Part-time faculty:** 570 total. **Class size:** 38% < 20, 54% 20-39, 7% 40-49, less than 1% 50-99.

Transfer out. Colleges most students transferred to 2015: California State University: San Bernardino, University of California: Riverside, California State University: San Marcos, San Diego State University, Azusa Pacific University.

Basis for selection. Open admission, but selective for some programs. Special requirements for nursing and diagnostic medical sonography programs and for concurrently enrolled high school students.

2015-2016 Annual costs. Tuition/fees: $1,394; $7,724 out-of-state. Per-credit charge: $46 in-state; $257 out-of-state. Books/supplies: $1,566. Personal expenses: $3,024.

Financial aid. Need-based: Need-based aid available for part-time students. Work-study available nights, weekends and for part-time students. **Non-need-based:** Scholarships awarded for academics, music/drama. **Additional information:** Board of Governors Grant Program for state residents to defray cost of enrollment fees.

Application procedures. Admission: Closing date 12/21 (receipt date). No application fee. **Financial aid:** Priority date 3/2; no closing date. FAFSA, institutional form required. Applicants notified on a rolling basis starting 5/1; must reply within 3 week(s) of notification.

Academics. Special study options: Cross-registration, distance learning, double major, dual enrollment of high school students, ESL, honors, independent study, internships, study abroad, weekend college. License preparation in nursing, paramedic, real estate. **Credit/placement by examination:** AP, CLEP, institutional tests. 12 credit hours maximum toward associate degree. **Support services:** Learning center, pre-admission summer program, reduced course load, remedial instruction, study skills assistance, tutoring, writing center.

Majors. Business: Business admin, real estate. **Computer sciences:** General. **Education:** Early childhood, physical. **Health services:** Nursing (RN), substance abuse counseling. **Liberal arts:** Arts/sciences. **Math:** General. **Protective services:** Police science. **Social sciences:** General. **Visual/performing arts:** Art, dance, dramatic, music, photography.

Technology on campus. 120 workstations in library, computer center. Commuter students can connect to campus network. Online course registration, online library, helpline, wireless network available.

Student life. Freshman orientation: Mandatory. Preregistration for classes offered. 2-hour orientation; online or group session. **Activities:** Bands, dance, drama, international student organizations, musical theater, radio station, student government, student newspaper.

Athletics. NAIA, NCAA. **Intercollegiate:** Baseball M, basketball, football (tackle) M, golf, soccer W, softball W, tennis, volleyball W. **Intramural:** Cheerleading, weight lifting. **Team name:** Eagles.

Student services. Adult student services, career counseling, services for economically disadvantaged, student employment services, financial aid counseling, minority student services, on-campus daycare, veterans' counselor. **Physically disabled:** Services for visually, speech, hearing impaired. **Transfer:** Pre-admission transcript evaluation for new students. Transfer center, transfer adviser, college fairs on campus for students transferring to 4-year colleges.

Contact. E-mail: enrollsvcs@msjc.edu
Phone: (951) 487-3215 Fax: (951) 654-6738
Susan Loomis, Associate Dean Student Services, Mount San Jacinto College, 1499 North State Street, San Jacinto, CA 92583

MTI College
Sacramento, California
www.mticollege.edu   CB code: 3543

- For-profit 2-year business and technical college
- Commuter campus in large city
- Interview required

General. Regionally accredited. **Enrollment:** 1,020 undergraduates. **Degrees:** 121 associate awarded. **Calendar:** Differs by program, extensive summer session. **Full-time faculty:** 12 total. **Part-time faculty:** 56 total.

Transfer out. Colleges most students transferred to 2015: University of Phoenix, Golden Gate University.

Basis for selection. Interview, talent, ability, character and personal qualities important.

2015-2016 Annual costs. Personal expenses: $444. **Additional information:** Diploma programs range from $12,050-$17,185, books and supplies range from $1,444-$2,773, Associates programs range from $12,325-$14,439, books and supplies range from $1,033-$2,098.

Financial aid. Need-based: Work-study available nights, weekends and for part-time students.

Application procedures. Admission: No deadline. $50 fee. Admission notification on a rolling basis.

Academics. Special study options: Cooperative education, distance learning, internships, liberal arts/career combination. **Credit/placement by examination:** AP, CLEP, institutional tests. **Support services:** Learning center, reduced course load, remedial instruction, study skills assistance, tutoring.

Majors. Business: Office management. **Computer sciences:** Networking.

Most popular majors. Business/marketing 9%, computer/information sciences 27%, legal studies 64%.

Technology on campus. 300 workstations in library, computer center.

Student life. Freshman orientation: Mandatory. Preregistration for classes offered.

Student services. Adult student services, career counseling, financial aid counseling, placement for graduates, veterans' counselor. **Transfer:** Pre-admission transcript evaluation for new students. College fairs on campus for students transferring to 4-year colleges.

Contact. Phone: (916) 339-1500 Fax: (916) 339-0305
Eric Patterson, Director of Admissions, MTI College, 5221 Madison Avenue, Sacramento, CA 95841

Napa Valley College
Napa, California
www.napavalley.edu   CB code: 4530

- Public 2-year community college
- Commuter campus in small city

General. Founded in 1940. Regionally accredited. **Enrollment:** 6,062 degree-seeking undergraduates. **Degrees:** 588 associate awarded. **Location:** 50 miles from San Francisco. **Calendar:** Semester, limited summer session. **Full-time faculty:** 98 total. **Part-time faculty:** 275 total. **Special facilities:** Nature preserve, working vineyard, telecommunications laboratory, performing arts center.

Basis for selection. Open admission, but selective for some programs. Special admission requirements for health occupations programs and athletic program applicants.

High school preparation. College-preparatory program required.

2015-2016 Annual costs. Tuition/fees: $1,414; $7,354 out-of-state. Per-credit charge: $46 in-state; $244 out-of-state. Books/supplies: $1,746. Personal expenses: $3,132.

Financial aid. Need-based: Work-study available nights, weekends and for part-time students. **Non-need-based:** Scholarships awarded for academics, athletics, leadership, state residency.

Application procedures. Admission: No deadline. No application fee. Admission notification on a rolling basis. College-administered placement tests recommended for students enrolling in English or mathematics. **Financial aid:** Closing date 5/29. FAFSA required. Applicants notified on a rolling basis starting 6/1; must reply within 3 week(s) of notification.

Academics. Culinary arts program available. **Special study options:** Cooperative education, distance learning, double major, dual enrollment of high school students, ESL, honors, independent study, internships, study abroad, weekend college. Exchange program with Tafe College, Tasmania. **Credit/placement by examination:** AP, CLEP, institutional tests. 12 credit hours maximum toward associate degree. **Support services:** GED preparation and test center, learning center, remedial instruction, study skills assistance, tutoring, writing center.

Majors. Business: General, accounting, administrative services, real estate. **Communications technology:** General. **Computer sciences:** General. **Conservation:** Wildlife/wilderness. **Education:** General, early childhood. **English:** English lit. **Health services:** Licensed practical nurse, nursing (RN), respiratory therapy technology. **Liberal arts:** Arts/sciences. **Protective services:** Police science. **Social sciences:** General.

Technology on campus. 30 workstations in library, computer center.

Student life. Freshman orientation: Mandatory. Preregistration for classes offered. **Activities:** Bands, choral groups, dance, drama, international student organizations, music ensembles, musical theater, student government, student newspaper, symphony orchestra, various religious, ethnic, social service, and special interest organizations including International Student Club, Amnesty International, Hispano-Americano Club.

Athletics. NJCAA. **Intercollegiate:** Baseball M, basketball, golf, soccer, softball W, tennis, volleyball W. **Team name:** Storm.

Student services. Adult student services, career counseling, services for economically disadvantaged, student employment services, financial aid counseling, health services, minority student services, on-campus daycare, personal counseling, veterans' counselor. **Physically disabled:** Services for visually, speech, hearing impaired. **Transfer:** Re-entry adviser for new students. Transfer center, transfer adviser, college fairs on campus for students transferring to 4-year colleges.

Contact. Phone: (707) 256-7200 Fax: (707) 253-3064
Jessica Millikan, Director of Admissions, Napa Valley College, 2277 Napa-Vallejo Highway, Napa, CA 94558

Norco College
Norco, California
www.norcocollege.edu   CB code: 6503

- Public 2-year community college
- Commuter campus in large town

General. Regionally accredited. **Enrollment:** 6,658 degree-seeking undergraduates. **Degrees:** 817 associate awarded. **Location:** 51 miles from Los Angeles. **Calendar:** Semester, limited summer session. **Full-time faculty:** 68 total; 32% have terminal degrees, 34% minority, 50% women. **Part-time faculty:** 186 total; 34% minority, 48% women.

Basis for selection. Open admission.

2015-2016 Annual costs. Tuition/fees: $1,416; $7,416 out-of-state. Per-credit charge: $46 in-state; $246 out-of-state. Books/supplies: $1,666. Personal expenses: $3,106.

Financial aid. Need-based: Work-study available nights, weekends and for part-time students.

Application procedures. Admission: No deadline. No application fee. Admission notification on a rolling basis. **Financial aid:** Closing date 3/1.

Academics. Special study options: Distance learning, dual enrollment of high school students, ESL, honors, study abroad, weekend college. **Credit/placement by examination:** AP, CLEP. **Support services:** Learning center, pre-admission summer program, remedial instruction, tutoring, writing center.

Majors. Architecture: Architecture. **Business:** General, accounting, marketing, real estate. **Communications:** General. **Computer sciences:** Programming. **Education:** Early childhood. **Foreign languages:** Spanish.

Most popular majors. Biological/life sciences 20%, liberal arts 19%, social sciences 38%, visual/performing arts 16%.

Technology on campus. Online course registration, online library, wireless network available.

Student life. Freshman orientation: Mandatory. Preregistration for classes offered. **Activities:** Student newspaper.

Athletics. Intercollegiate: Soccer. **Team name:** Mustangs.

Student services. Career counseling, services for economically disadvantaged, student employment services, financial aid counseling, health services, minority student services, personal counseling, veterans' counselor. **Physically disabled:** Services for visually, speech, hearing impaired. **Transfer:** Transfer center, transfer adviser, college fairs on campus for students transferring to 4-year colleges.

Contact. Phone: (951) 372-7003
Mark DeAsis, Dean, Admissions and Records, Norco College, 2001 Third Street, Norco, CA 92860

Ohlone College
Fremont, California
www.ohlone.edu CB code: 4579

▶ Public 2-year community college
▶ Commuter campus in large city

General. Founded in 1966. Regionally accredited. **Enrollment:** 7,105 degree-seeking undergraduates; 3,080 non-degree-seeking students. **Degrees:** 421 associate awarded. **ROTC:** Air Force. **Location:** 15 miles from San Jose, 40 miles from San Francisco. **Calendar:** Semester, extensive summer session. **Full-time faculty:** 119 total; 39% minority, 60% women. **Part-time faculty:** 375 total; 41% minority, 59% women. **Class size:** 36% < 20, 57% 20-39, 4% 40-49, 2% 50-99, less than 1% >100. **Special facilities:** Fine and performing arts center, business and technology center, Newark center for health sciences and technology.

Student profile. Among degree-seeking undergraduates, 64% enrolled in a transfer program, 14% enrolled in a vocational program, 1,008 enrolled as first-time, first-year students.

Part-time:	59%	Women:	52%
Out-of-state:	1%	25 or older:	28%

Transfer out. Colleges most students transferred to 2015: California State University: East Bay, San Jose State University, University of California: Berkeley, University of California: Davis, San Francisco State University.

Basis for selection. Open admission, but selective for some programs. Nursing, respiratory therapy and physical therapy assisting programs require basic competence in reading comprehension and English skills, basic knowledge of related sciences. All candidates who achieve minimum standards selected by lottery. High school diploma or equivalent not required if applicant is 18 years of age or older.

High school preparation. Nursing and physical therapy assisting programs require anatomy and physiology. Respiratory therapy program requires algebra and physics.

2015-2016 Annual costs. Tuition/fees: $1,418; $8,378 out-of-state. Per-credit charge: $46 in-state; $278 out-of-state. Books/supplies: $1,972. Personal expenses: $3,024.

2014-2015 Financial aid. Need-based: 93% of total undergraduate aid awarded as scholarships/grants, 7% as loans/jobs. Need-based aid available for part-time students. Work-study available nights, weekends and for part-time students.

Application procedures. Admission: No deadline. No application fee. **Financial aid:** No deadline. FAFSA required. Must reply within 2 week(s) of notification.

Academics. Special study options: Cooperative education, distance learning, double major, dual enrollment of high school students, ESL, independent study, internships, liberal arts/career combination, study abroad, weekend college. License preparation in nursing, physical therapy, real estate. **Credit/placement by examination:** AP, CLEP, IB, institutional tests. A student who has achieved knowledge elsewhere or who has an understanding equivalent to that required by one or more college courses may receive academic credit by successfully completing a comprehensive course examination. To apply for Credit by Examination a student must be registered at the institution and be in good academic standing. Not all courses are offered for Credit by Examination. Final determination of which courses are available for credit by examination will be made by the faculty member(s) who teaches the course and the appropriate division dean. Credit may only be granted for a course listed in the institution's catalog. **Support services:** Learning center, reduced course load, remedial instruction, study skills assistance, tutoring, writing center.

Majors. Biology: General. **Business:** General, accounting technology, administrative services, business admin, office management, real estate. **Communications:** Communications/speech/rhetoric, journalism, radio/TV. **Communications technology:** Animation/special effects. **Computer sciences:** Computer science, networking, security, support specialist. **Conservation:** Environmental studies. **Engineering:** Pre-engineering. **English:** English lit. **Foreign languages:** American Sign Language, sign language interpretation, Spanish. **Health services:** Athletic training, massage therapy, nursing (RN), physical therapy assistant, respiratory therapy technology. **History:** General. **Liberal arts:** Arts/sciences, humanities. **Math:** General. **Philosophy/religion:** Philosophy. **Physical sciences:** Chemistry, geology, physics. **Protective services:** Police science. **Psychology:** General. **Social sciences:** General, anthropology, economics, geography, sociology. **Visual/performing arts:** General, art, dramatic, graphic design, interior design, music, theater design. **Work/family studies:** Child care service.

Most popular majors. Business/marketing 21%, health sciences 8%, interdisciplinary studies 9%, liberal arts 7%, social sciences 44%.

Technology on campus. 450 workstations in library, computer center. Commuter students can connect to campus network. Online course registration, online library, wireless network available.

Student life. Freshman orientation: Mandatory. Preregistration for classes offered. **Activities:** Bands, choral groups, dance, drama, literary magazine, music ensembles, musical theater, radio station, student government, student newspaper, symphony orchestra, TV station, Abundant Life Christian Fellowship, Afghan Students Association, Asian Pacific Islanders Club, Chinese Culture Club, Muslim Student Association, Alpha Gamma Sigma Honor Society, Ohlone Women Engineers and Physical Scientists, Theater and Dance Alliance.

Athletics. Intercollegiate: Baseball M, basketball, soccer, softball W, swimming, volleyball W, water polo. **Team name:** Renegades.

Student services. Adult student services, career counseling, services for economically disadvantaged, student employment services, financial aid counseling, health services, personal counseling, placement for graduates, veterans' counselor. **Physically disabled:** Services for visually, hearing impaired. **Transfer:** Pre-admission transcript evaluation for new students. Transfer center, transfer adviser, college fairs on campus for students transferring to 4-year colleges.

Contact. E-mail: admissions@ohlone.edu
Phone: (510) 659-6100 Fax: (510) 659-7231
Laura Weaver, Dean, Enrollment Services, Ohlone College, 43600 Mission Boulevard, Fremont, CA 94539-0390

Orange Coast College
Costa Mesa, California
www.orangecoastcollege.edu CB code: 4584

▶ Public 2-year community college
▶ Commuter campus in small city

General. Founded in 1947. Regionally accredited. **Enrollment:** 16,150 degree-seeking undergraduates; 5,780 non-degree-seeking students. **Degrees:** 1,855 associate awarded. **Location:** 40 miles from Los Angeles. **Calendar:** Semester, limited summer session. **Full-time faculty:** 242 total; 27% minority, 51% women. **Part-time faculty:** 408 total; 26% minority, 53% women. **Class size:** 14% < 20, 52% 20-39, 18% 40-49, 10% 50-99, 6% >100. **Special facilities:** Plastination lab, sailing academy, international center.

Student profile. Among degree-seeking undergraduates, 2,609 enrolled as first-time, first-year students.

Part-time:	57%	Women:	48%
Out-of-state:	4%	25 or older:	28%

Transfer out. Colleges most students transferred to 2015: University of California: Irvine, California State University: Fullerton, California State University: Long Beach, UCLA.

Basis for selection. Open admission. **Home schooled:** Transcript of courses and grades required.

2015-2016 Annual costs. Tuition/fees: $1,418; $8,348 out-of-state. Per-credit charge: $46 in-state; $277 out-of-state. Books/supplies: $1,562. Personal expenses: $5,173.

Financial aid. Need-based: Need-based aid available for part-time students. Work-study available nights, weekends and for part-time students.

Application procedures. Admission: No deadline. No application fee. Admission notification on a rolling basis. Admission opens January for summer and fall semester, September for spring semester; dates establish registration priority. **Financial aid:** Priority date 3/2; no closing date. FAFSA required. Applicants notified on a rolling basis; must reply within 2 week(s) of notification.

Academics. Student Success Center (individual tutoring, drop-in tutoring, online tutoring, and study skills assistance) available. **Special study options:** Cooperative education, cross-registration, distance learning, ESL, honors, independent study, internships, liberal arts/career combination, student-designed major, study abroad. License preparation in aviation, dental hygiene, paramedic, radiology, real estate. **Credit/placement by examination:** AP, CLEP, institutional tests. 12 credit hours maximum toward associate degree. **Support services:** Learning center, pre-admission summer program, reduced course load, remedial instruction, study skills assistance, tutoring, writing center.

Honors college/program. Students complete a minimum of 18 units in honors courses for program certification.

Majors. Architecture: Technology. **Biology:** General, ecology. **Business:** General, accounting, administrative services, fashion, hospitality/recreation, international, management information systems, office technology, office/clerical, real estate, sales/distribution, selling, travel services. **Communications:** Advertising, journalism, media studies. **Computer sciences:** General, computer graphics, data entry, information systems, programming. **Education:** Drama/dance, early childhood, kindergarten/preschool, music. **Engineering:** General. **English:** English lit, rhetoric/composition, technical writing. **Foreign languages:** French, German, Italian, Japanese, Spanish. **General:** Maintenance, pipefitting, power transmission. **Health services:** Athletic training, cardiovascular technology, dental assistant, dietetic technician, electroencephalograph technology, health information technology, medical assistant, medical radiologic technology/radiation therapy, radiologic technology/medical imaging, respiratory therapy technology, sonography, speech-language pathology assistant. **History:** General. **Liberal arts:** Arts/sciences, humanities. **Math:** General. **Parks/recreation:** Health/fitness, sports admin. **Philosophy/religion:** Philosophy, religion. **Physical sciences:** Astronomy, chemistry, geology, physics. **Psychology:** General. **Social sciences:** General, anthropology, economics, geography, political science, sociology. **Visual/performing arts:** Art, cinematography, commercial photography, commercial/advertising art, dance, dramatic, fashion design, film/cinema/video, interior design, music, music management, photography, studio arts. **Work/family studies:** General, child care management, clothing/textiles, food/nutrition, institutional food production.

Most popular majors. Business/marketing 14%, communications/journalism 8%, health sciences 8%, liberal arts 25%, psychology 8%, social sciences 6%.

Technology on campus. 1,473 workstations in library, computer center, student center. Online course registration, online library, helpline, wireless network available.

Student life. Freshman orientation: Mandatory. Preregistration for classes offered. 3-hour sessions given year round. **Activities:** Bands, choral groups, dance, drama, film society, international student organizations, literary magazine, music ensembles, musical theater, student government, student newspaper, symphony orchestra, Associate Students of Orange Coast College, Doctors of Tomorrow, Circle K International, Spirit of Ability Club, Puente Club, EOPS Honors Club, honors student council, engineering club, Phi Theta Kappa International Honors Society.

Athletics. Intercollegiate: Baseball M, basketball, cheerleading, cross-country, diving, football (tackle) M, golf M, rowing (crew), soccer, softball W, swimming, tennis, track and field, volleyball, water polo. **Team name:** Pirates.

Student services. Adult student services, alcohol/substance abuse counseling, career counseling, services for economically disadvantaged, student employment services, financial aid counseling, health services, minority student services, on-campus daycare, personal counseling, placement for graduates, veterans' counselor. **Physically disabled:** Services for visually, speech, hearing impaired. **Transfer:** Re-entry adviser for new students. Transfer center, transfer adviser, college fairs on campus for students transferring to 4-year colleges.

Contact. E-mail: arinfo@mail.occ.cccd.edu
Phone: (714) 432-5072
Efren Galvan, Director of Admissions, Records & Enrollment
Technology, Orange Coast College, 2701 Fairview Road, Costa Mesa, CA 92628-5005

Oxnard College
Oxnard, California
www.oxnardcollege.edu   CB code: 4591

- Public 2-year community college
- Commuter campus in small city

General. Founded in 1975. Regionally accredited. **Enrollment:** 4,525 degree-seeking undergraduates. **Degrees:** 636 associate awarded. **Location:** 60 miles from Los Angeles. **Calendar:** Semester, limited summer session. **Full-time faculty:** 96 total. **Part-time faculty:** 186 total. **Special facilities:** Marine education center, performing arts center.

Basis for selection. Open admission.

2015-2016 Annual costs. Tuition/fees: $1,418; $8,738 out-of-state. Books/supplies: $1,746. Personal expenses: $3,134.

Financial aid. Need-based: Work-study available nights, weekends and for part-time students.

Application procedures. Admission: No deadline. No application fee. Admission notification on a rolling basis. **Financial aid:** Priority date 3/2, closing date 6/30. FAFSA required. Applicants notified on a rolling basis; must reply within 2 week(s) of notification.

Academics. Special study options: Cross-registration, distance learning, dual enrollment of high school students, ESL, independent study. First 2 years of bilingual (English-Spanish) teacher preparatory program, transfer certificates and AA/AS transfer degrees articulated with California State University and University of California systems. **Credit/placement by examination:** AP, CLEP, institutional tests. 12 credit hours maximum toward associate degree. **Support services:** Learning center, remedial instruction, study skills assistance, tutoring, writing center.

Majors. Biology: General, marine. **Business:** Administrative services, business admin. **Communications:** Radio/TV. **Computer sciences:** Networking. **English:** English lit. **Foreign languages:** Spanish. **Health services:** Dental hygiene, substance abuse counseling. **History:** General. **Liberal arts:** Arts/sciences, humanities. **Math:** General. **Philosophy/religion:** Philosophy. **Protective services:** Firefighting. **Psychology:** General. **Social sciences:** Anthropology, economics, political science, sociology. **Visual/performing arts:** Art, drawing, sculpture. **Work/family studies:** Child development.

Most popular majors. Business/marketing 10%, family/consumer sciences 6%, liberal arts 63%, security/protective services 9%.

Technology on campus. 57 workstations in library, student center. Online course registration available.

Student life. Freshman orientation: Mandatory. Preregistration for classes offered. **Activities:** Jazz band, choral groups, dance, student government, TV station, MECha, chemistry club, culinary arts club, auto club, chess club, NEMA (belly-dancing) club, poetry club, theater arts club, Phi Theta Kappa, philosophy club.

Athletics. Intercollegiate: Baseball M, cross-country, soccer, softball W. **Team name:** Condors.

Student services. Services for economically disadvantaged, student employment services, financial aid counseling, health services, on-campus daycare, personal counseling, veterans' counselor. **Physically disabled:** Services for visually, speech, hearing impaired. **Transfer:** Transfer center, transfer adviser, college fairs on campus for students transferring to 4-year colleges.

Contact. E-mail: ocadmissions@vcccd.edu
Phone: (805) 986-5810 Fax: (805) 986-5943
Joel Diaz, Director of Admissions, Oxnard College, 4000 South Rose Avenue, Oxnard, CA 93033

Pacific College of Oriental Medicine: San Diego
San Diego, California
www.pacificcollege.edu

- For-profit 2-year health science and career college
- Very large city

General. Regionally accredited; also accredited by ACCSC. **Enrollment:** 111 undergraduates. **Degrees:** 18 associate awarded; master's, professional offered. **Location:** Downtown. **Calendar:** Semester. **Full-time faculty:** 17 total. **Part-time faculty:** 64 total.

Basis for selection. Admission requirements vary by programs.

2015-2016 Annual costs. Program cost: Massage Therapist/Asian Bodywork (Certificate) $12,124, books and supplies $790. Associate of Science $21,747, books and supplies $1,280. Associate of Applied Science (AAS) $22,390, books and supplies $1,350.

Financial aid. Need-based: Work-study available nights, weekends and for part-time students.

Application procedures. Admission: $50 fee. **Financial aid:** Closing date 8/1.

Academics. Special study options: Distance learning. Bachelor's degree programs available on campus. **Credit/placement by examination:** AP, CLEP. **Support services:** Reduced course load, study skills assistance, tutoring.

Majors. Health services: Holistic, massage therapy.

Technology on campus. PC or laptop required.

Contact. E-mail: admissions-sd@pacificcollege.edu
Phone: (619) 574-6909 Toll-free number: (800) 729-0941
Reza Garajedaghi, Executive Director of Admissions, Pacific College of Oriental Medicine: San Diego, 7445 Mission Valley Road, Suite 105, San Diego, CA 92108

Palo Verde College
Blythe, California
www.paloverde.edu   **CB code: 4603**

◗ Public 2-year community college
◗ Commuter campus in large town

General. Founded in 1947. Regionally accredited. **Enrollment:** 450 degree-seeking undergraduates. **Degrees:** 148 associate awarded. **Location:** 120 miles from Palm Springs. **Calendar:** Semester, limited summer session. **Full-time faculty:** 41 total; 15% have terminal degrees. **Part-time faculty:** 95 total; 3% have terminal degrees.

Transfer out. Colleges most students transferred to 2015: CSU: San Bernardino, San Diego State University, University of California: Riverside, Brandman University, University of Phoenix.

Basis for selection. Open admission, but selective for some programs. Limited admission to nursing program. **Adult students:** SAT/ACT scores not required.

2015-2016 Annual costs. Tuition/fees: $1,380; $7,890 out-of-state. Per-credit charge: $46 in-state; $263 out-of-state. Books/supplies: $1,710. Personal expenses: $3,096.

Financial aid. All financial aid based on need. Need-based aid available for part-time students. Work-study available nights, weekends and for part-time students.

Application procedures. Admission: Closing date 9/2. No application fee. Application must be submitted online. Admission notification on a rolling basis. **Financial aid:** No deadline. FAFSA, institutional form required. Applicants notified on a rolling basis starting 7/1; must reply within 4 week(s) of notification.

Academics. Special study options: Cooperative education, distance learning, dual enrollment of high school students, ESL, independent study. License preparation in nursing, paramedic, real estate. **Credit/placement by examination:** AP, CLEP, institutional tests. 12 credit hours maximum toward associate degree. **Support services:** GED test center, learning center, remedial instruction, study skills assistance, tutoring, writing center.

Majors. Business: Accounting, business admin, office/clerical. **Computer sciences:** General. **English:** English lit. **History:** General. **Liberal arts:** Arts/sciences. **Protective services:** Firefighting, law enforcement admin. **Visual/performing arts:** Music. **Work/family studies:** Child development.

Most popular majors. Business/marketing 49%, liberal arts 38%, social sciences 6%.

Technology on campus. 125 workstations in library, computer center. Commuter students can connect to campus network. Online course registration, wireless network available.

Student life. Freshman orientation: Mandatory. Preregistration for classes offered. **Activities:** Literary magazine, student government.

Athletics. Team name: Pirates.

Student services. Career counseling, services for economically disadvantaged, student employment services, financial aid counseling, personal counseling, placement for graduates. **Physically disabled:** Services for visually, speech, hearing impaired. **Transfer:** Transfer center, transfer adviser, college fairs on campus for students transferring to 4-year colleges.

Contact. E-mail: mwalnoha@paloverde.edu
Phone: (760) 921-5500
Shelley Hamilton, Director of Admissions & Records, Palo Verde College, One College Drive, Blythe, CA 92225

Palomar College
San Marcos, California   **CB member**
www.palomar.edu   **CB code: 4602**

◗ Public 2-year community college
◗ Commuter campus in small city

General. Founded in 1946. Regionally accredited. Off-campus sites located throughout North San Diego County area. **Enrollment:** 12,286 degree-seeking undergraduates. **Degrees:** 1,883 associate awarded. **Location:** 40 miles from San Diego. **Calendar:** Semester, extensive summer session. **Full-time faculty:** 280 total. **Part-time faculty:** 1,025 total. **Special facilities:** Arboretum, observatory.

Transfer out. Colleges most students transferred to 2015: CSU: San Marcos, UC: San Diego, San Diego State University, University of Phoenix.

Basis for selection. Open admission, but selective for some programs. ASSET mathematics and English tests required for nursing applicants. **Adult students:** SAT/ACT scores not required.

2015-2016 Annual costs. Tuition/fees: $1,428; $7,428 out-of-state. Per-credit charge: $46 in-state; $246 out-of-state. Books/supplies: $1,764. Personal expenses: $1,392.

Financial aid. All financial aid based on need. Need-based aid available for part-time students. Work-study available nights, weekends and for part-time students.

Application procedures. Admission: No deadline. No application fee. Application deadlines for nursing program April 1 for fall semester, November 1 for spring semester. **Financial aid:** Priority date 4/1; no closing date. FAFSA, institutional form required. Applicants notified on a rolling basis starting 6/1.

Academics. Special study options: Cooperative education, distance learning, dual enrollment of high school students, ESL, internships, liberal arts/career combination, study abroad, weekend college. License preparation in nursing, paramedic, real estate. **Credit/placement by examination:** AP, CLEP, IB, institutional tests. 15 credit hours maximum toward associate degree. **Support services:** Learning center, pre-admission summer program, reduced course load, remedial instruction, tutoring, writing center.

Majors. Architecture: Technology. **Area/ethnic studies:** Women's. **Biology:** General. **Business:** General, accounting technology, administrative services, business admin, e-commerce, insurance, international, real estate. **Communications:** Advertising, communications/speech/rhetoric, journalism, radio/TV. **Communications technology:** Animation/special effects, desktop publishing, graphic/printing, photo/film/video. **Computer sciences:** Computer graphics, information technology, networking, programming, web page design. **Education:** General, early childhood special. **Engineering:** Pre-engineering. **English:** English lit. **Foreign languages:** General, French, sign language interpretation. **General:** Building inspection, carpentry, drywall, electrician, masonry. **Health services:** Dental assistant, EMT paramedic, medical secretary, nursing (RN), substance abuse counseling. **Human services:** General. **Liberal arts:** Arts/sciences, humanities, library assistant. **Math:** General. **Parks/recreation:** General, exercise sciences. **Physical sciences:** Astronomy, chemistry, geology. **Protective services:** Fire safety technology, forensics, homeland security, police science. **Psychology:** General. **Social sciences:** General, archaeology, economics, GIS/cartography, sociology. **Visual/performing arts:** Art, ceramics, commercial/advertising art, dance, design, dramatic, drawing, fashion design, film/cinema/video, graphic design, interior design, metal/jewelry, music, painting, sculpture. **Work/family studies:** General, apparel marketing, child care management, child care service, family/community services.

Technology on campus. 922 workstations in library, computer center, student center. Online course registration, online library, wireless network available.

Student life. Freshman orientation: Available. Preregistration for classes offered. **Activities:** Bands, choral groups, dance, drama, international student organizations, literary magazine, music ensembles, musical theater, radio station, student government, student newspaper, symphony orchestra, TV station.

Athletics. NJCAA. **Intercollegiate:** Baseball M, basketball, cross-country, diving, football (tackle) M, golf M, soccer, softball W, swimming, tennis, track and field M, volleyball, water polo, wrestling M. **Intramural:** Volleyball W. **Team name:** Comets.

Student services. Career counseling, services for economically disadvantaged, student employment services, financial aid counseling, health services, minority student services, on-campus daycare, personal counseling, placement for graduates, veterans' counselor. **Physically disabled:** Services for visually, speech, hearing impaired. **Transfer:** Transfer center, transfer adviser, college fairs on campus for students transferring to 4-year colleges.

Contact. E-mail: admissions@palomar.edu
Phone: (760) 744-1150 ext. 2164 Fax: (760) 761-3536
Kendyl Magnuson, Director of Enrollment Services, Palomar College, 1140 West Mission Road, San Marcos, CA 92069-1487

Pasadena City College
Pasadena, California
www.pasadena.edu   CB code: 4604

▶ Public 2-year community college
▶ Commuter campus in small city

General. Founded in 1924. Regionally accredited. **Enrollment:** 21,141 degree-seeking undergraduates. **Degrees:** 3,146 associate awarded. **Location:** 10 miles from downtown Los Angeles. **Calendar:** Semester, limited summer session. **Full-time faculty:** 398 total; 24% have terminal degrees. **Part-time faculty:** 658 total; 16% have terminal degrees. **Class size:** 6% < 20, 66% 20-39, 25% 40-49, 2% 50-99, 1% >100. **Special facilities:** Observatory.

Student profile.

Out-of-state: 3%   25 or older: 36%

Transfer out. Colleges most students transferred to 2015: California State University: Los Angeles, Long Beach, Northridge; California State Polytechnic Institute: Pomona.

Basis for selection. Open admission, but selective for some programs. Admission to RN, LVN, dental hygiene programs based on test scores, interview, high school record; minimum 2.0 high school GPA required. School and College Ability Tests, SAT, ACT, or California Achievement Test scores used for admission to some programs. Interview required of dental hygiene majors. Audition required of music majors.

2015-2016 Annual costs. Tuition/fees: $1,428; $8,268 out-of-state. Per-credit charge: $46 in-district; $274 out-of-district; $274 out-of-state. Books/supplies: $1,656. Personal expenses: $3,780. **Additional information:** $516 International Student Insurance per each 6 months.

Financial aid. All financial aid based on need. Work-study available nights, weekends and for part-time students.

Application procedures. Admission: Closing date 8/11. No application fee. Admission notification on a rolling basis beginning on or about 4/1. **Financial aid:** Priority date 5/13; no closing date. FAFSA required. Applicants notified on a rolling basis starting 6/1; must reply within 2 week(s) of notification.

Academics. Special study options: Accelerated study, distance learning, dual enrollment of high school students, ESL, independent study, liberal arts/career combination, study abroad. **Credit/placement by examination:** AP, CLEP, institutional tests. 12 credit hours maximum toward associate degree. **Support services:** Learning center, pre-admission summer program, reduced course load, remedial instruction, study skills assistance, tutoring, writing center.

Majors. Biology: General. **Business:** General, accounting, administrative services, banking/financial services, entrepreneurial studies, fashion, hospitality/recreation, management information systems, office/clerical, real estate, sales/distribution, tourism promotion. **Communications:** Broadcast journalism, communications/speech/rhetoric, journalism. **Communications technology:** General. **Computer sciences:** Applications programming, data processing, programming. **Education:** Early childhood. **English:** Rhetoric/composition. **General:** Carpentry, maintenance. **Health services:** Clinical lab technology, dental assistant, dental hygiene, dental lab technology, licensed practical nurse, medical assistant, medical radiologic technology/radiation therapy, medical secretary, nursing (RN), speech-language pathology assistant. **Liberal arts:** Arts/sciences, library assistant. **Parks/recreation:** General. **Protective services:** Firefighting, police science. **Psychology:** General. **Social sciences:** General. **Visual/performing arts:** Ceramics, commercial

photography, commercial/advertising art, crafts, drawing, music, painting, printmaking, sculpture, studio arts.

Technology on campus. 300 workstations in library, computer center, student center.

Student life. Freshman orientation: Available. Preregistration for classes offered. **Activities:** Bands, choral groups, dance, drama, film society, international student organizations, literary magazine, music ensembles, musical theater, radio station, student government, student newspaper, symphony orchestra, TV station, wide variety of religious, political, ethnic, and social service organizations.

Athletics. Intercollegiate: Badminton W, baseball M, basketball, cross-country, football (tackle) M, soccer, softball W, swimming, tennis W, track and field, volleyball W, water polo W. **Team name:** Lancers.

Student services. Career counseling, services for economically disadvantaged, student employment services, financial aid counseling, health services, on-campus daycare, personal counseling, placement for graduates, veterans' counselor. **Physically disabled:** Services for visually, speech, hearing impaired. **Transfer:** Transfer center, transfer adviser, college fairs on campus for students transferring to 4-year colleges.

Contact. Phone: (626) 578-7396 Fax: (626) 585-7915
Associate Dean of Admissions and Records, Pasadena City College, 1570 East Colorado Boulevard, Pasadena, CA 91106

Platt College: Los Angeles
Alhambra, California
www.plattcollege.edu   CB code: 3014

▶ For-profit 2-year visual arts and technical college
▶ Commuter campus in very large city
▶ Application essay, interview required

General. Accredited by ACCSC. **Enrollment:** 661 undergraduates. **Degrees:** 34 bachelor's, 226 associate awarded. **Location:** 10 miles from downtown Los Angeles. **Calendar:** Differs by program, extensive summer session. **Full-time faculty:** 6 total. **Part-time faculty:** 21 total. **Class size:** 85% < 20, 15% 20-39.

Transfer out. Colleges most students transferred to 2015: University of LaVerne, University of Phoenix.

Basis for selection. Must score at least 126 on CPAT for admissions. Multimedia program requires degree. MCSE program requires computer background. **Learning Disabled:** Students with learning disabilities allowed 30 extra minutes on CPAT examination.

2015-2016 Annual costs. Medical Sciences: certificate $1,795-$31,941; associate $26,913.50-$45,798; bachelor's $24,867.50-$66,858.50. Legal Studies: certificate/diploma $26,981-$31,515.50; associate $31,816-$37,919; Bachelor's $72,936.50-$78,939.50.

Financial aid. Need-based: Need-based aid available for part-time students. Work-study available nights, weekends and for part-time students.

Application procedures. Admission: No deadline. $75 fee. Admission notification on a rolling basis. **Financial aid:** Priority date 3/2; no closing date. FAFSA, institutional form required. Applicants notified on a rolling basis starting 1/1.

Academics. Special study options: Accelerated study, cooperative education, internships. Bachelor's degree programs available on campus. **Credit/placement by examination:** AP, CLEP, institutional tests. 48 credit hours maximum toward associate degree. **Support services:** Tutoring.

Majors. Computer sciences: General, computer graphics. **Visual/performing arts:** General, commercial/advertising art.

Technology on campus. 60 workstations in library.

Student life. Freshman orientation: Mandatory. Preregistration for classes offered. 2-hour program on or around first day of classes.

Student services. Adult student services, career counseling, student employment services, financial aid counseling, placement for graduates. **Transfer:** Re-entry adviser, pre-admission transcript evaluation for new students. Transfer adviser for students transferring to 4-year colleges.

Contact. E-mail: DHarper@PlattCollege.edu
Phone: (626) 300-5444 Toll-free number: (866) 752-8852
Fax: (626) 457-8295
Daryle Harper, Director of Admissions, Platt College: Los Angeles, 1000
South Fremont Avenue A9W, Alhambra, CA 91803

Porterville College
Porterville, California
www.portervillecollege.edu   CB code: 4608

▶ Public 2-year community college
▶ Commuter campus in large town

General. Founded in 1927. Regionally accredited. **Enrollment:** 2,742
degree-seeking undergraduates. **Degrees:** 367 associate awarded. **Location:**
75 miles from Fresno, 50 miles from Bakersfield. **Calendar:** Semester,
limited summer session. **Full-time faculty:** 69 total. **Part-time faculty:** 79
total. **Special facilities:** Anthropology library.

Basis for selection. Open admission.

2015-2016 Annual costs. Tuition/fees: $1,404; $7,614 out-of-state. Per-
credit charge: $46 in-state; $253 out-of-state. Books/supplies: $1,638. Per-
sonal expenses: $2,826.

Financial aid. Need-based: Work-study available nights, weekends and
for part-time students.

Application procedures. Admission: No deadline. No application fee.
Admission notification on a rolling basis. **Financial aid:** Priority date 3/1;
no closing date. FAFSA required. Applicants notified on a rolling basis; must
reply within 2 week(s) of notification.

Academics. Special study options: Double major, dual enrollment of high
school students. **Credit/placement by examination:** AP, CLEP, institutional
tests. 30 credit hours maximum toward associate degree. **Support services:**
Learning center, reduced course load, remedial instruction, tutoring.

Majors. Biology: General. **Business:** General, administrative services,
banking/financial services, business admin, office/clerical, real estate. **Computer sciences:** General. **Education:** General. **English:** English lit. **General:**
Carpentry. **Health services:** Licensed practical nurse. **Liberal arts:** Arts/
sciences. **Math:** General. **Physical sciences:** Chemistry. **Protective services:**
Police science. **Social sciences:** General, criminology. **Visual/performing
arts:** General, commercial/advertising art, music, studio arts. **Work/family
studies:** Child care management.

Technology on campus. 25 workstations in library, computer center.

Student life. Activities: Choral groups, drama, music ensembles, musical
theater, student government, Mexican-American Student Association.

Athletics. NJCAA. **Intercollegiate:** Baseball M, basketball, tennis, volleyball W. **Team name:** Pirates.

Student services. Career counseling, student employment services, health
services, on-campus daycare; personal counseling, placement for graduates,
veterans' counselor. **Physically disabled:** Services for visually, speech, hearing impaired. **Transfer:** Transfer adviser for students transferring to 4-
year colleges.

Contact. Phone: (209) 791-2220 Fax: (209) 784-4779
Virginia Gurrola, Vice President Student Services and Enrollment,
Porterville College, 100 East College Avenue, Porterville, CA 93257

Professional Golfers Career College
Temecula, California
www.golfcollege.edu   CB code: 3548

▶ For-profit 2-year golf academy
▶ Commuter campus in small city

General. Accredited by ACICS. **Enrollment:** 311 undergraduates.
Degrees: 122 associate awarded. **Location:** 60 miles from San Diego. **Calendar:** Semester. **Full-time faculty:** 6 total; 33% have terminal degrees. **Part-
time faculty:** 18 total; 11% women. **Special facilities:** Pro shop, video studio.

Basis for selection. Handicap of 20 or below, 3 letters of personal character reference, 1 letter of recommendation attesting to golf ability required.
Home schooled: Transcript of courses and grades, letter of recommendation
(nonparent) required.

2015-2016 Annual costs. Tuition/fees: $15,000. Books/supplies: $500.

Financial aid. Need-based: Work-study available nights, weekends and
for part-time students.

Application procedures. Admission: No deadline. $75 fee. Application
must be submitted on paper. Admission notification on a rolling basis. **Financial aid:** No deadline.

Academics. Special study options: Honors. **Credit/placement by examination:** AP, CLEP.

Majors. Parks/recreation: Facilities management.

Technology on campus. 12 workstations in computer center. Online
library, wireless network available.

Student life. Freshman orientation: Mandatory. Preregistration for
classes offered. **Policies:** PGCC performs a mandatory drug test on all students
in their first semester. The Student Handbook details college regulations
concerning drugs and alcohol.

Student services. Alcohol/substance abuse counseling, career counseling,
financial aid counseling, personal counseling, placement for graduates, veterans' counselor.

Contact. E-mail: admin@progolfed.com
Phone: (951) 719-2994 Toll-free number: (800) 877-4380
Fax: (951) 719-1643
Dan Lindsey, Admissions Director, Professional Golfers Career College,
26109 Ynez Road, Temecula, CA 92591

Reedley College
Reedley, California
www.reedleycollege.edu   CB code: 4655

▶ Public 2-year community college
▶ Commuter campus in large town

General. Founded in 1926. Regionally accredited. Courses also offered at
community campus sites in Madera, Clovis, and Oakhurst. **Enrollment:**
11,184 degree-seeking undergraduates. **Degrees:** 807 associate awarded.
Location: 25 miles from Fresno. **Calendar:** Semester, extensive summer
session. **Full-time faculty:** 165 total. **Part-time faculty:** 599 total.

Student profile.

25 or older:	35%	**Live on campus:** 4%

Transfer out. Colleges most students transferred to 2015: California
State University: Fresno, California State University: Long Beach.

Basis for selection. Open admission. **Home schooled:** If under 18, a
letter from parent required.

High school preparation. College-preparatory program recommended.

2015-2016 Annual costs. Tuition/fees: $1,420; $8,470 out-of-state. Per-
credit charge: $46 in-state; $281 out-of-state. Room/board: $6,668. Books/
supplies: $1,566. Personal expenses: $2,600.

Financial aid. All financial aid based on need. Need-based aid available
for part-time students. Work-study available nights, weekends and for part-
time students. **Additional information:** Board of Governors fee waiver
available for low-income students. Book voucher available for EOPS students.

Application procedures. Admission: No deadline. No application fee.
Admission notification on a rolling basis. **Financial aid:** Priority date 3/2;
no closing date. FAFSA required. Applicants notified on a rolling basis
starting 3/2; must reply within 3 week(s) of notification.

Academics. Special study options: Cooperative education, cross-
registration, distance learning, double major, dual enrollment of high school
students, ESL, honors, independent study, study abroad, weekend college.
License preparation in aviation, dental hygiene, nursing, occupational therapy.
Credit/placement by examination: AP, CLEP. 48 credit hours maximum
toward associate degree. **Support services:** Learning center, pre-admission
summer program, reduced course load, remedial instruction, study skills
assistance, tutoring, writing center.

Majors. Biology: General. **Business:** Accounting. **Computer sciences:**
General, computer science, information systems. **Conservation:** Forestry.

Education: Early childhood, physical. **English:** English lit. **Foreign languages:** General. **Health services:** Dental assistant. **Liberal arts:** Arts/sciences. **Math:** General. **Social sciences:** General. **Visual/performing arts:** Art, dramatic, music.

Most popular majors. Interdisciplinary studies 80%.

Technology on campus. 140 workstations in dormitories, library, computer center. Dormitories wired for high-speed internet access and linked to campus network. Commuter students can connect to campus network. Online course registration, online library, wireless network available.

Student life. Freshman orientation: Mandatory. Preregistration for classes offered. **Housing:** Single-sex dorms available. $140 deposit. **Activities:** Bands, choral groups, drama, music ensembles, musical theater, student government, student newspaper, symphony orchestra.

Athletics. NJCAA. **Intercollegiate:** Baseball M, basketball, equestrian, football (tackle) M, golf, softball W, tennis, volleyball W. **Team name:** Tigers.

Student services. Adult student services, alcohol/substance abuse counseling, career counseling, services for economically disadvantaged, student employment services, financial aid counseling, health services, minority student services, on-campus daycare, personal counseling, placement for graduates, veterans' counselor, women's services. **Physically disabled:** Services for visually, speech, hearing impaired. **Transfer:** Transfer adviser, college fairs on campus for students transferring to 4-year colleges.

Contact. Phone: (559) 638-0323 Fax: (559) 638-5040
Leticia Alvarez, Admissions and Records Manager, Reedley College, 995 North Reed Avenue, Reedley, CA 93654

Rio Hondo College
Whittier, California
www.riohondo.edu   **CB code: 4663**

- Public 2-year community college
- Commuter campus in small city

General. Founded in 1960. Regionally accredited. **Enrollment:** 9,113 degree-seeking undergraduates. **Degrees:** 1,159 associate awarded. **Location:** 15 miles from Los Angeles. **Calendar:** Semester, extensive summer session. **Full-time faculty:** 177 total; 49% minority, 50% women. **Part-time faculty:** 369 total; 47% minority, 50% women. **Special facilities:** Observatory, nature preserve.

Transfer out. Colleges most students transferred to 2015: California State University: Los Angeles, California State University: Fullerton, California State University: Long Beach, California State University: Pomona, California State University: Dominguez Hills.

Basis for selection. Open admission, but selective for some programs. Nursing program has special requirements. **Learning Disabled:** Disabled Services Program available to students with disabilities.

2015-2016 Annual costs. Tuition/fees: $1,452; $7,452 out-of-state. Per-credit charge: $46 in-state; $246 out-of-state. Books/supplies: $1,764. Personal expenses: $4,684.

2014-2015 Financial aid. Need-based: 98% of total undergraduate aid awarded as scholarships/grants, 2% as loans/jobs. Need-based aid available for part-time students. Work-study available nights, weekends and for part-time students.

Application procedures. Admission: No deadline. No application fee. Application must be submitted online. Admission notification on a rolling basis. **Financial aid:** Priority date 7/15; no closing date. FAFSA required. Applicants notified on a rolling basis.

Academics. Special study options: Accelerated study, distance learning, double major, dual enrollment of high school students, ESL, honors, independent study, study abroad, weekend college. License preparation in nursing. **Credit/placement by examination:** AP, CLEP, institutional tests. 12 credit hours maximum toward associate degree. **Support services:** Learning center, pre-admission summer program, remedial instruction, tutoring, writing center.

Majors. Architecture: Environmental design. **Biology:** General. **Business:** Accounting, business admin, international, sales/distribution. **Communications:** Journalism, media studies. **Communications technology:** General, graphic/printing. **Computer sciences:** General. **English:** English lit. **Health services:** Licensed practical nurse, nursing (RN). **Liberal arts:** Arts/sciences, library assistant. **Math:** General. **Philosophy/religion:** Philosophy. **Protective services:** Fire safety technology, police science. **Psychology:** General.

Social sciences: Sociology. **Visual/performing arts:** General, commercial/advertising art, dance, dramatic, music, photography. **Work/family studies:** Child care service.

Most popular majors. Business/marketing 16%, health sciences 16%, liberal arts 51%.

Technology on campus. Commuter students can connect to campus network. Online course registration, online library, wireless network available.

Student life. Freshman orientation: Available. Preregistration for classes offered. **Activities:** Jazz band, choral groups, dance, drama, film society, literary magazine, music ensembles, musical theater, radio station, student government, student newspaper, TV station.

Athletics. NJCAA. **Intercollegiate:** Baseball M, basketball, cross-country, soccer, softball W, swimming, tennis, track and field, volleyball W, water polo, wrestling M. **Team name:** Roadrunners.

Student services. Career counseling, student employment services, financial aid counseling, health services, on-campus daycare, personal counseling, veterans' counselor. **Physically disabled:** Services for visually, speech, hearing impaired. **Transfer:** Transfer center, transfer adviser, college fairs on campus for students transferring to 4-year colleges.

Contact. Phone: (562) 908-3415 ext. 3415 Fax: (562) 692-8318
Leigh Ann Unger, Director of Admissions and Records, Rio Hondo College, 3600 Workman Mill Road, Whittier, CA 90601-1699

Riverside City College
Riverside, California   **CB member**
www.rcc.edu   **CB code: 4658**

- Public 2-year community college
- Commuter campus in large city

General. Founded in 1916. Regionally accredited. **Enrollment:** 13,294 degree-seeking undergraduates. **Degrees:** 1,639 associate awarded. **ROTC:** Army, Naval, Air Force. **Location:** 60 miles from Los Angeles. **Calendar:** Semester, limited summer session. **Full-time faculty:** 215 total; 31% have terminal degrees, 30% minority, 50% women. **Part-time faculty:** 435 total; 32% minority, 58% women. **Special facilities:** Planetarium, aquatics complex.

Transfer out. Colleges most students transferred to 2015: University of California: Riverside, California State University: San Bernardino.

Basis for selection. Open admission, but selective for some programs. Limited admission to nursing program.

2015-2016 Annual costs. Tuition/fees: $1,416; $7,416 out-of-state. Per-credit charge: $46 in-state; $246 out-of-state. Books/supplies: $1,666. Personal expenses: $3,106.

Financial aid. Need-based: Need-based aid available for part-time students. Work-study available nights, weekends and for part-time students. **Non-need-based:** Scholarships awarded for academics, alumni affiliation, art, leadership, minority status, music/drama, state residency.

Application procedures. Admission: No deadline. No application fee. Admission notification on a rolling basis. **Financial aid:** Priority date 3/1; no closing date. FAFSA, institutional form required. Applicants notified on a rolling basis starting 7/1.

Academics. Special study options: Distance learning, dual enrollment of high school students, ESL, honors, study abroad, weekend college. License preparation in nursing. **Credit/placement by examination:** AP, CLEP, institutional tests. 30 credit hours maximum toward associate degree. **Support services:** Remedial instruction, tutoring, writing center.

Majors. Business: General, accounting, marketing, real estate. **Computer sciences:** General, programming. **Education:** Early childhood. **Foreign languages:** Sign language interpretation. **Health services:** Licensed practical nurse, nursing (RN). **Protective services:** Fire safety technology. **Visual/performing arts:** Photography. **Work/family studies:** General, food/nutrition.

Most popular majors. Health sciences 12%, interdisciplinary studies 76%.

Technology on campus. Online library, wireless network available.

Student life. Activities: Bands, choral groups, dance, drama, music ensembles, Model UN, musical theater, student government, student newspaper,

College Democrats, MECHA, Latter-day Saints student association, multicultural advisory council, African American student union.

Athletics. Intercollegiate: Baseball M, basketball, cross-country, diving, football (tackle) M, golf, soccer, softball W, swimming, tennis, track and field, volleyball W, water polo. **Intramural:** Badminton, baseball M, basketball, bowling, golf, racquetball, soccer, tennis, volleyball. **Team name:** Tigers.

Student services. Services for economically disadvantaged, student employment services, financial aid counseling, health services, on-campus daycare, placement for graduates, veterans' counselor. **Physically disabled:** Services for visually, speech, hearing impaired. **Transfer:** Transfer center, transfer adviser, college fairs on campus for students transferring to 4-year colleges.

Contact. E-mail: webmstr@rcc.edu
Phone: (951) 222-8600
Joy Chambers, Dean of Enrollment Services, Riverside City College, 4800 Magnolia Avenue, Riverside, CA 92506

Sacramento City College
Sacramento, California
www.scc.losrios.edu   CB code: 4670

- Public 2-year community college
- Commuter campus in large city

General. Founded in 1916. Regionally accredited. **Enrollment:** 15,932 degree-seeking undergraduates. **Degrees:** 1,626 associate awarded. **ROTC:** Army, Naval, Air Force. **Location:** 75 miles from San Francisco. **Calendar:** Semester, extensive summer session. **Full-time faculty:** 327 total. **Part-time faculty:** 494 total. **Special facilities:** Observatory.

Student profile.

Out-of-state:	5%	25 or older:	68%

Basis for selection. Open admission.

2015-2016 Annual costs. Tuition/fees: $1,416; $7,956 out-of-state. Per-credit charge: $46 in-state; $264 out-of-state. Books/supplies: $1,746. Personal expenses: $3,158.

Financial aid. Need-based: Need-based aid available for part-time students. Work-study available nights, weekends and for part-time students.

Application procedures. Admission: Priority date 7/28; no deadline. No application fee. Admission notification on a rolling basis. **Financial aid:** Priority date 3/2; no closing date. FAFSA required. Applicants notified on a rolling basis starting 7/1; must reply within 2 week(s) of notification.

Academics. Special study options: Accelerated study, cooperative education, cross-registration, distance learning, double major, dual enrollment of high school students, ESL, honors, independent study, internships, study abroad, weekend college. License preparation in aviation, dental hygiene, nursing, physical therapy, real estate. **Credit/placement by examination:** AP, CLEP, institutional tests. 15 credit hours maximum toward associate degree. **Support services:** Learning center, remedial instruction, study skills assistance, tutoring, writing center.

Majors. Area/ethnic studies: Women's. **Business:** General, accounting, administrative services, international marketing, management information systems, office/clerical, real estate. **Communications:** Journalism. **Communications technology:** Graphic/printing. **Computer sciences:** General. **Education:** Bilingual, special ed. **Health services:** Dental assistant, dental hygiene, licensed practical nurse, medical secretary, nursing (RN), occupational therapy assistant, physical therapy assistant. **Liberal arts:** Arts/sciences, library assistant. **Math:** General. **Protective services:** Corrections, police science. **Social sciences:** General. **Visual/performing arts:** General, commercial photography, dramatic, music, music management, studio arts. **Work/family studies:** General, child care management, clothing/textiles, family/community services.

Technology on campus. 350 workstations in library, computer center. Online course registration available.

Student life. Freshman orientation: Available. Preregistration for classes offered. **Activities:** Bands, choral groups, dance, drama, literary magazine, music ensembles, musical theater, student government, student newspaper, minority groups, professional associations, Bible club, gay and lesbian student alliance, special interest groups.

Athletics. Intercollegiate: Baseball M, basketball, cross-country, football (tackle) M, golf W, soccer W, softball W, swimming, tennis, track and field, volleyball W, water polo W, wrestling M. **Intramural:** Badminton, baseball

M, basketball, bowling, boxing M, fencing, football (tackle) M, golf, handball, racquetball, softball, swimming, table tennis, tennis, volleyball. **Team name:** Panthers.

Student services. Adult student services, career counseling, services for economically disadvantaged, student employment services, financial aid counseling, health services, on-campus daycare, personal counseling, placement for graduates, veterans' counselor. **Physically disabled:** Services for visually, speech, hearing impaired. **Transfer:** Transfer center, transfer adviser, college fairs on campus for students transferring to 4-year colleges.

Contact. E-mail: sccaeinfo@scc.losrios.edu
Phone: (916) 558-2351 Fax: (916) 558-2190
Catherine Fites, Dean of Enrollment and Student Services, Sacramento City College, 3835 Freeport Boulevard, Sacramento, CA 95822

Saddleback College
Mission Viejo, California
www.saddleback.edu   CB code: 4747

- Public 2-year community college
- Commuter campus in small city

General. Founded in 1967. Regionally accredited. **Enrollment:** 10,309 degree-seeking undergraduates. **Degrees:** 1,313 associate awarded. **Location:** 23 miles from Anaheim, 43 miles from Los Angeles. **Calendar:** Semester, extensive summer session. **Full-time faculty:** 242 total; 28% have terminal degrees, 15% minority, 57% women. **Part-time faculty:** 720 total; 11% have terminal degrees, 12% minority, 56% women. **Class size:** 49% 20-39, 47% 40-49, 2% 50-99, 2% >100. **Special facilities:** Solar observatory, outdoor environmental laboratory and greenhouse, golf driving range, archeology lab and on-campus dig site, three-camera television studio, student radio station, art gallery.

Student profile. Among degree-seeking undergraduates, 1,689 enrolled as first-time, first-year students.

Part-time:	56%	Hispanic/Latino:	12%
Out-of-state:	2%	Multi-racial, non-Hispanic:	19%
Women:	52%	International:	4%
African American:	3%	25 or older:	35%
Asian American:	7%		

Transfer out. 20% of students enrolled in the transfer program go on to 4-year colleges. **Colleges most students transferred to 2015:** California State University Fullerton, University of California Irvine, California State University Long Beach, University of California Los Angeles, Chapman University.

Basis for selection. Open admission, but selective for some programs. International applicants are not admitted to impacted programs, which include the Nursing and Paramedic programs. Students seeking admission to the Nursing program are required to show: proof of satisfactory completion of an accredited VN program or a current California VN license; completion of all core science courses with a grade of "C" or better; overall GPA of 2.5 in prerequisite courses; and completion of a minimum of one year of direct patient care. Students seeking admission to the Paramedic program are required to have a current EMT license and one year recent work experience. SAT/ACT recommended for placement and counseling.

2015-2016 Annual costs. Tuition/fees: $1,418; $8,678 out-of-state. Per-credit charge: $46 in-state; $288 out-of-state. Books/supplies: $1,791. Personal expenses: $3,177.

2014-2015 Financial aid. All financial aid based on need. 84% of total undergraduate aid awarded as scholarships/grants, 16% as loans/jobs. Need-based aid available for part-time students. Work-study available nights, weekends and for part-time students.

Application procedures. Admission: No deadline. No application fee. Admission notification on a rolling basis. **Financial aid:** Closing date 6/30. FAFSA required. Applicants notified on a rolling basis starting 4/1.

Academics. Special study options: Cooperative education, cross-registration, distance learning, double major, dual enrollment of high school students, ESL, honors, independent study, liberal arts/career combination, study abroad. License preparation in nursing, paramedic, real estate. **Credit/placement by examination:** AP, CLEP, IB, institutional tests. **Support services:** Learning center, pre-admission summer program, reduced course load, remedial instruction, study skills assistance, tutoring, writing center. The DSPS Program provides support services and specialized instruction for students with disabilities. Also available are mobility orientations and campus-accessibility maps; notetaking, reader, and transcription services; printed enlargement; alternative media production; adapted computer labs; sign-language interpreter services; and liaison with faculty and community agencies. In addition, DSPS offers specialized courses in strategy training, basic skills, and adapted computer and adapted kinesiology (formerly physical education).

Majors. Area/ethnic studies: Women's. **Biology:** General. **Business:** General, accounting, administrative services, business admin, fashion, marketing, office management, real estate, tourism/travel. **Communications:** Broadcast journalism, journalism. **Computer sciences:** General, computer science, programming. **Conservation:** General, environmental studies. **Education:** Early childhood, family/consumer sciences, mathematics, music, physical, social science. **Engineering:** General. **English:** British lit, English lit, rhetoric/composition. **Foreign languages:** General, sign language interpretation. **Health services:** Medical assistant, nursing (RN), surgical technology. **History:** General. **Liberal arts:** Arts/sciences. **Math:** General. **Parks/recreation:** Health/fitness. **Philosophy/religion:** Philosophy. **Physical sciences:** Astronomy, chemistry, geology, physics. **Psychology:** General. **Social sciences:** General, anthropology, economics, geography, international relations, political science, sociology. **Visual/performing arts:** Art, commercial photography, commercial/advertising art, dance, design, dramatic, fashion design, interior design, music, photography, studio arts. **Work/family studies:** General, food/nutrition.

Most popular majors. Business/marketing 13%, communications/journalism 6%, health sciences 16%, liberal arts 25%, natural resources/environmental science 7%, psychology 10%.

Technology on campus. 150 workstations in library, computer center, student center. Commuter students can connect to campus network. Online course registration, online library, wireless network available.

Student life. Freshman orientation: Available. Preregistration for classes offered. Online program available. **Activities:** Bands, choral groups, dance, drama, literary magazine, music ensembles, musical theater, radio station, student government, student newspaper, symphony orchestra, TV station, College Democrats club, College Republicans club, Christian club, ACLAMO, Black United Students, gay and Llesbian club, Amnesty International, Muslim Student Union, Environmental Awareness, California Nursing Students Association club.

Athletics. NJCAA. **Intercollegiate:** Baseball M, basketball, cheerleading W, cross-country, diving, football (tackle) M, golf, soccer W, softball W, swimming, tennis, track and field, volleyball W, water polo. **Team name:** Gauchos.

Student services. Adult student services, alcohol/substance abuse counseling, career counseling, services for economically disadvantaged, student employment services, financial aid counseling, health services, minority student services, on-campus daycare, personal counseling, placement for graduates, veterans' counselor, women's services. **Physically disabled:** Services for visually, speech, hearing impaired. **Transfer:** Re-entry adviser for new students. Transfer center, transfer adviser, college fairs on campus for students transferring to 4-year colleges.

Contact. E-mail: scadmissions@saddleback.edu
Phone: (949) 582-4555 Fax: (949) 347-8315
Christian Alvarado, Dean, Division of Enrollment Services, Saddleback College, 28000 Marguerite Parkway, Mission Viejo, CA 92692

Sage College
Moreno Valley, California
www.sagecollege.edu

♦ For-profit 2-year technical and career college
♦ Commuter campus in large city

General. Accredited by ACICS. Sage College offers exclusively Court Reporting or Paralegal Studies educational programs. **Enrollment:** 190 degree-seeking undergraduates. **Degrees:** 19 associate awarded. **Location:** 9 miles from Riverside. **Calendar:** Quarter, extensive summer session. **Full-time faculty:** 3 total. **Part-time faculty:** 14 total.

Basis for selection. Open admission. **Home schooled:** State high school equivalency certificate required.

2015-2016 Annual costs. Tuition/fees: $9,400. Books/supplies: $1,000. **Additional information:** Quoted figures are for court reporting program. Paralegal studies program: tuition, $10,238 (includes books) and required fees, $125. Charted figures above represent the three quarters of full-time Court Reporting Program. Total program cost for Paralegal Studies Diploma program is $20,500. Total program cost for Associate of Arts degree program is $32,250.

Financial aid. Need-based: Work-study available nights, weekends and for part-time students.

Application procedures. Admission: No deadline. $100 fee. Admission notification on a rolling basis.

Academics. Special study options: Distance learning. **Credit/placement by examination:** AP, CLEP.

Technology on campus. 79 workstations in library, computer center.

Student life. Freshman orientation: Mandatory. Preregistration for classes offered.

Student services. Career counseling, financial aid counseling, personal counseling, placement for graduates. **Transfer:** Pre-admission transcript evaluation for new students.

Contact. E-mail: admissions@sagecollege.edu
Phone: (951) 781-2727 Toll-free number: (888) 755-sage
Fax: (951) 781-0570
Lauren Somma, Executive Director, Sage College, 12125 Day Street, Building L, Moreno Valley, CA 92557-6720

Salvation Army College for Officer Training at Crestmont
Rancho Palos Verdes, California
www.crestmont.edu   CB code: 3890

♦ Private 2-year seminary college affiliated with the Christian Church
♦ Residential campus in small city
♦ Interview required

General. Regionally accredited. Christian education for Salvation Army officer candidates and others. Officers ordained ministers who manage human service programs and ministries in western US and overseas. Require applicants to have at least 1 year membership in local corps (church). Admissions inquiries should be directed to local Salvation Army community centers. **Enrollment:** 106 degree-seeking undergraduates. **Degrees:** 38 associate awarded. **Calendar:** Quarter. **Full-time faculty:** 20 total; 15% have terminal degrees, 35% women. **Part-time faculty:** 5 total; 20% have terminal degrees, 80% women. **Special facilities:** Salvation Army museum.

Basis for selection. Open admission, but selective for some programs. High school diploma, Salvation Army officer candidate status required.

High school preparation. College-preparatory program recommended.

2015-2016 Annual costs. Tuition/fees: $5,265. Books/supplies: $750. **Additional information:** No additional costs related to attendance.

Financial aid. Need-based: Work-study available nights, weekends and for part-time students.

Application procedures. Admission: No deadline. No application fee. **Financial aid:** No deadline.

Academics. Credit/placement by examination: AP, CLEP. **Support services:** Learning center, pre-admission summer program, reduced course load, study skills assistance, tutoring, writing center.

Majors. Theology: Missionary.

Technology on campus. PC or laptop required. Dormitories wired for high-speed internet access and linked to campus network. Online library, helpline, repair service, wireless network available.

Student life. Freshman orientation: Mandatory. Preregistration for classes offered. **Policies:** Religious observance required. Freshmen not permitted cars on campus. **Housing:** Apartments available. Housing for both students and families available. **Activities:** Concert band, campus ministries, choral groups, drama, music ensembles, TV station.

Student services. Adult student services, alcohol/substance abuse counseling, chaplain/spiritual director, career counseling, services for economically disadvantaged, on-campus daycare, personal counseling.

Contact. Phone: (310) 377-0481
Bob Louangamath, Director of Admissions, Salvation Army College for Officer Training at Crestmont, 30840 Hawthorne Boulevard, Rancho Palos Verdes, CA 90275

San Bernardino Valley College
San Bernardino, California
www.valleycollege.edu

CB code: 4679

- Public 2-year community college
- Small city

General. Founded in 1926. Regionally accredited. **Enrollment:** 8,307 degree-seeking undergraduates. **Degrees:** 980 associate awarded. **Location:** 60 miles from Los Angeles. **Calendar:** Semester, limited summer session. **Full-time faculty:** 154 total. **Part-time faculty:** 397 total. **Special facilities:** Planetarium.

Basis for selection. Open admission, but selective for some programs. Special requirements for nursing program. **Home schooled:** Transcript of courses and grades required.

2015-2016 Annual costs. Tuition/fees: $1,420; $7,232 out-of-state. Per-credit charge: $46 in-state; $232 out-of-state. Books/supplies: $1,638. Personal expenses: $2,000.

Financial aid. Need-based: Work-study available nights, weekends and for part-time students.

Application procedures. Admission: No deadline. No application fee. **Financial aid:** Priority date 5/25; no closing date. Applicants notified on a rolling basis starting 5/1; must reply within 2 week(s) of notification.

Academics. Special study options: Cooperative education, cross-registration, distance learning, double major, dual enrollment of high school students, ESL, honors, independent study, internships, liberal arts/career combination, weekend college. Service Members Opportunity College. **Credit/placement by examination:** AP, CLEP, institutional tests. **Support services:** GED preparation, learning center, pre-admission summer program, reduced course load, remedial instruction, study skills assistance, tutoring, writing center.

Majors. Biology: General. **Business:** Accounting, business admin, real estate. **Communications:** Communications/speech/rhetoric. **Computer sciences:** Computer science, systems analysis. **Human services:** Social work. **Liberal arts:** Arts/sciences, library assistant. **Math:** General. **Physical sciences:** Astronomy, chemistry, geology, physics. **Protective services:** Law enforcement admin. **Psychology:** General. **Social sciences:** Geography. **Visual/performing arts:** Commercial/advertising art.

Technology on campus. 180 workstations in library, computer center, student center.

Student life. Freshman orientation: Available. Preregistration for classes offered. **Activities:** Choral groups, drama, literary magazine, music ensembles, musical theater, radio station, student government, student newspaper, TV station, Campus Crusade for Christ, Newman Club, Baptist Student Union, Movimiento Estudiantil Chicano de Aztlan, Black Student Union, Young Democrats, Young Republicans.

Athletics. NCAA. **Intercollegiate:** Baseball M, basketball, cross-country, football (tackle) M, soccer, softball W, track and field, volleyball W. **Team name:** Wolverines.

Student services. Adult student services, career counseling, services for economically disadvantaged, student employment services, financial aid counseling, health services, on-campus daycare, personal counseling, placement for graduates, veterans' counselor. **Physically disabled:** Services for visually, speech, hearing impaired. **Transfer:** Pre-admission transcript evaluation for new students.

Contact. E-mail: admissions@valleycollege.edu
Phone: (909) 384-4401
Dan Angelo, Associate Dean of Enrollment, San Bernardino Valley College, 701 South Mount Vernon Avenue, San Bernardino, CA 92410

San Diego City College
San Diego, California
www.sdcity.edu

- Public 2-year community and junior college
- Commuter campus in very large city

General. Founded in 1914. Regionally accredited. **Enrollment:** 9,977 degree-seeking undergraduates. **Degrees:** 851 associate awarded. **ROTC:** Army, Air Force. **Location:** Downtown. **Calendar:** Semester, extensive summer session. **Full-time faculty:** 167 total; 41% have terminal degrees. **Part-time faculty:** 636 total; 9% have terminal degrees, 35% minority.

Special facilities: Computerized independent study and learning laboratories, vocational training centers, academic success center, veterans resource center, planetarium.

Transfer out. Colleges most students transferred to 2015: San Diego State University, University California San Diego, CSU San Marcos, National University.

Basis for selection. Open admission.

2015-2016 Annual costs. Tuition/fees: $1,418; $7,208 out-of-state. Per-credit charge: $46 in-state; $239 out-of-state. Books/supplies: $1,764. Personal expenses: $3,159.

2014-2015 Financial aid. All financial aid based on need. 90% of total undergraduate aid awarded as scholarships/grants, 10% as loans/jobs. Need-based aid available for part-time students. Work-study available nights, weekends and for part-time students.

Application procedures. Admission: No deadline. No application fee. High school students must submit an approved supplemental application certified by parents, principal, registrar, and/or school district official. International students must submit a pre-application prior to officially applying to the college. **Financial aid:** Priority date 4/15; no closing date. FAFSA required. Applicants notified on a rolling basis starting 7/1; must reply within 4 week(s) of notification.

Academics. Special study options: Accelerated study, cooperative education, cross-registration, double major, dual enrollment of high school students, honors, independent study, internships, liberal arts/career combination, student-designed major, study abroad, teacher certification program, weekend college. **Credit/placement by examination:** AP, CLEP, institutional tests. 15 credit hours maximum toward associate degree. **Support services:** Learning center, pre-admission summer program, reduced course load, remedial instruction, study skills assistance, tutoring, writing center. MESA program and first year services.

Majors. Area/ethnic studies: African, African-American, Latin American. **Biology:** General. **Business:** General, accounting, administrative services, business admin, labor relations, management information systems, management science, office technology, office/clerical, operations, purchasing, real estate, tourism promotion. **Communications:** Broadcast journalism. **Communications technology:** General. **Computer sciences:** General, applications programming, data entry, data processing, information systems, systems analysis. **Education:** Bilingual. **Engineering:** General. **English:** English lit, rhetoric/composition. **Foreign languages:** General, French, Italian, Spanish. **General:** Pipefitting, power transmission. **Health services:** Nursing (RN), substance abuse counseling. **History:** General. **Liberal arts:** Arts/sciences. **Math:** General, applied. **Parks/recreation:** Health/fitness. **Philosophy/religion:** Philosophy. **Physical sciences:** Chemistry, geology, physics. **Psychology:** General. **Social sciences:** General, anthropology, geography, political science. **Visual/performing arts:** General, art history/conservation, commercial/advertising art, dramatic, music, photography, studio arts.

Most popular majors. Biological/life sciences 10%, business/marketing 6%, foreign language 23%, health sciences 14%, social sciences 19%, trade and industry 7%, visual/performing arts 7%.

Technology on campus. 150 workstations in library, computer center, student center. Online course registration, online library, helpline, repair service, wireless network available.

Student life. Freshman orientation: Available. Preregistration for classes offered. **Activities:** Jazz band, choral groups, dance, drama, film society, musical theater, radio station, student government, student newspaper, symphony orchestra, TV station, Arabic club, Italian club, MECHA, National Society of Black Engineers, Society of Hispanic Professional Engineers, California Coalition Against Poverty, students for labor and solidarity, lesbian, gay, bisexual and transsexual student union.

Athletics. Intercollegiate: Baseball, basketball M, cross-country, football (tackle) M, golf, soccer, softball W, tennis, track and field, volleyball. **Intramural:** Archery, badminton, baseball M, basketball, bowling, racquetball, soccer, tennis, track and field, volleyball, weight lifting. **Team name:** Knights.

Student services. Adult student services, career counseling, student employment services, health services, on-campus daycare, personal counseling, placement for graduates, veterans' counselor. **Physically disabled:** Services for visually, speech, hearing impaired. **Transfer:** Pre-admission transcript evaluation for new students. Transfer center, transfer adviser, college fairs on campus for students transferring to 4-year colleges.

Contact. Phone: (619) 388-3475 ext. 6 Fax: (619) 388-3505
Lou Humphries, Student Services Supervisor II, San Diego City College, 1313 Park Boulevard, San Diego, CA 92101-4787

San Diego Mesa College
San Diego, California
www.sdmesa.edu

CB member
CB code: 4735

- Public 2-year community college
- Commuter campus in very large city

General. Founded in 1964. Regionally accredited. **Enrollment:** 15,343 degree-seeking undergraduates. **Degrees:** 1,488 associate awarded. **Calendar:** Semester, limited summer session. **Full-time faculty:** 226 total; 53% women. **Part-time faculty:** 735 total; 52% women. **Special facilities:** Anthropology museum, art museum, culinary arts operated cafe.

Student profile.

Out-of-state: 4%   25 or older: 19%

Transfer out. Colleges most students transferred to 2015: San Diego State University, University of California San Diego.

Basis for selection. Open admission. Students without high school diploma or equivalent admitted provisionally. **Learning Disabled:** Disabled Student Service Program (DSPS) available.

High school preparation. College-preparatory program recommended.

2015-2016 Annual costs. Tuition/fees: $1,418; $7,208 out-of-state. Per-credit charge: $46 in-state; $239 out-of-state. Books/supplies: $1,746. Personal expenses: $3,132.

Financial aid. All financial aid based on need. Need-based aid available for part-time students. Work-study available nights, weekends and for part-time students.

Application procedures. Admission: No deadline. No application fee. Application must be submitted online. Admission notification on a rolling basis. Applications not accepted by mail. **Financial aid:** Priority date 3/2; no closing date. FAFSA required. Applicants notified on a rolling basis starting 6/15; must reply within 3 week(s) of notification.

Academics. Special study options: Accelerated study, distance learning, double major, dual enrollment of high school students, honors, independent study, internships, liberal arts/career combination, student-designed major, study abroad, teacher certification program. License preparation in physical therapy, radiology, real estate. **Credit/placement by examination:** AP, CLEP, institutional tests. 15 credit hours maximum toward associate degree. Institutional test required for placement and counseling. **Support services:** Learning center, reduced course load, remedial instruction, study skills assistance, tutoring, writing center.

Majors. Architecture: Landscape. **Area/ethnic studies:** African, African-American, Chicano/Hispanic-American/Latino. **Biology:** General. **Business:** General, accounting, business admin, fashion, hotel/motel admin, real estate, tourism/travel. **Computer sciences:** Programming, web page design. **Education:** Physical, sales/marketing, speech. **Engineering:** General. **Foreign languages:** American Sign Language, French, Spanish. **Health services:** Dental assistant, dental lab technology, medical assistant, medical radiologic technology/radiation therapy, physical therapy assistant. **Liberal arts:** Arts/sciences. **Math:** General. **Philosophy/religion:** Philosophy. **Physical sciences:** Chemistry, physics. **Psychology:** General. **Social sciences:** General, anthropology, sociology. **Visual/performing arts:** Art, dramatic, interior design, music, studio arts. **Work/family studies:** Child development.

Most popular majors. Business/marketing 14%, health sciences 6%, psychology 10%.

Technology on campus. Commuter students can connect to campus network. Online library, wireless network available.

Student life. Freshman orientation: Available. Preregistration for classes offered. **Activities:** Bands, choral groups, dance, drama, international student organizations, music ensembles, musical theater, student government, student newspaper.

Athletics. Intercollegiate: Badminton W, baseball M, basketball, cross-country, diving, football (tackle) M, soccer, softball W, swimming, tennis, track and field, volleyball, water polo. **Team name:** Olympians.

Student services. Adult student services, career counseling, services for economically disadvantaged, financial aid counseling, health services, on-campus daycare, personal counseling, placement for graduates, veterans' counselor. **Physically disabled:** Services for visually, speech, hearing impaired. **Transfer:** Transfer center, transfer adviser, college fairs on campus for students transferring to 4-year colleges.

Contact. E-mail: csawyer@sdccd.edu
Phone: (619) 388-2682 Fax: (619) 388-2960
Ivonne Alvarez, Director of Admissions and Records, San Diego Mesa College, 7250 Mesa College Drive, San Diego, CA 92111

San Diego Miramar College
San Diego, California
www.sdmiramar.edu

CB member
CB code: 4728

- Public 2-year community college
- Commuter campus in very large city

General. Founded in 1969. Regionally accredited. **Enrollment:** 11,710 undergraduates. **Degrees:** 735 associate awarded. **Location:** 9 miles from downtown. **Calendar:** Semester, limited summer session. **Full-time faculty:** 73 total. **Part-time faculty:** 237 total.

Student profile. 56% enrolled in a transfer program, 1% enrolled in a vocational program, 8% already have a bachelor's degree or higher.

Out-of-state: 1%   25 or older: 45%

Basis for selection. Open admission.

2015-2016 Annual costs. Tuition/fees: $1,437; $7,227 out-of-state. Per-credit charge: $46 in-state; $239 out-of-state. Books/supplies: $1,710. Personal expenses: $4,275.

Financial aid. Need-based: Need-based aid available for part-time students. Work-study available nights, weekends and for part-time students. **Additional information:** Private scholarships available.

Application procedures. Admission: No deadline. No application fee. Admission notification on a rolling basis. **Financial aid:** Priority date 3/2, closing date 6/30. FAFSA required. Applicants notified on a rolling basis; must reply within 3 week(s) of notification.

Academics. Special study options: Accelerated study, cross-registration, distance learning, dual enrollment of high school students, honors, independent study, weekend college. **Credit/placement by examination:** AP, CLEP. 15 credit hours maximum toward associate degree. Institutional placement tests required. **Support services:** Learning center, remedial instruction, study skills assistance, tutoring.

Majors. Biology: General. **Business:** Accounting, administrative services, business admin, marketing, office/clerical. **Communications:** Communications/speech/rhetoric. **Computer sciences:** General. **Education:** Early childhood. **English:** English lit, rhetoric/composition. **History:** General. **Liberal arts:** Humanities. **Math:** General. **Parks/recreation:** Health/fitness. **Physical sciences:** Chemistry, physics. **Protective services:** Corrections, firefighting, law enforcement admin. **Psychology:** General. **Social sciences:** General. **Visual/performing arts:** Studio arts. **Work/family studies:** Family studies.

Most popular majors. Business/marketing 16%, legal studies 7%, liberal arts 33%, security/protective services 23%.

Technology on campus. 10 workstations in library, computer center.

Student life. Freshman orientation: Mandatory. Preregistration for classes offered. **Activities:** Student government, student newspaper, Amnesty International, Child Development Professionals, Filipino American Association, Latin American club, Miramar Associated Gaming Imagination Club (MAGIC), parent student advisory board, Phi Theta Kappa.

Athletics. Team name: Jets.

Student services. Career counseling, services for economically disadvantaged, health services, on-campus daycare, personal counseling, veterans' counselor. **Physically disabled:** Services for visually, hearing impaired. **Transfer:** Transfer adviser, college fairs on campus for students transferring to 4-year colleges.

Contact. E-mail: dstack@sdccd.edu
Phone: (619) 388-7844 Fax: (619) 388-7915
Dana Stack, Student Services Supervisor II, San Diego Miramar College, 10440 Black Mountain Road, San Diego, CA 92126-2999

San Joaquin Delta College
Stockton, California
www.deltacollege.edu

CB code: 4706

- Public 2-year community college
- Commuter campus in large city

General. Founded in 1935. Regionally accredited. Two off-campus sites located in service district: Manteca Farm and Mountain House. **Enrollment:** 14,373 degree-seeking undergraduates; 4,289 non-degree-seeking students. **Degrees:** 2,282 associate awarded. **Location:** 45 miles from Sacramento. **Calendar:** Semester, extensive summer session. **Full-time faculty:** 261 total; 38% women. **Part-time faculty:** 254 total; 42% women. **Class size:** 18% < 20, 48% 20-39, 11% 40-49, 21% 50-99, 2% >100. **Special facilities:** Electron microscopy laboratory, farm laboratory, natural resources laboratory, 3 theaters. **Partnerships:** Formal partnerships with Nissan, General Motors, Caterpillar, Cisco.

Student profile. Among degree-seeking undergraduates, 2,554 enrolled as first-time, first-year students.

Part-time:	58%	Women:	58%
Out-of-state:	4%	25 or older:	32%

Transfer out. Colleges most students transferred to 2015: California State University: Stanislaus, California State University: Sacramento, University of the Pacific, California State Polytechnic University, University of California: Davis.

Basis for selection. Open admission, but selective for some programs. Limited admission to registered nursing, psychiatric technician, radiological technician, and police academy programs.

2015-2016 Annual costs. Tuition/fees: $1,380; $7,950 out-of-state. Per-credit charge: $46 in-state; $265 out-of-state. Books/supplies: $1,764. Personal expenses: $3,159.

2014-2015 Financial aid. Need-based: 8,067 full-time freshmen applied for aid; 6,516 deemed to have need; 5,290 received aid. Average need met was 31%. Average scholarship/grant was $5,180; average loan $2,633. 96% of total undergraduate aid awarded as scholarships/grants, 4% as loans/jobs. Need-based aid available for part-time students. Work-study available nights, weekends and for part-time students. **Non-need-based:** Awarded to 5 full-time undergraduates, including 1 freshmen. Scholarships awarded for academics, athletics. **Additional information:** Enrollment fee waivers available for low-income California residents.

Application procedures. Admission: No deadline. No application fee. Application must be submitted online. **Financial aid:** Closing date 6/30. FAFSA, institutional form required. Applicants notified on a rolling basis starting 4/1; must reply within 3 week(s) of notification.

Academics. Special study options: Cooperative education, distance learning, dual enrollment of high school students, ESL, honors, independent study, internships, liberal arts/career combination, study abroad, weekend college. License preparation in nursing, radiology, real estate. **Credit/placement by examination:** AP, CLEP, IB, institutional tests. 15 credit hours maximum toward associate degree. All students taking more than one course must take ASSET or COMPASS for placement. AP and CLEP credit granted after 12 semester hours in residence completed. **Support services:** Learning center, reduced course load, remedial instruction, study skills assistance, tutoring, writing center.

Majors. Architecture: Technology. **Business:** General, accounting technology, banking/financial services, business admin, logistics, office management, real estate, retail management. **Communications:** Communications/speech/rhetoric, media studies, radio/TV. **Computer sciences:** Information technology, networking. **Engineering:** Pre-engineering. **English:** English lit. **Foreign languages:** Chinese, French, German, Italian, Japanese, Spanish. **Health services:** Mental health services, nursing (RN), radiologic technology/medical imaging. **History:** General. **Human services:** General. **Liberal arts:** Arts/sciences. **Math:** General. **Parks/recreation:** Health/fitness. **Physical sciences:** Geology, physics. **Protective services:** Corrections, fire safety technology, police science. **Psychology:** General. **Social sciences:** General. **Visual/performing arts:** Art, dance, dramatic, fashion design, graphic design, interior design, music, photography, theater design. **Work/family studies:** General, apparel marketing, child care service.

Most popular majors. Health sciences 6%, interdisciplinary studies 57%, social sciences 18%.

Technology on campus. 220 workstations in library, computer center. Commuter students can connect to campus network. Online course registration, online library, helpline, wireless network available.

Student life. Freshman orientation: Available. Preregistration for classes offered. **Activities:** Bands, choral groups, dance, drama, international student organizations, literary magazine, music ensembles, musical theater, radio station, student government, student newspaper, symphony orchestra, African-American Student Union, Movimiento Estudiantil Chicano de Aztlan, Japanese Club, Christians United For Israel (CUFI), Christians on Campus, San Joaquin Delta College Circle K International, Latino Medical Student Association.

Athletics. NJCAA. **Intercollegiate:** Baseball M, basketball, cross-country, diving, football (tackle) M, golf, soccer, softball W, swimming, track and field, volleyball W, water polo, wrestling M. **Team name:** Mustangs.

Student services. Adult student services, alcohol/substance abuse counseling, career counseling, services for economically disadvantaged, student employment services, financial aid counseling, legal services, minority student services, on-campus daycare, personal counseling, placement for graduates, veterans' counselor. **Physically disabled:** Services for visually, speech, hearing impaired. **Transfer:** Re-entry adviser for new students. Transfer center, transfer adviser, college fairs on campus for students transferring to 4-year colleges.

Contact. Phone: (209) 954-5151
Karen Sea, Registrar, San Joaquin Delta College, 5151 Pacific Avenue, Stockton, CA 95207-6370

San Joaquin Valley College
Visalia, California
www.sjvc.edu **CB code: 2052**

▶ For-profit 2-year junior college
▶ Commuter campus in small city
▶ Application essay, interview required

General. Regionally accredited. Additional campuses in Bakersfield, Fresno, Modesto, Rancho Cordova, and Rancho Cucamonga. Aviation campus located in Fresno. **Enrollment:** 1,892 undergraduates. **Degrees:** 2,206 associate awarded. **Calendar:** Semester, extensive summer session. **Full-time faculty:** 96 total. **Part-time faculty:** 73 total.

Basis for selection. Open admission, but selective for some programs. Selective admission to allied health programs. Various programs use either ACCUPLACER or Wonderlic for placement. ACCUPLACER for placement in Math and English.

2015-2016 Annual costs. Certificate programs range from $14,415-$40,500, Associates programs range from $28,830-$58,970, books and supplies included in tuition.

Financial aid. Need-based: Work-study available nights, weekends and for part-time students.

Application procedures. Admission: No deadline. No application fee. Admission notification on a rolling basis. **Financial aid:** No deadline. FAFSA, institutional form required.

Academics. Special study options: Independent study, internships, liberal arts/career combination. License preparation in aviation, dental hygiene, nursing. **Credit/placement by examination:** AP, CLEP. **Support services:** Learning center, remedial instruction, study skills assistance, tutoring.

Majors. Business: Business admin, construction management, human resources. **Computer sciences:** Support specialist. **Health services:** Dental assistant, dental hygiene, EMT paramedic, health care admin, health information management, insurance coding, licensed practical nurse, massage therapy, medical assistant, medical secretary, nursing (RN), office assistant, pharmacy assistant, physician assistant, respiratory therapy technology, surgical technology, veterinary technology/assistant. **Protective services:** Corrections.

Technology on campus. 100 workstations in library, computer center.

Student life. Freshman orientation: Mandatory. Preregistration for classes offered. Full day on Friday prior to start of classes, continues through first week. **Activities:** Student government, student newspaper.

Student services. Adult student services, career counseling, services for economically disadvantaged, student employment services, financial aid counseling, personal counseling, placement for graduates. **Transfer:** Pre-admission transcript evaluation for new students.

Contact. Phone: (559) 651-2500 Fax: (559) 651-0574
Susie Topjian, Enrollment Services Director, San Joaquin Valley College, 8400 West Mineral King Avenue, Visalia, CA 93291-9283

San Jose City College
San Jose, California
www.sjcc.edu **CB code: 4686**

▶ Public 2-year community college
▶ Commuter campus in very large city

General. Founded in 1921. Regionally accredited. **Enrollment:** 4,833 degree-seeking undergraduates. **Degrees:** 594 associate awarded. **Location:** 55 miles from San Francisco. **Calendar:** Semester, limited summer session. **Full-time faculty:** 124 total. **Part-time faculty:** 288 total. **Partnerships:** Formal partnerships with Intel (Manufacturing Technology program), Laser Electro-Optics Manufacturing Association (Laser Technology program), IntelSemiconductor (Mask Design Technology program).

Transfer out. **Colleges most students transferred to 2015:** San Jose State University, California State University: East Bay.

Basis for selection. Open admission.

High school preparation. College-preparatory program recommended.

2015-2016 Annual costs. Tuition/fees: $1,418; $7,538 out-of-state. Per-credit charge: $46 in-state; $250 out-of-state. Books/supplies: $1,764. Personal expenses: $3,159.

Financial aid. All financial aid based on need. Need-based aid available for part-time students. Work-study available nights, weekends and for part-time students. **Additional information:** Board of Governors Grant (fee waivers) available to all qualified applicants.

Application procedures. **Admission:** No deadline. No application fee. **Financial aid:** No deadline. FAFSA required. Applicants notified on a rolling basis; must reply within 4 week(s) of notification.

Academics. **Special study options:** Cross-registration, distance learning, dual enrollment of high school students, ESL, honors, independent study, liberal arts/career combination, weekend college. License preparation in real estate. **Credit/placement by examination:** AP, CLEP, IB, institutional tests. 30 credit hours maximum toward associate degree. **Support services:** Learning center, pre-admission summer program, reduced course load, remedial instruction, study skills assistance, tutoring, writing center.

Majors. **Business:** Accounting, administrative services, banking/financial services, entrepreneurial studies, labor studies, marketing, office technology, office/clerical, real estate. **Communications technology:** General. **Computer sciences:** General, applications programming, data entry, networking, programming. **Education:** Early childhood. **General:** Power transmission. **Health services:** Dental assistant, substance abuse counseling. **Liberal arts:** Arts/sciences. **Protective services:** Law enforcement admin. **Psychology:** General. **Social sciences:** General. **Visual/performing arts:** Music, studio arts.

Technology on campus. 250 workstations in library, computer center, student center. Online course registration, helpline, wireless network available.

Student life. **Freshman orientation:** Available. Preregistration for classes offered. **Activities:** Dance, drama, music ensembles, musical theater, radio station, student government, student newspaper.

Athletics. **Intercollegiate:** Basketball, cross-country, football (tackle) M, golf M, softball W, track and field, volleyball W. **Team name:** Jaguars.

Student services. Career counseling, services for economically disadvantaged, student employment services, financial aid counseling, health services, minority student services, personal counseling, veterans' counselor. **Physically disabled:** Services for visually, speech, hearing impaired. **Transfer:** Transfer center, transfer adviser, college fairs on campus for students transferring to 4-year colleges.

Contact. E-mail: takeo.kubo@sjcc.edu
Phone: (408) 288-3700 Fax: (408) 298-1935
Takeo Kubo, Dean of Enrollment Services, San Jose City College, 2100 Moorpark Avenue, San Jose, CA 95128-2798

Santa Ana College
Santa Ana, California
www.sac.edu

CB code: 4689

‣ Public 2-year community college
‣ Commuter campus in large city

General. Founded in 1915. Regionally accredited. **Enrollment:** 10,929 degree-seeking undergraduates. **Degrees:** 1,978 associate awarded. **Location:** 40 miles from Los Angeles. **Calendar:** Semester, extensive summer session. **Full-time faculty:** 221 total; 18% have terminal degrees, 37% minority. **Part-time faculty:** 707 total; 27% minority. **Class size:** 33% < 20, 38% 20-39, 16% 40-49, 10% 50-99, 2% >100. **Special facilities:** Planetarium, 2 art galleries, digital media center/digital incubator.

Transfer out. **Colleges most students transferred to 2015:** California State University: Fullerton, California State University: Long Beach, California State University: Irvine, University of Phoenix.

Basis for selection. Open admission. All students 18 years and older who can benefit from instruction are admitted. **Adult students:** SAT/ACT scores not required.

2015-2016 Annual costs. Tuition/fees: $1,418; $8,018 out-of-state. Per-credit charge: $46 in-state; $266 out-of-state. Books/supplies: $1,700. Personal expenses: $3,096.

Financial aid. **Need-based:** Work-study available nights, weekends and for part-time students.

Application procedures. **Admission:** Priority date 4/1; no deadline. No application fee. Admission notification on a rolling basis. **Financial aid:** Priority date 6/30; no closing date. FAFSA required. Applicants notified on a rolling basis starting 6/1; must reply within 2 week(s) of notification.

Academics. **Special study options:** Cooperative education, distance learning, double major, dual enrollment of high school students, ESL, honors, independent study, internships, liberal arts/career combination, study abroad, weekend college. **Credit/placement by examination:** AP, CLEP, institutional tests. 30 credit hours maximum toward associate degree. **Support services:** GED preparation, learning center, pre-admission summer program, reduced course load, remedial instruction, study skills assistance, tutoring.

Majors. **Area/ethnic studies:** General, African-American, Chicano/Hispanic-American/Latino, women's. **Biology:** General. **Business:** Accounting, business admin, entrepreneurial studies, fashion, insurance, international, management science, marketing. **Communications:** Advertising, broadcast journalism, communications/speech/rhetoric, journalism. **Computer sciences:** General, computer science, data processing. **Education:** Early childhood. **Engineering:** General. **English:** English lit. **Foreign languages:** General. **Health services:** Medical assistant, nursing (RN), occupational therapy assistant, pharmacy assistant. **History:** General. **Liberal arts:** Arts/sciences, library assistant. **Math:** General. **Parks/recreation:** Exercise sciences. **Philosophy/religion:** Philosophy. **Physical sciences:** Chemistry, geology, physics. **Protective services:** Fire safety technology, fire services admin, firefighting, police science. **Psychology:** General. **Social sciences:** General, anthropology, economics, geography, political science, sociology. **Visual/performing arts:** General, commercial/advertising art, dance, dramatic, fashion design, music, photography. **Work/family studies:** Family/community services, food/nutrition.

Most popular majors. Health sciences 11%, liberal arts 50%, security/protective services 9%.

Technology on campus. 66 workstations in library, computer center. Online course registration, wireless network available.

Student life. **Freshman orientation:** Available. Preregistration for classes offered. **Activities:** Bands, choral groups, dance, drama, international student organizations, literary magazine, music ensembles, musical theater, radio station, student government, student newspaper, TV station.

Athletics. NJCAA. **Intercollegiate:** Baseball M, basketball, cross-country, football (tackle) M, soccer, softball W, track and field, volleyball, water polo, wrestling M. **Team name:** Dons.

Student services. Adult student services, alcohol/substance abuse counseling, career counseling, services for economically disadvantaged, student employment services, financial aid counseling, health services, minority student services, on-campus daycare, personal counseling, veterans' student services, women's services. **Physically disabled:** Services for visually, speech, hearing impaired. **Transfer:** Re-entry adviser, pre-admission transcript evaluation for new students. Transfer center, transfer adviser, college fairs on campus for students transferring to 4-year colleges.

Contact. E-mail: adm_records@sac.edu
Phone: (714) 564-6042 Fax: (714) 564-6455
Mark Liang, Director, Admissions and Records, Santa Ana College, 1530 West 17th Street, Santa Ana, CA 92706

Santa Barbara Business College
Santa Barbara, California
www.sbbcollege.edu

‣ For-profit 2-year technical and career college
‣ Small city
‣ Interview required

General. Accredited by ACICS. Campuses located in Santa Barbara, Ventura, Santa Maria, Bakersfield, Rancho Mirage, and Online. **Enrollment:** 94 degree-seeking undergraduates. **Degrees:** 2 bachelor's, 15 associate awarded; master's offered. **Location:** 90 miles from Los Angeles. **Calendar:** Terms begin every 10 weeks. **Full-time faculty:** 5 total. **Part-time faculty:** 10 total.

Basis for selection. Admission decisions based on Wonderlic assessment and interview to determine interest and motivation of prospective student. **Home schooled:** Transcript of courses and grades required. Need to take ATB proctored test if unable to supply an official transcript.

2015-2016 Annual costs. Tuition/fees: $13,619. Per-credit charge: $375.54. **Additional information:** Costs posted are for all programs except AS Aviation Studies which are $20275 tuition + $31388 required fees.

Financial aid. **Need-based:** Work-study available nights, weekends and for part-time students.

Application procedures. **Admission:** No deadline. $25 fee. **Financial aid:** No deadline. FAFSA required. Applicants notified on a rolling basis.

Academics. **Special study options:** Bachelor's degree programs available on campus. **Credit/placement by examination:** AP, CLEP. **Support services:** Remedial instruction, study skills assistance, tutoring.

Majors. **Business:** General. **Health services:** Health information management, pharmacy assistant. **Protective services:** Criminal justice.

Technology on campus. Online library available.

Student life. **Freshman orientation:** Mandatory. Preregistration for classes offered.

Student services. Career counseling, financial aid counseling, placement for graduates.

Contact. E-mail: infodesk@sbbcollege.edu
Phone: (805) 967-9677 Fax: (805) 967-4248
Tamu Smith-Kohls, Director of Admissions, Santa Barbara Business College, 506 Chapala Street, Santa Barbara, CA 93101

Santa Barbara Business College: Bakersfield
Bakersfield, California
www.sbbcollege.edu

- For-profit 2-year technical and career college
- Commuter campus in large city
- Interview required

General. Accredited by ACICS. Campuses located in Santa Barbara, Ventura, Santa Maria, Rancho Mirage, and Online. **Enrollment:** 405 degree-seeking undergraduates. **Degrees:** 4 bachelor's, 98 associate awarded. **Calendar:** Terms begin every 10 weeks. **Full-time faculty:** 10 total. **Part-time faculty:** 20 total.

Basis for selection. Admissions decisions based on Wonderlic assessment and interview to determine interest and motivation of prospective student. **Home schooled:** Transcript of courses and grades required. Need to take ATB proctored test if unable to supply an official transcript.

2015-2016 Annual costs. Tuition/fees: $13,619. Per-credit charge: $375.54. **Additional information:** Costs posted are for all programs except AS Aviation STudies which are $20275 tuition + $31388 required fees.

Financial aid. **Need-based:** Work-study available nights, weekends and for part-time students.

Application procedures. **Admission:** No deadline. $25 fee. **Financial aid:** FAFSA required. Applicants notified on a rolling basis.

Academics. **Special study options:** Bachelor's degree programs available on campus. License preparation in nursing. **Credit/placement by examination:** AP, CLEP. **Support services:** GED preparation, remedial instruction, study skills assistance, tutoring.

Majors. **Business:** General. **Computer sciences:** LAN/WAN management. **Health services:** Health information management, medical assistant, office assistant, pharmacy assistant. **Protective services:** Criminal justice.

Technology on campus. Online library available.

Student life. **Freshman orientation:** Mandatory. Preregistration for classes offered.

Student services. Career counseling, financial aid counseling, placement for graduates.

Contact. Phone: (866) 749-7222
Tamu Smith-Kohls, Director of Admissions, Santa Barbara Business College: Bakersfield, 5300 California Avenue, Bakersfield, CA 93304

Santa Barbara Business College: Rancho Mirage
Rancho Mirage, California
www.sbbcollege.edu

- For-profit 2-year technical and career college
- Small city
- Interview required

General. Regionally accredited; also accredited by ACICS. Campuses also located in Bakersfield, Ventura, Santa Barbara, Santa Maria, and Online. **Enrollment:** 256 degree-seeking undergraduates. **Degrees:** 16 bachelor's, 70 associate awarded. **Calendar:** Differs by program. Terms begin every 10 weeks. **Part-time faculty:** 12 total.

Basis for selection. Open admission.

2015-2016 Annual costs. Tuition/fees: $13,619. Per-credit charge: $375.54.

Financial aid. **Need-based:** Work-study available nights, weekends and for part-time students.

Application procedures. **Admission:** No deadline. $25 fee. **Financial aid:** No deadline.

Academics. **Special study options:** Bachelor's degree programs available on campus. **Credit/placement by examination:** AP, CLEP. **Support services:** GED preparation, tutoring.

Majors. **Business:** Business admin. **Health services:** Health information management, medical assistant. **Protective services:** Criminal justice.

Technology on campus. Online library available.

Student life. **Freshman orientation:** Mandatory. Preregistration for classes offered. **Activities:** Student newspaper.

Student services. Career counseling, financial aid counseling, placement for graduates.

Contact. E-mail: infodesk@sbbcollege.edu
Phone: (866) 749-7222
Tamu Smith-Kohls, Director of Admissions, Santa Barbara Business College: Rancho Mirage, 34275 Monterey Avenue, Rancho Mirage, CA 92270

Santa Barbara Business College: Santa Maria
Santa Maria, California
www.sbbcollege.edu

- For-profit 2-year technical and career college
- Small city
- Interview required

General. Accredited by ACICS. Campuses located in Santa Barbara, Ventura, Bakersfield, Rancho Mirage, and Online. **Enrollment:** 222 degree-seeking undergraduates. **Degrees:** 3 bachelor's, 43 associate awarded. **Calendar:** Quarter. Terms begin every 10 weeks. **Full-time faculty:** 8 total. **Part-time faculty:** 12 total.

Basis for selection. Open admission, but selective for some programs. Admissions decisions based on Wonderlic assessment and interview to determine interest and motivation of prospective student. **Home schooled:** Transcript of courses and grades required. Need to take ATB proctored test if unable to supply an official transcript.

2015-2016 Annual costs. Tuition/fees: $13,619. Per-credit charge: $375.54.

Financial aid. **Need-based:** Work-study available nights, weekends and for part-time students.

Two-Year Colleges

Application procedures. Admission: No deadline. $25 fee. **Financial aid:** No deadline. FAFSA required. Applicants notified on a rolling basis.

Academics. Special study options: Bachelor's degree programs available on campus. License preparation in nursing. **Credit/placement by examination:** AP, CLEP. **Support services:** Remedial instruction, study skills assistance, tutoring.

Majors. Business: General. **Health services:** Health information technology, medical assistant, office assistant, pharmacy assistant. **Protective services:** Criminal justice.

Technology on campus. Online library available.

Student life. Freshman orientation: Mandatory. Preregistration for classes offered.

Student services. Career counseling, financial aid counseling, placement for graduates.

Contact. Phone: (866) 749-7222 Toll-free number: (866) 749-7222 Fax: (805) 346-1862
Tamu Smith-Kohls, Director of Admissions, Santa Barbara Business College: Santa Maria, 303 East Plaza Drive, Santa Maria, CA 93454

Santa Barbara Business College: Ventura
Ventura, California
www.sbbcollege.edu

▶ For-profit 2-year technical and career college
▶ Commuter campus in small city
▶ Interview required

General. Accredited by ACICS. Campuses located in Ventura, Santa Barbara, Santa Maria, Bakersfield, Rancho Mirage, and Online. **Enrollment:** 106 degree-seeking undergraduates. **Degrees:** 5 bachelor's, 15 associate awarded. **Location:** 40 miles from Los Angeles. **Calendar:** Quarter. Terms begin every 10 weeks. Extensive summer session. **Full-time faculty:** 4 total. **Part-time faculty:** 27 total.

Basis for selection. Admission decisions based on Wonderlic assessment and interview to determine interest and motivation of prospective student. Wonderlic Basic Skills Test required. **Home schooled:** Transcript of courses and grades required. Need to take ATB proctored test if unable to supply an official transcript.

2015-2016 Annual costs. Tuition/fees: $13,619. Per-credit charge: $375.54.

Financial aid. Need-based: Work-study available nights, weekends and for part-time students.

Application procedures. Admission: No deadline. $25 fee. **Financial aid:** No deadline. FAFSA required. Applicants notified on a rolling basis.

Academics. Credit/placement by examination: AP, CLEP. **Support services:** Learning center, remedial instruction, study skills assistance, tutoring.

Majors. Business: Business admin. **Health services:** Health information technology, medical assistant, office assistant. **Protective services:** Criminal justice.

Technology on campus. Online library available.

Student life. Freshman orientation: Mandatory. Preregistration for classes offered. **Activities:** Student newspaper.

Student services. Career counseling, financial aid counseling, placement for graduates.

Contact. E-mail: infodesk@sbbcollege.edu
Phone: (866) 749-7222 Fax: (805) 339-2994
Tamu Smith-Kohls, Director of Admissions, Santa Barbara Business College: Ventura, 4839 Market Street, Ventura, CA 93003

Santa Barbara City College
Santa Barbara, California
www.sbcc.edu CB code: 4690

▶ Public 2-year community college
▶ Commuter campus in small city

General. Founded in 1908. Regionally accredited. **Enrollment:** 13,699 degree-seeking undergraduates. **Degrees:** 1,854 associate awarded. **Location:** 90 miles from Los Angeles. **Calendar:** Semester, limited summer session. **Full-time faculty:** 254 total; 22% minority. **Part-time faculty:** 1,009 total; 10% minority. **Class size:** 19% < 20, 62% 20-39, 12% 40-49, 5% 50-99, 3% >100.

Student profile.

Out-of-state: 6% 25 or older: 29%

Transfer out. Colleges most students transferred to 2015: University of California: Santa Barbara, California State University: Northridge, San Francisco State University, San Diego State University, University of California: Los Angeles.

Basis for selection. Open admission, but selective for some programs. Special requirements for hotel/restaurant/culinary, nursing, radiography, early childhood education, cosmetology, marine diving technology programs. Criteria vary by program. Interview required of nursing, hotel and restaurant management, marine technology majors. Audition required of some music and theater majors. **Adult students:** English assessment test required for placement.

2015-2016 Annual costs. Tuition/fees: $1,478; $9,458 out-of-state. Per-credit charge: $46 in-state; $312 out-of-state. Books/supplies: $1,746. Personal expenses: $3,132.

Financial aid. Need-based: Need-based aid available for part-time students. Work-study available nights, weekends and for part-time students. **Additional information:** California residents may qualify for Board of Governor's Financial Assistance Program, which will allow institutions to waive enrollment fee.

Application procedures. Admission: Priority date 2/1; deadline 8/19 (receipt date). No application fee. Admission notification on a rolling basis beginning on or about 3/1. **Financial aid:** No deadline. FAFSA required. Applicants notified on a rolling basis starting 5/1; must reply within 2 week(s) of notification.

Academics. Special study options: Cooperative education, cross-registration, distance learning, double major, dual enrollment of high school students, ESL, honors, independent study, internships, study abroad. License preparation in nursing, paramedic, radiology, real estate. **Credit/placement by examination:** AP, CLEP, IB, institutional tests. 12 credit hours maximum toward associate degree. **Support services:** Learning center, pre-admission summer program, reduced course load, remedial instruction, study skills assistance, tutoring, writing center.

Majors. Area/ethnic studies: African-American, Chicano/Hispanic-American/Latino, Native American. **Biology:** General. **Business:** General, accounting, accounting technology, administrative services, banking/financial services, business admin, finance, hospitality/recreation, international, marketing, office management, real estate, sales/distribution, selling, small business admin. **Communications:** Communications/speech/rhetoric, digital media. **Communications technology:** General, computer typography. **Computer sciences:** General, computer science, data processing. **Conservation:** Environmental studies. **Education:** Early childhood, kindergarten/preschool, physical. **Engineering:** General, computer, marine. **English:** English lit, rhetoric/composition. **Foreign languages:** French, Spanish. **Health services:** Athletic training, licensed practical nurse, medical radiologic technology/radiation therapy, nursing (RN), recreational therapy, sonography, substance abuse counseling. **History:** General. **Human services:** General. **Liberal arts:** Arts/sciences. **Math:** General. **Parks/recreation:** General, exercise sciences, health/fitness. **Philosophy/religion:** Philosophy. **Physical sciences:** Chemistry, geology, physics. **Protective services:** Law enforcement admin. **Psychology:** General. **Social sciences:** Anthropology, economics, geography, political science, sociology. **Visual/performing arts:** Art, art history/conservation, commercial/advertising art, dramatic, film/cinema/video, interior design, multimedia, music, studio arts, theater design. **Work/family studies:** Child care management, institutional food production.

Most popular majors. English 7%, health sciences 12%, interdisciplinary studies 10%, liberal arts 40%, social sciences 8%.

Technology on campus. 1,340 workstations in library, computer center, student center. Commuter students can connect to campus network. Online library, helpline, wireless network available.

Student life. Freshman orientation: Mandatory. Preregistration for classes offered. 2-hour on-campus or on-line orientation. **Activities:** Bands, choral groups, dance, drama, literary magazine, music ensembles, musical theater, student government, student newspaper, symphony orchestra, Black Student Union, College Republicans, EOPS, Hillel Club, Latter Day Saint Student Association, Phi Theta Kappa, Shodo Japanese Calligraphy Club, Special Abilities Club, Students Left Alliance Party, Student Sustainability Club, Vaquero Christian Fellowship.

Athletics. Intercollegiate: Baseball M, basketball, cross-country, football (tackle) M, golf, soccer, softball W, tennis, track and field, volleyball. **Team name:** Vaqueros.

Student services. Adult student services, alcohol/substance abuse counseling, career counseling, services for economically disadvantaged, student employment services, financial aid counseling, health services, minority student services, on-campus daycare, personal counseling, placement for graduates, veterans' counselor, women's services. **Physically disabled:** Services for visually, speech, hearing impaired. **Transfer:** Transfer center, transfer adviser, college fairs on campus for students transferring to 4-year colleges.

Contact. E-mail: admissions@sbcc.edu
Phone: (805) 965-0581 ext. 2200 Fax: (805) 963-7222
Allison Curtis, Director of Admissions and Records, Santa Barbara City College, 721 Cliff Drive, Santa Barbara, CA 93109-2394

Santa Monica College
Santa Monica, California
www.smc.edu

CB member
CB code: 4691

◆ Public 2-year community college
◆ Commuter campus in small city

General. Founded in 1929. Regionally accredited. Off-campus program at Santa Monica College of Design. **Enrollment:** 24,770 degree-seeking undergraduates. **Degrees:** 2,221 associate awarded. **Location:** 18 miles from Los Angeles. **Calendar:** Semester, extensive summer session. **Full-time faculty:** 318 total; 32% minority, 58% women. **Part-time faculty:** 1,114 total; 22% minority, 54% women. **Special facilities:** Planetarium, photo gallery, humanities center, entertainment technology academy, digital learning studio, small business development center. **Partnerships:** Formal partnerships with DreamWorks, Disney Channel, Sony, 20th Century Fox, and other entertainment industry leaders (for Academy of Entertainment Technology students).

Transfer out. Colleges most students transferred to 2015: University of California at Los Angeles, California State University-Northridge, University of Southern California.

Basis for selection. Open admission, but selective for some programs. Music, theater arts, entertainment technology programs are competitive with various requirements. Nursing program has course requirements for admission. Audition and portfolio required for music, theater arts.

2015-2016 Annual costs. Tuition/fees: $1,444; $10,114 out-of-state. Per-credit charge: $46 in-state; $335 out-of-state. Books/supplies: $1,650. Personal expenses: $2,862.

Financial aid. Need-based: Need-based aid available for part-time students. Work-study available nights, weekends and for part-time students.

Application procedures. Admission: No deadline. No application fee. Admission notification on a rolling basis. **Financial aid:** No deadline. FAFSA, institutional form required. Applicants notified on a rolling basis starting 7/1; must reply within 2 week(s) of notification.

Academics. Special study options: Accelerated study, cooperative education, distance learning, dual enrollment of high school students, ESL, honors, independent study, internships, study abroad, weekend college. License preparation in nursing. **Credit/placement by examination:** AP, CLEP, institutional tests. 30 credit hours maximum toward associate degree. Math and English placement tests required for some students. **Support services:** Learning center, pre-admission summer program, remedial instruction, study skills assistance, tutoring, writing center.

Majors. Area/ethnic studies: General, women's. **Business:** Accounting, administrative services, business admin, insurance, logistics, selling. **Communications:** Digital media, journalism, radio/TV. **Communications technology:** General, animation/special effects. **Computer sciences:** Computer science, data entry, database management, programming. **Conservation:** Environmental science, environmental studies. **Education:** Early childhood special. **Health services:** Medical assistant, medical secretary, respiratory therapy technology. **Liberal arts:** Arts/sciences, humanities. **Math:** General. **Parks/recreation:** Health/fitness. **Visual/performing arts:** Art, commercial photography, dance, dramatic, fashion design, film/cinema/video, graphic design, interior design, music, photography. **Work/family studies:** Apparel marketing, child development.

Technology on campus. 600 workstations in library, computer center, student center. Commuter students can connect to campus network. Helpline available.

Student life. Freshman orientation: Mandatory. Preregistration for classes offered. **Activities:** Concert band, choral groups, dance, drama, literary magazine, music ensembles, musical theater, opera, radio station, student government, student newspaper.

Athletics. NJCAA. Intercollegiate: Basketball, cross-country M, diving, football (tackle) M, swimming, tennis, track and field, volleyball, water polo M. **Intramural:** Badminton. **Team name:** Corsairs.

Student services. Adult student services, career counseling, services for economically disadvantaged, student employment services, financial aid counseling, health services, minority student services, on-campus daycare, personal counseling, placement for graduates, veterans' counselor. **Physically disabled:** Services for visually, speech, hearing impaired. **Transfer:** Transfer center, transfer adviser, college fairs on campus for students transferring to 4-year colleges.

Contact. E-mail: Admissions@smc.edu
Phone: (310) 434-4380 Fax: (310) 434-3645
Esau Tovar, Dean, Enrollment Services, Santa Monica College, 1900 Pico Boulevard, Santa Monica, CA 90405-1628

Santa Rosa Junior College
Santa Rosa, California
www.santarosa.edu

CB code: 4692

◆ Public 2-year community college
◆ Commuter campus in small city

General. Founded in 1918. Regionally accredited. **Enrollment:** 12,640 degree-seeking undergraduates. **Degrees:** 1,865 associate awarded. **Location:** 55 miles from San Francisco. **Calendar:** Semester, extensive summer session. **Full-time faculty:** 279 total; 18% have terminal degrees, 18% minority, 58% women. **Part-time faculty:** 909 total; 10% have terminal degrees, 10% minority, 61% women. **Class size:** 19% < 20, 66% 20-39, 11% 40-49, 4% 50-99, less than 1% >100. **Special facilities:** Native American art museum, college farm, summer repertory theater, planetarium, culinary cafe.

Transfer out. Colleges most students transferred to 2015: Sonoma State University, San Francisco State University, University of California: Davis, California State University: Sacramento, University of California: Berkeley.

Basis for selection. Open admission, but selective for some programs. Audition recommended of music and theater performance courses, some physical education, some communications majors.

2015-2016 Annual costs. Tuition/fees: $1,420; $7,330 out-of-state. Per-credit charge: $46 in-state; $243 out-of-state. Books/supplies: $1,710. Personal expenses: $3,096.

Financial aid. Need-based: Need-based aid available for part-time students. Work-study available nights, weekends and for part-time students. **Non-need-based:** Scholarships awarded for academics, art, leadership, music/drama, state residency. **Additional information:** California's Board of Governors Program provides fee waivers for applicants with need.

Application procedures. Admission: No deadline. No application fee. **Financial aid:** Priority date 3/1; no closing date. FAFSA required. Applicants notified on a rolling basis starting 4/15.

Academics. Special study options: Cooperative education, cross-registration, distance learning, double major, dual enrollment of high school students, ESL, independent study, internships, liberal arts/career combination, study abroad, weekend college. License preparation in dental hygiene, nursing, paramedic, radiology, real estate. **Credit/placement by examination:** AP, CLEP, IB, institutional tests. 15 credit hours maximum toward associate degree. Credit will be granted to any student who satisfactorily passes an exam approved or conducted by proper authorities of the college. Such credit may be granted only to a student who is registered at the college and in good standing and only for a course listed in the College catalog. **Support services:** GED preparation and test center, learning center, pre-admission summer program, reduced course load, remedial instruction, study skills assistance, tutoring.

Majors. Area/ethnic studies: Latin American. **Biology:** General, physiology. **Business:** Business admin. **Computer sciences:** Computer science. **Conservation:** General, environmental studies. **Education:** General, early childhood. **Engineering:** General. **English:** English lit. **Foreign languages:** American Sign Language, Spanish. **Health services:** Dental assistant, dental hygiene, EMT paramedic, licensed practical nurse, medical radiologic technology/radiation therapy, mental health services, nursing (RN), nursing assistant, pharmacy assistant. **History:** General. **Liberal arts:** Arts/sciences. **Math:** General. **Parks/recreation:** General. **Philosophy/religion:** Philosophy. **Physical sciences:** Chemistry, physics. **Protective services:** Firefighting, police science. **Psychology:** General. **Social sciences:** Anthropology, economics, geography, political science, sociology. **Visual/performing arts:** Art, commercial/advertising art, dramatic, fashion design.

Most popular majors. Health sciences 16%, interdisciplinary studies 29%, security/protective services 6%, social sciences 29%.

Technology on campus. 1,900 workstations in library, computer center. Commuter students can connect to campus network. Online course registration, wireless network available.

Student life. Freshman orientation: Available. Preregistration for classes offered. Held year round as a drop-in program. Online program also available. **Activities:** Jazz band, choral groups, dance, drama, film society, international student organizations, music ensembles, musical theater, student government, student newspaper, symphony orchestra.

Athletics. NJCAA. **Intercollegiate:** Badminton W, baseball M, basketball, cross-country, diving, football (tackle) M, golf M, soccer, softball W, swimming, tennis, track and field, volleyball W, water polo, wrestling M. **Team name:** Bear Cubs.

Student services. Adult student services, alcohol/substance abuse counseling, career counseling, services for economically disadvantaged, student employment services, financial aid counseling, health services, on-campus daycare, personal counseling, placement for graduates, veterans' counselor. **Physically disabled:** Services for visually, speech, hearing impaired. **Transfer:** Re-entry adviser for new students. Transfer center, transfer adviser, college fairs on campus for students transferring to 4-year colleges.

Contact. E-mail: admininfo@santarosa.edu
Phone: (707) 527-4685 Toll-free number: (800) 564-7752
Fax: (707) 527-4798
Freyja Pereira, Director, Admissions , Records & Enrollment Devleopment, Santa Rosa Junior College, 1501 Mendocino Avenue, Santa Rosa, CA 95401-4395

Santiago Canyon College
Orange, California
www.sccollege.edu   **CB code: 2830**

♦ Public 2-year community college
♦ Commuter campus in small city

General. Regionally accredited. **Enrollment:** 4,662 degree-seeking undergraduates. **Degrees:** 1,694 associate awarded. **Location:** 30 miles from Los Angeles. **Calendar:** Semester, extensive summer session. **Full-time faculty:** 108 total; 33% minority. **Part-time faculty:** 288 total; 33% minority. **Class size:** 13% < 20, 58% 20-39, 19% 40-49, 8% 50-99, 1% >100.

Transfer out. Colleges most students transferred to 2015: California State University: Fullerton, University of California: Irvine, Chapman University, California State University: Long Beach, University of Phoenix.

Basis for selection. Open admission. **Adult students:** SAT/ACT scores not required. Placement tests for English, math, reading, and chemistry. **Home schooled:** Statement describing home school structure and mission required. Must show private school affidavit confirmation from the California Department of Education.

2015-2016 Annual costs. Tuition/fees: $1,418; $8,018 out-of-state. Per-credit charge: $46 in-state; $266 out-of-state. Books/supplies: $1,710. Personal expenses: $3,096.

Financial aid. All financial aid based on need. Need-based aid available for part-time students. Work-study available nights, weekends and for part-time students.

Application procedures. Admission: No application fee. **Financial aid:** Priority date 7/1; no closing date. FAFSA, institutional form required. Applicants notified on a rolling basis starting 6/1.

Academics. Special study options: Accelerated study, cooperative education, distance learning, double major, dual enrollment of high school students, ESL, honors, weekend college. License preparation in real estate. **Credit/placement by examination:** AP, CLEP, institutional tests. **Support services:** GED preparation and test center, learning center, remedial instruction, study skills assistance, tutoring, writing center.

Majors. Biology: General. **Business:** Accounting, business admin, managerial economics, marketing, selling, tourism/travel. **Communications:** Communications/speech/rhetoric. **Communications technology:** Graphics, photo/film/video. **Computer sciences:** Computer science, information systems, web page design. **Engineering:** General. **English:** English lit, rhetoric/

composition. **Foreign languages:** General, American Sign Language, French, Italian, Spanish. **General:** Carpentry, electrician. **Health services:** Medical assistant. **History:** General. **Liberal arts:** Arts/sciences, library assistant. **Math:** General. **Philosophy/religion:** Philosophy. **Physical sciences:** Chemistry, geology, hydrology, physics. **Protective services:** Fire safety technology. **Psychology:** General. **Social sciences:** General, anthropology, economics, geography, political science, sociology. **Visual/performing arts:** Art, commercial/advertising art, crafts, dance, fashion design, metal/jewelry, music. **Work/family studies:** General.

Most popular majors. Business/marketing 7%, liberal arts 74%.

Technology on campus. Online course registration, wireless network available.

Student life. Freshman orientation: Available. Preregistration for classes offered. **Activities:** Bands, choral groups, dance, drama, music ensembles, student government, student newspaper, TV station.

Athletics. Intercollegiate: Cross-country, golf, soccer, track and field. **Intramural:** Softball, track and field. **Team name:** Hawks. .

Student services. Adult student services, alcohol/substance abuse counseling, career counseling, services for economically disadvantaged, student employment services, financial aid counseling, health services, minority student services, on-campus daycare, personal counseling, veterans' counselor, women's services. **Physically disabled:** Services for visually, speech, hearing impaired. **Transfer:** Re-entry adviser, pre-admission transcript evaluation for new students. Transfer center, transfer adviser, college fairs on campus for students transferring to 4-year colleges.

Contact. E-mail: admissions@sccollege.edu
Phone: (714) 628-4901 Fax: (714) 628-4723
Linda Miskovic, Associate Dean of Admissions, Santiago Canyon College, 8045 East Chapman Avenue, Orange, CA 92869

Shasta College
Redding, California
www.shastacollege.edu   **CB code: 4696**

♦ Public 2-year community and junior college
♦ Commuter campus in small city

General. Founded in 1948. Regionally accredited. **Enrollment:** 6,056 degree-seeking undergraduates. **Degrees:** 583 associate awarded. **Location:** 160 miles from Sacramento. **Calendar:** Semester, extensive summer session. **Full-time faculty:** 141 total; 10% minority. **Part-time faculty:** 275 total; 8% minority. **Class size:** 41% < 20, 53% 20-39, 3% 40-49, 2% 50-99, less than 1% >100. **Special facilities:** Early childhood education center lab school, college farm.

Student profile.

Out-of-state:	1%	Live on campus:	1%
25 or older:	49%		

Transfer out. Colleges most students transferred to 2015: California State University: Chico, California State University: Sacramento, Humboldt State University, Simpson University, National University.

Basis for selection. Open admission, but selective for some programs. Applicants to the nursing and dental hygiene programs must have a high school diploma and complete a series of courses as outlined in college catalog. In addition, nursing program applicants must take the National League for Nursing examination.

2015-2016 Annual costs. Tuition/fees: $1,418; $7,718 out-of-state. Per-credit charge: $46 in-state; $256 out-of-state. Books/supplies: $1,746. Personal expenses: $3,134.

Financial aid. All financial aid based on need. Need-based aid available for part-time students. Work-study available nights, weekends and for part-time students.

Application procedures. Admission: No deadline. No application fee. Admission notification on a rolling basis. **Financial aid:** Priority date 3/2; no closing date. FAFSA, institutional form required. Applicants notified on a rolling basis starting 7/1.

Academics. On-campus programs leading to bachelor's degree from California State University: Chico offered. **Special study options:** Cooperative education, distance learning, double major, dual enrollment of high school students, ESL, honors, independent study, internships, liberal arts/career combination, study abroad, weekend college. Bachelor's degree programs available on campus. License preparation in dental hygiene, nursing, paramedic, real estate. **Credit/placement by examination:** AP, CLEP, institutional tests. 12 credit hours maximum toward associate degree. **Support services:** GED preparation, learning center, reduced course load, remedial instruction, study skills assistance, tutoring, writing center.

Majors. Biology: General. **Business:** General, accounting, administrative services, business admin, entrepreneurial studies, executive assistant, hotel/motel admin, management information systems, office management, office technology, office/clerical, restaurant/food services, sales/distribution. **Communications:** Communications/speech/rhetoric, journalism. **Computer sciences:** General, data processing, networking. **Education:** Early childhood, elementary, science. **Engineering:** General. **Foreign languages:** General. **Health services:** Dental hygiene, EMT paramedic, nursing (RN). **Liberal arts:** Humanities. **Math:** General. **Parks/recreation:** Health/fitness. **Physical sciences:** General, atmospheric science, climatology, geology, oceanography. **Protective services:** Criminal justice, fire safety technology, fire services admin, firefighting, law enforcement admin, police science. **Social sciences:** General. **Visual/performing arts:** Art, commercial/advertising art, dramatic, music, studio arts. **Work/family studies:** General, child care management, child development, family studies, institutional food production.

Most popular majors. Business/marketing 8%, health sciences 11%, liberal arts 56%.

Technology on campus. 191 workstations in library, computer center. Dormitories wired for high-speed internet access and linked to campus network. Commuter students can connect to campus network. Online course registration, online library, helpline, wireless network available.

Student life. Freshman orientation: Mandatory. Preregistration for classes offered. **Housing:** Single-sex dorms available. **Activities:** Bands, choral groups, dance, drama, international student organizations, music ensembles, musical theater, student government, student newspaper, symphony orchestra, Agriculture/Natural Resources Leaders Club, Amigos Unidos Club, Early Childhood Educators Network, Intercultural Club, Intervarsity Christian Fellowship, NATIVE (Native American Tradition in Valued Education) Club, Rotaract, science club, sustainability club, Veterans Organization.

Athletics. NJCAA. **Intercollegiate:** Baseball M, basketball, cross-country, football (tackle) M, golf M, soccer, softball W, swimming, tennis, track and field, volleyball W, wrestling M. **Team name:** Knights.

Student services. Career counseling, services for economically disadvantaged, student employment services, financial aid counseling, health services, on-campus daycare, personal counseling, veterans' counselor. **Physically disabled:** Services for visually, speech, hearing impaired. **Transfer:** Transfer center, transfer adviser, college fairs on campus for students transferring to 4-year colleges.

Contact. E-mail: Admissions@shastacollege.edu
Phone: (530) 242-7650 Fax: (530) 225-4995
Kevin O'Rorke, Dean, Enrollment Services, Shasta College, Box 496006, Redding, CA 96049-6006

Sierra College
Rocklin, California
www.sierracollege.edu
CB code: 4697

- Public 2-year community college
- Commuter campus in small city

General. Founded in 1914. Regionally accredited. **Enrollment:** 13,800 degree-seeking undergraduates. **Degrees:** 2,544 associate awarded. **Location:** 25 miles from Sacramento. **Calendar:** Semester, extensive summer session. **Full-time faculty:** 224 total. **Part-time faculty:** 665 total. **Special facilities:** Nature trail, planetarium, science museum displays, learning resource center, cross-country trail.

Student profile.

Out-of-state: 1% Live on campus: 1%

Transfer out. Colleges most students transferred to 2015: California State University: Sacramento, University of California: Davis, California State University: Chico, University of California: Berkeley, San Francisco State University.

Basis for selection. Open admission, but selective for some programs. **Adult students:** SAT/ACT scores not required.

2015-2016 Annual costs. Tuition/fees: $1,428; $7,428 out-of-state. Per-credit charge: $46 in-state; $245 out-of-state. Room/board: $7,400. Books/supplies: $2,224. Personal expenses: $3,096.

Financial aid. Need-based: Need-based aid available for part-time students. Work-study available nights, weekends and for part-time students.

Application procedures. Admission: No deadline. No application fee. Application must be submitted online. Applicants notified within 4 working days. **Financial aid:** Priority date 3/2; no closing date. FAFSA required. Applicants notified on a rolling basis starting 5/15.

Academics. Special study options: Cross-registration, distance learning, double major, dual enrollment of high school students, ESL, honors, independent study, internships, study abroad, weekend college. License preparation in nursing, real estate. **Credit/placement by examination:** AP, CLEP, institutional tests. 15 credit hours maximum toward associate degree. **Support services:** Learning center, pre-admission summer program, remedial instruction, study skills assistance, tutoring, writing center.

Majors. Area/ethnic studies: Deaf, women's. **Biology:** General. **Business:** General, accounting, administrative services, apparel, business admin, real estate, sales/distribution, small business admin. **Communications:** Digital media. **Computer sciences:** Data entry, information technology, networking, programming, system admin, web page design, webmaster. **Conservation:** Environmental studies. **Education:** Early childhood. **Engineering:** General. **English:** English lit, rhetoric/composition. **Foreign languages:** American Sign Language. **General:** Carpentry. **Health services:** Nursing (RN). **History:** General. **Liberal arts:** Arts/sciences, library assistant. **Math:** General. **Parks/recreation:** General, health/fitness. **Philosophy/religion:** Philosophy. **Physical sciences:** Chemistry, geology, physics. **Protective services:** Criminal justice, fire safety technology, firefighting, police science, security services. **Psychology:** General. **Social sciences:** General. **Visual/performing arts:** Art, dramatic, music performance, photography, studio arts. **Work/family studies:** General, child care management.

Most popular majors. Business/marketing 11%, liberal arts 44%, security/protective services 6%, social sciences 8%.

Technology on campus. 300 workstations in dormitories, library, computer center. Dormitories wired for high-speed internet access and linked to campus network. Commuter students can connect to campus network. Online course registration, online library, helpline, wireless network available.

Student life. Freshman orientation: Mandatory. Preregistration for classes offered. **Housing:** Coed dorms available. $250 fully refundable deposit. **Activities:** Concert band, choral groups, drama, international student organizations, music ensembles, student government, student newspaper, symphony orchestra, Persian Cultural Club, Rainbow Alliance, Contemporary Arts Club, Veteran Students Alliance, Environmentally Concerned Students, Freethinkers, Intervarsity Christian Fellowship, Law Club, Circle K International.

Athletics. Intercollegiate: Baseball M, basketball, cross-country W, diving, football (tackle) M, golf, soccer W, softball W, swimming, tennis, volleyball W, water polo W, wrestling M. **Intramural:** Archery, badminton, basketball, cheerleading W, football (non-tackle), golf, softball, tennis, volleyball. **Team name:** Wolverines.

Student services. Adult student services, alcohol/substance abuse counseling, career counseling, services for economically disadvantaged, student employment services, financial aid counseling, health services, on-campus daycare, personal counseling, veterans' counselor. **Physically disabled:** Services for visually, speech, hearing impaired. **Transfer:** Pre-admission transcript evaluation for new students. Transfer center, transfer adviser, college fairs on campus for students transferring to 4-year colleges.

Contact. Phone: (916) 660-7340 Toll-free number: (800) 242-4004
Fax: (916) 630-4500
Gail Modder, Admissions and Records Program Manager, Sierra College, 5000 Rocklin Road, Rocklin, CA 95677-3397

Skyline College
San Bruno, California
www.skylinecollege.edu
CB code: 4746

- Public 2-year community college
- Commuter campus in small city

General. Founded in 1969. Regionally accredited. **Enrollment:** 6,945 degree-seeking undergraduates. **Degrees:** 832 associate awarded. **Location:** 15 miles from San Francisco. **Calendar:** Semester, limited summer session. **Full-time faculty:** 143 total. **Part-time faculty:** 222 total.

Student profile.

Out-of-state: 2% **25 or older:** 24%

Transfer out. Colleges most students transferred to 2015: San Francisco State University, San Jose State University, California State University: East Bay, UC Berkeley, UC Davis.

Basis for selection. Open admission, but selective for some programs. Supplemental application must be submitted to automotive technology, cosmetology, and respiratory therapy programs. Selection is made by the department. Concurrent enrollment students must submit a high school permission form. SAT/ACT may be substituted for institutional placement tests. Interview required of respiratory therapy majors. Essay required of full-time international student applicants. **Adult students:** Assessment test required to determine placement for math and English courses. **Home schooled:** State high school equivalency certificate required. **Learning Disabled:** Students may request a skills assessment for best placement in courses.

High school preparation. College-preparatory program recommended.

2015-2016 Annual costs. Tuition/fees: $1,446; $8,076 out-of-state. Per-credit charge: $46 in-state; $267 out-of-state. Books/supplies: $1,764. Personal expenses: $3,159.

Financial aid. Need-based: Need-based aid available for part-time students. Work-study available nights, weekends and for part-time students.

Application procedures. Admission: No deadline. No application fee. Application must be submitted online. Admission notification on a rolling basis. **Financial aid:** Priority date 5/2; no closing date. FAFSA, institutional form required. Applicants notified on a rolling basis starting 5/1; must reply within 2 week(s) of notification.

Academics. Special study options: Accelerated study, cooperative education, cross-registration, distance learning, double major, dual enrollment of high school students, ESL, honors, independent study, internships, liberal arts/career combination, study abroad, weekend college. License preparation in paramedic, real estate. **Credit/placement by examination:** AP, CLEP, institutional tests. 12 credit hours maximum toward associate degree. **Support services:** Learning center, remedial instruction, study skills assistance, tutoring, writing center.

Majors. Area/ethnic studies: Asian. **Business:** Accounting, administrative services, business admin, hospitality admin, management information systems, office/clerical. **Communications:** General, journalism. **Communications technology:** General. **Computer sciences:** General, computer science, data processing, information systems, webmaster. **Education:** Early childhood. **English:** English lit, rhetoric/composition. **Foreign languages:** Spanish. **Health services:** Medical secretary, medical transcription, respiratory therapy technology, surgical technology. **Liberal arts:** Arts/sciences. **Math:** General. **Parks/recreation:** Exercise sciences, health/fitness. **Physical sciences:** Physics. **Protective services:** Law enforcement admin. **Psychology:** General. **Visual/performing arts:** General, art, dance, music. **Work/family studies:** General, business.

Most popular majors. Business/marketing 12%, health sciences 13%, interdisciplinary studies 12%, liberal arts 28%, psychology 10%.

Technology on campus. 220 workstations in library, computer center, student center. Online course registration, online library, helpline, repair service, wireless network available.

Student life. Freshman orientation: Available. Preregistration for classes offered. **Activities:** Bands, choral groups, dance, drama, student government, student newspaper.

Athletics. NJCAA. **Intercollegiate:** Badminton W, baseball M, basketball, soccer, volleyball W, wrestling M. **Team name:** Trojans.

Student services. Adult student services, career counseling, services for economically disadvantaged, student employment services, financial aid counseling, health services, minority student services, on-campus daycare, personal counseling, veterans' counselor, women's services. **Physically disabled:** Services for visually, speech, hearing impaired. **Transfer:** Transfer center, transfer adviser, college fairs on campus for students transferring to 4-year colleges.

Contact. E-mail: skyadmissions@smccd.edu
Phone: (650) 738-4251 Fax: (650) 738-4200
William Minnich, Dean of Enrollment Services, Skyline College, 3300 College Drive, San Bruno, CA 94066-1662

Solano Community College
Fairfield, California
www.solano.edu
CB code: 4930

- Public 2-year community college
- Commuter campus in small city

General. Founded in 1945. Regionally accredited. Additional campus centers in Vacaville, Vallejo, and Travis Air Force Base. **Enrollment:** 6,101 degree-seeking undergraduates. **Degrees:** 1,356 associate awarded. **ROTC:** Air Force. **Location:** 11 miles from Vallejo. **Calendar:** Semester, extensive summer session. **Full-time faculty:** 161 total. **Part-time faculty:** 305 total. **Partnerships:** Formal partnership with Workforce Investment Board of Solano County.

Basis for selection. Open admission, but selective for some programs. Special requirements for nursing program.

2015-2016 Annual costs. Tuition/fees: $1,406; $7,376 out-of-state. Per-credit charge: $46 in-state; $245 out-of-state. Books/supplies: $1,656. Personal expenses: $3,114.

Financial aid. Need-based: Work-study available nights, weekends and for part-time students.

Application procedures. Admission: No deadline. No application fee. Admission notification on a rolling basis. **Financial aid:** Priority date 3/1; no closing date. FAFSA required. Applicants notified on a rolling basis starting 7/1.

Academics. Special study options: Cooperative education, cross-registration, distance learning, double major, dual enrollment of high school students, ESL, honors, independent study, internships, liberal arts/career combination, weekend college. License preparation in nursing, real estate. **Credit/placement by examination:** AP, CLEP, institutional tests. 15 credit hours maximum toward associate degree. Credit-by-examination available for some non-remedial courses, as identified by the appropriate academic division. Credit granted may not exceed the amount listed for the specific course in the college catalog. **Support services:** Learning center, pre-admission summer program, reduced course load, remedial instruction, study skills assistance, tutoring, writing center.

Majors. Area/ethnic studies: African-American, Asian-American, Chicano/Hispanic-American/Latino, Native American. **Biology:** General. **Business:** Accounting, administrative services, banking/financial services, business admin, office management, real estate. **Communications:** Communications/speech/rhetoric, journalism. **Computer sciences:** General, programming. **Education:** Early childhood. **English:** English lit. **Foreign languages:** General, French, German, Spanish. **Health services:** Medical secretary, nursing (RN). **History:** General. **Liberal arts:** Arts/sciences. **Math:** General. **Parks/recreation:** Health/fitness, sports admin. **Physical sciences:** Chemistry, physics. **Protective services:** Firefighting, police science. **Psychology:** General. **Social sciences:** General, international relations, political science. **Visual/performing arts:** Commercial photography, commercial/advertising art, dramatic, drawing, interior design, music, painting, sculpture, studio arts. **Work/family studies:** General.

Technology on campus. 240 workstations in library, computer center, student center. Commuter students can connect to campus network. Online course registration, helpline, wireless network available.

Student life. Freshman orientation: Available. Preregistration for classes offered. **Policies:** Mandatory attendance at first meeting of class each semester for enrollment verification; failure to appear may result in withdrawal from class. Regular attendance and participation is required of all students. **Activities:** Bands, choral groups, dance, drama, international student organizations, literary magazine, music ensembles, musical theater, radio station, student government, student newspaper, symphony orchestra, Black Student Union, women's change, veterans organization, Sierra club, student nurses, Filipino club, Democratic club, Mathematics, Engineering & Science Achievement club, Asian-Pacific Islander club.

Athletics. Intercollegiate: Baseball M, basketball, diving, soccer W, softball W, swimming, volleyball W. **Team name:** Falcons.

Student services. Career counseling, student employment services, financial aid counseling, health services, on-campus daycare, personal counseling, placement for graduates, veterans' counselor. **Physically disabled:** Services for visually, speech, hearing impaired. **Transfer:** Transfer center for students transferring to 4-year colleges.

Contact. E-mail: admissions@solano.edu
Phone: (707) 864-7171 Fax: (707) 646-2053
Barbara Fountain, Associate Dean of Admissions, Assessment & Scheduling, Solano Community College, 4000 Suisun Valley Road, Fairfield, CA 94534-3197

South Coast College
Orange, California
www.southcoastcollege.com

- For-profit 2-year business and career college
- Small city

Two-Year Colleges

General. Accredited by ACICS. **Enrollment:** 342 undergraduates. **Degrees:** 39 associate awarded. **Location:** 20 miles from Los Angeles. **Calendar:** Quarter, extensive summer session. **Full-time faculty:** 4 total. **Part-time faculty:** 24 total. **Special facilities:** Computer training center.

Basis for selection. Open admission, but selective for some programs.

2015-2016 Annual costs. Tuition/fees: $10,569. Books/supplies: $700. Personal expenses: $3,105. **Additional information:** Certificate programs-Legal Administrative Assistant/Secretary - $10,524, Books and supplies, $1000, Medical/Clinical Assistant - $10,459, Books and supplies $550. Associates degree programs - Court Reporting - $52,849, Books and supplies $2211. Realtime: Steno-Interpreting - 39,150, Books and supplies $1811. Legal Assistant/Paralegal - $21,124, Books and supplies, $3,000.

Financial aid. **Need-based:** Work-study available nights, weekends and for part-time students.

Application procedures. **Admission:** Closing date 3/31. $99 fee.

Academics. **Special study options:** Bachelor's degree programs available on campus. **Credit/placement by examination:** AP, CLEP.

Majors. **Health services:** Medical transcription.

Contact. E-mail: requestinfo@southcoastcollege.com
Phone: (714) 867-5009 Toll-free number: (800) 337-8366
Kevin Magner, Dean of Admissions and Marketing, South Coast College, 2011 West Chapman Avenue, Orange, CA 92868

Southwestern College
Chula Vista, California
www.swccd.edu

CB member
CB code: 4726

- Public 2-year community college
- Commuter campus in small city

General. Founded in 1961. Regionally accredited. Medical occupation programs accredited by the National League for Nursing Accrediting Commission Inc. (NLNAC). **Enrollment:** 11,472 degree-seeking undergraduates. **Degrees:** 1,298 associate awarded. **Location:** 10 miles from San Diego. **Calendar:** Semester, extensive summer session. **Full-time faculty:** 249 total. **Part-time faculty:** 689 total. **Class size:** 36% < 20, 49% 20-39, 13% 40-49, 3% 50-99.

Transfer out. Colleges most students transferred to 2015: San Diego State University, University of California: San Diego.

Basis for selection. Open admission, but selective for some programs. Limited admission to nursing and dental hygiene programs.

2015-2016 Annual costs. Tuition/fees: $1,428; $7,218 out-of-state. Per-credit charge: $46 in-state; $239 out-of-state. Books/supplies: $1,710. Personal expenses: $3,096.

Financial aid. **Need-based:** Need-based aid available for part-time students. Work-study available nights, weekends and for part-time students.

Application procedures. **Admission:** No deadline. No application fee. Admission notification on a rolling basis. **Financial aid:** No deadline. FAFSA required. Applicants notified on a rolling basis starting 7/1.

Academics. Broad offerings of online and traditional courses. Online credit and non-credit courses available. **Special study options:** Cooperative education, cross-registration, distance learning, double major, dual enrollment of high school students, ESL, honors, independent study, internships, study abroad, weekend college. License preparation in dental hygiene, nursing, paramedic, real estate. **Credit/placement by examination:** AP, CLEP, IB, institutional tests. 15 credit hours maximum toward associate degree. In-house placement test required for some. **Support services:** Learning center, pre-admission summer program, remedial instruction, study skills assistance, tutoring, writing center.

Majors. **Architecture:** Landscape, technology. **Area/ethnic studies:** African-American, American, Asian-American, Chicano/Hispanic-American/Latino, women's. **Biology:** General, biotechnology. **Business:** Accounting, business admin, construction management, entrepreneurial studies, finance, financial planning, international, market research, office management, office/clerical, real estate, tourism promotion, tourism/travel. **Communications:** Broadcast journalism, communications/speech/rhetoric, journalism. **Communications technology:** General, radio/TV, recording arts. **Computer sciences:** General, applications programming, computer science, information systems, information technology, networking, programming, web page

design, webmaster. **Conservation:** Environmental studies. **Education:** General, early childhood, elementary, kindergarten/preschool, physical. **Engineering:** General. **English:** English lit. **Foreign languages:** French, Spanish. **General:** Building inspection, maintenance. **Health services:** Clinical lab technology, dental hygiene, EMT paramedic, health information management, health information technology, insurance coding, licensed practical nurse, medical transcription, nursing (RN), prenursing, surgical technology. **History:** General. **Human services:** Social work. **Liberal arts:** Arts/sciences, humanities. **Math:** General. **Parks/recreation:** General, health/fitness. **Philosophy/religion:** Philosophy. **Physical sciences:** Astronomy, chemistry, geology, physics. **Protective services:** Criminal justice, firefighting, forensics, law enforcement admin. **Psychology:** General. **Social sciences:** Anthropology, economics, geography, political science, sociology. **Visual/performing arts:** Art, cinematography, dance, dramatic, graphic design, music, photography. **Work/family studies:** Child care management, child care service, child development.

Technology on campus. 1,360 workstations in library, computer center. Online course registration, online library, helpline, student web hosting, wireless network available.

Student life. **Freshman orientation:** Available. Preregistration for classes offered. **Activities:** Jazz band, choral groups, dance, drama, literary magazine, music ensembles, musical theater, student government, student newspaper, over 40 student clubs and organizations available.

Athletics. **Intercollegiate:** Baseball M, basketball, cross-country, football (tackle) M, soccer, softball W, tennis, track and field, volleyball W, water polo. **Team name:** Jaguars.

Student services. Career counseling, services for economically disadvantaged, student employment services, financial aid counseling, health services, legal services, on-campus daycare, personal counseling, veterans' counselor, women's services. **Physically disabled:** Services for visually, speech, hearing impaired. **Transfer:** Pre-admission transcript evaluation for new students. Transfer center, transfer adviser, college fairs on campus for students transferring to 4-year colleges.

Contact. E-mail: admissions@swccd.edu
Phone: (619) 421-6700 ext. 5215 Fax: (619) 482-6489
Nicholas Montez, Director, Admissions & Records, Southwestern College, 900 Otay Lakes Road, Chula Vista, CA 91910-7297

Taft College
Taft, California
www.taftcollege.edu

CB code: 4820

- Public 2-year community college
- Commuter campus in small town

General. Founded in 1922. Regionally accredited. **Enrollment:** 2,284 degree-seeking undergraduates. **Degrees:** 340 associate awarded. **Location:** 35 miles from Bakersfield. **Calendar:** Semester, limited summer session. **Full-time faculty:** 55 total. **Part-time faculty:** 60 total.

Transfer out. Colleges most students transferred to 2015: California State University: Bakersfield, California State University: Fresno, California Polytechnic State University: San Luis Obispo, University of La Verne.

Basis for selection. Open admission. **Adult students:** SAT/ACT scores not required.

2015-2016 Annual costs. Tuition/fees: $1,380; $7,380 out-of-state. Per-credit charge: $46 in-state; $246 out-of-state. Room/board: $4,707. Books/supplies: $1,600.

Financial aid. **Need-based:** Need-based aid available for part-time students. Work-study available nights, weekends and for part-time students. **Non-need-based:** Scholarships awarded for academics.

Application procedures. **Admission:** No deadline. No application fee. Admission notification on a rolling basis. **Financial aid:** No deadline. FAFSA, institutional form required. Applicants notified on a rolling basis; must reply within 4 week(s) of notification.

Academics. **Special study options:** Distance learning, double major, dual enrollment of high school students, ESL, independent study. License preparation in dental hygiene, paramedic. **Credit/placement by examination:** AP, CLEP, institutional tests. 12 credit hours maximum toward associate degree. **Support services:** GED preparation and test center, learning center, pre-admission summer program, reduced course load, remedial instruction, study skills assistance, tutoring.

Two-Year Colleges

Majors. Business: General, accounting, business admin. **Education:** Early childhood. **English:** English lit. **Health services:** Dental hygiene. **History:** General. **Liberal arts:** Arts/sciences, humanities. **Math:** General. **Physical sciences:** General. **Protective services:** Corrections, criminal justice. **Psychology:** General. **Social sciences:** Sociology. **Visual/performing arts:** Art, music.

Technology on campus. 121 workstations in dormitories, library, computer center, student center. Dormitories wired for high-speed internet access. Online course registration, online library, helpline, wireless network available.

Student life. Freshman orientation: Mandatory. Preregistration for classes offered. Offered online or by video. **Housing:** Single-sex dorms, special housing for disabled available. $125 fully refundable deposit. **Activities:** Drama, international student organizations, student government, student newspaper, International club, Rotary club, MECHA club, Best Buddies.

Athletics. NJCAA. **Intercollegiate:** Baseball M, basketball W, soccer, softball W, volleyball W. **Team name:** Cougars.

Student services. Adult student services, career counseling, services for economically disadvantaged, student employment services, financial aid counseling, minority student services, on-campus daycare, personal counseling, veterans' counselor. **Physically disabled:** Services for visually, speech, hearing impaired. **Transfer:** Re-entry adviser, pre-admission transcript evaluation for new students. Transfer center, transfer adviser, college fairs on campus for students transferring to 4-year colleges.

Contact. E-mail: admissions@taftcollege.edu
Phone: (661) 763-7741 Toll-free number: (800) 379-6784
Fax: (661) 763-7758
Michelle Hines, Registrar/Director of Admissions, Taft College, 29 Cougar Court, Taft, CA 93268

Ventura College
Ventura, California
www.venturacollege.edu
CB code: 4931

- Public 2-year community college
- Commuter campus in small city

General. Founded in 1925. Regionally accredited. **Enrollment:** 8,951 degree-seeking undergraduates. **Degrees:** 1,356 associate awarded. **Location:** 60 miles from downtown Los Angeles. **Calendar:** Semester, limited summer session. **Full-time faculty:** 137 total. **Part-time faculty:** 323 total.

Basis for selection. Open admission, but selective for some programs. Limited admission to nursing program.

2015-2016 Annual costs. Tuition/fees: $1,418; $8,738 out-of-state. Per-credit charge: $46 in-state; $290 out-of-state. Books/supplies: $1,656. Personal expenses: $3,105.

Financial aid. Need-based: Need-based aid available for part-time students. Work-study available nights, weekends and for part-time students.

Application procedures. Admission: No deadline. No application fee. Admission notification on a rolling basis. **Financial aid:** Priority date 3/2; no closing date. FAFSA required. Applicants notified on a rolling basis.

Academics. Special study options: Cross-registration, distance learning, dual enrollment of high school students, ESL, independent study, study abroad. **Credit/placement by examination:** AP, CLEP, institutional tests. 12 credit hours maximum toward associate degree. **Support services:** Learning center, reduced course load, remedial instruction, tutoring.

Majors. Biology: General. **Business:** General, accounting, administrative services, business admin, fashion, office management, office/clerical. **Computer sciences:** General. **Conservation:** General. **Education:** Early childhood. **Engineering:** General. **General:** Maintenance. **Health services:** EMT paramedic, medical secretary, nursing (RN). **Protective services:** Criminal justice. **Social sciences:** International relations. **Visual/performing arts:** Ceramics, commercial/advertising art, dramatic, fashion design, music, photography, studio arts. **Work/family studies:** General, child development.

Technology on campus. Online course registration available.

Student life. Freshman orientation: Available. Preregistration for classes offered. **Housing:** Student housing available off-campus at nearby apartments. **Activities:** Jazz band, choral groups, dance, drama, international student organizations, music ensembles, student government, student newspaper, religious, ethnic, political, special interest organizations, international student club.

Athletics. Intercollegiate: Baseball M, basketball, cheerleading, cross-country, diving, football (tackle) M, golf M, softball W, swimming, tennis, track and field, volleyball M, water polo M. **Team name:** Pirates.

Student services. Adult student services, career counseling, services for economically disadvantaged, student employment services, health services, on-campus daycare, personal counseling, placement for graduates, veterans' counselor. **Physically disabled:** Services for visually, hearing impaired. **Transfer:** Transfer center, transfer adviser, college fairs on campus for students transferring to 4-year colleges.

Contact. Phone: (805) 654-6457 Fax: (805) 654-6357
Susan Bricker, Registrar, Ventura College, 4667 Telegraph Road, Ventura, CA 93003

Victor Valley College
Victorville, California
www.vvc.edu
CB code: 4932

- Public 2-year community college
- Small city

General. Founded in 1960. Regionally accredited. **Enrollment:** 7,283 degree-seeking undergraduates. **Degrees:** 900 associate awarded. **Location:** 38 miles from San Bernardino. **Calendar:** Semester. 2 Primary Semesters / 2 Intersessions. Limited summer session. **Full-time faculty:** 121 total. **Part-time faculty:** 401 total. **Class size:** 22% < 20, 69% 20-39, 7% 40-49, 2% 50-99, less than 1% >100. **Special facilities:** Planetarium, mock archaeological dig site.

Student profile. Among degree-seeking undergraduates, 1,284 enrolled as first-time, first-year students, 575 transferred in from other institutions.

Part-time:	62%	Women:	58%
Out-of-state:	3%	25 or older:	31%

Transfer out. Colleges most students transferred to 2015: California State University: San Bernardino.

Basis for selection. Open admission. **Adult students:** SAT/ACT scores not required. **Home schooled:** Must complete concurrent enrollment form with parent signature.

2015-2016 Annual costs. Tuition/fees: $1,390; $7,180 out-of-state. Per-credit charge: $46 in-state; $239 out-of-state. Books/supplies: $1,746. Personal expenses: $3,132.

Financial aid. Need-based: Need-based aid available for part-time students. Work-study available nights, weekends and for part-time students. **Additional information:** Board of Governors grant pays enrollment fee in full for low-income students.

Application procedures. Admission: No deadline. No application fee. Admission notification on a rolling basis. **Financial aid:** Priority date 3/2; no closing date. FAFSA, institutional form required. Applicants notified on a rolling basis starting 8/1; must reply within 4 week(s) of notification.

Academics. Special study options: Accelerated study, cooperative education, cross-registration, distance learning, double major, dual enrollment of high school students, ESL, honors, independent study, internships, semester at sea, study abroad, weekend college. License preparation in nursing, paramedic. **Credit/placement by examination:** AP, CLEP, institutional tests. 32 credit hours maximum toward associate degree. **Support services:** Learning center, pre-admission summer program, reduced course load, remedial instruction, study skills assistance, tutoring, writing center.

Majors. Business: General, administrative services, business admin, real estate. **General:** Carpentry. **Health services:** EMT paramedic, medical assistant, nursing (RN), respiratory therapy technology. **Liberal arts:** Arts/sciences. **Math:** General. **Protective services:** Fire safety technology, law enforcement admin. **Visual/performing arts:** Art.

Most popular majors. Business/marketing 12%, health sciences 10%, interdisciplinary studies 24%, liberal arts 31%, security/protective services 9%.

Technology on campus. 350 workstations in computer center, student center. Online course registration, online library, helpline available.

Student life. Freshman orientation: Available. Preregistration for classes offered. **Activities:** Bands, campus ministries, choral groups, dance, drama, music ensembles, Model UN, musical theater, student government, student newspaper, symphony orchestra.

Athletics. NJCAA. **Intercollegiate:** Baseball M, basketball, cross-country, football (tackle) M, golf M, soccer, softball W, tennis, track and field, volleyball W, wrestling M. **Team name:** Rams.

Student services. Career counseling, services for economically disadvantaged, student employment services, financial aid counseling, health services, on-campus daycare, personal counseling, placement for graduates, veterans' counselor. **Physically disabled:** Services for visually, speech, hearing impaired. **Transfer:** Re-entry adviser, pre-admission transcript evaluation for new students. College fairs on campus for students transferring to 4-year colleges.

Contact. E-mail: greta.moon@vvc.edu
Phone: (760) 245-4271 ext. 2373 Fax: (760) 843-7707
Greta Moon, Director, Admissions and Records, Victor Valley College, 18422 Bear Valley Road, Victorville, CA 92392-5850

West Hills College: Coalinga
Coalinga, California
www.westhillscollege.com   **CB code: 4056**

◗ Public 2-year community college
◗ Commuter campus in small town

General. Founded in 1932. Regionally accredited. **Enrollment:** 1,985 degree-seeking undergraduates. **Degrees:** 258 associate awarded. **Location:** 60 miles from Fresno. **Calendar:** Semester, limited summer session. **Full-time faculty:** 37 total; 16% minority, 46% women. **Part-time faculty:** 60 total; 32% minority, 57% women.

Student profile.

Out-of-state:	10%	Live on campus:	5%
25 or older:	28%		

Transfer out. Colleges most students transferred to 2015: California State University Fresno, California Polytechnic University SLO, University of Phoenix, Fresno Pacific University.

Basis for selection. Open admission. Grade 7-12 students admitted with parental permission and principal of the educational institution recommendation as special students. **Adult students:** SAT/ACT scores not required.

2015-2016 Annual costs. Tuition/fees: $1,380; $8,430 out-of-state. Per-credit charge: $46 in-state; $281 out-of-state. Room/board: $7,977. Books/supplies: $1,764. Personal expenses: $2,322.

Financial aid. Need-based: Need-based aid available for part-time students. Work-study available nights, weekends and for part-time students.

Application procedures. Admission: No deadline. No application fee. Application must be submitted online. Admission notification on a rolling basis. **Financial aid:** Priority date 3/2; no closing date. FAFSA required. Applicants notified on a rolling basis starting 6/1.

Academics. Special study options: Distance learning, double major, dual enrollment of high school students, ESL, honors, independent study, study abroad. **Credit/placement by examination:** AP, CLEP, institutional tests. 15 credit hours maximum toward associate degree. **Support services:** GED preparation, learning center, reduced course load, remedial instruction, tutoring.

Majors. Business: General, accounting, administrative services, business admin, management information systems, office technology, office/clerical. **Communications:** General. **Computer sciences:** General, applications programming. **Education:** Early childhood. **Liberal arts:** Arts/sciences. **Protective services:** Police science. **Psychology:** General. **Social sciences:** General, criminology, geography. **Visual/performing arts:** Art, commercial/advertising art, studio arts.

Most popular majors. Business/marketing 7%, family/consumer sciences 7%, health sciences 19%, liberal arts 49%, psychology 6%.

Technology on campus. 40 workstations in dormitories, library, computer center. Dormitories wired for high-speed internet access. Online course registration, helpline, wireless network available.

Student life. Freshman orientation: Available. Preregistration for classes offered. **Housing:** Single-sex dorms available. $125 fully refundable deposit. **Activities:** Drama, international student organizations, musical theater, student government.

Athletics. NJCAA. **Intercollegiate:** Baseball M, basketball M, football (tackle) M, rodeo, softball W, volleyball W. **Team name:** Falcons.

Student services. Adult student services, career counseling, services for economically disadvantaged, student employment services, financial aid counseling, on-campus daycare, personal counseling, veterans' counselor. **Physically disabled:** Services for visually, speech, hearing impaired. **Transfer:** Transfer center, transfer adviser, college fairs on campus for students transferring to 4-year colleges.

Contact. E-mail: admissions@whccd.edu
Phone: (559) 934-2300 Toll-free number: (800) 266-1114
Fax: (559) 934-2852
West Hills College: Coalinga, 300 Cherry Lane, Coalinga, CA 93210

West Hills College: Lemoore
Lemoore, California
www.westhillscollege.com   **CB code: 5500**

◗ Public 2-year community college
◗ Large town

General. Regionally accredited. **Enrollment:** 2,675 degree-seeking undergraduates. **Degrees:** 455 associate awarded. **Location:** 20 miles from Fresno. **Calendar:** Semester, limited summer session. **Full-time faculty:** 47 total; 23% minority, 45% women. **Part-time faculty:** 104 total; 24% minority, 44% women. **Class size:** 4% < 20, 96% 20-39.

Transfer out. Colleges most students transferred to 2015: California State University Fresno, California State University Bakersfield, California State University Chico.

Basis for selection. Open admission. Grades 7-12 students admitted with parental permission and principal of the educational institution recommendation as special students. **Adult students:** SAT/ACT scores not required.

2015-2016 Annual costs. Tuition/fees: $1,380; $8,430 out-of-state. Per-credit charge: $46 in-state; $281 out-of-state. Books/supplies: $1,764. Personal expenses: $3,160.

Financial aid. Need-based: Work-study available nights, weekends and for part-time students.

Application procedures. Admission: No deadline. No application fee. Application must be submitted online. Admission notification on a rolling basis. **Financial aid:** No deadline.

Academics. Special study options: Distance learning, dual enrollment of high school students, ESL, honors, independent study. **Credit/placement by examination:** AP, CLEP, institutional tests. 15 credit hours maximum toward associate degree. **Support services:** GED preparation, learning center, reduced course load, remedial instruction, tutoring.

Majors. Biology: General. **Business:** General, business admin. **Computer sciences:** General. **Engineering:** General. **Health services:** Nursing (RN). **Liberal arts:** Arts/sciences, humanities. **Math:** General. **Protective services:** Law enforcement admin. **Psychology:** General. **Social sciences:** General.

Most popular majors. Business/marketing 12%, health sciences 9%, liberal arts 55%, psychology 6%, security/protective services 13%.

Technology on campus. 60 workstations in library, computer center. Online course registration, wireless network available.

Student life. Freshman orientation: Available. Preregistration for classes offered. **Activities:** Student government, student newspaper.

Athletics. NJCAA. **Intercollegiate:** Cross-country, golf, soccer, wrestling M. **Team name:** Golden Eagles.

Student services. Adult student services, career counseling, services for economically disadvantaged, student employment services, financial aid counseling, on-campus daycare, personal counseling, veterans' counselor. **Physically disabled:** Services for visually, speech, hearing impaired. **Transfer:** Pre-admission transcript evaluation for new students. Transfer center, transfer adviser, college fairs on campus for students transferring to 4-year colleges.

Contact. E-mail: admissions@westhillscollege.com
Phone: (559) 925-3317 Toll-free number: (800) 266-1114
Fax: (559) 925-3837
Keith Stearns, Associate Vice Chancellor/Registrar, West Hills College: Lemoore, 555 College Avenue, Lemoore, CA 93245

West Los Angeles College
Culver City, California
www.wlac.edu   CB code: 4964

- Public 2-year community college
- Commuter campus in large town

General. Founded in 1968. Regionally accredited. **Enrollment:** 6,134 degree-seeking undergraduates. **Degrees:** 405 associate awarded. **Location:** 10 miles from Civic Center. **Calendar:** Semester, limited summer session. **Full-time faculty:** 102 total. **Part-time faculty:** 304 total.

Student profile.

Out-of-state: 1%   25 or older: 74%

Basis for selection. Open admission.

2015-2016 Annual costs. Tuition/fees: $1,404; $7,854 out-of-state. Per-credit charge: $46 in-state; $261 out-of-state. Books/supplies: $1,638. Personal expenses: $3,132.

Financial aid. All financial aid based on need. Need-based aid available for part-time students. Work-study available nights, weekends and for part-time students. **Additional information:** California residents may qualify for Board of Governors Grant Program.

Application procedures. Admission: No deadline. No application fee. Admission notification on a rolling basis. **Financial aid:** No deadline. FAFSA required. Applicants notified on a rolling basis; must reply within 4 week(s) of notification.

Academics. Special study options: Accelerated study, cooperative education, distance learning, dual enrollment of high school students, ESL, honors, independent study, internships, student-designed major, study abroad, weekend college. License preparation in aviation, dental hygiene, nursing, paramedic, real estate. **Credit/placement by examination:** AP, CLEP, institutional tests. 15 credit hours maximum toward associate degree. **Support services:** GED preparation, learning center, reduced course load, remedial instruction, study skills assistance, tutoring, writing center.

Majors. Biology: General. **Business:** General, accounting, administrative services, business admin, real estate. **Engineering:** General. **English:** English lit, rhetoric/composition. **Foreign languages:** French, Spanish. **Health services:** Dental hygiene. **History:** General. **Liberal arts:** Arts/sciences. **Parks/recreation:** Health/fitness. **Philosophy/religion:** Philosophy. **Physical sciences:** Chemistry, geology, physics. **Psychology:** General. **Social sciences:** Anthropology, economics, geography, political science, sociology. **Visual/performing arts:** Art, ceramics, music.

Technology on campus. Commuter students can connect to campus network. Online course registration, online library, wireless network available.

Student life. Freshman orientation: Available. Preregistration for classes offered. 2 hour session prior to start of each semester. **Activities:** Bands, choral groups, dance, drama, film society, student government, student newspaper, TV station.

Athletics. Intercollegiate: Baseball M, basketball, cross-country, football (tackle) M, track and field. **Team name:** Wildcats.

Student services. Adult student services, career counseling, services for economically disadvantaged, student employment services, financial aid counseling, health services, on-campus daycare, personal counseling, placement for graduates, veterans' counselor. **Physically disabled:** Services for visually, speech, hearing impaired.

Contact. Phone: (310) 287-4501
John Goltermann, Dean, West Los Angeles College, 9000 Overland Avenue, Culver City, CA 90230

West Valley College
Saratoga, California
www.westvalley.edu   CB code: 4958

- Public 2-year community college
- Large town

General. Founded in 1963. Regionally accredited. **Enrollment:** 3,854 degree-seeking undergraduates. **Degrees:** 738 associate awarded. **ROTC:** Army, Air Force. **Location:** 13 miles from downtown San Jose. **Calendar:** Semester, limited summer session. **Full-time faculty:** 176 total. **Part-time faculty:** 474 total. **Special facilities:** Planetarium, wireless campus center.

Transfer out. Colleges most students transferred to 2015: University of California: Davis, San Jose State University.

Basis for selection. Open admission.

2015-2016 Annual costs. Tuition/fees: $1,418; $7,568 out-of-state. Per-credit charge: $46 in-state; $251 out-of-state. Books/supplies: $2,460. Personal expenses: $3,096.

Financial aid. All financial aid based on need. Need-based aid available for part-time students. Work-study available nights, weekends and for part-time students.

Application procedures. Admission: Priority date 4/21; no deadline. No application fee. Admission notification on a rolling basis. **Financial aid:** Priority date 5/31; no closing date. FAFSA required. Applicants notified on a rolling basis starting 7/1.

Academics. Special study options: Distance learning, double major, dual enrollment of high school students, ESL, honors, independent study, teacher certification program. License preparation in real estate. **Credit/placement by examination:** AP, CLEP, institutional tests. 12 credit hours maximum toward associate degree. **Support services:** Learning center, pre-admission summer program, remedial instruction, study skills assistance, tutoring, writing center.

Majors. Architecture: Landscape. **Area/ethnic studies:** Women's. **Biology:** General. **Business:** General, accounting, administrative services, business admin, fashion, office management, office technology, office/clerical, real estate. **Computer sciences:** General, programming. **Education:** Early childhood. **Engineering:** General. **English:** English lit, rhetoric/composition. **Foreign languages:** General. **General:** Maintenance. **Health services:** Medical assistant. **History:** General. **Liberal arts:** Arts/sciences. **Math:** General. **Parks/recreation:** Facilities management. **Physical sciences:** Chemistry, geology, physics. **Protective services:** Criminal justice. **Psychology:** General. **Social sciences:** General, sociology. **Visual/performing arts:** Art, dramatic, fashion design, interior design, music. **Work/family studies:** Child care management.

Technology on campus. 150 workstations in library, computer center. Commuter students can connect to campus network. Online course registration, online library, wireless network available.

Student life. Freshman orientation: Available. Preregistration for classes offered. **Activities:** Bands, choral groups, drama, music ensembles, student government, student newspaper, symphony orchestra, TV station, Vietnamese student association, Unlimited Horizons (handicapped), Descendants of Africa, Latin American student association, Alpha Gamma Sigma, Latter-Day Saints, fashion design, Puente, JC Ministries (Christian).

Athletics. Intercollegiate: Baseball M, basketball, cross-country, field hockey W, football (tackle) M, gymnastics W, soccer M, softball W, swimming, tennis, track and field, volleyball, water polo M, wrestling M. **Intramural:** Badminton, basketball, bowling, swimming, tennis, volleyball. **Team name:** Vikings.

Student services. Adult student services, career counseling, student employment services, health services, on-campus daycare, personal counseling, veterans' counselor. **Physically disabled:** Services for visually, speech, hearing impaired. **Transfer:** Re-entry adviser for new students. Transfer center, transfer adviser, college fairs on campus for students transferring to 4-year colleges.

Contact. Phone: (408) 741-2001 Fax: (408) 867-5033
Herlisa Hamp, Director of Admissions, West Valley College, 14000 Fruitvale Avenue, Saratoga, CA 95070-5698

Westwood College: Los Angeles
Los Angeles, California
www.westwood.edu/locations/california/los-angeles-campus

- For-profit 2-year career college
- Very large city

General. Regionally accredited; also accredited by ACICS. This Westwood College campus offers a unique hands-on, career-focused curriculum providing associate degrees that can be earned in as little as three months and bachelor's degrees that can be earned in as little as three years. Degree programs are available in the fields of technology, healthcare, business, design and justice. **Enrollment:** 2,448 degree-seeking undergraduates. **Degrees:** 157

Two-Year Colleges

bachelor's, 56 associate awarded; master's offered. **Calendar:** Differs by program. **Full-time faculty:** 17 total. **Part-time faculty:** 253 total.

Basis for selection. Admissions decisions based on assessment test and interview. SAT or ACT recommended. Institutional test (ACCUPLACER) and interview most important. Developmental courses may be required for those who do not pass entrance examination.

2015-2016 Annual costs. Books/supplies: $1,106. **Additional information:** Electronics Technology: AOS $34,825. Information Technology: AOS $34,825. Business Administration: AAS $36,428. Construction Management: AAS $36,428. Criminal Justice: AAS $38,717. Graphic Design: AAS $40,278. Medical Assisting: AAS $27,251. Paralegal: AAS $33,250. Business Administration: Major in Healthcare Management: BS $72,856. Business Administration: Major in Management: BS $72,856. Business Administration: Major in Marketing Management: BS $72,856. Construction Management: BS $72,856. Criminal Justice: Major in Administration: BS $77,434. Graphic Design: Major in Visual Communications: BS $76,720. Information & Network Technologies: Major in Network Management: BS $69,650. Medical Assisting: DP $19,465. Master of Business Administration: MBA $27,354. Additional costs and fees such as books, tool kits, lab fee and online fees may apply.

Financial aid. **Need-based:** Work-study available nights, weekends and for part-time students.

Application procedures. **Admission:** No deadline. No application fee. Admission notification on a rolling basis. **Financial aid:** FAFSA required. Applicants notified on a rolling basis.

Academics. **Credit/placement by examination:** AP, CLEP.

Majors. **Business:** Business admin, construction management. **Computer sciences:** Networking. **Health services:** Medical assistant. **Protective services:** Law enforcement admin. **Visual/performing arts:** Graphic design.

Contact. E-mail: AdmissionsRepresentativesWW-Campus@westwood.edu
Phone: (213) 739-9999 Toll-free number: (866) 930-9256
Bob Fingerlin, Director of Admissions, Westwood College: Los Angeles, 3250 Wilshire Boulevard, Suite 400, Los Angeles, CA 90010

Woodland Community College
Woodland, California
http://wcc.yccd.edu

CB code: 5762

◗ Public 2-year community and junior college
◗ Small city

General. Regionally accredited. **Enrollment:** 1,159 degree-seeking undergraduates. **Degrees:** 280 associate awarded. **Calendar:** Semester. **Full-time faculty:** 39 total. **Part-time faculty:** 80 total.

Basis for selection. Open admission.

2015-2016 Annual costs. Tuition/fees: $1,400; $8,000 out-of-state. Per-credit charge: $46 in-state; $266 out-of-state. Books/supplies: $700.

Financial aid. **Need-based:** Work-study available nights, weekends and for part-time students.

Application procedures. **Admission:** No deadline. No application fee. **Financial aid:** Closing date 6/30.

Academics. **Credit/placement by examination:** AP, CLEP.

Majors. **Business:** Accounting, administrative services, business admin, small business admin. **Communications:** General. **Education:** Early childhood. **English:** English lit. **History:** General. **Math:** General. **Protective services:** Corrections, records/evidence management. **Psychology:** General. **Social sciences:** General, sociology.

Contact. E-mail: WCCAdmissionsinfo@yccd.edu
Phone: (530) 661-5700
Sonya Hord, Admissions Director, Woodland Community College, 2300 East Gibson Road, Building 700, Woodland, CA 95776

Yuba College
Marysville, California
http://yc.yccd.edu

◗ Public 2-year community college
◗ Commuter campus in small city

General. Founded in 1927. Regionally accredited. **Enrollment:** 6,461 degree-seeking undergraduates; 39 non-degree-seeking students. **Degrees:** 707 associate awarded. **Location:** 56 miles from Sacramento. **Calendar:** Semester, limited summer session. **Full-time faculty:** 92 total. **Part-time faculty:** 375 total. **Special facilities:** Peace officers standards and training academies, nursing training facilities, veterinary technical training clinic, manufacturing technology facilities, welding, automotive, theater. **Partnerships:** Formal partnerships with numerous local businesses.

Student profile. Among degree-seeking undergraduates, 1,266 enrolled as first-time, first-year students.

Part-time:	58%	25 or older:	44%
Women:	60%		

Transfer out. Colleges most students transferred to 2015: California State University Sacramento, California State University Chico, University of California Davis, American River College, University of Phoenix.

Basis for selection. Open admission, but selective for some programs. Limited admission to allied health programs. CPT tests recommended for counseling.

2015-2016 Annual costs. Tuition/fees: $1,400; $8,000 out-of-state. Per-credit charge: $46 in-state; $266 out-of-state. Books/supplies: $1,764. Personal expenses: $3,159.

Financial aid. **Need-based:** Need-based aid available for part-time students. Work-study available nights, weekends and for part-time students. **Non-need-based:** Scholarships awarded for academics, athletics, job skills, minority status, music/drama. **Additional information:** Tuition fee waiver based on Board of Governors Grant.

Application procedures. **Admission:** No deadline. No application fee. Application must be submitted online. Admission notification on a rolling basis beginning on or about 6/1. **Financial aid:** Priority date 8/7, closing date 3/1. FAFSA required. Applicants notified on a rolling basis starting 4/1.

Academics. **Special study options:** Cooperative education, distance learning, ESL, internships. License preparation in nursing, radiology. **Credit/placement by examination:** AP, CLEP, institutional tests. **Support services:** Learning center, remedial instruction, study skills assistance, tutoring, writing center.

Majors. **Biology:** General. **Business:** Accounting, administrative services, business admin, entrepreneurial studies, human resources, taxation. **Communications:** Journalism, media studies. **Computer sciences:** General, computer science. **Education:** Early childhood, physical. **English:** English lit. **Health services:** Medical radiologic technology/radiation therapy, medical transcription, nursing (RN), substance abuse counseling, veterinary technology/assistant. **History:** General. **Liberal arts:** Arts/sciences. **Math:** General. **Protective services:** Criminal justice, fire safety technology, police science. **Psychology:** General. **Social sciences:** General. **Visual/performing arts:** Art, dramatic, music, photography, studio arts. **Work/family studies:** Family/community services.

Technology on campus. 300 workstations in library, computer center. Commuter students can connect to campus network. Online course registration, online library, helpline, wireless network available.

Student life. Freshman orientation: Mandatory. Preregistration for classes offered. **Activities:** Bands, choral groups, drama, music ensembles, musical theater, student government, student newspaper, symphony orchestra, AD Nursing Students Association, Care Club, EOP&S Club, DECA/Marketing Club, Christian students association, Green Society, Future Teachers of America, speech team, photography guild, veterinary technicians association.

Athletics. Intercollegiate: Baseball M, basketball, cross-country, football (tackle) M, soccer, softball W, track and field, volleyball W. **Team name:** 49'ers.

Student services. Adult student services, career counseling, services for economically disadvantaged, student employment services, financial aid counseling, health services, minority student services, on-campus daycare, personal counseling, veterans' counselor, women's services. **Physically disabled:** Services for visually, speech, hearing impaired. **Transfer:** Transfer adviser, college fairs on campus for students transferring to 4-year colleges.

Contact. E-mail: admissions@yccd.edu
Phone: (530) 741-6720 Fax: (530) 741-6872
Sonya Horn, Director, Admissions and Enrollment Services, Yuba College, 2088 North Beale Road, Marysville, CA 95901

Colorado

Aims Community College
Greeley, Colorado   **CB member**
www.aims.edu   **CB code: 4204**

▶ Public 2-year community college
▶ Commuter campus in small city

General. Founded in 1967. Regionally accredited. **Enrollment:** 3,586 degree-seeking undergraduates; 1,597 non-degree-seeking students. **Degrees:** 521 associate awarded. **Location:** 55 miles from Denver. **Calendar:** Semester, extensive summer session. **Full-time faculty:** 111 total; 6% minority, 55% women. **Part-time faculty:** 236 total; 12% minority, 47% women. **Class size:** 80% < 20, 20% 20-39, less than 1% 40-49.

Student profile. Among degree-seeking undergraduates, 53% enrolled in a transfer program, 47% enrolled in a vocational program, 3% already have a bachelor's degree or higher, 752 enrolled as first-time, first-year students, 461 transferred in from other institutions.

Part-time:	52%	Asian American:	1%
Out-of-state:	3%	Hispanic/Latino:	36%
Women:	58%	Multi-racial, non-Hispanic:	2%
African American:	2%	25 or older:	41%

Transfer out. 46% of students enrolled in the transfer program go on to 4-year colleges. **Colleges most students transferred to 2015:** University of Northern Colorado, Front Range Community College, Colorado State University, Morgan Community College, Metropolitan State College.

Basis for selection. Open admission, but selective for some programs. Special admissions requirements for Aviation, Surgical Technology, Radiologic Technology, Peace Officer Academy, Paramedic, Fire Academy, and Nursing. All students must meet assessment requirement by taking computerized placement test, submitting ACT/SAT scores or showing proof of previous college experience.

High school preparation. College-preparatory program recommended. 17 units recommended. Recommended units include English 4, mathematics 4, social studies 3, science 3 (laboratory 3), foreign language 1 and academic electives 2.

2015-2016 Annual costs. Tuition/fees: $2,281; $3,432 out-of-district; $13,018 out-of-state. Per-credit charge: $67 in-district; $106 out-of-district; $425 out-of-state. Books/supplies: $1,475. Personal expenses: $3,402.

Financial aid. Need-based: Need-based aid available for part-time students. Work-study available nights, weekends and for part-time students.

Application procedures. Admission: No deadline. No application fee. Admission notification on a rolling basis. **Financial aid:** Priority date 3/15; no closing date. FAFSA required. Applicants notified on a rolling basis starting 6/1.

Academics. Special study options: Distance learning, double major, dual enrollment of high school students, ESL, honors, independent study, internships, liberal arts/career combination, student-designed major, weekend college. License preparation in aviation, nursing, paramedic, radiology, real estate. **Credit/placement by examination:** AP, CLEP, IB, institutional tests. 45 credit hours maximum toward associate degree. **Support services:** GED preparation and test center, learning center, remedial instruction, study skills assistance, tutoring, writing center.

Majors. Business: Accounting, management information systems, marketing, office technology. **Communications:** Digital media. **Communications technology:** Animation/special effects, graphics, photo/film/video, radio/TV, recording arts. **Computer sciences:** General. **Education:** Early childhood. **General:** Site management. **Health services:** EMT paramedic, management/clinical assistant, medical secretary, nursing (RN), office admin, radiologic technology/medical imaging, surgical technology. **Liberal arts:** Arts/sciences. **Protective services:** Firefighting, forest/wildland firefighting, law enforcement admin.

Most popular majors. Health sciences 14%, liberal arts 55%, trade and industry 10%.

Technology on campus. 1,915 workstations in library, computer center, student center. Online course registration, online library, wireless network available.

Student life. Freshman orientation: Available. Preregistration for classes offered. The orientation is provided online and is only required for degree or certificate seeking students, although all students are encouraged to participate. The orientation can be found on the Student tab in the student's myAims account. **Policies:** Student code of conduct, civility statement enforced; parking permits required. **Activities:** Campus ministries, film society, literary magazine, radio station, student government, student newspaper, TV station, Aims Ambassadors for Christ, Veterans National Honor Society, veterans club, Aims PRISM, League of United Latin American Citizens, Women in Transition Together, student advisory club, Helping Hands club, Phi Theta Kappa honor society.

Athletics. Intramural: Basketball, volleyball.

Student services. Adult student services, alcohol/substance abuse counseling, career counseling, services for economically disadvantaged, financial aid counseling, minority student services, personal counseling, veterans' counselor. **Physically disabled:** Services for visually, speech, hearing impaired. **Transfer:** Transfer adviser, college fairs on campus for students transferring to 4-year colleges.

Contact. E-mail: admissions.records@aims.edu
Phone: (970) 339-6440 Fax: (970) 506-6958
Jody Margheim, Director of Admissions, Registration and Recruitment, Aims Community College, 4911 West 20th Street, Greeley, CO 80634

Arapahoe Community College
Littleton, Colorado
www.arapahoe.edu   **CB code: 4014**

▶ Public 2-year community college
▶ Commuter campus in large town

General. Founded in 1965. Regionally accredited. Extension locations in Parker and Castle Rock, CO. **Enrollment:** 7,673 degree-seeking undergraduates; 1,943 non-degree-seeking students. **Degrees:** 703 associate awarded. **ROTC:** Army, Air Force. **Location:** 10 miles from Denver. **Calendar:** Semester, extensive summer session. **Full-time faculty:** 105 total; 66% women. **Part-time faculty:** 388 total; 60% women. **Class size:** 66% < 20, 34% 20-39, less than 1% 50-99. **Special facilities:** Colorado Gallery of the Arts. **Partnerships:** Formal partnerships with National Cable Telecommunications Institute, Swedish Medical Center, Porter Adventist Hospital, Skyridge Medical Center.

Student profile. Among degree-seeking undergraduates, 866 enrolled as first-time, first-year students.

Part-time:	76%	Hispanic/Latino:	15%
Out-of-state:	5%	Native American:	1%
Women:	57%	Multi-racial, non-Hispanic:	4%
African American:	3%	International:	1%
Asian American:	3%	25 or older:	41%

Basis for selection. Open admission, but selective for some programs. Allied health, nursing, automotive, legal assistant, and law enforcement programs require interviews and/or test scores.

2015-2016 Annual costs. Tuition/fees: $4,117; $16,264 out-of-state. Per-credit charge: $131 in-state; $535 out-of-state. Books/supplies: $1,749. Personal expenses: $3,375. **Additional information:** In-state tuition based upon assumption of Colorado Opportunity Fund waiver of $75 per-credit hour.

2014-2015 Financial aid. Need-based: Need-based aid available for part-time students. Work-study available nights, weekends and for part-time students. **Non-need-based:** Scholarships awarded for academics, alumni affiliation, art, leadership, minority status, music/drama, state residency.

Application procedures. Admission: No deadline. No application fee. Admission notification on a rolling basis. **Financial aid:** Priority date 4/1; no closing date. FAFSA required. Applicants notified on a rolling basis starting 4/15; must reply by 11/1.

Academics. Special study options: Accelerated study, cooperative education, distance learning, double major, dual enrollment of high school students, honors, independent study, internships, student-designed major, study abroad. License preparation in nursing, occupational therapy, paramedic, physical therapy. **Credit/placement by examination:** AP, CLEP, IB, institutional tests. No more than half of required credit can be fulfilled through credit for prior learning. **Support services:** GED preparation and test center, learning center, pre-admission summer program, reduced course load, remedial instruction, study skills assistance, tutoring, writing center.

Majors. Business: Accounting technology, administrative services, banking/financial services, hospitality admin, international, management information systems, marketing, office management, selling. **Communications:** Journalism. **Communications technology:** General. **Computer sciences:** Data entry, LAN/WAN management, networking, web page design. **General:** Building inspection. **Health services:** Clinical lab technology, health information technology, nursing (RN), occupational therapy assistant, office admin, physical therapy assistant. **Liberal arts:** Arts/sciences. **Parks/recreation:** Health/fitness. **Protective services:** Law enforcement admin. **Visual/performing arts:** Graphic design, interior design. **Work/family studies:** Child development.

Most popular majors. Health sciences 24%, liberal arts 44%, personal/culinary services 6%, visual/performing arts 6%.

Technology on campus. 110 workstations in library, computer center, student center. Online course registration, online library, helpline, wireless network available.

Student life. Freshman orientation: Mandatory. Preregistration for classes offered. **Activities:** Jazz band, choral groups, drama, literary magazine, music ensembles, student government, student newspaper.

Athletics. Team name: Coyotes.

Student services. Adult student services, career counseling, services for economically disadvantaged, student employment services, financial aid counseling, minority student services, on-campus daycare, placement for graduates, veterans' counselor. **Physically disabled:** Services for visually, speech, hearing impaired. **Transfer:** Pre-admission transcript evaluation for new students. Transfer adviser, college fairs on campus for students transferring to 4-year colleges.

Contact. E-mail: admissions@arapahoe.edu
Phone: (303) 797-5621 Fax: (303) 797-5970
Darcy Briggs-Jackson, Registrar-Director of Enrollment Services, Arapahoe Community College, PO Box 9002, Littleton, CO 80160-9002

Bel-Rea Institute of Animal Technology
Denver, Colorado
www.bel-rea.com   CB code: 0928

- For-profit 2-year technical college
- Commuter campus in very large city

General. Accredited by ACCSC. **Enrollment:** 489 undergraduates. **Degrees:** 182 associate awarded. **Calendar:** Differs by program. **Full-time faculty:** 16 total. **Part-time faculty:** 3 total.

Transfer out. Colleges most students transferred to 2015: University of Denver.

Basis for selection. Interview most important, followed by school achievement record. Recommendations considered. 2.5 GPA or GED required. Applicants with below 2.5 GPA or without GED must take entrance exam.

High school preparation. As much science and math as possible recommended. Algebra and chemistry recommended.

2015-2016 Annual costs. Books/supplies: $2,450. Personal expenses: $1,100.

Financial aid. All financial aid based on need. Work-study available nights, weekends and for part-time students.

Application procedures. Admission: No deadline. No application fee. Application must be submitted on paper. Admission notification on a rolling basis. **Financial aid:** Priority date 8/31; no closing date. FAFSA required. Applicants notified on a rolling basis starting 8/15.

Academics. Students intern at college-affiliated emergency veterinary hospital. **Special study options:** Accelerated study, internships. **Credit/placement by examination:** AP, CLEP. **Support services:** Reduced course load, study skills assistance, tutoring.

Majors. Health services: Veterinary technology/assistant.

Technology on campus. PC or laptop required. 20 workstations in student center. Wireless network available.

Student life. Freshman orientation: Mandatory. Preregistration for classes offered. **Activities:** Student government.

Student services. Career counseling, student employment services, personal counseling, placement for graduates, veterans' counselor.

Contact. E-mail: kaufman@bel-rea.com
Phone: (303) 751-8700 Toll-free number: (800) 950-8001
Fax: (303) 751-9969
Paulette Kaufman, Director, Bel-Rea Institute of Animal Technology, 1681 South Dayton Street, Denver, CO 80247

CollegeAmerica: Denver
Denver, Colorado
www.collegeamerica.edu

- Private 2-year nursing and technical college
- Commuter campus in very large city
- Application essay, interview required

General. Accredited by ACCSC. **Enrollment:** 204 degree-seeking undergraduates. **Degrees:** 30 bachelor's, 86 associate awarded. **Calendar:** Differs by program, extensive summer session. **Full-time faculty:** 7 total. **Part-time faculty:** 19 total.

Basis for selection. Open admission. Open admissions policy with exception of our nursing program. Admissions criteria for nursing can be found in our student catalog. **Home schooled:** Transcript of courses and grades, state high school equivalency certificate required.

2015-2016 Annual costs. Books/supplies: $101. Personal expenses: $1,000. **Additional information:** Tuition varies by program. Associate's programs range from $34,390 to $48,251 for the complete program. Bachelor's programs range from $55,800 to $74,753 for the complete program.

Financial aid. All financial aid based on need. Work-study available nights, weekends and for part-time students.

Application procedures. Admission: No deadline. $25 fee. Application must be submitted on paper. Admission notification on a rolling basis. **Financial aid:** No deadline. FAFSA, institutional form required. Applicants notified on a rolling basis; must reply within 4 week(s) of notification.

Academics. Special study options: Accelerated study, distance learning. Bachelor's degree programs available on campus. License preparation in nursing. **Credit/placement by examination:** AP, CLEP. **Support services:** GED preparation, remedial instruction, tutoring.

Majors. Business: Accounting/business management, business admin. **Computer sciences:** Computer graphics, networking.

Technology on campus. 50 workstations in library, computer center. Commuter students can connect to campus network. Online course registration, online library, helpline, repair service, wireless network available.

Student life. Freshman orientation: Mandatory. Preregistration for classes offered.

Student services. Adult student services, career counseling, services for economically disadvantaged, student employment services, financial aid counseling, placement for graduates.

Contact. Phone: (303) 300-8740 ext. 7001
Mary Gordy, Director of Admissions, CollegeAmerica: Denver, 1385 South Colorado Boulevard, 5th Floor, Denver, CO 80222-1912

Colorado Mountain College
Glenwood Springs, Colorado
www.coloradomtn.edu   CB code: 4112

- Public 2-year community and liberal arts college
- Residential campus in small town

General. Founded in 1965. Regionally accredited. Composed of 11 campuses. Three campuses have residential facilities: Alpine Campus in Steamboat Springs; Spring Valley Campus near Glenwood Springs; and Timberline Campus in Leadville. Commuter campuses located in: Aspen, Breckenridge, Buena Vista, Carbondale, Dillion, Edwards, Glenwood Springs and Rifle. **Enrollment:** 4,023 degree-seeking undergraduates; 153 non-degree-seeking students. **Degrees:** 102 bachelor's, 573 associate awarded. **Location:** 160 miles from Denver. **Calendar:** Semester, limited summer session. **Full-time faculty:** 109 total; 35% minority, 47% women. **Part-time faculty:** 435 total; 6% minority, 65% women. **Class size:** 88% < 20, 12% 20-39. **Special facilities:** Outdoor education center, farm for veterinarian technician program, climbing walls, ice climbing wall, community theater, 18 hole Frisbee golf, challenge course, analytical laboratory, entrepreneurship center.

Student profile. Among degree-seeking undergraduates, 482 enrolled as first-time, first-year students.

Part-time:	89%	25 or older:	52%
Out-of-state:	15%	Live on campus:	8%
Women:	56%		

Transfer out. Colleges most students transferred to 2015: University of Colorado-Boulder, Colorado State University, Mesa State University, Western State College, Fort Lewis College.

Basis for selection. Open admission, but selective for some programs. Special requirements for nursing and bachelor's degree applicants. The following programs have testing requirements: veterinary technology, photography, outdoor recreation leadership, culinary arts, paramedic, and ski area operations.

High school preparation. College-preparatory program recommended.

2015-2016 Annual costs. Tuition/fees: $2,010; $3,510 out-of-district; $11,490 out-of-state. Per-credit charge: $57 in-district; $107 out-of-district; $373 out-of-state. Room/board: $9,000. Books/supplies: $1,200. Personal expenses: $906.

Financial aid. All financial aid based on need. Need-based aid available for part-time students. Work-study available nights, weekends and for part-time students.

Application procedures. Admission: No deadline. No application fee. Admission notification on a rolling basis. **Financial aid:** Priority date 3/31; no closing date. FAFSA required. Applicants notified on a rolling basis; must reply within 4 week(s) of notification.

Academics. Special study options: Distance learning, dual enrollment of high school students, independent study, internships, liberal arts/career combination, study abroad. Bachelor's degree programs available on campus. License preparation in nursing. **Credit/placement by examination:** AP, CLEP, IB, SAT, ACT, institutional tests. 30 credit hours maximum toward associate degree. Also recognize and accept exam results for DANTES, Excelsior, Institutional Challenge Exams, and credit for life experiences. **Support services:** GED preparation and test center, learning center, reduced course load, remedial instruction, study skills assistance, tutoring.

Majors. Biology: General. **Business:** General, accounting, accounting technology, business admin, hospitality admin, hotel/motel admin, management information systems, real estate, resort management, tourism/travel. **Communications:** Photojournalism. **Communications technology:** Animation/special effects, graphic/printing, graphics, photo/film/video. **Computer sciences:** General, applications programming, computer graphics, information technology, networking, programming. **Conservation:** General, forestry. **Education:** General, bilingual, early childhood. **English:** English lit, rhetoric/composition. **Health services:** EMT paramedic, nursing (RN), office assistant, prenursing, veterinary technology/assistant. **Liberal arts:** Arts/sciences. **Math:** General. **Parks/recreation:** General, facilities management. **Physical sciences:** Chemistry, geology. **Protective services:** Criminal justice, firefighting. **Social sciences:** General. **Visual/performing arts:** General, art, commercial photography, commercial/advertising art, design, dramatic, graphic design, photography.

Most popular majors. Business/marketing 9%, health sciences 14%, liberal arts 65%.

Technology on campus. 30 workstations in dormitories, library, computer center, student center. Dormitories wired for high-speed internet access and linked to campus network. Online library, helpline, wireless network available.

Student life. Freshman orientation: Available. Preregistration for classes offered. **Policies:** All students living on-campus must follow housing policies. **Housing:** Guaranteed on-campus for freshmen. Coed dorms available. $300 fully refundable deposit. **Activities:** Drama, radio station, student government.

Athletics. NJCAA. **Intercollegiate:** Skiing, soccer. **Intramural:** Basketball, cross-country, skiing, soccer, softball, volleyball. **Team name:** Eagles.

Student services. Adult student services, career counseling, student employment services, financial aid counseling, health services, personal counseling, placement for graduates, veterans' counselor. **Physically disabled:** Services for visually, speech, hearing impaired. **Transfer:** Transfer center, transfer adviser, college fairs on campus for students transferring to 4-year colleges.

Contact. E-mail: joinus@coloradomtn.edu
Phone: (970) 945-8691 Toll-free number: (866) 271-2381
Shane Larson, Assistant Vice President, Enrollment Services, Colorado Mountain College, 802 Grand Avenue, Glenwood Springs, CO 81601

Colorado Northwestern Community College
Rangely, Colorado
www.cncc.edu   **CB code: 4665**

- Public 2-year community college
- Residential campus in rural community

General. Founded in 1962. Regionally accredited. Additional campus in Craig and 3 off-campus sites in Meeker, Hayden, Oak Creek. **Enrollment:** 649 degree-seeking undergraduates. **Degrees:** 119 associate awarded. **Location:** 300 miles from Denver, 90 miles from Grand Junction. **Calendar:** Semester, limited summer session. **Full-time faculty:** 46 total; 48% women. **Part-time faculty:** 59 total; 3% minority, 70% women. **Class size:** 83% < 20, 17% 20-39. **Special facilities:** Flight simulator, firearms training simulator, cadaver lab, computerized teaching mannequin for nursing.

Student profile.

Out-of-state:	18%	Live on campus:	24%
25 or older:	36%		

Transfer out. Colleges most students transferred to 2015: University of Northern Colorado, Colorado State University, Mesa State College.

Basis for selection. Open admission, but selective for some programs. Selective admissions to dental hygiene and nursing. Both programs have application deadline and pre-requisite requirements. Interview required of dental hygiene majors. Competitive entry scoring required of nursing majors.

High school preparation. Biological science and/or chemistry required for dental hygiene. Math/science desirable for aviation technology and aviation maintenance.

2015-2016 Annual costs. Tuition/fees: $4,210; $6,999 out-of-state. Per-credit charge: $131 in-state; $223 out-of-state. Room/board: $6,654. **Additional information:** In-state tuition based upon assumption of Colorado Opportunity Fund waiver of $75 per-credit hour.

2014-2015 Financial aid. Need-based: 56% of total undergraduate aid awarded as scholarships/grants, 44% as loans/jobs. Need-based aid available for part-time students. Work-study available nights, weekends and for part-time students. **Non-need-based:** Scholarships awarded for academics, athletics, leadership.

Application procedures. Admission: No deadline. No application fee. Admission notification on a rolling basis. Application closing date for dental hygiene program, March 15; for nursing program, April 15. **Financial aid:** Priority date 5/1; no closing date. FAFSA, institutional form required. Applicants notified on a rolling basis starting 5/15; must reply within 4 week(s) of notification.

Academics. Special study options: Distance learning, dual enrollment of high school students, honors, independent study, internships. License preparation in aviation, dental hygiene, nursing. **Credit/placement by examination:** AP, CLEP, institutional tests. 30 credit hours maximum toward associate degree. **Support services:** GED preparation and test center, learning center, remedial instruction, study skills assistance, tutoring, writing center.

Majors. Biology: Marine. **Business:** Accounting technology, banking/financial services, entrepreneurial studies, management information systems, office management. **Conservation:** General. **Education:** Early childhood. **General:** Power transmission. **Health services:** Dental hygiene, EMT paramedic, nursing (RN). **Liberal arts:** Arts/sciences. **Parks/recreation:** Outdoor education. **Work/family studies:** Child care management.

Most popular majors. Health sciences 43%, liberal arts 50%.

Technology on campus. 54 workstations in dormitories, library, computer center. Dormitories wired for high-speed internet access and linked to campus network. Online course registration, online library, wireless network available.

Student life. Freshman orientation: Mandatory. Preregistration for classes offered. Two sessions in July, one in August. **Housing:** Guaranteed on-campus for freshmen. Coed dorms available. $200 fully refundable deposit. **Activities:** Student government, student newspaper.

Athletics. NJCAA. **Intercollegiate:** Baseball M, basketball, rodeo, softball W, volleyball W. **Intramural:** Basketball, football (non-tackle), golf, racquetball, rodeo, soccer, softball, table tennis, volleyball. **Team name:** Spartans.

Student services. Adult student services, alcohol/substance abuse counseling, career counseling, student employment services, financial aid counseling, personal counseling, veterans' counselor. **Physically disabled:** Services for visually, hearing impaired. **Transfer:** Pre-admission transcript evaluation for new students. Transfer adviser, college fairs on campus for students transferring to 4-year colleges.

Contact. E-mail: infocentral@cncc.edu
Phone: (970) 675-3218 Toll-free number: (800) 562-1105
Fax: (970) 975-3343
Tresa England, Dean of Student Services/Registrar, Colorado Northwestern Community College, 500 Kennedy Drive, Rangely, CO 81648

Colorado School of Healing Arts
Lakewood, Colorado
www.csha.net

- For-profit 2-year career college
- Commuter campus in small city
- Application essay, interview required

General. Accredited by ACCSC. **Enrollment:** 176 undergraduates. **Degrees:** 63 associate awarded. **Location:** 7 miles from Denver. **Calendar:** Quarter, extensive summer session. **Part-time faculty:** 24 total. **Class size:** 84% < 20, 16% 20-39.

Basis for selection. Open admission. **Home schooled:** Interview required.

2015-2016 Annual costs. Books/supplies: $693.

Financial aid. All financial aid based on need. Need-based aid available for part-time students. Work-study available nights, weekends and for part-time students.

Application procedures. **Admission:** No deadline. $50 fee. Application must be submitted on paper. Admission notification on a rolling basis. **Financial aid:** No deadline. FAFSA required.

Academics. **Special study options:** Accelerated study. **Credit/placement by examination:** AP, CLEP. **Support services:** Learning center, tutoring.

Majors. **Health services:** Massage therapy.

Technology on campus. 2 workstations in library. Wireless network available.

Student life. **Freshman orientation:** Mandatory. Preregistration for classes offered. 4-hour program held prior to start of quarter.

Student services. Career counseling, financial aid counseling.

Contact. E-mail: rosa@csha.net
Phone: (303) 986-2320 Toll-free number: (800) 233-7114
Fax: (303) 980-6594
Rosa Torres, Admissions Representative, Colorado School of Healing Arts, 7655 West Mississippi Avenue, Suite 100, Lakewood, CO 80226

Colorado School of Trades
Lakewood, Colorado
www.schooloftrades.edu
CB code: 3211

- For-profit 2-year technical college
- Small city
- Application essay, interview required

General. Accredited by ACCSC. **Enrollment:** 153 degree-seeking undergraduates. **Degrees:** 124 associate awarded. **Calendar:** Differs by program, limited summer session. **Full-time faculty:** 15 total.

Basis for selection. Open admission.

2015-2016 Annual costs. Books/supplies: $3,500.

Financial aid. **Need-based:** Work-study available nights, weekends and for part-time students.

Application procedures. **Admission:** No deadline. $25 fee. Admission notification on a rolling basis. **Financial aid:** No deadline. FAFSA, institutional form required.

Academics. **Special study options:** Accelerated study. **Credit/placement by examination:** AP, CLEP. **Support services:** Learning center, remedial instruction, tutoring.

Majors. **Education:** Trade/industrial.

Technology on campus. 6 workstations in computer center.

Contact. E-mail: info@schooloftrades.edu
Phone: (800) 234-4594 ext. 45 Toll-free number: (800) 234-4594 ext. 45
Fax: (303) 233-4723
Evan Jones, Director of Admissions, Colorado School of Trades, 1575 Hoyt Street, Lakewood, CO 80215-2945

Community College of Aurora
Aurora, Colorado
www.ccaurora.edu
CB code: 0969

- Public 2-year community college
- Commuter campus in large city

General. Founded in 1983. Regionally accredited. **Enrollment:** 5,405 degree-seeking undergraduates; 1,538 non-degree-seeking students. **Degrees:** 604 associate awarded. **Location:** 9 miles from Denver. **Calendar:** Semester, extensive summer session. **Full-time faculty:** 51 total; 16% have terminal degrees, 14% minority, 61% women. **Part-time faculty:** 352 total; 8% have terminal degrees, 12% minority, 45% women. **Class size:** 41% < 20, 55% 20-39, 2% 40-49, 2% 50-99. **Special facilities:** Observatory, EMS simulator, simulation center.

Student profile. Among degree-seeking undergraduates, 688 enrolled as first-time, first-year students, 503 transferred in from other institutions.

Part-time:	79%	25 or older:	41%
Women:	57%		

Transfer out. **Colleges most students transferred to 2015:** Metropolitan State University, University of Colorado Denver, Colorado State University, University of Northern Colorado.

Basis for selection. Open admission.

2015-2016 Annual costs. Tuition/fees: $4,163; $16,310 out-of-state. Per-credit charge: $131 in-state; $535 out-of-state. Books/supplies: $1,800. Personal expenses: $3,546.

Financial aid. **Need-based:** Need-based aid available for part-time students. Work-study available nights, weekends and for part-time students. **Non-need-based:** Scholarships awarded for academics, minority status, music/drama, state residency.

Application procedures. **Admission:** No deadline. No application fee. Admission notification on a rolling basis. **Financial aid:** Priority date 6/1; no closing date. FAFSA required. Applicants notified on a rolling basis starting 7/15.

Academics. **Special study options:** Accelerated study, distance learning, dual enrollment of high school students, ESL, honors, independent study, internships, weekend college. License preparation in paramedic. **Credit/placement by examination:** AP, CLEP, IB. 30 credit hours maximum toward associate degree. **Support services:** GED preparation and test center, learning center, remedial instruction, tutoring, writing center.

Majors. **Biology:** General. **Business:** Accounting technology, business admin, human resources, marketing, office management. **Computer sciences:** General, computer science, networking, web page design. **Education:** Early childhood. **Health services:** EMT paramedic, respiratory therapy technology. **History:** General. **Liberal arts:** Arts/sciences. **Math:** General. **Philosophy/religion:** Philosophy. **Physical sciences:** Chemistry, physics. **Protective services:** Disaster management, fire services admin, firefighting, law enforcement admin. **Psychology:** General. **Social sciences:** Anthropology, criminology, political science, sociology. **Visual/performing arts:** Art, cinematography, illustration, studio arts.

Most popular majors. Liberal arts 75%, security/protective services 6%.

Technology on campus. Commuter students can connect to campus network. Online course registration, online library, helpline, wireless network available.

Student life. Freshman orientation: Mandatory. Preregistration for classes offered. **Housing:** $150 deposit. **Activities:** Jazz band, dance, drama, international student organizations, literary magazine, musical theater, student government.

Student services. Career counseling, services for economically disadvantaged, student employment services, minority student services. **Physically disabled:** Services for visually, speech, hearing impaired. **Transfer:** Transfer adviser, college fairs on campus for students transferring to 4-year colleges.

Contact. E-mail: OnlineAdvisor@ccaurora.edu
Phone: (303) 360-4700
Kristen Cusack, Registrar, Community College of Aurora, 16000 East CentreTech Parkway, Aurora, CO 80011-9036

Community College of Denver
Denver, Colorado
www.ccd.edu   CB code: 4137

- Public 2-year community college
- Commuter campus in very large city

General. Founded in 1970. Regionally accredited. Library, student center and physical education facilities shared with Metropolitan State College at Denver and University of Colorado/Health Sciences Center at Denver. **Enrollment:** 8,003 degree-seeking undergraduates. **Degrees:** 622 associate awarded. **ROTC:** Army. **Calendar:** Semester, limited summer session. **Full-time faculty:** 124 total. **Part-time faculty:** 393 total. **Class size:** 33% < 20, 64% 20-39, 2% 50-99.

Student profile.

Out-of-state: 2%   25 or older: 49%

Transfer out. Colleges most students transferred to 2015: Metropolitan State College of Denver, University of Colorado at Denver.

Basis for selection. Open admission, but selective for some programs. Special requirements for health occupations and computer information systems programs.

2015-2016 Annual costs. Tuition/fees: $4,916; $17,063 out-of-state. Per-credit charge: $130.5 in-state; $535.4 out-of-state. Books/supplies: $1,800. Personal expenses: $3,402. **Additional information:** In-state tuition based upon assumption of Colorado Opportunity Fund waiver of $75 per-credit hour.

Financial aid. Need-based: Need-based aid available for part-time students. Work-study available nights, weekends and for part-time students. **Non-need-based:** Scholarships awarded for academics, leadership, state residency.

Application procedures. Admission: Priority date 8/1; no deadline. No application fee. Admission notification on a rolling basis. **Financial aid:** Priority date 4/15; no closing date. FAFSA, institutional form required. Applicants notified on a rolling basis.

Academics. Special study options: Accelerated study, cooperative education, cross-registration, distance learning, double major, dual enrollment of high school students, ESL, external degree, honors, independent study, internships. **Credit/placement by examination:** AP, CLEP, institutional tests. 45 credit hours maximum toward associate degree. **Support services:** GED preparation and test center, learning center, pre-admission summer program, reduced course load, remedial instruction, study skills assistance, tutoring, writing center.

Majors. Biology: Biomedical sciences. **Business:** Accounting technology, administrative services, business admin, management information systems. **Computer sciences:** General, applications programming. **Education:** Teacher assistance. **Health services:** Dental hygiene, electroencephalograph technology, health aide, nursing (RN), radiologic technology/medical imaging, veterinary technology/assistant. **Liberal arts:** Arts/sciences. **Parks/recreation:** General, health/fitness. **Protective services:** Security services. **Visual/performing arts:** Graphic design. **Work/family studies:** Child development.

Most popular majors. Health sciences 31%, liberal arts 55%.

Technology on campus. 1,032 workstations in library, computer center, student center. Commuter students can connect to campus network. Online course registration available.

Student life. Freshman orientation: Mandatory. Preregistration for classes offered. **Housing:** Dormitory housing available at Lowry campus

through cooperative agreement. **Activities:** Choral groups, international student organizations, student government, student newspaper, Mexican-American student organization, African-American student organization, Amnesty International, nursing club.

Student services. Adult student services, career counseling, services for economically disadvantaged, student employment services, financial aid counseling, health services, legal services, minority student services, on-campus daycare, personal counseling, placement for graduates, veterans' counselor, women's services. **Physically disabled:** Services for visually, hearing impaired. **Transfer:** Re-entry adviser, pre-admission transcript evaluation for new students. Transfer center, transfer adviser, college fairs on campus for students transferring to 4-year colleges.

Contact. E-mail: enrollment_services@ccd.edu
Phone: (303) 556-2420 Fax: (303) 556-2431
Michael Rusk, Dean of Students, Community College of Denver, Campus Box 201, PO Box 173363, Denver, CO 80217-3363

Concorde Career College: Aurora
Aurora, Colorado
www.concorde.edu

- For-profit 2-year health science college
- Large city

General. Accredited by ACCSC. **Enrollment:** 761 undergraduates. **Degrees:** 148 associate awarded. **Calendar:** Differs by program. **Full-time faculty:** 32 total. **Part-time faculty:** 8 total.

Basis for selection. Wonderlic and CPAT exams used.

2015-2016 Annual costs. Diploma programs: medical assistant $14,748; practical nursing $25,100; dental assistant $14,493; surgical technologist $24,591; medical office administration $14,480. Associate programs: nursing $39,904; nursing bridge $30,624; dental hygiene $51,559; physical therapy assistant $27,524; radiologic technology $24,591; respiratory therapy $31,957. Books and supplies vary by program ranging from $1,243-$7,411.

Financial aid. Need-based: Work-study available nights, weekends and for part-time students.

Application procedures. Admission: No deadline. No application fee. Admission notification on a rolling basis. **Financial aid:** No deadline.

Academics. Credit/placement by examination: AP, CLEP.

Majors. Health services: Dental hygiene, medical radiologic technology/radiation therapy, nursing (RN), physical therapy assistant, respiratory therapy technology.

Contact. Phone: (303) 861-1151
Michael Como, Director of Admissions, Concorde Career College: Aurora, 111 North Havana Street, Aurora, CO 80010

Ecotech Institute
Aurora, Colorado
www.ecotechinstitute.com   CB code: 7244

- For-profit 2-year career college
- Large city

General. Regionally accredited; also accredited by ACICS. Ecotech Institute is a college entirely focused on careers in renewable energy and sustainability. **Enrollment:** 375 undergraduates. **Degrees:** 215 associate awarded. **Calendar:** Quarter. **Full-time faculty:** 15 total. **Part-time faculty:** 21 total.

Basis for selection. Open admission.

2015-2016 Annual costs. Associate degree programs range from $387 to $468 per credit-hour. Most programs require 96 credit hours to complete.

Financial aid. Need-based: Work-study available nights, weekends and for part-time students.

Academics. Credit/placement by examination: AP.

Majors. Engineering: General. **General:** Power transmission.

Front Range Community College
Westminster, Colorado
www.frontrange.edu

CB code: 4119

▸ Public 2-year community college
▸ Commuter campus in large city

General. Founded in 1968. Regionally accredited. Additional campuses in Brighton, Boulder County, Larimer County. **Enrollment:** 15,551 degree-seeking undergraduates; 3,210 non-degree-seeking students. **Degrees:** 1,634 associate awarded. **Location:** 12 miles from Denver. **Calendar:** Semester, limited summer session. **Full-time faculty:** 245 total. **Part-time faculty:** 769 total. **Class size:** 49% < 20, 51% 20-39, less than 1% 40-49. **Special facilities:** Observatories. **Partnerships:** Formal partnerships with local workforce centers for career training or retraining.

Student profile. Among degree-seeking undergraduates, 64% enrolled in a transfer program, 37% enrolled in a vocational program, 2,348 enrolled as first-time, first-year students, 1,753 transferred in from other institutions.

Part-time:	67%	Hispanic/Latino:	14%
Out-of-state:	2%	Native American:	1%
Women:	58%	Multi-racial, non-Hispanic:	4%
African American:	2%	International:	2%
Asian American:	3%	25 or older:	42%

Transfer out. Colleges most students transferred to 2015: Colorado State University, University of Colorado at Boulder, Metropolitan State College, University of Northern Colorado, University of Colorado at Denver Health Sciences.

Basis for selection. Open admission.

High school preparation. 12 units recommended. Recommended units include English 4, mathematics 3, history 3, science 2 (laboratory 1).

2015-2016 Annual costs. Tuition/fees: $4,310; $16,457 out-of-state. Per-credit charge: $131 in-state; $535 out-of-state. Books/supplies: $1,800. Personal expenses: $4,842. **Additional information:** In-state tuition based upon assumption of Colorado Opportunity Fund waiver of $75 per-credit hour.

2014-2015 Financial aid. Need-based: 59% of total undergraduate aid awarded as scholarships/grants, 41% as loans/jobs. Need-based aid available for part-time students. Work-study available nights, weekends and for part-time students. **Non-need-based:** Scholarships awarded for academics, job skills, leadership, state residency.

Application procedures. Admission: No deadline. No application fee. Admission notification on a rolling basis. **Financial aid:** Priority date 5/1; no closing date. FAFSA, institutional form required. Applicants notified on a rolling basis starting 4/15; must reply within 3 week(s) of notification.

Academics. Special study options: Accelerated study, cooperative education, cross-registration, distance learning, double major, dual enrollment of high school students, ESL, honors, independent study, internships, liberal arts/career combination, teacher certification program, weekend college. License preparation in dental hygiene, nursing, paramedic. **Credit/placement by examination:** AP, CLEP, institutional tests. 30 credit hours maximum toward associate degree. **Support services:** GED preparation and test center, learning center, remedial instruction, study skills assistance, tutoring, writing center.

Majors. Business: Accounting technology, business admin, hospitality admin. **Communications technology:** Animation/special effects. **Computer sciences:** General. **Conservation:** Wildlife/wilderness. **Education:** Early childhood. **Foreign languages:** Sign language interpretation. **Health services:** EMT paramedic, health information technology, nursing (RN), office assistant, veterinary technology/assistant. **Liberal arts:** Arts/sciences. **Visual/performing arts:** Interior design.

Most popular majors. Business/marketing 6%, health sciences 14%, liberal arts 66%.

Technology on campus. 233 workstations in library, computer center, student center. Commuter students can connect to campus network. Online course registration, helpline, wireless network available.

Student life. Freshman orientation: Available. Preregistration for classes offered. **Activities:** Campus ministries, dance, drama, international student organizations, music ensembles, student government, student newspaper, interpreters for the deaf, gay/straight alliance, pharmacy tech club, dance club, ski/snowboard club, Phi Theta Kappa, horticulture club, student vet tech association, Latino club, science club.

Student services. Adult student services, alcohol/substance abuse counseling, career counseling, services for economically disadvantaged, student employment services, financial aid counseling, minority student services, personal counseling, veterans' counselor, women's services. **Physically disabled:** Services for visually, speech, hearing impaired. **Transfer:** Transfer center, college fairs on campus for students transferring to 4-year colleges.

Contact. Phone: (303) 404-5414 Fax: (303) 404-5150
Kris Binard, Registrar, Front Range Community College, 3645 West 112th Avenue, Westminster, CO 80031

IBMC College: Fort Collins
Fort Collins, Colorado
www.ibmc.edu

CB code: 3566

▸ For-profit 2-year technical college
▸ Commuter campus in small city
▸ Application essay, interview required

General. Accredited by ACICS. Additional branch campuses in Greeley, Longmont and Cheyenne, WY. **Enrollment:** 897 degree-seeking undergraduates. **Degrees:** 421 associate awarded. **Location:** 60 miles from Denver; 45 miles from Cheyenne, WY. **Calendar:** Differs by program. **Full-time faculty:** 20 total; 15% minority, 85% women. **Part-time faculty:** 55 total; 6% minority, 73% women.

Transfer out. Colleges most students transferred to 2015: Colorado Christian University, Front Range Community College, Aims Community College.

Basis for selection. Open admission, but selective for some programs. Applicants must be able to prove graduation from high school or completion of GED. Students must present certain scores on entrance evaluation exam based on program of study. Institutional entrance exam required for placement. **Home schooled:** State high school equivalency certificate required.

Financial aid. Need-based: Work-study available nights, weekends and for part-time students.

Application procedures. Admission: No deadline. $75 fee. Admission notification on a rolling basis. **Financial aid:** No deadline.

Academics. Special study options: Accelerated study, internships. **Credit/placement by examination:** AP, CLEP, institutional tests. Up to 50% of total program credits may be obtained through transfer or test out. **Support services:** GED preparation, learning center, reduced course load, remedial instruction, study skills assistance, tutoring.

Majors. Business: Accounting technology, administrative services, business admin. **Computer sciences:** Support specialist. **Health services:** Dental assistant, massage therapy, medical assistant, medical secretary, pharmacy assistant.

Most popular majors. Business/marketing 8%, health sciences 88%.

Technology on campus. 24 workstations in library, student center. Commuter students can connect to campus network. Wireless network available.

Student life. Freshman orientation: Available. Preregistration for classes offered.

Student services. Career counseling, student employment services, financial aid counseling, placement for graduates. **Transfer:** Pre-admission transcript evaluation for new students.

Contact. E-mail: info@ibmc.edu
Phone: (970) 223-2669 Toll-free number: (800) 495-2669
Fax: (970) 223-2796
Jimmy Henig, Regional Director of Admissions, IBMC College: Fort Collins, 3842 South Mason Street, Fort Collins, CO 80525

IntelliTec College
Colorado Springs, Colorado
http://intelliteccollege.com

CB code: 2500

▸ For-profit 2-year technical college
▸ Commuter campus in large city

(Above, preceding Front Range entry:)

Contact. Toll-free number: (877) 326-5576
Kolby Chase, Director of Admissions, Ecotech Institute, 1400 South Abilene Street, Aurora, CO 80012

General. Founded in 1965. Accredited by ACCSC. **Enrollment:** 828 undergraduates. **Degrees:** 331 associate awarded. **Location:** 68 miles from Denver. **Calendar:** 6-week cycle. Extensive summer session. **Full-time faculty:** 27 total.

Transfer out. Colleges most students transferred to 2015: Pikes Peak Community College, Denver Technical College.

Basis for selection. Open admission.

2015-2016 Annual costs. Books/supplies: $1,200.

Financial aid. All financial aid based on need. Need-based aid available for part-time students. Work-study available nights, weekends and for part-time students.

Application procedures. Admission: No deadline. No application fee. Admission notification on a rolling basis. **Financial aid:** No deadline. FAFSA, institutional form required. Applicants notified on a rolling basis.

Academics. Special study options: Accelerated study, liberal arts/career combination. **Credit/placement by examination:** AP, CLEP. Maximum 50% of required credits may be awarded for prior work and/or life experience. Pre-admission interview required for placement into program. **Support services:** Learning center, tutoring.

Majors. Computer sciences: General, computer science, systems analysis.

Most popular majors. Computer/information sciences 13%, engineering/ engineering technologies 21%, trade and industry 66%.

Technology on campus. 125 workstations in library, computer center. Online library, repair service available.

Student life. Freshman orientation: Available. Preregistration for classes offered. **Activities:** Student newspaper.

Student services. Adult student services, career counseling, student employment services, financial aid counseling, personal counseling, placement for graduates, veterans' counselor. **Transfer:** Pre-admission transcript evaluation for new students.

Contact. E-mail: admcs@intelliteccollege.com
Phone: (719) 632-7626 Toll-free number: (800) 748-2282
Fax: (719) 632-7451
Stacey Snyder, Vice President of Admissions and Marketing, IntelliTec College, 2315 East Pikes Peak Avenue, Colorado Springs, CO 80909

IntelliTec College: Grand Junction
Grand Junction, Colorado
http://intelliteccollege.com　　　　　**CB code: 2489**

▶ For-profit 2-year technical college
▶ Commuter campus in small city
▶ Interview required

General. Accredited by ACCSC. **Enrollment:** 145 degree-seeking undergraduates. **Degrees:** 41 associate awarded. **Location:** 250 miles from Denver, 300 miles from Salt Lake City. **Calendar:** Differs by program, extensive summer session.

Basis for selection. Open admission. **Home schooled:** Interview required.

Financial aid. All financial aid based on need. Work-study available nights, weekends and for part-time students.

Application procedures. Admission: No deadline. No application fee. Admission notification on a rolling basis. **Financial aid:** No deadline. FAFSA required. Applicants notified on a rolling basis.

Academics. Special study options: Internships. **Credit/placement by examination:** AP, CLEP. **Support services:** GED test center, learning center, tutoring.

Majors. Business: Accounting/business management. **Health services:** Medical assistant.

Technology on campus. 81 workstations in library, student center. Online library, wireless network available.

Student life. Freshman orientation: Mandatory. Preregistration for classes offered.

Student services. Career counseling, student employment services, placement for graduates.

Contact. E-mail: frontdeskGJ@intellitec.edu
Phone: (970) 245-8101 Fax: (970) 243-8074
Carol Langan, Admissions Team Lead, IntelliTec College: Grand Junction, 772 Horizon Drive, Grand Junction, CO 81506

Lamar Community College
Lamar, Colorado
www.lamarcc.edu　　　　　**CB code: 4382**

▶ Public 2-year community college
▶ Commuter campus in small town

General. Founded in 1937. Regionally accredited. **Enrollment:** 476 degree-seeking undergraduates; 363 non-degree-seeking students. **Degrees:** 142 associate awarded. **Location:** 117 miles from Pueblo. **Calendar:** Semester, limited summer session. **Full-time faculty:** 16 total. **Part-time faculty:** 39 total. **Class size:** 81% < 20, 19% 20-39.

Student profile. Among degree-seeking undergraduates, 73% enrolled in a transfer program, 27% enrolled in a vocational program, 142 enrolled as first-time, first-year students, 48 transferred in from other institutions.

Part-time:	28%	Native American:	8%
Out-of-state:	9%	Native Hawaiian/Pacific islander:	61%
Women:	56%	Multi-racial, non-Hispanic:	3%
African American:	1%	International:	3%
Hispanic/Latino:	22%	25 or older:	16%

Transfer out. Colleges most students transferred to 2015: Adams State College, Otero Junior College, Colorado State University, Pueblo Community College, Pikes Peak Community College.

Basis for selection. Open admission, but selective for some programs. Admission criteria for horse training management based on riding skills; admission to nursing based on specific prerequisite course grades. Interview required of horse training and management, practical nursing majors.

2015-2016 Annual costs. Tuition/fees: $4,329; $7,118 out-of-state. Per-credit charge: $131 in-state; $223 out-of-state. Room/board: $6,070. Books/supplies: $1,800. Personal expenses: $4,842. **Additional information:** In-state tuition based upon assumption of Colorado Opportunity Fund waiver of $75 per-credit hour.

2014-2015 Financial aid. Need-based: 58% of total undergraduate aid awarded as scholarships/grants, 42% as loans/jobs. Need-based aid available for part-time students. Work-study available nights, weekends and for part-time students. **Non-need-based:** Scholarships awarded for academics, athletics, minority status, state residency.

Application procedures. Admission: No deadline. No application fee. Admission notification on a rolling basis. Applicants to horse training and management and LPN nursing program encouraged to apply early. **Financial aid:** Priority date 4/1; no closing date. FAFSA required. Applicants notified on a rolling basis starting 4/15.

Academics. Special study options: Distance learning, dual enrollment of high school students, ESL, internships. **Credit/placement by examination:** AP, CLEP, institutional tests. 16 credit hours maximum toward associate degree. **Support services:** GED preparation and test center, learning center, pre-admission summer program, remedial instruction, study skills assistance, tutoring.

Majors. Business: Executive assistant, marketing, office technology. **Computer sciences:** General, LAN/WAN management. **Health services:** Nursing (RN), office computer specialist. **Liberal arts:** Arts/sciences.

Most popular majors. Agriculture 15%, health sciences 20%, liberal arts 59%.

Technology on campus. 65 workstations in dormitories, library, computer center. Dormitories wired for high-speed internet access. Online course registration, online library, wireless network available.

Student life. Freshman orientation: Available. Preregistration for classes offered. **Policies:** All single freshmen under age 21 not living with parent, guardian, or relatives must live in dormitory. **Housing:** Guaranteed on-campus for freshmen. Coed dorms, single-sex dorms available. $150 partly refundable deposit, deadline 5/29. **Activities:** International student organizations, student government, Christian athletes, horse and rodeo club, Kosmetiques, LPN association, Phi Beta Lambda, nontraditional students club.

Athletics. NJCAA. **Intercollegiate:** Baseball M, basketball, golf M, softball W, volleyball W. **Team name:** Runnin Lopes.

Student services. Career counseling, student employment services, health services, personal counseling. **Transfer:** Transfer adviser, college fairs on campus for students transferring to 4-year colleges.

Contact. E-mail: admissions@lamarcc.edu
Phone: (719) 336-1590 Toll-free number: (800) 968-6920
Fax: (719) 336-2400
Amber Thompson, Admissions Counselor, Lamar Community College, 2401 South Main Street, Lamar, CO 81052-3999

Lincoln College of Technology: Denver
Denver, Colorado
www.lincolnedu.com
CB code: 3133

- For-profit 2-year technical and career college
- Commuter campus in very large city
- Interview required

General. Accredited by ACCSC. **Enrollment:** 900 undergraduates. **Degrees:** 72 associate awarded. **Calendar:** Differs by program, extensive summer session. **Full-time faculty:** 46 total. **Part-time faculty:** 7 total. **Special facilities:** Full automotive and diesel lab shops.

Basis for selection. Open admission. **Home schooled:** Statement describing home school structure and mission, transcript of courses and grades required.

2015-2016 Annual costs. Certificate programs: $15,627 to $16,229. Diploma programs: $21,274 to $32,387. Associate programs: $36,145 to $36,747. Costs include total tuition, materials, tool fees, and registration fee.

Financial aid. Need-based: Work-study available nights, weekends and for part-time students.

Application procedures. Admission: No deadline. $150 fee. Admission notification on a rolling basis. **Financial aid:** No deadline.

Academics. Credit/placement by examination: AP, CLEP.

Contact. Phone: (303) 722-5724 Toll-free number: (800) 347-3232
Jennifer Hash, Director of Admissions, Lincoln College of Technology: Denver, 11194 East 45th Ave, Denver, CO 80239

Morgan Community College
Fort Morgan, Colorado
www.morgancc.edu
CB code: 0444

- Public 2-year community college
- Commuter campus in large town

General. Founded in 1967. Regionally accredited. **Enrollment:** 1,172 degree-seeking undergraduates. **Degrees:** 181 associate awarded. **Location:** 81 miles from Denver. **Calendar:** Semester, limited summer session. **Full-time faculty:** 33 total; 61% women. **Part-time faculty:** 141 total. **Class size:** 69% < 20, 31% 20-39.

Student profile.

Out-of-state:	1%	25 or older:	35%

Basis for selection. Open admission, but selective for some programs. Special requirements for Physical Therapist Assistant and Nursing programs. Interview required of allied health majors.

2015-2016 Annual costs. Tuition/fees: $4,097; $16,244 out-of-state. Per-credit charge: $131 in-state; $535 out-of-state. Books/supplies: $675. Personal expenses: $3,564.

Financial aid. Need-based: Need-based aid available for part-time students. Work-study available nights, weekends and for part-time students.

Application procedures. Admission: No deadline. No application fee. Admission notification on a rolling basis. **Financial aid:** Closing date 4/2. FAFSA required. Applicants notified on a rolling basis.

Academics. Special study options: Distance learning, double major, dual enrollment of high school students, ESL, honors, independent study, internships, liberal arts/career combination. License preparation in nursing, physical therapy, radiology, real estate. **Credit/placement by examination:** AP, CLEP, institutional tests. 31 credit hours maximum toward associate degree. **Support services:** GED preparation and test center, learning center, reduced course load, remedial instruction, study skills assistance, tutoring.

Majors. Business: General, accounting. **Computer sciences:** Webmaster. **Education:** General. **Health services:** Nursing (RN), occupational therapy assistant, physical therapy assistant. **Liberal arts:** Arts/sciences. **Visual/performing arts:** Art.

Most popular majors. Health sciences 33%, liberal arts 61%.

Technology on campus. 50 workstations in library, computer center, student center. Commuter students can connect to campus network. Online course registration, online library, helpline, wireless network available.

Student life. Freshman orientation: Available. Preregistration for classes offered. **Activities:** Jazz band, choral groups, literary magazine, music ensembles, student government, student newspaper, occupational therapy association, vocational industrial collusion association, Phi Theta Kappa, science club, history club, student nursing association, Phi Beta Lambda, health occupation student organization, physical therapy association.

Student services. Career counseling, financial aid counseling. **Physically disabled:** Services for visually, hearing impaired. **Transfer:** Pre-admission transcript evaluation for new students.

Contact. Phone: (970) 542-3156
Toll-free number: (800) 622-0216 ext. 3167 Fax: (970) 542-3114
Kim Maxwell, Director of Admissions, Morgan Community College, 920 Barlow Road, Fort Morgan, CO 80701

Northeastern Junior College
Sterling, Colorado
www.njc.edu
CB code: 4537

- Public 2-year community and junior college
- Residential campus in large town

General. Founded in 1941. Regionally accredited. **Enrollment:** 1,063 degree-seeking undergraduates; 435 non-degree-seeking students. **Degrees:** 246 associate awarded. **Location:** 125 miles from Denver. **Calendar:** Semester, limited summer session. **Full-time faculty:** 49 total; 6% have terminal degrees, 6% minority, 59% women. **Part-time faculty:** 28 total; 4% have terminal degrees, 14% minority, 64% women. **Class size:** 71% < 20, 28% 20-39, less than 1% 40-49, less than 1% 50-99. **Special facilities:** Equine center, wind technology laboratory, automotive/diesel repair lab, nursing laboratories.

Student profile. Among degree-seeking undergraduates, 93% enrolled in a transfer program, 8% enrolled in a vocational program, 357 enrolled as first-time, first-year students.

Part-time:	19%	Native American:	1%
Out-of-state:	6%	Multi-racial, non-Hispanic:	3%
Women:	52%	International:	2%
African American:	6%	25 or older:	21%
Hispanic/Latino:	13%	Live on campus:	31%

Transfer out. Colleges most students transferred to 2015: Colorado State University, University of Northern Colorado, Metro State, University of Wyoming, Oklahoma State University.

Basis for selection. Open admission, but selective for some programs. Qualifications for programs with limited space, such as licensed practical nursing program, set individually by department. SAT or ACT required for some technical vocational programs. Assessment determination required using ACCUPLACER, minimum ACT or SAT scores in subject areas, or proof of previous successful college experience. Cooperative admission program with Colorado State University. **Adult students:** ACCUPLACER required. **Home schooled:** Transcript of courses and grades, state high school equivalency certificate required. **Learning Disabled:** IEP required.

2015-2016 Annual costs. Tuition/fees: $4,515; $7,304 out-of-state. Per-credit charge: $125 in-state; $223 out-of-state. Room/board: $7,504. Books/supplies: $1,749. Personal expenses: $3,546. **Additional information:** In-state tuition based upon assumption of Colorado Opportunity Fund waiver of $75 per-credit hour.

2014-2015 Financial aid. Need-based: 53% of total undergraduate aid awarded as scholarships/grants, 47% as loans/jobs. Need-based aid available for part-time students. Work-study available nights, weekends and for part-time students. **Non-need-based:** Scholarships awarded for academics, alumni affiliation, art, athletics, job skills, leadership, music/drama, state residency.

Additional information: Need-based financial aid available to part-time students taking 6 credits or more per semester.

Application procedures. Admission: No deadline. No application fee. Admission notification on a rolling basis. **Financial aid:** Priority date 3/1; no closing date. FAFSA, institutional form required. Applicants notified on a rolling basis starting 4/15; must reply within 3 week(s) of notification.

Academics. Special study options: Accelerated study, cooperative education, distance learning, double major, dual enrollment of high school students, ESL, honors, independent study, internships, liberal arts/career combination, study abroad, teacher certification program, weekend college. License preparation in nursing, paramedic. **Credit/placement by examination:** AP, CLEP, IB, institutional tests. 45 credit hours maximum toward associate degree. **Support services:** GED preparation and test center, learning center, pre-admission summer program, remedial instruction, study skills assistance, tutoring, writing center.

Majors. Business: Accounting technology, management information systems. **Education:** Early childhood. **Health services:** EMT paramedic, nursing (RN). **Liberal arts:** Arts/sciences. **Protective services:** Firefighting, forest/wildland firefighting, law enforcement admin. **Work/family studies:** Child development.

Most popular majors. Agriculture 8%, business/marketing 7%, engineering/engineering technologies 6%, health sciences 10%, liberal arts 63%.

Technology on campus. 302 workstations in library, computer center, student center. Dormitories wired for high-speed internet access and linked to campus network. Online course registration, helpline, student web hosting, wireless network available.

Student life. Freshman orientation: Mandatory. Preregistration for classes offered. **Policies:** No drugs, alcohol, or smoking on campus. **Housing:** Guaranteed on-campus for freshmen. Coed dorms, single-sex dorms available. $150 fully refundable deposit, deadline 8/19. Honors house available. **Activities:** Campus ministries, choral groups, dance, drama, literary magazine, music ensembles, student government, student newspaper, Christian Fellowship, Black Student Alliance, LEARN.

Athletics. NJCAA. **Intercollegiate:** Baseball M, basketball, golf, rodeo, soccer, softball W, volleyball W. **Intramural:** Badminton, baseball, basketball, bowling, cheerleading, football (non-tackle) M, racquetball, soccer, softball, tennis, ultimate frisbee, volleyball, weight lifting. **Team name:** Plainswomen, Plainsmen.

Student services. Adult student services, alcohol/substance abuse counseling, career counseling, student employment services, financial aid counseling, health services, personal counseling. **Physically disabled:** Services for visually, speech, hearing impaired. **Transfer:** Pre-admission transcript evaluation for new students. Transfer adviser, college fairs on campus for students transferring to 4-year colleges.

Contact. E-mail: admissions@njc.edu
Phone: (970) 521-7000 Toll-free number: (800) 626-4367
Fax: (970) 521-6715
Terry Ruch, Director of Admissions, Northeastern Junior College, 100 College Avenue, Sterling, CO 80751-2399

Otero Junior College
La Junta, Colorado
https://www.ojc.edu
CB code: 4588

- Public 2-year community and junior college
- Commuter campus in small town

General. Founded in 1941. Regionally accredited. **Enrollment:** 1,410 degree-seeking undergraduates. **Degrees:** 173 associate awarded. **Location:** 60 miles from Pueblo, 100 miles from Colorado Springs. **Calendar:** Semester, limited summer session. **Full-time faculty:** 35 total. **Part-time faculty:** 50 total. **Class size:** 74% < 20, 21% 20-39, 2% 40-49, 3% 50-99. **Special facilities:** Koshare Indian Kiva museum, Falcon Telescope observatory.

Student profile.

Out-of-state:	7%	Live on campus:	22%
25 or older:	30%		

Basis for selection. Open admission, but selective for some programs. Special admission requirements for nursing program.

2015-2016 Annual costs. Tuition/fees: $4,209; $6,998 out-of-state. Per-credit charge: $131 in-state; $223 out-of-state. Room/board: $6,306. Books/supplies: $1,700. Personal expenses: $2,500.

2014-2015 Financial aid. Need-based: 73% of total undergraduate aid awarded as scholarships/grants, 27% as loans/jobs. Need-based aid available for part-time students. Work-study available nights, weekends and for part-time students. **Non-need-based:** Scholarships awarded for academics, athletics, state residency.

Application procedures. Admission: Closing date 8/21. No application fee. Admission notification on a rolling basis. **Financial aid:** Priority date 4/1; no closing date. FAFSA required. Applicants notified on a rolling basis starting 4/1; must reply within 2 week(s) of notification.

Academics. Special study options: Dual enrollment of high school students. Bachelor's degree programs available on campus. **Credit/placement by examination:** AP, CLEP, institutional tests. 45 credit hours maximum toward associate degree. **Support services:** GED preparation and test center, learning center, reduced course load, remedial instruction, study skills assistance, tutoring.

Majors. Biology: General. **Business:** Administrative services, business admin. **Computer sciences:** General. **Education:** General, early childhood, elementary, secondary, teacher assistance. **Health services:** Medical secretary, nursing (RN), pharmacy assistant, predental, premedicine, prepharmacy, preveterinary, veterinary technology/assistant. **History:** General. **Liberal arts:** Arts/sciences. **Math:** General. **Physical sciences:** Chemistry. **Psychology:** General. **Social sciences:** Political science. **Visual/performing arts:** Dramatic.

Technology on campus. 100 workstations in dormitories, library, computer center, student center. Dormitories wired for high-speed internet access. Wireless network available.

Student life. Freshman orientation: Available. Preregistration for classes offered. **Housing:** Single-sex dorms available. $100 nonrefundable deposit. **Activities:** Choral groups, dance, drama, student government.

Athletics. NJCAA. **Intercollegiate:** Baseball M, basketball, golf, rodeo, soccer, softball W, volleyball W, wrestling M. **Intramural:** Basketball, volleyball. **Team name:** Rattlers.

Student services. Adult student services, career counseling, student employment services, financial aid counseling, on-campus daycare, personal counseling, placement for graduates, veterans' counselor. **Physically disabled:** Services for visually, hearing impaired. **Transfer:** Pre-admission transcript evaluation for new students. Transfer adviser, college fairs on campus for students transferring to 4-year colleges.

Contact. E-mail: rana.brown@ojc.edu
Phone: (719) 384-6831 Fax: (719) 384-6933
Rana Brown, Registrar, Otero Junior College, 1802 Colorado Avenue, La Junta, CO 81050

Pikes Peak Community College
Colorado Springs, Colorado
www.ppcc.edu
CB code: 4291

- Public 2-year community college
- Commuter campus in large city

General. Founded in 1967. Regionally accredited. **Enrollment:** 12,448 degree-seeking undergraduates; 889 non-degree-seeking students. **Degrees:** 1,374 associate awarded. **Location:** 70 miles from Denver. **Calendar:** Semester, extensive summer session. **Full-time faculty:** 194 total; 14% have terminal degrees, 10% minority, 63% women. **Part-time faculty:** 578 total; 7% have terminal degrees, 11% minority, 53% women. **Class size:** 70% < 20, 30% 20-39, less than 1% 40-49, less than 1% 50-99. **Partnerships:** Formal partnership with Cheyenne Mountain Zoo.

Student profile. Among degree-seeking undergraduates, 66% enrolled in a transfer program, 34% enrolled in a vocational program, 2,295 enrolled as first-time, first-year students, 859 transferred in from other institutions.

Part-time:	60%	Native American:	1%
Out-of-state:	19%	Native Hawaiian/Pacific islander:	1%
Women:	57%	Multi-racial, non-Hispanic:	7%
African American:	7%	International:	1%
Asian American:	3%	25 or older:	44%
Hispanic/Latino:	15%		

Transfer out. Colleges most students transferred to 2015: University of Colorado at Colorado Springs, Colorado State University, University Of Northern Colorado.

Basis for selection. Open admission.

High school preparation. College-preparatory program recommended.

2015-2016 Annual costs. Tuition/fees: $4,218; $16,365 out-of-state. Per-credit charge: $131 in-state; $535.4 out-of-state. Books/supplies: $1,800. Personal expenses: $3,564. **Additional information:** In-state tuition based upon assumption of Colorado Opportunity Fund waiver of $75 per-credit hour.

2014-2015 Financial aid. **Need-based:** Average need met was 40%. Average scholarship/grant was $4,200; average loan $3,000. 69% of total undergraduate aid awarded as scholarships/grants, 31% as loans/jobs. Need-based aid available for part-time students. Work-study available nights, weekends and for part-time students. **Non-need-based:** Awarded to 324 full-time undergraduates, including 25 freshmen.

Application procedures. Admission: No deadline. No application fee. Admission notification on a rolling basis. **Financial aid:** Priority date 3/31, closing date 7/1. FAFSA required. Applicants notified on a rolling basis; must reply within 2 week(s) of notification.

Academics. Special study options: Cooperative education, distance learning, double major, dual enrollment of high school students, ESL, external degree, independent study, internships, study abroad, weekend college. License preparation in nursing, paramedic, radiology, real estate. **Credit/placement by examination:** AP, CLEP, IB, institutional tests. Students may receive up to 75% of total credits for all types of prior learning (testing, work and/or life experience). **Support services:** GED test center, learning center, remedial instruction, study skills assistance, tutoring, writing center.

Majors. Business: Accounting technology, marketing, office management. **Communications technology:** Animation/special effects, radio/TV. **Computer sciences:** General, information systems, networking. **Conservation:** General. **Education:** Early childhood. **Foreign languages:** Sign language interpretation. **Health services:** Dental assistant, EMT paramedic, mental health services, nursing (RN), office admin, pharmacy assistant, radiologic technology/medical imaging. **Liberal arts:** Arts/sciences. **Protective services:** Firefighting, forest/wildland firefighting, homeland security, law enforcement admin. **Visual/performing arts:** Interior design, photography.

Most popular majors. Health sciences 13%, liberal arts 54%, security/protective services 6%.

Technology on campus. 233 workstations in library, computer center. Commuter students can connect to campus network. Online course registration, helpline, wireless network available.

Student life. Freshman orientation: Available. Preregistration for classes offered. **Policies:** Clubs must be open to all students, be run by students, have a constitution, and have an adviser. All Advisers must be full-time faculty or staff and must go through training. **Activities:** Bands, choral groups, dance, drama, music ensembles, radio station, student government, TV station, social services club, Phi Theta Kappa, Phi Beta Lambda, Multicultural Student Union, nursing club, dental assisting club, Sign Language club, para legal club, infinity math club, zoology club.

Athletics. Team name: Aardvarks.

Student services. Adult student services, career counseling, services for economically disadvantaged, student employment services, financial aid counseling, on-campus daycare, personal counseling, veterans' counselor. **Physically disabled:** Services for visually, speech, hearing impaired. **Transfer:** Re-entry adviser, pre-admission transcript evaluation for new students. Transfer adviser, college fairs on campus for students transferring to 4-year colleges.

Contact. E-mail: admissions@ppcc.edu
Phone: (719) 502-3000 Toll-free number: (800) 456-6847
Jeff Horner, Director of Admissions, Pikes Peak Community College, 5675 South Academy Boulevard, Colorado Springs, CO 80906-5498

Pueblo Community College
Pueblo, Colorado
www.pueblocc.edu   CB code: 4634

- Public 2-year community college
- Commuter campus in small city

General. Founded in 1933. Regionally accredited. **Enrollment:** 4,893 degree-seeking undergraduates; 825 non-degree-seeking students. **Degrees:** 713 associate awarded. **Location:** 50 miles from Colorado Springs, 100 miles from Denver. **Calendar:** Semester, extensive summer session. **Full-time faculty:** 76 total; 20% minority, 60% women. **Part-time faculty:** 308 total; 11% minority, 56% women. **Class size:** 76% < 20, 23% 20-39, less than 1% 40-49, less than 1% >100. **Special facilities:** STEM center, cadaver lab, downtown studio, advanced technology center, healthcare simulators, fire science, emergency medical services. **Partnerships:** Formal partnership with St. Mary Corwin Hospital.

Student profile. Among degree-seeking undergraduates, 58% enrolled in a transfer program, 42% enrolled in a vocational program, 2% already have a bachelor's degree or higher, 559 enrolled as first-time, first-year students, 488 transferred in from other institutions.

Part-time:	61%	Hispanic/Latino:	27%
Out-of-state:	1%	Native American:	2%
Women:	64%	Multi-racial, non-Hispanic:	5%
African American:	3%	International:	1%
Asian American:	1%	25 or older:	56%

Transfer out. Colleges most students transferred to 2015: Colorado State University-Pueblo.

Basis for selection. Open admission, but selective for some programs. Admission to health programs based on GPA, high school courses, test scores. ACT required of dental hygiene applicants; score report by May 1. Assessment testing required for all entering degree- and certificate-seeking students, unless ACT/SAT scores or transcripts showing successful completion of college-level English and math courses provided. Interview required of allied health majors only. **Learning Disabled:** Reasonable accommodations will be provided upon request for persons with disabilities. To make a request, please notify the Disability Resources Team.

2015-2016 Annual costs. Tuition/fees: $4,479; $16,626 out-of-state. Per-credit charge: $131 in-state; $535 out-of-state. Books/supplies: $1,869. Personal expenses: $3,606. **Additional information:** In-state tuition based upon assumption of Colorado Opportunity Fund waiver of $75 per-credit hour.

Financial aid. Need-based: Need-based aid available for part-time students. Work-study available nights, weekends and for part-time students. **Non-need-based:** Scholarships awarded for academics, art, job skills, leadership, music/drama.

Application procedures. Admission: Closing date 8/18 (receipt date). No application fee. Admission notification on a rolling basis beginning on or about 4/10. Foreign applicants must show evidence of resources sufficient to cover tuition/fees for full academic year before acceptance. Application closing date for allied health programs: 4/1. **Financial aid:** Priority date 3/15; no closing date. FAFSA required. Applicants notified on a rolling basis starting 4/1.

Academics. Special study options: Cooperative education, cross-registration, distance learning, double major, dual enrollment of high school students, ESL, honors, independent study, internships, liberal arts/career combination. License preparation in dental hygiene, nursing, occupational therapy, paramedic, physical therapy, radiology. **Credit/placement by examination:** AP, CLEP, IB, institutional tests. All but 15 hour residence requirement for certificate or associate degree may be from credit for prior learning. **Support services:** GED preparation and test center, learning center, reduced course load, remedial instruction, study skills assistance, tutoring, writing center. Integrated mentoring program.

Majors. Business: Accounting technology, business admin, entrepreneurial studies, office technology. **Communications technology:** General, animation/special effects. **Computer sciences:** General, web page design. **Education:** Early childhood. **Health services:** Dental assistant, dental hygiene, EMT paramedic, insurance coding, nursing (RN), occupational therapy assistant, office admin, physical therapy assistant, radiologic technology/medical imaging, respiratory therapy technology, surgical technology. **Liberal arts:** Arts/sciences, library assistant. **Protective services:** Firefighting, law enforcement admin.

Most popular majors. Health sciences 31%, liberal arts 42%, trade and industry 8%.

Technology on campus. 147 workstations in library, computer center, student center. Commuter students can connect to campus network. Online course registration, online library, helpline, wireless network available.

Student life. Freshman orientation: Available. Preregistration for classes offered. 1-day orientation held several times before the start of the fall, summer, and spring semesters. **Activities:** Choral groups, dance, drama, literary magazine, music ensembles, student government, student newspaper, TV station.

Athletics. Team name: Panthers.

Student services. Adult student services, alcohol/substance abuse counseling, career counseling, services for economically disadvantaged, student employment services, financial aid counseling, health services, personal counseling, placement for graduates, veterans' counselor. **Physically disabled:** Services for visually, speech, hearing impaired. **Transfer:** Transfer center, transfer adviser, college fairs on campus for students transferring to 4-year colleges.

Contact. E-mail: admissions@pueblocc.edu
Phone: (719) 549-3010 Toll-free number: (888) 642-6017
Fax: (719) 549-3012
Barbara Benedict, Director of Admissions and Records, Pueblo
Community College, 900 West Orman Avenue, Pueblo, CO 81004-1499

Red Rocks Community College
Lakewood, Colorado
www.rrcc.edu CB code: 4130

▶ Public 2-year community and career college
▶ Commuter campus in small city

General. Founded in 1969. Regionally accredited. **Enrollment:** 7,789 undergraduates. **Degrees:** 678 associate awarded. **ROTC:** Army, Air Force. **Location:** 10 miles from Denver. **Calendar:** Semester, extensive summer session. **Full-time faculty:** 94 total. **Part-time faculty:** 418 total. **Class size:** 66% < 20, 34% 20-39.

Student profile.

Out-of-state:	6%	25 or older: 53%

Basis for selection. Open admission.

2015-2016 Annual costs. Tuition/fees: $4,353; $16,499 out-of-state. Per-credit charge: $130.5 in-state; $535.4 out-of-state. Books/supplies: $1,800. Personal expenses: $3,546.

Financial aid. Need-based: Need-based aid available for part-time students. Work-study available nights, weekends and for part-time students. **Non-need-based:** Scholarships awarded for academics, leadership, minority status, state residency.

Application procedures. Admission: No deadline. No application fee. Admission notification on a rolling basis. **Financial aid:** Priority date 4/1; no closing date. FAFSA required. Applicants notified on a rolling basis starting 5/1.

Academics. Students in advanced ESL classes may begin some college-level courses early. Scholarships offered for outstanding ESL performance when funds are available. **Special study options:** Accelerated study, cross-registration, distance learning, dual enrollment of high school students, ESL, honors, independent study, internships, liberal arts/career combination, teacher certification program, weekend college. License preparation in paramedic, radiology, real estate. **Credit/placement by examination:** AP, CLEP, IB, institutional tests. **Support services:** GED preparation and test center, learning center, reduced course load, remedial instruction, study skills assistance, tutoring, writing center.

Majors. Business: Accounting technology, business admin, management information systems, real estate. **Communications:** Digital media. **Computer sciences:** Database management, networking, programming, web page design, webmaster. **Education:** Early childhood, educational technology. **General:** Building construction, electrician. **Health services:** EMT paramedic, health information technology, holistic, office admin, radiologic technology/medical imaging, sonography. **Liberal arts:** Arts/sciences. **Protective services:** Disaster management, firefighting, police science. **Visual/performing arts:** Cinematography, game design, interior design, photography, theater design.

Most popular majors. Business/marketing 10%, engineering/engineering technologies 16%, health sciences 22%, liberal arts 10%, security/protective services 16%, trade and industry 17%, visual/performing arts 6%.

Technology on campus. 128 workstations in library, computer center, student center. Online course registration, online library, helpline, wireless network available.

Student life. Freshman orientation: Available. Preregistration for classes offered. **Activities:** Campus ministries, dance, drama, film society, international student organizations, literary magazine, music ensembles, musical theater, student government.

Student services. Adult student services, career counseling, student employment services, health services, on-campus daycare, personal counseling, placement for graduates, veterans' counselor. **Physically disabled:** Services for visually, speech, hearing impaired. **Transfer:** Transfer adviser, college fairs on campus for students transferring to 4-year colleges.

Contact. E-mail: admissions@rrcc.edu
Phone: (303) 914-6348 Fax: (303) 989-6919
Dean Rathe, Director of Enrollment Services, Red Rocks Community
College, 13300 West Sixth Avenue, Lakewood, CO 80228-1255

Redstone College
Broomfield, Colorado
www.redstone.edu

▶ For-profit 2-year technical college
▶ Commuter campus in small city

General. Accredited by ACCSC. **Enrollment:** 552 undergraduates. **Degrees:** 296 associate awarded. **Location:** 15 miles from Denver and Boulder. **Calendar:** Differs by program. **Full-time faculty:** 35 total. **Part-time faculty:** 21 total.

Basis for selection. Open admission.

2015-2016 Annual costs. Tuition and fees for entire Associate degree program $33,455 to $40,219 depending on program.

Financial aid. All financial aid based on need. Work-study available nights, weekends and for part-time students.

Application procedures. Admission: No deadline. $25 fee. Admission notification on a rolling basis. **Financial aid:** No deadline. FAFSA required. Applicants notified on a rolling basis; must reply within 2 week(s) of notification.

Academics. Special study options: License preparation in aviation. **Credit/placement by examination:** AP, CLEP. **Support services:** Learning center, tutoring.

Technology on campus. 8 workstations in computer center.

Student life. Housing: Apartments available.

Student services. Career counseling, student employment services, placement for graduates, veterans' counselor.

Contact. Phone: (303) 466-1714 Toll-free number: (800) 460-0592
Fax: (303) 469-3797
Cate Clark, Director of Admissions, Redstone College, 10851 West 120th
Avenue, Broomfield, CO 80021-3401

Trinidad State Junior College
Trinidad, Colorado
www.trinidadstate.edu CB code: 4821

▶ Public 2-year community college
▶ Commuter campus in small town

General. Founded in 1925. Regionally accredited. TSJC operates two campuses and several additional sites. **Enrollment:** 1,216 degree-seeking undergraduates. **Degrees:** 293 associate awarded. **Location:** 15 miles from New Mexico border, 198 miles from Denver. **Calendar:** Semester, limited summer session. **Full-time faculty:** 49 total. **Part-time faculty:** 104 total. **Class size:** 88% < 20, 11% 20-39, less than 1% 40-49. **Special facilities:** Anthropology and geology museum, gunsmith laboratory, gun range, aquaculture farm, line tech field, welding and automotive labs, heavy equipment operating job site. **Partnerships:** Formal partnership with San Isabel Electric Association for the Lineman Technician program.

Student profile.

Out-of-state:	10%	Live on campus:	10%
25 or older:	44%		

Transfer out. Colleges most students transferred to 2015: Colorado State University-Pueblo, Adams State College, Colorado State University, University of Northern Colorado.

Basis for selection. Open admission, but selective for some programs. A background check is required for the nursing, gunsmith, emergency medical technician, line technician, administrative medical assistant, early childhood education, and massage therapy programs. The nursing and line technician programs also require a medical examination. Some programs have academic prerequisites. TSJC has an open-admissions policy. However, students must have a specified score on standardized tests, or college placement tests, to enroll in certain courses. There is also restricted admissions to some programs, such as the nursing and gunsmith programs. **Adult students:** ACT/SAT or ACCUPLACER required for placement.

High school preparation. 17 units required. Required units include English 4, mathematics 4, social studies 3, science 3, foreign language 1 and academic electives 2.

2015-2016 Annual costs. Tuition/fees: $4,353; $7,142 out-of-state. Per-credit charge: $130 in-state; $223 out-of-state. Room/board: $6,274. Books/supplies: $1,800. **Additional information:** In-state tuition based upon assumption of Colorado Opportunity Fund waiver of $75 per-credit hour.

Financial aid. Need-based: Need-based aid available for part-time students. Work-study available nights, weekends and for part-time students. **Non-need-based:** Scholarships awarded for academics, athletics, state residency.

Application procedures. Admission: Closing date 8/28 (receipt date). No application fee. Admission notification on a rolling basis. Enrollment can be postponed for one academic year after admission. If not enrolled within the year, applicant must resubmit an admission application. **Financial aid:** Priority date 5/1; no closing date. FAFSA required. Applicants notified on a rolling basis starting 6/15.

Academics. Special study options: Accelerated study, cooperative education, distance learning, double major, dual enrollment of high school students, ESL, independent study, internships, liberal arts/career combination. Bachelor's degree programs available on campus. License preparation in nursing, paramedic. **Credit/placement by examination:** AP, CLEP, institutional tests. 45 credit hours maximum toward associate degree. **Support services:** GED preparation and test center, learning center, reduced course load, remedial instruction, study skills assistance, tutoring, writing center.

Majors. Business: General, accounting, business admin. **Communications:** Advertising, journalism. **Computer sciences:** General, computer science, programming, word processing. **Conservation:** General, fisheries. **Engineering:** General. **General:** Lineworker. **Health services:** Massage therapy. **Liberal arts:** Arts/sciences. **Protective services:** Criminal justice, law enforcement admin, police science. **Social sciences:** Criminology. **Visual/performing arts:** Commercial/advertising art. **Work/family studies:** Child care management.

Most popular majors. Engineering/engineering technologies 7%, health sciences 11%, liberal arts 63%, trade and industry 10%.

Technology on campus. 260 workstations in dormitories, library, student center. Dormitories wired for high-speed internet access and linked to campus network. Commuter students can connect to campus network. Online course registration, helpline, wireless network available.

Student life. Freshman orientation: Available. Preregistration for classes offered. **Housing:** Guaranteed on-campus for all undergraduates. Single-sex dorms available. $150 partly refundable deposit. Special housing available for welding, line tech, and gunsmith students. **Activities:** Campus ministries, drama, student government, MECHA, black student alliance, Christian Challenge.

Athletics. NJCAA. **Intercollegiate:** Baseball M, basketball, soccer, softball W, volleyball W. **Intramural:** Baseball M, basketball, rifle, soccer, softball W, volleyball W. **Team name:** Trojans.

Student services. Adult student services, career counseling, services for economically disadvantaged, student employment services, financial aid counseling, placement for graduates. **Physically disabled:** Services for visually, speech, hearing impaired. **Transfer:** Transfer adviser, college fairs on campus for students transferring to 4-year colleges.

Contact. E-mail: bernadine.degarbo@trinidadstate.edu
Phone: (719) 846-5621 Toll-free number: (800) 621-8752
Fax: (719) 846-5620
Kerry Gabrielson, Vice President of Student and Academic Affairs,
Trinidad State Junior College, 600 Prospect Street, Trinidad, CO 81082

Connecticut

Asnuntuck Community College
Enfield, Connecticut   **CB member**
www.asnuntuck.edu   **CB code: 3656**

▶ Public 2-year community and technical college
▶ Commuter campus in large town

General. Founded in 1972. Regionally accredited. **Enrollment:** 1,295 degree-seeking undergraduates; 276 non-degree-seeking students. **Degrees:** 177 associate awarded. **Location:** 15 miles from Hartford; 10 miles from Springfield, Massachusetts. **Calendar:** Semester, extensive summer session. **Full-time faculty:** 27 total. **Part-time faculty:** 91 total. **Class size:** 38% < 20, 61% 20-39, less than 1% 40-49.

Student profile. Among degree-seeking undergraduates, 325 enrolled as first-time, first-year students.

Part-time:	52%	Hispanic/Latino:	10%
Women:	52%	Multi-racial, non-Hispanic:	3%
African American:	11%	25 or older:	23%
Asian American:	3%		

Transfer out. Colleges most students transferred to 2015: Eastern Connecticut State University, Central Connecticut State University, University of Connecticut, Western New England College.

Basis for selection. Open admission. Special waivers may be granted to applicants without high school diploma/GED who demonstrate the ability to perform academically at college level. **Home schooled:** Transcript of courses and grades required.

High school preparation. College-preparatory program recommended.

2015-2016 Annual costs. Tuition/fees: $4,052; $12,116 out-of-state. Per-credit charge: $150 in-state; $450 out-of-state. Books/supplies: $1,200. Personal expenses: $1,551.

Financial aid. Need-based: Need-based aid available for part-time students. Work-study available nights, weekends and for part-time students.

Application procedures. Admission: No deadline. $20 fee, may be waived for applicants with need. Admission notification on a rolling basis. **Financial aid:** Closing date 6/1. FAFSA, institutional form required. Applicants notified on a rolling basis starting 7/1; must reply within 2 week(s) of notification.

Academics. On-line tutoring available. **Special study options:** Cooperative education, cross-registration, distance learning, double major, dual enrollment of high school students, independent study, internships, liberal arts/career combination, weekend college. License preparation in paramedic, real estate. **Credit/placement by examination:** AP, CLEP, institutional tests. 48 credit hours maximum toward associate degree. **Support services:** Learning center, remedial instruction, study skills assistance, tutoring.

Majors. Business: Accounting, business admin, office technology. **Communications technology:** General, radio/TV. **Computer sciences:** General. **Education:** Early childhood. **Engineering:** Engineering science. **Health services:** Mental health services. **Liberal arts:** Arts/sciences. **Protective services:** Police science. **Work/family studies:** Child care management.

Most popular majors. Business/marketing 31%, family/consumer sciences 7%, liberal arts 47%, security/protective services 7%.

Technology on campus. 111 workstations in library, computer center. Online course registration, online library, wireless network available.

Student life. Freshman orientation: Available. Preregistration for classes offered. **Activities:** Drama, literary magazine, radio station, student government, TV station, human services club, Phi Theta Kappa.

Student services. Career counseling, student employment services, financial aid counseling, minority student services, on-campus daycare, personal counseling, placement for graduates, veterans' counselor. **Physically disabled:** Services for visually, speech, hearing impaired. **Transfer:** Pre-admission transcript evaluation for new students. Transfer adviser, college fairs on campus for students transferring to 4-year colleges.

Contact. E-mail: AS-Admissions@asnuntuck.edu
Phone: (860) 253-3000 ext. 3010 Toll-free number: (800) 501-3967
Fax: (860) 253-3014
Timothy St. James, Director of Enrollment Management, Asnuntuck Community College, 170 Elm Street, Enfield, CT 06082

Capital Community College
Hartford, Connecticut
www.ccc.commnet.edu   **CB code: 3421**

▶ Public 2-year community and technical college
▶ Commuter campus in small city

General. Founded in 1946. Regionally accredited. **Enrollment:** 3,110 degree-seeking undergraduates; 393 non-degree-seeking students. **Degrees:** 384 associate awarded. **ROTC:** Army, Naval, Air Force. **Calendar:** Semester, limited summer session. **Full-time faculty:** 69 total. **Part-time faculty:** 210 total. **Special facilities:** Math development center, computerized English as a Second Language lab, interactive videodisc instruction for nursing students, learning/writing center. **Partnerships:** Formal partnerships with high schools for Tech Prep program.

Student profile. Among degree-seeking undergraduates, 538 enrolled as first-time, first-year students.

Part-time:	74%	25 or older:	57%
Women:	71%		

Transfer out. Colleges most students transferred to 2015: University of Connecticut, Central Connecticut State University, University of Hartford, Eastern Connecticut State University.

Basis for selection. Open admission, but selective for some programs. SAT scores used to satisfy admission criteria for nursing, physical therapist assistant, and radiologic technology programs.

High school preparation. Algebra, biology, and chemistry required for nursing program. Physical therapy assistant, radiologic technology, and pre-nursing programs also have specific course requirements. Paramedic program has specific educational and training requirements.

2015-2016 Annual costs. Tuition/fees: $4,052; $12,116 out-of-state. Per-credit charge: $150 in-state; $450 out-of-state. Books/supplies: $850. Personal expenses: $1,965.

Financial aid. All financial aid based on need. Need-based aid available for part-time students. Work-study available nights, weekends and for part-time students.

Application procedures. Admission: No deadline. $20 fee, may be waived for applicants with need. Admission notification on a rolling basis. **Financial aid:** Closing date 7/15. FAFSA required. Applicants notified on a rolling basis starting 7/15; must reply within 2 week(s) of notification.

Academics. Special study options: Accelerated study, cross-registration, distance learning, double major, dual enrollment of high school students, ESL, independent study, internships, liberal arts/career combination, weekend college. Interdisciplinary summer program with Smith College. License preparation in nursing, paramedic, radiology. **Credit/placement by examination:** AP, CLEP, institutional tests. **Support services:** GED preparation, learning center, pre-admission summer program, remedial instruction, study skills assistance, tutoring, writing center.

Majors. Business: Accounting, administrative services, business admin. **Computer sciences:** General. **Education:** Early childhood. **Engineering:** Electrical. **Health services:** EMT paramedic, medical assistant, medical radiologic technology/radiation therapy, mental health services, nursing (RN), physical therapy assistant. **Liberal arts:** Arts/sciences, library assistant. **Protective services:** Fire safety technology.

Most popular majors. Business/marketing 18%, health sciences 40%, liberal arts 26%, public administration/social services 6%.

Technology on campus. 500 workstations in library, computer center, student center. Commuter students can connect to campus network. Online course registration, online library, wireless network available.

Student life. Freshman orientation: Available. Preregistration for classes offered. 3 day program held prior to start of semester. **Policies:** Policies against drugs and alcohol, violence, weapons, and sexual harassment on campus. **Activities:** Bands, choral groups, dance, drama, international student organizations, literary magazine, radio station, student government, TV station, Latin American students association, senior renewal club, early childhood club, pre-professional club, Phi Theta Kappa, nursing club, black student union.

Student services. Adult student services, chaplain/spiritual director, career counseling, services for economically disadvantaged, student employment services, financial aid counseling, minority student services, on-campus daycare, personal counseling, placement for graduates, veterans' counselor, women's services. **Physically disabled:** Services for visually, speech, hearing impaired. **Transfer:** College fairs on campus for students transferring to 4-year colleges.

Contact. E-mail: ggorneault@ccc.commnet.edu
Phone: (860) 906-5126 Toll-free number: (800) 894-6126
Gregg Gorneault, Director of Admissions, Capital Community College, 950 Main Street, Hartford, CT 06103-1207

Gateway Community College
New Haven, Connecticut   **CB member**
www.gatewayct.edu   **CB code: 3425**

- Public 2-year community college
- Commuter campus in small city
- Application essay, interview required

General. Founded in 1992. Regionally accredited. **Enrollment:** 6,542 degree-seeking undergraduates. **Degrees:** 708 associate awarded. **Location:** 75 miles from New York City, 130 miles from Boston. **Calendar:** Semester, limited summer session. **Full-time faculty:** 109 total. **Part-time faculty:** 480 total. **Class size:** 24% < 20, 71% 20-39, 4% 40-49, less than 1% 50-99. **Special facilities:** Early childhood learning center, day care center, student operated cafe, student art museum.

Student profile.

Out-of-state: 1% **25 or older:**   32%

Transfer out. Colleges most students transferred to 2015: Southern Connecticut State University, University of New Haven, Quinnipiac College.

Basis for selection. Open admission, but selective for some programs. Special requirements for radiology, nursing, nuclear medicine technology, diagnostic medical sonography, drug and alcohol rehabilitation counselor. Interview required of radiology, drug and alcohol counseling, nuclear medicine technology, diagnostic medical sonography, nursing majors. **Home schooled:** Transcript of courses and grades required.

2015-2016 Annual costs. Tuition/fees: $4,052; $12,116 out-of-state. Per-credit charge: $150 in-state; $450 out-of-state. Books/supplies: $1,200. Personal expenses: $1,748.

Financial aid. All financial aid based on need. Need-based aid available for part-time students. Work-study available nights, weekends and for part-time students.

Application procedures. Admission: Priority date 6/1; deadline 9/1. $20 fee, may be waived for applicants with need. Admission notification on a rolling basis beginning on or about 2/1. **Financial aid:** No deadline. FAFSA, institutional form required. Applicants notified on a rolling basis; must reply within 2 week(s) of notification.

Academics. Special study options: Accelerated study, cross-registration, distance learning, dual enrollment of high school students, ESL, independent study, internships, liberal arts/career combination, weekend college. License preparation in nursing, radiology. **Credit/placement by examination:** AP, CLEP, institutional tests. 30 credit hours maximum toward associate degree. **Support services:** GED preparation, learning center, pre-admission summer program, reduced course load, remedial instruction, study skills assistance, tutoring, writing center.

Majors. Business: Accounting, administrative services, business admin, fashion, hotel/motel admin, office/clerical, restaurant/food services, sales/distribution. **Computer sciences:** Computer science, data processing, information systems, networking, programming, word processing. **Conservation:** General, environmental science. **Education:** Early childhood, special ed. **Engineering:** Engineering science. **Health services:** Dental hygiene, dietetic technician, environmental health, medical radiologic technology/radiation therapy, medical secretary, nuclear medical technology, nursing (RN), radiologic technology/medical imaging, sonography, substance abuse counseling. **Liberal arts:** Arts/sciences. **Math:** General. **Parks/recreation:** Sports admin. **Protective services:** Fire services admin. **Visual/performing arts:** Graphic design, studio arts. **Work/family studies:** Aging, food/nutrition, institutional food production.

Most popular majors. Business/marketing 8%, engineering/engineering technologies 7%, health sciences 27%, liberal arts 49%.

Technology on campus. 650 workstations in library, computer center, student center. Online library, helpline, wireless network available.

Student life. Freshman orientation: Available. Preregistration for classes offered. **Activities:** Choral groups, drama, international student organizations, literary magazine, music ensembles, student government, student newspaper, Spanish-American club, math/science club, Phi Theta Kappa, art club, athletic club, veteran's club, biology club, Theater Goers, black student union.

Athletics. NJCAA. **Intercollegiate:** Baseball M, basketball. **Team name:** Ravens.

Student services. Adult student services, career counseling, student employment services, financial aid counseling, health services, on-campus daycare, personal counseling, placement for graduates, veterans' counselor, women's services. **Physically disabled:** Services for visually, speech, hearing impaired. **Transfer:** Transfer adviser for students transferring to 4-year colleges.

Contact. E-mail: Admissions@gwcc.commnet.edu
Phone: (203) 285-2010 Toll-free number: (800) 390-7723
Fax: (203) 285-2260
Carberry Tony, Director of Enrollment Management, Gateway Community College, 20 Church Street, New Haven, CT 06510

Goodwin College
East Hartford, Connecticut   **CB member**
www.goodwin.edu   **CB code: 5879**

- Private 2-year health science and career college
- Commuter campus in small city

General. Enrollment: 3,287 degree-seeking undergraduates; 153 non-degree-seeking students. **Degrees:** 99 bachelor's, 456 associate awarded. **Location:** 5 miles from Hartford. **Calendar:** Semester, extensive summer session. **Full-time faculty:** 90 total; 30% have terminal degrees, 20% minority, 70% women. **Part-time faculty:** 221 total; 17% have terminal degrees, 20% minority, 63% women. **Class size:** 74% < 20, 26% 20-39.

Student profile. Among degree-seeking undergraduates, 318 enrolled as first-time, first-year students.

Part-time: 82% **Women:**   82%
Out-of-state: 3%

Transfer out. Colleges most students transferred to 2015: Manchester Community College, Capital Community College, Central Connecticut State University, Tunxis Community College, University of Connecticut.

Basis for selection. Open admission, but selective for some programs. Applicants to nursing, respiratory therapist, and histology technician programs must have successfully completed prerequisite courses prior to application and submit completed application to program desired. Interviews may be required for some programs. **Home schooled:** State high school equivalency certificate required.

2015-2016 Annual costs. Books/supplies: $1,000. Personal expenses: $1,651.

Financial aid. All financial aid based on need. Need-based aid available for part-time students. Work-study available nights, weekends and for part-time students.

Application procedures. Admission: No deadline. $50 fee, may be waived for applicants with need. Admission notification on a rolling basis. **Financial aid:** No deadline. FAFSA, institutional form required. Applicants notified on a rolling basis starting 7/1.

Academics. Special study options: Cross-registration, distance learning, double major, ESL, internships. Bachelor's degree programs available on campus. License preparation in nursing, paramedic. **Credit/placement by examination:** AP, CLEP, institutional tests. 30 credit hours maximum toward associate degree, 30 toward bachelor's. **Support services:** Learning center, pre-admission summer program, reduced course load, remedial instruction, study skills assistance, tutoring, writing center.

Majors. Business: General, business admin, logistics, nonprofit/public, office management. **Conservation:** Environmental studies. **Health services:** Dental hygiene, histologic assistant, insurance specialist, medical assistant, nursing (RN), occupational therapy assistant, office admin, optician, respiratory therapy technology. **Protective services:** Homeland security, law enforcement admin. **Work/family studies:** Child care management, child care service, child development, family systems.

Most popular majors. Health sciences 84%, public administration/social services 6%.

Technology on campus. 100 workstations in library, computer center, student center. Commuter students can connect to campus network. Online course registration, online library, helpline, repair service, wireless network available.

Student life. Freshman orientation: Available. Preregistration for classes offered. **Activities:** Choral groups, literary magazine, student government.

Athletics. Intercollegiate: Basketball M, football (non-tackle) M, soccer M. **Intramural:** Basketball, soccer, volleyball. **Team name:** Navigators.

Student services. Adult student services, alcohol/substance abuse counseling, career counseling, student employment services, financial aid counseling, personal counseling, placement for graduates, veterans' counselor. **Physically disabled:** Services for visually impaired. **Transfer:** Re-entry adviser, pre-admission transcript evaluation for new students. Transfer adviser for students transferring to 4-year colleges.

Contact. E-mail: nlentino@goodwin.edu
Phone: (860) 528-4111 Toll-free number: (800) 889-3282
Fax: (860) 291-9550
Nicholas Lentino, Assistant Vice President for Admissions, Goodwin College, One Riverside Drive, East Hartford, CT 06118-9980

Housatonic Community College
Bridgeport, Connecticut
www.hcc.commnet.edu   CB code: 3446

◗ Public 2-year community college
◗ Commuter campus in small city

General. Founded in 1966. Regionally accredited. **Enrollment:** 4,808 degree-seeking undergraduates. **Degrees:** 492 associate awarded. **Location:** 60 miles from Hartford, 60 miles from New York City. **Calendar:** Semester, extensive summer session. **Full-time faculty:** 73 total. **Part-time faculty:** 325 total. **Class size:** 45% < 20, 53% 20-39, 2% 40-49, less than 1% 50-99. **Special facilities:** Art museum.

Basis for selection. Open admission, but selective for some programs. Special requirements for clinical lab science, physical therapist assistant, occupational therapy assistant, nursing programs. Interview required of allied health, computer program majors.

2015-2016 Annual costs. Tuition/fees: $4,042; $12,106 out-of-state. Per-credit charge: $150 in-state; $450 out-of-state. Books/supplies: $700.

Financial aid. All financial aid based on need. Need-based aid available for part-time students. Work-study available nights, weekends and for part-time students.

Application procedures. Admission: No deadline. $20 fee, may be waived for applicants with need. Admission notification on a rolling basis. Application period ends one week after start of classes. **Financial aid:** Priority date 11/1, closing date 5/1. FAFSA required. Applicants notified on a rolling basis starting 6/1.

Academics. Special study options: Cooperative education, distance learning, double major, dual enrollment of high school students, ESL, honors, independent study, internships, weekend college. License preparation in occupational therapy, real estate. **Credit/placement by examination:** AP, CLEP, institutional tests. 30 credit hours maximum toward associate degree. New Jersey Basic Skills Placement Test and/or ACCUPLACER used for advising and placement. **Support services:** GED preparation, learning center, reduced course load, remedial instruction, study skills assistance, tutoring, writing center.

Majors. Business: General, accounting, administrative services, business admin. **Computer sciences:** General. **Education:** Early childhood. **Health services:** Mental health services, nursing (RN), physical therapy assistant, substance abuse counseling. **Liberal arts:** Arts/sciences. **Protective services:** Police science. **Visual/performing arts:** Art, commercial/advertising art, dramatic, graphic design, photography, studio arts. **Work/family studies:** Child care management.

Most popular majors. Business/marketing 19%, education 9%, health sciences 8%, liberal arts 39%, security/protective services 11%.

Technology on campus. 140 workstations in library, computer center. Commuter students can connect to campus network. Online course registration, wireless network available.

Student life. Freshman orientation: Available. Preregistration for classes offered. **Activities:** Drama, literary magazine, student government, student newspaper.

Student services. Adult student services, career counseling, services for economically disadvantaged, student employment services, financial aid counseling, health services, minority student services, on-campus daycare, personal counseling, placement for graduates, veterans' counselor, women's services. **Physically disabled:** Services for visually, hearing impaired. **Transfer:** Transfer adviser, college fairs on campus for students transferring to 4-year colleges.

Contact. E-mail: ho-webadmissions@hcc.commnet.edu
Phone: (203) 332-5100 Fax: (203) 332-5123
Earl Graham, Director of Admissions, Housatonic Community College, 900 Lafayette Boulevard, Bridgeport, CT 06604-4704

Lincoln College of New England
Southington, Connecticut
www.lincolncollegene.edu   CB code: 0481

◗ For-profit 2-year culinary school and business college
◗ Residential campus in small town
◗ Application essay, interview required

General. Regionally accredited. Additional campus in Hartford. Students can complete degree program in 18-month accelerated format. Cost of attendance includes 6-month paid internship. **Enrollment:** 715 undergraduates. **Degrees:** 17 bachelor's, 139 associate awarded. **Location:** 50 miles from Hartford. **Calendar:** Differs by program, limited summer session. **Full-time faculty:** 44 total. **Part-time faculty:** 170 total. **Class size:** 95% < 20, 5% 20-39.

Student profile.

Out-of-state:	90%	Live on campus:	90%
25 or older:	40%		

Transfer out. Colleges most students transferred to 2015: Institut Hotelier Cesar Ritz (Switzerland).

Basis for selection. Open admission.

2015-2016 Annual costs. Tuition/fees: $19,940. Room/board: $9,200.

Financial aid. Need-based: Need-based aid available for part-time students. Work-study available nights, weekends and for part-time students. **Non-need-based:** Scholarships awarded for academics.

Application procedures. Admission: No deadline. $125 fee, may be waived for applicants with need. Admission notification on a rolling basis. **Financial aid:** No deadline. Applicants notified on a rolling basis starting 1/1.

Academics. Special study options: Accelerated study, cooperative education, internships, liberal arts/career combination, study abroad. Bachelor's degree programs available on campus. **Credit/placement by examination:** AP, CLEP, institutional tests. 18 credit hours maximum toward associate degree. **Support services:** Learning center, remedial instruction, study skills assistance, tutoring, writing center.

Majors. Business: Accounting technology, fashion, hospitality admin, hotel/motel admin.

Most popular majors. Business/marketing 68%, personal/culinary services 32%.

Technology on campus. 38 workstations in dormitories, library, computer center, student center. Dormitories wired for high-speed internet access and linked to campus network. Online library, helpline, wireless network available.

Student life. Freshman orientation: Mandatory. Preregistration for classes offered. Half of the first week devoted to orientation. **Housing:** Guaranteed on-campus for freshmen. Coed dorms, wellness housing available. $500 deposit. **Activities:** Film society, student government, Ritz Guild.

Athletics. Intramural: Basketball, soccer, table tennis, tennis, volleyball, weight lifting.

Student services. Adult student services, alcohol/substance abuse counseling, career counseling, student employment services, financial aid counseling, health services, placement for graduates. **Transfer:** Pre-admission transcript evaluation for new students.

Contact. E-mail: admissions@lincolncollegene.edu
Phone: (860) 628-4751 Toll-free number: (860) 628-4751
Rick Einstein, Director of Admissions, Lincoln College of New England, 2279 Mount Vernon Road, Southington, CT 06489-1057

Two-Year Colleges

Manchester Community College
Manchester, Connecticut
www.mcc.commnet.edu

CB member
CB code: 3544

▶ Public 2-year community college
▶ Commuter campus in small city

General. Founded in 1963. Regionally accredited. **Enrollment:** 5,952 degree-seeking undergraduates; 939 non-degree-seeking students. **Degrees:** 852 associate awarded. **Location:** 8 miles from Hartford. **Calendar:** Semester, extensive summer session. **Full-time faculty:** 108 total; 21% minority, 61% women. **Part-time faculty:** 378 total; 14% minority, 55% women.

Student profile. Among degree-seeking undergraduates, 1,163 enrolled as first-time, first-year students, 836 transferred in from other institutions.

Part-time:	62%	Hispanic/Latino:	19%
Women:	53%	Multi-racial, non-Hispanic:	2%
African American:	16%	25 or older:	31%
Asian American:	5%		

Transfer out. Colleges most students transferred to 2015: Central Connecticut State University, University of Connecticut, Eastern Connecticut State University.

Basis for selection. Open admission, but selective for some programs. Interview required of allied health, drug and alcohol rehabilitation counselor majors.

2015-2016 Annual costs. Tuition/fees: $4,042; $12,106 out-of-state. Per-credit charge: $150 in-state; $450 out-of-state. Books/supplies: $1,200. Personal expenses: $1,596.

2014-2015 Financial aid. Need-based: 96% of total undergraduate aid awarded as scholarships/grants, 4% as loans/jobs. Need-based aid available for part-time students. Work-study available nights, weekends and for part-time students.

Application procedures. Admission: No deadline. $20 fee, may be waived for applicants with need. Admission notification on a rolling basis. **Financial aid:** Priority date 5/15, closing date 8/13. FAFSA required. Applicants notified on a rolling basis starting 5/1; must reply within 2 week(s) of notification.

Academics. Special study options: Cooperative education, cross-registration, distance learning, double major, dual enrollment of high school students, ESL, honors, independent study, internships, semester at sea, student-designed major, weekend college. License preparation in occupational therapy, paramedic. **Credit/placement by examination:** AP, CLEP, SAT, ACT, institutional tests. 45 credit hours maximum toward associate degree. **Support services:** Learning center, reduced course load, remedial instruction, study skills assistance, tutoring, writing center.

Majors. Area/ethnic studies: Women's. **Business:** Accounting, administrative services, business admin, hospitality/recreation, management information systems. **Communications:** Digital media, journalism. **Computer sciences:** Data entry, information systems, networking. **Education:** Early childhood, teacher assistance. **Engineering:** Engineering science. **Health services:** Clinical lab technology, occupational therapy assistant, pharmacy assistant, physical therapy assistant, respiratory therapy technology, substance abuse counseling, surgical technology. **Human services:** Community org/advocacy. **Liberal arts:** Arts/sciences. **Parks/recreation:** Exercise sciences. **Visual/performing arts:** Commercial/advertising art, music. **Work/family studies:** Institutional food production.

Technology on campus. 310 workstations in library, computer center. Online course registration, online library, wireless network available.

Student life. Freshman orientation: Available. Preregistration for classes offered. **Activities:** Choral groups, dance, drama, student organization of Latinos, African American Males Achieving Excellence, Muslim student association, Spanish club, political union, PRIDE, Phi Theta Kappa, Veterans Empowering Themselves to Succeed.

Athletics. NJCAA. **Intercollegiate:** Baseball M, basketball W, soccer, softball W. **Team name:** Cougars.

Student services. Adult student services, career counseling, student employment services, health services, on-campus daycare, personal counseling, placement for graduates, veterans' counselor. **Physically disabled:** Services for visually, speech, hearing impaired. **Transfer:** Transfer adviser, college fairs on campus for students transferring to 4-year colleges.

Contact. Phone: (860) 512-3210 Fax: (860) 512-3221
Peter Harris, Director of Admissions, Manchester Community College, PO Box 1046, MS#12, Manchester, CT 06045-1046

Middlesex Community College
Middletown, Connecticut
www.mxcc.edu

CB member
CB code: 3551

▶ Public 2-year community college
▶ Commuter campus in large town

General. Founded in 1966. **Enrollment:** 2,534 degree-seeking undergraduates. **Degrees:** 349 associate awarded. **Location:** 20 miles from Hartford and New Haven. **Calendar:** Semester, limited summer session. **Full-time faculty:** 43 total; 19% have terminal degrees, 19% minority, 51% women. **Part-time faculty:** 170 total; 59% women. **Class size:** 43% < 20, 56% 20-39, 2% 40-49. **Special facilities:** Nature trails, art gallery.

Student profile.

Out-of-state:	1%	25 or older:	40%

Transfer out. Colleges most students transferred to 2015: Eastern Connecticut State University, Southern Connecticut State University, University of Connecticut, University of Hartford.

Basis for selection. Open admission, but selective for some programs. Special requirements for radiology technician, broadcast communications, human services, and drug and alcohol rehabilitation counselor programs. Interview recommended of mental health, radiology, drug and alcohol counseling program majors.

High school preparation. College-preparatory program recommended.

2015-2016 Annual costs. Tuition/fees: $4,052; $12,116 out-of-state. Per-credit charge: $150 in-state; $450 out-of-state. Books/supplies: $1,000. Personal expenses: $1,925.

Financial aid. All financial aid based on need. Need-based aid available for part-time students. Work-study available nights, weekends and for part-time students. **Additional information:** Tuition and/or fee waiver for veterans.

Application procedures. Admission: Priority date 7/1; deadline 8/1 (postmark date). $20 fee, may be waived for applicants with need. Admission notification on a rolling basis beginning on or about 1/1. **Financial aid:** Priority date 6/1; no closing date. FAFSA, institutional form required. Applicants notified on a rolling basis starting 7/1; must reply within 2 week(s) of notification.

Academics. Special study options: Cross-registration, dual enrollment of high school students, ESL, independent study, internships, student-designed major. License preparation in radiology. **Credit/placement by examination:** AP, CLEP, institutional tests. 48 credit hours maximum toward associate degree. **Support services:** Pre-admission summer program, reduced course load, remedial instruction, tutoring.

Majors. Biology: Biotechnology. **Business:** Accounting, administrative services, business admin, marketing. **Communications:** Broadcast journalism, communications/speech/rhetoric. **Communications technology:** Radio/TV. **Computer sciences:** Information systems. **Conservation:** Environmental science. **Education:** Early childhood. **Engineering:** Engineering science. **Health services:** Medical radiologic technology/radiation therapy, medical secretary, mental health services, ophthalmic lab technology, optician, substance abuse counseling, veterinary technology/assistant. **Liberal arts:** Arts/sciences. **Protective services:** Police science. **Visual/performing arts:** Art, metal/jewelry, studio arts. **Work/family studies:** Child care management.

Most popular majors. Business/marketing 16%, health sciences 9%, liberal arts 43%, public administration/social services 8%, security/protective services 9%.

Technology on campus. 472 workstations in library, computer center. Online library, helpline, wireless network available.

Student life. Freshman orientation: Available. Preregistration for classes offered. **Activities:** Drama, international student organizations, literary magazine, student government, student newspaper, Student Senate, poetry club, national scholastic honor society, student guild, computer club, Minority Opportunities in Education club, art club, human services organization.

Student services. Career counseling, student employment services, financial aid counseling, minority student services, on-campus daycare, personal counseling, placement for graduates, veterans' counselor. **Physically disabled:** Services for visually, hearing impaired. **Transfer:** Transfer adviser, college fairs on campus for students transferring to 4-year colleges.

Contact. E-mail: mshabazz@mxcc.commnet.edu
Phone: (860) 343-5719 Toll-free number: (800) 818-5501
Fax: (860) 344-7488
Gayle Barrett, Director of Admissions, Middlesex Community College,
100 Training Hill Road, Middletown, CT 06457-4889

Naugatuck Valley Community College
Waterbury, Connecticut CB member
www.nv.edu CB code: 3550

▶ Public 2-year community and technical college
▶ Commuter campus in small city

General. Founded in 1992. Regionally accredited. **Enrollment:** 6,302 degree-seeking undergraduates; 674 non-degree-seeking students. **Degrees:** 849 associate awarded. **Location:** 90 miles from New York City. **Calendar:** Semester, limited summer session. **Full-time faculty:** 105 total; 45% have terminal degrees, 15% minority, 50% women. **Part-time faculty:** 259 total; 32% have terminal degrees, 11% minority, 48% women. **Class size:** 30% < 20, 69% 20-39, less than 1% 40-49, less than 1% 50-99, less than 1% >100. **Special facilities:** Fine arts center, 2 theaters, music and dance studios, video studios, rehearsal rooms, fire sprinkler laboratory, automotive center, greenhouse laboratory, observatory, arboretum, nature trail, advanced manufacturing center.

Student profile. Among degree-seeking undergraduates, 1,434 enrolled as first-time, first-year students.

Part-time:	63%	25 or older:	35%
Women:	58%		

Transfer out. Colleges most students transferred to 2015: Western Connecticut State University, Southern Connecticut State University, Central Connecticut State University, University of Connecticut, Post University.

Basis for selection. Open admission, but selective for some programs. Admission to nursing, physical therapy assistant, radiology, respiratory care programs based on school achievement, recommendations, test scores. Interview required of physical therapy majors. Audition recommended of music majors. Portfolio recommended of art majors. **Home schooled:** Statement describing home school structure and mission, interview required. Placement test and interview required.

High school preparation. Recommended units include English 4, mathematics 3, social studies 2, history 2 and science 1. Most allied health programs require high school algebra, biology, chemistry. Engineering technologies require 2 years algebra, 1 year laboratory science (preferably physics or chemistry), and computer literacy.

2015-2016 Annual costs. Tuition/fees: $4,052; $12,116 out-of-state. Per-credit charge: $150 in-state; $450 out-of-state. Books/supplies: $1,600. Personal expenses: $3,720.

Financial aid. All financial aid based on need. Need-based aid available for part-time students. Work-study available nights, weekends and for part-time students.

Application procedures. Admission: Priority date 6/1; no deadline. $20 fee, may be waived for applicants with need. Admission notification on a rolling basis beginning on or about 9/1. **Financial aid:** Priority date 4/1; no closing date. FAFSA required. Applicants notified on a rolling basis starting 6/1.

Academics. Associates degree in General Studies and Liberal Arts available through distance learning. **Special study options:** Cooperative education, cross-registration, distance learning, double major, dual enrollment of high school students, ESL, honors, independent study. License preparation in aviation, nursing, paramedic, physical therapy, radiology, real estate. **Credit/placement by examination:** AP, CLEP, institutional tests. 45 credit hours maximum toward associate degree. **Support services:** Learning center, reduced course load, remedial instruction, study skills assistance, tutoring, writing center.

Majors. Biology: General. **Business:** Accounting technology, administrative services, banking/financial services, business admin, merchandising. **Communications:** Digital media. **Computer sciences:** General, networking, web page design. **Conservation:** Environmental science. **Health services:** Medical radiologic technology/radiation therapy, mental health services, nursing (RN), physical therapy assistant, respiratory therapy technology, substance abuse counseling. **Human services:** Social work. **Liberal arts:** Arts/sciences. **Physical sciences:** General. **Protective services:** Fire safety technology, police science. **Psychology:** General. **Visual/performing arts:** Art, dance, dramatic, multimedia, music. **Work/family studies:** Child development, facilities/event planning, institutional food production.

Most popular majors. Business/marketing 14%, engineering/engineering technologies 6%, health sciences 21%, liberal arts 40%, security/protective services 6%, trade and industry 8%.

Technology on campus. 1,100 workstations in library, computer center, student center. Commuter students can connect to campus network. Online course registration, online library, helpline, repair service, wireless network available.

Student life. Freshman orientation: Available. Preregistration for classes offered. **Activities:** Concert band, choral groups, dance, drama, literary magazine, student government, student newspaper, symphony orchestra, agro-bio club, allied health clubs, Alpha Beta Gamma, black students union, Hispanic students union, human services club, male encouragement network, Phi Theta Kappa, Veterans Oasis, women's center.

Student services. Adult student services, career counseling, student employment services, financial aid counseling, health services, personal counseling, placement for graduates, veterans' counselor, women's services. **Physically disabled:** Services for visually, speech, hearing impaired. **Transfer:** Re-entry adviser, pre-admission transcript evaluation for new students. Transfer adviser, college fairs on campus for students transferring to 4-year colleges.

Contact. E-mail: nvcc@nvcc.commnet.edu
Phone: (203) 575-8040 Fax: (203) 596-8766
Linda Stango, Director of Admissions, Naugatuck Valley Community College, 750 Chase Parkway, Waterbury, CT 06708-3089

Northwestern Connecticut Community College
Winsted, Connecticut
www.nwcc.commnet.edu CB code: 3652

▶ Public 2-year community and technical college
▶ Commuter campus in large town

General. Founded in 1965. Regionally accredited. **Enrollment:** 1,132 degree-seeking undergraduates. **Degrees:** 169 associate awarded. **Location:** 25 miles from Hartford, 25 miles from Waterbury. **Calendar:** Semester, limited summer session. **Full-time faculty:** 24 total. **Part-time faculty:** 76 total.

Basis for selection. Open admission, but selective for some programs. Special requirements for nursing.

2015-2016 Annual costs. Tuition/fees: $4,047; $12,111 out-of-state. Per-credit charge: $150 in-state; $450 out-of-state. Books/supplies: $600. Personal expenses: $1,000.

Financial aid. Need-based: Work-study available nights, weekends and for part-time students.

Application procedures. Admission: No deadline. $20 fee, may be waived for applicants with need. Admission notification on a rolling basis. **Financial aid:** Priority date 6/1; no closing date. FAFSA required. Applicants notified on a rolling basis starting 6/1.

Academics. Career education for the deaf program offers full range of services and participation in all majors by deaf and hearing impaired students. Interpreting major prepares hearing students for National Registry test for interpreters for the deaf. **Special study options:** Cooperative education, cross-registration, distance learning, double major, dual enrollment of high school students, ESL, independent study, internships. **Credit/placement by examination:** AP, CLEP, institutional tests. **Support services:** Learning center, reduced course load, remedial instruction, tutoring.

Majors. Business: Accounting, banking/financial services, business admin, hospitality admin, marketing. **Communications technology:** Animation/special effects, graphics. **Computer sciences:** Systems analysis. **Education:** Early childhood. **Foreign languages:** Sign language interpretation. **Health services:** Medical assistant, nursing (RN), physical therapy assistant, recreational therapy, veterinary technology/assistant. **Liberal arts:** Arts/sciences. **Protective services:** Law enforcement admin.

Student life. Freshman orientation: Available. Preregistration for classes offered. **Activities:** Literary magazine, student government, student newspaper.

Student services. Career counseling, student employment services, personal counseling, veterans' counselor. **Physically disabled:** Services for hearing impaired. **Transfer:** Transfer adviser, college fairs on campus for students transferring to 4-year colleges.

Two-Year Colleges

Contact. E-mail: dmartineau@nwcc.commnet.edu
Phone: (860) 738-6330 Fax: (860) 379-4465
Joanne Nardi, Director of Admissions, Northwestern Connecticut
Community College, Park Place East, Winsted, CT 06098

Norwalk Community College
Norwalk, Connecticut
http://norwalk.edu/default.asp **CB code: 3677**

◆ Public 2-year community college
◆ Commuter campus in small city

General. Founded in 1961. Regionally accredited. **Enrollment:** 4,714 degree-seeking undergraduates; 1,340 non-degree-seeking students. **Degrees:** 592 associate awarded. **Location:** 45 miles from New York City. **Calendar:** Semester, extensive summer session. **Full-time faculty:** 105 total; 57% women. **Part-time faculty:** 229 total; 56% women. **Special facilities:** Theater, rotating art and cultural exhibits, culinary arts facility, early childhood education lab/preschool.

Student profile. Among degree-seeking undergraduates, 877 enrolled as first-time, first-year students, 361 transferred in from other institutions.

Part-time:	58%	**Women:**	57%
Out-of-state:	1%		

Basis for selection. Open admission, but selective for some programs. Special requirements for nursing, legal assistant, respiratory care programs. ACCUPLACER placement test requirement waived for applicants with 450 SAT English and 550 SAT Math.

High school preparation. Recommended units include English 4, mathematics 3, (laboratory 2) and foreign language 2. Chemistry, biology and algebra required for nursing and respiratory therapy applicants. Nursing applicants must have taken chemistry within past 5 years.

2015-2016 Annual costs. Tuition/fees: $4,042; $12,106 out-of-state. Per-credit charge: $150 in-state; $450 out-of-state. Books/supplies: $1,200. Personal expenses: $3,934.

Financial aid. Need-based: Need-based aid available for part-time students. Work-study available nights, weekends and for part-time students. **Non-need-based:** Scholarships awarded for academics, alumni affiliation.

Application procedures. Admission: No deadline. , may be waived for applicants with need. No application fee. Admission notification on a rolling basis. Applicants to nursing program should apply by February 1. **Financial aid:** Priority date 7/7; no closing date. FAFSA required. Applicants notified on a rolling basis starting 7/1; must reply within 2 week(s) of notification.

Academics. Special 10-week sessions with longer class hours per day let students finish courses more quickly during fall and spring. Evening hours are limited for the Academic support services. **Special study options:** Cooperative education, cross-registration, distance learning, double major, dual enrollment of high school students, ESL, internships, liberal arts/career combination. Early childhood education credential training program. License preparation in nursing, paramedic, physical therapy, real estate. **Credit/placement by examination:** AP, CLEP, IB, institutional tests. 45 credit hours maximum toward associate degree. **Support services:** Pre-admission summer program, reduced course load, remedial instruction, study skills assistance, tutoring, writing center.

Majors. Business: General, accounting, business admin, financial planning, hospitality admin, marketing. **Communications:** Communications/speech/rhetoric, journalism, radio/TV. **Computer sciences:** General, applications programming, information systems, programming, systems analysis. **Education:** Early childhood. **Engineering:** General. **Health services:** Mental health services, nursing (RN), office admin, physical therapy assistant, respiratory therapy technology, veterinary technology/assistant. **Liberal arts:** Arts/sciences. **Parks/recreation:** General. **Protective services:** Law enforcement admin. **Visual/performing arts:** Commercial/advertising art, graphic design, interior design, studio arts.

Most popular majors. Business/marketing 19%, health sciences 18%, liberal arts 36%, security/protective services 6%.

Technology on campus. 90 workstations in library, computer center, student center. Commuter students can connect to campus network. Online library, helpline, wireless network available.

Student life. Freshman orientation: Available. Preregistration for classes offered. One-day held before start of semester. **Activities:** Choral groups, drama, film society, international student organizations, literary magazine, student government, student newspaper, African culture club, Hay Motivo,

Phi Theta Kappa, legal assistants club, early childhood education club, French club, Haitian student association, criminal justice club.

Athletics. Team name: Panthers.

Student services. Adult student services, career counseling, services for economically disadvantaged, student employment services, financial aid counseling, on-campus daycare, placement for graduates, veterans' counselor, women's services. **Physically disabled:** Services for visually, speech, hearing impaired. **Transfer:** Re-entry adviser, pre-admission transcript evaluation for new students. Transfer adviser, college fairs on campus for students transferring to 4-year colleges.

Contact. E-mail: admissions@ncc.commnet.edu
Phone: (203) 857-7068 Fax: (203) 857-3335
Chagnon William, Director of Admission, Norwalk Community College, 188 Richards Avenue, Norwalk, CT 06854-1655

Quinebaug Valley Community College
Danielson, Connecticut
www.qvcc.commnet.edu **CB code: 3716**

◆ Public 2-year community and technical college
◆ Commuter campus in large town

General. Founded in 1971. Regionally accredited. Instructional Center in downtown Willimantic. **Enrollment:** 1,530 degree-seeking undergraduates. **Degrees:** 227 associate awarded. **Location:** 50 miles from Hartford; 35 miles from Worcester, MA, and 25 miles from Providence, RI. **Calendar:** Semester, limited summer session. **Full-time faculty:** 29 total. **Part-time faculty:** 98 total. **Class size:** 30% < 20, 70% 20-39. **Special facilities:** Manufacturing center, art gallery.

Student profile.

Out-of-state:	1%	**25 or older:**	40%

Transfer out. Colleges most students transferred to 2015: Eastern Connecticut State University, University of Connecticut, Worcester State College.

Basis for selection. Open admission. Interview recommended. **Learning Disabled:** Meeting with the Coordinator of Learning Disability Services recommended, however there are no special admission requirements or procedures required for admission to the college.

2015-2016 Annual costs. Tuition/fees: $4,047; $12,111 out-of-state. Per-credit charge: $150 in-state; $450 out-of-state. Books/supplies: $1,300. Personal expenses: $1,200.

Financial aid. All financial aid based on need. Need-based aid available for part-time students. Work-study available nights, weekends and for part-time students.

Application procedures. Admission: No deadline. $20 fee, may be waived for applicants with need. Admission notification on a rolling basis. **Financial aid:** Closing date 8/1. FAFSA required. Applicants notified on a rolling basis starting 5/1.

Academics. Special study options: Distance learning, double major, dual enrollment of high school students, ESL, independent study, internships. License preparation in real estate. **Credit/placement by examination:** AP, CLEP, institutional tests. 30 credit hours maximum toward associate degree. **Support services:** Learning center, pre-admission summer program, reduced course load, remedial instruction, study skills assistance, tutoring, writing center.

Majors. Business: Accounting, administrative services, business admin, office technology. **Computer sciences:** General. **Education:** Early childhood. **Engineering:** Polymer. **Health services:** Community health services, medical assistant. **Liberal arts:** Arts/sciences. **Visual/performing arts:** Graphic design, photography, studio arts.

Most popular majors. Business/marketing 9%, liberal arts 40%, public administration/social services 33%.

Technology on campus. 115 workstations in library, computer center. Commuter students can connect to campus network. Online course registration, online library, helpline, wireless network available.

Student life. Freshman orientation: Available. Preregistration for classes offered. **Activities:** Student government, medical assisting association, Phi Theta Kappa, Alpha Beta Gamma.

Student services. Adult student services, career counseling, student employment services, financial aid counseling, minority student services, on-campus daycare, placement for graduates, veterans' counselor. **Physically disabled:** Services for visually, speech, hearing impaired. **Transfer:** Re-entry adviser, pre-admission transcript evaluation for new students. Transfer adviser, college fairs on campus for students transferring to 4-year colleges.

Contact. E-mail: admissions@qvcc.commnet.edu
Phone: (860) 932-4002
Susan Breault, Director of Enrollment Management, Quinebaug Valley Community College, 742 Upper Maple Street, Danielson, CT 06239-1440

St. Vincent's College
Bridgeport, Connecticut
www.stvincentscollege.edu   CB code: 3789

▶ Private 2-year health science college affiliated with the Roman Catholic Church
▶ Commuter campus in small city
▶ SAT or ACT (ACT writing optional) required

General. Regionally accredited. Majority of students are adult learners. Nursing and radiography programs highly competitive; pre-programs available. **Enrollment:** 669 degree-seeking undergraduates; 6 non-degree-seeking students. **Degrees:** 51 bachelor's, 138 associate awarded. **Location:** 55 miles from New York City. **Calendar:** Semester, limited summer session. **Full-time faculty:** 21 total. **Part-time faculty:** 53 total. **Special facilities:** Affiliated hospital with clinical opportunities adjacent to campus.

Student profile. Among degree-seeking undergraduates, 17% already have a bachelor's degree or higher, 14 enrolled as first-time, first-year students, 233 transferred in from other institutions.

Part-time:	93%	Asian American:	2%
Out-of-state:	1%	Hispanic/Latino:	13%
Women:	87%	25 or older:	69%
African American:	13%		

Basis for selection. High school record and GPA are most important. For students applying for the nursing program, TEAS scores are very important. **Adult students:** SAT/ACT scores not required if out of high school 1 year(s) or more. **Home schooled:** Transcript of courses and grades, letter of recommendation (nonparent) required.

High school preparation. College-preparatory program required. 16 units required. Required units include English 4, mathematics 3, social studies 3, science 3 and academic electives 6.

2015-2016 Annual costs. Tuition/fees: $17,850. Per-credit charge: $595. Books/supplies: $1,900. Personal expenses: $3,720.

Financial aid. All financial aid based on need. Need-based aid available for part-time students. Work-study available nights, weekends and for part-time students.

Application procedures. Admission: No deadline. No application fee. Application must be submitted online. Admission notification on a rolling basis beginning on or about 10/1. **Financial aid:** Priority date 3/15; no closing date.

Academics. Special study options: Distance learning, internships. Bachelor's degree programs available on campus. License preparation in nursing, radiology. **Credit/placement by examination:** AP, CLEP, institutional tests. **Support services:** Learning center, pre-admission summer program, reduced course load, remedial instruction, study skills assistance, tutoring, writing center.

Majors. Health services: Medical assistant, nursing (RN), radiologic technology/medical imaging.

Technology on campus. 40 workstations in computer center, student center. Commuter students can connect to campus network. Online library, wireless network available.

Student life. Freshman orientation: Mandatory. Preregistration for classes offered. Held for one-day each spring and fall.

Student services. Alcohol/substance abuse counseling, chaplain/spiritual director, career counseling, financial aid counseling, health services, personal counseling.

Contact. E-mail: admissions@stvincentscollege.edu
Phone: (203) 576-5513 Fax: (203) 576-5318
Joseph Marrone, Admissions Director, St. Vincent's College, 2800 Main Street, Bridgeport, CT 06606

Three Rivers Community College
Norwich, Connecticut   CB member
www.threerivers.edu   CB code: 3558

▶ Public 2-year community and technical college
▶ Commuter campus in large town

General. Founded in 1969. Regionally accredited. **Enrollment:** 3,949 degree-seeking undergraduates. **Degrees:** 510 associate awarded. **Location:** 45 miles from Hartford. **Calendar:** Semester, limited summer session. **Full-time faculty:** 82 total; 55% women. **Part-time faculty:** 203 total; 51% women. **Special facilities:** Nuclear reactor simulator, child development center.

Student profile.

Out-of-state:	1%	25 or older:	43%

Transfer out. Colleges most students transferred to 2015: Eastern Connecticut State University, University of Connecticut, Central Connecticut State University, Southern Illinois University, Sacred Heart University.

Basis for selection. Open admission, but selective for some programs. Admission for nursing program based on successful performance on ATI-TEAS Exam, completion of prerequisite courses, and 2.7 GPA. **Adult students:** SAT or basic skills tests in math and English required for placement unless student has completed college level math and English course. **Home schooled:** Student may take Ability to Benefit Test if standard documentation requirements are not met.

High school preparation. One unit chemistry, biology, and algebra required for nursing program.

2015-2016 Annual costs. Tuition/fees: $4,052; $12,116 out-of-state. Per-credit charge: $150 in-state; $450 out-of-state. Books/supplies: $1,200. Personal expenses: $1,000.

Financial aid. All financial aid based on need. Need-based aid available for part-time students. Work-study available nights, weekends and for part-time students.

Application procedures. Admission: No deadline. $20 fee, may be waived for applicants with need. Admission notification on a rolling basis beginning on or about 3/30. **Financial aid:** Priority date 5/1; no closing date. FAFSA required. Applicants notified on a rolling basis; must reply within 2 week(s) of notification.

Academics. Special study options: Distance learning, double major, dual enrollment of high school students, ESL, honors, independent study, internships, liberal arts/career combination. License preparation in nursing. **Credit/placement by examination:** AP, CLEP, institutional tests. 45 credit hours maximum toward associate degree. **Support services:** Learning center, pre-admission summer program, remedial instruction, study skills assistance, tutoring, writing center.

Majors. Architecture: Technology. **Business:** Accounting, banking/financial services, business admin, construction management, hospitality admin, office technology, restaurant/food services, tourism/travel. **Communications:** Public relations. **Computer sciences:** General, applications programming, information systems. **Conservation:** Environmental science. **Education:** Early childhood, special ed. **Health services:** Nursing (RN). **Liberal arts:** Arts/sciences, library assistant. **Physical sciences:** General. **Protective services:** Criminal justice, fire safety technology, law enforcement admin, police science. **Work/family studies:** Family studies.

Most popular majors. Business/marketing 13%, engineering/engineering technologies 11%, health sciences 16%, liberal arts 44%.

Technology on campus. 300 workstations in library, computer center, student center. Commuter students can connect to campus network. Online course registration, online library, helpline, wireless network available.

Student life. Freshman orientation: Available. Preregistration for classes offered. **Policies:** Student government controls student activity fees. **Activities:** Drama, student government, student newspaper, Spanish-American association, Afro-American association, student chapters of professional organizations, gay-straight alliance, volunteer club, golf club, student nurses association, environmentalists club, senior student ambassadors, veterans organization.

Student services. Career counseling, student employment services, financial aid counseling, on-campus daycare, personal counseling, veterans' counselor. **Physically disabled:** Services for visually, hearing impaired. **Transfer:** Re-entry adviser for new students. Transfer adviser, college fairs on campus for students transferring to 4-year colleges.

Contact. E-mail: admissions@threerivers.edu
Phone: (860) 215-9020
Stephan Finton, Director of Admissions, Three Rivers Community College, Admissions Office, Norwich, CT 06360-6598

Tunxis Community College
Farmington, Connecticut **CB member**
www.tunxis.edu **CB code: 3897**

◗ Public 2-year community college
◗ Commuter campus in large town

General. Founded in 1970. Regionally accredited. **Enrollment:** 3,517 degree-seeking undergraduates; 562 non-degree-seeking students. **Degrees:** 412 associate awarded. **ROTC:** Army, Naval, Air Force. **Location:** 15 miles from Hartford. **Calendar:** Semester, limited summer session. **Full-time faculty:** 66 total. **Part-time faculty:** 241 total. **Class size:** 29% < 20, 70% 20-39, less than 1% 40-49. **Special facilities:** Early childhood center, art gallery.

Student profile. Among degree-seeking undergraduates, 831 enrolled as first-time, first-year students.

Part-time:	55%	**Women:**	55%
Out-of-state:	1%	**25 or older:**	33%

Transfer out. Colleges most students transferred to 2015: Central Connecticut State University, Charter Oak College, St. Joseph College, University of Connecticut.

Basis for selection. Open admission, but selective for some programs. Special requirements for dental hygiene and dental assisting. Interview required for dental hygiene. **Home schooled:** Interview required. Placement test (ACCUPLACER) required. **Learning Disabled:** Contact Academic Support Center prior to placement testing if accommodations are necessary.

High school preparation. College-preparatory program recommended.

2015-2016 Annual costs. Tuition/fees: $4,052; $12,116 out-of-state. Per-credit charge: $150 in-state; $450 out-of-state. Books/supplies: $1,000. Personal expenses: $4,856.

Financial aid. Need-based: Need-based aid available for part-time students. Work-study available nights, weekends and for part-time students. **Non-need-based:** Scholarships awarded for academics. **Additional information:** Financial aid available to all students showing need. Part-time students encouraged to apply.

Application procedures. Admission: No deadline. $20 fee, may be waived for applicants with need. Admission notification on a rolling basis. Dental hygiene program closing date 1/1, notification by 3/1. **Financial aid:** Priority date 6/1; no closing date. FAFSA required. Applicants notified on a rolling basis starting 3/1.

Academics. Special study options: Cross-registration, distance learning, double major, dual enrollment of high school students, ESL, honors, independent study, internships, liberal arts/career combination. License preparation in dental hygiene. **Credit/placement by examination:** AP, CLEP, institutional tests. 30 credit hours maximum toward associate degree. **Support services:** Learning center, pre-admission summer program, reduced course load, remedial instruction, study skills assistance, tutoring, writing center.

Majors. Business: Accounting, administrative services, business admin, fashion, finance, office/clerical. **Computer sciences:** Applications programming, computer graphics. **Education:** Early childhood. **Engineering:** Engineering science. **Health services:** Dental hygiene, medical secretary, substance abuse counseling. **Liberal arts:** Arts/sciences. **Visual/performing arts:** General, commercial/advertising art.

Technology on campus. 200 workstations in library, computer center. Commuter students can connect to campus network. Wireless network available.

Student life. Freshman orientation: Available. Preregistration for classes offered. **Activities:** Jazz band, literary magazine, student government, student newspaper, minority student alliance, human services club, criminal justice club, dental hygiene group.

Student services. Career counseling, student employment services, financial aid counseling, health services, minority student services, on-campus daycare, personal counseling, placement for graduates. **Physically disabled:** Services for visually impaired. **Transfer:** Transfer adviser, college fairs on campus for students transferring to 4-year colleges.

Contact. E-mail: tx-admissions@txcc.commnet.edu
Phone: (860) 773-1490 Fax: (860) 606-9501
Tamika Davis, Director of Admissions, Tunxis Community College, 271 Scott Swamp Road, Farmington, CT 06032-3187

Two-Year Colleges

Delaware

Delaware College of Art and Design
Wilmington, Delaware
www.dcad.edu   CB code: 5161

▶ Private 2-year visual arts college
▶ Residential campus in large city
▶ Application essay required

General. Regionally accredited. **Enrollment:** 155 degree-seeking under-graduates. **Degrees:** 79 associate awarded. **Location:** 25 miles from Philadelphia. **Calendar:** Semester, limited summer session. **Full-time faculty:** 5 total. **Part-time faculty:** 25 total. **Class size:** 90% < 20, 10% 20-39.

Student profile. Among degree-seeking undergraduates, 67 enrolled as first-time, first-year students.

Part-time:	9%	Hispanic/Latino:	9%
Out-of-state:	64%	Native American:	1%
Women:	63%	Multi-racial, non-Hispanic:	8%
African American:	24%	International:	1%
Asian American:	1%	Live on campus:	74%

Transfer out. Colleges most students transferred to 2015: Pratt Institute, Corcoran College of Art and Design, University of the Arts, School of the Visual Arts, Moore College of Art and Design.

Basis for selection. Academic GPA and talent/ability most important. Standardized test scores are recommended but required. Visual art portfolio required. **Adult students:** SAT/ACT scores not required. **Home schooled:** Statement describing home school structure and mission, transcript of courses and grades, state high school equivalency certificate, letter of recommendation (nonparent) required. Portfolio of 15-20 images of art work.

High school preparation. College-preparatory program recommended. Recommended units include English 4, mathematics 3, social studies 4, history 2, science 3, foreign language 2, computer science 2 and visual/performing arts 4.

2015-2016 Annual costs. Tuition/fees: $23,945. Per-credit charge: $975. Room/board: $11,850. Books/supplies: $1,090. Personal expenses: $4,080.

Financial aid. Need-based: Need-based aid available for part-time students. Work-study available nights, weekends and for part-time students. **Non-need-based:** Scholarships awarded for academics, art.

Application procedures. Admission: Priority date 3/15; no deadline. $40 fee, may be waived for applicants with need. Admission notification on a rolling basis beginning on or about 12/15. Must reply by May 1 or within 2 week(s) if notified thereafter. **Financial aid:** Priority date 4/1; no closing date. FAFSA required. Applicants notified on a rolling basis; must reply within 2 week(s) of notification.

Academics. Credit/placement by examination: AP, CLEP, institutional tests. **Support services:** Reduced course load, study skills assistance, tutoring.

Majors. Communications technology: Animation/special effects. **Visual/performing arts:** Graphic design, illustration, interior design, photography, studio arts.

Technology on campus. 50 workstations in library, computer center. Dormitories wired for high-speed internet access. Wireless network available.

Student life. Freshman orientation: Mandatory. Preregistration for classes offered. **Housing:** Guaranteed on-campus for all undergraduates. Coed dorms, apartments available. $350 nonrefundable deposit, deadline 5/1. **Activities:** Literary magazine, student government.

Student services. Financial aid counseling. **Transfer:** Pre-admission transcript evaluation for new students. College fairs on campus for students transferring to 4-year colleges.

Contact. E-mail: admissions@dcad.edu
Phone: (302) 622-8000 ext. 118 Fax: (302) 622-8870
Tracy Stephanski, Director of Admissions, Delaware College of Art and Design, 600 North Market Street, Wilmington, DE 19801

Delaware Technical Community College: Jack F. Owens Campus
Georgetown, Delaware
https://www.dtcc.edu/our-campuses/georgetown
    CB code: 5169

▶ Public 2-year community and technical college
▶ Commuter campus in small town

General. Founded in 1967. Regionally accredited. **Enrollment:** 3,852 degree-seeking undergraduates. **Degrees:** 501 associate awarded. **Location:** 80 miles from Wilmington. **Calendar:** Semester, limited summer session. **Full-time faculty:** 115 total. **Part-time faculty:** 200 total. **Class size:** 67% < 20, 33% 20-39, less than 1% 40-49. **Special facilities:** Maritime exhibit.

Basis for selection. Open admission, but selective for some programs.

2015-2016 Annual costs. Tuition/fees: $3,568; $8,458 out-of-state. Per-credit charge: $136 in-state; $340 out-of-state. Books/supplies: $1,500. Personal expenses: $200.

Financial aid. All financial aid based on need. Need-based aid available for part-time students. Work-study available nights, weekends and for part-time students.

Application procedures. Admission: No deadline. $10 fee, may be waived for applicants with need. Admission notification on a rolling basis. **Financial aid:** Priority date 6/1; no closing date. FAFSA required. Applicants notified on a rolling basis starting 5/1; must reply within 2 week(s) of notification.

Academics. Special study options: Accelerated study, distance learning, dual enrollment of high school students, ESL, independent study, internships, study abroad. License preparation in nursing, occupational therapy, physical therapy, radiology, real estate. **Credit/placement by examination:** AP, CLEP, SAT, ACT, institutional tests. **Support services:** GED preparation and test center, learning center, pre-admission summer program, remedial instruction, study skills assistance, tutoring, writing center.

Majors. Biology: General. **Business:** General, accounting, construction management, customer service support, e-commerce, entrepreneurial studies, management information systems, marketing, office management, office technology. **Computer sciences:** General. **Education:** Early childhood, elementary, kindergarten/preschool, mathematics, middle, multi-level teacher. **Health services:** Clinical lab assistant, EMT paramedic, medical assistant, nursing (RN), occupational therapy assistant, physical therapy assistant, radiologic technology/medical imaging, respiratory therapy assistant, sonography, veterinary technology/assistant. **Protective services:** Law enforcement admin, police science.

Most popular majors. Business/marketing 17%, education 10%, engineering/engineering technologies 7%, health sciences 32%, public administration/social services 13%, security/protective services 9%.

Technology on campus. 728 workstations in library, computer center, student center. Commuter students can connect to campus network. Online course registration, online library, helpline, wireless network available.

Student life. Freshman orientation: Available. Preregistration for classes offered. **Activities:** Bands, campus ministries, choral groups, dance, drama, international student organizations, music ensembles, musical theater, student government, student newspaper.

Athletics. NJCAA. **Intercollegiate:** Baseball M, golf M. **Team name:** Road Runners.

Student services. Adult student services, career counseling, student employment services, financial aid counseling, personal counseling, placement for graduates, veterans' counselor. **Physically disabled:** Services for visually, hearing impaired. **Transfer:** Transfer adviser for students transferring to 4-year colleges.

Contact. E-mail: g-admissions@dtcc.edu
Phone: (302) 856-5400
Claire MacDonald, Admissions Coordinator, Delaware Technical Community College: Jack F. Owens Campus, 21179 College Drive, Georgetown, DE 19947

Two-Year Colleges

Delaware Technical Community College: Stanton/Wilmington Campus
Newark, Delaware
https://www.dtcc.edu/our-campuses/stanton   CB code: 5204

▶ Public 2-year community and technical college
▶ Commuter campus in small city

General. Founded in 1967. Regionally accredited. Multi-location institution. **Enrollment:** 6,076 degree-seeking undergraduates. **Degrees:** 705 associate awarded. **Location:** 30 miles from Philadelphia. **Calendar:** Semester, limited summer session. **Full-time faculty:** 175 total. **Part-time faculty:** 360 total. **Class size:** 81% < 20, 19% 20-39, less than 1% 40-49.

Basis for selection. Open admission, but selective for some programs. Admission to health technologies program restricted to state residents. Selective admission to allied health, nursing, and culinary arts programs.

2015-2016 Annual costs. Tuition/fees: $3,568; $8,458 out-of-state. Per-credit charge: $136 in-state; $340 out-of-state. Books/supplies: $1,500. Personal expenses: $200.

Financial aid. All financial aid based on need. Need-based aid available for part-time students. Work-study available nights, weekends and for part-time students.

Application procedures. Admission: No deadline. $10 fee, may be waived for applicants with need. Admission notification on a rolling basis. **Financial aid:** Priority date 6/1; no closing date. FAFSA required. Applicants notified on a rolling basis starting 5/1; must reply within 2 week(s) of notification.

Academics. Special study options: Accelerated study, distance learning, dual enrollment of high school students, ESL, independent study, internships, study abroad. License preparation in dental hygiene, nursing, occupational therapy, paramedic, physical therapy, radiology. **Credit/placement by examination:** AP, CLEP, SAT, ACT, institutional tests. **Support services:** GED preparation and test center, learning center, pre-admission summer program, remedial instruction, study skills assistance, tutoring, writing center.

Majors. Biology: General. **Business:** General, accounting, business admin, construction management, customer service, customer service support, hotel/motel admin, management information systems, management science, marketing, office management, office technology. **Computer sciences:** General, networking. **Education:** Early childhood, elementary, kindergarten/preschool, mathematics, middle, multi-level teacher. **Engineering:** Operations research. **Health services:** Cardiovascular technology, dental hygiene, electrocardiograph technology, EMT ambulance attendant, EMT paramedic, histologic technology, medical assistant, nuclear medical technology, nursing (RN), occupational therapy assistant, physical therapy assistant, radiologic technology/medical imaging, respiratory therapy assistant, sonography, substance abuse counseling. **Parks/recreation:** Exercise sciences. **Protective services:** Fire safety technology, fire services admin, firefighting, law enforcement admin, police science.

Most popular majors. Business/marketing 18%, education 7%, engineering/engineering technologies 12%, health sciences 37%, public administration/social services 6%, security/protective services 10%.

Technology on campus. 1,139 workstations in library, computer center. Commuter students can connect to campus network. Online course registration, online library, helpline, wireless network available.

Student life. Freshman orientation: Available. Preregistration for classes offered. **Activities:** Bands, campus ministries, choral groups, dance, drama, international student organizations, music ensembles, musical theater, student government, student newspaper.

Athletics. NJCAA. **Intercollegiate:** Basketball, soccer M, softball W. **Intramural:** Basketball, football (tackle), softball W, volleyball. **Team name:** Spirit.

Student services. Adult student services, career counseling, student employment services, financial aid counseling, health services, personal counseling, placement for graduates, veterans' counselor, women's services. **Physically disabled:** Services for visually, speech, hearing impaired. **Transfer:** Transfer adviser for students transferring to 4-year colleges.

Contact. E-mail: s-admissions@dtcc.edu
Phone: (302) 855-1619 Fax: (302) 453-3084
Rebecca Bailey-Bell, Admissions Representative, Delaware Technical Community College: Stanton/Wilmington Campus, 400 Stanton-Christiana Road, Newark, DE 19713

Delaware Technical Community College: Terry Campus
Dover, Delaware   CB member
https://www.dtcc.edu/our-campuses/dover   CB code: 5201

▶ Public 2-year community and technical college
▶ Commuter campus in large town

General. Founded in 1972. Regionally accredited. **Enrollment:** 2,732 degree-seeking undergraduates. **Degrees:** 1,549 associate awarded. **Location:** 90 miles from Baltimore, 75 miles from Philadelphia. **Calendar:** Semester, limited summer session. **Full-time faculty:** 80 total. **Part-time faculty:** 160 total. **Class size:** 79% < 20, 21% 20-39.

Basis for selection. Open admission, but selective for some programs. Special requirements for health/nursing programs.

2015-2016 Annual costs. Tuition/fees: $3,568; $8,458 out-of-state. Per-credit charge: $136 in-state; $340 out-of-state. Books/supplies: $1,500. Personal expenses: $200.

Financial aid. All financial aid based on need. Need-based aid available for part-time students. Work-study available nights, weekends and for part-time students.

Application procedures. Admission: No deadline. $10 fee, may be waived for applicants with need. Admission notification on a rolling basis. **Financial aid:** Priority date 6/1; no closing date. FAFSA required. Applicants notified on a rolling basis starting 5/1; must reply within 2 week(s) of notification.

Academics. Special study options: Accelerated study, distance learning, dual enrollment of high school students, ESL, independent study, internships, study abroad. License preparation in nursing, paramedic. **Credit/placement by examination:** AP, CLEP, SAT, ACT, institutional tests. **Support services:** GED preparation and test center, learning center, pre-admission summer program, remedial instruction, study skills assistance, tutoring, writing center.

Majors. Business: Accounting, business admin, e-commerce, entrepreneurial studies, hotel/motel admin, human resources, management information systems, marketing, office management. **Communications:** Digital media. **Computer sciences:** General, networking. **Education:** Bilingual, early childhood, elementary, kindergarten/preschool, mathematics, middle, multi-level teacher. **Health services:** EMT paramedic, medical assistant, nursing (RN), substance abuse counseling. **Protective services:** Law enforcement admin, police science. **Visual/performing arts:** Commercial/advertising art, interior design, photography.

Most popular majors. Business/marketing 11%, education 12%, engineering/engineering technologies 6%, health sciences 36%, personal/culinary services 6%, public administration/social services 8%, security/protective services 9%, visual/performing arts 7%.

Technology on campus. 423 workstations in library, computer center. Commuter students can connect to campus network. Online course registration, online library, helpline available.

Student life. Freshman orientation: Available. Preregistration for classes offered. **Activities:** Bands, campus ministries, choral groups, dance, drama, international student organizations, music ensembles, musical theater, student government, student newspaper.

Athletics. NJCAA. **Intercollegiate:** Lacrosse M, soccer, softball W. **Team name:** Hawks.

Student services. Adult student services, career counseling, student employment services, financial aid counseling, personal counseling, placement for graduates, veterans' counselor. **Physically disabled:** Services for visually, hearing impaired. **Transfer:** Transfer adviser for students transferring to 4-year colleges.

Contact. E-mail: terry-info@dtcc.edu
Phone: (302) 857-1029 Fax: (302) 739-6169
Maria Harris, Admissions Coordinator, Delaware Technical Community College: Terry Campus, 100 Campus Drive, Dover, DE 19901

management, medical radiologic technology/radiation therapy, nuclear medical technology, nursing (RN), ophthalmic lab technology, physical therapy assistant, predental, premedicine, prenursing, prepharmacy, preveterinary, recreational therapy, respiratory therapy technology, sonography. **History:** General. **Human services:** Social work. **Liberal arts:** Arts/sciences. **Math:** General. **Parks/recreation:** General. **Philosophy/religion:** Religion. **Physical sciences:** Chemistry, physics. **Protective services:** Criminal justice, firefighting, security services. **Psychology:** General. **Social sciences:** Anthropology, economics, geography, political science, sociology. **Visual/performing arts:** Art, dramatic, interior design, music, music history. **Work/family studies:** Child care management, food/nutrition.

Technology on campus. 3,635 workstations in library, computer center, student center. Commuter students can connect to campus network. Online course registration, online library, helpline, wireless network available.

Student life. Freshman orientation: Available. Preregistration for classes offered. **Activities:** Bands, choral groups, dance, drama, international student organizations, literary magazine, music ensembles, musical theater, opera, student government, student newspaper, symphony orchestra, Phi Theta Kappa, Phi Beta Lambda, African American student union, American Institute of Architecture Students, Catholic club, chess club, HIV peer educators, film club, French club.

Athletics. NJCAA. **Intercollegiate:** Baseball M, basketball, soccer, softball W, tennis W, volleyball W. **Team name:** Seahawks.

Student services. Adult student services, alcohol/substance abuse counseling, career counseling, student employment services, financial aid counseling, health services, on-campus daycare, personal counseling, placement for graduates, veterans' counselor, women's services. **Physically disabled:** Services for visually, speech, hearing impaired. **Transfer:** College fairs on campus for students transferring to 4-year colleges.

Contact. Phone: (954) 201-7471 Fax: (954) 201-7466
Willie Alexander, Associate Vice President for Student Affairs and Registrar, Broward College, 225 East Las Olas Boulevard, Fort Lauderdale, FL 33301

Broward College
Fort Lauderdale, Florida
www.broward.edu

CB code: 5074

- Public 2-year community college
- Commuter campus in small city

General. Founded in 1959. Regionally accredited. 3 main campuses and 9 centers as well as overseas centers. **Enrollment:** 38,127 degree-seeking undergraduates; 4,521 non-degree-seeking students. **Degrees:** 463 bachelor's, 5,981 associate awarded. **ROTC:** Army, Air Force. **Location:** 20 miles from Miami. **Calendar:** Semester, extensive summer session. **Full-time faculty:** 401 total; 31% have terminal degrees, 42% minority, 53% women. **Part-time faculty:** 1,309 total; 22% have terminal degrees, 37% minority, 50% women. **Class size:** 40% < 20, 58% 20-39, less than 1% 40-49, less than 1% 50-99, less than 1% >100. **Special facilities:** Concert hall, planetarium.

Student profile. Among degree-seeking undergraduates, 6,531 enrolled as first-time, first-year students, 1,431 transferred in from other institutions.

Part-time:	68%	Hispanic/Latino:	35%
Out-of-state:	1%	Multi-racial, non-Hispanic:	2%
Women:	59%	International:	4%
African American:	35%	25 or older:	38%
Asian American:	3%		

Transfer out. Colleges most students transferred to 2015: Florida Atlantic University, Florida International University.

Basis for selection. Open admission, but selective for some programs. Limited access and baccalaureate programs require secondary application process. **Home schooled:** Statement describing home school structure and mission required.

High school preparation. Required units include English 4, mathematics 3, science 2 and foreign language 2.

2015-2016 Annual costs. Tuition/fees: $3,405; $11,058 out-of-state. Per-credit charge: $113.5 in-state; $368.6 out-of-state. Books/supplies: $1,234. Personal expenses: $2,090. **Additional information:** Bachelor programs charged at higher tuition rates.

2015-2016 Financial aid. Need-based: 80% of total undergraduate aid awarded as scholarships/grants, 20% as loans/jobs. Need-based aid available for part-time students. Work-study available nights, weekends and for part-time students. **Non-need-based:** Scholarships awarded for academics, athletics, leadership, state residency.

Application procedures. Admission: No deadline. $35 fee, may be waived for applicants with need. Admission notification on a rolling basis beginning on or about 2/15. **Financial aid:** Priority date 4/15; no closing date. FAFSA, institutional form required. Applicants notified on a rolling basis starting 6/1.

Academics. Special study options: Accelerated study, cooperative education, distance learning, dual enrollment of high school students, ESL, exchange student, honors, independent study, internships, study abroad, teacher certification program, weekend college. Bachelor's degree programs available on campus. License preparation in aviation, dental hygiene, nursing, paramedic, physical therapy, radiology, real estate. **Credit/placement by examination:** AP, CLEP, IB, institutional tests. 30 credit hours maximum toward associate degree. **Support services:** Learning center, pre-admission summer program, reduced course load, remedial instruction, study skills assistance, tutoring, writing center.

Majors. Architecture: Landscape. **Biology:** General. **Business:** General, accounting, business admin, finance, hospitality admin, international, international marketing, management science, office/clerical, tourism/travel. **Communications:** Broadcast journalism, journalism. **Computer sciences:** General, computer graphics, computer science, data processing, information systems, programming, systems analysis. **Conservation:** Environmental science. **Education:** General, early childhood, elementary, mathematics, music, science, special ed. **Engineering:** General, civil, computer, electrical, software. **English:** English lit. **Foreign languages:** General. **Health services:** Athletic training, cardiovascular technology, clinical lab assistant, clinical lab technology, dental hygiene, EMT paramedic, health care admin, health information

Brown Mackie College: Miami
Miami, Florida
www.brownmackie.edu

- For-profit 2-year business and career college
- Commuter campus in very large city

General. Accredited by ACICS. **Enrollment:** 919 undergraduates. **Degrees:** 56 bachelor's, 276 associate awarded. **Location:** Downtown. **Calendar:** Quarter, extensive summer session. **Full-time faculty:** 13 total; 23% have terminal degrees, 85% minority, 38% women. **Part-time faculty:** 70 total; 6% have terminal degrees, 84% minority, 46% women. **Class size:** 79% < 20, 21% 20-39.

Basis for selection. Open admission. **Home schooled:** Transcript of courses and grades, state high school equivalency certificate required.

2015-2016 Annual costs. Tuition/fees: $19,145. Per-credit charge: $391. Books/supplies: $900. Personal expenses: $2,970.

Financial aid. Need-based: Work-study available nights, weekends and for part-time students. **Non-need-based:** Scholarships awarded for academics, state residency.

Application procedures. Admission: No deadline. No application fee.

Academics. Special study options: Double major, independent study, internships, liberal arts/career combination. Bachelor's degree programs available on campus. **Credit/placement by examination:** AP, CLEP, institutional tests. **Support services:** Learning center, remedial instruction, study skills assistance, tutoring.

Majors. Business: Accounting, business admin. **Health services:** Health services admin, medical secretary. **Protective services:** Law enforcement admin.

Most popular majors. Business/marketing 10%, health sciences 28%, legal studies 25%, security/protective services 31%.

Technology on campus. 300 workstations in library, computer center, student center. Commuter students can connect to campus network. Online library, wireless network available.

Student life. Freshman orientation: Mandatory. Preregistration for classes offered. **Activities:** Student newspaper.

Athletics. Team name: Lions.

Student services. Adult student services, alcohol/substance abuse counseling, career counseling, student employment services, financial aid counseling, personal counseling, placement for graduates, veterans' counselor. **Transfer:** Re-entry adviser, pre-admission transcript evaluation for new students. Transfer adviser, college fairs on campus for students transferring to 4-year colleges.

Contact. E-mail: bmmiadm@brownmackie.edu
Phone: (305) 341-6600 Toll-free number: (866) 505-0335
Fax: (305) 341-6649
Greg King, Director of Admissions, Brown Mackie College: Miami, One Herald Plaza, Miami, FL 33132

Chipola College
Marianna, Florida
www.chipola.edu   **CB code: 5106**

- Public 2-year community college
- Commuter campus in small town

General. Founded in 1947. Regionally accredited. **Enrollment:** 1,425 degree-seeking undergraduates; 722 non-degree-seeking students. **Degrees:** 78 bachelor's, 298 associate awarded. **Location:** 70 miles from Tallahassee. **Calendar:** Semester, limited summer session. **Full-time faculty:** 43 total; 33% have terminal degrees, 7% minority, 60% women. **Part-time faculty:** 111 total; 4% have terminal degrees, 21% minority, 45% women.

Student profile. Among degree-seeking undergraduates, 212 enrolled as first-time, first-year students.

Part-time:	47%	Women:	65%
Out-of-state:	10%	Live on campus:	5%

Transfer out. Colleges most students transferred to 2015: Florida State University, University of West Florida, University of Florida, Troy State University-Dothan.

Basis for selection. Open admission, but selective for some programs.

High school preparation. Recommended units include English 4, mathematics 3, social studies 3 and science 3.

2015-2016 Annual costs. Tuition/fees: $3,060; $8,891 out-of-state. Books/supplies: $800. Personal expenses: $1,500.

Financial aid. Need-based: Need-based aid available for part-time students. Work-study available nights, weekends and for part-time students. **Non-need-based:** Scholarships awarded for academics, alumni affiliation, art, athletics, job skills, leadership, minority status, music/drama.

Application procedures. Admission: Priority date 8/1; no deadline. No application fee. Admission notification on a rolling basis. **Financial aid:** Priority date 5/1; no closing date. FAFSA, institutional form required. Applicants notified on a rolling basis starting 1/2; must reply within 2 week(s) of notification.

Academics. Special study options: Accelerated study, cooperative education, distance learning, dual enrollment of high school students, honors, independent study, internships, liberal arts/career combination, teacher certification program. Bachelor's degree programs available on campus. License preparation in nursing, paramedic. **Credit/placement by examination:** AP, CLEP, IB. 45 credit hours maximum toward associate degree, 45 toward bachelor's. **Support services:** Remedial instruction, study skills assistance, tutoring, writing center.

Majors. Biology: General. **Business:** Business admin. **Communications:** Communications/speech/rhetoric, journalism. **Computer sciences:** General, computer science, information systems. **Conservation:** Forest sciences. **Education:** General. **Engineering:** General, computer. **Health services:** Nursing (RN). **History:** General. **Math:** General. **Parks/recreation:** General. **Protective services:** Firefighting, law enforcement admin.

Technology on campus. 150 workstations in library, computer center, student center. Dormitories linked to campus network. Online library available.

Student life. Freshman orientation: Mandatory. Preregistration for classes offered. **Housing:** Only men's and women's athletic dorms available. **Activities:** Jazz band, campus ministries, choral groups, dance, drama, musical theater, student government, student newspaper, TV station, black student union, Fellowship of Christian Athletes.

Athletics. NJCAA. **Intercollegiate:** Baseball M, basketball, softball W. **Team name:** Indians.

Student services. Career counseling, financial aid counseling, personal counseling, veterans' counselor. **Physically disabled:** Services for visually, speech, hearing impaired. **Transfer:** Pre-admission transcript evaluation for new students.

Contact. Phone: (850) 526-2761 ext. 2233 Fax: (850) 718-2287
Kathy Rehberg, Registrar, Chipola College, 3094 Indian Circle, Marianna, FL 32446

City College: Altamonte Springs
Casselberry, Florida
www.citycollege.edu

- Private 2-year career college
- Large town
- Interview required

General. Accredited by ACICS. **Enrollment:** 340 undergraduates. **Degrees:** 94 associate awarded. **Calendar:** Quarter, extensive summer session. **Full-time faculty:** 2 total. **Part-time faculty:** 33 total.

Basis for selection. Open admission.

2015-2016 Annual costs. Tuition/fees: $14,550. Per-credit charge: $320. **Additional information:** Additional program fees are charged per credit hour or per course.

Financial aid. Need-based: Work-study available nights, weekends and for part-time students.

Application procedures. Admission: No deadline. $25 fee. **Financial aid:** No deadline.

Academics. Credit/placement by examination: AP, CLEP.

Majors. Business: Business admin, marketing. **Computer sciences:** General. **Protective services:** Security management.

Contact. Phone: (407) 831-8466 Fax: (407) 831-1147
Abby Freeman, Director of Admissions, City College: Altamonte Springs, 853 Semoran Boulevard 436, Casselberry, FL 32707-5353

City College: Gainesville
Gainesville, Florida
www.citycollege.edu   **CB code: 3579**

- Private 2-year business and health science college
- Commuter campus in small city

General. Accredited by ACICS. **Enrollment:** 430 undergraduates. **Degrees:** 7 bachelor's, 108 associate awarded. **Location:** 55 miles from Orlando. **Calendar:** Differs by program. **Full-time faculty:** 1 total. **Part-time faculty:** 38 total.

Basis for selection. Open admission.

2015-2016 Annual costs. Tuition/fees: $14,550. Per-credit charge: $320. Books/supplies: $1,556. Personal expenses: $4,311. **Additional information:** Additional program fees are charged per credit hour or per course.

Financial aid. Need-based: Work-study available nights, weekends and for part-time students.

Application procedures. Admission: No deadline. $40 fee. **Financial aid:** No deadline.

Academics. Special study options: Bachelor's degree programs available on campus. **Credit/placement by examination:** AP, CLEP. **Support services:** Tutoring.

Majors. Business: Business admin. **Computer sciences:** General. **Health services:** EMT ambulance attendant. **Protective services:** Criminal justice, law enforcement admin.

Technology on campus. Repair service, wireless network available.

Student life. Freshman orientation: Mandatory. Preregistration for classes offered.

Student services. Career counseling, student employment services, financial aid counseling, placement for graduates. **Physically disabled:** Services for hearing impaired.

Contact. E-mail: kbowden@citycollege.edu
Phone: (352) 335-4000 ext. 410 Fax: (352) 335-4303
Kim Bowden, Director of Admissions, City College: Gainesville, 7001 NW 4th Boulevard, Gainesville, FL 32607

City College: Miami
Miami, Florida
www.citycollege.edu   CB code: 3580

▶ Private 2-year career college
▶ Large city

General. Accredited by ACICS. **Enrollment:** 228 degree-seeking undergraduates. **Degrees:** 12 bachelor's, 66 associate awarded. **Calendar:** Quarter, extensive summer session. **Full-time faculty:** 9 total; 56% minority, 78% women. **Part-time faculty:** 25 total.

Basis for selection. All non-nursing applicants required to pass TABE entrance exam. Nursing applicants required to pass Kaplan entrance exam.

2015-2016 Annual costs. Tuition/fees: $14,550. Per-credit charge: $320. **Additional information:** Additional program fees are charged per credit hour or per course.

Financial aid. All financial aid based on need. Need-based aid available for part-time students. Work-study available nights, weekends and for part-time students.

Application procedures. Admission: No deadline. $25 fee. Admission notification on a rolling basis. **Financial aid:** No deadline. FAFSA, institutional form required. Applicants notified on a rolling basis.

Academics. Special study options: Distance learning, independent study. Bachelor's degree programs available on campus. License preparation in nursing, paramedic. **Credit/placement by examination:** AP, CLEP.

Majors. Business: Business admin. **Health services:** EMT paramedic, medical assistant, nursing practice, office admin, surgical technology.

Contact. E-mail: dsinawi@citycollege.edu
Phone: (305) 666-9242 Fax: (305) 666-9243
Diane Sinawi, Director of Admissions, City College: Miami, 9300 South Dadeland Boulevard, Miami, FL 33156

College of Business and Technology: Cutler Bay
Cutler Bay, Florida
www.cbt.edu

▶ For-profit 2-year technical and career college
▶ Commuter campus in very large city
▶ Interview required

General. Regionally accredited; also accredited by ACICS. **Enrollment:** 78 degree-seeking undergraduates. **Degrees:** 37 associate awarded. **Location:** 20 miles from Miami. **Calendar:** Semester. **Full-time faculty:** 4 total; 25% have terminal degrees, 25% minority, 75% women. **Part-time faculty:** 8 total; 12% have terminal degrees, 100% minority, 50% women.

Student profile. Among degree-seeking undergraduates, 100% enrolled in a vocational program, 17 enrolled as first-time, first-year students.

Women: 71% 25 or older: 65%

Basis for selection. Open admission. **Home schooled:** Transcript of courses and grades, interview required.

2015-2016 Annual costs. Books/supplies: $300. Personal expenses: $95. **Additional information:** Tuition per semester credit $498; enrollment fee $150; student services fee $120; additional fees vary by program.

2014-2015 Financial aid. All financial aid based on need. 37% of total undergraduate aid awarded as scholarships/grants, 63% as loans/jobs. Need-based aid available for part-time students. Work-study available nights, weekends and for part-time students.

Application procedures. Admission: No deadline. $25 fee. Admission notification on a rolling basis. **Financial aid:** No deadline. FAFSA required.

Academics. Credit/placement by examination: AP, CLEP. No more than 12 semester hours towards a degree may be earned by credit by examination. Each application is subject to review and approval. **Support services:** Tutoring. CBT's student success center mission is to help students define, clarify and achieve their academic, professional and personal goals. The services offered include: tutoring, student success seminars, writing labs, study skills development, personal resources and academic success counseling.

Majors. Business: Business admin. **Health services:** Health information technology, medical assistant.

Most popular majors. Business/marketing 30%, health sciences 70%.

Technology on campus. Online library, repair service, wireless network available.

Student life. Freshman orientation: Mandatory. Preregistration for classes offered.

Student services. Career counseling, student employment services, financial aid counseling, placement for graduates.

Contact. E-mail: admissions@cbt.edu
Phone: (305) 273-4499 ext. 4-404 Toll-free number: (866) 626-8842
Fax: (305) 238-2302
Armando Alvarez, Regional Direcof Enrollment Operations, College of Business and Technology: Cutler Bay, 19151 South Dixie Highway, #203, Cutler Bay, FL 33157

College of Business and Technology: Flagler
Miami, Florida
www.cbt.edu

▶ For-profit 2-year technical and career college
▶ Commuter campus in very large city
▶ Interview required

General. Accredited by ACICS. **Enrollment:** 288 degree-seeking undergraduates. **Degrees:** 57 associate awarded. **Location:** 6 miles from downtown. **Calendar:** Semester. **Full-time faculty:** 8 total; 100% minority. **Part-time faculty:** 14 total; 100% minority, 29% women.

Student profile. Among degree-seeking undergraduates, 100% enrolled in a vocational program, 82 enrolled as first-time, first-year students.

Basis for selection. Open admission. **Home schooled:** Transcript of courses and grades, interview required.

2015-2016 Annual costs. Books/supplies: $350. Personal expenses: $95. **Additional information:** Tuition per semester credit $498; enrollment fee $150; student services fee $120; additional fees vary by program.

2014-2015 Financial aid. All financial aid based on need. 40% of total undergraduate aid awarded as scholarships/grants, 60% as loans/jobs. Need-based aid available for part-time students. Work-study available nights, weekends and for part-time students.

Application procedures. Admission: No deadline. $25 fee. Admission notification on a rolling basis. **Financial aid:** No deadline. FAFSA required.

Academics. Special study options: ESL. **Credit/placement by examination:** AP, CLEP. No more than 12 semester hours towards a degree may be earned by credit by examination. Each application is subject to review and approval. **Support services:** Tutoring. Personal coaching, student success seminars, writing labs, study skill development, personal resources and academic success counseling.

Majors. Business: Business admin. **Computer sciences:** Networking. **General:** Electrician.

Most popular majors. Business/marketing 7%, computer/information sciences 26%, trade and industry 67%.

Technology on campus. Online library, repair service, wireless network available.

Student life. Freshman orientation: Mandatory. Preregistration for classes offered.

Student services. Career counseling, student employment services, financial aid counseling, placement for graduates.

Contact. E-mail: admissions@cbt.edu
Phone: (305) 273-4499 ext. 2-204 Toll-free number: (866) 626-8842
Fax: (305) 485-4411
Armando Alvarez, Regional Director of Enrollment Operations, College of Business and Technology: Flagler, 8230 West Flagler Street, Miami, FL 33144

College of Business and Technology: Hialeah
Hialeah, Florida
www.cbt.edu

- For-profit 2-year technical and career college
- Commuter campus in large city
- Interview required

General. Accredited by ACICS. **Enrollment:** 200 degree-seeking undergraduates. **Degrees:** 40 associate awarded. **Location:** 10 miles from Miami. **Calendar:** Semester. **Full-time faculty:** 5 total; 100% minority. **Part-time faculty:** 12 total; 100% minority, 17% women.

Student profile. Among degree-seeking undergraduates, 100% enrolled in a vocational program, 85 enrolled as first-time, first-year students.

Women:	11%	25 or older:	84%

Basis for selection. Open admission. **Home schooled:** Transcript of courses and grades, interview required.

2015-2016 Annual costs. Books/supplies: $350. Personal expenses: $95. **Additional information:** Tuition per semester credit $498; enrollment fee $150; student services fee $120; additional fees vary by program.

2014-2015 Financial aid. All financial aid based on need. 43% of total undergraduate aid awarded as scholarships/grants, 57% as loans/jobs. Need-based aid available for part-time students. Work-study available nights, weekends and for part-time students.

Application procedures. Admission: No deadline. $25 fee. Admission notification on a rolling basis. **Financial aid:** No deadline. FAFSA required.

Academics. Special study options: ESL. **Credit/placement by examination:** AP, CLEP. No more than 12 semester hours towards a degree may be earned by credit by examination. Each application is subject to review and approval. **Support services:** Tutoring. Personal coaching, student success seminars, writing labs, study skill development, personal resources and academic success counseling.

Majors. General: Electrician.

Technology on campus. Online library, repair service, wireless network available.

Student life. Freshman orientation: Mandatory. Preregistration for classes offered.

Student services. Career counseling, student employment services, financial aid counseling, placement for graduates.

Contact. E-mail: admissions@cbt.edu
Phone: (786) 693-8842 Toll-free number: (866) 457-0073
Fax: (305) 827-9955
Armando Alvarez, Regional Director of Enrollment Operations, College of Business and Technology: Hialeah, 935 West 49th Street Suite 203, Hialeah, FL 33012-3436

College of Business and Technology: Kendall
Miami, Florida
www.cbt.edu

- For-profit 2-year technical and career college
- Commuter campus in very large city
- Interview required

General. Accredited by ACICS. **Enrollment:** 10 degree-seeking undergraduates. **Degrees:** 22 associate awarded. **Location:** 8 miles from downtown. **Calendar:** Semester. **Full-time faculty:** 3 total; 67% minority, 67% women.

Student profile. Among degree-seeking undergraduates, 100% enrolled in a vocational program, 1 enrolled as first-time, first-year students.

Women:	30%	25 or older:	76%

Basis for selection. Open admission. **Home schooled:** Transcript of courses and grades, interview required.

2015-2016 Annual costs. Books/supplies: $350. Personal expenses: $95. **Additional information:** Tuition per semester credit $498; enrollment fee $150; student services fee $120; additional fees vary by program.

2014-2015 Financial aid. All financial aid based on need. 67% of total undergraduate aid awarded as scholarships/grants, 33% as loans/jobs. Need-based aid available for part-time students. Work-study available nights, weekends and for part-time students.

Application procedures. Admission: No deadline. $25 fee. Admission notification on a rolling basis. **Financial aid:** No deadline. FAFSA required.

Academics. Special study options: ESL. Bachelor's degree programs available on campus. **Credit/placement by examination:** AP, CLEP. No more than 12 semester hours towards a degree may be earned through credit by examination. Each application subject to review and approval. **Support services:** Tutoring. Personal coaching, student success seminars, writing labs, study skill development, personal resources and academic success counseling.

Majors. Business: Accounting, business admin. **Computer sciences:** LAN/WAN management. **Visual/performing arts:** Graphic design.

Most popular majors. Business/marketing 31%, computer/information sciences 14%, visual/performing arts 55%.

Technology on campus. Online library, repair service, wireless network available.

Student life. Freshman orientation: Mandatory. Preregistration for classes offered.

Student services. Career counseling, student employment services, financial aid counseling, placement for graduates.

Contact. E-mail: admissions@cbt.edu
Phone: (305) 273-4499 ext. 1100 Toll-free number: (866) 442-8725
Fax: (305) 270-0779
Armando Alvarez, Regional Director of Enrollment Operations, College of Business and Technology: Kendall, 8700 W Flagler Street, Miami, FL 33174

College of Business and Technology: Miami Gardens
Miami Gardens, Florida
www.cbt.edu

- For-profit 2-year technical and career college
- Commuter campus in small city
- Interview required

General. Accredited by ACICS. **Enrollment:** 72 degree-seeking undergraduates. **Degrees:** 11 associate awarded. **Location:** 20 miles from downtown. **Calendar:** Semester. **Part-time faculty:** 13 total; 8% have terminal degrees, 85% minority, 62% women.

Student profile. Among degree-seeking undergraduates, 100% enrolled in a vocational program, 12 enrolled as first-time, first-year students.

Basis for selection. Open admission. **Home schooled:** Transcript of courses and grades, interview required.

2015-2016 Annual costs. Books/supplies: $350. Personal expenses: $95.

2014-2015 Financial aid. All financial aid based on need. 58% of total undergraduate aid awarded as scholarships/grants, 42% as loans/jobs. Need-based aid available for part-time students. Work-study available nights, weekends and for part-time students.

Application procedures. Admission: No deadline. $25 fee. Admission notification on a rolling basis. **Financial aid:** No deadline. FAFSA required.

Academics. Special study options: ESL. Bachelor's degree programs available on campus. **Credit/placement by examination:** AP. No more than 12 semester hours towards a degree may be earned by credit by examination. Each application is subject to review and approval. **Support services:** Tutoring. Personal coaching, student success seminars, writing labs, study skill development, personal resources and academic success counseling.

Majors. Business: Business admin. **Health services:** Health information technology, medical assistant. **Visual/performing arts:** Graphic design.

Most popular majors. Business/marketing 64%, computer/information sciences 18%, health sciences 18%.

Technology on campus. Online library, repair service, wireless network available.

Student life. Freshman orientation: Mandatory. Preregistration for classes offered.

Student services. Career counseling, student employment services, financial aid counseling, placement for graduates.

Contact. E-mail: admissions@cbt.edu
Phone: (305) 273-4499 ext. 6600 Toll-free number: (866) 442-8725
Armando Alvarez, Regional Director of Enrollment Operations, College of Business and Technology: Miami Gardens, 5190 NW 167th Street, Miami Gardens, FL 33014-6338

College of Central Florida
Ocala, Florida
www.cf.edu   **CB code: 5127**

▶ Public 2-year community college
▶ Commuter campus in small city

General. Founded in 1957. Regionally accredited. **Enrollment:** 6,937 degree-seeking undergraduates; 994 non-degree-seeking students. **Degrees:** 65 bachelor's, 1,207 associate awarded. **Location:** 72 miles from Orlando. **Calendar:** Semester, extensive summer session. **Full-time faculty:** 138 total; 19% have terminal degrees, 4% minority, 59% women. **Part-time faculty:** 236 total; 6% have terminal degrees, 2% minority, 43% women. **Special facilities:** Art museum.

Student profile. Among degree-seeking undergraduates, 1,503 enrolled as first-time, first-year students.

Part-time:	60%	Women:	64%
Out-of-state:	16%	25 or older:	39%

Transfer out. Colleges most students transferred to 2015: University of Florida, University of Central Florida, Florida State University.

Basis for selection. Open admission, but selective for some programs. Special requirements for registered nursing, dental assisting, physical therapy assistant, child care, criminal justice, surgical technology programs. **Home schooled:** Notarized home school affidavit required.

High school preparation. College-preparatory program recommended. 22 units recommended. Recommended units include English 4, mathematics 4, social studies 3, science 3 (laboratory 2), foreign language 2, computer science 1 and academic electives 2.

2015-2016 Annual costs. Tuition/fees: $3,213; $12,656 out-of-state. Per-credit charge: $107 in-state; $422 out-of-state. Books/supplies: $1,132. Personal expenses: $1,350. **Additional information:** Bachelor programs charged at higher tuition rates.

Financial aid. Need-based: Need-based aid available for part-time students. Work-study available nights, weekends and for part-time students. **Non-need-based:** Scholarships awarded for academics, athletics, minority status, music/drama, state residency.

Application procedures. Admission: Closing date 8/4 (receipt date). $30 fee, may be waived for applicants with need. Admission notification on a rolling basis. **Financial aid:** No deadline. FAFSA required.

Academics. Special study options: Accelerated study, cooperative education, distance learning, dual enrollment of high school students, ESL, honors, independent study, internships, liberal arts/career combination, study abroad, teacher certification program. Bachelor's degrees are available at CF or through the on-campus University Center. Corporate training is available through CF Institute. Bachelor's degree programs available on campus. License preparation in dental hygiene, nursing, occupational therapy, paramedic, physical therapy, radiology, real estate. **Credit/placement by examination:** AP, CLEP, IB, institutional tests. 21 credit hours maximum toward associate degree. **Support services:** GED preparation and test center, learning center, pre-admission summer program, reduced course load, remedial instruction, study skills assistance, tutoring, writing center.

Majors. Business: Accounting technology, business admin. **Computer sciences:** Information technology. **Education:** Early childhood. **Health services:** Dental assistant, EMT paramedic, health information technology, nursing (RN), physical therapy, physical therapy assistant. **Liberal arts:** Arts/sciences. **Protective services:** Law enforcement admin.

Most popular majors. Health sciences 12%, liberal arts 78%.

Technology on campus. 2,500 workstations in library, computer center, student center. Online library, helpline, wireless network available.

Student life. Freshman orientation: Mandatory. Preregistration for classes offered. Held prior to beginning of every term, also available online. **Housing:** Apartments available. College Square Student Residence Center is located near campus. **Activities:** Bands, choral groups, dance, drama, international student organizations, literary magazine, music ensembles, Model UN, musical theater, student government, student newspaper, symphony orchestra, African American Student Union, Hispanic-American Association, Club of Educational Opportunity, Pantheist, Agonostic, Non-Theist Society, international club, Federated College Republicans, Patriot Politics, Voicing Every Need Together, PREP Psychological Rehabilitation Education Program, environmental club.

Athletics. NJCAA. **Intercollegiate:** Baseball M, basketball, softball W, volleyball W. **Intramural:** Bowling, football (non-tackle), soccer. **Team name:** Patriots.

Student services. Adult student services, career counseling, services for economically disadvantaged, student employment services, financial aid counseling, on-campus daycare, personal counseling, placement for graduates, veterans' counselor. **Physically disabled:** Services for visually, speech, hearing impaired. **Transfer:** Transfer adviser, college fairs on campus for students transferring to 4-year colleges.

Contact. E-mail: admissions@cf.edu
Phone: (352) 873-5801 Fax: (352) 873-5875
Teri Little-Berry, Director of Admissions and Records, College of Central Florida, 3001 SW College Road, Ocala, FL 34474-4415

Daytona State College
Daytona Beach, Florida
www.daytonastate.edu   **CB code: 5159**

▶ Public 2-year community and technical college
▶ Commuter campus in large city

General. Founded in 1958. Regionally accredited. **Enrollment:** 10,856 degree-seeking undergraduates; 2,742 non-degree-seeking students. **Degrees:** 250 bachelor's, 1,678 associate awarded. **ROTC:** Army, Air Force. **Location:** 90 miles from Jacksonville, 65 miles from Orlando. **Calendar:** Semester, extensive summer session. **Full-time faculty:** 302 total; 30% have terminal degrees, 18% minority, 53% women. **Part-time faculty:** 574 total; 8% have terminal degrees, 19% minority, 47% women. **Class size:** 41% < 20, 53% 20-39, 3% 40-49, 3% 50-99. **Special facilities:** Museum of photography.

Student profile. Among degree-seeking undergraduates, 50% enrolled in a transfer program, 20% enrolled in a vocational program, 2% already have a bachelor's degree or higher, 1,683 enrolled as first-time, first-year students, 639 transferred in from other institutions.

Part-time:	58%	Hispanic/Latino:	14%
Out-of-state:	3%	Multi-racial, non-Hispanic:	2%
Women:	61%	International:	1%
African American:	13%	25 or older:	43%
Asian American:	2%		

Transfer out. Colleges most students transferred to 2015: University of Central Florida, University of Northern Florida, University of Florida, University of Southern Florida, Florida State University.

Basis for selection. Open admission, but selective for some programs. Special requirements for limited access programs including Bachelor's degree program. **Home schooled:** Signed Home-School Affidavit form. If student is attempting to obtain college credit for a home-schooled course, they must have a transcript with course work listed.

2015-2016 Annual costs. Tuition/fees: $3,134; $12,204 out-of-state. Books/supplies: $1,200. Personal expenses: $1,624. **Additional information:** Bachelor programs charged at higher tuition rates.

2014-2015 Financial aid. Need-based: 737 full-time freshmen applied for aid; 602 deemed to have need; 580 received aid. Average scholarship/grant was $4,346. 74% of total undergraduate aid awarded as scholarships/grants, 26% as loans/jobs. Need-based aid available for part-time students. Work-study available nights, weekends and for part-time students. **Non-need-based:** Awarded to 400 full-time undergraduates, including 66 freshmen. Scholarships awarded for academics, athletics, leadership, music/drama, state residency.

Application procedures. Admission: No deadline. No application fee. Admission notification on a rolling basis. **Financial aid:** Priority date 5/15;

Two-Year Colleges

no closing date. FAFSA required. Applicants notified on a rolling basis starting 3/15.

Academics. Special study options: Cooperative education, distance learning, dual enrollment of high school students, ESL, honors, independent study, internships, liberal arts/career combination, study abroad, teacher certification program, weekend college. Bachelor's degree programs available on campus. License preparation in dental hygiene, nursing, occupational therapy, paramedic, physical therapy, radiology. **Credit/placement by examination:** AP, CLEP, IB, institutional tests. 45 credit hours maximum toward associate degree, 45 toward bachelor's. Credit awarded for prior experiential learning shall not exceed 25% of the units required for completion of the program. The maximum number of credits that can be earned through the combined total of transfer, examination or experiential learning is 75% of the degree or certificate program. **Support services:** GED preparation and test center, learning center, pre-admission summer program, remedial instruction, study skills assistance, tutoring, writing center.

Majors. Architecture: Architecture. **Biology:** General, botany, marine, microbiology, zoology. **Business:** Accounting, accounting technology, banking/financial services, business admin, executive assistant, hospitality admin, management information systems, marketing, operations. **Communications technology:** Photo/film/video. **Computer sciences:** General, applications programming, systems analysis. **Education:** General, Deaf/hearing impaired. **Engineering:** General, computer. **Health services:** Dental hygiene, EMT paramedic, health information technology, medical radiologic technology/radiation therapy, mental health services, nursing (RN), occupational therapy assistant, physical therapy assistant, respiratory therapy technology, veterinary technology/assistant. **Human services:** Social work. **Liberal arts:** Arts/sciences. **Math:** General, statistics. **Philosophy/religion:** Philosophy. **Physical sciences:** General, astronomy, chemistry, meteorology. **Protective services:** Fire safety technology, law enforcement admin. **Psychology:** General. **Social sciences:** Economics, geography, political science, sociology. **Visual/performing arts:** General, acting, art, dance, graphic design, interior design, music, photography, studio arts. **Work/family studies:** Child care service.

Most popular majors. Health sciences 16%, liberal arts 70%.

Technology on campus. 3,200 workstations in library, computer center, student center. Online course registration, online library, helpline, wireless network available.

Student life. Freshman orientation: Mandatory. Preregistration for classes offered. Online Orientation must be taken before students can to register for courses. **Housing:** Off-campus housing available to international students and athletes. **Activities:** Bands, campus ministries, choral groups, dance, drama, international student organizations, music ensembles, musical theater, opera, student government, student newspaper, symphony orchestra, TV station, Campus Crusade for Christ, Global Friends, Phi Theta Kappa, Bachelor of Applied Science club.

Athletics. NJCAA. **Intercollegiate:** Baseball M, basketball, golf W, softball W, volleyball W. **Intramural:** Basketball, football (tackle), soccer, table tennis, tennis, volleyball, weight lifting. **Team name:** Falcons.

Student services. Adult student services, alcohol/substance abuse counseling, career counseling, student employment services, financial aid counseling, minority student services, on-campus daycare, personal counseling, placement for graduates, veterans' counselor, women's services. **Physically disabled:** Services for visually, speech, hearing impaired. **Transfer:** Transfer adviser, college fairs on campus for students transferring to 4-year colleges.

Contact. E-mail: admissions@daytonastate.edu
Phone: (386) 506-3059 ext. 3059 Fax: (386) 506-3940
Karen Sanders, Director of Admissions, Daytona State College,
Admissions Office Daytona State College, Daytona Beach, FL 32114

Eastern Florida State College
Cocoa, Florida
www.easternflorida.edu   CB code: 5073

▸ Public 2-year community college
▸ Commuter campus in very large city

General. Founded in 1960. Regionally accredited. Physical campuses in Cocoa, Melbourne, Palm Bay, Titusville. **Enrollment:** 12,736 degree-seeking undergraduates. **Degrees:** 42 bachelor's, 2,757 associate awarded. **ROTC:** Army, Air Force. **Location:** 50 miles from Orlando. **Calendar:** Semester, extensive summer session. **Full-time faculty:** 215 total; 20% have terminal degrees, 11% minority, 60% women. **Part-time faculty:** 822 total; 9% minority, 51% women. **Class size:** 56% < 20, 44% 20-39, less than 1% 40-49, less than 1% 50-99. **Special facilities:** Planetarium, observatory, performing arts center, multicultural center.

Transfer out. Colleges most students transferred to 2015: University of Central Florida.

Basis for selection. Open admission, but selective for some programs. Additional application and requirements for limited access programs such as health sciences, law enforcement and corrections programs. CPT, SAT or ACT required for admission but scores not used. California Achievement Tests, Stanford Test of Academic Skills, Test of Adult Basic Education required for health program applicants. **Home schooled:** Transcript of courses and grades required. Affidavit of home school completion required. **Learning Disabled:** Students may self-disclose with Office for Students with Disabilities.

High school preparation. Standard high school or equivalent required for degree seeking students. College prep courses required for students testing below college proficiency.

2015-2016 Annual costs. Tuition/fees: $3,130; $12,183 out-of-state. Per-credit charge: $104 in-state; $406 out-of-state. Books/supplies: $800. Personal expenses: $1,224.

Financial aid. Need-based: Need-based aid available for part-time students. Work-study available nights, weekends and for part-time students. **Non-need-based:** Scholarships awarded for academics, athletics.

Application procedures. Admission: No deadline. $30 fee, may be waived for applicants with need. Admission notification on a rolling basis. **Financial aid:** Priority date 4/15, closing date 6/30. FAFSA required. Applicants notified on a rolling basis starting 6/1; must reply within 2 week(s) of notification.

Academics. Special study options: Accelerated study, cooperative education, cross-registration, distance learning, double major, dual enrollment of high school students, ESL, honors, independent study, internships, study abroad. Bachelor's degree programs available on campus. License preparation in dental hygiene, nursing, paramedic, radiology, real estate. **Credit/placement by examination:** AP, CLEP, IB, institutional tests. 45 credit hours maximum toward associate degree. **Support services:** Learning center, reduced course load, remedial instruction, study skills assistance, tutoring, writing center.

Majors. Business: Administrative services, business admin, management information systems, office management. **Computer sciences:** Programming, systems analysis. **Education:** Early childhood. **Engineering:** General, computer. **Health services:** Clinical lab technology, dental hygiene, EMT paramedic, health information technology, medical radiologic technology/radiation therapy, nursing (RN). **Protective services:** Firefighting, police science. **Visual/performing arts:** Commercial/advertising art.

Technology on campus. 1,800 workstations in library, computer center, student center. Commuter students can connect to campus network. Online course registration, online library, helpline, student web hosting, wireless network available.

Student life. Freshman orientation: Mandatory. Preregistration for classes offered. **Activities:** Concert band, choral groups, dance, drama, international student organizations, literary magazine, music ensembles, musical theater, student government, TV station, Student Nurses Association of Florida, Phi Theta Kappa, African American student association, Phi Mu Alpha.

Athletics. NJCAA. **Intercollegiate:** Baseball M, basketball, golf M, soccer, softball W, tennis W, volleyball W. **Team name:** Titans.

Student services. Adult student services, career counseling, services for economically disadvantaged, student employment services, financial aid counseling, minority student services, on-campus daycare, personal counseling, placement for graduates, veterans' counselor. **Physically disabled:** Services for visually, speech, hearing impaired. **Transfer:** College fairs on campus for students transferring to 4-year colleges.

Contact. E-mail: loufekm@easternflorida.edu
Phone: (321) 632-1111 Toll-free number: (888) 747-2802
Fax: (321) 433-7357
Michelle Loufek, Associate Director, Collegewide Admissions, Eastern Florida State College, 1519 Clearlake Road, Cocoa, FL 32922-9987

Florida Career College: Hialeah
Hialeah, Florida
www.careercollege.edu

▸ For-profit 2-year junior and technical college
▸ Commuter campus in very large city

General. Accredited by ACICS. **Calendar:** Quarter.

Annual costs/financial aid. Total program costs including tuition, books and supplies: diploma, $14,475-$22,698; associate degree, $27,322-$44,003; Additional lab fees, supply fees, and technology fees vary by program. Books/supplies: $1,000.

Contact. Phone: (305) 825-3231
Director of Admissions, 3750 West 18th Avenue, Hialeah, FL 33012

Florida Career College: Miami
Miami, Florida
www.careercollege.edu   CB code: 3581

- For-profit 2-year business and technical college
- Large city

General. Accredited by ACICS. **Enrollment:** 6,227 undergraduates. **Degrees:** 1 bachelor's, 59 associate awarded. **Calendar:** Differs by program. **Full-time faculty:** 13 total. **Part-time faculty:** 16 total.

Basis for selection. Open admission.

2015-2016 Annual costs. Total program costs including tuition, books and supplies: diploma, $14,475-$22,698; associate degree, $27,322-$44,003; Additional lab fees, supply fees, and technology fees vary by program.

Financial aid. Need-based: Work-study available nights, weekends and for part-time students.

Application procedures. Admission: No deadline. $100 fee. **Financial aid:** No deadline.

Academics. Credit/placement by examination: AP, CLEP.

Majors. Computer sciences: General, webmaster. **Engineering:** Computer. **Health services:** Office admin.

Contact. Phone: (305) 553-6065
Heidi Cruz, Director of Admissions, Florida Career College: Miami, 1321 SW 107th Avenue, Suite 201B, Miami, FL 33174-2521

Florida Career College: Pembroke Pines
Pembroke Pines, Florida
www.careercollege.edu

- For-profit 2-year business and technical college
- Small city

General. Accredited by ACICS. **Calendar:** Differs by program.

Annual costs/financial aid. Total program costs including tuition, books and supplies: diploma, $14,475-$22,698; associate degree, $27,322-$44,003; Additional lab fees, supply fees, and technology fees vary by program.

Contact. Phone: (954) 965-7272
Director of Admissions, 7891 Pines Boulevard, Pembroke Pines, FL 33024

Florida Career College: West Palm Beach
West Palm Beach, Florida
www.careercollege.edu

- For-profit 2-year technical college
- Commuter campus in small city

General. Accredited by ACICS. **Calendar:** Differs by program.

Annual costs/financial aid. Total program costs including tuition, books and supplies: diploma, $14,475-$22,698; associate degree, $27,322-$44,003; Additional lab fees, supply fees, and technology fees vary by program.

Contact. Phone: (561) 689-0550
Director of Admissions, 6058 Okeechobee Boulevard, West Palm Beach, FL 33417

Florida College of Natural Health: Bradenton
Bradenton, Florida
www.fcnh.com   CB code: 5024

- For-profit 2-year health science and career college
- Commuter campus in small city

General. Accredited by ACCSC. **Enrollment:** 143 undergraduates. **Degrees:** 1 associate awarded. **Location:** 40 miles from Tampa. **Calendar:** Differs by program, extensive summer session. **Full-time faculty:** 2 total. **Part-time faculty:** 5 total.

Basis for selection. Open admission, but selective for some programs.

2015-2016 Annual costs. Books/supplies: $2,430. Personal expenses: $4,620. **Additional information:** Therapeutic Massage; $12,529, books & supplies; $870. Advanced Therapeutic Massage; $16,644, books & supplies $1,040. Advanced Paramedical Skin Care; $17,761, books & supplies; $1,934. A.S. Advanced Therapeutic Massage; $22,189, books & supplies; $1,629. A.S. Therapeutic Massage and Skin Care; $23,414, books & supplies; $2,502. A.S. Advanced Paramedical Skin Care; $23,307, books & supplies; $2,523.

Financial aid. All financial aid based on need. Work-study available nights, weekends and for part-time students.

Application procedures. Admission: No deadline. $50 fee. Admission notification on a rolling basis. **Financial aid:** No deadline. FAFSA required. Applicants notified on a rolling basis.

Academics. Credit/placement by examination: AP, CLEP. **Support services:** Tutoring.

Majors. Health services: Massage therapy.

Technology on campus. 2 workstations in library. Online library available.

Student life. Freshman orientation: Mandatory. Preregistration for classes offered.

Student services. Career counseling, financial aid counseling, placement for graduates.

Contact. E-mail: sarasota@fcnh.com
Phone: (941) 744-1244 Toll-free number: (800) 966-7117
Fax: (941) 744-1242
Admissions, Florida College of Natural Health: Bradenton, 616 67th Street Circle East, Bradenton, FL 34208

Florida College of Natural Health: Maitland
Maitland, Florida
www.fcnh.com   CB code: 5239

- For-profit 2-year health science and junior college
- Large town
- SAT or ACT required

General. Accredited by ACCSC. **Enrollment:** 418 undergraduates. **Degrees:** 16 associate awarded. **Calendar:** Differs by program. **Full-time faculty:** 6 total.

Basis for selection. Passing score on OLSAT entrance exam or 800 SAT (exclusive of Writing) or 17 ACT required of degree-seeking applicants.

2015-2016 Annual costs. Books/supplies: $2,379. Personal expenses: $2,464. **Additional information:** Therapeutic Massage $12,529, books & supplies $870. Advanced Therapeutic Massage $16,644, books & supplies $1,040. Skin Care and Electrology $10,379, books & supplies $1,755. Advanced Paramedical Skin Care $17,761, books & supplies $1,934. A.S. Advanced Therapeutic Massage $22,189, books & supplies $1,629. A.S. Therapeutic Massage and Skin Care $23,414, books & supplies $2,502. A.S. Advanced Paramedical Skin Care $23,307, books & supplies $2,523.

Financial aid. All financial aid based on need. Work-study available nights, weekends and for part-time students.

Application procedures. Admission: No deadline. No application fee. Admission notification on a rolling basis. **Financial aid:** No deadline. FAFSA required. Applicants notified on a rolling basis.

Academics. Credit/placement by examination: AP, CLEP.

Majors. Health services: Massage therapy.

Contact. E-mail: orlando@fcnh.com
Phone: (407) 261-0319 Toll-free number: (800) 393-7337
Fax: (407) 261-0342
Leonore Barfield, Director of Marketing, Florida College of Natural Health: Maitland, 2600 Lake Lucien Drive; Suite 240, Maitland, FL 32751

Florida College of Natural Health: Miami
Miami, Florida
www.fcnh.com   CB code: 5231

- For-profit 2-year branch campus and community college
- Very large city

General. Accredited by ACCSC. **Enrollment:** 202 undergraduates. **Degrees:** 17 associate awarded. **Calendar:** Differs by program. **Full-time faculty:** 1 total. **Part-time faculty:** 8 total.

Basis for selection. Open admission, but selective for some programs. OLSAT, SAT or ACT required for placement.

2015-2016 Annual costs. Books/supplies: $2,379. Personal expenses: $2,464. **Additional information:** Therapeutic Massage $12,533, books & supplies $870. Advanced Therapeutic Massage $16,649, books & supplies $1,040. Skin Care and Electrology $10,387, books & supplies $1,755. Advanced Paramedical Skin Care $17,771, books & supplies $1,934. A.S. Advanced Therapeutic Massage $22,198, books & supplies $1,629. A.S. Therapeutic Massage and Skin Care $23,427, books & supplies $2,502. A.S. Advanced Paramedical Skin Care $23,319, books & supplies $2,523.

Financial aid. All financial aid based on need. Work-study available nights, weekends and for part-time students.

Application procedures. Admission: No deadline. No application fee. Admission notification on a rolling basis. **Financial aid:** No deadline. FAFSA required. Applicants notified on a rolling basis.

Academics. Credit/placement by examination: AP, CLEP.

Majors. Health services: Massage therapy.

Contact. E-mail: miami@fcnh.com
Phone: (305) 597-9599 Toll-free number: (800) 599-9599
Fax: (305) 597-9110
Florida College of Natural Health: Miami, 7925 Northwest 12th Street, Suite 201, Miami, FL 33126

Florida College of Natural Health: Pompano Beach
Pompano Beach, Florida
www.fcnh.com   CB code: 5238

- For-profit 2-year junior college
- Very large city

General. Accredited by ACCSC. **Enrollment:** 203 undergraduates. **Degrees:** 7 associate awarded. **Calendar:** Differs by program. **Full-time faculty:** 5 total. **Part-time faculty:** 6 total.

Basis for selection. Open admission, but selective for some programs. OLSAT, SAT or ACT required for placement.

2015-2016 Annual costs. Books/supplies: $2,379. **Additional information:** Therapeutic Massage $12,525, books & supplies $870. Advanced Therapeutic Massage $16,639, books & supplies $1,040. Skin Care and Electrology $10,370, books & supplies $1,755. Advanced Paramedical Skin Care $17,752, books & supplies $1,934. A.S. Advanced Therapeutic Massage $22,181, books & supplies $1,629. A.S. Therapeutic Massage and Skin Care $23,402, books & supplies $2,502. A.S. Advanced Paramedical Skin Care $23,294, books & supplies $2,523.

Financial aid. All financial aid based on need. Work-study available nights, weekends and for part-time students.

Application procedures. Admission: No deadline. No application fee. Admission notification on a rolling basis. **Financial aid:** No deadline. FAFSA required. Applicants notified on a rolling basis.

Academics. Credit/placement by examination: AP, CLEP.

Majors. Health services: Massage therapy.

Contact. E-mail: ftlauderdale@fcnh.com
Phone: (954) 975-6400 Toll-free number: (800) 541-9299
Fax: (954) 975-9633
Jim Howard, Chief Operating Officer, Florida College of Natural Health: Pompano Beach, 2001 West Sample Road, Suite 100, Pompano Beach, FL 33064

Florida Gateway College
Lake City, Florida   **CB member**
www.fgc.edu   CB code: 5377

- Public 2-year community college
- Commuter campus in large town

General. Founded in 1947. Regionally accredited. **Enrollment:** 1,996 degree-seeking undergraduates; 864 non-degree-seeking students. **Degrees:** 11 bachelor's, 446 associate awarded. **Location:** 60 miles from Jacksonville, 45 miles from Gainesville. **Calendar:** Semester, limited summer session. **Full-time faculty:** 66 total. **Part-time faculty:** 110 total. **Special facilities:** Performing arts center, arboretum.

Student profile. Among degree-seeking undergraduates, 330 enrolled as first-time, first-year students.

Part-time:	65%	**Women:**	65%
Out-of-state:	1%	**25 or older:**	38%

Transfer out. Colleges most students transferred to 2015: University of Florida, Florida State University, University of North Florida, Saint Leo University.

Basis for selection. Open admission, but selective for some programs. Limited admission to allied health programs. Interview recommended for most allied health programs. **Home schooled:** Must supply home school affidavits and/or a GED transcript, and graduation date.

2015-2016 Annual costs. Tuition/fees: $3,100; $11,747 out-of-state. Books/supplies: $1,000. **Additional information:** Bachelor programs charged at higher tuition rates.

Financial aid. Need-based: Need-based aid available for part-time students. Work-study available nights, weekends and for part-time students. **Non-need-based:** Scholarships awarded for academics, leadership, minority status, music/drama, state residency.

Application procedures. Admission: Priority date 8/1; deadline 8/12 (receipt date). No application fee. Application must be submitted on paper. Admission notification on a rolling basis. Some technical programs reach maximum enrollment and close prior to 8/1. **Financial aid:** Priority date 6/1; no closing date. FAFSA, institutional form required. Applicants notified on a rolling basis starting 6/1; must reply within 2 week(s) of notification.

Academics. Special study options: Accelerated study, distance learning, dual enrollment of high school students, honors, independent study, teacher certification program. Bachelor's degree programs available on campus. License preparation in nursing, paramedic, physical therapy. **Credit/placement by examination:** AP, CLEP, IB, institutional tests. 45 credit hours maximum toward associate degree. Restrictions on credits awarded on exams administered prior to July 1, 2001. **Support services:** GED test center, learning center, pre-admission summer program, reduced course load, remedial instruction, study skills assistance, tutoring. Remedial Learning Groups.

Majors. Business: Business admin. **Computer sciences:** General, computer graphics, programming. **Conservation:** Environmental science. **Education:** Early childhood. **Health services:** EMT paramedic, health information technology, nursing (RN), physical therapy assistant, veterinary technology/assistant. **Liberal arts:** Arts/sciences. **Protective services:** Law enforcement admin. **Visual/performing arts:** Graphic design.

Technology on campus. 320 workstations in library, computer center, student center. Online course registration, online library, wireless network available.

Student life. Freshman orientation: Available. Preregistration for classes offered. **Activities:** Concert band, drama, literary magazine, music ensembles, student government, TV station, Florida Student Nurses Association, Phi Theta Kappa.

Athletics. Intramural: Basketball, football (non-tackle), soccer. **Team name:** Timberwolves.

Student services. Alcohol/substance abuse counseling, career counseling, student employment services, financial aid counseling, personal counseling, veterans' counselor. **Physically disabled:** Services for visually, speech, hearing impaired. **Transfer:** Transfer adviser, college fairs on campus for students transferring to 4-year colleges.

Contact. E-mail: admissions@fgc.edu
Phone: (386) 754-4287 Fax: (386) 754-4787
Sandra Johnston, Director Enrollment Management, Florida Gateway College, 149 SE College Place, Lake City, FL 32025-2007

Florida Keys Community College
Key West, Florida
www.fkcc.edu   CB code: 5236

▶ Public 2-year community college
▶ Commuter campus in large town

General. Founded in 1965. Regionally accredited. Branch campuses in Tavernier and Marathon. **Enrollment:** 819 degree-seeking undergraduates. **Degrees:** 157 associate awarded. **Location:** 150 miles from Miami; 90 miles from Havana, Cuba. **Calendar:** Semester, limited summer session. **Special facilities:** Fine arts center and theater, ceramics studio, marine propulsion technology center, welding lab, aquatic center, diving program underwater education complex, hyperbaric chamber.

Transfer out. Colleges most students transferred to 2015: University of Central Florida, Florida International University, University of Florida, Florida State University, St. Leo's College.

Basis for selection. Open admission, but selective for some programs. Special application, placement examination, pre-requisite courses and essay required for nursing technology applicants. Admission based on objective points system. Special application, placement examination, psychological test, polygraph test and additional documentation required for all law enforcement academies.

High school preparation. Recommended units include English 4, mathematics 3, social studies 3 and science 3.

2015-2016 Annual costs. Tuition/fees: $3,277; $13,162 out-of-state. Per-credit charge: $82.78 in-state; $331.11 out-of-state. Room only: $8,131. Books/supplies: $1,300.

Financial aid. Need-based: Need-based aid available for part-time students. Work-study available nights, weekends and for part-time students. **Non-need-based:** Scholarships awarded for academics, art, leadership, minority status.

Application procedures. Admission: No deadline. $30 fee. Admission notification on a rolling basis. **Financial aid:** Priority date 5/1; no closing date. FAFSA, institutional form required. Applicants notified on a rolling basis starting 6/15; must reply within 2 week(s) of notification.

Academics. Special study options: Distance learning, double major, dual enrollment of high school students, ESL, independent study, internships. License preparation in nursing, paramedic. **Credit/placement by examination:** AP, CLEP, IB, institutional tests. 45 credit hours maximum toward associate degree. **Support services:** GED test center, learning center, reduced course load, remedial instruction, tutoring, writing center.

Majors. Biology: Marine. **Business:** Business admin. **Computer sciences:** General, programming. **Health services:** Nursing (RN).

Technology on campus. 130 workstations in library, computer center, student center. Online course registration, online library, helpline, wireless network available.

Student life. Freshman orientation: Available. Preregistration for classes offered. **Housing:** Coed dorms available. **Activities:** Choral groups, student government, nurses pinning club, Florida nurses student association, Mud-Pi ceramics club, Phi Theta Kappa, cyber league, photo guild club, wreckers club, propmasters club.

Athletics. Team name: Wreckers.

Student services. Adult student services, career counseling, student employment services, financial aid counseling, placement for graduates, veterans' counselor. **Physically disabled:** Services for visually, speech, hearing impaired. **Transfer:** Transfer adviser, college fairs on campus for students transferring to 4-year colleges.

Contact. E-mail: admissions@fkcc.edu
Phone: (305) 809-3188 Fax: (305) 292-5163
Cheryl Malsheimer, Director of Enrollment Services/Registrar, Florida Keys Community College, 5901 College Road, Key West, FL 33040

Florida National University
Hialeah, Florida   CB member
www.fnu.edu   CB code: 2057

▶ For-profit 2-year junior college
▶ Commuter campus in very large city
▶ Interview required

General. Regionally accredited. **Enrollment:** 2,389 degree-seeking undergraduates; 67 non-degree-seeking students. **Degrees:** 125 bachelor's, 315 associate awarded; master's offered. **Location:** 12 miles from Miami. **Calendar:** Semester. **Full-time faculty:** 76 total; 16% have terminal degrees, 92% minority, 38% women. **Part-time faculty:** 54 total; 17% have terminal degrees, 85% minority, 46% women. **Class size:** 56% < 20, 44% 20-39.

Student profile. Among degree-seeking undergraduates, 28% enrolled in a vocational program, 1% already have a bachelor's degree or higher, 384 enrolled as first-time, first-year students.

Part-time:	10%	Hispanic/Latino:	86%
Women:	71%	International:	9%
African American:	3%		

Transfer out. Colleges most students transferred to 2015: Nova Southeastern University, Florida International University, American Intercontinental University, Miami Institute of Psychology, Carlos Albizu University.

Basis for selection. Open admission, but selective for some programs. Test of Essential Academic Skills required for Nursing program, Radiology Technology, and Diagnostic Medical Sonographer Teachnology.

2015-2016 Annual costs. Tuition/fees: $13,090. Per-credit charge: $525. Books/supplies: $1,000. Personal expenses: $1,982.

2014-2015 Financial aid. All financial aid based on need. 40% of total undergraduate aid awarded as scholarships/grants, 60% as loans/jobs. Need-based aid available for part-time students. Work-study available nights, weekends and for part-time students.

Application procedures. Admission: No deadline. No application fee. Admission notification on a rolling basis. **Financial aid:** No deadline. FAFSA, institutional form required. Applicants notified on a rolling basis.

Academics. Special study options: Accelerated study, cooperative education, distance learning, dual enrollment of high school students, ESL, independent study, internships. Bachelor's degree programs available on campus. License preparation in nursing, physical therapy, radiology. **Credit/placement by examination:** AP, CLEP, institutional tests. 9 credit hours maximum toward associate degree, 9 toward bachelor's. **Support services:** GED preparation, reduced course load, remedial instruction, study skills assistance, tutoring, writing center.

Majors. Business: Accounting, business admin, hospitality admin. **Computer sciences:** General, system admin, web page design. **Education:** General. **Health services:** Dental hygiene, dental lab technology, health services admin, medical assistant, physical therapy assistant, radiologic technology/medical imaging, respiratory therapy technology, sonography. **Human services:** General. **Protective services:** Criminal justice.

Most popular majors. Business/marketing 15%, health sciences 70%, security/protective services 8%.

Technology on campus. Online library, wireless network available.

Student life. Freshman orientation: Mandatory. Preregistration for classes offered. **Activities:** Student government.

Athletics. USCAA. **Intercollegiate:** Basketball M, soccer. **Team name:** Conquistadors.

Student services. Career counseling, student employment services, financial aid counseling, on-campus daycare, placement for graduates. **Transfer:** Re-entry adviser, pre-admission transcript evaluation for new students.

Contact. E-mail: admissions@fnu.edu
Phone: (305) 821-3333 Fax: (305) 362-0595
Robert Lopez, Director of Admissions, Florida National University, 4425 West Jose Regueiro (20th) Avenue, Hialeah, FL 33012

Florida SouthWestern State College
Fort Myers, Florida   CB member
www.fsw.edu   CB code: 5191

▶ Public 2-year liberal arts college
▶ Commuter campus in small city

General. Founded in 1961. Regionally accredited. Additional campus sites: Charlotte Campus, Collier Campus, Hendry Glades Center, FSW Online. **Enrollment:** 14,885 degree-seeking undergraduates; 857 non-degree-seeking students. **Degrees:** 341 bachelor's, 1,942 associate awarded. **Location:** 35 miles from Naples; 120 miles from Tampa; 150 miles from Miami. **Calendar:** Semester, limited summer session. **Full-time faculty:** 183 total; 49% have terminal degrees, 17% minority, 53% women. **Part-time faculty:** 418 total; 31% have terminal degrees, 15% minority, 53% women. **Class size:** 21% < 20, 74% 20-39, 4% 40-49, less than 1% 50-99. **Special facilities:** Performing arts hall, observatory, 3-hole instructional golf course, fine art gallery.

Student profile. Among degree-seeking undergraduates, 2,979 enrolled as first-time, first-year students, 548 transferred in from other institutions.

Part-time:	64%	Hispanic/Latino:	27%
Out-of-state:	2%	Multi-racial, non-Hispanic:	2%
Women:	61%	International:	2%
African American:	11%	25 or older:	28%
Asian American:	2%	Live on campus:	2%

Transfer out. Colleges most students transferred to 2015: University of South Florida, Florida Gulf Coast University, University of Central Florida, Florida State University, University of Florida.

Basis for selection. Open admission, but selective for some programs. Special requirements for allied health programs. **Home schooled:** Applicants must submit affidavit of completion.

High school preparation. College-preparatory program recommended. 24 units recommended. Recommended units include English 4, mathematics 4, social studies 3, history 2, science 3 (laboratory 3), foreign language 2, computer science 2, visual/performing arts 2 and academic electives 2.

2015-2016 Annual costs. Tuition/fees: $3,341; $13,039 out-of-state. Books/supplies: $1,650. Personal expenses: $4,518. **Additional information:** Bachelor programs charged at higher tuition rates.

2014-2015 Financial aid. Need-based: 1,570 full-time freshmen applied for aid; 1,318 deemed to have need; 1,248 received aid. Average need met was 48%. Average scholarship/grant was $5,307; average loan $3,011. 66% of total undergraduate aid awarded as scholarships/grants, 34% as loans/jobs. Need-based aid available for part-time students. Work-study available nights, weekends and for part-time students. **Non-need-based:** Awarded to 208 full-time undergraduates, including 112 freshmen. Scholarships awarded for academics, art, athletics, leadership, music/drama.

Application procedures. Admission: Closing date 8/17 (receipt date). $30 fee, may be waived for applicants with need. Admission notification on a rolling basis. **Financial aid:** Priority date 5/1, closing date 9/16. FAFSA, institutional form required. Applicants notified on a rolling basis starting 6/30.

Academics. Special study options: Distance learning, double major, dual enrollment of high school students, ESL, honors, independent study, internships, liberal arts/career combination, study abroad, teacher certification program. Bachelor's degree programs available on campus. **Credit/placement by examination:** AP, CLEP, IB, institutional tests. 45 credit hours maximum toward associate degree, 45 toward bachelor's. **Support services:** Learning center, remedial instruction, study skills assistance, tutoring, writing center. Math center, oral communication, English for Academic Purposes.

Majors. Architecture: Technology. **Business:** Accounting technology, business admin. **Computer sciences:** Networking, programming, system admin, web page design. **Education:** Early childhood. **Health services:** Cardiovascular technology, community health services, dental hygiene, EMT paramedic, health information technology, medical radiologic technology/radiation therapy, nursing (RN), optician, physical therapy assistant, respiratory therapy assistant, respiratory therapy technology, substance abuse counseling. **Liberal arts:** Arts/sciences. **Protective services:** Fire safety technology, forensics, law enforcement admin.

Most popular majors. Health sciences 17%, liberal arts 74%.

Technology on campus. Dormitories wired for high-speed internet access and linked to campus network. Online course registration, online library, helpline, repair service, wireless network available.

Student life. Freshman orientation: Mandatory. Preregistration for classes offered. **Housing:** Coed dorms available. $50 nonrefundable deposit. **Activities:** Concert band, campus ministries, choral groups, dance, drama, literary magazine, Model UN, student government, African American Student Association, Campus Activities Board, SCUBA club, National Student Nurses Association, Christian Fellowship Club, multicultural club, Republican club, Democrat club, Student Leadership Academy, Future Educators Association.

Athletics. NJCAA. **Intramural:** Basketball, football (non-tackle), soccer, volleyball. **Team name:** Buccaneers.

Student services. Alcohol/substance abuse counseling, career counseling, services for economically disadvantaged, student employment services, financial aid counseling, minority student services, on-campus daycare, personal counseling, veterans' counselor. **Physically disabled:** Services for visually, speech, hearing impaired.

Contact. E-mail: admissions@fsw.edu
Phone: (239) 489-9054 Toll-free number: (800) 749-2322
Fax: (239) 489-9094
Amber McCown, Director of Admissions, Florida SouthWestern State College, 8099 College Parkway, Fort Myers, FL 33919

Florida State College at Jacksonville
Jacksonville, Florida
www.fscj.edu   **CB code: 5232**

▶ Public 2-year community and junior college
▶ Commuter campus in very large city

General. Founded in 1963. Regionally accredited. 4 campus locations, 6 center sites, online campus. **Enrollment:** 21,565 degree-seeking undergraduates; 4,599 non-degree-seeking students. **Degrees:** 436 bachelor's, 2,821 associate awarded. **ROTC:** Army, Naval. **Calendar:** Semester, extensive summer session. **Full-time faculty:** 404 total. **Part-time faculty:** 816 total. **Class size:** 51% < 20, 49% 20-39, less than 1% 40-49, less than 1% 50-99. **Special facilities:** Performing arts theater, criminal justice center, advanced technology center, aviation center. **Partnerships:** Formal partnerships with Florida Construction Institute, Florida Home Builders Association, Navy Contracts, GM/ASEP contracts for non-credit (Education-To-Go), NE Florida Credit Union Association, Aviation Professional/Pilot Contract, Cisco Agreement with 2 schools in midwest.

Student profile. Among degree-seeking undergraduates, 67% enrolled in a transfer program, 33% enrolled in a vocational program, 3,286 enrolled as first-time, first-year students, 702 transferred in from other institutions.

Part-time:	69%	Hispanic/Latino:	8%
Out-of-state:	1%	Native Hawaiian/Pacific islander:	1%
Women:	59%	Multi-racial, non-Hispanic:	3%
African American:	25%	International:	1%
Asian American:	4%	25 or older:	49%

Transfer out. Colleges most students transferred to 2015: University of North Florida, Jacksonville University, University of Florida, Florida State University, University of Central Florida.

Basis for selection. Open admission, but selective for some programs. Special requirements for some associate of science programs and all baccalaureate programs. Additional program application may be required. SAT/ACT or Postsecondary Education Readiness Test (PERT) required for placement. **Home schooled:** Transcript of courses and grades required. Home school letter form required. **Learning Disabled:** Medical documentation required.

High school preparation. 24 units recommended. Recommended units include English 4, mathematics 4, social studies 3, science 4 (laboratory 2), foreign language 2, visual/performing arts 1 and academic electives 6. Social studies should be .5 US government, .5 economics, 1 US history, 1 world history.

2015-2016 Annual costs. Tuition/fees: $3,146; $12,038 out-of-state. Books/supplies: $1,920. Personal expenses: $1,120. **Additional information:** Bachelor programs charged at higher tuition rates.

Financial aid. Need-based: Need-based aid available for part-time students. Work-study available nights, weekends and for part-time students. **Non-need-based:** Scholarships awarded for academics, alumni affiliation, art, athletics, job skills, leadership, minority status, music/drama.

Application procedures. Admission: Priority date 7/27; no deadline. $25 fee. Admission notification on a rolling basis. **Financial aid:** Priority date 8/1; no closing date. FAFSA, institutional form required.

Academics. Special study options: Accelerated study, cooperative education, cross-registration, distance learning, double major, dual enrollment of high school students, ESL, exchange student, external degree, honors, independent study, internships, liberal arts/career combination, study abroad, teacher certification program, weekend college. Bachelor's degree programs available on campus. License preparation in aviation, dental hygiene, nursing, paramedic, physical therapy, radiology, real estate. **Credit/placement by examination:** AP, CLEP, institutional tests. 45 credit hours maximum toward associate degree. **Support services:** GED preparation and test center, learning center, reduced course load, remedial instruction, study skills assistance, tutoring.

Majors. Architecture: Environmental design, interior. **Biology:** Biomedical sciences. **Business:** Accounting, administrative services, banking/financial services, business admin, fashion, financial planning, hospitality admin, insurance, management information systems, office management, office technology, sales/distribution, tourism/travel. **Communications technology:** Graphic/printing. **Computer sciences:** General, applications programming, computer graphics, data processing, information systems, networking, programming, systems analysis. **Education:** Elementary. **Engineering:** General, civil, computer. **Foreign languages:** Sign language interpretation. **General:** Maintenance. **Health services:** Clinical lab technology, dental hygiene, EMT paramedic, health information technology, medical radiologic technology/radiation therapy, medical secretary, nursing (RN), physical therapy assistant, respiratory therapy technology, sonography, substance abuse counseling. **Protective services:** Criminal justice, fire safety technology, fire services admin, firefighting, law enforcement admin. **Visual/performing arts:** General, cinematography, commercial/advertising art, design, dramatic, interior design, theater design. **Work/family studies:** Clothing/textiles.

Most popular majors. Health sciences 11%, liberal arts 76%.

Technology on campus. 2,500 workstations in library, computer center, student center. Commuter students can connect to campus network. Online course registration, online library, helpline, repair service, student web hosting, wireless network available.

Student life. Freshman orientation: Mandatory. Preregistration for classes offered. **Housing:** Housing assistance available to qualified Talent Grant students. **Activities:** Bands, choral groups, dance, drama, international student organizations, literary magazine, music ensembles, musical theater, radio station, student government, student newspaper, TV station, Phi Theta Kappa, gospel and concert choir, Spanish club, diversity club, German student association.

Athletics. NJCAA. **Intercollegiate:** Baseball M, basketball, softball W, tennis W, volleyball W. **Intramural:** Badminton, basketball, bowling, football (non-tackle), golf, soccer, softball, table tennis, tennis, volleyball. **Team name:** Blue Wave.

Student services. Adult student services, alcohol/substance abuse counseling, career counseling, services for economically disadvantaged, student employment services, financial aid counseling, legal services, minority student services, on-campus daycare, personal counseling, placement for graduates, veterans' counselor, women's services. **Physically disabled:** Services for visually, speech, hearing impaired. **Transfer:** Transfer adviser, college fairs on campus for students transferring to 4-year colleges.

Contact. E-mail: info@fscj.edu
Phone: (904) 646-2300 Fax: (904) 633-5955
Rich Turner, Dean of Enrollment Management, Florida State College at Jacksonville, 501 West State Street, Jacksonville, FL 32202

Florida Technical College: Deland
Deland, Florida
www.ftccollege.edu   CB code: 3589

- For-profit 2-year junior and technical college
- Small city

General. Accredited by ACICS. **Location:** 30 miles from Orlando, 20 miles from Daytona Beach. **Calendar:** Quarter.

Annual costs/financial aid. Diploma programs $995-$22,635. Associate degree programs $31,555-$34,259. Bachelor's degree programs $58,985-$59,335. Other fees vary by program. Need-based financial aid available to full-time and part-time students.

Contact. Phone: (386) 734-3303
Director of Admissions, 1199 South Woodland Boulevard, Deland, FL 32720

Florida Technical College: Lakeland
Lakeland, Florida
www.ftccollege.edu   CB code: 3432

- For-profit 2-year business and junior college
- Large town

General. Accredited by ACICS. **Calendar:** Differs by program.

Annual costs/financial aid. Diploma programs $995-$22,635. Associate degree programs $31,555-$34,259. Bachelor's degree programs $58,985-$59,335. Other fees vary by program. Need-based financial aid available to full-time and part-time students.

Contact. Phone: (863) 967-8822
School Director, 4715 South Florida Avenue, Lakeland, FL 33813

Florida Technical College: Orlando
Orlando, Florida
www.ftccollege.edu   CB code: 3588

- For-profit 2-year junior and technical college
- Commuter campus in large city
- Interview required

General. Accredited by ACICS. **Enrollment:** 2,977 undergraduates. **Degrees:** 87 bachelor's, 398 associate awarded. **Location:** 13 miles from downtown. **Calendar:** Differs by program, extensive summer session. **Full-time faculty:** 132 total. **Part-time faculty:** 13 total.

Basis for selection. Open admission.

2015-2016 Annual costs. Diploma programs $995-$22,635. Associate degree programs $31,555-$34,259. Bachelor's degree programs $58,985-$59,335. Other fees vary by program.

Financial aid. All financial aid based on need. Need-based aid available for part-time students. Work-study available nights, weekends and for part-time students.

Application procedures. Admission: No deadline. $25 fee, may be waived for applicants with need. Application must be submitted on paper. Admission notification on a rolling basis. **Financial aid:** No deadline. FAFSA required. Applicants notified on a rolling basis.

Academics. Special study options: Independent study. **Credit/placement by examination:** AP, CLEP, institutional tests. **Support services:** Tutoring.

Majors. Business: Business admin. **Computer sciences:** Networking, programming, web page design. **Health services:** Medical assistant, medical secretary. **Protective services:** Law enforcement admin.

Technology on campus. 100 workstations in library, computer center. Online library, wireless network available.

Student life. Freshman orientation: Mandatory. Preregistration for classes offered.

Student services. Career counseling, student employment services, financial aid counseling, placement for graduates.

Contact. E-mail: dboothe@flatech.edu
Phone: (407) 447-7300 Toll-free number: (888) 678-2929
Fax: (407) 447-7301
Dane Boothe, Director, Florida Technical College: Orlando, 12900 Challenger Parkway, Orlando, FL 32826-2707

Fortis College: Orange Park
Orange Park, Florida
www.fortis.edu

- For-profit 2-year business and health science college
- Large city
- Interview required

General. Regionally accredited; also accredited by ACCSC. **Enrollment:** 312 undergraduates. **Degrees:** 24 associate awarded. **Calendar:** Continuous. **Full-time faculty:** 9 total. **Part-time faculty:** 16 total.

Basis for selection. Open admission. Interview required to discuss programs in relation to prospective student's career preferences, training needs, and individual motivation.

2015-2016 Annual costs. Diploma programs: Dental Assisting $18,500; Medical Assisting $14,995; Medical Assisting with Basic X-Ray Operation $18,500; Medical Billing and Coding $18,025; Medical Office Basic X-Ray Technician $18,500; Sterile Processing Technology $15,836. Associate degree programs: Criminal Justice $27,912; Healthcare Management $15,991; Surgical Technology $35,000; Nursing $47,332. All program costs include tuition, books, supplies, exams, and immunizations (where required).

Financial aid. Need-based: Work-study available nights, weekends and for part-time students.

Application procedures. Admission: No deadline. $67 fee.

Academics. Credit/placement by examination: AP, CLEP.

Majors. Business: Business admin. **Health services:** Insurance specialist, management/clinical assistant, pharmacy assistant. **Protective services:** Criminal justice.

Contact. Phone: (904) 269-7086
Fortis College: Orange Park, 560 Wells Road, Orange Park, FL 32073

Fortis College: Winter Park
Winter Park, Florida
www.fortis.edu

- For-profit 2-year technical college
- Very large city
- Interview required

General. Regionally accredited; also accredited by ACCSC. **Enrollment:** 14 undergraduates. **Calendar:** Differs by program, extensive summer session. **Full-time faculty:** 8 total. **Part-time faculty:** 7 total.

Basis for selection. Open admission.

2015-2016 Annual costs. Diploma programs: Dental Assisting $18,500; Medical Assisting $14,995; Medical Assisting with Basic X-Ray Operation $18,500; Medical Billing and Coding $18,025; Medical Office Basic X-Ray Technician $18,500; Sterile Processing Technology $15,836. Associate degree programs: Criminal Justice $27,912; Healthcare Management $15,991; Surgical Technology $35,000; Nursing $47,332. All program costs include tuition, books, supplies, exams, and immunizations (where required).

Financial aid. All financial aid based on need. Work-study available nights, weekends and for part-time students.

Application procedures. Admission: No deadline. $50 fee. Admission notification on a rolling basis. **Financial aid:** No deadline. FAFSA required.

Academics. Special study options: Distance learning, liberal arts/career combination. **Credit/placement by examination:** AP, CLEP. **Support services:** Study skills assistance.

Majors. Business: Accounting, business admin. **Health services:** Health information technology, insurance specialist, medical assistant. **Protective services:** Police science.

Most popular majors. Business/marketing 13%, health sciences 80%.

Technology on campus. 64 workstations in library, computer center. Online library available.

Contact. E-mail: admissions@centralfloridacollege.edu
Phone: (407) 843-3984
Bill Poulmear, Director, Fortis College: Winter Park, 1573 West Fairbanks Avenue, Suite 100, Winter Park, FL 32789

Golf Academy of America: Orlando
Apopka, Florida
www.golfacademy.edu

- For-profit 2-year community college
- Large town

General. Accredited by ACICS. **Enrollment:** 192 undergraduates. **Degrees:** 157 associate awarded. **Calendar:** Semester. **Full-time faculty:** 3 total. **Part-time faculty:** 20 total.

Basis for selection. Open admission, but selective for some programs.

2015-2016 Annual costs. Tuition/fees: $17,150.

Financial aid. Need-based: Work-study available nights, weekends and for part-time students.

Application procedures. Admission: No deadline. $50 fee. **Financial aid:** No deadline.

Academics. Credit/placement by examination: AP, CLEP.

Majors. Business: Business admin. **Parks/recreation:** Golf management.

Contact. E-mail: orlando.info@golfacademy.edu
Phone: (407) 699-1990 Toll-free number: (800) 342-7342
Angel Nguyen, Director of Admissions, Golf Academy of America: Orlando, 7373 North Scottsdale Road, Suite B-100, Scottsdale, AZ 85253

Gulf Coast State College
Panama City, Florida
www.gulfcoast.edu   **CB code: 5271**

- Public 2-year community college
- Commuter campus in small city

General. Founded in 1957. Regionally accredited. **Enrollment:** 4,258 degree-seeking undergraduates; 1,195 non-degree-seeking students. **Degrees:** 48 bachelor's, 888 associate awarded. **Location:** 100 miles from Tallahassee, 100 miles from Pensacola. **Calendar:** Semester, limited summer session. **Full-time faculty:** 105 total; 14% minority, 61% women. **Part-time faculty:** 278 total; 17% minority, 54% women. **Class size:** 58% < 20, 41% 20-39, less than 1% 40-49, less than 1% 50-99. **Partnerships:** Formal partnerships with local businesses.

Student profile. Among degree-seeking undergraduates, 62% enrolled in a transfer program, 30% enrolled in a vocational program, 184 enrolled as first-time, first-year students.

Part-time:	56%	Hispanic/Latino:	6%
Out-of-state:	4%	Native American:	1%
Women:	60%	Multi-racial, non-Hispanic:	4%
African American:	11%	25 or older:	41%
Asian American:	3%		

Transfer out. Colleges most students transferred to 2015: Florida State University, University of Florida, University of Central Florida, University of West Florida.

Basis for selection. Open admission, but selective for some programs. Admission to health science programs determined through high school transcripts, placement test performance and other admissions criteria. Interview required of allied health applicants. Audition recommended for music majors. **Home schooled:** Home School Affidavit must be submitted with parent's signature and notarized.

High school preparation. 13 units recommended. Recommended units include English 4, mathematics 3, social studies 3 and science 3.

2015-2016 Annual costs. Tuition/fees: $2,963; $10,791 out-of-state. Books/supplies: $1,035. Personal expenses: $1,200. **Additional information:** Bachelor programs charged at higher tuition rates.

2014-2015 Financial aid. Need-based: 73% of total undergraduate aid awarded as scholarships/grants, 27% as loans/jobs. Need-based aid available for part-time students. Work-study available nights, weekends and for part-time students. **Non-need-based:** Scholarships awarded for academics, athletics, job skills, leadership, minority status, music/drama, state residency.

Application procedures. Admission: No deadline. $20 fee. Admission notification on a rolling basis. Application deadline for nursing program 2/28; dental hygiene 1/19; EMT and paramedic 6/1; radiography 5/16; physical therapist assistant 5/9; surgical technology 6/1. **Financial aid:** Priority date 5/15, closing date 7/1. FAFSA required. Applicants notified on a rolling basis starting 7/1.

Academics. Special study options: Accelerated study, cooperative education, distance learning, dual enrollment of high school students, honors, independent study, internships, teacher certification program. Bachelor's degree programs available on campus. License preparation in dental hygiene, nursing, paramedic, physical therapy, radiology, real estate. **Credit/placement by examination:** AP, CLEP, IB, institutional tests. 45 credit hours maximum toward associate degree. **Support services:** Reduced course load, remedial instruction, study skills assistance, tutoring.

Majors. Business: Accounting technology, business admin, hospitality admin. **Computer sciences:** Applications programming, system admin. **Education:** Early childhood. **Health services:** Dental hygiene, EMT paramedic, medical radiologic technology/radiation therapy, nursing (RN), physical therapy assistant, respiratory therapy technology, sonography, surgical technology. **Liberal arts:** Arts/sciences. **Protective services:** Fire safety technology, law enforcement admin. **Visual/performing arts:** Cinematography.

Most popular majors. Health sciences 23%, liberal arts 67%.

Technology on campus. 560 workstations in library, computer center. Commuter students can connect to campus network. Online course registration, online library, helpline, wireless network available.

Student life. Freshman orientation: Mandatory. Preregistration for classes offered. Orientation is available online. **Activities:** Bands, campus ministries, choral groups, dance, drama, international student organizations, literary magazine, music ensembles, Model UN, musical theater, radio station, student government, student newspaper, TV station, African American Student Union, Armed Services Association, debate club, Gay Straight Alliance, National Society of Leadership and Success, Nursing Student Association, Spanish club, technology and engineering club, TRiO Society, Visionaries Ink.

Athletics. NJCAA. **Intercollegiate:** Baseball M, basketball, softball W, volleyball W. **Intramural:** Basketball. **Team name:** Commodores.

Student services. Adult student services, career counseling, services for economically disadvantaged, student employment services, financial aid counseling, minority student services, personal counseling, veterans' counselor, women's services. **Physically disabled:** Services for visually, speech, hearing impaired. **Transfer:** Pre-admission transcript evaluation for new students. Transfer adviser, college fairs on campus for students transferring to 4-year colleges.

Contact. Phone: (850) 872-3892 Toll-free number: (800) 311-3685 Fax: (850) 913-3308
Sharon Todd, Executive Director, Enrollment Services, Gulf Coast State College, 5230 West US Highway 98, Panama City, FL 32401-1041

Herzing University: Winter Park
Winter Park, Florida
www.herzing.edu   CB code: 3438

‣ For-profit 2-year business and health science college
‣ Commuter campus in very large city
‣ Interview required

General. Regionally accredited. **Enrollment:** 430 undergraduates. **Degrees:** 16 bachelor's, 103 associate awarded. **Calendar:** Semester, extensive summer session. **Full-time faculty:** 20 total. **Part-time faculty:** 14 total.

Basis for selection. Open admission, but selective for some programs. Entrance test and evaluation for all applicants.

2015-2016 Annual costs. Certificate programs: $13,670 to $26,820. Associate programs: $26,180 to $53,640. Bachelor's programs: $61,515 to $88,065.

Financial aid. Need-based: Work-study available nights, weekends and for part-time students.

Application procedures. Admission: No deadline. No application fee. Admission notification on a rolling basis.

Academics. Special study options: Distance learning. Bachelor's degree programs available on campus. **Credit/placement by examination:** AP, CLEP, IB, institutional tests. 52 credit hours maximum toward associate degree, 97 toward bachelor's. **Support services:** Reduced course load, remedial instruction, study skills assistance, tutoring.

Majors. Business: General, accounting, business admin. **Computer sciences:** Computer science, information technology, LAN/WAN management, networking, programming. **Health services:** Insurance coding, insurance specialist, massage therapy, medical assistant, nursing (RN), radiologic technology/medical imaging, surgical technology.

Technology on campus. 120 workstations in library, computer center. Online library, wireless network available.

Student life. Freshman orientation: Mandatory. Preregistration for classes offered.

Student services. Adult student services, student employment services, financial aid counseling. **Transfer:** Pre-admission transcript evaluation for new students.

Contact. E-mail: info@orl.herzing.edu
Phone: (407) 478-0500 Toll-free number: (800) 574-4446
Fax: (401) 418-0501
Todd Lasota, Director of Admissions, Herzing University: Winter Park, 1595 South Semoran Boulevard, Winter Park, FL 32792

Hillsborough Community College
Tampa, Florida   CB member
www.hccfl.edu   CB code: 5304

‣ Public 2-year community college
‣ Commuter campus in large city

General. Founded in 1968. Regionally accredited. **Enrollment:** 23,138 degree-seeking undergraduates; 3,433 non-degree-seeking students. **Degrees:** 1,843 associate awarded. **ROTC:** Army. **Calendar:** Semester, limited summer session. **Full-time faculty:** 310 total; 24% have terminal degrees, 22% minority, 56% women. **Part-time faculty:** 1,142 total; 13% have terminal degrees, 28% minority, 51% women. **Class size:** 34% < 20, 66% 20-39, less than 1% 40-49. **Special facilities:** Two environmental studies centers: English Creek, a 400 acre nature preserve, and Cockroach Bay, an estuary located on the South-Eastern shore of Tampa Bay.

Student profile. Among degree-seeking undergraduates, 4,781 enrolled as first-time, first-year students.

Part-time:	55%	Women:	56%
Out-of-state:	4%	25 or older:	35%

Transfer out. Colleges most students transferred to 2015: University of South Florida.

Basis for selection. Open admission, but selective for some programs. Certain health programs require a separate application and application fee ($53), 2.0 GPA, satisfactory background check, drug screening, physical exam. Course prerequisites in math, English, anatomy, microbiology, psychology, and sociology with minimum grade of C may be required. Applicants must be at least 18 by the first day of class. Degree-seeking students may need to provide assessment/placement scores from PERT, CPT, FCELPT, ACT, or SAT prior to registering for classes. Test scores may be no more than 2 years old. Exemptions made for active military service members, students graduating from a Florida Public high school with standard high-school diploma, and students who entered the 9th grade in a Florida Public high school during the 2003-2004 year or later. **Home schooled:** Signed affidavit affirming completion required. **Learning Disabled:** Students should contact Coordinator of Services for students with disabilities to discuss documentation guidelines at least 1 month prior to semester.

High school preparation. 24 units recommended. Recommended units include English 4, mathematics 3, science 3, foreign language 2 and academic electives 8.

2015-2016 Annual costs. Tuition/fees: $3,132; $11,388 out-of-state. Books/supplies: $1,320. Personal expenses: $1,944.

2014-2015 Financial aid. Need-based: 55% of total undergraduate aid awarded as scholarships/grants, 45% as loans/jobs. Need-based aid available for part-time students. Work-study available nights, weekends and for part-time students. **Non-need-based:** Scholarships awarded for academics, art, athletics, minority status, music/drama.

Application procedures. Admission: No application fee. Application must be submitted online. Admission notification on a rolling basis. **Financial aid:** FAFSA, institutional form required. Applicants notified on a rolling basis.

Academics. Selection of courses available in winter intersession between fall and spring terms. **Special study options:** Accelerated study, cooperative education, cross-registration, distance learning, double major, dual enrollment of high school students, ESL, honors, independent study, internships, liberal arts/career combination, study abroad, teacher certification program. Selected weekend courses available. License preparation in dental hygiene, nursing, paramedic, real estate. **Credit/placement by examination:** AP, CLEP, IB, institutional tests. 45 credit hours maximum toward associate degree. Approval required. **Support services:** GED preparation, learning center, remedial instruction, study skills assistance, tutoring, writing center. SmarThinking 24/7 online tutoring service.

Majors. Business: Accounting technology, business admin, executive assistant, hospitality admin, management information systems, operations, restaurant/food services. **Computer sciences:** Applications programming, system admin, systems analysis. **Education:** Deaf/hearing impaired. **Health services:** Dental hygiene, dietician assistant, EMT paramedic, medical radiologic technology/radiation therapy, mental health services, nuclear medical technology, nursing (RN), optician, optometric assistant, respiratory therapy technology, sonography, veterinary technology/assistant. **Liberal arts:** Arts/sciences. **Protective services:** Fire safety technology, law enforcement admin. **Visual/performing arts:** Cinematography. **Work/family studies:** Child care management.

Most popular majors. Health sciences 12%, liberal arts 78%.

Technology on campus. Dormitories wired for high-speed internet access. Commuter students can connect to campus network. Online course registration, online library, helpline, wireless network available.

Student life. Freshman orientation: Mandatory. Preregistration for classes offered. **Housing:** Apartments available. **Activities:** Bands, choral groups, dance, drama, international student organizations, literary magazine, music ensembles, radio station, student government, student newspaper, Active Minds, African-American Student Union, American Medical Student Club, Phi Theta Kappa, Music Club, National Society of Collegiate Scholars.

Athletics. NJCAA. **Intercollegiate:** Baseball M, basketball, softball W, tennis W, volleyball W. **Team name:** Hawks.

Student services. Career counseling, services for economically disadvantaged, student employment services, financial aid counseling, on-campus daycare, personal counseling. **Physically disabled:** Services for visually, speech, hearing impaired. **Transfer:** Transfer center, transfer adviser, college fairs on campus for students transferring to 4-year colleges.

Contact. E-mail: registrar@hccfl.edu
Phone: (813) 253-7000 Toll-free number: (877) 736-2575
Fax: (813) 253-7196
Jennifer Young, Registrar, Hillsborough Community College, Box 31127, Tampa, FL 33631-3127

Indian River State College
Fort Pierce, Florida   CB member
www.irsc.edu   CB code: 5322

▶ Public 2-year community college
▶ Commuter campus in small city

General. Founded in 1960. Regionally accredited. Branch campuses in Vero Beach, Stuart, Okeechobee, Port St. Lucie; Criminal Justice Academy, Marine Center in Fort Pierce. **Enrollment:** 14,044 degree-seeking undergraduates; 3,621 non-degree-seeking students. **Degrees:** 545 bachelor's, 2,330 associate awarded. **Location:** 65 miles from West Palm Beach. **Calendar:** Semester, limited summer session. **Full-time faculty:** 228 total; 42% have terminal degrees, 57% women. **Part-time faculty:** 646 total; 12% have terminal degrees, 62% women. **Special facilities:** Olympic-size pool complex, fine arts center, planetarium, public safety complex.

Student profile. Among degree-seeking undergraduates, 1,877 enrolled as first-time, first-year students.

Part-time:	64%	Women:	60%
Out-of-state:	2%	25 or older:	44%

Transfer out. Colleges most students transferred to 2015: University of Central Florida, University of South Florida, University of Florida, Florida State University, Florida Atlantic University.

Basis for selection. Open admission, but selective for some programs. Testing and academic records determine admission to health science programs.

High school preparation. 24 units recommended. Recommended units include English 4, mathematics 3, social studies 3, history 2, science 3, foreign language 2 and academic electives 7.

2015-2016 Annual costs. Tuition/fees: $3,115; $11,715 out-of-state. Books/supplies: $1,000. **Additional information:** Bachelor programs charged at higher tuition rates.

Financial aid. Need-based: Need-based aid available for part-time students. Work-study available nights, weekends and for part-time students. **Non-need-based:** Scholarships awarded for academics, athletics, minority status, music/drama, state residency.

Application procedures. Admission: No deadline. No application fee. Admission notification on a rolling basis. **Financial aid:** Priority date 7/18; no closing date. FAFSA, institutional form required. Applicants notified on a rolling basis starting 5/15.

Academics. Special study options: Accelerated study, distance learning, dual enrollment of high school students, ESL, honors, teacher certification program, weekend college. Bachelor's degree programs available on campus. License preparation in dental hygiene, nursing, paramedic, physical therapy, radiology, real estate. **Credit/placement by examination:** AP, CLEP, IB, institutional tests. 45 credit hours maximum toward associate degree. Degree-seeking students must achieve state-designated cutoff scores on placement test to enter college-level programs, or complete sequence of developmental courses. **Support services:** GED preparation and test center, learning center,

pre-admission summer program, reduced course load, remedial instruction, study skills assistance, tutoring.

Majors. Biology: General. **Business:** Accounting, administrative services, business admin, hospitality admin, management information systems, office management, sales/distribution. **Communications:** Public relations. **Communications technology:** Graphic/printing. **Computer sciences:** General, applications programming, computer graphics, information technology, programming, systems analysis, web page design. **Conservation:** Environmental studies. **Education:** General, early childhood, elementary, secondary. **Engineering:** General. **English:** English lit. **Foreign languages:** General. **Health services:** Clinical lab technology, dental hygiene, dental lab technology, EMT paramedic, health information management, health information technology, medical radiologic technology/radiation therapy, medical transcription, nursing (RN), physical therapy assistant, predental, premedicine, prepharmacy, preveterinary, respiratory therapy technology. **History:** General. **Liberal arts:** Arts/sciences, library assistant. **Math:** General. **Philosophy/religion:** Philosophy. **Physical sciences:** Chemistry, physics. **Protective services:** Criminal justice, fire safety technology. **Psychology:** General. **Social sciences:** Anthropology, economics, political science, sociology. **Visual/performing arts:** Art, commercial/advertising art, dance, dramatic, interior design, music.

Technology on campus. Online course registration, online library available.

Student life. Freshman orientation: Available. Preregistration for classes offered. **Housing:** Apartments available. **Activities:** Bands, choral groups, dance, drama, international student organizations, literary magazine, music ensembles, musical theater, radio station, student government, symphony orchestra, Distributive Education Clubs of America, Vocational International Clubs of America, cultural exchange club, human services club, ambassador club, Bacchus club, Phi Beta Lambda.

Athletics. NJCAA. **Intercollegiate:** Baseball M, basketball, diving, softball W, swimming, volleyball W. **Team name:** Pioneers.

Student services. Alcohol/substance abuse counseling, career counseling, services for economically disadvantaged, student employment services, financial aid counseling, health services, minority student services, on-campus daycare, placement for graduates, veterans' counselor, women's services. **Physically disabled:** Services for visually, speech, hearing impaired. **Transfer:** Transfer adviser, college fairs on campus for students transferring to 4-year colleges.

Contact. Phone: (772) 462-4740 Toll-free number: (866) 866-4722
Fax: (772) 462-4699
Karen Chapdelaine, Director of Admissions, Indian River State College, 3209 Virginia Avenue, Fort Pierce, FL 34981-5596

Key College
Dania Beach, Florida
www.keycollege.edu   CB code: 3577

▶ For-profit 2-year business and technical college
▶ Commuter campus in very large city
▶ Interview required

General. Regionally accredited; also accredited by ACICS. **Enrollment:** 59 undergraduates. **Calendar:** Quarter, extensive summer session. **Full-time faculty:** 7 total. **Part-time faculty:** 5 total.

Student profile.

Out-of-state:	6%	25 or older:	72%

Basis for selection. Admissions based on entrance exam and school record. SAT or ACT recommended. CPAT may be submitted in lieu of SAT/ACT. **Home schooled:** State high school equivalency certificate required.

2015-2016 Annual costs. Personal expenses: $3,621. **Additional information:** Total program costs: certificates $14,780-$25,865, books and supplies $1,839-$2,100; associates $22,170-$33,255, books and supplies; $2,000-$3,170.

Financial aid. All financial aid based on need. Need-based aid available for part-time students. Work-study available nights, weekends and for part-time students. **Additional information:** Federal Supplemental Educational Opportunities Grant (FSEOG), PELL grant, ACG, FFEL (federal loan program) available; direct loans offered.

Application procedures. Admission: No deadline. $35 fee. Application must be submitted on paper. Admission notification on a rolling basis. **Financial aid:** No deadline. FAFSA, institutional form required.

Academics. Credit/placement by examination: AP, CLEP, institutional tests. **Support services:** Remedial instruction, study skills assistance.

Majors. Health services: Medical secretary.

Most popular majors. Engineering/engineering technologies 27%, health sciences 9%, legal studies 64%.

Technology on campus. 65 workstations in library, computer center.

Student life. Freshman orientation: Mandatory. Preregistration for classes offered. Held one week prior to beginning of classes for approximately 3 hours. **Activities:** Student newspaper.

Student services. Career counseling, financial aid counseling, personal counseling, veterans' counselor.

Contact. E-mail: admissions@keycollege.edu
Phone: (954) 923-4440 Toll-free number: (800) 581-8292
Fax: (954) 923-9226
Steve Levine, Admissions Specialist, Key College, 225 East Dania Beach Boulevard, Dania Beach, FL 33004-3046

Lake-Sumter State College
Leesburg, Florida
www.lssc.edu   **CB code: 5376**

- Public 2-year community and junior college
- Commuter campus in small city

General. Founded in 1962. Regionally accredited. Campuses in Leesburg, South Lake (Clermont) and Sumter (Sumterville). **Enrollment:** 1,786 full-time, degree-seeking students. **Degrees:** 12 bachelor's, 653 associate awarded. **Location:** 35 miles from Orlando. **Calendar:** Semester, limited summer session. **Full-time faculty:** 78 total; 19% have terminal degrees, 8% minority, 68% women. **Part-time faculty:** 160 total; 11% minority, 53% women. **Class size:** 53% < 20, 47% 20-39. **Special facilities:** Veterans lounge, performing arts center, black box theater, nature trail, Math Emporium.

Student profile.

Out-of-state: 1%   25 or older: 26%

Transfer out. Colleges most students transferred to 2015: University of Central Florida, University of Florida, Florida State University, University of South Florida.

Basis for selection. Open admission, but selective for some programs. Special requirements for nursing program. Limited admission for BAS - Organizational Management. **Home schooled:** Home-schooled affidavit accepted in lieu of high school diploma or GED.

2015-2016 Annual costs. Tuition/fees: $3,172; $13,276 out-of-state. Books/supplies: $1,000. **Additional information:** Bachelor programs charged at higher tuition rates.

Financial aid. Need-based: Need-based aid available for part-time students. Work-study available nights, weekends and for part-time students. **Non-need-based:** Scholarships awarded for academics, art, athletics, leadership, minority status, state residency.

Application procedures. Admission: Closing date 8/15. $30 fee. Admission notification on a rolling basis. **Financial aid:** Priority date 5/29; no closing date. FAFSA, institutional form required. Applicants notified on a rolling basis.

Academics. Special study options: Cooperative education, distance learning, dual enrollment of high school students, independent study, liberal arts/career combination, teacher certification program. Bachelor's degree programs available on campus. License preparation in nursing. **Credit/placement by examination:** AP, CLEP, IB, institutional tests. 45 credit hours maximum toward associate degree. **Support services:** Learning center, reduced course load, remedial instruction, study skills assistance, tutoring, writing center.

Majors. Business: Business admin, executive assistant. **Computer sciences:** Information technology, programming, systems analysis. **Conservation:** Environmental science. **Education:** Early childhood. **Health services:** EMT paramedic, health information technology, nursing (RN). **Liberal arts:** Arts/sciences. **Protective services:** Fire safety technology, firefighting, law enforcement admin. **Visual/performing arts:** Commercial/advertising art. **Work/family studies:** Child care service.

Most popular majors. Health sciences 12%, liberal arts 81%.

Technology on campus. 1,000 workstations in library, computer center, student center. Commuter students can connect to campus network. Online course registration, online library, helpline, wireless network available.

Student life. Freshman orientation: Mandatory. Preregistration for classes offered. Day, evening, and online sessions available. **Activities:** Bands, campus ministries, choral groups, drama, literary magazine, music ensembles, student government, student newspaper, symphony orchestra, student ambassadors, Campus Diplomats, College Democrats, Fellowship of Christian Athletes, Florida Future Educators' Association, health information students association, nursing students association, Society for Advancement of Management, student government association.

Athletics. NJCAA. **Intercollegiate:** Baseball M, softball W, volleyball W. **Intramural:** Basketball, football (non-tackle), soccer, table tennis, volleyball. **Team name:** Lakehawks.

Student services. Adult student services, career counseling, services for economically disadvantaged, student employment services, financial aid counseling, minority student services, personal counseling, placement for graduates, veterans' counselor, women's services. **Physically disabled:** Services for visually, speech, hearing impaired. **Transfer:** Pre-admission transcript evaluation for new students. Transfer adviser, college fairs on campus for students transferring to 4-year colleges.

Contact. E-mail: AdmissionsOffice@lssc.edu
Phone: (352) 323-3665 Fax: (352) 365-3553
Bryan Anderson, Director of Admissions, Lake-Sumter State College, 9501 US Highway 441, Leesburg, FL 34788-8751

Le Cordon Bleu College of Culinary Arts: Miami
Hollywood, Florida
www.chefs.edu/Miami

- For-profit 2-year culinary school
- Small city

General. Regionally accredited; also accredited by ACCSC. **Enrollment:** 789 undergraduates. **Degrees:** 230 associate awarded. **Calendar:** Differs by program. **Full-time faculty:** 21 total. **Part-time faculty:** 5 total.

Basis for selection. Admission requirements will vary by program.

2015-2016 Annual costs. Certificate programs: $19,500. Associate programs: $40,000. Books and supplies are included.

Financial aid. Need-based: Work-study available nights, weekends and for part-time students.

Application procedures. Admission: No deadline. **Financial aid:** No deadline.

Academics. Credit/placement by examination: AP, CLEP.

Contact. Phone: (954) 438-8882 Toll-free number: (888) 569-3222
Le Cordon Bleu College of Culinary Arts: Miami, 3221 Enterprise Way, Miramar, FL 33025

Le Cordon Bleu College of Culinary Arts: Orlando
Orlando, Florida
www.chefs.edu/Orlando

- For-profit 2-year culinary school
- Very large city
- Application essay, interview required

General. Regionally accredited; also accredited by ACICS. **Enrollment:** 972 undergraduates. **Degrees:** 263 associate awarded. **Location:** Downtown. **Calendar:** Differs by program. **Full-time faculty:** 33 total. **Part-time faculty:** 6 total. **Special facilities:** 14 teaching kitchens, one open-to-the-public restaurant and cafe.

Basis for selection. Open admission.

2015-2016 Annual costs. Certificate programs: $19,500. Associate programs: $40,000. Books and supplies are included.

Financial aid. Need-based: Work-study available nights, weekends and for part-time students.

Application procedures. **Admission:** No deadline. $50 fee. Application must be submitted online. Admission notification on a rolling basis. **Financial aid:** No deadline.

Academics. **Credit/placement by examination:** AP, CLEP. **Support services:** Learning center, study skills assistance, tutoring.

Technology on campus. 60 workstations in computer center. Online library, wireless network available.

Contact. Phone: (407) 888-4000 Toll-free number: (866) 622-2433 Fax: (407) 888-4019
Le Cordon Bleu College of Culinary Arts: Orlando, 8511 Commodity Circle, Suite 100, Orlando, FL 32819

Lincoln College of Technology: West Palm Beach
West Palm Beach, Florida
www.lincolnedu.com   CB code: 0529

▸ For-profit 2-year technical college
▸ Commuter campus in small city

General. Founded in 1982. Accredited by ACICS. **Enrollment:** 713 undergraduates. **Degrees:** 33 bachelor's, 183 associate awarded. **Location:** 75 miles from Miami. **Calendar:** Quarter, extensive summer session. **Full-time faculty:** 26 total. **Part-time faculty:** 14 total. **Class size:** 75% < 20, 24% 20-39, 1% 40-49.

Basis for selection. Open admission. Applicants who do not have a high school diploma or GED may be admitted if they pass a standardized test approved by the Department of Education. Interview recommended.

2015-2016 Annual costs. Diploma programs: $16,281-$28,351. Associate programs: $18,994-$42,053. Bachelor programs: $55,681-$65,674. Costs include total tuition, materials, tool fees, and registration fee.

Financial aid. **Need-based:** Work-study available nights, weekends and for part-time students.

Application procedures. **Admission:** No deadline. $25 fee. Admission notification on a rolling basis. **Financial aid:** No deadline. FAFSA, institutional form required. Applicants notified on a rolling basis.

Academics. Courses are designed to provide a combination of theory and instruction that simulates real world experiences. **Special study options:** Double major, dual enrollment of high school students, internships. Bachelor's degree programs available on campus. **Credit/placement by examination:** AP, CLEP, institutional tests. **Support services:** GED preparation, learning center, remedial instruction, study skills assistance, tutoring.

Majors. **Business:** General, administrative services. **Computer sciences:** Information systems, networking, programming, system admin, web page design. **Parks/recreation:** Exercise sciences.

Technology on campus. 479 workstations in library, computer center, student center. Online library, helpline, repair service, student web hosting, wireless network available.

Student life. **Freshman orientation:** Mandatory. Preregistration for classes offered.

Student services. Adult student services, career counseling, student employment services, financial aid counseling, personal counseling, placement for graduates, veterans' counselor. **Physically disabled:** Services for visually, hearing impaired.

Contact. Phone: (561) 842-8324 Toll-free number: (800) 826-9986 Fax: (561) 842-9503
Don Cunningham, Admissions Director, Lincoln College of Technology: West Palm Beach, 2410 Metrocentre Boulevard, West Palm Beach, FL 33407

Miami Dade College
Miami, Florida   CB member
www.mdc.edu/main   CB code: 5457

▸ Public 2-year community college
▸ Commuter campus in very large city

General. Founded in 1959. Regionally accredited. **Enrollment:** 57,884 degree-seeking undergraduates; 4,448 non-degree-seeking students. **Degrees:** 1,106 bachelor's, 10,070 associate awarded. **ROTC:** Army, Air Force. **Calendar:** Semester, limited summer session. **Full-time faculty:** 736 total; 34% have terminal degrees, 66% minority, 53% women. **Part-time faculty:** 1,872 total; 19% have terminal degrees, 74% minority, 48% women. **Class size:** 25% < 20, 66% 20-39, 8% 40-49, less than 1% 50-99, less than 1% >100. **Special facilities:** Environmental demonstration center, bilingual center for dual degree program, greenhouse, fire science tower, fire science burn building, emerging technologies center of the Americas, center for the environment, horticulture center, firearms demonstration lab, earth science museum, studio theater, human patient simulator lab, flight simulator lab, child care labs, culinary institute, museum. **Partnerships:** Formal partnerships with Florida Power and Light's Electrical Power Technology Program, Disney, Center for Financial Training, Homeland Security-TSA, Institute for Civic Engagement and Democracy, Paying It Forward.

Student profile. Among degree-seeking undergraduates, 73% enrolled in a transfer program, 27% enrolled in a vocational program, 1% already have a bachelor's degree or higher, 11,807 enrolled as first-time, first-year students, 1,189 transferred in from other institutions.

Part-time:	58%	Asian American:	1%
Out-of-state:	5%	Hispanic/Latino:	69%
Women:	58%	International:	6%
African American:	15%	25 or older:	36%

Transfer out. 82% of students enrolled in the transfer program go on to 4-year colleges. **Colleges most students transferred to 2015:** Florida International University.

Basis for selection. Open admission, but selective for some programs. Special requirements for visual and performing arts, honors, allied health, and bachelor programs. Audition required of performing arts majors. Portfolio required of visual arts majors. **Learning Disabled:** ACCESS office provides, arranges and coordinates accommodations for students with documented disabilities.

High school preparation. 24 units required. Required units include English 4, mathematics 4, social studies 3, science 3 (laboratory 2), visual/performing arts 1 and academic electives 8. 1 unit physical education required. At least one course within the 24 credits required under this section must be completed through online learning.

2015-2016 Annual costs. Tuition/fees: $3,547; $12,075 out-of-state. Per-credit charge: $118 in-state; $403 out-of-state. Books/supplies: $1,500. Personal expenses: $2,628. **Additional information:** Bachelor programs charged at higher tuition rates.

2014-2015 Financial aid. **Need-based:** 6,866 full-time freshmen applied for aid; 6,865 deemed to have need; 6,864 received aid. Average need met was 64%. Average scholarship/grant was $5,370; average loan $2,244. 79% of total undergraduate aid awarded as scholarships/grants, 21% as loans/jobs. Need-based aid available for part-time students. Work-study available nights, weekends and for part-time students. **Non-need-based:** Awarded to 1,954 full-time undergraduates, including 367 freshmen. Scholarships awarded for academics, art, athletics, music/drama, state residency.

Application procedures. **Admission:** No deadline. $30 fee. Admission notification on a rolling basis. **Financial aid:** Priority date 3/15, closing date 6/30. FAFSA required. Applicants notified on a rolling basis starting 5/15.

Academics. **Special study options:** Accelerated study, cooperative education, cross-registration, distance learning, dual enrollment of high school students, ESL, honors, independent study, internships, study abroad, teacher certification program, weekend college. Bachelor's degree programs available on campus. License preparation in aviation, dental hygiene, nursing, paramedic, physical therapy, radiology, real estate. **Credit/placement by examination:** AP, CLEP, IB, institutional tests. 45 credit hours maximum toward associate degree, 45 toward bachelor's. Maximum number of credits accepted may not exceed 75% of degree program requirements. **Support services:** GED preparation and test center, learning center, reduced course load, remedial instruction, study skills assistance, tutoring, writing center.

Honors college/program. Combination of grades, test scores, recommendations, essay on assigned topic and personal interview most important. Priority date 2/1, deadline 4/1.

Majors. **Architecture:** Technology. **Area/ethnic studies:** American, Asian, Latin American. **Biology:** General, biotechnology. **Business:** Accounting, administrative services, banking/financial services, business admin, logistics, management science, office management, office/clerical, real estate, small business admin, tourism promotion, tourism/travel. **Communications:** Broadcast journalism, journalism. **Communications technology:** General, animation/special effects, graphic/printing, graphics, radio/TV. **Computer sciences:** General, applications programming, information systems, information technology, web page design. **Conservation:** Environmental science, forestry. **Education:** Early childhood, elementary, mathematics, physical, science, secondary, special ed, technology/industrial arts. **Engineering:** Architectural, civil, electrical. **English:** American lit, English lit, rhetoric/composition. **Foreign languages:** General, sign language interpretation, translation. **General:** Maintenance. **Health services:** Clinical lab technology, dental hygiene, EMT paramedic, health information management, histologic technology, medical assistant, medical radiologic technology/radiation therapy, medical secretary, nursing (RN), optician, physician assistant, predental, premedicine, prepharmacy, preveterinary, respiratory therapy technology, veterinary technology/assistant. **History:** General. **Human services:** General, social work. **Liberal arts:** Arts/sciences. **Math:** General. **Parks/recreation:** Exercise sciences. **Philosophy/religion:** Philosophy, religion. **Physical sciences:** Atmospheric science, chemistry, geology, physics. **Protective services:** Fire services admin, forensics, law enforcement admin. **Psychology:** General. **Social sciences:** Anthropology, economics, international relations, political science, sociology. **Visual/performing arts:** Cinematography, commercial/advertising art, dance, dramatic, music, studio arts. **Work/family studies:** Child development, food/nutrition.

Most popular majors. Health sciences 9%, liberal arts 86%.

Technology on campus. 8,000 workstations in library, computer center. Commuter students can connect to campus network. Online course registration, online library, helpline, wireless network available.

Student life. Freshman orientation: Mandatory. Preregistration for classes offered. Held before start of classes; must complete online component prior to orientation. **Policies:** Membership in clubs and organizations is contingent upon students being in clear academic and conduct standing. **Housing:** Assistance with locating rental housing available for athletes. **Activities:** Bands, campus ministries, choral groups, dance, drama, film society, international student organizations, literary magazine, music ensembles, Model UN, musical theater, radio station, student government, student newspaper, TV station, Patriot Batallion, Catholic Student Ministry, WAVES, Haitian Ibo, Chinese culture club, Unity for Christ, Black Male Initiative, MDC Cares, Haitian Boukan club, Diverse Student Organization.

Athletics. NJCAA. **Intercollegiate:** Baseball M, basketball, softball W, volleyball W. **Team name:** Sharks.

Student services. Adult student services, career counseling, services for economically disadvantaged, student employment services, financial aid counseling, health services, legal services, minority student services, on-campus daycare, personal counseling, placement for graduates, veterans' counselor. **Physically disabled:** Services for visually, speech, hearing impaired. **Transfer:** Transfer center, transfer adviser, college fairs on campus for students transferring to 4-year colleges.

Contact. E-mail: mdcinfo@mdc.edu
Phone: (305) 237-8888 Fax: (305) 237-2532
Ferne Creary, College Registrar, Miami Dade College, 11011 SW 104th Street, Miami, FL 33176-3393

North Florida Community College
Madison, Florida
www.nfcc.edu
CB code: 5503

- Public 2-year community college
- Commuter campus in rural community

General. Founded in 1958. Regionally accredited. **Enrollment:** 1,167 degree-seeking undergraduates. **Degrees:** 193 associate awarded. **Location:** 56 miles from Tallahassee. **Calendar:** Semester, limited summer session. **Full-time faculty:** 36 total. **Part-time faculty:** 18 total. **Special facilities:** Nature center.

Transfer out. Colleges most students transferred to 2015: Florida State University, Florida A&M University, Valdosta State University, University of Florida.

Basis for selection. Open admission, but selective for some programs. Limited enrollment for nursing, criminal justice, EMT. Background checks completed by Florida Department of Law Enforcement. Florida College Entry-Level Placement Tests required for all students; students with satisfactory ACT/SAT scores are exempt. **Home schooled:** Statement describing home school structure and mission required. Submit affidavit stating that home education complies with Florida law. **Learning Disabled:** Disabilities must have documentation.

High school preparation. 24 units recommended. Recommended units include English 4, mathematics 4, social studies 3, science 2 (laboratory 1) and foreign language 2. Algebra 1 recommended.

2015-2016 Annual costs. Tuition/fees: $3,084; $12,018 out-of-state. Books/supplies: $1,400. Personal expenses: $1,100.

Financial aid. All financial aid based on need. Need-based aid available for part-time students. Work-study available nights, weekends and for part-time students.

Application procedures. Admission: Priority date 7/1; no deadline. $20 fee, may be waived for applicants with need. Application must be submitted on paper. Admission notification on a rolling basis. **Financial aid:** Priority date 5/15; no closing date. FAFSA required. Applicants notified on a rolling basis starting 6/20; must reply within 2 week(s) of notification.

Academics. Special study options: Accelerated study, distance learning, dual enrollment of high school students, independent study, teacher certification program. Bachelor's degree programs available on campus. License preparation in nursing, paramedic, real estate. **Credit/placement by examination:** AP, CLEP, IB, institutional tests. 45 credit hours maximum toward associate degree. **Support services:** GED preparation and test center, reduced course load, remedial instruction, study skills assistance, tutoring, writing center.

Majors. Health services: Nursing assistant. **Liberal arts:** Arts/sciences.

Technology on campus. 65 workstations in library, computer center, student center. Online course registration, online library, wireless network available.

Student life. Freshman orientation: Available. Preregistration for classes offered. **Activities:** Jazz band, choral groups, drama, music ensembles, musical theater, student government, student newspaper, environmental awareness group, African-American Association, veterans club, ASL.

Athletics. NJCAA. **Intercollegiate:** Baseball M, basketball W, softball W. **Team name:** Sentinels.

Student services. Adult student services, career counseling, student employment services, health services, personal counseling, placement for graduates, veterans' counselor. **Physically disabled:** Services for hearing impaired. **Transfer:** Pre-admission transcript evaluation for new students. Transfer adviser, college fairs on campus for students transferring to 4-year colleges.

Contact. Phone: (850) 973-1622 Toll-free number: (866) 937-6322 Fax: (850) 973-1697
Mary Wheeler, Dean of Enrollment Services, North Florida Community College, 325 NW Turner Davis Drive, Madison, FL 32340

Northwest Florida State College
Niceville, Florida
www.nwfsc.edu
CB code: 5526

- Public 2-year technical college
- Commuter campus in large town

General. Founded in 1963. Regionally accredited. Additional teaching campuses/centers at Ft. Walton Beach, Eglin Air Force Base, Hurlburt Field, DeFuniak Springs, Crestview and South Walton County. **Enrollment:** 4,604 degree-seeking undergraduates. **Degrees:** 207 bachelor's, 1,188 associate awarded. **ROTC:** Army. **Location:** 58 miles from Pensacola. **Calendar:** Semester, extensive summer session. **Full-time faculty:** 98 total; 41% have terminal degrees, 57% women. **Part-time faculty:** 289 total; 11% have terminal degrees, 53% women. **Special facilities:** Fine and performing arts center with 2 theaters and 2 art galleries, observatory, sports complex, childcare center, criminal justice training center.

Transfer out. Colleges most students transferred to 2015: University of West Florida, University of Central Florida, Florida State University.

Basis for selection. Open admission. Applicants without high school diploma may be admitted to credit-bearing certificate programs. Some programs have additional admission requirements. **Home schooled:** Must complete an Affidavit for Home-Educated Students form verifying high school graduation. These forms may be obtained from the NWFSC Registrar's Office. **Learning Disabled:** Recommend self identification with Office of Disability Support Services to qualify for services.

High school preparation. College-preparatory program recommended. Recommended units include English 4, mathematics 4, social studies 3, science 3 (laboratory 2), foreign language 2 and visual/performing arts 1.

2015-2016 Annual costs. Tuition/fees: $3,120; $11,941 out-of-state. Books/supplies: $1,440. Personal expenses: $3,176. **Additional information:** Bachelor programs charged at higher tuition rate. Certificates and ATD diplomas charted at a lower tuition rate.

Financial aid. Need-based: Need-based aid available for part-time students. Work-study available nights, weekends and for part-time students. **Non-need-based:** Scholarships awarded for academics, leadership, minority status, ROTC, state residency.

Application procedures. Admission: Priority date 7/25; no deadline. No application fee. Admission notification on a rolling basis. **Financial aid:** Priority date 4/1; no closing date. FAFSA, institutional form required. Applicants notified on a rolling basis starting 2/1; must reply within 2 week(s) of notification.

Academics. Special study options: Accelerated study, cooperative education, cross-registration, distance learning, dual enrollment of high school students, ESL, independent study, internships, student-designed major, teacher certification program. Bachelor's degree programs available on campus. License preparation in nursing, paramedic, radiology. **Credit/placement by examination:** AP, CLEP. **Support services:** GED preparation and test center, learning center, reduced course load, remedial instruction, study skills assistance, tutoring, writing center.

Majors. Business: Accounting technology, business admin, executive assistant, operations. **Computer sciences:** Applications programming, systems analysis. **Health services:** EMT paramedic, health care admin, medical radiologic technology/radiation therapy, nursing (RN). **Human services:** General. **Liberal arts:** Arts/sciences. **Protective services:** Law enforcement admin. **Visual/performing arts:** General, art, commercial/advertising art, music. **Work/family studies:** Child care service.

Most popular majors. Business/marketing 10%, health sciences 6%, liberal arts 77%.

Technology on campus. 300 workstations in library, computer center, student center. Commuter students can connect to campus network. Online course registration, online library, helpline, wireless network available.

Student life. Freshman orientation: Mandatory. Preregistration for classes offered. Web-based orientation. **Activities:** Bands, campus ministries, choral groups, dance, drama, film society, literary magazine, music ensembles, musical theater, student government, symphony orchestra, African American student association, Asian Pop culture club, Campus Christian Fellowship, Circle K International, Early Childhood student association, Fellowship of Christian Athletes, Pre-Professional Educators association, Student Nurses' association, Society of American Military Engineers.

Athletics. NJCAA. **Intercollegiate:** Baseball M, basketball, cheerleading, softball W. **Intramural:** Football (tackle), golf, tennis, volleyball. **Team name:** Raiders.

Student services. Adult student services, career counseling, student employment services, financial aid counseling, on-campus daycare, personal counseling, placement for graduates, veterans' counselor, women's services. **Physically disabled:** Services for visually, speech, hearing impaired. **Transfer:** Pre-admission transcript evaluation for new students. Transfer adviser, college fairs on campus for students transferring to 4-year colleges.

Contact. E-mail: admissions@nwfsc.edu
Phone: (850) 729-4901 Fax: (850) 729-5206
Karyn Cooper, Director of Admissions, Northwest Florida State College, 100 College Boulevard, Niceville, FL 32578-1347

Palm Beach State College

Lake Worth, Florida
www.palmbeachstate.edu

CB member
CB code: 5531

▶ Public 2-year community college
▶ Commuter campus in large town

General. Founded in 1933. Regionally accredited. 4 campuses, numerous other locations throughout service area. **Enrollment:** 26,351 degree-seeking undergraduates; 3,265 non-degree-seeking students. **Degrees:** 279 bachelor's, 4,128 associate awarded. **Location:** 30 miles from Fort Lauderdale. **Calendar:** Semester, limited summer session. **Full-time faculty:** 282 total; 32% minority, 57% women. **Part-time faculty:** 903 total; 31% minority, 53% women. **Special facilities:** Performing arts centers at 3 campuses.

Student profile. Among degree-seeking undergraduates, 80% enrolled in a transfer program, 20% enrolled in a vocational program, 4,756 enrolled as first-time, first-year students, 1,129 transferred in from other institutions.

Part-time:	69%	**Hispanic/Latino:**	28%
Out-of-state:	6%	**Multi-racial, non-Hispanic:**	2%
Women:	56%	**International:**	2%
African American:	25%	**25 or older:**	40%
Asian American:	2%		

Transfer out. Colleges most students transferred to 2015: Florida Atlantic University, University of Florida, Florida State University, University of South Florida.

Basis for selection. Open admission, but selective for some programs. Special requirements for dental, nursing, dietetic, occupational therapy assistant programs. Admission to paramedic, radiography, respiratory care programs based on test scores and GPA. SAT/ACT required for nursing and dental programs. CPT or SAT/ACT used for placement for all. Interview required for nursing, dental, radiography, respiratory care, paramedic majors. Audition required of music majors. **Home schooled:** Home education program affidavit required.

2015-2016 Annual costs. Tuition/fees: $3,030; $10,890 out-of-state. Per-credit charge: $101 in-state; $363 out-of-state. Books/supplies: $1,000. Personal expenses: $400.

Financial aid. Need-based: Work-study available nights, weekends and for part-time students. **Non-need-based:** Scholarships awarded for academics, alumni affiliation, athletics, leadership, state residency.

Application procedures. Admission: Closing date 8/21. $40 fee. Admission notification on a rolling basis beginning on or about 3/1. **Financial aid:** Priority date 7/1; no closing date. FAFSA, institutional form required. Applicants notified on a rolling basis; must reply within 2 week(s) of notification.

Academics. Center for Personalized Instruction offers full assistance in all academic areas for students. **Special study options:** Cooperative education, distance learning, double major, dual enrollment of high school students, ESL, honors, independent study, internships, study abroad, weekend college. Bachelor's degree programs available on campus. License preparation in aviation, dental hygiene, nursing, paramedic, radiology, real estate. **Credit/placement by examination:** AP, CLEP, IB, institutional tests. 45 credit hours maximum toward associate degree. **Support services:** Learning center, pre-admission summer program, reduced course load, remedial instruction, study skills assistance, tutoring, writing center.

Majors. Architecture: Interior. **Biology:** General, zoology. **Business:** General, accounting, business admin, finance, hospitality admin, management information systems, marketing, sales/distribution. **Communications:** Broadcast journalism, journalism. **Communications technology:** Graphic/printing. **Computer sciences:** General, applications programming, information systems, programming, systems analysis. **Education:** Art, early childhood, elementary, health, health occupations, music, physical, sales/marketing, science, secondary, social science, voc/tech. **Engineering:** General, electrical. **English:** English lit. **General:** Maintenance. **Health services:** Clinical lab technology, dental hygiene, dietetics, EMT paramedic, massage therapy, medical radiologic technology/radiation therapy, nursing (RN), occupational therapy assistant, premedicine, respiratory therapy technology. **History:** General. **Human services:** Social work. **Liberal arts:** Arts/sciences. **Math:** General. **Parks/recreation:** General, health/fitness. **Philosophy/religion:** Philosophy. **Physical sciences:** Chemistry, physics. **Protective services:** Fire services admin, firefighting. **Psychology:** General. **Social sciences:** General, anthropology, geography, international relations, political science, sociology. **Visual/performing arts:** General, art history/conservation, cinematography, commercial/advertising art, dance, dramatic, interior design, jazz, music, photography, studio arts. **Work/family studies:** General, child care management.

Most popular majors. Biological/life sciences 10%, health sciences 10%, liberal arts 75%.

Technology on campus. 1,500 workstations in library, computer center. Online course registration, online library, helpline, wireless network available.

Student life. Freshman orientation: Mandatory. Preregistration for classes offered. **Activities:** Bands, choral groups, dance, drama, literary magazine, music ensembles, musical theater, student government, student newspaper, black student union, Students for International Understanding, ASPIRA, Christian Fellowship, Community Earth, Kiskeya Club.

Athletics. NJCAA. **Intercollegiate:** Baseball M, basketball, softball W, volleyball W. **Intramural:** Basketball, softball, volleyball. **Team name:** Panthers.

Student services. Adult student services, alcohol/substance abuse counseling, career counseling, student employment services, financial aid counseling, minority student services, personal counseling, placement for graduates, veterans' counselor. **Physically disabled:** Services for visually, speech, hearing impaired. **Transfer:** Transfer adviser, college fairs on campus for students transferring to 4-year colleges.

Contact. E-mail: admissions@palmbeachstate.edu
Phone: (561) 868-3300 Fax: (561) 868-3584
Chuck Zettler, Dean of Enrollment Management, Palm Beach State College, 4200 Congress Avenue, Lake Worth, FL 33461

Pasco-Hernando State College
New Port Richey, Florida
www.phsc.edu
CB code: 5578

- Public 2-year community college
- Commuter campus in large town

General. Founded in 1972. Regionally accredited. District covers counties of Pasco and Hernando with campuses located in New Port Richey, Brooksville, Spring Hill, Wesley Chapel, and Dade City. Distance learning courses offered for a variety of courses. **Enrollment:** 11,207 degree-seeking undergraduates; 368 non-degree-seeking students. **Degrees:** 1,556 associate awarded. **ROTC:** Army, Naval. **Location:** 35 miles from Tampa. **Calendar:** Semester, limited summer session. **Full-time faculty:** 156 total; 26% have terminal degrees, 17% minority, 66% women. **Part-time faculty:** 270 total; 15% have terminal degrees, 16% minority, 53% women. **Class size:** 31% < 20, 66% 20-39, 3% 40-49. **Special facilities:** Art gallery, performing arts center.

Student profile. Among degree-seeking undergraduates, 1,833 enrolled as first-time, first-year students, 255 transferred in from other institutions.

Part-time:	60%	Hispanic/Latino:	19%
Women:	62%	Multi-racial, non-Hispanic:	3%
African American:	5%	25 or older:	37%
Asian American:	3%		

Transfer out. Colleges most students transferred to 2015: University of South Florida, St. Leo University, University of Florida, University of Central Florida, St. Petersburg College.

Basis for selection. Open admission, but selective for some programs. Special requirements for law enforcement, registered nursing, practical nursing, radiography, paramedic, dental hygiene, dental assisting, BSN and BAS. SAT or ACT, SAT Subject Tests recommended. **Learning Disabled:** Appropriate documentation to Office of Disabilities Services required.

High school preparation. College-preparatory program recommended. Recommended units include English 4, mathematics 3, social studies 1, history 2, science 3, visual/performing arts 2, academic electives 7.5.

2015-2016 Annual costs. Tuition/fees: $3,155; $12,032 out-of-state. Books/supplies: $748. Personal expenses: $918. **Additional information:** Bachelor programs charged at higher tuition rates.

2014-2015 Financial aid. Need-based: 72% of total undergraduate aid awarded as scholarships/grants, 28% as loans/jobs. Need-based aid available for part-time students. Work-study available nights, weekends and for part-time students. **Non-need-based:** Scholarships awarded for academics, athletics, minority status. **Additional information:** Childcare assistance grants available to eligible students.

Application procedures. Admission: No deadline. $25 fee, may be waived for applicants with need. Application must be submitted online. Admission notification on a rolling basis. **Financial aid:** No deadline. FAFSA required. Applicants notified on a rolling basis.

Academics. Distance learning courses offered for a variety of courses. **Special study options:** Distance learning, dual enrollment of high school students, honors, independent study, internships, liberal arts/career combination, student-designed major, teacher certification program. Bachelor's degree programs available on campus. License preparation in dental hygiene, nursing, paramedic, radiology. **Credit/placement by examination:** AP, CLEP, IB, SAT, ACT, institutional tests. 45 credit hours maximum toward associate degree. **Support services:** GED preparation and test center, learning center, reduced course load, remedial instruction, study skills assistance, tutoring, writing center.

Majors. Business: Business admin, e-commerce. **Computer sciences:** Information technology, networking, programming, security, systems analysis. **Health services:** Dental hygiene, nursing (RN), radiologic technology/medical imaging. **Liberal arts:** Arts/sciences. **Protective services:** Law enforcement admin.

Most popular majors. Health sciences 15%, liberal arts 77%.

Technology on campus. Commuter students can connect to campus network. Online course registration, online library, helpline, wireless network available.

Student life. Freshman orientation: Mandatory. Preregistration for classes offered. Four-hour program held on a variety of days and nights. **Housing:** Housing for out of state athletes available. **Activities:** Campus ministries, choral groups, drama, literary magazine, music ensembles, student government, Coexist, Campus Crusade for Christ, Earth awareness organization, gay straight alliance, Men of Excellence, human rights awareness organization, veterans club, international club, human services club, Uhuru, women's resource group.

Athletics. NJCAA. **Intercollegiate:** Baseball M, basketball M, cheerleading, cross-country W, softball W, volleyball W. **Intramural:** Basketball, football (non-tackle), ultimate frisbee. **Team name:** Conquistadors.

Student services. Career counseling, services for economically disadvantaged, financial aid counseling, minority student services, on-campus daycare, personal counseling, placement for graduates, veterans' counselor. **Physically disabled:** Services for visually, speech, hearing impaired. **Transfer:** College fairs on campus for students transferring to 4-year colleges.

Contact. E-mail: admissions@phsc.edu
Phone: (727) 816-3371 Toll-free number: (800) 879-7422
Fax: (727) 816-3389
Pasco-Hernando State College, 10230 Ridge Road, New Port Richey, FL 34654-5199

Pensacola State College
Pensacola, Florida
www.pensacolastate.edu
CB member
CB code: 5535

- Public 2-year community college
- Commuter campus in small city

General. Founded in 1948. Regionally accredited. Additional campuses: Milton, Warrington, Downtown Center, South Santa Rosa Center, Century Center. **Enrollment:** 7,836 degree-seeking undergraduates; 2,004 non-degree-seeking students. **Degrees:** 109 bachelor's, 1,624 associate awarded. **ROTC:** Army. **Location:** 60 miles from Mobile, AL. **Calendar:** Semester, extensive summer session. **Full-time faculty:** 180 total; 18% have terminal degrees, 20% minority, 59% women. **Part-time faculty:** 419 total; 16% minority, 64% women. **Special facilities:** Planetarium, smart center for patient simulation training am research, center for visual arts.

Student profile. Among degree-seeking undergraduates, 1,489 enrolled as first-time, first-year students.

Part-time:	58%	Hispanic/Latino:	6%
Women:	60%	Native American:	1%
African American:	16%	Multi-racial, non-Hispanic:	5%
Asian American:	3%	International:	1%

Transfer out. Colleges most students transferred to 2015: University of West Florida, Florida State University, University of Florida, University of South Alabama.

Basis for selection. Open admission, but selective for some programs. Special requirements for some health programs. Post-secondary Educational Readiness test (PERT) must be taken for admission; student may submit SAT/ACT in its place. Scores used for placement only. **Home schooled:** State high school equivalency certificate required. Notarized affidavit with verification from school district office. **Learning Disabled:** Reasonable accommodations are made based on recommendations from the Office of Student Resource Services for ADA Compliance.

2015-2016 Annual costs. Tuition/fees: $3,137; $12,593 out-of-state. Books/supplies: $1,100. Personal expenses: $960. **Additional information:** Bachelor programs charged at higher tuition rates.

Financial aid. Need-based: Need-based aid available for part-time students. Work-study available nights, weekends and for part-time students. **Non-need-based:** Scholarships awarded for academics, athletics, leadership, music/drama, state residency.

Application procedures. Admission: No deadline. $30 fee. Admission notification on a rolling basis. **Financial aid:** Priority date 5/1; no closing date. FAFSA required. Applicants notified on a rolling basis starting 3/1; must reply within 2 week(s) of notification.

Academics. Special study options: Accelerated study, cooperative education, cross-registration, distance learning, double major, dual enrollment of high school students, ESL, honors, independent study, internships, study abroad, teacher certification program, weekend college. Bachelor's degree programs available on campus. License preparation in dental hygiene, nursing, paramedic, radiology. **Credit/placement by examination:** AP, CLEP, IB, institutional tests. No limit but student must earn 25% of program requirement with institutional courses. **Support services:** GED preparation and test center, learning center, reduced course load, remedial instruction, study skills assistance, tutoring, writing center.

Majors. Biology: General, biochemistry, botany, zoology. **Business:** General, accounting, administrative services, banking/financial services, business admin, hospitality/recreation, management information systems, management science, office management. **Communications:** Communications/speech/rhetoric, journalism. **Communications technology:** General, photo/film/video. **Computer sciences:** General, applications programming, computer science, information systems, programming, systems analysis. **Conservation:** Forest management, forest resources, forestry, management/policy. **Education:** General, art, early childhood, elementary, music, physical, special ed. **Engineering:** General, civil, computer, electrical. **English:** English lit. **General:** Maintenance. **Health services:** Dental hygiene, EMT paramedic, health care admin, health information management, medical radiologic technology/radiation therapy, nursing (RN), physical therapy assistant, predental, premedicine, prenursing, prepharmacy, preveterinary, sonography. **History:** General. **Liberal arts:** Arts/sciences. **Math:** General. **Parks/recreation:** General. **Philosophy/religion:** Ethics, philosophy, religion. **Physical sciences:** Chemistry, geology, physics. **Protective services:** Firefighting, law enforcement admin. **Psychology:** General. **Social sciences:** Sociology. **Visual/performing arts:** Art, commercial/advertising art, dramatic, music. **Work/family studies:** Advocacy, child care management, child care service, food/nutrition, institutional food production.

Technology on campus. 1,500 workstations in library, computer center. Online course registration, online library, helpline, wireless network available.

Student life. Freshman orientation: Available. Preregistration for classes offered. **Activities:** Bands, campus ministries, choral groups, dance, drama, international student organizations, literary magazine, music ensembles, musical theater, student government, student newspaper, symphony orchestra, TV station, African-American student association, Wesley Foundation, Phi Theta Kappa, campus activities board, students for multi-cultural society, Student Veterans Association.

Athletics. NJCAA. **Intercollegiate:** Baseball M, basketball, softball W, volleyball W. **Intramural:** Archery, badminton, basketball, bowling, racquetball, skin diving, soccer, softball W, table tennis, tennis, volleyball, water polo, weight lifting. **Team name:** Pirates.

Student services. Adult student services, alcohol/substance abuse counseling, career counseling, services for economically disadvantaged, student employment services, financial aid counseling, health services, minority student services, on-campus daycare, personal counseling, placement for graduates, veterans' counselor. **Physically disabled:** Services for visually, speech, hearing impaired. **Transfer:** Pre-admission transcript evaluation for new students. Transfer adviser, college fairs on campus for students transferring to 4-year colleges.

Contact. E-mail: askus@pensacolastate.edu
Phone: (850) 484-2544 Toll-free number: (888) 897-3605
Fax: (850) 484-1829
Susan Desbrow, Registrar, Pensacola State College, 1000 College Boulevard, Pensacola, FL 32504-8998

Polk State College
Winter Haven, Florida   CB member
www.polk.edu   CB code: 5548

- Public 2-year community college
- Commuter campus in large town

General. Founded in 1963. Regionally accredited. Branch campus in Lakeland. Additional locations in Lake Wales and Lakeland Airside. **Enrollment:** 8,436 degree-seeking undergraduates; 2,221 non-degree-seeking students. **Degrees:** 331 bachelor's, 1,420 associate awarded. **ROTC:** Army. **Location:** 60 miles from Tampa, 60 miles from Orlando. **Calendar:** Semester, extensive summer session. **Full-time faculty:** 158 total; 39% have terminal degrees, 15% minority, 53% women. **Part-time faculty:** 209 total; 18% have terminal degrees, 25% minority, 48% women. **Class size:** 51% < 20, 49% 20-39, less than 1% 40-49, less than 1% 50-99, less than 1% >100.

Student profile. Among degree-seeking undergraduates, 52% enrolled in a transfer program, 29% enrolled in a vocational program, 3% already have a bachelor's degree or higher, 940 enrolled as first-time, first-year students, 472 transferred in from other institutions.

Part-time:	66%	Hispanic/Latino:	20%
Out-of-state:	1%	Multi-racial, non-Hispanic:	2%
Women:	63%	International:	1%
African American:	17%	25 or older:	40%
Asian American:	2%		

Transfer out. Colleges most students transferred to 2015: University of South Florida, University of Central Florida, University of Florida, Florida State University.

Basis for selection. Open admission, but selective for some programs. Limited access to nursing, radiology, physical therapy assistant, occupational therapy assistant, respiratory therapy, paramedic programs, cardiovascular tech, medical sonography. Audition recommended for theater, music majors. Portfolio recommended for graphic arts majors. **Home schooled:** Adheres to FLDOE policy and Florida state statute: affidavit signed by guardian attesting to home school applicant completion required in place of high school diploma. **Learning Disabled:** Students needing classroom accommodations must provide documentation as required.

High school preparation. Recommended units include English 4, mathematics 4, social studies 3, science 3 and foreign language 2.

2015-2016 Annual costs. Tuition/fees: $3,367; $12,272 out-of-state. Books/supplies: $2,000. Personal expenses: $3,696. **Additional information:** Bachelor programs charged at higher tuition rates.

Financial aid. Need-based: Need-based aid available for part-time students. Work-study available nights, weekends and for part-time students. **Non-need-based:** Scholarships awarded for academics, athletics, leadership, state residency.

Application procedures. Admission: No deadline. No application fee. Admission notification on a rolling basis. **Financial aid:** Priority date 5/15; no closing date. FAFSA required. Applicants notified on a rolling basis.

Academics. Special study options: Cross-registration, distance learning, double major, dual enrollment of high school students, ESL, honors, independent study, internships. Bachelor's degree programs available on campus. License preparation in aviation, nursing, occupational therapy, paramedic, physical therapy, radiology. **Credit/placement by examination:** AP, CLEP, IB, institutional tests. 45 credit hours maximum toward associate degree, 45 toward bachelor's. **Support services:** Learning center, reduced course load, remedial instruction, study skills assistance, tutoring. Trio student support services which provides loaner textbooks, computers and other support.

Honors college/program. High school graduates with 3.5 GPA may apply for honors program and designated courses.

Majors. Business: Accounting technology, business admin, entrepreneurial studies, finance, office management, operations, transportation. **Computer sciences:** Programming, vendor certification, web page design. **Health services:** Cardiovascular technology, EMT paramedic, medical radiologic technology/radiation therapy, nursing (RN), occupational therapy assistant, physical therapy assistant, respiratory therapy technology, sonography. **Liberal arts:** Arts/sciences. **Protective services:** Fire safety technology, law enforcement admin, police science. **Work/family studies:** Child care management.

Most popular majors. Health sciences 15%, liberal arts 75%.

Technology on campus. 775 workstations in library, computer center, student center. Commuter students can connect to campus network. Online course registration, online library, helpline, wireless network available.

Student life. Freshman orientation: Available. Preregistration for classes offered. **Activities:** Bands, choral groups, drama, music ensembles, musical theater, student government.

Athletics. NJCAA. **Intercollegiate:** Baseball M, basketball M, soccer W, softball W, volleyball W. **Intramural:** Basketball, bowling, cheerleading, football (non-tackle), table tennis, volleyball. **Team name:** Eagles.

Student services. Adult student services, alcohol/substance abuse counseling, career counseling, services for economically disadvantaged, student employment services, financial aid counseling, minority student services, personal counseling, placement for graduates, veterans' counselor. **Physically disabled:** Services for visually, speech, hearing impaired. **Transfer:** Re-entry adviser for new students. Transfer adviser, college fairs on campus for students transferring to 4-year colleges.

Contact. E-mail: studentservices@polk.edu
Phone: (863) 297-1001 Fax: (863) 297-1023
Kathy Bucklew, Registrar, Polk State College, 999 Avenue H NE, Winter Haven, FL 33881-4299

Professional Golfers Career College: Orlando
Apopka, Florida
www.golfcollege.edu

- For-profit 2-year branch campus college
- Commuter campus in very large city

General. Accredited by ACICS. **Location:** 16 miles from Orlando. **Calendar:** Semester.

Annual costs/financial aid. Tuition/fees (2015-2016): $15,000. Books/supplies: $500.

Contact. Phone: (866) 407-7422
PO Box 892319, Temecula, CA 92589-2319

Rasmussen College: Pasco/Land O'Lakes
Land O'Lakes, Florida
www.rasmussen.edu

▶ For-profit 2-year career college
▶ Small city

General. Regionally accredited. **Enrollment:** 274 degree-seeking undergraduates. **Degrees:** 15 bachelor's, 19 associate awarded. **Calendar:** Quarter. **Full-time faculty:** 5 total. **Part-time faculty:** 27 total.

Basis for selection. Open admission, but selective for some programs.

2016-2017 Annual costs. Tuition/fees (projected): $13,455. Per-credit charge: $299.

Financial aid. Need-based: Work-study available nights, weekends and for part-time students.

Application procedures. Admission: No deadline. No application fee. Admission notification on a rolling basis. **Financial aid:** No deadline.

Academics. Credit/placement by examination: AP, CLEP.

Majors. Business: Accounting, business admin, human resources, management information systems, marketing. **Computer sciences:** Support specialist, web page design. **Education:** Early childhood. **Engineering:** Software. **Health services:** Health information technology, licensed practical nurse, medical assistant, medical secretary, pharmacy assistant. **Protective services:** Criminal justice. **Visual/performing arts:** Game design.

Contact. Susan Hammerstrom, Director of Admission, Rasmussen College: Pasco/Land O'Lakes, 18600 Fernview Street, Land O' Lakes, FL 34638

Saint Johns River State College
Palatka, Florida
www.sjrstate.edu
CB code: 5641

▶ Public 2-year community college
▶ Commuter campus in large town

General. Founded in 1957. Regionally accredited. The Florida School of the Arts, is part of St. Johns River State College and offers two year degrees in visual and performing arts. **Enrollment:** 4,962 degree-seeking undergraduates; 2,129 non-degree-seeking students. **Degrees:** 73 bachelor's, 902 associate awarded. **Location:** 55 miles from Jacksonville and Daytona Beach. **Calendar:** Semester, limited summer session. **Full-time faculty:** 113 total. **Part-time faculty:** 127 total.

Student profile. Among degree-seeking undergraduates, 69% enrolled in a transfer program, 23% enrolled in a vocational program, 1,136 enrolled as first-time, first-year students.

Part-time:	64%	Asian American:	2%
Out-of-state:	2%	Hispanic/Latino:	8%
Women:	63%	Native American:	1%
African American:	10%	Multi-racial, non-Hispanic:	3%

Basis for selection. Open admission, but selective for some programs. Interview, audition, and portfolio required for Florida School of Arts program. There are some limited access associate level allied health programs. Baccalaureate students should have appropriate associate degree. **Home schooled:** Provide proof of a home education program meeting requirements of Florida Statutes 1002.41.

High school preparation. 24 units recommended. Recommended units include English 4, mathematics 4, social studies 3 and science 3.

2015-2016 Annual costs. Tuition/fees: $3,180; $11,608 out-of-state. Books/supplies: $1,285. Personal expenses: $1,507. **Additional information:** Bachelor programs charged at higher tuition rates. Tuition and fees combined as fees are also variable based on in-state / out-of-state residency.

Financial aid. Need-based: Need-based aid available for part-time students. Work-study available nights, weekends and for part-time students.

Application procedures. Admission: Priority date 7/16; no deadline. $30 fee. Application must be submitted online. Admission notification on a rolling basis. **Financial aid:** Priority date 7/1; no closing date. FAFSA required. Applicants notified on a rolling basis.

Academics. Special study options: Distance learning, dual enrollment of high school students, honors, teacher certification program. Bachelor's degree programs available on campus. **Credit/placement by examination:** AP, CLEP, IB. 45 credit hours maximum toward associate degree. **Support services:** GED preparation and test center, learning center, remedial instruction, tutoring.

Majors. Business: Accounting technology, business admin, marketing, office management, operations. **Computer sciences:** Computer graphics, information technology, networking, programming, system admin, web page design. **Health services:** EMT paramedic, health care admin, health information technology, medical radiologic technology/radiation therapy, nursing (RN), respiratory therapy technology. **Liberal arts:** Arts/sciences. **Protective services:** Computer forensics, fire safety technology, law enforcement admin. **Visual/performing arts:** Theater design.

Most popular majors. Business/marketing 6%, health sciences 15%, liberal arts 70%.

Technology on campus. Online course registration, online library, helpline, wireless network available.

Student life. Freshman orientation: Mandatory. Preregistration for classes offered. **Activities:** Student government, Campus Crusade for Christ, Fellowship of Christian Athletes, Phi Theta Kappa, Mathematical Association of America, sailing club, riding club, nature/enrvironmental club.

Athletics. NJCAA. **Intercollegiate:** Baseball M, softball W, volleyball W. **Team name:** Vikings.

Student services. Career counseling, financial aid counseling, veterans' counselor. **Physically disabled:** Services for visually, hearing impaired. **Transfer:** College fairs on campus for students transferring to 4-year colleges.

Contact. Phone: (386) 312-4050 Fax: (386) 312-4048
Daniel Barkowitz, Director of Enrollment Management, Saint Johns River State College, 5001 St. Johns Avenue, Palatka, FL 32177-3897

Santa Fe College
Gainesville, Florida
www.sfcollege.edu
CB member
CB code: 5653

▶ Public 2-year community college
▶ Commuter campus in small city

General. Founded in 1965. Regionally accredited. Branch campuses located in Gainesville, Starke, Archer, Keystone Heights, and Alachua. **Enrollment:** 14,998 degree-seeking undergraduates. **Degrees:** 190 bachelor's, 2,988 associate awarded. **ROTC:** Army, Air Force. **Location:** 80 miles from Jacksonville, 110 miles from Orlando. **Calendar:** Semester, extensive summer session. **Full-time faculty:** 182 total; 18% minority, 59% women. **Part-time faculty:** 367 total; 14% minority, 52% women. **Class size:** 15% < 20, 85% 20-39, less than 1% 40-49, less than 1% 50-99, less than 1% >100. **Special facilities:** Teaching zoo, planetarium, rock cycle garden, laboratory preschool, fine arts hall.

Transfer out. Colleges most students transferred to 2015: University of Florida, University of Central Florida, University of South Florida, University of North Florida, Florida State University.

Basis for selection. Open admission, but selective for some programs. Separate application and requirements for nursing, interactive media production, law enforcement and correctional officer, paramedic and EMT, surgical technology, diagnostic medical sonography, computed tomography, dental assisting, certified nursing assistant, home health aide and patient care assisting programs.

High school preparation. 18 units required. Required and recommended units include English 4, mathematics 4, social studies 3, science 3 (laboratory 2), foreign language 2 and academic electives 2.

2015-2016 Annual costs. Tuition/fees: $3,203; $11,487 out-of-state. Books/supplies: $700. Personal expenses: $3,032. **Additional information:** Bachelor programs charged at higher tuition rates.

Financial aid. Need-based: Need-based aid available for part-time students. Work-study available nights, weekends and for part-time students. **Non-need-based:** Scholarships awarded for academics, art, athletics, leadership, minority status, music/drama, state residency.

Application procedures. Admission: No deadline. No application fee. Application must be submitted online. Admission notification on a rolling basis. High school diploma not required of applicants to most vocational programs. **Financial aid:** Priority date 3/15, closing date 6/30. FAFSA required. Applicants notified by 8/1.

Academics. Special study options: Cooperative education, cross-registration, distance learning, dual enrollment of high school students, ESL, honors, independent study, internships, study abroad, teacher certification program, weekend college. Bachelor's degree programs available on campus. License preparation in aviation, dental hygiene, nursing, paramedic, radiology, real estate. **Credit/placement by examination:** AP, CLEP, IB, institutional tests. 30 credit hours maximum toward associate degree. **Support services:** GED preparation, learning center, remedial instruction, tutoring, writing center.

Majors. Business: Business admin, office management, small business admin. **Computer sciences:** Networking, web page design. **Education:** Early childhood. **Health services:** Cardiovascular technology, dental hygiene, EMT paramedic, health information technology, medical radiologic technology/radiation therapy, nuclear medical technology, nursing (RN), respiratory therapy technology, sonography. **Liberal arts:** Arts/sciences. **Protective services:** Fire safety technology, law enforcement admin. **Work/family studies:** Child care service.

Most popular majors. Health sciences 10%, liberal arts 84%.

Technology on campus. 9 workstations in library, computer center, student center. Commuter students can connect to campus network. Online course registration, online library, helpline, wireless network available.

Student life. Freshman orientation: Mandatory. Preregistration for classes offered. **Policies:** Students expected to abide by student conduct code. **Activities:** Jazz band, choral groups, film society, international student organizations, music ensembles, Model UN, student government, student newspaper, Catholic Saints, Christian Student Association, Global Society, Hispanic Organization of Latino Activities, Black Student Union, Phi Theta Kappa, Circle K International, Collegiate Veterans Society, Organic Gardeners.

Athletics. NJCAA. **Intercollegiate:** Baseball M, basketball, softball W. **Intramural:** Basketball, football (non-tackle), golf, racquetball, soccer, ultimate frisbee, volleyball, weight lifting. **Team name:** Saints.

Student services. Adult student services, alcohol/substance abuse counseling, career counseling, services for economically disadvantaged, student employment services, financial aid counseling, health services, legal services, minority student services, on-campus daycare, personal counseling, placement for graduates, veterans' counselor, women's services. **Physically disabled:** Services for visually, speech, hearing impaired. **Transfer:** Transfer adviser, college fairs on campus for students transferring to 4-year colleges.

Contact. E-mail: admission@sfcollege.edu
Phone: (352) 395-7322 Fax: (352) 395-7300
Michael Hutley, Registrar, Santa Fe College, 3000 NW 83rd Street, R-112, Gainesville, FL 32606-6210

Seminole State College of Florida
Sanford, Florida
www.seminolestate.edu   CB code: 5662

‣ Public 2-year community college
‣ Commuter campus in large town

General. Founded in 1965. Regionally accredited. **Enrollment:** 15,792 degree-seeking undergraduates; 2,031 non-degree-seeking students. **Degrees:** 188 bachelor's, 2,775 associate awarded. **ROTC:** Army. **Location:** 21 miles from Orlando. **Calendar:** Semester, limited summer session. **Full-time faculty:** 223 total; 20% have terminal degrees, 19% minority, 60% women. **Part-time faculty:** 586 total; 14% have terminal degrees, 24% minority, 51% women. **Class size:** 38% < 20, 62% 20-39, less than 1% 40-49, less than 1% 50-99, less than 1% >100. **Special facilities:** Planetarium. **Partnerships:** Formal partnerships with Siemens/Stromberg, local businesses, Collegiate high school at Crooms Academy.

Student profile. Among degree-seeking undergraduates, 2,691 enrolled as first-time, first-year students.

Part-time:	62%	Women:	56%
Out-of-state:	3%	25 or older:	48%

Transfer out. Colleges most students transferred to 2015: University of Central Florida.

Basis for selection. Open admission, but selective for some programs. Limited access to associate of science degrees including nursing, physical therapy, and respiratory care. Interview recommended for respiratory therapy, nursing, and physical therapy. **Home schooled:** Transcript of courses and grades required. Affidavit of home school completion required.

High school preparation. College-preparatory program recommended.

2015-2016 Annual costs. Tuition/fees: $3,074; $11,399 out-of-state. Books/supplies: $1,430. Personal expenses: $900. **Additional information:** Bachelor programs charged at higher tuition rates.

Financial aid. Need-based: Need-based aid available for part-time students. Work-study available nights, weekends and for part-time students. **Non-need-based:** Scholarships awarded for academics, art, athletics, leadership, minority status, music/drama, state residency.

Application procedures. Admission: Closing date 8/12 (postmark date). No application fee. Admission notification on a rolling basis. **Financial aid:** Priority date 7/1; no closing date. FAFSA required. Applicants notified on a rolling basis starting 4/1.

Academics. Special study options: Accelerated study, cooperative education, cross-registration, distance learning, dual enrollment of high school students, ESL, honors, independent study, internships, study abroad, teacher certification program, weekend college. Bachelor's degree programs available on campus. **Credit/placement by examination:** AP, CLEP, IB, institutional tests. 15 credit hours maximum toward associate degree, 30 toward bachelor's. **Support services:** GED preparation and test center, learning center, reduced course load, remedial instruction, study skills assistance, tutoring.

Majors. Architecture: Interior. **Business:** Accounting technology, administrative services, banking/financial services, business admin, marketing, office management. **Communications technology:** General. **Computer sciences:** General, applications programming, computer graphics, computer science, data processing, information systems, networking, programming, systems analysis. **Education:** Kindergarten/preschool. **Health services:** EMT paramedic, health information technology, medical secretary, nursing (RN), pharmacy assistant, physical therapy assistant, respiratory therapy technology. **Liberal arts:** Arts/sciences. **Protective services:** Fire safety technology, firefighting, law enforcement admin. **Visual/performing arts:** Commercial/advertising art, interior design. **Work/family studies:** Child care management.

Most popular majors. Health sciences 12%, liberal arts 75%.

Technology on campus. 100 workstations in library, computer center. Commuter students can connect to campus network. Online course registration, online library, helpline, student web hosting, wireless network available.

Student life. Freshman orientation: Mandatory. Preregistration for classes offered. **Activities:** Bands, campus ministries, choral groups, dance, drama, film society, international student organizations, literary magazine, music ensembles, musical theater, student government, student newspaper, symphony orchestra, African American cultural forum, disabled student association, Hispanic student associations, Muslim student association, Unity Gay Straight Alliance, Fellowship of Christian Athletes, Campus Crusade for Christ, Intervarsity Christian Fellowship, Sigma Phi Gamma.

Athletics. NJCAA. **Intercollegiate:** Baseball M, golf W, softball W. **Intramural:** Basketball M, football (non-tackle) M, soccer, table tennis, tennis, volleyball. **Team name:** Raider.

Student services. Adult student services, alcohol/substance abuse counseling, career counseling, services for economically disadvantaged, student employment services, financial aid counseling, minority student services, personal counseling, placement for graduates, veterans' counselor. **Physically disabled:** Services for visually, speech, hearing impaired. **Transfer:** Pre-admission transcript evaluation for new students. Transfer adviser, college fairs on campus for students transferring to 4-year colleges.

Contact. E-mail: admissions@seminolestate.edu
Phone: (407) 708-2380 Fax: (407) 708-2395
Pamela Mennechey, Associate Vice President of Recruitment and Admissions, Seminole State College of Florida, 100 Weldon Boulevard, Sanford, FL 32773-6199

South Florida State College
Avon Park, Florida   CB member
www.southflorida.edu   CB code: 5666

‣ Public 2-year community and technical college
‣ Commuter campus in small town

General. Founded in 1965. Regionally accredited. **Enrollment:** 2,049 degree-seeking undergraduates; 610 non-degree-seeking students. **Degrees:** 28 bachelor's, 430 associate awarded. **Location:** 90 miles from Orlando. **Calendar:** Semester, limited summer session. **Full-time faculty:** 62 total; 27% have terminal degrees, 8% minority, 60% women. **Part-time faculty:** 84 total; 8% have terminal degrees, 11% minority, 51% women. **Class size:** 69% < 20, 30% 20-39, 1% 40-49. **Special facilities:** Museum of Florida Art and Culture, nature walk, center for performing arts.

Student profile. Among degree-seeking undergraduates, 342 enrolled as first-time, first-year students.

Part-time:	60%	Hispanic/Latino:	33%
Out-of-state:	2%	Multi-racial, non-Hispanic:	2%
Women:	62%	International:	2%
African American:	11%	25 or older:	23%
Asian American:	2%	Live on campus:	2%

Basis for selection. Open admission, but selective for some programs. Some programs have test and prerequisite requirements. Interview recommended for selected programs. **Home schooled:** Students must meet with registrar prior to admission. **Learning Disabled:** Recommend students seek assistance from campus disabilities specialist.

High school preparation. College-preparatory program recommended. 24 units recommended. Recommended units include English 4, mathematics 4, social studies 1, history 2, science 3 (laboratory 2), foreign language 2, visual/performing arts 1 and academic electives 5.

2015-2016 Annual costs. Tuition/fees: $3,136; $11,829 out-of-state. Books/supplies: $1,220. Personal expenses: $1,112. **Additional information:** Bachelor programs charged at higher tuition rates.

2014-2015 Financial aid. Need-based: 91% of total undergraduate aid awarded as scholarships/grants, 9% as loans/jobs. Need-based aid available for part-time students. Work-study available nights, weekends and for part-time students. **Non-need-based:** Scholarships awarded for academics, athletics, leadership, minority status, music/drama, state residency.

Application procedures. Admission: No deadline. $15 fee. Admission notification on a rolling basis. **Financial aid:** Priority date 4/15; no closing date. FAFSA required. Applicants notified on a rolling basis starting 4/1.

Academics. Special study options: Accelerated study, cooperative education, distance learning, double major, dual enrollment of high school students, ESL, external degree, honors, independent study, internships, teacher certification program. Bachelor's degree programs available on campus. License preparation in dental hygiene, nursing, paramedic, radiology. **Credit/placement by examination:** AP, CLEP, IB, institutional tests. 30 credit hours maximum toward associate degree. **Support services:** GED preparation and test center, learning center, reduced course load, remedial instruction, study skills assistance, tutoring, writing center.

Majors. Biology: General. **Business:** General, accounting technology, business admin, office management, operations, transportation. **Communications:** Public relations. **Computer sciences:** General, programming, system admin. **Education:** Elementary, English, science. **Engineering:** General. **English:** English lit. **Health services:** Dental hygiene, EMT paramedic, medical radiologic technology/radiation therapy, nursing (RN), prepharmacy. **Human services:** Social work. **Liberal arts:** Arts/sciences. **Math:** General. **Parks/recreation:** Exercise sciences. **Physical sciences:** Chemistry, physics. **Protective services:** Criminal justice, fire safety technology, law enforcement admin. **Psychology:** General. **Visual/performing arts:** Art, graphic design.

Most popular majors. Health sciences 17%, liberal arts 73%.

Technology on campus. 100 workstations in library, computer center, student center. Online course registration, online library, wireless network available.

Student life. Freshman orientation: Mandatory. Preregistration for classes offered. Online video with review quiz. **Housing:** Single-sex dorms, wellness housing available. **Activities:** Choral groups, drama, international student organizations, music ensembles, student government, student newspaper, African American association, campus Christian club, Circle K, College Democrats, College Republicans, Haitian student association, international student organization, ROTORACT.

Athletics. NJCAA. **Intercollegiate:** Baseball M, cross-country W, softball W, volleyball W. **Intramural:** Bowling, football (non-tackle), tennis, volleyball. **Team name:** Panthers.

Student services. Adult student services, career counseling, services for economically disadvantaged, student employment services, financial aid counseling, minority student services, personal counseling, placement for graduates, veterans' counselor, women's services. **Physically disabled:** Services for visually, speech, hearing impaired. **Transfer:** Transfer adviser, college fairs on campus for students transferring to 4-year colleges.

Contact. E-mail: deborah.fuschetti@southflorida.edu Phone: (863) 453-6661 ext. 7405 Fax: (863) 453-2365 Deborah Fuschetti, Registrar, South Florida State College, 600 West College Drive, Avon Park, FL 33825

Southeastern College: Greenacres
Greenacres, Florida
www.sec.edu

- For-profit 2-year business and health science college
- Commuter campus in small city

General. Regionally accredited; also accredited by ACCSC. **Enrollment:** 1,013 undergraduates. **Degrees:** 239 associate awarded. **Calendar:** Differs by program. **Full-time faculty:** 115 total. **Part-time faculty:** 187 total.

Basis for selection. Admissions based on school record and SAT/ACT or other test scores.

2015-2016 Annual costs. Total program costs vary by program. Associate degrees tuition and fees $33,712-$50,568; books and supplies $1,820-$4,240. Diploma programs tuition and fees $16,856-$33,712; books and supplies $876-$2,470.

Financial aid. Need-based: Work-study available nights, weekends and for part-time students.

Application procedures. Admission: No deadline. $50 fee. **Financial aid:** No deadline.

Academics. Credit/placement by examination: AP, CLEP.

Majors. Computer sciences: General. **Health services:** EMT paramedic, licensed practical nurse, massage therapy, medical assistant, nursing (RN), pharmacy assistant, sonography, surgical technology.

Contact. Phone: (561) 433-2330 Becky Anderson, Office of the President, Southeastern College: Greenacres, 6812 Forest Hill Boulevard, Greenacres, FL 33413

Southeastern College: Miami Lakes
Miami Lakes, Florida
www.sec.edu

- For-profit 2-year business and health science college
- Commuter campus in large town

General. Regionally accredited. **Calendar:** Differs by program.

Annual costs/financial aid. Total program costs vary by program. Associate degrees tuition and fees $33,712-$50,568; books and supplies $1,820-$4,240. Diploma programs tuition and fees $16,856-$33,712; books and supplies $876-$2,470.

Contact. Phone: (305) 820-5003 Office of the President, 17395 NW 59th Avenue, Miami Lakes, FL 33015

Southern Technical College
Fort Myers, Florida
www.southerntech.edu   CB code: 3445

- Private 2-year career college
- Commuter campus in large city

General. Regionally accredited; also accredited by ACICS. **Enrollment:** 15,389 undergraduates. **Degrees:** 84 bachelor's, 306 associate awarded. **Location:** 130 miles from Tampa. **Calendar:** Quarter, extensive summer session. **Class size:** 93% < 20, 7% 20-39.

Basis for selection. Open admission, but selective for some programs. Interview required for certain Allied Health programs.

2015-2016 Annual costs. Books/supplies: $1,110. Personal expenses: $1,968. **Additional information:** Full program costs: diplomas $11,346-$19,150, books and supplies $184; associates $33,570-$47,654, books and supplies up to $825; bachelor's $69,350-$74,975, books and supplies up to $825.

Financial aid. Need-based: Need-based aid available for part-time students. Work-study available nights, weekends and for part-time students.

Application procedures. Admission: No deadline. $25 fee. Application must be submitted on paper. Admission notification on a rolling basis. **Financial aid:** No deadline. FAFSA required. Applicants notified on a rolling basis.

Academics. Online academic assistance available to students enrolled in online courses. **Special study options:** Accelerated study, cooperative education, distance learning, internships, liberal arts/career combination, teacher certification program. Bachelor's degree programs available on campus. **Credit/placement by examination:** AP, CLEP, institutional tests. 24 credit hours maximum toward associate degree, 48 toward bachelor's. **Support services:** GED preparation, learning center, reduced course load, remedial instruction, study skills assistance, tutoring, writing center.

Majors. Business: Accounting, business admin. **Computer sciences:** Networking. **Education:** Early childhood. **Health services:** Health information technology, medical assistant, nursing (RN), sonography, staff services technology, surgical technology. **Protective services:** Law enforcement admin. **Visual/performing arts:** Interior design.

Most popular majors. Business/marketing 12%, computer/information sciences 16%, education 6%, health sciences 42%, security/protective services 18%.

Technology on campus. 195 workstations in library, computer center, student center. Commuter students can connect to campus network. Online library, repair service, wireless network available.

Student life. Freshman orientation: Mandatory. Preregistration for classes offered. Typically held the Saturday before classes begin and lasts approximately 1-2 hours. **Activities:** Student newspaper.

Student services. Adult student services, career counseling, services for economically disadvantaged, student employment services, financial aid counseling, placement for graduates. **Physically disabled:** Services for visually, speech, hearing impaired. **Transfer:** Re-entry adviser, pre-admission transcript evaluation for new students.

Contact. E-mail: pdennis@swfc.edu
Phone: (239) 939-4766 Toll-free number: (877) 493-5147
Fax: (239) 936-4040
Patti Dennis, Campus Director, Southern Technical College, 1685 Medical Lane, Ft. Myers, FL 33907-1108

Southwest Florida College: Tampa
Tampa, Florida
www.swfc.edu

▶ Private 2-year branch campus and junior college
▶ Commuter campus in very large city

General. Accredited by ACICS. Institution is a branch campus of Southwest Florida College, Ft. Myers. **Location:** 15 miles from downtown. **Calendar:** Quarter, extensive summer session. **Full-time faculty:** 15 total; 20% minority, 60% women. **Part-time faculty:** 22 total; 18% minority, 23% women. **Class size:** 77% < 20, 23% 20-39.

Basis for selection. Open admission.

2015-2016 Annual costs. Books/supplies: $1,110. **Additional information:** Full program costs: diplomas $11,346-$19,150, books and supplies $184; associates $33,570-$47,654, books and supplies up to $825; bachelor's $69,350-$74,975, books and supplies up to $825.

Financial aid. Need-based: Work-study available nights, weekends and for part-time students.

Application procedures. Admission: No deadline. $25 fee, may be waived for applicants with need. Admission notification on a rolling basis.

Academics. Special study options: Cooperative education, distance learning, double major, dual enrollment of high school students, internships. Bachelor's degree programs available on campus. **Credit/placement by examination:** AP, CLEP, institutional tests. 24 credit hours maximum toward associate degree. **Support services:** Learning center, reduced course load, remedial instruction, study skills assistance, tutoring, writing center.

Majors. Business: Accounting, marketing. **Computer sciences:** Computer graphics, information systems. **Education:** Early childhood. **Health services:** Medical assistant, office admin, pharmacy assistant, surgical technology. **Protective services:** Criminal justice.

Most popular majors. Business/marketing 8%, computer/information sciences 12%, engineering/engineering technologies 11%, health sciences 57%, legal studies 6%.

Technology on campus. Online library, wireless network available.

Student life. Freshman orientation: Mandatory. Preregistration for classes offered. **Activities:** Student newspaper.

Student services. Career counseling, student employment services, financial aid counseling, placement for graduates, veterans' counselor.

Contact. Phone: (813) 630-4401 Toll-free number: (877) 907-2456 Patrick McDermott, Vice President of Admissions, Southwest Florida College: Tampa, 3910 Riga Boulevard, Tampa, FL 33619

St. Petersburg College
Saint Petersburg, Florida
www.spcollege.edu

CB member
CB code: 5606

▶ Public 2-year community college
▶ Commuter campus in large city

General. Founded in 1927. Regionally accredited. Campuses include Clearwater, Seminole, St. Petersburg, Tarpon Springs. Health education center in Pinellas Park. Criminal justice/computer complex in St. Petersburg. Corporate training and Cisco at the Epicenter. Downtown and Midtown centers. **Enrollment:** 27,354 degree-seeking undergraduates. **Degrees:** 1,106 bachelor's, 3,871 associate awarded. **Location:** 20 miles from Tampa. **Calendar:** Semester, extensive summer session. **Full-time faculty:** 377 total. **Part-time faculty:** 1,419 total. **Special facilities:** Observatory, planetarium, firing range, college-operated museums, theater, nature preserves.

Student profile.

Out-of-state:	3%	**25 or older:**	50%

Basis for selection. Open admission, but selective for some programs. Limited enrollment to health-related programs. Interview recommended for allied health applicants. **Home schooled:** Transcript of courses and grades, state high school equivalency certificate required.

2015-2016 Annual costs. Tuition/fees: $3,353; $11,607 out-of-state. Books/supplies: $1,600. Personal expenses: $4,337. **Additional information:** Bachelor programs charged at higher tuition rates.

Financial aid. Need-based: Need-based aid available for part-time students. Work-study available nights, weekends and for part-time students. **Non-need-based:** Scholarships awarded for academics, art, athletics, minority status, music/drama.

Application procedures. Admission: No deadline. $40 fee. Admission notification on a rolling basis. **Financial aid:** Priority date 4/15; no closing date. FAFSA required. Applicants notified on a rolling basis starting 5/15; must reply within 2 week(s) of notification.

Academics. Special study options: Accelerated study, cooperative education, cross-registration, distance learning, dual enrollment of high school students, ESL, exchange student, honors, independent study, internships, liberal arts/career combination, study abroad, teacher certification program, weekend college. 2-year associate degree program in business and computer science for deaf students. Bachelor's degree programs available on campus. License preparation in dental hygiene, nursing, paramedic, physical therapy, radiology. **Credit/placement by examination:** AP, CLEP, IB, institutional tests. 45 credit hours maximum toward associate degree, 45 toward bachelor's. Florida CPT required for placement. **Support services:** GED preparation, learning center, reduced course load, remedial instruction, study skills assistance, tutoring.

Majors. Business: Banking/financial services, business admin, hospitality admin. **Computer sciences:** Programming, web page design, webmaster. **Education:** Early childhood. **Health services:** Clinical lab technology, dental hygiene, EMT paramedic, health information management, nursing (RN), physical therapy assistant, radiologic technology/medical imaging, respiratory therapy technology, substance abuse counseling, veterinary technology/assistant. **Liberal arts:** Arts/sciences. **Parks/recreation:** General. **Protective services:** Firefighting, forensics, law enforcement admin. **Visual/performing arts:** Music, photography.

Most popular majors. Health sciences 18%, liberal arts 74%.

Technology on campus. 4,110 workstations in library, computer center, student center. Commuter students can connect to campus network. Online course registration, online library, helpline, student web hosting, wireless network available.

Student life. Freshman orientation: Mandatory. Preregistration for classes offered. **Activities:** Jazz band, choral groups, dance, drama, film society, international student organizations, literary magazine, music ensembles, student government, student newspaper, Phi Theta Kappa, Harambee black culture club, ethics club, math and science club, American Sign Language club, Rotary club, College Democrats, College Republicans, digital artists in motion, hospitality club.

Athletics. NJCAA. **Intercollegiate:** Baseball M, basketball, softball W, tennis W, volleyball W. **Team name:** Titans.

Student services. Career counseling, services for economically disadvantaged, student employment services, financial aid counseling, health services, minority student services, personal counseling, placement for graduates, veterans' counselor, women's services. **Physically disabled:** Services for visually, speech, hearing impaired. **Transfer:** College fairs on campus for students transferring to 4-year colleges.

Contact. E-mail: information@spcollege.edu
Phone: (727) 341-4772
Susan Fell, Director of Admissions and Records, St. Petersburg College, Box 13489, St. Petersburg, FL 33733-3489

State College of Florida, Manatee-Sarasota
Bradenton, Florida   **CB member**
www.scf.edu   **CB code: 5427**

▶ Public 2-year nursing and community college
▶ Commuter campus in small city

General. Founded in 1957. Regionally accredited. **Enrollment:** 9,848 degree-seeking undergraduates; 242 non-degree-seeking students. **Degrees:** 207 bachelor's, 1,348 associate awarded. **Location:** 40 miles from Tampa, 20 miles from St. Petersburg. **Calendar:** Semester, extensive summer session. **Full-time faculty:** 186 total; 26% have terminal degrees, 12% minority, 60% women. **Part-time faculty:** 382 total; 12% have terminal degrees, 13% minority, 56% women.

Student profile. Among degree-seeking undergraduates, 1,579 enrolled as first-time, first-year students, 786 transferred in from other institutions.

Part-time:	60%	Women:	61%
Out-of-state:	3%	25 or older:	35%

Basis for selection. Open admission, but selective for some programs. Interview recommended for nursing, radiologic technology, respiratory therapy, occupational therapy assistant, physical therapist assistant, dental hygiene majors.

High school preparation. Recommended units include English 4, mathematics 3, social studies 2, history 1, science 3 and foreign language 2.

2015-2016 Annual costs. Tuition/fees: $3,074; $11,596 out-of-state. Books/supplies: $1,562. Personal expenses: $2,128. **Additional information:** Bachelor programs charged at higher tuition rates.

2015-2016 Financial aid. Need-based: 59% of total undergraduate aid awarded as scholarships/grants, 41% as loans/jobs. Need-based aid available for part-time students. Work-study available nights, weekends and for part-time students. **Non-need-based:** Scholarships awarded for academics, art, athletics, music/drama, state residency.

Application procedures. Admission: No deadline. No application fee. Admission notification on a rolling basis. **Financial aid:** Priority date 6/1, closing date 7/28. FAFSA required. Applicants notified on a rolling basis starting 3/15.

Academics. Special study options: Accelerated study, cooperative education, distance learning, dual enrollment of high school students, honors, independent study, teacher certification program. Bachelor's degree programs available on campus. License preparation in dental hygiene, nursing, occupational therapy, physical therapy, radiology. **Credit/placement by examination:** AP, CLEP. 30 credit hours maximum toward associate degree. SAT, ACT or CPT (Florida Placement Test) used for placement only. **Support services:** GED preparation, learning center, pre-admission summer program, remedial instruction, study skills assistance, tutoring.

Majors. Biology: Biotechnology. **Business:** Accounting, business admin, hospitality admin. **Computer sciences:** Networking, programming, systems analysis. **Education:** Early childhood. **Engineering:** Civil, computer, engineering science. **Health services:** Dental hygiene, EMT ambulance attendant, medical radiologic technology/radiation therapy, nursing (RN), occupational therapy assistant, physical therapy assistant. **Liberal arts:** Arts/sciences. **Protective services:** Criminal justice, firefighting. **Visual/performing arts:** Graphic design.

Technology on campus. 2,275 workstations in library, computer center, student center. Commuter students can connect to campus network. Online course registration, online library, helpline, repair service, wireless network available.

Student life. Freshman orientation: Mandatory. Preregistration for classes offered. **Activities:** Bands, campus ministries, choral groups, dance, drama, film society, international student organizations, literary magazine, music ensembles, musical theater, opera, student government, student newspaper, symphony orchestra, African-American student union, multicultural student club, art club, student Bible club, Manasota Geographic and Anthropological Society, American Chemical Society, student film club, Hispanic-American club.

Athletics. NJCAA. **Intercollegiate:** Baseball M, basketball M, softball W, volleyball W. **Intramural:** Basketball, golf, soccer, softball, volleyball, weight lifting. **Team name:** Manatees.

Student services. Adult student services, alcohol/substance abuse counseling, chaplain/spiritual director, career counseling, services for economically disadvantaged, student employment services, financial aid counseling, health services, minority student services, personal counseling, placement for graduates, veterans' counselor. **Physically disabled:** Services for visually, speech, hearing impaired. **Transfer:** Transfer adviser for students transferring to 4-year colleges.

Contact. E-mail: admissions@scf.edu
Phone: (941) 752-5031 Fax: (941) 727-6380
Marilynn Lewy, Registrar, State College of Florida, Manatee-Sarasota, Box 1849, Bradenton, FL 34206-1849

Stenotype Institute: Jacksonville
Jacksonville, Florida
www.stenotype.edu

▶ For-profit 2-year business and community college
▶ Very large city

General. Accredited by ACICS. **Enrollment:** 130 undergraduates. **Calendar:** Differs by program. **Full-time faculty:** 12 total. **Part-time faculty:** 3 total.

Basis for selection. Admission based on ability, ambition, and character. Prior experience with typing and word processing also important.

2015-2016 Annual costs. Tuition/fees: $16,100. Per-credit charge: $470.59. Books/supplies: $200. Personal expenses: $3,432. **Additional information:** Part-time evening classes 3 days a week for $12,000 per year offered. 25% discount on tuition offered to students who quality to pay cash.

Financial aid. Need-based: Work-study available nights, weekends and for part-time students.

Application procedures. Admission: Closing date 8/15. $100 fee.

Academics. Credit/placement by examination: AP, CLEP.

Contact. E-mail: info@thestenotypeinstitute.com
Phone: (904) 398-4141 Toll-free number: (800) 273-5090
Fax: (904) 398-7878
LaNell Derby, Director of Admissions, Stenotype Institute: Jacksonville, 3563 Phillips Highway, Building E, #501, Jacksonville, FL 32207

Tallahassee Community College
Tallahassee, Florida
www.tcc.fl.edu   **CB code: 5794**

▶ Public 2-year community college
▶ Commuter campus in small city

General. Founded in 1965. Regionally accredited. **Enrollment:** 11,357 degree-seeking undergraduates; 1,088 non-degree-seeking students. **Degrees:** 2,523 associate awarded. **ROTC:** Army, Naval, Air Force. **Location:** 164 miles from Jacksonville. **Calendar:** Semester, extensive summer session. **Full-time faculty:** 190 total; 90% have terminal degrees, 25% minority, 58% women. **Part-time faculty:** 378 total; 62% have terminal degrees, 25% minority, 46% women. **Class size:** 17% < 20, 54% 20-39, 24% 40-49, 5% 50-99. **Special facilities:** Center for healthcare education.

Student profile. Among degree-seeking undergraduates, 74% enrolled in a transfer program, 16% enrolled in a vocational program, 2,288 enrolled as first-time, first-year students, 1,180 transferred in from other institutions.

Part-time:	51%	Hispanic/Latino:	12%
Out-of-state:	1%	Multi-racial, non-Hispanic:	4%
Women:	52%	International:	1%
African American:	31%	25 or older:	22%
Asian American:	1%		

Transfer out. 77% of students enrolled in the transfer program go on to 4-year colleges. **Colleges most students transferred to 2015:** Florida State University, Florida Agricurtural and Mechanical University.

Basis for selection. Open admission, but selective for some programs. Special requirements for nursing, dental hygiene, emergency medical technology, radiologic technology and respiratory therapy programs. Each program requires specific course prerequisites or test scores or required GPA in addition to letters of recommendation. **Adult students:** Adult Ed students take TABE, GED Ready (formally Official Practice Text: OPT), and GED Test. **Home schooled:** Present affidavit verifying completion of high school requirements. **Learning Disabled:** If service or accommodations are needed, documentation required.

High school preparation. College-preparatory program recommended.

2015-2016 Annual costs. Tuition/fees: $3,025; $11,288 out-of-state. Books/supplies: $800. Personal expenses: $1,800.

2014-2015 Financial aid. Need-based: 1,561 full-time freshmen applied for aid; 1,079 deemed to have need; 1,050 received aid. Average scholarship/grant was $3,698. 46% of total undergraduate aid awarded as scholarships/grants, 54% as loans/jobs. Need-based aid available for part-time students. Work-study available nights, weekends and for part-time students. **Non-need-based:** Scholarships awarded for academics, art, athletics, leadership, music/drama, state residency.

Application procedures. Admission: No deadline. No application fee. Admission notification on a rolling basis. Separate application procedure for healthcare programs. **Financial aid:** Priority date 6/1; no closing date. FAFSA, institutional form required. Applicants notified on a rolling basis starting 6/1; must reply within 2 week(s) of notification.

Academics. Special study options: Accelerated study, cooperative education, cross-registration, distance learning, double major, dual enrollment of high school students, ESL, honors, independent study, liberal arts/career combination, study abroad. License preparation in dental hygiene, nursing, paramedic, radiology. **Credit/placement by examination:** AP, CLEP, IB, institutional tests. 45 credit hours maximum toward associate degree. **Support services:** GED preparation and test center, learning center, pre-admission summer program, reduced course load, remedial instruction, study skills assistance, tutoring, writing center.

Majors. Business: General, accounting, administrative services, banking/financial services, business admin, entrepreneurial studies, management information systems, sales/distribution. **Computer sciences:** Computer graphics, networking, programming. **Education:** Early childhood, health. **Engineering:** General, civil, software. **General:** Maintenance. **Health services:** Dental hygiene, EMT paramedic, medical radiologic technology/radiation therapy, nursing (RN), respiratory therapy technology, surgical technology. **Human services:** General. **Liberal arts:** Arts/sciences. **Parks/recreation:** Facilities management. **Protective services:** Criminal justice, law enforcement admin. **Social sciences:** General. **Visual/performing arts:** General, commercial/advertising art, film/cinema/video. **Work/family studies:** Child care service.

Most popular majors. Liberal arts 88%.

Technology on campus. 1,733 workstations in library, computer center, student center. Commuter students can connect to campus network. Online course registration, online library, helpline, wireless network available.

Student life. Freshman orientation: Mandatory. Preregistration for classes offered. All-day event held few days prior to start of term; includes small group meetings and advising. Online orientation also available. **Activities:** Bands, campus ministries, choral groups, dance, drama, international student organizations, literary magazine, music ensembles, musical theater, student government, student newspaper, TV station, Phi Theta Kappa, black student union, Returning Adults Valuing Education, Future Educators of America, students interested in legal careers, College Democrats, BACCHUS, student environmental action coalition.

Athletics. NJCAA. **Intercollegiate:** Baseball M, basketball, softball W. **Intramural:** Basketball, golf, soccer, softball, table tennis, tennis. **Team name:** Eagles.

Student services. Adult student services, career counseling, services for economically disadvantaged, financial aid counseling, minority student services, on-campus daycare, personal counseling, placement for graduates, veterans' counselor. **Physically disabled:** Services for visually, speech, hearing impaired. **Transfer:** Transfer adviser, college fairs on campus for students transferring to 4-year colleges.

Contact. E-mail: enrollment@tcc.fl.edu
Phone: (850) 201-6200 Fax: (850) 201-8474
Renee Green, College Registrar, Tallahassee Community College, 444 Appleyard Drive, Tallahassee, FL 32304

University of Southernmost Florida
Jacksonville, Florida
www.usmf.edu **CB code: 3590**

- For-profit 2-year technical college
- Very large city

General. Regionally accredited; also accredited by ACICS. **Enrollment:** 164 undergraduates. **Degrees:** 31 associate awarded. **Calendar:** Differs by program. **Full-time faculty:** 7 total. **Part-time faculty:** 3 total.

Basis for selection. Entrance exam (Wonderlic) required.

2015-2016 Annual costs. Associate programs: $22,000-$47,813. Bachelor's programs: $35,000-$48,000.

Financial aid. Need-based: Work-study available nights, weekends and for part-time students.

Application procedures. Admission: No deadline. $50 fee. **Financial aid:** No deadline. FAFSA required.

Academics. Credit/placement by examination: AP, CLEP.

Majors. Business: Business admin. **Computer sciences:** General.

Contact. E-mail: bdurden@flatech.edu
Phone: (904) 724-2229
Barry Durden, Campus Director, University of Southernmost Florida, 9550 Regency Square Boulevard, Jacksonville, FL 32225

Valencia College
Orlando, Florida
www.valenciacollege.edu **CB member / CB code: 5869**

- Public 2-year community college
- Commuter campus in very large city

General. Founded in 1967. Regionally accredited. **Enrollment:** 36,537 degree-seeking undergraduates. **Degrees:** 30 bachelor's, 7,625 associate awarded. **ROTC:** Army, Air Force. **Location:** Central Florida - 90 miles from Tampa, 145 miles from Jacksonville. **Calendar:** Semester, extensive summer session. **Full-time faculty:** 475 total; 26% have terminal degrees, 24% minority, 58% women. **Part-time faculty:** 1,075 total; 16% have terminal degrees, 34% minority, 53% women. **Class size:** 23% < 20, 77% 20-39, less than 1% 40-49, less than 1% 50-99. **Special facilities:** Performing arts center, black box theater.

Student profile.

Out-of-state:	3%	25 or older:	37%

Transfer out. Colleges most students transferred to 2015: University of Central Florida, University of Florida.

Basis for selection. Open admission, but selective for some programs. Special requirements for high school dual enrollment, criminal justice, fire science, dance performance, film production, health science programs and bachelor's degrees. **Home schooled:** Home school diplomas accepted with official home school verification affidavit.

High school preparation. College-preparatory program recommended. Recommended units include English 4, mathematics 4, social studies 3 and science 3.

2015-2016 Annual costs. Tuition/fees: $3,092; $11,729 out-of-state. Books/supplies: $1,266. Personal expenses: $3,387. **Additional information:** Bachelor programs charged at higher tuition rates.

Financial aid. Need-based: Need-based aid available for part-time students. Work-study available nights, weekends and for part-time students.

Application procedures. **Admission:** Closing date 8/12 (postmark date). $35 fee. Admission notification on a rolling basis beginning on or about 3/31. **Financial aid:** Closing date 3/15. FAFSA required. Applicants notified on a rolling basis starting 4/2; must reply within 2 week(s) of notification.

Academics. **Special study options:** Accelerated study, combined bachelor's/graduate degree, cooperative education, distance learning, double major, dual enrollment of high school students, ESL, exchange student, honors, independent study, internships, student-designed major, study abroad, weekend college. Bachelor's degree programs available on campus. License preparation in dental hygiene, nursing, paramedic, radiology. **Credit/placement by examination:** AP, CLEP, IB, institutional tests. 45 credit hours maximum toward associate degree. Less than 75 percent of a program's hours may be met with credit by examination and/or other acceleration mechanisms. **Support services:** Learning center, reduced course load, remedial instruction, study skills assistance, tutoring, writing center. Office of Students with Disabilities ensures reasonable and appropriate accommodations and modifications for qualified students with documented disabilities, to assist with self-advocacy, and to educate the Valencia community about disabilities.

Majors. **Business:** Accounting technology, business admin, executive assistant, hospitality admin, operations. **Communications technology:** General. **Computer sciences:** Systems analysis. **Health services:** Dental hygiene, health information technology, medical radiologic technology/radiation therapy, radiologic technology/medical imaging, respiratory therapy technology, sonography. **Liberal arts:** Arts/sciences. **Protective services:** Firefighting, law enforcement admin. **Visual/performing arts:** Cinematography, dance.

Most popular majors. Liberal arts 81%.

Technology on campus. 2,500 workstations in library, computer center, student center. Commuter students can connect to campus network. Online course registration, online library, helpline, wireless network available.

Student life. **Freshman orientation:** Mandatory. Preregistration for classes offered. Two-hour program. **Activities:** Bands, choral groups, dance, drama, international student organizations, literary magazine, music ensembles, musical theater, student government, student newspaper, symphony orchestra, African American cultural society, Brain Bowl, Latin American student organization, student nurses association, volunteer club, Phi Beta Lambda, Earth club, Muslim student organization, black high achievers club.

Student services. Career counseling, student employment services, financial aid counseling, health services, personal counseling, placement for graduates, veterans' counselor. **Physically disabled:** Services for visually, hearing impaired. **Transfer:** College fairs on campus for students transferring to 4-year colleges.

Contact. Phone: (407) 582-1507 Fax: (407) 582-1866
Renee Simpson, Director of Admissions and Records, Valencia College, PO Box 3028, Orlando, FL 32802-3028

Virginia College in Jacksonville
Jacksonville, Florida
www.jacksonville.vc.edu

- For-profit 2-year technical and career college
- Very large city

General. Regionally accredited; also accredited by ACICS. Jacksonville campus includes Culinard: The Culinary Institute of Virginia College, which offers 36-week programs in pastry and culinary arts. **Enrollment:** 687 undergraduates. **Degrees:** 109 associate awarded. **Calendar:** Quarter. **Full-time faculty:** 30 total. **Part-time faculty:** 46 total.

Basis for selection. Open admission.

2015-2016 Annual costs. Diploma programs $13,932-$23,220. Associate degree programs $37,152-$49,059. Cosmetology program $21,225.

Financial aid. **Need-based:** Work-study available nights, weekends and for part-time students.

Application procedures. **Admission:** $100 fee.

Academics. **Credit/placement by examination:** AP, CLEP.

Majors. **Business:** Business admin. **Computer sciences:** Networking. **Health services:** Health information management, insurance coding, medical assistant, nursing (RN), office assistant, surgical technology.

Contact. E-mail: jacksonville.info@vc.edu
Phone: (904) 520-7400
Virginia College in Jacksonville, 5940 Beach Boulevard, Jacksonville, FL 32207

Virginia College in Pensacola
Pensacola, Florida
www.vc.edu/pensacola

- For-profit 2-year business and health science college
- Commuter campus in small city

General. Accredited by ACICS. **Enrollment:** 384 undergraduates. **Degrees:** 61 associate awarded. **Calendar:** Quarter, extensive summer session. **Full-time faculty:** 13 total. **Part-time faculty:** 62 total.

Basis for selection. Open admission.

2015-2016 Annual costs. Diploma programs range from $13,932-$23,220. Associate degree programs $37,152-$39,072. Practical nursing clock hour diploma $24,375.

Financial aid. **Need-based:** Work-study available nights, weekends and for part-time students.

Application procedures. **Admission:** $100 fee.

Academics. **Credit/placement by examination:** AP, CLEP. **Support services:** Learning center, remedial instruction, tutoring.

Majors. **Business:** Administrative services, business admin, office management. **Health services:** Health information technology, medical assistant, medical claims examiner, office assistant, pharmacy assistant, surgical technology.

Technology on campus. 80 workstations in library, computer center. Online library available.

Contact. E-mail: melanie.parlier@vc.edu
Phone: (850) 436-8444 Toll-free number: (888) 208-6932
Fax: (850) 436-4838
Melanie Parlier, Director of Admissions, Virginia College in Pensacola, 19 West Garden Street, Pensacola, FL 32502

Georgia

Abraham Baldwin Agricultural College

Tifton, Georgia   CB member
www.abac.edu   CB code: 5001

- Public 2-year agricultural and nursing college
- Commuter campus in large town
- SAT or ACT (ACT writing optional) required

General. Founded in 1924. Regionally accredited. **Enrollment:** 3,458 degree-seeking undergraduates. **Degrees:** 165 bachelor's, 471 associate awarded. **Location:** 100 miles from Macon, 50 miles from Albany. **Calendar:** Semester, extensive summer session. **Full-time faculty:** 79 total. **Part-time faculty:** 60 total. **Class size:** 34% < 20, 56% 20-39, 7% 40-49, 3% 50-99. **Special facilities:** 200-acre farm.

Student profile. Among degree-seeking undergraduates, 1,017 enrolled as first-time, first-year students.

Out-of-state:	4%	Live on campus:	32%
25 or older:	18%		

Basis for selection. Admission based on prior academic achievement or potential, as well as GPA and SAT or ACT scores. Interview recommended for nursing majors. **Home schooled:** Statement describing home school structure and mission, transcript of courses and grades required. Specific application and portfolio procedures required of home schooled applicants.

High school preparation. College-preparatory program recommended. 16 units required. Required units include English 4, mathematics 4, social studies 3, science 3 and foreign language 2.

2015-2016 Annual costs. Tuition/fees: $4,066; $12,324 out-of-state. Per-credit charge: $102.13 in-state; $377.4 out-of-state. Room/board: $7,870. Books/supplies: $1,200.

Financial aid. Need-based: Work-study available nights, weekends and for part-time students. **Non-need-based:** Scholarships awarded for academics, athletics.

Application procedures. Admission: Closing date 8/1. $20 fee, may be waived for applicants with need. Admission notification on a rolling basis. **Financial aid:** Closing date 11/15. FAFSA, institutional form required. Applicants notified on a rolling basis starting 5/15; must reply within 2 week(s) of notification.

Academics. Special study options: Accelerated study, cooperative education, distance learning, dual enrollment of high school students, honors, internships, study abroad. Bachelor's degree programs available on campus. **Credit/placement by examination:** AP, CLEP, SAT, ACT, institutional tests. **Support services:** Learning center, remedial instruction, tutoring, writing center.

Majors. Conservation: Forest technology. **Health services:** Nursing (RN). **Liberal arts:** Arts/sciences. **Visual/performing arts:** Art.

Most popular majors. Agriculture 8%, health sciences 18%, liberal arts 63%, natural resources/environmental science 7%.

Technology on campus. 100 workstations in dormitories, library, computer center. Dormitories wired for high-speed internet access. Commuter students can connect to campus network. Online course registration, online library, wireless network available.

Student life. Freshman orientation: Mandatory, $40 fee. Preregistration for classes offered. **Housing:** Coed dorms, apartments available. $235 nonrefundable deposit. **Activities:** Bands, campus ministries, choral groups, drama, international student organizations, literary magazine, radio station, student government, student newspaper.

Athletics. NJCAA. **Intercollegiate:** Baseball M, golf M, rodeo, soccer W, softball W, tennis, volleyball W. **Intramural:** Badminton W, basketball, bowling, football (non-tackle) M, softball, tennis, volleyball. **Team name:** Stallions.

Student services. Adult student services, career counseling, student employment services, health services, minority student services, personal counseling, placement for graduates, veterans' counselor.

Contact. E-mail: admissions@abac.edu
Phone: (229) 391-5004 Toll-free number: (800) 733-3653
Fax: (229) 391-5002
Donna Webb, Director of Enrollment Services, Abraham Baldwin Agricultural College, ABAC 4, 2802 Moore Highway, Tifton, GA 31793-2601

Albany Technical College

Albany, Georgia
www.albanytech.edu   CB code: 3921

- Public 2-year technical college
- Commuter campus in small city

General. Regionally accredited. Traditional and distance education classes available. **Enrollment:** 3,894 degree-seeking undergraduates. **Degrees:** 316 associate awarded. **Location:** 3 miles from downtown Albany, 225 miles from Atlanta. **Calendar:** Semester, extensive summer session. **Full-time faculty:** 91 total. **Special facilities:** Logistics education center, culinary arts institute, firefighter training tower, health care and occupational labs.

Transfer out. Colleges most students transferred to 2015: Albany State University.

Basis for selection. Open admission, but selective for some programs. Limited admission to health technology programs. Under certain conditions, ACT or SAT scores may be accepted in lieu of taking the COMPASS or ASSET test.

High school preparation. College-preparatory program recommended. 22 units recommended. Recommended units include English 4, mathematics 3, social studies 3, science 3, foreign language 1 and academic electives 3. 4 tech prep, 1 health science recommended.

2015-2016 Annual costs. Tuition/fees: $3,182; $5,852 out-of-state. Per-credit charge: $89 in-state; $178 out-of-state. Books/supplies: $1,260.

Financial aid. Need-based: Need-based aid available for part-time students. Work-study available nights, weekends and for part-time students. **Non-need-based:** Scholarships awarded for academics, state residency.

Application procedures. Admission: No deadline. $23 fee, may be waived for applicants with need. Admission notification on a rolling basis beginning on or about 8/1. **Financial aid:** No deadline. FAFSA required. Applicants notified on a rolling basis starting 5/1.

Academics. Special study options: Distance learning, dual enrollment of high school students, weekend college. Associates + Bachelors, 2 + 2 agreements with Albany State University in accounting, business administrative technology, business management, computer information systems, early childhood care education, law enforcement, marketing. License preparation in nursing, paramedic, radiology. **Credit/placement by examination:** AP, CLEP, institutional tests. **Support services:** GED preparation and test center, remedial instruction, tutoring.

Majors. Business: Sales/distribution. **Computer sciences:** Data processing, networking. **Conservation:** Forestry. **Education:** Early childhood. **General:** Carpentry. **Health services:** Pharmacy assistant. **Protective services:** Criminal justice.

Most popular majors. Business/marketing 38%, computer/information sciences 8%, education 16%, health sciences 12%, security/protective services 15%, trade and industry 8%.

Technology on campus. Online library available.

Student life. Freshman orientation: Available. Preregistration for classes offered. **Activities:** Choral groups, student government.

Athletics. Intercollegiate: Basketball M. **Team name:** Titans.

Student services. Adult student services, career counseling, services for economically disadvantaged, student employment services, financial aid counseling, on-campus daycare, personal counseling, placement for graduates, veterans' counselor. **Physically disabled:** Services for visually, speech, hearing impaired. **Transfer:** Pre-admission transcript evaluation for new students.

Contact. Phone: (229) 430-3520 Fax: (229) 430-0652
Lisa DeJesus, Director of Admissions, Albany Technical College, 1704
South Slappy Boulevard, Albany, GA 31701-3514

Andrew College
Cuthbert, Georgia
www.andrewcollege.edu
CB code: 5009

▶ Private 2-year junior and liberal arts college affiliated with the United
Methodist Church

▶ Residential campus in small town

General. Founded in 1854. Regionally accredited. **Enrollment:** 307 degree-
seeking undergraduates; 6 non-degree-seeking students. **Degrees:** 45 associate awarded. **Location:** 60 miles from Columbus, 40 miles from Albany.
Calendar: Semester, limited summer session. **Full-time faculty:** 20 total.
Part-time faculty: 13 total. **Class size:** 70% < 20, 29% 20-39, less than
1% >100.

Student profile. Among degree-seeking undergraduates, 100% enrolled in
a transfer program, 152 enrolled as first-time, first-year students, 7 transferred
in from other institutions.

Part-time: 2% **Women:** 47%

Transfer out. Colleges most students transferred to 2015: Georgia Southwestern State University, Valdosta State University, Georgia Southern University, Columbus State University, Troy State University.

Basis for selection. High school academic record, test scores, school and
community activities important. SAT or ACT recommended. Essay recommended. Interview required of the academically weak. Audition required
of music majors. Portfolio recommended for art majors. **Home schooled:**
Transcript of courses and grades required.

High school preparation. College-preparatory program recommended.
18 units recommended.

2015-2016 Annual costs. Tuition/fees: $14,924. Room/board: $9,182.
Books/supplies: $600. Personal expenses: $1,200.

2014-2015 Financial aid. Need-based: 130 full-time freshmen applied
for aid; 113 deemed to have need; 113 received aid. Average scholarship/
grant was $7,500; average loan $5,500. 54% of total undergraduate aid
awarded as scholarships/grants, 46% as loans/jobs. Need-based aid available
for part-time students. Work-study available nights, weekends and for part-
time students. **Non-need-based:** Scholarships awarded for academics, alumni
affiliation, art, athletics, leadership, music/drama, religious affiliation,
state residency.

Application procedures. Admission: Priority date 6/1; deadline 8/1
(receipt date). $20 fee, may be waived for applicants with need. Admission
notification on a rolling basis. **Financial aid:** Priority date 4/1, closing date
8/1. FAFSA, institutional form required. Applicants notified on a rolling
basis starting 4/15.

Academics. Special study options: Distance learning, double major, dual
enrollment of high school students, ESL, honors, independent study, liberal
arts/career combination, study abroad. **Credit/placement by examination:**
AP, CLEP, institutional tests. 24 credit hours maximum toward associate
degree. **Support services:** Learning center, pre-admission summer program,
reduced course load, remedial instruction, study skills assistance, tutoring,
writing center.

Majors. Business: General. **Communications:** Communications/speech/
rhetoric. **Computer sciences:** Computer science. **Conservation:** Forestry.
Education: General. **Engineering:** General. **Health services:** Athletic training, predental, premedicine, prenursing, prepharmacy, preveterinary. **History:** General. **Liberal arts:** Arts/sciences. **Math:** General. **Parks/recrea-
tion:** Health/fitness. **Physical sciences:** General. **Psychology:** General. **Social
sciences:** General, sociology. **Visual/performing arts:** General, dramatic.

Most popular majors. Business/marketing 13%, health sciences 17%,
liberal arts 13%, parks/recreation 24%, security/protective services 13%,
social sciences 8%.

Technology on campus. 100 workstations in dormitories, library, computer center, student center. Dormitories wired for high-speed internet access
and linked to campus network. Commuter students can connect to campus
network. Online library, repair service, wireless network available.

Student life. Freshman orientation: Mandatory. Preregistration for
classes offered. Held selected weekends during summer and beginning of
fall term for 3-4 days. **Policies:** No alcohol/illegal drugs allowed on campus.

Housing: Guaranteed on-campus for all undergraduates. Coed dorms, single-
sex dorms available. $50 fully refundable deposit. **Activities:** Campus minis-
tries, choral groups, drama, international student organizations, literary magazine, music ensembles, musical theater, student government, student newspaper, Baptist Student Union, Wesley Fellowship, Unity, Community Service
group, Interdenominational Christian group.

Athletics. NJCAA. **Intercollegiate:** Baseball M, basketball W, golf M,
soccer, softball W, volleyball W. **Intramural:** Archery, badminton, basketball, cheerleading, football (non-tackle) M, racquetball, soccer, softball,
swimming, table tennis, tennis, volleyball W, weight lifting. **Team name:**
Fighting Tigers.

Student services. Alcohol/substance abuse counseling, chaplain/spiritual
director, career counseling, services for economically disadvantaged, financial aid counseling, health services, veterans' counselor. **Physically disabled:**
Services for speech impaired. **Transfer:** Transfer adviser, college fairs on
campus for students transferring to 4-year colleges.

Contact. E-mail: admissions@andrewcollege.edu
Phone: (800) 664-9250 Toll-free number: (800) 664-9250
Fax: (229) 732-2176
Andy Geeter, VP of Enrollment Management, Andrew College, 501
College Street, Cuthbert, GA 39840-1395

Ashworth College
Norcross, Georgia
www.ashworthcollege.edu
CB code: 3912

▶ For-profit 2-year community and career college

▶ Commuter campus in very large city

General. Accredited by DETC. **Enrollment:** 3,000 undergraduates.
Degrees: 456 bachelor's, 2,100 associate awarded; master's offered. **Location:** 18 miles from Atlanta. **Calendar:** Differs by program, extensive summer
session. **Full-time faculty:** 20 total. **Part-time faculty:** 43 total.

Transfer out. Colleges most students transferred to 2015: Ashford University, Phoenix University.

Basis for selection. Open admission. **Home schooled:** Statement describing home school structure and mission, transcript of courses and grades
required.

Financial aid. Need-based: Work-study available nights, weekends and
for part-time students.

Application procedures. Admission: No deadline. No application fee.
Admission notification on a rolling basis.

Academics. Special study options: Accelerated study, distance learning,
weekend college. Bachelor's degree programs available on campus. **Credit/
placement by examination:** AP, CLEP. 15 credit hours maximum toward
associate degree, 30 toward bachelor's. **Support services:** Reduced course
load, study skills assistance, tutoring.

Majors. Business: Accounting, business admin, finance, human resources,
marketing. **Education:** Early childhood. **General:** Site management. **Health
services:** Health care admin. **Protective services:** Criminal justice, security
management. **Psychology:** General.

Technology on campus. Online library available.

Student life. Freshman orientation: Available. Preregistration for
classes offered.

Student services. Transfer: Pre-admission transcript evaluation for new
students. Transfer adviser for students transferring to 4-year colleges.

Contact. E-mail: info@ashworthcollege.edu
Phone: (770) 729-8400 Toll-free number: (800) 223-4542
Fax: (770) 729-9389
Eric Ryall, Registrar, Ashworth College, 6625 The Corners Parkway,
Norcross, GA 30092-3406

Athens Technical College
Athens, Georgia
www.athenstech.edu
CB code: 0462

▶ Public 2-year community and technical college

▶ Commuter campus in small city

General. Founded in 1959. Regionally accredited. **Enrollment:** 4,563 degree-seeking undergraduates. **Degrees:** 389 associate awarded. **Location:** 65 miles from Atlanta. **Calendar:** Semester, extensive summer session. **Full-time faculty:** 97 total. **Part-time faculty:** 323 total. **Class size:** 61% < 20, 36% 20-39, 1% 40-49, 2% 50-99.

Transfer out. Colleges most students transferred to 2015: University of Georgia.

Basis for selection. Open admission, but selective for some programs. Special requirements for radiology, respiratory therapy, nursing, physical therapy assistant, dental hygiene, surgical technology, veterinary technology dental assisting, medical assisting, practical nursing and paramedicine. School record, recommendations, standardized test scores, essay, and interview required or recommended depending on program. Under certain conditions, ACT or SAT may be accepted in lieu of COMPASS or ASSET for placement. Interview required of radiology, respiratory therapy, nursing, physical therapy assistant, dental assisting, and dental hygiene majors. **Home schooled:** Must provide documentation of designated home study program activities.

High school preparation. College-preparatory program recommended. 22 units recommended. Recommended units include English 4, mathematics 3, social studies 3, science 3, foreign language 1 and academic electives 3. 4 tech prep and 1 health science recommended.

2015-2016 Annual costs. Tuition/fees: $3,218; $5,888 out-of-state. Per-credit charge: $89 in-state; $178 out-of-state. Books/supplies: $800. Personal expenses: $1,000.

Financial aid. Need-based: Need-based aid available for part-time students. Work-study available nights, weekends and for part-time students. **Non-need-based:** Scholarships awarded for academics, leadership.

Application procedures. Admission: Priority date 8/1; no deadline. $20 fee. Admission notification on a rolling basis. 2/1 deadline for nursing and dental hygiene; 3/1 deadline for dental assistance; 4/1 deadline for radiography, surgical technology, diagnostic medical sonography, nursing accelerated, and veterinary technology; 5/1 deadline for physical therapist assistant, practical nursing; 7/1 deadline for respiratory therapy; 8/1 deadline for medical assistance. **Financial aid:** No deadline. FAFSA required. Applicants notified on a rolling basis starting 6/15; must reply within 2 week(s) of notification.

Academics. Special study options: Distance learning, dual enrollment of high school students, weekend college. License preparation in real estate. **Credit/placement by examination:** AP, CLEP, institutional tests. **Support services:** GED preparation and test center, learning center, reduced course load, remedial instruction, study skills assistance, tutoring.

Majors. Biology: Biotechnology. **Business:** Accounting technology, administrative services, sales/distribution, travel services. **Computer sciences:** Applications programming, data processing, networking, programming. **Education:** Early childhood. **Health services:** Dental assistant, dental hygiene, nursing (RN), physical therapy assistant, radiologic technology/medical imaging, respiratory therapy technology, sonography, veterinary technology/assistant. **Human services:** Social work. **Protective services:** Law enforcement admin. **Visual/performing arts:** Interior design.

Most popular majors. Business/marketing 18%, computer/information sciences 7%, education 11%, health sciences 37%, security/protective services 7%.

Technology on campus. 346 workstations in computer center. Commuter students can connect to campus network. Online course registration, online library, wireless network available.

Student life. Freshman orientation: Mandatory. Preregistration for classes offered. **Activities:** Student government.

Athletics. Team name: Owls.

Student services. Adult student services, career counseling, student employment services, financial aid counseling, personal counseling, placement for graduates, veterans' counselor. **Physically disabled:** Services for visually, speech, hearing impaired. **Transfer:** Transfer adviser for students transferring to 4-year colleges.

Contact. E-mail: admissions@athenstech.edu
Phone: (706) 355-5008 Fax: (706) 369-5756
Lenzy Reid, Director of Admissions, Athens Technical College, 800 US Highway 29 North, Athens, GA 30601-1500

Atlanta Metropolitan College
Atlanta, Georgia
www.atlm.edu

CB member
CB code: 5725

◗ Public 2-year junior college
◗ Commuter campus in very large city

General. Founded in 1974. Regionally accredited. **Enrollment:** 2,700 degree-seeking undergraduates. **Degrees:** 19 bachelor's, 327 associate awarded. **Location:** 4 miles from downtown. **Calendar:** Semester, extensive summer session. **Full-time faculty:** 58 total. **Part-time faculty:** 60 total.

Student profile.

Out-of-state:	6%	**25 or older:**	26%

Basis for selection. Applicants who have followed college preparatory curriculum must have 2.0 GPA. Applicants who have followed technology/career curriculum must have 2.2 GPA. All applicants must meet immunization requirements. Applicants with 430 SAT verbal or 17 ACT English and completion of college preparatory curriculum in English exempt from taking COMPASS Placement Test in English and Reading. Applicants with 400 SAT math or 17 ACT math and completion of college preparatory curriculum in math exempt from taking COMPASS Placement Test in math. **Home schooled:** Transcript of courses and grades required.

High school preparation. 16 units required. Required units include English 4, mathematics 4, social studies 1, history 2, science 3 (laboratory 2) and foreign language 2.

2015-2016 Annual costs. Tuition/fees: $3,830; $11,752 out-of-state. Per-credit charge: $97 in-state; $361 out-of-state. Books/supplies: $1,300.

Financial aid. All financial aid based on need. Need-based aid available for part-time students. Work-study available nights, weekends and for part-time students.

Application procedures. Admission: Priority date 7/15; no deadline. $20 fee. Admission notification on a rolling basis. **Financial aid:** Closing date 6/1. FAFSA required. Applicants notified on a rolling basis; must reply by 6/30.

Academics. Academic and technological workshops provided. Tutorial services available in math, physics, chemistry, English, reading, accounting, and general science. **Special study options:** Distance learning, dual enrollment of high school students, ESL, external degree, honors, independent study, study abroad, weekend college. **Credit/placement by examination:** AP, CLEP. **Support services:** Learning center, remedial instruction, study skills assistance, tutoring, writing center.

Majors. Area/ethnic studies: African-American. **Biology:** General. **Business:** Business admin, office management. **Communications:** Communications/speech/rhetoric. **Computer sciences:** General, computer science. **Education:** Multi-level teacher. **English:** English lit, rhetoric/composition. **Foreign languages:** General. **Health services:** Health information management. **History:** General. **Human services:** Social work. **Math:** General. **Parks/recreation:** Health/fitness. **Physical sciences:** Chemistry, physics. **Protective services:** Law enforcement admin. **Psychology:** General. **Social sciences:** Political science. **Visual/performing arts:** Art, music.

Most popular majors. Liberal arts 94%.

Technology on campus. 580 workstations in library, computer center, student center. Commuter students can connect to campus network. Online course registration, online library, helpline, repair service, wireless network available.

Student life. Freshman orientation: Mandatory. Preregistration for classes offered. Daytime and evening sessions held each semester. **Housing:** Off-campus housing available for college athletes only. **Activities:** Choral groups, dance, drama, international student organizations, student government, student newspaper.

Athletics. NJCAA. **Intercollegiate:** Basketball. **Team name:** Red-Eyed Panthers.

Student services. Adult student services, career counseling, services for economically disadvantaged, financial aid counseling, minority student services, personal counseling, veterans' counselor. **Physically disabled:** Services for visually, speech, hearing impaired. **Transfer:** Pre-admission transcript evaluation for new students. College fairs on campus for students transferring to 4-year colleges.

Two-Year Colleges

Contact. E-mail: areid@atlm.edu
Phone: (404) 756-4004 Fax: (404) 756-4407
Audrey Reid, Director of Admissions, Atlanta Metropolitan College, 1630 Metropolitan Parkway, SW, Atlanta, GA 30310-4498

Atlanta Technical College
Atlanta, Georgia
www.atlantatech.edu   CB code: 5030

- Public 2-year community and technical college
- Commuter campus in very large city

General. Regionally accredited. **Enrollment:** 3,558 degree-seeking undergraduates; 231 non-degree-seeking students. **Degrees:** 261 associate awarded. **Location:** 2 miles from downtown Atlanta. **Calendar:** Semester, extensive summer session. **Full-time faculty:** 109 total; 8% have terminal degrees, 80% minority, 51% women. **Part-time faculty:** 227 total; 4% have terminal degrees, 91% minority, 60% women. **Partnerships:** BMW's Service Technician Education Program (STEP).

Student profile. Among degree-seeking undergraduates, 3% already have a bachelor's degree or higher, 604 enrolled as first-time, first-year students.

Part-time:	62%	Hispanic/Latino:	2%
Women:	66%	Multi-racial, non-Hispanic:	2%
African American:	91%	International:	1%
Asian American:	1%	25 or older:	67%

Transfer out. Colleges most students transferred to 2015: Atlanta Metropolitan College, Georgia Perimeter College, Georgia Piedmont Technical College, Ashford University, Georgia State University.

Basis for selection. Open admission, but selective for some programs. Requirements vary by program for selective admission majors. Under certain conditions, ACT or SAT may be accepted in lieu of COMPASS or ASSET for placement. **Home schooled:** Transcript of courses and grades, letter of recommendation (nonparent) required. Letter from superintendent's office confirming compliance with Georgia/TCSG policies and attendance and final exit exam scores from accredited national testing program required.

High school preparation. College-preparatory program recommended. 22 units recommended. Recommended units include English 4, mathematics 3, social studies 3, science 3, foreign language 2 and academic electives 3.

2015-2016 Annual costs. Tuition/fees: $3,274; $5,944 out-of-state. Per-credit charge: $89 in-state; $178 out-of-state. Books/supplies: $1,100.

2014-2015 Financial aid. Need-based: Average scholarship/grant was $5,002. 45% of total undergraduate aid awarded as scholarships/grants, 55% as loans/jobs. Need-based aid available for part-time students. Work-study available nights, weekends and for part-time students.

Application procedures. Admission: Closing date 7/18 (receipt date). $20 fee. Admission notification on a rolling basis. **Financial aid:** Priority date 3/1; no closing date. Applicants notified on a rolling basis starting 4/15.

Academics. Special study options: Distance learning, dual enrollment of high school students, ESL, internships, study abroad, weekend college. License preparation in aviation, dental hygiene, nursing, paramedic, physical therapy, radiology. **Credit/placement by examination:** AP, CLEP, IB, institutional tests. 50% of the total credit hours required for the program may be exempted. **Support services:** GED preparation and test center, learning center, remedial instruction, study skills assistance, tutoring. Instructional workshops.

Majors. Business: Accounting technology, administrative services, business admin, hospitality admin, logistics, marketing, sales/distribution. **Computer sciences:** General, database management, networking, programming, system admin. **Education:** Early childhood. **Health services:** Dental hygiene, health information technology, occupational therapy assistant, pharmacy assistant, radiologic technology/medical imaging, surgical technology. **Protective services:** Fire services admin. **Visual/performing arts:** Commercial/advertising art, design.

Most popular majors. Business/marketing 31%, computer/information sciences 8%, education 19%, health sciences 28%, legal studies 9%.

Technology on campus. 148 workstations in library. Online course registration, online library, wireless network available.

Student life. Freshman orientation: Mandatory. Preregistration for classes offered. **Activities:** Student government.

Student services. Career counseling, student employment services, financial aid counseling, on-campus daycare. **Physically disabled:** Services for visually, speech, hearing impaired. **Transfer:** Re-entry adviser for new students.

Contact. E-mail: admissions@atlantatech.edu
Phone: (404) 225-4400
Vory Billups, Director of Enrollment Management, Atlanta Technical College, 1560 Metropolitan Parkway, SW, Atlanta, GA 30310-4446

Augusta Technical College
Augusta, Georgia
www.augustatech.edu   CB code: 2620

- Public 2-year technical college
- Commuter campus in large city

General. Founded in 1961. Regionally accredited. Additional campuses in Grovetown, Thomson, and Waynesboro. **Enrollment:** 4,490 degree-seeking undergraduates. **Degrees:** 332 associate awarded. **Location:** 145 miles from Atlanta; 75 miles from Columbia, South Carolina. **Calendar:** Semester, extensive summer session. **Full-time faculty:** 136 total. **Part-time faculty:** 240 total.

Basis for selection. Open admission, but selective for some programs. Competitive admission to cardiovascular technology, respiratory therapy care, occupational therapy assistant, radiologic technology, and practical nursing. Requirements vary by program and may include required college courses, placement exam scores, interviews, essays, and GPA. **Home schooled:** Transcript of courses and grades required.

High school preparation. College-preparatory program recommended. 22 units recommended. Recommended units include English 4, mathematics 3, social studies 3, science 3, foreign language 1 and academic electives 3. Highly recommended that math units include algebra and trigonometry. 4 tech prep and 1 health science recommended.

2015-2016 Annual costs. Tuition/fees: $3,178; $5,848 out-of-state. Per-credit charge: $89 in-state; $178 out-of-state. Books/supplies: $450.

2014-2015 Financial aid. Need-based: Work-study available nights, weekends and for part-time students. **Non-need-based:** Scholarships awarded for state residency.

Application procedures. Admission: No deadline. $20 fee, may be waived for applicants with need. Application deadlines exist for competitive healthcare programs and vary by major. **Financial aid:** No deadline. FAFSA, institutional form required. Must reply within 2 week(s) of notification.

Academics. Special study options: Distance learning, dual enrollment of high school students, weekend college. **Credit/placement by examination:** AP, CLEP, institutional tests. **Support services:** GED preparation and test center, learning center, reduced course load, remedial instruction, tutoring.

Majors. Business: Accounting, administrative services, sales/distribution. **Computer sciences:** Applications programming. **Health services:** Cardiovascular technology, clinical lab technology, EMT paramedic, pharmacy assistant, respiratory therapy technology.

Most popular majors. Business/marketing 23%, computer/information sciences 8%, engineering/engineering technologies 11%, health sciences 32%, trade and industry 6%.

Technology on campus. Commuter students can connect to campus network. Online course registration, online library, wireless network available.

Student life. Freshman orientation: Available. Preregistration for classes offered. **Activities:** Student government.

Student services. Career counseling, student employment services, financial aid counseling, on-campus daycare, placement for graduates, veterans' counselor. **Physically disabled:** Services for visually, speech, hearing impaired. **Transfer:** Pre-admission transcript evaluation for new students.

Contact. E-mail: dwendt@augustatech.edu
Phone: (706) 771-4150 Fax: (706) 771-4034
Christine Ball, Director of Admissions, Augusta Technical College, 3200 Augusta Tech Drive, Augusta, GA 30906

Bainbridge State College

Bainbridge, Georgia
www.bainbridge.edu

CB member
CB code: 5062

- Public 2-year agricultural, community and technical college
- Commuter campus in large town

General. Founded in 1973. Regionally accredited. **Enrollment:** 2,401 degree-seeking undergraduates. **Degrees:** 228 associate awarded. **Location:** 43 miles of Tallahassee, Florida. **Calendar:** Semester, limited summer session. **Full-time faculty:** 57 total. **Part-time faculty:** 50 total. **Class size:** 62% < 20, 38% 20-39, less than 1% 40-49. **Special facilities:** Nature trail, commercial truck driving range.

Student profile. Among degree-seeking undergraduates, 2% already have a bachelor's degree or higher, 514 enrolled as first-time, first-year students, 982 transferred in from other institutions.

Part-time:	66%	Women:	69%
Out-of-state:	8%	25 or older:	38%

Transfer out. 87% of students enrolled in the transfer program go on to 4-year colleges. **Colleges most students transferred to 2015:** Valdosta State University, Albany State University, Georgia Southwestern University.

Basis for selection. College preparatory curriculum and a minimum High School GPA of 2.0 required for associate of arts degree-seeking students. Limited number admitted who do not meet admission standards. Applicants that score a 400 Math/430 Reading on SAT or 17 English/17 Math on ACT are exempt from the COMPASS placement exam. All other applicants excluding transfer applicants are required to take the COMPASS exam. Transfer applicants are reviewed by Admissions to determine whether COMPASS is needed. **Adult students:** SAT/ACT scores not required. Compass test required. **Home schooled:** Transcript of courses and grades required. Acceptable scores on COMPASS required.

High school preparation. College-preparatory program recommended. 17 units required. Required units include English 4, mathematics 4, social studies 3, science 4 and foreign language 2.

2015-2016 Annual costs. Tuition/fees: $3,772; $11,366 out-of-state. Per-credit charge: $91 in-state; $344 out-of-state. Books/supplies: $650. Personal expenses: $450.

Financial aid. All financial aid based on need. Need-based aid available for part-time students. Work-study available nights, weekends and for part-time students.

Application procedures. Admission: Closing date 8/10 (receipt date). No application fee. Admission notification on a rolling basis. **Financial aid:** Priority date 6/1, closing date 8/1. FAFSA, institutional form required. Applicants notified on a rolling basis starting 6/1; must reply within 2 week(s) of notification.

Academics. Special study options: Combined bachelor's/graduate degree, distance learning, double major, dual enrollment of high school students, honors, independent study, internships, study abroad, weekend college. 2-year registered nursing program. 2+2 Agreements with Thomas University, Georgia Southwestern University, and University of Georgia. Bachelor's degree programs available on campus. License preparation in nursing, paramedic, real estate. **Credit/placement by examination:** AP, CLEP, IB, institutional tests. 18 credit hours maximum toward associate degree. **Support services:** GED preparation and test center, learning center, reduced course load, remedial instruction, study skills assistance, tutoring.

Majors. Business: General, accounting, administrative services, management information systems, marketing. **Communications:** Communications/speech/rhetoric. **Computer sciences:** General. **Education:** General, early childhood, health, middle, physical, secondary. **English:** English lit. **Foreign languages:** General. **General:** Electrician. **Health services:** Health information technology, nursing (RN). **History:** General. **Math:** General. **Protective services:** Law enforcement admin, police science. **Psychology:** General. **Social sciences:** Political science.

Most popular majors. Business/marketing 27%, education 16%, health sciences 25%, security/protective services 13%.

Technology on campus. 350 workstations in library, computer center, student center. Online course registration, online library, helpline, wireless network available.

Student life. Freshman orientation: Mandatory. Preregistration for classes offered. Online and on-campus orientations held prior to start of semester. **Activities:** Choral groups, international student organizations, music ensembles, Model UN, student government, Delta club, service organizations, Phi Theta Kappa, Sigma Kappa Delta, Mu Alpha Theta.

Athletics. Intramural: Basketball, football (non-tackle), softball, table tennis, volleyball.

Student services. Adult student services, alcohol/substance abuse counseling, career counseling, services for economically disadvantaged, student employment services, financial aid counseling, health services, minority student services, personal counseling, placement for graduates, veterans' counselor. **Physically disabled:** Services for visually, speech, hearing impaired. **Transfer:** Transfer adviser, college fairs on campus for students transferring to 4-year colleges.

Contact. E-mail: melanie.cleveland@bainbridge.edu
Phone: (229) 243-6920 Fax: (229) 248-2623
Melanie Cleveland, Director of Admissions, Bainbridge State College, 2500 East Shotwell Street, Bainbridge, GA 39818-0990

Brown Mackie College: Atlanta

Atlanta, Georgia
www.brownmackie.edu

- For-profit 2-year business and health science college
- Very large city

General. Accredited by ACICS. **Enrollment:** 1,033 undergraduates. **Degrees:** 222 associate awarded. **Calendar:** Quarter. **Full-time faculty:** 7 total. **Part-time faculty:** 7 total.

Basis for selection. Open admission. **Home schooled:** Transcript of courses and grades, state high school equivalency certificate required.

2015-2016 Annual costs. Tuition/fees: $18,920. Per-credit charge: $381.

Financial aid. Need-based: Work-study available nights, weekends and for part-time students.

Application procedures. Admission: No deadline. No application fee. Application must be submitted on paper. Admission notification on a rolling basis.

Academics. Special study options: License preparation in occupational therapy. **Credit/placement by examination:** AP, CLEP. **Support services:** Remedial instruction, tutoring.

Majors. Business: Accounting, business admin. **Health services:** Medical assistant, occupational therapy assistant, surgical technology.

Technology on campus. 12 workstations in library.

Student services. Transfer: Re-entry adviser, pre-admission transcript evaluation for new students.

Contact. E-mail: bmcatadm@brownmackie.edu
Phone: (404) 799-4500 Toll-free number: (888) 301-3670
Embry McCray, Senior Director of Admissions, Brown Mackie College: Atlanta, 4370 Peachtree Road NE, Atlanta, GA 30319

Central Georgia Technical College

Warner Robins, Georgia
www.centralgatech.edu

CB code: 1709

- Public 2-year community and technical college
- Commuter campus in small city

General. Regionally accredited. **Enrollment:** 7,833 degree-seeking undergraduates. **Degrees:** 454 associate awarded. **Location:** 80 miles from Atlanta. **Calendar:** Semester, extensive summer session. **Full-time faculty:** 198 total. **Part-time faculty:** 324 total. **Class size:** 76% < 20, 24% 20-39, less than 1% 50-99. **Partnerships:** Formal partnerships with Cisco and local industries.

Student profile. Among degree-seeking undergraduates, 100% enrolled in a vocational program, 1% already have a bachelor's degree or higher.

Part-time:	66%	Asian American:	1%
Out-of-state:	1%	Hispanic/Latino:	4%
Women:	63%	Multi-racial, non-Hispanic:	1%
African American:	51%	25 or older:	50%

Transfer out. Colleges most students transferred to 2015: Middle Georgia State College, Georgia Military College, Fort Valley State University, Mercer University, Ashford University.

Basis for selection. Open admission, but selective for some programs. Placement test administered for accurate placement. Scores from the SAT, ACT or CPE from the past five years is accepted. Health and health related programs have varying admissions criteria. Under certain conditions, ACT or SAT may be accepted in lieu of COMPASS or ASSET for placement.

High school preparation. College-preparatory program recommended. 22 units recommended. Recommended units include English 4, mathematics 3, social studies 3, science 3, foreign language 1 and academic electives 3. 4 tech prep and 1 health science recommended.

2015-2016 Annual costs. Tuition/fees: $3,208; $5,878 out-of-state. Per-credit charge: $89 in-state; $178 out-of-state. Books/supplies: $750.

Financial aid. Need-based: Need-based aid available for part-time students. Work-study available nights, weekends and for part-time students. **Non-need-based:** Scholarships awarded for academics, athletics, state residency.

Application procedures. Admission: No deadline. $20 fee, may be waived for applicants with need. Admission notification on a rolling basis. Application closing date is one month prior to first day of attendance. **Financial aid:** Closing date 7/15. FAFSA, institutional form required.

Academics. Special study options: Cooperative education, distance learning, double major, dual enrollment of high school students, internships, study abroad, weekend college. License preparation in aviation, dental hygiene, nursing, paramedic, radiology, real estate. **Credit/placement by examination:** AP, CLEP, institutional tests. Dependent on approval by department/program. **Support services:** GED preparation and test center, reduced course load, remedial instruction, study skills assistance, tutoring, writing center.

Majors. Business: Accounting technology, administrative services, banking/financial services, business admin, construction management, hospitality admin, logistics, marketing. **Computer sciences:** Data processing, IT project management, programming, system admin, web page design. **Education:** Early childhood, teacher assistance. **General:** Carpentry. **Health services:** Cardiovascular technology, clinical lab technology, dental hygiene, EMT paramedic, medical assistant, MRI technology, nursing (RN), polysomnography, radiologic technology/medical imaging, sonography. **Protective services:** Criminal justice, disaster management. **Social sciences:** GIS/cartography. **Visual/performing arts:** Design. **Work/family studies:** Aging.

Most popular majors. Business/marketing 33%, computer/information sciences 11%, education 11%, health sciences 20%, security/protective services 10%, trade and industry 11%.

Technology on campus. 600 workstations in library, computer center. Commuter students can connect to campus network. Online course registration, online library, helpline, wireless network available.

Student life. Freshman orientation: Available. Preregistration for classes offered. Held prior to the registration period each semester and available online. **Activities:** Student government.

Athletics. NJCAA. **Intercollegiate:** Basketball, cross-country. **Team name:** Titans.

Student services. Adult student services, career counseling, services for economically disadvantaged, financial aid counseling, minority student services, on-campus daycare, placement for graduates, veterans' counselor. **Physically disabled:** Services for visually, speech, hearing impaired. **Transfer:** College fairs on campus for students transferring to 4-year colleges.

Contact. E-mail: admissionsoffice@centralgatech.edu
Phone: (478) 988-6850 Fax: (478) 988-6947
Dann Webb, Director of Admissions, Central Georgia Technical College, 80 Cohen Walker Drive, Warner Robins, GA 31088

Chattahoochee Technical College
Marietta, Georgia
www.chattahoocheetech.edu   CB code: 5441

▸ Public 2-year community and technical college
▸ Commuter campus in large city

General. Founded in 1961. Regionally accredited. **Enrollment:** 9,819 degree-seeking undergraduates. **Degrees:** 495 associate awarded. **Location:** 20 miles from Atlanta. **Calendar:** Semester, extensive summer session. **Full-time faculty:** 180 total. **Part-time faculty:** 400 total.

Transfer out. Colleges most students transferred to 2015: Kennesaw State University.

Basis for selection. Open admission, but selective for some programs. Special admissions requirements for health science programs and several technical programs. Under certain conditions, ACT or SAT may be accepted in lieu of COMPASS or ASSET for placement. **Home schooled:** Transcript of courses and grades required. Documentation of home school registration with state required; SAT/ACT may be required.

High school preparation. College-preparatory program recommended.

2015-2016 Annual costs. Tuition/fees: $3,216; $5,886 out-of-state. Per-credit charge: $89 in-state; $178 out-of-state.

Financial aid. Need-based: Need-based aid available for part-time students. Work-study available nights, weekends and for part-time students.

Application procedures. Admission: Closing date 7/24 (postmark date). $20 fee. Admission notification on a rolling basis. **Financial aid:** No deadline. FAFSA required. Applicants notified on a rolling basis.

Academics. Special study options: Distance learning, dual enrollment of high school students, internships, study abroad, weekend college. License preparation in nursing, paramedic. **Credit/placement by examination:** AP, CLEP, IB, institutional tests. **Support services:** GED preparation and test center, learning center, reduced course load, remedial instruction, study skills assistance, tutoring. Special populations, disability services, student navigator.

Majors. Business: Accounting, administrative services, business admin, logistics, marketing, office management, office technology. **Communications technology:** Animation/special effects, desktop publishing, radio/TV. **Computer sciences:** General, applications programming, LAN/WAN management, networking, programming. **Conservation:** Environmental science. **Education:** Early childhood, early childhood special. **Health services:** Clinical lab technology, EMT paramedic, health care admin, health information management, health information technology, insurance coding, medical secretary, nursing (RN), occupational therapy assistant, office assistant, physical therapy assistant, radiologic technology/medical imaging, receptionist, sterile processing technology, surgical technology. **Protective services:** Criminal justice, fire services admin. **Visual/performing arts:** Design, graphic design, interior design.

Most popular majors. Business/marketing 22%, computer/information sciences 11%, education 11%, engineering/engineering technologies 6%, health sciences 11%, natural resources/environmental science 6%, personal/culinary services 6%, security/protective services 6%, trade and industry 17%, visual/performing arts 6%.

Technology on campus. Online course registration, online library, wireless network available.

Student life. Freshman orientation: Available. Preregistration for classes offered. **Activities:** International student organizations, student government.

Athletics. NJCAA. **Intercollegiate:** Basketball. **Intramural:** Baseball, basketball, bowling, football (non-tackle), soccer, softball, tennis. **Team name:** Golden Eagles.

Student services. Career counseling, services for economically disadvantaged, student employment services, financial aid counseling, minority student services, placement for graduates, veterans' counselor. **Physically disabled:** Services for visually, speech, hearing impaired. **Transfer:** Re-entry adviser for new students. College fairs on campus for students transferring to 4-year colleges.

Contact. E-mail: enroll@chattahoocheetech.edu
Nate Beardsley, Director of Admissions, Chattahoochee Technical College, 980 South Cobb Drive, SE, Marietta, GA 30060-3300

Coastal Pines Technical College
Waycross, Georgia
www.coastalpines.edu   CB code: 0147

▸ Public 2-year community and technical college
▸ Commuter campus in large town

General. Regionally accredited. **Enrollment:** 714 degree-seeking undergraduates. **Degrees:** 69 associate awarded. **Location:** 100 miles from Savannah. **Calendar:** Semester, extensive summer session.

Basis for selection. Open admission. **Home schooled:** Transcript of courses and grades required. Letter from local school superintendent's office verifying the parent/legal guardian complied with state law concerning home schooling.

High school preparation. 22 units recommended. Recommended units include English 4, mathematics 3, social studies 3, science 3, foreign language 1 and academic electives 3. 4 tech prep, 1 health science recommended.

2015-2016 Annual costs. Tuition/fees: $3,166; $6,136 out-of-state. Per-credit charge: $89 in-state; $178 out-of-state.

Financial aid. Need-based: Work-study available nights, weekends and for part-time students.

Application procedures. Admission: No deadline. $24 fee. Admission notification on a rolling basis.

Academics. Special study options: Distance learning, dual enrollment of high school students, ESL. License preparation in nursing, paramedic, radiology. **Credit/placement by examination:** AP, CLEP. **Support services:** GED preparation and test center, learning center, remedial instruction, study skills assistance, tutoring.

Majors. Business: Accounting, business admin, marketing. **Computer sciences:** Networking, support specialist. **Conservation:** Forest technology. **Education:** Early childhood. **Engineering:** Electrical, mechanical. **Health services:** Medical radiologic technology/radiation therapy. **Protective services:** Police science. **Work/family studies:** Child care service.

Technology on campus. Online course registration, online library, wireless network available.

Student life. Freshman orientation: Mandatory. Preregistration for classes offered. Held the week before the start of the semester. **Activities:** Student government.

Athletics. Team name: Stingrays.

Student services. Career counseling, services for economically disadvantaged, financial aid counseling, personal counseling, placement for graduates. **Physically disabled:** Services for visually, speech, hearing impaired.

Contact. Phone: (912) 427-1958 Toll-free number: (800) 645-8284 Fax: (912) 427-1901
Chris Jeancake, Director of Admissions, Coastal Pines Technical College, 1777 West Cherry Street, Jesup, GA 31545

Columbus Technical College
Columbus, Georgia
www.columbustech.edu   **CB code: 5704**

- Public 2-year technical college
- Commuter campus in small city
- Interview required

General. Founded in 1961. Regionally accredited. **Enrollment:** 3,739 degree-seeking undergraduates. **Degrees:** 295 associate awarded. **Location:** 110 miles from Atlanta, 86 miles from Albany. **Calendar:** Semester, extensive summer session. **Full-time faculty:** 75 total. **Part-time faculty:** 155 total.

Basis for selection. Open admission, but selective for some programs. Special requirements for health programs. Under certain conditions, ACT or SAT may be accepted in lieu of COMPASS or ASSET for placement.

High school preparation. College-preparatory program recommended. 22 units recommended. Recommended units include English 4, mathematics 3, social studies 3, science 3, foreign language 1 and academic electives 3. 4 tech prep and 1 health science recommended.

2015-2016 Annual costs. Tuition/fees: $3,228; $5,898 out-of-state. Per-credit charge: $89 in-state; $178 out-of-state. Books/supplies: $1,600. Personal expenses: $1,100.

Financial aid. Need-based: Need-based aid available for part-time students. Work-study available nights, weekends and for part-time students.

Application procedures. Admission: No deadline. $25 fee. Notification before registration date. **Financial aid:** No deadline. FAFSA required. Applicants notified on a rolling basis.

Academics. Special study options: Distance learning, dual enrollment of high school students, weekend college. License preparation in dental hygiene, nursing, paramedic, radiology, real estate. **Credit/placement by examination:** AP, CLEP. **Support services:** Learning center, remedial instruction, study skills assistance, tutoring.

Majors. Biology: General. **Business:** Accounting, administrative services, business admin, hotel/motel/restaurant management, human resources. **Computer sciences:** Support specialist, system admin. **Education:** Early childhood. **Health services:** Cardiovascular technology, dental hygiene, licensed practical nurse, nursing (RN), pharmaceutical sciences, pharmacy assistant, radiologic technology/medical imaging, respiratory therapy technology, surgical technology. **Protective services:** Law enforcement admin.

Most popular majors. Business/marketing 18%, computer/information sciences 14%, health sciences 54%.

Technology on campus. 40 workstations in library, computer center. Online library available.

Student life. Freshman orientation: Mandatory. Preregistration for classes offered. Three-hour orientation held day before start of classes. **Activities:** Student government.

Student services. Career counseling, student employment services, financial aid counseling, personal counseling, placement for graduates, veterans' counselor. **Physically disabled:** Services for speech, hearing impaired.

Contact. E-mail: admissions@columbustech.edu
Phone: (706) 649-1901 Fax: (404) 649-1885
Nicole Kennedy, Director of Admissions, Columbus Technical College, 928 Manchester Expressway, Columbus, GA 31904-6572

Darton College
Albany, Georgia   **CB member**
www.darton.edu   **CB code: 5026**

- Public 2-year community college
- Commuter campus in small city

General. Founded in 1963. Regionally accredited. **Enrollment:** 5,990 degree-seeking undergraduates. **Degrees:** 46 bachelor's, 795 associate awarded. **Location:** 175 miles from Atlanta. **Calendar:** Semester, extensive summer session. **Full-time faculty:** 121 total; 63% women. **Part-time faculty:** 161 total; 53% women. **Class size:** 56% < 20, 41% 20-39, 2% 40-49, less than 1% 50-99, less than 1% >100. **Special facilities:** 50-foot Carolina tower and climbing wall, nature trail, indoor heated pool, bowling alley, racquetball courts.

Student profile.

25 or older:	49%	**Live on campus:**	7%

Transfer out. Colleges most students transferred to 2015: Georgia Southwestern State University, Albany State University, Florida State University, Valdosta State University.

Basis for selection. Open admission, but selective for some programs. Special requirements for nursing, diagnostic medical sonography, physical therapy, and respiratory care programs. Criminal background check required for all students. Interview, portfolios and essays considered when students do not meet minimum admission requirements but show promise. **Adult students:** Must take COMPASS test if out of high school or college for more than 5 years and do not have 30 transferrable credit hours. **Home schooled:** Transcript of courses and grades required.

High school preparation. College-preparatory program required. 16 units required. Required units include English 4, mathematics 4, social studies 3, science 3 and foreign language 2.

2015-2016 Annual costs. Tuition/fees: $3,940; $11,534 out-of-state. Per-credit charge: $91 in-state; $344 out-of-state. Room/board: $9,770. Books/supplies: $1,100.

Financial aid. Need-based: Need-based aid available for part-time students. Work-study available nights, weekends and for part-time students. **Non-need-based:** Scholarships awarded for academics, alumni affiliation, art, athletics, music/drama, state residency. **Additional information:** Auditions, portfolios, essays, extracurricular activities impact scholarship decisions.

Application procedures. Admission: Priority date 8/1; no deadline. $20 fee. Admission notification on a rolling basis. Applications must be received 10 days prior to registration. **Financial aid:** No deadline. FAFSA, institutional form required. Applicants notified on a rolling basis; must reply within 3 week(s) of notification.

Academics. Career and transfer programs available. Support services available online. **Special study options:** Accelerated study, cooperative education, cross-registration, distance learning, double major, dual enrollment of high school students, ESL, honors, independent study, liberal arts/career combination, weekend college. Bachelor's degree programs available on campus.

License preparation in dental hygiene, nursing, occupational therapy, paramedic, physical therapy. **Credit/placement by examination:** AP, CLEP, IB, institutional tests. 18 hours in residence required. **Support services:** Learning center, pre-admission summer program, reduced course load, remedial instruction, study skills assistance, tutoring, writing center.

Majors. Biology: General, biomedical sciences. **Business:** Administrative services, business admin, office management. **Communications:** Journalism. **Computer sciences:** General, computer science, information systems, networking. **Conservation:** Environmental studies, forestry. **Education:** Art, business, drama/dance, early childhood, English, foreign languages, mathematics, middle, multi-level teacher, music, science, social science, speech. **Engineering:** Pre-engineering. **English:** English lit. **Foreign languages:** General. **Health services:** Cardiovascular technology, clinical lab science, community health services, dental hygiene, EMT paramedic, health information management, health information technology, histologic assistant, histologic technology, licensed practical nurse, medical radiologic technology/radiation therapy, mental health services, nuclear medical technology, nursing (RN), occupational therapy assistant, physical therapy assistant, polysomnography, predental, premedicine, prepharmacy, prephysical therapy, preveterinary, respiratory therapy assistant, respiratory therapy technology, sonography. **History:** General. **Human services:** Social work. **Math:** General. **Parks/recreation:** General, exercise sciences, health/fitness, sports admin. **Philosophy/religion:** Philosophy. **Physical sciences:** Chemistry, physics. **Protective services:** Criminal justice, forensics. **Psychology:** General. **Social sciences:** Anthropology, economics, geography, political science, sociology. **Visual/performing arts:** Art, dance, dramatic, music.

Most popular majors. Health sciences 44%, liberal arts 50%.

Technology on campus. 420 workstations in library, computer center, student center. Dormitories wired for high-speed internet access and linked to campus network. Commuter students can connect to campus network. Online course registration, online library, helpline, wireless network available.

Student life. Freshman orientation: Available. Preregistration for classes offered. Held every semester; required of all students enrolled in learning support classes. **Policies:** All tobacco products banned on campus. **Housing:** Coed dorms, special housing for disabled available. $200 fully refundable deposit. **Activities:** Bands, choral groups, dance, drama, international student organizations, literary magazine, music ensembles, musical theater, student government, student newspaper, symphony orchestra, cultural exchange club, Democratic/Independent/Republican Team, honors club, Phi Theta Kappa.

Athletics. NJCAA. **Intercollegiate:** Baseball M, basketball W, cross-country, golf M, soccer, softball W, swimming, wrestling M. **Intramural:** Basketball, bowling, football (non-tackle), golf, racquetball, softball, table tennis, tennis, volleyball. **Team name:** Cavaliers.

Student services. Alcohol/substance abuse counseling, career counseling, student employment services, financial aid counseling, health services, minority student services, personal counseling, veterans' counselor. **Physically disabled:** Services for visually, speech, hearing impaired. **Transfer:** Pre-admission transcript evaluation for new students. Transfer adviser, college fairs on campus for students transferring to 4-year colleges.

Contact. E-mail: info@darton.edu
Phone: (229) 317-6740 Toll-free number: (866) 775-1214
Fax: (229) 317-6607
Susan Bowen, Director of Admission, Darton College, 2400 Gillionville Road, Albany, GA 31707-3098

East Georgia State College
Swainsboro, Georgia   **CB member**
www.ega.edu   **CB code: 5200**

▸ Public 2-year community and junior college
▸ Commuter campus in small town

General. Founded in 1973. Regionally accredited. **Enrollment:** 3,001 degree-seeking undergraduates. **Degrees:** 3 bachelor's, 182 associate awarded. **ROTC:** Army. **Location:** 85 miles from Savannah and Augusta. **Calendar:** Semester, limited summer session. **Full-time faculty:** 76 total; 42% have terminal degrees, 13% minority, 46% women. **Part-time faculty:** 56 total; 27% have terminal degrees, 12% minority, 52% women. **Class size:** 25% < 20, 73% 20-39, 1% 40-49. **Special facilities:** Outdoor exercise trail, community learning center, 5K trail run.

Student profile. Among degree-seeking undergraduates, 35 transferred in from other institutions.

Out-of-state: 6%   **25 or older:**   12%

Transfer out. Colleges most students transferred to 2015: Georgia Southern University.

Basis for selection. Graduation from accredited or approved high school or GED, complete 17 required high school curriculum, 2.0 GPA, and qualifying SAT, ACT or Compass Score. SAT or ACT recommended. **Home schooled:** Transcript of courses and grades required. SAT/ACT, home school portfolio, and letter of completion from primary teacher or program administrator with date of graduation required. GED scores and portfolio required of applicants with GED; SAT/ACT not required. COMPASS placement test may be required.

High school preparation. College-preparatory program recommended. 17 units required. Required and recommended units include English 4, mathematics 4, social studies 3, science 4 and foreign language 2.

2015-2016 Annual costs. Tuition/fees: $3,612; $12,092 out-of-state. Per-credit charge: $89 in-state; $344 out-of-state. Room/board: $7,542. Books/supplies: $1,400.

Financial aid. Need-based: Need-based aid available for part-time students. Work-study available nights, weekends and for part-time students. **Non-need-based:** Scholarships awarded for academics, leadership, state residency.

Application procedures. Admission: No deadline. $20 fee, may be waived for applicants with need. Admission notification on a rolling basis. **Financial aid:** Priority date 6/1; no closing date. FAFSA, institutional form required. Applicants notified on a rolling basis starting 6/1; must reply within 2 week(s) of notification.

Academics. Special study options: Distance learning, double major, dual enrollment of high school students, independent study, study abroad. Bachelor's degree programs available on campus. License preparation in nursing. **Credit/placement by examination:** AP, CLEP, IB, SAT, ACT, institutional tests. 30 credit hours maximum toward associate degree. **Support services:** Learning center, pre-admission summer program, reduced course load, remedial instruction, study skills assistance, tutoring, writing center.

Majors. Biology: General. **Business:** Business admin. **Communications:** General. **Computer sciences:** Computer science. **Education:** General, business, multi-level teacher. **English:** English lit. **Foreign languages:** Translation. **Health services:** Prenursing. **History:** General. **Liberal arts:** Arts/sciences. **Math:** General. **Parks/recreation:** General, exercise sciences, health/fitness. **Physical sciences:** Chemistry, geology. **Protective services:** Criminal justice. **Psychology:** General. **Social sciences:** Anthropology, criminology, political science, sociology. **Visual/performing arts:** Art. **Work/family studies:** General.

Most popular majors. Liberal arts 97%.

Technology on campus. 284 workstations in dormitories, library, computer center, student center. Dormitories wired for high-speed internet access and linked to campus network. Commuter students can connect to campus network. Online course registration, online library, helpline, wireless network available.

Student life. Freshman orientation: Mandatory, $25 fee. Preregistration for classes offered. Combined 1-day orientation and registration event. **Policies:** Substance-free campus. **Housing:** Coed dorms available. **Activities:** Campus ministries, choral groups, drama, international student organizations, literary magazine, musical theater, student government, student newspaper, Republican club, Democratic club, Afro-American union, Earth club, Students in Free Enterprise, Student Professional Association of Georgia Educators, art club, Circle K, non-traditional club, Geocachers, Baptist Collegiate Ministries.

Athletics. NJCAA. **Intercollegiate:** Baseball M, basketball, softball W. **Intramural:** Basketball, cheerleading, football (non-tackle), sand volleyball, softball, table tennis, tennis, volleyball. **Team name:** Bobcats.

Student services. Adult student services, alcohol/substance abuse counseling, career counseling, student employment services, financial aid counseling, health services, minority student services, personal counseling, veterans' counselor. **Physically disabled:** Services for visually, speech, hearing impaired. **Transfer:** Pre-admission transcript evaluation for new students. Transfer adviser, college fairs on campus for students transferring to 4-year colleges.

Contact. E-mail: admissions@ega.edu
Phone: (478) 289-2169 Fax: (478) 289-2353
Georgia Mathews, Director of Admissions, East Georgia State College, 131 College Circle, Swainsboro, GA 30401-2699

Georgia Highlands College
Rome, Georgia
www.highlands.edu

CB member
CB code: 5237

- Public 2-year community and liberal arts college
- Commuter campus in large town

General. Founded in 1968. Regionally accredited. Classes offered at Cartersville, Marietta, Paulding, Douglasville, and Rome. **Enrollment:** 5,748 degree-seeking undergraduates. **Degrees:** 23 bachelor's, 623 associate awarded. **Location:** 75 miles from Atlanta. **Calendar:** Semester, limited summer session. **Full-time faculty:** 123 total; 28% have terminal degrees, 10% minority, 57% women. **Part-time faculty:** 154 total; 14% have terminal degrees, 24% minority, 61% women. **Class size:** 30% < 20, 68% 20-39, less than 1% 40-49, less than 1% 50-99. **Special facilities:** Observatory, wetlands preserve, lake.

Student profile. Among degree-seeking undergraduates, 75% enrolled in a transfer program, 1% already have a bachelor's degree or higher, 1,378 enrolled as first-time, first-year students, 493 transferred in from other institutions.

Part-time:	53%	Asian American:	1%
Out-of-state:	1%	Hispanic/Latino:	11%
Women:	63%	Multi-racial, non-Hispanic:	3%
African American:	17%	25 or older:	24%

Transfer out. Colleges most students transferred to 2015: Kennesaw State University, University of West Georgia, Berry College, Shorter College, University of Georgia.

Basis for selection. 2.0 college prep GPA required. SAT/ACT required for nursing and dental hygiene programs. SAT or ACT recommended. SAT/ACT can be used to exempt COMPASS placement exams. **Home schooled:** Statement describing home school structure and mission, transcript of courses and grades, state high school equivalency certificate required. Must submit SAT that is equal to or greater than last year's freshman class average and provide completed home school college prep curriculum evaluation form; portfolio required. Interviews and letters of recommendations are required for students under 18 with GED. **Learning Disabled:** Foreign language college preparatory curriculum may be waived through Georgia Board of Regents Center of Learning Disabilities.

High school preparation. College-preparatory program recommended. 17 units recommended. Recommended units include English 4, mathematics 4, social studies 3, science 4 (laboratory 2) and foreign language 2. College preparatory program required for students planning to transfer to 4-year school.

2015-2016 Annual costs. Tuition/fees: $3,660; $12,188 out-of-state. Per-credit charge: $90.87 in-state; $344 out-of-state. Books/supplies: $1,200. Personal expenses: $550.

2014-2015 Financial aid. Need-based: 84% of total undergraduate aid awarded as scholarships/grants, 16% as loans/jobs. Need-based aid available for part-time students. Work-study available nights, weekends and for part-time students. **Non-need-based:** Scholarships awarded for academics, art. **Additional information:** All Federal Work Study students must be Pell eligible and taking a minimum of 6 credit hours.

Application procedures. Admission: Closing date 8/1 (receipt date). $30 fee. Admission notification on a rolling basis. **Financial aid:** Priority date 7/1, closing date 4/1. FAFSA required. Applicants notified on a rolling basis starting 4/1; must reply within 2 week(s) of notification.

Academics. Special study options: Accelerated study, combined bachelor's/graduate degree, cooperative education, distance learning, double major, dual enrollment of high school students, honors, independent study, liberal arts/career combination, study abroad, weekend college. Bachelor's degree programs available on campus. License preparation in dental hygiene, nursing. **Credit/placement by examination:** AP, CLEP, IB, SAT, ACT, institutional tests. No limit on credits awarded. **Support services:** Learning center, pre-admission summer program, remedial instruction, study skills assistance, tutoring, writing center.

Honors college/program. 3.5 GPA, 1100 SAT required.

Majors. Biology: General. **Business:** Managerial economics. **Communications:** Communications/speech/rhetoric, journalism. **Computer sciences:** General, information systems. **Education:** General. **Engineering:** Pre-engineering. **English:** English lit. **Foreign languages:** General. **Health services:** Clinical lab science, dental hygiene, health information management, nursing (RN), occupational therapy, physician assistant, prepharmacy, prephysical therapy, respiratory therapy technology. **History:** General. **Math:** General. **Philosophy/religion:** Philosophy. **Physical sciences:** Chemistry, geology, physics. **Protective services:** Police science. **Psychology:** General.

Social sciences: Economics, political science, sociology. **Visual/performing arts:** Art, music.

Most popular majors. Business/marketing 19%, education 11%, health sciences 30%, liberal arts 13%, psychology 10%.

Technology on campus. 1,100 workstations in library, computer center, student center. Commuter students can connect to campus network. Online course registration, online library, helpline, repair service, wireless network available.

Student life. Freshman orientation: Mandatory. Preregistration for classes offered. Held prior to each semester. **Housing:** Marietta campus housing available through Kennesaw State University. **Activities:** Pep band, literary magazine, music ensembles, student government, student newspaper, TV station, political science club, Brother 2 Brother, Equality Alliance, Green Highlands, Baptist student union, Phi Theta Kappa, Hispanic student association, Woman to Woman, Psi Beta, Alpha Beta Gamma.

Athletics. NJCAA. **Intercollegiate:** Baseball, basketball, softball. **Intramural:** Basketball, football (non-tackle), skiing, soccer, softball, table tennis, tennis, volleyball, weight lifting. **Team name:** Chargers.

Student services. Adult student services, alcohol/substance abuse counseling, career counseling, services for economically disadvantaged, student employment services, financial aid counseling, minority student services, personal counseling, placement for graduates, veterans' counselor. **Physically disabled:** Services for visually, speech, hearing impaired. **Transfer:** Re-entry adviser, pre-admission transcript evaluation for new students. College fairs on campus for students transferring to 4-year colleges.

Contact. E-mail: admitme@highlands.edu
Phone: (706) 295-6339 Toll-free number: (800) 332-2406 ext. 6339
Fax: (706) 295-6341
Sandie Davis, Director of Admissions, Georgia Highlands College, 3175 Cedartown Highway, Rome, GA 30161

Georgia Military College
Milledgeville, Georgia
www.gmc.edu

CB code: 5249

- Public 2-year community and military college
- Commuter campus in large town

General. Founded in 1879. Regionally accredited. Multiple locations: Augusta, Columbus, Dublin, Fairburn, Fayetteville, Madison, Milledgeville, Sandersville, Stone Mountain, Valdosta, Warner Robins, and Online. **Enrollment:** 6,840 degree-seeking undergraduates. **Degrees:** 1,472 associate awarded. **ROTC:** Army. **Location:** 90 miles from Atlanta, 30 miles from Macon. **Calendar:** Quarter, limited summer session. **Full-time faculty:** 111 total. **Part-time faculty:** 261 total. **Class size:** 51% < 20, 49% 20-39.

Student profile.

Out-of-state:	3%	Live on campus:	3%
25 or older:	32%		

Transfer out. Colleges most students transferred to 2015: Georgia College and State University, Macon State University, Georgia State University, Augusta State University, Valdosta State University.

Basis for selection. Open admission, but selective for some programs. ROTC applicants for early commissioning must have 920 SAT or 19 ACT and 2.0 GPA. Interview recommended for ROTC cadets. **Home schooled:** Transcript of courses and grades required. List of courses completed and bibliography of textbooks and/or assigned readings required. Must submit writing sample or show successful GED completion. **Learning Disabled:** Students with disabilities are encouraged to present documentation to the campus Disabilities Officer prior to enrollment.

2015-2016 Annual costs. Tuition/fees: $5,453; $5,453 out-of-state. Per-credit charge: $122. Books/supplies: $420. Personal expenses: $2,640.

Financial aid. Need-based: Need-based aid available for part-time students. Work-study available nights, weekends and for part-time students. **Non-need-based:** Scholarships awarded for athletics, leadership, ROTC, state residency. **Additional information:** Institutional aid offered to those enrolled in Cadet Corps who reside on campus.

Application procedures. Admission: No deadline. $35 fee, may be waived for applicants with need. Admission notification on a rolling basis. August 1 closing date for cadet applications. Students interested in attending ROTC Basic Camp must apply by May 1. **Financial aid:** No deadline. FAFSA required. Applicants notified on a rolling basis.

Academics. All academic courses contain an exercise on ethical reasoning to foster educated, contributing citizens. **Special study options:** Cross-registration, distance learning, double major, dual enrollment of high school students, external degree, independent study. **Credit/placement by examination:** AP, CLEP, IB, institutional tests. 45 credit hours maximum toward associate degree. **Support services:** Learning center, reduced course load, remedial instruction, study skills assistance, tutoring, writing center.

Majors. Biology: General. **Business:** General, logistics. **Communications:** Communications/speech/rhetoric, media studies. **Computer sciences:** Computer science, information technology, security. **Education:** Early childhood, health, middle, secondary. **English:** English lit. **Health services:** Prenursing. **History:** General. **Human services:** Social work. **Math:** General. **Protective services:** Homeland security, law enforcement admin. **Psychology:** General. **Social sciences:** Political science, sociology.

Most popular majors. Business/marketing 18%, education 9%, health sciences 17%, liberal arts 28%, security/protective services 8%.

Technology on campus. Dormitories wired for high-speed internet access and linked to campus network. Commuter students can connect to campus network. Online course registration, online library, wireless network available.

Student life. Freshman orientation: Available. Preregistration for classes offered. Two summer sessions, college athlete session, Early Commissioning session, State Service Scholarship sessions available. **Policies:** Resident programs are only available to members of the Corps of Cadets. **Housing:** $75 fully refundable deposit, deadline 9/1. Housing at the Milledgeville campus provided only for members of the Corps of Cadets. **Activities:** Marching band, choral groups, drama, literary magazine, music ensembles, student government, student newspaper, Circle-K, Phi Theta Kappa, Alpha Phi Omega, Ranger Challenge, drill team, drama club, officer Christians' fellowship, business club, math club, debate/speech organization.

Athletics. NJCAA. **Intercollegiate:** Cross-country, football (tackle) M, golf M, rifle, soccer, softball W. **Intramural:** Badminton, basketball, bowling, golf, softball, tennis, volleyball. **Team name:** Bulldogs.

Student services. Financial aid counseling, health services, veterans' counselor. **Physically disabled:** Services for visually, speech, hearing impaired. **Transfer:** College fairs on campus for students transferring to 4-year colleges.

Contact. E-mail: admissionsinfo@gmc.edu
Phone: (478) 387-4953 Toll-free number: (800) 342-0413
Fax: (478) 445-6520
Jody Yearwood, Vice President for Enrollment Management, Georgia Military College, 201 East Greene Street, Milledgeville, GA 31061

Georgia Northwestern Technical College
Rome, Georgia
www.gntc.edu

▶ Public 2-year technical college
▶ Commuter campus in large town

General. Regionally accredited. GNTC offers 5 campuses within a 9 county service area in Northwest Georgia. The main campus is located in Rome, Georgia. **Enrollment:** 5,876 degree-seeking undergraduates. **Degrees:** 629 associate awarded. **Location:** 70 miles from Atlanta. **Calendar:** Semester, extensive summer session. **Full-time faculty:** 123 total. **Part-time faculty:** 296 total.

Student profile. Among degree-seeking undergraduates, 100% enrolled in a vocational program, 1% already have a bachelor's degree or higher.

Out-of-state:	1%	Hispanic/Latino:	12%
African American:	8%	Multi-racial, non-Hispanic:	2%
Asian American:	1%	25 or older:	35%

Basis for selection. Open admission, but selective for some programs. COMPASS placement test or official transcripts showing satisfactory completion of appropriate English and math courses with 2.0 GPA required of applicants without SAT/ACT or ASSET. Under certain conditions, prior scores on the ACT or SAT may be accepted in lieu of COMPASS or ASSET test for placement. **Adult students:** SAT/ACT scores not required if applicant over 16. **Home schooled:** Transcript of courses and grades required.

High school preparation. College-preparatory program recommended. 22 units recommended. Recommended units include English 4, mathematics 3, social studies 3, science 3, foreign language 1 and academic electives 3.

2015-2016 Annual costs. Tuition/fees: $3,218; $5,888 out-of-state. Per-credit charge: $89 in-state; $178 out-of-state. Books/supplies: $1,000.

Financial aid. Need-based: Work-study available nights, weekends and for part-time students.

Application procedures. Admission: No deadline. $20 fee. Admission notification on a rolling basis. **Financial aid:** Closing date 9/1.

Academics. Special study options: Distance learning, double major, dual enrollment of high school students, internships. License preparation in aviation, nursing, occupational therapy, paramedic, radiology. **Credit/placement by examination:** AP, CLEP, institutional tests. **Support services:** GED preparation and test center, remedial instruction, study skills assistance, tutoring, writing center.

Majors. Business: Marketing. **Health services:** Management/clinical assistant. **Protective services:** Law enforcement admin.

Most popular majors. Business/marketing 22%, computer/information sciences 12%, education 10%, health sciences 35%, security/protective services 7%, trade and industry 10%.

Technology on campus. 500 workstations in library, computer center, student center. Commuter students can connect to campus network. Online course registration, online library, wireless network available.

Student life. Freshman orientation: Mandatory. Preregistration for classes offered. Online orientation required for all students. **Activities:** Student government.

Athletics. NJCAA. **Intercollegiate:** Basketball, cheerleading, golf M. **Intramural:** Bowling, football (non-tackle) M, golf M, softball, volleyball. **Team name:** Bobcats.

Student services. Alcohol/substance abuse counseling, career counseling, services for economically disadvantaged, student employment services, financial aid counseling, personal counseling, placement for graduates, veterans' counselor. **Physically disabled:** Services for hearing impaired.

Contact. E-mail: dhopper@gntc.edu
Phone: (706) 295-6933 Toll-free number: (866) 983-4682
Donna Hopper, Admissions Coordinator, Georgia Northwestern Technical College, One Maurice Culberson Drive, Rome, GA 30161

Georgia Perimeter College
Clarkston, Georgia
www.gpc.edu
CB member
CB code: 5711

▶ Public 2-year junior and liberal arts college
▶ Commuter campus in very large city

General. Founded in 1964. Regionally accredited. Additional campuses in Alpharetta, Clarkston, Dunwoody, Decatur, and Newton. Online course/program offerings also available. **Enrollment:** 18,678 degree-seeking undergraduates; 2,410 non-degree-seeking students. **Degrees:** 1,827 associate awarded. **Calendar:** Semester, extensive summer session. **Full-time faculty:** 433 total; 40% have terminal degrees, 28% minority, 58% women. **Part-time faculty:** 504 total; 27% have terminal degrees, 38% minority, 58% women. **Class size:** 33% < 20, 66% 20-39, less than 1% 40-49, less than 1% 50-99, less than 1% >100. **Special facilities:** Botanical gardens, observatory.

Student profile. Among degree-seeking undergraduates, 3,312 enrolled as first-time, first-year students, 1,137 transferred in from other institutions.

Part-time:	62%	Hispanic/Latino:	9%
Out-of-state:	4%	Multi-racial, non-Hispanic:	4%
Women:	59%	International:	6%
African American:	45%	25 or older:	33%
Asian American:	9%		

Transfer out. Colleges most students transferred to 2015: Georgia State University, University of Georgia.

Basis for selection. Any college preparatory curriculum deficiencies must be satisfied by placement testing or substituting college coursework. Admission to nursing program is competitive; GPA in general education and biology, TEAS scores most important. SAT or ACT recommended. SAT/ACT required for dual enrollment. Interview required for top 50 dental hygiene applicants. **Home schooled:** Transcript of courses and grades required. Detailed portfolio and SAT/ACT required.

High school preparation. College-preparatory program recommended. 16 units required. Required units include English 4, mathematics 4, social studies 3, science 4 (laboratory 4) and foreign language 2.

2015-2016 Annual costs. Tuition/fees: $3,758; $11,352 out-of-state. Per-credit charge: $91 in-state; $344 out-of-state. Books/supplies: $1,400. Personal expenses: $1,200.

2014-2015 Financial aid. Need-based: 1,686 full-time freshmen applied for aid; 1,543 deemed to have need; 1,543 received aid. Average need met was 52%. Average scholarship/grant was $4,587; average loan $2,996. 66% of total undergraduate aid awarded as scholarships/grants, 34% as loans/jobs. Need-based aid available for part-time students. Work-study available nights, weekends and for part-time students. **Non-need-based:** Awarded to 1,689 full-time undergraduates, including 635 freshmen. Scholarships awarded for academics, alumni affiliation, art, athletics, job skills, leadership, minority status, music/drama, religious affiliation, ROTC, state residency.

Application procedures. Admission: Closing date 7/1 (postmark date). $20 fee, may be waived for applicants with need. Admission notification on a rolling basis. **Financial aid:** Closing date 6/1. FAFSA required. Applicants notified on a rolling basis; must reply within 3 week(s) of notification.

Academics. Special study options: Accelerated study, distance learning, dual enrollment of high school students, ESL, honors, independent study, liberal arts/career combination, study abroad, weekend college. License preparation in dental hygiene, nursing. **Credit/placement by examination:** AP, CLEP, IB, SAT, ACT, institutional tests. 21 credit hours maximum toward associate degree. **Support services:** Learning center, remedial instruction, study skills assistance, tutoring, writing center.

Majors. Biology: General. **Business:** Business admin. **Communications:** Communications/speech/rhetoric, journalism. **Computer sciences:** Computer science. **Education:** General, health, physical. **Engineering:** General. **English:** English lit. **Foreign languages:** General, sign language interpretation. **Health services:** Dental hygiene, nursing (RN), predental, premedicine, prepharmacy. **History:** General. **Liberal arts:** Library assistant. **Math:** General. **Philosophy/religion:** Philosophy. **Physical sciences:** Chemistry, geology, physics. **Protective services:** Homeland security, law enforcement admin. **Psychology:** General. **Social sciences:** Anthropology, political science, sociology. **Visual/performing arts:** Art, dramatic, film/cinema/video, music.

Most popular majors. Business/marketing 33%, education 6%, health sciences 21%, liberal arts 6%, psychology 8%.

Technology on campus. Commuter students can connect to campus network. Online course registration, online library, helpline, wireless network available.

Student life. Freshman orientation: Mandatory, $15 fee. Preregistration for classes offered. 2.5 hour orientations begin one month prior to beginning of term. **Activities:** Bands, choral groups, drama, international student organizations, literary magazine, music ensembles, Model UN, musical theater, student government, student newspaper, symphony orchestra.

Athletics. NJCAA. **Intercollegiate:** Baseball M, basketball, soccer, softball W, tennis. **Team name:** Jaguars.

Student services. Adult student services, career counseling, services for economically disadvantaged, financial aid counseling, minority student services, personal counseling, veterans' counselor. **Physically disabled:** Services for visually, hearing impaired. **Transfer:** Transfer adviser, college fairs on campus for students transferring to 4-year colleges.

Contact. E-mail: gpcrec@gpc.edu
Phone: (404) 631-6585 Toll-free number: (888) 696-2780
Fax: (678) 891-3211
Richard Beaubien, Director of Recruitment & Admissions, Georgia Perimeter College, 555 North Indian Creek Drive, Clarkston, GA 30021-2361

Transfer out. Colleges most students transferred to 2015: Georgia State University, Southern Polytechnic State University, DeVry University, Clayton College and State University, Georgia Perimeter College.

Basis for selection. Open admission, but selective for some programs. Limited admission to health technologies programs. Under certain conditions, ACT or SAT may be accepted in lieu of COMPASS or ASSET for placement. Interview recommended.

High school preparation. College-preparatory program recommended. 22 units recommended. Recommended units include English 4, mathematics 3, social studies 3, science 3, foreign language 1 and academic electives 3. 4 tech prep and 1 health science recommended.

2015-2016 Annual costs. Tuition/fees: $3,374; $6,044 out-of-state. Per-credit charge: $89 in-state; $178 out-of-state. Books/supplies: $1,200. Personal expenses: $900.

Financial aid. Need-based: Need-based aid available for part-time students. Work-study available nights, weekends and for part-time students. **Non-need-based:** Scholarships awarded for academics, minority status.

Application procedures. Admission: Closing date 8/22 (receipt date). $25 fee. Admission notification on a rolling basis. **Financial aid:** Closing date 8/20. FAFSA required. Applicants notified on a rolling basis.

Academics. Special study options: Distance learning, dual enrollment of high school students, ESL, internships, weekend college. License preparation in nursing, paramedic, real estate. **Credit/placement by examination:** AP, CLEP, institutional tests. 35 credit hours maximum toward associate degree. **Support services:** GED preparation and test center, learning center, reduced course load, remedial instruction, study skills assistance, tutoring.

Majors. Business: Accounting technology, administrative services, banking/financial services, business admin, human resources, marketing. **Computer sciences:** General, networking, programming, support specialist, system admin. **Education:** Early childhood. **Engineering:** Computer, electrical. **Health services:** Clinical lab technology, ophthalmic lab technology. **Protective services:** Criminal justice.

Most popular majors. Business/marketing 31%, computer/information sciences 11%, education 15%, security/protective services 12%, trade and industry 19%.

Technology on campus. 500 workstations in computer center. Online course registration, online library, helpline, repair service, wireless network available.

Student life. Freshman orientation: Mandatory. Preregistration for classes offered. **Activities:** Student government, student newspaper, Delta Epsilon Chi, Collegiate Secretaries International, Noon Net-Working of New Connections, Phi Beta Lambda, Student Optical Society, Licensed Practical Nurses Association, Vocational Industrial Clubs of America, Epsilon Delta Phi Honorary Society, Phi Theta Kappa Honor Society.

Student services. Adult student services, career counseling, services for economically disadvantaged, student employment services, financial aid counseling, minority student services, placement for graduates, veterans' counselor, women's services. **Physically disabled:** Services for visually, speech, hearing impaired. **Transfer:** Pre-admission transcript evaluation for new students.

Contact. E-mail: parkerc@gptc.edu
Phone: (404) 297-9522 ext. 1602
Corey Parker, Director, Admissions and Records, Georgia Piedmont Technical College, 495 North Indian Creek Drive, Clarkston, GA 30021-2397

Georgia Piedmont Technical College
Clarkston, Georgia
www.gptc.edu
CB code: 3226

▸ Public 2-year technical college
▸ Commuter campus in large city

General. Founded in 1961. Regionally accredited. Additional campus located in Covington. **Enrollment:** 4,050 degree-seeking undergraduates. **Degrees:** 365 associate awarded. **Location:** 12 miles from Atlanta. **Calendar:** Semester, extensive summer session. **Full-time faculty:** 76 total; 54% minority, 55% women. **Part-time faculty:** 237 total; 67% minority, 58% women. **Class size:** 77% < 20, 22% 20-39, less than 1% 40-49, less than 1% 50-99. **Partnerships:** Formal partnerships with MARTA; Fulton County Government; DeKalb, Rockdale, Newton, Morgan County, Decatur City Schools.

Gordon State College
Barnesville, Georgia
www.gordonstate.edu
CB code: 5256

▸ Public 2-year liberal arts college
▸ Commuter campus in small town

General. Founded in 1852. Regionally accredited. **Enrollment:** 4,084 degree-seeking undergraduates. **Degrees:** 148 bachelor's, 395 associate awarded. **Location:** 60 miles from Atlanta. **Calendar:** Semester, limited summer session. **Full-time faculty:** 120 total; 68% have terminal degrees, 22% minority, 49% women. **Part-time faculty:** 83 total; 19% have terminal degrees, 20% minority, 64% women. **Class size:** 23% < 20, 73% 20-39, 2% 40-49, 3% 50-99. **Special facilities:** Georgia book collection, performance theater, indoor pool, ropes course, walking trail, amphitheatre.

Student profile.

Out-of-state:	1%	**Live on campus:**	24%
25 or older:	19%		

Transfer out. Colleges most students transferred to 2015: Clayton State University, Georgia State University, Griffin Technical College, University of Georgia, University of West Georgia.

Basis for selection. Test scores and GPA considered. Additional requirements for associate degree in nursing and bachelor's of science in education. SAT or ACT, SAT Subject Tests recommended. Interview required for nursing program. Applicants may be asked to interview for admission to B.S. in Education program. **Adult students:** COMPASS placement test used if applicant presents SAT/ACT scores lower than minimum required or if applicant lacks scores. **Home schooled:** Statement describing home school structure and mission required. Portfolio demonstrating completion of college prep curriculum required. Include the following for each course: course descriptions, list of assignments, work samples and grades, and list of educational resources (textbooks and other materials).

High school preparation. College-preparatory program recommended. 16 units recommended. Recommended units include English 4, mathematics 4, social studies 3, science 3 (laboratory 2) and foreign language 2. Foreign language units must be in same language.

2015-2016 Annual costs. Tuition/fees: $4,164; $12,422 out-of-state. Per-credit charge: $103 in-state; $378 out-of-state. Room/board: $6,210. Books/supplies: $1,336. Personal expenses: $7,406.

2014-2015 Financial aid. Need-based: Need-based aid available for part-time students. Work-study available nights, weekends and for part-time students. **Non-need-based:** Scholarships awarded for academics, athletics, music/drama, state residency.

Application procedures. Admission: No deadline. $30 fee. Admission notification on a rolling basis. **Financial aid:** Priority date 5/1, closing date 6/1. FAFSA required. Applicants notified on a rolling basis starting 4/1.

Academics. Special study options: Distance-learning, dual enrollment of high school students, ESL, honors, liberal arts/career combination, study abroad, teacher certification program, weekend college. Bachelor's degree programs available on campus. License preparation in nursing. **Credit/placement by examination:** AP, CLEP, IB, SAT, ACT, institutional tests. 42 credit hours maximum toward associate degree. **Support services:** Tutoring, writing center.

Majors. Biology: General. **Business:** Business admin. **Communications:** Communications/speech/rhetoric. **Computer sciences:** Computer science, information systems. **Conservation:** Environmental science, forestry. **Education:** Multi-level teacher. **Engineering:** Pre-engineering. **English:** English lit. **Foreign languages:** General. **Health services:** Dental hygiene, health information management, nursing (RN), physician assistant, preoccupational therapy, prepharmacy, prephysical therapy, radiologic technology/medical imaging, respiratory therapy assistant. **History:** General. **Human services:** Social work. **Math:** General. **Parks/recreation:** Health/fitness. **Physical sciences:** Astronomy, chemistry, physics. **Protective services:** Criminal justice. **Psychology:** General. **Social sciences:** Political science, sociology. **Visual/performing arts:** Art, dramatic, music.

Most popular majors. Health sciences 20%, liberal arts 80%.

Technology on campus. 242 workstations in dormitories, library, computer center, student center. Dormitories wired for high-speed internet access and linked to campus network. Commuter students can connect to campus network. Online course registration, online library, student web hosting, wireless network available.

Student life. Freshman orientation: Mandatory. Preregistration for classes offered. Approximately 5-6 hours in length; held twice prior to start of semester, for students and parents. **Housing:** Coed dorms, single-sex dorms, apartments, themed housing, wellness housing available. $250 partly refundable deposit, deadline 7/1. **Activities:** Bands, campus ministries, choral groups, dance, drama, international student organizations, literary magazine, music ensembles, musical theater, student government, student newspaper, Baptist Collegiate Ministries, Gordon Christian Fellowship, Association of Nursing Students, art club, education association, Driftwood literary club, Phi Theta Kappa (honor society), science club, history club.

Athletics. NJCAA. **Intercollegiate:** Baseball M, basketball M, cheerleading W, cross-country, soccer W, softball W. **Intramural:** Basketball M, football (non-tackle), soccer W, softball W, table tennis, tennis. **Team name:** Highlanders.

Student services. Alcohol/substance abuse counseling, career counseling, student employment services, financial aid counseling, health services, minority student services, personal counseling, veterans' counselor. **Physically**

disabled: Services for visually, speech, hearing impaired. **Transfer:** College fairs on campus for students transferring to 4-year colleges.

Contact. E-mail: admissions@gordonstate.edu
Phone: (678) 359-5021 Toll-free number: (800) 282-6504
Fax: (678) 359-5080
Ben Ferguson, Director of Admissions, Gordon State College, 419 College Drive, Barnesville, GA 30204

Gupton Jones College of Funeral Service
Decatur, Georgia
www.gupton-jones.edu   CB code: 6200

- Private 2-year technical college
- Commuter campus in very large city

General. Founded in 1920. Accredited by American Board of Funeral Service Education. **Enrollment:** 212 undergraduates. **Degrees:** 98 associate awarded. **Location:** 18 miles from Atlanta. **Calendar:** Quarter. **Full-time faculty:** 7 total; 29% women.

Student profile.

Out-of-state:	65%	**25 or older:**	50%

Basis for selection. Open admission.

2015-2016 Annual costs. Tuition/fees: $11,100. Per-credit charge: $250. Personal expenses: $600. **Additional information:** Books are included in tuition.

Financial aid. All financial aid based on need. Need-based aid available for part-time students. Work-study available nights, weekends and for part-time students.

Application procedures. Admission: No deadline. $50 fee. Admission notification on a rolling basis. **Financial aid:** No deadline. FAFSA required. Applicants notified on a rolling basis.

Academics. Special study options: Distance learning. Distance learning for General Studies courses only. **Credit/placement by examination:** AP, CLEP.

Technology on campus. 23 workstations in library, computer center.

Student life. Freshman orientation: Mandatory. Preregistration for classes offered.

Student services. Career counseling, personal counseling, placement for graduates.

Contact. E-mail: fsmith@gupton-jones.edu
Phone: (770) 593-2257 Fax: (770) 593-1891
Patty Hutcheson, President, Gupton Jones College of Funeral Service, 5141 Snapfinger Woods Drive, Decatur, GA 30035

Gwinnett College
Lilburn, Georgia
www.gwinnettcollege.edu

- For-profit 2-year junior and career college
- Commuter campus in large city

General. Accredited by ACICS. Additional locations in Sandy Springs, Georgia; Sarasota, Florida; Raleigh, North Carolina. **Enrollment:** 352 degree-seeking undergraduates. **Degrees:** 65 associate awarded. **Location:** 20 miles from Atlanta. **Calendar:** Quarter, extensive summer session. **Full-time faculty:** 8 total. **Part-time faculty:** 35 total.

Transfer out. Colleges most students transferred to 2015: DeVry University, Argosy University, University of Phoenix, Colorado Tech Online, Strayer University.

Basis for selection. Open admission, but selective for some programs. Aptitude testing required for some programs. **Home schooled:** Transcript of courses and grades required.

High school preparation. College-preparatory program recommended.

2015-2016 Annual costs. Tuition/fees: $9,850. Books/supplies: $900. Personal expenses: $220.

Financial aid. Need-based: Need-based aid available for part-time students. Work-study available nights, weekends and for part-time students.

Application procedures. Admission: No deadline. No application fee. Application must be submitted on paper. **Financial aid:** No deadline. FAFSA required. Applicants notified on a rolling basis.

Academics. Special study options: Double major, internships. **Credit/placement by examination:** AP, CLEP. **Support services:** Reduced course load.

Majors. Business: Business admin. **Computer sciences:** Information technology. **Health services:** Medical assistant, medical secretary.

Technology on campus. PC or laptop required. 100 workstations in library, computer center. Wireless network available.

Student services. Adult student services, financial aid counseling, placement for graduates. **Transfer:** Re-entry adviser, pre-admission transcript evaluation for new students.

Contact. E-mail: admissions@gwinnettcollege.edu
Phone: (770) 381-7200 Fax: (770) 381-0454
Lee Cates, Director of Admissions, Gwinnett College, 4230 Highway 29, Lilburn, GA 30047

Gwinnett Technical College
Lawrenceville, Georgia
www.gwinnetttech.edu

CB member
CB code: 5168

- Public 2-year technical college
- Commuter campus in large town

General. Founded in 1984. Regionally accredited. **Enrollment:** 7,234 degree-seeking undergraduates. **Degrees:** 589 associate awarded. **Calendar:** Semester. **Full-time faculty:** 104 total. **Part-time faculty:** 249 total.

Basis for selection. Open admission, but selective for some programs. Admission to some programs, primarily in health sciences, based on a combination of factors that may include required college courses (prerequisites), placement examination scores, interviews, essays, and grade point average. In addition, these programs may have file completion deadlines. Under certain circumstances, ACT or SAT may be accepted in lieu of COMPASS or ASSET for placement.

High school preparation. College-preparatory program recommended. 22 units recommended. Recommended units include English 4, mathematics 3, social studies 3, science 3 and foreign language 1. 4 units tech prep, 1 unit health science recommended.

2015-2016 Annual costs. Tuition/fees: $3,238; $5,908 out-of-state. Per-credit charge: $89 in-state; $178 out-of-state.

Financial aid. Need-based: Need-based aid available for part-time students. Work-study available nights, weekends and for part-time students.

Application procedures. Admission: Closing date 6/3 (receipt date). $20 fee, may be waived for applicants with need. Admission notification on a rolling basis. **Financial aid:** Closing date 7/8. FAFSA required.

Academics. Special study options: Distance learning, double major, dual enrollment of high school students, internships, weekend college. License preparation in dental hygiene, nursing, paramedic, radiology. **Credit/placement by examination:** AP, CLEP. **Support services:** GED preparation and test center, learning center, remedial instruction, study skills assistance, tutoring, writing center.

Majors. Business: Accounting technology, administrative services, business admin, construction management, hospitality admin, marketing, sales/distribution. **Computer sciences:** Networking, programming, security, system admin, web page design. **Education:** Early childhood. **Health services:** Cardiovascular technology, EMT paramedic, health information technology, licensed practical nurse, nursing (RN), radiologic technology/medical imaging, respiratory therapy technology, sonography, veterinary technology/assistant. **Parks/recreation:** Facilities management. **Protective services:** Criminal justice, fire services admin. **Visual/performing arts:** Commercial photography, interior design.

Most popular majors. Business/marketing 27%, computer/information sciences 19%, education 6%, health sciences 17%, personal/culinary services 7%, security/protective services 6%, trade and industry 6%.

Student life. Activities: Student government, student newspaper.

Contact. E-mail: admissions@gwinnetttech.edu
Phone: (678) 762-7580 ext. 434
Gwinnett Technical College, 5150 Sugarloaf Parkway, Lawrenceville, GA 30043-5702

ITT Technical Institute: Kennesaw
Kennesaw, Georgia
www.itt-tech.edu

- For-profit 2-year business and technical college
- Large town

General. Accredited by ACICS. **Enrollment:** 351 undergraduates. **Degrees:** 21 bachelor's, 110 associate awarded. **Calendar:** Quarter. **Full-time faculty:** 9 total. **Part-time faculty:** 33 total.

Basis for selection. Admission requirements will vary by program.

2015-2016 Annual costs. Per-credit-hour charge, $493, will vary depending on program level and course of study. Academic fee, $300. Some programs require purchase of tools, which could cost an additional $100 to $500. All costs subject to change.

Financial aid. Need-based: Work-study available nights, weekends and for part-time students.

Academics. Credit/placement by examination: AP, CLEP.

Majors. Computer sciences: Information technology, networking, web page design. **Protective services:** Law enforcement admin. **Visual/performing arts:** Design, game design.

Contact. Toll-free number: (877) 231-6415
ITT Technical Institute: Kennesaw, 2065 ITT Tech Way NW, Kennesaw, GA 30144

Le Cordon Bleu College of Culinary Arts: Atlanta
Tucker, Georgia
www.chefs.edu/Atlanta

- For-profit 2-year branch campus and technical college
- Commuter campus in very large city
- Interview required

General. Regionally accredited; also accredited by ACCSC. **Enrollment:** 1,108 undergraduates. **Degrees:** 299 associate awarded. **Location:** 10 miles from Atlanta. **Calendar:** Differs by program. **Full-time faculty:** 38 total. **Part-time faculty:** 2 total.

Basis for selection. Open admission. Documentation of high school graduation or GED only requirement.

2015-2016 Annual costs. Certificate programs: $19,500; Associate degree programs: $40,000. Costs include books and supplies.

Financial aid. Need-based: Work-study available nights, weekends and for part-time students.

Application procedures. Admission: No deadline. $50 fee. Application must be submitted on paper. Admission notification on a rolling basis.

Academics. Credit/placement by examination: AP, CLEP. **Support services:** Study skills assistance, tutoring.

Technology on campus. Online library available.

Student life. Freshman orientation: Mandatory. Preregistration for classes offered.

Student services. Adult student services, career counseling, student employment services, financial aid counseling, placement for graduates. **Transfer:** Re-entry adviser for new students.

Contact. Phone: (770) 938-4711 Toll-free number: (866) 315-2433 Fax: (773) 938-4571
Terri Holte, Vice President of Admissions, Le Cordon Bleu College of Culinary Arts: Atlanta, 1927 Lakeside Parkway, Tucker, GA 30084

North Georgia Technical College
Clarkesville, Georgia
www.northgatech.edu
CB code: 5507

- Public 2-year community and technical college
- Commuter campus in small town

General. Regionally accredited. **Enrollment:** 2,414 degree-seeking undergraduates; 249 non-degree-seeking students. **Degrees:** 183 associate awarded. **Location:** 75 miles from Atlanta. **Calendar:** Semester, extensive summer session. **Full-time faculty:** 61 total; 5% have terminal degrees, 7% minority, 52% women. **Part-time faculty:** 79 total; 5% have terminal degrees, 1% minority, 52% women. **Class size:** 60% < 20, 39% 20-39, less than 1% 40-49, less than 1% 50-99.

Student profile. Among degree-seeking undergraduates, 629 enrolled as first-time, first-year students.

Part-time:	61%	25 or older:	50%
Out-of-state:	2%	Live on campus:	9%
Women:	58%		

Basis for selection. Open admission, but selective for some programs. Additional requirement for some allied health programs. Under certain conditions, ACT/SAT may be accepted in lieu of COMPASS or ASSET for placement. **Home schooled:** Statement describing home school structure and mission, transcript of courses and grades required. **Learning Disabled:** Documentation of IEP required.

High school preparation. College-preparatory program recommended. 22 units recommended. Recommended units include English 4, mathematics 3, social studies 3, history 2, science 3, foreign language 1 and academic electives 3.

2015-2016 Annual costs. Tuition/fees: $3,218; $5,888 out-of-state. Per-credit charge: $89 in-state; $178 out-of-state. Room/board: $4,000. Books/supplies: $825. Personal expenses: $3,628.

2014-2015 Financial aid. **Need-based:** 64% of total undergraduate aid awarded as scholarships/grants, 36% as loans/jobs. Need-based aid available for part-time students. Work-study available nights, weekends and for part-time students.

Application procedures. **Admission:** Closing date 12/1 (receipt date). $20 fee. Admission notification on a rolling basis. **Financial aid:** No deadline. FAFSA required. Applicants notified on a rolling basis.

Academics. **Special study options:** Distance learning, dual enrollment of high school students. License preparation in nursing, paramedic. **Credit/placement by examination:** AP, CLEP, institutional tests. **Support services:** GED preparation and test center, learning center, remedial instruction, tutoring.

Majors. **Business:** Accounting, business admin, office technology. **Computer sciences:** Networking. **Conservation:** Environmental science. **Health services:** Clinical lab technology, EMT paramedic, medical assistant, pharmacy assistant. **Protective services:** Law enforcement admin. **Visual/performing arts:** Commercial photography.

Most popular majors. Business/marketing 37%, computer/information sciences 15%, health sciences 11%, security/protective services 14%, trade and industry 6%, visual/performing arts 6%.

Technology on campus. 1,169 workstations in library, computer center, student center. Dormitories wired for high-speed internet access and linked to campus network. Commuter students can connect to campus network. Online course registration, online library, wireless network available.

Student life. **Freshman orientation:** Mandatory. Preregistration for classes offered. **Housing:** Coed dorms available.

Athletics. NJCAA. **Intercollegiate:** Cross-country. **Intramural:** Basketball, football (tackle), softball. **Team name:** Wolves.

Student services. Career counseling, services for economically disadvantaged, financial aid counseling, placement for graduates. **Physically disabled:** Services for visually, speech, hearing impaired.

Contact. E-mail: admissions@northgatech.edu
Phone: (706) 754-7725 Fax: (706) 754-7777
Michele Shirley, Director of Admissions, North Georgia Technical College, 1500 Highway 197 North, Clarkesville, GA 30523

Oxford College of Emory University
Oxford, Georgia
CB member
www.oxford.emory.edu
CB code: 5186

- Private 2-year branch campus and liberal arts college affiliated with the United Methodist Church
- Residential campus in large town
- SAT or ACT with writing, application essay required

General. Founded in 1836. Regionally accredited. One of nine schools within Emory University. Students continue to Emory College of Arts & Sciences or School of Nursing after freshman and sophomore years to complete their bachelor's degree. Selective continuation to Emory School of Business. **Enrollment:** 935 degree-seeking undergraduates; 1 non-degree-seeking students. **Degrees:** 465 associate awarded. **ROTC:** Army, Naval, Air Force. **Location:** 38 miles from Atlanta. **Calendar:** Semester, extensive summer session. **Full-time faculty:** 50 total; 22% minority, 72% women. **Part-time faculty:** 21 total; 52% have terminal degrees, 14% minority, 67% women. **Class size:** 50% < 20, 49% 20-39, less than 1% 40-49, less than 1% 50-99. **Special facilities:** Center for international studies, two hospitals, regional primate center, Center for Disease Control, museum, park, ethics center.

Student profile. Among degree-seeking undergraduates, 485 enrolled as first-time, first-year students.

Out-of-state:	75%	Hispanic/Latino:	7%
Women:	57%	Multi-racial, non-Hispanic:	4%
African American:	8%	International:	16%
Asian American:	27%	Live on campus:	99%

Basis for selection. GED not accepted. GPA, high school curriculum and transcript most important, standardized test scores, letters of recommendation, extracurricular activities, and essays also important. Demonstrated interest also considered. **Adult students:** SAT/ACT scores not required if out of high school 5 year(s) or more. **Home schooled:** Transcript of courses and grades, state high school equivalency certificate required. 3 SAT Subject Tests, including math, required.

High school preparation. College-preparatory program recommended. 22 units recommended. Recommended units include English 4, mathematics 4, social studies 3, science 3 (laboratory 3) and foreign language 2. Math units should include geometry and algebra II.

2016-2017 Annual costs. Tuition/fees (projected): $43,254. Per-credit charge: $1,775. Room/board: $12,006. Books/supplies: $1,224. Personal expenses: $1,486.

Financial aid. **Need-based:** Need-based aid available for part-time students. Work-study available nights, weekends and for part-time students. **Non-need-based:** Scholarships awarded for academics, leadership, religious affiliation, state residency. **Additional information:** Loan reduction program for families with annual assessed incomes of $100,000 or less who demonstrate need.

Application procedures. **Admission:** Closing date 1/1 (postmark date). $75 fee, may be waived for applicants with need. Application must be submitted online. Admission notification by 4/1. Must reply by May 1 or within 3 week(s) if notified thereafter. 11/15 deadline for academic scholarship program. **Financial aid:** Priority date 2/15, closing date 3/1. FAFSA, CSS PROFILE required. Applicants notified on a rolling basis starting 4/1; must reply by 5/1.

Academics. **Special study options:** Dual enrollment of high school students, ESL, honors, independent study, internships, study abroad. **Credit/placement by examination:** AP, CLEP, IB, institutional tests. 16 credit hours maximum toward associate degree. **Support services:** Reduced course load, study skills assistance, tutoring, writing center. All academic services that are conducted outside of the classroom are provided by students.

Majors. **Liberal arts:** Arts/sciences.

Technology on campus. 80 workstations in dormitories, library, computer center, student center. Dormitories wired for high-speed internet access and linked to campus network. Commuter students can connect to campus network. Online course registration, online library, helpline, repair service, student web hosting, wireless network available.

Student life. **Freshman orientation:** Mandatory, $100 fee. Preregistration for classes offered. Six-day orientation program held directly prior to start of school year. **Policies:** Dry campus since all students are under 21. Students required to live on campus both years. All residence halls co-ed by floor or wing. **Housing:** Guaranteed on-campus for all undergraduates. Coed dorms, single-sex dorms, special housing for disabled available. $75 nonrefundable deposit, deadline 5/1. **Activities:** Campus ministries, choral groups, dance, drama, international student organizations, literary magazine, music ensembles, student government, student newspaper, volunteer club, Christian Fellowship, College Republicans, Circle K, Jewish student union, Catholic student union, Muslim student association, Young Democrats, Hindu student council.

Athletics. NJCAA. **Intercollegiate:** Basketball M, soccer W, tennis. **Intramural:** Badminton, basketball, football (non-tackle), golf, table tennis, volleyball. **Team name:** Eagles.

Student services. Alcohol/substance abuse counseling, chaplain/spiritual director, career counseling, financial aid counseling, health services, minority student services, personal counseling, placement for graduates. **Physically disabled:** Services for visually, speech, hearing impaired.

Contact. E-mail: oxadmission@emory.edu
Phone: (770) 784-8328 Toll-free number: (800) 723-8328
Fax: (770) 784-8359
Kelley Lips, Dean of Enrollment Services, Oxford College of Emory University, 122 Few Circle, Oxford, GA 30054-1418

Savannah Technical College
Savannah, Georgia
www.savannahtech.edu   CB code: 3741

- Public 2-year technical college
- Commuter campus in large city

General. Regionally accredited. Classes offered at satellite campuses in Liberty and Effingham Counties. **Enrollment:** 4,784 degree-seeking undergraduates. **Degrees:** 275 associate awarded. **Location:** 250 miles from Atlanta. **Calendar:** Semester, extensive summer session. **Full-time faculty:** 87 total. **Part-time faculty:** 224 total. **Class size:** 100% < 20, 50% 20-39.

Transfer out. Colleges most students transferred to 2015: Savannah State University, Armstrong Atlantic State University.

Basis for selection. Open admission, but selective for some programs. Competitive admissions for allied health programs. Under certain conditions, ACT or SAT may be accepted in lieu of COMPASS or ASSET for placement. **Learning Disabled:** Must meet with disability coordinator.

High school preparation. 22 units recommended. Recommended units include English 4, mathematics 3, social studies 3, science 3, foreign language 1 and academic electives 3. 4 tech prep and 1 science recommended.

2015-2016 Annual costs. Tuition/fees: $3,188; $5,858 out-of-state. Per-credit charge: $89 in-state; $178 out-of-state. Books/supplies: $1,500.

Financial aid. Need-based: Need-based aid available for part-time students. Work-study available nights, weekends and for part-time students. **Non-need-based:** Scholarships awarded for academics, leadership, minority status, state residency.

Application procedures. Admission: No deadline. $20 fee. Application must be submitted on paper. Admission notification on a rolling basis. **Financial aid:** No deadline. FAFSA required. Applicants notified on a rolling basis.

Academics. Special study options: Distance learning, dual enrollment of high school students, weekend college. License preparation in dental hygiene, nursing, paramedic. **Credit/placement by examination:** AP, CLEP, institutional tests. **Support services:** GED preparation and test center, learning center, reduced course load, remedial instruction, study skills assistance, tutoring.

Majors. Business: Accounting technology, administrative services, construction management, office technology, operations, sales/distribution. **Computer sciences:** Data processing, networking. **Education:** Early childhood. **General:** Power transmission. **Health services:** Dental hygiene, EMT paramedic, surgical technology. **Protective services:** Criminal justice, firefighting. **Work/family studies:** Child care service.

Most popular majors. Business/marketing 29%, computer/information sciences 15%, education 6%, engineering/engineering technologies 8%, health sciences 17%, personal/culinary services 8%, security/protective services 6%.

Technology on campus. 100 workstations in library, computer center. Online course registration, online library, helpline, wireless network available.

Student life. Freshman orientation: Available. Preregistration for classes offered. **Activities:** Student government.

Student services. Career counseling, services for economically disadvantaged, student employment services, financial aid counseling, personal counseling, placement for graduates. **Physically disabled:** Services for visually, hearing impaired. **Transfer:** Re-entry adviser, pre-admission transcript evaluation for new students.

Contact. E-mail: gmoore@savannahtech.edu
Phone: (912) 443-5711 Toll-free number: (800) 769-6362
Fax: (912) 443-5705
Gwen Moore, Director of Admissions, Savannah Technical College, 5717 White Bluff Road, Savannah, GA 31401-5521

Southeastern Technical College
Vidalia, Georgia
www.southeasterntech.edu   CB code: 5652

- Public 2-year technical college
- Commuter campus in large town

General. Regionally accredited. **Enrollment:** 1,665 undergraduates. **Degrees:** 57 associate awarded. **Location:** 73 miles from Savannah. **Calendar:** Semester. **Full-time faculty:** 57 total. **Part-time faculty:** 36 total. **Class size:** 79% < 20, 17% 20-39, 2% 40-49, 2% 50-99.

Basis for selection. Open admission, but selective for some programs. Special requirements for dental hygiene, practical nursing and radiologic technology programs. Under certain conditions, ACT or SAT may be accepted in lieu of COMPASS or ASSET for placement.

High school preparation. College-preparatory program recommended. 22 units recommended. Recommended units include English 4, mathematics 3, social studies 3, science 3, foreign language 1 and academic electives 3. 4 tech prep, 1 health science recommended.

2015-2016 Annual costs. Tuition/fees: $3,308; $5,978 out-of-state. Per-credit charge: $89 in-state; $178 out-of-state. Books/supplies: $1,072.

Financial aid. Need-based: Need-based aid available for part-time students. Work-study available nights, weekends and for part-time students. **Non-need-based:** Scholarships awarded for state residency.

Application procedures. Admission: No deadline. $25 fee. **Financial aid:** No deadline. FAFSA required. Applicants notified on a rolling basis starting 4/6.

Academics. Special study options: Combined bachelor's/graduate degree, distance learning, dual enrollment of high school students, internships. License preparation in dental hygiene, nursing, paramedic, radiology. **Credit/placement by examination:** AP, CLEP, institutional tests. **Support services:** GED preparation and test center, learning center, remedial instruction, study skills assistance, tutoring.

Majors. Business: Accounting, business admin, marketing. **Computer sciences:** LAN/WAN management, networking, support specialist. **Conservation:** Wildlife/wilderness. **Education:** Early childhood. **General:** Electrician. **Health services:** Clinical lab assistant, clinical lab technology, dental hygiene, nursing (RN), radiologic technology/medical imaging. **Protective services:** Law enforcement admin.

Most popular majors. Business/marketing 26%, computer/information sciences 12%, health sciences 37%, security/protective services 9%, trade and industry 10%.

Technology on campus. 1,400 workstations in library, computer center, student center. Commuter students can connect to campus network. Online library, wireless network available.

Student life. Freshman orientation: Mandatory. Preregistration for classes offered. **Activities:** Student government.

Athletics. Team name: Patriots.

Student services. Career counseling, student employment services, financial aid counseling, placement for graduates, veterans' counselor. **Physically disabled:** Services for visually, speech, hearing impaired. **Transfer:** Pre-admission transcript evaluation for new students.

Contact. E-mail: admissions@southeasterntech.edu
Phone: (912) 538-3142 Fax: (912) 538-3156
Brad Hart, Director of Enrollment Services, Southeastern Technical College, 3001 East First Street, Vidalia, GA 30474

Southern Crescent Technical College
Griffin, Georgia
www.sctech.edu   CB code: 5670

- Public 2-year technical college
- Small city

General. Regionally accredited. **Enrollment:** 4,898 degree-seeking undergraduates. **Degrees:** 320 associate awarded. **Calendar:** Semester. **Full-time faculty:** 106 total. **Part-time faculty:** 246 total.

Basis for selection. Open admission, but selective for some programs. Admission criteria vary by program. Under certain circumstances, ACT or SAT may be accepted in lieu of COMPASS or ASSET for placement.

High school preparation. College-preparatory program recommended. 22 units recommended. Recommended units include English 4, mathematics 3, social studies 3, science 4, foreign language 2 and academic electives 3. 4 tech prep, 1 health science recommended.

2015-2016 Annual costs. Tuition/fees: $3,226; $5,896 out-of-state. Per-credit charge: $89 in-state; $178 out-of-state. Books/supplies: $150. Personal expenses: $587.

Financial aid. Need-based: Work-study available nights, weekends and for part-time students.

Application procedures. Admission: No deadline. $20 fee. Admission notification on a rolling basis. **Financial aid:** FAFSA, institutional form required. Applicants notified on a rolling basis.

Academics. Special study options: Distance learning, dual enrollment of high school students, weekend college. **Credit/placement by examination:** AP, CLEP. **Support services:** GED preparation and test center.

Majors. Business: Accounting, administrative services, business admin, management science. **Computer sciences:** General, information systems. **Health services:** Radiologic technology/medical imaging. **Protective services:** Law enforcement admin.

Most popular majors. Business/marketing 26%, computer/information sciences 11%, education 6%, health sciences 21%, security/protective services 13%, trade and industry 10%.

Athletics. Team name: Tigers.

Student services. Career counseling, services for economically disadvantaged, financial aid counseling, placement for graduates, veterans' counselor.

Contact. E-mail: admissions@sctech.edu
Phone: (770) 228-7348 Fax: (770) 229-3227
Jasper Foust, Director of Enrollment Services, Southern Crescent Technical College, 501 Varsity Road, Griffin, GA 30223

Southern Regional Technical College
Thomasville, Georgia
www.southernregional.edu   CB code: 3627

- Public 2-year technical college
- Commuter campus in large town

General. Regionally accredited. **Enrollment:** 2,277 degree-seeking undergraduates. **Degrees:** 202 associate awarded. **Location:** 35 miles from Tallahassee, Florida. **Calendar:** Semester, extensive summer session. **Full-time faculty:** 116 total. **Part-time faculty:** 85 total. **Special facilities:** Virtual hospital, surgical suite-veterinary technology, operating room-surgical technology, fire arms simulation lab. **Partnerships:** Formal partnership with John Deere.

Basis for selection. Open admission, but selective for some programs. Most health science programs are selective due to class size limitations. The selection process may include required certifications, additional standardized testing, and prerequisite courses. Under certain conditions, prior official scores on the ACT or SAT may be accepted in lieu of COMPASS or ASSET test results for placement. **Learning Disabled:** Students seeking accommodations should provide documentation of learning disability.

High school preparation. College-preparatory program recommended. 22 units recommended. Recommended units include English 4, mathematics 3, social studies 3, science 3, foreign language 1 and academic electives 3. 4 tech prep and 1 health science recommended.

2015-2016 Annual costs. Tuition/fees: $3,148; $5,818 out-of-state. Per-credit charge: $89 in-state; $178 out-of-state. Books/supplies: $900. Personal expenses: $4,400.

Financial aid. Need-based: Need-based aid available for part-time students. Work-study available nights, weekends and for part-time students. **Non-need-based:** Scholarships awarded for state residency.

Application procedures. Admission: No deadline. $20 fee. Admission notification on a rolling basis. **Financial aid:** No deadline. FAFSA required. Applicants notified on a rolling basis starting 7/1.

Academics. Special study options: Distance learning, dual enrollment of high school students, weekend college. License preparation in nursing, paramedic, radiology. **Credit/placement by examination:** AP, CLEP, institutional tests. **Support services:** GED preparation and test center, remedial instruction, tutoring.

Majors. Business: Accounting technology, administrative services, business admin. **Computer sciences:** Data processing, system admin. **Education:** Early childhood. **Health services:** Clinical lab technology, EMT paramedic, health information technology, medical assistant, nursing (RN), radiologic technology/medical imaging, respiratory therapy technology, surgical technology, veterinary technology/assistant. **Protective services:** Criminal justice, police science.

Most popular majors. Business/marketing 10%, health sciences 70%, public administration/social services 6%, security/protective services 6%.

Technology on campus. 42 workstations in library. Online course registration, online library available.

Student life. Freshman orientation: Mandatory. Preregistration for classes offered. Held each semester. **Activities:** Student government, National Vocational honor society, Phi Beta Lambda, SkillsUSA.

Student services. Adult student services, career counseling, services for economically disadvantaged, student employment services, financial aid counseling, personal counseling, placement for graduates. **Physically disabled:** Services for visually, hearing impaired. **Transfer:** Pre-admission transcript evaluation for new students.

Contact. Phone: (229) 225-5060 Fax: (229) 227-2666
Wanda Hancock, Director of Admissions, Southern Regional Technical College, 15689 US Highway 19 North, Thomasville, GA 31792-9960

Virginia College in Augusta
Augusta, Georgia
www.vc.edu/campus/augusta-georgia-college.cfm

- For-profit 2-year health science and career college
- Large city
- Interview required

General. Regionally accredited; also accredited by ACICS. **Enrollment:** 902 undergraduates. **Degrees:** 180 associate awarded. **Calendar:** Quarter. **Full-time faculty:** 14 total. **Part-time faculty:** 45 total.

Basis for selection. Open admission. High school record, interview and essay evaluated. **Home schooled:** Diploma and transcript required. **Learning Disabled:** Documentation for untimed testing required.

2015-2016 Annual costs. Certificate programs: $13,932-$23,220. Associate programs: $37,152-$40,700. Clock hour certificate program: Cosmetology $21,225.

Financial aid. Need-based: Work-study available nights, weekends and for part-time students.

Application procedures. Admission: No deadline. $100 fee. Admission notification on a rolling basis. **Financial aid:** No deadline.

Academics. Special study options: Distance learning, independent study. **Credit/placement by examination:** AP, CLEP, institutional tests. 45 credit hours maximum toward associate degree. **Support services:** Learning center, study skills assistance, tutoring.

Majors. Business: Business admin, office management. **Health services:** Health information management, medical assistant, office admin, surgical technology.

Technology on campus. Online library, repair service available.

Student life. Freshman orientation: Mandatory. Preregistration for classes offered.

Student services. Career counseling, student employment services, financial aid counseling, placement for graduates, veterans' counselor. **Transfer:** Transfer adviser for students transferring to 4-year colleges.

Contact. E-mail: augusta.info@vc.edu
Phone: (706) 288-2500 Fax: (706) 288-2599
Troy Jenkens, Director of Admissions, Virginia College in Augusta, 2807 Wylds Road, Augusta, GA 30909

Virginia College in Columbus
Columbus, Georgia
www.vc.edu/college/columbus-georgia-colleges.cfm

⬩ For-profit 2-year health science and career college
⬩ Small city

General. Regionally accredited; also accredited by ACICS. **Enrollment:** 741 undergraduates. **Degrees:** 152 associate awarded. **Calendar:** Quarter.

Basis for selection. Open admission.

2015-2016 Annual costs. Certificate programs: $13,932-$23,220. Associate programs: $37,152-$40,700. Clock hour certificate program: Cosmetology $21,225; Therapeutic Massage $15,435.

Financial aid. Need-based: Work-study available nights, weekends and for part-time students.

Application procedures. Admission: $100 fee.

Academics. Credit/placement by examination: AP, CLEP.

Majors. Business: Business admin. **Health services:** Health information management.

Contact. E-mail: columbus.info@vc.edu
Phone: (762) 207-1600
Brian Ashton, Director of Admissions, Virginia College in Columbus, 5601 Veterans Parkway, Columbus, GA 31904

Virginia College in Macon
Macon, Georgia
www.vc.edu/campus/macon-georgia-college.cfm

⬩ For-profit 2-year health science and career college
⬩ Small city

General. Accredited by ACICS. **Enrollment:** 451 undergraduates. **Degrees:** 86 associate awarded. **Calendar:** Quarter. **Full-time faculty:** 9 total. **Part-time faculty:** 23 total.

Basis for selection. Open admission.

2015-2016 Annual costs. Certificate programs: $13,932-$23,220. Associate programs: $37,152-$39,072. Clock hour certificate program: Cosmetology $21,225.

Financial aid. Need-based: Work-study available nights, weekends and for part-time students.

Application procedures. Admission: No deadline. $100 fee.

Academics. Credit/placement by examination: AP, CLEP.

Majors. Business: Business admin. **Health services:** Health information management, surgical technology.

Contact. E-mail: macon.info@vc.edu
Phone: (478) 803-4600
Tanya Meggs, Director of Admissions, Virginia College in Macon, 1901 Paul Walsh Drive, Macon, GA 31206

Virginia College in Savannah
Savannah, Georgia
www.vc.edu/campus/savannah-georgia-college.cfm

⬩ For-profit 2-year culinary school and career college
⬩ Large city

General. Regionally accredited; also accredited by ACICS. Savannah campus includes Culinard: The Culinary Institute of Virginia College, which offers 36-week programs in pastry and culinary arts. **Enrollment:** 620 undergraduates. **Degrees:** 76 associate awarded. **Calendar:** Quarter.

Basis for selection. Open admission.

2015-2016 Annual costs. Certificate programs: $13,932-$23,220. Associate programs: $37,152-$40,700. Clock hour certificate program: Cosmetology $21,225; Therapeutic Massage $15,435.

Financial aid. Need-based: Work-study available nights, weekends and for part-time students.

Application procedures. Admission: $100 fee.

Academics. Credit/placement by examination: AP, CLEP.

Majors. Business: Business admin, executive assistant. **Health services:** Health information management, surgical technology.

Contact. E-mail: savannah.info@vc.edu
Phone: (912) 721-5600
Michelle Anderson, Director of Admissions, Virginia College in Savannah, 14045 Abercorn Street, Suite 1503, Savannah, GA 31419

West Georgia Technical College
Waco, Georgia
www.westgatech.edu   CB code: 3632

⬩ Public 2-year technical college
⬩ Commuter campus in small city

General. Regionally accredited. **Enrollment:** 6,431 undergraduates. **Degrees:** 348 associate awarded. **Location:** 60 miles from Atlanta. **Calendar:** Semester, limited summer session. **Full-time faculty:** 126 total. **Part-time faculty:** 356 total. **Class size:** 80% < 20, 20% 20-39.

Basis for selection. Open admission, but selective for some programs. Applicants to diploma and associate degree health sciences programs must complete a competitive selection process prior to admission to program. Under certain circumstances, ACT/SAT may be accepted in lieu of COMPASS or ASSET for placement. **Home schooled:** Transcript of courses and grades required. Must provide satisfactory documentation indicating the homeschool is approved. **Learning Disabled:** Disabilities must be documented with the on-site coordinator to receive consideration for accommodation.

High school preparation. College-preparatory program recommended. 22 units recommended. Recommended units include English 4, mathematics 3, social studies 3, science 3, foreign language 1 and academic electives 3. 4 tech prep and 1 health science recommended.

2015-2016 Annual costs. Tuition/fees: $3,288; $5,958 out-of-state. Per-credit charge: $89 in-state; $178 out-of-state. Books/supplies: $1,283. Personal expenses: $1,300.

Financial aid. Need-based: Need-based aid available for part-time students. Work-study available nights, weekends and for part-time students. **Non-need-based:** Scholarships awarded for state residency.

Application procedures. Admission: No deadline. $25 fee. Admission notification on a rolling basis. **Financial aid:** No deadline. FAFSA, institutional form required. Applicants notified on a rolling basis; must reply within 1 week(s) of notification.

Academics. Tutorial program available. **Special study options:** Distance learning, dual enrollment of high school students. License preparation in paramedic, radiology, real estate. **Credit/placement by examination:** AP, CLEP. 15 credit hours maximum toward associate degree. **Support services:** GED preparation and test center, learning center, study skills assistance, tutoring.

Majors. Business: Accounting, administrative services, business admin, executive assistant, management science. **Computer sciences:** General, data entry, networking, web page design. **Education:** Early childhood. **Health services:** Health information technology, pharmacy assistant. **Protective services:** Criminal justice, firefighting.

Most popular majors. Business/marketing 26%, computer/information sciences 12%, education 7%, health sciences 31%, security/protective services 17%.

Technology on campus. 100 workstations in library, computer center. Online library available.

Student life. Freshman orientation: Mandatory. Preregistration for classes offered. **Activities:** Student government, TV station, Phi Beta Lambda.

Student services. Adult student services, career counseling, student employment services, financial aid counseling, on-campus daycare, placement for graduates, veterans' counselor, women's services. **Physically disabled:** Services for visually, hearing impaired.

Contact. E-mail: lbasham@westgatech.edu
Phone: (770) 537-5719
Mary Aderhold, Director of Admission, West Georgia Technical College, 176 Murphy Campus Boulevard, Waco, GA 30182

Wiregrass Georgia Technical College
Valdosta, Georgia
www.wiregrass.edu   **CB code: 4557**

♦   Public 2-year technical college
♦   Commuter campus in small city

General. Regionally accredited. **Enrollment:** 499 degree-seeking undergraduates. **Degrees:** 184 associate awarded. **Location:** 120 miles from Macon; 80 miles from Tallahassee, FL. **Calendar:** Semester, extensive summer session. **Full-time faculty:** 116 total; 3% have terminal degrees, 21% minority, 62% women. **Part-time faculty:** 139 total; 18% minority, 57% women. **Class size:** 100% 20-39.

Student profile. Among degree-seeking undergraduates, 99% enrolled in a vocational program, 1% already have a bachelor's degree or higher.

Transfer out. Colleges most students transferred to 2015: South Georgia College, Georgia Military College, Abraham Baldwin Agricultural College, Valdosta State University.

Basis for selection. Open admission, but selective for some programs. Acceptable entrance scores from the ACT, SAT, or other state approved placement tests such as COMPASS or Accuplacer are used for general program admission. Background checks required for health programs and early childhood education; drug screens required for commercial truck driving; HESI testing required for competitive admission programs in allied health areas. Under certain conditions, prior official scores on the ACT or SAT may be accepted in lieu of COMPASS or ASSET test for placement. **Home schooled:** Transcript of courses and grades required. Letter of intent required.

High school preparation. College-preparatory program recommended. 22 units recommended. Recommended units include English 4, mathematics 3, social studies 3, science 3, foreign language 1 and academic electives 3. 4 tech prep and 1 health science recommended.

2015-2016 Annual costs. Tuition/fees: $3,268; $5,938 out-of-state. Per-credit charge: $89 in-state; $178 out-of-state. Books/supplies: $1,276.

Financial aid. Need-based: Need-based aid available for part-time students. Work-study available nights, weekends and for part-time students. **Non-need-based:** Scholarships awarded for academics, job skills, state residency.

Application procedures. Admission: Priority date 7/11; no deadline. $25 fee, may be waived for applicants with need. Admission notification on a rolling basis. **Financial aid:** No deadline. FAFSA, institutional form required. Applicants notified on a rolling basis starting 6/1.

Academics. Special study options: Distance learning, double major, dual enrollment of high school students, ESL, internships, teacher certification program. License preparation in dental hygiene, nursing, paramedic, radiology, real estate. **Credit/placement by examination:** AP, CLEP, IB, institutional tests. 12 credit hours maximum toward associate degree. **Support services:** GED preparation and test center, learning center, reduced course load, remedial instruction, study skills assistance, tutoring, writing center.

Majors. Business: Accounting, banking/financial services, business admin, marketing, office technology. **Communications technology:** Graphic/printing. **Computer sciences:** General. **Education:** Early childhood. **Engineering:** General, computer, electrical, mechanical, telecommunications. **General:** Site management. **Health services:** Clinical lab technology, radiologic technology/medical imaging. **Protective services:** Firefighting.

Most popular majors. Business/marketing 30%, computer/information sciences 18%, education 7%, health sciences 22%, security/protective services 18%.

Technology on campus. 250 workstations in library, computer center, student center. Online course registration, online library, helpline, repair service, wireless network available.

Student life. Freshman orientation: Mandatory. Preregistration for classes offered. **Activities:** Campus ministries, literary magazine, student government, Wiregrass Georgia Collegiate Fellowship.

Student services. Adult student services, alcohol/substance abuse counseling, career counseling, services for economically disadvantaged, student employment services, financial aid counseling, health services, personal counseling, placement for graduates, veterans' counselor. **Physically disabled:** Services for visually, speech, hearing impaired. **Transfer:** Pre-admission transcript evaluation for new students. College fairs on campus for students transferring to 4-year colleges.

Contact. E-mail: admissions@wiregrass.edu
Phone: (229) 333-2105 Fax: (229) 333-2153
Shannon Pollock, Dean of Student Affairs, Wiregrass Georgia Technical College, 4089 Val Tech Road, Valdosta, GA 31602

Hawaii

Hawaii Tokai International College
Kapolei, Hawaii
www.hawaiitokai.edu
CB code: 2588

- Private 2-year junior and liberal arts college
- Residential campus in large town
- Application essay required

General. Regionally accredited. Students can study abroad in China, Japan or Korea. Students have the opportunity to complete a certificate program in Peace Studies. **Enrollment:** 79 degree-seeking undergraduates. **Degrees:** 54 associate awarded. **Location:** 20 miles from Honolulu. **Calendar:** Quarter, limited summer session. **Full-time faculty:** 11 total; 18% have terminal degrees, 36% minority, 82% women. **Part-time faculty:** 15 total; 20% have terminal degrees, 60% minority, 60% women. **Class size:** 100% < 20.

Student profile. Among degree-seeking undergraduates, 1 transferred in from other institutions.

Out-of-state:	23%	International:	84%
Women:	49%	25 or older:	3%
Asian American:	6%	Live on campus:	85%
Native Hawaiian/Pacific islander:			
	4%		

Transfer out. 87% of students enrolled in the transfer program go on to 4-year colleges. **Colleges most students transferred to 2015:** University of Hawaii at Manoa, Tokai University (Japan).

Basis for selection. Academic GPA, personal statement, commitment to studies are important. Letters of recommendation are considered but not required. SAT or ACT recommended. **Home schooled:** State high school equivalency certificate required. **Learning Disabled:** Students needing disability support are expected to identify themselves to the College. The College requires documentation regarding the nature and extent of the disability and recommendations for reasonable accommodations. Requests should be received at least six weeks prior to the start of the term.

2016-2017 Annual costs. Tuition/fees: $12,225. Room/board: $8,700. Books/supplies: $1,200. Personal expenses: $600.

Financial aid. Need-based: Work-study available nights, weekends and for part-time students. **Non-need-based:** Scholarships awarded for academics, leadership.

Application procedures. Admission: Closing date 8/1 (postmark date). $50 fee, may be waived for applicants with need. Admission notification on a rolling basis. **Financial aid:** No deadline. Institutional form required. Applicants notified on a rolling basis.

Academics. Special study options: Cross-registration, ESL, study abroad. **Credit/placement by examination:** AP, CLEP, IB, institutional tests. **Support services:** Learning center, study skills assistance, tutoring, writing center.

Majors. Liberal arts: Arts/sciences.

Technology on campus. 60 workstations in library, computer center. Dormitories wired for high-speed internet access and linked to campus network. Commuter students can connect to campus network. Online library, wireless network available.

Student life. Freshman orientation: Mandatory. Preregistration for classes offered. Normally held on the Monday, Tuesday and Wednesday before classes begin on Thursday. **Policies:** Students must maintain 2.75 GPA in order to participate in any clubs and organizations. **Housing:** Guaranteed on-campus for freshmen. Coed dorms, apartments, wellness housing available. $100 fully refundable deposit. **Activities:** Student government.

Student services. Alcohol/substance abuse counseling, career counseling, financial aid counseling, health services, personal counseling. **Transfer:** Re-entry adviser, pre-admission transcript evaluation for new students. Transfer center, transfer adviser, college fairs on campus for students transferring to 4-year colleges.

Contact. E-mail: admissions@tokai.edu
Phone: (808) 983-4202 Fax: (808) 983-4107
Darrell Kicker, Director of Admissions and Recruitment, Hawaii Tokai International College, 91-971 Farrington Highway, Kapolei, HI 96707-2657

Remington College: Honolulu
Honolulu, Hawaii
http://honolulu.remingtoncollege.edu
CB code: 3507

- Private 2-year career college
- Commuter campus in very large city
- Interview required

General. Regionally accredited; also accredited by ACCSC. **Enrollment:** 763 undergraduates. **Degrees:** 27 bachelor's, 128 associate awarded. **Calendar:** Quarter. **Full-time faculty:** 18 total. **Part-time faculty:** 36 total.

Basis for selection. Interview most important; CPAT assessment test score also important. CPAT entrance examination required. **Home schooled:** Statement describing home school structure and mission, transcript of courses and grades required.

2015-2016 Annual costs. Diploma programs: cosmetology $24,000; massage therapy $15,995. Associate programs: business administration $33,900; clinical medical assisting $33,900; criminal justice $33,900. Bahelor's programs: criminal justice $37,500; organizational management $37,500.

Financial aid. Need-based: Work-study available nights, weekends and for part-time students.

Application procedures. Admission: No deadline. $50 fee. Admission notification on a rolling basis. **Financial aid:** No deadline.

Academics. Special study options: Bachelor's degree programs available on campus. **Credit/placement by examination:** AP, CLEP.

Majors. Business: International. **Computer sciences:** General, networking. **Health services:** Medical assistant. **Protective services:** Criminal justice.

Technology on campus. Online library available.

Student life. Activities: International club.

Student services. Transfer: Pre-admission transcript evaluation for new students.

Contact. Phone: (808) 772-5978
Louis LaMair, Director of Admissions, Remington College: Honolulu, 1111 Bishop Street, Suite 400, Honolulu, HI 96813-2811

University of Hawaii: Hawaii Community College
Hilo, Hawaii
www.hawaii.hawaii.edu
CB code: 1801

- Public 2-year community college
- Residential campus in small city

General. Founded in 1969. Regionally accredited. **Enrollment:** 2,354 degree-seeking undergraduates. **Degrees:** 486 associate awarded. **Location:** 200 miles from Honolulu. **Calendar:** Semester, limited summer session. **Full-time faculty:** 86 total. **Part-time faculty:** 121 total.

Student profile.

Out-of-state:	1%	Live on campus:	35%
25 or older:	42%		

Basis for selection. Open admission. **Home schooled:** Transcript of courses and grades required.

2015-2016 Annual costs. Tuition/fees: $3,660; $9,900 out-of-state. Per-credit charge: $120 in-state; $328 out-of-state. Books/supplies: $672. Personal expenses: $953.

Financial aid. All financial aid based on need. Need-based aid available for part-time students. Work-study available nights, weekends and for part-time students. **Additional information:** Hawaii student incentive grants and tuition waivers (merit and need-based) available to Hawaii residents.

Application procedures. Admission: Closing date 8/1 (postmark date). No application fee in-state; $25 out-of-state. Admission notification on a rolling basis. **Financial aid:** Priority date 4/1; no closing date. FAFSA required. Applicants notified on a rolling basis starting 2/1; must reply within 2 week(s) of notification.

Academics. Special study options: Combined bachelor's/graduate degree, cooperative education, cross-registration, distance learning, dual enrollment of high school students, ESL, honors, independent study, internships, liberal arts/career combination, teacher certification program. **Credit/placement by examination:** AP, CLEP, institutional tests. 15 credit hours maximum toward associate degree. **Support services:** Learning center, reduced course load, remedial instruction, study skills assistance, tutoring.

Majors. Business: Accounting, administrative services, market research, marketing, operations. **Computer sciences:** Information systems. **Conservation:** Management/policy. **Education:** Early childhood. **General:** Carpentry, power transmission. **Health services:** Nursing (RN). **Liberal arts:** Arts/sciences. **Protective services:** Firefighting, law enforcement admin.

Most popular majors. Business/marketing 14%, liberal arts 8%, security/protective services 8%, trade and industry 36%.

Technology on campus. 1,256 workstations in library, computer center, student center. Dormitories wired for high-speed internet access. Commuter students can connect to campus network. Online course registration, online library, helpline, wireless network available.

Student life. Freshman orientation: Mandatory. Preregistration for classes offered. **Housing:** Coed dorms, special housing for disabled, apartments available. $100 fully refundable deposit, deadline 7/26. **Activities:** Dance, drama, literary magazine, music ensembles, radio station, student government, student newspaper, TV station, Phi Theta Kappa honors society.

Athletics. Team name: Hawaii Hawks (i'eo).

Student services. Adult student services, alcohol/substance abuse counseling, career counseling, services for economically disadvantaged, student employment services, financial aid counseling, health services, on-campus daycare, personal counseling, veterans' counselor, women's services. **Physically disabled:** Services for visually, speech, hearing impaired. **Transfer:** Transfer adviser, college fairs on campus for students transferring to 4-year colleges.

Contact. E-mail: hawccinf@hawaii.edu
Phone: (808) 934-2710 Fax: (808) 934-2501
Dorinna Manuel-Cortez, Registrar/Admiss & Recs Mgr, University of Hawaii: Hawaii Community College, 200 West Kawili Street, Hilo, HI 96720-4091

University of Hawaii: Honolulu Community College
Honolulu, Hawaii
www2.honolulu.hawaii.edu   CB code: 4350

- Public 2-year community and technical college
- Commuter campus in very large city

General. Founded in 1920. Regionally accredited. **Enrollment:** 3,261 degree-seeking undergraduates. **Degrees:** 504 associate awarded. **ROTC:** Army, Air Force. **Calendar:** Semester, limited summer session. **Full-time faculty:** 130 total. **Part-time faculty:** 86 total. **Class size:** 50% < 20, 49% 20-39, less than 1% 50-99.

Student profile.

Out-of-state: 5%   **25 or older:**   39%

Transfer out. Colleges most students transferred to 2015: University of Hawaii at Manoa, University of Hawaii at Hilo, University of Hawaii West Oahu, Chaminade University, Hawaii Pacific University.

Basis for selection. Open admission, but selective for out-of-state students. Out-of-state and foreign applicants subject to non-resident quota. High school diploma required for cosmetology program.

2015-2016 Annual costs. Tuition/fees: $3,630; $9,870 out-of-state. Per-credit charge: $120 in-state; $328 out-of-state. Books/supplies: $773. Personal expenses: $1,166.

Financial aid. Need-based: Need-based aid available for part-time students. Work-study available nights, weekends and for part-time students. **Non-need-based:** Scholarships awarded for academics, state residency. **Additional information:** Hawaii student incentive grants and tuition waivers

---

(merit and need-based) available to Hawaii residents at participating institutions.

Application procedures. Admission: Priority date 7/1; no deadline. No application fee in-state; $25 out-of-state. Admission notification on a rolling basis beginning on or about 3/1. **Financial aid:** Priority date 4/1; no closing date. FAFSA required. Applicants notified on a rolling basis starting 7/1; must reply within 3 week(s) of notification.

Academics. Special study options: Cooperative education, cross-registration, distance learning, dual enrollment of high school students, ESL, independent study, internships, student-designed major. License preparation in aviation. **Credit/placement by examination:** AP, CLEP, institutional tests. 30 credit hours maximum toward associate degree. **Support services:** Learning center, remedial instruction, study skills assistance, tutoring, writing center.

Majors. Business: Fashion. **Communications technology:** Graphic/printing. **Computer sciences:** General, computer graphics, information systems. **Education:** Early childhood, technology/industrial arts, voc/tech. **Engineering:** Computer, polymer. **General:** Carpentry, electrician. **Health services:** Occupational health. **Human services:** Community org/advocacy, social work. **Liberal arts:** Arts/sciences. **Protective services:** Criminal justice, fire safety technology, fire services admin, firefighting, law enforcement admin, police science. **Visual/performing arts:** Commercial/advertising art, fashion design. **Work/family studies:** Child care management, institutional food production.

Most popular majors. Engineering/engineering technologies 30%, liberal arts 22%, personal/culinary services 6%, security/protective services 9%, trade and industry 19%.

Technology on campus. 135 workstations in library, computer center, student center. Commuter students can connect to campus network. Online course registration, wireless network available.

Student life. Freshman orientation: Mandatory. Preregistration for classes offered. **Housing:** Dorms and apartments available at University of Hawaii at Manoa campus. **Activities:** Literary magazine, student government, student newspaper, Pacific Islander association, Filipino club.

Student services. Alcohol/substance abuse counseling, career counseling, student employment services, financial aid counseling, health services, on-campus daycare, personal counseling, placement for graduates, veterans' counselor. **Physically disabled:** Services for visually, speech, hearing impaired. **Transfer:** Pre-admission transcript evaluation for new students. Transfer center, transfer adviser, college fairs on campus for students transferring to 4-year colleges.

Contact. E-mail: honcc@hawaii.edu
Phone: (808) 845-9129 Fax: (808) 847-9829
Admissions Counselor, University of Hawaii: Honolulu Community College, 874 Dillingham Boulevard, Honolulu, HI 96817

University of Hawaii: Kapiolani Community College
Honolulu, Hawaii
www.kcc.hawaii.edu   CB code: 4377

- Public 2-year community college
- Commuter campus in very large city

General. Founded in 1957. Regionally accredited. **Enrollment:** 7,994 undergraduates. **Degrees:** 1,083 associate awarded. **Calendar:** Semester, limited summer session. **Full-time faculty:** 197 total. **Part-time faculty:** 184 total. **Class size:** 55% < 20, 45% 20-39, less than 1% 40-49, less than 1% 50-99.

Student profile.

Out-of-state: 7%   **25 or older:**   41%

Transfer out. Colleges most students transferred to 2015: University of Hawaii at Manoa.

Basis for selection. Open admission, but selective for some programs. Special requirements for health science and nursing programs. High school diploma required for allied health and nursing programs and for students under age 18. Essay recommended. Interview required of allied health, legal assistant, and nursing programs.

2015-2016 Annual costs. Tuition/fees: $3,660; $9,900 out-of-state. Per-credit charge: $120 in-state; $328 out-of-state. Books/supplies: $725. Personal expenses: $1,143.

Financial aid. All financial aid based on need. Need-based aid available for part-time students. Work-study available nights, weekends and for part-time students.

Application procedures. **Admission:** Closing date 7/17 (postmark date). $25 fee. Application must be submitted on paper. Admission notification on a rolling basis. Application deadline 4/1 for allied health and legal assistant programs; 2/1 for registered nursing program. **Financial aid:** Priority date 4/1; no closing date. FAFSA required. Applicants notified on a rolling basis starting 4/1; must reply within 2 week(s) of notification.

Academics. **Special study options:** Cross-registration, distance learning, double major, dual enrollment of high school students, ESL, exchange student, external degree, honors, independent study, internships, study abroad, teacher certification program, weekend college. Service learning. License preparation in nursing, paramedic. **Credit/placement by examination:** AP, CLEP, institutional tests. **Support services:** Learning center, remedial instruction, tutoring.

Majors. **Business:** General, accounting, hospitality/recreation, office technology, sales/distribution. **Computer sciences:** Data processing. **Health services:** Clinical lab technology, dental assistant, dental hygiene, EMT paramedic, licensed practical nurse, medical assistant, medical radiologic technology/radiation therapy, nursing (RN), nursing assistant, occupational therapy assistant, physical therapy assistant, physician assistant, respiratory therapy technology, sonography. **Liberal arts:** Arts/sciences. **Work/family studies:** Institutional food production.

Most popular majors. Business/marketing 30%, computer/information sciences 6%, health sciences 21%, liberal arts 38%.

Technology on campus. 150 workstations in library, computer center, student center. Commuter students can connect to campus network. Online course registration, online library, student web hosting, wireless network available.

Student life. **Freshman orientation:** Mandatory. Preregistration for classes offered. Two-hour sessions available. **Housing:** Housing available through University of Hawaii system. **Activities:** Choral groups, dance, drama, literary magazine, music ensembles, student government, student newspaper, international students club, marketing association, music club, Phi Theta Kappa, nursing association, Japanese, Chinese and Korean club, Catholic Ministry Association, pre-engineering club.

Student services. Career counseling, services for economically disadvantaged, student employment services, financial aid counseling, minority student services, on-campus daycare, personal counseling, placement for graduates, veterans' counselor. **Physically disabled:** Services for visually, speech, hearing impaired.

Contact. E-mail: kapinfo@hawaii.edu
Phone: (808) 734-9555 Fax: (808) 734-9896
Jerilynn Enokawa, Registrar, University of Hawaii: Kapiolani Community College, 4303 Diamond Head Road, Honolulu, HI 96816-4421

University of Hawaii: Kauai Community College
Lihue, Hawaii
www.kauai.hawaii.edu   **CB code: 4378**

▶ Public 2-year community college
▶ Commuter campus in small city

General. Founded in 1928. Regionally accredited. **Enrollment:** 1,098 degree-seeking undergraduates. **Degrees:** 187 associate awarded. **Location:** 100 miles from Honolulu. **Calendar:** Semester, limited summer session. **Full-time faculty:** 55 total. **Part-time faculty:** 50 total. **Special facilities:** Botanical facilities.

Basis for selection. Open admission, but selective for out-of-state students. Special requirements for out-of-state residents in nursing, electrical installation and maintenance technology, facilities engineering technology, nurse's aide, electronics technology programs, and culinary arts.

2015-2016 Annual costs. Tuition/fees: $3,708; $9,948 out-of-state. Per-credit charge: $120 in-state; $328 out-of-state. Books/supplies: $900.

Financial aid. **Need-based:** Work-study available nights, weekends and for part-time students. **Additional information:** Hawaii student incentive grants and tuition waivers (merit and need-based) available to Hawaii residents.

Application procedures. **Admission:** Priority date 8/1; no deadline. Admission notification on a rolling basis beginning on or about 3/1. Institutional placement test. **Financial aid:** Priority date 3/1, closing date 5/1.

FAFSA, institutional form required. Applicants notified on a rolling basis starting 5/1.

Academics. **Special study options:** Cooperative education, cross-registration, distance learning, ESL, internships. **Credit/placement by examination:** AP, CLEP, institutional tests. **Support services:** Learning center, tutoring, writing center.

Majors. **Business:** Accounting, hospitality admin, office/clerical. **Education:** Early childhood. **General:** Carpentry, electrician. **Health services:** Nursing (RN). **Liberal arts:** Arts/sciences.

Technology on campus. 150 workstations in computer center.

Student life. **Freshman orientation:** Available. Preregistration for classes offered. **Activities:** Concert band, choral groups, international student organizations, music ensembles, student government, Hawaiian club, Pamantasan club, Hawaiian performing arts club, Japanese club, environmental club.

Athletics. **Intramural:** Basketball.

Student services. Adult student services, career counseling, student employment services, financial aid counseling, health services, on-campus daycare, personal counseling, placement for graduates, veterans' counselor. **Physically disabled:** Services for visually, speech, hearing impaired. **Transfer:** Transfer adviser, college fairs on campus for students transferring to 4-year colleges.

Contact. E-mail: arkauai@hawaii.edu
Phone: (808) 245-8225 Fax: (808) 245-8297
Kailana Soto, Registrar, University of Hawaii: Kauai Community College, 3-1901 Kaumualii Highway, Lihue, HI 96766-9500

University of Hawaii: Leeward Community College
Pearl City, Hawaii
www.lcc.hawaii.edu   **CB code: 4410**

▶ Public 2-year community college
▶ Commuter campus in large town

General. Founded in 1968. Regionally accredited. **Enrollment:** 5,789 degree-seeking undergraduates. **Degrees:** 898 associate awarded. **Location:** 10 miles from Honolulu. **Calendar:** Semester, limited summer session. **Special facilities:** Observatory.

Basis for selection. Open admission.

2015-2016 Annual costs. Tuition/fees: $3,655; $9,895 out-of-state. Per-credit charge: $120 in-state; $328 out-of-state. Books/supplies: $948. Personal expenses: $1,356.

Financial aid. **Need-based:** Need-based aid available for part-time students. Work-study available nights, weekends and for part-time students. **Additional information:** Leveraging Educational Assistance Partnership (LEAP) funds or tuition waivers available to students with financial need.

Application procedures. **Admission:** Closing date 7/15 (postmark date). No application fee in-state; $25 out-of-state. Admission notification on a rolling basis. **Financial aid:** Priority date 4/15; no closing date. FAFSA required. Applicants notified on a rolling basis starting 6/1; must reply within 2 week(s) of notification.

Academics. **Special study options:** Accelerated study, cross-registration, distance learning, dual enrollment of high school students, ESL, honors, independent study, internships, liberal arts/career combination, teacher certification program, weekend college. **Credit/placement by examination:** AP, CLEP, IB, institutional tests. 21 credit hours maximum toward associate degree. **Support services:** Learning center, pre-admission summer program, remedial instruction, study skills assistance, tutoring, writing center.

Majors. **Business:** Accounting, accounting technology, administrative services, business admin, office/clerical. **Communications technology:** Animation/special effects, radio/TV. **Computer sciences:** General. **Education:** Multi-level teacher. **Liberal arts:** Arts/sciences.

Technology on campus. 200 workstations in library, computer center, student center. Commuter students can connect to campus network. Online library, helpline, wireless network available.

Student life. **Freshman orientation:** Mandatory. Preregistration for classes offered. **Activities:** Campus ministries, dance, international student organizations, literary magazine, music ensembles, student government, student newspaper, Filipino ethnic organization, club for physically handicapped, human services club.

Athletics. Intramural: Soccer, volleyball.

Student services. Adult student services, career counseling, student employment services, financial aid counseling, health services, minority student services, on-campus daycare, personal counseling, placement for graduates, veterans' counselor. **Physically disabled:** Services for visually, speech, hearing impaired. **Transfer:** Transfer adviser, college fairs on campus for students transferring to 4-year colleges.

Contact. E-mail: lccar@hawaii.edu
Phone: (808) 455-0642 Fax: (808) 454-8804
Grant Helgeson, Coordinator of Admissions and Records, University of Hawaii: Leeward Community College, 96-045 Ala Ike, Pearl City, HI 96782

University of Hawaii: Maui College
Kahului, Hawaii
www.maui.hawaii.edu   CB code: 4510

▶ Public 2-year community college
▶ Commuter campus in small city

General. Founded in 1931. Regionally accredited. Branch campuses on Molokai, Lanai, Lahaina and Hana. **Enrollment:** 3,149 degree-seeking undergraduates; 427 non-degree-seeking students. **Degrees:** 8 bachelor's, 488 associate awarded. **Location:** 150 miles from Honolulu. **Calendar:** Semester, limited summer session. **Full-time faculty:** 124 total. **Part-time faculty:** 1 total.

Student profile. Among degree-seeking undergraduates, 568 enrolled as first-time, first-year students.

Part-time:	61%	Women:	63%
Out-of-state:	1%	Live on campus:	1%

Basis for selection. Open admission, but selective for some programs. Special requirements for nursing program. Interview required of nursing majors.

2015-2016 Annual costs. Tuition/fees: $3,726; $9,966 out-of-state. Per-credit charge: $120 in-state; $328 out-of-state. Books/supplies: $976. Personal expenses: $1,422.

Financial aid. Need-based: Need-based aid available for part-time students. Work-study available nights, weekends and for part-time students.

Application procedures. Admission: Priority date 7/31; no deadline. No application fee in-state; $25 out-of-state. Admission notification on a rolling basis. **Financial aid:** Closing date 4/1. FAFSA, institutional form required. Applicants notified on a rolling basis starting 6/1; must reply within 4 week(s) of notification.

Academics. Special study options: Cooperative education, distance learning, dual enrollment of high school students, ESL, independent study, liberal arts/career combination, weekend college. **Credit/placement by examination:** AP, CLEP, institutional tests. 30 credit hours maximum toward associate degree. **Support services:** Learning center, pre-admission summer program, reduced course load, remedial instruction, tutoring.

Majors. Business: General, accounting, tourism/travel. **Education:** Early childhood. **General:** Carpentry. **Liberal arts:** Arts/sciences. **Work/family studies:** Apparel marketing, food/nutrition.

Technology on campus. Commuter students can connect to campus network. Online course registration, helpline available.

Student life. Freshman orientation: Available. Preregistration for classes offered. **Activities:** Student government, student newspaper, TV station.

Student services. Career counseling, student employment services, health services, on-campus daycare, personal counseling, veterans' counselor. **Physically disabled:** Services for visually, speech, hearing impaired. **Transfer:** Transfer adviser for students transferring to 4-year colleges.

Contact. Phone: (808) 984-3500 Toll-free number: (800) 479-6692
Fax: (808) 984-3872
Flora Mora, Admissions Officer/Registrar, University of Hawaii: Maui College, 310 West Kaahumanu Avenue, Kahului, HI 96732-1617

University of Hawaii: Windward Community College
Kaneohe, Hawaii
www.wcc.hawaii.edu   CB code: 4976

▶ Public 2-year community college
▶ Commuter campus in small city

General. Founded in 1972. Regionally accredited. **Enrollment:** 2,460 degree-seeking undergraduates. **Degrees:** 309 associate awarded. **ROTC:** Army. **Location:** 10 miles from Honolulu. **Calendar:** Semester, limited summer session. **Full-time faculty:** 49 total. **Part-time faculty:** 56 total. **Special facilities:** Planetarium, greenhouse, observatory, NASA lab, biomedicinal garden, theater.

Student profile.

Out-of-state:	9%	25 or older:	38%

Basis for selection. Open admission.

2015-2016 Annual costs. Tuition/fees: $3,640; $9,880 out-of-state. Per-credit charge: $120 in-state; $328 out-of-state. Books/supplies: $987. Personal expenses: $1,730.

Financial aid. Need-based: Need-based aid available for part-time students. Work-study available nights, weekends and for part-time students. **Non-need-based:** Scholarships awarded for academics. **Additional information:** Hawaii student incentive grants and tuition waivers (merit and need-based) available to Hawaii residents.

Application procedures. Admission: Priority date 8/1; no deadline. No application fee in-state; $25 out-of-state. Admission notification on a rolling basis. Out-of-state military dependents not required to pay application fee. **Financial aid:** Priority date 4/1; no closing date. FAFSA required. Applicants notified on a rolling basis starting 3/15; must reply within 2 week(s) of notification.

Academics. Special study options: Cooperative education, distance learning, double major, dual enrollment of high school students, independent study, internships, student-designed major, study abroad. **Credit/placement by examination:** AP, CLEP, institutional tests. **Support services:** Learning center, reduced course load, remedial instruction, study skills assistance, tutoring.

Majors. Liberal arts: Arts/sciences.

Technology on campus. 100 workstations in library, computer center, student center. Commuter students can connect to campus network. Online course registration, helpline, wireless network available.

Student life. Freshman orientation: Mandatory. Preregistration for classes offered. **Activities:** Choral groups, drama, literary magazine, student government, student newspaper.

Student services. Adult student services, career counseling, services for economically disadvantaged, student employment services, financial aid counseling, minority student services, personal counseling, placement for graduates, veterans' counselor. **Physically disabled:** Services for visually, speech, hearing impaired. **Transfer:** Pre-admission transcript evaluation for new students. Transfer adviser, college fairs on campus for students transferring to 4-year colleges.

Contact. E-mail: wccinfo@hawaii.edu
Phone: (808) 235-7432 Fax: (808) 235-9148
Geri Imai, Registrar, University of Hawaii: Windward Community College, 45-720 Kea'ahala Road, Kaneohe, HI 96744

Idaho

Broadview University: Boise
Meridian, Idaho
www.broadviewuniversity.edu

- For-profit 2-year career college
- Commuter campus in large town
- Interview required

General. Regionally accredited; also accredited by ACICS. **Enrollment:** 142 undergraduates. **Degrees:** 1 bachelor's, 24 associate awarded. **Calendar:** Quarter, extensive summer session.

Basis for selection. Open admission. **Adult students:** SAT/ACT scores not required.

2015-2016 Annual costs. Tuition/fees: $18,027. Per-credit charge: $372. Books/supplies: $1,260.

Financial aid. Need-based: Need-based aid available for part-time students. Work-study available nights, weekends and for part-time students.

Application procedures. Admission: No deadline. $50 fee. Admission notification on a rolling basis. **Financial aid:** No deadline. FAFSA, institutional form required. Applicants notified on a rolling basis starting 7/1; must reply within 2 week(s) of notification.

Academics. Special study options: Distance learning, independent study, internships, liberal arts/career combination. **Credit/placement by examination:** AP, CLEP. **Support services:** Remedial instruction, study skills assistance, tutoring, writing center.

Majors. Business: Accounting, business admin, marketing. **Computer sciences:** Networking. **Health services:** Massage therapy, medical assistant, medical secretary, veterinary technology/assistant. **Protective services:** Law enforcement admin.

Most popular majors. Business/marketing 11%, computer/information sciences 22%, health sciences 56%, legal studies 11%.

Technology on campus. 60 workstations in library, computer center, student center. Commuter students can connect to campus network. Online library, helpline, student web hosting, wireless network available.

Student life. Freshman orientation: Mandatory. Preregistration for classes offered. Day and evening sessions available the week prior to classes starting. **Activities:** Literary magazine.

Student services. Career counseling, student employment services, financial aid counseling, placement for graduates. **Transfer:** Re-entry adviser for new students.

Contact. Phone: (208) 577-2900 Toll-free number: (877) 572-5757 Michael McAllister, Campus Director, Broadview University: Boise, 2750 East Gala Court, Meridian, ID 83642

Carrington College: Boise
Boise, Idaho
www.carrington.edu

- For-profit 2-year career college
- Very large city

General. Regionally accredited; also accredited by ACICS. **Enrollment:** 494 degree-seeking undergraduates. **Degrees:** 114 associate awarded. **Calendar:** Differs by program. **Full-time faculty:** 26 total. **Part-time faculty:** 25 total.

Basis for selection. Admission requirements will vary by program.

2015-2016 Annual costs. Tuition costs vary by program. Total program cost for the largest program (Dental Hygiene-Assoc.) is $58,204.

Financial aid. Need-based: Work-study available nights, weekends and for part-time students.

Application procedures. Admission: No deadline. No application fee. **Financial aid:** No deadline.

Academics. Credit/placement by examination: AP, CLEP.

Majors. Health services: Dental assistant, dental hygiene, health services admin, insurance coding, insurance specialist, licensed practical nurse, massage therapy, medical assistant, office admin, pharmacy assistant, physical therapy assistant.

Contact. Phone: (888) 720-5014 Director of Enrollment Services, Carrington College: Boise, 1122 North Liberty Street, Boise, ID 83704-8742

College of Southern Idaho
Twin Falls, Idaho
www.csi.edu   CB code: 4114

- Public 2-year community and junior college
- Commuter campus in large town

General. Founded in 1964. Regionally accredited. **Enrollment:** 9,300 undergraduates. **Degrees:** 845 associate awarded. **Location:** 130 miles from Boise. **Calendar:** Semester, limited summer session. **Full-time faculty:** 162 total. **Part-time faculty:** 76 total. **Special facilities:** Museum and planetarium including anthropology, archeology, fine arts collections.

Student profile.

Out-of-state:	5%	Live on campus:	5%
25 or older:	52%		

Transfer out. Colleges most students transferred to 2015: Boise State University, University of Idaho, Idaho State University, Utah State University, Albertsons College.

Basis for selection. Open admission, but selective for some programs. ACT recommended; letters of reference, letter of intent, and special tests required for applicants to registered nursing program. Interview required of registered nursing, technical majors.

2015-2016 Annual costs. Tuition/fees: $3,600; $5,100 out-of-district; $8,400 out-of-state. Per-credit charge: $120 in-district; $170 out-of-district; $280 out-of-state. Room/board: $5,540. Books/supplies: $990. Personal expenses: $1,900.

Financial aid. Need-based: Need-based aid available for part-time students. Work-study available nights, weekends and for part-time students. **Additional information:** Out-of-state tuition waivers based on GPA and activities.

Application procedures. Admission: No deadline. No application fee. Admission notification on a rolling basis. **Financial aid:** Priority date 3/1; no closing date. FAFSA required. Applicants notified on a rolling basis starting 4/30; must reply within 3 week(s) of notification.

Academics. Special study options: Distance learning, dual enrollment of high school students, ESL, honors. License preparation in real estate. **Credit/placement by examination:** AP, CLEP. 21 credit hours maximum toward associate degree. **Support services:** GED preparation and test center, learning center, reduced course load, remedial instruction, study skills assistance, tutoring, writing center.

Majors. Biology: General. **Business:** General, accounting, hospitality/recreation, real estate, tourism promotion. **Communications:** Communications/speech/rhetoric. **Computer sciences:** Computer graphics, computer science, LAN/WAN management. **Conservation:** General, forestry, water/wetlands/marine, wildlife/wilderness. **Education:** Bilingual, early childhood, elementary, physical, secondary. **Engineering:** Civil, computer, electrical. **English:** English lit. **Foreign languages:** General, sign language interpretation. **Health services:** Dental hygiene, EMT paramedic, nursing (RN), pharmacy assistant, predental, premedicine, prepharmacy, preveterinary, respiratory therapy technology, veterinary technology/assistant. **History:** General. **Liberal arts:** Arts/sciences, library assistant. **Math:** General. **Parks/recreation:** Health/fitness. **Physical sciences:** Chemistry, geology, physics. **Protective services:** Fire safety technology, law enforcement admin. **Psychology:** General. **Social sciences:** Anthropology, economics, geography, political science, sociology. **Visual/performing arts:** Art, commercial/advertising art, dramatic, music, photography.

Technology on campus. 350 workstations in dormitories, library, computer center, student center. Dormitories wired for high-speed internet access

and linked to campus network. Commuter students can connect to campus network. Online course registration, online library, helpline, student web hosting, wireless network available.

Student life. Housing: Coed dorms, apartments, wellness housing available. $100 fully refundable deposit. **Activities:** Pep band, campus ministries, choral groups, drama, international student organizations, student government, student newspaper, Christian Fellowship, Latter-day Saints student association, Ambassadors, Latinos Unidos, Golden Eagle Native Americans, Chi Alpha, accent club.

Athletics. NJCAA. **Intercollegiate:** Baseball M, basketball, equestrian, rodeo, softball, volleyball W. **Intramural:** Basketball, bowling, football (non-tackle), golf, racquetball, soccer, softball, tennis, volleyball. **Team name:** Eagles.

Student services. Adult student services, alcohol/substance abuse counseling, career counseling, student employment services, financial aid counseling, health services, minority student services, on-campus daycare, personal counseling, veterans' counselor. **Physically disabled:** Services for visually, hearing impaired. **Transfer:** Re-entry adviser, pre-admission transcript evaluation for new students. College fairs on campus for students transferring to 4-year colleges.

Contact. Phone: (208) 732-6792 Fax: (208) 736-3014
Gail Schull, Director of Admissions, College of Southern Idaho, Box 1238, Twin Falls, ID 83303-1238

College of Western Idaho
Nampa, Idaho
www.cwidaho.cc

CB member
CB code: 7924

▶ Public 2-year community and technical college
▶ Commuter campus in large city

General. Candidate for regional accreditation. **Enrollment:** 8,376 degree-seeking undergraduates. **Degrees:** 898 associate awarded. **Calendar:** Semester, limited summer session. **Full-time faculty:** 117 total; 3% minority, 48% women. **Part-time faculty:** 416 total; 10% minority, 55% women. **Class size:** 17% < 20, 72% 20-39, 6% 40-49, 4% 50-99.

Student profile. Among degree-seeking undergraduates, 91% enrolled in a transfer program, 9% enrolled in a vocational program.

Out-of-state: 1% **25 or older:** 37%

Transfer out. Colleges most students transferred to 2015: Boise State University, Idaho State University, University of Idaho, Lewis-Clark State College, Northwest Nazarene University.

Basis for selection. Open admission, but selective for some programs. Limited-enrollment programs may include special admission criteria or space limitations. **Home schooled:** Transcript of courses and grades required. Home-schooled students are asked to provide a transcript of their homeschool coursework.

2015-2016 Annual costs. Tuition/fees: $4,080; $5,080 out-of-district; $9,000 out-of-state. Per-credit charge: $136 in-district; $186 out-of-district; $300 out-of-state. Books/supplies: $768. Personal expenses: $1,118.

Financial aid. Need-based: Need-based aid available for part-time students. Work-study available nights, weekends and for part-time students. **Non-need-based:** Scholarships awarded for academics, leadership, minority status.

Application procedures. Admission: No deadline. $25 fee, may be waived for applicants with need. Admission notification on a rolling basis. **Financial aid:** Priority date 7/15; no closing date. FAFSA required. Applicants notified on a rolling basis starting 3/1; must reply within 4 week(s) of notification.

Academics. Special study options: Distance learning, double major, dual enrollment of high school students, ESL, independent study, internships. **Credit/placement by examination:** AP, CLEP, institutional tests. 21 credit hours maximum toward associate degree. **Support services:** GED preparation and test center, learning center, reduced course load, remedial instruction, study skills assistance, tutoring, writing center.

Majors. Biology: General. **Business:** General, accounting, accounting technology, administrative services, marketing. **Communications:** General. **Computer sciences:** LAN/WAN management, networking, security, support specialist, system admin, web page design. **Education:** Early childhood, elementary, physical. **English:** English lit. **Health services:** Dental assistant, nursing (RN), office assistant, prepharmacy, surgical technology. **History:** General. **Liberal arts:** Arts/sciences. **Parks/recreation:** Exercise sciences,

sports admin. **Physical sciences:** Geology. **Protective services:** Criminal justice, firefighting, forest/wildland firefighting. **Psychology:** General. **Social sciences:** Anthropology, geography, political science, sociology. **Work/family studies:** Child care management.

Most popular majors. Biological/life sciences 8%, business/marketing 12%, computer/information sciences 8%, health sciences 6%, liberal arts 29%, security/protective services 7%, social sciences 9%.

Technology on campus. 94 workstations in library, computer center. Online course registration, online library, helpline, wireless network available.

Student life. Freshman orientation: Mandatory. Preregistration for classes offered. **Activities:** Student government.

Student services. Adult student services, career counseling, services for economically disadvantaged, student employment services, financial aid counseling, health services, personal counseling, placement for graduates, veterans' counselor. **Physically disabled:** Services for visually, speech, hearing impaired. **Transfer:** Transfer center, transfer adviser, college fairs on campus for students transferring to 4-year colleges.

Contact. E-mail: onestop@cwidaho.cc
Phone: (208) 562-3000 Fax: (888) 562-3216
Luis Caloca, Director of Admissions, College of Western Idaho, MS 3000, Nampa, ID 83653

Eastern Idaho Technical College
Idaho Falls, Idaho
www.eitc.edu

CB code: 0975

▶ Public 2-year technical college
▶ Commuter campus in small city

General. Founded in 1969. Regionally accredited. **Enrollment:** 553 degree-seeking undergraduates. **Degrees:** 97 associate awarded. **Location:** 286 miles from Boise, 230 miles from Salt Lake City. **Calendar:** Semester, limited summer session. **Full-time faculty:** 30 total. **Part-time faculty:** 16 total.

Basis for selection. Open admission, but selective for some programs. COMPASS required of all applicants. Students who score below acceptable level must complete developmental classes before enrolling in degree program. Entrance exam, essay required for nursing.

High school preparation. Recommended units include English 8, mathematics 6 and science 4.

2015-2016 Annual costs. Tuition/fees: $2,334; $8,550 out-of-state. Per-credit charge: $103 in-state; $205 out-of-state. Books/supplies: $1,171. Personal expenses: $1,606.

Financial aid. Need-based: Need-based aid available for part-time students. Work-study available nights, weekends and for part-time students. **Non-need-based:** Scholarships awarded for academics, job skills, state residency.

Application procedures. Admission: No deadline. $15 fee. Admission notification on a rolling basis. **Financial aid:** Priority date 6/1; no closing date. FAFSA, institutional form required. Applicants notified on a rolling basis starting 6/6.

Academics. Special study options: Distance learning, ESL. License preparation in dental hygiene, nursing. **Credit/placement by examination:** AP, CLEP, institutional tests. **Support services:** GED preparation and test center, learning center, remedial instruction, study skills assistance, tutoring, writing center.

Majors. Business: Accounting, administrative services, marketing. **Computer sciences:** Networking, web page design. **Health services:** Medical assistant, nursing (RN), surgical technology. **Protective services:** Firefighting.

Most popular majors. Business/marketing 14%, computer/information sciences 19%, health sciences 50%, legal studies 11%.

Technology on campus. 100 workstations in library, computer center. Online library, helpline, wireless network available.

Student life. Freshman orientation: Mandatory. Preregistration for classes offered. **Activities:** Student government.

Student services. Adult student services, alcohol/substance abuse counseling, career counseling, services for economically disadvantaged, student

employment services, financial aid counseling, personal counseling, placement for graduates, veterans' counselor, women's services. **Physically disabled:** Services for visually, speech, hearing impaired. **Transfer:** Preadmission transcript evaluation for new students.

Contact. E-mail: pamala.levan@my.eitc.edu
Phone: (208) 524-3000 ext. 3390
Toll-free number: (800) 662-0261 ext. 3390 Fax: (208) 525-7026
RaeLynn Patterson, Director of Admissions, Eastern Idaho Technical College, 1600 South 25th East, Idaho Falls, ID 83404-5788

North Idaho College
Coeur d'Alene, Idaho
www.nic.edu
CB code: 4539

▶ Public 2-year community college
▶ Commuter campus in large town

General. Founded in 1933. Regionally accredited. **Enrollment:** 5,779 undergraduates. **Degrees:** 676 associate awarded. **ROTC:** Army. **Location:** 30 miles from Spokane, Washington. **Calendar:** Semester, limited summer session. **Full-time faculty:** 162 total; 13% have terminal degrees, 4% minority, 48% women. **Part-time faculty:** 358 total; 8% have terminal degrees, 6% minority, 55% women. **Partnerships:** Formal partnerships with local businesses.

Transfer out. Colleges most students transferred to 2015: University of Idaho, Lewis-Clark State College, Boise State University, Eastern Washington University, Spokane Community College.

Basis for selection. RN, LPN and other allied health program applicants must submit 3 references and supplemental statement. Professional technical applicants should be interviewed by counselor. Interview recommended for professional technical majors. **Home schooled:** GED highly recommended. **Learning Disabled:** Contact Disability Support Services at time of application.

High school preparation. Algebra, biology, 2 years chemistry with laboratory, or 1 year chemistry and 1 year physics, with cumulative 2.50 GPA required for registered nursing applicants. Physics, advanced algebra recommended for nursing applicants.

2015-2016 Annual costs. Tuition/fees: $4,012; $5,282 out-of-district; $9,952 out-of-state. Room/board: $7,450. Books/supplies: $1,250. Personal expenses: $1,512.

Financial aid. Need-based: Need-based aid available for part-time students. Work-study available nights, weekends and for part-time students. **Non-need-based:** Scholarships awarded for academics, art, athletics, leadership, minority status, music/drama, state residency.

Application procedures. Admission: No deadline. $25 fee, may be waived for applicants with need. Admission notification on a rolling basis. **Financial aid:** Priority date 3/15; no closing date. FAFSA required. Applicants notified on a rolling basis starting 4/1; must reply within 2 week(s) of notification.

Academics. Special study options: Distance learning, dual enrollment of high school students, independent study, internships. Lewis Clark State College and University of Idaho upper division and graduate classes on campus. Bachelor's degree programs available on campus. License preparation in nursing. **Credit/placement by examination:** AP, CLEP, SAT, ACT, institutional tests. 24 credit hours maximum toward associate degree. **Support services:** GED preparation and test center, learning center, reduced course load, remedial instruction, study skills assistance, tutoring, writing center.

Majors. Area/ethnic studies: Native American. **Biology:** General, botany, zoology. **Business:** Administrative services, business admin. **Communications:** Communications/speech/rhetoric, journalism, public relations. **Computer sciences:** General, applications programming, programming. **Conservation:** Fisheries, forestry, wildlife/wilderness. **Education:** General, business, early childhood, elementary, secondary. **Engineering:** General, chemical, civil, electrical. **English:** English lit. **Foreign languages:** General. **General:** Carpentry. **Health services:** Clinical lab assistant, medical assistant, medical secretary, medical transcription, mental health services, nursing (RN), pharmacy assistant, physical therapy assistant, predental, premedicine, prepharmacy, preveterinary. **History:** General. **Liberal arts:** Arts/sciences. **Math:** General. **Parks/recreation:** Health/fitness. **Philosophy/religion:** Philosophy. **Physical sciences:** Astronomy, chemistry, geology, physics. **Protective services:** Criminal justice, police science. **Psychology:** General. **Social sciences:** General, anthropology, political science, sociology. **Visual/performing arts:** Commercial/advertising art, music, music performance, music theory/composition, studio arts.

Technology on campus. 150 workstations in dormitories, library, computer center, student center. Dormitories wired for high-speed internet access and linked to campus network. Commuter students can connect to campus network. Online course registration, helpline, repair service, wireless network available.

Student life. Freshman orientation: Available. Preregistration for classes offered. **Housing:** Coed dorms available. $200 deposit. Apartment complex adjacent to campus available. **Activities:** Bands, choral groups, dance, drama, film society, international student organizations, literary magazine, music ensembles, musical theater, student government, student newspaper, Students for Human Equality, creative writers club, nursing student association, veterans club.

Athletics. NJCAA. **Intercollegiate:** Basketball, cheerleading, soccer, softball W, volleyball W, wrestling M. **Intramural:** Basketball, bowling, football (non-tackle), golf, softball, table tennis, tennis, volleyball. **Team name:** Cardinals.

Student services. Adult student services, alcohol/substance abuse counseling, career counseling, services for economically disadvantaged, student employment services, financial aid counseling, health services, legal services, minority student services, on-campus daycare, personal counseling, placement for graduates, veterans' counselor, women's services. **Physically disabled:** Services for visually, speech, hearing impaired. **Transfer:** Transfer adviser, college fairs on campus for students transferring to 4-year colleges.

Contact. E-mail: admit@nic.edu
Phone: (208) 769-3311 Toll-free number: (877) 404-4536
Fax: (208) 769-3399
Tami Haft, Registrar and Director of Admissions, North Idaho College, 1000 West Garden Avenue, Coeur d'Alene, ID 83814-2199

Stevens-Henager College: Boise
Boise, Idaho
www.stevenshenager.edu

▶ For-profit 2-year technical and career college
▶ Commuter campus in small city
▶ Application essay, interview required

General. Enrollment: 350 undergraduates. **Degrees:** 13 bachelor's, 91 associate awarded. **Calendar:** Differs by program, extensive summer session. **Full-time faculty:** 12 total. **Part-time faculty:** 34 total.

Student profile.

Out-of-state:	1%	25 or older:	70%

Basis for selection. Open admission, but selective for some programs. All applicants must complete a personal interview and submit a personal statement. Students applying for Respiratory Program must complete Wonderlic test and interview with the Program director. **Adult students:** SAT/ACT scores not required. **Home schooled:** Transcript of courses and grades, interview required.

High school preparation. 11 units required; 15 recommended. Required and recommended units include English 4, mathematics 2-3, social studies 1, history 2, science 2-3, foreign language 1 and computer science 1.

2015-2016 Annual costs. Associate programs: $42,387-$58,692. Bachelor's programs: $31,620-$74,778. Amounts are for the entire program and include books and supplies.

Financial aid. All financial aid based on need. Work-study available nights, weekends and for part-time students.

Application procedures. Admission: No deadline. $75 fee. Application must be submitted on paper. Admission notification on a rolling basis. **Financial aid:** No deadline. FAFSA required.

Academics. Special study options: Accelerated study, distance learning, external degree, liberal arts/career combination. Bachelor's degree programs available on campus. **Credit/placement by examination:** AP, CLEP. **Support services:** GED preparation, learning center, remedial instruction, study skills assistance, tutoring, writing center.

Majors. Business: Accounting, business admin. **Computer sciences:** General. **Health services:** Office assistant. **Visual/performing arts:** Graphic design.

Technology on campus. 35 workstations in library, computer center, student center. Commuter students can connect to campus network. Online library, helpline, repair service, wireless network available.

Student life. Freshman orientation: Mandatory. Preregistration for classes offered. **Activities:** Student newspaper.

Student services. Adult student services, career counseling, student employment services, financial aid counseling, placement for graduates, veterans' counselor. **Transfer:** Pre-admission transcript evaluation for new students. Transfer adviser for students transferring to 4-year colleges.

Contact. E-mail: jaime.davis@stevenshenager.edu
Phone: (208) 383-4540 Toll-free number: (888) 842-7990
Fax: (208) 345-6999
David Breck, Director of Admissions, Stevens-Henager College: Boise, 1444 S Entertainment Avenue, Boise, ID 83709

Illinois

Benedictine University at Springfield
Springfield, Illinois
www.ben.edu/springfield   CB code: 1734

- Private 2-year branch campus college affiliated with the Roman Catholic Church
- Commuter campus in small city
- SAT or ACT (ACT writing optional) required

General. Founded in 1929. Regionally accredited. **Enrollment:** 771 degree-seeking undergraduates. **Degrees:** 187 bachelor's, 2 associate awarded; master's, professional offered. **Location:** 200 miles from Chicago, 100 miles from St. Louis. **Calendar:** Semester, limited summer session. **Full-time faculty:** 31 total; 39% have terminal degrees, 3% minority, 68% women. **Part-time faculty:** 91 total; 3% have terminal degrees, 9% minority, 56% women. **Class size:** 87% < 20, 13% 20-39.

Student profile.

Out-of-state:	3%	Live on campus:	11%
25 or older:	47%		

Transfer out. Colleges most students transferred to 2015: Southern Illinois University-Edwardsville, University of Illinois-Springfield, Illinois State University, Eastern Illinois University, Southern Illinois University-Carbondale.

Basis for selection. High school course work, test scores, GPA, class rank are required criteria. Test scores may determine if additional placement testing for advising is necessary. Interview may be recommended for academically weak applicants. **Adult students:** SAT/ACT scores not required if applicant over 24. **Home schooled:** Transcript of courses and grades, state high school equivalency certificate required. GED required to qualify for federal and state financial aid. **Learning Disabled:** Students with learning disabilities required to disclose in order to receive accommodations.

High school preparation. Recommended units include English 4, mathematics 3, social studies 2, science 2 and academic electives 2. Mathematics and physical science recommended for all applicants, foreign language for some.

2015-2016 Annual costs. Books/supplies: $1,450. Personal expenses: $2,450.

Financial aid. Need-based: Need-based aid available for part-time students. Work-study available nights, weekends and for part-time students. **Non-need-based:** Scholarships awarded for academics, art, athletics, leadership, religious affiliation.

Application procedures. Admission: No deadline. $20 fee, may be waived for applicants with need. Admission notification on a rolling basis. **Financial aid:** Priority date 4/15; no closing date. FAFSA required. Applicants notified on a rolling basis starting 4/15; must reply within 2 week(s) of notification.

Academics. Special study options: Accelerated study, combined bachelor's/graduate degree, cooperative education, cross-registration, double major, dual enrollment of high school students, exchange student, honors, independent study, internships, study abroad, teacher certification program. Bachelor's degree programs available on campus. **Credit/placement by examination:** AP, CLEP, ACT, institutional tests. 15 credit hours maximum toward associate degree, 30 toward bachelor's. **Support services:** Learning center, reduced course load, remedial instruction, study skills assistance, tutoring, writing center.

Technology on campus. 113 workstations in library, computer center, student center. Dormitories wired for high-speed internet access and linked to campus network. Commuter students can connect to campus network. Online course registration, online library, helpline, wireless network available.

Student life. Freshman orientation: Mandatory. Preregistration for classes offered. Held Friday before classes begin. **Policies:** Alcohol and other drugs prohibited. **Housing:** Coed dorms, single-sex dorms, special housing for disabled, apartments, wellness housing available. $300 nonrefundable deposit. **Activities:** Campus ministries, choral groups, international student organizations, literary magazine, student government, student newspaper,

Student Ambassadors, art club, chem club, student activity council, arts and cultural events club, Alpha Sigma Lambda.

Athletics. NAIA. **Intercollegiate:** Baseball M, basketball, cheerleading, cross-country, golf, soccer, softball W, volleyball W. **Team name:** Bulldogs.

Student services. Adult student services, alcohol/substance abuse counseling, chaplain/spiritual director, career counseling, student employment services, financial aid counseling, personal counseling, veterans' counselor. **Physically disabled:** Services for visually, speech, hearing impaired. **Transfer:** Pre-admission transcript evaluation for new students. Transfer adviser for students transferring to 4-year colleges.

Contact. E-mail: springadm@ben.edu
Phone: (217) 525-1420 Toll-free number: (800) 635-7289
Fax: (217) 525-1497
Kevin Broeckling, Associate VP of Enrollment & Student Life, Benedictine University at Springfield, 1500 North Fifth Street, Springfield, IL 62702-2694

Black Hawk College
Moline, Illinois
www.bhc.edu   CB code: 1483

- Public 2-year community college
- Commuter campus in large town

General. Founded in 1946. Regionally accredited. **Enrollment:** 3,441 degree-seeking undergraduates; 1,830 non-degree-seeking students. **Degrees:** 571 associate awarded. **Location:** 160 miles from Chicago, 60 miles from Iowa City. **Calendar:** Semester, limited summer session. **Full-time faculty:** 126 total; 16% have terminal degrees, 9% minority, 57% women. **Part-time faculty:** 152 total; 8% have terminal degrees, 7% minority, 61% women. **Class size:** 68% < 20, 31% 20-39, less than 1% 40-49, less than 1% 50-99. **Special facilities:** Sustainable technologies building, wind turbine, agriculture arena, horse barn.

Student profile. Among degree-seeking undergraduates, 56% enrolled in a transfer program, 44% enrolled in a vocational program, 4% already have a bachelor's degree or higher, 552 enrolled as first-time, first-year students, 163 transferred in from other institutions.

Part-time:	47%	Asian American:	2%
Out-of-state:	8%	Hispanic/Latino:	6%
Women:	61%	Multi-racial, non-Hispanic:	13%
African American:	9%	25 or older:	30%

Transfer out. 63% of students enrolled in the transfer program go on to 4-year colleges. **Colleges most students transferred to 2015:** Western Illinois University, St. Ambrose University, Augustana College, University of Illinois, University of Iowa.

Basis for selection. Open admission, but selective for some programs. Special requirements for health care related programs, such as nursing, licensed practical nursing, and physical therapy assistant. **Learning Disabled:** Students with any disability (physical, mental, or learning), wanting services from the College, must register with the College's Disability Services department. The student must provide documentation of disability and will be evaluated to determine which services would be appropriate for their situation.

High school preparation. 15 units recommended. Recommended units include English 4, mathematics 3, social studies 3 and science 3. 2 years of foreign language, music, or art.

2015-2016 Annual costs. Tuition/fees: $4,050; $7,500 out-of-district; $7,650 out-of-state. Per-credit charge: $135 in-district; $250 out-of-district; $255 out-of-state. Books/supplies: $1,060. Personal expenses: $2,179. **Additional information:** Tuition for five contiguous counties is $180 per credit hour. Online courses are $150 per credit hour in-state;$175 per credit hour out-of-state.

2014-2015 Financial aid. Need-based: 480 full-time freshmen applied for aid; 320 deemed to have need; 292 received aid. Average need met was 72%. Average scholarship/grant was $2,306; average loan $1,614. 84% of total undergraduate aid awarded as scholarships/grants, 16% as loans/jobs. Need-based aid available for part-time students. Work-study available nights, weekends and for part-time students. **Non-need-based:** Awarded to 416 full-time undergraduates, including 142 freshmen. Scholarships awarded for academics, art, athletics, leadership, music/drama, state residency. **Additional information:** 5/15 deadline for scholarships.

Application procedures. Admission: No deadline. No application fee. Admission notification on a rolling basis beginning on or about 3/1. **Financial aid:** Priority date 5/15; no closing date. FAFSA required. Applicants notified on a rolling basis starting 5/1.

Academics. Free online tutoring from Tutor.com. Expert tutors are available 24/7 to help with math, science, English, and history. **Special study options:** Accelerated study, distance learning, dual enrollment of high school students, ESL, honors, independent study, internships, study abroad, weekend college. License preparation in nursing, physical therapy. **Credit/placement by examination:** AP, CLEP, institutional tests. 30 credit hours maximum toward associate degree. Most CLEP credit awarded to students pursuing associate degree in liberal studies. **Support services:** GED preparation, learning center, reduced course load, remedial instruction, study skills assistance, tutoring. Free workshops on a variety of topics.

Majors. Business: Accounting, administrative services, banking/financial services, office technology, retailing, small business admin. **Education:** Early childhood, mathematics, special ed. **General:** Carpentry. **Health services:** EMT paramedic, health information technology, nursing (RN), physical therapy assistant, radiologic technology/medical imaging, veterinary technology/assistant. **Liberal arts:** Arts/sciences. **Protective services:** Fire services admin, police science. **Visual/performing arts:** Art, design. **Work/family studies:** Child care service.

Most popular majors. Agriculture 11%, health sciences 16%, interdisciplinary studies 21%, liberal arts 41%.

Technology on campus. 950 workstations in library, computer center. Commuter students can connect to campus network. Online course registration, online library, wireless network available.

Student life. Freshman orientation: Available. Preregistration for classes offered. **Housing:** There are privately-owned apartment complexes adjacent to both campuses: The Villas at the Quad City Campus and Prairie Pointe Apartments at the East Campus. **Activities:** Jazz band, choral groups, drama, international student organizations, music ensembles, student government, student newspaper, Association of Latin-American Students, Clean Sphere, College Republicans, student wellness club, Sisterhood on Campus, Unity Alliance, Military students and veterans club, African Student Association, College Democrats, International Student Association.

Athletics. NJCAA. **Intercollegiate:** Baseball M, basketball, golf M, softball W, volleyball W. **Team name:** Braves.

Student services. Career counseling, services for economically disadvantaged, student employment services, financial aid counseling, minority student services, personal counseling, placement for graduates, veterans' counselor, women's services. **Physically disabled:** Services for visually, speech, hearing impaired. **Transfer:** Pre-admission transcript evaluation for new students. Transfer center, transfer adviser, college fairs on campus for students transferring to 4-year colleges.

Contact. E-mail: registrar@bhc.edu
Phone: (309) 796-5300 Toll-free number: (800) 334-1311
Fax: (309) 796-5209
Heather Bjorgan, Registrar, Black Hawk College, 6600-34th Avenue, Moline, IL 61265-5899

Carl Sandburg College
Galesburg, Illinois
www.sandburg.edu
CB code: 1982

- Public 2-year community college
- Commuter campus in large town

General. Founded in 1966. Regionally accredited. Branch center in Carthage, extension center in Bushnell. **Enrollment:** 1,516 degree-seeking undergraduates. **Degrees:** 178 associate awarded. **ROTC:** Army. **Location:** 198 miles from Chicago, 47 miles from Peoria. **Calendar:** Semester, limited summer session. **Full-time faculty:** 52 total. **Part-time faculty:** 145 total. **Class size:** 94% < 20, 6% 20-39, less than 1% 40-49, less than 1% 50-99. **Special facilities:** Greenhouse, 22-acre agriculture experience plot.

Student profile.

Out-of-state:	3%	25 or older:	39%

Transfer out. Colleges most students transferred to 2015: Western Illinois University, Illinois State University.

Basis for selection. Open admission, but selective for some programs. Special requirements for allied health programs. Interview recommended for radiologic technology, mortuary science, and physical therapy assistant majors.

High school preparation. 15 units recommended. Recommended units include English 4, mathematics 3, social studies 2, science 2 (laboratory 2) and academic electives 2.

2015-2016 Annual costs. Tuition/fees: $4,650; $6,540 out-of-district; $7,680 out-of-state. Per-credit charge: $150 in-district; $213 out-of-district; $251 out-of-state. Books/supplies: $756. Personal expenses: $840.

Financial aid. Need-based: Work-study available nights, weekends and for part-time students. **Non-need-based:** Scholarships awarded for academics, art, athletics, music/drama.

Application procedures. Admission: No deadline. No application fee. Admission notification on a rolling basis. **Financial aid:** Priority date 5/1; no closing date. FAFSA, institutional form required. Applicants notified on a rolling basis starting 5/1; must reply by 8/25 or within 2 week(s) of notification.

Academics. Special study options: Cross-registration, dual enrollment of high school students, ESL, honors, independent study, internships, student-designed major, study abroad, teacher certification program. License preparation in dental hygiene, nursing, paramedic, radiology. **Credit/placement by examination:** AP, CLEP, institutional tests. 20 credit hours maximum toward associate degree. **Support services:** GED preparation and test center, learning center, remedial instruction, tutoring.

Majors. Business: Accounting, administrative services, banking/financial services, business admin, operations. **Computer sciences:** General. **Health services:** Nursing (RN). **Protective services:** Firefighting, law enforcement admin. **Work/family studies:** Child care management.

Most popular majors. Business/marketing 8%, health sciences 31%, interdisciplinary studies 17%, liberal arts 32%.

Technology on campus. 69 workstations in library, computer center. Commuter students can connect to campus network. Online library, helpline, wireless network available.

Student life. Activities: Bands, choral groups, drama, literary magazine, music ensembles, student government.

Athletics. NJCAA. **Intercollegiate:** Baseball M, basketball, softball W, volleyball W. **Team name:** Chargers.

Student services. Career counseling, services for economically disadvantaged, student employment services, on-campus daycare, personal counseling, placement for graduates, veterans' counselor. **Physically disabled:** Services for visually, hearing impaired. **Transfer:** Transfer adviser, college fairs on campus for students transferring to 4-year colleges.

Contact. Phone: (309) 344-2518 Fax: (309) 344-3526
Carol Kreider, Dean of Student Support Services, Carl Sandburg College, 2400 Tom L. Wilson Boulevard, Galesburg, IL 61401

City Colleges of Chicago: Harold Washington College
Chicago, Illinois
www.ccc.edu
CB code: 1089

- Public 2-year community college
- Commuter campus in very large city

General. Founded in 1962. Regionally accredited. **Enrollment:** 7,943 degree-seeking undergraduates. **Degrees:** 1,057 associate awarded. **Calendar:** Semester, limited summer session. **Full-time faculty:** 114 total. **Part-time faculty:** 292 total.

Transfer out. Colleges most students transferred to 2015: University of Illinois-Chicago, DePaul University, Northeastern Illinois University, Columbia College, Roosevelt University.

Basis for selection. Open admission, but selective for some programs. Special requirements for physicians assistant and police programs. All incoming freshmen required to take placement tests.

2015-2016 Annual costs. Tuition/fees: $3,506; $9,206 out-of-district; $11,906 out-of-state.

Financial aid. All financial aid based on need. Need-based aid available for part-time students. Work-study available nights, weekends and for part-time students.

Application procedures. Admission: No deadline. No application fee. **Financial aid:** FAFSA required. Applicants notified on a rolling basis.

Academics. Credit/placement by examination: AP, CLEP, institutional tests. **Support services:** GED preparation, learning center, reduced course load, remedial instruction, study skills assistance, tutoring.

Majors. Business: Accounting, hotel/motel admin. **Communications technology:** Animation/special effects. **Computer sciences:** Information technology. **Education:** Art, early childhood, ESL, music, teacher assistance. **Engineering:** General. **Health services:** Substance abuse counseling. **Human services:** Social work. **Liberal arts:** Arts/sciences. **Math:** General. **Protective services:** Criminal justice, firefighting. **Visual/performing arts:** Art, music. **Work/family studies:** Child care service.

Most popular majors. Business/marketing 12%, computer/information sciences 7%, family/consumer sciences 17%, interdisciplinary studies 29%, security/protective services 7%.

Student life. Freshman orientation: Mandatory. Preregistration for classes offered. One hour overview. **Activities:** Music ensembles, black student union, Organization of Latin American Students, Berean Bible club, Circle K.

Student services. Adult student services, career counseling, services for economically disadvantaged, student employment services, financial aid counseling, minority student services, personal counseling, placement for graduates, veterans' counselor. **Physically disabled:** Services for visually, speech, hearing impaired.

Contact. Phone: (312) 553-6071 Fax: (312) 553-6077
Courtney O'Brien, Registrar, City Colleges of Chicago: Harold Washington College, 30 East Lake Street, Chicago, IL 60601

City Colleges of Chicago: Harry S. Truman College
Chicago, Illinois
www.ccc.edu
CB code: 1111

- Public 2-year community college
- Commuter campus in very large city

General. Founded in 1956. Regionally accredited. **Enrollment:** 4,135 degree-seeking undergraduates. **Degrees:** 698 associate awarded. **Calendar:** Semester, limited summer session. **Full-time faculty:** 96 total. **Part-time faculty:** 117 total. **Special facilities:** Art gallery for Chicago artists, performing arts theater. **Partnerships:** Formal partnerships with Chamber of Commerce and aldermanic representative for our ward.

Transfer out. Colleges most students transferred to 2015: University of Illinois Chicago, Northeastern Illinois University, DePaul University, Loyola University, Columbia College.

Basis for selection. Open admission, but selective for some programs. Test scores, essay considered for nursing and certain allied health programs. ACT required of nursing applicants. Applicants without high school diploma must obtain GED prior to graduation.

2015-2016 Annual costs. Tuition/fees: $3,506; $9,206 out-of-district; $11,906 out-of-state.

Financial aid. All financial aid based on need. Need-based aid available for part-time students. Work-study available nights, weekends and for part-time students.

Application procedures. Admission: No deadline. No application fee. Admission notification on a rolling basis. **Financial aid:** No deadline. FAFSA required. Applicants notified on a rolling basis.

Academics. Credit/placement by examination: AP, CLEP, institutional tests. 30 credit hours maximum toward associate degree. **Support services:** GED preparation and test center.

Majors. Business: Accounting, business admin. **Computer sciences:** Information technology, networking. **Education:** Mathematics. **Engineering:** General. **Health services:** Nursing (RN). **Liberal arts:** Arts/sciences. **Protective services:** Criminal justice. **Visual/performing arts:** Art. **Work/family studies:** Child care service.

Most popular majors. Health sciences 41%, interdisciplinary studies 8%, liberal arts 38%.

Student life. Freshman orientation: Available. Preregistration for classes offered. **Activities:** Latin American center, refugee center, Native American center.

Contact. Phone: (773) 907-6814 Fax: (773) 907-4757
Mylinh Tran, Registrar, City Colleges of Chicago: Harry S. Truman College, 1145 West Wilson Avenue, Chicago, IL 60640

City Colleges of Chicago: Kennedy-King College
Chicago, Illinois
www.ccc.edu
CB code: 1910

- Public 2-year community college
- Commuter campus in very large city

General. Founded in 1935. Regionally accredited. **Enrollment:** 2,821 degree-seeking undergraduates. **Degrees:** 565 associate awarded. **Calendar:** Semester, limited summer session. **Full-time faculty:** 83 total. **Part-time faculty:** 106 total.

Basis for selection. Open admission. Applicants admitted without high school diploma must pass GED by end of first school year.

2015-2016 Annual costs. Tuition/fees: $3,506; $9,206 out-of-district; $11,906 out-of-state.

Financial aid. All financial aid based on need. Need-based aid available for part-time students. Work-study available nights, weekends and for part-time students.

Application procedures. Admission: No deadline. No application fee. **Financial aid:** No deadline. FAFSA required. Applicants notified on a rolling basis; must reply within 2 week(s) of notification.

Academics. Credit/placement by examination: AP, CLEP, institutional tests. **Support services:** GED preparation.

Majors. Business: Accounting, administrative services, business admin, construction management. **Communications:** Radio/TV. **Communications technology:** Platemaker/imager. **Computer sciences:** Information technology. **Education:** Early childhood, early childhood special. **Health services:** Dental hygiene, nursing (RN), substance abuse counseling. **Human services:** Social work. **Liberal arts:** Arts/sciences. **Protective services:** Criminal justice. **Visual/performing arts:** Dramatic. **Work/family studies:** Child care service.

Most popular majors. Family/consumer sciences 6%, health sciences 20%, liberal arts 52%, personal/culinary services 7%.

Student life. Freshman orientation: Available. Preregistration for classes offered.

Athletics. Team name: Statesman, Lady Statesman.

Contact. Phone: (773) 602-5273 Fax: (773) 602-5247
Eric Hayes, Registrar, City Colleges of Chicago: Kennedy-King College, 6301 South Halsted Street, Chicago, IL 60621

City Colleges of Chicago: Malcolm X College
Chicago, Illinois
www.ccc.edu
CB code: 1144

- Public 2-year community college
- Commuter campus in very large city

General. Founded in 1911. Regionally accredited. **Enrollment:** 4,027 degree-seeking undergraduates. **Degrees:** 530 associate awarded. **Location:** 3 miles from downtown. **Calendar:** Semester, limited summer session. **Full-time faculty:** 86 total. **Part-time faculty:** 98 total.

Basis for selection. Open admission, but selective for some programs. Test scores, essay considered for nursing and certain allied health programs. ACT required of nursing applicants.

2015-2016 Annual costs. Tuition/fees: $3,506; $9,206 out-of-district; $11,906 out-of-state.

Financial aid. All financial aid based on need. Need-based aid available for part-time students. Work-study available nights, weekends and for part-time students.

Application procedures. Admission: No deadline. No application fee. Admission notification on a rolling basis. **Financial aid:** No deadline. FAFSA, institutional form required. Applicants notified on a rolling basis; must reply within 2 week(s) of notification.

Academics. Credit/placement by examination: AP, CLEP, institutional tests. 30 credit hours maximum toward associate degree. **Support services:** GED preparation.

Majors. Computer sciences: Information technology. **Health services:** Dialysis technology, EMT paramedic, nursing (RN), physician assistant, radiologic technology/medical imaging, respiratory therapy technology, surgical technology. **Liberal arts:** Arts/sciences. **Work/family studies:** Child care service.

Most popular majors. Health sciences 47%, liberal arts 43%.

Student life. Freshman orientation: Available. Preregistration for classes offered.

Contact. Phone: (312) 850-7126 Fax: (312) 850-7092
Jeffrey Wonders, Registrar, City Colleges of Chicago: Malcolm X College, 1900 West Van Buren Street, Chicago, IL 60612

City Colleges of Chicago: Olive-Harvey College
Chicago, Illinois
www.ccc.edu   CB code: 1584

▶ Public 2-year community college
▶ Commuter campus in very large city

General. Founded in 1970. Regionally accredited. **Enrollment:** 2,149 degree-seeking undergraduates. **Degrees:** 406 associate awarded. **Location:** 16 miles from downtown. **Calendar:** Semester, limited summer session. **Full-time faculty:** 53 total. **Part-time faculty:** 57 total.

Basis for selection. Open admission, but selective for some programs.

2015-2016 Annual costs. Tuition/fees: $3,506; $9,206 out-of-district; $11,906 out-of-state.

Financial aid. Need-based: Need-based aid available for part-time students. Work-study available nights, weekends and for part-time students.

Application procedures. Admission: No deadline. No application fee. Admission notification on a rolling basis. **Financial aid:** No deadline. FAFSA required. Applicants notified on a rolling basis.

Academics. Credit/placement by examination: AP, CLEP, institutional tests.

Majors. Business: Accounting, business admin. **Computer sciences:** Information technology. **Health services:** Ophthalmic technology, respiratory therapy technology. **Liberal arts:** Arts/sciences. **Protective services:** Criminal justice. **Work/family studies:** Child care service, family studies.

Most popular majors. Family/consumer sciences 17%, health sciences 7%, interdisciplinary studies 12%, liberal arts 60%.

Student life. Freshman orientation: Available. Preregistration for classes offered.

Contact. Phone: (773) 291-6384 Fax: (773) 291-6185
Dorian Thomas, Registrar, City Colleges of Chicago: Olive-Harvey College, 10001 South Woodlawn Avenue, Chicago, IL 60628

City Colleges of Chicago: Richard J. Daley College
Chicago, Illinois
www.ccc.edu   CB code: 1093

▶ Public 2-year community college
▶ Commuter campus in very large city

General. Founded in 1960. Regionally accredited. **Enrollment:** 3,953 degree-seeking undergraduates. **Degrees:** 622 associate awarded. **Calendar:** Semester, limited summer session. **Full-time faculty:** 53 total. **Part-time faculty:** 109 total.

Basis for selection. Open admission, but selective for some programs. Test scores, essay considered for nursing and certain allied health programs. ACT required of nursing applicants.

2015-2016 Annual costs. Tuition/fees: $3,506; $9,206 out-of-district; $11,906 out-of-state.

Financial aid. Need-based: Work-study available nights, weekends and for part-time students.

Application procedures. Admission: No deadline. No application fee. Admission notification on a rolling basis. **Financial aid:** No deadline. FAFSA required. Applicants notified on a rolling basis.

Academics. Credit/placement by examination: AP, CLEP, institutional tests. 30 credit hours maximum toward associate degree.

Majors. Business: Accounting, business admin, sales/distribution. **Computer sciences:** Information technology, networking. **Engineering:** General. **General:** Electrician. **Health services:** Nursing (RN). **Liberal arts:** Arts/sciences. **Protective services:** Criminal justice. **Work/family studies:** Child care service.

Most popular majors. Family/consumer sciences 9%, health sciences 30%, liberal arts 33%, security/protective services 12%, trade and industry 7%.

Technology on campus. 250 workstations in library, computer center.

Student life. Freshman orientation: Available. Preregistration for classes offered.

Contact. Phone: (773) 838-7606 Fax: (773) 838-7605
Cynthia Moreno, Director of Admission, City Colleges of Chicago: Richard J. Daley College, 7500 South Pulaski Road, Chicago, IL 60652

City Colleges of Chicago: Wilbur Wright College
Chicago, Illinois
www.ccc.edu   CB code: 1925

▶ Public 2-year community college
▶ Commuter campus in very large city

General. Founded in 1934. Regionally accredited. **Enrollment:** 7,691 degree-seeking undergraduates. **Degrees:** 1,066 associate awarded. **Location:** 15 miles from downtown. **Calendar:** Semester, limited summer session. **Full-time faculty:** 107 total. **Part-time faculty:** 223 total.

Basis for selection. Open admission.

2015-2016 Annual costs. Tuition/fees: $3,506; $9,206 out-of-district; $11,906 out-of-state.

Financial aid. Need-based: Need-based aid available for part-time students. Work-study available nights, weekends and for part-time students.

Application procedures. Admission: No deadline. No application fee. Admission notification on a rolling basis. **Financial aid:** No deadline. FAFSA, institutional form required. Applicants notified on a rolling basis.

Academics. Credit/placement by examination: AP, CLEP, IB, institutional tests. **Support services:** GED preparation and test center.

Majors. Business: Accounting, business admin, sales/distribution. **Computer sciences:** Information technology. **Engineering:** General. **Health services:** Nursing (RN), occupational therapy assistant, radiologic technology/medical imaging. **Human services:** Social work. **Liberal arts:** Arts/sciences, library assistant. **Visual/performing arts:** Music.

Most popular majors. Interdisciplinary studies 11%, liberal arts 75%, security/protective services 6%.

Student life. Freshman orientation: Available. Preregistration for classes offered.

Athletics. Intercollegiate: Wrestling M.

Contact. Phone: (773) 481-8259 Fax: (773) 481-8053
Mai Aly, Registrar, City Colleges of Chicago: Wilbur Wright College, 4300 North Narragansett Avenue, Chicago, IL 60634-4276

College of DuPage
Glen Ellyn, Illinois
www.cod.edu   CB code: 1083

▶ Public 2-year community college
▶ Commuter campus in large town

General. Founded in 1966. Regionally accredited. **Enrollment:** 16,535 degree-seeking undergraduates; 12,142 non-degree-seeking students.

Degrees: 2,892 associate awarded. **Location:** 25 miles from Chicago. **Calendar:** Semester, extensive summer session. **Full-time faculty:** 284 total; 32% have terminal degrees, 44% minority, 48% women. **Part-time faculty:** 1,199 total; 16% have terminal degrees, 11% minority, 58% women. **Special facilities:** Older adult institute, prairie-marsh nature preserve, arts center, community recreation center, state of the art homeland security center, on-site restaurant and hotel for hospitality and culinary arts students, simulation center for nursing students.

Student profile. Among degree-seeking undergraduates, 34% enrolled in a transfer program, 59% enrolled in a vocational program, 7% already have a bachelor's degree or higher, 3,181 enrolled as first-time, first-year students.

Part-time:	56%	Hispanic/Latino:	21%
Women:	53%	Native American:	1%
African American:	9%	Native Hawaiian/Pacific islander:	1%
Asian American:	10%	International:	1%

Transfer out. Colleges most students transferred to 2015: Northern Illinois University, Illinois State University, University of Illinois at Chicago, Elmhurst College, Benedictine University.

Basis for selection. Open admission, but selective for some programs. Special requirements for allied health programs.

2015-2016 Annual costs. Tuition/fees: $4,320; $9,930 out-of-district; $12,030 out-of-state. Per-credit charge: $144 in-district; $331 out-of-district; $401 out-of-state. Books/supplies: $1,587. Personal expenses: $1,596.

2014-2015 Financial aid. Need-based: 1,964 full-time freshmen applied for aid; 1,124 deemed to have need; 1,043 received aid. Average scholarship/grant was $4,817; average loan $2,652. 68% of total undergraduate aid awarded as scholarships/grants, 32% as loans/jobs. Need-based aid available for part-time students. Work-study available nights, weekends and for part-time students. **Non-need-based:** Awarded to 522 full-time undergraduates, including 169 freshmen. Scholarships awarded for academics, art, leadership, minority status, music/drama, state residency.

Application procedures. Admission: No deadline. $20 fee, may be waived for applicants with need. Admission notification on a rolling basis. **Financial aid:** Priority date 4/30; no closing date. FAFSA required. Applicants notified on a rolling basis starting 6/1; must reply within 2 week(s) of notification.

Academics. Special study options: Accelerated study, cooperative education, cross-registration, distance learning, double major, dual enrollment of high school students, ESL, honors, independent study, internships, student-designed major, study abroad, weekend college. Adult fast-track program for students over 21. 2+2 and 3+1 programs leading to Bachelor's degrees in association with other colleges and universities in the area. Bachelor's degree programs available on campus. License preparation in dental hygiene, nursing, paramedic, real estate. **Credit/placement by examination:** AP, CLEP, institutional tests. 65 credit hours maximum toward associate degree. **Support services:** GED preparation and test center, learning center, pre-admission summer program, reduced course load, remedial instruction, study skills assistance, tutoring, writing center.

Majors. Architecture: Architecture. **Business:** Accounting, accounting technology, administrative services, business admin, fashion, office management, real estate, sales/distribution, tourism promotion. **Communications technology:** General, graphic/printing. **Computer sciences:** Applications programming. **Education:** Early childhood. **Engineering:** General. **General:** Maintenance. **Health services:** Dental hygiene, EMT paramedic, health information technology, medical radiologic technology/radiation therapy, nursing (RN), occupational therapy assistant, physical therapy assistant, respiratory therapy technology, speech-language pathology assistant, substance abuse counseling, surgical technology. **Human services:** Social work. **Liberal arts:** Arts/sciences, library assistant. **Protective services:** Fire safety technology, firefighting, homeland security, police science. **Visual/performing arts:** Art, commercial photography, design, music. **Work/family studies:** Child care management.

Most popular majors. Health sciences 25%, interdisciplinary studies 6%, liberal arts 43%, security/protective services 7%.

Technology on campus. 2,450 workstations in library, computer center, student center. Commuter students can connect to campus network. Online course registration, online library, helpline, repair service, wireless network available.

Student life. Freshman orientation: Available. Preregistration for classes offered. Held close to start of term; parents encouraged to attend. **Housing:** Housing available in cooperation with nearby private college. **Activities:** Bands, choral groups, dance, drama, international student organizations, literary magazine, music ensembles, opera, radio station, student government, student newspaper, symphony orchestra, InterVarsity Christian Fellowship, Endowment for Future Generations, Brothers and Sisters in Christ, Black Student union, Latino ethnic awareness association, Japanese culture club, La Rencontre Francaise, Muslim student association, Safe Zone for LGBT students.

Athletics. NJCAA. **Intercollegiate:** Baseball M, basketball, cross-country, football (tackle) M, golf M, soccer, softball W, tennis, track and field, volleyball W. **Intramural:** Basketball, softball. **Team name:** Chaparrels.

Student services. Adult student services, career counseling, student employment services, financial aid counseling, health services, on-campus daycare, personal counseling, placement for graduates, veterans' counselor. **Physically disabled:** Services for visually, speech, hearing impaired. **Transfer:** Transfer center, transfer adviser, college fairs on campus for students transferring to 4-year colleges.

Contact. E-mail: admissions@cod.edu
Phone: (630) 942-2482 Fax: (630) 790-2686
Coordinator of Admission and Outreach, College of DuPage, 425 Fawell Boulevard, Glen Ellyn, IL 60137-6599

College of Lake County
Grayslake, Illinois
www.clcillinois.edu

CB member
CB code: 1983

▶ Public 2-year community college
▶ Commuter campus in large town

General. Founded in 1967. Regionally accredited. **Enrollment:** 11,466 degree-seeking undergraduates. **Degrees:** 1,388 associate awarded. **Location:** 40 miles from Chicago, 45 miles from Milwaukee. **Calendar:** Semester, extensive summer session. **Full-time faculty:** 205 total; 25% have terminal degrees, 22% minority, 55% women. **Part-time faculty:** 695 total; 12% have terminal degrees, 15% minority, 53% women. **Special facilities:** CAD/CAM center, automated industrial center, performing arts center, child care center.

Student profile.

Out-of-state:	1%	25 or older:	43%

Transfer out. Colleges most students transferred to 2015: Northern Illinois University, University of Wisconsin at Parkside, Northeastern Illinois University, Southern Illinois University, University of Illinois at Chicago.

Basis for selection. Open admission, but selective for some programs. Open admission for certificate and associate of applied science. College-preparatory high school program required for associate of arts and science. Selective admission for health career programs: academic record, class rank, test scores important; recommendations, interview considered. **Learning Disabled:** Accommodations provided when taking proficiency exams.

High school preparation. 15 units recommended. Recommended units include English 4, mathematics 3, social studies 3, (laboratory 3) and academic electives 2. 2 biology and 1 chemistry required for nursing program, mathematics for medical laboratory technician program, chemistry for radiology program. Recommended electives include foreign language, music, vocational education or art.

2015-2016 Annual costs. Tuition/fees: $3,870; $8,955 out-of-district; $11,855 out-of-state. Per-credit charge: $99 in-district; $256 out-of-district; $345 out-of-state. Books/supplies: $1,568. Personal expenses: $1,512.

Financial aid. Need-based: Need-based aid available for part-time students. Work-study available nights, weekends and for part-time students. **Non-need-based:** Scholarships awarded for academics, alumni affiliation, art, athletics, leadership, minority status, music/drama.

Application procedures. Admission: No deadline. No application fee. Admission notification on a rolling basis. Application deadlines vary for health career programs. **Financial aid:** Priority date 6/3; no closing date. FAFSA required. Applicants notified on a rolling basis starting 6/15; must reply within 2 week(s) of notification.

Academics. High school distribution requirement for associate degree applicants may be fulfilled at college. **Special study options:** Accelerated study, cooperative education, cross-registration, distance learning, dual enrollment of high school students, ESL, honors, independent study, internships, student-designed major, study abroad. License preparation in dental hygiene, nursing, paramedic, radiology, real estate. **Credit/placement by examination:** AP, CLEP, institutional tests. 30 credit hours maximum toward associate degree. **Support services:** GED preparation and test center, learning center, reduced course load, remedial instruction, study skills assistance, tutoring, writing center.

Majors. Business: Accounting technology, administrative services, business admin, office technology. **Computer sciences:** Artificial intelligence, networking, web page design. **Conservation:** Management/policy. **Education:**

Music. **Engineering:** General. **English:** Technical writing. **General:** Electrician. **Health services:** Dental hygiene, medical radiologic technology/radiation therapy, nursing (RN), office admin, substance abuse counseling, surgical technology. **Human services:** Social work. **Liberal arts:** Arts/sciences, library assistant. **Protective services:** Fire safety technology, police science. **Visual/performing arts:** Art, music.

Most popular majors. Health sciences 15%, interdisciplinary studies 11%, liberal arts 54%.

Technology on campus. 800 workstations in library, computer center. Online course registration, online library, helpline, wireless network available.

Student life. Freshman orientation: Available. Preregistration for classes offered. **Policies:** Alcohol-free campus, smoking allowed only outside the building. **Activities:** Bands, campus ministries, choral groups, dance, drama, international student organizations, literary magazine, music ensembles, musical theater, radio station, student government, student newspaper, 11 academic organizations, 6 ethnic organizations, 4 religious organizations, 6 health and fitness organizations available.

Athletics. NJCAA. **Intercollegiate:** Baseball M, basketball, cross-country, golf, soccer, softball W, tennis, volleyball W. **Intramural:** Basketball, golf, soccer, table tennis, tennis, volleyball. **Team name:** Lancers.

Student services. Alcohol/substance abuse counseling, career counseling, services for economically disadvantaged, student employment services, financial aid counseling, health services, minority student services, on-campus daycare, personal counseling, placement for graduates, veterans' counselor, women's services. **Physically disabled:** Services for visually, speech, hearing impaired. **Transfer:** Re-entry adviser for new students. Transfer center, transfer adviser, college fairs on campus for students transferring to 4-year colleges.

Contact. E-mail: info@clcillinois.edu
Phone: (847) 543-2061 Fax: (847) 543-3061
Karen Hlavin, Associate Vice President, College of Lake County, 19351 West Washington Street, Grayslake, IL 60030-1198

College of Office Technology
Chicago, Illinois
www.cot.edu
CB code: 3527

▶ For-profit 2-year career college
▶ Commuter campus in very large city

General. Accredited by ACICS. **Calendar:** Differs by program.

Annual costs/financial aid. Personal expenses: $4,600. Need-based financial aid available to full-time and part-time students.

Contact. Phone: (773) 278-0042
Director of Admissions, 1520 West Division Street, Chicago, IL 60622-3312

Coyne College
Chicago, Illinois
www.coynecollege.edu

▶ For-profit 2-year technical and career college
▶ Commuter campus in very large city

General. Regionally accredited; also accredited by ACCSC. **Enrollment:** 590 undergraduates. **Degrees:** 134 associate awarded. **Location:** 1 mile from downtown. **Calendar:** Differs by program. **Full-time faculty:** 25 total. **Part-time faculty:** 16 total.

Basis for selection. Open admission.

Financial aid. Need-based: Work-study available nights, weekends and for part-time students.

Academics. Externships are required for courses in the Allied Health programs. Construction trades programs do practical training at school labs in addition to the theory part of the curriculum. **Credit/placement by examination:** AP, CLEP, institutional tests.

Majors. Health services: Medical assistant.

Technology on campus. Wireless network available.

Student life. Freshman orientation: Available. Preregistration for classes offered. **Activities:** Student newspaper.

Contact. E-mail: ppauletti@coynecollege.edu
Phone: (773) 577-8102 Toll-free number: (800) 999-5220
Fax: (312) 226-3818
Peter Pauletti, Director of Admissions, Coyne College, 330 North Green Street, Chicago, IL 60607

Danville Area Community College
Danville, Illinois
www.dacc.edu
CB code: 1160

▶ Public 2-year community college
▶ Commuter campus in large town

General. Founded in 1946. Regionally accredited. **Enrollment:** 1,885 degree-seeking undergraduates. **Degrees:** 303 associate awarded. **Location:** 150 miles from Chicago, 90 miles from Indianapolis. **Calendar:** Semester, limited summer session. **Full-time faculty:** 66 total; 15% have terminal degrees, 12% minority, 52% women. **Part-time faculty:** 121 total; 7% have terminal degrees, 9% minority, 50% women.

Student profile. Among degree-seeking undergraduates, 35% enrolled in a transfer program, 65% enrolled in a vocational program, 417 enrolled as first-time, first-year students.

Part-time:	47%	25 or older:	34%
Women:	62%		

Transfer out. 85% of students enrolled in the transfer program go on to 4-year colleges. **Colleges most students transferred to 2015:** Eastern Illinois University, Illinois State University, Southern Illinois University at Carbondale, University of Illinois at Urbana/Champaign.

Basis for selection. Open admission.

High school preparation. College-preparatory program recommended. 15 units recommended. Recommended units include English 4, mathematics 3, social studies 2, science 2 and academic electives 4.

2015-2016 Annual costs. Tuition/fees: $3,900; $6,150 out-of-district; $6,150 out-of-state. Per-credit charge: $115 in-district; $190 out-of-district; $190 out-of-state. Books/supplies: $700. Personal expenses: $1,575.

2014-2015 Financial aid. Need-based: 86% of total undergraduate aid awarded as scholarships/grants, 14% as loans/jobs. Need-based aid available for part-time students. Work-study available nights, weekends and for part-time students. **Non-need-based:** Scholarships awarded for academics, art, athletics, leadership, minority status, music/drama, state residency.

Application procedures. Admission: No deadline. No application fee. Application must be submitted on paper. Admission notification on a rolling basis. **Financial aid:** Priority date 7/1; no closing date. FAFSA, institutional form required. Applicants notified on a rolling basis starting 4/1.

Academics. Special study options: Distance learning, double major, dual enrollment of high school students, ESL, independent study, internships, liberal arts/career combination, study abroad. License preparation in nursing, radiology. **Credit/placement by examination:** AP, CLEP, IB, institutional tests. 45 credit hours maximum toward associate degree. **Support services:** GED preparation and test center, learning center, remedial instruction, study skills assistance, tutoring, writing center.

Majors. Business: Accounting technology, executive assistant, office technology, selling. **Computer sciences:** Applications programming, networking. **Education:** Teacher assistance. **Engineering:** General. **General:** Electrician. **Health services:** Health information technology, medical secretary, nursing (RN), radiologic technology/medical imaging. **Liberal arts:** Arts/sciences. **Protective services:** Corrections, firefighting, juvenile corrections, police science. **Work/family studies:** Child care service.

Most popular majors. Business/marketing 6%, health sciences 20%, liberal arts 56%, trade and industry 6%.

Technology on campus. 600 workstations in library, computer center, student center. Commuter students can connect to campus network. Online course registration, helpline, wireless network available.

Student life. Freshman orientation: Mandatory. Preregistration for classes offered. **Activities:** Choral groups, drama, literary magazine, student government, Fellowship of Christian Athletes, Hispanic student association, Power House Collegiate Ministries, A-MALE.

Athletics. NJCAA. **Intercollegiate:** Baseball M, basketball, cheerleading W, cross-country, softball W. **Team name:** Jaguars.

Student services. Adult student services, career counseling, student employment services, financial aid counseling, on-campus daycare, personal counseling, placement for graduates, veterans' counselor. **Physically disabled:** Services for visually, speech, hearing impaired. **Transfer:** Preadmission transcript evaluation for new students. Transfer adviser, college fairs on campus for students transferring to 4-year colleges.

Contact. E-mail: admissions@dacc.edu
Phone: (217) 443-8800 Fax: (217) 443-8337
Cindy Peck, Director, Admissions & Records/Registrar, Danville Area Community College, 2000 East Main Street, Danville, IL 61832

Elgin Community College
Elgin, Illinois
www.elgin.edu

CB member
CB code: 1203

- Public 2-year community college
- Commuter campus in small city

General. Founded in 1949. Regionally accredited. **Enrollment:** 8,167 degree-seeking undergraduates; 2,169 non-degree-seeking students. **Degrees:** 1,199 associate awarded. **Location:** 35 miles from Chicago. **Calendar:** Semester, extensive summer session. **Full-time faculty:** 133 total; 24% have terminal degrees, 15% minority, 50% women. **Part-time faculty:** 468 total; 9% have terminal degrees, 4% minority, 60% women. **Class size:** 62% < 20, 38% 20-39, less than 1% 40-49, less than 1% 50-99, less than 1% >100. **Special facilities:** Greenhouse, business conference center, visual and performing arts center, student-run gourmet restaurant.

Student profile. Among degree-seeking undergraduates, 1,343 enrolled as first-time, first-year students, 443 transferred in from other institutions.

Part-time:	61%	Hispanic/Latino:	34%
Women:	52%	Multi-racial, non-Hispanic:	3%
African American:	5%	25 or older:	35%
Asian American:	6%		

Transfer out. Colleges most students transferred to 2015: Northern Illinois University, Illinois State University, Southern Illinois University-Carbondale, University of Illinois, University of Illinois at Chicago.

Basis for selection. Open admission, but selective for some programs. Additional requirements for nursing and some health professions programs.

High school preparation. College-preparatory program recommended.

2015-2016 Annual costs. Tuition/fees: $3,580; $13,030 out-of-district; $14,950 out-of-state. Per-credit charge: $119 in-district; $434 out-of-district; $498 out-of-state. Books/supplies: $1,700. Personal expenses: $4,130.

Financial aid. Need-based: Need-based aid available for part-time students. Work-study available nights, weekends and for part-time students. **Non-need-based:** Scholarships awarded for academics, alumni affiliation, art, athletics, job skills, leadership, minority status, music/drama, religious affiliation, ROTC, state residency.

Application procedures. Admission: No deadline. No application fee. Admission notification on a rolling basis. **Financial aid:** Priority date 6/1; no closing date. FAFSA, institutional form required. Applicants notified on a rolling basis starting 4/6; must reply within 3 week(s) of notification.

Academics. Special study options: Accelerated study, distance learning, double major, dual enrollment of high school students, ESL, external degree, honors, independent study, internships, study abroad, teacher certification program. Dual admission with selected 4-year schools. Bachelor's degree programs available on campus. License preparation in dental hygiene, nursing, paramedic, physical therapy, radiology. **Credit/placement by examination:** AP, CLEP, institutional tests. 30 credit hours maximum toward associate degree. **Support services:** GED preparation and test center, learning center, reduced course load, remedial instruction, study skills assistance, tutoring, writing center.

Honors college/program. Top 20% of class, 3.5 GPA, or 25 ACT/1140 SAT required. Offers smaller class sizes and innovative learning experiences, including multidisciplinary approaches.

Majors. Business: Accounting, administrative services, business admin, entrepreneurial studies, executive assistant, marketing, retailing. **Communications technology:** Animation/special effects. **Computer sciences:** Data entry, networking, security. **Engineering:** General. **Health services:** Clinical lab technology, nursing (RN), physical therapy assistant, radiologic technology/medical imaging. **Human services:** Social work. **Liberal arts:** Arts/

sciences. **Parks/recreation:** Health/fitness. **Protective services:** Fire services admin, police science. **Visual/performing arts:** Design, graphic design.

Most popular majors. Health sciences 11%, interdisciplinary studies 21%, liberal arts 51%.

Technology on campus. 800 workstations in library, computer center, student center. Online course registration, wireless network available.

Student life. Freshman orientation: Mandatory. Preregistration for classes offered. **Activities:** Bands, choral groups, dance, literary magazine, music ensembles, musical theater, student government, student newspaper, Phi Theta Kappa, Alpha Beta Gamma, Latin American organization, United Students of All Cultures, black student association, single parents student group, Advocacy for Disabled and Abled Persons Together, Amnesty International, gay/lesbian/bi-sexual, Earth First.

Athletics. NJCAA. **Intercollegiate:** Baseball M, basketball, cross-country, golf M, soccer, softball W, tennis, volleyball W. **Team name:** Spartans.

Student services. Adult student services, career counseling, services for economically disadvantaged, student employment services, financial aid counseling, health services, legal services, minority student services, on-campus daycare, personal counseling, placement for graduates, veterans' counselor. **Physically disabled:** Services for visually, speech, hearing impaired. **Transfer:** Transfer center, transfer adviser, college fairs on campus for students transferring to 4-year colleges.

Contact. E-mail: admissions@elgin.edu
Phone: (847) 214-7385 Fax: (847) 608-5458
Jennifer McClure, Managing Director of Enrollment Services, Elgin Community College, 1700 Spartan Drive, Elgin, IL 60123-7193

Fox College
Bedford Park, Illinois
www.foxcollege.edu

CB code: 2670

- For-profit 2-year junior and technical college
- Commuter campus in very large city

General. Additional degree site in Tinley Park. **Enrollment:** 387 undergraduates. **Degrees:** 247 associate awarded. **Calendar:** Semester. **Full-time faculty:** 20 total. **Part-time faculty:** 15 total.

Basis for selection. Open admission, but selective for some programs. GED/High school academic record, writing sample, and interview considered for selective programs.

2015-2016 Annual costs. Diploma programs: $18,900-$19,380, books and supplies $2,002-$3,177. Associate programs: $26,064-$34,390, books and supplies $1,960-$3,177.

Financial aid. Need-based: Work-study available nights, weekends and for part-time students.

Application procedures. Admission: No deadline. $50 fee. **Financial aid:** No deadline.

Academics. Credit/placement by examination: AP, CLEP.

Majors. Business: Accounting technology, administrative services, hotel/motel admin, retailing. **Health services:** Medical assistant, physical therapy assistant, veterinary technology/assistant.

Student services. Career counseling, financial aid counseling, placement for graduates.

Contact. E-mail: admissions@foxcollege.edu
Phone: (708) 444-4500
Director of Admission, Fox College, 6640 South Cicero Avenue, Bedford Park, IL 60638

Harper College
Palatine, Illinois
www.harpercollege.edu

CB member
CB code: 1932

- Public 2-year community college
- Commuter campus in small city

General. Founded in 1965. Regionally accredited. Program for hearing-impaired offered. **Enrollment:** 11,636 degree-seeking undergraduates.

Degrees: 1,620 associate awarded. **Location:** 30 miles from Chicago. **Calendar:** Semester, extensive summer session. **Full-time faculty:** 205 total; 11% minority, 60% women. **Part-time faculty:** 622 total; 4% minority, 49% women. **Special facilities:** Observatory. **Partnerships:** Formal partnership with Achieving the Dream - Student Success Initiative.

Student profile.

Out-of-state:	1%	25 or older: 38%

Transfer out. Colleges most students transferred to 2015: Northern Illinois University, Roosevelt University, Northeastern University, DePaul University, University of Illinois at Chicago.

Basis for selection. Open admission, but selective for some programs. Selective admission to cardiac technology, dental hygiene, emergency medical technician, certified nursing assistant, electrocardiograph technology, emergency medical service paramedic, and diagnostic medical sonography. Pre-nursing examinations for nursing applicants. Critical thinking test for legal technology applicants.

High school preparation. 17 units recommended. Recommended units include English 4, mathematics 4, social studies 2 and science 2.

2015-2016 Annual costs. Tuition/fees: $4,007; $11,717 out-of-district; $13,982 out-of-state. Per-credit charge: $113.75 in-district; $370.75 out-of-district; $446.25 out-of-state. Books/supplies: $1,000. Personal expenses: $182.

Financial aid. Need-based: Need-based aid available for part-time students. Work-study available nights, weekends and for part-time students. **Non-need-based:** Scholarships awarded for academics, art, leadership, minority status, music/drama, state residency.

Application procedures. Admission: No deadline. $25 fee, may be waived for applicants with need. Admission notification on a rolling basis. Priority given to applications to nursing program received by 12/1. Priority given to applications received by 2/1 for all other limited-enrollment programs. **Financial aid:** Closing date 3/1. FAFSA required. Applicants notified on a rolling basis starting 3/1; must reply within 2 week(s) of notification.

Academics. Cooperative career program with in-district high schools. Students begin specialized training in high school and continue in colleges. Team-taught interdisciplinary courses and courseloads offered each semester. **Special study options:** Accelerated study, cooperative education, distance learning, dual enrollment of high school students, ESL, honors, independent study, internships, study abroad, weekend college. Dual enrollment programs with Northeastern University, Northern Illinois University, Roosevelt University, Western Illinois University. License preparation in dental hygiene, nursing, paramedic, radiology, real estate. **Credit/placement by examination:** AP, CLEP, institutional tests. 30 credit hours maximum toward associate degree. Maximum of 50% total hours in any degree program may be earned through credit by examination. **Support services:** GED preparation and test center, learning center, pre-admission summer program, reduced course load, remedial instruction, study skills assistance, tutoring, writing center.

Majors. Business: Accounting, banking/financial services, business admin, fashion, fashion modeling, hospitality admin, international, sales/distribution, selling, small business admin. **Computer sciences:** General, applications programming, computer science, programming, web page design. **Engineering:** General. **English:** English lit. **Health services:** Cardiovascular technology, dental hygiene, dietetic technician, EMT paramedic, medical secretary, nursing (RN), radiologic technology/medical imaging, sonography. **Liberal arts:** Arts/sciences. **Math:** General. **Philosophy/religion:** Philosophy. **Physical sciences:** General. **Protective services:** Computer forensics, firefighting, homeland security, police science. **Visual/performing arts:** Music, studio arts. **Work/family studies:** Child care service, fashion consultant, institutional food production.

Most popular majors. Biological/life sciences 7%, health sciences 11%, interdisciplinary studies 8%, liberal arts 64%.

Technology on campus. 1,698 workstations in library, computer center, student center. Online course registration, online library, helpline, wireless network available.

Student life. Freshman orientation: Mandatory. Preregistration for classes offered. Two-day program includes tour, assessment tests, academic advising. Optional for part-time students. **Activities:** Bands, campus ministries, choral groups, dance, drama, international student organizations, literary magazine, music ensembles, musical theater, radio station, student government, student newspaper, black student union, Latinos Unidos, pride club, Indian-Pakistani student association, access & disabilities success club, deaf club, Campus Crusade for Christ, Circle K-Kiwanis, Fufilled club, Harper Catholics.

Athletics. NJCAA. **Intercollegiate:** Baseball M, basketball, cross-country, soccer, softball W, track and field, volleyball W, wrestling M. **Intramural:** Baseball M, basketball M, football (non-tackle) M, soccer, softball, table tennis, tennis, volleyball. **Team name:** Hawks.

Student services. Adult student services, career counseling, services for economically disadvantaged, student employment services, financial aid counseling, health services, legal services, minority student services, on-campus daycare, personal counseling, veterans' counselor, women's services. **Physically disabled:** Services for visually, speech, hearing impaired. **Transfer:** Transfer adviser, college fairs on campus for students transferring to 4-year colleges.

Contact. E-mail: admissions@harpercollege.edu
Phone: (847) 925-6707 Fax: (847) 925-6044
Robert Parzy, Director Student Recruitment & Outreach, Harper College, 1200 West Algonquin Road, Palatine, IL 60067-7398

Heartland Community College
Normal, Illinois
www.heartland.edu   CB code: 1361

▶ Public 2-year community college
▶ Commuter campus in small city

General. Regionally accredited. Green construction and technology employed in construction projects. Commercial grade wind turbine provides half the electricity used on campus. **Enrollment:** 3,354 degree-seeking undergraduates; 1,684 non-degree-seeking students. **Degrees:** 602 associate awarded. **Calendar:** Semester, limited summer session. **Full-time faculty:** 91 total; 23% have terminal degrees, 9% minority, 54% women. **Part-time faculty:** 211 total; 10% have terminal degrees, 8% minority, 62% women. **Class size:** 56% < 20, 44% 20-39.

Student profile. Among degree-seeking undergraduates, 74% enrolled in a transfer program, 26% enrolled in a vocational program, 4% already have a bachelor's degree or higher, 480 enrolled as first-time, first-year students.

Part-time:	46%	Hispanic/Latino:	6%
Out-of-state:	2%	Multi-racial, non-Hispanic:	4%
Women:	54%	International:	1%
African American:	12%	25 or older:	22%
Asian American:	2%		

Transfer out. 19% of students enrolled in the transfer program go on to 4-year colleges. **Colleges most students transferred to 2015:** Illinois State University, Illinois Central College, Lincoln College-Normal, University of Illinois - Urbana-Champaign, Illinois Wesleyan University.

Basis for selection. Open admission, but selective for some programs. Special requirements for nursing, radiography, and physical therapy assistant programs. Placement testing required to determine readiness in reading, English, and math. Developmental courses may be required before proceeding to college-level courses.

High school preparation. Recommended units include English 4, mathematics 3, social studies 2, science 2 and foreign language 2. Social studies units should include history and government.

2015-2016 Annual costs. Tuition/fees: $4,260; $8,520 out-of-district; $12,780 out-of-state. Per-credit charge: $142 in-district; $284 out-of-district; $426 out-of-state. Books/supplies: $1,200. Personal expenses: $1,000.

Financial aid. Need-based: Need-based aid available for part-time students. Work-study available nights, weekends and for part-time students. **Non-need-based:** Scholarships awarded for academics, alumni affiliation, athletics, job skills, leadership, minority status, state residency.

Application procedures. Admission: Priority date 6/1; no deadline. No application fee. Admission notification on a rolling basis. May defer admission up to one year. Early admission of high school students with recommendation of high school officials. **Financial aid:** Priority date 4/1; no closing date. FAFSA, institutional form required. Applicants notified on a rolling basis starting 5/15; must reply within 2 week(s) of notification.

Academics. Special study options: Distance learning, double major, dual enrollment of high school students, ESL, honors, independent study, internships, liberal arts/career combination, study abroad. License preparation in nursing, paramedic, physical therapy, radiology, real estate. **Credit/placement by examination:** AP, CLEP, institutional tests. 15 credit hours maximum toward associate degree. **Support services:** GED preparation and test center, learning center, remedial instruction, study skills assistance, tutoring, writing center.

Majors. Business: Administrative services. **Computer sciences:** Information technology, networking. **Education:** Teacher assistance. **Engineering:** General. **General:** Electrician, site management. **Health services:** Nursing

(RN), physical therapy assistant, radiologic technology/medical imaging. **Liberal arts:** Arts/sciences. **Parks/recreation:** Sports admin. **Protective services:** Criminal justice. **Visual/performing arts:** Design. **Work/family studies:** Child care service.

Most popular majors. Health sciences 6%, interdisciplinary studies 22%, liberal arts 66%.

Technology on campus. 75 workstations in library, computer center, student center. Commuter students can connect to campus network. Online course registration, online library, helpline, wireless network available.

Student life. Freshman orientation: Mandatory. Preregistration for classes offered. Multiple half-day sessions for full-time students; reservations required. Online session required for part-time students. **Activities:** Dance, international student organizations, student government, student newspaper, Phi Theta Kappa, Sigma Kappa Delta, Alpha Beta Gamma, PRIDE, Moms Moving Forward, M.E.N. Male Empowerment Network, Toastmasters, international student clubs, environmental club, game club.

Athletics. NJCAA. Intercollegiate: Baseball M, soccer, softball W. **Intramural:** Basketball, softball, volleyball. **Team name:** Hawks.

Student services. Adult student services, alcohol/substance abuse counseling, career counseling, services for economically disadvantaged, student employment services, financial aid counseling, minority student services, on-campus daycare, personal counseling, placement for graduates, veterans' counselor. **Physically disabled:** Services for visually, speech, hearing impaired. **Transfer:** Pre-admission transcript evaluation for new students. Transfer adviser, college fairs on campus for students transferring to 4-year colleges.

Contact. E-mail: admissions@heartland.edu
Phone: (309) 268-8010 Fax: (309) 268-7971
Candace Brownlee, Dean of Student Services, Heartland Community College, 1500 West Raab Road, Normal, IL 61761

Highland Community College
Freeport, Illinois
www.highland.edu
CB code: 1233

- Public 2-year community college
- Commuter campus in large town

General. Founded in 1961. Regionally accredited. **Enrollment:** 1,511 degree-seeking undergraduates; 293 non-degree-seeking students. **Degrees:** 275 associate awarded. **Location:** 100 miles from Chicago, 38 miles from Rockford. **Calendar:** Semester, limited summer session. **Full-time faculty:** 48 total; 8% minority, 44% women. **Part-time faculty:** 72 total; 3% minority, 58% women. **Class size:** 79% < 20, 19% 20-39, 1% 40-49, less than 1% 50-99. **Special facilities:** Regional arboretum, YMCA on campus, wind turbine training facility.

Student profile. Among degree-seeking undergraduates, 404 enrolled as first-time, first-year students, 54 transferred in from other institutions.

Part-time:	40%	Women:	62%
Out-of-state:	3%	25 or older:	30%

Transfer out. Colleges most students transferred to 2015: Illinois State University, University of Wisconsin-Platteville, Northern Illinois University, Western Illinois University, Columbia College.

Basis for selection. Open admission, but selective for some programs. Special criteria for acceptance into nursing program: based on points accumulated by taking prerequisite courses, class rank, and test scores considered. Special criteria for wind turbine program: based on pre-requisites, GPA, and letters of recommendation. **Home schooled:** Transcript of courses and grades required.

High school preparation. College-preparatory program recommended. 15 units recommended. Recommended units include English 4, mathematics 3, social studies 2, science 2 (laboratory 2) and academic electives 4.

2015-2016 Annual costs. Tuition/fees: $4,290; $6,510 out-of-district; $6,780 out-of-state. Per-credit charge: $123 in-district; $197 out-of-district; $206 out-of-state.

2014-2015 Financial aid. Need-based: 285 full-time freshmen applied for aid; 236 deemed to have need; 222 received aid. Average need met was 34%. Average scholarship/grant was $5,038; average loan $2,686. Need-based aid available for part-time students. Work-study available nights, weekends and for part-time students. **Non-need-based:** Awarded to 171 full-time undergraduates, including 44 freshmen. Scholarships awarded for academics, athletics.

Application procedures. Admission: No deadline. No application fee. Admission notification on a rolling basis. **Financial aid:** No deadline. FAFSA, institutional form required. Applicants notified on a rolling basis starting 8/1; must reply within 2 week(s) of notification.

Academics. Special study options: Distance learning, dual enrollment of high school students, ESL, honors, internships, liberal arts/career combination, student-designed major. Bachelor's degree programs available on campus. License preparation in nursing, real estate. **Credit/placement by examination:** AP, CLEP, institutional tests. 21 credit hours maximum toward associate degree. **Support services:** GED preparation, learning center, remedial instruction, study skills assistance, tutoring, writing center.

Majors. Business: Accounting, administrative services. **Computer sciences:** Information technology. **Education:** Early childhood, learning disabled, mathematics. **Engineering:** General. **Health services:** EMT paramedic, health information technology, medical assistant, nursing (RN). **Liberal arts:** Arts/sciences. **Visual/performing arts:** Graphic design. **Work/family studies:** Child care service.

Most popular majors. Health sciences 19%, interdisciplinary studies 29%, liberal arts 39%.

Technology on campus. 366 workstations in library, computer center, student center. Commuter students can connect to campus network. Online course registration, online library, helpline, repair service, wireless network available.

Student life. Freshman orientation: Available. Preregistration for classes offered. **Activities:** Bands, campus ministries, choral groups, dance, drama, international student organizations, literary magazine, music ensembles, Model UN, musical theater, radio station, student government, student newspaper, current issues club, environmental awareness, religious fellowship, People of Color, pride club, student senate.

Athletics. NJCAA. Intercollegiate: Baseball M, basketball, golf M, softball W, volleyball W. **Intramural:** Basketball, volleyball. **Team name:** Cougars.

Student services. Adult student services, alcohol/substance abuse counseling, career counseling, services for economically disadvantaged, student employment services, financial aid counseling, on-campus daycare, personal counseling, veterans' counselor. **Physically disabled:** Services for visually, speech, hearing impaired. **Transfer:** Pre-admission transcript evaluation for new students. Transfer center, transfer adviser, college fairs on campus for students transferring to 4-year colleges.

Contact. E-mail: registration@highland.edu
Phone: (815) 235-6121 ext. 3414 Fax: (815) 235-6130
Jeremy Bradt, Director of Enrollment and Records, Highland Community College, 2998 West Pearl City Road, Freeport, IL 61032-9341

Illinois Central College
East Peoria, Illinois
www.icc.edu
CB code: 1312

- Public 2-year community college
- Commuter campus in large town

General. Founded in 1966. Regionally accredited. **Enrollment:** 7,425 degree-seeking undergraduates; 2,280 non-degree-seeking students. **Degrees:** 1,253 associate awarded. **Location:** 150 miles from Chicago, 5 miles from Peoria. **Calendar:** Semester, extensive summer session. **Full-time faculty:** 178 total; 88% have terminal degrees, 10% minority, 54% women. **Part-time faculty:** 370 total; 56% have terminal degrees, 8% minority, 65% women. **Class size:** 69% < 20, 30% 20-39, less than 1% 40-49, less than 1% 50-99, less than 1% >100. **Partnerships:** Formal partnerships with Caterpillar Tractor Company and General Motors.

Student profile. Among degree-seeking undergraduates, 53% enrolled in a transfer program, 26% enrolled in a vocational program, 3% already have a bachelor's degree or higher, 1,052 enrolled as first-time, first-year students, 209 transferred in from other institutions.

Part-time:	55%	Asian American:	2%
Out-of-state:	1%	Hispanic/Latino:	4%
Women:	55%	Multi-racial, non-Hispanic:	3%
African American:	11%	25 or older:	33%

Transfer out. Colleges most students transferred to 2015: Illinois State University, Bradley University, Western Illinois University, Methodist College, University of Illinois: Springfield.

Basis for selection. Open admission, but selective for some programs. Special requirements for health occupation programs and diesel mechanics.

Some programs require ACT for admission and placement. Audition required of music majors. **Home schooled:** Transcript of courses and grades required.

High school preparation. 15 units recommended. Recommended units include English 4, mathematics 3, social studies 2, science 2, foreign language 1, visual/performing arts 1 and academic electives 2.

2015-2016 Annual costs. Tuition/fees: $4,050; $10,050 out-of-state. Per-credit charge: $135 in-state; $290 out-of-state. Books/supplies: $1,200. Personal expenses: $2,000.

Financial aid. Need-based: Need-based aid available for part-time students. Work-study available nights, weekends and for part-time students. **Non-need-based:** Scholarships awarded for academics, athletics, minority status, music/drama, state residency.

Application procedures. Admission: No deadline. No application fee. **Financial aid:** Priority date 6/1; no closing date. FAFSA required. Applicants notified on a rolling basis starting 5/1; must reply within 2 week(s) of notification.

Academics. Team-taught, multidisciplinary program available for transfers. **Special study options:** Distance learning, ESL, honors, independent study, internships, study abroad, weekend college. Bachelor's degree programs available on campus. License preparation in dental hygiene, nursing, occupational therapy, paramedic, physical therapy, radiology, real estate. **Credit/placement by examination:** AP, CLEP, institutional tests. 30 credit hours maximum toward associate degree. **Support services:** GED preparation, learning center, reduced course load, remedial instruction, study skills assistance, tutoring, writing center.

Majors. Architecture: Interior. **Business:** General, accounting, accounting technology, administrative services, banking/financial services, business admin, real estate, retailing. **Communications:** Broadcast journalism, journalism. **Communications technology:** Animation/special effects, platemaker/imager. **Computer sciences:** Networking, programming, web page design, webmaster. **Conservation:** General. **Education:** Elementary, physical, secondary, special ed, teacher assistance. **Engineering:** General, electrical. **English:** English lit, rhetoric/composition. **Foreign languages:** General, sign language interpretation. **Health services:** Clinical lab technology, community health services, dental hygiene, EMT paramedic, health care admin, health information technology, mental health counseling, mental health services, nursing (RN), occupational therapy assistant, physical therapy assistant, predental, premedicine, prepharmacy, preveterinary, radiologic technology/medical imaging, respiratory therapy technology, substance abuse counseling, surgical technology. **Liberal arts:** Arts/sciences, humanities, library assistant. **Math:** General. **Parks/recreation:** Health/fitness. **Physical sciences:** Chemistry, geology, physics, planetary. **Protective services:** Corrections, firefighting, juvenile corrections, police science, security services. **Visual/performing arts:** Dance, design, dramatic, graphic design, music, studio arts. **Work/family studies:** General, child care management, child care service, food/nutrition.

Most popular majors. Health sciences 14%, liberal arts 64%.

Technology on campus. 500 workstations in library, computer center. Wireless network available.

Student life. Freshman orientation: Available. Preregistration for classes offered. **Housing:** Apartments available. **Activities:** Bands, campus ministries, choral groups, dance, drama, international student organizations, literary magazine, music ensembles, radio station, student government, student newspaper, TV station, College Democrats, Campus Crusade for Christ, Chi Alpha Fellowship, Areopagus.

Athletics. NJCAA. **Intercollegiate:** Baseball M, basketball, cross-country, golf M, soccer, softball W, volleyball W. **Intramural:** Basketball, bowling, football (non-tackle), ultimate frisbee. **Team name:** Cougars.

Student services. Adult student services, career counseling, services for economically disadvantaged, student employment services, financial aid counseling, health services, minority student services, on-campus daycare, personal counseling, placement for graduates, veterans' counselor. **Physically disabled:** Services for visually, speech, hearing impaired. **Transfer:** Transfer center, transfer adviser, college fairs on campus for students transferring to 4-year colleges.

Contact. E-mail: enroll@icc.edu
Phone: (309) 694-5354 Fax: (309) 694-8461
Beth McClain, Dean of Enrollment Management, Illinois Central College, 1 College Drive, East Peoria, IL 61635-0001

Illinois Eastern Community Colleges: Frontier Community College
Fairfield, Illinois
www.iecc.edu/fcc   CB code: 1894

- Public 2-year community college
- Commuter campus in small town

General. Founded in 1976. Regionally accredited. **Enrollment:** 341 degree-seeking undergraduates; 1,888 non-degree-seeking students. **Degrees:** 104 associate awarded. **Location:** 110 miles from St. Louis. **Calendar:** Semester, extensive summer session. **Full-time faculty:** 6 total. **Part-time faculty:** 89 total.

Student profile. Among degree-seeking undergraduates, 48% enrolled in a transfer program, 52% enrolled in a vocational program, 101 enrolled as first-time, first-year students.

Part-time:	48%	**Women:**	64%
Out-of-state:	1%	**25 or older:**	57%

Basis for selection. Open admission, but selective for some programs. Special requirements for nursing and radiography programs. Preference given to regional residents. Interview recommended for nursing and radiography technology.

High school preparation. Recommended units include English 3, mathematics 2 and science 1.

2015-2016 Annual costs. Tuition/fees: $2,950; $8,512 out-of-district; $10,378 out-of-state. Per-credit charge: $83 in-district; $268 out-of-district; $330 out-of-state. Books/supplies: $1,000. Personal expenses: $1,120.

Financial aid. Need-based: Need-based aid available for part-time students. Work-study available nights, weekends and for part-time students. **Non-need-based:** Scholarships awarded for academics, athletics, state residency.

Application procedures. Admission: No deadline. No application fee. Admission notification on a rolling basis beginning on or about 8/1. **Financial aid:** No deadline. FAFSA, institutional form required. Applicants notified on a rolling basis starting 8/1; must reply within 2 week(s) of notification.

Academics. Students, with counselors' aid, design own academic programs through nontraditional alternatives to classroom study. **Special study options:** Distance learning, double major, dual enrollment of high school students, ESL, honors, independent study, internships, student-designed major, study abroad, teacher certification program, weekend college. License preparation in nursing, paramedic. **Credit/placement by examination:** AP, CLEP, institutional tests. 32 credit hours maximum toward associate degree. **Support services:** GED preparation, learning center, remedial instruction, study skills assistance, tutoring.

Majors. Business: Administrative services, executive assistant, office technology. **Computer sciences:** General. **Engineering:** General. **Health services:** EMT ambulance attendant, health information technology. **Liberal arts:** Arts/sciences. **Parks/recreation:** Sports admin. **Protective services:** Firefighting.

Most popular majors. Health sciences 16%, liberal arts 65%.

Technology on campus. 40 workstations in library, computer center. Commuter students can connect to campus network. Helpline available.

Student life. Freshman orientation: Available. Preregistration for classes offered. Freshman orientation strongly recommended. **Activities:** Bands, choral groups, drama, music ensembles, musical theater, student government, student newspaper.

Athletics. NJCAA. **Intercollegiate:** Golf, softball W. **Intramural:** Softball W, volleyball W. **Team name:** Bobcats.

Student services. Adult student services, career counseling, services for economically disadvantaged, student employment services, financial aid counseling, minority student services, personal counseling, placement for graduates, veterans' counselor. **Physically disabled:** Services for visually, speech, hearing impaired. **Transfer:** Pre-admission transcript evaluation for new students. Transfer adviser, college fairs on campus for students transferring to 4-year colleges.

Contact. Phone: (618) 842-3711 Toll-free number: (877) 464-3687
Fax: (618) 842-6340
Amy Loss, Coordinator, Registration & Record, Illinois Eastern Community Colleges: Frontier Community College, Two Frontier Drive, Fairfield, IL 62837-9801

Illinois Eastern Community Colleges: Lincoln Trail College

Robinson, Illinois
www.iecc.edu/ltc   CB code: 0758

◆ Public 2-year community college
◆ Commuter campus in small town

General. Founded in 1969. Regionally accredited. **Enrollment:** 546 degree-seeking undergraduates; 464 non-degree-seeking students. **Degrees:** 163 associate awarded. **Location:** 200 miles from Indianapolis, 110 miles from St. Louis. **Calendar:** Semester, extensive summer session. **Full-time faculty:** 16 total. **Part-time faculty:** 48 total.

Student profile. Among degree-seeking undergraduates, 60% enrolled in a transfer program, 40% enrolled in a vocational program, 163 enrolled as first-time, first-year students.

Part-time:	26%	Women:	58%
Out-of-state:	5%	25 or older:	36%

Basis for selection. Open admission, but selective for some programs.

High school preparation. Recommended units include English 3, mathematics 2 and science 1.

2015-2016 Annual costs. Tuition/fees: $2,950; $8,512 out-of-district; $10,378 out-of-state. Per-credit charge: $83 in-district; $268 out-of-district; $330 out-of-state. Books/supplies: $1,000. Personal expenses: $1,120.

Financial aid. Need-based: Need-based aid available for part-time students. Work-study available nights, weekends and for part-time students. **Non-need-based:** Scholarships awarded for academics, athletics, state residency.

Application procedures. Admission: No deadline. No application fee. Admission notification on a rolling basis beginning on or about 8/1. **Financial aid:** No deadline. FAFSA, institutional form required. Applicants notified on a rolling basis starting 8/1; must reply within 2 week(s) of notification.

Academics. Students (with counselors' aid) design academic programs through nontraditional alternatives to classroom study. **Special study options:** Distance learning, double major, dual enrollment of high school students, ESL, honors, independent study, internships, student-designed major, study abroad, weekend college. License preparation in nursing. **Credit/placement by examination:** AP, CLEP, institutional tests. 32 credit hours maximum toward associate degree. **Support services:** GED preparation, learning center, remedial instruction, study skills assistance, tutoring.

Majors. Business: Office technology. **Computer sciences:** General, networking. **Education:** Teacher assistance. **Engineering:** General. **General:** Power transmission. **Health services:** Clinical lab technology, medical assistant. **Liberal arts:** Arts/sciences. **Parks/recreation:** Sports admin.

Most popular majors. Engineering/engineering technologies 22%, interdisciplinary studies 10%, liberal arts 62%.

Technology on campus. 91 workstations in library, computer center. Commuter students can connect to campus network. Helpline available.

Student life. Freshman orientation: Available. Preregistration for classes offered. **Activities:** Bands, choral groups, drama, music ensembles, musical theater, student government, student newspaper.

Athletics. NJCAA. **Intercollegiate:** Baseball M, basketball, softball W. **Intramural:** Basketball, softball. **Team name:** Statesmen.

Student services. Career counseling, services for economically disadvantaged, student employment services, financial aid counseling, minority student services, personal counseling, placement for graduates, veterans' counselor. **Physically disabled:** Services for visually, speech, hearing impaired. **Transfer:** Pre-admission transcript evaluation for new students. Transfer adviser, college fairs on campus for students transferring to 4-year colleges.

Contact. Phone: (618) 544-8657 Toll-free number: (866) 582-4322
Fax: (618) 544-3957
Megan Scott, Assistant Dean of Student Services, Illinois Eastern Community Colleges: Lincoln Trail College, 11220 State Highway 1, Robinson, IL 62454-5707

Illinois Eastern Community Colleges: Olney Central College

Olney, Illinois
www.iecc.edu/occ   CB code: 0827

◆ Public 2-year community college
◆ Commuter campus in small town

General. Founded in 1962. Regionally accredited. **Enrollment:** 805 degree-seeking undergraduates; 490 non-degree-seeking students. **Degrees:** 269 associate awarded. **Location:** 200 miles from St. Louis. **Calendar:** Semester, extensive summer session. **Full-time faculty:** 43 total. **Part-time faculty:** 54 total.

Student profile. Among degree-seeking undergraduates, 57% enrolled in a transfer program, 43% enrolled in a vocational program, 206 enrolled as first-time, first-year students.

Part-time:	26%	Women:	59%
Out-of-state:	1%	25 or older:	36%

Basis for selection. Open admission, but selective for some programs. Special requirements for nursing, radiology programs. Preference given to Illinois Eastern Community College region residents. Interview recommended for nursing, radiology technology majors.

High school preparation. Recommended units include English 3, mathematics 2 and science 1.

2015-2016 Annual costs. Tuition/fees: $2,950; $8,512 out-of-district; $10,378 out-of-state. Per-credit charge: $83 in-district; $268 out-of-district; $330 out-of-state. Books/supplies: $1,000. Personal expenses: $1,120.

Financial aid. Need-based: Need-based aid available for part-time students. Work-study available nights, weekends and for part-time students. **Non-need-based:** Scholarships awarded for academics, athletics, state residency.

Application procedures. Admission: No deadline. No application fee. Admission notification on a rolling basis beginning on or about 8/1. **Financial aid:** No deadline. FAFSA, institutional form required. Applicants notified on a rolling basis starting 8/1; must reply within 2 week(s) of notification.

Academics. Students design academic programs with aid of counselors through nontraditional alternatives to classroom study. **Special study options:** Distance learning, double major, dual enrollment of high school students, ESL, honors, independent study, internships, student-designed major, study abroad, weekend college. License preparation in nursing, radiology. **Credit/placement by examination:** AP, CLEP, institutional tests. 32 credit hours maximum toward associate degree. **Support services:** GED preparation, learning center, remedial instruction, study skills assistance, tutoring.

Majors. Business: Accounting, administrative services, business admin, human resources, office technology. **Computer sciences:** Information technology. **Engineering:** General. **Health services:** Medical radiologic technology/radiation therapy, medical secretary. **Liberal arts:** Arts/sciences. **Parks/recreation:** Sports admin.

Most popular majors. Health sciences 37%, liberal arts 51%, trade and industry 6%.

Technology on campus. 125 workstations in library, computer center. Commuter students can connect to campus network. Helpline available.

Student life. Freshman orientation: Available. Preregistration for classes offered. **Activities:** Bands, choral groups, drama, music ensembles, musical theater, student government, student newspaper.

Athletics. NJCAA. **Intercollegiate:** Baseball M, basketball, softball W. **Intramural:** Basketball, softball. **Team name:** Blue Knights.

Student services. Career counseling, services for economically disadvantaged, student employment services, financial aid counseling, minority student services, on-campus daycare, personal counseling, placement for graduates, veterans' counselor. **Physically disabled:** Services for visually, speech, hearing impaired. **Transfer:** Pre-admission transcript evaluation for new students. Transfer adviser, college fairs on campus for students transferring to 4-year colleges.

Contact. Phone: (618) 395-7777 Toll-free number: (866) 622-4322
Fax: (618) 392-3293
Adam Greathouse, Assistant Dean of Student Services, Illinois Eastern Community Colleges: Olney Central College, 305 North West Street, Olney, IL 62450

Illinois Eastern Community Colleges: Wabash Valley College
Mount Carmel, Illinois
www.iecc.edu/wvc   CB code: 1936

▶ Public 2-year community college
▶ Commuter campus in small town

General. Founded in 1960. Regionally accredited. **Enrollment:** 702 degree-seeking undergraduates; 3,572 non-degree-seeking students. **Degrees:** 196 associate awarded. **Location:** 40 miles from Evansville, IN. **Calendar:** Semester, extensive summer session. **Full-time faculty:** 35 total. **Part-time faculty:** 45 total.

Student profile. Among degree-seeking undergraduates, 50% enrolled in a transfer program, 50% enrolled in a vocational program, 255 enrolled as first-time, first-year students.

Part-time:	30%	**Women:**	49%
Out-of-state:	3%	**25 or older:**	50%

Basis for selection. Open admission, but selective for some programs. Special requirements for nursing, radiology programs. Preference given to Illinois Eastern Community College region residents. Interview recommended for nursing, radiology technology majors.

High school preparation. Recommended units include English 3, mathematics 2 and science 1.

2015-2016 Annual costs. Tuition/fees: $2,950; $8,512 out-of-district; $10,378 out-of-state. Per-credit charge: $83 in-district; $268 out-of-district; $330 out-of-state. Books/supplies: $1,000. Personal expenses: $1,120.

Financial aid. Need-based: Need-based aid available for part-time students. Work-study available nights, weekends and for part-time students. **Non-need-based:** Scholarships awarded for academics, athletics, state residency.

Application procedures. Admission: No deadline. No application fee. Admission notification on a rolling basis beginning on or about 8/1. **Financial aid:** No deadline. FAFSA, institutional form required. Applicants notified on a rolling basis starting 8/1; must reply within 2 week(s) of notification.

Academics. Students, with counselor's aid, design own academic programs through nontraditional alternatives to classroom study. **Special study options:** Distance learning, double major, dual enrollment of high school students, ESL, honors, independent study, internships, student-designed major, study abroad, weekend college. License preparation in nursing, real estate. **Credit/placement by examination:** AP, CLEP, institutional tests. 32 credit hours maximum toward associate degree. **Support services:** GED preparation, learning center, remedial instruction, study skills assistance, tutoring.

Majors. Business: Accounting technology, office technology. **Communications:** Broadcast journalism. **Engineering:** General. **Human services:** Social work. **Liberal arts:** Arts/sciences. **Parks/recreation:** Sports admin. **Visual/performing arts:** Music. **Work/family studies:** Child care management.

Most popular majors. Agriculture 13%, business/marketing 6%, interdisciplinary studies 24%, liberal arts 31%, trade and industry 15%.

Technology on campus. 100 workstations in library, computer center. Commuter students can connect to campus network. Helpline available.

Student life. Freshman orientation: Available. Preregistration for classes offered. **Activities:** Bands, choral groups, drama, music ensembles, musical theater, radio station, student government, student newspaper, TV station.

Athletics. NJCAA. **Intercollegiate:** Baseball M, basketball, softball W. **Intramural:** Basketball, softball. **Team name:** Warriors.

Student services. Career counseling, services for economically disadvantaged, student employment services, financial aid counseling, minority student services, on-campus daycare, personal counseling, placement for graduates, veterans' counselor. **Physically disabled:** Services for visually, speech, hearing impaired. **Transfer:** Pre-admission transcript evaluation for new students. Transfer adviser, college fairs on campus for students transferring to 4-year colleges.

Contact. Phone: (618) 262-8641 Toll-free number: (866) 982-4322 Fax: (618) 262-8647
Diana Spear, Assistant Dean for Student Services, Illinois Eastern Community Colleges: Wabash Valley College, 2200 College Drive, Mount Carmel, IL 62863-2657

Illinois Valley Community College
Oglesby, Illinois   CB member
www.ivcc.edu   CB code: 1397

▶ Public 2-year community college
▶ Commuter campus in small town

General. Founded in 1966. Regionally accredited. **Enrollment:** 2,572 degree-seeking undergraduates. **Degrees:** 464 associate awarded. **Location:** 60 miles from Peoria, 95 miles from Chicago. **Calendar:** Semester, extensive summer session. **Full-time faculty:** 79 total. **Part-time faculty:** 137 total.

Transfer out. Colleges most students transferred to 2015: Illinois State University, Northern Illinois University, Western Illinois University, University of Illinois/Urbana-Champaign, Eastern Illinois University.

Basis for selection. Open admission, but selective for some programs. Nursing program applicants generally have 2.0 GPA for LPN, and 2.5 GPA for RN, and are selected based on completion and grades in five core pre-nursing courses and a pre-nursing assessment exam; dental assisting must have 2.0 GPA. **Home schooled:** Transcript of courses and grades required.

2015-2016 Annual costs. Tuition/fees: $3,580; $9,944 out-of-district; $10,752 out-of-state. Per-credit charge: $111.6 in-district; $323.72 out-of-district; $350.65 out-of-state. Books/supplies: $1,400. Personal expenses: $1,350.

Financial aid. Need-based: Need-based aid available for part-time students. Work-study available nights, weekends and for part-time students. **Non-need-based:** Scholarships awarded for academics, art, athletics, leadership, music/drama.

Application procedures. Admission: No deadline. No application fee. Admission notification on a rolling basis. **Financial aid:** Priority date 3/1; no closing date. FAFSA required. Applicants notified on a rolling basis starting 3/1.

Academics. Special study options: Cross-registration, distance learning, dual enrollment of high school students, honors, independent study, internships, study abroad. License preparation in nursing, real estate. **Credit/placement by examination:** AP, CLEP, institutional tests. 16 credit hours maximum toward associate degree. **Support services:** GED preparation and test center, learning center, pre-admission summer program, reduced course load, remedial instruction, study skills assistance, tutoring, writing center.

Majors. Biology: General. **Business:** Accounting, business admin, management science, office technology, selling. **Communications:** Communications/speech/rhetoric, journalism. **Computer sciences:** General, applications programming, information systems, system admin. **Education:** General, early childhood, teacher assistance. **Engineering:** General. **English:** American lit, English lit, rhetoric/composition, writing. **Foreign languages:** General. **General:** Electrician. **Health services:** Athletic training, massage therapy, nursing (RN). **History:** General. **Human services:** Social work. **Liberal arts:** Arts/sciences. **Math:** General. **Parks/recreation:** Health/fitness, sports admin. **Physical sciences:** Chemistry, geology, oceanography, physics, planetary. **Protective services:** Corrections, forensics, juvenile corrections, law enforcement admin, police science. **Psychology:** General. **Social sciences:** General, political science, sociology. **Visual/performing arts:** General, art, art history/conservation, dramatic, graphic design, music, music history, music performance, studio arts. **Work/family studies:** Child care management, child care service.

Most popular majors. Health sciences 12%, interdisciplinary studies 46%, liberal arts 17%, trade and industry 9%.

Technology on campus. 242 workstations in library, computer center. Commuter students can connect to campus network. Online course registration, online library, helpline, wireless network available.

Student life. Freshman orientation: Available. Preregistration for classes offered. Sessions held in spring and fall. **Activities:** Bands, choral groups, drama, literary magazine, music ensembles, musical theater, student government, student newspaper, Amnesty International, gay/straight alliance, People of the World End Racism (POWER), student nurses association, Young Republicans.

Athletics. NJCAA. **Intercollegiate:** Baseball M, basketball, golf M, softball W, tennis, volleyball W. **Intramural:** Basketball, softball, volleyball. **Team name:** Eagles.

Student services. Career counseling, student employment services, financial aid counseling, on-campus daycare, personal counseling, placement for graduates, veterans' counselor. **Physically disabled:** Services for visually, hearing impaired. **Transfer:** Transfer adviser for students transferring to 4-year colleges.

Two-Year Colleges

Contact. E-mail: mark_grzybowski@ivcc.edu
Phone: (815) 224-0439 Fax: (815) 224-6091
Mark Gryzbowski, Director of Admissions and Records, Illinois Valley Community College, 815 North Orlando Smith Avenue, Oglesby, IL 61348-9693

John A. Logan College
Carterville, Illinois
www.jalc.edu   **CB code: 1357**

- Public 2-year community college
- Commuter campus in small town

General. Founded in 1967. Regionally accredited. **Enrollment:** 2,600 degree-seeking undergraduates. **Degrees:** 542 associate awarded. **ROTC:** Army, Air Force. **Location:** 10 miles from Carbondale. **Calendar:** Semester, limited summer session. **Full-time faculty:** 95 total. **Part-time faculty:** 188 total. **Class size:** 53% < 20, 44% 20-39, less than 1% 40-49, less than 1% 50-99, less than 1% >100.

Student profile.

Out-of-state: 1%   **25 or older:**   47%

Transfer out. Colleges most students transferred to 2015: Southern Illinois University at Carbondale.

Basis for selection. Open admission, but selective for some programs. Admission to allied health programs competitive, unique criteria depending on program. ASSET and/or COMPASS accepted in place of SAT or ACT.

High school preparation. College preparatory program required of 2-year transfer degree applicants. Must have 15 high school course units: 4 English, 3 math, 3 laboratory science, 3 social science, 2 electives.

2015-2016 Annual costs. Books/supplies: $1,234. Personal expenses: $617.

Financial aid. All financial aid based on need. Need-based aid available for part-time students. Work-study available nights, weekends and for part-time students.

Application procedures. Admission: No deadline. No application fee. Admission notification on a rolling basis. **Financial aid:** Priority date 5/1; no closing date. FAFSA, institutional form required. Applicants notified on a rolling basis starting 5/1.

Academics. Special study options: Distance learning, double major, dual enrollment of high school students, liberal arts/career combination, study abroad. Bachelor's degree programs available on campus. License preparation in dental hygiene, nursing, occupational therapy, paramedic, real estate. **Credit/placement by examination:** AP, CLEP, institutional tests. 30 credit hours maximum toward associate degree. **Support services:** GED preparation and test center, remedial instruction, study skills assistance, tutoring, writing center.

Majors. Biology: General. **Business:** Accounting technology, business admin, executive assistant, office management. **Communications:** Journalism. **Computer sciences:** General, data entry, information technology. **Education:** Art, early childhood, elementary, history, mathematics, physical, secondary, social studies, special ed, teacher assistance. **Engineering:** General. **English:** English lit. **General:** Carpentry. **Health services:** Clinical lab technology, dental hygiene, health information technology, nursing (RN), occupational therapy assistant, prepharmacy, sonography. **Human services:** Social work. **Liberal arts:** Arts/sciences. **Math:** General. **Physical sciences:** Chemistry, physics. **Protective services:** Corrections, criminal justice. **Psychology:** General. **Social sciences:** Economics, international relations, political science, sociology. **Visual/performing arts:** Art, dramatic, music.

Most popular majors. Business/marketing 15%, health sciences 13%, interdisciplinary studies 9%, liberal arts 23%, security/protective services 6%, trade and industry 14%.

Technology on campus. Commuter students can connect to campus network. Online course registration, wireless network available.

Student life. Freshman orientation: Available. Preregistration for classes offered. **Housing:** Housing available at Southern Illinois University - Carbondale. **Activities:** Concert band, choral groups, drama, music ensembles, musical theater, student government, student newspaper.

Athletics. NJCAA. **Intercollegiate:** Baseball M, basketball, golf, softball W, volleyball W. **Team name:** Volunteers.

Student services. Adult student services, career counseling, student employment services, financial aid counseling, minority student services, on-campus daycare, placement for graduates, veterans' counselor. **Physically disabled:** Services for visually, hearing impaired. **Transfer:** Transfer center, college fairs on campus for students transferring to 4-year colleges.

Contact. E-mail: terrycrain@jalc.edu
Phone: (618) 985-3741 ext. 8298 Fax: (618) 985-4433
Lauralyn Cima, Dean for Student Services, John A. Logan College, 700 Logan College Road, Carterville, IL 62918

John Wood Community College
Quincy, Illinois
www.jwcc.edu   **CB code: 1374**

- Public 2-year community college
- Commuter campus in large town

General. Founded in 1974. Regionally accredited. Additional extension sites in Pittsfield, Perry and Mt. Sterling. **Enrollment:** 1,612 degree-seeking undergraduates. **Degrees:** 310 associate awarded. **Location:** 140 miles from St. Louis, 100 miles from Springfield. **Calendar:** Semester, extensive summer session. **Full-time faculty:** 54 total. **Part-time faculty:** 200 total. **Class size:** 59% < 20, 41% 20-39. **Special facilities:** Workforce development center, truck driver training facility, greenhouse, agricultural center, G.E.D. center.

Student profile.

Out-of-state: 7%   **25 or older:**   38%

Transfer out. Colleges most students transferred to 2015: Western Illinois University, Eastern Illinois University, University of Illinois-Springfield, Quincy University.

Basis for selection. Open admission, but selective for some programs. Limited enrollment in certificate programs in dietary management, practical nursing, nurse assistant and surgical technology, and in associate degree programs in nursing and radiologic technology.

High school preparation. Recommended units include English 4, mathematics 3, social studies 3 and science 4.

2015-2016 Annual costs. Tuition/fees: $4,614; $7,914 out-of-state. Per-credit charge: $147 in-state; $257 out-of-state. Books/supplies: $1,200. Personal expenses: $898.

Financial aid. Need-based: Need-based aid available for part-time students. Work-study available nights, weekends and for part-time students.

Application procedures. Admission: No deadline. No application fee. Admission notification on a rolling basis. **Financial aid:** No deadline. FAFSA required. Applicants notified on a rolling basis starting 3/1.

Academics. Special study options: Distance learning, dual enrollment of high school students, ESL, independent study, internships, liberal arts/career combination, student-designed major, study abroad. License preparation in nursing, paramedic, radiology, real estate. **Credit/placement by examination:** AP, CLEP, institutional tests. 30 credit hours maximum toward associate degree. **Support services:** GED preparation and test center, learning center, reduced course load, remedial instruction, study skills assistance, tutoring, writing center.

Majors. Biology: General. **Business:** General, accounting, accounting technology, administrative services, business admin, executive assistant, sales/distribution. **Communications:** Communications/speech/rhetoric. **Engineering:** General. **Foreign languages:** Spanish. **General:** Electrician. **Health services:** Clinical lab technology, EMT paramedic, medical radiologic technology/radiation therapy, medical secretary, nursing (RN). **History:** General. **Liberal arts:** Arts/sciences. **Math:** General. **Parks/recreation:** Health/fitness. **Physical sciences:** General, physics. **Protective services:** Fire safety technology, homeland security, police science. **Psychology:** General. **Social sciences:** Economics, sociology. **Visual/performing arts:** Art, graphic design, music. **Work/family studies:** Child care management.

Most popular majors. Health sciences 20%, liberal arts 58%.

Technology on campus. 400 workstations in library, computer center. Commuter students can connect to campus network. Online course registration, online library, helpline, wireless network available.

Student life. Freshman orientation: Mandatory. Preregistration for classes offered. **Activities:** Bands, choral groups, drama, music ensembles, musical theater, student government, service organizations, honor society, Phi Theta Kappa, Campus Crusade for Christ.

Athletics. NJCAA. **Intercollegiate:** Baseball M, basketball, cheerleading, softball W. **Intramural:** Basketball, bowling, football (non-tackle), volleyball. **Team name:** Trail Blazers.

Student services. Adult student services, career counseling, services for economically disadvantaged, student employment services, financial aid counseling, minority student services, veterans' counselor. **Physically disabled:** Services for visually, speech, hearing impaired. **Transfer:** Transfer adviser, college fairs on campus for students transferring to 4-year colleges.

Contact. E-mail: admissions@jwcc.edu
Phone: (217) 641-4338 Fax: (217) 224-4208
Rachel Buhr, Director of Admissions, John Wood Community College, 1301 South 48th Street, Quincy, IL 62305-8736

Joliet Junior College
Joliet, Illinois
www.jjc.edu
CB code: 1346

- Public 2-year community and junior college
- Commuter campus in small city

General. Founded in 1901. Regionally accredited. **Enrollment:** 11,945 degree-seeking undergraduates. **Degrees:** 1,641 associate awarded. **Location:** 45 miles from Chicago. **Calendar:** Semester, extensive summer session. **Full-time faculty:** 219 total. **Part-time faculty:** 673 total. **Class size:** 48% < 20, 51% 20-39, less than 1% 40-49, less than 1% 50-99, less than 1% >100. **Special facilities:** Planetarium, nature trail, arboretum, working farm, fitness center.

Student profile.

Out-of-state:	1%	25 or older:	42%

Transfer out. Colleges most students transferred to 2015: Northern Illinois University, Illinois State University, University of St. Francis, Lewis University, Governors State University.

Basis for selection. Open admission, but selective for some programs and for out-of-state students. Special requirements for nursing, veterinary medical technology, radiologic technology, international students, early-entry students from high school, high school dual credit, and those pursuing dual admissions with a four-year college or university. Interview recommended for some.

High school preparation. 15 units recommended. Recommended units include English 4, mathematics 3, social studies 3, science 3 and academic electives 2.

2015-2016 Annual costs. Tuition/fees: $3,450; $10,530 out-of-district; $11,190 out-of-state. Per-credit charge: $115 in-district; $320 out-of-district; $342 out-of-state. Personal expenses: $1,500.

Financial aid. Need-based: Need-based aid available for part-time students. Work-study available nights, weekends and for part-time students. **Non-need-based:** Scholarships awarded for academics.

Application procedures. Admission: No deadline. No application fee. Admission notification on a rolling basis. **Financial aid:** Closing date 6/12. FAFSA, institutional form required. Applicants notified on a rolling basis starting 5/15.

Academics. Special study options: Cooperative education, distance learning, dual enrollment of high school students, ESL, honors, independent study, internships, study abroad. License preparation in nursing, paramedic, radiology, real estate. **Credit/placement by examination:** AP, CLEP, institutional tests. 45 credit hours maximum toward associate degree. **Support services:** GED preparation, learning center, pre-admission summer program, reduced course load, remedial instruction, study skills assistance, tutoring, writing center.

Majors. Biology: General. **Business:** Accounting, administrative services, business admin, office management, office technology, office/clerical. **Computer sciences:** General, information systems, programming. **Education:** Early childhood, elementary, secondary, special ed, teacher assistance. **Engineering:** Electrical. **English:** English lit. **Health services:** Medical secretary, nursing (RN), veterinary technology/assistant. **History:** General. **Liberal arts:** Arts/sciences. **Math:** General. **Physical sciences:** Chemistry. **Protective services:** Law enforcement admin. **Psychology:** General. **Social sciences:** Political science, sociology. **Visual/performing arts:** Art, interior design, music. **Work/family studies:** Clothing/textiles.

Most popular majors. Business/marketing 7%, health sciences 15%, liberal arts 49%.

Technology on campus. Helpline, repair service available.

Student life. Freshman orientation: Available. Preregistration for classes offered. **Activities:** Bands, campus ministries, choral groups, drama, literary magazine, music ensembles, musical theater, student government, student newspaper, black student organization, Intervarsity Christian Fellowship, Latinos Unidos, Latter-day Saints association, unity club.

Athletics. NJCAA. **Intercollegiate:** Baseball M, basketball, cross-country, football (tackle) M, soccer, softball W, tennis, volleyball W. **Team name:** Wolves.

Student services. Career counseling, services for economically disadvantaged, student employment services, financial aid counseling, minority student services, on-campus daycare, personal counseling, placement for graduates, veterans' counselor, women's services. **Physically disabled:** Services for visually, speech, hearing impaired. **Transfer:** Transfer center, transfer adviser for students transferring to 4-year colleges.

Contact. E-mail: jkloberd@jjc.edu
Phone: (815) 729-9020 Fax: (815) 744-5507
Jennifer Kloberdanz, Director of Admissions and Recruitment, Joliet Junior College, 1215 Houbolt Road, Joliet, IL 60431-8938

Kankakee Community College
Kankakee, Illinois
www.kcc.edu
CB member
CB code: 1380

- Public 2-year community college
- Commuter campus in large town

General. Founded in 1966. Regionally accredited. **Enrollment:** 2,539 degree-seeking undergraduates; 767 non-degree-seeking students. **Degrees:** 456 associate awarded. **ROTC:** Army. **Location:** 60 miles from Chicago. **Calendar:** Semester, extensive summer session. **Full-time faculty:** 59 total; 12% have terminal degrees, 5% minority, 73% women. **Part-time faculty:** 186 total; 3% have terminal degrees, 9% minority, 54% women. **Class size:** 68% < 20, 30% 20-39, less than 1% 40-49, 1% 50-99. **Special facilities:** Greenhouse.

Student profile. Among degree-seeking undergraduates, 59% enrolled in a transfer program, 41% enrolled in a vocational program, 4% already have a bachelor's degree or higher, 334 enrolled as first-time, first-year students.

Part-time:	64%	Asian American:	1%
Out-of-state:	2%	Hispanic/Latino:	12%
Women:	62%	Multi-racial, non-Hispanic:	1%
African American:	15%	25 or older:	44%

Transfer out. Colleges most students transferred to 2015: Illinois State University, Governors State University, Olivet Nazarene University, Northern Illinois University, Eastern Illinois University.

Basis for selection. Open admission, but selective for some programs. Criteria for health career programs may include prerequisite coursework, high school record and test scores; separate application and COMPASS required. COMPASS or ACT test required of all students for placement. **Adult students:** COMPASS test required.

High school preparation. 15 units recommended. Recommended units include English 4, mathematics 3, social studies 2, science 2 (laboratory 1) and academic electives 4.

2015-2016 Annual costs. Tuition/fees: $4,080; $9,120 out-of-district; $17,760 out-of-state. Per-credit charge: $122 in-district; $290 out-of-district; $578 out-of-state. Books/supplies: $1,090. Personal expenses: $1,300.

Financial aid. Need-based: Need-based aid available for part-time students. Work-study available nights, weekends and for part-time students. **Non-need-based:** Scholarships awarded for athletics.

Application procedures. Admission: No deadline. No application fee. Admission notification on a rolling basis. **Financial aid:** Closing date 7/13. FAFSA required. Applicants notified on a rolling basis; must reply within 4 week(s) of notification.

Academics. Special study options: Cross-registration, distance learning, dual enrollment of high school students, ESL, honors, independent study, internships, study abroad, teacher certification program. License preparation in aviation, nursing, paramedic, physical therapy, radiology. **Credit/placement by examination:** AP, CLEP, institutional tests. 16 credit hours maximum toward associate degree. **Support services:** GED preparation and test center, learning center, reduced course load, remedial instruction, study skills assistance, tutoring, writing center.

Majors. Biology: General. **Business:** Administrative services, business admin, construction management. **Communications technology:** Desktop publishing. **Education:** General, early childhood, elementary, mathematics, secondary, special ed, teacher assistance. **Engineering:** General. **English:** English lit. **Health services:** Clinical lab technology, EMT paramedic, medical assistant, nursing (RN), office assistant, physical therapy assistant, radiologic technology/medical imaging, respiratory therapy technology. **History:** General. **Math:** General. **Physical sciences:** Chemistry, physics. **Protective services:** Law enforcement admin, police science. **Psychology:** General. **Social sciences:** Political science, sociology. **Visual/performing arts:** General, art.

Most popular majors. Business/marketing 9%, health sciences 34%; liberal arts 29%, trade and industry 7%.

Technology on campus. 1,200 workstations in library, computer center, student center. Commuter students can connect to campus network. Online course registration, online library, helpline, wireless network available.

Student life. Freshman orientation: Mandatory. Preregistration for classes offered. Two-hour orientation class held multiple dates and times at beginning of term. **Activities:** Radio station, student government.

Athletics. NJCAA. **Intercollegiate:** Baseball M, basketball, soccer M, softball W, volleyball W. **Intramural:** Basketball, golf. **Team name:** Cavaliers.

Student services. Adult student services, career counseling, services for economically disadvantaged, student employment services, financial aid counseling, minority student services, on-campus daycare, placement for graduates, veterans' counselor. **Physically disabled:** Services for visually, speech, hearing impaired. **Transfer:** Pre-admission transcript evaluation for new students. Transfer center, transfer adviser, college fairs on campus for students transferring to 4-year colleges.

Contact. E-mail: admissions@kcc.edu
Phone: (815) 802-8520 Fax: (815) 802-8521
David Hermann, Registrar/Director Admissions & Registration, Kankakee Community College, 100 College Drive, Kankakee, IL 60901-6505

Kaskaskia College
Centralia, Illinois
www.kaskaskia.edu   **CB code: 1108**

▶ Public 2-year community college
▶ Commuter campus in large town

General. Founded in 1966. Regionally accredited. Season of Entertainment and Guest Artists Speaker Series throughout the year. **Enrollment:** 2,370 degree-seeking undergraduates; 2,102 non-degree-seeking students. **Degrees:** 596 associate awarded. **ROTC:** Army. **Location:** 60 miles from St. Louis. **Calendar:** Semester, limited summer session. **Full-time faculty:** 76 total; 9% have terminal degrees, 5% minority, 51% women. **Part-time faculty:** 130 total; 4% have terminal degrees, 5% minority, 59% women. **Class size:** 84% < 20, 15% 20-39, less than 1% 40-49, less than 1% 50-99. **Special facilities:** Fitness trail, fitness center. **Partnerships:** Formal partnerships with local businesses, hospitals, factories/industries, correctional institutions.

Student profile. Among degree-seeking undergraduates, 51% enrolled in a transfer program, 49% enrolled in a vocational program, 2% already have a bachelor's degree or higher, 265 enrolled as first-time, first-year students, 48 transferred in from other institutions.

Part-time:	43%	Hispanic/Latino:	1%
Out-of-state:	1%	Multi-racial, non-Hispanic:	2%
Women:	63%	25 or older:	35%
African American:	8%		

Transfer out. Colleges most students transferred to 2015: Southern Illinois University at Carbondale, Southern Illinois University at Edwardsville, Greenville College, McKendree University, Eastern Illinois University.

Basis for selection. Open admission, but selective for some programs. English and math placement tests are required for all special admit health-related programs which include: nursing (RN), practical nursing, nursing assistant, radiologic technology, diagnostic medical sonography, respiratory therapy, paramedicine, physical therapy assistant, massage therapy, surgical technology, medical laboratory technology, occupational therapy assistant and veterinary technician. Nursing (RN) also requires the Test of Essential Academic Skills (TEAS) test for acceptance. Interview required of allied health majors.

High school preparation. 15 units recommended. Recommended units include English 4, mathematics 3, social studies 3, science 3, foreign language 2 and academic electives 2. Specific requirements for allied health.

2015-2016 Annual costs. Tuition/fees: $3,930; $6,990 out-of-district; $12,330 out-of-state. Per-credit charge: $115 in-district; $217 out-of-district; $395 out-of-state.

2015-2016 Financial aid. Need-based: 118 full-time freshmen applied for aid; 118 deemed to have need; 102 received aid. Average need met was 65%. Average scholarship/grant was $1,308. 21% of total undergraduate aid awarded as scholarships/grants, 79% as loans/jobs. Need-based aid available for part-time students. Work-study available nights, weekends and for part-time students. **Non-need-based:** Scholarships awarded for academics, athletics, state residency.

Application procedures. Admission: No deadline. No application fee. Admission notification on a rolling basis. Allied health programs have specific closing dates. **Financial aid:** Priority date 5/15; no closing date. FAFSA required. Applicants notified on a rolling basis starting 4/1; must reply within 2 week(s) of notification.

Academics. Learning communities available. **Special study options:** Accelerated study, cooperative education, distance learning, double major, dual enrollment of high school students, ESL, honors, independent study, internships, liberal arts/career combination, student-designed major, weekend college. License preparation in nursing, paramedic, physical therapy, radiology. **Credit/placement by examination:** AP, CLEP, institutional tests. 30 credit hours maximum toward associate degree. **Support services:** GED preparation and test center, learning center, reduced course load, remedial instruction, study skills assistance, tutoring.

Majors. Business: General, accounting, construction management, executive assistant, office technology. **Computer sciences:** Information systems, system admin, webmaster. **Education:** Mathematics, teacher assistance. **Engineering:** General. **General:** Carpentry, electrician. **Health services:** Clinical lab technology, EMT paramedic, health information technology, nursing (RN), occupational therapy assistant, physical therapy assistant, radiologic technology/medical imaging, respiratory therapy technology, veterinary technology/assistant. **Liberal arts:** Arts/sciences, library assistant. **Protective services:** Juvenile corrections, law enforcement admin. **Visual/performing arts:** Music. **Work/family studies:** Child care service.

Most popular majors. Agriculture 6%, health sciences 24%, liberal arts 44%.

Technology on campus. 191 workstations in library, computer center, student center. Commuter students can connect to campus network. Online library, helpline, wireless network available.

Student life. Freshman orientation: Available. Preregistration for classes offered. Two-hour program held several times throughout each semester. Individuals may choose to attend the program on the main Kaskaskia College campus or one of the six education centers. Participants may register by calling 618.545.3063, emailing KCNSO@kaskaskia.edu, online through www.kaskaskia.edu/nso or through registration at any of the seven college locations. **Activities:** Bands, choral groups, drama, international student organizations, music ensembles, student government, student newspaper, Brothers and Sisters in Christ, Black Student Association.

Athletics. NJCAA. **Intercollegiate:** Baseball M, basketball, cross-country, golf, soccer, softball W, tennis, volleyball W. **Team name:** Blue Devils.

Student services. Adult student services, career counseling, services for economically disadvantaged, student employment services, financial aid counseling, minority student services, on-campus daycare, personal counseling, placement for graduates, veterans' counselor. **Physically disabled:** Services for visually, speech, hearing impaired. **Transfer:** Pre-admission transcript evaluation for new students. Transfer center, transfer adviser, college fairs on campus for students transferring to 4-year colleges.

Contact. E-mail: kcadmissions@kaskaskia.edu
Phone: (618) 545-3040 Fax: (618) 545-3393
Cheryl Boehne, Director of Admissions and Registration, Kaskaskia College, 27210 College Road, Centralia, IL 62801

Kishwaukee College
Malta, Illinois
www.kishwaukeecollege.edu   **CB code: 0511**

▶ Public 2-year community college
▶ Commuter campus in rural community

General. Founded in 1967. Regionally accredited. **Enrollment:** 4,900 undergraduates. **Degrees:** 451 associate awarded. **ROTC:** Army. **Location:** 7 miles from DeKalb. **Calendar:** Semester, limited summer session. **Full-time faculty:** 73 total. **Part-time faculty:** 163 total.

Student profile.

Out-of-state: 1% 25 or older: 32%

Transfer out. Colleges most students transferred to 2015: Northern Illinois University.

Basis for selection. Open admission, but selective for some programs. Special requirements, including interview, for nursing, radiologic technology and therapeutic massage programs. Portfolio recommended for art majors. **Learning Disabled:** Students with learning disabilities should contact disabilities service office at least 30 days before enrollment to assist student with reasonable accommodations.

High school preparation. 15 units recommended. Recommended units include English 4, mathematics 3, social studies 3, science 3 and foreign language 2. High school diploma or equivalency required for nursing, radiologic technology, and therapeutic massage applicants.

2015-2016 Annual costs. Tuition/fees: $3,930; $9,690 out-of-district; $15,390 out-of-state. Per-credit charge: $119 in-district; $311 out-of-district; $501 out-of-state. Books/supplies: $1,000. Personal expenses: $1,000.

Financial aid. Need-based: Need-based aid available for part-time students. Work-study available nights, weekends and for part-time students. **Non-need-based:** Scholarships awarded for academics, athletics, leadership, music/drama, state residency.

Application procedures. Admission: No deadline. No application fee. Admission notification on a rolling basis. **Financial aid:** Priority date 5/1; no closing date. FAFSA, institutional form required. Applicants notified on a rolling basis starting 5/1; must reply within 2 week(s) of notification.

Academics. Cross-registration with Northern Illinois University and nearby community colleges. Distance Learning Consortium, member Illinois Virtual College (IVC). **Special study options:** Cross-registration, distance learning, double major, dual enrollment of high school students, ESL, independent study, internships, study abroad. License preparation in aviation, nursing, radiology, real estate. **Credit/placement by examination:** AP, CLEP, institutional tests. 48 credit hours maximum toward associate degree. Must complete 15 hours residency prior to posting proficiency credit. **Support services:** GED preparation and test center, learning center, pre-admission summer program, reduced course load, remedial instruction, study skills assistance, tutoring.

Majors. Architecture: Landscape. **Business:** General, accounting, human resources, management information systems, office management, office/clerical, operations. **Communications:** Communications/speech/rhetoric, journalism. **Computer sciences:** Applications programming. **Education:** General, early childhood, elementary, physical, secondary, special ed. **Engineering:** General. **English:** English lit. **Foreign languages:** General, French, Spanish. **Health services:** Medical radiologic technology/radiation therapy, nursing (RN), predental, premedicine, prenursing, prepharmacy, preveterinary. **History:** General. **Human services:** Social work. **Liberal arts:** Arts/sciences. **Math:** General. **Parks/recreation:** Health/fitness. **Physical sciences:** Astronomy, chemistry, physics. **Protective services:** Fire safety technology, firefighting, police science. **Psychology:** General. **Social sciences:** General, criminology, economics, political science, sociology. **Visual/performing arts:** General, art, dramatic, music. **Work/family studies:** General, child care management.

Most popular majors. Agriculture 7%, health sciences 10%, interdisciplinary studies 51%, liberal arts 29%.

Technology on campus. 376 workstations in library, computer center. Online library, helpline available.

Student life. Freshman orientation: Available. Preregistration for classes offered. Five sessions held during summer. **Activities:** Choral groups, drama, literary magazine, music ensembles, musical theater, student government, student newspaper, international student club, Nurses Christian Fellowship, Phi Theta Kappa, black student union, Vocational Industrial Clubs of America, Christian Fellowship, agriculture club, horticulture club, student nurses organization, student radiographers association.

Athletics. NJCAA. **Intercollegiate:** Baseball M, basketball, golf, soccer M, softball W, volleyball W. **Intramural:** Badminton, basketball, softball, volleyball. **Team name:** Kougars.

Student services. Adult student services, career counseling, services for economically disadvantaged, student employment services, financial aid counseling, health services, minority student services, on-campus daycare, personal counseling, placement for graduates, veterans' counselor, women's services. **Physically disabled:** Services for visually, speech, hearing impaired. **Transfer:** Re-entry adviser, pre-admission transcript evaluation for new students. Transfer center, transfer adviser, college fairs on campus for students transferring to 4-year colleges.

Contact. Phone: (815) 825-2086 ext. 218 Fax: (815) 825-2306 Jill Bier, Director of Admissions, Registration and Records, Kishwaukee College, 21193 Malta Road, Malta, IL 60150-9699

Lake Land College
Mattoon, Illinois
www.lakelandcollege.edu CB code: 1424

- Public 2-year community college
- Commuter campus in large town

General. Founded in 1966. Regionally accredited. **Enrollment:** 3,387 degree-seeking undergraduates. **Degrees:** 976 associate awarded. **Location:** 45 miles from Decatur, 45 miles from Champaign. **Calendar:** Semester, extensive summer session. **Full-time faculty:** 116 total. **Part-time faculty:** 362 total. **Class size:** 55% < 20, 45% 20-39.

Student profile. Among degree-seeking undergraduates, 43% enrolled in a transfer program, 57% enrolled in a vocational program, 1,088 enrolled as first-time, first-year students.

Out-of-state: 3% 25 or older: 46%

Transfer out. Colleges most students transferred to 2015: Eastern Illinois University, Southern Illinois University, University of Illinois.

Basis for selection. Open admission, but selective for some programs. Special requirements for dental hygiene, nursing, physical therapist assistant, John Deere agricultural technology, massage therapy, and cosmetology programs. ACT required of dental hygiene applicants for placement only. **Adult students:** Assessment battery test required.

High school preparation. Recommended units include English 4, mathematics 3, social studies 3, history 3, science 3 (laboratory 3), foreign language 2 and academic electives 2. Math and biology required for dental hygiene and nursing applicants.

2015-2016 Annual costs. Tuition/fees: $3,507; $7,328 out-of-district; $13,130 out-of-state. Books/supplies: $318.

Financial aid. Need-based: Need-based aid available for part-time students. Work-study available nights, weekends and for part-time students. **Non-need-based:** Scholarships awarded for academics, athletics.

Application procedures. Admission: No deadline. No application fee. Admission notification on a rolling basis. **Financial aid:** Priority date 5/1; no closing date. FAFSA required. Applicants notified on a rolling basis starting 6/1.

Academics. Special study options: Accelerated study, cooperative education, distance learning, dual enrollment of high school students, ESL, honors, independent study, internships, study abroad, weekend college. License preparation in dental hygiene, nursing, paramedic, physical therapy. **Credit/placement by examination:** AP, CLEP, institutional tests. 32 credit hours maximum toward associate degree. **Support services:** GED preparation, learning center, reduced course load, remedial instruction, study skills assistance, tutoring.

Majors. Business: General, administrative services, human resources. **Communications:** Broadcast journalism, journalism. **Computer sciences:** LAN/WAN management, networking. **Conservation:** Wildlife/wilderness. **Education:** General, mathematics, social science. **Engineering:** General, civil. **English:** Rhetoric/composition. **Health services:** Dental hygiene, nursing (RN), physical therapy assistant, premedicine, prepharmacy, preveterinary. **Liberal arts:** Arts/sciences. **Math:** General. **Protective services:** Police science. **Psychology:** General. **Social sciences:** General, economics. **Visual/performing arts:** Studio arts. **Work/family studies:** General, child care management.

Technology on campus. 500 workstations in library, computer center. Online course registration available.

Student life. Freshman orientation: Available. Preregistration for classes offered. Mandatory for degree-seeking students; approximately 4 hours in length. **Activities:** Choral groups, radio station, student government, student newspaper, Phi Theta Kappa.

Athletics. NJCAA. **Intercollegiate:** Baseball M, basketball, softball W, volleyball W. **Team name:** Lakers.

Student services. Career counseling, student employment services, health services, on-campus daycare, personal counseling, placement for graduates, veterans' counselor. **Physically disabled:** Services for visually, speech, hearing impaired. **Transfer:** Transfer adviser, college fairs on campus for students transferring to 4-year colleges.

Contact. E-mail: admissions@lakeland.cc.il.us
Phone: (217) 234-5434 Fax: (217) 234-5390
Jon VanDyke, Dean of Admission Services, Lake Land College, 5001
Lake Land Boulevard, Mattoon, IL 61938-9366

Le Cordon Bleu College of Culinary Arts: Chicago
Chicago, Illinois
www.chefs.edu/Chicago   CB code: 2564

- For-profit 2-year culinary school
- Commuter campus in very large city
- Interview required

General. Regionally accredited. Affiliated with Le Cordon Bleu. **Enrollment:** 958 undergraduates. **Degrees:** 72 associate awarded. **Location:** Downtown. **Calendar:** Differs by program, extensive summer session. **Full-time faculty:** 27 total. **Part-time faculty:** 24 total. **Special facilities:** Student-run restaurant.

Student profile.

Out-of-state: 29%   25 or older: 46%

Basis for selection. Open admission. **Home schooled:** Portfolio required. **Learning Disabled:** Documentation of learning disability and special accommodations needed must be provided.

2015-2016 Annual costs. Personal expenses: $2,116. **Additional information:** Certificate programs: $19,500. Associate programs: $40,000. Books and supplies are included.

Financial aid. Need-based: Need-based aid available for part-time students. Work-study available nights, weekends and for part-time students.

Application procedures. Admission: No deadline. $50 fee. Admission notification on a rolling basis. **Financial aid:** No deadline. FAFSA, institutional form required. Applicants notified on a rolling basis.

Academics. All levels of developmental learning provided. **Special study options:** All programs contain an externship course. **Credit/placement by examination:** AP, CLEP. 12 credit hours maximum toward associate degree. **Support services:** Learning center, remedial instruction, tutoring.

Technology on campus. 70 workstations in library, computer center, student center. Commuter students can connect to campus network. Online library, wireless network available.

Student life. Freshman orientation: Mandatory. Preregistration for classes offered. **Activities:** Student newspaper.

Student services. Career counseling, student employment services, financial aid counseling, placement for graduates, veterans' counselor.

Contact. Phone: (312) 944-0882 Toll-free number: (877) 828-7772
Fax: (312) 944-8557
Christopher Heath, Senior Director of Admissions, Le Cordon Bleu College of Culinary Arts: Chicago, 361 West Chestnut, Chicago, IL 60610-3050

Lewis and Clark Community College
Godfrey, Illinois   CB member
www.lc.edu   CB code: 0623

- Public 2-year community college
- Commuter campus in large town

General. Founded in 1970. Regionally accredited. **Enrollment:** 3,599 degree-seeking undergraduates. **Degrees:** 828 associate awarded. **ROTC:** Army. **Location:** 30 miles from St. Louis. **Calendar:** Semester, limited summer session. **Full-time faculty:** 105 total. **Part-time faculty:** 250 total.

Transfer out. Colleges most students transferred to 2015: Southern Illinois University: Edwardsville.

Basis for selection. Open admission, but selective for some programs. Special requirements for nursing and other allied health programs. Admission is based on GPA, completion of prerequisite courses, and admission tests. Interview required for radio broadcasting, music majors. Audition required for music majors.

High school preparation. Recommended units include English 4, mathematics 3 and science 2.

2015-2016 Annual costs. Tuition/fees: $4,440; $10,920 out-of-district; $14,160 out-of-state. Per-credit charge: $108 in-district; $324 out-of-district; $432 out-of-state. Books/supplies: $1,008. Personal expenses: $2,583.

Financial aid. Need-based: Need-based aid available for part-time students. Work-study available nights, weekends and for part-time students.

Application procedures. Admission: No deadline. No application fee. Admission notification on a rolling basis. **Financial aid:** Priority date 6/1; no closing date. FAFSA required. Applicants notified on a rolling basis starting 8/1; must reply within 3 week(s) of notification.

Academics. Special study options: Cooperative education, cross-registration, distance learning, double major, dual enrollment of high school students, internships, liberal arts/career combination, student-designed major. Bachelor's degree programs available on campus. License preparation in dental hygiene, nursing, occupational therapy, paramedic, real estate. **Credit/placement by examination:** AP, CLEP, institutional tests. 32 credit hours maximum toward associate degree. **Support services:** GED preparation, learning center, remedial instruction, study skills assistance, tutoring, writing center.

Majors. Business: General, accounting, banking/financial services, business admin, office/clerical. **Communications:** Radio/TV. **Computer sciences:** General, computer graphics, computer science, data processing, information technology, LAN/WAN management, web page design, webmaster. **Education:** General, early childhood, teacher assistance. **Health services:** Dental hygiene, nursing (RN), occupational therapy assistant, predental, premedicine, prenursing, prepharmacy. **Liberal arts:** Arts/sciences. **Protective services:** Criminal justice, firefighting. **Visual/performing arts:** Music, studio arts. **Work/family studies:** Child care management.

Technology on campus. 300 workstations in library, computer center. Online course registration, online library, wireless network available.

Student life. Freshman orientation: Mandatory. Preregistration for classes offered. Approximately 3 hours long and held every Monday, Wednesday and Friday after open registration begins. **Activities:** Bands, choral groups, dance, drama, music ensembles, radio station, student government, student newspaper, TV station, veterans organization, Christian Campus Fellowship, disabled students organization, black student association, political action club.

Athletics. NJCAA. **Intercollegiate:** Baseball M, basketball, golf M, soccer, softball W, tennis, volleyball W. **Team name:** Trailblazers.

Student services. Adult student services, career counseling, student employment services, health services, on-campus daycare, personal counseling, placement for graduates, veterans' counselor. **Physically disabled:** Services for visually, hearing impaired. **Transfer:** Pre-admission transcript evaluation for new students. Transfer center, transfer adviser, college fairs on campus for students transferring to 4-year colleges.

Contact. E-mail: enroll@lc.edu
Phone: (618) 468-2222 Toll-free number: (800) 500-5222
Fax: (618) 468-2310
Kim Widman, Assistant Director of Admissions and Registration, Lewis and Clark Community College, 5800 Godfrey Road, Godfrey, IL 62035-2466

Lincoln College
Lincoln, Illinois
www.lincolncollege.edu   CB code: 1406

- Private 2-year junior and liberal arts college
- Residential campus in large town
- SAT or ACT (ACT writing optional) required

General. Founded in 1865. Regionally accredited. Associate in liberal arts and science degree programs and two bachelor's degree programs offered at Lincoln campus. Bachelor's degree and vocational programs available at Normal campus. **Enrollment:** 1,200 degree-seeking undergraduates. **Degrees:** 99 bachelor's, 168 associate awarded. **Location:** 185 miles from Chicago, 125 miles from St. Louis. **Calendar:** Semester, limited summer session. **Full-time faculty:** 40 total. **Part-time faculty:** 86 total. **Class size:** 67% <20, 32% 20-39, 1% 40-49. **Special facilities:** Lincoln heritage museum, museum of the presidents.

Transfer out. Colleges most students transferred to 2015: Illinois State University, Southern Illinois University, Eastern Illinois University, Northern Illinois University, Western Illinois University.

Basis for selection. Test scores and high school transcripts are given the most weight. Letters of recommendation and/or personal statement or interview may be required. Normal campus requires 18 ACT score for resident students. Interview and personal statement recommended for applicants whom do not meet the minimum admissions requirement of a 16 ACT, 2.0 GPA. **Adult students:** SAT/ACT scores not required if applicant over 23. **Home schooled:** Transcript of courses and grades, state high school equivalency certificate required. **Learning Disabled:** Upon acceptance students may submit documentation to the Office of Disability Services for consideration for the ACCESS program or to receive services through the Office of Disability Services.

High school preparation. College-preparatory program recommended. Recommended units include English 4, mathematics 3, social studies 2, history 2, science 3 (laboratory 1), foreign language 2 and computer science 2.

2015-2016 Annual costs. Tuition/fees: $17,900. Room/board: $7,100. Personal expenses: $1,886.

2014-2015 Financial aid. Need-based: 581 full-time freshmen applied for aid; 559 deemed to have need; 542 received aid. Average need met was 46%. Average scholarship/grant was $125. 51% of total undergraduate aid awarded as scholarships/grants, 49% as loans/jobs. Need-based aid available for part-time students. Work-study available nights, weekends and for part-time students. **Non-need-based:** Awarded to 70 full-time undergraduates, including 34 freshmen. Scholarships awarded for academics, alumni affiliation, art, athletics, leadership, music/drama. **Additional information:** Auditions recommended for music, speech, theater, broadcasting, and dance scholarship candidates, portfolios recommended for art and technical theater scholarship candidates.

Application procedures. Admission: Priority date 7/1; no deadline. $25 fee, may be waived for applicants with need. Admission notification on a rolling basis. Upon receipt of official high school transcripts and ACT scores, application can be reviewed. Additional information may be requested by the Director of Admissions. **Financial aid:** Priority date 4/1; no closing date. FAFSA required. Applicants notified on a rolling basis starting 6/1; must reply within 3 week(s) of notification.

Academics. Special study options: Dual enrollment of high school students, honors, independent study, study abroad. Bachelor's degree programs available on campus. **Credit/placement by examination:** AP, CLEP, SAT, ACT, institutional tests. 15 credit hours maximum toward associate degree. **Support services:** Learning center, pre-admission summer program, reduced course load, remedial instruction, study skills assistance, tutoring.

Majors. Biology: General. **Business:** General, accounting, business admin, tourism promotion, tourism/travel. **Communications:** Communications/speech/rhetoric, journalism. **Computer sciences:** Computer science. **Conservation:** General, environmental studies. **Education:** General, art, elementary, multi-level teacher. **English:** American lit, English lit, rhetoric/composition, writing. **History:** General. **Liberal arts:** Arts/sciences. **Math:** General. **Parks/recreation:** Health/fitness. **Philosophy/religion:** Philosophy, religion. **Physical sciences:** Chemistry, physics. **Protective services:** Law enforcement admin, police science. **Psychology:** General. **Social sciences:** General, economics, geography, sociology. **Visual/performing arts:** General, art, art history/conservation, ceramics, dance, dramatic, drawing, jazz, music, music history, music performance, music theory/composition, painting, photography, piano/keyboard, sculpture, studio arts, theater design, voice/opera.

Technology on campus. 130 workstations in library, computer center, student center. Dormitories wired for high-speed internet access and linked to campus network. Commuter students can connect to campus network. Helpline available.

Student life. Freshman orientation: Mandatory. Preregistration for classes offered. 1-day event for freshman and transfers held in May, June, and July. **Housing:** Guaranteed on-campus for all undergraduates. Single-sex dorms available. $125 fully refundable deposit, deadline 8/1. **Activities:** Bands, choral groups, dance, drama, literary magazine, music ensembles, musical theater, radio station, student government, student newspaper, Black Student Union, Rotaract, Mosaic (Christian group), Phi Theta Kappa.

Athletics. NJCAA. **Intercollegiate:** Baseball M, basketball, cross-country, diving, golf, soccer, softball W, swimming, track and field, volleyball W, wrestling M. **Intramural:** Baseball M, basketball, football (non-tackle), soccer, softball, table tennis, volleyball. **Team name:** Lynx.

Student services. Adult student services, alcohol/substance abuse counseling, career counseling, financial aid counseling, health services, personal counseling, placement for graduates. **Transfer:** Pre-admission transcript evaluation for new students. Transfer center, transfer adviser, college fairs on campus for students transferring to 4-year colleges.

Contact. E-mail: admissions@lincolncollege.edu
Phone: (800) 569-0556 Fax: (217) 732-7715
Gretchen Bree, Director of Admissions, Lincoln College, 300 Keokuk Street, Lincoln, IL 62656

Lincoln Land Community College
Springfield, Illinois
www.llcc.edu

CB code: 1428

- Public 2-year community and junior college
- Commuter campus in small city

General. Founded in 1967. Regionally accredited. **Enrollment:** 3,831 degree-seeking undergraduates. **Degrees:** 1,048 associate awarded. **ROTC:** Army, Naval, Air Force. **Location:** 180 miles from Chicago, 96 miles from St. Louis. **Calendar:** Semester, extensive summer session. **Full-time faculty:** 129 total; 21% have terminal degrees, 7% minority, 51% women. **Part-time faculty:** 253 total; 6% have terminal degrees, 5% minority, 49% women. **Class size:** 74% < 20, 25% 20-39, less than 1% 40-49, less than 1% 50-99. **Special facilities:** Museum.

Transfer out. Colleges most students transferred to 2015: University of Illinois: Springfield, Southern Illinois University: Carbondale, Eastern Illinois University, Western Illinois University, Illinois State University.

Basis for selection. Open admission, but selective for some programs. Nursing and allied health program applicants must rank in top half of high school class and have 20 ACT. Admissions assessment not required of students with 22 ACT or above.

High school preparation. Recommended units include English 4, mathematics 3, social studies 2, science 2 (laboratory 2) and academic electives 2.

2015-2016 Annual costs. Tuition/fees: $3,630; $6,930 out-of-district; $10,230 out-of-state. Per-credit charge: $110 in-district; $220 out-of-district; $330 out-of-state. Books/supplies: $888. Personal expenses: $1,035.

Financial aid. Need-based: Need-based aid available for part-time students. Work-study available nights, weekends and for part-time students. **Non-need-based:** Scholarships awarded for academics, athletics, minority status, state residency.

Application procedures. Admission: No deadline. No application fee. Application must be submitted on paper. Admission notification on a rolling basis. **Financial aid:** Closing date 6/30. FAFSA, institutional form required. Applicants notified on a rolling basis starting 4/15; must reply within 2 week(s) of notification.

Academics. Special study options: Accelerated study, cooperative education, distance learning, double major, dual enrollment of high school students, ESL, honors, independent study, internships, liberal arts/career combination, study abroad, United Nations semester. License preparation in nursing, occupational therapy, paramedic, physical therapy, radiology, real estate. **Credit/placement by examination:** AP, CLEP, institutional tests. 30 credit hours maximum toward associate degree. **Support services:** GED preparation, learning center, reduced course load, remedial instruction, study skills assistance, tutoring, writing center.

Majors. Business: General, accounting, administrative services, hospitality admin, office technology. **Computer sciences:** Applications programming, networking, programming. **Education:** Teacher assistance. **Engineering:** General. **General:** Maintenance. **Health services:** Nursing (RN), occupational therapy assistant, office assistant, radiologic technology/medical imaging. **Liberal arts:** Arts/sciences. **Protective services:** Firefighting, police science. **Visual/performing arts:** Graphic design, music, studio arts. **Work/family studies:** Child care service.

Most popular majors. Health sciences 16%, interdisciplinary studies 28%, liberal arts 48%.

Technology on campus. 325 workstations in library, computer center, student center. Commuter students can connect to campus network. Online course registration, online library, helpline, wireless network available.

Student life. Freshman orientation: Available. Preregistration for classes offered. Half-day program offered at beginning of semester. **Activities:** Bands, choral groups, dance, drama, international student organizations, literary magazine, music ensembles, musical theater, student government, student newspaper.

Athletics. NJCAA. **Intercollegiate:** Baseball M, basketball, cheerleading W, soccer M, softball W, volleyball W. **Team name:** Loggers.

Student services. Adult student services, career counseling, services for economically disadvantaged, student employment services, financial aid counseling, minority student services, on-campus daycare, personal counseling, placement for graduates, veterans' counselor. **Physically disabled:** Services for visually, speech, hearing impaired. **Transfer:** Pre-admission transcript evaluation for new students. Transfer adviser, college fairs on campus for students transferring to 4-year colleges.

Contact. E-mail: ron.gregoire@llcc.cc.il.us
Phone: (217) 786-2290 Toll-free number: (800) 727-4161
Fax: (217) 786-2492
Ron Gregoire, Director of Admissions and Records, Lincoln Land
Community College, 5250 Shepherd Road, Springfield, IL 62794-9256

MacCormac College

Chicago, Illinois — CB member
www.maccormac.edu — CB code: 1520

- Private 2-year community and junior college
- Commuter campus in very large city
- SAT or ACT (ACT writing recommended), interview required

General. Founded in 1904. Regionally accredited. **Enrollment:** 198 degree-seeking undergraduates. **Degrees:** 20 associate awarded. **Calendar:** Semester, extensive summer session. **Full-time faculty:** 6 total; 17% have terminal degrees, 67% women. **Part-time faculty:** 19 total; 37% have terminal degrees, 47% minority, 63% women.

Student profile.

Out-of-state:	1%	25 or older:	30%

Transfer out. Colleges most students transferred to 2015: National-Louis University, Robert Morris University, Loyola University, DePaul University, Roosevelt University.

Basis for selection. High school academic transcripts and/or GED scores; and ACT, SAT or ASSET scores. Students applying for admissions to the Court Reporting program are required to have a keyboarding speed of 30 wpm before entry into the traditional program and a keyboarding speed of 50 wpm before entry to the FAST TRACK program. On-site testing is required. SAT or ACT recommended. **Home schooled:** Transcript of courses and grades required.

High school preparation. 13 units required; 15 recommended. Required and recommended units include English 4, mathematics 2-3, social studies 3-4, history 1, science 2 (laboratory 1).

2015-2016 Annual costs. Tuition/fees: $12,820. Books/supplies: $1,250. Personal expenses: $2,750.

Financial aid. Need-based: Need-based aid available for part-time students. Work-study available nights, weekends and for part-time students. **Non-need-based:** Scholarships awarded for academics, leadership.

Application procedures. Admission: No deadline. $20 fee ($20 out-of-state), may be waived for applicants with need. Admission notification on a rolling basis. **Financial aid:** Closing date 8/15. FAFSA required. Must reply within 2 week(s) of notification.

Academics. Special study options: Distance learning, double major, dual enrollment of high school students, internships. **Credit/placement by examination:** AP, CLEP, IB, institutional tests. **Support services:** Remedial instruction, study skills assistance, tutoring.

Majors. Business: General, business admin, office management. **Health services:** Medical transcription.

Most popular majors. Business/marketing 23%, computer/information sciences 9%, health sciences 27%, legal studies 41%.

Technology on campus. 100 workstations in library, computer center.

Student life. Freshman orientation: Mandatory. Preregistration for classes offered. **Activities:** Student government, student newspaper, student activities committee, Phi Theta Kappa.

Student services. Career counseling, student employment services, financial aid counseling, personal counseling, placement for graduates. **Transfer:** Re-entry adviser, pre-admission transcript evaluation for new students. Transfer adviser for students transferring to 4-year colleges.

Contact. E-mail: admissions@maccormac.edu
Phone: (312) 922-1884 ext. 202 Fax: (312) 922-4286
Roberto Torres, Dean of Enrollment Management and Student Services,
MacCormac College, 29 East Madison Street, Chicago, IL 60602

McHenry County College

Crystal Lake, Illinois
www.mchenry.edu — CB code: 1525

- Public 2-year community college
- Commuter campus in large town

General. Founded in 1967. Regionally accredited. **Enrollment:** 4,486 degree-seeking undergraduates; 2,075 non-degree-seeking students. **Degrees:** 988 associate awarded. **Location:** 50 miles from Chicago. **Calendar:** Semester, limited summer session. **Full-time faculty:** 97 total; 92% have terminal degrees, 7% minority, 53% women. **Part-time faculty:** 263 total; 62% have terminal degrees, 10% minority, 58% women. **Special facilities:** Planetarium, weather cam, art galleries, black box theatre, greenhouse, robotics/manufacturing laboratory, zen garden, fire science building.

Student profile. Among degree-seeking undergraduates, 58% enrolled in a transfer program, 43% enrolled in a vocational program, 1% already have a bachelor's degree or higher, 1,011 enrolled as first-time, first-year students.

Part-time:	55%	Asian American:	1%
Out-of-state:	1%	Hispanic/Latino:	16%
Women:	53%	Multi-racial, non-Hispanic:	2%
African American:	1%	25 or older:	30%

Transfer out. Colleges most students transferred to 2015: Northern Illinois University, Illinois State University, University of Illinois at Chicago, Southern Illinois University, Columbia College.

Basis for selection. Open admission, but selective for some programs. Selective admission to RN program. **Adult students:** SAT/ACT scores not required. **Learning Disabled:** Students requesting accommodations from the Special Needs Department must present appropriate documentation during an intake appointment.

High school preparation. College-preparatory program required. 18 units recommended. Recommended units include English 4, mathematics 3, social studies 3, science 3 (laboratory 3) and academic electives 2. 2 units in foreign language, music, vocational education, or art recommended.

2016-2017 Annual costs. Tuition/fees (projected): $3,314; $10,666 out-of-district; $13,497 out-of-state. Per-credit charge: $101 in-district; $346 out-of-district; $440 out-of-state. Books/supplies: $1,200. Personal expenses: $1,540.

Financial aid. Need-based: Need-based aid available for part-time students. Work-study available nights, weekends and for part-time students. **Non-need-based:** Scholarships awarded for academics, athletics, leadership, music/drama, state residency. **Additional information:** Students can apply throughout the award year for federal and state aid. Students with physical handicaps or learning disabilities may apply for special needs scholarship.

Application procedures. Admission: No deadline. $15 fee. Admission notification on a rolling basis. **Financial aid:** Priority date 6/1; no closing date. FAFSA, institutional form required. Applicants notified on a rolling basis starting 5/1.

Academics. Special study options: Accelerated study, cooperative education, distance learning, dual enrollment of high school students, ESL, honors, independent study, internships, liberal arts/career combination, study abroad. Cooperative programs (tech prep) with Education for Employment. License preparation in nursing, occupational therapy, paramedic, real estate. **Credit/placement by examination:** AP, CLEP, institutional tests. 30 credit hours maximum toward associate degree. Local proficiency exams available for occupational course credit, DANTES exams accepted. **Support services:** GED preparation and test center, learning center, pre-admission summer program, reduced course load, remedial instruction, study skills assistance, tutoring, writing center.

Majors. Business: Accounting technology, administrative services, business admin, operations, real estate, selling. **Computer sciences:** Applications programming. **Engineering:** General. **General:** Building inspection. **Health services:** EMT paramedic, nursing (RN). **Liberal arts:** Arts/sciences. **Protective services:** Firefighting, police science. **Visual/performing arts:** Art, music. **Work/family studies:** Child care service.

Most popular majors. Business/marketing 20%, engineering/engineering technologies 6%, health sciences 45%, security/protective services 6%, trade and industry 7%.

Technology on campus. 153 workstations in library, computer center, student center. Commuter students can connect to campus network. Online course registration, online library, wireless network available.

Student life. Freshman orientation: Available. Preregistration for classes offered. Admitted students from local high schools invited to participate in orientation and preregistration during April and May. **Activities:** Bands, campus ministries, choral groups, drama, literary magazine, music ensembles, radio station, student government, student newspaper, Latinos Unidos, Phi Theta Kappa, campus activities board, campus Christian fellowship, Club Concordia, Pride Alliance, black student alliance, Latter-day Saint student association, Special Needs Action Program.

Athletics. NJCAA. **Intercollegiate:** Baseball M, basketball, soccer M, softball W, tennis, volleyball W. **Intramural:** Basketball. **Team name:** Scots.

Student services. Adult student services, career counseling, student employment services, financial aid counseling, minority student services, on-campus daycare, personal counseling, placement for graduates, veterans' counselor. **Physically disabled:** Services for visually, speech, hearing impaired. **Transfer:** Pre-admission transcript evaluation for new students. Transfer center, transfer adviser, college fairs on campus for students transferring to 4-year colleges.

Contact. E-mail: admissions@mchenry.edu
Phone: (815) 455-8530 Fax: (815) 455-3766
Kellie Carper-Sowiak, Manager of New Student Transitions, McHenry County College, 8900 US Highway 14, Crystal Lake, IL 60012-2738

Moraine Valley Community College
Palos Hills, Illinois
www.morainevalley.edu   CB code: 1524

▶ Public 2-year community and junior college
▶ Commuter campus in large town

General. Founded in 1967. Regionally accredited. **Enrollment:** 11,235 degree-seeking undergraduates; 3,781 non-degree-seeking students. **Degrees:** 1,727 associate awarded. **Location:** 25 miles from Chicago. **Calendar:** Semester, extensive summer session. **Full-time faculty:** 196 total; 13% have terminal degrees, 12% minority, 58% women. **Part-time faculty:** 763 total; 10% have terminal degrees, 16% minority, 51% women. **Class size:** 47% < 20, 53% 20-39. **Special facilities:** Nature study area, center for contemporary technology, fine and performing arts center, business and conference center, health and fitness center.

Student profile. Among degree-seeking undergraduates, 68% enrolled in a transfer program, 24% enrolled in a vocational program, 3% already have a bachelor's degree or higher, 2,250 enrolled as first-time, first-year students, 402 transferred in from other institutions.

Part-time:	47%	Hispanic/Latino:	23%
Women:	51%	Multi-racial, non-Hispanic:	2%
African American:	8%	International:	2%
Asian American:	2%	25 or older:	23%

Transfer out. Colleges most students transferred to 2015: Governors State University, University of Illinois Chicago, St. Xavier University, Lewis University, Illinois State, Northern Illinois University.

Basis for selection. Open admission, but selective for some programs. Some health science programs have special admission requirements and limited enrollment. Placement tests may be waived for students with specified ACT scores. COMPASS tests required of all full-time students. **Learning Disabled:** Students should register with Center for Disability Services before 5/1.

High school preparation. College-preparatory program recommended. 15 units required. Required units include English 4, mathematics 2, social studies 2, science 2 (laboratory 2) and academic electives 5.

2015-2016 Annual costs. Tuition/fees: $3,996; $8,916 out-of-district; $10,326 out-of-state. Per-credit charge: $116 in-district; $280 out-of-district; $327 out-of-state. Books/supplies: $1,608. Personal expenses: $1,820.

2014-2015 Financial aid. Need-based: 88% of total undergraduate aid awarded as scholarships/grants, 12% as loans/jobs. Need-based aid available for part-time students. Work-study available nights, weekends and for part-time students. **Non-need-based:** Scholarships awarded for academics, alumni affiliation, athletics, leadership, state residency.

Application procedures. Admission: No deadline. No application fee. Admission notification on a rolling basis. **Financial aid:** Priority date 5/1; no closing date. FAFSA, institutional form required. Applicants notified on a rolling basis starting 6/15; must reply within 2 week(s) of notification.

Academics. Special study options: Accelerated study, cooperative education, distance learning, double major, dual enrollment of high school students, ESL, honors, independent study, internships, liberal arts/career combination, study abroad, weekend college. License preparation in paramedic. **Credit/placement by examination:** AP, CLEP, institutional tests. **Support services:**

GED preparation and test center, learning center, reduced course load, remedial instruction, study skills assistance, tutoring, writing center.

Majors. Biology: General. **Business:** General, administrative services, business admin, hospitality admin, human resources, management information systems, retailing, small business admin, tourism/travel. **Computer sciences:** Computer graphics, computer science, LAN/WAN management, security, system admin, webmaster. **Education:** Early childhood, elementary, learning disabled, mathematics, science, teacher assistance. **Engineering:** General. **English:** English lit. **Health services:** EMT paramedic, health information technology, movement therapy, nursing (RN), polysomnography, radiologic technology/medical imaging, respiratory therapy technology, substance abuse counseling. **History:** General. **Liberal arts:** Arts/sciences. **Math:** General. **Parks/recreation:** Facilities management. **Physical sciences:** Physics. **Protective services:** Fire safety technology, firefighting, law enforcement admin, police science. **Psychology:** General. **Social sciences:** Political science, sociology. **Visual/performing arts:** General, design, music. **Work/family studies:** Child care service.

Most popular majors. Health sciences 9%, interdisciplinary studies 50%, liberal arts 23%.

Technology on campus. 1,751 workstations in library, computer center, student center. Commuter students can connect to campus network. Online course registration, online library, helpline, wireless network available.

Student life. Freshman orientation: Mandatory. Preregistration for classes offered. Students registering for 12 or more credit hours required to participate in orientation program prior to first registration. **Activities:** Bands, choral groups, dance, drama, international student organizations, literary magazine, music ensembles, musical theater, student government, student newspaper, Action social and political empowerment club, Alliance of Latin American Students, Arab student union, Asian diversity club, Black Student Association, Christian Fellowship, Gender and Sexuality Progress, Go Green club, International Student Ambassadors, international student club, international women's club, student government association, Women in Action.

Athletics. NJCAA. **Intercollegiate:** Baseball M, basketball, cross-country, golf M, soccer, softball W, tennis, volleyball W. **Intramural:** Badminton, basketball, football (non-tackle), soccer, volleyball. **Team name:** Cyclones.

Student services. Adult student services, career counseling, services for economically disadvantaged, student employment services, financial aid counseling, minority student services, on-campus daycare, personal counseling, veterans' counselor, women's services. **Physically disabled:** Services for visually, speech, hearing impaired. **Transfer:** Transfer center, transfer adviser, college fairs on campus for students transferring to 4-year colleges.

Contact. E-mail: admissions@morainevalley.edu
Phone: (708) 974-2110 Fax: (708) 974-0974
Beatriz Ruiz, Director of Registrtion & Records, Moraine Valley Community College, 9000 West College Parkway, Palos Hills, IL 60465-2478

Morrison Institute of Technology
Morrison, Illinois
www.morrisontech.edu   CB code: 1269

▶ Private 2-year technical college
▶ Residential campus in small town

General. Founded in 1973. Accredited by Technology Accreditation Commission of Accreditation Board of Engineering and Technology, ABET, and COE. **Enrollment:** 91 degree-seeking undergraduates. **Degrees:** 32 associate awarded. **Location:** 100 miles from Chicago, 50 miles from Davenport, Iowa. **Calendar:** Semester, limited summer session. **Full-time faculty:** 8 total; 100% have terminal degrees, 25% women. **Part-time faculty:** 2 total; 100% have terminal degrees, 50% minority, 50% women. **Class size:** 46% < 20, 54% 20-39. **Special facilities:** 4 computer-aided design (CAD) laboratories.

Student profile. Among degree-seeking undergraduates, 55 enrolled as first-time, first-year students.

Transfer out. Colleges most students transferred to 2015: Bradley University, University of Wisconsin at Platteville.

Basis for selection. Open admission. Interview recommended. **Home schooled:** Transcript of courses and grades required.

High school preparation. College-preparatory program recommended. Recommended units include mathematics 2 and science 1. Algebra, geometry and drafting recommended.

2015-2016 Annual costs. Tuition/fees: $15,590. Room only: $3,900. Books/supplies: $1,050. Personal expenses: $900.

Financial aid. Need-based: Need-based aid available for part-time students. Work-study available nights, weekends and for part-time students. **Non-need-based:** Scholarships awarded for academics.

Application procedures. Admission: Priority date 8/1; no deadline. $30 fee. Admission notification on a rolling basis. **Financial aid:** No deadline. FAFSA, institutional form required. Applicants notified on a rolling basis; must reply within 2 week(s) of notification.

Academics. Special study options: Double major. **Credit/placement by examination:** AP, CLEP, IB, institutional tests. 25 credit hours maximum toward associate degree. SOC approved guidelines. **Support services:** Reduced course load, tutoring.

Majors. Architecture: Technology. **Computer sciences:** LAN/WAN management.

Most popular majors. Computer/information sciences 10%, engineering/engineering technologies 90%.

Technology on campus. 80 workstations in library, computer center. Dormitories wired for high-speed internet access and linked to campus network. Wireless network available.

Student life. Freshman orientation: Mandatory. Preregistration for classes offered. Five 1-hour presentations during first 5 weeks of semester. **Housing:** Guaranteed on-campus for all undergraduates. Coed dorms, special housing for disabled, wellness housing available. $100 deposit. **Activities:** Student government, student newspaper, professional societies, student chapters.

Student services. Career counseling, student employment services, personal counseling, placement for graduates. **Transfer:** Transfer adviser, college fairs on campus for students transferring to 4-year colleges.

Contact. E-mail: admissions@morrisontech.edu
Phone: (815) 772-7218 ext. 206 Fax: (815) 772-7548
Jim Prombo, Director of Admissions, Morrison Institute of Technology, 701 Portland Avenue, Morrison, IL 61270-2959

Morton College
Cicero, Illinois
www.morton.edu　　　　　　　　　　**CB code: 1489**

▶ Public 2-year community college
▶ Commuter campus in small city

General. Founded in 1924. Regionally accredited. **Enrollment:** 3,008 degree-seeking undergraduates; 1,525 non-degree-seeking students. **Degrees:** 504 associate awarded. **Location:** 6 miles from Chicago Loop. **Calendar:** Semester, limited summer session. **Full-time faculty:** 57 total; 10% minority, 51% women. **Part-time faculty:** 200 total; 22% minority, 52% women. **Class size:** 44% < 20, 55% 20-39, less than 1% 40-49, less than 1% 50-99, less than 1% >100. **Special facilities:** Planetarium, natural history museum, aquarium, Western Electric museum, internet cafe. **Partnerships:** Formal partnership with UPS.

Student profile. Among degree-seeking undergraduates, 53% enrolled in a transfer program, 47% enrolled in a vocational program, 713 enrolled as first-time, first-year students, 1,343 transferred in from other institutions.

Part-time:	58%	Women:	54%
Out-of-state:	1%	25 or older:	25%

Transfer out. Colleges most students transferred to 2015: University of Illinois at Chicago, Northeastern Illinois University, Triton Community College, Benedictine University, Moraine Valley Community College.

Basis for selection. Open admission, but selective for some programs and for out-of-state students. Nursing and physical therapist assistant programs have limited space. Preference given to in-district applicants using class rank, math and science course prerequisites, and placement tests as guides.

High school preparation. 15 units required. Required units include English 4, mathematics 3, social studies 3, science 3 and academic electives 2.

2015-2016 Annual costs. Tuition/fees: $3,440; $7,280 out-of-district; $9,200 out-of-state. Per-credit charge: $88 in-district; $216 out-of-district; $280 out-of-state. Books/supplies: $1,600.

Financial aid. Need-based: Need-based aid available for part-time students. Work-study available nights, weekends and for part-time students.

Application procedures. Admission: No deadline. $10 fee. Admission notification on a rolling basis. **Financial aid:** Priority date 6/1; no closing date. FAFSA, institutional form required. Applicants notified on a rolling basis starting 8/3.

Academics. Special study options: Distance learning, double major, dual enrollment of high school students, ESL, internships, weekend college. License preparation in nursing, physical therapy. **Credit/placement by examination:** AP, CLEP, IB, institutional tests. 30 credit hours maximum toward associate degree. **Support services:** GED preparation, learning center, pre-admission summer program, remedial instruction, study skills assistance, tutoring, writing center. College Study Seminar offered to support development of academic and personal skills needed to make college experience successful.

Majors. Business: Accounting, administrative services, business admin. **Computer sciences:** Information technology, vendor certification, web page design. **Education:** Early childhood. **Health services:** Massage therapy, nursing (RN), physical therapy assistant. **Liberal arts:** Arts/sciences. **Protective services:** Police science. **Visual/performing arts:** Studio arts. **Work/family studies:** Child care service.

Most popular majors. Health sciences 20%, interdisciplinary studies 18%, liberal arts 46%, security/protective services 7%.

Technology on campus. 314 workstations in library, computer center, student center. Commuter students can connect to campus network. Online course registration, helpline, wireless network available.

Student life. Freshman orientation: Available. Preregistration for classes offered. **Activities:** Jazz band, choral groups, dance, drama, music ensembles, musical theater, radio station, student government, student newspaper, nursing students association, Phi Theta Kappa, College Bowl, film club, Anime Gamers Union, belly dance club, Broadway club, Kosho Ryu Kempo, language and culture club, Morton Ambassador Program.

Athletics. NJCAA. **Intercollegiate:** Baseball M, basketball, cross-country, soccer M, softball W, volleyball W. **Team name:** Panthers.

Student services. Career counseling, services for economically disadvantaged, student employment services, financial aid counseling, on-campus daycare, personal counseling, placement for graduates. **Physically disabled:** Services for visually, speech, hearing impaired. **Transfer:** Pre-admission transcript evaluation for new students. Transfer center, transfer adviser, college fairs on campus for students transferring to 4-year colleges.

Contact. E-mail: enroll@morton.edu
Phone: (708) 656-8000 ext. 346 Fax: (708) 656-9592
Marlena Avalos-Thompson, Director of Student Development, Morton College, 3801 South Central Avenue, Cicero, IL 60804-4398

Northwestern College
Chicago, Illinois
www.nc.edu　　　　　　　　　　**CB code: 2433**

▶ For-profit 2-year technical and career college
▶ Commuter campus in very large city
▶ Interview required

General. Founded in 1902. Regionally accredited. Additional campus in Bridgeview, Illinois. **Enrollment:** 973 degree-seeking undergraduates; 47 non-degree-seeking students. **Degrees:** 230 associate awarded. **Calendar:** Quarter, extensive summer session. **Full-time faculty:** 35 total; 3% have terminal degrees, 43% minority, 66% women. **Part-time faculty:** 57 total; 16% have terminal degrees, 49% minority, 56% women.

Student profile. Among degree-seeking undergraduates, 212 enrolled as first-time, first-year students.

Part-time:	66%	Hispanic/Latino:	19%
Women:	85%	Native American:	1%
African American:	44%	Multi-racial, non-Hispanic:	11%
Asian American:	1%		

Basis for selection. Open admission, but selective for some programs. Students must have a 15 ACT, 740 SAT or achieve an established score on placement exam. ACT score of 21 in Reading and 20 Math or SAT score of 510 in Reading and Math required for Nursing. ACT composite of 20 or higher required for Radiologic Technology. COMPASS or ASSET used for placement. **Home schooled:** State high school equivalency certificate required.

2015-2016 Annual costs. Tuition/fees: $21,195. Per-credit charge: $465. Books/supplies: $500. Personal expenses: $1,593.

Financial aid. Need-based: Need-based aid available for part-time students. Work-study available nights, weekends and for part-time students. **Non-need-based:** Scholarships awarded for academics, alumni affiliation. **Additional information:** State grant programs for Illinois residents and alternative loans offered.

Application procedures. Admission: No deadline. $25 fee. Admission notification on a rolling basis. **Financial aid:** Priority date 2/15, closing date 6/30. FAFSA, institutional form required. Applicants notified on a rolling basis starting 1/2; must reply within 4 week(s) of notification.

Academics. Special study options: Distance learning, honors, internships. **Credit/placement by examination:** AP, CLEP, institutional tests. 45 credit hours maximum toward associate degree. No more than 50 percent of the credits in the major may be earned through proficiency examinations. **Support services:** Learning center, reduced course load, remedial instruction, study skills assistance, tutoring.

Majors. Business: Accounting, business admin. **Health services:** Health information technology, massage therapy, medical assistant, nursing (RN), radiologic technology/medical imaging. **Protective services:** Police science.

Most popular majors. Business/marketing 19%, health sciences 56%, legal studies 9%, security/protective services 16%.

Technology on campus. PC or laptop required. 330 workstations in library, computer center, student center. Commuter students can connect to campus network. Online library, wireless network available.

Student life. Freshman orientation: Mandatory. Preregistration for classes offered. Three-hour program offered day and evening.

Student services. Alcohol/substance abuse counseling, career counseling, student employment services, financial aid counseling, personal counseling, placement for graduates. **Physically disabled:** Services for visually, speech, hearing impaired. **Transfer:** Pre-admission transcript evaluation for new students. College fairs on campus for students transferring to 4-year colleges.

Contact. E-mail: admissionsdepartment@nc.edu
Phone: (773) 777-4220 Toll-free number: (888) 205-2283
Fax: (773) 777-2861
Director of Admissions, Northwestern College, 4811 N. Milwaukee Avenue, STE 203, Chicago, IL 60630

Oakton Community College
Des Plaines, Illinois
www.oakton.edu   **CB code: 1573**

- Public 2-year community college
- Commuter campus in small city

General. Founded in 1969. Regionally accredited. **Enrollment:** 2,788 full-time, degree-seeking students. **Degrees:** 744 associate awarded. **Location:** 15 miles from Chicago. **Calendar:** Semester, limited summer session. **Full-time faculty:** 161 total. **Part-time faculty:** 520 total. **Special facilities:** Wildlife preserve, visual arts center, performing arts center.

Student profile.

Out-of-state:	7%	25 or older:	45%

Transfer out. Colleges most students transferred to 2015: University of Illinois-Chicago, Northeastern Illinois University, DePaul University, Loyola University-Chicago.

Basis for selection. Open admission, but selective for some programs. Special requirements for health career programs and international students. Interview required of non-nursing health career majors. **Learning Disabled:** After applying for admission, students provide documentation of disability and arrange meetings for testing and registration.

2015-2016 Annual costs. Tuition/fees: $3,518; $9,510 out-of-district; $11,640 out-of-state. Per-credit charge: $111 in-district; $311 out-of-district; $382 out-of-state. Books/supplies: $1,300. Personal expenses: $1,800.

2014-2015 Financial aid. Need-based: 95% of total undergraduate aid awarded as scholarships/grants, 5% as loans/jobs. Need-based aid available for part-time students. Work-study available nights, weekends and for part-time students. **Non-need-based:** Scholarships awarded for academics, art, athletics, leadership, minority status, music/drama, state residency.

Application procedures. Admission: No deadline. $25 fee. Admission notification on a rolling basis. **Financial aid:** Priority date 3/1; no closing date. FAFSA, institutional form required. Applicants notified on a rolling basis starting 3/1; must reply within 2 week(s) of notification.

Academics. Special study options: Accelerated study, distance learning, dual enrollment of high school students, exchange student, honors, independent study, internships, study abroad, teacher certification program, weekend college. License preparation in nursing. **Credit/placement by examination:** AP, CLEP, institutional tests. 30 credit hours maximum toward associate degree. **Support services:** GED preparation, learning center, remedial instruction, study skills assistance, tutoring, writing center.

Majors. Business: Accounting, business admin, international, office management. **Computer sciences:** General, data processing. **Education:** Early childhood. **Engineering:** General. **General:** Maintenance. **Health services:** Clinical lab assistant, health information technology, nursing (RN), physical therapy assistant. **Liberal arts:** Arts/sciences. **Protective services:** Firefighting, police science. **Visual/performing arts:** Commercial/advertising art, music.

Technology on campus. 1,200 workstations in library, computer center, student center. Commuter students can connect to campus network. Online course registration, online library, helpline, wireless network available.

Student life. Freshman orientation: Mandatory. Preregistration for classes offered. **Activities:** Jazz band, choral groups, drama, literary magazine, music ensembles, student government, student newspaper, Christian student association, Indian student association, political science forum, black student union, Hillel, Japanese club, desktop publishing club.

Athletics. NJCAA. **Intercollegiate:** Baseball M, basketball, cross-country, golf M, soccer, softball W, tennis, track and field, volleyball W. **Intramural:** Basketball, volleyball. **Team name:** Raiders.

Student services. Adult student services, alcohol/substance abuse counseling, career counseling, student employment services, financial aid counseling, health services, minority student services, on-campus daycare, personal counseling, placement for graduates, veterans' counselor. **Transfer:** College fairs on campus for students transferring to 4-year colleges.

Contact. E-mail: admiss@oakton.edu
Phone: (847) 635-1700 Fax: (847) 635-1706
Michele Brown, Director of Student Recruitment & Outreach, Oakton Community College, Enrollment Center, Des Plaines, IL 60016

Parkland College
Champaign, Illinois
www.parkland.edu   **CB code: 1619**

- Public 2-year community college
- Commuter campus in small city

General. Founded in 1966. Regionally accredited. Students have access to resources at University of Illinois and within certain guidelines may enroll in University of Illinois classes. **Enrollment:** 7,958 degree-seeking undergraduates. **Degrees:** 730 associate awarded. **ROTC:** Army, Naval, Air Force. **Location:** 136 miles from Chicago, 122 miles from Indianapolis. **Calendar:** Semester, extensive summer session. **Full-time faculty:** 174 total. **Part-time faculty:** 317 total. **Class size:** 64% < 20, 34% 20-39, less than 1% 40-49, less than 1% 50-99, less than 1% >100. **Special facilities:** Applied technology center, planetarium, theatre, gallery, tv station, radio station, nature preserve, agricultural technology applications center, land laboratory. **Partnerships:** Formal partnerships with local businesses including CISCO Systems, Case Corporation, Microsoft, Ford ASSET, LINUX Professional Institute.

Transfer out. Colleges most students transferred to 2015: University of Illinois at Urbana-Champaign, Eastern Illinois University, Illinois State University, Southern Illinois University-Carbondale, Southern Illinois University-Edwardsville.

Basis for selection. Open admission, but selective for some programs. Acceptance does not ensure admission into particular major or enrollment in specific course. Special requirements for certain health profession and trade union programs. Selective health programs require either ACT scores or 15 hours of college level courses. **Home schooled:** Recommended that students meet with admissions adviser. **Learning Disabled:** Encouraged to contact learning disabilities specialist prior to enrolling.

High school preparation. 15 units required. Required units include English 4, mathematics 3, social studies 2, science 2, foreign language 2 and academic electives 2.

2015-2016 Annual costs. Tuition/fees: $4,215; $10,095 out-of-district; $14,985 out-of-state. Per-credit charge: $125 in-district; $321 out-of-district; $484 out-of-state. Books/supplies: $1,200. Personal expenses: $1,500.

Two-Year Colleges

Financial aid. Need-based: Work-study available nights, weekends and for part-time students. **Non-need-based:** Scholarships awarded for academics, art, athletics, leadership, minority status, music/drama, state residency.

Application procedures. Admission: No deadline. No application fee. Admission notification on a rolling basis. **Financial aid:** Closing date 3/1. FAFSA, institutional form required. Applicants notified on a rolling basis starting 6/1; must reply within 2 week(s) of notification.

Academics. Special study options: Accelerated study, cross-registration, distance learning, double major, dual enrollment of high school students, ESL, honors, independent study, internships, student-designed major, study abroad. Bachelor's degree programs available on campus. License preparation in aviation, dental hygiene, nursing, occupational therapy, paramedic, radiology, real estate. **Credit/placement by examination:** AP, CLEP, SAT, ACT, institutional tests. 25 credit hours maximum toward associate degree. Institutionally-prepared proficiency exams are available. **Support services:** GED preparation and test center, learning center, reduced course load, remedial instruction, study skills assistance, tutoring, writing center.

Majors. Business: General, accounting, business admin, construction management, executive assistant, hotel/motel admin, resort management, restaurant/food services, selling. **Communications:** Digital media, radio/TV. **Communications technology:** Photo/film/video, radio/TV. **Computer sciences:** Applications programming, data entry, system admin. **Education:** Multi-level teacher, music, teacher assistance. **Engineering:** General. **Health services:** Dental hygiene, dietetic technician, EMT paramedic, massage therapy, nursing (RN), occupational therapy assistant, radiologic technology/medical imaging, respiratory therapy technology, surgical technology, veterinary technology/assistant. **Human services:** Social work. **Liberal arts:** Arts/sciences. **Protective services:** Firefighting, police science. **Visual/performing arts:** Graphic design, music, studio arts, theater design. **Work/family studies:** Child care service.

Most popular majors. Business/marketing 14%, education 7%, health sciences 18%, interdisciplinary studies 20%, liberal arts 14%.

Technology on campus. 1,425 workstations in library, computer center. Online course registration, helpline, wireless network available.

Student life. Freshman orientation: Mandatory. Preregistration for classes offered. **Policies:** Students may take part in activities at University of Illinois. **Housing:** Housing available at University of Illinois facilities. **Activities:** Bands, choral groups, dance, drama, international student organizations, literary magazine, music ensembles, musical theater, radio station, student government, student newspaper, TV station, black student association, Phi Theta Kappa, student nurses association, veterinary technology association, Christian Fellowship, Colours, dental assisting association, dental hygienists association.

Athletics. NJCAA. **Intercollegiate:** Baseball M, basketball, golf M, soccer, softball W, volleyball W. **Intramural:** Basketball, bowling, softball, tennis, volleyball. **Team name:** Cobras.

Student services. Adult student services, career counseling, services for economically disadvantaged, student employment services, financial aid counseling, minority student services, on-campus daycare, personal counseling, placement for graduates, veterans' counselor, women's services. **Physically disabled:** Services for visually, speech, hearing impaired. **Transfer:** Re-entry adviser, pre-admission transcript evaluation for new students. Transfer center, transfer adviser, college fairs on campus for students transferring to 4-year colleges.

Contact. E-mail: admissions@parkland.edu
Phone: (217) 351-2482 Fax: (217) 353-2640
Tim Wendt, Director of Enrollment Services, Parkland College, 2400 West Bradley Avenue, Champaign, IL 61821-1899

Prairie State College
Chicago Heights, Illinois
www.prairiestate.edu
CB code: 1077

◗ Public 2-year community college
◗ Commuter campus in large town

General. Founded in 1957. Regionally accredited. **Enrollment:** 4,571 undergraduates. **Degrees:** 424 associate awarded. **Location:** 30 miles from Chicago. **Calendar:** Semester, limited summer session. **Full-time faculty:** 76 total. **Part-time faculty:** 408 total.

Transfer out. Colleges most students transferred to 2015: Governors State University, University of Illinois - Urbana, Eastern Illinois University, University of Illinois - Chicago, Chicago State University.

Basis for selection. Open admission, but selective for some programs. Admission to nursing and dental hygiene programs based on GPA in required courses and test scores.

High school preparation. One unit each of chemistry and algebra required for nursing and dental programs, plus 1 unit biology for nursing.

2015-2016 Annual costs. Tuition/fees: $4,290; $9,750 out-of-district; $11,550 out-of-state. Per-credit charge: $121 in-district; $303 out-of-district; $363 out-of-state. Books/supplies: $2,500. Personal expenses: $3,268.

Financial aid. Need-based: Need-based aid available for part-time students. Work-study available nights, weekends and for part-time students.

Application procedures. Admission: No deadline. $10 fee, may be waived for applicants with need. Admission notification on a rolling basis. **Financial aid:** Closing date 7/1. FAFSA, institutional form required. Applicants notified on a rolling basis; must reply within 2 week(s) of notification.

Academics. Students completing an Associate in Arts or Science degree are guaranteed their classes will transfer to other Illinois colleges. **Special study options:** Cross-registration, distance learning, dual enrollment of high school students, ESL, honors, independent study, internships, study abroad, weekend college. License preparation in dental hygiene, nursing. **Credit/placement by examination:** AP, CLEP, institutional tests. 45 credit hours maximum toward associate degree. **Support services:** GED preparation and test center, learning center, pre-admission summer program, reduced course load, remedial instruction, study skills assistance, tutoring.

Majors. Business: Business admin. **Communications technology:** Graphics. **Computer sciences:** Information technology. **Education:** Mathematics, teacher assistance. **General:** Electrician. **Health services:** Dental hygiene, EMT ambulance attendant, nursing (RN). **Liberal arts:** Arts/sciences. **Parks/recreation:** Exercise sciences. **Protective services:** Firefighting, police science. **Visual/performing arts:** Commercial photography, studio arts. **Work/family studies:** Child care service.

Most popular majors. Business/marketing 12%, education 7%, health sciences 29%, liberal arts 19%, public administration/social services 7%.

Technology on campus. 248 workstations in library, computer center, student center. Helpline available.

Student life. Freshman orientation: Available. Preregistration for classes offered. **Activities:** Jazz band, choral groups, dance, drama, musical theater, student government, student newspaper, symphony orchestra, All Latin Alliance, Black Student Union.

Athletics. Intercollegiate: Baseball M, basketball, cheerleading W, cross-country, golf M, soccer M, softball W, tennis M, volleyball W. **Team name:** Pioneers.

Student services. Career counseling, services for economically disadvantaged, student employment services, financial aid counseling, minority student services, on-campus daycare, personal counseling, placement for graduates, veterans' counselor. **Physically disabled:** Services for visually, speech, hearing impaired. **Transfer:** Transfer center, transfer adviser, college fairs on campus for students transferring to 4-year colleges.

Contact. Phone: (708) 709-3516
Jaime Miller, Director of Admissions, Prairie State College, 202 South Halsted Street, Chicago Heights, IL 60411

Rasmussen College: Aurora
Aurora, Illinois
www.rasmussen.edu

◗ For-profit 2-year branch campus and career college
◗ Small city

General. Regionally accredited. **Enrollment:** 369 degree-seeking undergraduates. **Degrees:** 39 bachelor's, 52 associate awarded. **Calendar:** Quarter. **Full-time faculty:** 3 total. **Part-time faculty:** 13 total.

Basis for selection. Open admission, but selective for some programs.

2016-2017 Annual costs. Tuition/fees (projected): $13,455. Per-credit charge: $299.

Financial aid. Need-based: Need-based aid available for part-time students. Work-study available nights, weekends and for part-time students.

Application procedures. Admission: No deadline. No application fee. **Financial aid:** No deadline. FAFSA, institutional form required. Applicants notified on a rolling basis.

Academics. Special study options: Bachelor's degree programs available on campus. **Credit/placement by examination:** AP, CLEP.

Majors. Business: Accounting, business admin, human resources, management information systems, marketing. **Computer sciences:** Support specialist, web page design. **Education:** Teacher assistance. **Engineering:** Software. **Health services:** Health information technology, medical assistant, medical secretary, pharmacy assistant. **Protective services:** Criminal justice. **Visual/performing arts:** Game design.

Contact. Phone: (630) 888-3500
Susan Hammerstrom, Director of Admissions, Rasmussen College: Aurora, 2363 Sequoia Drive, Suite 131, Aurora, IL 60506

Rasmussen College: Rockford
Rockford, Illinois
www.rasmussen.edu   **CB code: 5753**

▶ For-profit 2-year career college
▶ Small city

General. Regionally accredited. **Enrollment:** 587 degree-seeking undergraduates. **Degrees:** 53 bachelor's, 115 associate awarded. **Calendar:** Quarter. **Full-time faculty:** 12 total. **Part-time faculty:** 42 total.

Basis for selection. Open admission, but selective for some programs.

2016-2017 Annual costs. Tuition/fees (projected): $13,455. Per-credit charge: $299.

Financial aid. Need-based: Need-based aid available for part-time students. Work-study available nights, weekends and for part-time students.

Application procedures. Admission: No deadline. No application fee. Admission notification on a rolling basis. **Financial aid:** No deadline. FAFSA, institutional form required. Applicants notified on a rolling basis.

Academics. Credit/placement by examination: AP, CLEP.

Majors. Business: Accounting, business admin, human resources, management information systems, marketing. **Computer sciences:** Support specialist, web page design. **Education:** Teacher assistance. **Engineering:** Software. **Health services:** Health information technology, medical assistant, medical secretary, pharmacy assistant. **Protective services:** Criminal justice. **Visual/performing arts:** Game design.

Contact. Phone: (815) 316-4800
Susan Hammerstrom, Director of Admissions, Rasmussen College: Rockford, 6000 East State Street, Fourth Floor, Rockford, IL 61108-2513

Rasmussen College: Romeoville/Joliet
Romeoville, Illinois
www.rasmussen.edu

▶ For-profit 2-year career college
▶ Large town

General. Regionally accredited. **Enrollment:** 532 degree-seeking undergraduates. **Degrees:** 35 bachelor's, 100 associate awarded. **Calendar:** Quarter. **Full-time faculty:** 10 total. **Part-time faculty:** 45 total.

Basis for selection. Open admission, but selective for some programs.

2016-2017 Annual costs. Tuition/fees (projected): $13,455. Per-credit charge: $299.

Financial aid. Need-based: Need-based aid available for part-time students. Work-study available nights, weekends and for part-time students.

Application procedures. Admission: No deadline. No application fee. Admission notification on a rolling basis. **Financial aid:** No deadline. FAFSA, institutional form required. Applicants notified on a rolling basis.

Academics. Credit/placement by examination: AP, CLEP.

Majors. Business: Accounting, business admin, human resources, management information systems, marketing. **Computer sciences:** Support specialist, web page design. **Education:** Teacher assistance. **Engineering:** Software.

Health services: Health information technology, medical assistant, medical secretary, pharmacy assistant. **Protective services:** Criminal justice, firefighting. **Visual/performing arts:** Game design.

Contact. Phone: (815) 306-2600
Susan Hammerstrom, Director of Admissions, Rasmussen College: Romeoville/Joliet, 400 West Normantown Road, Romeoville, IL 60446

Rend Lake College
Ina, Illinois
www.rlc.edu   **CB code: 1673**

▶ Public 2-year community college
▶ Commuter campus in rural community

General. Founded in 1955. Regionally accredited. Satellite campuses located in Mt. Vernon and Pinckneyville. **Enrollment:** 1,424 degree-seeking undergraduates; 879 non-degree-seeking students. **Degrees:** 603 associate awarded. **Location:** 45 miles from Carbondale, 85 miles from St. Louis. **Calendar:** Semester, limited summer session. **Full-time faculty:** 67 total; 4% have terminal degrees, 2% minority, 58% women. **Part-time faculty:** 162 total; 3% have terminal degrees, 2% minority, 46% women. **Class size:** 79% < 20, 19% 20-39, 1% 40-49, less than 1% 50-99, less than 1% >100. **Special facilities:** Aquatics center, walking/bicycle paths, mock mine for coal mining program, nursing training center, criminal justice shooting range, concealed carry classes. **Partnerships:** Formal partnerships to provide technical training for employees of General Tire (Mt. Vernon) and Walgreens Distribution Center; mandated federal training provided to Department of Natural Resources-Mines and Minerals.

Student profile. Among degree-seeking undergraduates, 62% enrolled in a transfer program, 145% already have a bachelor's degree or higher, 469 enrolled as first-time, first-year students, 75 transferred in from other institutions.

Part-time:	27%	African American:	6%
Out-of-state:	2%	Asian American:	1%
Women:	53%	Hispanic/Latino:	1%

Transfer out. Colleges most students transferred to 2015: Southern Illinois University-Carbondale, Southern Illinois University-Edwardsville, Eastern Illinois University, Southeast Missouri State University, Murray State University.

Basis for selection. Open admission, but selective for some programs. Special requirements for allied health programs. SAT, ACT, ASSET, or COMPASS scores required for degree-seeking students for placement. **Home schooled:** Provide certified documentation stating the student has never had or has officially severed his or her connection with the school system.

High school preparation. College-preparatory program required. 15 units required. Required units include English 4, mathematics 3, social studies 3, science 3 (laboratory 3) and academic electives 2. Social studies units should include history and government. Electives may include foreign language, vocational education, music, or art. Lowest level math accepted is algebra 1.

2015-2016 Annual costs. Tuition/fees: $3,300; $4,905 out-of-district; $4,950 out-of-state. Per-credit charge: $95 in-district; $148 out-of-district; $150 out-of-state. Books/supplies: $1,800. Personal expenses: $2,000.

2014-2015 Financial aid. Need-based: Need-based aid available for part-time students. Work-study available nights, weekends and for part-time students. **Non-need-based:** Scholarships awarded for academics, art, athletics, leadership, music/drama, state residency.

Application procedures. Admission: No deadline. No application fee. Admission notification on a rolling basis. **Financial aid:** No deadline. FAFSA required. Applicants notified on a rolling basis starting 3/15; must reply within 4 week(s) of notification.

Academics. Special study options: Combined bachelor's/graduate degree, cooperative education, distance learning, double major, dual enrollment of high school students, ESL, honors, independent study, internships, study abroad, teacher certification program. License preparation in nursing, occupational therapy, paramedic, radiology, real estate. **Credit/placement by examination:** AP, CLEP, institutional tests. 16 credit hours maximum toward associate degree. Credits awarded for CLEP, proficiency exams and AP scores. **Support services:** GED preparation, learning center, remedial instruction, study skills assistance, tutoring, writing center.

Majors. Architecture: Technology. **Business:** Administrative services, business admin. **Computer sciences:** Applications programming, LAN/WAN management, programming. **Engineering:** General. **Health services:** Clinical lab technology, EMT paramedic, health information technology, medical radiologic technology/radiation therapy, nursing (RN), occupational therapy assistant, staff services technology, veterinary technology/assistant. **Liberal arts:** Arts/sciences. **Protective services:** Corrections, fire services admin, police science. **Visual/performing arts:** Art, commercial/advertising art, graphic design. **Work/family studies:** Child care service, child development.

Most popular majors. Agriculture 26%, engineering/engineering technologies 12%, health sciences 20%, personal/culinary services 8%, trade and industry 21%.

Technology on campus. 605 workstations in library, computer center, student center. Commuter students can connect to campus network. Online library, helpline, wireless network available.

Student life. Freshman orientation: Mandatory. Preregistration for classes offered. **Activities:** Bands, choral groups, drama, music ensembles, musical theater, student government, student newspaper, symphony orchestra, culinary arts club, Active College Christians, practical nursing club, automotive club, horticulture club, art league, criminal justice club.

Athletics. NJCAA. **Intercollegiate:** Baseball M, basketball, golf, softball W, tennis W, volleyball W. **Team name:** Warriors.

Student services. Adult student services, career counseling, services for economically disadvantaged, student employment services, financial aid counseling, on-campus daycare, personal counseling, placement for graduates, veterans' counselor. **Physically disabled:** Services for visually, speech, hearing impaired. **Transfer:** Pre-admission transcript evaluation for new students. Transfer adviser, college fairs on campus for students transferring to 4-year colleges.

Contact. E-mail: admissions@rlc.edu
Phone: (618) 437-5321 ext. 1230 Toll-free number: (800) 369-5321
Fax: (618) 437-5677
Kelly Downes, Director of Student Records/Registrar, Rend Lake College, 468 North Ken Gray Parkway, Ina, IL 62846

Richland Community College
Decatur, Illinois
www.richland.edu
CB member
CB code: 0738

- Public 2-year community college
- Commuter campus in small city

General. Founded in 1971. Regionally accredited. **Enrollment:** 2,855 degree-seeking undergraduates. **Degrees:** 354 associate awarded. **Location:** 180 miles from Chicago, 120 miles from St. Louis. **Calendar:** Semester, limited summer session. **Full-time faculty:** 76 total. **Part-time faculty:** 106 total. **Class size:** 76% < 20, 24% 20-39, less than 1% 40-49. **Special facilities:** Human patient simulators for allied health students, National Sequestration Education Center, Center for Sustainability and Innovation.

Transfer out. Colleges most students transferred to 2015: Illinois State University, Millikin University, Southern Illinois University-Carbondale, Eastern Illinois University, University of Illinois-Springfield.

Basis for selection. Open admission, but selective for some programs. Special requirements for allied health programs.

High school preparation. Required units include English 4, mathematics 3, social studies 3, science 3 and foreign language 2.

2015-2016 Annual costs. Tuition/fees: $3,732; $5,757 out-of-district; $13,662 out-of-state. Per-credit charge: $114 in-district; $181.5 out-of-district; $445 out-of-state. Books/supplies: $1,000.

Financial aid. Need-based: Need-based aid available for part-time students. Work-study available nights, weekends and for part-time students. **Non-need-based:** Scholarships awarded for academics, art, leadership, music/drama.

Application procedures. Admission: No deadline. No application fee. Admission notification on a rolling basis. **Financial aid:** Priority date 7/25; no closing date. FAFSA required. Applicants notified on a rolling basis starting 3/20.

Academics. Special study options: Accelerated study, cooperative education, distance learning, double major, dual enrollment of high school students, ESL, honors, independent study, internships, liberal arts/career combination, study abroad, teacher certification program. Bachelor's degree programs available on campus. License preparation in nursing, paramedic, radiology. **Credit/placement by examination:** AP, CLEP, institutional tests. **Support services:** GED preparation, learning center, reduced course load, remedial instruction, study skills assistance, tutoring, writing center.

Majors. Biology: General. **Business:** General, accounting, hospitality admin, management information systems. **Communications:** Journalism. **Computer sciences:** General, computer graphics, computer science, data entry, programming. **Education:** General. **Engineering:** General. **English:** American lit, English lit, rhetoric/composition, writing. **Foreign languages:** French, German, Spanish. **General:** Electrician. **Health services:** EMT paramedic, nursing (RN), radiologic technology/medical imaging, surgical technology. **History:** General. **Liberal arts:** Arts/sciences. **Math:** General. **Philosophy/religion:** Philosophy. **Physical sciences:** Planetary. **Protective services:** Criminal justice, firefighting, police science. **Psychology:** General. **Social sciences:** General, anthropology, archaeology, economics, geography, political science, sociology. **Visual/performing arts:** General, art, art history/conservation, ceramics, drawing, music, painting, sculpture.

Most popular majors. Health sciences 26%, interdisciplinary studies 24%, liberal arts 27%.

Technology on campus. 245 workstations in library, computer center. Commuter students can connect to campus network. Online course registration, online library, helpline, wireless network available.

Student life. Freshman orientation: Mandatory. Preregistration for classes offered. 2 hours, includes registering for courses, variety of times available. **Activities:** Jazz band, dance, drama, literary magazine, radio station, student government, student newspaper.

Student services. Adult student services, career counseling, services for economically disadvantaged, student employment services, financial aid counseling, minority student services, on-campus daycare, personal counseling, placement for graduates, veterans' counselor, women's services. **Physically disabled:** Services for visually, speech, hearing impaired. **Transfer:** Pre-admission transcript evaluation for new students. Transfer center, transfer adviser, college fairs on campus for students transferring to 4-year colleges.

Contact. E-mail: admissions@richland.edu
Phone: (217) 875-7200 ext. 257 Fax: (217) 875-7783
Cathy Sebok, Director of Admissions, Richland Community College, One College Park, Decatur, IL 62521

Rock Valley College
Rockford, Illinois
www.rockvalleycollege.edu
CB member
CB code: 1674

- Public 2-year community college
- Commuter campus in small city

General. Founded in 1964. Regionally accredited. **Enrollment:** 6,922 degree-seeking undergraduates. **Degrees:** 1,028 associate awarded. **Location:** 85 miles from Chicago. **Calendar:** Semester, limited summer session. **Full-time faculty:** 159 total; 8% minority, 54% women. **Part-time faculty:** 303 total; 8% minority, 53% women. **Special facilities:** Outdoor theater with retractable roof.

Transfer out. Colleges most students transferred to 2015: Northern Illinois University, Illinois State University, Judson University, Southern Illinois University at Carbondale, Rockford University.

Basis for selection. Open admission, but selective for some programs. Special requirements for nursing, respiratory therapy, dental hygiene, and surgical technology programs. **Adult students:** Must submit ACT/SAT, proof of successful performance in college, or complete ACCUPLACER placement test. **Learning Disabled:** Students encouraged to access services through the coordinator of disability services.

High school preparation. College-preparatory program recommended. 15 units required. Required units include English 4, mathematics 3, social studies 3, science 3 and academic electives 2.

2015-2016 Annual costs. Tuition/fees: $3,044; $8,264 out-of-district; $15,374 out-of-state. Per-credit charge: $91 in-district; $265 out-of-district; $502 out-of-state. Books/supplies: $1,204. Personal expenses: $668.

Financial aid. Need-based: Need-based aid available for part-time students. Work-study available nights, weekends and for part-time students.

Application procedures. Admission: No deadline. No application fee. Admission notification on a rolling basis. **Financial aid:** Priority date 5/1; no closing date. FAFSA, institutional form required. Applicants notified on a rolling basis; must reply within 4 week(s) of notification.

Academics. Special study options: Accelerated study, cooperative education, distance learning, dual enrollment of high school students, ESL, honors, independent study, internships, study abroad. License preparation in aviation, dental hygiene, nursing. **Credit/placement by examination:** AP, CLEP, institutional tests. 39 credit hours maximum toward associate degree. **Support services:** GED preparation, learning center, reduced course load, remedial instruction, study skills assistance, tutoring, writing center.

Majors. Business: Accounting, administrative services, business admin, construction management, office technology. **Communications technology:** Graphic/printing. **Computer sciences:** Information technology, networking, security. **Education:** Teacher assistance. **Engineering:** General. **General:** Electrician. **Health services:** Dental hygiene, nursing (RN), respiratory therapy technology. **Liberal arts:** Arts/sciences. **Parks/recreation:** Health/fitness. **Protective services:** Firefighting, police science. **Work/family studies:** Child care management.

Most popular majors. Health sciences 7%, interdisciplinary studies 16%, liberal arts 56%.

Technology on campus. 225 workstations in library, computer center, student center. Commuter students can connect to campus network. Online course registration, online library, helpline, wireless network available.

Student life. Freshman orientation: Available. Preregistration for classes offered. Two-part process with educational planning session followed by a multi-week College Success course. **Activities:** Bands, choral groups, dance, drama, international student organizations, literary magazine, music ensembles, Model UN, musical theater, student government, student newspaper, symphony orchestra, TV station, Association of Latin American Students, black student alliance, Intervarsity Christian Fellowship, Islamic awareness association, Latter Day Saints Student Association, multicultural club, Phi Theta Kappa honor society, student veterans association.

Athletics. NJCAA. **Intercollegiate:** Baseball M, basketball, golf M, soccer, softball W, tennis, volleyball W. **Team name:** Golden Eagles.

Student services. Adult student services, career counseling, student employment services, financial aid counseling, minority student services, personal counseling, placement for graduates, veterans' counselor. **Physically disabled:** Services for visually, speech, hearing impaired. **Transfer:** Preadmission transcript evaluation for new students. Transfer center, transfer adviser, college fairs on campus for students transferring to 4-year colleges.

Contact. E-mail: RVC-Admissions@rockvalleycollege.edu
Phone: (815) 921-4250 Fax: (815) 921-4269
Jennifer Thompson, Admissions Director, Rock Valley College, 3301 North Mulford Road, Rockford, IL 61114-5699

Rockford Career College
Rockford, Illinois
www.rockfordcareercollege.edu   CB code: 2459

▶ For-profit 2-year career college
▶ Commuter campus in small city
▶ Interview required

General. Founded in 1862. Regionally accredited; also accredited by ACCSC. **Enrollment:** 484 undergraduates. **Degrees:** 130 associate awarded. **Location:** 90 miles from Chicago, 75 miles from Madison, Wisconsin. **Calendar:** Quarter, extensive summer session. **Full-time faculty:** 19 total. **Part-time faculty:** 38 total. **Class size:** 88% < 20, 11% 20-39, 1% 40-49.

Transfer out. Colleges most students transferred to 2015: Upper Iowa University, Judson University.

Basis for selection. Open admission.

2015-2016 Annual costs. Books/supplies: $800. Personal expenses: $2,880.

Financial aid. All financial aid based on need. Need-based aid available for part-time students. Work-study available nights, weekends and for part-time students.

Application procedures. Admission: No deadline. $150 fee. Application must be submitted on paper. Admission notification on a rolling basis. **Financial aid:** No deadline. FAFSA required. Applicants notified on a rolling basis.

Academics. Special study options: Distance learning, independent study, internships. **Credit/placement by examination:** AP, CLEP, IB, institutional tests. 50 credit hours maximum toward associate degree. **Support services:** Study skills assistance, tutoring.

Majors. Business: Accounting, business admin, marketing. **Computer sciences:** General, data processing, information systems. **Health services:** Massage therapy, medical assistant, medical secretary, pharmacy assistant, veterinary technology/assistant.

Most popular majors. Business/marketing 14%, computer/information sciences 8%, health sciences 46%.

Technology on campus. 75 workstations in library, computer center. Online library, repair service, wireless network available.

Student life. Freshman orientation: Mandatory. Preregistration for classes offered. **Activities:** Student newspaper.

Student services. Career counseling, student employment services, financial aid counseling, placement for graduates. **Transfer:** Pre-admission transcript evaluation for new students.

Contact. E-mail: info@rockfordcareercollege.edu
Phone: (815) 965-8616 Toll-free number: (866) 722-4632
Fax: (815) 965-0360
David Julius, Director of Admissions, Rockford Career College, 1130 South Alpine Road, Rockford, IL 61108

Sauk Valley Community College
Dixon, Illinois
www.svcc.edu   CB code: 1780

▶ Public 2-year community college
▶ Commuter campus in large town

General. Founded in 1965. Regionally accredited. **Enrollment:** 1,532 degree-seeking undergraduates; 404 non-degree-seeking students. **Degrees:** 305 associate awarded. **Location:** 110 miles from Chicago. **Calendar:** Semester, limited summer session. **Full-time faculty:** 44 total; 25% have terminal degrees, 2% minority, 54% women. **Part-time faculty:** 90 total; 6% have terminal degrees, 8% minority, 51% women. **Class size:** 67% < 20, 30% 20-39, 2% 40-49, less than 1% 50-99. **Special facilities:** Prairie grass preserves. **Partnerships:** Formal partnership with Workforce Council meetings to regularly connect with local businesses.

Student profile. Among degree-seeking undergraduates, 53% enrolled in a transfer program, 47% enrolled in a vocational program, 1% already have a bachelor's degree or higher, 400 enrolled as first-time, first-year students.

Part-time:	46%	Asian American:	1%
Women:	62%	Hispanic/Latino:	10%
African American:	5%	25 or older:	34%

Transfer out. Colleges most students transferred to 2015: Northern Illinois University, Ashford University, Western Illinois University, Illinois State University, Aurora University.

Basis for selection. Open admission, but selective for some programs. Special requirements for health programs: academic record, state residency important; class rank, test scores considered. Placement exam required of all students who plan to enroll in college level English or math courses. **Home schooled:** Transcript of courses and grades required.

High school preparation. College-preparatory program required. 15 units recommended. Recommended units include English 4, mathematics 3, social studies 2, science 2 (laboratory 2) and academic electives 4. Special course requirements for health programs.

2016-2017 Annual costs. Tuition/fees (projected): $3,258; $9,110 out-of-district; $9,716 out-of-state. Books/supplies: $1,829. Personal expenses: $1,488.

2014-2015 Financial aid. Need-based: 145 full-time freshmen applied for aid; 113 deemed to have need; 103 received aid. Average need met was 23%. Average scholarship/grant was $4,814; average loan $2,117. 82% of total undergraduate aid awarded as scholarships/grants, 18% as loans/jobs. Need-based aid available for part-time students. Work-study available nights, weekends and for part-time students. **Non-need-based:** Awarded to 343 full-time undergraduates, including 133 freshmen. Scholarships awarded for academics, athletics, minority status, state residency.

Application procedures. Admission: No deadline. No application fee. Admission notification on a rolling basis. **Financial aid:** Priority date 8/5; no closing date. FAFSA, institutional form required. Applicants notified on a rolling basis starting 3/20; must reply within 4 week(s) of notification.

Academics. Special study options: Cooperative education, distance learning, dual enrollment of high school students, ESL, honors, independent study, internships. License preparation in nursing, radiology. **Credit/placement by examination:** AP, CLEP, institutional tests. 30 credit hours maximum toward associate degree. Both CLEP and DANTES exams are used. **Support services:** GED preparation and test center, learning center, pre-admission summer program, reduced course load, remedial instruction, study skills assistance, tutoring, writing center.

Majors. Biology: General. **Business:** General, accounting, accounting/business management, administrative services, management science, marketing. **Communications:** Communications/speech/rhetoric, media studies. **Communications technology:** Desktop publishing. **Computer sciences:** Data entry, LAN/WAN management, system admin. **Education:** Early childhood, elementary, mathematics, physical, secondary, special ed, teacher assistance. **Engineering:** General. **English:** English lit. **Foreign languages:** General. **Health services:** Athletic training, EMT paramedic, nursing (RN), occupational therapy assistant, premedicine, radiologic technology/medical imaging. **History:** General. **Human services:** Social work. **Liberal arts:** Arts/sciences. **Math:** General. **Parks/recreation:** Health/fitness. **Physical sciences:** Chemistry, physics. **Protective services:** Corrections, firefighting, police science. **Psychology:** General. **Social sciences:** Economics, political science, sociology. **Visual/performing arts:** Art, music, studio arts. **Work/family studies:** Child care service.

Most popular majors. Business/marketing 10%, health sciences 21%, interdisciplinary studies 38%, liberal arts 17%.

Technology on campus. 100 workstations in library, computer center, student center. Online course registration, online library, helpline, wireless network available.

Student life. Freshman orientation: Mandatory. Preregistration for classes offered. Day and evening program to allow students to explore curriculum and services of the college. **Activities:** Bands, choral groups, drama, literary magazine, music ensembles, musical theater, student government, symphony orchestra, Association of Latin American Students, Campus Crusade for Christ, Phi Theta Kappa, social justice club.

Athletics. NJCAA. **Intercollegiate:** Baseball M, basketball, cheerleading, cross-country, golf M, softball W, tennis, volleyball W. **Intramural:** Basketball M. **Team name:** Skyhawks.

Student services. Adult student services, career counseling, services for economically disadvantaged, student employment services, financial aid counseling, minority student services, personal counseling, placement for graduates, veterans' counselor. **Physically disabled:** Services for visually, speech, hearing impaired. **Transfer:** Pre-admission transcript evaluation for new students. Transfer center, transfer adviser, college fairs on campus for students transferring to 4-year colleges.

Contact. E-mail: admissionsvc@svcc.edu
Phone: (815) 835-6273 Fax: (815) 288-3190
Pamela Medema, Registrar, Sauk Valley Community College, 173 Illinois Route 2, Dixon, IL 61021-9112

Shawnee Community College
Ullin, Illinois
www.shawneecc.edu
CB code: 0882

- Public 2-year community college
- Commuter campus in rural community

General. Founded in 1967. Regionally accredited. Extension centers in Anna, Cairo, and Metropolis. **Enrollment:** 1,819 degree-seeking undergraduates. **Degrees:** 243 associate awarded. **ROTC:** Army, Naval, Air Force. **Location:** 40 miles from Paducah, Kentucky. **Calendar:** Semester, extensive summer session. **Full-time faculty:** 39 total; 3% have terminal degrees, 3% minority, 72% women. **Part-time faculty:** 135 total. **Class size:** 86% < 20, 11% 20-39, 2% 40-49, less than 1% 50-99, less than 1% >100.

Transfer out. Colleges most students transferred to 2015: SIU-C, SEMO, Murray.

Basis for selection. Open admission, but selective for some programs. Applicants for allied health programs selected on basis of entrance examination score. ACT recommended for placement and counseling. Interview recommended for art, music, speech majors. Audition recommended for speech and music majors. Portfolio recommended for art majors.

High school preparation. 15 units recommended. Recommended units include English 4, mathematics 3, social studies 3, science 3 and foreign language 2. 2 units recommended in foreign language, music, or art. Transfer program applicants must have state mandated high school course requirements or demonstrate proficiency through placement tests.

2016-2017 Annual costs. Tuition/fees (projected): $2,970; $4,920 out-of-district; $4,980 out-of-state. Per-credit charge: $99 in-district; $164 out-of-district; $166 out-of-state. Books/supplies: $1,126. Personal expenses: $1,442.

Financial aid. All financial aid based on need. Need-based aid available for part-time students. Work-study available nights, weekends and for part-time students.

Application procedures. Admission: No deadline. No application fee. Admission notification on a rolling basis beginning on or about 1/15. **Financial aid:** Priority date 9/1; no closing date. FAFSA required. Applicants notified on a rolling basis; must reply within 2 week(s) of notification.

Academics. Special study options: Cooperative education, distance learning, dual enrollment of high school students, honors, independent study, internships, liberal arts/career combination. License preparation in nursing, occupational therapy, paramedic, real estate. **Credit/placement by examination:** AP, CLEP, institutional tests. 15 credit hours maximum toward associate degree. **Support services:** GED preparation and test center, learning center, pre-admission summer program, remedial instruction, study skills assistance, tutoring, writing center.

Majors. Business: General, accounting, management science. **Conservation:** Forestry, wildlife/wilderness. **Health services:** Health information technology, medical secretary. **Liberal arts:** Arts/sciences. **Work/family studies:** Family/community services, food/nutrition.

Technology on campus. 120 workstations in library, computer center, student center. Online course registration, online library, helpline, wireless network available.

Student life. Freshman orientation: Mandatory. Preregistration for classes offered. **Activities:** Concert band, choral groups, dance, drama, music ensembles, musical theater, student government, student newspaper.

Athletics. NJCAA. **Intercollegiate:** Baseball M, basketball, softball W, volleyball W. **Intramural:** Baseball M, basketball, volleyball. **Team name:** Saints.

Student services. Career counseling, services for economically disadvantaged, student employment services, financial aid counseling, on-campus daycare, personal counseling, placement for graduates, veterans' counselor. **Physically disabled:** Services for visually, speech, hearing impaired. **Transfer:** Pre-admission transcript evaluation for new students. Transfer center, transfer adviser, college fairs on campus for students transferring to 4-year colleges.

Contact. E-mail: admissions@shawneecc.edu
Phone: (618) 634-3298 Fax: (618) 634-3346
Dee Blakely, Dean of Student Services, Shawnee Community College, 8364 Shawnee College Road, Ullin, IL 62992

South Suburban College of Cook County
South Holland, Illinois
www.ssc.edu
CB code: 1806

- Public 2-year community college
- Commuter campus in large town

General. Founded in 1927. Regionally accredited. **Enrollment:** 4,401 undergraduates. **Degrees:** 315 associate awarded. **Location:** 20 miles from Chicago. **Calendar:** Semester, limited summer session. **Full-time faculty:** 114 total. **Part-time faculty:** 399 total.

Student profile.

Out-of-state:	5%	25 or older:	54%

Transfer out. Colleges most students transferred to 2015: Governors State University, University of Illinois-Chicago, Purdue University-Calumet, Chicago State University.

Basis for selection. Open admission, but selective for some programs. Separate requirements for some allied health and nursing programs. Audition recommended for music majors. **Home schooled:** Transcript of courses and grades required. **Learning Disabled:** Students need to self-declare with counseling center. Accommodations provided as needed.

High school preparation. 15 units required; 18 recommended. Required and recommended units include English 4, mathematics 2-3, social studies 2, science 2 (laboratory 1) and academic electives 4.

2016-2017 Annual costs. Tuition/fees (projected): $4,583; $10,523 out-of-district; $12,173 out-of-state. Per-credit charge: $135 in-district; $333 out-of-district; $358 out-of-state. Books/supplies: $1,200. Personal expenses: $1,200.

2014-2015 Financial aid. Need-based: 671 full-time freshmen applied for aid; 629 deemed to have need; 629 received aid. Average need met was

65%. Average scholarship/grant was $4,740. 98% of total undergraduate aid awarded as scholarships/grants, 2% as loans/jobs. Need-based aid available for part-time students. Work-study available nights, weekends and for part-time students. **Non-need-based:** Scholarships awarded for academics, art, athletics, music/drama, state residency.

Application procedures. Admission: No deadline. No application fee. Application must be submitted on paper. Admission notification on a rolling basis. **Financial aid:** Priority date 6/30; no closing date. FAFSA required. Applicants notified on a rolling basis starting 5/1.

Academics. Special study options: Distance learning, double major, dual enrollment of high school students, ESL, honors, internships, liberal arts/career combination, study abroad. License preparation in nursing, occupational therapy, paramedic, radiology, real estate. **Credit/placement by examination:** AP, CLEP, institutional tests. DANTES, CLEP, AP credit accepted. **Support services:** GED preparation and test center, learning center, reduced course load, remedial instruction, study skills assistance, tutoring, writing center.

Majors. Biology: General, biomedical sciences. **Business:** General, accounting, administrative services, fashion, finance, marketing, office management. **Computer sciences:** General. **Education:** General, early childhood, special ed, teacher assistance. **Engineering:** General, engineering science. **English:** English lit. **Foreign languages:** Spanish. **General:** Maintenance. **Health services:** Medical radiologic technology/radiation therapy, nursing (RN), occupational therapy assistant, pharmacy assistant. **History:** General. **Liberal arts:** Arts/sciences. **Math:** General. **Parks/recreation:** Health/fitness, sports admin. **Philosophy/religion:** Philosophy. **Physical sciences:** Astronomy, chemistry, geology, physics. **Protective services:** Criminal justice. **Psychology:** General. **Social sciences:** Anthropology, economics, geography, political science, sociology. **Visual/performing arts:** Dramatic, music, studio arts.

Technology on campus. 300 workstations in library, computer center, student center. Online course registration, online library, helpline, repair service, wireless network available.

Student life. Freshman orientation: Available. Preregistration for classes offered. Continuous orientation program; specialized high school student success program in summer. **Activities:** Bands, campus ministries, choral groups, drama, music ensembles, student government, TV station, business professionals, veterans organization, paralegal association, occupational therapy organization, human service club, Creative Dimensions, nursing club.

Athletics. NJCAA. **Intercollegiate:** Baseball M, basketball, soccer M, softball W, volleyball W. **Intramural:** Baseball M, basketball, softball, volleyball. **Team name:** Bulldogs.

Student services. Career counseling, student employment services, financial aid counseling, on-campus daycare, personal counseling, veterans' counselor. **Physically disabled:** Services for visually, speech, hearing impaired. **Transfer:** Transfer center, transfer adviser, college fairs on campus for students transferring to 4-year colleges.

Contact. E-mail: Admissions@ssc.edu
Phone: (708) 596-2000 ext. 2330 Fax: (708) 225-5806
Robin Rihacek, Director of Enrollment Services, South Suburban College of Cook County, 15800 South State Street, South Holland, IL 60473

Southeastern Illinois College
Harrisburg, Illinois
www.sic.edu   CB code: 1777

▶ Public 2-year community college
▶ Commuter campus in small town

General. Founded in 1960. Regionally accredited. **Enrollment:** 1,004 degree-seeking undergraduates; 1,030 non-degree-seeking students. **Degrees:** 276 associate awarded. **Location:** 45 miles from Carbondale; 65 miles from Evansville, Indiana. **Calendar:** Semester, extensive summer session. **Full-time faculty:** 45 total. **Part-time faculty:** 209 total. **Class size:** 77% < 20, 21% 20-39, 1% 40-49, less than 1% 50-99, less than 1% >100. **Special facilities:** Shooting complex, archery range, fire science center, burn tunnel. **Partnerships:** Formal partnership with Cummins Corporation for diesel technology.

Student profile. Among degree-seeking undergraduates, 47% enrolled in a transfer program, 53% enrolled in a vocational program, 4% already have a bachelor's degree or higher, 224 enrolled as first-time, first-year students.

Part-time:	30%	Hispanic/Latino:	2%
Women:	62%	25 or older:	60%
African American:	5%		

Transfer out. Colleges most students transferred to 2015: Southern Illinois University at Carbondale.

Basis for selection. Open admission, but selective for some programs. Special requirements for nursing, medical records, health information technology, surgical nurse, occupational therapy assistant, and conservation game management programs. Psychological Services Bureau-Health Occupations Examination required for medical laboratory technician, ASSET for health information systems. TEAS test required for associate degree and practical nursing programs. **Home schooled:** Transcript of courses and grades required.

High school preparation. 15 units recommended. Recommended units include English 4, mathematics 3, social studies 3, science 3 and academic electives 2.

2015-2016 Annual costs. Tuition/fees: $3,120; $4,800 out-of-district; $5,040 out-of-state. Books/supplies: $450. Personal expenses: $1,357.

2014-2015 Financial aid. Need-based: 138 full-time freshmen applied for aid; 125 deemed to have need; 125 received aid. Average need met was 35%. Average scholarship/grant was $4,677. 98% of total undergraduate aid awarded as scholarships/grants, 2% as loans/jobs. Need-based aid available for part-time students. Work-study available nights, weekends and for part-time students. **Non-need-based:** Awarded to 40 full-time undergraduates, including 26 freshmen. Scholarships awarded for academics, alumni affiliation, art, athletics, music/drama.

Application procedures. Admission: No deadline. No application fee. Admission notification on a rolling basis beginning on or about 5/1. **Financial aid:** Priority date 2/15; no closing date. FAFSA required. Applicants notified on a rolling basis starting 3/1; must reply within 2 week(s) of notification.

Academics. Special study options: Cross-registration, distance learning, double major, dual enrollment of high school students, independent study, internships, student-designed major. Bachelor's degree programs available on campus. License preparation in nursing. **Credit/placement by examination:** AP, CLEP, institutional tests. 29 credit hours maximum toward associate degree. **Support services:** GED preparation and test center, learning center, pre-admission summer program, reduced course load, remedial instruction, tutoring.

Majors. Business: Administrative services, business admin, office technology. **Computer sciences:** Information systems, LAN/WAN management. **Conservation:** Wildlife/wilderness. **Education:** General. **Health services:** Clinical lab technology, health information technology, nursing (RN), occupational therapy assistant, office assistant. **Liberal arts:** Arts/sciences. **Math:** General. **Protective services:** Police science. **Work/family studies:** Child care management.

Most popular majors. Health sciences 14%, trade and industry 13%.

Technology on campus. 75 workstations in library, computer center. Online course registration, repair service, wireless network available.

Student life. Freshman orientation: Available. Preregistration for classes offered. **Activities:** Concert band, choral groups, drama, music ensembles, musical theater, student government, student newspaper, art club, math and science club, BASIC, Students in Free Enterprise, Phi Theta Kappa, Phi Beta Lambda, Theta Sigma Phi, Student Association of Family and Consumer Sciences, forensics club.

Athletics. NJCAA. **Intercollegiate:** Baseball M, basketball, softball W. **Intramural:** Basketball. **Team name:** Falcons.

Student services. Career counseling, student employment services, financial aid counseling, on-campus daycare, personal counseling, placement for graduates, veterans' counselor. **Physically disabled:** Services for visually, hearing impaired. **Transfer:** Transfer adviser, college fairs on campus for students transferring to 4-year colleges.

Contact. E-mail: admissions@sic.edu
Phone: (618) 252-5400 ext. 2441 Toll-free number: (866) 338-2742
Fax: (618) 252-3062
Kyla Burford, Director of Enrollment Services/Registrar, Southeastern Illinois College, 3575 College Road, Harrisburg, IL 62946

Southwestern Illinois College
Belleville, Illinois
www.swic.edu   CB code: 1057

▶ Public 2-year community college
▶ Commuter campus in small city

General. Founded in 1946. Regionally accredited. **Enrollment:** 9,028 degree-seeking undergraduates; 915 non-degree-seeking students. **Degrees:** 1,423 associate awarded. **ROTC:** Army, Air Force. **Location:** 20 miles from St. Louis. **Calendar:** Semester, extensive summer session. **Full-time faculty:** 148 total; 8% have terminal degrees, 53% women. **Part-time faculty:** 598 total; 6% have terminal degrees, 42% women. **Special facilities:** Greenhouse solar collector, native tree arboretum, interactive video classrooms, art center.

Student profile. Among degree-seeking undergraduates, 39% enrolled in a transfer program, 38% enrolled in a vocational program, 4% already have a bachelor's degree or higher, 1,256 enrolled as first-time, first-year students.

Part-time:	55%	Asian American:	2%
Women:	57%	Hispanic/Latino:	4%
African American:	23%	25 or older:	41%

Basis for selection. Open admission, but selective for some programs. Special requirements for health career programs and associate degrees in arts, fine arts, teaching, science, or engineering science. All applicants required to take COMPASS and ASSET tests. **Home schooled:** Placement test or ACT/SAT required.

High school preparation. 15 units recommended. Recommended units include English 4, mathematics 2, social studies 3, science 3 (laboratory 2) and academic electives 2. 1 unit foreign language, music, art, or vocational education recommended.

2015-2016 Annual costs. Tuition/fees: $3,420; $12,120 out-of-district; $15,750 out-of-state. Per-credit charge: $109 in-district; $399 out-of-district; $520 out-of-state. Books/supplies: $1,500. Personal expenses: $2,000.

Financial aid. Need-based: Need-based aid available for part-time students. Work-study available nights, weekends and for part-time students. **Non-need-based:** Scholarships awarded for academics, art, athletics, leadership, minority status, music/drama, ROTC.

Application procedures. Admission: No deadline. No application fee. **Financial aid:** Priority date 8/1, closing date 5/31. FAFSA, institutional form required. Applicants notified on a rolling basis starting 4/1; must reply within 2 week(s) of notification.

Academics. Special study options: Accelerated study, distance learning, double major, dual enrollment of high school students, ESL, independent study, internships, study abroad, weekend college. License preparation in aviation, nursing, paramedic. **Credit/placement by examination:** AP, CLEP, institutional tests. 16 credit hours maximum toward associate degree. 30 hours of credit may be awarded for successful completion of CLEP tests. **Support services:** GED preparation, learning center, reduced course load, remedial instruction, study skills assistance, tutoring, writing center.

Majors. Biology: General. **Business:** General, accounting, business admin, hospitality admin, management information systems, management science, office/clerical, sales/distribution. **Communications:** Communications/speech/rhetoric. **Communications technology:** General. **Computer sciences:** General, applications programming, computer science, data processing, information systems, programming. **Education:** Early childhood, elementary, middle, secondary. **Engineering:** General. **English:** English lit, rhetoric/composition. **Foreign languages:** General. **General:** Carpentry, electrician, maintenance, masonry, power transmission. **Health services:** Clinical lab assistant, clinical lab technology, EMT paramedic, health information technology, medical assistant, medical radiologic technology/radiation therapy, nursing (RN), physical therapy assistant, premedicine, prepharmacy, preveterinary, respiratory therapy technology. **History:** General. **Human services:** Social work. **Liberal arts:** Arts/sciences. **Math:** General. **Parks/recreation:** Health/fitness. **Philosophy/religion:** Philosophy. **Physical sciences:** Astronomy, chemistry, physics. **Protective services:** Firefighting, police science, security services. **Psychology:** General. **Social sciences:** Anthropology, archaeology, economics, geography, political science, sociology. **Visual/performing arts:** Art, dramatic, music, photography, studio arts. **Work/family studies:** Child care management.

Technology on campus. 250 workstations in library, computer center. Commuter students can connect to campus network. Online course registration, helpline, wireless network available.

Student life. Freshman orientation: Available. Preregistration for classes offered. **Activities:** Bands, choral groups, drama, international student organizations, literary magazine, music ensembles, musical theater, student government, student newspaper, Black Affairs Council, physically challenged organization, Campus Christian Fellowship.

Athletics. NJCAA. **Intercollegiate:** Baseball M, basketball, soccer, softball W, volleyball W. **Intramural:** Basketball. **Team name:** Blue Storm.

Student services. Adult student services, career counseling, student employment services, financial aid counseling, minority student services, on-campus daycare, personal counseling, placement for graduates, veterans' counselor. **Physically disabled:** Services for visually, speech, hearing impaired. **Transfer:** Transfer adviser, college fairs on campus for students transferring to 4-year colleges.

Contact. E-mail: admissions@swic.edu
Phone: (618) 235-2700 ext. 5526
Toll-free number: (866) 942-7942 ext. 5526 Fax: (618) 222-9768
Michelle Birk, Dean of Enrollment Services, Southwestern Illinois College, 2500 Carlyle Avenue, Belleville, IL 62221-5899

Spoon River College
Canton, Illinois
www.src.edu
CB code: 1154

- Public 2-year community college
- Commuter campus in large town

General. Founded in 1959. Regionally accredited. **Enrollment:** 1,161 degree-seeking undergraduates; 504 non-degree-seeking students. **Degrees:** 140 associate awarded. **ROTC:** Army. **Location:** 35 miles from Peoria. **Calendar:** Semester, limited summer session. **Full-time faculty:** 37 total. **Part-time faculty:** 85 total. **Special facilities:** Natural arboretum, walking trail, agricultural test plots.

Student profile. Among degree-seeking undergraduates, 5% already have a bachelor's degree or higher, 406 enrolled as first-time, first-year students, 81 transferred in from other institutions.

Part-time:	37%	25 or older:	32%
Women:	60%		

Transfer out. Colleges most students transferred to 2015: Western Illinois University, Illinois State University, University of Illinois: Springfield.

Basis for selection. Open admission, but selective for some programs. Special requirements for nursing program. All students must take COMPASS exam for placement; if score indicates, student must be remediated before taking college-level courses. College-preparatory program recommended for transfer degree programs. Vocational students not required to have specific high school courses.

High school preparation. College-preparatory program recommended. 15 units recommended. Recommended units include English 4, mathematics 3, social studies 3, science 3 (laboratory 3) and academic electives 2.

2015-2016 Annual costs. Tuition/fees: $4,200; $9,240 out-of-district; $10,020 out-of-state. Per-credit charge: $120 in-district; $288 out-of-district; $314 out-of-state. Books/supplies: $850. Personal expenses: $900.

2014-2015 Financial aid. Need-based: 68% of total undergraduate aid awarded as scholarships/grants, 32% as loans/jobs. Need-based aid available for part-time students. Work-study available nights, weekends and for part-time students. **Non-need-based:** Scholarships awarded for academics, art, athletics, music/drama, state residency. **Additional information:** Students who have submitted all required forms by the processing deadline are guaranteed to have aid eligibility established by the tuition deadline. All forms submitted after the processing deadline are processed in the order received on a continuing basis.

Application procedures. Admission: No deadline. No application fee. Admission notification on a rolling basis. **Financial aid:** Priority date 6/21, closing date 7/1. FAFSA required. Applicants notified on a rolling basis starting 5/15.

Academics. Special study options: Accelerated study, distance learning, dual enrollment of high school students, ESL, internships. License preparation in nursing, paramedic. **Credit/placement by examination:** AP, CLEP, IB, institutional tests. 32 credit hours maximum toward associate degree. Maximum 50% of credit hours toward degree may be awarded through CLEP. **Support services:** GED preparation, learning center, reduced course load, remedial instruction, study skills assistance, tutoring, writing center.

Majors. Biology: General. **Business:** General, administrative services, managerial economics. **Communications:** General. **Computer sciences:** Information technology, web page design. **Conservation:** Management/policy. **Education:** General, early childhood, elementary, elementary special ed, ESL, secondary. **English:** English lit. **Health services:** Geriatric nursing, health care admin. **History:** General. **Math:** General. **Physical sciences:** General. **Protective services:** Law enforcement admin. **Psychology:** General. **Social sciences:** Sociology. **Visual/performing arts:** Art.

Most popular majors. Agriculture 10%, health sciences 7%, liberal arts 78%, trade and industry 11%.

Technology on campus. 100 workstations in library, computer center, student center. Online course registration, online library, helpline, wireless network available.

Student life. Freshman orientation: Available. Preregistration for classes offered. Offered prior to fall semester and online. **Activities:** Drama, literary magazine, student government, Agriculture Fraternity, International Honor Society, Peer Ambassador Program, Diesel Fraternity, Intramurals, Environmental Organization, Habitat for Humanity.

Athletics. NJCAA. **Intercollegiate:** Baseball M, cross-country, softball W. **Intramural:** Table tennis. **Team name:** Snappers.

Student services. Adult student services, career counseling, services for economically disadvantaged, student employment services, financial aid counseling, placement for graduates, veterans' counselor. **Physically disabled:** Services for visually, speech, hearing impaired. **Transfer:** Pre-admission transcript evaluation for new students. Transfer adviser, college fairs on campus for students transferring to 4-year colleges.

Contact. E-mail: admissions@src.edu
Phone: (309) 649-7020 Toll-free number: (800) 334-7337
Fax: (309) 649-6393
Janet Munson, Director of Enrollment Services, Spoon River College, 23235 North County Road 22, Canton, IL 61520

Taylor Business Institute
Chicago, Illinois
www.tbiil.edu   CB code: 2488

▶ For-profit 2-year business college
▶ Very large city

General. Accredited by ACICS. **Enrollment:** 257 undergraduates. **Degrees:** 31 associate awarded. **Calendar:** Differs by program. **Full-time faculty:** 6 total. **Part-time faculty:** 22 total.

Basis for selection. Admissions assessment based on individual strengths; CPAT used. CPAT required for placement and assessment after admission.

2015-2016 Annual costs. Books/supplies: $450.

Financial aid. Need-based: Work-study available nights, weekends and for part-time students.

Application procedures. Admission: No deadline. $25 fee, may be waived for applicants with need. **Financial aid:** FAFSA, institutional form required.

Academics. Credit/placement by examination: AP, CLEP.

Majors. Business: Accounting. **Health services:** Insurance coding. **Protective services:** Law enforcement admin.

Student life. Freshman orientation: Available. Preregistration for classes offered.

Student services. Alcohol/substance abuse counseling, career counseling, services for economically disadvantaged, student employment services, financial aid counseling, minority student services, personal counseling, placement for graduates, veterans' counselor, women's services.

Contact. Phone: (312) 658-5100
Franklin Parker, Vice President, Taylor Business Institute, 318 West Adams Street, 5th Floor, Chicago, IL 60606

Triton College
River Grove, Illinois   CB member
www.triton.edu   CB code: 1821

▶ Public 2-year community and junior college
▶ Commuter campus in large town

General. Founded in 1964. Regionally accredited. **Enrollment:** 8,561 degree-seeking undergraduates; 3,123 non-degree-seeking students. **Degrees:** 786 associate awarded. **Location:** 5 miles from Chicago. **Calendar:** Semester, extensive summer session. **Full-time faculty:** 101 total; 26% have terminal degrees, 23% minority, 60% women. **Part-time faculty:** 652 total; 10% have terminal degrees, 24% minority, 53% women. **Class size:** 57% < 20, 43% 20-39, less than 1% 40-49. **Special facilities:** Earth and space center with planetarium, theater, performing arts center, botanical gardens, educational

technology resource center, culinary arts operated dining facility. **Partnerships:** Formal partnerships with General Motors, hospitals and health care providers in Chicago area.

Student profile. Among degree-seeking undergraduates, 1,393 enrolled as first-time, first-year students.

Part-time:	64%	**Women:** 53%
Out-of-state:	1%	

Transfer out. Colleges most students transferred to 2015: Northern Illinois University, Northeastern Illinois University, University of Illinois at Chicago, DePaul University, Eastern Illinois University.

Basis for selection. Open admission, but selective for some programs. Special requirements for most health programs and two manufacturer-related automotive programs. Applicants to allied health program must attend information session. **Learning Disabled:** Students must self-identify.

High school preparation. 15 units required. Required units include English 4, mathematics 3, social studies 3, science 3 and academic electives 2. Biology, chemistry, or algebra required for most allied health programs. 15 specified units required for university transfer programs.

2015-2016 Annual costs. Tuition/fees: $3,870; $9,370 out-of-district; $11,629 out-of-state. Per-credit charge: $113 in-district; $296 out-of-district; $371 out-of-state. Books/supplies: $1,322. Personal expenses: $1,436.

Financial aid. Need-based: Need-based aid available for part-time students. Work-study available nights, weekends and for part-time students. **Non-need-based:** Scholarships awarded for academics, athletics.

Application procedures. Admission: No deadline. No application fee. Admission notification on a rolling basis. **Financial aid:** Priority date 4/15; no closing date. FAFSA, institutional form required. Applicants notified on a rolling basis starting 4/1; must reply within 2 week(s) of notification.

Academics. Special study options: Accelerated study, cooperative education, cross-registration, distance learning, dual enrollment of high school students, ESL, exchange student, external degree, honors, independent study, internships, liberal arts/career combination, study abroad, teacher certification program, weekend college. Bachelor's degree programs available on campus. License preparation in nursing, paramedic, radiology, real estate. **Credit/placement by examination:** AP, CLEP, institutional tests. 30 credit hours maximum toward associate degree. **Support services:** GED preparation, learning center, reduced course load, remedial instruction, study skills assistance, tutoring, writing center.

Honors college/program. 25 ACT and/or 3.35 GPA required; about 25 admitted each year.

Majors. Business: Accounting, business admin, construction management, financial planning, hospitality admin, hotel/motel admin, human resources, restaurant/food services. **Computer sciences:** Information systems, networking. **Education:** General, early childhood, mathematics, teacher assistance. **Foreign languages:** General, French, Italian, Spanish. **General:** Site management. **Health services:** Clinical lab technology, EMT paramedic, medical assistant, nuclear medical technology, nursing (RN), ophthalmic technology, radiologic technology/medical imaging, respiratory therapy technology, sonography, substance abuse counseling. **Liberal arts:** Arts/sciences. **Parks/recreation:** Facilities management. **Protective services:** Firefighting, law enforcement admin, police science. **Visual/performing arts:** Commercial photography, design, interior design, music, studio arts. **Work/family studies:** Child care service.

Most popular majors. Health sciences 18%, interdisciplinary studies 18%, liberal arts 42%.

Technology on campus. 946 workstations in library, computer center. Commuter students can connect to campus network. Online course registration, online library, helpline, wireless network available.

Student life. Freshman orientation: Available. Preregistration for classes offered. Sessions held throughout summer months. **Activities:** Jazz band, campus ministries, choral groups, dance, drama, international student organizations, music ensembles, Model UN, musical theater, radio station, student government, student newspaper, over 30 clubs and organizations available.

Athletics. NJCAA. **Intercollegiate:** Baseball M, basketball, soccer, softball W, volleyball W, wrestling M. **Team name:** Trojans.

Student services. Career counseling, services for economically disadvantaged, student employment services, financial aid counseling, health services, minority student services, on-campus daycare, personal counseling, placement for graduates, veterans' counselor. **Physically disabled:** Services for visually, speech, hearing impaired. **Transfer:** Pre-admission transcript evaluation for new students. Transfer center, transfer adviser, college fairs on campus for students transferring to 4-year colleges.

Contact. E-mail: triton@triton,edu
Phone: (708) 456-0300 ext. 3130 Fax: (708) 583-3162
Amanda Turner, Dean, Enrollment Services, Triton College, 2000 North
Fifth Avenue, River Grove, IL 60171

Vatterott College: Quincy
Quincy, Illinois
www.vatterott.edu   CB code: 3640

▶ For-profit 2-year technical college
▶ Commuter campus in small city

General. Accredited by ACCSC. **Enrollment:** 200 undergraduates.
Degrees: 12 associate awarded. **Calendar:** Differs by program. **Full-time
faculty:** 15 total. **Part-time faculty:** 30 total.

Basis for selection. Open admission.

2015-2016 Annual costs. Diploma programs: (60 weeks) $27,620-
$28,420. Associate programs: (80 weeks) $35,808-$38,432. Costs include
fees, books and supplies.

Financial aid. Need-based: Work-study available nights, weekends and
for part-time students.

Application procedures. Admission: No deadline. No application fee.

Academics. Credit/placement by examination: AP, CLEP.

Majors. Computer sciences: Computer science. **Health services:** Medical assistant.

Contact. Phone: (217) 224-0600 Toll-free number: (800) 438-5621
Fax: (217) 223-6771
Mark Thomas, Director of Admissions, Vatterott College: Quincy, 3609
North Marx Drive, Quincy, IL 62305

Waubonsee Community College
Sugar Grove, Illinois
www.waubonsee.edu   CB code: 1938

▶ Public 2-year community and junior college
▶ Commuter campus in small town

General. Founded in 1966. Regionally accredited. Comprehensive community college. **Enrollment:** 8,055 degree-seeking undergraduates. **Degrees:**
1,094 associate awarded. **ROTC:** Army. **Location:** 9 miles from Aurora.
Calendar: Semester, extensive summer session. **Special facilities:** Observatory, nature trail. **Partnerships:** Formal partnership with Valley Education
for Employment System.

Transfer out. Colleges most students transferred to 2015: Northern Illinois University, Illinois State University, Aurora University-Illinois, University of Illinois at Urbana-Champaign, University of Illinois at Chicago.

Basis for selection. Open admission, but selective for some programs.
Limited enrollment to certain programs based on specific assessment testing
and/or successful completion of prerequisite coursework.

High school preparation. College-preparatory program recommended.
15 units recommended. Recommended units include English 4, mathematics
3, social studies 3, science 3 and academic electives 2.

2015-2016 Annual costs. Tuition/fees: $3,540; $8,753 out-of-district;
$9,483 out-of-state. Books/supplies: $1,560. Personal expenses: $1,440.

Financial aid. Need-based: Need-based aid available for part-time students. Work-study available nights, weekends and for part-time students.
Non-need-based: Scholarships awarded for academics, art, athletics, leadership, minority status, music/drama, state residency.

Application procedures. Admission: No deadline. No application fee.
Admission notification on a rolling basis. **Financial aid:** Priority date 3/1;
no closing date. FAFSA required. Applicants notified on a rolling basis
starting 4/1.

Academics. Review classes offered for various levels of math, english,
and reading. **Special study options:** Accelerated study, distance learning,
dual enrollment of high school students, ESL, honors, independent study,
internships, liberal arts/career combination, study abroad, weekend college.
License preparation in nursing. **Credit/placement by examination:** AP,

CLEP, institutional tests. 30 credit hours maximum toward associate degree.
Student must be enrolled before scores can be recorded on transcript. Recording fee may apply. **Support services:** GED preparation and test center,
learning center, reduced course load, remedial instruction, study skills assistance, tutoring, writing center.

Majors. Business: Accounting, business admin, construction management,
executive assistant, human resources, office technology, small business
admin. **Communications technology:** Radio/TV. **Computer sciences:** Programming, web page design. **Education:** Teacher assistance. **Engineering:**
General. **Foreign languages:** Sign language interpretation. **General:** Electrician. **Health services:** Community health services, EMT ambulance attendant, health information technology, nursing (RN). **Human services:** Social
work. **Liberal arts:** Arts/sciences, library assistant. **Parks/recreation:**
Health/fitness. **Protective services:** Firefighting, police science. **Visual/per-
forming arts:** Graphic design, music. **Work/family studies:** Child care
service.

Most popular majors. Health sciences 10%, interdisciplinary studies 47%,
liberal arts 28%.

Technology on campus. 140 workstations in library, computer center,
student center. Commuter students can connect to campus network. Online
course registration, helpline, wireless network available.

Student life. Freshman orientation: Available. Preregistration for classes
offered. Three hour orientation for new students and mandatory 45 minute
online tutorial for registration and planning. **Activities:** Bands, choral groups,
dance, drama, literary magazine, music ensembles, musical theater, student
government, student newspaper, Latinos Unidos, Christian Fellowship, Black
Student Alliance, Students for a Diverse Society, Students Organizing Sustainability, Christian Athlete's Club, Spectrum, Veterans Club/SALUTE,
Womyn For Womyn Alliance.

Athletics. NJCAA. **Intercollegiate:** Baseball M, basketball, cheerleading,
cross-country, golf M, soccer, softball W, tennis, volleyball W. **Intramural:**
Basketball, table tennis, volleyball. **Team name:** Chiefs.

Student services. Career counseling, services for economically disadvantaged, student employment services, financial aid counseling, minority student
services, on-campus daycare, personal counseling, veterans' counselor. **Physically disabled:** Services for visually, speech, hearing impaired. **Transfer:**
Transfer adviser, college fairs on campus for students transferring to 4-
year colleges.

Contact. E-mail: admissions@waubonsee.edu
Phone: (630) 466-7900 ext. 5756 Fax: (630) 466-6663
Joy Sanders, Admissions Manager, Waubonsee Community College,
Route 47 at Waubonsee Drive, Sugar Grove, IL 60554-9454

Indiana

American National University: Fort Wayne
Fort Wayne, Indiana
www.national-college.edu

▶ For-profit 2-year career college
▶ Large city

General. Regionally accredited; also accredited by ACICS. **Enrollment:** 26 degree-seeking undergraduates. **Degrees:** 6 associate awarded. **Calendar:** Quarter. **Full-time faculty:** 2 total. **Part-time faculty:** 8 total.

Basis for selection. Open admission.

2016-2017 Annual costs. Tuition/fees: $15,411. Per-credit charge: $317. Personal expenses: $1,956.

Financial aid. Need-based: Work-study available nights, weekends and for part-time students.

Application procedures. Admission: No deadline. $50 fee. **Financial aid:** No deadline.

Academics. Credit/placement by examination: AP, CLEP.

Majors. Business: Accounting, business admin. **Computer sciences:** Information systems. **Health services:** Health information technology, medical assistant, pharmacy assistant.

Contact. Phone: (260) 483-1605
Trent Ramey, Regional Director of Admissions, American National University: Fort Wayne, 6131 N. Clinton St., Fort Wayne, IN 46825

American National University: Indianapolis
Indianapolis, Indiana
https://www.an.edu

▶ For-profit 2-year branch campus college
▶ Very large city

General. Regionally accredited; also accredited by ACICS. **Enrollment:** 128 degree-seeking undergraduates. **Degrees:** 1 bachelor's, 33 associate awarded. **Calendar:** Quarter. **Full-time faculty:** 6 total. **Part-time faculty:** 11 total.

Basis for selection. Open admission, but selective for some programs.

2016-2017 Annual costs. Tuition/fees: $15,411. Per-credit charge: $317. Personal expenses: $1,956.

Financial aid. Need-based: Work-study available nights, weekends and for part-time students.

Application procedures. Admission: No deadline. $50 fee.

Academics. Credit/placement by examination: AP, CLEP.

Majors. Business: Accounting/business management, administrative services, business admin. **Health services:** Health information technology, medical assistant, pharmacy assistant, surgical technology.

Contact. Phone: (317) 578-7353
Christina Shoaf, Director of Admissions, American National University: Indianapolis, 6060 Castleway Drive West, Indianapolis, IN 46250

American National University: South Bend
South Bend, Indiana
www.national-college.edu

▶ For-profit 2-year career college
▶ Large city

General. Regionally accredited; also accredited by ACICS. **Enrollment:** 63 degree-seeking undergraduates. **Degrees:** 8 associate awarded. **Calendar:** Quarter. **Full-time faculty:** 7 total. **Part-time faculty:** 7 total.

Basis for selection. Open admission.

2016-2017 Annual costs. Tuition/fees: $15,411. Per-credit charge: $317. Personal expenses: $1,956.

Financial aid. Need-based: Work-study available nights, weekends and for part-time students.

Application procedures. Admission: No deadline. $50 fee.

Academics. Credit/placement by examination: AP, CLEP.

Majors. Business: Accounting, business admin. **Computer sciences:** Information systems. **Health services:** Health information technology, medical assistant, pharmacy assistant.

Contact. Phone: (574) 307-7100
Trent Ramey, Regional Director of Admissions, American National University: South Bend, 1030 East Jefferson Boulevard, South Bend, IN 46617

Ancilla College
Donaldson, Indiana
www.ancilla.edu   CB code: 1015

▶ Private 2-year junior and liberal arts college affiliated with the Roman Catholic Church
▶ Residential campus in rural community

General. Founded in 1937. Regionally accredited. **Enrollment:** 468 degree-seeking undergraduates; 36 non-degree-seeking students. **Degrees:** 62 associate awarded. **Location:** 30 miles from South Bend, 7 miles from Plymouth. **Calendar:** Semester, limited summer session. **Full-time faculty:** 18 total; 11% have terminal degrees, 67% women. **Part-time faculty:** 33 total; 9% have terminal degrees, 58% women.

Student profile. Among degree-seeking undergraduates, 213 enrolled as first-time, first-year students, 72 transferred in from other institutions.

Part-time:	19%	**25 or older:**	23%
Out-of-state:	5%	**Live on campus:**	23%
Women:	57%		

Transfer out. Colleges most students transferred to 2015: Indiana University South Bend, Indiana-Purdue University Indianapolis, Ball State University, Indiana University Kokomo, Bethel College.

Basis for selection. Open admission, but selective for some programs. Academic record including test scores, courses taken and GPA along with college's placement test most important. **Adult students:** SAT/ACT scores not required. **Home schooled:** Transcript of courses and grades required. Submit either SAT or ACT test scores and/or take college placement test.

High school preparation. College-preparatory program recommended. Recommended units include English 4, mathematics 3, social studies 2, science 2 and foreign language 3.

2015-2016 Annual costs. Tuition/fees: $14,330. Per-credit charge: $470. Room/board: $8,500. Books/supplies: $1,420. Personal expenses: $870.

2014-2015 Financial aid. Need-based: 151 full-time freshmen applied for aid; 149 deemed to have need; 149 received aid. 77% of total undergraduate aid awarded as scholarships/grants, 23% as loans/jobs. Need-based aid available for part-time students. Work-study available nights, weekends and for part-time students. **Non-need-based:** Scholarships awarded for academics, athletics, job skills, leadership.

Application procedures. Admission: No deadline. No application fee. Admission notification on a rolling basis. **Financial aid:** Closing date 3/10. FAFSA required. Applicants notified on a rolling basis starting 3/10; must reply within 2 week(s) of notification.

Academics. Special study options: Double major, dual enrollment of high school students, independent study, internships, liberal arts/career combination. **Credit/placement by examination:** AP, CLEP, institutional tests. 12 credit hours maximum toward associate degree. **Support services:** Learning center, reduced course load, remedial instruction, study skills assistance, tutoring, writing center.

Majors. Business: Business admin, hospitality admin, logistics. **Communications:** Communications/speech/rhetoric, media studies. **Computer sciences:** Information technology. **Conservation:** Environmental studies. **Education:** General, early childhood, elementary, secondary. **Health services:** Nursing (RN). **History:** General. **Parks/recreation:** Exercise sciences. **Protective services:** Criminal justice. **Social sciences:** General, criminology.

Most popular majors. Business/marketing 16%, education 10%, health sciences 26%, liberal arts 37%, social sciences 11%.

Technology on campus. 53 workstations in library, computer center. Dormitories wired for high-speed internet access and linked to campus network. Online library, wireless network available.

Student life. Freshman orientation: Mandatory. Preregistration for classes offered. **Housing:** Coed dorms, single-sex dorms available. On campus housing available. **Activities:** Campus ministries, dance, student government, Student ambassadors, Phi Theta Kappa Society, Leaders for Life, Collegiate FFA, intramurals.

Athletics. NJCAA. **Intercollegiate:** Baseball M, basketball, bowling, cheerleading, cross-country, golf, lacrosse, soccer, softball W, tennis, track and field, volleyball W, wrestling M. **Team name:** Chargers.

Student services. Chaplain/spiritual director, career counseling, financial aid counseling, personal counseling. **Transfer:** Pre-admission transcript evaluation for new students. Transfer adviser, college fairs on campus for students transferring to 4-year colleges.

Contact. E-mail: admissions@ancilla.edu
Phone: (574) 936-8898 ext. 330
Toll-free number: (866) 262-4552 ext. 330 Fax: (574) 935-1773
Eric Wignall, Vice-President Enrollment Management, Ancilla College,
9601 Union Road, Donaldson, IN 46513

Brown Mackie College: Fort Wayne
Fort Wayne, Indiana
www.brownmackie.edu   **CB code: 3379**

- For-profit 2-year branch campus and business college
- Large city

General. Accredited by ACICS. **Enrollment:** 507 undergraduates. **Degrees:** 20 bachelor's, 166 associate awarded. **Calendar:** Quarter. **Full-time faculty:** 15 total. **Part-time faculty:** 50 total.

Basis for selection. Open admission.

2015-2016 Annual costs. Tuition/fees: $16,490. Per-credit charge: $327. Books/supplies: $600. Personal expenses: $2,946.

Financial aid. Need-based: Work-study available nights, weekends and for part-time students.

Application procedures. Admission: No deadline. $20 fee.

Academics. Special study options: Bachelor's degree programs available on campus. **Credit/placement by examination:** AP, CLEP.

Majors. Business: General, office management. **Computer sciences:** General. **Health services:** Health care admin, medical assistant, occupational therapy assistant. **Parks/recreation:** Health/fitness.

Contact. E-mail: ktaboh@brownmackie.edu
Phone: (260) 484-4400 Toll-free number: (866) 433-2289
Fax: (260) 484-2678
Phil Hooks, Director of Admissions, Brown Mackie College: Fort Wayne,
3000 Coliseum Boulevard, Suite 100, Fort Wayne, IN 46805

Brown Mackie College: Merrillville
Merrillville, Indiana
www.brownmackie.edu   **CB code: 7115**

- For-profit 2-year business college
- Commuter campus in small city

General. Accredited by ACICS. **Enrollment:** 512 undergraduates. **Degrees:** 10 bachelor's, 135 associate awarded. **Calendar:** Differs by program. **Full-time faculty:** 9 total. **Part-time faculty:** 30 total.

Basis for selection. Interview, test scores and school achievement record important.

2015-2016 Annual costs. Tuition/fees: $16,490. Per-credit charge: $327. Books/supplies: $600. Personal expenses: $2,946.

Financial aid. Need-based: Work-study available nights, weekends and for part-time students.

Application procedures. Admission: No deadline. $20 fee.

Academics. Credit/placement by examination: AP, CLEP.

Majors. Business: General. **Computer sciences:** Data entry. **Health services:** Medical assistant, occupational therapy assistant, office admin. **Protective services:** Criminal justice.

Contact. E-mail: bmcmeadm@brownmackie.edu
Phone: (219) 769-3321 Toll-free number: (800) 258-3321
Charles Woods, Director of Admissions, Brown Mackie College:
Merrillville, 1000 East 80th Place, Suite 101N, Merrillville, IN 46410

Brown Mackie College: Michigan City
Michigan City, Indiana
www.brownmackie.edu   **CB code: 3345**

- For-profit 2-year branch campus college
- Commuter campus in small city
- Interview required

General. Accredited by ACICS. **Enrollment:** 112 undergraduates. **Degrees:** 4 bachelor's, 31 associate awarded. **Calendar:** Differs by program. **Full-time faculty:** 4 total. **Part-time faculty:** 26 total.

Transfer out. Colleges most students transferred to 2015: Tri-State University.

Basis for selection. Open admission. **Home schooled:** GED or equivalent required.

2015-2016 Annual costs. Tuition/fees: $15,680. Per-credit charge: $314. Books/supplies: $1,500. Personal expenses: $2,970.

Financial aid. Need-based: Work-study available nights, weekends and for part-time students.

Application procedures. Admission: No deadline. No application fee.

Academics. Credit/placement by examination: AP, CLEP.

Majors. Business: Accounting technology. **Computer sciences:** Data entry. **Education:** Early childhood special. **Health services:** Health care admin, massage therapy, medical assistant, medical secretary, office admin, surgical technology, veterinary technology/assistant. **Protective services:** Criminal justice.

Contact. Phone: (219) 877-3100
Nancy Spenny, Director of Admissions, Brown Mackie College: Michigan City, 325 East US Highway 20, Michigan City, IN 46360-7362

Brown Mackie College: South Bend
South Bend, Indiana
www.brownmackie.edu   **CB code: 3140**

- For-profit 2-year community and technical college
- Commuter campus in small city
- Application essay, interview required

General. Founded in 1882. Accredited by ACICS. **Enrollment:** 340 undergraduates. **Degrees:** 15 bachelor's, 129 associate awarded. **Location:** 90 miles from Chicago, 150 miles from Indianapolis. **Calendar:** Quarter, extensive summer session. **Full-time faculty:** 17 total. **Part-time faculty:** 57 total. **Class size:** 81% < 20, 19% 20-39.

Student profile.

Out-of-state:	7%	25 or older:	45%

Basis for selection. Open admission.

2015-2016 Annual costs. Tuition/fees: $16,490. Per-credit charge: $327. Books/supplies: $600. Personal expenses: $2,946.

Financial aid. All financial aid based on need. Need-based aid available for part-time students. Work-study available nights, weekends and for part-time students.

Application procedures. Admission: No deadline. No application fee. Must reply by May 1 or within 1 week(s) if notified thereafter. **Financial aid:** No deadline. FAFSA required. Applicants notified on a rolling basis; must reply within 1 week(s) of notification.

Academics. Four-day academic week. Optional Friday tutorial sessions available. **Special study options:** Accelerated study, double major, independent study, internships. **Credit/placement by examination:** AP, CLEP. 28 credit hours maximum toward associate degree. **Support services:** Remedial instruction, study skills assistance, tutoring.

Majors. Business: General, accounting technology. **Computer sciences:** Support specialist. **Health services:** Medical assistant, occupational therapy assistant, physical therapy assistant, veterinary technology/assistant. **Protective services:** Criminal justice.

Technology on campus. 60 workstations in computer center.

Student life. Freshman orientation: Mandatory. Preregistration for classes offered. Two-hour sessions held Thursday before class starts. **Housing:** Students are referred to local apartment complexes.

Student services. Career counseling, student employment services, personal counseling, placement for graduates, veterans' counselor. **Transfer:** Transfer adviser for students transferring to 4-year colleges.

Contact. E-mail: bmcsbadm@brownmackie.edu
Phone: (574) 237-0774 Toll-free number: (800) 743-2447
Amy Wolf, Director of Admissions, Brown Mackie College: South Bend, 3454 Douglas Road, South Bend, IN 46635

College of Court Reporting
Hobart, Indiana
www.ccr.edu   CB code: 3532

▶ For-profit 2-year business and technical college
▶ Commuter campus in small city

General. Accredited by ACICS. **Enrollment:** 239 undergraduates. **Degrees:** 12 associate awarded. **Calendar:** Semester, extensive summer session. **Part-time faculty:** 24 total.

Basis for selection. Open admission. **Home schooled:** Transcript of courses and grades, state high school equivalency certificate required.

High school preparation. College-preparatory program recommended.

2015-2016 Annual costs. Books/supplies: $600. **Additional information:** Tuition for online students is $350 per-credit; tuition for onsite students is $175 per-credit. Cost of books ranges $16-$300 per semester and there is a $300 technology fee per semester. All costs are subject to change.

Financial aid. Need-based: Work-study available nights, weekends and for part-time students.

Application procedures. Admission: Closing date 9/30 (receipt date). $50 fee. Application must be submitted on paper. Admission notification on a rolling basis.

Academics. Special study options: Distance learning, internships. **Credit/placement by examination:** AP, CLEP.

Majors. Business: Office technology. **Health services:** Medical transcription.

Technology on campus. PC or laptop required. Online library, helpline, wireless network available.

Student life. Freshman orientation: Mandatory. Preregistration for classes offered. **Activities:** Student newspaper.

Student services. Adult student services, student employment services, financial aid counseling, placement for graduates. **Transfer:** Pre-admission transcript evaluation for new students.

Contact. E-mail: information@ccr.edu
Phone: (219) 942-1459 Toll-free number: (866) 294-3974
Fax: (219) 942-1631
Nicky Rodriguez, Director of Admissions, College of Court Reporting, 111 West 10th Street, Suite 111, Hobart, IN 46342

Fortis College: Indianapolis
Indianapolis, Indiana
www.fortis.edu

▶ For-profit 2-year career college
▶ Very large city

General. Regionally accredited; also accredited by ACCSC. **Enrollment:** 231 undergraduates. **Degrees:** 9 associate awarded. **Calendar:** Quarter. **Full-time faculty:** 8 total. **Part-time faculty:** 12 total.

Basis for selection. Open admission.

2015-2016 Annual costs. Books/supplies: $2,258. Personal expenses: $3,046. **Additional information:** Tuition and fees vary by program. Associate's Degree in Nursing; $45,352. Diploma/certificate programs range $14,376-$17,941. Books and supplies range $559-$2,423 depending on program and level.

Financial aid. Need-based: Work-study available nights, weekends and for part-time students.

Application procedures. Admission: No deadline. $25 fee. **Financial aid:** No deadline.

Academics. Credit/placement by examination: AP, CLEP.

Majors. Health services: Nursing (RN).

Contact. Phone: (317) 808-4800 Toll-free number: (855) 436-7847
James Cox, Campus President, Fortis College: Indianapolis, 9001 North Wesleyan Road, Suite 101, Indianapolis, IN 46268

Harrison College: Indianapolis
Indianapolis, Indiana
www.harrison.edu   CB code: 2317

▶ For-profit 2-year business and health science college
▶ Commuter campus in very large city

General. Founded in 1902. Accredited by ACICS. This group of Harrison College campuses includes an online division and on-ground campuses in the Indiana cities of Anderson, Columbus, Elkhart, Evansville, Ft. Wayne, Indianapolis, Lafayette, and Terre Haute. Other campuses located in Columbus, OH and Morrisville, NC. **Enrollment:** 3,498 undergraduates. **Degrees:** 189 bachelor's, 888 associate awarded. **Calendar:** Quarter, extensive summer session. **Full-time faculty:** 54 total. **Part-time faculty:** 236 total.

Basis for selection. Open admission, but selective for some programs. **Home schooled:** State high school equivalency certificate required.

2015-2016 Annual costs. Tuition varies by program. Per-credit-hour charges; $100-$475; program fees (including books); $275-$975. All costs are subject to change.

Financial aid. Need-based: Work-study available nights, weekends and for part-time students. **Additional information:** Work-study programs available.

Application procedures. Admission: No deadline. No application fee. Admission notification on a rolling basis.

Academics. Special study options: Distance learning, double major, internships, weekend college. Bachelor's degree programs available on campus. License preparation in nursing. **Credit/placement by examination:** AP, CLEP, institutional tests. A student may receive credit through successful completion of selected examinations offered through the Dantes Subject Standardized Tests (DSST) tests and through Defense Language Proficiency Tests (DLPT). **Support services:** Learning center, reduced course load, study skills assistance, tutoring. Academic/career counseling services.

Majors. Business: Accounting, administrative services, business admin, human resources, organizational leadership. **Computer sciences:** Networking. **Health services:** Clinical lab science, insurance specialist, massage therapy, medical assistant, surgical technology, veterinary technology/assistant. **Protective services:** Law enforcement admin.

Most popular majors. Business/marketing 19%, health sciences 61%, personal/culinary services 11%, security/protective services 7%.

Technology on campus. Commuter students can connect to campus network. Online course registration, online library, helpline, wireless network available.

Student life. Freshman orientation: Available. Preregistration for classes offered.

Student services. Adult student services, career counseling, student employment services, financial aid counseling, legal services, personal counseling, placement for graduates. **Transfer:** Re-entry adviser for new students.

Contact. Phone: (317) 264-5656 Toll-free number: (888) 544-4422 Fax: (317) 264-5650
Jason Howanec, Vice President of Enrollment, Harrison College: Indianapolis, 550 East Washington Street, Indianapolis, IN 46204

International Business College: Indianapolis
Indianapolis, Indiana
www.ibcindianapolis.edu   **CB code: 3374**

▶ For-profit 2-year business college
▶ Commuter campus in very large city

General. Accredited by ACICS. Branch campus of International Business College. **Enrollment:** 399 undergraduates. **Degrees:** 179 associate awarded. **Calendar:** Differs by program.

Basis for selection. Interview and Wonderlic evaluation are main admission criteria.

2015-2016 Annual costs. Tuition/fees: $13,920. Room only: $6,720. **Additional information:** Estimated cost of books and supplies vary depending upon degree program. All costs are subject to change.

Financial aid. Need-based: Work-study available nights, weekends and for part-time students.

Application procedures. Admission: No deadline. $50 fee.

Academics. Credit/placement by examination: AP, CLEP.

Majors. Business: Accounting technology, hotel/motel admin. **Computer sciences:** Networking, programming. **Health services:** Dental assistant, medical assistant, veterinary technology/assistant. **Visual/performing arts:** Graphic design.

Most popular majors. Business/marketing 11%, health sciences 70%, visual/performing arts 12%.

Contact. Phone: (317) 841-6400 Toll-free number: (800) 589-6500 International Business College: Indianapolis, 7205 Shadeland Station, Indianapolis, IN 46256

ITT Technical Institute: Newburgh
Newburgh, Indiana
www.itt-tech.edu   **CB code: 7311**

▶ For-profit 2-year business and technical college
▶ Commuter campus in small town

General. Accredited by ACICS. **Enrollment:** 222 undergraduates. **Degrees:** 14 bachelor's, 92 associate awarded. **Calendar:** Quarter. **Full-time faculty:** 14 total. **Part-time faculty:** 30 total.

Basis for selection. Selective admissions to certain programs.

2015-2016 Annual costs. Per-credit-hour charge, $493; academic fee, $200. Some programs require purchase of tools, which could cost an additional $500. All costs subject to change.

Financial aid. Need-based: Work-study available nights, weekends and for part-time students.

Academics. Credit/placement by examination: AP, CLEP.

Majors. Computer sciences: Networking, programming, web page design. **Health services:** Nursing (RN). **Protective services:** Law enforcement admin. **Visual/performing arts:** Design.

Contact. Toll-free number: (800) 832-4488
ITT Technical Institute: Newburgh, 10999 Stahl Road, Newburgh, IN 47630

Ivy Tech Community College: Bloomington
Bloomington, Indiana
www.ivytech.edu   **CB code: 1455**

▶ Public 2-year community college
▶ Commuter campus in small city

General. Enrollment: 4,023 degree-seeking undergraduates. **Degrees:** 515 associate awarded. **Calendar:** Semester, extensive summer session. **Full-time faculty:** 84 total. **Part-time faculty:** 309 total.

Student profile.

Out-of-state:	1%	25 or older:	39%

Transfer out. Colleges most students transferred to 2015: Indiana University-Bloomington.

Basis for selection. Open admission, but selective for some programs. Special requirements for human services and health technology programs based on test scores and prior academic work.

2015-2016 Annual costs. Tuition/fees: $4,115; $7,992 out-of-state. Per-credit charge: $133.15 in-state; $262.4 out-of-state.

Financial aid. Need-based: Need-based aid available for part-time students. Work-study available nights, weekends and for part-time students.

Application procedures. Admission: No deadline. No application fee. Admission notification on a rolling basis. Application closing date for international students at least 60 days prior to start of semester. **Financial aid:** Closing date 3/1. FAFSA required. Applicants notified on a rolling basis starting 7/1.

Academics. Special study options: Distance learning, dual enrollment of high school students, internships, liberal arts/career combination, teacher certification program, weekend college. License preparation in nursing. **Credit/placement by examination:** AP, CLEP, institutional tests. 45 credit hours maximum toward associate degree. 15 credits must be earned in residence. **Support services:** Learning center, reduced course load, remedial instruction, tutoring.

Majors. Business: Accounting technology, administrative services, business admin, hospitality admin, logistics, transportation. **Computer sciences:** General, computer science, information systems, information technology. **Education:** General, early childhood. **General:** Electrician, maintenance, pipefitting, plumbing. **Health services:** EMT paramedic, health aide, health information technology, medical radiologic technology/radiation therapy, nursing (RN), respiratory therapy technology. **Liberal arts:** Arts/sciences, library assistant. **Parks/recreation:** Exercise sciences. **Protective services:** Criminal justice. **Visual/performing arts:** Studio arts.

Most popular majors. Business/marketing 20%, computer/information sciences 11%, engineering/engineering technologies 6%, health sciences 18%, liberal arts 28%, security/protective services 7%.

Technology on campus. 884 workstations in library, computer center. Online course registration, online library, helpline, repair service, student web hosting available.

Student life. Freshman orientation: Available. Preregistration for classes offered. **Activities:** Student government, Phi Theta Kappa, College Democrats, student leadership academy, Christian Challenge, computer club, cultural awareness.

Student services. Adult student services, career counseling, student employment services, financial aid counseling, minority student services, placement for graduates, veterans' counselor. **Physically disabled:** Services for visually, speech, hearing impaired. **Transfer:** Transfer center, transfer adviser, college fairs on campus for students transferring to 4-year colleges.

Contact. E-mail: vclay@ivytech.edu
Phone: (812) 330-6023 Toll-free number: (800) 447-0700 ext. 6350
Fax: (812) 330-106
Vonda Clay, Director of Enrollment Services, Ivy Tech Community College: Bloomington, 200 Daniels Way, Bloomington, IN 47404-1511

Ivy Tech Community College: Central Indiana
Indianapolis, Indiana
www.ivytech.edu   CB code: 1311

◗ Public 2-year community college
◗ Commuter campus in very large city

General. Founded in 1966. Regionally accredited. Branch location at Lawrence. **Enrollment:** 16,828 degree-seeking undergraduates. **Degrees:** 1,800 associate awarded. **Location:** 2 miles from downtown. **Calendar:** Semester, extensive summer session. **Full-time faculty:** 187 total. **Part-time faculty:** 749 total.

Student profile.

Out-of-state: 1% 25 or older: 49%

Transfer out. Colleges most students transferred to 2015: Indiana University-Purdue University Indianapolis, Vincennes University, Indiana University-Bloomington, Purdue University-West Lafayette, Ball State University.

Basis for selection. Open admission, but selective for some programs. Special requirements for human services and health technology programs based on test scores and prior academic work.

2015-2016 Annual costs. Tuition/fees: $4,115; $7,992 out-of-state. Per-credit charge: $133.15 in-state; $262.4 out-of-state.

Financial aid. Need-based: Need-based aid available for part-time students. Work-study available nights, weekends and for part-time students.

Application procedures. Admission: No deadline. No application fee. Admission notification on a rolling basis. Application closing date for undergraduate international students at least 60 days prior to start of semester. **Financial aid:** Closing date 3/1. FAFSA required. Applicants notified on a rolling basis starting 7/1.

Academics. Special study options: Cooperative education, distance learning, dual enrollment of high school students, ESL, internships, liberal arts/career combination, teacher certification program, weekend college. License preparation in nursing, radiology. **Credit/placement by examination:** AP, CLEP, institutional tests. 45 credit hours maximum toward associate degree. 15 credits must be earned in residence. **Support services:** GED preparation and test center, learning center, reduced course load, remedial instruction, tutoring.

Majors. Business: Accounting technology, administrative services, business admin, hospitality admin, logistics, transportation. **Computer sciences:** General, computer science, information systems, information technology. **Education:** General, early childhood. **Engineering:** Pre-engineering. **General:** Carpentry, electrician, glazier, maintenance, masonry, painting, pipefitting. **Health services:** Electroencephalograph technology, EMT paramedic, health aide, health information technology, medical assistant, nursing (RN), radiologic technology/medical imaging, respiratory therapy technology, surgical technology. **Liberal arts:** Arts/sciences, library assistant. **Protective services:** Criminal justice, homeland security. **Visual/performing arts:** Design, studio arts.

Most popular majors. Business/marketing 18%, computer/information sciences 6%, education 6%, health sciences 20%, liberal arts 17%, public administration/social services 8%, security/protective services 6%.

Technology on campus. 1,599 workstations in library, computer center. Online course registration, online library, helpline, repair service, student web hosting, wireless network available.

Student life. Freshman orientation: Available. Preregistration for classes offered. **Activities:** Student government, Phi Theta Kappa, accounting association, human service club, radiology technology club, student leadership academy, black student union, Veterans Association.

Student services. Adult student services, career counseling, student employment services, financial aid counseling, minority student services, placement for graduates, veterans' counselor. **Physically disabled:** Services for visually, speech, hearing impaired. **Transfer:** Transfer center, transfer adviser, college fairs on campus for students transferring to 4-year colleges.

Contact. E-mail: tfunk@ivytech.edu
Phone: (317) 921-4882 Toll-free number: (800) 732-1470
Fax: (317) 921-4753
Tracy Funk, Director of Admissions, Ivy Tech Community College: Central Indiana, 50 West Fall Creek Parkway North Drive, Indianapolis, IN 46208-5752

Ivy Tech Community College: Columbus
Columbus, Indiana
www.ivytech.edu   CB code: 1286

◗ Public 2-year community college
◗ Commuter campus in large town

General. Founded in 1963. Regionally accredited. **Enrollment:** 2,248 degree-seeking undergraduates. **Degrees:** 376 associate awarded. **Location:** 40 miles from Indianapolis. **Calendar:** Semester, extensive summer session. **Full-time faculty:** 53 total. **Part-time faculty:** 230 total. **Special facilities:** Visual communications gallery.

Student profile.

Out-of-state: 1% 25 or older: 45%

Transfer out. Colleges most students transferred to 2015: Indiana University-Purdue University Indianapolis, Indiana University-Bloomington, Purdue University, Vincennes University, Indiana State University.

Basis for selection. Open admission, but selective for some programs. Special requirements for human services and health technology programs based on test scores and prior academic work.

2015-2016 Annual costs. Tuition/fees: $4,115; $7,992 out-of-state. Per-credit charge: $133.15 in-state; $262.4 out-of-state.

Financial aid. Need-based: Need-based aid available for part-time students. Work-study available nights, weekends and for part-time students.

Application procedures. Admission: No deadline. No application fee. Admission notification on a rolling basis. Application closing date for international students at least 60 days prior to start of semester. **Financial aid:** Closing date 3/1. FAFSA required. Applicants notified on a rolling basis starting 7/1.

Academics. Special study options: Distance learning, dual enrollment of high school students, internships, liberal arts/career combination, teacher certification program, weekend college. License preparation in dental hygiene, nursing, paramedic, radiology. **Credit/placement by examination:** AP, CLEP, institutional tests. 45 credit hours maximum toward associate degree. 15 credits must be earned in residence. **Support services:** Learning center, reduced course load, remedial instruction, tutoring.

Majors. Business: Accounting technology, administrative services, business admin, hospitality admin, logistics. **Computer sciences:** General, computer science, information systems, information technology. **Education:** General, early childhood. **General:** Maintenance, masonry. **Health services:** EMT paramedic, health aide, health information technology, medical assistant, medical radiologic technology/radiation therapy, nursing (RN), surgical technology. **Liberal arts:** Arts/sciences, library assistant. **Protective services:** Criminal justice. **Visual/performing arts:** Design, interior design.

Most popular majors. Business/marketing 17%, computer/information sciences 7%, engineering/engineering technologies 6%, health sciences 29%, liberal arts 14%, security/protective services 6%, visual/performing arts 7%.

Technology on campus. 524 workstations in library, computer center. Online course registration, online library, helpline, repair service, student web hosting available.

Student life. Freshman orientation: Available. Preregistration for classes offered. **Activities:** Student government, student newspaper, Phi Theta Kappa, student leadership academy.

Student services. Adult student services, career counseling, student employment services, financial aid counseling, minority student services, placement for graduates, veterans' counselor. **Physically disabled:** Services for visually, speech, hearing impaired. **Transfer:** Transfer adviser, college fairs on campus for students transferring to 4-year colleges.

Contact. E-mail: adeck@ivytech.edu
Phone: (812) 374-5129 Toll-free number: (800) 922-4838
Fax: (812) 372-0311
Alisa Deck, Director of Admissions, Ivy Tech Community College: Columbus, 4475 Central Avenue, Columbus, IN 47203-1868

Ivy Tech Community College: East Central
Muncie, Indiana
www.ivytech.edu/eastcentral   CB code: 1279

◗ Public 2-year community college
◗ Commuter campus in small city

General. Founded in 1968. Regionally accredited. Campuses also at Anderson and Marion. **Enrollment:** 5,295 degree-seeking undergraduates. **Degrees:** 870 associate awarded. **Location:** 50 miles from Indianapolis. **Calendar:** Semester, extensive summer session. **Full-time faculty:** 110 total. **Part-time faculty:** 455 total.

Student profile.

Out-of-state:	1%	25 or older:	44%

Transfer out. Colleges most students transferred to 2015: Ball State University, Purdue University-West Lafayette, Indiana University-Kokomo.

Basis for selection. Open admission, but selective for some programs. Special requirements for human services and health technology programs based on test scores and prior academic work. **Adult students:** SAT/ACT scores not required.

2015-2016 Annual costs. Tuition/fees: $4,115; $7,992 out-of-state. Per-credit charge: $133.15 in-state; $262.4 out-of-state.

Financial aid. Need-based: Need-based aid available for part-time students. Work-study available nights, weekends and for part-time students. **Additional information:** Higher Education Aid (HEA), Child of Disabled/Deceased Veterans (CDV), Ivy Tech Scholarships (IVTC) and grants, vocational rehabilitation and veteran's assistance available. None require repayment.

Application procedures. Admission: No deadline. No application fee. Admission notification on a rolling basis. Application closing date for international students at least 60 days prior to start of semester. **Financial aid:** Closing date 3/1. FAFSA required. Applicants notified on a rolling basis starting 7/1.

Academics. Special study options: Distance learning, dual enrollment of high school students, internships, liberal arts/career combination, teacher certification program, weekend college. License preparation in dental hygiene, nursing, physical therapy, radiology. **Credit/placement by examination:** AP, CLEP, institutional tests. 45 credit hours maximum toward associate degree. 15 credits must be earned in residence. **Support services:** GED preparation and test center, learning center, reduced course load, remedial instruction, tutoring.

Majors. Business: Accounting technology, administrative services, business admin, hospitality admin, logistics, transportation. **Computer sciences:** General, computer science, information systems, information technology. **Education:** General, early childhood. **General:** Carpentry, electrician, maintenance, masonry, painting, pipefitting. **Health services:** Dental hygiene, health aide, health information technology, medical assistant, nursing (RN), physical therapy assistant, radiologic technology/medical imaging, respiratory therapy technology, surgical technology. **Liberal arts:** Arts/sciences, library assistant. **Protective services:** Criminal justice.

Most popular majors. Business/marketing 17%, computer/information sciences 6%, health sciences 35%, liberal arts 13%, public administration/social services 7%, security/protective services 8%.

Technology on campus. 1,481 workstations in library, computer center. Online course registration, online library, helpline, repair service, student web hosting available.

Student life. Freshman orientation: Available. Preregistration for classes offered. **Activities:** Student government, Phi Theta Kappa, Skills USA-VICA, early childhood education club, human services club, student leadership academy.

Student services. Adult student services, career counseling, student employment services, financial aid counseling, minority student services, placement for graduates, veterans' counselor. **Physically disabled:** Services for visually, speech, hearing impaired. **Transfer:** Transfer center, transfer adviser, college fairs on campus for students transferring to 4-year colleges.

Contact. E-mail: csharp@ivytech.edu
Phone: (765) 289-2291 ext. 1479 Toll-free number: (800) 589-8324
Fax: (765) 289-2292 ext. 502
Corey Sharp, Director of Enrollment Management, Ivy Tech Community College: East Central, 4301 South Cowan Road, Muncie, IN 47302-9448

Ivy Tech Community College: Kokomo
Kokomo, Indiana
www.ivytech.edu	CB code: 1329

- Public 2-year community college
- Commuter campus in large town

General. Founded in 1968. Regionally accredited. Campus also at Logansport. Branch location at Wabash. **Enrollment:** 2,557 degree-seeking undergraduates. **Degrees:** 473 associate awarded. **Location:** 50 miles from Indianapolis. **Calendar:** Semester, extensive summer session. **Full-time faculty:** 76 total. **Part-time faculty:** 253 total.

Student profile.

Out-of-state:	1%	25 or older:	56%

Transfer out. Colleges most students transferred to 2015: Indiana University-Kokomo, Purdue University-West Lafayette, Ball State University.

Basis for selection. Open admission, but selective for some programs. Special requirements for human services and health technology programs based on test scores and prior academic work.

2015-2016 Annual costs. Tuition/fees: $4,115; $7,992 out-of-state. Per-credit charge: $133.15 in-state; $262.4 out-of-state.

Financial aid. Need-based: Need-based aid available for part-time students. Work-study available nights, weekends and for part-time students.

Application procedures. Admission: No deadline. No application fee. Admission notification on a rolling basis. Application closing date for international students at least 60 days prior to start of semester. **Financial aid:** Closing date 3/1. FAFSA required. Applicants notified on a rolling basis starting 7/1.

Academics. Special study options: Distance learning, dual enrollment of high school students, independent study, internships, liberal arts/career combination, teacher certification program, weekend college. License preparation in nursing, paramedic, physical therapy. **Credit/placement by examination:** AP, CLEP, institutional tests. 45 credit hours maximum toward associate degree. 15 credits must be earned in residence. **Support services:** Learning center, reduced course load, remedial instruction, tutoring.

Majors. Business: Accounting technology, administrative services, business admin, logistics. **Communications:** Communications/speech/rhetoric. **Computer sciences:** General, computer science, information systems, information technology. **Education:** General, early childhood. **General:** Electrician, maintenance, site management. **Health services:** Dental hygiene, EMT paramedic, health aide, health information technology, medical assistant, nursing (RN), physical therapy assistant, surgical technology. **Liberal arts:** Arts/sciences, library assistant. **Protective services:** Criminal justice. **Visual/performing arts:** Design.

Most popular majors. Business/marketing 15%, computer/information sciences 6%, education 6%, health sciences 30%, liberal arts 11%, public administration/social services 8%, trade and industry 6%.

Technology on campus. 699 workstations in library, computer center. Online course registration, online library, helpline, repair service, student web hosting available.

Student life. Freshman orientation: Available. Preregistration for classes offered. **Activities:** Student government, Phi Theta Kappa, student leadership academy, business administration student organization, professional and trade organization.

Student services. Adult student services, career counseling, student employment services, financial aid counseling, minority student services, placement for graduates, veterans' counselor. **Physically disabled:** Services for visually, speech, hearing impaired. **Transfer:** Transfer adviser, college fairs on campus for students transferring to 4-year colleges.

Contact. E-mail: mfedersp@ivytech.edu
Phone: (765) 459-0561 ext. 318 Toll-free number: (800) 459-0561
Fax: (765) 454-5111
Mike Federspill, Director of Admissions, Ivy Tech Community College: Kokomo, 1815 East Morgan Street, Kokomo, IN 46903-1373

Ivy Tech Community College: Lafayette
Lafayette, Indiana
www.ivytech.edu	CB code: 1282

- Public 2-year community college
- Commuter campus in large town

General. Founded in 1968. Regionally accredited. **Enrollment:** 4,106 degree-seeking undergraduates. **Degrees:** 683 associate awarded. **Location:** 60 miles from Indianapolis. **Calendar:** Semester, extensive summer session. **Full-time faculty:** 98 total. **Part-time faculty:** 341 total. **Special facilities:** Multimedia laboratory.

Student profile.

Out-of-state: 1% **25 or older:** 39%

Transfer out. Colleges most students transferred to 2015: Purdue University-West Lafayette, Indiana University-Purdue University Indianapolis.

Basis for selection. Open admission, but selective for some programs. Special requirements for human services and health technology programs based on test scores and prior academic work.

2015-2016 Annual costs. Tuition/fees: $4,115; $7,992 out-of-state. Per-credit charge: $133.15 in-state; $262.4 out-of-state.

Financial aid. Need-based: Need-based aid available for part-time students. Work-study available nights, weekends and for part-time students.

Application procedures. Admission: No deadline. No application fee. Admission notification on a rolling basis. Application closing date for international students at least 60 days prior to start of semester. **Financial aid:** Closing date 3/1. FAFSA required. Applicants notified on a rolling basis starting 7/1.

Academics. Special study options: Distance learning, dual enrollment of high school students, internships, liberal arts/career combination, teacher certification program, weekend college. License preparation in dental hygiene, nursing. **Credit/placement by examination:** AP, CLEP, institutional tests. 45 credit hours maximum toward associate degree. 15 credits must be earned in residence. **Support services:** Learning center, reduced course load, remedial instruction, tutoring.

Majors. Biology: Biotechnology. **Business:** Accounting technology, administrative services, business admin, transportation. **Computer sciences:** General, computer science, information systems, information technology. **Education:** General, early childhood. **Engineering:** Pre-engineering. **General:** Carpentry, electrician, lineworker, maintenance, masonry, painting. **Health services:** Health aide, health information technology, medical assistant, nursing (RN), respiratory therapy technology, surgical technology. **Liberal arts:** Arts/sciences, library assistant. **Protective services:** Criminal justice.

Most popular majors. Business/marketing 16%, computer/information sciences 6%, education 6%, engineering/engineering technologies 8%, health sciences 23%, liberal arts 16%, security/protective services 7%, trade and industry 7%.

Technology on campus. 1,313 workstations in library, computer center. Online course registration, online library, helpline, repair service, student web hosting available.

Student life. Freshman orientation: Available. Preregistration for classes offered. **Activities:** Student government, Phi Theta Kappa, American Chemical Society, Dental Assistant Society, Respiratory Care Society, student leadership academy, culture club.

Student services. Adult student services, career counseling, student employment services, financial aid counseling, minority student services, placement for graduates, veterans' counselor. **Physically disabled:** Services for visually, speech, hearing impaired. **Transfer:** Transfer center, transfer adviser for students transferring to 4-year colleges.

Contact. E-mail: ihernand@ivytech.edu
Phone: (765) 269-5200 Toll-free number: (800) 669-4882 ext. 5200
Fax: (765) 772-9293
Ivan Hernandez, Director of Admissions, Ivy Tech Community College: Lafayette, 3101 South Creasy Lane, Lafayette, IN 47905-6299

Ivy Tech Community College: North Central
South Bend, Indiana
www.ivytech.edu
CB code: 1280

- Public 2-year community college
- Commuter campus in small city

General. Founded in 1968. Regionally accredited. Campuses also at Warsaw and Elkhart. **Enrollment:** 4,911 degree-seeking undergraduates. **Degrees:** 667 associate awarded. **Location:** 100 miles from Chicago. **Calendar:** Semester, extensive summer session. **Full-time faculty:** 108 total. **Part-time faculty:** 307 total.

Student profile.

Out-of-state: 2% **25 or older:** 55%

Transfer out. Colleges most students transferred to 2015: Indiana University-South Bend, Indiana University-Purdue University Fort Wayne, Purdue University-West Lafayette, Purdue University-North Central.

Basis for selection. Open admission, but selective for some programs. Special requirements for human services and health technology programs based on test scores and prior academic work. Comparative Guidance and Placement Program required for admission of allied health applicants. Interview required of allied health majors. Portfolio recommended for photographic technology and graphic arts technology majors.

High school preparation. Medical laboratory assistant program requires 1 chemistry and 1 algebra.

2015-2016 Annual costs. Tuition/fees: $4,115; $7,992 out-of-state. Per-credit charge: $133.15 in-state; $262.4 out-of-state.

Financial aid. Need-based: Need-based aid available for part-time students. Work-study available nights, weekends and for part-time students.

Application procedures. Admission: No deadline. No application fee. Admission notification on a rolling basis. **Financial aid:** Closing date 3/1. FAFSA required. Applicants notified on a rolling basis starting 7/1.

Academics. Industrial training division offers customized courses and seminars to companies and corporations in surrounding community. **Special study options:** Distance learning, dual enrollment of high school students, ESL, internships, liberal arts/career combination, teacher certification program, weekend college. License preparation in nursing. **Credit/placement by examination:** AP, CLEP, institutional tests. 45 credit hours maximum toward associate degree. 15 credits must be earned in residence. **Support services:** Learning center, reduced course load, remedial instruction, tutoring.

Majors. Business: Accounting technology, administrative services, business admin, hospitality admin, logistics, transportation. **Computer sciences:** General, computer science, information systems, information technology. **Education:** General, early childhood. **Engineering:** Pre-engineering. **General:** Carpentry, electrician, maintenance, masonry, painting, pipefitting, plumbing, roofing. **Health services:** Clinical lab technology, dental hygiene, EMT paramedic, health aide, health information technology, medical assistant, nursing (RN), respiratory therapy technology, surgical technology. **Liberal arts:** Arts/sciences, library assistant. **Protective services:** Criminal justice. **Visual/performing arts:** Design, interior design.

Most popular majors. Business/marketing 21%, computer/information sciences 7%, health sciences 29%, liberal arts 7%, public administration/social services 8%, trade and industry 9%.

Technology on campus. 1,178 workstations in library, computer center. Online course registration, online library, helpline, repair service, student web hosting available.

Student life. Freshman orientation: Available. Preregistration for classes offered. **Activities:** Student government, Phi Theta Kappa, student leadership academy, student ad club.

Student services. Adult student services, career counseling, student employment services, financial aid counseling, minority student services, placement for graduates, veterans' counselor. **Physically disabled:** Services for visually, speech, hearing impaired. **Transfer:** Transfer adviser, college fairs on campus for students transferring to 4-year colleges.

Contact. E-mail: jaustin@ivytech.edu
Phone: (574) 289-7001 Toll-free number: (888) 489-5463
Fax: (574) 236-7177
Janice Austin, Director of Admissions, Ivy Tech Community College: North Central, 220 Dean Johnson Boulevard, South Bend, IN 46601-3415

Ivy Tech Community College: Northeast
Fort Wayne, Indiana
www.ivytech.edu
CB code: 1278

- Public 2-year community college
- Commuter campus in small city

General. Founded in 1963. Regionally accredited. **Enrollment:** 7,128 degree-seeking undergraduates. **Degrees:** 823 associate awarded. **Location:** 120 miles from Indianapolis. **Calendar:** Semester, extensive summer session. **Full-time faculty:** 133 total. **Part-time faculty:** 408 total.

Student profile.

Out-of-state: 1% **25 or older:** 48%

Transfer out. Colleges most students transferred to 2015: Indiana University, Purdue University-Ft. Wayne, Ball State University.

Basis for selection. Open admission, but selective for some programs. Special requirements for human services and health technology programs based on test scores and prior academic work.

2015-2016 Annual costs. Tuition/fees: $4,115; $7,992 out-of-state. Per-credit charge: $133.15 in-state; $262.4 out-of-state.

Financial aid. Need-based: Need-based aid available for part-time students. Work-study available nights, weekends and for part-time students.

Application procedures. Admission: No deadline. No application fee. Admission notification on a rolling basis. Application closing dates for international students at least 60 days prior to start of semester. **Financial aid:** Closing date 3/1. FAFSA required. Applicants notified on a rolling basis starting 7/1.

Academics. Special study options: Distance learning, dual enrollment of high school students, ESL, internships, liberal arts/career combination, teacher certification program, weekend college. License preparation in nursing. **Credit/placement by examination:** AP, CLEP, institutional tests. 45 credit hours maximum toward associate degree. 15 credits must be completed in residence. **Support services:** GED preparation and test center, learning center, reduced course load, remedial instruction, tutoring.

Majors. Business: Accounting technology, administrative services, business admin, hospitality admin, logistics, transportation. **Computer sciences:** General, computer science, information systems, information technology. **Education:** General, early childhood. **Engineering:** Pre-engineering. **General:** Electrician, maintenance, masonry, painting, pipefitting, site management. **Health services:** EMT paramedic, health aide, health information technology, massage therapy, medical assistant, nursing (RN), respiratory therapy technology. **Liberal arts:** Arts/sciences, library assistant. **Protective services:** Criminal justice. **Visual/performing arts:** Design.

Most popular majors. Business/marketing 23%, computer/information sciences 6%, health sciences 32%, liberal arts 9%, security/protective services 6%, trade and industry 7%.

Technology on campus. 1,511 workstations in library, computer center. Online course registration, online library, helpline, repair service, student web hosting available.

Student life. Freshman orientation: Available. Preregistration for classes offered. **Activities:** Student government, student newspaper, Phi Theta Kappa, multi-cultural organization, Society of Manufacturing Engineers, student leadership academy, Association of Construction Technology Students.

Student services. Adult student services, career counseling, student employment services, financial aid counseling, minority student services, placement for graduates, veterans' counselor. **Physically disabled:** Services for visually, speech, hearing impaired. **Transfer:** Transfer center, transfer adviser, college fairs on campus for students transferring to 4-year colleges.

Contact. E-mail: rboss1@ivytech.edu
Phone: (260) 480-4221 Toll-free number: (800) 859-4882 ext. 4268
Fax: (260) 480-2053
Robyn Boss, Director of Admissions, Ivy Tech Community College: Northeast, 3800 North Anthony Boulevard, Fort Wayne, IN 46805-1489

Ivy Tech Community College: Northwest
Gary, Indiana
www.ivytech.edu   **CB code: 1281**

▶ Public 2-year community college
▶ Commuter campus in small city

General. Founded in 1968. Regionally accredited. Campuses also at East Chicago, Valparaiso, and Michigan City. **Enrollment:** 7,551 degree-seeking undergraduates; 615 non-degree-seeking students. **Degrees:** 950 associate awarded. **Location:** 30 miles from Chicago. **Calendar:** Semester, extensive summer session. **Full-time faculty:** 126 total. **Part-time faculty:** 410 total.

Student profile. Among degree-seeking undergraduates, 1,421 enrolled as first-time, first-year students.

Part-time:	65%	**Women:**	60%
Out-of-state:	1%	**25 or older:**	51%

Transfer out. Colleges most students transferred to 2015: Purdue University- Calumet, Indiana University-Northwest, Purdue University-North Central.

Basis for selection. Open admission, but selective for some programs. Special requirements for human services and health technology programs based on test scores and prior academic work.

2015-2016 Annual costs. Tuition/fees: $4,115; $7,992 out-of-state. Per-credit charge: $133.15 in-state; $262.4 out-of-state.

Financial aid. Need-based: Need-based aid available for part-time students. Work-study available nights, weekends and for part-time students.

Application procedures. Admission: No deadline. No application fee. Admission notification on a rolling basis. Application closing date for international students at least 60 days prior to start of semester. **Financial aid:** Closing date 3/1. FAFSA required. Applicants notified on a rolling basis starting 7/1.

Academics. Special study options: Distance learning, dual enrollment of high school students, internships, liberal arts/career combination, teacher certification program, weekend college. License preparation in nursing, physical therapy, real estate. **Credit/placement by examination:** AP, CLEP, institutional tests. 45 credit hours maximum toward associate degree. 15 credits must be earned in residence. **Support services:** Learning center, reduced course load, remedial instruction, tutoring.

Majors. Business: Accounting technology, administrative services, business admin, hospitality admin, logistics, transportation. **Computer sciences:** General, computer science, information systems, information technology. **Education:** General, early childhood. **Engineering:** General. **General:** Carpentry, electrician, maintenance, masonry, painting, pipefitting, site management. **Health services:** EMT paramedic, health aide, health information technology, medical assistant, nursing (RN), physical therapy assistant, radiologic technology/medical imaging, respiratory therapy technology, surgical technology. **Liberal arts:** Arts/sciences, library assistant. **Protective services:** Criminal justice.

Most popular majors. Business/marketing 18%, engineering/engineering technologies 9%, health sciences 25%, liberal arts 6%, security/protective services 6%, trade and industry 23%.

Technology on campus. 419 workstations in library, computer center. Online course registration, online library, helpline, repair service, student web hosting, wireless network available.

Student life. Freshman orientation: Available. Preregistration for classes offered. **Activities:** Student government, Phi Theta Kappa, computer club, business club, culinary arts club, medical assistants, mortuary science club, student leadership academy, early childhood development club, nursing club.

Student services. Adult student services, career counseling, student employment services, financial aid counseling, minority student services, placement for graduates, veterans' counselor. **Physically disabled:** Services for visually, speech, hearing impaired. **Transfer:** Transfer adviser, college fairs on campus for students transferring to 4-year colleges.

Contact. E-mail: jpjohnso@ivytech.edu
Phone: (219) 981-1111 ext. 2216 Toll-free number: (888) 489-5463
Fax: (219) 981-4415
John Johnson, Director of Admissions, Ivy Tech Community College: Northwest, 1440 East 35th Avenue, Gary, IN 46409-1499

Ivy Tech Community College: Richmond
Richmond, Indiana
www.ivytech.edu   **CB code: 1283**

▶ Public 2-year community college
▶ Commuter campus in large town

General. Founded in 1968. Regionally accredited. Branch location at Connersville. **Enrollment:** 1,980 degree-seeking undergraduates. **Degrees:** 373 associate awarded. **Location:** 70 miles from Indianapolis; 45 miles from Dayton, Ohio. **Calendar:** Semester, extensive summer session. **Full-time faculty:** 40 total. **Part-time faculty:** 158 total. **Special facilities:** Student-operated restaurant.

Transfer out. Colleges most students transferred to 2015: Indiana University East, Purdue University-West Lafayette.

Basis for selection. Open admission, but selective for some programs. Special requirements for human services and health technology programs based on test scores and prior academic work.

2015-2016 Annual costs. Tuition/fees: $4,115; $7,992 out-of-state. Per-credit charge: $133.15 in-state; $262.4 out-of-state.

Financial aid. Need-based: Need-based aid available for part-time students. Work-study available nights, weekends and for part-time students.

Application procedures. Admission: No deadline. No application fee. Admission notification on a rolling basis. Application closing date for international students at least 60 days prior to start of semester. **Financial aid:** Closing date 3/1. FAFSA required. Applicants notified on a rolling basis starting 7/1.

Academics. Special study options: Distance learning, dual enrollment of high school students, independent study, internships, liberal arts/career combination, teacher certification program, weekend college. License preparation in nursing. **Credit/placement by examination:** AP, CLEP, institutional tests. 45 credit hours maximum toward associate degree. 15 credits must be earned in residence. **Support services:** Learning center, reduced course load, remedial instruction, tutoring.

Majors. Business: Accounting technology, administrative services, business admin, logistics. **Computer sciences:** General, computer science, information systems, information technology. **Education:** General, early childhood. **General:** Electrician, maintenance, plumbing. **Health services:** EMT paramedic, health aide, health information technology, medical assistant, nursing (RN), radiologic technology/medical imaging, respiratory therapy technology. **Liberal arts:** Arts/sciences, library assistant. **Protective services:** Criminal justice.

Most popular majors. Business/marketing 16%, health sciences 43%, liberal arts 13%.

Technology on campus. 857 workstations in library, computer center. Online course registration, online library, helpline, repair service, student web hosting available.

Student life. Freshman orientation: Available. Preregistration for classes offered. **Activities:** Student government, Phi Theta Kappa, Business Professionals of America, student computer association, Student Chapter of the Institute of Management Accounts, Refrigeration Service Engineers Society, student leadership academy, multicultural student organization.

Student services. Adult student services, career counseling, student employment services, financial aid counseling, minority student services, placement for graduates, veterans' counselor. **Physically disabled:** Services for visually, speech, hearing impaired. **Transfer:** Transfer adviser for students transferring to 4-year colleges.

Contact. E-mail: crethlake@ivytech.edu
Phone: (765) 966-2656 ext. 1212 Toll-free number: (800) 659-4562
Fax: (765) 962-8741
Christine Seger, Director of Admissions, Ivy Tech Community College: Richmond, 2357 Chester Boulevard, Richmond, IN 47374-1298

Ivy Tech Community College: South Central
Sellersburg, Indiana
www.ivytech.edu   CB code: 1273

- Public 2-year community college
- Commuter campus in small town

General. Founded in 1968. Regionally accredited. **Enrollment:** 4,090 degree-seeking undergraduates. **Degrees:** 495 associate awarded. **Location:** 10 miles from Louisville, Kentucky. **Calendar:** Semester, extensive summer session. **Full-time faculty:** 58 total. **Part-time faculty:** 220 total.

Student profile.

Out-of-state:	27%	25 or older: 55%

Transfer out. Colleges most students transferred to 2015: Indiana University Southeast.

Basis for selection. Open admission, but selective for some programs. Special requirements for human services and health technology programs based on test scores and prior academic work.

2015-2016 Annual costs. Tuition/fees: $4,115; $7,992 out-of-state. Per-credit charge: $133.15 in-state; $262.4 out-of-state.

Financial aid. Need-based: Need-based aid available for part-time students. Work-study available nights, weekends and for part-time students.

Application procedures. Admission: No deadline. No application fee. Admission notification on a rolling basis. Application closing date for international students at least 60 days prior to start of semester. **Financial aid:** Closing date 3/1. FAFSA required. Applicants notified on a rolling basis starting 7/1.

Academics. Special study options: Cooperative education, distance learning, dual enrollment of high school students, internships, liberal arts/career combination, teacher certification program, weekend college. License preparation in nursing, real estate. **Credit/placement by examination:** AP, CLEP, institutional tests. 45 credit hours maximum toward associate degree. 15 credits must be earned in residence. **Support services:** GED preparation and test center, learning center, reduced course load, remedial instruction, tutoring.

Majors. Business: Accounting technology, administrative services, business admin, logistics. **Computer sciences:** General, computer science, information systems, information technology. **Education:** General, early childhood. **General:** Carpentry, electrician, maintenance, masonry, pipefitting. **Health services:** Clinical lab technology, EMT paramedic, health aide, medical assistant, nursing (RN), radiologic technology/medical imaging, respiratory therapy technology. **Liberal arts:** Arts/sciences, library assistant. **Protective services:** Criminal justice. **Visual/performing arts:** Design.

Most popular majors. Business/marketing 12%, computer/information sciences 6%, health sciences 29%, liberal arts 11%, security/protective services 7%, trade and industry 16%.

Technology on campus. 505 workstations in library, computer center. Online course registration, online library, helpline, repair service, student web hosting available.

Student life. Freshman orientation: Mandatory. Preregistration for classes offered. **Activities:** Student government, student newspaper, Phi Theta Kappa, art club, Christian Student Fellowship, C.A.R.E. Club, ASN Club, Business Professionals of America, human services club, computer information club, student leadership academy.

Student services. Career counseling, student employment services, financial aid counseling, minority student services, placement for graduates, veterans' counselor. **Transfer:** Transfer center, transfer adviser, college fairs on campus for students transferring to 4-year colleges.

Contact. E-mail: bharris88@ivytech.edu
Phone: (812) 246-3301 ext. 4136 Toll-free number: (800) 321-9021
Fax: (812) 246-9905
Ben Harris, Director of Enrollment Services, Ivy Tech Community College: South Central, 8204 Highway 311, Sellersburg, IN 47172-1897

Ivy Tech Community College: Southeast
Madison, Indiana
www.ivytech.edu   CB code: 1334

- Public 2-year community college
- Commuter campus in large town

General. Founded in 1968. Regionally accredited. Branch in Lawrenceburg. **Enrollment:** 1,849 degree-seeking undergraduates. **Degrees:** 298 associate awarded. **Location:** 46 miles from Columbus, Ohio; 88 miles from Indianapolis. **Calendar:** Semester, extensive summer session. **Full-time faculty:** 49 total. **Part-time faculty:** 177 total. **Special facilities:** Gaming training center in Aurora, Indiana.

Transfer out. Colleges most students transferred to 2015: Indiana University-Southeast.

Basis for selection. Open admission, but selective for some programs. Special requirements for human services and health technology programs based on test scores and prior academic work.

2015-2016 Annual costs. Tuition/fees: $4,115; $7,992 out-of-state. Per-credit charge: $133.15 in-state; $262.4 out-of-state.

Financial aid. Need-based: Need-based aid available for part-time students. Work-study available nights, weekends and for part-time students.

Application procedures. Admission: No deadline. No application fee. Admission notification on a rolling basis. Application closing date for international students at least 60 days prior to start of semester. **Financial aid:** Closing date 3/1. FAFSA required. Applicants notified on a rolling basis starting 7/1.

Academics. Special study options: Distance learning, dual enrollment of high school students, internships, liberal arts/career combination, teacher certification program, weekend college. License preparation in nursing. **Credit/placement by examination:** AP, CLEP, institutional tests. 45 credit hours maximum toward associate degree. 15 credit hours must be earned in residence. **Support services:** Learning center, reduced course load, remedial instruction, tutoring.

Majors. Business: Accounting technology, administrative services, business admin, logistics. **Computer sciences:** General, computer science, information systems, information technology. **Education:** General, early childhood. **Health services:** Health aide, health information technology, medical assistant, nursing (RN), radiologic technology/medical imaging. **Liberal arts:** Arts/sciences, library assistant. **Protective services:** Criminal justice.

Most popular majors. Business/marketing 18%, education 6%, health sciences 42%, liberal arts 10%, security/protective services 9%.

Technology on campus. 710 workstations in library, computer center. Online course registration, online library, helpline, repair service, student web hosting available.

Student life. Freshman orientation: Available. Preregistration for classes offered. **Activities:** Student government, Phi Theta Kappa, student leadership academy, computer club, fitness club.

Student services. Career counseling, student employment services, financial aid counseling, minority student services, placement for graduates, veterans' counselor. **Physically disabled:** Services for visually, speech, hearing impaired. **Transfer:** Transfer adviser, college fairs on campus for students transferring to 4-year colleges.

Contact. E-mail: chutcher@ivytech.edu
Phone: (812) 265-2580 ext. 4142 Toll-free number: (800) 403-2190
Fax: (812) 265-4028
Cindy Hutcherson, Assistant Director of Admission/Career Services, Ivy Tech Community College: Southeast, 590 Ivy Tech Drive, Madison, IN 47250-1881

Ivy Tech Community College: Southwest
Evansville, Indiana
www.ivytech.edu   **CB code: 1277**

- Public 2-year community college
- Commuter campus in small city

General. Founded in 1968. Regionally accredited. Branch location at Tell City. **Enrollment:** 4,260 degree-seeking undergraduates. **Degrees:** 747 associate awarded. **Location:** 180 miles from Indianapolis; 112 miles from Louisville, Kentucky. **Calendar:** Semester, extensive summer session. **Full-time faculty:** 85 total. **Part-time faculty:** 259 total. **Special facilities:** Plastics lab, computer integrated manufacturing lab.

Student profile.

Out-of-state: 1%   **25 or older:**   54%

Transfer out. Colleges most students transferred to 2015: University of Southern Indiana, Vincennes University, Indiana State University.

Basis for selection. Open admission, but selective for some programs. Special requirements for human services and health technology programs based on test scores and prior academic work.

2015-2016 Annual costs. Tuition/fees: $4,115; $7,992 out-of-state. Per-credit charge: $133.15 in-state; $262.4 out-of-state.

Financial aid. Need-based: Need-based aid available for part-time students. Work-study available nights, weekends and for part-time students.

Application procedures. Admission: No deadline. No application fee. Admission notification on a rolling basis. Application closing date for international students at least 60 days prior to start of semester. **Financial aid:** Closing date 3/1. FAFSA required. Applicants notified on a rolling basis starting 7/1.

Academics. Special study options: Cooperative education, distance learning, dual enrollment of high school students, independent study, internships, liberal arts/career combination, teacher certification program, weekend college. License preparation in nursing, paramedic. **Credit/placement by examination:** AP, CLEP, institutional tests. 45 credit hours maximum toward associate degree. 15 credit hours must be earned in residence. **Support services:** Learning center, reduced course load, remedial instruction, tutoring.

Majors. Biology: Biotechnology. **Business:** Accounting technology, administrative services, business admin, hospitality admin, logistics. **Computer sciences:** General, computer science, information systems, information technology. **Education:** General, early childhood. **Engineering:** Pre-engineering. **General:** Carpentry, electrician, maintenance, masonry, painting, pipefitting, site management. **Health services:** EMT paramedic, health aide, health information technology, medical assistant, nursing (RN), surgical technology. **Liberal arts:** Arts/sciences, library assistant. **Protective services:** Criminal justice. **Visual/performing arts:** Design, interior design.

Most popular majors. Business/marketing 17%, computer/information sciences 6%, education 8%, engineering/engineering technologies 7%, health sciences 23%, liberal arts 7%, trade and industry 17%.

Technology on campus. 1,021 workstations in library, computer center. Online course registration, online library, helpline, repair service, student web hosting available.

Student life. Freshman orientation: Available. Preregistration for classes offered. **Housing:** Housing available at University of Southern Indiana. **Activities:** Student government, Phi Theta Kappa, American Institute of Architectural Students, National Association of Industrial Technicians, International Association of Administrative Professionals, human services club, student leadership academy, art and design club.

Student services. Adult student services, career counseling, student employment services, financial aid counseling, minority student services, placement for graduates, veterans' counselor. **Physically disabled:** Services for visually, speech, hearing impaired. **Transfer:** Transfer adviser, college fairs on campus for students transferring to 4-year colleges.

Contact. E-mail: ajohnson@ivytech.edu
Phone: (812) 429-1430 Toll-free number: (888) 489-5463
Fax: (812) 429-9878
Denise Johnson-Kincaid, Director of Admissions, Ivy Tech Community College: Southwest, 3501 First Avenue, Evansville, IN 47710-3398

Ivy Tech Community College: Wabash Valley
Terre Haute, Indiana
www.ivytech.edu   **CB code: 1284**

- Public 2-year community college
- Commuter campus in small city

General. Founded in 1966. Regionally accredited. Branch location at Greencastle. **Enrollment:** 3,247 degree-seeking undergraduates. **Degrees:** 583 associate awarded. **Location:** 80 miles from Indianapolis. **Calendar:** Semester, extensive summer session. **Full-time faculty:** 93 total. **Part-time faculty:** 189 total. **Special facilities:** Plastics productivity center.

Student profile.

Out-of-state: 3%   **25 or older:**   48%

Transfer out. Colleges most students transferred to 2015: Indiana State University, Vincennes University, Purdue University-West Lafayette.

Basis for selection. Open admission, but selective for some programs. Special requirements for human services and health technology programs based on test scores and prior academic work.

2015-2016 Annual costs. Tuition/fees: $4,115; $7,992 out-of-state. Per-credit charge: $133.15 in-state; $262.4 out-of-state.

Financial aid. Need-based: Need-based aid available for part-time students. Work-study available nights, weekends and for part-time students.

Application procedures. Admission: No deadline. No application fee. Admission notification on a rolling basis. Application closing date for international students is at least 60 days prior to start of semester. **Financial aid:** Closing date 3/1. FAFSA required. Applicants notified on a rolling basis starting 7/1.

Academics. Special study options: Distance learning, dual enrollment of high school students, internships, liberal arts/career combination, teacher certification program, weekend college. License preparation in aviation, nursing, paramedic, radiology. **Credit/placement by examination:** AP, CLEP, institutional tests. 45 credit hours maximum toward associate degree. 15 credits must be earned in residence. **Support services:** Learning center, reduced course load, remedial instruction, tutoring.

Majors. Business: Accounting technology, administrative services, business admin, logistics, transportation. **Computer sciences:** General, computer science, information systems, information technology. **Education:** General, early childhood. **General:** Carpentry, electrician, maintenance, masonry, painting, pipefitting. **Health services:** Clinical lab technology, health aide, health information technology, medical assistant, nursing (RN), radiologic technology/medical imaging, respiratory therapy technology, surgical technology. **Liberal arts:** Arts/sciences, library assistant. **Protective services:** Criminal justice. **Visual/performing arts:** Design.

Most popular majors. Business/marketing 14%, engineering/engineering technologies 7%, health sciences 36%, liberal arts 8%, trade and industry 8%.

Technology on campus. 1,589 workstations in library, computer center. Online course registration, online library, helpline, repair service, student web hosting, wireless network available.

Student life. Freshman orientation: Available. Preregistration for classes offered. **Activities:** Student government, Phi Theta Kappa, student leadership academy, practical nurses class organization.

Student services. Adult student services, career counseling, student employment services, financial aid counseling, minority student services, on-campus daycare, placement for graduates, veterans' counselor. **Physically disabled:** Services for visually, speech, hearing impaired. **Transfer:** Transfer center, transfer adviser, college fairs on campus for students transferring to 4-year colleges.

Contact. E-mail: mfisher@ivytech.edu
Phone: (812) 298-2300 Toll-free number: (800) 377-4882
Fax: (812) 299-5723
Michael Fisher, Director of Admissions, Ivy Tech Community College: Wabash Valley, 8000 South Education Drive, Terre Haute, IN 47802-4898

Kaplan College: Hammond
Hammond, Indiana
www.kaplan.com   CB code: 2461

- For-profit 2-year business and technical college
- Commuter campus in small city
- Interview required

General. Founded in 1969. Accredited by ACICS. Branch campus in Merrillville. **Enrollment:** 299 undergraduates. **Degrees:** 3 associate awarded. **Location:** 30 miles from Chicago, 15 miles from Merrillville. **Calendar:** Quarter, extensive summer session. **Full-time faculty:** 7 total. **Part-time faculty:** 20 total.

Basis for selection. Personal interview with admissions representative and passing score on entrance examination required.

2015-2016 Annual costs. Additional information: Applied Business Fundamentals: $11,010. Basic Life Support for Healthcare Providers (CPR): $75. Clinical Massage Therapy: $16,285.70. Dental Assistant: $14,930. Medical Assistant: $16,285. Medical Billing and Coding Specialist: $16,075. OSHA 30 Construction: $810. OSHA 10 General Industry: $310. OSHA 30 General Industry: $810. Personal Trainer Certification: $802.97. Spanish for Healthcare Workers: $510.

Financial aid. Need-based: Work-study available nights, weekends and for part-time students.

Application procedures. Admission: No deadline. $10 fee. Admission notification on a rolling basis. **Financial aid:** No deadline. FAFSA required. Applicants notified on a rolling basis.

Academics. Special study options: Internships. **Credit/placement by examination:** AP, CLEP, institutional tests. 24 credit hours maximum toward associate degree. Institutional placement test score must be at least 81%. **Support services:** Remedial instruction, study skills assistance, tutoring.

Majors. Health services: Massage therapy, medical assistant.

Most popular majors. Business/marketing 48%, computer/information sciences 52%.

Technology on campus. 70 workstations in computer center.

Student life. Activities: Student newspaper.

Student services. Career counseling, student employment services, personal counseling, placement for graduates. **Transfer:** Pre-admission transcript evaluation for new students.

Contact. Phone: (219) 844-0100 Fax: (219) 844-0105
Rodger Schilling, Admissions Director, Kaplan College: Hammond, 7833 Indianapolis Boulevard, Hammond, IN 46324

Kaplan College: Indianapolis
Indianapolis, Indiana
www.kaplancollege.com   CB code: 7700

- For-profit 2-year health science and nursing college
- Commuter campus in very large city
- Application essay, interview required

General. Accredited by ACCSC. **Enrollment:** 501 undergraduates. **Degrees:** 21 associate awarded. **Calendar:** Differs by program. **Full-time faculty:** 8 total. **Part-time faculty:** 15 total.

Basis for selection. Open admission, but selective for some programs. Interview most important. Class rank, school record, recommendations, standardized test scores, and essay also important.

2015-2016 Annual costs. Criminal Justice: $31,365. Dental Assistant: $16,450. Electrical Technician: $21,904. Medical Assistant: $16,465. Medical Office Specialist: $16,735. Practical Nursing: $23,340. Spanish for Healthcare Workers: $510.

Financial aid. All financial aid based on need. Work-study available nights, weekends and for part-time students.

Application procedures. Admission: No deadline. $10 fee. Admission notification on a rolling basis.

Academics. Special study options: Accelerated study, internships. **Credit/placement by examination:** AP, CLEP.

Technology on campus. 30 workstations in library, computer center.

Student services. Financial aid counseling, placement for graduates.

Contact. E-mail: rmagaruh@kaplan.edu
Phone: (317) 299-6001 Fax: (317) 298-6342
Jerry Rasberry, Director of Admissions, Kaplan College: Indianapolis, 7302 Woodland Drive, Indianapolis, IN 46278-1736

Lincoln College of Technology: Indianapolis
Indianapolis, Indiana
www.lincolntech.com   CB code: 3058

- For-profit 2-year technical college
- Very large city

General. Accredited by ACCSC. **Enrollment:** 1,199 undergraduates. **Degrees:** 192 associate awarded. **Calendar:** Differs by program. **Full-time faculty:** 39 total. **Part-time faculty:** 9 total.

Basis for selection. Open admission.

2015-2016 Annual costs. Diploma programs; $8,107-$31,967. Certificate programs; $9,850-$14,843. Associate Degree Programs; $28,510-$36,025. Tuition, fees, books, uniforms, and tools included in program cost. All costs are subject to change.

Financial aid. Need-based: Work-study available nights, weekends and for part-time students.

Application procedures. Admission: No deadline. $100 fee.

Academics. Credit/placement by examination: AP, CLEP.

Contact. Phone: (317) 632-5553 Toll-free number: (800) 554-4465
Fax: (317) 634-1089
David Cahill, Vice President of Admissions, Lincoln College of Technology: Indianapolis, 7225 Winton Drive, Building 128, Indianapolis, IN 46268

Mid-America College of Funeral Service
Jeffersonville, Indiana
www.mid-america.edu   CB code: 0644

- Private 2-year school of mortuary science
- Commuter campus in large town

General. Founded in 1905. **Enrollment:** 60 undergraduates. **Degrees:** 11 bachelor's, 35 associate awarded. **Location:** 5 miles from Louisville, KY. **Calendar:** Quarter. **Full-time faculty:** 4 total. **Part-time faculty:** 3 total.

Basis for selection. Open admission. **Home schooled:** Transcript of courses and grades required.

2015-2016 Annual costs. Personal expenses: $2,520.

Financial aid. Need-based: Work-study available nights, weekends and for part-time students.

Application procedures. Admission: No deadline. $50 fee. Admission notification on a rolling basis. **Financial aid:** No deadline. FAFSA required. Applicants notified on a rolling basis.

Academics. Credit/placement by examination: AP, CLEP.

Technology on campus. 15 workstations in library, computer center.

Student life. Activities: Student government.

Student services. Student employment services, personal counseling, placement for graduates. **Transfer:** Pre-admission transcript evaluation for new students.

Contact. E-mail: macfs@mindspring.com
Phone: (812) 288-8878 Toll-free number: (800) 221-6158
Fax: (812) 288-5942
Amanda Christiansen, Director of Admissions, Mid-America College of Funeral Service, 3111 Hamburg Pike, Jeffersonville, IN 47130

Vincennes University
Vincennes, Indiana
www.vinu.edu

CB member
CB code: 1877

▶ Public 2-year junior college
▶ Residential campus in large town

General. Founded in 1801. Regionally accredited. Additional campuses/sites: Center for technology, innovation, and manufacturing at Jasper; aviation technology center at the Indianapolis International Airport; American Sign Language program at Indiana School for the Deaf; Indiana Center for Applied Technology; Gibson County Center for Advanced Manufacturing and Logistics; Plainfield logistics training and education center. **Enrollment:** 7,940 degree-seeking undergraduates; 10,771 non-degree-seeking students. **Degrees:** 152 bachelor's, 1,708 associate awarded. **ROTC:** Army, Air Force. **Location:** 55 miles from Evansville; 120 miles from Indianapolis. **Calendar:** Semester, extensive summer session. **Full-time faculty:** 226 total; 4% minority, 47% women. **Part-time faculty:** 1,064 total; 9% minority, 43% women. **Class size:** 74% < 20, 26% 20-39, less than 1% 40-49, less than 1% 50-99. **Special facilities:** Performing arts center, center for art and design, center for applied technology, physical education complex, student recreation and aquatics center, center for science, engineering, and mathematics. **Partnerships:** Formal partnerships with Toyota/TMMI, Hurco, Lincoln Electric, ABB Robotics, John Deere, Haas, Subaru/SIA, Associated Builders and Contractors, and Kimball International.

Student profile. Among degree-seeking undergraduates, 2,889 enrolled as first-time, first-year students.

Part-time:	35%	Hispanic/Latino:	3%
Out-of-state:	5%	Multi-racial, non-Hispanic:	3%
Women:	43%	International:	1%
African American:	12%	25 or older:	14%
Asian American:	1%	Live on campus:	41%

Transfer out. Colleges most students transferred to 2015: Indiana University, Indiana State University, Purdue University, University of Southern Indiana, Ball State University.

Basis for selection. Open admission, but selective for some programs. Admission to health occupation programs is based primarily on high school transcripts, test scores, school and community activities, and special talents/skills. Audition required of music majors. Portfolio recommended for fine arts, commercial art, design majors, and graduates of non-traditional high schools. **Adult students:** SAT/ACT scores not required. **Home schooled:** Statement describing home school structure and mission, transcript of courses and grades required. Documentation should include course/curriculum descriptions and an academic portfolio. **Learning Disabled:** Students requesting special accommodations required to submit psychometric testing indicating diagnosis of a specific disability along with a list of any special services required.

High school preparation. College-preparatory program recommended. Recommended units include English 4, mathematics 3, social studies 2, history 2, science 3 (laboratory 2) and foreign language 2.

2015-2016 Annual costs. Tuition/fees: $5,374; $12,710 out-of-state. Per-credit charge: $171.14 in-state; $415.62 out-of-state. Room/board: $8,732. Books/supplies: $1,248. Personal expenses: $1,076. **Additional information:** Students from Illinois are charged the in-state tuition rate.

2014-2015 Financial aid. Need-based: 2,389 full-time freshmen applied for aid; 2,234 deemed to have need; 2,234 received aid. 51% of total undergraduate aid awarded as scholarships/grants, 49% as loans/jobs. Need-based aid available for part-time students. Work-study available nights, weekends

and for part-time students. **Non-need-based:** Scholarships awarded for academics, art, athletics, job skills, leadership, music/drama, state residency.

Application procedures. Admission: No deadline. $20 fee, may be waived for applicants with need. Admission notification on a rolling basis. **Financial aid:** Priority date 3/1; no closing date. FAFSA required. Applicants notified on a rolling basis starting 5/1; must reply by 8/24.

Academics. The College of Extended studies offers 27 online degree programs and VU's Military Education Program is available at over 40 sites across the US. **Special study options:** Accelerated study, distance learning, double major, dual enrollment of high school students, ESL, external degree, honors, independent study, internships. Bachelor's degree programs available on campus. License preparation in aviation, nursing, paramedic, radiology, real estate. **Credit/placement by examination:** AP, CLEP, IB, institutional tests. **Support services:** GED test center, learning center, pre-admission summer program, reduced course load, remedial instruction, study skills assistance, tutoring, writing center. Student Success Center focused on student retention and outreach strategies.

Honors college/program. Have a minimum 1100 SAT (exclusive of Writing) or 25 ACT score, leadership qualities, writing sample, 3 references. 20 students admitted for fall.

Majors. Biology: General, biochemistry, biotechnology. **Business:** General, accounting technology, administrative services, business admin, fashion, hospitality admin, hotel/motel admin, logistics. **Communications:** Journalism, photojournalism, public relations. **Communications technology:** Graphic/printing, radio/TV, recording arts. **Computer sciences:** General, computer science, networking, programming, webmaster. **Conservation:** General. **Education:** Art, business, chemistry, early childhood, elementary, English, family/consumer sciences, health, mathematics, music, physical, secondary, special ed, speech, technology/industrial arts. **Engineering:** Agricultural, civil, electrical, mechanical, surveying. **English:** English lit. **Foreign languages:** General, American Sign Language. **Health services:** Art therapy, dietetics, EMT paramedic, environmental health, health information technology, medical radiologic technology/radiation therapy, nursing (RN), pharmacy assistant, physical therapy assistant, predental, premedicine, prepharmacy, preveterinary, surgical technology. **History:** General. **Human services:** General, social work. **Liberal arts:** Arts/sciences. **Math:** General. **Parks/recreation:** Health/fitness, sports admin. **Philosophy/religion:** Philosophy. **Physical sciences:** Chemistry, geology, physics. **Protective services:** Firefighting, police science, security management, security services. **Psychology:** General. **Social sciences:** General, anthropology, economics, geography, political science, sociology. **Visual/performing arts:** Art, commercial/advertising art, dramatic, music performance, theater design. **Work/family studies:** General, child care management.

Most popular majors. Business/marketing 8%, engineering/engineering technologies 8%, health sciences 12%, liberal arts 33%, security/protective services 6%, trade and industry 10%.

Technology on campus. 1,500 workstations in dormitories, library, computer center, student center. Dormitories wired for high-speed internet access and linked to campus network. Commuter students can connect to campus network. Online library, wireless network available.

Student life. Freshman orientation: Available. Preregistration for classes offered. Held the weekend prior to first day of classes; includes study skills, social activities, both student and parent sessions, tours, move-in, and entertainment. **Policies:** Tobacco use is only permitted in designated areas. Facilities and grounds are tobacco-free zones. **Housing:** Coed dorms, single-sex dorms, special housing for disabled, apartments, cooperative housing, fraternity/sorority housing, wellness housing available. $150 partly refundable deposit. **Activities:** Bands, campus ministries, choral groups, dance, drama, international student organizations, literary magazine, music ensembles, musical theater, radio station, student government, student newspaper, TV station, Black Male Initiative, College Republicans, Christian Campus Fellowship, Democrat Club, Today's Black Women, Women of Essence and Gospel Choir, Embracing Latino Heritage, VU Pride (GLBT).

Athletics. NJCAA. **Intercollegiate:** Baseball M, basketball, bowling, cheerleading, cross-country, golf M, track and field, volleyball W. **Intramural:** Badminton, baseball M, basketball, bowling, cross-country, football (non-tackle) M, golf, gymnastics, handball, racquetball, skiing, softball, swimming, table tennis, track and field, ultimate frisbee, volleyball, wrestling M. **Team name:** Trailblazers.

Student services. Adult student services, alcohol/substance abuse counseling, chaplain/spiritual director, career counseling, services for economically disadvantaged, student employment services, financial aid counseling, health services, minority student services, personal counseling, placement for graduates, veterans' counselor. **Physically disabled:** Services for visually, speech, hearing impaired. **Transfer:** Pre-admission transcript evaluation for new students. Transfer adviser for students transferring to 4-year colleges.

Contact. E-mail: vuadmit@vinu.edu
Phone: (812) 888-4313 Toll-free number: (800) 742-9198
Fax: (812) 888-5707
Heidi Whitehead, Director of Admissions, Vincennes University, 1002
North First Street, Vincennes, IN 47591

Iowa

Clinton Community College
Clinton, Iowa
www.eicc.edu
CB code: 6100

▶ Public 2-year community college
▶ Commuter campus in large town

General. Founded in 1946. Regionally accredited. **Enrollment:** 1,909 undergraduates. **Degrees:** 153 associate awarded. **Location:** 40 miles from Davenport, 140 miles from Chicago. **Calendar:** Semester, extensive summer session. **Full-time faculty:** 57 total. **Part-time faculty:** 89 total. **Class size:** 80% < 20, 19% 20-39, less than 1% 40-49, less than 1% 50-99. **Special facilities:** Arboretum.

Transfer out. Colleges most students transferred to 2015: Ashford University, University of Iowa, Iowa State University, University of Northern Iowa, St. Ambrose University.

Basis for selection. Open admission, but selective for some programs. Special requirements for nursing program.

High school preparation. College-preparatory program recommended.

2015-2016 Annual costs. Tuition/fees: $4,200; $6,210 out-of-state. Per-credit charge: $140 in-state; $207 out-of-state. Books/supplies: $1,600. Personal expenses: $3,042. **Additional information:** Online course tuition is $162 per credit hour. Tuition for nearby Illinois counties is $162 per credit hour.

Financial aid. Need-based: Work-study available nights, weekends and for part-time students.

Application procedures. Admission: No deadline. No application fee. Admission notification on a rolling basis beginning on or about 9/1. **Financial aid:** Priority date 4/1; no closing date. FAFSA, institutional form required. Applicants notified on a rolling basis starting 5/15; must reply within 2 week(s) of notification.

Academics. Special study options: Accelerated study, cooperative education, cross-registration, distance learning, double major, dual enrollment of high school students, ESL, honors, independent study, study abroad, weekend college. License preparation in nursing, paramedic, real estate. **Credit/placement by examination:** AP, CLEP, institutional tests. 30 credit hours maximum toward associate degree. **Support services:** GED preparation and test center, learning center, reduced course load, remedial instruction, study skills assistance, tutoring, writing center.

Majors. Biology: General. **Business:** Administrative services, business admin. **Communications:** Journalism. **Communications technology:** Graphic/printing, graphics. **Computer sciences:** Applications programming, networking, web page design. **Education:** General. **English:** English lit. **Health services:** EMT paramedic, nursing (RN). **History:** General. **Liberal arts:** Arts/sciences. **Math:** General. **Physical sciences:** General. **Protective services:** Firefighting, police science. **Psychology:** General. **Social sciences:** General.

Most popular majors. Engineering/engineering technologies 9%, health sciences 18%, liberal arts 61%.

Technology on campus. 55 workstations in library, computer center. Commuter students can connect to campus network. Online course registration, helpline, wireless network available.

Student life. Freshman orientation: Mandatory. Preregistration for classes offered. **Activities:** Drama, literary magazine, student government, student newspaper, Phi Beta Lambda, Phi Theta Kappa, student senate, peer ambassadors, fine arts club, S.N.A.P., drafting club, nursing club, graphic arts/printer club.

Athletics. Intercollegiate: Volleyball W. **Intramural:** Basketball, bowling, softball, table tennis, tennis, volleyball. **Team name:** Cougars.

Student services. Career counseling, student employment services, financial aid counseling, personal counseling, placement for graduates, veterans' counselor. **Physically disabled:** Services for visually, speech, hearing impaired. **Transfer:** Transfer adviser, college fairs on campus for students transferring to 4-year colleges.

Contact. E-mail: eiccinfo@eicc.edu
Phone: (888) 336-3907 Toll-free number: (888) 336-3907
Fax: (563) 244-7107
Erin Snyder, Director of Enrollment Management, Clinton Community College, 1000 Lincoln Boulevard, Clinton, IA 52732

Des Moines Area Community College
Ankeny, Iowa
www.dmacc.edu
CB code: 6177

▶ Public 2-year community college
▶ Commuter campus in large town

General. Founded in 1966. Regionally accredited. Multilocation institution with campuses at Boone, Des Moines, West Des Moines, Carroll, and Newton. Ankeny campus is primary location and administrative center. **Enrollment:** 12,798 degree-seeking undergraduates; 2,136 non-degree-seeking students. **Degrees:** 2,512 associate awarded. **Location:** 15 miles from downtown Des Moines, 25 miles from Ames. **Calendar:** Semester, extensive summer session. **Full-time faculty:** 340 total. **Part-time faculty:** 3 total. **Special facilities:** Wireless computer technology campus, career academies.

Student profile. Among degree-seeking undergraduates, 32% enrolled in a transfer program, 68% enrolled in a vocational program, 951 enrolled as first-time, first-year students.

Part-time:	50%	Hispanic/Latino:	7%
Women:	56%	Multi-racial, non-Hispanic:	3%
African American:	8%	25 or older:	24%
Asian American:	3%	Live on campus:	1%

Transfer out. Colleges most students transferred to 2015: Iowa State University, Grand View College, University of Northern Iowa.

Basis for selection. Open admission, but selective for some programs. Special requirements for dental hygiene, commercial art, nursing, CAP programs. Interview required of dental hygiene, commercial art majors. Portfolio required of commercial art majors.

High school preparation. Recommended units include English 4, mathematics 3 and science 3.

2015-2016 Annual costs. Tuition/fees: $4,290; $8,580 out-of-state. Per-credit charge: $139 in-state; $278 out-of-state. Books/supplies: $1,316. Personal expenses: $2,078.

Financial aid. Need-based: Need-based aid available for part-time students. Work-study available nights, weekends and for part-time students. **Non-need-based:** Scholarships awarded for academics, athletics, state residency.

Application procedures. Admission: No deadline. No application fee. Admission notification on a rolling basis. **Financial aid:** Priority date 4/1; no closing date. FAFSA required. Applicants notified on a rolling basis starting 4/1; must reply within 2 week(s) of notification.

Academics. Special study options: Cooperative education, cross-registration, distance learning, dual enrollment of high school students, ESL, honors, independent study, internships, liberal arts/career combination, study abroad, weekend college. Bachelor's degree programs available on campus. License preparation in dental hygiene, nursing, paramedic, real estate. **Credit/placement by examination:** AP, CLEP, institutional tests. 28 credit hours maximum toward associate degree. **Support services:** GED preparation and test center, learning center, pre-admission summer program, reduced course load, remedial instruction, study skills assistance, tutoring, writing center.

Majors. Biology: Biotechnology. **Business:** Accounting, accounting technology, apparel, business admin, hospitality admin, marketing, office management, sales/distribution. **Communications technology:** Desktop publishing. **Computer sciences:** Information technology, webmaster. **Engineering:** Surveying. **Foreign languages:** Translation. **Health services:** Clinical lab technology, dental hygiene, health care admin, health information technology, medical secretary, nursing (RN), respiratory therapy technology, veterinary technology/assistant. **Human services:** Community org/advocacy. **Liberal arts:** Arts/sciences. **Parks/recreation:** Sports admin. **Protective services:** Fire safety technology, police science. **Visual/performing arts:** Commercial/advertising art. **Work/family studies:** Child care service.

Most popular majors. Health sciences 8%, liberal arts 68%.

Technology on campus. 200 workstations in library, computer center. Dormitories wired for high-speed internet access and linked to campus network. Commuter students can connect to campus network. Online course registration, online library, helpline, wireless network available.

Student life. Freshman orientation: Available. Preregistration for classes offered. Half-day program offered. **Policies:** Student Action Board responsible for many on-campus professional and social activities. **Activities:** Choral groups, drama, literary magazine, student government, student newspaper.

Athletics. NJCAA. **Intercollegiate:** Baseball M, basketball, volleyball W. **Intramural:** Badminton, basketball, bowling, football (non-tackle), golf, softball, table tennis, tennis, volleyball. **Team name:** Bears (Boone campus only).

Student services. Adult student services, career counseling, student employment services, financial aid counseling, health services, on-campus daycare, personal counseling, placement for graduates, veterans' counselor. **Physically disabled:** Services for visually, speech, hearing impaired. **Transfer:** Transfer adviser, college fairs on campus for students transferring to 4-year colleges.

Contact. E-mail: admissions@dmacc.edu
Phone: (515) 964-6241 Toll-free number: (800) 362-2127 ext. 6241
Fax: (515) 964-6391
Michael Lentsch, Director of Enrollment Management, Des Moines Area Community College, 2006 South Ankeny Boulevard, Ankeny, IA 50023-3993

Ellsworth Community College
Iowa Falls, Iowa
www.iavalley.cc.ia.us/ecc   **CB code: 5528**

▶ Public 2-year community college
▶ Residential campus in small town

General. Founded in 1890. Regionally accredited. **Enrollment:** 709 full-time, degree-seeking students. **Degrees:** 170 associate awarded. **Location:** 70 miles from Des Moines. **Calendar:** Semester, limited summer session. **Full-time faculty:** 32 total. **Special facilities:** 80-acre wildlife area.

Transfer out. Colleges most students transferred to 2015: University of Northern Iowa, Buena Vista University, Iowa State University, Wartburg College, University of Iowa.

Basis for selection. Open admission, but selective for some programs. Special requirements for some nursing programs.

2015-2016 Annual costs. Tuition/fees: $5,520; $6,480 out-of-state. Per-credit charge: $158 in-state; $190 out-of-state. Room/board: $6,464. Books/supplies: $700. Personal expenses: $1,400.

Financial aid. Need-based: Need-based aid available for part-time students. Work-study available nights, weekends and for part-time students. **Non-need-based:** Scholarships awarded for academics, art, athletics, leadership, minority status, music/drama.

Application procedures. Admission: No deadline. No application fee. Admission notification on a rolling basis. COMPASS required of applicants without SAT or ACT. **Financial aid:** Closing date 4/1. FAFSA, institutional form required. Applicants notified on a rolling basis starting 2/15; must reply within 4 week(s) of notification.

Academics. Special study options: Cooperative education, cross-registration, distance learning, double major, dual enrollment of high school students, ESL, honors, independent study, internships, liberal arts/career combination. Bachelor's degree programs available on campus. License preparation in nursing. **Credit/placement by examination:** AP, CLEP, institutional tests. 24 credit hours maximum toward associate degree. **Support services:** GED preparation and test center, learning center, remedial instruction, study skills assistance, tutoring, writing center.

Majors. Biology: General, biotechnology. **Business:** General, accounting, administrative services, fashion, insurance, office technology, office/clerical. **Communications:** Communications/speech/rhetoric. **Computer sciences:** General, computer graphics, computer science, data processing, information systems, LAN/WAN management, programming. **Conservation:** General, wildlife/wilderness. **Education:** General, agricultural, biology, business, chemistry, elementary, family/consumer sciences, history, mathematics, middle, multi-level teacher, physical, physics, science, secondary, social science, social studies, teacher assistance. **Engineering:** General. **English:** English lit. **General:** Carpentry. **Health services:** Athletic training, medical secretary, nursing (RN), predental, premedicine, prepharmacy, preveterinary. **History:** General. **Human services:** Social work. **Liberal arts:** Arts/sciences.

Math: General. **Parks/recreation:** Health/fitness. **Physical sciences:** Chemistry, physics. **Protective services:** Criminal justice, law enforcement admin. **Psychology:** General. **Social sciences:** General, criminology, sociology. **Visual/performing arts:** Art, commercial/advertising art, dramatic, studio arts. **Work/family studies:** General, clothing/textiles, family/community services.

Most popular majors. Business/marketing 10%, health sciences 10%, liberal arts 59%.

Technology on campus. 100 workstations in dormitories, library, computer center, student center. Dormitories wired for high-speed internet access and linked to campus network. Commuter students can connect to campus network. Online library, repair service, wireless network available.

Student life. Freshman orientation: Mandatory. Preregistration for classes offered. Various dates to chose from for orientation, advising, and preregistration. **Housing:** Guaranteed on-campus for freshmen. Single-sex dorms available. $200 deposit. **Activities:** Bands, choral groups, dance, drama, international student organizations, literary magazine, music ensembles, musical theater, student government, student newspaper, Young Democrats, Young Republicans, minority student organization, human services club, agricultural science club, criminal justice club.

Athletics. NJCAA. **Intercollegiate:** Baseball M, basketball, cross-country, football (tackle) M, golf, softball W, volleyball W, wrestling M. **Intramural:** Badminton, basketball, bowling, football (non-tackle), handball, racquetball, swimming, tennis, volleyball. **Team name:** Panthers.

Student services. Adult student services, alcohol/substance abuse counseling, career counseling, services for economically disadvantaged, student employment services, financial aid counseling, health services, personal counseling, placement for graduates, veterans' counselor. **Transfer:** Pre-admission transcript evaluation for new students. Transfer adviser, college fairs on campus for students transferring to 4-year colleges.

Contact. Phone: (641) 648-4611 ext. 431
Toll-free number: (800) 322-9253 Fax: (641) 648-3128
Annie Kalous, Director of Admissions, Ellsworth Community College, 1100 College Avenue, Iowa Falls, IA 50126

Hawkeye Community College
Waterloo, Iowa
www.hawkeyecollege.edu   **CB code: 6288**

▶ Public 2-year community and technical college
▶ Commuter campus in small city

General. Founded in 1966. Regionally accredited. **Enrollment:** 3,903 degree-seeking undergraduates; 1,388 non-degree-seeking students. **Degrees:** 853 associate awarded. **ROTC:** Army, Naval, Air Force. **Location:** 120 miles from Des Moines, 70 miles from Cedar Rapids. **Calendar:** Semester, limited summer session. **Full-time faculty:** 118 total; 13% have terminal degrees, 4% minority, 46% women. **Part-time faculty:** 224 total; 8% have terminal degrees, 8% minority, 56% women.

Student profile. Among degree-seeking undergraduates, 45% enrolled in a transfer program, 55% enrolled in a vocational program, 1,041 enrolled as first-time, first-year students, 727 transferred in from other institutions.

Part-time:	33%	Hispanic/Latino:	3%
Out-of-state:	1%	Multi-racial, non-Hispanic:	2%
Women:	56%	International:	1%
African American:	10%	25 or older:	28%
Asian American:	1%		

Transfer out. Colleges most students transferred to 2015: University of Northern Iowa, University of Iowa, Iowa State University.

Basis for selection. Open admission, but selective for some programs. Selective admission to health, engineering and information systems programs. ACT required for admission to medical laboratory technician and dental hygiene programs. Specific placement scores may be required in reading, writing and math for selective programs. **Home schooled:** Transcript of courses and grades required.

High school preparation. 1 year biology for nursing and medical laboratory technicians. 1 year chemistry for nursing, 1 semester physics for physical therapist assistant.

2015-2016 Annual costs. Tuition/fees: $4,785; $5,535 out-of-state. Per-credit charge: $152 in-state; $177 out-of-state.

Financial aid. Need-based: Work-study available nights, weekends and for part-time students. **Non-need-based:** Scholarships awarded for academics, state residency.

Two-Year Colleges

Application procedures. Admission: No deadline. No application fee. Application must be submitted online. Admission notification on a rolling basis. Accepted students asked to pay first-semester tuition in August to confirm fall enrollment or enter into a tuition payment plan. **Financial aid:** Priority date 7/1; no closing date. FAFSA required. Applicants notified on a rolling basis starting 5/1; must reply within 2 week(s) of notification.

Academics. Special study options: Cooperative education, distance learning, dual enrollment of high school students, external degree, independent study, internships, liberal arts/career combination, study abroad. License preparation in dental hygiene, nursing, occupational therapy, paramedic, physical therapy. **Credit/placement by examination:** AP, CLEP, institutional tests. 30 credit hours maximum toward associate degree. **Support services:** GED preparation and test center, learning center, reduced course load, remedial instruction, study skills assistance, tutoring.

Majors. Business: Accounting, executive assistant, hospitality admin, human resources, sales/distribution. **Communications:** Digital media. **Communications technology:** Graphics. **Computer sciences:** Networking, web page design. **Conservation:** Management/policy. **General:** Carpentry. **Health services:** Clinical lab technology, dental hygiene, EMT paramedic, insurance coding, medical secretary, nursing (RN), occupational therapy assistant, physical therapy assistant, respiratory therapy technology. **Liberal arts:** Arts/sciences. **Protective services:** Firefighting, police science. **Visual/performing arts:** Commercial photography, interior design. **Work/family studies:** Child care service.

Most popular majors. Agriculture 8%, health sciences 18%, liberal arts 43%.

Technology on campus. 2,239 workstations in library, computer center, student center. Commuter students can connect to campus network. Online course registration, wireless network available.

Student life. Freshman orientation: Mandatory. Preregistration for classes offered. Held week before classes begin. **Activities:** Choral groups, dance, international student organizations, student government.

Athletics. Intramural: Badminton, basketball, bowling, football (non-tackle), softball, table tennis. **Team name:** Red Tails.

Student services. Alcohol/substance abuse counseling, career counseling, services for economically disadvantaged, student employment services, financial aid counseling, health services, on-campus daycare, personal counseling, placement for graduates, veterans' counselor. **Physically disabled:** Services for visually, speech, hearing impaired. **Transfer:** Pre-admission transcript evaluation for new students. Transfer center, transfer adviser, college fairs on campus for students transferring to 4-year colleges.

Contact. E-mail: admission@hawkeyecollege.edu
Phone: (319) 296-4000 Toll-free number: (800) 670-4769 ext. 4000
Fax: (319) 296-1651
David Ball, Director of Admissions & Recruiting, Hawkeye Community College, Box 8015, Waterloo, IA 50704-8015

Iowa Central Community College
Fort Dodge, Iowa
www.iowacentral.edu   **CB code: 6217**

◗ Public 2-year community college
◗ Commuter campus in large town

General. Founded in 1966. Regionally accredited. Courses available at 2 branch campuses: Webster City and Storm Lake. **Enrollment:** 3,454 degree-seeking undergraduates; 2,180 non-degree-seeking students. **Degrees:** 774 associate awarded. **Location:** 90 miles from Des Moines. **Calendar:** Semester, limited summer session. **Full-time faculty:** 87 total. **Part-time faculty:** 350 total. **Special facilities:** Broadcasting suite, criminal justice simulator, Willow Ridge Golf Course (for turf grass, culinary arts and restaurant management), simulation center.

Student profile. Among degree-seeking undergraduates, 1,244 enrolled as first-time, first-year students, 297 transferred in from other institutions.

Part-time: 20% **Women:**   50%

Transfer out. Colleges most students transferred to 2015: Buena Vista University, Iowa State University, University of Northern Iowa.

Basis for selection. Open admission, but selective for some programs. Some majors in health science have an additional application and selection process.

2015-2016 Annual costs. Tuition/fees: $5,130; $7,275 out-of-state. Per-credit charge: $157 in-state; $229 out-of-state. Room/board: $6,150. Books/supplies: $1,040. Personal expenses: $1,300.

2015-2016 Financial aid. Need-based: Average need met was 76%. Average scholarship/grant was $1,167; average loan $1,610. 55% of total undergraduate aid awarded as scholarships/grants, 45% as loans/jobs. Need-based aid available for part-time students. Work-study available nights, weekends and for part-time students. **Non-need-based:** Scholarships awarded for academics, art, athletics, leadership, music/drama.

Application procedures. Admission: No deadline. No application fee. Admission notification on a rolling basis. **Financial aid:** Priority date 3/15; no closing date. FAFSA required. Applicants notified on a rolling basis starting 4/15.

Academics. Special study options: Accelerated study, cooperative education, cross-registration, distance learning, dual enrollment of high school students, ESL, external degree, independent study, internships, study abroad. 2 Plus 2 Agreements with Iowa State University and the University of Iowa and University of Northern Iowa, University of Iowa College of Nursing RN-BSN program. License preparation in dental hygiene, nursing, paramedic, radiology. **Credit/placement by examination:** AP, CLEP. 30 credit hours maximum toward associate degree. **Support services:** GED preparation and test center, learning center, pre-admission summer program, reduced course load, remedial instruction, study skills assistance, tutoring, writing center. Retention center.

Majors. Business: Accounting, administrative services, business admin, hospitality admin, logistics, operations. **Communications technology:** General, desktop publishing, radio/TV. **Computer sciences:** Web page design, webmaster. **Health services:** Clinical lab technology, dental hygiene, EMT paramedic, health care admin, medical assistant, medical radiologic technology/radiation therapy, nursing (RN), occupational therapy assistant, physical therapy assistant, premedicine, prepharmacy, preveterinary, radiologic technology/medical imaging. **Human services:** Social work. **Liberal arts:** Arts/sciences. **Protective services:** Firefighting, police science.

Technology on campus. 500 workstations in library, computer center, student center. Dormitories wired for high-speed internet access and linked to campus network. Commuter students can connect to campus network. Online course registration, helpline, repair service, wireless network available.

Student life. Freshman orientation: Available. Preregistration for classes offered. **Housing:** Coed dorms, single-sex dorms, special housing for disabled, apartments available. $100 nonrefundable deposit. **Activities:** Bands, choral groups, dance, drama, music ensembles, musical theater, radio station, student government, student newspaper, symphony orchestra.

Athletics. NJCAA. Intercollegiate: Baseball M, basketball, bowling, cross-country, football (tackle) M, golf, rifle, rodeo, soccer, softball W, swimming, tennis, track and field, volleyball W, wrestling M. **Intramural:** Basketball, bowling, golf, volleyball. **Team name:** Tritons.

Student services. Career counseling, services for economically disadvantaged, student employment services, financial aid counseling, health services, minority student services, personal counseling, placement for graduates, veterans' counselor. **Physically disabled:** Services for visually, speech, hearing impaired. **Transfer:** Pre-admission transcript evaluation for new students. Transfer adviser, college fairs on campus for students transferring to 4-year colleges.

Contact. E-mail: scharf_s@iowacentral.edu
Phone: (515) 576-7201 ext. 1008
Toll-free number: (800) 362-2793 ext. 1008 Fax: (515) 576-7724
Sara Condon, Director of Admissions, Iowa Central Community College, One Triton Circle, Fort Dodge, IA 50501

Iowa Lakes Community College
Estherville, Iowa
www.iowalakes.edu   **CB code: 6196**

◗ Public 2-year community college
◗ Commuter campus in small town

General. Founded in 1967. Regionally accredited. 3 campuses with dormitories and food service operating in Emmetsburg, Estherville and Spencer. Classes also offered at campuses located in Algona and Spirit Lake. **Enrollment:** 1,307 degree-seeking undergraduates; 997 non-degree-seeking students. **Degrees:** 447 associate awarded. **Location:** 100 miles from Mason City; 100 miles from Sioux Falls, SD. **Calendar:** Semester, limited summer session. **Full-time faculty:** 91 total; 47% women. **Part-time faculty:** 86 total; 66% women. **Special facilities:** 360-acre farm, print collection, wind turbine.

Student profile. Among degree-seeking undergraduates, 62% enrolled in a transfer program, 38% enrolled in a vocational program, 25% already have a bachelor's degree or higher, 383 enrolled as first-time, first-year students, 399 transferred in from other institutions.

Part-time:	20%	25 or older:	23%
Out-of-state:	15%	Live on campus:	15%
Women:	48%		

Transfer out. Colleges most students transferred to 2015: University of Northern Iowa, Iowa State University, University of Iowa, South Dakota State University, Buena Vista University.

Basis for selection. Open admission, but selective for some programs. Special requirements for nursing, aviation/airport management, wind turbine technology programs. ACT required for nursing students. Interview required of career programs. Audition recommended for music majors. Portfolio recommended for advertising design majors. **Home schooled:** Transcript of courses and grades, state high school equivalency certificate required.

High school preparation. College-preparatory program recommended.

2015-2016 Annual costs. Tuition/fees: $5,322; $5,652 out-of-state. Room/board: $5,850. Books/supplies: $1,300. Personal expenses: $3,400.

Financial aid. All financial aid based on need. Need-based aid available for part-time students. Work-study available nights, weekends and for part-time students.

Application procedures. Admission: No deadline. No application fee. Admission notification on a rolling basis. **Financial aid:** Priority date 4/22; no closing date. FAFSA, institutional form required. Applicants notified on a rolling basis starting 4/15.

Academics. Special study options: Cooperative education, cross-registration, distance learning, dual enrollment of high school students, ESL, honors, independent study, internships, liberal arts/career combination, weekend college. Evening college. License preparation in aviation, nursing, paramedic, real estate. **Credit/placement by examination:** AP, CLEP, institutional tests. 30 credit hours maximum toward associate degree. **Support services:** GED preparation and test center, learning center, reduced course load, remedial instruction, study skills assistance, tutoring.

Majors. Business: Accounting, business admin, hotel/motel admin, office management, restaurant/food services, sales/distribution. **Communications:** Journalism. **Computer sciences:** Applications programming, networking. **Conservation:** Environmental studies. **Engineering:** Agricultural. **Health services:** EMT paramedic, health care admin, nursing (RN). **Liberal arts:** Arts/sciences. **Parks/recreation:** Facilities management. **Protective services:** Police science. **Social sciences:** GIS/cartography. **Visual/performing arts:** Commercial/advertising art, photography. **Work/family studies:** Child care service.

Most popular majors. Agriculture 7%, business/marketing 8%, health sciences 23%, liberal arts 41%, trade and industry 6%.

Technology on campus. 800 workstations in library, computer center, student center. Dormitories wired for high-speed internet access and linked to campus network. Online course registration, online library, helpline, repair service, wireless network available.

Student life. Freshman orientation: Mandatory. Preregistration for classes offered. **Housing:** Coed dorms, special housing for disabled, apartments available. **Activities:** Bands, campus ministries, choral groups, dance, drama, international student organizations, literary magazine, music ensembles, musical theater, radio station, student government, TV station.

Athletics. NJCAA. **Intercollegiate:** Baseball M, basketball, cross-country, golf, soccer, softball W, swimming, volleyball W, wrestling M. **Intramural:** Basketball, bowling, racquetball, skiing, softball, table tennis, volleyball. **Team name:** Lakers.

Student services. Adult student services, alcohol/substance abuse counseling, career counseling, services for economically disadvantaged, financial aid counseling, personal counseling, placement for graduates, veterans' counselor, women's services. **Transfer:** Pre-admission transcript evaluation for new students. Transfer adviser, college fairs on campus for students transferring to 4-year colleges.

Contact. E-mail: info@iowalakes.edu
Phone: (712) 362-7945 Toll-free number: (800) 521-5054
Julie Williams, Dean of Students, Iowa Lakes Community College, 300 South 18th Street, Estherville, IA 51334-2725

Iowa Western Community College
Council Bluffs, Iowa
www.iwcc.edu
CB code: 6302

▶ Public 2-year community and technical college
▶ Commuter campus in small city

General. Founded in 1966. Regionally accredited. Centers in Harlan, Clarinda, and Atlantic, Iowa offer evening programs in liberal arts and business administration. Practical nursing offered at Harlan. Design Technology program offered at Atlantic. **Enrollment:** 4,645 degree-seeking undergraduates; 312 non-degree-seeking students. **Degrees:** 900 associate awarded. **ROTC:** Army, Air Force. **Location:** 5 miles from Omaha. **Calendar:** Semester, extensive summer session. **Full-time faculty:** 129 total. **Part-time faculty:** 233 total. **Special facilities:** Center for advanced nursing and allied health programs, engineering technology and advanced manufacturing building, cyber library, arts center, athletic complex.

Student profile. Among degree-seeking undergraduates, 58% enrolled in a transfer program, 42% enrolled in a vocational program, 1,865 enrolled as first-time, first-year students.

Part-time:	29%	Hispanic/Latino:	7%
Out-of-state:	40%	Native American:	2%
Women:	57%	International:	2%
African American:	13%	25 or older:	29%
Asian American:	1%	Live on campus:	27%

Transfer out. Colleges most students transferred to 2015: Bellevue University, University of Nebraska at Lincoln, University of Iowa, Iowa State University, Northwest Missouri State University.

Basis for selection. Open admission, but selective for some programs. Limited admission to some vocational-technical programs, including nursing, dental hygiene, automotive technology, veterinary technology, medical assisting, surgical technology, design technology, and dental assisting. COMPASS or ACT/SAT required for placement. Academic enrichment courses available. **Home schooled:** Transcript of courses and grades required.

High school preparation. College-preparatory program recommended. Specific subject requirements for some career programs.

2015-2016 Annual costs. Tuition/fees: $4,888; $5,038 out-of-state. Per-credit charge: $149 in-state; $154 out-of-state. Room/board: $6,040. Books/supplies: $1,040. Personal expenses: $1,782.

Financial aid. Need-based: Need-based aid available for part-time students. Work-study available nights, weekends and for part-time students. **Non-need-based:** Scholarships awarded for athletics, music/drama.

Application procedures. Admission: No deadline. No application fee. Admission notification on a rolling basis. Applicants for limited-enrollment programs considered on first applied, first accepted basis. **Financial aid:** No deadline. FAFSA required. Applicants notified on a rolling basis starting 3/1; must reply within 3 week(s) of notification.

Academics. Special study options: Cooperative education, distance learning, dual enrollment of high school students, ESL, independent study, internships, student-designed major. License preparation in aviation, dental hygiene, nursing, paramedic. **Credit/placement by examination:** AP, CLEP, institutional tests. 40 credit hours maximum toward associate degree. **Support services:** GED preparation and test center, learning center, reduced course load, remedial instruction, study skills assistance, tutoring, writing center.

Majors. Area/ethnic studies: Spanish/Iberian. **Biology:** General, botany, microbiology, molecular. **Business:** Business admin, fashion, hotel/motel/restaurant management, human resources, marketing, office management, sales/distribution. **Communications:** General, broadcast journalism, media studies, radio/TV, sports. **Communications technology:** Graphic/printing. **Computer sciences:** Computer science, programming, security, system admin, web page design. **Education:** General. **English:** General lit. **Foreign languages:** Sign language interpretation. **Health services:** Athletic training, dental hygiene, nursing (RN), premedicine, preoccupational therapy, prepharmacy, prephysical therapy, substance abuse counseling, surgical technology, veterinary technology/assistant. **Human services:** Social work. **Liberal arts:** Arts/sciences. **Math:** General. **Physical sciences:** Chemistry. **Protective services:** Firefighting, forensics. **Psychology:** General. **Social sciences:** General, political science, sociology. **Visual/performing arts:** Art, music, theater arts management. **Work/family studies:** Child care management, institutional food production.

Technology on campus. 250 workstations in dormitories, library, computer center, student center. Dormitories wired for high-speed internet access and linked to campus network. Commuter students can connect to campus network. Online course registration, online library, helpline, wireless network available.

Two-Year Colleges

Student life. Freshman orientation: Mandatory. Preregistration for classes offered. **Housing:** Coed dorms, single-sex dorms, apartments, gender-neutral housing available. $200 fully refundable deposit. **Activities:** Bands, choral groups, dance, drama, international student organizations, literary magazine, music ensembles, musical theater, radio station, student government, student newspaper, TV station, Christian Fellowship, special interest clubs, Phi Theta Kappa, multicultural student alliance.

Athletics. NJCAA. **Intercollegiate:** Baseball M, basketball, cheerleading, cross-country, football (tackle) M, golf, soccer, softball W, track and field, volleyball W, wrestling M. **Intramural:** Basketball, bowling, football (non-tackle), softball, table tennis, tennis, volleyball. **Team name:** Reivers.

Student services. Career counseling, services for economically disadvantaged, student employment services, financial aid counseling, health services, on-campus daycare, personal counseling, placement for graduates, veterans' counselor. **Physically disabled:** Services for visually, speech, hearing impaired. **Transfer:** Pre-admission transcript evaluation for new students. Transfer center, transfer adviser, college fairs on campus for students transferring to 4-year colleges.

Contact. E-mail: admissions@iwcc.edu
Phone: (712) 325-3277 Toll-free number: (800) 432-5852
Fax: (712) 325-3720
Chris LaFerla, Dean of Admissions and Records, Iowa Western Community College, 2700 College Road, Council Bluffs, IA 51502-3004

Kaplan University: Cedar Rapids
Cedar Rapids, Iowa
www.kaplanuniversity.edu/cedar-rapids-iowa.aspx

CB code: 3384

- For-profit 2-year liberal arts college
- Commuter campus in small city
- Application essay, interview required

General. Regionally accredited. **Enrollment:** 483 undergraduates. **Degrees:** 76 bachelor's, 133 associate awarded; master's offered. **Calendar:** Continuous, extensive summer session. **Full-time faculty:** 9 total. **Part-time faculty:** 24 total. **Class size:** 49% < 20, 51% 20-39.

Basis for selection. Open admission, but selective for some programs. **Home schooled:** State high school equivalency certificate required.

2015-2016 Annual costs. Diploma programs: $11,501-$23,410. Associate programs: $30,654-$35,763. Bachelor's programs: $35,763-$66,417.

Financial aid. Need-based: Need-based aid available for part-time students. Work-study available nights, weekends and for part-time students. **Non-need-based:** Scholarships awarded for academics.

Application procedures. Admission: No deadline. $20 fee. Application must be submitted on paper. Admission notification on a rolling basis. **Financial aid:** Priority date 6/30; no closing date. FAFSA, institutional form required. Applicants notified on a rolling basis.

Academics. Special study options: Accelerated study, distance learning, honors, independent study, internships. Bachelor's degree programs available on campus. License preparation in nursing. **Credit/placement by examination:** AP, CLEP, institutional tests. Combined credit by examination and for life/work experiences shall not exceed 25% of program requirements. **Support services:** Learning center, remedial instruction, tutoring.

Majors. Business: Accounting, business admin. **Computer sciences:** Information technology. **Health services:** Medical assistant. **Protective services:** Criminal justice.

Most popular majors. Business/marketing 19%, computer/information sciences 14%, health sciences 34%, security/protective services 19%.

Technology on campus. 207 workstations in library. Commuter students can connect to campus network. Online library available.

Student life. Freshman orientation: Mandatory, $20 fee. Preregistration for classes offered.

Student services. Adult student services, career counseling, student employment services, financial aid counseling, placement for graduates. **Physically disabled:** Services for visually, hearing impaired. **Transfer:** Reentry adviser for new students.

Contact. Phone: (319) 363-0481 Toll-free number: (800) 728-0481
Fax: (319) 363-3812
Dave Ruddy, Director of Admissions, Kaplan University: Cedar Rapids, 3165 Edgewood Parkway, SW, Cedar Rapids, IA 52404

Kirkwood Community College
Cedar Rapids, Iowa
www.kirkwood.edu

CB code: 6027

- Public 2-year community college
- Commuter campus in small city

General. Founded in 1966. Regionally accredited. Off-campus sites in Iowa City, Coralville, Vinton, Tipton, Williamsburg, Monticello, Washington, Belle Plaine, Cedar Rapids. **Enrollment:** 9,453 degree-seeking undergraduates. **Degrees:** 1,935 associate awarded. **Location:** 128 miles from Des Moines. **Calendar:** Semester, extensive summer session. **Full-time faculty:** 301 total. **Part-time faculty:** 574 total. **Class size:** 53% < 20, 44% 20-39, 2% 40-49, less than 1% 50-99. **Special facilities:** Raptor center, equestrian center, hotel, authorized Apple campus store, jazz station, healthcare simulation center.

Student profile.

Out-of-state:	2%	**25 or older:**	25%

Transfer out. Colleges most students transferred to 2015: University of Iowa, University of Northern Iowa, Iowa State University, Mount Mercy College, Coe College.

Basis for selection. Open admission, but selective for some programs. Some health science programs require minimum scores on COMPASS exam for admission to program. A program conference is required of some vocational-technical applicants.

2015-2016 Annual costs. Tuition/fees: $4,490; $5,390 out-of-state. Per-credit charge: $148 in-state; $178 out-of-state.

Financial aid. Need-based: Need-based aid available for part-time students. Work-study available nights, weekends and for part-time students. **Non-need-based:** Scholarships awarded for art, athletics, leadership, music/drama.

Application procedures. Admission: No deadline. No application fee. Admission notification on a rolling basis. **Financial aid:** Closing date 6/30. FAFSA required. Applicants notified on a rolling basis starting 4/1.

Academics. Special study options: Accelerated study, cooperative education, cross-registration, distance learning, dual enrollment of high school students, ESL, exchange student, external degree, honors, independent study, internships, liberal arts/career combination, student-designed major, study abroad, weekend college. License preparation in dental hygiene, nursing, occupational therapy, paramedic, real estate. **Credit/placement by examination:** AP, CLEP, IB, institutional tests. 18 credit hours maximum toward associate degree. **Support services:** GED preparation and test center, learning center, pre-admission summer program, reduced course load, remedial instruction, study skills assistance, tutoring, writing center.

Majors. Biology: Biotechnology. **Business:** Accounting, administrative services, apparel, business admin, construction management, finance, hospitality admin, marketing. **Communications technology:** Graphics. **Computer sciences:** Applications programming, system admin, web page design. **Conservation:** General. **Engineering:** Surveying. **Health services:** Dental assistant, dental hygiene, dental lab technology, electroencephalograph technology, EMT paramedic, health information technology, management/clinical assistant, medical assistant, nursing (RN), occupational therapy assistant, physical therapy assistant, respiratory therapy technology, surgical technology, veterinary technology/assistant. **Liberal arts:** Arts/sciences. **Protective services:** Firefighting. **Visual/performing arts:** Interior design. **Work/family studies:** Child care service.

Technology on campus. 1,000 workstations in library, computer center, student center. Commuter students can connect to campus network. Online course registration, online library, helpline, repair service, wireless network available.

Student life. Freshman orientation: Available. Preregistration for classes offered. One-day sessions held June-August and December-January. **Activities:** Bands, campus ministries, choral groups, dance, drama, literary magazine, music ensembles, musical theater, student government, student newspaper, over 50 organizations.

Athletics. NJCAA. **Intercollegiate:** Baseball M, basketball, cheerleading W, golf M, softball W, volleyball W. **Intramural:** Badminton, basketball, cheerleading, football (tackle), golf, racquetball, soccer, table tennis, tennis, ultimate frisbee, volleyball. **Team name:** Eagles.

Student services. Adult student services, alcohol/substance abuse counseling, career counseling, services for economically disadvantaged, student employment services, financial aid counseling, health services, minority student services, personal counseling, placement for graduates, veterans' counselor. **Physically disabled:** Services for visually, speech, hearing impaired. **Transfer:** Pre-admission transcript evaluation for new students. Transfer center, transfer adviser, college fairs on campus for students transferring to 4-year colleges.

Contact. E-mail: info@kirkwood.edu
Phone: (319) 398-5517 Toll-free number: (800) 332-2055 ext. 5517
Fax: (319) 398-1244
Doug Bannon, Director of Admissions Services, Kirkwood Community College, 6301 Kirkwood Boulevard SW, Cedar Rapids, IA 52404-2068

Marshalltown Community College
Marshalltown, Iowa
www.iavalley.edu/mcc/   CB code: 6394

▶ Public 2-year community college
▶ Residential campus in large town

General. Founded in 1927. Regionally accredited. **Enrollment:** 2,101 undergraduates. **Degrees:** 199 associate awarded. **Location:** 50 miles from Des Moines. **Calendar:** Semester, limited summer session. **Full-time faculty:** 37 total. **Part-time faculty:** 4 total. **Special facilities:** Prairie, challenge course.

Transfer out. Colleges most students transferred to 2015: Iowa State University, University of Northern Iowa, University of Iowa.

Basis for selection. Open admission, but selective for some programs. Special requirements for health career programs. Interview recommended for health careers majors.

2015-2016 Annual costs. Books/supplies: $425. Personal expenses: $760.

Financial aid. Need-based: Work-study available nights, weekends and for part-time students.

Application procedures. Admission: No deadline. No application fee. Admission notification on a rolling basis. **Financial aid:** Closing date 3/1. Institutional form required. Applicants notified on a rolling basis starting 6/1; must reply within 2 week(s) of notification.

Academics. Special study options: Accelerated study, cooperative education, cross-registration, distance learning, dual enrollment of high school students, ESL, honors, independent study, internships, liberal arts/career combination, study abroad. Bachelor's degree programs available on campus. License preparation in nursing, real estate. **Credit/placement by examination:** AP, CLEP, institutional tests. 30 credit hours maximum toward associate degree. **Support services:** GED preparation and test center, learning center, reduced course load, remedial instruction, study skills assistance, tutoring, writing center.

Majors. Biology: General, botany. **Business:** General, accounting, administrative services, business admin. **Communications:** Journalism. **Communications technology:** General. **Computer sciences:** General, networking, systems analysis. **Conservation:** Forestry. **Education:** General, elementary, physical, secondary. **Engineering:** General. **English:** English lit. **Foreign languages:** Spanish. **Health services:** Nursing (RN), predental, premedicine, prenursing, prepharmacy, preveterinary, surgical technology. **Human services:** Community org/advocacy. **Liberal arts:** Arts/sciences. **Math:** General. **Protective services:** Law enforcement admin, police science. **Psychology:** General. **Social sciences:** General. **Visual/performing arts:** General, music, studio arts. **Work/family studies:** General, child care management.

Most popular majors. Computer/information sciences 7%, education 8%, health sciences 10%, liberal arts 65%.

Technology on campus. 250 workstations in dormitories, library, computer center. Commuter students can connect to campus network. Online library, helpline available.

Student life. Freshman orientation: Available. Preregistration for classes offered. **Housing:** Special housing for disabled, apartments available. $300 deposit. **Activities:** Concert band, choral groups, drama, international student organizations, radio station, student government, student newspaper, TV station.

Athletics. NJCAA. **Intercollegiate:** Baseball M, basketball, golf, soccer M, softball W. **Intramural:** Basketball, racquetball. **Team name:** Tigers.

Student services. Adult student services, career counseling, services for economically disadvantaged, student employment services, financial aid counseling, health services, on-campus daycare, personal counseling, placement for graduates, veterans' counselor. **Physically disabled:** Services for visually, speech, hearing impaired. **Transfer:** College fairs on campus for students transferring to 4-year colleges.

Contact. Phone: (641) 752-7106 ext. 216 Fax: (641) 752-8149
Angela Redmond, Director of Admissions, Marshalltown Community College, 3700 South Center Street, Marshalltown, IA 50158

Muscatine Community College
Muscatine, Iowa
www.eicc.edu   CB code: 6422

▶ Public 2-year community college
▶ Commuter campus in large town

General. Founded in 1929. Regionally accredited. **Enrollment:** 1,600 undergraduates. **Degrees:** 916 associate awarded. **Location:** 30 miles from Davenport. **Calendar:** Semester, extensive summer session. **Full-time faculty:** 34 total. **Part-time faculty:** 100 total. **Class size:** 28% < 20, 4% 20-39, 68% 40-49.

Student profile.

Out-of-state:	94%	Live on campus:	8%
25 or older:	24%		

Basis for selection. Open admission, but selective for some programs. Special requirements for nursing program.

High school preparation. College-preparatory program recommended.

2015-2016 Annual costs. Tuition/fees: $4,200; $6,210 out-of-state. Per-credit charge: $140 in-state; $207 out-of-state. Room only: $4,570. Books/supplies: $1,600. **Additional information:** Online course tuition is $162 per credit hour.

Financial aid. Need-based: Work-study available nights, weekends and for part-time students.

Application procedures. Admission: No deadline. No application fee. Admission notification on a rolling basis. **Financial aid:** Priority date 4/20; no closing date. FAFSA required. Applicants notified on a rolling basis starting 5/15; must reply within 2 week(s) of notification.

Academics. Special study options: Accelerated study, cooperative education, cross-registration, distance learning, double major, dual enrollment of high school students, ESL, honors, independent study, internships, study abroad. License preparation in nursing, real estate. **Credit/placement by examination:** AP, CLEP, institutional tests. 30 credit hours maximum toward associate degree. **Support services:** GED preparation and test center, learning center, reduced course load, remedial instruction, tutoring.

Majors. Business: Accounting, administrative services, business admin, logistics. **Computer sciences:** Applications programming. **Conservation:** General. **Health services:** EMT paramedic, veterinary technology/assistant. **Liberal arts:** Arts/sciences. **Protective services:** Firefighting, police science. **Work/family studies:** Child care service.

Most popular majors. Agriculture 11%, liberal arts 82%.

Technology on campus. 60 workstations in library, computer center. Dormitories wired for high-speed internet access and linked to campus network. Commuter students can connect to campus network. Online course registration, online library, helpline, wireless network available.

Student life. Freshman orientation: Mandatory. Preregistration for classes offered. **Housing:** Coed dorms, apartments available. **Activities:** Choral groups, drama, film society, music ensembles, musical theater, student government, student newspaper, TV station, Agriculture tech club, All Kinds of People, veterinary tech club, Business Professionals of America, Phi Theta Kappa, Silver & Blue Volunteers, Student Veterans of America, Online Gaming Association, Entrepreneurs Organization.

Athletics. NJCAA. **Intercollegiate:** Baseball M, softball W. **Intramural:** Bowling, football (non-tackle), golf, skiing, soccer, table tennis, ultimate frisbee, volleyball. **Team name:** Cardinals.

Student services. Adult student services, career counseling, student employment services, financial aid counseling, on-campus daycare, placement for graduates. **Physically disabled:** Services for visually, speech, hearing impaired. **Transfer:** Transfer adviser, college fairs on campus for students transferring to 4-year colleges.

Contact. Phone: (563) 288-6000 Toll-free number: (888) 336-3907
Fax: (563) 264-8341
Ben Huntington, Admissions Officer, Muscatine Community College, 152
Colorado Street, Muscatine, IA 52761-5396

North Iowa Area Community College
Mason City, Iowa
www.niacc.edu | **CB code: 6400**

▶ Public 2-year community college
▶ Commuter campus in large town

General. Founded in 1918. Regionally accredited. **Enrollment:** 1,930
degree-seeking undergraduates. **Degrees:** 482 associate awarded. **Location:**
120 miles from Des Moines, 120 miles from Minneapolis-St. Paul. **Calendar:**
Semester, limited summer session. **Full-time faculty:** 141 total; 4% have
terminal degrees, less than 1% minority, 54% women. **Part-time faculty:**
121 total; less than 1% have terminal degrees, less than 1% minority, 51%
women. **Class size:** 64% < 20, 34% 20-39, 2% 40-49. **Special facilities:**
Health simulation center, manufacturing technology center, entrepreneurial
center, community auditorium, business incubator, recreation center.

Student profile.

Out-of-state:	7%	Multi-racial, non-Hispanic:	2%
African American:	6%	International:	2%
Asian American:	1%	25 or older:	20%
Hispanic/Latino:	5%	Live on campus:	10%

Transfer out. Colleges most students transferred to 2015: University of
Northern Iowa, Iowa State University, University of Iowa.

Basis for selection. Open admission, but selective for some programs.
Nursing and physical therapy assistant programs have additional requirements. Applicants missing requirements accepted as pre-major students until
all requirements are met.

2015-2016 Annual costs. Tuition/fees: $4,792; $6,798 out-of-state.
Room/board: $6,518. Books/supplies: $955. Personal expenses: $1,932.

2014-2015 Financial aid. Need-based: 490 full-time freshmen applied
for aid; 380 deemed to have need; 380 received aid. Average need met was
25%. Average scholarship/grant was $4,415; average loan $2,499. 52% of
total undergraduate aid awarded as scholarships/grants, 48% as loans/jobs.
Need-based aid available for part-time students. Work-study available nights,
weekends and for part-time students. **Non-need-based:** Scholarships awarded
for academics, art, athletics, leadership.

Application procedures. Admission: No deadline. No application fee.
Admission notification on a rolling basis. **Financial aid:** Priority date 3/1;
no closing date. FAFSA, institutional form required. Applicants notified on
a rolling basis starting 4/1; must reply within 2 week(s) of notification.

Academics. Special study options: Cooperative education, distance learning, dual enrollment of high school students, ESL, honors, independent study,
internships, liberal arts/career combination, student-designed major. Bachelor's degree programs available on campus. **Credit/placement by examination:** AP, CLEP, institutional tests. 30 credit hours maximum toward associate
degree. **Support services:** GED preparation and test center, learning center,
remedial instruction, study skills assistance, tutoring, writing center.

Majors. Business: Accounting, administrative services, business admin,
entrepreneurial studies, hospitality admin. **Computer sciences:** System
admin. **Education:** General, early childhood, physical, secondary. **Health
services:** Clinical lab technology, EMT paramedic, nursing (RN), physical
therapy assistant. **Liberal arts:** Arts/sciences. **Parks/recreation:** Sports
admin. **Protective services:** Fire services admin, police science. **Social sciences:** General, criminology, geography, political science, sociology. **Work/
family studies:** General.

Most popular majors. Agriculture 6%, health sciences 10%, liberal arts
68%, trade and industry 8%.

Technology on campus. 400 workstations in dormitories, library, computer center. Dormitories wired for high-speed internet access and linked to
campus network. Commuter students can connect to campus network. Online
course registration, online library, helpline, wireless network available.

Student life. Freshman orientation: Mandatory. Preregistration for
classes offered. **Housing:** Coed dorms, apartments, wellness housing available. $50 partly refundable deposit. **Activities:** Concert band, choral groups,
international student organizations, literary magazine, music ensembles, student government, student newspaper, symphony orchestra.

Athletics. NJCAA. **Intercollegiate:** Baseball M, basketball, cross-country,
golf, soccer M, softball W, track and field, volleyball W, wrestling M. **Team
name:** Trojans.

Student services. Adult student services, alcohol/substance abuse counseling, career counseling, student employment services, financial aid counseling, health services, personal counseling, placement for graduates, veterans'
counselor. **Physically disabled:** Services for visually, speech, hearing
impaired. **Transfer:** Transfer adviser, college fairs on campus for students
transferring to 4-year colleges.

Contact. E-mail: admisoff@niacc.edu
Phone: (641) 422-4245 Toll-free number: (888) 466-4222
Fax: (641) 422-4385
Rachel McGuire, Director of Admissions, North Iowa Area Community
College, 500 College Drive, Mason City, IA 50401

Northeast Iowa Community College
Calmar, Iowa
www.nicc.edu | **CB member** **CB code: 6754**

▶ Public 2-year community college
▶ Commuter campus in rural community

General. Founded in 1966. Regionally accredited. Branch campus in Peosta.
Enrollment: 2,431 degree-seeking undergraduates; 2,434 non-degree-
seeking students. **Degrees:** 554 associate awarded. **Location:** 75 miles from
Waterloo, 13 miles from Dubuque. **Calendar:** Semester, extensive summer
session. **Full-time faculty:** 116 total; less than 1% have terminal degrees,
2% minority, 53% women. **Part-time faculty:** 238 total; 60% women. **Class
size:** 69% < 20, 31% 20-39. **Special facilities:** Nature preserve, prairie,
wetland. **Partnerships:** Formal partnership with John Deere.

Student profile. Among degree-seeking undergraduates, 621 enrolled as
first-time, first-year students, 204 transferred in from other institutions.

Part-time:	43%	Hispanic/Latino:	2%
Out-of-state:	14%	Native Hawaiian/Pacific islander:	1%
Women:	63%	Multi-racial, non-Hispanic:	5%
African American:	4%	25 or older:	35%
Asian American:	1%		

Transfer out. Colleges most students transferred to 2015: University of
Northern Iowa-Cedar Falls, Upper Iowa University, University of Dubuque,
University of Iowa, Clarke College.

Basis for selection. Open admission, but selective for some programs.
Health students required to meet program specific admission criteria. Students
admitted to the electrical program must have high school diploma or GED.
All degree-seeking students required to submit placement test scores.

2015-2016 Annual costs. Tuition/fees: $5,010; $5,010 out-of-state. Per-
credit charge: $154. Books/supplies: $1,600. Personal expenses: $1,652.

Financial aid. Need-based: Need-based aid available for part-time students. Work-study available nights, weekends and for part-time students.
Non-need-based: Scholarships awarded for academics, leadership, state residency.

Application procedures. Admission: No deadline. No application fee.
Admission notification on a rolling basis. **Financial aid:** Priority date 7/1;
no closing date. FAFSA required. Applicants notified on a rolling basis
starting 5/1.

Academics. Dental assisting certification exam given on-campus. **Special
study options:** Distance learning, double major, dual enrollment of high
school students, external degree, internships, liberal arts/career combination.
License preparation in nursing, paramedic, radiology. **Credit/placement by
examination:** AP, CLEP. **Support services:** GED preparation and test center,
learning center, reduced course load, remedial instruction, study skills assistance, tutoring, writing center.

Majors. Business: Accounting, administrative services, business admin,
office technology, sales/distribution. **Communications technology:** Desktop
publishing. **Computer sciences:** Applications programming. **General:** Carpentry, electrician, plumbing. **Health services:** Clinical lab technology, EMT
paramedic, health information technology, nursing (RN), radiologic technol-
ogy/medical imaging, respiratory therapy technology. **Human services:**
Social work. **Liberal arts:** Arts/sciences. **Protective services:** Firefighting.

Most popular majors. Agriculture 16%, business/marketing 10%, health
sciences 27%, liberal arts 35%, trade and industry 6%.

Technology on campus. Commuter students can connect to campus network. Online course registration, helpline, repair service, wireless network available.

Student life. Freshman orientation: Mandatory. Preregistration for classes offered. One-day program with different interest sessions available. **Policies:** Smoke-free campuses. **Housing:** Adjacent apartment complex available. **Activities:** Choral groups, student government.

Athletics. Intramural: Basketball, bowling, football (non-tackle) M, golf, skiing, softball, volleyball. **Team name:** Cougars.

Student services. Adult student services, career counseling, services for economically disadvantaged, student employment services, financial aid counseling, on-campus daycare, personal counseling, placement for graduates. **Physically disabled:** Services for visually, speech, hearing impaired. **Transfer:** Pre-admission transcript evaluation for new students. Transfer adviser, college fairs on campus for students transferring to 4-year colleges.

Contact. Phone: (563) 362-5263
Toll-free number: (800) 728-2256 ext. 307 Fax: (563) 562-4369
Kristi Strief, Admissions Manager, Northeast Iowa Community College, PO Box 400, Calmar, IA 52132

Northwest Iowa Community College
Sheldon, Iowa
www.nwicc.edu   CB code: 1359

▶ Public 2-year community college
▶ Commuter campus in small town

General. Founded in 1966. Regionally accredited. **Enrollment:** 775 degree-seeking undergraduates. **Degrees:** 202 associate awarded. **Location:** 60 miles from Sioux City; 65 miles from Sioux Falls, South Dakota. **Calendar:** Semester, extensive summer session. **Full-time faculty:** 40 total; 32% women. **Part-time faculty:** 95 total; 2% minority, 58% women.

Basis for selection. Open admission, but selective for some programs. 2.0 GPA and 2 science required for LPN and Radiologic Technology programs. Minimum COMPASS scores for ADN, Radiologic Technology, and Powerline programs. **Home schooled:** Transcript of courses and grades required.

2015-2016 Annual costs. Tuition/fees: $5,550; $5,850 out-of-state. Per-credit charge: $150 in-state; $160 out-of-state. Room/board: $4,942. Books/supplies: $1,134. Personal expenses: $1,350.

Financial aid. Need-based: Need-based aid available for part-time students. Work-study available nights, weekends and for part-time students.

Application procedures. Admission: No deadline. No application fee. Admission notification on a rolling basis. **Financial aid:** Priority date 4/1; no closing date. FAFSA, institutional form required. Applicants notified on a rolling basis starting 5/1.

Academics. Special study options: Cooperative education, distance learning, dual enrollment of high school students, ESL, independent study, liberal arts/career combination. Bachelor's degree programs available on campus. License preparation in nursing, radiology. **Credit/placement by examination:** AP, CLEP, institutional tests. 30 credit hours maximum toward associate degree. **Support services:** GED preparation and test center, learning center, reduced course load, remedial instruction, study skills assistance, tutoring.

Majors. Business: Accounting, business admin. **Computer sciences:** Networking, system admin. **Conservation:** General. **General:** Carpentry, lineworker. **Health services:** Health information technology, nursing (RN), radiologic technology/medical imaging. **Liberal arts:** Arts/sciences.

Technology on campus. 433 workstations in dormitories, library, computer center, student center. Dormitories wired for high-speed internet access. Online course registration, online library, helpline, repair service, wireless network available.

Student life. Freshman orientation: Available. Preregistration for classes offered. **Policies:** Student housing is non-smoking; no alcohol allowed. **Housing:** $175 fully refundable deposit. **Activities:** Campus ministries, student government, student newspaper, Campus Crusade for Christ, multi-cultural association, business club.

Athletics. Intramural: Basketball, bowling, football (non-tackle) M, softball, volleyball. **Team name:** Thunder.

Student services. Student employment services, financial aid counseling, personal counseling, veterans' counselor. **Physically disabled:** Services for

---

visually, speech, hearing impaired. **Transfer:** Pre-admission transcript evaluation for new students. Transfer adviser, college fairs on campus for students transferring to 4-year colleges.

Contact. E-mail: studentservices@nwicc.edu
Phone: (712) 324-5061 ext. 115
Toll-free number: (800) 352-4907 ext. 115 Fax: (712) 324-4136
Lisa Story, Director of Enrollment, Northwest Iowa Community College, 603 West Park Street, Sheldon, IA 51201

Scott Community College
Bettendorf, Iowa
www.eicc.edu   CB code: 0282

▶ Public 2-year community college
▶ Commuter campus in small city

General. Founded in 1966. Regionally accredited. **Enrollment:** 2,571 degree-seeking undergraduates. **Degrees:** 558 associate awarded. **Location:** 175 miles from Chicago. **Calendar:** Semester, extensive summer session. **Full-time faculty:** 73 total. **Part-time faculty:** 255 total. **Class size:** 80% < 20, 20% 20-39, less than 1% 40-49, less than 1% 50-99. **Special facilities:** Nahant Marsh, 265-acre preserve on the Mississippi River, home of 150 species of birds and 400 species of plants.

Student profile.

Out-of-state:	12%	25 or older:	39%

Transfer out. Colleges most students transferred to 2015: University of Iowa, Iowa State University, University of Northern Iowa, St. Ambrose University, Western Illinois University.

Basis for selection. Open admission, but selective for some programs. Admission to some programs, particularly health occupations, based on academic achievement and previous courses. Interview required for radiologic technology and medical laboratory technician; recommended for nursing, sonography, electroneurodiagnostic technology and pharmacy technician.

2015-2016 Annual costs. Tuition/fees: $4,200; $6,210 out-of-state. Per-credit charge: $140 in-state; $207 out-of-state. Books/supplies: $1,140. Personal expenses: $1,090. **Additional information:** Online course tuition is $162 per credit hour. Tuition for nearby Illinois counties is $162 per credit hour.

Financial aid. Need-based: Work-study available nights, weekends and for part-time students.

Application procedures. Admission: No deadline. No application fee. Admission notification on a rolling basis. **Financial aid:** Priority date 4/20; no closing date. FAFSA required. Applicants notified on a rolling basis starting 5/15; must reply within 2 week(s) of notification.

Academics. Special study options: Accelerated study, cooperative education, cross-registration, distance learning, double major, dual enrollment of high school students, ESL, honors, independent study, liberal arts/career combination, study abroad, weekend college. License preparation in nursing, paramedic, radiology, real estate. **Credit/placement by examination:** AP, CLEP, institutional tests. 30 credit hours maximum toward associate degree. **Support services:** GED preparation and test center, learning center, reduced course load, remedial instruction, tutoring.

Majors. Business: General, accounting, administrative services, hospitality admin, logistics. **Computer sciences:** Applications programming, networking. **Conservation:** General. **Foreign languages:** Sign language interpretation. **Health services:** Dental hygiene, electroencephalograph technology, EMT paramedic, health information technology, nursing (RN), polysomnography, radiologic technology/medical imaging, radiologist assistant, sonography, surgical technology. **Liberal arts:** Arts/sciences. **Protective services:** Police science. **Visual/performing arts:** Interior design. **Work/family studies:** Child care service.

Most popular majors. Business/marketing 8%, health sciences 18%, liberal arts 58%, trade and industry 6%.

Technology on campus. 125 workstations in library, computer center. Commuter students can connect to campus network. Online course registration, online library, helpline, wireless network available.

Student life. Freshman orientation: Mandatory. Preregistration for classes offered. **Activities:** Drama, international student organizations, literary magazine, student government, Phi Theta Kappa, Black Student Union, creative writing club, fine arts club, student veterans association, volunteer club, fashion club.

Athletics. NJCAA. **Intercollegiate:** Cross-country, soccer. **Intramural:** Bowling, table tennis, ultimate frisbee. **Team name:** Eagles.

Student services. Career counseling, student employment services, financial aid counseling, on-campus daycare, personal counseling, placement for graduates, veterans' counselor. **Physically disabled:** Services for visually, speech, hearing impaired. **Transfer:** Transfer adviser, college fairs on campus for students transferring to 4-year colleges.

Contact. Phone: (563) 441-4004 Toll-free number: (888) 336-3907
Fax: (563) 441-4101
Kelsey VenHorst, Admissions Officer, Scott Community College, 500 Belmont Road, Bettendorf, IA 52722-6804

Southeastern Community College
West Burlington, Iowa
www.scciowa.edu   **CB code: 6048**

- Public 2-year community and junior college
- Commuter campus in large town

General. Founded in 1966. Regionally accredited. Campuses in West Burlington, Keokuk, Mt. Pleasant, and Ft. Madison. **Enrollment:** 1,732 degree-seeking undergraduates; 1,136 non-degree-seeking students. **Degrees:** 144 associate awarded. **Location:** 200 miles from Des Moines, 300 miles from Chicago. **Calendar:** Semester, limited summer session. **Full-time faculty:** 42 total; 14% have terminal degrees, 7% minority, 19% women. **Part-time faculty:** 96 total; 6% have terminal degrees, 5% minority, 32% women. **Class size:** 75% < 20, 24% 20-39, less than 1% 40-49, less than 1% 50-99. **Special facilities:** Greenhouse, college operated farm.

Student profile. Among degree-seeking undergraduates, 410 enrolled as first-time, first-year students, 50 transferred in from other institutions.

Part-time:	29%	Native American:	1%
Out-of-state:	15%	Multi-racial, non-Hispanic:	3%
Women:	61%	International:	1%
African American:	6%	25 or older:	22%
Asian American:	1%	Live on campus:	4%
Hispanic/Latino:	5%		

Transfer out. Colleges most students transferred to 2015: University of Iowa, Western Illinois University, Iowa State University, University of Northern Iowa, Iowa Wesleyan College.

Basis for selection. Open admission, but selective for some programs. Special requirements for nursing, electronic technology, medical assistant, medical coding and billing, medical transcription, chemical dependency counselor, EMT-paramedic, and respiratory care.

2015-2016 Annual costs. Tuition/fees: $5,000; $5,150 out-of-state. Per-credit charge: $165 in-state; $170 out-of-state. Room/board: $6,216. Books/supplies: $1,188. Personal expenses: $1,846.

2015-2016 Financial aid. Need-based: 316 full-time freshmen applied for aid; 297 deemed to have need; 293 received aid. Average scholarship/grant was $4,021; average loan $2,840. 69% of total undergraduate aid awarded as scholarships/grants, 31% as loans/jobs. Need-based aid available for part-time students. Work-study available nights, weekends and for part-time students. **Non-need-based:** Scholarships awarded for academics, art, athletics, minority status.

Application procedures. Admission: No deadline. No application fee. Admission notification on a rolling basis. **Financial aid:** No deadline. FAFSA required. Applicants notified on a rolling basis starting 3/1; must reply within 4 week(s) of notification.

Academics. Special study options: Cooperative education, cross-registration, distance learning, dual enrollment of high school students, ESL, honors, independent study, internships, student-designed major, study abroad. Bachelor's degree programs available on campus. License preparation in dental hygiene, nursing, occupational therapy, paramedic, physical therapy, radiology, real estate. **Credit/placement by examination:** AP, CLEP, institutional tests. 30 credit hours maximum toward associate degree. **Support services:** GED preparation and test center, learning center, pre-admission summer program, reduced course load, remedial instruction, study skills assistance, tutoring.

Majors. Business: General, accounting, administrative services, business admin, construction management, executive assistant, office management, office technology, office/clerical, receptionist. **Communications:** Digital media, journalism. **Communications technology:** Desktop publishing, graphics. **Computer sciences:** Computer graphics, data processing, networking, programming, web page design. **Engineering:** Electrical, engineering mechanics. **General:** Carpentry, maintenance. **Health services:** EMT-

paramedic, medical assistant, medical radiologic technology/radiation therapy, nursing (RN), substance abuse counseling. **Liberal arts:** Arts/sciences. **Protective services:** Law enforcement admin. **Work/family studies:** Child care management.

Most popular majors. Business/marketing 8%, health sciences 16%, liberal arts 57%.

Technology on campus. 100 workstations in library, computer center. Dormitories wired for high-speed internet access. Helpline, wireless network available.

Student life. Freshman orientation: Mandatory. Preregistration for classes offered. Two-hour session offered both day and evening before term begins. **Housing:** Coed dorms, single-sex dorms, special housing for disabled, apartments available. $300 partly refundable deposit. **Activities:** Choral groups, drama, international student organizations, music ensembles, musical theater, student government, student newspaper, Campus Crusade for Christ, multicultural club.

Athletics. NJCAA. **Intercollegiate:** Baseball M, basketball, golf, softball W, volleyball W. **Intramural:** Basketball, bowling, cheerleading, football (non-tackle), softball, volleyball. **Team name:** Black Hawks.

Student services. Career counseling, services for economically disadvantaged, student employment services, financial aid counseling, minority student services, on-campus daycare, personal counseling, placement for graduates, veterans' counselor. **Physically disabled:** Services for visually, speech, hearing impaired. **Transfer:** Pre-admission transcript evaluation for new students. Transfer adviser, college fairs on campus for students transferring to 4-year colleges.

Contact. E-mail: admoff@scciowa.edu
Phone: (319) 208-5010 Toll-free number: (866) 722-4692 ext. 5012
Fax: (319) 758-6725
Dana Chrisman, Senior Enrollment Officer, Southeastern Community College, 1500 West Agency Road, West Burlington, IA 52655-0605

Southwestern Community College
Creston, Iowa
www.swcciowa.edu   **CB code: 6122**

- Public 2-year community college
- Commuter campus in small town

General. Founded in 1966. Regionally accredited. **Enrollment:** 935 degree-seeking undergraduates. **Degrees:** 223 associate awarded. **Location:** 75 miles from Des Moines; 110 miles from Omaha, Nebraska. **Calendar:** Semester, limited summer session. **Full-time faculty:** 43 total. **Part-time faculty:** 73 total. **Class size:** 79% < 20, 18% 20-39, 2% 40-49, 1% 50-99. **Special facilities:** Recording studio.

Student profile.

Out-of-state:	4%	Live on campus:	5%
25 or older:	38%		

Transfer out. Colleges most students transferred to 2015: Northwest Missouri State University, Buena Vista University, Iowa State University, Graceland College, University of Northern Iowa.

Basis for selection. Open admission, but selective for some programs. Special requirements for nursing. LPN criteria includes date nursing application is received and date COMPASS test scores are achieved. ADN requirements contingent upon application, COMPASS test scores, and ranking selection process. **Adult students:** Students must take COMPASS test for placement.

High school preparation. One chemistry required for health programs.

2015-2016 Annual costs. Tuition/fees: $4,920; $5,130 out-of-state. Per-credit charge: $152 in-state; $159 out-of-state. Room/board: $6,450. Books/supplies: $1,230. Personal expenses: $1,766.

2014-2015 Financial aid. Need-based: 58% of total undergraduate aid awarded as scholarships/grants, 42% as loans/jobs. Need-based aid available for part-time students. Work-study available nights, weekends and for part-time students. **Non-need-based:** Scholarships awarded for academics, athletics, leadership, music/drama, state residency.

Application procedures. Admission: Priority date 8/1; no deadline. No application fee. Admission notification on a rolling basis. **Financial aid:** Closing date 7/1. FAFSA required. Applicants notified on a rolling basis starting 6/1; must reply within 2 week(s) of notification.

Academics. Special study options: Cooperative education, distance learning, double major, dual enrollment of high school students, independent study, internships, liberal arts/career combination. License preparation in nursing. **Credit/placement by examination:** AP, CLEP. 30 credit hours maximum toward associate degree. Arts and science students without 19 ACT required to take ASSET exam. **Support services:** GED preparation and test center, learning center, reduced course load, remedial instruction, study skills assistance, tutoring.

Majors. Business: General, accounting, administrative services, marketing. **Computer sciences:** Applications programming, information systems, webmaster. **Education:** General. **General:** Carpentry. **Health services:** Medical transcription, nursing (RN). **Liberal arts:** Arts/sciences. **Visual/performing arts:** Music performance.

Most popular majors. Business/marketing 10%, computer/information sciences 6%, health sciences 20%, liberal arts 43%, trade and industry 12%.

Technology on campus. 140 workstations in dormitories, library, computer center, student center. Dormitories wired for high-speed internet access and linked to campus network. Helpline, repair service, wireless network available.

Student life. Freshman orientation: Mandatory. Preregistration for classes offered. **Housing:** Coed dorms, single-sex dorms, wellness housing available. $100 deposit. **Activities:** Bands, choral groups, music ensembles, student government, student newspaper.

Athletics. NJCAA. **Intercollegiate:** Baseball M, basketball, cross-country, golf M, softball W, volleyball W. **Intramural:** Basketball, table tennis, tennis, volleyball. **Team name:** Spartans.

Student services. Adult student services, career counseling, services for economically disadvantaged, student employment services, health services, legal services, personal counseling, placement for graduates, veterans' counselor. **Physically disabled:** Services for visually, speech, hearing impaired. **Transfer:** Pre-admission transcript evaluation for new students. Transfer adviser, college fairs on campus for students transferring to 4-year colleges.

Contact. Phone: (641) 782-7081 ext. 421
Toll-free number: (800) 247-4023 Fax: (641) 782-3312
Caitlyn Lesan, Director of Admissions, Southwestern Community College, 1501 West Townline Street, Creston, IA 50801

St. Luke's College
Sioux City, Iowa
www.stlukescollege.edu   CB code: 3625

- Private 2-year health science and nursing college
- Commuter campus in small city
- SAT or ACT (ACT writing optional), application essay, interview required

General. Regionally accredited. Offers hospital-based health care provider programs. **Enrollment:** 245 degree-seeking undergraduates. **Degrees:** 6 bachelor's, 90 associate awarded. **Location:** 90 miles from Omaha. **Calendar:** Semester, limited summer session. **Full-time faculty:** 29 total; 7% have terminal degrees, 3% minority, 90% women. **Part-time faculty:** 21 total; 14% have terminal degrees, 81% women. **Class size:** 65% < 20, 35% 20-39.

Student profile. Among degree-seeking undergraduates, 30% enrolled in a transfer program, 70% enrolled in a vocational program, 4% already have a bachelor's degree or higher, 11 enrolled as first-time, first-year students, 16 transferred in from other institutions.

Part-time:	46%	**Women:**	89%
Out-of-state:	35%	**25 or older:**	38%

Transfer out. Colleges most students transferred to 2015: Morningside College, Briar Cliff College, Western Iowa Tech Community College, Dordt College.

Basis for selection. Degree programs require 2.5 GPA or GED and 19 ACT. Equivalent coursework considered for transfer credit. **Learning Disabled:** Job shadowing recommended.

High school preparation. 8 units recommended. Recommended units include English 4, mathematics 2 and science 2. Electives recommended include psychology, computer operations, typing or keyboarding.

2016-2017 Annual costs. Tuition/fees: $20,460. Per-credit charge: $525. Books/supplies: $1,188. Personal expenses: $1,900.

2015-2016 Financial aid. Need-based: Average need met was 75%. Average scholarship/grant was $3,096; average loan $4,250. 48% of total undergraduate aid awarded as scholarships/grants, 52% as loans/jobs. Need-based aid available for part-time students. Work-study available nights, weekends and for part-time students. **Non-need-based:** Scholarships awarded for academics, job skills, leadership.

Application procedures. Admission: No deadline. $50 fee, may be waived for applicants with need. Admission notification on a rolling basis. Must reply within 2 weeks of acceptance. **Financial aid:** Priority date 3/1; no closing date. FAFSA required. Applicants notified on a rolling basis starting 4/15; must reply within 2 week(s) of notification.

Academics. Special study options: Combined bachelor's/graduate degree, internships. Bachelor's degree programs available on campus. License preparation in nursing, radiology. **Credit/placement by examination:** AP, CLEP. 22 credit hours maximum toward associate degree. **Support services:** Reduced course load, study skills assistance, tutoring.

Majors. Health services: Nursing (RN), radiologic technology/medical imaging, respiratory therapy technology.

Technology on campus. 12 workstations in library, computer center, student center. Commuter students can connect to campus network. Online library, helpline, wireless network available.

Student life. Freshman orientation: Mandatory, $20 fee. Preregistration for classes offered. Held prior to classes. **Policies:** Alcohol- and drug-free campus. **Activities:** Community service participation.

Student services. Alcohol/substance abuse counseling, chaplain/spiritual director, student employment services, financial aid counseling, health services, personal counseling, veterans' counselor. **Transfer:** Pre-admission transcript evaluation for new students.

Contact. E-mail: sherry.mccarthy@stlukescollege.edu
Phone: (712) 279-3158 Toll-free number: (800) 352-4660 ext. 3158
Fax: (712) 233-8017
Sherry McCarthy, Enrollment Coordinator, St. Luke's College, 2800 Pierce Street Suite 410, Sioux City, IA 51104

Vatterott College: Des Moines
Des Moines, Iowa
www.vatterott-college.edu   CB code: 2909

- For-profit 2-year health science and technical college
- Commuter campus in large city
- Interview required

General. Accredited by ACCSC. **Enrollment:** 239 undergraduates. **Degrees:** 40 associate awarded. **Calendar:** Differs by program, extensive summer session. **Full-time faculty:** 6 total. **Part-time faculty:** 18 total.

Basis for selection. Open admission.

2015-2016 Annual costs. Certificate program: (5 weeks) $4,250. Diploma programs: (40 weeks) $20,384-$21,500; (50 weeks) $24,440. Associate programs: (70 weeks) $31,260-$39,090; (80 weeks) $38,280. Costs include fees, books and supplies.

Financial aid. All financial aid based on need. Work-study available nights, weekends and for part-time students.

Application procedures. Admission: No deadline. No application fee. Admission notification on a rolling basis. School tour, interview with admissions representative, financial clearance, completion of placement evaluation, application, and enrollment forms required. **Financial aid:** No deadline. FAFSA required. Applicants notified on a rolling basis.

Academics. Credit/placement by examination: AP, CLEP, institutional tests. 24 credit hours maximum toward associate degree. Credits may be counted toward diploma if student passes and is awarded credit for previous training. **Support services:** Remedial instruction, tutoring.

Majors. Computer sciences: Networking, programming.

Technology on campus. 125 workstations in library, computer center.

Student life. Freshman orientation: Mandatory. Preregistration for classes offered.

Student services. Financial aid counseling, placement for graduates. **Transfer:** Pre-admission transcript evaluation for new students.

Contact. E-mail: desmoines@vatterott-college.edu
Phone: (515) 309-9000 Toll-free number: (800) 353-7264
Fax: (515) 309-0366
Maureen Shay, Director of Admissions, Vatterott College: Des Moines,
7000 Fleur Drive, Des Moines, IA 50321

Western Iowa Tech Community College

Sioux City, Iowa   **CB member**
www.witcc.edu   **CB code: 6950**

▶ Public 2-year community college
▶ Commuter campus in small city

General. Founded in 1966. Regionally accredited. **Enrollment:** 3,288
degree-seeking undergraduates. **Degrees:** 556 associate awarded. **Location:**
200 miles from Des Moines; 90 miles from Omaha, NE. **Calendar:** Semester,
extensive summer session. **Full-time faculty:** 77 total; 9% have terminal
degrees, 4% minority, 51% women. **Part-time faculty:** 296 total; 7% have
terminal degrees, 4% minority, 56% women. **Class size:** 73% < 20, 25% 20-
39, less than 1% 40-49, less than 1% 50-99, less than 1% >100.

Transfer out. Colleges most students transferred to 2015: University
of South Dakota, Bellevue University, Briar Cliff University, Buena Vista
University, Morningside College.

Basis for selection. Open admission, but selective for some programs.
Special requirements for nursing, surgical technician, dental assistant, physical therapy assistant, childcare supervision and management, emergency
medical technician, police science, forensics, corrections, emergency disaster
management, emergency medical services, and business.

High school preparation. Recommended units include English 4, mathematics 3, social studies 3, history 2, science 3 and foreign language 1.

2015-2016 Annual costs. Tuition/fees: $5,130; $5,160 out-of-state. Per-
credit charge: $139 in-state; $140 out-of-state. Room/board: $4,800. Books/
supplies: $1,200. Personal expenses: $1,206.

Financial aid. Need-based: Need-based aid available for part-time students. Work-study available nights, weekends and for part-time students.
Non-need-based: Scholarships awarded for academics, art, leadership,
minority status, music/drama.

Application procedures. Admission: No deadline. No application fee.
Admission notification on a rolling basis. **Financial aid:** No deadline. FAFSA
required. Applicants notified on a rolling basis starting 4/1.

Academics. Special study options: Accelerated study, cooperative education, distance learning, double major, dual enrollment of high school students,
ESL, external degree, honors, independent study, internships, liberal arts/
career combination, study abroad, weekend college. License preparation in
dental hygiene, nursing, paramedic, physical therapy. **Credit/placement by
examination:** AP, CLEP, institutional tests. **Support services:** GED preparation and test center, learning center, pre-admission summer program, reduced
course load, remedial instruction, study skills assistance, tutoring.

Majors. Biology: Biotechnology. **Business:** Accounting, administrative services, business admin, finance, human resources, office technology, sales/
distribution. **Communications technology:** Animation/special effects, desktop publishing, recording arts. **Computer sciences:** Web page design. **Health
services:** Dental hygiene, EMT paramedic, medical secretary, office admin,
physical therapy assistant, surgical technology. **Liberal arts:** Arts/sciences.
Protective services: Firefighting, police science, security management. **Vis-
ual/performing arts:** Cinematography, interior design. **Work/family studies:** Child care service.

Most popular majors. Business/marketing 13%, health sciences 20%,
liberal arts 32%, security/protective services 6%, trade and industry 6%.

Technology on campus. 1,500 workstations in dormitories, library, computer center, student center. Dormitories wired for high-speed internet access
and linked to campus network. Commuter students can connect to campus
network. Online course registration, online library, helpline, wireless network available.

Student life. Freshman orientation: Mandatory. Preregistration for
classes offered. **Housing:** Coed dorms, apartments available. $145 nonrefund-
able deposit. **Activities:** Jazz band, choral groups, dance, drama, international
student organizations, music ensembles, radio station, student government,
Cherokee Garden, Habitat for Humanity, CRU, Harmony and Discord, inter-
national/multi-cultural club, Military and Veterans, Young Democrats,
Young Republicans.

Athletics. Intramural: Basketball, bowling M, football (non-tackle), rugby
M, soccer, softball, volleyball. **Team name:** Comets.

Student services. Adult student services, alcohol/substance abuse counseling, career counseling, services for economically disadvantaged, student
employment services, financial aid counseling, minority student services,
personal counseling, placement for graduates, veterans' counselor. **Physically
disabled:** Services for visually, speech, hearing impaired. **Transfer:** Transfer
center, transfer adviser, college fairs on campus for students transferring to
4-year colleges.

Contact. E-mail: Admissions@witcc.edu
Phone: (712) 274-6403 Toll-free number: (800) 352-4649 ext. 6403
Fax: (712) 274-6441
Lora VanderZwaag, Director of Admissions & Advising, Western Iowa
Tech Community College, Box 5199, Sioux City, IA 51102-5199

Kansas

Allen County Community College
Iola, Kansas
www.allencc.edu CB code: 6305

- Public 2-year community college
- Commuter campus in small town

General. Founded in 1923. Regionally accredited. **Enrollment:** 2,854 undergraduates. **Degrees:** 250 associate awarded. **Location:** 100 miles from Kansas City. **Calendar:** Semester, limited summer session. **Full-time faculty:** 36 total. **Part-time faculty:** 145 total.

Student profile.

Out-of-state:	3%	Live on campus:	20%
25 or older:	31%		

Transfer out. Colleges most students transferred to 2015: Pittsburg State University, Kansas State University, Emporia State University, University of Kansas, Washburn University.

Basis for selection. Open admission. TOEFL score of 520 or higher required for admission of non-English-speaking students. **Home schooled:** Transcript of courses and grades required. Placement test required (ACT, COMPASS or ASSET). **Learning Disabled:** Copies of a high school IEP are helpful, but not required.

2015-2016 Annual costs. Tuition/fees: $2,250; $2,250 out-of-district; $2,250 out-of-state. Per-credit charge: $57 in-district; $57 out-of-district; $57 out-of-state. Room/board: $4,550. Books/supplies: $300. Personal expenses: $1,620.

Financial aid. Need-based: Need-based aid available for part-time students. Work-study available nights, weekends and for part-time students. **Non-need-based:** Scholarships awarded for academics, art, athletics, music/drama, state residency. **Additional information:** Scholarships for livestock judging, cheerleading, choir, dance, drama, art, academic challenge, and student ambassadors.

Application procedures. Admission: No deadline. No application fee. Admission notification on a rolling basis. **Financial aid:** Closing date 6/1. FAFSA required. Applicants notified on a rolling basis starting 6/1; must reply within 2 week(s) of notification.

Academics. Special study options: Cooperative education, distance learning, double major, dual enrollment of high school students, independent study, internships, liberal arts/career combination, student-designed major, weekend college. Bachelor's degree programs available on campus. **Credit/placement by examination:** AP, CLEP, institutional tests. 12 credit hours maximum toward associate degree. **Support services:** GED preparation and test center, learning center, reduced course load, remedial instruction, study skills assistance, tutoring, writing center.

Majors. Biology: General. **Business:** Accounting, administrative services, business admin, office management, sales/distribution. **Computer sciences:** General, computer science. **Education:** Mathematics, music, secondary. **Engineering:** Electrical. **Health services:** EMT paramedic, nursing assistant. **History:** General. **Liberal arts:** Library assistant. **Math:** General. **Physical sciences:** Chemistry, physics. **Protective services:** Police science. **Social sciences:** Economics, geography, sociology. **Visual/performing arts:** Art, ceramics, crafts, drawing, music, painting, studio arts, voice/opera.

Technology on campus. 100 workstations in dormitories, library, computer center, student center. Dormitories wired for high-speed internet access. Online library, repair service, wireless network available.

Student life. Freshman orientation: Mandatory. Preregistration for classes offered. **Housing:** Coed dorms, apartments available. $125 fully refundable deposit. **Activities:** Bands, choral groups, dance, drama, music ensembles, musical theater, student government, student newspaper, Aggie club, biology club, Phi Theta Kappa, Academic Challenge, student senate, Allen Flame.

Athletics. NJCAA. **Intercollegiate:** Baseball M, basketball, cheerleading, cross-country, golf M, soccer, softball W, track and field, volleyball W.

Intramural: Basketball, football (non-tackle), softball, table tennis, tennis, volleyball. **Team name:** Red Devils.

Student services. Adult student services, alcohol/substance abuse counseling, career counseling, services for economically disadvantaged, student employment services, financial aid counseling, minority student services, personal counseling, placement for graduates, veterans' counselor, women's services. **Physically disabled:** Services for visually, hearing impaired. **Transfer:** Pre-admission transcript evaluation for new students. Transfer adviser, college fairs on campus for students transferring to 4-year colleges.

Contact. E-mail: admissions@allencc.edu
Phone: (620) 365-5116 ext. 268 Fax: (620) 365-3284
Rebecca Bilderback, Director of Admissions and Marketing, Allen County Community College, 1801 North Cottonwood, Iola, KS 66749

Barton County Community College
Great Bend, Kansas
www.bartonccc.edu CB code: 0784

- Public 2-year community college
- Commuter campus in large town

General. Founded in 1965. Regionally accredited. **Enrollment:** 2,646 degree-seeking undergraduates. **Degrees:** 521 associate awarded. **Location:** 125 miles from Wichita. **Calendar:** Semester, limited summer session. **Full-time faculty:** 71 total; 8% have terminal degrees, 7% minority, 44% women. **Part-time faculty:** 162 total; 2% have terminal degrees, 4% minority. **Class size:** 85% < 20, 14% 20-39, less than 1% 40-49. **Special facilities:** Natatorium, planetarium.

Student profile.

Out-of-state:	5%	Live on campus:	8%
25 or older:	46%		

Transfer out. Colleges most students transferred to 2015: Fort Hays State University, Kansas State University, University of Kansas, Wichita State University, Emporia State University.

Basis for selection. Open admission, but selective for some programs. Special requirements for medical laboratory technician, nursing, and mobile intensive care technician programs. ACT, SAT, ASSET or ACCUPLACER required for placement in math or English courses. Interview required of nursing majors.

2015-2016 Annual costs. Tuition/fees: $2,910; $3,840 out-of-state. Per-credit charge: $65 in-district; $65 out-of-district; $65 out-of-state. Room/board: $5,379. Books/supplies: $1,270. Personal expenses: $2,041.

Financial aid. Need-based: Need-based aid available for part-time students. Work-study available nights, weekends and for part-time students. **Non-need-based:** Scholarships awarded for academics, athletics.

Application procedures. Admission: No deadline. No application fee. Application must be submitted on paper. Admission notification on a rolling basis. **Financial aid:** Priority date 3/1; no closing date. FAFSA required. Applicants notified on a rolling basis starting 6/1; must reply within 4 week(s) of notification.

Academics. Special study options: Accelerated study, cooperative education, distance learning, dual enrollment of high school students, ESL, honors, independent study, internships. License preparation in nursing, paramedic, real estate. **Credit/placement by examination:** AP, CLEP, IB, institutional tests. ACT, SAT, ASSET, or ACCUPLACER is required for enrollment in Math or English coursework. **Support services:** GED preparation and test center, learning center, remedial instruction, tutoring.

Majors. Biology: General, wildlife. **Business:** General, accounting, accounting technology, administrative services, business admin, human resources, operations. **Communications:** Communications/speech/rhetoric, journalism. **Computer sciences:** Computer science, information systems, networking. **Conservation:** Forestry. **Education:** General. **Engineering:** General. **English:** English lit. **Foreign languages:** General. **Health services:** Athletic training, clinical lab technology, dietetics, EMT paramedic, health information management, medical assistant, nursing (RN), office assistant, predental, premedicine, prenursing, prepharmacy, preveterinary. **History:** General. **Human services:** General, social work. **Liberal arts:** Arts/sciences. **Math:** General. **Parks/recreation:** Exercise sciences, health/fitness, sports admin. **Philosophy/religion:** Philosophy. **Physical sciences:** General, chemistry, physics. **Protective services:** Corrections, firefighting, police science, security management. **Psychology:** General. **Social sciences:** Anthropology, economics, political science, sociology. **Visual/performing arts:** Art, dance, dramatic, graphic design, music. **Work/family studies:** Child care management.

Most popular majors. Health sciences 15%, liberal arts 72%.

Technology on campus. 350 workstations in dormitories, library, computer center, student center. Dormitories wired for high-speed internet access and linked to campus network. Commuter students can connect to campus network. Online course registration, online library, helpline, wireless network available.

Student life. Freshman orientation: Mandatory. Preregistration for classes offered. **Housing:** Guaranteed on-campus for freshmen. Coed dorms, wellness housing available. $120 fully refundable deposit. **Activities:** Bands, choral groups, dance, drama, literary magazine, music ensembles, musical theater, student government, student newspaper, Newman Club, Fellowship of Christian Athletes, Campus Christian Fellowship, Student Ambassadors.

Athletics. NJCAA. **Intercollegiate:** Baseball M, basketball, cheerleading, cross-country, golf, soccer, softball W, tennis, track and field, volleyball W, wrestling M. **Intramural:** Baseball M, basketball, football (non-tackle), softball, table tennis, tennis, volleyball. **Team name:** Cougars.

Student services. Adult student services, alcohol/substance abuse counseling, career counseling, services for economically disadvantaged, student employment services, financial aid counseling, health services, on-campus daycare, personal counseling, placement for graduates, veterans' counselor. **Physically disabled:** Services for hearing impaired. **Transfer:** Pre-admission transcript evaluation for new students. Transfer adviser, college fairs on campus for students transferring to 4-year colleges.

Contact. E-mail: admissions@bartonccc.edu
Phone: (620) 792-2701 ext. 286 Toll-free number: (800) 722-6842
Fax: (620) 786-1160
Tana Cooper, Director of Admissions, Barton County Community College, 245 North East 30th Road, Great Bend, KS 67530-9283

Brown Mackie College: Salina
Salina, Kansas
www.brownmackie.edu/Salina/   CB code: 3366

▶ For-profit 2-year junior college
▶ Commuter campus in large town

General. Regionally accredited. Branch campus in Kansas City. **Enrollment:** 560 undergraduates. **Degrees:** 7 bachelor's, 118 associate awarded. **Location:** 90 miles from Wichita, 108 miles from Topeka. **Calendar:** Quarter, extensive summer session. **Full-time faculty:** 12 total. **Part-time faculty:** 32 total.

Transfer out. Colleges most students transferred to 2015: Kansas Wesleyan University, Kansas State University.

Basis for selection. Open admission. **Home schooled:** Transcript of courses and grades required. Home-school must be registered by state department of education.

2015-2016 Annual costs. Tuition/fees: $16,490. Per-credit charge: $327. Books/supplies: $1,500. Personal expenses: $1,520.

Financial aid. Need-based: Work-study available nights, weekends and for part-time students.

Application procedures. Admission: No deadline. No application fee. Application must be submitted on paper. Admission notification on a rolling basis. **Financial aid:** No deadline. Applicants notified on a rolling basis.

Academics. Special study options: Internships, weekend college. License preparation in nursing. **Credit/placement by examination:** AP, CLEP, institutional tests. **Support services:** Remedial instruction, study skills assistance, tutoring.

Majors. Business: Accounting, business admin, selling. **Computer sciences:** Information technology, networking. **Health services:** Office admin. **Protective services:** Law enforcement admin.

Technology on campus. 134 workstations in library, computer center.

Student life. Freshman orientation: Mandatory. Preregistration for classes offered. Part-day program held prior to start of classes. **Activities:** Student government, student newspaper.

Athletics. NJCAA. **Intercollegiate:** Baseball M, basketball, softball W. **Intramural:** Softball. **Team name:** Lions.

Student services. Career counseling, student employment services, placement for graduates.

Contact. E-mail: dheath@brownmackie.edu
Phone: (785) 825-5422 Toll-free number: (800) 365-0433
Fax: (785) 827-7623
Diann Heath, Director of Admissions, Brown Mackie College: Salina, 2106 South Ninth Street, Salina, KS 67401

Bryan University: Topeka
Topeka, Kansas
www.bryancolleges.edu

▶ For-profit 2-year technical and career college
▶ Small city

General. Regionally accredited; also accredited by ACICS. **Enrollment:** 63 undergraduates. **Degrees:** 31 associate awarded. **Calendar:** Quarter. **Full-time faculty:** 1 total. **Part-time faculty:** 10 total.

Basis for selection. Secondary school record required.

2015-2016 Annual costs. Books/supplies: $2,625. **Additional information:** Diploma programs range from $19,430-$21,765; Associates programsrange from $31,955- $34,097. Books, supplies, fees range depending on program level and course of study. All costs are subject to change.

Financial aid. Need-based: Work-study available nights, weekends and for part-time students.

Application procedures. Admission: $50 fee.

Academics. Credit/placement by examination: AP, CLEP.

Majors. Business: Business admin. **Computer sciences:** Networking. **Health services:** Clinical lab technology, medical assistant, medical secretary. **Protective services:** Criminal justice.

Contact. E-mail: csollars@bryancc.edu
Phone: (785) 272-0889
Carolynn Sollars, Director of Admission, Bryan University: Topeka, 1527 SW Fairlawn Road, Topeka, KS 66604

Butler Community College
El Dorado, Kansas
www.butlercc.edu   CB code: 6191

▶ Public 2-year community college
▶ Commuter campus in large town

General. Founded in 1927. Regionally accredited. Off-campus sites at Andover, McConnell, Augusta, Flint Hills, Rose Hill and 20 other smaller locations. **Enrollment:** 9,363 undergraduates. **Degrees:** 1,141 associate awarded. **Location:** 25 miles from Wichita. **Calendar:** Semester, extensive summer session. **Full-time faculty:** 152 total. **Part-time faculty:** 484 total. **Class size:** 70% < 20, 30% 20-39, less than 1% 40-49, less than 1% 50-99.

Student profile.

Out-of-state:	1%	Live on campus:	2%
25 or older:	38%		

Transfer out. Colleges most students transferred to 2015: Wichita State University, Kansas State University, Emporia State University, University of Kansas, Kansas Newman College.

Basis for selection. Open admission, but selective for some programs. Nursing applicants admitted based on GPA in prerequisite courses.

2015-2016 Annual costs. Tuition/fees: $2,640; $2,970 out-of-district; $4,770 out-of-state. Per-credit charge: $69 in-district; $80 out-of-district; $140 out-of-state. Room/board: $5,650. Books/supplies: $1,000. Personal expenses: $1,350.

Financial aid. Need-based: Need-based aid available for part-time students. Work-study available nights, weekends and for part-time students. **Non-need-based:** Scholarships awarded for academics, art, athletics, music/drama.

Application procedures. Admission: No deadline. No application fee. Admission notification on a rolling basis. **Financial aid:** Priority date 4/1; no closing date. FAFSA, institutional form required. Applicants notified on a rolling basis starting 5/1; must reply within 2 week(s) of notification.

Academics. **Special study options:** Accelerated study, cooperative education, distance learning, dual enrollment of high school students, ESL, honors, independent study, internships, liberal arts/career combination, weekend college. License preparation in nursing, paramedic. **Credit/placement by examination:** AP, CLEP, institutional tests. 30 credit hours maximum toward associate degree. **Support services:** GED preparation, learning center, reduced course load, remedial instruction, study skills assistance, tutoring, writing center.

Majors. **Business:** Accounting, business admin, hospitality admin, hospitality/recreation, office/clerical. **Communications:** Journalism. **Computer sciences:** General, computer science. **Education:** Business, early childhood, elementary, physical, secondary, teacher assistance. **Engineering:** General. **English:** Rhetoric/composition, writing. **Foreign languages:** General, Spanish. **Health services:** Licensed practical nurse, nursing (RN), premedicine. **History:** General. **Human services:** Social work. **Liberal arts:** Arts/sciences. **Math:** General. **Physical sciences:** Chemistry, physics. **Protective services:** Criminal justice, firefighting, police science. **Psychology:** General. **Social sciences:** Economics, political science. **Visual/performing arts:** Art, dramatic, music. **Work/family studies:** Child care management.

Most popular majors. Health sciences 15%, liberal arts 75%.

Technology on campus. 130 workstations in dormitories, library, computer center, student center. Dormitories wired for high-speed internet access and linked to campus network. Commuter students can connect to campus network. Online course registration, online library, helpline, repair service available.

Student life. **Freshman orientation:** Mandatory. Preregistration for classes offered. **Housing:** Coed dorms, single-sex dorms, special housing for disabled, wellness housing available. $75 fully refundable deposit. **Activities:** Bands, choral groups, dance, drama, literary magazine, music ensembles, musical theater, radio station, student government, student newspaper, TV station, international student association, Campus Crusade for Christ.

Athletics. NJCAA. **Intercollegiate:** Baseball M, basketball, cross-country, football (tackle) M, soccer W, softball W, track and field, volleyball W. **Intramural:** Basketball, bowling, soccer, softball, table tennis, volleyball. **Team name:** Grizzlies.

Student services. Adult student services, career counseling, student employment services, financial aid counseling, health services, on-campus daycare, personal counseling, placement for graduates, veterans' counselor. **Physically disabled:** Services for visually, speech, hearing impaired. **Transfer:** Pre-admission transcript evaluation for new students. Transfer adviser, college fairs on campus for students transferring to 4-year colleges.

Contact. E-mail: admissions@butlercc.edu
Phone: (316) 322-3255 Fax: (316) 322-3316
Kirsten Allen, Director of Enrollment Management, Butler Community College, 901 South Haverhill Road, El Dorado, KS 67042-3280

Cloud County Community College
Concordia, Kansas
www.cloud.edu   **CB code: 6137**

▶ Public 2-year community college
▶ Commuter campus in small town

General. Founded in 1965. Regionally accredited. **Enrollment:** 1,196 degree-seeking undergraduates. **Degrees:** 245 associate awarded. **Location:** 200 miles from Kansas City, 140 miles from Topeka. **Calendar:** Semester, limited summer session. **Full-time faculty:** 42 total; 14% have terminal degrees, 2% minority, 38% women. **Part-time faculty:** 214 total; 7% minority, 68% women. **Class size:** 84% < 20, 16% 20-39, less than 1% 40-49. **Special facilities:** Theater, observatory, children's center, human cadaver lab.

Student profile. Among degree-seeking undergraduates, 537 enrolled as first-time, first-year students.

Part-time:	40%	25 or older:	24%
Women:	61%	Live on campus:	14%

Transfer out. **Colleges most students transferred to 2015:** Kansas State University, Fort Hays State University, Wichita State University, Kansas Wesleyan University, University of Kansas.

Basis for selection. Open admission.

High school preparation. 18 units recommended. Recommended units include English 4, mathematics 3, social studies 2 and science 4.

2015-2016 Annual costs. Tuition/fees: $2,820; $2,970 out-of-district; $3,120 out-of-state. Per-credit charge: $72 in-district; $79 out-of-district;

$133 out-of-state. Room/board: $5,750. Books/supplies: $1,200. Personal expenses: $1,650.

2014-2015 Financial aid. **Need-based:** 59% of total undergraduate aid awarded as scholarships/grants, 41% as loans/jobs. Need-based aid available for part-time students. Work-study available nights, weekends and for part-time students.

Application procedures. **Admission:** No deadline. No application fee. Admission notification on a rolling basis. **Financial aid:** Priority date 4/1; no closing date. FAFSA required. Applicants notified on a rolling basis starting 5/1; must reply within 4 week(s) of notification.

Academics. **Special study options:** Cooperative education, distance learning, dual enrollment of high school students, ESL, honors, independent study, internships. License preparation in nursing. **Credit/placement by examination:** AP, CLEP, institutional tests. 30 credit hours maximum toward associate degree. **Support services:** GED preparation and test center, learning center, pre-admission summer program, remedial instruction, study skills assistance, tutoring, writing center.

Majors. **Business:** Administrative services, business admin. **Communications:** Journalism. **Communications technology:** Radio/TV. **Computer sciences:** LAN/WAN management, web page design. **Health services:** Nursing (RN). **Liberal arts:** Arts/sciences. **Protective services:** Police science. **Visual/performing arts:** Graphic design. **Work/family studies:** Child care management.

Most popular majors. Health sciences 11%, liberal arts 69%, trade and industry 9%.

Technology on campus. 294 workstations in library, computer center. Dormitories wired for high-speed internet access and linked to campus network. Commuter students can connect to campus network. Online course registration, online library, helpline, wireless network available.

Student life. **Freshman orientation:** Mandatory. Preregistration for classes offered. One-day prior to classes each fall semester, from 9am to 3pm. **Housing:** Single-sex dorms, apartments available. $100 fully refundable deposit. **Activities:** Bands, choral groups, dance, drama, international student organizations, music ensembles, radio station, student government, Fellowship of Christian Athletes.

Athletics. NJCAA. **Intercollegiate:** Baseball M, basketball, cheerleading, cross-country, soccer M, softball W, track and field, volleyball W. **Intramural:** Basketball, football (non-tackle), ultimate frisbee, volleyball. **Team name:** Thunderbirds.

Student services. Career counseling, services for economically disadvantaged, student employment services, financial aid counseling, health services, on-campus daycare, personal counseling, veterans' counselor. **Physically disabled:** Services for visually, hearing impaired. **Transfer:** Pre-admission transcript evaluation for new students. Transfer center, transfer adviser, college fairs on campus for students transferring to 4-year colleges.

Contact. E-mail: admit@cloud.edu
Phone: (785) 243-1435 ext. 212
Toll-free number: (800) 729-5101 ext. 212 Fax: (785) 243-9380
Shane Olson, Director of Admissions, Cloud County Community College, 2221 Campus Drive, Concordia, KS 66901-1002

Coffeyville Community College
Coffeyville, Kansas
www.coffeyville.edu   **CB code: 6102**

▶ Public 2-year community and technical college
▶ Commuter campus in large town

General. Founded in 1923. Regionally accredited. **Enrollment:** 1,067 degree-seeking undergraduates; 673 non-degree-seeking students. **Degrees:** 252 associate awarded. **Location:** 75 miles from Tulsa, Oklahoma, 137 miles from Wichita. **Calendar:** Semester, limited summer session. **Full-time faculty:** 50 total. **Part-time faculty:** 25 total. **Class size:** 64% < 20, 33% 20-39, less than 1% 40-49, 3% 50-99. **Special facilities:** Greenhouse, commercial television station.

Student profile. Among degree-seeking undergraduates, 70% enrolled in a transfer program, 23% enrolled in a vocational program, 484 enrolled as first-time, first-year students, 56 transferred in from other institutions.

Part-time:	10%	Native American:	5%
Out-of-state:	15%	Multi-racial, non-Hispanic:	7%
Women:	43%	International:	3%
African American:	24%	Live on campus:	31%
Hispanic/Latino:	7%		

Transfer out. Colleges most students transferred to 2015: Pittsburg State University, Kansas State University, University of Kansas.

Basis for selection. Open admission. Home schooled: Transcript of courses and grades required. ACT or placement test required for placement. **Learning Disabled:** Require IEP.

High school preparation. 20 units recommended. Recommended units include English 4, mathematics 4, social studies 3, history 2, science 3 (laboratory 2), foreign language 1, computer science 1 and visual/performing arts 1.

2015-2016 Annual costs. Tuition/fees: $2,160; $3,630 out-of-state. Per-credit charge: $35 in-state; $84 out-of-state. Room/board: $5,551. Books/supplies: $800. Personal expenses: $1,200.

Financial aid. Need-based: Need-based aid available for part-time students. Work-study available nights, weekends and for part-time students. **Non-need-based:** Scholarships awarded for academics, alumni affiliation, art, athletics, leadership, music/drama, state residency.

Application procedures. Admission: No deadline. No application fee. Admission notification on a rolling basis. **Financial aid:** Priority date 7/1; no closing date. FAFSA required. Applicants notified on a rolling basis starting 6/20.

Academics. Special study options: Distance learning, dual enrollment of high school students, independent study, internships, liberal arts/career combination. License preparation in nursing, paramedic. **Credit/placement by examination:** AP, CLEP, institutional tests. **Support services:** Learning center, reduced course load, remedial instruction, study skills assistance, tutoring.

Honors college/program. Application for Presidential Scholarship, minimum ACT score of 24, minimum 3.5 high school GPA, essay required. Top 12-15 applicants accepted each fall.

Majors. Biology: General. **Business:** General, accounting, administrative services, business admin, entrepreneurial studies, management information systems, office management, office/clerical, retailing. **Communications:** Broadcast journalism, communications/speech/rhetoric, journalism. **Communications technology:** General. **Computer sciences:** General, networking. **Education:** General, early childhood, elementary, multi-level teacher, physical, secondary, speech. **Engineering:** General. **English:** English lit, rhetoric/composition. **Foreign languages:** General, Spanish. **Health services:** Athletic training, EMT paramedic, nursing assistant, predental, premedicine, prenursing, prepharmacy, preveterinary. **History:** General. **Human services:** Social work. **Liberal arts:** Arts/sciences. **Math:** General. **Parks/recreation:** Health/fitness. **Physical sciences:** Chemistry, physics. **Psychology:** General. **Social sciences:** General, economics, political science, sociology. **Visual/performing arts:** General, art, dramatic, music, studio arts. **Work/family studies:** General, institutional food production.

Technology on campus. 100 workstations in dormitories, library, computer center, student center. Dormitories wired for high-speed internet access. Online course registration, wireless network available.

Student life. Freshman orientation: Mandatory. Preregistration for classes offered. **Housing:** Single-sex dorms, apartments available. $100 non-refundable deposit. **Activities:** Bands, choral groups, dance, drama, film society, international student organizations, music ensembles, musical theater, student government, TV station, Phi Theta Kappa, agriculture club.

Athletics. NJCAA. **Intercollegiate:** Baseball M, basketball, cheerleading, cross-country, football (tackle) M, golf, rodeo, soccer, softball W, track and field, volleyball W. **Intramural:** Basketball, bowling, golf, table tennis, volleyball. **Team name:** Red Ravens.

Student services. Adult student services, alcohol/substance abuse counseling, career counseling, student employment services, financial aid counseling, health services, personal counseling, veterans' counselor. **Physically disabled:** Services for visually, speech, hearing impaired. **Transfer:** Transfer adviser, college fairs on campus for students transferring to 4-year colleges.

Contact. E-mail: admissions@coffeyville.edu
Phone: (620) 252-7047 Toll-free number: (877) 517-2836
Fax: (620) 252-7098
Kristin Horner, Admissions Coordinator, Coffeyville Community College, 400 West 11th Street, Coffeyville, KS 67337-5064

Colby Community College
Colby, Kansas
www.colbycc.edu

CB code: 6129

▶ Public 2-year community college
▶ Commuter campus in small town

General. Founded in 1964. Regionally accredited. **Enrollment:** 1,311 undergraduates. **Degrees:** 282 associate awarded. **Location:** 100 miles from Hays, 200 miles from Denver. **Calendar:** Semester, limited summer session. **Full-time faculty:** 65 total. **Part-time faculty:** 75 total. **Class size:** 72% < 20, 26% 20-39, less than 1% 40-49, less than 1% 50-99. **Special facilities:** Cultural arts center, fitness laboratory, college swimming pool.

Student profile.

Out-of-state:	30%	**Live on campus:**	30%
25 or older:	12%		

Transfer out. Colleges most students transferred to 2015: Fort Hays State University, Kansas State University, University of Kansas.

Basis for selection. Open admission, but selective for some programs. Interview required for physical therapist assistant, veterinary technology, dental hygiene, and nursing programs. Audition recommended for music majors. Portfolios recommended for art majors. **Adult students:** COMPASS required if 2 or more years since ACT/SAT was taken. **Home schooled:** Transcript of courses and grades, state high school equivalency certificate required.

2015-2016 Annual costs. Tuition/fees: $3,150; $4,920 out-of-state. Per-credit charge: $65 in-state; $124 out-of-state. Room/board: $4,460. Books/supplies: $900. Personal expenses: $850.

Financial aid. Need-based: Need-based aid available for part-time students. Work-study available nights, weekends and for part-time students. **Non-need-based:** Scholarships awarded for academics, athletics, leadership, music/drama.

Application procedures. Admission: No deadline. No application fee. Admission notification on a rolling basis. **Financial aid:** Priority date 6/1; no closing date. FAFSA required. Applicants notified on a rolling basis starting 5/1.

Academics. Special study options: Cooperative education, distance learning, dual enrollment of high school students, independent study, internships, liberal arts/career combination. License preparation in dental hygiene, nursing. **Credit/placement by examination:** AP, CLEP, institutional tests. 15 credit hours maximum toward associate degree. **Support services:** GED preparation and test center, learning center, pre-admission summer program, reduced course load, remedial instruction, study skills assistance, tutoring, writing center.

Majors. Biology: General, wildlife. **Business:** Administrative services, business admin. **Communications:** General, journalism, media studies, persuasive communications, radio/TV. **Computer sciences:** General. **Conservation:** Forestry, wildlife/wilderness. **Education:** General, agricultural, art, business, elementary, health, mathematics, middle, multi-level teacher, music, physical, sales/marketing, secondary. **English:** English lit. **Health services:** Dental hygiene, nursing (RN), physical therapy assistant, substance abuse counseling, veterinary technology/assistant. **History:** General. **Human services:** Social work. **Liberal arts:** Arts/sciences. **Math:** General. **Parks/recreation:** Exercise sciences, health/fitness. **Philosophy/religion:** Philosophy. **Physical sciences:** General, chemistry, geology, physics. **Protective services:** Police science. **Psychology:** General. **Social sciences:** General, sociology. **Visual/performing arts:** General, graphic design. **Work/family studies:** Child care management.

Most popular majors. Health sciences 20%, liberal arts 67%.

Technology on campus. 100 workstations in dormitories, library, computer center, student center. Dormitories wired for high-speed internet access. Online course registration, online library, helpline, repair service, wireless network available.

Student life. Freshman orientation: Mandatory, $15 fee. Preregistration for classes offered. **Housing:** Coed dorms, special housing for disabled, wellness housing available. $100 fully refundable deposit. **Activities:** Bands, choral groups, dance, international student organizations, literary magazine, music ensembles, musical theater, radio station, student government, student newspaper, OPTIC (Ordinary People Together in Christ), Catholic Youth.

Athletics. NJCAA. **Intercollegiate:** Baseball M, basketball, cheerleading, cross-country, equestrian, golf, rodeo, softball W, track and field, volleyball W, wrestling M. **Intramural:** Basketball, softball, volleyball. **Team name:** Trojans.

Student services. Adult student services, alcohol/substance abuse counseling, career counseling, services for economically disadvantaged, student employment services, financial aid counseling, health services, personal counseling, placement for graduates, veterans' counselor. **Physically disabled:** Services for visually, speech, hearing impaired. **Transfer:** Pre-admission transcript evaluation for new students. Transfer adviser, college fairs on campus for students transferring to 4-year colleges.

Contact. E-mail: admissions@colbycc.edu
Phone: (785) 460-4690 Toll-free number: (888) 634-9350
Fax: (785) 460-4691
Nikol Nolan, Director of Admissions, Colby Community College, 1255
South Range Avenue, Colby, KS 67701

Cowley County Community College
Arkansas City, Kansas
www.cowley.edu   **CB code: 6008**

- Public 2-year community and technical college
- Commuter campus in large town

General. Founded in 1922. Regionally accredited. **Enrollment:** 3,569
degree-seeking undergraduates. **Degrees:** 575 associate awarded. **Location:**
50 miles from Wichita. **Calendar:** Semester, limited summer session. **Full-
time faculty:** 51 total; 6% minority, 49% women. **Part-time faculty:** 227
total; 8% minority, 58% women. **Class size:** 70% < 20, 28% 20-39, less than
1% 40-49, less than 1% 50-99, less than 1% >100.

Student profile.

Out-of-state:	9%	Live on campus:	13%
25 or older:	42%		

Transfer out. Colleges most students transferred to 2015: Wichita State
University, Southwestern College, University of Kansas, Kansas State University, Oklahoma State University.

Basis for selection. Open admission, but selective for some programs.
Special requirements for mobile intensive care training program. **Home
schooled:** Transcript of courses and grades required.

2015-2016 Annual costs. Tuition/fees: $2,520; $2,820 out-of-district;
$4,230 out-of-state. Per-credit charge: $55 in-district; $65 out-of-district;
$112 out-of-state. Room/board: $4,625. Books/supplies: $1,000. Personal
expenses: $900. **Additional information:** Oklahoma residents $75 per credit
hour for tuition, $29 per credit hour for fees.

Financial aid. Need-based: Need-based aid available for part-time students. Work-study available nights, weekends and for part-time students.
Non-need-based: Scholarships awarded for academics, alumni affiliation,
art, athletics, leadership, music/drama, state residency.

Application procedures. Admission: No deadline. No application fee.
Admission notification on a rolling basis. **Financial aid:** Priority date 4/15;
no closing date. FAFSA required. Applicants notified on a rolling basis
starting 1/15; must reply within 2 week(s) of notification.

Academics. Special study options: Cooperative education, distance learning, double major, dual enrollment of high school students, independent
study, internships, teacher certification program. Area vocational-technical
school programs available. **Credit/placement by examination:** AP, CLEP.
15 credit hours maximum toward associate degree. Students must complete
12 credit hours with a GPA of 2.0 or higher before CLEP credit is listed on
the transcript. **Support services:** GED preparation and test center, learning
center, reduced course load, remedial instruction, study skills assistance,
tutoring.

Majors. Biology: General. **Business:** General, accounting, administrative
services, business admin, customer service support, entrepreneurial studies,
office/clerical, organizational behavior. **Communications:** Communications/
speech/rhetoric, journalism, media studies. **Computer sciences:** General,
database management, information technology, networking, security, web
page design. **Education:** General, early childhood, elementary, secondary.
Engineering: General, pre-engineering, robotics. **English:** Creative writing,
English lit. **Foreign languages:** General, sign language interpretation. **Health
services:** EMT ambulance attendant, EMT paramedic, health information
technology, medical transcription, nursing assistant, premedicine, prenursing,
prepharmacy, preveterinary. **History:** General. **Human services:** Social
work. **Liberal arts:** Arts/sciences. **Math:** General. **Parks/recreation:** Golf
management, sports admin. **Philosophy/religion:** Philosophy, religion. **Physical sciences:** General, chemistry. **Protective services:** Corrections, law
enforcement admin, police science. **Psychology:** General. **Social sciences:**
General, anthropology, sociology. **Visual/performing arts:** General, art,
design, dramatic, music, studio arts. **Work/family studies:** Child care management.

Most popular majors. Liberal arts 86%.

Technology on campus. 100 workstations in dormitories, library, computer center, student center. Dormitories wired for high-speed internet access
and linked to campus network. Commuter students can connect to campus
network. Online course registration, online library, wireless network available.

Student life. Freshman orientation: Available. Preregistration for classes
offered. **Housing:** Single-sex dorms, wellness housing available. $75 nonre-
fundable deposit. **Activities:** Bands, choral groups, drama, music ensembles,
student government, student newspaper, Academic Civic Engagement
through Service, Fellowship of Christian Athletes, Creative Claws, Art and
Design Club, Act One Drama Club, Phi Beta Lambda, Mu Alpha Sigma
Chi, Film Club, KNEA.

Athletics. NJCAA. **Intercollegiate:** Baseball M, basketball, cheerleading,
cross-country, soccer, softball W, tennis, track and field, volleyball W. **Intramural:** Basketball, football (non-tackle), softball, volleyball. **Team name:**
Tigers.

Student services. Career counseling, student employment services, health
services, personal counseling, veterans' counselor.

Contact. E-mail: admissions@cowley.edu
Phone: (620) 442-0430 Toll-free number: (800) 593-2222
Fax: (620) 441-5350
Terri Hutchinson, Admissions Secretary, Cowley County Community
College, PO Box 1147, Arkansas City, KS 67005-1147

Dodge City Community College
Dodge City, Kansas
www.dc3.edu   **CB code: 6166**

- Public 2-year community and technical college
- Commuter campus in large town

General. Founded in 1935. Regionally accredited. **Enrollment:** 1,105
degree-seeking undergraduates. **Degrees:** 211 associate awarded. **Location:**
150 miles from Wichita. **Calendar:** Semester, limited summer session. **Full-
time faculty:** 60 total. **Part-time faculty:** 130 total. **Class size:** 25% < 20,
75% 20-39. **Special facilities:** Federal depository of books and documents,
horse barn, rodeo practice arena.

Student profile.

Out-of-state:	5%	Live on campus:	33%
25 or older:	45%		

Transfer out. Colleges most students transferred to 2015: Kansas State
University, Fort Hays State University, University of Kansas, Pittsburg State
University, Wichita State University.

Basis for selection. Open admission, but selective for some programs.
Special requirements for nursing program. CELSEA assessment test given
to ESL students. Interview recommended for nursing majors. Audition recommended for music majors. Portfolio recommended for art majors. **Home
schooled:** Transcript of courses and grades required. **Learning Disabled:**
Students must self identify.

High school preparation. Recommended units include English 4, mathematics 3, social studies 3 and science 3.

2015-2016 Annual costs. Tuition/fees: $2,620; $2,770 out-of-district;
$3,070 out-of-state. Per-credit charge: $35 in-district; $40 out-of-district; $50
out-of-state. Room/board: $5,720. Books/supplies: $800. Personal
expenses: $1,000.

Financial aid. Need-based: Need-based aid available for part-time students. Work-study available nights, weekends and for part-time students.
Non-need-based: Scholarships awarded for academics, athletics, music/
drama, state residency.

Application procedures. Admission: No deadline. No application fee.
Admission notification on a rolling basis. **Financial aid:** Priority date 3/15;
no closing date. FAFSA, institutional form required. Applicants notified on
a rolling basis; must reply within 2 week(s) of notification.

Academics. Special study options: Distance learning, double major, dual
enrollment of high school students, ESL, independent study. License preparation in nursing. **Credit/placement by examination:** AP, CLEP. 30 credit
hours maximum toward associate degree. **Support services:** GED preparation
and test center, learning center, reduced course load, remedial instruction,
tutoring, writing center.

Majors. Biology: General. **Business:** General, accounting, banking/finan-
cial services, management information systems, office management. **Communications:** Broadcast journalism, journalism. **Computer sciences:** General, computer science, data processing. **Education:** General, elementary,
secondary. **Engineering:** General. **Health services:** Athletic training, health
information technology, licensed practical nurse, nursing (RN), nursing assistant, premedicine, prepharmacy, preveterinary, substance abuse counseling.

Two-Year Colleges

Math: General. **Parks/recreation:** Health/fitness. **Physical sciences:** Chemistry. **Protective services:** Firefighting. **Social sciences:** General, economics, sociology. **Visual/performing arts:** Art, music. **Work/family studies:** Child care management.

Technology on campus. 125 workstations in dormitories, library, computer center, student center. Dormitories wired for high-speed internet access. Online library, wireless network available.

Student life. Freshman orientation: Mandatory. Preregistration for classes offered. Held 2 days before classes begins. **Housing:** Guaranteed on-campus for freshmen. Single sex dorms, wellness housing available. **Activities:** Bands, choral groups, dance, drama, music ensembles, radio station, student government, student newspaper, TV station, Black student union, Fellowship of Christian Athletes, Hispanic American leadership organization.

Athletics. NJCAA. **Intercollegiate:** Baseball M, basketball, cross-country, football (tackle) M, golf, soccer, softball W, track and field, volleyball W. **Intramural:** Basketball, softball W. **Team name:** Conquistadors.

Student services. Adult student services, career counseling, services for economically disadvantaged, student employment services, financial aid counseling, personal counseling, veterans' counselor. **Physically disabled:** Services for visually, speech, hearing impaired. **Transfer:** Transfer adviser, college fairs on campus for students transferring to 4-year colleges.

Contact. E-mail: admit@dc3.edu
Phone: (620) 227-9207 Toll-free number: (800) 367-3222
Fax: (620) 227-9350
Alisha Ontiberos, Director of Admissions, Dodge City Community College, 2501 North 14th Avenue, Dodge City, KS 67801-2399

Donnelly College
Kansas City, Kansas
www.donnelly.edu   CB code: 6167

▶ Private 2-year junior and liberal arts college affiliated with the Roman Catholic Church
▶ Commuter campus in small city

General. Founded in 1949. Regionally accredited. **Enrollment:** 262 degree-seeking undergraduates. **Degrees:** 6 bachelor's, 30 associate awarded. **Location:** 5 miles from downtown. **Calendar:** Semester, limited summer session. **Full-time faculty:** 21 total; 19% minority, 62% women. **Part-time faculty:** 24 total; 33% minority, 58% women. **Class size:** 93% < 20, 7% 20-39.

Student profile. Among degree-seeking undergraduates, 5% enrolled in a vocational program, 3% already have a bachelor's degree or higher, 73 enrolled as first-time, first-year students, 12 transferred in from other institutions.

Part-time:	25%	Hispanic/Latino:	48%
Out-of-state:	24%	Multi-racial, non-Hispanic:	5%
Women:	68%	International:	5%
African American:	29%	25 or older:	34%
Asian American:	5%		

Transfer out. Colleges most students transferred to 2015: University of Kansas, University of Missouri-Kansas City, Kansas City Kansas Community College, Kansas State, Johnson County Community College.

Basis for selection. Open admission.

High school preparation. College-preparatory program required.

2015-2016 Annual costs. Tuition/fees: $8,340. Per-credit charge: $275. Room/board: $7,020. Books/supplies: $830.

2015-2016 Financial aid. Need-based: 61 full-time freshmen applied for aid; 57 deemed to have need; 57 received aid. Average need met was 97%. Average scholarship/grant was $2,526; average loan $3,286. 75% of total undergraduate aid awarded as scholarships/grants, 25% as loans/jobs. Need-based aid available for part-time students. Work-study available nights, weekends and for part-time students. **Non-need-based:** Awarded to 98 full-time undergraduates, including 67 freshmen. Scholarships awarded for academics, religious affiliation.

Application procedures. Admission: No deadline. No application fee. Admission notification on a rolling basis. **Financial aid:** Priority date 4/1, closing date 4/1. FAFSA, institutional form required. Applicants notified on a rolling basis starting 7/1.

Academics. Special study options: Distance learning, double major, dual enrollment of high school students, ESL, honors, liberal arts/career combination, weekend college. Bachelor's degree programs available on campus.

Credit/placement by examination: AP, CLEP, IB, institutional tests. 20 credit hours maximum toward associate degree, 20 toward bachelor's. **Support services:** GED preparation, learning center, reduced course load, remedial instruction, study skills assistance, tutoring, writing center.

Majors. Computer sciences: Information technology.

Technology on campus. 75 workstations in library, computer center. Dormitories wired for high-speed internet access and linked to campus network. Commuter students can connect to campus network. Online course registration, online library, helpline, wireless network available.

Student life. Freshman orientation: Mandatory. Preregistration for classes offered. **Housing:** Single-sex dorms available. $100 nonrefundable deposit, deadline 8/1. **Activities:** Campus ministries, organization of student leadership.

Student services. Chaplain/spiritual director, career counseling, services for economically disadvantaged, student employment services, financial aid counseling, personal counseling, placement for graduates, veterans' counselor. **Physically disabled:** Services for visually, speech, hearing impaired. **Transfer:** Pre-admission transcript evaluation for new students. Transfer adviser, college fairs on campus for students transferring to 4-year colleges.

Contact. E-mail: admissions@donnelly.edu
Phone: (913) 621-8700 Fax: (913) 621-8719
Elora Thomas, Director of Admissions, Donnelly College, 608 North 18th Street, Kansas City, KS 66102-4210

Fort Scott Community College
Fort Scott, Kansas
www.fortscott.edu   CB code: 6219

▶ Public 2-year community college
▶ Commuter campus in small town

General. Founded in 1919. Regionally accredited. **Enrollment:** 1,702 degree-seeking undergraduates. **Degrees:** 216 associate awarded. **Location:** Approximately 90 miles of Kansas City. **Calendar:** Semester, limited summer session. **Full-time faculty:** 48 total. **Part-time faculty:** 81 total. **Special facilities:** Indoor and outdoor rodeo training facilities, museum.

Student profile. Among degree-seeking undergraduates, 130 transferred in from other institutions.

Basis for selection. Open admission.

High school preparation. College-preparatory program required.

2015-2016 Annual costs. Tuition/fees: $2,825; $2,915 out-of-district; $4,595 out-of-state. Per-credit charge: $50 in-district; $53 out-of-district; $109 out-of-state. Room/board: $5,580. Books/supplies: $1,200. Personal expenses: $1,200.

2014-2015 Financial aid. Need-based: 51% of total undergraduate aid awarded as scholarships/grants, 49% as loans/jobs. Need-based aid available for part-time students. Work-study available nights, weekends and for part-time students.

Application procedures. Admission: No deadline. No application fee. Application must be submitted online. Admission notification on a rolling basis. **Financial aid:** Priority date 7/1; no closing date. FAFSA required. Applicants notified on a rolling basis starting 10/1.

Academics. Special study options: Cooperative education, distance learning, dual enrollment of high school students, ESL, independent study, internships, weekend college. **Credit/placement by examination:** AP, CLEP. 24 credit hours maximum toward associate degree. **Support services:** GED test center, learning center, pre-admission summer program, remedial instruction, study skills assistance, tutoring.

Majors. Business: Administrative services. **General:** Carpentry. **Health services:** Nursing (RN). **History:** General. **Liberal arts:** Arts/sciences. **Protective services:** Police science.

Technology on campus. Dormitories wired for high-speed internet access. Wireless network available.

Student life. Freshman orientation: Mandatory. Preregistration for classes offered. **Housing:** Coed dorms available. $125 deposit, deadline 8/1. **Activities:** Bands, choral groups, dance, drama, music ensembles, musical theater, symphony orchestra, Christians on Campus, Phi Theta Kappa.

Athletics. NJCAA. **Intercollegiate:** Baseball M, basketball, cheerleading W, football (tackle) M, rodeo, softball W, volleyball W. **Team name:** Greyhounds.

Student services. Adult student services, alcohol/substance abuse counseling, services for economically disadvantaged, student employment services, financial aid counseling. **Transfer:** Transfer adviser, college fairs on campus for students transferring to 4-year colleges.

Contact. E-mail: admissions@fortscott.edu
Phone: (620) 223-2700 ext. 3530
Toll-free number: (800) 874-3722 ext. 3530 Fax: (620) 223-4927
Josh Budd, Director of Admissions, Fort Scott Community College, 2108 S Horton St, Fort Scott, KS 66701

Garden City Community College
Garden City, Kansas
www.gcccks.edu   CB code: 6246

- Public 2-year community college
- Commuter campus in large town

General. Founded in 1919. Regionally accredited. **Enrollment:** 1,953 degree-seeking undergraduates. **Degrees:** 292 associate awarded. **Location:** 200 miles from Wichita, 335 miles from Denver, CO. **Calendar:** Semester, limited summer session. **Full-time faculty:** 64 total. **Part-time faculty:** 63 total. **Class size:** 69% < 20, 31% 20-39, less than 1% 50-99, less than 1% >100. **Special facilities:** Cadaver lab, fire arms training system, fire training tower, welding lab. **Partnerships:** Formal partnerships with John Deere Company and dealers.

Student profile. Among degree-seeking undergraduates, 75% enrolled in a transfer program, 25% enrolled in a vocational program, 2% already have a bachelor's degree or higher.

Out-of-state:	17%	Live on campus:	38%
25 or older:	16%		

Transfer out. Colleges most students transferred to 2015: Fort Hays State University, Kansas State University, Kansas University, Wichita State University, National American University at Garden City Community College.

Basis for selection. Open admission, but selective for some programs. Additional requirements and/or an additional application is required for Nursing, Cosmetology, Automotive Technology, Industrial Maintenance Technology, Emergency Medical Services Technology, Information Technology, and John Deere Agricultural Technology programs. Students must take the COMPASS test on-campus or submit ACT scores for mandatory placement into courses. Audition recommended for music majors. Portfolio recommended for art and photography majors. **Home schooled:** The home-school must be in compliance with the regulations set forth by the state in which it is located.

High school preparation. College-preparatory program recommended. Recommended units include English 4, mathematics 3, social studies 2, history 2, science 3 (laboratory 1), visual/performing arts 1 and academic electives 6.

2015-2016 Annual costs. Tuition/fees: $2,816; $3,424 out-of-state. Per-credit charge: $57 in-state; $76 out-of-state. Room/board: $5,250. Books/supplies: $1,100. Personal expenses: $1,722. **Additional information:** Border State Tuition Rate extended to residents of the following states: CO, MO, NE, NM, OK, TX.

Financial aid. **Need-based:** Need-based aid available for part-time students. Work-study available nights, weekends and for part-time students. **Non-need-based:** Scholarships awarded for academics, art, athletics, job skills, leadership, minority status, music/drama, state residency.

Application procedures. Admission: No deadline. No application fee. Admission notification on a rolling basis. **Financial aid:** Priority date 3/1; no closing date. FAFSA, institutional form required. Applicants notified on a rolling basis starting 4/15; must reply within 2 week(s) of notification.

Academics. Special study options: Cross-registration, distance learning, dual enrollment of high school students, ESL, internships, liberal arts/career combination, student-designed major. Bachelor's degree programs available on campus. License preparation in nursing, paramedic. **Credit/placement by examination:** AP, CLEP. 30 credit hours maximum toward associate degree. **Support services:** GED preparation and test center, learning center, remedial instruction, study skills assistance, tutoring, writing center.

Majors. Biology: General, wildlife. Business: General, accounting, business admin, entrepreneurial studies, hospitality admin, marketing, restaurant/food

services. **Communications:** Communications/speech/rhetoric, digital media, journalism, media studies, persuasive communications, photojournalism. **Computer sciences:** General, computer science, networking. **Conservation:** Forestry, wildlife/wilderness. **Education:** General, agricultural, art, biology, business, chemistry, drama/dance, early childhood, earth science, elementary, geography, health, history, mathematics, middle, music, physical, physics, psychology, reading, science, secondary, social science, social studies, speech. **Engineering:** General, engineering science. **English:** English lit. **Health services:** Athletic training, EMT paramedic, nursing (RN), prechiropractic, predental, premedicine, prenursing, prepharmacy, prephysical therapy, preveterinary, substance abuse counseling. **Human services:** Social work. **Liberal arts:** Arts/sciences, humanities. **Math:** General. **Parks/recreation:** Health/fitness. **Physical sciences:** General, chemistry. **Protective services:** Firefighting, law enforcement admin, police science. **Psychology:** General. **Social sciences:** General. **Visual/performing arts:** General, art, ceramics, design, dramatic, drawing, music, painting, printmaking, sculpture. **Work/family studies:** General, food/nutrition.

Most popular majors. Agriculture 11%, business/marketing 18%, education 8%, health sciences 21%, liberal arts 18%.

Technology on campus. 325 workstations in dormitories, library. Dormitories wired for high-speed internet access and linked to campus network. Commuter students can connect to campus network. Wireless network available.

Student life. Freshman orientation: Mandatory. Preregistration for classes offered. Held prior to start of classes. **Policies:** Smoke free buildings. **Housing:** Coed dorms, apartments, wellness housing available. $300 partly refundable deposit, deadline 8/1. **Activities:** Bands, choral groups, drama, literary magazine, music ensembles, musical theater, radio station, student government, student newspaper, Newman Club, Hispanic American Leadership Organization.

Athletics. NJCAA. **Intercollegiate:** Baseball M, basketball, cheerleading, cross-country, football (tackle) M, golf M, rodeo, soccer, softball W, track and field, volleyball W. **Intramural:** Basketball, bowling, football (non-tackle) M, handball, racquetball, rifle, sand volleyball, soccer, softball, table tennis, tennis, volleyball. **Team name:** Broncbusters.

Student services. Alcohol/substance abuse counseling, career counseling, services for economically disadvantaged, student employment services, financial aid counseling, health services, personal counseling, veterans' counselor, women's services. **Physically disabled:** Services for visually, speech, hearing impaired. **Transfer:** Transfer adviser, college fairs on campus for students transferring to 4-year colleges.

Contact. E-mail: admission@gcccks.edu
Phone: (620) 276-9608 Fax: (620) 276-9650
Tammy Tabor, Director of Enrollment Management, Garden City Community College, 801 Campus Drive, Garden City, KS 67846-6333

Hesston College
Hesston, Kansas
www.hesston.edu   CB code: 6274

- Private 2-year junior and liberal arts college affiliated with the Mennonite Church
- Residential campus in small town

General. Founded in 1909. Regionally accredited. **Enrollment:** 408 degree-seeking undergraduates; 1 non-degree-seeking students. **Degrees:** 143 associate awarded. **Location:** 35 miles from Wichita. **Calendar:** Semester, limited summer session. **Full-time faculty:** 37 total; 16% have terminal degrees, 11% minority, 46% women. **Part-time faculty:** 15 total; 7% have terminal degrees, 7% minority, 73% women. **Class size:** 76% < 20, 19% 20-39, 3% 40-49, 2% 50-99. **Special facilities:** Arboretum, retreat center. **Partnerships:** Formal partnerships with schools in the Mennonite Secondary Education Council.

Student profile. Among degree-seeking undergraduates, 156 enrolled as first-time, first-year students, 52 transferred in from other institutions.

Part-time:	13%	Hispanic/Latino:	11%
Out-of-state:	44%	Multi-racial, non-Hispanic:	3%
Women:	62%	International:	11%
African American:	6%	25 or older:	16%
Asian American:	2%	Live on campus:	72%

Transfer out. Colleges most students transferred to 2015: Eastern Mennonite University, Goshen College, Wichita State University, Bethel College.

Basis for selection. Open admission, but selective for some programs. Special requirements for nursing program. A supplementary application is required for admission to the nursing and pastoral ministries programs. **Home schooled:** Must provide ACT, SAT, ASSET, or COMPASS scores.

High school preparation. Recommended units include English 4, mathematics 3, social studies 3 and science 3.

2015-2016 Annual costs. Tuition/fees: $25,234. Room/board: $8,144. Books/supplies: $1,100. Personal expenses: $2,000.

2015-2016 Financial aid. Need-based: 123 full-time freshmen applied for aid; 111 deemed to have need; 111 received aid. Need-based aid available for part-time students. Work-study available nights, weekends and for part-time students. **Non-need-based:** Awarded to 173 full-time undergraduates, including 74 freshmen. Scholarships awarded for academics, alumni affiliation, art, athletics, job skills, music/drama.

Application procedures. Admission: Priority date 6/1; no deadline. No application fee. Admission notification on a rolling basis. **Financial aid:** Closing date 4/1. FAFSA required. Applicants notified on a rolling basis starting 2/1; must reply within 4 week(s) of notification.

Academics. Special study options: Cooperative education, ESL, independent study, internships, liberal arts/career combination. Bachelor's degree programs available on campus. License preparation in aviation, nursing. **Credit/placement by examination:** AP, CLEP, IB, institutional tests. 12 credit hours maximum toward associate degree. **Support services:** Learning center, reduced course load, remedial instruction, study skills assistance, tutoring, writing center.

Majors. Education: Early childhood. **Health services:** Nursing (RN). **Liberal arts:** Arts/sciences.

Most popular majors. Health sciences 36%, liberal arts 53%, theological studies 6%.

Technology on campus. 142 workstations in library, computer center, student center. Dormitories wired for high-speed internet access and linked to campus network. Commuter students can connect to campus network. Online course registration, online library, helpline, repair service, wireless network available.

Student life. Freshman orientation: Mandatory. Preregistration for classes offered. One day prior to the beginning of classes. All new first-time students are required to enroll during the first semester in either College Orientation/Success or College Learning Strategies. **Policies:** Use of alcohol, drugs, smoking and possession of firearms/fireworks prohibited. Decency in dress and appearance is expected. Chapel attendance is required. Religious observance required. **Housing:** Guaranteed on-campus for all undergraduates. Single-sex dorms, wellness housing available. $50 deposit. **Activities:** Bands, campus ministries, choral groups, drama, international student organizations, music ensembles, musical theater, student newspaper, symphony orchestra, peace and service club, International Christian Fellowship, Students for Responsible Citizenship.

Athletics. NJCAA. **Intercollegiate:** Baseball M, basketball, cross-country, soccer, softball W, tennis, volleyball W. **Intramural:** Basketball, cross-country, soccer, ultimate frisbee, volleyball. **Team name:** Larks.

Student services. Alcohol/substance abuse counseling, chaplain/spiritual director, career counseling, financial aid counseling, minority student services, personal counseling, veterans' counselor. **Physically disabled:** Services for hearing impaired. **Transfer:** Pre-admission transcript evaluation for new students. Transfer adviser, college fairs on campus for students transferring to 4-year colleges.

Contact. E-mail: admissions@hesston.edu
Phone: (620) 327-8222 Toll-free number: (800) 995-2757
Fax: (620) 327-8300
Rachel Swartzendruber, Vice President of Admissions, Hesston College, Box 3000, Hesston, KS 67062-2093

Highland Community College
Highland, Kansas
www.highlandcc.edu   CB code: 6276

- Public 2-year community college
- Residential campus in rural community

General. Founded in 1857. Regionally accredited. **Enrollment:** 1,876 degree-seeking undergraduates; 1,467 non-degree-seeking students. **Degrees:** 259 associate awarded. **Location:** 26 miles from St. Joseph, Missouri. **Calendar:** Semester, limited summer session. **Full-time faculty:** 38 total; 8% have terminal degrees, 3% minority, 50% women. **Part-time faculty:** 192 total; 5% have terminal degrees, 4% minority, 55% women. **Class size:** 90%

< 20, 9% 20-39, less than 1% 40-49, less than 1% 50-99. **Special facilities:** Photography studio, sports medicine/athletic trainer facilities, learning skills center, communication technology complex, wellness/fitness center, college farm, restored historic barn as meeting center, mud run/obstacle course.

Student profile. Among degree-seeking undergraduates, 654 enrolled as first-time, first-year students.

Part-time:	40%	Hispanic/Latino:	4%
Out-of-state:	7%	Native American:	3%
Women:	57%	Multi-racial, non-Hispanic:	4%
African American:	9%	25 or older:	29%
Asian American:	2%	Live on campus:	19%

Transfer out. Colleges most students transferred to 2015: Kansas State University, Emporia State University, University of Kansas, Washburn University, Missouri Western State College.

Basis for selection. Open admission, but selective for out-of-state students. Out-of-state applicants must be in top two-thirds of graduating class or have 14 ACT or 660 SAT (exclusive of Writing). Placement tests determine program eligibility. **Adult students:** Full Compass Placement. **Home schooled:** Transcript of courses and grades required. **Learning Disabled:** Students are asked to self-identify if they have an IEP or other verified disability. There are no special requirements or procedures.

High school preparation. College-preparatory program recommended. 11 units recommended. Recommended units include English 3, mathematics 2, social studies 2 and science 4.

2015-2016 Annual costs. Tuition/fees: $2,910; $3,300 out-of-district; $3,300 out-of-state. Per-credit charge: $55 in-district; $68 out-of-district; $68 out-of-state. Room/board: $5,506. Books/supplies: $600. Personal expenses: $1,800.

Financial aid. Need-based: Need-based aid available for part-time students. Work-study available nights, weekends and for part-time students. **Non-need-based:** Scholarships awarded for academics, alumni affiliation, art, athletics, job skills, leadership, music/drama. **Additional information:** Auditions and portfolios important for certain scholarship candidates.

Application procedures. Admission: No deadline. No application fee. Admission notification on a rolling basis beginning on or about 4/1. Application deadline for out-of-state applicants August 1, must reply within 2 weeks. SAT or ACT recommended, ACT preferred. Score report by August 1. **Financial aid:** Priority date 4/1; no closing date. FAFSA required. Applicants notified on a rolling basis starting 4/15; must reply within 4 week(s) of notification.

Academics. Special study options: Cooperative education, distance learning, double major, dual enrollment of high school students, independent study, internships, liberal arts/career combination. License preparation in nursing, paramedic. **Credit/placement by examination:** AP, CLEP. 15 credit hours maximum toward associate degree. **Support services:** GED preparation and test center, reduced course load, remedial instruction, study skills assistance, tutoring.

Majors. Business: Accounting technology, administrative services, business admin. **Computer sciences:** Data processing, networking. **Health services:** Medical secretary, nursing (RN), ward clerk. **Math:** General. **Protective services:** Police science, security services. **Visual/performing arts:** Commercial photography, commercial/advertising art. **Work/family studies:** Child care management.

Most popular majors. Business/marketing 8%, health sciences 14%, liberal arts 67%.

Technology on campus. 96 workstations in library, computer center. Dormitories linked to campus network. Commuter students can connect to campus network. Online course registration, online library, helpline, repair service, wireless network available.

Student life. Freshman orientation: Mandatory. Preregistration for classes offered. **Housing:** Coed dorms, single-sex dorms, apartments, themed housing, wellness housing available. $150 fully refundable deposit. **Activities:** Bands, campus ministries, choral groups, dance, drama, music ensembles, musical theater, student government, campus Christian fellowship, Gay/Straight Alliance.

Athletics. NJCAA. **Intercollegiate:** Baseball M, basketball, cheerleading, cross-country, football (tackle) M, softball W, track and field, volleyball W. **Intramural:** Basketball, football (non-tackle), softball, table tennis, tennis, volleyball. **Team name:** Scotties.

Student services. Adult student services, alcohol/substance abuse counseling, career counseling, services for economically disadvantaged, financial aid counseling, personal counseling. **Physically disabled:** Services for visually, speech, hearing impaired. **Transfer:** Transfer adviser, college fairs on campus for students transferring to 4-year colleges.

Contact. E-mail: jpeden@highlandcc.edu
Phone: (785) 442-6020 Fax: (785) 442-6106
Cheryl Rasmussen, Vice President for Student Services, Highland Community College, 606 West Main Street, Highland, KS 66035

Hutchinson Community College
Hutchinson, Kansas
www.hutchcc.edu   CB code: 6281

- Public 2-year community college
- Commuter campus in large town

General. Founded in 1928. Regionally accredited. Additional centers in Newton and McPherson. **Enrollment:** 5,172 degree-seeking undergraduates; 374 non-degree-seeking students. **Degrees:** 796 associate awarded. **Location:** 45 miles from Wichita; 200 miles from Kansas City. **Calendar:** Semester, limited summer session. **Full-time faculty:** 111 total; 13% have terminal degrees, less than 1% minority, 42% women. **Part-time faculty:** 295 total; less than 1% have terminal degrees, 45% women. **Class size:** 81% < 20, 18% 20-39, less than 1% 40-49. **Special facilities:** Cosmosphere space center, Kansas state fair, underground salt mine museum (Strataca).

Student profile. Among degree-seeking undergraduates, 36% enrolled in a transfer program, 64% enrolled in a vocational program, 1% already have a bachelor's degree or higher, 1,015 enrolled as first-time, first-year students, 327 transferred in from other institutions.

Part-time:	59%	Native American:	1%
Out-of-state:	8%	Multi-racial, non-Hispanic:	3%
Women:	55%	International:	1%
African American:	6%	25 or older:	27%
Asian American:	1%	Live on campus:	10%
Hispanic/Latino:	10%		

Transfer out. 75% of students enrolled in the transfer program go on to 4-year colleges. **Colleges most students transferred to 2015:** Kansas State University, University of Kansas, Wichita State University, Emporia State University, Fort Hays State University.

Basis for selection. Open admission, but selective for some programs. Special requirements for nursing, radiology, emergency medical sciences paramedic, health information management, licensed practical nursing, physical therapy assistant, and surgical technology. C-NET exam required for nursing program applicants. Interview required for nursing, radiology, paramedic, health information technology, physical therapy assistant, and surgical technology programs. **Home schooled:** Provide home school/high school diploma or GED.

2015-2016 Annual costs. Tuition/fees: $2,670; $2,970 out-of-district; $3,900 out-of-state. Per-credit charge: $70 in-district; $80 out-of-district; $111 out-of-state. Room/board: $5,430. Books/supplies: $1,000. Personal expenses: $1,368. **Additional information:** Residence Hall students pay a $50 social fee.

2014-2015 Financial aid. Need-based: 695 full-time freshmen applied for aid; 504 deemed to have need; 490 received aid. Average need met was 41%. Average scholarship/grant was $3,774; average loan $2,447. 68% of total undergraduate aid awarded as scholarships/grants, 32% as loans/jobs. Need-based aid available for part-time students. Work-study available nights, weekends and for part-time students. **Non-need-based:** Awarded to 1,139 full-time undergraduates, including 669 freshmen. Scholarships awarded for academics, art, athletics, leadership, minority status, music/drama, state residency.

Application procedures. Admission: No deadline. No application fee. Admission notification on a rolling basis. Priority application dates: Practical Nursing 1/15, Nursing 1/30, Physical Therapy Assistant 5/21, Radiology 5/24. **Financial aid:** Priority date 2/1; no closing date. FAFSA, institutional form required. Applicants notified on a rolling basis starting 4/1; must reply within 2 week(s) of notification.

Academics. Special study options: Accelerated study, distance learning, double major, dual enrollment of high school students, honors, independent study, internships. Bachelor's degree programs available on campus. License preparation in nursing, paramedic, physical therapy, radiology. **Credit/placement by examination:** AP, CLEP, IB, institutional tests. Credit by examination hours not limited. **Support services:** GED preparation and test center, learning center, remedial instruction, study skills assistance, tutoring, writing center.

Majors. Biology: General, zoology. **Business:** General, accounting technology, administrative services, retailing, small business admin. **Communications:** Communications/speech/rhetoric. **Communications technology:** Radio/TV. **Computer sciences:** General, networking, systems analysis, web page design. **Conservation:** Management/policy. **Education:** General, drama/dance. **Engineering:** General. **English:** English lit. **Foreign languages:** General. **General:** Carpentry. **Health services:** EMT paramedic, health information technology, medical radiologic technology/radiation therapy, nursing (RN), physical therapy assistant, radiologic technology/medical imaging, respiratory therapy technology, surgical technology. **Liberal arts:** Arts/sciences. **Math:** General. **Parks/recreation:** Sports admin. **Physical sciences:** General, meteorology. **Protective services:** Fire safety technology, police science. **Psychology:** General. **Social sciences:** General. **Visual/performing arts:** General, design. **Work/family studies:** General, child care management.

Most popular majors. Health sciences 26%, liberal arts 54%, security/protective services 6%.

Technology on campus. 200 workstations in library. Dormitories wired for high-speed internet access. Online course registration, helpline, wireless network available.

Student life. Freshman orientation: Available. Preregistration for classes offered. **Housing:** Single-sex dorms available. $100 fully refundable deposit, deadline 6/1. Apartment style college housing available. **Activities:** Bands, choral groups, dance, drama, international student organizations, literary magazine, music ensembles, student government, student newspaper, symphony orchestra, Black Leadership League, Hispanic American Leadership Organization, SPARK, College Democrats, College Republicans, Fellowship of Christian Athletes.

Athletics. NJCAA. **Intercollegiate:** Baseball M, basketball, cross-country, football (tackle) M, golf M, soccer W, softball W, track and field, volleyball W. **Intramural:** Basketball, soccer, softball, tennis, volleyball. **Team name:** Blue Dragons.

Student services. Adult student services, career counseling, student employment services, financial aid counseling, health services, on-campus daycare, personal counseling, veterans' counselor. **Physically disabled:** Services for visually, speech, hearing impaired. **Transfer:** Pre-admission transcript evaluation for new students. Transfer adviser, college fairs on campus for students transferring to 4-year colleges.

Contact. E-mail: admissions@hutchcc.edu
Phone: (620) 665-3536 Toll-free number: (800) 289-3501 ext. 3536
Fax: (620) 665-3301
Corbin Strobel, Director of Admissions, Hutchinson Community College, 1300 North Plum, Hutchinson, KS 67501

Independence Community College
Independence, Kansas
www.indycc.edu   CB code: 6304

- Public 2-year community college
- Commuter campus in large town

General. Founded in 1925. Regionally accredited. **Enrollment:** 642 degree-seeking undergraduates; 33 non-degree-seeking students. **Degrees:** 86 associate awarded. **Location:** 110 miles from Tulsa, Oklahoma. **Calendar:** Semester, extensive summer session. **Full-time faculty:** 35 total; 14% have terminal degrees, 17% minority, 54% women. **Part-time faculty:** 51 total. **Class size:** 75% < 20, 25% 20-39.

Student profile. Among degree-seeking undergraduates, 287 enrolled as first-time, first-year students.

Part-time:	12%	25 or older:	15%
Out-of-state:	23%	Live on campus:	48%
Women:	48%		

Transfer out. Colleges most students transferred to 2015: Pittsburg State University, Emporia State University, Wichita State University, Kansas State University, University of Kansas.

Basis for selection. Open admission. **Adult students:** SAT/ACT scores not required.

High school preparation. 17 units recommended. Recommended units include English 4, mathematics 4, social studies 2, history 2, science 2 (laboratory 1) and foreign language 2.

2015-2016 Annual costs. Tuition/fees: $3,045; $3,225 out-of-district; $4,425 out-of-state. Per-credit charge: $54 in-district; $60 out-of-district; $100 out-of-state. Room/board: $4,950. Books/supplies: $200.

Financial aid. Need-based: Need-based aid available for part-time students. Work-study available nights, weekends and for part-time students. **Non-need-based:** Scholarships awarded for academics, art, athletics, music/drama, state residency. **Additional information:** Student labor grants awarded to students not eligible for Federal Work-Study. Students may apply by completing Student Employment Application. Student Support Services (SSS) grants available to eligible participants of the SSS program. Tuition waiver to all persons residing in college's taxing district.

Application procedures. Admission: No deadline. No application fee. Admission notification on a rolling basis beginning on or about 5/1. **Financial aid:** Priority date 4/1; no closing date. FAFSA required. Applicants notified on a rolling basis.

Academics. Special study options: Combined bachelor's/graduate degree, distance learning, double major, dual enrollment of high school students. Bachelor's degree programs available on campus. License preparation in paramedic. **Credit/placement by examination:** AP, CLEP, institutional tests. **Support services:** GED preparation and test center, learning center, reduced course load, remedial instruction, study skills assistance, tutoring, writing center.

Majors. Biology: General. **Business:** Accounting technology, administrative services, business admin, small business admin. **Communications:** Communications/speech/rhetoric. **Computer sciences:** Computer science, networking, programming, web page design, word processing. **Education:** Elementary, secondary. **English:** English lit. **Foreign languages:** General. **Health services:** Athletic training, office assistant, veterinary technology/assistant. **History:** General. **Liberal arts:** Arts/sciences. **Math:** General. **Parks/recreation:** Health/fitness. **Physical sciences:** General. **Protective services:** Corrections. **Psychology:** General. **Social sciences:** General, sociology. **Visual/performing arts:** Art, dramatic, music. **Work/family studies:** Child care management.

Most popular majors. Health sciences 12%, liberal arts 58%.

Technology on campus. 130 workstations in dormitories, library, computer center, student center. Online course registration, online library, helpline, wireless network available.

Student life. Freshman orientation: Mandatory, $10 fee. Preregistration for classes offered. 12-week, 1 credit hour course during the summer months. **Policies:** All first-year, full-time, non-married students between the ages of 18 and 24, whose permanent address is outside a 50-mile radius of the institution, are required to live on campus. **Housing:** Coed dorms available. $150 deposit. **Activities:** Bands, choral groups, drama, international student organizations, music ensembles, musical theater, student government.

Athletics. NJCAA. **Intercollegiate:** Baseball M, basketball, football (tackle) M, softball W, volleyball W. **Team name:** Pirates.

Student services. Services for economically disadvantaged, financial aid counseling. **Physically disabled:** Services for visually, speech, hearing impaired. **Transfer:** Pre-admission transcript evaluation for new students. Transfer adviser, college fairs on campus for students transferring to 4-year colleges.

Contact. E-mail: bthornton@indycc.edu
Phone: (620) 331-5495 Toll-free number: (800) 842-6063 ext. 5400
Fax: (620) 331-5344
Brittany Thornton, Director, Independence Community College, 1057 West College Avenue, Independence, KS 67301

Johnson County Community College
Overland Park, Kansas
www.jccc.edu   **CB code: 6325**

◗ Public 2-year community college
◗ Commuter campus in very large city

General. Founded in 1967. Regionally accredited. **Enrollment:** 11,608 degree-seeking undergraduates. **Degrees:** 2,189 associate awarded. **Location:** 20 miles from Kansas City. **Calendar:** Semester, extensive summer session. **Full-time faculty:** 330 total. **Part-time faculty:** 555 total. **Special facilities:** National academy of railroad sciences.

Student profile. Among degree-seeking undergraduates, 1,397 transferred in from other institutions.

Out-of-state: 7% **25 or older:**   34%

Transfer out. Colleges most students transferred to 2015: Kansas University, Kansas State University.

Basis for selection. Open admission, but selective for some programs. Special requirements for some allied health programs. ACT required for admission for nursing and dental hygiene applicants. Interview required for nursing, dental hygiene, emergency medical intensive care technician, respiratory therapy, and paralegal programs. Portfolio required of art majors. **Adult students:** SAT/ACT scores not required. **Home schooled:** Transcript of courses and grades required. **Learning Disabled:** Access services office assists students with documented disabilities.

2015-2016 Annual costs. Tuition/fees: $2,730; $3,180 out-of-district; $6,420 out-of-state. Per-credit charge: $75 in-district; $90 out-of-district; $198 out-of-state. Books/supplies: $1,000. Personal expenses: $1,500.

Financial aid. Need-based: Need-based aid available for part-time students. Work-study available nights, weekends and for part-time students. **Non-need-based:** Scholarships awarded for academics.

Application procedures. Admission: No deadline. No application fee. Admission notification on a rolling basis. **Financial aid:** Priority date 4/1; no closing date. FAFSA required. Applicants notified on a rolling basis starting 4/15; must reply within 2 week(s) of notification.

Academics. Wide variety of telecourses and courses offered by special arrangement. **Special study options:** Cooperative education, cross-registration, distance learning, double major, dual enrollment of high school students, ESL, exchange student, honors, independent study, internships, study abroad, weekend college. License preparation in dental hygiene, nursing, paramedic, radiology, real estate. **Credit/placement by examination:** AP, CLEP, institutional tests. 30 credit hours maximum toward associate degree. **Support services:** GED preparation and test center, learning center, reduced course load, remedial instruction, tutoring, writing center.

Majors. Business: Accounting, administrative services, business admin, entrepreneurial studies, logistics, sales/distribution. **Communications technology:** Animation/special effects. **Computer sciences:** Applications programming, modeling/simulation, networking. **Education:** Early childhood. **Foreign languages:** Sign language interpretation. **General:** Power transmission. **Health services:** Dental assistant, dental hygiene, EMT paramedic, health information technology, medical radiologic technology/radiation therapy, nursing (RN), occupational therapy assistant, physical therapy assistant, respiratory therapy technology, surgical technology, veterinary technology/assistant. **Liberal arts:** Arts/sciences. **Protective services:** Firefighting, police science. **Visual/performing arts:** Commercial/advertising art, fashion design, game design, graphic design, interior design. **Work/family studies:** Child care management, institutional food production.

Most popular majors. Business/marketing 7%, family/consumer sciences 8%, health sciences 12%, liberal arts 60%.

Technology on campus. 800 workstations in library, computer center, student center. Online course registration, online library, helpline, wireless network available.

Student life. Freshman orientation: Available. Preregistration for classes offered. **Activities:** Bands, choral groups, dance, drama, international student organizations, literary magazine, Model UN, radio station, student government, student newspaper.

Athletics. NJCAA. **Intercollegiate:** Baseball M, basketball, cross-country, golf M, soccer M, softball W, tennis, track and field, volleyball W. **Intramural:** Basketball M, bowling, handball, racquetball, softball M, table tennis M, tennis M, volleyball M. **Team name:** Cavaliers.

Student services. Adult student services, career counseling, student employment services, on-campus daycare, personal counseling, placement for graduates, veterans' counselor. **Physically disabled:** Services for visually, hearing impaired. **Transfer:** Transfer adviser, college fairs on campus for students transferring to 4-year colleges.

Contact. E-mail: jcccadmissions@jccc.edu
Phone: (913) 469-3803 Toll-free number: (866) 896-5893
Fax: (913) 469-2524
Pete Belk, Director of Admission, Johnson County Community College, 12345 College Boulevard, Overland Park, KS 66210-1299

Kansas City Kansas Community College
Kansas City, Kansas   **CB member**
www.kckcc.edu   **CB code: 6333**

◗ Public 2-year community and career college
◗ Commuter campus in very large city

General. Founded in 1923. Regionally accredited. **Enrollment:** 4,768 degree-seeking undergraduates. **Degrees:** 648 associate awarded. **Calendar:**

Semester, extensive summer session. **Full-time faculty:** 154 total; 23% minority, 51% women. **Part-time faculty:** 238 total; 12% minority, 48% women. **Class size:** 87% < 20, 12% 20-39, less than 1% 40-49, less than 1% 50-99. **Partnerships:** Formal partnership with American Hotel and Lodging Educational Institute.

Student profile. Among degree-seeking undergraduates, 920 enrolled as first-time, first-year students, 56 transferred in from other institutions.

Part-time:	61%	Hispanic/Latino:	15%
Out-of-state:	5.6%	Native American:	1%
Women:	61%	Multi-racial, non-Hispanic:	4%
African American:	25%	International:	3%
Asian American:	3%	25 or older:	39%

Basis for selection. Open admission, but selective for some programs. Special requirements for nursing program. **Home schooled:** Interview required. Admission based on ACT, SAT, or GED scores and interview.

High school preparation. 21 units recommended. Recommended units include English 4, mathematics 4, social studies 4, history 4, science 3 and foreign language 2.

2015-2016 Annual costs. Tuition/fees: $2,640; $6,660 out-of-state. Per-credit charge: $73 in-state; $207 out-of-state. Room/board: $4,800. Books/supplies: $1,146.

2014-2015 Financial aid. Need-based: 73% of total undergraduate aid awarded as scholarships/grants, 27% as loans/jobs. Need-based aid available for part-time students. Work-study available nights, weekends and for part-time students. **Non-need-based:** Scholarships awarded for academics, art, athletics, music/drama.

Application procedures. Admission: No deadline. No application fee. Admission notification on a rolling basis. **Financial aid:** No deadline. FAFSA required. Applicants notified on a rolling basis starting 5/1; must reply within 4 week(s) of notification.

Academics. Extensive online classes. **Special study options:** Cooperative education, distance learning, dual enrollment of high school students, ESL, external degree, honors, internships, liberal arts/career combination, weekend college. **Credit/placement by examination:** AP, CLEP, IB, institutional tests. 15 credit hours maximum toward associate degree. **Support services:** GED preparation and test center, learning center, reduced course load, remedial instruction, study skills assistance, tutoring, writing center.

Majors. Business: Accounting/business management, administrative services, business admin, marketing. **Communications technology:** Desktop publishing, recording arts. **Computer sciences:** Networking. **Health services:** EMT paramedic, nursing (RN), physical therapy assistant, respiratory therapy assistant, respiratory therapy technology, substance abuse counseling. **Liberal arts:** Arts/sciences. **Protective services:** Corrections, fire safety technology, firefighting, police science. **Work/family studies:** Child care management.

Most popular majors. Health sciences 32%, liberal arts 49.1%, security/protective services 6%.

Technology on campus. 900 workstations in library, computer center. Commuter students can connect to campus network. Online course registration, online library, helpline, wireless network available.

Student life. Freshman orientation: Available. Preregistration for classes offered. **Housing:** Apartments available. **Activities:** Bands, choral groups, drama, international student organizations, music ensembles, musical theater, student government, student newspaper, TV station, African American Student Union, International Student Organization, Campus Forum, Christian Student Union, Phi Theta Kappa, Student Senate, Out Questioning & Straight Diversity Club, Student Organization of Latinos, Economics Club, Students in Free Enterprise.

Athletics. NJCAA. **Intercollegiate:** Baseball M, basketball, cross-country, golf M, soccer M, softball W, track and field, volleyball W. **Team name:** Blue Devils.

Student services. Adult student services, alcohol/substance abuse counseling, career counseling, services for economically disadvantaged, student employment services, financial aid counseling, health services, on-campus daycare, personal counseling, veterans' counselor, women's services. **Physically disabled:** Services for visually, speech, hearing impaired. **Transfer:** Transfer adviser, college fairs on campus for students transferring to 4-year colleges.

Contact. E-mail: admiss@kckcc.edu
Phone: (913) 288-7600 Fax: (913) 288-7648
Tami Bartunek, Director of Admission, Kansas City Kansas Community College, 7250 State Avenue, Kansas City, KS 66112

Labette Community College
Parsons, Kansas
www.labette.edu   CB code: 6576

▸ Public 2-year community college
▸ Commuter campus in large town

General. Founded in 1923. Regionally accredited. **Enrollment:** 1,574 undergraduates. **Degrees:** 159 associate awarded. **Location:** 130 miles from Kansas City, 50 miles from Tulsa, Oklahoma. **Calendar:** Semester, extensive summer session. **Full-time faculty:** 34 total. **Part-time faculty:** 117 total. **Class size:** 78% < 20, 22% 20-39, less than 1% 40-49. **Partnerships:** Formal partnerships with local businesses.

Student profile.

Out-of-state:	5%	Live on campus:	3%
25 or older:	41%		

Transfer out. Colleges most students transferred to 2015: Pittsburg State, Emporia State, Wichita State, Kansas University, Kansas State University.

Basis for selection. Open admission, but selective for some programs. Special requirements for health care programs. ACT, school and College Ability Tests required of nursing applicants. COMPASS also used to measure language proficiency. Interview required for nursing, radiology, respiratory therapy programs, and commercial music programs. **Home schooled:** Transcript of courses and grades required. GED and ACT scores may be considered. Placement testing available. **Learning Disabled:** Student must notify campus ADA coordinator at least 30 days prior to first day of classes (earlier in special circumstances).

2015-2016 Annual costs. Tuition/fees: $2,700; $3,450 out-of-state. Per-credit charge: $48 in-state; $73 out-of-state. Books/supplies: $1,050. Personal expenses: $2,500.

Financial aid. Need-based: Need-based aid available for part-time students. Work-study available nights, weekends and for part-time students. **Non-need-based:** Scholarships awarded for academics, leadership.

Application procedures. Admission: No deadline. No application fee. Admission notification on a rolling basis. **Financial aid:** No deadline. FAFSA required. Applicants notified on a rolling basis starting 4/4; must reply within 2 week(s) of notification.

Academics. Extensive PLATO learning system available. Four-year bachelor's program with Emporia State University, Washburn University. **Special study options:** Distance learning, dual enrollment of high school students, liberal arts/career combination. License preparation in nursing, radiology. **Credit/placement by examination:** AP, CLEP, institutional tests. 12 credit hours maximum toward associate degree. **Support services:** GED preparation and test center, learning center, remedial instruction, study skills assistance, tutoring, writing center.

Majors. Biology: General. **Business:** Accounting, business admin, office/clerical. **Communications:** Journalism. **Computer sciences:** General, data processing, LAN/WAN management, networking, programming. **Education:** General, business, early childhood, elementary, music, secondary. **English:** English lit. **Health services:** Medical secretary, nursing (RN), radiologic technology/medical imaging, respiratory therapy technology. **History:** General. **Liberal arts:** Arts/sciences. **Protective services:** Corrections, firefighting, law enforcement admin. **Psychology:** General. **Social sciences:** General, political science. **Visual/performing arts:** Commercial/advertising art, music, music management, studio arts.

Most popular majors. Business/marketing 11%, education 15%, health sciences 53%.

Technology on campus. 150 workstations in library, computer center, student center. Commuter students can connect to campus network. Online library, helpline, student web hosting, wireless network available.

Student life. Freshman orientation: Mandatory. Preregistration for classes offered. **Activities:** Bands, choral groups, dance, drama, music ensembles, student government, Christian Club, Phi Beta Lambda, Phi Theta Kappa.

Athletics. NJCAA. **Intercollegiate:** Baseball M, basketball, cheerleading, softball W, tennis W, volleyball W, wrestling M. **Team name:** Cardinals.

Student services. Adult student services, career counseling, services for economically disadvantaged, student employment services, financial aid counseling, personal counseling, placement for graduates, veterans' counselor. **Physically disabled:** Services for visually, speech, hearing impaired. **Transfer:** Transfer adviser, college fairs on campus for students transferring to 4-year colleges.

Contact. Phone: (620) 421-6700 Toll-free number: (888) 522-3883
Fax: (620) 421-0180
Kylie Lucas, Director of Admissions, Labette Community College, 200
South 14th Street, Parsons, KS 67357

Manhattan Area Technical College
Manhattan, Kansas
www.manhattantech.edu

- Public 2-year technical college
- Commuter campus in large town

General. **Enrollment:** 446 degree-seeking undergraduates; 424 non-degree-seeking students. **Degrees:** 139 associate awarded. **Location:** 125 miles of Kansas City. **Calendar:** Semester, limited summer session. **Full-time faculty:** 28 total. **Part-time faculty:** 56 total. **Class size:** 67% < 20, 29% 20-39, 4% 40-49.

Student profile. Among degree-seeking undergraduates, 100% enrolled in a vocational program, 62 enrolled as first-time, first-year students, 106 transferred in from other institutions.

Part-time:	22%	Hispanic/Latino:	6%
Women:	43%	Multi-racial, non-Hispanic:	4%
African American:	5%	25 or older:	30%
Asian American:	2%		

Basis for selection. Open admission, but selective for some programs. Practical Nursing applicants must meet testing requirements and be KS licensed Certified Nurse Aide; Associate Degree/Registered Nurse applicants must be KS licensed Practical Nurses; Electric Power & Distribution applicants must be 18 years of age prior to June 1 of their year of enrollment and have or be eligible to receive a Commercial Drivers License by the same date. **Adult students:** SAT/ACT scores not required.

2015-2016 Annual costs. Tuition/fees: $3,897; $3,897 out-of-state. Per-credit charge: $100. Books/supplies: $2,000. Personal expenses: $2,500.

2014-2015 Financial aid. **Need-based:** 80 full-time freshmen applied for aid; 65 deemed to have need; 63 received aid. Average need met was 38%. Average scholarship/grant was $5,026; average loan $2,867. 44% of total undergraduate aid awarded as scholarships/grants, 56% as loans/jobs. Need-based aid available for part-time students. Work-study available nights, weekends and for part-time students. **Non-need-based:** Awarded to 6 full-time undergraduates, including 1 freshmen. Scholarships awarded for academics, leadership.

Application procedures. **Admission:** No deadline. $40 fee. Admission notification on a rolling basis. **Financial aid:** Priority date 7/1; no closing date. FAFSA, institutional form required. Applicants notified on a rolling basis.

Academics. **Special study options:** Cooperative education, dual enrollment of high school students, internships. License preparation in dental hygiene, nursing. **Credit/placement by examination:** AP, CLEP, institutional tests. 9 credit hours maximum toward associate degree. **Support services:** Learning center, reduced course load, study skills assistance, tutoring.

Majors. **Business:** Administrative services, executive assistant. **Computer sciences:** General. **General:** Carpentry, power transmission. **Health services:** Clinical lab technology, dental hygiene, medication aide, nursing (RN).

Most popular majors. Health sciences 21%, trade and industry 13%.

Technology on campus. 16 workstations in library, student center. Commuter students can connect to campus network. Online library, wireless network available.

Student life. **Freshman orientation:** Mandatory. Preregistration for classes offered. Approximately 6-8 weeks prior to beginning of semester. Half day sessions include pre-enrollment, and pre-testing. **Activities:** Student government.

Student services. Career counseling, financial aid counseling, personal counseling, placement for graduates. **Transfer:** Pre-admission transcript evaluation for new students.

Contact. E-mail: nicolefischer@matc.net
Phone: (785) 320-4560 Toll-free number: (800) 352-7575
Fax: (785) 587-2804
Neil Ross, Director of Admissions, Manhattan Area Technical College,
3136 Dickens Avenue, Manhattan, KS 66503-2499

Neosho County Community College
Chanute, Kansas
www.neosho.edu   CB code: 6093

- Public 2-year community college
- Commuter campus in small town

General. Founded in 1936. Regionally accredited. **Enrollment:** 2,259 degree-seeking undergraduates. **Degrees:** 320 associate awarded. **Location:** Approximately 100 miles from both Kansas City, Missouri and Wichita. **Calendar:** Semester, limited summer session. **Full-time faculty:** 53 total. **Part-time faculty:** 140 total.

Student profile.

Out-of-state:	14%	Live on campus:	28%

Transfer out. **Colleges most students transferred to 2015:** Pittsburg State University, Emporia State University, Kansas State University, University of Kansas, Wichita State University.

Basis for selection. Open admission, but selective for some programs. Nursing entrance test (TEAS) required. **Home schooled:** Must take GED or have ACT score of 20 or SAT score of 850.

High school preparation. College-preparatory program required.

2015-2016 Annual costs. Tuition/fees: $2,850; $2,850 out-of-district; $2,850 out-of-state. Per-credit charge: $64 in-district; $64 out-of-district; $64 out-of-state. Room/board: $5,900. Books/supplies: $480. Personal expenses: $800.

Financial aid. **Need-based:** Need-based aid available for part-time students. Work-study available nights, weekends and for part-time students. **Non-need-based:** Scholarships awarded for academics, art, athletics, job skills, leadership, music/drama, state residency.

Application procedures. **Admission:** Priority date 8/15; no deadline. No application fee. Admission notification on a rolling basis. **Financial aid:** Priority date 4/1; no closing date. FAFSA required. Applicants notified on a rolling basis; must reply within 6 week(s) of notification.

Academics. **Special study options:** Cooperative education, distance learning, dual enrollment of high school students, honors, independent study, liberal arts/career combination, weekend college. License preparation in nursing. **Credit/placement by examination:** AP, CLEP, institutional tests. 15 credit hours maximum toward associate degree. **Support services:** GED preparation and test center, learning center, reduced course load, remedial instruction, study skills assistance, tutoring, writing center.

Majors. **Biology:** General. **Business:** Accounting, administrative services, banking/financial services, business admin, office management. **Communications:** Communications/speech/rhetoric. **Computer sciences:** General. **Education:** General, secondary. **English:** English lit. **Foreign languages:** General. **Health services:** Athletic training, health care admin, licensed practical nurse, nursing (RN). **Human services:** Social work. **Liberal arts:** Arts/sciences. **Math:** General. **Parks/recreation:** Exercise sciences. **Physical sciences:** Chemistry. **Psychology:** General. **Social sciences:** General. **Visual/performing arts:** Art, dramatic, music, studio arts. **Work/family studies:** General.

Technology on campus. 120 workstations in dormitories, library, computer center, student center. Dormitories wired for high-speed internet access. Online library, helpline, wireless network available.

Student life. **Freshman orientation:** Mandatory. Preregistration for classes offered. **Housing:** Guaranteed on-campus for freshmen. Coed dorms available. $125 nonrefundable deposit. Home stays with host families for international students available. **Activities:** Choral groups, dance, drama, international student organizations, music ensembles, musical theater, student government.

Athletics. NJCAA. **Intercollegiate:** Baseball M, basketball, cheerleading, cross-country, soccer, softball W, track and field, volleyball W, wrestling M. **Team name:** Panthers.

Student services. Adult student services, career counseling, student employment services, financial aid counseling, personal counseling, veterans' counselor. **Physically disabled:** Services for visually, speech, hearing impaired. **Transfer:** Pre-admission transcript evaluation for new students. Transfer adviser, college fairs on campus for students transferring to 4-year colleges.

Contact. E-mail: admissions@neosho.edu
Phone: (620) 431-2820 ext. 233 Toll-free number: (800) 729-6222
Fax: (620) 431-6056
Leslie Beddo, Director of Admission, Neosho County Community
College, 800 West 14th Street, Chanute, KS 66720

North Central Kansas Technical College
Beloit, Kansas
www.ncktc.edu   CB code: 2616

▸ Public 2-year technical college
▸ Small town

General. Regionally accredited. **Enrollment:** 785 degree-seeking undergraduates. **Degrees:** 121 associate awarded. **Location:** 107 miles from Hays,
175 miles from Topeka. **Calendar:** Semester, limited summer session. **Full-
time faculty:** 45 total. **Part-time faculty:** 12 total.

Basis for selection. Open admission. **Home schooled:** Transcript of
courses and grades required. **Learning Disabled:** Students must present
written documentation from certified professional identifying disability with
recommendations for accommodations.

2015-2016 Annual costs. Tuition/fees: $3,488; $3,488 out-of-state. Per-
credit charge: $109. Room/board: $5,094. Books/supplies: $1,550. Personal
expenses: $1,275.

2015-2016 Financial aid. Need-based: 35% of total undergraduate aid
awarded as scholarships/grants, 65% as loans/jobs. Need-based aid available
for part-time students. Work-study available nights, weekends and for part-
time students. **Non-need-based:** Scholarships awarded for academics,
state residency.

Application procedures. Admission: Priority date 12/15; no deadline.
$50 fee. Admission notification on a rolling basis. **Financial aid:** No deadline.
FAFSA required.

Academics. Credit/placement by examination: AP, CLEP. **Support services:** Learning center, remedial instruction, tutoring.

Majors. Business: General. **Computer sciences:** Information technology,
networking. **Health services:** Nursing (RN). **Social sciences:** GIS/cartog-
raphy.

Technology on campus. 50 workstations in library, computer center.
Dormitories wired for high-speed internet access. Repair service, wireless
network available.

Student life. Freshman orientation: Mandatory. Preregistration for
classes offered. **Housing:** Coed dorms available. $140 deposit. **Activities:**
Student government.

Athletics. Intramural: Basketball M, football (non-tackle) M, volleyball.

Student services. Career counseling, financial aid counseling, placement
for graduates.

Contact. E-mail: aprescott@ncktc.edu
Phone: (800) 658-4655 Toll-free number: (800) 658-4655
Fax: (785) 738-2903
Angel Prescott, Admissions Director, North Central Kansas Technical
College, PO Box 507, Beloit, KS 67420

Northwest Kansas Technical College
Goodland, Kansas
www.nwktc.edu

▸ Public 2-year technical college
▸ Residential campus in small town

General. Regionally accredited. **Enrollment:** 626 undergraduates.
Degrees: 232 associate awarded. **Location:** 200 miles from Denver, CO.
Calendar: Semester, limited summer session. **Full-time faculty:** 32 total;
16% minority, 25% women. **Part-time faculty:** 4 total; 50% women. **Special
facilities:** Rodeo practice arena.

Transfer out. Colleges most students transferred to 2015: Pittsburg State
University, Fort Hays State University, Kansas State University.

Basis for selection. Open admission, but selective for some programs.
Test scores required to confirm placement level. **Home schooled:** Transcript
of courses and grades required.

High school preparation. College-preparatory program required.

2015-2016 Annual costs. Tuition/fees: $8,200; $8,200 out-of-state.

Financial aid. All financial aid based on need. Need-based aid available
for part-time students. Work-study available nights, weekends and for part-
time students.

Application procedures. Admission: No deadline. $25 fee. Admission
notification on a rolling basis. **Financial aid:** Closing date 8/1.

Academics. Special study options: Distance learning, dual enrollment of
high school students, ESL, internships. **Credit/placement by examination:**
AP, CLEP, institutional tests. **Support services:** Learning center, pre-
admission summer program, remedial instruction, study skills assistance,
tutoring.

Majors. Communications technology: General. **Computer sciences:**
Computer graphics.

Technology on campus. 250 workstations in library, computer center,
student center. Dormitories wired for high-speed internet access and linked to
campus network. Online course registration, helpline, repair service, wireless
network available.

Student life. Freshman orientation: Mandatory. Preregistration for
classes offered. Held 5 times prior to the beginning of the fall semester.
Housing: Guaranteed on-campus for freshmen. Single-sex dorms, special
housing for disabled, apartments, wellness housing available. $200 fully
refundable deposit. **Activities:** Campus ministries, dance, student government, student newspaper.

Athletics. NJCAA. **Intercollegiate:** Basketball, cheerleading, cross-
country, golf, rodeo, soccer, track and field, wrestling. **Intramural:** Badminton, baseball, football (non-tackle), racquetball, softball, ultimate frisbee,
volleyball, weight lifting. **Team name:** Mavericks.

Student services. Adult student services, alcohol/substance abuse counseling, career counseling, services for economically disadvantaged, student
employment services, financial aid counseling, on-campus daycare, personal
counseling, placement for graduates. **Physically disabled:** Services for hearing impaired. **Transfer:** Pre-admission transcript evaluation for new students.
Transfer adviser for students transferring to 4-year colleges.

Contact. E-mail: admissions@nwktc.edu
Phone: (785) 890-3641 Toll-free number: (800) 316-4127
Fax: (785) 899-5711
Reina Branum, Assistant Vice President for Student Affairs, Northwest
Kansas Technical College, 1209 Harrison, Goodland, KS 67735

Pratt Community College
Pratt, Kansas
www.prattcc.edu   CB code: 6581

▸ Public 2-year community and technical college
▸ Commuter campus in small town

General. Founded in 1938. Regionally accredited. **Enrollment:** 673 full-
time, degree-seeking students. **Degrees:** 267 associate awarded. **Location:**
70 miles from Wichita. **Calendar:** Semester, limited summer session. **Full-
time faculty:** 41 total. **Part-time faculty:** 78 total. **Class size:** 64% < 20,
33% 20-39, 2% 40-49, less than 1% 50-99. **Special facilities:** Indoor and
outdoor rodeo facilities, electrical powerlineman training facility.

Student profile.

Out-of-state:	11%	Live on campus:	40%
25 or older:	20%		

Transfer out. Colleges most students transferred to 2015: Fort Hays
State University, Emporia State University, Kansas State University.

Basis for selection. Open admission, but selective for some programs.
Special requirements for nursing, agriculture power technology, and electrical
power distribution programs. Interview required of nursing majors. Audition
required of music and drama majors. Portfolio recommended for art majors.
Home schooled: Transcript of courses and grades required. **Learning Disabled:** IEP's must be submitted to admissions before initial enrollment and
request of services.

2015-2016 Annual costs. Tuition/fees: $2,970; $3,210 out-of-state. Per-
credit charge: $58 in-state; $66 out-of-state. Room/board: $5,422. Books/
supplies: $900. Personal expenses: $1,000.

Financial aid. Need-based: Need-based aid available for part-time students. Work-study available nights, weekends and for part-time students. **Non-need-based:** Scholarships awarded for academics, art, athletics, leadership, minority status, music/drama, state residency.

Application procedures. Admission: No deadline. No application fee. Admission notification on a rolling basis beginning on or about 1/1. **Financial aid:** Priority date 5/1, closing date 8/1. FAFSA, institutional form required. Applicants notified on a rolling basis starting 2/1; must reply within 2 week(s) of notification.

Academics. Special study options: Distance learning, dual enrollment of high school students, honors, independent study, internships, liberal arts/career combination. Bachelor's degree programs available on campus. License preparation in nursing. **Credit/placement by examination:** AP, CLEP, IB, institutional tests. 15 credit hours maximum toward associate degree. **Support services:** Learning center, remedial instruction, tutoring.

Majors. Biology: General, botany. **Business:** Accounting, business admin, entrepreneurial studies, office management, office technology, office/clerical. **Communications:** Communications/speech/rhetoric, journalism. **Conservation:** Wildlife/wilderness. **Education:** General, early childhood, elementary, secondary. **Engineering:** General. **English:** English lit, rhetoric/composition. **Health services:** Licensed practical nurse, medical secretary, nursing (RN), predental, premedicine, prepharmacy, preveterinary. **History:** General. **Liberal arts:** Arts/sciences. **Math:** General. **Physical sciences:** Chemistry. **Psychology:** General. **Social sciences:** General, political science, sociology. **Visual/performing arts:** General, ceramics, commercial/advertising art, dramatic, drawing, music, painting, studio arts.

Most popular majors. Health sciences 45%, liberal arts 6%.

Technology on campus. 125 workstations in dormitories, library, computer center. Dormitories wired for high-speed internet access and linked to campus network. Commuter students can connect to campus network. Online course registration, online library, helpline, wireless network available.

Student life. Freshman orientation: Available. Preregistration for classes offered. One to 2 days before classes begin in each fall and spring semester. **Policies:** 2 MMR (Measle, Mumps, Rubella) inoculations and Meningitis inoculations required for dorm students. **Housing:** Coed dorms, single-sex dorms, wellness housing available. $200 deposit. **Activities:** Bands, choral groups, dance, drama, international student organizations, literary magazine, music ensembles, musical theater, student government, student newspaper, Christian Challenge, Student Senate, Student Ambassadors, Rotaract.

Athletics. NJCAA. **Intercollegiate:** Baseball M, basketball, cheerleading, cross-country, rodeo, soccer, softball W, track and field, volleyball W, wrestling M. **Intramural:** Basketball, football (non-tackle), rodeo, softball, table tennis, volleyball. **Team name:** Beavers.

Student services. Adult student services, career counseling, student employment services, financial aid counseling, health services, personal counseling, placement for graduates, veterans' counselor. **Physically disabled:** Services for visually, speech, hearing impaired. **Transfer:** College fairs on campus for students transferring to 4-year colleges.

Contact. E-mail: pccadmissions@prattcc.edu
Phone: (620) 672-5641 ext. 217
Toll-free number: (800) 794-3091 ext. 217 Fax: (620) 672-5247
Frank Stahl, Director of Admissions, Pratt Community College, 348 Northeast State Route 61, Pratt, KS 67124-8317

Seward County Community College
Liberal, Kansas
www.sccc.edu   CB code: 0286

▶ Public 2-year community and technical college
▶ Commuter campus in large town

General. Founded in 1967. Regionally accredited. Off-campus classes offered in 7 locations, adult learning center with ESL classes, interactive television classrooms to off-site locations, GED classes/testing available. **Enrollment:** 1,629 degree-seeking undergraduates. **Degrees:** 215 associate awarded. **Location:** 210 miles from Wichita; 160 miles from Amarillo; 260 miles from Oklahoma City; 320 miles from Colorado Springs. **Calendar:** Semester, limited summer session. **Full-time faculty:** 62 total. **Part-time faculty:** 85 total. **Class size:** 83% < 20, 16% 20-39, less than 1% 40-49, less than 1% 50-99.

Student profile. Among degree-seeking undergraduates, 429 enrolled as first-time, first-year students.

Out-of-state: 19% **Live on campus:** 15%

Transfer out. Colleges most students transferred to 2015: Kansas State University, Texas Christian University, University of Texas-Arlington, University of Central Oklahoma, Fort Hays State University.

Basis for selection. Open admission. **Adult students:** SAT/ACT scores not required. Students may take the COMPASS placement test on campus if no recent SAT/ACT scores are available.

High school preparation. 20 units recommended. Recommended units include English 4, mathematics 3, social studies 2, science 2 and foreign language 1.

2015-2016 Annual costs. Tuition/fees: $2,520; $2,640 out-of-district; $3,660 out-of-state. Per-credit charge: $51 in-district; $55 out-of-district; $89 out-of-state. Room/board: $4,680. Books/supplies: $800. Personal expenses: $1,000.

Financial aid. Need-based: Need-based aid available for part-time students. Work-study available nights, weekends and for part-time students. **Non-need-based:** Scholarships awarded for academics, athletics.

Application procedures. Admission: No deadline. No application fee. Admission notification on a rolling basis. **Financial aid:** Priority date 4/1; no closing date. FAFSA, institutional form required. Applicants notified on a rolling basis starting 6/15; must reply within 4 week(s) of notification.

Academics. Special study options: Cooperative education, cross-registration, distance learning, double major, dual enrollment of high school students, external degree, independent study, internships, liberal arts/career combination. Bachelor's degree programs available on campus. License preparation in nursing, paramedic. **Credit/placement by examination:** AP, CLEP, institutional tests. 24 credit hours maximum toward associate degree. **Support services:** GED preparation and test center, learning center, remedial instruction, study skills assistance, tutoring, writing center.

Majors. Biology: General. **Business:** General, accounting, administrative services, business admin, fashion, finance, hospitality admin, office management, office technology, office/clerical, sales/distribution. **Communications:** Communications/speech/rhetoric, journalism. **Computer sciences:** General, applications programming, computer graphics, computer science, data entry, data processing, information technology, programming. **Conservation:** Forestry, wildlife/wilderness. **Education:** General, teacher assistance. **Engineering:** General. **English:** English lit. **Health services:** Athletic training, clinical lab assistant, clinical lab technology, dental hygiene, medical secretary, nursing (RN), predental, premedicine, prenursing, prepharmacy, preveterinary, respiratory therapy technology. **History:** General. **Human services:** Social work. **Liberal arts:** Arts/sciences, library assistant. **Math:** General. **Parks/recreation:** General, exercise sciences, health/fitness. **Philosophy/religion:** Religion. **Physical sciences:** Chemistry, physics. **Protective services:** Law enforcement admin, police science. **Psychology:** General. **Social sciences:** General, economics, sociology. **Visual/performing arts:** General, art, ceramics, dramatic, music, music performance, painting, studio arts, voice/opera.

Most popular majors. Business/marketing 15%, health sciences 35%, liberal arts 17%.

Technology on campus. 50 workstations in dormitories, library, computer center, student center. Dormitories wired for high-speed internet access. Commuter students can connect to campus network. Online course registration, online library, repair service, wireless network available.

Student life. Freshman orientation: Mandatory. Preregistration for classes offered. **Housing:** Coed dorms available. $100 deposit, deadline 6/30. **Activities:** Bands, choral groups, drama, film society, international student organizations, literary magazine, music ensembles, musical theater, student government, student newspaper, symphony orchestra, TV station.

Athletics. NJCAA. **Intercollegiate:** Baseball M, basketball, softball W, tennis, volleyball W. **Intramural:** Basketball, bowling, football (non-tackle), golf, soccer, swimming, table tennis, volleyball. **Team name:** Saints.

Student services. Adult student services, career counseling, student employment services, financial aid counseling, personal counseling, veterans' counselor. **Transfer:** Transfer adviser, college fairs on campus for students transferring to 4-year colleges.

Contact. E-mail: admissions@sccc.edu
Phone: (620) 417-1100 Toll-free number: (800) 373-9951 ext. 1100
Fax: (620) 417-1079
Bert Luallen, Director of Admissions, Seward County Community College, 1801 North Kansas Avenue, Liberal, KS 67905-1137

Wichita Area Technical College
Wichita, Kansas
www.watc.edu

- Public 2-year technical college
- Commuter campus in large city

General. Regionally accredited. **Enrollment:** 1,482 degree-seeking undergraduates. **Degrees:** 103 associate awarded. **Location:** 200 miles from Kansas City, Missouri, 162 miles from Oklahoma City. **Calendar:** Semester, extensive summer session. **Full-time faculty:** 60 total; 12% minority, 48% women. **Part-time faculty:** 242 total; 16% minority, 56% women. **Class size:** 91% < 20, 8% 20-39, less than 1% 40-49, less than 1% 50-99.

Transfer out. Colleges most students transferred to 2015: Wichita State University, Pratt Community College, Butler Community College, Newman University, Cowley County Community College.

Basis for selection. Open admission, but selective for some programs. Some programs have specific admission requirements. **Adult students:** SAT/ACT scores not required.

2015-2016 Annual costs. Tuition/fees: $2,940; $3,360 out-of-state. Per-credit charge: $67 in-state; $81 out-of-state. Books/supplies: $1,850. **Additional information:** Tuition for general education courses is $67 per credit hour and fees are $31 per credit hour. Tuition costs vary by program.

Financial aid. All financial aid based on need. Need-based aid available for part-time students. Work-study available nights, weekends and for part-time students.

Application procedures. Admission: No deadline. No application fee. Application must be submitted online. Admission notification on a rolling basis. **Financial aid:** No deadline. FAFSA, institutional form, CSS PROFILE required. Applicants notified on a rolling basis starting 1/1.

Academics. Special study options: Distance learning, dual enrollment of high school students, internships. License preparation in aviation, nursing. **Credit/placement by examination:** AP, CLEP, institutional tests. 15 credit hours maximum toward associate degree. Combined life experience/credit by exam may not exceed 15 hours for an associate degree. **Support services:** GED preparation, remedial instruction, study skills assistance, tutoring, writing center.

Majors. Business: Business admin, office/clerical, operations. **Health services:** Dental assistant, licensed practical nurse, medical assistant, surgical technology. **Visual/performing arts:** Interior design.

Most popular majors. Business/marketing 7%, engineering/engineering technologies 13%, health sciences 10%, trade and industry 59%, visual/performing arts 7%.

Technology on campus. 200 workstations in computer center. Commuter students can connect to campus network. Online course registration, online library, helpline, wireless network available.

Student life. Freshman orientation: Available. Preregistration for classes offered.

Student services. Career counseling, student employment services, financial aid counseling, placement for graduates, veterans' counselor. **Physically disabled:** Services for visually, speech, hearing impaired.

Contact. E-mail: info@watc.edu
Phone: (316) 677-9400 Toll-free number: (866) 296-4031
Andy McFayden, Director, Marketing & Community Outreach, Wichita Area Technical College, 4004 North Webb Road, Suite 100, Wichita, KS 67226

Wright Career College: Overland Park
Overland Park, Kansas
www.wrightcc.edu

- Private 2-year career college
- Large city

General. Regionally accredited; also accredited by ACICS. **Enrollment:** 116 undergraduates. **Degrees:** 53 bachelor's, 339 associate awarded. **Calendar:** Continuous.

Basis for selection. Open admission.

2015-2016 Annual costs. Tuition/fees: $12,550.

Financial aid. Need-based: Work-study available nights, weekends and for part-time students.

Application procedures. Admission: No deadline.

Academics. Credit/placement by examination: AP.

Majors. Business: Business admin. **Health services:** Insurance coding. **Parks/recreation:** Sports admin.

Contact. Phone: (913) 385-7700
Wright Career College: Overland Park, 10700 Metcalf Avenue, Overland Park, KS 66210

Wright Career College: Wichita
Wichita, Kansas
www.wrightcc.edu

- Private 2-year career college
- Very large city

General. Regionally accredited; also accredited by ACICS. **Enrollment:** 128 undergraduates. **Degrees:** 41 associate awarded. **Calendar:** Continuous.

Basis for selection. Open admission.

2015-2016 Annual costs. Tuition/fees: $12,550.

Financial aid. Need-based: Work-study available nights, weekends and for part-time students.

Academics. Credit/placement by examination: AP.

Majors. Business: Accounting, business admin. **Health services:** Insurance coding, medical assistant, nursing practice, surgical technology. **Parks/recreation:** Exercise sciences.

Contact. Phone: (316) 927-7000
Wright Career College: Wichita, 7700 East Kellogg, Wichita, KY 67207

Kentucky

Ashland Community and Technical College
Ashland, Kentucky
www.ashland.kctcs.edu
CB code: 0703

▶ Public 2-year community college
▶ Commuter campus in large town

General. Founded in 1957. Regionally accredited. Off-campus classes in surrounding counties. **Enrollment:** 1,852 degree-seeking undergraduates. **Degrees:** 373 associate awarded. **Location:** 120 miles from Lexington; 15 miles from Huntington, WV. **Calendar:** Semester, limited summer session. **Full-time faculty:** 95 total. **Part-time faculty:** 106 total. **Special facilities:** Three open computer labs, learning assistance center, early intervention program for students at risk.

Student profile.

Out-of-state: 26% 25 or older: 43%

Transfer out. Colleges most students transferred to 2015: Morehead State University, Marshall University, Shawnee State University.

Basis for selection. Open admission, but selective for some programs. Admission to nursing program based on test scores and academic record. Interview recommended.

High school preparation. 11 units recommended. Recommended units include English 4, mathematics 3, social studies 2, science 2 (laboratory 2).

2015-2016 Annual costs. Tuition/fees: $4,650; $15,690 out-of-state. Per-credit charge: $147 in-state; $515 out-of-state. Books/supplies: $1,000. Personal expenses: $800. **Additional information:** Nonresident students living in contiguous counties are charged a discounted non-resident rate of $294 per credit hour.

Financial aid. Need-based: Work-study available nights, weekends and for part-time students. **Non-need-based:** Scholarships awarded for academics, job skills, leadership, minority status, music/drama. **Additional information:** In-state 100% disabled or deceased veterans' children receive tuition waiver from state.

Application procedures. Admission: Closing date 8/5. No application fee. Admission notification on a rolling basis. Nursing applications due by 3/1. **Financial aid:** Priority date 3/15; no closing date. FAFSA, institutional form required. Applicants notified on a rolling basis starting 5/1; must reply within 3 week(s) of notification.

Academics. Special study options: Cooperative · education, cross-registration, distance learning, dual enrollment of high school students, honors, internships, liberal arts/career combination, weekend college. **Credit/placement by examination:** AP, CLEP, institutional tests. 40 credit hours maximum toward associate degree. **Support services:** GED test center, learning center, pre-admission summer program, reduced course load, remedial instruction, study skills assistance, tutoring.

Honors college/program. Participants have option of taking selected honors courses.

Majors. Business: Business admin. **Computer sciences:** General. **Health services:** EMT paramedic, medical secretary, nursing (RN), respiratory therapy technology. **Liberal arts:** Arts/sciences. **Protective services:** Firefighting, law enforcement admin. **Work/family studies:** Child care service.

Most popular majors. Business/marketing 6%, health sciences 17%, interdisciplinary studies 22%, liberal arts 40%, security/protective services 6%.

Technology on campus. 138 workstations in library, computer center. Commuter students can connect to campus network. Online course registration, helpline available.

Student life. Freshman orientation: Mandatory. Preregistration for classes offered. **Activities:** Campus ministries, drama, musical theater, student government, student newspaper, Baptist Campus Ministry/students for Christ, Circle K, drama club, multicultural student affairs, Phi Theta Kappa, students in free enterprise.

Student services. Adult student services, career counseling, services for economically disadvantaged, student employment services, financial aid counseling, health services, minority student services, on-campus daycare, placement for graduates, veterans' counselor. **Physically disabled:** Services for visually, speech, hearing impaired. **Transfer:** Re-entry adviser for new students. Transfer center, transfer adviser for students transferring to 4-year colleges.

Contact. E-mail: steve.woodburn@kctcs.net
Phone: (606) 326-2000 Toll-free number: (800) 370-7191
Fax: (606) 325-8124
Steve Woodburn, Dean for Student Affairs, Ashland Community and Technical College, 1400 College Drive, Ashland, KY 41101-3683

Big Sandy Community and Technical College
Prestonsburg, Kentucky
www.bigsandy.kctcs.edu
CB code: 0869

▶ Public 2-year community and technical college
▶ Commuter campus in small town

General. Founded in 1964. Regionally accredited. Four campuses located at Hager Hill, Paintsville, Pikeville, and Prestonsburg. **Enrollment:** 3,250 degree-seeking undergraduates. **Degrees:** 506 associate awarded. **Location:** 120 miles from Lexington. **Calendar:** Semester, limited summer session. **Full-time faculty:** 122 total. **Part-time faculty:** 71 total. **Special facilities:** East Kentucky Science Center, planetarium, nature trail.

Student profile.

Out-of-state: 1% 25 or older: 36%

Basis for selection. Open admission, but selective for some programs. 21 ACT required for nursing and dental hygiene programs. All others required to submit COMPASS, ASSET, ACT or SAT for placement.

2015-2016 Annual costs. Tuition/fees: $4,650; $15,690 out-of-state. Per-credit charge: $147 in-state; $515 out-of-state. Books/supplies: $550. Personal expenses: $3,000. **Additional information:** Nonresident students living in contiguous counties are charged a discounted non-resident rate of $294 per credit hour.

Financial aid. Need-based: Need-based aid available for part-time students. Work-study available nights, weekends and for part-time students. **Non-need-based:** Scholarships awarded for academics.

Application procedures. Admission: No deadline. No application fee. Admission notification on a rolling basis. Must have completed junior year of high school prior to enrolling full-time; may audit courses as sophomores or juniors. **Financial aid:** Priority date 4/1; no closing date. FAFSA required. Applicants notified on a rolling basis; must reply within 2 week(s) of notification.

Academics. Special study options: Cooperative education, distance learning, dual enrollment of high school students, independent study, internships, liberal arts/career combination, weekend college. Bachelor's degree programs available on campus. **Credit/placement by examination:** AP, CLEP, institutional tests. 36 credit hours maximum toward associate degree. **Support services:** GED preparation and test center, learning center, remedial instruction, study skills assistance, tutoring, writing center.

Majors. Business: Accounting, administrative services, management information systems, management science, real estate. **Computer sciences:** Information technology, networking, programming, webmaster. **Health services:** Dental hygiene, nursing (RN). **Liberal arts:** Arts/sciences. **Protective services:** Police science.

Technology on campus. 575 workstations in library, computer center, student center. Online course registration, online library, wireless network available.

Student life. Freshman orientation: Available. Preregistration for classes offered. **Activities:** Choral groups, drama, literary magazine, student government, Baptist Student Union, Phi Theta Kappa, Phi Beta Lambda, Kentucky Association of Nursing Students, CARE, law enforcement club.

Student services. Career counseling, services for economically disadvantaged, financial aid counseling, personal counseling, veterans' counselor. **Physically disabled:** Services for visually, speech, hearing impaired. **Transfer:** Pre-admission transcript evaluation for new students. Transfer center, transfer adviser, college fairs on campus for students transferring to 4-year colleges.

Contact. E-mail: jimmy.wright@kctcs.edu
Phone: (606) 886-3863 ext. 67366
Toll-free number: (888) 641-4132 ext. 67366 Fax: (606) 886-6943
Jimmy Wright, Dean of Admissions, Big Sandy Community and
Technical College, One Bert T. Combs Drive, Prestonsburg, KY 41653

Bluegrass Community and Technical College
Lexington, Kentucky
www.bluegrass.kctcs.edu   CB code: 0645

❧ Public 2-year community and technical college
❧ Commuter campus in large city

General. Founded in 1965. Regionally accredited. Locations include Danville, Georgetown, Lawrenceburg, Lexington, Nicholasville, and Winchester. **Enrollment:** 10,392 undergraduates. **Degrees:** 716 associate awarded. **Location:** 90 miles from Cincinnati, 75 miles from Louisville. **Calendar:** Semester, extensive summer session. **Full-time faculty:** 248 total. **Part-time faculty:** 425 total. **Special facilities:** North American Racing Academy located at Kentucky Horse Park. **Partnerships:** Industrial maintenance internship with Toyota; pre-hire assessments conducted for local companies; short-term training offered for local businesses (computer skills, HVAC skills, etc.).

Student profile.

Out-of-state: 1%   25 or older: 47%

Transfer out. Colleges most students transferred to 2015: University of Kentucky, Eastern Kentucky University, Midway College, Morehead University, University of Phoenix.

Basis for selection. Open admission, but selective for some programs. Special requirements for computer information systems, health technologies, nursing, nuclear medicine, radiography, respiratory care, dental hygiene, dental laboratory technology. ACT required for admission to some health programs. NLN preadmission test may be used for nursing rather than ACT. **Home schooled:** ACT/SAT scores (or COMPASS) and transcript including grading scale required.

High school preparation. Students strongly encouraged to follow state pre-college curriculum.

2015-2016 Annual costs. Tuition/fees: $4,650; $15,690 out-of-state. Per-credit charge: $147 in-state; $515 out-of-state. Books/supplies: $1,000. Personal expenses: $800. **Additional information:** Nonresident students living in contiguous counties are charged a discounted non-resident rate of $294 per credit hour.

Financial aid. Need-based: Need-based aid available for part-time students. Work-study available nights, weekends and for part-time students. **Non-need-based:** Scholarships awarded for academics, minority status, state residency.

Application procedures. Admission: Closing date 8/1 (receipt date). No application fee. Admission notification on a rolling basis. **Financial aid:** Priority date 4/15; no closing date. FAFSA, institutional form required. Applicants notified on a rolling basis starting 6/5; must reply within 3 week(s) of notification.

Academics. Six nationally accredited programs offered in allied health and nursing. **Special study options:** Cooperative education, distance learning, double major, dual enrollment of high school students, ESL, exchange student, internships, study abroad, weekend college. License preparation in dental hygiene, nursing, radiology, real estate. **Credit/placement by examination:** AP, CLEP, institutional tests. **Support services:** GED preparation and test center, learning center, remedial instruction, study skills assistance, tutoring, writing center.

Majors. Architecture: Landscape. **Area/ethnic studies:** Latin American, Russian/Slavic. **Biology:** General, biochemistry. **Business:** Administrative services, business admin, executive assistant. **Communications:** Communications/speech/rhetoric, journalism, radio/TV. **Computer sciences:** General, data processing, informatics, information technology. **Conservation:** General, forest sciences, wildlife/wilderness. **Education:** Teacher assistance. **English:** English lit, rhetoric/composition. **Foreign languages:** French, German, Italian, linguistics, Russian, Spanish. **General:** Carpentry, electrician. **Health services:** Dental hygiene, dental lab technology, medical assistant, medical radiologic technology/radiation therapy, medical secretary, nuclear medical technology, nursing (RN), respiratory therapy technology, surgical technology. **Human services:** Social work. **Liberal arts:** Arts/sciences. **Math:** General. **Philosophy/religion:** Philosophy, religion. **Physical sciences:** General, chemistry, geology, physics. **Protective services:** Fire safety technology, firefighting. **Psychology:** General. **Visual/performing arts:**

General, art history/conservation, commercial/advertising art, dramatic, interior design, music, music history, music performance, music theory/composition, studio arts, studio arts management. **Work/family studies:** Child care service.

Most popular majors. Business/marketing 9%, health sciences 23%, interdisciplinary studies 6%, liberal arts 43%, trade and industry 6%.

Technology on campus. 370 workstations in library, computer center. Commuter students can connect to campus network. Online course registration, online library, helpline, repair service, wireless network available.

Student life. Freshman orientation: Mandatory. Preregistration for classes offered. Four-hour session held periodically throughout summer. **Housing:** Coed dorms, single-sex dorms, apartments available. Students apply for and are assigned housing at University of Kentucky. Applications submitted to Office of Student Housing, University of Kentucky. **Activities:** Choral groups, drama, international student organizations, student government, student newspaper, Christian Fellowship, College Republicans, Students for Peace and Earth Justice.

Athletics. Intramural: Basketball, soccer.

Student services. Adult student services, alcohol/substance abuse counseling, career counseling, services for economically disadvantaged, student employment services, financial aid counseling, health services, minority student services, on-campus daycare, personal counseling, placement for graduates, veterans' counselor. **Physically disabled:** Services for visually, speech, hearing impaired. **Transfer:** Pre-admission transcript evaluation for new students. Transfer center, transfer adviser, college fairs on campus for students transferring to 4-year colleges.

Contact. E-mail: shelbie.hugle@kctcs.edu
Phone: (859) 246-6210 Toll-free number: (866) 774-4872 ext. 56210
Fax: (859) 246-4666
Shelbie Hugle, Director of Admissions, Bluegrass Community and
Technical College, 200 Oswald Building, Cooper Drive, Lexington, KY
40506-0235

Brown Mackie College: Hopkinsville
Hopkinsville, Kentucky
www.brownmackie.edu   CB code: 5375

❧ For-profit 2-year business and junior college
❧ Large town

General. Accredited by ACICS. **Enrollment:** 222 undergraduates. **Degrees:** 55 associate awarded. **Calendar:** Quarter. **Full-time faculty:** 3 total. **Part-time faculty:** 7 total.

Basis for selection. Open admission.

2015-2016 Annual costs. Tuition/fees: $16,490. Per-credit charge: $327. Books/supplies: $1,500. Personal expenses: $2,970.

Financial aid. Need-based: Work-study available nights, weekends and for part-time students.

Application procedures. Admission: No deadline. $20 fee. Admission notification on a rolling basis. High school diploma not required for those entering certificate/diploma programs. **Financial aid:** No deadline. FAFSA required. Applicants notified on a rolling basis.

Academics. Credit/placement by examination: AP, CLEP.

Majors. Business: Accounting, business admin, management information systems. **Health services:** Medical assistant.

Contact. Phone: (270) 886-1302 Toll-free number: (800) 359-4753
Fax: (270) 886-3544
Brown Mackie College: Hopkinsville, 4001 Fort Campbell Boulevard,
Hopkinsville, KY 42240

Brown Mackie College: Louisville
Louisville, Kentucky
www.brownmackie.edu   CB code: 0305

❧ For-profit 2-year technical college
❧ Commuter campus in large city
❧ Interview required

General. Founded in 1972. Accredited by ACICS. **Enrollment:** 1,120 undergraduates. **Degrees:** 18 bachelor's, 359 associate awarded. **Calendar:** Quarter, extensive summer session. **Full-time faculty:** 36 total. **Part-time faculty:** 25 total.

Student profile.

Out-of-state: 9% 25 or older: 59%

Basis for selection. Open admission.

2015-2016 Annual costs. Tuition/fees: $16,490. Per-credit charge: $327. Books/supplies: $1,500. Personal expenses: $2,970.

Financial aid. All financial aid based on need. Work-study available nights, weekends and for part-time students.

Application procedures. Admission: No deadline. No application fee. Admission notification on a rolling basis. **Financial aid:** No deadline. FAFSA required. Applicants notified on a rolling basis.

Academics. Credit/placement by examination: AP, CLEP. 16 hours of credit by CLEP Engineering Technologies examination may be counted toward associate degree. **Support services:** Tutoring.

Majors. Computer sciences: General.

Technology on campus. 12 workstations in library, computer center.

Student life. Freshman orientation: Mandatory. Preregistration for classes offered. **Activities:** Student government, student newspaper.

Athletics. Intercollegiate: Softball M.

Student services. Career counseling, student employment services, personal counseling, placement for graduates.

Contact. Phone: (502) 968-7191 Toll-free number: (888) 476-1266 Fax: (502) 968-1727
George Nosko, Admissions Director, Brown Mackie College: Louisville, 3605 Fern Valley Road, Louisville, KY 40219

Brown Mackie College: North Kentucky
Fort Mitchell, Kentucky
www.brownmackie.edu   **CB code: 3419**

⬧ For-profit 2-year business and health science college
⬧ Small town

General. Accredited by ACICS. **Enrollment:** 306 undergraduates. **Degrees:** 15 bachelor's, 120 associate awarded. **Location:** 8 miles from Cincinnati. **Calendar:** Differs by program. **Full-time faculty:** 15 total; 27% have terminal degrees, 67% women. **Part-time faculty:** 24 total; 46% women.

Basis for selection. Open admission.

2015-2016 Annual costs. Tuition/fees: $15,680. Per-credit charge: $314. Books/supplies: $1,500. Personal expenses: $2,970.

Financial aid. Need-based: Work-study available nights, weekends and for part-time students.

Application procedures. Admission: No deadline. No application fee. Admission notification on a rolling basis.

Academics. Special study options: License preparation in nursing, occupational therapy. **Credit/placement by examination:** AP, CLEP. **Support services:** Remedial instruction, tutoring.

Majors. Business: Accounting technology, business admin. **Computer sciences:** General.

Technology on campus. 16 workstations in library.

Student life. Freshman orientation: Mandatory. Preregistration for classes offered.

Contact. Phone: (859) 341-5627 Toll-free number: (800) 888-1445 Fax: (859) 341-6483
Brown Mackie College: North Kentucky, 309 Buttermilk Pike, Fort Mitchell, KY 41017

Daymar College: Bowling Green
Bowling Green, Kentucky
www.daymarcollege.edu   **CB code: 3399**

⬧ For-profit 2-year branch campus and career college
⬧ Commuter campus in small city

General. Regionally accredited; also accredited by ACICS. **Enrollment:** 225 degree-seeking undergraduates. **Degrees:** 15 bachelor's, 108 associate awarded. **Location:** 90 miles from Louisville; 60 miles from Nashville, TN. **Calendar:** Quarter, extensive summer session. **Full-time faculty:** 12 total; 17% have terminal degrees, 8% minority, 75% women. **Part-time faculty:** 11 total; 9% minority, 64% women. **Class size:** 92% < 20, 8% 20-39.

Student profile.

Out-of-state: 1% 25 or older: 80%

Transfer out. Colleges most students transferred to 2015: Western Kentucky University, Bowling Green Technical College.

Basis for selection. Open admission. **Home schooled:** Transcript of courses and grades required.

2015-2016 Annual costs. Diploma programs: $22,000-$26,500. Associate programs: $33,000.

Financial aid. All financial aid based on need. Need-based aid available for part-time students. Work-study available nights, weekends and for part-time students.

Application procedures. Admission: No deadline. No application fee. Admission notification on a rolling basis. **Financial aid:** No deadline. FAFSA required.

Academics. Special study options: Distance learning, double major, internships. Bachelor's degree programs available on campus. **Credit/placement by examination:** AP, CLEP, SAT, ACT, institutional tests. 16 credit hours maximum toward associate degree. **Support services:** Learning center, reduced course load, remedial instruction, tutoring.

Majors. Business: Accounting technology, business admin. **Computer sciences:** General, system admin, webmaster. **Health services:** Cardiovascular technology, insurance coding, medical assistant, medical secretary, pharmacy assistant. **Protective services:** Law enforcement admin.

Most popular majors. Business/marketing 20%, computer/information sciences 10%, health sciences 64%, legal studies 6%, security/protective services 9%.

Technology on campus. 75 workstations in library, computer center. Online library, wireless network available.

Student life. Freshman orientation: Mandatory. Preregistration for classes offered. One-day session held 1 week prior to beginning of quarter. **Activities:** Student newspaper.

Student services. Adult student services, career counseling, financial aid counseling, personal counseling, placement for graduates. **Transfer:** Re-entry adviser, pre-admission transcript evaluation for new students. Transfer adviser for students transferring to 4-year colleges.

Contact. E-mail: thenderson@daymarcollege.edu
Phone: (270) 843-6750 Toll-free number: (800) 541-0296
Fax: (270) 843-6976
Traci Henderson, Admissions, Daymar College: Bowling Green, 2421 Fitzgerald Industrial Drive, Bowling Green, KY 42101

Daymar College: Louisville
Louisville, Kentucky
www.daymarcollege.edu   **CB code: 3407**

⬧ For-profit 2-year business college
⬧ Large city

General. Accredited by ACICS. **Enrollment:** 68 undergraduates. **Degrees:** 6 bachelor's, 55 associate awarded. **Calendar:** Quarter. **Full-time faculty:** 7 total. **Part-time faculty:** 28 total.

Basis for selection. Open admission. SAT, ACT, or Wonderlic Scholastic Level Exam required for placement.

2015-2016 Annual costs. Books/supplies: $3,000. **Additional information:** Diploma programs: $22,000-$26,500. Associate programs: $33,000.

Financial aid. Need-based: Work-study available nights, weekends and for part-time students.

Application procedures. Admission: No deadline. No application fee.

Academics. Credit/placement by examination: AP, CLEP.

Majors. Business: Business admin. **Computer sciences:** Networking. **Health services:** Health information technology, office assistant, pharmacy assistant.

Student life. Freshman orientation: Available. Preregistration for classes offered.

Contact. Phone: (502) 495-1040
Shawn Wantland, Director of Admissions, Daymar College: Louisville, 4112 Fern Valley Road, Louisville, KY 40219-1973

Daymar College: Owensboro
Owensboro, Kentucky
www.daymarcollege.edu   **CB code: 0772**

- For-profit 2-year business and junior college
- Commuter campus in small city
- Interview required

General. Founded in 1963. Accredited by ACICS. Provides hands-on training with practical theory. Medical assisting-clinical track students have 3 classes at Owensboro Medical Health System. **Enrollment:** 94 undergraduates. **Degrees:** 2 bachelor's, 63 associate awarded. **Location:** 120 miles from Louisville; 35 miles from Evansville, IN. **Calendar:** Quarter, extensive summer session. **Full-time faculty:** 7 total. **Part-time faculty:** 54 total.

Basis for selection. Open admission. Must have diploma or GED. SAT, ACT, or Wonderlic Scholastic Level Exam required for placement. **Learning Disabled:** Copy of IEP required.

High school preparation. Recommended units include English 3, mathematics 1, social studies 1 and science 1. One human relations also recommended.

2015-2016 Annual costs. Books/supplies: $3,000. **Additional information:** Diploma programs: $22,000-$26,500. Associate programs: $33,000-$48,000.

Financial aid. All financial aid based on need. Need-based aid available for part-time students. Work-study available nights, weekends and for part-time students.

Application procedures. Admission: No deadline. No application fee. Admission notification on a rolling basis. **Financial aid:** No deadline. FAFSA required. Applicants notified on a rolling basis.

Academics. Special study options: Cooperative education, distance learning, double major, dual enrollment of high school students, honors, independent study, internships. **Credit/placement by examination:** AP, CLEP, institutional tests. 12 credit hours maximum toward associate degree. **Support services:** GED preparation, remedial instruction, tutoring.

Majors. Business: Administrative services, business admin, office management, office technology, office/clerical, operations. **Computer sciences:** General, data processing, information systems, networking, systems analysis. **Health services:** Medical assistant, medical secretary, pharmacy assistant.

Most popular majors. Business/marketing 14%, computer/information sciences 36%, health sciences 32%, legal studies 19%.

Technology on campus. 115 workstations in library, computer center.

Student life. Freshman orientation: Mandatory. Preregistration for classes offered. **Activities:** Student newspaper.

Student services. Alcohol/substance abuse counseling, career counseling, student employment services, financial aid counseling, personal counseling, placement for graduates. **Physically disabled:** Services for visually, hearing impaired. **Transfer:** Re-entry adviser, pre-admission transcript evaluation for new students. Transfer adviser for students transferring to 4-year colleges.

Contact. Phone: (270) 926-4040 Toll-free number: (800) 960-4090
Fax: (270) 685-4090
Latasha Shemwell, Director of Admissions, Daymar College: Owensboro, 3361 Buckland Square, Owensboro, KY 42301

Daymar College: Paducah
Paducah, Kentucky
www.daymarcollege.edu   **CB code: 0669**

- For-profit 2-year technical college
- Commuter campus in small city
- Interview required

General. Founded in 1964. Accredited by ACICS. Associate program completes 3 academic years in 2 calendar years. **Enrollment:** 47 undergraduates. **Degrees:** 11 bachelor's, 39 associate awarded. **Location:** 150 miles from St. Louis and Nashville, TN. **Calendar:** Quarter, extensive summer session. **Full-time faculty:** 10 total. **Part-time faculty:** 15 total.

Basis for selection. Open admission.

2015-2016 Annual costs. Books/supplies: $3,000. **Additional information:** Diploma programs: $22,000-$26,500. Associate programs: $33,000.

Financial aid. Need-based: Work-study available nights, weekends and for part-time students.

Application procedures. Admission: No deadline. No application fee. Admission notification on a rolling basis. **Financial aid:** No deadline. FAFSA, CSS PROFILE required. Applicants notified on a rolling basis; must reply within 3 week(s) of notification.

Academics. Special study options: Distance learning, internships. **Credit/placement by examination:** AP, CLEP. **Support services:** Learning center, tutoring.

Majors. Engineering: Electrical. **Health services:** Insurance coding, insurance specialist, pharmacy assistant.

Technology on campus. 50 workstations in library, computer center. Commuter students can connect to campus network. Online library, helpline, wireless network available.

Student life. Freshman orientation: Mandatory. Preregistration for classes offered.

Student services. Alcohol/substance abuse counseling, career counseling, student employment services, financial aid counseling, personal counseling, placement for graduates, veterans' counselor. **Transfer:** Pre-admission transcript evaluation for new students.

Contact. Phone: (270) 444-9676 Toll-free number: (800) 995-4438
Fax: (270) 441-7202
Connie Holley, Director of Admission, Daymar College: Paducah, 509 South 30th Street, Paducah, KY 42001

Elizabethtown Community and Technical College
Elizabethtown, Kentucky
www.elizabethtown.kctcs.edu   **CB code: 1211**

- Public 2-year community and technical college
- Commuter campus in large town

General. Founded in 1964. Regionally accredited. Off-campus locations at Fort Knox, Bardstown, Leitchfield, Hardinsburg, and Brandenburg. **Enrollment:** 4,485 degree-seeking undergraduates. **Degrees:** 896 associate awarded. **ROTC:** Army. **Location:** 40 miles from Louisville. **Calendar:** Semester, limited summer session. **Full-time faculty:** 141 total. **Part-time faculty:** 180 total. **Special facilities:** Regional Home for the Arts center.

Student profile.

Out-of-state:	1%
25 or older:	52%

Transfer out. Colleges most students transferred to 2015: Western Kentucky University, University of Louisville, University of Kentucky.

Basis for selection. Open admission, but selective for some programs. All nursing, radiography and dental hygiene programs have selective criteria. Enrolled freshmen must take ACT, ACT/Career Planning Profile or ASSET by start of second semester. **Learning Disabled:** ADA counselor assists those with special needs or disabilities.

High school preparation. College-preparatory program recommended.

2015-2016 Annual costs. Tuition/fees: $4,770; $15,810 out-of-state. Per-credit charge: $147 in-state; $515 out-of-state. Books/supplies: $1,358.

Financial aid. All financial aid based on need. Need-based aid available for part-time students. Work-study available nights, weekends and for part-time students.

Application procedures. Admission: No deadline. No application fee. Admission notification on a rolling basis. Early admission available for specially qualified high school students on part-time basis. **Financial aid:** Priority date 8/1; no closing date. FAFSA required. Applicants notified on a rolling basis starting 6/1; must reply within 2 week(s) of notification.

Academics. Special study options: Cooperative education, distance learning, dual enrollment of high school students, honors, internships, liberal arts/career combination, teacher certification program, weekend college. Bachelor's degree programs available on campus. License preparation in dental hygiene, nursing, radiology, real estate. **Credit/placement by examination:** AP, CLEP, institutional tests. 6 credit hours maximum toward associate degree. **Support services:** GED test center, learning center, remedial instruction, study skills assistance, tutoring, writing center.

Majors. Business: Business admin, executive assistant, real estate. **Computer sciences:** General. **Education:** Early childhood, teacher assistance. **General:** Electrician. **Health services:** Dental hygiene, medical radiologic technology/radiation therapy, medical secretary, nursing (RN). **Human services:** Social work. **Liberal arts:** Arts/sciences. **Protective services:** Firefighting, law enforcement admin. **Work/family studies:** Child care service.

Technology on campus. 87 workstations in library, computer center, student center. Online library, helpline, wireless network available.

Student life. Freshman orientation: Available. Preregistration for classes offered. Online orientation or on-campus orientation available. **Activities:** Choral groups, drama, literary magazine, student government, student newspaper, Baptist campus ministry, Association of Nursing Students, Phi Theta Kappa, Phi Beta Lambda, gay straight alliance, Students in Free Enterprise, Skills USA, Phoenix club.

Student services. Adult student services, career counseling, services for economically disadvantaged, financial aid counseling, personal counseling, placement for graduates, veterans' counselor, women's services. **Physically disabled:** Services for visually, speech, hearing impaired. **Transfer:** Transfer adviser, college fairs on campus for students transferring to 4-year colleges.

Contact. E-mail: Elizabethtown-Admissions@kctcs.edu
Phone: (270) 769-1632 Toll-free number: (877) 246-2322
Fax: (270) 769-1618
Bryan Smith, Registrar, Elizabethtown Community and Technical College, 600 College Street Road, Elizabethtown, KY 42701

Gateway Community and Technical College
Florence, Kentucky
www.gateway.kctcs.edu   **CB code: 0596**

▶ Public 2-year community and technical college
▶ Commuter campus in large city

General. Regionally accredited. **Enrollment:** 3,001 degree-seeking undergraduates. **Degrees:** 419 associate awarded. **Location:** 10 miles from Cincinnati, OH. **Calendar:** Semester, limited summer session. **Full-time faculty:** 91 total. **Part-time faculty:** 166 total. **Class size:** 70% < 20, 30% 20-39, less than 1% 40-49.

Student profile. Among degree-seeking undergraduates, 40% enrolled in a transfer program, 60% enrolled in a vocational program, 398 enrolled as first-time, first-year students, 211 transferred in from other institutions.

Part-time:	64%	Asian American:	1%
Out-of-state:	5%	Hispanic/Latino:	3%
Women:	57%	Multi-racial, non-Hispanic:	2%
African American:	9%	25 or older:	44%

Basis for selection. Open admission, but selective for some programs. Selective admission is used for the Registered Nurse program only. ACT COMPASS used for placement.

2015-2016 Annual costs. Tuition/fees: $4,450; $15,490 out-of-state. Per-credit charge: $147 in-state; $515 out-of-state. Books/supplies: $1,000.

Financial aid. Need-based: Work-study available nights, weekends and for part-time students.

Application procedures. Admission: No deadline. No application fee.

Academics. Special study options: Cooperative education, distance learning, dual enrollment of high school students, independent study, internships. **Credit/placement by examination:** AP, CLEP, institutional tests. **Support services:** GED preparation and test center, remedial instruction, tutoring.

Majors. Business: Business admin, executive assistant. **Computer sciences:** Information technology. **Education:** Early childhood, educational technology. **General:** Electrician. **Health services:** EMT paramedic, health information technology, medical assistant, medical secretary, nursing (RN). **Human services:** Social work. **Protective services:** Criminal justice. **Visual/performing arts:** Graphic design. **Work/family studies:** Child care service.

Most popular majors. Business/marketing 7%, health sciences 23%, interdisciplinary studies 16%, liberal arts 29%, security/protective services 6%.

Technology on campus. Online library, helpline, repair service, wireless network available.

Student life. Freshman orientation: Available. Preregistration for classes offered. **Activities:** Student government.

Student services. Career counseling, services for economically disadvantaged, financial aid counseling, personal counseling, placement for graduates, veterans' counselor. **Transfer:** Pre-admission transcript evaluation for new students. Transfer center, transfer adviser, college fairs on campus for students transferring to 4-year colleges.

Contact. Phone: (859) 442-1134 Fax: (859) 442-1107
Andre Washington, Dean of Enrollment Services, Gateway Community and Technical College, 790 Thomas More Parkway, Edgewood, KY 41017

Hazard Community and Technical College
Hazard, Kentucky
www.hazard.kctcs.edu   **CB code: 0815**

▶ Public 2-year community and technical college
▶ Commuter campus in small town

General. Founded in 1968. Regionally accredited. **Enrollment:** 1,803 degree-seeking undergraduates. **Degrees:** 352 associate awarded. **Location:** 100 miles from Lexington. **Calendar:** Semester, limited summer session. **Full-time faculty:** 87 total. **Part-time faculty:** 31 total.

Transfer out. Colleges most students transferred to 2015: Morehead State University, Eastern Kentucky University, University of Kentucky, Lindsey Wilson College.

Basis for selection. Open admission, but selective for some programs and for out-of-state students. GPA, ACT/COMPASS, and pre-admissions conference required for applicants to allied health programs. Out-of-state applicants must rank in top 50% of high school class or have 3.0 GPA.

High school preparation. 11 units recommended. Recommended units include English 4, mathematics 3, social studies 1, history 1 and science 2.

2015-2016 Annual costs. Tuition/fees: $4,650; $9,060 out-of-district; $15,690 out-of-state. Per-credit charge: $147 in-district; $294 out-of-district; $515 out-of-state. Books/supplies: $1,000. Personal expenses: $800.

Financial aid. All financial aid based on need. Need-based aid available for part-time students. Work-study available nights, weekends and for part-time students.

Application procedures. Admission: Priority date 8/1; no deadline. No application fee. Admission notification on a rolling basis beginning on or about 6/15. **Financial aid:** Priority date 4/1; no closing date. FAFSA required. Applicants notified on a rolling basis starting 6/15; must reply within 2 week(s) of notification.

Academics. Special study options: Cooperative education, distance learning, dual enrollment of high school students, honors, independent study, internships, liberal arts/career combination. 2+2 bachelor's degree programs in business administration, elementary education and University Studies with Morehead State University; 2+2 bachelor's degree program in criminal justice, Individualized studies, nursing and social work with Eastern Kentucky University; 2+2 bachelor's degree in Arts/Human Services and Counseling with Lindsey Wilson and a Master of Education in Mental Health Counseling with Lindsey Wilson. Bachelor's degree programs available on campus. **Credit/**

placement by examination: AP, CLEP, institutional tests. **Support services:** GED test center, learning center, remedial instruction, study skills assistance, tutoring, writing center.

Majors. Business: Marketing. **Computer sciences:** General. **Education:** Early childhood. **Health services:** Medical radiologic technology/radiation therapy, nursing (RN), physical therapy assistant. **Liberal arts:** Arts/sciences.

Technology on campus. 494 workstations in library, computer center, student center.

Student life. Freshman orientation: Available. Preregistration for classes offered. **Activities:** Student government.

Student services. Physically disabled: Services for visually, speech, hearing impaired. **Transfer:** Pre-admission transcript evaluation for new students. College fairs on campus for students transferring to 4-year colleges.

Contact. Phone: (606) 436-5721 ext. 73525 Toll-free number: (800) 246-7521 ext. 73525 Fax: (606) 666-4312 Scott Gross, Director of Admissions, Hazard Community and Technical College, One Community College Drive, Hazard, KY 41701

Henderson Community College
Henderson, Kentucky
www.henderson.kctcs.edu
CB code: 1307

- Public 2-year community college
- Commuter campus in large town

General. Founded in 1960. Regionally accredited. **Enrollment:** 1,300 degree-seeking undergraduates. **Degrees:** 197 associate awarded. **Location:** 10 miles from Evansville, IN. **Calendar:** Semester, limited summer session. **Full-time faculty:** 48 total. **Part-time faculty:** 78 total. **Special facilities:** Fine arts center hosting variety of social and cultural activities in visual and performing arts.

Transfer out. Colleges most students transferred to 2015: Western Kentucky University, Murray State University, University of Kentucky, University of Southern Indiana.

Basis for selection. Open admission, but selective for some programs. Dental Hygiene, Dental Assisting, and Nursing are designated as Selective Admission Programs; test scores and high school GPA important admissions criteria. Interview required for nursing program.

2015-2016 Annual costs. Tuition/fees: $4,650; $15,690 out-of-state. Per-credit charge: $147 in-state; $515 out-of-state. Books/supplies: $1,250.

Financial aid. Need-based: Work-study available nights, weekends and for part-time students.

Application procedures. Admission: Closing date 8/1 (receipt date). No application fee. Application must be submitted online. Admission notification on a rolling basis beginning on or about 3/1. **Financial aid:** Closing date 7/15. FAFSA required. Applicants notified on a rolling basis starting 5/1.

Academics. Special study options: Cooperative education, distance learning, dual enrollment of high school students, honors, independent study, liberal arts/career combination, weekend college. Bachelor's degree programs available on campus. License preparation in dental hygiene, nursing. **Credit/placement by examination:** AP, CLEP, institutional tests. **Support services:** GED preparation and test center, learning center, pre-admission summer program, reduced course load, remedial instruction, study skills assistance, tutoring, writing center.

Majors. Business: Administrative services, business admin, management information systems. **Computer sciences:** Data processing. **Education:** Early childhood. **Health services:** Clinical lab technology. **Liberal arts:** Arts/sciences.

Technology on campus. 99 workstations in library, computer center, student center. Commuter students can connect to campus network. Online course registration, online library, helpline, repair service, wireless network available.

Student life. Freshman orientation: Mandatory. Preregistration for classes offered. Required of all new students. Sessions offered at various times throughout the entire academic year. **Activities:** Drama, literary magazine, student government, student newspaper, CROSS, unity coalition, Henderson Pride, green river area development district, vocational rehabilitation.

Student services. Career counseling, financial aid counseling, minority student services, on-campus daycare, personal counseling, placement for

graduates, veterans' counselor. **Transfer:** Re-entry adviser, pre-admission transcript evaluation for new students. Transfer center, transfer adviser, college fairs on campus for students transferring to 4-year colleges.

Contact. Phone: (270) 831-9739 Toll-free number: (855) 464-2244 Fax: (270) 831-9612 Cary Conley, Associate Dean of Enrollment Management, Henderson Community College, 2660 South Green Street, Henderson, KY 42420

Hopkinsville Community College
Hopkinsville, Kentucky
www.hopkinsville.kctcs.edu
CB code: 1274

- Public 2-year community college
- Commuter campus in small city

General. Founded in 1965. Regionally accredited. **Enrollment:** 3,165 degree-seeking undergraduates. **Degrees:** 536 associate awarded. **Location:** 70 miles from Nashville, 25 miles from Clarksville. **Calendar:** Semester, limited summer session. **Class size:** 65% < 20, 34% 20-39, less than 1% 40-49, less than 1% 50-99.

Student profile. Among degree-seeking undergraduates, 70% enrolled in a transfer program, 30% enrolled in a vocational program.

Out-of-state:	35% **25 or older:**	48%

Transfer out. Colleges most students transferred to 2015: Murray State University, Austin Peay State University, Western Kentucky University, Kentucky State University, University of Kentucky.

Basis for selection. Open admission, but selective for some programs. Selective admissions to practical and registered nursing programs. **Learning Disabled:** Must be documented to receive services.

High school preparation. College-preparatory program recommended.

2015-2016 Annual costs. Tuition/fees: $4,650; $9,060 out-of-district; $15,690 out-of-state. Per-credit charge: $147 in-district; $297 out-of-district; $515 out-of-state. Books/supplies: $1,000. Personal expenses: $2,820.

Financial aid. Need-based: Need-based aid available for part-time students. Work-study available nights, weekends and for part-time students. **Non-need-based:** Scholarships awarded for academics, leadership, minority status, state residency. **Additional information:** ACT required for academic scholarships.

Application procedures. Admission: No deadline. No application fee. Admission notification on a rolling basis. **Financial aid:** Priority date 7/15; no closing date. FAFSA required. Applicants notified on a rolling basis starting 7/1.

Academics. Special study options: Cooperative education, distance learning, dual enrollment of high school students, independent study, internships. License preparation in nursing. **Credit/placement by examination:** AP, CLEP, institutional tests. **Support services:** GED preparation and test center, learning center, remedial instruction, study skills assistance, tutoring, writing center.

Majors. Architecture: Architecture. **Business:** Business admin, executive assistant, office management. **Communications:** Communications/speech/rhetoric, journalism. **Computer sciences:** General. **Conservation:** Forest sciences. **Health services:** Dental hygiene, nuclear medical technology, nursing (RN), pharmacy assistant, physical therapy. **Human services:** Social work. **Liberal arts:** Arts/sciences. **Protective services:** Law enforcement admin. **Work/family studies:** Child care service.

Most popular majors. Business/marketing 8%, health sciences 11%, liberal arts 67%.

Technology on campus. Online course registration, online library, helpline, wireless network available.

Student life. Freshman orientation: Mandatory. Preregistration for classes offered. Held prior to start of semester. **Activities:** Campus ministries, literary magazine, student government, student newspaper, Ag Tech, Phi Theta Kappa, ballroom dance, Baptist campus ministries, Black Men United, College Democrats, College Republicans, criminal justice organization, Pi Gamma Epsilon, Donovan Scholars.

Student services. Adult student services, career counseling, services for economically disadvantaged, student employment services, financial aid counseling, minority student services, personal counseling, placement for graduates, veterans' counselor. **Physically disabled:** Services for visually, speech, hearing impaired. **Transfer:** Transfer adviser for students transferring to 4-year colleges.

Contact. E-mail: melissa.stevenson@kctcs.edu
Phone: (270) 707-3810 Fax: (270) 886-0237
Melissa Stevenson, Registrar, Hopkinsville Community College, PO Box 2100, Hopkinsville, KY 42241-2100

Jefferson Community and Technical College
Louisville, Kentucky
www.jefferson.kctcs.edu   **CB code: 1328**

- Public 2-year community and technical college
- Commuter campus in large city
- Interview required

General. Founded in 1968. Regionally accredited. 3 other campuses: southwestern Jefferson County, Shelby County and Carrollton. Courses also offered off-campus and online. **Enrollment:** 11,588 degree-seeking undergraduates. **Degrees:** 1,398 associate awarded. **ROTC:** Army. **Location:** Downtown. **Calendar:** Semester, extensive summer session. **Full-time faculty:** 330 total. **Part-time faculty:** 310 total. **Class size:** 54% < 20, 40% 20-39, 2% 40-49, 2% 50-99, less than 1% >100. **Special facilities:** Classes taught at local zoo, local pottery, local truck manufacturing plant, multimedia allied health lab, machine shop lab. **Partnerships:** Formal partnerships with United Parcel Service, Ford Motor Company, Norton Hospital, Jewish Hospital, St. Mary's Health Care System and local area technology centers.

Student profile.

Out-of-state:	4%	25 or older:	45%

Transfer out. Colleges most students transferred to 2015: University of Louisville, Spalding University, University of Kentucky, Bellarmine University.

Basis for selection. Open admission, but selective for some programs. Special requirements for nursing and other allied health programs. Entering freshmen required to take ACT for placement before start of second semester. Interview required for allied health programs: nursing, respiratory therapy, radiology, nuclear medicine, health information technology, occupational therapy, physical therapy, surgical technology, and practical nursing.

2015-2016 Annual costs. Tuition/fees: $4,650; $15,690 out-of-state. Per-credit charge: $147 in-state; $515 out-of-state. Books/supplies: $1,000. Personal expenses: $800.

Financial aid. Need-based: Need-based aid available for part-time students. Work-study available nights, weekends and for part-time students. **Non-need-based:** Scholarships awarded for academics, art, minority status.

Application procedures. Admission: No deadline. No application fee. Admission notification on a rolling basis. **Financial aid:** Priority date 3/15; no closing date. FAFSA, institutional form required. Applicants notified on a rolling basis starting 6/15; must reply within 3 week(s) of notification.

Academics. Special study options: Cooperative education, cross-registration, distance learning, dual enrollment of high school students, ESL, honors, independent study, internships, teacher certification program, weekend college. License preparation in aviation, nursing, occupational therapy, physical therapy, radiology, real estate. **Credit/placement by examination:** AP, CLEP, IB, institutional tests. STEP test, challenge exams available. **Support services:** GED preparation and test center, learning center, reduced course load, remedial instruction, study skills assistance, tutoring, writing center.

Majors. Business: Accounting technology, business admin, executive assistant, real estate. **Communications technology:** General. **Computer sciences:** General, data processing. **Education:** Teacher assistance. **Health services:** Electrocardiograph technology, health information technology, nuclear medical technology, nursing (RN), occupational therapy assistant, physical therapy assistant, respiratory therapy technology, sonography. **Human services:** Social work. **Liberal arts:** Arts/sciences. **Protective services:** Firefighting. **Work/family studies:** Child care service.

Most popular majors. Health sciences 30%, interdisciplinary studies 7%, liberal arts 43%.

Technology on campus. 1,500 workstations in library, computer center, student center. Commuter students can connect to campus network. Online course registration, online library, helpline available.

Student life. Freshman orientation: Mandatory. Preregistration for classes offered. **Activities:** Drama, literary magazine, student government,

student newspaper, black student union, Baptist student union, Earth-ecology club, Aspire, international student club, WOW.

Student services. Adult student services, career counseling, services for economically disadvantaged, student employment services, financial aid counseling, health services, minority student services, on-campus daycare, personal counseling, placement for graduates, veterans' counselor, women's services. **Physically disabled:** Services for visually, speech, hearing impaired. **Transfer:** Re-entry adviser, pre-admission transcript evaluation for new students. Transfer adviser, college fairs on campus for students transferring to 4-year colleges.

Contact. Phone: (502) 213-5333
Denise Gray-Lackey, Dean of Student Affairs, Jefferson Community and Technical College, 109 East Broadway, Louisville, KY 40202

Lincoln College of Technology: Florence
Florence, Kentucky
www.swcollege.net   **CB code: 2482**

- For-profit 2-year health science and career college
- Residential campus in small city
- Interview required

General. Accredited by ACICS. **Enrollment:** 222 undergraduates. **Degrees:** 44 associate awarded. **Location:** 5 miles from Cincinnati. **Calendar:** Quarter, extensive summer session. **Full-time faculty:** 10 total; 50% have terminal degrees, 20% minority, 60% women. **Part-time faculty:** 14 total.

Transfer out. Colleges most students transferred to 2015: Brown Mackie, Beckfield, Northern Kentucky University, Gateway Technical Community College.

Basis for selection. Open admission. **Home schooled:** State high school equivalency certificate required.

High school preparation. College-preparatory program required.

2015-2016 Annual costs. Certificate programs: $10,255. Diploma programs: $15,320 to $30,045. Associate programs: $30,515 to $33,048. Costs include total tuition, materials, tool fees, and registration fee.

Financial aid. All financial aid based on need. Need-based aid available for part-time students. Work-study available nights, weekends and for part-time students.

Application procedures. Admission: No deadline. $125 fee. Application must be submitted on paper. Admission notification on a rolling basis. **Financial aid:** No deadline. FAFSA required. Applicants notified on a rolling basis.

Academics. Special study options: Independent study, liberal arts/career combination. **Credit/placement by examination:** AP, CLEP. **Support services:** GED preparation, study skills assistance, tutoring.

Majors. Business: Business admin. **Computer sciences:** General. **Health services:** Medical assistant. **Protective services:** Law enforcement admin.

Technology on campus. 50 workstations in library, computer center. Online library available.

Student life. Freshman orientation: Mandatory. Preregistration for classes offered. Held on campus before each quarter in mornings and evenings. **Activities:** Student government, student newspaper.

Student services. Career counseling, services for economically disadvantaged, student employment services, financial aid counseling, placement for graduates. **Transfer:** Pre-admission transcript evaluation for new students.

Contact. E-mail: mdurkin@swcollege.net
Phone: (859) 282-9999 Fax: (859) 282-7940
Melissa Durkin, Director of Admissions, Lincoln College of Technology: Florence, 8095 Connector Drive, Florence, KY 41042

Madisonville Community College
Madisonville, Kentucky
www.madisonville.kctcs.edu   **CB code: 1606**

- Public 2-year community college
- Commuter campus in large town

General. Founded in 1968. Regionally accredited. Campuses include: North Campus, Health Sciences Campus, and Muhlenberg County Campus. **Enrollment:** 2,265 degree-seeking undergraduates. **Degrees:** 412 associate awarded. **Location:** 50 miles from Evansville, IN. **Calendar:** Semester, extensive summer session. **Full-time faculty:** 112 total. **Part-time faculty:** 146 total. **Special facilities:** Center for the arts.

Student profile.

Out-of-state: 1%   25 or older: 50%

Transfer out. Colleges most students transferred to 2015: Murray State University, Western Kentucky University, University of Kentucky.

Basis for selection. Open admission, but selective for some programs. ACT or Compass required for placement/counseling. Special requirements for nursing, physical therapy assistant, radiography, respiratory, occupational therapy assistant, clinical lab technology. **Adult students:** ACT or COMPASS placement scores must be less than 5 years old. **Home schooled:** Encouraged to apply for early admissions status prior to completion of high school credential.

High school preparation. 14 units recommended. Recommended units include English 4, mathematics 3, social studies 2, history 2, science 2 (laboratory 1).

2015-2016 Annual costs. Tuition/fees: $4,650; $9,060 out-of-district; $15,690 out-of-state. Per-credit charge: $147 in-district; $294 out-of-district; $515 out-of-state. Personal expenses: $1,000.

Financial aid. Need-based: Need-based aid available for part-time students. Work-study available nights, weekends and for part-time students. **Non-need-based:** Scholarships awarded for minority status.

Application procedures. Admission: Closing date 8/1 (receipt date). No application fee. Admission notification on a rolling basis. **Financial aid:** Priority date 7/1; no closing date. FAFSA, institutional form required. Applicants notified on a rolling basis; must reply within 3 week(s) of notification.

Academics. Adult and continuing education programs available both on- and off-campus. Tech prep and school-to-work programs available. Classes also offered at area high schools and other off-campus locations, including KET telecourses and online. **Special study options:** Cooperative education, distance learning, double major, dual enrollment of high school students, honors, independent study, internships, liberal arts/career combination, weekend college. Bachelor's degree programs available on campus. License preparation in nursing, occupational therapy, paramedic, physical therapy, radiology, real estate. **Credit/placement by examination:** AP, CLEP, institutional tests. **Support services:** GED preparation and test center, learning center, remedial instruction, study skills assistance, tutoring, writing center.

Majors. Business: Accounting, administrative services, business admin, finance, management information systems, real estate, sales/distribution. **Computer sciences:** General. **Education:** General, early childhood. **Health services:** Clinical lab science, clinical lab technology, medical radiologic technology/radiation therapy, medical secretary, nursing (RN), occupational therapy assistant, physical therapy assistant, respiratory therapy technology. **Liberal arts:** Arts/sciences. **Protective services:** Law enforcement admin. **Work/family studies:** Child care service.

Most popular majors. Business/marketing 14%, health sciences 39%, liberal arts 36%.

Technology on campus. 200 workstations in library, computer center, student center. Commuter students can connect to campus network. Online course registration, online library, helpline, wireless network available.

Student life. Freshman orientation: Mandatory. Preregistration for classes offered. First Semester Experience held throughout June and July for new students. **Activities:** Campus ministries, choral groups, drama, literary magazine, musical theater, student government, student newspaper, multicultural student organization, Lions Club, student ambassadors, Socratic Society, Phi Theta Kappa, Baptist student union.

Student services. Adult student services, career counseling, services for economically disadvantaged, student employment services, financial aid counseling, health services, minority student services, personal counseling, placement for graduates, veterans' counselor. **Physically disabled:** Services for visually, speech, hearing impaired. **Transfer:** Pre-admission transcript evaluation for new students. Transfer center, transfer adviser, college fairs on campus for students transferring to 4-year colleges.

Contact. Phone: (270) 821-2250 Toll-free number: (866) 227-4812 Fax: (270) 825-8553
Aimee Wilkerson, Director of Enrollment Management, Madisonville Community College, 2000 College Drive, Madisonville, KY 42431

Maysville Community and Technical College
Maysville, Kentucky
www.maysville.kctcs.edu   CB code: 0693

- Public 2-year community and technical college
- Commuter campus in small town

General. Founded in 1968. Regionally accredited. Access to Kentucky Virtual Library. **Enrollment:** 3,184 undergraduates. **Degrees:** 331 associate awarded. **Location:** 60 miles from Lexington, 60 miles from Cincinnati. **Calendar:** Semester, limited summer session. **Full-time faculty:** 95 total. **Part-time faculty:** 90 total.

Basis for selection. Open admission, but selective for some programs. ACT considered for nursing program. Some occupational/technical programs have additional requirements. ACT or COMPASS may be required for placement in degree-seeking programs. Interview required of nursing majors. **Home schooled:** Transcript of courses and grades required.

High school preparation. College-preparatory program recommended. Recommended units include English 4, mathematics 3, social studies 2, history 1, science 2 (laboratory 1), foreign language 2 and academic electives 5.

2015-2016 Annual costs. Tuition/fees: $4,650; $15,690 out-of-state. Per-credit charge: $147 in-state; $515 out-of-state. Books/supplies: $4,000. **Additional information:** Nonresident students living in contiguous counties are charged a discounted non-resident rate of $294 per credit hour.

Financial aid. Need-based: Need-based aid available for part-time students. Work-study available nights, weekends and for part-time students. **Non-need-based:** Scholarships awarded for academics.

Application procedures. Admission: No deadline. No application fee. Admission notification on a rolling basis. 3/1 priority date for nursing applicants. **Financial aid:** Priority date 4/1; no closing date. FAFSA, institutional form required. Applicants notified on a rolling basis starting 3/1; must reply within 3 week(s) of notification.

Academics. Special study options: Cooperative education, distance learning, double major, dual enrollment of high school students, honors, independent study, internships. Bachelor's degree programs available on campus. License preparation in nursing, real estate. **Credit/placement by examination:** AP, CLEP, institutional tests. **Support services:** GED preparation and test center, learning center, reduced course load, remedial instruction, study skills assistance, tutoring, writing center.

Majors. Business: General, accounting, business admin, e-commerce, executive assistant, office management. **Computer sciences:** General. **Education:** Early childhood. **Engineering:** Industrial, manufacturing. **Health services:** Medical secretary, nursing (RN). **Liberal arts:** Arts/sciences.

Technology on campus. 375 workstations in library, computer center. Commuter students can connect to campus network. Online library, wireless network available.

Student life. Freshman orientation: Mandatory. Preregistration for classes offered. **Activities:** Student government, Phi Theta Kappa, Phi Beta Lambda, Christian student fellowship.

Student services. Adult student services, career counseling, services for economically disadvantaged, financial aid counseling. **Physically disabled:** Services for hearing impaired. **Transfer:** Transfer adviser, college fairs on campus for students transferring to 4-year colleges.

Contact. E-mail: jessica.kern@kctcs.edu
Phone: (606) 759-7141 ext. 66186 Fax: (606) 759-5818
Lori Gaunce, Associate Dean of Student Development/Registrar/Admissions Officer, Maysville Community and Technical College, 1755 US HIghway 68, Maysville, KY 41056

National College: Danville
Danville, Kentucky
www.national-college.edu   CB code: 3413

- For-profit 2-year business college
- Commuter campus in large town

General. Accredited by ACICS. **Enrollment:** 81 degree-seeking undergraduates. **Degrees:** 27 associate awarded. **Calendar:** Quarter, extensive summer session. **Full-time faculty:** 3 total. **Part-time faculty:** 9 total.

Basis for selection. Open admission. Interviews highly recommended.

2016-2017 Annual costs. Tuition/fees: $14,460. Per-credit charge: $317. Books/supplies: $1,500.

Financial aid. All financial aid based on need. Need-based aid available for part-time students. Work-study available nights, weekends and for part-time students.

Application procedures. Admission: No deadline. $50 fee, may be waived for applicants with need. Admission notification on a rolling basis. **Financial aid:** No deadline. FAFSA required. Applicants notified on a rolling basis.

Academics. Special study options: Double major, internships, liberal arts/career combination. **Credit/placement by examination:** AP, CLEP, institutional tests. **Support services:** Learning center, remedial instruction, tutoring.

Majors. Business: Accounting, administrative services, business admin. **Computer sciences:** Computer science. **Health services:** Medical assistant, medical secretary, physician assistant.

Technology on campus. 35 workstations in library, computer center.

Student life. Freshman orientation: Mandatory. Preregistration for classes offered. **Activities:** Student government.

Student services. Career counseling, student employment services, financial aid counseling, personal counseling, placement for graduates, veterans' counselor.

Contact. E-mail: market@educorp.edu
Phone: (859) 236-6991 Toll-free number: (800) 664-1886
Fax: (859) 236-1063
Trent Ramey, Regional Director of Admissions, National College: Danville, 115 East Lexington Avenue, Danville, KY 40422

National College: Florence
Florence, Kentucky
www.national-college.edu　　　CB code: 3408

- For-profit 2-year business college
- Commuter campus in large town

General. Accredited by ACICS. **Enrollment:** 40 degree-seeking undergraduates. **Degrees:** 26 associate awarded. **Calendar:** Quarter, limited summer session. **Full-time faculty:** 4 total. **Part-time faculty:** 13 total.

Basis for selection. Open admission. Interview highly recommended.

2016-2017 Annual costs. Tuition/fees: $14,460. Per-credit charge: $317. Books/supplies: $1,500.

Financial aid. All financial aid based on need. Need-based aid available for part-time students. Work-study available nights, weekends and for part-time students.

Application procedures. Admission: No deadline. $50 fee. Admission notification on a rolling basis. **Financial aid:** No deadline. FAFSA required. Applicants notified on a rolling basis.

Academics. Special study options: Double major, internships. **Credit/placement by examination:** AP, CLEP, institutional tests. **Support services:** Learning center, remedial instruction, tutoring.

Majors. Business: Accounting, administrative services, business admin. **Computer sciences:** Computer science. **Health services:** Medical assistant, medical secretary.

Technology on campus. 35 workstations in library, computer center.

Student life. Freshman orientation: Mandatory. Preregistration for classes offered. **Activities:** Student government.

Student services. Career counseling, student employment services, financial aid counseling, personal counseling, placement for graduates, veterans' counselor.

Contact. E-mail: market@educorp.edu
Phone: (606) 525-6510 Fax: (606) 525-8961
Trent Ramey, Regional Director of Admissions, National College: Florence, 8095 Connector Drive, Florence, KY 41042

National College: Lexington
Lexington, Kentucky
www.national-college.edu　　　CB code: 0987

- For-profit 2-year business and junior college
- Commuter campus in small city

General. Founded in 1941. Accredited by ACICS. **Enrollment:** 98 degree-seeking undergraduates. **Degrees:** 7 bachelor's, 43 associate awarded. **Location:** 100 miles from Cincinnati. **Calendar:** Quarter, limited summer session. **Full-time faculty:** 5 total. **Part-time faculty:** 14 total.

Basis for selection. Open admission, but selective for some programs. Interview recommended.

2016-2017 Annual costs. Tuition/fees: $14,460. Per-credit charge: $317. Books/supplies: $1,500.

Financial aid. All financial aid based on need. Need-based aid available for part-time students. Work-study available nights, weekends and for part-time students.

Application procedures. Admission: No deadline. $50 fee, may be waived for applicants with need. Admission notification on a rolling basis. **Financial aid:** No deadline. FAFSA required. Applicants notified on a rolling basis.

Academics. Special study options: Double major, internships. **Credit/placement by examination:** AP, CLEP, institutional tests. **Support services:** Learning center, remedial instruction, tutoring.

Majors. Business: Accounting, administrative services, business admin, office management, office/clerical. **Computer sciences:** Computer science. **Health services:** Medical assistant, medical secretary, physician assistant.

Technology on campus. 35 workstations in library, computer center.

Student life. Freshman orientation: Mandatory. Preregistration for classes offered. **Activities:** Student government.

Student services. Career counseling, student employment services, personal counseling, placement for graduates, veterans' counselor.

Contact. E-mail: market@educorp.edu
Phone: (859) 253-0621 Toll-free number: (800) 664-1886
Fax: (859) 233-3054
Trent Ramey, Regional Director of Admissions, National College: Lexington, 2376 Sir Barton Way, Lexington, KY 40509

National College: Louisville
Louisville, Kentucky
www.national-college.edu　　　CB code: 3415

- For-profit 2-year business college
- Commuter campus in large city

General. Accredited by ACICS. **Enrollment:** 158 degree-seeking undergraduates. **Degrees:** 4 bachelor's, 34 associate awarded. **Calendar:** Quarter, limited summer session. **Full-time faculty:** 7 total. **Part-time faculty:** 15 total.

Basis for selection. Open admission, but selective for some programs. Interviews highly recommended.

2016-2017 Annual costs. Tuition/fees: $14,460. Per-credit charge: $317. Books/supplies: $1,500.

Financial aid. All financial aid based on need. Need-based aid available for part-time students. Work-study available nights, weekends and for part-time students.

Application procedures. Admission: No deadline. $50 fee, may be waived for applicants with need. Admission notification on a rolling basis. **Financial aid:** No deadline. FAFSA required. Applicants notified on a rolling basis.

Academics. Special study options: Internships. **Credit/placement by examination:** AP, CLEP, institutional tests. **Support services:** Learning center, remedial instruction, tutoring.

Majors. Business: Accounting, administrative services, business admin. **Computer sciences:** Computer science. **Health services:** Medical assistant, medical secretary.

Technology on campus. 35 workstations in library, computer center.

Student life. Freshman orientation: Mandatory. Preregistration for classes offered. **Activities:** Student government.

Student services. Career counseling, student employment services, personal counseling, placement for graduates, veterans' counselor.

Contact. E-mail: market@educorp.edu
Phone: (502) 447-7634 Toll-free number: (800) 664-1886
Fax: (502) 447-7665
Virgie Douglas, Director of Admissions, National College: Louisville, 4205 Dixie Highway, Louisville, KY 40216

National College: Pikeville
Pikeville, Kentucky
www.national-college.edu   **CB code: 3412**

◆   For-profit 2-year business college
◆   Commuter campus in large town

General. Accredited by ACICS. **Enrollment:** 137 degree-seeking undergraduates. **Degrees:** 38 associate awarded. **Calendar:** Quarter, extensive summer session. **Full-time faculty:** 4 total. **Part-time faculty:** 15 total.

Basis for selection. Open admission, but selective for some programs. Interviews highly recommended.

2016-2017 Annual costs. Tuition/fees: $14,460. Per-credit charge: $317. Books/supplies: $1,500.

Financial aid. All financial aid based on need. Need-based aid available for part-time students. Work-study available nights, weekends and for part-time students.

Application procedures. Admission: No deadline. $50 fee, may be waived for applicants with need. Admission notification on a rolling basis. **Financial aid:** No deadline. FAFSA required.

Academics. Special study options: Double major, internships. **Credit/placement by examination:** AP, CLEP, institutional tests. **Support services:** Learning center, remedial instruction, tutoring.

Majors. Business: Accounting, administrative services, business admin. **Health services:** Medical assistant, medical secretary.

Technology on campus. 35 workstations in library, computer center.

Student life. Freshman orientation: Mandatory. Preregistration for classes offered. **Activities:** Student government.

Student services. Career counseling, student employment services, financial aid counseling, personal counseling, placement for graduates, veterans' counselor.

Contact. E-mail: market@educorp.edu
Phone: (606) 432-5477 Toll-free number: (800) 664-1886
Fax: (606) 437-4952
Leigh Ann Harris, Director of Admissions, National College: Pikeville, 50 National Collge Boulevard, Pikeville, KY 41501

National College: Richmond
Richmond, Kentucky
www.national-college.edu   **CB code: 3414**

◆   For-profit 2-year business college
◆   Commuter campus in large town

General. Accredited by ACICS. **Enrollment:** 61 degree-seeking undergraduates. **Degrees:** 41 associate awarded. **Calendar:** Quarter, limited summer session. **Full-time faculty:** 4 total. **Part-time faculty:** 10 total.

Basis for selection. Open admission. Interviews highly recommended.

2016-2017 Annual costs. Tuition/fees: $14,460. Per-credit charge: $317. Books/supplies: $1,500.

Financial aid. All financial aid based on need. Need-based aid available for part-time students. Work-study available nights, weekends and for part-time students.

Application procedures. Admission: No deadline. $50 fee, may be waived for applicants with need. Admission notification on a rolling basis. **Financial aid:** No deadline. FAFSA required. Applicants notified on a rolling basis.

Academics. Special study options: Double major, internships. **Credit/placement by examination:** AP, CLEP, institutional tests. **Support services:** Learning center, remedial instruction, tutoring.

Majors. Business: Accounting, administrative services, business admin. **Computer sciences:** Computer science. **Health services:** Medical assistant, medical secretary.

Technology on campus. 35 workstations in library, computer center.

Student life. Freshman orientation: Mandatory. Preregistration for classes offered. **Activities:** Student government.

Student services. Career counseling, student employment services, financial aid counseling, personal counseling, placement for graduates, veterans' counselor.

Contact. E-mail: market@educorp.edu
Phone: (859) 623-8956 Toll-free number: (800) 664-1886
Fax: (859) 624-5544
Trent Ramey, Regional Director of Admissions, National College: Richmond, 125 South Killarney Lane, Richmond, KY 40475

Owensboro Community and Technical College
Owensboro, Kentucky
www.owensboro.kctcs.edu   **CB code: 0613**

◆   Public 2-year community and technical college
◆   Commuter campus in small city

General. Founded in 1986. Regionally accredited. **Enrollment:** 2,615 degree-seeking undergraduates; 1,370 non-degree-seeking students. **Degrees:** 553 associate awarded. **ROTC:** Army. **Location:** 120 miles from Louisville; 40 miles from Evansville, IN. **Calendar:** Semester, extensive summer session. **Full-time faculty:** 82 total; 15% have terminal degrees, 5% minority, 50% women. **Part-time faculty:** 79 total; 4% have terminal degrees, 4% minority, 46% women. **Class size:** 56% < 20, 40% 20-39, 3% 40-49, less than 1% 50-99. **Special facilities:** Outdoor classroom/nature area.

Student profile. Among degree-seeking undergraduates, 43% enrolled in a transfer program, 57% enrolled in a vocational program, 583 enrolled as first-time, first-year students.

Part-time:	46%	Asian American:	1%
Out-of-state:	3%	Hispanic/Latino:	2%
Women:	60%	Multi-racial, non-Hispanic:	2%
African American:	3%	25 or older:	29%

Transfer out. Colleges most students transferred to 2015: Western Kentucky University, Kentucky Wesleyan College, Brescia University, University of Southern Indiana, University of Kentucky.

Basis for selection. Open admission, but selective for some programs. ACT or COMPASS scores, pre-admission conferences, or personal interviews may be required for the nursing, radiography, surgical technology, and veterinary technology programs. **Home schooled:** Documentation of courses required.

High school preparation. 11 units recommended. Recommended units include English 4, mathematics 3, social studies 2, science 2 (laboratory 2).

2015-2016 Annual costs. Tuition/fees: $4,650; $15,690 out-of-state. Per-credit charge: $147 in-state; $515 out-of-state. Books/supplies: $1,550. Personal expenses: $800.

2014-2015 Financial aid. Need-based: 67% of total undergraduate aid awarded as scholarships/grants, 33% as loans/jobs. Need-based aid available for part-time students. Work-study available nights, weekends and for part-time students. **Non-need-based:** Scholarships awarded for academics, art, minority status, music/drama, state residency.

Application procedures. Admission: Priority date 4/1; deadline 8/15 (receipt date). No application fee. Admission notification on a rolling basis beginning on or about 3/1. **Financial aid:** Priority date 4/1; no closing date. FAFSA required. Must reply within 2 week(s) of notification.

Academics. Special study options: Cooperative education, distance learning, dual enrollment of high school students, independent study, internships, study abroad. License preparation in nursing, paramedic, radiology. **Credit/placement by examination:** AP, CLEP, institutional tests. **Support services:**

GED preparation and test center, learning center, remedial instruction, study skills assistance, tutoring.

Majors. Business: Business admin, executive assistant. **Computer sciences:** General. **Education:** Teacher assistance. **General:** Carpentry, electrician. **Health services:** EMT paramedic, medical secretary, nursing (RN), radiologic technology/medical imaging, surgical technology, veterinary technology/assistant. **Liberal arts:** Arts/sciences. **Protective services:** Firefighting, law enforcement admin. **Visual/performing arts:** Dramatic, studio arts. **Work/family studies:** Child care service.

Most popular majors. Business/marketing 6%, health sciences 14%, liberal arts 58%, trade and industry 7%.

Technology on campus. 350 workstations in library, computer center, student center. Commuter students can connect to campus network. Online course registration, online library, helpline, wireless network available.

Student life. Freshman orientation: Mandatory. Preregistration for classes offered. 75 minutes on campus before classes start. **Activities:** Choral groups, drama, literary magazine, student government, TV station.

Student services. Career counseling, services for economically disadvantaged, student employment services, financial aid counseling, minority student services, on-campus daycare, personal counseling, placement for graduates, veterans' counselor. **Physically disabled:** Services for visually, speech, hearing impaired. **Transfer:** Transfer center, transfer adviser, college fairs on campus for students transferring to 4-year colleges.

Contact. E-mail: octc.admissions@kctcs.edu
Phone: (270) 686-4527 Toll-free number: (866) 546-6282
Fax: (270) 686-4648
Kevin Beardmore, Vice President of Student Affairs, Owensboro Community and Technical College, 4800 New Hartford Road, Owensboro, KY 42303-1899

Somerset Community College
Somerset, Kentucky
www.somerset.kctcs.edu   CB code: 1779

◗ Public 2-year community and technical college
◗ Commuter campus in large town

General. Founded in 1965. Regionally accredited. One of 16 community colleges and 12 technical colleges consolidated under one administration. **Enrollment:** 6,995 degree-seeking undergraduates. **Degrees:** 752 associate awarded. **Location:** 70 miles from Lexington. **Calendar:** Semester, limited summer session. **Full-time faculty:** 187 total. **Part-time faculty:** 133 total. **Class size:** 54% < 20, 39% 20-39, 2% 40-49, 4% 50-99, less than 1% >100.

Transfer out. Colleges most students transferred to 2015: Morehead State University, University of Kentucky, Western Kentucky University, Eastern Kentucky University.

Basis for selection. Open admission, but selective for some programs. Test scores, letters of recommendation, and interview required for limited enrollment programs in allied health. ACT required in admissions process but not ordinarily used as selective criterion.

High school preparation. 20 units recommended. Recommended units include English 4, mathematics 3, social studies 2, science 2 and academic electives 9.

2015-2016 Annual costs. Tuition/fees: $4,650; $15,690 out-of-state. Per-credit charge: $147 in-state; $515 out-of-state. Books/supplies: $1,000. Personal expenses: $800. **Additional information:** Nonresident students living in contiguous counties are charged a discounted non-resident rate of $294 per credit hour.

Financial aid. All financial aid based on need. Need-based aid available for part-time students. Work-study available nights, weekends and for part-time students.

Application procedures. Admission: No deadline. No application fee. Admission notification on a rolling basis. Admitted students in nursing, clinical laboratory techniques, and physical therapy assisting must reply within 10 days. **Financial aid:** Priority date 3/1; no closing date. FAFSA required. Applicants notified on a rolling basis starting 5/1; must reply within 2 week(s) of notification.

Academics. Special study options: Cooperative education, distance learning, dual enrollment of high school students, ESL, external degree, independent study, internships, liberal arts/career combination. Bachelor's degree programs available on campus. License preparation in aviation, nursing, physical

therapy, radiology, real estate. **Credit/placement by examination:** AP, CLEP. 12 credit hours maximum toward associate degree. **Support services:** GED preparation and test center, learning center, reduced course load, remedial instruction, study skills assistance, tutoring, writing center.

Majors. Business: Business admin, executive assistant. **Communications technology:** Graphics, printing management. **Computer sciences:** General. **Education:** General, teacher assistance. **General:** Carpentry, electrician, masonry, pipefitting, plumbing. **Health services:** Clinical lab assistant, clinical lab technology, licensed practical nurse, medical assistant, medical secretary, nursing (RN), physical therapy assistant. **Liberal arts:** Arts/sciences. **Protective services:** Law enforcement admin, police science. **Work/family studies:** Child care management, child care service.

Technology on campus. 947 workstations in library, computer center, student center. Commuter students can connect to campus network. Online course registration, online library, repair service, wireless network available.

Student life. Freshman orientation: Available. Preregistration for classes offered. **Activities:** Drama, film society, student government, student newspaper, Baptist Student Union, Student Government Association, Students for Free Enterprise, Phi Beta Lambda, Phi Theta Kappa, criminal justice student organization.

Athletics. Team name: Cougars.

Student services. Adult student services, career counseling, services for economically disadvantaged, student employment services, financial aid counseling, minority student services, personal counseling, placement for graduates, veterans' counselor. **Physically disabled:** Services for visually, speech, hearing impaired. **Transfer:** Pre-admission transcript evaluation for new students. Transfer center, transfer adviser, college fairs on campus for students transferring to 4-year colleges.

Contact. E-mail: somerset-admissions@kctcs.edu
Phone: (606) 451-6630 Toll-free number: (877) 629-9722
Fax: (606) 679-4369
Tracy Casada, Dean of Student Affairs, Somerset Community College, 808 Monticello Street, Somerset, KY 42501

Southeast Kentucky Community and Technical College
Cumberland, Kentucky
www.southeast.kctcs.edu   CB code: 1770

◗ Public 2-year community and technical college
◗ Commuter campus in small town

General. Founded in 1960. Regionally accredited. Branch campuses at Harlan, Middlesboro, Pineville and Whitesburg. **Enrollment:** 2,376 degree-seeking undergraduates; 1,441 non-degree-seeking students. **Degrees:** 447 associate awarded. **Location:** 150 miles from Lexington. **Calendar:** Semester, limited summer session. **Full-time faculty:** 109 total; 14% have terminal degrees, 12% minority, 46% women. **Part-time faculty:** 90 total; 3% have terminal degrees, 4% minority, 40% women. **Class size:** 31% < 20, 55% 20-39, 10% 40-49, 4% 50-99. **Special facilities:** Appalachian archives.

Student profile. Among degree-seeking undergraduates, 292 enrolled as first-time, first-year students.

Part-time:	28%	**Women:**	62%
Out-of-state:	4%	**25 or older:**	40%

Transfer out. Colleges most students transferred to 2015: Lincoln Memorial University, University of Louisville, Eastern Kentucky University.

Basis for selection. Open admission, but selective for some programs. ACT required for nursing, radiography, respiratory care and physical therapy programs. **Home schooled:** Transcript of courses and grades required.

High school preparation. 12 units recommended. Recommended units include English 4, mathematics 3, history 2, science 2 (laboratory 1).

2015-2016 Annual costs. Tuition/fees: $4,650; $15,690 out-of-state. Per-credit charge: $147 in-state; $515 out-of-state. Books/supplies: $650. Personal expenses: $1,100. **Additional information:** Nonresident students living in contiguous counties are charged a discounted non-resident rate of $294 per credit hour.

Financial aid. All financial aid based on need. Need-based aid available for part-time students. Work-study available nights, weekends and for part-time students. **Additional information:** March 15 deadline for state financial aid.

Application procedures. Admission: No deadline. No application fee. Admission notification on a rolling basis. **Financial aid:** Priority date 3/15; no closing date. FAFSA required. Must reply within 2 week(s) of notification.

Academics. Special study options: Cross-registration, distance learning, dual enrollment of high school students, internships, liberal arts/career combination. License preparation in nursing. **Credit/placement by examination:** AP, CLEP, institutional tests. 30 credit hours maximum toward associate degree. **Support services:** GED preparation and test center, learning center, pre-admission summer program, reduced course load, remedial instruction, study skills assistance, tutoring, writing center.

Majors. Business: Administrative services, banking/financial services, business admin, finance, management information systems. **Computer sciences:** General, data processing. **Health services:** Clinical lab assistant, medical radiologic technology/radiation therapy, nursing (RN), physical therapy assistant, respiratory therapy technology. **Liberal arts:** Arts/sciences. **Protective services:** Police science.

Most popular majors. Business/marketing 10%, health sciences 30%, liberal arts 50%.

Technology on campus. 60 workstations in library, computer center. Commuter students can connect to campus network. Online course registration, wireless network available.

Student life. Freshman orientation: Mandatory. Preregistration for classes offered. **Activities:** Choral groups, dance, drama, student government, student newspaper, Christian student union, black student union, Professional Business Leaders, wilderness club, nursing club.

Student services. Adult student services, career counseling, financial aid counseling, personal counseling, placement for graduates, veterans' counselor. **Physically disabled:** Services for visually impaired. **Transfer:** Transfer adviser, college fairs on campus for students transferring to 4-year colleges.

Contact. Phone: (606) 589-2145 Toll-free number: (888) 274-7332 Fax: (606) 589-5423
Veria Baldwin, Director of Admissions, Southeast Kentucky Community and Technical College, 700 College Road, Cumberland, KY 40823

Spencerian College
Louisville, Kentucky
www.spencerian.edu   **CB code: 3422**

▶ For-profit 2-year career college
▶ Commuter campus in large city

General. Accredited by ACICS. **Enrollment:** 466 degree-seeking undergraduates; 34 non-degree-seeking students. **Degrees:** 73 associate awarded. **Location:** 10 miles from downtown. **Calendar:** Quarter, extensive summer session. **Full-time faculty:** 46 total. **Part-time faculty:** 53 total. **Special facilities:** Radiology digital lab, X-ray lab, surgical technology lab, massage therapy lab, medical laboratory technology lab.

Student profile. Among degree-seeking undergraduates, 81 enrolled as first-time, first-year students.

Part-time: 39% **Women:**   87%

Basis for selection. Open admission, but selective for some programs. Requirements vary for medical programs. Minimum entrance test scores required for some programs and other admission criteria specific to certain programs. Interview may be required for selective programs such as nursing, medical laboratory technology, invasive cardiovascular technology, respiratory care, and surgical technology programs. **Home schooled:** Transcript of courses and grades required. Students may be asked to provide copies of letters notifying school district for each year they were home schooled. Students must provide transcripts of courses and grades received.

2015-2016 Annual costs. Books/supplies: $2,100. Personal expenses: $3,559. **Additional information:** Certificate programs range from $13,225-$38,905, books and supplies range from $900-$3,300, room and board ranges from $5,950-$17,850. Associates programs range from $32,485-$52,625, books and supplies range from $2,400-$4,000, room and board ranges from $14,875-$23,800.

2014-2015 Financial aid. Need-based: 54% of total undergraduate aid awarded as scholarships/grants, 46% as loans/jobs. Need-based aid available for part-time students. Work-study available nights, weekends and for part-time students. **Non-need-based:** Scholarships awarded for academics.

Application procedures. Admission: $50 fee. Admission notification on a rolling basis. **Financial aid:** No deadline. FAFSA, institutional form required.

Academics. Special study options: Distance learning, internships. **Credit/placement by examination:** AP, CLEP, institutional tests. **Support services:** Learning center, tutoring.

Majors. Health services: Clinical lab technology, insurance coding, massage therapy, medical secretary, nursing (RN), radiologic technology/medical imaging, respiratory therapy technology, surgical technology. **Parks/recreation:** Physical fitness technician.

Most popular majors. Health sciences 98%.

Technology on campus. 86 workstations in library. Commuter students can connect to campus network.

Student life. Freshman orientation: Mandatory. Preregistration for classes offered. One day and one evening session held week before classes begin. Make-up orientation held second week of quarter. **Housing:** $95 deposit.

Student services. Career counseling, financial aid counseling, placement for graduates. **Transfer:** Pre-admission transcript evaluation for new students.

Contact. Phone: (502) 447-1000 Toll-free number: (800) 264-1799 Fax: (502) 447-4574
Charmaine Powell, Director of Admissions, Spencerian College, 4627 Dixie Highway, Louisville, KY 40216

Spencerian College: Lexington
Lexington, Kentucky
www.spencerian.edu   **CB code: 3424**

▶ For-profit 2-year branch campus college
▶ Commuter campus in small city
▶ Interview required

General. Accredited by ACICS. **Enrollment:** 76 degree-seeking undergraduates. **Degrees:** 32 associate awarded. **Location:** 72 miles from Louisville. **Calendar:** Quarter, limited summer session. **Full-time faculty:** 13 total. **Part-time faculty:** 5 total. **Class size:** 100% < 20.

Transfer out. Colleges most students transferred to 2015: Lexington Community College, University of Kentucky, Eastern Kentucky University.

Basis for selection. Open admission, but selective for some programs. 17 ACT or passing score on ASSET required for selective programs. HOBET required for certain programs. **Home schooled:** Transcript of courses and grades, state high school equivalency certificate required. **Learning Disabled:** Potential students need to submit IEP or 504.

2015-2016 Annual costs. Tuition/fees: $19,260. Per-credit charge: $299. Room only: $5,940. Books/supplies: $1,500. Personal expenses: $1,250.

2014-2015 Financial aid. All financial aid based on need. Need-based aid available for part-time students. Work-study available nights, weekends and for part-time students.

Application procedures. Admission: No deadline. $50 fee, may be waived for applicants with need. Application must be submitted on paper. Admission notification on a rolling basis. **Financial aid:** No deadline. FAFSA, institutional form required. Applicants notified on a rolling basis starting 1/1.

Academics. Special study options: Cooperative education, double major, independent study, internships. License preparation in radiology. **Credit/placement by examination:** AP, CLEP, IB. 23 credit hours maximum toward associate degree. **Support services:** Reduced course load, study skills assistance, tutoring.

Majors. Health services: Office assistant.

Most popular majors. Architecture 9%, computer/information sciences 13%, engineering/engineering technologies 19%, health sciences 59%.

Technology on campus. PC or laptop required. 170 workstations in library, computer center. Commuter students can connect to campus network. Online library, helpline, wireless network available.

Student life. Freshman orientation: Mandatory. Preregistration for classes offered. Four-hour session held at beginning of quarter. **Policies:** Students must be under the age of 21 to live in dorm. **Housing:** Guaranteed on-campus for freshmen. Coed dorms, special housing for disabled, apartments available. $95 nonrefundable deposit. **Activities:** Student newspaper, Healing Hands student organization, Skeleton Crew (radiography), CADD student organization, allied health student organization.

Student services. Adult student services, career counseling, student employment services, financial aid counseling, placement for graduates, veterans' counselor. **Physically disabled:** Services for visually, speech, hearing impaired. **Transfer:** Pre-admission transcript evaluation for new students.

Contact. Phone: (859) 223-9608 ext. 5460
Toll-free number: (800) 456-3253 ext. 5460 Fax: (859) 977-5435
Innessa Savchuk, Associate Director of Admissions, Spencerian College: Lexington, 2355 Harrodsburg Rd, Lexington, KY 40504

Sullivan College of Technology and Design
Louisville, Kentucky
www.sctd.edu   CB code: 1501

▶ For-profit 2-year visual arts, technical and career college
▶ Commuter campus in very large city
▶ Interview required

General. Founded in 1961. Regionally accredited; also accredited by ACICS. **Enrollment:** 395 degree-seeking undergraduates. **Degrees:** 27 bachelor's, 109 associate awarded. **Location:** 7 miles from Louisville. **Calendar:** Quarter, extensive summer session. **Full-time faculty:** 25 total; 8% minority, 40% women. **Part-time faculty:** 48 total; 6% minority, 33% women. **Class size:** 98% < 20, 2% 20-39. **Special facilities:** Laboratories for computer-aided graphics, web development, computer-aided design drafting, electronics, computer networking, computer security and forensics, robotics, and heating-ventilation-air conditioning-refrigeration.

Student profile.

Out-of-state:	13%	Live on campus:	4%
25 or older:	49%		

Transfer out. **Colleges most students transferred to 2015:** Sullivan University.

Basis for selection. Entrance test, previous school records, interview and complete a tour are very important. Equivalent ACT/SAT scores may be accepted in place of COMPASS. **Home schooled:** State high school equivalency certificate required. In-state applicants must have certificate of completion or high school diploma provided by local public school district. Applicants from other states must have certificate of completion or high school diploma provided by local school district or state's Department of Education. Applicants who cannot meet these requirements must obtain GED. **Learning Disabled:** Students seeking special accommodations must provide documentation of professional assessment indicating nature and level of disability and types of recommended accommodations.

High school preparation. Recommended units include English 4, mathematics 4, social studies 2, science 3, computer science 1 and visual/performing arts 1.

2015-2016 Annual costs. Books/supplies: $1,500. Personal expenses: $3,559. **Additional information:** Full-program tuition cost ranges from $38,160-$44,520 depending on the program of study. The per-credit-hour tuition rate ranges from $450-$525 also depending on the program of study. The approximate cost of books and supplies per academic year varies by program of study. Required fees are a $200 general fee per quarter plus a fee of $240 for online courses. Rent for a semi-private room is $660 per month or $5,940 for the academic year (9 months/3 quarters). The required meal plan for all housing students includes three meals a day Mon-Fri and brunch and dinner on Sat-Sun (19 meals) and costs $2,985 per academic year. Total room and board for an academic year is $8,925.

2014-2015 Financial aid. **Need-based:** 67% of total undergraduate aid awarded as scholarships/grants, 33% as loans/jobs. Need-based aid available for part-time students. Work-study available nights, weekends and for part-time students. **Non-need-based:** Scholarships awarded for academics, art, job skills.

Application procedures. **Admission:** No deadline. $50 fee. Admission notification on a rolling basis. **Financial aid:** No deadline. FAFSA required. Applicants notified on a rolling basis; must reply within 2 week(s) of notification.

Academics. **Special study options:** Accelerated study, cooperative education, double major, dual enrollment of high school students, internships. Bachelor's degree programs available on campus. **Credit/placement by examination:** AP, CLEP, SAT, ACT, institutional tests. 75 credit hours maximum toward associate degree, 145 toward bachelor's. **Support services:** Learning center, reduced course load, remedial instruction, study skills assistance, tutoring.

Majors. **Architecture:** Interior. **Communications technology:** Animation/special effects, desktop publishing, graphics. **Computer sciences:** Computer

graphics, information systems, information technology, LAN/WAN management, security, system admin, vendor certification, web page design. **Engineering:** Architectural. **Visual/performing arts:** Graphic design, interior design.

Most popular majors. Computer/information sciences 40%, engineering/engineering technologies 46%, visual/performing arts 14%.

Technology on campus. 250 workstations in dormitories, library, computer center. Dormitories wired for high-speed internet access and linked to campus network. Commuter students can connect to campus network. Online library, helpline, repair service, wireless network available.

Student life. Freshman orientation: Mandatory. Preregistration for classes offered. Three-hour program held at start of quarter. College Success Strategies is a required course for all entering students who do not already have successful college experience. **Housing:** Guaranteed on-campus for freshmen. Coed dorms, apartments, wellness housing available. $95 nonrefundable deposit. **Activities:** SkillsUSA student chapter, American Design Drafting Association, American Society of Interior Designers, International Interior Design Association, ad federation, greener living club.

Student services. Adult student services, career counseling, services for economically disadvantaged, student employment services, financial aid counseling, placement for graduates, veterans' counselor. **Physically disabled:** Services for speech, hearing impaired. **Transfer:** Re-entry adviser, pre-admission transcript evaluation for new students.

Contact. E-mail: hcunningham@sctd.edu
Phone: (502) 456-6509 Toll-free number: (800) 844-6528
Fax: (502) 456-2341
Heather Cunningham, Director of Admissions, Sullivan College of Technology and Design, 3901 Atkinson Square Drive, Louisville, KY 40218-4524

West Kentucky Community and Technical College
Paducah, Kentucky
www.westkentucky.kctcs.edu   CB code: 1620

▶ Public 2-year community and technical college
▶ Commuter campus in large town

General. Founded in 1932. Regionally accredited. **Enrollment:** 4,668 degree-seeking undergraduates. **Degrees:** 690 associate awarded. **Location:** 140 miles from Nashville, TN. **Calendar:** Semester, limited summer session. **Full-time faculty:** 137 total. **Part-time faculty:** 166 total.

Student profile.

Out-of-state:	4%	25 or older:	39%

Basis for selection. Open admission, but selective for some programs. Special requirements for nursing and allied health programs. Interview required of nursing applicants.

High school preparation. 20 units recommended. Recommended units include English 4, mathematics 3, social studies 2 and science 2.

2015-2016 Annual costs. Tuition/fees: $4,650; $15,690 out-of-state. Per-credit charge: $147 in-state; $515 out-of-state. Books/supplies: $1,200. Personal expenses: $425. **Additional information:** Nonresident students living in contiguous counties are charged a discounted non-resident rate of $294 per credit hour.

Financial aid. **Need-based:** Need-based aid available for part-time students. Work-study available nights, weekends and for part-time students.

Application procedures. **Admission:** No deadline. No application fee. Admission notification on a rolling basis beginning on or about 4/1. **Financial aid:** Priority date 4/1, closing date 7/15. FAFSA required. Applicants notified on a rolling basis starting 7/15; must reply within 4 week(s) of notification.

Academics. **Special study options:** Accelerated study, cooperative education, distance learning, dual enrollment of high school students, ESL, honors, weekend college. License preparation in real estate. **Credit/placement by examination:** AP, CLEP. **Support services:** GED preparation and test center, learning center, reduced course load, remedial instruction, tutoring.

Majors. **Business:** Accounting, administrative services, banking/financial services, business admin, management information systems, office technology, real estate. **Communications:** Communications/speech/rhetoric. **Computer sciences:** General, applications programming. **General:** Electrician. **Health services:** Clinical lab technology, medical radiologic technology/

Two-Year Colleges

radiation therapy, nursing (RN), physical therapy assistant, physics/radiologic health, respiratory therapy technology, sonography. **Liberal arts:** Arts/sciences.

Technology on campus. 70 workstations in library, computer center.

Student life. Freshman orientation: Mandatory. Preregistration for classes offered. **Activities:** Choral groups, drama, musical theater, radio station, student government, student newspaper, TV station.

Athletics. Intramural: Basketball M, golf, volleyball.

Student services. Adult student services, career counseling, student employment services, personal counseling, placement for graduates, veterans' counselor. **Physically disabled:** Services for visually, speech, hearing impaired. **Transfer:** Transfer adviser for students transferring to 4-year colleges.

Contact. Phone: (270) 534-3264 Fax: (270) 534-6304
Jess Puffenbarger, Director of Admissions, West Kentucky Community and Technical College, 4810 Alben Barkley Drive, Paducah, KY 42002-7380

Louisiana

Baton Rouge Community College
Baton Rouge, Louisiana
www.mybrcc.edu

CB code: 6023

▶ Public 2-year community college
▶ Commuter campus in large city

General. Regionally accredited. **Enrollment:** 7,843 degree-seeking undergraduates; 2,855 non-degree-seeking students. **Degrees:** 426 associate awarded. **Location:** 60 miles from New Orleans. **Calendar:** Semester, extensive summer session. **Full-time faculty:** 133 total. **Part-time faculty:** 162 total. **Special facilities:** Sonography lab, process technology glass lab, health and wellness facility with full-sized basketball court, rock climbing wall, weight room, dance and fitness rooms, academic learning center, black box theater, gaming and animation center, green house, student success center.

Student profile. Among degree-seeking undergraduates, 2,058 enrolled as first-time, first-year students.

| Part-time: | 42% | **Women:** | 59% |

Transfer out. Colleges most students transferred to 2015: Louisiana State University, Southern University, Southeastern University.

Basis for selection. Open admission. **Home schooled:** GED or documentation from state verifying completion of SBESE-approved home study program required. **Learning Disabled:** Students self-identify with disability services.

2015-2016 Annual costs. Tuition/fees: $4,054; $8,132 out-of-state. Books/supplies: $1,200. Personal expenses: $4,464.

Financial aid. Need-based: Need-based aid available for part-time students. Work-study available nights, weekends and for part-time students. **Non-need-based:** Scholarships awarded for academics, athletics, leadership, minority status, state residency.

Application procedures. Admission: Closing date 8/18 (receipt date). $7 fee. Admission notification on a rolling basis. **Financial aid:** Priority date 4/15, closing date 6/30. FAFSA, institutional form required. Applicants notified on a rolling basis.

Academics. Special study options: Cross-registration, distance learning, double major, dual enrollment of high school students, honors, internships, study abroad, teacher certification program, weekend college. License preparation in aviation, nursing. **Credit/placement by examination:** AP, CLEP, institutional tests. **Support services:** Learning center, remedial instruction, study skills assistance, tutoring, writing center.

Majors. Business: General, accounting technology, construction management, office technology. **Computer sciences:** General. **Education:** General. **Health services:** Nursing (RN). **Liberal arts:** Arts/sciences. **Protective services:** Police science. **Visual/performing arts:** Cinematography.

Most popular majors. Business/marketing 22%, engineering/engineering technologies 18%, health sciences 20%, liberal arts 21%, visual/performing arts 6%.

Technology on campus. 175 workstations in library, computer center, student center. Online course registration, online library, helpline, wireless network available.

Student life. Freshman orientation: Mandatory. Preregistration for classes offered. **Policies:** All student club members must maintain 2.0 GPA to be active in campus clubs. All student government association officers must maintain 2.5 GPA to remain in office. **Activities:** Jazz band, dance, drama, international student organizations, literary magazine, music ensembles, student government, student newspaper, Christian student association, future educators club, center for peace, peer advisors and leaders, poetry club, self-esteem club, twenty-five plus society, student government association, production assistance club, Christian student association.

Athletics. NJCAA. **Intercollegiate:** Baseball M, basketball. **Intramural:** Football (non-tackle) M, soccer, volleyball. **Team name:** Bears.

Student services. Career counseling, student employment services, financial aid counseling, personal counseling, placement for graduates, veterans'

counselor. **Physically disabled:** Services for visually, speech, hearing impaired. **Transfer:** College fairs on campus for students transferring to 4-year colleges.

Contact. Phone: (225) 216-8700 Toll-free number: (800) 601-4558 Shontelle Blake, Executive Director of Enrollment Services, Baton Rouge Community College, 201 Community College Drive, Baton Rouge, LA 70806

Baton Rouge School of Computers
Baton Rouge, Louisiana
www.brsc.edu

CB code: 3197

▶ For-profit 2-year technical college
▶ Small city

General. Accredited by ACCSC. **Enrollment:** 78 undergraduates. **Degrees:** 41 associate awarded. **Calendar:** Differs by program. **Full-time faculty:** 2 total.

Basis for selection. Open admission.

2015-2016 Annual costs. Books/supplies: $300. **Additional information:** Diploma Programs include Microcomputer Literacy, Webmaster, PC Desktop Support. Tuition and fees - $16,504. Associate Degree in Network Engineer Computer Information Systems - $33,008.

Financial aid. Need-based: Work-study available nights, weekends and for part-time students.

Application procedures. Admission: No deadline. $25 fee, may be waived for applicants with need.

Academics. Credit/placement by examination: AP, CLEP.

Majors. Business: General. **Computer sciences:** General.

Student life. Freshman orientation: Mandatory. Preregistration for classes offered.

Contact. Phone: (225) 923-2525 Fax: (225) 923-2979 Brenda Boss, Director of Admissions, Baton Rouge School of Computers, 10425 Plaza Americana, Baton Rouge, LA 70816

Blue Cliff College: Metairie
Metairie, Louisiana
www.bluecliffcollege.com

▶ For-profit 2-year technical college
▶ Commuter campus in large town

General. Accredited by ACCSC. **Enrollment:** 892 undergraduates. **Calendar:** Quarter. **Full-time faculty:** 15 total. **Part-time faculty:** 32 total.

Basis for selection. Open admission. Wonderlic test given as skills assessment before enrollment.

2015-2016 Annual costs. Diploma programs: Cosmetology $18,080. Dental Assisting $16,155; books and supplies $1,550. Massage Therapy $13,144; books and supplies $1,250. Dialysis Technician $17,450; books and supplies $1,850. Midical/clinical assistant $12,985; books and supplies $1,850.

Financial aid. Need-based: Work-study available nights, weekends and for part-time students.

Application procedures. Admission: No deadline. No application fee.

Academics. Credit/placement by examination: AP, CLEP.

Majors. Health services: Massage therapy. **Protective services:** Criminal justice.

Student services. Transfer: Pre-admission transcript evaluation for new students.

Contact. E-mail: pattyr@bluecliffcollege.com Phone: (504) 456-3141 Toll-free number: (800) 517-8176 Fax: (504) 456-7849 Lisa Prince, Admissions Officer, Blue Cliff College: Metairie, 3200 Cleary Avenue, Metairie, LA 70002

Blue Cliff College: Shreveport
Shreveport, Louisiana
www.bluecliffcollege.com

▶ For-profit 2-year technical college
▶ Commuter campus in small city

General. Accredited by ACCSC. **Enrollment:** 253 undergraduates. **Calendar:** Quarter. **Full-time faculty:** 14 total. **Part-time faculty:** 11 total.

Basis for selection. Open admission.

2015-2016 Annual costs. Diploma programs: Cosmetology $18,080. Cosmetology instructor training $8,850. Aesthetician $8,600; books and supplies $2,050. Massage therapy $13,144; books and supplies $1,250. Dialysis technician $17,450; books and supplies $1,850. Medical assistant $12,985; books and supplies $1,850. Associate program: Massage therapy $13,144; books and supplies $1,250.

Financial aid. Need-based: Work-study available nights, weekends and for part-time students.

Application procedures. Admission: No deadline. $25 fee. Admission notification on a rolling basis.

Academics. Credit/placement by examination: AP, CLEP.

Majors. Health services: Massage therapy, medical assistant.

Contact. Phone: (318) 425-7941
Admissions Representative, Blue Cliff College: Shreveport, 8731 Park Plaza Drive, Shreveport, LA 71105-5682

Bossier Parish Community College
Bossier City, Louisiana
www.bpcc.edu/index.html   CB code: 0787

▶ Public 2-year community college
▶ Commuter campus in small city

General. Founded in 1966. Regionally accredited. **Enrollment:** 5,393 degree-seeking undergraduates; 1,230 non-degree-seeking students. **Degrees:** 713 associate awarded. **Location:** 6 miles from downtown Shreveport. **Calendar:** Semester, extensive summer session. **Full-time faculty:** 134 total; 8% have terminal degrees, 9% minority, 61% women. **Part-time faculty:** 152 total; 7% have terminal degrees, 27% minority, 67% women. **Class size:** 63% < 20, 36% 20-39, less than 1% 40-49. **Partnerships:** Formal partnerships with General Motors, Libby Glass.

Student profile. Among degree-seeking undergraduates, 1,116 enrolled as first-time, first-year students, 279 transferred in from other institutions.

Part-time:	35%	Hispanic/Latino:	6%
Out-of-state:	3%	Native American:	1%
Women:	66%	Multi-racial, non-Hispanic:	2%
African American:	38%	25 or older:	57%
Asian American:	1%		

Transfer out. Colleges most students transferred to 2015: Louisiana State University in Shreveport, Northwestern State University of Louisiana, Louisiana Tech University, Southern Arkansas University, Grambling State University.

Basis for selection. Open admission. **Home schooled:** Students generally expected to complete requirements for GED.

High school preparation. College-preparatory program recommended.

2015-2016 Annual costs. Tuition/fees: $3,971; $8,648 out-of-state.

2014-2015 Financial aid. Need-based: 1,106 full-time freshmen applied for aid; 1,011 deemed to have need; 978 received aid. Average need met was 31%. Average scholarship/grant was $2,038; average loan $2,072. 54% of total undergraduate aid awarded as scholarships/grants, 46% as loans/jobs. Need-based aid available for part-time students. Work-study available nights, weekends and for part-time students. **Non-need-based:** Awarded to 22 full-time undergraduates, including 26 freshmen. Scholarships awarded for academics, athletics, leadership, minority status, music/drama.

Application procedures. Admission: $15 fee ($25 out-of-state). Admission notification on a rolling basis. **Financial aid:** Priority date 6/1; no closing date. FAFSA required. Applicants notified on a rolling basis starting 4/1; must reply within 3 week(s) of notification.

Academics. Special study options: Accelerated study, distance learning, dual enrollment of high school students, ESL, internships. License preparation in nursing, paramedic. **Credit/placement by examination:** AP, CLEP, institutional tests. 30 credit hours maximum toward associate degree. **Support services:** GED preparation, learning center, remedial instruction, study skills assistance, tutoring, writing center.

Majors. Business: General. **Computer sciences:** Information systems. **Education:** General. **Engineering:** General. **Health services:** EMT paramedic, facilities admin, medical assistant, nursing (RN), occupational therapy assistant, pharmacy assistant, physical therapy assistant, respiratory therapy technology. **Protective services:** Criminal justice. **Work/family studies:** Child care service.

Most popular majors. Business/marketing 13%, communication technologies 7%, computer/information sciences 6%, health sciences 20%, interdisciplinary studies 10%, liberal arts 23%, security/protective services 10%.

Technology on campus. 120 workstations in library. Online course registration, online library, wireless network available.

Student life. Freshman orientation: Available. Preregistration for classes offered. **Activities:** Bands, campus ministries, choral groups, dance, drama, literary magazine, musical theater, radio station, student government, student newspaper, TV station, Maroon Jackets, Americans with Disabilities and Accessible Personal Training Services, Gospel Choir, Student Government Association, Baptist Collegiate Ministry, Cavalier Express Student Recruiting Team, global connection club, Military Student Organization.

Athletics. NJCAA. **Intercollegiate:** Baseball M, basketball M, cheerleading, softball W. **Intramural:** Basketball W. **Team name:** Cavaliers.

Student services. Career counseling, student employment services, financial aid counseling, personal counseling, placement for graduates, veterans' counselor. **Physically disabled:** Services for visually, speech, hearing impaired. **Transfer:** Re-entry adviser, pre-admission transcript evaluation for new students. College fairs on campus for students transferring to 4-year colleges.

Contact. E-mail: admissions@bpcc.edu
Phone: (318) 678-6004 Fax: (318) 678-6390
Richard Cockerham, Admissions Officer, Bossier Parish Community College, 6220 East Texas Street, Bossier City, LA 71111-6922

Delgado Community College
New Orleans, Louisiana
www.dcc.edu   CB code: 6176

▶ Public 2-year community college
▶ Commuter campus in large city

General. Founded in 1921. Regionally accredited. **Enrollment:** 17,152 undergraduates. **Degrees:** 1,344 associate awarded. **Calendar:** Semester, extensive summer session. **Full-time faculty:** 411 total; 26% minority, 62% women. **Part-time faculty:** 447 total; 35% minority, 53% women. **Class size:** 60% < 20, 39% 20-39, 1% 40-49, less than 1% 50-99. **Special facilities:** Ship simulator, fine arts gallery, culinary arts facility, nursing clinic, maritime, fire and industrial training facility, cosmetology classrooms.

Student profile.

Out-of-state:	4%	25 or older:	50%

Transfer out. Colleges most students transferred to 2015: University of New Orleans, Southeastern Louisiana University, Southern University at New Orleans, Louisiana State University.

Basis for selection. Open admission, but selective for some programs. Special requirements for health-related programs. **Adult students:** SAT/ACT scores not required if applicant over 25. Adult students without high school diploma or GED required to pass Ability to Benefit Exam. **Home schooled:** Applicants who have not completed state or regionally approved program required to have GED or successfully pass Ability to Benefit Exam.

2015-2016 Annual costs. Tuition/fees: $3,911; $8,200 out-of-state. Books/supplies: $1,200. Personal expenses: $3,626.

Financial aid. Need-based: Need-based aid available for part-time students. Work-study available nights, weekends and for part-time students. **Non-need-based:** Scholarships awarded for academics, athletics, leadership, music/drama, state residency.

Application procedures. Admission: No deadline. $25 fee. Admission notification on a rolling basis. **Financial aid:** Priority date 5/1, closing date

7/15. FAFSA, institutional form required. Applicants notified on a rolling basis starting 4/1; must reply within 2 week(s) of notification.

Academics. **Special study options:** Accelerated study, combined bachelor's/graduate degree, cooperative education, cross-registration, distance learning, double major, dual enrollment of high school students, ESL, honors, independent study, internships, liberal arts/career combination, student-designed major, weekend college. License preparation in nursing, occupational therapy, paramedic, physical therapy, radiology, real estate. **Credit/placement by examination:** AP, CLEP, institutional tests. 24 credit hours maximum toward associate degree. **Support services:** GED preparation and test center, learning center, pre-admission summer program, remedial instruction, tutoring, writing center.

Majors. **Business:** General, accounting technology, business admin, hospitality admin. **Computer sciences:** Data processing, networking. **Education:** General. **Foreign languages:** Sign language interpretation. **Health services:** Clinical lab technology, dietetic technician, EMT paramedic, health information technology, medical radiologic technology/radiation therapy, nuclear medical technology, nursing (RN), occupational therapy assistant, physical therapy assistant, polysomnography, radiologic technology/medical imaging, respiratory therapy technology, sonography, veterinary technology/assistant. **Protective services:** Firefighting, police science. **Visual/performing arts:** Graphic design, interior design. **Work/family studies:** Child care service.

Most popular majors. Business/marketing 24%, health sciences 29%, liberal arts 17%, security/protective services 6%.

Technology on campus. 555 workstations in library, computer center, student center. Online library, helpline, wireless network available.

Student life. **Freshman orientation:** Available. Preregistration for classes offered. **Activities:** Concert band, choral groups, dance, drama, film society, international student organizations, music ensembles, musical theater, radio station, student government, student newspaper, religious organizations available.

Athletics. NJCAA. **Intercollegiate:** Baseball M, basketball W. **Intramural:** Baseball M, basketball, football (non-tackle) M, soccer, softball, volleyball. **Team name:** Dolphins.

Student services. Adult student services, career counseling, services for economically disadvantaged, student employment services, financial aid counseling, health services, on-campus daycare, personal counseling, placement for graduates, veterans' counselor, women's services. **Physically disabled:** Services for visually, speech, hearing impaired. **Transfer:** Re-entry adviser for new students. Transfer center, transfer adviser, college fairs on campus for students transferring to 4-year colleges.

Contact. E-mail: enroll@dcc.edu
Phone: (504) 671-5012
Gwen Boutte, Director of Admissions & Enrollment Services, Delgado Community College, 615 City Park Avenue, New Orleans, LA 70119

Delta College of Arts & Technology
Baton Rouge, Louisiana
www.deltacollege.com   **CB code: 3131**

‣ For-profit 2-year visual arts and technical college
‣ Large city

General. Accredited by ACCSC. **Enrollment:** 316 degree-seeking undergraduates. **Degrees:** 12 associate awarded. **Calendar:** Differs by program. **Full-time faculty:** 23 total. **Part-time faculty:** 32 total.

Student profile. Among degree-seeking undergraduates, 100% enrolled in a vocational program, 2% already have a bachelor's degree or higher, 19 enrolled as first-time, first-year students.

Women:	94%	**Asian American:**	1%
African American:	70%	**Hispanic/Latino:**	2%

Basis for selection. Open admission.

2015-2016 Annual costs. Program cost (including books & supplies): Business Office Administration $11,500. Dental Assistant $11,500. Graphic Design $23,200. Medical Assistant $11,500. Medical Office Assistant $11,500. Practical Nurse (LPN) $24,000. Registration fee $100.

2014-2015 Financial aid. **Need-based:** Work-study available nights, weekends and for part-time students.

Application procedures. **Admission:** No deadline. $100 fee. Admission notification on a rolling basis. **Financial aid:** No deadline.

Academics. **Credit/placement by examination:** AP, CLEP.

Majors. **Health services:** Licensed practical nurse. **Visual/performing arts:** General.

Student life. **Freshman orientation:** Available, $100 fee. Preregistration for classes offered.

Contact. E-mail: admissions@deltacollege.com
Phone: (225) 928-7770 Fax: (225) 927-9096
David Clark, General Manager, Delta College of Arts & Technology, 7380 Exchange Place, Baton Rouge, LA 70806

Delta School of Business & Technology
Lake Charles, Louisiana
www.deltatech.edu   **CB code: 2252**

‣ For-profit 2-year business and technical college
‣ Small city

General. Founded in 1970. Accredited by ACICS. **Enrollment:** 208 undergraduates. **Degrees:** 82 associate awarded. **Location:** 128 miles from Baton Rouge. **Calendar:** Differs by program. **Full-time faculty:** 22 total. **Part-time faculty:** 13 total.

Student profile.

Out-of-state:	10%	**25 or older:**	40%

Basis for selection. Open admission.

2015-2016 Annual costs. Business Management: $23,970, Dental Assistant: $11,785, Medical Assistant: $22,970, Administrative Assistant: $22,970, Information Technology: $22,970, Paralegal Studies: $25,570, Accounting: $23,970. Books and supplies are included in tuition.

Financial aid. **Need-based:** Work-study available nights, weekends and for part-time students.

Application procedures. **Admission:** No deadline. No application fee. Admission notification on a rolling basis.

Academics. **Special study options:** Accelerated study, distance learning, double major, honors, internships. **Credit/placement by examination:** AP, CLEP. **Support services:** Reduced course load, tutoring.

Majors. **Business:** Accounting, business admin. **Health services:** Medical assistant.

Technology on campus. 30 workstations in computer center.

Student services. Career counseling, student employment services, placement for graduates.

Contact. E-mail: barbara@deltatech.edu
Phone: (337) 439-5765 Toll-free number: (800) 259-5627
Fax: (337) 436-5151
Barbara Holt, Director of Admissions, Delta School of Business & Technology, 517 Broad Street, Lake Charles, LA 70601

ITI Technical College
Baton Rouge, Louisiana
www.iticollege.edu

‣ For-profit 2-year technical and career college
‣ Commuter campus in large city
‣ Interview required

General. Accredited by ACCSC. **Enrollment:** 536 degree-seeking undergraduates. **Degrees:** 131 associate awarded. **Calendar:** Continuous. **Full-time faculty:** 22 total; 9% have terminal degrees, 23% minority, 23% women. **Part-time faculty:** 35 total; 3% have terminal degrees, 29% minority, 34% women.

Student profile.

Out-of-state:	1%	**25 or older:**	49%

Basis for selection. Open admission, but selective for some programs. Applicant completes application, must interview and tour campus, complete entrance evaluation, settle funding, sign enrollment agreement. **Home schooled:** Students must have acceptable certificate or diploma at time of enrollment. **Learning Disabled:** Students must meet with school director regarding special needs and referral for assistance.

2015-2016 Annual costs. Full-time tuition varies by program from $10,550-$27,950. Registration fee $150. Estimated average total books and supplies from $1,875-$3,925.

Financial aid. All financial aid based on need. Work-study available nights, weekends and for part-time students.

Application procedures. Admission: No deadline. No application fee. Admission notification on a rolling basis. **Financial aid:** No deadline. FAFSA required.

Academics. Special study options: Internships. **Credit/placement by examination:** AP, CLEP. **Support services:** Study skills assistance, tutoring.

Majors. Business: Administrative services, business admin, executive assistant, office management, office technology. **Communications technology:** General. **Computer sciences:** Data processing, information systems. **Health services:** Health information management, health information technology, insurance coding, insurance specialist, medical secretary, medical transcription, office admin, office assistant, office computer specialist, receptionist.

Most popular majors. Business/marketing 14%, computer/information sciences 14%, engineering/engineering technologies 52%, science technologies 14%.

Technology on campus. 15 workstations in library. Repair service available.

Student life. Freshman orientation: Mandatory. Preregistration for classes offered.

Student services. Career counseling, financial aid counseling, placement for graduates.

Contact. E-mail: admissions@iticollege.edu
Phone: (225) 752-4233 Toll-free number: (800) 467-4484
Fax: (225) 756-0903
Marcia Stevens, Director of Admissions, ITI Technical College, 13944 Airline Highway, Baton Rouge, LA 70817

Louisiana State University at Eunice
Eunice, Louisiana
www.lsue.edu   CB code: 6386

- Public 2-year nursing and junior college
- Commuter campus in large town

General. Founded in 1964. Regionally accredited. **Enrollment:** 2,673 degree-seeking undergraduates. **Degrees:** 296 associate awarded. **Location:** 40 miles from Lafayette, 90 miles from Baton Rouge. **Calendar:** Semester, limited summer session. **Full-time faculty:** 71 total. **Part-time faculty:** 56 total.

Transfer out. Colleges most students transferred to 2015: Louisiana State University-Baton Rouge, University of Louisiana at Lafayette, McNeese State University, Southern University.

Basis for selection. Open admission, but selective for some programs. Test scores, school achievement record, interview considered for admission to nursing and respiratory care programs. **Home schooled:** Transcript of courses and grades required.

2015-2016 Annual costs. Tuition/fees: $3,828; $9,192 out-of-state. Books/supplies: $1,300. Personal expenses: $1,838.

Financial aid. Need-based: Need-based aid available for part-time students. Work-study available nights, weekends and for part-time students.

Application procedures. Admission: Closing date 8/21 (receipt date). $25 fee. Application must be submitted online. Admission notification on a rolling basis. **Financial aid:** Priority date 6/1; no closing date. FAFSA, institutional form required. Applicants notified on a rolling basis starting 4/1; must reply within 2 week(s) of notification.

Academics. Special study options: Accelerated study, distance learning, dual enrollment of high school students, honors, independent study, liberal arts/career combination. Bachelor's degree programs available on campus.

License preparation in nursing, physical therapy, radiology. **Credit/placement by examination:** AP, CLEP, institutional tests. 30 credit hours maximum toward associate degree. **Support services:** Learning center, remedial instruction, study skills assistance, tutoring.

Majors. Biology: General. **Business:** General, administrative services. **Communications:** Media studies. **Computer sciences:** General. **Education:** Early childhood. **Health services:** Licensed practical nurse, medical radiologic technology/radiation therapy, respiratory therapy technology. **Liberal arts:** Arts/sciences. **Physical sciences:** General. **Protective services:** Criminal justice, fire safety technology. **Social sciences:** General. **Visual/performing arts:** Studio arts.

Technology on campus. 150 workstations in library, computer center, student center. Dormitories wired for high-speed internet access. Commuter students can connect to campus network. Online course registration, online library, helpline, wireless network available.

Student life. Freshman orientation: Mandatory, $15 fee. Preregistration for classes offered. **Housing:** Apartments available. **Activities:** Campus ministries, drama, student government, student newspaper, Baptist collegiate ministry, Newman club, Rotoract, African American student alliance, Students in Free Enterprise, Catholic student center.

Athletics. NJCAA. **Intercollegiate:** Baseball M, basketball W, softball W. **Team name:** Bengals.

Student services. Adult student services, alcohol/substance abuse counseling, chaplain/spiritual director, career counseling, services for economically disadvantaged, student employment services, financial aid counseling, health services, personal counseling, placement for graduates, veterans' counselor. **Physically disabled:** Services for visually, speech, hearing impaired. **Transfer:** Pre-admission transcript evaluation for new students. Transfer adviser, college fairs on campus for students transferring to 4-year colleges.

Contact. E-mail: admissions@lsue.edu
Phone: (337) 550-1305 Toll-free number: (888) 367-5783
Fax: (337) 550-1306
Jason Sampler, Registrar and Director of Admissions, Louisiana State University at Eunice, Box 1129, Eunice, LA 70535

Nunez Community College
Chalmette, Louisiana
www.nunez.edu   CB code: 0295

- Public 2-year community and technical college
- Commuter campus in large town

General. Founded in 1992. Regionally accredited. **Enrollment:** 1,551 degree-seeking undergraduates; 1,061 non-degree-seeking students. **Degrees:** 229 associate awarded. **Location:** 11 miles from New Orleans. **Calendar:** Semester, limited summer session. **Full-time faculty:** 47 total; 11% minority, 51% women. **Part-time faculty:** 52 total; 23% minority, 44% women. **Class size:** 56% < 20, 43% 20-39, 1% 40-49. **Special facilities:** Methanol plant for industrial/process technology students.

Student profile. Among degree-seeking undergraduates, 5% enrolled in a transfer program, 243 enrolled as first-time, first-year students, 289 transferred in from other institutions.

Part-time:	48%	Hispanic/Latino:	6%
Women:	60%	Native American:	1%
African American:	47%	Multi-racial, non-Hispanic:	2%
Asian American:	2%	25 or older:	33%

Transfer out. Colleges most students transferred to 2015: University of New Orleans, Southern University of New Orleans, Louisiana State University-Baton Rouge, Our Lady of Holy Cross College, Loyola University of New Orleans.

Basis for selection. Open admission, but selective for some programs. Additional requirements for Practical Nursing, Emergency Medical Technician and Associate of Science in Teaching (Grades 1-5).

2015-2016 Annual costs. Tuition/fees: $3,946; $7,444 out-of-state. Books/supplies: $1,200. Personal expenses: $1,970.

2014-2015 Financial aid. Need-based: 62% of total undergraduate aid awarded as scholarships/grants, 38% as loans/jobs. Need-based aid available for part-time students. Work-study available nights, weekends and for part-time students. **Additional information:** Pell Grants, Stafford Loans, campus work-study, and tuition waiver scholarships available. Louisiana National Guard tuition exemption, teacher tuition exemption, dependents of injured fire-police tuition waivers available.

Application procedures. Admission: Priority date 8/1; no deadline. $20 fee. Admission notification on a rolling basis. **Financial aid:** Priority date 6/1, closing date 8/1. FAFSA required.

Academics. Special study options: Cooperative education, cross-registration, distance learning, double major, dual enrollment of high school students, honors, independent study, internships, student-designed major. License preparation in nursing, paramedic. **Credit/placement by examination:** AP, CLEP, institutional tests. 24 credit hours maximum toward associate degree. **Support services:** Learning center, reduced course load, remedial instruction, study skills assistance, tutoring.

Majors. Business: General. **Education:** General. **Work/family studies:** Child care service.

Most popular majors. Business/marketing 13%, engineering/engineering technologies 47%, liberal arts 28%.

Technology on campus. 75 workstations in library, computer center, student center. Online course registration, online library, helpline, wireless network available.

Student life. Freshman orientation: Mandatory. Preregistration for classes offered. Two-hour orientation offered during registration period. **Activities:** Drama, student government.

Athletics. Team name: Pelicans.

Student services. Career counseling, financial aid counseling, health services, personal counseling, placement for graduates, veterans' counselor. **Physically disabled:** Services for visually, hearing impaired. **Transfer:** Transfer adviser, college fairs on campus for students transferring to 4-year colleges.

Contact. E-mail: bmaillet@nunez.edu
Phone: (504) 278-6467 Fax: (504) 278-6487
Becky Maillet, Director of Admissions and Registration, Nunez Community College, 3710 Paris Road, Chalmette, LA 70043

Remington College: Baton Rouge
Baton Rouge, Louisiana
http://baton-rouge.remingtoncollege.edu   **CB code: 3428**

- Private 2-year technical college
- Commuter campus in large city
- Interview required

General. Regionally accredited; also accredited by ACCSC. **Enrollment:** 547 undergraduates. **Degrees:** 18 associate awarded. **Calendar:** Quarter. **Full-time faculty:** 20 total. **Part-time faculty:** 7 total.

Basis for selection. Open admission, but selective for some programs.

2015-2016 Annual costs. Total program tuition: diplomas $15,995-$21,700; associates $33,900.

Financial aid. All financial aid based on need. Work-study available nights, weekends and for part-time students.

Application procedures. Admission: No deadline. $50 fee. Admission notification on a rolling basis. **Financial aid:** No deadline. FAFSA required. Applicants notified on a rolling basis; must reply within 1 week(s) of notification.

Academics. Special study options: Liberal arts/career combination. **Credit/placement by examination:** AP, CLEP. **Support services:** Tutoring.

Majors. Computer sciences: General, information systems, LAN/WAN management.

Technology on campus. PC or laptop required.

Student life. Freshman orientation: Mandatory. Preregistration for classes offered. **Activities:** Student government.

Student services. Financial aid counseling, placement for graduates.

Contact. Phone: (225) 240-7049
Monica Butler-Johnson, Director of Admissions, Remington College: Baton Rouge, 10551 Coursey Boulevard, Baton Rouge, LA 70816

Remington College: Lafayette
Lafayette, Louisiana
http://lafayette.remingtoncollege.edu   **CB code: 7117**

- Private 2-year junior college
- Commuter campus in small city
- Interview required

General. Founded in 1940. Regionally accredited; also accredited by ACCSC. **Enrollment:** 585 undergraduates. **Degrees:** 19 associate awarded. **Location:** 50 miles from Baton Rouge. **Calendar:** Quarter, extensive summer session. **Full-time faculty:** 19 total. **Part-time faculty:** 10 total.

Basis for selection. Open admission, but selective for some programs. **Home schooled:** State high school equivalency certificate required.

2015-2016 Annual costs. Total program tuition: diplomas $15,995-$21,700; associates $33,900.

Financial aid. All financial aid based on need. Work-study available nights, weekends and for part-time students.

Application procedures. Admission: No deadline. $50 fee. Application must be submitted on paper. Admission notification on a rolling basis. **Financial aid:** No deadline. FAFSA, institutional form required.

Academics. Laptop computer provided to each student. **Special study options:** Accelerated study, independent study, liberal arts/career combination. **Credit/placement by examination:** AP, CLEP. **Support services:** GED preparation, tutoring.

Majors. Business: Business admin. **Computer sciences:** General. **Protective services:** Law enforcement admin.

Technology on campus. 110 workstations in library, computer center. Online library, helpline, repair service available.

Student life. Freshman orientation: Mandatory. Preregistration for classes offered. **Activities:** National Vocational Technical Society (associate degree honors society), Nightingale Medical Honor Society (diploma honors society).

Student services. Student employment services, financial aid counseling, placement for graduates. **Transfer:** Pre-admission transcript evaluation for new students.

Contact. E-mail: admissions@remingtoncollege.edu
Phone: (337) 246-5126
Joseph Howanski, Director of Admissions, Remington College: Lafayette, 303 Rue Louis XIV, Lafayette, LA 70508

Remington College: Shreveport
Shreveport, Louisiana
http://shreveport.remingtoncollege.edu

- Private 2-year technical college
- Small city

General. Regionally accredited; also accredited by ACCSC. **Enrollment:** 582 undergraduates. **Degrees:** 38 associate awarded. **Calendar:** Differs by program. **Full-time faculty:** 28 total. **Part-time faculty:** 5 total.

Basis for selection. Open admission, but selective for some programs.

2015-2016 Annual costs. Total program tuition: diplomas $15,995-$20,995; associates $33,900; bachelor's $24,700.

Financial aid. Need-based: Work-study available nights, weekends and for part-time students.

Application procedures. Admission: No deadline. $50 fee. **Financial aid:** No deadline.

Academics. Credit/placement by examination: AP, CLEP.

Majors. Business: Business admin. **Protective services:** Law enforcement admin.

Contact. E-mail: admissions@remingtoncollege.edu
Phone: (318) 239-4309
Jason Stanley, Director of Admissions, Remington College: Shreveport, 2106 W Bert Kouns Industrial Loop, Shreveport, LA 71118

River Parishes Community College
Sorrento, Louisiana
www.rpcc.edu

▶ Public 2-year community college
▶ Commuter campus in rural community

General. Regionally accredited. **Enrollment:** 3,561 undergraduates. **Degrees:** 202 associate awarded. **Location:** 20 miles from Baton Rouge, 40 miles from New Orleans. **Calendar:** Semester, extensive summer session. **Full-time faculty:** 48 total. **Part-time faculty:** 51 total.

Student profile.

Out-of-state: 1% 25 or older: 27%

Basis for selection. Open admission, but selective for some programs. **Home schooled:** Transcript of courses and grades required.

2015-2016 Annual costs. Tuition/fees: $3,911; $7,955 out-of-state. Books/supplies: $1,200. Personal expenses: $1,726.

Financial aid. Need-based: Work-study available nights, weekends and for part-time students.

Application procedures. Admission: $10 fee. Admission notification on a rolling basis. **Financial aid:** Priority date 4/15; no closing date. FAFSA required. Applicants notified on a rolling basis starting 3/1.

Academics. Credit/placement by examination: AP, CLEP, SAT, ACT.

Majors. Liberal arts: Arts/sciences.

Most popular majors. Liberal arts 96%.

Technology on campus. Online library, wireless network available.

Student life. Freshman orientation: Mandatory. Preregistration for classes offered. Orientation held prior to each semester.

Student services. Personal counseling, veterans' counselor. **Physically disabled:** Services for visually, speech, hearing impaired.

Contact. Phone: (225) 743-8500 Fax: (225) 675-5478
Dianna Gilbert, Admissions Director, River Parishes Community College, PO Box 310, Sorrento, LA 70778

South Louisiana Community College
Lafayette, Louisiana
www.solacc.edu   CB code: 4521

▶ Public 2-year community college
▶ Commuter campus in small city

General. Regionally accredited. Additional campus in New Iberia; Franklin, Opelousas, St. Martinville, Crowley, Abbeville, and Ville Platte. **Enrollment:** 5,640 degree-seeking undergraduates. **Degrees:** 376 associate awarded. **Calendar:** Semester, extensive summer session. **Full-time faculty:** 145 total. **Part-time faculty:** 137 total. **Class size:** 67% < 20, 31% 20-39, less than 1% 40-49, less than 1% 50-99.

Student profile.

Out-of-state: 5% 25 or older: 21%

Basis for selection. Open admission, but selective for some programs. Specific admissions criteria for selected Nursing and Allied Health programs.

High school preparation. College-preparatory program recommended.

2015-2016 Annual costs. Tuition/fees: $4,037; $7,642 out-of-state. Books/supplies: $1,200. Personal expenses: $2,025.

Financial aid. Need-based: Need-based aid available for part-time students. Work-study available nights, weekends and for part-time students. **Non-need-based:** Scholarships awarded for academics, leadership, state residency.

Application procedures. Admission: Priority date 7/1; no deadline. No application fee. Application must be submitted on paper. Admission notification on a rolling basis. **Financial aid:** Priority date 5/15; no closing date. FAFSA, institutional form required.

Academics. Special study options: Cross-registration, distance learning, double major, dual enrollment of high school students, independent study, internships. **Credit/placement by examination:** AP, CLEP, IB, institutional tests. **Support services:** Learning center, remedial instruction, study skills assistance, tutoring, writing center.

Majors. Business: General. **Computer sciences:** Networking, programming, web page design. **Health services:** Clinical lab technology, EMT paramedic, nursing (RN), surgical technology. **Protective services:** Criminal justice.

Technology on campus. 50 workstations in library, student center. Online course registration, online library, helpline, wireless network available.

Student life. Freshman orientation: Mandatory. Preregistration for classes offered. **Activities:** Literary magazine, student government.

Student services. Career counseling, student employment services, financial aid counseling, personal counseling. **Physically disabled:** Services for visually, speech, hearing impaired. **Transfer:** Pre-admission transcript evaluation for new students. College fairs on campus for students transferring to 4-year colleges.

Contact. E-mail: admissions@solacc.edu
Phone: (337) 521-9000 Fax: (337) 262-2101
Director of Admissions, South Louisiana Community College, 1101 Bertrand Dr., Lafayette, LA 70506-4124

Southern University at Shreveport
Shreveport, Louisiana
www.susla.edu   CB code: 0322

▶ Public 2-year community college
▶ Commuter campus in small city

General. Founded in 1964. Regionally accredited. **Enrollment:** 2,450 degree-seeking undergraduates. **Degrees:** 260 associate awarded. **Calendar:** Semester, limited summer session. **Full-time faculty:** 92 total. **Part-time faculty:** 86 total.

Student profile. Among degree-seeking undergraduates, 742 enrolled as first-time, first-year students, 3,174 transferred in from other institutions.

Out-of-state: 1% 25 or older: 25%
African American: 85% Live on campus: 4%
International: 7%

Basis for selection. Open admission, but selective for some programs. Students may only apply to selective programs once enrolled and after general education credits are complete.

2015-2016 Annual costs. Tuition/fees: $3,994; $7,296 out-of-state. Room/board: $9,650. Books/supplies: $1,200.

Financial aid. Need-based: Work-study available nights, weekends and for part-time students.

Application procedures. Admission: Priority date 7/1; no deadline. $20 fee ($15 out-of-state), may be waived for applicants with need. Application must be submitted online. Admission notification on a rolling basis. **Financial aid:** Priority date 4/1; no closing date. FAFSA required. Applicants notified on a rolling basis.

Academics. Special study options: Cross-registration, distance learning, dual enrollment of high school students, internships. License preparation in dental hygiene, nursing, radiology. **Credit/placement by examination:** AP, CLEP, institutional tests. 3 credit hours maximum toward associate degree. **Support services:** GED preparation, learning center, remedial instruction, study skills assistance, tutoring, writing center.

Majors. Biology: General. **Business:** Accounting, banking/financial services, business admin. **Computer sciences:** Computer science. **Health services:** Clinical lab technology, dental hygiene, health information technology, nursing (RN), polysomnography, radiologic technology/medical imaging, respiratory therapy technology, substance abuse counseling, surgical technology. **Protective services:** Law enforcement admin.

Most popular majors. Business/marketing 20%, education 9%, health sciences 41%, liberal arts 15%.

Technology on campus. 50 workstations in dormitories, library, computer center, student center. Dormitories wired for high-speed internet access and linked to campus network. Commuter students can connect to campus network. Online course registration, online library, helpline, wireless network available.

Two-Year Colleges

Student life. Freshman orientation: Mandatory. Preregistration for classes offered. **Housing:** Coed dorms available. $200 nonrefundable deposit. **Activities:** Choral groups, dance, student government, student newspaper, Baptist student union, Afro-American society.

Athletics. NJCAA. **Intercollegiate:** Basketball. **Team name:** Jaguars.

Student services. Health services, personal counseling, placement for graduates, veterans' counselor. **Transfer:** Transfer adviser for students transferring to 4-year colleges.

Contact. E-mail: admissions@susla.edu
Phone: (318) 674-3342 Fax: (318) 674-3489
Annie Moss, Director of Admissions, Southern University at Shreveport, 3050 Martin Luther King, Jr. Drive, Shreveport, LA 71107

Virginia College in Baton Rouge
Baton Rouge, Louisiana
www.vc.edu/campus/baton-rouge-louisiana-college.cfm

▸ For-profit 2-year health science and career college
▸ Very large city

General. Regionally accredited; also accredited by ACICS. **Enrollment:** 589 undergraduates. **Degrees:** 78 associate awarded. **Calendar:** Quarter.

Basis for selection. Open admission.

2015-2016 Annual costs. Certificate programs: $13,932-$23,220. Associate programs: $37,152-$39,072. Clock hour certificate program: Cosmetology $21,225.

Financial aid. Need-based: Work-study available nights, weekends and for part-time students.

Application procedures. Admission: No deadline. $100 fee. **Financial aid:** No deadline.

Academics. Credit/placement by examination: AP, CLEP.

Majors. Business: Office management. **Health services:** Insurance specialist, medical assistant, office admin, surgical technology.

Contact. E-mail: batonrouge.info@vc.edu
Phone: (225) 236-3900 Fax: (225) 236-3999
June Urein, Director of Admissions, Virginia College in Baton Rouge, 9501 Cortana Place, Baton Rouge, LA 70815

Virginia College in Shreveport
Bossier City, Louisiana
www.vc.edu/shreveport

▸ For-profit 2-year career college
▸ Small city

General. Regionally accredited; also accredited by ACICS. **Enrollment:** 264 undergraduates. **Degrees:** 9 associate awarded. **Calendar:** Quarter.

Basis for selection. Open admission.

2015-2016 Annual costs. Total program tuition cost: Diploma programs range from $12,060 to $20,100; Associate's degree programs range from $32,160 to $35,600.

Financial aid. Need-based: Work-study available nights, weekends and for part-time students.

Academics. Credit/placement by examination: AP.

Majors. Business: Business admin, executive assistant. **Health services:** Medical assistant, office assistant.

Contact. E-mail: shreveport.info@vc.edu
Toll-free number: (888) 342-0014
Mark Godfrey, Director of Admissions, Virginia College in Shreveport, 2950 East Texas Street, Suite C, Bossier City, LA 71111

Maine

Beal College
Bangor, Maine
www.bealcollege.edu   CB code: 3114

- For-profit 2-year junior and career college
- Commuter campus in large town

General. Founded in 1891. Accredited by ACICS. **Enrollment:** 429 undergraduates. **Degrees:** 125 associate awarded. **Location:** 250 miles from Boston. **Calendar:** Six 8-week modules per year. Extensive summer session. **Full-time faculty:** 8 total. **Part-time faculty:** 16 total. **Class size:** 59% < 20, 41% 20-39.

Basis for selection. Open admission. Interview recommended. **Home schooled:** Students who earned high school diploma through home school education must provide passing GED scores.

High school preparation. Recommended units include English 4, mathematics 4 and science 1.

2015-2016 Annual costs. Tuition/fees: $7,800. Per-credit charge: $260. Books/supplies: $1,200. Personal expenses: $700.

Financial aid. Need-based: Work-study available nights, weekends and for part-time students.

Application procedures. Admission: No deadline. $30 fee, may be waived for applicants with need. Admission notification on a rolling basis. **Financial aid:** No deadline. FAFSA, institutional form required. Applicants notified on a rolling basis starting 6/15; must reply within 2 week(s) of notification.

Academics. Students in medical assisting program must complete 160-hour practicum. **Special study options:** Accelerated study, double major, independent study. Externships. **Credit/placement by examination:** AP, CLEP, institutional tests. 30 credit hours maximum toward associate degree. **Support services:** Tutoring.

Majors. Business: Accounting, administrative services, business admin, office management, sales/distribution, tourism promotion. **Education:** Early childhood. **Health services:** Health information technology, medical assistant, medical secretary, office assistant. **Protective services:** Police science. **Work/family studies:** Child care service, family/community services.

Technology on campus. 45 workstations in library, computer center. Wireless network available.

Student life. Freshman orientation: Available. Preregistration for classes offered.

Student services. Adult student services, career counseling, student employment services, placement for graduates, veterans' counselor. **Transfer:** Pre-admission transcript evaluation for new students.

Contact. E-mail: admissions@bealcollege.edu
Phone: (207) 947-4591 Fax: (207) 947-0208
Erin Leighton, Director of Admissions, Beal College, 99 Farm Road, Bangor, ME 04401

Central Maine Community College
Auburn, Maine   CB member
www.cmcc.edu   CB code: 3309

- Public 2-year community and technical college
- Commuter campus in small city

General. Founded in 1964. Regionally accredited. **Enrollment:** 2,354 degree-seeking undergraduates; 630 non-degree-seeking students. **Degrees:** 465 associate awarded. **Location:** One mile from downtown. **Calendar:** Semester, limited summer session. **Full-time faculty:** 55 total. **Part-time faculty:** 154 total. **Class size:** 71% < 20, 29% 20-39, less than 1% 40-49, less than 1% 50-99. **Partnerships:** Formal partnership with Ford Motor Company.

Student profile. Among degree-seeking undergraduates, 629 enrolled as first-time, first-year students.

Part-time:	47%	25 or older:	35%
Out-of-state:	2%	Live on campus:	13%
Women:	58%		

Transfer out. Colleges most students transferred to 2015: University of Maine System.

Basis for selection. Open admission, but selective for some programs. Special requirements for nursing. Many other academic programs have specific academic prerequisites but are not selective in terms of admission to the program. **Home schooled:** Transcript of courses and grades required. A copy of the state department of education correspondence granting approval of homeschooling program and the most recent teacher certification recognizing student's grade level and/or appropriate test results required. **Learning Disabled:** Applicants with documented disabilities should contact the college's disability coordinator.

High school preparation. Recommended units include English 4, mathematics 2, social studies 1, history 1 and science 2.

2015-2016 Annual costs. Tuition/fees: $3,480; $6,180 out-of-state. Per-credit charge: $90 in-state; $180 out-of-state. Room/board: $7,978. Books/supplies: $1,200. Personal expenses: $1,400.

2015-2016 Financial aid. Need-based: Average need met was 67%. Average scholarship/grant was $5,175; average loan $5,613. 56% of total undergraduate aid awarded as scholarships/grants, 44% as loans/jobs. Need-based aid available for part-time students. Work-study available nights, weekends and for part-time students. **Additional information:** Tuition and/or fee waivers may be available to orphans, Native Americans, fire fighters, police, disabled veterans, dependents or survivors of veterans killed in line of duty.

Application procedures. Admission: No deadline. $20 fee, may be waived for applicants with need. Admission notification on a rolling basis beginning on or about 10/1. **Financial aid:** Priority date 5/1; no closing date. FAFSA required. Applicants notified on a rolling basis starting 2/15.

Academics. Special study options: Distance learning, dual enrollment of high school students, ESL, independent study, internships, liberal arts/career combination. License preparation in nursing. **Credit/placement by examination:** AP, CLEP, IB, institutional tests. Up to 75% of credits may meet curriculum requirements; 25% of credits must be completed in residence. **Support services:** Learning center, reduced course load, remedial instruction, study skills assistance, tutoring, writing center.

Majors. Business: Accounting, business admin, hospitality admin, management information systems. **Communications technology:** Graphic/printing. **Computer sciences:** LAN/WAN management. **Education:** Early childhood. **General:** Maintenance. **Health services:** Insurance coding, medical assistant, nursing (RN). **Liberal arts:** Arts/sciences. **Protective services:** Law enforcement admin.

Most popular majors. Business/marketing 17%, computer/information sciences 7%, engineering/engineering technologies 6%, health sciences 14%, liberal arts 24%, public administration/social services 6%, security/protective services 8%, trade and industry 13%.

Technology on campus. 400 workstations in library, computer center. Dormitories wired for high-speed internet access and linked to campus network. Commuter students can connect to campus network. Online course registration, online library, helpline, wireless network available.

Student life. Freshman orientation: Available. Preregistration for classes offered. **Policies:** Student code of conduct observed. **Housing:** Coed dorms, single-sex dorms, apartments available. $50 nonrefundable deposit. **Activities:** Drama, literary magazine, student government, CRU, international club, human services club.

Athletics. USCAA. **Intercollegiate:** Baseball M, basketball, cross-country M, lacrosse M, soccer, softball W. **Intramural:** Basketball, skiing. **Team name:** Mustangs.

Student services. Career counseling, services for economically disadvantaged, student employment services, financial aid counseling, personal counseling, placement for graduates, veterans' counselor, women's services. **Physically disabled:** Services for visually, speech, hearing impaired. **Transfer:** Transfer adviser, college fairs on campus for students transferring to 4-year colleges.

Contact. E-mail: enroll@cmcc.edu
Phone: (207) 755-5273 Toll-free number: (800) 891-2002 ext. 273
Fax: (207) 755-5493
Andrew Morong, Director of Admissions, Central Maine Community College, 1250 Turner Street, Auburn, ME 04210-6498

Two-Year Colleges

Eastern Maine Community College
Bangor, Maine
www.emcc.edu

CB member
CB code: 3372

- Public 2-year community and technical college
- Commuter campus in large town
- Application essay required

General. Founded in 1966. Regionally accredited. **Enrollment:** 1,988 degree-seeking undergraduates. **Degrees:** 351 associate awarded. **ROTC:** Army. **Location:** 250 miles from Boston, 130 miles from Portland. **Calendar:** Semester, limited summer session. **Full-time faculty:** 59 total. **Part-time faculty:** 112 total.

Transfer out. Colleges most students transferred to 2015: University of Maine-Orono, Husson College.

Basis for selection. Open admission, but selective for some programs. School record, recommendations, and essays most important. Entrance requirements vary by program. SAT required for engineering technologies, registered nursing, and medical radiography applicants; score report preferred by April 30. Interview recommended for some majors.

High school preparation. Recommended units include English 4, mathematics 3 and science 2. Academic requirements vary by program.

2015-2016 Annual costs. Tuition/fees: $3,675; $6,375 out-of-state. Per-credit charge: $90 in-state; $180 out-of-state. Room/board: $8,134. Books/supplies: $800. Personal expenses: $1,500.

Financial aid. All financial aid based on need. Need-based aid available for part-time students. Work-study available nights, weekends and for part-time students.

Application procedures. Admission: No deadline. $20 fee, may be waived for applicants with need. Admission notification on a rolling basis. Must reply by May 1 or within 4 week(s) if notified thereafter. Deposit refundable up to 60 days before program begins. **Financial aid:** Priority date 5/1; no closing date. FAFSA required. Applicants notified on a rolling basis starting 5/1; must reply within 3 week(s) of notification.

Academics. Special study options: Distance learning, dual enrollment of high school students, ESL, external degree, internships, student-designed major, study abroad. **Credit/placement by examination:** AP, CLEP, institutional tests. Maximum of 40% of required credit total in student's field of study may be obtained through credit by examination. **Support services:** Learning center, reduced course load, remedial instruction, study skills assistance, tutoring.

Majors. Business: General, administrative services, banking/financial services, business admin, office management. **Education:** Early childhood. **General:** Carpentry, pipefitting, power transmission. **Health services:** Medical radiologic technology/radiation therapy, nursing (RN), preop/surgical nursing. **Liberal arts:** Arts/sciences. **Protective services:** Firefighting.

Most popular majors. Business/marketing 36%, computer/information sciences 17%, health sciences 22%, interdisciplinary studies 11%, personal/culinary services 14%.

Technology on campus. 150 workstations in dormitories, library, computer center. Dormitories wired for high-speed internet access. Commuter students can connect to campus network. Online course registration, online library, helpline, wireless network available.

Student life. Freshman orientation: Available. Preregistration for classes offered. **Housing:** Coed dorms available. $50 nonrefundable deposit, deadline 7/1. **Activities:** Student government, student newspaper, Student Veterans Association, International Club, Phi Theta Kappa.

Athletics. Intercollegiate: Basketball, golf, soccer. **Intramural:** Badminton, basketball, bowling, cheerleading, ice hockey M, skiing, softball, table tennis, volleyball. **Team name:** Golden Eagles.

Student services. Adult student services, alcohol/substance abuse counseling, career counseling, student employment services, financial aid counseling, health services, on-campus daycare, personal counseling, placement for graduates, veterans' counselor.

Contact. E-mail: admissions@emcc.edu
Phone: (207) 974-4680 Toll-free number: (800) 286-9357
Fax: (207) 974-4683
Stacy Green, Director of Admissions, Eastern Maine Community College, 354 Hogan Road, Bangor, ME 04401

Kaplan University: South Portland
South Portland, Maine
www.kaplanuniversity.edu

CB code: 0688

- For-profit 2-year business and junior college
- Commuter campus in small city
- Interview required

General. Founded in 1966. Regionally accredited. **Enrollment:** 400 degree-seeking undergraduates. **Degrees:** 112 bachelor's, 221 associate awarded; master's offered. **Location:** 115 miles from Boston. **Calendar:** Quarter, extensive summer session. **Full-time faculty:** 12 total. **Part-time faculty:** 40 total. **Class size:** 98% < 20, 2% 20-39.

Transfer out. Colleges most students transferred to 2015: University of Southern Maine.

Basis for selection. Open admission, but selective for some programs. Students must take entrance assessment and receive a minimum score to gain entrance. **Home schooled:** Transcript of courses and grades, state high school equivalency certificate, interview required. **Learning Disabled:** Must submit documentation to the Director of the Academic Center.

2015-2016 Annual costs. Diploma programs: $9,145-$16,815. Associate programs: $26,550-$27,140. Bachelor's programs: $26,550-$57,330.

Financial aid. All financial aid based on need. Work-study available nights, weekends and for part-time students. **Additional information:** Work-study positions available.

Application procedures. Admission: No deadline. $20 fee. **Financial aid:** No deadline. FAFSA required. Applicants notified on a rolling basis.

Academics. Special study options: Accelerated study, cooperative education, distance learning, independent study, internships, liberal arts/career combination. **Credit/placement by examination:** AP, CLEP, institutional tests. 12 credit hours maximum toward associate degree. **Support services:** Learning center, reduced course load, remedial instruction, study skills assistance, tutoring, writing center.

Majors. Business: Accounting, administrative services, business admin, hospitality admin, hospitality/recreation, office management, office technology, office/clerical, tourism promotion, tourism/travel. **Computer sciences:** General, computer science, data processing, programming. **Education:** Early childhood, teacher assistance. **Health services:** Health information management, health information technology, medical assistant, medical secretary, medical transcription. **Protective services:** Criminal justice, law enforcement admin, police science.

Technology on campus. 90 workstations in library, computer center, student center. Helpline, wireless network available.

Student life. Freshman orientation: Mandatory, $20 fee. Preregistration for classes offered. **Activities:** Student newspaper, Phi Beta Lambda, C.O.P.S. (criminal justice), APPEAL paralegal professionals, college student advisors.

Student services. Adult student services, career counseling, student employment services, financial aid counseling, personal counseling, placement for graduates. **Physically disabled:** Services for hearing impaired. **Transfer:** Pre-admission transcript evaluation for new students.

Contact. E-mail: enroll@andovercollege.edu
Phone: (207) 774-6126 Toll-free number: (800) 639-3110
Fax: (207) 774-1715
Kashina Bourque-Micklon, Director of Admissions, Kaplan University: South Portland, 265 Western Avenue, South Portland, ME 04106

Kennebec Valley Community College
Fairfield, Maine
www.kvcc.me.edu

CB code: 3475

- Public 2-year community, liberal arts and technical college
- Commuter campus in small town

General. Founded in 1969. Regionally accredited. **Enrollment:** 1,600 degree-seeking undergraduates. **Degrees:** 303 associate awarded. **Location:** 24 miles from Augusta, 75 miles from Portland. **Calendar:** Semester, limited summer session. **Full-time faculty:** 40 total; 5% have terminal degrees, 5% minority, 65% women. **Part-time faculty:** 117 total; 5% have terminal degrees, 2% minority, 51% women. **Class size:** 71% < 20, 29% 20-39, less than 1% 40-49.

Basis for selection. Open admission, but selective for some programs. Special requirements for nursing and allied health programs. **Adult students:** SAT/ACT scores not required. **Home schooled:** Transcript of courses and grades required.

2015-2016 Annual costs. Tuition/fees: $3,355; $6,055 out-of-state. Per-credit charge: $90 in-state; $180 out-of-state. Books/supplies: $1,098. **Additional information:** Additional lab and technology fees apply to specific programs and courses.

Financial aid. All financial aid based on need. Need-based aid available for part-time students. Work-study available nights, weekends and for part-time students.

Application procedures. Admission: No deadline. $20 fee, may be waived for applicants with need. Admission notification on a rolling basis. Only allied health programs have application deadline. **Financial aid:** Priority date 4/1; no closing date. FAFSA, institutional form required. Applicants notified on a rolling basis starting 5/1.

Academics. Special study options: Cooperative education, cross-registration, distance learning, dual enrollment of high school students, internships, liberal arts/career combination. License preparation in nursing, occupational therapy, paramedic, physical therapy, radiology. **Credit/placement by examination:** AP, CLEP. **Support services:** Learning center, reduced course load, remedial instruction, study skills assistance, tutoring, writing center.

Majors. Biology: General. **Business:** Accounting technology, management information systems, marketing. **Conservation:** Forest technology. **Education:** Teacher assistance. **General:** Electrician. **Health services:** EMT paramedic, health information technology, medical assistant, nursing (RN), occupational therapy assistant, physical therapy assistant, radiologic technology/medical imaging, respiratory therapy technology. **Liberal arts:** Arts/sciences. **Work/family studies:** Child development.

Most popular majors. Business/marketing 16%, health sciences 53%, liberal arts 11%, trade and industry 7%.

Technology on campus. 400 workstations in library, computer center, student center. Commuter students can connect to campus network. Online course registration, online library, helpline, wireless network available.

Student life. Freshman orientation: Mandatory, $30 fee. Preregistration for classes offered. **Activities:** Choral groups, student government.

Athletics. Intramural: Basketball, bowling, cross-country, football (non-tackle), golf, softball, ultimate frisbee, volleyball. **Team name:** Lynx.

Student services. Career counseling, services for economically disadvantaged, student employment services, financial aid counseling, on-campus daycare, personal counseling, placement for graduates. **Transfer:** Transfer center, transfer adviser, college fairs on campus for students transferring to 4-year colleges.

Contact. E-mail: cmckenna@kvcc.me.edu
Phone: (207) 453-5131 Toll-free number: (800) 528-5882
Fax: (207) 453-5010
Jim Bourgoin, Director of Admissions, Kennebec Valley Community College, 92 Western Avenue, Fairfield, ME 04937-1367

Landing School of Boatbuilding and Design
Arundel, Maine
www.landingschool.edu

- Private 2-year career college
- Commuter campus in small town
- Application essay, interview required

General. Regionally accredited; also accredited by ACCSC. **Enrollment:** 73 degree-seeking undergraduates. **Degrees:** 11 associate awarded. **Location:** 20 miles from Portland, 30 miles from Portsmouth, NH. **Calendar:** Semester. **Full-time faculty:** 9 total.

Student profile. Among degree-seeking undergraduates, 73% enrolled in a vocational program.

Basis for selection. Open admission, but selective for some programs.

2016-2017 Annual costs. Tuition/fees (projected): $22,296. Books/supplies: $2,300. Personal expenses: $2,000. **Additional information:** Program fees vary by program.

2014-2015 Financial aid. All financial aid based on need. 11 full-time freshmen applied for aid; 11 deemed to have need; 11 received aid. Average

scholarship/grant was $4,151; average loan $8,428. 40% of total undergraduate aid awarded as scholarships/grants, 60% as loans/jobs. Work-study available nights, weekends and for part-time students.

Application procedures. Admission: No deadline. No application fee. Admission notification on a rolling basis. **Financial aid:** Priority date 4/1; no closing date. FAFSA required. Applicants notified on a rolling basis starting 3/1; must reply within 3 week(s) of notification.

Academics. Credit/placement by examination: AP, CLEP. **Support services:** Learning center, tutoring.

Technology on campus. 8 workstations in library. Wireless network available.

Contact. E-mail: info@landingschool.edu
Phone: (207) 985-7976
Wendy West, Admissions Representative, Landing School of Boatbuilding and Design, 286 River Road, Arundel, ME 04046

Maine College of Health Professions
Lewiston, Maine   CB member
www.mchp.edu   CB code: 3302

- Private 2-year health science and nursing college
- Commuter campus in large town
- SAT or ACT (ACT writing optional), application essay required

General. Founded in 1891. Regionally accredited. **Enrollment:** 184 degree-seeking undergraduates; 15 non-degree-seeking students. **Degrees:** 64 associate awarded. **Location:** 35 miles from Portland. **Calendar:** Semester, limited summer session. **Full-time faculty:** 18 total; 6% have terminal degrees, 94% women. **Part-time faculty:** 8 total; 75% women.

Student profile. Among degree-seeking undergraduates, 12% already have a bachelor's degree or higher, 3 enrolled as first-time, first-year students.

Part-time:	68%	Native American:	1%
Out-of-state:	2%	Native Hawaiian/Pacific islander:	1%
Women:	89%	25 or older:	58%
Asian American:	2%	Live on campus:	4%
Hispanic/Latino:	1%		

Basis for selection. Test scores required. Essay, academic ability very important. SAT or ACT may be waived if applicant has completed 12 academic college credits with minimum grade of 2.0. **Home schooled:** High school diploma or GED required.

High school preparation. College-preparatory program recommended. Required units include mathematics 2 and science 2.

2015-2016 Annual costs. Tuition/fees: $10,900. Per-credit charge: $266. Room only: $1,900. Books/supplies: $1,200.

2015-2016 Financial aid. All financial aid based on need. 26% of total undergraduate aid awarded as scholarships/grants, 74% as loans/jobs. Need-based aid available for part-time students. Work-study available nights, weekends and for part-time students.

Application procedures. Admission: Closing date 1/15 (receipt date). $50 fee, may be waived for applicants with need. Application must be submitted on paper. Admission notification by 3/15. Must reply by 4/1. **Financial aid:** No deadline. FAFSA required. Applicants notified on a rolling basis starting 4/1; must reply within 2 week(s) of notification.

Academics. Special study options: Distance learning, internships. License preparation in nursing, radiology. **Credit/placement by examination:** AP, CLEP. 15 credit hours maximum toward associate degree. **Support services:** Learning center, remedial instruction, study skills assistance, tutoring.

Majors. Health services: Nuclear medical technology, nursing (RN), radiologic technology/medical imaging.

Technology on campus. PC or laptop required. 20 workstations in computer center. Commuter students can connect to campus network. Wireless network available.

Student life. Freshman orientation: Mandatory. Preregistration for classes offered. One-day program held in June. **Policies:** Entire campus is smoke-free; zero tolerance for alcohol, drugs, weapons. **Housing:** Coed dorms, wellness housing available. Single rooms available at extra cost. **Activities:** Student government.

Student services. Financial aid counseling, health services, personal counseling, veterans' counselor. **Transfer:** Pre-admission transcript evaluation for new students.

Contact. E-mail: watsoner@cmhc.org
Phone: (207) 795-2843 Fax: (207) 795-2849
Erica Watson, Director of Admissions, Maine College of Health Professions, 70 Middle Street, Lewiston, ME 04240

Northern Maine Community College
Presque Isle, Maine
www.nmcc.edu   CB code: 3631

♦ Public 2-year community and technical college
♦ Commuter campus in small town
♦ Application essay, interview required

General. Founded in 1961. Regionally accredited. **Enrollment:** 626 degree-seeking undergraduates; 305 non-degree-seeking students. **Degrees:** 200 associate awarded. **Location:** 165 miles from Bangor. **Calendar:** Semester, limited summer session. **Full-time faculty:** 47 total. **Part-time faculty:** 44 total.

Student profile. Among degree-seeking undergraduates, 15% enrolled in a transfer program, 85% enrolled in a vocational program, 120 enrolled as first-time, first-year students.

Part-time:	36%	Live on campus:	19%
Women:	54%		

Transfer out. 5% of students enrolled in the transfer program go on to 4-year colleges.

Basis for selection. School achievement record and test scores important.

High school preparation. Required units include English 4 and mathematics 2.

2015-2016 Annual costs. Tuition/fees: $3,398; $6,098 out-of-state. Per-credit charge: $90 in-state; $180 out-of-state. Room/board: $7,106. Books/supplies: $1,400. Personal expenses: $1,200. **Additional information:** Additional lab and technology fees may apply to specific programs and courses.

2015-2016 Financial aid. **Need-based:** 98 full-time freshmen applied for aid; 90 deemed to have need; 90 received aid. Average need met was 50%. Average scholarship/grant was $6,270; average loan $3,006. 60% of total undergraduate aid awarded as scholarships/grants, 40% as loans/jobs. Need-based aid available for part-time students. Work-study available nights, weekends and for part-time students. **Non-need-based:** Awarded to 22 full-time undergraduates, including 11 freshmen.

Application procedures. **Admission:** No deadline. $20 fee, may be waived for applicants with need. Admission notification on a rolling basis. **Financial aid:** Priority date 5/1; no closing date. FAFSA, institutional form required. Applicants notified on a rolling basis starting 4/15; must reply within 2 week(s) of notification.

Academics. **Special study options:** Cross-registration, double major, internships, liberal arts/career combination. **Credit/placement by examination:** AP, CLEP. 15 credit hours maximum toward associate degree. **Support services:** Learning center, pre-admission summer program, reduced course load, remedial instruction, tutoring.

Majors. **Business:** Accounting, administrative services, business admin, management information systems, office management, office technology, operations. **Computer sciences:** Applications programming, data processing, programming. **Education:** Early childhood. **General:** Carpentry, electrician, pipefitting, power transmission. **Health services:** Health information technology, medical secretary, nursing (RN).

Technology on campus. Commuter students can connect to campus network.

Student life. **Freshman orientation:** Mandatory, $35 fee. Preregistration for classes offered. Held both in fall and spring semester. **Housing:** Coed dorms, apartments available. $25 deposit. **Activities:** Student government, student newspaper.

Athletics. **Intercollegiate:** Basketball M, golf, ice hockey, soccer. **Intramural:** Archery, badminton, baseball M, basketball M, racquetball, softball, table tennis, tennis, volleyball. **Team name:** Falcons.

Student services. Adult student services, alcohol/substance abuse counseling, career counseling, student employment services, financial aid counseling, health services, personal counseling, placement for graduates, veterans'

counselor. **Transfer:** Transfer adviser for students transferring to 4-year colleges.

Contact. E-mail: nemcclus@nmcc.edu
Phone: (207) 768-2785 Toll-free number: (800) 535-6682
Fax: (207) 768-2848
Eugene McCluskey, Director of Admissions, Northern Maine Community College, 33 Edgemont Drive, Presque Isle, ME 04769

Southern Maine Community College
South Portland, Maine   CB member
www.smccme.edu   CB code: 3535

♦ Public 2-year community and technical college
♦ Commuter campus in large town

General. Founded in 1946. Regionally accredited. **Enrollment:** 5,233 degree-seeking undergraduates; 812 non-degree-seeking students. **Degrees:** 815 associate awarded. **Location:** 3 miles from Portland, 120 miles from Boston. **Calendar:** Semester, extensive summer session. **Full-time faculty:** 109 total. **Part-time faculty:** 368 total. **Special facilities:** Spring Point Ledge Light House and Willard Beach are accessible from the campus.

Student profile. Among degree-seeking undergraduates, 1,251 enrolled as first-time, first-year students, 633 transferred in from other institutions.

Part-time:	50%	Hispanic/Latino:	3%
Women:	51%	Native American:	1%
African American:	7%	Multi-racial, non-Hispanic:	2%
Asian American:	2%	Live on campus:	5%

Basis for selection. Open admission, but selective for some programs. Additional requirements for admission into allied health science programs. Must have prerequisites completed prior to being accepted into the programs.

High school preparation. College-preparatory program recommended. Recommended units include English 4, mathematics 3, science 1 (laboratory 1).

2015-2016 Annual costs. Tuition/fees: $3,485; $6,185 out-of-state. Per-credit charge: $90 in-state; $180 out-of-state. Room/board: $8,688. Books/supplies: $1,400. Personal expenses: $1,972.

2014-2015 Financial aid. All financial aid based on need. 44% of total undergraduate aid awarded as scholarships/grants, 56% as loans/jobs. Need-based aid available for part-time students. Work-study available nights, weekends and for part-time students.

Application procedures. **Admission:** Priority date 7/15; no deadline. $20 fee, may be waived for applicants with need. Admission notification on a rolling basis. Must reply by May 1 or within 4 week(s) if notified thereafter. **Financial aid:** Priority date 5/1; no closing date. FAFSA required. Applicants notified on a rolling basis.

Academics. **Special study options:** Cross-registration, distance learning, double major, dual enrollment of high school students, honors, independent study, internships, liberal arts/career combination. License preparation in nursing, paramedic, radiology. **Credit/placement by examination:** AP, CLEP, institutional tests. **Support services:** Learning center, reduced course load, remedial instruction, study skills assistance, tutoring, writing center.

Majors. **Biology:** Biotechnology, marine. **Business:** Business admin, hospitality admin. **Communications:** Digital media. **Computer sciences:** Computer science, security, system admin. **Education:** Early childhood. **Engineering:** General, materials. **General:** Building construction, plumbing. **Health services:** Cardiovascular technology, dietetic technician, EMT paramedic, health information technology, medical assistant, medical radiologic technology/radiation therapy, nursing (RN), radiologic technology/medical imaging, respiratory therapy technology, surgical technology. **Protective services:** Criminal justice, firefighting.

Most popular majors. Business/marketing 12%, health sciences 23%, liberal arts 22%, security/protective services 8%, trade and industry 7%.

Technology on campus. 400 workstations in library, computer center, student center. Dormitories wired for high-speed internet access and linked to campus network. Commuter students can connect to campus network. Online course registration, online library, helpline, wireless network available.

Student life. **Freshman orientation:** Mandatory. Preregistration for classes offered. **Housing:** Coed dorms, single-sex dorms available. $250 fully refundable deposit. **Activities:** Choral groups, drama, international student organizations, literary magazine, student government, student newspaper.

Athletics. USCAA. **Intercollegiate:** Baseball M, basketball, golf, soccer, softball W. **Intramural:** Basketball, ice hockey M, soccer, volleyball. **Team name:** Seawolves.

Student services. Career counseling, student employment services, financial aid counseling, on-campus daycare, personal counseling, placement for graduates, veterans' counselor. **Physically disabled:** Services for visually, speech, hearing impaired. **Transfer:** Pre-admission transcript evaluation for new students. Transfer center, transfer adviser, college fairs on campus for students transferring to 4-year colleges.

Contact. E-mail: admissions@smccME.edu
Phone: (207) 741-5800 Toll-free number: (877) 282-2182
Fax: (207) 741-5760
Amy Lee, Director of Admissions, Southern Maine Community College, 2 Fort Road, South Portland, ME 04106

Washington County Community College
Calais, Maine
www.wccc.me.edu   CB code: 3961

▶ Public 2-year community and technical college
▶ Commuter campus in small town

General. Founded in 1969. Regionally accredited. **Enrollment:** 332 degree-seeking undergraduates. **Degrees:** 61 associate awarded. **Location:** 98 miles from Bangor, 75 miles from St. John, Canada. **Calendar:** Semester, limited summer session. **Full-time faculty:** 22 total. **Part-time faculty:** 19 total.

Student profile.

Out-of-state:	2%	Live on campus:	20%
25 or older:	41%		

Transfer out. Colleges most students transferred to 2015: University of Maine at Machias, University of Maine at Augusta, Husson College.

Basis for selection. Open admission, but selective for some programs. Algebra I required or placement in the equivalent of MAT106 on ACCUPLACER exam for Residential and Commercial Electricity program. **Home schooled:** Applicants required to take GED exam or equivalent.

High school preparation. 20 units recommended. Recommended units include English 4, mathematics 2, social studies 1, history 2 and science 2. Program-specific requirements apply in some areas.

2015-2016 Annual costs. Tuition/fees: $3,380; $6,080 out-of-state. Per-credit charge: $90 in-state; $180 out-of-state. Room/board: $5,340. Books/supplies: $1,900. Personal expenses: $1,669.

Financial aid. Need-based: Need-based aid available for part-time students. Work-study available nights, weekends and for part-time students. **Non-need-based:** Scholarships awarded for academics.

Application procedures. Admission: Closing date 8/29 (receipt date). $20 fee, may be waived for applicants with need. Admission notification on a rolling basis. **Financial aid:** Priority date 4/1, closing date 5/1. FAFSA, institutional form required. Applicants notified on a rolling basis starting 5/1; must reply within 2 week(s) of notification.

Academics. Special study options: Cooperative education, distance learning, double major, dual enrollment of high school students, independent study, liberal arts/career combination. Offer license preparation program in heating and plumbing. **Credit/placement by examination:** AP, CLEP, IB. **Support services:** GED preparation and test center, learning center, reduced course load, remedial instruction, study skills assistance, tutoring, writing center.

Majors. Business: Business admin, small business admin. **Education:** Early childhood. **Health services:** Medical assistant. **Liberal arts:** Arts/sciences. **Social sciences:** General.

Technology on campus. 117 workstations in dormitories, library, computer center, student center. Dormitories wired for high-speed internet access and linked to campus network. Helpline, wireless network available.

Student life. Freshman orientation: Mandatory. Preregistration for classes offered. **Policies:** Drug/alcohol/tobacco free apartments. **Housing:** Guaranteed on-campus for all undergraduates. Special housing for disabled, apartments available. $150 fully refundable deposit. **Activities:** Drama, student government, student senate, Skills USA, Phi Theta Kappa.

Athletics. Intercollegiate: Wrestling. **Intramural:** Baseball M, basketball, golf, rifle, skiing, soccer, volleyball, wrestling. **Team name:** Polar Bears.

Student services. Adult student services, alcohol/substance abuse counseling, career counseling, services for economically disadvantaged, student employment services, financial aid counseling, on-campus daycare, personal counseling, placement for graduates, veterans' counselor. **Physically disabled:** Services for visually, speech, hearing impaired. **Transfer:** Pre-admission transcript evaluation for new students. College fairs on campus for students transferring to 4-year colleges.

Contact. E-mail: admissions@wccc.me.edu
Phone: (207) 454-1000 Toll-free number: (800) 210-6932
Fax: (207) 454-1092
Susan Mingo, Dean for Enrollment Management and Student Services, Washington County Community College, One College Drive, Calais, ME 04619

York County Community College
Wells, Maine   CB member
www.yccc.edu   CB code: 3990

▶ Public 2-year community and technical college
▶ Commuter campus in small town

General. Regionally accredited. **Enrollment:** 1,391 degree-seeking undergraduates; 367 non-degree-seeking students. **Degrees:** 198 associate awarded. **Location:** 30 miles from Portland, 75 miles from Boston, MA. **Calendar:** Semester, extensive summer session. **Full-time faculty:** 25 total; 24% have terminal degrees, 44% women. **Part-time faculty:** 127 total; 9% have terminal degrees, 58% women. **Class size:** 84% < 20, 16% 20-39. **Partnerships:** Formal partnerships with Portsmouth Naval Shipyard, Hussey Seating.

Student profile. Among degree-seeking undergraduates, 210 enrolled as first-time, first-year students, 251 transferred in from other institutions.

Part-time:	67%	Hispanic/Latino:	3%
Out-of-state:	2%	Native American:	1%
Women:	67%	Multi-racial, non-Hispanic:	3%
African American:	1%	25 or older:	38%
Asian American:	2%		

Transfer out. Colleges most students transferred to 2015: University of Southern Maine, University of New England, Southern New Hampshire University, Husson University, Southern Maine Community College.

Basis for selection. Open admission. **Home schooled:** Statement describing home school structure and mission, transcript of courses and grades, state high school equivalency certificate required.

2015-2016 Annual costs. Tuition/fees: $3,330; $6,030 out-of-state. Per-credit charge: $90 in-state; $180 out-of-state. Books/supplies: $1,350. Personal expenses: $3,230. **Additional information:** Additional lab and technology fees may apply to specific programs and courses.

2014-2015 Financial aid. Need-based: 78 full-time freshmen applied for aid; 61 deemed to have need; 58 received aid. Average need met was 44%. Average scholarship/grant was $5,129; average loan $2,590. 70% of total undergraduate aid awarded as scholarships/grants, 30% as loans/jobs. Need-based aid available for part-time students. Work-study available nights, weekends and for part-time students. **Non-need-based:** Awarded to 15 full-time undergraduates, including 9 freshmen. Scholarships awarded for academics, alumni affiliation, art, job skills, leadership, state residency.

Application procedures. Admission: No deadline. $20 fee, may be waived for applicants with need. Admission notification on a rolling basis. **Financial aid:** Priority date 5/1; no closing date. FAFSA required. Must reply within 2 week(s) of notification.

Academics. Special study options: Cross-registration, distance learning, dual enrollment of high school students, independent study, internships, liberal arts/career combination. License preparation in nursing. **Credit/placement by examination:** AP, CLEP, institutional tests. 45 credit hours maximum toward associate degree. **Support services:** Learning center, pre-admission summer program, remedial instruction, study skills assistance, tutoring, writing center. Pre-admission summer program is a Summer Academy for Math and English remediation.

Majors. Business: Accounting, business admin. **Communications technology:** Animation/special effects. **Computer sciences:** Computer science, system admin. **Education:** General, early childhood. **Health services:** Health information technology, medical assistant, veterinary technology/assistant. **Liberal arts:** Arts/sciences. **Protective services:** Criminal justice.

Most popular majors. Business/marketing 13%, communication technologies 9%, computer/information sciences 7%, health sciences 16%, liberal arts 19%, personal/culinary services 6%, public administration/social services 9%, security/protective services 8%.

Technology on campus. 160 workstations in library, computer center, student center. Commuter students can connect to campus network. Online course registration, online library, helpline, wireless network available.

Student life. **Freshman orientation:** Available. Preregistration for classes offered. **Activities:** Student government.

Athletics. Intramural: Basketball, ice hockey, soccer, volleyball. **Team name:** Coyotes.

Student services. Adult student services, career counseling, services for economically disadvantaged, student employment services, financial aid counseling, personal counseling, veterans' counselor. **Physically disabled:** Services for visually, speech, hearing impaired. **Transfer:** Pre-admission transcript evaluation for new students. Transfer center, transfer adviser, college fairs on campus for students transferring to 4-year colleges.

Contact. E-mail: admissions@yccc.edu
Phone: (207) 216-4409 Toll-free number: (800) 580-3820
Fax: (207) 641-0837
Fred Quistgard, Director of Admissions, York County Community College, 112 College Drive, Wells, ME 04090

Maryland

Allegany College of Maryland
Cumberland, Maryland
www.allegany.edu

CB code: 5028

- Public 2-year community college
- Commuter campus in large town

General. Founded in 1961. Regionally accredited. **Enrollment:** 2,461 degree-seeking undergraduates. **Degrees:** 532 associate awarded. **ROTC:** Army. **Location:** 150 miles from Baltimore; 150 miles from Washington, DC. **Calendar:** Semester, limited summer session. **Full-time faculty:** 108 total. **Part-time faculty:** 199 total. **Class size:** 74% < 20, 24% 20-39, 1% 40-49, less than 1% 50-99, less than 1% >100. **Special facilities:** Greenhouse, arboretum, wetlands, Appalachian room, labyrinth, serenity garden.

Student profile.

Out-of-state:	47%	Live on campus:	7%
25 or older:	33%		

Transfer out. Colleges most students transferred to 2015: Frostburg State University, Shippensburg University, University of Pittsburgh at Johnstown.

Basis for selection. Open admission, but selective for some programs. Admission to allied health programs based on high school records, course performance, test scores.

2015-2016 Annual costs. Tuition/fees: $3,665; $6,665 out-of-district; $7,955 out-of-state. Per-credit charge: $114 in-district; $214 out-of-district; $257 out-of-state. Books/supplies: $1,400. Personal expenses: $2,041.

Financial aid. Need-based: Need-based aid available for part-time students. Work-study available nights, weekends and for part-time students. **Non-need-based:** Scholarships awarded for academics, athletics, leadership, state residency.

Application procedures. Admission: No deadline. No application fee. Admission notification on a rolling basis. High school and/or college transcript and placement tests in English, reading, and mathematics required. **Financial aid:** Priority date 3/1; no closing date. FAFSA, institutional form required. Applicants notified on a rolling basis starting 4/15; must reply within 2 week(s) of notification.

Academics. Special study options: Accelerated study, distance learning, double major, dual enrollment of high school students, ESL, honors, independent study, internships, liberal arts/career combination. License preparation in dental hygiene, nursing, occupational therapy, physical therapy, radiology, real estate. **Credit/placement by examination:** AP, CLEP, institutional tests. 30 credit hours maximum toward associate degree. **Support services:** Learning center, reduced course load, remedial instruction, study skills assistance, tutoring.

Majors. Biology: General. **Business:** General, accounting, accounting technology, administrative services, business admin, hospitality admin, hospitality/recreation, management information systems, managerial economics, marketing. **Communications:** Communications/speech/rhetoric. **Communications technology:** General. **Computer sciences:** General, computer science, information systems. **Conservation:** Forest management. **Education:** Early childhood, elementary, health, physical, secondary. **Engineering:** General. **English:** English lit. **Foreign languages:** Spanish. **Health services:** Clinical lab technology, dental hygiene, massage therapy, medical assistant, medical radiologic technology/radiation therapy, medical secretary, medical transcription, mental health services, nursing (RN), occupational therapy assistant, physical therapy assistant, prepharmacy, respiratory therapy technology. **History:** General. **Human services:** Social work. **Liberal arts:** Arts/sciences. **Math:** General. **Parks/recreation:** Facilities management. **Physical sciences:** Chemistry, physics. **Protective services:** Police science. **Psychology:** General. **Social sciences:** General, economics, political science, sociology. **Visual/performing arts:** Art.

Most popular majors. Business/marketing 14%, health sciences 45%, liberal arts 23%.

Technology on campus. 450 workstations in library, computer center. Online course registration, online library, student web hosting, wireless network available.

Student life. Freshman orientation: Available, $4 fee. Preregistration for classes offered. **Housing:** Apartments, wellness housing available. $300 partly refundable deposit, deadline 8/26. **Activities:** Choral groups, dance, literary magazine, student government, forestry club, Older and Wiser club, Phi Theta Kappa-Honors Society, Christian Fellowship, chess club, respiratory therapy club, dental hygiene club, medical laboratory technology club.

Athletics. NJCAA. **Intercollegiate:** Baseball M, basketball, golf M, soccer M, softball W, volleyball W. **Team name:** Trojans.

Student services. Career counseling, student employment services, financial aid counseling, on-campus daycare, personal counseling, placement for graduates, veterans' counselor, women's services. **Physically disabled:** Services for visually, speech, hearing impaired. **Transfer:** Pre-admission transcript evaluation for new students. Transfer adviser, college fairs on campus for students transferring to 4-year colleges.

Contact. E-mail: cnolan@allegany.edu
Phone: (301) 784-5199 Fax: (301) 784-5027
Cathy Nolan, Director of Admissions and Registration, Allegany College of Maryland, 12401 Willowbrook Road, SE, Cumberland, MD 21502

Anne Arundel Community College
Arnold, Maryland
www.aacc.edu

CB member
CB code: 5019

- Public 2-year community college
- Commuter campus in large town

General. Founded in 1964. Regionally accredited. 3 off-campus academic/student services centers: Fort Meade Army Education Center, Glen Burnie Town Center and Arundel Mills. Hospitality, Culinary Arts and Tourism Institute, Entrepreneurial Studies Institute. **Enrollment:** 12,601 degree-seeking undergraduates; 2,088 non-degree-seeking students. **Degrees:** 1,852 associate awarded. **ROTC:** Army, Air Force. **Location:** 20 miles from Baltimore, 8 miles from Annapolis. **Calendar:** Semester, limited summer session. **Class size:** 57% < 20, 41% 20-39, 2% 40-49, less than 1% 50-99. **Special facilities:** Off-campus workforce center at Baltimore-Washington international airport, environmental center, astronomy laboratory, center for performing arts, fine arts academic center, allied health/public services center, technology center, STEM center and cyber center.

Student profile. Among degree-seeking undergraduates, 2,361 enrolled as first-time, first-year students.

Part-time:	66%	Hispanic/Latino:	7%
Out-of-state:	1%	Multi-racial, non-Hispanic:	4%
Women:	59%	International:	1%
African American:	18%	25 or older:	35%
Asian American:	4%		

Transfer out. Colleges most students transferred to 2015: University of Maryland-Baltimore County, Towson University, University of Maryland-College Park, Salisbury University, University of Maryland University College.

Basis for selection. Open admission, but selective for some programs. Special requirements for certain allied health programs. International students must provide certification of finances. Interview recommended for applicants to nursing, human services, radiologic technology, physician's assistant programs, EMT, physical therapy assistant.

2015-2016 Annual costs. Tuition/fees: $3,920; $6,830 out-of-district; $11,480 out-of-state. Per-credit charge: $105 in-district; $202 out-of-district; $357 out-of-state. Books/supplies: $1,581. Personal expenses: $1,966.

2014-2015 Financial aid. Need-based: 71% of total undergraduate aid awarded as scholarships/grants, 29% as loans/jobs. Need-based aid available for part-time students. Work-study available nights, weekends and for part-time students.

Application procedures. Admission: No deadline. No application fee. Admission notification on a rolling basis. **Financial aid:** Priority date 5/15; no closing date. FAFSA, institutional form required. Applicants notified on a rolling basis starting 7/1; must reply within 2 week(s) of notification.

Academics. Special study options: Distance learning, dual enrollment of high school students, ESL, honors, independent study, internships, teacher certification program, weekend college. License preparation in nursing, paramedic, radiology, real estate. **Credit/placement by examination:** AP, CLEP, IB, institutional tests. 15 credit hours maximum toward associate degree. **Support services:** GED preparation, learning center, pre-admission summer program, reduced course load, remedial instruction, study skills assistance, tutoring, writing center.

Majors. Business: General, accounting technology, entrepreneurial studies, hotel/motel admin, management information systems. **Computer sciences:** General, networking, security. **Education:** Chemistry, early childhood, English, mathematics, physics, Spanish. **Engineering:** General, electrical, robotics. **Health services:** Clinical lab technology, health information technology, medical assistant, medical radiologic technology/radiation therapy, medical secretary, mental health services, nursing (RN), physical therapy assistant, substance abuse counseling, surgical technology. **Liberal arts:** Arts/sciences. **Math:** General. **Parks/recreation:** Health/fitness. **Protective services:** Fire safety technology, law enforcement admin, police science. **Visual/performing arts:** Graphic design. **Work/family studies:** Child care management.

Most popular majors. Business/marketing 18%, computer/information sciences 7%, health sciences 13%, liberal arts 49%.

Technology on campus. 2,008 workstations in library, computer center, student center. Commuter students can connect to campus network. Online library, helpline, wireless network available.

Student life. Freshman orientation: Mandatory. Preregistration for classes offered. One day program. **Activities:** Bands, campus ministries, choral groups, dance, drama, international student organizations, literary magazine, music ensembles, musical theater, opera, student government, student newspaper, symphony orchestra, TV station, American Sign Language Club, Center for Study of Local Issues, Human Services Club, Japanese Language Club, Spanish Club, Apostolic Campus Ministries, Arabic Club, Baptist Campus Ministries, Black Student Union, Gay/Straight Alliance.

Athletics. NJCAA. **Intercollegiate:** Baseball M, basketball, cross-country W, golf M, lacrosse, soccer, softball W, volleyball W. **Intramural:** Weight lifting. **Team name:** Riverhawks.

Student services. Adult student services, alcohol/substance abuse counseling, career counseling, services for economically disadvantaged, student employment services, financial aid counseling, health services, minority student services, on-campus daycare, personal counseling, placement for graduates, veterans' counselor. **Physically disabled:** Services for visually, speech, hearing impaired. **Transfer:** Transfer center, transfer adviser, college fairs on campus for students transferring to 4-year colleges.

Contact. E-mail: admissions@aacc.edu
Phone: (410) 777-2831 Fax: (410) 777-2018
Thomas McGinn, Director of Enrollment Development and Admissions, Anne Arundel Community College, 101 College Parkway, Arnold, MD 21012-1895

Baltimore City Community College
Baltimore, Maryland
www.bccc.edu   **CB code: 5051**

▶ Public 2-year community college
▶ Commuter campus in very large city

General. Founded in 1947. Regionally accredited. Numerous sites throughout Baltimore. **Enrollment:** 4,857 degree-seeking undergraduates. **Degrees:** 440 associate awarded. **Location:** 50 miles from Washington, DC; 75 miles from Philadelphia. **Calendar:** Semester, extensive summer session. **Full-time faculty:** 117 total. **Part-time faculty:** 331 total. **Special facilities:** Greenhouse, planetarium.

Student profile.

Out-of-state:	1%	25 or older:	58%

Transfer out. Colleges most students transferred to 2015: Coppin State University, Morgan State University, University of Baltimore, Towson University, University of Maryland Baltimore County.

Basis for selection. Open admission, but selective for some programs. Special requirements for nursing and allied health programs. SAT/ACT may be used in place of reading, math, and English proficiency tests required of all first-time students. Interview recommended for applicants to allied health, paralegal, emergency medical services programs. Portfolio recommended for art, fashion design majors.

2015-2016 Annual costs. Tuition/fees: $3,062; $7,172 out-of-state. Per-credit charge: $88 in-state; $225 out-of-state. Books/supplies: $700.

Financial aid. All financial aid based on need. Need-based aid available for part-time students. Work-study available nights, weekends and for part-time students.

Application procedures. Admission: Closing date 8/27. $10 fee, may be waived for applicants with need. Admission notification on a rolling basis.

Financial aid: Priority date 6/1; no closing date. FAFSA, institutional form required. Applicants notified on a rolling basis starting 7/1; must reply within 2 week(s) of notification.

Academics. Adults without diploma or GED become eligible for degree programs after successfully completing 15 college-level credits. **Special study options:** Cooperative education, distance learning, double major, dual enrollment of high school students, ESL, honors, independent study, internships, liberal arts/career combination, study abroad, teacher certification program, weekend college. License preparation in dental hygiene, nursing, paramedic, physical therapy. **Credit/placement by examination:** AP, CLEP, IB, institutional tests. 15 credit hours maximum toward associate degree. **Support services:** GED preparation, learning center, pre-admission summer program, reduced course load, remedial instruction, study skills assistance, tutoring, writing center.

Majors. Biology: Biotechnology. **Business:** General, accounting, administrative services, business admin, fashion, hospitality admin, management information systems, marketing, office management, office technology. **Computer sciences:** General, computer graphics, computer science, information systems, systems analysis. **Education:** General, early childhood, multi-level teacher. **Engineering:** General. **Health services:** Dental hygiene, EMT paramedic, health care admin, health information management, health information technology, licensed practical nurse, medical secretary, nursing (RN), physical therapy assistant, respiratory therapy technology. **Human services:** Social work. **Liberal arts:** Arts/sciences. **Protective services:** Corrections, law enforcement admin, police science. **Visual/performing arts:** Art, fashion design, music. **Work/family studies:** Clothing/textiles.

Most popular majors. Business/marketing 22%, health sciences 32%, liberal arts 27%.

Technology on campus. 926 workstations in library, computer center, student center. Online library, wireless network available.

Student life. Freshman orientation: Mandatory. Preregistration for classes offered. **Activities:** Choral groups, drama, international student organizations, musical theater, radio station, student government, student newspaper, fashion club, human services club, media club, civic organizations, computer club.

Athletics. NJCAA. **Intercollegiate:** Baseball M, basketball, volleyball W. **Team name:** Panthers.

Student services. Career counseling, student employment services, financial aid counseling, health services, on-campus daycare, personal counseling, placement for graduates, veterans' counselor. **Physically disabled:** Services for visually, speech, hearing impaired. **Transfer:** Pre-admission transcript evaluation for new students. Transfer adviser, college fairs on campus for students transferring to 4-year colleges.

Contact. E-mail: admissions@bccc.edu
Phone: (410) 462-8300 Toll-free number: (888) 203-1261
Fax: (410) 462-8345
Deneen Dangerfield, Director of Admissions, Baltimore City Community College, 2901 Liberty Heights Avenue, Baltimore, MD 21215-7893

Carroll Community College
Westminster, Maryland
www.carrollcc.edu   **CB code: 5797**

▶ Public 2-year community college
▶ Commuter campus in large town

General. Founded in 1993. Regionally accredited. **Enrollment:** 3,154 degree-seeking undergraduates; 395 non-degree-seeking students. **Degrees:** 622 associate awarded. **Location:** 30 miles from Baltimore. **Calendar:** Semester, extensive summer session. **Full-time faculty:** 79 total; 20% have terminal degrees, 5% minority, 73% women. **Part-time faculty:** 184 total; 9% minority, 63% women. **Class size:** 55% < 20, 43% 20-39, 1% 40-49. **Special facilities:** Theater, amphitheater.

Student profile. Among degree-seeking undergraduates, 82% enrolled in a transfer program, 18% enrolled in a vocational program, 5% already have a bachelor's degree or higher, 737 enrolled as first-time, first-year students, 203 transferred in from other institutions.

Part-time:	60%	Asian American:	2%
Out-of-state:	3%	Hispanic/Latino:	4%
Women:	61%	Multi-racial, non-Hispanic:	2%
African American:	4%	25 or older:	27%

Transfer out. Colleges most students transferred to 2015: Towson University, McDaniel College, University of Maryland College Park, University of Maryland Baltimore County, Stevenson University.

Basis for selection. Open admission, but selective for some programs. Selective admission programs; Register Nursing, Physical Therapy Assistant, and Emergency Medical Services - Paramedic (intended to serve firefighters).

2015-2016 Annual costs. Tuition/fees: $4,596; $6,684 out-of-district; $9,312 out-of-state. Per-credit charge: $153 in-district; $223 out-of-district; $310 out-of-state. Books/supplies: $1,500. Personal expenses: $1,000.

2014-2015 Financial aid. Need-based: 57% of total undergraduate aid awarded as scholarships/grants, 43% as loans/jobs. Need-based aid available for part-time students. Work-study available nights, weekends and for part-time students. **Non-need-based:** Scholarships awarded for academics, art, job skills, leadership, state residency.

Application procedures. Admission: No deadline. No application fee. Admission notification on a rolling basis. **Financial aid:** Priority date 3/1; no closing date. FAFSA required. Must reply within 2 week(s) of notification.

Academics. Special study options: Distance learning, dual enrollment of high school students, ESL, honors, independent study, teacher certification program. Associate of Arts in Teaching (AAT) provides a seamless transer to Maryland state and private colleges to complete the Teacher certificate program. License preparation in nursing, paramedic, physical therapy. **Credit/placement by examination:** AP, CLEP, institutional tests. 30 credit hours maximum toward associate degree. **Support services:** GED preparation and test center, learning center, remedial instruction, study skills assistance, tutoring, writing center.

Honors college/program. The Hill Scholars Program is a selective admission, honors cohort program. Highly motivated students who are within the top 15% of their class, have a GPA over 3.20, SAT scores of 550+ are invited to apply to this cohort program which includes honors courses and seminars. This program consists of 20-24 students per year.

Majors. Business: General, accounting technology, international, management information systems. **Computer sciences:** Computer graphics. **Education:** General, chemistry, early childhood, elementary, English, mathematics, secondary, Spanish. **Engineering:** Computer, electrical. **Health services:** EMT ambulance attendant, health information technology, nuclear medical technology, nursing (RN), physical therapy assistant, prenursing, radiologic technology/medical imaging, respiratory therapy technology, sonography, surgical technology. **Liberal arts:** Arts/sciences. **Parks/recreation:** Exercise sciences. **Protective services:** Forensics, police science. **Psychology:** General. **Visual/performing arts:** Music, studio arts, theater design. **Work/family studies:** Child care management.

Most popular majors. Business/marketing 9%, education 6%, health sciences 18%, liberal arts 59%.

Technology on campus. 684 workstations in library, computer center, student center. Commuter students can connect to campus network. Online library, helpline, wireless network available.

Student life. Freshman orientation: Available. Preregistration for classes offered. Held prior to start of semester; all new students expected to attend. **Policies:** Smoke free campus. **Activities:** Jazz band, choral groups, drama, literary magazine, music ensembles, musical theater, student government, symphony orchestra, animal science, art, chess, Cru, drama, gaming, Leadership Challenge, campus activities board, Green Team, multicultural, veteran's clubs.

Athletics. Intramural: Basketball, soccer, volleyball.

Student services. Career counseling, student employment services, financial aid counseling, on-campus daycare. **Physically disabled:** Services for visually, speech, hearing impaired. **Transfer:** Re-entry adviser, pre-admission transcript evaluation for new students. Transfer center, transfer adviser, college fairs on campus for students transferring to 4-year colleges.

Contact. E-mail: admissions@carrollcc.edu
Phone: (410) 386-8430 Toll-free number: (888) 221-9748
Fax: (410) 386-8446
Candace Edwards, Coordinator of Admissions, Carroll Community College, 1601 Washington Road, Westminster, MD 21157

Cecil College
North East, Maryland
www.my.cecil.edu   CB code: 5091

◗ Public 2-year community college
◗ Commuter campus in large town

General. Founded in 1968. Regionally accredited. **Enrollment:** 2,402 degree-seeking undergraduates. **Degrees:** 324 associate awarded. **Location:**

50 miles from Baltimore, 50 miles from Philadelphia. **Calendar:** Semester, limited summer session. **Full-time faculty:** 52 total; 31% have terminal degrees, 6% minority, 62% women. **Part-time faculty:** 221 total; 7% minority. **Class size:** 86% < 20, 13% 20-39, less than 1% 40-49, less than 1% 50-99.

Student profile.

Out-of-state: 9% 25 or older: 33%

Basis for selection. Open admission, but selective for some programs. Admission to nursing programs based on high school record, test scores, required interview. All students must take Cecil College placement tests.

High school preparation. College-preparatory program recommended.

2015-2016 Annual costs. Tuition/fees: $3,630; $6,330 out-of-district; $7,680 out-of-state. Per-credit charge: $100 in-district; $190 out-of-district; $235 out-of-state. Books/supplies: $1,900. Personal expenses: $1,000.

Financial aid. Need-based: Work-study available nights, weekends and for part-time students. **Non-need-based:** Scholarships awarded for academics, alumni affiliation, athletics, job skills, state residency.

Application procedures. Admission: No deadline. No application fee. Admission notification on a rolling basis. Application deadline for nursing program March 1. **Financial aid:** Priority date 8/1; no closing date. FAFSA required. Applicants notified on a rolling basis; must reply within 2 week(s) of notification.

Academics. Special study options: Accelerated study, cooperative education, distance learning, double major, dual enrollment of high school students, ESL, honors, independent study, internships, teacher certification program, weekend college. Bachelor's degree programs available on campus. License preparation in aviation, nursing. **Credit/placement by examination:** AP, CLEP, institutional tests. 45 credit hours maximum toward associate degree. **Support services:** Learning center, reduced course load, remedial instruction, tutoring, writing center.

Majors. Biology: General. **Business:** General, business admin, human resources, logistics, management information systems, marketing, purchasing, transportation. **Communications technology:** Animation/special effects. **Computer sciences:** Web page design. **Education:** General, elementary, English. **Health services:** EMT paramedic, nursing (RN). **Liberal arts:** Arts/sciences. **Math:** General. **Parks/recreation:** Outdoor education. **Protective services:** Firefighting, police science. **Visual/performing arts:** Commercial photography, design, drawing, photography, studio arts. **Work/family studies:** Child care management.

Most popular majors. Business/marketing 19%, health sciences 18%, liberal arts 38%, visual/performing arts 16%.

Technology on campus. 302 workstations in library, computer center, student center. Commuter students can connect to campus network. Online course registration, online library available.

Student life. Freshman orientation: Available. Preregistration for classes offered. **Activities:** Drama, musical theater, student government, student newspaper.

Athletics. NJCAA. **Intercollegiate:** Baseball M, basketball, cheerleading W, golf M, lacrosse M, soccer, softball W, tennis, volleyball W. **Team name:** Seahawks.

Student services. Adult student services, alcohol/substance abuse counseling, career counseling, student employment services, financial aid counseling, legal services, minority student services, personal counseling, placement for graduates, veterans' counselor. **Transfer:** Transfer adviser, college fairs on campus for students transferring to 4-year colleges.

Contact. E-mail: cmishoe@cecil.edu
Phone: (410) 287-6060 Fax: (410) 287-1091
Diane Lane, Vice President of Student Services, Cecil College, One Seahawk Drive, North East, MD 21901

Chesapeake College
Wye Mills, Maryland
www.chesapeake.edu   CB code: 5143

◗ Public 2-year community college
◗ Commuter campus in rural community

General. Founded in 1965. Regionally accredited. Bachelor and graduate degree programs offered on site by Salisbury University, University of Maryland-University College, University of Maryland-Eastern Shore, Stevenson University, Notre Dame University of Maryland, and Gratz College of

Pennsylvania through the Eastern Shore Higher Education Center. **Enrollment:** 1,975 degree-seeking undergraduates; 292 non-degree-seeking students. **Degrees:** 272 associate awarded. **Location:** 15 miles from Stevensville, 7 miles from Centreville. **Calendar:** Semester, limited summer session. **Full-time faculty:** 53 total; 30% have terminal degrees, 11% minority, 70% women. **Part-time faculty:** 67 total; 13% have terminal degrees, 8% minority, 51% women. **Class size:** 61% < 20, 39% 20-39. **Special facilities:** Health professions and athletic center, performing arts center, higher education center, theater.

Student profile. Among degree-seeking undergraduates, 5% already have a bachelor's degree or higher, 543 enrolled as first-time, first-year students, 88 transferred in from other institutions.

Part-time:	65%	Hispanic/Latino:	4%
Out-of-state:	1%	Native American:	1%
Women:	66%	Multi-racial, non-Hispanic:	2%
African American:	18%	International:	1%
Asian American:	1%	25 or older:	32%

Transfer out. 48% of students enrolled in the transfer program go on to 4-year colleges. **Colleges most students transferred to 2015:** Salisbury University, University of Maryland-University College, University of Maryland-College Park, Towson University, University of Maryland-Baltimore County.

Basis for selection. Open admission, but selective for some programs. Admission to radiological technology, surgical technology, physical therapist assistant and nursing programs based on specific high school courses, GPA, and/or test scores. In keeping with its philosophy of putting postsecondary education with the reach of all citizens, Chesapeake College has adopted an Open Door policy. Regular admission will be granted to any student, age 16 and older. **Adult students:** Accuplacer required, unless the student can show proficiency in English or math through earned college credit, SAT, ACT, or AP test scores.

2015-2016 Annual costs. Tuition/fees: $4,520; $6,560 out-of-district; $8,870 out-of-state. Per-credit charge: $115 in-district; $183 out-of-district; $260 out-of-state. Books/supplies: $943. Personal expenses: $600.

2014-2015 Financial aid. Need-based: 97% of total undergraduate aid awarded as scholarships/grants, 3% as loans/jobs. Need-based aid available for part-time students. Work-study available nights, weekends and for part-time students. **Non-need-based:** Scholarships awarded for academics, art, athletics, state residency.

Application procedures. Admission: No deadline. No application fee. Early application advised for radiologic technology and nursing programs. **Financial aid:** Priority date 5/1; no closing date. FAFSA, institutional form required. Applicants notified on a rolling basis starting 5/5; must reply within 2 week(s) of notification.

Academics. Special study options: Cooperative education, cross-registration, distance learning, dual enrollment of high school students, ESL, honors, independent study, internships, student-designed major. Bachelor's degree programs available on campus. License preparation in nursing, paramedic, physical therapy, radiology. **Credit/placement by examination:** AP, CLEP, institutional tests. 32 credit hours maximum toward associate degree. **Support services:** GED preparation and test center, learning center, reduced course load, remedial instruction, study skills assistance, tutoring, writing center.

Majors. Architecture: Landscape. **Business:** General, accounting technology, business admin, hotel/motel/restaurant management. **Computer sciences:** Security, web page design. **Conservation:** Environmental science. **Education:** Chemistry, early childhood, elementary, English, mathematics, physics. **Health services:** EMT paramedic, medical radiologic technology/radiation therapy, mental health counseling, nursing (RN), physical therapy assistant, substance abuse counseling. **Liberal arts:** Arts/sciences. **Parks/recreation:** Sports admin. **Protective services:** Law enforcement admin, police science. **Work/family studies:** Child care management.

Most popular majors. Business/marketing 10%, health sciences 31%, liberal arts 45%.

Technology on campus. 700 workstations in library, student center. Commuter students can connect to campus network. Online course registration, online library, helpline, wireless network available.

Student life. Freshman orientation: Available. Preregistration for classes offered. **Activities:** Campus ministries, choral groups, drama, literary magazine, student government, Student Government Association, Community Outreach Group, Gay/Straight Alliance, Green Team, Phi Theta Kappa Honor Society, Outdoors Club, Peake Players, Student Educators Association, UHURU, Veterans Club.

Athletics. NJCAA. **Intercollegiate:** Baseball M, basketball, soccer M, softball W, volleyball W. **Team name:** Skipjacks.

Student services. Adult student services, career counseling, student employment services, financial aid counseling, minority student services, on-campus daycare, placement for graduates, veterans' counselor. **Physically disabled:** Services for visually, speech, hearing impaired. **Transfer:** Transfer adviser, college fairs on campus for students transferring to 4-year colleges.

Contact. E-mail: kpetrichenko@chesapeake.edu
Phone: (410) 822-5400 ext. 2287 Fax: (410) 827-5878
Joan Seitzer, Dean of Retention, Chesapeake College, Box 8, Wye Mills, MD 21679-0008

College of Southern Maryland
La Plata, Maryland
www.csmd.edu — CB code: 5144

- Public 2-year community college
- Commuter campus in large town

General. Founded in 1958. Regionally accredited. Additional campuses located in Charles County, Calvert County, and St. Mary's County. **Enrollment:** 8,358 degree-seeking undergraduates. **Degrees:** 1,193 associate awarded. **Location:** 30 miles from Washington, DC. **Calendar:** Semester, limited summer session. **Full-time faculty:** 125 total; 22% have terminal degrees, 18% minority, 54% women. **Part-time faculty:** 404 total; 8% have terminal degrees, 21% minority, 61% women. **Class size:** 39% < 20, 61% 20-39, less than 1% 40-49. **Special facilities:** Twilight Performance Series during spring and summer.

Transfer out. Colleges most students transferred to 2015: University of Maryland: University College, University of Maryland: College Park, Towson University, Salisbury University, Prince Georges Community College.

Basis for selection. Open admission, but selective for some programs. Specific requirements for clinical nursing courses include a high school diploma or GED; minimum 2.0 weighted high school GPA for students with less than 12 credits from an accredited college or university; or minimum 2.0 cumulative college GPA for students with 12 or more credits from an accredited college; or university Skills Assessment Survey scores at the ENG 1010 and college general education math levels as well as placement out of reading; or completion of the appropriate developmental courses to achieve these levels; ACT composite raw score of 20 or greater or SAT total critical reading and math score must equal to 950 or greater. Interview required of early admission and nursing applicants. **Adult students:** SAT/ACT scores not required.

2015-2016 Annual costs. Tuition/fees: $4,428; $7,638 out-of-district; $9,889 out-of-state. Per-credit charge: $120 in-district; $207 out-of-district; $268 out-of-state. Books/supplies: $1,667. Personal expenses: $1,700.

Financial aid. Need-based: Need-based aid available for part-time students. Work-study available nights, weekends and for part-time students. **Non-need-based:** Scholarships awarded for academics, athletics, leadership.

Application procedures. Admission: No deadline. No application fee. Applicants notified at time of application. **Financial aid:** Priority date 3/1; no closing date. FAFSA required. Applicants notified on a rolling basis starting 6/15.

Academics. Special study options: Accelerated study, cooperative education, distance learning, dual enrollment of high school students, honors, independent study, liberal arts/career combination, study abroad, weekend college. License preparation in nursing, paramedic, physical therapy, radiology. **Credit/placement by examination:** AP, CLEP, institutional tests. 30 credit hours maximum toward associate degree. **Support services:** Learning center, reduced course load, remedial instruction, study skills assistance, tutoring.

Majors. Business: General, accounting technology, business admin, hospitality admin. **Computer sciences:** General, information technology, programming, security. **Education:** General, early childhood, elementary. **Engineering:** General. **General:** Electrician, lineworker. **Health services:** Clinical lab technology, EMT paramedic, licensed practical nurse, massage therapy, nursing (RN), physical therapy assistant. **Liberal arts:** Arts/sciences. **Parks/recreation:** Health/fitness. **Protective services:** Firefighting, law enforcement admin. **Work/family studies:** Child care management.

Most popular majors. Business/marketing 16%, engineering/engineering technologies 8%, health sciences 10%, liberal arts 51%.

Technology on campus. 1,200 workstations in library, computer center. Commuter students can connect to campus network. Online course registration, online library, helpline, wireless network available.

Student life. Freshman orientation: Available. Preregistration for classes offered. **Activities:** Jazz band, campus ministries, choral groups, dance, drama, film society, literary magazine, music ensembles, musical theater, student government, student newspaper, TV station, BACCHUS Peer Education Network, Black Student Union, Association of Future Educators, nursing student association, Phi Theta Kappa, Fellowship of Christian Athletes, English Honor Society, National Society of Leadership and Success, student ambassador club, veterans club.

Athletics. NJCAA. **Intercollegiate:** Baseball M, basketball, golf, soccer, softball W, tennis, volleyball W. **Team name:** Hawks.

Student services. Adult student services, career counseling, student employment services, financial aid counseling, personal counseling, placement for graduates, veterans' counselor. **Physically disabled:** Services for visually, speech, hearing impaired. **Transfer:** Re-entry adviser for new students. Transfer adviser, college fairs on campus for students transferring to 4-year colleges.

Contact. E-mail: askme@csmd.edu
Phone: (301) 934-7765 Toll-free number: (800) 933-9177 ext. 7765
Fax: (301) 539-4789
Brian Hammond, Director of Admission, College of Southern Maryland, College of Southern Maryland-AOD, La Plata, MD 20646-0910

Community College of Baltimore County
Baltimore, Maryland   CB member
www.ccbcmd.edu   CB code: 5137

▶ Public 2-year community college
▶ Commuter campus in very large city

General. Founded in 1956. Regionally accredited. 3 campuses-Catonsville, Dundalk and Essex; 3 extension centers in Owings Mills, Hunt Valley, and Randallstown. **Enrollment:** 20,630 degree-seeking undergraduates; 1,769 non-degree-seeking students. **Degrees:** 2,200 associate awarded. **Location:** 8 miles from Baltimore City. **Calendar:** Semester, limited summer session. **Special facilities:** Planetarium, occupational training center, performing arts theater, computer integrated manufacturing center.

Student profile. Among degree-seeking undergraduates, 4,157 enrolled as first-time, first-year students.

Part-time:	70%	Hispanic/Latino:	5%
Women:	60%	Multi-racial, non-Hispanic:	4%
African American:	40%	International:	4%
Asian American:	6%	25 or older:	42%

Transfer out. Colleges most students transferred to 2015: Towson University, University of Maryland - Baltimore County, University of Baltimore, University of Maryland - University College, Stevenson University.

Basis for selection. Open admission, but selective for some programs. Additional requirements for admission into programs under the School of Health Professions. Interview recommended for applicants under age 16 and early admission applicants. **Adult students:** SAT/ACT scores not required.

High school preparation. 21 units recommended. Recommended units include English 4, mathematics 3, social studies 4, science 3, foreign language 2 and academic electives 6.

2015-2016 Annual costs. Tuition/fees: $4,252; $7,342 out-of-district; $10,582 out-of-state. Per-credit charge: $113 in-district; $216 out-of-district; $324 out-of-state. Books/supplies: $1,400. Personal expenses: $1,510. **Additional information:** In-State, Out-of-District tuition and fees are $7,342.

Financial aid. Need-based: Need-based aid available for part-time students. Work-study available nights, weekends and for part-time students. **Non-need-based:** Scholarships awarded for academics, athletics, state residency. **Additional information:** On-campus employment typically available.

Application procedures. Admission: No deadline. No application fee. Admission notification on a rolling basis. **Financial aid:** Priority date 1/9; no closing date. FAFSA required. Applicants notified on a rolling basis starting 2/27; must reply within 2 week(s) of notification.

Academics. Special study options: Cooperative education, cross-registration, distance learning, dual enrollment of high school students, ESL, honors, independent study, internships, liberal arts/career combination, study abroad, teacher certification program. Weekend Courses available. License preparation in aviation, dental hygiene, nursing, occupational therapy, paramedic. **Credit/placement by examination:** AP, CLEP, institutional tests. 30 credit hours maximum toward associate degree. **Support services:** GED preparation, learning center, reduced course load, remedial instruction, tutoring.

Majors. Business: General, accounting technology, administrative services, business admin, hotel/motel admin, management information systems. **Computer sciences:** General, networking, security. **Education:** General, chemistry, early childhood, elementary, mathematics, physics, Spanish. **Engineering:** General, computer, electrical. **Foreign languages:** Sign language interpretation. **General:** Site management. **Health services:** Clinical lab technology, dental hygiene, EMT paramedic, massage therapy, medical informatics, medical radiologic technology/radiation therapy, medical secretary, mental health services, nursing (RN), occupational therapy, respiratory therapy technology, substance abuse counseling, veterinary technology/assistant. **Liberal arts:** Arts/sciences. **Parks/recreation:** General. **Protective services:** Police science. **Social sciences:** Geography. **Visual/performing arts:** General, commercial/advertising art. **Work/family studies:** Child care management.

Technology on campus. Online course registration, online library, wireless network available.

Student life. Freshman orientation: Mandatory. Preregistration for classes offered. **Activities:** Choral groups, dance, drama, international student organizations, literary magazine, music ensembles, musical theater, student government, student newspaper, Black Student Union, Christian Fellowship, International Student Association, Rainbow Club; Gay Straight Alliance, Multicultural Student Association, Student Government Association, Student Veteran Association, Muslim Student Association.

Athletics. NJCAA. **Intercollegiate:** Baseball M, basketball, cross-country W, lacrosse, soccer, softball W, track and field W, volleyball W. **Team name:** Catonsville Cardinals, Dundalk Lions, Essex Knights.

Student services. Career counseling, services for economically disadvantaged, student employment services, financial aid counseling, minority student services, on-campus daycare, personal counseling, placement for graduates, veterans' counselor. **Physically disabled:** Services for visually, speech, hearing impaired. **Transfer:** Pre-admission transcript evaluation for new students. Transfer adviser, college fairs on campus for students transferring to 4-year colleges.

Contact. E-mail: ccbcadmissionsoffice@ccbcmd.edu
Phone: (443) 840-4304 Fax: (443) 840-4433
Diane Drake, Director of Admissions, Community College of Baltimore County, 800 South Rolling Road, Baltimore, MD 21228-5317

Frederick Community College
Frederick, Maryland   CB member
www.frederick.edu   CB code: 5230

▶ Public 2-year community college
▶ Commuter campus in small city

General. Founded in 1957. Regionally accredited. **Enrollment:** 5,043 degree-seeking undergraduates. **Degrees:** 897 associate awarded. **Location:** 40 miles from Washington, DC; 40 miles from Baltimore. **Calendar:** Semester, extensive summer session. **Full-time faculty:** 102 total; 26% have terminal degrees, 19% minority, 57% women. **Part-time faculty:** 427 total; 13% have terminal degrees, 12% minority, 55% women. **Special facilities:** Culinary arts institute, advanced workforce training center.

Student profile.

Out-of-state:	3%	Multi-racial, non-Hispanic:	4%
African American:	14%	International:	1%
Asian American:	5%	25 or older:	49%
Hispanic/Latino:	11%		

Transfer out. Colleges most students transferred to 2015: Hood College, Mount St. Mary's University, Towson University, University of Maryland: College Park, Frostburg University.

Basis for selection. Open admission, but selective for some programs. All nursing, respiratory therapy, and surgical technology programs have special requirements. Students must show successful completion of appropriate general education requirements. 550 SAT math or verbal will exempt student from appropriate assessment. Interview required of nursing, respiratory therapy applicants. **Home schooled:** Transcript of courses and grades required. **Learning Disabled:** Meet with Office of Services for Students with Disabilities staff prior to testing/registration.

2015-2016 Annual costs. Tuition/fees: $4,165; $8,245 out-of-district; $10,945 out-of-state. Per-credit charge: $116 in-district; $252 out-of-district; $342 out-of-state. Books/supplies: $1,200. Personal expenses: $1,000.

2014-2015 Financial aid. Need-based: 77% of total undergraduate aid awarded as scholarships/grants, 23% as loans/jobs. Need-based aid available

for part-time students. Work-study available nights, weekends and for part-time students. **Non-need-based:** Scholarships awarded for academics, athletics, state residency.

Application procedures. Admission: No deadline. No application fee. Admission notification on a rolling basis beginning on or about 1/1. Application deadline for nursing applicants 12/15, surgical technology and emergency medical services applicants 2/1. **Financial aid:** Priority date 6/1; no closing date. FAFSA, institutional form required. Applicants notified on a rolling basis starting 5/15; must reply within 2 week(s) of notification.

Academics. Special study options: Cooperative education, distance learning, dual enrollment of high school students, ESL, honors, independent study, internships, liberal arts/career combination, study abroad, teacher certification program, weekend college. License preparation in nursing, real estate. **Credit/placement by examination:** AP, CLEP, institutional tests. 30 credit hours maximum toward associate degree. **Support services:** GED preparation, learning center, pre-admission summer program, reduced course load, remedial instruction, study skills assistance, tutoring, writing center.

Majors. Biology: General. **Business:** Accounting, banking/financial services, business admin, hospitality admin, international. **Communications:** Communications/speech/rhetoric. **Communications technology:** General. **Computer sciences:** General, applications programming, computer science, information systems, information technology, system admin, systems analysis. **Education:** General, early childhood, multi-level teacher, physical, Spanish. **Engineering:** General. **English:** English lit, rhetoric/composition. **Health services:** Nuclear medical technology, nursing (RN), prenursing, prepharmacy, respiratory therapy technology, surgical technology. **History:** General. **Liberal arts:** Arts/sciences. **Math:** General. **Philosophy/religion:** Philosophy. **Physical sciences:** Chemistry. **Protective services:** Criminal justice, fire services admin, homeland security, police science. **Psychology:** General. **Social sciences:** Economics, political science, sociology. **Visual/performing arts:** Art, dramatic. **Work/family studies:** Child care management.

Most popular majors. Business/marketing 17%, health sciences 14%, liberal arts 56%.

Technology on campus. 230 workstations in library, computer center. Commuter students can connect to campus network. Online course registration, online library, wireless network available.

Student life. Freshman orientation: Mandatory. Preregistration for classes offered. Held throughout summer; include advisement and preregistration. **Activities:** Jazz band, choral groups, dance, drama, film society, international student organizations, literary magazine, music ensembles, student government, student newspaper, multicultural student union, Christian students club, chess club, community service club, environmental awareness club, honors student association, gay/lesbian/bisexual group, nursing club, Young Democrats, Young Republicans.

Athletics. NJCAA. **Intercollegiate:** Baseball M, basketball, golf, soccer, softball W, volleyball W. **Team name:** Cougars.

Student services. Adult student services, alcohol/substance abuse counseling, career counseling, student employment services, financial aid counseling, minority student services, on-campus daycare, personal counseling, placement for graduates, veterans' counselor, women's services. **Physically disabled:** Services for visually, speech, hearing impaired. **Transfer:** Transfer center, transfer adviser, college fairs on campus for students transferring to 4-year colleges.

Contact. E-mail: Lfreel@frederick.edu
Phone: (301) 624-2716 Fax: (301) 624-2799
Laura Mears, Associate Vice President/Enrollment Management, Frederick Community College, 7932 Opossumtown Pike, Frederick, MD 21702

Garrett College
McHenry, Maryland
www.garrettcollege.edu
CB code: 5279

- Public 2-year community college
- Commuter campus in rural community

General. Founded in 1971. Regionally accredited. **Enrollment:** 548 degree-seeking undergraduates. **Degrees:** 107 associate awarded. **Location:** 45 miles from Cumberland. **Calendar:** Semester, limited summer session. **Full-time faculty:** 24 total; 25% have terminal degrees, 8% minority, 38% women. **Part-time faculty:** 58 total; 57% women. **Class size:** 34% < 20, 65% 20-39, 2% 40-49. **Special facilities:** Community aquatic and recreational complex.

Student profile.

Out-of-state:	26%	Live on campus:	29%
25 or older:	12%		

Transfer out. Colleges most students transferred to 2015: Frostburg State University, Allegany College of Maryland, West Virginia University.

Basis for selection. Open admission. SAT or ACT recommended. **Home schooled:** Transcript of courses and grades, state high school equivalency certificate required. **Learning Disabled:** Student encouraged to register as a 504 student with Associate Dean of Academic Affairs.

2015-2016 Annual costs. Tuition/fees: $3,890; $7,550 out-of-district; $8,750 out-of-state. Per-credit charge: $98 in-district; $220 out-of-district; $260 out-of-state. Room/board: $5,910. Books/supplies: $1,400. Personal expenses: $2,000. **Additional information:** Room and board is for Garrett Hall. Laker Hall charged at a higher rate.

Financial aid. Need-based: Need-based aid available for part-time students. Work-study available nights, weekends and for part-time students. **Non-need-based:** Scholarships awarded for academics, athletics, leadership. **Additional information:** Many merit and need-based local scholarships available.

Application procedures. Admission: No deadline. No application fee. Admission notification on a rolling basis. **Financial aid:** Priority date 3/1; no closing date. FAFSA required. Applicants notified on a rolling basis starting 6/1; must reply within 2 week(s) of notification.

Academics. Special study options: Distance learning, double major, dual enrollment of high school students, honors, independent study, internships, semester at sea. License preparation in paramedic. **Credit/placement by examination:** AP, CLEP, institutional tests. 30 credit hours maximum toward associate degree. **Support services:** GED preparation and test center, learning center, pre-admission summer program, reduced course load, remedial instruction, study skills assistance, tutoring, writing center.

Majors. Business: General, business admin, management information systems, office technology. **Computer sciences:** Security. **Conservation:** Wildlife/wilderness. **Education:** General, early childhood, elementary. **Engineering:** Electrical. **Liberal arts:** Arts/sciences. **Parks/recreation:** Sports admin.

Most popular majors. Business/marketing 26%, education 13%, liberal arts 40%, parks/recreation 8%, security/protective services 7%.

Technology on campus. 48 workstations in library. Dormitories wired for high-speed internet access. Commuter students can connect to campus network. Online library, wireless network available.

Student life. Freshman orientation: Available. Preregistration for classes offered. **Housing:** Coed dorms, special housing for disabled, wellness housing available. $200 fully refundable deposit. **Activities:** Campus ministries, choral groups, drama, international student organizations, student government.

Athletics. NJCAA. **Intercollegiate:** Baseball M, basketball, golf M, softball W, volleyball W. **Intramural:** Basketball. **Team name:** Lakers.

Student services. Alcohol/substance abuse counseling, career counseling, services for economically disadvantaged, student employment services, financial aid counseling, health services, personal counseling, veterans' counselor. **Physically disabled:** Services for visually, speech, hearing impaired. **Transfer:** Transfer center, transfer adviser, college fairs on campus for students transferring to 4-year colleges.

Contact. E-mail: admissions@garrettcollege.edu
Phone: (301) 387-3044 Toll-free number: (866) 554-2773
Fax: (301) 387-3038
Rachelle Davis, Director of Admission, Garrett College, 687 Mosser Road, McHenry, MD 21541

Hagerstown Community College
Hagerstown, Maryland
www.hagerstowncc.edu
CB code: 5290

- Public 2-year community college
- Commuter campus in small city

General. Founded in 1946. Regionally accredited. **Enrollment:** 3,396 degree-seeking undergraduates. **Degrees:** 634 associate awarded. **Location:** 70 miles from Baltimore. **Calendar:** Semester, extensive summer session. **Full-time faculty:** 80 total. **Part-time faculty:** 166 total. **Special facilities:** Technology center, amphitheater, biotechnology/wet labs.

Student profile.

Out-of-state:	19%	25 or older:	31%

Transfer out. Colleges most students transferred to 2015: Frostburg State University, Towson State University, Shepherd University, Shippensburg University, University of Maryland.

Basis for selection. Open admission, but selective for some programs. Additional requirements for LPN, RN, radiography, dental hygiene and paramedic emergency services/EMT programs.

High school preparation. College-preparatory program recommended. 16 units recommended. Recommended units include English 4, mathematics 3, social studies 1, history 1, science 3 (laboratory 2) and academic electives 2. 1 chemistry, 1 biology, 2 algebra required of nursing applicants; 1 physics, 1 chemistry, 2 algebra required of radiologic technologies applicants.

2015-2016 Annual costs. Tuition/fees: $3,930; $5,910 out-of-district; $7,650 out-of-state. Per-credit charge: $117 in-district; $183 out-of-district; $241 out-of-state. Books/supplies: $2,100. Personal expenses: $1,400.

2014-2015 Financial aid. All financial aid based on need. 257 full-time freshmen applied for aid; 207 deemed to have need; 194 received aid. Average need met was 45%. Average scholarship/grant was $4,247; average loan $2,702. 52% of total undergraduate aid awarded as scholarships/grants, 48% as loans/jobs. Need-based aid available for part-time students. Work-study available nights, weekends and for part-time students.

Application procedures. Admission: No deadline. No application fee. Admission notification on a rolling basis. **Financial aid:** Priority date 5/30; no closing date. FAFSA required. Applicants notified on a rolling basis starting 4/15.

Academics. Special study options: Accelerated study, cooperative education, cross-registration, distance learning, double major, dual enrollment of high school students, ESL, honors, independent study, internships, liberal arts/career combination, weekend college. License preparation in dental hygiene, nursing, paramedic, radiology, real estate. **Credit/placement by examination:** AP, CLEP, institutional tests. 30 credit hours maximum toward associate degree. **Support services:** GED preparation and test center, learning center, pre-admission summer program, reduced course load, remedial instruction, study skills assistance, tutoring.

Majors. Business: General, accounting technology, business admin, management information systems, transportation. **Computer sciences:** General, security, web page design. **Education:** General, early childhood, elementary, English. **Engineering:** General. **Health services:** Dental hygiene, EMT paramedic, medical radiologic technology/radiation therapy, medical secretary, mental health services, nursing (RN). **Liberal arts:** Arts/sciences. **Protective services:** Police science. **Visual/performing arts:** Commercial/advertising art. **Work/family studies:** Child care management.

Most popular majors. Business/marketing 20%, education 6%, health sciences 19%, liberal arts 42%.

Technology on campus. 500 workstations in library, computer center, student center. Commuter students can connect to campus network. Online course registration, online library, helpline, repair service, wireless network available.

Student life. Freshman orientation: Available. Preregistration for classes offered. **Activities:** Jazz band, choral groups, dance, drama, international student organizations, literary magazine, musical theater, student government, student newspaper.

Athletics. NJCAA. **Intercollegiate:** Baseball M, basketball, cheerleading, cross-country, golf, soccer, softball W, tennis, track and field, volleyball W. **Team name:** Hawks.

Student services. Adult student services, career counseling, services for economically disadvantaged, student employment services, financial aid counseling, health services, on-campus daycare, personal counseling, placement for graduates, veterans' counselor. **Physically disabled:** Services for visually, speech, hearing impaired. **Transfer:** Pre-admission transcript evaluation for new students. Transfer adviser, college fairs on campus for students transferring to 4-year colleges.

Contact. E-mail: admissions@hagerstowncc.edu
Phone: (240) 500-2238 Toll-free number: (301) 766-4422
Fax: (301) 791-9165
Robin Becker-Cornblatt, Director of Admissions, Records and Registration, Hagerstown Community College, 11400 Robinwood Drive, Hagerstown, MD 21742-6514

Harford Community College
Bel Air, Maryland
www.harford.edu
CB code: 5303

- Public 2-year community college
- Commuter campus in small city

General. Founded in 1957. Regionally accredited. **Enrollment:** 5,546 degree-seeking undergraduates; 974 non-degree-seeking students. **Degrees:** 997 associate awarded. **Location:** 25 miles from Baltimore. **Calendar:** Semester, limited summer session. **Full-time faculty:** 101 total; 19% have terminal degrees, 10% minority, 58% women. **Part-time faculty:** 243 total; 10% have terminal degrees, 10% minority, 59% women. **Special facilities:** Observatory, theater, arena, fitness center, pool. **Partnerships:** Formal partnerships with local employers who provide co-op opportunities.

Student profile. Among degree-seeking undergraduates, 65% enrolled in a transfer program, 35% enrolled in a vocational program, 5% already have a bachelor's degree or higher, 1,271 enrolled as first-time, first-year students, 255 transferred in from other institutions.

Part-time:	59%	Hispanic/Latino:	5%
Out-of-state:	3%	Multi-racial, non-Hispanic:	3%
Women:	58%	International:	1%
African American:	16%	25 or older:	29%
Asian American:	2%		

Transfer out. Colleges most students transferred to 2015: Towson University, University of Baltimore, University of Maryland - College Park, UMBC, University of Maryland University College.

Basis for selection. Open admission, but selective for some programs. Some restrictions apply for applicants under 16 and international students. Nursing program has specific selection criteria. Students with a SAT score of 500 or higher in the critical reading portion or the math section will be exempt from the corresponding ACCUPLACER section of the assessment. **Home schooled:** If under 16, Assessment Testing with a qualified college-level score and an interview. **Learning Disabled:** Students with disabilities should contact Disability Support Services (DIS) before the term begins.

High school preparation. 14 units recommended. Recommended units include English 4, mathematics 4, social studies 3 and science 3.

2015-2016 Annual costs. Tuition/fees: $4,176; $6,786 out-of-district; $9,396 out-of-state. Per-credit charge: $116 in-district; $203 out-of-district; $290 out-of-state. Books/supplies: $1,300. Personal expenses: $2,000.

2014-2015 Financial aid. Need-based: 659 full-time freshmen applied for aid; 437 deemed to have need; 402 received aid. 85% of total undergraduate aid awarded as scholarships/grants, 15% as loans/jobs. Need-based aid available for part-time students. Work-study available nights, weekends and for part-time students. **Non-need-based:** Awarded to 136 full-time undergraduates, including 66 freshmen.

Application procedures. Admission: No deadline. No application fee. Admission notification on a rolling basis. Application deadline for nursing 6/1. Notification within 30 days. **Financial aid:** Priority date 3/15; no closing date. FAFSA, institutional form required. Applicants notified on a rolling basis starting 4/1; must reply within 2 week(s) of notification.

Academics. Special study options: Cooperative education, distance learning, double major, dual enrollment of high school students, ESL, honors, independent study, internships, study abroad, teacher certification program. License preparation in nursing. **Credit/placement by examination:** AP, CLEP, IB, institutional tests. 30 credit hours maximum toward associate degree. **Support services:** GED preparation and test center, learning center, pre-admission summer program, remedial instruction, study skills assistance, tutoring, writing center. Disability Support Services.

Majors. Biology: General. **Business:** General, accounting technology, business admin, entrepreneurial studies, human resources, marketing. **Communications:** Advertising, media studies. **Computer sciences:** General, computer science, security. **Conservation:** Environmental science, environmental studies. **Education:** General, chemistry, early childhood, elementary, English, mathematics, physics, secondary, Spanish. **Engineering:** General. **English:** English lit. **Health services:** Electroencephalograph technology, medical assistant, nursing (RN). **History:** General. **Human services:** Social work. **Liberal arts:** Arts/sciences. **Math:** General. **Parks/recreation:** Golf management. **Philosophy/religion:** Philosophy. **Physical sciences:** Chemistry, physics. **Protective services:** Police science. **Psychology:** General. **Social sciences:** Anthropology, international relations, political science, sociology. **Visual/performing arts:** General, design, digital arts, graphic design, interior design, music, photography, studio arts, theater design.

Most popular majors. Business/marketing 17%, health sciences 16%, liberal arts 47%.

Two-Year Colleges

Technology on campus. 750 workstations in library, computer center, student center. Commuter students can connect to campus network. Online course registration, online library, helpline, student web hosting, wireless network available.

Student life. Freshman orientation: Available. Preregistration for classes offered. **Activities:** Bands, choral groups, dance, drama, international student organizations, musical theater, radio station, student government, student newspaper, TV station, Phi Theta Kappa, Multicultural Student Association, social empowerment club, Rainbow Alliance, The Warriors, Student Government Association, Student Veterans Club, Improv Club, Future Educators of America.

Athletics. NJCAA. **Intercollegiate:** Baseball M, basketball, cross-country, golf M, lacrosse, soccer, softball W, tennis, volleyball W. **Intramural:** Badminton, basketball, cheerleading, football (non-tackle), soccer, softball, swimming, tennis, volleyball. **Team name:** Fighting Owls.

Student services. Career counseling, student employment services, financial aid counseling, on-campus daycare, personal counseling, placement for graduates, veterans' counselor. **Physically disabled:** Services for visually, speech, hearing impaired. **Transfer:** Transfer adviser, college fairs on campus for students transferring to 4-year colleges.

Contact. E-mail: sendinfo@harford.edu
Phone: (443) 412-2109 Fax: (443) 412-2169
Megan Cornett, Director of Admissions, Harford Community College, 401 Thomas Run Road, Bel Air, MD 21015

Howard Community College
Columbia, Maryland
www.howardcc.edu   **CB code: 5308**

▶ Public 2-year community college
▶ Commuter campus in small city

General. Founded in 1966. Regionally accredited. **Enrollment:** 9,333 degree-seeking undergraduates; 602 non-degree-seeking students. **Degrees:** 1,165 associate awarded. **Location:** 20 miles from Baltimore. **Calendar:** Semester, extensive summer session. **Full-time faculty:** 193 total; 34% have terminal degrees, 26% minority, 67% women. **Part-time faculty:** 612 total; 14% have terminal degrees, 31% minority, 63% women. **Class size:** 53% < 20, 45% 20-39, 1% 40-49, less than 1% 50-99. **Special facilities:** Professional art gallery, practice rooms, recital hall, black box theater, art and dance studios, clinical simulation laboratory suites, child care facility, center for entrepreneurial and business excellence, wellness center, mediation and conflict resolution center, World Languages Institute, transfer center, Howard County African American cultural center research library and archives. **Partnerships:** Formal partnerships with Microsoft Authorized Academic Training Program, Certiport, Comp Tia Authorized Education Partner, Regional Cisco Networking Academy, Castle Worldwide, Pearson VUE.

Student profile. Among degree-seeking undergraduates, 67% enrolled in a transfer program, 33% enrolled in a vocational program, 12% already have a bachelor's degree or higher, 1,813 enrolled as first-time, first-year students.

Part-time:	61%	Hispanic/Latino:	10%
Women:	57%	Multi-racial, non-Hispanic:	5%
African American:	29%	International:	4%
Asian American:	12%	25 or older:	36%

Transfer out. 70% of students enrolled in the transfer program go on to 4-year colleges. **Colleges most students transferred to 2015:** University of Maryland-College Park, University of Maryland-Baltimore County, Towson University, Salisbury University.

Basis for selection. Open admission, but selective for some programs. Competitive admission to honors programs. Special requirements for cardiovascular technology, clinical nursing, dental hygiene, diagnostic medical sonography, emergency medical services, medical laboratory technician, physical therapist assistant, radiologic technology applicants. SAT or ACT required for admission to Scholars Program. Mandatory assessment policy. Most students must complete placement testing before completing 12 credits. Placement test exemptions allowed based on SAT/ACT scores. Interview and portfolio recommended for some selective admissions programs. **Adult students:** SAT/ACT scores not required.

High school preparation. Recommended units include English 4, mathematics 4, social studies 4, history 3, science 3 (laboratory 2) and foreign language 3. Computer related course involving skills such as word-processing, databases and spreadsheets, as well as the Internet.

2015-2016 Annual costs. Tuition/fees: $4,623; $7,113 out-of-district; $8,463 out-of-state. Per-credit charge: $132 in-district; $215 out-of-district; $260 out-of-state. Books/supplies: $2,000. Personal expenses: $1,600.

2014-2015 Financial aid. Need-based: 81% of total undergraduate aid awarded as scholarships/grants, 19% as loans/jobs. Need-based aid available for part-time students. Work-study available nights, weekends and for part-time students.

Application procedures. Admission: No deadline. $25 fee, may be waived for applicants with need. Admission notification on a rolling basis. Specific deadlines may apply for applications to honors programs, clinical nursing program and most allied health programs. **Financial aid:** Priority date 3/1; no closing date. FAFSA required. Applicants notified on a rolling basis starting 5/1.

Academics. Pre-admission summer program for disabled students only. **Special study options:** Accelerated study, cooperative education, distance learning, dual enrollment of high school students, ESL, external degree, honors, independent study, internships, liberal arts/career combination, study abroad, teacher certification program, weekend college. Service learning. License preparation in dental hygiene, nursing, paramedic, radiology. **Credit/placement by examination:** AP, CLEP, IB, institutional tests. 30 credit hours maximum toward associate degree. **Support services:** GED preparation, learning center, pre-admission summer program, reduced course load, remedial instruction, study skills assistance, tutoring, writing center.

Majors. Area/ethnic studies: Asian, women's. **Biology:** Bioinformatics, biotechnology. **Business:** Accounting technology, actuarial science, business admin, entrepreneurial studies, hospitality admin, international, office technology. **Communications:** General. **Computer sciences:** Computer science, LAN/WAN management, programming, security, web page design. **Conservation:** Environmental science. **Education:** Chemistry, early childhood, early childhood special, elementary, elementary special ed, English, mathematics, physics, Spanish. **Engineering:** General, biomedical, computer, electrical. **English:** English lit. **Foreign languages:** Arabic, Spanish. **Health services:** Cardiovascular technology, clinical lab technology, dental hygiene, dietetics, EMT paramedic, licensed practical nurse, nursing (RN), physical therapy assistant, premedicine, prepharmacy, public health ed, radiologic technology/medical imaging, sonography. **Liberal arts:** Arts/sciences. **Math:** General. **Philosophy/religion:** General. **Physical sciences:** General. **Protective services:** Computer forensics, criminal justice, fire services admin. **Social sciences:** General. **Visual/performing arts:** Art, dance, dramatic, film/cinema/video, game design, music.

Most popular majors. Business/marketing 8%, health sciences 18%, liberal arts 63%.

Technology on campus. 262 workstations in library, computer center, student center. Commuter students can connect to campus network. Online course registration, online library, helpline, student web hosting, wireless network available.

Student life. Freshman orientation: Available. Preregistration for classes offered. 3-4 hour day or evening program the week before start of fall and spring semesters or optional online orientation. **Policies:** Tobacco, drug- and alcohol-free campus; code of conduct, academic honesty. **Activities:** Jazz band, campus ministries, choral groups, dance, drama, international student organizations, literary magazine, music ensembles, musical theater, radio station, student government, student newspaper, TV station, Gay Straight Alliance, Student Veterans Organization, Society for Women Engineers, Pre-Med Club, International Student Association, Baha'i Peace Club, Campus Disciples, Genki Japanese Club, Jewish Student Union, South Asian Club.

Athletics. NJCAA. **Intercollegiate:** Basketball, cross-country, lacrosse, soccer, track and field, volleyball W. **Team name:** Dragons.

Student services. Adult student services, career counseling, services for economically disadvantaged, student employment services, financial aid counseling, minority student services, on-campus daycare, personal counseling, placement for graduates, veterans' counselor, women's services. **Physically disabled:** Services for visually, speech, hearing impaired. **Transfer:** Pre-admission transcript evaluation for new students. Transfer center, transfer adviser, college fairs on campus for students transferring to 4-year colleges.

Contact. E-mail: admissions@howardcc.edu
Phone: (443) 518-1200 Fax: (443) 518-4589
Christine Palmer, Assistant Director of Admissions (Outreach), Howard Community College, 10901 Little Patuxent Parkway, Columbia, MD 21044-3197

Kaplan University: Hagerstown
Hagerstown, Maryland
www.hagerstown.kaplanuniversity.edu   **CB code: 0804**

▶ For-profit 2-year business and junior college
▶ Commuter campus in large town
▶ Interview required

General. Founded in 1938. Regionally accredited. **Enrollment:** 854 undergraduates. **Degrees:** 68 bachelor's, 156 associate awarded; master's offered. **Location:** 70 miles from Baltimore, 70 miles from Washington, DC. **Calendar:** Quarter, limited summer session. **Full-time faculty:** 11 total. **Part-time faculty:** 31 total. **Special facilities:** Firearms training simulator, forensic recovery and evidence detection lab.

Student profile.

Out-of-state:	60%	Live on campus:	3%
25 or older:	55%		

Basis for selection. Open admission, but selective for some programs.

2015-2016 Annual costs. Personal expenses: $960. **Additional information:** Diploma programs: $11,501-$21,147. Associate programs: $33,390-$35,987. Bachelor's programs: $28,350-$66,780.

Financial aid. Need-based: Need-based aid available for part-time students. Work-study available nights, weekends and for part-time students.

Application procedures. Admission: No deadline. $20 fee. Admission notification on a rolling basis. **Financial aid:** No deadline. FAFSA, institutional form required. Applicants notified on a rolling basis starting 6/1; must reply within 2 week(s) of notification.

Academics. College includes allied health, legal, business, criminal justice, computer forensics and information technology divisions. Several bachelor's programs offered in online courses. **Special study options:** Distance learning, double major, internships. Bachelor's degree programs available on campus. **Credit/placement by examination:** AP, CLEP, institutional tests. 15 credit hours maximum toward associate degree. **Support services:** Reduced course load, remedial instruction, tutoring.

Majors. Business: Accounting, administrative services, business admin, office technology. **Computer sciences:** Computer graphics, data processing, LAN/WAN management, system admin, webmaster. **Health services:** Health information technology, medical assistant, medical secretary, medical transcription. **Protective services:** Criminal justice, forensics, law enforcement admin.

Most popular majors. Business/marketing 22%, computer/information sciences 28%, health sciences 39%, legal studies 11%.

Technology on campus. 85 workstations in library, computer center.

Student life. Freshman orientation: Mandatory. Preregistration for classes offered. **Housing:** Coed dorms available. $150 deposit. Residence hall space is limited, assignments will be made on a first-come, first-served basis. **Activities:** Student government.

Student services. Career counseling, student employment services, financial aid counseling, personal counseling, placement for graduates.

Contact. E-mail: info@ku-hagerstown.edu
Phone: (301) 739-2670 Toll-free number: (800) 422-2670
Fax: (301) 791-7661
Jim Klein, Director of Admissions, Kaplan University: Hagerstown, 18618 Crestwood Drive, Hagerstown, MD 21742

Montgomery College
Rockville, Maryland **CB member**
www.montgomerycollege.edu **CB code: 5440**

▶ Public 2-year community college
▶ Commuter campus in very large city

General. Founded in 1946. Regionally accredited. Campuses in Takoma Park/Silver Spring, Rockville, and Germantown. **Enrollment:** 19,096 degree-seeking undergraduates. **Degrees:** 2,662 associate awarded. **Location:** 5 miles from Washington, DC. **Calendar:** Semester, extensive summer session. **Full-time faculty:** 536 total. **Part-time faculty:** 864 total. **Class size:** 36% < 20, 62% 20-39, less than 1% 40-49, 2% 50-99. **Special facilities:** Performing arts center, child care center, planetarium.

Student profile.

Out-of-state:	4%	25 or older:	36%

Transfer out. Colleges most students transferred to 2015: University of Maryland: College Park, University of Maryland: Baltimore County, Towson State University, University of Maryland: University College, Salisbury University.

Basis for selection. Open admission, but selective for some programs. Admission to allied medical health programs considers standardized test scores, secondary school record, geographical residence, and state residence. Montgomery County residents get first priority; GPA rank within residency category is important. Audition required for music majors and School of Art & Design admissions process requires a portfolio review/interview.

High school preparation. College-preparatory program recommended.

2015-2016 Annual costs. Tuition/fees: $4,728; $9,156 out-of-district; $12,432 out-of-state. Per-credit charge: $118 in-district; $241 out-of-district; $332 out-of-state. Books/supplies: $1,200. Personal expenses: $1,380.

Financial aid. Need-based: Need-based aid available for part-time students. Work-study available nights, weekends and for part-time students. **Non-need-based:** Scholarships awarded for academics, alumni affiliation, art, athletics, leadership, minority status, music/drama, state residency.

Application procedures. Admission: No deadline. $25 fee, may be waived for applicants with need. Admission notification on a rolling basis. **Financial aid:** Priority date 5/15; no closing date. FAFSA, institutional form required. Applicants notified on a rolling basis starting 5/30.

Academics. Special study options: Accelerated study, cooperative education, distance learning, double major, dual enrollment of high school students, ESL, honors, independent study, internships, study abroad, teacher certification program. License preparation in nursing, physical therapy, radiology, real estate. **Credit/placement by examination:** AP, CLEP, institutional tests. 45 credit hours maximum toward associate degree. **Support services:** GED preparation, learning center, pre-admission summer program, remedial instruction, study skills assistance, tutoring, writing center.

Majors. Architecture: Technology. **Biology:** Biochemistry. **Business:** General, accounting technology, business admin, construction management, hospitality admin, hotel/motel admin, international, management information systems. **Communications:** Advertising, broadcast journalism. **Communications technology:** Desktop publishing, graphic/printing, graphics. **Computer sciences:** General, computer graphics, computer science, information systems, programming. **Education:** General, early childhood, science. **Engineering:** General, civil. **Foreign languages:** American Sign Language. **Health services:** Health information technology, medical radiologic technology/radiation therapy, nursing (RN), physical therapy assistant, predental, premedicine, prepharmacy, sonography, surgical technology. **Liberal arts:** Arts/sciences. **Math:** General. **Parks/recreation:** Exercise sciences. **Physical sciences:** Physics. **Protective services:** Firefighting, law enforcement admin. **Visual/performing arts:** General, art history/conservation, commercial photography, commercial/advertising art, dance, game design, interior design, music, photography, studio arts, theater design. **Work/family studies:** Child care management, institutional food production.

Most popular majors. Business/marketing 18%, engineering/engineering technologies 6%, health sciences 11%, liberal arts 52%.

Technology on campus. 400 workstations in library, computer center. Commuter students can connect to campus network. Online course registration, online library, helpline, wireless network available.

Student life. Freshman orientation: Available. Preregistration for classes offered. **Activities:** Concert band, choral groups, dance, drama, international student organizations, music ensembles, musical theater, radio station, student government, student newspaper, TV station, Jewish student association, progressive student alliance, Christian fellowship, lesbian student alliance, Students Against Driving Drunk, African-American student organization, Hispanic student organization, Asian student organization.

Athletics. NJCAA. **Intercollegiate:** Baseball M, basketball, soccer M, softball W, tennis, track and field, volleyball W. **Intramural:** Basketball.

Student services. Adult student services, career counseling, services for economically disadvantaged, student employment services, financial aid counseling, minority student services, on-campus daycare, personal counseling, placement for graduates, veterans' counselor. **Physically disabled:** Services for visually, speech, hearing impaired. **Transfer:** Re-entry adviser, pre-admission transcript evaluation for new students. Transfer center, transfer adviser, college fairs on campus for students transferring to 4-year colleges.

Contact. Phone: (240) 567-5034 Fax: (240) 567-5037
Rochelle Moore, Director of Enrollment Management, Montgomery College, 51 Mannakee Street, Rockville, MD 20850

Prince George's Community College
Largo, Maryland **CB member**
www.pgcc.edu **CB code: 5545**

▶ Public 2-year community college
▶ Commuter campus in very large city

General. Founded in 1958. Regionally accredited. Extension center at Andrews Air Force Base serves both military and civilian personnel. **Enrollment:** 12,617 degree-seeking undergraduates. **Degrees:** 908 associate awarded. **ROTC:** Army, Air Force. **Location:** 10 miles from Washington, DC. **Calendar:** Semester, limited summer session. **Full-time faculty:** 240 total. **Part-time faculty:** 697 total. **Class size:** 64% < 20, 35% 20-39, less than 1% 40-49, less than 1% 50-99. **Special facilities:** Natatorium, art gallery.

Student profile.

Out-of-state:	4%	25 or older:	47%

Transfer out. Colleges most students transferred to 2015: University of Maryland-College Park, Bowie State University, University of Maryland-University College, Morgan State University, Howard University.

Basis for selection. Open admission, but selective for some programs. Special requirements for health technology programs and for international students. Health technology program requires high school diploma or GED. For some scholarships or honors program consideration, 1050 SAT (exclusive of writing) required. SAT/ACT may be used in place of college's placement tests.

High school preparation. Recommended units include English 4, mathematics 4, social studies 3, history 3, science 3 (laboratory 2) and academic electives 4. One computer literacy recommended.

2015-2016 Annual costs. Tuition/fees: $4,550; $7,190 out-of-district; $10,100 out-of-state. Per-credit charge: $105 in-district; $193 out-of-district; $290 out-of-state. Books/supplies: $723.

Financial aid. All financial aid based on need. Need-based aid available for part-time students. Work-study available nights, weekends and for part-time students.

Application procedures. Admission: No deadline. $25 fee. Admission notification on a rolling basis. **Financial aid:** Priority date 6/1; no closing date. FAFSA, institutional form required. Applicants notified on a rolling basis starting 6/1; must reply within 2 week(s) of notification.

Academics. Special study options: Cooperative education, distance learning, double major, dual enrollment of high school students, ESL, honors, independent study, liberal arts/career combination, teacher certification program, weekend college. License preparation in nursing, paramedic, radiology, real estate. **Credit/placement by examination:** AP, CLEP, institutional tests. 30 credit hours maximum toward associate degree. **Support services:** GED preparation, learning center, reduced course load, remedial instruction, study skills assistance, tutoring, writing center.

Majors. Area/ethnic studies: African-American, American, women's. **Biology:** General. **Business:** Accounting, administrative services, business admin, marketing, office management, office technology. **Computer sciences:** General, computer science, information technology, programming, systems analysis. **Education:** Business, elementary, health, mathematics, physical, science, secondary. **Engineering:** General. **Health services:** EMT paramedic, health information management, health information technology, medical radiologic technology/radiation therapy, medical secretary, nuclear medical technology, nursing (RN), premedicine, prepharmacy, respiratory therapy technology. **Liberal arts:** Arts/sciences. **Physical sciences:** Chemistry. **Protective services:** Criminal justice, forensics. **Psychology:** General. **Visual/performing arts:** Commercial/advertising art, music, studio arts. **Work/family studies:** Child care management.

Technology on campus. 950 workstations in library, computer center, student center. Commuter students can connect to campus network. Online course registration, helpline, repair service available.

Student life. Freshman orientation: Available. Preregistration for classes offered. **Activities:** Choral groups, drama, film society, international student organizations, literary magazine, music ensembles, musical theater, opera, student government, student newspaper, TV station, Union of Black Scholars, Active Seniors (for senior citizens), student program board, Spanish club, French club, Caribbean students club, Muslim society, women's Bible study.

Athletics. NJCAA. **Intercollegiate:** Baseball M, basketball, bowling, golf, soccer, softball W, tennis M, volleyball W. **Intramural:** Basketball, bowling, golf, racquetball, soccer, table tennis, volleyball. **Team name:** Owls.

Student services. Adult student services, career counseling, services for economically disadvantaged, student employment services, financial aid counseling, health services, minority student services, on-campus daycare, personal counseling, placement for graduates, veterans' counselor. **Physically disabled:** Services for visually, speech, hearing impaired. **Transfer:** Re-entry adviser for new students. Transfer center, transfer adviser, college fairs on campus for students transferring to 4-year colleges.

Contact. E-mail: enrollmentservices@pgcc.edu
Phone: (301) 322-0801 Fax: (301) 322-0119
Vera Bagley, Director of Admissions and Records, Prince George's Community College, 301 Largo Road, Largo, MD 20774

TESST College of Technology: Baltimore
Baltimore, Maryland
www.tesst.com/tesstPortal

- For-profit 2-year technical college
- Very large city

General. Regionally accredited; also accredited by ACCSC. **Enrollment:** 582 undergraduates. **Degrees:** 10 associate awarded. **Calendar:** Semester. **Full-time faculty:** 1 total. **Part-time faculty:** 30 total.

Basis for selection. Open admission, but selective for some programs. Institutional evaluation test may be accepted in lieu of SAT/ACT for placement.

Financial aid. Need-based: Work-study available nights, weekends and for part-time students.

Application procedures. Admission: No deadline. $10 fee. Admission notification on a rolling basis. **Financial aid:** No deadline.

Academics. Credit/placement by examination: AP, CLEP.

Majors. Computer sciences: Information systems.

Contact. Phone: (410) 644-6400 Toll-free number: (800) 988-2650
Fax: (410) 644-6481
William Scott, Director of Admissions, TESST College of Technology: Baltimore, 1520 South Caton Avenue, Baltimore, MD 21227-1063

TESST College of Technology: Beltsville
Beltsville, Maryland
www.tesst.com

- For-profit 2-year technical college
- Large town

General. Accredited by ACCSC. **Enrollment:** 388 undergraduates. **Degrees:** 27 associate awarded. **Calendar:** Semester. **Full-time faculty:** 2 total. **Part-time faculty:** 28 total.

Basis for selection. Open admission.

Financial aid. Need-based: Work-study available nights, weekends and for part-time students.

Application procedures. Admission: No deadline. $10 fee. **Financial aid:** No deadline.

Academics. Credit/placement by examination: AP, CLEP.

Majors. Computer sciences: Data entry, information systems.

Contact. E-mail: dedmonds@tesst.com
Phone: (301) 937-8448 Toll-free number: (800) 935-1857
Cathy McKinney, Director of Admissions, TESST College of Technology: Beltsville, 4600 Powder Mill Road, Beltsville, MD 20705

TESST College of Technology: Towson
Towson, Maryland
www.tesst.com

- For-profit 2-year technical college
- Small city
- Interview required

General. Accredited by ACCSC. **Enrollment:** 318 undergraduates. **Degrees:** 50 associate awarded. **Location:** 15 miles from Baltimore. **Calendar:** Semester. **Full-time faculty:** 3 total. **Part-time faculty:** 21 total.

Basis for selection. Open admission, but selective for some programs. **Adult students:** CPAT for all students.

2015-2016 Annual costs. A+ Certification Preparation: $2,295. Computer Networking Technology: $32,364. Computer Support Technician: $16,892. Criminal Justice: $32,379. Medical Assistant: $15,867. Medical Billing and Coding Specialist: $15,455. Network+ Certification Preparation: $2,095. Phlebotomy Technician: $958. Security+ Certification Preparation: $2,095.

Financial aid. Need-based: Work-study available nights, weekends and for part-time students.

Application procedures. Admission: No deadline. $10 fee. Admission notification on a rolling basis. **Financial aid:** No deadline.

Academics. Credit/placement by examination: AP, CLEP. **Support services:** Tutoring.

Majors. Business: Management information systems. **Protective services:** Law enforcement admin.

Student life. Freshman orientation: Mandatory. Preregistration for classes offered.

Student services. Career counseling, student employment services, financial aid counseling, placement for graduates, veterans' counselor.

Contact. Phone: (410) 296-5350 Toll-free number: (800) 935-1857 Fax: (410) 296-5356
Nicholaus Buzzard, Director of Admissions, TESST College of Technology: Towson, 803 Glen Eagles Court, Towson, MD 21286

Wor-Wic Community College
Salisbury, Maryland
www.worwic.edu   CB code: 1613

▶ Public 2-year community college
▶ Commuter campus in large town

General. Founded in 1975. Regionally accredited. **Enrollment:** 2,775 degree-seeking undergraduates; 362 non-degree-seeking students. **Degrees:** 368 associate awarded. **Location:** 110 miles from Baltimore, 120 miles from Washington, DC. **Calendar:** Semester, limited summer session. **Full-time faculty:** 69 total; 26% have terminal degrees, 10% minority, 71% women. **Part-time faculty:** 99 total; 9% have terminal degrees, 12% minority, 64% women. **Class size:** 47% < 20, 49% 20-39, 4% 40-49, less than 1% 50-99. **Partnerships:** Formal partnership with local medical center to provide financial and clinical support to the college's health programs.

Student profile. Among degree-seeking undergraduates, 59% enrolled in a transfer program, 41% enrolled in a vocational program, 613 enrolled as first-time, first-year students, 232 transferred in from other institutions.

Part-time:	69%	Asian American:	1%
Out-of-state:	3%	Hispanic/Latino:	4%
Women:	66%	Multi-racial, non-Hispanic:	4%
African American:	23%	25 or older:	42%

Transfer out. 56% of students enrolled in the transfer program go on to 4-year colleges. **Colleges most students transferred to 2015:** Salisbury University, University of Maryland Eastern Shore, University of Maryland College Park, University of Maryland University College, Wilmington University.

Basis for selection. Open admission, but selective for some programs. Special requirements for emergency medical services, nursing, occupational therapy assistant, physical therapist assistant and radiologic technology programs.

High school preparation. College-preparatory program recommended.

2015-2016 Annual costs. Tuition/fees: $3,600; $7,440 out-of-district; $9,030 out-of-state. Per-credit charge: $103 in-district, $231 out-of-district; $284 out-of-state. Books/supplies: $1,600. Personal expenses: $2,000.

Financial aid. Need-based: Need-based aid available for part-time students. Work-study available nights, weekends and for part-time students. **Non-need-based:** Scholarships awarded for academics, state residency.

Application procedures. Admission: No deadline. No application fee. Application must be submitted online. Admission notification on a rolling basis. **Financial aid:** Priority date 6/1; no closing date. FAFSA, institutional form required. Applicants notified on a rolling basis starting 4/1.

Academics. Special study options: Distance learning, double major, dual enrollment of high school students, ESL, honors, internships. License preparation in nursing, occupational therapy, paramedic, physical therapy, radiology.

Credit/placement by examination: AP, CLEP, institutional tests. 30 credit hours maximum toward associate degree. **Support services:** GED preparation and test center, learning center, reduced course load, remedial instruction, study skills assistance, tutoring, writing center.

Majors. Business: General, accounting technology, administrative services, business admin, hospitality admin. **Computer sciences:** General, systems analysis. **Education:** General, early childhood, elementary. **Health services:** EMT paramedic, medical radiologic technology/radiation therapy, nursing (RN), occupational therapy assistant, physical therapy assistant, substance abuse counseling. **Liberal arts:** Arts/sciences. **Protective services:** Police science. **Work/family studies:** Child care management.

Most popular majors. Business/marketing 18%, health sciences 28%, liberal arts 34%.

Technology on campus. 710 workstations in library, computer center, student center. Commuter students can connect to campus network. Online library, helpline, wireless network available.

Student life. Freshman orientation: Available. Preregistration for classes offered. **Activities:** Drama, literary magazine, student government, gay-straight alliance, veterans and military association, Wor-Wic Christian community.

Student services. Career counseling, student employment services, financial aid counseling, on-campus daycare, personal counseling, placement for graduates, veterans' counselor. **Physically disabled:** Services for visually, speech, hearing impaired. **Transfer:** College fairs on campus for students transferring to 4-year colleges.

Contact. E-mail: admissions@worwic.edu
Phone: (410) 334-2895 Fax: (410) 334-2954
Richard Webster, Director of Admissions, Wor-Wic Community College, 32000 Campus Drive, Salisbury, MD 21804

Massachusetts

Bay State College
Boston, Massachusetts
www.baystate.edu   CB code: 3120

▶ For-profit 2-year nursing and career college
▶ Commuter campus in very large city
▶ Interview required

General. Founded in 1946. Regionally accredited. **Enrollment:** 1,070 degree-seeking undergraduates; 9 non-degree-seeking students. **Degrees:** 124 bachelor's, 163 associate awarded. **Calendar:** Continuous, extensive summer session. **Full-time faculty:** 25 total. **Part-time faculty:** 98 total.

Student profile. Among degree-seeking undergraduates, 6% already have a bachelor's degree or higher, 155 enrolled as first-time, first-year students, 106 transferred in from other institutions.

Part-time:	38%	International:	7%
Out-of-state:	12%	25 or older:	43%
Women:	67%	Live on campus:	9%
African American:	16%		

Basis for selection. Students must meet acceptance criteria for specific majors and interview with admissions.

High school preparation. Recommended units include English 4, mathematics 4, social studies 4, history 4, science 4 (laboratory 1).

2015-2016 Annual costs. Tuition/fees: $26,780. Per-credit charge: $876. Room/board: $13,000. Books/supplies: $1,200. Personal expenses: $3,000. **Additional information:** Tuition is based 30 credits per academic year. Bay State College charges by the credit to offer personalized flexibility on course loads. Online and Evening programs are offered at a considerably reduced rate.

2014-2015 Financial aid. Need-based: 37% of total undergraduate aid awarded as scholarships/grants, 63% as loans/jobs. Need-based aid available for part-time students. Work-study available nights, weekends and for part-time students. **Non-need-based:** Scholarships awarded for academics, alumni affiliation, job skills, leadership.

Application procedures. Admission: No deadline. $50 fee, may be waived for applicants with need. Admission notification on a rolling basis. **Financial aid:** Priority date 3/15, closing date 6/30. FAFSA required. Applicants notified on a rolling basis starting 2/1.

Academics. Special study options: Accelerated study, distance learning, double major, honors, independent study, internships, study abroad. License preparation in nursing, physical therapy. **Credit/placement by examination:** AP, CLEP, IB, institutional tests. 30 credit hours maximum toward associate degree, 30 toward bachelor's. **Support services:** Learning center, reduced course load, remedial instruction, study skills assistance, tutoring, writing center. Student Success Coordinators who provide outreach to students at risk.

Majors. Business: Business admin, fashion, hospitality/recreation, retailing. **Computer sciences:** Information technology. **Education:** Early childhood. **Health services:** General, licensed practical nurse, medical assistant, physical therapy assistant. **Protective services:** Criminal justice. **Visual/performing arts:** Fashion design, music management.

Most popular majors. Business/marketing 26%, health sciences 50%, security/protective services 10%, visual/performing arts 11%.

Technology on campus. 62 workstations in dormitories, library, computer center, student center. Dormitories wired for high-speed internet access and linked to campus network. Commuter students can connect to campus network. Online course registration, online library, helpline, repair service, student web hosting, wireless network available.

Student life. Freshman orientation: Mandatory, $25 fee. Preregistration for classes offered. Held few days prior to the start of the semester. **Policies:** Freshmen not permitted cars on campus. **Housing:** Coed dorms available. $300 nonrefundable deposit. **Activities:** International student organizations, radio station, student government, Community Organizers (Community O's), Justice Society, Alternative Spring Break, Trip/Habitat for Humanity.

Student services. Adult student services, alcohol/substance abuse counseling, career counseling, services for economically disadvantaged, student employment services, financial aid counseling, minority student services, personal counseling, placement for graduates, veterans' counselor, women's services. **Transfer:** Re-entry adviser, pre-admission transcript evaluation for new students. Transfer adviser, college fairs on campus for students transferring to 4-year colleges.

Contact. E-mail: admissions@baystate.edu
Phone: (617) 217-9000 Toll-free number: (800) 815-3276
Fax: (617) 249-0400
Clancy Krueger, Director of College-Wide Admissions, Bay State College, 122 Commonwealth Avenue, Boston, MA 02116

Benjamin Franklin Institute of Technology
Boston, Massachusetts   CB member
www.bfit.edu   CB code: 3394

▶ Private 2-year technical college
▶ Commuter campus in very large city
▶ Application essay required

General. Founded in 1908. Regionally accredited. Prepares students for careers in automotive, computer, industrial, and engineering technologies. **Enrollment:** 485 degree-seeking undergraduates; 8 non-degree-seeking students. **Degrees:** 16 bachelor's, 113 associate awarded. **Calendar:** Semester, limited summer session. **Full-time faculty:** 35 total; 9% have terminal degrees, 9% minority, 31% women. **Part-time faculty:** 27 total; 11% have terminal degrees, 15% minority, 30% women. **Class size:** 96% < 20, 4% 20-39. **Special facilities:** Extensive learning laboratories for automotive, architecture, computer, electronic, electrical, optician, pharmacy, and mechanical engineering technologies.

Student profile. Among degree-seeking undergraduates, 210 enrolled as first-time, first-year students.

Part-time:	12%	25 or older:	21%
Out-of-state:	6%	Live on campus:	8%
Women:	10%		

Transfer out. Colleges most students transferred to 2015: University of Massachusetts at Lowell, Wentworth Institute, Boston Architectural College, University of Massachusetts at Dartmouth, University of Massachusetts at Boston.

Basis for selection. High school academic performance and motivation most important. After conditional admission, all students required to take placement testing to determine English and math-level placement. Math requirements vary by academic program. SAT or ACT recommended. Interview recommended. **Home schooled:** State high school equivalency certificate, letter of recommendation (nonparent) required.

High school preparation. 17 units required; 20 recommended. Required and recommended units include English 4, mathematics 3-4, social studies 2, history 1, science 3 (laboratory 2), foreign language 2 and computer science 2. Level of math and science required varies by program.

2015-2016 Annual costs. Tuition/fees: $16,950. Per-credit charge: $707. Room/board: $13,900. Books/supplies: $900. Personal expenses: $550.

Financial aid. Need-based: Need-based aid available for part-time students. Work-study available nights, weekends and for part-time students. **Non-need-based:** Scholarships awarded for academics, leadership, state residency.

Application procedures. Admission: Priority date 6/1; no deadline. $25 fee, may be waived for applicants with need, free for online applicants. Admission notification on a rolling basis beginning on or about 11/15. **Financial aid:** Priority date 3/1; no closing date. FAFSA required. Applicants notified on a rolling basis starting 3/1; must reply within 3 week(s) of notification.

Academics. Special study options: Accelerated study, cross-registration, dual enrollment of high school students, ESL, independent study, internships. Bachelor's degree programs available on campus. **Credit/placement by examination:** AP, CLEP, IB, institutional tests. **Support services:** Learning center, pre-admission summer program, reduced course load, remedial instruction, study skills assistance, tutoring.

Majors. Architecture: Technology. **Biology:** Biomedical sciences. **Computer sciences:** General, programming. **General:** Electrician. **Health services:** Ophthalmic technology, optician.

Most popular majors. Health sciences 6%, library sciences 45%, trade and industry 49%.

Technology on campus. 120 workstations in library, computer center. Dormitories wired for high-speed internet access and linked to campus network. Commuter students can connect to campus network. Online library, helpline, wireless network available.

Student life. Freshman orientation: Mandatory. Preregistration for classes offered. Two-day program held in late-August or early-September prior to first day of class. **Housing:** Coed dorms available. $200 fully refundable deposit, deadline 6/1. **Activities:** Student government.

Athletics. NJCAA. **Intercollegiate:** Soccer M. **Intramural:** Basketball, football (non-tackle), skiing, table tennis. **Team name:** Shockers.

Student services. Career counseling, student employment services, financial aid counseling, personal counseling, placement for graduates, veterans' counselor, women's services. **Transfer:** Pre-admission transcript evaluation for new students. Transfer adviser, college fairs on campus for students transferring to 4-year colleges.

Contact. E-mail: admissions@bfit.edu
Phone: (617) 423-4630 ext. 121
Toll-free number: (877) 400-2348 ext. 121 Fax: (617) 778-6499
Marvin Loiseau, Dean of Admissions, Benjamin Franklin Institute of Technology, 41 Berkeley Street, Boston, MA 02116

Berkshire Community College
Pittsfield, Massachusetts **CB member**
www.berkshirecc.edu **CB code: 3102**

- Public 2-year community college
- Commuter campus in large town

General. Founded in 1960. Regionally accredited. **Enrollment:** 1,781 degree-seeking undergraduates; 330 non-degree-seeking students. **Degrees:** 265 associate awarded. **Location:** 45 miles from Albany, NY. **Calendar:** Semester, limited summer session. **Full-time faculty:** 56 total; 23% have terminal degrees, 7% minority, 62% women. **Part-time faculty:** 159 total; 14% have terminal degrees, 2% minority, 56% women. **Class size:** 75% < 20, 24% 20-39, less than 1% 50-99. **Special facilities:** Global positioning laboratory, nature trails, renewable energy technology resource training center, public recreational facility. **Partnerships:** Formal partnerships with Plastics Network, Applied Technology Council, Berkshire Works, Tech-Prep programs, service learning programs.

Student profile. Among degree-seeking undergraduates, 37% enrolled in a transfer program, 63% enrolled in a vocational program, 434 enrolled as first-time, first-year students, 164 transferred in from other institutions.

Part-time:	60%	Asian American:	2%
Out-of-state:	3%	Hispanic/Latino:	7%
Women:	59%	Multi-racial, non-Hispanic:	2%
African American:	7%	25 or older:	43%

Transfer out. Colleges most students transferred to 2015: University of Massachusetts-Amherst, Massachusetts College of Liberal Arts, Westfield State University, Sage College, Elms College.

Basis for selection. Open admission, but selective for some programs. Special requirements for nursing and allied health programs. **Home schooled:** State high school equivalency certificate required.

High school preparation. 1 chemistry, 1 biology, 1 algebra, demonstrated college level English skills required for nursing and health program applicants.

2015-2016 Annual costs. Tuition/fees: $6,060; $13,080 out-of-state. Per-credit charge: $26 in-state; $260 out-of-state. Books/supplies: $1,260. Personal expenses: $3,660.

Financial aid. Need-based: Need-based aid available for part-time students. Work-study available nights, weekends and for part-time students. **Non-need-based:** Scholarships awarded for academics, job skills, leadership, minority status, state residency.

Application procedures. Admission: No deadline. No application fee. Admission notification on a rolling basis. High school students may enroll in Dual Enrollment program and may take full time credit load (12 credits or more). **Financial aid:** No deadline. FAFSA required. Applicants notified on a rolling basis starting 6/1.

Academics. Special study options: Cross-registration, distance learning, dual enrollment of high school students, ESL, honors, independent study, internships, liberal arts/career combination. License preparation in nursing. **Credit/placement by examination:** AP, CLEP, IB, institutional tests. 51 credit hours maximum toward associate degree. **Support services:** GED test

---

center, learning center, pre-admission summer program, reduced course load, remedial instruction, study skills assistance, tutoring, writing center.

Majors. Business: General, business admin, hospitality admin, office technology. **Computer sciences:** General. **Conservation:** Environmental science. **Engineering:** General. **Health services:** Nursing (RN), physical therapy assistant, respiratory therapy technology. **Human services:** Community org/advocacy. **Liberal arts:** Arts/sciences. **Physical sciences:** Atmospheric science. **Protective services:** Criminal justice, firefighting. **Social sciences:** General. **Visual/performing arts:** General.

Most popular majors. Business/marketing 13%, engineering/engineering technologies 7%, health sciences 31%, liberal arts 25%, public administration/social services 8%, security/protective services 7%.

Technology on campus. 360 workstations in library, computer center, student center. Commuter students can connect to campus network. Online course registration, online library, helpline, wireless network available.

Student life. Freshman orientation: Mandatory. Preregistration for classes offered. Variety of options, including 1-day orientation/registration and 2-week summer transition program. **Policies:** Alcohol- and smoke-free campus. **Activities:** Jazz band, choral groups, dance, drama, international student organizations, literary magazine, music ensembles, musical theater, student government, Phi Theta Kappa honor society.

Student services. Adult student services, alcohol/substance abuse counseling, career counseling, services for economically disadvantaged, student employment services, financial aid counseling, minority student services, on-campus daycare, personal counseling, placement for graduates, veterans' counselor, women's services. **Physically disabled:** Services for visually, speech, hearing impaired. **Transfer:** Re-entry adviser, pre-admission transcript evaluation for new students. Transfer adviser, college fairs on campus for students transferring to 4-year colleges.

Contact. E-mail: admissions@berkshirecc.edu
Phone: (413) 236-1630 Toll-free number: (800) 816-1233 ext. 1630
Fax: (413) 496-9511
Christina Barrett, Director of Marketing and Student Recruitment, Berkshire Community College, 1350 West Street, Pittsfield, MA 01201-5786

Bristol Community College
Fall River, Massachusetts **CB member**
www.bristolcc.edu **CB code: 3110**

- Public 2-year community college
- Commuter campus in small city

General. Founded in 1965. Regionally accredited. **Enrollment:** 8,046 degree-seeking undergraduates. **Degrees:** 1,291 associate awarded. **Location:** 48 miles from Boston; 17 miles from Providence, Rhode Island. **Calendar:** Semester, extensive summer session. **Full-time faculty:** 131 total; 98% have terminal degrees, 11% minority, 70% women. **Part-time faculty:** 555 total; 75% have terminal degrees, 6% minority, 52% women. **Special facilities:** Planetarium, greenhouse, robotics laboratory, aquaculture laboratory, cyber cafe. **Partnerships:** Formal partnerships with local businesses and non-profit organizations.

Student profile.

Out-of-state:	15%	25 or older:	49%

Basis for selection. Open admission, but selective for some programs. Special requirements for health science and culinary arts programs. Essay or personal statement required for applicants to occupational therapy assistant program. **Home schooled:** Transcript of courses and grades required. Letter from student's school committee or Superintendent approving home-school program.

2015-2016 Annual costs. Tuition/fees: $5,505; $11,685 out-of-state. Per-credit charge: $24 in-state; $230 out-of-state. Books/supplies: $1,600. Personal expenses: $6,006.

Financial aid. Need-based: Need-based aid available for part-time students. Work-study available nights, weekends and for part-time students. **Non-need-based:** Scholarships awarded for academics, art, leadership, minority status, music/drama.

Application procedures. Admission: No deadline. $10 fee ($35 out-of-state), may be waived for applicants with need, free for online applicants. Admission notification on a rolling basis beginning on or about 12/1. Must reply by May 1 or within 2 week(s) if notified thereafter. **Financial aid:**

Two-Year Colleges

Priority date 5/1; no closing date. FAFSA, institutional form required. Applicants notified on a rolling basis starting 5/1; must reply within 2 week(s) of notification.

Academics. Students must complete general education requirement core curriculum prior to graduation. **Special study options:** Accelerated study, cooperative education, cross-registration, distance learning, dual enrollment of high school students, ESL, honors, independent study, internships, student-designed major, weekend college. License preparation in nursing, occupational therapy. **Credit/placement by examination:** AP, CLEP, institutional tests. 30 credit hours maximum toward associate degree. **Support services:** GED preparation and test center, learning center, pre-admission summer program, reduced course load, remedial instruction, study skills assistance, tutoring, writing center.

Majors. Business: General, accounting, banking/financial services, business admin, entrepreneurial studies, marketing, real estate, receptionist. **Communications:** Communications/speech/rhetoric. **Computer sciences:** General, computer science, data processing, information systems, networking, programming, systems analysis. **Conservation:** Environmental studies. **Education:** Elementary, kindergarten/preschool. **Engineering:** General, engineering science, environmental, manufacturing, mechanical, structural, water resource. **Foreign languages:** American Sign Language. **Health services:** Clinical lab technology, dental hygiene, health information technology, medical secretary, nursing (RN), occupational therapy assistant. **Human services:** Social work. **Liberal arts:** Arts/sciences, humanities. **Protective services:** Criminal justice, firefighting. **Social sciences:** General. **Visual/performing arts:** Design, graphic design, multimedia, studio arts. **Work/family studies:** Child care management.

Technology on campus. 1,000 workstations in library, computer center, student center. Commuter students can connect to campus network. Online course registration, online library, helpline, wireless network available.

Student life. Freshman orientation: Available. Preregistration for classes offered. **Activities:** Campus ministries, drama, international student organizations, radio station, student government, student newspaper, TV station, Christian Fellowship, International club, Portuguese club, Latino club, Nursing, Occupational Therapy, Photography club, Academic Support club, Asian student association, Bio Technology club.

Athletics. NJCAA. **Intercollegiate:** Basketball, soccer, tennis. **Team name:** Bristol Bees.

Student services. Adult student services, alcohol/substance abuse counseling, chaplain/spiritual director, career counseling, student employment services, financial aid counseling, health services, minority student services, on-campus daycare, personal counseling, placement for graduates, veterans' counselor. **Physically disabled:** Services for visually, speech, hearing impaired. **Transfer:** Transfer adviser, college fairs on campus for students transferring to 4-year colleges.

Contact. E-mail: admissions@bristolcc.edu
Phone: (508) 678-2811 ext. 2516 Toll-free number: (800) 462-0035
Fax: (508) 730-3265
Shilo Henriques, Dean of Admissions, Bristol Community College, 777 Elsbree Street, Fall River, MA 02720-7395

Bunker Hill Community College

Boston, Massachusetts — CB member
www.bhcc.edu — CB code: 3123

▸ Public 2-year community college
▸ Commuter campus in very large city

General. Founded in 1973. Regionally accredited. **Enrollment:** 13,187 degree-seeking undergraduates; 860 non-degree-seeking students. **Degrees:** 1,198 associate awarded. **Location:** 5 miles from downtown. **Calendar:** Semester, extensive summer session. **Full-time faculty:** 156 total. **Part-time faculty:** 612 total. **Class size:** 43% < 20, 57% 20-39, less than 1% 40-49. **Special facilities:** The Mary L. Fifield Art Gallery at Bunker Hill Community College provides the College and local communities opportunities to view high-caliber art exhibitions, exposure to a diversity of ideas and artistic media and access to forums with emerging and established Boston-based artists.

Student profile. Among degree-seeking undergraduates, 1,678 enrolled as first-time, first-year students, 1,067 transferred in from other institutions.

Part-time: 69% **Women:** 56%

Transfer out. Colleges most students transferred to 2015: University of Massachusetts Boston, Northeastern University, Salem State College, Suffolk University, Lesley Univeristy.

Basis for selection. Open admission, but selective for some programs. Limited admissions to Nursing program, Medical Radiography, Surgical Technology, Electric Power Utility Program (NSTAR), Medical Assistant, Central Processing, Practical Nursing, Patient Care Technician, Medical Laboratory Technician, Pharmacy Technician, Paralegal, Paramedic Program, Taxation. **Home schooled:** Transcript of courses and grades required. Must submit evidence that program was approved by school district's superintendent or school committee. If under the age of 16, a letter from school district's superintendent or school committee required as well.

2015-2016 Annual costs. Tuition/fees: $4,470; $10,650 out-of-state. Per-credit charge: $24 in-state; $230 out-of-state. Books/supplies: $1,800. Personal expenses: $1,800.

Financial aid. Need-based: Need-based aid available for part-time students. Work-study available nights, weekends and for part-time students. **Non-need-based:** Scholarships awarded for academics.

Application procedures. Admission: No deadline. No application fee. Admission notification on a rolling basis. **Financial aid:** Priority date 5/1; no closing date. FAFSA required. Applicants notified on a rolling basis starting 6/1; must reply within 2 week(s) of notification.

Academics. Some courses taught off-campus in the community. **Special study options:** Cross-registration, distance learning, double major, dual enrollment of high school students, ESL, external degree, honors, independent study, internships, liberal arts/career combination, study abroad, weekend college. License preparation in nursing, paramedic, radiology, real estate. **Credit/placement by examination:** AP, CLEP, institutional tests. 45 credit hours maximum toward associate degree. **Support services:** GED preparation, learning center, pre-admission summer program, reduced course load, remedial instruction, study skills assistance, tutoring, writing center.

Majors. Biology: General, biotechnology. **Business:** Accounting, business admin, finance, hospitality admin, international, office/clerical, operations, tourism/travel. **Communications:** Communications/speech/rhetoric. **Computer sciences:** Applications programming, computer science, data entry, networking, security, system admin, web page design, word processing. **Education:** General. **Engineering:** General, biomedical. **English:** English lit. **Foreign languages:** General. **Health services:** Cardiovascular technology, medical secretary, nuclear medical technology, nursing (RN), respiratory therapy technology, sonography. **History:** General. **Math:** General. **Physical sciences:** Chemistry, physics. **Protective services:** Corrections, law enforcement admin, security management. **Psychology:** General. **Social sciences:** Sociology. **Visual/performing arts:** Art, design, dramatic, music.

Most popular majors. Business/marketing 24%, computer/information sciences 6%, health sciences 16%, liberal arts 16%, security/protective services 6%.

Technology on campus. 1,674 workstations in library, computer center. Commuter students can connect to campus network. Online course registration, online library, helpline, wireless network available.

Student life. Freshman orientation: Available. Preregistration for classes offered. **Activities:** Jazz band, choral groups, drama, film society, international student organizations, music ensembles, radio station, student government, African American cultural society, African students club, Arab students association, Asian students association, Brazilian club, criminal justice society, multicultural club, Veterans of All Nations club, sustainability club, student success club.

Athletics. NJCAA. **Intercollegiate:** Baseball M, basketball, soccer. **Intramural:** Basketball, soccer, volleyball. **Team name:** Bulldogs.

Student services. Adult student services, career counseling, services for economically disadvantaged, student employment services, financial aid counseling, health services, on-campus daycare, personal counseling, placement for graduates, veterans' counselor. **Physically disabled:** Services for visually, speech, hearing impaired. **Transfer:** Re-entry adviser, pre-admission transcript evaluation for new students. Transfer center, transfer adviser, college fairs on campus for students transferring to 4-year colleges.

Contact. E-mail: admissions@bhcc.mass.edu
Phone: (617) 228-3398 Fax: (617) 228-3481
Vanessa Rowley, Director of Enrollment Management and Admissions, Bunker Hill Community College, 250 New Rutherford Avenue, Boston, MA 02129-2925

Cape Cod Community College

West Barnstable, Massachusetts — CB member
www.capecod.edu — CB code: 3289

▸ Public 2-year community college
▸ Commuter campus in small town

General. Founded in 1961. Regionally accredited. **Enrollment:** 3,057 degree-seeking undergraduates. **Degrees:** 448 associate awarded. **Location:** 79 miles from Boston; 80 miles from Providence, Rhode Island. **Calendar:** Semester, limited summer session. **Full-time faculty:** 68 total; 18% minority, 34% women. **Part-time faculty:** 247 total. **Class size:** 36% < 20, 63% 20-39, less than 1% 40-49, less than 1% 50-99. **Special facilities:** Source collection for Cape Cod history, marshland nature preserve, maritime studies collection, art gallery.

Transfer out. Colleges most students transferred to 2015: Bridgewater State College, University of Massachusetts (Amherst, Boston, Dartmouth), Suffolk University.

Basis for selection. Open admission, but selective for some programs. Special requirements for dental hygiene, massage therapy and nursing programs; priority given to Massachusetts residents. Interview recommended for dental hygiene and nursing programs. **Home schooled:** Ability To Benefit assessment required.

High school preparation. Chemistry with lab and algebra required for dental hygiene and nursing programs. Nursing also requires biology with anatomy and physiology unit labs.

2015-2016 Annual costs. Tuition/fees: $7,620; $11,250 out-of-state. Per-credit charge: $24 in-state; $230 out-of-state. Books/supplies: $1,200. Personal expenses: $6,956.

Financial aid. Need-based: Need-based aid available for part-time students. Work-study available nights, weekends and for part-time students. **Non-need-based:** Scholarships awarded for academics, art, job skills, leadership, music/drama, state residency.

Application procedures. Admission: Priority date 8/10; no deadline. No application fee. Admission notification on a rolling basis. Must reply by May 1 or within 4 week(s) if notified thereafter. January 5 application priority date for nursing, February 1 for dental hygiene. **Financial aid:** Priority date 5/1; no closing date. FAFSA required. Applicants notified on a rolling basis starting 5/1.

Academics. Special study options: Accelerated study, combined bachelor's/graduate degree, cooperative education, distance learning, dual enrollment of high school students, ESL, honors, independent study, internships, study abroad. Bachelor's degree programs available on campus. License preparation in aviation, dental hygiene, nursing, paramedic, real estate. **Credit/placement by examination:** AP, CLEP, institutional tests. 30 credit hours maximum toward associate degree. **Support services:** GED preparation and test center, learning center, reduced course load, remedial instruction, study skills assistance, tutoring, writing center.

Honors college/program. Students invited based on GPA at end of first semester or CPT results.

Majors. Business: Accounting, accounting/business management, administrative services, business admin, executive assistant, hotel/motel admin, management science, marketing, office management, office/clerical. **Communications:** Communications/speech/rhetoric, journalism, media studies, public relations. **Computer sciences:** General, applications programming, computer science, information systems, information technology, LAN/WAN management, networking, web page design, webmaster. **Conservation:** General, environmental science, environmental studies. **Education:** General, early childhood, kindergarten/preschool. **Engineering:** General. **English:** English lit. **Foreign languages:** General. **Health services:** Dental hygiene, EMT paramedic, medical secretary, nursing (RN), predental, prenursing. **History:** General. **Liberal arts:** Arts/sciences. **Math:** General. **Philosophy/religion:** Philosophy. **Physical sciences:** General. **Protective services:** Criminal justice, fire safety technology, firefighting, law enforcement admin. **Psychology:** General. **Social sciences:** General, sociology. **Visual/performing arts:** General, commercial/advertising art, dance, dramatic, graphic design, music.

Most popular majors. Computer/information sciences 19%, education 29%, English 7%, interdisciplinary studies 21%, liberal arts 93%.

Technology on campus. 400 workstations in library, computer center, student center. Commuter students can connect to campus network. Online library, helpline, wireless network available.

Student life. Freshman orientation: Mandatory. Preregistration for classes offered. Half-day program includes meeting with assigned adviser. **Policies:** All clubs must perform one item of community service in order to maintain recognition. **Activities:** Jazz band, choral groups, dance, drama, literary magazine, music ensembles, musical theater, radio station, student government, student newspaper, TV station, Phi Theta Kappa honor society, service learning, unity club, academic support club, recycling club, rotary club, sustainability club, gay-straight alliance.

Athletics. Intramural: Basketball, racquetball, table tennis, tennis, volleyball. **Team name:** Helmsmen.

Student services. Adult student services, alcohol/substance abuse counseling, career counseling, services for economically disadvantaged, student employment services, financial aid counseling, health services, minority student services, on-campus daycare, personal counseling, placement for graduates, veterans' counselor. **Physically disabled:** Services for visually, speech, hearing impaired. **Transfer:** Re-entry adviser, pre-admission transcript evaluation for new students. Transfer adviser, college fairs on campus for students transferring to 4-year colleges.

Contact. E-mail: admiss@capecod.edu
Phone: (508) 362-2131 ext. 4311
Toll-free number: (877) 846-3672 ext. 4311 Fax: (508) 375-4089
Mathew Cormier, Director of Admissions, Cape Cod Community College, 2240 Iyannough Road, West Barnstable, MA 02668-1599

Dean College
Franklin, Massachusetts
www.dean.edu

CB member
CB code: 3352

▶ Private 2-year liberal arts and performing arts college
▶ Residential campus in large town

General. Founded in 1865. Regionally accredited. Arch program for students with diagnosed learning disabilities (12% of student population), Honors Program available (5% of student population). **Enrollment:** 1,113 degree-seeking undergraduates. **Degrees:** 97 bachelor's, 191 associate awarded. **Location:** 30 miles from Boston; 30 miles from Providence, Rhode Island. **Calendar:** Semester, limited summer session. **Full-time faculty:** 31 total; 64% have terminal degrees, 16% minority, 55% women. **Part-time faculty:** 107 total; 19% have terminal degrees, 51% women. **Class size:** 56% < 20, 44% 20-39, less than 1% 40-49. **Special facilities:** Radio station, telecommunications center, childcare center, state of the art theatre, 3D science lab. **Partnerships:** Formal partnerships with Putnam Investments (students may earn associate degree while working), EMC, and the Kraft Sports Group.

Student profile. Among degree-seeking undergraduates, 497 enrolled as first-time, first-year students, 51 transferred in from other institutions.

Out-of-state:	53%	Native American:	1%
Women:	46%	Multi-racial, non-Hispanic:	4%
African American:	21%	25 or older:	1%
Asian American:	3%	Live on campus:	86%

Transfer out. Colleges most students transferred to 2015: Suffolk University, Northeastern University, University of Massachusetts Amherst, Emerson College, Bridgewater State University.

Basis for selection. School achievement record, recommendations most important. Dean College is a test optional school. We encourage submitting your scores, they will never be used as a reason to deny admission. Interview recommended. Students applying to a performing arts major must complete an audition or portfolio review. **Home schooled:** Statement describing home school structure and mission, transcript of courses and grades required. **Learning Disabled:** Arch program applicants must submit appropriate materials that identify and describe the student's learning abilities and any issues relevant to successful completion of a college program.

High school preparation. College-preparatory program recommended. Required and recommended units include English 4, mathematics 3, social studies 3, science 3 and foreign language 1.

2015-2016 Annual costs. Tuition/fees: $35,720. Room/board: $15,200. Books/supplies: $1,000. Personal expenses: $500.

2015-2016 Financial aid. Need-based: 394 full-time freshmen applied for aid; 372 deemed to have need; 372 received aid. Average need met was 70%. Average scholarship/grant was $25,206; average loan $3,112. 69% of total undergraduate aid awarded as scholarships/grants, 31% as loans/jobs. Need-based aid available for part-time students. Work-study available nights, weekends and for part-time students. **Non-need-based:** Awarded to 1,252 full-time undergraduates, including 581 freshmen. Scholarships awarded for academics, alumni affiliation, art, athletics, leadership, music/drama.

Application procedures. Admission: Priority date 3/15; deadline 8/30. No application fee. Application must be submitted online. Admission notification on a rolling basis beginning on or about 11/1. Must reply by May 1 or within 2 week(s) if notified thereafter. **Financial aid:** Priority date 3/15; no closing date. FAFSA required. Applicants notified on a rolling basis starting 2/25; must reply by 5/1 or within 2 week(s) of notification.

Academics. Special study options: Accelerated study, cross-registration, distance learning, double major, ESL, exchange student, honors, independent study, internships, student-designed major, study abroad, teacher certification program, Washington semester. Bachelor's degree programs available on campus. **Credit/placement by examination:** AP, CLEP, IB, SAT, ACT.

Support services: Learning center, reduced course load, study skills assistance, tutoring, writing center.

Majors. Biology: General. **Business:** Business admin. **Communications:** Communications/speech/rhetoric. **Conservation:** Environmental science. **Education:** Elementary. **English:** English lit. **History:** General. **Math:** General. **Parks/recreation:** Sports admin. **Protective services:** Criminal justice. **Psychology:** General. **Social sciences:** Sociology. **Visual/performing arts:** Dance, dramatic.

Most popular majors. Business/marketing 14%, education 7%, liberal arts 35%, parks/recreation 15%, security/protective services 8%, visual/performing arts 7%.

Technology on campus. PC or laptop required. Online library, helpline, wireless network available.

Student life. Freshman orientation: Mandatory. Preregistration for classes offered. **Policies:** Freshmen not permitted cars on campus. **Housing:** Guaranteed on-campus for all undergraduates. Coed dorms, single-sex dorms, apartments, themed housing, wellness housing available. $500 nonrefundable deposit, deadline 1/1. Off-campus condos available. **Activities:** Choral groups, dance, drama, international student organizations, music ensembles, musical theater, radio station, student government, Fellowship for christian students, Jewish community club, community outreach, National Society of Leadership and Success, Student Leadership Network.

Athletics. USCAA. Intercollegiate: Baseball M, basketball, cross-country, football (tackle) M, golf, lacrosse, soccer, softball W, volleyball M. **Intramural:** Basketball W, soccer, softball W. **Team name:** Bulldogs.

Student services. Adult student services, alcohol/substance abuse counseling, career counseling, student employment services, financial aid counseling, health services, on-campus daycare, personal counseling, placement for graduates, veterans' counselor. **Physically disabled:** Services for visually, speech, hearing impaired. **Transfer:** Transfer center, transfer adviser, college fairs on campus for students transferring to 4-year colleges.

Contact. E-mail: admissions@dean.edu
Phone: (508) 541-1508 Toll-free number: (877) 879-3326
Fax: (508) 541-8726
Iris Godes, Associate Vice President of Enrollment/Dean of Admissions, Dean College, 99 Main Street, Franklin, MA 02038-1994

Greenfield Community College
Greenfield, Massachusetts
www.gcc.mass.edu

CB member
CB code: 3420

- Public 2-year community college
- Commuter campus in large town

General. Founded in 1962. Regionally accredited. Students may enroll in credit courses taught at Smith College, Veterans Hospital (Northampton), Massachusetts College of Art. **Enrollment:** 1,850 degree-seeking undergraduates. **Degrees:** 314 associate awarded. **Location:** 40 miles from Springfield. **Calendar:** Semester, limited summer session. **Full-time faculty:** 62 total. **Part-time faculty:** 121 total. **Class size:** 75% < 20, 24% 20-39, less than 1% 40-49, less than 1% 50-99. **Special facilities:** Zero net energy greenhouse.

Transfer out. Colleges most students transferred to 2015: University of Massachusetts: Amherst, Westfield State College, Massachusetts College of Liberal Arts, Smith College, Elms College.

Basis for selection. Open admission, but selective for some programs. Special entrance requirements for nursing, paramedic, and outdoor leadership programs. **Home schooled:** State high school equivalency certificate required. Evidence that home school program was approved by student's school district's superintendent or school committee must be submitted at time of application. If under compulsory age, additional letter from student's school district's superintendent or school committee stating the student is not considered truant also required.

High school preparation. College-preparatory program recommended. Students from public high schools in the Commonwealth must be MCAS graduates, or demonstrate an ability to benefit.

2015-2016 Annual costs. Tuition/fees: $6,482; $14,132 out-of-state. Per-credit charge: $26 in-state; $281 out-of-state. Books/supplies: $850. Personal expenses: $1,560.

Financial aid. All financial aid based on need. Need-based aid available for part-time students. Work-study available nights, weekends and for part-time students.

Application procedures. Admission: No deadline. No application fee. Admission notification on a rolling basis. Limited space available in nursing and outdoor leadership programs. Application priority date 2/1. **Financial aid:** Priority date 4/15; no closing date. FAFSA, institutional form required. Applicants notified on a rolling basis starting 5/1; must reply within 2 week(s) of notification.

Academics. Special study options: Cross-registration, distance learning, double major, dual enrollment of high school students, ESL, independent study, internships, liberal arts/career combination. License preparation in nursing, paramedic, real estate. **Credit/placement by examination:** AP, CLEP, institutional tests. 15 credit hours maximum toward associate degree. **Support services:** GED test center, learning center, reduced course load, remedial instruction, study skills assistance, tutoring, writing center.

Majors. Business: General, accounting, administrative services, business admin. **Computer sciences:** General. **Conservation:** General, environmental science. **Education:** Early childhood. **Engineering:** Engineering science. **Health services:** Nursing (RN), occupational therapy assistant. **Liberal arts:** Arts/sciences. **Protective services:** Police science. **Visual/performing arts:** Commercial/advertising art.

Most popular majors. Business/marketing 8%, health sciences 15%, liberal arts 58%, security/protective services 9%.

Technology on campus. 272 workstations in library, computer center, student center. Commuter students can connect to campus network. Online library, helpline, wireless network available.

Student life. Freshman orientation: Available. Preregistration for classes offered. **Activities:** Jazz band, choral groups, dance, drama, international student organizations, music ensembles, student government.

Student services. Adult student services, alcohol/substance abuse counseling, career counseling, services for economically disadvantaged, student employment services, financial aid counseling, personal counseling, placement for graduates, veterans' counselor, women's services. **Physically disabled:** Services for visually, speech, hearing impaired. **Transfer:** Re-entry adviser, pre-admission transcript evaluation for new students. Transfer adviser, college fairs on campus for students transferring to 4-year colleges.

Contact. E-mail: admission@gcc.mass.edu
Phone: (413) 775-1801 Fax: (413) 775-1827
Colleen Kucinski, Director of Admission, Greenfield Community College, One College Drive, Greenfield, MA 01301

Holyoke Community College
Holyoke, Massachusetts
www.hcc.edu

CB member
CB code: 3437

- Public 2-year community college
- Commuter campus in large town

General. Founded in 1946. Regionally accredited. **Enrollment:** 5,851 degree-seeking undergraduates; 434 non-degree-seeking students. **Degrees:** 861 associate awarded. **ROTC:** Army, Air Force. **Location:** 8 miles from Springfield. **Calendar:** Semester, extensive summer session. **Full-time faculty:** 131 total; 41% have terminal degrees, 12% minority, 65% women. **Part-time faculty:** 355 total; 20% have terminal degrees, 11% minority, 59% women. **Class size:** 59% < 20, 41% 20-39, less than 1% 40-49, less than 1% 50-99.

Student profile. Among degree-seeking undergraduates, 1,416 enrolled as first-time, first-year students, 6,285 transferred in from other institutions.

Part-time:	51%	Hispanic/Latino:	24%
Out-of-state:	1%	Multi-racial, non-Hispanic:	3%
Women:	61%	International:	1%
African American:	6%	25 or older:	33%
Asian American:	2%		

Transfer out. Colleges most students transferred to 2015: University of Massachusetts-Amherst, Western New England College, American International College, Westfield State College, Elms College.

Basis for selection. Open admission, but selective for some programs. Special requirements for nursing, radiography, animal sciences, practical nursing, medical assistant, medical coding, graphic art certificate, and culinary programs. Audition required of music majors. Portfolio required of fine arts majors. **Home schooled:** Transcript of courses and grades required. Letter required from Superintendent stating student is approved to be home schooled.

2015-2016 Annual costs. Tuition/fees: $5,270; $11,450 out-of-state. Per-credit charge: $24 in-state; $230 out-of-state. Books/supplies: $1,600. Personal expenses: $1,280.

2014-2015 Financial aid. Need-based: 77% of total undergraduate aid awarded as scholarships/grants, 23% as loans/jobs. Need-based aid available for part-time students. Work-study available nights, weekends and for part-time students. **Non-need-based:** Scholarships awarded for academics, art, leadership, music/drama.

Application procedures. Admission: No deadline. No application fee. Admission notification on a rolling basis. **Financial aid:** Priority date 5/1; no closing date. FAFSA required. Applicants notified on a rolling basis starting 5/1; must reply within 2 week(s) of notification.

Academics. Special study options: Accelerated study, combined bachelor's/graduate degree, cooperative education, cross-registration, distance learning, double major, dual enrollment of high school students, ESL, honors, independent study, internships, liberal arts/career combination, student-designed major, study abroad, teacher certification program, weekend college. License preparation in nursing, radiology. **Credit/placement by examination:** AP, CLEP, institutional tests. 30 credit hours maximum toward associate degree. **Support services:** GED preparation and test center, learning center, reduced course load, remedial instruction, study skills assistance, tutoring, writing center.

Majors. Biology: General, biotechnology. **Business:** Accounting technology, administrative services, business admin, hospitality admin, human resources, restaurant/food services, retailing. **Computer sciences:** Applications programming. **Engineering:** General. **Health services:** Medical radiologic technology/radiation therapy, nursing (RN), public health ed, veterinary technology/assistant. **Human services:** Social work. **Liberal arts:** Arts/sciences. **Math:** General. **Parks/recreation:** Health/fitness, sports admin. **Physical sciences:** Chemistry, physics. **Protective services:** Criminal justice. **Visual/performing arts:** Art, music. **Work/family studies:** Child care management.

Most popular majors. Business/marketing 19%, health sciences 8%, liberal arts 47%, security/protective services 8%.

Technology on campus. 160 workstations in library, computer center, student center. Commuter students can connect to campus network. Online course registration, online library, helpline, wireless network available.

Student life. Freshman orientation: Mandatory. Preregistration for classes offered. **Activities:** Jazz band, choral groups, drama, international student organizations, literary magazine, music ensembles, musical theater, radio station, student government, student newspaper, symphony orchestra, more than 30 clubs and organizations available.

Athletics. NJCAA. **Intercollegiate:** Baseball M, basketball, cross-country, golf, soccer, volleyball W. **Team name:** Cougars.

Student services. Adult student services, alcohol/substance abuse counseling, career counseling, services for economically disadvantaged, student employment services, financial aid counseling, health services, minority student services, on-campus daycare, personal counseling, placement for graduates, veterans' counselor, women's services. **Physically disabled:** Services for visually, speech, hearing impaired. **Transfer:** Transfer adviser, college fairs on campus for students transferring to 4-year colleges.

Contact. E-mail: admissions@hcc.edu
Phone: (413) 552-2321 Fax: (413) 552-2045
Renee Tastad, Dean of Enrollment Management, Holyoke Community College, 303 Homestead Avenue, Holyoke, MA 01040

ITT Technical Institute: Norwood
Norwood, Massachusetts
www.itt-tech.edu
CB code: 2699

▶ For-profit 2-year technical college
▶ Commuter campus in small city
▶ Interview required

General. Accredited by ACICS. **Enrollment:** 455 undergraduates. **Degrees:** 33 bachelor's, 119 associate awarded. **Calendar:** Quarter, extensive summer session. **Full-time faculty:** 3 total. **Part-time faculty:** 50 total.

Basis for selection. Satisfactory scores from on-site tests in English and math required.

2015-2016 Annual costs. Per-credit-hour charge, $493, will vary depending on program level and course of study. Academic fee, $200. Some programs require purchase of tools, which could cost an additional $500. All costs subject to change.

Financial aid. Need-based: Work-study available nights, weekends and for part-time students.

Application procedures. Admission: No deadline. No application fee. Admission notification on a rolling basis. **Financial aid:** No deadline. FAFSA, institutional form required. Applicants notified on a rolling basis.

Academics. Credit/placement by examination: AP, CLEP. **Support services:** Learning center, tutoring.

Majors. Computer sciences: LAN/WAN management, networking, programming, web page design, webmaster.

Technology on campus. Online library available.

Student life. Freshman orientation: Available. Preregistration for classes offered.

Student services. Career counseling, student employment services, placement for graduates.

Contact. Phone: (781) 278-7200 Toll-free number: (800) 879-8324 Tom Ryan, Director of Recruitment, ITT Technical Institute: Norwood, 333 Providence Highway, Norwood, MA 02062

ITT Technical Institute: Wilmington
Wilmington, Massachusetts
www.itt-tech.edu
CB member
CB code: 7989

▶ For-profit 2-year technical and career college
▶ Commuter campus in large town

General. Regionally accredited; also accredited by ACICS. **Enrollment:** 347 undergraduates. **Degrees:** 33 bachelor's, 91 associate awarded. **Calendar:** Quarter. **Full-time faculty:** 4 total. **Part-time faculty:** 40 total.

Basis for selection. Satisfactory scores from on-site tests in English and math required.

2015-2016 Annual costs. Per-credit-hour charge, $493, will vary depending on program level and course of study. Academic fee, $200. Some programs require purchase of tools, which could cost an additional $500. All costs subject to change.

Financial aid. Need-based: Work-study available nights, weekends and for part-time students.

Application procedures. Admission: No deadline.

Academics. Credit/placement by examination: AP, CLEP.

Majors. Computer sciences: Networking, web page design.

Contact. ITT Technical Institute: Wilmington, 200 Ballardvale Street, Building 1 Suite 200, Wilmington, MA 01887

Laboure College
Milton, Massachusetts
www.laboure.edu
CB code: 3287

▶ Private 2-year health science and nursing college affiliated with the Roman Catholic Church
▶ Commuter campus in large town

General. Founded in 1971. Regionally accredited. 100% health care education focused. Program start dates three times per year. Affiliated with more than 50 health care agencies. **Enrollment:** 808 degree-seeking undergraduates. **Degrees:** 15 bachelor's, 142 associate awarded. **Location:** 7 miles from Boston, MA. **Calendar:** Semester, limited summer session. **Full-time faculty:** 27 total; 22% have terminal degrees, 4% minority, 82% women. **Part-time faculty:** 52 total; 14% have terminal degrees, 12% minority, 79% women. **Class size:** 68% < 20, 32% 20-39. **Special facilities:** Center for student success and teaching excellence, nursing simulation laboratory.

Student profile. Among degree-seeking undergraduates, 5% already have a bachelor's degree or higher, 9 enrolled as first-time, first-year students, 189 transferred in from other institutions.

Part-time:	93%	Asian American:	2%
Out-of-state:	5%	Hispanic/Latino:	8%
Women:	92%	Multi-racial, non-Hispanic:	1%
African American:	30%	25 or older:	75%

Basis for selection. Overall GPA of at least 2.0 and transcripts required from both high school and college (if applicable). SAT scores may be submitted to waive placement testing. **Home schooled:** Transcript of courses and grades, state high school equivalency certificate required.

High school preparation. College-preparatory program recommended. 10 units required; 16 recommended. Required and recommended units include English 4, mathematics 2, science 1-2 (laboratory 1).

2015-2016 Annual costs. Tuition/fees: $34,405. Per-credit charge: $930. Books/supplies: $1,250. Personal expenses: $1,000.

2014-2015 Financial aid. Need-based: 3 full-time freshmen applied for aid; 3 deemed to have need; 3 received aid. Average need met was 80%. Average scholarship/grant was $5,000; average loan $3,500. 19% of total undergraduate aid awarded as scholarships/grants, 81% as loans/jobs. Need-based aid available for part-time students. Work-study available nights, weekends and for part-time students. **Non-need-based:** Scholarships awarded for academics, alumni affiliation, leadership, religious affiliation.

Application procedures. Admission: Priority date 6/1; no deadline. $50 fee, may be waived for applicants with need. Admission notification on a rolling basis. Must reply and submit deposit within a specified time noted in their acceptance packet. **Financial aid:** Priority date 5/1; no closing date. FAFSA required. Applicants notified on a rolling basis starting 1/15; must reply within 2 week(s) of notification.

Academics. Flexible scheduling, hybrid and online options, personal faculty attention. **Special study options:** Accelerated study, combined bachelor's/graduate degree, distance learning, independent study. Bachelor's degree programs available on campus. License preparation in nursing. **Credit/placement by examination:** AP, CLEP, SAT, institutional tests. 17 credit hours maximum toward associate degree, 15 toward bachelor's. **Support services:** Learning center, reduced course load, remedial instruction, study skills assistance, tutoring. Academic Support Services such as advising, tutoring, study skills and career advising are conveniently located on campus for all students in The Center for Student Success and Teaching Excellence. Students enrolled in online programs are encouraged to contact The Center about accessing these services.

Majors. Health services: Dietetics, health information technology, medical radiologic technology/radiation therapy, nursing (RN).

Technology on campus. 60 workstations in library, computer center, student center. Commuter students can connect to campus network. Online course registration, online library, helpline, wireless network available.

Student life. Freshman orientation: Available. Preregistration for classes offered. One afternoon/evening orientation held prior to fall and spring semesters. Online programs conduct a career-specific online orientation. **Policies:** Policies in effect: student conduct policy (academic and non-academic); compliance policy (health and safety); Title IX policy. **Activities:** Campus ministries, student government, student newspaper, Laboure College Chapter of the National Student Nurses Association.

Student services. Adult student services, chaplain/spiritual director, career counseling, financial aid counseling, personal counseling. **Physically disabled:** Services for hearing impaired. **Transfer:** Pre-admission transcript evaluation for new students.

Contact. E-mail: admissions@laboure.edu
Phone: (617) 202-3491 Fax: (617) 296-7947
Erin Hanlon, Director of Admissions, Laboure College, 303 Adams Street, Milton, MA 02186

Marian Court College
Swampscott, Massachusetts
www.mariancourt.edu   **CB code: 9100**

- Private 2-year business and liberal arts college affiliated with the Roman Catholic Church
- Commuter campus in large town

General. Founded in 1964. Regionally accredited. **Location:** 12 miles from Boston. **Calendar:** Semester.

Annual costs/financial aid. Tuition/fees (2015-2016): $16,500. Books/supplies: $1,000. Need-based financial aid available to full-time and part-time students.

Contact. Phone: (781) 309-5200
Assistant VP of Enrollment Management, 35 Little's Point Road, Swampscott, MA 01907-2896

Massachusetts Bay Community College
Wellesley Hills, Massachusetts   **CB member**
www.massbay.edu   **CB code: 3294**

- Public 2-year community college
- Commuter campus in large town

General. Founded in 1961. Regionally accredited. Study abroad opportunities in Asia, Europe, and the Americas. **Enrollment:** 3,859 degree-seeking undergraduates. **Degrees:** 472 associate awarded. **Location:** 13 miles from Boston. **Calendar:** Semester, extensive summer session. **Full-time faculty:** 87 total; 62% women. **Part-time faculty:** 259 total; 53% women. **Class size:** 42% < 20, 57% 20-39, less than 1% 40-49, less than 1% 50-99. **Special facilities:** Technology and health science laboratories. **Partnerships:** Formal partnerships with Toyota, Chrysler, General Motors, EMC2.

Student profile.

Out-of-state: 1%   **25 or older:** 38%

Transfer out. Colleges most students transferred to 2015: Framingham State College, University of Massachusetts-Boston, Northeastern University, Bentley College.

Basis for selection. Open admission, but selective for some programs. Special requirements for nursing, radiologic technology, paramedic, respiratory therapy programs.

High school preparation. Some programs require special academic preparation.

2015-2016 Annual costs. Tuition/fees: $5,220; $11,400 out-of-state. Per-credit charge: $24 in-state; $230 out-of-state. Books/supplies: $1,200. Personal expenses: $3,638.

Financial aid. Need-based: Need-based aid available for part-time students. Work-study available nights, weekends and for part-time students.

Application procedures. Admission: No deadline. $20 fee, may be waived for applicants with need. Admission notification on a rolling basis. **Financial aid:** Priority date 5/1; no closing date. FAFSA required. Applicants notified on a rolling basis starting 4/1.

Academics. Special study options: Cooperative education, distance learning, dual enrollment of high school students, honors, internships, liberal arts/career combination, study abroad. License preparation in nursing, paramedic, physical therapy, radiology. **Credit/placement by examination:** AP, CLEP, IB, institutional tests. 30 credit hours maximum toward associate degree. **Support services:** Learning center, reduced course load, remedial instruction, study skills assistance, tutoring, writing center.

Majors. Biology: Marine. **Business:** General, accounting, business admin, hospitality admin. **Communications:** Communications/speech/rhetoric. **Computer sciences:** General, computer science, information systems. **Health services:** Medical informatics, medical radiologic technology/radiation therapy, nursing (RN), physical therapy assistant, respiratory therapy technology. **Liberal arts:** Arts/sciences. **Protective services:** Forensics, law enforcement admin. **Social sciences:** General. **Work/family studies:** Child care management.

Most popular majors. Business/marketing 18%, health sciences 17%, liberal arts 38%, security/protective services 6%, trade and industry 7%.

Technology on campus. 550 workstations in library, computer center, student center. Commuter students can connect to campus network. Wireless network available.

Student life. Freshman orientation: Available. Preregistration for classes offered. **Activities:** Drama, student government, student newspaper, volunteer service corps, Christian Fellowship, Hillel, New World club, Latino club, sexual orientation support group.

Athletics. NJCAA. **Intercollegiate:** Baseball M, basketball, cheerleading W, golf, soccer, softball W. **Intramural:** Ice hockey M. **Team name:** Buccaneers.

Student services. Adult student services, career counseling, student employment services, financial aid counseling, health services, minority student services, personal counseling, placement for graduates, veterans' counselor. **Physically disabled:** Services for visually, speech, hearing impaired. **Transfer:** Pre-admission transcript evaluation for new students. Transfer adviser, college fairs on campus for students transferring to 4-year colleges.

Contact. E-mail: info@massbay.edu
Phone: (781) 239-2500 Fax: (781) 239-1047
Lisa Slavin, Director for Admissions, Massachusetts Bay Community
College, 50 Oakland Street, Wellesley Hills, MA 02481

Massasoit Community College

Brockton, Massachusetts   **CB member**
www.massasoit.mass.edu   **CB code: 3549**

- Public 2-year community college
- Commuter campus in small city

General. Founded in 1966. Regionally accredited. Second campus located
in Canton, 10 miles from Boston. **Enrollment:** 6,738 degree-seeking undergraduates; 1,167 non-degree-seeking students. **Degrees:** 913 associate
awarded. **Location:** 25 miles from Boston. **Calendar:** Semester, extensive
summer session. **Full-time faculty:** 116 total. **Part-time faculty:** 568 total.
Special facilities: Theater, conference center, art museums.

Student profile. Among degree-seeking undergraduates, 1,715 enrolled as
first-time, first-year students.

Part-time:	51%	Women:	56%
Out-of-state:	1%	25 or older:	42%

Transfer out. Colleges most students transferred to 2015: Bridgewater
State University, University of Massachusetts Boston, University of Massachusetts Amherst, Stonehill College, Northeastern University.

Basis for selection. Open admission, but selective for some programs.
Special requirements for allied health programs.

2015-2016 Annual costs. Tuition/fees: $5,610; $11,790 out-of-state. Per-
credit charge: $24 in-state; $230 out-of-state. Books/supplies: $1,000. Per-
sonal expenses: $1,800.

Financial aid. All financial aid based on need. Need-based aid available
for part-time students. Work-study available nights, weekends and for part-
time students.

Application procedures. Admission: No deadline. No application fee.
Application must be submitted on paper. Admission notification on a rolling
basis. Application priority date of 2/1 for nursing and radiologic technology
programs. Application priority date of 6/15 for respiratory care program.
Financial aid: Priority date 4/15; no closing date. FAFSA required. Applicants notified on a rolling basis starting 6/1.

Academics. Special study options: Accelerated study, distance learning,
double major, dual enrollment of high school students, ESL, honors, independent study, internships, liberal arts/career combination, weekend college.
License preparation in nursing, paramedic, radiology, real estate. **Credit/
placement by examination:** AP, CLEP, institutional tests. 30 credit hours
maximum toward associate degree. **Support services:** GED preparation and
test center, learning center, pre-admission summer program, reduced course
load, remedial instruction, study skills assistance, tutoring, writing center.

Majors. Business: Accounting, business admin, hospitality admin, marketing, office management. **Communications:** Media studies. **Computer sciences:** General, programming. **Education:** Elementary. **Health services:**
Nursing (RN), radiologic technology/medical imaging, respiratory therapy
technology. **Liberal arts:** Arts/sciences. **Protective services:** Firefighting,
police science. **Visual/performing arts:** Dramatic, graphic design, studio
arts. **Work/family studies:** Child care management, child care service.

Most popular majors. Business/marketing 16%, health sciences 18%,
interdisciplinary studies 12%, liberal arts 23%, security/protective services
10%.

Technology on campus. Commuter students can connect to campus
network. Online library, helpline, repair service, student web hosting, wireless
network available.

Student life. Freshman orientation: Available. Preregistration for classes
offered. **Activities:** Choral groups, dance, drama, international student organizations, music ensembles, musical theater, radio station, student government,
student newspaper, Phi Theta Kappa, art and museum association, Helping
Hands, International Touch, senior center, women's resource center, Hearts
for Haiti, unity club.

Athletics. NJCAA. **Intercollegiate:** Baseball M, basketball, soccer, softball
W. **Intramural:** Racquetball, swimming, weight lifting. **Team name:** Warriors.

Student services. Adult student services, alcohol/substance abuse counseling, career counseling, services for economically disadvantaged, student
employment services, financial aid counseling, health services, minority student services, on-campus daycare, personal counseling, placement for graduates, veterans' counselor, women's services. **Physically disabled:** Services
for visually, speech, hearing impaired. **Transfer:** Transfer adviser, college
fairs on campus for students transferring to 4-year colleges.

Contact. E-mail: admoffice@massasoit.mass.edu
Phone: (508) 588-9100 ext. 1411 Fax: (508) 427-1257
Michelle Hughes, Director of Admissions, Massasoit Community College,
One Massasoit Boulevard, Brockton, MA 02302-3996

Middlesex Community College

Bedford, Massachusetts   **CB member**
www.middlesex.mass.edu   **CB code: 3554**

- Public 2-year community college
- Commuter campus in small city

General. Founded in 1969. Regionally accredited. Second main campus
located in Lowell. **Enrollment:** 8,353 degree-seeking undergraduates; 661
non-degree-seeking students. **Degrees:** 1,251 associate awarded. **ROTC:**
Army, Air Force. **Location:** 16 miles from Boston. **Calendar:** Semester,
limited summer session. **Full-time faculty:** 141 total. **Part-time faculty:**
426 total. **Special facilities:** Dental clinic, law center. **Partnerships:** Formal
partnerships with business and industry links.

Student profile. Among degree-seeking undergraduates, 1,839 enrolled as
first-time, first-year students.

Part-time:	60%	Women:	57%
Out-of-state:	4%	25 or older:	33%

Transfer out. Colleges most students transferred to 2015: University of
Massachusetts Lowell, Salem State College, Northern Essex Community
College, University of Massachusetts Boston, Bunker Hill Community Col-
lege.

Basis for selection. Open admission, but selective for some programs.
Admission to some health programs based on prerequisite courses in math
and science and placement test or program specific test scores. Some health,
counseling, and biotechnology programs require essays, letters of reference
and meeting with program coordinator. **Home schooled:** Must have successfully completed approved home school program in accordance with state laws.

High school preparation. For some health programs, 1 unit each of
biology and chemistry required in addition to 2 units of math at Algebra I
level and above.

2015-2016 Annual costs. Tuition/fees: $5,580; $11,760 out-of-state. Per-
credit charge: $181 in-state; $387 out-of-state. Books/supplies: $1,150. Per-
sonal expenses: $1,980.

Financial aid. All financial aid based on need. Need-based aid available
for part-time students. Work-study available nights, weekends and for part-
time students. **Additional information:** Application priority date 5/1 for
Massachusetts state funds.

Application procedures. Admission: No deadline. No application fee.
Admission notification on a rolling basis. Closing date first Friday in December for dental hygiene, radiologic technology and diagnostic medical sonography. Applications received later considered on space-available basis. Applicants must reply within 2 weeks of acceptance. **Financial aid:** Priority date
5/1; no closing date. FAFSA, institutional form required. Applicants notified
on a rolling basis starting 6/1; must reply within 2 week(s) of notification.

Academics. Academic support available online. **Special study options:**
Accelerated study, cooperative education, cross-registration, distance learning, dual enrollment of high school students, ESL, exchange student, honors,
independent study, internships, liberal arts/career combination, study abroad,
weekend college. License preparation in dental hygiene, nursing, paramedic,
radiology. **Credit/placement by examination:** AP, CLEP, institutional tests.
45 credit hours maximum toward associate degree. **Support services:** GED
preparation, learning center, pre-admission summer program, reduced course
load, remedial instruction, study skills assistance, tutoring, writing center.

Majors. Biology: General. **Business:** Business admin, fashion, hotel/motel
admin, office/clerical. **Computer sciences:** General. **Education:** Elementary,
kindergarten/preschool. **Health services:** Clinical lab technology, dental
assistant, dental hygiene, dental lab technology, environmental health, medical assistant, medical radiologic technology/radiation therapy, mental health
services, nursing (RN), sonography. **Liberal arts:** Arts/sciences. **Physical
sciences:** General. **Protective services:** Criminal justice, fire safety technology, forensics. **Psychology:** General. **Social sciences:** General. **Visual/per-
forming arts:** Commercial/advertising art, studio arts.

Most popular majors. Biological/life sciences 8%, business/marketing 17%, health sciences 15%, liberal arts 36%, security/protective services 8%.

Technology on campus. 350 workstations in library, computer center. Commuter students can connect to campus network. Online course registration, online library, helpline, wireless network available.

Student life. Freshman orientation: Available. Preregistration for classes offered. Held the day before classes begin. **Activities:** Choral groups, dance, drama, international student organizations, musical theater, student government, international club, student activities, mental health club, early childhood education club, art club, MassPIRG.

Athletics. Intramural: Basketball, bowling, football (non-tackle), soccer, volleyball.

Student services. Adult student services, alcohol/substance abuse counseling, career counseling, services for economically disadvantaged, student employment services, financial aid counseling, health services, legal services, minority student services, personal counseling, placement for graduates, veterans' counselor. **Physically disabled:** Services for visually, speech, hearing impaired. **Transfer:** Re-entry adviser, pre-admission transcript evaluation for new students. Transfer adviser, college fairs on campus for students transferring to 4-year colleges.

Contact. E-mail: admissions@middlesex.mass.edu
Phone: (978) 656-3207 Toll-free number: (800) 818-3434
Fax: (978) 656-3322
Marilynn Gallagan, Dean of Admissions, Middlesex Community College, 33 Kearney Square, Lowell, MA 01852-1987

Mount Wachusett Community College
Gardner, Massachusetts — CB member
www.mwcc.edu — CB code: 3545

- Public 2-year community college
- Commuter campus in large town

General. Founded in 1963. Regionally accredited. **Enrollment:** 3,648 degree-seeking undergraduates; 426 non-degree-seeking students. **Degrees:** 605 associate awarded. **ROTC:** Army. **Location:** 59 miles from Boston. **Calendar:** Semester, extensive summer session. **Full-time faculty:** 74 total; 8% minority, 65% women. **Part-time faculty:** 322 total; 7% minority, 54% women. **Class size:** 60% < 20, 39% 20-39, less than 1% 40-49, less than 1% 50-99. **Special facilities:** On-site child-care facility, theater, fitness and wellness center, pool. **Partnerships:** Formal partnership with Tech Prep (high school articulation programs), Nypro, Adams and Associates.

Student profile. Among degree-seeking undergraduates, 796 enrolled as first-time, first-year students, 252 transferred in from other institutions.

Part-time:	60%	Hispanic/Latino:	15%
Out-of-state:	4%	Native American:	1%
Women:	65%	Multi-racial, non-Hispanic:	2%
African American:	8%	25 or older:	43%
Asian American:	2%		

Transfer out. Colleges most students transferred to 2015: Fitchburg State College, University of Massachusetts Amherst, Worcester State College, University of Massachusetts Lowell.

Basis for selection. Open admission, but selective for some programs. Special requirements for all health science programs with emphasis on college level academic coursework, life science or other science programs, other academic preparation and work experience. Interview required for early admission of high school students. Portfolio recommended for art programs. **Home schooled:** Statement describing home school structure and mission, transcript of courses and grades, interview required. Applicants must submit copies of curriculum approvals from local secondary school district. **Learning Disabled:** Students advised to meet with coordinator of disabilities services during admissions process.

High school preparation. 16 units recommended. Recommended units include English 4, mathematics 3, social studies 1, history 1, science 2 (laboratory 2), foreign language 2 and academic electives 3.

2015-2016 Annual costs. Tuition/fees: $6,400; $12,550 out-of-state. Books/supplies: $1,200. Personal expenses: $2,000.

2014-2015 Financial aid. All financial aid based on need. 482 full-time freshmen applied for aid; 398 deemed to have need; 395 received aid. Average need met was 96%. Average scholarship/grant was $5,071; average loan $1,787. 66% of total undergraduate aid awarded as scholarships/grants, 34% as loans/jobs. Need-based aid available for part-time students. Work-study available nights, weekends and for part-time students.

Application procedures. Admission: No deadline. No application fee. Nursing, Dental Hygiene must apply by February 1. Clinical Laboratory Science, Physical Therapy Assistant, and Massage Therapy must apply by March 1. **Financial aid:** Priority date 5/1; no closing date. FAFSA required. Applicants notified on a rolling basis starting 3/15; must reply within 2 week(s) of notification.

Academics. Special study options: Accelerated study, cross-registration, distance learning, double major, dual enrollment of high school students, ESL, external degree, honors, independent study, liberal arts/career combination. License preparation in dental hygiene, nursing, physical therapy. **Credit/placement by examination:** AP, CLEP, IB, institutional tests. 30 credit hours maximum toward associate degree. **Support services:** GED preparation and test center, learning center, pre-admission summer program, reduced course load, remedial instruction, study skills assistance, tutoring, writing center.

Majors. Biology: Biotechnology. **Business:** General, business admin. **Communications technology:** Radio/TV. **Computer sciences:** General, computer graphics, web page design. **Conservation:** Environmental studies. **Engineering:** General. **Health services:** Clinical lab technology, dental hygiene, medical assistant, mental health services, nursing (RN), physical therapy assistant, yoga therapy. **Liberal arts:** Arts/sciences. **Protective services:** Corrections, fire safety technology, law enforcement admin. **Visual/performing arts:** Art. **Work/family studies:** Child care management, child development.

Most popular majors. Business/marketing 15%, computer/information sciences 6%, health sciences 30%, liberal arts 19%, public administration/social services 7%, security/protective services 6%.

Technology on campus. 415 workstations in library, computer center. Commuter students can connect to campus network. Online course registration, online library, helpline, wireless network available.

Student life. Freshman orientation: Available. Preregistration for classes offered. One-day session held week before start of classes. **Housing:** Limited housing available on campus of Fitchburg State College. **Activities:** Campus ministries, dance, drama, international student organizations, literary magazine, music ensembles, musical theater, student government, student newspaper, art club, nursing clubs, student government association, pride club, dental hygiene club, green society, Campus Crusade for Christ, campus activities team for students, MassPIRG, ALANA club.

Athletics. Intramural: Badminton, basketball, football (tackle), soccer, softball, table tennis, volleyball, water polo. **Team name:** Mountain Lions.

Student services. Adult student services, alcohol/substance abuse counseling, chaplain/spiritual director, career counseling, services for economically disadvantaged, student employment services, financial aid counseling, health services, minority student services, on-campus daycare, personal counseling, placement for graduates, veterans' counselor, women's services. **Physically disabled:** Services for visually, speech, hearing impaired. **Transfer:** Pre-admission transcript evaluation for new students. Transfer adviser, college fairs on campus for students transferring to 4-year colleges.

Contact. E-mail: admissions@mwcc.mass.edu
Phone: (978) 630-9110 Fax: (978) 630-9554
Ryan Forsythe, Admissions Director, Mount Wachusett Community College, 444 Green Street, Gardner, MA 01440-1000

New England College of Business and Finance
Boston, Massachusetts
www.necb.edu — CB code: 3376

- For-profit 2-year business college
- Large city

General. Founded in 1909. Regionally accredited. Programs designed for adult learners. Undergraduate courses delivered in 8-week format; graduate courses delivered in 5-week format. **Enrollment:** 690 undergraduates. **Degrees:** 110 bachelor's, 65 associate awarded; master's offered. **Calendar:** Differs by program, extensive summer session. **Full-time faculty:** 4 total. **Part-time faculty:** 47 total. **Partnerships:** Formal partnerships with several financial services companies.

Basis for selection. Open admission, but selective for some programs. Placement exams or equivalent completion of applicable college credits required.

2015-2016 Annual costs. Books/supplies: $800. **Additional information:** Certificate programs: Basic Accounting $7,140; Intermediate Accounting $7,140; Digital Marketing $5,100. Associate program: Business Administration $20,400. Bachelor's programs: Business Administration $40,800; Digital Marketing $40,800; International Business $40,800.

Financial aid. Need-based: Work-study available nights, weekends and for part-time students. **Additional information:** No college-administered financial aid. 90% of students receive tuition reimbursement from employer.

Application procedures. Admission: No deadline. $50 fee, may be waived for applicants with need. Application must be submitted online. Admission notification on a rolling basis.

Academics. Special study options: Accelerated study, distance learning, dual enrollment of high school students, independent study. Bachelor's degree programs available on campus. **Credit/placement by examination:** AP, CLEP, IB, institutional tests. **Support services:** Remedial instruction, tutoring.

Majors. Business: General, banking/financial services, business admin.

Technology on campus. PC or laptop required. Online library available.

Student life. Activities: Literary magazine.

Student services. Career counseling, financial aid counseling, personal counseling. **Transfer:** Pre-admission transcript evaluation for new students. Transfer adviser for students transferring to 4-year colleges.

Contact. Phone: (617) 951-2350 Fax: (617) 951-2533
Pamela Dellaporta, Director of Admissions and Student Services, New England College of Business and Finance, 10 High Street, Suite 204, Boston, MA 02110

North Shore Community College

Danvers, Massachusetts	**CB member**
www.northshore.edu	**CB code: 3651**

- Public 2-year community college
- Commuter campus in small city

General. Founded in 1965. Regionally accredited. Additional campus in Lynn, corporate training center in Beverly. **Enrollment:** 6,197 degree-seeking undergraduates; 764 non-degree-seeking students. **Degrees:** 880 associate awarded. **Location:** 25 miles from Boston. **Calendar:** Semester, limited summer session. **Full-time faculty:** 131 total. **Part-time faculty:** 384 total. **Class size:** 44% < 20, 55% 20-39, less than 1% 40-49, less than 1% 50-99. **Special facilities:** Agricultural facility, culinary arts and cosmetology centers. **Partnerships:** Formal partnership with Verizon, area high schools for Tech Prep, consortium providing distance learning opportunities.

Student profile. Among degree-seeking undergraduates, 1,244 enrolled as first-time, first-year students, 548 transferred in from other institutions.

Part-time:	61%	Asian American:	5%
Out-of-state:	2%	Hispanic/Latino:	25%
Women:	60%	Multi-racial, non-Hispanic:	3%
African American:	9%	25 or older:	40%

Transfer out. Colleges most students transferred to 2015: Salem State College, University of Massachusetts-Boston, University of Massachusetts-Lowell, Suffolk University, Northeastern University, Lesley College.

Basis for selection. Open admission, but selective for some programs. School achievement record considered for health, engineering, computer science programs; some prerequisite course requirements exist. Pre-Nursing Assessment Test required for pre-nursing program; Nurse Entrance Exam required for LPN program. Essay and/or interview may be required in some programs, including health and human services. **Home schooled:** Home program must be affiliated with accredited agency or local school system. **Learning Disabled:** Students must identify disability, individual test administration available.

High school preparation. One algebra, 1 biology, and 1 chemistry required for some health programs and for biotechnology. Trigonometry, physics, chemistry required for engineering. Trigonometry, computer literacy required for computer science.

2015-2016 Annual costs. Tuition/fees: $6,420; $13,380 out-of-state. Per-credit charge: $25 in-state; $257 out-of-state. Books/supplies: $1,200. Personal expenses: $1,500. **Additional information:** Health Professions Programs have a 150.00 fee per semester. Culinary Arts programs have a 100.00 fee per semester.

Financial aid. All financial aid based on need. Need-based aid available for part-time students. Work-study available nights, weekends and for part-time students.

Application procedures. Admission: No deadline. No application fee. Admission notification on a rolling basis. We accept high school seniors as conditional students. Once the student provides proof of high school graduation, the conditional status will be removed. **Financial aid:** Priority date 4/15; no closing date. FAFSA required. Applicants notified on a rolling basis starting 4/1; must reply within 2 week(s) of notification.

Academics. Participation in state dual enrollment program which allows high school juniors and seniors to take credit courses contingent upon approval of high school principal. Tuition and fees paid by state. **Special study options:** Accelerated study, cross-registration, distance learning, double major, dual enrollment of high school students, ESL, honors, independent study, internships, student-designed major, study abroad, weekend college. License preparation in aviation, nursing, occupational therapy, physical therapy, radiology, real estate. **Credit/placement by examination:** AP, CLEP, institutional tests. 45 credit hours maximum toward associate degree. DANTES, Excelsior, CLEP tests accepted. CLEP tests in Freshman Composition and Analyzing and Interpreting Literature must be accompanied by essay; lab credit not awarded for Biology and Chemistry tests. **Support services:** GED preparation and test center, learning center, reduced course load, remedial instruction, study skills assistance, tutoring, writing center.

Majors. Business: Accounting technology, business admin, executive assistant, hospitality admin, hotel/motel admin, marketing. **Computer sciences:** General, computer science, programming. **Education:** Early childhood, elementary, kindergarten/preschool, teacher assistance. **Engineering:** General. **Health services:** Dietetic technician, medical secretary, mental health services, nursing (RN), occupational therapy assistant, physical therapy assistant, radiologic technology/medical imaging, respiratory therapy technology, substance abuse counseling, veterinary technology/assistant. **Liberal arts:** Arts/sciences. **Protective services:** Criminal justice, fire safety technology. **Visual/performing arts:** Graphic design. **Work/family studies:** Aging, child care service.

Most popular majors. Business/marketing 10%, family/consumer sciences 6%, health sciences 27%, liberal arts 25%, security/protective services 16%.

Technology on campus. 300 workstations in library, computer center, student center. Commuter students can connect to campus network. Online course registration, online library, helpline, wireless network available.

Student life. Freshman orientation: Available. Preregistration for classes offered. All-day event includes placement testing, adviser assistance. **Activities:** Campus ministries, drama, literary magazine, Model UN, musical theater, student government, student newspaper, students against drug abuse, early childhood club, marketing club, engineering club, women in transition club, multicultural society, poets and writers club, gerontology club, occupational therapy assistant club.

Athletics. Intramural: Basketball, soccer. **Team name:** Seahawks.

Student services. Adult student services, career counseling, services for economically disadvantaged, student employment services, financial aid counseling, health services, on-campus daycare, personal counseling, placement for graduates, veterans' counselor, women's services. **Physically disabled:** Services for visually, speech, hearing impaired. **Transfer:** Pre-admission transcript evaluation for new students. Transfer adviser, college fairs on campus for students transferring to 4-year colleges.

Contact. E-mail: info@northshore.edu
Phone: (978) 762-4188 Fax: (978) 762-4015
Kimberly Odusami, Director of Admissions, North Shore Community College, One Ferncroft Road, Danvers, MA 01923-0840

Northern Essex Community College

Haverhill, Massachusetts	**CB member**
www.necc.mass.edu	**CB code: 3674**

- Public 2-year community and junior college
- Commuter campus in small city

General. Founded in 1960. Regionally accredited. Additional campus in Lawrence. **Enrollment:** 6,010 degree-seeking undergraduates; 618 non-degree-seeking students. **Degrees:** 768 associate awarded. **Location:** 30 miles from Boston. **Calendar:** Semester, extensive summer session. **Full-time faculty:** 114 total; 14% minority, 63% women. **Part-time faculty:** 510 total; 11% minority, 57% women.

Student profile. Among degree-seeking undergraduates, 1,330 enrolled as first-time, first-year students.

Part-time:	63%	Hispanic/Latino:	41%
Women:	61%	Multi-racial, non-Hispanic:	1%
African American:	4%	International:	1%
Asian American:	2%		

Basis for selection. Open admission, but selective for some programs. Health and Human Services are criteria based programs. Criteria may include info sessions, interviews, background forms, TEAS (scores vary), Accuplacer, high school or equivalent and 2.0 GPA in the case of transfer students.

High school preparation. Health and technologies programs have specific math and/or science requirements.

2015-2016 Annual costs. Tuition/fees: $5,700; $12,930 out-of-state. Per-credit charge: $25 in-state; $266 out-of-state. Books/supplies: $800. Personal expenses: $850.

Financial aid. Need-based: Need-based aid available for part-time students. Work-study available nights, weekends and for part-time students. **Non-need-based:** Scholarships awarded for academics.

Application procedures. Admission: Priority date 2/1; no deadline. Admission notification on a rolling basis. **Financial aid:** Priority date 5/1; no closing date. FAFSA, institutional form required. Must reply within 2 week(s) of notification.

Academics. Special study options: Accelerated study, combined bachelor's/graduate degree, cooperative education, cross-registration, distance learning, double major, dual enrollment of high school students, exchange student, honors, internships, liberal arts/career combination, study abroad, weekend college. **Credit/placement by examination:** AP, CLEP, institutional tests. 36 credit hours maximum toward associate degree. **Support services:** GED preparation and test center, learning center, pre-admission summer program, reduced course load, remedial instruction, study skills assistance, tutoring, writing center.

Majors. Biology: General. **Business:** General, accounting, administrative services, business admin, logistics, office management, office technology. **Communications:** Journalism. **Computer sciences:** General, information technology. **Education:** Business, early childhood. **Engineering:** Engineering science. **Foreign languages:** Sign language interpretation. **Health services:** EMT paramedic, health information management, nursing (RN), radiologic technology/medical imaging, respiratory therapy technology, substance abuse counseling. **Liberal arts:** Arts/sciences. **Parks/recreation:** Sports admin. **Protective services:** Criminal justice. **Psychology:** General. **Visual/performing arts:** Commercial/advertising art, design. **Work/family studies:** Child care management.

Technology on campus. 600 workstations in library, computer center, student center. Commuter students can connect to campus network. Online course registration, online library, helpline, wireless network available.

Student life. Freshman orientation: Mandatory. Preregistration for classes offered. **Activities:** Choral groups, dance, drama, literary magazine, music ensembles, musical theater, student government, student newspaper, American Sign Language club, Hispanic cultural club, women's resource network, social club (students with disabilities), Bible club.

Athletics. NJCAA. **Intercollegiate:** Baseball M, basketball, softball W, track and field, volleyball W. **Intramural:** Basketball, football (non-tackle), soccer, table tennis, ultimate frisbee, volleyball. **Team name:** Knights.

Student services. Adult student services, career counseling, services for economically disadvantaged, student employment services, financial aid counseling, health services, on-campus daycare, placement for graduates, veterans' counselor, women's services. **Physically disabled:** Services for visually, speech, hearing impaired. **Transfer:** Pre-admission transcript evaluation for new students. Transfer adviser, college fairs on campus for students transferring to 4-year colleges.

Contact. E-mail: admissions@necc.mass.edu
Phone: (978) 556-3600
Daniel Richer, Director of Admissions and Recruitment, Northern Essex Community College, 100 Elliott Street, Haverhill, MA 01830-2399

Quincy College
Quincy, Massachusetts
www.quincycollege.edu

CB member
CB code: 3713

▸ Public 2-year community college
▸ Commuter campus in small city

General. Founded in 1956. Regionally accredited. Branch campus in Plymouth. **Enrollment:** 4,135 degree-seeking undergraduates; 597 non-degree-seeking students. **Degrees:** 560 associate awarded. **Location:** 10 miles from downtown Boston. **Calendar:** Semester, extensive summer session. **Full-time faculty:** 69 total. **Part-time faculty:** 286 total. **Class size:** 62% < 20, 37% 20-39, less than 1% 40-49.

Student profile. Among degree-seeking undergraduates, 624 enrolled as first-time, first-year students, 657 transferred in from other institutions.

Part-time:	57%	Hispanic/Latino:	7%
Out-of-state:	1%	Multi-racial, non-Hispanic:	2%
Women:	67%	International:	8%
African American:	25%	25 or older:	48%
Asian American:	6%		

Basis for selection. Open admission, but selective for some programs. Admission to health career programs based on test scores, class rank and high school record. College-preparatory program with Anatomy and Physiology I with lab or Biology with lab and Introductory or General Chemistry with lab required for Associate Degree in Nursing program.

2015-2016 Annual costs. Tuition/fees: $6,496; $6,496 out-of-state. Books/supplies: $2,000. Personal expenses: $1,700.

Financial aid. Need-based: Work-study available nights, weekends and for part-time students.

Application procedures. Admission: No deadline. $30 fee, may be waived for applicants with need. Admission notification on a rolling basis. **Financial aid:** No deadline. FAFSA required. Applicants notified on a rolling basis starting 5/1; must reply within 2 week(s) of notification.

Academics. Special study options: Accelerated study, distance learning, dual enrollment of high school students, independent study, internships. **Credit/placement by examination:** AP, CLEP, institutional tests. 30 credit hours maximum toward associate degree. **Support services:** GED test center, learning center, reduced course load, remedial instruction, tutoring.

Majors. Biology: Exercise physiology. **Business:** Accounting, business admin. **Computer sciences:** Computer science. **Education:** Early childhood, elementary. **Health services:** Clinical lab technology, health services admin, nursing (RN). **Liberal arts:** Arts/sciences. **Protective services:** Law enforcement admin. **Visual/performing arts:** Studio arts.

Most popular majors. Business/marketing 18%, health sciences 34%, liberal arts 20%, security/protective services 7%.

Technology on campus. 312 workstations in library, computer center, student center. Commuter students can connect to campus network. Online library, helpline, wireless network available.

Student life. Freshman orientation: Available. Preregistration for classes offered. **Activities:** Drama, international student organizations, student government, student newspaper.

Student services. Adult student services, alcohol/substance abuse counseling, career counseling, student employment services, financial aid counseling, minority student services, personal counseling. **Transfer:** Pre-admission transcript evaluation for new students. Transfer adviser, college fairs on campus for students transferring to 4-year colleges.

Contact. E-mail: admissions@quincycollege.edu
Phone: (617) 984-1710 Toll-free number: (800) 698-1700
Fax: (617) 984-1794
Director of Admissions, Quincy College, 1250 Hancock Street, Quincy, MA 02169

Quinsigamond Community College
Worcester, Massachusetts
www.qcc.edu

CB member
CB code: 3714

▸ Public 2-year community college
▸ Commuter campus in small city

General. Founded in 1963. Regionally accredited. Additional locations: Downtown Worcester Campus, Worcester Senior Center, Southbridge, Marlborough. **Enrollment:** 7,224 degree-seeking undergraduates; 840 non-degree-seeking students. **Degrees:** 1,017 associate awarded. **ROTC:** Army, Air Force. **Location:** 45 miles from Boston. **Calendar:** Semester, extensive summer session. **Full-time faculty:** 140 total; 19% have terminal degrees, 21% minority, 69% women. **Part-time faculty:** 442 total; 13% have terminal degrees, 13% minority, 54% women. **Special facilities:** Dental hygiene clinic, child care center, food lab. **Partnerships:** Formal partnerships with Intel Corporation, Verizon, National Grid.

Student profile. Among degree-seeking undergraduates, 1,639 enrolled as first-time, first-year students, 558 transferred in from other institutions.

Part-time:	60%	Women:	58%
Out-of-state:	2%	25 or older:	39%

Transfer out. Colleges most students transferred to 2015: Worcester State University, University of Massachusetts-Amherst, Nichols College, Becker College, Assumption College.

Basis for selection. Open admission, but selective for some programs. Students without high school diploma may be considered for admission under Ability to Benefit. **Home schooled:** Transcript of courses and grades required. Letter from district superintendent approving home school curriculum required. **Learning Disabled:** Students encouraged to contact Disability Services office prior to enrollment.

High school preparation. College-preparatory program recommended. Recommended units include English 4, mathematics 3, social studies 2, history 1, science 3 (laboratory 2), foreign language 2 and computer science 1. English, college math, and laboratory sciences required for health programs. English and math required for business, technology, and early childhood education.

2015-2016 Annual costs. Tuition/fees: $6,540; $12,720 out-of-state. Per-credit charge: $24 in-state; $230 out-of-state. Books/supplies: $1,200. Personal expenses: $1,566.

2014-2015 Financial aid. Need-based: 65% of total undergraduate aid awarded as scholarships/grants, 35% as loans/jobs. Need-based aid available for part-time students. Work-study available nights, weekends and for part-time students. **Non-need-based:** Scholarships awarded for academics, leadership, minority status. **Additional information:** All Pell Grant eligible students applying by May 1 will receive enough grant aid to cover tuition, fees and books.

Application procedures. Admission: No deadline. $20 fee ($50 out-of-state), may be waived for applicants with need, free for online applicants. Admission notification on a rolling basis beginning on or about 10/1. Must reply by May 1 or within 2 week(s) if notified thereafter. **Financial aid:** Priority date 4/1; no closing date. FAFSA required. Applicants notified on a rolling basis starting 4/1.

Academics. Specialized academic support to those with disabilities. Online academic tutoring available in most subjects. **Special study options:** Accelerated study, cooperative education, cross-registration, distance learning, double major, dual enrollment of high school students, ESL, honors, independent study, internships, liberal arts/career combination, weekend college. Member of Worcester Consortium. License preparation in dental hygiene, nursing, occupational therapy, paramedic, radiology. **Credit/placement by examination:** AP, CLEP, IB, institutional tests. **Support services:** GED preparation and test center, learning center, reduced course load, remedial instruction, study skills assistance, tutoring, writing center.

Majors. Area/ethnic studies: Deaf. **Biology:** General, biotechnology. **Business:** General, business admin, executive assistant, hospitality admin, restaurant/food services. **Computer sciences:** General, applications programming, computer graphics, computer science, database management, security, systems analysis, web page design. **Conservation:** Environmental science. **Education:** Elementary, kindergarten/preschool, trade/industrial. **Engineering:** Biomedical. **Health services:** Community health, dental hygiene, EMT paramedic, health information technology, medical secretary, nursing (RN), occupational therapy assistant, prepharmacy, radiologic technology/medical imaging, respiratory therapy technology. **Liberal arts:** Arts/sciences. **Physical sciences:** Chemistry. **Protective services:** Fire services admin, police science. **Visual/performing arts:** Directing/producing, game design, music.

Most popular majors. Business/marketing 21%, education 6%, engineering/engineering technologies 7%, health sciences 22%, liberal arts 24%, security/protective services 9%.

Technology on campus. 1,023 workstations in library, computer center, student center. Helpline, wireless network available.

Student life. Freshman orientation: Available. Preregistration for classes offered. Half-day program; some academic majors hold specialized orientation programs. **Activities:** Campus ministries, choral groups, drama, literary magazine, student government, student newspaper, multicultural club, several occupational groups, academic clubs.

Athletics. NJCAA. **Intercollegiate:** Baseball M, basketball, softball W. **Intramural:** Basketball, football (non-tackle), soccer, volleyball. **Team name:** Wyverns.

Student services. Chaplain/spiritual director, career counseling, student employment services, financial aid counseling, minority student services, on-campus daycare, personal counseling, placement for graduates, veterans' counselor. **Physically disabled:** Services for visually, speech, hearing impaired. **Transfer:** Transfer center, transfer adviser, college fairs on campus for students transferring to 4-year colleges.

Contact. E-mail: admissions@qcc.mass.edu
Phone: (508) 854-4262 Fax: (508) 854-7525
Mishawn Davis-Eyene, Director of Admissions, Quinsigamond Community College, 670 West Boylston Street, Worcester, MA 01606

Roxbury Community College
Roxbury Crossing, Massachusetts   **CB member**
www.rcc.mass.edu   **CB code: 3740**

▶ Public 2-year community college
▶ Commuter campus in very large city

General. Founded in 1973. Regionally accredited. **Enrollment:** 2,216 degree-seeking undergraduates. **Degrees:** 302 associate awarded. **ROTC:** Army. **Calendar:** Semester, extensive summer session. **Full-time faculty:** 49 total. **Part-time faculty:** 170 total. **Class size:** 73% < 20, 27% 20-39. **Special facilities:** Indoor track and field facilities. **Partnerships:** Formal partnerships with local employers.

Basis for selection. Open admission, but selective for some programs. Specific admissions criteria for nursing and radiologic technology programs.

2015-2016 Annual costs. Tuition/fees: $4,980; $11,610 out-of-state. Per-credit charge: $26 in-state; $387 out-of-state. Books/supplies: $800. Personal expenses: $1,800.

Financial aid. All financial aid based on need. Need-based aid available for part-time students. Work-study available nights, weekends and for part-time students.

Application procedures. Admission: No deadline. $10 fee ($35 out-of-state), may be waived for applicants with need. Admission notification on a rolling basis. **Financial aid:** Closing date 5/1. FAFSA, institutional form required. Applicants notified on a rolling basis starting 6/15; must reply within 2 week(s) of notification.

Academics. Special study options: Cross-registration, double major, dual enrollment of high school students, ESL, honors, independent study, internships, liberal arts/career combination. License preparation in nursing. **Credit/placement by examination:** AP, CLEP, institutional tests. **Support services:** GED preparation and test center, learning center, remedial instruction, study skills assistance, tutoring, writing center.

Majors. Architecture: Technology. **Biology:** General. **Business:** Accounting, administrative services, business admin, hospitality/recreation, management information systems, office management, office technology. **Communications technology:** Radio/TV. **Computer sciences:** General, applications programming. **Conservation:** General. **Education:** Early childhood. **English:** English lit. **Foreign languages:** French. **Health services:** Medical secretary, nursing (RN), prenursing. **Liberal arts:** Arts/sciences, humanities. **Math:** General. **Physical sciences:** General. **Protective services:** Law enforcement admin. **Social sciences:** General. **Visual/performing arts:** General, music. **Work/family studies:** Child care management.

Most popular majors. Business/marketing 28%, health sciences 28%, liberal arts 30%, security/protective services 11%.

Technology on campus. 150 workstations in library, computer center.

Student life. Freshman orientation: Available. Preregistration for classes offered. **Activities:** Choral groups, dance, drama, student government, student newspaper, Union Estudiantil Latina, Christian ministry.

Athletics. NJCAA. **Intercollegiate:** Basketball, soccer M. **Team name:** Tigers.

Student services. Career counseling, student employment services, financial aid counseling, health services, on-campus daycare, personal counseling, placement for graduates. **Transfer:** Transfer adviser, college fairs on campus for students transferring to 4-year colleges.

Contact. Phone: (617) 541-5310 Fax: (617) 541-5316
Charles Diggs, Director of Admissions, Roxbury Community College, 1234 Columbus Avenue, Roxbury Crossing, MA 02120-3400

Springfield Technical Community College
Springfield, Massachusetts   **CB member**
www.stcc.edu   **CB code: 3791**

▶ Public 2-year community and technical college
▶ Commuter campus in small city

General. Founded in 1967. Regionally accredited. **Enrollment:** 5,658 degree-seeking undergraduates; 628 non-degree-seeking students. **Degrees:** 935 associate awarded. **Location:** 90 miles from Boston; 30 miles from Hartford, Connecticut. **Calendar:** Semester, limited summer session. **Full-time faculty:** 141 total. **Part-time faculty:** 333 total. **Special facilities:** Springfield Armory Museum (national historic site). **Partnerships:** Formal partnerships with Verizon, Microsoft, Novell, A+, Cisco, IBM.

Student profile. Among degree-seeking undergraduates, 2% already have a bachelor's degree or higher, 1,342 enrolled as first-time, first-year students, 378 transferred in from other institutions.

Part-time:	53%	Hispanic/Latino:	29%
Out-of-state:	3%	Native American:	1%
Women:	58%	Multi-racial, non-Hispanic:	2%
African American:	16%	International:	1%
Asian American:	3%	25 or older:	40%

Transfer out. Colleges most students transferred to 2015: University of Massachusetts-Amherst, Westfield State University, Elms College, American International College, Springfield College.

Basis for selection. Open admission, but selective for some programs. Special requirements for certain health, engineering and science programs. SAT required for selective health and engineering programs. **Home schooled:** Letter of approval of home schooled program from student's school district's superintendent or school committee.

High school preparation. Math, chemistry, biology and/or physics required for many competitive programs.

2015-2016 Annual costs. Tuition/fees: $5,436; $11,946 out-of-state. Per-credit charge: $25 in-state; $242 out-of-state. Books/supplies: $1,200. Personal expenses: $3,321. **Additional information:** New England reciprocal annual tuition and fees $5811.

2014-2015 Financial aid. Need-based: 77% of total undergraduate aid awarded as scholarships/grants, 23% as loans/jobs. Need-based aid available for part-time students. Work-study available nights, weekends and for part-time students.

Application procedures. Admission: No deadline. No application fee. Admission notification on a rolling basis beginning on or about 3/1. Applicants must reply within 3 weeks of notification of admission. **Financial aid:** Priority date 5/1; no closing date. FAFSA required. Applicants notified on a rolling basis starting 4/1.

Academics. Special study options: Cooperative education, cross-registration, distance learning, dual enrollment of high school students, ESL, honors, independent study, internships, liberal arts/career combination. License preparation in nursing, radiology. **Credit/placement by examination:** AP, CLEP, institutional tests. 45 credit hours maximum toward associate degree. **Support services:** GED preparation and test center, learning center, reduced course load, remedial instruction, study skills assistance, tutoring, writing center.

Majors. Architecture: Building sciences. **Biology:** General, biotechnology. **Business:** General, accounting, administrative services, business admin, marketing, small business admin. **Communications technology:** Animation/special effects, radio/TV, recording arts. **Computer sciences:** Applications programming, computer science, security. **Education:** Early childhood, elementary, secondary. **Engineering:** General, architectural. **Health services:** Clinical lab technology, dental hygiene, insurance coding, massage therapy, medical assistant, medical secretary, nursing (RN), occupational therapy assistant, physical therapy assistant, premedicine, radiologic technology/medical imaging, respiratory therapy technology, sonography, surgical technology. **Liberal arts:** Arts/sciences. **Math:** General. **Parks/recreation:** Sports admin. **Physical sciences:** Chemistry, physics. **Protective services:** Fire safety technology, police science. **Visual/performing arts:** Commercial photography, commercial/advertising art, studio arts.

Most popular majors. Business/marketing 10%, engineering/engineering technologies 10%, health sciences 22%, liberal arts 30%, security/protective services 10%.

Technology on campus. 1,743 workstations in library, student center. Commuter students can connect to campus network. Online course registration, online library, helpline, wireless network available.

Student life. Freshman orientation: Available. Preregistration for classes offered. Half-day session held 3 weeks before start of classes. **Policies:** No alcohol permitted. **Activities:** Drama, student government, student newspaper, TV station, student government association, student ambassadors, Latino culture club, gay/lesbian/bisexual/transgender alliance, Christian Fellowship, Phi Theta Kappa, Campus Civitan, Gallery Players.

Athletics. NJCAA. **Intercollegiate:** Basketball, golf, soccer, wrestling. **Team name:** Rams.

Student services. Adult student services, alcohol/substance abuse counseling, career counseling, services for economically disadvantaged, student employment services, financial aid counseling, health services, on-campus daycare, personal counseling, placement for graduates, veterans' counselor, women's services. **Physically disabled:** Services for visually, speech, hearing impaired. **Transfer:** Pre-admission transcript evaluation for new students. Transfer center, transfer adviser, college fairs on campus for students transferring to 4-year colleges.

Contact. E-mail: admissions@stcc.edu
Phone: (413) 755-3333
Louisa Davis-Freeman, Dean of Admissions, Springfield Technical Community College, One Armory Square, Springfield, MA 01102-9000

Urban College of Boston
Boston, Massachusetts
www.urbancollege.edu
CB code: 3630

- Private 2-year community college
- Commuter campus in very large city

General. Regionally accredited. **Enrollment:** 405 degree-seeking undergraduates. **Degrees:** 106 associate awarded. **Calendar:** Semester, limited summer session. **Full-time faculty:** 2 total. **Part-time faculty:** 34 total. **Class size:** 57% < 20, 43% 20-39.

Transfer out. Colleges most students transferred to 2015: Lesley College, Springfield College, Cambridge College.

Basis for selection. Open admission.

2015-2016 Annual costs. Tuition/fees: $8,900. Books/supplies: $1,100. Personal expenses: $2,860.

Financial aid. All financial aid based on need. Need-based aid available for part-time students. Work-study available nights, weekends and for part-time students.

Application procedures. Admission: No deadline. $10 fee, may be waived for applicants with need. Admission notification on a rolling basis. **Financial aid:** Priority date 12/10; no closing date. FAFSA required. Applicants notified on a rolling basis starting 4/15.

Academics. Special study options: Independent study, internships. **Credit/placement by examination:** AP, CLEP, IB. **Support services:** Learning center, study skills assistance, tutoring.

Majors. Education: Early childhood. **Liberal arts:** Arts/sciences.

Most popular majors. Education 82%, public administration/social services 15%.

Technology on campus. 2 workstations in library, computer center.

Student life. Freshman orientation: Available. Preregistration for classes offered. **Policies:** Drug and alcohol use prohibited.

Student services. Career counseling, services for economically disadvantaged, financial aid counseling, minority student services, personal counseling, placement for graduates. **Transfer:** Transfer adviser for students transferring to 4-year colleges.

Contact. E-mail: information@urbancollege.edu
Phone: (617) 348-6359 Fax: (617) 423-4758
Avanti Seymour, Dean of Enrollment Services, Urban College of Boston, 178 Tremont Street, Seventh Floor, Boston, MA 02111

Michigan

Alpena Community College
Alpena, Michigan
www.alpenacc.edu   CB code: 1011

‣ Public 2-year community college
‣ Commuter campus in large town

General. Founded in 1952. Regionally accredited. **Enrollment:** 2,000 degree-seeking undergraduates. **Degrees:** 307 associate awarded. **Location:** 240 miles from Detroit. **Calendar:** Semester, limited summer session. **Full-time faculty:** 54 total. **Part-time faculty:** 94 total. **Special facilities:** Museum, planetarium.

Student profile.

Out-of-state:	1%	Live on campus:	3%
25 or older:	48%		

Transfer out. Colleges most students transferred to 2015: Lake Superior State University, Central Michigan University, Michigan State University, Ferris State University, Saginaw Valley State University.

Basis for selection. Open admission, but selective for some programs. Special requirements for practical nursing, registered nursing, and utility technician programs. ACT may be used for scholarship consideration or as basis for corroboration of institutional placement exam results. Placement test requirement waived for applicants with 20 ACT.

High school preparation. High school diploma or equivalent required for nursing applicants.

2015-2016 Annual costs. Tuition/fees: $4,170; $6,210 out-of-district; $6,210 out-of-state. Per-credit charge: $121 in-district; $189 out-of-district; $189 out-of-state. Books/supplies: $1,000. Personal expenses: $600.

Financial aid. Need-based: Need-based aid available for part-time students. Work-study available nights, weekends and for part-time students. **Non-need-based:** Scholarships awarded for academics, art, athletics, job skills, leadership, music/drama.

Application procedures. Admission: Priority date 6/15; no deadline. No application fee. Admission notification on a rolling basis beginning on or about 2/15. **Financial aid:** Priority date 8/1; no closing date. FAFSA required. Applicants notified on a rolling basis starting 5/15; must reply within 3 week(s) of notification.

Academics. Special study options: Distance learning, double major, dual enrollment of high school students, internships, liberal arts/career combination. Bachelor's degree programs available on campus. License preparation in nursing. **Credit/placement by examination:** AP, CLEP, institutional tests. 30 credit hours maximum toward associate degree. **Support services:** Learning center, reduced course load, remedial instruction, study skills assistance, tutoring, writing center.

Majors. Business: Accounting, business admin, management information systems. **Communications technology:** Graphic/printing. **Computer sciences:** General, information systems, LAN/WAN management, networking. **Education:** General. **Engineering:** General. **Health services:** Medical assistant, nursing (RN). **Liberal arts:** Arts/sciences. **Protective services:** Corrections, law enforcement admin.

Technology on campus. 75 workstations in library, computer center. Commuter students can connect to campus network. Online library available.

Student life. Freshman orientation: Available. Preregistration for classes offered. One-day program during week prior to start of each semester. **Housing:** Apartments available. $410 deposit, deadline 8/1. **Activities:** Jazz band, dance, drama, musical theater, student government, student newspaper.

Athletics. NJCAA. **Intercollegiate:** Basketball, golf M, softball W, volleyball W. **Intramural:** Basketball, bowling, softball, volleyball. **Team name:** Lumberjacks.

Student services. Adult student services, alcohol/substance abuse counseling, career counseling, student employment services, financial aid counseling, personal counseling, placement for graduates, veterans' counselor,

women's services. **Transfer:** Pre-admission transcript evaluation for new students. Transfer adviser, college fairs on campus for students transferring to 4-year colleges.

Contact. E-mail: kollienm@alpenacc.edu
Phone: (989) 358-7339 Toll-free number: (888) 468-6222
Fax: (989) 358-7540
Michael Kollien, Director of Admissions, Alpena Community College, 665 Johnson Street, Alpena, MI 49707

Bay College
Escanaba, Michigan
www.baycollege.edu   CB code: 1049

‣ Public 2-year community college
‣ Commuter campus in large town

General. Founded in 1962. Regionally accredited. **Enrollment:** 1,497 degree-seeking undergraduates; 356 non-degree-seeking students. **Degrees:** 327 associate awarded. **Location:** 110 miles from Green Bay, WI. **Calendar:** Semester, limited summer session. **Full-time faculty:** 47 total. **Part-time faculty:** 100 total. **Class size:** 78% < 20, 22% 20-39. **Special facilities:** Center for performing arts.

Student profile. Among degree-seeking undergraduates, 40% enrolled in a transfer program, 60% enrolled in a vocational program, 337 enrolled as first-time, first-year students.

Part-time:	53%	Native American:	3%
Out-of-state:	3%	Multi-racial, non-Hispanic:	4%
Women:	61%	25 or older:	29%
Asian American:	1%	Live on campus:	2%
Hispanic/Latino:	2%		

Transfer out. 25% of students enrolled in the transfer program go on to 4-year colleges. **Colleges most students transferred to 2015:** Northern Michigan University, Michigan Technological University, Northeast Wisconsin Technical College, Central Michigan University, Ferris State University.

Basis for selection. Open admission, but selective for some programs. Special requirements for nursing program.

High school preparation. College-preparatory program recommended.

2015-2016 Annual costs. Tuition/fees: $4,290; $6,720 out-of-district; $10,980 out-of-state. Room only: $3,000. Books/supplies: $1,200. Personal expenses: $1,028.

Financial aid. Need-based: Need-based aid available for part-time students. Work-study available nights, weekends and for part-time students. **Non-need-based:** Scholarships awarded for academics.

Application procedures. Admission: Closing date 8/15. No application fee. Admission notification on a rolling basis. **Financial aid:** Priority date 4/1; no closing date. FAFSA required. Applicants notified on a rolling basis starting 2/1; must reply within 2 week(s) of notification.

Academics. Special study options: Cooperative education, distance learning, dual enrollment of high school students, honors, independent study, internships, liberal arts/career combination. Bachelor's degree programs available on campus. License preparation in nursing. **Credit/placement by examination:** AP, CLEP, institutional tests. 40 credit hours maximum toward associate degree. **Support services:** Learning center, pre-admission summer program, reduced course load, remedial instruction, study skills assistance, tutoring, writing center.

Majors. Biology: Biotechnology. **Business:** General, accounting, accounting technology, administrative services, business admin, hospitality admin, small business admin. **Computer sciences:** Networking. **Conservation:** General. **Engineering:** Pre-engineering. **Health services:** EMT paramedic, medical secretary, nursing (RN), premedicine. **Liberal arts:** Arts/sciences. **Protective services:** Criminal justice, law enforcement admin. **Visual/performing arts:** Studio arts. **Work/family studies:** Child care management.

Most popular majors. Business/marketing 18%, engineering/engineering technologies 13%, health sciences 22%, liberal arts 32%.

Technology on campus. 535 workstations in library, computer center. Dormitories wired for high-speed internet access and linked to campus network. Commuter students can connect to campus network. Online course registration, online library, helpline, wireless network available.

Student life. Freshman orientation: Available. Preregistration for classes offered. Students meet with counselors, financial aid officers, student services representatives to determine course of study and expenses. **Housing:** Apartments available. $150 partly refundable deposit, deadline 8/15. **Activities:** Campus ministries, drama, literary magazine, student government, student volunteer association, nurses association, student activities board, history club, water tech club, art club.

Student services. Adult student services, career counseling, student employment services, financial aid counseling, on-campus daycare, personal counseling, veterans' counselor. **Physically disabled:** Services for visually, hearing impaired. **Transfer:** Transfer adviser, college fairs on campus for students transferring to 4-year colleges.

Contact. E-mail: admissions@baycollege.edu
Phone: (906) 217-4010 Toll-free number: (800) 221-2001
Fax: (906) 217-1714
Jessica LaMarch, Director of Admissions, Bay College, 2001 North Lincoln Road, Escanaba, MI 49829-2511

Bay Mills Community College
Brimley, Michigan
www.bmcc.edu   CB code: 2101

- Public 2-year community college
- Commuter campus in rural community

General. Regionally accredited. **Enrollment:** 461 degree-seeking undergraduates. **Degrees:** 51 associate awarded. **Location:** 20 miles from Sault Ste. Marie. **Calendar:** Semester, limited summer session. **Full-time faculty:** 15 total.

Transfer out. **Colleges most students transferred to 2015:** Lake Superior State University.

Basis for selection. Open admission. All newly admitted degree-seeking students must complete the COMPASS test or provide results of previous testing or have successfully completed college courses in math and English. **Home schooled:** Transcript of courses and grades required. **Learning Disabled:** Students with documented disabilities must contact the Student Services Office to receive assistance and accommodations.

2015-2016 Annual costs. Tuition/fees: $3,250; $3,250 out-of-state. Per-credit charge: $95. Books/supplies: $700.

Financial aid. **Need-based:** Work-study available nights, weekends and for part-time students.

Application procedures. **Admission:** Closing date 8/26 (receipt date). No application fee. Admission notification on a rolling basis. **Financial aid:** Priority date 6/30; no closing date. FAFSA required.

Academics. **Special study options:** Cooperative education, distance learning, double major, dual enrollment of high school students, independent study, internships. License preparation in paramedic. **Credit/placement by examination:** AP, CLEP, institutional tests. 60% of credits required for any degree or certificate program must be earned in residence. **Support services:** GED preparation and test center, learning center, remedial instruction, study skills assistance, tutoring.

Majors. **Area/ethnic studies:** Native American. **Business:** Business admin. **Computer sciences:** Information technology. **Education:** Early childhood. **Parks/recreation:** Health/fitness. **Protective services:** Corrections.

Technology on campus. 30 workstations in library, computer center. Online library, repair service, wireless network available.

Student life. **Freshman orientation:** Mandatory. Preregistration for classes offered. **Activities:** Student government.

Student services. Career counseling, financial aid counseling. **Transfer:** Pre-admission transcript evaluation for new students. College fairs on campus for students transferring to 4-year colleges.

Contact. E-mail: elehre@bmcc.edu
Phone: (906) 248-3354 ext. 8422 Toll-free number: (800) 844-2622
Fax: (906) 248-3351
Elaine Lehre, Admissions Officer, Bay Mills Community College, 12214 West Lakeshore Drive, Brimley, MI 49715

Delta College
University Center, Michigan
www.delta.edu   CB code: 1816

- Public 2-year community college
- Commuter campus in small city

General. Founded in 1957. Regionally accredited. Classes offered at 21 off-campus sites, including 3 major off-campus facilities. **Enrollment:** 9,291 degree-seeking undergraduates. **Degrees:** 1,510 associate awarded. **Location:** 10 miles from Saginaw, 12 miles from Midland. **Calendar:** Semester, limited summer session. **Class size:** 44% < 20, 55% 20-39, less than 1% 40-49, less than 1% 50-99. **Special facilities:** Planetarium, on-site dental clinic.

Student profile.

Out-of-state:	9%	25 or older:	31.2%

Transfer out. **Colleges most students transferred to 2015:** Central Michigan University, Saginaw Valley State University, Northwood University, University of Michigan, Michigan State University.

Basis for selection. Open admission. ACT, ASSET or COMPASS required of all students for counseling purposes.

2015-2016 Annual costs. Tuition/fees: $3,495; $5,370 out-of-district; $9,870 out-of-state. Per-credit charge: $97 in-district; $159 out-of-district; $309 out-of-state. Books/supplies: $1,500. Personal expenses: $882.

Financial aid. **Need-based:** Need-based aid available for part-time students. Work-study available nights, weekends and for part-time students. **Non-need-based:** Scholarships awarded for academics, athletics.

Application procedures. **Admission:** No deadline. No application fee. Admission notification on a rolling basis. **Financial aid:** No deadline. FAFSA required. Applicants notified on a rolling basis; must reply within 2 week(s) of notification.

Academics. **Special study options:** Cooperative education, distance learning, double major, dual enrollment of high school students, honors, independent study, internships, liberal arts/career combination, student-designed major, study abroad, weekend college. License preparation in dental hygiene, nursing, occupational therapy, physical therapy, radiology, real estate. **Credit/placement by examination:** AP, CLEP, IB, institutional tests. 38 credit hours maximum toward associate degree. **Support services:** GED preparation and test center, learning center, reduced course load, remedial instruction, study skills assistance, tutoring, writing center.

Majors. **Architecture:** Technology. **Biology:** General, biotechnology. **Business:** General, accounting, administrative services, business admin, construction management, international, marketing, merchandising, office management, office technology, small business admin. **Communications:** Journalism. **Communications technology:** General, graphic/printing. **Computer sciences:** General, computer science, information systems, information technology, networking, programming, web page design, webmaster. **Conservation:** General, environmental science, forestry, water/wetlands/marine. **Education:** Art, business, elementary, kindergarten/preschool, music, physical, secondary, special ed, technology/industrial arts. **Engineering:** General, architectural, mechanical. **English:** English lit. **Foreign languages:** General. **General:** Carpentry, electrician, maintenance, pipefitting, plumbing. **Health services:** Clinical lab science, dental assistant, dental hygiene, dietetics, licensed practical nurse, medical assistant, medical radiologic technology/radiation therapy, medical secretary, nursing (RN), office assistant, optometric assistant, pharmacy assistant, physical therapy assistant, physics/radiologic health, predental, premedicine, prenursing, prepharmacy, preveterinary, respiratory therapy assistant, respiratory therapy technology, sonography, surgical technology. **Human services:** Social work. **Liberal arts:** Arts/sciences. **Math:** General. **Parks/recreation:** Health/fitness. **Physical sciences:** General, chemistry, geology. **Protective services:** Corrections, fire safety technology, fire services admin, firefighting, law enforcement admin, police science. **Psychology:** General. **Social sciences:** Economics, geography, sociology. **Visual/performing arts:** Art, dramatic, graphic design, interior design, music, photography. **Work/family studies:** Child development.

Technology on campus. 350 workstations in library, computer center, student center. Commuter students can connect to campus network. Online course registration, online library, helpline, wireless network available.

Student life. **Freshman orientation:** Mandatory. Preregistration for classes offered. General campus overview and individual academic counseling/advising. Assessment required prior to orientation. **Activities:** Choral groups, drama, radio station, student government, student newspaper, TV station.

Athletics. NJCAA. **Intercollegiate:** Basketball, golf M, soccer W, softball W. **Team name:** Pioneers.

Student services. Adult student services, career counseling, services for economically disadvantaged, student employment services, financial aid counseling, minority student services, personal counseling, placement for graduates, veterans' counselor. **Physically disabled:** Services for visually, speech, hearing impaired. **Transfer:** Transfer center, transfer adviser, college fairs on campus for students transferring to 4-year colleges.

Contact. E-mail: admit@delta.edu
Phone: (989) 686-9093 Toll-free number: (800) 285-1704
Fax: (989) 667-2202
Zachary Ward, Director of Admissions and Recruitment, Delta College, 1961 Delta Road D101, University Center, MI 48710

Glen Oaks Community College
Centreville, Michigan **CB member**
www.glenoaks.edu **CB code: 1261**

- Public 2-year community college
- Commuter campus in rural community

General. Founded in 1965. Regionally accredited. **Enrollment:** 680 degree-seeking undergraduates. **Degrees:** 154 associate awarded. **Location:** 35 miles from Kalamazoo. **Calendar:** Semester, limited summer session. **Full-time faculty:** 34 total. **Part-time faculty:** 31 total. **Special facilities:** Fitness center, nature trails and habitat.

Student profile.

Out-of-state: 18% 25 or older: 82%

Transfer out. Colleges most students transferred to 2015: Western Michigan University, Grand Valley State University, Kalamazoo Valley Community College, Kellogg Community College, Michigan State University.

Basis for selection. Open admission, but selective for some programs. Admission to nursing program based on pre-admission test, high school grades, and health form. ACCUPLACER test requested for certain programs. ACT/SAT may be considered in lieu of ACCUPLACER.

2015-2016 Annual costs. Tuition/fees: $3,960; $5,610 out-of-district; $6,870 out-of-state. Books/supplies: $1,556. Personal expenses: $980.

Financial aid. Need-based: Need-based aid available for part-time students. Work-study available nights, weekends and for part-time students. **Non-need-based:** Scholarships awarded for academics, art, athletics, leadership.

Application procedures. Admission: No deadline. No application fee. Admission notification on a rolling basis. **Financial aid:** No deadline. FAFSA, institutional form required. Applicants notified on a rolling basis.

Academics. Special study options: Accelerated study, distance learning, double major, dual enrollment of high school students, independent study, internships, liberal arts/career combination. Bachelor's degree programs available on campus. License preparation in nursing. **Credit/placement by examination:** AP, CLEP, institutional tests. 47 credit hours maximum toward associate degree. **Support services:** Learning center, pre-admission summer program, remedial instruction, study skills assistance, tutoring.

Majors. Business: General. **Education:** Early childhood. **Engineering:** Engineering science. **Health services:** Nursing (RN). **Liberal arts:** Arts/sciences. **Work/family studies:** Child care management.

Most popular majors. Business/marketing 26%, engineering/engineering technologies 6%, health sciences 27%, liberal arts 38%.

Technology on campus. 150 workstations in library, computer center, student center. Commuter students can connect to campus network. Online course registration, online library, wireless network available.

Student life. Freshman orientation: Mandatory. Preregistration for classes offered. **Activities:** Choral groups, student government, academic honorary society, Phi Theta Kappa, veterans club.

Athletics. NJCAA. **Intercollegiate:** Baseball M, basketball, cross-country, golf, softball W. **Intramural:** Table tennis. **Team name:** Vikings.

Student services. Adult student services, career counseling, services for economically disadvantaged, student employment services, financial aid counseling, personal counseling, women's services. **Physically disabled:** Services for visually, speech, hearing impaired. **Transfer:** Transfer adviser, college fairs on campus for students transferring to 4-year colleges.

Contact. E-mail: thowden@glenoaks.edu
Phone: (269) 294-4230 Toll-free number: (888) 994-7818 ext. 320
Fax: (269) 467-9068
Adrienne Skinner, Director of Admissions, Glen Oaks Community College, 62249 Shimmel Road, Centreville, MI 49032-9719

Gogebic Community College
Ironwood, Michigan
www.gogebic.edu **CB code: 1250**

- Public 2-year community college
- Commuter campus in small town

General. Founded in 1932. Regionally accredited. **Enrollment:** 771 degree-seeking undergraduates; 287 non-degree-seeking students. **Degrees:** 174 associate awarded. **Location:** 100 miles from Duluth, Minnesota, 150 miles from Marquette. **Calendar:** Semester, limited summer session. **Full-time faculty:** 35 total. **Part-time faculty:** 48 total. **Class size:** 81% < 20, 19% 20-39. **Special facilities:** Arboretum, ski hill, terrain park, tubing park, cross-country ski trails, snowshoeing trails.

Student profile. Among degree-seeking undergraduates, 36% enrolled in a transfer program, 37% enrolled in a vocational program, 215 enrolled as first-time, first-year students.

Part-time:	33%	Hispanic/Latino:	1%
Out-of-state:	16%	Native American:	3%
Women:	60%	Multi-racial, non-Hispanic:	2%
African American:	2%		

Transfer out. Colleges most students transferred to 2015: Northern Michigan University, University of Wisconsin-Superior, Northland College, Michigan Technological University.

Basis for selection. Open admission, but selective for some programs. Students applying to nursing programs required to show competency in biology and chemistry. Admission based on assessment test scores and academic achievement. Interview recommended. **Home schooled:** Interview required.

High school preparation. Nursing applicants must have background in chemistry, math, and biology.

2015-2016 Annual costs. Tuition/fees: $4,344; $5,708 out-of-district; $6,607 out-of-state. Per-credit charge: $106 in-district; $150 out-of-district; $179 out-of-state. Room/board: $5,804. Books/supplies: $1,000. Personal expenses: $7,604.

Financial aid. Need-based: Need-based aid available for part-time students. Work-study available nights, weekends and for part-time students. **Non-need-based:** Scholarships awarded for academics, art, athletics, job skills, leadership, music/drama, state residency.

Application procedures. Admission: Closing date 8/14 (receipt date). $10 fee, may be waived for applicants with need. Admission notification on a rolling basis. **Financial aid:** Priority date 5/1; no closing date. FAFSA required. Applicants notified on a rolling basis starting 3/15; must reply within 2 week(s) of notification.

Academics. Special study options: Cooperative education, distance learning, double major, dual enrollment of high school students, honors, internships, student-designed major. License preparation in nursing, paramedic. **Credit/placement by examination:** AP, CLEP, institutional tests. 12 credit hours maximum toward associate degree. AP exam scores not listed in policy evaluated on individual basis. **Support services:** Learning center, reduced course load, remedial instruction, study skills assistance, tutoring.

Majors. Biology: General. **Business:** General, accounting, business admin, entrepreneurial studies, office management, office technology. **Computer sciences:** General, information technology, networking, programming, security, system admin. **Conservation:** General, forestry. **Education:** General, early childhood, elementary, secondary, special ed, teacher assistance. **Engineering:** General. **Health services:** Clinical lab science, EMT paramedic, nursing (RN), predental, premedicine, prenursing, prepharmacy, preveterinary. **History:** General. **Human services:** Social work. **Liberal arts:** Arts/sciences. **Math:** General. **Parks/recreation:** Facilities management. **Physical sciences:** General, chemistry, physics. **Protective services:** Law enforcement admin. **Psychology:** General. **Social sciences:** Sociology. **Visual/performing arts:** Art, commercial/advertising art.

Technology on campus. 240 workstations in dormitories, library, computer center, student center. Dormitories wired for high-speed internet access and linked to campus network. Commuter students can connect to campus network. Wireless network available.

Student life. Freshman orientation: Mandatory. Preregistration for classes offered. Early orientation held in April for accepted students who have completed assessment. Other orientation programs in August and June. **Housing:** Coed dorms available. $200 fully refundable deposit. **Activities:** Campus ministries, drama, music ensembles, student government, student newspaper, student senate, student nurses association.

Athletics. NJCAA. **Intercollegiate:** Basketball, cross-country, volleyball M. **Team name:** Samsons.

Student services. Alcohol/substance abuse counseling, career counseling, services for economically disadvantaged, student employment services, financial aid counseling, personal counseling, placement for graduates, veterans' counselor. **Physically disabled:** Services for visually, hearing impaired. **Transfer:** Re-entry adviser for new students. Transfer adviser, college fairs on campus for students transferring to 4-year colleges.

Contact. E-mail: debbiej@gogebic.edu
Phone: (906) 932-4231 ext. 207
Toll-free number: (800) 682-5910 ext. 207 Fax: (906) 932-2339
Kim Zeckovich, Director of Admissions and Public Relations, Gogebic Community College, E4946 Jackson Road, Ironwood, MI 49938

Grand Rapids Community College
Grand Rapids, Michigan
www.grcc.edu

CB member
CB code: 1254

▶ Public 2-year community college
▶ Commuter campus in small city

General. Founded in 1914. Regionally accredited. Courses offered at several off-campus sites in Western Michigan. **Enrollment:** 13,840 degree-seeking undergraduates; 1,086 non-degree-seeking students. **Degrees:** 2,133 associate awarded. **Location:** 70 miles from Lansing, 180 miles from Chicago. **Calendar:** Semester, extensive summer session. **Full-time faculty:** 246 total. **Part-time faculty:** 518 total. **Class size:** 31% < 20, 69% 20-39, less than 1% 40-49.

Student profile. Among degree-seeking undergraduates, 56% enrolled in a transfer program, 44% enrolled in a vocational program, 2,856 enrolled as first-time, first-year students.

Part-time:	68%	Women:	51%
Out-of-state:	1%	25 or older:	35%

Transfer out. Colleges most students transferred to 2015: Grand Valley State University, Ferris State University, Western Michigan University, Michigan State University, Davenport University.

Basis for selection. Open admission, but selective for some programs. Certain health-related programs require 2.5 high school GPA and completion of certain math and science courses before admission. **Home schooled:** Assessment exam required.

High school preparation. College-preparatory program recommended. Recommended units include English 4, mathematics 4, social studies 3 and science 4.

2015-2016 Annual costs. Tuition/fees: $3,699; $7,419 out-of-district; $10,779 out-of-state. Per-credit charge: $108 in-district; $232 out-of-district; $344 out-of-state. Books/supplies: $1,661. Personal expenses: $1,618.

2014-2015 Financial aid. Need-based: 54% of total undergraduate aid awarded as scholarships/grants, 46% as loans/jobs. Need-based aid available for part-time students. Work-study available nights, weekends and for part-time students. **Non-need-based:** Scholarships awarded for academics. **Additional information:** Tuition reimbursement and/or child-care services for single parents and displaced homemakers who meet Perkins guidelines.

Application procedures. Admission: No deadline. No application fee. Admission notification on a rolling basis. **Financial aid:** Priority date 4/1; no closing date. FAFSA required. Applicants notified on a rolling basis starting 5/1; must reply within 3 week(s) of notification.

Academics. Liberal arts and pre-professional curricula along with extensive work-force training and technical seminars offered. **Special study options:** Cooperative education, distance learning, dual enrollment of high school students, ESL, honors, independent study, internships, study abroad. License preparation in dental hygiene, nursing, occupational therapy, radiology. **Credit/placement by examination:** AP, CLEP, institutional tests. 47 credit hours maximum toward associate degree. **Support services:** GED test center, learning center, pre-admission summer program, reduced course load, remedial instruction, study skills assistance, tutoring, writing center.

Majors. Architecture: Architecture. **Biology:** General. **Business:** General, accounting technology, business admin, executive assistant, fashion, sales/

distribution. **Communications:** Journalism. **Computer sciences:** General, applications programming, LAN/WAN management, programming, webmaster. **Conservation:** General, forestry. **Education:** Elementary, multi-level teacher, music, physical, teacher assistance. **Engineering:** General. **English:** English lit, rhetoric/composition. **Foreign languages:** General. **Health services:** Clinical lab science, dental assistant, dental hygiene, licensed practical nurse, medical radiologic technology/radiation therapy, nursing (RN), occupational therapy, occupational therapy assistant, physical therapy, predental, premedicine, prepharmacy, preveterinary, surgical technology. **Human services:** Social work. **Liberal arts:** Arts/sciences, library assistant. **Math:** General. **Physical sciences:** Chemistry, geology, oceanography, physics. **Protective services:** Corrections, law enforcement admin, police science. **Psychology:** General. **Social sciences:** Economics, geography, political science, sociology. **Visual/performing arts:** Art, commercial/advertising art, dramatic, interior design, music, music management, music performance, photography, piano/keyboard, studio arts, voice/opera. **Work/family studies:** Child care management.

Most popular majors. Business/marketing 12%, health sciences 11%, liberal arts 51%.

Technology on campus. 1,500 workstations in library, computer center, student center. Commuter students can connect to campus network. Online course registration, online library, helpline, wireless network available.

Student life. Freshman orientation: Available. Preregistration for classes offered. Provides campus tours and general information about the college. **Policies:** No smoking on campus. **Activities:** Bands, choral groups, dance, drama, film society, international student organizations, literary magazine, music ensembles, musical theater, student government, student newspaper, TV station, Black student organization, Hispanic student organization, Native American student organization, Vietnamese student organization, Christian Fellowship, content area student organizations, service learning.

Athletics. NJCAA. **Intercollegiate:** Baseball M, basketball, cross-country, golf M, softball W, volleyball W. **Team name:** Raiders.

Student services. Adult student services, career counseling, student employment services, financial aid counseling, on-campus daycare, personal counseling. **Physically disabled:** Services for visually, speech, hearing impaired. **Transfer:** Pre-admission transcript evaluation for new students. Transfer adviser, college fairs on campus for students transferring to 4-year colleges.

Contact. E-mail: admissions@grcc.edu
Phone: (616) 234-3300 Fax: (616) 234-4107
Diane Patrick, Director of Admissions, Grand Rapids Community College, 143 Bostwick Avenue NE, Grand Rapids, MI 49503-3295

Henry Ford Community College
Dearborn, Michigan
www.hfcc.edu

CB code: 1293

▶ Public 2-year community college
▶ Commuter campus in small city

General. Founded in 1938. Regionally accredited. **Enrollment:** 11,129 degree-seeking undergraduates; 1,626 non-degree-seeking students. **Degrees:** 1,412 associate awarded. **Location:** 8 miles from downtown. **Calendar:** Semester, extensive summer session. **Full-time faculty:** 176 total. **Part-time faculty:** 632 total.

Student profile. Among degree-seeking undergraduates, 2,334 enrolled as first-time, first-year students.

Part-time:	61%	Hispanic/Latino:	2%
Out-of-state:	1%	Native American:	1%
Women:	55%	Multi-racial, non-Hispanic:	2%
African American:	22%	International:	2%
Asian American:	2%	25 or older:	34%

Transfer out. Colleges most students transferred to 2015: University of Michigan-Dearborn, Wayne State University, Eastern Michigan University, Michigan State University.

Basis for selection. Open admission, but selective for some programs. Special requirements for specific allied health programs.

High school preparation. College-preparatory program recommended. Recommended units include English 4, mathematics 4, social studies 3, science 4, foreign language 1 and computer science 1. For allied health programs: 1 year high school biology, chemistry, and algebra.

2015-2016 Annual costs. Tuition/fees: $3,360; $5,340 out-of-district; $7,350 out-of-state. Per-credit charge: $92 in-district; $158 out-of-district; $225 out-of-state. Books/supplies: $1,464.

2014-2015 Financial aid. Need-based: 67% of total undergraduate aid awarded as scholarships/grants, 33% as loans/jobs. Work-study available nights, weekends and for part-time students. **Non-need-based:** Scholarships awarded for academics, athletics.

Application procedures. Admission: No deadline. No application fee. Admission notification on a rolling basis. **Financial aid:** Priority date 6/5; no closing date. FAFSA required. Applicants notified on a rolling basis starting 5/15.

Academics. Special study options: Cooperative education, distance learning, dual enrollment of high school students, ESL, honors, independent study, study abroad, weekend college. License preparation in nursing, paramedic, physical therapy, radiology. **Credit/placement by examination:** AP, CLEP, ACT, institutional tests. 20 credit hours maximum toward associate degree. **Support services:** Learning center, pre-admission summer program, reduced course load, remedial instruction, study skills assistance, tutoring, writing center.

Majors. Architecture: Technology. **Business:** General, accounting, business admin, executive assistant, hospitality admin, management science, office/clerical, real estate. **Communications:** Broadcast journalism. **Communications technology:** Animation/special effects. **Computer sciences:** General, security. **Conservation:** Environmental studies. **Education:** Early childhood, elementary, secondary, special ed. **Engineering:** General. **Health services:** EMT paramedic, health information technology, licensed practical nurse, management/clinical assistant, nursing (RN), office admin, physical therapy assistant, prepharmacy, radiologic technology/medical imaging, respiratory therapy technology, surgical technology. **Liberal arts:** Arts/sciences. **Parks/recreation:** Exercise sciences. **Philosophy/religion:** Religion. **Physical sciences:** Chemistry. **Protective services:** Firefighting, law enforcement admin, security management. **Visual/performing arts:** Art, commercial/advertising art, dramatic, interior design, studio arts. **Work/family studies:** Child development.

Most popular majors. Business/marketing 14%, health sciences 24%, liberal arts 33%, security/protective services 6%.

Technology on campus. Commuter students can connect to campus network. Online course registration, online library, helpline, wireless network available.

Student life. Freshman orientation: Available. Preregistration for classes offered. **Housing:** Housing referrals. **Activities:** Bands, campus ministries, choral groups, dance, drama, international student organizations, radio station, student government, student newspaper, Muslim student association, African American association, community service club, Campus Crusade for Christ, Students for a Democratic Society, Crazy Antics club, Yemen student association, multicultural club, diversity club.

Athletics. NJCAA. **Intercollegiate:** Baseball M, basketball, golf, softball W, volleyball W. **Intramural:** Basketball, bowling, golf, table tennis, tennis, track and field, volleyball. **Team name:** Hawks.

Student services. Adult student services, career counseling, services for economically disadvantaged, student employment services, financial aid counseling, on-campus daycare, personal counseling, placement for graduates, veterans' counselor. **Physically disabled:** Services for visually, hearing impaired. **Transfer:** Re-entry adviser, pre-admission transcript evaluation for new students. Transfer center, transfer adviser, college fairs on campus for students transferring to 4-year colleges.

Contact. Phone: (313) 845-6403 Toll-free number: (800) 585-4322 Fax: (313) 845-9891
Holly Diamond, Director of Enrollment Management, Henry Ford Community College, 5101 Evergreen Road, Dearborn, MI 48128

ITT Technical Institute: Canton
Canton, Michigan
www.itt-tech.edu

▶ For-profit 2-year business and technical college
▶ Commuter campus in small city

General. Accredited by ACICS. **Enrollment:** 415 undergraduates. **Degrees:** 38 bachelor's, 125 associate awarded. **Calendar:** Quarter. **Full-time faculty:** 18 total. **Part-time faculty:** 66 total.

Basis for selection. Selective admissions to some programs.

2015-2016 Annual costs. Per-credit-hour charge, $493; academic fee, $200. Certain programs require purchase of tools, which range from $150 to $700. All costs subject to change.

Financial aid. Need-based: Work-study available nights, weekends and for part-time students.

Academics. Credit/placement by examination: AP, CLEP.

Majors. Business: Business admin. **Computer sciences:** General, networking, web page design. **Health services:** Nursing (RN). **Protective services:** Law enforcement admin. **Visual/performing arts:** Design.

Contact. ITT Technical Institute: Canton, 1905 South Haggerty Road, Canton, MI 48188

ITT Technical Institute: Troy
Troy, Michigan
www.itt-tech.edu   CB code: 2784

▶ For-profit 2-year technical college
▶ Commuter campus in small city
▶ Interview required

General. Accredited by ACICS. **Enrollment:** 466 undergraduates. **Degrees:** 67 bachelor's, 166 associate awarded. **Calendar:** Quarter, extensive summer session. **Full-time faculty:** 12 total. **Part-time faculty:** 108 total.

Basis for selection. Satisfactory scores from on-site tests in English and mathematics required.

2015-2016 Annual costs. Per-credit-hour charge, $493; academic fee, $200. Certain programs require purchase of tools, which range from $100 to $500. All costs subject to change.

Financial aid. Need-based: Work-study available nights, weekends and for part-time students.

Application procedures. Admission: No deadline. No application fee. Admission notification on a rolling basis. **Financial aid:** No deadline. FAFSA, institutional form required. Applicants notified on a rolling basis.

Academics. Credit/placement by examination: AP, CLEP. **Support services:** Learning center, tutoring.

Majors. Business: Business admin. **Computer sciences:** Networking, programming, web page design. **Protective services:** Law enforcement admin. **Visual/performing arts:** Design.

Technology on campus. Online library available.

Student life. Freshman orientation: Available. Preregistration for classes offered.

Student services. Career counseling, student employment services, placement for graduates.

Contact. Phone: (248) 524-1800 Toll-free number: (800) 832-6817 Fax: (248) 524-1965
Patricia Hyman, Director of Recruitment, ITT Technical Institute: Troy, 1522 East Big Beaver Road, Troy, MI 48083-1905

Jackson College
Jackson, Michigan   CB member
www.jccmi.edu   CB code: 1340

▶ Public 2-year community college
▶ Commuter campus in small city

General. Founded in 1928. Regionally accredited. Off-campus locations in Hillsdale County and Lenawee County. **Enrollment:** 5,180 degree-seeking undergraduates. **Degrees:** 628 associate awarded. **Location:** 6 miles from downtown. **Calendar:** Semester, limited summer session. **Full-time faculty:** 87 total; 7% minority, 55% women. **Part-time faculty:** 320 total; 6% minority, 60% women. **Class size:** 57% < 20, 43% 20-39, less than 1% 40-49. **Partnerships:** Formal partnership with Foote Health University to provide education and training for employees.

Student profile.

Out-of-state:	2%	25 or older:	39%

Transfer out. Colleges most students transferred to 2015: Michigan State University, Spring Arbor University, Eastern Michigan University, Siena Heights University, Western Michigan University.

Basis for selection. Open admission, but selective for some programs. Special requirements for allied health programs and nursing program. ACT used for placement if submitted. Students not submitting ACT required to take college-administered placement tests. Second admit programs require interviews and specific academic prerequisites.

2015-2016 Annual costs. Tuition/fees: $4,890; $6,300 out-of-district; $8,640 out-of-state. Per-credit charge: $125 in-district; $172 out-of-district; $250 out-of-state. Books/supplies: $672.

Financial aid. Need-based: Need-based aid available for part-time students. Work-study available nights, weekends and for part-time students. **Non-need-based:** Scholarships awarded for academics, art, athletics, leadership.

Application procedures. Admission: No deadline. No application fee. Admission notification on a rolling basis. **Financial aid:** Priority date 6/15; no closing date. FAFSA, institutional form required. Applicants notified on a rolling basis starting 3/1.

Academics. Extensive on-line offerings. Students may also complete bachelor's degrees on-campus from partner universities. **Special study options:** Accelerated study, distance learning, dual enrollment of high school students, ESL, honors, independent study, internships, liberal arts/career combination, study abroad. Bachelor's degree programs available on campus. License preparation in aviation, nursing, paramedic, radiology. **Credit/placement by examination:** AP, CLEP, IB, institutional tests. 30 credit hours maximum toward associate degree. **Support services:** GED preparation and test center, learning center, pre-admission summer program, remedial instruction, study skills assistance, tutoring, writing center.

Majors. Business: General, accounting, business admin, finance. **Computer sciences:** Applications programming, computer graphics, data processing, programming, web page design. **Education:** Early childhood. **General:** Electrician. **Health services:** EMT paramedic, medical assistant, medical transcription, nursing (RN), radiologic technology/medical imaging, sonography. **Liberal arts:** Arts/sciences. **Protective services:** Criminal justice. **Visual/performing arts:** Graphic design.

Most popular majors. Business/marketing 12%, health sciences 28%, liberal arts 39%, trade and industry 9%.

Technology on campus. 356 workstations in library, computer center, student center. Online course registration, helpline available.

Student life. Freshman orientation: Available. Preregistration for classes offered. Two- to 3-hour program prior to semester. **Activities:** Concert band, choral groups, dance, drama, student government, student newspaper.

Athletics. Intramural: Basketball M, football (non-tackle) M, soccer M. **Team name:** Golden Jets.

Student services. Adult student services, career counseling, services for economically disadvantaged, financial aid counseling, minority student services, on-campus daycare. **Physically disabled:** Services for visually, speech, hearing impaired. **Transfer:** Pre-admission transcript evaluation for new students. Transfer center, transfer adviser, college fairs on campus for students transferring to 4-year colleges.

Contact. E-mail: admissions@jccmi.edu
Phone: (517) 796-8425 Toll-free number: (888) 522-7344
Fax: (517) 796-8631
Karen Cuzdlo, Director of Admissions, Jackson College, 2111 Emmons Road, Jackson, MI 49201-8399

Kalamazoo Valley Community College
Kalamazoo, Michigan
www.kvcc.edu
CB code: 1378

- Public 2-year community college
- Commuter campus in small city

General. Founded in 1966. Regionally accredited. Additional campus downtown. **Enrollment:** 7,479 degree-seeking undergraduates; 1,357 non-degree-seeking students. **Degrees:** 956 associate awarded. **Location:** 130 miles from Detroit, 150 miles from Chicago. **Calendar:** Semester, limited summer session. **Full-time faculty:** 133 total. **Part-time faculty:** 431 total. **Class size:** 30% < 20, 59% 20-39, 10% 40-49, less than 1% 50-99. **Special facilities:** Museum, nature trails.

Student profile. Among degree-seeking undergraduates, 1,498 enrolled as first-time, first-year students.

Part-time:	61%	Hispanic/Latino:	4%
Out-of-state:	1%	Native American:	1%
Women:	52%	Multi-racial, non-Hispanic:	3%
African American:	14%	International:	1%
Asian American:	1%	25 or older:	50%

Transfer out. Colleges most students transferred to 2015: Western Michigan University.

Basis for selection. Open admission.

2015-2016 Annual costs. Tuition/fees: $3,060; $5,100 out-of-district; $6,810 out-of-state. Per-credit charge: $95 in-district; $163 out-of-district; $220 out-of-state. Books/supplies: $1,350. Personal expenses: $1,282.

Financial aid. Need-based: Need-based aid available for part-time students. Work-study available nights, weekends and for part-time students. **Non-need-based:** Scholarships awarded for academics, athletics.

Application procedures. Admission: No deadline. No application fee. Admission notification on a rolling basis. **Financial aid:** Priority date 6/1; no closing date. FAFSA, institutional form required. Applicants notified on a rolling basis starting 5/1; must reply within 2 week(s) of notification.

Academics. Special study options: Cooperative education, cross-registration, distance learning, dual enrollment of high school students, ESL, honors, independent study, internships, liberal arts/career combination, weekend college. License preparation in dental hygiene, nursing. **Credit/placement by examination:** AP, CLEP, institutional tests. 32 credit hours maximum toward associate degree. Michigan Language Assessment Battery may be used for placement. **Support services:** Learning center, reduced course load, remedial instruction, study skills assistance, tutoring, writing center.

Majors. Business: Accounting, administrative services, business admin, management information systems. **Communications technology:** General. **Computer sciences:** Computer graphics, data processing, programming. **Education:** General. **Engineering:** General. **Health services:** Dental hygiene, licensed practical nurse, medical assistant, medical secretary, nursing (RN), respiratory therapy technology. **Liberal arts:** Arts/sciences. **Physical sciences:** General. **Protective services:** Firefighting, law enforcement admin, police science. **Visual/performing arts:** Commercial/advertising art. **Work/family studies:** Family studies.

Most popular majors. Business/marketing 11%, education 11%, engineering/engineering technologies 7%, health sciences 12%, liberal arts 43%.

Technology on campus. 1,000 workstations in library, computer center, student center. Online course registration, wireless network available.

Student life. Freshman orientation: Mandatory. Preregistration for classes offered. **Activities:** Choral groups, dance, Fellowship of Christian Athletes, Student American Dental Hygiene Association, data processing association, African American association, Latino student association, Native American association, deaf student association.

Athletics. NJCAA. Intercollegiate: Baseball M, basketball, softball W, volleyball W. **Intramural:** Basketball M, volleyball W. **Team name:** Cougars.

Student services. Adult student services, career counseling, services for economically disadvantaged, student employment services, financial aid counseling, personal counseling, placement for graduates, veterans' counselor, women's services. **Physically disabled:** Services for visually, speech, hearing impaired. **Transfer:** Transfer adviser, college fairs on campus for students transferring to 4-year colleges.

Contact. E-mail: admissions@kvcc.edu
Phone: (269) 488-4400 Fax: (269) 488-4161
Sarah Hubbeli, Director of Admissions, Registration and Records, Kalamazoo Valley Community College, 6767 West O Avenue, Kalamazoo, MI 49003-4070

Kellogg Community College
Battle Creek, Michigan
www.kellogg.edu
CB code: 1375

- Public 2-year community college
- Commuter campus in small city

General. Founded in 1956. Regionally accredited. Academic centers in Coldwater, Hastings and Albion. Regional Manufacturing Technical Center with open entry/open exit programs in several different technical areas.

Enrollment: 3,943 degree-seeking undergraduates; 1,138 non-degree-seeking students. **Degrees:** 901 associate awarded. **Location:** 20 miles from Kalamazoo, 40 miles from Lansing. **Calendar:** Semester, limited summer session. **Full-time faculty:** 87 total; 15% have terminal degrees, 8% minority, 52% women. **Part-time faculty:** 360 total; less than 1% have terminal degrees, 6% minority, 54% women. **Class size:** 76% < 20, 23% 20-39, less than 1% 50-99.

Student profile. Among degree-seeking undergraduates, 33% enrolled in a transfer program, 67% enrolled in a vocational program, 436 enrolled as first-time, first-year students.

Part-time:	69%	Hispanic/Latino:	5%
Women:	67%	Native American:	1%
African American:	11%	Multi-racial, non-Hispanic:	4%
Asian American:	2%	25 or older:	34%

Transfer out. Colleges most students transferred to 2015: Western Michigan University, Michigan State University, Ferris State University, Grand Valley State University, Central Michigan University.

Basis for selection. Open admission, but selective for some programs. Allied health and nursing program applicants must supply high school record, previous college transcripts, ACT/SAT, and meet specific academic criteria.

High school preparation. College-preparatory program recommended. Recommended units include English 4, mathematics 4, social studies 2, history 1, science 4 (laboratory 1) and academic electives 6.

2015-2016 Annual costs. Tuition/fees: $3,375; $5,228 out-of-district; $7,313 out-of-state. Per-credit charge: $100 in-district; $161 out-of-district; $231 out-of-state. Books/supplies: $1,500. Personal expenses: $5,514. **Additional information:** Current Military Service members pay in-district rates regardless of residency status. Health programs charged at higher rates.

2014-2015 Financial aid. Need-based: Need-based aid available for part-time students. Work-study available nights, weekends and for part-time students. **Non-need-based:** Scholarships awarded for academics, art, athletics, music/drama, state residency.

Application procedures. Admission: No deadline. No application fee. Admission notification on a rolling basis. **Financial aid:** Priority date 4/1; no closing date. FAFSA, institutional form required. Applicants notified on a rolling basis starting 3/13.

Academics. Special study options: Accelerated study, cooperative education, dual enrollment of high school students, honors, independent study, internships, liberal arts/career combination. License preparation in dental hygiene, nursing, paramedic, physical therapy, radiology. **Credit/placement by examination:** AP, CLEP, IB, institutional tests. Must be 2.0 or above for credit. **Support services:** GED test center, learning center, remedial instruction, study skills assistance, tutoring, writing center.

Majors. Business: Accounting technology, business admin, executive assistant. **Communications technology:** Animation/special effects. **Computer sciences:** Data entry, word processing. **Education:** Elementary. **General:** Electrician, pipefitting. **Health services:** Clinical lab technology, dental hygiene, EMT paramedic, medical radiologic technology/radiation therapy, medical secretary, nursing (RN), physical therapy assistant. **Human services:** Community org/advocacy. **Liberal arts:** Arts/sciences. **Protective services:** Corrections, law enforcement admin. **Visual/performing arts:** Graphic design. **Work/family studies:** Child care management.

Most popular majors. Business/marketing 10%, health sciences 25%, liberal arts 46%.

Technology on campus. 1,000 workstations in library, computer center, student center. Commuter students can connect to campus network. Online course registration, online library, helpline, wireless network available.

Student life. Freshman orientation: Available. Preregistration for classes offered. **Activities:** Bands, campus ministries, choral groups, drama, film society, international student organizations, literary magazine, music ensembles, musical theater, student newspaper, Military student support group, Bruin Christian Fellowship, Phi Theta Kappa, Kampus Activities Board, Spectrum, film club, Art League, Encore Theatre Company, human services club, international studies club, community garden.

Athletics. NJCAA. **Intercollegiate:** Baseball M, basketball, softball W, volleyball W. **Team name:** Bruins.

Student services. Adult student services, alcohol/substance abuse counseling, career counseling, student employment services, financial aid counseling, personal counseling, placement for graduates, veterans' counselor. **Physically disabled:** Services for visually, speech, hearing impaired. **Transfer:** Pre-admission transcript evaluation for new students. Transfer adviser, college fairs on campus for students transferring to 4-year colleges.

Contact. E-mail: admissions@kellogg.edu
Phone: (269) 965-4153 Fax: (269) 565-2085
Meredith Stravers, Director of Admissions, Kellogg Community College, 450 North Avenue, Battle Creek, MI 49017-3397

Kirtland Community College
Roscommon, Michigan
www.kirtland.edu
CB code: 1382

▶ Public 2-year community college
▶ Commuter campus in rural community

General. Founded in 1966. Regionally accredited. Additional locations in Grayling, West Branch and Gaylord. **Enrollment:** 1,220 degree-seeking undergraduates; 408 non-degree-seeking students. **Degrees:** 238 associate awarded. **Location:** 192 miles from Detroit, 150 miles from Grand Rapids. **Calendar:** Semester, extensive summer session. **Full-time faculty:** 33 total; 9% have terminal degrees, 12% minority, 52% women. **Part-time faculty:** 95 total; 20% minority, 46% women. **Class size:** 80% < 20, 20% 20-39. **Special facilities:** Fitness and nature trail, firing range, Michigan Technical Education Center.

Student profile. Among degree-seeking undergraduates, 26% enrolled in a transfer program, 74% enrolled in a vocational program, 185 enrolled as first-time, first-year students, 121 transferred in from other institutions.

Part-time:	58%	25 or older:	36%
Women:	62%		

Transfer out. Colleges most students transferred to 2015: Central Michigan University, Saginaw Valley State University, Lake Superior State University, Ferris State University, Grand Valley State University.

Basis for selection. Open admission, but selective for some programs. Special requirements for nursing, criminal justice administration, criminal justice pre-services, police academy, emergency medical services, cardiovascular sonography, and surgical technology programs. **Home schooled:** Transcript or record of courses and grades requested.

High school preparation. 10 units recommended. Recommended units include English 4, mathematics 3, social studies 3 and science 3.

2015-2016 Annual costs. Tuition/fees: $3,725; $4,955 out-of-district; $7,625 out-of-state. Per-credit charge: $105 in-district; $146 out-of-district; $235 out-of-state. Books/supplies: $1,300. Personal expenses: $1,847.

2014-2015 Financial aid. Need-based: 115 full-time freshmen applied for aid; 108 deemed to have need; 108 received aid. Average need met was 47%. Average scholarship/grant was $5,354; average loan $1,783. 59% of total undergraduate aid awarded as scholarships/grants; 41% as loans/jobs. Need-based aid available for part-time students. Work-study available nights, weekends and for part-time students. **Non-need-based:** Awarded to 20 full-time undergraduates, including 10 freshmen. Scholarships awarded for academics, athletics, minority status. **Additional information:** Federal and institutional work-study programs available.

Application procedures. Admission: No deadline. No application fee. Admission notification on a rolling basis. **Financial aid:** Priority date 5/1; no closing date. FAFSA required. Applicants notified on a rolling basis.

Academics. Special study options: Cooperative education, distance learning, dual enrollment of high school students, honors, independent study, internships. License preparation in nursing, paramedic. **Credit/placement by examination:** AP, CLEP, institutional tests. 45 credit hours maximum toward associate degree. **Support services:** GED test center, learning center, reduced course load, remedial instruction, study skills assistance, tutoring, writing center.

Majors. Business: Administrative services, business admin, management information systems. **Health services:** Cardiovascular technology, EMT paramedic, health information technology, medical secretary, nursing (RN), sonography. **Liberal arts:** Arts/sciences, humanities. **Protective services:** Law enforcement admin, police science. **Visual/performing arts:** Graphic design, industrial design.

Most popular majors. Business/marketing 9%, health sciences 48%, liberal arts 29%, security/protective services 7%.

Technology on campus. 100 workstations in library, student center. Commuter students can connect to campus network. Online course registration, online library, helpline, wireless network available.

Student life. Freshman orientation: Mandatory. Preregistration for classes offered. Held in July and August for students and parents for those enrolling fall semester. Held in November and December for students and parents for those enrolling winter semester. **Activities:** Student government, student senate, Phi Theta Kappa, student activities committee, criminal justice club, veterans club.

Athletics. NJCAA. **Intercollegiate:** Bowling, cross-country, golf. **Team name:** Firebirds.

Student services. Adult student services, career counseling, services for economically disadvantaged, student employment services, financial aid counseling, personal counseling, placement for graduates, veterans' counselor. **Physically disabled:** Services for visually, speech, hearing impaired. **Transfer:** Re-entry adviser for new students. Transfer adviser, college fairs on campus for students transferring to 4-year colleges.

Contact. E-mail: admissions@kirtland.edu
Phone: (989) 275-5000 ext. 280 Fax: (989) 275-6727
Tammy Mendyk, Admissions Coordinator, Kirtland Community College, 10775 North Saint Helen Road, Roscommon, MI 48653

Lake Michigan College
Benton Harbor, Michigan
www.lakemichigancollege.edu CB code: 1137

▸ Public 2-year community college
▸ Commuter campus in large town

General. Founded in 1946. Regionally accredited. Additional campuses located in South Haven and Bertrand Crossing in Niles, Michigan. Technical Education Center (M-TEC) located in Benton Harbor. **Enrollment:** 2,812 degree-seeking undergraduates; 1,360 non-degree-seeking students. **Degrees:** 421 associate awarded. **Location:** 80 miles from Grand Rapids, 40 miles from South Bend, IN. **Calendar:** Semester, limited summer session. **Full-time faculty:** 54 total; 28% have terminal degrees, 4% minority, 54% women. **Part-time faculty:** 269 total; 7% have terminal degrees, 11% minority, 62% women. **Class size:** 77% < 20, 23% 20-39, less than 1% 40-49. **Special facilities:** Video production facility, nature area, event center. **Partnerships:** Formal partnerships with Four Winds Casino for Casino Management program, Whirlpool Corporation for Best Ticket Program, American Electric Power for Energy Program.

Student profile. Among degree-seeking undergraduates, 709 enrolled as first-time, first-year students.

| Part-time: | 60% | Women: | 61% |
| Out-of-state: | 2% | 25 or older: | 43% |

Transfer out. **Colleges most students transferred to 2015:** Western Michigan University, Grand Valley State University, Michigan State University, Ferris State University, Siena Heights University.

Basis for selection. Open admission, but selective for some programs. Admission to health sciences programs based on GPA ranking in specific courses. Interview required for dental assistant, radiologic technology, nursing majors. **Home schooled:** Transcript of courses and grades required.

2015-2016 Annual costs. Tuition/fees: $4,140; $5,685 out-of-district; $5,685 out-of-state. Per-credit charge: $94 in-district; $145 out-of-district; $145 out-of-state. Room only: $7,000. Books/supplies: $1,800. Personal expenses: $1,400.

Financial aid. **Need-based:** Need-based aid available for part-time students. Work-study available nights, weekends and for part-time students.

Application procedures. **Admission:** No deadline. No application fee. Admission notification on a rolling basis. **Financial aid:** Priority date 3/1; no closing date. FAFSA required. Applicants notified on a rolling basis starting 4/1; must reply within 2 week(s) of notification.

Academics. **Special study options:** Cooperative education, cross-registration, distance learning, double major, dual enrollment of high school students, honors, independent study, internships, liberal arts/career combination. Bachelor's degree programs available on campus. License preparation in nursing, paramedic, radiology. **Credit/placement by examination:** AP, CLEP, institutional tests. 30 credit hours maximum toward associate degree. **Support services:** GED test center, learning center, remedial instruction, study skills assistance, tutoring, writing center.

Majors. **Biology:** General. **Business:** Accounting technology, administrative services, business admin, casino management, hospitality admin, marketing, restaurant/food services. **Communications:** General. **Computer sciences:** Computer science, information technology, programming, system admin, web page design. **Conservation:** Environmental science. **Education:** Early childhood, elementary, secondary. **Engineering:** Pre-engineering. **English:** English lit. **Foreign languages:** General. **Health services:** Dental assistant, EMT paramedic, MRI technology, nursing (RN), office assistant,

---

prechiropractic, predental, premedicine, preoptometry, prepharmacy, prephysical therapy, preveterinary, radiologic technology/medical imaging, sonography. **History:** General. **Liberal arts:** Arts/sciences, humanities. **Math:** General. **Parks/recreation:** Health/fitness. **Philosophy/religion:** Philosophy. **Physical sciences:** General, chemistry, geology, physics. **Protective services:** Corrections, police science. **Psychology:** General. **Social sciences:** Geography, political science, sociology. **Visual/performing arts:** Art, dramatic, graphic design, music.

Most popular majors. Business/marketing 20%, engineering/engineering technologies 10%, health sciences 24%, interdisciplinary studies 9%, liberal arts 22%.

Technology on campus. 200 workstations in dormitories, library, student center. Dormitories wired for high-speed internet access and linked to campus network. Commuter students can connect to campus network. Online course registration, online library, helpline, wireless network available.

Student life. **Freshman orientation:** Available. Preregistration for classes offered. Offered fall, spring and summer. **Policies:** Each club must do at least one community service project per academic year to maintain charter status. **Housing:** Coed dorms available. $250 nonrefundable deposit. **Activities:** Bands, choral groups, drama, music ensembles, student government, creationist club, Young Americans for Liberty, Political Fact club, LMC Circle K.

Athletics. NJCAA. **Intercollegiate:** Baseball M, basketball, soccer, softball W, volleyball W. **Team name:** Red Hawks.

Student services. Adult student services, career counseling, services for economically disadvantaged, student employment services, financial aid counseling, on-campus daycare, placement for graduates, veterans' counselor. **Physically disabled:** Services for visually, hearing impaired. **Transfer:** Transfer center, college fairs on campus for students transferring to 4-year colleges.

Contact. E-mail: admissions@lakemichigancollege.edu
Phone: (269) 927-8626 Toll-free number: (800) 252-1562
Fax: (269) 927-6718
Larissa Hunt, Director, Enrollment Management, Lake Michigan College, 2755 East Napier Avenue, Benton Harbor, MI 49022-1899

Lansing Community College
Lansing, Michigan
www.lcc.edu CB member
 CB code: 1414

▸ Public 2-year community college
▸ Commuter campus in small city

General. Founded in 1957. Regionally accredited. **Enrollment:** 12,528 degree-seeking undergraduates; 2,344 non-degree-seeking students. **Degrees:** 1,778 associate awarded. **ROTC:** Army, Air Force. **Location:** 90 miles from Detroit. **Calendar:** Semester, extensive summer session. **Full-time faculty:** 199 total; 20% minority, 54% women. **Part-time faculty:** 1,175 total; 12% minority, 57% women. **Class size:** 54% < 20, 45% 20-39, less than 1% 40-49, less than 1% 50-99, less than 1% >100. **Special facilities:** Planetarium, science concepts laboratory, computer-integrated manufacturing institute, in-depth photography institute, technical library, amphitheater, fitness center and weight room, 3D theater, Shigematsu memorial garden.

Student profile. Among degree-seeking undergraduates, 2,968 enrolled as first-time, first-year students.

Part-time:	61%	Hispanic/Latino:	7%
Out-of-state:	1%	Native American:	1%
Women:	54%	Multi-racial, non-Hispanic:	3%
African American:	11%	International:	1%
Asian American:	3%	25 or older:	35%

Transfer out. **Colleges most students transferred to 2015:** Michigan State University, Central Michigan University, Ferris State University, Siena Heights University, University of Michigan-Flint.

Basis for selection. Open admission, but selective for some programs. Special requirements for dental hygienist, diagnostic medical sonography, nursing, paramedic, radiologic technology, surgical technology, music, police and fire academy programs. Interview required of health program applicants and international applicants. Audition recommended for music, dance, theater majors. Portfolio recommended for art majors.

2015-2016 Annual costs. Tuition/fees: $3,020; $5,660 out-of-district; $8,300 out-of-state. Per-credit charge: $88 in-district; $176 out-of-district; $264 out-of-state. Books/supplies: $1,160. Personal expenses: $2,000.

2014-2015 Financial aid. Need-based: Need-based aid available for part-time students. Work-study available nights, weekends and for part-time students. **Non-need-based:** Scholarships awarded for academics, athletics.

Application procedures. Admission: Closing date 8/10 (receipt date). No application fee. Admission notification on a rolling basis. SAT/ACT recommended for assessment waivers and counseling. **Financial aid:** Closing date 7/19. FAFSA required. Applicants notified on a rolling basis starting 2/11.

Academics. Several 4-year degree course studies available, students complete 3 years in residence and 4th year at a 4-year degree institution. **Special study options:** Accelerated study, cooperative education, cross-registration, distance learning, double major, dual enrollment of high school students, ESL, exchange student, honors, independent study, internships, study abroad, teacher certification program, weekend college. University Center (partnership between Lansing Community College and six four-year universities). Bachelor's degree programs available on campus. License preparation in aviation, dental hygiene, nursing, paramedic, radiology, real estate. **Credit/placement by examination:** AP, CLEP, IB, institutional tests. 40 credit hours maximum toward associate degree. **Support services:** GED preparation, learning center, pre-admission summer program, reduced course load, remedial instruction, study skills assistance, tutoring, writing center.

Majors. Architecture: Technology. **Area/ethnic studies:** African-American, American. **Biology:** General, biotechnology. **Business:** General, accounting technology, banking/financial services, business admin, construction management, customer service support, e-commerce, fashion, hotel/motel admin, human resources, international, management information systems, real estate, sales/distribution, selling. **Communications:** Broadcast journalism, communications/speech/rhetoric. **Communications technology:** Animation/special effects. **Computer sciences:** General, applications programming, networking. **Education:** Teacher assistance. **Engineering:** Applied physics. **English:** Creative writing, English lit. **Foreign languages:** French, Germanic, Japanese, sign language interpretation, Spanish. **General:** Carpentry, electrician, power transmission. **Health services:** Dental hygiene, EMT paramedic, histologic assistant, licensed practical nurse, MRI technology, nursing (RN), premedicine, radiologic technology/medical imaging, sonography, surgical technology, veterinary technology/assistant. **History:** General. **Human services:** Community org/advocacy. **Liberal arts:** Arts/sciences, humanities. **Math:** General. **Parks/recreation:** Health/fitness, physical fitness technician. **Philosophy/religion:** Philosophy, religion. **Physical sciences:** Chemistry. **Protective services:** Corrections, firefighting, juvenile corrections, police science. **Psychology:** General. **Social sciences:** General, anthropology, economics, geography, international relations, political science, sociology. **Visual/performing arts:** Art, art history/conservation, cinematography, dramatic, graphic design, music, music performance, photography. **Work/family studies:** Child care service.

Most popular majors. Business/marketing 11%, health sciences 15%, liberal arts 44%.

Technology on campus. 2,500 workstations in library, computer center, student center. Commuter students can connect to campus network. Online course registration, online library, helpline, wireless network available.

Student life. Freshman orientation: Mandatory. Preregistration for classes offered. Four-hour sessions offered select days during registration; online orientation also available during these times. **Activities:** Bands, choral groups, dance, drama, international student organizations, music ensembles, musical theater, TV station, Student Veterans Association, Native American Student Alliance, Gay-Straight Alliance, international club, Latinos Unidos, Campus Disciples, Rise Up.

Athletics. NJCAA. **Intercollegiate:** Baseball M, basketball, cross-country, softball W, track and field, volleyball W. **Team name:** Stars.

Student services. Adult student services, career counseling, services for economically disadvantaged, student employment services, financial aid counseling, minority student services, on-campus daycare, personal counseling, placement for graduates, veterans' counselor, women's services. **Physically disabled:** Services for visually, speech, hearing impaired. **Transfer:** Transfer adviser, college fairs on campus for students transferring to 4-year colleges.

Contact. E-mail: Admissions@lcc.edu
Phone: (517) 483-1200 Toll-free number: (800) 644-4522 ext. 2
Fax: (517) 483-1170
Tammy Grossbauer, Director of Admissions, Lansing Community College, 1121 Enrollment Services, Lansing, MI 48901-7210

Macomb Community College
Warren, Michigan
www.macomb.edu   **CB code: 1722**

- Public 2-year community college
- Commuter campus in small city

General. Founded in 1954. Regionally accredited. **Enrollment:** 15,955 degree-seeking undergraduates; 6,227 non-degree-seeking students. **Degrees:** 2,632 associate awarded. **Location:** 20 miles from Detroit. **Calendar:** Semester, extensive summer session. **Full-time faculty:** 202 total. **Part-time faculty:** 797 total. **Special facilities:** Nature preserves, center for performing arts.

Student profile. Among degree-seeking undergraduates, 3,435 enrolled as first-time, first-year students.

Part-time:	68%	Native American:	1%
Women:	52%	Multi-racial, non-Hispanic:	2%
African American:	12%	International:	2%
Asian American:	4%	25 or older:	39%
Hispanic/Latino:	3%		

Transfer out. Colleges most students transferred to 2015: Central Michigan University, Oakland University, Walsh College, Wayne State University, Michigan State University.

Basis for selection. Open admission, but selective for some programs. Special requirements for nursing, physical therapy assistant, occupational therapy assistant, respiratory therapy assistant, veterinarian technician programs; combination of GPA and test scores considered.

2015-2016 Annual costs. Tuition/fees: $3,070; $5,050 out-of-district; $6,430 out-of-state. Per-credit charge: $94 in-district; $160 out-of-district; $206 out-of-state. Books/supplies: $1,556.

Financial aid. Need-based: Need-based aid available for part-time students. Work-study available nights, weekends and for part-time students. **Non-need-based:** Scholarships awarded for academics, athletics, leadership, music/drama, state residency.

Application procedures. Admission: No deadline. No application fee. Admission notification on a rolling basis. January 31 closing date for nursing and physical therapy assistant programs. **Financial aid:** Priority date 4/15; no closing date. FAFSA, institutional form required. Applicants notified on a rolling basis starting 5/15; must reply within 2 week(s) of notification.

Academics. Courses toward bachelor's degrees offered on campus by University of Detroit, Walsh College of Accountancy and Business Administration, Wayne State University, Central Michigan University, Oakland University, University of Detroit Mercy, Davenport University, Rochester College. On-line degree program with Franklin University. **Special study options:** Cooperative education, cross-registration, distance learning, dual enrollment of high school students, ESL, independent study, internships, liberal arts/career combination, study abroad, weekend college. **Credit/placement by examination:** AP, CLEP, institutional tests. 47 credit hours maximum toward associate degree. **Support services:** Learning center, reduced course load, remedial instruction, tutoring.

Majors. Biology: General. **Business:** General, accounting, administrative services, business admin, marketing, office technology, operations. **Communications:** Broadcast journalism, communications/speech/rhetoric, public relations. **Communications technology:** Graphic/printing. **Computer sciences:** General, data entry, networking, programming, web page design. **Health services:** EMT paramedic, medical assistant, medical secretary, nursing (RN), occupational therapy assistant, physical therapy assistant, respiratory therapy technology, surgical technology, veterinary technology/assistant. **Liberal arts:** Arts/sciences. **Math:** General. **Physical sciences:** Chemistry. **Protective services:** Fire safety technology, firefighting, forensics, police science. **Visual/performing arts:** Commercial/advertising art, music. **Work/family studies:** Child care management.

Most popular majors. Business/marketing 12%, engineering/engineering technologies 6%, health sciences 13%, liberal arts 51%.

Technology on campus. 1,800 workstations in library, computer center. Commuter students can connect to campus network.

Student life. Freshman orientation: Available. Preregistration for classes offered. Held beginning of semester. **Activities:** Bands, choral groups, dance, drama, music ensembles, musical theater, symphony orchestra, student activities board, College Republicans, service learning and volunteerism, Newman Club, Campus Crusade for Christ, Young Democrats, African American alliance, Phi Theta Kappa.

Athletics. NJCAA. **Intercollegiate:** Baseball M, basketball, cross-country, soccer M, softball W, volleyball W.

Student services. Chaplain/spiritual director, career counseling, student employment services, financial aid counseling, health services, personal counseling, placement for graduates. **Physically disabled:** Services for visually, speech, hearing impaired. **Transfer:** Transfer advisor, college fairs on campus for students transferring to 4-year colleges.

Contact. E-mail: answer@macomb.edu
Phone: (586) 445-7999 Toll-free number: (866) 622-6621
Fax: (586) 445-7157
Carrie Jeffers, Director of Enrollment Services, Macomb Community College, 14500 East Twelve Mile Road, Warren, MI 48088-3896

Mid Michigan Community College
Harrison, Michigan
www.midmich.edu
CB code: 1523

▶ Public 2-year community college
▶ Commuter campus in small town

General. Founded in 1965. Regionally accredited. Mt. Pleasant Campus offers full student services and academic programs. **Enrollment:** 2,942 degree-seeking undergraduates. **Degrees:** 481 associate awarded. **Location:** 30 miles from Mount Pleasant, 100 miles from Lansing. **Calendar:** Semester, limited summer session. **Full-time faculty:** 43 total. **Part-time faculty:** 162 total.

Transfer out. Colleges most students transferred to 2015: Central Michigan University, Ferris State University, Saginaw Valley State University.

Basis for selection. Open admission, but selective for some programs. Admission for health occupation majors based on prerequisite course completion and grades. High school diploma or GED recommended. Interview required of health program applicants. **Learning Disabled:** Students referred to counselor to address special needs.

High school preparation. Recommended units include English 4, mathematics 4, social studies 2, history 1, science 3 (laboratory 2) and foreign language 1. One unit chemistry, 1 algebra, 1 biology required for health occupations majors.

2015-2016 Annual costs. Tuition/fees: $3,580; $6,400 out-of-district; $6,400 out-of-state. Per-credit charge: $104 in-district; $188 out-of-district; $188 out-of-state. Books/supplies: $1,248. Personal expenses: $1,850.

Financial aid. Need-based: Need-based aid available for part-time students. Work-study available nights, weekends and for part-time students. **Non-need-based:** Scholarships awarded for academics, art.

Application procedures. Admission: No deadline. No application fee. Admission notification on a rolling basis. **Financial aid:** Priority date 5/1; no closing date. FAFSA, institutional form required. Applicants notified on a rolling basis starting 4/1; must reply within 2 week(s) of notification.

Academics. Special study options: Distance learning, double major, dual enrollment of high school students, independent study, internships, liberal arts/career combination. License preparation in nursing, physical therapy, radiology. **Credit/placement by examination:** AP, CLEP, institutional tests. 15 credit hours maximum toward associate degree. **Support services:** Learning center, reduced course load, remedial instruction, study skills assistance, tutoring, writing center.

Majors. Biology: General. **Business:** Accounting technology, administrative services, business admin, entrepreneurial studies, hospitality admin, marketing. **Computer sciences:** Applications programming, computer science, networking, programming. **Education:** Early childhood, elementary, secondary. **Health services:** Health information technology, medical assistant, medical radiologic technology/radiation therapy, medical secretary, medical transcription, nursing (RN), physical therapy assistant. **Liberal arts:** Arts/sciences. **Math:** General. **Physical sciences:** Chemistry. **Protective services:** Corrections, firefighting, police science. **Psychology:** General. **Social sciences:** Sociology. **Visual/performing arts:** General, dramatic, graphic design.

Technology on campus. 450 workstations in library, computer center. Commuter students can connect to campus network. Online library, helpline, wireless network available.

Student life. Freshman orientation: Available. Preregistration for classes offered. Scheduled before each semester. **Housing:** Community-wide housing bulletin available on request. **Activities:** Drama, student government, Phi Theta Kappa.

Athletics. NJCAA. **Intercollegiate:** Basketball, soccer. **Team name:** Lakers.

Student services. Adult student services, career counseling, services for economically disadvantaged, student employment services, financial aid counseling, personal counseling, veterans' counselor. **Physically disabled:** Services for visually, speech, hearing impaired. **Transfer:** Pre-admission transcript evaluation for new students. Transfer adviser, college fairs on campus for students transferring to 4-year colleges.

Contact. E-mail: admissions@midmich.edu
Phone: (989) 386-6661 Fax: (989) 386-6613
Jessica Gordon, Director of Marketing and Admissions, Mid Michigan Community College, 1375 South Clare Avenue, Harrison, MI 48625-9442

Monroe County Community College
Monroe, Michigan
www.monroeccc.edu
CB code: 1514

▶ Public 2-year community college
▶ Commuter campus in large town
▶ Interview required

General. Founded in 1964. Regionally accredited. Off-campus site at Whitman Center. **Enrollment:** 1,500 full-time, degree-seeking students. **Degrees:** 442 associate awarded. **Location:** 45 miles from Detroit, 20 miles from Toledo, Ohio. **Calendar:** Semester, limited summer session. **Full-time faculty:** 62 total. **Part-time faculty:** 125 total.

Student profile. Among full-time, degree-seeking students, 54% enrolled in a transfer program, 46% enrolled in a vocational program.

Out-of-state:	4%	**25 or older:**	42%

Transfer out. Colleges most students transferred to 2015: Eastern Michigan University, University of Toledo, Siena Heights University, Western Michigan University, University of Michigan.

Basis for selection. Open admission, but selective for some programs. Special requirements for nursing, respiratory therapy, medical assistance and culinary skills program. Baseline test scores required for most courses. Interview required for culinary program applicants.

High school preparation. Recommended units include English 4, mathematics 4, social studies 3, history 1 and science 3. Nursing and respiratory therapy applicants must have 1 unit chemistry and 1 biology. Strong science background highly recommended.

2015-2016 Annual costs. Tuition/fees: $3,730; $5,980 out-of-district; $6,580 out-of-state. Per-credit charge: $122 in-district; $197 out-of-district; $217 out-of-state. Books/supplies: $1,300. Personal expenses: $560.

Financial aid. Need-based: Need-based aid available for part-time students. Work-study available nights, weekends and for part-time students. **Non-need-based:** Scholarships awarded for academics, alumni affiliation, art, leadership, music/drama, state residency.

Application procedures. Admission: Priority date 5/1; no deadline. No application fee. Admission notification on a rolling basis. Closing date for nursing and respiratory therapy applications: first Monday in June. **Financial aid:** Priority date 4/1; no closing date. FAFSA, institutional form required. Applicants notified on a rolling basis starting 4/1; must reply within 2 week(s) of notification.

Academics. Special study options: Accelerated study, cooperative education, dual enrollment of high school students, independent study. Bachelor's degree programs available on campus. License preparation in nursing, paramedic, real estate. **Credit/placement by examination:** AP, CLEP, institutional tests. 30 credit hours maximum toward associate degree. **Support services:** Learning center, reduced course load, remedial instruction, tutoring, writing center.

Majors. Business: Accounting, administrative services, banking/financial services, business admin, office technology, office/clerical. **Computer sciences:** General, applications programming, programming. **Education:** Early childhood. **Engineering:** Electrical. **Health services:** Medical secretary, nursing (RN), respiratory therapy technology. **Liberal arts:** Arts/sciences. **Visual/performing arts:** Studio arts. **Work/family studies:** Child care management.

Technology on campus. 150 workstations in library, computer center, student center. Helpline, wireless network available.

Student life. Freshman orientation: Available. Preregistration for classes offered. **Activities:** Concert band, choral groups, drama, international student organizations, radio station, student government, student newspaper, symphony orchestra, respiratory therapy club, nursing club, Society of Automotive Engineers, campus Bible study.

Athletics. Team name: Huskies.

Student services. Career counseling, student employment services, on-campus daycare, personal counseling, placement for graduates. **Physically disabled:** Services for visually, speech, hearing impaired. **Transfer:** Transfer adviser, college fairs on campus for students transferring to 4-year colleges.

Contact. E-mail: mhall@monroeccc.edu
Phone: (734) 384-4104 Toll-free number: (877) 937-6222
Fax: (734) 384-4170
Mark Hall, Director of Admissions and Guidance Services, Monroe County Community College, 1555 South Raisinville Road, Monroe, MI 48161-9746

Montcalm Community College
Sidney, Michigan
www.montcalm.edu
CB code: 1522

- Public 2-year community and liberal arts college
- Commuter campus in rural community

General. Founded in 1965. Regionally accredited. Off-campus centers in Ionia, Howard City, and Greenville. **Enrollment:** 1,496 degree-seeking undergraduates. **Degrees:** 228 associate awarded. **Location:** 50 miles from Grand Rapids, 65 miles from Lansing. **Calendar:** Semester, limited summer session. **Full-time faculty:** 29 total; 10% have terminal degrees, 55% women. **Part-time faculty:** 89 total; 2% have terminal degrees, 4% minority, 65% women. **Class size:** 67% < 20, 33% 20-39. **Special facilities:** Marked nature preserves and trails, barn theatre.

Transfer out. Colleges most students transferred to 2015: Central Michigan University, Ferris State University, Grand Valley State University, Davenport University.

Basis for selection. Open admission, but selective for some programs. Applicants to nursing program must score at least 44 on COMPASS pre-algebra and 82 on COMPASS reading.

2015-2016 Annual costs. Tuition/fees: $3,540; $6,150 out-of-district; $8,880 out-of-state. Per-credit charge: $100 in-district; $187 out-of-district; $278 out-of-state. Books/supplies: $996. Personal expenses: $1,416.

Financial aid. Need-based: Need-based aid available for part-time students. Work-study available nights, weekends and for part-time students. **Non-need-based:** Scholarships awarded for academics, state residency.

Application procedures. Admission: No deadline. No application fee. Admission notification on a rolling basis. **Financial aid:** Priority date 2/15; no closing date. FAFSA, institutional form required. Applicants notified on a rolling basis starting 4/15; must reply within 2 week(s) of notification.

Academics. Special study options: Distance learning, double major, dual enrollment of high school students, internships. License preparation in nursing, paramedic. **Credit/placement by examination:** AP, CLEP, institutional tests. **Support services:** GED test center, learning center, reduced course load, remedial instruction, study skills assistance, tutoring.

Majors. Business: Accounting, administrative services, business admin, construction management, entrepreneurial studies, executive assistant, information resources management, management information systems, office technology. **Computer sciences:** General, data processing. **Education:** Teacher assistance. **Health services:** Medical secretary, nursing (RN). **Liberal arts:** Arts/sciences. **Protective services:** Criminal justice. **Visual/performing arts:** Music. **Work/family studies:** Child care management.

Most popular majors. Business/marketing 17%, education 6%, health sciences 22%, liberal arts 46%.

Technology on campus. 450 workstations in library, computer center. Online course registration, helpline, wireless network available.

Student life. Freshman orientation: Available. Preregistration for classes offered. **Activities:** Choral groups, Phi Theta Kappa, future business professionals club, Native American club, nursing club, judo club.

Athletics. Intramural: Volleyball.

Student services. Career counseling, financial aid counseling. **Physically disabled:** Services for visually, speech, hearing impaired. **Transfer:** Pre-admission transcript evaluation for new students. Transfer adviser, college fairs on campus for students transferring to 4-year colleges.

Contact. E-mail: admissions@montcalm.edu
Phone: (989) 328-1277 Toll-free number: (877) 328-2111
Fax: (989) 328-1203
Debra Alexander, Associate Dean of Student Services, Montcalm Community College, 2800 College Drive, Sidney, MI 48885

Mott Community College
Flint, Michigan
www.mcc.edu
CB member
CB code: 1225

- Public 2-year community college
- Commuter campus in small city

General. Founded in 1923. Regionally accredited. Satellite locations in Fenton, Lapeer, Howell and Clio. **Enrollment:** 7,556 degree-seeking undergraduates; 1,061 non-degree-seeking students. **Degrees:** 2,040 associate awarded. **Location:** 66 miles from Detroit. **Calendar:** Semester, extensive summer session. **Full-time faculty:** 142 total; 25% have terminal degrees, 17% minority, 57% women. **Part-time faculty:** 312 total; 5% have terminal degrees, 16% minority, 59% women. **Special facilities:** Geology museum, regional technology center, dental hygiene clinic, visual arts and design center, salon, automotive service lab, institute for medical simulation (satellite campus at Southern Lakes Branch Center).

Student profile. Among degree-seeking undergraduates, 32% enrolled in a transfer program, 68% enrolled in a vocational program, 1,549 enrolled as first-time, first-year students.

Part-time:	71%	Hispanic/Latino:	4%
Women:	59%	Native American:	1%
African American:	19%	Multi-racial, non-Hispanic:	4%
Asian American:	1%	25 or older:	42%

Transfer out. Colleges most students transferred to 2015: University of Michigan-Flint, Central Michigan University, Grand Valley State University, University of Phoenix, Northwood University.

Basis for selection. Open admission, but selective for some programs. Special requirements for nursing and allied health programs. Audition recommended for music majors. **Learning Disabled:** Students must request assistance, provide documentation of disabilities, and register with Disability Services before classes begin.

2016-2017 Annual costs. Tuition/fees (projected): $4,666; $6,260 out-of-district; $8,598 out-of-state. Per-credit charge: $130 in-district; $183 out-of-district; $261 out-of-state. Books/supplies: $998. Personal expenses: $1,818.

2014-2015 Financial aid. Need-based: Need-based aid available for part-time students. Work-study available nights, weekends and for part-time students. **Non-need-based:** Scholarships awarded for academics, alumni affiliation, art, athletics, leadership, minority status, music/drama, state residency.

Application procedures. Admission: No deadline. No application fee. Admission notification on a rolling basis. **Financial aid:** Priority date 6/1; no closing date. FAFSA required. Applicants notified on a rolling basis starting 5/1.

Academics. Special study options: Cooperative education, distance learning, double major, dual enrollment of high school students, honors, independent study, internships, liberal arts/career combination. Bachelor's degree programs available on campus. License preparation in dental hygiene, nursing, occupational therapy, physical therapy. **Credit/placement by examination:** AP, CLEP, institutional tests. 16 credit hours maximum toward associate degree. **Support services:** GED preparation, learning center, remedial instruction, study skills assistance, tutoring, writing center.

Majors. Biology: General. **Business:** General, accounting technology, business admin, entrepreneurial studies, marketing. **Communications technology:** General. **Computer sciences:** Applications programming, networking, programming, web page design. **Education:** Early childhood. **Foreign languages:** Sign language interpretation. **Health services:** Community health services, dental assistant, dental hygiene, EMT paramedic, histologic assistant, medical radiologic technology/radiation therapy, nursing (RN), occupational therapy assistant, physical therapy assistant, respiratory therapy technology. **Liberal arts:** Arts/sciences. **Protective services:** Corrections, fire safety technology, police science. **Visual/performing arts:** General, cinematography, graphic design, music technology, photography. **Work/family studies:** Child care service, institutional food production.

Most popular majors. Biological/life sciences 8%, health sciences 13%, liberal arts 62%.

Technology on campus. 1,400 workstations in library, computer center, student center. Commuter students can connect to campus network. Online course registration, online library, helpline, student web hosting, wireless network available.

Student life. Freshman orientation: Mandatory. Preregistration for classes offered. Sessions last approximately 3 hours. **Activities:** Bands, choral groups, dance, music ensembles, student government, Ballroomers/Steppers, dental hygiene club, Respiratory Care Student Society, social work club, Student Nurses Association, Otaku, Cutting Edge Campus Ministry, First Generation.

Athletics. NJCAA. **Intercollegiate:** Baseball M, basketball, cross-country, golf M, softball W, volleyball W. **Team name:** Bears.

Student services. Career counseling, services for economically disadvantaged, student employment services, financial aid counseling, health services, personal counseling, placement for graduates, veterans' counselor. **Physically disabled:** Services for visually, speech, hearing impaired. **Transfer:** Pre-admission transcript evaluation for new students. Transfer adviser, college fairs on campus for students transferring to 4-year colleges.

Contact. Phone: (810) 762-0315 Toll-free number: (800) 852-8614 Fax: (810) 232-9442
Jennifer McDonald, Executive Director, Admissions & Recruitment, Mott Community College, 1401 East Court Street, Flint, MI 48503-2089

Muskegon Community College
Muskegon, Michigan
www.muskegoncc.edu   CB code: 1495

- Public 2-year community college
- Commuter campus in small city

General. Founded in 1926. Regionally accredited. Bachelor's and graduate programs offered on-campus with participating 4-year institutions. **Enrollment:** 3,587 degree-seeking undergraduates; 919 non-degree-seeking students. **Degrees:** 484 associate awarded. **Location:** 41 miles from Grand Rapids. **Calendar:** Semester, limited summer session. **Full-time faculty:** 100 total. **Part-time faculty:** 218 total. **Special facilities:** Planetarium, nature preserve, herbal garden, observatory.

Student profile. Among degree-seeking undergraduates, 802 enrolled as first-time, first-year students, 303 transferred in from other institutions.

Part-time: 62% **Women:**   55%

Transfer out. Colleges most students transferred to 2015: Grand Valley State University, Central Michigan University, Ferris State University, Western Michigan University.

Basis for selection. Open admission, but selective for some programs. Reading proficiency required for select programs and courses. High school diploma, GED or completion of 15 credits with at least a C average required for degree-seeking candidates. Additional prerequisites required for nursing applicants. **Adult students:** SAT/ACT scores not required. **Home schooled:** Transcript of courses and grades required.

High school preparation. College-preparatory program recommended.

2015-2016 Annual costs. Tuition/fees: $3,790; $6,340 out-of-district; $8,500 out-of-state. Per-credit charge: $99 in-district; $184 out-of-district; $256 out-of-state. Books/supplies: $1,100. Personal expenses: $644.

2014-2015 Financial aid. Need-based: 76% of total undergraduate aid awarded as scholarships/grants, 24% as loans/jobs. Need-based aid available for part-time students. Work-study available nights, weekends and for part-time students.

Application procedures. Admission: Priority date 5/12; no deadline. No application fee. Admission notification on a rolling basis. **Financial aid:** Priority date 5/1; no closing date. FAFSA required. Applicants notified on a rolling basis starting 6/1; must reply within 2 week(s) of notification.

Academics. Special study options: Combined bachelor's/graduate degree, cooperative education, cross-registration, distance learning, double major, dual enrollment of high school students, honors, independent study, internships, liberal arts/career combination. Bachelor's degree programs available on campus. License preparation in nursing, real estate. **Credit/placement by examination:** AP, CLEP, institutional tests. 30 credit hours maximum

toward associate degree. **Support services:** Learning center, remedial instruction, study skills assistance, tutoring, writing center. Supplemental instruction is offered each semester in various academic areas at pre-arranged times.

Majors. Business: Accounting, administrative services, international, marketing. **Communications technology:** Graphic/printing. **Computer sciences:** General, data processing. **Education:** Early childhood. **Health services:** Licensed practical nurse, medical secretary, nursing (RN), respiratory therapy technology. **Protective services:** Law enforcement admin. **Visual/performing arts:** Commercial/advertising art.

Technology on campus. 88 workstations in library, computer center, student center. Online course registration, helpline, wireless network available.

Student life. Freshman orientation: Mandatory. Preregistration for classes offered. Offered year-round. **Activities:** Bands, choral groups, dance, drama, international student organizations, music ensembles, musical theater, student government, student newspaper, TV station, Christian Fellowship, Black student alliance, Gay Straight Alliance, Hispanic Students, Veteran Students.

Athletics. NJCAA. **Intercollegiate:** Baseball M, basketball, cross-country, golf, soccer, softball W, volleyball W, wrestling M. **Intramural:** Baseball M, basketball, bowling, golf, softball W, table tennis. **Team name:** Jayhawks.

Student services. Adult student services, career counseling, student employment services, financial aid counseling, health services, personal counseling, veterans' counselor. **Physically disabled:** Services for visually, speech, hearing impaired. **Transfer:** Pre-admission transcript evaluation for new students. College fairs on campus for students transferring to 4-year colleges.

Contact. E-mail: johnathon.skidmore@muskegoncc.edu
Phone: (231) 777-0366 Toll-free number: (866) 711-4622
Fax: (231) 777-0443
Cindy Reuss, Dean of Admissions, Muskegon Community College, 221 South Quarterline Road, Muskegon, MI 49442

North Central Michigan College
Petoskey, Michigan
www.ncmich.edu   CB code: 1569

- Public 2-year community college
- Commuter campus in small town

General. Founded in 1958. Regionally accredited. **Enrollment:** 2,581 undergraduates. **Degrees:** 311 associate awarded. **Location:** 40 miles from Mackinaw City, 60 miles from Traverse City. **Calendar:** Semester, limited summer session. **Full-time faculty:** 29 total. **Part-time faculty:** 32 total. **Class size:** 100% 20-39. **Special facilities:** Nature preserve.

Student profile.

Out-of-state: 5% **Live on campus:**   5%
25 or older: 57%

Transfer out. Colleges most students transferred to 2015: Lake Superior State University, Grand Valley State University, Central Michigan University, Northern Michigan University, Ferris State University.

Basis for selection. Open admission, but selective for some programs. All degree-seeking students must provide ACT, SAT or COMPASS scores for mandatory placement. Special requirements for most health science/allied health programs.

High school preparation. Recommended units include English 3, mathematics 3 and science 3. Chemistry recommended for nursing applicants.

2015-2016 Annual costs. Tuition/fees: $3,708; $5,725 out-of-district; $7,195 out-of-state. Per-credit charge: $103 in-district; $170 out-of-district; $219 out-of-state. Room/board: $6,250. Books/supplies: $1,050. Personal expenses: $650.

Financial aid. Need-based: Need-based aid available for part-time students. Work-study available nights, weekends and for part-time students.

Application procedures. Admission: No deadline. No application fee. Application must be submitted online. Admission notification on a rolling basis. **Financial aid:** No deadline. FAFSA, institutional form required. Applicants notified on a rolling basis starting 4/30.

Academics. Special study options: Cooperative education, cross-registration, distance learning, dual enrollment of high school students, independent study, internships. Bachelor's degree programs available on campus. **Credit/placement by examination:** AP, CLEP, IB. 15 credit hours maximum toward associate degree. **Support services:** Learning center, remedial instruction, tutoring.

Majors. Business: General, accounting, administrative services, business admin, office/clerical. **Computer sciences:** General. **Education:** Early childhood. **Health services:** EMT paramedic, nursing (RN). **Liberal arts:** Arts/sciences.

Most popular majors. Health sciences 21%, liberal arts 71%.

Technology on campus. 133 workstations in dormitories, library, computer center, student center. Dormitories wired for high-speed internet access and linked to campus network. Commuter students can connect to campus network. Online course registration, wireless network available.

Student life. Freshman orientation: Available. Preregistration for classes offered. Held in summer before classes begin. **Housing:** Coed dorms available. $50 deposit. **Activities:** Student government, student newspaper, nursing student association, Phi Theta Kappa, Campus Crusade.

Athletics. Intramural: Basketball, volleyball.

Student services. Career counseling, services for economically disadvantaged, financial aid counseling, personal counseling, veterans' counselor, women's services. **Physically disabled:** Services for visually, speech, hearing impaired. **Transfer:** Transfer adviser, college fairs on campus for students transferring to 4-year colleges.

Contact. E-mail: advisor@ncmich.edu
Phone: (231) 348-6600 Toll-free number: (888) 298-6605
Fax: (231) 348-6672
Renee DeYoung, Director Enrollment Management, North Central Michigan College, 1515 Howard Street, Petoskey, MI 49770

Northwestern Michigan College
Traverse City, Michigan
www.nmc.edu   CB code: 1564

‣ Public 2-year community and maritime college
‣ Commuter campus in large town

General. Founded in 1951. Regionally accredited. **Enrollment:** 3,938 degree-seeking undergraduates. **Degrees:** 34 bachelor's, 602 associate awarded. **Location:** 180 miles from Lansing, 265 miles from Detroit. **Calendar:** Semester, extensive summer session. **Full-time faculty:** 93 total; 38% women. **Part-time faculty:** 3 total; 67% women. **Class size:** 100% 20-39. **Special facilities:** Maritime academy, pilot training center, observatory, museum, fresh water studies institute, renewable energy facilities, automotive with hybrid repair and welding.

Student profile.

Out-of-state:	5%	Live on campus:	3%
25 or older:	64%		

Transfer out. Colleges most students transferred to 2015: Michigan State University, Grand Valley State University, Ferris State University, Central Michigan University.

Basis for selection. Open admission, but selective for some programs. Admission to maritime, nursing, dental assistant and aviation programs based on school GPA, recommendation and test scores. ACT/SAT required for maritime program. **Home schooled:** Transcript of courses and grades required. **Learning Disabled:** COMPASS testing to show ability to benefit.

2015-2016 Annual costs. Tuition/fees: $3,950; $6,783 out-of-district; $8,522 out-of-state. Per-credit charge: $96 in-district; $191 out-of-district; $249 out-of-state. Room/board: $9,850. Books/supplies: $1,500. Personal expenses: $1,000.

Financial aid. Need-based: Need-based aid available for part-time students. Work-study available nights, weekends and for part-time students. **Non-need-based:** Scholarships awarded for academics, art, job skills, leadership, minority status, music/drama, ROTC, state residency.

Application procedures. Admission: No deadline. $20 fee, may be waived for applicants with need. Admission notification on a rolling basis. **Financial aid:** Priority date 4/1; no closing date. FAFSA required. Applicants notified on a rolling basis starting 5/1; must reply within 2 week(s) of notification.

Academics. Great Lakes Maritime Academy (4-year deck officer and maritime engineer training program) for service in shipping industry on campus. 9 months spent aboard commercial vessels. Bachelor's degree awarded to maritime academy graduates in conjunction with Ferris State University.

Special study options: Cooperative education, cross-registration, distance learning, dual enrollment of high school students, ESL, honors, independent study, internships, liberal arts/career combination, study abroad. Bachelor's degree programs available on campus. License preparation in aviation, nursing. **Credit/placement by examination:** AP, CLEP, institutional tests. 32 credit hours maximum toward associate degree. **Support services:** Learning center, pre-admission summer program, reduced course load, remedial instruction, study skills assistance, tutoring, writing center.

Majors. Biology: General. **Business:** General, accounting, accounting technology, business admin, management information systems, office technology. **Communications:** Communications/speech/rhetoric. **Computer sciences:** Information systems. **Education:** General. **Engineering:** General. **English:** English lit. **General:** Carpentry, plumbing. **Health services:** Dental assistant, nursing (RN), respiratory therapy assistant. **Liberal arts:** Arts/sciences. **Math:** General. **Physical sciences:** General. **Protective services:** Law enforcement admin, police science. **Social sciences:** General. **Visual/performing arts:** Art, commercial/advertising art, dramatic, music, piano/keyboard, studio arts, voice/opera.

Most popular majors. Business/marketing 6%, health sciences 14%, liberal arts 60%, personal/culinary services 6%.

Technology on campus. 675 workstations in dormitories, library, computer center, student center. Dormitories wired for high-speed internet access and linked to campus network. Commuter students can connect to campus network. Online course registration, online library, helpline, wireless network available.

Student life. Freshman orientation: Mandatory. Preregistration for classes offered. Multiple one-day sessions prior to start of semester. **Housing:** Coed dorms, single-sex dorms, special housing for disabled, apartments available. $250 fully refundable deposit. **Activities:** Bands, campus ministries, choral groups, dance, drama, international student organizations, literary magazine, music ensembles, musical theater, radio station, student government, student newspaper, symphony orchestra, residence hall council, propeller club, Phi Theta Kappa, engineering club, botany club, diverse student body group, Native American student group.

Athletics. Team name: Hawk Owls.

Student services. Adult student services, career counseling, student employment services, health services, minority student services, personal counseling, placement for graduates, veterans' counselor. **Physically disabled:** Services for visually, speech, hearing impaired. **Transfer:** Re-entry adviser, pre-admission transcript evaluation for new students. Transfer adviser, college fairs on campus for students transferring to 4-year colleges.

Contact. E-mail: cgarvin@nmc.edu
Phone: (231) 995-1054 Toll-free number: (800) 748-0566
Fax: (231) 995-1339
Cathryn Claerhout, Director of Admissions, Northwestern Michigan College, 1701 East Front Street, Traverse City, MI 49686

Oakland Community College
Bloomfield Hills, Michigan
www.oaklandcc.edu   CB code: 1607

‣ Public 2-year community college
‣ Commuter campus in very large city

General. Founded in 1964. Regionally accredited. Multicampus institution with locations in Auburn Hills, Farmington Hills, Southfield, Royal Oak, and Waterford. CREST (Combined Regional Emergency Services Training Center) located in Auburn Hills. **Enrollment:** 12,202 degree-seeking undergraduates. **Degrees:** 2,505 associate awarded. **Location:** 30 miles from Detroit. **Calendar:** Semester, limited summer session. **Full-time faculty:** 243 total; 14% minority, 52% women. **Part-time faculty:** 1,215 total; 17% minority, 56% women. **Class size:** 21% < 20, 79% 20-39.

Student profile.

Out-of-state:	1%	25 or older:	47%

Transfer out. Colleges most students transferred to 2015: Oakland University, Wayne State University, Central Michigan University, Macomb Community College, Michigan State University.

Basis for selection. Open admission. Interview recommended. **Home schooled:** English and math placement testing mandatory.

2015-2016 Annual costs. Tuition/fees: $2,710; $5,200 out-of-district; $7,270 out-of-state. Per-credit charge: $88 in-district; $171 out-of-district; $240 out-of-state. Books/supplies: $2,700. Personal expenses: $600.

Financial aid. Need-based: Need based aid available for part-time students. Work-study available nights, weekends and for part-time students. **Non-need-based:** Scholarships awarded for academics, athletics, job skills.

Application procedures. Admission: No deadline. No application fee. Admission notification on a rolling basis. **Financial aid:** Priority date 4/15; no closing date. FAFSA required. Applicants notified on a rolling basis starting 4/15.

Academics. Special study options: Cooperative education, distance learning, dual enrollment of high school students, ESL, internships, study abroad. Saturday classes offered. License preparation in dental hygiene, nursing, occupational therapy, paramedic, physical therapy, radiology. **Credit/placement by examination:** AP, CLEP, institutional tests. Last 15 credit hours toward degree program must be satisfied with institution's coursework, not credit by exam. **Support services:** Learning center, reduced course load, remedial instruction, study skills assistance, tutoring, writing center.

Majors. Biology: Biotechnology. **Business:** Accounting technology, accounting/business management, business admin, construction management, entrepreneurial studies, fashion, hotel/motel admin, international, management information systems, office management, office technology, restaurant/food services, retail management. **Communications technology:** Photo/film/video, radio/TV. **Computer sciences:** Data processing, programming, security, systems analysis. **Engineering:** General. **Foreign languages:** Sign language interpretation. **General:** Carpentry, electrician, pipefitting. **Health services:** Community health services, dental hygiene, electroencephalograph technology, EMT paramedic, health care admin, histologic assistant, histologic technology, massage therapy, medical assistant, medical radiologic technology/radiation therapy, medical transcription, nuclear medical technology, nursing (RN), occupational therapy assistant, pharmacy assistant, physical therapy assistant, respiratory therapy technology, sonography, surgical technology, veterinary technology/assistant. **Liberal arts:** Arts/sciences, library assistant. **Parks/recreation:** Exercise sciences. **Protective services:** Corrections, criminalistics, firefighting, law enforcement admin, police science. **Visual/performing arts:** Art, ceramics, commercial/advertising art, film/cinema/video, graphic design, illustration, interior design, music performance, music theory/composition, photography, voice/opera. **Work/family studies:** Aging, child care management, child care service.

Most popular majors. Business/marketing 11%, health sciences 13%, liberal arts 56%.

Technology on campus. 2,501 workstations in library, computer center, student center. Commuter students can connect to campus network. Online course registration, online library, helpline, wireless network available.

Student life. Freshman orientation: Available. Preregistration for classes offered. Held in the first two weeks of class. **Activities:** Bands, choral groups, dance, drama, film society, international student organizations, literary magazine, music ensembles, student government, symphony orchestra, PTK, film society, Writers Block, student mentor program, dance team, Rhythm of the Cultures, anime club, Gamers Guild, psychology club.

Athletics. NJCAA. **Intercollegiate:** Basketball, cross-country, golf M, softball W, tennis W, volleyball W. **Intramural:** Cross-country, racquetball. **Team name:** Raiders.

Student services. Career counseling, services for economically disadvantaged, student employment services, financial aid counseling, on-campus daycare, personal counseling, placement for graduates, veterans' counselor, women's services. **Physically disabled:** Services for visually, speech, hearing impaired. **Transfer:** Pre-admission transcript evaluation for new students. Transfer center, transfer adviser, college fairs on campus for students transferring to 4-year colleges.

Contact. Phone: (248) 341-2200 Fax: (248) 341-2099
Stephen Linden, College Registrar, Oakland Community College, 2480 Opdyke Road, Bloomfield Hills, MI 48304-2266

Saginaw Chippewa Tribal College
Mount Pleasant, Michigan
www.sagchip.edu

- Public 2-year community college
- Commuter campus in large town

General. Enrollment: 128 degree-seeking undergraduates. **Degrees:** 11 associate awarded. **Calendar:** Semester, limited summer session. **Full-time faculty:** 7 total; 29% have terminal degrees, 29% minority, 57% women. **Part-time faculty:** 12 total; 17% minority, 67% women.

Transfer out. Colleges most students transferred to 2015: Mid Michigan Community College, Central Michigan University.

Basis for selection. Open admission.

2015-2016 Annual costs. Tuition/fees: $2,550. Per-credit charge: $60. Books/supplies: $1,200.

Financial aid. Need-based: Work-study available nights, weekends and for part-time students.

Application procedures. Admission: No deadline. $25 fee. Application must be submitted on paper. Admission notification on a rolling basis. **Financial aid:** No deadline.

Academics. Special study options: Dual enrollment of high school students. **Credit/placement by examination:** AP, CLEP, institutional tests. **Support services:** GED preparation, learning center, remedial instruction, tutoring.

Majors. Area/ethnic studies: Native American. **Business:** Business admin.

Technology on campus. Commuter students can connect to campus network. Wireless network available.

Student life. Freshman orientation: Available. Preregistration for classes offered. **Activities:** Student government.

Student services. Adult student services, financial aid counseling, minority student services. **Transfer:** Transfer adviser, college fairs on campus for students transferring to 4-year colleges.

Contact. E-mail: flaugher.amanda@sagchip.edu
Phone: (989) 775-4123 Fax: (989) 775-4528
Amanda Flaugher, Admissions Officer/Registrar, Saginaw Chippewa Tribal College, 2274 Enterprise Drive, Mount Pleasant, MI 48858

Schoolcraft College
Livonia, Michigan
www.schoolcraft.edu

CB member
CB code: 1764

- Public 2-year culinary school and community college
- Commuter campus in small city

General. Founded in 1961. Regionally accredited. **Enrollment:** 10,474 degree-seeking undergraduates; 1,213 non-degree-seeking students. **Degrees:** 1,405 associate awarded. **Location:** 20 miles from Ann Arbor, approximately 25 miles from Detroit. **Calendar:** Semester, limited summer session. **Full-time faculty:** 99 total. **Part-time faculty:** 439 total. **Special facilities:** Scanning electron microscope, biotech center, simulation lab for health professions, public safety training complex, fitness center, culinary restaurant, conference center.

Student profile. Among degree-seeking undergraduates, 2,174 enrolled as first-time, first-year students, 2,899 transferred in from other institutions.

Part-time:	71%	**25 or older:** 34%
Women:	54%	

Transfer out. Colleges most students transferred to 2015: Wayne State University, Eastern Michigan University, Michigan State University, Madonna University, University of Michigan-Dearborn.

Basis for selection. Open admission, but selective for some programs. Some programs require separate enrollment applications and requirements. International students advised to start application process 3 months prior to start date of semester. **Home schooled:** Interview required.

High school preparation. College-preparatory program required.

2015-2016 Annual costs. Tuition/fees: $3,564; $4,854 out-of-district; $6,834 out-of-state. Per-credit charge: $96 in-district; $139 out-of-district; $205 out-of-state.

2014-2015 Financial aid. Need-based: Need-based aid available for part-time students. Work-study available nights, weekends and for part-time students. **Non-need-based:** Scholarships awarded for academics, athletics, leadership, music/drama, state residency.

Application procedures. Admission: No deadline. No application fee. Admission notification on a rolling basis. **Financial aid:** No deadline. FAFSA required. Applicants notified on a rolling basis starting 6/1.

Academics. Special study options: Accelerated study, cooperative education, distance learning, double major, dual enrollment of high school students, ESL, external degree, honors, independent study, internships, liberal arts/career combination, teacher certification program, weekend college. Bachelor's degree programs available on campus. License preparation in nursing, paramedic. **Credit/placement by examination:** AP, CLEP, institutional tests. 30 credit hours maximum toward associate degree. **Support services:** GED preparation and test center, learning center, remedial instruction, study skills assistance, tutoring, writing center.

Honors college/program. 3.5 GPA, writing sample, personal interview and 2 letters of recommendation required.

Majors. Business: General, accounting technology, business admin, executive assistant, marketing, office technology, small business admin. **Communications technology:** Radio/TV, recording arts. **Computer sciences:** Applications programming, computer graphics, programming, web page design. **Education:** General. **Engineering:** General. **Health services:** EMT paramedic, health information technology, massage therapy, nursing (RN), prepharmacy. **Protective services:** Firefighting, police science. **Work/family studies:** Child development.

Technology on campus. 930 workstations in library, computer center, student center. Commuter students can connect to campus network. Online course registration, online library, helpline, wireless network available.

Student life. Freshman orientation: Available. Preregistration for classes offered. **Activities:** Bands, choral groups, dance, drama, film society, international student organizations, literary magazine, music ensembles, musical theater, student newspaper, symphony orchestra, international students club, student activities board, Phi Theta Kappa, Honors Society, video production club, environmental awareness group, Students of AMF, LGBTQI Alliance, Native American club, Civil Rights Action club.

Athletics. NJCAA. **Intercollegiate:** Baseball M, basketball, bowling, cross-country, golf M, soccer, softball W, volleyball W. **Team name:** Ocelots.

Student services. Adult student services, career counseling, services for economically disadvantaged, student employment services, financial aid counseling, health services, legal services, on-campus daycare, personal counseling, placement for graduates, veterans' counselor, women's services. **Physically disabled:** Services for visually, speech, hearing impaired. **Transfer:** Transfer adviser, college fairs on campus for students transferring to 4-year colleges.

Contact. E-mail: admissions@schoolcraft.edu
Phone: (734) 462-4683
Stacey Stover, Associate Dean of Admissions and Student Engagement, Schoolcraft College, 18600 Haggerty Road, Livonia, MI 48152-2696

Southwestern Michigan College
Dowagiac, Michigan
www.swmich.edu   CB code: 1783

▶ Public 2-year community college
▶ Commuter campus in small town

General. Founded in 1964. Regionally accredited. Bachelor's degree programs offered in agreement with 4-year colleges and universities including Bethel College, Ferris State University and Michigan State University. **Enrollment:** 1,951 degree-seeking undergraduates; 397 non-degree-seeking students. **Degrees:** 373 associate awarded. **Location:** 30 miles from South Bend, Indiana. **Calendar:** Semester, extensive summer session. **Full-time faculty:** 51 total; 31% have terminal degrees, 49% women. **Part-time faculty:** 98 total; 16% have terminal degrees, 11% minority, 52% women.

Student profile. Among degree-seeking undergraduates, 38% enrolled in a transfer program, 62% enrolled in a vocational program, 638 enrolled as first-time, first-year students, 159 transferred in from other institutions.

Part-time:	43%	Hispanic/Latino:	6%
Out-of-state:	15%	Native American:	1%
Women:	58%	Multi-racial, non-Hispanic:	5%
African American:	12%	25 or older:	22%
Asian American:	1%	Live on campus:	20%

Transfer out. Colleges most students transferred to 2015: Western Michigan University, Ferris State University, Indiana University of South Bend, Bethel College, Grand Valley State University.

Basis for selection. Open admission, but selective for some programs. Students who test below a specific score on basic assessment tests in reading, writing, and math will be admitted as provisional students only and will be advised to demonstrate competency. Students may be exempted based on ACT/SAT. Special requirements for nursing programs. Interview required for nursing applicants.

2015-2016 Annual costs. Tuition/fees: $4,763; $5,776 out-of-district; $6,166 out-of-state. Per-credit charge: $113 in-district; $147 out-of-district; $160 out-of-state. Room only: $5,980.

Financial aid. Need-based: Need-based aid available for part-time students. Work-study available nights, weekends and for part-time students. **Non-need-based:** Scholarships awarded for academics, art, leadership, music/drama.

Application procedures. Admission: No deadline. No application fee. Admission notification on a rolling basis. **Financial aid:** Priority date 7/1; no closing date. FAFSA, institutional form required. Applicants notified on a rolling basis starting 4/1; must reply within 2 week(s) of notification.

Academics. Special study options: Accelerated study, dual enrollment of high school students, ESL, independent study, internships. Bachelor's degree programs available on campus. License preparation in nursing. **Credit/placement by examination:** AP, CLEP, institutional tests. 13 credit hours maximum toward associate degree. Credit for specific courses may be earned through ACE (Achieved Credit by Examination) testing. **Support services:** Learning center, reduced course load, remedial instruction, study skills assistance, tutoring, writing center.

Majors. Business: Accounting technology, business admin. **Computer sciences:** Networking, programming. **Education:** Early childhood. **English:** Technical writing. **General:** Carpentry. **Health services:** Health information technology, medical assistant, nursing (RN), prenursing. **Human services:** Social work. **Liberal arts:** Arts/sciences. **Parks/recreation:** Sports admin. **Protective services:** Criminal justice, firefighting. **Visual/performing arts:** Graphic design.

Most popular majors. Business/marketing 8%, health sciences 20%, liberal arts 53%.

Technology on campus. 73 workstations in dormitories, library, computer center, student center. Dormitories wired for high-speed internet access and linked to campus network. Commuter students can connect to campus network. Online course registration, online library, helpline, repair service, wireless network available.

Student life. Freshman orientation: Available. Preregistration for classes offered. Full- or half-day programs held each fall. **Housing:** Coed dorms, themed housing, wellness housing available. $200 nonrefundable deposit, deadline 7/1. **Activities:** Bands, choral groups, drama, music ensembles, musical theater, Advocates for All, Alpha Kappa Omega, business club, criminal justice club, Phi Theta Kappa.

Athletics. Intramural: Basketball, football (non-tackle), soccer, softball, tennis, volleyball.

Student services. Career counseling, services for economically disadvantaged, financial aid counseling. **Physically disabled:** Services for visually, speech, hearing impaired. **Transfer:** Pre-admission transcript evaluation for new students. Transfer center, transfer adviser, college fairs on campus for students transferring to 4-year colleges.

Contact. E-mail: enrollment@swmich.edu
Phone: (269) 782-1499 Toll-free number: (800) 456-8675 ext. 1499
Fax: (269) 783-2162
Angela Palsak, Executive Director of Student Services, Southwestern Michigan College, 58900 Cherry Grove Road, Dowagiac, MI 49047-9793

St. Clair County Community College
Port Huron, Michigan
www.sc4.edu   CB code: 1628

▶ Public 2-year community college
▶ Commuter campus in large town

General. Founded in 1923. Regionally accredited. **Enrollment:** 3,466 degree-seeking undergraduates. **Degrees:** 697 associate awarded. **Location:** 55 miles from Detroit. **Calendar:** Semester, limited summer session. **Full-time faculty:** 74 total. **Part-time faculty:** 201 total. **Special facilities:** Fine arts facility, natural history museum.

Student profile.

Out-of-state:	1%	25 or older:	29%

Transfer out. Colleges most students transferred to 2015: Central Michigan University, Saginaw Valley Sate University, Ferris State University, University of Michigan-Flint, Walsh College.

Basis for selection. Open admission, but selective for some programs. Special requirements for nursing, health information technology, and radiologic technology.

Two-Year Colleges

2015-2016 Annual costs. Tuition/fees: $3,600; $6,480 out-of-district; $9,240 out-of-state. Per-credit charge: $102 in-district; $198 out-of-district; $290 out-of-state. Books/supplies: $1,156. Personal expenses: $572.

Financial aid. Need-based: Work-study available nights, weekends and for part-time students.

Application procedures. Admission: No deadline. No application fee. Admission notification on a rolling basis. **Financial aid:** Priority date 6/1; no closing date. FAFSA required. Applicants notified on a rolling basis starting 5/15; must reply within 2 week(s) of notification.

Academics. Special study options: Accelerated study, cooperative education, cross-registration, distance learning, double major, dual enrollment of high school students, honors, internships, weekend college. Bachelor's degree programs available on campus. License preparation in nursing, radiology. **Credit/placement by examination:** AP, CLEP, institutional tests. 47 credit hours maximum toward associate degree. **Support services:** Learning center, reduced course load, remedial instruction, study skills assistance, tutoring, writing center.

Majors. Business: General, accounting technology, executive assistant, marketing, office management. **Computer sciences:** Data processing, networking, programming, webmaster. **Engineering:** General. **Health services:** Health information technology, massage therapy, medical radiologic technology/radiation therapy, medical secretary, nursing (RN). **Liberal arts:** Arts/sciences. **Protective services:** Corrections, firefighting, law enforcement admin. **Visual/performing arts:** Commercial/advertising art, studio arts. **Work/family studies:** Child care management.

Technology on campus. 300 workstations in library, computer center, student center. Online course registration, online library, helpline, wireless network available.

Student life. Freshman orientation: Mandatory. Preregistration for classes offered. **Activities:** Concert band, choral groups, drama, music ensembles, radio station, student government, student newspaper, symphony orchestra, global awareness club.

Athletics. NJCAA. **Intercollegiate:** Baseball M, basketball, golf M, softball W, volleyball W. **Team name:** Skippers.

Student services. Career counseling, services for economically disadvantaged, student employment services, financial aid counseling, minority student services, personal counseling, placement for graduates, veterans' counselor. **Physically disabled:** Services for visually, speech, hearing impaired. **Transfer:** Pre-admission transcript evaluation for new students. Transfer adviser, college fairs on campus for students transferring to 4-year colleges.

Contact. E-mail: enrollment@sc4.edu
Phone: (810) 989-5500 Fax: (810) 984-4730
Carrie Bearss, Registrar, St. Clair County Community College, 323 Erie Street, Port Huron, MI 48061-5015

Washtenaw Community College
Ann Arbor, Michigan CB member
www.wccnet.edu CB code: 1935

▶ Public 2-year community college
▶ Commuter campus in small city

General. Founded in 1965. Regionally accredited. Classes taught in Brighton, Saline, Chelsea, Ypsilanti and Hartland. **Enrollment:** 12,190 degree-seeking undergraduates. **Degrees:** 1,137 associate awarded. **ROTC:** Army. **Location:** 40 miles from Detroit. **Calendar:** Semester, extensive summer session. **Full-time faculty:** 171 total. **Part-time faculty:** 724 total.

Transfer out. Colleges most students transferred to 2015: Eastern Michigan University, University of Michigan.

Basis for selection. Open admission, but selective for some programs. Special requirements for health service technologies programs and some computer technology programs.

High school preparation. 15 units recommended. Recommended units include English 4, mathematics 4, social studies 2, science 4 and foreign language 1. Biology, chemistry, and algebra required for health programs. Trigonometry and drafting required for technical programs.

2015-2016 Annual costs. Tuition/fees: $3,030; $4,770 out-of-district; $6,270 out-of-state. Per-credit charge: $94 in-district; $152 out-of-district; $202 out-of-state. Books/supplies: $600. Personal expenses: $2,000.

Financial aid. Need-based: Work-study available nights, weekends and for part-time students. **Non-need-based:** Scholarships awarded for academics.

Application procedures. Admission: Priority date 8/12; no deadline. No application fee. Admission notification on a rolling basis beginning on or about 2/20. **Financial aid:** Priority date 6/1, closing date 7/1. FAFSA, institutional form required. Applicants notified on a rolling basis.

Academics. Special study options: Cooperative education, cross-registration, distance learning, dual enrollment of high school students, ESL, honors, independent study, internships, liberal arts/career combination, weekend college. **Credit/placement by examination:** AP, CLEP, institutional tests. 45 credit hours maximum toward associate degree. **Support services:** GED preparation and test center, learning center, remedial instruction, study skills assistance, tutoring, writing center.

Majors. Architecture: Technology. **Business:** Accounting, administrative services, business admin. **Communications technology:** Graphic/printing. **Computer sciences:** General, applications programming, computer graphics, computer science, data processing, information systems, LAN/WAN management, networking, programming, security, web page design. **Education:** Early childhood, elementary, secondary. **Engineering:** General, engineering mechanics, engineering science. **English:** Technical writing. **General:** Maintenance. **Health services:** Health information management, medical radiologic technology/radiation therapy, nursing (RN), premedicine, respiratory therapy technology, substance abuse counseling. **Liberal arts:** Arts/sciences. **Protective services:** Corrections, law enforcement admin, police science. **Social sciences:** General. **Visual/performing arts:** Commercial photography, photography.

Technology on campus. 211 workstations in library, computer center, student center. Commuter students can connect to campus network. Online course registration, online library, helpline, repair service, student web hosting, wireless network available.

Student life. Freshman orientation: Mandatory. Preregistration for classes offered. **Activities:** Jazz band, choral groups, dance, drama, literary magazine, musical theater, radio station, student government, student newspaper, African-American student association, Christian Challenge Student Advisory Council, international student association, Phi Theta Kappa, student assembly.

Student services. Adult student services, alcohol/substance abuse counseling, career counseling, services for economically disadvantaged, student employment services, financial aid counseling, minority student services, on-campus daycare, personal counseling, placement for graduates, veterans' counselor, women's services. **Physically disabled:** Services for visually, speech, hearing impaired. **Transfer:** Pre-admission transcript evaluation for new students. Transfer center, transfer adviser, college fairs on campus for students transferring to 4-year colleges.

Contact. E-mail: studrec@wccnet.org
Phone: (734) 973-3543 Fax: (734) 677-5414
Sukanya Jett, Director of Admissions, Washtenaw Community College, 4800 East Huron River Drive, Ann Arbor, MI 48105-4800

Wayne County Community College
Detroit, Michigan
www.wcccd.edu CB code: 1937

▶ Public 2-year community college
▶ Commuter campus in very large city

General. Founded in 1967. Regionally accredited. Five campuses and extension site. **Enrollment:** 11,937 degree-seeking undergraduates; 4,717 non-degree-seeking students. **Degrees:** 1,853 associate awarded. **Calendar:** Semester, extensive summer session. **Full-time faculty:** 77 total. **Part-time faculty:** 859 total. **Special facilities:** Educational and performing arts center, art galleries, Michigan Institute for Public Safety Education.

Student profile. Among degree-seeking undergraduates, 2,992 enrolled as first-time, first-year students.

Part-time:	75%	Hispanic/Latino:	2%
Women:	65%	Multi-racial, non-Hispanic:	10%
African American:	58%	25 or older:	48%
Asian American:	1%		

Transfer out. Colleges most students transferred to 2015: Wayne State University, University of Michigan Dearborn, University of Detroit Mercy, Eastern Michigan University, Oakland University.

Basis for selection. Open admission, but selective for some programs. Competitive career programs require interviews and prerequisite classes. **Adult students:** COMPASS placement exam required. **Home schooled:**

Transcript of courses and grades, state high school equivalency certificate required. **Learning Disabled:** To obtain services/accommodations, students should be admitted through the regular admissions process and after being admitted, visit the Disability Services/ACCESS department and complete certain requirements.

2016-2017 Annual costs. Tuition/fees (projected): $3,460; $3,790 out-of-district; $4,690 out-of-state. Per-credit charge: $105 in-district; $116 out-of-district; $146 out-of-state. Books/supplies: $1,720. Personal expenses: $1,290.

Financial aid. Need-based: Need-based aid available for part-time students. Work-study available nights, weekends and for part-time students.

Application procedures. Admission: No deadline. No application fee. **Financial aid:** Priority date 5/1; no closing date. FAFSA required. Applicants notified on a rolling basis starting 5/1.

Academics. Special study options: Accelerated study, distance learning, double major, dual enrollment of high school students, ESL, honors, internships, liberal arts/career combination, study abroad, weekend college. License preparation in dental hygiene, nursing, occupational therapy, paramedic. **Credit/placement by examination:** AP, CLEP, institutional tests. **Support services:** GED preparation, learning center, remedial instruction, study skills assistance, tutoring, writing center. Smarthinking Online Tutoring Program, Language Institute, TRIO Student Support Services, ACCESS Student Support Services (Disability Services), Adult Education Program.

Majors. Business: Accounting technology, business admin, e-commerce, office management. **Communications:** Digital media. **Computer sciences:** Programming. **Education:** Elementary. **Engineering:** Pre-engineering. **General:** Maintenance. **Health services:** Dental hygiene, EMT paramedic, home attendant, nursing (RN), pharmacy assistant, physician assistant, surgical technology, veterinary technology/assistant. **Human services:** Social work. **Liberal arts:** Arts/sciences. **Protective services:** Corrections, fire safety technology, police science. **Social sciences:** General. **Visual/performing arts:** Art. **Work/family studies:** Child care management, institutional food production.

Most popular majors. Health sciences 13%, liberal arts 72%.

Technology on campus. Commuter students can connect to campus network. Online course registration, online library, helpline, wireless network available.

Student life. Freshman orientation: Available. Preregistration for classes offered. An online orientation is available and includes information about college policies, procedures, programs, and services. It is interactive and recommended for all new students. **Policies:** Students must follow student code of conduct. **Activities:** Student government.

Athletics. NJCAA. **Intercollegiate:** Basketball, cross-country, golf M. **Team name:** Wild Cats.

Student services. Adult student services, career counseling, services for economically disadvantaged, student employment services, financial aid counseling, on-campus daycare, personal counseling, placement for graduates, veterans' counselor. **Physically disabled:** Services for visually, speech, hearing impaired. **Transfer:** Re-entry adviser, pre-admission transcript evaluation for new students. Transfer adviser, college fairs on campus for students transferring to 4-year colleges.

Contact. Phone: (313) 496-2634
Brian Singleton, Vice Chancellor of Student Services, Wayne County Community College, 801 West Fort Street, Detroit, MI 48226

West Shore Community College
Scottville, Michigan
www.westshore.edu   **CB code: 1941**

♦ Public 2-year community college
♦ Commuter campus in rural community

General. Founded in 1967. Regionally accredited. **Enrollment:** 815 degree-seeking undergraduates. **Degrees:** 174 associate awarded. **Location:** 54 miles from Muskegon. **Calendar:** Semester, limited summer session. **Full-time faculty:** 24 total. **Part-time faculty:** 83 total. **Special facilities:** Performing arts stage, art gallery, music/recording rooms, pottery and drawing/painting studios, ice arena, disc golf course. **Partnerships:** Formal partnership with ASM Tech Early College High School.

Transfer out. Colleges most students transferred to 2015: Grand Valley State University, Ferris State University, Davenport College, Central Michigan University.

Basis for selection. Open admission, but selective for some programs. Applicants to nursing program must complete prerequisite course work with 2.7 GPA; criminal justice program must complete prerequisite course work with 2.0 GPA.

2015-2016 Annual costs. Tuition/fees: $3,052; $5,122 out-of-district; $6,772 out-of-state. Books/supplies: $1,000. Personal expenses: $1,000.

Financial aid. Need-based: Need-based aid available for part-time students. Work-study available nights, weekends and for part-time students.

Application procedures. Admission: No deadline. $15 fee, may be waived for applicants with need. Application must be submitted online. Admission notification on a rolling basis. Applicants for associate degree in nursing must apply by January 1, practical nursing applicants by June 1. **Financial aid:** Priority date 6/1; no closing date. FAFSA, institutional form required. Applicants notified on a rolling basis starting 5/15; must reply within 2 week(s) of notification.

Academics. Special study options: Distance learning, dual enrollment of high school students, ESL, honors, independent study, internships. Bachelor's degree programs available on campus. License preparation in nursing. **Credit/placement by examination:** AP, CLEP, institutional tests. 10 credit hours maximum toward associate degree. **Support services:** GED test center, learning center, reduced course load, remedial instruction, study skills assistance, tutoring, writing center.

Majors. Biology: General. **Business:** General, accounting, administrative services, management information systems, marketing, office technology, office/clerical. **Computer sciences:** Data processing, system admin. **Education:** General, early childhood. **Engineering:** Computer, engineering chemistry, pre-engineering. **Health services:** EMT paramedic, nursing (RN), nursing assistant. **Liberal arts:** Arts/sciences. **Math:** General. **Protective services:** Law enforcement admin.

Technology on campus. 300 workstations in library, computer center, student center. Commuter students can connect to campus network. Online course registration, helpline, wireless network available.

Student life. Freshman orientation: Mandatory. Preregistration for classes offered. **Activities:** Bands, choral groups, drama, music ensembles, musical theater, radio station, student government, student newspaper, symphony orchestra, Phi Theta Kappa Honor Society, law enforcement club, art club, LARP club, future business leaders, entrepreneurship club, sustainability movement, additional special interest clubs.

Athletics. Intramural: Basketball, football (non-tackle), racquetball, softball, ultimate frisbee, volleyball.

Student services. Career counseling, student employment services, financial aid counseling, personal counseling, placement for graduates, veterans' counselor, women's services. **Physically disabled:** Services for visually, speech, hearing impaired. **Transfer:** Pre-admission transcript evaluation for new students. Transfer adviser, college fairs on campus for students transferring to 4-year colleges.

Contact. E-mail: admissions@westshore.edu
Phone: (231) 845-6211 ext. 5503
Toll-free number: (800) 848-9722 ext. 5503 Fax: (231) 845-0808
Marcus Crook, Director of Enrollment Management, West Shore Community College, 3000 North Stiles Road, Scottville, MI 49454-0277

Two-Year Colleges

Minnesota

Academy College
Bloomington, Minnesota
www.academycollege.edu
CB code: 3311

♦ For-profit 2-year technical and career college
♦ Commuter campus in large city
♦ Interview required

General. Accredited by ACICS. **Enrollment:** 116 degree-seeking under-graduates; 8 non-degree-seeking students. **Degrees:** 11 bachelor's, 16 associate awarded. **Calendar:** Quarter, extensive summer session.

Student profile. Among degree-seeking undergraduates, 10 enrolled as first-time, first-year students.

Part-time:	70%	Hispanic/Latino:	5%
Out-of-state:	4%	Native American:	3%
Women:	26%	Multi-racial, non-Hispanic:	3%
African American:	17%	25 or older:	68%
Asian American:	11%		

Basis for selection. Open admission.

2015-2016 Annual costs. Per-credit-hour charge starts at $355, may vary depending on program level and course of study. There is a one-time student activity fee of $280; annual technology fee $120; estimated books and supplies vary by program and range from $750 to $1,500. All costs are subject to change.

2014-2015 Financial aid. Need-based: 33% of total undergraduate aid awarded as scholarships/grants, 67% as loans/jobs. Need-based aid available for part-time students. Work-study available nights, weekends and for part-time students.

Application procedures. Admission: No deadline. $40 fee. Application must be submitted on paper. Admission notification on a rolling basis. **Financial aid:** No deadline. FAFSA, institutional form required. Applicants notified on a rolling basis.

Academics. Special study options: Distance learning, dual enrollment of high school students, internships. License preparation in aviation. **Credit/placement by examination:** AP, CLEP, IB. **Support services:** Learning center, reduced course load, study skills assistance, tutoring.

Majors. Business: Accounting, business admin. **Communications technology:** Animation/special effects. **Computer sciences:** Programming, system admin, web page design.

Technology on campus. PC or laptop required. 50 workstations in library, computer center. Online library, wireless network available.

Student life. Freshman orientation: Mandatory. Preregistration for classes offered.

Student services. Adult student services, career counseling, student employment services, financial aid counseling, placement for graduates, veterans' counselor. **Transfer:** Re-entry adviser, pre-admission transcript evaluation for new students.

Contact. E-mail: admissions@academycollege.edu
Phone: (952) 851-0066 Toll-free number: (800) 292-9149
Fax: (952) 851-0094
Tracey Schantz, Director of Enrollment and Career Services, Academy College, 1600 W 82nd St, Bloomington, MN 55431

Alexandria Technical and Community College
Alexandria, Minnesota
www.alextech.edu
CB code: 0771

♦ Public 2-year community and technical college
♦ Commuter campus in large town
♦ Interview required

General. Founded in 1961. Regionally accredited. **Enrollment:** 1,628 degree-seeking undergraduates. **Degrees:** 452 associate awarded. **Location:** 135 miles from Minneapolis-St. Paul. **Calendar:** Semester, limited summer session. **Full-time faculty:** 66 total; 3% have terminal degrees, 44% women. **Part-time faculty:** 36 total; 6% have terminal degrees, 56% women.

Student profile.

Out-of-state:	4%	25 or older:	20%

Basis for selection. Open admission, but selective for some programs. Application, high school transcript/GED required. Mechanical Reasoning test required for Diesel and Marine, Motorcycle & Powersports students; physical agility test required for Law Enforcement students. Additional requirement for the Practical Nursing and Nursing programs. Applicants considered in order of applications received. Portfolio required for communications art and design students.

2015-2016 Annual costs. Tuition/fees: $5,402; $5,402 out-of-state. Books/supplies: $1,200. Personal expenses: $2,500.

2014-2015 Financial aid. All financial aid based on need. 40% of total undergraduate aid awarded as scholarships/grants, 60% as loans/jobs. Need-based aid available for part-time students. Work-study available nights, weekends and for part-time students.

Application procedures. Admission: Priority date 8/1; no deadline. $20 fee, may be waived for applicants with need. Admission notification on a rolling basis. **Financial aid:** Priority date 5/1; no closing date. FAFSA required. Applicants notified on a rolling basis starting 6/30; must reply within 2 week(s) of notification.

Academics. Special study options: Cross-registration, distance learning, double major, independent study, internships, liberal arts/career combination, student-designed major. License preparation in nursing. **Credit/placement by examination:** AP, CLEP, IB, institutional tests. No separate limits on CLEP and credit by exam. **Support services:** Reduced course load, remedial instruction, study skills assistance, tutoring, writing center.

Majors. Business: Accounting, business admin, fashion, office management, sales/distribution. **Computer sciences:** Information systems, networking. **Education:** Early childhood. **Engineering:** Pre-engineering. **Health services:** Clinical lab technology, medical secretary, nursing (RN), speech-language pathology assistant. **Liberal arts:** Arts/sciences. **Parks/recreation:** Physical fitness technician. **Protective services:** Police science. **Visual/performing arts:** Commercial/advertising art, interior design.

Most popular majors. Business/marketing 13%, engineering/engineering technologies 8%, health sciences 15%, liberal arts 14%, security/protective services 22%, visual/performing arts 6%.

Technology on campus. 563 workstations in library, computer center. Online course registration, online library, helpline, repair service, wireless network available.

Student life. Freshman orientation: Available. Preregistration for classes offered. **Activities:** Campus ministries, international student organizations, student government, Phi Theta Kappa, Business Professionals of America, Delta Epsilon Chi, Skills USA, student senate.

Athletics. Intramural: Basketball, football (tackle), softball, volleyball.

Student services. Alcohol/substance abuse counseling, career counseling, services for economically disadvantaged, student employment services, financial aid counseling, health services, minority student services, personal counseling, placement for graduates, veterans' counselor. **Physically disabled:** Services for visually, speech, hearing impaired. **Transfer:** Pre-admission transcript evaluation for new students. Transfer adviser, college fairs on campus for students transferring to 4-year colleges.

Contact. E-mail: admissionsrep@alextech.edu
Phone: (320) 762-4520 Toll-free number: (888) 234-1222
Fax: (320) 762-4603
Scott Berger, Director of Admissions, Alexandria Technical and Community College, 1601 Jefferson Street, Alexandria, MN 56308-3799

Anoka Technical College
Anoka, Minnesota
www.anokatech.edu
CB code: 6084

♦ Public 2-year technical college
♦ Commuter campus in large town

General. Regionally accredited. **Enrollment:** 2,095 undergraduates. **Degrees:** 289 associate awarded. **Location:** 25 miles from Minneapolis-St.

Paul. **Calendar:** Semester, limited summer session. **Full-time faculty:** 58 total. **Part-time faculty:** 49 total.

Basis for selection. Open admission, but selective for some programs. Testing and score requirements for admission to the Surgical Technology, Occupational Therapy Assistant, and Practical Nursing Programs. If seeking an associate's degree in the Practical Nursing Program, additional biology requirement needed. All new students required to take Accuplacer to determine skill level in mathematics, reading and writing or meet exemption criteria as described on the college's website. The student may begin a program regardless of test scores unless the program requires placement testing as a program pre-requisite. **Adult students:** SAT/ACT scores not required.

2015-2016 Annual costs. Tuition/fees: $5,585; $5,585 out-of-state. Per-credit charge: $167. Books/supplies: $1,600. Personal expenses: $2,250.

Financial aid. All financial aid based on need. Need-based aid available for part-time students. Work-study available nights, weekends and for part-time students.

Application procedures. Admission: No deadline. No application fee. Admission notification on a rolling basis. **Financial aid:** No deadline. FAFSA required. Applicants notified on a rolling basis starting 7/1.

Academics. Special study options: Distance learning, dual enrollment of high school students, internships, liberal arts/career combination. License preparation in nursing, occupational therapy. **Credit/placement by examination:** AP, CLEP, institutional tests. **Support services:** GED preparation and test center, learning center, reduced course load, remedial instruction, study skills assistance, tutoring, writing center.

Majors. Business: Accounting, administrative services, office management. **Health services:** Health information technology, licensed practical nurse, medical assistant, medical secretary, occupational therapy assistant, surgical technology. **Parks/recreation:** Golf management. **Work/family studies:** Developmental services.

Most popular majors. Business/marketing 9%, engineering/engineering technologies 21%, health sciences 57%.

Technology on campus. 511 workstations in library, computer center, student center. Online library, wireless network available.

Student life. Freshman orientation: Mandatory. Preregistration for classes offered. **Activities:** Student government.

Student services. Career counseling, student employment services, financial aid counseling, health services, personal counseling, placement for graduates, veterans' counselor. **Physically disabled:** Services for visually, speech, hearing impaired.

Contact. E-mail: EnrollmentServices@anokatech.edu
Phone: (763) 576-7710 Fax: (763) 576-4756
Director of Admission, Anoka Technical College, 1355 West Highway 10, Anoka, MN 55303

Anoka-Ramsey Community College
Coon Rapids, Minnesota
www.anokaramsey.edu   CB code: 6024

- Public 2-year community college
- Commuter campus in small city

General. Founded in 1965. Regionally accredited. Two campus locations in Minnesota: Cambridge and Coon Rapids. Additionally courses are available at 15 off-site locations in East Central Minnesota and the North Metro of the Twin Cities. **Enrollment:** 8,972 undergraduates. **Degrees:** 1,051 associate awarded. **ROTC:** Army, Naval, Air Force. **Location:** 20 miles from Minneapolis-St. Paul. **Calendar:** Semester, extensive summer session. **Full-time faculty:** 131 total. **Part-time faculty:** 143 total. **Special facilities:** Glass-blowing studio, native prairie grounds/nature area.

Transfer out. Colleges most students transferred to 2015: University of Minnesota-Twin Cities, St. Cloud State University, Metropolitan State University.

Basis for selection. Open admission, but selective for some programs. Special requirements for nursing and physical therapist assistant programs. **Learning Disabled:** Recommend students connect with our Coordinator of Disability Services to discuss accommodation needs.

2015-2016 Annual costs. Tuition/fees: $5,014; $5,014 out-of-state. Per-credit charge: $144.96.

Financial aid. All financial aid based on need. Need-based aid available for part-time students. Work-study available nights, weekends and for part-time students.

Application procedures. Admission: No deadline. No application fee. Admission notification on a rolling basis. **Financial aid:** Priority date 4/1; no closing date. FAFSA, institutional form required. Applicants notified on a rolling basis; must reply within 2 week(s) of notification.

Academics. Special study options: Combined bachelor's/graduate degree, cooperative education, cross-registration, distance learning, double major, dual enrollment of high school students, ESL, honors, independent study, internships, study abroad, weekend college. Bachelor's degree programs available on campus. **Credit/placement by examination:** AP, CLEP, IB, institutional tests. 10 credit hours maximum toward associate degree. **Support services:** GED preparation, learning center, reduced course load, remedial instruction, study skills assistance, tutoring, writing center.

Majors. Biology: General. **Business:** General, accounting, accounting technology, business admin, human resources, sales/distribution. **Communications:** General. **Computer sciences:** Computer science, networking, system admin. **Conservation:** Environmental science. **Education:** General. **Engineering:** Pre-engineering. **English:** Creative writing. **Health services:** Community health, holistic, nursing (RN), physical therapy assistant. **Liberal arts:** Arts/sciences. **Psychology:** General. **Visual/performing arts:** Dramatic, music, studio arts.

Most popular majors. Business/marketing 11%, health sciences 23%, liberal arts 58%.

Technology on campus. 989 workstations in library, computer center. Commuter students can connect to campus network. Online course registration, student web hosting, wireless network available.

Student life. Freshman orientation: Available. Preregistration for classes offered. **Activities:** Bands, choral groups, drama, international student organizations, literary magazine, music ensembles, musical theater, student government, student newspaper, symphony orchestra, Phi Theta Kappa, Gay Straight Alliance.

Athletics. NJCAA. **Intercollegiate:** Baseball M, basketball, soccer, softball W, volleyball W. **Intramural:** Badminton, baseball M, basketball, bowling, football (tackle), golf, soccer, softball, tennis, volleyball. **Team name:** Golden Rams.

Student services. Adult student services, career counseling, student employment services, financial aid counseling, personal counseling, veterans' counselor. **Physically disabled:** Services for visually, speech, hearing impaired. **Transfer:** Transfer adviser, college fairs on campus for students transferring to 4-year colleges.

Contact. E-mail: admissions@anokaramsey.edu
Phone: (763) 433-1300
Director of Enrollment Services, Anoka-Ramsey Community College, 11200 Mississippi Boulevard NW, Coon Rapids, MN 55433

Central Lakes College
Brainerd, Minnesota
www.clcmn.edu   CB code: 6045

- Public 2-year community and technical college
- Commuter campus in large town

General. Founded in 1938. Regionally accredited. Access to 1.5 million book titles through participation in online catalog system with 28 other libraries. **Enrollment:** 2,806 degree-seeking undergraduates. **Degrees:** 585 associate awarded. **Location:** 125 miles from Minneapolis-St. Paul. **Calendar:** Semester, limited summer session. **Full-time faculty:** 104 total; 3% have terminal degrees, 5% minority, 43% women. **Part-time faculty:** 72 total; 1% minority, 51% women. **Class size:** 54% < 20, 40% 20-39, 5% 40-49, less than 1% 50-99. **Special facilities:** Conservatory, American Indian studies center.

Student profile. Among degree-seeking undergraduates, 52% enrolled in a transfer program, 47% enrolled in a vocational program, 142 transferred in from other institutions.

Basis for selection. Open admission, but selective for some programs. Applicants to mobility nursing program must have graduate license in practical nursing (LPN). Practical nurse program grades and college grades considered. Instructor and employer references, practical to registered nursing mobility profile, and mathematics test scores also considered.

2015-2016 Annual costs. Tuition/fees: $5,384; $5,384 out-of-state. Books/supplies: $1,000. Personal expenses: $2,546.

Financial aid. Need-based: Need-based aid available for part-time students. Work-study available nights, weekends and for part-time students.

Application procedures. Admission: No deadline. $20 fee. Admission notification on a rolling basis. **Financial aid:** Priority date 6/1; no closing date. FAFSA required. Applicants notified on a rolling basis starting 6/10; must reply within 2 week(s) of notification.

Academics. Special study options: Distance learning, dual enrollment of high school students, honors, independent study, internships, liberal arts/career combination. Bachelor's degree programs available on campus. License preparation in nursing. **Credit/placement by examination:** AP, CLEP, IB, institutional tests. **Support services:** Learning center, remedial instruction, study skills assistance, tutoring, writing center.

Majors. Business: Accounting, administrative services, business admin, tourism/travel. **Communications technology:** Photo/film/video. **Computer sciences:** Data processing, networking, programming. **Conservation:** General. **Education:** Teacher assistance. **Engineering:** General. **Health services:** Medical secretary, nursing (RN). **Liberal arts:** Arts/sciences. **Protective services:** Criminal justice, criminalistics, police science. **Visual/performing arts:** Commercial/advertising art. **Work/family studies:** Child care management.

Most popular majors. Health sciences 17%, liberal arts 61%.

Technology on campus. 150 workstations in library, computer center. Commuter students can connect to campus network. Online course registration, online library, helpline, repair service, wireless network available.

Student life. Freshman orientation: Mandatory. Preregistration for classes offered. Online orientation required. Orientation also held in-person throughout spring and summer. **Activities:** Bands, choral groups, drama, international student organizations, music ensembles, musical theater, student government, student newspaper, Anishinabe Student Association, campus ambassadors, law enforcement club, mentoring, theater club, Phi Theta Kappa, Spanish club, minority student forum.

Athletics. NJCAA. **Intercollegiate:** Baseball M, basketball, football (tackle) M, golf, softball W, volleyball W. **Intramural:** Baseball M, basketball, bowling, golf, softball, volleyball. **Team name:** Raiders.

Student services. Adult student services, career counseling, services for economically disadvantaged, financial aid counseling, health services, minority student services, on-campus daycare, personal counseling, placement for graduates, veterans' counselor, women's services. **Physically disabled:** Services for visually, speech, hearing impaired. **Transfer:** Pre-admission transcript evaluation for new students. Transfer adviser, college fairs on campus for students transferring to 4-year colleges.

Contact. E-mail: jbrose@clcmn.edu
Phone: (218) 855-8037 Toll-free number: (800) 933-0346
Fax: (218) 855-8230
Jennifer Brose, Director of Admissions, Central Lakes College, 501 West College Drive, Brainerd, MN 56401

Century College
White Bear Lake, Minnesota
www.century.edu
CB code: 6388

‣ Public 2-year community and technical college
‣ Commuter campus in large town

General. Founded in 1967. Regionally accredited. **Enrollment:** 8,202 degree-seeking undergraduates; 719 non-degree-seeking students. **Degrees:** 1,183 associate awarded. **ROTC:** Air Force. **Location:** 16 miles from Minneapolis-St. Paul. **Calendar:** Semester, limited summer session. **Full-time faculty:** 177 total; 10% minority, 55% women. **Part-time faculty:** 183 total; 10% minority, 50% women. **Class size:** 41% < 20, 53% 20-39, 4% 40-49, 2% 50-99. **Special facilities:** 92-acre nature area, walking trail.

Student profile. Among degree-seeking undergraduates, 39% enrolled in a transfer program, 61% enrolled in a vocational program, 3% already have a bachelor's degree or higher, 1,246 enrolled as first-time, first-year students, 867 transferred in from other institutions.

Part-time:	58%	Hispanic/Latino:	8%
Out-of-state:	5%	Multi-racial, non-Hispanic:	5%
Women:	55%	International:	2%
African American:	11%	25 or older:	39%
Asian American:	18%		

Transfer out. Colleges most students transferred to 2015: Metropolitan State University, University of Minnesota Twin Cities, University of Wisconsin-River Falls, Concordia University, St. Cloud University.

Basis for selection. Open admission, but selective for some programs. Special requirements for medical assistant, nursing, radiology, orthotics, paramedic, prosthetics, dental assist and dental hygiene programs. LOEP used to determine English proficiency. **Learning Disabled:** Documentation of disability must be provided within the first semester of service.

2015-2016 Annual costs. Tuition/fees: $5,391; $5,391 out-of-state. Per-credit charge: $161. Books/supplies: $1,200. Personal expenses: $2,066.

Financial aid. All financial aid based on need. Need-based aid available for part-time students. Work-study available nights, weekends and for part-time students.

Application procedures. Admission: No deadline. $20 fee, may be waived for applicants with need. Admission notification on a rolling basis. **Financial aid:** Priority date 5/1; no closing date. FAFSA required. Applicants notified on a rolling basis starting 5/15.

Academics. Special study options: Distance learning, dual enrollment of high school students, ESL, honors, independent study, internships, liberal arts/career combination, student-designed major. License preparation in dental hygiene, nursing, paramedic, radiology. **Credit/placement by examination:** AP, CLEP, IB, institutional tests. **Support services:** Learning center, remedial instruction, study skills assistance, tutoring, writing center.

Majors. Business: Accounting, administrative services, business admin, e-commerce, marketing. **Communications technology:** Animation/special effects. **Computer sciences:** Computer science, information systems, networking, security, web page design. **Education:** General, teacher assistance. **Engineering:** Pre-engineering. **Foreign languages:** Translation. **General:** Maintenance. **Health services:** Dental assistant, dental hygiene, EMT paramedic, medical secretary, nursing (RN), orthotics/prosthetics, radiologic technology/medical imaging, substance abuse counseling. **Liberal arts:** Arts/sciences. **Protective services:** Computer forensics, criminal justice, police science. **Visual/performing arts:** Interior design, music, studio arts.

Most popular majors. Business/marketing 7%, health sciences 23%, liberal arts 41%, security/protective services 6%.

Technology on campus. 1,650 workstations in library, computer center. Commuter students can connect to campus network. Online course registration, helpline, wireless network available.

Student life. Freshman orientation: Mandatory. Preregistration for classes offered. Two-part orientation includes advising/registration session, welcome day/workshops, tours and speakers. **Activities:** Bands, choral groups, drama, literary magazine, student government, student newspaper, symphony orchestra, Student Senate, Muslim student association, Alpha Omega, Phi Theta Kappa, social change club, African American student association, Asian student association, Movimiento Latino, Epic Movement, Spanish club.

Athletics. NJCAA. **Intercollegiate:** Baseball M, soccer, softball W. **Intramural:** Archery, badminton, basketball, bowling, football (non-tackle), golf, ice hockey, sand volleyball, skiing, soccer, softball, table tennis, ultimate frisbee, volleyball. **Team name:** Wood Ducks.

Student services. Adult student services, career counseling, student employment services, financial aid counseling, health services, minority student services, on-campus daycare, personal counseling. **Physically disabled:** Services for visually, speech, hearing impaired. **Transfer:** Transfer adviser, college fairs on campus for students transferring to 4-year colleges.

Contact. E-mail: admissions@century.edu
Phone: (651) 779-1700 Toll-free number: (800) 228-1978
Fax: (651) 779-1796
Robert Beaver, Assistant Director of Admissions, Century College, 3300 Century Avenue North, White Bear Lake, MN 55110

Dakota County Technical College
Rosemount, Minnesota
www.dctc.edu
CB code: 7149

‣ Public 2-year technical college
‣ Commuter campus in large town

General. Regionally accredited. **Enrollment:** 2,359 degree-seeking undergraduates; 301 non-degree-seeking students. **Degrees:** 514 associate awarded. **Location:** 20 miles from Minneapolis-St. Paul. **Calendar:** Semester, limited summer session. **Full-time faculty:** 80 total; 12% have terminal degrees,

4% minority, 40% women. **Part-time faculty:** 74 total; 14% have terminal degrees, 3% minority, 58% women. **Class size:** 63% < 20, 36% 20-39, less than 1% 40-49. **Special facilities:** Skid pad. **Partnerships:** Formal partnership with General Motors for Automotive Service Education Program/Body Service Education Program.

Student profile. Among degree-seeking undergraduates, 871 enrolled as first-time, first-year students.

Part-time:	44%	Hispanic/Latino:	5%
Women:	42%	Native American:	1%
African American:	10%	International:	1%
Asian American:	4%	25 or older:	50%

Transfer out. Colleges most students transferred to 2015: St. Mary's University, Metropolitan State University, Concordia University.

Basis for selection. Open admission, but selective for some programs. Students must achieve qualifying scores on the ACUPLACER Assessment for entrance into Medical Assistant and Practical Nursing programs. TOEFL required for international students. Admissions visit including meeting with the program instructor(s) not required but strongly recommended. **Home schooled:** Transcript of courses and grades required. **Learning Disabled:** Recommended students meet with disability support staff prior to admissions.

2015-2016 Annual costs. Tuition/fees: $5,713; $5,713 out-of-state. Per-credit charge: $169. Books/supplies: $1,200. Personal expenses: $2,250.

Financial aid. Need-based: Need-based aid available for part-time students. Work-study available nights, weekends and for part-time students. **Non-need-based:** Scholarships awarded for academics, athletics, leadership.

Application procedures. Admission: No deadline. $20 fee, may be waived for applicants with need. Admission notification on a rolling basis. **Financial aid:** No deadline. FAFSA required. Applicants notified on a rolling basis starting 3/15.

Academics. Special study options: Distance learning, double major, internships, liberal arts/career combination, student-designed major. License preparation in nursing. **Credit/placement by examination:** AP, CLEP, IB, institutional tests. **Support services:** Learning center, pre-admission summer program, reduced course load, remedial instruction, study skills assistance, tutoring, writing center.

Majors. Business: Accounting, business admin, event planning, executive assistant, management information systems, marketing, office management, real estate, resort management, sales/distribution. **Computer sciences:** Database management, networking, programming, system admin, web page design, webmaster. **General:** Electrician, lineworker. **Health services:** Dental assistant, licensed practical nurse, medical assistant, medical secretary. **Parks/recreation:** Physical fitness technician. **Visual/performing arts:** Commercial/advertising art, graphic design, interior design, photography. **Work/family studies:** Child care management, child care service, child development.

Most popular majors. Business/marketing 28%, computer/information sciences 10%, engineering/engineering technologies 10%, health sciences 16%, trade and industry 15%, visual/performing arts 9%.

Technology on campus. 200 workstations in library, computer center, student center. Online course registration, online library, helpline, wireless network available.

Student life. Freshman orientation: Mandatory. Preregistration for classes offered. **Activities:** Campus ministries, international student organizations, student government, Multicultural Student Leadership Association, veterans center, student senate, Christians on Campus, Lion's Club, Student Ambassadors, Gay Straight Alliance, Skills USA, Phi Theta Kappa, Business Professionals of America.

Athletics. NJCAA. **Intercollegiate:** Baseball M, basketball M, soccer, softball W, volleyball W. **Team name:** Blue Knights.

Student services. Career counseling, services for economically disadvantaged, student employment services, financial aid counseling, health services, minority student services, personal counseling, placement for graduates, veterans' counselor. **Physically disabled:** Services for visually, speech, hearing impaired. **Transfer:** Re-entry adviser, pre-admission transcript evaluation for new students. College fairs on campus for students transferring to 4-year colleges.

Contact. E-mail: admissions@dctc.edu
Phone: (651) 423-8300 Toll-free number: (877) 937-3282
Fax: (651) 423-8775
Anne Buesgens, Admissions Coordinator, Dakota County Technical College, 1300 145th Street East, Rosemount, MN 55068

Duluth Business University
Duluth, Minnesota
www.dbumn.edu   CB code: 3312

- For-profit 2-year business, health science and career college
- Residential campus in small city
- Interview required

General. Accredited by ACICS. **Enrollment:** 144 degree-seeking undergraduates. **Degrees:** 1 bachelor's, 42 associate awarded. **Location:** 150 miles from Minneapolis-St. Paul. **Calendar:** Quarter, extensive summer session. **Full-time faculty:** 7 total; 14% have terminal degrees, 100% women. **Part-time faculty:** 19 total; 5% have terminal degrees, 53% women. **Class size:** 100% < 20.

Student profile. Among degree-seeking undergraduates, 5% already have a bachelor's degree or higher, 18 enrolled as first-time, first-year students.

Part-time:	44%	Asian American:	1%
Out-of-state:	10%	Hispanic/Latino:	1%
Women:	90%	Native American:	3%
African American:	2%	Native Hawaiian/Pacific islander:	1%

Basis for selection. High school diploma or GED and interview required.

2015-2016 Annual costs. Books/supplies: $1,500. **Additional information:** General program classes per-credit: $380; Veterinary Technology technical classes per-credit: $390. Lab fees vary by program. All costs are subject to change.

Financial aid. Need-based: Work-study available nights, weekends and for part-time students.

Application procedures. Admission: No deadline. $35 fee. Application must be submitted on paper. Admission notification on a rolling basis. **Financial aid:** No deadline.

Academics. Special study options: Distance learning, internships. **Credit/placement by examination:** AP, CLEP. **Support services:** Remedial instruction, tutoring.

Majors. Business: Business admin. **Health services:** Health information technology, massage therapy, medical assistant, phlebotomy, veterinary technology/assistant. **Visual/performing arts:** Commercial/advertising art.

Most popular majors. Business/marketing 27%, health sciences 27%.

Technology on campus. 60 workstations in library, student center. Online library, helpline, wireless network available.

Student life. Freshman orientation: Mandatory. Preregistration for classes offered.

Student services. Career counseling. **Transfer:** Re-entry adviser, pre-admission transcript evaluation for new students.

Contact. E-mail: info@dbumn.edu
Phone: (218) 722-4000 Toll-free number: (800) 777-8406
Fax: (218) 628-2127
Bonnie Kupczynski, Campus Director, Duluth Business University, 4727 Mike Colalillo Drive, Duluth, MN 55807

Dunwoody College of Technology
Minneapolis, Minnesota
www.dunwoody.edu   CB code: 2265

- Private 2-year technical college
- Commuter campus in very large city
- Application essay, interview required

General. Founded in 1914. Regionally accredited. **Enrollment:** 1,043 degree-seeking undergraduates; 51 non-degree-seeking students. **Degrees:** 47 bachelor's, 295 associate awarded. **Calendar:** Semester, limited summer session. **Full-time faculty:** 81 total; 10% have terminal degrees, 14% minority, 27% women. **Part-time faculty:** 47 total; 17% have terminal degrees, 13% minority, 8% women. **Class size:** 89% < 20, 11% 20-39.

Student profile. Among degree-seeking undergraduates, 100% enrolled in a vocational program, 188 enrolled as first-time, first-year students, 236 transferred in from other institutions.

Part-time:	18%	Hispanic/Latino:	2%
Out-of-state:	2%	Native American:	1%
Women:	15%	Multi-racial, non-Hispanic:	2%
African American:	6%	25 or older:	48%
Asian American:	6%		

Transfer out. Colleges most students transferred to 2015: Minneapolis Community and Technical College, Normandale Community College, University of Minnesota-Twin Cities, Inver Hills Community College, Century College.

Basis for selection. Selective admission based on a compilation of objective (GPA & test scores) and subjective (essay & personal interview). Essay or personal statement required at time of admissions testing. **Home schooled:** Transcript of courses and grades required. **Learning Disabled:** Students must submit official documentation.

High school preparation. College-preparatory program recommended.

2015-2016 Annual costs. Tuition/fees: $24,230.

2014-2015 Financial aid. Need-based: 164 full-time freshmen applied for aid; 146 deemed to have need; 146 received aid. Average need met was 31%. Average scholarship/grant was $5,494; average loan $3,379. 31% of total undergraduate aid awarded as scholarships/grants, 69% as loans/jobs. Need-based aid available for part-time students. Work-study available nights, weekends and for part-time students. **Non-need-based:** Awarded to 30 full-time undergraduates, including 13 freshmen.

Application procedures. Admission: No deadline. $50 fee, may be waived for applicants with need. Admission notification on a rolling basis. **Financial aid:** Priority date 6/1; no closing date. FAFSA required. Applicants notified on a rolling basis starting 3/1.

Academics. Special study options: Distance learning, independent study, internships, study abroad. Bachelor's degree programs available on campus. **Credit/placement by examination:** AP, CLEP, IB, institutional tests. **Support services:** Learning center, reduced course load, remedial instruction, study skills assistance, tutoring, writing center.

Majors. Architecture: Technology. **Communications technology:** Desktop publishing. **Computer sciences:** Networking, web page design. **General:** Electrician, site management. **Health services:** Medical radiologic technology/radiation therapy. **Visual/performing arts:** Graphic design.

Most popular majors. Architecture 6%, computer/information sciences 10%, engineering/engineering technologies 33%, health sciences 6%, trade and industry 40%.

Technology on campus. PC or laptop required. 1,900 workstations in library, computer center. Commuter students can connect to campus network. Online library, helpline, repair service, wireless network available.

Student life. Freshman orientation: Mandatory. Preregistration for classes offered. One-day program, offered multiple times. **Activities:** Student government.

Student services. Career counseling, student employment services, financial aid counseling, minority student services, personal counseling, placement for graduates, veterans' counselor, women's services. **Physically disabled:** Services for speech, hearing impaired. **Transfer:** Re-entry adviser, pre-admission transcript evaluation for new students. Transfer adviser for students transferring to 4-year colleges.

Contact. E-mail: info@dunwoody.edu
Phone: (612) 381-3041 Toll-free number: (800) 292-4625
Fax: (612) 377-3131
Cindy Olson, Director of Admissions, Dunwoody College of Technology, 818 Dunwoody Boulevard, Minneapolis, MN 55403-1192

Fond du Lac Tribal and Community College
Cloquet, Minnesota
www.fdltcc.edu   CB code: 2047

▸ Public 2-year community college
▸ Commuter campus in small town

General. Founded in 1987. Regionally accredited. **Enrollment:** 895 degree-seeking undergraduates; 524 non-degree-seeking students. **Degrees:** 235 associate awarded. **Location:** 16 miles from Duluth and two hours from Minneapolis-St. Paul. **Calendar:** Semester, limited summer session. **Full-time faculty:** 40 total; 2% have terminal degrees, 25% minority, 55% women. **Part-time faculty:** 85 total; 13% have terminal degrees, 8% minority, 49% women. **Special facilities:** 21,000 acre environmental study area, day care.

Student profile. Among degree-seeking undergraduates, 334 enrolled as first-time, first-year students, 407 transferred in from other institutions.

Part-time:	40%	Hispanic/Latino:	1%
Out-of-state:	5%	Native American:	23%
Women:	56%	25 or older:	34%
African American:	9%	Live on campus:	8%
Asian American:	1%		

Transfer out. Colleges most students transferred to 2015: College of St. Scholastica, University of Wisconsin Superior, University of Minnesota Duluth.

Basis for selection. Open admission. ACT, SAT, and Accuplacer (English, Reading, and Math) placement test results accepted.

High school preparation. Recommended units include English 4, mathematics 3 and foreign language 4.

2015-2016 Annual costs. Tuition/fees: $5,258; $5,258 out-of-state. Per-credit charge: $159. Room only: $3,508. Books/supplies: $1,114.

2014-2015 Financial aid. Need-based: 65% of total undergraduate aid awarded as scholarships/grants, 35% as loans/jobs. Need-based aid available for part-time students. Work-study available nights, weekends and for part-time students. **Non-need-based:** Scholarships awarded for academics.

Application procedures. Admission: No deadline. $20 fee, may be waived for applicants with need. Admission notification on a rolling basis. **Financial aid:** Priority date 3/16; no closing date. FAFSA required. Applicants notified on a rolling basis starting 4/16.

Academics. Special study options: Cooperative education, distance learning, double major, dual enrollment of high school students, independent study, internships, liberal arts/career combination, weekend college. Bachelor's degree programs available on campus. License preparation in nursing. **Credit/placement by examination:** AP, CLEP, IB, institutional tests. 24 credit hours maximum toward associate degree. **Support services:** GED test center, learning center, pre-admission summer program, remedial instruction, study skills assistance, tutoring, writing center.

Majors. Business: Finance. **Conservation:** Environmental science. **General:** Power transmission. **Health services:** Nursing (RN). **Liberal arts:** Arts/sciences. **Parks/recreation:** Physical fitness technician. **Protective services:** Police science. **Visual/performing arts:** Studio arts.

Most popular majors. Health sciences 13%, liberal arts 65%, security/protective services 19%.

Technology on campus. 100 workstations in dormitories, library, computer center, student center. Dormitories wired for high-speed internet access and linked to campus network. Commuter students can connect to campus network. Online course registration, wireless network available.

Student life. Freshman orientation: Mandatory. Preregistration for classes offered. **Housing:** Coed dorms available. $150 fully refundable deposit, deadline 6/15. **Activities:** Choral groups, drama, music ensembles, student government, student newspaper, Phi Theta Kappa Honor Society, law enforcement club, human services club, Anishinaabe Congress, math club, veterans group, American Indian Business Leaders, rocket and robotics club, GIS club.

Athletics. NJCAA. **Intercollegiate:** Baseball M, basketball, football (tackle) M, softball W. **Team name:** Thunder.

Student services. Adult student services, alcohol/substance abuse counseling, career counseling, services for economically disadvantaged, student employment services, financial aid counseling, minority student services, on-campus daycare, personal counseling, placement for graduates, veterans' counselor. **Physically disabled:** Services for visually, speech, hearing impaired. **Transfer:** Pre-admission transcript evaluation for new students. Transfer adviser, college fairs on campus for students transferring to 4-year colleges.

Contact. E-mail: admissions@fdltcc.edu
Phone: (218) 879-0808 Toll-free number: (800) 657-3712
Fax: (218) 879-0814
Susan Bumann, AdmissionsOfficer, Fond du Lac Tribal and Community College, 2101 14th Street, Cloquet, MN 55720

Hennepin Technical College
Brooklyn Park, Minnesota
www.hennepintech.edu   CB code: 6290

▸ Public 2-year technical college
▸ Commuter campus in small city

General. Regionally accredited. **Enrollment:** 5,052 degree-seeking undergraduates. **Degrees:** 721 associate awarded. **Location:** 10 miles from Minneapolis-St. Paul. **Calendar:** Semester, limited summer session. **Full-time faculty:** 138 total. **Part-time faculty:** 172 total. **Class size:** 38% < 20, 59% 20-39, 2% 40-49.

Student profile. Among degree-seeking undergraduates, 612 enrolled as first-time, first-year students.

Part-time:	62%	25 or older:	47%
Women:	39%		

Basis for selection. Open admission, but selective for some programs. Special requirements for nursing and dental program. ACCUPLACER for placement only.

2015-2016 Annual costs. Tuition/fees: $5,159; $5,159 out-of-state. Per-credit charge: $157. Books/supplies: $2,000.

Financial aid. All financial aid based on need. Need-based aid available for part-time students. Work-study available nights, weekends and for part-time students.

Application procedures. Admission: No deadline. No application fee. Admission notification on a rolling basis. **Financial aid:** No deadline. FAFSA, institutional form required. Applicants notified on a rolling basis starting 3/1.

Academics. Special study options: Accelerated study, cross-registration, distance learning, dual enrollment of high school students, ESL, honors, independent study, internships, student-designed major. License preparation in nursing. **Credit/placement by examination:** AP, CLEP, IB. **Support services:** Learning center, reduced course load, remedial instruction, study skills assistance, tutoring, writing center.

Majors. Business: Accounting, accounting technology, office technology, office/clerical. **Communications:** Advertising, digital media, publishing. **Communications technology:** General, desktop publishing, graphic/printing, graphics, photo/film/video, printing press operator, recording arts. **Computer sciences:** General, applications programming, computer graphics, data processing, information systems, programming, security, systems analysis, web page design. **General:** Carpentry, electrician, maintenance. **Health services:** Dental assistant, EMT paramedic, licensed practical nurse, medical secretary, office admin, ward clerk. **Protective services:** Fire safety technology. **Work/family studies:** Child development.

Technology on campus. 150 workstations in library, computer center, student center. Commuter students can connect to campus network. Online course registration, online library, wireless network available.

Student life. Freshman orientation: Mandatory. Preregistration for classes offered. A week before school starts. **Activities:** Student government.

Student services. Career counseling, student employment services, financial aid counseling, personal counseling, placement for graduates, veterans' counselor. **Physically disabled:** Services for visually, speech, hearing impaired. **Transfer:** Pre-admission transcript evaluation for new students. Transfer adviser, college fairs on campus for students transferring to 4-year colleges.

Contact. E-mail: info@hennepintech.edu
Phone: (763) 488-2500 Toll-free number: (800) 345-4655
Fax: (763) 488-2944
Hennepin Technical College, 9000 Brooklyn Boulevard, Brooklyn Park, MN 55445

Herzing University: Minneapolis
Minneapolis, Minnesota
www.herzing.edu

▸ For-profit 2-year technical college
▸ Commuter campus in large city

General. Regionally accredited. **Enrollment:** 350 undergraduates. **Degrees:** 33 bachelor's, 44 associate awarded. **Calendar:** Semester. **Full-time faculty:** 19 total. **Part-time faculty:** 31 total.

Basis for selection. Open admission, but selective for some programs. Admissions decisions based on applicant's interest, professional attitude, and performance on standardized tests. Applicants who don't submit SAT or ACT scores must complete an entrance examination for admission.

2015-2016 Annual costs. Certificate programs: $13,670 to $26,820. Associate programs: $26,180 to $53,640. Bachelor's programs: $61,515 to $88,065.

Financial aid. Need-based: Work-study available nights, weekends and for part-time students.

Application procedures. Admission: No deadline. No application fee. Admission notification on a rolling basis. **Financial aid:** No deadline.

Academics. Credit/placement by examination: AP, CLEP.

Majors. Business: Business admin. **Health services:** Dental assistant, dental hygiene, insurance coding, medical assistant, occupational therapy assistant, office admin, surgical technology.

Most popular majors. Health sciences 97%.

Contact. E-mail: info@mpls.herzing.edu
Phone: (763) 535-3000
Shelly Larson, Director of Admissions, Herzing University: Minneapolis, 5700 West Broadway, Minneapolis, MN 55428

Hibbing Community College
Hibbing, Minnesota
www.hibbing.edu   CB code: 6275

▸ Public 2-year community and technical college
▸ Commuter campus in large town

General. Founded in 1916. Regionally accredited. **Enrollment:** 770 full-time, degree-seeking students. **Degrees:** 239 associate awarded. **Location:** 75 miles from Duluth. **Calendar:** Semester, limited summer session. **Full-time faculty:** 113 total. **Part-time faculty:** 60 total.

Student profile.

Out-of-state:	13%	Live on campus:	10%
25 or older:	40%		

Transfer out. Colleges most students transferred to 2015: Bemidji State University, University of Minnesota: Duluth, College of St. Scholastica, University of Wisconsin-Superior, University of North Dakota.

Basis for selection. Open admission, but selective for some programs. Academic placement test required. Special requirements for nursing, dental assistant and law enforcement programs. **Home schooled:** Transcript of courses and grades required.

2015-2016 Annual costs. Tuition/fees: $5,310; $6,492 out-of-state. Room only: $3,000. Books/supplies: $900.

Financial aid. Need-based: Work-study available nights, weekends and for part-time students.

Application procedures. Admission: No deadline. $20 fee, may be waived for applicants with need. Admission notification on a rolling basis. **Financial aid:** Priority date 7/1; no closing date. FAFSA required. Applicants notified on a rolling basis starting 6/30; must reply within 2 week(s) of notification.

Academics. Special study options: Cooperative education, cross-registration, distance learning, dual enrollment of high school students, honors, independent study, internships, liberal arts/career combination. Bachelor's degree programs available on campus. License preparation in nursing. **Credit/placement by examination:** AP, CLEP, institutional tests. 12 credit hours maximum toward associate degree. **Support services:** GED preparation and test center, learning center, pre-admission summer program, reduced course load, remedial instruction, study skills assistance, tutoring, writing center.

Majors. Business: Administrative services, business admin, office/clerical. **Computer sciences:** General, security. **Education:** General. **Engineering:** General. **English:** English lit. **Health services:** Clinical lab technology, dental assistant, medical secretary, nursing (RN). **Liberal arts:** Arts/sciences. **Protective services:** Police science.

Technology on campus. 100 workstations in dormitories, library, computer center. Dormitories wired for high-speed internet access. Commuter students can connect to campus network. Online course registration, online library, wireless network available.

Student life. Freshman orientation: Available. Preregistration for classes offered. Registration orientation held throughout summer; all-student orientation held before fall & spring classes begin. **Housing:** Apartments available. $250 fully refundable deposit. **Activities:** Choral groups, student government, Phi Theta Kappa.

Athletics. NJCAA. **Intercollegiate:** Baseball M, basketball, golf, softball W, volleyball W. **Team name:** Cardinals.

Student services. Adult student services, career counseling, services for economically disadvantaged, student employment services, financial aid counseling, personal counseling, veterans' counselor. **Physically disabled:** Services for visually, speech, hearing impaired. **Transfer:** Transfer adviser, college fairs on campus for students transferring to 4-year colleges.

Contact. E-mail: admissions@hibbing.edu
Phone: (218) 262-7207 Toll-free number: (800) 224-4422
Fax: (218) 263-2992
Rick Kangas, Dean of Student Services, Hibbing Community College, 1515 East 25th Street, Hibbing, MN 55746

Institute of Production and Recording
Minneapolis, Minnesota
www.ipr.edu
CB code: 6461

- For-profit 2-year career college
- Commuter campus in large city
- Interview required

General. Regionally accredited; also accredited by ACCSC. **Enrollment:** 243 undergraduates. **Degrees:** 92 associate awarded. **Location:** Located in downtown Minneapolis. **Calendar:** Quarter.

Basis for selection. Open admission. **Adult students:** SAT/ACT scores not required.

2015-2016 Annual costs. Tuition/fees: $20,450. Per-credit charge: $390. Books/supplies: $1,260. **Additional information:** Per-credit hour charge for 1 to 13 hours, $460; for 14 to 16 hours, $390. Course fees: $10 to $400 per course.

Financial aid. Need-based: Need-based aid available for part-time students. Work-study available nights, weekends and for part-time students.

Application procedures. Admission: No deadline. $50 fee. Admission notification on a rolling basis. **Financial aid:** No deadline. FAFSA, institutional form required. Applicants notified on a rolling basis starting 7/1; must reply within 2 week(s) of notification.

Academics. Special study options: Internships, liberal arts/career combination. **Credit/placement by examination:** AP, CLEP. **Support services:** Remedial instruction, study skills assistance, tutoring, writing center.

Majors. Communications technology: Recording arts. **Visual/performing arts:** Music management.

Most popular majors. Communication technologies 45%, visual/performing arts 55%.

Technology on campus. 119 workstations in library, computer center, student center. Commuter students can connect to campus network. Online library, helpline, student web hosting, wireless network available.

Student life. Freshman orientation: Mandatory. Preregistration for classes offered. Day and evening sessions available the week prior to classes starting.

Student services. Career counseling, student employment services, financial aid counseling, placement for graduates. **Transfer:** Re-entry adviser for new students.

Contact. E-mail: sferkingstad@ipr.edu
Phone: (612) 244-2800 Toll-free number: (866) 477-4840
Sue Ferkingstad, Director of Admissions, Institute of Production and Recording, 300 North 1st Avenue, Suite 500, Minneapolis, MN 55401

Inver Hills Community College
Inver Grove Heights, Minnesota
www.inverhills.edu
CB code: 6300

- Public 2-year community college
- Commuter campus in large town

General. Founded in 1967. Regionally accredited. **Enrollment:** 4,112 degree-seeking undergraduates; 1,292 non-degree-seeking students. **Degrees:** 841 associate awarded. **ROTC:** Army, Air Force. **Location:** 6 miles from Minneapolis-St. Paul. **Calendar:** Semester, limited summer session. **Full-time faculty:** 103 total. **Part-time faculty:** 88 total. **Class size:** 34% < 20, 63% 20-39, 3% 40-49, less than 1% 50-99. **Special facilities:** Large communal garden and apple orchard where all produce grown is donated to food shelves and non-profit organizations; offer 10' X 10' plots to students and community members, awarded by lottery each spring.

Student profile. Among degree-seeking undergraduates, 682 enrolled as first-time, first-year students, 499 transferred in from other institutions.

Part-time:	58%	Asian American:	7%
Out-of-state:	2%	Hispanic/Latino:	8%
Women:	60%	Native American:	1%
African American:	14%	25 or older:	42%

Transfer out. Colleges most students transferred to 2015: Metro State University, University of Minnesota-Twin Cities, Dakota County Technical College, Hennepin Technical College, Century College.

Basis for selection. Open admission, but selective for some programs. Special requirements for nursing and emergency medical service programs, computer and networking technology, and international students. **Adult students:** SAT/ACT scores not required.

2015-2016 Annual costs. Tuition/fees: $5,288; $5,288 out-of-state. Per-credit charge: $159. Books/supplies: $1,500.

2014-2015 Financial aid. All financial aid based on need. 56% of total undergraduate aid awarded as scholarships/grants, 44% as loans/jobs. Need-based aid available for part-time students. Work-study available nights, weekends and for part-time students.

Application procedures. Admission: Closing date 8/18 (receipt date). No application fee. Admission notification on a rolling basis. **Financial aid:** No deadline. FAFSA required. Applicants notified on a rolling basis starting 4/1.

Academics. Special study options: Accelerated study, cross-registration, distance learning, double major, dual enrollment of high school students, ESL, honors, independent study, internships, liberal arts/career combination, student-designed major, study abroad. Bachelor's degree programs available on campus. License preparation in nursing, paramedic. **Credit/placement by examination:** AP, CLEP, IB, institutional tests. 40 credit hours maximum toward associate degree. Accept ACE, DSST, TCEP, Excelsior Exams, NYUFLP, NOCTI, and other forms of credits earned through non-formal learning. **Support services:** GED test center, learning center, reduced course load, remedial instruction, study skills assistance, tutoring, writing center.

Majors. Biology: General. **Business:** General, accounting, business admin, construction management, international. **Computer sciences:** Computer science, networking, programming, support specialist. **Education:** General, physical. **Engineering:** Pre-engineering. **Health services:** EMT paramedic, nursing (RN). **Liberal arts:** Arts/sciences. **Parks/recreation:** Exercise sciences. **Physical sciences:** Chemistry. **Protective services:** Criminal justice, police science. **Visual/performing arts:** Dramatic, music, studio arts.

Most popular majors. Business/marketing 11%, health sciences 10%, interdisciplinary studies 7%, liberal arts 49%, security/protective services 6%.

Technology on campus. 85 workstations in library, computer center, student center. Commuter students can connect to campus network. Online course registration, online library, helpline, wireless network available.

Student life. Freshman orientation: Mandatory. Preregistration for classes offered. Orientation is held prior to start of the semester. Online orientation also available. **Activities:** Campus ministries, choral groups, dance, drama, international student organizations, literary magazine, music ensembles, musical theater, student government, Young Americans for Liberty, black student union, Ethiopian student association, Muslim student association, Somali student club, Spanish club, Volunteering Individuals Bring Empowerment, Christian Fellowship club, international club.

Athletics. Intramural: Basketball, bowling, football (non-tackle), golf, ice hockey, lacrosse, soccer, softball, table tennis, ultimate frisbee, volleyball.

Student services. Adult student services, career counseling, services for economically disadvantaged, student employment services, financial aid counseling, health services, minority student services, personal counseling, placement for graduates, veterans' counselor. **Physically disabled:** Services for visually, speech, hearing impaired. **Transfer:** Pre-admission transcript evaluation for new students. Transfer center, transfer adviser, college fairs on campus for students transferring to 4-year colleges.

Contact. E-mail: admissions@inverhills.edu
Phone: (651) 450-3503 Fax: (651) 450-3677
Scott Klaehn, Director of Enrollment Services, Inver Hills Community
College, 2500 80th Street East, Inver Grove Heights, MN 55076-3224

Itasca Community College
Grand Rapids, Minnesota
www.itascacc.edu

CB code: 6309

- Public 2-year community college
- Residential campus in large town

General. Founded in 1922. Regionally accredited. Scenic Northwoods location. Over 70 percent of our graduates receive an associate degree and transfer to a 4-year college. **Enrollment:** 1,008 degree-seeking undergraduates; 214 non-degree-seeking students. **Degrees:** 257 associate awarded. **Location:** 80 miles from Duluth, 180 miles from Minneapolis-St. Paul. **Calendar:** Semester, limited summer session. **Full-time faculty:** 28 total; 7% minority, 50% women. **Part-time faculty:** 40 total; 2% minority, 52% women. **Special facilities:** Educational wetland habitat, University of Minnesota agricultural station, U.S. Forest Service shared campus, 500-acre experimental forest. **Partnerships:** Formal partnerships with local businesses for training, partnership council with area high schools.

Student profile. Among degree-seeking undergraduates, 232 enrolled as first-time, first-year students.

Part-time: 25% Women: 43%

Transfer out. Colleges most students transferred to 2015: Bemidji State University, College of St. Scholastica, University of Minnesota: Duluth, St. Cloud State University, University of North Dakota.

Basis for selection. Open admission, but selective for some programs. College-level reading and English testing required for teacher education program. Prerequisite classes are required for the practical nursing program. **Adult students:** SAT/ACT scores not required.

High school preparation. College-preparatory program recommended. 12 units recommended. Recommended units include English 4, mathematics 2, social studies 2, science 2 and foreign language 2. Computer skills recommended.

2015-2016 Annual costs. Tuition/fees: $5,325; $6,507 out-of-state. Room/board: $5,340. Books/supplies: $775. Personal expenses: $2,052.

2014-2015 Financial aid. Need-based: 66% of total undergraduate aid awarded as scholarships/grants, 34% as loans/jobs. Need-based aid available for part-time students. Work-study available nights, weekends and for part-time students. **Non-need-based:** Scholarships awarded for academics, leadership, state residency.

Application procedures. Admission: Priority date 8/1; deadline 8/15 (receipt date). $20 fee, may be waived for applicants with need. Admission notification on a rolling basis. **Financial aid:** Priority date 5/1; no closing date. FAFSA required. Applicants notified on a rolling basis starting 4/20.

Academics. Special study options: Cooperative education, double major, dual enrollment of high school students, independent study, internships, liberal arts/career combination, study abroad. Bachelor's degree programs available on campus. License preparation in nursing. **Credit/placement by examination:** AP, CLEP, IB, institutional tests. 10 credit hours maximum toward associate degree. **Support services:** GED test center, learning center, pre-admission summer program, reduced course load, remedial instruction, study skills assistance, tutoring, writing center.

Majors. Area/ethnic studies: Native American. **Business:** Accounting, business admin. **Conservation:** General, forestry. **Education:** General, early childhood. **Engineering:** General. **Health services:** Prenursing. **Human services:** Social work. **Liberal arts:** Arts/sciences. **Protective services:** Counterterrorism. **Psychology:** General. **Social sciences:** Geography.

Technology on campus. 275 workstations in dormitories, library, computer center, student center. Dormitories wired for high-speed internet access and linked to campus network. Commuter students can connect to campus network. Online course registration, online library, wireless network available.

Student life. Freshman orientation: Available. Preregistration for classes offered. Full day event held the day before classes begin. **Housing:** Coed dorms available. $200 nonrefundable deposit, deadline 6/30. Apartment complex adjacent to campus housing available for ICC students. It is not owned by the campus. **Activities:** Literary magazine, student government, Circle-K, business club, Student Ambassadors, Global Ed, engineering club, psychology club, leadership club, natural resources club, GSA, minority student club.

Athletics. NJCAA. **Intercollegiate:** Baseball M, basketball, football (tackle) M, softball W, volleyball W, wrestling M. **Intramural:** Basketball M, bowling, football (non-tackle), soccer, softball, table tennis, volleyball. **Team name:** Vikings.

Student services. Adult student services, career counseling, services for economically disadvantaged, financial aid counseling, minority student services, personal counseling, veterans' counselor. **Physically disabled:** Services for visually, speech, hearing impaired. **Transfer:** Transfer adviser, college fairs on campus for students transferring to 4-year colleges.

Contact. E-mail: info@itascacc.edu
Phone: (218) 322-2340 ext. 2340 Toll-free number: (800) 996-6422
Fax: (218) 322-2332
Bill Marshall, Director of Enrollment Services, Itasca Community
College, 1851 Highway 169 East, Grand Rapids, MN 55744

ITT Technical Institute: Eden Prairie
Eden Prairie, Minnesota
www.itt-tech.edu

- For-profit 2-year technical college
- Commuter campus in small city

General. Accredited by ACICS. **Enrollment:** 216 undergraduates. **Degrees:** 9 bachelor's, 41 associate awarded. **Calendar:** Quarter. **Full-time faculty:** 7 total. **Part-time faculty:** 46 total.

Basis for selection. To be admitted into a program of study offered by ITT Technical Institute, an individual must satisfy all of the admission requirements applicable to that program of study.

2015-2016 Annual costs. Per-credit-hour charge, $493; academic fee, $200. Some programs require purchase of tools, which could cost an additional $150 to $500. All costs subject to change.

Financial aid. Need-based: Work-study available nights, weekends and for part-time students.

Application procedures. Admission: No application fee.

Academics. Credit/placement by examination: AP, CLEP. **Support services:** Remedial instruction.

Majors. Business: General. **Computer sciences:** LAN/WAN management, networking, programming, web page design. **Protective services:** Criminalistics, law enforcement admin. **Visual/performing arts:** Design, graphic design.

Most popular majors. Computer/information sciences 60%, engineering/engineering technologies 21%, security/protective services 6%, visual/performing arts 14%.

Student services. Career counseling, student employment services, placement for graduates.

Contact. Phone: (952) 914-5300 Toll-free number: (888) 488-9646
ITT Technical Institute: Eden Prairie, 7905 Golden Triangle Drive, Eden
Prairie, MN 55344

Lake Superior College
Duluth, Minnesota
www.lsc.edu

CB code: 6352

- Public 2-year community and technical college
- Commuter campus in small city

General. Regionally accredited. **Enrollment:** 3,349 degree-seeking undergraduates; 1,101 non-degree-seeking students. **Degrees:** 681 associate awarded. **Location:** 150 miles from Minneapolis-St. Paul. **Calendar:** Semester, limited summer session. **Full-time faculty:** 102 total; 5% have terminal degrees, 7% minority, 54% women. **Part-time faculty:** 140 total; 7% have terminal degrees, 6% minority, 51% women. **Class size:** 53% < 20, 46% 20-39, 1% 40-49. **Special facilities:** 100 acre wooded site, interpretative hiking and snowshoe trails, trout stream, disc golf course adjacent to campus.

Student profile. Among degree-seeking undergraduates, 50% enrolled in a transfer program, 50% enrolled in a vocational program, 514 enrolled as first-time, first-year students, 502 transferred in from other institutions.

Part-time:	47%	Hispanic/Latino:	3%
Out-of-state:	14%	Native American:	2%
Women:	55%	Multi-racial, non-Hispanic:	4%
African American:	3%	25 or older:	40%
Asian American:	1%		

Basis for selection. Open admission, but selective for some programs. Many health programs have special requirements including coursework and GPA. Nursing program has competitive admissions. After admission, the ACCUPLACER computerized placement test is required for all students unless transcript shows completion of college-level math and English composition. **Home schooled:** Ability to Benefit test required for Wisconsin home schooled applicants.

High school preparation. College-preparatory program recommended.

2015-2016 Annual costs. Tuition/fees: $5,126; $9,543 out-of-state. Books/supplies: $1,500. Personal expenses: $3,237.

Financial aid. Need-based: Need-based aid available for part-time students. Work-study available nights, weekends and for part-time students. **Non-need-based:** Scholarships awarded for academics.

Application procedures. Admission: No deadline. $20 fee, may be waived for applicants with need. Admission notification on a rolling basis. **Financial aid:** No deadline. FAFSA required. Applicants notified on a rolling basis.

Academics. Special study options: Accelerated study, distance learning, double major, dual enrollment of high school students, independent study, internships, liberal arts/career combination, study abroad. License preparation in aviation, dental hygiene, nursing, paramedic, physical therapy, radiology. **Credit/placement by examination:** AP, CLEP, institutional tests. 30 credit hours maximum toward associate degree. **Support services:** Learning center, pre-admission summer program, reduced course load, remedial instruction, study skills assistance, tutoring, writing center.

Majors. Business: Accounting, business admin, management information systems, office management, office technology. **Computer sciences:** System admin, web page design. **General:** Electrician. **Health services:** Clinical lab technology, dental hygiene, medical secretary, nursing (RN), physical therapy assistant, radiologic technology/medical imaging, respiratory therapy technology, surgical technology. **Liberal arts:** Arts/sciences. **Protective services:** Fire safety technology. **Visual/performing arts:** Studio arts.

Most popular majors. Business/marketing 7%, engineering/engineering technologies 6%, health sciences 28%, liberal arts 47%.

Technology on campus. 514 workstations in library, computer center, student center. Commuter students can connect to campus network. Online course registration, online library, helpline, repair service, student web hosting, wireless network available.

Student life. Freshman orientation: Mandatory. Preregistration for classes offered. Less than one-half day. **Policies:** Students have a role in the allocation of student activity fees. Students are involved in the College's decision making processes through shared governance. **Activities:** Choral groups, international student organizations, student government, Environmental Club, Intervarsity Christian Fellowship, Phi Theta Kappa, Teachers of Tomorrow, United Students/Intercultural Club, Art Club, Business Professionals of America, Nursing Club, Physical Therapy Assistant Club, Unity/GLBT Club.

Athletics. NJCAA. **Intercollegiate:** Soccer. **Intramural:** Basketball, football (non-tackle), table tennis, volleyball. **Team name:** Ice Hawks.

Student services. Adult student services, career counseling, services for economically disadvantaged, student employment services, financial aid counseling, minority student services, on-campus daycare, personal counseling, placement for graduates, veterans' counselor. **Physically disabled:** Services for visually, speech, hearing impaired. **Transfer:** Pre-admission transcript evaluation for new students. Transfer center, transfer adviser, college fairs on campus for students transferring to 4-year colleges.

Contact. E-mail: enroll@lsc.edu
Phone: (218) 733-7601 Toll-free number: (800) 432-2884
Fax: (218) 733-5945
Melissa Leno, Director of Admissions, Lake Superior College, 2101 Trinity Road, Duluth, MN 55811

Le Cordon Bleu College of Culinary Arts: Minneapolis-St. Paul
Mendota Heights, Minnesota
www.chefs.edu/Minneapolis-St-Paul

- For-profit 2-year culinary school and career college
- Commuter campus in very large city
- Interview required

General. Accredited by ACCSC. **Enrollment:** 382 degree-seeking undergraduates. **Degrees:** 131 associate awarded. **Location:** 12 miles from Minneapolis-St. Paul. **Calendar:** Quarter, extensive summer session. **Full-time faculty:** 18 total. **Part-time faculty:** 6 total.

Basis for selection. Open admission. **Home schooled:** Statement describing home school structure and mission, transcript of courses and grades, interview required. **Learning Disabled:** Current IEP.

High school preparation. College-preparatory program recommended. Recommended units include English 3, mathematics 2, social studies 1, history 1 and science 1.

2015-2016 Annual costs. Tuition for both culinary and patisserie associate degree programs for residents: $40,000; $42,500 for non-resident students. Tuition for both culinary arts and patisserie certificate programs: $19,500. Tuition charges include books, supplies, and uniforms. All fees are subject to change.

Financial aid. Need-based: Work-study available nights, weekends and for part-time students. **Non-need-based:** Scholarships awarded for academics, job skills, leadership.

Application procedures. Admission: No deadline. $50 fee, may be waived for applicants with need. Admission notification on a rolling basis. **Financial aid:** No deadline.

Academics. Special study options: Internships. **Credit/placement by examination:** AP, CLEP. **Support services:** Remedial instruction, study skills assistance, tutoring.

Technology on campus. 40 workstations in library, computer center. Online library, wireless network available.

Student life. Freshman orientation: Mandatory. Preregistration for classes offered. Several options for orientation including the Friday prior to beginning of classes. **Activities:** Student government.

Student services. Adult student services, alcohol/substance abuse counseling, career counseling, student employment services, financial aid counseling, placement for graduates, veterans' counselor. **Physically disabled:** Services for hearing impaired. **Transfer:** Re-entry adviser, pre-admission transcript evaluation for new students.

Contact. E-mail: dpeterson@msp.chefs.edu
Phone: (651) 675-4700 ext. 4787
Toll-free number: (800) 528-4575 ext. 4787 Fax: (651) 452-5282
David Peterson, Director of Admissions, Le Cordon Bleu College of Culinary Arts: Minneapolis-St. Paul, 1315 Mendota Heights Road, Mendota Heights, MN 55120-1129

Leech Lake Tribal College
Cass Lake, Minnesota
www.lltc.edu CB code: 3931

- Public 2-year community college
- Commuter campus in small town

General. Regionally accredited. Chartered by the Leech Lake Band of Ojibwe. **Enrollment:** 328 degree-seeking undergraduates. **Degrees:** 26 associate awarded. **Location:** 15 miles from Bemidji. **Calendar:** Semester, limited summer session. **Full-time faculty:** 19 total; 5% have terminal degrees, 32% minority, 42% women. **Part-time faculty:** 13 total; 85% minority, 54% women. **Class size:** 100% < 20.

Transfer out. Colleges most students transferred to 2015: Bemidji State University.

Basis for selection. Open admission. Students must have a GED or High School Diploma. **Home schooled:** Documentation of high school classes required.

High school preparation. College-preparatory program required.

2015-2016 Annual costs. Tuition/fees: $4,920; $4,920 out-of-state. Per-credit charge: $154. Books/supplies: $800. Personal expenses: $2,000.

Financial aid. Need-based: Need-based aid available for part-time students. Work-study available nights, weekends and for part-time students.

Application procedures. Admission: Closing date 8/1 (postmark date). $15 fee. Application must be submitted online. Admission notification on a rolling basis. **Financial aid:** No deadline. FAFSA, institutional form required. Applicants notified on a rolling basis; must reply within 4 week(s) of notification.

Academics. Special study options: Double major, independent study, internships, liberal arts/career combination, teacher certification program, weekend college. **Credit/placement by examination:** AP, CLEP, institutional tests. **Support services:** GED preparation and test center, learning center, reduced course load, remedial instruction, study skills assistance, tutoring.

Majors. Area/ethnic studies: Native American. **Business:** Business admin. **Conservation:** Forest management. **Education:** Early childhood. **Liberal arts:** Arts/sciences. **Protective services:** Police science.

Most popular majors. Business/marketing 24%, education 6%, liberal arts 62%.

Technology on campus. 31 workstations in library, computer center, student center.

Student life. Freshman orientation: Available. Preregistration for classes offered. **Activities:** Choral groups, student government.

Athletics. Intercollegiate: Basketball. **Team name:** Leech Lakers.

Student services. Adult student services, financial aid counseling, on-campus daycare, personal counseling. **Transfer:** Transfer adviser for students transferring to 4-year colleges.

Contact. E-mail: admissions@lltc.edu
Phone: (218) 335-4222 Fax: (218) 335-4217
Stacey Lundberg, Registrar, Leech Lake Tribal College, 6945 Little Wolf Road NW, Cass Lake, MN 56633

Mesabi Range College
Virginia, Minnesota
www.mesabirange.edu   CB code: 6432

- Public 2-year community and technical college
- Commuter campus in large town

General. Founded in 1918. Regionally accredited. Career/technical programs offered at Eveleth campus. **Enrollment:** 1,373 undergraduates. **Degrees:** 163 associate awarded. **Location:** 60 miles from Duluth. **Calendar:** Semester, limited summer session. **Full-time faculty:** 47 total; 15% minority. **Part-time faculty:** 42 total. **Special facilities:** Iron Range Engineering.

Student profile.

Out-of-state:	9%	Live on campus:	8%
25 or older:	26%		

Transfer out. Colleges most students transferred to 2015: University of Minnesota-Duluth, Bemidji State University, St. Cloud State University, Mankato State University, University of Minnesota-Minneapolis.

Basis for selection. Open admission.

2015-2016 Annual costs. Tuition/fees: $5,311; $6,493 out-of-state. Per-credit charge: $177.03 in-state; $197.02 out-of-state. Room only: $4,036. Books/supplies: $1,000. Personal expenses: $1,000.

Financial aid. Need-based: Need-based aid available for part-time students. Work-study available nights, weekends and for part-time students. **Non-need-based:** Scholarships awarded for state residency.

Application procedures. Admission: No deadline. $20 fee. Admission notification on a rolling basis beginning on or about 1/1. **Financial aid:** Priority date 4/22; no closing date. FAFSA, institutional form required. Applicants notified on a rolling basis starting 5/1; must reply within 2 week(s) of notification.

Academics. Special study options: Dual enrollment of high school students, independent study, internships, liberal arts/career combination, study abroad. Bachelor's degree programs available on campus. License preparation

in nursing, paramedic. **Credit/placement by examination:** AP, CLEP, institutional tests. **Support services:** Learning center, reduced course load, remedial instruction, study skills assistance, tutoring.

Majors. Biology: General. **Business:** General, administrative services, marketing, office technology. **Communications technology:** Graphic/printing. **Computer sciences:** General, programming, systems analysis. **Education:** General, teacher assistance. **Engineering:** Computer. **General:** Carpentry. **Health services:** Substance abuse counseling. **Liberal arts:** Arts/sciences. **Parks/recreation:** Exercise sciences.

Technology on campus. Dormitories linked to campus network. Online course registration, helpline, wireless network available.

Student life. Freshman orientation: Mandatory. Preregistration for classes offered. **Housing:** Apartments available. $300 fully refundable deposit, deadline 9/1. **Activities:** Bands, choral groups, dance, drama, literary magazine, music ensembles, musical theater, student government, student newspaper, symphony orchestra.

Athletics. NJCAA. **Intercollegiate:** Baseball M, basketball, football (tackle) M, golf, softball W, volleyball W. **Intramural:** Badminton, basketball, bowling, field hockey W, ice hockey, softball, table tennis, volleyball. **Team name:** Norseman.

Student services. Career counseling, student employment services, minority student services, on-campus daycare, personal counseling, placement for graduates. **Physically disabled:** Services for visually, hearing impaired. **Transfer:** Pre-admission transcript evaluation for new students.

Contact. E-mail: s.twaddle@mr.mnscu.edu
Phone: (218) 749-0315 Fax: (218) 749-0318
Brenda Kochevar, Director of Enrollment Services, Mesabi Range College, 1001 Chestnut Street West, Virginia, MN 55792-3448

Minneapolis Business College
Roseville, Minnesota
www.minneapolisbusinesscollege.edu   CB code: 7126

- For-profit 2-year business and technical college
- Residential campus in very large city

General. Founded in 1874. Accredited by ACICS. **Enrollment:** 235 undergraduates. **Degrees:** 101 associate awarded. **Location:** 10 miles from Minneapolis-St. Paul. **Calendar:** Semester, limited summer session.

Student profile.

Out-of-state:	20%	Live on campus:	12%

Basis for selection. Open admission. Interview recommended. **Adult students:** SAT/ACT scores not required. **Home schooled:** Transcript of courses and grades required.

2015-2016 Annual costs. Tuition/fees: $14,720. Room only: $6,960.

Financial aid. All financial aid based on need. Work-study available nights, weekends and for part-time students. **Additional information:** Individual financial planning available for all students to meet the cost of education.

Application procedures. Admission: No deadline. $50 fee. Admission notification on a rolling basis beginning on or about 7/1. **Financial aid:** No deadline. FAFSA required. Applicants notified on a rolling basis.

Academics. Externships related to career available. 16-month associate of applied science degree options. **Credit/placement by examination:** AP, CLEP. **Support services:** Study skills assistance.

Majors. Business: Accounting, administrative services, hospitality admin, management information systems, office management, tourism/travel. **Computer sciences:** Applications programming. **Health services:** Medical assistant. **Visual/performing arts:** Commercial/advertising art.

Student life. Freshman orientation: Mandatory. Preregistration for classes offered. **Housing:** Single-sex dorms available. $100 partly refundable deposit. **Activities:** Student government, student newspaper.

Student services. Career counseling, financial aid counseling, placement for graduates.

Contact. Phone: (651) 636-7406 Toll-free number: (800) 279-5200
Fax: (651) 636-8185
Lisa Stuart, Admissions Supervisor, Minneapolis Business College, 1711 West County Road B, Roseville, MN 55113

Minneapolis Community and Technical College
Minneapolis, Minnesota
www.minneapolis.edu CB code: 6434

◆ Public 2-year community and technical college
◆ Commuter campus in large city

General. Founded in 1965. Regionally accredited. **Enrollment:** 8,187 degree-seeking undergraduates. **Degrees:** 992 associate awarded. **Location:** Downtown Minneapolis. **Calendar:** Semester, limited summer session. **Full-time faculty:** 185 total; 31% have terminal degrees, 21% minority, 57% women. **Part-time faculty:** 171 total; 13% have terminal degrees, 26% minority, 57% women. **Class size:** 47% < 20, 43% 20-39, 7% 40-49, 4% 50-99.

Basis for selection. Open admission, but selective for some programs. Admission to the college does not guarantee admission to a career program/major. Some programs have additional requirements for admission.

2015-2016 Annual costs. Tuition/fees: $5,366; $5,366 out-of-state. Books/supplies: $1,400. Personal expenses: $4,500.

Financial aid. All financial aid based on need. Need-based aid available for part-time students. Work-study available nights, weekends and for part-time students.

Application procedures. Admission: No deadline. $20 fee, may be waived for applicants with need. Admission notification on a rolling basis. **Financial aid:** Priority date 7/12; no closing date. FAFSA required. Applicants notified on a rolling basis starting 7/1.

Academics. Special study options: Accelerated study, cross-registration, distance learning, dual enrollment of high school students, ESL, honors, independent study, internships, liberal arts/career combination, teacher certification program, weekend college. License preparation in dental hygiene, nursing. **Credit/placement by examination:** AP, CLEP, IB, institutional tests. **Support services:** Learning center, reduced course load, remedial instruction, study skills assistance, tutoring, writing center. Math center, TRIO.

Majors. Biology: General, biotechnology. **Business:** Accounting technology, business admin, office technology, restaurant/food services. **Communications technology:** Animation/special effects, recording arts. **Computer sciences:** Programming, security, system admin, web page design. **Education:** General. **Health services:** Electroencephalograph technology, nursing (RN), polysomnography, substance abuse counseling. **Human services:** Community org/advocacy. **Liberal arts:** Arts/sciences, library assistant. **Math:** General. **Philosophy/religion:** Philosophy. **Physical sciences:** Chemistry. **Protective services:** Criminal justice, police science. **Visual/performing arts:** Cinematography, commercial photography, design, dramatic, play/screenwriting, studio arts. **Work/family studies:** Child development.

Most popular majors. Business/marketing 12%, computer/information sciences 7%, health sciences 10%, liberal arts 34%, security/protective services 7%, trade and industry 6%, visual/performing arts 11%.

Technology on campus. 279 workstations in library, computer center, student center. Online course registration, online library, helpline, repair service, wireless network available.

Student life. Freshman orientation: Mandatory. Preregistration for classes offered. **Activities:** Bands, choral groups, dance, drama, film society, international student organizations, literary magazine, music ensembles, student government, student newspaper, Phi Theta Kappa Honor Society, Skills USA, Association of Black Collegiates, Student Nurses Association, United Nations of Indian Tribes for Education, Bicycle Collective, Chicanos Latinos Unidos, Three-Legged Frog Environmental Club.

Athletics. Team name: Mavericks.

Student services. Adult student services, career counseling, services for economically disadvantaged, student employment services, financial aid counseling, health services, legal services, minority student services, personal counseling, placement for graduates, veterans' counselor. **Physically disabled:** Services for visually, speech, hearing impaired. **Transfer:** Pre-admission transcript evaluation for new students. Transfer adviser, college fairs on campus for students transferring to 4-year colleges.

Contact. E-mail: admissions.office@minneapolis.edu
Phone: (612) 659-6200 Toll-free number: (800) 247-0911
Fax: (612) 659-6210
Minneapolis Community and Technical College, 1501 Hennepin Avenue, Minneapolis, MN 55403-1710

Minnesota School of Business: Brooklyn Center
Brooklyn Center, Minnesota
www.msbcollege.edu CB code: 3314

◆ For-profit 2-year career college
◆ Commuter campus in large town
◆ Interview required

General. Accredited by ACICS. **Enrollment:** 109 undergraduates. **Degrees:** 25 bachelor's, 30 associate awarded. **Location:** 7.6 miles from Minneapolis. **Calendar:** Quarter, extensive summer session. **Full-time faculty:** 8 total. **Part-time faculty:** 7 total. **Partnerships:** Microsoft Developers Network Academic Alliance (MSDNAA).

Basis for selection. Open admission. **Adult students:** SAT/ACT scores not required.

2015-2016 Annual costs. Tuition/fees: $18,702. Per-credit charge: $390. Books/supplies: $1,260. **Additional information:** Per-credit hour charge for 1 to 11 hours, $460; for 12 to 16 hours, $390. Course fees: $10 to $400 per course.

Financial aid. Need-based: Need-based aid available for part-time students. Work-study available nights, weekends and for part-time students.

Application procedures. Admission: No deadline. $50 fee. Admission notification on a rolling basis. **Financial aid:** No deadline. FAFSA, institutional form required. Applicants notified on a rolling basis starting 7/1; must reply within 2 week(s) of notification.

Academics. Special study options: Distance learning, independent study, internships, liberal arts/career combination. Bachelor's degree programs available on campus. **Credit/placement by examination:** AP, CLEP. **Support services:** Remedial instruction, study skills assistance, tutoring, writing center.

Majors. Business: Accounting, business admin, marketing. **Computer sciences:** Networking. **Health services:** Massage therapy, medical assistant, medical secretary. **Protective services:** Law enforcement admin. **Visual/performing arts:** Music management.

Most popular majors. Business/marketing 19%, computer/information sciences 19%, health sciences 44%, legal studies 7%, security/protective services 6%, visual/performing arts 6%.

Technology on campus. 60 workstations in library, computer center, student center. Commuter students can connect to campus network. Online library, helpline, student web hosting, wireless network available.

Student life. Freshman orientation: Mandatory. Preregistration for classes offered. Day and evening sessions available the week prior to classes starting. **Activities:** Literary magazine.

Student services. Career counseling, student employment services, financial aid counseling, placement for graduates. **Transfer:** Re-entry adviser for new students.

Contact. Phone: (763) 566-7777 Toll-free number: (800) 231-9154 Kelly O'Brien, Director of Admissions, Minnesota School of Business: Brooklyn Center, 5910 Shingle Creek Parkway, Brooklyn Center, MN 55430

Minnesota State College - Southeast Technical
Winona, Minnesota
www.southeastmn.edu CB code: 7123

◆ Public 2-year technical college
◆ Commuter campus in large town

General. Founded in 1949. Regionally accredited. Unique programs include: musical string instrument repair, band instrument repair, mobile electronics installation. **Enrollment:** 1,538 degree-seeking undergraduates; 465 non-degree-seeking students. **Degrees:** 260 associate awarded. **Location:** 55 miles from Rochester. **Calendar:** Semester, limited summer session. **Full-time faculty:** 63 total; 6% have terminal degrees, 51% women. **Part-time faculty:** 43 total; 5% minority, 51% women. **Class size:** 87% < 20, 13% 20-39.

Student profile. Among degree-seeking undergraduates, 252 enrolled as first-time, first-year students, 260 transferred in from other institutions.

Part-time:	45%	Hispanic/Latino:	4%
Out-of-state:	29%	Native American:	1%
Women:	57%	Multi-racial, non-Hispanic:	3%
African American:	6%	25 or older:	49%
Asian American:	2%		

Transfer out. Colleges most students transferred to 2015: Rochester Community and Technical College, Winona State University, Metropolitan State University.

Basis for selection. Open admission, but selective for some programs. Nursing, radiography, and truck driving have requirements for admission to program. **Home schooled:** Transcript of courses and grades required. **Learning Disabled:** Disability documentation required to receive accommodations.

High school preparation. College-preparatory program recommended. 7 units recommended. Recommended units include English 4, mathematics 2 and science 1.

2015-2016 Annual costs. Tuition/fees: $5,615; $5,615 out-of-state. Books/supplies: $1,000.

2014-2015 Financial aid. Need-based: 128 full-time freshmen applied for aid; 113 deemed to have need; 111 received aid. Average need met was 36%. Average scholarship/grant was $4,585; average loan $3,178. 51% of total undergraduate aid awarded as scholarships/grants, 49% as loans/jobs. Need-based aid available for part-time students. Work-study available nights, weekends and for part-time students. **Non-need-based:** Awarded to 106 full-time undergraduates, including 23 freshmen. Scholarships awarded for academics, leadership.

Application procedures. Admission: No deadline. $20 fee, may be waived for applicants with need. Admission notification on a rolling basis. **Financial aid:** No deadline. FAFSA, institutional form required. Applicants notified on a rolling basis; must reply within 3 week(s) of notification.

Academics. Special study options: Distance learning, double major, dual enrollment of high school students, internships, liberal arts/career combination. **Credit/placement by examination:** AP, CLEP, IB, institutional tests. **Support services:** Learning center, pre-admission summer program, remedial instruction, tutoring.

Majors. Business: Accounting, accounting technology, administrative services, business admin, retailing, sales/distribution, selling. **Computer sciences:** Networking, programming, web page design. **Education:** Early childhood. **General:** Carpentry. **Health services:** Massage therapy, medical secretary, nursing (RN), radiologic technology/medical imaging. **Protective services:** Criminal justice.

Most popular majors. Business/marketing 13%, computer/information sciences 8%, engineering/engineering technologies 9%, health sciences 46%, interdisciplinary studies 8%, security/protective services 6%.

Technology on campus. 100 workstations in library. Online course registration, online library, wireless network available.

Student life. Freshman orientation: Mandatory. Preregistration for classes offered. **Housing:** Cooperative housing available. For Winona campus students, dormitories are available at Winona State University. For Red Wing campus students, a privately-owned dormitory near college is available. **Activities:** Student government, student newspaper, Student Senate, Business Professionals of America, Skills USA, Delta Epsilon Chi, Guild of American Luthiers, Association of Stringed Instrument Artisans, Violin Society of America, Musical Instrument Technicians Association, National Association of Professional Band Instrument Repair Technicians, Data Processing Management Association.

Student services. Adult student services, alcohol/substance abuse counseling, career counseling, services for economically disadvantaged, student employment services, financial aid counseling, health services, minority student services, personal counseling, placement for graduates, veterans' counselor. **Physically disabled:** Services for visually, speech, hearing impaired. **Transfer:** Re-entry adviser, pre-admission transcript evaluation for new students.

Contact. E-mail: enrollmentservices@southeastmn.edu
Phone: (507) 453-2700 Toll-free number: (877) 853-8324
Fax: (507) 453-2715
Gale Lanning, Director of Admissions, Minnesota State College - Southeast Technical, 1250 Homer Road, Winona, MN 55987-0409

Minnesota State Community and Technical College
Fergus Falls, Minnesota
www.minnesota.edu   **CB code: 2110**

- Public 2-year community and technical college
- Commuter campus in large town

General. Founded in 1960. Regionally accredited. Campuses in Detroit Lakes, Fergus Falls, Moorhead, and Wadena. Online programs available through E campus and we offer credit and non-credit courses through customized training/CTS and our Business Entrepreneur Center. **Enrollment:** 4,491 degree-seeking undergraduates; 1,876 non-degree-seeking students. **Degrees:** 1,035 associate awarded. **Location:** 180 miles from Minneapolis-St. Paul, 60 miles from Fargo, ND. **Calendar:** Semester, limited summer session. **Full-time faculty:** 154 total. **Part-time faculty:** 122 total. **Partnerships:** Formal partnerships with local high schools and local and national corporations.

Student profile. Among degree-seeking undergraduates, 1,077 enrolled as first-time, first-year students.

Part-time:	44%	Women:	58%
Out-of-state:	33%	Live on campus:	10%

Transfer out. Colleges most students transferred to 2015: Minnesota State University: Moorhead, St. Cloud State University, Bemidji State University, Minnesota State University: Mankato, University of Minnesota: Twin Cities, North Dakota State University.

Basis for selection. Open admission. **Home schooled:** Transcript of courses and grades required. **Learning Disabled:** Special accommodations available for students during placement assessment tests.

2015-2016 Annual costs. Tuition/fees: $5,361; $5,361 out-of-state. Per-credit charge: $160.8 in-state; $160.8 out-of-state. Room only: $3,000. **Additional information:** Students can buy a meal card with a starting balance of $900 per semester ($1,800) per academic year.

Financial aid. Need-based: Need-based aid available for part-time students. Work-study available nights, weekends and for part-time students. **Non-need-based:** Scholarships awarded for academics, art, leadership, minority status, music/drama, state residency.

Application procedures. Admission: $20 fee, may be waived for applicants with need. Admission notification on a rolling basis. **Financial aid:** Priority date 6/1; no closing date. FAFSA required. Applicants notified on a rolling basis starting 7/1.

Academics. Special study options: Accelerated study, distance learning, double major, dual enrollment of high school students, ESL, independent study, internships, liberal arts/career combination. License preparation in dental hygiene, nursing, radiology. **Credit/placement by examination:** AP, CLEP, IB, institutional tests. **Support services:** Learning center, pre-admission summer program, reduced course load, remedial instruction, study skills assistance, tutoring, writing center.

Majors. Biology: General. **Business:** General, accounting, administrative services, business admin, construction management, entrepreneurial studies, human resources, management information systems, marketing, office technology, sales/distribution. **Computer sciences:** Information technology, networking, programming, security, web page design. **Conservation:** Environmental studies. **Education:** Teacher assistance. **Engineering:** General. **Foreign languages:** Sign language interpretation. **General:** Carpentry, lineworker, plumbing, site management. **Health services:** Clinical lab technology, dental assistant, dental hygiene, health information technology, licensed practical nurse, medical secretary, nursing (RN), pharmacy assistant, radiologic technology/medical imaging, surgical technology. **Liberal arts:** Arts/sciences. **Protective services:** Criminal justice. **Visual/performing arts:** Graphic design, music, studio arts.

Most popular majors. Business/marketing 13%, health sciences 34%, liberal arts 33%.

Technology on campus. 600 workstations in dormitories, library, computer center, student center. Dormitories wired for high-speed internet access and linked to campus network. Commuter students can connect to campus network. Online course registration, online library, helpline, repair service, wireless network available.

Student life. Freshman orientation: Mandatory. Preregistration for classes offered. 3-5 hour session held in summer. **Policies:** Alcoholic beverages prohibited in dorms. **Housing:** Coed dorms, apartments available. $200 deposit, deadline 7/1. **Activities:** Bands, choral groups, dance, drama, music ensembles, musical theater, student government, student newspaper, CACTUS (campus diversity organization), United for Africa, Phi Theta Kappa,

Two-Year Colleges

Business Professionals of America, Ignite (Campus Crusade for Christ), Delta Epsilon Chi, nursing student organizations, Skills USA.

Athletics. NJCAA. **Intercollegiate:** Baseball M, basketball, football (tackle) M, golf, softball W, volleyball W. **Intramural:** Basketball, bowling, football (non-tackle), football (tackle) M, golf, soccer, softball, table tennis, volleyball. **Team name:** Spartans.

Student services. Adult student services, alcohol/substance abuse counseling, career counseling, student employment services, financial aid counseling, minority student services, personal counseling, placement for graduates, veterans' counselor, women's services. **Physically disabled:** Services for visually, speech, hearing impaired. **Transfer:** Transfer adviser, college fairs on campus for students transferring to 4-year colleges.

Contact. E-mail: enroll@minnesota.edu
Toll-free number: (877) 450-3322 Fax: (218) 736-1510
Kyle Johnston, Director of Admissions, Minnesota State Community and Technical College, 405 Colfax Avenue SW, Wadena, MN 56482-1447

Minnesota West Community and Technical College
Pipestone, Minnesota
www.mnwest.edu   CB code: 6945

▸ Public 2-year community and technical college
▸ Commuter campus in large town

General. Founded in 1936. Regionally accredited. Campuses at Canby, Granite Falls, Jackson, Pipestone, and Worthington; learning centers in Luverne and Marshall. **Enrollment:** 1,753 degree-seeking undergraduates. **Degrees:** 390 associate awarded. **Location:** 200 miles from Minneapolis-St. Paul, 60 miles from Sioux Falls, South Dakota. **Calendar:** Semester, extensive summer session. **Full-time faculty:** 81 total. **Part-time faculty:** 9 total.

Transfer out. Colleges most students transferred to 2015: Southwest Minnesota State University, Minnesota State University - Mankato, South Dakota State University.

Basis for selection. Open admission, but selective for some programs. PSB-Aptitude for Practical Nursing Examination required of nursing applicants. Test scores not required for continuing education students. Interview recommended. **Home schooled:** Transcript of courses and grades required.

2015-2016 Annual costs. Tuition/fees: $5,677; $5,677 out-of-state. Per-credit charge: $172. Books/supplies: $1,200. Personal expenses: $1,908.

2014-2015 Financial aid. Need-based: 62% of total undergraduate aid awarded as scholarships/grants, 38% as loans/jobs. Need-based aid available for part-time students. Work-study available nights, weekends and for part-time students.

Application procedures. Admission: No deadline. $20 fee. Admission notification on a rolling basis. Priority deadline for practical nursing applicants is 2/15. **Financial aid:** Priority date 6/9; no closing date. FAFSA required. Applicants notified on a rolling basis starting 4/9; must reply within 2 week(s) of notification.

Academics. Special study options: Cooperative education, cross-registration, distance learning, double major, dual enrollment of high school students, independent study, internships, liberal arts/career combination, student-designed major. License preparation in nursing, radiology. **Credit/placement by examination:** AP, CLEP, IB, institutional tests. **Support services:** GED test center, learning center, pre-admission summer program, reduced course load, remedial instruction, study skills assistance, tutoring.

Majors. Biology: General. **Business:** General, accounting, accounting/business management, accounting/finance, administrative services, business admin, executive assistant, office management. **Communications:** Communications/speech/rhetoric, media studies. **Computer sciences:** General. **Education:** General, business, elementary, physical, secondary, special ed. **Engineering:** General. **English:** English lit. **General:** Electrician, lineworker, power transmission. **Health services:** Clinical lab technology, dental assistant, medical assistant, medical secretary, nursing (RN), predental, premedicine, prenursing, prepharmacy, preveterinary, radiologic technology/medical imaging. **History:** General. **Liberal arts:** Arts/sciences. **Math:** General. **Philosophy/religion:** Philosophy. **Physical sciences:** Chemistry, physics. **Protective services:** Corrections, law enforcement admin, police science. **Psychology:** General. **Social sciences:** Economics, geography, political science, sociology. **Visual/performing arts:** General, art, music. **Work/family studies:** Child care management.

Technology on campus. Online course registration, online library, helpline, wireless network available.

Student life. Freshman orientation: Mandatory. Preregistration for classes offered. Orientation is provided at each campus location and generally takes 3 hours to complete. Online orientation available for off-campus students. **Housing:** Subsidized apartments adjacent to campus. **Activities:** Jazz band, choral groups, drama, music ensembles, musical theater, student government, TV station, non-traditional student club, student senate, Phi Beta Kappa.

Athletics. NJCAA. **Intercollegiate:** Basketball, cheerleading, football (tackle) M, golf, softball W, volleyball W, wrestling M. **Team name:** Blue Jays.

Student services. Adult student services, career counseling, services for economically disadvantaged, student employment services, financial aid counseling, minority student services, veterans' counselor. **Physically disabled:** Services for visually, speech, hearing impaired. **Transfer:** Pre-admission transcript evaluation for new students. Transfer adviser, college fairs on campus for students transferring to 4-year colleges.

Contact. Phone: (800) 658-2330 Toll-free number: (800) 658-2330
Fax: (507) 825-4656
Dean of Admissions, Minnesota West Community and Technical College, 1314 North Hiawatha Avenue, Pipestone, MN 56164

Normandale Community College
Bloomington, Minnesota
www.normandale.edu   CB code: 6501

▸ Public 2-year community college
▸ Commuter campus in very large city

General. Founded in 1968. Regionally accredited. **Enrollment:** 8,516 degree-seeking undergraduates. **Degrees:** 1,127 associate awarded. **Location:** 12 miles from Minneapolis-St. Paul. **Calendar:** Semester, extensive summer session. **Full-time faculty:** 199 total; 11% minority, 51% women. **Part-time faculty:** 171 total; 9% minority, 57% women. **Special facilities:** Japanese garden, career and academic planning center, tutoring center, classroom technology, language and learning labs, hiking trails, fitness center, library.

Student profile.

Out-of-state:	1% **25 or older:**	35%

Transfer out. Colleges most students transferred to 2015: University of Minnesota, University of St. Thomas, Minnesota State University: Mankato, St. Cloud State University, Metropolitan State University.

Basis for selection. Open admission, but selective for some programs. Admission to health-related programs (dental hygiene, nursing, dietetic technology) based on cumulative GPA of college level courses and completion of specific course requirements. In-house placement tests in English, mathematics, reading may also be required. **Adult students:** SAT/ACT scores not required. **Home schooled:** Must provide immunization information. **Learning Disabled:** No special requirement for admission. For those seeking accommodations, once admitted must make an appointment with the Office for Students with Disabilities for an intake interview and to present documentation of the disability. Accommodations determined on a case by case basis.

2015-2016 Annual costs. Tuition/fees: $5,736; $5,736 out-of-state. Per-credit charge: $162 in-state; $162 out-of-state. Books/supplies: $1,458. Personal expenses: $4,406.

Financial aid. Need-based: Need-based aid available for part-time students. Work-study available nights, weekends and for part-time students. **Non-need-based:** Scholarships awarded for academics, art, leadership, music/drama, state residency.

Application procedures. Admission: Closing date 8/10 (postmark date). $20 fee, may be waived for applicants with need. Admission notification on a rolling basis. **Financial aid:** Priority date 4/1; no closing date. FAFSA required. Applicants notified on a rolling basis starting 4/15.

Academics. Special study options: Accelerated study, cooperative education, distance learning, double major, dual enrollment of high school students, ESL, honors, independent study, internships, liberal arts/career combination, study abroad, teacher certification program. Bachelor's degree programs available on campus. License preparation in dental hygiene, nursing. **Credit/placement by examination:** AP, CLEP, IB, institutional tests. No limit to the number of credits that can be applied toward a student's degree, provided the student meets the college's credits-in-residence requirement. **Support services:** Learning center, reduced course load, remedial instruction, study skills assistance, tutoring, writing center. Tutoring provided by faculty, professional staff and peer tutors. Online tutoring service available 24/7 for selected subjects. Supplemental instruction study sessions (informal student seminars in which students review notes, discuss readings, learn study sills and prepare for exams) also available.

Majors. Business: Accounting, hospitality admin, management information systems, marketing. **Computer sciences:** Computer science. **Education:** Elementary, special ed. **Engineering:** Pre-engineering. **English:** Creative writing. **Health services:** Dental hygiene, dietetic technician, nursing (RN), office computer specialist, radiologic technology/medical imaging. **Liberal arts:** Arts/sciences. **Protective services:** Criminal justice, police science. **Visual/performing arts:** Dramatic, music, studio arts, theater design.

Most popular majors. Health sciences 11%, liberal arts 71%.

Technology on campus. 575 workstations in library, computer center, student center. Commuter students can connect to campus network. Online course registration, online library, helpline, wireless network available.

Student life. Freshman orientation: Mandatory, $25 fee. Preregistration for classes offered. Advising and registration session held prior to the beginning of fall and spring semesters. Required for all degree seeking students for first time registration. Approximately 2 hours in length. Separate sessions for first-year, transfer, ESL and high school dual enrollment students. Review of academic programs and assistance with course selection and registration. **Activities:** Bands, choral groups, drama, literary magazine, music ensembles, musical theater, student government, student newspaper, Black Student Alliance, Campus Crusade for Christ, College Democrats, diversity student club, Ethiopian student union, Gay and Straight Alliance, InterVarsity Christian Fellowship, Latter-day Saints association, Muslim student association, Somali student association, Club Latino.

Athletics. Intramural: Archery, badminton, baseball, basketball, bowling, boxing, cross-country, fencing, field hockey, football (non-tackle), golf, handball, ice hockey, judo, racquetball, skiing, soccer, softball, table tennis, tennis, volleyball, weight lifting.

Student services. Adult student services, career counseling, services for economically disadvantaged, student employment services, financial aid counseling, on-campus daycare, personal counseling, placement for graduates, veterans' counselor. **Physically disabled:** Services for visually, speech, hearing impaired. **Transfer:** Pre-admission transcript evaluation for new students. Transfer adviser, college fairs on campus for students transferring to 4-year colleges.

Contact. E-mail: admissions@normandale.edu
Phone: (952) 358-8201 Toll-free number: (866) 880-8740
Fax: (952) 358-8230
Nancy Pates, Director of Admissions, Normandale Community College, 9700 France Avenue South, Bloomington, MN 55431

North Hennepin Community College
Brooklyn Park, Minnesota
www.nhcc.edu   CB code: 6498

▶ Public 2-year community college
▶ Commuter campus in small city

General. Founded in 1966. Regionally accredited. Member of the Minnesota State Colleges and Universities (MnSCU) system. **Enrollment:** 6,173 degree-seeking undergraduates; 674 non-degree-seeking students. **Degrees:** 844 associate awarded. **ROTC:** Army, Naval, Air Force. **Location:** 14 miles from downtown Minneapolis. **Calendar:** Semester, limited summer session. **Full-time faculty:** 132 total; 11% minority, 68% women. **Part-time faculty:** 159 total; 14% minority, 48% women. **Class size:** 41% < 20, 51% 20-39, 6% 40-49, 2% 50-99. **Special facilities:** Greenhouse, undergraduate research facilities in science programs.

Student profile. Among degree-seeking undergraduates, 1,114 enrolled as first-time, first-year students.

Part-time:	68%	Women:	58%
Out-of-state:	1%		

Transfer out. Colleges most students transferred to 2015: University of MN-TC, Metropolitan State University, St. Cloud State University.

Basis for selection. Open admission, but selective for some programs. Nursing, Medical Laboratory Technology, Histotechnology, and Paralegal programs have additional program admission requirements to complete after a student has been accepted. **Home schooled:** State high school equivalency certificate required.

High school preparation. College-preparatory program recommended.

2015-2016 Annual costs. Tuition/fees: $5,383; $5,383 out-of-state. Per-credit charge: $165. Books/supplies: $1,000.

2014-2015 Financial aid. Need-based: 56% of total undergraduate aid awarded as scholarships/grants, 44% as loans/jobs. Need-based aid available

for part-time students. Work-study available nights, weekends and for part-time students. **Non-need-based:** Scholarships awarded for academics, art, leadership. **Additional information:** Computerized financial aid application.

Application procedures. Admission: No deadline. $20 fee, may be waived for applicants with need. Admission notification on a rolling basis. Application deadline for regular start courses is one week before term begins. **Financial aid:** Priority date 4/15; no closing date. FAFSA required. Applicants notified on a rolling basis starting 6/1.

Academics. Special study options: Accelerated study, cross-registration, distance learning, double major, dual enrollment of high school students, ESL, honors, independent study, internships, student-designed major, study abroad, weekend college. Bachelor's degree programs available on campus. License preparation in nursing. **Credit/placement by examination:** AP, CLEP, IB, institutional tests. 30 credit hours maximum toward associate degree. **Support services:** GED test center, learning center, reduced course load, remedial instruction, study skills assistance, tutoring, writing center.

Majors. Biology: General. **Business:** Accounting, accounting technology, business admin, construction management, entrepreneurial studies, finance, management information systems, marketing. **Computer sciences:** Computer science. **Education:** General, physical. **Engineering:** Pre-engineering. **English:** Creative writing. **Health services:** Clinical lab technology, histologic assistant, nursing (RN). **Liberal arts:** Arts/sciences. **Math:** General. **Parks/recreation:** Health/fitness. **Physical sciences:** Chemistry. **Protective services:** Criminal justice, police science. **Visual/performing arts:** Dramatic, graphic design, music, studio arts.

Most popular majors. Business/marketing 16%, health sciences 16%, liberal arts 44%, security/protective services 11%.

Technology on campus. 1,060 workstations in library, computer center, student center. Online course registration, online library, wireless network available.

Student life. Freshman orientation: Mandatory. Preregistration for classes offered. Three-hour sessions held prior to the start of each term. **Activities:** Bands, choral groups, drama, international student organizations, literary magazine, musical theater, student government, symphony orchestra.

Athletics. Intramural: Basketball, bowling, football (non-tackle), lacrosse, soccer, softball, table tennis, volleyball, weight lifting.

Student services. Career counseling, services for economically disadvantaged, student employment services, financial aid counseling, legal services, minority student services, personal counseling, placement for graduates, veterans' counselor. **Physically disabled:** Services for visually, speech, hearing impaired. **Transfer:** Transfer adviser, college fairs on campus for students transferring to 4-year colleges.

Contact. E-mail: admission@nhcc.edu
Phone: (763) 424-0724 Toll-free number: (800) 818-0395
Fax: (763) 493-0563
Sean Olson, Associate Director of Admissions & Outreach, North Hennepin Community College, 7411 85th Avenue North, Brooklyn Park, MN 55445

Northland Community & Technical College
Thief River Falls, Minnesota
www.northlandcollege.edu   CB code: 6500

▶ Public 2-year community and technical college
▶ Commuter campus in small town

General. Founded in 1965. Regionally accredited. Campuses in East Grand Forks and Thief River Falls. An aerospace campus at the Thief River Falls Airport. **Enrollment:** 2,310 degree-seeking undergraduates; 1,182 non-degree-seeking students. **Degrees:** 612 associate awarded. **Calendar:** Semester, limited summer session. **Full-time faculty:** 91 total; 7% have terminal degrees, 3% minority, 50% women. **Part-time faculty:** 58 total; 2% minority, 48% women. **Class size:** 56% < 20, 41% 20-39, 3% 40-49.

Student profile. Among degree-seeking undergraduates, 45% enrolled in a transfer program, 55% enrolled in a vocational program, 450 enrolled as first-time, first-year students.

Part-time:	46%	Women:	56%
Out-of-state:	33%		

Transfer out. Colleges most students transferred to 2015: University of North Dakota, North Dakota State University, Bemidji State University, University of Minnesota - Crookston, Minnesota State University-Moorhead.

Two-Year Colleges

Basis for selection. Open admission, but selective for some programs. Special requirements for some programs such as cardiovascular technology, firefighter-paramedic, nursing, occupational therapy assistant, intensive care paramedic, pharmacy technology, physical therapist assistant, practical nursing, radiology, respiratory therapy, and surgical technology. Students are required to go through the ACCUPLACER assessment program to determine their level of mathematics, reading and English skills for course placement purposes if not exempt by completion of college coursework or ACT scores. **Home schooled:** Transcript of courses and grades required.

2015-2016 Annual costs. Tuition/fees: $5,534; $5,534 out-of-state. Per-credit charge: $165 in-state; $165 out-of-state. Books/supplies: $1,000. Personal expenses: $1,800.

Financial aid. All financial aid based on need. Need-based aid available for part-time students. Work-study available nights, weekends and for part-time students.

Application procedures. Admission: No deadline. $20 fee, may be waived for applicants with need. Admission notification on a rolling basis. **Financial aid:** Priority date 5/1; no closing date. FAFSA required. Applicants notified on a rolling basis starting 5/15.

Academics. Special study options: Distance learning, double major, dual enrollment of high school students, external degree, internships, liberal arts/career combination. License preparation in aviation, nursing, occupational therapy, paramedic, physical therapy, radiology. **Credit/placement by examination:** AP, CLEP, IB, institutional tests. 45 credit hours maximum toward associate degree. **Support services:** GED preparation and test center, learning center, reduced course load, remedial instruction, study skills assistance, tutoring, writing center.

Majors. Business: Accounting technology, administrative services, business admin, sales/distribution, special products marketing. **Computer sciences:** Networking, support specialist. **Education:** Teacher assistance. **Health services:** Dietetic technician, EMT paramedic, insurance coding, licensed practical nurse, medical secretary, nursing (RN), occupational therapy assistant, pharmacy assistant, physical therapy assistant, radiologic technology/medical imaging, respiratory therapy technology, surgical technology. **Liberal arts:** Arts/sciences. **Military:** Geospatial intel. **Protective services:** Fire safety technology, police science.

Most popular majors. Business/marketing 7%, health sciences 44%, liberal arts 33%.

Technology on campus. 356 workstations in library, computer center, student center. Commuter students can connect to campus network. Online course registration, online library, helpline, repair service, wireless network available.

Student life. Freshman orientation: Mandatory. Preregistration for classes offered. **Activities:** Bands, choral groups, dance, music ensembles, musical theater, radio station, student government, Phi Theta Kappa honor society, student senate, various program clubs.

Athletics. NJCAA. **Intercollegiate:** Baseball M, basketball, football (tackle) M, softball W, volleyball W, wrestling M. **Intramural:** Basketball, bowling, golf, ice hockey M, softball, tennis, volleyball. **Team name:** Pioneers.

Student services. Career counseling, financial aid counseling, minority student services, personal counseling, veterans' counselor, women's services. **Physically disabled:** Services for visually, speech, hearing impaired. **Transfer:** Re-entry adviser, pre-admission transcript evaluation for new students. Transfer adviser, college fairs on campus for students transferring to 4-year colleges.

Contact. E-mail: admissions@northlandcollege.edu
Phone: (218) 793-2389 Toll-free number: (800) 959-6282
Fax: (218) 793-2857
Holly Bergh, Admissions, Northland Community & Technical College, 2022 Central Avenue NE, East Grand Forks, MN 56721

Northwest Technical College
Bemidji, Minnesota
www.ntcmn.edu

CB code: 3626

▶ Public 2-year technical college
▶ Commuter campus in large town

General. Regionally accredited. Northwest Technical College is affiliated with Bemidji State University. **Enrollment:** 712 degree-seeking undergraduates; 402 non-degree-seeking students. **Degrees:** 152 associate awarded. **Location:** 229 miles from Minneapolis-St. Paul, 152 miles from Duluth.

Calendar: Semester, limited summer session. **Full-time faculty:** 28 total; 4% minority, 68% women. **Part-time faculty:** 45 total; 62% women. **Class size:** 77% < 20, 23% 20-39. **Special facilities:** American Indian resource center.

Student profile. Among degree-seeking undergraduates, 104 enrolled as first-time, first-year students, 140 transferred in from other institutions.

Part-time:	54%	Native American:	8%
Out-of-state:	7%	Multi-racial, non-Hispanic:	7%
Women:	71%	25 or older:	56%
African American:	2%	Live on campus:	4%
Hispanic/Latino:	2%		

Transfer out. Colleges most students transferred to 2015: Bemidji State University, Northland Community and Technical College, Minnesota State Community and Technical College.

Basis for selection. Open admission, but selective for some programs. Health programs require a background check. **Learning Disabled:** Learners with learning disabilities are encouraged to have an IEP on file with the Learning Services Coordinator and meet with the coordinator prior to the start of the semester to develop a Personal Education Plan.

2015-2016 Annual costs. Tuition/fees: $5,480; $5,480 out-of-state. Per-credit charge: $173 in-state; $173 out-of-state. Room/board: $7,690. Books/supplies: $1,600. Personal expenses: $1,600.

2014-2015 Financial aid. All financial aid based on need. 62% of total undergraduate aid awarded as scholarships/grants, 38% as loans/jobs. Need-based aid available for part-time students. Work-study available nights, weekends and for part-time students.

Application procedures. Admission: No deadline. $20 fee, may be waived for applicants with need. Admission notification on a rolling basis. **Financial aid:** Priority date 6/1; no closing date. FAFSA required. Applicants notified on a rolling basis starting 3/1.

Academics. NTC learners can take General Education courses from Bemidji State University and/or online from a regional consortium of colleges in fulfillment of general education requirements of degrees at NTC. **Special study options:** Cooperative education, cross-registration, distance learning, double major, dual enrollment of high school students, ESL, internships, liberal arts/career combination, student-designed major. Study abroad options are available through our partnership with Bemidji State University. License preparation in nursing. **Credit/placement by examination:** AP, CLEP, IB, institutional tests. A maximum of 25% of the required credits for a program major is allowed for credit for experiential learning. **Support services:** Learning center, reduced course load, remedial instruction, study skills assistance, tutoring.

Majors. Business: Accounting technology, administrative services, office management, sales/distribution. **Computer sciences:** Networking. **Health services:** Dental assistant, insurance coding, licensed practical nurse, medical secretary, nursing (RN), office admin. **Work/family studies:** Child care service, child development.

Most popular majors. Business/marketing 20%, health sciences 67%, trade and industry 8%.

Technology on campus. PC or laptop required. 140 workstations in dormitories, library, computer center, student center. Dormitories wired for high-speed internet access. Commuter students can connect to campus network. Online course registration, online library, helpline, repair service, wireless network available.

Student life. Freshman orientation: Mandatory. Preregistration for classes offered. One day orientation/registration sessions are held periodically during the 6 months prior to the start of fall and spring semesters. **Housing:** Coed dorms, special housing for disabled, apartments, themed housing available. $150 partly refundable deposit, deadline 8/1. Students may reside in Bemidji State University residence halls. **Activities:** Student government, Phi Theta Kappa, Skills USA.

Student services. Adult student services, career counseling, services for economically disadvantaged, student employment services, financial aid counseling, health services, minority student services, personal counseling, placement for graduates, veterans' counselor. **Physically disabled:** Services for visually, speech, hearing impaired. **Transfer:** Re-entry adviser, pre-admission transcript evaluation for new students. Transfer adviser, college fairs on campus for students transferring to 4-year colleges.

Contact. Phone: (218) 333-6647 Toll-free number: (800) 942-8324
Fax: (218) 333-6697
Michael Heitkamp, Associate VP for Admissions & Enrollment, Northwest Technical College, 905 Grant Avenue Southeast, Bemidji, MN 56601-4907

Pine Technical & Community College
Pine City, Minnesota
www.pine.edu

CB code: 7118

- Public 2-year technical college
- Commuter campus in small town

General. Regionally accredited. **Enrollment:** 1,083 undergraduates. **Degrees:** 78 associate awarded. **Location:** 60 miles from Minneapolis-St. Paul. **Calendar:** Semester, limited summer session. **Full-time faculty:** 29 total; 3% have terminal degrees, 66% women. **Part-time faculty:** 28 total; 14% minority, 50% women.

Transfer out. Colleges most students transferred to 2015: St. Cloud Technical College, Anoka-Ramsey Community College, Lake Superior Community College, Mesabi Community College, North Hennepin College.

Basis for selection. Open admission, but selective for some programs. Additional requirements for some majors; criminal history check. **Home schooled:** State high school equivalency certificate required.

High school preparation. College-preparatory program required.

2015-2016 Annual costs. Tuition/fees: $5,081; $9,676 out-of-state. Books/supplies: $1,150.

Financial aid. Need-based: Need-based aid available for part-time students. Work-study available nights, weekends and for part-time students. **Non-need-based:** Scholarships awarded for academics, state residency.

Application procedures. Admission: No deadline. No application fee. Admission notification on a rolling basis. **Financial aid:** Priority date 5/5; no closing date. FAFSA required. Applicants notified on a rolling basis starting 6/5.

Academics. Special study options: Cross-registration, distance learning, double major, dual enrollment of high school students, independent study, internships, liberal arts/career combination, student-designed major. License preparation in nursing. **Credit/placement by examination:** AP, CLEP, institutional tests. 35 credit hours maximum toward associate degree. **Support services:** Learning center, reduced course load, remedial instruction, study skills assistance, tutoring.

Majors. Business: Accounting, business admin. **Computer sciences:** Data processing, information systems, programming. **Work/family studies:** Child care management.

Technology on campus. 100 workstations in library, computer center, student center. Commuter students can connect to campus network. Online course registration, online library, helpline, wireless network available.

Student life. Freshman orientation: Mandatory. Preregistration for classes offered. Registration takes place after orientation. **Activities:** Student government.

Athletics. Team name: Pines.

Student services. Career counseling, services for economically disadvantaged, student employment services, financial aid counseling, on-campus daycare, personal counseling, placement for graduates. **Physically disabled:** Services for visually, hearing impaired. **Transfer:** Pre-admission transcript evaluation for new students. Transfer adviser, college fairs on campus for students transferring to 4-year colleges.

Contact. E-mail: information@pinetech.edu
Phone: (320) 629-5100 Toll-free number: (800) 521-7463
Fax: (320) 629-5101
Shawnda Schelinder, Director of Marketing and Enrollment, Pine Technical & Community College, 900 Fourth Street SE, Pine City, MN 55063

Rainy River Community College
International Falls, Minnesota
www.rainyriver.edu

CB code: 1637

- Public 2-year community and technical college
- Commuter campus in small town

General. Founded in 1967. Regionally accredited. **Enrollment:** 278 degree-seeking undergraduates. **Degrees:** 69 associate awarded. **Location:** 300 miles from Minneapolis-St. Paul, 150 miles from Duluth. **Calendar:** Semester, limited summer session. **Full-time faculty:** 8 total; 38% women. **Part-time faculty:** 15 total; 7% have terminal degrees, 13% minority, 33% women.

Student profile.

Part-time: 18% **Women:** 58%

Transfer out. Colleges most students transferred to 2015: St. Cloud State University, Bemidji State University, University of Minnesota-Duluth.

Basis for selection. Open admission.

2015-2016 Annual costs. Tuition/fees: $5,325; $6,507 out-of-state. Room/board: $3,840. Books/supplies: $800. Personal expenses: $1,800.

2015-2016 Financial aid. Need-based: 54% of total undergraduate aid awarded as scholarships/grants, 46% as loans/jobs. Need-based aid available for part-time students. Work-study available nights, weekends and for part-time students. **Non-need-based:** Scholarships awarded for academics, alumni affiliation, leadership, minority status, state residency. **Additional information:** Many scholarship and employment opportunities for applicants showing little or no need.

Application procedures. Admission: No deadline. $20 fee. Admission notification on a rolling basis. **Financial aid:** Priority date 6/1; no closing date. FAFSA, institutional form required. Applicants notified on a rolling basis starting 5/1; must reply within 3 week(s) of notification.

Academics. Special study options: Distance learning, dual enrollment of high school students, honors, independent study, internships, liberal arts/career combination. License preparation in nursing. **Credit/placement by examination:** AP, CLEP, IB, institutional tests. **Support services:** Learning center, pre-admission summer program, reduced course load, remedial instruction, study skills assistance, tutoring, writing center.

Majors. Area/ethnic studies: Native American. **Education:** Science. **Liberal arts:** Arts/sciences. **Math:** General.

Most popular majors. Liberal arts 99%.

Technology on campus. 100 workstations in dormitories, library, computer center, student center. Dormitories wired for high-speed internet access. Online course registration available.

Student life. Freshman orientation: Mandatory. Preregistration for classes offered. **Housing:** Special housing for disabled, apartments available. $200 deposit. Student housing lobby equipped with computers, wireless available throughout building. **Activities:** Choral groups, drama, literary magazine, music ensembles, musical theater, student government, Black Student Association club, Native Student club, environment club.

Athletics. NJCAA. **Intercollegiate:** Baseball M, basketball, ice hockey W, softball W, volleyball W. **Intramural:** Archery, badminton, bowling, cheerleading, cross-country, golf, racquetball, skiing, softball, table tennis, tennis, volleyball. **Team name:** Voyageurs.

Student services. Adult student services, career counseling, services for economically disadvantaged, student employment services, financial aid counseling, minority student services, personal counseling, placement for graduates, veterans' counselor. **Physically disabled:** Services for visually, speech, hearing impaired. **Transfer:** Re-entry adviser, pre-admission transcript evaluation for new students. Transfer adviser, college fairs on campus for students transferring to 4-year colleges.

Contact. E-mail: admissions@rainyriver.edu
Phone: (218) 285-2207 Toll-free number: (800) 456-3996
Fax: (218) 285-2314
Berta Hagen, Registrar, Rainy River Community College, 1501 Highway 71, International Falls, MN 56649

Rasmussen College: Bloomington
Bloomington, Minnesota
www.rasmussen.edu

CB member
CB code: 2448

- For-profit 2-year branch campus and career college
- Commuter campus in small city

General. Regionally accredited. **Enrollment:** 809 degree-seeking undergraduates. **Degrees:** 50 bachelor's, 134 associate awarded. **Location:** 10 miles from Minneapolis-St. Paul. **Calendar:** Quarter. **Full-time faculty:** 11 total. **Part-time faculty:** 41 total.

Basis for selection. Open admission, but selective for some programs. Programs in allied health, justice studies, and education require students to complete a background check. **Adult students:** SAT/ACT scores not required.

2016-2017 Annual costs. Tuition/fees (projected): $13,455. Per-credit charge: $299. Personal expenses: $2,214.

Financial aid. Need-based: Need-based aid available for part-time students. Work-study available nights, weekends and for part-time students.

Application procedures. Admission: No deadline. No application fee. Admission notification on a rolling basis. **Financial aid:** No deadline. FAFSA, institutional form required. Applicants notified on a rolling basis.

Academics. Special study options: Distance learning, double major, honors, independent study, internships. **Credit/placement by examination:** AP, CLEP. 45 credit hours maximum toward associate degree, 90 toward bachelor's. Credit limited to specific programs and to courses for which examinations are available. 50% of the student's program credits must be completed through coursework at Rasmussen College. **Support services:** Learning center, remedial instruction, study skills assistance, tutoring, writing center.

Majors. Business: Accounting, business admin, human resources, management information systems, marketing. **Computer sciences:** Support specialist, web page design. **Education:** Teacher assistance. **Engineering:** Software. **Health services:** Health information technology, medical assistant, medical secretary, nursing (RN), pharmacy assistant. **Protective services:** Criminal justice. **Visual/performing arts:** Game design.

Technology on campus. 100 workstations in library, computer center, student center. Online course registration, online library, helpline, wireless network available.

Student life. Freshman orientation: Mandatory. Preregistration for classes offered.

Student services. Adult student services, career counseling, services for economically disadvantaged, student employment services, financial aid counseling, placement for graduates.

Contact. Phone: (952) 545-2000 Toll-free number: (800) 852-0929 Susan Hammerstrom, Director of Admissions, Rasmussen College: Bloomington, 4400 West 78th Street, Bloomington, MN 55435

Rasmussen College: Brooklyn Park
Brooklyn Park, Minnesota
www.rasmussen.edu   CB code: 6730

- For-profit 2-year branch campus and career college
- Commuter campus in small city

General. Regionally accredited. **Enrollment:** 654 degree-seeking undergraduates. **Degrees:** 74 bachelor's, 133 associate awarded. **Location:** 10 miles from Minneapolis-St. Paul. **Calendar:** Quarter. **Full-time faculty:** 13 total. **Part-time faculty:** 35 total.

Basis for selection. Open admission, but selective for some programs. Programs in allied health, justice studies, and education require students to complete a background check. **Adult students:** SAT/ACT scores not required.

2016-2017 Annual costs. Tuition/fees (projected): $13,455. Per-credit charge: $299. Personal expenses: $2,214.

Financial aid. Need-based: Need-based aid available for part-time students. Work-study available nights, weekends and for part-time students.

Application procedures. Admission: No deadline. No application fee. Admission notification on a rolling basis. **Financial aid:** No deadline. FAFSA, institutional form required. Applicants notified on a rolling basis.

Academics. Special study options: Distance learning, double major, honors, independent study, internships. **Credit/placement by examination:** AP, CLEP, institutional tests. 45 credit hours maximum toward associate degree, 90 toward bachelor's. Credit limited to specific programs and to courses for which examinations are available. 50% of a student's program credits must be completed through coursework at Rasmussen College. **Support services:** Learning center, remedial instruction, study skills assistance, tutoring, writing center.

Majors. Business: Accounting, business admin, human resources, management information systems, marketing. **Computer sciences:** Support specialist, web page design. **Education:** Teacher assistance. **Engineering:** Software. **Health services:** Health information technology, licensed practical nurse, massage therapy, medical assistant, medical secretary, pharmacy assistant, surgical technology. **Protective services:** Criminal justice. **Visual/performing arts:** Game design.

Technology on campus. 100 workstations in library, computer center, student center. Online course registration, online library, helpline, wireless network available.

Student life. Freshman orientation: Mandatory. Preregistration for classes offered.

Student services. Adult student services, career counseling, services for economically disadvantaged, student employment services, financial aid counseling, placement for graduates.

Contact. Phone: (763) 493-4500 Toll-free number: (877) 495-4500 Susan Hammerstrom, Director of Admissions, Rasmussen College: Brooklyn Park, 8301 93rd Avenue North, Brooklyn Park, MN 55445

Rasmussen College: Eagan
Eagan, Minnesota
www.rasmussen.edu   CB code: 2449

- For-profit 2-year career college
- Commuter campus in small city

General. Regionally accredited. **Enrollment:** 629 degree-seeking undergraduates. **Degrees:** 70 bachelor's, 88 associate awarded. **Location:** 12 miles from Minneapolis-St. Paul. **Calendar:** Quarter. **Full-time faculty:** 14 total. **Part-time faculty:** 71 total.

Basis for selection. Open admission, but selective for some programs. Programs in health sciences, justice studies, nursing, and education require students to complete a background check. **Adult students:** SAT/ACT scores not required.

2016-2017 Annual costs. Tuition/fees (projected): $13,455. Per-credit charge: $299. Personal expenses: $2,214.

Financial aid. Need-based: Need-based aid available for part-time students. Work-study available nights, weekends and for part-time students.

Application procedures. Admission: No deadline. No application fee. Admission notification on a rolling basis. **Financial aid:** No deadline. FAFSA, institutional form required. Applicants notified on a rolling basis.

Academics. Special study options: Distance learning, double major, honors, independent study, internships. **Credit/placement by examination:** AP, CLEP, institutional tests. 45 credit hours maximum toward associate degree, 90 toward bachelor's. Credit limited to specific programs and to courses for which examinations are available. 50% of the student's program credits must be completed through coursework at Rasmussen College. **Support services:** Learning center, remedial instruction, study skills assistance, tutoring, writing center.

Majors. Business: Accounting, business admin, human resources, management information systems, marketing. **Computer sciences:** Support specialist, web page design. **Education:** Teacher assistance. **Engineering:** Software. **Health services:** Health information technology, licensed practical nurse, medical assistant, medical secretary, pharmacy assistant. **Protective services:** Criminal justice. **Visual/performing arts:** Game design.

Technology on campus. 100 workstations in library, computer center, student center. Online course registration, online library, helpline, wireless network available.

Student life. Freshman orientation: Mandatory. Preregistration for classes offered.

Student services. Adult student services, career counseling, services for economically disadvantaged, student employment services, financial aid counseling, placement for graduates.

Contact. Phone: (651) 687-9000 Toll-free number: (800) 852-6367 Fax: (651) 687-0507 Susan Hammerstrom, Director of Admissions, Rasmussen College: Eagan, 3500 Federal Drive, Eagan, MN 55122

Rasmussen College: Mankato
Mankato, Minnesota
www.rasmussen.edu   CB code: 2453

- For-profit 2-year career college
- Commuter campus in large town

General. Founded in 1983. Regionally accredited. **Enrollment:** 672 degree-seeking undergraduates. **Degrees:** 64 bachelor's, 176 associate awarded. **Location:** 60 miles from Minneapolis-St. Paul. **Calendar:** Quarter. **Full-time faculty:** 19 total. **Part-time faculty:** 40 total.

Basis for selection. Open admission, but selective for some programs. The Medical Laboratory Technician and Practical Nursing AAS programs have selective admissions requirements, including entrance examinations, background checks, and health screenings. Some additional programs in health sciences, justice studies, and education require students to complete a background check. **Adult students:** SAT/ACT scores not required.

2016-2017 Annual costs. Tuition/fees (projected): $13,455. Per-credit charge: $299. Personal expenses: $2,214.

Financial aid. Need-based: Need-based aid available for part-time students. Work-study available nights, weekends and for part-time students.

Application procedures. Admission: No deadline. No application fee. Admission notification on a rolling basis. **Financial aid:** No deadline. FAFSA, institutional form required. Applicants notified on a rolling basis.

Academics. Special study options: Distance learning, double major, honors, independent study, internships. **Credit/placement by examination:** AP, CLEP, IB, institutional tests. 45 credit hours maximum toward associate degree, 90 toward bachelor's. Credit limited to specific programs and to courses for which examinations are available. 50% of the student's program must be completed through coursework at Rasmussen College. **Support services:** Learning center, remedial instruction, study skills assistance, tutoring, writing center.

Majors. Business: Accounting, business admin, human resources, management information systems, marketing. **Computer sciences:** Support specialist, web page design. **Education:** Teacher assistance. **Engineering:** Software. **Health services:** Clinical lab technology, health information technology, licensed practical nurse, massage therapy, medical assistant, medical secretary, nursing (RN), pharmacy assistant. **Protective services:** Criminal justice. **Visual/performing arts:** Game design.

Technology on campus. 100 workstations in library, computer center, student center. Online course registration, online library, helpline available.

Student life. Freshman orientation: Mandatory. Preregistration for classes offered.

Student services. Adult student services, career counseling, services for economically disadvantaged, student employment services, financial aid counseling, placement for graduates.

Contact. Phone: (507) 625-6556 Toll-free number: (800) 657-6767 Fax: (507) 625-6557
Susan Hammerstrom, Director of Admissions, Rasmussen College: Mankato, 130 Saint Andrews Drive, Mankato, MN 56001

Rasmussen College: St. Cloud
St. Cloud, Minnesota
www.rasmussen.edu   CB code: 3315

▶ For-profit 2-year career college
▶ Commuter campus in small city

General. Regionally accredited. **Enrollment:** 834 degree-seeking undergraduates. **Degrees:** 52 bachelor's, 201 associate awarded. **Location:** 60 miles from Minneapolis-St. Paul. **Calendar:** Quarter. **Full-time faculty:** 16 total. **Part-time faculty:** 50 total.

Basis for selection. Open admission, but selective for some programs. Medical Laboratory Technician, Surgical Technologist, and Practical Nursing AAS programs have additional requirements, including entrance examinations, background checks, and health screenings. Other programs in health science, justice studies, and education require students to complete a background check. **Adult students:** SAT/ACT scores not required.

2016-2017 Annual costs. Tuition/fees (projected): $13,455. Per-credit charge: $299. Personal expenses: $2,214.

Financial aid. Need-based: Need-based aid available for part-time students. Work-study available nights, weekends and for part-time students.

Application procedures. Admission: No deadline. No application fee. Admission notification on a rolling basis. **Financial aid:** No deadline. FAFSA, institutional form required. Applicants notified on a rolling basis.

Academics. Special study options: Distance learning, double major, honors, independent study, internships. **Credit/placement by examination:** AP, CLEP, institutional tests. 45 credit hours maximum toward associate degree, 90 toward bachelor's. Credit limited to specific programs and to courses for which examinations are available. 50% of a student's program credits must be completed through coursework at Rasmussen College. **Support services:**

Learning center, remedial instruction, study skills assistance, tutoring, writing center.

Majors. Business: Accounting, business admin, human resources, management information systems, marketing. **Computer sciences:** Support specialist, web page design. **Education:** Teacher assistance. **Engineering:** Software. **Health services:** Clinical lab technology, health information technology, licensed practical nurse, medical assistant, medical secretary, nursing (RN), pharmacy assistant, surgical technology. **Protective services:** Criminal justice, police science. **Visual/performing arts:** Game design.

Technology on campus. 100 workstations in library, computer center, student center. Online course registration, online library, helpline, wireless network available.

Student life. Freshman orientation: Mandatory. Preregistration for classes offered.

Student services. Adult student services, career counseling, services for economically disadvantaged, student employment services, financial aid counseling, placement for graduates.

Contact. Phone: (320) 251-5600 Toll-free number: (800) 852-0460 Fax: (320) 251-3702
Susan Hammerstrom, Director of Admissions, Rasmussen College: St. Cloud, 226 Park Avenue South, St. Cloud, MN 56301-3713

Ridgewater College
Willmar, Minnesota
www.ridgewater.edu   CB code: 4924

▶ Public 2-year community and technical college
▶ Commuter campus in large town

General. Founded in 1961. Regionally accredited. Two campuses: Willmar and Hutchinson. **Enrollment:** 3,438 undergraduates. **Degrees:** 631 associate awarded. **Location:** 100 miles from Minneapolis-St. Paul. **Calendar:** Semester, limited summer session. **Special facilities:** Natural wooded prairie and wetlands areas for biological study, nursing simulation centers.

Basis for selection. Open admission, but selective for some programs. Special requirements for practical nursing, registered nursing, chemical dependency counseling, veterinary technology, and post-secondary programs. An interview is recommended for the law enforcement, nursing, and veterinary technology programs.

High school preparation. Chemistry and mathematics are recommended for mathematics, science, and health science majors.

2015-2016 Annual costs. Tuition/fees: $5,402; $5,402 out-of-state.

Financial aid. Need-based: Need-based aid available for part-time students. Work-study available nights, weekends and for part-time students. **Additional information:** Special funds are available for adult transfer students returning or continuing education after a 7-year absence from academic training. ALLISS grants provide reimbursement for one class, up to five credits for one semester.

Application procedures. Admission: Priority date 8/1; no deadline. $20 fee. Admission notification on a rolling basis. **Financial aid:** No deadline. FAFSA, institutional form required. Applicants notified on a rolling basis.

Academics. Special study options: Combined bachelor's/graduate degree, cooperative education, distance learning, dual enrollment of high school students, internships, liberal arts/career combination, student-designed major, study abroad. Bachelor's degree programs available on campus. License preparation in nursing, paramedic. **Credit/placement by examination:** AP, CLEP, institutional tests. **Support services:** Learning center, pre-admission summer program, reduced course load, remedial instruction, study skills assistance, tutoring.

Majors. Biology: General, conservation. **Business:** General, accounting, management information systems, marketing, retailing, sales/distribution. **Communications:** Communications/speech/rhetoric, journalism, media studies, publishing. **Communications technology:** Desktop publishing. **Computer sciences:** General, computer science, networking, web page design, webmaster. **Education:** General, art, business, educational technology, elementary, health, mathematics, middle, multi-level teacher, music, physical, science, secondary, special ed, teacher assistance, voc/tech. **English:** English lit, rhetoric/composition. **General:** Carpentry, electrician. **Health services:** Athletic training, health care admin, health information technology, medical assistant, medical radiologic technology/radiation therapy, medical secretary, nursing (RN), substance abuse counseling, veterinary technology/assistant. **History:** General. **Human services:** Social work. **Liberal arts:** Arts/sciences.

Math: General. **Parks/recreation:** General, health/fitness. **Physical sciences:** Chemistry, geology. **Protective services:** Criminal justice, police science. **Psychology:** General. **Social sciences:** General, criminology, economics, political science, sociology, urban studies. **Visual/performing arts:** Art, commercial photography, music, photography, studio arts. **Work/family studies:** Family studies.

Technology on campus. 1,000 workstations in library, computer center. Commuter students can connect to campus network. Online course registration, online library, helpline, repair service, wireless network available.

Student life. Freshman orientation: Mandatory. Preregistration for classes offered. **Housing:** Apartment buildings are adjacent to campus. **Activities:** Choral groups, drama, music ensembles, musical theater, student government, Multicultural club, Phi Theta Kappa, PRISM (LGBTQ organization).

Athletics. NJCAA. **Intercollegiate:** Volleyball W. **Team name:** Warriors.

Student services. Adult student services, alcohol/substance abuse counseling, career counseling, services for economically disadvantaged, student employment services, financial aid counseling, health services, minority student services, personal counseling, placement for graduates, veterans' counselor. **Physically disabled:** Services for visually, speech, hearing impaired. **Transfer:** Transfer adviser, college fairs on campus for students transferring to 4-year colleges.

Contact. E-mail: info@ridgewater.edu
Phone: (320) 222-5976 Toll-free number: (800) 722-1151
Fax: (320) 222-5216
Sally Kerfeld, Director of Admissions, Ridgewater College, 2101 15th Avenue Northwest, Willmar, MN 56201

Riverland Community College
Austin, Minnesota
www.riverland.edu
CB code: 6017

• Public 2-year community and technical college
• Commuter campus in large town

General. Founded in 1996. Regionally accredited. **Enrollment:** 2,173 degree-seeking undergraduates. **Degrees:** 410 associate awarded. **Location:** 90 miles from Minneapolis-St. Paul. **Calendar:** Semester, limited summer session. **Full-time faculty:** 82 total. **Part-time faculty:** 69 total. **Class size:** 68% < 20, 29% 20-39, 2% 40-49, less than 1% 50-99. **Special facilities:** Several programs include simulation labs (nursing/healthcare, law enforcement, emergency medical/fire, other), customer service labs (cosmetology, massage, automotive, collision, diesel, other), nursing clinicals with the Mayo health system.

Student profile.

Out-of-state:	2%	Live on campus: 3%
25 or older:	46%	

Transfer out. Colleges most students transferred to 2015: Mankato State University, Winona State University, Southwest Minnesota State University.

Basis for selection. Open admission, but selective for some programs. Special requirements for human services, nursing, corrections, radiography, massage therapy, construction electrician, and wind turbine technician programs. **Home schooled:** Transcript of courses and grades required.

High school preparation. Chemistry required of nursing applicants.

2015-2016 Annual costs. Tuition/fees: $5,539; $5,539 out-of-state. Per-credit charge: $165. Room only: $3,000. Books/supplies: $1,000. Personal expenses: $4,346.

2014-2015 Financial aid. Need-based: 44% of total undergraduate aid awarded as scholarships/grants, 56% as loans/jobs. Need-based aid available for part-time students. Work-study available nights, weekends and for part-time students. **Additional information:** One class tuition-free for Minnesota residents over 25 who have not attended college for at least 7 years.

Application procedures. Admission: No deadline. $20 fee, may be waived for applicants with need. Admission notification on a rolling basis. **Financial aid:** Priority date 5/15; no closing date. FAFSA required. Applicants notified on a rolling basis; must reply within 5 week(s) of notification.

Academics. Special study options: Cross-registration, distance learning, double major, dual enrollment of high school students, ESL, independent study, internships, liberal arts/career combination, study abroad. Bachelor's degree programs available on campus. License preparation in nursing, radiology. **Credit/placement by examination:** AP, CLEP, IB, institutional tests.

Support services: Learning center, pre-admission summer program, reduced course load, remedial instruction, study skills assistance, tutoring, writing center.

Majors. Business: Accounting, administrative services, management science. **Computer sciences:** General, LAN/WAN management. **Engineering:** Software. **Health services:** Medical radiologic technology/radiation therapy, medical secretary, nursing (RN). **Liberal arts:** Arts/sciences. **Protective services:** Police science.

Most popular majors. Business/marketing 8%, health sciences 23%, liberal arts 51%, security/protective services 6%.

Technology on campus. 250 workstations in library, computer center, student center. Online course registration, online library, helpline, wireless network available.

Student life. Freshman orientation: Mandatory. Preregistration for classes offered. **Housing:** $350 partly refundable deposit, deadline 9/1. College foundation-owned student housing available; alcohol/drug/smoke-free. **Activities:** Concert band, choral groups, drama, international student organizations, music ensembles, musical theater, student government, student newspaper, Diversity club, DEEDS (Human Service) club, Criminal Justice Society, GLBTQ, Amnesty International, Student Ambassadors, Older, Wiser Learners, Phi Theta Kappa.

Athletics. NJCAA. **Intercollegiate:** Baseball M, basketball, soccer M, softball W, volleyball W. **Intramural:** Basketball, football (tackle) M, weight lifting. **Team name:** Blue Devils.

Student services. Alcohol/substance abuse counseling, career counseling, services for economically disadvantaged, student employment services, financial aid counseling, minority student services, on-campus daycare, personal counseling, placement for graduates, veterans' counselor, women's services. **Physically disabled:** Services for visually, speech, hearing impaired. **Transfer:** Transfer adviser, college fairs on campus for students transferring to 4-year colleges.

Contact. E-mail: admissions@riverland.edu
Phone: (507) 433-0600 Toll-free number: (800) 247-5039
Fax: (507) 433-0515
Sue Jech, Director of Enrollment Services/Registrar, Riverland Community College, 1900 Eighth Avenue, NW, Austin, MN 55912-1407

Rochester Community and Technical College
Rochester, Minnesota
www.rctc.edu
CB code: 6610

• Public 2-year community and technical college
• Commuter campus in small city

General. Founded in 1915. Regionally accredited. **Enrollment:** 6,062 undergraduates. **Degrees:** 829 associate awarded. **Location:** 80 miles from Minneapolis-St. Paul. **Calendar:** Semester, limited summer session. **Full-time faculty:** 131 total. **Part-time faculty:** 149 total. **Class size:** 57% < 20, 42% 20-39, less than 1% 40-49, less than 1% 50-99, less than 1% >100. **Special facilities:** Observatory, dental clinic, horticulture technology facility, regional sports center.

Student profile.

Out-of-state:	5%	25 or older: 37%

Transfer out. Colleges most students transferred to 2015: Winona State University, Minnesota State College: Mankato, University of Minnesota.

Basis for selection. Open admission, but selective for some programs. Admission to allied health and technology programs based on course work, class rank, institutional placement test scores. **Adult students:** SAT/ACT scores not required.

High school preparation. Biology, chemistry, algebra and/or English required for some programs.

2015-2016 Annual costs. Tuition/fees: $5,637; $5,637 out-of-state. Per-credit charge: $164. Books/supplies: $1,600. Personal expenses: $5,200.

Financial aid. Need-based: Need-based aid available for part-time students. Work-study available nights, weekends and for part-time students.

Application procedures. Admission: Priority date 6/1; deadline 8/10 (postmark date). $20 fee, may be waived for applicants with need. Admission notification on a rolling basis. **Financial aid:** Priority date 4/15; no closing date. FAFSA required. Applicants notified on a rolling basis.

Academics. Special study options: Distance learning, dual enrollment of high school students, honors, independent study, internships, study abroad. 2+2 and other career pathways spanning certificate to master's degree programs through a partnership with Winona State University and other 4-year institutions. Bachelor's degree programs available on campus. License preparation in dental hygiene, nursing, paramedic. **Credit/placement by examination:** AP, CLEP, institutional tests. 16 credit hours maximum toward associate degree. **Support services:** Learning center, reduced course load, remedial instruction, study skills assistance, tutoring, writing center.

Majors. Biology: Biomedical sciences. **Business:** Accounting, administrative services, business admin, office management, retailing, special products marketing. **Communications:** Digital media, media studies. **Computer sciences:** Computer science, information systems, web page design. **Conservation:** Environmental science. **Education:** Music. **Engineering:** General. **General:** Maintenance. **Health services:** Cardiovascular technology, dental assistant, dental hygiene, electroencephalograph technology, EMT paramedic, health information technology, medical secretary, mental health services, nursing (RN), radiologic technology/medical imaging, surgical technology, veterinary technology/assistant. **Liberal arts:** Arts/sciences. **Parks/recreation:** Sports admin. **Protective services:** Criminal justice, police science. **Visual/performing arts:** Graphic design, music management, music technology, music theory/composition, studio arts. **Work/family studies:** Child care management, child development.

Most popular majors. Business/marketing 7%, health sciences 30%, interdisciplinary studies 11%, liberal arts 32%.

Technology on campus. 450 workstations in library, computer center. Commuter students can connect to campus network. Online course registration, online library, helpline available.

Student life. Freshman orientation: Available. Preregistration for classes offered. **Housing:** Non-college-affiliated student-only housing available near campus. **Activities:** Bands, choral groups, dance, drama, international student organizations, music ensembles, musical theater, radio station, student government, student newspaper, student senate, ECHO (student newspaper), Asian student association, African student organization, Muslim student association, environmentalism club, Armed Forces and Veterans club, Circle of Friends-GLBTQA, international student association, law enforcement club.

Athletics. NJCAA. Intercollegiate: Baseball M, basketball, football (tackle) M, golf, soccer W, softball W, volleyball W, wrestling M. **Intramural:** Badminton, basketball, football (non-tackle), golf, soccer, softball, volleyball. **Team name:** Yellowjackets.

Student services. Alcohol/substance abuse counseling, career counseling, services for economically disadvantaged, financial aid counseling, health services, minority student services, on-campus daycare, personal counseling, veterans' counselor. **Physically disabled:** Services for visually, speech, hearing impaired. **Transfer:** Pre-admission transcript evaluation for new students. Transfer adviser, college fairs on campus for students transferring to 4-year colleges.

Contact. E-mail: getinfo@rctc.roch.edu
Phone: (507) 285-7265 Toll-free number: (800) 247-1296
Fax: (507) 280-3529
Holly Bigelow, Registrar, Rochester Community and Technical College, 851 30th Avenue SE, Rochester, MN 55904-4999

South Central College
North Mankato, Minnesota
www.southcentral.edu CB code: 7124

- Public 2-year community and technical college
- Commuter campus in large town

General. Founded in 1946. Regionally accredited. Campuses in North Mankato and Faribault, MN. **Enrollment:** 2,907 undergraduates. **Degrees:** 478 associate awarded. **Location:** 80 miles from Minneapolis-St. Paul. **Calendar:** Semester, limited summer session. **Full-time faculty:** 98 total; 8% have terminal degrees, 46% women. **Part-time faculty:** 98 total; 4% have terminal degrees, 5% minority, 66% women.

Basis for selection. Open admission. **Home schooled:** State high school equivalency certificate required.

High school preparation. College-preparatory program recommended.

2015-2016 Annual costs. Tuition/fees: $5,015; $5,015 out-of-state.

Financial aid. Need-based: Need-based aid available for part-time students. Work-study available nights, weekends and for part-time students.

Application procedures. Admission: Priority date 8/15; no deadline. $20 fee. Admission notification on a rolling basis. **Financial aid:** Priority date 5/1; no closing date. FAFSA required. Applicants notified on a rolling basis starting 6/1.

Academics. Special study options: Distance learning, dual enrollment of high school students, honors, independent study, internships, liberal arts/career combination. License preparation in nursing, paramedic. **Credit/placement by examination:** AP, CLEP, IB, institutional tests. **Support services:** GED preparation and test center, learning center, reduced course load, remedial instruction, study skills assistance, tutoring, writing center.

Majors. Architecture: Building sciences. **Biology:** General. **Business:** Accounting, accounting technology, administrative services, business admin, marketing, office management, restaurant/food services. **Communications technology:** Animation/special effects, graphics. **Computer sciences:** Data processing, information technology, LAN/WAN management, networking. **General:** Carpentry. **Health services:** Clinical lab technology, dental assistant, EMT paramedic, medical assistant, nursing (RN), pharmacy assistant. **Liberal arts:** Arts/sciences. **Visual/performing arts:** Studio arts. **Work/family studies:** Child care management, child development.

Technology on campus. 100 workstations in library, computer center, student center. Commuter students can connect to campus network. Online course registration, online library, helpline, wireless network available.

Student life. Freshman orientation: Mandatory. Preregistration for classes offered. **Activities:** Student government, student newspaper.

Athletics. Team name: Fighting Black Squirrels.

Student services. Alcohol/substance abuse counseling, career counseling, student employment services, financial aid counseling, placement for graduates, veterans' counselor. **Physically disabled:** Services for visually, speech, hearing impaired. **Transfer:** Pre-admission transcript evaluation for new students. Transfer adviser for students transferring to 4-year colleges.

Contact. E-mail: admissions@southcentral.edu
Phone: (507) 389-7451 Toll-free number: (800) 722-9359
Fax: (507) 388-9951
Anthony Riesberg, Admissions Director, South Central College, 1920 Lee Boulevard, North Mankato, MN 56003

St. Cloud Technical and Community College
St Cloud, Minnesota
www.sctcc.edu CB code: 1986

- Public 2-year community and technical college
- Commuter campus in small city

General. Founded in 1948. Regionally accredited. **Enrollment:** 4,010 degree-seeking undergraduates. **Degrees:** 866 associate awarded. **Location:** 65 miles from Minneapolis-St. Paul. **Calendar:** Semester, limited summer session. **Full-time faculty:** 102 total; 4% have terminal degrees, 2% minority, 40% women. **Part-time faculty:** 143 total; 6% have terminal degrees, 3% minority, 51% women. **Class size:** 18% < 20, 76% 20-39, 6% 40-49, less than 1% 50-99.

Student profile.

Out-of-state:	15% **25 or older:**	29%

Transfer out. Colleges most students transferred to 2015: St. Cloud State University, Southwest MN State University, Bemidji State University, University of Minnesota.

Basis for selection. Open admission, but selective for some programs. Paramedicine applicants must complete EMT basic and emergency cardiac care courses prior to acceptance. Sonography, cardiovascular technician, practical and registered nursing, dental assisting, and dental hygiene all require prerequisite courses to be completed prior to admission to the major. Programs such as echocardiography, sonography and cardiovascular technician require that students are interviewed as part of the acceptance process. **Home schooled:** Proof of high school graduation required. **Learning Disabled:** Students with developmental disabilities may take the course placement test with accommodations.

High school preparation. Recommended units include English 2, mathematics 2, science 1 (laboratory 1). Mathematics and science classes recommended for technical programs; algebra required for civil engineering; dental hygiene applicants must have all science and nutrition coursework completed; anatomy and physiology, college algebra, and physics required for echocardiography, sonography, and cardiovascular technology.

2015-2016 Annual costs. Tuition/fees: $5,325; $5,325 out-of-state. Per-credit charge: $159. Books/supplies: $1,200.

2014-2015 Financial aid. Need-based: 64% of total undergraduate aid awarded as scholarships/grants, 36% as loans/jobs. Need-based aid available for part-time students. Work-study available nights, weekends and for part-time students. **Non-need-based:** Scholarships awarded for academics, leadership, state residency.

Application procedures. Admission: Closing date 8/7 (postmark date). $20 fee. Admission notification on a rolling basis beginning on or about 10/7. **Financial aid:** No deadline. FAFSA required. Applicants notified on a rolling basis starting 6/1.

Academics. Special study options: Cooperative education, cross-registration, distance learning, double major, dual enrollment of high school students, ESL, independent study, internships, liberal arts/career combination. License preparation in dental hygiene, nursing, paramedic. **Credit/placement by examination:** AP, CLEP, institutional tests. **Support services:** Learning center, pre-admission summer program, reduced course load, remedial instruction, study skills assistance, tutoring, writing center.

Majors. Business: Accounting, administrative services, business admin, credit management, sales/distribution. **Communications:** Advertising, digital media. **Computer sciences:** Networking, programming, support specialist. **Education:** Teacher assistance. **General:** Carpentry, electrician, plumbing. **Health services:** Cardiovascular technology, dental assistant, dental hygiene, EMT paramedic, health information technology, licensed practical nurse, nursing (RN), office computer specialist, sonography, surgical technology. **Liberal arts:** Arts/sciences. **Work/family studies:** Child care management.

Most popular majors. Business/marketing 13%, engineering/engineering technologies 9%, health sciences 33%, liberal arts 26%.

Technology on campus. 486 workstations in library, computer center, student center. Commuter students can connect to campus network. Online course registration, online library, helpline, repair service, wireless network available.

Student life. Freshman orientation: Mandatory. Preregistration for classes offered. **Housing:** Privately-owned dormitory next to campus. Housing also available at St. Cloud State University. **Activities:** Student government, student newspaper, TV station, Student senate, Beta Xi Gamma, Somali student club, student veterans club.

Athletics. NJCAA. **Intercollegiate:** Baseball M, basketball, softball W, volleyball W. **Intramural:** Basketball, football (non-tackle), football (tackle), golf, ice hockey, racquetball, soccer, softball, tennis, track and field, volleyball. **Team name:** Cyclones.

Student services. Adult student services, career counseling, student employment services, financial aid counseling, on-campus daycare, personal counseling, placement for graduates, veterans' counselor. **Physically disabled:** Services for visually, speech, hearing impaired. **Transfer:** Pre-admission transcript evaluation for new students. Transfer adviser for students transferring to 4-year colleges.

Contact. E-mail: enroll@sctcc.edu
Phone: (320) 308-5089 Toll-free number: (800) 222-1009 ext. 5089
Fax: (320) 308-5981
Jodi Elness, Director of Enrollment Management, St. Cloud Technical and Community College, 1540 Northway Drive, St. Cloud, MN 56303

St. Paul College
Saint Paul, Minnesota
www.saintpaul.edu

CB code: 0534

▶ Public 2-year community and technical college
▶ Commuter campus in large city

General. Founded in 1919. Regionally accredited. **Enrollment:** 5,674 degree-seeking undergraduates. **Degrees:** 618 associate awarded. **Calendar:** Semester, limited summer session. **Full-time faculty:** 114 total. **Part-time faculty:** 140 total. **Class size:** 35% < 20, 61% 20-39, 4% 40-49, less than 1% 50-99.

Student profile.

Out-of-state:	1%	**25 or older:** 54%

Transfer out. Colleges most students transferred to 2015: Metropolitan State University, University of Minnesota, St. Mary's University of Minnesota, Concordia University, St. Paul, Augsburg College.

Basis for selection. Open admission, but selective for some programs. ACT considered for placement if submitted; scores must be received by July 1. Limited enrollment and additional requirements for the Medical Laboratory Technician, Respiratory Care Practitioner, and Practical Nursing programs. The $20 application fee is non-refundable, however due to challenging economic times this fee is waived until further notice. Interview recommended for selected programs. **Home schooled:** Transcript of courses and grades required.

High school preparation. College-preparatory program recommended. Recommended units include English 3, mathematics 2, social studies 3 and history 3.

2015-2016 Annual costs. Tuition/fees: $5,479; $5,479 out-of-state. Books/supplies: $800. Personal expenses: $1,640.

Financial aid. Need-based: Need-based aid available for part-time students. Work-study available nights, weekends and for part-time students. **Non-need-based:** Scholarships awarded for leadership.

Application procedures. Admission: Priority date 7/1; no deadline. $20 fee. Application must be submitted online. Admission notification on a rolling basis. **Financial aid:** No deadline. FAFSA required. Applicants notified on a rolling basis starting 6/1.

Academics. Special study options: Cross-registration, distance learning, dual enrollment of high school students, ESL, internships, weekend college. License preparation in nursing. **Credit/placement by examination:** AP, CLEP, IB, institutional tests. **Support services:** Learning center, reduced course load, remedial instruction, study skills assistance, tutoring, writing center.

Majors. Business: General, accounting, administrative services, business admin, entrepreneurial studies, hospitality admin, human resources, international marketing, logistics, management information systems, office management. **Communications technology:** Animation/special effects. **Computer sciences:** Computer graphics, networking, programming. **Foreign languages:** Sign language interpretation. **General:** Electrician. **Health services:** Athletic training, clinical lab technology, health information technology, licensed practical nurse, massage therapy, office assistant, respiratory therapy technology. **Liberal arts:** Arts/sciences. **Visual/performing arts:** Digital arts, game design. **Work/family studies:** Child care management, child development.

Most popular majors. Business/marketing 19%, computer/information sciences 8%, health sciences 26%, liberal arts 30%.

Technology on campus. 1,250 workstations in library, computer center. Commuter students can connect to campus network. Online course registration, online library, helpline, wireless network available.

Student life. Freshman orientation: Available. Preregistration for classes offered. **Activities:** Drama, student government, Phi Theta Kappa, Environmental Action Society, Muslim Student Association, American Sign Language Interpreting Association, Counter Culture Christian Club, Ethiopian Student Association, Somali Student Association, Students in Recovery, Student Senate, Skills USA.

Student services. Adult student services, alcohol/substance abuse counseling, career counseling, student employment services, financial aid counseling, on-campus daycare, personal counseling, placement for graduates, veterans' counselor. **Physically disabled:** Services for visually, speech, hearing impaired. **Transfer:** Pre-admission transcript evaluation for new students. Transfer center, transfer adviser, college fairs on campus for students transferring to 4-year colleges.

Contact. E-mail: admissions@saintpaul.edu
Phone: (651) 846-1555 Toll-free number: (800) 227-6029
Fax: (651) 846-1703
Ger Vue, Director of Enrollment Services, St. Paul College, 235 Marshall Avenue, Saint Paul, MN 55102-1800

Vermilion Community College
Ely, Minnesota
www.vcc.edu

CB code: 6194

▶ Public 2-year community and technical college
▶ Residential campus in small town

General. Founded in 1922. Regionally accredited. **Enrollment:** 696 degree-seeking undergraduates. **Degrees:** 142 associate awarded. **Location:** 100 miles from Duluth. **Calendar:** Semester, limited summer session. **Full-time faculty:** 18 total. **Part-time faculty:** 15 total. **Special facilities:** 40-acre outdoor learning center near Boundary Waters Canoe Area.

Student profile.

Out-of-state: 5% **Live on campus:** 40%
25 or older: 18%

Basis for selection. Open admission. Interview required for law enforcement, natural resources, parks and recreation students.

2015-2016 Annual costs. Tuition/fees: $5,325; $6,507 out-of-state. Room/board: $5,660. Books/supplies: $1,000. Personal expenses: $1,972.

Financial aid. Need-based: Need-based aid available for part-time students. Work-study available nights, weekends and for part-time students.

Application procedures. Admission: No deadline. $20 fee, may be waived for applicants with need. Admission notification on a rolling basis beginning on or about 1/1. **Financial aid:** Priority date 4/15; no closing date. FAFSA, institutional form required. Applicants notified on a rolling basis starting 4/1.

Academics. Special study options: Cooperative education, cross-registration, dual enrollment of high school students, honors, independent study, internships, liberal arts/career combination. **Credit/placement by examination:** AP, CLEP. **Support services:** Learning center, pre-admission summer program, reduced course load, remedial instruction, tutoring.

Majors. Business: General. **Conservation:** General, enforcement, land use planning, wildlife/wilderness. **History:** General. **Liberal arts:** Arts/sciences. **Parks/recreation:** Facilities management, sports admin. **Physical sciences:** Hydrology. **Protective services:** Police science.

Technology on campus. 110 workstations in dormitories, library, computer center, student center. Dormitories wired for high-speed internet access and linked to campus network. Helpline, wireless network available.

Student life. Freshman orientation: Mandatory. Preregistration for classes offered. 6 different programs from April through start of classes. **Housing:** Coed dorms available. $200 partly refundable deposit. On-campus, apartment style student housing available. **Activities:** Choral groups, drama, musical theater, student government, student newspaper, Campus Crusaders, GLBT Allies.

Athletics. NJCAA. **Intercollegiate:** Baseball M, basketball, football (tackle) M, softball W, volleyball W. **Intramural:** Basketball, bowling, softball, tennis, volleyball. **Team name:** Ironmen, Ironwomen.

Student services. Alcohol/substance abuse counseling, career counseling, student employment services, personal counseling, placement for graduates, veterans' counselor. **Physically disabled:** Services for visually, speech, hearing impaired. **Transfer:** Transfer adviser, college fairs on campus for students transferring to 4-year colleges.

Contact. E-mail: admissions@vcc.edu
Phone: (218) 235-2191 Toll-free number: (800) 657-3608
Fax: (218) 235-2173
Jeff Nelson, Director of Enrollment Services, Vermilion Community College, 1900 East Camp Street, Ely, MN 55731-9989

White Earth Tribal and Community College
Mahnomen, Minnesota
www.wetcc.edu

▶ Private 2-year community college
▶ Commuter campus in rural community

General. Anishinaabe-controlled, the school is one of three operating tribal colleges in Minnesota. **Enrollment:** 87 undergraduates. **Degrees:** 9 associate awarded. **Location:** 70 miles from Fargo/Moorhead. **Calendar:** Semester, limited summer session. **Full-time faculty:** 14 total. **Part-time faculty:** 7 total. **Class size:** 82% < 20, 18% 20-39. **Special facilities:** USDA Extension office.

Basis for selection. Open admission. **Learning Disabled:** Required to take ACCUPLACER exam.

High school preparation. College-preparatory program recommended.

2016-2017 Annual costs. Tuition/fees (projected): $3,315. Per-credit charge: $101. Books/supplies: $850. Personal expenses: $1,725.

Financial aid. Need-based: Work-study available nights, weekends and for part-time students.

Application procedures. Admission: No application fee. Application must be submitted on paper. Admission notification on a rolling basis. **Financial aid:** No deadline. FAFSA, institutional form required. Applicants notified on a rolling basis.

Academics. Special study options: Double major, liberal arts/career combination. **Credit/placement by examination:** AP, CLEP, institutional tests. **Support services:** GED preparation and test center, remedial instruction, study skills assistance, tutoring.

Majors. Area/ethnic studies: Native American. **Business:** Business admin. **Computer sciences:** General. **Conservation:** Environmental studies. **Education:** General, early childhood, kindergarten/preschool. **Liberal arts:** Humanities.

Most popular majors. Natural resources/environmental science 40%, public administration/social services 20%, social sciences 40%.

Technology on campus. 50 workstations in library, computer center, student center. Online library, wireless network available.

Student life. Freshman orientation: Mandatory. Preregistration for classes offered. **Activities:** Student government.

Student services. Adult student services, financial aid counseling, minority student services, personal counseling, veterans' counselor. **Transfer:** College fairs on campus for students transferring to 4-year colleges.

Contact. E-mail: Loreen.Estey@wetcc.edu
Phone: (218) 935-0417 ext. 322 Fax: (218) 936-5736
Loreen Estey, Admission, White Earth Tribal and Community College, PO Box 478, Mahnomen, MN 56557

Two-Year Colleges

Mississippi

Antonelli College: Hattiesburg
Hattiesburg, Mississippi
www.antonellicollege.edu   CB code: 3195

▶ For-profit 2-year branch campus and technical college
▶ Commuter campus in large town
▶ Interview required

General. Accredited by ACCSC. **Enrollment:** 209 undergraduates. **Degrees:** 126 associate awarded. **Location:** 90 miles from Jackson. **Calendar:** Quarter, extensive summer session. **Full-time faculty:** 14 total. **Part-time faculty:** 14 total.

Transfer out. Colleges most students transferred to 2015: Jones County Junior College, Pearl River Community College, University of Southern Mississippi.

Basis for selection. Open admission. **Home schooled:** Transcript of courses and grades, state high school equivalency certificate, interview required.

2015-2016 Annual costs. Books/supplies: $1,200. **Additional information:** Diploma program: $19,975. Associate programs: $31,960.

Financial aid. Need-based: Work-study available nights, weekends and for part-time students.

Application procedures. Admission: No deadline. $50 fee, may be waived for applicants with need. Application must be submitted on paper. Admission notification on a rolling basis.

Academics. Special study options: Distance learning, internships. **Credit/placement by examination:** AP, CLEP. **Support services:** GED preparation, tutoring.

Majors. Computer sciences: General.

Technology on campus. PC or laptop required. 7 workstations in library, computer center. Commuter students can connect to campus network. Online library, repair service, student web hosting, wireless network available.

Student life. Freshman orientation: Mandatory. Preregistration for classes offered.

Student services. Career counseling, student employment services, financial aid counseling. **Transfer:** Re-entry adviser, pre-admission transcript evaluation for new students. Transfer adviser for students transferring to 4-year colleges.

Contact. E-mail: steve.bryant@antonellicollege.edu
Phone: (601) 583-4100 Fax: (601) 583-0839
Jarita Large, Director of Admissions, Antonelli College: Hattiesburg, 1500 North 31st Avenue, Hattiesburg, MS 39401

Antonelli College: Jackson
Jackson, Mississippi
www.antonellicollege.edu   CB code: 3193

▶ For-profit 2-year technical and career college
▶ Commuter campus in small city
▶ Interview required

General. Accredited by ACCSC. **Enrollment:** 352 undergraduates. **Degrees:** 153 associate awarded. **Calendar:** Quarter. **Full-time faculty:** 17 total. **Part-time faculty:** 22 total.

Basis for selection. Open admission. **Home schooled:** Transcript of courses and grades required.

2015-2016 Annual costs. Books/supplies: $1,200. **Additional information:** Diploma program: $19,975. Associate programs: $31,960.

Financial aid. Need-based: Work-study available nights, weekends and for part-time students.

Application procedures. Admission: No deadline. No application fee. **Financial aid:** No deadline.

Academics. Special study options: Distance learning, double major, honors, internships. **Credit/placement by examination:** AP, CLEP, institutional tests. 14 credit hours maximum toward associate degree. **Support services:** Study skills assistance, tutoring.

Majors. Business: Accounting, office technology. **Computer sciences:** Computer graphics, data entry, networking, security, web page design, webmaster. **Health services:** Insurance coding, massage therapy, medical assistant, medical transcription. **Visual/performing arts:** Graphic design, interior design.

Technology on campus. PC or laptop required. 100 workstations in library, computer center. Commuter students can connect to campus network. Online course registration, online library, repair service, wireless network available.

Student life. Freshman orientation: Mandatory. Preregistration for classes offered. 2 days prior to start of class. **Activities:** Student newspaper.

Student services. Student employment services, financial aid counseling, placement for graduates.

Contact. E-mail: jackson.admissions@antonellicollege.edu
Phone: (601) 362-9991
Lou Bellson, Director of Admissions, Antonelli College: Jackson, 2323 Lakeland Drive, Jackson, MS 39232

Blue Cliff College: Gulfport
Gulfport, Mississippi
www.bluecliffcollege.edu

▶ For-profit 2-year career college
▶ Commuter campus in small city
▶ Interview required

General. Accredited by ACCSC. Medical assisting program graduates eligible to sit for the AMA exam. Massage therapy program graduates eligible for provisional license for up to six months until they take national boards. Fees for these exams included in tuition. **Enrollment:** 274 undergraduates. **Degrees:** 7 associate awarded. **Calendar:** Quarter, extensive summer session. **Full-time faculty:** 19 total. **Part-time faculty:** 11 total. **Class size:** 87% < 20, 13% 20-39.

Basis for selection. Requires High School Diploma or GED, admissions test, and campus tour. WONDERLIC test required. **Home schooled:** Transcript of courses and grades required.

2015-2016 Annual costs. Diploma programs: Cosmetology $18,080. Massage therapy $13,144; books and supplies $1,250. Dialysis technician $17,450; books and supplies $1,850. Midical/clinical assistant $12,985; books and supplies $1,850. Associate program: Massage therapy $13,144; books and supplies $1,250.

Financial aid. All financial aid based on need. Need-based aid available for part-time students. Work-study available nights, weekends and for part-time students.

Application procedures. Admission: No deadline. No application fee. Application must be submitted on paper. Admission notification on a rolling basis. **Financial aid:** FAFSA required.

Academics. Credit/placement by examination: AP, CLEP. **Support services:** Study skills assistance, tutoring.

Majors. Health services: Massage therapy, office assistant.

Technology on campus. 20 workstations in library, computer center. Online library, wireless network available.

Student life. Freshman orientation: Mandatory. Preregistration for classes offered.

Student services. Adult student services, career counseling, student employment services, financial aid counseling.

Contact. E-mail: AlbertF@BlueCliffCollege.com
Phone: (288) 896-9727 Toll-free number: (800) 514-0469
Fax: (228) 896-8659
Albert Frazier, Director of Admissions, Blue Cliff College: Gulfport,
12251 Bernard Parkway, Gulfport, MS 39503

Coahoma Community College
Clarksdale, Mississippi
www.coahomacc.edu   CB code: 1126

- Public 2-year community college
- Commuter campus in large town

General. Founded in 1949. Regionally accredited. **Enrollment:** 1,957
degree-seeking undergraduates. **Degrees:** 274 associate awarded. **Location:**
65 miles from Memphis, Tennessee. **Calendar:** Semester, limited summer
session. **Full-time faculty:** 72 total. **Part-time faculty:** 58 total.

Transfer out. Colleges most students transferred to 2015: Alcorn State
University, Delta State University, Jackson State University, Mississippi
Valley State University, University of Mississippi.

Basis for selection. Open admission, but selective for some programs.
High school record most important for admission to degree programs. Open
admissions to vocational programs. Limited admission to associate degree
nursing, licensed practical nursing, and respiratory therapy. ACT/SAT
required for nursing. Interview required for nursing students; audition required
for music students. **Home schooled:** Transcript of courses and grades, letter
of recommendation (nonparent) required.

High school preparation. College-preparatory program required. Recommended units include English 4, mathematics 3, social studies 2, science 3
(laboratory 3) and foreign language 1.

2015-2016 Annual costs. Tuition/fees: $2,440; $3,240 out-of-state.
Room/board: $4,220. Books/supplies: $800. Personal expenses: $700.

Financial aid. All financial aid based on need. Need-based aid available
for part-time students. Work-study available nights, weekends and for part-
time students.

Application procedures. Admission: No deadline. No application fee.
Admission notification on a rolling basis. **Financial aid:** Priority date 4/1;
no closing date. FAFSA, institutional form required. Applicants notified on
a rolling basis starting 7/1.

Academics. Special study options: Distance learning, dual enrollment of
high school students. License preparation in nursing. **Credit/placement by
examination:** AP, CLEP. **Support services:** GED preparation and test center,
reduced course load, remedial instruction, tutoring, writing center.

Majors. Biology: General. **Business:** General, accounting, hotel/motel
admin, office technology. **Communications:** Broadcast journalism, journalism. **Computer sciences:** General, computer science. **Education:** General,
art, business, early childhood, elementary, health, mathematics, music, physical, science, social science. **Health services:** Clinical lab science, EMT
paramedic, health information management, nursing (RN), predental, premedicine, prenursing, prepharmacy, preveterinary, respiratory therapy technology. **Human services:** Social work. **Math:** General. **Parks/recreation:**
Sports admin. **Physical sciences:** Chemistry. **Protective services:** Criminal
justice. **Social sciences:** General. **Visual/performing arts:** General. **Work/
family studies:** Child care management.

Most popular majors. Business/marketing 16%, education 41%, health
sciences 15%, public administration/social services 11%.

Technology on campus. Dormitories wired for high-speed internet
access and linked to campus network. Online course registration, online
library, helpline, wireless network available.

Student life. Freshman orientation: Mandatory. Preregistration for
classes offered. Semester-long course offered each semester. **Housing:** Single-sex dorms, special housing for disabled, wellness housing available. $100
deposit, deadline 8/1. **Activities:** Bands, choral groups, music ensembles,
student government, student newspaper, Baptist student union, Wesley Foundation, Black literary society.

Athletics. NJCAA. **Intercollegiate:** Baseball M, basketball, football (tackle) M, softball W. **Intramural:** Badminton, basketball, bowling, cheerleading W, football (non-tackle) M, football (tackle) M, softball, table tennis,
volleyball. **Team name:** Tigers.

Student services. Career counseling, services for economically disadvantaged, financial aid counseling, health services, personal counseling. **Physically disabled:** Services for visually, speech, hearing impaired. **Transfer:**
Pre-admission transcript evaluation for new students. Transfer adviser, college
fairs on campus for students transferring to 4-year colleges.

Contact. E-mail: mhouston@coahomacc.edu
Phone: (662) 621-4696 Toll-free number: (866) 470-1222
Michael Houston, Director of Admissions, Coahoma Community College,
3240 Friars Point Road, Clarksdale, MS 38614-9799

Copiah-Lincoln Community College
Wesson, Mississippi
www.colin.edu   CB code: 1142

- Public 2-year community college
- Commuter campus in small town

General. Founded in 1928. Regionally accredited. Full commuter campus
in Natchez, and center in Simpson County. **Enrollment:** 2,662 degree-seeking
undergraduates; 376 non-degree-seeking students. **Degrees:** 662 associate
awarded. **Location:** 45 miles from Jackson. **Calendar:** Semester, limited
summer session. **Full-time faculty:** 122 total. **Part-time faculty:** 77 total.
Special facilities: Nature trail, veterans memorial gardens, public golf course,
conference/workforce training center. **Partnerships:** Formal partnerships
with over 300 local businesses and industries, health occupation affiliates,
government agencies, and public service groups.

Student profile. Among degree-seeking undergraduates, 798 enrolled as
first-time, first-year students.

Part-time:	12%	25 or older:	29%
Out-of-state:	6%	Live on campus:	18%
Women:	61%		

Transfer out. Colleges most students transferred to 2015: University of
Southern Mississippi, Alcorn State University, University of Mississippi,
Mississippi State University, Jackson State University.

Basis for selection. Open admission, but selective for some programs.
ACT required for certain technology and health occupation programs. **Adult
students:** If ACT score not available, placement test required. **Home
schooled:** Transcript of courses and grades required. ACT required.

2015-2016 Annual costs. Tuition/fees: $2,730; $4,730 out-of-state.
Room/board: $3,400. Books/supplies: $2,000.

Financial aid. Need-based: Need-based aid available for part-time students. Work-study available nights, weekends and for part-time students.
Non-need-based: Scholarships awarded for academics, art, athletics, job
skills, leadership, music/drama, state residency.

Application procedures. Admission: No deadline. No application fee.
Application must be submitted on paper. Admission notification on a rolling
basis. **Financial aid:** Closing date 4/1. FAFSA required. Applicants notified
on a rolling basis starting 4/1; must reply within 2 week(s) of notification.

Academics. Special study options: Accelerated study, distance learning,
dual enrollment of high school students, honors. License preparation in nursing, radiology. **Credit/placement by examination:** AP, CLEP, institutional
tests. 24 credit hours maximum toward associate degree. **Support services:**
GED preparation and test center, learning center, remedial instruction, study
skills assistance, tutoring, writing center.

Majors. Business: Accounting technology, business admin, hotel/motel/
restaurant management, marketing, office technology. **Computer sciences:**
Data entry, networking. **Health services:** Clinical lab science, clinical lab
technology, medical radiologic technology/radiation therapy, nursing (RN),
respiratory therapy technology. **Liberal arts:** Arts/sciences. **Work/family
studies:** Child care management.

Technology on campus. 519 workstations in library, computer center.
Dormitories wired for high-speed internet access and linked to campus network. Commuter students can connect to campus network. Online course
registration, online library, helpline, student web hosting, wireless network
available.

Student life. Freshman orientation: Mandatory. Preregistration for
classes offered. Each freshman required to take an online or on-campus
orientation course. **Housing:** Guaranteed on-campus for all undergraduates.
Single-sex dorms, special housing for disabled, wellness housing available.
$50 nonrefundable deposit. **Activities:** Bands, campus ministries, choral
groups, dance, literary magazine, music ensembles, student government, student newspaper, Baptist student union, Wesley Foundation, student Christian
association, African-American Studies Club, College Republicans.

Athletics. NJCAA. **Intercollegiate:** Baseball M, basketball, chccrlcading, football (tackle) M, golf, soccer, softball W, tennis, track and field M. **Intramural:** Basketball, softball M, volleyball. **Team name:** Wolves.

Student services. Chaplain/spiritual director, career counseling, services for economically disadvantaged, financial aid counseling, health services, on-campus daycare, personal counseling, veterans' counselor. **Physically disabled:** Services for visually, speech, hearing impaired. **Transfer:** Pre-admission transcript evaluation for new students. College fairs on campus for students transferring to 4-year colleges.

Contact. E-mail: gay.langham@colin.edu
Phone: (601) 643-8307 Fax: (601) 643-8225
Christopher Warren, Director of Admissions, Copiah-Lincoln Community College, PO Box 649, Wesson, MS 39191

East Central Community College
Decatur, Mississippi
www.eccc.edu   CB code: 1196

▸ Public 2-year community college
▸ Commuter campus in rural community

General. Founded in 1928. Regionally accredited. **Enrollment:** 2,172 degree-seeking undergraduates. **Degrees:** 480 associate awarded. **Location:** 30 miles from Meridian, 90 milers from Jackson. **Calendar:** Semester, limited summer session. **Full-time faculty:** 75 total; 5% have terminal degrees, 4% minority, 68% women. **Part-time faculty:** 54 total; 4% minority, 68% women. **Class size:** 50% < 20, 44% 20-39, 4% 40-49, less than 1% 50-99, less than 1% >100.

Student profile. Among degree-seeking undergraduates, 68% enrolled in a transfer program, 32% enrolled in a vocational program.

Out-of-state:	2%	Live on campus:	30%
25 or older:	32%		

Basis for selection. Open admission, but selective for some programs. Special requirements for nursing program. **Home schooled:** Statement describing home school structure and mission, transcript of courses and grades required.

High school preparation. Recommended units include English 4 and mathematics 4.

2015-2016 Annual costs. Tuition/fees: $2,190; $4,290 out-of-state. Room/board: $3,340. Books/supplies: $1,280. Personal expenses: $1,220.

Financial aid. **Need-based:** Need-based aid available for part-time students. Work-study available nights, weekends and for part-time students. **Non-need-based:** Scholarships awarded for academics, art, athletics, leadership, music/drama, state residency.

Application procedures. **Admission:** No deadline. No application fee. Admission notification on a rolling basis. **Financial aid:** Priority date 4/1; no closing date. FAFSA required. Applicants notified on a rolling basis starting 7/31; must reply within 2 week(s) of notification.

Academics. **Special study options:** Distance learning, dual enrollment of high school students. **Credit/placement by examination:** AP, CLEP, institutional tests. 6 credit hours maximum toward associate degree. **Support services:** GED preparation and test center, learning center, remedial instruction, study skills assistance, tutoring. Free tutoring provided by full-time and part-time faculty in every subject matter.

Majors. **Computer sciences:** General, applications programming, data processing, programming. **Education:** General. **Health services:** Nursing (RN), surgical technology. **Liberal arts:** Arts/sciences.

Most popular majors. Family/consumer sciences 9%, health sciences 18%, liberal arts 55%, trade and industry 6%.

Technology on campus. 250 workstations in library, computer center, student center. Dormitories wired for high-speed internet access and linked to campus network. Commuter students can connect to campus network. Online course registration, wireless network available.

Student life. **Freshman orientation:** Mandatory. Preregistration for classes offered. **Housing:** Guaranteed on-campus for freshmen. Single-sex dorms, apartments available. $60 fully refundable deposit, deadline 8/1. **Activities:** Bands, campus ministries, choral groups, dance, drama, literary magazine, music ensembles, musical theater, student government, student newspaper, Newman Catholic Society, Baptist Student Union, Wesley Methodist Foundation, gospel choir.

Athletics. NJCAA. **Intercollegiate:** Baseball M, basketball, cheerleading, football (tackle) M, golf, soccer, softball W, tennis. **Intramural:** Baseball, basketball, football (non-tackle), soccer, softball, table tennis, ultimate frisbee, volleyball. **Team name:** Warriors.

Student services. Chaplain/spiritual director, career counseling, financial aid counseling, health services, on-campus daycare, personal counseling, veterans' counselor. **Transfer:** College fairs on campus for students transferring to 4-year colleges.

Contact. E-mail: admissions@eccc.edu
Phone: (601) 635-2111 ext. 392 Toll-free number: (877) 462-3222
Fax: (601) 635-4060
Deanna Rush, Director of Admissions, East Central Community College, Box 129, Decatur, MS 39327

East Mississippi Community College
Scooba, Mississippi
www.eastms.edu   CB code: 1197

▸ Public 2-year community college
▸ Residential campus in rural community

General. Founded in 1927. Regionally accredited. **Enrollment:** 4,296 degree-seeking undergraduates. **Degrees:** 743 associate awarded. **ROTC:** Army, Air Force. **Location:** 37 miles from Meridian, MS. **Calendar:** Semester, extensive summer session. **Full-time faculty:** 99 total. **Part-time faculty:** 154 total.

Student profile. Among degree-seeking undergraduates, 1,292 enrolled as first-time, first-year students.

Part-time:	30%	Women:	55%

Basis for selection. Open admission, but selective for some programs. Special requirements for associate degree nursing, practical nursing, cosmetology, funeral service technology. Most career and technical programs require a minimum ACT or COMPASS score, and most programs in the Manufacturing Technology and Engineering Division also required a Silver Certificate on the WorkKeys exam. **Adult students:** SAT/ACT scores not required if applicant over 21.

2015-2016 Annual costs. Tuition/fees: $2,840; $5,240 out-of-state. Room/board: $4,400. Books/supplies: $1,200. Personal expenses: $1,665.

2015-2016 Financial aid. **Need-based:** 52% of total undergraduate aid awarded as scholarships/grants, 48% as loans/jobs. Need-based aid available for part-time students. Work-study available nights, weekends and for part-time students. **Non-need-based:** Scholarships awarded for academics, alumni affiliation, art, athletics, leadership, music/drama, state residency.

Application procedures. **Admission:** No deadline. No application fee. Application must be submitted online. **Financial aid:** Priority date 4/1; no closing date. FAFSA, institutional form required. Applicants notified on a rolling basis starting 4/1; must reply within 2 week(s) of notification.

Academics. On-line classes offered in conjunction with the Mississippi Virtual Community College (MSVCC) enable students to take on-line courses with any of the 15 community colleges in the state. **Special study options:** Distance learning, double major, dual enrollment of high school students, honors, internships, study abroad. Work-based learning in major field of study. License preparation in nursing, paramedic. **Credit/placement by examination:** AP, CLEP, institutional tests. **Support services:** GED preparation and test center, learning center, reduced course load, remedial instruction, study skills assistance, tutoring, writing center.

Majors. **Architecture:** Architecture. **Area/ethnic studies:** African-American. **Biology:** General, biochemistry. **Business:** General, accounting, administrative services, banking/financial services, hospitality admin, hotel/motel admin, international, marketing, office management, office technology. **Communications:** General, advertising, journalism. **Computer sciences:** General, networking. **Conservation:** Forest technology, forestry, wildlife/wilderness. **Education:** Elementary, physical, secondary, special ed. **Engineering:** General, biomedical, software. **English:** English lit. **Foreign languages:** General, classics, Spanish. **General:** Electrician. **Health services:** Athletic training, clinical lab science, dental hygiene, EMT paramedic, nursing (RN), optician, pharmaceutical sciences, prenursing. **History:** General. **Human services:** Social work. **Liberal arts:** Arts/sciences, library assistant. **Math:** General. **Parks/recreation:** Exercise sciences, facilities management. **Physical sciences:** Atmospheric science, chemistry, physics, polymer chemistry. **Protective services:** Forensics, police science. **Psychology:** General, educational. **Social sciences:** General, economics, political science, sociology. **Visual/performing arts:** General, music. **Work/family studies:** Family systems.

Technology on campus. 60 workstations in library, computer center. Dormitories wired for high-speed internet access. Commuter students can connect to campus network. Online course registration, online library, helpline, wireless network available.

Student life. Freshman orientation: Mandatory. Preregistration for classes offered. **Housing:** Single-sex dorms available. **Activities:** Marching band, choral groups, drama, literary magazine, music ensembles, musical theater, radio station, student government, student newspaper, Gospel choir, interdenominational Christian fellowship group, Fellowship of Christian Athletes.

Athletics. NJCAA. **Intercollegiate:** Baseball M, basketball, cheerleading, football (tackle) M, golf, rodeo, softball W. **Team name:** Lions.

Student services. Adult student services, career counseling, services for economically disadvantaged, financial aid counseling, health services, personal counseling, placement for graduates, veterans' counselor. **Transfer:** Pre-admission transcript evaluation for new students. Transfer adviser, college fairs on campus for students transferring to 4-year colleges.

Contact. E-mail: kbriggs@eastms.edu
Phone: (662) 476-5040 Fax: (662) 476-5038
Karen Briggs, Director of Admissions, East Mississippi Community College, Admissions Office, Scooba, MS 39358

Hinds Community College
Raymond, Mississippi
www.hindscc.edu   CB code: 1296

- Public 2-year branch campus and community college
- Commuter campus in small town

General. Founded in 1917. Regionally accredited. Six locations: Raymond, Utica, Rankin (Pearl), Jackson Academic/Technical Center, Nursing/Allied Health Center (Jackson), and Vicksburg-Warren County Center. **Enrollment:** 10,198 degree-seeking undergraduates; 1,316 non-degree-seeking students. **Degrees:** 1,687 associate awarded. **ROTC:** Army. **Location:** Ten miles from Jackson, MS. **Calendar:** Semester, extensive summer session. **Full-time faculty:** 377 total; 34% minority, 68% women. **Part-time faculty:** 442 total; 39% minority, 66% women.

Student profile. Among degree-seeking undergraduates, 67% enrolled in a transfer program, 33% enrolled in a vocational program, 2,831 enrolled as first-time, first-year students.

Part-time:	29%	Hispanic/Latino:	2%
Out-of-state:	3%	Multi-racial, non-Hispanic:	2%
Women:	61%	25 or older:	32%
African American:	59%	Live on campus:	13%
Asian American:	1%		

Transfer out. Colleges most students transferred to 2015: Mississippi State University, University of Southern Mississippi, Jackson State University, Alcorn State University, Mississippi College.

Basis for selection. Open admission, but selective for some programs. Special requirements for allied health and data processing programs. ACT not required for placement in vocational programs. Interview required for allied health and some vocational majors. **Home schooled:** Transcript of courses and grades required.

2015-2016 Annual costs. Tuition/fees: $2,500; $5,100 out-of-state. Per-credit charge: $100 in-state; $200 out-of-state. Room/board: $3,960. Books/supplies: $1,600. Personal expenses: $477.

2014-2015 Financial aid. Need-based: 68% of total undergraduate aid awarded as scholarships/grants, 32% as loans/jobs. Need-based aid available for part-time students. Work-study available nights, weekends and for part-time students. **Non-need-based:** Scholarships awarded for academics, art, athletics, job skills, leadership, minority status, music/drama, state residency.

Application procedures. Admission: No deadline. No application fee. Admission notification on a rolling basis. **Financial aid:** Priority date 3/15; no closing date. FAFSA required. Applicants notified on a rolling basis.

Academics. Special study options: Accelerated study, cooperative education, distance learning, dual enrollment of high school students, honors, independent study, internships, study abroad, teacher certification program. License preparation in aviation, nursing, paramedic. **Credit/placement by examination:** AP, CLEP, institutional tests. 18 credit hours maximum toward associate degree. **Support services:** GED preparation and test center, learning center, reduced course load, remedial instruction, study skills assistance, tutoring, writing center.

Honors college/program. Incoming first time students must have a 3.5 GPA and a minimum of 25 on their ACT. Honors classes typically enroll 15-20 students and are taught by the top teaching faculty. Students receive specialized advising, priority enrollment, opportunities for cultural events and travel, and scholarship opportunities. The program promotes community service and giving back to the college and community. 60-80 freshman usually admitted each fall.

Majors. Architecture: Architecture, landscape. **Biology:** General. **Business:** General, accounting, accounting technology, administrative services, banking/financial services, fashion, hospitality admin, marketing, office technology, real estate, tourism/travel. **Communications:** Communications/speech/rhetoric, digital media, journalism, radio/TV. **Communications technology:** Photo/film/video, radio/TV. **Computer sciences:** General, networking, programming, security. **Conservation:** Forestry. **Education:** Business, elementary, physical, secondary, technology/industrial arts. **Engineering:** General. **English:** English lit. **Foreign languages:** Sign language interpretation. **General:** Electrician, plumbing. **Health services:** Clinical lab science, clinical lab technology, dental assistant, dental hygiene, EMT paramedic, health information management, health information technology, medical assistant, nursing (RN), occupational therapy, physical therapy, physical therapy assistant, predental, premedicine, prenursing, prepharmacy, preveterinary, radiologic technology/medical imaging, respiratory therapy technology, sonography, surgical technology, veterinary technology/assistant. **History:** General. **Math:** General. **Physical sciences:** General, chemistry, geology. **Protective services:** Criminal justice. **Psychology:** General. **Social sciences:** General, GIS/cartography, political science, sociology. **Visual/performing arts:** Art, dance, dramatic, game design, graphic design, music. **Work/family studies:** General, child care service.

Most popular majors. Health sciences 26%, liberal arts 50%.

Technology on campus. 214 workstations in dormitories, library, computer center, student center. Dormitories wired for high-speed internet access. Commuter students can connect to campus network. Online course registration, online library, helpline, repair service, wireless network available.

Student life. Freshman orientation: Available, $65 fee. Preregistration for classes offered. **Housing:** Coed dorms, single-sex dorms, special housing for disabled, wellness housing available. $50 nonrefundable deposit, deadline 6/15. **Activities:** Bands, campus ministries, choral groups, dance, drama, international student organizations, music ensembles, student government, student newspaper, Baptist student union, Afro-American Cultural Society, Catholic student organization, College Independents, College Republicans, Fellowship of Christian Athletes, Class/Leadership/Authority and Womanhood, Campus Christian Fellowship, IDEAL Woman.

Athletics. NJCAA. **Intercollegiate:** Baseball M, basketball, cheerleading, football (tackle) M, golf M, soccer, softball W, tennis, track and field. **Intramural:** Basketball, football (non-tackle), golf, softball, swimming, tennis, track and field, triathlon, volleyball. **Team name:** Eagles.

Student services. Adult student services, career counseling, services for economically disadvantaged, student employment services, financial aid counseling, minority student services, on-campus daycare, personal counseling, placement for graduates, veterans' counselor, women's services. **Physically disabled:** Services for visually, speech, hearing impaired. **Transfer:** Pre-admission transcript evaluation for new students. Transfer adviser, college fairs on campus for students transferring to 4-year colleges.

Contact. E-mail: records@hindscc.edu
Phone: (601) 857-3212
Randall Harris, Director of Admissions and Records, Hinds Community College, HCC Office of Admissions and Records, Raymond, MS 39154-1100

Holmes Community College
Goodman, Mississippi
www.holmescc.edu   CB code: 1299

- Public 2-year community college
- Residential campus in rural community

General. Founded in 1925. Regionally accredited. Additional campuses in Ridgeland and Grenada. **Enrollment:** 6,186 degree-seeking undergraduates. **Degrees:** 1,083 associate awarded. **Location:** 40 miles from Jackson. **Calendar:** Semester, extensive summer session. **Full-time faculty:** 149 total. **Part-time faculty:** 186 total. **Special facilities:** Observatory.

Student profile.

Out-of-state:	5%	Live on campus:	25%
25 or older:	33%		

Transfer out. Colleges most students transferred to 2015: Mississippi State University, University of Mississippi, Delta State University, University of Southern Mississippi.

Basis for selection. Open admission, but selective for some programs. Associate degree nursing applicants required to have ACT composite score of 18, and 17 math sub-score and 18 reading sub-score. Practical nurse applicants must have composite ACT score of 16 with math and reading sub-scores of 12. Adjustments made for scores pre-dating October 1989. ACT or SAT is required for placement. **Adult students:** SAT/ACT scores not required if applicant over 21. **Home schooled:** Transcript of courses and grades required.

High school preparation. College-preparatory program required. 21 units required. Required units include English 4, mathematics 4, social studies 1, history 2, science 3, computer science 1, visual/performing arts 1, academic electives 4.5. .5 unit in health.

2015-2016 Annual costs. Tuition/fees: $2,450; $5,030 out-of-state. Room/board: $2,950. Books/supplies: $1,500. Personal expenses: $3,800.

2014-2015 Financial aid. Need-based: 76% of total undergraduate aid awarded as scholarships/grants, 24% as loans/jobs. Work-study available nights, weekends and for part-time students. **Non-need-based:** Scholarships awarded for academics, athletics.

Application procedures. Admission: No deadline. No application fee. Admission notification on a rolling basis. **Financial aid:** Priority date 6/1; no closing date. FAFSA, institutional form required. Applicants notified on a rolling basis.

Academics. Special study options: Cooperative education, distance learning, dual enrollment of high school students, honors, internships, liberal arts/career combination, weekend college. License preparation in nursing, paramedic. **Credit/placement by examination:** AP, CLEP, institutional tests. **Support services:** GED test center, learning center, reduced course load, remedial instruction, study skills assistance, tutoring, writing center.

Majors. Business: Administrative services, business admin, fashion. **Computer sciences:** General, computer science, programming. **Conservation:** Forestry. **Education:** Elementary, secondary. **Engineering:** General, architectural, electrical. **Health services:** Predental, premedicine, prepharmacy, preveterinary. **Liberal arts:** Arts/sciences. **Math:** General.

Technology on campus. 400 workstations in library, computer center. Dormitories linked to campus network. Commuter students can connect to campus network. Online course registration, online library, helpline, repair service, wireless network available.

Student life. Freshman orientation: Available. Preregistration for classes offered. **Housing:** Single-sex dorms available. $50 partly refundable deposit. **Activities:** Bands, campus ministries, choral groups, dance, drama, literary magazine, music ensembles, musical theater, student government, student newspaper, Baptist Student Union, Wesley Foundation, College Republican Club, Fellowship of Christian Athletes.

Athletics. NJCAA. **Intercollegiate:** Baseball M, basketball, cheerleading, football (tackle) M, golf M, soccer, softball W, tennis, track and field. **Intramural:** Basketball, football (tackle) M, soccer M, softball, track and field M, volleyball. **Team name:** Bulldogs.

Student services. Adult student services, career counseling, services for economically disadvantaged, personal counseling, veterans' counselor. **Physically disabled:** Services for visually, speech, hearing impaired. **Transfer:** Pre-admission transcript evaluation for new students. Transfer adviser, college fairs on campus for students transferring to 4-year colleges.

Contact. E-mail: progers@holmescc.edu
Phone: (662) 472-9073 Toll-free number: (800) 465-6374
Fax: (662) 472-9152
Joshua Guest, Director of Admissions and Records, Holmes Community College, Box 398, Goodman, MS 39079

Itawamba Community College
Fulton, Mississippi
www.iccms.edu
CB code: 1326

- Public 2-year community and technical college
- Commuter campus in small town

General. Founded in 1948. Regionally accredited. Additional campuses in Fulton, Tupelo, as well as online instruction. **Enrollment:** 5,037 degree-seeking undergraduates; 617 non-degree-seeking students. **Degrees:** 1,254 associate awarded. **Location:** 115 miles from Memphis, Tennessee, 135 miles

from Birmingham, Alabama. **Calendar:** Semester, limited summer session. **Full-time faculty:** 185 total. **Part-time faculty:** 215 total. **Class size:** 51% < 20, 43% 20-39, 5% 40-49, 1% 50-99.

Student profile. Among degree-seeking undergraduates, 1,336 enrolled as first-time, first-year students.

Part-time:	25%	Live on campus:	18%
Women:	59%		

Transfer out. Colleges most students transferred to 2015: Mississippi State University, University of Mississippi.

Basis for selection. Open admission, but selective for some programs. Special requirements for health science programs, including minimum test scores on ACT or other discipline-specific tests and grade of at least 2.0 in program prerequisite courses. **Home schooled:** Must complete GED or appeal to Admissions and Guidance Committee. **Learning Disabled:** Developmental courses recommended. Assistance provided by special needs counselor.

2015-2016 Annual costs. Tuition/fees: $2,420; $4,620 out-of-state. Room/board: $3,150. Books/supplies: $900. Personal expenses: $180.

Financial aid. Need-based: Need-based aid available for part-time students. Work-study available nights, weekends and for part-time students. **Non-need-based:** Scholarships awarded for academics, art, athletics, leadership, music/drama, state residency.

Application procedures. Admission: No deadline. No application fee. Admission notification on a rolling basis. **Financial aid:** No deadline. FAFSA, institutional form required. Applicants notified on a rolling basis starting 4/15.

Academics. Special study options: Accelerated study, cooperative education, distance learning, double major, dual enrollment of high school students, ESL, honors, independent study, internships. License preparation in nursing, paramedic, physical therapy, radiology, real estate. **Credit/placement by examination:** AP, CLEP, institutional tests. 15 credit hours maximum toward associate degree. **Support services:** GED preparation and test center, learning center, reduced course load, remedial instruction, study skills assistance, tutoring, writing center.

Majors. Business: General, accounting, administrative services, management information systems, office/clerical. **Communications:** Broadcast journalism, journalism, public relations. **Computer sciences:** General, computer science, data processing, programming. **Conservation:** Forestry. **Education:** Art, biology, business, chemistry, elementary, French, health, history, mathematics, music, physical, physics, science, secondary, social studies, Spanish, special ed, speech. **Engineering:** General, electrical. **Foreign languages:** French, sign language interpretation, Spanish. **General:** Electrician. **Health services:** EMT paramedic, health information management, health information technology, medical radiologic technology/radiation therapy, nursing (RN), occupational health, physical therapy assistant, predental, premedicine, prepharmacy, preveterinary, respiratory therapy technology, sonography, surgical technology. **History:** General. **Human services:** Social work. **Liberal arts:** Arts/sciences, library assistant. **Math:** General. **Philosophy/religion:** Philosophy. **Physical sciences:** Chemistry, geology, physics. **Protective services:** Criminal justice. **Psychology:** General. **Social sciences:** Economics, sociology. **Visual/performing arts:** Art, music. **Work/family studies:** General, child care management.

Most popular majors. Business/marketing 11%, family/consumer sciences 6%, health sciences 36%, liberal arts 42%.

Technology on campus. 600 workstations in dormitories, library, computer center. Dormitories wired for high-speed internet access and linked to campus network. Commuter students can connect to campus network. Online course registration, online library, helpline, wireless network available.

Student life. Freshman orientation: Available. Preregistration for classes offered. **Housing:** Single-sex dorms, wellness housing available. $50 deposit. **Activities:** Bands, choral groups, dance, drama, literary magazine, music ensembles, musical theater, student government, student newspaper.

Athletics. NJCAA. **Intercollegiate:** Baseball M, basketball, cheerleading, football (tackle) M, golf M, soccer M, softball W. **Intramural:** Basketball. **Team name:** Indians.

Student services. Alcohol/substance abuse counseling, chaplain/spiritual director, career counseling, services for economically disadvantaged, student employment services, financial aid counseling, minority student services, on-campus daycare, placement for graduates, veterans' counselor, women's services. **Physically disabled:** Services for visually, hearing impaired. **Transfer:** Transfer adviser, college fairs on campus for students transferring to 4-year colleges.

Two-Year Colleges

Contact. E-mail: hgjefcoat@iccms.edu
Phone: (662) 862-8031 Fax: (662) 862-8036
Cay Lollar, Director of Admissions, Itawamba Community College, 602
West Hill Street, Fulton, MS 38843-1099

Jones County Junior College
Ellisville, Mississippi
www.jcjc.edu   **CB code: 1347**

> Public 2-year community and junior college
> Commuter campus in small town

General. Founded in 1927. Regionally accredited. College operates four
learning centers within the eight-county district; Clarke County Learning
Center, Greene County Learning Center, Jasper County Learning Center,
and Wayne County Learning Center. **Enrollment:** 4,066 degree-seeking
undergraduates. **Degrees:** 793 associate awarded. **ROTC:** Army. **Location:** 7
miles from Laurel, 20 miles from Hattiesburg. **Calendar:** Semester, extensive
summer session. **Special facilities:** Visual arts center, advanced technology
center, simulation center.

Transfer out. **Colleges most students transferred to 2015:** University of
Southern Mississippi, Mississippi State University, University of Mississippi,
William Carey College.

Basis for selection. Open admission, but selective for some programs.
Minimum ACT scores for College Algebra (19 or above) and English Composition I (17 or above). Minimum ACT composite score of 16 required for
practical nursing program, 17 for radiologic technology program, and 18
for associate degree nursing program. Interview required for health majors;
audition required for band, music majors; portfolio required for art majors.

2015-2016 Annual costs. Tuition/fees: $2,722; $4,722 out-of-state.
Room/board: $3,600. Books/supplies: $600. Personal expenses: $1,299.

Financial aid. **Need-based:** Need-based aid available for part-time students. Work-study available nights, weekends and for part-time students.
Non-need-based: Scholarships awarded for academics, athletics, state residency.

Application procedures. **Admission:** No deadline. No application fee.
Admission notification on a rolling basis beginning on or about 2/1. **Financial
aid:** Priority date 4/1; no closing date. FAFSA, institutional form required.
Applicants notified on a rolling basis starting 6/1; must reply within 2 week(s)
of notification.

Academics. **Special study options:** Cooperative education, distance learning, double major, dual enrollment of high school students, honors. License
preparation in nursing, paramedic, physical therapy, radiology, real estate.
Credit/placement by examination: AP, CLEP, institutional tests. 30 credit
hours maximum toward associate degree. **Support services:** GED preparation
and test center, learning center, reduced course load, remedial instruction,
study skills assistance, tutoring, writing center.

Majors. **Liberal arts:** Arts/sciences.

Technology on campus. 500 workstations in dormitories, library, computer center, student center. Dormitories wired for high-speed internet access
and linked to campus network. Commuter students can connect to campus
network. Online course registration, online library, helpline, wireless network available.

Student life. **Freshman orientation:** Mandatory. Preregistration for
classes offered. **Housing:** Single-sex dorms available. $100 deposit. **Activi-
ties:** Bands, campus ministries, choral groups, dance, drama, literary magazine, music ensembles, musical theater, student government, student newspaper, Wesley Foundation, Association of African-American Students.

Athletics. NJCAA. **Intercollegiate:** Baseball M, basketball, football (tackle) M, golf, soccer, softball W, tennis. **Intramural:** Archery, basketball,
racquetball, soccer, softball, table tennis, tennis, volleyball. **Team name:**
Bobcats.

Student services. Adult student services, alcohol/substance abuse counseling, career counseling, student employment services, financial aid counseling, health services, on-campus daycare, personal counseling, placement
for graduates, veterans' counselor, women's services. **Physically disabled:**
Services for visually, speech, hearing impaired. **Transfer:** Transfer adviser
for students transferring to 4-year colleges.

Contact. E-mail: admissions@jcjc.edu
Phone: (601) 477-4025 Fax: (601) 477-4017
Rick Hamilton, Director of Admissions & Records, Jones County Junior
College, 900 South Court Street, Ellisville, MS 39437

Meridian Community College
Meridian, Mississippi   **CB member**
www.meridiancc.edu   **CB code: 1461**

> Public 2-year community college
> Commuter campus in large town

General. Founded in 1937. Regionally accredited. On-line degree programs.
Enrollment: 3,188 degree-seeking undergraduates. **Degrees:** 545 associate
awarded. **Location:** 90 miles from Jackson, 90 miles from Tuscaloosa, AL.
Calendar: Semester, extensive summer session. **Full-time faculty:** 162 total.
Part-time faculty: 57 total. **Special facilities:** Fitness center & natatorium,
workforce development center, student success center.

Basis for selection. Open admission, but selective for some programs.
Specific programs may have admission criteria required for entrance to the
program. Test scores, recommendations, background checks, prerequisite
coursework all considered for health education applicants. Interview recommended for broadcast technology, data processing, graphic communication
technology, and health programs majors. **Adult students:** SAT/ACT scores
not required. ACCUPLACER given for placement if no SAT/ACT test scores
are available,.

High school preparation. Recommended units include English 4, mathematics 3, social studies 3, science 3 and academic electives 2. Unit computer
applications .5.

2015-2016 Annual costs. Tuition/fees: $2,350; $3,630 out-of-state. Per-
credit charge: $100 in-state; $157 out-of-state. Room/board: $3,450.

Financial aid. **Need-based:** Need-based aid available for part-time students. Work-study available nights, weekends and for part-time students.
Non-need-based: Scholarships awarded for academics, art, athletics, leadership, music/drama, state residency.

Application procedures. **Admission:** No deadline. No application fee.
Admission notification on a rolling basis. **Financial aid:** Priority date 6/1;
no closing date. FAFSA, institutional form required. Applicants notified on
a rolling basis starting 5/15; must reply within 2 week(s) of notification.

Academics. **Special study options:** Accelerated study, distance learning,
dual enrollment of high school students, ESL, independent study, internships,
weekend college. License preparation in dental hygiene, nursing, occupational
therapy, physical therapy, radiology, real estate. **Credit/placement by examination:** AP, CLEP. 45 credit hours maximum toward associate degree. **Support services:** GED preparation and test center, learning center, remedial
instruction, study skills assistance, tutoring.

Majors. **Business:** Administrative services, hotel/motel/restaurant management, marketing. **Communications technology:** Graphics, radio/TV. **Computer sciences:** General, LAN/WAN management, programming. **Education:** Early childhood. **Health services:** Clinical lab technology, dental
hygiene, health information technology, insurance coding, insurance specialist, medical radiologic technology/radiation therapy, medical secretary, nursing (RN), physical therapy assistant, radiologic technology/medical imaging,
respiratory therapy assistant, respiratory therapy technology. **Protective services:** Firefighting.

Technology on campus. 85 workstations in library, computer center.
Dormitories wired for high-speed internet access and linked to campus network. Commuter students can connect to campus network. Online course
registration, online library, helpline, repair service, wireless network available.

Student life. **Freshman orientation:** Mandatory. Preregistration for
classes offered. Orientation sessions specific to certain programs and for
first-time freshmen available. **Housing:** Single-sex dorms, special housing
for disabled, apartments, wellness housing available. $100 fully refundable
deposit. **Activities:** Bands, campus ministries, choral groups, drama, international student organizations, literary magazine, music ensembles, musical
theater, radio station, student government, student newspaper, TV station,
Baptist Student Union, T.J. Harris Organization, Wesley Foundation, Fellowship of Christian Athletes, Phi Theta Kappa, multicultural student association,
Future Teachers of America, health occupation organizations, HOSA.

Athletics. NJCAA. **Intercollegiate:** Baseball M, basketball, cheerleading,
golf, soccer, softball W, tennis. **Intramural:** Basketball, softball W, tennis,
volleyball. **Team name:** Eagles.

Student services. Career counseling, student employment services, financial aid counseling, personal counseling, placement for graduates, veterans'
counselor. **Physically disabled:** Services for visually, speech, hearing
impaired. **Transfer:** Pre-admission transcript evaluation for new students.
Transfer adviser, college fairs on campus for students transferring to 4-
year colleges.

Contact. E-mail: apayne@meridiancc.edu
Phone: (601) 484-8895 Toll-free number: (800) 622-8431
Fax: (601) 484-8838
Angela Payne, Director of Admissions, Meridian Community College, 910 Highway 19 North, Meridian, MS 39307-5890

Mississippi Delta Community College
Moorhead, Mississippi
www.msdelta.edu

CB code: 1742

- Public 2-year community college
- Commuter campus in rural community

General. Founded in 1926. Regionally accredited. **Enrollment:** 2,479 degree-seeking undergraduates. **Degrees:** 430 associate awarded. **Location:** 20 miles from Greenwood. **Calendar:** Semester, limited summer session. **Full-time faculty:** 116 total. **Part-time faculty:** 113 total.

Student profile.

Out-of-state: 3% Live on campus: 25%

Transfer out. Colleges most students transferred to 2015: Delta State University, Mississippi State University, University of Mississippi, University of Southern Mississippi, Mississippi Valley State University.

Basis for selection. Open admission, but selective for some programs. Test scores most important. Open admission to vocational programs. Limited admission to health occupations and computer technology curriculum.

High school preparation. 19 units recommended. Recommended units include English 3, mathematics 3, social studies 3, science 3, foreign language 3 and academic electives 4. 12 of the recommended units may be distributed in any combination in mathematics, science, foreign language, social studies, and history.

2015-2016 Annual costs. Tuition/fees: $2,490; $4,098 out-of-state. Per-credit charge: $125. Room/board: $2,740. Books/supplies: $450. Personal expenses: $400.

Financial aid. Need-based: Work-study available nights, weekends and for part-time students. **Non-need-based:** Scholarships awarded for academics, athletics, state residency.

Application procedures. Admission: No application fee. Admission notification on a rolling basis beginning on or about 5/30. **Financial aid:** Closing date 8/1. FAFSA, institutional form required. Applicants notified on a rolling basis; must reply within 2 week(s) of notification.

Academics. Special study options: Distance learning, dual enrollment of high school students. License preparation in dental hygiene, nursing, radiology. **Credit/placement by examination:** AP, CLEP, institutional tests. 15 credit hours maximum toward associate degree. **Support services:** GED preparation and test center, learning center, reduced course load, remedial instruction, study skills assistance, tutoring.

Majors. Area/ethnic studies: American. **Biology:** General. **Business:** Accounting, administrative services. **Communications:** Advertising, communications/speech/rhetoric. **Computer sciences:** Programming. **Conservation:** Forestry. **Education:** General, art, business, elementary, health, physical, secondary, special ed, speech. **Engineering:** General. **English:** English lit. **General:** Maintenance. **Health services:** Clinical lab technology, dental hygiene, EMT paramedic, health information management, medical radiologic technology/radiation therapy, predental, prepharmacy, preveterinary. **History:** General. **Human services:** Social work. **Liberal arts:** Arts/sciences. **Protective services:** Law enforcement admin. **Psychology:** General. **Social sciences:** General, sociology. **Visual/performing arts:** Music, studio arts. **Work/family studies:** General.

Technology on campus. Dormitories wired for high-speed internet access and linked to campus network. Commuter students can connect to campus network. Online course registration, wireless network available.

Student life. Freshman orientation: Available. Preregistration for classes offered. **Housing:** Single-sex dorms available. $75 nonrefundable deposit, deadline 6/15. **Activities:** Bands, campus ministries, choral groups, dance, drama, student government, student newspaper, Baptist Student Union, Wesley Foundation, Vocational Industrial Clubs of America.

Athletics. NJCAA. **Intercollegiate:** Baseball M, basketball, football (tackle) M, golf M, soccer M, softball W, tennis, track and field M. **Intramural:** Basketball, softball, tennis, track and field, volleyball.

Student services. Adult student services, career counseling, student employment services, financial aid counseling, health services, minority student services, personal counseling, placement for graduates, veterans' counselor. **Transfer:** Re-entry adviser, pre-admission transcript evaluation for new students. Transfer adviser, college fairs on campus for students transferring to 4-year colleges.

Contact. E-mail: admissions@msdelta.edu
Phone: (662) 246-6306 Fax: (662) 246-6321
J. Gregory, Associate Vice President of Instruction for Enrollment Management/Director of Admissions, Mississippi Delta Community College, Box 668, Moorhead, MS 38761

Mississippi Gulf Coast Community College
Perkinston, Mississippi
www.mgccc.edu

CB member
CB code: 1353

- Public 2-year community college
- Commuter campus in large city

General. Founded in 1965. Regionally accredited. 3 campuses and 4 centers. **Enrollment:** 8,975 degree-seeking undergraduates. **Degrees:** 2,087 associate awarded. **Location:** 30 miles from Biloxi, 90 miles from New Orleans. **Calendar:** Semester, limited summer session. **Full-time faculty:** 308 total. **Part-time faculty:** 230 total.

Student profile.

Out-of-state: 3% Live on campus: 8%
25 or older: 36%

Transfer out. Colleges most students transferred to 2015: University of Southern Mississippi, Mississippi State University, University of South Alabama.

Basis for selection. Open admission, but selective for some programs. Background check and substance tests, reading and math proficiency required for nursing.

High school preparation. 19 units recommended. Recommended units include English 3, mathematics 3 and science 3.

2015-2016 Annual costs. Tuition/fees: $2,800; $4,646 out-of-state. Room/board: $4,100. Books/supplies: $860. Personal expenses: $1,050.

Financial aid. All financial aid based on need. Work-study available nights, weekends and for part-time students.

Application procedures. Admission: No deadline. No application fee. **Financial aid:** Priority date 6/1; no closing date. FAFSA, institutional form required. Applicants notified on a rolling basis starting 7/1.

Academics. Special study options: Accelerated study, cooperative education, distance learning, dual enrollment of high school students, honors, weekend college. License preparation in nursing, paramedic, radiology. **Credit/placement by examination:** AP, CLEP, institutional tests. 32 credit hours maximum toward associate degree. **Support services:** GED preparation and test center, learning center, reduced course load, remedial instruction, study skills assistance, tutoring.

Majors. Biology: General. **Business:** General, accounting, administrative services, banking/financial services, business admin, management information systems, marketing, office technology. **Communications:** Communications/speech/rhetoric. **Computer sciences:** General. **Conservation:** Fisheries, forestry. **Education:** General, art, business, elementary, mathematics, multi-level teacher, science, secondary, trade/industrial. **Engineering:** General. **General:** Lineworker, pipefitting, power transmission. **Health services:** Clinical lab science, clinical lab technology, EMT paramedic, health information management, medical radiologic technology/radiation therapy, medical secretary, nursing (RN), veterinary technology/assistant. **Human services:** Social work. **Liberal arts:** Arts/sciences. **Math:** General. **Protective services:** Criminal justice, fire safety technology. **Psychology:** General. **Visual/performing arts:** Art, commercial/advertising art, interior design, music, sculpture. **Work/family studies:** Child development, institutional food production.

Most popular majors. Business/marketing 13%, education 15%, engineering/engineering technologies 7%, health sciences 18%, liberal arts 32%.

Technology on campus. 750 workstations in library, computer center, student center. Dormitories wired for high-speed internet access and linked to campus network. Commuter students can connect to campus network. Online course registration, wireless network available.

Student life. Freshman orientation: Mandatory. Preregistration for classes offered. **Housing:** Single-sex dorms, special housing for disabled available. $50 nonrefundable deposit. **Activities:** Bands, campus ministries, choral groups, dance, drama, music ensembles, musical theater, student government, student newspaper, Baptist student union, Wesley Foundation, Newman Club, A.D.U.L.T.

Athletics. NJCAA. **Intercollegiate:** Baseball M, basketball, cheerleading, football (tackle) M, golf M, soccer, softball, tennis. **Intramural:** Baseball, basketball, football (tackle), softball, tennis. **Team name:** Bulldogs.

Student services. Adult student services, career counseling, student employment services, financial aid counseling, health services, on-campus daycare, personal counseling, placement for graduates, veterans' counselor. **Physically disabled:** Services for visually, hearing impaired. **Transfer:** Transfer adviser, college fairs on campus for students transferring to 4-year colleges.

Contact. E-mail: michelle.sekul@mgccc.edu
Phone: (601) 928-6333 Toll-free number: (866) 735-1122
Fax: (601) 928-6345
Michelle Sekul, College Registrar, Mississippi Gulf Coast Community College, PO Box 548, Perkinston, MS 39573

Northeast Mississippi Community College
Booneville, Mississippi
www.nemcc.edu   CB code: 1557

- Public 2-year community college
- Commuter campus in small town

General. Founded in 1948. Regionally accredited. **Enrollment:** 3,568 degree-seeking undergraduates. **Degrees:** 610 associate awarded. **ROTC:** Army. **Location:** 30 miles from Tupelo, 110 miles from Memphis, TN. **Calendar:** Semester, extensive summer session. **Full-time faculty:** 120 total; 13% have terminal degrees, 7% minority, 67% women. **Part-time faculty:** 36 total; 3% have terminal degrees, 69% women.

Student profile.

Out-of-state: 2% **25 or older:**   5%

Transfer out. Colleges most students transferred to 2015: University of Mississippi, Mississippi State University, Blue Mountain College, Mississippi University for Women, University of North Alabama.

Basis for selection. Open admission, but selective for some programs. Admission to nursing, dental hygiene, medical laboratory, medical assisting, practical nursing, radiologic technology, and respiratory technician programs based on test scores and other criteria. Interview required for dental hygiene, medical laboratory technology, and nursing students.

2015-2016 Annual costs. Tuition/fees: $2,452; $4,702 out-of-state. Room/board: $3,650. Books/supplies: $1,600. Personal expenses: $1,650.

2014-2015 Financial aid. Need-based: 73% of total undergraduate aid awarded as scholarships/grants, 27% as loans/jobs. Need-based aid available for part-time students. Work-study available nights, weekends and for part-time students. **Non-need-based:** Scholarships awarded for academics, alumni affiliation, athletics, leadership, music/drama.

Application procedures. Admission: No deadline. No application fee. Application must be submitted on paper. Admission notification on a rolling basis. **Financial aid:** Priority date 4/1; no closing date. FAFSA, institutional form required. Applicants notified on a rolling basis.

Academics. Special study options: Distance learning, dual enrollment of high school students, study abroad. License preparation in dental hygiene, nursing, occupational therapy, radiology. **Credit/placement by examination:** AP, CLEP, institutional tests. 18 credit hours maximum toward associate degree. **Support services:** GED preparation and test center, learning center, pre-admission summer program, reduced course load, remedial instruction, study skills assistance, tutoring, writing center.

Majors. Architecture: Building sciences. **Biology:** General. **Business:** Accounting, accounting technology, administrative services, business admin, hospitality admin, marketing, office technology. **Communications:** Communications/speech/rhetoric, journalism. **Computer sciences:** General, programming, web page design. **Education:** Agricultural, art, business, elementary, English, family/consumer sciences, foreign languages, mathematics, music, physical, science, social science, special ed. **Engineering:** General, geological. **English:** Writing. **Foreign languages:** General. **Health services:** Athletic training, clinical lab technology, dental hygiene, health information management, medical assistant, nursing (RN), premedicine, prepharmacy, preveterinary, radiologic technology/medical imaging, respiratory therapy

technology. **History:** General. **Human services:** Social work. **Liberal arts:** Arts/sciences, library assistant. **Math:** General. **Physical sciences:** Chemistry, physics. **Protective services:** Criminal justice. **Psychology:** General. **Social sciences:** Political science, sociology. **Theology:** Theology. **Visual/performing arts:** Art, interior design, music, music performance, musical theater, photography. **Work/family studies:** General, child care service, clothing/textiles.

Technology on campus. Dormitories wired for high-speed internet access and linked to campus network. Commuter students can connect to campus network. Online course registration, online library, helpline, wireless network available.

Student life. Freshman orientation: Available, $25 fee. Preregistration for classes offered. Two one-day sessions; students attend sessions according to major. **Housing:** Coed dorms, single-sex dorms available. $100 fully refundable deposit. **Activities:** Bands, choral groups, dance, drama, film society, literary magazine, music ensembles, musical theater, radio station, student government, student newspaper, Baptist student union, Wesley House.

Athletics. NJCAA. **Intercollegiate:** Baseball M, basketball, cheerleading W, football (tackle) M, golf M, softball W, tennis. **Intramural:** Basketball, softball, table tennis, volleyball. **Team name:** Tigers.

Student services. Adult student services, career counseling, student employment services, financial aid counseling, health services, minority student services, on-campus daycare, personal counseling, placement for graduates, veterans' counselor. **Physically disabled:** Services for visually, speech, hearing impaired. **Transfer:** Transfer adviser, college fairs on campus for students transferring to 4-year colleges.

Contact. E-mail: admitme@nemcc.edu
Phone: (662) 720-7290 Toll-free number: (800) 555-2154
Fax: (662) 728-1165
Chassie Kelly, Director of Enrollment Services/Registrar, Northeast Mississippi Community College, 101 Cunningham Boulevard, Booneville, MS 38829

Northwest Mississippi Community College
Senatobia, Mississippi
www.northwestms.edu   CB code: 1562

- Public 2-year community college
- Commuter campus in small town

General. Founded in 1927. Regionally accredited. **Enrollment:** 8,220 undergraduates. **Degrees:** 988 associate awarded. **ROTC:** Air Force. **Location:** 30 miles from Memphis, Tennessee. **Calendar:** Semester, extensive summer session. **Full-time faculty:** 206 total. **Part-time faculty:** 176 total. **Class size:** 45% < 20, 49% 20-39, 6% 40-49, less than 1% 50-99.

Student profile.

Out-of-state: 10% **Live on campus:**   14%

Transfer out. Colleges most students transferred to 2015: University of Mississippi; Mississippi State.

Basis for selection. Open admission, but selective for some programs. Special requirements for some technical programs. **Adult students:** SAT/ACT scores not required if applicant over 21.

High school preparation. 17 units recommended. Recommended units include English 4, mathematics 3, social studies 4 and science 2.

2015-2016 Annual costs. Tuition/fees: $2,550; $4,950 out-of-state. Per-credit charge: $110 in-state; $210 out-of-state. Room/board: $3,400. Books/supplies: $750.

Financial aid. Need-based: Work-study available nights, weekends and for part-time students.

Application procedures. Admission: No deadline. No application fee. Application must be submitted on paper. Admission notification on a rolling basis beginning on or about 7/1. **Financial aid:** Priority date 4/1; no closing date. FAFSA required. Applicants notified by 8/16.

Academics. Special study options: Accelerated study, distance learning, dual enrollment of high school students. Bachelor's degree programs available on campus. License preparation in aviation, nursing, paramedic, real estate. **Credit/placement by examination:** AP, CLEP, institutional tests. **Support services:** GED preparation and test center, reduced course load, remedial instruction, tutoring.

Majors. Business: Accounting, business admin, fashion, hospitality/recreation, management information systems, office technology. **Communications:** Broadcast journalism, journalism, public relations. **Communications technology:** General, graphic/printing. **Computer sciences:** General, applications programming, data processing, networking, programming. **Education:** General, art, business, elementary, family/consumer sciences, mathematics, music, physical, sales/marketing, science, secondary, social science, social studies, special ed. **Health services:** Medical secretary, respiratory therapy technology. **Liberal arts:** Arts/sciences. **Visual/performing arts:** Commercial/advertising art.

Most popular majors. Business/marketing 31%, computer/information sciences 23%, education 15%, health sciences 31%.

Technology on campus. Dormitories wired for high-speed internet access and linked to campus network. Commuter students can connect to campus network. Online library, helpline, wireless network available.

Student life. Freshman orientation: Available. Preregistration for classes offered. **Housing:** Single-sex dorms available. **Activities:** Bands, campus ministries, choral groups, drama, music ensembles, musical theater, student government, student newspaper.

Athletics. NJCAA. **Intercollegiate:** Baseball M, basketball, cheerleading W, football (tackle) M, golf M, rodeo, soccer, softball W, tennis. **Intramural:** Badminton, basketball, football (non-tackle), softball, tennis, volleyball. **Team name:** Rangers.

Student services. Alcohol/substance abuse counseling, career counseling, services for economically disadvantaged, personal counseling, veterans' counselor. **Physically disabled:** Services for visually, speech, hearing impaired.

Contact. E-mail: jlsimpson@northwestms.edu
Phone: (601) 562-3200 ext. 3219 Fax: (662) 562-3221
Larry Simpson, Registrar, Northwest Mississippi Community College, 4975 Highway 51 North, Senatobia, MS 38668

Pearl River Community College
Poplarville, Mississippi
www.prcc.edu CB code: 1622

- Public 2-year community college
- Commuter campus in small town

General. Founded in 1921. Regionally accredited. **Enrollment:** 4,900 degree-seeking undergraduates. **Degrees:** 730 associate awarded. **Location:** 35 miles from Hattiesburg, 70 miles from New Orleans. **Calendar:** Semester, limited summer session. **Full-time faculty:** 200 total. **Part-time faculty:** 50 total.

Student profile.

Out-of-state: 9% Live on campus: 25%
25 or older: 23%

Basis for selection. Open admission, but selective for some programs. Special requirements for health occupation programs. Interview recommended for nursing majors.

2015-2016 Annual costs. Tuition/fees: $2,900; $5,298 out-of-state. Room/board: $4,500. Books/supplies: $500.

Financial aid. Need-based: Need-based aid available for part-time students. Work-study available nights, weekends and for part-time students. **Non-need-based:** Scholarships awarded for academics, alumni affiliation, athletics, leadership, music/drama, state residency.

Application procedures. Admission: No deadline. No application fee. Admission notification on a rolling basis. **Financial aid:** Priority date 4/17; no closing date. FAFSA, institutional form required. Applicants notified on a rolling basis.

Academics. Special study options: Cooperative education, dual enrollment of high school students. License preparation in dental hygiene, nursing, occupational therapy, physical therapy, radiology. **Credit/placement by examination:** AP, CLEP, ACT. 30 credit hours maximum toward associate degree. **Support services:** GED preparation and test center, learning center, reduced course load, remedial instruction, tutoring.

Majors. Business: Business admin, management information systems, office technology. **Computer sciences:** Applications programming, data processing. **Education:** Multi-level teacher. **General:** Carpentry, masonry, power transmission. **Health services:** Licensed practical nurse, medical secretary, respiratory therapy technology. **Liberal arts:** Arts/sciences.

Technology on campus. 150 workstations in library, computer center. Dormitories wired for high-speed internet access and linked to campus network. Commuter students can connect to campus network. Online course registration, helpline, wireless network available.

Student life. Freshman orientation: Available, $25 fee. Preregistration for classes offered. **Housing:** Single-sex dorms, special housing for disabled available. **Activities:** Bands, choral groups, drama, music ensembles, student government, student newspaper, Black Student Union, Wesley and Newman Clubs, Phi Theta Kappa, Afro-American Club, Baptist Student Union.

Athletics. NJCAA. **Intercollegiate:** Baseball M, basketball, football (tackle) M, golf M, softball W, tennis. **Intramural:** Badminton, basketball, softball, table tennis, tennis, volleyball. **Team name:** Wildcats.

Student services. Career counseling, student employment services, health services, personal counseling, placement for graduates, veterans' counselor.

Contact. E-mail: tmoody@prcc.edu
Phone: (601) 403-1214 Fax: (601) 403-1060
Dow Ford, Vice President for Enrollment Management, Pearl River Community College, 101 Highway 11 North, Poplarville, MS 39470

Southwest Mississippi Community College
Summit, Mississippi
www.smcc.edu CB code: 1729

- Public 2-year community college
- Commuter campus in rural community

General. Founded in 1918. Regionally accredited. **Enrollment:** 1,771 degree-seeking undergraduates. **Degrees:** 403 associate awarded. **Location:** 76 miles from Jackson, 100 miles from New Orleans. **Calendar:** Semester, limited summer session. **Full-time faculty:** 120 total. **Part-time faculty:** 9 total. **Class size:** 56% < 20, 35% 20-39, 8% 40-49, 1% 50-99. **Special facilities:** Observatory.

Student profile.

Out-of-state: 10% Live on campus: 20%
25 or older: 28%

Transfer out. Colleges most students transferred to 2015: University of Southern Mississippi, Southeastern Louisiana University, Mississippi State University, University of Mississippi, Jackson State University.

Basis for selection. Open admission, but selective for some programs. Some career-technical programs have additional requirements for admission, such as minimum ACT scores and/or sufficient grades in prerequisite courses. For ability to benefit from career programs, high school graduation or GED preferred. **Home schooled:** Transcript of courses and grades required. ACT scores highly recommended.

High school preparation. College-preparatory program recommended.

2015-2016 Annual costs. Tuition/fees: $2,720; $5,420 out-of-state. Per-credit charge: $115 in-state; $120 out-of-state. Room/board: $3,600. Books/supplies: $1,000. Personal expenses: $1,300.

Financial aid. Need-based: Need-based aid available for part-time students. Work-study available nights, weekends and for part-time students.

Application procedures. Admission: Priority date 8/1; no deadline. No application fee. Application must be submitted on paper. Admission notification on a rolling basis. **Financial aid:** No deadline. FAFSA required. Applicants notified on a rolling basis.

Academics. Special study options: Distance learning, dual enrollment of high school students. License preparation in nursing. **Credit/placement by examination:** AP, CLEP. 24 credit hours maximum toward associate degree. **Support services:** GED preparation and test center, learning center, reduced course load, remedial instruction, tutoring.

Majors. Business: Marketing, office/clerical. **Computer sciences:** Data processing. **Health services:** Health information management, health information technology, insurance specialist, nursing (RN). **Liberal arts:** Arts/sciences.

Most popular majors. Business/marketing 9%, engineering/engineering technologies 9%, health sciences 26%, liberal arts 42%.

Technology on campus. 150 workstations in library, computer center. Dormitories wired for high-speed internet access. Online course registration, wireless network available.

Student life. Freshman orientation: Mandatory. Preregistration for classes offered. 4-hour sessions offered during summer and week before class begins. **Housing:** Single-sex dorms available. $60 partly refundable deposit, deadline 8/1. **Activities:** Bands, campus ministries, choral groups, dance, music ensembles, student government, student newspaper, Baptist student union, Wesley Foundation.

Athletics. NJCAA. **Intercollegiate:** Baseball M, basketball, football (tackle) M, soccer, softball W. **Intramural:** Basketball, football (non-tackle), table tennis, tennis M, volleyball. **Team name:** Bears.

Student services. Career counseling, health services, personal counseling, placement for graduates, veterans' counselor. **Physically disabled:** Services for visually, speech, hearing impaired. **Transfer:** Transfer adviser, college fairs on campus for students transferring to 4-year colleges.

Contact. E-mail: mattc@smcc.edu
Phone: (601) 276-2001 Fax: (601) 276-3888
Matthew Calhoun, Vice President of Admissions, Southwest Mississippi Community College, 1156 College Drive, Summit, MS 39666

Virginia College in Biloxi
Biloxi, Mississippi
www.vc.edu/college/biloxi-colleges-mississippi.cfm

▶ For-profit 2-year business and health science college
▶ Commuter campus in small city

General. Accredited by ACICS. **Enrollment:** 470 undergraduates. **Degrees:** 82 associate awarded. **Calendar:** Quarter. **Full-time faculty:** 17 total. **Part-time faculty:** 26 total.

Basis for selection. Admission requirements vary by program.

2015-2016 Annual costs. Certificate programs: $13,932-$23,220. Associate programs: $37,152-$40,700. Clock hour certificate program: Cosmetology $21,225; Therapeutic Massage $15,435.

Financial aid. Need-based: Work-study available nights, weekends and for part-time students.

Application procedures. Admission: No deadline. $100 fee.

Academics. Credit/placement by examination: AP, CLEP.

Majors. Business: Business admin, office management. **Health services:** Medical assistant, office admin, office assistant, surgical technology.

Contact. Phone: (228) 392-2994 Fax: (228) 392-2039
Betina Yurkus, Director of Admissions, Virginia College in Biloxi, 920 Cedar Lake Road, Biloxi, MS 39532

Virginia College in Jackson
Jackson, Mississippi
www.vc.edu

▶ For-profit 2-year community college
▶ Commuter campus in small city

General. Regionally accredited; also accredited by ACICS. **Enrollment:** 376 undergraduates. **Degrees:** 13 associate awarded. **Calendar:** Quarter. **Full-time faculty:** 23 total. **Part-time faculty:** 33 total.

Basis for selection. Passing score on CPAT exam required.

2015-2016 Annual costs. Certificate programs: $13,932-$23,220. Associate programs: $37,152-$40,700. Clock hour certificate program: Cosmetology $16,920.

Financial aid. Need-based: Work-study available nights, weekends and for part-time students.

Application procedures. Admission: No deadline. $100 fee.

Academics. Credit/placement by examination: AP, CLEP.

Majors. Business: Business admin, office management. **Computer sciences:** LAN/WAN management, networking, system admin. **Health services:** Office admin, surgical technology.

Contact. E-mail: mtlittle@vc.edu
Phone: (601) 977-0960 Fax: (601) 977-2719
Lawrence Brown, Director of Admissions, Virginia College in Jackson, 4795 Interstate 55 North, Jackson, MS 39206

Missouri

Bolivar Technical College
Bolivar, Missouri
www.bolivarcollege.org

♦ Private 2-year branch campus and technical college
♦ Commuter campus in small town
♦ Application essay required

General. Accredited by ACICS. Home campus in Houston Missouri. **Enrollment:** 86 degree-seeking undergraduates. **Degrees:** 55 associate awarded. **Location:** 120 miles from Kansas City. **Calendar:** Semester, limited summer session. **Full-time faculty:** 7 total; 100% women. **Part-time faculty:** 13 total; 8% have terminal degrees, 69% women.

Transfer out. Colleges most students transferred to 2015: Missouri State University, Ozarks Technical Community College.

Basis for selection. Open admission, but selective for some programs. Admission requires a minimum passing score on each section of the wonderlic exam. Wonderlic exam administered to all admitted students; additional testing for nursing students. **Home schooled:** Transcript of courses and grades required. ACT score of 18 or higher required. **Learning Disabled:** High school IEP from the junior or senior year allowed; adult diagnosis of special needs required if out of high school 2 or more years.

2015-2016 Annual costs. Tuition/fees: $12,982. Books/supplies: $2,000.

2014-2015 Financial aid. All financial aid based on need. 16 full-time freshmen applied for aid; 16 deemed to have need; 16 received aid. Average scholarship/grant was $2,888. 71% of total undergraduate aid awarded as scholarships/grants, 29% as loans/jobs. Need-based aid available for part-time students. Work-study available nights, weekends and for part-time students.

Application procedures. Admission: No deadline. $50 fee. Application must be submitted on paper. Admission notification on a rolling basis. **Financial aid:** Priority date 4/1; no closing date. FAFSA, institutional form required.

Academics. Special study options: Internships. License preparation in nursing. **Credit/placement by examination:** AP, CLEP, institutional tests. **Support services:** Remedial instruction, study skills assistance, tutoring.

Majors. Health services: Medical secretary, nursing (RN).

Technology on campus. 40 workstations in library, computer center. Online library available.

Student life. Freshman orientation: Mandatory. Preregistration for classes offered. **Activities:** Student newspaper.

Student services. Career counseling, financial aid counseling. **Transfer:** Pre-admission transcript evaluation for new students.

Contact. E-mail: info@bolivarcollege.org
Phone: (417) 777-5062 Toll-free number: (800) 440-6135
Fax: (417) 777-8908
Nancy Brannon, Admissions Director, Bolivar Technical College, PO Box 592, Bolivar, MO 65613

Brown Mackie College: St. Louis
Fenton, Missouri
www.brownmackie.edu

♦ For-profit 2-year career college
♦ Very large city

General. Regionally accredited; also accredited by ACICS. **Enrollment:** 634 undergraduates. **Degrees:** 1 bachelor's, 130 associate awarded. **Calendar:** Quarter. **Full-time faculty:** 2 total. **Part-time faculty:** 21 total.

Basis for selection. Open admission.

2015-2016 Annual costs. Tuition/fees: $16,490. Per-credit charge: $327.

Financial aid. Need-based: Work-study available nights, weekends and for part-time students.

Academics. Credit/placement by examination: AP, CLEP.

Majors. Business: Accounting technology. **Computer sciences:** Support specialist. **Health services:** Health care admin, medical assistant, occupational therapy assistant, pharmacy assistant, surgical technology. **Protective services:** Criminal justice.

Contact. Phyllis Hutto, Director of Admissions, Brown Mackie College: St. Louis, #2 Soccer Park Road, Fenton, MO 63026

Concorde Career College: Kansas City
Kansas City, Missouri
www.concorde.edu/kansas   CB code: 3126

♦ For-profit 2-year business and health science college
♦ Large city

General. Accredited by ACCSC. **Enrollment:** 783 undergraduates. **Degrees:** 130 associate awarded. **Calendar:** Differs by program. **Full-time faculty:** 20 total. **Part-time faculty:** 11 total.

Basis for selection. Open admission, but selective for some programs.

2015-2016 Annual costs. Books/supplies: $348. **Additional information:** Diploma programs: medical assistant $14,296; practical nursing $28,040; dental assistant $15,466; medical office administration $14,686; pharmacy technician $11,040. Associate programs: dental hygiene $56,214; physical therapy assistant $31,017; respiratory therapy $34,458; health information management $35,145. Books and supplies vary by program ranging from $751-$7,547.

Financial aid. Need-based: Work-study available nights, weekends and for part-time students.

Application procedures. Admission: $100 fee.

Academics. Credit/placement by examination: AP, CLEP.

Majors. Business: Business admin. **Health services:** Licensed practical nurse, respiratory therapy assistant.

Contact. E-mail: dcrow@concorde.edu
Phone: (816) 531-5223 Toll-free number: (800) 464-1212
Fax: (816) 756-3231
Deborah Crow, Campus Director, Concorde Career College: Kansas City, 3239 Broadway, Kansas City, MO 64111

Cottey College
Nevada, Missouri   CB member
www.cottey.edu   CB code: 6120

♦ Private 2-year liberal arts college for women
♦ Residential campus in small town
♦ SAT or ACT (ACT writing optional) required

General. Founded in 1884. Regionally accredited. Sponsored and supported by P.E.O. Sisterhood, nonsectarian philanthropic educational organization. College owned and supported by women for women. **Enrollment:** 317 degree-seeking undergraduates. **Degrees:** 12 bachelor's, 90 associate awarded. **Location:** 100 miles from Kansas City, 60 miles from Joplin. **Calendar:** Semester. **Full-time faculty:** 37 total; 84% have terminal degrees, 14% minority, 65% women. **Part-time faculty:** 10 total; 60% women. **Class size:** 92% < 20, 8% 20-39. **Special facilities:** 33-acre wooded area with lodge for outings and nature laboratory, women's leadership center.

Student profile.

Out-of-state: 90% **Live on campus:**   99%

Transfer out. Colleges most students transferred to 2015: Smith College, Hood College, Truman State University, Boston University, Mount Holyoke College.

Basis for selection. High school course of study most important; GPA and test scores also important. Recommendations, essay and interviews considered when other criteria not met. Interview recommended for all students. Audition recommended for music students; portfolio recommended for art students. Essay requested sometimes. **Home schooled:** Statement describing home school structure and mission, transcript of courses and grades required. Students should take GED examination.

High school preparation. College-preparatory program required. 15 units required. Required units include English 4, mathematics 3, social studies 2, science 2 (laboratory 2) and foreign language 2. Mathematics should include algebra I, algebra II, geometry.

2015-2016 Annual costs. Tuition/fees: $19,300. Room/board: $7,000. Books/supplies: $1,100. Personal expenses: $1,350.

Financial aid. Need-based: Need-based aid available for part-time students. Work-study available nights, weekends and for part-time students. **Non-need-based:** Scholarships awarded for academics, alumni affiliation, art, athletics, leadership, music/drama.

Application procedures. Admission: Priority date 3/1; no deadline. $20 fee, may be waived for applicants with need. Admission notification on a rolling basis. Tuition deposit of $100 required to reserve spot in class and in student housing. **Financial aid:** Priority date 3/1; no closing date. FAFSA required. Applicants notified on a rolling basis starting 4/1; must reply within 2 week(s) of notification.

Academics. Special study options: Cross-registration, dual enrollment of high school students, independent study, internships. Bachelor's degree programs available on campus. **Credit/placement by examination:** AP, CLEP, IB, SAT, ACT, institutional tests. **Support services:** Reduced course load, study skills assistance, tutoring, writing center.

Majors. Liberal arts: Arts/sciences. **Physical sciences:** General. **Visual/performing arts:** Dance, music, studio arts, theater arts management.

Technology on campus. 62 workstations in dormitories, library, computer center, student center. Commuter students can connect to campus network. Wireless network available.

Student life. Freshman orientation: Mandatory. Preregistration for classes offered. Held in late August, 5 days prior to the first day of class. **Housing:** Guaranteed on-campus for all undergraduates. Wellness housing available. $100 fully refundable deposit, deadline 5/1. **Activities:** Jazz band, campus ministries, choral groups, dance, drama, international student organizations, literary magazine, music ensembles, opera, student government, student newspaper, 35 campus service and social organizations available.

Athletics. NJCAA. **Intercollegiate:** Basketball W, softball W, volleyball W. **Intramural:** Basketball W, golf W, softball W, swimming W, synchronized swimming W, table tennis W, tennis W, volleyball W. **Team name:** Comets.

Student services. Alcohol/substance abuse counseling, chaplain/spiritual director, career counseling, student employment services, financial aid counseling, health services, personal counseling. **Transfer:** Pre-admission transcript evaluation for new students. Transfer center, transfer adviser, college fairs on campus for students transferring to 4-year colleges.

Contact. E-mail: enrollmgt@cottey.edu
Phone: (417) 667-8181 Toll-free number: (888) 526-8839
Fax: (417) 448-1025
Judi Steege, Director of Admission, Cottey College, 1000 West Austin Boulevard, Nevada, MO 64772

Crowder College
Neosho, Missouri
www.crowder.edu   CB code: 6138

▸ Public 2-year community and liberal arts college
▸ Commuter campus in small town

General. Founded in 1963. Regionally accredited. Water resource school with active/passive solar program. **Enrollment:** 3,923 degree-seeking undergraduates; 1,661 non-degree-seeking students. **Degrees:** 680 associate awarded. **Location:** 70 miles from Springfield, 28 miles from Joplin. **Calendar:** Semester, limited summer session. **Full-time faculty:** 100 total; 10% have terminal degrees, 3% minority, 60% women. **Part-time faculty:** 438 total; 7% have terminal degrees, 2% minority, 60% women. **Class size:** 76% < 20, 23% 20-39, less than 1% 40-49, less than 1% 50-99.

Student profile. Among degree-seeking undergraduates, 1,125 enrolled as first-time, first-year students.

Part-time:	40%	Native American:	3%
Women:	63%	Multi-racial, non-Hispanic:	3%
African American:	2%	International:	1%
Asian American:	2%	Live on campus:	10%
Hispanic/Latino:	10%		

Transfer out. Colleges most students transferred to 2015: Missouri Southern State College, Pittsburg State University, Southwest Missouri State University.

Basis for selection. Open admission, but selective for some programs. Interview, 2.75 GPA, and minimum 19 ACT score required for nursing program. **Home schooled:** Must pass GED.

High school preparation. Recommended units include English 4, mathematics 3 and science 3.

2016-2017 Annual costs. Tuition/fees (projected): $2,940; $4,140 out-of-district; $4,140 out-of-state. Per-credit charge: $82 in-district; $122 out-of-district; $122 out-of-state. Room/board: $5,002. Books/supplies: $900.

2014-2015 Financial aid. Need-based: 77% of total undergraduate aid awarded as scholarships/grants, 23% as loans/jobs. Need-based aid available for part-time students. Work-study available nights, weekends and for part-time students. **Non-need-based:** Scholarships awarded for academics, art, athletics, leadership, minority status, music/drama, state residency.

Application procedures. Admission: No deadline. $25 fee, may be waived for applicants with need. Admission notification on a rolling basis. **Financial aid:** Priority date 7/1; no closing date. FAFSA, institutional form required. Applicants notified on a rolling basis starting 5/15; must reply within 4 week(s) of notification.

Academics. Special study options: Distance learning, dual enrollment of high school students, ESL, honors, independent study, internships, liberal arts/career combination, study abroad, weekend college. License preparation in nursing, occupational therapy, paramedic. **Credit/placement by examination:** AP, CLEP, institutional tests. 15 credit hours maximum toward associate degree. **Support services:** GED preparation and test center, learning center, reduced course load, remedial instruction, study skills assistance, tutoring.

Majors. Biology: General. **Business:** General, administrative services, office/clerical. **Communications:** Journalism, public relations. **Computer sciences:** General, system admin. **Education:** Elementary, physical, secondary. **Engineering:** General. **Foreign languages:** Spanish. **Health services:** Environmental health, nursing (RN), office assistant. **History:** General. **Liberal arts:** Arts/sciences. **Math:** General. **Physical sciences:** General, chemistry, physics. **Psychology:** General. **Social sciences:** General. **Visual/performing arts:** Art, music, theater arts management.

Most popular majors. Business/marketing 14%, education 6%, health sciences 19%, liberal arts 48%.

Technology on campus. 1,000 workstations in dormitories, library, computer center. Dormitories wired for high-speed internet access. Online library, helpline, wireless network available.

Student life. Freshman orientation: Mandatory. Preregistration for classes offered. **Housing:** Guaranteed on-campus for all undergraduates. Single-sex dorms, wellness housing available. $150 deposit. **Activities:** Bands, choral groups, dance, drama, literary magazine, music ensembles, musical theater, student government, student newspaper, Aggies (agricultural club), art club, Baptist student union, Students in Free Enterprise, Student-Missouri State Teacher's Association, Phi Theta Kappa, Latino union, Habitat for Humanity.

Athletics. NJCAA. **Intercollegiate:** Baseball M, basketball W, soccer M, softball W. **Team name:** Roughriders.

Student services. Career counseling, student employment services, financial aid counseling, personal counseling, placement for graduates. **Transfer:** Transfer adviser, college fairs on campus for students transferring to 4-year colleges.

Contact. E-mail: admissions@crowder.edu
Phone: (417) 455-5718 Toll-free number: (866) 238-7788
Fax: (417) 455-2439
Jim Riggs, Director of Admission, Crowder College, 601 Laclede Avenue, Neosho, MO 64850

East Central College
Union, Missouri   CB member
www.eastcentral.edu   CB code: 0845

▸ Public 2-year community college
▸ Commuter campus in large town

General. Founded in 1968. Regionally accredited. **Enrollment:** 2,543 degree-seeking undergraduates; 679 non-degree-seeking students. **Degrees:**

440 associate awarded. **Location:** 45 miles from St. Louis. **Calendar:** Semester, limited summer session. **Full-time faculty:** 73 total; 58% women. **Part-time faculty:** 110 total; 52% women. **Special facilities:** Learning and assessment center, observatory, natural prairie.

Student profile. Among degree-seeking undergraduates, 686 enrolled as first-time, first-year students.

Part-time:	42%	Hispanic/Latino:	2%
Women:	62%	Native American:	1%
African American:	1%	25 or older:	30%

Basis for selection. Open admission, but selective for some programs. Special requirements for nursing and teaching programs. Compass Test required for placement for all associate degree and most certificate programs. **Home schooled:** Transcript of courses and grades required. Transcript must be notarized.

2016-2017 Annual costs. Tuition/fees (projected): $2,850; $3,900 out-of-district; $5,610 out-of-state. Per-credit charge: $76 in-district; $111 out-of-district; $168 out-of-state. Books/supplies: $1,500. Personal expenses: $1,575.

Financial aid. Need-based: Need-based aid available for part-time students. Work-study available nights, weekends and for part-time students. **Non-need-based:** Scholarships awarded for academics, alumni affiliation, art, athletics, music/drama, state residency.

Application procedures. Admission: No deadline. No application fee. Admission notification on a rolling basis. **Financial aid:** Priority date 3/15; no closing date. FAFSA required. Applicants notified on a rolling basis starting 4/1.

Academics. Special study options: Distance learning, dual enrollment of high school students, honors, independent study, internships, liberal arts/career combination. Central Methodist University classes offered on campus and may count toward 4-year degree. Bachelor's degree programs available on campus. License preparation in nursing, paramedic, radiology. **Credit/placement by examination:** AP, CLEP, institutional tests. **Support services:** GED preparation and test center, learning center, reduced course load, remedial instruction, study skills assistance, tutoring, writing center.

Majors. Business: General, accounting technology, administrative services, management information systems. **Computer sciences:** Networking. **Education:** General, voc/tech. **Engineering:** General. **Health services:** EMT paramedic, health information technology, medical assistant, medical radiologic technology/radiation therapy, nursing (RN), occupational therapy assistant, respiratory therapy technology. **Protective services:** Firefighting. **Visual/performing arts:** Commercial/advertising art, music, studio arts. **Work/family studies:** Child care management.

Most popular majors. Business/marketing 6%, health sciences 28%, liberal arts 47%.

Technology on campus. Online course registration, online library, wireless network available.

Student life. Freshman orientation: Mandatory. Preregistration for classes offered. Held prior to start of classes, includes tours, seminars, advisor activities, social activities. **Activities:** Bands, choral groups, drama, music ensembles, musical theater, student government, student newspaper, TV station, Phi Theta Kappa honor society, AHERO club, art club, R&R club, variety of religious and social clubs.

Athletics. NJCAA. **Intercollegiate:** Soccer M, softball W, volleyball W. **Team name:** Falcons.

Student services. Adult student services, career counseling, student employment services, financial aid counseling, personal counseling, placement for graduates, veterans' counselor. **Physically disabled:** Services for visually, hearing impaired. **Transfer:** Pre-admission transcript evaluation for new students. Transfer adviser, college fairs on campus for students transferring to 4-year colleges.

Contact. E-mail: admissions@eastcentral.edu
Phone: (636) 584-6588 Fax: (636) 584-7347
Nathaniel Mitchell, Director of Admissions, East Central College, 1964 Prairie Dell Road, Union, MO 63084-0529

ITT Technical Institute: Kansas City
Kansas City, Missouri
www.itt-tech.edu

▶ For-profit 2-year business and technical college
▶ Commuter campus in large city

General. Accredited by ACICS. **Enrollment:** 231 undergraduates. **Degrees:** 33 bachelor's, 76 associate awarded. **Calendar:** Quarter. **Full-time faculty:** 10 total. **Part-time faculty:** 53 total.

Basis for selection. Admission requirements will vary by program.

2015-2016 Annual costs. Per-credit-hour charge, $493, will vary depending on program level and course of study. Academic fee, $200. Some programs require purchase of tools, which could cost between $100 to $500. All costs subject to change.

Financial aid. Need-based: Work-study available nights, weekends and for part-time students.

Academics. Credit/placement by examination: AP, CLEP. **Support services:** Remedial instruction.

Majors. Business: General. **Computer sciences:** LAN/WAN management, networking, programming. **Protective services:** Criminalistics, forensics, law enforcement admin. **Visual/performing arts:** Design, graphic design.

Student services. Placement for graduates.

Contact. Toll-free number: (877) 488-1442
ITT Technical Institute: Kansas City, 9150 East 41st Terrace, Kansas City, MO 64133

Jefferson College
Hillsboro, Missouri
www.jeffco.edu — **CB code: 6320**

▶ Public 2-year community and technical college
▶ Commuter campus in rural community

General. Founded in 1963. Regionally accredited. Serves as county area vocational/technical school. **Enrollment:** 4,563 degree-seeking undergraduates; 142 non-degree-seeking students. **Degrees:** 698 associate awarded. **Location:** 30 miles from St Louis. **Calendar:** Semester, limited summer session. **Full-time faculty:** 100 total; 16% have terminal degrees, 6% minority, 57% women. **Part-time faculty:** 253 total; 7% have terminal degrees, 5% minority, 47% women. **Class size:** 64% < 20, 35% 20-39, less than 1% 40-49, less than 1% 50-99, less than 1% >100. **Special facilities:** Facility for computer-related technologies, veterinary technology clinic, health occupation program labs, law enforcement academy, emergency medical technician lab/classroom, CNA lab/classroom, olympic size pool, business and technology training center.

Student profile. Among degree-seeking undergraduates, 55% enrolled in a transfer program, 45% enrolled in a vocational program, 1% already have a bachelor's degree or higher, 980 enrolled as first-time, first-year students, 256 transferred in from other institutions.

Part-time:	50%	Asian American:	1%
Women:	59%	Native American:	1%
African American:	2%	Live on campus:	2%

Transfer out. Colleges most students transferred to 2015: University of Missouri: St. Louis, Missouri Baptist University, Southeast Missouri State University.

Basis for selection. Open admission, but selective for some programs. Special requirements for the nursing program, veterinary technology program, health and occupational programs, law enforcement academy, and emergency medical technician. Interview required for health occupational technology students. **Home schooled:** Minimum placement test scores if high school transcript is not from an approved accrediting body. **Learning Disabled:** Students should meet with Disability Support Services Coordinator prior to enrollment.

High school preparation. College-preparatory program required. Elementary algebra required for electronics; chemistry required for nursing and veterinary technology.

2015-2016 Annual costs. Tuition/fees: $3,090; $4,560 out-of-district; $6,000 out-of-state. Room/board: $5,644. Books/supplies: $915. Personal expenses: $621.

2014-2015 Financial aid. Need-based: 886 full-time freshmen applied for aid; 667 deemed to have need; 640 received aid. Average need met was 52%. Average scholarship/grant was $2,452; average loan $2,746. 63% of total undergraduate aid awarded as scholarships/grants, 37% as loans/jobs. Need-based aid available for part-time students. Work-study available nights, weekends and for part-time students. **Non-need-based:** Awarded to 698 full-time undergraduates, including 269 freshmen. Scholarships awarded for academics, art, athletics, leadership, music/drama, state residency.

Application procedures. Admission: No deadline. $25 fee, may be waived for applicants with need. Admission notification on a rolling basis. **Financial aid:** Priority date 4/1; no closing date. FAFSA required. Applicants notified on a rolling basis starting 4/15.

Academics. Special study options: Cooperative education, distance learning, dual enrollment of high school students, ESL, honors, independent study, internships, liberal arts/career combination, teacher certification program. Bachelor's degree programs available on campus. License preparation in nursing, occupational therapy, paramedic, physical therapy, radiology. **Credit/placement by examination:** AP, CLEP, IB, institutional tests. 30 credit hours maximum toward associate degree. **Support services:** GED preparation and test center, learning center, remedial instruction, study skills assistance, tutoring, writing center.

Majors. Business: General, administrative services, office/clerical. **Computer sciences:** Networking, web page design. **Education:** General, early childhood. **Engineering:** General. **Health services:** EMT paramedic, health information technology, medical secretary, nursing (RN), occupational therapy assistant, physical therapy assistant, radiologic technology/medical imaging, respiratory therapy technology, veterinary technology/assistant. **Liberal arts:** Arts/sciences. **Protective services:** Computer forensics, fire safety technology, law enforcement admin. **Work/family studies:** Child care management.

Most popular majors. Education 6%, health sciences 17%, liberal arts 51%, security/protective services 6%.

Technology on campus. 250 workstations in dormitories, library, computer center, student center. Dormitories wired for high-speed internet access and linked to campus network. Commuter students can connect to campus network. Online course registration, online library, helpline, wireless network available.

Student life. Freshman orientation: Mandatory. Preregistration for classes offered. **Housing:** Apartments, wellness housing available. $200 partly refundable deposit. **Activities:** Jazz band, choral groups, drama, literary magazine, music ensembles, musical theater, student government, student newspaper, TV station, Phi Theta Kappa, College Ambassadors, Habitat for Humanity, academic clubs, cultural clubs, Missouri Student National Educational Association, National Technical Honors Society.

Athletics. NJCAA. **Intercollegiate:** Baseball M, basketball W, soccer M, softball W, volleyball W. **Team name:** Vikings.

Student services. Adult student services, alcohol/substance abuse counseling, career counseling, services for economically disadvantaged, student employment services, financial aid counseling, on-campus daycare, personal counseling, placement for graduates, veterans' counselor. **Physically disabled:** Services for visually, speech, hearing impaired. **Transfer:** Re-entry adviser, pre-admission transcript evaluation for new students. Transfer adviser, college fairs on campus for students transferring to 4-year colleges.

Contact. E-mail: admissions@jeffco.edu
Phone: (636) 481-3217 Fax: (636) 789-5103
Kimberly Harvey, Senior Director of Enrollment Services-Registrar, Jefferson College, 1000 Viking Drive, Hillsboro, MO 63050-2441

L'Ecole Culinaire
St. Louis, Missouri
www.lecoleculinaire.com

- For-profit 2-year culinary school
- Commuter campus in large city

General. Accredited by ACCSC. **Enrollment:** 269 undergraduates. **Degrees:** 98 associate awarded. **Calendar:** Quarter. **Full-time faculty:** 31 total. **Part-time faculty:** 2 total.

Basis for selection. Open admission.

2015-2016 Annual costs. Diploma program: Culinary Fundamentals (40 weeks) $22,100. Associate program: Culinary & Restaurant Management (70 weeks) $37,300.

Financial aid. Need-based: Work-study available nights, weekends and for part-time students.

Academics. Credit/placement by examination: AP, CLEP.

Student life. Activities: Ambassador's Club honorary society, outdoors club, garden club.

Contact. Phone: (314) 587-2433 Toll-free number: (866) 532-6532
Michelle Dorsett, Director of Admissions, L'Ecole Culinaire, 9811 South Outer Forty Drive, St. Louis, MO 63124

Metro Business College
Cape Girardeau, Missouri
www.metrobusinesscollege.edu
CB code: 3316

- For-profit 2-year career college
- Commuter campus in large town
- Interview required

General. Accredited by ACICS. **Enrollment:** 118 undergraduates. **Degrees:** 28 associate awarded. **Location:** 125 miles from St. Louis. **Calendar:** Differs by program. **Full-time faculty:** 9 total. **Part-time faculty:** 4 total.

Basis for selection. Open admission. **Home schooled:** State high school equivalency certificate required.

2015-2016 Annual costs. Certificate programs: $10,325-$13,725. Associate programs: $17,875-$21,125.

Financial aid. Need-based: Work-study available nights, weekends and for part-time students.

Application procedures. Admission: No deadline. $25 fee.

Academics. Credit/placement by examination: AP, CLEP. **Support services:** Study skills assistance, tutoring.

Majors. Business: Business admin.

Technology on campus. Online library available.

Student life. Freshman orientation: Mandatory. Preregistration for classes offered.

Student services. Adult student services, alcohol/substance abuse counseling, career counseling, services for economically disadvantaged, student employment services, financial aid counseling, minority student services, personal counseling, placement for graduates, veterans' counselor. **Physically disabled:** Services for visually impaired.

Contact. E-mail: denise@metrobusinesscollege.edu
Phone: (573) 334-9181 Toll-free number: (800) 467-0785
Fax: (573) 334-0617
Denise Acey, Director of Admissions, Metro Business College, 1732 North Kingshighway, Cape Girardeau, MO 63701

Metro Business College: Jefferson City
Jefferson City, Missouri
www.metrobusinesscollege.edu
CB code: 3318

- For-profit 2-year health science and career college
- Commuter campus in large town
- Interview required

General. Accredited by ACICS. **Enrollment:** 80 degree-seeking undergraduates. **Degrees:** 49 associate awarded. **Location:** 35 miles from Columbia. **Calendar:** Differs by program, limited summer session. **Full-time faculty:** 6 total; 83% women. **Part-time faculty:** 7 total; 14% have terminal degrees, 14% minority, 100% women. **Class size:** 100% 40-49.

Student profile. Among degree-seeking undergraduates, 100% enrolled in a vocational program, 1% already have a bachelor's degree or higher, 9 enrolled as first-time, first-year students.

Part-time:	15%	Asian American:	1%
Women:	94%	Native American:	1%
African American:	19%	25 or older:	40%

Transfer out. 2% of students enrolled in the transfer program go on to 4-year colleges. **Colleges most students transferred to 2015:** Columbia College.

Basis for selection. Open admission, but selective for some programs. Students must take entrance exam. Required scores vary by program. **Adult students:** SAT/ACT scores not required. **Home schooled:** Transcript of courses and grades required.

2016-2017 Annual costs. Tuition/fees (projected): $11,375. Per-credit charge: $230.

Financial aid. Need-based: Need-based aid available for part-time students. Work-study available nights, weekends and for part-time students.

Application procedures. Admission: No deadline. $25 fee. Application must be submitted on paper. Admission notification on a rolling basis. **Financial aid:** No deadline. FAFSA, institutional form required. Applicants notified on a rolling basis.

Academics. Special study options: Internships. **Credit/placement by examination:** AP, CLEP. **Support services:** Reduced course load, remedial instruction, study skills assistance, tutoring.

Majors. Business: Business admin. **Computer sciences:** Data entry. **Health services:** Office assistant.

Most popular majors. Computer/information sciences 19%, health sciences 31%.

Technology on campus. 98 workstations in library, computer center. Online library, repair service, wireless network available.

Student life. Freshman orientation: Mandatory. Preregistration for classes offered. **Activities:** Student government.

Student services. Adult student services, alcohol/substance abuse counseling, career counseling, services for economically disadvantaged, student employment services, financial aid counseling, personal counseling, placement for graduates. **Transfer:** Pre-admission transcript evaluation for new students. College fairs on campus for students transferring to 4-year colleges.

Contact. E-mail: infojeff@metrobusinesscollege.edu
Phone: (573) 635-6600 Toll-free number: (888) 436-3876
Fax: (573) 635-6999
Shawn Nesbitt, Admissions Representative, Metro Business College: Jefferson City, 210 El Mercado Plaza, Jefferson City, MO 65109

Metro Business College: Rolla
Rolla, Missouri
www.metrobusinesscollege.edu
CB code: 3317

‣ For-profit 2-year business college
‣ Commuter campus in large town

General. Accredited by ACICS. **Enrollment:** 76 undergraduates. **Degrees:** 27 associate awarded. **Calendar:** Differs by program. **Full-time faculty:** 7 total. **Part-time faculty:** 2 total.

Basis for selection. Open admission.

2015-2016 Annual costs. Certificate programs: $10,325-$13,725. Associate programs: $17,875-$21,125.

Financial aid. Need-based: Work-study available nights, weekends and for part-time students.

Application procedures. Admission: No deadline. $25 fee.

Academics. Credit/placement by examination: AP, CLEP.

Majors. Business: Accounting, office technology. **Health services:** Insurance coding, office computer specialist.

Contact. E-mail: dana@metrobusinesscollege.edu
Phone: (573) 364-8464 Toll-free number: (888) 436-3876
Fax: (573) 364-8077
Karla Lindeman, Director, Metro Business College: Rolla, 1202 East Highway 72, Rolla, MO 65401

Metropolitan Community College - Kansas City
Kansas City, Missouri
www.mcckc.edu
CB code: 6324

‣ Public 2-year community college
‣ Commuter campus in large city

General. Regionally accredited. **Enrollment:** 15,547 degree-seeking undergraduates. **Degrees:** 2,032 associate awarded. **ROTC:** Army. **Location:** 2

miles from downtown. **Calendar:** Semester, extensive summer session. **Full-time faculty:** 233 total; 18% minority, 53% women. **Part-time faculty:** 1,163 total; 13% minority, 51% women. **Class size:** 36% < 20, 62% 20-39, 1% 40-49, less than 1% 50-99.

Student profile.

Out-of-state: 2%   25 or older: 35%

Basis for selection. Open admission, but selective for some programs. Special requirements for allied health programs. ACT or ASSET required for placement and counseling. **Home schooled:** Statement describing home school structure and mission, transcript of courses and grades, interview required. Students under 16 must meet with Dean of Student Development.

High school preparation. 16 units recommended. Recommended units include English 4, mathematics 3, social studies 3, science 3 and foreign language 2. One unit visual/performing arts recommended.

2015-2016 Annual costs. Tuition/fees: $2,870; $5,270 out-of-district; $6,890 out-of-state. Books/supplies: $2,160. Personal expenses: $5,202.

Financial aid. Need-based: Work-study available nights, weekends and for part-time students. **Non-need-based:** Scholarships awarded for academics, athletics, leadership.

Application procedures. Admission: No deadline. No application fee. Admission notification on a rolling basis. **Financial aid:** Priority date 5/30, closing date 6/30. FAFSA, institutional form required. Applicants notified on a rolling basis starting 4/8.

Academics. Special study options: Cross-registration, distance learning, dual enrollment of high school students, ESL, honors, independent study, internships, liberal arts/career combination, weekend college. Cooperative programs in allied health with Johnson County Community College and Kansas City Kansas Community College. License preparation in dental hygiene, nursing, occupational therapy, paramedic, physical therapy, radiology. **Credit/placement by examination:** AP, CLEP, IB, institutional tests. 30 credit hours maximum toward associate degree. **Support services:** GED test center, learning center, reduced course load, remedial instruction, study skills assistance, tutoring, writing center.

Majors. Business: General, accounting, administrative services, business admin, customer service support, fashion, office management, office technology, sales/distribution. **Computer sciences:** General, programming. **Education:** General. **Engineering:** General. **Foreign languages:** Sign language interpretation. **Health services:** Dental assistant, EMT paramedic, medical radiologic technology/radiation therapy, mental health services, nursing (RN), occupational therapy assistant, physical therapy assistant, respiratory therapy technology, veterinary technology/assistant. **Liberal arts:** Arts/sciences. **Protective services:** Corrections, criminal justice, law enforcement admin. **Visual/performing arts:** Commercial/advertising art, fashion design, graphic design. **Work/family studies:** Child care management.

Most popular majors. Engineering/engineering technologies 6%, health sciences 13%, liberal arts 66%.

Technology on campus. 2,798 workstations in library, computer center. Online course registration, online library, helpline, wireless network available.

Student life. Freshman orientation: Mandatory. Preregistration for classes offered. **Activities:** Bands, choral groups, drama, music ensembles, student government, student newspaper, Black Student Association, Los Americanos.

Athletics. NJCAA. **Intercollegiate:** Baseball M, basketball, cross-country W, soccer, softball W, volleyball W.

Student services. Adult student services, career counseling, student employment services, financial aid counseling, on-campus daycare, personal counseling, placement for graduates, veterans' counselor. **Physically disabled:** Services for visually, speech, hearing impaired.

Contact. Phone: (816) 604-1000 Fax: (816) 759-1149
Karen Goos, Director of Enrollment Services, Metropolitan Community College - Kansas City, 3200 Broadway, Kansas City, MO 64111

Mineral Area College
Park Hills, Missouri
www.mineralarea.edu
CB code: 6323

‣ Public 2-year community college
‣ Commuter campus in small town

General. Founded in 1922. Regionally accredited. **Enrollment:** 2,157 degree-seeking undergraduates; 42 non-degree-seeking students. **Degrees:** 641 associate awarded. **Location:** 60 miles from St. Louis. **Calendar:** Semester, limited summer session. **Full-time faculty:** 74 total. **Part-time faculty:** 322 total. **Class size:** 49% < 20, 51% 20-39.

Student profile. Among degree-seeking undergraduates, 525 enrolled as first-time, first-year students.

Part-time:	26%	25 or older:	35%
Out-of-state:	1%	Live on campus:	4%
Women:	61%		

Transfer out. **Colleges most students transferred to 2015:** Central Methodist College at Park Hills, Southeast Missouri State University, Southwest Missouri State University, University of Missouri - St. Louis, University of Missouri - Columbia.

Basis for selection. Open admission, but selective for some programs. Special requirements for nursing program. Interview required for health majors and law enforcement academy. **Home schooled:** Must submit documentation as required by Missouri State Statute 167.031.

2016-2017 Annual costs. Tuition/fees (projected): $3,220; $4,240 out-of-district; $5,620 out-of-state. Room/board: $6,994. Books/supplies: $1,600.

2014-2015 Financial aid. **Need-based:** 74% of total undergraduate aid awarded as scholarships/grants, 26% as loans/jobs. Need-based aid available for part-time students. Work-study available nights, weekends and for part-time students. **Non-need-based:** Scholarships awarded for academics, alumni affiliation, art, athletics, leadership, music/drama, state residency.

Application procedures. **Admission:** Priority date 8/1; no deadline. $15 fee. Admission notification on a rolling basis beginning on or about 2/15. **Financial aid:** Closing date 4/1. FAFSA required. Applicants notified on a rolling basis starting 2/15; must reply within 4 week(s) of notification.

Academics. **Special study options:** Cross-registration, distance learning, dual enrollment of high school students, honors, independent study, internships, liberal arts/career combination, study abroad. Bachelor's degree programs available on campus. License preparation in nursing, paramedic. **Credit/placement by examination:** AP, CLEP, institutional tests. 30 credit hours maximum toward associate degree. Credit held in escrow for 1 semester. **Support services:** GED test center, learning center, pre-admission summer program, reduced course load, remedial instruction, study skills assistance, tutoring, writing center.

Majors. **Business:** General, accounting, administrative services, banking/financial services, business admin. **Communications technology:** Graphic/printing. **Computer sciences:** Networking, programming. **Education:** Voc/tech. **English:** English lit. **Health services:** Clinical lab technology, nursing (RN), respiratory therapy technology. **Liberal arts:** Arts/sciences. **Protective services:** Firefighting, police science. **Social sciences:** General. **Work/family studies:** Child development.

Technology on campus. Dormitories wired for high-speed internet access. Commuter students can connect to campus network. Online course registration, helpline available.

Student life. **Freshman orientation:** Mandatory. Preregistration for classes offered. One-day program for students and parents. **Housing:** Coed dorms, wellness housing available. $200 deposit. Privatized housing available. **Activities:** Bands, choral groups, drama, music ensembles, musical theater, student government, Young Democrats, Young Republicans, Baptist Youth.

Athletics. NJCAA. **Intercollegiate:** Baseball M, basketball, volleyball W. **Team name:** Cardinals.

Student services. Adult student services, career counseling, student employment services, financial aid counseling, personal counseling, placement for graduates, veterans' counselor. **Physically disabled:** Services for visually, speech, hearing impaired. **Transfer:** Pre-admission transcript evaluation for new students. Transfer adviser, college fairs on campus for students transferring to 4-year colleges.

Contact. E-mail: admissions@mineralarea.edu
Phone: (573) 518-2206 Fax: (573) 518-2166
Julie Sheets, Admissions Officer, Mineral Area College, PO Box 1000, Park Hills, MO 63601-1000

Missouri College
Brentwood, Missouri
www.missouricollege.com   CB code: 3074

▸ For-profit 2-year technical college
▸ Commuter campus in large city
▸ Interview required

General. Accredited by ACCSC. **Enrollment:** 553 undergraduates. **Degrees:** 10 bachelor's, 68 associate awarded. **Calendar:** Differs by program. **Full-time faculty:** 14 total. **Part-time faculty:** 20 total. **Class size:** 59% < 20, 41% 20-39.

Basis for selection. Open admission, but selective for some programs. Dental hygiene is limited enrollment program with additional requirements, including entrance exam.

2015-2016 Annual costs. Diploma programs: $10,250-$15,050. Associate programs: $2,200-$35,501. Bachelor's programs: $37,270.

Financial aid. **Need-based:** Need-based aid available for part-time students. Work-study available nights, weekends and for part-time students.

Application procedures. **Admission:** No deadline. $35 fee. Admission notification on a rolling basis. **Financial aid:** No deadline. FAFSA required.

Academics. **Special study options:** Distance learning. Bachelor's degree programs available on campus. **Credit/placement by examination:** AP, CLEP.

Majors. **Business:** Business admin. **Health services:** Dental assistant, dietician assistant, massage therapy, medical assistant.

Most popular majors. Business/marketing 20%, health sciences 80%.

Student life. **Freshman orientation:** Mandatory. Preregistration for classes offered.

Student services. Career counseling, financial aid counseling, personal counseling, placement for graduates. **Physically disabled:** Services for visually impaired.

Contact. E-mail: kjefferson@missouricollege.com
Phone: (314) 821-7700 Toll-free number: (800) 216-6732
Karl Jefferson, Director of Admissions, Missouri College, 1405 South Hanley Road, Brentwood, MO 63144

Missouri State University: West Plains
West Plains, Missouri
www.wp.missouristate.edu   CB code: 6662

▸ Public 2-year branch campus and liberal arts college
▸ Commuter campus in large town

General. Regionally accredited. The open admissions 2-year campus in Missouri State University system. **Enrollment:** 1,554 degree-seeking undergraduates. **Degrees:** 293 associate awarded. **Location:** 110 miles from Springfield. **Calendar:** Semester, limited summer session. **Full-time faculty:** 39 total; 15% have terminal degrees, 15% minority, 56% women. **Part-time faculty:** 78 total; 6% have terminal degrees, 6% minority, 63% women. **Class size:** 49% < 20, 49% 20-39, 2% 40-49. **Partnerships:** Partnership with West Plains High School.

Student profile.

Out-of-state:	9%	Live on campus:	3%
25 or older:	38%		

Transfer out. **Colleges most students transferred to 2015:** Missouri State University: Springfield.

Basis for selection. Open admission, but selective for some programs. Nursing and respiratory therapy programs require separate application and applicants are considered competitively. **Home schooled:** Transcript of courses and grades required. Must submit ACT score (minimum 18) or official GED transcript.

2015-2016 Annual costs. Tuition/fees: $3,880; $7,450 out-of-state. Per-credit charge: $119 in-state; $238 out-of-state. Room/board: $5,590. Books/supplies: $950. Personal expenses: $2,701.

Financial aid. **Need-based:** Need-based aid available for part-time students. Work-study available nights, weekends and for part-time students. **Non-need-based:** Scholarships awarded for academics, athletics, state residency.

Application procedures. **Admission:** Closing date 8/20 (receipt date). $15 fee, may be waived for applicants with need. Admission notification on a rolling basis. **Financial aid:** Priority date 3/31; no closing date. FAFSA, institutional form required. Applicants notified on a rolling basis; must reply by 4/15.

Academics. Special study options: Distance learning, dual enrollment of high school students, honors, independent study, internships, liberal arts/career combination, student-designed major, study abroad. Early degree for High School students to earn high school diploma and A.A. degree concurrently. Bachelor's degree programs available on campus. License preparation in nursing. **Credit/placement by examination:** AP, CLEP, IB, institutional tests. 15 credit hours maximum toward associate degree. **Support services:** GED test center, learning center, remedial instruction, study skills assistance, tutoring, writing center.

Majors. Business: General, entrepreneurial studies. **Communications technology:** Animation/special effects. **Computer sciences:** General, information technology. **Education:** General. **Health services:** Nursing (RN), respiratory therapy technology. **Liberal arts:** Arts/sciences. **Protective services:** Firefighting, police science. **Work/family studies:** Child care management.

Most popular majors. Agriculture 6%, biological/life sciences 7%, business/marketing 6%, education 21%, English 7%, history 6%, liberal arts 35%, mathematics 7%.

Technology on campus. 120 workstations in dormitories, library, computer center, student center. Dormitories wired for high-speed internet access and linked to campus network. Commuter students can connect to campus network. Online course registration, online library, helpline, repair service, wireless network available.

Student life. Freshman orientation: Mandatory. Preregistration for classes offered. Half-day sessions held throughout summer. **Housing:** Coed dorms, special housing for disabled, wellness housing available. $100 fully refundable deposit. **Activities:** Campus ministries, choral groups, drama, international student organizations, student government, Campus Crusade for Christ, Christian Campus House, Wesley Club, College Democrats, College Republicans,.

Athletics. NJCAA. **Intercollegiate:** Basketball M, volleyball W. **Team name:** Grizzlies.

Student services. Career counseling, services for economically disadvantaged, student employment services, financial aid counseling, health services, legal services, minority student services, personal counseling, placement for graduates, veterans' counselor. **Physically disabled:** Services for visually, hearing impaired. **Transfer:** Transfer adviser, college fairs on campus for students transferring to 4-year colleges.

Contact. E-mail: wpadmissions@missouristate.edu
Phone: (417) 255-7955 Toll-free number: (888) 466-7897
Fax: (417) 255-7959
Melissa Jett, Coordinator of Admissions, Missouri State University: West Plains, 128 Garfield Avenue, West Plains, MO 65775-2715

Moberly Area Community College
Moberly, Missouri
www.macc.edu   CB code: 6414

- Public 2-year community college
- Commuter campus in large town

General. Founded in 1927. Regionally accredited. **Enrollment:** 5,800 undergraduates. **Degrees:** 711 associate awarded. **Location:** 35 miles from Columbia. **Calendar:** Semester, extensive summer session. **Full-time faculty:** 72 total. **Part-time faculty:** 239 total. **Special facilities:** Multimedia/instructional television center, graphic arts/fine arts gallery, alumni museum.

Student profile.

Out-of-state:	2%	Live on campus:	2%
25 or older:	24%		

Transfer out. Colleges most students transferred to 2015: Central Methodist University, Columbia College, University of Missouri.

Basis for selection. Open admission, but selective for some programs. Special requirements for allied health and law enforcement programs. ACT scores required for admission to nursing programs. Degree-seeking students, or those taking 14 or more credits, must have ACT or ASSET score for placement purposes; tests also required for students enrolling in English or math courses. **Home schooled:** Transcript of courses and grades, state high school equivalency certificate required. Applicants must provide transcript outlining educational process or take GED.

2015-2016 Annual costs. Tuition/fees: $3,060; $4,590 out-of-district; $6,120 out-of-state. Per-credit charge: $86 in-district; $137 out-of-district; $188 out-of-state. Room/board: $4,600. Books/supplies: $800. Personal expenses: $1,500.

Financial aid. Need-based: Need-based aid available for part-time students. Work-study available nights, weekends and for part-time students. **Non-need-based:** Scholarships awarded for academics, alumni affiliation, art, athletics, leadership, music/drama.

Application procedures. Admission: No deadline. No application fee. Admission notification on a rolling basis. **Financial aid:** Priority date 4/1; no closing date. FAFSA required. Applicants notified on a rolling basis starting 4/1; must reply by 7/15 or within 2 week(s) of notification.

Academics. Special study options: Cooperative education, distance learning, dual enrollment of high school students, honors, internships, study abroad, teacher certification program. License preparation in nursing, paramedic. **Credit/placement by examination:** AP, CLEP, IB, institutional tests. 30 credit hours maximum toward associate degree. **Support services:** GED preparation and test center, learning center, remedial instruction, study skills assistance, tutoring.

Majors. Business: Accounting technology, marketing, office/clerical. **Communications:** Journalism. **Communications technology:** Graphic/printing. **Computer sciences:** Programming. **Education:** Voc/tech. **Engineering:** General. **Health services:** Nursing (RN). **Liberal arts:** Arts/sciences. **Work/family studies:** Child care management.

Most popular majors. Business/marketing 6%, liberal arts 74%.

Technology on campus. 750 workstations in dormitories, library, computer center. Dormitories wired for high-speed internet access. Commuter students can connect to campus network. Online library, helpline, repair service, wireless network available.

Student life. Freshman orientation: Available. Preregistration for classes offered. Half-day program held during late summer. **Housing:** Single-sex dorms, wellness housing available. $150 partly refundable deposit, deadline 8/20. Limited housing available. **Activities:** Choral groups, drama, literary magazine, student government, student newspaper, Phi Theta Kappa, Association for the Education of Young Children, Brothers OX, service organizations, multicultural club.

Athletics. NJCAA. **Intercollegiate:** Basketball, cheerleading. **Intramural:** Basketball, volleyball. **Team name:** Greyhounds.

Student services. Adult student services, career counseling, services for economically disadvantaged, student employment services, financial aid counseling, placement for graduates. **Physically disabled:** Services for visually, speech, hearing impaired. **Transfer:** Pre-admission transcript evaluation for new students. Transfer adviser, college fairs on campus for students transferring to 4-year colleges.

Contact. E-mail: info@macc.edu
Phone: (660) 263-4110 ext. 270
Toll-free number: (800) 622-2070 ext. 270 Fax: (660) 263-2406
James Grant, Dean of Student Services, Moberly Area Community College, 101 College Avenue, Moberly, MO 65270-1304

North Central Missouri College
Trenton, Missouri
www.ncmissouri.edu   CB code: 6830

- Public 2-year community college
- Commuter campus in small town

General. Founded in 1925. Regionally accredited. Evening classes offered at outreach sites in many area communities. **Enrollment:** 1,085 degree-seeking undergraduates. **Degrees:** 302 associate awarded. **Location:** 90 miles from Kansas City. **Calendar:** Semester, limited summer session. **Full-time faculty:** 38 total. **Part-time faculty:** 57 total.

Student profile.

Out-of-state:	2%	Live on campus:	8%
25 or older:	28%		

Transfer out. Colleges most students transferred to 2015: Missouri Western State College, Northwest Missouri State University, Missouri State University, University of Central Missouri.

Basis for selection. Open admission, but selective for some programs. Special requirements for associate and certificate programs in nursing, occupational therapy assistant. Interview required for nursing students. **Home schooled:** Statement describing home school structure and mission required.

2015-2016 Annual costs. Tuition/fees: $3,180; $4,170 out-of-district; $5,340 out-of-state. Per-credit charge: $76 in-district; $109 out-of-district;

$148 out-of-state. Room/board: $5,734. Books/supplies: $954. Personal expenses: $1,400.

Financial aid. **Need-based:** Need-based aid available for part-time students. Work-study available nights, weekends and for part-time students. **Non-need-based:** Scholarships awarded for academics, athletics, leadership.

Application procedures. **Admission:** Closing date 8/3 (receipt date). $20 fee. Application must be submitted online. Admission notification on a rolling basis beginning on or about 2/1. **Financial aid:** Priority date 7/1; no closing date. FAFSA, institutional form required. Applicants notified on a rolling basis starting 3/15.

Academics. **Special study options:** Distance learning, dual enrollment of high school students, internships, liberal arts/career combination. Bachelor's degree programs available on campus. License preparation in nursing, occupational therapy, paramedic, radiology. **Credit/placement by examination:** AP, CLEP, institutional tests. 30 credit hours maximum toward associate degree. **Support services:** Learning center, reduced course load, remedial instruction, study skills assistance, tutoring.

Majors. **Business:** Accounting, business admin, office technology, office/clerical. **Education:** General. **General:** Maintenance. **Health services:** EMT paramedic, health care admin, medical radiologic technology/radiation therapy, medical secretary, nursing (RN), office assistant, pharmacy assistant, physical therapy assistant, surgical technology. **Liberal arts:** Arts/sciences. **Protective services:** Criminal justice. **Work/family studies:** Child care service.

Most popular majors. Business/marketing 9%, health sciences 38%, liberal arts 40%.

Technology on campus. 163 workstations in dormitories, library, computer center, student center. Dormitories wired for high-speed internet access. Online course registration, helpline, wireless network available.

Student life. **Freshman orientation:** Mandatory. Preregistration for classes offered. **Housing:** Single-sex dorms, wellness housing available. $100 partly refundable deposit. **Activities:** Student government, Baptist student union, Fellowship of Christian Athletes.

Athletics. NJCAA. **Intercollegiate:** Baseball M, basketball, softball W. **Team name:** Pirates.

Student services. Career counseling, student employment services, financial aid counseling, veterans' counselor. **Physically disabled:** Services for visually, speech, hearing impaired. **Transfer:** Transfer adviser, college fairs on campus for students transferring to 4-year colleges.

Contact. E-mail: admissions@mail.ncmissouri.edu
Phone: (660) 359-3948 ext. 1414 Fax: (660) 359-2211
Karla McCollum, Admission Director, North Central Missouri College, 1301 Main Street, Trenton, MO 64683

Ozarks Technical Community College
Springfield, Missouri
www.otc.edu   CB code: 2583

- Public 2-year community and technical college
- Commuter campus in small city

General. Regionally accredited. **Enrollment:** 13,614 undergraduates. **Degrees:** 1,901 associate awarded. **Location:** 160 miles from Kansas City, 250 miles from St. Louis. **Calendar:** Semester, extensive summer session. **Full-time faculty:** 188 total. **Part-time faculty:** 700 total.

Transfer out. **Colleges most students transferred to 2015:** Drury University, Evangel University, Missouri State University.

Basis for selection. Open admission, but selective for some programs. Special requirements for some allied health programs.

2015-2016 Annual costs. Tuition/fees: $3,600; $5,070 out-of-district; $6,540 out-of-state. Per-credit charge: $98 in-district; $147 out-of-district; $196 out-of-state. Books/supplies: $800.

2014-2015 Financial aid. All financial aid based on need. 63% of total undergraduate aid awarded as scholarships/grants, 37% as loans/jobs. Need-based aid available for part-time students. Work-study available nights, weekends and for part-time students.

Application procedures. **Admission:** No deadline. No application fee. Admission notification on a rolling basis. **Financial aid:** Closing date 3/31.

FAFSA, institutional form required. Applicants notified on a rolling basis starting 5/16.

Academics. **Special study options:** Cooperative education, distance learning, dual enrollment of high school students, ESL, honors, independent study, internships, study abroad. License preparation in dental hygiene, nursing, paramedic. **Credit/placement by examination:** AP, CLEP, IB, institutional tests. **Support services:** GED preparation and test center, learning center, reduced course load, remedial instruction, study skills assistance, tutoring, writing center.

Honors college/program. 27 ACT; 3.75 GPA; 2 letters of recommendation required.

Majors. **Biology:** General. **Business:** Accounting technology, administrative services, management information systems, marketing. **Communications technology:** General, graphic/printing, graphics. **Computer sciences:** Networking, programming. **Education:** Voc/tech. **Engineering:** General. **Health services:** Dental assistant, dental hygiene, EMT paramedic, health information technology, hearing instrument specialist, nursing (RN), occupational therapy assistant, physical therapy assistant, respiratory therapy technology, surgical technology. **Liberal arts:** Arts/sciences. **Physical sciences:** Chemistry. **Protective services:** Firefighting. **Work/family studies:** Child care service.

Technology on campus. 325 workstations in library, computer center. Commuter students can connect to campus network. Online course registration, online library, helpline, repair service, wireless network available.

Student life. **Freshman orientation:** Mandatory. Preregistration for classes offered. **Activities:** Choral groups, drama, international student organizations, student newspaper, Phi Theta Kappa, National Honor Society, Women in Construction, nursing students groups, Phi Beta Lambda, national business organizations, electronics club, Society of Manufacturing Engineers.

Athletics. **Team name:** Eagles.

Student services. Career counseling, student employment services, financial aid counseling, health services, on-campus daycare, personal counseling, placement for graduates, veterans' counselor. **Physically disabled:** Services for visually, speech, hearing impaired. **Transfer:** Re-entry adviser for new students. Transfer adviser, college fairs on campus for students transferring to 4-year colleges.

Contact. E-mail: admissions@otc.edu
Phone: (417) 447-6900 Fax: (417) 447-6906
Joan Barrett, Associate Vice Chancellor for Student Affairs, Ozarks Technical Community College, 1001 East Chestnut Expressway, Springfield, MO 65802

Pinnacle Career Institute: Kansas City
Kansas City, Missouri
www.pcitraining.edu   CB code: 2271

- For-profit 2-year technical and career college
- Commuter campus in very large city
- Interview required

General. Accredited by ACICS. Second campus in Kansas City, in addition to the main location, and campus in Lawrence, KS. Offer distance education programs. **Enrollment:** 807 degree-seeking undergraduates. **Degrees:** 177 associate awarded. **Location:** Downtown. **Calendar:** Quarter, limited summer session. **Full-time faculty:** 12 total. **Part-time faculty:** 16 total. **Class size:** 100% >100.

Student profile. Among degree-seeking undergraduates, 100% enrolled in a vocational program, 5% already have a bachelor's degree or higher, 480 enrolled as first-time, first-year students.

Basis for selection. Open admission. **Home schooled:** Transcript of courses and grades, state high school equivalency certificate, interview required.

2015-2016 Annual costs. Books/supplies: $1,500. Personal expenses: $2,241.

Financial aid. **Need-based:** Work-study available nights, weekends and for part-time students.

Application procedures. **Admission:** No deadline. No application fee. Admission notification on a rolling basis. **Financial aid:** No deadline.

Academics. **Special study options:** Distance learning, weekend college. **Credit/placement by examination:** AP, CLEP, institutional tests. 12 credit hours maximum toward associate degree. **Support services:** Study skills assistance, tutoring.

Majors. Business: Executive assistant. **Computer sciences:** Information technology. **Health services:** Medical assistant. **Parks/recreation:** Exercise sciences.

Most popular majors. Health sciences 57%, physical sciences 24%, trade and industry 15%.

Technology on campus. 30 workstations in computer center. Online library, helpline, wireless network available.

Student life. Freshman orientation: Mandatory. Preregistration for classes offered. **Activities:** Student newspaper.

Student services. Career counseling, services for economically disadvantaged, student employment services, financial aid counseling, placement for graduates, veterans' counselor. **Transfer:** Pre-admission transcript evaluation for new students.

Contact. E-mail: bricks@pcitraining.edu
Phone: (816) 331-5700 Toll-free number: (800) 676-7912
Fax: (816) 331-2026
Elton Ladd, Director of Admissions, Pinnacle Career Institute: Kansas City, 1001 East 101st Terrace, Suite 325, Kansas City, MO 64131-3367

Ranken Technical College
St. Louis, Missouri
www.ranken.edu
CB code: 7028

- Private 2-year technical college
- Commuter campus in very large city

General. Founded in 1907. Regionally accredited. **Enrollment:** 1,929 degree-seeking undergraduates. **Degrees:** 43 bachelor's, 424 associate awarded. **Location:** 3 miles from downtown. **Calendar:** Semester, limited summer session. **Full-time faculty:** 76 total. **Part-time faculty:** 80 total. **Partnerships:** Partnerships with General Motors, JM&A Group, Customer Direct, bioMerieux, Toyota Technical Education Network, National Automotive Technicians Education Foundation, National Institute for Automotive Service Excellence, Shearwater High School, Hunter Engineering, American Honda Motor Company.

Student profile.

Out-of-state:	43%	Live on campus:	3%
25 or older:	23%		

Transfer out. Colleges most students transferred to 2015: Webster University, Lindenwood, University of Missouri: St. Louis, Southern Illinois University.

Basis for selection. Open admission. Institutional placement test, counseling session, and tour recommended. Interviews recommended. **Home schooled:** State high school equivalency certificate required. **Learning Disabled:** Special accommodations available with appropriate documentation.

High school preparation. College-preparatory program recommended. Recommended units include English 4 and mathematics 3. Recommend industrial arts elective.

2015-2016 Annual costs. Books/supplies: $1,700. Personal expenses: $1,774.

Financial aid. Need-based: Need-based aid available for part-time students. Work-study available nights, weekends and for part-time students.

Application procedures. Admission: No deadline. $25 fee, may be waived for applicants with need, free for online applicants. Admission notification on a rolling basis. Interview and tour recommended for new applicants. **Financial aid:** Priority date 4/1; no closing date. FAFSA, institutional form required. Applicants notified on a rolling basis starting 4/1.

Academics. Special study options: Accelerated study, cooperative education, distance learning, double major, dual enrollment of high school students, independent study, internships, study abroad. Bachelor's degree programs available on campus. **Credit/placement by examination:** AP, CLEP, IB, institutional tests. Enrolled students are reviewed on an individual case basis. **Support services:** Learning center, pre-admission summer program, reduced course load, remedial instruction, study skills assistance, tutoring, writing center.

Majors. Architecture: Environmental design. **Communications technology:** General. **Computer sciences:** General, LAN/WAN management, webmaster. **General:** Carpentry.

Technology on campus. 100 workstations in dormitories, library, computer center, student center. Dormitories wired for high-speed internet access and linked to campus network. Commuter students can connect to campus network. Online course registration, online library, helpline, repair service, wireless network available.

Student life. Freshman orientation: Mandatory. Preregistration for classes offered. Four hour session held the week before classes begin. **Housing:** Guaranteed on-campus for all undergraduates. Coed dorms, special housing for disabled available. $150 fully refundable deposit. **Activities:** Student government, Women's support program, Phi Theta Kappa.

Athletics. Intramural: Baseball, basketball, football (non-tackle).

Student services. Adult student services, alcohol/substance abuse counseling, career counseling, services for economically disadvantaged, student employment services, financial aid counseling, minority student services, personal counseling, placement for graduates, veterans' counselor, women's services. **Physically disabled:** Services for visually, speech, hearing impaired. **Transfer:** Pre-admission transcript evaluation for new students. Transfer adviser, college fairs on campus for students transferring to 4-year colleges.

Contact. E-mail: admissions@ranken.edu
Phone: (314) 286-4809 Toll-free number: (866) 472-6536
Fax: (314) 371-0241
Abe Brummett, Director of Admissions, Ranken Technical College, 4431 Finney Avenue, St. Louis, MO 63113

Southeast Missouri Hospital College of Nursing and Health Sciences
Cape Girardeau, Missouri
www.sehcollege.edu
CB code: 4459

- Private 2-year health science and nursing college
- Commuter campus in large town
- Application essay required

General. Hands-on laboratory and clinical experiences. **Enrollment:** 210 undergraduates. **Degrees:** 81 associate awarded. **Location:** 100 miles from St. Louis. **Calendar:** Semester, limited summer session. **Full-time faculty:** 20 total. **Part-time faculty:** 2 total.

Basis for selection. Open admission, but selective for some programs. Competitive admission to all programs. **Adult students:** SAT/ACT scores not required if out of high school 5 year(s) or more. Compass test required for those out of high school 5 or more years. **Home schooled:** Transcript of courses and grades, letter of recommendation (nonparent) required.

High school preparation. College-preparatory program recommended.

2015-2016 Annual costs. Tuition/fees: $12,330. Books/supplies: $1,000.

Financial aid. Need-based: Work-study available nights, weekends and for part-time students.

Application procedures. Admission: No deadline. $100 fee, may be waived for applicants with need. Application must be submitted on paper. Admission notification on a rolling basis. Must reply by May 1 or within 2 week(s) if notified thereafter.

Academics. Special study options: Accelerated study. Bachelor's degree programs available on campus. License preparation in nursing, radiology. **Credit/placement by examination:** AP, CLEP. 6 credit hours maximum toward associate degree. **Support services:** Remedial instruction, tutoring.

Majors. Health services: Nursing (RN), radiologic technology/medical imaging.

Technology on campus. Online library, helpline, wireless network available.

Student life. Freshman orientation: Mandatory. Preregistration for classes offered. Orientation 2 months before program entry date. **Activities:** Student government.

Student services. Financial aid counseling. **Transfer:** Pre-admission transcript evaluation for new students.

Contact. E-mail: dhowey@sehcollege.edu
Phone: (573) 334-6825 ext. 23 Fax: (573) 339-7805
Debbie Howey, Registrar, Southeast Missouri Hospital College of Nursing and Health Sciences, 2001 William Street, Cape Girardeau, MO 63703

St. Charles Community College
Cottleville, Missouri
www.stchas.edu   CB code: 0168

- Public 2-year community college
- Commuter campus in small city

General. Founded in 1986. Regionally accredited. **Enrollment:** 6,301 degree-seeking undergraduates; 629 non-degree-seeking students. **Degrees:** 931 associate awarded. **Location:** 35 miles from St. Louis. **Calendar:** Semester, limited summer session. **Full-time faculty:** 105 total; 26% have terminal degrees, 7% minority, 62% women. **Part-time faculty:** 281 total; 17% have terminal degrees, 9% minority, 59% women. **Class size:** 46% < 20, 53% 20-39, less than 1% 40-49, less than 1% 50-99.

Student profile. Among degree-seeking undergraduates, 86% enrolled in a transfer program, 14% enrolled in a vocational program, 1,504 enrolled as first-time, first-year students.

Part-time:	47%	Hispanic/Latino:	4%
Women:	56%	Multi-racial, non-Hispanic:	3%
African American:	6%	International:	1%
Asian American:	2%	25 or older:	24%

Transfer out. Colleges most students transferred to 2015: University of Missouri: St. Louis, Lindenwood University, University of Missouri: Columbia.

Basis for selection. Open admission, but selective for some programs. Must submit ACT scores for allied health and nursing programs. **Home schooled:** Transcript of courses and grades required.

2016-2017 Annual costs. Tuition/fees (projected): $3,090; $4,560 out-of-district; $6,600 out-of-state. Per-credit charge: $98 in-district; $147 out-of-district; $215 out-of-state. Books/supplies: $1,200. Personal expenses: $1,800.

2014-2015 Financial aid. Need-based: 79% of total undergraduate aid awarded as scholarships/grants, 21% as loans/jobs. Need-based aid available for part-time students. Work-study available nights, weekends and for part-time students. **Non-need-based:** Scholarships awarded for academics, art, athletics, leadership, music/drama.

Application procedures. Admission: No deadline. $20 fee. Application must be submitted online. Admission notification on a rolling basis. **Financial aid:** Priority date 6/1; no closing date. FAFSA, institutional form required. Applicants notified on a rolling basis starting 4/1; must reply by 8/1.

Academics. Special study options: Distance learning, double major, dual enrollment of high school students, ESL, honors, independent study, internships, liberal arts/career combination, study abroad. License preparation in nursing, occupational therapy. **Credit/placement by examination:** AP, CLEP, institutional tests. 49 credit hours maximum toward associate degree. **Support services:** Learning center, pre-admission summer program, remedial instruction, study skills assistance, tutoring, writing center.

Honors college/program. For high school students, ACT score of 30 or above, submit two essays or writing samples written for high school classes. ACT score of 26-29, submit two essays or writing samples written for high school classes, and two letters of recommendation from teachers. For current or former college students, complete 12 hours or more of college classes, achieve a GPA of 3.5 or higher, submit two letters of recommendation from college teachers, submit two essays or writing samples written for college classes.

Majors. Biology: General. **Business:** Accounting technology, marketing, office management. **Computer sciences:** Applications programming, programming. **Education:** Teacher assistance. **Engineering:** General, civil, mechanical, pre-engineering. **Health services:** EMT paramedic, health information technology, nursing (RN), occupational therapy assistant. **Human services:** Social work. **Liberal arts:** Arts/sciences. **Physical sciences:** Chemistry. **Protective services:** Police science. **Visual/performing arts:** Commercial/advertising art, dramatic, music history. **Work/family studies:** Child care management.

Most popular majors. Education 6%, health sciences 12%, liberal arts 74%.

Technology on campus. 131 workstations in library, computer center, student center. Commuter students can connect to campus network. Online course registration, online library, helpline, wireless network available.

Student life. Freshman orientation: Available. Preregistration for classes offered. One credit hour, multiple formats, with online campus tour. **Activities:** Bands, campus ministries, choral groups, drama, international student organizations, literary magazine, music ensembles, musical theater, student government, student newspaper, CRU, Fellowship of Christian Athletes, Global Student Network, SCC Young Democrats, Cougars Care, Tau Upsilon Alpha, Revolution Campus Ministry.

Athletics. NJCAA. **Intercollegiate:** Baseball M, soccer, softball W. **Team name:** Cougars.

Student services. Adult student services, alcohol/substance abuse counseling, career counseling, student employment services, financial aid counseling, on-campus daycare, personal counseling, placement for graduates, veterans' counselor. **Physically disabled:** Services for visually, speech, hearing impaired. **Transfer:** Pre-admission transcript evaluation for new students. Transfer center, transfer adviser, college fairs on campus for students transferring to 4-year colleges.

Contact. Phone: (636) 922-8237 Fax: (636) 922-8236
Kathy Brockgreitens-Gober, Dean of Enrollment Services, St. Charles Community College, 4601 Mid Rivers Mall Drive, Cottleville, MO 63376

St. Louis Community College
Saint Louis, Missouri
www.stlcc.edu   CB member
                                           CB code: 6226

- Public 2-year community and junior college
- Commuter campus in large city

General. Founded in 1962. Regionally accredited. Four campus locations: Forest Park (St. Louis), Florissant Valley (Ferguson), Meramec (Kirkwood), and Wildwood (Wildwood). **Enrollment:** 8,820 undergraduates. **Degrees:** 2,067 associate awarded. **Calendar:** Semester, extensive summer session. **Full-time faculty:** 132 total. **Part-time faculty:** 401 total.

Student profile.

Out-of-state:	4%	25 or older:	52%

Transfer out. Colleges most students transferred to 2015: St. Louis University, Washington University, University of Missouri: St. Louis, University of Missouri: Columbia, Webster University.

Basis for selection. Open admission.

2015-2016 Annual costs. Tuition/fees: $3,090; $4,470 out-of-district; $6,150 out-of-state. Per-credit charge: $103 in-district; $149 out-of-district; $205 out-of-state. Books/supplies: $800. Personal expenses: $2,100.

Financial aid. Need-based: Need-based aid available for part-time students. Work-study available nights, weekends and for part-time students. **Non-need-based:** Scholarships awarded for academics, art, athletics, leadership, music/drama.

Application procedures. Admission: No deadline. No application fee. Admission notification on a rolling basis beginning on or about 4/1. **Financial aid:** Priority date 4/15; no closing date. FAFSA required. Applicants notified on a rolling basis starting 4/1.

Academics. Special study options: Cross-registration, distance learning, double major, dual enrollment of high school students, ESL, honors, independent study, liberal arts/career combination, study abroad, weekend college. License preparation in dental hygiene, nursing, paramedic, radiology, real estate. **Credit/placement by examination:** AP, CLEP, institutional tests. 30 credit hours maximum toward associate degree. **Support services:** GED preparation and test center, learning center, remedial instruction, study skills assistance, tutoring, writing center.

Majors. Biology: General. **Business:** General, accounting, administrative services, banking/financial services, international, organizational behavior, tourism/travel. **Communications:** Communications/speech/rhetoric. **Communications technology:** Graphic/printing. **Computer sciences:** General, data processing, programming, systems analysis. **Education:** Teacher assistance. **Engineering:** General. **General:** Carpentry, electrician, maintenance, pipefitting. **Health services:** Clinical lab science, dental assistant, dental hygiene, EMT paramedic, medical radiologic technology/radiation therapy, respiratory therapy technology, sonography, surgical technology. **Liberal arts:** Arts/sciences. **Math:** General. **Physical sciences:** Chemistry, physics. **Protective services:** Fire safety technology. **Psychology:** General. **Social sciences:** General. **Visual/performing arts:** Music, photography, studio arts.

Work/family studies: Child care management, food/nutrition, institutional food production.

Most popular majors. Business/marketing 7%, computer/information sciences 9%, health sciences 20%, liberal arts 34%, personal/culinary services 12%.

Technology on campus. Commuter students can connect to campus network. Online course registration, online library available.

Student life. Freshman orientation: Available. Preregistration for classes offered. **Activities:** Choral groups, drama, literary magazine, musical theater, student government, student newspaper, TV station.

Athletics. NJCAA. **Intercollegiate:** Baseball M, basketball, soccer M, softball W. **Team name:** Highlanders.

Student services. Career counseling, services for economically disadvantaged, student employment services, financial aid counseling, health services, on-campus daycare, personal counseling, placement for graduates, veterans' counselor. **Physically disabled:** Services for visually, speech, hearing impaired. **Transfer:** Transfer adviser, college fairs on campus for students transferring to 4-year colleges.

Contact. E-mail: gmarshall@stlcc.edu
Phone: (314) 644-9127 Fax: (314) 644-9375
Glenn Marshall, Manager, Admissions/Registration, St. Louis Community College, 300 South Broadway, St. Louis, MO 63102-2800

St. Louis Community College at Florissant Valley
St. Louis, Missouri
www.stlcc.edu   CB code: 6225

▸ Public 2-year branch campus and community college
▸ Commuter campus in large city

General. Founded in 1962. Regionally accredited. **Location:** 17 miles from downtown. **Calendar:** Semester.

Annual costs/financial aid. Tuition/fees (2015-2016): $3,090; $4,470 out-of-district; $6,150 out-of-state. Books/supplies: $1,000. Personal expenses: $2,100.

Contact. Phone: (314) 513-4244
Manager of Admissions/Registration, 3400 Pershall Road, St. Louis, MO 63135

St. Louis Community College at Meramec
St. Louis, Missouri
www.stlcc.edu   CB code: 6430

▸ Public 2-year community college
▸ Commuter campus in large city

General. Founded in 1963. Regionally accredited. **Location:** 15 miles from St. Louis. **Calendar:** Semester.

Annual costs/financial aid. Tuition/fees (2015-2016): $3,090; $4,470 out-of-district; $6,150 out-of-state. Books/supplies: $800. Personal expenses: $2,100. Need-based financial aid available to full-time and part-time students.

Contact. Phone: (314) 984-7601
Director of Admission, 11333 Big Bend Road, Kirkwood, MO 63122-5799

State Fair Community College
Sedalia, Missouri
www.sfccmo.edu   CB code: 6709

▸ Public 2-year community college
▸ Commuter campus in large town

General. Founded in 1966. Regionally accredited. Academic Quality Improvement Program (AQIP) institution. **Enrollment:** 4,050 degree-seeking undergraduates. **Degrees:** 676 associate awarded. **ROTC:** Army. **Location:** 78 miles from Kansas City. **Calendar:** Semester, limited summer session.

Full-time faculty: 78 total. **Part-time faculty:** 311 total. **Special facilities:** Contemporary art museum.

Student profile.

Out-of-state:	2%	Live on campus:	3%
25 or older:	41%		

Transfer out. Colleges most students transferred to 2015: University of Central Missouri, Missouri State University.

Basis for selection. Open admission, but selective for some programs. Special requirements for Associate Degree Nursing, Practical Nursing, Occupational Therapy Assistant, Radiologic Technology, Dental Hygiene and Medical Sonography. ACT, ASSET, or COMPASS score current within the last five years required of full-time students and all degree-seeking students. Mechanical knowledge test required for auto mechanics program. Interview required for radiologic technology program applicants. **Learning Disabled:** Students encouraged to establish documentation two weeks prior to first day of semester to receive accommodations.

2015-2016 Annual costs. Tuition/fees: $3,000; $4,200 out-of-district; $6,000 out-of-state. Per-credit charge: $100 in-district; $140 out-of-district; $200 out-of-state. Room/board: $5,100. Books/supplies: $698. Personal expenses: $693.

Financial aid. Need-based: Need-based aid available for part-time students. Work-study available nights, weekends and for part-time students. **Non-need-based:** Scholarships awarded for academics, art, athletics, music/drama, state residency.

Application procedures. Admission: No deadline. No application fee. Application must be submitted online. Admission notification on a rolling basis. **Financial aid:** Priority date 7/1; no closing date. FAFSA required. Applicants notified on a rolling basis starting 7/15; must reply within 3 week(s) of notification.

Academics. Special study options: Cooperative education, cross-registration, distance learning, dual enrollment of high school students, ESL, internships. License preparation in dental hygiene, nursing, occupational therapy, radiology. **Credit/placement by examination:** AP, CLEP, institutional tests. 30 credit hours maximum toward associate degree. Students may earn a maximum of 30 hours in combination from credit by exam or nontraditional credit toward an AA or AAS degree. **Support services:** GED preparation, learning center, reduced course load, remedial instruction, study skills assistance, tutoring, writing center.

Majors. Business: Accounting, business admin, special products marketing. **Computer sciences:** Applications programming, networking. **Education:** Teacher assistance. **Engineering:** General. **General:** Power transmission, site management. **Health services:** Dental hygiene, health information technology, nursing (RN), occupational therapy assistant, radiologic technology/medical imaging, sonography. **Liberal arts:** Arts/sciences. **Physical sciences:** Chemistry. **Protective services:** Police science. **Work/family studies:** Child care management.

Most popular majors. Business/marketing 9%, health sciences 20%, liberal arts 53%.

Technology on campus. 520 workstations in dormitories, library, computer center, student center. Dormitories wired for high-speed internet access and linked to campus network. Commuter students can connect to campus network. Online course registration, online library, helpline, wireless network available.

Student life. Freshman orientation: Available. Preregistration for classes offered. **Housing:** Coed dorms, wellness housing available. $100 nonrefundable deposit. **Activities:** Jazz band, choral groups, drama, music ensembles, student government.

Athletics. NJCAA. **Intercollegiate:** Basketball, cheerleading W. **Intramural:** Basketball, football (tackle), softball, table tennis, volleyball. **Team name:** Roadrunners.

Student services. Career counseling, services for economically disadvantaged, student employment services, financial aid counseling, minority student services, on-campus daycare, personal counseling, placement for graduates, veterans' counselor. **Physically disabled:** Services for visually, speech, hearing impaired. **Transfer:** Pre-admission transcript evaluation for new students. Transfer adviser, college fairs on campus for students transferring to 4-year colleges.

Contact. E-mail: admissions@sfccmo.edu
Phone: (660) 530-5833 Toll-free number: (877) 311-7322
Amanda Stoecklein, Director of Admissions and Outreach, State Fair Community College, 3201 West 16th Street, Sedalia, MO 65301-2199

State Technical College of Missouri
Linn, Missouri
www.statetechmo.edu

- Public 2-year technical college
- Commuter campus in rural community

General. Educational sites and cooperatives in Jefferson City, Mexico, Poplar Bluff, St. Charles, Trenton, MO. **Enrollment:** 1,171 degree-seeking undergraduates; 103 non-degree-seeking students. **Degrees:** 421 associate awarded. **Location:** 30 miles from Jefferson City. **Calendar:** Semester, limited summer session. **Full-time faculty:** 94 total; 37% women. **Part-time faculty:** 10 total; 20% women. **Class size:** 78% < 20, 17% 20-39, 4% 40-49, less than 1% 50-99. **Special facilities:** Airport, hangars, fueling station, hard surface runway, fixed base operations. **Partnerships:** Formal partnerships with Caterpillar Incorporated, the Heartland International Dealers Association, Haas Technical Education Center, Cisco Systems, Toyota Bodine.

Student profile. Among degree-seeking undergraduates, 100% enrolled in a vocational program, 507 enrolled as first-time, first-year students.

Part-time:	9%	Multi-racial, non-Hispanic:	1%
Out-of-state:	5%	25 or older:	11%
Women:	15%	Live on campus:	11%
African American:	1%		

Transfer out. 1% of students enrolled in the transfer program go on to 4-year colleges.

Basis for selection. Open admission, but selective for some programs. Some programs have additional requirements and are filled on a competitive basis. Some programs require essays, interviews and other information. **Learning Disabled:** Students with learning disabilities must meet entrance requirements established for each program. Accommodations are available if a student provides proper documentation.

High school preparation. College-preparatory program recommended. 24 units recommended. Recommended units include English 4, mathematics 3, social studies 3, science 3 (laboratory 1), visual/performing arts 1 and academic electives 7. 1 practical arts, 1 physical education, .5 health education, .5 personal finance recommended.

2016-2017 Annual costs. Tuition/fees (projected): $5,873; $10,665 out-of-state. Per-credit charge: $159.75 in-state; $319.5 out-of-state. Room/board: $5,300. Books/supplies: $1,360. Personal expenses: $1,600.

2014-2015 Financial aid. **Need-based:** 464 full-time freshmen applied for aid; 371 deemed to have need; 371 received aid. Average need met was 9%. Average scholarship/grant was $4,809; average loan $2,913. 69% of total undergraduate aid awarded as scholarships/grants, 31% as loans/jobs. Need-based aid available for part-time students. Work-study available nights, weekends and for part-time students. **Non-need-based:** Scholarships awarded for academics, alumni affiliation, state residency.

Application procedures. **Admission:** No deadline. No application fee. Admission notification on a rolling basis. **Financial aid:** Priority date 4/1; no closing date. FAFSA required. Applicants notified on a rolling basis starting 4/1; must reply within 3 week(s) of notification.

Academics. **Special study options:** Distance learning, double major, dual enrollment of high school students, independent study, internships. License preparation in aviation, nursing, physical therapy, radiology. **Credit/placement by examination:** AP, CLEP, institutional tests. **Support services:** Learning center, remedial instruction, study skills assistance, tutoring, writing center. Academic and technical class tutoring provided at no cost.

Majors. **Business:** Office management. **Computer sciences:** Networking, programming. **General:** Electrician, lineworker. **Health services:** Physical therapy assistant, radiologic technology/medical imaging.

Most popular majors. Engineering/engineering technologies 10%, health sciences 11%, science technologies 8%, trade and industry 60%.

Technology on campus. 51 workstations in library, student center. Dormitories wired for high-speed internet access. Helpline, wireless network available.

Student life. **Freshman orientation:** Mandatory. Preregistration for classes offered. Sessions offered simultaneously with registration sessions throughout summer. One day orientation also available day before classes start. **Policies:** Drug- and alcohol-free campus. **Housing:** Coed dorms available. $350 fully refundable deposit. **Activities:** Student government.

Athletics. **Intramural:** Archery, badminton, basketball, football (non-tackle), golf, sand volleyball, softball, table tennis, ultimate frisbee, volleyball. **Team name:** Eagles.

Student services. Financial aid counseling, placement for graduates. **Transfer:** Pre-admission transcript evaluation for new students. College fairs on campus for students transferring to 4-year colleges.

Contact. E-mail: admissions@statetechmo.edu
Phone: (573) 897-5000 Toll-free number: (800) 743-8324
Fax: (573) 897-5026
Kathy Scheulen, Assistant Dean of Enrollment Management, State Technical College of Missouri, One Technology Drive, Linn, MO 65051

Stevens Institute of Business & Arts
St. Louis, Missouri
www.siba.edu   **CB code: 3319**

- For-profit 2-year business and liberal arts college
- Commuter campus in very large city
- Application essay, interview required

General. Regionally accredited; also accredited by ACICS. **Enrollment:** 61 undergraduates. **Degrees:** 49 bachelor's, 30 associate awarded. **Location:** Downtown. **Calendar:** Quarter, extensive summer session. **Full-time faculty:** 8 total. **Part-time faculty:** 19 total. **Class size:** 97% < 20, 3% 20-39.

Student profile. 61 enrolled as first-time, first-year students.

Out-of-state:	26%	25 or older:	39%

Transfer out. **Colleges most students transferred to 2015:** Fontbonne University, Lindenwood University, Maryville University, University of Phoenix, Webster University.

Basis for selection. Open admission, but selective for some programs. SAT or ACT scores are only required of students enrolling in a bachelor's degree program with less than 90 quarter hours in transfer credits. SAT or ACT scores are not required for students enrolling in an AAS program. **Home schooled:** Statement describing home school structure and mission, transcript of courses and grades, state high school equivalency certificate, interview required.

Financial aid. All financial aid based on need. Need-based aid available for part-time students. Work-study available nights, weekends and for part-time students.

Application procedures. **Admission:** No deadline. $25 fee. Application must be submitted on paper. Admission notification on a rolling basis. **Financial aid:** No deadline. FAFSA required. Applicants notified on a rolling basis.

Academics. **Special study options:** Accelerated study, independent study, internships, liberal arts/career combination. Bachelor's degree programs available on campus. **Credit/placement by examination:** AP, CLEP. **Support services:** Reduced course load, study skills assistance, tutoring.

Majors. **Business:** Business admin, fashion, hospitality admin, retailing, tourism/travel, travel services. **Visual/performing arts:** Interior design.

Most popular majors. Business/marketing 23%.

Technology on campus. 42 workstations in library, computer center, student center. Commuter students can connect to campus network. Online library, wireless network available.

Student life. **Freshman orientation:** Mandatory. Preregistration for classes offered. Held each quarter before start of classes. **Policies:** Dress code and attendance policies enforced.

Student services. Adult student services, alcohol/substance abuse counseling, career counseling, student employment services, financial aid counseling, placement for graduates. **Transfer:** Pre-admission transcript evaluation for new students. Transfer adviser, college fairs on campus for students transferring to 4-year colleges.

Contact. E-mail: admissions@siba.edu
Phone: (314) 421-0949 ext. 1119
Toll-free number: (800) 871-0949 ext. 1119 Fax: (314) 421-0304
John Willmon, Director of Admissions, Stevens Institute of Business & Arts, 1521 Washington Avenue, St. Louis, MO 63103

Texas County Technical College
Houston, Missouri
www.texascountytech.edu

- Private 2-year nursing and technical college
- Commuter campus in small town
- Application essay required

General. Accredited by ACICS. Located in the Missouri Ozarks. **Enrollment:** 17 degree-seeking undergraduates. **Degrees:** 22 associate awarded. **Location:** 97 miles from Springfield. **Calendar:** Semester. **Full-time faculty:** 11 total; 100% women. **Part-time faculty:** 18 total; 11% have terminal degrees, 83% women.

Basis for selection. Open admission. **Home schooled:** Transcript of courses and grades required.

2015-2016 Annual costs. Tuition/fees: $13,348. Per-credit charge: $428. Books/supplies: $3,550. Personal expenses: $1,200. **Additional information:** Annual fees cost range by the program from $450-$2,794.

2014-2015 Financial aid. All financial aid based on need. Need-based aid available for part-time students. Work-study available nights, weekends and for part-time students.

Application procedures. Admission: No deadline. $50 fee. Application must be submitted on paper. Admission notification on a rolling basis. **Financial aid:** No deadline. FAFSA, institutional form required.

Academics. Special study options: License preparation in nursing. **Credit/placement by examination:** AP, CLEP. **Support services:** Remedial instruction, study skills assistance, tutoring.

Majors. Health services: Medical secretary, nursing (RN).

Most popular majors. Health sciences 27%.

Technology on campus. 50 workstations in library, computer center.

Student life. Freshman orientation: Mandatory. Preregistration for classes offered. **Activities:** Student newspaper.

Student services. Career counseling, financial aid counseling. **Transfer:** Pre-admission transcript evaluation for new students.

Contact. E-mail: info@texascountytech.edu
Phone: (417) 967-5466 Toll-free number: (800) 835-1130
Fax: (417) 967-4604
Clarice Casebeer, Director of Admissions, Texas County Technical College, 6915 South Highway 63, Houston, MO 65483

Three Rivers Community College
Poplar Bluff, Missouri
www.trcc.edu
CB code: 6836

▶ Public 2-year community college
▶ Commuter campus in large town

General. Founded in 1966. Regionally accredited. Selected courses offered at area high schools, vocational schools and other off-campus facilities. **Enrollment:** 3,087 degree-seeking undergraduates. **Degrees:** 490 associate awarded. **Location:** 160 miles from St. Louis. **Calendar:** Semester, limited summer session. **Full-time faculty:** 63 total. **Part-time faculty:** 114 total.

Student profile.

Out-of-state:	2%	Live on campus:	6%
25 or older:	35%		

Transfer out. Colleges most students transferred to 2015: Southeast Missouri State University, Arkansas State University, Southwest Missouri State University.

Basis for selection. Open admission, but selective for some programs. Special requirements for allied health programs and nursing. **Home schooled:** Statement describing home school structure and mission required.

2015-2016 Annual costs. Tuition/fees: $3,420; $4,890 out-of-district; $5,970 out-of-state. Per-credit charge: $85 in-district; $134 out-of-district; $170 out-of-state. Room only: $3,440.

Financial aid. Need-based: Need-based aid available for part-time students. Work-study available nights, weekends and for part-time students. **Non-need-based:** Scholarships awarded for academics, athletics, state residency.

Application procedures. Admission: No deadline. No application fee. Application must be submitted on paper. Admission notification on a rolling basis. **Financial aid:** Priority date 4/1; no closing date. FAFSA, institutional form required. Applicants notified on a rolling basis starting 6/1; must reply within 2 week(s) of notification.

Academics. Special study options: Accelerated study, distance learning, dual enrollment of high school students, independent study, internships, liberal arts/career combination. Bachelor's degree programs available on campus. License preparation in nursing, paramedic. **Credit/placement by examination:** AP, CLEP. 30 credit hours maximum toward associate degree. **Support services:** GED test center, learning center, remedial instruction, study skills assistance, tutoring, writing center.

Majors. Biology: General. **Business:** Accounting, administrative services, entrepreneurial studies, management information systems, marketing. **Education:** General. **English:** English lit, rhetoric/composition. **Foreign languages:** General. **Health services:** Clinical lab technology, nursing (RN), premedicine, prepharmacy, preveterinary. **History:** General. **Liberal arts:** Arts/sciences, library assistant. **Math:** General. **Parks/recreation:** Health/fitness. **Philosophy/religion:** Philosophy. **Physical sciences:** Chemistry. **Protective services:** Police science. **Psychology:** General. **Social sciences:** Economics, geography, political science, sociology. **Visual/performing arts:** Music, studio arts.

Most popular majors. Business/marketing 8%, education 7%, health sciences 18%, liberal arts 50%.

Technology on campus. 100 workstations in dormitories, library, computer center, student center. Dormitories wired for high-speed internet access.

Student life. Freshman orientation: Available. Preregistration for classes offered. Mini orientation activities are held for incoming freshmen during registration. Orientation for new students offered at beginning of each semester for students, family and friends. **Housing:** Apartments, wellness housing available. $200 partly refundable deposit. **Activities:** Concert band, choral groups, drama, music ensembles, student government, Student Senate, Phi Theta Kappa, Marketing Management Association,.

Athletics. NJCAA. **Intercollegiate:** Baseball M, basketball, softball W. **Team name:** Raiders.

Student services. Career counseling, student employment services, placement for graduates, veterans' counselor. **Transfer:** Transfer adviser, college fairs on campus for students transferring to 4-year colleges.

Contact. E-mail: mfields@trcc.edu
Phone: (573) 840-9605 Toll-free number: (877) 879-8722 ext. 605
Fax: (573) 840-9058
Chris Adams, Director of Admissions, Three Rivers Community College, 2080 Three Rivers Boulevard, Poplar Bluff, MO 63901-1308

Vatterott College: Berkeley
Berkeley, Missouri
www.vatterott-college.edu
CB code: 2507

▶ For-profit 2-year technical college
▶ Large city
▶ Interview required

General. Accredited by ACCSC. **Enrollment:** 1,344 undergraduates. **Degrees:** 156 associate awarded. **Location:** 20 miles from St. Louis, 310 miles from Chicago. **Calendar:** Differs by program. **Full-time faculty:** 30 total. **Part-time faculty:** 30 total.

Basis for selection. Open admission. High school achievement, interview, and institutional testing used to determine admission.

2015-2016 Annual costs. Diploma programs (60 weeks) $28,034-$28,536. Associate programs (70 weeks) $30,559-$35,386; (90 weeks) $40,650-$42,422. Costs include fees, books and supplies.

Financial aid. Need-based: Work-study available nights, weekends and for part-time students.

Application procedures. Admission: No deadline. $25 fee. Admission notification on a rolling basis. **Financial aid:** No deadline. Institutional form required.

Academics. Special study options: Bachelor's degree programs available on campus. **Credit/placement by examination:** AP, CLEP. **Support services:** Remedial instruction, tutoring.

Majors. Computer sciences: Programming, system admin. **General:** Electrician.

Student life. Activities: Literary magazine, TV station.

Contact. E-mail: adm@vatterot-college.edu
Phone: (314) 264-1040 Toll-free number: (866) 314-6454
Fax: (314) 522-6174
Ann Farajallah, Director of Admissions, Vatterott College: Berkeley, 8580 Evans Avenue, Berkeley, MO 63134

Vatterott College: Joplin
Joplin, Missouri
www.vatterott.edu   CB code: 3635

- For-profit 2-year technical college
- Large town

General. Accredited by ACCSC. **Enrollment:** 236 undergraduates. **Degrees:** 45 associate awarded. **Calendar:** Differs by program. **Full-time faculty:** 8 total. **Part-time faculty:** 17 total.

Basis for selection. Open admission.

2015-2016 Annual costs. Diploma programs: (40 weeks) $19,800; (50 weeks) $21,050-$24,050; (60 weeks) $28,034-$28,640. Associate programs: (70 weeks) $30,559-$34,900; (80 weeks) $38,400; (90 weeks) $40,974-$43,178. Costs include fees, books and supplies.

Financial aid. Need-based: Work-study available nights, weekends and for part-time students.

Academics. Credit/placement by examination: AP, CLEP.

Majors. Computer sciences: General. **Health services:** Medical assistant, pharmacy assistant.

Contact. Phone: (417) 781-5633
Nancy Marlow, Director of Admissions, Vatterott College: Joplin, 809 Illinois Avenue, Joplin, MO 64801

Vatterott College: Kansas City
Kansas City, Missouri
www.vatterott.edu   CB code: 2893

- For-profit 2-year technical college
- Large city

General. Accredited by ACCSC. **Enrollment:** 540 undergraduates. **Degrees:** 128 associate awarded. **Calendar:** Differs by program. **Full-time faculty:** 27 total. **Part-time faculty:** 3 total.

Basis for selection. Open admission.

2015-2016 Annual costs. Diploma programs: (40 weeks) $18,900-$18,950; (50 weeks) $20,800-$20,850; (60 weeks) $21,050-$28,034. Associate programs: (70 weeks) $30,552-$37,450; (90 weeks) $40,650-$41,878. Costs include fees, books and supplies.

Financial aid. Need-based: Work-study available nights, weekends and for part-time students.

Academics. Credit/placement by examination: AP, CLEP.

Majors. Business: Business admin. **Computer sciences:** General, information systems.

Contact. E-mail: kc@yatterott-college.edu
Phone: (816) 861-1000 Toll-free number: (800) 466-3997
Fax: (816) 861-1400
Valerie Johnson, Director of Admissions, Vatterott College: Kansas City, 8955 East 38th Terrace, Kansas City, MO 64129

Vatterott College: O'Fallon
Saint Charles, Missouri
www.vatterott-college.edu

- For-profit 2-year branch campus and technical college
- Small city

General. Accredited by ACCSC. **Enrollment:** 305 undergraduates. **Degrees:** 42 associate awarded. **Location:** 30 miles from St. Louis. **Calendar:** Differs by program. **Full-time faculty:** 8 total. **Part-time faculty:** 6 total.

Basis for selection. Open admission.

2015-2016 Annual costs. Diploma programs: (40 weeks) $19,800-$21,500; (50 weeks) $20,850-$21,050; (60 weeks) $28,436-$28,464. Associate programs: (70 weeks) $30,559-$34,900; (90 weeks) $41,406-$41,806. Costs include fees, books and supplies.

Financial aid. Need-based: Work-study available nights, weekends and for part-time students.

Academics. Credit/placement by examination: AP, CLEP.

Majors. Computer sciences: Networking. **Health services:** Medical assistant.

Contact. E-mail: ofallon@vatterott-college.edu
Phone: (636) 978-7488 Toll-free number: (888) 766-3601
Fax: (636) 978-5121
Gertrude Bogan-Jones, Director of Admissions, Vatterott College: O'Fallon, 3350 West Clay Street, St. Charles, MO 63301

Vatterott College: Springfield
Springfield, Missouri
www.vatterott.edu   CB code: 2895

- For-profit 2-year branch campus and technical college
- Commuter campus in small city
- Application essay, interview required

General. Accredited by ACCSC. **Enrollment:** 312 undergraduates. **Degrees:** 69 associate awarded. **Calendar:** Quarter. **Full-time faculty:** 30 total. **Part-time faculty:** 10 total.

Basis for selection. Open admission. **Adult students:** SAT/ACT scores not required. **Home schooled:** Transcript of courses and grades, state high school equivalency certificate required.

2015-2016 Annual costs. Books/supplies: $2,388. Personal expenses: $2,289. **Additional information:** Certificate program: (5 weeks) $4,250. Diploma programs: (40 weeks) $18,242-$21,500; (60 weeks) $28,034-$28,448. Associate programs: (70 weeks) $30,559-$41,050; (90 weeks) $41,050. Costs include fees, books and supplies.

Financial aid. All financial aid based on need. Work-study available nights, weekends and for part-time students.

Application procedures. Admission: No deadline. No application fee. Application must be submitted on paper. Admission notification on a rolling basis. **Financial aid:** No deadline. FAFSA required.

Academics. Credit/placement by examination: AP, CLEP, institutional tests. 36 credit hours maximum toward associate degree. **Support services:** Tutoring.

Majors. Health services: Medical assistant, pharmacy assistant.

Technology on campus. 2 workstations in library, computer center.

Student life. Freshman orientation: Mandatory. Preregistration for classes offered. Held the week before class term is scheduled to start.

Student services. Adult student services, student employment services, financial aid counseling, placement for graduates, veterans' counselor.

Contact. E-mail: springfield@vatterott-college.edu
Phone: (417) 831-8116 Toll-free number: (800) 766-5829
Fax: (417) 831-5099
Melissa Cornelius, Director of Admissions, Vatterott College: Springfield, 3850 South Campbell, Springfield, MO 65807

Vatterott College: St. Joseph
Saint Joseph, Missouri
www.vatterott-college.edu   CB code: 2896

- For-profit 2-year branch campus and technical college
- Commuter campus in small city

General. Accredited by ACCSC. **Enrollment:** 231 undergraduates. **Degrees:** 44 associate awarded. **Location:** 50 miles from Kansas City. **Calendar:** Quarter, extensive summer session. **Full-time faculty:** 5 total. **Part-time faculty:** 12 total.

Basis for selection. Open admission.

2015-2016 Annual costs. Personal expenses: $1,288. **Additional information:** Diploma programs: (30 weeks) $13,350; (40 weeks) $19,800; (50 weeks) $20,800; (60 weeks) $21,050. Associate programs: (70 weeks) $30,559-$34,900. Costs include fees, books and supplies.

Financial aid. Need-based: Need-based aid available for part-time students. Work-study available nights, weekends and for part-time students.

Application procedures. Admission: No deadline. No application fee. **Financial aid:** No deadline. FAFSA required.

Academics. Credit/placement by examination: AP, CLEP, institutional tests. 36 credit hours maximum toward associate degree. **Support services:** Tutoring.

Majors. Computer sciences: General. **Health services:** Medical secretary.

Student life. Freshman orientation: Mandatory. Preregistration for classes offered. Held first day of classes. Students are briefed on policies and procedures and are introduced to the directors, career services, instructors and financial aid paperwork.

Student services. Career counseling, student employment services, financial aid counseling, placement for graduates, veterans' counselor.

Contact. E-mail: jaymi.evans@vatterott-college.edu
Phone: (816) 364-5399 Toll-free number: (800) 282-5327
Fax: (816) 364-1593
Jaymi Evans, Director of Admissions, Vatterott College: St. Joseph, 3131 Frederick Avenue, St. Joseph, MO 64506

Vatterott College: Sunset Hills
Sunset Hills, Missouri
www.vatterott.edu   CB code: 2898

▸ For-profit 2-year branch campus and technical college
▸ Very large city

General. Accredited by ACCSC. **Enrollment:** 624 undergraduates. **Degrees:** 4 bachelor's, 144 associate awarded. **Calendar:** Differs by program. **Full-time faculty:** 23 total. **Part-time faculty:** 17 total.

Basis for selection. Open admission, but selective for some programs.

2015-2016 Annual costs. Diploma programs: (40 weeks) $19,800-$21,500; (60 weeks) $27,508-$28,940. Associate programs: (70 weeks) $31,220-$35,990; (80 weeks) $36,300; (90 weeks) $40,690-$41,922. Bachelor's program: (170 weeks) $78,329-$78,629. Costs include fees, books and supplies.

Financial aid. Need-based: Work-study available nights, weekends and for part-time students.

Application procedures. Admission: No deadline. No application fee. **Financial aid:** No deadline.

Academics. Special study options: Bachelor's degree programs available on campus. **Credit/placement by examination:** AP, CLEP.

Majors. Computer sciences: General, networking.

Contact. E-mail: jessalyn.mckeown@vatterott-college.edu
Phone: (314) 843-4200 Toll-free number: (888) 553-6627
Director, Vatterott College: Sunset Hills, 12900 Maurer Industrial Drive, Sunset Hills, MO 63127

Wentworth Military Junior College
Lexington, Missouri   CB member
www.wma.edu   CB code: 6934

▸ Private 2-year junior and military college
▸ Commuter campus in small town
▸ Interview required

General. Founded in 1880. Regionally accredited. Adult evening program open to both men and women. **Enrollment:** 343 degree-seeking undergraduates. **Degrees:** 130 associate awarded. **ROTC:** Army. **Location:** 40 miles from Kansas City. **Calendar:** Semester, extensive summer session. **Full-time faculty:** 13 total. **Part-time faculty:** 30 total. **Class size:** 100% < 20.

Special facilities: Nature trail, military history library, indoor rifle range, athletic facilities.

Student profile.

Out-of-state:	55%	Live on campus:	23%
25 or older:	30%		

Transfer out. Colleges most students transferred to 2015: Central Missouri State University, Texas A&M University, University of Kansas, Kansas State University, University of Missouri.

Basis for selection. Open admission, but selective for some programs. Admittees to senior ROTC programs must meet ROTC admission criteria. **Home schooled:** Transcript of courses and grades, letter of recommendation (nonparent) required.

High school preparation. 24 units recommended. Recommended units include English 4, mathematics 3, social studies 3, science 2 (laboratory 2), foreign language 2 and academic electives 8.

2015-2016 Annual costs. Tuition/fees: $20,900. Per-credit charge: $180. Room/board: $6,800. Books/supplies: $1,500. Personal expenses: $2,200.

Financial aid. All financial aid based on need. Work-study available nights, weekends and for part-time students.

Application procedures. Admission: Closing date 8/15. No application fee. Admission notification on a rolling basis. **Financial aid:** Closing date 4/30. FAFSA required. Applicants notified on a rolling basis.

Academics. Service academy preparatory program. **Special study options:** Accelerated study, distance learning, dual enrollment of high school students, ESL, independent study, liberal arts/career combination. License preparation in nursing. **Credit/placement by examination:** AP, CLEP, institutional tests. 30 credit hours maximum toward associate degree. **Support services:** Tutoring.

Majors. Liberal arts: Arts/sciences.

Technology on campus. 50 workstations in library, computer center. Dormitories wired for high-speed internet access and linked to campus network. Commuter students can connect to campus network. Helpline, wireless network available.

Student life. Freshman orientation: Available. Preregistration for classes offered. **Policies:** Religious observance required. **Housing:** Single-sex dorms available. $1,500 deposit, deadline 6/30. **Activities:** Bands, choral groups, dance, drama, music ensembles, student government, student newspaper.

Athletics. NJCAA. **Intercollegiate:** Cross-country, rifle M, track and field, wrestling M. **Intramural:** Baseball M, basketball M, cheerleading W, football (non-tackle) M, golf, racquetball, rifle, soccer, swimming, tennis, volleyball, weight lifting M. **Team name:** Red Dragons.

Student services. Career counseling, financial aid counseling, health services, personal counseling. **Transfer:** Transfer adviser, college fairs on campus for students transferring to 4-year colleges.

Contact. E-mail: admissions@wma.edu
Phone: (660) 259-2221 Toll-free number: (800) 962-7682
Fax: (660) 259-2677
Connie McNeill, Admissions Director, Wentworth Military Junior College, 1880 Washington Avenue, Lexington, MO 64067-1799

Montana

Aaniiih Nakoda College
Harlem, Montana
www.ancollege.edu

Two-Year Colleges

- Public 2-year community college
- Commuter campus in rural community

General. Regionally accredited. Tribal college. **Enrollment:** 220 undergraduates. **Degrees:** 25 associate awarded. **Location:** On Fort Belknap Reservation. **Calendar:** Semester. **Full-time faculty:** 18 total. **Part-time faculty:** 3 total. **Special facilities:** Native American cultural center.

Transfer out. Colleges most students transferred to 2015: University of Missoula.

Basis for selection. Open admission. COMPASS Placement Test required. **Home schooled:** Transcript of courses and grades, state high school equivalency certificate required.

2015-2016 Annual costs. Tuition/fees: $2,410; $2,410 out-of-state. Per-credit charge: $70. Books/supplies: $910. Personal expenses: $960.

Financial aid. Need-based: Work-study available nights, weekends and for part-time students.

Application procedures. Admission: No deadline. $10 fee. Admission notification on a rolling basis. **Financial aid:** No deadline. Applicants notified on a rolling basis.

Academics. Special study options: Dual enrollment of high school students. **Credit/placement by examination:** AP, CLEP. **Support services:** GED preparation, learning center, tutoring.

Majors. Area/ethnic studies: Native American. **Business:** General, office technology. **Computer sciences:** General. **Education:** Early childhood, elementary. **Liberal arts:** Arts/sciences.

Most popular majors. Biological/life sciences 21%, business/marketing 7%, computer/information sciences 29%, education 7%, liberal arts 7%, natural resources/environmental science 21%, psychology 7%.

Student life. Freshman orientation: Mandatory. Preregistration for classes offered. **Activities:** Student government.

Student services. Career counseling, financial aid counseling.

Contact. Phone: (406) 353-2607 Fax: (406) 353-2898
Dixie Brockie, Registrar/Admissions Officer, Aaniiih Nakoda College, Box 159, Harlem, MT 59526-0159

Blackfeet Community College
Browning, Montana
www.bfcc.edu   CB code: 0379

- Public 2-year tribal community college
- Commuter campus in small town

General. Founded in 1976. Regionally accredited. Tribally controlled college located on Blackfeet Indian reservation. **Enrollment:** 462 degree-seeking undergraduates. **Degrees:** 65 associate awarded. **Location:** 126 miles from Great Falls. **Calendar:** Semester, limited summer session. **Full-time faculty:** 24 total. **Part-time faculty:** 13 total. **Class size:** 77% < 20, 22% 20-39, less than 1% 40-49.

Student profile. Among degree-seeking undergraduates, 198 enrolled as first-time, first-year students.

Part-time:	27%	Women:	65%
Out-of-state:	2%		

Basis for selection. Open admission. **Home schooled:** State high school equivalency certificate required.

2015-2016 Annual costs. Tuition/fees: $2,810; $2,810 out-of-state. Per-credit charge: $95. Books/supplies: $2,000. Personal expenses: $1,200.

2015-2016 Financial aid. Need-based: 92 full-time freshmen applied for aid; 92 deemed to have need; 92 received aid. Average need met was 53%. Average scholarship/grant was $1,530. 98% of total undergraduate aid awarded as scholarships/grants, 2% as loans/jobs. Need-based aid available for part-time students. Work-study available nights, weekends and for part-time students. **Non-need-based:** Scholarships awarded for academics, minority status, state residency.

Application procedures. Admission: No deadline. $30 fee. Application must be submitted on paper. Admission notification on a rolling basis. **Financial aid:** No deadline. FAFSA, institutional form required. Applicants notified on a rolling basis starting 8/1; must reply by 3/1.

Academics. Special study options: Distance learning, double major, internships. 2-2 teacher training program with Montana University System. **Credit/placement by examination:** AP, CLEP. 3 credit hours maximum toward associate degree. **Support services:** GED test center, learning center, pre-admission summer program, remedial instruction, tutoring, writing center.

Majors. Area/ethnic studies: Native American. **Biology:** General. **Business:** Business admin, entrepreneurial studies, hospitality admin, office management, small business admin. **Computer sciences:** General, networking. **Conservation:** Environmental science, management/policy. **Education:** Bilingual, early childhood, elementary. **Engineering:** General. **General:** Building construction. **Health services:** General, prenursing, substance abuse counseling. **Human services:** Social work. **Liberal arts:** Arts/sciences. **Math:** General. **Parks/recreation:** Health/fitness. **Protective services:** Criminal justice. **Work/family studies:** Family studies.

Most popular majors. Business/marketing 18%, education 19%, health sciences 25%, parks/recreation 7%.

Technology on campus. 5 workstations in library, computer center, student center.

Student life. Freshman orientation: Mandatory. Preregistration for classes offered. **Activities:** Literary magazine, student government, student newspaper.

Athletics. Intercollegiate: Basketball, rodeo. **Intramural:** Basketball. **Team name:** Thunder.

Student services. Adult student services, career counseling, financial aid counseling, personal counseling. **Transfer:** Transfer adviser for students transferring to 4-year colleges.

Contact. E-mail: helen_morris@bfcc.edu
Phone: (406) 338-5421 ext. 2243 Toll-free number: (800) 549-7457
Fax: (406) 338-3272
Deana McNabb, Registrar/Admissions Officer, Blackfeet Community College, 504 SE Boundary, Browning, MT 59417

Chief Dull Knife College
Lame Deer, Montana
www.cdkc.edu   CB code: 5938

- Public 2-year junior college
- Commuter campus in rural community

General. Regionally accredited. **Enrollment:** 26 degree-seeking undergraduates. **Degrees:** 35 associate awarded. **Location:** 110 miles from Billings. **Calendar:** Semester, limited summer session. **Full-time faculty:** 12 total.

Basis for selection. Open admission.

2015-2016 Annual costs. Tuition/fees: $2,260; $2,260 out-of-state. Per-credit charge: $70. Books/supplies: $1,000. Personal expenses: $4,000.

Financial aid. Need-based: Need-based aid available for part-time students. Work-study available nights, weekends and for part-time students. **Non-need-based:** Scholarships awarded for academics.

Application procedures. Admission: No deadline. No application fee. Application must be submitted on paper. Admission notification on a rolling basis. **Financial aid:** Priority date 3/1; no closing date. FAFSA, institutional form required. Applicants notified on a rolling basis; must reply within 2 week(s) of notification.

Academics. Special study options: Cooperative education, double major, internships. Bachelor's degree programs available on campus. **Credit/placement by examination:** AP, CLEP, institutional tests. 9 credit hours maximum toward associate degree. **Support services:** GED preparation and test center, learning center, remedial instruction, tutoring.

Majors. Business: Business admin, office management.

Most popular majors. Liberal arts 95%.

Technology on campus. 25 workstations in library, computer center. Online library available.

Student life. Freshman orientation: Mandatory. Preregistration for classes offered. **Activities:** Student government, student newspaper.

Athletics. Intramural: Basketball.

Student services. Career counseling, financial aid counseling, on-campus daycare, personal counseling, veterans' counselor. **Transfer:** Transfer adviser for students transferring to 4-year colleges.

Contact. E-mail: zspang@cdkc.edu
Phone: (406) 477-6215 Fax: (406) 477-6219
Zane Spang, Dean of Student Affairs, Chief Dull Knife College, Box 98, Lame Deer, MT 59043

Dawson Community College
Glendive, Montana
www.dawson.edu
CB code: 4280

▶ Public 2-year community college
▶ Commuter campus in small town

General. Founded in 1940. Regionally accredited. **Enrollment:** 216 degree-seeking undergraduates; 87 non-degree-seeking students. **Degrees:** 72 associate awarded. **Location:** 220 miles from Billings, 200 miles from Bismarck, North Dakota. **Calendar:** Semester, limited summer session. **Full-time faculty:** 16 total; 12% have terminal degrees, 50% women. **Part-time faculty:** 13 total; 31% women. **Class size:** 95% < 20, 5% 20-39.

Student profile. Among degree-seeking undergraduates, 69% enrolled in a transfer program, 30% enrolled in a vocational program, 79 enrolled as first-time, first-year students.

Part-time:	26%	Women:	55%
Out-of-state:	20%	Live on campus:	55%

Transfer out. Colleges most students transferred to 2015: Dickinson State University, Montana State University-Bozeman, Montana State University-Billings, University of Montana.

Basis for selection. Open admission.

2015-2016 Annual costs. Tuition/fees: $3,570; $5,005 out-of-district; $10,815 out-of-state. Per-credit charge: $65 in-district; $111.5 out-of-district; $306.5 out-of-state. Room/board: $5,575. Books/supplies: $1,200. Personal expenses: $1,200.

Financial aid. Need-based: Work-study available nights, weekends and for part-time students. **Non-need-based:** Scholarships awarded for academics, art, athletics, music/drama.

Application procedures. Admission: No deadline. $30 fee. Admission notification on a rolling basis. **Financial aid:** Priority date 3/1; no closing date. FAFSA required. Applicants notified on a rolling basis starting 5/15; must reply within 2 week(s) of notification.

Academics. Special study options: Distance learning, double major, dual enrollment of high school students, independent study, internships. **Credit/placement by examination:** AP, CLEP, IB, institutional tests. 15 credit hours maximum toward associate degree. **Support services:** GED preparation and test center, learning center, reduced course load, remedial instruction, study skills assistance, tutoring.

Majors. Business: General, administrative services. **Education:** Early childhood. **Health services:** Substance abuse counseling. **Liberal arts:** Arts/sciences. **Protective services:** Law enforcement admin, police science. **Visual/performing arts:** Music technology.

Most popular majors. Business/marketing 6%, education 11%, liberal arts 67%, security/protective services 8%.

Technology on campus. 70 workstations in dormitories, library, computer center. Dormitories wired for high-speed internet access and linked to campus network. Wireless network available.

Student life. Freshman orientation: Mandatory. Preregistration for classes offered. Held during June and July. **Housing:** Coed dorms available. $150 fully refundable deposit. Student dormitories include kitchen facilities. **Activities:** Bands, choral groups, drama, music ensembles, musical theater, student government, law enforcement club, Intervarsity Christian Fellowship, rodeo club, associated student body government.

Athletics. NJCAA. **Intercollegiate:** Baseball M, basketball, rodeo, softball W. **Intramural:** Basketball, bowling, golf, racquetball, softball, table tennis, tennis, volleyball. **Team name:** Buccaneers.

Student services. Adult student services, career counseling, student employment services, placement for graduates, veterans' counselor. **Physically disabled:** Services for visually, speech, hearing impaired. **Transfer:** Pre-admission transcript evaluation for new students. College fairs on campus for students transferring to 4-year colleges.

Contact. E-mail: myers@dawson.edu
Phone: (406) 377-3396 ext. 410
Toll-free number: (800) 821-8320 ext. 410 Fax: (406) 377-8132
John Bole, Vice President of Student Services, Dawson Community College, 300 College Drive, Glendive, MT 59330

Flathead Valley Community College
Kalispell, Montana
www.fvcc.edu
CB code: 4317

▶ Public 2-year community college
▶ Commuter campus in large town

General. Founded in 1967. Regionally accredited. **Enrollment:** 2,206 undergraduates. **Degrees:** 369 associate awarded. **Location:** 238 miles from Spokane, Washington. **Calendar:** Semester, limited summer session. **Full-time faculty:** 51 total. **Part-time faculty:** 129 total. **Class size:** 75% < 20, 25% 20-39. **Partnerships:** Formal partnerships with area high schools for Early College programs.

Student profile.

Out-of-state:	2%	25 or older:	51%

Transfer out. 8% of students enrolled in the transfer program go on to 4-year colleges. **Colleges most students transferred to 2015:** Montana State University, University of Montana.

Basis for selection. Open admission, but selective for some programs. Culinary Arts Program requires COMPASS scores of 78 in reading, 71 in writing, and 47 in pre-algebra, or completion of appropriate remedial coursework. Heavy Equipment Operator students must pass a physical and drug screen. Paramedicine requires a valid EMT-B License, Basic A&P and college level math, entrance exam, interview with selection committee, and a background check. Practical Nursing requires the completion of specific courses, with grades of C or higher; GPA of at least 2.75 in all prerequisite courses. Pharmacy Technology requires COMPASS scores of 30 in Algebra and 74 in Reading or completion of appropriate remedial coursework. Comprehensive background check required. Associate of Science in Nursing requires a grade of C or better in all prerequisite courses and is a competitive application process. Application essay and letter of reference required for Culinary Arts Program. Essay, references, and interview required for Radiologic and Surgical Technology students. **Home schooled:** Applicants must have GED or COMPASS test scores.

2015-2016 Annual costs. Tuition/fees: $3,965; $5,337 out-of-district; $11,105 out-of-state. Books/supplies: $1,000. Personal expenses: $2,240.

Financial aid. Need-based: Need-based aid available for part-time students. Work-study available nights, weekends and for part-time students. **Non-need-based:** Scholarships awarded for academics, athletics.

Application procedures. Admission: No deadline. $15 fee. Admission notification on a rolling basis. **Financial aid:** Priority date 3/1; no closing date. FAFSA required. Applicants notified on a rolling basis starting 4/15; must reply within 2 week(s) of notification.

Academics. Special study options: Distance learning, dual enrollment of high school students, honors, independent study, internships, liberal arts/career combination, study abroad. Bachelor's degree programs available on campus. License preparation in nursing, paramedic, radiology. **Credit/placement by examination:** AP, CLEP, IB, institutional tests. There is no limit to the number of credits that may be granted. **Support services:** GED preparation and test center, learning center, reduced course load, remedial instruction, study skills assistance, tutoring, writing center.

Two-Year Colleges

Honors college/program. Competitive admissions process; factors influencing the admissions decision include high school grades, an essay, letters of reference, and standardized test scores. 20 students admitted each year.

Majors. Business: Accounting, business admin, executive assistant, small business admin. **Computer sciences:** Information technology, web page design. **Conservation:** Management/policy. **Education:** Early childhood. **General:** Electrician. **Health services:** EMT paramedic, licensed practical nurse, medical assistant, medical radiologic technology/radiation therapy, medical secretary, nursing (RN), office assistant, physical therapy assistant, receptionist, substance abuse counseling, surgical technology. **Liberal arts:** Arts/sciences, humanities. **Protective services:** Criminal justice. **Visual/performing arts:** Graphic design, metal/jewelry.

Most popular majors. Health sciences 14%, liberal arts 65%, trade and industry 7%.

Technology on campus. 456 workstations in library, computer center. Commuter students can connect to campus network. Online course registration, online library, helpline, wireless network available.

Student life. Freshman orientation: Available. Preregistration for classes offered. 4 half-day summer advising and registration programs. **Housing:** $150 deposit. **Activities:** Campus ministries, choral groups, drama, student government, student newspaper, Phi Theta Kappa, veterans organization, forestry club, Bitta club (Native American), human service club, international student association.

Athletics. NJCAA. **Intercollegiate:** Cross-country. **Intramural:** Basketball, bowling, skiing, soccer, softball, table tennis, volleyball. **Team name:** Eagles.

Student services. Adult student services, career counseling, services for economically disadvantaged, student employment services, financial aid counseling, health services, minority student services, on-campus daycare, personal counseling, placement for graduates, veterans' counselor. **Physically disabled:** Services for visually, hearing impaired. **Transfer:** Pre-admission transcript evaluation for new students. Transfer adviser, college fairs on campus for students transferring to 4-year colleges.

Contact. E-mail: mstoltz@fvcc.edu
Phone: (406) 756-3846 Toll-free number: (800) 313-3822
Fax: (406) 756-3965
Marlene Stoltz, Registrar/Admissions and Records Coordinator, Flathead Valley Community College, 777 Grandview Drive, Kalispell, MT 59901

Fort Peck Community College
Poplar, Montana
www.fpcc.edu

▸ Public 2-year community college
▸ Residential campus in rural community

General. Regionally accredited. Tribally controlled college. Transfer degrees and Vocational Degrees also offered. **Enrollment:** 323 degree-seeking undergraduates. **Degrees:** 28 associate awarded. **Location:** 70 miles from Williston, North Dakota; 320 miles from Billings. **Calendar:** Semester, limited summer session. **Full-time faculty:** 24 total; 12% have terminal degrees, 50% minority, 42% women. **Part-time faculty:** 27 total; 44% minority, 56% women.

Student profile.

25 or older:	22%	Live on campus:	5%

Transfer out. Colleges most students transferred to 2015: Montana State University - Billings, University of Montana, Montana State University - Bozeman, Williston State University.

Basis for selection. Open admission. Interview recommended. **Home schooled:** State high school equivalency certificate required.

2015-2016 Annual costs. Tuition/fees: $2,250; $2,250 out-of-state. Per-credit charge: $70. Room only: $1,350. Books/supplies: $700.

Financial aid. Need-based: Need-based aid available for part-time students. Work-study available nights, weekends and for part-time students. **Non-need-based:** Scholarships awarded for academics, minority status, state residency.

Application procedures. Admission: No deadline. $15 fee. Application must be submitted on paper. Admission notification on a rolling basis. **Financial aid:** No deadline. FAFSA, institutional form required. Applicants notified on a rolling basis starting 5/1; must reply within 3 week(s) of notification.

Academics. Special study options: Distance learning, dual enrollment of high school students, independent study, internships. **Credit/placement by examination:** AP, CLEP. **Support services:** GED preparation and test center, learning center, remedial instruction, study skills assistance, tutoring.

Majors. Area/ethnic studies: Native American. **Biology:** Biomedical sciences. **Business:** General, business admin. **Computer sciences:** Computer graphics, data processing, information technology. **Conservation:** General. **Education:** General, science. **Health services:** Prenursing, substance abuse counseling. **Social sciences:** General, sociology.

Most popular majors. Business/marketing 29%, education 7%, history 7%, liberal arts 18%, social sciences 18%, trade and industry 18%.

Technology on campus. 65 workstations in dormitories, library, computer center, student center. Dormitories wired for high-speed internet access and linked to campus network. Wireless network available.

Student life. Freshman orientation: Available. Preregistration for classes offered. **Housing:** Coed dorms available. $75 nonrefundable deposit, deadline 8/30. **Activities:** Student government, American Indian Business Leaders.

Athletics. Intercollegiate: Basketball. **Intramural:** Basketball. **Team name:** Buffalo Chasers.

Student services. Adult student services, career counseling, student employment services, on-campus daycare, personal counseling, placement for graduates, veterans' counselor. **Transfer:** Pre-admission transcript evaluation for new students. Transfer adviser, college fairs on campus for students transferring to 4-year colleges.

Contact. Phone: (406) 768-6300 Fax: (406) 738-6301
Linda Hansen, Registrar, Fort Peck Community College, Box 398, 605 Indian, Poplar, MT 59255-0398

Great Falls College Montana State University
Great Falls, Montana
www.gfcmsu.edu   CB code: 4482

▸ Public 2-year community college
▸ Commuter campus in small city

General. Founded in 1969. Regionally accredited. **Enrollment:** 1,398 degree-seeking undergraduates. **Degrees:** 290 associate awarded. **Location:** 200 miles from Billings, 150 miles from Missoula. **Calendar:** Semester, limited summer session. **Full-time faculty:** 46 total; 15% have terminal degrees, 9% minority, 65% women. **Part-time faculty:** 95 total; 13% have terminal degrees, 4% minority, 60% women. **Class size:** 57% < 20, 43% 20-39. **Special facilities:** Simulated hospital, remote access science lab.

Student profile. Among degree-seeking undergraduates, 132 transferred in from other institutions.

Out-of-state:	4%	25 or older:	54%

Transfer out. Colleges most students transferred to 2015: Montana State University, Montana State University - Northern, Montana State University - Billings, University of Great Falls.

Basis for selection. Open admission, but selective for some programs. Special admissions requirements for dental assistant, dental hygiene, radiologic technology, practical nursing, dental assistant, surgical technology, EMS, diet tech, and physical therapist assistant programs. **Adult students:** COMPASS test used to determine placement in courses. All placement tests must have been taken within the past three years. **Home schooled:** Transcript of courses and grades, letter of recommendation (nonparent) required. Notarized copy of the home school curriculum, 2 letters of recommendation from non-family members, parental approval form if under 18 required.

2015-2016 Annual costs. Tuition/fees: $3,130; $9,382 out-of-state. Per-credit charge: $104 in-state; $364 out-of-state. Books/supplies: $1,500. Personal expenses: $3,430.

Financial aid. Need-based: Need-based aid available for part-time students. Work-study available nights, weekends and for part-time students. **Non-need-based:** Scholarships awarded for academics, leadership.

Application procedures. Admission: No deadline. $30 fee. Admission notification on a rolling basis. **Financial aid:** Priority date 3/1; no closing date. FAFSA, institutional form required. Applicants notified on a rolling basis starting 4/15.

Academics. Special study options: Distance learning, dual enrollment of high school students, ESL, independent study, internships. License preparation in dental hygiene, nursing, paramedic, physical therapy, radiology.

Credit/placement by examination: AP, CLEP, institutional tests. 45 credit hours maximum toward associate degree. **Support services:** Learning center, remedial instruction, study skills assistance, tutoring.

Majors. Business: Accounting, business admin, entrepreneurial studies. **Computer sciences:** Information technology, networking, web page design. **Health services:** Dental hygiene, EMT paramedic, health information management, insurance specialist, licensed practical nurse, medical assistant, medical transcription, nursing (RN), physical therapy assistant, radiologic technology/medical imaging, respiratory therapy assistant, respiratory therapy technology, surgical technology. **Visual/performing arts:** Graphic design, interior design.

Most popular majors. Business/marketing 7%, computer/information sciences 6%, health sciences 40%, liberal arts 44%.

Technology on campus. 465 workstations in library, computer center. Commuter students can connect to campus network. Online course registration, online library, helpline, wireless network available.

Student life. Freshman orientation: Available. Preregistration for classes offered. Held prior to the fall and spring semesters. Students attend mandatory sessions selected by the college and then have optional sections to choose from. Students able to choose the days and times for their sessions; sessions will be offered in the week prior to the beginning of the semester. **Activities:** Radio station, student government, Phi Theta Kappa, Health Occupations Students of America, interior design club, Student Association of Dental Hygiene, Native American student group, Christian Bible study group, Veterans Center, Anime club, Lambda COT.

Student services. Career counseling, services for economically disadvantaged, student employment services, financial aid counseling, placement for graduates, veterans' counselor. **Physically disabled:** Services for visually, speech, hearing impaired. **Transfer:** Pre-admission transcript evaluation for new students. Transfer adviser, college fairs on campus for students transferring to 4-year colleges.

Contact. E-mail: admissions@gfcmsu.edu
Phone: (406) 771-4420 Toll-free number: (800) 446-2698
Fax: (406) 771-4329
Joe Simonsen, Director of Admissions, Great Falls College Montana State University, 2100 16th Avenue South, Great Falls, MT 59405

Helena College University of Montana
Helena, Montana
www.umhelena.edu   CB code: 2022

▶ Public 2-year community and technical college
▶ Commuter campus in large town

General. Founded in 1939. Regionally accredited. **Enrollment:** 1,063 degree-seeking undergraduates. **Degrees:** 202 associate awarded. **Location:** 90 miles from Great Falls. **Calendar:** Semester, limited summer session. **Full-time faculty:** 40 total. **Part-time faculty:** 105 total. **Class size:** 77% < 20, 23% 20-39.

Student profile.

Out-of-state: 1%   25 or older: 37%

Basis for selection. Open admission. **Home schooled:** May be required to provide GED scores or meet Ability to Benefit Requirements.

2015-2016 Annual costs. Tuition/fees: $3,062; $8,358 out-of-state. Per-credit charge: $79 in-state; $255 out-of-state. Books/supplies: $1,200.

Financial aid. Need-based: Need-based aid available for part-time students. Work-study available nights, weekends and for part-time students.

Application procedures. Admission: No deadline. $30 fee. Admission notification on a rolling basis. **Financial aid:** Priority date 3/1; no closing date. FAFSA, institutional form required. Applicants notified on a rolling basis starting 5/1.

Academics. Special study options: Distance learning, dual enrollment of high school students, external degree, honors, independent study, internships. Bachelor's degree programs available on campus. License preparation in aviation, nursing, paramedic. **Credit/placement by examination:** AP, CLEP, institutional tests. Total credits by examination cannot exceed 25% of the credits required for a degree. **Support services:** GED preparation and test center, learning center, pre-admission summer program, remedial instruction, study skills assistance, tutoring, writing center.

Majors. Business: Accounting, administrative services. **Computer sciences:** Programming. **Health services:** Licensed practical nurse, nursing

(RN), office assistant. **Liberal arts:** Arts/sciences. **Protective services:** Fire-fighting. **Visual/performing arts:** Interior design.

Most popular majors. Business/marketing 18%, computer/information sciences 8%, health sciences 24%, liberal arts 16%, security/protective services 7%, trade and industry 25%.

Technology on campus. 160 workstations in library, computer center. Commuter students can connect to campus network. Online course registration, online library, helpline, wireless network available.

Student life. Freshman orientation: Mandatory, $15 fee. Preregistration for classes offered. **Activities:** Student government, Circle K, Student Government Association, College Christian Fellowship.

Student services. Adult student services, career counseling, services for economically disadvantaged, student employment services, financial aid counseling, personal counseling, placement for graduates, veterans' counselor. **Physically disabled:** Services for visually, speech, hearing impaired. **Transfer:** Transfer adviser, college fairs on campus for students transferring to 4-year colleges.

Contact. E-mail: admissions@umhelena.edu
Phone: (406) 447-6900 Fax: (406) 447-6392
Sarah Dellwo, Director of Admissions & Records, Helena College University of Montana, 1115 North Roberts Street, Helena, MT 59601-3098

Little Big Horn College
Crow Agency, Montana
www.lbhc.edu   CB code: 0536

▶ Private 2-year community college
▶ Commuter campus in rural community

General. Founded in 1980. Regionally accredited. Provides education for Crow Indian community. Crow lifeways, economic environment, history, language, and culture emphasized with standard curriculum. **Enrollment:** 236 degree-seeking undergraduates. **Degrees:** 53 associate awarded. **Location:** 60 miles from Billings. **Calendar:** Semester, limited summer session. **Full-time faculty:** 17 total. **Part-time faculty:** 12 total.

Basis for selection. Open admission.

2015-2016 Annual costs. Tuition/fees: $2,860. Per-credit charge: $85. Books/supplies: $600. Personal expenses: $600.

2014-2015 Financial aid. All financial aid based on need. 99% of total undergraduate aid awarded as scholarships/grants, 1% as loans/jobs. Need-based aid available for part-time students. Work-study available nights, weekends and for part-time students.

Application procedures. Admission: No deadline. No application fee. Admission notification on a rolling basis. **Financial aid:** No deadline. FAFSA, institutional form required. Applicants notified on a rolling basis.

Academics. Bilingual methodologies approach in some course work. **Special study options:** Distance learning, exchange student, internships. **Credit/placement by examination:** AP, CLEP, institutional tests. **Support services:** Remedial instruction, tutoring.

Majors. Biology: General. **Business:** Business admin, management information systems. **Conservation:** General. **Education:** General. **Health services:** Community health services, environmental health, premedicine, prenursing. **Liberal arts:** Arts/sciences. **Math:** General.

Most popular majors. Education 13%, health sciences 23%, history 40%, liberal arts 19%.

Student life. Policies: Native religious ceremonies offered. **Activities:** Student government.

Athletics. Intercollegiate: Basketball. **Team name:** RAMS.

Student services. Career counseling, student employment services, personal counseling. **Transfer:** Transfer adviser, college fairs on campus for students transferring to 4-year colleges.

Contact. E-mail: dawesa@lbhc.edu
Phone: (406) 638-3116 Fax: (406) 638-3169
Arlene Dawes, Admissions Clerk, Little Big Horn College, Box 370, Crow Agency, MT 59022

Miles Community College
Miles City, Montana
www.milescc.edu

CB code: 4081

- Public 2-year community college
- Commuter campus in small town

General. Founded in 1939. Regionally accredited. **Enrollment:** 367 degree-seeking undergraduates; 114 non-degree-seeking students. **Degrees:** 101 associate awarded. **Location:** 150 miles from Billings. **Calendar:** Semester, limited summer session. **Full-time faculty:** 21 total. **Part-time faculty:** 25 total.

Student profile. Among degree-seeking undergraduates, 121 enrolled as first-time, first-year students, 60 transferred in from other institutions.

Part-time:	26%	Hispanic/Latino:	4%
Out-of-state:	6%	Native American:	5%
Women:	63%	International:	1%
African American:	3%	25 or older:	30%
Asian American:	2%	Live on campus:	35%

Transfer out. Colleges most students transferred to 2015: Montana State University-Billings, Montana State University-Bozeman, Dickinson State University, University of Montana, South Dakota State University.

Basis for selection. Open admission, but selective for some programs. Special requirements for nursing program: National League for Nursing Pre-Admission Examination and nurse's aide certification required. COMPASS or Placement testing required for all students. **Home schooled:** Minimum COMPASS scores: Writing, 32; Reading, 62; Pre-Algebra/Number Skills, 25; may be used in lieu of high school diploma or GED.

2015-2016 Annual costs. Tuition/fees: $3,945; $5,085 out-of-district; $8,085 out-of-state. Room/board: $5,880. Books/supplies: $1,100. Personal expenses: $1,400.

Financial aid. Need-based: Need-based aid available for part-time students. Work-study available nights, weekends and for part-time students. **Non-need-based:** Scholarships awarded for academics, athletics, leadership.

Application procedures. Admission: No deadline. $30 fee. Admission notification on a rolling basis. **Financial aid:** Priority date 3/1; no closing date. FAFSA required. Applicants notified on a rolling basis starting 4/15; must reply within 4 week(s) of notification.

Academics. Special study options: Cooperative education, cross-registration, distance learning, dual enrollment of high school students, ESL, independent study, internships. License preparation in nursing. **Credit/placement by examination:** AP, CLEP, IB, institutional tests. 15 credit hours maximum toward associate degree. **Support services:** Learning center, pre-admission summer program, reduced course load, remedial instruction, study skills assistance, tutoring, writing center.

Majors. Biology: General. **Business:** Administrative services, business admin, office management, office/clerical. **Computer sciences:** General, computer graphics, data processing. **Conservation:** General, forestry, wildlife/wilderness. **Education:** General. **Engineering:** General. **General:** Maintenance. **Health services:** Nursing (RN), prenursing. **Liberal arts:** Arts/sciences. **Parks/recreation:** Health/fitness.

Technology on campus. 90 workstations in library, computer center. Dormitories wired for high-speed internet access. Commuter students can connect to campus network. Online course registration, helpline, wireless network available.

Student life. Freshman orientation: Mandatory. Preregistration for classes offered. **Housing:** Coed dorms available. $200 deposit. **Activities:** Campus ministries, choral groups, dance, drama, international student organizations, student government, Phi Theta Kappa, rodeo club, student senate, student ambassadors.

Athletics. NJCAA. **Intercollegiate:** Baseball M, basketball, cheerleading, golf, rodeo. **Intramural:** Basketball, bowling, fencing, golf, handball, ice hockey, racquetball, soccer, tennis, volleyball, weight lifting. **Team name:** Pioneers.

Student services. Adult student services, career counseling, student employment services, financial aid counseling, placement for graduates, veterans' counselor. **Transfer:** Pre-admission transcript evaluation for new students. College fairs on campus for students transferring to 4-year colleges.

Contact. Phone: (406) 874-6217 Toll-free number: (800) 541-9281 Fax: (406) 874-6283
Jessie Dufner, Vice President of Student Success, Miles Community College, 2715 Dickinson Street, Miles City, MT 59301

Stone Child College
Box Elder, Montana
www.stonechild.edu

CB code: 7044

- Public 2-year community and junior college
- Commuter campus in rural community

General. Founded in 1984. Regionally accredited. Tribally-controlled college located on the Rocky Boys Indian Reservation. **Enrollment:** 289 degree-seeking undergraduates. **Degrees:** 32 associate awarded. **Location:** 26 miles from Havre, 100 miles from Great Falls. **Calendar:** Semester, limited summer session. **Full-time faculty:** 9 total; 11% have terminal degrees, 22% minority, 33% women. **Part-time faculty:** 22 total; 100% minority, 64% women. **Class size:** 80% < 20, 20% 20-39.

Student profile. Among degree-seeking undergraduates, 40 enrolled as first-time, first-year students, 1 transferred in from other institutions.

Part-time:	45%	25 or older:	35%
Women:	64%		

Transfer out. 45% of students enrolled in the transfer program go on to 4-year colleges. **Colleges most students transferred to 2015:** Montana State University-Northern, Montana State University-Billings, University of Montana, University of Great Falls, Salish Kootenai College.

Basis for selection. Open admission. **Adult students:** ACCUPLACER testing required of all incoming students. **Home schooled:** Transcript of courses and grades, state high school equivalency certificate required.

High school preparation. College-preparatory program recommended. 22 units recommended. Recommended units include English 4, mathematics 3, social studies 3, history 4, science 3, foreign language 1 and academic electives 4.

2015-2016 Annual costs. Tuition/fees: $2,645; $2,645 out-of-state. Books/supplies: $1,000. Personal expenses: $1,520.

2015-2016 Financial aid. Need-based: 36% of total undergraduate aid awarded as scholarships/grants, 64% as loans/jobs. Need-based aid available for part-time students. Work-study available nights, weekends and for part-time students. **Additional information:** Scholarships available to high school and GED graduates who apply for college admission during the first term after graduation.

Application procedures. Admission: No deadline. $10 fee. Application must be submitted on paper. **Financial aid:** Priority date 3/1; no closing date. FAFSA required. Applicants notified on a rolling basis.

Academics. Special study options: Double major, dual enrollment of high school students, independent study. **Credit/placement by examination:** AP, CLEP. **Support services:** Learning center, remedial instruction, tutoring.

Majors. Area/ethnic studies: Native American. **Business:** General, management information systems, office/clerical. **Computer sciences:** Information systems. **Conservation:** General. **Education:** Elementary. **Health services:** Substance abuse counseling. **Liberal arts:** Arts/sciences. **Math:** General.

Most popular majors. Area/ethnic studies 13%, business/marketing 26%, family/consumer sciences 16%, health sciences 13%, liberal arts 19%, natural resources/environmental science 6%.

Technology on campus. 35 workstations in library, computer center, student center. Online library, wireless network available.

Student life. Freshman orientation: Available. Preregistration for classes offered. Half-day program held before regular registration, introduces new students to programs and services. **Activities:** Student government.

Athletics. Intercollegiate: Basketball. **Team name:** Bear Paws.

Student services. Career counseling, financial aid counseling, on-campus daycare. **Transfer:** College fairs on campus for students transferring to 4-year colleges.

Contact. Phone: (406) 395-4875 ext. 262 Fax: (406) 395-4836
Gaile Torres, Registrar, Stone Child College, 8294 Upper Box Elder Road, Box Elder, MT 59521

Nebraska

Central Community College
Grand Island, Nebraska
www.cccneb.edu

▶ Public 2-year community and technical college
▶ Commuter campus in large town

General. Founded in 1966. Regionally accredited. Multi-campus institution with campuses in Columbus, Grand Island, and Hastings. Learning Centers located in Holdrege, Kearney, and Lexington. Multiple starting dates for most programs and courses. **Enrollment:** 3,965 degree-seeking undergraduates; 2,267 non-degree-seeking students. **Degrees:** 762 associate awarded. **Location:** 100 miles from Lincoln. **Calendar:** Semester, extensive summer session. **Full-time faculty:** 171 total; 5% have terminal degrees, 2% minority, 52% women. **Part-time faculty:** 211 total; less than 1% have terminal degrees, 61% women.

Student profile. Among degree-seeking undergraduates, 37% enrolled in a transfer program, 63% enrolled in a vocational program, 808 enrolled as first-time, first-year students.

Part-time:	49%	Asian American:	1%
Out-of-state:	1%	Hispanic/Latino:	19%
Women:	62%	Multi-racial, non-Hispanic:	1%
African American:	3%	25 or older:	27%

Transfer out. Colleges most students transferred to 2015: University of Nebraska-Kearney, University of Nebraska-Lincoln, University of Nebraska-Omaha, Bellevue University.

Basis for selection. Open admission. Interview required for some programs.

2015-2016 Annual costs. Tuition/fees: $2,820; $4,050 out-of-state. Per-credit charge: $82 in-state; $123 out-of-state. Room/board: $6,878. Books/supplies: $1,500. Personal expenses: $1,398.

2014-2015 Financial aid. Need-based: 531 full-time freshmen applied for aid; 429 deemed to have need; 410 received aid. Average need met was 78%. Average scholarship/grant was $2,426; average loan $1,431. 76% of total undergraduate aid awarded as scholarships/grants, 24% as loans/jobs. Need-based aid available for part-time students. Work-study available nights, weekends and for part-time students. **Non-need-based:** Awarded to 922 full-time undergraduates, including 306 freshmen. Scholarships awarded for academics, art, athletics, job skills, leadership, music/drama. **Additional information:** All students are eligible to apply for a Pell Grant. Students enrolled for at least six semester hours (half-time) are eligible to apply for grants, loans, work study, and scholarships. To be considered for full-time benefits, students must be enrolled for at least 12 credit hours during the semester.

Application procedures. Admission: No deadline. No application fee. Admission notification on a rolling basis. Application deadlines for the following programs only: February 1 for Dental Hygiene and April 15th for Occupational Therapy Assistant. **Financial aid:** Priority date 3/1; no closing date. FAFSA, institutional form required. Applicants notified on a rolling basis starting 2/1; must reply within 2 week(s) of notification.

Academics. Special study options: Accelerated study, cooperative education, distance learning, double major, dual enrollment of high school students, ESL, honors, independent study, internships, weekend college. License preparation in dental hygiene, nursing, occupational therapy, real estate. **Credit/placement by examination:** AP, CLEP, institutional tests. 48 credit hours maximum toward associate degree. **Support services:** GED preparation and test center, learning center, reduced course load, remedial instruction, study skills assistance, tutoring.

Majors. Business: Administrative services, business admin, vehicle parts marketing. **Communications:** Digital media. **Computer sciences:** General. **General:** Electrician. **Health services:** Clinical lab technology, dental assistant, dental hygiene, health information technology, licensed practical nurse, medical assistant, nursing (RN). **Liberal arts:** Arts/sciences. **Protective services:** Criminal justice. **Visual/performing arts:** Commercial/advertising art. **Work/family studies:** General, child care management.

Most popular majors. Business/marketing 14%, health sciences 22%, liberal arts 29%, trade and industry 18%.

Technology on campus. Dormitories linked to campus network. Commuter students can connect to campus network. Online course registration, online library, helpline, wireless network available.

Student life. Freshman orientation: Available. Preregistration for classes offered. **Housing:** Coed dorms, single-sex dorms, apartments, wellness housing available. $150 partly refundable deposit. **Activities:** Jazz band, choral groups, dance, drama, music ensembles, musical theater, radio station, student government, student newspaper, Multicultural Student Association, FOCUS (Friendships of Culturally Unique Students), Campus Crusade for Christ.

Athletics. NJCAA. **Intercollegiate:** Basketball M, golf M, softball W, volleyball W. **Intramural:** Basketball, bowling, table tennis, volleyball, weight lifting. **Team name:** Raiders.

Student services. Adult student services, career counseling, services for economically disadvantaged, student employment services, financial aid counseling, health services, minority student services, on-campus daycare, personal counseling, placement for graduates, veterans' counselor, women's services. **Physically disabled:** Services for visually, speech, hearing impaired. **Transfer:** Pre-admission transcript evaluation for new students. Transfer adviser, college fairs on campus for students transferring to 4-year colleges.

Contact. E-mail: admissions@cccneb.edu
Phone: (308) 398-7406 Toll-free number: (877) 222-0780
Fax: (308) 398-7398
Michelle Lubken, Admissions Director, Central Community College, 3134 West Highway 34, P.O.Box 4903, Grand Island, NE 68802-4903

Kaplan University: Lincoln
Lincoln, Nebraska
www.lincoln.kaplanuniversity.edu   CB code: 3385

▶ For-profit 2-year branch campus college
▶ Commuter campus in small city

General. Founded in 1884. **Enrollment:** 548 undergraduates. **Degrees:** 43 bachelor's, 125 associate awarded; master's offered. **Calendar:** Differs by program, extensive summer session. **Full-time faculty:** 10 total. **Part-time faculty:** 49 total. **Class size:** 83% < 20, 17% 20-39.

Student profile.

Out-of-state:	2%	25 or older:	54%

Transfer out. Colleges most students transferred to 2015: Southeast Community College.

Basis for selection. Open admission, but selective for some programs. CPAt required of all applicants. Students must pass entrance exam.

2015-2016 Annual costs. Personal expenses: $2,096. **Additional information:** Bachelor's degree programs - $66,417, Associate's degree programs range from $30,654-$35,763, Certificate programs range from $11,501-$22,368. Some programs have additional associated fees that are not included in the price of tuition.

Financial aid. All financial aid based on need. Need-based aid available for part-time students. Work-study available nights, weekends and for part-time students.

Application procedures. Admission: No deadline. $20 fee. Admission notification on a rolling basis. **Financial aid:** No deadline. FAFSA, institutional form required. Applicants notified on a rolling basis starting 2/1.

Academics. Special study options: Internships. Bachelor's degree programs available on campus. License preparation in nursing. **Credit/placement by examination:** AP, CLEP. **Support services:** Learning center, study skills assistance, tutoring.

Majors. Business: Accounting, administrative services, business admin. **Computer sciences:** Information technology. **Health services:** Medical assistant. **Protective services:** Criminal justice.

Most popular majors. Business/marketing 20%, computer/information sciences 11%, health sciences 31%, legal studies 9%, security/protective services 23%.

Technology on campus. 70 workstations in library, computer center.

Student life. Freshman orientation: Mandatory. Preregistration for classes offered. Orientation held on first day of classes for all new students. **Housing:** $150 deposit. **Activities:** Tour and travel club, medical club, Association of Information Technology Professionals, business club, legal assisting club.

Student services. Career counseling, student employment services, financial aid counseling, placement for graduates, veterans' counselor. **Physically disabled:** Services for visually, hearing impaired. **Transfer:** Pre-admission transcript evaluation for new students.

Contact. E-mail: kfrette@kaplan.edu
Phone: (402) 474-5315 Toll-free number: (800) 742-7738
Fax: (402) 474-0896
Michael Klacik, Director of Admissions, Kaplan University: Lincoln, 1821 K Street, Lincoln, NE 68508

Kaplan University: Omaha
Omaha, Nebraska
www.omaha.kaplanuniversity.edu   CB code: 3326

▶ For-profit 2-year career college
▶ Commuter campus in large city
▶ Interview required

General. **Enrollment:** 549 undergraduates. **Degrees:** 69 bachelor's, 155 associate awarded; master's offered. **Calendar:** Quarter, extensive summer session. **Full-time faculty:** 16 total. **Part-time faculty:** 48 total. **Class size:** 54% < 20, 46% 20-39. **Special facilities:** Firearms training simulator, dental assisting lab with 4 operatories, nursing lab.

Basis for selection. Open admission, but selective for some programs. **Home schooled:** Transcript of courses and grades, state high school equivalency certificate required.

High school preparation. College-preparatory program required.

2015-2016 Annual costs. Bachelor's degree programs - $66,417, Associate's degree programs range from $30,654-$35,763, Certificate programs range from $11,501-$22,368. Some programs have additional associated fees that are not included in the price of tuition.

Financial aid. All financial aid based on need. Need-based aid available for part-time students. Work-study available nights, weekends and for part-time students.

Application procedures. **Admission:** No deadline. $20 fee. Application must be submitted on paper. Admission notification on a rolling basis. **Financial aid:** No deadline. FAFSA, institutional form required. Applicants notified on a rolling basis.

Academics. **Special study options:** Accelerated study, distance learning, internships, liberal arts/career combination. Bachelor's degree programs available on campus. License preparation in nursing. **Credit/placement by examination:** AP, CLEP, institutional tests. 32 credit hours maximum toward associate degree. **Support services:** Learning center, reduced course load, remedial instruction, study skills assistance, tutoring, writing center.

Majors. **Business:** Accounting, business admin. **Computer sciences:** Data processing. **Health services:** Medical assistant. **Protective services:** Criminal justice.

Technology on campus. 120 workstations in library, computer center, student center. Commuter students can connect to campus network. Online course registration, online library, helpline, wireless network available.

Student life. **Freshman orientation:** Mandatory. Preregistration for classes offered. **Activities:** Student government, student newspaper.

Student services. Adult student services, career counseling, services for economically disadvantaged, student employment services, financial aid counseling, placement for graduates, veterans' counselor. **Physically disabled:** Services for visually, speech, hearing impaired. **Transfer:** Pre-admission transcript evaluation for new students.

Contact. E-mail: zlorenzen@kaplan.edu
Phone: (402) 431-6100 Toll-free number: (800) 642-1456
Fax: (402) 573-6482
Zac Lorenzen, Director of Admissions, Kaplan University: Omaha, 5425 North 103rd Street, Omaha, NE 68134

Little Priest Tribal College
Winnebago, Nebraska
www.littlepriest.edu   CB code: 3616

▶ Private 2-year community college
▶ Commuter campus in rural community

General. Regionally accredited. **Enrollment:** 104 degree-seeking undergraduates; 28 non-degree-seeking students. **Degrees:** 11 associate awarded. **Location:** 20 miles from Sioux City, Iowa. **Calendar:** Semester, limited summer session. **Full-time faculty:** 7 total; 14% have terminal degrees, 14% minority, 43% women. **Part-time faculty:** 7 total; 14% have terminal degrees, 71% minority, 71% women. **Class size:** 91% < 20, 7% 20-39, 2% 40-49.

Student profile. Among degree-seeking undergraduates, 3% enrolled in a transfer program, 18 enrolled as first-time, first-year students, 9 transferred in from other institutions.

Part-time:	35%	African American:	8%
Out-of-state:	4%	Hispanic/Latino:	1%
Women:	57%	Native American:	90%

Transfer out. 5% of students enrolled in the transfer program go on to 4-year colleges. **Colleges most students transferred to 2015:** Wayne State College, University of Nebraska-Lincoln, Haskell Indian Nations University.

Basis for selection. Open admission. **Home schooled:** State high school equivalency certificate required. **Learning Disabled:** There are no special requirements for students with disabilities. Student must self-identify so that they may be accommodated.

High school preparation. College-preparatory program recommended. 11 units recommended. Recommended units include English 4, mathematics 4, social studies 3, science 3 and computer science 1.

2015-2016 Annual costs. Books/supplies: $500.

Financial aid. **Need-based:** Need-based aid available for part-time students. Work-study available nights, weekends and for part-time students.

Application procedures. **Admission:** Closing date 8/1. $25 fee. **Financial aid:** No deadline. FAFSA, institutional form required.

Academics. **Special study options:** Distance learning, double major, dual enrollment of high school students, independent study. **Credit/placement by examination:** AP, CLEP, institutional tests. **Support services:** GED test center, learning center, reduced course load, remedial instruction, study skills assistance, tutoring.

Majors. **Area/ethnic studies:** Native American. **Business:** General. **Conservation:** Environmental science. **Education:** General. **Liberal arts:** Arts/sciences.

Most popular majors. Computer/information sciences 42%, interdisciplinary studies 7%, natural resources/environmental science 42%.

Technology on campus. 30 workstations in computer center, student center. Commuter students can connect to campus network. Online library, wireless network available.

Student life. **Freshman orientation:** Mandatory. Preregistration for classes offered. **Activities:** Student government.

Athletics. NJCAA. **Intercollegiate:** Basketball. **Team name:** Warriors.

Student services. Adult student services, financial aid counseling, personal counseling. **Transfer:** Pre-admission transcript evaluation for new students. College fairs on campus for students transferring to 4-year colleges.

Contact. E-mail: cheise@littlepriest.edu
Phone: (402) 878-3307
Cherie Heise, Director of Admissions and Student Records, Little Priest Tribal College, PO Box 270, Winnebago, NE 68071

Metropolitan Community College
Omaha, Nebraska
www.mccneb.edu   CB code: 5755

▶ Public 2-year community and technical college
▶ Commuter campus in large city

General. Founded in 1974. Regionally accredited. Additional locations: Fort Omaha, Elkhorn Valley, South Omaha, Applied Technology Center, Fremont Area Center, Sarpy Center in La Vista. **Enrollment:** 12,662 degree-seeking undergraduates. **Degrees:** 1,523 associate awarded. **Location:** 50 miles from Lincoln. **Calendar:** Quarter, extensive summer session. **Full-time faculty:** 247 total. **Part-time faculty:** 838 total. **Class size:** 63% < 20, 37% 20-39, less than 1% 40-49, less than 1% 50-99. **Special facilities:** CAD/CAM and electronic graphics facilities.

Student profile.

Out-of-state:	3%	Live on campus:	1%
25 or older:	46%		

Transfer out. Colleges most students transferred to 2015: University of Nebraska-Omaha, Bellevue University.

Basis for selection. Open admission, but selective for some programs. Admission to nursing and allied health programs based on test scores and references. Assessment testing and standardized RN entrance examination required for nursing associate degree programs. Human services programs require a "C" and approval from Human Services Faculty Review Committee. Certain programs may require preparatory work before attending classes. Interview required for nursing and allied health programs.

High school preparation. High school diploma or GED required of nursing and allied health applicants.

2015-2016 Annual costs. Tuition/fees: $2,775; $4,035 out-of-state. Per-credit charge: $56 in-state; $84 out-of-state. Room/board: $6,255. Books/supplies: $1,350. Personal expenses: $900.

Financial aid. Need-based: Need-based aid available for part-time students. Work-study available nights, weekends and for part-time students. **Non-need-based:** Scholarships awarded for academics.

Application procedures. Admission: No deadline. No application fee. Admission notification on a rolling basis. **Financial aid:** Priority date 3/15; no closing date. FAFSA, institutional form required. Applicants notified on a rolling basis starting 4/15.

Academics. Individualized, self-paced instruction. Degree through online available. **Special study options:** Cooperative education, distance learning, double major, dual enrollment of high school students, ESL, honors, independent study, internships, weekend college. License preparation in nursing. **Credit/placement by examination:** AP, CLEP, institutional tests. 81 credit hours maximum toward associate degree. **Support services:** GED preparation and test center, learning center, remedial instruction, tutoring, writing center.

Majors. Architecture: Interior. **Business:** General, accounting, administrative services, business admin, management information systems. **Communications technology:** Graphic/printing. **Computer sciences:** General, networking. **Foreign languages:** Sign language interpretation. **General:** Maintenance, power transmission. **Health services:** Nursing (RN), respiratory therapy technology. **Human services:** Social work. **Liberal arts:** Arts/sciences. **Protective services:** Fire services admin, police science. **Visual/performing arts:** Commercial photography, commercial/advertising art, studio arts, theater arts management. **Work/family studies:** Child care management, institutional food production.

Most popular majors. Business/marketing 16%, health sciences 15%, liberal arts 29%, security/protective services 6%, trade and industry 9%, visual/performing arts 7%.

Technology on campus. 1,550 workstations in library, computer center. Dormitories wired for high-speed internet access. Commuter students can connect to campus network. Online course registration, online library, helpline available.

Student life. Freshman orientation: Available. Preregistration for classes offered. **Housing:** Coed dorms, single-sex dorms, wellness housing available. $200 fully refundable deposit. **Activities:** Phi Theta Kappa scholastic honor society.

Student services. Adult student services, career counseling, services for economically disadvantaged, student employment services, financial aid counseling, minority student services, personal counseling, placement for graduates, veterans' counselor, women's services. **Physically disabled:** Services for visually, speech, hearing impaired. **Transfer:** Transfer adviser for students transferring to 4-year colleges.

Contact. E-mail: info@mccneb.edu
Phone: (402) 457-2422 Toll-free number: (800) 228-9553
Fax: (402) 457-2616
Maria Vazquez, Associate Vice President for Student Affairs,
Metropolitan Community College, Box 3777, Omaha, NE 68103-0777

Mid-Plains Community College
North Platte, Nebraska
www.mpcc.edu   CB code: 6497

◗ Public 2-year community and technical college
◗ Commuter campus in large town

General. Founded in 1964. Regionally accredited. Three main campus sites in North Platte and McCook; extended campus sites in Broken Bow, Imperial, Ogallala, and Valentine. **Enrollment:** 1,209 degree-seeking undergraduates; 1,026 non-degree-seeking students. **Degrees:** 308 associate awarded. **Location:** 230 miles from Lincoln, 250 miles from Denver, CO. **Calendar:** Semester, limited summer session. **Full-time faculty:** 66 total; 11% have terminal degrees, 6% minority, 50% women. **Part-time faculty:** 239 total; 4% minority, 61% women. **Partnerships:** Formal partnership with Union Pacific Railroad for apprenticeships, technical training, continuing education.

Student profile. Among degree-seeking undergraduates, 63% enrolled in a transfer program, 37% enrolled in a vocational program, 2% already have a bachelor's degree or higher, 480 enrolled as first-time, first-year students.

Part-time:	37%	Native American:	1%
Out-of-state:	14%	Multi-racial, non-Hispanic:	2%
Women:	63%	International:	2%
African American:	4%	25 or older:	34%
Asian American:	1%	Live on campus:	25%
Hispanic/Latino:	9%		

Transfer out. Colleges most students transferred to 2015: University of Nebraska at Lincoln, University of Nebraska at Kearney, Chadron State College.

Basis for selection. Open admission, but selective for some programs. Psychological Corporation Pre-Nursing Examination required of applicants to nursing program. Minimum ACT score of 17 required for licensed practical nursing and 21 for associate degree nursing. Minimum ASSET score of 40 in all areas required for medical laboratory technology program. **Adult students:** SAT/ACT scores not required. **Home schooled:** State high school equivalency certificate required. **Learning Disabled:** Student should have physician's documentation of learning disability.

High school preparation. College-preparatory program recommended. Recommended units include English 4, mathematics 4, social studies 1, history 1, science 2, foreign language 1, computer science 1 and visual/performing arts 1.

2015-2016 Annual costs. Tuition/fees: $2,880; $3,600 out-of-state. Per-credit charge: $81 in-state; $105 out-of-state. Room/board: $5,896. Books/supplies: $1,200. Personal expenses: $830.

2014-2015 Financial aid. Need-based: 292 full-time freshmen applied for aid; 219 deemed to have need; 218 received aid. Average need met was 84%. Average scholarship/grant was $4,591; average loan $2,064. 72% of total undergraduate aid awarded as scholarships/grants, 28% as loans/jobs. Need-based aid available for part-time students. Work-study available nights, weekends and for part-time students. **Non-need-based:** Awarded to 242 full-time undergraduates, including 126 freshmen. Scholarships awarded for academics, art, athletics, music/drama.

Application procedures. Admission: No deadline. No application fee. Admission notification on a rolling basis. **Financial aid:** Priority date 5/1; no closing date. FAFSA, institutional form required. Applicants notified on a rolling basis starting 5/1; must reply within 3 week(s) of notification.

Academics. Special study options: Cooperative education, distance learning, dual enrollment of high school students, ESL, exchange student, honors, independent study, internships, liberal arts/career combination. Bachelor's degree programs available on campus. License preparation in dental hygiene, nursing, paramedic, real estate. **Credit/placement by examination:** AP, CLEP. 20 credit hours maximum toward associate degree. **Support services:** GED preparation and test center, learning center, remedial instruction, study skills assistance, tutoring, writing center. Math lab, online tutoring, exam proctoring, placement assessments, scheduled study groups as needed, career services, disability services, mentoring program.

Majors. Business: Administrative services, business admin. **Computer sciences:** General, information technology. **General:** Electrician. **Health services:** Clinical lab technology, dental assistant, EMT paramedic, nursing (RN). **Liberal arts:** Arts/sciences. **Protective services:** Firefighting, police science. **Visual/performing arts:** Graphic design. **Work/family studies:** Child care management.

Most popular majors. Business/marketing 10%, health sciences 15%, liberal arts 64%, trade and industry 7%.

Technology on campus. 100 workstations in dormitories, library, computer center, student center. Dormitories wired for high-speed internet access and linked to campus network. Commuter students can connect to campus network. Online course registration, online library, helpline, wireless network available.

Student life. Freshman orientation: Available. Preregistration for classes offered. **Policies:** Drugs, alcohol, tobacco and weapons strictly prohibited. **Housing:** Coed dorms, single-sex dorms, special housing for disabled available. $200 deposit, deadline 8/15. **Activities:** Bands, campus ministries, choral groups, dance, drama, international student organizations, music ensembles, musical theater, student government, student newspaper, Phi Beta Lambda-Greek Life Business Chapter, Phi Theta Kappa-Greek Life Honor Society, Gay Straight Alliance, International Club, Campus Crusade for Christ (CRU), Fellowship of Christian Athletes.

Athletics. NJCAA. **Intercollegiate:** Baseball M, basketball, golf M, rodeo, softball W, volleyball W. **Intramural:** Basketball, volleyball. **Team name:** McCook Indians & North Platte Knights.

Student services. Adult student services, alcohol/substance abuse counseling, career counseling, services for economically disadvantaged, student employment services, financial aid counseling, on-campus daycare, personal counseling, placement for graduates. **Physically disabled:** Services for visually, speech, hearing impaired. **Transfer:** Transfer adviser for students transferring to 4-year colleges.

Contact. E-mail: simsh@mpcc.edu
Phone: (308) 535-3609 Toll-free number: (800) 658-4308 ext. 3609
Fax: (308) 534-5767
Hillary Sims, Admissions Coordinator, Mid-Plains Community College, 1101 Halligan Drive, North Platte, NE 69101

Myotherapy Institute
Lincoln, Nebraska
www.myotherapy.edu

- For-profit 2-year health science and community college
- Commuter campus in small city

General. Accredited by ACCSC. **Enrollment:** 15 undergraduates. **Degrees:** 18 associate awarded. **Calendar:** Differs by program. **Part-time faculty:** 6 total.

Basis for selection. Open admission.

2015-2016 Annual costs. Books/supplies: $750. **Additional information:** Associates Degree of Applied Science in Message Therapy program $16,000, books and supplies $800. Massage Therapy Diploma Program $14,500, books and supplies $800. Tuition subject to change without notice.

Financial aid. Need-based: Work-study available nights, weekends and for part-time students.

Application procedures. Admission: $150 fee.

Academics. Credit/placement by examination: AP, CLEP.

Majors. Health services: Massage therapy.

Contact. E-mail: info@myotherapy.edu
Phone: (402) 421-7410 Toll-free number: (800) 896-3363
Sue Kosizek, Director, Myotherapy Institute, 4001 Pioneer Woods Drive, Lincoln, NE 68516

Nebraska College of Technical Agriculture
Curtis, Nebraska
www.ncta.unl.edu   CB code: 1305

- Public 2-year agricultural college
- Residential campus in rural community

General. Founded in 1965. Regionally accredited. **Enrollment:** 253 degree-seeking undergraduates; 259 non-degree-seeking students. **Degrees:** 67 associate awarded. **Location:** 40 miles from North Platte, 40 miles from McCook. **Calendar:** Semester, extensive summer session. **Full-time faculty:** 14 total; 29% have terminal degrees, 50% women. **Part-time faculty:** 8 total; 12% have terminal degrees, 50% women. **Class size:** 69% < 20, 20% 20-39, 7% 40-49, 4% 50-99. **Special facilities:** Farm, community golf course, land lab, cattle working facilities, indoor arena, horticulture greenhouse, vet tech surgery and lab facilities.

Student profile. Among degree-seeking undergraduates, 5% enrolled in a transfer program, 94% enrolled in a vocational program, 92 enrolled as first-time, first-year students, 8 transferred in from other institutions.

Part-time:	6%	Multi-racial, non-Hispanic:	4%
Out-of-state:	22%	25 or older:	5%
Women:	60%	Live on campus:	25%

Transfer out. Colleges most students transferred to 2015: University of Nebraska-Lincoln, University of Nebraska-Kearney, Chadron State.

Basis for selection. Open admission. **Home schooled:** Transcript of courses and grades, state high school equivalency certificate required.

High school preparation. College-preparatory program recommended. 14 units recommended. Recommended units include English 4, mathematics 3, social studies 3, science 3 (laboratory 1).

2015-2016 Annual costs. Tuition/fees: $4,679; $9,175 out-of-state. Per-credit charge: $118 in-state; $250.25 out-of-state. Room/board: $6,956. Books/supplies: $1,000. Personal expenses: $3,600.

2014-2015 Financial aid. Need-based: Average need met was 69%. Average scholarship/grant was $6,385; average loan $3,147. 66% of total undergraduate aid awarded as scholarships/grants, 34% as loans/jobs. Need-based aid available for part-time students. Work-study available nights, weekends and for part-time students. **Non-need-based:** Scholarships awarded for academics, leadership, state residency.

Application procedures. Admission: Priority date 3/1; no deadline. $25 fee, may be waived for applicants with need. Admission notification on a rolling basis. **Financial aid:** Priority date 4/1; no closing date. FAFSA required. Applicants notified on a rolling basis starting 5/1; must reply within 2 week(s) of notification.

Academics. Special study options: Cooperative education, distance learning, double major, dual enrollment of high school students, internships. Bachelor's degree programs available on campus. **Credit/placement by examination:** AP, CLEP, institutional tests. **Support services:** Reduced course load, remedial instruction, study skills assistance, tutoring, writing center.

Majors. Health services: Veterinary technology/assistant.

Technology on campus. 99 workstations in dormitories, library, computer center, student center, student center. Dormitories wired for high-speed internet access and linked to campus network. Online course registration, online library, repair service, wireless network available.

Student life. Freshman orientation: Mandatory. Preregistration for classes offered. 2-day program. **Housing:** Guaranteed on-campus for freshmen. Coed dorms, single-sex dorms, wellness housing available. $250 fully refundable deposit, deadline 7/1. **Activities:** Student government, student newspaper.

Athletics. Intercollegiate: Equestrian, rodeo, volleyball W. **Intramural:** Basketball, football (non-tackle), softball, volleyball. **Team name:** Aggies.

Student services. Alcohol/substance abuse counseling, career counseling, student employment services, financial aid counseling, health services, personal counseling, placement for graduates, veterans' counselor. **Transfer:** Pre-admission transcript evaluation for new students. Transfer adviser, college fairs on campus for students transferring to 4-year colleges.

Contact. E-mail: tsmith24@unl.edu
Phone: (308) 367-4124 Toll-free number: (800) 328-7847
Fax: (308) 367-5212
Ron Rosati, Dean, Nebraska College of Technical Agriculture, 404 East 7th Street, Curtis, NE 69025-0069

Nebraska Indian Community College
Macy, Nebraska
www.thenicc.edu   CB code: 1431

- Public 2-year community college
- Commuter campus in rural community

General. Founded in 1979. Regionally accredited. **Enrollment:** 132 degree-seeking undergraduates. **Degrees:** 17 associate awarded. **Location:** 70 miles from Omaha, 30 miles from Sioux City, Iowa. **Calendar:** Semester, limited summer session. **Full-time faculty:** 10 total; 40% minority, 50% women. **Part-time faculty:** 8 total; 38% minority, 62% women. **Class size:** 99% < 20, 1% 20-39.

Student profile. Among degree-seeking undergraduates, 98% enrolled in a transfer program, 8% enrolled in a vocational program, 67 enrolled as first-time, first-year students, 6 transferred in from other institutions.

Out-of-state:	15%	25 or older:	65%
Native American:	99%		

Transfer out. 75% of students enrolled in the transfer program go on to 4-year colleges. **Colleges most students transferred to 2015:** Wayne State University, Northeast Community College, University of South Dakota, University of Nebraska Lincoln.

Basis for selection. Open admission. High school transcripts and pre-testing on entrance required.

High school preparation. College-preparatory program required. Strong background in English, mathematics, and science recommended.

2016-2017 Annual costs. Tuition/fees (projected): $5,150. Per-credit charge: $170. Personal expenses: $2,836.

2014-2015 Financial aid. All financial aid based on need. 18 full-time freshmen applied for aid; 18 deemed to have need; 18 received aid. 99% of total undergraduate aid awarded as scholarships/grants, 1% as loans/jobs. Need-based aid available for part-time students. Work-study available nights, weekends and for part-time students.

Application procedures. Admission: No deadline. $50 fee, may be waived for applicants with need. Application must be submitted on paper. Admission notification on a rolling basis. **Financial aid:** Priority date 9/1; no closing date. FAFSA required.

Academics. Special study options: Accelerated study, combined bachelor's/graduate degree, distance learning, double major, dual enrollment of high school students, independent study, internships. Bachelor's degree programs available on campus. License preparation in nursing. **Credit/placement by examination:** AP, CLEP, institutional tests. 15 credit hours maximum toward associate degree. **Support services:** GED preparation and test center, learning center, remedial instruction, study skills assistance, tutoring, writing center.

Majors. Area/ethnic studies: Native American. **Business:** Business admin. **Conservation:** General. **Education:** Early childhood. **General:** Carpentry. **Human services:** Social work. **Liberal arts:** Arts/sciences.

Most popular majors. Area/ethnic studies 6%, biological/life sciences 6%, business/marketing 35%, education 6%, liberal arts 41%, public administration/social services 6%.

Technology on campus. 40 workstations in library, computer center. Online library, wireless network available.

Student life. Freshman orientation: Available. Preregistration for classes offered. Held one week before classes start. **Activities:** Radio station, student government, student newspaper.

Student services. Adult student services, career counseling, student employment services, financial aid counseling, minority student services. **Transfer:** Pre-admission transcript evaluation for new students. Transfer adviser, college fairs on campus for students transferring to 4-year colleges.

Contact. E-mail: tmunhofen@thenicc.edu
Phone: (402) 494-2311 Fax: (402) 837-4183
Troy Munhofen, Registrar, Nebraska Indian Community College, PO Box 428, Macy, NE 68039-0428

Northeast Community College
Norfolk, Nebraska
www.northeast.edu   CB code: 6473

▶ Public 2-year community college
▶ Residential campus in large town

General. Founded in 1973. Regionally accredited. **Enrollment:** 2,726 degree-seeking undergraduates. **Degrees:** 793 associate awarded. **Location:** 110 miles from Omaha. **Calendar:** Semester, limited summer session. **Full-time faculty:** 110 total. **Part-time faculty:** 290 total. **Class size:** 78% < 20, 22% 20-39, less than 1% 40-49, less than 1% >100. **Special facilities:** College farm.

Student profile.

Out-of-state:	5%	Live on campus:	20%
25 or older:	40%		

Transfer out. Colleges most students transferred to 2015: Wayne State College, University of Nebraska-Lincoln, University of Nebraska-Omaha, University of Nebraska-Kearney, University of South Dakota.

Basis for selection. Open admission, but selective for some programs. Special requirements for nursing programs, physical therapy assistant program, and veterinary technician program. ACT or ASSET scores required for placement for students enrolling in 6 or more credit hours.

2015-2016 Annual costs. Tuition/fees: $3,165; $4,215 out-of-state. Per-credit charge: $86 in-state; $121 out-of-state. Room/board: $7,200. Books/supplies: $1,413. Personal expenses: $900.

Financial aid. Need-based: Need-based aid available for part-time students. Work-study available nights, weekends and for part-time students. **Non-need-based:** Scholarships awarded for academics, athletics, music/drama.

Application procedures. Admission: No deadline. No application fee. Admission notification on a rolling basis. **Financial aid:** No deadline. FAFSA, institutional form required. Applicants notified on a rolling basis; must reply within 2 week(s) of notification.

Academics. Off-campus credit classes available. Lifelong Learning Center offers students opportunity to earn advanced degrees on NECC campus. **Special study options:** Accelerated study, cooperative education, cross-registration, distance learning, dual enrollment of high school students, ESL, independent study, internships, liberal arts/career combination. License preparation in nursing, paramedic, physical therapy, real estate. **Credit/placement by examination:** AP, CLEP, institutional tests. **Support services:** GED preparation and test center, learning center, reduced course load, remedial instruction, study skills assistance, tutoring, writing center.

Majors. Biology: General. **Business:** Accounting, administrative services, banking/financial services, business admin, entrepreneurial studies, international, marketing, merchandising, office/clerical, real estate. **Communications:** Journalism. **Communications technology:** Radio/TV, recording arts. **Computer sciences:** General, computer science, programming, support specialist. **Education:** Early childhood, elementary, music, secondary. **Engineering:** General. **English:** English lit, rhetoric/composition. **General:** Electrician, lineworker. **Health services:** Dietetics, EMT paramedic, health information technology, medical radiologic technology/radiation therapy, medical secretary, nursing (RN), physical therapy assistant, predental, premedicine, prenursing, prepharmacy, preveterinary, surgical technology, veterinary technology/assistant. **Liberal arts:** Arts/sciences, library assistant. **Math:** General. **Parks/recreation:** Health/fitness. **Physical sciences:** Chemistry, physics. **Protective services:** Corrections. **Psychology:** General. **Social sciences:** General. **Visual/performing arts:** Art, dramatic, music, music management, music performance.

Most popular majors. Agriculture 10%, business/marketing 12%, education 7%, engineering/engineering technologies 8%, health sciences 19%, liberal arts 8%, trade and industry 21%.

Technology on campus. 300 workstations in dormitories, library, computer center, student center. Dormitories linked to campus network. Online course registration, online library, helpline, wireless network available.

Student life. Freshman orientation: Mandatory. Preregistration for classes offered. **Housing:** Coed dorms, special housing for disabled, apartments, wellness housing available. $25 nonrefundable deposit. **Activities:** Bands, choral groups, dance, drama, music ensembles, musical theater, radio station, student government, student newspaper, symphony orchestra, TV station, Habitat for Humanity, HOPE, multicultural club, Campus Crusade for Christ, Christian Student Fellowship.

Athletics. NJCAA. **Intercollegiate:** Basketball. **Intramural:** Basketball, soccer, softball. **Team name:** Hawks.

Student services. Adult student services, career counseling, student employment services, financial aid counseling, health services, minority student services, on-campus daycare, personal counseling, placement for graduates, veterans' counselor. **Physically disabled:** Services for visually, speech, hearing impaired. **Transfer:** Pre-admission transcript evaluation for new students. Transfer adviser for students transferring to 4-year colleges.

Contact. E-mail: admission@northeast.edu
Phone: (402) 844-7260 Toll-free number: (800) 348-9033
Fax: (402) 844-7400
Sandy Hilliges, Coordinator of Admissions Services, Northeast Community College, 801 East Benjamin Avenue, Norfolk, NE 68702-0469

Southeast Community College
Lincoln, Nebraska
www.southeast.edu   CB code: 1189

▶ Public 2-year community college
▶ Commuter campus in small city

General. Founded in 1973. Regionally accredited. Extensive adult and continuing education programs, both credit and noncredit. Additional campuses in Beatrice and Milford. **Enrollment:** 6,537 degree-seeking undergraduates. **Degrees:** 1,379 associate awarded. **Location:** 50 miles from Omaha. **Calendar:** Quarter, extensive summer session. **Full-time faculty:** 310 total; 4% minority, 47% women. **Part-time faculty:** 397 total; 3% minority, 61% women. **Special facilities:** Fire service training facility.

Student profile. Among degree-seeking undergraduates, 28% enrolled in a transfer program, 43% enrolled in a vocational program.

Out-of-state:	2%	25 or older:	26%

Transfer out. Colleges most students transferred to 2015: University of Nebraska, Doane-Lincoln College, College of St. Mary, Nebraska Wesleyan, University of Nebraska-Kearney.

Basis for selection. Open admission. The college has an open admission policy. Applications are made to a specific program and some programs have additional requirements as outlined on the college's website. Generally, students must score at a minimum level in the areas of math, reading and writing to be admitted to a program. However, the college has foundations coursework available to those who do not score at a high enough level. **Home schooled:** Transcript of courses and grades, state high school equivalency certificate required.

2015-2016 Annual costs. Tuition/fees: $2,779; $3,409 out-of-state. Per-credit charge: $60.5 in-state; $74.5 out-of-state. Room/board: $4,647. Books/supplies: $1,650.

Financial aid. Need-based: Need-based aid available for part-time students. Work-study available nights, weekends and for part-time students. **Non-need-based:** Scholarships awarded for academics, leadership, minority status, state residency.

Application procedures. Admission: No deadline. No application fee. Admission notification on a rolling basis. **Financial aid:** No deadline. FAFSA, institutional form required. Applicants notified on a rolling basis; must reply within 2 week(s) of notification.

Academics. Academic transfer courses (liberal arts) offered on Saturdays. **Special study options:** Cooperative education, distance learning, dual enrollment of high school students, independent study, internships, liberal arts/career combination. License preparation in nursing, paramedic, physical therapy, radiology, real estate. **Credit/placement by examination:** AP, CLEP, institutional tests. 30 credit hours maximum toward associate degree. Most applicants required to take COMPASS or Accuplacer for placement purposes. ACT may be substituted for ASSET. **Support services:** GED preparation and test center, learning center, reduced course load, remedial instruction, study skills assistance, tutoring, writing center.

Majors. Business: Administrative services, business admin. **Computer sciences:** Information systems. **Health services:** Clinical lab technology, medical radiologic technology/radiation therapy, nursing (RN), respiratory therapy technology, surgical technology. **Liberal arts:** Arts/sciences. **Protective services:** Criminal justice, fire safety technology. **Visual/performing arts:** Commercial/advertising art. **Work/family studies:** Child care management.

Most popular majors. Agriculture 6%, business/marketing 18%, engineering/engineering technologies 12%, health sciences 14%, liberal arts 18%, trade and industry 19%.

Technology on campus. Dormitories wired for high-speed internet access and linked to campus network. Online course registration, online library, helpline, wireless network available.

Student life. Freshman orientation: Mandatory. Preregistration for classes offered. **Housing:** Single-sex dorms, apartments available. $100 fully refundable deposit. **Activities:** Choral groups, drama, student government, student newspaper, multicultural student organization.

Athletics. NJCAA. **Intercollegiate:** Baseball M, basketball, cross-country, golf M, soccer, softball W, volleyball W. **Intramural:** Baseball M, basketball, softball W, table tennis, tennis, volleyball. **Team name:** Storm.

Student services. Career counseling, student employment services, financial aid counseling, on-campus daycare, placement for graduates, veterans' counselor. **Physically disabled:** Services for visually, speech, hearing impaired. **Transfer:** Transfer adviser, college fairs on campus for students transferring to 4-year colleges.

Contact. Phone: (402) 437-2600 Toll-free number: (800) 642-4075 Fax: (402) 437-2402
Kat Kreikemeier, Administrative Director of Admissions, Southeast Community College, 8800 O Street, Lincoln, NE 68520

Vatterott College: Spring Valley
Omaha, Nebraska
www.vatterott.edu

◗ For-profit 2-year community and technical college
◗ Commuter campus in large city

General. Accredited by ACCSC. **Enrollment:** 145 undergraduates. **Degrees:** 43 associate awarded. **Calendar:** Quarter. **Full-time faculty:** 12 total. **Part-time faculty:** 19 total.

Basis for selection. Interview most important. High school record also important.

Financial aid. Need-based: Work-study available nights, weekends and for part-time students.

Application procedures. Admission: No application fee.

Academics. Credit/placement by examination: AP, CLEP.

Majors. Business: General. **Computer sciences:** Computer graphics, system admin. **Health services:** Medical assistant, medical secretary, pharmacy assistant, substance abuse counseling, veterinary technology/assistant. **Visual/performing arts:** Graphic design.

Contact. Phone: (402) 891-9411 Toll-free number: (888) 886-3856 Fax: (402) 891-9413
Derek Handel, Director of Admissions, Vatterott College: Spring Valley, 11818 I Street, Omaha, NE 68137

Western Nebraska Community College
Scottsbluff, Nebraska
www.wncc.edu   CB code: 6648

◗ Public 2-year community college
◗ Commuter campus in large town

General. Founded in 1926. Regionally accredited. Additional campuses at Sidney and Alliance. Advanced Technology Center in Scottsbluff. **Enrollment:** 1,232 degree-seeking undergraduates; 316 non-degree-seeking students. **Degrees:** 233 associate awarded. **Location:** 100 miles from Cheyenne, Wyoming. **Calendar:** Semester, extensive summer session. **Full-time faculty:** 71 total; 13% have terminal degrees, 4% minority, 45% women. **Part-time faculty:** 54 total; 4% minority, 44% women. **Class size:** 87% < 20, 13% 20-39.

Student profile. Among degree-seeking undergraduates, 76% enrolled in a transfer program, 24% enrolled in a vocational program, 390 enrolled as first-time, first-year students, 79 transferred in from other institutions.

Part-time:	37%	Native American:	1%
Out-of-state:	18%	Native Hawaiian/Pacific islander:	1%
Women:	63%	International:	6%
African American:	3%	25 or older:	34%
Asian American:	1%	Live on campus:	20%
Hispanic/Latino:	20%		

Transfer out. 47% of students enrolled in the transfer program go on to 4-year colleges. **Colleges most students transferred to 2015:** Chadron State College, University of Nebraska-Lincoln, University of Wyoming.

Basis for selection. Open admission, but selective for some programs. Special requirements for practical nursing, Associate Degree-Nursing, and radiologic technologies programs. **Adult students:** ECOMPASS used for proper course placement in writing, mathematics, and classes with a reading prerequisite; ACT, SAT, or ASSET accepted in lieu of eCOMPASS. **Home schooled:** Transcript of courses and grades required. **Learning Disabled:** Students should contact the Director of Counseling to discuss the process required to request assistance and arrange for reasonable accommodations.

High school preparation. College-preparatory program recommended. Recommended units include English 4, mathematics 4, social studies 3, history 3, science 4 (laboratory 2) and foreign language 1.

2016-2017 Annual costs. Tuition/fees (projected): $3,270; $3,660 out-of-state. Per-credit charge: $91.5 in-state; $104.5 out-of-state. Room/board: $7,010. Books/supplies: $1,400. Personal expenses: $1,618. **Additional information:** Border state students from Colorado, Wyoming, and South Dakota pay in-state tuition rates.

2015-2016 Financial aid. Need-based: 237 full-time freshmen applied for aid; 178 deemed to have need; 173 received aid. Average need met was 92%. Average scholarship/grant was $4,859; average loan $3,194. 79% of total undergraduate aid awarded as scholarships/grants, 21% as loans/jobs. Need-based aid available for part-time students. Work-study available nights, weekends and for part-time students. **Non-need-based:** Awarded to 510 full-time undergraduates, including 273 freshmen. Scholarships awarded for academics, art, athletics, leadership, music/drama, state residency.

Application procedures. Admission: No deadline. No application fee. Application must be submitted online. Admission notification on a rolling basis. **Financial aid:** Priority date 3/1; no closing date. FAFSA required. Applicants notified on a rolling basis starting 4/1.

Academics. Special study options: Cooperative education, distance learning, double major, dual enrollment of high school students, ESL, independent study, internships, liberal arts/career combination, student-designed major. Radiological technology program at Regional West Medical Center. License preparation in aviation, nursing, paramedic, radiology, real estate. **Credit/placement by examination:** AP, CLEP, IB, institutional tests. 25 credit hours maximum toward associate degree. **Support services:** GED preparation and test center, learning center, pre-admission summer program, reduced course load, remedial instruction, study skills assistance, tutoring, writing center.

Majors. Biology: General. **Business:** General, accounting, administrative services, business admin, office/clerical. **Communications:** Journalism. **Computer sciences:** General, computer science, programming. **Conservation:** Forestry. **Education:** General, art, early childhood, elementary, music, physical, secondary. **Engineering:** General. **English:** English lit. **Foreign languages:** French, Spanish. **General:** Lineworker. **Health services:** Athletic training, health information technology, medical radiologic technology/radiation therapy, nursing (RN), predental, premedicine, prenursing, prepharmacy, preveterinary. **History:** General. **Human services:** Social work. **Liberal arts:** Arts/sciences. **Math:** General. **Physical sciences:** Chemistry, physics. **Protective services:** Police science. **Psychology:** General. **Social sciences:** Economics, geography, political science, sociology. **Visual/performing arts:** Art, music performance. **Work/family studies:** Food/nutrition.

Most popular majors. Business/marketing 13%, health sciences 27%, liberal arts 32%, trade and industry 7%.

Technology on campus. 518 workstations in dormitories, library, computer center. Dormitories wired for high-speed internet access and linked to campus network. Commuter students can connect to campus network. Online course registration, online library, helpline, wireless network available.

Student life. Freshman orientation: Available. Preregistration for classes offered. 6 hours held the weekday before classes begin. **Policies:** All buildings are smoke-free. **Housing:** Coed dorms, wellness housing available. $180 partly refundable deposit, deadline 8/15. **Activities:** Jazz band, choral groups, drama, international student organizations, literary magazine, music ensembles, musical theater, student government, student newspaper, Campus Ventures, College Republicans, Student Ambassadors, United Leaders for Cultural Diversity, student senate, student council.

Athletics. NJCAA. **Intercollegiate:** Baseball M, basketball, soccer, softball W, volleyball W. **Intramural:** Basketball, football (non-tackle), volleyball. **Team name:** Cougars.

Student services. Adult student services, alcohol/substance abuse counseling, career counseling, student employment services, financial aid counseling, minority student services, on-campus daycare, personal counseling, placement for graduates, veterans' counselor. **Physically disabled:** Services for visually, speech, hearing impaired. **Transfer:** Pre-admission transcript evaluation for new students. Transfer adviser, college fairs on campus for students transferring to 4-year colleges.

Contact. E-mail: admissions@wncc.edu
Phone: (308) 635-6183 Toll-free number: (800) 348-4435 ext. 6183
Fax: (308) 635-6732
Gretchen Foster, Admissions Director, Western Nebraska Community College, 1601 East 27th Street, Scottsbluff, NE 69361

Wright Career College: Omaha
Omaha, Nebraska
www.wrightcc.edu

▶ Private 2-year career college
▶ Very large city

General. Regionally accredited; also accredited by ACICS. **Enrollment:** 91 undergraduates. **Degrees:** 2 associate awarded. **Calendar:** Continuous.

Basis for selection. Open admission.

2015-2016 Annual costs. Program Tuition and Fees: Health Care Administration (BS) $68,973.08, (AS) $35,030.94. Medical Assisting (AAS) 35,235.40, Medical Insurance Coding (AAS) $34,940.56, Administrative Medical Assistant (Diploma) 21,467.27, Medical Insurance Coding (Diploma) $21,338.47, Medical Assistant (Diploma) $21,096.21, Accounting (BS) $69,581.18, (AS) $34,168.98, Business Administration (BS) $69,065.14, (AS) $34,256.49, Entrepreneurship and Small Business Management (AAS) $33,544.83, Accounting (Diploma) $20,833.48, Administrative Assistant (Diploma) $20,945.87, Personal Training and Fitness (AAS) $36,708.58,

Computer Information Systems & Analysis (BS) $68,875.28, Computer Information Systems-Software Development (AS) $35,230.52, PC Support & Administration (AS) $35,390, Network Administration & Security (AS) $35,383.82, Software Administration (Diploma) $21,442.87.

Financial aid. Need-based: Work-study available nights, weekends and for part-time students.

Academics. Credit/placement by examination: AP.

Majors. Business: Business admin. **Computer sciences:** System admin. **Health services:** Athletic training, insurance coding.

Contact. Phone: (402) 514-2500
Wright Career College: Omaha, 3000 South 84th Street, Omaha, NE 68124

Nevada

Career College of Northern Nevada
Sparks, Nevada
www.ccnn.edu
CB code: 3202

- For-profit 2-year career college
- Commuter campus in large city
- Interview required

General. Accredited by ACCSC. **Enrollment:** 581 undergraduates. **Degrees:** 189 associate awarded. **Calendar:** Quarter, extensive summer session. **Full-time faculty:** 24 total. **Part-time faculty:** 12 total. **Class size:** 82% < 20, 18% 20-39.

Basis for selection. Open admission. Must pass Wonderlic or CPAt. **Home schooled:** State high school equivalency certificate required.

2015-2016 Annual costs. Books/supplies: $1,500. Personal expenses: $1,832.

Financial aid. All financial aid based on need. Work-study available nights, weekends and for part-time students.

Application procedures. Admission: No deadline. $25 fee. Application must be submitted on paper. Admission notification on a rolling basis. **Financial aid:** No deadline. FAFSA required. Applicants notified on a rolling basis.

Academics. Special study options: Accelerated study, cooperative education, internships, liberal arts/career combination. **Credit/placement by examination:** AP, CLEP. **Support services:** Remedial instruction, study skills assistance, tutoring.

Majors. Computer sciences: System admin. **Health services:** Health information technology, insurance coding, insurance specialist, medical assistant, medical secretary.

Most popular majors. Computer/information sciences 14%, engineering/engineering technologies 19%, health sciences 62%, legal studies 6%.

Technology on campus. 78 workstations in computer center, student center.

Student life. Freshman orientation: Mandatory. Preregistration for classes offered. Held Saturday morning before classes begin.

Student services. Adult student services, career counseling, financial aid counseling, placement for graduates.

Contact. E-mail: mbuendia@ccnn4u.com
Phone: (775) 856-2266
Maria Buendia, Director of Admissions, Career College of Northern Nevada, 1421 Pullman Drive, Sparks, NV 89434

Carrington College: Las Vegas
Las Vegas, Nevada
www.carrington.edu

- For-profit 2-year career college
- Very large city

General. Regionally accredited; also accredited by ACICS. **Enrollment:** 325 degree-seeking undergraduates. **Degrees:** 64 associate awarded. **Calendar:** Differs by program. **Full-time faculty:** 10 total. **Part-time faculty:** 12 total.

Basis for selection. Admission requirements vary by program.

2015-2016 Annual costs. Tuition costs vary by program. Total program cost for the largest program (Respiratory Care-Assoc.) is $44,563.

Financial aid. Need-based: Work-study available nights, weekends and for part-time students.

Application procedures. Admission: No deadline. No application fee. **Financial aid:** No deadline.

Academics. Credit/placement by examination: AP, CLEP.

Majors. Health services: Physical therapy assistant, respiratory therapy assistant, respiratory therapy technology.

Contact. Phone: (888) 720-5014
Director of Enrollment Services, Carrington College: Las Vegas, 5740 South Eastern Avenue, Las Vegas, NV 89119-1642

Carrington College: Reno
Reno, Nevada
www.carrington.edu

- For-profit 2-year nursing college
- Large city

General. Regionally accredited; also accredited by ACICS. **Enrollment:** 343 degree-seeking undergraduates. **Degrees:** 105 associate awarded. **Calendar:** Semester. **Full-time faculty:** 17 total. **Part-time faculty:** 16 total.

Basis for selection. Admission requirements vary by program.

2015-2016 Annual costs. Tuition costs vary by program. Total program cost for the largest program (Registered Nursing-Assoc.) is $50,599.

Financial aid. Need-based: Work-study available nights, weekends and for part-time students.

Application procedures. Admission: No deadline. No application fee. **Financial aid:** Priority date 8/27; no closing date.

Academics. Credit/placement by examination: AP, CLEP.

Majors. Health services: Nursing (RN).

Contact. E-mail: brossini@carrington.edu
Phone: (888) 720-5014
Director of Enrollment Services, Carrington College: Reno, 5580 Kietzke Lane, Reno, NV 89511

College of Southern Nevada
Las Vegas, Nevada
www.csn.edu
CB code: 4136

- Public 2-year community college
- Commuter campus in very large city

General. Founded in 1971. Regionally accredited. Three major campuses and seven High-Tech/Academic & Learning Centers. **Enrollment:** 28,685 degree-seeking undergraduates; 4,628 non-degree-seeking students. **Degrees:** 32 bachelor's, 2,833 associate awarded. **ROTC:** Army. **Location:** 6 miles from downtown. **Calendar:** Semester, limited summer session. **Full-time faculty:** 508 total. **Part-time faculty:** 616 total. **Special facilities:** Planetarium, ornamental horticulture demonstration facilities, culinary facilities, telecommunications/multimedia center, automotive technology center, occupational therapy labs, dental practice.

Student profile. Among degree-seeking undergraduates, 4,100 enrolled as first-time, first-year students.

Part-time:	70%	Native American:	1%
Out-of-state:	2%	Native Hawaiian/Pacific islander:	2%
Women:	58%	Multi-racial, non-Hispanic:	5%
African American:	12%	International:	1%
Asian American:	10%	25 or older:	54%
Hispanic/Latino:	29%		

Transfer out. Colleges most students transferred to 2015: University of Nevada Las Vegas, Nevada State College.

Basis for selection. Open admission, but selective for some programs. Special requirements for nursing, dental hygiene, and health professions programs. Associate degree and certification required for bachelor's dental hygiene program. **Adult students:** SAT/ACT scores not required. All degree-seeking students must either take placement tests, provide SAT or ACT scores, or other proof of accomplishment to enter college-level math and English. **Learning Disabled:** Degree-seeking students must provide HS graduation info (diploma, transcripts, etc) or GED equivalent.

2015-2016 Annual costs. Tuition/fees: $2,805; $9,450 out-of-state. Per-credit charge: $88. Books/supplies: $1,020. Personal expenses: $1,836.

Financial aid. Need-based: Work-study available nights, weekends and for part-time students. **Non-need-based:** Scholarships awarded for state residency.

Application procedures. Admission: No deadline. $10 fee, may be waived for applicants with need. Admission notification on a rolling basis. **Financial aid:** Priority date 5/1, closing date 6/30. FAFSA required. Applicants notified on a rolling basis starting 7/15; must reply within 2 week(s) of notification.

Academics. Special study options: Cooperative education, distance learning, dual enrollment of high school students, ESL, honors, independent study, internships, liberal arts/career combination. Bachelor's degree programs available on campus. License preparation in aviation, dental hygiene, nursing, occupational therapy, paramedic, physical therapy, radiology, real estate. **Credit/placement by examination:** AP, CLEP, institutional tests. 15 credit hours maximum toward associate degree. **Support services:** GED preparation and test center, learning center, remedial instruction, study skills assistance, tutoring, writing center.

Majors. Area/ethnic studies: Women's. **Biology:** General. **Business:** General, accounting, administrative services, banking/financial services, business admin, hospitality admin, hospitality/recreation, management information systems, office management, real estate, sales/distribution. **Communications:** Communications/speech/rhetoric, journalism. **Communications technology:** Animation/special effects. **Computer sciences:** Database management, information technology, LAN/WAN management. **Education:** Deaf/hearing impaired, early childhood, kindergarten/preschool. **Engineering:** Electrical, software. **English:** English lit. **Health services:** Clinical lab assistant, clinical lab technology, dental hygiene, EMT paramedic, health information technology, nursing (RN), optician, orthotics/prosthetics, physical therapy assistant. **Liberal arts:** Arts/sciences. **Protective services:** Corrections, criminal justice, fire safety technology, firefighting, police science, security services. **Psychology:** General. **Social sciences:** General. **Visual/performing arts:** Art, commercial photography, commercial/advertising art, studio arts.

Technology on campus. 650 workstations in library, computer center. Commuter students can connect to campus network. Online course registration, online library, helpline, wireless network available.

Student life. Freshman orientation: Mandatory. Preregistration for classes offered. Mandatory for degree-seeking students only. **Activities:** Bands, choral groups, dance, drama, international student organizations, literary magazine, music ensembles, musical theater, student government, student newspaper.

Athletics. NJCAA. **Intercollegiate:** Baseball M, softball W. **Intramural:** Baseball W, softball W. **Team name:** Coyotes.

Student services. Adult student services, career counseling, student employment services, financial aid counseling, on-campus daycare, personal counseling, placement for graduates, veterans' counselor, women's services. **Physically disabled:** Services for visually, speech, hearing impaired. **Transfer:** Re-entry adviser, pre-admission transcript evaluation for new students. Transfer center, transfer adviser, college fairs on campus for students transferring to 4-year colleges.

Contact. E-mail: admrec@csn.edu
Phone: (702) 651-5610 Fax: (702) 651-4811
Patricia Zozaya, Registrar, College of Southern Nevada, 6375 West Charleston Boulevard, Las Vegas, NV 89146-1164

Kaplan College: Las Vegas
Las Vegas, Nevada
www.kaplancollege.com   **CB code: 3167**

- For-profit 2-year career college
- Commuter campus in very large city
- Interview required

General. Accredited by ACCSC. **Enrollment:** 944 undergraduates. **Degrees:** 176 associate awarded. **Calendar:** Differs by program. **Full-time faculty:** 19 total. **Part-time faculty:** 35 total.

Basis for selection. Open admission, but selective for some programs. Clean legal record required for pharmacy technician, practical nursing and criminal justice programs. Wonderlic SLE exam required for all applicants; cut-off scores vary by program. **Adult students:** All students must take a Wonderlic Scholastic Level Exam.

2015-2016 Annual costs. Personal expenses: $2,925. **Additional information:** Criminal Justice: $292.22 quarter unit credit (95 Credit Hours), total $30,805. Health Information Technology: $293.89 quarter unit credit (94 Credit Hours), total $30,805. Medical Assistant: $297.03 quarter unit credit (51 Credit Hours), total $15,663. Medical Assistant X-Ray Technician: $291.51 quarter unit credit (70 Credit Hours), total $22,045. Medical Billing and Coding Specialist: $289.09 quarter unit credit (51 Credit Hours), total $15,663. Pharmacy Technician: $258.31 quarter unit credit (57 Credit Hours), total $15,663. Phlebotomy Technician: total $995. Practical Nursing: $313.39 quarter unit credit (89 Credit Hours), total $29,731.

Financial aid. Need-based: Need-based aid available for part-time students. Work-study available nights, weekends and for part-time students.

Application procedures. Admission: No deadline. $10 fee. **Financial aid:** No deadline. FAFSA, institutional form required.

Academics. Credit/placement by examination: AP, CLEP. **Support services:** Learning center, study skills assistance, tutoring.

Majors. Health services: Insurance coding, office assistant, pharmacy assistant. **Protective services:** Law enforcement admin.

Technology on campus. 90 workstations in library, computer center. Online library available.

Student life. Freshman orientation: Available. Preregistration for classes offered. Held one week to a few days before start of class; on-campus; attendance strongly encouraged. **Activities:** Student government.

Student services. Adult student services, career counseling, student employment services, financial aid counseling, placement for graduates.

Contact. Phone: (702) 368-2338 Toll-free number: (888) 727-7863
Fax: (702) 368-3853
Derrick Perry, Director of Admissions, Kaplan College: Las Vegas, 3535 West Sahara Avenue, Las Vegas, NV 89102

Truckee Meadows Community College
Reno, Nevada
www.tmcc.edu   **CB code: 1096**

- Public 2-year community and technical college
- Commuter campus in large city

General. Founded in 1971. Regionally accredited. Classes offered at over 30 sites in Reno-Sparks area. **Enrollment:** 8,861 degree-seeking undergraduates; 2,723 non-degree-seeking students. **Degrees:** 1,174 associate awarded. **ROTC:** Army. **Location:** 9 miles from downtown. **Calendar:** Semester, limited summer session. **Full-time faculty:** 172 total; 11% minority. **Part-time faculty:** 409 total; 10% minority. **Class size:** 29% < 20, 69% 20-39, 2% 40-49, less than 1% 50-99.

Student profile. Among degree-seeking undergraduates, 1,277 enrolled as first-time, first-year students, 267 transferred in from other institutions.

Part-time:	72%	Women:	56%
Out-of-state:	9%		

Transfer out. Colleges most students transferred to 2015: University of Nevada-Reno, University of Nevada-Las Vegas.

Basis for selection. Open admission, but selective for some programs. High school diploma or GED required for degree seeking students. Competitive admissions to nursing, dental assistant, and radiological technician programs. **Home schooled:** Statement describing home school structure and mission required. **Learning Disabled:** Applicants must contact Disabled Students Office. Accommodations provided according to documentation.

2015-2016 Annual costs. Tuition/fees: $2,805; $9,450 out-of-state. Per-credit charge: $88. Books/supplies: $1,548. Personal expenses: $860.

Financial aid. Need-based: Work-study available nights, weekends and for part-time students. **Non-need-based:** Scholarships awarded for academics, art, leadership, minority status, music/drama, state residency. **Additional information:** Institutional grants to state residents, short-term emergency loans available. Work-study applications must reply within 10 days of notification.

Application procedures. Admission: No deadline. $10 fee. Admission notification on a rolling basis. Application fee is paid at time of registration for first class. **Financial aid:** Priority date 1/15; no closing date. FAFSA, institutional form required.

Academics. Special study options: Cooperative education, distance learning, dual enrollment of high school students, ESL, honors, internships, liberal arts/career combination, weekend college. License preparation in dental hygiene, nursing, radiology, real estate. **Credit/placement by examination:** AP, CLEP, IB, institutional tests. 15 credit hours maximum toward associate degree. **Support services:** GED preparation and test center, learning center, reduced course load, remedial instruction, study skills assistance, tutoring, writing center.

Majors. Architecture: Landscape. **Business:** General, accounting, administrative services, business admin, office management, office technology, real estate. **Computer sciences:** General, data processing, programming. **Conservation:** Environmental studies. **Education:** Early childhood, elementary, secondary. **General:** Carpentry, maintenance, masonry, pipefitting, power transmission. **Health services:** Dental assistant, dental hygiene, medical radiologic technology/radiation therapy, medical secretary, nursing (RN), radiologic technology/medical imaging, substance abuse counseling. **Parks/recreation:** Facilities management. **Protective services:** Corrections, criminal justice, firefighting, juvenile corrections, law enforcement admin, police science. **Social sciences:** Anthropology. **Visual/performing arts:** Design, dramatic, music. **Work/family studies:** Child care management, institutional food production.

Most popular majors. Health sciences 11%, liberal arts 58%, physical sciences 9%, security/protective services 7%.

Technology on campus. 558 workstations in library, computer center, student center. Commuter students can connect to campus network. Online course registration, online library, helpline, repair service, wireless network available.

Student life. Freshman orientation: Mandatory. Preregistration for classes offered. **Housing:** Housing available 2 miles away at University of Nevada: Reno for students enrolled for 12 or more credits. **Activities:** Concert band, choral groups, drama, literary magazine, music ensembles, student government, student newspaper, symphony orchestra, social organization for handicapped students.

Student services. Adult student services, career counseling, student employment services, financial aid counseling, health services, on-campus daycare, personal counseling, placement for graduates, veterans' counselor. **Physically disabled:** Services for visually, speech, hearing impaired. **Transfer:** Re-entry adviser for new students. Transfer adviser, college fairs on campus for students transferring to 4-year colleges.

Contact. E-mail: admissions@tmcc.edu
Phone: (775) 673-7042 Fax: (775) 673-7028
Andrew Hughes, Director of Admissions and Records, Truckee Meadows Community College, 7000 Dandini Boulevard, Reno, NV 89512

Western Nevada College
Carson City, Nevada
www.wnc.edu   CB code: 4972

▶ Public 2-year community college
▶ Commuter campus in small city

General. Founded in 1971. Regionally accredited. Three campuses and additional class locations. **Enrollment:** 3,327 degree-seeking undergraduates; 512 non-degree-seeking students. **Degrees:** 2 bachelor's, 518 associate awarded. **Location:** 30 miles from Reno. **Calendar:** Semester, limited summer session. **Special facilities:** Observatory, fitness center, baseball field. **Partnerships:** Formal partnerships with selected high schools for dual credit.

Student profile. Among degree-seeking undergraduates, 623 enrolled as first-time, first-year students, 137 transferred in from other institutions.

Part-time:	59%	Women:	60%
Out-of-state:	3%	25 or older:	48%

Transfer out. Colleges most students transferred to 2015: University of Nevada-Reno.

Basis for selection. Open admission, but selective for some programs. SAT/ACT accepted, but not required, for math and English placement. Special requirements for nursing program.

2015-2016 Annual costs. Tuition/fees: $2,805; $9,450 out-of-state. Per-credit charge: $88. Books/supplies: $1,400. Personal expenses: $2,160.

2014-2015 Financial aid. Need-based: 203 full-time freshmen applied for aid; 185 deemed to have need; 185 received aid. 62% of total undergraduate aid awarded as scholarships/grants, 38% as loans/jobs. Need-based aid available for part-time students. Work-study available nights, weekends and for part-time students. **Non-need-based:** Awarded to 268 full-time undergraduates, including 146 freshmen. Scholarships awarded for academics, athletics, state residency.

Application procedures. Admission: No deadline. $15 fee. Application must be submitted online. No notification sent to applicants except by request. **Financial aid:** Priority date 4/1; no closing date. FAFSA required. Applicants notified on a rolling basis; must reply within 3 week(s) of notification.

Academics. Special study options: Accelerated study, distance learning, double major, dual enrollment of high school students, ESL, honors, independent study, internships. Bachelor's degree programs available on campus. License preparation in nursing, paramedic, real estate. **Credit/placement by examination:** AP, CLEP, institutional tests. 30 credit hours maximum toward associate degree, 30 toward bachelor's. **Support services:** GED preparation and test center, learning center, remedial instruction, study skills assistance, tutoring.

Majors. Area/ethnic studies: Deaf. **Business:** Accounting, business admin, management science, office technology. **Communications technology:** Graphics. **Computer sciences:** General, LAN/WAN management, webmaster. **General:** Site management. **Health services:** Nursing (RN). **Liberal arts:** Arts/sciences. **Protective services:** Police science.

Most popular majors. Business/marketing 8%, health sciences 8%, liberal arts 51%, physical sciences 11%.

Technology on campus. 568 workstations in library, computer center, student center. Commuter students can connect to campus network. Online course registration, online library, student web hosting, wireless network available.

Student life. Freshman orientation: Available. Preregistration for classes offered. **Activities:** Bands, choral groups, dance, drama, musical theater, student government.

Athletics. NJCAA. **Intercollegiate:** Baseball M, softball W. **Team name:** Wildcats.

Student services. Adult student services, alcohol/substance abuse counseling, career counseling, services for economically disadvantaged, student employment services, financial aid counseling, minority student services, on-campus daycare, personal counseling, placement for graduates, veterans' counselor, women's services. **Physically disabled:** Services for visually, speech, hearing impaired. **Transfer:** Pre-admission transcript evaluation for new students. Transfer center, transfer adviser for students transferring to 4-year colleges.

Contact. E-mail: admissions.records@wnc.edu
Phone: (775) 445-3277 Fax: (775) 887-3147
Dianne Hilliard, Director, Admissions and Records, Western Nevada College, 2201 West College Parkway, Carson City, NV 89703-7399

New Hampshire

Great Bay Community College
Portsmouth, New Hampshire
www.greatbay.edu   CB code: 3661

▶ Public 2-year community and technical college
▶ Commuter campus in small town

General. Founded in 1945. Regionally accredited. **Enrollment:** 1,887 degree-seeking undergraduates. **Degrees:** 189 associate awarded. **Location:** 45 miles from Boston. **Calendar:** Semester, limited summer session. **Full-time faculty:** 36 total. **Part-time faculty:** 169 total. **Special facilities:** Biotechnology lab.

Transfer out. Colleges most students transferred to 2015: University of New Hampshire, Southern New Hampshire University, Keene State College, Plymouth State University, Granite State College.

Basis for selection. Open admission, but selective for some programs. Selective admission to allied health and automotive programs. National League for Nursing Pre-Admission Assessment for Registered Nursing required for applicants to RN program. ACT-PEP Nursing Fundamentals Test required for admission to associate degree nursing program as advanced standing students. Career Guidance Placement Test given to technical majors on selected basis. Interview required for allied health and education applicants.

High school preparation. Recommended units include English 4, mathematics 2, social studies 2 and science 2. High school vocational and college-preparatory courses recommended. For mechanical-technical majors, algebra I and II and geometry recommended. For associate nursing applicants and surgical technology, biology, chemistry, algebra I required. For vet tech, algebra, biology and chemistry are required. For business management, typing or keyboarding skills required.

2015-2016 Annual costs. Tuition/fees: $6,660; $14,310 out-of-state. Per-credit charge: $200 in-state; $455 out-of-state. Books/supplies: $600. **Additional information:** New England Regional tuition: $300 per credit hour; Graduation Fee $100.

Financial aid. All financial aid based on need. Need-based aid available for part-time students. Work-study available nights, weekends and for part-time students.

Application procedures. Admission: No deadline. $20 fee, may be waived for applicants with need, free for online applicants. Admission notification on a rolling basis. **Financial aid:** No deadline. FAFSA, institutional form required. Applicants notified on a rolling basis; must reply within 2 week(s) of notification.

Academics. Special study options: Accelerated study, distance learning, double major, dual enrollment of high school students, ESL, independent study, internships, liberal arts/career combination. License preparation in nursing. **Credit/placement by examination:** AP, CLEP, institutional tests. **Support services:** GED preparation, learning center, pre-admission summer program, reduced course load, remedial instruction, study skills assistance, tutoring, writing center.

Majors. Biology: Biotechnology. **Business:** General, accounting, administrative services, business admin, hospitality admin, management science, marketing. **Computer sciences:** Information systems, programming, web page design. **Education:** Early childhood, social science. **Health services:** Massage therapy, nursing (RN), surgical technology, veterinary technology/assistant. **Liberal arts:** Arts/sciences. **Protective services:** Law enforcement admin. **Work/family studies:** Child care management.

Technology on campus. 140 workstations in library, computer center. Online library, helpline, wireless network available.

Student life. Freshman orientation: Available. Preregistration for classes offered. **Activities:** Literary magazine, student government, student senate, Phi Theta Kappa.

Student services. Career counseling, student employment services, placement for graduates. **Transfer:** Pre-admission transcript evaluation for new students. Transfer adviser, college fairs on campus for students transferring to 4-year colleges.

Contact. E-mail: askgreatbay@ccsnh.edu
Phone: (603) 772-1194 Toll-free number: (800) 522-1194
Fax: (603) 772-1198
Sandy Ho, Admissions Coordinator, Great Bay Community College, 320 Corporate Drive, Portsmouth, NH 03801

Lakes Region Community College
Laconia, New Hampshire
www.lrcc.edu   CB code: 3850

▶ Public 2-year community and technical college
▶ Commuter campus in small city

General. Founded in 1967. Regionally accredited. Numerous satellite programs at various locations. **Enrollment:** 894 degree-seeking undergraduates. **Degrees:** 150 associate awarded. **Location:** 95 miles from Boston, 25 miles from Concord. **Calendar:** Semester, limited summer session. **Full-time faculty:** 44 total. **Part-time faculty:** 34 total. **Special facilities:** Student operated restaurant.

Basis for selection. Open admission, but selective for some programs. Competitive admission to nursing program.

High school preparation. College-preparatory program recommended. Required and recommended units include English 4, mathematics 2-3, social studies 2 and science 4.

2015-2016 Annual costs. Tuition/fees: $6,180; $13,830 out-of-state. Per-credit charge: $200 in-state; $455 out-of-state. Books/supplies: $800. **Additional information:** New England Regional tuition: $300 per credit hour.

Financial aid. Need-based: Need-based aid available for part-time students. Work-study available nights, weekends and for part-time students.

Application procedures. Admission: No deadline. $20 fee, may be waived for applicants with need, free for online applicants. Admission notification on a rolling basis beginning on or about 10/1. Must reply by May 1 or within 4 week(s) if notified thereafter. **Financial aid:** Priority date 5/1; no closing date. FAFSA, institutional form required.

Academics. Special study options: Cooperative education, distance learning, double major, honors, independent study, internships, liberal arts/career combination. **Credit/placement by examination:** AP, CLEP, IB, institutional tests. 12 credit hours maximum toward associate degree. **Support services:** Learning center, reduced course load, remedial instruction, study skills assistance, tutoring.

Majors. Business: Accounting, business admin, hospitality/recreation. **Communications technology:** Graphic/printing. **Computer sciences:** General, data processing, programming. **Education:** Early childhood. **General:** Electrician. **Human services:** Social work. **Liberal arts:** Arts/sciences. **Protective services:** Fire safety technology, fire services admin, firefighting. **Visual/performing arts:** Commercial/advertising art, studio arts.

Technology on campus. 100 workstations in library, computer center. Online course registration, wireless network available.

Student life. Freshman orientation: Mandatory, $30 fee. Preregistration for classes offered. **Activities:** Literary magazine, student government.

Athletics. NJCAA. **Intercollegiate:** Basketball M, golf, track and field. **Intramural:** Soccer, table tennis. **Team name:** Centurions.

Student services. Career counseling, student employment services, financial aid counseling, personal counseling, placement for graduates, veterans' counselor. **Physically disabled:** Services for hearing impaired. **Transfer:** Pre-admission transcript evaluation for new students. Transfer adviser, college fairs on campus for students transferring to 4-year colleges.

Contact. E-mail: wfraser@ccsnh.edu
Phone: (603) 524-3207 ext. 767 Toll-free number: (800) 357-2992
Fax: (603) 524-8084
Wayne Fraser, Director of Admissions, Lakes Region Community College, 379 Belmont Road, Laconia, NH 03246-9204

Manchester Community College
Manchester, New Hampshire   CB member
www.mccnh.edu   CB code: 3660

▶ Public 2-year community and technical college
▶ Commuter campus in small city

General. Founded in 1945. Regionally accredited. **Enrollment:** 3,075 degree-seeking undergraduates. **Degrees:** 307 associate awarded. **Location:** 50 miles from Boston. **Calendar:** Semester, limited summer session. **Full-time faculty:** 56 total. **Part-time faculty:** 276 total. **Partnerships:** Formal partnerships with local businesses.

Basis for selection. Open admission, but selective for some programs. National League for Nursing Pre-Admission Examination-RN required for nursing applicants. **Learning Disabled:** A Disabilities Counselor is available for students with learning and other disabilities.

High school preparation. Recommended units include English 4, mathematics 3 and science 2. Chemistry, algebra, geometry and biology required for some programs.

2015-2016 Annual costs. Tuition/fees: $6,420; $14,070 out-of-state. Per-credit charge: $200 in-state; $455 out-of-state. Books/supplies: $550. **Additional information:** New England Regional tuition: $300 per credit hour.

Financial aid. All financial aid based on need. Need-based aid available for part-time students. Work-study available nights, weekends and for part-time students.

Application procedures. Admission: No deadline. $20 fee, may be waived for applicants with need. Admission notification on a rolling basis. **Financial aid:** Priority date 5/1; no closing date. FAFSA, institutional form required. Applicants notified on a rolling basis starting 4/15; must reply within 2 week(s) of notification.

Academics. Special study options: Cooperative education, cross-registration, distance learning, double major, dual enrollment of high school students, ESL, external degree, independent study, internships, liberal arts/career combination, student-designed major. License preparation in nursing. **Credit/placement by examination:** AP, CLEP, institutional tests. 32 credit hours maximum toward associate degree. **Support services:** Learning center, reduced course load, remedial instruction, study skills assistance, tutoring, writing center.

Majors. Business: Accounting, administrative services, business admin, management science, marketing, office management. **Communications technology:** Desktop publishing, graphics. **Computer sciences:** General. **Education:** Early childhood. **General:** Maintenance. **Health services:** Health information technology, medical assistant, nursing (RN), prenursing. **Liberal arts:** Arts/sciences. **Parks/recreation:** Exercise sciences. **Visual/performing arts:** Commercial/advertising art, interior design.

Technology on campus. 75 workstations in library, computer center. Online library, helpline, wireless network available.

Student life. Freshman orientation: Available, $25 fee. Preregistration for classes offered. **Activities:** Literary magazine, student government, student newspaper, honor society, community service club, Alternative Spring Break, international club, student senate, medical assisting club, business honor society.

Athletics. Intramural: Skiing, soccer, volleyball.

Student services. Career counseling, services for economically disadvantaged, financial aid counseling, minority student services, on-campus daycare. **Physically disabled:** Services for visually, hearing impaired. **Transfer:** Pre-admission transcript evaluation for new students. Transfer adviser, college fairs on campus for students transferring to 4-year colleges.

Contact. E-mail: maxisa@ccsnh.edu
Phone: (603) 206-8100 Toll-free number: (800) 924-3445
Fax: (603) 668-5354
Manchester Community College, 1066 Front Street, Manchester, NH 03102-8518

Nashua Community College
Nashua, New Hampshire
www.nashuacc.edu
CB member
CB code: 3643

- Public 2-year community and technical college
- Commuter campus in small city

General. Founded in 1967. Regionally accredited. **Enrollment:** 1,830 degree-seeking undergraduates. **Degrees:** 283 associate awarded. **Location:** 20 miles from Lowell, Massachusetts. **Calendar:** Semester, limited summer session.

Transfer out. Colleges most students transferred to 2015: University of Southern New Hampshire, University of New Hampshire, Keene State College, Plymouth State College.

Basis for selection. Open admission, but selective for some programs. Prerequisite courses, references, exam required for nursing program. Clean driving record required for Honda program.

High school preparation. One unit algebra required for business and technical programs, 2 for computer/engineering technology.

2015-2016 Annual costs. Tuition/fees: $6,480; $14,130 out-of-state. Per-credit charge: $200 in-state; $455 out-of-state. Books/supplies: $1,400. Personal expenses: $1,800. **Additional information:** New England Regional tuition: $300 per credit hour.

Financial aid. All financial aid based on need. Need-based aid available for part-time students. Work-study available nights, weekends and for part-time students.

Application procedures. Admission: No deadline. $20 fee, may be waived for applicants with need. Admission notification on a rolling basis. Application deadline of 1/31 for nursing applicants. **Financial aid:** Priority date 5/1; no closing date. FAFSA required. Applicants notified on a rolling basis starting 3/1; must reply within 2 week(s) of notification.

Academics. Special study options: Distance learning, double major, dual enrollment of high school students, ESL, honors, internships. License preparation in aviation, nursing. **Credit/placement by examination:** AP, CLEP, institutional tests. 16 credit hours maximum toward associate degree. **Support services:** Learning center, pre-admission summer program, reduced course load, remedial instruction, study skills assistance, tutoring, writing center.

Majors. Business: Accounting, business admin, marketing, restaurant/food services. **Computer sciences:** Applications programming, networking, web page design. **Education:** General, early childhood, speech impaired. **Health services:** Nursing (RN), somatic bodywork. **Liberal arts:** Arts/sciences. **Protective services:** Law enforcement admin.

Technology on campus. 150 workstations in library, computer center. Online course registration, student web hosting, wireless network available.

Student life. Freshman orientation: Mandatory, $30 fee. Preregistration for classes offered. One-day session held prior to beginning of each semester. **Policies:** All activities open to all students. **Housing:** Student housing available near campus. **Activities:** Drama, student government, Phi Theta Kappa, Rotaract.

Athletics. Intercollegiate: Volleyball W. **Team name:** Jaguars.

Student services. Career counseling, financial aid counseling, veterans' counselor. **Transfer:** Pre-admission transcript evaluation for new students. Transfer adviser, college fairs on campus for students transferring to 4-year colleges.

Contact. E-mail: nashua@ccsnh.edu
Phone: (603) 578-8908 Fax: (603) 882-8690
Lizbeth Gonzalez, Vice President of Student and Community Affairs, Nashua Community College, 505 Amherst Street, Nashua, NH 03063-1026

NHTI-Concord's Community College
Concord, New Hampshire
www.nhti.edu
CB code: 3647

- Public 2-year community and technical college
- Commuter campus in large town

General. Founded in 1965. Regionally accredited. **Enrollment:** 3,642 degree-seeking undergraduates; 707 non-degree-seeking students. **Degrees:** 608 associate awarded. **Location:** 75 miles from Boston. **Calendar:** Semester, extensive summer session. **Full-time faculty:** 105 total; 10% have terminal degrees. **Part-time faculty:** 300 total. **Special facilities:** Planetarium, wellness center, child care clinic, dental clinic, nature trails. **Partnerships:** Formal partnerships with New Hampshire businesses for internships, practicums, and clinicals.

Student profile. Among degree-seeking undergraduates, 951 enrolled as first-time, first-year students.

Part-time:	51%	25 or older:	30%
Out-of-state:	2%	Live on campus:	8%
Women:	55%		

Transfer out. Colleges most students transferred to 2015: University of New Hampshire, Southern New Hampshire University, Plymouth State College, Keene State College, Granite State College.

Basis for selection. Open admission, but selective for some programs. Requirements vary by program. Nursing and allied health programs require special testing and interviews. National League for Nursing Pre-Nursing Test, special challenge test for practical nursing required. Institutional assessment test required of all students. Interview required for health program applicants, early child education programs, and recommended for some others. **Home schooled:** Transcript of courses and grades required. Must submit portfolio of work approved by school district.

High school preparation. Recommended units include English 4, mathematics 3 and science 2. High school academic subject requirements vary according to program. Strong background in mathematics and natural sciences recommended.

2015-2016 Annual costs. Tuition/fees: $6,660; $14,310 out-of-state. Per-credit charge: $200 in-state; $455 out-of-state. Room/board: $8,754. Books/supplies: $600. Personal expenses: $1,600. **Additional information:** New England Regional tuition: $300 per credit hour.

2014-2015 Financial aid. All financial aid based on need. 690 full-time freshmen applied for aid; 583 deemed to have need; 549 received aid. Average need met was 58%. Average scholarship/grant was $4,419; average loan $3,016. 48% of total undergraduate aid awarded as scholarships/grants, 52% as loans/jobs. Need-based aid available for part-time students. Work-study available nights, weekends and for part-time students. **Additional information:** 60% of students who apply receive some form of financial aid. State school; all financial aid need-based, primarily from federal sources. No scholarships awarded.

Application procedures. Admission: No deadline. $20 fee. Admission notification on a rolling basis. Must reply by May 1 or within 4 week(s) if notified thereafter. Applicants must make a $100 deposit within 30 days of acceptance. **Financial aid:** Priority date 5/1; no closing date. FAFSA required. Applicants notified on a rolling basis starting 6/1; must reply within 2 week(s) of notification.

Academics. Special study options: Distance learning, double major, dual enrollment of high school students, ESL, honors, internships, teacher certification program. License preparation in dental hygiene, nursing, paramedic, radiology, real estate. **Credit/placement by examination:** AP, CLEP, IB, institutional tests. **Support services:** Learning center, pre-admission summer program, reduced course load, remedial instruction, study skills assistance, tutoring, writing center.

Majors. Architecture: Landscape. **Business:** Accounting, business admin, hospitality admin, hospitality/recreation, marketing, tourism promotion, tourism/travel. **Communications technology:** General. **Computer sciences:** Information technology. **Conservation:** Environmental science. **Education:** General, early childhood, special ed. **Health services:** Dental hygiene, EMT paramedic, nursing (RN), radiologic technology/medical imaging, sonography, substance abuse counseling. **Liberal arts:** Arts/sciences. **Parks/recreation:** Sports admin. **Protective services:** Law enforcement admin.

Most popular majors. Business/marketing 11%, computer/information sciences 9%, engineering/engineering technologies 10%, health sciences 31%, liberal arts 16%, security/protective services 8%.

Technology on campus. 225 workstations in dormitories, library, computer center. Dormitories wired for high-speed internet access. Helpline, wireless network available.

Student life. Freshman orientation: Mandatory, $30 fee. Preregistration for classes offered. Session held before start of semester. **Housing:** Coed dorms, wellness housing available. $300 fully refundable deposit. **Activities:** Drama, literary magazine, musical theater, student government, NHTI alliance, environmental action, Phi Theta Kappa, student nurses association, human service club, alternative spring break, criminal justice club, Christian club, cultural exchange club.

Athletics. USCAA. **Intercollegiate:** Baseball M, basketball, bowling, cross-country, golf, soccer, softball W, volleyball. **Intramural:** Basketball, football (non-tackle) M, volleyball. **Team name:** Lynx.

Student services. Alcohol/substance abuse counseling, career counseling, student employment services, financial aid counseling, health services, on-campus daycare, personal counseling, placement for graduates, veterans' counselor. **Physically disabled:** Services for visually, speech, hearing impaired. **Transfer:** Pre-admission transcript evaluation for new students. Transfer adviser, college fairs on campus for students transferring to 4-year colleges.

Contact. E-mail: nhtiadm@ccsnh.edu
Phone: (603) 271-6484 ext. 4011
Toll-free number: (800) 247-0179 ext. 4011 Fax: (603) 230-9302
Charles Lloyd, Director of Admissions, NHTI-Concord's Community College, 31 College Drive, Concord, NH 03301

River Valley Community College
Claremont, New Hampshire
www.rivervalley.edu

CB code: 3684

- Public 2-year community college
- Commuter campus in large town

General. Founded in 1967. Regionally accredited. **Enrollment:** 719 degree-seeking undergraduates. **Degrees:** 102 associate awarded. **Location:** 50 miles from Concord. **Calendar:** Semester, limited summer session. **Full-time faculty:** 26 total. **Part-time faculty:** 74 total.

Basis for selection. Open admission, but selective for some programs. ACCUPLACER test used for placement. Special requirements for nursing program.

High school preparation. Typing required for medical assistant, chemistry required for nursing and medical laboratory programs. Algebra recommended for all applicants.

2015-2016 Annual costs. Tuition/fees: $6,150; $13,800 out-of-state. Per-credit charge: $200 in-state; $455 out-of-state. Books/supplies: $550. Personal expenses: $1,100. **Additional information:** New England Regional tuition: $300 per credit hour.

Financial aid. All financial aid based on need. Need-based aid available for part-time students. Work-study available nights, weekends and for part-time students.

Application procedures. Admission: No deadline. $20 fee, may be waived for applicants with need. Admission notification on a rolling basis. **Financial aid:** Closing date 4/1. FAFSA required. Applicants notified on a rolling basis; must reply within 2 week(s) of notification.

Academics. Special study options: Accelerated study, cooperative education, distance learning, double major, independent study, internships, student-designed major. Joint associate degree program in restaurant management with Les Roches, 2-2 program in teacher education with Keene State College. **Credit/placement by examination:** AP, CLEP, institutional tests. 16 credit hours maximum toward associate degree. **Support services:** Learning center, reduced course load, study skills assistance, tutoring.

Majors. Business: General, accounting, office technology. **Health services:** Clinical lab technology, nursing (RN), occupational therapy assistant, physical therapy assistant, respiratory therapy technology. **Liberal arts:** Arts/sciences. **Parks/recreation:** General. **Work/family studies:** General, child care service.

Most popular majors. Health sciences 87%.

Technology on campus. 45 workstations in library, computer center. Wireless network available.

Student life. Freshman orientation: Available, $30 fee. Preregistration for classes offered. **Activities:** Student government.

Student services. Adult student services, student employment services, financial aid counseling, veterans' counselor.

Contact. Phone: (603) 542-7744 Toll-free number: (800) 837-0658 Fax: (603) 543-1844
Kathleen Carlson, Associate Vice President of Student Services, River Valley Community College, One College Drive, Claremont, NH 03743-9707

White Mountains Community College
Berlin, New Hampshire
www.wmcc.edu

CB code: 3646

- Public 2-year community college
- Commuter campus in large town

General. Founded in 1966. Regionally accredited. **Enrollment:** 627 degree-seeking undergraduates. **Degrees:** 91 associate awarded. **Location:** 110 miles from Concord; 100 miles from Portland, Maine. **Calendar:** Semester, limited summer session. **Full-time faculty:** 25 total. **Part-time faculty:** 150 total.

Basis for selection. Open admission, but selective for some programs. Pre-admission exam required for nursing students; ACCUPLACER required for placement for all others. **Home schooled:** Statement describing home school structure and mission, transcript of courses and grades, state high school equivalency certificate required.

2015-2016 Annual costs. Tuition/fees: $6,510; $14,160 out-of-state. Per-credit charge: $200 in-state; $455 out-of-state. Books/supplies: $1,500. **Additional information:** New England Regional tuition: $300 per credit hour.

Financial aid. All financial aid based on need. Need-based aid available for part-time students. Work-study available nights, weekends and for part-time students.

Application procedures. Admission: No deadline. $20 fee, may be waived for applicants with need. Admission notification on a rolling basis. **Financial aid:** Priority date 5/1; no closing date. FAFSA, institutional form required. Applicants notified on a rolling basis starting 5/1; must reply within 2 week(s) of notification.

Academics. Special study options: Cooperative education, double major, dual enrollment of high school students, independent study, internships, student-designed major. Bachelor's degree programs available on campus. **Credit/placement by examination:** AP, CLEP, institutional tests. **Support services:** Learning center, reduced course load, remedial instruction, study skills assistance, tutoring.

Majors. Business: Accounting, administrative services, business admin, office management, office technology, office/clerical, restaurant/food services. **Computer sciences:** General. **Conservation:** Environmental science. **Education:** Early childhood, multi-level teacher. **Health services:** Medical assistant, nursing (RN), office admin. **Liberal arts:** Arts/sciences. **Protective services:** Law enforcement admin.

Technology on campus. 45 workstations in library, computer center. Online course registration, online library, wireless network available.

Student life. Freshman orientation: Mandatory, $30 fee. Preregistration for classes offered. **Activities:** Student government.

Student services. Adult student services, career counseling, financial aid counseling, on-campus daycare, personal counseling, veterans' counselor. **Physically disabled:** Services for visually, hearing impaired. **Transfer:** Transfer adviser for students transferring to 4-year colleges.

Contact. E-mail: wmcc@ccsnh.edu
Phone: (603) 752-1113 ext. 3000
Toll-free number: (800) 445-4525 ext. 3000 Fax: (603) 752-6335
White Mountains Community College, 2020 Riverside Drive, Berlin, NH 03570

New Jersey

Assumption College for Sisters
Denville, New Jersey
www.acs350.org   CB code: 2009

▶ Private 2-year junior and liberal arts college for women affiliated with the Roman Catholic Church
▶ Residential campus in small town
▶ Application essay required

General. Founded in 1953. Regionally accredited. **Enrollment:** 31 degree-seeking undergraduates. **Degrees:** 9 associate awarded. **Location:** 35 miles from New York City. **Calendar:** Semester, limited summer session. **Part-time faculty:** 11 total; 18% have terminal degrees, 82% women. **Class size:** 100% < 20.

Student profile. Among degree-seeking undergraduates, 11 enrolled as first-time, first-year students.

Part-time: 29%   Live on campus: 65%
Women: 97%

Basis for selection. Interview, recommendations, school achievement record, test scores, commitment to obligations of religious vocation as well as acceptance of applicant by a religious community important.

High school preparation. 16 units required. Required and recommended units include English 4, mathematics 2-3, history 2, science 2-3, foreign language 2, visual/performing arts 1 and academic electives 4.

2015-2016 Annual costs. Tuition/fees: $5,439. Per-credit charge: $165. Books/supplies: $110.

Financial aid. Need-based: Work-study available nights, weekends and for part-time students.

Application procedures. Admission: No deadline. $50 fee, may be waived for applicants with need. Admission notification on a rolling basis. **Financial aid:** No deadline.

Academics. Special study options: ESL. **Credit/placement by examination:** AP, CLEP, SAT. **Support services:** Reduced course load, remedial instruction, study skills assistance, tutoring.

Majors. Liberal arts: Arts/sciences. **Theology:** Theology.

Technology on campus. 21 workstations in library, computer center, student center. Online library, helpline, repair service, wireless network available.

Student life. Freshman orientation: Mandatory. Preregistration for classes offered. **Policies:** Religious observance required. **Housing:** Students reside with their religious congregations or with the Sisters of Christian Charity.

Student services. Transfer: Pre-admission transcript evaluation for new students. Transfer adviser for students transferring to 4-year colleges.

Contact. E-mail: academicdean@acs350.org
Phone: (973) 957-0188 ext. 106 Fax: (973) 957-0190
Sr. Mary Slattery, Academic Dean, Assumption College for Sisters, 200 A Morris Avenue, Denville, NJ 07834

Atlantic Cape Community College
Mays Landing, New Jersey   CB member
www.atlantic.edu   CB code: 2024

▶ Public 2-year culinary school and community college
▶ Commuter campus in small town

General. Founded in 1964. Regionally accredited. Instruction and student/academic support services delivered at all 3 campuses (Mays Landing, Atlantic City, Cape May). **Enrollment:** 3,675 full-time, degree-seeking students. **Degrees:** 812 associate awarded. **Location:** 15 miles from Atlantic City, 49 miles from Philadelphia. **Calendar:** Semester, limited summer session. **Full-time faculty:** 80 total. **Part-time faculty:** 374 total. **Class size:** 53% < 20, 47% 20-39, less than 1% 40-49, less than 1% 50-99. **Special facilities:** Gourmet student-run restaurant.

Transfer out. Colleges most students transferred to 2015: Richard Stockton College of New Jersey, Rowan University, Rutgers University.

Basis for selection. Open admission, but selective for some programs. Admission to allied health and nursing programs based upon entrance exam scores and GPA. ACCUPLACER exam used for placement only. All students must take college basic skills exam after completing 12th credit or when they officially matriculate. Students who score 500 SAT Verbal and 470 SAT Math exempt from basic skills testing. **Home schooled:** Students must be in certified program. Letter from certifying school district approving courses required. **Learning Disabled:** Student must self-identify.

2015-2016 Annual costs. Tuition/fees: $4,266; $5,946 out-of-district; $7,536 out-of-state. Per-credit charge: $116 in-district; $172 out-of-district; $225 out-of-state. Books/supplies: $1,900. **Additional information:** Higher tuition for culinary arts program; Installment plan available.

Financial aid. Need-based: Need-based aid available for part-time students. Work-study available nights, weekends and for part-time students.

Application procedures. Admission: No deadline. $35 fee, may be waived for applicants with need. Admission notification on a rolling basis. **Financial aid:** Priority date 5/1; no closing date. FAFSA, institutional form required. Applicants notified on a rolling basis starting 5/1.

Academics. 15 associate degrees available through distance education. **Special study options:** Cooperative education, distance learning, double major, dual enrollment of high school students, ESL, independent study, internships, liberal arts/career combination. Bachelor's degree programs available on campus. License preparation in nursing, paramedic, real estate. **Credit/placement by examination:** AP, CLEP, institutional tests. 32 credit hours maximum toward associate degree. **Support services:** GED preparation and test center, learning center, pre-admission summer program, reduced course load, remedial instruction, study skills assistance, tutoring, writing center.

Majors. Business: Accounting, administrative services, business admin, hotel/motel admin, management information systems. **Computer sciences:** Data processing, programming. **Health services:** Nursing (RN), respiratory therapy technology. **Liberal arts:** Arts/sciences. **Protective services:** Police science.

Most popular majors. Business/marketing 15%, education 6%, health sciences 12%, liberal arts 27%, psychology 6%, security/protective services 9%.

Technology on campus. 635 workstations in library, computer center, student center. Commuter students can connect to campus network. Online course registration, online library, helpline, wireless network available.

Student life. Freshman orientation: Available. Preregistration for classes offered. Online orientation available. **Activities:** Choral groups, drama, international student organizations, literary magazine, music ensembles, radio station, student government, student newspaper, human services club, African American coalition, Jewish association of students, Phi Theta Kappa, Alpha and Omega Christian clubs, Shades of Brown of Atlantic City.

Athletics. NJCAA. **Intercollegiate:** Archery, baseball M, basketball, soccer M, softball W, volleyball W. **Intramural:** Basketball, bowling, soccer, softball, volleyball. **Team name:** Buccaneers.

Student services. Adult student services, career counseling, student employment services, health services, on-campus daycare, personal counseling, placement for graduates, veterans' counselor. **Physically disabled:** Services for visually, speech, hearing impaired. **Transfer:** Pre-admission transcript evaluation for new students. Transfer adviser, college fairs on campus for students transferring to 4-year colleges.

Contact. E-mail: accadmit@atlantic.edu
Phone: (609) 343-5000 Fax: (609) 343-4921
Regina Skinner, Director, Admission and College Recruitment, Atlantic Cape Community College, 5100 Black Horse Pike, Mays Landing, NJ 08330-2699

Bergen Community College
Paramus, New Jersey
www.bergen.edu   CB code: 2032

▶ Public 2-year community college
▶ Commuter campus in large town

General. Founded in 1965. Regionally accredited. Center for Deaf Education with counselors and specialized equipment. **Enrollment:** 13,575 degree-seeking undergraduates. **Degrees:** 2,440 associate awarded. **Location:** 12 miles from New York City. **Calendar:** Semester, extensive summer session.

Transfer out. Colleges most students transferred to 2015: Montclair State University, William Paterson University, Rutgers University, Ramapo College.

Basis for selection. Open admission, but selective for some programs. Admission to allied health programs based on academic record and specific courses taken. Priority given to county residents. High school diploma not required for students over 18 years old. **Learning Disabled:** Students must provide documentation of disability to Office of Specialized Services.

High school preparation. Math, biology, chemistry required for most allied health programs.

2015-2016 Annual costs. Tuition/fees: $5,340; $9,600 out-of-district; $10,050 out-of-state. Per-credit charge: $135 in-district; $277 out-of-district; $292 out-of-state. Books/supplies: $1,400.

Financial aid. Need-based: Work-study available nights, weekends and for part-time students.

Application procedures. Admission: No deadline. No application fee. Admission notification on a rolling basis. Application closing date for nursing and dental hygiene 3/1. **Financial aid:** No deadline. FAFSA required. Applicants notified on a rolling basis starting 6/1.

Academics. Special study options: Cooperative education, distance learning, dual enrollment of high school students, ESL, honors, internships, study abroad. **Credit/placement by examination:** AP, CLEP, institutional tests. **Support services:** Learning center, pre-admission summer program, reduced course load, remedial instruction, tutoring, writing center.

Majors. Area/ethnic studies: Women's. **Biology:** General, biotechnology. **Business:** Accounting technology, administrative services, banking/financial services, hotel/motel admin, marketing, sales/distribution, special products marketing. **Communications:** Communications/speech/rhetoric, journalism. **Communications technology:** Animation/special effects, radio/TV, recording arts. **Computer sciences:** General, applications programming, computer graphics, information technology, system admin. **Conservation:** Environmental science. **Education:** General, early childhood. **Engineering:** General. **English:** English lit. **Foreign languages:** General. **Health services:** Clinical lab technology, dental hygiene, medical assistant, medical radiologic technology/radiation therapy, nursing (RN), physical therapy assistant, respiratory therapy technology, sonography, veterinary technology/assistant. **History:** General. **Liberal arts:** Arts/sciences. **Math:** General. **Philosophy/religion:** Philosophy, religion. **Physical sciences:** General, chemistry, physics. **Protective services:** Corrections, police science. **Psychology:** General. **Social sciences:** Economics, sociology. **Visual/performing arts:** General, commercial/advertising art, film/cinema/video, music, theater arts management.

Most popular majors. Health sciences 10%, liberal arts 82%.

Student life. Freshman orientation: Available. Preregistration for classes offered. **Activities:** Choral groups, dance, drama, literary magazine, music ensembles, musical theater, student government, student newspaper, TV station.

Athletics. NJCAA. **Intercollegiate:** Baseball M, basketball, cross-country, golf M, soccer M, softball W, tennis M, track and field, volleyball W, wrestling M. **Team name:** Bulldogs.

Student services. Career counseling, student employment services, financial aid counseling, health services, on-campus daycare, personal counseling, placement for graduates, veterans' counselor. **Physically disabled:** Services for visually, speech, hearing impaired. **Transfer:** Transfer adviser, college fairs on campus for students transferring to 4-year colleges.

Contact. E-mail: admissions@bergen.edu
Phone: (201) 447-7195 Fax: (201) 670-7973
Office of Enrollment Services, Bergen Community College, 400 Paramus Road, Paramus, NJ 07652-1595

Brookdale Community College
Lincroft, New Jersey
www.brookdalecc.edu

CB member
CB code: 2181

- Public 2-year community college
- Commuter campus in small city

General. Founded in 1967. Regionally accredited. **Enrollment:** 12,077 degree-seeking undergraduates. **Degrees:** 2,054 associate awarded. **ROTC:** Army, Air Force. **Location:** 5 miles from Red Bank, 25 miles from New Brunswick. **Calendar:** Semester, extensive summer session. **Full-time faculty:** 234 total; 11% minority, 57% women. **Part-time faculty:** 722 total; 11% minority, 58% women.

Student profile.

Out-of-state:	1%	25 or older:	38%

Transfer out. Colleges most students transferred to 2015: Monmouth University, Rutgers University, Kean University, Georgian Court University, and New Jersey City University.

Basis for selection. Open admission, but selective for some programs. Special requirements for culinary, dental hygiene, nursing, respiratory therapy, radiologic technology, diagnostic medical sonography, medical laboratory technology, and automotive technology. Applicants 18 or older may be admitted without high school diploma or GED. **Home schooled:** Documentation of age-appropriate learning skills.

High school preparation. One unit high school or college algebra, 1 chemistry, 1 biology required for allied health programs.

2015-2016 Annual costs. Tuition/fees: $4,567; $8,249 out-of-district; $8,999 out-of-state. Per-credit charge: $123 in-district; $246 out-of-district; $271 out-of-state. Books/supplies: $1,200. Personal expenses: $4,370.

Financial aid. Need-based: Need-based aid available for part-time students. Work-study available nights, weekends and for part-time students. **Non-need-based:** Scholarships awarded for academics, athletics.

Application procedures. Admission: No deadline. $25 fee. Admission notification on a rolling basis. **Financial aid:** Priority date 5/1; no closing date. FAFSA, institutional form required. Applicants notified on a rolling basis starting 5/1; must reply within 2 week(s) of notification.

Academics. Special study options: Cooperative education, distance learning, dual enrollment of high school students, ESL, honors, independent study, internships, study abroad. License preparation in dental hygiene, nursing, radiology. **Credit/placement by examination:** AP, CLEP, institutional tests. **Support services:** GED preparation and test center, reduced course load, remedial instruction, tutoring, writing center.

Majors. Architecture: Architecture. **Business:** General, accounting technology, business admin, fashion, marketing. **Communications technology:** Animation/special effects, radio/TV. **Computer sciences:** General, system admin. **Education:** General, teacher assistance. **Engineering:** General. **General:** Lineworker. **Health services:** Clinical lab technology, dental hygiene, health information technology, medical radiologic technology/radiation therapy, nursing (RN), respiratory therapy technology, sonography. **Human services:** Social work. **Liberal arts:** Arts/sciences. **Protective services:** Police science. **Social sciences:** General. **Visual/performing arts:** Graphic design, interior design, music technology, studio arts.

Most popular majors. Business/marketing 22%, education 11%, health sciences 10%, interdisciplinary studies 6%, liberal arts 15%, security/protective services 9%, social sciences 14%.

Technology on campus. 1,100 workstations in library, computer center. Commuter students can connect to campus network. Helpline, wireless network available.

Student life. Freshman orientation: Available. Preregistration for classes offered. **Activities:** Dance, drama, film society, international student organizations, literary magazine, musical theater, radio station, student government, student newspaper, TV station.

Athletics. NJCAA. **Intercollegiate:** Baseball M, basketball, cross-country, soccer, softball W, tennis. **Intramural:** Basketball, golf M, volleyball. **Team name:** Jersey Blues.

Student services. Career counseling, student employment services, financial aid counseling, health services, on-campus daycare, personal counseling, placement for graduates, veterans' counselor. **Physically disabled:** Services for visually, speech, hearing impaired. **Transfer:** Transfer adviser for students transferring to 4-year colleges.

Contact. E-mail: recruitment@brookdalecc.edu
Phone: (732) 224-2375 Fax: (732) 224-2271
Kim Heuser, Registrar, Brookdale Community College, 765 Newman Springs Road, Lincroft, NJ 07738

Two-Year Colleges

Camden County College
Blackwood, New Jersey
www.camdencc.edu

CB code: 2121

- Public 2-year community college
- Commuter campus in large town

General. Founded in 1966. Regionally accredited. Additional campus locations in Camden and Cherry Hill. **Enrollment:** 10,284 degree-seeking undergraduates; 979 non-degree-seeking students. **Degrees:** 1,354 associate awarded. **Location:** 15 miles from Philadelphia, 13 miles from Camden. **Calendar:** Semester, extensive summer session. **Full-time faculty:** 135 total. **Part-time faculty:** 662 total. **Special facilities:** Integrated manufacturing building, laser technology institute for education and research, computer graphics laboratories.

Student profile. Among degree-seeking undergraduates, 2,073 enrolled as first-time, first-year students.

Part-time:	47%	Women:	58%
Out-of-state:	1%	25 or older:	39%

Transfer out. Colleges most students transferred to 2015: Rowan University, Rutgers University-Camden, Temple University, Widener University.

Basis for selection. Open admission, but selective for some programs. Special requirements for allied health, dental, and nursing programs. Interview recommended for various health programs and the General Motors programs.

2016-2017 Annual costs. Tuition/fees (projected): $4,320; $4,440 out-of-district; $4,440 out-of-state. Per-credit charge: $107 in-district; $111 out-of-district; $111 out-of-state.

Financial aid. Need-based: Need-based aid available for part-time students. Work-study available nights, weekends and for part-time students. **Non-need-based:** Scholarships awarded for academics, state residency.

Application procedures. Admission: No deadline. No application fee. Admission notification on a rolling basis beginning on or about 2/3. **Financial aid:** Priority date 5/1; no closing date. FAFSA, institutional form required. Applicants notified on a rolling basis starting 7/1.

Academics. Strong program in robotics, laser/electro optics technology, and computer graphics. **Special study options:** Cooperative education, cross-registration, distance learning, double major, dual enrollment of high school students, ESL, honors, independent study, internships, liberal arts/career combination, weekend college. General Motors automotive service education program. Bachelor's degree programs available on campus. License preparation in dental hygiene, nursing, paramedic, real estate. **Credit/placement by examination:** AP, CLEP, institutional tests. 30 credit hours maximum toward associate degree. New Jersey College Basic Skills placement test required. **Support services:** GED preparation and test center, learning center, pre-admission summer program, reduced course load, remedial instruction, study skills assistance, tutoring.

Majors. Business: Accounting, banking/financial services, business admin, management information systems, marketing, sales/distribution. **Computer sciences:** General, computer graphics. **Engineering:** Engineering science. **Foreign languages:** Sign language interpretation. **Health services:** Clinical lab technology, dental assistant, dental hygiene, nursing (RN), optician, respiratory therapy technology, veterinary technology/assistant. **Human services:** Social work. **Liberal arts:** Arts/sciences. **Protective services:** Fire safety technology, police science. **Visual/performing arts:** Photography.

Technology on campus. 800 workstations in library, computer center. Online course registration, online library, wireless network available.

Student life. Freshman orientation: Available. Preregistration for classes offered. **Activities:** Concert band, choral groups, dance, drama, international student organizations, literary magazine, music ensembles, radio station, student government, student newspaper.

Athletics. NJCAA. **Intercollegiate:** Baseball M, basketball, soccer, softball W. **Team name:** Cougars.

Student services. Career counseling, student employment services, financial aid counseling, health services, on-campus daycare, placement for graduates, veterans' counselor. **Physically disabled:** Services for visually, speech, hearing impaired. **Transfer:** Re-entry adviser, pre-admission transcript evaluation for new students. Transfer center, transfer adviser, college fairs on campus for students transferring to 4-year colleges.

Contact. E-mail: admissions@camdencc.edu
Phone: (856) 227-7200 ext. 4200 Toll-free number: (888) 228-2466
Fax: (856) 374-4917
James Canonica, Executive Dean, Enrollment and Student Services, Camden County College, Box 200, Blackwood, NJ 08012

County College of Morris
Randolph, New Jersey
www.ccm.edu

CB member
CB code: 2124

- Public 2-year community college
- Commuter campus in large town

General. Founded in 1965. Regionally accredited. Courses available at off-campus sites. **Enrollment:** 7,170 degree-seeking undergraduates. **Degrees:** 1,176 associate awarded. **Location:** 40 miles from New York City. **Calendar:** Semester, extensive summer session. **Full-time faculty:** 157 total. **Part-time faculty:** 370 total. **Special facilities:** Planetarium.

Transfer out. Colleges most students transferred to 2015: Montclair State University, William Paterson University of New Jersey, Rutgers University, Kean University, Fairleigh Dickinson University, New Jersey Institute of Technology.

Basis for selection. Open admission, but selective for some programs. Restricted admissions to nursing, medical lab technology, radiography, respiratory therapy, and veterinary technology on space-available basis. SAT required for honors programs. Students who submit 500 SAT section scores are exempt from basic skills placement test. Audition required for music programs. **Learning Disabled:** Students may apply to Horizons program if they want accommodations.

High school preparation. 16 units recommended. Some programs require 2 to 4 units math and 1 to 2 units laboratory science.

2015-2016 Annual costs. Tuition/fees: $4,570; $8,200 out-of-district; $11,290 out-of-state. Per-credit charge: $121 in-district; $242 out-of-district; $345 out-of-state. Books/supplies: $1,400. Personal expenses: $1,220.

Financial aid. Need-based: Need-based aid available for part-time students. Work-study available nights, weekends and for part-time students. **Non-need-based:** Scholarships awarded for athletics.

Application procedures. Admission: No deadline. $30 fee. Admission notification on a rolling basis. **Financial aid:** Priority date 3/1; no closing date. FAFSA required. Applicants notified on a rolling basis starting 5/1.

Academics. Special study options: Accelerated study, cooperative education, distance learning, double major, dual enrollment of high school students, ESL, exchange student, external degree, honors, independent study, internships, liberal arts/career combination, study abroad, teacher certification program, weekend college. License preparation in aviation, nursing, radiology. **Credit/placement by examination:** AP, CLEP, institutional tests. **Support services:** GED preparation, learning center, pre-admission summer program, reduced course load, remedial instruction, study skills assistance, tutoring, writing center.

Majors. Business: Business admin, management information systems. **Communications:** Journalism. **Communications technology:** General. **Computer sciences:** General. **Education:** Biology, chemistry, drama/dance, early childhood, French, German, history, physics, Spanish. **Engineering:** Engineering science. **Health services:** Clinical lab technology, nursing (RN), respiratory therapy technology. **Human services:** General. **Liberal arts:** Arts/sciences. **Math:** General. **Parks/recreation:** Health/fitness. **Protective services:** Police science. **Social sciences:** General. **Visual/performing arts:** General.

Technology on campus. 650 workstations in library, computer center. Commuter students can connect to campus network. Online course registration, online library, helpline, wireless network available.

Student life. Freshman orientation: Available. Preregistration for classes offered. Half-day sessions held 1 week prior to start of academic year. **Activities:** Bands, campus ministries, choral groups, dance, drama, international student organizations, literary magazine, music ensembles, musical theater, radio station, student government, student newspaper, symphony orchestra, Phi Theta Kappa, United Latino organization, student ambassadors, black student union, Asian students association, Jewish students association, Christian Fellowship, IEEE, Muslim student club, Alpha Beta Gamma.

Athletics. NJCAA. **Intercollegiate:** Baseball M, basketball, golf, lacrosse, soccer, softball W, volleyball W. **Intramural:** Badminton, basketball, bowling, soccer, table tennis, tennis, volleyball. **Team name:** Titans.

Student services. Adult student services, alcohol/substance abuse counseling, career counseling, services for economically disadvantaged, student employment services, financial aid counseling, health services, minority student services, on-campus daycare, personal counseling, placement for graduates, veterans' counselor, women's services. **Physically disabled:** Services for visually, hearing impaired. **Transfer:** Pre-admission transcript evaluation for new students. Transfer adviser, college fairs on campus for students transferring to 4-year colleges.

Contact. E-mail: admiss@ccm.edu
Phone: (973) 328-5100 Fax: (973) 328-5199
Eugene Soltys, Director of Admissions, County College of Morris, 214 Center Grove Road, Randolph, NJ 07869-2086

Cumberland County College
Vineland, New Jersey   CB member
www.cccnj.edu   CB code: 2118

- Public 2-year community college
- Commuter campus in small city

General. Founded in 1963. Regionally accredited. **Enrollment:** 3,453 degree-seeking undergraduates. **Degrees:** 573 associate awarded. **Location:** 35 miles from Philadelphia. **Calendar:** Semester, extensive summer session. **Full-time faculty:** 46 total. **Part-time faculty:** 250 total. **Special facilities:** Fine and performing arts center, conference center.

Transfer out. Colleges most students transferred to 2015: Rowan University, Stockton State College, Rutgers University, University of Delaware.

Basis for selection. Open admission, but selective for some programs. Special requirements for nursing program; ATI TEAS-V and radiography; HOAE.

High school preparation. College-preparatory program recommended.

2015-2016 Annual costs. Tuition/fees: $4,290; $6,540 out-of-district; $14,460 out-of-state. Per-credit charge: $113 in-district; $188 out-of-district; $452 out-of-state. Books/supplies: $1,920. Personal expenses: $2,248. **Additional information:** In-state, out-of-district students will be charged $123 per-credit-hour with appropriate chargeback documentation.

Financial aid. Need-based: Need-based aid available for part-time students. Work-study available nights, weekends and for part-time students. **Non-need-based:** Scholarships awarded for academics.

Application procedures. Admission: No deadline. No application fee. Admission notification on a rolling basis. **Financial aid:** No deadline. FAFSA required. Applicants notified on a rolling basis; must reply within 3 week(s) of notification.

Academics. Special study options: Accelerated study, distance learning, double major, dual enrollment of high school students, ESL, honors, independent study. Project Assist for students with learning disabilities. Bachelor's degree programs available on campus. License preparation in nursing, radiology, real estate. **Credit/placement by examination:** AP, CLEP, institutional tests. 32 credit hours maximum toward associate degree. **Support services:** GED preparation, learning center, pre-admission summer program, reduced course load, remedial instruction, study skills assistance, tutoring, writing center.

Majors. Biology: Biomedical sciences. **Business:** Accounting, administrative services, business admin, hospitality/recreation, management information systems, marketing, office management, operations, tourism/travel. **Communications:** Journalism, radio/TV. **Computer sciences:** General, computer science, information technology, LAN/WAN management, networking, vendor certification. **Education:** Art, early childhood, multi-level teacher. **Engineering:** General. **English:** English lit. **Foreign languages:** General. **General:** Site management. **Health services:** Health information management, medical radiologic technology/radiation therapy, nursing (RN), respiratory therapy assistant. **History:** General. **Human services:** General, social work. **Liberal arts:** Arts/sciences, humanities. **Math:** General. **Protective services:** Corrections, criminal justice, forensics, homeland security, police science. **Social sciences:** General. **Visual/performing arts:** Acting, art, ceramics, cinematography, commercial/advertising art, dramatic, graphic design, music, studio arts.

Technology on campus. 400 workstations in library, computer center, student center. Commuter students can connect to campus network. Online course registration, online library, helpline, wireless network available.

Student life. Freshman orientation: Mandatory. Preregistration for classes offered. **Policies:** Comprehensive support center for learning disabled students. **Activities:** Choral groups, drama, literary magazine, musical theater, student government, student newspaper, symphony orchestra, multicultural club, Latin American club, African American club.

Athletics. NJCAA. **Intercollegiate:** Baseball M, basketball, cross-country, soccer, softball W, track and field. **Intramural:** Cross-country. **Team name:** Dukes, Lady Dukes.

Student services. Adult student services, career counseling, services for economically disadvantaged, student employment services, financial aid counseling, personal counseling, placement for graduates, veterans' counselor. **Physically disabled:** Services for visually, speech, hearing impaired. **Transfer:** Pre-admission transcript evaluation for new students. Transfer adviser, college fairs on campus for students transferring to 4-year colleges.

Contact. Phone: (856) 691-8986 Fax: (856) 691-6157
Anne Daly-Eimer, Senior Director, Admissions and Registration, Cumberland County College, PO Box 1500, Vineland, NJ 08362-9912

Eastern International College
Jersey City, New Jersey
www.eicollege.edu   CB code: 7930

- For-profit 2-year health science and nursing college
- Commuter campus in very large city

General. Regionally accredited. **Enrollment:** 433 degree-seeking undergraduates. **Degrees:** 110 associate awarded. **Calendar:** Semester. **Full-time faculty:** 6 total; 83% have terminal degrees, 50% minority, 50% women. **Part-time faculty:** 12 total; 83% have terminal degrees, 50% minority, 50% women.

Student profile. Among degree-seeking undergraduates, 100% enrolled in a vocational program, 6% already have a bachelor's degree or higher, 153 enrolled as first-time, first-year students.

Part-time: 26% **Women:**   91%

Basis for selection. Open admission.

2015-2016 Annual costs. Books/supplies: $2,000. Personal expenses: $651. **Additional information:** Associate degree programs annual tuition: Nursing $15,100, lab and supply fees $2,000; Dental Hygiene $17,100, lab and supply fees $3,000; Diagnostic Medical Sonography $15,100, lab and supply fees $400; Medical Assistant $9,500, lab and supply fees $400; Cardiovascular Technology $13,600, lab and supply fees $400. Bachelor degree annual tuition: Diagnostic Medical Sonography $15,100, lab and supply fees $600. Registration fee $100.

2014-2015 Financial aid. Need-based: 156 full-time freshmen applied for aid; 119 deemed to have need; 119 received aid. Average need met was 89%. Average scholarship/grant was $17,811; average loan $5,250. 63% of total undergraduate aid awarded as scholarships/grants, 37% as loans/jobs. Need-based aid available for part-time students. Work-study available nights, weekends and for part-time students. **Non-need-based:** Scholarships awarded for academics.

Application procedures. Admission: No deadline. $125 fee. **Financial aid:** Closing date 6/1. FAFSA required. Applicants notified on a rolling basis; must reply within 2 week(s) of notification.

Academics. Credit/placement by examination: AP, CLEP.

Majors. Health services: Cardiovascular technology, dental hygiene, medical assistant, nursing (RN), sonography.

Contact. E-mail: admissions@eicollege.edu
Phone: (201) 216-9901 Fax: (201) 216-9225
Ruth Zayas, Director of Admissions, Eastern International College, 684 Newark Avenue, Jersey City, NJ 07306

Eastwick College
Ramsey, New Jersey
www.eastwick.edu   CB code: 5829

- For-profit 2-year nursing college
- Commuter campus in large town

General. Regionally accredited; also accredited by ACICS. **Enrollment:** 865 undergraduates. **Degrees:** 346 associate awarded. **Calendar:** Differs by program. **Full-time faculty:** 75 total. **Part-time faculty:** 75 total.

Basis for selection. Open admission.

2015-2016 Annual costs. Total program costs for associate degrees: Diagnostic Cardiovascular Sonography $35,970, books and supplies $2,950; Health Science $28,320, books and supplies $2,700; Health Information Technology $28,320, books and supplies $2,950; Occupational Therapy Assistant $30,625, books and supplies $2,550; Surgical Technology $32,125, books and supplies $1,950; AAS in Nursing (LPN-to-RN Bridge program)

$32,995, books and supplies $1,900. Total program costs for certificates/diplomas: Licensed Practical Nursing $28,325, books and supplies $1,800; Medical Assisting $16,150, books and supplies $1,500.

Financial aid. Need-based: Work-study available nights, weekends and for part-time students.

Application procedures. Admission: No deadline. $100 fee. **Financial aid:** No deadline.

Academics. Special study options: Accelerated study, cooperative education. License preparation in nursing, occupational therapy, physical therapy, real estate. **Credit/placement by examination:** AP, CLEP. **Support services:** GED preparation and test center.

Majors. Health services: Health information technology, nursing (RN), sonography.

Contact. E-mail: admissions2@eastwick.edu
Phone: (201) 327-8877
Ruth Zayas, Director of Admissions, Eastwick College, 10 South Franklin Turnpike, Ramsey, NJ 07446

Eastwick College: Hackensack
Hackensack, New Jersey
www.eastwickcollege.edu   CB code: 7463

▶ For-profit 2-year school of mortuary science and career college
▶ Very large city

General. Regionally accredited; also accredited by ACICS. Diploma programs available in Bilingual Licensed Practical Nursing, Licensed Practical Nursing, and Medical Assisting. **Enrollment:** 324 degree-seeking undergraduates. **Degrees:** 40 associate awarded. **Calendar:** Quarter. **Full-time faculty:** 17 total. **Part-time faculty:** 27 total.

Basis for selection. Students interview with admission staff, submit proof of high school completion or GED equivalency, and take an admission examination. The vice president for admissions reviews all information to make admission determination.

2015-2016 Annual costs. Books/supplies: $1,147. **Additional information:** Total program costs for associate degrees: Health Science $28,320, books and supplies $2,700; Health Information Technology $28,320, books and supplies $2,950; Business and Entrepreneurship $27,115, books and supplies $3,000; Mortuary Science $37,255, books and supplies $2,700. Total program costs for certificates/diplomas: Bilingual Licensed Practical Nursing $36,740, books and supplies $2,000; Licensed Practical Nursing $28,325, books and supplies $1,800; Medical Assisting $16,150, books and supplies $1,500; Medical Assisting with Patient Care Technician $16,150, books and supplies $1,500; Medical Billing and Coding $15,735, books and supplies $1,950; Business Administration with Computerized Accounting/Bookkeeping $13,740, books and supplies $1,900; Computer Concepts and Applications $3,675, books and supplies $350.

Financial aid. Need-based: Work-study available nights, weekends and for part-time students.

Application procedures. Admission: No deadline. $25 fee.

Academics. Credit/placement by examination: AP.

Majors. Business: Entrepreneurial studies.

Contact. E-mail: rzayas@eastwick.edu
Phone: (201) 488-9400
Ruth Zayas, Director of Admissions, Eastwick College: Hackensack, 250 Moore Street, Hackensack, NJ 07601

Essex County College
Newark, New Jersey
www.essex.edu   CB code: 2237

▶ Public 2-year community college
▶ Commuter campus in large city

General. Founded in 1966. Regionally accredited. Classes also held at West Caldwell campus and several locations in Essex County and Newark. **Enrollment:** 9,828 degree-seeking undergraduates; 1,126 non-degree-seeking students. **Degrees:** 1,316 associate awarded. **Location:** 12 miles

from New York City. **Calendar:** Semester, limited summer session. **Full-time faculty:** 115 total; 59% minority, 49% women. **Part-time faculty:** 608 total. **Class size:** 28% < 20, 72% 20-39, less than 1% 40-49, less than 1% 50-99, less than 1% >100. **Special facilities:** Public safety academy, Africana institute, urban issues institute.

Student profile. Among degree-seeking undergraduates, 86% enrolled in a transfer program, 14% enrolled in a vocational program, 1% already have a bachelor's degree or higher, 2,276 enrolled as first-time, first-year students, 318 transferred in from other institutions.

Part-time:	45%	Hispanic/Latino:	25%
Out-of-state:	1%	Multi-racial, non-Hispanic:	1%
Women:	59%	International:	8%
African American:	50%	25 or older:	39%
Asian American:	3%		

Transfer out. 53% of students enrolled in the transfer program go on to 4-year colleges. **Colleges most students transferred to 2015:** Rutgers University at Newark, Montclair University, Kean University, New Jersey Institute of Technology, New Jersey City University.

Basis for selection. Open admission, but selective for some programs. Special requirements for allied health programs. National League for Nursing test required of nursing students. Priority given to allied health program applications received by 4/15. Interview recommended for nursing, ophthalmic science, physical therapy programs. **Adult students:** Companion Placement Test required.

2015-2016 Annual costs. Tuition/fees: $4,680; $8,175 out-of-district; $8,175 out-of-state. Per-credit charge: $116.5 in-district; $233 out-of-district; $233 out-of-state. Books/supplies: $2,400. Personal expenses: $1,860.

Financial aid. Need-based: Need-based aid available for part-time students. Work-study available nights, weekends and for part-time students.

Application procedures. Admission: No deadline. $25 fee, may be waived for applicants with need. Admission notification on a rolling basis. **Financial aid:** Priority date 6/30; no closing date. FAFSA, institutional form required. Applicants notified on a rolling basis starting 6/15; must reply within 3 week(s) of notification.

Academics. Special study options: Cooperative education, cross-registration, distance learning, double major, dual enrollment of high school students, ESL, honors, independent study, internships, study abroad, teacher certification program, weekend college. Cross-registration with other institutions in Council of Higher Education in Newark; civil construction engineering program with New Jersey Institute of Technology; criminal justice program with Rutgers: State University of New Jersey. License preparation in nursing, physical therapy, radiology. **Credit/placement by examination:** AP, CLEP, institutional tests. 30 credit hours maximum toward associate degree. Maximum credits accepted must be 30 credits less than number required for degree in residence; may not include more than half credits required in major field. **Support services:** GED preparation and test center, learning center, reduced course load, remedial instruction, study skills assistance, tutoring, writing center.

Majors. Biology: General. **Business:** Accounting, accounting technology, administrative services, business admin, hospitality admin, office technology, tourism/travel. **Communications:** Journalism, media studies. **Computer sciences:** General, programming. **Education:** General, elementary, kindergarten/preschool, music, physical, secondary. **Engineering:** General, civil, electrical. **Health services:** Dental hygiene, EMT paramedic, health care admin, medical radiologic technology/radiation therapy, medical secretary, nursing (RN), optician, physical therapy assistant, premedicine, respiratory therapy technology. **Human services:** Social work. **Liberal arts:** Arts/sciences. **Math:** General. **Physical sciences:** Chemistry. **Protective services:** Criminal justice, firefighting, law enforcement admin, police science. **Social sciences:** General. **Visual/performing arts:** Art, commercial/advertising art, dramatic, music, studio arts, theater design.

Most popular majors. Business/marketing 16%, education 10%, engineering/engineering technologies 6%, health sciences 29%, liberal arts 9%, security/protective services 6%, social sciences 10%.

Technology on campus. 870 workstations in library, computer center. Commuter students can connect to campus network. Online course registration available.

Student life. Freshman orientation: Available. Preregistration for classes offered. **Activities:** Choral groups, drama, music ensembles, musical theater, student government, student newspaper, French club, Islamic student organization, Latin student union, Distributive Education Club of America, criminal justice organization, black student association, social science club, fashion entertainment board, Phi Theta Kappa.

Athletics. NJCAA. **Intercollegiate:** Basketball, soccer M, track and field. **Intramural:** Basketball, table tennis, volleyball. **Team name:** Wolverines.

Student services. Alcohol/substance abuse counseling, career counseling, student employment services, financial aid counseling, on-campus daycare, personal counseling, placement for graduates, veterans' counselor, women's services. **Physically disabled:** Services for visually, speech, hearing impaired. **Transfer:** Transfer center, transfer adviser, college fairs on campus for students transferring to 4-year colleges.

Contact. Phone: (973) 877-3100
Marva Mack, Associate Dean of Retention & Academic Advisement, Essex County College, 303 University Avenue, Newark, NJ 07102

Hudson County Community College
Jersey City, New Jersey
www.hccc.edu
CB code: 2291

- Public 2-year community college
- Commuter campus in small city

General. Founded in 1974. Regionally accredited. HACU Hispanic-serving institution. **Enrollment:** 8,510 degree-seeking undergraduates; 541 non-degree-seeking students. **Degrees:** 952 associate awarded. **Location:** 10 miles from New York City. **Calendar:** Semester, limited summer session. **Full-time faculty:** 92 total. **Part-time faculty:** 409 total. **Special facilities:** Culinary arts classroom, conference center.

Student profile. Among degree-seeking undergraduates, 2,283 enrolled as first-time, first-year students, 396 transferred in from other institutions.

Part-time:	31%	Hispanic/Latino:	57%
Women:	58%	Native Hawaiian/Pacific islander:	1%
African American:	13%	Multi-racial, non-Hispanic:	2%
Asian American:	7%		

Transfer out. Colleges most students transferred to 2015: New Jersey City University, St. Peter's College.

Basis for selection. Open admission, but selective for some programs. High school diploma required if applicant is less than 18 years of age. Special requirements for nursing, paramedic science, respiratory care, and health science programs.

2015-2016 Annual costs. Tuition/fees: $5,083; $8,743 out-of-district; $12,403 out-of-state. Per-credit charge: $122 in-district; $244 out-of-district; $366 out-of-state. Books/supplies: $1,500. Personal expenses: $1,500.

2014-2015 Financial aid. All financial aid based on need. 2,580 full-time freshmen applied for aid; 2,580 deemed to have need; 2,099 received aid. Average need met was 36%. Average scholarship/grant was $4,968; average loan $2,745. 85% of total undergraduate aid awarded as scholarships/grants, 15% as loans/jobs. Need-based aid available for part-time students. Work-study available nights, weekends and for part-time students.

Application procedures. Admission: No deadline. $25 fee, may be waived for applicants with need. Admission notification on a rolling basis. **Financial aid:** Priority date 7/15; no closing date. FAFSA required. Applicants notified on a rolling basis starting 6/1; must reply within 1 week(s) of notification.

Academics. Students may earn second degree by completing 24 additional credits, including all requirements for second major. **Special study options:** Cross-registration, distance learning, dual enrollment of high school students, ESL, honors, independent study, internships, liberal arts/career combination, teacher certification program, weekend college. License preparation in nursing, occupational therapy, paramedic. **Credit/placement by examination:** AP, CLEP, IB, institutional tests. 12 credit hours maximum toward associate degree. **Support services:** Pre-admission summer program, reduced course load, remedial instruction, study skills assistance, tutoring, writing center.

Majors. Biology: General. **Business:** Accounting, administrative services, business admin, hospitality admin, management information systems. **Computer sciences:** Computer science, data processing. **Conservation:** Environmental studies. **Education:** Early childhood. **Engineering:** Engineering science. **Health services:** Health information technology, medical assistant, nursing (RN), respiratory therapy technology. **History:** General. **Liberal arts:** Arts/sciences. **Math:** General. **Physical sciences:** Chemistry. **Protective services:** Criminal justice. **Psychology:** General. **Social sciences:** Sociology. **Visual/performing arts:** Studio arts. **Work/family studies:** Child care management.

Most popular majors. Business/marketing 9%, health sciences 12%, interdisciplinary studies 7%, liberal arts 56%, personal/culinary services 7%.

Technology on campus. 645 workstations in library, computer center. Commuter students can connect to campus network. Online library, wireless network available.

Student life. Freshman orientation: Mandatory. Preregistration for classes offered. **Activities:** Drama, film society, international student organizations, literary magazine, student government, student newspaper, South Asian society, black history and art society, law club, French club, Hispanos Unidos para el Progreso, women's awareness organization, hospitality club, health information and technology club, medical assisting club.

Student services. Adult student services, career counseling, student employment services, financial aid counseling, personal counseling, placement for graduates, veterans' counselor. **Physically disabled:** Services for visually, speech, hearing impaired. **Transfer:** Pre-admission transcript evaluation for new students. Transfer center, transfer adviser, college fairs on campus for students transferring to 4-year colleges.

Contact. E-mail: admissions@hccc.edu
Phone: (201) 714-7200 Fax: (201) 714-2136
Peter Vida, Director of Admissions, Hudson County Community College, 70 Sip Avenue, 1st Floor, Jersey City, NJ 07306

Mercer County Community College
Trenton, New Jersey
www.mccc.edu
CB member
CB code: 2444

- Public 2-year community college
- Commuter campus in small city

General. Founded in 1966. Regionally accredited. Courses also available at downtown Trenton location. External degree program for military service members. **Enrollment:** 7,012 degree-seeking undergraduates; 967 non-degree-seeking students. **Degrees:** 861 associate awarded. **Location:** 35 miles from Philadelphia, 60 miles from New York City. **Calendar:** Semester, extensive summer session. **Full-time faculty:** 124 total. **Part-time faculty:** 520 total. **Class size:** 48% < 20, 50% 20-39, less than 1% 40-49, less than 1% 50-99. **Special facilities:** CAD laboratory, computer graphics laboratory, greenhouse complex, mortuary science lab.

Student profile. Among degree-seeking undergraduates, 1,748 enrolled as first-time, first-year students.

Part-time:	57%	Women:	51%
Out-of-state:	2%	25 or older:	29%

Transfer out. Colleges most students transferred to 2015: College of New Jersey, Rider University, Rutgers University, Rowan University, Thomas Edison State College.

Basis for selection. Open admission. Applicants without high school diploma or GED must be 18 or older and have completed the New Jersey Basic Skills Placement Examination. Interview required for nursing and funeral service programs; recommended for all others. **Home schooled:** State high school equivalency certificate required.

2015-2016 Annual costs. Tuition/fees: $4,610; $6,035 out-of-district; $8,675 out-of-state. Per-credit charge: $118.5 in-district; $166 out-of-district; $254 out-of-state. Books/supplies: $1,320. Personal expenses: $2,232.

Financial aid. Need-based: Need-based aid available for part-time students. Work-study available nights, weekends and for part-time students. **Non-need-based:** Scholarships awarded for academics, athletics, state residency.

Application procedures. Admission: No deadline. No application fee. Admission notification on a rolling basis. **Financial aid:** Closing date 5/1. FAFSA required. Applicants notified on a rolling basis.

Academics. Cross-registration with area hospitals for nursing. **Special study options:** Cooperative education, cross-registration, distance learning, double major, dual enrollment of high school students, ESL, external degree, independent study, internships, liberal arts/career combination, weekend college. Bachelor's degree programs available on campus. License preparation in aviation, nursing, occupational therapy, physical therapy, radiology. **Credit/placement by examination:** AP, CLEP, institutional tests. 45 credit hours maximum toward associate degree. **Support services:** GED preparation and test center, learning center, pre-admission summer program, reduced course load, remedial instruction, study skills assistance, tutoring, writing center.

Majors. Biology: General. **Business:** General, accounting, administrative services, business admin, hotel/motel admin, management information systems, restaurant/food services. **Communications technology:** Radio/TV. **Computer sciences:** Networking, programming. **Health services:** Clinical lab technology, medical radiologic technology/radiation therapy, nursing (RN), physical therapy assistant, respiratory therapy technology. **Liberal arts:** Arts/sciences. **Math:** General. **Parks/recreation:** Exercise sciences. **Protective services:** Fire safety technology, police science. **Visual/performing arts:** General, commercial/advertising art.

Most popular majors. Business/marketing 18%, health sciences 22%, liberal arts 29%, security/protective services 8%, visual/performing arts 7%.

Technology on campus. 1,100 workstations in library, computer center. Commuter students can connect to campus network. Online course registration, online library, helpline, wireless network available.

Student life. Freshman orientation: Available. Preregistration for classes offered. **Activities:** Bands, choral groups, dance, drama, international student organizations, literary magazine, music ensembles, musical theater, radio station, student government, student newspaper, TV station, Christian Fellowship, bilingual club, African-American student organization, Fuerza Latina, ecology club, educational opportunity fund club, gay/straight alliance.

Athletics. NJCAA. **Intercollegiate:** Baseball M, basketball, soccer, softball W, tennis, track and field. **Intramural:** Basketball, softball, volleyball. **Team name:** Vikings.

Student services. Adult student services, career counseling, services for economically disadvantaged, student employment services, financial aid counseling, minority student services, personal counseling, placement for graduates, veterans' counselor. **Physically disabled:** Services for visually, speech, hearing impaired. **Transfer:** Transfer center, transfer adviser, college fairs on campus for students transferring to 4-year colleges.

Contact. E-mail: admiss@mccc.edu
Phone: (609) 570-3795 Fax: (609) 570-3861
Savita Bambhrolia, Director of Admissions, Mercer County Community College, PO Box B, Trenton, NJ 08690-1099

Middlesex County College
Edison, New Jersey
www.middlesexcc.edu

CB member
CB code: 2441

- Public 2-year community college
- Commuter campus in small city

General. Founded in 1964. Regionally accredited. **Enrollment:** 10,675 degree-seeking undergraduates. **Degrees:** 1,560 associate awarded. **ROTC:** Army. **Location:** 5 miles from New Brunswick, 30 miles from New York City. **Calendar:** Semester, extensive summer session. **Special facilities:** Ecological walking path, performing arts center, child care center.

Student profile. Among degree-seeking undergraduates, 373 transferred in from other institutions.

Transfer out. Colleges most students transferred to 2015: Rutgers State University, New Jersey Institute of Technology, Montclair State University, Kean University, Farleigh Dickinson University.

Basis for selection. Open admission, but selective for some programs. Special requirements for dental hygiene, nursing, radiography, respiratory care, psychosocial rehabilitation and treatment, medical laboratory technology, automotive technology programs. **Learning Disabled:** Must submit separate application to Project Connections Office to be eligible for learning disabilities program.

High school preparation. Recommended units include English 4, mathematics 3, social studies 2, history 2, science 3 (laboratory 3) and foreign language 2. Math and science units required for some programs.

2015-2016 Annual costs. Tuition/fees: $4,301; $8,516 out-of-state. Per-credit charge: $106 in-state; $212 out-of-state.

Financial aid. Need-based: Need-based aid available for part-time students. Work-study available nights, weekends and for part-time students.

Application procedures. Admission: Priority date 8/1; no deadline. $25 fee, may be waived for applicants with need. Admission notification on a rolling basis. **Financial aid:** Priority date 4/1; no closing date. FAFSA, institutional form required. Applicants notified on a rolling basis starting 5/4.

Academics. Special study options: Cooperative education, cross-registration, distance learning, double major, dual enrollment of high school students, ESL, independent study, internships, study abroad. License preparation in dental hygiene, nursing. **Credit/placement by examination:** AP, CLEP, institutional tests. 45 credit hours maximum toward associate degree. **Support services:** Learning center, pre-admission summer program, reduced course load, remedial instruction, tutoring, writing center.

Majors. Business: Accounting, business admin, fashion, office management. **Communications:** Communications/speech/rhetoric, journalism. **Computer sciences:** General, computer graphics, programming. **Education:** General, teacher assistance. **Engineering:** Civil, engineering science. **Health**

services: Clinical lab technology, dental hygiene, nursing (RN), pharmacy assistant, respiratory therapy technology. **Parks/recreation:** Health/fitness. **Physical sciences:** Chemistry, physics. **Protective services:** Corrections, firefighting, law enforcement admin. **Social sciences:** Political science, sociology. **Visual/performing arts:** Commercial photography, commercial/advertising art, dance, dramatic, music performance, studio arts.

Technology on campus. 1,921 workstations in library, computer center. Commuter students can connect to campus network. Online library, helpline, wireless network available.

Student life. Freshman orientation: Available. Preregistration for classes offered. One-day program scheduled 1 week prior to start of classes. **Activities:** Jazz band, choral groups, dance, drama, literary magazine, music ensembles, musical theater, radio station, student government, student newspaper, Third World student association, Hispanic club, foreign student association.

Athletics. NJCAA. **Intercollegiate:** Baseball M, basketball, cross-country, golf, soccer, softball W, track and field, wrestling M. **Team name:** Blue Colts.

Student services. Alcohol/substance abuse counseling, career counseling, student employment services, financial aid counseling, health services, minority student services, on-campus daycare, personal counseling, placement for graduates, veterans' counselor. **Physically disabled:** Services for visually, speech, hearing impaired. **Transfer:** Transfer adviser, college fairs on campus for students transferring to 4-year colleges.

Contact. E-mail: admissions@middlesexcc.edu
Phone: (732) 906-4243 Toll-free number: (888) 968-4622
Fax: (732) 956-7728
Dean of Enrollment Management, Middlesex County College, 2600 Woodbridge Avenue, Edison, NJ 08818-3050

Ocean County College
Toms River, New Jersey
www.ocean.edu

CB member
CB code: 2630

- Public 2-year community college
- Commuter campus in small city

General. Founded in 1964. Regionally accredited. Off campus classes offered at Southern Educational Center and several other sites in Ocean County. **Enrollment:** 7,535 degree-seeking undergraduates; 1,128 non-degree-seeking students. **Degrees:** 1,555 associate awarded. **Location:** 60 miles from Philadelphia, 80 miles from New York City. **Calendar:** Semester, extensive summer session. **Full-time faculty:** 97 total; 24% have terminal degrees, 11% minority, 58% women. **Part-time faculty:** 458 total; 11% have terminal degrees, 7% minority, 55% women. **Class size:** 31% < 20, 69% 20-39, less than 1% 40-49. **Special facilities:** Planetarium, Grunin Center for the Arts.

Student profile. Among degree-seeking undergraduates, 1,841 enrolled as first-time, first-year students, 494 transferred in from other institutions.

Part-time:	40%	**25 or older:**	25%
Women:	55%		

Transfer out. Colleges most students transferred to 2015: Kean University, Rutgers University, Georgian Court University, Rowan University, Richard Stockton College of New Jersey.

Basis for selection. Open admission, but selective for some programs. Special requirements for nursing program. SAT/ACT required for nursing and honors program; score report due by 5/30. **Learning Disabled:** Students invited to share learning disability needs with Disability Services, which then makes appropriate accommodations.

High school preparation. Algebra, chemistry, biology required of nursing applicants.

2015-2016 Annual costs. Tuition/fees: $4,255; $5,035 out-of-district; $7,735 out-of-state. Per-credit charge: $109 in-district; $135 out-of-district; $225 out-of-state. Books/supplies: $2,150. Personal expenses: $1,500.

2014-2015 Financial aid. Need-based: 56% of total undergraduate aid awarded as scholarships/grants, 44% as loans/jobs. Need-based aid available for part-time students. Work-study available nights, weekends and for part-time students. **Non-need-based:** Scholarships awarded for academics, state residency.

Application procedures. Admission: No deadline. No application fee. Application must be submitted online. Admission notification on a rolling basis. **Financial aid:** Priority date 5/31, closing date 10/1. FAFSA required. Applicants notified on a rolling basis starting 7/15; must reply within 1 week(s) of notification.

Academics. Special study options: Distance learning, dual enrollment of high school students, ESL, honors, internships, liberal arts/career combination, study abroad, teacher certification program, weekend college. Bachelor's degree programs available on campus. License preparation in dental hygiene, nursing, occupational therapy. **Credit/placement by examination:** AP, CLEP, institutional tests. 32 credit hours maximum toward associate degree. **Support services:** GED preparation and test center, learning center, pre-admission summer program, reduced course load, remedial instruction, study skills assistance, tutoring, writing center.

Majors. Business: General, business admin. **Communications:** Broadcast journalism. **Computer sciences:** General. **Conservation:** Environmental science. **Engineering:** General. **Foreign languages:** Sign language interpretation. **Health services:** Dental assistant, dental hygiene, nursing (RN), occupational therapy assistant, respiratory therapy technology. **Liberal arts:** Arts/sciences. **Protective services:** Fire safety technology, police science. **Visual/performing arts:** General.

Most popular majors. Health sciences 10%, liberal arts 76%, security/protective services 6%.

Technology on campus. 210 workstations in library, computer center. Commuter students can connect to campus network. Online course registration, online library, helpline, wireless network available.

Student life. Freshman orientation: Mandatory. Preregistration for classes offered. **Activities:** Concert band, choral groups, dance, drama, literary magazine, music ensembles, musical theater, radio station, student government, student newspaper, TV station, EOF Alliance, Circle K, organization for black unity, East Asian student alliance, sign language society, Student Alliance for Latino Unity and Achievement, students learning about politics, veterans club, single parenting, Native American studies society.

Athletics. NJCAA. **Intercollegiate:** Baseball M, basketball, cross-country, golf, lacrosse M, soccer, softball W, swimming, tennis. **Intramural:** Basketball, soccer, volleyball. **Team name:** Vikings.

Student services. Adult student services, alcohol/substance abuse counseling, career counseling, services for economically disadvantaged, student employment services, financial aid counseling, health services, minority student services, on-campus daycare, personal counseling, veterans' counselor. **Physically disabled:** Services for visually, speech, hearing impaired. **Transfer:** Re-entry adviser, pre-admission transcript evaluation for new students. Transfer adviser, college fairs on campus for students transferring to 4-year colleges.

Contact. Phone: (732) 255-0400 ext. 2013 Fax: (732) 255-0444 Lisa Kasper, Director of Admissions, Ocean County College, College Drive, Toms River, NJ 08754-2001

Passaic County Community College
Paterson, New Jersey
www.pccc.edu

CB member
CB code: 2694

- Public 2-year community college
- Commuter campus in small city

General. Founded in 1968. Regionally accredited. **Enrollment:** 8,389 undergraduates. **Degrees:** 746 associate awarded. **Location:** 15 miles from New York City. **Calendar:** Semester, limited summer session. **Full-time faculty:** 100 total. **Part-time faculty:** 409 total. **Special facilities:** Art galleries, playhouse, poetry center, theater.

Student profile.

Out-of-state:	.3%	25 or older:	41%

Transfer out. Colleges most students transferred to 2015: William Paterson University, Rutgers University, Montclair State University, Kean University.

Basis for selection. Open admission, but selective for some programs. Special requirements for nursing and other allied health programs. Interview recommended.

2015-2016 Annual costs. Tuition/fees: $4,410; $5,115 out-of-district; $7,755 out-of-state. Per-credit charge: $112 in-district; $135 out-of-district; $223 out-of-state. Books/supplies: $1,150.

Financial aid. Need-based: Need-based aid available for part-time students. Work-study available nights, weekends and for part-time students. **Non-need-based:** Scholarships awarded for academics. **Additional information:** Limited scholarship funds available for low income students eligible for federal or state aid.

Application procedures. Admission: No deadline. No application fee. Admission notification on a rolling basis. Early admissions available to high school students based on decisions made by high school guidance counselor and college's director of admissions. **Financial aid:** Priority date 8/1; no closing date. FAFSA required. Applicants notified on a rolling basis starting 8/1; must reply within 2 week(s) of notification.

Academics. Special study options: Accelerated study, cooperative education, cross-registration, distance learning, double major, dual enrollment of high school students, ESL, honors, independent study, internships, liberal arts/career combination, weekend college. License preparation in nursing, occupational therapy, paramedic, radiology. **Credit/placement by examination:** AP, CLEP, institutional tests. 12 credit hours maximum toward associate degree. New Jersey Basic Skills test required for placement. **Support services:** Learning center, reduced course load, remedial instruction, study skills assistance, tutoring, writing center.

Majors. Biology: Environmental. **Business:** General, accounting technology, hospitality admin, international, management information systems, marketing, sales/distribution, selling. **Communications:** General, journalism. **Communications technology:** Desktop publishing. **Computer sciences:** General, support specialist, system admin, web page design. **Education:** Early childhood, multi-level teacher. **Engineering:** Engineering science. **English:** English lit. **Health services:** Medical radiologic technology/radiation therapy, nursing (RN), nursing education, occupational therapy assistant, prenursing. **Liberal arts:** Arts/sciences, humanities. **Math:** General. **Protective services:** Corrections, fire safety technology, homeland security, police science. **Psychology:** General. **Social sciences:** Sociology. **Visual/performing arts:** Music, theater arts management.

Most popular majors. Business/marketing 15%, health sciences 18%, liberal arts 47%, public administration/social services 9%.

Technology on campus. 900 workstations in library, computer center. Online library available.

Student life. Freshman orientation: Available. Preregistration for classes offered. **Activities:** Dance, drama, student government, student newspaper, Organization of African Ancestry, Christian Fellowship Club, LGBT club, Muslim Student Association.

Athletics. NJCAA. **Intercollegiate:** Basketball, soccer M, volleyball W. **Team name:** Panthers.

Student services. Adult student services, career counseling, services for economically disadvantaged, student employment services, financial aid counseling, minority student services, on-campus daycare, personal counseling, placement for graduates, veterans' counselor, women's services. **Physically disabled:** Services for visually, hearing impaired. **Transfer:** Transfer adviser, college fairs on campus for students transferring to 4-year colleges.

Contact. E-mail: admissions@pccc.edu Phone: (973) 684-6868 Fax: (973) 684-6778 Stephanie Decker, Director of Admissions, Passaic County Community College, One College Boulevard, Paterson, NJ 07505-1179

Raritan Valley Community College
Branchburg, New Jersey
www.raritanval.edu

CB member
CB code: 2867

- Public 2-year community college
- Commuter campus in large town

General. Founded in 1966. Regionally accredited. **Enrollment:** 6,722 degree-seeking undergraduates; 1,377 non-degree-seeking students. **Degrees:** 1,043 associate awarded. **ROTC:** Army, Air Force. **Location:** 36 miles from New York City. **Calendar:** Semester, extensive summer session. **Full-time faculty:** 124 total; 11% minority, 56% women. **Part-time faculty:** 339 total; 18% minority, 52% women. **Special facilities:** Planetarium, professional theater, pool, fitness center.

Student profile. Among degree-seeking undergraduates, 77% enrolled in a transfer program, 23% enrolled in a vocational program, 1,403 enrolled as first-time, first-year students, 345 transferred in from other institutions.

Part-time:	51%	Asian American:	6%
Out-of-state:	1%	Hispanic/Latino:	20%
Women:	50%	Multi-racial, non-Hispanic:	2%
African American:	10%	International:	2%

Transfer out. Colleges most students transferred to 2015: Rutgers State University, Kean University, Montclair State University, William Paterson University, Rider University.

Basis for selection. Open admission, but selective for some programs. Special requirements for nursing program; interview recommended. Matriculated students must take ACCUPLACER test. **Adult students:** SAT/ACT scores not required; however, based on scores, students may be exempt from taking college's placement test. **Home schooled:** Must provide home school portfolio.

High school preparation. College-preparatory program recommended.

2015-2016 Annual costs. Tuition/fees: $5,034; $5,934 out-of-district; $5,934 out-of-state. Per-credit charge: $137 in-district; $167 out-of-district; $167 out-of-state. Books/supplies: $2,000. Personal expenses: $500.

Financial aid. Need-based: Need-based aid available for part-time students. Work-study available nights, weekends and for part-time students. **Non-need-based:** Scholarships awarded for academics.

Application procedures. Admission: No deadline. $25 fee, may be waived for applicants with need. Admission notification on a rolling basis. **Financial aid:** No deadline. FAFSA required. Applicants notified on a rolling basis starting 4/1.

Academics. Special study options: Accelerated study, cooperative education, distance learning, double major, dual enrollment of high school students, ESL, external degree, honors, independent study, weekend college. Service learning. Bachelor's degree programs available on campus. License preparation in nursing. **Credit/placement by examination:** AP, CLEP, institutional tests. 45 credit hours maximum toward associate degree. **Support services:** GED test center, learning center, pre-admission summer program, remedial instruction, study skills assistance, tutoring, writing center.

Majors. Biology: Biotechnology. **Business:** General, accounting technology, business admin, management information systems, marketing. **Communications:** Digital media. **Communications technology:** Animation/special effects. **Computer sciences:** Information technology. **Education:** Kindergarten/preschool. **Engineering:** Engineering science. **English:** English lit. **General:** Lineworker. **Health services:** Dental hygiene, health information technology, medical assistant, nursing (RN), occupational therapy, optician, respiratory therapy technology. **Liberal arts:** Arts/sciences. **Parks/recreation:** Exercise sciences. **Protective services:** Law enforcement admin. **Visual/performing arts:** Dance, interior design, music, studio arts.

Most popular majors. Business/marketing 14%, health sciences 12%, interdisciplinary studies 15%, liberal arts 29%, security/protective services 8%.

Technology on campus. 844 workstations in library, computer center, student center. Commuter students can connect to campus network. Online course registration, online library, helpline, wireless network available.

Student life. Freshman orientation: Available. Preregistration for classes offered. Three-hour sessions available. **Activities:** Choral groups, dance, drama, international student organizations, music ensembles, musical theater, radio station, student government, student newspaper, Black Student Association, Student Nurses Association, students for environmental awareness, BLGT club, Christian Fellowship, Islamic culture association, performing artist club, Orgullo Latino/Latin pride club, social justice club.

Athletics. NJCAA. **Intercollegiate:** Baseball M, basketball, golf, soccer, softball W. **Intramural:** Basketball, softball W, volleyball. **Team name:** Golden Lions.

Student services. Adult student services, alcohol/substance abuse counseling, career counseling, student employment services, financial aid counseling, on-campus daycare, personal counseling, placement for graduates, veterans' counselor. **Physically disabled:** Services for visually, speech, hearing impaired. **Transfer:** Re-entry adviser, pre-admission transcript evaluation for new students. Transfer center, transfer adviser, college fairs on campus for students transferring to 4-year colleges.

Contact. E-mail: registrar@raritanval.edu
Phone: (908) 526-1200 ext. 8935 Fax: (908) 704-3442
Jache Williams, Director of Admissions and Recruitment, Raritan Valley Community College, 118 Lamington Road, Branchburg, NJ 08876-1265

Rowan College at Burlington County
Pemberton, New Jersey
www.bcc.edu/rcbc
CB member
CB code: 2180

- Public 2-year community college
- Commuter campus in small town

General. Founded in 1966. Regionally accredited. Credit courses offered at four main campuses in Pemberton, Mount Laurel, Willingboro Center, Mount Holly Center; educational centers at Bordentown Regional High School and McGuire AFB, various other county high schools. **Enrollment:** 8,014 degree-seeking undergraduates; 748 non-degree-seeking students. **Degrees:** 1,326 associate awarded. **Location:** 30 miles from Philadelphia, 80 miles from New York City. **Calendar:** Semester, limited summer session. **Full-time faculty:** 64 total; 19% minority, 58% women. **Part-time faculty:** 592 total; 21% minority, 55% women. **Class size:** 56% < 20, 39% 20-39, 2% 40-49, 3% 50-99. **Special facilities:** Culinary arts, hospitality and tourism facility, sculpture garden, outdoor amphitheatre, small business science and high technology incubators, NASA laboratory. **Partnerships:** Formal partnerships with the Police Academy, Global Corporate College.

Student profile. Among degree-seeking undergraduates, 1,864 enrolled as first-time, first-year students, 2,139 transferred in from other institutions.

Part-time:	48%	Women:	57%
Out-of-state:	1%	25 or older:	38%

Transfer out. Colleges most students transferred to 2015: Rutgers University, Richard Stockton College of New Jersey, Rowan University, Drexel University.

Basis for selection. Open admission, but selective for some programs. Academic high school background required of nursing program applicants. Criminal background check required for all allied health students.

2016-2017 Annual costs. Tuition/fees (projected): $4,065; $4,545 out-of-district; $6,495 out-of-state. Per-credit charge: $100 in-district; $116 out-of-district; $181 out-of-state. Books/supplies: $1,200. Personal expenses: $1,610.

2014-2015 Financial aid. All financial aid based on need. Need-based aid available for part-time students. Work-study available nights, weekends and for part-time students.

Application procedures. Admission: No deadline. $20 fee, may be waived for applicants with need, free for online applicants. Admission notification on a rolling basis. **Financial aid:** No deadline. FAFSA required. Applicants notified on a rolling basis.

Academics. Special study options: Cooperative education, distance learning, double major, dual enrollment of high school students, ESL, external degree, independent study, study abroad, weekend college. Bachelor's degree programs available on campus. License preparation in dental hygiene, nursing, radiology. **Credit/placement by examination:** AP, CLEP, institutional tests. 30 credit hours maximum toward associate degree. **Support services:** GED preparation and test center, learning center, pre-admission summer program, reduced course load, remedial instruction, study skills assistance, tutoring, writing center.

Majors. Biology: Biotechnology. **Business:** General, accounting, accounting technology, business admin, casino management, hospitality admin, management information systems, real estate, restaurant/food services, sales/distribution. **Communications technology:** Animation/special effects, photo/film/video. **Computer sciences:** Computer graphics, computer science, data processing, information systems. **Foreign languages:** Sign language interpretation. **Health services:** Dental hygiene, health information technology, medical radiologic technology/radiation therapy, nursing (RN), respiratory therapy technology, sonography. **Liberal arts:** Arts/sciences. **Physical sciences:** General. **Protective services:** Firefighting, police science. **Social sciences:** GIS/cartography. **Visual/performing arts:** Art, fashion design, graphic design, music, photography.

Most popular majors. Health sciences 13%, liberal arts 70%, security/protective services 7%.

Technology on campus. 1,447 workstations in library, computer center, student center. Commuter students can connect to campus network. Online library, helpline, wireless network available.

Student life. Freshman orientation: Available. Preregistration for classes offered. **Activities:** Concert band, choral groups, dance, drama, international student organizations, literary magazine, music ensembles, musical theater, radio station, student government, Multicultural Student Union, veterans club, Phi Theta Kappa, Student Nurses Association, philosophy club, psychology club, Campus Crusade for Christ, human services club, GLASS, international club.

Athletics. NJCAA. **Intercollegiate:** Baseball M, basketball, golf, soccer, softball W. **Team name:** Barons.

Student services. Adult student services, career counseling, services for economically disadvantaged, student employment services, financial aid counseling, health services, minority student services, placement for graduates, veterans' counselor. **Physically disabled:** Services for visually, speech, hearing impaired. **Transfer:** Transfer center, transfer adviser, college fairs on campus for students transferring to 4-year colleges.

Contact. Phone: (609) 894-9311 ext. 1200 Fax: (609) 894-8356
Misun Phillips, Associate Dean of Admissions and Registration, Rowan
College at Burlington County, 601 Pemberton Browns Mills Road,
Pemberton, NJ 08068-1599

Contact. E-mail: admissions@rcgc.edu
Phone: (856) 415-2209 Fax: (856) 468-8498
Michael Chando, Executive Director, Admissions and Financial Aid,
Rowan College at Gloucester, 1400 Tanyard Road, Sewell, NJ 08080

Rowan College at Gloucester
Sewell, New Jersey
www.rcgc.edu

CB member
CB code: 2281

- Public 2-year community and liberal arts college
- Commuter campus in large town

General. Founded in 1966. Regionally accredited. **Enrollment:** 6,128
degree-seeking undergraduates. **Degrees:** 870 associate awarded. **Location:**
13 miles from Camden, 16 miles from Philadelphia, PA. **Calendar:** Semester,
limited summer session. **Full-time faculty:** 72 total. **Part-time faculty:**
278 total.

Basis for selection. Open admission, but selective for some programs.
Nursing and Allied Health as well as automotive technology are selective
admission programs and have special admissions requirements. Special-need
students and deaf or hearing-impaired students are evaluated on an individual
basis to determine the most appropriate support the college can offer. Institutional placement tests may be used. **Home schooled:** Eligible, but admission
is determined on individual basis.

High school preparation. Biology and chemistry required for nursing
applicants. Algebra also required for respiratory therapy, nuclear medicine,
and diagnostic medical sonography applicants.

2015-2016 Annual costs. Tuition/fees: $4,125; $4,815 out-of-district;
$8,415 out-of-state. Per-credit charge: $97 in-district; $120 out-of-district;
$240 out-of-state. Books/supplies: $2,000. Personal expenses: $2,482.

Financial aid. Need-based: Need-based aid available for part-time students. Work-study available nights, weekends and for part-time students.

Application procedures. Admission: No deadline. $20 fee, may be
waived for applicants with need, free for online applicants. Admission notification on a rolling basis beginning on or about 2/28. Application closing
dates for selective admission programs vary by program. **Financial aid:**
Priority date 5/1; no closing date. FAFSA, institutional form required. Applicants notified on a rolling basis starting 3/20.

Academics. Special study options: Distance learning, dual enrollment of
high school students, independent study. License preparation in nursing.
Credit/placement by examination: AP, CLEP, institutional tests. 16 credit
hours maximum toward associate degree. **Support services:** GED preparation
and test center, learning center, pre-admission summer program, reduced
course load, remedial instruction, study skills assistance, tutoring.

Majors. Biology: General, marine. **Business:** Accounting technology, business admin, marketing. **Computer sciences:** General, computer graphics,
computer science, web page design. **Education:** General, physical, special
ed. **Engineering:** General. **Health services:** Nuclear medical technology,
nursing (RN), respiratory therapy technology, sonography. **Liberal arts:**
Arts/sciences. **Parks/recreation:** Exercise sciences. **Physical sciences:**
Chemistry. **Protective services:** Police science.

Technology on campus. 750 workstations in library, computer center.
Commuter students can connect to campus network. Online course registration, online library, wireless network available.

Student life. Freshman orientation: Available. Preregistration for classes
offered. **Activities:** Campus ministries, choral groups, drama, literary magazine, musical theater, student government, student newspaper, Student Government Association, Humanities Club, Jesus is Lord Club, Multicultural
Club, Phi Theta Kappa, Paralegal Club, Student Veterans Organization, Gay
Straight Alliance, Psychology Club, DECA.

Athletics. NJCAA. **Intercollegiate:** Baseball M, basketball, cross-country,
soccer, softball W, tennis, track and field, wrestling M. **Team name:**
Road Runners.

Student services. Career counseling, services for economically disadvantaged, financial aid counseling, health services, personal counseling, veterans'
counselor. **Physically disabled:** Services for visually, speech, hearing
impaired. **Transfer:** Pre-admission transcript evaluation for new students.
Transfer adviser, college fairs on campus for students transferring to 4-
year colleges.

Salem Community College
Carneys Point, New Jersey
www.salemcc.edu

CB member
CB code: 2868

- Public 2-year community and junior college
- Commuter campus in small town

General. Founded in 1972. Regionally accredited. Known for glass education; is site for the International Flameworking Conference, held early spring
each academic year. **Enrollment:** 1,025 degree-seeking undergraduates.
Degrees: 196 associate awarded. **Location:** 12 miles from Wilmington,
Delaware. **Calendar:** Semester, limited summer session. **Full-time faculty:**
22 total; 14% have terminal degrees, 18% minority, 54% women. **Part-
time faculty:** 74 total. **Special facilities:** Glass education center, science
laboratories, computer graphic arts lab, sustainable energy center, PSEG
energy and environmental resource center, nursing center.

Student profile.

Out-of-state:	19%	**25 or older:** 30%

Transfer out. Colleges most students transferred to 2015: Wilmington
University, Rowan University.

Basis for selection. Open admission, but selective for some programs.
Acceptance into nursing, nuclear energy technology and glass programs, is
contingent upon specific application deadline procedures, as well as space
availability. Interview suggested for scientific glassblowing and glass art
programs. **Learning Disabled:** Students must file release form and documentation of disability to be granted special accommodations.

2015-2016 Annual costs. Tuition/fees: $4,104; $4,794 out-of-district;
$5,544 out-of-state. Per-credit charge: $102 in-district; $125 out-of-district;
$150 out-of-state. Books/supplies: $975. Personal expenses: $1,150. **Addi-
tional information:** Special Program costs as required.

Financial aid. Need-based: Need-based aid available for part-time students. Work-study available nights, weekends and for part-time students.
Non-need-based: Scholarships awarded for academics, athletics, state residency.

Application procedures. Admission: No deadline. $27 fee, may be
waived for applicants with need. Admission notification on a rolling basis.
Financial aid: Priority date 6/1; no closing date. FAFSA, institutional form
required. Applicants notified on a rolling basis starting 4/1; must reply within
2 week(s) of notification.

Academics. Special study options: Cooperative education, double major,
dual enrollment of high school students, independent study, internships,
liberal arts/career combination, weekend college. License preparation in nursing. **Credit/placement by examination:** AP, CLEP, institutional tests. 30
credit hours maximum toward associate degree. **Support services:** GED
preparation and test center, learning center, reduced course load, remedial
instruction, study skills assistance, tutoring, writing center.

Majors. Biology: Biotechnology. **Business:** Business admin. **Communications:** Journalism. **Computer sciences:** Computer graphics, computer science. **Education:** General, early childhood. **English:** English lit. **Health
services:** Nursing (RN). **History:** General. **Human services:** Community org/
advocacy. **Liberal arts:** Arts/sciences, humanities. **Math:** General. **Parks/
recreation:** Health/fitness. **Physical sciences:** Chemistry, physics. **Protective services:** Forensics. **Psychology:** General. **Social sciences:** General,
criminology, political science, sociology. **Visual/performing arts:** Industrial design.

Most popular majors. Education 9%, engineering/engineering technologies 20%, health sciences 24%, liberal arts 17%, security/protective services 9%.

Technology on campus. 50 workstations in library, computer center.
Online course registration, online library, helpline, wireless network available.

Student life. Freshman orientation: Available. Preregistration for classes
offered. Held at beginning of semester. **Activities:** Choral groups, student
government, Chi Alpha Epsilon, Educational Opportunity Fund Students,
Institutional Diversity Committee, Phi Theta Kappa, multicultural club, Gay-
Straight Alliance.

Athletics. NJCAA. **Intercollegiate:** Baseball M, basketball, golf M, soccer
W, softball W. **Team name:** Oaks.

Student services. Adult student services, career counseling, services for economically disadvantaged, student employment services, financial aid counseling, minority student services, personal counseling, veterans' counselor. **Physically disabled:** Services for visually, speech, hearing impaired. **Transfer:** Re-entry adviser, pre-admission transcript evaluation for new students. Transfer center, transfer adviser, college fairs on campus for students transferring to 4-year colleges.

Contact. E-mail: sccinfo@salemcc.edu
Phone: (856) 351-2703 Fax: (856) 299-9193
Kevin Catalfamo, Executive Director of Enrollment Management and Marketing, Salem Community College, 460 Hollywood Avenue, Carneys Point, NJ 08069-2799

Sussex County Community College
Newton, New Jersey — CB member
www.sussex.edu — CB code: 2711

- Public 2-year community college
- Commuter campus in small town

General. Founded in 1981. Regionally accredited. Extension sites at Sussex County Technical School, several area high schools, and other locations. **Enrollment:** 2,482 degree-seeking undergraduates. **Degrees:** 494 associate awarded. **Location:** 70 miles from New York City. **Calendar:** Semester, limited summer session. **Full-time faculty:** 44 total. **Part-time faculty:** 206 total. **Special facilities:** 10 computer laboratories (including graphic design).

Transfer out. Colleges most students transferred to 2015: Montclair State University, William Paterson University of New Jersey, Rutgers University, Ramapo College of New Jersey, Centenary College.

Basis for selection. Open admission, but selective for some programs. Special requirements for nursing program. Incoming freshmen must pass ACCUPLACER placement test for admission to program of study; those failing any part of test must satisfactorily complete remedial study in appropriate areas before being admitted to program.

2015-2016 Annual costs. Tuition/fees: $6,000; $7,950 out-of-district; $9,900 out-of-state. Books/supplies: $2,000. Personal expenses: $2,400.

Financial aid. All financial aid based on need. Need-based aid available for part-time students. Work-study available nights, weekends and for part-time students.

Application procedures. Admission: No deadline. $25 fee, may be waived for applicants with need. Admission notification on a rolling basis. **Financial aid:** Closing date 6/1. FAFSA required. Applicants notified on a rolling basis starting 5/1; must reply within 2 week(s) of notification.

Academics. Special study options: Distance learning, double major, dual enrollment of high school students, ESL, independent study, internships, teacher certification program. Bachelor's degree programs available on campus. License preparation in nursing, paramedic. **Credit/placement by examination:** AP, CLEP, IB, institutional tests. 30 credit hours maximum toward associate degree. **Support services:** GED preparation and test center, learning center, reduced course load, remedial instruction, study skills assistance, tutoring.

Majors. Biology: General. **Business:** Accounting, business admin. **Communications:** Journalism. **Computer sciences:** General, applications programming. **Conservation:** Environmental studies. **Education:** Early childhood, elementary, secondary. **English:** English lit. **Health services:** Clinical lab technology, predental, premedicine, prepharmacy, respiratory therapy technology. **Human services:** Social work. **Liberal arts:** Arts/sciences. **Math:** General. **Physical sciences:** Chemistry. **Protective services:** Criminal justice, firefighting. **Psychology:** General. **Social sciences:** General. **Visual/performing arts:** Art, commercial/advertising art, studio arts.

Technology on campus. 250 workstations in library, computer center, student center. Commuter students can connect to campus network. Online course registration, online library, wireless network available.

Student life. Freshman orientation: Available. Preregistration for classes offered. Half-day program held 2 days before start of classes. **Activities:** Concert band, campus ministries, choral groups, dance, drama, international student organizations, literary magazine, music ensembles, musical theater, opera, student government, student newspaper, symphony orchestra, TV station, student ambassadors, arts club, broadcasting club, criminal justice club, law & justice society, Phi Theta Kappa, Rainbows in the Dark, psychology club, University Mothers Against Drunk Driving, Strengths Without Violence.

Athletics. NJCAA. **Intercollegiate:** Baseball M, basketball M, soccer, softball W. **Intramural:** Archery, badminton, basketball, soccer, softball, table tennis, volleyball. **Team name:** Skylanders.

Student services. Adult student services, career counseling, student employment services, financial aid counseling, personal counseling, placement for graduates, veterans' counselor, women's services. **Physically disabled:** Services for visually, speech, hearing impaired. **Transfer:** Pre-admission transcript evaluation for new students. Transfer adviser, college fairs on campus for students transferring to 4-year colleges.

Contact. E-mail: tpoltersdorf@sussex.edu
Phone: (973) 300-2253 Fax: (973) 579-5226
Todd Poltersdorf, Director of Admissions, Sussex County Community College, One College Hill Road, Newton, NJ 07860

Union County College
Cranford, New Jersey
www.ucc.edu — CB code: 2921

- Public 2-year community college
- Commuter campus in large town

General. Founded in 1933. Regionally accredited. Union operates major campuses in Cranford, Elizabeth, Plainfield and Scotch Plains. **Enrollment:** 10,745 degree-seeking undergraduates; 475 non-degree-seeking students. **Degrees:** 1,425 associate awarded. **ROTC:** Air Force. **Location:** 25 miles from New York City. **Calendar:** Semester, extensive summer session. **Class size:** 32% < 20, 67% 20-39, less than 1% 40-49, less than 1% 50-99. **Special facilities:** Astronomical observatory. **Partnerships:** Union offers a business program, in partnership with Walt Disney World, through the Disney College Program.

Student profile. Among degree-seeking undergraduates, 83% enrolled in a transfer program, 17% enrolled in a vocational program, 2,168 enrolled as first-time, first-year students, 693 transferred in from other institutions.

Part-time:	56%	Hispanic/Latino:	34%
Out-of-state:	3%	Multi-racial, non-Hispanic:	1%
Women:	62%	International:	2%
African American:	28%	25 or older:	41%
Asian American:	4%		

Transfer out. Colleges most students transferred to 2015: Kean University; Montclair State University; and Rutgers, the State University of New Jersey.

Basis for selection. Open admission, but selective for some programs. Admission is open to all high school graduates, those holding high school equivalency diploma, or those persons eighteen years of age or older. Cooperative Nursing and Allied Health programs have additional admission requirements. **Home schooled:** Applicants must provide a signed form by the parent who conducted the home-schooled education. In the case of home-schooled applicants, who are affiliated with a local high school, the form will be signed by the Principal.

High school preparation. College-preparatory program recommended. 19 units recommended. Recommended units include English 4, mathematics 3, history 3, science 2 (laboratory 2), foreign language 2 and academic electives 5. Candidates for STEM (Science, Technology, Engineering, Mathematics) programs are expected to have taken elementary and intermediate algebra, plane geometry, and pre-calculus.

2015-2016 Annual costs. Tuition/fees: $4,450; $8,900 out-of-district; $8,900 out-of-state. Per-credit charge: $177 in-district; $354 out-of-district; $354 out-of-state. Books/supplies: $1,200. Personal expenses: $1,000.

Financial aid. All financial aid based on need. Need-based aid available for part-time students. Work-study available nights, weekends and for part-time students.

Application procedures. Admission: No deadline. No application fee. Admission notification on a rolling basis. **Financial aid:** Priority date 5/1; no closing date. FAFSA, institutional form required. Must reply within 2 week(s) of notification.

Academics. Special study options: Distance learning, dual enrollment of high school students, ESL, honors, independent study, internships, liberal arts/career combination. License preparation in nursing, paramedic, physical therapy. **Credit/placement by examination:** AP, CLEP, institutional tests. CLEP credits not accepted for Biology, Chemistry or Natural Sciences. **Support services:** GED preparation and test center, learning center, remedial instruction, study skills assistance, tutoring, writing center. The Academic Learning Centers provide academic support through tutoring and computer assisted instruction at three campus locations.

Majors. Biology: General. **Business:** General, accounting technology, business admin, hospitality admin, marketing. **Communications:** Media studies. **Communications technology:** Animation/special effects. **Computer sciences:** Computer science, information technology. **Engineering:** General. **Foreign languages:** American Sign Language, sign language interpretation. **Health services:** Dental hygiene, EMT paramedic, medical radiologic technology/radiation therapy, nuclear medical technology, nursing (RN), physical therapy assistant, radiologic technology/medical imaging, respiratory therapy technology, sonography. **History:** General. **Liberal arts:** Arts/sciences. **Math:** General. **Parks/recreation:** Sports admin. **Physical sciences:** Chemistry. **Protective services:** Fire safety technology, law enforcement admin.

Most popular majors. Business/marketing 14%, health sciences 19%, liberal arts 43%.

Technology on campus. 1,375 workstations in library, student center. Commuter students can connect to campus network. Online library, helpline, wireless network available.

Student life. Freshman orientation: Available. Preregistration for classes offered. **Activities:** International student organizations, literary magazine, radio station, student government, student newspaper, Art Society, Black Heritage Student Organization, Business Association, criminal justice club, Gaming and Animation Society, hospitality club, history club, Sexuality and Gender Alliance, and SIGN club (ASL-English).

Athletics. NJCAA. **Intercollegiate:** Baseball M, basketball, cross-country, golf, lacrosse M, soccer, track and field, volleyball W. **Team name:** Owls; Lady Owls.

Student services. Career counseling, services for economically disadvantaged, student employment services, financial aid counseling, minority student services, personal counseling, placement for graduates, veterans' counselor. **Physically disabled:** Services for visually, speech, hearing impaired. **Transfer:** Re-entry adviser, pre-admission transcript evaluation for new students. Transfer adviser, college fairs on campus for students transferring to 4-year colleges.

Contact. Phone: (908) 709-7596 Fax: (908) 709-7125
Nina Hernandez, Director of Admissions, Records, and Registration, Union County College, 1033 Springfield Avenue, Cranford, NJ 07016-1528

Warren County Community College
Washington, New Jersey
www.warren.edu
CB code: 2722

▸ Public 2-year community college
▸ Commuter campus in small town

General. Founded in 1981. Regionally accredited. **Enrollment:** 1,257 degree-seeking undergraduates; 1,499 non-degree-seeking students. **Degrees:** 285 associate awarded. **Location:** 10 miles from Phillipsburg; 20 miles from Easton, PA. **Calendar:** Semester, extensive summer session. **Full-time faculty:** 26 total; 27% have terminal degrees, 15% minority, 62% women. **Part-time faculty:** 111 total.

Student profile. Among degree-seeking undergraduates, 299 enrolled as first-time, first-year students, 77 transferred in from other institutions.

Part-time:	49%	Women:	58%
Out-of-state:	11%	25 or older:	27%

Transfer out. Colleges most students transferred to 2015: Centenary College, Rutgers-New Brunswick, East Stroudsburg University.

Basis for selection. Open admission, but selective for some programs. Admission to nursing program based on academic success in prerequisite college coursework. Interview recommended.

High school preparation. High school diploma or GED strongly recommended.

2015-2016 Annual costs. Tuition/fees: $4,410; $4,710 out-of-district; $5,310 out-of-state. Per-credit charge: $127 in-district; $137 out-of-district; $157 out-of-state. Books/supplies: $1,200. Personal expenses: $1,000.

Financial aid. All financial aid based on need. Need-based aid available for part-time students. Work-study available nights, weekends and for part-time students.

Application procedures. Admission: No deadline. $25 fee, may be waived for applicants with need. Application must be submitted on paper. Admission notification on a rolling basis. Early admission students ages 16-18 must provide written permission from parent/guardian and high school official. **Financial aid:** Closing date 7/1. FAFSA, institutional form required. Applicants notified on a rolling basis; must reply within 2 week(s) of notification.

Academics. Special study options: Cooperative education, cross-registration, distance learning, double major, dual enrollment of high school students, ESL, independent study, internships, liberal arts/career combination, weekend college. License preparation in dental hygiene, nursing, real estate. **Credit/placement by examination:** AP, CLEP, IB, institutional tests. Challenge exams. **Support services:** Learning center, pre-admission summer program, reduced course load, remedial instruction, study skills assistance, tutoring, writing center.

Majors. Biology: General. **Business:** General, accounting, entrepreneurial studies. **Computer sciences:** General. **Conservation:** General, environmental studies. **Education:** General, early childhood. **English:** English lit. **Health services:** Nursing (RN). **Liberal arts:** Arts/sciences. **Physical sciences:** Chemistry. **Protective services:** Criminal justice. **Social sciences:** General. **Visual/performing arts:** Studio arts.

Most popular majors. Health sciences 12%, liberal arts 61%, physical sciences 7%, security/protective services 8%.

Technology on campus. 100 workstations in library, computer center. Commuter students can connect to campus network. Online library, helpline, wireless network available.

Student life. Freshman orientation: Mandatory. Preregistration for classes offered. **Activities:** Literary magazine, student government, student newspaper, Phi Theta Kappa honor society, criminal justice association.

Athletics. Team name: Golden Eagles.

Student services. Adult student services, career counseling, student employment services, financial aid counseling, personal counseling, placement for graduates, veterans' counselor. **Physically disabled:** Services for visually, speech, hearing impaired. **Transfer:** Transfer adviser, college fairs on campus for students transferring to 4-year colleges.

Contact. Phone: (908) 835-9222 Fax: (908) 689-5824
Shannon Horwath, Associate Director of Admissions, Warren County Community College, 475 Route 57 West, Washington, NJ 07882-4343

New Mexico

Brookline College: Albuquerque
Albuquerque, New Mexico
www.brooklinecollege.edu

- For-profit 2-year branch campus and career college
- Commuter campus in large city
- Interview required

General. Accredited by ACICS. Additional campuses in Phoenix, Tempe, Tucson, and Oklahoma City. **Enrollment:** 357 undergraduates. **Degrees:** 27 bachelor's, 34 associate awarded. **Calendar:** Differs by program, extensive summer session. **Full-time faculty:** 10 total. **Part-time faculty:** 6 total.

Basis for selection. Open admission. **Home schooled:** Letter of attestation is required.

2015-2016 Annual costs. Personal expenses: $5,880. **Additional information:** Diploma programs: $15,225;Associate degree programs:$30,000; Bachelor's degree programs:$49,467-$85,000. Fees vary by course and program. All fees are subject to change.

Financial aid. All financial aid based on need. Work-study available nights, weekends and for part-time students.

Application procedures. Admission: No deadline. No application fee. Admission notification on a rolling basis. **Financial aid:** No deadline. FAFSA, institutional form required.

Academics. Special study options: Accelerated study. **Credit/placement by examination:** AP, CLEP, institutional tests. **Support services:** GED preparation and test center, learning center, remedial instruction, tutoring.

Majors. Business: Accounting, business admin. **Protective services:** Law enforcement admin.

Most popular majors. Business/marketing 35%, legal studies 30%, security/protective services 35%.

Technology on campus. Commuter students can connect to campus network. Online library available.

Student life. Freshman orientation: Mandatory. Preregistration for classes offered.

Student services. Career counseling, services for economically disadvantaged, financial aid counseling, placement for graduates. **Transfer:** Pre-admission transcript evaluation for new students.

Contact. E-mail: awebb@brooklinecollege.edu
Phone: (505) 880-2877 Toll-free number: (888) 660-2428
Fax: (505) 352-0199
Andrew Webb, Campus Director, Brookline College: Albuquerque, 4201 Central Avenue NW, Suite J, Albuquerque, NM 87105-1649

Carrington College: Albuquerque
Albuquerque, New Mexico
www.carrington.edu

- For-profit 2-year career college
- Commuter campus in very large city

General. Regionally accredited; also accredited by ACICS. **Enrollment:** 586 degree-seeking undergraduates. **Degrees:** 90 associate awarded. **Calendar:** Differs by program. **Full-time faculty:** 19 total. **Part-time faculty:** 53 total.

Basis for selection. Applicants must be at least 18 in New Mexico by the first day of classes, have a high school diploma or its equivalent, interview with an Enrollment Services Representative, complete admission testing, and fulfill additional program-specific requirements.

2015-2016 Annual costs. Tuition costs vary by program. Total program cost for the largest program (Medical Assisting-Cert.) is $14,833.

Financial aid. Need-based: Work-study available nights, weekends and for part-time students.

Academics. Credit/placement by examination: AP, CLEP.

Majors. Health services: Health care admin, nursing (RN), office admin, physical therapy assistant.

Contact. Phone: (888) 720-5014
Carrington College: Albuquerque, 1001 Menaul Boulevard, N.E., Albuquerque, NM 87107-1642

Central New Mexico Community College
Albuquerque, New Mexico
www.cnm.edu

CB member
CB code: 3387

- Public 2-year community and technical college
- Commuter campus in very large city

General. Founded in 1965. Regionally accredited. **Enrollment:** 24,171 degree-seeking undergraduates; 1,717 non-degree-seeking students. **Degrees:** 4,974 associate awarded. **ROTC:** Army, Naval, Air Force. **Calendar:** Trimester, extensive summer session. **Full-time faculty:** 358 total; 25% minority, 57% women. **Part-time faculty:** 726 total; 28% minority, 58% women. **Class size:** 30% < 20, 66% 20-39, 3% 40-49, less than 1% 50-99.

Student profile. Among degree-seeking undergraduates, 2,886 enrolled as first-time, first-year students, 1,289 transferred in from other institutions.

Part-time:	67%	Hispanic/Latino:	50%
Women:	56%	Native American:	7%
African American:	3%	Multi-racial, non-Hispanic:	2%
Asian American:	2%	25 or older:	43%

Transfer out. Colleges most students transferred to 2015: University of New Mexico.

Basis for selection. Open admission.

2015-2016 Annual costs. Tuition/fees: $1,484; $6,740 out-of-state. Per-credit charge: $51 in-state; $270 out-of-state. Books/supplies: $800. **Additional information:** CNM is a 100% commuter campus. There is no on-campus room and board.

2014-2015 Financial aid. Need-based: 1,711 full-time freshmen applied for aid; 1,445 deemed to have need; 1,385 received aid. Average scholarship/grant was $2,433; average loan $3,063. 72% of total undergraduate aid awarded as scholarships/grants, 28% as loans/jobs. Need-based aid available for part-time students. Work-study available nights, weekends and for part-time students. **Non-need-based:** Awarded to 1,715 full-time undergraduates, including 642 freshmen.

Application procedures. Admission: No deadline. No application fee. Admission notification on a rolling basis. **Financial aid:** Priority date 5/1; no closing date. FAFSA required. Applicants notified on a rolling basis starting 5/1.

Academics. Special study options: Dual enrollment of high school students, ESL, independent study, internships, liberal arts/career combination, teacher certification program. Apprenticeships. License preparation in aviation, dental hygiene, nursing, paramedic, radiology, real estate. **Credit/placement by examination:** AP, CLEP, institutional tests. **Support services:** GED preparation and test center, learning center, remedial instruction, study skills assistance, tutoring, writing center.

Majors. Biology: General, biotechnology. **Business:** General, accounting, administrative services, business admin, construction management, hospitality admin, human resources, office/clerical. **Communications:** General. **Computer sciences:** General, data processing, information systems, systems analysis. **Education:** Early childhood, multi-level teacher, secondary, technology/industrial arts. **Engineering:** Environmental, pre-engineering, surveying. **English:** English lit. **General:** Building construction, plumbing. **Health services:** Clinical lab technology, EMT paramedic, health information management, licensed practical nurse, medical radiologic technology/radiation therapy, nursing (RN), radiologic technology/medical imaging, respiratory therapy technology, sonography, veterinary technology/assistant. **History:** General. **Liberal arts:** Arts/sciences. **Physical sciences:** Physics. **Protective services:** Firefighting, law enforcement admin. **Psychology:** General. **Social sciences:** Anthropology, criminology, GIS/cartography, political science, sociology. **Work/family studies:** Family studies.

Most popular majors. Business/marketing 8%, health sciences 12%, liberal arts 50%, trade and industry 6%.

Technology on campus. Commuter students can connect to campus network. Online course registration, online library, student web hosting, wireless network available.

Student life. Freshman orientation: Mandatory. Preregistration for classes offered. **Activities:** Literary magazine, student government, student newspaper.

Student services. Adult student services, career counseling, services for economically disadvantaged, student employment services, financial aid counseling, health services, minority student services, placement for graduates. **Physically disabled:** Services for visually, speech, hearing impaired.

Contact. Phone: (505) 224-3160 Fax: (505) 224-3237
Glenn Damiani, Registrar/Director of Enrollment Services, Central New Mexico Community College, 525 Buena Vista Drive, SE, Albuquerque, NM 87106

Clovis Community College
Clovis, New Mexico
www.clovis.edu
CB member
CB code: 4921

▶ Public 2-year community and junior college
▶ Commuter campus in large town

General. Founded in 1990. Regionally accredited. **Enrollment:** 1,850 degree-seeking undergraduates; 1,856 non-degree-seeking students. **Degrees:** 387 associate awarded. **Location:** 200 miles from Albuquerque, 100 miles from Lubbock, Texas. **Calendar:** Semester, limited summer session. **Full-time faculty:** 52 total; 71% women. **Part-time faculty:** 77 total; 77% women. **Class size:** 65% < 20, 33% 20-39, less than 1% 40-49, less than 1% 50-99. **Special facilities:** Cultures of New Mexico art collection.

Student profile. Among degree-seeking undergraduates, 60% enrolled in a vocational program, 259 enrolled as first-time, first-year students.

Part-time:	68%	Hispanic/Latino:	36%
Women:	72%	Native American:	1%
African American:	6%	Multi-racial, non-Hispanic:	2%
Asian American:	2%		

Transfer out. Colleges most students transferred to 2015: Eastern New Mexico University, New Mexico State University, University of New Mexico, Texas Tech University, West Texas A&M University.

Basis for selection. Open admission, but selective for some programs. Nursing, PTA and radiologic technology are selective; criteria include GPA, performance in related science courses. Test of Adult Basic Education (TABE) or ACCUPLACER required for vocational programs. **Home schooled:** Students required to present documented grade level status from a nationally accredited home school curriculum provider. **Learning Disabled:** Students with learning disabilities encouraged to register with Office of Special Services to obtain appropriate diagnostic services and modifications.

2015-2016 Annual costs. Tuition/fees: $1,176; $1,248 out-of-district; $2,376 out-of-state. Books/supplies: $1,326. Personal expenses: $1,247.

Financial aid. Need-based: Need-based aid available for part-time students. Work-study available nights, weekends and for part-time students. **Non-need-based:** Scholarships awarded for academics, state residency. **Additional information:** Endowment of over $1,000,000 to assist nursing students.

Application procedures. Admission: No deadline. No application fee. Admission notification on a rolling basis. **Financial aid:** Priority date 9/1; no closing date. FAFSA required. Applicants notified on a rolling basis starting 4/15.

Academics. Special study options: Cooperative education, distance learning, double major, dual enrollment of high school students, ESL, independent study, internships, weekend college. License preparation in nursing, paramedic, radiology. **Credit/placement by examination:** AP, CLEP, institutional tests. 32 credit hours maximum toward associate degree. **Support services:** GED preparation and test center, learning center, remedial instruction, study skills assistance, tutoring, writing center.

Majors. Business: Management information systems, office management, office/clerical. **Computer sciences:** General, system admin, web page design. **Education:** Early childhood, teacher assistance. **Health services:** EMT ambulance attendant, health information technology, nursing (RN), physical therapy assistant, radiologist assistant. **Liberal arts:** Arts/sciences. **Parks/recreation:** Health/fitness. **Protective services:** Firefighting, police science. **Psychology:** General. **Visual/performing arts:** Commercial/advertising art, studio arts.

Most popular majors. Psychology 50%, security/protective services 50%.

Technology on campus. 280 workstations in library, computer center, student center. Online course registration, online library, helpline, wireless network available.

Student life. Freshman orientation: Available. Preregistration for classes offered. Held for 3 hours prior to start of semester. **Activities:** Drama, literary magazine, musical theater, student government, Hispanic advisory council, Phi Theta Kappa, social committee, international awareness organization, student ambassadors.

Student services. Adult student services, career counseling, services for economically disadvantaged, student employment services, financial aid counseling, minority student services, personal counseling, placement for graduates, veterans' counselor. **Physically disabled:** Services for visually, speech, hearing impaired. **Transfer:** Re-entry adviser for new students. Transfer adviser, college fairs on campus for students transferring to 4-year colleges.

Contact. E-mail: admissions@clovis.edu
Phone: (575) 769-4025 Fax: (575) 769-4190
Kimberly Tate, Director of Admissions/Registrar, Clovis Community College, 417 Schepps Boulevard, Clovis, NM 88101-8381

Dona Ana Community College of New Mexico State University
Las Cruces, New Mexico
www.dacc.nmsu.edu
CB member
CB code: 6296

▶ Public 2-year branch campus and community college
▶ Commuter campus in small city

General. Founded in 1973. Regionally accredited. Access to New Mexico State University facilities and activities. **Enrollment:** 9,280 undergraduates. **Degrees:** 1,078 associate awarded. **ROTC:** Army, Air Force. **Location:** 42 miles from El Paso, Texas. **Calendar:** Semester, limited summer session. **Full-time faculty:** 130 total. **Part-time faculty:** 386 total.

Basis for selection. Open admission, but selective for some programs. Applicants to radiology technology, EMT-paramedic, and respiratory care programs selected on basis of COMPASS scores, Health Occupations Aptitude Test scores, resume, 3 letters of recommendation, clinical observation, and interview. Applicants to nursing program selected on basis of nursing entrance exam scores and completion of requirements. COMPASS required for placement if ACT or SAT not taken.

2015-2016 Annual costs. Tuition/fees: $1,632; $1,968 out-of-district; $5,184 out-of-state. Per-credit charge: $68 in-district; $82 out-of-district; $216 out-of-state. Room/board: $5,784. Books/supplies: $1,060. Personal expenses: $2,286.

Financial aid. Need-based: Need-based aid available for part-time students. Work-study available nights, weekends and for part-time students.

Application procedures. Admission: No deadline. $20 fee, may be waived for applicants with need. Admission notification on a rolling basis. February 15th application deadline for radiology technology, EMT-paramedic, nursing, and respiratory care programs. **Financial aid:** Priority date 3/1; no closing date. FAFSA required. Applicants notified on a rolling basis starting 5/1.

Academics. Special study options: Cooperative education, cross-registration, distance learning, double major, dual enrollment of high school students, ESL, independent study, internships. License preparation in dental hygiene, nursing, paramedic, radiology. **Credit/placement by examination:** AP, CLEP, institutional tests. 30 credit hours maximum toward associate degree. **Support services:** GED preparation and test center, learning center, pre-admission summer program, remedial instruction, study skills assistance, tutoring.

Majors. Business: Administrative services, business admin, fashion, hospitality admin, marketing, office management. **Computer sciences:** Computer graphics, computer science, data processing. **Education:** General, early childhood. **Engineering:** Electrical. **General:** Electrician, lineworker, maintenance. **Health services:** EMT paramedic, medical radiologic technology/radiation therapy, medical secretary, nursing (RN), respiratory therapy technology. **Liberal arts:** Library assistant. **Protective services:** Firefighting.

Most popular majors. Liberal arts 97%.

Technology on campus. 460 workstations in library, computer center. Commuter students can connect to campus network. Online course registration, online library, helpline, repair service, wireless network available.

Student life. Freshman orientation: Available. Preregistration for classes offered. **Housing:** Coed dorms, single-sex dorms, special housing for disabled, apartments available. Housing available on adjacent New Mexico State University campus. **Activities:** Student government, student newspaper, Vocational Industrial Clubs of America, Distributive Education Clubs of America, Phi Theta Kappa, fraternities and sororities available through New Mexico State University.

Student services. Adult student services, career counseling, student employment services, health services, personal counseling, placement for graduates, veterans' counselor. **Physically disabled:** Services for visually, speech, hearing impaired. **Transfer:** Transfer adviser, college fairs on campus for students transferring to 4-year colleges.

Contact. E-mail: admissions@dacc.nmsu.edu
Phone: (575) 527-7710 Fax: (575) 527-7515
Geraldine Martinez, Director, Admissions, Dona Ana Community College of New Mexico State University, MSC-3DA, Las Cruces, NM 88003-8001

Eastern New Mexico University: Roswell
Roswell, New Mexico
www.roswell.enmu.edu   CB code: 4662

▶ Public 2-year branch campus and community college
▶ Commuter campus in large town

General. Founded in 1958. Regionally accredited. Online and on-site classes available from main campus, allowing students to continue upper-division classes without travel. **Enrollment:** 1,878 degree-seeking undergraduates. **Degrees:** 265 associate awarded. **Location:** 200 miles from Albuquerque. **Calendar:** Semester, limited summer session. **Full-time faculty:** 51 total; 8% have terminal degrees, 20% minority, 51% women. **Part-time faculty:** 115 total; 3% have terminal degrees, 13% minority, 53% women. **Class size:** 73% < 20, 23% 20-39, 2% 40-49, 2% 50-99.

Student profile.

Out-of-state: 7% Live on campus: 5%
25 or older: 43%

Transfer out. Colleges most students transferred to 2015: Eastern New Mexico University-Portales, New Mexico State University, University of New Mexico, New Mexico Highlands University.

Basis for selection. Open admission, but selective for some programs. Students must pass university skills placement test to enroll in math or English courses. Student may be exempt based on ACT scores. Some health services programs require completion of a pre-admission series of courses, have minimum course grades and GPAs. **Adult students:** SAT/ACT scores not required. Some programs require completion of placement testing as prerequisite. **Home schooled:** High School GPA of 2.5 or above and ACT score of 15. **Learning Disabled:** Services based on need and disability documentation. Students requiring special services are asked to provide information on needs as soon as possible to avoid delays in receiving service.

2015-2016 Annual costs. Tuition/fees: $1,752; $1,860 out-of-district; $4,356 out-of-state. Room/board: $8,090. Books/supplies: $1,066. Personal expenses: $2,471.

Financial aid. Need-based: Need-based aid available for part-time students. Work-study available nights, weekends and for part-time students. **Non-need-based:** Scholarships awarded for academics.

Application procedures. Admission: No deadline. No application fee. Admission notification on a rolling basis. **Financial aid:** Priority date 4/1; no closing date. FAFSA required. Applicants notified on a rolling basis starting 4/1; must reply within 3 week(s) of notification.

Academics. Special study options: Combined bachelor's/graduate degree, distance learning, dual enrollment of high school students, ESL, independent study, internships, liberal arts/career combination. Bachelor's degree programs available on campus. License preparation in aviation, nursing, occupational therapy, paramedic, radiology. **Credit/placement by examination:** AP, CLEP, IB, institutional tests. 30 credit hours maximum toward associate degree. Credits earned through CLEP and Advanced Placement must be mutually exclusive. **Support services:** GED preparation and test center, learning center, remedial instruction, study skills assistance, tutoring, writing center.

Majors. Biology: General. **Business:** Accounting, business admin. **Computer sciences:** Data processing. **Education:** General, health occupations. **Engineering:** Industrial. **Health services:** Dental hygiene, EMT paramedic, medical assistant, nursing (RN), occupational therapy assistant, office admin, radiologic technology/medical imaging, respiratory therapy technology.

Human services: Social work. **Math:** General. **Protective services:** Criminal justice, disaster management, fire safety technology, firefighting, police science. **Visual/performing arts:** Cinematography, design, graphic design. **Work/family studies:** Child care management.

Most popular majors. Business/marketing 7%, health sciences 38%, liberal arts 10%, trade and industry 25%.

Technology on campus. 700 workstations in dormitories, library, computer center, student center. Dormitories wired for high-speed internet access. Commuter students can connect to campus network. Online course registration, online library, helpline, wireless network available.

Student life. Freshman orientation: Available. Preregistration for classes offered. One-day program before classes commence. **Housing:** Coed dorms, apartments available. $150 fully refundable deposit, deadline 8/1. **Activities:** Concert band, drama, student government, art club, ski club, computer club, Spanish club, science club, Student Nurses Association, residence hall council, psychology club, electronics club, occupational therapy assistants, SkillsUSA club.

Athletics. Intramural: Basketball, football (non-tackle), racquetball, volleyball.

Student services. Career counseling, services for economically disadvantaged, student employment services, financial aid counseling, health services, personal counseling, placement for graduates, veterans' counselor. **Physically disabled:** Services for visually, speech, hearing impaired. **Transfer:** College fairs on campus for students transferring to 4-year colleges.

Contact. E-mail: admissions@roswell.enmu.edu
Phone: (575) 624-7142 Toll-free number: (800) 243-6687 ext. 142
Fax: (575) 624-7144
Griselda Aubert, Supervisor of Admissions, Eastern New Mexico University: Roswell, PO Box 6000, Roswell, NM 88202-6000

Luna Community College
Las Vegas, New Mexico
www.luna.edu   CB code: 2591

▶ Public 2-year community and liberal arts college
▶ Commuter campus in large town

General. Regionally accredited. **Enrollment:** 1,739 undergraduates. **Degrees:** 84 associate awarded. **Location:** 60 miles from Santa Fe. **Calendar:** Semester, extensive summer session. **Class size:** 86% < 20, 14% 20-39, less than 1% 40-49, less than 1% >100.

Student profile.

Out-of-state: 6% 25 or older: 43%

Basis for selection. Open admission, but selective for some programs and for out-of-state students. Nursing program requires a 2.7 college GPA in nursing prerequisite courses and passing scores on approved nursing entrance exam. **Adult students:** SAT/ACT scores not required. Placement testing for students that do not have ACT test scores. **Home schooled:** State high school equivalency certificate required.

2015-2016 Annual costs. Tuition/fees: $886; $1,198 out-of-district; $2,230 out-of-state. Per-credit charge: $35 in-district; $48 out-of-district; $91 out-of-state. Books/supplies: $1,000. Personal expenses: $2,204.

Financial aid. Need-based: Work-study available nights, weekends and for part-time students. **Non-need-based:** Scholarships awarded for academics, athletics, state residency.

Application procedures. Admission: No deadline. No application fee. Admission notification on a rolling basis.

Academics. Special study options: Accelerated study, distance learning, double major, dual enrollment of high school students, ESL, liberal arts/career combination. License preparation in dental hygiene, nursing. **Credit/placement by examination:** AP, CLEP, institutional tests. **Support services:** GED preparation, learning center, remedial instruction, tutoring.

Majors. Biology: General. **Business:** Accounting, administrative services, business admin. **Computer sciences:** General. **Education:** Early childhood, multi-level teacher. **Engineering:** General. **Health services:** Nursing (RN). **Liberal arts:** Arts/sciences. **Parks/recreation:** Sports studies. **Protective services:** Criminal justice, firefighting. **Visual/performing arts:** Cinematography.

Most popular majors. Business/marketing 10%, education 14%, health sciences 30%, liberal arts 18%, security/protective services 17%.

Technology on campus. 100 workstations in library, computer center, student center. Commuter students can connect to campus network. Online course registration, online library, helpline, repair service, wireless network available.

Student life. Freshman orientation: Mandatory. Preregistration for classes offered. **Activities:** Student government, student newspaper.

Athletics. NJCAA. **Intercollegiate:** Baseball M, softball W. **Team name:** Rough Riders.

Student services. Career counseling, financial aid counseling, minority student services, on-campus daycare.

Contact. E-mail: mmarquez@luna.edu
Phone: (505) 454-2550 Toll-free number: (800) 588-7232
Fax: (505) 454-5338
Moses Marquez, Director of Admissions, Luna Community College, 366 Luna Drive, Las Vegas, NM 87701

Mesalands Community College
Tucumcari, New Mexico
www.mesalands.edu   CB code: 3618

◗ Public 2-year community and technical college
◗ Commuter campus in small town

General. Regionally accredited. **Enrollment:** 770 degree-seeking undergraduates. **Degrees:** 54 associate awarded. **Location:** 175 miles from Albuquerque, 110 miles from Amarillo, Texas. **Calendar:** Semester, extensive summer session. **Full-time faculty:** 15 total. **Part-time faculty:** 33 total. **Special facilities:** Museum, foundry, production wind turbine, farrier, equine science facility.

Basis for selection. Open admission, but selective for some programs. COMPASS placement test must be taken by all incoming students. Associate of applied science degree in wind energy technology requires certain levels of math and English proficiency. **Home schooled:** Ability to Benefit Test or GED required. **Learning Disabled:** Students must submit an IEP.

2015-2016 Annual costs. Tuition/fees: $2,115; $3,225 out-of-state. Per-credit charge: $50 in-state; $91 out-of-state. Books/supplies: $1,336.

Financial aid. Need-based: Need-based aid available for part-time students. Work-study available nights, weekends and for part-time students. **Non-need-based:** Scholarships awarded for academics, athletics, leadership, minority status, state residency.

Application procedures. Admission: No deadline. No application fee. Admission notification on a rolling basis. **Financial aid:** Priority date 3/31; no closing date. FAFSA required. Applicants notified on a rolling basis starting 4/1; must reply within 3 week(s) of notification.

Academics. Special study options: Distance learning, dual enrollment of high school students, ESL, independent study, internships. Bachelor's degree programs available on campus. **Credit/placement by examination:** AP, CLEP, institutional tests. 18 credit hours maximum toward associate degree. **Support services:** GED preparation and test center, learning center, remedial instruction, study skills assistance, tutoring.

Majors. Business: Business admin. **Education:** General. **Engineering:** General. **Liberal arts:** Arts/sciences. **Physical sciences:** Geology, paleontology. **Protective services:** Law enforcement admin.

Technology on campus. 48 workstations in library, computer center. Online course registration, wireless network available.

Student life. Freshman orientation: Mandatory. Preregistration for classes offered. **Activities:** Student government.

Athletics. NCAA. **Intercollegiate:** Rodeo. **Team name:** Stampede.

Student services. Adult student services, financial aid counseling. **Physically disabled:** Services for visually, hearing impaired.

Contact. Phone: (575) 461-4413
E. Amber Trujillo-McClure, Director of Admissions, Mesalands Community College, 911 South Tenth Street, Tucumcari, NM 88401

Navajo Technical University
Crownpoint, New Mexico   CB member
www.navajotech.edu

◗ Public 2-year college
◗ Commuter campus in rural community

General. Enrollment: 1,383 degree-seeking undergraduates. **Degrees:** 10 bachelor's, 78 associate awarded; master's offered. **Location:** 28 miles from Thoreau, NM and 71 miles from Farmington, NM. **Calendar:** Semester, limited summer session. **Full-time faculty:** 44 total; 59% minority, 27% women. **Partnerships:** Formal partnerships with TeraGrid, SC08, Navajo Head Start, University of New Mexico, New Mexico Computing Applications Center, Navajo Rural Systemic Initiative, Navajo Workforce Development, Office of Dine Youth, Lewis and Clark University (Illinois), Southern University (Louisiana), National Museum of the American Indian, UNM Telemedicine Consortium, New Mexico State University's Extension Program, Sandia National Laboratories.

Student profile.

Out-of-state:	39%	**Live on campus:**	20%
25 or older:	70%		

Basis for selection. Open admission. ACCUPLACER required for all first-year students. **Home schooled:** Statement describing home school structure and mission, transcript of courses and grades, interview required. **Learning Disabled:** Special needs assessment conducted if disability is declared.

High school preparation. College-preparatory program recommended.

2015-2016 Annual costs. Tuition/fees: $2,460; $4,170 out-of-district. Per-credit charge: $71.25 in-district; $142.5 out-of-district. Room/board: $6,270. Books/supplies: $1,200. Personal expenses: $500.

2014-2015 Financial aid. Need-based: 242 full-time freshmen applied for aid; 220 deemed to have need; 220 received aid. Average need met was 55%. Average scholarship/grant was $6,502. 99% of total undergraduate aid awarded as scholarships/grants, 1% as loans/jobs. Need-based aid available for part-time students. Work-study available nights, weekends and for part-time students. **Non-need-based:** Awarded to 273 full-time undergraduates, including 50 freshmen. Scholarships awarded for academics.

Application procedures. Admission: Closing date 6/25 (postmark date). No application fee. Application must be submitted on paper. Admission notification by 9/9. Admission notification on a rolling basis. Must reply by May 1 or within 1 week(s) if notified thereafter. Serves a 98% Navajo population and local scholarship agencies require a June 25th deadline. However, non-Navajo and non-American Indian applicants can apply up to the last week of August. **Financial aid:** Priority date 6/30; no closing date. FAFSA, institutional form required. Applicants notified on a rolling basis starting 8/5; must reply by 11/30 or within 4 week(s) of notification.

Academics. Special study options: Accelerated study, distance learning, double major, dual enrollment of high school students, honors, independent study, internships, teacher certification program, weekend college. Bachelor's degree programs available on campus. License preparation in nursing. **Credit/placement by examination:** AP, CLEP. **Support services:** GED preparation and test center, remedial instruction, study skills assistance, tutoring.

Majors. Business: Accounting, administrative services. **Computer sciences:** General, information technology. **Conservation:** Environmental science. **Education:** Early childhood. **Foreign languages:** Native American. **Health services:** Nursing (RN), nursing assistant, veterinary technology/assistant. **Human services:** General.

Most popular majors. Agriculture 6%, business/marketing 16%, computer/information sciences 22%, education 10%, health sciences 6%, legal studies 28%, personal/culinary services 8%.

Technology on campus. 68 workstations in dormitories, library, computer center, student center. Dormitories wired for high-speed internet access and linked to campus network. Commuter students can connect to campus network. Online course registration, online library, helpline, repair service, wireless network available.

Student life. Freshman orientation: Mandatory. Preregistration for classes offered. 3 day event held one week before classes start. First time applicants must attend orientation before registering for classes. **Housing:** Guaranteed on-campus for all undergraduates. Single-sex dorms, special housing for disabled, apartments available. $250 fully refundable deposit, deadline 9/29. **Activities:** Drama, film society, international student organizations, student government, student newspaper, Native American Church, Christian Club, Alcoholics Anonymous.

Athletics. USCAA. **Intercollegiate:** Cross-country, rodeo. **Intramural:** Archery, basketball, softball, volleyball. **Team name:** Skyhawks.

Student services. Adult student services, alcohol/substance abuse counseling, career counseling, services for economically disadvantaged, student employment services, financial aid counseling, on-campus daycare, personal counseling, placement for graduates, veterans' counselor. **Physically disabled:** Services for visually, speech, hearing impaired. **Transfer:** Pre-admission transcript evaluation for new students. Transfer adviser for students transferring to 4-year colleges.

Contact. E-mail: tbegay@navajotech.edu
Phone: (505) 786-4326 Fax: (505) 786-5644
Delores Becenti, Dean of Student Services, Navajo Technical University, PO Box 849, Crownpoint, NM 87313

New Mexico Junior College
Hobbs, New Mexico
www.nmjc.edu
CB code: 4553

- Public 2-year community and technical college
- Commuter campus in large town

General. Founded in 1965. Regionally accredited. **Enrollment:** 2,949 undergraduates. **Degrees:** 251 associate awarded. **Location:** 110 miles from Roswell, 100 miles from Lubbock, Texas. **Calendar:** Semester, extensive summer session. **Full-time faculty:** 71 total; 11% have terminal degrees, 7% minority, 56% women. **Part-time faculty:** 120 total. **Class size:** 39% < 20, 61% 20-39. **Special facilities:** Western Heritage Museum, Cowboy Hall of Fame.

Student profile.

Out-of-state:	10%	Live on campus:	8%
25 or older:	51%		

Transfer out. Colleges most students transferred to 2015: College of the Southwest, Eastern New Mexico University, Texas Tech University, University of New Mexico, New Mexico State University.

Basis for selection. Open admission, but selective for some programs. Special requirements for nursing, law enforcement, and automotive service education programs. Applicants admitted without high school diploma or GED must pass GED before completion of degree program. Interview required for nursing, medical laboratory technician, automotive service education programs. **Home schooled:** Transcript of courses and grades required.

High school preparation. 18 units recommended. Recommended units include English 4, mathematics 3, social studies 4, science 2 and academic electives 5.

2015-2016 Annual costs. Tuition/fees: $1,248; $1,704 out-of-district; $1,896 out-of-state. Per-credit charge: $35 in-district; $54 out-of-district; $62 out-of-state. Room/board: $4,150. Books/supplies: $1,000. Personal expenses: $1,575.

Financial aid. Need-based: Need-based aid available for part-time students. Work-study available nights, weekends and for part-time students. **Non-need-based:** Scholarships awarded for academics, art, athletics, leadership, music/drama.

Application procedures. Admission: No deadline. No application fee. Admission notification on a rolling basis. **Financial aid:** Priority date 6/1; no closing date. FAFSA required. Applicants notified on a rolling basis; must reply within 2 week(s) of notification.

Academics. Special study options: Cooperative education, cross-registration, distance learning, dual enrollment of high school students, ESL, honors, internships, weekend college. Bachelor's degree programs available on campus. License preparation in nursing, paramedic, real estate. **Credit/placement by examination:** AP, CLEP, institutional tests. 30 credit hours maximum toward associate degree. **Support services:** GED preparation and test center, learning center, pre-admission summer program, remedial instruction, study skills assistance, tutoring, writing center.

Majors. Biology: General. **Business:** General, accounting, administrative services, banking/financial services, business admin, office management, office technology, real estate. **Communications:** Communications/speech/rhetoric. **Computer sciences:** General, applications programming, computer graphics, programming. **Education:** General, early childhood, elementary, middle, physical, secondary. **Engineering:** General. **Foreign languages:** Spanish. **Health services:** Athletic training, clinical lab assistant, clinical lab technology, EMT paramedic, medical radiologic technology/radiation therapy, predental, premedicine, prepharmacy. **Liberal arts:** Arts/sciences. **Math:** General. **Physical sciences:** Chemistry, physics. **Protective services:**

Criminal justice, police science. **Psychology:** General. **Social sciences:** General. **Visual/performing arts:** Commercial/advertising art, music, studio arts.

Most popular majors. Agriculture 6%, business/marketing 11%, education 13%, health sciences 24%, liberal arts 10%, mathematics 7%, trade and industry 13%.

Technology on campus. 275 workstations in dormitories, library, computer center, student center. Dormitories wired for high-speed internet access. Commuter students can connect to campus network. Helpline available.

Student life. Freshman orientation: Mandatory. Preregistration for classes offered. **Housing:** Single-sex dorms, special housing for disabled, wellness housing available. **Activities:** Concert band, choral groups, drama, music ensembles, student government, Young Republicans, Young Democrats, student nurses, ambassadors.

Athletics. NJCAA. **Intercollegiate:** Baseball M, basketball, golf M. **Intramural:** Badminton, basketball, bowling, golf, handball, racquetball, skiing, soccer, softball, swimming, table tennis, tennis, volleyball. **Team name:** Thunderbirds.

Student services. Career counseling, student employment services, financial aid counseling, health services, personal counseling, placement for graduates, veterans' counselor. **Physically disabled:** Services for visually, speech, hearing impaired. **Transfer:** Pre-admission transcript evaluation for new students. Transfer adviser, college fairs on campus for students transferring to 4-year colleges.

Contact. Phone: (575) 392-5113 Toll-free number: (800) 657-6260 Fax: (575) 392-0322
Michele Clingman, Dean of Enrollment Management, New Mexico Junior College, 5317 Lovington Highway, Hobbs, NM 88240

New Mexico Military Institute
Roswell, New Mexico
www.nmmi.edu
CB member
CB code: 4534

- Public 2-year junior and military college
- Residential campus in small city
- SAT or ACT (ACT writing optional) required

General. Founded in 1891. Regionally accredited. Nation's only state-supported, nationally accredited military junior college with embedded service academy preparatory program that serves all five national service academies and offers the US Army ROTC 2-Year Early Commissioning Program (ECP). **Enrollment:** 428 degree-seeking undergraduates. **Degrees:** 112 associate awarded. **ROTC:** Army. **Location:** 200 miles from Albuquerque, 200 miles from El Paso, Texas. **Calendar:** Semester, limited summer session. **Full-time faculty:** 82 total. **Part-time faculty:** 1 total. **Class size:** 64% < 20, 34% 20-39, 3% 40-49. **Special facilities:** Leadership center, museum, high and low ropes courses, leader reaction course, fitness factory, obstacle course, golf course, paint ball course, rappel tower.

Student profile. Among degree-seeking undergraduates, 315 enrolled as first-time, first-year students.

Out-of-state:	77%	Live on campus:	100%
Women:	20%		

Transfer out. Colleges most students transferred to 2015: University of New Mexico, New Mexico State University, Texas A&M University, University of Colorado.

Basis for selection. Applicants undergo a holistic review that includes GPA, test score and other considerations to be admitted. Additionally, students must be under 22 years of age at the time of matriculation, can never have been married, nor have any children.

High school preparation. College-preparatory program recommended. 21 units recommended. Recommended units include English 4, mathematics 3, social studies 1, history 2, science 2 (laboratory 2), foreign language 2 and academic electives 5. Computer science 0.5 unit recommended.

2015-2016 Annual costs. Tuition/fees: $7,454; $12,725 out-of-state. Room/board: $5,170. Books/supplies: $800. Personal expenses: $1,000.

Financial aid. Need-based: Work-study available nights, weekends and for part-time students. **Non-need-based:** Scholarships awarded for academics, alumni affiliation, athletics, leadership, minority status, music/drama, ROTC, state residency.

Application procedures. Admission: No deadline. $85 fee, may be waived for applicants with need, free for online applicants. Admission notification on a rolling basis beginning on or about 9/1. Advanced Army ROTC

New Mexico *New Mexico Military Institute*

applicants must pass Army physical examination. **Financial aid:** Priority date 2/1; no closing date. FAFSA required. Applicants notified on a rolling basis starting 2/1; must reply within 3 week(s) of notification.

Academics. **Special study options:** Dual enrollment of high school students. **Credit/placement by examination:** AP, CLEP, institutional tests. 30 credit hours maximum toward associate degree. **Support services:** Learning center, remedial instruction, tutoring, writing center.

Majors. **Liberal arts:** Arts/sciences.

Technology on campus. 100 workstations in dormitories, library, computer center, student center. Dormitories linked to campus network. Helpline, repair service available.

Student life. **Freshman orientation:** Mandatory. Preregistration for classes offered. **Policies:** Student life governed by the Cadet Rules and Regulations and the Cadet Honor Code. All students must live in college housing. **Housing:** Guaranteed on-campus for all undergraduates. Single-sex dorms available. $350 nonrefundable deposit. **Activities:** Bands, campus ministries, choral groups, film society, literary magazine, music ensembles, student government, student newspaper, symphony orchestra, Fellowship of Christian Athletes, African-American club, Native American club, Mexican club, Pacific Islander club, Corps of Cadets Community Service.

Athletics. NJCAA. **Intercollegiate:** Baseball M, basketball M, fencing, football (tackle) M, golf, rifle, tennis, track and field, volleyball W. **Intramural:** Fencing, football (tackle) M, handball, racquetball, skiing, soccer, softball, swimming, tennis, track and field, volleyball. **Team name:** Broncos.

Student services. Alcohol/substance abuse counseling, chaplain/spiritual director, career counseling, financial aid counseling, health services, personal counseling. **Transfer:** Pre-admission transcript evaluation for new students.

Contact. E-mail: admissions@nmmi.edu
Phone: (575) 624-8435 Toll-free number: (800) 421-5376
Fax: (575) 624-8058
LTC. Steve Davis, Director of Admissions, New Mexico Military Institute, 101 West College Boulevard, Roswell, NM 88201-5173

New Mexico State University at Alamogordo
Alamogordo, New Mexico
www.nmsua.edu   CB code: 4012

▶ Public 2-year branch campus college
▶ Commuter campus in large town

General. Founded in 1958. Regionally accredited. **Enrollment:** 1,849 degree-seeking undergraduates; 65 non-degree-seeking students. **Degrees:** 183 associate awarded. **ROTC:** Air Force. **Location:** 65 miles from Las Cruces, 85 miles from El Paso, Texas. **Calendar:** Semester, limited summer session. **Full-time faculty:** 46 total; 15% have terminal degrees, 24% minority, 65% women. **Part-time faculty:** 86 total; 2% have terminal degrees, 17% minority, 50% women. **Class size:** 64% < 20, 36% 20-39. **Special facilities:** Planetarium.

Student profile. Among degree-seeking undergraduates, 65% enrolled in a transfer program, 15% enrolled in a vocational program, 5% already have a bachelor's degree or higher, 243 enrolled as first-time, first-year students, 76 transferred in from other institutions.

Part-time:	48%	Hispanic/Latino:	43%
Out-of-state:	16%	Native American:	3%
Women:	64%	Multi-racial, non-Hispanic:	2%
African American:	4%	International:	2%
Asian American:	2%	25 or older:	47%

Transfer out. Colleges most students transferred to 2015: New Mexico State University.

Basis for selection. Open admission, but selective for some programs. **Home schooled:** State high school equivalency certificate required.

2015-2016 Annual costs. Tuition/fees: $2,064; $2,424 out-of-district; $5,376 out-of-state. Per-credit charge: $78 in-district; $93 out-of-district; $216 out-of-state. Books/supplies: $1,206. Personal expenses: $96.

Financial aid. **Need-based:** Need-based aid available for part-time students. Work-study available nights, weekends and for part-time students. **Non-need-based:** Scholarships awarded for academics, state residency.

Application procedures. **Admission:** No deadline. $20 fee. Admission notification on a rolling basis. High School students are admitted as non-degree dual credit students. **Financial aid:** Priority date 3/1; no closing date. FAFSA, institutional form required.

Academics. **Special study options:** Cooperative education, cross-registration, distance learning, double major, dual enrollment of high school students, ESL, independent study, internships, liberal arts/career combination, study abroad, weekend college. Bachelor's degree programs available on campus. License preparation in paramedic. **Credit/placement by examination:** AP, CLEP, institutional tests. **Support services:** GED preparation and test center, learning center, reduced course load, remedial instruction, study skills assistance, tutoring, writing center.

Majors. **Business:** General, administrative services, office/clerical. **Communications technology:** Animation/special effects, photo/film/video. **Computer sciences:** Data processing, information technology, programming, webmaster. **Education:** General, early childhood. **Engineering:** Pre-engineering. **Health services:** EMT paramedic. **Protective services:** Criminal justice. **Visual/performing arts:** Graphic design, studio arts.

Most popular majors. Business/marketing 11%, education 9%, health sciences 13%, liberal arts 48%, security/protective services 7%.

Technology on campus. 225 workstations in library, computer center, student center. Commuter students can connect to campus network. Online library, helpline, repair service, wireless network available.

Student life. **Freshman orientation:** Mandatory. Preregistration for classes offered. Held various times prior to class start each semester. **Activities:** Drama, student government, League of United Latin American Citizens (LULAC), Native American student group, social science club, Advocates for Children and Education (ACE), Campus Christian Fellowship (CCF), The National Society of Leadership and Success (NSLS).

Student services. Career counseling, student employment services, financial aid counseling, personal counseling, placement for graduates, veterans' counselor. **Physically disabled:** Services for visually, speech, hearing impaired. **Transfer:** Transfer adviser, college fairs on campus for students transferring to 4-year colleges.

Contact. E-mail: admissions@nmsua.nmsu.edu
Phone: (575) 439-3700
Rose Pena, Admissions Coordinator, New Mexico State University at Alamogordo, 2400 North Scenic Drive, Alamogordo, NM 88310

New Mexico State University at Carlsbad
Carlsbad, New Mexico
www.cavern.nmsu.edu   CB code: 4547

▶ Public 2-year branch campus and community college
▶ Commuter campus in large town

General. Founded in 1950. Regionally accredited. **Enrollment:** 1,360 degree-seeking undergraduates. **Degrees:** 102 associate awarded. **Location:** 165 miles from El Paso, Texas. **Calendar:** Semester, limited summer session. **Full-time faculty:** 41 total. **Part-time faculty:** 55 total. **Partnerships:** Formal partnership with Intrepid Potash, Mosaic Company.

Student profile.

Out-of-state:	3%	25 or older:	28%

Transfer out. Colleges most students transferred to 2015: New Mexico State University.

Basis for selection. Open admission, but selective for some programs. Special admission process for nursing and surgical tech applicants; HESI and prerequisite courses required. **Adult students:** SAT/ACT scores not required. **Home schooled:** Copy of document verifying registration as homeschooled student and academic transcript outlining 9th-12th grade courses and grades required.

High school preparation. 10 units recommended. Recommended units include English 4, mathematics 3, science 2 and foreign language 1.

2015-2016 Annual costs. Tuition/fees: $1,208; $1,952 out-of-district; $3,968 out-of-state. Per-credit charge: $42 in-district; $73 out-of-district. Books/supplies: $1,206. Personal expenses: $2,400.

Financial aid. **Need-based:** Need-based aid available for part-time students. Work-study available nights, weekends and for part-time students. **Non-need-based:** Scholarships awarded for academics, state residency.

Application procedures. **Admission:** No deadline. No application fee. Admission notification on a rolling basis. **Financial aid:** Priority date 3/1; no closing date. FAFSA required. Applicants notified on a rolling basis starting 5/1; must reply within 4 week(s) of notification.

Academics. Special study options: Distance learning, double major, dual enrollment of high school students, ESL, independent study, internships, student-designed major. Bachelor's degree programs available on campus. License preparation in nursing. **Credit/placement by examination:** AP, CLEP, institutional tests. 30 credit hours maximum toward associate degree. **Support services:** GED preparation and test center, learning center, reduced course load, remedial instruction, study skills assistance, tutoring, writing center.

Majors. Business: General, administrative services, office/clerical. **Education:** General, early childhood, teacher assistance. **Engineering:** General. **Health services:** Nursing (RN), prenursing. **Protective services:** Criminal justice.

Most popular majors. Business/marketing 11%, health sciences 22%, liberal arts 50%, security/protective services 7%.

Technology on campus. 365 workstations in library, computer center. Commuter students can connect to campus network. Online course registration, online library, helpline, wireless network available.

Student life. Freshman orientation: Available. Preregistration for classes offered. **Activities:** Choral groups, literary magazine, student government, student newspaper, student nursing association, criminal justice association, Phi Theta Kappa, MEChA.

Athletics. Team name: Aggies.

Student services. Career counseling, services for economically disadvantaged, student employment services, financial aid counseling, health services, minority student services, personal counseling. **Physically disabled:** Services for visually, speech, hearing impaired. **Transfer:** Transfer adviser, college fairs on campus for students transferring to 4-year colleges.

Contact. E-mail: mcleary@nmsu.edu
Phone: (575) 234-9223 Toll-free number: (888) 888-2199
Fax: (575) 885-4951
Michael Cleary, Vice President for Student Services, New Mexico State University at Carlsbad, 1500 University Drive, Carlsbad, NM 88220

New Mexico State University at Grants
Grants, New Mexico
www.grants.nmsu.edu
CB code: 0461

- Public 2-year branch campus and community college
- Commuter campus in small town

General. Founded in 1968. Regionally accredited. **Enrollment:** 821 degree-seeking undergraduates. **Degrees:** 65 associate awarded. **Location:** 75 miles from Albuquerque. **Calendar:** Semester, limited summer session. **Full-time faculty:** 19 total. **Part-time faculty:** 48 total.

Basis for selection. Open admission.

High school preparation. 15 units recommended. Recommended units include English 3, mathematics 3, social studies 1 and science 1.

2015-2016 Annual costs. Tuition/fees: $1,896; $2,112 out-of-district; $3,936 out-of-state. Books/supplies: $400.

Financial aid. Need-based: Need-based aid available for part-time students. Work-study available nights, weekends and for part-time students.

Application procedures. Admission: Closing date 8/28. $20 fee, may be waived for applicants with need. Admission notification on a rolling basis beginning on or about 8/3. **Financial aid:** Priority date 3/5; no closing date. FAFSA, institutional form required. Applicants notified on a rolling basis starting 6/15; must reply by 8/28.

Academics. Special study options: Distance learning, double major, dual enrollment of high school students, student-designed major, weekend college. Bachelor's degree programs available on campus. License preparation in nursing. **Credit/placement by examination:** AP, CLEP, institutional tests. 30 credit hours maximum toward associate degree. **Support services:** GED preparation and test center, learning center, reduced course load, remedial instruction, tutoring.

Majors. Business: General, office management. **Communications:** Digital media. **Computer sciences:** Programming. **Education:** General. **Protective services:** Law enforcement admin. **Visual/performing arts:** Art.

Most popular majors. Business/marketing 12%, interdisciplinary studies 13%, liberal arts 52%, public administration/social services 11%.

Technology on campus. 230 workstations in computer center. Online library available.

Student life. Freshman orientation: Available. Preregistration for classes offered. **Activities:** Student government, student newspaper.

Athletics. Team name: Aggies.

Student services. Adult student services, career counseling, student employment services, personal counseling, veterans' counselor. **Transfer:** Pre-admission transcript evaluation for new students. Transfer adviser, college fairs on campus for students transferring to 4-year colleges.

Contact. E-mail: barmstead@nmsu.edu
Phone: (505) 287-7981 Toll-free number: (888) 450-6678
Fax: (505) 287-2329
Beth Armstead, Vice President for Student Services, New Mexico State University at Grants, 1500 North Third Street, Grants, NM 87020

San Juan College
Farmington, New Mexico
www.sanjuancollege.edu
CB member
CB code: 4732

- Public 2-year community and technical college
- Commuter campus in large town

General. Founded in 1956. Regionally accredited. **Enrollment:** 5,669 degree-seeking undergraduates. **Degrees:** 684 associate awarded. **Location:** 183 miles from Albuquerque. **Calendar:** Semester, limited summer session. **Full-time faculty:** 160 total. **Part-time faculty:** 217 total. **Special facilities:** Planetarium, Southwestern books and materials collection, geographic information system, art gallery and performance hall, fire tower for specialized training, commercial truck driving training range, drilling rig, clean room for instrumentation training, plant operations equipment, complete dental facility, School of Energy well simulation software and computer trainers, 3-D printer, and outdoor learning center. **Partnerships:** Formal partnerships with General Motors, Chrysler, Toyota, Public Service Company of New Mexico.

Student profile.

Out-of-state: 18% **25 or older:** 58%

Transfer out. Colleges most students transferred to 2015: University of New Mexico, New Mexico Highlands University, University of Phoenix, Central New Mexico Community College, Fort Lewis College.

Basis for selection. Open admission. **Home schooled:** Transcript of courses and grades required. Minimum score on ACCUPLACER showing ability to benefit required.

High school preparation. 13 units recommended. Recommended units include English 4, mathematics 3, social studies 3, science 2 and foreign language 1.

2015-2016 Annual costs. Tuition/fees: $1,750; $4,990 out-of-state. Per-credit charge: $46 in-state; $146 out-of-state. Books/supplies: $1,200. Personal expenses: $1,350.

Financial aid. Need-based: Need-based aid available for part-time students. Work-study available nights, weekends and for part-time students. **Non-need-based:** Scholarships awarded for academics, state residency.

Application procedures. Admission: No deadline. $10 fee. Admission notification on a rolling basis. High school students may enroll as Early Admit or Dual Credit students. **Financial aid:** No deadline. FAFSA, institutional form required. Applicants notified on a rolling basis starting 7/1; must reply within 2 week(s) of notification.

Academics. Special study options: Combined bachelor's/graduate degree, cooperative education, distance learning, double major, dual enrollment of high school students, ESL, external degree, honors, independent study, internships, liberal arts/career combination, teacher certification program. Bachelor's degree programs available on campus. License preparation in dental hygiene, nursing, occupational therapy, paramedic, physical therapy. **Credit/placement by examination:** AP, CLEP, institutional tests. 30 credit hours maximum toward associate degree. **Support services:** GED preparation and test center, learning center, remedial instruction, study skills assistance, tutoring, writing center. Student achievement center, SMART Lab.

Majors. Area/ethnic studies: Native American. **Biology:** General. **Business:** Accounting technology, business admin. **Computer sciences:** Data processing. **Education:** Elementary, secondary, special ed. **Engineering:** General. **General:** Carpentry. **Health services:** Clinical lab technology, dental hygiene, EMT paramedic, health information technology, nursing (RN), physical therapy assistant, premedicine, respiratory therapy technology, surgical technology, veterinary technology/assistant. **Human services:** Social work. **Liberal arts:** Arts/sciences. **Math:** General. **Parks/recreation:** General, health/fitness. **Physical sciences:** General, chemistry, geology, physics. **Protective services:** Firefighting. **Psychology:** General. **Visual/performing arts:** Commercial/advertising art, theater design. **Work/family studies:** Child care service.

Most popular majors. Business/marketing 8%, engineering/engineering technologies 11%, health sciences 27%, liberal arts 19%, public administration/social services 6%, trade and industry 17%.

Technology on campus. 1,233 workstations in library, computer center, student center. Commuter students can connect to campus network. Online course registration, online library, helpline, wireless network available.

Student life. Freshman orientation: Mandatory. Preregistration for classes offered. One-day session held prior to beginning of semester. **Activities:** Bands, choral groups, dance, drama, music ensembles, musical theater, radio station, student government, symphony orchestra, Nations United Club, Student Ambassadors, Phi Theta Kappa honor society, Latino club, SJC OUT, American Indian Science and Engineering Society, Society for Advancement of Hispanic/Chicanos & Native Americans in Science, All Great Accomplishments Value Equality, Latter-Day Saints Student Association, SJC Legalize Cannibis Now Club.

Athletics. Intramural: Basketball, handball, softball, table tennis, ultimate frisbee, volleyball.

Student services. Alcohol/substance abuse counseling, career counseling, services for economically disadvantaged, student employment services, financial aid counseling, minority student services, on-campus daycare, personal counseling, placement for graduates, veterans' counselor. **Physically disabled:** Services for visually, speech, hearing impaired. **Transfer:** Transfer adviser, college fairs on campus for students transferring to 4-year colleges.

Contact. E-mail: admissions@sanjuancollege.edu
Phone: (505) 566-3545 Fax: (505) 566-3500
Jon Betz, Senior Director of Enrollment Management, San Juan College, 4601 College Boulevard, Farmington, NM 87402-4699

Santa Fe Community College

Santa Fe, New Mexico
www.sfcc.edu

CB member
CB code: 4816

- Public 2-year community college
- Commuter campus in small city

General. Founded in 1983. Regionally accredited. LEED certified new construction and 90% bio-fueled heating system. **Enrollment:** 4,437 degree-seeking undergraduates. **Degrees:** 452 associate awarded. **Location:** 50 miles from Albuquerque. **Calendar:** Semester, limited summer session. **Full-time faculty:** 84 total. **Part-time faculty:** 340 total. **Class size:** 50% < 20, 47% 20-39, 3% 40-49, less than 1% 50-99. **Special facilities:** Planetarium, art galleries, fine arts studios, fitness center, swimming pools, child development center, trades and advanced technology center. **Partnerships:** Formal partnerships with businesses and state agencies.

Student profile.

Out-of-state:	11% 25 or older:	60%

Transfer out. Colleges most students transferred to 2015: University of New Mexico, New Mexico State University.

Basis for selection. Open admission, but selective for some programs. Selective admissions to nursing program. A minimum GPA of 2.75 in all prerequisite courses, a minimum GPA of 2.75 in the science courses, a current CPR certificate and Test of Essential Academic Skills (TEAS) test scores (minimum score of 64.7%) required. Math and science courses must have been completed within five years prior to the nursing program. Essay and interview required for international students. **Home schooled:** State high school equivalency certificate required.

2015-2016 Annual costs. Tuition/fees: $1,196; $1,484 out-of-district; $2,600 out-of-state. Per-credit charge: $44.5 in-district; $56.5 out-of-district; $103 out-of-state. Books/supplies: $1,196. Personal expenses: $3,219.

Financial aid. Need-based: Need-based aid available for part-time students. Work-study available nights, weekends and for part-time students. **Non-need-based:** Scholarships awarded for academics, state residency.

Application procedures. Admission: No deadline. No application fee. Admission notification on a rolling basis. **Financial aid:** Priority date 5/1;

---

no closing date. FAFSA, institutional form required. Applicants notified on a rolling basis starting 6/1; must reply within 4 week(s) of notification.

Academics. Special study options: Accelerated study, cooperative education, cross-registration, distance learning, double major, dual enrollment of high school students, ESL, honors, independent study, internships, liberal arts/career combination, teacher certification program. Bachelor's degree programs available on campus. License preparation in nursing, paramedic. **Credit/placement by examination:** AP, CLEP, institutional tests. 30 credit hours maximum toward associate degree. **Support services:** GED preparation and test center, reduced course load, remedial instruction, study skills assistance, tutoring, writing center.

Majors. Area/ethnic studies: Regional. **Biology:** General. **Business:** Accounting, banking/financial services, business admin. **Computer sciences:** General. **Conservation:** Environmental studies. **Education:** General, kindergarten/preschool. **Engineering:** General. **Foreign languages:** Sign language interpretation, Spanish. **Health services:** Dental assistant, nursing (RN), respiratory therapy technology. **Human services:** Social work. **Liberal arts:** Arts/sciences. **Parks/recreation:** Health/fitness. **Physical sciences:** General. **Protective services:** Criminal justice, police science. **Psychology:** General. **Visual/performing arts:** Art, art history/conservation, design, interior design, studio arts management.

Most popular majors. Business/marketing 21%, education 6%, health sciences 23%, liberal arts 6%, public administration/social services 8%, visual/performing arts 13%.

Technology on campus. 200 workstations in library, computer center, student center. Commuter students can connect to campus network. Online course registration, online library, helpline, wireless network available.

Student life. Freshman orientation: Mandatory. Preregistration for classes offered. **Activities:** Choral groups, drama, film society, international student organizations, literary magazine, music ensembles, radio station, student government, TV station, Phi Theta Kappa, Native American student association, student nursing association, student council, Movimiento Estudiantil Chiemo de Aztlan, fine arts club, Los Tournants, sign language interpreters club, student ambassadors, veterans club.

Student services. Adult student services, career counseling, services for economically disadvantaged, student employment services, financial aid counseling, minority student services, on-campus daycare, personal counseling, placement for graduates, veterans' counselor, women's services. **Physically disabled:** Services for visually, speech, hearing impaired. **Transfer:** Transfer adviser, college fairs on campus for students transferring to 4-year colleges.

Contact. E-mail: enroll@sfcc.edu
Phone: (505) 428-1278 Fax: (505) 428-1468
Cheryl Fields, Assistant VP for Enrollment Management, Santa Fe Community College, 6401 Richards Avenue, Santa Fe, NM 87508-4887

Southwestern Indian Polytechnic Institute

Albuquerque, New Mexico
www.sipi.edu

CB code: 7047

- Public 2-year community and technical college
- Residential campus in large city

General. Founded in 1971. Regionally accredited. National Indian Community College serving American Indians from federally recognized tribes across the United States. Students must show membership by either a certificate of Indian blood or tribal enrollment card. **Enrollment:** 397 degree-seeking undergraduates; 5 non-degree-seeking students. **Degrees:** 84 associate awarded. **Calendar:** Trimester, extensive summer session. **Full-time faculty:** 19 total; 10% have terminal degrees, 68% minority, 53% women. **Part-time faculty:** 29 total; 21% have terminal degrees, 31% minority, 62% women. **Class size:** 90% < 20, 10% 20-39.

Student profile. Among degree-seeking undergraduates, 48% enrolled in a vocational program, 95 enrolled as first-time, first-year students.

Part-time:	13%	Women:	55%
Out-of-state:	85%	25 or older:	35%

Transfer out. Colleges most students transferred to 2015: University of New Mexico, New Mexico State University, New Mexico Highlands University, Northern Arizona University.

Basis for selection. Open admission. Applicants must have valid membership in U.S. federally recognized Indian tribe. ACT-COMPASS and TABE required for placement of new students. **Home schooled:** Transcript of courses and grades, state high school equivalency certificate required.

High school preparation. College-preparatory program recommended.

2016-2017 Annual costs. Tuition/fees (projected): $730. Room/board: $450. Books/supplies: $800. Personal expenses: $2,400.

2014-2015 Financial aid. **Need-based:** 192 full-time freshmen applied for aid; 192 deemed to have need; 192 received aid. Average need met was 30%. Average scholarship/grant was $1,292. 98% of total undergraduate aid awarded as scholarships/grants, 2% as loans/jobs. Need-based aid available for part-time students. Work-study available nights, weekends and for part-time students. **Non-need-based:** Awarded to 298 full-time undergraduates, including 10 freshmen. Scholarships awarded for academics, leadership, minority status. **Additional information:** Students with valid membership in recognized Indian tribe attend tuition-free.

Application procedures. **Admission:** Closing date 7/31 (receipt date). No application fee. Admission notification on a rolling basis. **Financial aid:** Closing date 3/1. FAFSA, institutional form required. Applicants notified on a rolling basis starting 9/30.

Academics. **Special study options:** Cooperative education, distance learning, double major, honors, liberal arts/career combination. **Credit/placement by examination:** AP, CLEP. **Support services:** GED preparation, learning center, remedial instruction, study skills assistance, tutoring.

Majors. **Business:** General, accounting technology, business admin. **Computer sciences:** LAN/WAN management. **Education:** Early childhood. **Engineering:** General. **Health services:** Optician. **Liberal arts:** Arts/sciences. **Social sciences:** GIS/cartography.

Most popular majors. Business/marketing 29%, computer/information sciences 10%, education 6%, engineering/engineering technologies 6%, health sciences 11%, liberal arts 22%, natural resources/environmental science 6%, personal/culinary services 7%.

Technology on campus. 15 workstations in dormitories, library, computer center, student center. Dormitories linked to campus network. Wireless network available.

Student life. **Freshman orientation:** Mandatory. Preregistration for classes offered. Held week prior to start of classes. **Policies:** Zero tolerance policy on alcohol and drugs. **Housing:** Single-sex dorms available. $275 fully refundable deposit, deadline 7/30. **Activities:** Dance, student government, natural resources club, Phi Theta Kappa, dance club, AISES, intertribal pow-wow club, music and art club, Four Winds and Golden Eagle Lodge Council.

Athletics. **Intramural:** Basketball, softball, volleyball, weight lifting. **Team name:** Eagles.

Student services. Alcohol/substance abuse counseling, career counseling, student employment services, financial aid counseling, health services, personal counseling, placement for graduates. **Transfer:** Pre-admission transcript evaluation for new students. Transfer adviser, college fairs on campus for students transferring to 4-year colleges.

Contact. E-mail: joseph.carpio@bie.edu
Phone: (505) 346-2338 Toll-free number: (800) 586-7474
Fax: (505) 346-2373
Joseph Carpio, Director Admissions/Financial Aid, Southwestern Indian Polytechnic Institute, PO Box 10146, Albuquerque, NM 87184

New York

Adirondack Community College
Queensbury, New York
www.sunyacc.edu

CB member
CB code: 2017

▸ Public 2-year community college
▸ Commuter campus in large town

General. Founded in 1960. Regionally accredited. **Enrollment:** 3,300 degree-seeking undergraduates. **Degrees:** 723 associate awarded. **Location:** 50 miles from Albany, 1 mile from Glens Falls. **Calendar:** Semester, limited summer session. **Full-time faculty:** 94 total. **Part-time faculty:** 199 total. **Special facilities:** Culinary arts facility, new media center, Cisco facility, business resource center, challenge course, pond preserve, arboretum, simulation lab for nursing program, local history collection of unique or rare books, documents and scrap books.

Student profile.

Out-of-state:	1%	Live on campus:	9%
25 or older:	21%		

Basis for selection. Open admission, but selective for some programs. Minimum GPA of 2.8 for acceptance into nursing program. Must be eligible to take college level Math and English classes (as determined by placement test) and BIO 107 (human anatomy and physiology). **Home schooled:** State high school equivalency certificate required.

High school preparation. College-preparatory program recommended. 22 units recommended. Recommended units include English 4, mathematics 3, social studies 4, history 2, science 3, foreign language 1 and academic electives 5. Allied health programs require Regents biology, chemistry examinations. Engineering requires Regents biology, chemistry and mathematics through pre-calculus. Computer science, mechanical and electrical technology require mathematics through advanced algebra. Forestry requires Regents biology, chemistry, and mathematics through intermediate algebra.

2015-2016 Annual costs. Tuition/fees: $4,419; $8,403 out-of-state. Per-credit charge: $166 in-state; $332 out-of-state. Room/board: $10,460. Books/supplies: $1,400. Personal expenses: $976.

Financial aid. Need-based: Need-based aid available for part-time students. Work-study available nights, weekends and for part-time students. **Non-need-based:** Scholarships awarded for academics, state residency.

Application procedures. Admission: No deadline. $35 fee, may be waived for applicants with need. Admission notification on a rolling basis. **Financial aid:** Priority date 4/15; no closing date. FAFSA, institutional form required. Applicants notified on a rolling basis starting 5/1.

Academics. Special study options: Cross-registration, distance learning, double major, dual enrollment of high school students, independent study, internships, liberal arts/career combination. Bachelor's degree programs available on campus. **Credit/placement by examination:** AP, CLEP, IB, institutional tests. 34 credit hours maximum toward associate degree. **Support services:** Learning center, reduced course load, remedial instruction, study skills assistance, tutoring, writing center.

Majors. Business: Accounting technology, business admin, hospitality admin. **Communications technology:** Radio/TV. **Computer sciences:** Computer science, information technology, networking. **Engineering:** General. **English:** Creative writing. **Health services:** Nursing (RN), radiologic technology/medical imaging, substance abuse counseling. **Liberal arts:** Arts/sciences. **Protective services:** Police science. **Visual/performing arts:** Design, music performance.

Most popular majors. Business/marketing 12%, health sciences 25%, liberal arts 41%, security/protective services 7%.

Technology on campus. 600 workstations in library, computer center, student center. Dormitories wired for high-speed internet access. Commuter students can connect to campus network. Online course registration, online library, wireless network available.

Student life. Freshman orientation: Mandatory. Preregistration for classes offered. **Housing:** Coed dorms available. $250 nonrefundable deposit.

Activities: Bands, choral groups, dance, drama, literary magazine, music ensembles, musical theater, radio station, student government, TV station.

Athletics. NJCAA. **Intercollegiate:** Baseball M, basketball, bowling, golf, soccer M, softball W, tennis, volleyball W. **Intramural:** Badminton, basketball, football (non-tackle), softball, volleyball. **Team name:** Timberwolves.

Student services. Adult student services, career counseling, financial aid counseling, on-campus daycare, personal counseling, placement for graduates, veterans' counselor. **Physically disabled:** Services for visually, speech, hearing impaired. **Transfer:** Transfer adviser, college fairs on campus for students transferring to 4-year colleges.

Contact. E-mail: admission@sunyacc.edu
Phone: (518) 743-2264 Toll-free number: (888) 786-9235
Fax: (518) 832-7602
Sara Jane Linehan, Director of Admissions, Adirondack Community College, 640 Bay Road, Queensbury, NY 12804

American Academy McAllister Institute of Funeral Service
New York, New York
www.funeraleducation.org

CB code: 0774

▸ Private 2-year school of mortuary science
▸ Commuter campus in very large city
▸ Interview required

General. Founded in 1926. **Enrollment:** 493 degree-seeking undergraduates. **Degrees:** 141 associate awarded. **Calendar:** Semester, extensive summer session. **Part-time faculty:** 25 total; 4% have terminal degrees, 12% minority, 48% women. **Class size:** 61% < 20, 37% 20-39, less than 1% 40-49, less than 1% 50-99.

Student profile. Among degree-seeking undergraduates, 15% already have a bachelor's degree or higher, 76 enrolled as first-time, first-year students, 94 transferred in from other institutions.

Part-time:	77%	Hispanic/Latino:	11%
Out-of-state:	26%	Native American:	1%
Women:	66%	Native Hawaiian/Pacific islander:	1%
African American:	26%	25 or older:	39%
Asian American:	1%		

Basis for selection. Interview, character/personal qualities, state residency, and level of interest most important. **Home schooled:** Transcript of courses and grades required.

2016-2017 Annual costs. Tuition/fees (projected): $14,410. Per-credit charge: $475. Books/supplies: $700. Personal expenses: $2,635.

Financial aid. All financial aid based on need. Work-study available nights, weekends and for part-time students. **Additional information:** Financial aid application due 30 days before start of semester.

Application procedures. Admission: Priority date 7/17; no deadline. $50 fee. Admission notification on a rolling basis. **Financial aid:** No deadline. FAFSA required. Applicants notified on a rolling basis starting 7/1; must reply by 9/1 or within 3 week(s) of notification.

Academics. Special study options: Cross-registration, distance learning. **Credit/placement by examination:** AP, CLEP.

Technology on campus. 10 workstations in library.

Student life. Freshman orientation: Mandatory. Preregistration for classes offered.

Student services. Transfer: Pre-admission transcript evaluation for new students.

Contact. E-mail: info@funeraleducation.org
Phone: (212) 757-1190 Toll-free number: (866) 932-2264
Fax: (212) 765-5923
Alan Loveder, Director of Admissions and Enrollment Management, American Academy McAllister Institute of Funeral Service, 619 West 54th Street, 2nd Floor, New York, NY 10019-3602

American Academy of Dramatic Arts
New York, New York
www.aada.edu   CB code: 2603

- Private 2-year junior and performing arts college
- Commuter campus in very large city
- Application essay, interview required

General. Founded in 1884. Regionally accredited. Offers practical conservatory and training. Additional campus in Hollywood, CA. **Enrollment:** 290 degree-seeking undergraduates. **Degrees:** 93 associate awarded. **Location:** Midtown Manhattan. **Calendar:** Semester, limited summer session. **Full-time faculty:** 8 total. **Part-time faculty:** 18 total. **Class size:** 100% < 20. **Special facilities:** 3 theaters, dance studio, costume department, property/production areas, audio/visual center, state-of-the-art television studio.

Student profile.

Out-of-state:	67%	25 or older:	11%

Basis for selection. Dramatic ability or potential, academic qualifications, maturity and motivation. Audition required; regional audition/interview may be arranged. **Home schooled:** Transcript of courses and grades, interview, letter of recommendation (nonparent) required.

2015-2016 Annual costs. Tuition/fees: $30,650. Books/supplies: $700. Personal expenses: $1,400.

Financial aid. All financial aid based on need. Work-study available nights, weekends and for part-time students. **Additional information:** Need-based incentive grants of $200-$2,000 for first-year students.

Application procedures. Admission: No deadline. $50 fee. Admission notification on a rolling basis. **Financial aid:** No deadline. FAFSA, institutional form required. Applicants notified on a rolling basis.

Academics. 2-year professional actor training program offered with associate of occupational studies degree. Third year, available by faculty invitation, forms showcase Academy Company. **Special study options:** Students may study 1 year at each of 2 campuses. **Credit/placement by examination:** AP, CLEP. **Support services:** Tutoring.

Majors. Visual/performing arts: Acting.

Technology on campus. 6 workstations in library.

Student life. Freshman orientation: Mandatory. Preregistration for classes offered. **Activities:** Drama, student government, student newspaper, various arts-related organizations available.

Student services. Career counseling, student employment services, placement for graduates.

Contact. E-mail: admissions-ny@aada.org
Phone: (212) 686-9244 Toll-free number: (800) 463-8990
Fax: (212) 685-8093
Kerin Reilly, Director of Admissions, American Academy of Dramatic Arts, 120 Madison Avenue, New York, NY 10016

ASA College
Brooklyn, New York
www.asa.edu

- For-profit 2-year technical and career college
- Commuter campus in very large city
- Interview required

General. Regionally accredited; also accredited by ACICS. Externships are included in every program. **Enrollment:** 4,551 degree-seeking undergraduates. **Degrees:** 1,179 associate awarded. **Calendar:** Semester, extensive summer session. **Full-time faculty:** 81 total. **Part-time faculty:** 270 total. **Class size:** 57% < 20, 43% 20-39.

Student profile. Among degree-seeking undergraduates, 1,223 enrolled as first-time, first-year students.

Part-time:	6%	Hispanic/Latino:	39%
Out-of-state:	12%	Multi-racial, non-Hispanic:	1%
Women:	63%	International:	15%
African American:	32%	25 or older:	48%
Asian American:	8%	Live on campus:	1%

Transfer out. **Colleges most students transferred to 2015:** St. Joseph's College.

Basis for selection. Open admission. Candidates accorded individual consideration through assessment testing results. **Learning Disabled:** Meet with Director, Office of Students with Disability Services.

2015-2016 Annual costs. Tuition/fees: $12,898. Per-credit charge: $520. Room/board: $9,200. Books/supplies: $1,500.

Financial aid. Need-based: Need-based aid available for part-time students. Work-study available nights, weekends and for part-time students. **Non-need-based:** Scholarships awarded for academics, alumni affiliation, athletics, leadership, state residency.

Application procedures. Admission: Priority date 10/12; no deadline. $25 fee. Application must be submitted on paper. **Financial aid:** No deadline. FAFSA required. Applicants notified on a rolling basis starting 7/13; must reply by 10/13.

Academics. Special study options: Accelerated study, distance learning, ESL, internships. **Credit/placement by examination:** AP, CLEP. **Support services:** GED preparation, learning center, reduced course load, remedial instruction, study skills assistance, tutoring, writing center.

Majors. Business: Accounting/business management, business admin. **Computer sciences:** Networking, programming. **Health services:** Health care admin, health information management, massage therapy, medical assistant, nursing practice, pharmacy assistant. **Protective services:** Criminal justice.

Most popular majors. Business/marketing 17%, computer/information sciences 8%, health sciences 52%, legal studies 23%.

Technology on campus. 700 workstations in dormitories, library, computer center. Online library, helpline available.

Student life. Freshman orientation: Mandatory. Preregistration for classes offered. **Housing:** Coed dorms available. $200 fully refundable deposit. **Activities:** Drama, literary magazine, student government.

Athletics. NJCAA. **Intercollegiate:** Basketball, soccer M. **Team name:** Avengers.

Student services. Adult student services, career counseling, services for economically disadvantaged, student employment services, financial aid counseling, personal counseling, placement for graduates.

Contact. E-mail: vkostyukov@asa.edu
Phone: (718) 522-9073 Toll-free number: (877) 679-8772
Fax: (718) 532-1432
Victoria Kostyukov, Vice President of Marketing and Admissions, ASA College, 81 Willoughby Street, Brooklyn, NY 11201

Bramson ORT College
Forest Hills, New York
www.bramsonort.edu   CB code: 0944

- Private 2-year junior and technical college affiliated with the Jewish faith
- Commuter campus in very large city

General. Founded in 1977. Regionally accredited. Extensions in Brooklyn and Queens. **Enrollment:** 508 undergraduates. **Degrees:** 203 associate awarded. **Calendar:** Semester, extensive summer session. **Full-time faculty:** 11 total. **Part-time faculty:** 61 total.

Basis for selection. High school diploma and placement examination required. English and mathematics placement tests required. Interview recommended.

2015-2016 Annual costs. Tuition/fees: $11,280. Per-credit charge: $450. Books/supplies: $900. Personal expenses: $1,026.

Financial aid. Need-based: Work-study available nights, weekends and for part-time students.

Application procedures. Admission: No deadline. $50 fee. Admission notification on a rolling basis. **Financial aid:** No deadline. Institutional form required. Applicants notified on a rolling basis; must reply within 3 week(s) of notification.

Academics. Special study options: Accelerated study, double major, ESL, internships. **Credit/placement by examination:** AP, CLEP, institutional tests. 50% of total hours needed for degree may be maximum of earned by examination. **Support services:** Learning center, pre-admission summer program, reduced course load, remedial instruction, tutoring.

Majors. Business: Accounting, administrative services, business admin, financial planning, management information systems. **Computer sciences:** General, applications programming, data processing, programming. **Engineering:** Electrical.

Technology on campus. 87 workstations in library, computer center.

Student life. Activities: Student government, student newspaper.

Student services. Adult student services, career counseling, student employment services, personal counseling, placement for graduates, veterans' counselor. **Physically disabled:** Services for visually, speech, hearing impaired.

Contact. Phone: (718) 261-5800 Fax: (718) 575-5118
Aleksandra Kagan, Director of Admissions, Bramson ORT College, 6930 Austin Street, Forest Hills, NY 11375

Broome Community College
Binghamton, New York
www.sunybroome.edu

CB member
CB code: 2048

◗ Public 2-year community college
◗ Commuter campus in small city

General. Founded in 1946. Regionally accredited. SUNY institution. **Enrollment:** 5,539 degree-seeking undergraduates. **Degrees:** 1,013 associate awarded. **Location:** 3 miles from downtown. **Calendar:** Semester, extensive summer session. **Full-time faculty:** 156 total. **Part-time faculty:** 297 total. **Class size:** 67% < 20, 31% 20-39, less than 1% 40-49, less than 1% 50-99, less than 1% >100. **Special facilities:** College-operated ice rink.

Student profile.

Out-of-state:	4%	25 or older: 28%

Transfer out. Colleges most students transferred to 2015: Binghamton University, Rochester Institute of Technology, State University of New York Cortland, State University of New York Utica-Rome, Ithaca College.

Basis for selection. Open admission, but selective for some programs. Entry into certain health sciences programs (nursing, physical therapy assistant, medical lab technology, medical assistant, radiologic technology, health information technology, dental hygiene) based on a competitive admissions process. Interview recommended for computer science and health science programs. **Home schooled:** Provide either 1) letter from superintendent of the school district in which student resides attesting to completion of program meeting requirements of Section 100.10 of the Regulations of the Commissioner of Education or 2) a passing score on GED (and diploma itself when available). Also may be admitted on ability-to-benefit basis.

2015-2016 Annual costs. Tuition/fees: $4,811; $9,035 out-of-state. Per-credit charge: $176 in-state; $352 out-of-state. Room/board: $10,362. Books/supplies: $1,400. Personal expenses: $1,004.

Financial aid. Need-based: Need-based aid available for part-time students. Work-study available nights, weekends and for part-time students.

Application procedures. Admission: No deadline. $50 fee. Admission notification on a rolling basis. Health Science students should apply and have all transcripts sent by March 1 prior to the fall semester. Deadline for all other students is the Friday before classes begin. **Financial aid:** Priority date 3/1; no closing date. FAFSA required. Applicants notified on a rolling basis starting 3/15; must reply within 2 week(s) of notification.

Academics. Special study options: Cooperative education, distance learning, dual enrollment of high school students, ESL, exchange student, honors, independent study, internships, student-designed major, study abroad, weekend college. License preparation in dental hygiene, nursing, paramedic, physical therapy, radiology, real estate. **Credit/placement by examination:** AP, CLEP, institutional tests. Contact division dean for assessment of experiential learning or portfolio assessment. **Support services:** Learning center, reduced course load, remedial instruction, study skills assistance, tutoring, writing center.

Majors. Business: Accounting technology, business admin, executive assistant, financial planning, hotel/motel admin, international finance. **Communications:** Communications/speech/rhetoric. **Computer sciences:** General, data processing, information systems. **Engineering:** Engineering science. **Health services:** Clinical lab technology, dental hygiene, EMT paramedic, health information technology, medical assistant, medical radiologic

technology/radiation therapy, nursing (RN), physical therapy assistant, substance abuse counseling. **Liberal arts:** Arts/sciences. **Protective services:** Corrections, firefighting, police science. **Work/family studies:** Child care management.

Most popular majors. Business/marketing 17%, engineering/engineering technologies 8%, health sciences 19%, liberal arts 40%.

Technology on campus. 500 workstations in library, computer center. Commuter students can connect to campus network. Online course registration, helpline, wireless network available.

Student life. Freshman orientation: Available. Preregistration for classes offered. **Activities:** Bands, campus ministries, choral groups, dance, drama, international student organizations, music ensembles, musical theater, student government, student newspaper, black student union, Phi Theta Kappa, Ski Extreme, writing club, chess club, Alpha Beta Gamma, computer club, music association.

Athletics. NJCAA. **Intercollegiate:** Baseball M, basketball, cheerleading, cross-country, golf M, ice hockey M, lacrosse M, soccer, tennis M, volleyball W. **Intramural:** Badminton, basketball, bowling, golf, soccer, tennis, volleyball. **Team name:** Hornets.

Student services. Adult student services, career counseling, services for economically disadvantaged, student employment services, financial aid counseling, health services, on-campus daycare, personal counseling, placement for graduates, veterans' counselor. **Physically disabled:** Services for visually, speech, hearing impaired. **Transfer:** Transfer adviser, college fairs on campus for students transferring to 4-year colleges.

Contact. E-mail: admissions@sunybroome.edu
Phone: (607) 778-5001 Toll-free number: (800) 836-0689
Fax: (607) 778-5310
Jenae Norris, Director of Admissions, Broome Community College, Box 1017, Binghamton, NY 13902

Bryant & Stratton College: Albany
Albany, New York
www.bryantstratton.edu

CB code: 2018

◗ For-profit 2-year business and career college
◗ Commuter campus in small city
◗ Application essay, interview required

General. Founded in 1854. Regionally accredited. **Enrollment:** 481 degree-seeking undergraduates. **Degrees:** 9 bachelor's, 154 associate awarded. **Location:** 2 miles from Albany, 28 miles from Saratoga. **Calendar:** Semester, extensive summer session. **Full-time faculty:** 20 total. **Part-time faculty:** 37 total.

Basis for selection. High school record, entrance examination score, personal interview and personal essay considered. Portfolio recommended. **Home schooled:** State high school equivalency certificate required.

High school preparation. Business courses recommended. Mathematics concentration preferred.

2015-2016 Annual costs. Tuition/fees: $17,190. Per-credit charge: $573. **Additional information:** Tuition and fees may vary by program.

Financial aid. All financial aid based on need. Need-based aid available for part-time students. Work-study available nights, weekends and for part-time students.

Application procedures. Admission: Closing date 9/22. $35 fee. Admission notification on a rolling basis. **Financial aid:** Closing date 9/17. FAFSA required. Applicants notified on a rolling basis.

Academics. Special study options: Distance learning, double major, independent study, internships. Bachelor's degree programs available on campus. **Credit/placement by examination:** AP, CLEP. 31 credit hours maximum toward associate degree. **Support services:** GED preparation, learning center, reduced course load, remedial instruction, study skills assistance, tutoring, writing center.

Majors. Business: Accounting, administrative services, business admin, human resources. **Computer sciences:** General. **Health services:** Medical assistant. **Protective services:** Law enforcement admin.

Most popular majors. Business/marketing 24%, computer/information sciences 10%, health sciences 34%, legal studies 11%, security/protective services 21%.

Technology on campus. 210 workstations in library, computer center. Wireless network available.

Student life. Freshman orientation: Mandatory. Preregistration for classes offered.

Student services. Alcohol/substance abuse counseling, career counseling, student employment services, financial aid counseling, personal counseling, placement for graduates, veterans' counselor. **Physically disabled:** Services for visually impaired. **Transfer:** Pre-admission transcript evaluation for new students. Transfer adviser, college fairs on campus for students transferring to 4-year colleges.

Contact. E-mail: rpferrell@bryantstratton.edu
Phone: (518) 437-1802 ext. 203 Fax: (518) 437-1049
Robert Ferrell, Director of Admissions, Bryant & Stratton College: Albany, 1259 Central Avenue, Albany, NY 12205

Bryant & Stratton College: Amherst
Getzville, New York
www.bryantstratton.edu   CB code: 3331

- For-profit 2-year business and career college
- Small town

General. Regionally accredited. **Enrollment:** 340 degree-seeking undergraduates. **Degrees:** 15 bachelor's, 122 associate awarded. **Calendar:** Trimester. **Full-time faculty:** 12 total. **Part-time faculty:** 31 total.

Basis for selection. Students conditionally accepted if all admissions requirements are received except for the official transcripts as long as a College official is able to verbally verify the graduation status or receipt of the GED from the granting institution.

2015-2016 Annual costs. Tuition/fees: $17,190. Per-credit charge: $573. Books/supplies: $1,200. **Additional information:** Tuition and fees may vary by program.

Financial aid. Need-based: Work-study available nights, weekends and for part-time students.

Application procedures. Admission: Closing date 9/22. $35 fee. **Financial aid:** Closing date 9/17.

Academics. Special study options: Distance learning, internships. Bachelor's degree programs available on campus. **Credit/placement by examination:** AP, CLEP. **Support services:** Learning center.

Majors. Business: Business admin. **Computer sciences:** General. **Visual/performing arts:** General.

Technology on campus. Wireless network available.

Student life. Freshman orientation: Available. Preregistration for classes offered.

Student services. Placement for graduates.

Contact. Phone: (716) 625-6300 Fax: (716) 689-6078
Nathan Cole, Director of Admissions, Bryant & Stratton College: Amherst, 3650 Millersport Highway, Getzville, NY 14068

Bryant & Stratton College: Buffalo
Buffalo, New York
www.bryantstratton.edu   CB code: 2058

- For-profit 2-year business and career college
- Commuter campus in large city
- Interview required

General. Founded in 1854. Regionally accredited. Branch campuses in Amherst (NY) and Orchard Park. **Enrollment:** 671 degree-seeking undergraduates. **Degrees:** 16 bachelor's, 185 associate awarded. **Calendar:** Semester, extensive summer session. **Full-time faculty:** 19 total. **Part-time faculty:** 44 total.

Transfer out. Colleges most students transferred to 2015: Erie Community College.

Basis for selection. Open admission. **Learning Disabled:** Students with special needs are invited to discuss their needs with their student services

advisor prior to registration. Students requesting accommodations are required to provide current documentation in order to determine reasonable accommodations where appropriate.

2015-2016 Annual costs. Tuition/fees: $17,190. Per-credit charge: $573. **Additional information:** Tuition and fees may vary by program.

Financial aid. Need-based: Work-study available nights, weekends and for part-time students.

Application procedures. Admission: Closing date 9/22. $35 fee, may be waived for applicants with need. Admission notification on a rolling basis. **Financial aid:** Closing date 9/17. Applicants notified on a rolling basis.

Academics. Special study options: Distance learning, internships, weekend college. Bachelor's degree programs available on campus. **Credit/placement by examination:** AP, CLEP, institutional tests. **Support services:** Learning center, remedial instruction, study skills assistance, tutoring, writing center.

Majors. Business: General, administrative services. **Computer sciences:** General. **Health services:** Medical assistant.

Technology on campus. 150 workstations in library, computer center. Online library, repair service, wireless network available.

Student life. Freshman orientation: Mandatory. Preregistration for classes offered. **Activities:** Student government, student newspaper, numerous special interest clubs.

Athletics. Intramural: Bowling, skiing, softball, swimming.

Student services. Career counseling, student employment services, financial aid counseling, personal counseling, placement for graduates. **Physically disabled:** Services for visually, hearing impaired. **Transfer:** Re-entry adviser, pre-admission transcript evaluation for new students. Transfer adviser, college fairs on campus for students transferring to 4-year colleges.

Contact. E-mail: mbrobinson@bryantstratton.edu
Phone: (716) 884-9120 Fax: (716) 884-0091
Philip Struebel, Director of Admissions, Bryant & Stratton College: Buffalo, 465 Main Street, Suite 400, Buffalo, NY 14203

Bryant & Stratton College: Henrietta
Rochester, New York
www.bryantstratton.edu

- For-profit 2-year business college
- Commuter campus in small city

General. Enrollment: 393 degree-seeking undergraduates. **Degrees:** 88 associate awarded. **Calendar:** Semester. **Full-time faculty:** 17 total. **Part-time faculty:** 37 total.

Basis for selection. Interview, entrance evaluation important.

2015-2016 Annual costs. Tuition/fees: $17,190. Per-credit charge: $573. **Additional information:** Tuition and fees may vary by program.

Financial aid. Need-based: Work-study available nights, weekends and for part-time students.

Application procedures. Admission: Closing date 9/22. $35 fee. **Financial aid:** Closing date 9/17.

Academics. Credit/placement by examination: AP, CLEP.

Majors. Business: Accounting, administrative services, human resources. **Computer sciences:** Information technology. **Health services:** Medical assistant, medical secretary. **Protective services:** Law enforcement admin. **Visual/performing arts:** Graphic design.

Contact. Phone: (585) 292-5627
Kevin Leonard, Admissions Director, Bryant & Stratton College: Henrietta, 1225 Jefferson Road, Rochester, NY 14623

Bryant & Stratton College: Rochester
Rochester, New York
www.bryantstratton.edu   CB code: 7327

- For-profit 2-year business and career college
- Commuter campus in large city
- Interview required

General. Founded in 1973. Regionally accredited. Two campuses in Rochester. Degree program runs 4 consecutive semesters. **Enrollment:** 401 degree-seeking undergraduates. **Degrees:** 3 bachelor's, 78 associate awarded. **Calendar:** Differs by program, extensive summer session. **Full-time faculty:** 2 total. **Part-time faculty:** 28 total.

Basis for selection. Character, previous scholastic record, and counselor recommendation important. CPAt required for admission.

2015-2016 Annual costs. Tuition/fees: $17,190. Per-credit charge: $573. Books/supplies: $1,000. **Additional information:** Tuition and fees may vary by program.

Financial aid. **Need-based:** Work-study available nights, weekends and for part-time students.

Application procedures. **Admission:** Closing date 9/22. $35 fee. Admission notification on a rolling basis. **Financial aid:** Closing date 9/17. FAFSA required. Applicants notified on a rolling basis.

Academics. **Special study options:** Accelerated study, distance learning, double major, internships. **Credit/placement by examination:** AP, CLEP. **Support services:** Learning center, reduced course load, study skills assistance, tutoring.

Majors. **Business:** Accounting, administrative services, business admin, customer service, office technology. **Computer sciences:** Information technology, webmaster. **Health services:** Office admin. **Visual/performing arts:** Design.

Technology on campus. 10 workstations in computer center. Commuter students can connect to campus network.

Student life. **Freshman orientation:** Available. Preregistration for classes offered. **Activities:** Student government, professional interest clubs.

Athletics. **Team name:** Bobcats.

Student services. Career counseling, financial aid counseling, personal counseling, placement for graduates. **Transfer:** Pre-admission transcript evaluation for new students. Transfer adviser for students transferring to 4-year colleges.

Contact. Phone: (585) 292-5627
Angel Gonzalez, Director of Admissions, Bryant & Stratton College: Rochester, 1225 Jefferson Road, Rochester, NY 14623

Bryant & Stratton College: Southtowns
Orchard Park, New York
www.bryantstratton.edu   **CB code: 3328**

- For-profit 2-year business college
- Commuter campus in large town

General. Regionally accredited. **Enrollment:** 2,330 degree-seeking undergraduates. **Degrees:** 77 bachelor's, 426 associate awarded. **Location:** 11 miles from downtown Buffalo. **Calendar:** Differs by program, extensive summer session. **Full-time faculty:** 34 total. **Part-time faculty:** 207 total.

Basis for selection. Open admission.

2015-2016 Annual costs. Tuition/fees: $17,190. Per-credit charge: $573. Books/supplies: $1,200. **Additional information:** Tuition and fees may vary by program.

Financial aid. **Need-based:** Work-study available nights, weekends and for part-time students.

Application procedures. **Admission:** Closing date 9/22. $35 fee. **Financial aid:** Closing date 9/17.

Academics. **Special study options:** Distance learning, double major. **Credit/placement by examination:** AP, CLEP. **Support services:** Learning center, study skills assistance, tutoring.

Majors. **Business:** Business admin. **Computer sciences:** General.

Technology on campus. Online library available.

Student life. **Freshman orientation:** Mandatory. Preregistration for classes offered. **Activities:** Student government, student newspaper.

Student services. Career counseling, student employment services, financial aid counseling. **Physically disabled:** Services for visually, hearing impaired. **Transfer:** Pre-admission transcript evaluation for new students.

Contact. E-mail: prkehr@bryantstratton.edu
Phone: (716) 677-9500 Fax: (716) 677-9599
Liliana Mateo, Director of Admissions, Bryant & Stratton College: Southtowns, 200 Redtail, Orchard Park, NY 14127

Bryant & Stratton College: Syracuse
Syracuse, New York
www.bryantstratton.edu   **CB code: 0654**

- For-profit 2-year business and junior college
- Commuter campus in small city

General. Founded in 1854. Regionally accredited. **Enrollment:** 503 degree-seeking undergraduates. **Degrees:** 138 associate awarded. **Location:** 75 miles from Rochester. **Calendar:** Trimester, extensive summer session. **Full-time faculty:** 19 total. **Part-time faculty:** 32 total. **Class size:** 54% < 20, 46% 20-39.

Student profile.

Out-of-state:	2%	Live on campus:	10%
25 or older:	45%		

Basis for selection. Open admission.

2015-2016 Annual costs. Tuition/fees: $17,190. Per-credit charge: $573. Room/board: $8,880. Books/supplies: $700.

Financial aid. All financial aid based on need. Work-study available nights, weekends and for part-time students.

Application procedures. **Admission:** Closing date 9/22. $35 fee. Application must be submitted on paper. Admission notification on a rolling basis. **Financial aid:** Closing date 9/17. FAFSA required. Applicants notified on a rolling basis starting 10/1.

Academics. **Special study options:** Cross-registration, distance learning, honors, internships. **Credit/placement by examination:** AP, CLEP. **Support services:** Learning center, reduced course load, remedial instruction, study skills assistance, tutoring.

Majors. **Business:** Accounting, administrative services, business admin, hotel/motel admin, marketing, office management, sales/distribution, tourism promotion, tourism/travel. **Computer sciences:** General. **Health services:** Medical assistant, medical secretary. **Protective services:** Police science.

Most popular majors. Business/marketing 61%, health sciences 35%.

Technology on campus. 230 workstations in dormitories, library, computer center. Dormitories wired for high-speed internet access and linked to campus network. Commuter students can connect to campus network. Online library available.

Student life. **Freshman orientation:** Mandatory. Preregistration for classes offered. **Housing:** Single-sex dorms available. $100 fully refundable deposit. **Activities:** Student newspaper.

Athletics. NJCAA. **Intercollegiate:** Soccer. **Team name:** Bobcats.

Student services. Career counseling, student employment services, financial aid counseling, personal counseling, placement for graduates. **Physically disabled:** Services for visually, speech, hearing impaired. **Transfer:** Re-entry adviser, pre-admission transcript evaluation for new students. Transfer adviser, college fairs on campus for students transferring to 4-year colleges.

Contact. Phone: (315) 472-6603 Fax: (315) 474-4383
Jon Bristol, Director of Admissions, Bryant & Stratton College: Syracuse, 953 James Street, Syracuse, NY 13203

Bryant & Stratton College: Syracuse North
Liverpool, New York
www.bryantstratton.edu

- For-profit 2-year career college
- Commuter campus in small city
- Interview required

General. **Enrollment:** 466 degree-seeking undergraduates. **Degrees:** 12 bachelor's, 126 associate awarded. **Location:** 5 miles from Syracuse. **Calendar:** Semester, extensive summer session. **Full-time faculty:** 14 total. **Part-time faculty:** 27 total.

Transfer out. Colleges most students transferred to 2015: Onondaga Community College.

Basis for selection. Acceptance based on the completion of the required admissions paperwork. This process includes the admissions application, interview, and entrance evaluation. **Home schooled:** State high school equivalency certificate, interview required. **Learning Disabled:** Testing accommodations made when students disclose they have a learning disability.

High school preparation. College-preparatory program recommended.

2015-2016 Annual costs. Tuition/fees: $17,190. Per-credit charge: $573. Room/board: $8,880.

Financial aid. All financial aid based on need. Need-based aid available for part-time students. Work-study available nights, weekends and for part-time students.

Application procedures. Admission: Closing date 9/22. $35 fee. Application must be submitted on paper. Admission notification on a rolling basis beginning on or about 9/20. **Financial aid:** Closing date 9/17. FAFSA, institutional form required.

Academics. Special study options: Accelerated study, internships. **Credit/placement by examination:** AP, CLEP. **Support services:** GED preparation, learning center, study skills assistance, tutoring.

Majors. Business: General, accounting, administrative services. **Computer sciences:** System admin. **Health services:** Medical assistant, medical secretary. **Visual/performing arts:** Graphic design.

Technology on campus. Online library available.

Student life. Freshman orientation: Mandatory. Preregistration for classes offered.

Athletics. NJCAA. **Intercollegiate:** Cross-country, soccer. **Team name:** Bobcats.

Student services. Career counseling, financial aid counseling, placement for graduates. **Transfer:** Pre-admission transcript evaluation for new students. College fairs on campus for students transferring to 4-year colleges.

Contact. Phone: (315) 652-6500
Heather Macknick, Admissions Director, Bryant & Stratton College: Syracuse North, 8687 Carling Road, Liverpool, NY 13090

Business Informatics Center
Valley Stream, New York
www.thecollegeforbusiness.com

- For-profit 2-year business and community college
- Commuter campus in large town
- Interview required

General. Accredited by ACCSC. **Enrollment:** 59 degree-seeking undergraduates. **Degrees:** 12 associate awarded. **Calendar:** Quarter. **Full-time faculty:** 2 total. **Part-time faculty:** 6 total. **Class size:** 92% < 20, 8% 20-39.

Transfer out. Colleges most students transferred to 2015: Briarcliff College, Katharine Gibbs.

Basis for selection. Open admission.

2015-2016 Annual costs. Tuition/fees: $13,375.

Financial aid. Need-based: Work-study available nights, weekends and for part-time students.

Application procedures. Admission: No deadline. $75 fee, may be waived for applicants with need. Admission notification on a rolling basis. **Financial aid:** No deadline.

Academics. Credit/placement by examination: AP, CLEP, institutional tests. **Support services:** Tutoring.

Majors. Business: Office technology.

Most popular majors. Business/marketing 77%, legal studies 23%.

Technology on campus. 50 workstations in library, computer center.

Student life. Freshman orientation: Mandatory. Preregistration for classes offered. **Activities:** Student government.

Student services. Financial aid counseling, placement for graduates. **Transfer:** Transfer center for students transferring to 4-year colleges.

Contact. Phone: (516) 561-0050
Bernard Price, Admissions Director, Business Informatics Center, 134 South Central Avenue, Valley Stream, NY 11580-5431

Cayuga Community College
Auburn, New York
www.cayuga-cc.edu

CB member
CB code: 2010

- Public 2-year community college
- Commuter campus in large town

General. Founded in 1953. Regionally accredited. **Enrollment:** 2,527 degree-seeking undergraduates; 1,903 non-degree-seeking students. **Degrees:** 501 associate awarded. **Location:** 30 miles from Syracuse. **Calendar:** Semester, limited summer session. **Full-time faculty:** 50 total; 24% have terminal degrees, 6% minority, 52% women. **Part-time faculty:** 179 total; 8% have terminal degrees, less than 1% minority, 51% women. **Class size:** 68% < 20, 32% 20-39. **Special facilities:** Nature trail, multitrack recording studio and video-editing suites.

Student profile. Among degree-seeking undergraduates, 69% enrolled in a transfer program, 31% enrolled in a vocational program, 563 enrolled as first-time, first-year students, 295 transferred in from other institutions.

Part-time:	29%	Asian American:	1%
Out-of-state:	1%	Hispanic/Latino:	4%
Women:	62%	Multi-racial, non-Hispanic:	3%
African American:	7%	25 or older:	39%

Transfer out. Colleges most students transferred to 2015: SUNY Oswego, SUNY Cortland, SUNY Brockport, Rochester Institute of Technology, SUNY Institute of Technology.

Basis for selection. Open admission, but selective for some programs. Special requirements for nursing; interview required. All students who apply for financial aid or matriculation into a degree or certificate program may be required to take placement tests in English and mathematics. Any non-degree-seeking student who wishes to take an English or mathematics course must take the placement test prior to registering. Students who have successfully transferred an acceptable college course in English and/or completed four years of English with an average of 80 or higher and/or math from another college will not be required to take that portion of the exam. **Home schooled:** 1) official final high school transcript from student's school district indicating graduation or 2) letter on district letterhead from relevant district superintendent certifying that student has documented satisfactory completion of equivalent of 4-year high school program or 3) taking college's placement test; and if Ability to Benefit scores set by college met/exceeded, may matriculate and be considered for financial aid and work toward satisfying 24-credit option prescribed by New York State Education Department.

High school preparation. Recommended units include English 4, mathematics 2, social studies 3 and science 1.

2015-2016 Annual costs. Tuition/fees: $4,742; $9,068 out-of-state. Per-credit charge: $178 in-state; $356 out-of-state. Books/supplies: $1,250. Personal expenses: $1,009.

2014-2015 Financial aid. All financial aid based on need. 56% of total undergraduate aid awarded as scholarships/grants, 44% as loans/jobs. Need-based aid available for part-time students. Work-study available nights, weekends and for part-time students.

Application procedures. Admission: No deadline. No application fee. Admission notification on a rolling basis. **Financial aid:** Priority date 5/1; no closing date. FAFSA required. Applicants notified on a rolling basis starting 4/1.

Academics. Special study options: Accelerated study, cross-registration, distance learning, double major, dual enrollment of high school students, honors, independent study, internships, liberal arts/career combination, study abroad, weekend college. License preparation in nursing. **Credit/placement by examination:** AP, CLEP, institutional tests. 30 credit hours maximum toward associate degree. **Support services:** Learning center, pre-admission summer program, reduced course load, remedial instruction, study skills assistance, tutoring, writing center.

Majors. Biology: General. **Business:** Accounting technology, business admin. **Communications:** Broadcast journalism, radio/TV. **Communications technology:** General, photo/film/video, recording arts. **Computer sciences:** General, computer science, web page design. **Education:** Early childhood. **Health services:** Nursing (RN). **Liberal arts:** Arts/sciences. **Math:**

General. **Physical sciences:** Chemistry, geology. **Protective services:** Corrections, police science. **Social sciences:** GIS/cartography. **Visual/performing arts:** Art, studio arts.

Most popular majors. Biological/life sciences 7%, business/marketing 14%, health sciences 10%, liberal arts 37%, security/protective services 15%.

Technology on campus. 450 workstations in library, computer center. Online library, wireless network available.

Student life. Freshman orientation: Available. Preregistration for classes offered. Held week before classes begin. **Activities:** Choral groups, drama, musical theater, radio station, student government, student newspaper, TV station, honor fraternity, business society, nursing club, multicultural association, criminal justice club, alumni association, diversity club.

Athletics. NJCAA. **Intercollegiate:** Basketball, bowling, golf, soccer, softball W, volleyball W. **Intramural:** Racquetball, skiing, volleyball. **Team name:** Spartans.

Student services. Chaplain/spiritual director, career counseling, student employment services, financial aid counseling, health services, on-campus daycare, personal counseling, placement for graduates, veterans' counselor. **Transfer:** Pre-admission transcript evaluation for new students. Transfer adviser, college fairs on campus for students transferring to 4-year colleges.

Contact. E-mail: admissions@cayuga-cc.edu
Phone: (315) 255-1743 ext. 2241 Fax: (315) 283-2075
Bruce Blodgett, Director of Admissions, Cayuga Community College, 197 Franklin Street, Auburn, NY 13021-3099

City University of New York: Borough of Manhattan Community College

New York, New York — CB member
www.bmcc.cuny.edu — CB code: 2063

- Public 2-year community college
- Commuter campus in very large city

General. Founded in 1963. Regionally accredited. **Enrollment:** 26,560 degree-seeking undergraduates; 749 non-degree-seeking students. **Degrees:** 3,435 associate awarded. **Calendar:** Semester, limited summer session. **Full-time faculty:** 508 total; 61% have terminal degrees, 46% minority, 55% women. **Part-time faculty:** 1,031 total; 19% have terminal degrees, 47% minority, 44% women. **Class size:** 10% < 20, 90% 20-39, less than 1% 40-49, less than 1% 50-99. **Special facilities:** Two theaters, media center, gymnasium with intercollegiate-size swimming pool.

Student profile. Among degree-seeking undergraduates, 6,812 enrolled as first-time, first-year students, 1,533 transferred in from other institutions.

Part-time:	32%	Asian American:	13%
Out-of-state:	2%	Hispanic/Latino:	40%
Women:	57%	International:	6%
African American:	30%	25 or older:	25%

Transfer out. Colleges most students transferred to 2015: Baruch College, Brooklyn College, City College, Hunter College, Lehman College.

Basis for selection. Open admission, but selective for some programs. Special requirements for associate degree programs in nursing; admission to clinical sequence of AAS degree programs competitive, based on college GPA. SAT or ACT recommended.

High school preparation. 16 units recommended. Recommended units include English 4, mathematics 3, social studies 4, science 2 (laboratory 2) and foreign language 2. One unit of fine arts recommended.

2015-2016 Annual costs. Tuition/fees: $5,169; $9,969 out-of-state. Per-credit charge: $210 in-state; $320 out-of-state. Books/supplies: $1,304. Personal expenses: $1,798.

2014-2015 Financial aid. All financial aid based on need. 4,760 full-time freshmen applied for aid; 4,760 deemed to have need; 4,668 received aid. 92% of total undergraduate aid awarded as scholarships/grants, 8% as loans/jobs. Need-based aid available for part-time students. Work-study available nights, weekends and for part-time students.

Application procedures. Admission: Priority date 2/1; no deadline. $65 fee, may be waived for applicants with need. Admission notification on a rolling basis beginning on or about 2/1. All CUNY schools operate on a rolling admission basis; therefore colleges and programs may close before the deadline date. **Financial aid:** Priority date 5/1; no closing date. FAFSA, institutional form required. Applicants notified on a rolling basis starting 4/15.

Academics. Special study options: Accelerated study, cooperative education, cross-registration, distance learning, dual enrollment of high school students, ESL, exchange student, honors, independent study, internships, liberal arts/career combination, study abroad, weekend college. License preparation in nursing. **Credit/placement by examination:** AP, CLEP, institutional tests. 30 credit hours maximum toward associate degree. **Support services:** GED preparation and test center, learning center, pre-admission summer program, remedial instruction, study skills assistance, tutoring, writing center.

Majors. Biology: Biomedical sciences. **Business:** Accounting technology, administrative services, business admin, small business admin. **Computer sciences:** General, computer science, networking, web page design. **Education:** Teacher assistance. **Engineering:** General. **English:** English lit. **Health services:** EMT paramedic, health information technology, nursing (RN), respiratory therapy assistant. **Human services:** Community org/advocacy. **Liberal arts:** Arts/sciences. **Math:** General. **Physical sciences:** General. **Protective services:** Forensics, police science. **Visual/performing arts:** General.

Most popular majors. Business/marketing 23%, computer/information sciences 6%, health sciences 6%, liberal arts 34%, security/protective services 11%.

Technology on campus. 1,500 workstations in library, computer center, student center. Commuter students can connect to campus network. Online course registration, online library, wireless network available.

Student life. Freshman orientation: Available. Preregistration for classes offered. **Activities:** Campus ministries, choral groups, dance, drama, international student organizations, literary magazine, musical theater, student government, numerous organizations.

Athletics. NJCAA. **Intercollegiate:** Baseball, basketball, soccer M, volleyball. **Intramural:** Basketball, cricket, football (non-tackle), soccer, table tennis, triathlon, volleyball. **Team name:** Panthers.

Student services. Alcohol/substance abuse counseling, career counseling, services for economically disadvantaged, student employment services, financial aid counseling, health services, legal services, on-campus daycare, personal counseling, placement for graduates, veterans' counselor, women's services. **Physically disabled:** Services for visually, speech, hearing impaired. **Transfer:** Pre-admission transcript evaluation for new students. Transfer center, transfer adviser, college fairs on campus for students transferring to 4-year colleges.

Contact. E-mail: admissions@bmcc.cuny.edu
Phone: (212) 220-1265 Toll-free number: (866) 583-5729
Fax: (212) 220-2366
Eugenio Barrios, Director of Enrollment Management, City University of New York: Borough of Manhattan Community College, 199 Chambers Street, New York, NY 10007

City University of New York: Bronx Community College

Bronx, New York — CB member
www.bcc.cuny.edu — CB code: 2051

- Public 2-year community college
- Commuter campus in very large city

General. Founded in 1957. Regionally accredited. **Enrollment:** 11,434 degree-seeking undergraduates. **Degrees:** 1,543 associate awarded. **Calendar:** Semester, limited summer session. **Full-time faculty:** 336 total; 48% have terminal degrees, 55% minority, 50% women. **Part-time faculty:** 492 total; 13% have terminal degrees, 61% minority, 43% women. **Special facilities:** Hall of Fame for Great Americans.

Transfer out. Colleges most students transferred to 2015: Lehman College, City College, Baruch College, Hunter College, John Jay College of Criminal Justice.

Basis for selection. Open admission. Units recommended for admission must be acquired before graduation from any CUNY community college.

High school preparation. College-preparatory program recommended. 9 units recommended. Recommended units include English 3, mathematics 2 and science 1.

2015-2016 Annual costs. Tuition/fees: $5,205; $10,005 out-of-state. Per-credit charge: $210 in-state; $320 out-of-state. Books/supplies: $652. Personal expenses: $2,432.

Financial aid. All financial aid based on need. Need-based aid available for part-time students. Work-study available nights, weekends and for part-time students.

Application procedures. Admission: $65 fee. Admission notification on a rolling basis beginning on or about 2/1. All CUNY schools operate on a rolling admission basis; therefore colleges and programs may close before the deadline date. **Financial aid:** Closing date 6/30. FAFSA required. Applicants notified on a rolling basis starting 8/1.

Academics. Special study options: Cooperative education, cross-registration, distance learning, double major, dual enrollment of high school students, ESL, external degree, honors, independent study, internships, liberal arts/career combination, student-designed major, study abroad, weekend college. License preparation in nursing. **Credit/placement by examination:** AP, CLEP, IB, institutional tests. 30 credit hours maximum toward associate degree. **Support services:** GED preparation and test center, learning center, pre-admission summer program, reduced course load, remedial instruction, study skills assistance, tutoring, writing center.

Majors. Business: General, accounting, administrative services, management information systems, office technology. **Computer sciences:** Computer science, data processing. **Education:** Teacher assistance. **Health services:** Clinical lab technology, medical assistant, medical radiologic technology/radiation therapy, nuclear medical technology, nursing (RN). **Liberal arts:** Arts/sciences. **Visual/performing arts:** Commercial/advertising art.

Most popular majors. Business/marketing 21%, computer/information sciences 6%, health sciences 14%, liberal arts 27%, public administration/social services 15%.

Technology on campus. 490 workstations in library, computer center, student center. Commuter students can connect to campus network. Online course registration, online library, wireless network available.

Student life. Freshman orientation: Available. Preregistration for classes offered. **Activities:** Choral groups, dance, drama, literary magazine, music ensembles, radio station, student government, student newspaper.

Athletics. Intercollegiate: Baseball M, basketball, cheerleading, soccer M, track and field. **Team name:** BCC Broncos.

Student services. Chaplain/spiritual director, career counseling, student employment services, financial aid counseling, health services, on-campus daycare, personal counseling, placement for graduates, veterans' counselor. **Physically disabled:** Services for visually, speech impaired. **Transfer:** Transfer adviser, college fairs on campus for students transferring to 4-year colleges.

Contact. E-mail: admission@bcc.cuny.edu
Phone: (718) 289-5895 Fax: (718) 289-6352
Patricia Ramos, Director of Admissions, City University of New York: Bronx Community College, 2155 University Avenue, Bronx, NY 10453

City University of New York: Guttman Community College
New York, New York
www.guttman.cuny.edu

▸ Public 2-year community college
▸ Commuter campus in very large city

General. Regionally accredited. **Enrollment:** 691 degree-seeking undergraduates. **Degrees:** 158 associate awarded. **Location:** Midtown Manhattan in New York City. **Calendar:** Semester. **Full-time faculty:** 36 total. **Part-time faculty:** 30 total. **Class size:** 25% < 20, 75% 20-39.

Basis for selection. Guttman Community College is an open admissions college. Applicants who have a high school diploma or high school equivalency, including undocumented immigrants, are welcome to apply. Enrollment of new first-year students in the fall semester only.

High school preparation. College-preparatory program recommended. Required and recommended units include English 4, mathematics 3-4, social studies 3-4, (laboratory 2-3), foreign language 2 and computer science 1.

2015-2016 Annual costs. Tuition/fees: $5,193; $9,993 out-of-state. Per-credit charge: $210 in-state; $320 out-of-state. Books/supplies: $1,304. Personal expenses: $3,066.

Financial aid. Need-based: Need-based aid available for part-time students. Work-study available nights, weekends and for part-time students.

Application procedures. Admission: Closing date 2/1. $65 fee, may be waived for applicants with need. Application must be submitted online.

Admission notification on a rolling basis beginning on or about 2/1. Must reply by 5/1. Application deadline 2/1, however all applications considered until enrollment is full. **Financial aid:** Closing date 6/30. FAFSA required. Applicants notified on a rolling basis starting 4/1.

Academics. Full-time attendance required in the first year. First-year students attend classes in a block schedule, five days a week, approximately four hours per day. The first-year core curriculum integrates developmental work with credit-bearing content to build college-level reading, writing, and math skills and interdisciplinary thinking and reasoning skills. **Special study options:** Internships. Community Days for community-based learning and academic service-learning. **Credit/placement by examination:** AP. **Support services:** Pre-admission summer program, study skills assistance, tutoring. Integrated support through instructional teams and learning communities. Peer mentors assist students with study skills, test taking skills, time management, and general academic competencies. Subject-area "Meet-Ups" provide additional help with coursework and skills development. LABSS (Learning About Being a Successful Student) is a weekly advisement seminar.

Majors. Business: Business admin. **Computer sciences:** Information technology. **Health services:** Health information technology. **Liberal arts:** Arts/sciences. **Social sciences:** Urban studies.

Technology on campus. 517 workstations in library, computer center. Online library, helpline, wireless network available.

Student life. Freshman orientation: Mandatory. Preregistration for classes offered. Orientation is typically in July and August and is a half-day event for students. Parents also invited to attend. Formal overview of college requirements and services and informal time to meet other students. Email accounts are issued and student ID card photos taken. **Activities:** Student government, student newspaper.

Athletics. Intramural: Basketball, soccer, table tennis, track and field.

Student services. Career counseling, services for economically disadvantaged, student employment services, financial aid counseling, personal counseling. **Physically disabled:** Services for visually, speech, hearing impaired.

Contact. E-mail: admissions@guttman.cuny.edu
Phone: (646) 313-8010
Sophea So, Director of College Admissions and Access, City University of New York: Guttman Community College, 50 West 40th Street, New York, NY 10018

City University of New York: Hostos Community College
Bronx, New York
www.hostos.cuny.edu

CB code: 2303

▸ Public 2-year community college
▸ Commuter campus in very large city

General. Founded in 1970. Regionally accredited. Bilingual Spanish/English liberal arts program. **Enrollment:** 6,427 degree-seeking undergraduates. **Degrees:** 920 associate awarded. **Calendar:** Semester, limited summer session. **Full-time faculty:** 191 total; 56% have terminal degrees, 56% minority, 54% women. **Part-time faculty:** 328 total; 23% have terminal degrees, 68% minority, 47% women.

Student profile.

Out-of-state:	1% **25 or older:**	35%

Transfer out. Colleges most students transferred to 2015: CUNY Lehman College, CUNY City College, CUNY John Jay College.

Basis for selection. Open admission, but selective for some programs. Admission to allied health programs based on Freshman Skills Assessment and subsequent performance in courses.

High school preparation. 16 units recommended. Recommended units include English 4, mathematics 3, social studies 4, science 2 and foreign language 2. 2 fine arts required. High school biology, chemistry, math required of allied health applicants.

2015-2016 Annual costs. Tuition/fees: $5,206; $10,006 out-of-state. Per-credit charge: $210 in-state; $320 out-of-state.

Financial aid. Need-based: Need-based aid available for part-time students. Work-study available nights, weekends and for part-time students.

Application procedures. Admission: $65 fee, may be waived for applicants with need. Admission notification on a rolling basis beginning on or about 2/1. All CUNY schools operate on a rolling admission basis; therefore colleges and programs may close before the deadline date. **Financial aid:** Priority date 7/1; no closing date. FAFSA required. Applicants notified on a rolling basis; must reply within 3 week(s) of notification.

Academics. Dual enrollment programs with City College, John Jay College. **Special study options:** Cooperative education, distance learning, dual enrollment of high school students, ESL, honors, independent study, internships, liberal arts/career combination, student-designed major, study abroad, weekend college. Serrano scholars program. License preparation in dental hygiene, nursing, radiology. **Credit/placement by examination:** AP, CLEP, institutional tests. **Support services:** GED preparation and test center, learning center, pre-admission summer program, remedial instruction, study skills assistance, tutoring, writing center.

Majors. Business: General, accounting, administrative services, business admin, office technology. **Education:** Early childhood. **Engineering:** Chemical, electrical. **Health services:** Community health, dental hygiene, medical radiologic technology/radiation therapy, medical secretary, nursing (RN). **Human services:** General. **Liberal arts:** Arts/sciences. **Math:** General. **Protective services:** Criminal justice, forensics. **Visual/performing arts:** Digital arts.

Most popular majors. Business/marketing 14%, education 19%, health sciences 13%, legal studies 12%, liberal arts 34%.

Technology on campus. 1,000 workstations in library, computer center, student center. Commuter students can connect to campus network. Online course registration, online library, helpline, wireless network available.

Student life. **Freshman orientation:** Available. Preregistration for classes offered. Held once a week each semester. **Activities:** Marching band, dance, drama, student government, student newspaper, TV station, Puerto Rican club, Christian club, black student union, Dominican association, South American student union, Ecuadorean student association, dental hygiene club, nursing club, Mexican club, Cuban club.

Athletics. NJCAA. **Intercollegiate:** Baseball M, basketball, soccer, volleyball W. **Intramural:** Basketball, volleyball W. **Team name:** Caimans.

Student services. Alcohol/substance abuse counseling, chaplain/spiritual director, career counseling, services for economically disadvantaged, student employment services, financial aid counseling, health services, on-campus daycare, personal counseling, placement for graduates, veterans' counselor, women's services. **Physically disabled:** Services for visually, speech, hearing impaired. **Transfer:** Re-entry adviser, pre-admission transcript evaluation for new students. Transfer adviser, college fairs on campus for students transferring to 4-year colleges.

Contact. E-mail: admissions@hostos.cuny.edu
Phone: (718) 518-4405 Fax: (718) 518-6643
Roland Velez, Director of Admissions/Recruitment, City University of New York: Hostos Community College, 500 Grand Concourse, Bronx, NY 10451

City University of New York: Kingsborough Community College
Brooklyn, New York   **CB member**
www.kbcc.cuny.edu   **CB code: 2358**

- Public 2-year community college
- Commuter campus in very large city

General. Founded in 1963. Regionally accredited. **Enrollment:** 12,847 degree-seeking undergraduates. **Degrees:** 2,817 associate awarded. **Location:** 10 miles from midtown. **Calendar:** Semester, extensive summer session. **Full-time faculty:** 357 total. **Part-time faculty:** 617 total. **Class size:** 36% < 20, 53% 20-39, 11% 40-49. **Special facilities:** Private beach on campus. **Partnerships:** Formal partnership with College Now program for high school seniors.

Student profile.

Out-of-state: 1%   **25 or older:**   24%

Transfer out. Colleges most students transferred to 2015: City University of New York: Brooklyn College, Long Island University, Pace University, City University of New York: College of Staten Island, City University of New York: Baruch College.

Basis for selection. Open admission. Units recommended for admission must be acquired before graduation from any CUNY community college.

High school preparation. 16 units recommended. Recommended units include English 4, mathematics 3, social studies 4, science 2 and foreign language 2. One unit fine arts.

2015-2016 Annual costs. Tuition/fees: $5,201; $10,001 out-of-state. Per-credit charge: $210 in-state; $320 out-of-state. Books/supplies: $1,179. Personal expenses: $2,912.

Financial aid. All financial aid based on need. Need-based aid available for part-time students. Work-study available nights, weekends and for part-time students.

Application procedures. Admission: $65 fee, may be waived for applicants with need. Admission notification on a rolling basis beginning on or about 2/1. All CUNY schools operate on a rolling admission basis; therefore colleges and programs may close before the deadline date. **Financial aid:** Closing date 4/30. FAFSA required. Applicants notified on a rolling basis; must reply within 2 week(s) of notification.

Academics. Special study options: Accelerated study, cross-registration, dual enrollment of high school students, ESL, honors, independent study, internships, student-designed major. My Turn Program for senior citizens, New Start Program for students academically dismissed from 4-year institutions. License preparation in nursing. **Credit/placement by examination:** AP, CLEP, institutional tests. 16 credit hours maximum toward associate degree. **Support services:** GED preparation, learning center, pre-admission summer program, reduced course load, remedial instruction, tutoring, writing center.

Majors. Biology: General. **Business:** Accounting, business admin, fashion, office management, tourism promotion, tourism/travel. **Communications:** Broadcast journalism, journalism. **Computer sciences:** Computer science, data processing. **Education:** Early childhood, elementary, teacher assistance. **Engineering:** General. **Health services:** Community health services, mental health services, nursing (RN), physical therapy assistant, prenursing, surgical technology. **Liberal arts:** Arts/sciences. **Math:** General. **Parks/recreation:** General, exercise sciences. **Physical sciences:** Chemistry, physics. **Protective services:** Law enforcement admin. **Visual/performing arts:** General, commercial/advertising art, studio arts.

Most popular majors. Business/marketing 15%, health sciences 13%, liberal arts 39%, security/protective services 7%.

Technology on campus. 900 workstations in library, computer center. Online course registration available.

Student life. Freshman orientation: Available. Preregistration for classes offered. **Activities:** Bands, choral groups, dance, drama, film society, literary magazine, music ensembles, musical theater, opera, radio station, student government, student newspaper, symphony orchestra, over 60 ethnic, academic, religious, and political groups.

Athletics. NJCAA. **Intercollegiate:** Baseball M, basketball, soccer M, softball W, tennis, track and field, volleyball W. **Intramural:** Basketball, bowling, football (non-tackle), racquetball, soccer, softball, swimming, table tennis, tennis, volleyball, weight lifting.

Student services. Adult student services, career counseling, student employment services, health services, on-campus daycare, personal counseling, placement for graduates, veterans' counselor. **Physically disabled:** Services for visually, speech, hearing impaired. **Transfer:** Transfer adviser for students transferring to 4-year colleges.

Contact. E-mail: info@kbcc.cuny.edu
Phone: (718) 368-4600 Fax: (718) 368-5356
Javier Morgades, Admissions Information Center Director, City University of New York: Kingsborough Community College, 2001 Oriental Boulevard, Brooklyn, NY 11235

City University of New York: LaGuardia Community College
Long Island City, New York
www.lagcc.cuny.edu   **CB code: 2246**

- Public 2-year community college
- Commuter campus in very large city

General. Founded in 1970. Regionally accredited. **Enrollment:** 16,062 degree-seeking undergraduates; 3,270 non-degree-seeking students. **Degrees:** 2,426 associate awarded. **Calendar:** Semester, extensive summer session. **Full-time faculty:** 407 total; 58% have terminal degrees, 42% minority, 58% women. **Part-time faculty:** 719 total; 14% have terminal degrees, 42% minority, 46% women. **Class size:** 24% < 20, 76% 20-39, less than 1% 40-49, less than 1% 50-99. **Special facilities:** LaGuardia and Wagner archives.

Student profile. Among degree-seeking undergraduates, 76% enrolled in a transfer program, 24% enrolled in a vocational program, 2,950 enrolled as first-time, first-year students, 1,410 transferred in from other institutions.

Part-time:	35%	Hispanic/Latino:	42%
Out-of-state:	1%	Multi-racial, non-Hispanic:	1%
Women:	58%	International:	4%
African American:	15%	25 or older:	35%
Asian American:	12%		

Transfer out. Colleges most students transferred to 2015: Queens College, Baruch College, Hunter College, York College, John Jay College.

Basis for selection. Open admission. **Adult students:** SAT/ACT scores not required. **Home schooled:** Transcript of courses and grades required. Submit a letter from their school district superintendent confirming that all high school graduation requirements of the district have been met. **Learning Disabled:** Students are encouraged to contact the office for Students with Disabilities before completing the application to ensure accommodations are addressed throughout the application and matriculation process.

High school preparation. 13 units recommended. Recommended units include English 4, mathematics 2, social studies 2, science 1 and academic electives 4.

2015-2016 Annual costs. Tuition/fees: $5,217; $10,017 out-of-state. Per-credit charge: $210 in-state; $320 out-of-state. Books/supplies: $1,304. Personal expenses: $1,798.

2014-2015 Financial aid. All financial aid based on need. 2,364 full-time freshmen applied for aid; 2,279 deemed to have need; 1,945 received aid. Average need met was 32%. Average scholarship/grant was $4,307; average loan $1,415. 91% of total undergraduate aid awarded as scholarships/grants, 9% as loans/jobs. Need-based aid available for part-time students. Work-study available nights, weekends and for part-time students.

Application procedures. Admission: $65 fee, may be waived for applicants with need. Admission notification on a rolling basis beginning on or about 2/1. All CUNY schools operate on a rolling admission basis; therefore colleges and programs may close before the deadline date. **Financial aid:** Closing date 4/15. FAFSA, institutional form required. Applicants notified on a rolling basis starting 3/1; must reply within 4 week(s) of notification.

Academics. Special study options: Accelerated study, cooperative education, cross-registration, distance learning, dual enrollment of high school students, ESL, honors, independent study, internships, liberal arts/career combination, student-designed major, study abroad. Summer program with Vassar College. License preparation in nursing, occupational therapy, paramedic, physical therapy, radiology. **Credit/placement by examination:** AP, CLEP, institutional tests. 10 credit hours maximum toward associate degree. **Support services:** GED preparation and test center, learning center, pre-admission summer program, reduced course load, remedial instruction, tutoring, writing center.

Majors. Biology: General. **Business:** Accounting technology, administrative services, business admin, restaurant/food services, tourism/travel. **Communications:** Communications/speech/rhetoric. **Communications technology:** Recording arts. **Computer sciences:** Computer science, data entry, networking, programming. **Conservation:** Environmental science. **Education:** Teacher assistance. **Engineering:** Civil, electrical, mechanical. **English:** English lit. **Foreign languages:** Spanish. **Health services:** Dietetic technician, EMT paramedic, medical radiologic technology/radiation therapy, mental health services, nursing (RN), occupational therapy assistant, physical therapy assistant, veterinary technology/assistant. **Liberal arts:** Arts/sciences. **Philosophy/religion:** Philosophy. **Physical sciences:** General. **Protective services:** Law enforcement admin. **Psychology:** General. **Visual/performing arts:** Commercial photography, dramatic, industrial design, studio arts. **Work/family studies:** Aging.

Most popular majors. Business/marketing 23%, computer/information sciences 6%, health sciences 12%, legal studies 12%, liberal arts 21%, visual/performing arts 6%.

Technology on campus. 1,414 workstations in library, computer center. Commuter students can connect to campus network. Online course registration, online library, helpline, wireless network available.

Student life. Freshman orientation: Available. Preregistration for classes offered. **Activities:** Dance, drama, film society, international student organizations, literary magazine, music ensembles, Model UN, radio station, student government, student newspaper, TV station, Muslim, Christian, Buddhist, Phi Theta Kappa, Jewish, Catholic clubs.

Athletics. Intercollegiate: Basketball. **Intramural:** Basketball, handball, soccer, softball, swimming, table tennis, volleyball.

Student services. Adult student services, career counseling, services for economically disadvantaged, student employment services, financial aid

counseling, health services, legal services, minority student services, on-campus daycare, personal counseling, placement for graduates, veterans' counselor, women's services. **Physically disabled:** Services for visually, speech, hearing impaired. **Transfer:** Transfer center, transfer adviser, college fairs on campus for students transferring to 4-year colleges.

Contact. E-mail: admissions@lagcc.cuny.edu
Phone: (718) 482-7206 Fax: (718) 482-2033
LaVora Desvigne, Director of Admissions, City University of New York: LaGuardia Community College, 31-10 Thomson Avenue, Long Island City, NY 11101

City University of New York: Queensborough Community College
Bayside, New York
www.qcc.cuny.edu   CB code: 2751

◗ Public 2-year community college
◗ Commuter campus in very large city

General. Founded in 1958. Regionally accredited. **Enrollment:** 13,692 degree-seeking undergraduates; 1,801 non-degree-seeking students. **Degrees:** 2,129 associate awarded. **Location:** 10 miles from midtown Manhattan. **Calendar:** Semester, limited summer session. **Full-time faculty:** 395 total; 82% have terminal degrees, 31% minority, 51% women. **Part-time faculty:** 560 total; 30% have terminal degrees, 33% minority, 47% women. **Class size:** 25% < 20, 73% 20-39, 2% 40-49, 1% 50-99. **Special facilities:** Resource center for Holocaust studies, observatory, art museum. **Partnerships:** Formal partnership with Verizon for Next Step associate degree program in telecommunication technology for Verizon employees.

Student profile. Among degree-seeking undergraduates, 3,354 enrolled as first-time, first-year students, 1,081 transferred in from other institutions.

Part-time:	32%	Native American:	1%
Women:	53%	Native Hawaiian/Pacific islander:	1%
African American:	22%	Multi-racial, non-Hispanic:	1%
Asian American:	23%	International:	6%
Hispanic/Latino:	32%		

Transfer out. Colleges most students transferred to 2015: CUNY Queens College, St. John's University.

Basis for selection. Open admission. Candidates for admission who hold a regular or local high school diploma, or a New York State Equivalency Diploma (GED) and who have not yet attended college or any post-secondary institution including business, trade or technical school must file the Freshman application for admission. Units recommended for admission must be acquired before graduation from CUNY. **Home schooled:** Transcript of courses and grades required.

High school preparation. Recommended units include English 4, mathematics 3, social studies 2, science 2 (laboratory 2) and academic electives 4.

2015-2016 Annual costs. Tuition/fees: $5,209; $10,009 out-of-state. Per-credit charge: $210 in-state; $320 out-of-state. Books/supplies: $1,304. Personal expenses: $2,946.

Financial aid. Need-based: Work-study available nights, weekends and for part-time students.

Application procedures. Admission: Closing date 2/1 (postmark date). $65 fee, may be waived for applicants with need. Admission notification on a rolling basis beginning on or about 2/1. All CUNY schools operate on a rolling admission basis; therefore colleges and programs may close before the deadline date. **Financial aid:** No deadline. FAFSA, institutional form required. Applicants notified on a rolling basis starting 7/15.

Academics. Special study options: Distance learning, ESL, honors, student-designed major, weekend college. License preparation in nursing. **Credit/placement by examination:** AP, CLEP, institutional tests. **Support services:** GED preparation, learning center, pre-admission summer program, remedial instruction, tutoring, writing center.

Majors. Biology: General. **Business:** General, accounting, administrative services, business admin, office management. **Communications technology:** General, recording arts. **Computer sciences:** General, data processing, information systems, programming. **Engineering:** Computer. **Health services:** Clinical lab technology, environmental health, nursing (RN). **History:** General. **Liberal arts:** Arts/sciences. **Physical sciences:** Chemistry. **Psychology:** General. **Social sciences:** Political science, sociology. **Visual/performing arts:** General, art, dance, dramatic, music history, photography.

Most popular majors. Business/marketing 18%, engineering/engineering technologies 6%, health sciences 13%, liberal arts 39%, physical sciences 6%, security/protective services 9%.

Technology on campus. 143 workstations in library, computer center. Online course registration, helpline, wireless network available.

Student life. Freshman orientation: Available. Preregistration for classes offered. **Activities:** Choral groups, drama, international student organizations, musical theater, opera, architecture club, Asian society, biology club, Chi Alpha Christian, drama society, future teachers society, Hillel club, Muslim student association, Newman club.

Athletics. NJCAA. **Intercollegiate:** Baseball M, basketball, cross-country, soccer M, softball W, tennis, track and field, volleyball. **Intramural:** Badminton, basketball, soccer, softball, swimming, table tennis, tennis, track and field, volleyball. **Team name:** Tigers.

Student services. Adult student services, career counseling, student employment services, health services, on-campus daycare, personal counseling, placement for graduates, veterans' counselor. **Physically disabled:** Services for visually, speech, hearing impaired. **Transfer:** Transfer adviser, college fairs on campus for students transferring to 4-year colleges.

Contact. E-mail: admissions@qcc.cuny.edu
Phone: (718) 281-5000
Laura Bruno, Director, City University of New York: Queensborough Community College, 222-05 56th Avenue, Bayside, NY 11364-1497

Clinton Community College
Plattsburgh, New York
www.clinton.edu   CB code: 2135

- Public 2-year community and career college
- Commuter campus in large town

General. Founded in 1966. Regionally accredited. SUNY (State University of New York) institution. **Enrollment:** 937 degree-seeking undergraduates; 26 non-degree-seeking students. **Degrees:** 305 associate awarded. **Location:** 60 miles from Montreal, Canada; 30 miles from Burlington, Vermont; 50 miles from Lake Placid. **Calendar:** Semester, limited summer session. **Full-time faculty:** 51 total. **Part-time faculty:** 72 total. **Class size:** 66% < 20, 33% 20-39, less than 1% 50-99. **Special facilities:** Science and technology center, wind energy and turbine technology lab.

Student profile. Among degree-seeking undergraduates, 380 enrolled as first-time, first-year students, 81 transferred in from other institutions.

Part-time: 3% **Women:**   58%

Transfer out. Colleges most students transferred to 2015: SUNY at Plattsburgh.

Basis for selection. Open admission, but selective for some programs and for out-of-state students. Selective program for Nursing requires an essay, recommendations; TEAS examination. A college committee determines top candidates to enroll. Test scores of a certain level may exempt students from taking placement test. SAT or ACT recommended. We offer our own placement testing in reading, writing and math. Exemption crtieria used to determine if a student needs the entire exam. SAT Math, Reading, Writing: 500+, ACT Math 20+, Reading 21+, English 21+ are eligible for exemption. **Adult students:** SAT/ACT scores not required. **Home schooled:** State high school equivalency certificate required.

High school preparation. Recommended units include English 4, mathematics 3, social studies 4, history 4, science 2 (laboratory 2) and foreign language 2. Chemistry and Biology high school level courses recommended for Nursing applicants.

2015-2016 Annual costs. Tuition/fees: $5,122; $10,122 out-of-state. Per-credit charge: $175 in-state; $383 out-of-state. Room/board: $9,518. Books/supplies: $850. Personal expenses: $1,260.

Financial aid. All financial aid based on need. Need-based aid available for part-time students. Work-study available nights, weekends and for part-time students.

Application procedures. Admission: Closing date 9/1. No application fee. Admission notification by 9/1. Admission notification on a rolling basis beginning on or about 9/15. **Financial aid:** Priority date 6/12; no closing date. FAFSA required. Applicants notified on a rolling basis starting 4/12; must reply within 2 week(s) of notification.

Academics. Special study options: Combined bachelor's/graduate degree, cross-registration, distance learning, dual enrollment of high school students,

---

honors, independent study, internships, liberal arts/career combination, student-designed major. Remedial Basic skills program. **Credit/placement by examination:** AP, CLEP, IB, SAT, ACT, institutional tests. 30 credit hours maximum toward associate degree. **Support services:** Remedial instruction, study skills assistance, tutoring, writing center.

Majors. Business: Accounting, business admin. **Computer sciences:** General. **Conservation:** Environmental science. **Health services:** Nursing (RN). **Liberal arts:** Arts/sciences. **Protective services:** Law enforcement admin.

Technology on campus. 350 workstations in dormitories, library, computer center. Dormitories wired for high-speed internet access and linked to campus network. Commuter students can connect to campus network. Online library, helpline, wireless network available.

Student life. Freshman orientation: Mandatory. Preregistration for classes offered. Held for about 3 hours and takes place during the 2 weeks before classes begin. **Housing:** Guaranteed on-campus for freshmen. Coed dorms, special housing for disabled available. $200 nonrefundable deposit. Pets allowed in dorm rooms. **Activities:** Choral groups, drama, international student organizations, musical theater, student government, student newspaper.

Athletics. NJCAA. **Intercollegiate:** Baseball M, basketball, soccer, softball W. **Team name:** Cougars.

Student services. Adult student services, alcohol/substance abuse counseling, career counseling, financial aid counseling, health services, on-campus daycare, personal counseling, placement for graduates, veterans' counselor. **Physically disabled:** Services for visually, speech, hearing impaired. **Transfer:** Transfer adviser, college fairs on campus for students transferring to 4-year colleges.

Contact. E-mail: admissions@clinton.edu
Phone: (518) 562-4170 Toll-free number: (800) 552-1160
Fax: (518) 562-4373
Lauren Currie, Registrar, Clinton Community College, 136 Clinton Point Drive, Plattsburgh, NY 12901

Cochran School of Nursing
Yonkers, New York
www.cochranschoolofnursing.us   CB code: 2894

- Private 2-year nursing college
- Commuter campus in small city

General. Founded in 1894. **Enrollment:** 89 degree-seeking undergraduates. **Degrees:** 28 associate awarded. **Location:** 20 miles from New York City. **Calendar:** Semester, limited summer session. **Full-time faculty:** 9 total; 33% minority, 100% women. **Part-time faculty:** 2 total; 100% women. **Class size:** 100% < 20. **Special facilities:** Clinical facilities at St. John's Riverside Hospital, skills lab with several mechanical simulators.

Student profile.

Part-time:	87%	**Hispanic/Latino:**	28%
Women:	85%	**Multi-racial, non-Hispanic:**	3%
African American:	22%	**25 or older:**	81%
Asian American:	7%		

Transfer out. Colleges most students transferred to 2015: Mercy College, College of New Rochelle, College of Mount St. Vincent, Adelphi University, Westchester Community College.

Basis for selection. School achievement record, test scores, interview most important. Completion of prerequisite with C+ grade or better. Writing sample required. Essay questions is given after applicant completes entrance exam. **Learning Disabled:** Must submit necessary documentation of disabilities at time of admission to disability officer.

High school preparation. Math units should include 1 algebra, science units should include 1 biology and 1 chemistry. 2 units of laboratory recommended.

2015-2016 Annual costs. Tuition/fees: $11,132. Per-credit charge: $563. Books/supplies: $450.

2015-2016 Financial aid. All financial aid based on need. 25% of total undergraduate aid awarded as scholarships/grants, 75% as loans/jobs. Need-based aid available for part-time students. Work-study available nights, weekends and for part-time students.

Application procedures. Admission: Closing date 6/1 (postmark date). $35 fee. Admission notification on a rolling basis. Application deadline for

January enrollment is October 1. **Financial aid:** Closing date 4/30. FAFSA required. Applicants notified on a rolling basis.

Academics. Special testing program facilitates career goals of LPNs who want to become RNs. **Special study options:** Combined bachelor's/graduate degree, internships, liberal arts/career combination. License preparation in nursing. **Credit/placement by examination:** AP, CLEP, IB, institutional tests. 27 credit hours maximum toward associate degree.

Majors. Health services: Nursing (RN).

Technology on campus. 35 workstations in library, computer center, student center. Online course registration, online library, wireless network available.

Student life. Freshman orientation: Mandatory. Preregistration for classes offered. **Policies:** Freshmen not permitted cars on campus. **Activities:** Student government, student newspaper.

Student services. Adult student services, career counseling, health services, personal counseling. **Transfer:** Pre-admission transcript evaluation for new students.

Contact. E-mail: admissions@cochranschoolofnursing.us
Phone: (914) 964-4296 Fax: (914) 964-4796
Drew Thompson, Admissions Counselor, Cochran School of Nursing, 967 North Broadway, Yonkers, NY 10701

College of Westchester
White Plains, New York
www.cw.edu   CB code: 1023

- For-profit 2-year business and career college
- Commuter campus in small city
- Interview required

General. Founded in 1915. Regionally accredited. **Enrollment:** 962 degree-seeking undergraduates; 105 non-degree-seeking students. **Degrees:** 81 bachelor's, 258 associate awarded. **Location:** 30 miles from New York City. **Calendar:** Semester, extensive summer session. **Full-time faculty:** 41 total. **Part-time faculty:** 44 total. **Class size:** 76% < 20, 24% 20-39. **Partnerships:** Formal partnerships with local corporations and businesses for internship and co-op work experience programs.

Student profile. Among degree-seeking undergraduates, 211 enrolled as first-time, first-year students.

Part-time:	12%	Asian American:	2%
Out-of-state:	3%	Hispanic/Latino:	41%
Women:	64%	Multi-racial, non-Hispanic:	2%
African American:	39%	25 or older:	41%

Basis for selection. Interview, prior academic performance, recommendations most important. Activities considered. Test scores considered when available. Institution-administered assessments used for academic placement.

High school preparation. College-preparatory program recommended. Recommended units include English 4 and mathematics 3.

2016-2017 Annual costs. Tuition/fees (projected): $23,350. Books/supplies: $1,000.

2014-2015 Financial aid. Need-based: 65% of total undergraduate aid awarded as scholarships/grants, 35% as loans/jobs. Need-based aid available for part-time students. Work-study available nights, weekends and for part-time students. **Non-need-based:** Scholarships awarded for academics, alumni affiliation.

Application procedures. Admission: No deadline. $40 fee, may be waived for applicants with need. Admission notification on a rolling basis. **Financial aid:** No deadline. FAFSA, institutional form required. Applicants notified on a rolling basis starting 2/7; must reply within 2 week(s) of notification.

Academics. Special study options: Accelerated study, cooperative education, distance learning, double major, honors, internships. Bachelor's degree programs available on campus. **Credit/placement by examination:** AP, CLEP, IB, SAT, institutional tests. 12 credit hours maximum toward associate degree. **Support services:** Learning center, pre-admission summer program, reduced course load, remedial instruction, study skills assistance, tutoring, writing center.

Majors. Business: Accounting, business admin. **Computer sciences:** General, LAN/WAN management, web page design. **Health services:** Insurance

specialist, medical assistant. **Visual/performing arts:** Commercial/advertising art.

Most popular majors. Business/marketing 39%, computer/information sciences 27%, health sciences 34%.

Technology on campus. 290 workstations in library, computer center. Commuter students can connect to campus network. Online library, helpline, repair service, wireless network available.

Student life. Freshman orientation: Mandatory. Preregistration for classes offered. **Activities:** Dance, student government, student newspaper, accounting society, allied health club, business club, Caribbean student association, Digital media club, Just Dance Crew, network technologies association, Phi Beta Kappa, Sigma Beta Delta.

Student services. Adult student services, career counseling, student employment services, financial aid counseling, personal counseling, placement for graduates, veterans' counselor. **Transfer:** Re-entry adviser, pre-admission transcript evaluation for new students. Transfer adviser for students transferring to 4-year colleges.

Contact. E-mail: admissions@cw.edu
Phone: (914) 831-0200 Toll-free number: (800) 333-4924
Fax: (914) 948-5441
Matt Curtis, Director of Admissions, College of Westchester, 325 Central Avenue, White Plains, NY 10606

Columbia-Greene Community College
Hudson, New York   CB member
www.sunycgcc.edu   CB code: 2138

- Public 2-year community college
- Commuter campus in small town

General. Founded in 1966. Regionally accredited. SUNY institution. **Enrollment:** 1,261 degree-seeking undergraduates; 516 non-degree-seeking students. **Degrees:** 329 associate awarded. **Location:** 40 miles from Albany. **Calendar:** Semester, limited summer session.

Student profile. Among degree-seeking undergraduates, 310 enrolled as first-time, first-year students.

Part-time:	44%	Women:	65%

Transfer out. Colleges most students transferred to 2015: SUNY Albany, SUNY New Paltz, College of Saint Rose.

Basis for selection. Admission to some programs based on school achievement record, test scores, and recommendations. Interview recommended. **Adult students:** SAT/ACT scores not required. **Home schooled:** Transcript of courses and grades, interview required.

2015-2016 Annual costs. Tuition/fees: $4,552; $8,752 out-of-state. Per-credit charge: $175 in-state; $350 out-of-state. Books/supplies: $1,200. Personal expenses: $950.

Financial aid. Need-based: Need-based aid available for part-time students. Work-study available nights, weekends and for part-time students.

Application procedures. Admission: No deadline. No application fee. Admission notification on a rolling basis. **Financial aid:** No deadline. FAFSA, institutional form required.

Academics. Special study options: Cooperative education, cross-registration, distance learning, dual enrollment of high school students, ESL, honors, independent study, internships, student-designed major. License preparation in nursing. **Credit/placement by examination:** AP, CLEP, institutional tests. **Support services:** GED preparation, learning center, pre-admission summer program, remedial instruction, study skills assistance, tutoring, writing center.

Honors college/program. Program offers the opportunity to work closely with faculty, conduct research, and participate in seminars and conferences with an interdisciplinary focus.

Majors. Business: Accounting technology, administrative services, business admin. **Computer sciences:** General, information technology. **Conservation:** Environmental studies. **Education:** Multi-level teacher. **Health services:** Medical assistant, nursing (RN). **Liberal arts:** Arts/sciences, humanities. **Parks/recreation:** Health/fitness. **Protective services:** Computer forensics, law enforcement admin. **Visual/performing arts:** Art.

Technology on campus. 150 workstations in library, computer center. Commuter students can connect to campus network. Online library, wireless network available.

Student life. Freshman orientation: Mandatory. Preregistration for classes offered. Held 1 week prior to start of fall classes. Online version is also available. **Activities:** Campus ministries, international student organizations, radio station, student government.

Athletics. NJCAA. **Intercollegiate:** Baseball M, basketball M, bowling, cross-country, golf, softball W, volleyball W. **Intramural:** Basketball, bowling, volleyball. **Team name:** Twins.

Student services. Adult student services, career counseling, student employment services, financial aid counseling, health services, on-campus daycare, personal counseling, placement for graduates, veterans' counselor. **Physically disabled:** Services for visually, hearing impaired. **Transfer:** Transfer adviser, college fairs on campus for students transferring to 4-year colleges.

Contact. E-mail: rachel.kappel@sunycgcc.edu
Phone: (518) 828-4181 ext. 3427 Fax: (518) 828-8543
Rachel Kappel, Acting Director of Admissions, Columbia-Greene Community College, 4400 Route 23, Hudson, NY 12534

Corning Community College
Corning, New York
www.corning-cc.edu   CB code: 2106

▶ Public 2-year community college
▶ Commuter campus in large town

General. Founded in 1956. Regionally accredited. SUNY institution. **Enrollment:** 2,558 degree-seeking undergraduates; 1,414 non-degree-seeking students. **Degrees:** 609 associate awarded. **Location:** 70 miles from Binghamton. **Calendar:** Semester, limited summer session. **Full-time faculty:** 89 total; 1% have terminal degrees, 6% minority, 40% women. **Part-time faculty:** 121 total; 2% have terminal degrees, 6% minority, 60% women. **Class size:** 59% < 20, 38% 20-39, less than 1% 40-49, 2% 50-99, less than 1% >100. **Special facilities:** 200-acre nature center, observatory with historic working model of Hale telescope, planetarium.

Student profile. Among degree-seeking undergraduates, 745 enrolled as first-time, first-year students, 131 transferred in from other institutions.

Part-time:	30%	25 or older:	30%
Out-of-state:	5%	Live on campus:	6%
Women:	59%		

Transfer out. Colleges most students transferred to 2015: Mansfield University, Keuka College, Rochester Institute of Technology, SUNY Empire State College, Elmira College.

Basis for selection. Open admission, but selective for some programs. Applicants without diploma or GED evaluated on individual basis. **Adult students:** SAT/ACT scores not required. **Home schooled:** Ability to Benefit testing required. **Learning Disabled:** Students should contact disability services to arrange accommodations, including accommodations for placement tests.

High school preparation. Recommended units include English 4, mathematics 1, social studies 4, science 1 (laboratory 1). 4 math and 4 science required of engineering science applicants.

2015-2016 Annual costs. Tuition/fees: $4,774; $9,004 out-of-state. Per-credit charge: $177 in-state; $354 out-of-state. Room/board: $9,000. Books/supplies: $1,000. Personal expenses: $1,200.

2014-2015 Financial aid. All financial aid based on need. Need-based aid available for part-time students. Work-study available nights, weekends and for part-time students.

Application procedures. Admission: No deadline. No application fee. Admission notification on a rolling basis. **Financial aid:** No deadline. FAFSA, CSS PROFILE required. Applicants notified on a rolling basis starting 4/1; must reply within 4 week(s) of notification.

Academics. Special study options: Distance learning, double major, dual enrollment of high school students, honors, independent study, internships, liberal arts/career combination, student-designed major, study abroad, weekend college. License preparation in nursing, paramedic. **Credit/placement by examination:** AP, CLEP, institutional tests. 30 credit hours maximum toward associate degree. **Support services:** Learning center, reduced course load, remedial instruction, study skills assistance, tutoring, writing center.

Majors. Biology: Environmental. **Business:** Accounting, administrative services, business admin. **Computer sciences:** General, information systems, networking, system admin. **Education:** Early childhood, elementary, health, physical. **Engineering:** Engineering science. **Health services:** EMT paramedic, nursing (RN), substance abuse counseling. **Liberal arts:** Arts/sciences, humanities. **Math:** General. **Parks/recreation:** Health/fitness. **Physical sciences:** General. **Protective services:** Law enforcement admin. **Social sciences:** General. **Work/family studies:** Child care management.

Most popular majors. Business/marketing 15%, health sciences 15%, liberal arts 42%, public administration/social services 6%.

Technology on campus. 400 workstations in library, computer center, student center. Online course registration, online library, helpline, wireless network available.

Student life. Freshman orientation: Available. Preregistration for classes offered. One-day transition course offered in January, end of August. **Housing:** Coed dorms available. $250 nonrefundable deposit, deadline 4/1. **Activities:** Campus ministries, choral groups, drama, international student organizations, literary magazine, music ensembles, radio station, student government, student newspaper, Christian club, Veteran's Association, service club, Red Cross club, My Brother's and Sister's Keeper, Environmental Protection Information Coalition.

Athletics. NJCAA. **Intercollegiate:** Baseball M, basketball, bowling, golf, soccer, softball W, volleyball W. **Intramural:** Badminton, basketball, soccer, volleyball. **Team name:** Red Barons.

Student services. Adult student services, alcohol/substance abuse counseling, chaplain/spiritual director, career counseling, services for economically disadvantaged, student employment services, financial aid counseling, health services, personal counseling, placement for graduates, veterans' counselor. **Physically disabled:** Services for visually, speech, hearing impaired. **Transfer:** Transfer center, transfer adviser, college fairs on campus for students transferring to 4-year colleges.

Contact. E-mail: admissions@corning-cc.edu
Phone: (607) 962-9151 Toll-free number: (800) 358-7171
Fax: (607) 962-9582
Karen Brown, Director of Admissions, Corning Community College, One Academic Drive, Corning, NY 14830

Dutchess Community College
Poughkeepsie, New York   CB member
www.sunydutchess.edu   CB code: 2198

▶ Public 2-year community college
▶ Commuter campus in large town

General. Founded in 1957. Regionally accredited. Extension programs at 2 sites. **Enrollment:** 6,327 degree-seeking undergraduates; 3,217 non-degree-seeking students. **Degrees:** 1,090 associate awarded. **Location:** 70 miles from New York City. **Calendar:** Semester, limited summer session. **Full-time faculty:** 125 total; 26% have terminal degrees, 19% minority, 52% women. **Part-time faculty:** 382 total; 56% women. **Special facilities:** Biological experimentation site on Hudson River.

Student profile. Among degree-seeking undergraduates, 80% enrolled in a transfer program, 20% enrolled in a vocational program, 1,853 enrolled as first-time, first-year students, 311 transferred in from other institutions.

Part-time:	34%	25 or older:	15%
Out-of-state:	1%	Live on campus:	5%
Women:	53%		

Transfer out. Colleges most students transferred to 2015: State University of New York at New Paltz, Marist College, Mount St. Mary's College, State University of New York at Albany, Mercy College.

Basis for selection. Open admission, but selective for some programs. Special requirements for nursing and engineering programs. **Home schooled:** Students must supply a superintendent's letter stating he/she has met the requirements of a public high school for graduation.

High school preparation. Recommended units include English 4, mathematics 3, social studies 4, science 3 and foreign language 2.

2015-2016 Annual costs. Tuition/fees: $3,900; $7,260 out-of-state. Per-credit charge: $140 in-state; $280 out-of-state. Room/board: $9,750. Books/supplies: $1,350. Personal expenses: $1,500.

2014-2015 Financial aid. Need-based: 73% of total undergraduate aid awarded as scholarships/grants, 27% as loans/jobs. Need-based aid available

for part-time students. Work-study available nights, weekends and for part-time students. **Non-need-based:** Scholarships awarded for academics.

Application procedures. Admission: No deadline. No application fee. Admission notification on a rolling basis. **Financial aid:** Priority date 5/1; no closing date. FAFSA required. Applicants notified on a rolling basis starting 5/15; must reply within 2 week(s) of notification.

Academics. Special study options: Cooperative education, cross-registration, distance learning, dual enrollment of high school students, ESL, honors, independent study, internships, liberal arts/career combination. Combined degree in education with SUNY at New Paltz. License preparation in aviation, nursing, paramedic. **Credit/placement by examination:** AP, CLEP, institutional tests. 40 credit hours maximum toward associate degree. **Support services:** GED preparation and test center, learning center, pre-admission summer program, reduced course load, remedial instruction, study skills assistance, tutoring, writing center.

Majors. Business: Accounting technology, business admin. **Communications:** Communications/speech/rhetoric. **Computer sciences:** General, information systems. **Education:** Biology, chemistry, early childhood, elementary, English, French, German, kindergarten/preschool, mathematics, middle, physical, science, secondary, social studies, Spanish. **Engineering:** General. **Foreign languages:** Sign language interpretation. **General:** Electrician. **Health services:** Clinical lab technology, EMT paramedic, nursing (RN). **Liberal arts:** Arts/sciences, humanities. **Parks/recreation:** Facilities management. **Protective services:** Fire services admin, police science. **Visual/performing arts:** General, art, commercial/advertising art. **Work/family studies:** Child care management.

Most popular majors. Business/marketing 17%, communication technologies 6%, education 9%, health sciences 15%, liberal arts 30%, security/protective services 7%.

Technology on campus. 1,606 workstations in dormitories, library, computer center. Dormitories wired for high-speed internet access and linked to campus network. Commuter students can connect to campus network. Online course registration, online library, helpline, repair service, wireless network available.

Student life. Freshman orientation: Available. Preregistration for classes offered. **Housing:** Coed dorms available. $350 partly refundable deposit. **Activities:** Jazz band, choral groups, dance, drama, film society, international student organizations, literary magazine, music ensembles, Model UN, musical theater, radio station, student government, student newspaper, TV station, political science club, black student union, anthropology club, fire science club, nursing club, early education club, human services club, Society for German Culture, christian fellowship.

Athletics. NJCAA. **Intercollegiate:** Baseball M, basketball, cross-country, soccer M, softball W, volleyball W. **Team name:** Falcons.

Student services. Adult student services, career counseling, services for economically disadvantaged, student employment services, financial aid counseling, health services, minority student services, on-campus daycare, personal counseling, placement for graduates, veterans' counselor. **Physically disabled:** Services for visually, speech, hearing impaired. **Transfer:** Pre-admission transcript evaluation for new students. Transfer adviser, college fairs on campus for students transferring to 4-year colleges.

Contact. E-mail: admissions@sunydutchess.edu
Phone: (845) 431-8010 Toll-free number: (800) 378-9707
Fax: (845) 431-8605
Michael Roe, Associate Dean of Enrollment Management, Dutchess Community College, 53 Pendell Road, Poughkeepsie, NY 12601-1595

Elmira Business Institute
Elmira, New York
www.ebi-college.com   CB code: 3332

- For-profit 2-year business, health science, technical and career college
- Commuter campus in large town
- Interview required

General. Accredited by ACICS. **Enrollment:** 196 degree-seeking undergraduates. **Degrees:** 104 associate awarded. **Calendar:** Semester. **Full-time faculty:** 15 total. **Part-time faculty:** 26 total.

Basis for selection. Open admission. **Home schooled:** State high school equivalency certificate required.

2015-2016 Annual costs. Books/supplies: $4,000.

Financial aid. All financial aid based on need. Need-based aid available for part-time students. Work-study available nights, weekends and for part-time students.

Application procedures. Admission: No deadline. No application fee. Admission notification on a rolling basis. **Financial aid:** Priority date 5/1; no closing date. FAFSA required. Applicants notified on a rolling basis starting 1/1; must reply within 1 week(s) of notification.

Academics. Special study options: Honors, internships, weekend college. **Credit/placement by examination:** AP, CLEP, institutional tests. **Support services:** Learning center, reduced course load, remedial instruction, study skills assistance, tutoring, writing center.

Majors. Business: Accounting. **Health services:** Clinical lab assistant, health information management, health information technology, insurance coding, medical assistant, medical secretary, medical transcription.

Technology on campus. 100 workstations in library, computer center. Wireless network available.

Student life. Freshman orientation: Mandatory. Preregistration for classes offered.

Student services. Career counseling, student employment services, financial aid counseling, personal counseling, placement for graduates. **Transfer:** Pre-admission transcript evaluation for new students. College fairs on campus for students transferring to 4-year colleges.

Contact. E-mail: sgalilei@ebi-college.com
Phone: (607) 733-7177 Toll-free number: (800) 843-1812
Fax: (607) 733-7178
Scott Galilie, Regional Director of Admissions, Elmira Business Institute, 303 North Main Street, Elmira, NY 14901

Elmira Business Institute: Vestal
Vestal, New York
www.elmirabusinessinstitute.edu

- For-profit 2-year business, health science, technical and career college
- Commuter campus in small city
- Interview required

General. Accredited by ACICS. **Enrollment:** 400 degree-seeking undergraduates. **Degrees:** 120 associate awarded. **Calendar:** Semester, extensive summer session. **Full-time faculty:** 14 total. **Part-time faculty:** 20 total.

Transfer out. Colleges most students transferred to 2015: Broome Community College.

Basis for selection. Open admission. **Home schooled:** Statement describing home school structure and mission required. Must have a letter from school superintendent or principal.

2015-2016 Annual costs. Personal expenses: $1,688.

Financial aid. All financial aid based on need. Need-based aid available for part-time students. Work-study available nights, weekends and for part-time students.

Application procedures. Admission: No deadline. No application fee. **Financial aid:** No deadline. FAFSA required. Applicants notified on a rolling basis starting 1/1; must reply within 1 week(s) of notification.

Academics. Credit/placement by examination: AP, CLEP, institutional tests. **Support services:** Reduced course load, remedial instruction, study skills assistance, tutoring.

Majors. Business: Accounting technology. **Health services:** Clinical lab assistant, insurance coding.

Technology on campus. Online library available.

Student life. Freshman orientation: Mandatory. Preregistration for classes offered.

Student services. Transfer: Pre-admission transcript evaluation for new students.

Contact. Phone: (607) 729-8915
Scott Galilei, Associate Director of Admissions, Elmira Business Institute: Vestal, 4100 Vestal Road, Vestal, NY 13850

Erie Community College
Buffalo, New York
www.ecc.edu

CB member
CB code: 2213

- Public 2-year community college
- Commuter campus in large city

General. Founded in 1971. Regionally accredited. SUNY institution. Main campus located in Buffalo. Additional campuses in Williamsville and Orchard Park. **Enrollment:** 10,027 degree-seeking undergraduates; 1,995 non-degree-seeking students. **Degrees:** 2,090 associate awarded. **ROTC:** Army. **Calendar:** Semester, limited summer session. **Special facilities:** Natatorium (City Campus), Vehicle Technical Training Center (South Campus), ECC One-Stop Center (North Campus), ECC One Stop Center Satellite office (South Campus), dental hygiene clinic (North Campus), gourmet restaurant (City and North Campus), Green Building Technology Center (South Campus), child care centers (all campuses). **Partnerships:** Formal partnerships with Ford Motor Company, Daimler Chrysler, Verizon.

Student profile. Among degree-seeking undergraduates, 48% enrolled in a transfer program, 52% enrolled in a vocational program, 2,661 enrolled as first-time, first-year students, 784 transferred in from other institutions.

Part-time:	22%	Hispanic/Latino:	5%
Out-of-state:	1%	Native American:	1%
Women:	49%	Multi-racial, non-Hispanic:	3%
African American:	15%	International:	4%
Asian American:	3%	25 or older:	32%

Transfer out. Colleges most students transferred to 2015: SUNY College at Buffalo, SUNY College at Fredonia, SUNY College at Brockport, SUNY Buffalo.

Basis for selection. Open admission, but selective for some programs. Special requirements for nursing and radiologic technology programs, occupational therapy, dental hygiene and dental lab tech; interview required. Students scoring 500 or higher on SAT Critical Reading waived from English placement test; students scoring 500 or higher on SAT Math waived from Math placement test. International students must be at least 17 years of age. Interview required for nursing, radiologic technology, occupational therapy, dental hygiene and dental laboratory technology. **Home schooled:** Applicants follow same criteria as applicants with GED.

2015-2016 Annual costs. Tuition/fees: $5,188; $9,783 out-of-state. Per-credit charge: $192 in-state; $384 out-of-state. Books/supplies: $1,300. Personal expenses: $512.

2014-2015 Financial aid. All financial aid based on need. 83% of total undergraduate aid awarded as scholarships/grants, 17% as loans/jobs. Need-based aid available for part-time students. Work-study available nights, weekends and for part-time students.

Application procedures. Admission: Priority date 8/1; no deadline. $25 fee. Admission notification on a rolling basis. **Financial aid:** Priority date 5/1; no closing date. FAFSA required. Applicants notified on a rolling basis starting 4/1; must reply within 2 week(s) of notification.

Academics. Special study options: Cooperative education, cross-registration, distance learning, double major, dual enrollment of high school students, ESL, exchange student, honors, independent study, internships, liberal arts/career combination, student-designed major, study abroad, teacher certification program, weekend college. Dual admissions with 4-year institutions. License preparation in dental hygiene, nursing, occupational therapy, paramedic, radiology. **Credit/placement by examination:** AP, CLEP, institutional tests. **Support services:** GED preparation and test center, learning center, pre-admission summer program, reduced course load, remedial instruction, study skills assistance, tutoring, writing center.

Majors. Business: Business admin, office management, restaurant/food services. **Communications:** Communications/speech/rhetoric. **Communications technology:** Graphic/printing. **Computer sciences:** General, information technology. **Conservation:** Environmental science. **Engineering:** General. **General:** Maintenance, site management. **Health services:** General, clinical lab technology, dental hygiene, dental lab technology, dietician assistant, EMT paramedic, health information technology, medical radiologic technology/radiation therapy, medical secretary, nursing (RN), occupational therapy assistant, optician, respiratory therapy technology, substance abuse counseling. **Liberal arts:** Arts/sciences, humanities. **Parks/recreation:** Health/fitness. **Protective services:** Disaster management, fire services admin, law enforcement admin, police science. **Work/family studies:** Child care management.

Most popular majors. Business/marketing 12%, health sciences 17%, liberal arts 41%, security/protective services 8%, trade and industry 6%.

Technology on campus. 1,260 workstations in library, computer center, student center. Commuter students can connect to campus network. Online course registration, online library, helpline, student web hosting, wireless network available.

Student life. Freshman orientation: Mandatory, $50 fee. Preregistration for classes offered. **Activities:** Bands, campus ministries, choral groups, dance, drama, international student organizations, literary magazine, music ensembles, musical theater, radio station, student government, student newspaper, honors association, Phi Theta Kappa, veterans club.

Athletics. NJCAA. **Intercollegiate:** Baseball M, basketball, bowling, cheerleading W, football (tackle) M, ice hockey M, lacrosse W, soccer, softball W, volleyball W. **Team name:** Kats.

Student services. Adult student services, career counseling, services for economically disadvantaged, student employment services, financial aid counseling, health services, minority student services, on-campus daycare, personal counseling, placement for graduates, veterans' counselor, women's services. **Physically disabled:** Services for visually, speech, hearing impaired. **Transfer:** Pre-admission transcript evaluation for new students. Transfer adviser, college fairs on campus for students transferring to 4-year colleges.

Contact. E-mail: admissions@ecc.edu
Phone: (716) 851-1455 Fax: (716) 270-2961
Director of Admissions, Erie Community College, 6205 Main Street, Williamsville, NY 14221-7095

Finger Lakes Community College
Canandaigua, New York
www.flcc.edu

CB code: 2134

- Public 2-year community college
- Commuter campus in small town

General. Founded in 1965. Regionally accredited. SUNY institution. **Enrollment:** 3,906 degree-seeking undergraduates; 2,855 non-degree-seeking students. **Degrees:** 813 associate awarded. **Location:** 25 miles from Rochester. **Calendar:** Semester, extensive summer session. **Full-time faculty:** 119 total; 4% minority, 48% women. **Part-time faculty:** 222 total; 2% minority, 58% women. **Class size:** 66% < 20, 32% 20-39, less than 1% 40-49, less than 1% 50-99. **Special facilities:** Outdoor classrooms, nature trails, music recording studio, performing arts center. **Partnerships:** Formal partnerships with local hospitals for nursing clinics; more informally for cooperative studies and placement of interns.

Student profile. Among degree-seeking undergraduates, 64% enrolled in a transfer program, 36% enrolled in a vocational program, 1,272 enrolled as first-time, first-year students, 315 transferred in from other institutions.

Part-time:	25%	Hispanic/Latino:	5%
Out-of-state:	1%	Multi-racial, non-Hispanic:	3%
Women:	56%	25 or older:	21%
African American:	7%	Live on campus:	5%
Asian American:	1%		

Transfer out. Colleges most students transferred to 2015: SUNY at Brockport, SUNY at Geneseo, St. John Fisher College, Keuka College, Rochester Institute of Technology.

Basis for selection. Open admission, but selective for some programs. Admission to nursing program based on high school curriculum and GPA; and for current college students on college coursework and GPA. Competitive admission to therapeutic massage/integrated health care program. **Home schooled:** State high school equivalency certificate required.

High school preparation. 1 each biology, chemistry, and algebra required of nursing applicants. Students without high school diploma or GED/TASC must pass entrance test prior to acceptance. 1 biology required for therapeutic massage/integrated health care applicants.

2015-2016 Annual costs. Tuition/fees: $4,704; $8,884 out-of-state. Per-credit charge: $168 in-state; $336 out-of-state. Books/supplies: $900. Personal expenses: $944.

2014-2015 Financial aid. All financial aid based on need. 1,179 full-time freshmen applied for aid; 1,001 deemed to have need; 929 received aid. 67% of total undergraduate aid awarded as scholarships/grants, 33% as loans/jobs. Need-based aid available for part-time students. Work-study available nights, weekends and for part-time students.

Application procedures. Admission: $20 fee, may be waived for applicants with need. Application must be submitted online. Admission notification on a rolling basis beginning on or about 10/1. Must reply by May 1 or within 4 week(s) if notified thereafter. Application closing date for Nursing and

Therapeutic Massage programs is February 1. **Financial aid:** Priority date 3/15; no closing date. FAFSA required. Applicants notified on a rolling basis starting 4/1; must reply within 2 week(s) of notification.

Academics. Special study options: Cooperative education, cross-registration, distance learning, double major, dual enrollment of high school students, ESL, honors, independent study, internships. Credit-bearing travel opportunities. License preparation in nursing, paramedic. **Credit/placement by examination:** AP, CLEP, IB, institutional tests. 32 credit hours maximum toward associate degree. **Support services:** GED preparation, learning center, pre-admission summer program, reduced course load, remedial instruction, study skills assistance, tutoring, writing center.

Majors. Biology: Biotechnology. **Business:** General, accounting, administrative services, business admin, e-commerce, hospitality/recreation, hotel/motel admin, marketing, sales/distribution, tourism promotion. **Communications:** Broadcast journalism, communications/speech/rhetoric. **Communications technology:** Recording arts. **Computer sciences:** General, computer science, information systems, programming. **Conservation:** General, environmental studies, wildlife/wilderness. **Education:** Elementary, physical. **Engineering:** General, engineering science. **Health services:** Athletic training, EMT paramedic, massage therapy, nursing (RN), substance abuse counseling. **Liberal arts:** Arts/sciences. **Math:** General. **Parks/recreation:** Sports admin. **Physical sciences:** Chemistry. **Protective services:** Criminal justice. **Social sciences:** General. **Visual/performing arts:** Commercial/advertising art, dramatic, music, studio arts.

Most popular majors. Business/marketing 19%, health sciences 11%, liberal arts 30%, natural resources/environmental science 8%, visual/performing arts 8%.

Technology on campus. 700 workstations in library, computer center, student center. Commuter students can connect to campus network. Online course registration, online library, helpline, student web hosting, wireless network available.

Student life. Freshman orientation: Available. Preregistration for classes offered. One-day program with faculty and student leaders. **Policies:** Student code of conduct policy, grievance procedures, procedures for services for students with disabilities. **Housing:** Coed dorms available. **Activities:** Bands, choral groups, drama, music ensembles, musical theater, student government, TV station, Phi Theta Kappa international honor society, Sigma Alpha Pi, nursing club, social science/human services club, College Democrats, Finger Lakes Environmental Action, veterans club, massage therapy club, ASL club, viticulture club, horticulture club.

Athletics. NJCAA. **Intercollegiate:** Baseball M, basketball, cross-country, lacrosse M, soccer, softball W, track and field, volleyball W. **Intramural:** Badminton, basketball, football (non-tackle), soccer, softball, tennis, volleyball, weight lifting.

Student services. Adult student services, career counseling, services for economically disadvantaged, student employment services, financial aid counseling, health services, legal services, on-campus daycare, personal counseling, placement for graduates, veterans' counselor. **Physically disabled:** Services for visually, speech, hearing impaired. **Transfer:** Pre-admission transcript evaluation for new students. Transfer center, transfer adviser, college fairs on campus for students transferring to 4-year colleges.

Contact. E-mail: admissions@flcc.edu
Phone: (585) 785-1279 Fax: (585) 742-6353
Bonnie Ritts, Admissions Office, Finger Lakes Community College, 3325 Marvin Sands Drive, Canandaigua, NY 14424-8395

Fulton-Montgomery Community College
Johnstown, New York
www.fmcc.suny.edu
CB code: 2254

- Public 2-year community college
- Commuter campus in large town

General. Founded in 1963. Regionally accredited. **Enrollment:** 1,961 degree-seeking undergraduates. **Degrees:** 449 associate awarded. **Location:** 40 miles from Albany, 200 miles from New York City. **Calendar:** Semester, extensive summer session. **Full-time faculty:** 54 total. **Part-time faculty:** 81 total. **Class size:** 44% < 20, 53% 20-39, 3% 40-49, less than 1% 50-99. **Special facilities:** Clean room for nano scale chip manufacturing, an advanced manufacturing lab and a high-tech nursing lab with programmable mannequins capable of simulating symptoms.

Student profile.

25 or older:	26%	Live on campus:	11%

Transfer out. Colleges most students transferred to 2015: State University of New York at Plattsburgh, College of Saint Rose, SUNY College at Oneonta, University at Albany.

Basis for selection. Open admission, but selective for some programs. Admission to Nursing and Radiologic Technology programs based on high school GPA, class rank, any college experience and meeting program prerequisites. COMPASS test used for placement in math and English. Focal Skills Test used for ESL placement. Interview recommended. **Home schooled:** Applicants applying for financial aid may be required to complete Ability to Benefit Test. Applicants from accredited home school who have received or will receive diploma may not be required to take test.

2015-2016 Annual costs. Tuition/fees: $4,420; $8,320 out-of-state. Per-credit charge: $163 in-state; $326 out-of-state. Room/board: $11,000.

Financial aid. Need-based: Need-based aid available for part-time students. Work-study available nights, weekends and for part-time students. **Non-need-based:** Scholarships awarded for academics.

Application procedures. Admission: No deadline. No application fee. Admission notification on a rolling basis. **Financial aid:** Priority date 6/1; no closing date. FAFSA required. Applicants notified on a rolling basis starting 6/15; must reply within 2 week(s) of notification.

Academics. Career-oriented individual studies program (COCAL) where students learn career skills in fields in which jobs are available locally. Students can also complete bachelor's degree online through Empire State College (SUNY). Advising for this is available on campus. **Special study options:** Accelerated study, cooperative education, cross-registration, distance learning, double major, dual enrollment of high school students, ESL, external degree, honors, independent study, internships, student-designed major, study abroad. Bachelor's degree programs available on campus. License preparation in nursing, radiology. **Credit/placement by examination:** AP, CLEP, institutional tests. 30 credit hours maximum toward associate degree. **Support services:** Learning center, reduced course load, remedial instruction, study skills assistance, tutoring, writing center.

Majors. Business: General, accounting technology, administrative services, business admin. **Communications:** Communications/speech/rhetoric, journalism. **Communications technology:** Graphic/printing. **Computer sciences:** General, information systems. **Education:** Elementary, kindergarten/preschool, secondary. **Engineering:** General. **Health services:** Medical radiologic technology/radiation therapy, nursing (RN), office admin. **Liberal arts:** Arts/sciences. **Parks/recreation:** Health/fitness. **Protective services:** Criminal justice. **Visual/performing arts:** Art, commercial/advertising art. **Work/family studies:** Child care management.

Most popular majors. Business/marketing 16%, engineering/engineering technologies 7%, health sciences 13%, liberal arts 40%, security/protective services 8%.

Technology on campus. 400 workstations in library, computer center, student center. Dormitories wired for high-speed internet access. Commuter students can connect to campus network. Online library, helpline, wireless network available.

Student life. Freshman orientation: Available. Preregistration for classes offered. A one-day orientation is held just before classes begin. **Housing:** Coed dorms available. $300 nonrefundable deposit. **Activities:** Choral groups, drama, musical theater, student government, student newspaper.

Athletics. NJCAA. **Intercollegiate:** Baseball M, basketball, soccer, softball W, volleyball W. **Intramural:** Volleyball. **Team name:** Raiders.

Student services. Adult student services, career counseling, student employment services, financial aid counseling, on-campus daycare, personal counseling, veterans' counselor. **Physically disabled:** Services for visually, speech, hearing impaired. **Transfer:** Pre-admission transcript evaluation for new students. Transfer center, college fairs on campus for students transferring to 4-year colleges.

Contact. E-mail: geninfo@fmcc.suny.edu
Phone: (518) 736-3622 ext. 8301
Laura LaPorte, Associate Dean of Enrollment Management, Fulton-Montgomery Community College, 2805 State Highway 67, Johnstown, NY 12095

Genesee Community College
Batavia, New York
www.genesee.edu
CB code: 2272

- Public 2-year community college
- Commuter campus in large town

General. Founded in 1966. Regionally accredited. SUNY institution. Mall-type campus, suited to disabled. Seven campus sites in Genesee, Livingston, Orleans, and Wyoming counties. **Enrollment:** 3,715 degree-seeking undergraduates; 2,806 non-degree-seeking students. **Degrees:** 799 associate awarded. **ROTC:** Army. **Location:** 35 miles from Buffalo, 35 miles from Rochester. **Calendar:** Semester, limited summer session. **Full-time faculty:** 87 total. **Part-time faculty:** 281 total. **Special facilities:** Nature trail, center for the arts.

Student profile. Among degree-seeking undergraduates, 988 enrolled as first-time, first-year students, 326 transferred in from other institutions.

Part-time:	28%	Hispanic/Latino:	5%
Out-of-state:	2%	Native American:	1%
Women:	66%	Multi-racial, non-Hispanic:	2%
African American:	10%	International:	4%
Asian American:	1%	25 or older:	41%

Transfer out. Colleges most students transferred to 2015: SUNY: Brockport, Buffalo State, Geneseo, University of Buffalo, Empire State College.

Basis for selection. Open admission, but selective for some programs. Admission to nursing, physical therapist assistant, paralegal, respiratory care, polysomnographic technology and veterinary technology programs based on academic achievement, test scores, interview, and school and community activities. ACT and COMPASS used for placement. Although SAT not used as placement test, students scoring above 500 on each part exempted from remedial courses. Portfolio recommended for digital art program. **Home schooled:** State high school equivalency certificate required. District certificate from school superintendent.

High school preparation. Recommended units include English 4, mathematics 3, social studies 4, science 3 and foreign language 2. Additional units of math and science recommended for students planning to transfer to 4-year programs. 18 units, including biology and chemistry, required for nursing applicants. 18 units, including biology and physics, required for physical therapist assistant applicants.

2015-2016 Annual costs. Tuition/fees: $4,410; $5,010 out-of-state. Room/board: $8,475. Books/supplies: $1,108. Personal expenses: $1,054.

2014-2015 Financial aid. Need-based: 733 full-time freshmen applied for aid; 550 deemed to have need; 550 received aid. Average need met was 80%. Average scholarship/grant was $5,155; average loan $3,750. 74% of total undergraduate aid awarded as scholarships/grants, 26% as loans/jobs. Need-based aid available for part-time students. Work-study available nights, weekends and for part-time students. **Non-need-based:** Awarded to 165 full-time undergraduates, including 97 freshmen. Scholarships awarded for academics, alumni affiliation, athletics, leadership, state residency.

Application procedures. Admission: No deadline. No application fee. Admission notification on a rolling basis beginning on or about 11/15. **Financial aid:** Priority date 3/1, closing date 5/1. FAFSA required. Applicants notified on a rolling basis starting 4/15; must reply within 2 week(s) of notification.

Academics. Special study options: Cooperative education, cross-registration, distance learning, double major, dual enrollment of high school students, ESL, honors, independent study, internships, liberal arts/career combination, student-designed major, study abroad. License preparation in nursing, physical therapy. **Credit/placement by examination:** AP, CLEP, IB, institutional tests. 31 credit hours maximum toward associate degree. **Support services:** GED preparation, learning center, reduced course load, remedial instruction, study skills assistance, tutoring, writing center.

Majors. Biology: General. **Business:** Accounting, accounting technology, administrative services, business admin, customer service, fashion, retailing, tourism/travel. **Communications:** Communications/speech/rhetoric. **Computer sciences:** Information systems, webmaster. **Conservation:** Environmental studies. **Education:** Physical, teacher assistance. **Engineering:** Pre-engineering. **Health services:** General, medical secretary, nursing (RN), physical therapy assistant, polysomnography, recreational therapy, respiratory therapy technology, substance abuse counseling, veterinary technology/assistant. **Human services:** Community org/advocacy. **Liberal arts:** Arts/sciences, humanities. **Protective services:** Financial forensics, law enforcement admin. **Visual/performing arts:** Art, dramatic, theater design.

Most popular majors. Business/marketing 15%, health sciences 32%, liberal arts 30%, public administration/social services 6%, security/protective services 7%.

Technology on campus. 350 workstations in dormitories, library, computer center, student center. Dormitories wired for high-speed internet access and linked to campus network. Commuter students can connect to campus network. Online course registration, online library, helpline, wireless network available.

Student life. Freshman orientation: Mandatory. Preregistration for classes offered. Day-long orientation before classes begin. **Policies:** Residence life regulations covered in housing license signed by students. **Housing:** Single-sex dorms, special housing for disabled, themed housing, wellness housing available. Global living community, quiet building available. **Activities:** Choral groups, dance, drama, film society, international student organizations, literary magazine, musical theater, radio station, student government, student newspaper, African American student union, Native American student organization, Christian Students United, New Age Circle, Phi Theta Kappa, Distribution Education Clubs of America, Habitat for Humanity.

Athletics. NJCAA. **Intercollegiate:** Baseball M, basketball, diving, golf, lacrosse, soccer, softball W, swimming, volleyball W. **Intramural:** Basketball, cheerleading, football (non-tackle), golf, soccer, softball, table tennis, tennis, volleyball. **Team name:** Cougars.

Student services. Adult student services, career counseling, student employment services, financial aid counseling, health services, on-campus daycare, personal counseling, placement for graduates, veterans' counselor. **Physically disabled:** Services for visually, speech, hearing impaired. **Transfer:** Re-entry adviser for new students. Transfer center, transfer adviser, college fairs on campus for students transferring to 4-year colleges.

Contact. E-mail: tmlanemartin@genesee.edu
Phone: (585) 345-6800 Toll-free number: (866) 225-5422
Fax: (585) 345-6842
Tanya Lane-Martin, Director of Admissions and Recruitment/Assistant Dean for Enrollment Services, Genesee Community College, One College Road, Batavia, NY 14020-9704

Helene Fuld College of Nursing
New York, New York
www.helenefuld.edu   **CB code: 2327**

▸ Private 2-year nursing and junior college
▸ Commuter campus in very large city

General. Founded in 1945. Regionally accredited. One-year, full-time associate degree program accredited by National League for Nursing Accrediting Commission and Middle States Association of Colleges and Schools. Career ladder for LPNs. Part-time accredited study also offered. **Enrollment:** 448 degree-seeking undergraduates. **Degrees:** 22 bachelor's, 151 associate awarded. **Location:** Uptown. **Calendar:** Quarter, limited summer session. **Full-time faculty:** 13 total. **Class size:** 6% < 20, 47% 20-39, 29% 40-49, 18% 50-99.

Student profile.

Part-time:	55%	Asian American:	8%
Out-of-state:	3%	Hispanic/Latino:	9%
Women:	88%	Multi-racial, non-Hispanic:	1%
African American:	77%		

Basis for selection. Must be licensed practical nurse with 1 year work experience. Require satisfactory performance on pre-entrance exams on practical nursing equivalent, mathematics, and English and completion of a prerequisite chemistry and mathematics course. After all entrance requirements fulfilled, including successful completion of testing, 18 credits granted for practical nursing. ATI testing required for entrance to nursing program.

2015-2016 Annual costs. Tuition/fees: $19,099. Per-credit charge: $341. Books/supplies: $2,252. Personal expenses: $2,688.

Financial aid. All financial aid based on need. Need-based aid available for part-time students. Work-study available nights, weekends and for part-time students.

Application procedures. Admission: No deadline. $110 fee. Admission notification on a rolling basis. **Financial aid:** Closing date 6/30. FAFSA required. Applicants notified on a rolling basis.

Academics. Special study options: Accelerated study, liberal arts/career combination. License preparation in nursing. **Credit/placement by examination:** AP, CLEP, institutional tests. **Support services:** Learning center, reduced course load, study skills assistance, tutoring.

Majors. Health services: Nursing (RN).

Technology on campus. 24 workstations in library, computer center. Commuter students can connect to campus network. Wireless network available.

Student life. Freshman orientation: Mandatory. Preregistration for classes offered. 2 weeks before term starts. **Activities:** Student government.

Student services. Adult student services, career counseling, financial aid counseling, personal counseling. **Transfer:** Pre-admission transcript evaluation for new students. College fairs on campus for students transferring to 4-year colleges.

Contact. E-mail: sandra.senior@helenefuld.edu
Phone: (212) 616-7200
Gladys Pineda, Assistant Director of Student Services, Helene Fuld College of Nursing, 24 East 120th Street, New York, NY 10035

Herkimer County Community College
Herkimer, New York
www.herkimer.edu
CB code: 2316

‣ Public 2-year community college
‣ Commuter campus in small town

General. Founded in 1966. Regionally accredited. **Enrollment:** 2,125 degree-seeking undergraduates; 894 non-degree-seeking students. **Degrees:** 576 associate awarded. **ROTC:** Army. **Location:** 10 miles from Utica, 55 miles from Syracuse. **Calendar:** Semester, limited summer session. **Full-time faculty:** 51 total; 8% have terminal degrees, 4% minority, 47% women. **Part-time faculty:** 109 total; 9% have terminal degrees, 2% minority, 44% women. **Special facilities:** Art gallery, natural history museum, archaeology museum, nature center, veterans memorial park.

Student profile. Among degree-seeking undergraduates, 793 enrolled as first-time, first-year students, 208 transferred in from other institutions.

Part-time:	18%	25 or older:	27%
Out-of-state:	4%	Live on campus:	28%
Women:	58%		

Transfer out. Colleges most students transferred to 2015: SUNY Polytechnic Institute, SUNY Oneonta, SUNY Brockport, SUNY Oswego, SUNY Cortland.

Basis for selection. Open admission, but selective for some programs. SAT and ACT scores may be used to waive required college placement test. Students from Herkimer County must have proof of graduation or a GED certificate. Students from outside Herkimer County must have a 68 GPA or 2400 or higher on the GED. ACCUPLACER used to help determine placement into developmental courses. Interview recommended for emergency medical technician, occupational/physical therapy assistant programs. Audition required for performance and sound engineering majors. **Home schooled:** Transcript of courses and grades, letter of recommendation (nonparent) required. Letter from superintendent of home district stating student meets the requirements.

High school preparation. Physical/occupational therapist assistant applicants should contact admissions office to review high school course requirements.

2015-2016 Annual costs. Tuition/fees: $4,640; $7,700 out-of-state. Per-credit charge: $139 in-state; $278 out-of-state. Room/board: $9,550. Books/supplies: $1,200. Personal expenses: $710.

Financial aid. Need-based: Need-based aid available for part-time students. Work-study available nights, weekends and for part-time students.

Application procedures. Admission: Closing date 8/29. No application fee. Admission notification on a rolling basis. **Financial aid:** Closing date 4/1. FAFSA required. Applicants notified on a rolling basis starting 4/1; must reply within 2 week(s) of notification.

Academics. Online tutoring and late night writing lab (via Angel) available after 6:00. Regular Academic Support Center open weekdays. **Special study options:** Cross-registration, distance learning, dual enrollment of high school students, ESL, honors, independent study, internships, liberal arts/career combination. License preparation in paramedic, physical therapy. **Credit/placement by examination:** AP, CLEP, institutional tests. 32 credit hours maximum toward associate degree. **Support services:** Learning center, reduced course load, remedial instruction, study skills assistance, tutoring.

Honors college/program. Applicants need high school average of 88. Students must maintain GPA of 3.5.

Majors. Business: Accounting technology, business admin, entrepreneurial studies, fashion, human resources, international, travel services. **Communications:** Broadcast journalism, digital media. **Communications technology:** Photo/film/video. **Computer sciences:** General, support specialist. **Education:** Kindergarten/preschool. **Engineering:** General. **Health services:** EMT paramedic, physical therapy assistant. **Human services:** Community org/

advocacy. **Liberal arts:** Arts/sciences, humanities. **Parks/recreation:** Facilities management. **Protective services:** Criminal justice, forensics, law enforcement admin. **Visual/performing arts:** General, art.

Most popular majors. Business/marketing 27%, health sciences 6%, liberal arts 36%, security/protective services 12%.

Technology on campus. 317 workstations in dormitories, library, computer center, student center. Dormitories wired for high-speed internet access and linked to campus network. Commuter students can connect to campus network. Online library, helpline, wireless network available.

Student life. Freshman orientation: Mandatory. Preregistration for classes offered. **Housing:** Coed dorms available. $350 partly refundable deposit. **Activities:** Pep band, dance, drama, literary magazine, musical theater, radio station, student government, TV station, Amnesty International, Black Latino Student Union, Campus Christian Fellowship, Gay Straight Alliance, International Student Association, National Alliance for Mental Illness On-Campus, Phi Theta Kappa, Students Against Destructive Decisions, Student Government Association, Women's club.

Athletics. NJCAA. **Intercollegiate:** Baseball M, basketball, cross-country, diving, field hockey W, lacrosse, soccer, softball W, swimming, tennis, track and field, volleyball W. **Intramural:** Badminton, baseball M, basketball, bowling, lacrosse, soccer, softball, swimming, tennis, volleyball. **Team name:** Generals.

Student services. Adult student services, alcohol/substance abuse counseling, career counseling, student employment services, financial aid counseling, on-campus daycare, personal counseling, placement for graduates, veterans' counselor. **Physically disabled:** Services for visually, hearing impaired. **Transfer:** Re-entry adviser, pre-admission transcript evaluation for new students. Transfer adviser, college fairs on campus for students transferring to 4-year colleges.

Contact. E-mail: admissions@herkimer.edu
Phone: (315) 866-0300 ext. 8278
Toll-free number: (844) 464-7375 ext. 8278 Fax: (315) 866-0062
Rebecca Kohler, Director of Admissions, Herkimer County Community College, 100 Reservoir Road, Herkimer, NY 13350-1598

Hudson Valley Community College
Troy, New York
CB member
www.hvcc.edu
CB code: 2300

‣ Public 2-year community college
‣ Commuter campus in small city

General. Founded in 1953. Regionally accredited. SUNY institution. **Enrollment:** 13,750 undergraduates. **Degrees:** 1,870 associate awarded. **ROTC:** Army, Air Force. **Location:** 10 miles from Albany. **Calendar:** Semester, limited summer session. **Full-time faculty:** 271 total. **Part-time faculty:** 406 total. **Special facilities:** Language laboratory, computer laboratories.

Basis for selection. Open admission, but selective for some programs. Admission to some programs based on school achievement record and test scores. Interview also considered for some programs.

High school preparation. Requirements vary for selective programs.

2015-2016 Annual costs. Tuition/fees: $5,016; $13,216 out-of-state. Per-credit charge: $171 in-state; $513 out-of-state. Books/supplies: $1,200.

Financial aid. Need-based: Work-study available nights, weekends and for part-time students.

Application procedures. Admission: No deadline. $30 fee, may be waived for applicants with need. Admission notification on a rolling basis. **Financial aid:** Priority date 5/30; no closing date. FAFSA required. Applicants notified on a rolling basis starting 5/1; must reply within 2 week(s) of notification.

Academics. Special study options: Accelerated study, cooperative education, cross-registration, distance learning, double major, internships, student-designed major. License preparation in dental hygiene, nursing, paramedic, radiology. **Credit/placement by examination:** AP, CLEP. 30 credit hours maximum toward associate degree. **Support services:** GED preparation, learning center, pre-admission summer program, reduced course load, remedial instruction, tutoring.

Majors. Business: General, accounting, administrative services, business admin, finance, insurance, international, office technology, real estate. **Computer sciences:** Data processing, networking. **Conservation:** Environmental studies. **Education:** Physical. **Engineering:** General, engineering science. **General:** Carpentry, maintenance. **Health services:** Clinical lab science, clinical lab technology, dental hygiene, medical radiologic technology/radiation therapy, medical secretary, nursing (RN), physician assistant, respiratory therapy technology, substance abuse counseling. **Human services:** Community org/advocacy, social work. **Physical sciences:** Chemistry. **Protective services:** Forensics. **Social sciences:** General. **Work/family studies:** Child care management.

Technology on campus. 1,000 workstations in library, computer center.

Student life. Activities: Drama, radio station, student government, student newspaper, TV station.

Athletics. NJCAA. **Intercollegiate:** Baseball M, basketball, bowling, cross-country, football (tackle) M, golf, ice hockey M, lacrosse M, soccer, softball W, tennis, track and field, volleyball W. **Intramural:** Baseball M, basketball, bowling, cross-country, field hockey W, golf, ice hockey, lacrosse, racquetball, skiing, soccer, softball, table tennis, tennis, track and field, volleyball, wrestling M.

Student services. Adult student services, career counseling, student employment services, health services, on-campus daycare, personal counseling, placement for graduates, veterans' counselor. **Physically disabled:** Services for visually, speech, hearing impaired.

Contact. E-mail: admissions@hvcc.edu
Phone: (518) 629-7309 Toll-free number: (877) 325-4822
Fax: (518) 629-4576
Mary Bauer, Director of Admissions, Hudson Valley Community College, 80 Vandenburgh Avenue, Troy, NY 12180

Institute of Design and Construction
Brooklyn, New York
www.idc.edu   **CB code: 0677**

- Private 2-year junior and technical college
- Commuter campus in very large city

General. Founded in 1947. Regionally accredited. **Enrollment:** 65 degree-seeking undergraduates. **Degrees:** 11 associate awarded. **Calendar:** Semester, limited summer session. **Part-time faculty:** 20 total; 70% have terminal degrees, 15% minority, 5% women. **Class size:** 93% < 20, 7% 20-39.

Student profile.

Out-of-state:	3%	25 or older:	60%

Transfer out. Colleges most students transferred to 2015: CUNY colleges including New York City College of Technology, John Jay College of Criminal Justice, College of Staten Island.

Basis for selection. Open admission. Interview recommended. **Adult students:** SAT/ACT scores not required. **Home schooled:** Statement describing home school structure and mission, transcript of courses and grades required.

High school preparation. Recommended units include English 4, mathematics 4, science 3 and foreign language 4. One unit of drafting or architecture recommended.

2015-2016 Annual costs. Tuition/fees: $10,950. Per-credit charge: $355. Books/supplies: $900. Personal expenses: $750.

Financial aid. All financial aid based on need. Need-based aid available for part-time students. Work-study available nights, weekends and for part-time students.

Application procedures. Admission: No deadline. $30 fee, may be waived for applicants with need. Admission notification on a rolling basis. Must reply by May 1 or within 4 week(s) if notified thereafter. **Financial aid:** No deadline. FAFSA, institutional form required. Applicants notified on a rolling basis starting 3/1; must reply within 4 week(s) of notification.

Academics. Work and study plan available. Students can spend 2 full-time semesters in accelerated study, then complete degree through part-time evening study while working during the day in the architecture/construction industries. **Special study options:** Double major. Classes and seminars available for candidates preparing for Architect Registration Exam. **Credit/placement by examination:** AP, CLEP, institutional tests. **Support services:** Learning center, reduced course load, remedial instruction, tutoring.

Majors. General: Building construction.

Most popular majors. Engineering/engineering technologies 19%, trade and industry 81%.

Technology on campus. 18 workstations in library, computer center. Online library, wireless network available.

Student life. Freshman orientation: Available. Preregistration for classes offered.

Student services. Career counseling, student employment services, financial aid counseling, personal counseling, placement for graduates, veterans' counselor. **Transfer:** Pre-admission transcript evaluation for new students. Transfer adviser for students transferring to 4-year colleges.

Contact. E-mail: ebattista@idc.edu
Phone: (718) 855-3661 Fax: (718) 852-5889
Elizabeth Battista, Director of Communications, Institute of Design and Construction, 141 Willoughby Street, Brooklyn, NY 11201-5380

Island Drafting and Technical Institute
Amityville, New York
www.idti.edu   **CB code: 3048**

- For-profit 2-year technical and career college
- Commuter campus in large town
- Interview required

General. Accredited by ACCSC. **Enrollment:** 110 undergraduates. **Degrees:** 47 associate awarded. **Location:** 25 miles from New York City. **Calendar:** Semester, extensive summer session. **Full-time faculty:** 5 total. **Part-time faculty:** 3 total.

Basis for selection. Open admission, but selective for some programs. School-administered test for CADD/Architecture students. **Home schooled:** Interview required.

High school preparation. Recommended units include English 2 and mathematics 2.

2015-2016 Annual costs. Tuition/fees: $16,200. Per-credit charge: $525. Books/supplies: $600.

Financial aid. All financial aid based on need. Work-study available nights, weekends and for part-time students.

Application procedures. Admission: No deadline. $25 fee. Application must be submitted on paper. Admission notification on a rolling basis. **Financial aid:** No deadline. Applicants notified on a rolling basis.

Academics. Credit/placement by examination: AP, CLEP, institutional tests.

Majors. Computer sciences: Computer graphics. **Engineering:** Electrical.

Technology on campus. 100 workstations in library, computer center. Wireless network available.

Student life. Freshman orientation: Mandatory. Preregistration for classes offered.

Student services. Alcohol/substance abuse counseling, career counseling, student employment services, financial aid counseling, personal counseling, placement for graduates, veterans' counselor.

Contact. E-mail: info@idti.edu
Phone: (631) 691-8733 Fax: (631) 691-8738
Patricia Hausfeld, Assistant to President, Island Drafting and Technical Institute, 128 Broadway, Amityville, NY 11701-2704

ITT Technical Institute: Albany
Albany, New York
www.itt-tech.edu   **CB code: 2689**

- For-profit 2-year technical college
- Commuter campus in large city
- Interview required

General. Accredited by ACICS. **Enrollment:** 232 undergraduates. **Degrees:** 75 associate awarded. **Calendar:** Quarter, extensive summer session. **Full-time faculty:** 4 total. **Part-time faculty:** 30 total.

Basis for selection. Satisfactory scores from on-site tests in English and mathematics required.

2015-2016 Annual costs. Per-credit-hour charge, $493; academic fee, $200. Certain programs require purchase of tools, which could cost an additional $500. All costs are subject to change.

Financial aid. Need-based: Work-study available nights, weekends and for part-time students.

Application procedures. Admission: No deadline. No application fee. Admission notification on a rolling basis. **Financial aid:** No deadline. FAFSA, institutional form required. Applicants notified on a rolling basis.

Academics. Credit/placement by examination: AP, CLEP. **Support services:** Learning center, tutoring.

Majors. Computer sciences: Networking, web page design. **Visual/performing arts:** Design.

Technology on campus. Online library available.

Student life. Freshman orientation: Available. Preregistration for classes offered.

Student services. Career counseling, student employment services, placement for graduates.

Contact. Phone: (518) 452-9300 Toll-free number: (800) 489-1191 Fax: (518) 452-9393
John Henebry, Director of Recruitment, ITT Technical Institute: Albany, 13 Airline Drive, Albany, NY 12205

ITT Technical Institute: Getzville
Getzville, New York
www.itt-tech.edu   CB code: 2704

- For-profit 2-year technical college
- Commuter campus in rural community
- Interview required

General. Accredited by ACICS. **Enrollment:** 326 undergraduates. **Degrees:** 112 associate awarded. **Calendar:** Quarter, extensive summer session. **Full-time faculty:** 6 total. **Part-time faculty:** 34 total.

Basis for selection. Satisfactory scores from on-site tests in English and mathematics required.

2015-2016 Annual costs. Per-credit-hour charge, $493. Academic fee, $200. Some programs require purchase of tools, which could cost an additional $100 to $500. All costs subject to change.

Financial aid. Need-based: Work-study available nights, weekends and for part-time students.

Application procedures. Admission: No deadline. No application fee. Admission notification on a rolling basis. **Financial aid:** No deadline. FAFSA, institutional form required. Applicants notified on a rolling basis.

Academics. Credit/placement by examination: AP, CLEP. **Support services:** Learning center, tutoring.

Majors. Computer sciences: Networking, web page design. **Protective services:** Law enforcement admin. **Visual/performing arts:** Design.

Technology on campus. Online library available.

Student services. Career counseling, student employment services, placement for graduates.

Contact. Phone: (716) 689-2200 Toll-free number: (800) 469-7593 Fax: (716) 689-2828
Scott Jaskier, Director of Recruitment, ITT Technical Institute: Getzville, 2295 Millersport Highway, PO Box 327, Getzville, NY 14068

ITT Technical Institute: Liverpool
Liverpool, New York
www.itt-tech.edu   CB code: 2725

- For-profit 2-year technical college
- Commuter campus in small town
- Interview required

General. Accredited by ACICS. **Enrollment:** 215 undergraduates. **Degrees:** 84 associate awarded. **Calendar:** Quarter, extensive summer session. **Full-time faculty:** 4 total. **Part-time faculty:** 21 total.

Basis for selection. Satisfactory scores from on-site tests in English and mathematics required.

2015-2016 Annual costs. Books/supplies: $3,300. **Additional information:** Per-credit-hour charge, $493; academic fee, $200. Certain programs require purchase of tools, which could cost an additional $100 to $500. All costs are subject to change.

Financial aid. Need-based: Work-study available nights, weekends and for part-time students.

Application procedures. Admission: No deadline. Admission notification on a rolling basis. **Financial aid:** No deadline. FAFSA, institutional form required. Applicants notified on a rolling basis.

Academics. Credit/placement by examination: AP, CLEP. **Support services:** Learning center, tutoring.

Majors. Computer sciences: Networking, web page design. **Visual/performing arts:** Design.

Technology on campus. Online library available.

Student life. Freshman orientation: Available. Preregistration for classes offered.

Student services. Career counseling, student employment services, placement for graduates.

Contact. Phone: (315) 461-8000 Toll-free number: (877) 488-0011 Fax: (315) 461-8008
Terry Riesel, Director of Recruitment, ITT Technical Institute: Liverpool, 235 Greenfield Parkway, Liverpool, NY 13088-6651

Jamestown Business College
Jamestown, New York
www.jamestownbusinesscollege.edu   CB code: 2346

- For-profit 2-year business and junior college
- Commuter campus in large town
- Application essay, interview required

General. Founded in 1886. Regionally accredited. JBC offers programming outside of general curriculum to enhance student and professional experiences. **Enrollment:** 296 degree-seeking undergraduates. **Degrees:** 27 bachelor's, 83 associate awarded. **Location:** 80 miles from Buffalo, 60 miles from Erie, Pennsylvania. **Calendar:** Quarter, limited summer session. **Full-time faculty:** 7 total; 14% minority. **Part-time faculty:** 22 total; 4% have terminal degrees, 9% minority.

Student profile. Among degree-seeking undergraduates, 95 enrolled as first-time, first-year students, 36 transferred in from other institutions.

Part-time:	3%	Hispanic/Latino:	14%
Women:	74%	Native American:	3%
African American:	3%	Multi-racial, non-Hispanic:	5%

Basis for selection. Class rank and admissions test. College uses Comparative Guidance and Placement program in admission process.

2015-2016 Annual costs. Tuition/fees: $12,300.

Financial aid. Need-based: Need-based aid available for part-time students. Work-study available nights, weekends and for part-time students. **Non-need-based:** Scholarships awarded for academics.

Application procedures. Admission: No deadline. $25 fee. Application must be submitted on paper. Admission notification on a rolling basis. **Financial aid:** No deadline. FAFSA required. Applicants notified on a rolling basis starting 2/15.

Academics. Special study options: Bachelor's degree programs available on campus. **Credit/placement by examination:** AP, CLEP, institutional tests. **Support services:** Reduced course load, study skills assistance, tutoring.

Majors. Business: Accounting, administrative services, business admin, marketing. **Computer sciences:** General, data processing. **Health services:** Medical secretary.

Technology on campus. 100 workstations in library, computer center. Commuter students can connect to campus network. Online library, wireless network available.

Student life. Freshman orientation: Mandatory. Preregistration for classes offered.

Student services. Adult student services, career counseling, student employment services, financial aid counseling, placement for graduates. **Transfer:** Pre-admission transcript evaluation for new students. Transfer adviser for students transferring to 4-year colleges.

Contact. E-mail: admissions@jamestownbusinesscollege.edu
Phone: (716) 664-5100 Fax: (716) 664-3144
Brenda Salemme, Director of Admissions, Jamestown Business College, 7 Fairmount Avenue, Jamestown, NY 14701-0429

Jamestown Community College
Jamestown, New York
www.sunyjcc.edu   **CB code: 2335**

▶ Public 2-year community college
▶ Commuter campus in large town

General. Founded in 1950. Regionally accredited. SUNY institution. Branch campus in Olean, NY for Cattaraugus County. Extensions in Dunkirk, NY and Warren, PA. **Enrollment:** 2,889 degree-seeking undergraduates; 149 non-degree-seeking students. **Degrees:** 764 associate awarded. **Location:** 80 miles from Buffalo, 50 miles from Erie, PA. **Calendar:** Semester, extensive summer session. **Full-time faculty:** 86 total; 20% have terminal degrees, 5% minority, 62% women. **Part-time faculty:** 264 total; 6% minority, 54% women. **Class size:** 54% < 20, 45% 20-39, less than 1% 40-49, less than 1% 50-99. **Special facilities:** Roger Tory Peterson Institute of Natural History, manufacturing technology institute. **Partnerships:** Formal partnerships with Jones Memorial Hospital, Bradford Regional Medical Center, Olean General Hospital, WCA Hospital.

Student profile. Among degree-seeking undergraduates, 65% enrolled in a transfer program, 35% enrolled in a vocational program, 929 enrolled as first-time, first-year students, 204 transferred in from other institutions.

Part-time:	23%	Native American:	1%
Out-of-state:	8%	Multi-racial, non-Hispanic:	3%
Women:	58%	International:	1%
African American:	5%	25 or older:	28%
Asian American:	1%	Live on campus:	11%
Hispanic/Latino:	8%		

Transfer out. 54% of students enrolled in the transfer program go on to 4-year colleges. **Colleges most students transferred to 2015:** SUNY Fredonia, Daemen College, SUNY Empire State College, University at Buffalo, Pennsylvania State University.

Basis for selection. Open admission, but selective for some programs. Preference given to area students in highly subscribed programs. Competitive admission to Nursing and Occupational Therapy Assistant programs with school achievement record very important. ACT and ASSET scores used for placement.

2015-2016 Annual costs. Tuition/fees: $5,152; $9,622 out-of-state. Per-credit charge: $188 in-state; $377 out-of-state. Room/board: $10,740. Books/supplies: $1,100. Personal expenses: $800.

2015-2016 Financial aid. Need-based: 816 full-time freshmen applied for aid; 680 deemed to have need; 679 received aid. 66% of total undergraduate aid awarded as scholarships/grants, 34% as loans/jobs. Need-based aid available for part-time students. Work-study available nights, weekends and for part-time students. **Non-need-based:** Awarded to 154 full-time undergraduates, including 90 freshmen. Scholarships awarded for academics, alumni affiliation, art, athletics, music/drama, state residency.

Application procedures. Admission: No deadline. No application fee. Admission notification on a rolling basis. Must reply by May 1 or within 2 week(s) if notified thereafter. **Financial aid:** Priority date 3/1; no closing date. FAFSA required. Applicants notified on a rolling basis starting 4/15.

Academics. Special study options: Cross-registration, distance learning, dual enrollment of high school students, ESL, honors, independent study, internships, liberal arts/career combination, study abroad. License preparation in nursing, occupational therapy. **Credit/placement by examination:** AP, CLEP, institutional tests. 36 credit hours maximum toward associate degree. **Support services:** Learning center, pre-admission summer program, reduced course load, remedial instruction, study skills assistance, tutoring.

Majors. Business: Accounting technology, administrative services, business admin. **Communications:** Communications/speech/rhetoric. **Computer sciences:** General, information systems, information technology. **Conservation:** Environmental science. **Education:** Teacher assistance. **Engineering:** General. **Health services:** Health information technology, nursing (RN), occupational therapy assistant. **Liberal arts:** Arts/sciences, humanities. **Parks/recreation:** Health/fitness. **Protective services:** Police science. **Visual/performing arts:** Music, studio arts.

Most popular majors. Business/marketing 10%, health sciences 22%, liberal arts 40%, public administration/social services 6%, security/protective services 9%.

Technology on campus. 671 workstations in library, computer center, student center. Dormitories wired for high-speed internet access and linked to campus network. Commuter students can connect to campus network. Online course registration, online library, helpline, wireless network available.

Student life. Freshman orientation: Available. Preregistration for classes offered. **Housing:** Coed dorms available. $200 nonrefundable deposit. Suite-style dorms available to students. **Activities:** Bands, choral groups, dance, drama, music ensembles, musical theater, student government, Black Student Union, criminal justice club, IMPACT Club, Interweave Gay-Straight Alliance, sign language club, Brothers & Sisters in Christ, Student Occupational Therapy Association, nursing club, teacher education club.

Athletics. NJCAA. **Intercollegiate:** Baseball M, basketball, diving, golf, soccer, softball W, swimming, volleyball W, wrestling M. **Intramural:** Basketball, bowling, cross-country, football (non-tackle), volleyball. **Team name:** Jayhawks, Jaguars.

Student services. Adult student services, alcohol/substance abuse counseling, career counseling, services for economically disadvantaged, student employment services, financial aid counseling, health services, personal counseling, placement for graduates, veterans' counselor. **Physically disabled:** Services for visually, speech, hearing impaired. **Transfer:** Transfer adviser, college fairs on campus for students transferring to 4-year colleges.

Contact. E-mail: admissions@mail.sunyjcc.edu
Phone: (716) 338-1001 Toll-free number: (800) 388-8557
Fax: (716) 338-1450
Wendy Present, Director of Admissions, Jamestown Community College, 525 Falconer Street, Jamestown, NY 14702-0020

Jefferson Community College
Watertown, New York
www.sunyjefferson.edu   **CB member**
     CB code: 2345

▶ Public 2-year community college
▶ Commuter campus in large town

General. Founded in 1961. Regionally accredited. **Enrollment:** 3,009 degree-seeking undergraduates; 871 non-degree-seeking students. **Degrees:** 687 associate awarded. **Location:** 70 miles from Syracuse. **Calendar:** Semester, limited summer session. **Full-time faculty:** 80 total. **Part-time faculty:** 166 total.

Student profile. Among degree-seeking undergraduates, 882 enrolled as first-time, first-year students.

Part-time:	29%	25 or older:	35%
Out-of-state:	1%	Live on campus:	7%
Women:	60%		

Transfer out. Colleges most students transferred to 2015: SUNY Empire State College, SUNY Oswego, SUNY Potsdam.

Basis for selection. Open admission, but selective for some programs. Admission to some programs based on grades, class rank, test scores, school recommendation, personal interview. Waiting list available for nursing program. Interview recommended for engineering science, nursing programs.

High school preparation. Strong background in math and science required for engineering science, computer science, nursing, and science laboratory technologies programs.

2015-2016 Annual costs. Tuition/fees: $4,739; $7,019 out-of-state. Per-credit charge: $174 in-state; $269 out-of-state. Room/board: $10,050. Books/supplies: $1,300. Personal expenses: $1,000.

Financial aid. All financial aid based on need. Need-based aid available for part-time students. Work-study available nights, weekends and for part-time students.

Application procedures. Admission: No deadline. No application fee. Admission notification on a rolling basis. **Financial aid:** Priority date 4/1, closing date 8/15. FAFSA, institutional form required. Applicants notified on a rolling basis starting 4/15; must reply within 2 week(s) of notification.

Academics. Students in engineering science, computer science, and computer information systems programs required to purchase or lease microcomputers. **Special study options:** Cooperative education, distance learning, double major, dual enrollment of high school students, honors, independent study, internships, student-designed major, teacher certification program, weekend college. Bachelor's degree programs available on campus. **Credit/placement by examination:** AP, CLEP, IB, institutional tests. 30 credit hours maximum toward associate degree. **Support services:** Learning center, reduced course load, remedial instruction, study skills assistance, tutoring.

Majors. Business: Accounting technology, administrative services, business admin, tourism promotion. **Computer sciences:** General, computer science, information systems. **Engineering:** General. **Health services:** EMT paramedic, medical secretary, nursing (RN). **Human services:** Community org/advocacy. **Liberal arts:** Arts/sciences. **Protective services:** Fire services admin, law enforcement admin.

Most popular majors. Business/marketing 20%, health sciences 10%, liberal arts 45%, security/protective services 9%.

Technology on campus. 354 workstations in library, computer center, student center. Online course registration, online library, helpline, wireless network available.

Student life. Freshman orientation: Available. Preregistration for classes offered. Half-day program held in August and January. **Housing:** Privately owned apartments available. **Activities:** Bands, choral groups, drama, literary magazine, music ensembles, student government, student newspaper, veterans club, multicultural club, human services club, environmental club, European excursion club, business club, office technology association, political clubs, Brothers and Sisters in Christ.

Athletics. NJCAA. **Intercollegiate:** Baseball M, basketball, golf, lacrosse, soccer, softball W, tennis W, volleyball W. **Intramural:** Badminton, basketball, soccer, softball, volleyball. **Team name:** Cannoneers.

Student services. Adult student services, chaplain/spiritual director, career counseling, student employment services, financial aid counseling, health services, on-campus daycare, personal counseling, placement for graduates, veterans' counselor. **Physically disabled:** Services for visually, speech, hearing impaired. **Transfer:** Transfer adviser, college fairs on campus for students transferring to 4-year colleges.

Contact. E-mail: admissions@sunyjefferson.edu
Phone: (315) 786-2277 Fax: (315) 786-2459
Rosanne Weir, Director of Admissions, Jefferson Community College, 1220 Coffeen Street, Watertown, NY 13601

Long Island Business Institute
Flushing, New York
www.libi.edu

- For-profit 2-year business and career college
- Commuter campus in very large city
- Interview required

General. Regionally accredited; also accredited by ACICS. Additional campus in Commack, Long Island. Additional extension site on Broadway in Manhattan. **Enrollment:** 1,104 degree-seeking undergraduates; 249 non-degree-seeking students. **Degrees:** 229 associate awarded. **Location:** 8 miles from Manhattan, Long Island Campus 38 miles from Manhattan. **Calendar:** Semester, extensive summer session. **Full-time faculty:** 25 total; 40% minority, 44% women. **Part-time faculty:** 106 total; 3% have terminal degrees, 55% minority, 59% women. **Class size:** 76% < 20, 24% 20-39. **Special facilities:** ESL Language lab, computer learning center, student business club owned and operated cafe.

Student profile. Among degree-seeking undergraduates, 190 enrolled as first-time, first-year students, 33 transferred in from other institutions.

Part-time:	15%	Hispanic/Latino:	20%
Women:	74%	International:	4%
African American:	18%	25 or older:	66%
Asian American:	41%		

Basis for selection. High school diploma or GED are required for admissions. Applicants without U.S. high school diploma or GED are required to pass COMPASS or CELSA exams. Some programs have additional admissions requirements. CELSA is used for placement purpose for ESL applicants. **Home schooled:** State high school equivalency certificate required.

2016-2017 Annual costs. Tuition/fees (projected): $14,769. Books/supplies: $600.

2015-2016 Financial aid. Need-based: Average scholarship/grant was $2,380; average loan $1,500. 91% of total undergraduate aid awarded as scholarships/grants, 9% as loans/jobs. Need-based aid available for part-time students. Work-study available nights, weekends and for part-time students. **Non-need-based:** Scholarships awarded for academics.

Application procedures. Admission: No deadline. No application fee. Admission notification on a rolling basis. **Financial aid:** Closing date 5/1. FAFSA required. Applicants notified by 1/1; must reply by 4/30.

Academics. Special study options: ESL. **Credit/placement by examination:** AP, CLEP, institutional tests. 15 credit hours maximum toward associate degree. **Support services:** Learning center, reduced course load, remedial instruction, study skills assistance, tutoring.

Majors. Business: Accounting, business admin, hospitality admin, office/clerical. **Protective services:** Homeland security.

Most popular majors. Business/marketing 82%, security/protective services 16%.

Technology on campus. 400 workstations in library, computer center, student center.

Student life. Freshman orientation: Available. Preregistration for classes offered. **Activities:** Student newspaper.

Student services. Career counseling, student employment services, financial aid counseling, placement for graduates, veterans' counselor.

Contact. E-mail: admissions@libi.edu
Phone: (718) 939-5100 Fax: (718) 939-9235
Michael Talarico, Vice Presideht of Admissiohs, Long Island Business Institute, 136-18 39th Avenue, 5th Floor, Flushing, NY 11354

Maria College
Albany, New York
www.mariacollege.edu
CB member
CB code: 2434

- Private 2-year health science and liberal arts college
- Commuter campus in small city
- SAT or ACT (ACT writing optional), application essay, interview required

General. Founded in 1958. Regionally accredited. **Enrollment:** 770 degree-seeking undergraduates; 38 non-degree-seeking students. **Degrees:** 15 bachelor's, 201 associate awarded. **ROTC:** Army, Naval, Air Force. **Location:** 150 miles from New York City and Boston. **Calendar:** Semester, limited summer session. **Full-time faculty:** 34 total. **Part-time faculty:** 41 total. **Class size:** 67% < 20, 26% 20-39, 2% 40-49, 5% 50-99.

Student profile. Among degree-seeking undergraduates, 64 enrolled as first-time, first-year students, 274 transferred in from other institutions.

Part-time:	62%	Hispanic/Latino:	3%
Out-of-state:	3%	Native American:	1%
Women:	85%	Multi-racial, non-Hispanic:	2%
African American:	10%	25 or older:	70%
Asian American:	3%		

Basis for selection. School achievement record, test scores, interviews, recommendations important. Test required for students with scores on SAT Verbal less than 480, Math less than 490, or ACT Composite less than 19. **Adult students:** Applicants who did not take SAT or ACT may be required to take an admissions test, which may be waived based on prior college credit. **Home schooled:** Transcript of courses and grades, state high school equivalency certificate, interview, letter of recommendation (nonparent) required. SAT or ACT scores required or applicant must take college admissions test for placement purposes. Qualified Nursing applicants (Associate Degree and Practical Nurse certificate) must take Test of Essential Academic Skills and score at required level.

High school preparation. College-preparatory program recommended. 21 units recommended. Recommended units include English 4, mathematics 3, social studies 4, science 3 (laboratory 3). Requirements vary with program.

2015-2016 Annual costs. Tuition/fees: $13,570. Per-credit charge: $555. Books/supplies: $1,000. Personal expenses: $500.

2014-2015 Financial aid. All financial aid based on need. 48% of total undergraduate aid awarded as scholarships/grants, 52% as loans/jobs. Need-based aid available for part-time students. Work-study available nights, weekends and for part-time students.

Application procedures. Admission: $35 fee, may be waived for applicants with need. Admission notification on a rolling basis. Must reply by May 1 or within 4 week(s) if notified thereafter. **Financial aid:** No deadline. FAFSA required. Applicants notified on a rolling basis starting 3/1; must reply within 2 week(s) of notification.

Academics. Special study options: Cross-registration, distance learning, dual enrollment of high school students, independent study, internships, liberal arts/career combination, weekend college. Advanced placement program in nursing for licensed practical nurse and New York State LPN to ADN Nursing Bridge Course. Bachelors Completion Program in Nursing. Bachelor's degree programs available on campus. License preparation in nursing, occupational therapy. **Credit/placement by examination:** AP, CLEP, IB, SAT, ACT, institutional tests. 16 credit hours maximum toward associate degree. **Support services:** Learning center, pre-admission summer program, reduced course load, remedial instruction, study skills assistance, tutoring.

Majors. Business: General, accounting, business admin. **Education:** Early childhood, teacher assistance. **Health services:** Nursing (RN), occupational therapy assistant. **Liberal arts:** Arts/sciences.

Most popular majors. Health sciences 91%, liberal arts 7%.

Technology on campus. 72 workstations in library, computer center. Commuter students can connect to campus network. Online course registration, online library, wireless network available.

Student life. Freshman orientation: Mandatory. Preregistration for classes offered. Held one day prior to the beginning of the semester. **Housing:** Community based housing is available on a first-come, first-served basis for students attending local colleges, within 2 miles of Maria College. **Activities:** Campus ministries.

Student services. Adult student services, alcohol/substance abuse counseling, chaplain/spiritual director, career counseling, student employment services, financial aid counseling, personal counseling, placement for graduates. **Physically disabled:** Services for visually impaired. **Transfer:** Re-entry adviser, pre-admission transcript evaluation for new students. Transfer adviser, college fairs on campus for students transferring to 4-year colleges.

Contact. E-mail: admissions@mariacollege.edu
Phone: (518) 861-2517 Fax: (518) 453-1366
John Ramoska, Director of Admissions, Maria College, 700 New Scotland Avenue, Albany, NY 12208

Mildred Elley: Albany
Albany, New York
www.mildred-elley.edu
CB code: 3335

- For-profit 2-year junior and career college
- Commuter campus in small city
- Interview required

General. Accredited by ACICS. **Enrollment:** 748 undergraduates. **Degrees:** 123 associate awarded. **Location:** 147 miles from New York City. **Calendar:** Semester, extensive summer session. **Full-time faculty:** 16 total; 19% have terminal degrees, 19% minority, 69% women. **Part-time faculty:** 31 total; 13% have terminal degrees, 32% minority, 61% women. **Class size:** 72% < 20, 25% 20-39, 2% 40-49, less than 1% 50-99.

Student profile.

Out-of-state: 2% 25 or older: 65%

Basis for selection. Open admission, but selective for some programs. Additional requirements for Massage Therapy and Practical Nursing programs. Applicants without a high school diploma or GED may be eligible for admission as ability-to-benefit students upon receiving a passing score on an approved national examination. **Home schooled:** Transcript of courses and grades, state high school equivalency certificate required.

2015-2016 Annual costs. Books/supplies: $2,700.

Financial aid. All financial aid based on need. Need-based aid available for part-time students. Work-study available nights, weekends and for part-time students.

Application procedures. Admission: No deadline. $25 fee, may be waived for applicants with need. Application must be submitted on paper. Admission notification on a rolling basis. **Financial aid:** No deadline. FAFSA required. Applicants notified on a rolling basis starting 7/16; must reply within 2 week(s) of notification.

Academics. Special study options: Accelerated study, distance learning, independent study, internships, liberal arts/career combination, weekend college. License preparation in nursing. **Credit/placement by examination:** AP, CLEP, institutional tests. **Support services:** GED preparation, learning center, remedial instruction, study skills assistance, tutoring, writing center.

Majors. Business: Business admin, office technology, tourism/travel. **Communications technology:** Animation/special effects. **Computer sciences:** Information technology, web page design. **Health services:** Massage therapy, medical assistant.

Most popular majors. Business/marketing 30%, communication technologies 9%, computer/information sciences 12%, health sciences 39%, legal studies 10%.

Technology on campus. 100 workstations in library, computer center, student center. Commuter students can connect to campus network. Online library, helpline, repair service, wireless network available.

Student life. Freshman orientation: Mandatory. Preregistration for classes offered. **Activities:** Student government.

Student services. Adult student services, alcohol/substance abuse counseling, career counseling, financial aid counseling, legal services, personal counseling, placement for graduates, veterans' counselor, women's services. **Transfer:** Re-entry adviser, pre-admission transcript evaluation for new students. College fairs on campus for students transferring to 4-year colleges.

Contact. E-mail: admissions@mildred-elley.edu
Phone: (518) 786-3171 Toll-free number: (800) 622-6327
Fax: (518) 786-0011
Stacy Laniewski, Admissions Director, Mildred Elley: Albany, 855 Central Avenue, Albany, NY 12206-1513

Mildred Elley: New York City
New York, New York
www.mildred-elley.edu

- For-profit 2-year junior and career college
- Commuter campus in very large city
- Interview required

General. Regionally accredited; also accredited by ACICS. **Enrollment:** 590 undergraduates. **Degrees:** 130 associate awarded. **Location:** Located in lower Manhattan. **Calendar:** Semester, extensive summer session. **Full-time faculty:** 15 total; 53% have terminal degrees, 53% minority, 47% women. **Part-time faculty:** 30 total; 50% have terminal degrees, 57% minority, 53% women. **Class size:** 53% < 20, 30% 20-39, 3% 40-49, 14% 50-99.

Student profile.

Out-of-state: 1% 25 or older: 62%

Basis for selection. Open admission. Applicants without a high school diploma or GED may be admitted as Ability-to-Benefit (ATB) students, upon receiving a passing score on an approved national examination. **Home schooled:** Transcript of courses and grades, state high school equivalency certificate required.

2015-2016 Annual costs. Books/supplies: $1,350.

Financial aid. All financial aid based on need. Need-based aid available for part-time students. Work-study available nights, weekends and for part-time students.

Application procedures. Admission: No deadline. $25 fee, may be waived for applicants with need. Admission notification on a rolling basis. **Financial aid:** No deadline. FAFSA required.

Academics. Special study options: Accelerated study, distance learning, independent study, internships, weekend college. License preparation in nursing. **Credit/placement by examination:** AP, institutional tests. **Support services:** GED preparation, learning center, remedial instruction, study skills assistance, tutoring, writing center.

Majors. Health services: Medical assistant.

Technology on campus. 60 workstations in library, computer center, student center. Commuter students can connect to campus network. Online library, helpline, repair service, wireless network available.

Student life. Freshman orientation: Mandatory. Preregistration for classes offered.

Student services. Adult student services, alcohol/substance abuse counseling, career counseling, financial aid counseling, legal services, personal counseling, placement for graduates, veterans' counselor, women's services. **Transfer:** Re-entry adviser, pre-admission transcript evaluation for new students. College fairs on campus for students transferring to 4-year colleges.

Contact. E-mail: admissions@mildred-elley.edu
Phone: (212) 380-9004 Toll-free number: (800) 622-6327
Bernard Price, Director of Admissions, Mildred Elley: New York City, 25 Broadway, 16th Floor, New York, NY 10004

Mohawk Valley Community College
Utica, New York.
www.mvcc.edu
CB code: 2414

▶ Public 2-year community college
▶ Commuter campus in small city

General. Founded in 1946. Regionally accredited. SUNY institution. Branch campus in Rome, New York. **Enrollment:** 4,613 degree-seeking undergraduates; 2,062 non-degree-seeking students. **Degrees:** 1,129 associate awarded. **ROTC:** Army, Air Force. **Location:** 55 miles from Syracuse, 95 miles from Albany. **Calendar:** Semester, limited summer session. **Full-time faculty:** 140 total; 19% have terminal degrees, 11% minority, 43% women. **Part-time faculty:** 369 total; 9% have terminal degrees, 5% minority, 50% women. **Class size:** 60% < 20, 38% 20-39, 2% 40-49, less than 1% 50-99. **Special facilities:** Human cadaver lab, welding facilities, airframe and powerplant hangar facilities.

Student profile. Among degree-seeking undergraduates, 47% enrolled in a transfer program, 53% enrolled in a vocational program, 1% already have a bachelor's degree or higher, 1,279 enrolled as first-time, first-year students, 325 transferred in from other institutions.

Part-time:	23%	Multi-racial, non-Hispanic:	3%
Women:	53%	International:	1%
African American:	8%	25 or older:	29%
Asian American:	6%	Live on campus:	10%
Hispanic/Latino:	9%		

Transfer out. 50% of students enrolled in the transfer program go on to 4-year colleges. **Colleges most students transferred to 2015:** Utica College, SUNY Institute of Technology, SUNY Oswego, Morrisville, SUNY Albany.

Basis for selection. Open admission, but selective for some programs. Applicants' records reviewed for completion of program-specific prerequisites to determine regular or underprepared acceptance to program. Interview recommended for all, required for Airframe & Powerplant Tech and Radiologic Tech applicants. **Home schooled:** State high school equivalency certificate required. Must pass Academic Opportunity Assessment (AOA) test prior to acceptance if the state high school equivalency certificate letter is not provided. **Learning Disabled:** Learning-disabled applicants should forward copy of IEP to Coordinator of Disabilities Services.

High school preparation. College-preparatory program recommended. 15 units recommended. Recommended units include English 4, mathematics 2, social studies 4, science 2, foreign language 1 and academic electives 2. Requirements vary for admission to nursing and certain other programs.

2015-2016 Annual costs. Tuition/fees: $4,600; $8,560 out-of-state. Per-credit charge: $160 in-state; $320 out-of-state. Room/board: $10,090.

2015-2016 Financial aid. Need-based: 1,134 full-time freshmen applied for aid; 629 deemed to have need; 629 received aid. Average need met was 94%. Average scholarship/grant was $6,517; average loan $3,563. 81% of total undergraduate aid awarded as scholarships/grants, 19% as loans/jobs. Need-based aid available for part-time students. Work-study available nights, weekends and for part-time students. **Non-need-based:** Awarded to 123 full-time undergraduates, including 71 freshmen. **Additional information:** First year students must attend an orientation to receive Federal Work Study funds.

Application procedures. Admission: No deadline. No application fee. Admission notification on a rolling basis beginning on or about 12/1. Fall applicants accepted prior to March 15 should return the form by April 1. Applicants requesting on-campus housing should return the form as soon as possible after acceptance (housing is limited). Fall applicants accepted after March 15 (or Spring or Summer applicants) should return the form within 2 weeks from the date listed on the acceptance letter. **Financial aid:** Priority date 4/15; no closing date. FAFSA required. Applicants notified on a rolling basis starting 3/1; must reply within 2 week(s) of notification.

Academics. Special study options: Cross-registration, distance learning, double major, dual enrollment of high school students, ESL, honors, independent study, internships, student-designed major. Bachelor's degree programs available on campus. License preparation in aviation, nursing, radiology. **Credit/placement by examination:** AP, CLEP, institutional tests. Each center has its own policy for the awarding of credit. **Support services:** Learning center, reduced course load, remedial instruction, study skills assistance, tutoring, writing center. Supplemental Instruction.

Majors. Business: Accounting technology, administrative services, banking/financial services, business admin, hotel/motel admin, operations. **Communications:** Advertising. **Computer sciences:** General, programming, security, web page design. **Engineering:** General. **Foreign languages:** Sign language interpretation. **Health services:** Dietetic technician, EMT ambulance attendant, medical assistant, medical radiologic technology/radiation therapy, nursing (RN), respiratory therapy technology, substance abuse counseling. **Liberal arts:** Arts/sciences, humanities. **Parks/recreation:** Facilities management. **Protective services:** Fire services admin, investigation and interviewing, law enforcement admin. **Visual/performing arts:** Art, commercial photography, commercial/advertising art, digital arts.

Most popular majors. Business/marketing 13%, health sciences 14%, liberal arts 37%, security/protective services 9%, trade and industry 6%.

Technology on campus. 145 workstations in dormitories, library, computer center. Dormitories wired for high-speed internet access and linked to campus network. Commuter students can connect to campus network. Online course registration, online library, helpline, wireless network available.

Student life. Freshman orientation: Mandatory. Preregistration for classes offered. Orientation mandatory for residence hall students, with a $45 charge. Orientation for commuter students now part of the overall advising process. **Housing:** Coed dorms, special housing for disabled, wellness housing available. $100 fully refundable deposit. Housing eligibility based on academic standing for initial acceptance and continued eligibility. All halls nonsmoking; 1 residence hall has extended quiet hours. Limited visitation suites available. On-campus housing is on first-come, first-served basis. **Activities:** Concert band, drama, international student organizations, literary magazine, musical theater, student government, student newspaper, Catalyst, chemical dependency club, Kidz-N-Coaches, Phi Theta Kappa, gay/straight alliance, IF, Latino student union, returning adult student association, human service and psychology club, Student Veteran Association.

Athletics. NJCAA. **Intercollegiate:** Baseball M, basketball, bowling, cross-country, golf, ice hockey M, lacrosse, soccer, softball W, tennis, track and field, volleyball W. **Intramural:** Badminton, basketball, football (non-tackle), volleyball. **Team name:** Hawks.

Student services. Adult student services, alcohol/substance abuse counseling, career counseling, student employment services, financial aid counseling, health services, personal counseling, placement for graduates, veterans' counselor. **Physically disabled:** Services for visually, speech, hearing impaired. **Transfer:** Pre-admission transcript evaluation for new students. Transfer center, transfer adviser, college fairs on campus for students transferring to 4-year colleges.

Contact. E-mail: admissions@mvcc.edu
Phone: (315) 792-5354 Toll-free number: (800) 733-6822
Fax: (315) 792-5527
Daniel Ianno, Director of Admissions, Mohawk Valley Community College, 1101 Sherman Drive, Utica, NY 13501-5394

Monroe Community College
Rochester, New York
CB member
www.monroecc.edu
CB code: 2429

▶ Public 2-year community college
▶ Commuter campus in large city

General. Founded in 1961. Regionally accredited. SUNY institution. Off-campus extension centers in 4 area high schools, branch campus in downtown Rochester. Applied technology center. **Enrollment:** 13,385 degree-seeking undergraduates; 1,201 non-degree-seeking students. **Degrees:** 2,394 associate awarded. **ROTC:** Army, Naval, Air Force. **Location:** 4 miles from downtown. **Calendar:** Semester, limited summer session. **Full-time faculty:** 307 total; 18% have terminal degrees, 19% minority, 57% women. **Part-time faculty:** 501 total; 11% have terminal degrees, 12% minority, 51% women. **Class size:** 31% < 20, 48% 20-39, 21% 40-49, less than 1% 50-99. **Special facilities:** Human ecology habitat, human performance laboratory, electronic learning center. **Partnerships:** Formal partnerships with Xerox, Kodak, Frontier, Wegman's.

Student profile. Among degree-seeking undergraduates, 3,272 enrolled as first-time, first-year students.

Part-time:	34%	Hispanic/Latino:	9%
Out-of-state:	2%	Multi-racial, non-Hispanic:	4%
Women:	54%	International:	1%
African American:	21%	25 or older:	40%
Asian American:	4%		

Transfer out. Colleges most students transferred to 2015: SUNY College at Brockport, Rochester Institute of Technology, St. John Fisher College, SUNY College at Geneseo, Nazareth College.

Basis for selection. Open admission, but selective for some programs. Admissions to certain programs based on high school records, with preference given to county residents. Applicants to engineering and computer science must have precalculus, chemistry and physics. **Home schooled:** Transcript of courses and grades required. Must meet Federal Ability to Benefit guidelines on placement exam if not issued a regular high school diploma.

High school preparation. College-preparatory program recommended. Individual programs have specific math and science requirements.

2015-2016 Annual costs. Tuition/fees: $4,043; $7,843 out-of-state. Per-credit charge: $159 in-state; $318 out-of-state. Room only: $6,170. Books/supplies: $1,000.

Financial aid. All financial aid based on need. Need-based aid available for part-time students. Work-study available nights, weekends and for part-time students.

Application procedures. Admission: Closing date 8/18. No application fee. Admission notification by 8/31. Admission notification on a rolling basis beginning on or about 10/1. Application deadline for healthcare programs: 1/31 for fall term, 10/31 for spring term. Applicants to nursing program are encouraged to apply 1 year prior to registration. **Financial aid:** Priority date 3/30; no closing date. FAFSA required. Applicants notified on a rolling basis starting 3/15; must reply within 2 week(s) of notification.

Academics. Special study options: Dual enrollment of high school students, ESL, external degree. License preparation in aviation, dental hygiene, nursing, paramedic, radiology. **Credit/placement by examination:** AP, CLEP, institutional tests. 30 credit hours maximum toward associate degree. **Support services:** Learning center, pre-admission summer program, reduced course load, remedial instruction, study skills assistance, tutoring, writing center.

Majors. Architecture: Landscape. **Biology:** General. **Business:** General, accounting, administrative services, international, marketing, sales/distribution, tourism promotion, tourism/travel. **Communications:** Advertising, communications/speech/rhetoric, public relations. **Communications technology:** General, radio/TV. **Computer sciences:** Computer science, information technology, networking, programming, systems analysis. **Education:** Health, music, physical. **Engineering:** Engineering science. **Health services:** Dental hygiene, health information technology, nursing (RN), physics/radiologic health. **History:** General. **Liberal arts:** Arts/sciences. **Math:** General. **Parks/recreation:** Health/fitness. **Physical sciences:** Chemistry, optics, physics. **Protective services:** Corrections, criminal justice, fire safety technology, police science. **Social sciences:** General, political science. **Visual/performing arts:** Commercial/advertising art, interior design, music performance, photography, studio arts. **Work/family studies:** Child care service, institutional food production.

Most popular majors. Business/marketing 14%, engineering/engineering technologies 6%, health sciences 11%, liberal arts 42%.

Technology on campus. 150 workstations in library, computer center, student center. Dormitories wired for high-speed internet access and linked to campus network. Commuter students can connect to campus network. Helpline, wireless network available.

Student life. Freshman orientation: Available. Preregistration for classes offered. Held 1 week prior to beginning of semester. **Housing:** Coed dorms, single-sex dorms, apartments available. **Activities:** Bands, choral groups, drama, literary magazine, musical theater, radio station, student government, student newspaper, symphony orchestra, Christian, Jewish, and Christian Science groups; Latin American, Italian-American, Black, and international student organizations; veterans and handicapped student clubs; honor society.

Athletics. NJCAA. **Intercollegiate:** Baseball M, basketball, diving, golf M, ice hockey M, lacrosse M, soccer, softball W, swimming, tennis, volleyball W. **Intramural:** Archery, basketball, bowling, cheerleading W, cross-country, diving, lacrosse, racquetball, rugby M, skiing, soccer, softball, swimming, tennis, volleyball, water polo M. **Team name:** Tribunes.

Student services. Adult student services, career counseling, student employment services, financial aid counseling, health services, on-campus daycare, personal counseling, placement for graduates, veterans' counselor.

Physically disabled: Services for visually, hearing impaired. **Transfer:** Transfer center, transfer adviser, college fairs on campus for students transferring to 4-year colleges.

Contact. Phone: (585) 292-2200 Fax: (585) 292-3860
Andrew Freeman, Director of Admissions, Monroe Community College, Office of Admissions-Monroe Community College, Rochester, NY 14692-8908

Nassau Community College
Garden City, New York   **CB member**
www.ncc.edu   **CB code: 2563**

▶ Public 2-year community college
▶ Commuter campus in large town

General. Founded in 1959. Regionally accredited. SUNY institution. Students may attend some courses at off-campus locations. **Enrollment:** 19,448 degree-seeking undergraduates; 2,008 non-degree-seeking students. **Degrees:** 3,422 associate awarded. **Location:** 25 miles from New York City. **Calendar:** Semester, extensive summer session. **Full-time faculty:** 473 total; 37% have terminal degrees, 14% minority, 59% women. **Part-time faculty:** 910 total; 26% have terminal degrees, 14% minority, 44% women. **Class size:** 27% < 20, 72% 20-39, less than 1% 40-49. **Special facilities:** Firehouse gallery. **Partnerships:** Formal partnerships with local businesses and industry to provide on-site training to employees.

Student profile. Among degree-seeking undergraduates, 4,325 enrolled as first-time, first-year students.

Part-time:	36%	Asian American:	6%
Women:	49%	Hispanic/Latino:	25%
African American:	23%	International:	1%

Transfer out. Colleges most students transferred to 2015: Hofstra University, Adelphi University, SUNY Old Westbury, SUNY Stony Brook, Dowling College.

Basis for selection. Open admission, but selective for some programs. Class rank and fulfillment of mathematics and science requirements important for admission to accounting, business, engineering, nursing, allied health, mortuary science, civil technology, computer information systems, computer science, electrical technology, paralegal, and telecommunications technology programs. Students without high school diploma or equivalent may apply for GED after successful completion of 24 college credits. SAT scores may result in exemption from placement testing. Interview required for allied health programs; audition required for music program; portfolio review required for fashion apparel design program. **Adult students:** Placement test in reading, English, and math required unless applicant has prior associate or bachelor's degree or prior college credit for English composition and college-level math. **Home schooled:** Transcript of courses and grades, state high school equivalency certificate required. **Learning Disabled:** Students must submit a copy of their IEP in order to get services through the Center for Students with Disabilities.

High school preparation. Recommended units include English 4, mathematics 4, social studies 4, science 4 (laboratory 4), foreign language 3 and academic electives 4.

2015-2016 Annual costs. Tuition/fees: $4,888; $9,422 out-of-state. Per-credit charge: $189 in-state; $378 out-of-state. Books/supplies: $1,400. Personal expenses: $2,200.

Financial aid. Need-based: Need-based aid available for part-time students. Work-study available nights, weekends and for part-time students. **Non-need-based:** Scholarships awarded for academics, minority status.

Application procedures. Admission: Closing date 8/15 (receipt date). $50 fee. Application must be submitted on paper. Admission notification on a rolling basis beginning on or about 2/15. **Financial aid:** Priority date 6/7; no closing date. FAFSA required. Applicants notified on a rolling basis; must reply within 1 week(s) of notification.

Academics. Special study options: Cooperative education, cross-registration, distance learning, ESL, honors, internships, study abroad, weekend college. Cooperative programs with SUNY College of Technology at Utica-Rome and SUNY at New Paltz, New York State Chiropractic College, Fashion Institute of Technology, Adelphi University; joint admissions with SUNY at Stony Brook and SUNY College at Old Westbury. License preparation in nursing, physical therapy, radiology. **Credit/placement by examination:** AP, CLEP, IB, institutional tests. 33 credit hours maximum toward associate degree. **Support services:** GED preparation and test center, learning center, reduced course load, remedial instruction, study skills assistance, tutoring, writing center.

Honors college/program. Honors applicants must rank in the top 20% of their graduating class and have 3 years of Regents math, English, science and high grades in each.

Majors. Area/ethnic studies: African. **Business:** Accounting, administrative services, business admin, fashion, management information systems, sales/distribution. **Communications:** Communications/speech/rhetoric, media studies. **Computer sciences:** General, computer science, programming. **Education:** Early childhood, elementary, middle, secondary. **Engineering:** General, electrical. **Foreign languages:** American Sign Language. **Health services:** Medical radiologic technology/radiation therapy, medical secretary, nursing (RN), physical therapy assistant, respiratory therapy technology, surgical technology. **Liberal arts:** Arts/sciences. **Math:** General. **Protective services:** Disaster management, firefighting, law enforcement admin. **Visual/performing arts:** Art, digital arts, graphic design, interior design, music performance, photography. **Work/family studies:** Food/nutrition.

Most popular majors. Business/marketing 15%, health sciences 9%, liberal arts 50%, security/protective services 7%.

Technology on campus. 1,300 workstations in library, computer center. Commuter students can connect to campus network. Online course registration, online library, helpline, wireless network available.

Student life. Freshman orientation: Available. Preregistration for classes offered. Full-day program. **Activities:** Bands, choral groups, dance, drama, literary magazine, music ensembles, musical theater, radio station, student government, student newspaper, symphony orchestra, TV station, Haraya Caribbean students organizations, Asian American society, Irish American club, NYPIRG, women center, Association Catholic Community, Jewish students organization, organization of Latinos, multicultural club, Intervarsity Christian Fellowship.

Athletics. NJCAA. **Intercollegiate:** Baseball M, basketball, bowling, cross-country, football (tackle) M, golf, lacrosse, soccer, softball W, tennis, track and field, volleyball W, wrestling M. **Intramural:** Badminton, baseball M, basketball, football (non-tackle) M, handball, judo, racquetball, soccer, softball, swimming, table tennis, tennis, volleyball. **Team name:** Lions.

Student services. Adult student services, career counseling, student employment services, financial aid counseling, health services, minority student services, on-campus daycare, personal counseling, placement for graduates, veterans' counselor, women's services. **Physically disabled:** Services for visually, speech, hearing impaired. **Transfer:** Pre-admission transcript evaluation for new students. Transfer center, transfer adviser, college fairs on campus for students transferring to 4-year colleges.

Contact. E-mail: admissions@ncc.edu
Phone: (516) 572-7345 Fax: (516) 572-9743
David Follick, Dean of Academic Student Services, Nassau Community College, One Education Drive, Garden City, NY 11530

New York Career Institute
New York, New York
www.nyci.edu   CB code: 5324

▸ For-profit 2-year career college
▸ Commuter campus in very large city
▸ Interview required

General. Accredited by New York State Board of Regents. **Enrollment:** 420 degree-seeking undergraduates. **Degrees:** 84 associate awarded. **Calendar:** Trimester, extensive summer session. **Full-time faculty:** 8 total. **Part-time faculty:** 30 total.

Basis for selection. Open admission. All applicants take English and math placement examinations (CPAt). **Adult students:** SAT/ACT scores not required.

2016-2017 Annual costs. Tuition/fees (projected): $13,700. Books/supplies: $1,545. Personal expenses: $4,000.

Financial aid. All financial aid based on need. Need-based aid available for part-time students. Work-study available nights, weekends and for part-time students.

Application procedures. Admission: No deadline. $50 fee, may be waived for applicants with need. Admission notification on a rolling basis. **Financial aid:** No deadline. Applicants notified on a rolling basis.

Academics. Special study options: Distance learning, internships. **Credit/placement by examination:** AP, CLEP, institutional tests. **Support services:** Learning center, remedial instruction, study skills assistance, tutoring.

Majors. Health services: Medical secretary.

Technology on campus. 125 workstations in library, computer center. Online course registration, online library, repair service available.

Student life. Freshman orientation: Mandatory. Preregistration for classes offered.

Student services. Career counseling, student employment services, financial aid counseling, personal counseling, placement for graduates. **Transfer:** Pre-admission transcript evaluation for new students.

Contact. E-mail: lstieglitz@nyci.edu
Phone: (212) 962-0002 ext. 100 Fax: (212) 385-7574
Larry Steiglitz, Director of Admissions, New York Career Institute, 11 Park Place, New York, NY 10007

Niagara County Community College
Sanborn, New York   CB member
www.niagaracc.suny.edu   CB code: 2568

▸ Public 2-year community college
▸ Commuter campus in rural community

General. Founded in 1962. Regionally accredited. SUNY institution. **Enrollment:** 4,701 degree-seeking undergraduates; 1,432 non-degree-seeking students. **Degrees:** 969 associate awarded. **ROTC:** Army. **Location:** 10 miles from Niagara Falls. **Calendar:** Semester, limited summer session. **Full-time faculty:** 104 total; 32% have terminal degrees, 11% minority, 56% women. **Part-time faculty:** 256 total; 6% have terminal degrees, 6% minority, 64% women. **Special facilities:** Biofeedback laboratory.

Student profile. Among degree-seeking undergraduates, 1,301 enrolled as first-time, first-year students.

Part-time:	23%	Asian American:	1%
Out-of-state:	1%	Hispanic/Latino:	4%
Women:	58%	Native American:	1%
African American:	14%	Live on campus:	5%

Transfer out. Colleges most students transferred to 2015: Buffalo State College, Niagara University, SUNY Buffalo, Brockport, Fredonia.

Basis for selection. Open admission, but selective for some programs. Admission to nursing, physical therapist assistant, radiologic technology, and surgical technology programs based on school achievement record and test scores, on a space-available basis. SAT/ACT reviewed for placement if submitted. Interview recommended.

High school preparation. 1 drafting required for drafting applicants; 1 biology or chemistry required for nursing applicants; 3 mathematics for engineering technology; 1 biology, 1 chemistry and 2 mathematics for physical therapist assistant; 1 chemistry, 1 biology, 2 mathematics for radiologic technology; 1 biology for surgical technician; 3 mathematics for business administration.

2015-2016 Annual costs. Tuition/fees: $4,370; $10,310 out-of-state. Per-credit charge: $165 in-state; $412.5 out-of-state. Books/supplies: $1,000. Personal expenses: $650.

2014-2015 Financial aid. All financial aid based on need. 43% of total undergraduate aid awarded as scholarships/grants, 57% as loans/jobs. Need-based aid available for part-time students. Work-study available nights, weekends and for part-time students. **Additional information:** Assistance offered with placing students in part-time employment through the Job Locator office. Students can charge books and food coupons.

Application procedures. Admission: Closing date 8/31. No application fee. Admission notification on a rolling basis beginning on or about 8/1. Must reply by May 1 or within 4 week(s) if notified thereafter. **Financial aid:** Priority date 4/1; no closing date. FAFSA required. Applicants notified on a rolling basis starting 5/1; must reply within 2 week(s) of notification.

Academics. Orientation program for Distance Learning students. **Special study options:** Cooperative education, cross-registration, distance learning, double major, dual enrollment of high school students, honors, independent study, internships, study abroad. License preparation in nursing. **Credit/placement by examination:** AP, CLEP, IB, institutional tests. 30 credit hours maximum toward associate degree. **Support services:** Learning center, pre-admission summer program, reduced course load, remedial instruction, study skills assistance, tutoring, writing center.

Majors. Business: Accounting, administrative services, business admin, casino management, hospitality admin, retailing, tourism/travel. **Communications:** Communications/speech/rhetoric, digital media. **Computer sciences:** General, computer science. **Conservation:** Environmental studies. **Education:** Elementary. **Health services:** Massage therapy, medical assistant, medical radiologic technology/radiation therapy, nursing (RN), physical therapy assistant, surgical technology. **Liberal arts:** Arts/sciences, humanities. **Parks/recreation:** General, health/fitness, sports admin. **Protective services:** Criminalistics, law enforcement admin. **Visual/performing arts:** Dramatic, music, studio arts.

Most popular majors. Business/marketing 16%, health sciences 27%, liberal arts 24%, security/protective services 8%.

Technology on campus. 500 workstations in library, computer center, student center. Dormitories wired for high-speed internet access and linked to campus network. Commuter students can connect to campus network. Online course registration, online library, helpline, student web hosting, wireless network available.

Student life. Freshman orientation: Available. Preregistration for classes offered. One-day orientation in August. **Housing:** Guaranteed on-campus for all undergraduates. Coed dorms available. $275 partly refundable deposit. **Activities:** Jazz band, choral groups, dance, drama, international student organizations, music ensembles, musical theater, radio station, student government, student newspaper, disabled student association, comeback club, African American student association, Native American club, human services club, international club, outdoor adventure club, student ambassadors, student nurses association, tanzen dance club.

Athletics. NJCAA. **Intercollegiate:** Baseball M, basketball, golf, soccer, softball W, volleyball W, wrestling M. **Intramural:** Basketball, ice hockey M, racquetball, soccer, tennis. **Team name:** Thunderwolves.

Student services. Adult student services, alcohol/substance abuse counseling, career counseling, student employment services, financial aid counseling, health services, on-campus daycare, personal counseling, placement for graduates, veterans' counselor. **Physically disabled:** Services for visually, speech, hearing impaired. **Transfer:** Pre-admission transcript evaluation for new students. Transfer adviser, college fairs on campus for students transferring to 4-year colleges.

Contact. E-mail: admissions@niagaracc.suny.edu
Phone: (716) 614-6200 Fax: (716) 614-6820
James Trimboli, Director of Admissions, Niagara County Community College, 3111 Saunders Settlement Road, Sanborn, NY 14132-9460

North Country Community College
Saranac Lake, New York   **CB member**
www.nccc.edu   **CB code: 2571**

- Public 2-year community college
- Commuter campus in small town

General. Founded in 1967. Regionally accredited. SUNY institution. Campuses in Saranac Lake, Malone, and Ticonderoga. **Enrollment:** 2,680 undergraduates. **Degrees:** 234 associate awarded. **Location:** 150 miles from Albany, 50 miles from Plattsburgh. **Calendar:** Semester, limited summer session. **Full-time faculty:** 42 total. **Part-time faculty:** 91 total. **Class size:** 75% < 20, 24% 20-39, 1% 40-49. **Partnerships:** Formal partnerships with local high schools through College Bridge Program.

Student profile.

Out-of-state:	2%	Live on campus:	6%
25 or older:	26%		

Transfer out. Colleges most students transferred to 2015: SUNY Colleges at Plattsburgh, Potsdam, Cobleskill, Geneseo; SUNY at Buffalo.

Basis for selection. Open admission, but selective for some programs. Special requirements for nursing, radiologic technology, and massage therapy. SAT or ACT and placement tests recommended for competitive programs. **Home schooled:** Must complete and score in appropriate ranges on College Board Descriptive Tests System in math, English, and reading.

High school preparation. 16 units recommended. Recommended units include English 4, mathematics 3, social studies 4, science 3 (laboratory 1) and foreign language 3. 5 units of math and science recommended (3 math and 2 science or 2 math and 3 science).

2015-2016 Annual costs. Tuition/fees: $5,212; $11,362 out-of-state. Per-credit charge: $185 in-state; $441 out-of-state. Room/board: $9,480. Books/supplies: $800. Personal expenses: $800. **Additional information:** Annual

room rate based on single-occupancy bedroom within suite; no double-occupancy rooms available.

Financial aid. All financial aid based on need. Need-based aid available for part-time students. Work-study available nights, weekends and for part-time students.

Application procedures. Admission: Priority date 2/1; no deadline. No application fee. Admission notification on a rolling basis. Must reply by May 1 or within 4 week(s) if notified thereafter. **Financial aid:** Priority date 4/1; no closing date. FAFSA required. Applicants notified on a rolling basis starting 4/1; must reply within 3 week(s) of notification.

Academics. 23-42 credit hours required in major, 62-70 required for graduation depending on field of study. **Special study options:** Distance learning, double major, dual enrollment of high school students, internships, liberal arts/career combination, student-designed major. License preparation in nursing, radiology. **Credit/placement by examination:** AP, CLEP, institutional tests. 31 credit hours maximum toward associate degree. **Support services:** Learning center, reduced course load, remedial instruction, study skills assistance, tutoring.

Majors. Business: General, business admin, office/clerical. **Computer sciences:** Computer graphics. **Health services:** Massage therapy, medical radiologic technology/radiation therapy, nursing (RN). **Liberal arts:** Arts/sciences. **Parks/recreation:** Facilities management. **Protective services:** Criminal justice.

Technology on campus. 200 workstations in dormitories, library, computer center, student center. Dormitories linked to campus network. Commuter students can connect to campus network. Online library, helpline, wireless network available.

Student life. Freshman orientation: Mandatory. Preregistration for classes offered. Day-long session held 1 day prior to start of classes. **Housing:** Coed dorms, wellness housing available. $250 nonrefundable deposit. **Activities:** Drama, literary magazine, music ensembles, student government, student newspaper.

Athletics. NJCAA. **Intercollegiate:** Basketball M, ice hockey M, soccer, softball W. **Intramural:** Badminton, basketball, bowling, golf, soccer, softball, swimming, volleyball, weight lifting. **Team name:** Saints.

Student services. Adult student services, alcohol/substance abuse counseling, career counseling, student employment services, financial aid counseling, personal counseling, placement for graduates. **Physically disabled:** Services for visually, speech, hearing impaired. **Transfer:** Pre-admission transcript evaluation for new students. Transfer adviser, college fairs on campus for students transferring to 4-year colleges.

Contact. E-mail: info@nccc.edu
Phone: (518) 891-2915 ext. 233 Toll-free number: (888) 879-6222
Fax: (518) 891-0898
Edwin Trathen, Vice President for Enrollment and Student Services, North Country Community College, 23 Santanoni Avenue, Saranac Lake, NY 12983

Onondaga Community College
Syracuse, New York   **CB member**
www.sunyocc.edu   **CB code: 2627**

- Public 2-year community college
- Commuter campus in small city

General. Founded in 1962. Regionally accredited. **Enrollment:** 8,009 degree-seeking undergraduates. **Degrees:** 1,243 associate awarded. **ROTC:** Army, Air Force. **Location:** 4 miles from downtown Syracuse. **Calendar:** Semester, extensive summer session. **Full-time faculty:** 177 total; 8% minority, 58% women. **Part-time faculty:** 468 total; 5% minority, 50% women. **Class size:** 52% < 20, 47% 20-39, less than 1% 40-49, less than 1% 50-99, less than 1% >100. **Special facilities:** Children's learning center, The Gallery at the Ann Felton Multicultural Center, Furnace Brook Retreat Center, Southwest YMCA. **Partnerships:** Formal partnerships with Syracuse public schools, Manufacturers Association of Central New York, Disney.

Student profile. Among degree-seeking undergraduates, 72% enrolled in a transfer program, 28% enrolled in a vocational program, 2,260 enrolled as first-time, first-year students, 531 transferred in from other institutions.

Part-time:	28%	25 or older:	21%
Out-of-state:	1%	Live on campus:	7%
Women:	51%		

Transfer out. Colleges most students transferred to 2015: SUNY Oswego, SUNY Cortland, SUNY Buffalo, Le Moyne College, Syracuse University.

Basis for selection. Open admission, but selective for some programs. Admission to some programs based on high school GPA, test scores, and specific program prerequisites. Mandatory developmental skills courses required as condition of acceptance for students lacking adequate academic background. School achievement record, test scores, special talents considered for placement only. Information session required for nursing and recommended for physical therapy assistant; audition required for music. **Adult students:** SAT/ACT scores not required. **Home schooled:** State high school equivalency certificate required. Letter of substantial equivalency from local school district.

High school preparation. 15 units recommended. Recommended units include English 4, mathematics 3, science 3 and foreign language 2. Algebra, biology, chemistry required of respiratory care, surgical technology, nursing applicants. 4 math required for engineering, science, computer science and physical therapy assistant applicants. Language required for humanities.

2015-2016 Annual costs. Tuition/fees: $5,014; $9,444 out-of-state. Per-credit charge: $184 in-state; $368 out-of-state. Room/board: $8,900. Books/supplies: $1,230. Personal expenses: $700.

2014-2015 Financial aid. All financial aid based on need. 2,045 full-time freshmen applied for aid; 1,822 deemed to have need; 1,665 received aid. Average need met was 56%. Average scholarship/grant was $5,814; average loan $2,974. 76% of total undergraduate aid awarded as scholarships/grants, 24% as loans/jobs. Need-based aid available for part-time students. Work-study available nights, weekends and for part-time students.

Application procedures. Admission: No application fee. Admission notification on a rolling basis. **Financial aid:** No deadline. FAFSA required. Applicants notified on a rolling basis; must reply within 4 week(s) of notification.

Academics. Special study options: Accelerated study, cooperative education, cross-registration, distance learning, double major, dual enrollment of high school students, honors, independent study, internships, liberal arts/career combination, New York semester, study abroad. License preparation in nursing, physical therapy. **Credit/placement by examination:** AP, CLEP, institutional tests. 62 credit hours maximum toward associate degree. **Support services:** GED preparation, learning center, pre-admission summer program, reduced course load, remedial instruction, study skills assistance, tutoring, writing center. PowerStart new student advising.

Majors. Architecture: Technology. **Business:** Accounting technology, business admin, hospitality admin. **Communications:** Communications/speech/rhetoric, radio/TV. **Computer sciences:** General, computer science. **Education:** Multi-level teacher. **Engineering:** Engineering science. **Foreign languages:** American Sign Language. **Health services:** Health information technology, nursing (RN), physical therapy assistant. **Liberal arts:** Humanities. **Parks/recreation:** General. **Protective services:** Criminal justice, fire safety technology, forensics, law enforcement admin, police science. **Visual/performing arts:** Interior design, music.

Most popular majors. Business/marketing 12%, engineering/engineering technologies 8%, health sciences 9%, liberal arts 32%, public administration/social services 9%, security/protective services 10%, visual/performing arts 7%.

Technology on campus. 1,200 workstations in library, computer center, student center. Dormitories wired for high-speed internet access and linked to campus network. Commuter students can connect to campus network. Online course registration, online library, helpline, repair service, student web hosting, wireless network available.

Student life. Freshman orientation: Available. Preregistration for classes offered. Programs held for half day in fall and spring prior to start of classes. **Policies:** Dorms are alcohol free. **Housing:** Coed dorms, wellness housing available. $300 nonrefundable deposit. Suite-style housing available. **Activities:** Bands, campus ministries, choral groups, drama, international student organizations, music ensembles, musical theater, radio station, student government, student newspaper, TV station, Emergency Services Organization, Phi Theta Kappa, Whole Earth club, Campus Connect Ministries, Residence Hall Association, indoor marching percussion ensemble, American Sign Language Club, veterans' association.

Athletics. NJCAA. **Intercollegiate:** Baseball M, basketball, cross-country, lacrosse, soccer, softball W, tennis, volleyball W. **Intramural:** Badminton, basketball, golf, skiing, swimming, table tennis, tennis, track and field, volleyball. **Team name:** Lazers.

Student services. Alcohol/substance abuse counseling, chaplain/spiritual director, career counseling, services for economically disadvantaged, student employment services, financial aid counseling, health services, minority student services, on-campus daycare, personal counseling, placement for graduates, veterans' counselor. **Physically disabled:** Services for visually, speech, hearing impaired. **Transfer:** Pre-admission transcript evaluation for new students. Transfer adviser, college fairs on campus for students transferring to 4-year colleges.

Contact. E-mail: OCCadmissions@sunyocc.edu
Phone: (315) 498-2202 Fax: (315) 498-2107
Denny Nicholson, Associate Vice President, Onondaga Community College, 4585 West Seneca Turnpike, Syracuse, NY 13215-4585

Orange County Community College
Middletown, New York
www.sunyorange.edu CB code: 2625

- Public 2-year community college
- Commuter campus in large town

General. Founded in 1950. Regionally accredited. **Enrollment:** 5,353 degree-seeking undergraduates; 1,541 non-degree-seeking students. **Degrees:** 842 associate awarded. **Location:** 60 miles from New York City. **Calendar:** Semester, limited summer session. **Full-time faculty:** 158 total. **Part-time faculty:** 284 total. **Class size:** 57% < 20, 43% 20-39, less than 1% 40-49. **Partnerships:** Formal partnerships with over 220 local and national companies.

Student profile. Among degree-seeking undergraduates, 76% enrolled in a transfer program, 24% enrolled in a vocational program, 1,303 enrolled as first-time, first-year students, 297 transferred in from other institutions.

Part-time:	41%	Hispanic/Latino:	30%
Women:	59%	Multi-racial, non-Hispanic:	3%
African American:	12%	25 or older:	22%
Asian American:	2%		

Transfer out. Colleges most students transferred to 2015: SUNY College at New Paltz, Mount Saint Mary College, SUNY Oneonta, SUNY Albany, SUNY Oswego.

Basis for selection. Open admission, but selective for some programs. Admission to allied health and nursing programs are based on program GPA, credits complete towards program, science credits complete. For Nursing students, the TEAS exam will also be factored into the admissions process. OTA and PTA students will look at all the above information, without the TEAS exam, and will also factor in observation hours, quality of essay, and interview. **Home schooled:** Must have letter from school district supervisor attesting that the student has completed 4 years of high school study.

High school preparation. Regents chemistry is recommended for Dental Hygiene and Nursing.

2015-2016 Annual costs. Tuition/fees: $5,088; $9,574 out-of-state. Per-credit charge: $187 in-state; $374 out-of-state. Books/supplies: $1,500. Personal expenses: $1,766.

2014-2015 Financial aid. Need-based: 57% of total undergraduate aid awarded as scholarships/grants, 43% as loans/jobs. Need-based aid available for part-time students. Work-study available nights, weekends and for part-time students.

Application procedures. Admission: Closing date 8/20 (receipt date). $30 fee, may be waived for applicants with need. Admission notification on a rolling basis beginning on or about 1/4. Must reply by May 1 or within 2 week(s) if notified thereafter. Notification my March 15, must reply within 2 weeks. Honors students by May 1st, must reply within 2 weeks. February 1 application closing date for allied health/nursing program. **Financial aid:** Priority date 4/15, closing date 7/1. FAFSA, institutional form required. Applicants notified on a rolling basis starting 4/1; must reply within 4 week(s) of notification.

Academics. Special study options: Cooperative education, cross-registration, distance learning, double major, dual enrollment of high school students, ESL, honors, independent study, internships, student-designed major. License preparation in dental hygiene, nursing, radiology. **Credit/placement by examination:** AP, CLEP, institutional tests. 30 credit hours maximum toward associate degree. **Support services:** GED preparation and test center, learning center, pre-admission summer program, reduced course load, remedial instruction, study skills assistance, tutoring, writing center.

Honors college/program. Students must have 90 GPA or better or 1200+ SAT in Math and Reading.

Majors. Business: General, accounting, administrative services, business admin, e-commerce, finance, office technology, sales/distribution. **Communications:** Communications/speech/rhetoric. **Computer sciences:** General, data processing. **Education:** General, elementary. **Engineering:** General. **Foreign languages:** General, French, Spanish. **Health services:** Clinical lab science, clinical lab technology, dental hygiene, medical radiologic technology/radiation therapy, occupational therapy assistant, physical therapy assistant. **Liberal arts:** Arts/sciences. **Math:** General. **Parks/recreation:** Exercise sciences, facilities management. **Protective services:** Criminal justice, police science. **Work/family studies:** Child care management.

Technology on campus. 300 workstations in library, computer center, student center. Online course registration, online library, helpline, wireless network available.

Student life. Freshman orientation: Mandatory. Preregistration for classes offered. **Activities:** Bands, choral groups, drama, international student organizations, music ensembles, musical theater, student government, Black and Latino organization, Helping Hands, social service organization, Habitat for Humanity, LGBQ Organization.

Athletics. NJCAA. **Intercollegiate:** Baseball M, basketball, cross-country, golf, soccer, softball W, volleyball W. **Intramural:** Badminton, basketball, racquetball, soccer, softball, volleyball, wrestling M. **Team name:** Colts.

Student services. Adult student services, alcohol/substance abuse counseling, career counseling, services for economically disadvantaged, student employment services, financial aid counseling, health services, on-campus daycare, personal counseling, placement for graduates, veterans' counselor. **Physically disabled:** Services for visually, speech, hearing impaired. **Transfer:** Transfer adviser, college fairs on campus for students transferring to 4-year colleges.

Contact. E-mail: apply@sunyorange.edu
Phone: (845) 341-4030 Fax: (845) 342-8662
Maynard Schmidt, Director of Admissions, Orange County Community College, 115 South Street, Middletown, NY 10940-0115

Phillips Beth Israel School of Nursing
New York, New York
www.pbisn.edu   CB code: 2031

- Private 2-year nursing college
- Commuter campus in very large city
- Application essay, interview required

General. Founded in 1904. **Enrollment:** 252 degree-seeking undergraduates. **Degrees:** 109 associate awarded. **Calendar:** Semester, limited summer session. **Full-time faculty:** 11 total; 18% have terminal degrees, 36% minority, 100% women. **Part-time faculty:** 29 total; 14% have terminal degrees, 66% minority, 93% women. **Class size:** 10% < 20, 67% 20-39, 18% 40-49, 5% 50-99.

Student profile.

Out-of-state:	15%	**25 or older:** 50%

Transfer out. Colleges most students transferred to 2015: Pace University, New York University, New York City College of Technology, Excelsior College.

Basis for selection. For AAS Program: Academic achievement, aptitude test scores, personal interview, recommendations, and prior experience of primary consideration. Mandatory score of 102 or better on National League for Nursing Preadmission Examination-RN. Standing in top half of high school class recommended. High school minimum average of 75 percent required, college GPA of 2.5 or better, GED minimum score of 250. For RN-BSN Program: Associates degree or diploma in nursing from a state-registered nursing program, unrestricted and unencumbered current license and registration to practice as a registered nurse in NY State, minimum college GPA of 2.5, a "C" or higher in all science and math courses, "C+" or higher in all nursing courses; satisfactory completion of prerequisite general education courses. **Home schooled:** Statement describing home school structure and mission, transcript of courses and grades, state high school equivalency certificate required.

High school preparation. College-preparatory program recommended. 16 units required. Required and recommended units include English 4, mathematics 2, social studies 2, history 2, science 2 (laboratory 2), foreign language 2 and academic electives 2. Chemistry and biology required.

2015-2016 Annual costs. Tuition/fees: $24,120. Per-credit charge: $500. Books/supplies: $2,650.

Financial aid. Need-based: Need-based aid available for part-time students. Work-study available nights, weekends and for part-time students.

Application procedures. Admission: Closing date 3/1 (postmark date). $50 fee, may be waived for applicants with need. Application must be submitted on paper. Admission notification on a rolling basis beginning on or about 2/1. Must reply by May 1 or within 2 week(s) if notified thereafter. **Financial aid:** Closing date 6/30. FAFSA, institutional form required. Applicants notified by 8/1; must reply within 3 week(s) of notification.

Academics. Special study options: Honors, weekend college. Bachelor's degree programs available on campus. License preparation in nursing. **Credit/placement by examination:** AP, CLEP, institutional tests. 24 credit hours maximum toward associate degree, 5 toward bachelor's. **Support services:** Learning center, pre-admission summer program, reduced course load, remedial instruction, study skills assistance, tutoring.

Majors. Health services: Nursing (RN).

Technology on campus. PC or laptop required. 45 workstations in library, computer center. Commuter students can connect to campus network. Online course registration, wireless network available.

Student life. Freshman orientation: Mandatory. Preregistration for classes offered. 2 full days the week before classes start. **Activities:** Choral groups, student government, student newspaper, National Student Nurses Association Chapter.

Student services. Alcohol/substance abuse counseling, career counseling, financial aid counseling, health services, personal counseling. **Physically disabled:** Services for visually, speech, hearing impaired. **Transfer:** Pre-admission transcript evaluation for new students. Transfer adviser, college fairs on campus for students transferring to 4-year colleges.

Contact. E-mail: pbisn@chpnet.org
Phone: (212) 614-6114 Fax: (212) 614-6109
Bernice Pass-Stern, Assistant Dean, Phillips Beth Israel School of Nursing, 776 Sixth Avenue, Fourth Floor, New York, NY 10001

Plaza College
Forest Hills, New York
www.plazacollege.edu   CB code: 0545

- For-profit 2-year business and health science college
- Commuter campus in very large city
- Application essay, interview required

General. Founded in 1916. Regionally accredited. **Enrollment:** 739 degree-seeking undergraduates. **Degrees:** 38 bachelor's, 87 associate awarded. **Calendar:** Semester, limited summer session. **Full-time faculty:** 15 total. **Part-time faculty:** 50 total. **Special facilities:** Specialized medical assisting labs.

Basis for selection. Prospective students must attend a career planning session with an Admissions counselor and write an admissions essay. Essay, interview, and test scores are taken into account to reach admission decisions. Wonderlic and college-administered writing test required of all students.

2015-2016 Annual costs. Tuition/fees: $11,350. Books/supplies: $1,500. Personal expenses: $5,102. **Additional information:** 3 semesters required in academic year; costs quoted for 2 of 3 semesters.

Financial aid. Need-based: Work-study available nights, weekends and for part-time students.

Application procedures. Admission: No deadline. $100 fee, may be waived for applicants with need. Application must be submitted on paper. Admission notification on a rolling basis. **Financial aid:** No deadline. FAFSA, institutional form required. Applicants notified on a rolling basis.

Academics. Special study options: Accelerated study, internships. Bachelor's degree programs available on campus. **Credit/placement by examination:** AP, CLEP, institutional tests. 30 credit hours maximum toward associate degree. **Support services:** Learning center, reduced course load, remedial instruction, study skills assistance, tutoring, writing center.

Majors. Business: Accounting, business admin. **Computer sciences:** Information systems. **Health services:** Medical assistant.

Technology on campus. 200 workstations in library, computer center, student center. Commuter students can connect to campus network. Online library, wireless network available.

Student life. Freshman orientation: Mandatory. Preregistration for classes offered. **Activities:** Literary magazine.

Student services. Career counseling, financial aid counseling, personal counseling, placement for graduates. **Transfer:** Transfer adviser for students transferring to 4-year colleges.

Contact. E-mail: info@plazacollege.edu
Phone: (718) 505-4188 Fax: (718) 779-7423
Vanessa Lopez, Dean of Admissions, Plaza College, 118-33 Queens Boulevard, Forest Hills, NY 11375

Rockland Community College
Suffern, New York   CB member
www.sunyrockland.edu   CB code: 2767

- Public 2-year community college
- Commuter campus in large town

General. Founded in 1959. Regionally accredited. SUNY institution. **Enrollment:** 6,040 degree-seeking undergraduates. **Degrees:** 1,043 associate awarded. **Location:** 35 miles from New York City. **Calendar:** Semester, extensive summer session. **Full-time faculty:** 113 total. **Part-time faculty:** 377 total. **Class size:** 40% < 20, 60% 20-39, less than 1% 40-49.

Student profile.

Out-of-state:	1%	25 or older:	35%

Transfer out. Colleges most students transferred to 2015: SUNY New Paltz, Ramapo College, Dominican College.

Basis for selection. Open admission. Students required to take assessment examination before enrolling full-time. **Adult students:** SAT/ACT scores not required. **Home schooled:** Mathematics and English placement exams. **Learning Disabled:** Students with disabilities encouraged to self-report to our Disabilities Services Office, which arranges for appropriate accommodations with faculty.

High school preparation. 18 units recommended. Recommended units include English 4, mathematics 2, social studies 4, history 4, science 2, foreign language 1 and academic electives 4.

2015-2016 Annual costs. Tuition/fees: $4,654; $8,953 out-of-state. Per-credit charge: $180 in-state; $360 out-of-state. Books/supplies: $1,320. Personal expenses: $1,180.

Financial aid. Need-based: Need-based aid available for part-time students. Work-study available nights, weekends and for part-time students.

Application procedures. Admission: Priority date 8/1; no deadline. $30 fee, may be waived for applicants with need. Admission notification on a rolling basis. **Financial aid:** Priority date 5/31; no closing date. FAFSA, institutional form required. Applicants notified on a rolling basis starting 6/1.

Academics. Special study options: Accelerated study, distance learning, double major, dual enrollment of high school students, ESL, honors, independent study, internships, liberal arts/career combination, teacher certification program. License preparation in nursing. **Credit/placement by examination:** AP, CLEP, IB. 45 credit hours maximum toward associate degree. **Support services:** Learning center, remedial instruction, study skills assistance, tutoring, writing center.

Honors college/program. Mentor/Talented honors program. Business honors degree requires minimum combined SAT score of 1100 (exclusive of Writing) and at least 90 average; interviews, auditions and portfolios recommended.

Majors. Business: Accounting, accounting technology, business admin, entrepreneurial studies, hospitality admin, international, marketing, office technology, tourism promotion, tourism/travel. **Communications:** Communications/speech/rhetoric. **Communications technology:** Photo/film/video. **Computer sciences:** Computer graphics, data processing, information systems, programming, security, support specialist. **Conservation:** Environmental science. **Education:** Early childhood special, elementary, physical. **Engineering:** General. **General:** Maintenance. **Health services:** EMT paramedic, nursing (RN), occupational therapy assistant. **Liberal arts:** Arts/sciences. **Protective services:** Fire safety technology, fire services admin, police science, security management. **Visual/performing arts:** Commercial photography, commercial/advertising art, dramatic, music, photography, studio arts.

Most popular majors. Business/marketing 13%, health sciences 11%, liberal arts 54%, security/protective services 8%.

Technology on campus. 177 workstations in library, computer center. Commuter students can connect to campus network. Online library, wireless network available.

Student life. Freshman orientation: Available. Preregistration for classes offered. **Activities:** Bands, campus ministries, choral groups, dance, drama, international student organizations, literary magazine, music ensembles, radio station, student government, student newspaper, TV station, special interest clubs.

Athletics. NJCAA. **Intercollegiate:** Baseball M, basketball, bowling, golf M, soccer, softball W, table tennis, tennis, volleyball W. **Intramural:** Basketball, bowling, racquetball, soccer, softball, table tennis, track and field, volleyball. **Team name:** Hawks.

Student services. Adult student services, alcohol/substance abuse counseling, chaplain/spiritual director, career counseling, services for economically disadvantaged, student employment services, financial aid counseling, health services, minority student services, on-campus daycare, personal counseling, placement for graduates, veterans' counselor. **Physically disabled:** Services for visually, speech, hearing impaired. **Transfer:** Pre-admission transcript evaluation for new students. Transfer adviser, college fairs on campus for students transferring to 4-year colleges.

Contact. E-mail: info@sunyrockland.edu
Phone: (845) 574-4462 Toll-free number: (800) 722-7666
Fax: (845) 574-4433
Dana Stilley, Dean of Enrollment Management, Rockland Community College, 145 College Road, Suffern, NY 10901-3699

Schenectady County Community College
Schenectady, New York
www.sunysccc.edu   CB code: 2879

- Public 2-year community college
- Commuter campus in small city

General. Founded in 1968. Regionally accredited. SUNY institution. **Enrollment:** 3,293 degree-seeking undergraduates; 2,862 non-degree-seeking students. **Degrees:** 477 associate awarded. **ROTC:** Air Force. **Location:** 150 miles from New York City, 20 miles from Albany. **Calendar:** Semester, limited summer session. **Full-time faculty:** 72 total. **Part-time faculty:** 246 total.

Student profile. Among degree-seeking undergraduates, 844 enrolled as first-time, first-year students.

Part-time:	34%	Hispanic/Latino:	8%
Out-of-state:	1%	Native American:	1%
Women:	54%	Native Hawaiian/Pacific islander:	1%
African American:	19%	Multi-racial, non-Hispanic:	3%
Asian American:	5%	25 or older:	22%

Transfer out. Colleges most students transferred to 2015: SUNY Albany, College of Saint Rose, Siena College, Sage College of Albany.

Basis for selection. Open admission, but selective for some programs. Special requirements for music program. Interview recommended for all; audition required for music, music merchandising programs. **Home schooled:** Letter from school district superintendent where they reside attesting to home school equivalency of public system.

High school preparation. Certain programs have specific mathematics and science prerequisites.

2015-2016 Annual costs. Tuition/fees: $3,934; $7,462 out-of-state. Per-credit charge: $147 in-state; $294 out-of-state. Books/supplies: $1,200. Personal expenses: $1,020.

2014-2015 Financial aid. All financial aid based on need. 58% of total undergraduate aid awarded as scholarships/grants, 42% as loans/jobs. Need-based aid available for part-time students. Work-study available nights, weekends and for part-time students. **Additional information:** Federal Work Study for full time students.

Application procedures. Admission: No deadline. No application fee. Admission notification on a rolling basis. **Financial aid:** Priority date 5/1; no closing date. FAFSA required. Applicants notified on a rolling basis starting 3/1; must reply by 8/31.

Academics. 25-32 credit hours required in major depending on program. 60-66 credit hours required for graduation depending on program. **Special study options:** Cross-registration, distance learning, double major, dual enrollment of high school students, ESL, honors, independent study, internships, liberal arts/career combination, teacher certification program, weekend college. License preparation in aviation. **Credit/placement by examination:** AP, CLEP, institutional tests. 30 credit hours maximum toward associate degree. **Support services:** GED preparation, learning center, reduced course load, remedial instruction, study skills assistance, tutoring, writing center.

Majors. Business: General, tourism promotion, travel services. **Computer sciences:** General, computer science, programming. **Education:** Early childhood, multi-level teacher. **Liberal arts:** Arts/sciences. **Physical sciences:** General. **Protective services:** Criminal justice, security services. **Social sciences:** General. **Visual/performing arts:** Music.

Most popular majors. Business/marketing 32%, computer/information sciences 7%, engineering/engineering technologies 6%, liberal arts 13%, public administration/social services 10%, security/protective services 12%, trade and industry 10%.

Technology on campus. 800 workstations in library, computer center, student center. Online library, wireless network available.

Student life. Freshman orientation: Available. Preregistration for classes offered. **Housing:** Cooperative housing available. Washington Square, located adjacent to campus, offers apartment-style suites for college students. **Activities:** Bands, choral groups, drama, literary magazine, music ensembles, student government, student newspaper, Black and Latino student alliance, Christian Fellowship, human services club, disabled student awareness committee, culinary club.

Athletics. NJCAA. **Intercollegiate:** Baseball M, basketball, bowling, rowing (crew) W. **Team name:** The Royals.

Student services. Adult student services, alcohol/substance abuse counseling, career counseling, services for economically disadvantaged, student employment services, financial aid counseling, minority student services, on-campus daycare, personal counseling, placement for graduates, veterans' counselor. **Physically disabled:** Services for visually, speech, hearing impaired. **Transfer:** Transfer adviser, college fairs on campus for students transferring to 4-year colleges.

Contact. E-mail: sampsodg@sunysccc.edu
Phone: (518) 381-1366 Fax: (518) 346-0379
David Sampson, Director of Admissions, Schenectady County Community College, 78 Washington Avenue, Schenectady, NY 12305

St. Elizabeth College of Nursing
Utica, New York
www.secon.edu   CB code: 2847

◗ Private 2-year nursing college affiliated with the Roman Catholic Church
◗ Commuter campus in small city
◗ SAT or ACT (ACT writing optional) required

General. Regionally accredited. **Enrollment:** 206 degree-seeking undergraduates. **Degrees:** 64 associate awarded. **Location:** 90 miles from Albany, 50 miles from Syracuse. **Calendar:** Semester. **Full-time faculty:** 17 total; 94% women. **Part-time faculty:** 2 total; 100% women.

Student profile. Among degree-seeking undergraduates, 13% already have a bachelor's degree or higher, 10 enrolled as first-time, first-year students, 89 transferred in from other institutions.

Part-time:	54%	Hispanic/Latino:	1%
Women:	89%	Multi-racial, non-Hispanic:	1%
African American:	1%	International:	3%
Asian American:	2%	25 or older:	44%

Basis for selection. Rigor of high school record, test scores most important. SAT Subject Tests recommended. **Adult students:** SAT/ACT scores not required. **Home schooled:** Transcript of courses and grades, state high school equivalency certificate, letter of recommendation (nonparent) required. Strong math and science background required, including coursework in chemistry, biology and equivalent of Math Level 1 and 2. **Learning Disabled:** Self-reporting highly recommended. Learning disabilities coordinator on campus.

High school preparation. Required and recommended units include English 4, mathematics 2-3, social studies 4, history 4, science 2 (laboratory 2) and foreign language 1.

2015-2016 Annual costs. Tuition/fees: $14,864. Per-credit charge: $412. Books/supplies: $1,750. Personal expenses: $1,300.

Financial aid. Need-based: Need-based aid available for part-time students. Work-study available nights, weekends and for part-time students.

Application procedures. Admission: Priority date 12/31; deadline 3/31 (receipt date). $65 fee. Application must be submitted on paper. Admission notification on a rolling basis. Must reply by May 1 or within 2 week(s) if notified thereafter. Admission application fee $50 if submitted before February 1. **Financial aid:** No deadline. FAFSA required. Applicants notified on a rolling basis starting 1/1; must reply within 2 week(s) of notification.

Academics. One 6-week summer session at end of first year. **Special study options:** Combined bachelor's/graduate degree, distance learning, dual enrollment of high school students, liberal arts/career combination, weekend college. Articulation agreements with upper division BSN colleges. License preparation in nursing. **Credit/placement by examination:** AP, CLEP. **Support services:** Remedial instruction, study skills assistance, tutoring.

Majors. Health services: Nursing (RN).

Technology on campus. 42 workstations in library, computer center, student center. Commuter students can connect to campus network. Online library, helpline, wireless network available.

Student life. Freshman orientation: Mandatory. Preregistration for classes offered. Held week prior to classes. **Housing:** Option of staying on campus at affiliated college available. **Activities:** Student government.

Student services. Alcohol/substance abuse counseling, chaplain/spiritual director, career counseling, financial aid counseling, health services, on-campus daycare, personal counseling, veterans' counselor. **Transfer:** Pre-admission transcript evaluation for new students. Transfer center, transfer adviser, college fairs on campus for students transferring to 4-year colleges.

Contact. E-mail: conadmis@stemc.org
Phone: (315) 801-8347 Fax: (315) 801-8271
Sherry Wojnas, Director of Finance & Enrollment, St. Elizabeth College of Nursing, 2215 Genesee Street, Utica, NY 13501

St. Joseph's College of Nursing
Syracuse, New York
www.sjhcon.edu   CB code: 2825

◗ Private 2-year nursing college affiliated with the Roman Catholic Church
◗ Commuter campus in small city
◗ SAT or ACT (ACT writing optional), application essay, interview required

General. Founded in 1898. Practice in a variety of settings including medical/surgical, maternity, pediatrics, oncology, psychiatry, ambulatory care clinics, and home care and outpatient experiences. **Enrollment:** 153 degree-seeking undergraduates; 135 non-degree-seeking students. **Degrees:** 158 associate awarded. **Calendar:** Semester, limited summer session. **Full-time faculty:** 24 total; 96% women. **Part-time faculty:** 7 total; 14% have terminal degrees, 100% women. **Class size:** 7% < 20, 50% 20-39, 14% 40-49, 29% 50-99. **Special facilities:** Cardiovascular lab, electro-physiology lab, home care, outpatient services, 462-bed teaching hospital.

Student profile. Among degree-seeking undergraduates, 16% already have a bachelor's degree or higher, 1 enrolled as first-time, first-year students, 91 transferred in from other institutions.

Part-time:	18%	Live on campus:	30%
Women:	91%		

Transfer out. Colleges most students transferred to 2015: SUNY New York Upstate Medical University, SUNY College of Technology at Utica-Rome, Le Moyne College.

Basis for selection. High school record, SAT/ACT test scores, and personal interview very important. **Adult students:** SAT/ACT scores not required. **Home schooled:** Transcript of courses and grades, state high school equivalency certificate, letter of recommendation (nonparent) required.

High school preparation. College-preparatory program recommended. 13 units required. Required and recommended units include English 4, mathematics 2-4, social studies 4 and science 2-4. Science units must be in biology and chemistry; advanced biology and/or physics recommended.

2016-2017 Annual costs. Tuition/fees (projected): $20,420. Per-credit charge: $530. Room only: $5,500. Books/supplies: $2,000. Personal expenses: $4,656.

2014-2015 Financial aid. All financial aid based on need. 31% of total undergraduate aid awarded as scholarships/grants, 69% as loans/jobs. Need-based aid available for part-time students. Work-study available nights, weekends and for part-time students.

Application procedures. Admission: Closing date 1/1 (postmark date). $50 fee. Admission notification on a rolling basis. **Financial aid:** Priority date 3/1; no closing date. FAFSA required. Applicants notified on a rolling basis starting 6/15.

Academics. Weekend program meets every Wednesday evening and every other Friday, Saturday and Sunday year-round for 18 months. **Special study**

options: Accelerated study, liberal arts/career combination, weekend college. License preparation in nursing. **Credit/placement by examination:** AP, CLEP. **Support services:** Reduced course load, study skills assistance, tutoring.

Majors. **Health services:** Nursing (RN).

Technology on campus. 31 workstations in dormitories, library, computer center. Dormitories wired for high-speed internet access and linked to campus network. Commuter students can connect to campus network. Online library, helpline, wireless network available.

Student life. Freshman orientation: Mandatory. Preregistration for classes offered. Two days of orientation one month prior to the start of classes. Additional orientation is completed at the beginning of the academic year. **Housing:** Guaranteed on-campus for all undergraduates. Coed dorms, wellness housing available. $200 fully refundable deposit. **Activities:** Student government.

Student services. Adult student services, alcohol/substance abuse counseling, chaplain/spiritual director, career counseling, student employment services, financial aid counseling, health services, personal counseling, placement for graduates, veterans' counselor. **Physically disabled:** Services for visually, speech, hearing impaired. **Transfer:** Pre-admission transcript evaluation for new students. Transfer adviser, college fairs on campus for students transferring to 4-year colleges.

Contact. E-mail: admissions@sjhcon.org
Phone: (315) 448-5040 Fax: (315) 448-5745
Felicia Corp, Coordinator for Admissions and Recruitment, St. Joseph's College of Nursing, 206 Prospect Avenue, Syracuse, NY 13203-1892

Suffolk County Community College
Selden, New York　　　　　　　　　　　　CB member
www.sunysuffolk.edu　　　　　　　　　　CB code: 2827

▶ Public 2-year community college
▶ Commuter campus in large town

General. Founded in 1959. Regionally accredited. 3 campuses in Suffolk County: Brentwood, Selden, Riverhead. Downtown center in Sayville dedicated to nursing, downtown center in Riverhead dedicated to culinary arts. **Enrollment:** 26,600 undergraduates. **Degrees:** 3,596 associate awarded. **Location:** 60 miles from New York City. **Calendar:** Semester, extensive summer session. **Full-time faculty:** 326 total. **Part-time faculty:** 1,303 total. **Special facilities:** Planetarium.

Student profile.

Out-of-state:	2%	25 or older:	51%

Transfer out. Colleges most students transferred to 2015: SUNY Stony Brook, Hofstra University, St. Joseph's College, Dowling College, Adelphi University.

Basis for selection. Open admission, but selective for some programs. Admission tests may be used for admission or placement in certain programs in conjunction with high school record. Portfolio required for visual arts program; interview recommended for broadcast telecommunications, fine arts, health career, and paralegal assistant programs. Audition recommended for performing arts programs. **Home schooled:** State high school equivalency certificate required. Appropriate scores on the CPT test to indicate Ability To Benefit.

High school preparation. Special course requirements vary by program.

2015-2016 Annual costs. Tuition/fees: $5,280; $9,850 out-of-state. Per-credit charge: $191 in-state; $392 out-of-state. Books/supplies: $1,370. Personal expenses: $2,600.

Financial aid. Need-based: Need-based aid available for part-time students. Work-study available nights, weekends and for part-time students. **Non-need-based:** Scholarships awarded for academics, art, leadership, minority status, music/drama, state residency.

Application procedures. Admission: No deadline. $40 fee, may be waived for applicants with need. Admission notification on a rolling basis. **Financial aid:** Priority date 4/15, closing date 6/1. FAFSA required. Applicants notified on a rolling basis starting 4/15; must reply within 2 week(s) of notification.

Academics. Special study options: Cooperative education, distance learning, dual enrollment of high school students, ESL, honors, independent study, internships, study abroad, weekend college. Joint admission with other SUNY

schools and private institutions. License preparation in nursing. **Credit/placement by examination:** AP, CLEP, IB, institutional tests. 30 credit hours maximum toward associate degree. **Support services:** GED preparation and test center, learning center, pre-admission summer program, reduced course load, remedial instruction, study skills assistance, tutoring, writing center.

Majors. Architecture: Environmental design, interior. **Area/ethnic studies:** Women's. **Biology:** General. **Business:** General, accounting, business admin, finance, human resources, management science, marketing, office management, office technology, sales/distribution. **Communications:** Broadcast journalism, communications/speech/rhetoric. **Communications technology:** General. **Computer sciences:** General, computer graphics, computer science, information systems, information technology, webmaster. **Conservation:** Environmental science, environmental studies. **Education:** Early childhood, secondary. **Engineering:** Electrical, engineering science. **Foreign languages:** Sign language interpretation. **Health services:** Athletic training, clinical lab science, dietetic technician, EMT paramedic, health information technology, nursing (RN), occupational therapy assistant, physical therapy assistant, substance abuse counseling, veterinary technology/assistant. **History:** General. **Liberal arts:** Arts/sciences. **Math:** General. **Physical sciences:** Astronomy, chemistry, geology, meteorology, physics, planetary. **Protective services:** Firefighting. **Psychology:** General. **Social sciences:** General, economics, political science. **Visual/performing arts:** Commercial/advertising art, dramatic, interior design, music, studio arts, theater design. **Work/family studies:** Food/nutrition.

Technology on campus. 1,785 workstations in library, computer center, student center. Commuter students can connect to campus network. Online course registration, online library, helpline, wireless network available.

Student life. Freshman orientation: Available. Preregistration for classes offered. **Activities:** Bands, choral groups, drama, international student organizations, literary magazine, music ensembles, musical theater, radio station, student government, student newspaper, over 60 clubs available.

Athletics. NJCAA. **Intercollegiate:** Baseball M, basketball, bowling M, cross-country, golf M, lacrosse M, soccer M, softball, tennis, track and field, triathlon W. **Intramural:** Basketball, bowling, softball.

Student services. Adult student services, career counseling, services for economically disadvantaged, student employment services, financial aid counseling, health services, minority student services, on-campus daycare, personal counseling, placement for graduates, veterans' counselor. **Physically disabled:** Services for visually, speech, hearing impaired. **Transfer:** Pre-admission transcript evaluation for new students. Transfer adviser, college fairs on campus for students transferring to 4-year colleges.

Contact. E-mail: admissions@sunysuffolk.edu
Phone: (631) 451-4000 Fax: (631) 451-4415
Joanne Braxton, College Dean of Enrollment Management, Suffolk County Community College, 533 College Road, Selden, NY 11784

Sullivan County Community College
Loch Sheldrake, New York
www.sunysullivan.edu　　　　　　　　　　CB code: 2855

▶ Public 2-year community college
▶ Commuter campus in small town

General. Founded in 1962. Regionally accredited. **Enrollment:** 1,079 degree-seeking undergraduates; 516 non-degree-seeking students. **Degrees:** 279 associate awarded. **Location:** 100 miles from New York City, 90 miles from Binghamton. **Calendar:** Semester, limited summer session. **Full-time faculty:** 47 total; 28% have terminal degrees, 6% minority, 55% women. **Part-time faculty:** 58 total; 5% have terminal degrees, 10% minority, 64% women. **Class size:** 73% < 20, 26% 20-39, less than 1% 40-49. **Special facilities:** Complete kitchens, dining room for hospitality programs, computer graphics labs, TV studio for communications and media arts program.

Student profile. Among degree-seeking undergraduates, 53% enrolled in a transfer program, 47% enrolled in a vocational program, 291 enrolled as first-time, first-year students, 77 transferred in from other institutions.

Part-time:	27%	Hispanic/Latino:	22%
Out-of-state:	1%	Multi-racial, non-Hispanic:	3%
Women:	53%	International:	1%
African American:	25%	25 or older:	24%
Asian American:	1%	Live on campus:	15%

Transfer out. Colleges most students transferred to 2015: SUNY New Paltz, SUNY Oneonta, SUNY at Albany, SUNY Empire State College, SUNY Binghamton.

Basis for selection. Open admission, but selective for some programs. Special requirements for nursing program and university parallel business administration program. Out of county applicants must have a high school grade point average of 72 or better. SAT or ACT recommended for placement and counseling. Interview recommended.

High school preparation. Liberal arts applicants entering science programs should have 3 each in math and science. Computer science applicants, 3 math and 1 chemistry or physics. Nursing applicants, 1 laboratory biology. Engineering science, 3.5 math and 1 chemistry or physics.

2015-2016 Annual costs. Tuition/fees: $5,500; $10,174 out-of-state. Per-credit charge: $195 in-state; $312 out-of-state. Room/board: $9,350. Books/supplies: $1,400. Personal expenses: $1,000.

2014-2015 Financial aid. Need-based: 79% of total undergraduate aid awarded as scholarships/grants, 21% as loans/jobs. Need-based aid available for part-time students. Work-study available nights, weekends and for part-time students. **Additional information:** 60% of students hold part-time jobs locally.

Application procedures. Admission: No deadline. No application fee. Admission notification on a rolling basis. Recommended priority application date for nursing department is December 1. **Financial aid:** Priority date 4/15; no closing date. FAFSA required. Applicants notified on a rolling basis starting 5/15; must reply within 2 week(s) of notification.

Academics. Practical experience in class laboratory situations emphasized in technical programs. **Special study options:** Distance learning, dual enrollment of high school students, exchange student, honors, independent study, internships. License preparation in nursing. **Credit/placement by examination:** AP, CLEP, institutional tests. 31 credit hours maximum toward associate degree. **Support services:** Learning center, pre-admission summer program, reduced course load, remedial instruction, study skills assistance, tutoring, writing center.

Majors. Business: Accounting technology, administrative services, business admin, hospitality admin, management information systems, office technology, tourism/travel. **Communications:** Broadcast journalism, communications/speech/rhetoric. **Computer sciences:** General, computer graphics, data processing, programming. **Conservation:** General. **Health services:** Medical assistant, nursing (RN), respiratory therapy technology. **Human services:** Community org/advocacy. **Liberal arts:** Arts/sciences, humanities. **Parks/recreation:** General, facilities management, health/fitness. **Protective services:** Disaster management, fire safety technology, forensics, police science. **Psychology:** General. **Visual/performing arts:** General, commercial photography, commercial/advertising art, game design.

Most popular majors. Business/marketing 15%, health sciences 15%, liberal arts 35%, security/protective services 8%.

Technology on campus. 80 workstations in library, computer center. Dormitories wired for high-speed internet access. Online course registration, wireless network available.

Student life. Freshman orientation: Mandatory, $30 fee. Preregistration for classes offered. **Housing:** Guaranteed on-campus for freshmen. Coed dorms available. $500 partly refundable deposit. College-approved housing adjacent to campus. **Activities:** Drama, radio station, student government, student newspaper, TV station, Latin America student organization, black student league, gay straight alliance, international relations club, BASIC (Brothers and Sisters in Christ), SERVE (Students Engaged in outReach, Volunteering, and Education), Youth Ministries.

Athletics. NJCAA. **Intercollegiate:** Baseball M, basketball, cheerleading, cross-country, golf, track and field, wrestling M. **Intramural:** Archery, badminton, baseball M, basketball, bowling, cheerleading, handball, racquetball, soccer, softball W, table tennis, tennis, volleyball. **Team name:** Generals.

Student services. Adult student services, career counseling, student employment services, financial aid counseling, health services, personal counseling, placement for graduates, veterans' counselor. **Transfer:** Transfer adviser, college fairs on campus for students transferring to 4-year colleges.

Contact. E-mail: admissions@sunysullivan.edu
Phone: (845) 434-5750 ext. 4287 Toll-free number: (800) 577-5243
Fax: (845) 434-0923
Sari Rosenheck, Director of Admissions and Registration Services, Sullivan County Community College, 112 College Road, Loch Sheldrake, NY 12759-5151

SUNY College of Agriculture and Technology at Cobleskill
Cobleskill, New York
www.cobleskill.edu
CB code: 2524

◆ Public 2-year agricultural and technical college
◆ Residential campus in small town

General. Founded in 1911. Regionally accredited. **Enrollment:** 2,419 degree-seeking undergraduates; 27 non-degree-seeking students. **Degrees:** 365 bachelor's, 263 associate awarded. **Location:** 35 miles from Albany, 29 miles from Oneonta. **Calendar:** Semester, limited summer session. **Full-time faculty:** 103 total; 41% have terminal degrees, 5% minority, 38% women. **Part-time faculty:** 72 total; 8% have terminal degrees, 3% minority, 49% women. **Class size:** 41% < 20, 50% 20-39, 4% 40-49, 4% 50-99. **Special facilities:** Arboretum, 14 greenhouses, livestock pavilion, 350-acre farm, 200-cow dairy facility, modern chemical and biological technology laboratories, student-operated restaurant, fish hatchery, ski area, equestrian center, child care and development center. **Partnerships:** Formal partnership with John Deere Company for agricultural engineering.

Student profile. Among degree-seeking undergraduates, 761 enrolled as first-time, first-year students, 199 transferred in from other institutions.

Part-time:	4%	Hispanic/Latino:	8%
Out-of-state:	7%	Native American:	1%
Women:	53%	International:	1%
African American:	13%	25 or older:	9%
Asian American:	1%	Live on campus:	59%

Transfer out. Colleges most students transferred to 2015: Cornell University, College of St. Rose, SUNY Albany, SUNY Oneonta, SUNY Plattsburgh.

Basis for selection. Strength of high school curriculum most important. GPA and SAT/ACT scores considered. Letters of recommendation and an interview recommended. SAT scores required for all applicants to a degree-seeking bachelor's program. **Home schooled:** Transcript of courses and grades, letter of recommendation (nonparent) required. Letter of certification from local high school required.

High school preparation. College-preparatory program recommended. 13 units required. Required and recommended units include English 4, mathematics 2-3, social studies 4, history 3, science 2-3 (laboratory 1-3) and foreign language 1.

2015-2016 Annual costs. Tuition/fees: $7,951; $17,301 out-of-state. Per-credit charge: $269.58 in-state; $680 out-of-state. Room/board: $12,606. Books/supplies: $1,200. Personal expenses: $1,092.

Financial aid. Need-based: Need-based aid available for part-time students. Work-study available nights, weekends and for part-time students. **Non-need-based:** Scholarships awarded for academics, alumni affiliation, leadership, minority status, state residency. **Additional information:** Application deadline for scholarships March 15. Separate application required, available through admissions office.

Application procedures. Admission: No deadline. $50 fee, may be waived for applicants with need. Admission notification on a rolling basis beginning on or about 11/1. Must reply by May 1 or within 4 week(s) if notified thereafter. **Financial aid:** Priority date 2/15; no closing date. FAFSA required. Applicants notified on a rolling basis starting 3/15; must reply within 2 week(s) of notification.

Academics. Special study options: Accelerated study, cross-registration, distance learning, ESL, honors, independent study, internships, study abroad, weekend college. Bachelor's degree programs available on campus. **Credit/placement by examination:** AP, CLEP, SAT, ACT, institutional tests. 33 credit hours maximum toward associate degree, 60 toward bachelor's. **Support services:** Learning center, reduced course load, remedial instruction, study skills assistance, tutoring, writing center.

Majors. Business: Accounting technology, business admin. **Communications:** Communications/speech/rhetoric. **Computer sciences:** General. **Conservation:** General, fisheries. **Health services:** EMT paramedic, histologic assistant. **Human services:** Social work. **Liberal arts:** Arts/sciences, humanities. **Math:** General. **Physical sciences:** General. **Social sciences:** General. **Visual/performing arts:** Graphic design.

Most popular majors. Agriculture 17%, business/marketing 9%, engineering/engineering technologies 7%, family/consumer sciences 8%, health sciences 6%, liberal arts 16%, personal/culinary services 14%, public administration/social services 6%.

Technology on campus. 320 workstations in dormitories, library, computer center, student center. Dormitories wired for high-speed internet access and linked to campus network. Commuter students can connect to campus network. Online course registration, online library, helpline, repair service, student web hosting, wireless network available.

Student life. Freshman orientation: Mandatory. Preregistration for classes offered. Held for two days during the first week of classes. **Housing:** Guaranteed on-campus for freshmen. Coed dorms, special housing for disabled, wellness housing available. $100 fully refundable deposit, deadline 5/29. **Activities:** Jazz band, campus ministries, choral groups, drama, international student organizations, student government, student newspaper, Phi Theta

Kappa, activities team, community club, Student Christian Fellowship, student medical response team, X-Pressions of Kolor, Black and Latino alliance.

Athletics. NCAA. **Intercollegiate:** Basketball, cross-country, diving, golf, lacrosse M, soccer, softball W, swimming, track and field, volleyball W. **Intramural:** Bowling, football (non-tackle), soccer, softball. **Team name:** Tigers.

Student services. Alcohol/substance abuse counseling, career counseling, student employment services, financial aid counseling, health services, on-campus daycare, personal counseling, placement for graduates, veterans' counselor. **Physically disabled:** Services for visually, speech, hearing impaired. **Transfer:** Pre-admission transcript evaluation for new students. College fairs on campus for students transferring to 4-year colleges.

Contact. E-mail: admissions@cobleskill.edu
Phone: (518) 255-5525 Toll-free number: (800) 295-8988
Fax: (518) 255-6769
Robert Blanchet, Director of Admissions, SUNY College of Agriculture and Technology at Cobleskill, Knapp Hall, Cobleskill, NY 12043

SUNY College of Technology at Alfred
Alfred, New York
www.alfredstate.edu   **CB code: 2522**

♦ Public 2-year liberal arts and technical college
♦ Residential campus in rural community
♦ Application essay required

General. Founded in 1908. Regionally accredited. School of Applied Technology located in Wellsville. **Enrollment:** 3,669 degree-seeking undergraduates; 30 non-degree-seeking students. **Degrees:** 260 bachelor's, 812 associate awarded. **ROTC:** Army. **Location:** 75 miles from Rochester, 90 miles from Buffalo. **Calendar:** Semester, limited summer session. **Full-time faculty:** 175 total; 33% have terminal degrees, 6% minority, 30% women. **Part-time faculty:** 51 total; 10% have terminal degrees, 2% minority, 61% women. **Class size:** 48% < 20, 45% 20-39, 3% 40-49, 3% 50-99, less than 1% >100. **Special facilities:** 750-acre working farm, motorsports facility, center for organic and sustainable agriculture.

Student profile. Among degree-seeking undergraduates, 21% enrolled in a vocational program, 1,058 enrolled as first-time, first-year students, 328 transferred in from other institutions.

Part-time:	8%	Hispanic/Latino:	7%
Out-of-state:	4%	Multi-racial, non-Hispanic:	2%
Women:	38%	International:	2%
African American:	10%	25 or older:	14%
Asian American:	1%	Live on campus:	64%

Transfer out. Colleges most students transferred to 2015: Alfred University, Clarkson University, SUNY Brockport, SUNY Fredonia, SUNY Oswego.

Basis for selection. School achievement record most important, test scores, class rank, school and community service considered. SAT or ACT recommended. SAT or ACT required for students applying for baccalaureate degree programs, some scholarship considerations, and for those students interested in intercollegiate athletics. Recommended for associate degree programs. Interview, essay is required on supplemental application, and letters of reference recommended. **Adult students:** SAT/ACT scores not required if applicant has graduated high school and completed at least one semester of college. **Home schooled:** Applicant must provide one of the following: letter from superintendent of home school district; passing score on GED exam; 24 college credit hours in appropriate courses; college degree; or passed 5 Regents exams (NY).

High school preparation. Recommended units include English 4, mathematics 4, social studies 4 and science 4. Course requirements vary depending on program.

2015-2016 Annual costs. Tuition/fees: $8,057; $11,327 out-of-state. Per-credit charge: $270 in-state; $406 out-of-state. Room/board: $11,430. Books/supplies: $1,200. Personal expenses: $1,300. **Additional information:** Tuition for Out-of-State Full-time Bachelor's degree-seeking students is $16,320; per credit hour is $680.

2015-2016 Financial aid. Need-based: 1,017 full-time freshmen applied for aid; 890 deemed to have need; 877 received aid. Average need met was 58%. Average scholarship/grant was $8,007; average loan $3,635. 29% of total undergraduate aid awarded as scholarships/grants, 71% as loans/jobs. Need-based aid available for part-time students. Work-study available nights, weekends and for part-time students. **Non-need-based:** Awarded to 942

full-time undergraduates, including 353 freshmen. Scholarships awarded for academics, alumni affiliation, job skills, music/drama, state residency.

Application procedures. Admission: No deadline. $50 fee, may be waived for applicants with need. Admission notification on a rolling basis beginning on or about 10/1. Must reply by May 1 or within 4 week(s) if notified thereafter. Reply within 30 days of acceptance; full refund of deposit if requested in writing by May 1. Early application recommended for applied technology programs. **Financial aid:** No deadline. FAFSA required. Applicants notified on a rolling basis starting 3/1; must reply within 4 week(s) of notification.

Academics. Special study options: Accelerated study, cooperative education, cross-registration, distance learning, double major, ESL, honors, independent study, internships, liberal arts/career combination, student-designed major, study abroad. Bachelor's degree programs available on campus. License preparation in nursing. **Credit/placement by examination:** AP, CLEP, IB, SAT, ACT, institutional tests. **Support services:** Learning center, reduced course load, remedial instruction, study skills assistance, tutoring, writing center.

Majors. Biology: General. **Business:** Accounting technology, business admin, sales/distribution. **Communications technology:** Animation/special effects. **Computer sciences:** General, information systems. **Engineering:** General. **General:** Masonry, power transmission. **Health services:** Health information technology, nursing (RN), radiologic technology/medical imaging, veterinary technology/assistant. **Liberal arts:** Arts/sciences, humanities. **Parks/recreation:** Sports admin. **Social sciences:** Criminology. **Visual/performing arts:** Interior design.

Most popular majors. Business/marketing 6%, engineering/engineering technologies 12%, health sciences 14%, liberal arts 7%, public administration/social services 7%, trade and industry 38%.

Technology on campus. 100 workstations in dormitories, library, student center. Dormitories wired for high-speed internet access and linked to campus network. Commuter students can connect to campus network. Online course registration, online library, helpline, repair service, student web hosting, wireless network available.

Student life. Freshman orientation: Mandatory, $100 fee. Preregistration for classes offered. Day-long summer program in mid-July, followed by pre-entry orientation/Welcome Week in August. Parallel January program for mid-year entrants. **Housing:** Guaranteed on-campus for all undergraduates. Coed dorms, special housing for disabled, apartments, fraternity/sorority housing, themed housing, wellness housing available. $50 nonrefundable deposit. Pets allowed in dorm rooms. Townhouse complex, extended stay, quiet study, over 21, over 24, single-room options available, gender Inclusive housing available. **Activities:** Bands, campus ministries, choral groups, dance, drama, international student organizations, literary magazine, music ensembles, musical theater, radio station, student government, student newspaper, sustainability club, international club, Ujima, disaster response team, Cultural Kaleidoscope, student senate, Caribbean student association, African student association.

Athletics. NCAA, USCAA. **Intercollegiate:** Baseball M, basketball, cross-country, diving, equestrian, football (tackle) M, lacrosse M, soccer, softball W, swimming, track and field, volleyball W, wrestling M. **Intramural:** Basketball, football (non-tackle), football (tackle) M, golf, handball, soccer, softball, tennis, ultimate frisbee, volleyball. **Team name:** Pioneers.

Student services. Adult student services, alcohol/substance abuse counseling, chaplain/spiritual director, career counseling, services for economically disadvantaged, student employment services, financial aid counseling, health services, minority student services, personal counseling, placement for graduates, veterans' counselor, women's services. **Physically disabled:** Services for visually, hearing impaired. **Transfer:** Pre-admission transcript evaluation for new students. Transfer center, transfer adviser, college fairs on campus for students transferring to 4-year colleges.

Contact. E-mail: admissions@alfredstate.edu
Phone: (607) 587-4215 Toll-free number: (800) 425-3733 ext. 1
Fax: (607) 587-4299
Deb Goodrich, Associate Vice President for Enrollment Management, SUNY College of Technology at Alfred, Huntington Administration Building, Alfred, NY 14802-1196

SUNY College of Technology at Canton
Canton, New York
www.canton.edu   **CB code: 2523**

♦ Public 2-year technical college
♦ Commuter campus in small town

Two-Year Colleges

General. Founded in 1906. Regionally accredited. Approximately 111 veterans, National Guard Members, reservists and veteran dependents are enrolled. **Enrollment:** 3,040 degree-seeking undergraduates; 143 non-degree-seeking students. **Degrees:** 413 bachelor's, 496 associate awarded. **ROTC:** Army, Air Force. **Location:** 135 miles from Syracuse, 77 miles from Ottawa. **Calendar:** Semester, limited summer session. **Full-time faculty:** 124 total; 52% have terminal degrees, 14% minority, 45% women. **Part-time faculty:** 118 total; 13% have terminal degrees, 8% minority, 46% women. **Class size:** 52% < 20, 43% 20-39, 2% 40-49, 3% 50-99. **Special facilities:** Cross-country trails. **Partnerships:** Formal partnerships with Polaris and Subaru.

Student profile. Among degree-seeking undergraduates, 3% already have a bachelor's degree or higher, 650 enrolled as first-time, first-year students, 353 transferred in from other institutions.

Part-time:	13%	Native American:	1%
Out-of-state:	3%	Multi-racial, non-Hispanic:	2%
Women:	56%	International:	2%
African American:	14%	25 or older:	24%
Asian American:	1%	Live on campus:	38%
Hispanic/Latino:	10%		

Basis for selection. High school record most important. Admission requirements vary according to program of study. Some enrolled freshmen must complete ACCUPLACER placement test on campus before classes begin. Students notified of testing dates and whether they need ACCUPLACER. SAT or ACT required of bachelor's degree program applicants. SAT, ACT, SAT Subject Test scores received on rolling basis. Interview recommended. **Home schooled:** Transcript of courses and grades required. Applicants must do 1 of following: present letter from superintendent from school district they reside in indicating completion of program equivalent to high school diploma; take GED exam; take 5 Regents Exams indicated in SUNY policy; complete 30 credit-hour program to earn GED. **Learning Disabled:** Students with documented needs should request accommodations through coordinator of Accommodative Services.

High school preparation. College-preparatory program recommended. 15 units required; 21 recommended. Required and recommended units include English 4, mathematics 3, social studies 4, science 3 (laboratory 1-3), foreign language 3, visual/performing arts 1 and academic electives 1-3. Required high school courses vary with major. Engineering science technologies, health, and life sciences stress math and science; business technologies stress algebra.

2015-2016 Annual costs. Tuition/fees: $7,855; $12,245 out-of-state. Per-credit charge: $270 in-state; $453 out-of-state. Room/board: $11,800. Books/supplies: $1,300. Personal expenses: $1,200.

2014-2015 Financial aid. Need-based: 705 full-time freshmen applied for aid; 625 deemed to have need; 617 received aid. Average need met was 17%. Average scholarship/grant was $8,060; average loan $3,461. 48% of total undergraduate aid awarded as scholarships/grants, 52% as loans/jobs. Need-based aid available for part-time students. Work-study available nights, weekends and for part-time students. **Non-need-based:** Awarded to 279 full-time undergraduates, including 91 freshmen. Scholarships awarded for academics, alumni affiliation, leadership, minority status, state residency. **Additional information:** Students can apply after the priority deadline has passed, but not all types of aid will be available.

Application procedures. Admission: No deadline. $50 fee, may be waived for applicants with need. Admission notification on a rolling basis beginning on or about 10/1. Must reply by 5/1. **Financial aid:** Priority date 3/1; no closing date. FAFSA required. Applicants notified on a rolling basis starting 2/15; must reply within 4 week(s) of notification.

Academics. Special study options: Cooperative education, cross-registration, distance learning, dual enrollment of high school students, honors, independent study, internships, student-designed major, study abroad. Criminal justice students can complete Police Academy during spring semester of senior year. License preparation in dental hygiene, nursing, physical therapy. **Credit/placement by examination:** AP, CLEP, IB, SAT, ACT, institutional tests. Student must take at least 15 credit hours at the in College to earn an associate degree and 30 hours to earn a bachelor's degree. Maximum number of credits awarded for life experience is 30 credits for a bachelor's degree and 15 credits for an associate degree. **Support services:** Learning center, reduced course load, remedial instruction, study skills assistance, tutoring, writing center. EOP summer program, engineering tutoring lab, math tutoring lab, business/accounting tutoring lab.

Majors. Business: Accounting technology, business admin. **Computer sciences:** Information systems. **Engineering:** General. **General:** Site management. **Health services:** Dental hygiene, nursing (RN), physical therapy assistant, veterinary technology/assistant. **Protective services:** Police science. **Work/family studies:** Child care management.

Most popular majors. Business/marketing 8%, engineering/engineering technologies 8%, health sciences 36%, liberal arts 19%, security/protective services 19%.

Technology on campus. 876 workstations in library, computer center, student center. Dormitories wired for high-speed internet access. Online course registration, online library, helpline, wireless network available.

Student life. Freshman orientation: Mandatory, $60 fee. Preregistration for classes offered. For students entering in the fall, 2-day orientation for traditional students, 1-day orientation for non-traditional students. 1-day orientation for students entering in the spring. **Policies:** Restricted tobacco use on campus. **Housing:** Guaranteed on-campus for freshmen. Coed dorms, special housing for disabled, apartments, fraternity/sorority housing, themed housing available. $55 fully refundable deposit, deadline 5/1. Pets allowed in dorm rooms. Some all-male or all-female floors and wings available; pet wing available. **Activities:** Campus ministries, choral groups, dance, drama, international student organizations, student government, African Student Union, Anointed Voices of Praise Gospel Choir, Brother 2 Brother, Caribbean United, Habitat for Humanity, Hispanic Unity, Newman Club, Peer Educators, Sister 2 Sister, Spectrum.

Athletics. NCAA, USCAA. **Intercollegiate:** Baseball M, basketball, cross-country, golf M, ice hockey, lacrosse, soccer, softball W, volleyball W. **Intramural:** Basketball, football (non-tackle), soccer, softball, volleyball. **Team name:** Kangaroos.

Student services. Adult student services, alcohol/substance abuse counseling, chaplain/spiritual director, career counseling, services for economically disadvantaged, student employment services, financial aid counseling, health services, minority student services, personal counseling, placement for graduates, veterans' counselor. **Physically disabled:** Services for visually, speech, hearing impaired. **Transfer:** Pre-admission transcript evaluation for new students. Transfer adviser, college fairs on campus for students transferring to 4-year colleges.

Contact. E-mail: admissions@canton.edu
Phone: (315) 386-7123 Toll-free number: (800) 388-7123
Fax: (315) 386-7929
Melissa Evans, Director of Admissions, SUNY College of Technology at Canton, 34 Cornell Drive, Canton, NY 13617-1098

SUNY College of Technology at Delhi
Delhi, New York
www.delhi.edu   **CB code: 2525**

▶ Public 2-year liberal arts and technical college
▶ Residential campus in rural community

General. Founded in 1913. Regionally accredited. Students can earn bachelor degrees in selected programs on main campus as well as at remote sites and online. **Enrollment:** 3,392 degree-seeking undergraduates; 32 non-degree-seeking students. **Degrees:** 351 bachelor's, 572 associate awarded; master's offered. **Location:** 70 miles from Albany and Binghamton. **Calendar:** Semester, limited summer session. **Full-time faculty:** 147 total; 23% have terminal degrees, 6% minority, 49% women. **Part-time faculty:** 94 total; 20% have terminal degrees, 2% minority, 65% women. **Class size:** 44% < 20, 51% 20-39, 1% 40-49, 3% 50-99, less than 1% >100. **Special facilities:** Demonstration forest and arboretum, student-operated restaurant, veterinary science laboratories, golf course, CAD laboratory, architecture laboratories, golf swing lab.

Student profile. Among degree-seeking undergraduates, 828 enrolled as first-time, first-year students, 417 transferred in from other institutions.

Part-time:	25%	Asian American:	4%
Out-of-state:	4%	Hispanic/Latino:	14%
Women:	54%	25 or older:	27%
African American:	16%	Live on campus:	49%

Basis for selection. Special requirements for 4-year programs. Enrollment limits in some programs. Once a program is full, academically admissible students can defer admission to the next available semester. Interview recommended. **Home schooled:** Transcript of courses and grades, state high school equivalency certificate required.

High school preparation. College-preparatory program recommended. Required and recommended units include English 4, mathematics 3-4, social studies 4, science 3 (laboratory 1-2), foreign language 1, visual/performing arts 1, academic electives 3.5. Requirements vary by program.

2015-2016 Annual costs. Tuition/fees: $8,075; $12,445 out-of-state. Per-credit charge: $270 in-state; $452 out-of-state. Room/board: $11,436. Books/supplies: $1,400. Personal expenses: $1,474. **Additional information:** Out of State tuition listed is for Associate Programs only; the rate for Bachelor's Programs is: $16,320.

Financial aid. Need-based: Need-based aid available for part-time students. Work-study available nights, weekends and for part-time students.

Application procedures. Admission: Priority date 8/1; no deadline. $50 fee, may be waived for applicants with need. Admission notification on a rolling basis beginning on or about 11/1. Deposit is required within four weeks of acceptance and is fully refundable until May 1st. **Financial aid:** Priority date 2/15; no closing date. FAFSA required. Applicants notified on a rolling basis starting 3/1; must reply within 2 week(s) of notification.

Academics. Special study options: Accelerated study, cross-registration, distance learning, double major, dual enrollment of high school students, ESL, honors, independent study, internships, study abroad. Bachelor's degree programs available on campus. License preparation in nursing. **Credit/placement by examination:** AP, CLEP, IB, institutional tests. 50 credit hours maximum toward associate degree, 50 toward bachelor's. Maximum of 50 percent of credits required for degree may be earned by combination of transfer, life experience and credit by examination. **Support services:** Learning center, reduced course load, remedial instruction, study skills assistance, tutoring, writing center.

Majors. Architecture: Landscape, technology. **Business:** Accounting, administrative services, business admin, management information systems, marketing, tourism promotion, tourism/travel. **Computer sciences:** Data processing. **Education:** Early childhood, elementary, physical, secondary. **General:** Carpentry, electrician, masonry. **Health services:** Nursing (RN), veterinary technology/assistant. **Liberal arts:** Arts/sciences. **Math:** General. **Parks/recreation:** Facilities management. **Work/family studies:** Institutional food production.

Most popular majors. Business/marketing 12%, engineering/engineering technologies 10%, health sciences 15%, liberal arts 21%, security/protective services 8%, trade and industry 19%.

Technology on campus. 230 workstations in library, computer center. Dormitories wired for high-speed internet access and linked to campus network. Commuter students can connect to campus network. Online course registration, online library, helpline, repair service, student web hosting, wireless network available.

Student life. Freshman orientation: Available, $75 fee. Preregistration for classes offered. Several pre-orientation dates throughout the spring and summer. In addition, students take part in a 3-day orientation immediately prior to the beginning of the fall semester. **Housing:** Guaranteed on-campus for freshmen. Coed dorms, apartments, themed housing, wellness housing available. $100 nonrefundable deposit, deadline 6/1. **Activities:** Bands, campus ministries, choral groups, dance, drama, international student organizations, literary magazine, musical theater, radio station, student government, student newspaper, TV station, Delhi Interfaith Council, black student union, Latin student association, West Indian coalition.

Athletics. NAIA, NJCAA. **Intercollegiate:** Basketball, cross-country, golf, lacrosse M, soccer, softball W, swimming, tennis, track and field, volleyball W. **Intramural:** Badminton, basketball, bowling, boxing, football (non-tackle) M, golf, handball, racquetball, soccer, softball, swimming, table tennis, tennis, ultimate frisbee, volleyball. **Team name:** Broncos.

Student services. Adult student services, alcohol/substance abuse counseling, chaplain/spiritual director, career counseling, services for economically disadvantaged, student employment services, financial aid counseling, health services, minority student services, on-campus daycare, personal counseling, placement for graduates, veterans' counselor, women's services. **Physically disabled:** Services for visually, hearing impaired. **Transfer:** Pre-admission transcript evaluation for new students. Transfer adviser, college fairs on campus for students transferring to 4-year colleges.

Contact. E-mail: enroll@delhi.edu
Phone: (607) 746-4550 Toll-free number: (800) 963-3544
Fax: (607) 746-4104
Robert Piurowski, Director of Admissions, SUNY College of Technology at Delhi, 2 Main Street, Delhi, NY 13753-1190

Swedish Institute
New York, New York
www.swedishinstitute.edu

- For-profit 2-year health science college
- Commuter campus in very large city
- Interview required

General. Accredited by ACCSC. **Enrollment:** 700 degree-seeking undergraduates. **Degrees:** 291 associate awarded. **Calendar:** Semester, extensive summer session. **Full-time faculty:** 17 total. **Part-time faculty:** 35 total.

Basis for selection. GPA and recommendations are strongly considered. **Home schooled:** Transcript of courses and grades, state high school equivalency certificate, interview, letter of recommendation (nonparent) required.

2015-2016 Annual costs. Books/supplies: $500. **Additional information:** Nursing: $568 per credit; 68 semester credits. Massage Therapy: $484 per credit; 64 semester credits. Advanced Personal Training: $493 per credit; 62 semester credits. Personal Training: $493 per credit; 37 semester credits. Clinical and Administrative Medical Assistant: $304 per credit; 90 quarter credits. Surgical Technologist: $368 per credit; 94.5 quarter credits. Medical Billing and Coding: $304 per credit; 48 quarter credits. One-time registration fee: $100. Program fees vary per term: ranges from $188 to $705.

Financial aid. All financial aid based on need. Need-based aid available for part-time students. Work-study available nights, weekends and for part-time students.

Application procedures. Admission: No deadline. $100 fee, may be waived for applicants with need. **Financial aid:** No deadline. FAFSA, institutional form required.

Academics. Special study options: Internships. License preparation in nursing, occupational therapy. **Credit/placement by examination:** AP, CLEP, institutional tests. **Support services:** Reduced course load, study skills assistance, tutoring.

Majors. Health services: Asian bodywork therapy, massage therapy.

Technology on campus. 100 workstations in library, computer center, student center. Commuter students can connect to campus network. Student web hosting, wireless network available.

Student life. Freshman orientation: Mandatory. Preregistration for classes offered. **Activities:** Student government.

Student services. Career counseling, student employment services, financial aid counseling, health services, personal counseling, veterans' counselor. **Physically disabled:** Services for visually, speech, hearing impaired. **Transfer:** Re-entry adviser, pre-admission transcript evaluation for new students. College fairs on campus for students transferring to 4-year colleges.

Contact. E-mail: admissions@swedishinstitute.edu
Phone: (212) 924-5900 ext. 199
Stacy Jameson, Director of Admissions, Swedish Institute, 151 West 26th Street, New York, NY 10001

Technical Career Institutes
New York, New York
www.tcicollege.edu
CB code: 2755

- For-profit 2-year technical and career college
- Commuter campus in very large city

General. Founded in 1909. Regionally accredited. **Enrollment:** 2,081 degree-seeking undergraduates. **Degrees:** 805 associate awarded. **Calendar:** Trimester, extensive summer session. **Full-time faculty:** 69 total. **Part-time faculty:** 79 total.

Student profile. Among degree-seeking undergraduates, 346 enrolled as first-time, first-year students.

Part-time:	15% **Women:**	33%

Basis for selection. Open admission. **Home schooled:** Transcript of courses and grades, state high school equivalency certificate, interview required.

2015-2016 Annual costs. Tuition/fees: $13,800. Per-credit charge: $548. Books/supplies: $1,600. Personal expenses: $2,490.

Financial aid. Need-based: Need-based aid available for part-time students. Work-study available nights, weekends and for part-time students. **Non-need-based:** Scholarships awarded for academics, alumni affiliation.

Application procedures. Admission: No deadline. No application fee. Admission notification on a rolling basis. **Financial aid:** No deadline. FAFSA, institutional form required. Applicants notified on a rolling basis.

Academics. Special study options: ESL, independent study, internships. **Credit/placement by examination:** AP, CLEP, institutional tests. **Support services:** Learning center, reduced course load, remedial instruction.

Majors. Business: Accounting technology, business admin. **Communications:** Digital media. **General:** Maintenance. **Health services:** Health information technology, optometric assistant. **Protective services:** Security management.

Most popular majors. Business/marketing 7%, engineering/engineering technologies 33%, health sciences 16%, public administration/social services 16%, trade and industry 16%.

Technology on campus. Commuter students can connect to campus network. Online library, wireless network available.

Student life. Freshman orientation: Available. Preregistration for classes offered. **Activities:** Student government, Student chapter of Institute of Electrical and Electronics Engineering, Electronics Technicians Association, Tau Alpha Pi Honor Fraternity for Engineering Technology, Future Business Leaders, Society of Women Engineers, Dare to Dream Volunteer Project, and American Society of Heating, Refrigeration & Air Conditioning Engineers.

Student services. Adult student services, career counseling, financial aid counseling, personal counseling, placement for graduates.

Contact. E-mail: admissions@tcicollege.edu
Phone: (212) 594-4000 Toll-free number: (800) 878-8246
Fax: (212) 629-3937
Michael Gall, Executive Vice President for Enrollment Management, Technical Career Institutes, 320 West 31st Street, New York, NY 10001

Tompkins Cortland Community College
Dryden, New York   **CB member**
www.TC3.edu   **CB code: 2904**

- Public 2-year community college
- Commuter campus in small town

General. Founded in 1968. Regionally accredited. State University of New York (SUNY) institution. **Enrollment:** 2,706 degree-seeking undergraduates; 379 non-degree-seeking students. **Degrees:** 703 associate awarded. **Location:** 45 miles from Syracuse, 12 miles from Ithaca. **Calendar:** Semester, extensive summer session. **Full-time faculty:** 64 total. **Part-time faculty:** 254 total. **Class size:** 62% < 20, 38% 20-39, less than 1% 40-49, less than 1% 50-99. **Special facilities:** On-campus organic farm, restaurant/culinary center.

Student profile. Among degree-seeking undergraduates, 62% enrolled in a transfer program, 38% enrolled in a vocational program, 820 enrolled as first-time, first-year students, 249 transferred in from other institutions.

Part-time:	22%	Hispanic/Latino:	11%
Out-of-state:	2%	Multi-racial, non-Hispanic:	4%
Women:	55%	International:	2%
African American:	14%	25 or older:	27%
Asian American:	1%	Live on campus:	24%

Transfer out. Colleges most students transferred to 2015: SUNY Cortland, SUNY Binghamton, Empire State College, Cornell University, Ithaca College.

Basis for selection. Open admission, but selective for some programs. Special requirements for nursing students. Nursing requires high school average of B or better, plus math and science prerequisites, and ACT. Interview recommended for nursing. **Home schooled:** Letter of recommendation (non-parent) required. Completion of an IHIP pursuant to section 100.10 of the Regulations of the Commissions of Education required.

High school preparation. College-preparatory program recommended.

2015-2016 Annual costs. Tuition/fees: $5,636; $10,586 out-of-state. Per-credit charge: $164 in-state; $338 out-of-state. Room/board: $10,980. Books/supplies: $1,200. Personal expenses: $1,500.

Financial aid. Need-based: Need-based aid available for part-time students. Work-study available nights, weekends and for part-time students. **Non-need-based:** Scholarships awarded for academics.

Application procedures. Admission: No deadline. $15 fee, may be waived for applicants with need, free for online applicants. Admission notification on a rolling basis. **Financial aid:** Priority date 4/15; no closing date. FAFSA, institutional form required. Applicants notified on a rolling basis starting 3/15; must reply within 4 week(s) of notification.

Academics. Special study options: Accelerated study, cooperative education, cross-registration, distance learning, dual enrollment of high school students, ESL, honors, independent study, internships, liberal arts/career combination, study abroad. Bachelor's degree programs available on campus. License preparation in nursing. **Credit/placement by examination:** AP, CLEP, IB, institutional tests. 45 credit hours maximum toward associate degree. **Support services:** GED preparation, learning center, reduced course load, remedial instruction, study skills assistance, tutoring, writing center.

Honors college/program. All applicants to the honors college will be individually evaluated based on their academic achievement and potential for further achievement.

Majors. Business: Accounting technology, business admin, entrepreneurial studies, hotel/motel admin, international. **Communications:** Communications/speech/rhetoric, digital media. **Communications technology:** Photo/film/video, radio/TV. **Computer sciences:** General, information systems, support specialist. **Conservation:** Environmental studies. **Education:** Early childhood, kindergarten/preschool, secondary. **Engineering:** General. **English:** Creative writing. **Health services:** Nursing (RN), substance abuse counseling. **Human services:** Community org/advocacy. **Liberal arts:** Arts/sciences, humanities. **Parks/recreation:** General, facilities management, sports admin. **Protective services:** Law enforcement admin, police science. **Visual/performing arts:** Commercial/advertising art, photography. **Work/family studies:** Child care management.

Most popular majors. Business/marketing 21%, health sciences 10%, liberal arts 34%, security/protective services 7%.

Technology on campus. 400 workstations in library, computer center, student center. Dormitories wired for high-speed internet access and linked to campus network. Commuter students can connect to campus network. Online course registration, online library, helpline, wireless network available.

Student life. Freshman orientation: Available. Preregistration for classes offered. Held prior to each semester. Multiple sessions offered: new students, international students, and adult students. **Policies:** All campus organizations must apply for recognition, must have a staff advisor, and are funded by the activity fee through the Faculty-Student Association and student government. **Housing:** Coed dorms, special housing for disabled, apartments, gender-neutral housing, themed housing, wellness housing available. $250 fully refundable deposit, deadline 5/16. **Activities:** Choral groups, dance, drama, film society, international student organizations, literary magazine, radio station, student government, Student Government Association, Accounting and Business Association, Alpha Omega Christian Fellowship, African Latin society, Drama Club, Hotel and Restaurant Association, Early Childhood Club, Cinema Club, Active Minds.

Athletics. NJCAA. **Intercollegiate:** Baseball M, basketball, golf, lacrosse M, soccer, softball W, volleyball W. **Intramural:** Archery, badminton, basketball, bowling, football (non-tackle), golf, handball, lacrosse, racquetball, skiing, soccer, softball, squash, swimming, table tennis, tennis, ultimate frisbee, volleyball, water polo, weight lifting, wrestling. **Team name:** Panthers.

Student services. Adult student services, alcohol/substance abuse counseling, career counseling, services for economically disadvantaged, student employment services, financial aid counseling, health services, minority student services, on-campus daycare, personal counseling, placement for graduates, veterans' counselor. **Physically disabled:** Services for visually, speech, hearing impaired. **Transfer:** Re-entry adviser, pre-admission transcript evaluation for new students. Transfer center, transfer adviser, college fairs on campus for students transferring to 4-year colleges.

Contact. E-mail: admissions@tc3.edu
Phone: (607) 844-6580 Toll-free number: (888) 567-8211
Fax: (607) 844-6541
Sandy Drumluk, Director of Admissions, Tompkins Cortland Community College, 170 North Street, Dryden, NY 13053-0139

Trocaire College
Buffalo, New York
www.trocaire.edu   **CB code: 2856**

- Private 2-year health science and career college affiliated with the Roman Catholic Church
- Commuter campus in large city

General. Founded in 1958. Regionally accredited. Affiliated with the Sisters of Mercy. Although offering primarily 2-year degrees, Trocaire does offer several 4-year Bachelor's degree programs. **Enrollment:** 1,230 degree-seeking undergraduates; 139 non-degree-seeking students. **Degrees:** 20 bachelor's, 274 associate awarded. **Calendar:** Semester, limited summer session. **Full-time faculty:** 52 total. **Part-time faculty:** 108 total.

Student profile. Among degree-seeking undergraduates, 117 enrolled as first-time, first-year students.

Part-time:	50%	Women:	89%

Basis for selection. Open admission, but selective for some programs. Special requirements for health-related fields.

High school preparation. 16 units required. Laboratory science and mathematics required for some programs.

Two-Year Colleges

2015-2016 Annual costs. Tuition/fees: $16,290. Per-credit charge: $660. Books/supplies: $1,000. Personal expenses: $1,000.

Financial aid. Need-based: Need-based aid available for part-time students. Work-study available nights, weekends and for part-time students. **Non-need-based:** Scholarships awarded for academics, alumni affiliation.

Application procedures. Admission: No deadline. $25 fee, may be waived for applicants with need, free for online applicants. Admission notification on a rolling basis. Must reply by May 1 or within 4 week(s) if notified thereafter. **Financial aid:** Priority date 3/15; no closing date. FAFSA required. Applicants notified on a rolling basis starting 3/1; must reply within 2 week(s) of notification.

Academics. Special study options: Cross-registration, dual enrollment of high school students, independent study, internships. Bachelor's degree programs available on campus. License preparation in nursing, radiology. **Credit/placement by examination:** AP, CLEP, institutional tests. 30 credit hours maximum toward associate degree. **Support services:** Learning center, reduced course load, remedial instruction, study skills assistance, tutoring.

Majors. Business: Hospitality admin, human resources. **Computer sciences:** Networking. **Health services:** Dietetic technician, health information technology, massage therapy, medical assistant, medical informatics, nursing (RN), radiologic technology/medical imaging, surgical technology. **Liberal arts:** Arts/sciences.

Technology on campus. 114 workstations in library, computer center, student center. Commuter students can connect to campus network. Helpline, wireless network available.

Student life. Freshman orientation: Mandatory. Preregistration for classes offered. **Activities:** Campus ministries, student government.

Student services. Adult student services, chaplain/spiritual director, career counseling, student employment services, financial aid counseling, health services, personal counseling, placement for graduates, veterans' counselor. **Physically disabled:** Services for visually, hearing impaired. **Transfer:** Pre-admission transcript evaluation for new students. Transfer center, transfer adviser, college fairs on campus for students transferring to 4-year colleges.

Contact. E-mail: info@trocaire.edu
Phone: (716) 827-2545 Fax: (716) 828-6107
Mollie Ballaro, Dean of Admissions and Workforce Development, Trocaire College, 360 Choate Avenue, Buffalo, NY 14220

Ulster County Community College
Stone Ridge, New York
www.sunyulster.edu   CB code: 2938

- Public 2-year community college
- Commuter campus in small town

General. Founded in 1963. Regionally accredited. SUNY institution. **Enrollment:** 1,907 degree-seeking undergraduates; 1,604 non-degree-seeking students. **Degrees:** 444 associate awarded. **Location:** 8 miles from Kingston. **Calendar:** Semester, extensive summer session. **Full-time faculty:** 65 total. **Part-time faculty:** 150 total. **Class size:** 71% < 20, 28% 20-39, less than 1% 40-49, less than 1% 50-99. **Special facilities:** Computer art graphics laboratory, small-business incubator, Health and Safety Institute, Advanced Technology Center. **Partnerships:** Formal partnership with Cisco Networking Academy, the Microsoft IT Academy program.

Student profile. Among degree-seeking undergraduates, 78% enrolled in a transfer program, 22% enrolled in a vocational program, 506 enrolled as first-time, first-year students, 150 transferred in from other institutions.

Part-time:	32%	Hispanic/Latino:	12%
Women:	59%	Multi-racial, non-Hispanic:	2%
African American:	6%	International:	2%
Asian American:	1%	25 or older:	25%

Transfer out. Colleges most students transferred to 2015: SUNY New Paltz, SUNY Albany, Marist College, Mount St. Mary's College, College of Saint Rose.

Basis for selection. Open admission, but selective for some programs. Special requirements for nursing, veterinary technology, and honors programs, with school achievement record very important. SAT or ACT recommended for all applicants. Entry into nursing program is competitive and based on the results of the ATI - TEAS exam. Within the veterinary technology program, students must complete the Health Occupations Basic Entrance Test (HOBET V) and prerequisite courses before enrolling in the veterinary technology coursework. Interview required for nursing, honors program, early

admissions applicants; recommended for others. Portfolio recommended for graphic arts.

High school preparation. 18 units recommended. Recommended units include English 4 and social studies 4. 3 math and 3 science, including chemistry and physics, required of engineering applicants. 4 English, 3 math, 3 language required of honors program applicants.

2015-2016 Annual costs. Tuition/fees: $5,010; $9,240 out-of-state. Per-credit charge: $159 in-state; $318 out-of-state. Books/supplies: $1,000. Personal expenses: $1,000.

2014-2015 Financial aid. Need-based: 68% of total undergraduate aid awarded as scholarships/grants, 32% as loans/jobs. Need-based aid available for part-time students. Work-study available nights, weekends and for part-time students.

Application procedures. Admission: No deadline. No application fee. Admission notification on a rolling basis. **Financial aid:** Priority date 6/1; no closing date. FAFSA required. Applicants notified on a rolling basis starting 6/1; must reply within 2 week(s) of notification.

Academics. Special study options: Cooperative education, cross-registration, distance learning, double major, dual enrollment of high school students, ESL, honors, independent study, internships, student-designed major. License preparation in nursing. **Credit/placement by examination:** AP, CLEP, institutional tests. 30 credit hours maximum toward associate degree. **Support services:** GED preparation, learning center, pre-admission summer program, reduced course load, remedial instruction, study skills assistance, tutoring, writing center.

Majors. Business: General, accounting technology, business admin, entrepreneurial studies, managerial economics, office/clerical. **Communications;** Communications/speech/rhetoric. **Computer sciences:** Computer science, system admin. **Conservation:** Environmental studies. **Education:** Biology, chemistry, elementary, English, kindergarten/preschool, mathematics, middle, science, social studies, Spanish. **Engineering:** General. **Health services:** EMT paramedic, nursing (RN), substance abuse counseling, veterinary technology/assistant. **Human services:** Community org/advocacy. **Liberal arts:** Arts/sciences, humanities. **Math:** General. **Protective services:** Homeland security, law enforcement admin. **Social sciences:** General. **Visual/performing arts:** General, commercial/advertising art, dramatic, fashion design, music.

Most popular majors. Business/marketing 7%, health sciences 17%, liberal arts 45%, security/protective services 11%, visual/performing arts 7%.

Technology on campus. 600 workstations in library, computer center, student center. Wireless network available.

Student life. Freshman orientation: Mandatory. Preregistration for classes offered. **Activities:** Bands, choral groups, drama, music ensembles, musical theater, student government, child care club, environmental awareness club, business club, improv club, Phi Theta Kappa, LGBTA, vet tech club, tomorrow's teachers, psychology club, nursing club, biology club.

Athletics. NJCAA. **Intercollegiate:** Baseball M, basketball M, cross-country, golf, soccer, softball W, tennis, volleyball W. **Intramural:** Basketball M. **Team name:** Senators.

Student services. Adult student services, career counseling, services for economically disadvantaged, student employment services, financial aid counseling, health services, on-campus daycare, personal counseling, placement for graduates, veterans' counselor. **Physically disabled:** Services for visually, speech, hearing impaired. **Transfer:** Transfer adviser, college fairs on campus for students transferring to 4-year colleges.

Contact. E-mail: admissions@sunyulster.edu
Phone: (845) 687-5022 Toll-free number: (800) 724-5022
Fax: (845) 687-5090
Matthew Green, Director of Admissions, Ulster County Community College, Cottekill Road, Stone Ridge, NY 12484

Utica School of Commerce
Utica, New York
www.uscny.edu   CB code: 0343

- For-profit 2-year business college
- Commuter campus in small city
- Interview required

General. Founded in 1896. Regionally accredited. Branch campuses in Oneonta and Canastota. **Enrollment:** 324 degree-seeking undergraduates.

Degrees: 72 associate awarded. **Location:** 50 miles from Syracuse. **Calendar:** Semester, extensive summer session. **Full-time faculty:** 15 total. **Part-time faculty:** 41 total. **Special facilities:** Museum of business education.

Student profile.

Out-of-state: 1% 25 or older: 30%

Transfer out. Colleges most students transferred to 2015: SUNY College of Technology, St. Rose College, SUNY at Oneonta.

Basis for selection. Open admission. Admissions interview required. High School diploma or GED required.

2015-2016 Annual costs. Tuition/fees: $13,500. Per-credit charge: $540. Books/supplies: $1,400.

Financial aid. All financial aid based on need. Work-study available nights, weekends and for part-time students.

Application procedures. Admission: No deadline. No application fee. Admission notification on a rolling basis. Must reply by May 1 or within 3 week(s) if notified thereafter. **Financial aid:** No deadline. FAFSA, institutional form required. Applicants notified on a rolling basis.

Academics. Special study options: Accelerated study, dual enrollment of high school students, liberal arts/career combination. Joint admissions with SUNY Institute of Technology. **Credit/placement by examination:** AP, CLEP, institutional tests. 30 credit hours maximum toward associate degree. **Support services:** Learning center, reduced course load, remedial instruction, tutoring.

Majors. Business: General, accounting, administrative services, business admin, executive assistant, management information systems, nonprofit/public, retailing, sales/distribution. **Computer sciences:** General, data processing, programming, word processing. **Health services:** Health care admin, health information technology, medical secretary.

Most popular majors. Business/marketing 81%, computer/information sciences 19%.

Technology on campus. 168 workstations in library, computer center.

Student life. Freshman orientation: Mandatory. Preregistration for classes offered. **Activities:** Student government, student newspaper, future secretaries association, accounting association.

Student services. Career counseling, student employment services, personal counseling, placement for graduates, veterans' counselor. **Physically disabled:** Services for visually, hearing impaired. **Transfer:** Transfer adviser, college fairs on campus for students transferring to 4-year colleges.

Contact. E-mail: admissions@uscny.edu
Phone: (315) 733-2307 Toll-free number: (800) 321-4872
Fax: (315) 733-9281
Leslie Crosley, Director of Admissions, Utica School of Commerce, 201 Bleecker Street, Utica, NY 13501

Villa Maria College of Buffalo
Buffalo, New York
www.villa.edu
CB code: 2962

- Private 2-year visual arts and music college affiliated with the Roman Catholic Church
- Commuter campus in large city
- Interview required

General. Founded in 1960. Regionally accredited. **Enrollment:** 541 degree-seeking undergraduates; 2 non-degree-seeking students. **Degrees:** 46 bachelor's, 46 associate awarded. **Location:** 2 miles from downtown. **Calendar:** Semester, limited summer session. **Full-time faculty:** 28 total; 54% have terminal degrees, 7% minority, 57% women. **Part-time faculty:** 61 total; 30% have terminal degrees, 5% minority, 38% women. **Class size:** 83% < 20, 17% 20-39. **Special facilities:** Interior design resource center, recording studio, recital hall, digital photography lab, art shop, photography studio, apparel construction lab, computer animation lab, stop action lab.

Student profile. Among degree-seeking undergraduates, 9% already have a bachelor's degree or higher, 137 enrolled as first-time, first-year students, 95 transferred in from other institutions.

Part-time:	23%	Asian American:	1%
Out-of-state:	2%	Hispanic/Latino:	7%
Women:	63%	Multi-racial, non-Hispanic:	6%
African American:	26%	25 or older:	21%

Transfer out. Colleges most students transferred to 2015: SUNY at Buffalo, Buffalo State College, Medaille College, Hilbert College, Canisius College.

Basis for selection. Academic records, learning experience, and assessment and advisement program results where applicable. Interview, recommendations also considered. Physical therapist assistant program requires 3.5 GPA. Portfolio reviews also required for select programs. Music programs may require auditions. Animation requires interview with program personnel. Interview and audition required for associate and bachelor's level music programs. Essay, portfolio and interview with faculty required for all BFA programs and associate level interior design program. **Adult students:** SAT/ACT scores not required. **Home schooled:** Statement describing home school structure and mission, transcript of courses and grades, interview required. Letter required verifying completion of all requirements from the school district in which applicant resides, or a passing GED score. **Learning Disabled:** Must submit all documentation to Coordinator for Students with Disabilities. Coordinator follows through with placement and accommodations.

High school preparation. Required and recommended units include English 1-3, mathematics 1-3, social studies 1, history 1, science 1-3 and foreign language 1. General physics with lab required for physical therapist assistant applicants.

2015-2016 Annual costs. Tuition/fees: $19,910. Per-credit charge: $645. Books/supplies: $1,000. Personal expenses: $1,000.

2014-2015 Financial aid. Need-based: 59% of total undergraduate aid awarded as scholarships/grants, 41% as loans/jobs. Need-based aid available for part-time students. Work-study available nights, weekends and for part-time students. **Non-need-based:** Scholarships awarded for academics, alumni affiliation, art, leadership.

Application procedures. Admission: No deadline. No application fee. Admission notification on a rolling basis beginning on or about 10/1. **Financial aid:** No deadline. FAFSA required. Applicants notified on a rolling basis starting 2/15; must reply within 2 week(s) of notification.

Academics. Special study options: Cross-registration, double major, dual enrollment of high school students, honors, internships, liberal arts/career combination, study abroad. Bachelor's degree programs available on campus. License preparation in physical therapy. **Credit/placement by examination:** AP, CLEP, SAT, ACT, institutional tests. 30 credit hours maximum toward associate degree, 30 toward bachelor's. **Support services:** Learning center, pre-admission summer program, reduced course load, study skills assistance, tutoring. Student Success Center with academic coaches; specialized advisement for first year students; college wide mentorship program. Implemented Adviser/Advisee Action Plan provides early identification of students encountering difficulty with scheduling, finances, academic skills, personal problems, and employment.

Majors. Business: Business admin. **Health services:** Occupational therapy assistant, physical therapy assistant. **Visual/performing arts:** Graphic design, interior design, jazz, music management, music performance, photography, studio arts.

Most popular majors. Health sciences 54%, liberal arts 7%, visual/performing arts 39%.

Technology on campus. 200 workstations in library, computer center. Commuter students can connect to campus network. Online library, wireless network available.

Student life. Freshman orientation: Mandatory, $50 fee. Preregistration for classes offered. One-day program for first-time students and their parents; half day for transfer students. **Housing:** $300 fully refundable deposit. Housing is available at Collegiate Village, located 2.5 miles off-campus. Van service to/from campus is available. No on-campus housing available. **Activities:** Jazz band, campus ministries, choral groups, literary magazine, music ensembles, student government, Helping Adults' New Dreams Succeed, Students Actively Striving for Success, Students Against Destructive Decision Making.

Athletics. Team name: Vikings.

Student services. Adult student services, alcohol/substance abuse counseling, chaplain/spiritual director, career counseling, services for economically disadvantaged, student employment services, financial aid counseling, health services, personal counseling, placement for graduates, veterans' counselor. **Transfer:** Pre-admission transcript evaluation for new students. Transfer adviser for students transferring to 4-year colleges.

Contact. E-mail: admissions@villa.edu
Phone: (716) 896-0700 ext. 1805 Fax: (716) 896-0705
Kevin Donovan, Director of Admissions, Villa Maria College of Buffalo, 240 Pine Ridge Road, Buffalo, NY 14225-3999

Westchester Community College
Valhalla, New York
www.sunywcc.edu

CB member
CB code: 2972

- Public 2-year community college
- Commuter campus in large town

General. Founded in 1946. Regionally accredited. SUNY institution. **Enrollment:** 11,689 degree-seeking undergraduates; 1,277 non-degree-seeking students. **Degrees:** 1,552 associate awarded. **Location:** 30 miles from New York City, 6 miles from White Plains. **Calendar:** Semester, extensive summer session. **Full-time faculty:** 173 total; 30% have terminal degrees, 18% minority, 50% women. **Part-time faculty:** 881 total; 19% minority, 54% women. **Special facilities:** On-campus child care center.

Student profile. Among degree-seeking undergraduates, 2,235 enrolled as first-time, first-year students, 748 transferred in from other institutions.

Part-time:	41%	25 or older:	27%
Women:	52%		

Transfer out. Colleges most students transferred to 2015: CUNY Lehman, Mercy College, SUNY Purchase, Pace University, Iona College.

Basis for selection. Open admission, but selective for some programs. Competitive programs in allied health curricula. High school diploma or GED required of applicants 18 years of age or older. Interview recommended. **Home schooled:** Statement describing home school structure and mission required. Students must submit letter from superintendent of district in which they reside certifying that home instruction program is equivalent of high school program.

2015-2016 Annual costs. Tuition/fees: $4,723; $12,213 out-of-state. Per-credit charge: $179 in-state; $493 out-of-state. Books/supplies: $2,000. Personal expenses: $600.

2014-2015 Financial aid. **Need-based:** 1,617 full-time freshmen applied for aid; 1,254 deemed to have need; 1,201 received aid. Average scholarship/grant was $3,905; average loan $1,583. 93% of total undergraduate aid awarded as scholarships/grants, 7% as loans/jobs. Need-based aid available for part-time students. Work-study available nights, weekends and for part-time students. **Non-need-based:** Awarded to 179 full-time undergraduates, including 13 freshmen. Scholarships awarded for academics, leadership.

Application procedures. **Admission:** No deadline. $35 fee, may be waived for applicants with need. Admission notification on a rolling basis beginning on or about 2/1. **Financial aid:** Priority date 6/30; no closing date. FAFSA required. Applicants notified on a rolling basis starting 4/1; must reply within 4 week(s) of notification.

Academics. Extensive ESL program and online tutoring. **Special study options:** Cooperative education, distance learning, double major, dual enrollment of high school students, ESL, honors, independent study, internships, study abroad. Cambridge University summer program; Italian language study program in Italy. License preparation in nursing, paramedic, radiology, real estate. **Credit/placement by examination:** AP, CLEP, IB, institutional tests. 32 credit hours maximum toward associate degree. **Support services:** Learning center, reduced course load, remedial instruction, study skills assistance, tutoring, writing center.

Majors. **Business:** Accounting, administrative services, business admin, international, marketing, merchandising, office/clerical, sales/distribution. **Communications:** Communications/speech/rhetoric. **Computer sciences:** General, computer science, information systems, LAN/WAN management, security. **Education:** Early childhood. **Engineering:** General, engineering science. **Health services:** EMT paramedic, medical radiologic technology/radiation therapy, nursing (RN), nursing assistant, respiratory therapy technology, substance abuse counseling. **Human services:** Social work. **Liberal arts:** Arts/sciences. **Physical sciences:** General. **Protective services:** Corrections, police science. **Social sciences:** General. **Visual/performing arts:** General, dramatic, music performance. **Work/family studies:** Child care management, food/nutrition, institutional food production.

Most popular majors. Business/marketing 18%, health sciences 8%, liberal arts 39%, security/protective services 6%.

Technology on campus. 3,303 workstations in library, computer center, student center. Online library, helpline, wireless network available.

Student life. **Freshman orientation:** Available. Preregistration for classes offered. **Activities:** Jazz band, campus ministries, choral groups, dance, drama, film society, international student organizations, literary magazine, music ensembles, Model UN, musical theater, radio station, student government, student newspaper, international friendship club, black student union, Brazilian club, El Club Hispano Americano, Jamaican club, Il Club Italiano,

Gays, Lesbian & Others of Westchester, Friends of Jewish Culture, Muslim student club, Asian society.

Athletics. NJCAA. **Intercollegiate:** Baseball M, basketball, bowling, cheerleading W, golf M, soccer M, softball W, volleyball W. **Intramural:** Basketball M, soccer M, softball, volleyball. **Team name:** Westcos.

Student services. Adult student services, career counseling, services for economically disadvantaged, financial aid counseling, health services, legal services, on-campus daycare, personal counseling, veterans' counselor, women's services. **Physically disabled:** Services for visually, speech, hearing impaired. **Transfer:** Pre-admission transcript evaluation for new students. Transfer center, transfer adviser, college fairs on campus for students transferring to 4-year colleges.

Contact. E-mail: admissions@sunywcc.edu
Phone: (914) 606-6735 Fax: (914) 606-6540
Gloria Leon, Director of Admissions, Westchester Community College, 75 Grasslands Road, Valhalla, NY 10595

Wood Tobe-Coburn School
New York, New York
www.woodtobecoburn.edu

CB code: 2913

- For-profit 2-year career college
- Commuter campus in very large city
- Interview required

General. Founded in 1879. Regionally accredited. **Enrollment:** 476 degree-seeking undergraduates. **Degrees:** 225 associate awarded. **Calendar:** Semester. **Full-time faculty:** 5 total. **Part-time faculty:** 15 total.

Student profile.

Out-of-state:	5%	25 or older:	5%

Basis for selection. Evaluation of high school or college transcript and/or GED. Portfolio recommended.

2015-2016 Annual costs. Books/supplies: $1,165. Personal expenses: $2,110. **Additional information:** Tuition per semester, Fall 2015: $8,410, Spring 2016: $8,430. Lab fees vary from $330 to $350 per semester. Books and supplies vary from semester to semester, ranging from $390 to $1,710 per semester.

Financial aid. **Need-based:** Work-study available nights, weekends and for part-time students.

Application procedures. **Admission:** No deadline. $50 fee, may be waived for applicants with need. Application must be submitted on paper. Admission notification on a rolling basis. **Financial aid:** No deadline. Applicants notified on a rolling basis.

Academics. 16-month accelerated program available for fashion students, and 8 weeks of supervised on-the-job training each year. **Special study options:** Accelerated study, internships. Externships. **Credit/placement by examination:** AP, CLEP.

Majors. **Business:** Accounting technology, administrative services, fashion, hotel/motel admin. **Computer sciences:** Networking, programming. **Health services:** Medical assistant. **Visual/performing arts:** Fashion design, graphic design.

Most popular majors. Business/marketing 59%, visual/performing arts 41%.

Technology on campus. 154 workstations in library, computer center.

Student life. **Freshman orientation:** Mandatory. Preregistration for classes offered.

Student services. Career counseling, student employment services, placement for graduates.

Contact. Phone: (212) 686-9040 Toll-free number: (800) 394-9663 Fax: (212) 686-9171
Sandra Andujar-Wendland, Director of Admissions, Wood Tobe-Coburn School, 8 East 40th Street, New York, NY 10016-0190

North Carolina

Alamance Community College
Graham, North Carolina
www.alamancecc.edu   CB code: 5790

▶ Public 2-year community college
▶ Commuter campus in large town

General. Founded in 1958. Regionally accredited. **Enrollment:** 4,042 degree-seeking undergraduates; 378 non-degree-seeking students. **Degrees:** 453 associate awarded. **Location:** 4 miles from Burlington, 30 miles from Greensboro. **Calendar:** Semester, extensive summer session. **Full-time faculty:** 115 total; 6% have terminal degrees, 10% minority, 64% women. **Part-time faculty:** 320 total; 1% have terminal degrees, 13% minority, 53% women. **Class size:** 81% < 20, 19% 20-39.

Student profile. Among degree-seeking undergraduates, 35% enrolled in a transfer program, 65% enrolled in a vocational program, 785 enrolled as first-time, first-year students.

| Part-time: | 38% | Women: | 61% |
| Out-of-state: | 1% | 25 or older: | 54% |

Transfer out. Colleges most students transferred to 2015: University of North Carolina System.

Basis for selection. Open admission, but selective for some programs. Special admission requirements for Dental and Nursing. Acceptable SAT or ACT scores, or certain high school GPAs (coupled with specific math course completion in high school), may waive required placement testing. Portfolio recommended for advertising design, commercial art majors. **Learning Disabled:** Disabilities must be documented with special needs counselor. Contact Student Success Office.

High school preparation. 21 units recommended. Recommended units include English 4, mathematics 3, social studies 2, history 1, science 3 (laboratory 1), foreign language 2 and academic electives 6. Biology, chemistry required for nursing.

2015-2016 Annual costs. Tuition/fees: $2,190; $7,950 out-of-state. Per-credit charge: $72 in-state; $264 out-of-state. Books/supplies: $800. Personal expenses: $800.

2014-2015 Financial aid. Need-based: 94% of total undergraduate aid awarded as scholarships/grants, 6% as loans/jobs. Need-based aid available for part-time students. Work-study available nights, weekends and for part-time students. **Non-need-based:** Scholarships awarded for academics, state residency.

Application procedures. Admission: No deadline. No application fee. Application must be submitted online. Admission notification on a rolling basis. **Financial aid:** Priority date 5/15; no closing date. FAFSA required. Applicants notified on a rolling basis starting 3/15; must reply within 2 week(s) of notification.

Academics. Special study options: Cooperative education, distance learning, double major, dual enrollment of high school students, ESL, independent study, internships, weekend college. License preparation in nursing. **Credit/placement by examination:** AP, CLEP, IB, institutional tests. 18 credit hours maximum toward associate degree. Maximum 25% of hours for degree by examination. **Support services:** GED preparation and test center, learning center, reduced course load, remedial instruction, study skills assistance, tutoring.

Majors. Biology: Biotechnology. **Business:** General, accounting, administrative services, banking/financial services, business admin, management science, office management, sales/distribution. **Computer sciences:** Information systems. **Education:** Early childhood. **Engineering:** Electrical. **Health services:** Clinical lab assistant, clinical lab technology, health information management, medical secretary, nursing (RN). **Liberal arts:** Arts/sciences. **Protective services:** Criminal justice, firefighting, law enforcement admin. **Visual/performing arts:** Music.

Most popular majors. Business/marketing 21%, health sciences 21%, liberal arts 20%.

Technology on campus. 152 workstations in library, computer center, student center. Wireless network available.

Student life. Freshman orientation: Available. Preregistration for classes offered. General orientation available; some programs have additional orientations. **Activities:** Choral groups, student government, student newspaper, ethnic student association, marketing club, Phi Beta Lambda (service organization), criminal justice club, early childhood education club, Phi Theta Kappa, nursing club, medical assisting club, Sigma Psi, animal care club, biotechnology, college transfer student club.

Student services. Career counseling, student employment services, financial aid counseling, health services, on-campus daycare, personal counseling, placement for graduates, veterans' counselor. **Physically disabled:** Services for visually, speech, hearing impaired. **Transfer:** Pre-admission transcript evaluation for new students. Transfer adviser, college fairs on campus for students transferring to 4-year colleges.

Contact. E-mail: admissions@alamancecc.edu
Phone: (336) 506-4270 Fax: (336) 506-4264
Elizabeth Brehler, Director of Enrollment Management, Alamance Community College, Box 8000, Graham, NC 27253

Asheville-Buncombe Technical Community College
Asheville, North Carolina   CB member
www.abtech.edu   CB code: 5033

▶ Public 2-year community and technical college
▶ Commuter campus in small city

General. Founded in 1959. Regionally accredited. Certain credit courses offered at the Enka, South and Madison Sites. **Enrollment:** 4,491 degree-seeking undergraduates. **Degrees:** 909 associate awarded. **Location:** 115 miles from Charlotte. **Calendar:** Semester, limited summer session. **Full-time faculty:** 175 total; 6% have terminal degrees, 1% minority. **Part-time faculty:** 514 total; 4% have terminal degrees, 8% minority.

Student profile.

| Out-of-state: | 2% | 25 or older: | 47% |

Basis for selection. Open admission, but selective for some programs. NC Diagnostic Assessment and Placement (NC DAP) administered by college. SAT and/or ACT scores may be used in lieu of CPT for English and math placement. For allied health programs, tests used to earn admission through point system. Provisional or unconditional admission to individual programs will be determined by scores on the test requirements. Placement interview required of all entering students; interview required for all medical programs.

High school preparation. 8 units recommended. Recommended units include English 4, mathematics 2 and science 2. Algebra I and algebra II or geometry for engineering; algebra I, chemistry and biology for nursing, medical laboratory and dental programs; algebra I for radiologic technology; biology and 1 mathematics for practical nursing.

2015-2016 Annual costs. Tuition/fees: $2,396; $8,540 out-of-state. Per-credit charge: $72 in-state; $264 out-of-state. Books/supplies: $1,000. Personal expenses: $7,367.

Financial aid. Need-based: Work-study available nights, weekends and for part-time students. **Non-need-based:** Scholarships awarded for academics, leadership.

Application procedures. Admission: No deadline. No application fee. **Financial aid:** Priority date 3/15, closing date 3/31. FAFSA required. Applicants notified on a rolling basis starting 5/1; must reply within 2 week(s) of notification.

Academics. Special study options: Cooperative education, cross-registration, distance learning, double major, dual enrollment of high school students, independent study, internships, liberal arts/career combination. License preparation in dental hygiene, nursing. **Credit/placement by examination:** AP, CLEP, institutional tests. **Support services:** GED preparation and test center, learning center, pre-admission summer program, reduced course load, remedial instruction, tutoring.

Majors. Business: Accounting, administrative services, business admin, management information systems, office technology, office/clerical, operations, sales/distribution. **Computer sciences:** Applications programming. **Health services:** Clinical lab technology, dental hygiene, EMT paramedic, medical radiologic technology/radiation therapy, nursing (RN). **Human services:** Social work. **Liberal arts:** Arts/sciences. **Protective services:** Police science. **Work/family studies:** Child care management, institutional food production.

Most popular majors. Business/marketing 13%, computer/information sciences 9%, engineering/engineering technologies 14%, health sciences 29%, liberal arts 9%, trade and industry 13%.

Technology on campus. 300 workstations in library, computer center.

Student life. Activities: Drama, literary magazine, student government, student newspaper.

Student services. Career counseling, student employment services, on-campus daycare, personal counseling, placement for graduates, veterans' counselor. **Physically disabled:** Services for visually, speech, hearing impaired. **Transfer:** Transfer adviser, college fairs on campus for students transferring to 4-year colleges.

Contact. E-mail: admissions@abtech.edu
Phone: (828) 398-7900 Fax: (828) 251-6718
Lisa Bush, Director of Enrollment Services, Asheville-Buncombe Technical Community College, 340 Victoria Road, Asheville, NC 28801-4897

Beaufort County Community College
Washington, North Carolina
www.beaufortccc.edu
CB code: 7307

▸ Public 2-year community college
▸ Commuter campus in small town

General. Founded in 1967. Regionally accredited. **Enrollment:** 1,385 degree-seeking undergraduates. **Degrees:** 271 associate awarded. **Location:** 23 miles from Greenville. **Calendar:** Semester, limited summer session. **Full-time faculty:** 64 total. **Part-time faculty:** 138 total. **Special facilities:** Fitness trail.

Student profile. Among degree-seeking undergraduates, 78 transferred in from other institutions.

Transfer out. Colleges most students transferred to 2015: East Carolina University.

Basis for selection. Open admission, but selective for some programs. Special admission requirements for allied health programs and basic law enforcement training. **Adult students:** SAT/ACT scores may be substituted for College Placement Testing (Accuplacer). **Home schooled:** Must provide proof that the home school is registered with the appropriate state agencies.

High school preparation. One unit chemistry required for nursing and medical technology applicants.

2015-2016 Annual costs. Tuition/fees: $2,224; $7,984 out-of-state. Per-credit charge: $72 in-state; $264 out-of-state. Books/supplies: $944. Personal expenses: $2,247.

2014-2015 Financial aid. Need-based: 99% of total undergraduate aid awarded as scholarships/grants, 1% as loans/jobs. Need-based aid available for part-time students. Work-study available nights, weekends and for part-time students. **Non-need-based:** Scholarships awarded for academics.

Application procedures. Admission: No deadline. No application fee. Admission notification on a rolling basis. **Financial aid:** Closing date 8/1. FAFSA, institutional form required. Applicants notified on a rolling basis starting 5/1; must reply within 2 week(s) of notification.

Academics. Special study options: Cooperative education, distance learning, dual enrollment of high school students, ESL, internships, liberal arts/career combination, study abroad. Bachelor's degree programs available on campus. License preparation in nursing. **Credit/placement by examination:** AP, CLEP, institutional tests. **Support services:** GED preparation and test center, learning center, remedial instruction, study skills assistance, tutoring, writing center.

Majors. Business: Administrative services, business admin. **Computer sciences:** Applications programming, information systems, networking, programming, vendor certification. **Education:** General, early childhood. **General:** Electrician. **Health services:** Clinical lab technology, medical secretary, nursing (RN), office admin. **Liberal arts:** Arts/sciences. **Protective services:** Criminal justice. **Work/family studies:** Child care management, child development.

Technology on campus. Commuter students can connect to campus network. Online library, wireless network available.

Student life. Freshman orientation: Available. Preregistration for classes offered. **Activities:** Campus ministries, literary magazine, student government, Gamma Beta Phi, running club, service club, Waves, Jeremiah 29, LGBT, chess club.

Student services. Career counseling, services for economically disadvantaged, student employment services, financial aid counseling, personal counseling, placement for graduates, veterans' counselor. **Physically disabled:** Services for visually, speech, hearing impaired. **Transfer:** Pre-admission transcript evaluation for new students. Transfer adviser, college fairs on campus for students transferring to 4-year colleges.

Contact. E-mail: michele.mayo@beaufortccc.edu
Phone: (252) 940-6237 Fax: (252) 940-6393
Michele Mayo, Director of Admissions and Recruitment, Beaufort County Community College, Box 1069, Washington, NC 27889

Bladen Community College
Dublin, North Carolina
www.bladencc.edu
CB code: 3082

▸ Public 2-year community college
▸ Commuter campus in rural community

General. Founded in 1967. Regionally accredited. **Enrollment:** 1,360 degree-seeking undergraduates. **Degrees:** 110 associate awarded. **Location:** 35 miles from Fayetteville. **Calendar:** Semester, limited summer session. **Full-time faculty:** 56 total; 5% have terminal degrees, 20% minority. **Part-time faculty:** 36 total; 11% have terminal degrees, 44% minority. **Class size:** 82% < 20, 18% 20-39.

Transfer out. Colleges most students transferred to 2015: University of North Carolina-Wilmington, University of North Carolina-Pembroke, Fayetteville State University, East Carolina University, North Carolina State University.

Basis for selection. Open admission, but selective for some programs. Practical nursing program requires submission of appropriate test results and completion of high school biology and algebra courses with grade of C or better. ADN program requires biology and algebra, plus general chemistry. Biology and chemistry must be within last 5 years for ADN.

High school preparation. 26 units recommended. Recommended units include English 4, mathematics 3, social studies 1, history 2, science 3 (laboratory 1), foreign language 2, computer science 1 and academic electives 10.

2015-2016 Annual costs. Tuition/fees: $2,226; $7,986 out-of-state. Per-credit charge: $72 in-state; $264 out-of-state. Books/supplies: $850. Personal expenses: $850.

Financial aid. Need-based: Need-based aid available for part-time students. Work-study available nights, weekends and for part-time students.

Application procedures. Admission: Priority date 8/15; no deadline. No application fee. Admission notification on a rolling basis beginning on or about 6/15. **Financial aid:** Priority date 6/1, closing date 7/1. FAFSA required. Applicants notified on a rolling basis starting 8/1; must reply within 2 week(s) of notification.

Academics. Special study options: Cooperative education, distance learning, double major, dual enrollment of high school students, ESL, independent study, internships, liberal arts/career combination, weekend college. Bachelor's degree programs available on campus. **Credit/placement by examination:** AP, CLEP, institutional tests. 10 credit hours maximum toward associate degree. **Support services:** GED preparation and test center, learning center, reduced course load, remedial instruction, study skills assistance, tutoring, writing center.

Majors. Biology: Biotechnology. **Business:** Business admin, office technology, office/clerical. **Computer sciences:** General, applications programming, programming. **Education:** General. **Health services:** Nursing (RN). **Liberal arts:** Arts/sciences. **Protective services:** Law enforcement admin. **Work/family studies:** Child care service.

Technology on campus. 100 workstations in library, computer center, student center. Online course registration, helpline, wireless network available.

Student life. Freshman orientation: Mandatory. Preregistration for classes offered. **Activities:** Drama, literary magazine, student government, student newspaper.

Athletics. Team name: Eagles.

Student services. Adult student services, alcohol/substance abuse counseling, career counseling, services for economically disadvantaged, student employment services, financial aid counseling, minority student services, personal counseling, placement for graduates, veterans' counselor. **Physically disabled:** Services for visually, speech, hearing impaired. **Transfer:** Pre-admission transcript evaluation for new students. Transfer center, transfer adviser, college fairs on campus for students transferring to 4-year colleges.

Contact. E-mail: lmclean@bladencc.edu
Phone: (910) 879-5593 Fax: (910) 879-5564
Carlton Bryan, Dean of Enrollment Management, Bladen Community College, Post Office Box 266, Dublin, NC 28332-0266

Blue Ridge Community College
Flat Rock, North Carolina
www.blueridge.edu   CB code: 5644

- Public 2-year community and technical college
- Commuter campus in large town

General. Founded in 1969. Regionally accredited. **Enrollment:** 1,327 degree-seeking undergraduates. **Degrees:** 611 associate awarded. **Location:** 25 miles from Asheville. **Calendar:** Semester, limited summer session. **Full-time faculty:** 72 total. **Part-time faculty:** 246 total. **Class size:** 81% < 20, 19% 20-39, less than 1% 40-49. **Special facilities:** CAVE - virtual reality training center.

Student profile.

Out-of-state: 2%   25 or older: 29%

Basis for selection. Open admission, but selective for some programs. Mathematics and science requirements for allied health programs in surgical technology, pharmacy technology, nursing.

High school preparation. 3 units of science, one of which must be lab, required for allied health programs only.

2015-2016 Annual costs. Tuition/fees: $2,245; $8,005 out-of-state. Per-credit charge: $72 in-state; $264 out-of-state. Books/supplies: $1,200.

Financial aid. Need-based: Need-based aid available for part-time students. Work-study available nights, weekends and for part-time students. **Non-need-based:** Scholarships awarded for academics, athletics, leadership, minority status, state residency.

Application procedures. Admission: No deadline. No application fee. Admission notification on a rolling basis. **Financial aid:** Priority date 6/30; no closing date. FAFSA, institutional form required. Applicants notified on a rolling basis starting 2/1; must reply within 4 week(s) of notification.

Academics. Special study options: Cooperative education, distance learning, double major, dual enrollment of high school students, ESL, study abroad, teacher certification program. Bachelor's degree programs available on campus. License preparation in dental hygiene, nursing, paramedic, physical therapy, real estate. **Credit/placement by examination:** AP, CLEP, institutional tests. Maximum of 50% of credit hours by examination may be counted toward degree. **Support services:** GED preparation and test center, learning center, reduced course load, remedial instruction, study skills assistance, tutoring.

Majors. Business: General, accounting, administrative services, personal/financial services, sales/distribution, tourism promotion. **Computer sciences:** Information systems, information technology, programming. **Conservation:** General. **Engineering:** Electrical. **Foreign languages:** Sign language interpretation, translation. **Health services:** Dental hygiene, EMT paramedic, nursing (RN), physical therapy, surgical technology. **Liberal arts:** Arts/sciences. **Protective services:** Fire safety technology, police science. **Visual/performing arts:** Dramatic, game design, music. **Work/family studies:** Child care management.

Most popular majors. Business/marketing 17%, computer/information sciences 27%, health sciences 12%, liberal arts 23%.

Technology on campus. 200 workstations in library, computer center. Commuter students can connect to campus network. Online course registration, helpline, wireless network available.

Student life. Freshman orientation: Mandatory. Preregistration for classes offered. **Activities:** Drama, literary magazine, student government, Circle-K, Rotaract, Phi Theta Kappa, National Vocational-Technical Honor Society.

Athletics. NJCAA. **Intercollegiate:** Bowling M, volleyball W. **Team name:** Bears.

Student services. Adult student services, career counseling, student employment services, financial aid counseling, on-campus daycare, personal counseling, placement for graduates, veterans' counselor. **Physically disabled:** Services for visually, speech, hearing impaired. **Transfer:** Pre-admission transcript evaluation for new students. Transfer adviser, college fairs on campus for students transferring to 4-year colleges.

Contact. E-mail: kirstenb@blueridge.edu
Phone: (828) 694-1800 Fax: (828) 694-1693
Marcia Stoneman, Dean for Student Services, Blue Ridge Community College, 180 West Campus Drive, Flat Rock, NC 28731-9624

Brunswick Community College
Bolivia, North Carolina
www.brunswickcc.edu   CB code: 7314

- Public 2-year community college
- Commuter campus in small town

General. Founded in 1979. Regionally accredited. **Enrollment:** 1,468 degree-seeking undergraduates. **Degrees:** 247 associate awarded. **Location:** 25 miles from Wilmington and 30 miles from Myrtle Beach, SC. **Calendar:** Semester, limited summer session. **Full-time faculty:** 42 total; 24% have terminal degrees, 7% minority, 64% women. **Part-time faculty:** 113 total; 8% have terminal degrees, 8% minority, 62% women. **Class size:** 74% < 20, 26% 20-39. **Special facilities:** Nature trail, fitness and aquatics center.

Transfer out. Colleges most students transferred to 2015: University of North Carolina Wilmington.

Basis for selection. Open admission, but selective for some programs. Phlebotomy, basic law enforcement technology, practical nursing, associate degree nursing, and health information technology program applicants must have completed specific course work before they are considered. Limited slots. May also enter based on test scores. No interview necessary. **Adult students:** SAT/ACT scores not required. **Home schooled:** Transcript of courses and grades, state high school equivalency certificate required. **Learning Disabled:** Requests for any accommodations should be made at least 2 weeks prior to beginning of applicant's first semester.

2015-2016 Annual costs. Tuition/fees: $2,260; $8,020 out-of-state. Per-credit charge: $72 in-state; $264 out-of-state. Books/supplies: $1,500. Personal expenses: $3,307.

Financial aid. Need-based: Need-based aid available for part-time students. Work-study available nights, weekends and for part-time students. **Non-need-based:** Scholarships awarded for academics, state residency. **Additional information:** Attendance required at financial aid orientation session for those receiving federal student aid.

Application procedures. Admission: No deadline. No application fee. Admission notification on a rolling basis. **Financial aid:** Priority date 6/1, closing date 6/15. FAFSA, institutional form required. Applicants notified on a rolling basis starting 3/1; must reply by 6/30 or within 2 week(s) of notification.

Academics. Special study options: Cooperative education, distance learning, double major, dual enrollment of high school students, internships. License preparation in nursing, paramedic, real estate. **Credit/placement by examination:** AP, CLEP, SAT, institutional tests. No limits on credit by examination hours that may be applied toward an associate degree. **Support services:** GED preparation and test center, learning center, reduced course load, remedial instruction, study skills assistance, tutoring.

Majors. Business: Administrative services, business admin, small business admin. **Computer sciences:** Information systems, programming. **Education:** Early childhood. **Health services:** Health information technology, nursing (RN). **Liberal arts:** Arts/sciences.

Most popular majors. Agriculture 9%, business/marketing 11%, computer/information sciences 6%, education 8%, health sciences 22%, liberal arts 44%.

Technology on campus. 146 workstations in library, computer center. Helpline, wireless network available.

Student life. Freshman orientation: Available. Preregistration for classes offered. **Policies:** All facilities are nonsmoking. Smoking allowed in designated outdoor areas only. **Activities:** Dance, drama, radio station, student government, student newspaper, National Technical Honor Society, Phi Theta Kappa, science club, journalism club, drama club, art club.

Athletics. NJCAA. **Intercollegiate:** Baseball M, basketball, volleyball W. **Team name:** Dolphins.

Student services. Alcohol/substance abuse counseling, career counseling, student employment services, financial aid counseling, minority student services, on-campus daycare, personal counseling, placement for graduates, veterans' counselor. **Physically disabled:** Services for visually, speech, hearing impaired. **Transfer:** Pre-admission transcript evaluation for new students. Transfer adviser, college fairs on campus for students transferring to 4-year colleges.

Contact. E-mail: admissions@brunswickcc.edu
Phone: (910) 755-7320 Toll-free number: (800) 754-1050 ext. 324
Fax: (910) 754-9609
Christine Dye, Director of Records & Enrollment Services, Brunswick Community College, 50 College Road NE, Bolivia, NC 28422

Caldwell Community College and Technical Institute
Hudson, North Carolina
www.cccti.edu   **CB code: 5146**

♦ Public 2-year community and technical college
♦ Commuter campus in small town

General. Founded in 1964. Regionally accredited. **Enrollment:** 3,940 degree-seeking undergraduates. **Degrees:** 495 associate awarded. **Location:** 90 miles from Charlotte. **Calendar:** Semester, limited summer session. **Full-time faculty:** 130 total. **Part-time faculty:** 290 total. **Class size:** 68% < 20, 31% 20-39, 1% 40-49, less than 1% 50-99, less than 1% >100. **Special facilities:** Civic center.

Student profile.

Out-of-state:	2%	25 or older:	43%

Basis for selection. Open admission, but selective for some programs. Limited number of applicants are admitted to health science programs. These students are accepted based on competitive admissions.

2015-2016 Annual costs. Tuition/fees: $2,236; $7,996 out-of-state. Per-credit charge: $72 in-state; $264 out-of-state. Books/supplies: $1,100. Personal expenses: $1,350.

Financial aid. All financial aid based on need. Need-based aid available for part-time students. Work-study available nights, weekends and for part-time students.

Application procedures. Admission: No deadline. No application fee. Admission notification on a rolling basis. **Financial aid:** Closing date 5/1. FAFSA required. Applicants notified on a rolling basis starting 6/30.

Academics. Special study options: Cooperative education, distance learning, dual enrollment of high school students, independent study. Bachelor's degree programs available on campus. License preparation in aviation, nursing, paramedic, physical therapy, radiology. **Credit/placement by examination:** AP, CLEP, institutional tests. 16 credit hours maximum toward associate degree. **Support services:** GED preparation and test center, learning center, reduced course load, remedial instruction, study skills assistance, tutoring, writing center.

Majors. Business: Accounting, administrative services, business admin. **Computer sciences:** Applications programming, data processing, programming. **Education:** Early childhood. **Health services:** Cardiovascular technology, medical radiologic technology/radiation therapy, medical secretary, nuclear medical technology, nursing (RN), physical therapy assistant, sonography, speech-language pathology assistant. **Liberal arts:** Arts/sciences. **Math:** General. **Visual/performing arts:** Art, music.

Most popular majors. Business/marketing 23%, computer/information sciences 12%, health sciences 38%, liberal arts 16%.

Technology on campus. 750 workstations in library, computer center. Commuter students can connect to campus network. Online course registration, online library, helpline, wireless network available.

Student life. Freshman orientation: Mandatory. Preregistration for classes offered. Day/evening sessions held during the early registration time over a one week period each semester. **Activities:** Choral groups, drama, literary magazine, student government, student newspaper, TV station, Ebony Kinship, Phi Theta Kappa, Alpha Omega (non-denominational religious organization), special interest clubs.

Athletics. NJCAA. **Intercollegiate:** Basketball. **Team name:** Cobras.

Student services. Adult student services, career counseling, services for economically disadvantaged, student employment services, financial aid

counseling, minority student services, personal counseling, placement for graduates, veterans' counselor. **Physically disabled:** Services for visually, speech, hearing impaired. **Transfer:** Pre-admission transcript evaluation for new students. Transfer center, transfer adviser, college fairs on campus for students transferring to 4-year colleges.

Contact. E-mail: CCCTIAdmissions@cccti.edu
Phone: (828) 726-2200 Fax: (828) 726-2709
Dennis Seagle, Director, Enrollment Management Services, Caldwell Community College and Technical Institute, 2855 Hickory Boulevard, Hudson, NC 28638-2672

Cape Fear Community College
Wilmington, North Carolina
www.cfcc.edu   **CB code: 5094**

♦ Public 2-year community college
♦ Commuter campus in small city

General. Founded in 1959. Regionally accredited. Additional campuses in Burgaw, Castle Hayne, and Surf City. **Enrollment:** 8,067 degree-seeking undergraduates; 784 non-degree-seeking students. **Degrees:** 1,262 associate awarded. **Location:** 125 miles from Raleigh. **Calendar:** Semester, limited summer session. **Full-time faculty:** 301 total. **Part-time faculty:** 455 total. **Special facilities:** Research vessel.

Student profile. Among degree-seeking undergraduates, 44% enrolled in a transfer program, 56% enrolled in a vocational program, 1,625 enrolled as first-time, first-year students, 947 transferred in from other institutions.

Part-time:	52%	Hispanic/Latino:	7%
Women:	53%	Native American:	1%
African American:	13%	Multi-racial, non-Hispanic:	3%
Asian American:	1%		

Transfer out. Colleges most students transferred to 2015: University of North Carolina at Wilmington, North Carolina State University, East Carolina University.

Basis for selection. Open admission, but selective for some programs. Special requirements for health science programs: Psychological Services Bureau Examination and interview required. **Home schooled:** A copy of approval from North Carolina Department of Non-Public Instruction required or similar documents from states other than North Carolina. **Learning Disabled:** Students must register with Disability Services.

2015-2016 Annual costs. Tuition/fees: $2,498; $8,258 out-of-state. Per-credit charge: $76 in-state; $268 out-of-state. Books/supplies: $1,325. Personal expenses: $3,236.

2015-2016 Financial aid. Need-based: 59% of total undergraduate aid awarded as scholarships/grants, 41% as loans/jobs. Need-based aid available for part-time students. Work-study available nights, weekends and for part-time students. **Non-need-based:** Scholarships awarded for academics, athletics, leadership.

Application procedures. Admission: No deadline. No application fee. Admission notification on a rolling basis. **Financial aid:** Priority date 6/1; no closing date. FAFSA required. Applicants notified on a rolling basis starting 4/1; must reply within 2 week(s) of notification.

Academics. Special study options: Cooperative education, distance learning, dual enrollment of high school students, ESL, independent study, internships. Bachelor's degree programs available on campus. License preparation in dental hygiene, nursing, occupational therapy, paramedic, radiology, real estate. **Credit/placement by examination:** AP, CLEP, IB, institutional tests. **Support services:** GED preparation and test center, learning center, remedial instruction, study skills assistance, tutoring.

Majors. Architecture: Interior, landscape, urban/community planning. **Business:** Accounting technology, administrative services, business admin, hospitality admin, hotel/motel admin, restaurant/food services. **Computer sciences:** Informatics, information technology. **Conservation:** General. **Education:** General. **Foreign languages:** Translation. **General:** Electrician, site management. **Health services:** Dental hygiene, EMT paramedic, medical radiologic technology/radiation therapy, nursing (RN), occupational therapy assistant, pharmacy assistant, sonography. **Liberal arts:** Arts/sciences. **Physical sciences:** Oceanography. **Protective services:** Police science. **Visual/performing arts:** Cinematography, interior design. **Work/family studies:** Child care management, institutional food production.

Most popular majors. Health sciences 14%, liberal arts 64%.

Technology on campus. 2,000 workstations in library, computer center. Online course registration, helpline, wireless network available.

Student life. Freshman orientation: Mandatory. Preregistration for classes offered. Held in July and December. **Policies:** CFCC is a smoke-free campus. **Activities:** Student government, student newspaper, Phi Theta Kappa Honor Society.

Athletics. NJCAA. **Intercollegiate:** Basketball, golf, volleyball W. **Intramural:** Cheerleading, soccer. **Team name:** Sea Devils.

Student services. Alcohol/substance abuse counseling, career counseling, student employment services, financial aid counseling, on-campus daycare, personal counseling, placement for graduates, veterans' counselor. **Physically disabled:** Services for visually, speech, hearing impaired. **Transfer:** Pre-admission transcript evaluation for new students. Transfer adviser, college fairs on campus for students transferring to 4-year colleges.

Contact. E-mail: admissions@cfcc.edu
Phone: (910) 362-7557 Fax: (910) 362-7080
Linda Kasyan, Director of Enrollment Management, Cape Fear
Community College, 411 North Front Street, Wilmington, NC 28401-3910

Carolinas College of Health Sciences
Charlotte, North Carolina
www.carolinascollege.edu   CB code: 6211

- Public 2-year health science college
- Commuter campus in very large city

General. Regionally accredited. The institution is supported by Carolinas Medical Center and specializes in health careers such as nursing, radiologic technology, radiation therapy, surgical technology and medical laboratory sciences. **Enrollment:** 474 degree-seeking undergraduates. **Degrees:** 131 associate awarded. **Calendar:** Semester, extensive summer session. **Full-time faculty:** 24 total. **Part-time faculty:** 20 total. **Special facilities:** Simulation center, a collection of human patient simulators and procedural task trainers.

Student profile. Among degree-seeking undergraduates, 21 enrolled as first-time, first-year students.

Part-time:	88%	Asian American:	3%
Women:	89%	Hispanic/Latino:	2%
African American:	9%	Multi-racial, non-Hispanic:	3%

Transfer out. Colleges most students transferred to 2015: Queens University of Charlotte, University of North Carolina at Charlotte, Winston-Salem State University, Central Piedmont Community College, Mercy School of Nursing.

Basis for selection. Open admission, but selective for some programs. Selection based on SAT/ACT test scores, high school GPA, college GPA. A number ranking system is used. Only students with permanent resident status will be considered for enrollment.

High school preparation. College-preparatory program recommended. 15 units required. Required units include English 4, mathematics 1, social studies 2, history 2, science 2 (laboratory 2) and foreign language 2. Algebra, biology, chemistry required.

2015-2016 Annual costs. Tuition/fees: $9,630; $9,630 out-of-state. Per-credit charge: $323. Books/supplies: $1,400. Personal expenses: $3,510.

2014-2015 Financial aid. Need-based: 2 full-time freshmen applied for aid; 2 deemed to have need; 2 received aid. Average need met was 75%. Average scholarship/grant was $3,326; average loan $5,443. 43% of total undergraduate aid awarded as scholarships/grants, 57% as loans/jobs. Need-based aid available for part-time students. Work-study available nights, weekends and for part-time students. **Non-need-based:** Scholarships awarded for academics. **Additional information:** The College offers the Carolinas HealthCare System Educational Forgiveness Loan that allows students in a 2-year program to borrow up to $10,000 and up to $5,000 in a 1-year program. The loan may be forgiven if the student obtains an eligible full-time position after graduation.

Application procedures. Admission: Closing date 12/1 (receipt date). $50 fee. Application must be submitted online. Admission notification on a rolling basis beginning on or about 3/15. Must reply by May 1 or within 4 week(s) if notified thereafter. Application deadlines vary by program. **Financial aid:** Priority date 5/1; no closing date. FAFSA required. Applicants notified on a rolling basis starting 5/1.

Academics. Special study options: Combined bachelor's/graduate degree, distance learning, double major, independent study, liberal arts/career combination, study abroad. License preparation in nursing, radiology. **Credit/placement by examination:** AP, CLEP. **Support services:** Learning center, study skills assistance, tutoring.

Majors. Health services: Medical radiologic technology/radiation therapy, nursing (RN), radiologic technology/medical imaging.

Technology on campus. 40 workstations in library, computer center. Commuter students can connect to campus network. Online course registration, online library, wireless network available.

Student life. Freshman orientation: Mandatory. Preregistration for classes offered. **Housing:** Apartments available. **Activities:** Student government.

Student services. Alcohol/substance abuse counseling, chaplain/spiritual director, career counseling, student employment services, financial aid counseling, health services, personal counseling, placement for graduates, veterans' counselor. **Transfer:** Pre-admission transcript evaluation for new students. College fairs on campus for students transferring to 4-year colleges.

Contact. E-mail: cchsinformation@carolinas.org
Phone: (704) 355-5583 Fax: (704) 355-9336
Rhoda Rillorta, Admissions Coordinator, Carolinas College of Health
Sciences, PO Box 32861, Charlotte, NC 28232-2861

Carteret Community College
Morehead City, North Carolina
www.carteret.edu   CB code: 5092

- Public 2-year community and technical college
- Commuter campus in small town

General. Founded in 1963. Regionally accredited. Aquaculture technology and marine technical trades programs. **Enrollment:** 1,382 degree-seeking undergraduates. **Degrees:** 208 associate awarded. **Location:** 150 miles from Raleigh, 87 miles from Wilmington. **Calendar:** Semester, limited summer session. **Full-time faculty:** 95 total; 43% have terminal degrees, 5% minority, 48% women. **Part-time faculty:** 84 total; 36% have terminal degrees, 12% minority, 67% women. **Special facilities:** Carteret County historical research center, center for marine science and technology, North Carolina marine technical education center. **Partnerships:** Formal partnerships with the North Carolina State Department of Public Instruction and the North Carolina Community College System.

Transfer out. Colleges most students transferred to 2015: University of North Carolina at Wilmington, East Carolina University, North Carolina State University, Pitt Community College, Cape Fear Community College.

Basis for selection. Open admission, but selective for some programs. General college acceptance to all applicants with complete admissions files. Specific admissions programs have additional requirements. **Home schooled:** Transcript of courses and grades required. **Learning Disabled:** Students must present proper documentation and follow the procedures to request reasonable accommodations.

High school preparation. College-preparatory program recommended. Extensive science and mathematics recommended for allied health programs, particularly respiratory therapy, radiography, and nursing.

2015-2016 Annual costs. Tuition/fees: $2,252; $8,012 out-of-state. Per-credit charge: $72 in-state; $264 out-of-state. Books/supplies: $950.

Financial aid. Need-based: Need-based aid available for part-time students. Work-study available nights, weekends and for part-time students. **Non-need-based:** Scholarships awarded for academics, leadership, minority status, state residency. **Additional information:** Institutional student loan program administered by college. Student may charge up to $600 for books, supplies and tuition per quarter. Repayment due by 11th week of semester.

Application procedures. Admission: No deadline. No application fee. Application must be submitted online. Admission notification on a rolling basis. **Financial aid:** No deadline. FAFSA, institutional form required. Must reply within 2 week(s) of notification.

Academics. Special study options: Cooperative education, cross-registration, distance learning, double major, dual enrollment of high school students, ESL, independent study, internships, liberal arts/career combination. License preparation in nursing, paramedic, radiology, real estate. **Credit/placement by examination:** AP, CLEP, institutional tests. **Support services:** GED preparation and test center, learning center, reduced course load, remedial instruction, study skills assistance, tutoring, writing center.

Majors. Biology: Biotechnology. **Business:** General, administrative services, hotel/motel admin, office/clerical. **Communications:** Photojournalism. **Communications technology:** Photo/film/video. **Computer sciences:** General, information technology, LAN/WAN management, web page design, webmaster, word processing. **Education:** General, teacher assistance. **Health**

services: EMT ambulance attendant, massage therapy, medical radiologic technology/radiation therapy, office admin, predental, premedicine, prenursing, prepharmacy, preveterinary, radiologic technology/medical imaging, recreational therapy, respiratory therapy technology. **Liberal arts:** Arts/sciences. **Math:** General. **Protective services:** Criminal justice, police science. **Psychology:** General. **Visual/performing arts:** General, interior design, photography. **Work/family studies:** Child care management, child care service, child development.

Technology on campus. 225 workstations in library, computer center, student center. Commuter students can connect to campus network. Online course registration, online library, helpline, repair service, student web hosting, wireless network available.

Student life. Freshman orientation: Mandatory. Preregistration for classes offered. **Activities:** Drama, literary magazine, student government, student newspaper, Psi Beta (honorary society for psychology majors), Phi Beta Lambda (business organization), Sigma Kappa Delta (honorary society for English majors), Phi Theta Kappa - Beta Delta Pi (honors fraternity).

Student services. Adult student services, alcohol/substance abuse counseling, career counseling, services for economically disadvantaged, student employment services, financial aid counseling, minority student services, personal counseling, placement for graduates, veterans' counselor. **Physically disabled:** Services for visually, speech, hearing impaired. **Transfer:** Pre-admission transcript evaluation for new students. Transfer center, transfer adviser, college fairs on campus for students transferring to 4-year colleges.

Contact. E-mail: admissions@carteret.edu
Phone: (252) 222-6154 Fax: (252) 222-6265
Martin Nichols, Admissions Officer, Carteret Community College, 3505 Arendell Street, Morehead City, NC 28557-2989

Catawba Valley Community College
Hickory, North Carolina
www.cvcc.edu
CB code: 5098

- Public 2-year community college
- Commuter campus in large town

General. Founded in 1960. Regionally accredited. **Enrollment:** 4,165 degree-seeking undergraduates. **Degrees:** 710 associate awarded. **ROTC:** Air Force. **Location:** 50 miles from Charlotte. **Calendar:** Semester, limited summer session. **Full-time faculty:** 157 total; 3% minority, 50% women. **Part-time faculty:** 385 total; 7% minority, 55% women. **Class size:** 63% < 20, 37% 20-39, less than 1% >100. **Special facilities:** Regional simulated hospital.

Basis for selection. Open admission, but selective for some programs. Special requirements for nursing, emergency medical science, surgical technology, respiratory care, health information technology, dental hygiene, speech-language pathology assistant, advertising and graphic design, electroneurodiagnostic technology, polysomnography, radiography, basic law enforcement. Interview required for health program applicants, advertising and graphic design applicants, and photography applicants; recommended for all others. **Home schooled:** Transcript of courses and grades, state high school equivalency certificate required.

2015-2016 Annual costs. Tuition/fees: $2,280; $8,040 out-of-state. Per-credit charge: $72 in-state; $264 out-of-state. Books/supplies: $1,550. Personal expenses: $4,244.

Financial aid. Need-based: Need-based aid available for part-time students. Work-study available nights, weekends and for part-time students. **Non-need-based:** Scholarships awarded for academics, leadership, music/drama.

Application procedures. Admission: No deadline. No application fee. Admission notification on a rolling basis. **Financial aid:** Closing date 3/15. FAFSA required. Applicants notified on a rolling basis starting 5/15.

Academics. Special study options: Cooperative education, distance learning, double major, dual enrollment of high school students, ESL, honors, independent study, student-designed major, teacher certification program, weekend college. License preparation in dental hygiene, nursing, paramedic, real estate. **Credit/placement by examination:** AP, CLEP, IB, institutional tests. Maximum of 65 percent of total credit hours required for degree may be obtained by examination. **Support services:** GED preparation and test center, learning center, reduced course load, remedial instruction, study skills assistance, tutoring.

Majors. Business: Accounting technology, banking/financial services, business admin, customer service, e-commerce, management information systems, office management, operations, real estate. **Communications technology:** Photo/film/video. **Computer sciences:** Information systems, information technology, LAN/WAN management, programming. **Education:** Early childhood. **Health services:** Dental hygiene, electroencephalograph technology, EMT paramedic, health information technology, medical radiologic technology/radiation therapy, nursing (RN), office admin, respiratory therapy technology. **Liberal arts:** Arts/sciences. **Protective services:** Criminal justice, fire safety technology, forensics. **Visual/performing arts:** Commercial/advertising art.

Most popular majors. Business/marketing 12%, engineering/engineering technologies 6%, health sciences 22%, liberal arts 38%, security/protective services 6%.

Technology on campus. 1,550 workstations in library, computer center. Commuter students can connect to campus network. Online course registration, online library, helpline, repair service, wireless network available.

Student life. Freshman orientation: Available. Preregistration for classes offered. Held a few days prior to the first day of semester. Lasts 3-4 hours. **Activities:** Choral groups, drama, international student organizations, music ensembles, musical theater, student government, Phi Theta Kappa, association of nursing students, Certifiable club, Rotaract club, Student American Dental Hygiene Association, Students in Free Enterprise, theater arts club, student photographic society club, Seeds of Service, Hmong student association.

Athletics. NJCAA. **Intercollegiate:** Baseball M, basketball, volleyball W. **Team name:** Buccaneers.

Student services. Career counseling, services for economically disadvantaged, student employment services, financial aid counseling, minority student services, personal counseling, placement for graduates, veterans' counselor, women's services. **Physically disabled:** Services for visually, hearing impaired. **Transfer:** Pre-admission transcript evaluation for new students. Transfer adviser, college fairs on campus for students transferring to 4-year colleges.

Contact. E-mail: admissions@cvcc.edu
Phone: (828) 327-7000 Fax: (828) 327-7276
Laurie Wegner, Director of Admissions, Catawba Valley Community College, 2550 Highway 70 SE, Hickory, NC 28602

Central Carolina Community College
Sanford, North Carolina
www.cccc.edu
CB code: 5147

- Public 2-year community college
- Commuter campus in large town

General. Founded in 1958. Regionally accredited. **Enrollment:** 3,656 degree-seeking undergraduates; 1,321 non-degree-seeking students. **Degrees:** 534 associate awarded. **Location:** 45 miles from Raleigh. **Calendar:** Semester, limited summer session. **Full-time faculty:** 162 total; 9% have terminal degrees, 15% minority, 55% women. **Part-time faculty:** 358 total; 8% have terminal degrees, 20% minority, 60% women. **Class size:** 76% < 20, 24% 20-39, less than 1% 40-49.

Student profile. Among degree-seeking undergraduates, 29% enrolled in a transfer program, 71% enrolled in a vocational program, 782 enrolled as first-time, first-year students.

Part-time:	48%	Hispanic/Latino:	14%
Out-of-state:	2%	Native American:	1%
Women:	63%	Multi-racial, non-Hispanic:	2%
African American:	24%	25 or older:	38%
Asian American:	1%		

Transfer out. Colleges most students transferred to 2015: East Carolina University, NC State University, University of NC-Greensboro, University of NC-Chapel Hill, Appalachian State University.

Basis for selection. Open admission, but selective for some programs. Specific admission requirements for Basic Law Enforcement Training, Cosmetology Instructor, Dental Assisting, Dental Hygiene, Health Information Technology, Medical Assisting, Motorcycle Mechanics, Nursing, Paralegal Technology, and Veterinary Medical Technology. ACT/SAT scores may exempt student from placement tests. **Adult students:** Adult students pursuing a program that contains English and/or Math will need to submit appropriate placement test scores within five years. Exemption from placement testing may occur if appropriate credit is transferred. **Home schooled:** Transcript of courses and grades required. Must be registered with NC Department of Non-Public Education office; must submit documentation of the last 2 years of standardized testing, official home school transcript signed by the home school administrator showing official graduation date. **Learning Disabled:** Students should identify with the Special Populations Office in order to receive accommodations and services.

High school preparation. Recommended units include English 4, mathematics 4, social studies 1, history 1, science 4, foreign language 2, computer science 1 and visual/performing arts 1. Strong background in mathematics, biology, and chemistry required for the majors of Veterinary Medical Technology, Dental, and Nursing.

2015-2016 Annual costs. Tuition/fees: $2,268; $8,028 out-of-state. Per-credit charge: $72 in-state; $264 out-of-state. Books/supplies: $1,660.

2014-2015 Financial aid. **Need-based:** Need-based aid available for part-time students. Work-study available nights, weekends and for part-time students. **Non-need-based:** Scholarships awarded for academics, state residency.

Application procedures. **Admission:** No deadline. No application fee. Admission notification on a rolling basis. **Financial aid:** Priority date 6/1; no closing date. FAFSA required. Applicants notified on a rolling basis; must reply within 2 week(s) of notification.

Academics. **Special study options:** Accelerated study, cooperative education, distance learning, double major, dual enrollment of high school students, independent study, internships, liberal arts/career combination. License preparation in dental hygiene, nursing. **Credit/placement by examination:** AP, CLEP, institutional tests. AP, CLEP, and Dantes credit accepted for scores earned within the last 10 years. **Support services:** GED preparation, learning center, reduced course load, remedial instruction, study skills assistance, tutoring, writing center. Minority male mentoring program, TRIO - veterans upward bound, TRIO - student support services.

Majors. **Business:** Accounting, business admin, human resources. **Communications technology:** Radio/TV. **Computer sciences:** General, information systems, information technology, system admin. **Conservation:** General. **Education:** General, early childhood. **General:** Building construction. **Health services:** Athletic training, dental hygiene, health care admin, health information technology, massage therapy, medical assistant, nursing (RN), office assistant, veterinary technology/assistant. **Liberal arts:** Archival admin, arts/sciences. **Protective services:** Criminal justice, forensics. **Work/family studies:** Child care management.

Most popular majors. Business/marketing 12%, education 6%, engineering/engineering technologies 7%, health sciences 24%, liberal arts 30%, security/protective services 6%.

Technology on campus. Online course registration, online library, helpline, wireless network available.

Student life. **Freshman orientation:** Available. Preregistration for classes offered. Half-day orientation held prior to the beginning of the fall and spring semesters. **Activities:** Radio station, student government, TV station, Student nurses association, student ambassador program, veterinary medical technician student organization, social work club.

Athletics. NJCAA. **Intercollegiate:** Basketball, golf M, volleyball W. **Team name:** Cougars.

Student services. Career counseling, student employment services, financial aid counseling, on-campus daycare, personal counseling, placement for graduates, veterans' counselor. **Physically disabled:** Services for visually, speech, hearing impaired. **Transfer:** Transfer adviser, college fairs on campus for students transferring to 4-year colleges.

Contact. E-mail: admissions@cccc.edu
Phone: (919) 775-5401 ext. 7300
Toll-free number: (800) 682-8353 ext. 7300 Fax: (919) 718-7412
Jamee Stiffler, Dean of Admissions, Central Carolina Community College, 1105 Kelly Drive, Sanford, NC 27330

Central Piedmont Community College

Charlotte, North Carolina   **CB member**
www.cpcc.edu   **CB code: 5102**

▶ Public 2-year community college
▶ Commuter campus in very large city

General. Founded in 1963. Regionally accredited. **Enrollment:** 18,092 degree-seeking undergraduates; 1,503 non-degree-seeking students. **Degrees:** 1,878 associate awarded. **Location:** 247 miles from Atlanta. **Calendar:** Semester, extensive summer session. **Full-time faculty:** 382 total. **Part-time faculty:** 1,400 total.

Student profile. Among degree-seeking undergraduates, 3,201 enrolled as first-time, first-year students.

Part-time:	63%	Hispanic/Latino:	11%
Out-of-state:	4%	Multi-racial, non-Hispanic:	3%
Women:	55%	International:	6%
African American:	31%	25 or older:	37%
Asian American:	4%		

Transfer out. **Colleges most students transferred to 2015:** University of North Carolina at Charlotte.

Basis for selection. Open admission, but selective for some programs. Placement test scores used for admission to some programs with specific requirements.

High school preparation. Recommended units include English 4, mathematics 3, social studies 3 and science 3.

2015-2016 Annual costs. Tuition/fees: $2,326; $8,086 out-of-state. Per-credit charge: $72 in-state; $264 out-of-state. Books/supplies: $1,750. Personal expenses: $2,835.

2014-2015 Financial aid. **Need-based:** Need-based aid available for part-time students. Work-study available nights, weekends and for part-time students. **Non-need-based:** Scholarships awarded for academics, minority status.

Application procedures. **Admission:** No deadline. No application fee. Admission notification on a rolling basis. **Financial aid:** Priority date 4/1, closing date 6/1. FAFSA required. Applicants notified on a rolling basis.

Academics. **Special study options:** Cooperative education, cross-registration, distance learning, double major, dual enrollment of high school students, ESL, honors, independent study, internships, study abroad, weekend college. License preparation in dental hygiene, nursing, occupational therapy, paramedic. **Credit/placement by examination:** AP, CLEP, institutional tests. **Support services:** GED preparation and test center, learning center, reduced course load, remedial instruction, study skills assistance, tutoring, writing center.

Majors. **Business:** Accounting, accounting technology, administrative services, business admin, hospitality admin, hotel/motel/restaurant management, human resources, international, management information systems, marketing, office management, real estate, retailing, tourism/travel. **Communications technology:** Animation/special effects, graphic/printing, graphics. **Computer sciences:** Data processing, database management, information systems, information technology, LAN/WAN management, networking, programming, security, webmaster. **Education:** Early childhood. **Engineering:** Pre-engineering, robotics. **Foreign languages:** Sign language interpretation. **General:** Electrician, maintenance. **Health services:** Cardiovascular technology, clinical lab assistant, cytotechnology, dental hygiene, health information technology, medical assistant, mental health services, nursing (RN), physical therapy assistant, respiratory therapy technology, substance abuse counseling. **Liberal arts:** Arts/sciences. **Parks/recreation:** Facilities management. **Protective services:** Corrections, criminal justice, fire safety technology. **Visual/performing arts:** Commercial/advertising art, game design, graphic design, interior design. **Work/family studies:** Child care management.

Most popular majors. Business/marketing 8%, health sciences 15%, liberal arts 55%.

Technology on campus. 4,499 workstations in library, computer center, student center. Commuter students can connect to campus network. Online course registration, helpline, wireless network available.

Student life. **Freshman orientation:** Available. Preregistration for classes offered. **Activities:** Bands, campus ministries, choral groups, dance, drama, film society, international student organizations, literary magazine, music ensembles, musical theater, opera, radio station, student government, student newspaper, symphony orchestra, TV station, African Student Association, chess club, Phi Theta Kappa, Model United Nations, service club, Student Veterans Association, Peer Mentor Association.

Athletics. NJCAA. **Intramural:** Soccer.

Student services. Adult student services, chaplain/spiritual director, career counseling, student employment services, financial aid counseling, personal counseling, placement for graduates, veterans' counselor, women's services. **Physically disabled:** Services for visually, speech, hearing impaired. **Transfer:** Re-entry adviser, pre-admission transcript evaluation for new students. Transfer center, transfer adviser, college fairs on campus for students transferring to 4-year colleges.

Contact. E-mail: Student.Admissions@cpcc.edu
Phone: (704) 330-2722 Fax: (704) 330-6007
Greg Stanley, Associate Dean of Admissions & Registration, Central Piedmont Community College, PO Box 35009, Charlotte, NC 28235-5009

Two-Year Colleges

Chef's Academy
Morrisville, North Carolina
www.harrison.edu

▶ For-profit 2-year culinary school
▶ Commuter campus in large town

General. Regionally accredited; also accredited by ACICS. This campus is part of Harrison College, which has several campuses in Indiana and one in Ohio. **Enrollment:** 200 degree-seeking undergraduates. **Degrees:** 26 associate awarded. **Calendar:** Quarter, extensive summer session. **Full-time faculty:** 5 total. **Part-time faculty:** 9 total.

Basis for selection. Open admission, but selective for some programs. High school diploma required. **Adult students:** SAT/ACT scores not required.

2015-2016 Annual costs. Personal expenses: $2,400. **Additional information:** Tuition varies by program. Per-credit-hour charges; $100-$475; program fees (including books); $275-$975. All costs are subject to change.

Financial aid. Need-based: Work-study available nights, weekends and for part-time students.

Application procedures. Admission: No deadline. No application fee. Admission notification on a rolling basis.

Academics. Special study options: Distance learning, double major, internships, weekend college. **Credit/placement by examination:** AP, institutional tests. **Support services:** Learning center, reduced course load, study skills assistance, tutoring.

Technology on campus. Commuter students can connect to campus network. Online course registration, online library, helpline, wireless network available.

Student life. Freshman orientation: Mandatory. Preregistration for classes offered.

Student services. Adult student services, career counseling, student employment services, financial aid counseling, legal services, personal counseling, placement for graduates. **Transfer:** Re-entry adviser for new students.

Contact. E-mail: ashley.hanslits@thechefsacademy.com
Toll-free number: (800) 919-2500
Ashley Hanslits, Director of Admissions, Chef's Academy, 2001 Carrington Mill Boulevard, Morrisville, NC 27560

Cleveland Community College
Shelby, North Carolina   **CB member**
www.clevelandcc.edu   **CB code: 5140**

▶ Public 2-year community college
▶ Commuter campus in large town

General. Founded in 1965. Regionally accredited. **Enrollment:** 2,476 degree-seeking undergraduates. **Degrees:** 274 associate awarded. **Location:** 45 miles from Charlotte. **Calendar:** Semester, limited summer session. **Full-time faculty:** 76 total. **Part-time faculty:** 183 total.

Transfer out. Colleges most students transferred to 2015: Gardner-Webb University, University of North Carolina-Charlotte, Appalachian State University, Western Carolina University, North Carolina State University.

Basis for selection. Open admission, but selective for some programs. Special requirements for allied health programs. Interview required for nursing, radiography, surgical technology, and phlebotomy programs. **Home schooled:** Transcript of courses and grades required.

2015-2016 Annual costs. Tuition/fees: $2,252; $8,012 out-of-state. Per-credit charge: $72 in-state; $264 out-of-state. Books/supplies: $1,000. Personal expenses: $400.

Financial aid. Need-based: Need-based aid available for part-time students. Work-study available nights, weekends and for part-time students. **Non-need-based:** Scholarships awarded for academics.

Application procedures. Admission: No deadline. No application fee. Applicants notified immediately except for allied health applicants. **Financial aid:** Priority date 6/27; no closing date. FAFSA required. Applicants notified on a rolling basis starting 3/15.

Academics. Special study options: Accelerated study, cooperative education, cross-registration, distance learning, double major, dual enrollment of high school students, ESL, independent study, internships, liberal arts/career combination. Bachelor's degree programs available on campus. License preparation in nursing, paramedic. **Credit/placement by examination:** AP, CLEP, IB, institutional tests. Credit determined on individual basis. Students may not receive Credit By Exam for more than 20 percent of the total number of credits required for program. **Support services:** GED preparation and test center, learning center, reduced course load, remedial instruction, study skills assistance, tutoring.

Majors. Biology: Biotechnology. **Business:** Accounting, banking/financial services, business admin, entrepreneurial studies, marketing, office management, operations. **Communications technology:** Radio/TV. **Computer sciences:** Information systems, information technology, networking, security. **Education:** Early childhood, elementary. **Foreign languages:** Translation. **General:** Electrician. **Health services:** EMT paramedic, medical assistant, nursing (RN), office admin, radiologic technology/medical imaging. **Liberal arts:** Arts/sciences. **Protective services:** Criminal justice, fire safety technology.

Technology on campus. Online library, wireless network available.

Student life. Freshman orientation: Available. Preregistration for classes offered. **Activities:** Drama, student government, student newspaper, TV station, Beta Iota Phi of Phi Theta Kappa, Campus Crusade for Christ, Gamma Beta Phi Honor Society.

Student services. Adult student services, career counseling, student employment services, financial aid counseling, placement for graduates, veterans' counselor. **Physically disabled:** Services for visually, speech, hearing impaired. **Transfer:** Transfer adviser, college fairs on campus for students transferring to 4-year colleges.

Contact. E-mail: admissions@clevelandcc.edu
Phone: (704) 669-4103 Fax: (704) 669-4204
Emily Arey, Admissions Coordinator, Cleveland Community College, 137 South Post Road, Shelby, NC 28152-6224

Coastal Carolina Community College
Jacksonville, North Carolina
www.coastalcarolina.edu   **CB code: 5134**

▶ Public 2-year community college
▶ Commuter campus in small city

General. Founded in 1964. Regionally accredited. Off-campus classes available at Camp Lejeune Marine Corps Base and New River Marine Corps Air Station. **Enrollment:** 3,930 degree-seeking undergraduates; 256 non-degree-seeking students. **Degrees:** 697 associate awarded. **Location:** 100 miles from Raleigh. **Calendar:** Semester, extensive summer session. **Full-time faculty:** 134 total; 15% have terminal degrees, 16% minority, 54% women. **Part-time faculty:** 191 total; 14% have terminal degrees, 10% minority, 60% women. **Class size:** 41% < 20, 58% 20-39, less than 1% 40-49, less than 1% 50-99.

Student profile. Among degree-seeking undergraduates, 781 enrolled as first-time, first-year students.

Part-time:	47%	Women:	57%
Out-of-state:	31%	25 or older:	44%

Transfer out. Colleges most students transferred to 2015: University of North Carolina - Wilmington, East Carolina University, North Carolina State University.

Basis for selection. Open admission, but selective for some programs. Admission to limited enrollment programs based on examination. **Adult students:** SAT/ACT scores not required. **Home schooled:** Transcript of courses and grades required.

High school preparation. 20 units recommended. Recommended units include English 4, mathematics 3, social studies 2, history 1, science 3 (laboratory 1) and academic electives 6. Recommended units may vary by college.

2015-2016 Annual costs. Tuition/fees: $2,190; $7,950 out-of-state. Per-credit charge: $72 in-state; $264 out-of-state. Books/supplies: $1,688.

Financial aid. Need-based: Need-based aid available for part-time students. Work-study available nights, weekends and for part-time students. **Non-need-based:** Scholarships awarded for academics, state residency.

Application procedures. Admission: No deadline. No application fee. Admission notification on a rolling basis beginning on or about 2/15. **Financial aid:** Priority date 5/15; no closing date. FAFSA, institutional form required. Applicants notified on a rolling basis starting 5/15; must reply within 2 week(s) of notification.

Academics. Special study options: Cooperative education, distance learning, dual enrollment of high school students, independent study, internships, liberal arts/career combination. License preparation in dental hygiene, nursing, paramedic. **Credit/placement by examination:** AP, CLEP, IB, institutional tests. 30 credit hours maximum toward associate degree. **Support services:** GED preparation and test center, learning center, reduced course load, remedial instruction, tutoring.

Majors. Business: Accounting technology, administrative services, financial planning, hospitality admin, information resources management. **Computer sciences:** Information systems. **Education:** Early childhood. **Health services:** Clinical lab technology, dental hygiene, EMT paramedic, nursing (RN). **Liberal arts:** Arts/sciences. **Protective services:** Fire safety technology, police science.

Most popular majors. Health sciences 19%, liberal arts 61%, security/protective services 6%.

Technology on campus. 720 workstations in library, computer center, student center. Commuter students can connect to campus network. Online library, helpline available.

Student life. Freshman orientation: Available. Preregistration for classes offered. Orientation sessions available throughout the month prior to start of each term. **Activities:** Concert band, choral groups, drama, music ensembles, student government, Phi Theta Kappa, Star of Life, Association of Nursing Students, social science club, Practical Nursing Students, fine arts society, Extreme Science.

Student services. Adult student services, alcohol/substance abuse counseling, career counseling, services for economically disadvantaged, student employment services, financial aid counseling, minority student services, personal counseling, placement for graduates, veterans' counselor. **Physically disabled:** Services for visually, speech, hearing impaired. **Transfer:** Transfer adviser, college fairs on campus for students transferring to 4-year colleges.

Contact. E-mail: admissions@coastalcarolina.edu
Phone: (910) 938-6332 Fax: (910) 455-2767
Don Herring, Division Chair for Admissions, Coastal Carolina Community College, 444 Western Boulevard, Jacksonville, NC 28546-6816

College of the Albemarle
Elizabeth City, North Carolina
www.albemarle.edu   CB code: 5133

▶ Public 2-year branch campus and community college
▶ Commuter campus in large town

General. Founded in 1960. Regionally accredited. The college has campuses in Elizabeth City, Manteo/Roanoke Island (Dare County), Edenton (Chowan County) with a center Currituck County for Aviation Technologies. **Enrollment:** 1,473 degree-seeking undergraduates; 579 non-degree-seeking students. **Degrees:** 270 associate awarded. **Location:** 45 miles from Norfolk, Virginia. **Calendar:** Semester, limited summer session. **Full-time faculty:** 79 total. **Part-time faculty:** 184 total. **Special facilities:** Community center auditorium.

Student profile. Among degree-seeking undergraduates, 42% enrolled in a transfer program, 34% enrolled in a vocational program, 411 enrolled as first-time, first-year students.

| Part-time: | 55% | Women: | 64% |
| Out-of-state: | 3% | 25 or older: | 40% |

Transfer out. Colleges most students transferred to 2015: Elizabeth City State University, East Carolina University, North Carolina State University, UNC-Chapel Hill, UNC-Wilmington.

Basis for selection. Open admission, but selective for some programs. All degree-seeking students required to take placement test. Students may waive placement test if scores for SAT or ACT are acceptable. Limited enrollment programs have additional admissions criteria. Admission limited to fall semester for associate degree in nursing, practical nursing, associate degree nursing, electrical/electronics technology, AC/HR, machining technology, surgical technology, medical assisting, and phlebotomy. New students admitted to cosmetology program as spaces become available. Interview required for allied health programs.

High school preparation. Recommended units include English 4, mathematics 3, social studies 3, history 3, science 3 and academic electives 6.

2015-2016 Annual costs. Tuition/fees: $2,287; $8,047 out-of-state. Per-credit charge: $72 in-state; $264 out-of-state. Books/supplies: $1,000.

Financial aid. Need-based: Need-based aid available for part-time students. Work-study available nights, weekends and for part-time students. **Non-need-based:** Scholarships awarded for academics, art, leadership, minority status, music/drama, state residency. **Additional information:** Separate application must be submitted for COA Private Scholarships.

Application procedures. Admission: No deadline. No application fee. Admission notification on a rolling basis. Application deadline for allied health January 15 prior to fall semester. **Financial aid:** Priority date 3/15, closing date 6/1. FAFSA required. Applicants notified on a rolling basis starting 5/1; must reply within 2 week(s) of notification.

Academics. Special study options: Cooperative education, distance learning, double major, dual enrollment of high school students, ESL, honors, independent study, internships, liberal arts/career combination. Agreement with Elizabeth City State University to offer the first 2 years of Elementary Education. License preparation in nursing, real estate. **Credit/placement by examination:** AP, CLEP, institutional tests. 30 credit hours maximum toward associate degree. Credit by examination not granted until examinee has enrolled at COA and passed 12 credit hours with 2.0 or better grade point average. **Support services:** GED preparation and test center, learning center, reduced course load, remedial instruction, study skills assistance, tutoring, writing center.

Majors. Architecture: Technology. **Business:** Administrative services, business admin, office/clerical. **Computer sciences:** General, applications programming, information systems, networking, programming. **Education:** General, early childhood. **Engineering:** Computer. **Health services:** Clinical lab science, medical assistant, medical secretary, nursing (RN), office admin. **Liberal arts:** Arts/sciences. **Protective services:** Law enforcement admin. **Visual/performing arts:** Art, dramatic, music.

Technology on campus. 553 workstations in library, computer center, student center. Commuter students can connect to campus network. Online course registration, online library, helpline, wireless network available.

Student life. Freshman orientation: Mandatory. Preregistration for classes offered. Monthly information sessions held for all COA programs. **Activities:** Bands, drama, literary magazine, musical theater, student government, Phi Theta Kappa, environmental club, literacy round table, nursing club, SADD, Spanish club.

Athletics. Intramural: Archery, badminton, baseball, basketball, bowling, football (non-tackle), golf, racquetball, sailing, soccer, softball, swimming, tennis, volleyball, weight lifting M. **Team name:** Dolphins.

Student services. Adult student services, career counseling, services for economically disadvantaged, student employment services, financial aid counseling, personal counseling, placement for graduates, veterans' counselor. **Physically disabled:** Services for visually, speech, hearing impaired. **Transfer:** Pre-admission transcript evaluation for new students. College fairs on campus for students transferring to 4-year colleges.

Contact. Phone: (252) 335-0821 ext. 2290 Fax: (252) 335-2011
Angie Godfrey-Dawson, Director, Admissions and Financial Aid, College of the Albemarle, 1208 North Road Street, Elizabeth City, NC 27909

Craven Community College
New Bern, North Carolina
www.cravencc.edu   CB code: 5148

▶ Public 2-year community college
▶ Commuter campus in large town

General. Founded in 1965. Campuses in New Bern and Havelock. **Enrollment:** 2,840 degree-seeking undergraduates. **Degrees:** 435 associate awarded. **Location:** 100 miles from Raleigh, 45 miles from Greenville. **Calendar:** Semester, limited summer session. **Full-time faculty:** 63 total. **Part-time faculty:** 127 total. **Special facilities:** Nursing simulation laboratory, Institute of Aeronautical Technology, advanced manufacturing, robotics.

Transfer out. Colleges most students transferred to 2015: East Carolina University, University of North Carolina: Wilmington, North Carolina State University.

Basis for selection. Open admission, but selective for some programs. Open admission policy except for Nursing, Practical Nursing, Health Information Technology, Pharmacy Technology, and Physical Therapist Assistant programs.

2015-2016 Annual costs. Tuition/fees: $2,326; $8,086 out-of-state. Per-credit charge: $72 in-state; $264 out-of-state. Books/supplies: $1,300. Personal expenses: $3,910.

Financial aid. Need-based: Need-based aid available for part-time students. Work-study available nights, weekends and for part-time students.

Application procedures. Admission: No deadline. No application fee. Admission notification on a rolling basis. **Financial aid:** Closing date 6/1. FAFSA required. Applicants notified on a rolling basis.

Academics. Special study options: Cooperative education, distance learning, dual enrollment of high school students, ESL, independent study, teacher certification program. Bachelor's degree programs available on campus. License preparation in aviation, nursing, paramedic, physical therapy, real estate. **Credit/placement by examination:** AP, CLEP, institutional tests. **Support services:** GED preparation and test center, learning center, reduced course load, remedial instruction, study skills assistance, tutoring, writing center.

Majors. Business: Accounting, business admin, entrepreneurial studies, operations. **Computer sciences:** Information technology. **Education:** Early childhood, elementary. **Engineering:** Pre-engineering. **Health services:** Health information technology, medical assistant, nursing (RN), office admin, physical therapy assistant. **Liberal arts:** Arts/sciences. **Protective services:** Criminal justice.

Technology on campus. Online library, helpline, wireless network available.

Student life. Freshman orientation: Mandatory. Preregistration for classes offered. **Activities:** Choral groups, radio station, student government.

Athletics. Team name: Panthers.

Student services. Career counseling, financial aid counseling, personal counseling, veterans' counselor. **Transfer:** Pre-admission transcript evaluation for new students. Transfer center, college fairs on campus for students transferring to 4-year colleges.

Contact. Phone: (252) 638-7200 Fax: (252) 638-4649
Zomar Peter, Executive Director of Enrollment & Retention, Craven Community College, 800 College Court, New Bern, NC 28562

Davidson County Community College
Lexington, North Carolina
www.davidsonccc.edu
CB code: 5170

- Public 2-year community college
- Commuter campus in large town

General. Founded in 1958. Regionally accredited. Davie Campus in Mocksville has 3 buildings and an emergency services training facility on 45 acres. **Enrollment:** 3,521 degree-seeking undergraduates. **Degrees:** 600 associate awarded. **Location:** 30 miles from Greensboro. **Calendar:** Semester, limited summer session. **Full-time faculty:** 97 total. **Part-time faculty:** 133 total. **Class size:** 59% < 20, 39% 20-39, less than 1% 40-49, less than 1% 50-99.

Student profile.

Out-of-state:	1%	**25 or older:**	46%

Transfer out. Colleges most students transferred to 2015: University of North Carolina-Greensboro, University of North Carolina-Charlotte, High Point University, Winston-Salem State University, Catawba College.

Basis for selection. Open admission, but selective for some programs. Admission to the nursing program, certain other allied health programs, and selected programs of study are based on test scores, grades, and other factors which vary by program.

High school preparation. Recommended units include English 4, mathematics 3, social studies 2, history 2, science 3 and foreign language 2.

2015-2016 Annual costs. Tuition/fees: $2,312; $8,072 out-of-state. Per-credit charge: $72 in-state; $264 out-of-state. Books/supplies: $1,600. Personal expenses: $1,800.

Financial aid. Need-based: Need-based aid available for part-time students. Work-study available nights, weekends and for part-time students. **Non-need-based:** Scholarships awarded for academics, leadership.

Application procedures. Admission: Priority date 8/1; no deadline. No application fee. Admission notification on a rolling basis. Nursing program deadline 1/31, Allied Health program deadlines 3/15 to 5/15. **Financial aid:** Priority date 6/30; no closing date. FAFSA, institutional form required. Applicants notified on a rolling basis starting 7/31; must reply within 2 week(s) of notification.

Academics. Special study options: Distance learning, dual enrollment of high school students, ESL, independent study. License preparation in nursing, paramedic, real estate. **Credit/placement by examination:** AP, CLEP, institutional tests. Students must complete 25% of hours required for graduation in residence. **Support services:** GED preparation and test center, learning center, pre-admission summer program, reduced course load, remedial instruction, study skills assistance, tutoring, writing center.

Majors. Biology: Zoology. **Business:** Accounting, business admin, human resources. **Computer sciences:** Information technology, networking, programming. **Education:** Early childhood. **Health services:** Clinical lab technology, EMT paramedic, health information technology, medical assistant, nursing (RN). **Liberal arts:** Arts/sciences. **Protective services:** Criminal justice, fire safety technology.

Technology on campus. 450 workstations in library, computer center. Commuter students can connect to campus network. Helpline available.

Student life. Freshman orientation: Mandatory. Preregistration for classes offered. **Activities:** Literary magazine, student government, criminal justice club, association of nursing students, Phi Theta Kappa, Rotaract, spanish club, cosmetology club, Christian organization, computer system technology association, future educators club.

Athletics. NJCAA. **Intercollegiate:** Basketball M. **Team name:** Storm.

Student services. Career counseling, student employment services, financial aid counseling, on-campus daycare, personal counseling, placement for graduates, veterans' counselor. **Physically disabled:** Services for visually, speech, hearing impaired. **Transfer:** Pre-admission transcript evaluation for new students. Transfer adviser, college fairs on campus for students transferring to 4-year colleges.

Contact. E-mail: admissions@davidsonccc.edu
Phone: (336) 249-8186 ext. 6731 Fax: (336) 224-0240
Lori Blevins, Director of Admissions, Davidson County Community College, P O Box 1287, Lexington, NC 27293-1287

Durham Technical Community College
Durham, North Carolina
www.durhamtech.edu
CB code: 5172

- Public 2-year community and technical college
- Commuter campus in small city

General. Founded in 1958. Regionally accredited. Most programs are structured to begin in fall and continue for 5 or 6 consecutive semesters. Satellite sites in northern Durham and Orange Counties. **Enrollment:** 5,120 degree-seeking undergraduates. **Degrees:** 450 associate awarded. **Location:** 25 miles from Raleigh, 50 miles from Greensboro. **Calendar:** Semester, limited summer session. **Full-time faculty:** 172 total. **Part-time faculty:** 640 total.

Transfer out. Colleges most students transferred to 2015: University of North Carolina - Chapel Hill, North Carolina Central University, North Carolina State University.

Basis for selection. Open admission, but selective for some programs. Placement testing required. ASSET, COMPASS, ACCUPLACER, ACT/SAT scores are used. Admission to some allied health programs based on placement test and completion of prerequisite courses. **Home schooled:** Documentation of state recognition of home school required.

High school preparation. College-preparatory program required. Algebra, chemistry, and biology required for allied health programs. Algebra and science courses recommended for most associate degree programs.

2015-2016 Annual costs. Tuition/fees: $2,252; $8,012 out-of-state. Per-credit charge: $72 in-state; $264 out-of-state. Books/supplies: $1,300. Personal expenses: $562.

2015-2016 Financial aid. Need-based: 58% of total undergraduate aid awarded as scholarships/grants, 42% as loans/jobs. Need-based aid available

for part-time students. Work-study available nights, weekends and for part-time students. **Non-need-based:** Scholarships awarded for academics, minority status, state residency. **Additional information:** Special funds available to single parents for tuition, fees, books, supplies and child care expenses.

Application procedures. Admission: Priority date 4/15; deadline 8/11 (receipt date). No application fee. Application must be submitted online. Admission notification on a rolling basis. **Financial aid:** FAFSA required. Applicants notified on a rolling basis starting 1/31; must reply within 3 week(s) of notification.

Academics. Special study options: Distance learning, dual enrollment of high school students, ESL, honors, student-designed major, weekend college. License preparation in nursing, occupational therapy, paramedic, real estate. **Credit/placement by examination:** AP, CLEP, institutional tests. Maximum of 10% of total curriculum hours of credit by examination may be counted toward degree. **Support services:** GED preparation and test center, learning center, remedial instruction, study skills assistance, tutoring.

Majors. Architecture: Technology. **Biology:** Biotechnology. **Business:** Accounting, administrative services, business admin, operations. **Computer sciences:** Applications programming, data processing, information technology, networking, programming, security, systems analysis. **Education:** Early childhood, teacher assistance. **Engineering:** Electrical. **Health services:** Dental lab technology, environmental health, health information management, medical secretary, nursing (RN), occupational health, occupational therapy assistant, office admin, optician, respiratory therapy assistant, respiratory therapy technology. **Liberal arts:** Arts/sciences.

Technology on campus. Commuter students can connect to campus network. Online course registration, online library, wireless network available.

Student life. Freshman orientation: Mandatory. Preregistration for classes offered. **Activities:** Drama, international student organizations, literary magazine, student government.

Student services. Career counseling, services for economically disadvantaged, financial aid counseling, minority student services, personal counseling, veterans' counselor. **Physically disabled:** Services for visually, speech, hearing impaired. **Transfer:** Pre-admission transcript evaluation for new students. Transfer center, college fairs on campus for students transferring to 4-year colleges.

Contact. E-mail: admissions@durhamtech.edu
Phone: (919) 536-7202 Fax: (919) 686-3669
Leigh Forell, Director of Admissions, Durham Technical Community College, 1637 Lawson Street, Durham, NC 27703

Edgecombe Community College
Tarboro, North Carolina — **CB member**
www.edgecombe.edu — **CB code: 5199**

- Public 2-year community college
- Commuter campus in large town

General. Founded in 1967. Regionally accredited. Branch campus in Rocky Mount. **Enrollment:** 2,002 degree-seeking undergraduates. **Degrees:** 301 associate awarded. **Location:** 75 miles from Raleigh. **Calendar:** Semester, limited summer session. **Full-time faculty:** 85 total; 11% have terminal degrees, 45% minority. **Part-time faculty:** 125 total; 6% have terminal degrees, 31% minority. **Class size:** 77% < 20, 20% 20-39, 2% 40-49, less than 1% 50-99. **Special facilities:** Wildlife preserve.

Student profile.

Out-of-state:	1% **25 or older:**	46%

Transfer out. Colleges most students transferred to 2015: East Carolina University, Pitt Community College, NC Wesleyan College, North Carolina Agricultural and Technical State University.

Basis for selection. Open admission, but selective for some programs. Special requirements for allied health programs and networking technology. TEAS Nursing Test required for nursing applicants.

2015-2016 Annual costs. Tuition/fees: $2,253; $8,053 out-of-state. Per-credit charge: $75 in-state; $265 out-of-state. Books/supplies: $1,500. Personal expenses: $2,000.

Financial aid. All financial aid based on need. Need-based aid available for part-time students. Work-study available nights, weekends and for part-time students.

Application procedures. Admission: No deadline. No application fee. Admission notification on a rolling basis. **Financial aid:** No deadline. FAFSA, institutional form required. Applicants notified on a rolling basis starting 8/15; must reply within 3 week(s) of notification.

Academics. Special study options: Cooperative education, distance learning, double major, dual enrollment of high school students, ESL, independent study. License preparation in nursing, radiology. **Credit/placement by examination:** AP, CLEP, institutional tests. 24 credit hours maximum toward associate degree. **Support services:** GED preparation and test center, learning center, reduced course load, remedial instruction, study skills assistance, tutoring.

Majors. Business: Accounting, administrative services, business admin. **Computer sciences:** General, information systems, networking. **Education:** Early childhood, teacher assistance. **Engineering:** Manufacturing. **Health services:** Health information technology, medical assistant, medical radiologic technology/radiation therapy, nursing (RN), respiratory therapy technology. **Liberal arts:** Arts/sciences. **Protective services:** Criminal justice. **Work/family studies:** Child care management.

Most popular majors. Business/marketing 13%, education 14%, health sciences 48%, liberal arts 13%.

Technology on campus. 120 workstations in library, computer center. Online library, helpline available.

Student life. Activities: Drama, student government.

Athletics. Team name: Eagles.

Student services. Alcohol/substance abuse counseling, career counseling, student employment services, financial aid counseling, minority student services, personal counseling, placement for graduates, veterans' counselor. **Physically disabled:** Services for visually, hearing impaired. **Transfer:** Pre-admission transcript evaluation for new students. Transfer adviser, college fairs on campus for students transferring to 4-year colleges.

Contact. Phone: (252) 823-5166 ext. 254 Fax: (252) 823-6817
Tony Rook, Dean of Enrollment, Edgecombe Community College, 2009 West Wilson Street, Tarboro, NC 27886

Fayetteville Technical Community College
Fayetteville, North Carolina — **CB member**
www.faytechcc.edu — **CB code: 5208**

- Public 2-year community and technical college
- Commuter campus in large city

General. Founded in 1961. Regionally accredited. **Enrollment:** 9,645 degree-seeking undergraduates; 1,899 non-degree-seeking students. **Degrees:** 1,580 associate awarded. **Location:** 60 miles from Raleigh, 20 miles from Lumberton. **Calendar:** Semester, limited summer session. **Full-time faculty:** 274 total; 12% have terminal degrees, 27% minority, 57% women. **Part-time faculty:** 282 total; 31% minority, 64% women. **Class size:** 60% < 20, 40% 20-39. **Special facilities:** Center for applied technology, virtual college center, horticulture educational center, Spring Lake campus, collision repair and refinishing (ICAR) facility. **Partnerships:** Formal partnerships with ITCAP, FTCC Special Warfare Center, Enterprise Rent-A-Car, NC Cumberland County Commissioners, Cumberland County Workforce Development Center, Career and College Promise.

Student profile. Among degree-seeking undergraduates, 33% enrolled in a transfer program, 50% enrolled in a vocational program, .3% already have a bachelor's degree or higher, 1,865 enrolled as first-time, first-year students, 972 transferred in from other institutions.

Part-time:	54%	**Women:**	60%
Out-of-state:	22%	**25 or older:**	59%

Transfer out. Colleges most students transferred to 2015: Fayetteville State University, University of North Carolina at Pembroke, Norwich University, University of North Carolina at Chapel Hill, Campbell University.

Basis for selection. Open admission, but selective for some programs. Admission of health applicants based upon transcripts, academic average, interview, institutional assessment of reading, writing, and math, or credit for prior learning. Group interview required for allied health programs. **Home schooled:** Transcript of courses and grades required. Must submit a copy of the home school's approved registration from the state in which they are registered and an official transcript including the graduation date and documentation of completion of competency. **Learning Disabled:** Documentation of disability required if applicant desires any academic accommodations.

High school preparation. Engineering and College Transfer programs require the successful completion of two high school algebra courses or their college equivalent. Allied health programs require the successful completion of up to two high school algebra courses, one biology course, one chemistry course, or their college equivalent.

2015-2016 Annual costs. Tuition/fees: $2,370; $8,130 out-of-state. Per-credit charge: $76 in-state; $268 out-of-state. Books/supplies: $1,750. Personal expenses: $270.

2014-2015 Financial aid. Need-based: 966 full-time freshmen applied for aid; 807 deemed to have need; 780 received aid. Average need met was 100%. Average scholarship/grant was $1,352; average loan $2,811. 63% of total undergraduate aid awarded as scholarships/grants, 37% as loans/jobs. Need-based aid available for part-time students. Work-study available nights, weekends and for part-time students.

Application procedures. Admission: No deadline. No application fee. Application must be submitted online. Admission notification on a rolling basis. Deadline for Allied Health program applicants is January 30. Applicants admitted into these programs must reply immediately upon notification. High school students enroll only on a part-time basis while simultaneously attending high school. **Financial aid:** No deadline. FAFSA required. Applicants notified on a rolling basis starting 4/1.

Academics. FTCC offers the only funeral services curriculum in the North Carolina Community College System. Military students can receive credit for prior learning and military occupational specialty credit toward an Associate in General Education. **Special study options:** Accelerated study, combined bachelor's/graduate degree, cooperative education, distance learning, double major, dual enrollment of high school students, ESL, independent study, liberal arts/career combination, student-designed major, weekend college. Work-based learning. License preparation in dental hygiene, nursing, paramedic, physical therapy, radiology. **Credit/placement by examination:** AP, CLEP, IB, institutional tests. 49 credit hours maximum toward associate degree. Up to 49 credit hours allowed, however, students must complete at least 25% of program requirements at Fayetteville Technical Community College. **Support services:** GED preparation and test center, learning center, reduced course load, remedial instruction, study skills assistance, tutoring, writing center.

Majors. Business: Accounting, banking/financial services, business admin, hotel/motel/restaurant management, human resources, logistics, marketing, office management, operations. **Computer sciences:** Information systems, information technology, networking, programming, security. **Education:** Early childhood, elementary. **General:** Electrician. **Health services:** Dental hygiene, EMT paramedic, health information technology, nuclear medical technology, nursing (RN), office admin, pharmacy assistant, physical therapy assistant, radiologic technology/medical imaging, respiratory therapy technology, speech-language pathology assistant, surgical technology. **Human services:** General. **Liberal arts:** Arts/sciences. **Protective services:** Criminal justice, disaster management, fire safety technology, forensics. **Visual/performing arts:** Commercial/advertising art, game design.

Most popular majors. Business/marketing 10%, health sciences 15%, liberal arts 49%, security/protective services 6%.

Technology on campus. 1,450 workstations in library, computer center, student center. Commuter students can connect to campus network. Online course registration, online library, helpline, wireless network available.

Student life. Freshman orientation: Available. Preregistration for classes offered. Two-hour program held by curriculum divisions before the beginning of each major term (Fall and Spring). Online orientation is also available. **Activities:** Choral groups, drama, international student organizations, student government, TV station, African-American Heritage Club, Spanish Club, Parents for Higher Education, Students Against Destructive Decisions, Intercultural Club, Student Veterans Club of America.

Athletics. Intramural: Badminton, basketball, bowling, football (non-tackle), soccer, tennis. **Team name:** Trojan.

Student services. Alcohol/substance abuse counseling, career counseling, student employment services, financial aid counseling, health services, minority student services, on-campus daycare, personal counseling, placement for graduates, veterans' counselor. **Physically disabled:** Services for visually, speech, hearing impaired. **Transfer:** Pre-admission transcript evaluation for new students. Transfer adviser, college fairs on campus for students transferring to 4-year colleges.

Contact. E-mail: Admissions@faytechcc.edu
Phone: (910) 678-8473 Fax: (910) 678-0085
Louanna Castleman, Director of Admissions, Fayetteville Technical Community College, 2201 Hull Road, Fayetteville, NC 28303-0236

Forsyth Technical Community College
Winston-Salem, North Carolina **CB member**
www.forsythtech.edu **CB code: 5234**

◆ Public 2-year community and technical college
◆ Commuter campus in small city

General. Founded in 1964. Regionally accredited. **Enrollment:** 7,482 degree-seeking undergraduates; 914 non-degree-seeking students. **Degrees:** 947 associate awarded. **Location:** 32 miles from Greensboro, 85 miles from Charlotte. **Calendar:** Semester, extensive summer session. **Full-time faculty:** 250 total; 13% have terminal degrees, 21% minority, 58% women. **Part-time faculty:** 808 total; 7% have terminal degrees, 31% minority, 60% women. **Class size:** 75% < 20, 24% 20-39, less than 1% 40-49, less than 1% 50-99.

Student profile. Among degree-seeking undergraduates, 1,256 enrolled as first-time, first-year students.

Part-time:	57%	Native American:	2%
Out-of-state:	1%	Native Hawaiian/Pacific islander:	2%
Women:	59%	Multi-racial, non-Hispanic:	1%
African American:	57%	International:	10%
Hispanic/Latino:	27%	25 or older:	43%

Transfer out. Colleges most students transferred to 2015: Winston-Salem State University, Gardner-Webb University, High Point University, Appalachian State University, North Carolina A&T State University.

Basis for selection. Open admission, but selective for some programs. Admission to health program based on school record and test scores. Health information session attendance required. SAT or ACT used for admission to health and developmental programs and for placement in other programs. **Home schooled:** NCDPI registration information or similar information from the respective state's department of education authorizing the home school to provide instruction.

High school preparation. College-preparatory program recommended. Algebra I required for allied health and engineering programs. Biology and chemistry required for allied health programs.

2015-2016 Annual costs. Tuition/fees: $2,326; $8,086 out-of-state. Per-credit charge: $72 in-state; $264 out-of-state. Books/supplies: $1,210.

2014-2015 Financial aid. Need-based: 86% of total undergraduate aid awarded as scholarships/grants, 14% as loans/jobs. Need-based aid available for part-time students. Work-study available nights, weekends and for part-time students. **Non-need-based:** Scholarships awarded for academics, alumni affiliation, leadership, state residency. **Additional information:** Apply for aid as close to January 1 as possible for best consideration.

Application procedures. Admission: No deadline. No application fee. Admission notification on a rolling basis. **Financial aid:** Priority date 6/1, closing date 6/1. FAFSA required. Applicants notified on a rolling basis starting 5/1.

Academics. Special study options: Cooperative education, distance learning, double major, dual enrollment of high school students, ESL, study abroad, weekend college. License preparation in dental hygiene, nursing, radiology, real estate. **Credit/placement by examination:** AP, CLEP, institutional tests. **Support services:** GED preparation and test center, learning center, pre-admission summer program, reduced course load, remedial instruction, study skills assistance, tutoring, writing center.

Majors. Biology: Biophysics. **Business:** Accounting, banking/financial services, business admin, executive assistant, international, logistics, office/clerical. **Computer sciences:** General, applications programming, information technology, networking. **Education:** Early childhood, science, special ed. **Health services:** Cardiovascular technology, dental hygiene, EMT paramedic, licensed practical nurse, massage therapy, medical assistant, medical radiologic technology/radiation therapy, nuclear medical technology, nursing (RN), office admin, radiologic technology/medical imaging, respiratory therapy technology, sonography. **Liberal arts:** Arts/sciences. **Protective services:** Criminal justice, fire safety technology, forensics. **Visual/performing arts:** Graphic design, interior design.

Most popular majors. Business/marketing 8%, health sciences 29%, liberal arts 37%.

Technology on campus. 400 workstations in library, computer center. Online library, helpline, wireless network available.

Student life. Freshman orientation: Available. Preregistration for classes offered. **Activities:** Drama, international student organizations, literary magazine, radio station, student government, student newspaper, Circle-K, Afro-American Society, minority male mentoring program, women's center, veterans' programs.

Athletics. Intercollegiate: Basketball M, softball. **Intramural:** Basketball, bowling, golf, softball, volleyball. **Team name:** Tech Tigers.

Student services. Adult student services, alcohol/substance abuse counseling, career counseling, services for economically disadvantaged, student employment services, financial aid counseling, health services, minority student services, personal counseling, placement for graduates, veterans' counselor, women's services. **Physically disabled:** Services for visually, speech, hearing impaired. **Transfer:** Transfer adviser, college fairs on campus for students transferring to 4-year colleges.

Contact. E-mail: admissions@forsythtech.edu
Phone: (336) 734-7253 Fax: (336) 734-7291
Jean Groome, Dean of Enrollment Management, Forsyth Technical
Community College, 2100 Silas Creek Parkway, Winston-Salem, NC
27103

Gaston College
Dallas, North Carolina
www.gaston.edu   CB code: 5262

▶ Public 2-year community college
▶ Commuter campus in small town

General. Founded in 1963. Regionally accredited. Branch campus at Lincolnton. **Enrollment:** 5,603 degree-seeking undergraduates. **Degrees:** 717 associate awarded. **Location:** 25 miles from Charlotte. **Calendar:** Semester, limited summer session. **Full-time faculty:** 161 total. **Part-time faculty:** 410 total.

Student profile.

Out-of-state: 1%   25 or older: 54%

Basis for selection. Open admission, but selective for some programs. Admission to health services programs, including nursing, based on ACT scores and interview. Basic literacy must be demonstrated, after admission, in order to take certain courses. Interview recommended for emergency medical technician, medical assistant, nursing programs; audition recommended for music programs; portfolio recommended for art programs.

2015-2016 Annual costs. Tuition/fees: $2,577; $8,722 out-of-state. Books/supplies: $1,200. Personal expenses: $1,504.

Financial aid. Need-based: Work-study available nights, weekends and for part-time students. **Non-need-based:** Scholarships awarded for academics, state residency. **Additional information:** Grants/scholarships available for women pursuing nontraditional roles.

Application procedures. Admission: No deadline. No application fee. Admission notification on a rolling basis. **Financial aid:** Priority date 3/15, closing date 6/30. FAFSA, institutional form required. Applicants notified on a rolling basis.

Academics. Special study options: Cooperative education, cross-registration, distance learning, double major, dual enrollment of high school students, ESL, independent study, internships, weekend college. **Credit/placement by examination:** AP, CLEP, institutional tests. 18 credit hours maximum toward associate degree. **Support services:** GED preparation and test center, learning center, reduced course load, remedial instruction, study skills assistance, tutoring, writing center.

Majors. Architecture: Technology. **Business:** Accounting, administrative services, business admin. **Communications:** Broadcast journalism. **Computer sciences:** Applications programming, information technology, programming. **Education:** Early childhood. **Health services:** Dietetic technician, EMT paramedic, massage therapy, medical assistant, medical secretary, nursing (RN), office admin, veterinary technology/assistant. **Human services:** Social work. **Liberal arts:** Arts/sciences. **Protective services:** Fire safety technology.

Technology on campus. 233 workstations in library, computer center.

Student life. Freshman orientation: Available. Preregistration for classes offered. **Activities:** Literary magazine, music ensembles, radio station, student government.

Student services. Adult student services, career counseling, student employment services, financial aid counseling, on-campus daycare, placement for graduates, veterans' counselor. **Physically disabled:** Services for visually, speech, hearing impaired. **Transfer:** Transfer adviser, college fairs on campus for students transferring to 4-year colleges.

Contact. E-mail: wray.michelle@gaston.edu
Phone: (704) 922-6214 Fax: (704) 922-2344
Terry Bracier, Director of Admissions/Enrollment Management, Gaston
College, 201 Highway 321 South, Dallas, NC 28034-1499

Guilford Technical Community College
Jamestown, North Carolina
www.gtcc.edu   CB code: 5275

▶ Public 2-year community and technical college
▶ Commuter campus in large city

General. Founded in 1958. Regionally accredited. Campuses in Greensboro and High Point. **Enrollment:** 11,292 degree-seeking undergraduates; 232 non-degree-seeking students. **Degrees:** 1,334 associate awarded. **Location:** 2 miles from Greensboro, 5 miles from High Point. **Calendar:** Semester, limited summer session. **Full-time faculty:** 365 total; 51% have terminal degrees, 17% minority, 51% women. **Part-time faculty:** 312 total; 28% have terminal degrees, 24% minority, 58% women. **Special facilities:** Observatory.

Student profile. Among degree-seeking undergraduates, 63% enrolled in a transfer program, 39% enrolled in a vocational program, 1,849 enrolled as first-time, first-year students, 1,849 transferred in from other institutions.

Part-time:	54%	Hispanic/Latino:	8%
Out-of-state:	1%	Native American:	1%
Women:	56%	Multi-racial, non-Hispanic:	2%
African American:	39%	25 or older:	50%
Asian American:	5%		

Transfer out. Colleges most students transferred to 2015: University of North Carolina-Greensboro, University of North Carolina-Charlotte, North Carolina A&T, University of North Carolina-Wilmington, and Winston-Salem State University.

Basis for selection. Open admission, but selective for some programs. Admission to allied health programs is highly competitive. Each program has specific requirements that must be met to be considered for admission. **Home schooled:** Proof of NC home-school registry from the NC Department of Non-Public Instruction. **Learning Disabled:** Contact Disability Access Services office.

High school preparation. Allied health programs have specific course requirements that vary according to program.

2015-2016 Annual costs. Tuition/fees: $2,251; $8,011 out-of-state. Per-credit charge: $72 in-state; $264 out-of-state. Books/supplies: $1,208. Personal expenses: $8,316.

Financial aid. Need-based: Need-based aid available for part-time students. Work-study available nights, weekends and for part-time students. **Non-need-based:** Scholarships awarded for academics, athletics, leadership, minority status, state residency.

Application procedures. Admission: No deadline. No application fee. Admission notification on a rolling basis. Applicants for limited enrollment programs (nursing, aviation maintenance/mechanic, dental hygiene, dental assistant, medical assistant, Pharmacy Technology, Physical Therapist Assistant, Radiography, surgical technology, cosmetology, emergency medical science) advised to apply before 12/31. **Financial aid:** Priority date 3/15, closing date 7/25. FAFSA required. Applicants notified on a rolling basis starting 7/1; must reply within 2 week(s) of notification.

Academics. Special study options: Cooperative education, cross-registration, distance learning, double major, dual enrollment of high school students, ESL, internships, liberal arts/career combination, teacher certification program. License preparation in aviation, dental hygiene, nursing, paramedic, physical therapy, radiology, real estate. **Credit/placement by examination:** AP, CLEP, IB, institutional tests. 60 credit hours maximum toward associate degree. **Support services:** GED preparation and test center, learning center, reduced course load, remedial instruction, study skills assistance, tutoring, writing center.

Majors. Business: Accounting technology, business admin, executive assistant, human resources, management information systems. **Communications technology:** Recording arts. **Computer sciences:** Information systems. **Education:** General, early childhood. **General:** Electrician, maintenance. **Health services:** Dental hygiene, EMT paramedic, medical assistant, mental health services, nursing (RN), physical therapy assistant, substance abuse counseling, surgical technology. **Liberal arts:** Arts/sciences. **Protective services:** Criminal justice, fire safety technology. **Visual/performing arts:** Commercial/advertising art, music management.

Most popular majors. Business/marketing 8%, computer/information sciences 6%, health sciences 21%, liberal arts 34%, trade and industry 13%.

Technology on campus. 130 workstations in library, computer center. Commuter students can connect to campus network. Online course registration, online library, helpline, wireless network available.

Student life. Freshman orientation: Mandatory. Preregistration for classes offered. **Activities:** Campus ministries, choral groups, drama, international student organizations, music ensembles, Model UN, student government, Ambassadors for Christ, American Muslim student association, Nurses Christian Fellowship, Fellowship of Christian Athletes, political science club, Rotaract, Phi Theta Kappa, veterans and civilians organized network.

Athletics. NJCAA. **Intercollegiate:** Baseball M, basketball, cheerleading, volleyball W. **Team name:** Titans.

Student services. Alcohol/substance abuse counseling, career counseling, services for economically disadvantaged, student employment services, financial aid counseling, minority student services, on-campus daycare, personal counseling, placement for graduates, veterans' counselor, women's services. **Physically disabled:** Services for visually, speech, hearing impaired. **Transfer:** Pre-admission transcript evaluation for new students. Transfer adviser, college fairs on campus for students transferring to 4-year colleges.

Contact. E-mail: jlcross@gtcc.edu
Phone: (336) 334-4822 ext. 31125 Fax: (336) 819-2022
Jesse Cross, Director of Admissions, Guilford Technical Community College, PO Box 309, Jamestown, NC 27282

Halifax Community College
Weldon, North Carolina
www.halifaxcc.edu   CB code: 0621

- Public 2-year community college
- Commuter campus in small town

General. Founded in 1967. Regionally accredited. **Enrollment:** 1,154 degree-seeking undergraduates. **Degrees:** 150 associate awarded. **Location:** 83 miles from Raleigh. **Calendar:** Semester, limited summer session. **Full-time faculty:** 62 total; 6% have terminal degrees, 32% minority, 48% women. **Part-time faculty:** 122 total; 2% have terminal degrees, 43% minority, 45% women. **Class size:** 91% < 20, 9% 20-39. **Special facilities:** Performing arts auditorium. **Partnerships:** Formal partnerships with Small Business Center and Continuing Ed Workforce Development. Early College Program- Northampton and Halifax Counties High Schools and Weldon City High School.

Student profile. Among degree-seeking undergraduates, 37% enrolled in a transfer program, 63% enrolled in a vocational program.

Transfer out. Colleges most students transferred to 2015: Elizabeth City State University, North Carolina Central State University, North Carolina Wesleyan.

Basis for selection. Open admission, but selective for some programs. Special requirements for nursing and allied health programs. **Adult students:** SAT/ACT scores not required but if provided, scores cannot be more than 5 years old or applicant will be required to take a placement test. **Home schooled:** Transcript of courses and grades required.

High school preparation. High school chemistry or equivalent and developmental mathematics required for nursing applicants.

2015-2016 Annual costs. Tuition/fees: $2,292; $8,052 out-of-state. Per-credit charge: $72 in-state; $264 out-of-state. Books/supplies: $1,400.

2014-2015 Financial aid. Need-based: 99% of total undergraduate aid awarded as scholarships/grants, 1% as loans/jobs. Need-based aid available for part-time students. Work-study available nights, weekends and for part-time students. **Non-need-based:** Scholarships awarded for academics.

Application procedures. Admission: No deadline. No application fee. Admission notification on a rolling basis. **Financial aid:** Priority date 6/1; no closing date. FAFSA required. Applicants notified on a rolling basis starting 8/1; must reply within 2 week(s) of notification.

Academics. Special study options: Combined bachelor's/graduate degree, distance learning, dual enrollment of high school students, ESL, independent study, internships, teacher certification program. Career and College Promise Pathways. License preparation in dental hygiene, nursing. **Credit/placement by examination:** AP, CLEP, institutional tests. Hours of credit by examination may be counted towards associate degree cannot exceed 25% of the required credits for degree/diploma. **Support services:** GED preparation and test center, learning center, remedial instruction, study skills assistance, tutoring, writing center. Student Support Services Program, PRIDE Male Mentoring Program.

Majors. Business: Business admin, office management, office/clerical. **Computer sciences:** General. **Education:** Early childhood. **Health services:** Clinical lab technology, dental hygiene, medical secretary, nursing (RN). **Liberal arts:** Arts/sciences. **Protective services:** Police science. **Visual/performing arts:** Commercial/advertising art. **Work/family studies:** Child care management.

Most popular majors. Business/marketing 7%, education 9%, health sciences 41%, liberal arts 18%, social sciences 6%.

Technology on campus. 100 workstations in library, computer center, student center. Commuter students can connect to campus network. Online library, wireless network available.

Student life. Freshman orientation: Mandatory. Preregistration for classes offered. **Activities:** Student government.

Student services. Career counseling, services for economically disadvantaged, financial aid counseling, health services, minority student services, on-campus daycare, personal counseling, veterans' counselor. **Physically disabled:** Services for visually, speech, hearing impaired. **Transfer:** Pre-admission transcript evaluation for new students. Transfer adviser, college fairs on campus for students transferring to 4-year colleges.

Contact. E-mail: jwashington660@halifaxcc.edu
Phone: (252) 536-7220 Fax: (252) 538-4311
James Washington, Director of Admissions and Recruitment, Halifax Community College, 100 College Drive, Drawer 809, Weldon, NC 27890

Haywood Community College
Clyde, North Carolina
www.haywood.edu   CB code: 5289

- Public 2-year community and technical college
- Commuter campus in rural community

General. Founded in 1965. Regionally accredited. **Enrollment:** 1,614 degree-seeking undergraduates. **Degrees:** 276 associate awarded. **Location:** 25 miles from Asheville. **Calendar:** Semester, extensive summer session. **Full-time faculty:** 80 total. **Part-time faculty:** 183 total. **Class size:** 85% < 20, 14% 20-39, less than 1% 40-49.

Student profile.

Out-of-state:	14%	**25 or older:**	39%

Transfer out. Colleges most students transferred to 2015: Western Carolina University, Appalachian State University, University of North Carolina - Asheville.

Basis for selection. Open admission, but selective for some programs. Completion of ACCUPLACER, SAT score of 500 or higher on each section, ACT composite score of 21 or higher, or official transcript with "C" or better in college-level English and algebra required. Admission to nursing program based on admission test scores, high school record, GPA, prerequisite courses, and health occupations aptitude examination. Informational interview required for electrical engineering technology, manufacturing engineering technology, cosmetology, and professional crafts programs. **Home schooled:** Transcript of courses and grades required. Evidence that the home school is registered with the state. Home school transcript must be notarized. **Learning Disabled:** Accommodations made upon request.

High school preparation. College-preparatory program required. Algebra, biology and chemistry required for nursing. Algebra recommended for electrical and manufacturing engineering, microcomputer systems and college transfer.

2015-2016 Annual costs. Tuition/fees: $2,263; $8,023 out-of-state. Per-credit charge: $72 in-state; $264 out-of-state. Books/supplies: $1,200. Personal expenses: $1,665.

Financial aid. Need-based: Need-based aid available for part-time students. Work-study available nights, weekends and for part-time students. **Non-need-based:** Scholarships awarded for academics. **Additional information:** Complete FAFSA by priority filing date for consideration for institutional scholarships.

Application procedures. Admission: No deadline. No application fee. Admission notification on a rolling basis. **Financial aid:** Priority date 6/1; no closing date. FAFSA required. Applicants notified on a rolling basis starting 4/15; must reply within 2 week(s) of notification.

Academics. Special study options: Cooperative education, distance learning, dual enrollment of high school students, independent study, internships. **Credit/placement by examination:** AP, CLEP, institutional tests. 18 credit hours maximum toward associate degree. **Support services:** GED preparation and test center, learning center, reduced course load, remedial instruction, tutoring.

Majors. Business: Accounting, administrative services, business admin. **Computer sciences:** Applications programming, networking. **Conservation:** Fisheries, forest resources, forestry, wildlife/wilderness, wood science. **Engineering:** Computer. **General:** Electrician, maintenance. **Health services:** Medical assistant, nursing (RN). **Liberal arts:** Arts/sciences. **Protective services:** Criminal justice. **Visual/performing arts:** Ceramics, fiber arts, metal/jewelry. **Work/family studies:** Child care management.

Most popular majors. Agriculture 6%, business/marketing 10%, engineering/engineering technologies 7%, family/consumer sciences 6%, health sciences 10%, liberal arts 15%, natural resources/environmental science 19%, trade and industry 8%, visual/performing arts 8%.

Technology on campus. 10 workstations in library.

Student life. Freshman orientation: Available. Preregistration for classes offered. **Activities:** Student government, Phi Theta Kappa, Phi Beta Lambda.

Student services. Career counseling, student employment services, financial aid counseling, on-campus daycare, personal counseling, placement for graduates, veterans' counselor. **Physically disabled:** Services for visually, speech, hearing impaired. **Transfer:** Transfer adviser for students transferring to 4-year colleges.

Contact. E-mail: enrollment@haywood.edu
Phone: (828) 627-4505 Toll-free number: (866) 468-6422
Fax: (828) 627-4513
Jennifer Herrera, Director of Enrollment Management, Haywood Community College, 185 Freelander Drive, Clyde, NC 28721-9454

Isothermal Community College
Spindale, North Carolina
www.isothermal.edu   CB code: 5319

- Public 2-year community college
- Commuter campus in small town

General. Founded in 1964. Regionally accredited. **Enrollment:** 2,067 degree-seeking undergraduates. **Degrees:** 225 associate awarded. **Location:** 65 miles from Charlotte, 48 miles from Asheville. **Calendar:** Semester, extensive summer session. **Full-time faculty:** 69 total. **Part-time faculty:** 109 total. **Class size:** 69% < 20, 31% 20-39. **Special facilities:** College-operated public, radio station, WNCW, located on the Spindale campus. **Partnerships:** Formal partnership with Rutherford County Schools.

Basis for selection. Open admission, but selective for some programs. Special requirements for Basic Law Enforcement Training, LPN, RN, and Surgical Technology programs. The Basic Law Enforcement Training program utilizes a check sheet of requirements that must be met before a student is enrolled in the program. **Home schooled:** Transcript of courses and grades required. Copy of license to operate as provided by the state required.

2015-2016 Annual costs. Tuition/fees: $2,214; $7,974 out-of-state. Per-credit charge: $72 in-state; $264 out-of-state. Books/supplies: $837. Personal expenses: $927.

Financial aid. Need-based: Need-based aid available for part-time students. Work-study available nights, weekends and for part-time students. **Non-need-based:** Scholarships awarded for academics, job skills, leadership, minority status, music/drama, state residency.

Application procedures. Admission: Priority date 5/31; no deadline. No application fee. Admission notification on a rolling basis. **Financial aid:** Priority date 5/31, closing date 7/1. FAFSA, institutional form required. Applicants notified on a rolling basis starting 4/30; must reply within 4 week(s) of notification.

Academics. Special study options: Cooperative education, distance learning, dual enrollment of high school students, ESL, independent study. License preparation in nursing, real estate. **Credit/placement by examination:** AP, CLEP, institutional tests. 12 credit hours maximum toward associate degree. **Support services:** GED preparation and test center, learning center, reduced course load, remedial instruction, tutoring, writing center.

Majors. Business: Banking/financial services, business admin, customer service support, e-commerce, entrepreneurial studies, marketing, office management, operations. **Communications technology:** Radio/TV. **Computer sciences:** Information systems, information technology, LAN/WAN management, networking, programming, security. **Education:** Early childhood, elementary, trade/industrial. **General:** Electrician. **Health services:** Nursing

(RN), office admin. **Liberal arts:** Arts/sciences. **Protective services:** Criminal justice. **Visual/performing arts:** Commercial/advertising art.

Most popular majors. Business/marketing 13%, education 6%, engineering/engineering technologies 10%, health sciences 17%, liberal arts 43%.

Technology on campus. 44 workstations in library, computer center. Commuter students can connect to campus network. Online library, helpline, wireless network available.

Student life. Freshman orientation: Available. Preregistration for classes offered. **Activities:** Literary magazine, radio station, student government, TV station, art and computer design club, Afro-American club, chess club, Student Nurses' Association, International Association of Administrative Professionals, Isothermal Education Society, math club, Phi Theta Kappa, Phi Beta Lambda, Twin Phoenix Karate Club.

Athletics. Intramural: Basketball, football (non-tackle), table tennis, volleyball. **Team name:** Patriots.

Student services. Career counseling, financial aid counseling, personal counseling, placement for graduates, veterans' counselor. **Physically disabled:** Services for visually, speech, hearing impaired. **Transfer:** Transfer adviser, college fairs on campus for students transferring to 4-year colleges.

Contact. E-mail: admissions@isothermal.edu
Phone: (828) 395-1442 Fax: (828) 286-8109
Alice McCluney, Director, Enrollment Management, Isothermal Community College, PO Box 804, Spindale, NC 28160-0804

James Sprunt Community College
Kenansville, North Carolina
www.jamessprunt.edu   CB code: 6256

- Public 2-year community college
- Commuter campus in rural community

General. Founded in 1964. Regionally accredited. **Enrollment:** 806 degree-seeking undergraduates; 389 non-degree-seeking students. **Degrees:** 173 associate awarded. **Location:** 75 miles from Raleigh, 45 miles from Wilmington. **Calendar:** Semester, limited summer session. **Full-time faculty:** 31 total; 6% have terminal degrees, 13% minority, 81% women. **Part-time faculty:** 34 total; 9% minority, 50% women. **Class size:** 80% < 20, 19% 20-39, less than 1% 40-49, less than 1% 50-99.

Student profile. Among degree-seeking undergraduates, 32% enrolled in a transfer program, 68% enrolled in a vocational program, 1% already have a bachelor's degree or higher, 151 enrolled as first-time, first-year students, 65 transferred in from other institutions.

Part-time:	44%	Women:	71%
Out-of-state:	1%	25 or older:	32%

Transfer out. 43% of students enrolled in the transfer program go on to 4-year colleges. **Colleges most students transferred to 2015:** University of North Carolina at Wilmington, East Carolina University, Mount Olive College, North Carolina State University, Fayetteville State University.

Basis for selection. Open admission, but selective for some programs. Test of Essential Academic Skills (TEAS), 2.0 GPA in biology, chemistry, and algebra required for nursing applicants. SAT or ACT accepted in lieu of academic placement tests. Credit may be awarded for graphic arts classes based on portfolio. **Home schooled:** Letter from State Board of Education giving approval for home school, operating legally on a regular schedule for at least 9 calendar months, submit transcript and testing information. **Learning Disabled:** Submit letter from professional stating disabilities.

2015-2016 Annual costs. Tuition/fees: $2,230; $7,990 out-of-state. Per-credit charge: $72 in-state; $264 out-of-state. Books/supplies: $1,800. Personal expenses: $1,500.

2014-2015 Financial aid. Need-based: 130 full-time freshmen applied for aid; 125 deemed to have need; 106 received aid. Average scholarship/grant was $4,711. 99% of total undergraduate aid awarded as scholarships/grants, 1% as loans/jobs. Need-based aid available for part-time students. Work-study available nights, weekends and for part-time students. **Non-need-based:** Scholarships awarded for academics, state residency.

Application procedures. Admission: Priority date 8/1; no deadline. No application fee. **Financial aid:** Priority date 7/15, closing date 7/1. FAFSA, institutional form required. Applicants notified on a rolling basis starting 5/15; must reply within 2 week(s) of notification.

Academics. Special study options: Cooperative education, distance learning, double major, dual enrollment of high school students, ESL, independent study, internships, liberal arts/career combination. License preparation in nursing. **Credit/placement by examination:** AP, CLEP, institutional tests. 16 credit hours maximum toward associate degree. **Support services:** GED preparation and test center, learning center, pre-admission summer program, reduced course load, remedial instruction, study skills assistance, tutoring.

Majors. Business: Accounting, business admin, office management. **Computer sciences:** Information technology. **Education:** Early childhood, elementary. **Health services:** Medical assistant, nursing (RN). **Liberal arts:** Arts/sciences. **Protective services:** Criminal justice. **Visual/performing arts:** Commercial/advertising art.

Most popular majors. Business/marketing 8%, computer/information sciences 7%, education 15%, health sciences 12%, liberal arts 45%.

Technology on campus. 310 workstations in library, computer center. Online library, helpline, wireless network available.

Student life. Freshman orientation: Mandatory. Preregistration for classes offered. Held prior to regular registration day; students must pre-register with counselors. **Activities:** Student government, student newspaper, Phi Theta Kappa, Student Nurses Association, National Vocational-Technical Honor Society, Ambassador Program, Criminal Justice Club.

Athletics. Intercollegiate: Volleyball W. **Intramural:** Soccer. **Team name:** Spartans.

Student services. Career counseling, services for economically disadvantaged, student employment services, financial aid counseling, personal counseling, placement for graduates, veterans' counselor. **Physically disabled:** Services for visually, hearing impaired. **Transfer:** Pre-admission transcript evaluation for new students. Transfer adviser, college fairs on campus for students transferring to 4-year colleges.

Contact. E-mail: wedwards@jamessprunt.edu
Phone: (910) 296-2500 Fax: (910) 296-1222
Wanda Edwards, Admissions Specialist, James Sprunt Community College, PO Box 398, Kenansville, NC 28349-0398

Johnston Community College
Smithfield, North Carolina
www.johnstoncc.edu
CB code: 0727

+ Public 2-year community and technical college
+ Commuter campus in large town

General. Founded in 1969. Regionally accredited. **Enrollment:** 2,855 degree-seeking undergraduates; 1,114 non-degree-seeking students. **Degrees:** 563 associate awarded. **Location:** 30 miles from Raleigh. **Calendar:** Semester, limited summer session. **Full-time faculty:** 141 total; 41% minority, 53% women. **Part-time faculty:** 273 total; 26% minority, 51% women. **Class size:** 74% < 20, 26% 20-39. **Special facilities:** Howell woods.

Student profile. Among degree-seeking undergraduates, 57% enrolled in a transfer program, 43% enrolled in a vocational program, 613 enrolled as first-time, first-year students.

Part-time:	46%	Hispanic/Latino:	11%
Out-of-state:	1%	Native American:	1%
Women:	66%	Multi-racial, non-Hispanic:	1%
African American:	16%	International:	1%
Asian American:	1%		

Transfer out. Colleges most students transferred to 2015: East Carolina University, University of North Carolina at Wilmington, North Carolina State University.

Basis for selection. Open admission, but selective for some programs. Admission to health programs based on test scores, high school record and related completed courses. PSB required for admission to nursing and radiologic technology programs. Placement interview required for all applicants; interview required for health programs.

2015-2016 Annual costs. Tuition/fees: $2,257; $8,017 out-of-state. Per-credit charge: $72 in-state; $264 out-of-state. Books/supplies: $1,350. Personal expenses: $2,465.

2014-2015 Financial aid. All financial aid based on need. 92% of total undergraduate aid awarded as scholarships/grants, 8% as loans/jobs. Need-based aid available for part-time students. Work-study available nights, weekends and for part-time students.

Application procedures. Admission: Priority date 8/1; no deadline. No application fee. Admission notification on a rolling basis. **Financial aid:**

Priority date 5/31; no closing date. FAFSA required. Applicants notified on a rolling basis starting 6/1; must reply within 2 week(s) of notification.

Academics. Special study options: Cross-registration, distance learning, double major, dual enrollment of high school students, internships. **Credit/placement by examination:** AP, CLEP, IB, institutional tests. **Support services:** GED preparation and test center, learning center, pre-admission summer program, reduced course load, remedial instruction, tutoring, writing center.

Majors. Business: Accounting, business admin, office management. **Computer sciences:** Networking, programming. **Education:** Early childhood, teacher assistance. **Foreign languages:** Translation. **Health services:** Cardio-pulmonary technology, cardiovascular technology, medical assistant, nuclear medical technology, nursing (RN), office admin, pharmacy assistant, radiologic technology/medical imaging. **Liberal arts:** Arts/sciences. **Protective services:** Criminal justice. **Visual/performing arts:** Commercial/advertising art.

Most popular majors. Business/marketing 11%, health sciences 23%, legal studies 12%, liberal arts 30%, trade and industry 7%.

Technology on campus. 115 workstations in library, computer center. Commuter students can connect to campus network. Online course registration available.

Student life. Freshman orientation: Mandatory. Preregistration for classes offered. **Activities:** Jazz band, choral groups, student government.

Athletics. NJCAA. **Intercollegiate:** Basketball M, golf M, volleyball W. **Team name:** Jaguars.

Student services. Chaplain/spiritual director, career counseling, student employment services, financial aid counseling, minority student services, on-campus daycare, personal counseling, placement for graduates, veterans' counselor. **Physically disabled:** Services for visually, speech, hearing impaired. **Transfer:** Pre-admission transcript evaluation for new students. College fairs on campus for students transferring to 4-year colleges.

Contact. Phone: (919) 209-2128 Fax: (919) 989-7862
Joan McLendon, Director of Admissions and Counseling, Johnston Community College, PO Box 2350, Smithfield, NC 27577

King's College
Charlotte, North Carolina
www.kingscollegecharlotte.edu
CB code: 5361

+ For-profit 2-year career college
+ Large city

General. Accredited by ACICS. **Enrollment:** 381 undergraduates. **Degrees:** 161 associate awarded. **Calendar:** Semester. **Full-time faculty:** 10 total. **Part-time faculty:** 15 total.

Basis for selection. Interview and rigor of secondary school record very important, class rank and standardized test scores important.

2015-2016 Annual costs. Diploma programs:$14,330-$21,470, books and supplies $1,539-$3,562, room and board $6,500-$9,750. Associate programs: $28,610-$29,460, books and supplies $2,189-$4,878, room and board $13,000.

Financial aid. Need-based: Work-study available nights, weekends and for part-time students.

Application procedures. Admission: No deadline. $50 fee. Admission notification on a rolling basis.

Academics. Credit/placement by examination: AP, CLEP.

Majors. Business: Accounting technology, administrative services, hotel/motel admin. **Computer sciences:** Networking, programming. **Health services:** Medical assistant. **Visual/performing arts:** Graphic design.

Student life. Freshman orientation: Mandatory. Preregistration for classes offered.

Student services. Career counseling, financial aid counseling, placement for graduates.

Contact. Phone: (704) 372-0266 Toll-free number: (800) 768-2255 Fax: (704) 348-2029
Diane Ryon, Director of Admissions, King's College, 322 Lamar Avenue, Charlotte, NC 28204

Lenoir Community College
Kinston, North Carolina
www.lenoircc.edu   **CB code: 5378**

▶ Public 2-year community college
▶ Commuter campus in large town

General. Founded in 1958. Regionally accredited. Extension campuses in Jones and Greene Counties. **Enrollment:** 1,754 degree-seeking undergraduates; 1,003 non-degree-seeking students. **Degrees:** 318 associate awarded. **Location:** 75 miles from Raleigh, 25 miles from Greenville. **Calendar:** Semester, extensive summer session. **Full-time faculty:** 93 total; 8% have terminal degrees, 16% minority, 57% women. **Part-time faculty:** 42 total; 5% have terminal degrees, 14% minority, 36% women. **Class size:** 88% < 20, 12% 20-39, less than 1% 40-49, less than 1% 50-99. **Special facilities:** Facility for local history, genealogy collection.

Student profile. Among degree-seeking undergraduates, 36% enrolled in a transfer program, 48% enrolled in a vocational program, 336 enrolled as first-time, first-year students, 217 transferred in from other institutions.

Part-time:	47%	Hispanic/Latino:	6%
Out-of-state:	8%	Native American:	1%
Women:	61%	Multi-racial, non-Hispanic:	1%
African American:	35%	International:	1%
Asian American:	1%		

Transfer out. Colleges most students transferred to 2015: East Carolina University, University of North Carolina at Wilmington, North Carolina State University.

Basis for selection. Open admission, but selective for some programs. Special requirements for Health Science programs. Interview required for Surgical Technology program.

High school preparation. Recommended units include English 4, mathematics 2, social studies 2, history 1, science 2 (laboratory 1). One biology, 1 chemistry required for registered nursing program.

2015-2016 Annual costs. Tuition/fees: $2,279; $8,039 out-of-state. Per-credit charge: $72 in-state; $264 out-of-state. Books/supplies: $1,800.

2015-2016 Financial aid. Need-based: 96% of total undergraduate aid awarded as scholarships/grants, 4% as loans/jobs. Need-based aid available for part-time students. Work-study available nights, weekends and for part-time students. **Non-need-based:** Scholarships awarded for academics, athletics, leadership, state residency.

Application procedures. Admission: No deadline. No application fee. Admission notification on a rolling basis. Separate application required for Health Science programs. January 31 is deadline for most programs. **Financial aid:** Priority date 7/1, closing date 8/15. FAFSA required. Applicants notified on a rolling basis starting 8/1; must reply within 2 week(s) of notification.

Academics. Special study options: Cooperative education, distance learning, double major, dual enrollment of high school students, honors, liberal arts/career combination. License preparation in aviation, nursing, paramedic, radiology, real estate. **Credit/placement by examination:** AP, CLEP, IB, institutional tests. **Support services:** GED preparation and test center, learning center, pre-admission summer program, reduced course load, remedial instruction, tutoring, writing center.

Majors. Business: Accounting, business admin, logistics, marketing, office management, operations. **Computer sciences:** Information technology, networking. **Education:** Early childhood, trade/industrial. **Engineering:** Pre-engineering. **Health services:** EMT paramedic, massage therapy, medical assistant, nursing (RN), office admin, polysomnography, prenursing, radiologic technology/medical imaging. **Human services:** General. **Liberal arts:** Arts/sciences. **Protective services:** Criminal justice. **Visual/performing arts:** Graphic design.

Most popular majors. Business/marketing 14%, computer/information sciences 6%, education 6%, engineering/engineering technologies 11%, health sciences 22%, liberal arts 6%, personal/culinary services 6%, trade and industry 20%.

Technology on campus. 100 workstations in library, computer center, student center. Commuter students can connect to campus network. Online course registration, wireless network available.

Student life. Freshman orientation: Available. Preregistration for classes offered. Held in July for fall freshmen. **Policies:** Tobacco-free campus and no weapons on campus. **Activities:** Student government, student newspaper, Phi Theta Kappa, various clubs related to major fields of study.

Athletics. NJCAA. **Intercollegiate:** Baseball M, basketball, volleyball W. **Team name:** Lancers.

Student services. Adult student services, career counseling, student employment services, financial aid counseling, health services, minority student services, personal counseling, placement for graduates, veterans' counselor. **Physically disabled:** Services for visually, hearing impaired. **Transfer:** Pre-admission transcript evaluation for new students. Transfer adviser, college fairs on campus for students transferring to 4-year colleges.

Contact. E-mail: krhill01@lenoircc.edu
Phone: (252) 527-6223 ext. 301 Fax: (252) 233-6879 ext. 323
Kim Hill, Enrollment Management Coordinator, Lenoir Community College, PO Box 188, Kinston, NC 28502-0188

Louisburg College
Louisburg, North Carolina   **CB member**
www.louisburg.edu   **CB code: 5369**

▶ Private 2-year junior college affiliated with the United Methodist Church
▶ Residential campus in small town
▶ SAT or ACT (ACT writing optional) required

General. Founded in 1787. Regionally accredited. Small classes with individual approach. **Enrollment:** 704 degree-seeking undergraduates; 1 non-degree-seeking students. **Degrees:** 120 associate awarded. **Location:** 25 miles from Raleigh. **Calendar:** Semester, limited summer session. **Full-time faculty:** 31 total; 19% have terminal degrees, 58% women. **Part-time faculty:** 24 total; 8% have terminal degrees, 25% minority, 71% women.

Student profile. Among degree-seeking undergraduates, 99% enrolled in a transfer program, 351 enrolled as first-time, first-year students, 50 transferred in from other institutions.

Out-of-state:	21%	Native American:	1%
Women:	37%	Multi-racial, non-Hispanic:	4%
African American:	59%	25 or older:	1%
Asian American:	1%	Live on campus:	92%

Transfer out. Colleges most students transferred to 2015: North Carolina State University, East Carolina University, Appalachian State University, University of North Carolina at Wilmington, University of North Carolina at Greensboro.

Basis for selection. School achievement most important, followed by test scores and recommendations. Interview recommended for some applicants. Submission of SAT verbal and mathematics scores or ACT scores is required. **Adult students:** SAT/ACT scores not required if out of high school 1 year(s) or more. **Home schooled:** Transcript of courses and grades required. **Learning Disabled:** Comprehensive tutorial program available for learning-disabled students. Interested students must contact the Learning Partners program for testing and consideration.

High school preparation. College-preparatory program required. 20 units recommended. Recommended units include English 4, mathematics 3, social studies 3, science 2 and foreign language 2.

2015-2016 Annual costs. Tuition/fees: $17,346. Room/board: $10,709. Books/supplies: $100.

Financial aid. Need-based: Work-study available nights, weekends and for part-time students. **Non-need-based:** Scholarships awarded for academics, art, athletics, leadership, minority status, music/drama, religious affiliation, state residency. **Additional information:** Job location and development program helps students obtain work in the community.

Application procedures. Admission: Priority date 7/1; deadline 8/15 (postmark date). $25 fee, may be waived for applicants with need. Application must be submitted online. Admission notification on a rolling basis. Must reply by May 1 or within 2 week(s) if notified thereafter. **Financial aid:** Priority date 3/1; no closing date. FAFSA required.

Academics. Special study options: Cooperative education, dual enrollment of high school students, honors, independent study. Louisburg Learning Partners for Students with Learning Differences. **Credit/placement by examination:** AP, CLEP, institutional tests. 32 credit hours maximum toward associate degree. Computer Literacy and Internet Literacy. **Support services:** Learning center, pre-admission summer program, reduced course load, remedial instruction, study skills assistance, tutoring, writing center.

Majors. Biology: General. **Business:** General. **Liberal arts:** Arts/sciences.

Most popular majors. Biological/life sciences 10%, business/marketing 14%, liberal arts 76%.

Technology on campus. 151 workstations in dormitories, library, computer center, student center. Dormitories wired for high-speed internet access and linked to campus network. Online library, helpline, wireless network available.

Student life. Freshman orientation: Mandatory. Preregistration for classes offered. **Policies:** Non-resident undergraduates under 21 must live on campus or at home. **Housing:** Guaranteed on-campus for all undergraduates. Single-sex dorms available. $200 partly refundable deposit, deadline 7/1. **Activities:** Campus ministries, choral groups, dance, drama, literary magazine, music ensembles, musical theater, student government, Christian Life Council, Spanish Club, Workers Actively Volunteering Energetic Services, Phi Theta Kappa, Ecological Concerns Club.

Athletics. NJCAA. **Intercollegiate:** Baseball M, basketball, cheerleading, cross-country, soccer, softball W, volleyball W. **Intramural:** Basketball, football (tackle), soccer, softball, table tennis, volleyball. **Team name:** Hurricanes.

Student services. Adult student services, alcohol/substance abuse counseling, chaplain/spiritual director, career counseling, student employment services, financial aid counseling, health services, personal counseling, veterans' counselor. **Transfer:** Transfer adviser, college fairs on campus for students transferring to 4-year colleges.

Contact. E-mail: admissions@louisburg.edu
Phone: (919) 497-3222 Toll-free number: (800) 775-0208
Fax: (919) 496-1788
Stephanie Tolbert, Vice President of Enrollment Management, Louisburg College, 501 North Main Street, Louisburg, NC 27549

Martin Community College
Williamston, North Carolina **CB member**
www.martincc.edu **CB code: 5445**

▶ Public 2-year community and technical college
▶ Commuter campus in small town

General. Founded in 1967. Regionally accredited. **Enrollment:** 875 undergraduates. **Degrees:** 72 associate awarded. **Location:** 30 miles from Greenville, 100 miles from Raleigh. **Calendar:** Semester, limited summer session. **Full-time faculty:** 23 total; 4% have terminal degrees, 13% minority, 65% women. **Part-time faculty:** 33 total; 3% have terminal degrees, 9% minority, 61% women. **Special facilities:** Equine arena, rodeo.

Transfer out. Colleges most students transferred to 2015: East Carolina University.

Basis for selection. Open admission, but selective for some programs. Limited enrollment in physical therapy assistant program. Selection based on high school record, placement test results, completion of required courses and interview. Selection of Dental Assisting applications includes high school record, completion of required courses, and an interview. COMPASS required of some students. Interview required for physical therapist assistant applicants and dental assisting applicants. **Home schooled:** Statement describing home school structure and mission, transcript of courses and grades required.

High school preparation. 22 units recommended. Recommended units include English 4, mathematics 3, social studies 2, history 1, science 3 (laboratory 1) and academic electives 9.

2015-2016 Annual costs. Tuition/fees: $2,198; $7,958 out-of-state. Per-credit charge: $72 in-state; $264 out-of-state. Books/supplies: $1,000. Personal expenses: $400.

Financial aid. Need-based: Need-based aid available for part-time students. Work-study available nights, weekends and for part-time students. **Non-need-based:** Scholarships awarded for academics.

Application procedures. Admission: No deadline. No application fee. Admission notification on a rolling basis. **Financial aid:** No deadline. FAFSA required. Applicants notified on a rolling basis starting 5/1.

Academics. Special study options: Cooperative education, distance learning, double major, dual enrollment of high school students, ESL, independent study, internships, liberal arts/career combination, teacher certification program. License preparation in paramedic, physical therapy, real estate. **Credit/placement by examination:** AP, CLEP, institutional tests. No more than half of credits required in program of study may be earned through credit by exam (including CLEP). **Support services:** GED preparation and test center, learning center, reduced course load, remedial instruction, study skills assistance, tutoring.

Majors. Business: Accounting technology, business admin, executive assistant, management information systems. **Computer sciences:** Information systems. **Education:** General, early childhood, elementary, secondary. **General:** Electrician. **Health services:** Medical assistant, medical secretary, physical therapy assistant. **Liberal arts:** Arts/sciences.

Most popular majors. Business/marketing 7%, education 7%, health sciences 45%, liberal arts 24%, trade and industry 11%.

Technology on campus. 31 workstations in library, computer center. Commuter students can connect to campus network. Wireless network available.

Student life. Freshman orientation: Available. Preregistration for classes offered. Offered on registration day. **Activities:** Student government, physical therapist assistant club, Phi Theta Kappa, equine club, medical assisting club, Alpha Beta Gamma.

Student services. Career counseling, services for economically disadvantaged, student employment services, financial aid counseling, on-campus daycare, personal counseling, placement for graduates, veterans' counselor. **Transfer:** Pre-admission transcript evaluation for new students. Transfer adviser, college fairs on campus for students transferring to 4-year colleges.

Contact. E-mail: admissions@martincc.edu
Phone: (252) 798-0268 Fax: (252) 792-0826
Brian Busch, Director of Student Services, Martin Community College, 1161 Kehukee Park Road, Williamston, NC 27892-9988

Mayland Community College
Spruce Pine, North Carolina **CB member**
www.mayland.edu **CB code: 0795**

▶ Public 2-year community college
▶ Commuter campus in rural community

General. Founded in 1971. Regionally accredited. **Enrollment:** 1,119 degree-seeking undergraduates; 9 non-degree-seeking students. **Degrees:** 109 associate awarded. **Location:** 50 miles from Asheville. **Calendar:** Semester, limited summer session. **Full-time faculty:** 32 total; 3% have terminal degrees, 69% women. **Part-time faculty:** 38 total; 5% have terminal degrees, 63% women. **Class size:** 89% < 20, 11% 20-39. **Special facilities:** Observatory.

Student profile. Among degree-seeking undergraduates, 27% enrolled in a transfer program, 73% enrolled in a vocational program, 123 enrolled as first-time, first-year students.

Part-time:	67%	Hispanic/Latino:	4%
Women:	56%	25 or older:	24%
African American:	1%		

Transfer out. Colleges most students transferred to 2015: Appalachian State University, University of North Carolina-Asheville, Western Carolina University, East Tennessee State University, Gardner-Webb University.

Basis for selection. Open admission, but selective for some programs. Placement assessment required of all degree-seeking students. Admission to associate degree nursing program based on competitive ranking system. Medical assisting admissions based on completion of requirements and timely application. Basic Law Enforcement Training students must meet entrance requirements set forth by the North Carolina Criminal Justice Education and Training Standards Commission. **Home schooled:** Transcript of courses and grades required.

2015-2016 Annual costs. Tuition/fees: $2,449; $8,609 out-of-state. Per-credit charge: $72 in-state; $264 out-of-state. Books/supplies: $1,185. Personal expenses: $1,792.

2014-2015 Financial aid. Need-based: 99% of total undergraduate aid awarded as scholarships/grants, 1% as loans/jobs. Need-based aid available for part-time students. Work-study available nights, weekends and for part-time students.

Application procedures. Admission: No deadline. No application fee. Admission notification on a rolling basis beginning on or about 3/1. **Financial aid:** Priority date 3/15, closing date 6/30. FAFSA, institutional form required. Applicants notified on a rolling basis starting 6/15.

Academics. Special study options: Cooperative education, cross-registration, distance learning, double major, dual enrollment of high school students, ESL, independent study, internships, liberal arts/career combination. License preparation in nursing, real estate. **Credit/placement by examination:** AP, CLEP, institutional tests. Maximum 25% of program hours can be earned via credit by examination. **Support services:** GED preparation and test center, learning center, pre-admission summer program, reduced course load, remedial instruction, study skills assistance, tutoring, writing center.

Majors. Business: Business admin. **Computer sciences:** General. **Education:** Early childhood. **Engineering:** Electrical. **Health services:** Medical secretary, nursing (RN). **Liberal arts:** Arts/sciences. **Protective services:** Police science. **Work/family studies:** Child care management.

Most popular majors. Business/marketing 10%, computer/information sciences 11%, engineering/engineering technologies 7%, health sciences 31%, liberal arts 22%, security/protective services 12%.

Technology on campus. 150 workstations in library, computer center, student center. Commuter students can connect to campus network. Online course registration, online library, helpline, student web hosting, wireless network available.

Student life. Freshman orientation: Available. Preregistration for classes offered. **Activities:** Literary magazine, student government, Association of Student Medical Assistants, Circle K club, early childhood club, Human Services Student Organization, Student Ambassador Program, Student Government Association, Student Nurses' Association, First & Second Year.

Student services. Career counseling, services for economically disadvantaged, student employment services, financial aid counseling, health services, personal counseling, placement for graduates, veterans' counselor. **Physically disabled:** Services for visually, speech, hearing impaired. **Transfer:** Re-entry adviser, pre-admission transcript evaluation for new students. Transfer center, transfer adviser, college fairs on campus for students transferring to 4-year colleges.

Contact. E-mail: jforbes@mayland.edu
Phone: (828) 766-1234 Toll-free number: (800) 462-9526 ext. 1234
Fax: (828) 765-0728
Michelle Musich, Dean of Students, Mayland Community College, PO Box 547, Spruce Pine, NC 28777

McDowell Technical Community College
Marion, North Carolina
www.mcdowelltech.edu   **CB code: 0789**

- Public 2-year community and technical college
- Commuter campus in small town

General. Founded in 1964. Regionally accredited. **Enrollment:** 1,323 degree-seeking undergraduates. **Degrees:** 124 associate awarded. **Location:** 35 miles from Asheville. **Calendar:** Semester, limited summer session. **Full-time faculty:** 49 total. **Part-time faculty:** 95 total; 2% minority. **Special facilities:** Color and black/white photography laboratories.

Student profile.

Out-of-state: 2%   25 or older: 58%

Basis for selection. Open admission, but selective for some programs. Special requirements for allied health programs. Interview required for some allied health programs. **Adult students:** Must take required placement tests. **Home schooled:** Transcript of courses and grades required.

2015-2016 Annual costs. Tuition/fees: $2,213; $7,973 out-of-state. Per-credit charge: $72 in-state; $264 out-of-state. Books/supplies: $1,200. Personal expenses: $3,316.

Financial aid. All financial aid based on need. Need-based aid available for part-time students. Work-study available nights, weekends and for part-time students.

Application procedures. Admission: No deadline. No application fee. Application must be submitted on paper. Admission notification on a rolling basis. **Financial aid:** Priority date 3/15; no closing date. FAFSA, institutional form required. Applicants notified on a rolling basis starting 7/1.

Academics. Special study options: Cooperative education, distance learning, double major, dual enrollment of high school students, independent study, internships, liberal arts/career combination. Bachelor's degree programs available on campus. License preparation in nursing. **Credit/placement by examination:** AP, CLEP, institutional tests. 20 credit hours maximum toward associate degree. **Support services:** GED preparation and test center, learning center, reduced course load, remedial instruction, study skills assistance, tutoring.

Majors. Business: General, accounting, office/clerical. **Communications technology:** Graphic/printing. **Computer sciences:** Applications programming, programming. **Education:** General. **Health services:** Nursing (RN).

Liberal arts: Arts/sciences. **Visual/performing arts:** Commercial photography, commercial/advertising art.

Most popular majors. Business/marketing 13%, computer/information sciences 6%, education 16%, health sciences 25%, liberal arts 14%, trade and industry 20%.

Technology on campus. 80 workstations in library, computer center.

Student life. Freshman orientation: Available. Preregistration for classes offered. Two-hour orientation held one day prior to registration day. **Activities:** Student government.

Student services. Adult student services, career counseling, student employment services, on-campus daycare, personal counseling, placement for graduates, veterans' counselor. **Physically disabled:** Services for visually, speech, hearing impaired. **Transfer:** Transfer adviser for students transferring to 4-year colleges.

Contact. E-mail: wingatecain@mcdowelltech.edu
Phone: (828) 652-0632 Fax: (828) 652-1014
Wingate Cain, Director of Admissions, McDowell Technical Community College, 54 College Drive, Marion, NC 28752

Miller-Motte College: Cary
Cary, North Carolina
www.miller-motte.edu

- For-profit 2-year technical and career college
- Commuter campus in small city

General. Regionally accredited; also accredited by ACICS. **Enrollment:** 316 undergraduates. **Degrees:** 63 associate awarded. **Location:** 10 miles from downtown Raleigh. **Calendar:** Quarter. **Full-time faculty:** 15 total. **Part-time faculty:** 23 total.

Basis for selection. Open admission, but selective for some programs. High school diploma is required and GED is accepted. **Home schooled:** Interview required.

2015-2016 Annual costs. Certificate programs: $10,560-$19,897, books and supplies $400-$4,800. Associate programs: $28,059-$28,248, books and supplies $5,400-$6,400.

Financial aid. Need-based: Work-study available nights, weekends and for part-time students.

Application procedures. Admission: No deadline. $40 fee. **Financial aid:** No deadline.

Academics. Credit/placement by examination: AP, CLEP. **Support services:** Tutoring.

Majors. Health services: Insurance coding, massage therapy, medical assistant, surgical technology.

Technology on campus. 25 workstations in library.

Student life. Freshman orientation: Preregistration for classes offered.

Student services. Physically disabled: Services for visually impaired.

Contact. Toll-free number: (888) 800-3049
Tim VanHorn, Admissions Director, Miller-Motte College: Cary, 2205 Walnut Street, Cary, NC 27518

Miller-Motte College: Fayetteville
Fayetteville, North Carolina
www.miller-motte.edu

- For-profit 2-year branch campus and technical college
- Large city

General. Regionally accredited; also accredited by ACICS. **Enrollment:** 741 undergraduates. **Degrees:** 127 associate awarded. **Calendar:** Quarter. **Full-time faculty:** 5 total. **Part-time faculty:** 38 total.

Basis for selection. Admission requirements vary by programs.

2015-2016 Annual costs. Certificate programs: $10,560-$20,788, books and supplies $400-$3,600. Associate programs: $26,202-$28,272, books and supplies $3,600-$4,800.

Financial aid. Need-based: Work-study available nights, weekends and for part-time students.

Application procedures. Admission: $40 fee.

Academics. Credit/placement by examination: AP, CLEP.

Majors. Health services: Medical assistant. **Protective services:** Law enforcement admin.

Contact. Toll-free number: (800) 705-9182
Brian Dow, Director of Admissions, Miller-Motte College: Fayetteville, 3725 Ramsey Street, Suite 103A, Fayetteville, NC 28311

Mitchell Community College
Statesville, North Carolina **CB member**
www.mitchellcc.edu **CB code: 5412**

▶ Public 2-year community college
▶ Commuter campus in large town

General. Founded in 1852. Regionally accredited. **Enrollment:** 2,672 degree-seeking undergraduates. **Degrees:** 417 associate awarded. **Location:** 40 miles from Charlotte, 40 miles from Winston-Salem. **Calendar:** Semester, limited summer session. **Full-time faculty:** 97 total. **Part-time faculty:** 238 total.

Student profile.

Out-of-state: 8% 25 or older: 40%

Transfer out. Colleges most students transferred to 2015: University of North Carolina-Charlotte, Appalachian State University, Gardner-Webb University, Lenoir-Rhyne University.

Basis for selection. Open admission, but selective for some programs. Special requirements for Nursing and Medical Assisting programs. Applicants for competitive entry programs are ranked based on completed courses, GPA, prior degrees earned, and performance on standardized tests.

2015-2016 Annual costs. Tuition/fees: $2,228; $7,988 out-of-state. Per-credit charge: $72 in-state; $264 out-of-state. Books/supplies: $1,100. Personal expenses: $3,160.

Financial aid. Need-based: Need-based aid available for part-time students. Work-study available nights, weekends and for part-time students.

Application procedures. Admission: No deadline. No application fee. Admission notification on a rolling basis. **Financial aid:** No deadline. FAFSA, institutional form required. Applicants notified on a rolling basis starting 3/1; must reply within 2 week(s) of notification.

Academics. Special study options: Cooperative education, distance learning, dual enrollment of high school students, independent study, weekend college. License preparation in nursing, paramedic, real estate. **Credit/placement by examination:** AP, CLEP, institutional tests. 20 credit hours maximum toward associate degree. **Support services:** GED preparation and test center, learning center, reduced course load, remedial instruction, tutoring.

Majors. Business: Accounting, administrative services, business admin, operations. **Computer sciences:** Information systems. **Education:** Early childhood, teacher assistance. **Engineering:** Electrical. **Health services:** Nursing (RN), predental, premedicine, prepharmacy, preveterinary. **Liberal arts:** Arts/sciences. **Protective services:** Police science. **Visual/performing arts:** Studio arts.

Most popular majors. Business/marketing 15%, computer/information sciences 13%, engineering/engineering technologies 6%, health sciences 26%, liberal arts 18%, personal/culinary services 8%.

Technology on campus. 45 workstations in library, computer center.

Student life. Freshman orientation: Available. Preregistration for classes offered. Usually held immediately prior to fall semester for approximately 2.5 hours. **Activities:** Concert band, choral groups, literary magazine, student government, Circle-K, Christian Student Fellowship, Ebony Kinship.

Student services. Chaplain/spiritual director, career counseling, student employment services, financial aid counseling, personal counseling, placement for graduates, veterans' counselor. **Physically disabled:** Services for

---

visually, hearing impaired. **Transfer:** College fairs on campus for students transferring to 4-year colleges.

Contact. E-mail: kmoore@mitchellcc.edu
Phone: (704) 878-3243 Fax: (704) 878-0872
Kirby Moore, Director of Admissions and Records, Mitchell Community College, 500 West Broad Street, Statesville, NC 28677

Montgomery Community College
Troy, North Carolina
www.montgomery.edu **CB code: 0785**

▶ Public 2-year community college
▶ Commuter campus in small town

General. Founded in 1967. Regionally accredited. **Enrollment:** 809 undergraduates. **Degrees:** 74 associate awarded. **Location:** 50 miles from Greensboro, 62 miles from Charlotte. **Calendar:** Semester, limited summer session. **Full-time faculty:** 36 total. **Part-time faculty:** 34 total. **Special facilities:** Rifle/pistol firing range.

Student profile. 15% enrolled in a transfer program, 82% enrolled in a vocational program, 3% already have a bachelor's degree or higher.

Out-of-state: 1% 25 or older: 38%

Transfer out. Colleges most students transferred to 2015: Pfeiffer University, Gardner-Webb University, University of North Carolina at Greensboro.

Basis for selection. Open admission, but selective for some programs. Special requirements for allied health programs. Secondary school record and test scores considered. **Home schooled:** Home school must provide copy of "Notification of intent to operate" card from NC Department of Non-Public Education. **Learning Disabled:** Requests for accommodations should be made at least 1 month prior to registration to allow time for review and arrangements. To determine eligibility for services, documentation of disability may be required.

High school preparation. Required units include English 4, mathematics 4, social studies 4, science 3 and academic electives 7.

2015-2016 Annual costs. Tuition/fees: $2,277; $8,037 out-of-state. Per-credit charge: $72 in-state; $264 out-of-state. Books/supplies: $1,404. Personal expenses: $1,224.

Financial aid. Need-based: Need-based aid available for part-time students. Work-study available nights, weekends and for part-time students. **Non-need-based:** Scholarships awarded for academics, minority status, state residency.

Application procedures. Admission: No deadline. No application fee. Application must be submitted online. Admission notification on a rolling basis. Application deadlines are in place for allied health programs. **Financial aid:** Closing date 7/1. FAFSA, institutional form required. Applicants notified on a rolling basis starting 3/15; must reply by 7/1.

Academics. Special study options: Distance learning, dual enrollment of high school students. Bachelor's degree programs available on campus. License preparation in nursing. **Credit/placement by examination:** AP, CLEP, institutional tests. 16 credit hours maximum toward associate degree. **Support services:** GED preparation and test center, learning center, reduced course load, remedial instruction, study skills assistance, tutoring, writing center.

Majors. Business: Business admin, office management. **Computer sciences:** Information technology. **Conservation:** Forest technology. **Education:** Early childhood. **General:** Electrician. **Health services:** Medical assistant. **Liberal arts:** Arts/sciences. **Protective services:** Criminal justice.

Most popular majors. Business/marketing 12%, education 8%, health sciences 16%, liberal arts 18%, natural resources/environmental science 20%, trade and industry 21%.

Technology on campus. 125 workstations in library, computer center. Commuter students can connect to campus network. Helpline, wireless network available.

Student life. Freshman orientation: Available. Preregistration for classes offered. **Activities:** Student government, human serivces club, phi beta lambda, practical nursing club, medical assisting club.

Athletics. Team name: Trailblazers.

Student services. Career counseling, financial aid counseling, personal counseling, veterans' counselor. **Physically disabled:** Services for visually, speech, hearing impaired. **Transfer:** Transfer adviser, college fairs on campus for students transferring to 4-year colleges.

Contact. E-mail: housleyt@montgomery.edu
Phone: (910) 576-6222 ext. 220 Toll-free number: (800) 839-6222
Fax: (910) 576-2176
Karen Frye, Enrollment Coordinator, Montgomery Community College, 1011 Page Street, Troy, NC 27371

Nash Community College
Rocky Mount, North Carolina
www.nashcc.edu

CB member
CB code: 5881

▶ Public 2-year community and technical college
▶ Commuter campus in small city

General. Founded in 1967. Regionally accredited. **Enrollment:** 1,939 degree-seeking undergraduates; 691 non-degree-seeking students. **Degrees:** 327 associate awarded. **Location:** 55 miles from Raleigh. **Calendar:** Semester, limited summer session. **Full-time faculty:** 100 total. **Part-time faculty:** 150 total. **Class size:** 54% < 20, 46% 20-39. **Special facilities:** Nature trail. **Partnerships:** Formal partnership with high schools to provide students opportunity to earn college credit.

Student profile. Among degree-seeking undergraduates, 30% enrolled in a transfer program, 70% enrolled in a vocational program, 15% already have a bachelor's degree or higher, 494 enrolled as first-time, first-year students.

Part-time:	46%	Native American:	1%
Out-of-state:	1%	International:	1%
Women:	62%	25 or older:	52%
African American:	28%		

Transfer out. 75% of students enrolled in the transfer program go on to 4-year colleges. **Colleges most students transferred to 2015:** University of North Carolina system universities.

Basis for selection. Open admission, but selective for some programs. Special requirements for nursing, physical therapy assistant, phlebotomy, cosmetology programs. **Adult students:** College recommends ASSET or COMPASS placement test if student does not have SAT scores. **Home schooled:** Transcript of courses and grades required.

High school preparation. Appropriate biology courses required for nursing and physical therapist assistant programs.

2015-2016 Annual costs. Tuition/fees: $2,776; $8,966 out-of-state. Per-credit charge: $72 in-state; $264 out-of-state. Books/supplies: $1,500. Personal expenses: $2,000.

Financial aid. Need-based: Need-based aid available for part-time students. Work-study available nights, weekends and for part-time students. **Non-need-based:** Scholarships awarded for academics.

Application procedures. Admission: No deadline. No application fee. Admission notification on a rolling basis. **Financial aid:** Priority date 6/30; no closing date. FAFSA, institutional form required. Applicants notified on a rolling basis starting 7/15.

Academics. Special study options: Accelerated study, distance learning, dual enrollment of high school students, ESL, honors, liberal arts/career combination. License preparation in nursing, paramedic, physical therapy, real estate. **Credit/placement by examination:** AP, CLEP, IB, institutional tests. 20 credit hours maximum toward associate degree. **Support services:** GED preparation and test center, learning center, reduced course load, remedial instruction, study skills assistance, tutoring, writing center.

Majors. Architecture: Technology. **Business:** Accounting, administrative services, business admin, hotel/motel admin, management information systems. **Computer sciences:** Information systems. **Education:** General, early childhood, teacher assistance. **Engineering:** Electrical. **General:** Lineworker. **Health services:** Licensed practical nurse, medical secretary, nursing (RN). **Liberal arts:** Arts/sciences. **Protective services:** Police science. **Work/family studies:** Child care management.

Most popular majors. Business/marketing 18%, computer/information sciences 8%, engineering/engineering technologies 16%, health sciences 21%, liberal arts 21%, social sciences 7%.

Technology on campus. PC or laptop required. 110 workstations in library, computer center, student center. Commuter students can connect to campus network. Online library, helpline, repair service, wireless network available.

Student life. Freshman orientation: Mandatory. Preregistration for classes offered. **Activities:** Campus ministries, choral groups, drama, radio station, student government, TV station.

Athletics. Team name: NightHawk.

Student services. Adult student services, alcohol/substance abuse counseling, career counseling, services for economically disadvantaged, student employment services, financial aid counseling, legal services, minority student services, on-campus daycare, personal counseling, placement for graduates, veterans' counselor, women's services. **Physically disabled:** Services for visually, speech, hearing impaired. **Transfer:** Pre-admission transcript evaluation for new students. Transfer adviser, college fairs on campus for students transferring to 4-year colleges.

Contact. E-mail: sgeanes@nashcc.edu
Phone: (252) 451-8257 Fax: (252) 451-8401
Stephanie Geanes, Admissions Officer, Nash Community College, Box 7488, Rocky Mount, NC 27804-0488

Pamlico Community College
Grantsboro, North Carolina
www.pamlicocc.edu

CB code: 0864

▶ Public 2-year community college
▶ Commuter campus in rural community
▶ Interview required

General. Founded in 1962. Regionally accredited. **Enrollment:** 504 degree-seeking undergraduates. **Degrees:** 32 associate awarded. **Location:** 20 miles from New Bern. **Calendar:** Semester, limited summer session. **Full-time faculty:** 29 total. **Part-time faculty:** 55 total.

Transfer out. Colleges most students transferred to 2015: Craven Community College.

Basis for selection. Open admission. Students talk to admission counselor and adviser. **Home schooled:** Transcript of courses and grades required.

High school preparation. College-preparatory program recommended. 24 units required.

2015-2016 Annual costs. Tuition/fees: $2,203; $7,963 out-of-state. Per-credit charge: $72 in-state; $264 out-of-state. Books/supplies: $1,220. Personal expenses: $1,630.

Financial aid. Need-based: Work-study available nights, weekends and for part-time students.

Application procedures. Admission: No deadline. No application fee. Application must be submitted on paper. Admission notification on a rolling basis. **Financial aid:** Closing date 6/1. FAFSA required. Applicants notified on a rolling basis.

Academics. Special study options: Cooperative education, distance learning, dual enrollment of high school students, ESL, independent study, internships. **Credit/placement by examination:** AP, CLEP, institutional tests. **Support services:** GED preparation and test center, learning center, reduced course load, remedial instruction, tutoring.

Majors. Business: Accounting, business admin, office/clerical. **Conservation:** General. **Education:** General, early childhood. **Engineering:** Electrical.

Technology on campus. 40 workstations in library. Online library, helpline, wireless network available.

Student life. Freshman orientation: Available. Preregistration for classes offered. **Activities:** Student government.

Student services. Career counseling, student employment services, financial aid counseling, personal counseling, placement for graduates, veterans' counselor. **Transfer:** Pre-admission transcript evaluation for new students. College fairs on campus for students transferring to 4-year colleges.

Contact. E-mail: cwarner@pamlicocc.edu
Phone: (252) 249-1851 Fax: (252) 249-2377
Cristy Lewis, Counselor, Pamlico Community College, PO Box 185, Grantsboro, NC 28529

Piedmont Community College
Roxboro, North Carolina
www.piedmontcc.edu

CB code: 5518

- Public 2-year community college
- Commuter campus in small town

General. Founded in 1970. Regionally accredited. Branch campus in Caswell County. Correctional education in foodservice technology and carpentry offered in Hillsborough. **Enrollment:** 1,020 degree-seeking undergraduates. **Degrees:** 155 associate awarded. **Location:** 30 miles from Durham, 45 miles from Chapel Hill. **Calendar:** Semester, limited summer session. **Special facilities:** 4-mile nature trail.

Student profile. Among degree-seeking undergraduates, 231 enrolled as first-time, first-year students.

Basis for selection. Open admission, but selective for some programs. Admission for nursing based on test scores, interview and recommendations. Nursing applicants must provide health data.

2015-2016 Annual costs. Tuition/fees: $2,232; $7,992 out-of-state. Per-credit charge: $72 in-state; $264 out-of-state. Books/supplies: $1,850. Personal expenses: $3,100.

2014-2015 Financial aid. Need-based: 99% of total undergraduate aid awarded as scholarships/grants, 1% as loans/jobs. Need-based aid available for part-time students. Work-study available nights, weekends and for part-time students.

Application procedures. Admission: No deadline. No application fee. Admission notification on a rolling basis. Certain certificate programs do not require high school diploma. **Financial aid:** Priority date 4/1; no closing date. FAFSA required. Applicants notified on a rolling basis starting 4/15; must reply within 2 week(s) of notification.

Academics. Special study options: Cooperative education, distance learning, double major, dual enrollment of high school students, independent study, internships, study abroad. License preparation in nursing. **Credit/placement by examination:** AP, CLEP, institutional tests. Maximum of 50% of coursework may be completed through credit by examination. **Support services:** GED preparation and test center, learning center, reduced course load, remedial instruction, study skills assistance, tutoring.

Majors. Business: Accounting, administrative services, business admin, office management. **Communications technology:** Animation/special effects, photo/film/video. **Computer sciences:** General. **Education:** Early childhood. **General:** Power transmission. **Health services:** Medical assistant, nursing (RN), office admin. **Liberal arts:** Arts/sciences. **Protective services:** Criminal justice. **Visual/performing arts:** General, cinematography.

Technology on campus. 140 workstations in library, computer center.

Student life. Freshman orientation: Available. Preregistration for classes offered. **Activities:** Choral groups, dance, drama, student government, student newspaper, Phi Theta Kappa, Student Nursing Assoc., C.A.R.E. (Human Services), Film/Video Production Technology club, ACM Student Siggraph Chapter, criminal justice club, Phi Beta Lambda, PCC Engage (Warriors for Christ), Minority Male Mentoring Initiative (3MI), athletic club.

Athletics. Team name: Pacers.

Student services. Career counseling, services for economically disadvantaged, student employment services, financial aid counseling, on-campus daycare, personal counseling, placement for graduates, veterans' counselor. **Physically disabled:** Services for visually, hearing impaired. **Transfer:** Pre-admission transcript evaluation for new students. Transfer center, transfer adviser, college fairs on campus for students transferring to 4-year colleges.

Contact. Phone: (336) 599-1181 Fax: (336) 598-9283
Gene Ritter, Director, Enrollment Management, Piedmont Community College, 1715 College Drive, Roxboro, NC 27573-1197

Pitt Community College
Greenville, North Carolina
www.pittcc.edu

CB member
CB code: 5556

- Public 2-year community and technical college
- Commuter campus in small city

General. Founded in 1961. Regionally accredited. **Enrollment:** 8,521 undergraduates. **Degrees:** 1,161 associate awarded. **ROTC:** Army. **Location:** 85 miles from Raleigh. **Calendar:** Semester, limited summer session. **Full-time faculty:** 226 total. **Part-time faculty:** 429 total. **Class size:** 66% < 20, 34% 20-39, less than 1% 40-49, less than 1% 50-99.

Student profile. 1,005 transferred in from other institutions.

Out-of-state: 2% **25 or older:** 39%

Transfer out. Colleges most students transferred to 2015: East Carolina University, University of North Carolina at Wilmington, Barton College.

Basis for selection. Open admission, but selective for some programs. Special admission requirements for some allied health programs. SAT and/or ACT may be used in lieu of the college's placement test for placement into English and Math courses.

2015-2016 Annual costs. Tuition/fees: $2,234; $7,994 out-of-state. Per-credit charge: $72 in-state; $264 out-of-state. Books/supplies: $1,200.

Financial aid. Need-based: Need-based aid available for part-time students. Work-study available nights, weekends and for part-time students. **Non-need-based:** Scholarships awarded for academics, athletics, ROTC.

Application procedures. Admission: No deadline. No application fee. Admission notification on a rolling basis. **Financial aid:** Priority date 3/15, closing date 5/15. FAFSA required. Applicants notified on a rolling basis starting 2/1.

Academics. Special study options: Cooperative education, distance learning, double major, dual enrollment of high school students, ESL, independent study, internships, weekend college. License preparation in nursing, occupational therapy, paramedic, radiology, real estate. **Credit/placement by examination:** AP, CLEP, institutional tests. 40 credit hours maximum toward associate degree. Credit by examination can not be included in the 25% residency requirement. **Support services:** GED preparation and test center, learning center, remedial instruction, tutoring.

Majors. Architecture: Technology. **Business:** Accounting technology, administrative services, business admin, e-commerce, entrepreneurial studies, human resources, marketing, office management, office/clerical, operations, retail management, sales/distribution, training/development. **Computer sciences:** Applications programming, information systems, information technology, security, vendor certification. **Education:** Early childhood. **General:** Building construction, electrician. **Health services:** Cardiovascular technology, electrocardiograph technology, EMT paramedic, health care admin, health information technology, licensed practical nurse, mammography technology, massage therapy, medical assistant, medical radiologic technology/radiation therapy, medical secretary, mental health services, nuclear medical technology, occupational therapy assistant, office admin, polysomnography, radiologic technology/medical imaging, radiologist assistant, recreational therapy, respiratory therapy assistant, respiratory therapy technology, sonography, substance abuse counseling. **Liberal arts:** Arts/sciences. **Protective services:** Criminal justice, police science. **Visual/performing arts:** Graphic design, studio arts. **Work/family studies:** Child care service.

Most popular majors. Business/marketing 10%, computer/information sciences 10%, engineering/engineering technologies 10%, health sciences 33%, liberal arts 20%, trade and industry 15%.

Technology on campus. 50 workstations in library, computer center. Helpline available.

Student life. Freshman orientation: Available. Preregistration for classes offered. **Activities:** Student government, Gamma Beta Phi, student government association, Southern Organization of Human Services Organization, Society of Advancement of Management, Delta Epsilon Chi, multicultural/international Club, Students Monitoring Students.

Athletics. NJCAA. **Intercollegiate:** Baseball M, basketball M, golf M, softball W, volleyball W. **Intramural:** Basketball M. **Team name:** Bulldogs.

Student services. Adult student services, alcohol/substance abuse counseling, career counseling, services for economically disadvantaged, student employment services, financial aid counseling, minority student services, on-campus daycare, personal counseling, veterans' counselor. **Physically disabled:** Services for visually, speech, hearing impaired. **Transfer:** Transfer adviser, college fairs on campus for students transferring to 4-year colleges.

Contact. E-mail: pittadm@email.pittcc.edu
Phone: (252) 493-7232 Fax: (252) 321-4209
Joanne Ceres, Director of Admissions and Records, Pitt Community College, PO Drawer 7007, Greenville, NC 27835-7007

Randolph Community College
Asheboro, North Carolina
www.randolph.edu
CB code: 5585

- Public 2-year community and technical college
- Commuter campus in large town

General. Founded in 1962. Regionally accredited. **Enrollment:** 2,813 degree-seeking undergraduates. **Degrees:** 447 associate awarded. **ROTC:** Air Force. **Location:** 65 miles from Charlotte, 26 miles from Greensboro. **Calendar:** Semester, limited summer session. **Full-time faculty:** 85 total. **Part-time faculty:** 169 total.

Transfer out. Colleges most students transferred to 2015: University of North Carolina-Greensboro, High Point University, Guilford College, University of North Carolina-Charlotte.

Basis for selection. Open admission, but selective for some programs. Selective admission to Allied Health programs. **Home schooled:** Transcript of courses and grades required. Copy of certificate of home school operation or a Notice of Intent (to operate a home school) is required to have been sent to the North Carolina Non-Public Education Office.

High school preparation. College-preparatory program recommended.

2015-2016 Annual costs. Tuition/fees: $2,228; $7,988 out-of-state. Per-credit charge: $72 in-state; $264 out-of-state. Books/supplies: $1,091. Personal expenses: $2,700.

Financial aid. Need-based: Need-based aid available for part-time students. Work-study available nights, weekends and for part-time students. **Non-need-based:** Scholarships awarded for academics, leadership, minority status, state residency.

Application procedures. Admission: No deadline. No application fee. Admission notification on a rolling basis. Students are required to complete placement testing, sign a placement assessment waiver, or send official placement test scores taken within the last 5 years prior to enrolling in addition to submitting transcripts (high school and college if applicable). **Financial aid:** No deadline. FAFSA required. Applicants notified on a rolling basis starting 3/1.

Academics. Special study options: Cooperative education, distance learning, double major, dual enrollment of high school students, ESL, independent study, internships, liberal arts/career combination, weekend college. Bachelor's degree programs available on campus. **Credit/placement by examination:** AP, CLEP, IB, institutional tests. 16 credit hours maximum toward associate degree. **Support services:** GED preparation and test center, learning center, remedial instruction, study skills assistance, tutoring, writing center.

Majors. Business: Accounting, business admin, entrepreneurial studies, human resources, logistics, office management. **Communications:** Photojournalism. **Communications technology:** Photo/film/video. **Computer sciences:** Information technology, networking. **Education:** Early childhood. **General:** Electrician. **Health services:** Medical assistant, nursing (RN), office admin, radiologic technology/medical imaging. **Liberal arts:** Arts/sciences. **Protective services:** Criminal justice. **Visual/performing arts:** Commercial photography, commercial/advertising art, interior design.

Most popular majors. Business/marketing 11%, education 6%, family/consumer sciences 6%, health sciences 19%, liberal arts 31%, security/protective services 7%, trade and industry 9%, visual/performing arts 8%.

Technology on campus. Online course registration, online library, wireless network available.

Student life. Freshman orientation: Available. Preregistration for classes offered. **Activities:** Student government.

Athletics. Team name: Armadillos.

Student services. Adult student services, career counseling, financial aid counseling, minority student services, personal counseling, veterans' counselor. **Physically disabled:** Services for visually, speech, hearing impaired. **Transfer:** Pre-admission transcript evaluation for new students. Transfer adviser, college fairs on campus for students transferring to 4-year colleges.

Contact. E-mail: rccreg@randolph.edu
Phone: (336) 633-0239 Fax: (336) 629-4695
Brandi Hagerman, Director of Enrollment Management / Registrar, Randolph Community College, 629 Industrial Park Avenue, Asheboro, NC 27205

Richmond Community College
Hamlet, North Carolina
CB member
www.richmondcc.edu
CB code: 5588

- Public 2-year community college
- Commuter campus in small town

General. Founded in 1964. Regionally accredited. **Enrollment:** 2,321 undergraduates. **Degrees:** 298 associate awarded. **Location:** 75 miles from Charlotte. **Calendar:** Semester, limited summer session. **Full-time faculty:** 68 total. **Part-time faculty:** 5 total. **Special facilities:** Health science building with exam rooms and simulation areas.

Transfer out. Colleges most students transferred to 2015: UNC-Pembroke, Gardner-Webb University, UNC-Charlotte, Fayetteville State.

Basis for selection. Open admission, but selective for some programs. Admission to nursing program based on academic record and completion of admission requirements, interview required. **Home schooled:** Transcript of courses and grades required.

2015-2016 Annual costs. Tuition/fees: $2,224; $7,984 out-of-state. Per-credit charge: $72 in-state; $264 out-of-state. Books/supplies: $600. Personal expenses: $900.

Financial aid. Need-based: Need-based aid available for part-time students. Work-study available nights, weekends and for part-time students. **Non-need-based:** Scholarships awarded for academics, leadership.

Application procedures. Admission: No deadline. No application fee. Admission notification on a rolling basis. **Financial aid:** Closing date 7/25. FAFSA, institutional form required. Applicants notified on a rolling basis starting 7/8; must reply within 2 week(s) of notification.

Academics. Special study options: Cooperative education, cross-registration, distance learning, double major, dual enrollment of high school students, ESL, independent study, internships, student-designed major, teacher certification program. Bachelor's degree programs available on campus. License preparation in nursing. **Credit/placement by examination:** AP, CLEP, institutional tests. 15 credit hours maximum toward associate degree. Interview required for placement and counseling. **Support services:** GED preparation and test center, learning center, reduced course load, remedial instruction, study skills assistance, tutoring, writing center.

Majors. Business: Accounting, administrative services, business admin, management information systems. **Computer sciences:** Information systems, networking. **Engineering:** Electrical. **Health services:** Medical assistant, mental health services, nursing (RN). **Human services:** Social work. **Liberal arts:** Arts/sciences. **Work/family studies:** Child care management.

Technology on campus. 250 workstations in library, computer center.

Student life. Freshman orientation: Mandatory. Preregistration for classes offered. **Activities:** Drama, student government, student newspaper.

Student services. Career counseling, student employment services, financial aid counseling, health services, minority student services, personal counseling, placement for graduates, veterans' counselor. **Physically disabled:** Services for visually, hearing impaired. **Transfer:** Transfer adviser, college fairs on campus for students transferring to 4-year colleges.

Contact. Phone: (910) 410-1736 Fax: (910) 582-7102
Director of Admissions, Richmond Community College, Box 1189, Hamlet, NC 28345

Roanoke-Chowan Community College
Ahoskie, North Carolina
www.roanokechowan.edu
CB code: 5564

- Public 2-year community college
- Commuter campus in small town

General. Founded in 1967. Regionally accredited. **Enrollment:** 903 degree-seeking undergraduates. **Degrees:** 77 associate awarded. **Location:** 60 miles from Greenville, 65 miles from Norfolk, VA. **Calendar:** Semester, limited summer session. **Full-time faculty:** 33 total. **Part-time faculty:** 39 total. **Class size:** 70% < 20, 29% 20-39, 2% 40-49. **Special facilities:** Arboretum/environmental science outdoor laboratory.

Student profile. Among degree-seeking undergraduates, 36 transferred in from other institutions.

Two-Year Colleges

Transfer out. Colleges most students transferred to 2015: Elizabeth City State University, Pitt Community College, East Carolina University.

Basis for selection. Open admission, but selective for some programs. Special requirements for nursing applicants. **Adult students:** SAT/ACT scores not required. **Home schooled:** Statement describing home school structure and mission, transcript of courses and grades required.

2015-2016 Annual costs. Tuition/fees: $2,261; $8,021 out-of-state. Per-credit charge: $72 in-state; $264 out-of-state. Books/supplies: $800. Personal expenses: $1,555.

2014-2015 Financial aid. Need-based: 56 full-time freshmen applied for aid; 56 deemed to have need; 56 received aid. Average need met was 95%. Average scholarship/grant was $4,841; average loan $1,364. 98% of total undergraduate aid awarded as scholarships/grants, 2% as loans/jobs. Need-based aid available for part-time students. Work-study available nights, weekends and for part-time students. **Non-need-based:** Scholarships awarded for academics.

Application procedures. Admission: No deadline. No application fee. Admission notification on a rolling basis. **Financial aid:** Priority date 3/15; no closing date. FAFSA required. Applicants notified on a rolling basis starting 7/1.

Academics. Special study options: Accelerated study, cooperative education, distance learning, dual enrollment of high school students, ESL, independent study, internships. License preparation in nursing, paramedic. **Credit/placement by examination:** AP, CLEP, institutional tests. **Support services:** GED preparation and test center, learning center, reduced course load, remedial instruction, study skills assistance, tutoring.

Majors. Business: Administrative services, business admin. **Computer sciences:** Information systems, webmaster. **Conservation:** Environmental science. **Education:** Early childhood. **Health services:** Mental health services, nursing (RN), substance abuse counseling. **Liberal arts:** Arts/sciences. **Protective services:** Criminal justice.

Most popular majors. Business/marketing 11%, computer/information sciences 7%, health sciences 24%, liberal arts 39%, security/protective services 6%.

Technology on campus. 200 workstations in library, computer center. Commuter students can connect to campus network. Online library, wireless network available.

Student life. Freshman orientation: Available. Preregistration for classes offered. **Activities:** Choral groups, student government, student newspaper.

Athletics. Team name: Waves.

Student services. Career counseling, services for economically disadvantaged, student employment services, financial aid counseling, minority student services, personal counseling, veterans' counselor, women's services. **Transfer:** Pre-admission transcript evaluation for new students.

Contact. Phone: (252) 862-1200 Fax: (252) 862-1355
Amy Wiggins, Director of Enrollment Services, Roanoke-Chowan Community College, 109 Community College Road, Ahoskie, NC 27910-9522

Robeson Community College
Lumberton, North Carolina
www.robeson.edu
CB code: 5594

- Public 2-year community college
- Commuter campus in large town

General. Founded in 1965. Regionally accredited. **Enrollment:** 1,867 degree-seeking undergraduates. **Degrees:** 165 associate awarded. **Location:** 30 miles from Fayetteville. **Calendar:** Semester, limited summer session.

Basis for selection. Open admission, but selective for some programs. Special admissions requirements for health science programs. Interview recommended. **Adult students:** SAT/ACT scores not required.

2015-2016 Annual costs. Tuition/fees: $2,285; $8,045 out-of-state. Per-credit charge: $72 in-state; $264 out-of-state.

Financial aid. Need-based: Need-based aid available for part-time students. Work-study available nights, weekends and for part-time students.

Application procedures. Admission: Closing date 7/12. No application fee. Admission notification on a rolling basis. **Financial aid:** Priority date

5/15; no closing date. FAFSA required. Applicants notified on a rolling basis starting 7/31.

Academics. Special study options: Distance learning, double major, dual enrollment of high school students, honors. License preparation in nursing, paramedic, radiology. **Credit/placement by examination:** AP, CLEP, IB, institutional tests. 40 credit hours maximum toward associate degree. **Support services:** GED preparation and test center, learning center, reduced course load, remedial instruction, study skills assistance, tutoring, writing center.

Majors. Business: Business admin, office management. **Computer sciences:** Information technology. **Education:** Early childhood. **General:** Electrician. **Health services:** EMT paramedic, nursing (RN), office admin, radiologic technology/medical imaging, respiratory therapy technology. **Liberal arts:** Arts/sciences. **Protective services:** Criminal justice.

Technology on campus. 50 workstations in library. Commuter students can connect to campus network. Online course registration, online library, helpline, wireless network available.

Student life. Freshman orientation: Mandatory. Preregistration for classes offered. **Activities:** Student government.

Student services. Adult student services, career counseling, services for economically disadvantaged, student employment services, financial aid counseling, personal counseling, placement for graduates, veterans' counselor. **Physically disabled:** Services for visually, hearing impaired. **Transfer:** Pre-admission transcript evaluation for new students. Transfer center, transfer adviser, college fairs on campus for students transferring to 4-year colleges.

Contact. E-mail: rlocklear@robeson.edu
Phone: (910) 272-3347 Fax: (910) 618-5686
Ronnie Locklear, Director of Admissions, Robeson Community College, PO Box 1420, Lumberton, NC 28359

Rockingham Community College
Wentworth, North Carolina
www.rockinghamcc.edu
CB code: 5582

- Public 2-year community college
- Commuter campus in rural community

General. Founded in 1963. Regionally accredited. **Enrollment:** 1,860 undergraduates. **Degrees:** 189 associate awarded. **Location:** 26 miles from Greensboro. **Calendar:** Semester, extensive summer session. **Full-time faculty:** 62 total. **Part-time faculty:** 65 total.

Transfer out. Colleges most students transferred to 2015: University of North Carolina at Greensboro, North Carolina A&T University.

Basis for selection. Open admission, but selective for some programs. All allied health programs and some other programs require all or some of the following: qualifying high school and college GPA, placement testing, specific high school courses, professional certification, other exams. Interview required for nursing and occupational therapy assistant programs. **Home schooled:** Need complete record of all courses taken in grades 9-12.

High school preparation. Recommended units include English 4, mathematics 3, social studies 2, history 1, science 3 (laboratory 1) and foreign language 2.

2015-2016 Annual costs. Tuition/fees: $2,256; $8,016 out-of-state. Per-credit charge: $72 in-state; $264 out-of-state. Books/supplies: $1,500. Personal expenses: $4,100.

Financial aid. Need-based: Need-based aid available for part-time students. Work-study available nights, weekends and for part-time students. **Non-need-based:** Scholarships awarded for academics.

Application procedures. Admission: No deadline. No application fee. Admission notification on a rolling basis. **Financial aid:** Priority date 3/15; no closing date. FAFSA, institutional form required. Must reply within 2 week(s) of notification.

Academics. Special study options: Cooperative education, distance learning, dual enrollment of high school students, independent study. Preengineering program leading to transfer to North Carolina State University, North Carolina Agricultural and Technical State University, or University of North Carolina at Charlotte. License preparation in nursing. **Credit/placement by examination:** AP, CLEP, institutional tests. **Support services:** GED preparation and test center, learning center, reduced course load, remedial instruction, study skills assistance, tutoring.

Majors. Biology: Biotechnology. **Business:** Accounting, business admin, financial planning, office technology, office/clerical. **Computer sciences:** Information systems. **Education:** Early childhood. **Engineering:** Electrical. **Health services:** Medical secretary, nursing (RN), respiratory therapy technology. **Liberal arts:** Arts/sciences. **Protective services:** Law enforcement admin. **Visual/performing arts:** Studio arts.

Most popular majors. Health sciences 15%, liberal arts 53%, security/protective services 8%, trade and industry 6%.

Technology on campus. 1,022 workstations in library, computer center. Wireless network available.

Student life. Freshman orientation: Available. Preregistration for classes offered. **Activities:** Student government, student newspaper, Phi Theta Kappa, art club, criminal justice club, early childhood educators club, musicians guild, NC Association of Nursing Students, practical nursing club, science club, Sigma Kappa Delta, Students in Free Enterprise.

Athletics. NJCAA. **Intercollegiate:** Baseball M, volleyball W. **Intramural:** Basketball, table tennis, tennis, volleyball. **Team name:** Eagles.

Student services. Career counseling, services for economically disadvantaged, student employment services, financial aid counseling, personal counseling, placement for graduates, veterans' counselor. **Physically disabled:** Services for visually, hearing impaired. **Transfer:** Transfer adviser, college fairs on campus for students transferring to 4-year colleges.

Contact. E-mail: admissions@rockinghamcc.edu
Phone: (336) 342-4261 ext. 2333 Fax: (336) 342-1809
Derrick Satterfield, Director of Enrollment Services, Rockingham Community College, Box 38, Wentworth, NC 27375-0038

Rowan-Cabarrus Community College
Salisbury, North Carolina
www.rccc.edu
CB code: 5589

▶ Public 2-year community and technical college
▶ Commuter campus in large town

General. Founded in 1961. Regionally accredited. **Enrollment:** 5,536 degree-seeking undergraduates. **Degrees:** 828 associate awarded. **Location:** 40 miles from Charlotte. **Calendar:** Semester, extensive summer session. **Full-time faculty:** 157 total. **Part-time faculty:** 437 total. **Class size:** 58% < 20, 39% 20-39, 2% 40-49, less than 1% 50-99.

Transfer out. Colleges most students transferred to 2015: University of North Carolina-Charlotte, Pfeiffer University, Catawba College.

Basis for selection. Open admission, but selective for some programs. Interview required for allied health programs.

2015-2016 Annual costs. Tuition/fees: $2,289; $8,049 out-of-state. Per-credit charge: $72 in-state; $264 out-of-state. Books/supplies: $900.

Financial aid. Need-based: Need-based aid available for part-time students. Work-study available nights, weekends and for part-time students. **Non-need-based:** Scholarships awarded for academics, job skills, state residency.

Application procedures. Admission: No deadline. No application fee. Admission notification on a rolling basis. **Financial aid:** Priority date 3/15; no closing date. FAFSA required. Applicants notified on a rolling basis starting 5/1; must reply within 3 week(s) of notification.

Academics. Special study options: Cooperative education, distance learning, dual enrollment of high school students, ESL, liberal arts/career combination, teacher certification program. License preparation in nursing, radiology, real estate. **Credit/placement by examination:** AP, CLEP, institutional tests. 75 credit hours maximum toward associate degree. Student must complete 25% of credits required for graduation in resident classes. **Support services:** GED preparation and test center, learning center, reduced course load, remedial instruction, tutoring, writing center.

Majors. Business: Accounting, business admin, office technology. **Computer sciences:** Information systems, programming. **Education:** Early childhood. **Health services:** Nursing (RN), radiologic technology/medical imaging. **Protective services:** Criminal justice, fire safety technology.

Student life. Freshman orientation: Available. Preregistration for classes offered. Fall and spring orientation. **Activities:** Student government.

Student services. Career counseling, student employment services, on-campus daycare, personal counseling, placement for graduates, veterans'

counselor. **Physically disabled:** Services for visually, speech, hearing impaired. **Transfer:** Pre-admission transcript evaluation for new students. College fairs on campus for students transferring to 4-year colleges.

Contact. Phone: (704) 216-3602 Fax: (704) 633-6804
Rob Dunnam, Director, Admissions and Recruitment, Rowan-Cabarrus Community College, Box 1595, Salisbury, NC 28145

Sampson Community College
Clinton, North Carolina
www.sampsoncc.edu
CB code: 0505

▶ Public 2-year community and technical college
▶ Commuter campus in small town
▶ Interview required

General. Founded in 1965. Regionally accredited. **Enrollment:** 1,539 degree-seeking undergraduates. **Degrees:** 192 associate awarded. **Location:** 30 miles from Fayetteville. **Calendar:** Semester, limited summer session. **Full-time faculty:** 76 total. **Part-time faculty:** 53 total.

Student profile.

Out-of-state:	1% 25 or older:	47%

Transfer out. Colleges most students transferred to 2015: Fayetteville State University, UNC-Wilmington, Campbell University, Mt. Olive College, East Carolina University.

Basis for selection. Open admission, but selective for some programs. Special requirements for nursing and practical nursing; secondary school record and test scores important. Interview required for nursing programs.

High school preparation. 15 units recommended. Recommended units include English 4, mathematics 3, social studies 3, science 4 and foreign language 2. Algebra, chemistry and biology required for nursing programs.

2015-2016 Annual costs. Tuition/fees: $2,237; $7,997 out-of-state. Per-credit charge: $72 in-state; $264 out-of-state. Books/supplies: $600. Personal expenses: $900.

Financial aid. Need-based: Need-based aid available for part-time students. Work-study available nights, weekends and for part-time students. **Non-need-based:** Scholarships awarded for academics, state residency.

Application procedures. Admission: Priority date 5/1; no deadline. No application fee. Admission notification on a rolling basis. **Financial aid:** Priority date 5/1; no closing date. FAFSA required. Applicants notified on a rolling basis starting 7/15; must reply within 2 week(s) of notification.

Academics. Special study options: Cooperative education, distance learning, dual enrollment of high school students, independent study, internships, liberal arts/career combination, weekend college. License preparation in nursing. **Credit/placement by examination:** AP, CLEP, institutional tests. 15 credit hours maximum toward associate degree. **Support services:** GED preparation and test center, learning center, pre-admission summer program, reduced course load, remedial instruction, study skills assistance, tutoring.

Majors. Business: Accounting, administrative services, business admin, office/clerical. **Computer sciences:** General, applications programming, information systems. **Education:** General, early childhood. **General:** Carpentry. **Health services:** Licensed practical nurse, nursing (RN).

Technology on campus. 110 workstations in library, computer center.

Student life. Freshman orientation: Mandatory. Preregistration for classes offered. **Activities:** Student government, student newspaper.

Student services. Adult student services, career counseling, student employment services, financial aid counseling, personal counseling, placement for graduates, veterans' counselor. **Physically disabled:** Services for visually, speech, hearing impaired. **Transfer:** Pre-admission transcript evaluation for new students. Transfer adviser, college fairs on campus for students transferring to 4-year colleges.

Contact. E-mail: admissions@sampsoncc.edu
Phone: (910) 592-8081 Fax: (910) 592-8048
Oscar Rodriguez, Director of Admissions, Sampson Community College, PO Box 318, Clinton, NC 28329

Sandhills Community College
Pinehurst, North Carolina
www.sandhills.edu   CB code: 5649

- Public 2-year community college
- Commuter campus in large town

General. Founded in 1963. Regionally accredited. **Enrollment:** 2,889 degree-seeking undergraduates. **Degrees:** 579 associate awarded. **Location:** 41 miles from Fayetteville, 71 miles from Raleigh. **Calendar:** Semester, limited summer session. **Full-time faculty:** 128 total. **Part-time faculty:** 185 total. **Class size:** 51% < 20, 46% 20-39, 1% 40-49, 2% 50-99. **Special facilities:** Student maintained 30-acre garden, culinary arts lab.

Student profile.

Out-of-state: 1%   25 or older: 41%

Transfer out. Colleges most students transferred to 2015: University of North Carolina-Chapel Hill, University of North Carolina-Charlotte, University of North Carolina-Pembroke, North Carolina State University, Appalachian State University.

Basis for selection. Open admission, but selective for some programs. Placement testing required for all students who wish to enroll in curriculum programs and all non-degree seeking students who enroll in English, mathematics, or other restricted courses. Students with a minimum SAT score of 500 Writing, 500 Critical Reading, 500 Math or ACT score of 21 Writing, 21 Reading, 21 Math may be placed into college level English and math classes without taking a placement test. **Adult students:** SAT/ACT scores not required. **Home schooled:** Transcript of courses and grades required. Copy of state registration required. **Learning Disabled:** Students with learning disabilities recommended to take classes in Continuing Education Program first.

2015-2016 Annual costs. Tuition/fees: $2,326; $8,086 out-of-state. Per-credit charge: $72 in-state; $264 out-of-state. Books/supplies: $1,250. Personal expenses: $924.

2015-2016 Financial aid. Need-based: 95% of total undergraduate aid awarded as scholarships/grants, 5% as loans/jobs. Need-based aid available for part-time students. Work-study available nights, weekends and for part-time students. **Non-need-based:** Scholarships awarded for academics, state residency.

Application procedures. Admission: No deadline. No application fee. Admission notification on a rolling basis. **Financial aid:** Closing date 7/14. FAFSA required. Applicants notified on a rolling basis starting 5/1; must reply by 8/1 or within 4 week(s) of notification.

Academics. Weekend support services held at satellite campus. **Special study options:** Cooperative education, distance learning, double major, dual enrollment of high school students, ESL, honors, independent study, internships, liberal arts/career combination, teacher certification program. Third and fourth year courses offered on campus evenings by St. Andrews Presbyterian College and UNC Pembroke. Bachelor's degree programs available on campus. License preparation in nursing, paramedic, radiology. **Credit/placement by examination:** AP, CLEP, institutional tests. **Support services:** GED preparation and test center, learning center, reduced course load, remedial instruction, study skills assistance, tutoring.

Majors. Architecture: Technology. **Biology:** General. **Business:** Accounting, administrative services, business admin, e-commerce, hotel/motel admin, restaurant/food services. **Computer sciences:** General, applications programming, computer science, information systems, programming, webmaster. **Education:** Biology, chemistry, early childhood, elementary, history, science, secondary, social science, social studies, teacher assistance. **Health services:** Clinical lab technology, EMT ambulance attendant, EMT paramedic, health information management, massage therapy, medical radiologic technology/radiation therapy, nursing (RN), predental, premedicine, prenursing, prepharmacy, preveterinary, respiratory therapy technology, substance abuse counseling, surgical technology. **Human services:** Social work. **Liberal arts:** Arts/sciences. **Math:** General. **Parks/recreation:** Health/fitness. **Protective services:** Criminal justice. **Psychology:** General. **Social sciences:** General. **Visual/performing arts:** Art, music. **Work/family studies:** Child care management.

Most popular majors. Business/marketing 8%, computer/information sciences 6%, health sciences 42%, liberal arts 11%, trade and industry 11%.

Technology on campus. 400 workstations in library, computer center, student center. Commuter students can connect to campus network. Wireless network available.

Student life. Freshman orientation: Available. Preregistration for classes offered. 2-hour information session, course planning, and registration. **Activities:** Bands, choral groups, music ensembles, student government, student newspaper, symphony orchestra, Minority Students for Academic and Cultural Enrichment, Circle-K, Young Democrats, Young Republicans, Phi Theta Kappa, Nursing Club, Rotaract.

Athletics. NJCAA. **Intercollegiate:** Basketball M, golf, volleyball W. **Intramural:** Ultimate frisbee. **Team name:** Flyers.

Student services. Adult student services, alcohol/substance abuse counseling, career counseling, services for economically disadvantaged, student employment services, financial aid counseling, minority student services, personal counseling, placement for graduates, veterans' counselor. **Physically disabled:** Services for visually, hearing impaired. **Transfer:** Pre-admission transcript evaluation for new students. Transfer adviser, college fairs on campus for students transferring to 4-year colleges.

Contact. E-mail: greenec@sandhills.edu
Phone: (910) 692-6185 Toll-free number: (800) 338-3944
Fax: (910) 695-3981
Cary Greene, Director of Admissions, Sandhills Community College, 3395 Airport Road, Pinehurst, NC 28374

South College
Asheville, North Carolina
www.southcollegenc.edu   CB code: 0508

- For-profit 2-year health science and career college
- Commuter campus in small city
- Interview required

General. Founded in 1905. Regionally accredited; also accredited by ACICS. **Enrollment:** 263 degree-seeking undergraduates. **Degrees:** 4 bachelor's, 75 associate awarded. **Location:** 4 miles from downtown. **Calendar:** Quarter, extensive summer session. **Full-time faculty:** 21 total; 19% have terminal degrees, 71% women. **Part-time faculty:** 41 total; 24% have terminal degrees, 49% women. **Class size:** 92% < 20, 8% 20-39.

Transfer out. Colleges most students transferred to 2015: Asheville-Buncombe Technical Community College, Blue Ridge Community College, Mars Hill College, Montreat College.

Basis for selection. Open admission, but selective for some programs. College-administered exam required of all applicants. Scores used for admission and program placement. **Home schooled:** Copy of homeschool diploma required.

2015-2016 Annual costs. Books/supplies: $2,000. Personal expenses: $3,069. **Additional information:** Bachelor programs: Legal Studies $75,725, books and supplies $4,245. Radiological Sciences $75,725, books and supplies $5,243. Associate programs: Accounting $46,600, books and supplies $3,459. Business Administration $46,600, books and supplies $2,755. Criminal Justice $46,600, books and supplies $3,713. Medical Assisting $46,600, books and supplies $2,672. Nursing $50,300, books and supplies $3,485. Occupational Therapy Assistant $49,800, books and supplies $3,473. Paralegal Studies $46,600, books and supplies $4,359. Physical Therapist Assistant $49,800, books and supplies $3,473. Radiologic Technology $4,800, books and supplies $4,821. Certificate programs: Medical Assisting $23,300, books and supplies $1,336. Surgical Technology $2,125, books and supplies $2,313.

Financial aid. Need-based: Need-based aid available for part-time students. Work-study available nights, weekends and for part-time students.

Application procedures. Admission: No deadline. $50 fee, may be waived for applicants with need. Application must be submitted on paper. Admission notification on a rolling basis. **Financial aid:** No deadline. FAFSA, institutional form required. Applicants notified on a rolling basis; must reply within 4 week(s) of notification.

Academics. Special study options: Internships, liberal arts/career combination. Bachelor's degree programs available on campus. License preparation in nursing, occupational therapy, physical therapy, radiology. **Credit/placement by examination:** AP, CLEP, institutional tests. Students may not earn more than 60% of their total credits or 50% of their major credits through credit by examination, transfer credit, or a combination thereof. **Support services:** Reduced course load, study skills assistance, tutoring, writing center.

Majors. Business: Accounting, business admin. **Health services:** Medical assistant, nursing (RN), physical therapy assistant, radiologic technology/medical imaging. **Protective services:** Law enforcement admin.

Most popular majors. Health sciences 96%.

Technology on campus. 28 workstations in library, computer center. Online library, wireless network available.

Student life. Freshman orientation: Mandatory. Preregistration for classes offered. Orientation is held prior to each quarter. **Policies:** No smoking on campus.

Student services. Career counseling, student employment services, financial aid counseling, placement for graduates, veterans' counselor. **Transfer:** Pre-admission transcript evaluation for new students.

Contact. Phone: (828) 398-2500 Fax: (828) 277-6151
Elisa Jacobs, Director of Admissions, South College, 140 Sweeten Creek Road, Asheville, NC 28803

South Piedmont Community College
Polkton, North Carolina
www.spcc.edu   CB code: 3623

▶ Public 2-year community college
▶ Commuter campus in small city

General. Founded in 1962. Regionally accredited. Multiple campus locations near Charlotte. **Enrollment:** 1,747 degree-seeking undergraduates. **Degrees:** 281 associate awarded. **Location:** 60 miles from Charlotte. **Calendar:** Semester, limited summer session. **Full-time faculty:** 61 total. **Part-time faculty:** 74 total.

Student profile.

Out-of-state:	1%	25 or older:	57%

Basis for selection. Open admission, but selective for some programs. Special requirements for health technology programs. **Home schooled:** Students should have state certification number, successful completion of competency exam, registered with local board of education, copy of transcript and diploma.

2015-2016 Annual costs. Tuition/fees: $2,305; $8,065 out-of-state. Books/supplies: $1,278. Personal expenses: $3,268.

Financial aid. Need-based: Need-based aid available for part-time students. Work-study available nights, weekends and for part-time students. **Additional information:** Small amount of non-federal scholarship aid available. FAFSA applications received before June 1 will receive first priority.

Application procedures. Admission: No deadline. No application fee. Admission notification on a rolling basis. **Financial aid:** Priority date 6/1; no closing date. FAFSA required. Applicants notified on a rolling basis.

Academics. Special study options: Cooperative education, distance learning, dual enrollment of high school students, independent study. **Credit/placement by examination:** AP, CLEP, institutional tests. **Support services:** GED preparation and test center, learning center, reduced course load, remedial instruction, study skills assistance, tutoring.

Majors. Business: Accounting, business admin. **Computer sciences:** General. **Education:** Early childhood, elementary. **Health services:** Massage therapy, medical assistant, nursing (RN), office assistant, sonography. **Liberal arts:** Arts/sciences. **Protective services:** Criminal justice. **Visual/performing arts:** Commercial/advertising art. **Work/family studies:** Child care service.

Technology on campus. 200 workstations in library, computer center. Wireless network available.

Student life. Freshman orientation: Available. Preregistration for classes offered. **Activities:** Student government, student newspaper, Phi Beta Lambda business organization, criminal justice student association, social services club, Phi Theta Kappa.

Athletics. Team name: Patriots.

Student services. Alcohol/substance abuse counseling, career counseling, student employment services, financial aid counseling, personal counseling, placement for graduates, veterans' counselor. **Physically disabled:** Services for visually, hearing impaired. **Transfer:** Transfer adviser for students transferring to 4-year colleges.

Contact. E-mail: admissions@spcc.edu
Phone: (704) 272-5325 Toll-free number: (800) 766-0319
Fax: (704) 272-5303
Amanda Secrest, Assistant Director of Admissions, South Piedmont Community College, PO Box 126, Polkton, NC 28135

Southeastern Community College
Whiteville, North Carolina
www.sccnc.edu   CB code: 5651

▶ Public 2-year community college
▶ Commuter campus in small town

General. Founded in 1964. Regionally accredited. **Enrollment:** 1,044 degree-seeking undergraduates; 304 non-degree-seeking students. **Degrees:** 143 associate awarded. **Location:** 50 miles from Wilmington. **Calendar:** Semester, extensive summer session. **Full-time faculty:** 60 total. **Part-time faculty:** 41 total. **Special facilities:** Hardwood and pine forest with signed nature trail, greenhouses. **Partnerships:** Formal partnership with Columbus County School System - Early College High School.

Student profile. Among degree-seeking undergraduates, 279 enrolled as first-time, first-year students.

Part-time:	42%	Women:	68%
Out-of-state:	1%	25 or older:	42%

Transfer out. Colleges most students transferred to 2015: University of North Carolina at Wilmington, University of North Carolina at Pembroke, Fayetteville State University, East Carolina University.

Basis for selection. Open admission, but selective for some programs. Basic law Enforcement Training: Age 21 and Reading test requirements. Allied Health: Reading, Math, CNA 1 certification, points requirements. SAT may be substituted for placement test. **Home schooled:** Transcript of courses and grades required. Documentation from state showing authorization. **Learning Disabled:** Applicant must provide proof of disability from specialist, and list of required accommodations from specialist, and list of requested accommodations from student.

High school preparation. Recommended units include English 6, mathematics 6, social studies 6 and science 6.

2015-2016 Annual costs. Tuition/fees: $2,288; $8,048 out-of-state. Per-credit charge: $72 in-state; $264 out-of-state. Books/supplies: $1,400. Personal expenses: $1,350.

Financial aid. Need-based: Need-based aid available for part-time students. Work-study available nights, weekends and for part-time students. **Non-need-based:** Scholarships awarded for academics, athletics, leadership, music/drama, state residency.

Application procedures. Admission: No deadline. No application fee. Admission notification on a rolling basis. **Financial aid:** Priority date 4/1; no closing date. FAFSA required. Applicants notified on a rolling basis starting 6/1; must reply within 2 week(s) of notification.

Academics. Special study options: Cooperative education, distance learning, dual enrollment of high school students, independent study. License preparation in nursing. **Credit/placement by examination:** AP, CLEP, institutional tests. Credit by exam, in combination with credits transferred from other post-secondary institutions, should not exceed 25% of degree awarded. **Support services:** GED preparation and test center, learning center, reduced course load, remedial instruction, study skills assistance, tutoring.

Majors. Biology: General. **Business:** Business admin, office management. **Communications:** Communications/speech/rhetoric. **Communications technology:** Radio/TV. **Computer sciences:** General, information technology, networking, web page design. **Conservation:** Environmental science, forest technology. **Education:** Early childhood, elementary, secondary. **English:** English lit. **Health services:** Clinical lab technology, massage therapy, nursing assistant, prenursing. **History:** General. **Liberal arts:** Arts/sciences. **Math:** General. **Physical sciences:** Chemistry. **Protective services:** Law enforcement admin. **Psychology:** General. **Social sciences:** General. **Visual/performing arts:** Music performance, studio arts. **Work/family studies:** Child care management.

Technology on campus. 395 workstations in library, computer center. Online library, helpline, wireless network available.

Student life. Freshman orientation: Available. Preregistration for classes offered. **Activities:** Concert band, choral groups, literary magazine, student government, student newspaper, Student Ambassadors, Environmental Action Club, Phi Beta Lambda, early childhood organization, medical lab, technology club, Spanish club, Student Nurses Association, cosmetology club, art club.

Athletics. NJCAA. **Intercollegiate:** Baseball M, volleyball W. **Team name:** Rams.

Student services. Career counseling, services for economically disadvantaged, student employment services, financial aid counseling, on-campus daycare, veterans' counselor. **Physically disabled.** Services for visually, speech, hearing impaired. **Transfer:** Pre-admission transcript evaluation for new students. Transfer center, college fairs on campus for students transferring to 4-year colleges.

Contact. Phone: (910) 642-7141 ext. 265 Fax: (910) 642-1267 Julia Roberts, Director, Student Success Center, Southeastern Community College, 4564 Chadbourn Highway, Whiteville, NC 28472-0151

Southwestern Community College
Sylva, North Carolina
www.southwesterncc.edu   CB code: 5667

- Public 2-year community college
- Commuter campus in rural community

General. Founded in 1964. Regionally accredited. Five off-campus sites serve two adjoining counties. **Enrollment:** 1,760 degree-seeking undergraduates; 709 non-degree-seeking students. **Degrees:** 382 associate awarded. **Location:** 48 miles from Asheville. **Calendar:** Semester, limited summer session. **Full-time faculty:** 83 total. **Part-time faculty:** 184 total.

Student profile. Among degree-seeking undergraduates, 329 enrolled as first-time, first-year students.

Part-time:	54%	Women:	65%

Transfer out. Colleges most students transferred to 2015: Western Carolina University.

Basis for selection. Open admission, but selective for some programs. Admission to allied health programs based on test scores, academic record, interview, and recommendations. Interview required for allied health applicants; recommended for all others.

High school preparation. Algebra, biology, and chemistry required for allied health program applicants.

2015-2016 Annual costs. Tuition/fees: $2,251; $8,011 out-of-state. Per-credit charge: $72 in-state; $264 out-of-state. Books/supplies: $1,100. Personal expenses: $1,080.

Financial aid. Need-based: Need-based aid available for part-time students. Work-study available nights, weekends and for part-time students.

Application procedures. Admission: No deadline. No application fee. Admission notification on a rolling basis. **Financial aid:** Closing date 6/30. FAFSA required. Applicants notified on a rolling basis starting 5/1; must reply within 2 week(s) of notification.

Academics. Special study options: Cooperative education, distance learning, double major, dual enrollment of high school students, ESL, honors, independent study, internships, liberal arts/career combination. License preparation in nursing, occupational therapy, paramedic, physical therapy, radiology. **Credit/placement by examination:** AP, CLEP, institutional tests. **Support services:** GED preparation and test center, learning center, reduced course load, remedial instruction, tutoring.

Majors. Business: Accounting, administrative services, business admin, marketing. **Computer sciences:** General, networking, programming. **Education:** General, early childhood, trade/industrial. **Engineering:** Computer, electrical. **Health services:** Clinical lab science, clinical lab technology, EMT paramedic, health information technology, medical radiologic technology/radiation therapy, mental health services, nursing (RN), occupational therapy assistant, physical therapy assistant, respiratory therapy assistant, respiratory therapy technology, sonography, substance abuse counseling. **Liberal arts:** Arts/sciences. **Parks/recreation:** General. **Protective services:** Criminal justice. **Visual/performing arts:** Commercial/advertising art. **Work/family studies:** Child care management.

Most popular majors. Business/marketing 7%, computer/information sciences 7%, engineering/engineering technologies 13%, health sciences 27%, liberal arts 16%, personal/culinary services 7%, security/protective services 6%.

Technology on campus. 200 workstations in library, computer center. Commuter students can connect to campus network. Helpline, wireless network available.

Student life. Freshman orientation: Mandatory. Preregistration for classes offered. One-day live orientation held on Jackson Campus at beginning of Fall Semester for all students enrolling for first time. New students enrolling in Spring or Summer semesters take on-line orientation program. **Activities:** Literary magazine, student government, Phi Theta Kappa, Native American

Society, nursing, outdoor leadership, environmental, culinary arts, journalism, Spanish clubs.

Student services. Career counseling, services for economically disadvantaged, student employment services, financial aid counseling, personal counseling, placement for graduates, veterans' counselor. **Physically disabled:** Services for visually, speech, hearing impaired. **Transfer:** Pre-admission transcript evaluation for new students. Transfer adviser for students transferring to 4-year colleges.

Contact. Phone: (828) 339-4352 Toll-free number: (800) 447-4091 Cheryl Contino-Conner, Dean of Student Services, Southwestern Community College, 447 College Drive, Sylva, NC 28779

Stanly Community College
Albemarle, North Carolina
www.stanly.edu   CB code: 0496

- Public 2-year community college
- Commuter campus in large town

General. Founded in 1971. Regionally accredited. **Enrollment:** 2,368 degree-seeking undergraduates; 276 non-degree-seeking students. **Degrees:** 477 associate awarded. **Location:** 30 miles from Charlotte. **Calendar:** Semester, limited summer session. **Full-time faculty:** 100 total. **Part-time faculty:** 230 total.

Student profile. Among degree-seeking undergraduates, 401 enrolled as first-time, first-year students.

Part-time:	69%	Asian American:	3%
Women:	69%	Hispanic/Latino:	2%
African American:	16%	Native American:	1%

Transfer out. Colleges most students transferred to 2015: University of North Carolina at Charlotte, Pfeiffer University.

Basis for selection. Open admission, but selective for some programs. Special requirements for nursing, radiography, respiratory therapy, and medical lab assistant majors. **Learning Disabled:** Written verification of disability, no more than five years old, required at least 60 days prior to enrollment.

2015-2016 Annual costs. Tuition/fees: $2,326; $8,086 out-of-state. Per-credit charge: $72 in-state; $264 out-of-state. Books/supplies: $1,168. Personal expenses: $4,208.

2014-2015 Financial aid. All financial aid based on need. Average need met was 40%. Average scholarship/grant was $4,892. 98% of total undergraduate aid awarded as scholarships/grants, 2% as loans/jobs. Need-based aid available for part-time students. Work-study available nights, weekends and for part-time students.

Application procedures. Admission: No deadline. No application fee. Admission notification on a rolling basis. **Financial aid:** No deadline. FAFSA, institutional form required. Applicants notified on a rolling basis starting 6/1; must reply within 2 week(s) of notification.

Academics. Special study options: Distance learning, dual enrollment of high school students, ESL, weekend college. **Credit/placement by examination:** AP, CLEP, institutional tests. **Support services:** GED preparation and test center, remedial instruction, study skills assistance, tutoring.

Majors. Business: Accounting, business admin, human resources. **Computer sciences:** Computer graphics, information systems, information technology, LAN/WAN management, networking, security. **Education:** Early childhood, elementary, special ed. **Health services:** Clinical lab assistant, EMT paramedic, medical assistant, nursing (RN), radiologic technology/medical imaging, respiratory therapy technology. **Liberal arts:** Arts/sciences. **Protective services:** Computer forensics, criminal justice. **Visual/performing arts:** Game design, graphic design. **Work/family studies:** General.

Most popular majors. Business/marketing 11%, computer/information sciences 6%, education 13%, health sciences 32%, liberal arts 18%, security/protective services 12%.

Technology on campus. 100 workstations in library, computer center, student center. Commuter students can connect to campus network. Online library, helpline, wireless network available.

Student life. Freshman orientation: Available. Preregistration for classes offered. **Activities:** Student government.

Athletics. Team name: Eagles.

Student services. Adult student services, alcohol/substance abuse counseling, career counseling, services for economically disadvantaged, student employment services, financial aid counseling, minority student services, personal counseling, placement for graduates, veterans' counselor, women's services. **Transfer:** Pre-admission transcript evaluation for new students. Transfer adviser, college fairs on campus for students transferring to 4-year colleges.

Contact. E-mail: sccadmissions@stanly.edu
Phone: (704) 991-0226 Fax: (704) 991-0255
Jeania Martin, Director of Admissions, Stanly Community College, 141 College Drive, Albemarle, NC 28001

Surry Community College
Dobson, North Carolina
www.surry.edu   CB code: 5656

- Public 2-year community college
- Commuter campus in rural community

General. Founded in 1964. Regionally accredited. **Enrollment:** 2,171 degree-seeking undergraduates; 1,214 non-degree-seeking students. **Degrees:** 511 associate awarded. **Location:** 40 miles from Winston-Salem. **Calendar:** Semester, limited summer session. **Full-time faculty:** 100 total; 10% have terminal degrees, 5% minority, 62% women. **Part-time faculty:** 267 total; 4% have terminal degrees, 2% minority, 45% women. **Class size:** 81% < 20, 18% 20-39, less than 1% 40-49, less than 1% 50-99. **Special facilities:** Working vineyard and wine-making facilities, center for viticulture and enology.

Student profile. Among degree-seeking undergraduates, 30% enrolled in a transfer program, 70% enrolled in a vocational program, 1% already have a bachelor's degree or higher, 531 enrolled as first-time, first-year students.

Part-time:	44%	Hispanic/Latino:	9%
Out-of-state:	2%	Multi-racial, non-Hispanic:	1%
Women:	58%	International:	1%
African American:	4%	25 or older:	21%

Transfer out. Colleges most students transferred to 2015: Appalachian State University, Gardner-Webb University, Lees-McRae University, University of North Carolina-Greensboro, Winston-Salem State University.

Basis for selection. Open admission, but selective for some programs. Competitive admission to associate degree nursing program (RN) and practical nursing program (LPN) based primarily on academic standing; test scores considered. Special admissions also required for Physical Therapy Assistant and Medical Assisting Program. Teas test required as part of RN, LPN and PTA programs. Portfolio required for advertising and graphic design programs. **Home schooled:** Proof of homeschool registration from the state of NC required.

2015-2016 Annual costs. Tuition/fees: $2,257; $8,017 out-of-state. Per-credit charge: $72 in-state; $264 out-of-state. Books/supplies: $1,700. Personal expenses: $1,650.

Financial aid. Need-based: Need-based aid available for part-time students. Work-study available nights, weekends and for part-time students. **Non-need-based:** Scholarships awarded for academics.

Application procedures. Admission: No deadline. No application fee. Admission notification on a rolling basis. **Financial aid:** Closing date 5/1. FAFSA, institutional form required. Applicants notified on a rolling basis starting 6/1; must reply within 2 week(s) of notification.

Academics. Special study options: Accelerated study, cooperative education, distance learning, double major, dual enrollment of high school students, ESL, independent study, internships, weekend college. Bachelor's degree programs available on campus. License preparation in nursing, paramedic, physical therapy. **Credit/placement by examination:** AP, CLEP, institutional tests. **Support services:** GED preparation and test center, learning center, reduced course load, remedial instruction, study skills assistance, tutoring.

Majors. Business: Accounting, business admin, office/clerical. **Computer sciences:** Information systems. **Education:** Early childhood, early childhood special. **Engineering:** Computer, electrical. **Foreign languages:** Translation. **General:** Carpentry, site management. **Health services:** Medical assistant, nursing (RN), office admin, physical therapy assistant. **Liberal arts:** Arts/sciences. **Protective services:** Law enforcement admin. **Visual/performing arts:** Commercial/advertising art, game design.

Most popular majors. Business/marketing 13%, health sciences 17%, liberal arts 43%, trade and industry 7%.

Technology on campus. 500 workstations in library, computer center. Online library, helpline, wireless network available.

Student life. Freshman orientation: Mandatory. Preregistration for classes offered. **Activities:** Choral groups, literary magazine, student government.

Athletics. NJCAA. **Intercollegiate:** Baseball M, golf, softball W, volleyball W. **Intramural:** Basketball M. **Team name:** Knights.

Student services. Adult student services, chaplain/spiritual director, career counseling, services for economically disadvantaged, student employment services, financial aid counseling, personal counseling, placement for graduates, veterans' counselor. **Physically disabled:** Services for visually, hearing impaired. **Transfer:** Transfer adviser, college fairs on campus for students transferring to 4-year colleges.

Contact. E-mail: hazelwoodr@surry.edu
Phone: (336) 386-3392 Fax: (336) 386-8951
Renita Hazelwood, Director of Admissions, Surry Community College, ATTN: Admissions Offfice 630 South Main Street, Dobson, NC 27017

Tri-County Community College
Murphy, North Carolina
www.tricountycc.edu   CB code: 5785

- Public 2-year community college
- Commuter campus in rural community

General. Founded in 1964. Regionally accredited. **Enrollment:** 1,003 degree-seeking undergraduates. **Degrees:** 192 associate awarded. **Location:** 110 miles from Asheville, 96 miles from Chattanooga, TN, 120 miles from Atlanta GA. **Calendar:** Semester, extensive summer session. **Full-time faculty:** 32 total. **Part-time faculty:** 138 total. **Class size:** 22% < 20, 57% 20-39, 20% 40-49, 1% 50-99.

Student profile.

Out-of-state:	9%	25 or older:	54%

Transfer out. Colleges most students transferred to 2015: Western Carolina University, Southwestern Community College.

Basis for selection. Open admission. **Home schooled:** Transcript of courses and grades, state high school equivalency certificate required. **Learning Disabled:** ADA Compliant; Request for Accommodations Form available at Student Success Services.

2015-2016 Annual costs. Tuition/fees: $2,219; $7,979 out-of-state. Per-credit charge: $72 in-state; $264 out-of-state. Books/supplies: $1,019. Personal expenses: $2,242.

2014-2015 Financial aid. All financial aid based on need. 99% of total undergraduate aid awarded as scholarships/grants, 1% as loans/jobs. Need-based aid available for part-time students. Work-study available nights, weekends and for part-time students.

Application procedures. Admission: No deadline. No application fee. Admission notification on a rolling basis. **Financial aid:** Priority date 6/30; no closing date. FAFSA required. Applicants notified on a rolling basis starting 6/1; must reply within 4 week(s) of notification.

Academics. Special study options: Accelerated study, distance learning, double major, dual enrollment of high school students, ESL, independent study, internships. License preparation in nursing, paramedic, real estate. **Credit/placement by examination:** AP, CLEP, institutional tests. 6 credit hours maximum toward associate degree. **Support services:** GED preparation and test center, learning center, reduced course load, remedial instruction, study skills assistance, tutoring, writing center.

Majors. Business: Accounting, administrative services, business admin. **Computer sciences:** Information systems. **Education:** Early childhood. **General:** Electrician. **Health services:** EMT paramedic, medical assistant, nursing (RN). **Liberal arts:** Arts/sciences.

Most popular majors. Business/marketing 24%, liberal arts 43%, trade and industry 35%.

Technology on campus. 42 workstations in library, computer center, student center. Online course registration, online library, wireless network available.

Student life. Freshman orientation: Mandatory. Preregistration for classes offered. **Activities:** Student government, student newspaper, honor society.

Student services. Adult student services, career counseling, services for economically disadvantaged, student employment services, financial aid counseling, personal counseling, placement for graduates, veterans' counselor. **Physically disabled:** Services for visually, speech, hearing impaired. **Transfer:** Pre-admission transcript evaluation for new students. Transfer adviser, college fairs on campus for students transferring to 4-year colleges.

Contact. E-mail: lbeal@tricountycc.edu
Phone: (828) 837-6810 Fax: (828) 837-3266
Lee Beal, Director of Enrollment Management, Tri-County Community College, 21 Campus Circle, Murphy, NC 28906

Vance-Granville Community College
Henderson, North Carolina — **CB member**
www.vgcc.edu — **CB code: 0617**

- Public 2-year community college
- Commuter campus in large town

General. Founded in 1969. Regionally accredited. 4 rural counties served with satellite campuses in Warrenton, Butner and Louisburg. **Enrollment:** 2,322 degree-seeking undergraduates. **Degrees:** 505 associate awarded. **Location:** 42 miles from Raleigh. **Calendar:** Semester, limited summer session. **Full-time faculty:** 119 total. **Part-time faculty:** 246 total.

Basis for selection. Open admission, but selective for some programs. Admission to nursing, radiologic technology, and medical assisting is based on academic record, health education aptitude test, and other criteria. Interview recommended for nursing, radiologic technology programs.

2015-2016 Annual costs. Tuition/fees: $2,279; $8,039 out-of-state. Per-credit charge: $72 in-state; $264 out-of-state. Books/supplies: $1,200.

2014-2015 Financial aid. Need-based: 97% of total undergraduate aid awarded as scholarships/grants, 3% as loans/jobs. Need-based aid available for part-time students. Work-study available nights, weekends and for part-time students. **Non-need-based:** Scholarships awarded for academics, leadership, music/drama, state residency.

Application procedures. Admission: No deadline. No application fee. Admission notification on a rolling basis. Application deadlines apply and may vary for Allied Health programs. College placement examinations required of all students, unless acceptable scores on SAT/ACT or special students. **Financial aid:** Priority date 3/15; no closing date. FAFSA required. Applicants notified on a rolling basis starting 5/1; must reply within 2 week(s) of notification.

Academics. Special study options: Cooperative education, distance learning, double major, dual enrollment of high school students, ESL, independent study, internships. License preparation in nursing, radiology, real estate. **Credit/placement by examination:** AP, CLEP, institutional tests. **Support services:** GED preparation and test center, learning center, pre-admission summer program, reduced course load, remedial instruction, study skills assistance, tutoring.

Majors. Business: Accounting, administrative services, business admin, entrepreneurial studies, logistics, office management, office technology. **Computer sciences:** Information systems, information technology, networking, security, web page design. **Education:** General, early childhood, elementary, teacher assistance. **Engineering:** Electrical. **Health services:** Medical assistant, medical radiologic technology/radiation therapy, nursing (RN), office admin, pharmacy assistant, radiologic technology/medical imaging, recreational therapy, substance abuse counseling. **Liberal arts:** Arts/sciences. **Parks/recreation:** General. **Protective services:** Criminal justice, law enforcement admin. **Work/family studies:** Child care management.

Most popular majors. Business/marketing 14%, education 6%, health sciences 21%, liberal arts 39%.

Technology on campus. 48 workstations in library, computer center.

Student life. Activities: Drama, student government, departmental clubs.

Student services. Adult student services, career counseling, student employment services, financial aid counseling, on-campus daycare, personal counseling, placement for graduates, veterans' counselor. **Physically disabled:** Services for visually, hearing impaired. **Transfer:** Transfer adviser for students transferring to 4-year colleges.

Contact. E-mail: waddlet@vgcc.edu
Phone: (252) 492-2061 Fax: (252) 430-0460
Tonya Waddle, Director of Admissions and Records, Vance-Granville Community College, Box 917, Henderson, NC 27536

Virginia College In Greensboro
Greensboro, North Carolina
www.vc.edu/greensboro

- For-profit 2-year career college
- Large city

General. Regionally accredited; also accredited by ACICS. **Enrollment:** 468 undergraduates. **Calendar:** Quarter.

Basis for selection. Open admission.

2015-2016 Annual costs. Total program tuition: Certificate programs range from $13,932 to $15,891; Diploma programs, $23,220; Associate's programs range from $37,152 to $43,956; Bachelor's programs $69,66.

Financial aid. Need-based: Work-study available nights, weekends and for part-time students.

Academics. Credit/placement by examination: AP.

Contact. E-mail: greensboro.info@vc.edu
Phone: (336) 398-5400
Heather Robbins, Director of Admissions, Virginia College in Greensboro, 3740 S. Holden Road, Greensboro, NC 27406

Wake Technical Community College
Raleigh, North Carolina
www.waketech.edu — **CB code: 5928**

- Public 2-year community and technical college
- Commuter campus in large city

General. Founded in 1958. Regionally accredited. **Enrollment:** 21,268 degree-seeking undergraduates; 690 non-degree-seeking students. **Degrees:** 2,171 associate awarded. **ROTC:** Army. **Location:** 10 miles from Raleigh. **Calendar:** Semester, extensive summer session. **Full-time faculty:** 577 total. **Part-time faculty:** 956 total.

Student profile. Among degree-seeking undergraduates, 50% enrolled in a transfer program, 50% enrolled in a vocational program, 4,084 enrolled as first-time, first-year students.

Part-time:	66%	25 or older:	42%
Women:	54%		

Transfer out. Colleges most students transferred to 2015: North Carolina State University, University of North Carolina at Chapel Hill, East Carolina University, University of North Carolina at Greensboro, Appalachian State University.

Basis for selection. Open admission, but selective for some programs. Admission to health programs based on standardized test scores, post-secondary coursework. Placement tests required of all degree and diploma students with SAT scores below 520 verbal or 600 math, or below ACT math 21, reading 21, and writing 21. Interview recommended. **Home schooled:** Must include transcript and test scores.

High school preparation. Recommended units include English 4 and mathematics 4. 1 chemistry required for health sciences associate degree programs.

2015-2016 Annual costs. Tuition/fees: $2,490; $8,250 out-of-state. Per-credit charge: $72 in-state; $264 out-of-state. Books/supplies: $1,500. Personal expenses: $1,494.

Financial aid. Need-based: Need-based aid available for part-time students. Work-study available nights, weekends and for part-time students. **Non-need-based:** Scholarships awarded for academics, job skills, leadership, ROTC, state residency.

Application procedures. Admission: No deadline. No application fee. Admission notification on a rolling basis. Application fee for international students requesting issuance of I-20. **Financial aid:** Priority date 3/15; no closing date. FAFSA, institutional form required. Applicants notified on a rolling basis starting 4/1; must reply within 2 week(s) of notification.

Academics. Special study options: Cooperative education, distance learning, double major, dual enrollment of high school students, ESL, honors, liberal arts/career combination, study abroad. License preparation in dental hygiene, nursing, paramedic, radiology. **Credit/placement by examination:** AP, CLEP, IB, institutional tests. 25% of degree requirement must be taken in residence. **Support services:** GED preparation and test center, learning center, pre-admission summer program, reduced course load, remedial instruction, study skills assistance, tutoring, writing center.

Majors. Architecture: Landscape. **Business:** Accounting, business admin, hotel/motel/restaurant management, human resources, logistics, management science, office management. **Computer sciences:** General, applications programming, computer graphics, programming. **Conservation:** General. **Education:** Early childhood. **Engineering:** Pre-engineering. **General:** Power transmission. **Health services:** Clinical lab technology, dental hygiene, EMT paramedic, health information technology, medical assistant, medical radiologic technology/radiation therapy, medical secretary, nursing (RN). **Liberal arts:** Arts/sciences. **Protective services:** Police science. **Visual/performing arts:** Commercial/advertising art, game design, interior design.

Most popular majors. Business/marketing 12%, computer/information sciences 7%, engineering/engineering technologies 6%, health sciences 19%, liberal arts 40%.

Technology on campus. 62 workstations in library, computer center, student center. Online course registration, helpline, wireless network available.

Student life. Freshman orientation: Available. Preregistration for classes offered. Held on first day of class. **Activities:** Choral groups, drama, international student organizations, student government, student newspaper.

Athletics. NJCAA. **Intercollegiate:** Baseball M, basketball, cheerleading, cross-country, golf, soccer, softball W, volleyball W. **Team name:** Eagles.

Student services. Career counseling, student employment services, financial aid counseling, minority student services, personal counseling, placement for graduates, veterans' counselor. **Physically disabled:** Services for visually, speech, hearing impaired. **Transfer:** Transfer adviser, college fairs on campus for students transferring to 4-year colleges.

Contact. E-mail: admissions@waketech.edu
Phone: (919) 866-5500 Fax: (919) 661-0117
Santrell Caison, Associate Dean of Admissions, Wake Technical Community College, 9101 Fayetteville Road, Raleigh, NC 27603

Wayne Community College
Goldsboro, North Carolina
www.waynecc.edu   **CB code: 5926**

▸ Public 2-year community college
▸ Commuter campus in large town

General. Founded in 1957. Regionally accredited. **Enrollment:** 2,773 degree-seeking undergraduates. **Degrees:** 557 associate awarded. **Location:** 55 miles from Raleigh. **Calendar:** Semester, limited summer session.

Student profile.

Out-of-state:	4%	25 or older:	5%

Transfer out. Colleges most students transferred to 2015: East Carolina University, University of Mount Olive, Campbell University, North Carolina State.

Basis for selection. Open admission, but selective for some programs.

2015-2016 Annual costs. Tuition/fees: $2,252; $8,012 out-of-state. Per-credit charge: $72 in-state; $264 out-of-state. Books/supplies: $1,560. Personal expenses: $1,100.

Financial aid. Need-based: Need-based aid available for part-time students. Work-study available nights, weekends and for part-time students. **Non-need-based:** Scholarships awarded for academics.

Application procedures. Admission: No deadline. No application fee. Admission notification on a rolling basis. For limited admission programs only. **Financial aid:** Priority date 3/15, closing date 5/1. FAFSA required. Applicants notified on a rolling basis starting 6/1; must reply within 2 week(s) of notification.

Academics. Special study options: Cooperative education, distance learning, double major, dual enrollment of high school students, honors, teacher certification program. License preparation in aviation, dental hygiene, nursing, paramedic, real estate. **Credit/placement by examination:** AP, CLEP, IB, institutional tests. **Support services:** GED preparation and test center, learning center, reduced course load, remedial instruction, study skills assistance, tutoring, writing center.

Majors. Business: Accounting, business admin, office management, operations. **Computer sciences:** Information technology, networking. **Conservation:** Forest technology. **Education:** Early childhood. **Health services:** Dental hygiene, medical assistant, nursing (RN), office admin. **Liberal arts:** Arts/sciences. **Protective services:** Criminal justice, disaster management, forensics, police science. **Visual/performing arts:** Game design.

Technology on campus. 75 workstations in library, computer center. Online course registration, online library, helpline, wireless network available.

Student life. Freshman orientation: Available. Preregistration for classes offered. Available year-round online. **Activities:** Choral groups, international student organizations, literary magazine, student government, Minority male mentoring group, human services club, nursing club, criminal justice club, Phi Theta Kappa.

Athletics. Intramural: Football (tackle). **Team name:** Bisons.

Student services. Alcohol/substance abuse counseling, career counseling, student employment services, financial aid counseling, minority student services, on-campus daycare, personal counseling, veterans' counselor. **Physically disabled:** Services for visually, speech, hearing impaired. **Transfer:** Re-entry adviser, pre-admission transcript evaluation for new students. Transfer center, transfer adviser, college fairs on campus for students transferring to 4-year colleges.

Contact. E-mail: jbmayo@waynecc.edu
Phone: (919) 739-6720 Fax: (919) 736-9425
Jennifer Mayo, Director of Admissions and Records, Wayne Community College, PO Box 8002, Goldsboro, NC 27533-8002

Western Piedmont Community College
Morganton, North Carolina
www.wpcc.edu   **CB code: 5922**

▸ Public 2-year community and technical college
▸ Commuter campus in large town

General. Founded in 1964. Regionally accredited. **Enrollment:** 2,153 degree-seeking undergraduates. **Degrees:** 322 associate awarded. **Location:** 60 miles from Charlotte, 55 miles from Asheville. **Calendar:** Semester, extensive summer session. **Full-time faculty:** 79 total; 6% have terminal degrees, 5% minority. **Part-time faculty:** 354 total; less than 1% have terminal degrees, 5% minority. **Special facilities:** Greenhouses, fitness and nature trails, alpine climbing tower, Senator Sam J. Ervin Jr. library and museum.

Transfer out. Colleges most students transferred to 2015: Appalachian State University, Gardner-Webb University, Western Carolina University, Lenoir-Rhyne College, Lees McRae.

Basis for selection. Open admission, but selective for some programs. All students must submit official high school/GED transcripts, as well as transcripts from any other college or university attended. Placement tests required for all programs. Special requirements for certain programs. **Home schooled:** Transcript of courses and grades required. Submission of homeschool certification required. **Learning Disabled:** The Office of Disability Services coordinates accommodations and support services to all students with a qualifying disability.

2015-2016 Annual costs. Tuition/fees: $2,259; $8,019 out-of-state. Per-credit charge: $72 in-state; $264 out-of-state. Books/supplies: $1,160. Personal expenses: $3,476.

Financial aid. Need-based: Need-based aid available for part-time students. Work-study available nights, weekends and for part-time students. **Non-need-based:** Scholarships awarded for academics.

Application procedures. Admission: No deadline. No application fee. Notified 2-3 weeks after the application is received. Application closing date for allied health programs varies for fall admission. **Financial aid:** Priority date 6/1; no closing date. FAFSA required. Applicants notified on a rolling basis starting 6/15; must reply within 2 week(s) of notification.

Academics. Special study options: Combined bachelor's/graduate degree, cooperative education, distance learning, double major, dual enrollment of high school students, internships. Bachelor's degree programs available on campus. License preparation in nursing. **Credit/placement by examination:** AP, CLEP, IB, institutional tests. 15 credit hours maximum toward associate degree. **Support services:** GED preparation and test center, learning center, reduced course load, remedial instruction, study skills assistance, tutoring, writing center.

Majors. Biology: General. **Business:** Accounting, administrative services, business admin, office technology, office/clerical, operations, sales/distribution. **Communications:** General. **Computer sciences:** Computer science, data processing, information systems, systems analysis. **Conservation:** General. **Education:** Early childhood, elementary, special ed. **Engineering:** General, civil, computer, electrical. **English:** English lit. **General:** Maintenance. **Health services:** Clinical lab assistant, medical assistant, nursing (RN), nursing education, office admin, recreational therapy. **History:** General. **Liberal arts:** Arts/sciences. **Math:** General. **Physical sciences:** General, chemistry. **Protective services:** Criminal justice. **Psychology:** General. **Social sciences:** Political science, sociology. **Visual/performing arts:** Art, dramatic, interior design, studio arts. **Work/family studies:** Child care management.

Most popular majors. Business/marketing 24%, education 6%, health sciences 28%, liberal arts 30%, security/protective services 9%.

Technology on campus. 280 workstations in library, computer center. Commuter students can connect to campus network. Online library, wireless network available.

Student life. Freshman orientation: Mandatory. Preregistration for classes offered. Held prior to the fall semester. **Activities:** Drama, student government, Phi Beta Lambda, Phi Theta Kappa, Criminal Justice, Global Village, Rotaract, Students for Christ.

Athletics. Intramural: Basketball. **Team name:** Pioneers.

Student services. Adult student services, career counseling, services for economically disadvantaged, student employment services, financial aid counseling, personal counseling, placement for graduates, veterans' counselor. **Physically disabled:** Services for visually, speech, hearing impaired. **Transfer:** Transfer adviser, college fairs on campus for students transferring to 4-year colleges.

Contact. E-mail: jpropst@wpcc.edu
Phone: (828) 448-6051 Fax: (828) 448-6170
Jennifer Propst, Director, Enrollment Management, Western Piedmont Community College, 1001 Burkemont Avenue, Morganton, NC 28655-4504

Wilkes Community College
Wilkesboro, North Carolina
www.wilkescc.edu   CB code: 5921

- Public 2-year community college
- Commuter campus in small town

General. Founded in 1965. Regionally accredited. **Enrollment:** 2,999 undergraduates. **Degrees:** 447 associate awarded. **Location:** 50 miles from Winston-Salem. **Calendar:** Semester, limited summer session. **Full-time faculty:** 84 total. **Part-time faculty:** 261 total. **Class size:** 80% < 20, 19% 20-39, 1% 40-49, less than 1% 50-99. **Special facilities:** Community center.

Student profile.

Out-of-state: 1%   25 or older: 39%

Transfer out. Colleges most students transferred to 2015: Appalachian State University, Gardner-Webb University, Winston-Salem State University.

Basis for selection. Open admission, but selective for some programs. High school diploma or its equivalency required. Special requirements for nursing program.

High school preparation. 20 units recommended. Recommended units include English 4, mathematics 4, social studies 3, history 2, science 3 (laboratory 1), foreign language 2 and academic electives 2.

2015-2016 Annual costs. Tuition/fees: $2,300; $8,060 out-of-state. Per-credit charge: $72 in-state; $264 out-of-state. Books/supplies: $1,200. Personal expenses: $500.

2014-2015 Financial aid. Need-based: 1,900 full-time freshmen applied for aid; 1,640 deemed to have need; 1,510 received aid. Average need met was 45%. Average scholarship/grant was $600; average loan $1,250. 79% of total undergraduate aid awarded as scholarships/grants, 21% as loans/jobs. Need-based aid available for part-time students. Work-study available nights, weekends and for part-time students. **Non-need-based:** Scholarships awarded for academics, art, job skills, leadership, minority status, music/drama, state residency.

Application procedures. Admission: No deadline. No application fee. Admission notification on a rolling basis. **Financial aid:** Priority date 5/15, closing date 5/15. FAFSA required. Applicants notified by 5/30; Applicants notified on a rolling basis starting 5/1; must reply by 8/1.

Academics. Special study options: Cooperative education, distance learning, double major, dual enrollment of high school students, ESL, independent study, internships. Bachelor's degree programs available on campus. License preparation in nursing, paramedic, real estate. **Credit/placement by examination:** AP, CLEP, IB, institutional tests. 16 credit hours maximum toward associate degree. **Support services:** GED preparation and test center, learning center, pre-admission summer program, reduced course load, remedial instruction, study skills assistance, tutoring, writing center.

Majors. Business: Accounting, business admin, marketing, office management. **Communications technology:** Radio/TV. **Computer sciences:** Computer graphics, information systems, information technology, LAN/WAN management, programming. **Education:** Early childhood, elementary. **General:** Electrician. **Health services:** Medical assistant, nursing (RN). **Liberal arts:** Arts/sciences. **Protective services:** Criminal justice.

Most popular majors. Business/marketing 18%, education 7%, engineering/engineering technologies 11%, health sciences 16%, liberal arts 26%, trade and industry 9%.

Technology on campus. 150 workstations in library, computer center, student center.

Student life. Freshman orientation: Mandatory. Preregistration for classes offered. **Activities:** Choral groups, drama, literary magazine, music ensembles, musical theater, radio station, student government, student newspaper, Baptist student union, Ye Hosts food service club, camera club, Phi Theta Kappa, Association of Information Technology Professionals, Rotaract, human services club, medical assisting club, student government association, Student Ambassadors.

Athletics. NJCAA. Intercollegiate: Baseball M, basketball, volleyball W. **Intramural:** Basketball, table tennis, tennis, volleyball. **Team name:** Cougars.

Student services. Adult student services, career counseling, services for economically disadvantaged, student employment services, financial aid counseling, minority student services, personal counseling, placement for graduates, veterans' counselor. **Physically disabled:** Services for visually, speech, hearing impaired. **Transfer:** Pre-admission transcript evaluation for new students. Transfer adviser, college fairs on campus for students transferring to 4-year colleges.

Contact. E-mail: elisabeth.blevins@wilkescc.edu
Phone: (336) 838-6135 Fax: (336) 838-6547
Elisabeth Blevins, Director of Admissions, Wilkes Community College, 1328 South Collegiate Drive, Wilkesboro, NC 28697-0120

Wilson Community College
Wilson, North Carolina
www.wilsoncc.edu   CB code: 5930

- Public 2-year community college
- Commuter campus in large town
- Interview required

General. Founded in 1958. Regionally accredited. **Enrollment:** 1,786 degree-seeking undergraduates. **Degrees:** 237 associate awarded. **Location:** 50 miles from Raleigh. **Calendar:** Semester, limited summer session. **Full-time faculty:** 50 total; 10% have terminal degrees, 14% minority. **Part-time faculty:** 187 total; 22% minority. **Special facilities:** Student services green building featuring sustainable energy technologies such as a vertical axis wind turbine and photovoltaic solar panels.

Student profile.

Out-of-state: 1%   25 or older: 51%

Basis for selection. Open admission, but selective for some programs. Admission for nursing based on test scores, high school record, skills, and experience. Health requirement for emergency medical technology. **Adult students:** SAT/ACT scores not required.

High school preparation. High school diploma not required for certificate programs.

2015-2016 Annual costs. Tuition/fees: $2,727; $8,055 out-of-state. Books/supplies: $1,100. Personal expenses: $1,500.

Financial aid. Need-based: Need-based aid available for part-time students. Work-study available nights, weekends and for part-time students. **Non-need-based:** Scholarships awarded for academics.

Application procedures. Admission: No deadline. No application fee. Admission notification on a rolling basis beginning on or about 1/1. Applicants accepted to nursing program must reply by May 1. **Financial aid:** Priority date 3/15; no closing date. FAFSA, institutional form required. Applicants notified on a rolling basis.

Academics. Special program assistance for hearing-impaired students. **Special study options:** Cooperative education, distance learning, double major, dual enrollment of high school students, ESL, liberal arts/career combination. License preparation in nursing. **Credit/placement by examination:** AP, CLEP, institutional tests. **Support services:** GED preparation and test center, learning center, reduced course load, remedial instruction, study skills assistance, tutoring.

Majors. Business: Accounting, business admin, executive assistant, office management. **Computer sciences:** Information technology, networking, security. **Education:** Early childhood, elementary. **Foreign languages:** Sign language interpretation, translation. **General:** Electrician. **Health services:** Nursing (RN), office admin, surgical technology. **Liberal arts:** Arts/sciences. **Protective services:** Criminal justice, fire safety technology. **Visual/performing arts:** Game design.

Most popular majors. Business/marketing 16%, education 11%, health sciences 25%, liberal arts 22%, security/protective services 12%.

Technology on campus. 42 workstations in library, computer center. Online course registration, helpline, wireless network available.

Student life. Freshman orientation: Available. Preregistration for classes offered. **Activities:** Choral groups, literary magazine, student government.

Student services. Career counseling, services for economically disadvantaged, student employment services, veterans' counselor. **Physically disabled:** Services for hearing impaired. **Transfer:** Pre-admission transcript evaluation for new students. Transfer adviser, college fairs on campus for students transferring to 4-year colleges.

Contact. E-mail: slackner@wilsoncc.edu
Phone: (252) 246-1285 Fax: (252) 246-1384
Sandra Lackner, Director of Admissions/Student Activities, Wilson Community College, Box 4305, Wilson, NC 27893-0305

North Dakota

Bismarck State College
Bismarck, North Dakota
www.bismarckstate.edu
CB code: 6041

▶ Public 2-year community college
▶ Commuter campus in small city

General. Founded in 1939. Regionally accredited. **Enrollment:** 3,175 degree-seeking undergraduates; 903 non-degree-seeking students. **Degrees:** 62 bachelor's, 922 associate awarded. **Location:** 200 miles from Fargo. **Calendar:** Semester, limited summer session. **Full-time faculty:** 133 total; less than 1% have terminal degrees, 2% minority, 39% women. **Part-time faculty:** 224 total; less than 1% have terminal degrees, 2% minority, 38% women. **Class size:** 71% < 20, 29% 20-39, less than 1% 40-49, less than 1% 50-99.

Student profile. Among degree-seeking undergraduates, 36% enrolled in a transfer program, 55% enrolled in a vocational program, 848 enrolled as first-time, first-year students, 176 transferred in from other institutions.

Part-time:	29%	Hispanic/Latino:	3%
Out-of-state:	25%	Native American:	2%
Women:	39%	Multi-racial, non-Hispanic:	3%
African American:	4%	25 or older:	36%
Asian American:	1%	Live on campus:	11%

Basis for selection. Open admission, but selective for some programs. Test scores required for selective admission programs in air conditioning, heating and refrigeration, automotive technology, automotive collision technology, carpentry, electronics technology, line worker (electrical), power plant technology, process plant technology, welding, commercial art. Interview recommended for some programs; portfolio recommended for graphic arts program. **Adult students:** Students aged 25 or older must submit COMPASS assessment scores in the areas of English, math, and reading. The assessment may be waived if the student has completed college level reading, English, or math classes.

High school preparation. Recommended units include English 4, mathematics 3, social studies 3, science 3 (laboratory 1) and foreign language 2.

2015-2016 Annual costs. Tuition/fees: $4,319; $10,292 out-of-state. Per-credit charge: $119 in-state; $318 out-of-state. Room/board: $6,578. Books/supplies: $1,000. Personal expenses: $2,230.

Financial aid. All financial aid based on need. Need-based aid available for part-time students. Work-study available nights, weekends and for part-time students.

Application procedures. Admission: No deadline. $35 fee. Admission notification on a rolling basis beginning on or about 1/1. **Financial aid:** Priority date 4/15; no closing date. FAFSA required. Applicants notified on a rolling basis starting 5/1.

Academics. Academic advising focus over the summer with 20+ sessions offered to students who are enrolling for the following fall session. Online academic support services available. **Special study options:** Cooperative education, distance learning, dual enrollment of high school students, independent study, internships, liberal arts/career combination, study abroad. Bachelor's degree programs available on campus. License preparation in nursing, paramedic. **Credit/placement by examination:** AP, CLEP, institutional tests. 45 credit hours maximum toward associate degree, 60 toward bachelor's. The number of credits that may be awarded for prior work/life experiences or credit by examination toward a degree are combined for a limitation of 45 credits for an associate degree and 60 for a bachelor's degree. **Support services:** Learning center, remedial instruction, study skills assistance, tutoring, writing center.

Majors. Business: General, administrative services, office technology, transportation. **Communications:** Public relations. **Communications technology:** Recording arts. **Computer sciences:** Networking, web page design. **General:** Carpentry, lineworker. **Health services:** Clinical lab technology, EMT paramedic, medical secretary, nursing (RN), surgical technology. **Liberal arts:** Arts/sciences. **Protective services:** Criminal justice. **Visual/performing arts:** Commercial/advertising art.

Most popular majors. Engineering/engineering technologies 33%, liberal arts 44%.

Technology on campus. 430 workstations in library, computer center, student center. Dormitories wired for high-speed internet access. Commuter students can connect to campus network. Online course registration, online library, helpline, wireless network available.

Student life. Freshman orientation: Available. Preregistration for classes offered. **Housing:** Coed dorms, single-sex dorms, special housing for disabled, wellness housing available. $100 partly refundable deposit. **Activities:** Bands, choral groups, drama, music ensembles, musical theater, radio station, student government, student newspaper.

Athletics. NJCAA. **Intercollegiate:** Baseball M, basketball, golf, soccer, softball W, volleyball W. **Intramural:** Basketball, bowling, football (non-tackle), golf, soccer, softball, table tennis, volleyball. **Team name:** Mystics.

Student services. Adult student services, alcohol/substance abuse counseling, career counseling, student employment services, financial aid counseling, health services, minority student services, personal counseling, placement for graduates, veterans' counselor. **Physically disabled:** Services for visually, speech, hearing impaired. **Transfer:** Pre-admission transcript evaluation for new students. Transfer adviser, college fairs on campus for students transferring to 4-year colleges.

Contact. E-mail: BSC.Admissions@bismarckstate.edu
Phone: (701) 224-5429 Toll-free number: (800) 445-5073
Fax: (701) 224-5643
Karen Erickson, Director of Admissions and Enrollment Services, Bismarck State College, PO Box 5587, Bismarck, ND 58506-5587

Cankdeska Cikana Community College
Fort Totten, North Dakota
www.littlehoop.edu
CB code: 1306

▶ Public 2-year community college
▶ Residential campus in rural community

General. Founded in 1974. Regionally accredited. **Enrollment:** 161 degree-seeking undergraduates. **Degrees:** 18 associate awarded. **Location:** 13 miles from Devils Lake. **Calendar:** Semester, limited summer session. **Full-time faculty:** 20 total. **Part-time faculty:** 11 total.

Basis for selection. Open admission.

2015-2016 Annual costs. Tuition/fees: $3,300; $3,300 out-of-state. Room/board: $5,750. Books/supplies: $700.

Financial aid. All financial aid based on need. Need-based aid available for part-time students. Work-study available nights, weekends and for part-time students.

Application procedures. Admission: No deadline. No application fee. **Financial aid:** Priority date 4/15, closing date 8/20. FAFSA, institutional form required. Applicants notified on a rolling basis.

Academics. Special study options: Cooperative education, independent study, internships. **Credit/placement by examination:** AP, CLEP. **Support services:** GED preparation and test center, learning center, remedial instruction, study skills assistance, tutoring.

Majors. Area/ethnic studies: Native American. **Business:** General, administrative services, auditing, business admin, office technology. **Computer sciences:** General, applications programming. **Conservation:** Management/policy. **Education:** Early childhood. **Engineering:** Pre-engineering. **General:** Carpentry. **Health services:** Medical assistant, prenursing. **Human services:** General. **Liberal arts:** Arts/sciences. **Visual/performing arts:** Digital arts, studio arts.

Technology on campus. 30 workstations in library, computer center. Repair service, wireless network available.

Student life. Freshman orientation: Available. Preregistration for classes offered. **Activities:** Student government, Indian organization.

Athletics. Intramural: Volleyball.

Student services. Career counseling, financial aid counseling, on-campus daycare, personal counseling. **Transfer:** Transfer adviser, college fairs on campus for students transferring to 4-year colleges.

Contact. E-mail: Ermen_Brown@littlehoop.edu
Phone: (701) 766-1342 Fax: (701) 766-1344
Ermen Brown, Registrar, Cankdeska Cikana Community College, Box 269, Fort Totten, ND 58335

Dakota College at Bottineau
Bottineau, North Dakota
www.dakotacollege.edu   CB code: 1540

◆ Public 2-year nursing and junior college
◆ Residential campus in small town

General. Founded in 1907. Regionally accredited. **Enrollment:** 411 degree-seeking undergraduates. **Degrees:** 113 associate awarded. **Location:** 80 miles from Minot. **Calendar:** Semester, limited summer session. **Full-time faculty:** 28 total; 7% have terminal degrees, 46% women. **Part-time faculty:** 60 total; 5% have terminal degrees.

Student profile.

Out-of-state:	23%	Live on campus:	24%
25 or older:	33%		

Basis for selection. Open admission. **Adult students:** SAT/ACT scores not required if applicant over 25. Must take Math and English placement tests.

2015-2016 Annual costs. Tuition/fees: $4,181; $5,872 out-of-state. Per-credit charge: $141 in-state; $211 out-of-state. Room/board: $6,486. Books/supplies: $1,100. Personal expenses: $3,400. **Additional information:** Full-time annual tuition for residents of South Dakota, Montana-$4,230; All Canadian Provinces $3,384.

Financial aid. Need-based: Need-based aid available for part-time students. Work-study available nights, weekends and for part-time students. **Non-need-based:** Scholarships awarded for academics, alumni affiliation, athletics, minority status, state residency.

Application procedures. Admission: No deadline. $35 fee. Application must be submitted online. Admission notification on a rolling basis. **Financial aid:** Priority date 4/15; no closing date. FAFSA required. Applicants notified on a rolling basis starting 6/1; must reply within 2 week(s) of notification.

Academics. Special study options: Cooperative education, distance learning, double major, dual enrollment of high school students, independent study, internships, liberal arts/career combination. License preparation in nursing, paramedic. **Credit/placement by examination:** AP, CLEP, institutional tests. **Support services:** Learning center, reduced course load, remedial instruction, study skills assistance, tutoring.

Majors. Biology: General, botany, wildlife, zoology. **Business:** Accounting technology, accounting/business management, administrative services, business admin, office/clerical, receptionist. **Communications:** Advertising. **Computer sciences:** Information technology, webmaster. **Conservation:** General, environmental studies, wildlife/wilderness. **Education:** General, teacher assistance. **Engineering:** Surveying. **English:** English lit. **Health services:** EMT paramedic, medical assistant, medical secretary, nursing (RN), premedicine, prenursing, prepharmacy, preveterinary. **History:** General. **Liberal arts:** Arts/sciences. **Math:** General. **Parks/recreation:** General, facilities management, health/fitness. **Physical sciences:** General. **Psychology:** General. **Social sciences:** General. **Visual/performing arts:** Photography. **Work/family studies:** Child care service.

Most popular majors. Biological/life sciences 6%, business/marketing 6%, education 6%, health sciences 21%, liberal arts 50%.

Technology on campus. 60 workstations in library, computer center, student center. Dormitories wired for high-speed internet access. Online course registration, online library, repair service, wireless network available.

Student life. Freshman orientation: Mandatory. Preregistration for classes offered. **Housing:** Guaranteed on-campus for all undergraduates. Single-sex dorms, wellness housing available. $50 nonrefundable deposit. **Activities:** Campus ministries, drama, student government.

Athletics. NJCAA. **Intercollegiate:** Baseball M, basketball, football (tackle) M, ice hockey M, softball W, volleyball W. **Intramural:** Badminton, basketball, bowling, football (non-tackle), golf, racquetball, skiing, soccer, softball, table tennis, volleyball. **Team name:** Lumberjacks and Ladyjacks.

Student services. Adult student services, alcohol/substance abuse counseling, career counseling, student employment services, financial aid counseling, health services, personal counseling, veterans' counselor. **Transfer:** Transfer adviser, college fairs on campus for students transferring to 4-year colleges.

Contact. E-mail: admissions@dakotacollege.edu
Phone: (701) 228-5488 Toll-free number: (800) 542-6866
Fax: (701) 228-5499
Dan Davis, Associate Dean, Dakota College at Bottineau, 105 Simrall Boulevard, Bottineau, ND 58318-1198

Fort Berthold Community College
New Town, North Dakota
www.fortbertholdcc.edu   CB code: 7304

◆ Public 2-year community college
◆ Small town

General. Founded in 1973. Regionally accredited. Affiliated with American Indian Higher Education Consortium. **Enrollment:** 205 undergraduates. **Degrees:** 5 bachelor's, 15 associate awarded. **Location:** 80 miles from Minot, 150 miles from Bismarck. **Calendar:** Semester, limited summer session. **Full-time faculty:** 21 total. **Part-time faculty:** 6 total.

Basis for selection. Open admission.

2015-2016 Annual costs. Tuition/fees: $4,910. Room only: $7,000. Books/supplies: $400.

Financial aid. Need-based: Work-study available nights, weekends and for part-time students.

Application procedures. Admission: No deadline. $25 fee.

Academics. Special study options: Double major, independent study. **Credit/placement by examination:** AP, CLEP. **Support services:** GED preparation and test center, remedial instruction, tutoring.

Majors. Area/ethnic studies: Native American. **Business:** Business admin, office technology. **Education:** Elementary. **Health services:** Medical secretary, nursing assistant. **Human services:** General.

Student life. Activities: Drama, student government.

Athletics. Intercollegiate: Basketball, cross-country.

Student services. Adult student services, personal counseling, veterans' counselor. **Transfer:** Transfer adviser for students transferring to 4-year colleges.

Contact. E-mail: taulau@fbcc.bia.edu
Phone: (701) 627-4738 ext. 286 Fax: (701) 627-4790
Kathy Kraft, Registrar, Fort Berthold Community College, Box 490, New Town, ND 58763

Lake Region State College
Devils Lake, North Dakota
www.lrsc.edu   CB code: 6163

◆ Public 2-year community and technical college
◆ Commuter campus in small town

General. Founded in 1941. Regionally accredited. Course and program offerings at the Grand Forks Air Force Base and University of North Dakota. **Enrollment:** 663 degree-seeking undergraduates; 1,286 non-degree-seeking students. **Degrees:** 183 associate awarded. **Location:** 90 miles from Grand Forks, 122 miles from Minot. **Calendar:** Semester, limited summer session.

Student profile. Among degree-seeking undergraduates, 35% enrolled in a transfer program, 65% enrolled in a vocational program, 201 enrolled as first-time, first-year students.

Part-time:	24%	Native American:	4%
Women:	56%	Native Hawaiian/Pacific islander:	1%
African American:	4%	Multi-racial, non-Hispanic:	4%
Asian American:	1%	International:	6%
Hispanic/Latino:	5%		

Transfer out. Colleges most students transferred to 2015: Mayville State University, Minot State University, North Dakota State University, University of North Dakota, Valley City State University.

Basis for selection. Open admission, but selective for some programs. Special program requirements for nursing, peace officer training, and speech language pathology assistant. **Adult students:** SAT/ACT scores not required if applicant over 25. COMPASS test may be required. **Home schooled:** Transcript of courses and grades required.

High school preparation. Recommended units include English 4, mathematics 3, social studies 3, science 3 (laboratory 2) and foreign language 2.

2015-2016 Annual costs. Tuition/fees: $4,138; $4,138 out-of-state. Per-credit charge: $136. Room/board: $6,055.

2015-2016 Financial aid. **Need-based:** 145 full-time freshmen applied for aid; 112 deemed to have need; 110 received aid. Average need met was 82%. Average scholarship/grant was $6,076; average loan $4,704. 54% of total undergraduate aid awarded as scholarships/grants, 46% as loans/jobs. Need-based aid available for part-time students. Work-study available nights, weekends and for part-time students. **Non-need-based:** Awarded to 110 full-time undergraduates, including 64 freshmen. Scholarships awarded for academics, athletics, leadership, minority status, music/drama.

Application procedures. **Admission:** No deadline. $35 fee. Admission notification on a rolling basis. **Financial aid:** Priority date 4/15; no closing date. FAFSA required. Applicants notified on a rolling basis starting 5/15; must reply within 4 week(s) of notification.

Academics. **Special study options:** Combined bachelor's/graduate degree, cooperative education, distance learning, dual enrollment of high school students, ESL, liberal arts/career combination. License preparation in nursing. **Credit/placement by examination:** AP, CLEP, institutional tests. 15 credit hours maximum toward associate degree. **Support services:** GED preparation and test center, reduced course load, remedial instruction, study skills assistance, tutoring.

Majors. **Business:** Administrative services, business admin, management information systems. **Foreign languages:** Translation. **Health services:** Nursing (RN). **Liberal arts:** Arts/sciences. **Parks/recreation:** Physical fitness technician. **Protective services:** Police science. **Work/family studies:** Child care service.

Most popular majors. Business/marketing 17%, family/consumer sciences 8%, health sciences 12%, liberal arts 48%, security/protective services 8%.

Technology on campus. 250 workstations in dormitories, library, computer center, student center. Dormitories wired for high-speed internet access and linked to campus network. Commuter students can connect to campus network. Online course registration, online library, helpline, wireless network available.

Student life. **Freshman orientation:** Mandatory. Preregistration for classes offered. **Policies:** Smoke and alcohol-free campus. **Housing:** Single-sex dorms, special housing for disabled, apartments, wellness housing available. $50 nonrefundable deposit, deadline 9/1. **Activities:** Bands, campus ministries, choral groups, drama, literary magazine, music ensembles, musical theater, student government, symphony orchestra, Collegiate DECA, Skills USA, Phi Beta Lambda, student nurse organization, Campus Crusade for Christ, Phi Theta Kappa, LGBTQIA.

Athletics. NJCAA. **Intercollegiate:** Baseball M, basketball, golf, softball W, volleyball W. **Intramural:** Basketball, cheerleading, rifle, soccer, swimming, volleyball. **Team name:** Royals.

Student services. Career counseling, services for economically disadvantaged, student employment services, financial aid counseling, on-campus daycare, personal counseling. **Physically disabled:** Services for hearing impaired. **Transfer:** Transfer adviser, college fairs on campus for students transferring to 4-year colleges.

Contact. E-mail: lrsc.admissions@lrsc.edu
Phone: (701) 662-1514 Toll-free number: (800) 443-1313 ext. 1514
Fax: (701) 662-1581
Stephanie Shock, Director of Admissions and Enrollment Management, Lake Region State College, 1801 College Drive North, Devils Lake, ND 58301-1598

North Dakota State College of Science
Wahpeton, North Dakota
www.ndscs.edu   CB code: 6476

- Public 2-year junior and technical college
- Residential campus in small town

General. Founded in 1903. Regionally accredited. **Enrollment:** 2,095 degree-seeking undergraduates; 1,028 non-degree-seeking students. **Degrees:** 579 associate awarded. **Location:** 50 miles from Fargo, 200 miles from Sioux Falls, South Dakota. **Calendar:** Semester, limited summer session. **Full-time faculty:** 116 total; 4% have terminal degrees, 2% minority, 40% women. **Part-time faculty:** 223 total; 8% have terminal degrees, 4% minority, 56% women. **Class size:** 69% < 20, 28% 20-39, 3% 40-49, 1% 50-99. **Partnerships:** Formal partnerships with Butler Machinery, Caterpillar, F-M Ambulance, John Deere, ND Case IH Regional Dealers, Butler, Emerson Process Management, Haas, PPG Industries, RDO Integrated Controls, Snap-on Industrial, Bell State Bank & Trust, Nodak Mutual Insurance Company, North Dakota Society of Professional Land Surveyors, RSES.

Student profile. Among degree seeking undergraduates, 715 enrolled as first-time, first-year students.

Part-time:	20%	Native American:	1%
Out-of-state:	42%	Multi-racial, non-Hispanic:	3%
Women:	41%	International:	2%
African American:	8%	25 or older:	15%
Asian American:	1%	Live on campus:	59%
Hispanic/Latino:	2%		

Transfer out. **Colleges most students transferred to 2015:** Minnesota State University Moorhead, North Dakota State University, University of North Dakota, Valley City State University.

Basis for selection. Open admission, but selective for some programs. Special requirements for allied health programs. **Adult students:** SAT/ACT scores not required if applicant over 25.

High school preparation. Chemistry, English, and anatomy & physiology required for dental hygiene.

2015-2016 Annual costs. Tuition/fees: $4,571; $11,129 out-of-state. Per-credit charge: $123 in-state; $328 out-of-state. Room/board: $6,448. Books/supplies: $1,000. Personal expenses: $2,268.

2014-2015 Financial aid. **Need-based:** 625 full-time freshmen applied for aid; 457 deemed to have need; 446 received aid. Average need met was 69%. Average scholarship/grant was $4,921; average loan $5,386. 45% of total undergraduate aid awarded as scholarships/grants, 55% as loans/jobs. Need-based aid available for part-time students. Work-study available nights, weekends and for part-time students. **Non-need-based:** Awarded to 164 full-time undergraduates, including 77 freshmen. Scholarships awarded for academics, alumni affiliation, athletics, leadership, minority status, music/drama, state residency.

Application procedures. **Admission:** No deadline. $35 fee. Admission notification on a rolling basis. **Financial aid:** Priority date 4/15, closing date 4/15. FAFSA required. Applicants notified on a rolling basis starting 6/1; must reply within 2 week(s) of notification.

Academics. **Special study options:** Cooperative education, distance learning, dual enrollment of high school students, ESL, independent study, internships, liberal arts/career combination. License preparation in dental hygiene, nursing, occupational therapy, paramedic. **Credit/placement by examination:** AP, CLEP, institutional tests. 32 credit hours maximum toward associate degree. **Support services:** Learning center, pre-admission summer program, reduced course load, remedial instruction, study skills assistance, tutoring, writing center.

Majors. **Business:** Administrative services, business admin, e-commerce. **Computer sciences:** General, data entry, networking, programming. **Health services:** Dental hygiene, EMT paramedic, insurance coding, licensed practical nurse, nursing (RN), occupational therapy assistant, pharmacy assistant. **Liberal arts:** Arts/sciences.

Most popular majors. Agriculture 14%, engineering/engineering technologies 15%, health sciences 22%, liberal arts 17%, trade and industry 24%.

Technology on campus. 550 workstations in dormitories, library, computer center, student center. Dormitories wired for high-speed internet access and linked to campus network. Commuter students can connect to campus network. Online course registration, online library, helpline, wireless network available.

Student life. **Freshman orientation:** Mandatory, $25 fee. Preregistration for classes offered. Orientation held the day before classes start. **Housing:** Guaranteed on-campus for freshmen. Coed dorms, single-sex dorms, special housing for disabled, apartments available. $25 fully refundable deposit. Honors floor available. **Activities:** Bands, campus ministries, choral groups, drama, music ensembles, student government, Intervarsity Christian Fellowship.

Athletics. NJCAA. **Intercollegiate:** Basketball, football (tackle) M, volleyball W. **Intramural:** Basketball, racquetball, softball, volleyball. **Team name:** Wildcats.

Student services. Alcohol/substance abuse counseling, career counseling, student employment services, financial aid counseling, health services, on-campus daycare, personal counseling, placement for graduates, veterans' counselor. **Physically disabled:** Services for visually, hearing impaired. **Transfer:** Pre-admission transcript evaluation for new students. Transfer adviser, college fairs on campus for students transferring to 4-year colleges.

Contact. E-mail: ndscs.admissions@ndscs.edu
Phone: (701) 671-2203 Toll-free number: (800) 342-4325 ext. 32203
Fax: (701) 671-2332
Barb Mund, Director of Admissions and Records, North Dakota State College of Science, 800 North 6th Street, Wahpeton, ND 58076-0001

Rasmussen College: Bismarck
Bismarck, North Dakota
www.rasmussen.edu

◗ For-profit 2-year career college
◗ Commuter campus in small city

General. **Enrollment:** 15 degree-seeking undergraduates. **Degrees:** 19 bachelor's, 37 associate awarded. **Calendar:** Quarter. **Full-time faculty:** 1 total. **Part-time faculty:** 3 total.

Basis for selection. Open admission, but selective for some programs. Placement exams required for some programs. **Adult students:** SAT/ACT scores not required.

2016-2017 Annual costs. Tuition/fees (projected): $13,455. Per-credit charge: $299. Personal expenses: $2,214.

Financial aid. **Need-based:** Need-based aid available for part-time students. Work-study available nights, weekends and for part-time students.

Application procedures. **Admission:** No deadline. No application fee. Admission notification on a rolling basis. **Financial aid:** No deadline. FAFSA, institutional form required. Applicants notified on a rolling basis.

Academics. **Special study options:** Distance learning, double major, honors, independent study, internships. **Credit/placement by examination:** AP, CLEP, institutional tests. 45 credit hours maximum toward associate degree, 90 toward bachelor's. Credit limited to specific programs, and to courses for which examinations are available. 50% of the student's program must be completed through coursework at institution. **Support services:** Learning center, remedial instruction, study skills assistance, tutoring, writing center.

Majors. **Business:** Accounting, business admin, human resources, management information systems, marketing. **Computer sciences:** Support specialist, web page design. **Engineering:** Software. **Health services:** Health information technology, medical assistant, medical secretary. **Protective services:** Criminal justice. **Visual/performing arts:** Game design.

Technology on campus. 100 workstations in library, computer center, student center. Online course registration, online library, helpline, wireless network available.

Student life. **Freshman orientation:** Mandatory. Preregistration for classes offered.

Student services. Adult student services, career counseling, services for economically disadvantaged, student employment services, financial aid counseling, placement for graduates.

Contact. Phone: (701) 530-9600 Toll-free number: (877) 530-9600 Fax: (701) 530-9604
Susan Hammerstrom, Director of Admissions, Rasmussen College: Bismarck, 1701 East Century Avenue, Bismarck, ND 58503

Sitting Bull College
Fort Yates, North Dakota
www.sittingbull.edu   **CB code: 0310**

◗ Public 2-year community college
◗ Commuter campus in small town

General. Founded in 1971. Regionally accredited. **Enrollment:** 234 degree-seeking undergraduates. **Degrees:** 7 bachelor's, 30 associate awarded. **Location:** 75 miles from Bismarck, 60 miles from Mobridge, South Dakota. **Calendar:** Semester, limited summer session. **Full-time faculty:** 25 total. **Part-time faculty:** 22 total. **Class size:** 99% < 20, 1% 20-39.

Transfer out. **Colleges most students transferred to 2015:** Northern State College, Black Hills State College, Bismarck State College, United Tribes Technical College.

Basis for selection. Open admission. High school students may enroll with approval of Vice President of Academic Affairs and parents; letters of recommendation from high school counselor or principal required. COMPASS test required of students without 2-year college degree. **Adult students:** COMPASS required for placement in math and English.

2015-2016 Annual costs. Tuition/fees: $3,910; $3,910 out-of-state. Books/supplies: $1,200. Personal expenses: $2,000.

Financial aid. **Need-based:** Need-based aid available for part-time students. Work-study available nights, weekends and for part-time students.

Application procedures. **Admission:** No deadline. $25 fee. Application must be submitted on paper. Admission notification on a rolling basis. **Financial aid:** Priority date 5/1; no closing date. FAFSA, institutional form required. Applicants notified on a rolling basis starting 7/15; must reply within 6 week(s) of notification.

Academics. **Special study options:** Dual enrollment of high school students, independent study. Bachelor's degree programs available on campus. **Credit/placement by examination:** AP, CLEP. **Support services:** GED preparation and test center, learning center, remedial instruction, study skills assistance, tutoring, writing center.

Majors. **Area/ethnic studies:** Native American. **Business:** Business admin, entrepreneurial studies, office technology. **Computer sciences:** Applications programming. **Conservation:** Environmental science, wildlife/wilderness. **Education:** Early childhood, elementary, multi-level teacher. **General:** Carpentry. **Health services:** Licensed practical nurse. **Protective services:** Law enforcement admin.

Most popular majors. Business/marketing 30%, computer/information sciences 8%, education 15%, liberal arts 15%, natural resources/environmental science 12%, public administration/social services 8%.

Technology on campus. 75 workstations in library, computer center, student center. Online course registration, wireless network available.

Student life. **Housing:** Very limited housing available for single parents or married students. **Activities:** Model UN, student government, culture club, rodeo club.

Athletics. **Team name:** Suns.

Student services. Career counseling, student employment services, on-campus daycare, personal counseling, placement for graduates, veterans' counselor. **Transfer:** Transfer adviser for students transferring to 4-year colleges.

Contact. E-mail: melodya@sbci.edu
Phone: (701) 854-8020 Fax: (701) 854-3403
Melody Azure, Director of Admissions/Registrar, Sitting Bull College, 9299 Hwy 24, Fort Yates, ND 58538

Turtle Mountain Community College
Belcourt, North Dakota
www.tm.edu   **CB code: 0352**

◗ Private 2-year community college
◗ Commuter campus in rural community

General. Regionally accredited. **Enrollment:** 550 degree-seeking undergraduates. **Degrees:** 16 bachelor's, 72 associate awarded. **Calendar:** Semester. **Full-time faculty:** 35 total. **Part-time faculty:** 22 total.

Basis for selection. Open admission, but selective for some programs. Special requirements for Bachelor of Science Elementary Education program.

2015-2016 Annual costs. Tuition/fees: $2,220. Books/supplies: $400.

2014-2015 Financial aid. **Need-based:** 123 full-time freshmen applied for aid; 123 deemed to have need; 123 received aid. Average scholarship/grant was $4,520. 99% of total undergraduate aid awarded as scholarships/grants, 1% as loans/jobs. Need-based aid available for part-time students. Work-study available nights, weekends and for part-time students. **Non-need-based:** Awarded to 142 full-time undergraduates, including 81 freshmen. Scholarships awarded for academics, athletics, job skills, leadership, minority status.

Application procedures. **Admission:** No deadline. No application fee. Admission notification on a rolling basis. **Financial aid:** Priority date 4/15; no closing date. FAFSA, institutional form required.

Academics. **Special study options:** Bachelor's degree programs available on campus. **Credit/placement by examination:** AP, CLEP.

Majors. **Business:** Business admin. **Computer sciences:** Computer science. **Education:** Early childhood. **Health services:** Insurance coding.

Student life. **Activities:** Student government.

Athletics. **Team name:** Mighty Mikinock.

Contact. E-mail: jlafontaine@tm.edu
Phone: (701) 477-7862 Fax: (701) 477-7892
Joni LaFontaine, Admissions/Records Officer, Turtle Mountain
Community College, PO Box 340, Belcourt, ND 58316

United Tribes Technical College
Bismarck, North Dakota
www.uttc.edu   CB code: 4915

▶ Private 2-year technical college
▶ Residential campus in small city

General. Regionally accredited. Native American college. **Enrollment:** 394 degree-seeking undergraduates. **Degrees:** 9 bachelor's, 56 associate awarded. **Location:** One mile from Bismarck. **Calendar:** Semester, limited summer session. **Full-time faculty:** 50 total. **Part-time faculty:** 34 total. **Special facilities:** Elementary school on campus.

Basis for selection. Open admission, but selective for some programs. Some programs have limited enrollment and/or more stringent academic, medical, and legal requirements. Admittance priority given to those who are members of recognized tribe. **Home schooled:** Statement describing home school structure and mission, transcript of courses and grades, state high school equivalency certificate required.

2015-2016 Annual costs. Tuition/fees: $3,650. Books/supplies: $1,200. Personal expenses: $1,880.

Financial aid. **Need-based:** Need-based aid available for part-time students. Work-study available nights, weekends and for part-time students.

Application procedures. **Admission:** No deadline. No application fee. Application must be submitted on paper. Admission notification on a rolling basis. **Financial aid:** Priority date 5/29, closing date 6/30. FAFSA required. Applicants notified on a rolling basis starting 5/29; must reply within 2 week(s) of notification.

Academics. **Special study options:** Accelerated study, distance learning. Bachelor's degree programs available on campus. **Credit/placement by examination:** AP, CLEP. **Support services:** Learning center, remedial instruction, study skills assistance, tutoring.

Majors. **Biology:** Environmental. **Business:** Administrative services, business admin, office/clerical, sales/distribution. **Computer sciences:** Networking. **Education:** General, early childhood, elementary. **Health services:** Licensed practical nurse. **Protective services:** Law enforcement admin. **Visual/performing arts:** Studio arts management.

Technology on campus. 40 workstations in computer center. Commuter students can connect to campus network. Online course registration, repair service available.

Student life. **Freshman orientation:** Mandatory. Preregistration for classes offered. **Housing:** Coed dorms, single-sex dorms, wellness housing available. **Activities:** Student newspaper.

Athletics. NJCAA. **Intercollegiate:** Basketball, cross-country. **Team name:** Thunderbirds.

Student services. Adult student services, alcohol/substance abuse counseling, chaplain/spiritual director, career counseling, financial aid counseling, health services, on-campus daycare, personal counseling, placement for graduates, women's services. **Transfer:** Pre-admission transcript evaluation for new students.

Contact. E-mail: dlambert@uttc.edu
Phone: (701) 255-3285 ext. 1334 Toll-free number: (800) 643-8882
Fax: (701) 530-0640
Donovan Lambert, Director of Admissions, United Tribes Technical College, 3315 University Drive, Bismarck, ND 58504

Williston State College
Williston, North Dakota
www.willistonstate.edu   CB code: 6905

▶ Public 2-year community and junior college
▶ Commuter campus in large town

General. Founded in 1957. Regionally accredited. Baccalaureate, postbaccalaureate programs from other campuses available on-campus, all via interactive video network. **Enrollment:** 738 degree seeking undergraduates;

300 non-degree-seeking students. **Degrees:** 151 associate awarded. **Location:** 250 miles from Bismarck, 130 miles from Minot. **Calendar:** Semester, limited summer session. **Full-time faculty:** 28 total; 4% have terminal degrees, 4% minority, 54% women. **Part-time faculty:** 2 total; 50% women. **Class size:** 76% < 20, 22% 20-39, 1% 40-49.

Student profile. Among degree-seeking undergraduates, 302 enrolled as first-time, first-year students, 99 transferred in from other institutions.

Part-time:	19%	25 or older:	24%
Women:	61%	Live on campus:	20%

Transfer out. **Colleges most students transferred to 2015:** University of North Dakota, Minot State University, Dickinson State University, North Dakota State University, Montana State University-Bozeman.

Basis for selection. Open admission, but selective for some programs. Special requirements for practical nursing, speech language pathology assistant, mental health addictions technician, and massage therapy programs. **Adult students:** Degree seeking students must submit placement scores. Other types of students (non-degree, collaborative, etc.) must submit test scores for placement into Math and English courses. **Home schooled:** Transcript of courses and grades required. **Learning Disabled:** A student is recommended to contact the Disability Support Service office to self-disclose disability, fill out the Application Packet and provide documentation of disability from a qualified professional.

High school preparation. 15 units recommended. Recommended units include English 4, mathematics 3, social studies 3, science 3 (laboratory 1) and foreign language 1.

2015-2016 Annual costs. Tuition/fees: $5,233; $5,233 out-of-state. Room/board: $9,866. Books/supplies: $1,100. Personal expenses: $2,230.

2014-2015 Financial aid. **Need-based:** Need-based aid available for part-time students. Work-study available nights, weekends and for part-time students. **Non-need-based:** Scholarships awarded for academics, athletics, music/drama.

Application procedures. **Admission:** No deadline. $35 fee. Admission notification on a rolling basis. **Financial aid:** Priority date 3/15; no closing date. FAFSA required. Applicants notified on a rolling basis starting 5/15.

Academics. **Special study options:** Cooperative education, crossregistration, distance learning, double major, dual enrollment of high school students, internships, liberal arts/career combination, student-designed major, study abroad. Bachelor's degree programs available on campus. License preparation in nursing. **Credit/placement by examination:** AP, CLEP, IB, institutional tests. 15 credit hours maximum toward associate degree. **Support services:** GED preparation and test center, learning center, reduced course load, remedial instruction, study skills assistance, tutoring, writing center.

Majors. **Business:** Accounting technology, business admin. **Computer sciences:** System admin. **Health services:** Massage therapy, mental health services, nursing (RN), speech-language pathology assistant. **Liberal arts:** Arts/sciences.

Most popular majors. Health sciences 28%, liberal arts 60%.

Technology on campus. 70 workstations in dormitories, library, computer center. Dormitories wired for high-speed internet access and linked to campus network. Online course registration, online library, helpline, wireless network available.

Student life. **Freshman orientation:** Mandatory. Preregistration for classes offered. Activities take place on the day prior to first day of fall semester. **Housing:** Coed dorms, single-sex dorms, apartments available. $200 partly refundable deposit. **Activities:** Bands, campus ministries, choral groups, dance, drama, literary magazine, music ensembles, student government, student newspaper, Campus Crusade.

Athletics. NJCAA. **Intercollegiate:** Baseball M, basketball, ice hockey M, softball W, volleyball W. **Team name:** Tetons.

Student services. Alcohol/substance abuse counseling, career counseling, services for economically disadvantaged, student employment services, financial aid counseling, minority student services, personal counseling, veterans' counselor. **Physically disabled:** Services for visually, speech, hearing impaired. **Transfer:** Pre-admission transcript evaluation for new students. Transfer adviser, college fairs on campus for students transferring to 4-year colleges.

Contact. E-mail: wsc.admission@willistonstate.edu
Phone: (701) 771-4200 Toll-free number: (888) 863-9455
Fax: (701) 774-4211
Leah Windnagle, Director for Enrollment Services, Williston State College, 1410 University Avenue, Williston, ND 58801

Ohio

Antonelli College: Cincinnati
Cincinnati, Ohio
www.antonellicollege.edu

- For-profit 2-year visual arts and technical college
- Commuter campus in large city
- Interview required

General. Founded in 1947. Regionally accredited; also accredited by ACCSC. **Enrollment:** 173 undergraduates. **Degrees:** 47 associate awarded. **Location:** 55 miles from Dayton; 90 miles from Lexington, Kentucky. **Calendar:** Quarter. **Full-time faculty:** 8 total. **Part-time faculty:** 29 total. **Special facilities:** Computer graphics laboratory, complete darkroom and commercial studio facilities.

Student profile.

| Out-of-state: | 25% | Live on campus: | 11% |
| 25 or older: | 25% | | |

Basis for selection. Interview and portfolio reviewed to determine interest, motivation, and ability. Portfolio required for commercial art program.

2015-2016 Annual costs. Diploma program: $19,975. Associate programs: $31,960.

Financial aid. Need-based: Work-study available nights, weekends and for part-time students.

Application procedures. Admission: No deadline. $35 fee. Admission notification on a rolling basis. **Financial aid:** No deadline. FAFSA required. Applicants notified on a rolling basis.

Academics. Special study options: Internships. **Credit/placement by examination:** AP, CLEP, institutional tests. **Support services:** Pre-admission summer program, reduced course load, tutoring.

Majors. Computer sciences: General, information systems. **Visual/performing arts:** Commercial photography, commercial/advertising art, interior design, photography.

Most popular majors. Health sciences 29%, visual/performing arts 66%.

Technology on campus. 44 workstations in library, computer center.

Student life. Freshman orientation: Available. Preregistration for classes offered. **Housing:** Off-campus coeducational dormitory housing available at nearby College of Mount St. Joseph. **Activities:** Student newspaper, Alpha Beta Kappa honor society.

Student services. Adult student services, career counseling, student employment services, personal counseling, placement for graduates, veterans' counselor. **Transfer:** Pre-admission transcript evaluation for new students.

Contact. Phone: (513) 241-4338 Toll-free number: (800) 505-4338 Fax: (513) 241-9396
Shawnya Amendola, Registrar, Antonelli College: Cincinnati, 124 East Seventh Street, Cincinnati, OH 45202

Art Institute of Cincinnati
Cincinnati, Ohio
www.aic-arts.edu
CB code: 3181

- For-profit 2-year visual arts college
- Commuter campus in large city
- Application essay, interview required

General. Accredited by ACCSC. **Enrollment:** 47 degree-seeking undergraduates. **Degrees:** 13 bachelor's, 11 associate awarded. **Location:** 12 miles from downtown. **Calendar:** Semester. **Full-time faculty:** 5 total; 20% minority, 20% women. **Part-time faculty:** 6 total; 17% have terminal degrees, 17% minority, 67% women.

Student profile. Among degree-seeking undergraduates, 12 enrolled as first-time, first-year students.

Part-time:	11%	African American:	19%
Out-of-state:	23%	Hispanic/Latino:	2%
Women:	62%	25 or older:	13%

Basis for selection. Admission determined by applicant's artistic ability. SAT or ACT recommended. SAT/ACT scores are recommended to determine your need for placement testing for remedial English and Math courses. Students who have not submitted scores will be automatically schedule for placement testing. Portfolio, letter of recommendation from art teacher required. **Adult students:** SAT/ACT scores not required if applicant over 25. **Home schooled:** Statement describing home school structure and mission, transcript of courses and grades, state high school equivalency certificate, interview, letter of recommendation (nonparent) required. Portfolio presentation of at least 10 pieces of art with variety of media and subject matter. Statement from the state or school district certifying the home-school.

High school preparation. College-preparatory program recommended. Required and recommended units include English 2-3, mathematics 1, social studies 1, history 1, science 1, foreign language 1 and visual/performing arts 3.

2016-2017 Annual costs. Tuition/fees (projected): $16,834. Books/supplies: $905.

2014-2015 Financial aid. Need-based: 7 full-time freshmen applied for aid; 7 deemed to have need; 7 received aid. Average need met was 90%. Average scholarship/grant was $5,595. 41% of total undergraduate aid awarded as scholarships/grants, 59% as loans/jobs. Work-study available nights, weekends and for part-time students. **Non-need-based:** Scholarships awarded for academics, art.

Application procedures. Admission: No deadline. $100 fee, may be waived for applicants with need. Application must be submitted on paper. Admission notification on a rolling basis. **Financial aid:** No deadline. FAFSA, institutional form required. Applicants notified on a rolling basis starting 9/1; must reply within 1 week(s) of notification.

Academics. Special study options: Accelerated study. Bachelor's degree programs available on campus. **Credit/placement by examination:** AP, CLEP, SAT, ACT, institutional tests. **Support services:** Pre-admission summer program, remedial instruction, study skills assistance, writing center.

Majors. Computer sciences: Computer graphics. **Visual/performing arts:** Graphic design.

Technology on campus. 20 workstations in library, computer center, student center. Online library, student web hosting, wireless network available.

Student life. Freshman orientation: Mandatory. Preregistration for classes offered. **Activities:** Student government.

Student services. Career counseling, financial aid counseling, personal counseling, placement for graduates. **Transfer:** Pre-admission transcript evaluation for new students.

Contact. E-mail: admissions@aic-arts.edu
Phone: (513) 751-1206 Fax: (513) 751-1209
Cyndi Mendell, Vice President, Admissions, Art Institute of Cincinnati, 1171 East Kemper Road, Cincinnati, OH 45246

ATS Institute of Technology
Highland Heights, Ohio
www.atsinstitute.com

- For-profit 2-year nursing and technical college
- Commuter campus in very large city

General. Accredited by ACICS. **Enrollment:** 459 undergraduates. **Calendar:** Semester. **Full-time faculty:** 43 total. **Part-time faculty:** 30 total.

Basis for selection. Open admission, but selective for some programs. Selective admissions to allied health programs.

2015-2016 Annual costs. Tuition/fees: $9,500. Books/supplies: $900.

Financial aid. Need-based: Work-study available nights, weekends and for part-time students.

Application procedures. Admission: No deadline. $30 fee. **Financial aid:** FAFSA required. Applicants notified on a rolling basis.

Academics. Special study options: Accelerated study. License preparation in nursing. **Credit/placement by examination:** AP, CLEP. **Support services:** Remedial instruction, tutoring.

Majors. Health services: Nursing (RN).

Technology on campus. 30 workstations in library, computer center.

Contact. E-mail: info@atsinstitute.com
Phone: (440) 449-1700 Fax: (440) 442-9876
Yelena Bykov, Academic Director, ATS Institute of Technology, 325 Alpha Park, Highland Heights, OH 44143

Aultman College of Nursing and Health Sciences
Canton, Ohio
www.aultmancollege.edu   CB code: 3203

▶ Private 2-year health science and nursing college
▶ Commuter campus in small city
▶ SAT or ACT (ACT writing optional) required

General. Regionally accredited. Affiliated with Aultman Hospital, a community hospital serving Stark, Wayne, Tuscarawas, and Carroll counties. **Enrollment:** 362 degree-seeking undergraduates; 10 non-degree-seeking students. **Degrees:** 18 bachelor's, 109 associate awarded. **Location:** 50 miles from Cleveland. **Calendar:** Semester, limited summer session. **Full-time faculty:** 17 total; 18% have terminal degrees, 12% minority, 88% women. **Part-time faculty:** 41 total; 15% have terminal degrees, 12% minority, 78% women. **Class size:** 68% < 20, 32% 20-39.

Student profile. Among degree-seeking undergraduates, 13 enrolled as first-time, first-year students, 109 transferred in from other institutions.

Part-time:	82%	**Native American:**	1%
Women:	87%	**Native Hawaiian/Pacific islander:**	1%
African American:	4%	**Multi-racial, non-Hispanic:**	2%
Hispanic/Latino:	1%	25 or older:	62%

Transfer out. Colleges most students transferred to 2015: Stark State College of Technology, University of Akron, Kent State University.

Basis for selection. High School Applicants: 1) must have a high school GPA of 3.00 or better, or GED score of 2250 or better, and 2) an ACT score of 20 or better or SAT combined score or 950 or better; 3) if completed dual enrollment/post-secondary coursework, please refer to the Transfer Applicant's requirements. Transfer Applicants: Must have a college GPA of 2.5 or greater with 6 credit hours or more of coursework based on most recent college transcript. COMPASS math placement testing required.

2016-2017 Annual costs. Tuition/fees (projected): $15,915. Per-credit charge: $523. Books/supplies: $2,000. Personal expenses: $3,060.

2014-2015 Financial aid. All financial aid based on need. 31% of total undergraduate aid awarded as scholarships/grants, 69% as loans/jobs. Need-based aid available for part-time students. Work-study available nights, weekends and for part-time students.

Application procedures. Admission: Closing date 2/1 (receipt date). $45 fee, may be waived for applicants with need. Must reply by May 1 or within 2 week(s) if notified thereafter. **Financial aid:** Priority date 3/1, closing date 10/1. FAFSA, institutional form required. Applicants notified on a rolling basis starting 6/15; must reply within 2 week(s) of notification.

Academics. Special study options: Double major, dual enrollment of high school students. Bachelor's degree programs available on campus. License preparation in nursing, radiology. **Credit/placement by examination:** AP, CLEP, institutional tests. 6 credit hours maximum toward associate degree, 6 toward bachelor's. **Support services:** Learning center, reduced course load, remedial instruction, study skills assistance, tutoring, writing center.

Majors. Health services: Nursing (RN), radiologic technology/medical imaging.

Technology on campus. PC or laptop required. 173 workstations in library, computer center. Commuter students can connect to campus network. Online course registration, online library, helpline, wireless network available.

Student life. Freshman orientation: Mandatory. Preregistration for classes offered. One-day program held in Fall, Spring, and Summer. **Activities:** Student government.

Student services. Chaplain/spiritual director, career counseling, financial aid counseling, health services.

Contact. E-mail: linda.celik@aultman.com
Phone: (330) 363-5075 Fax: (330) 580-6654
Wendy Davis, Director of Finance and Enrollment Services, Aultman College of Nursing and Health Sciences, 2600 Sixth Street SW, Canton, OH 44710-1799

Belmont College
St Clairsville, Ohio
www.belmontcollege.edu   CB code: 1072

▶ Public 2-year community and technical college
▶ Commuter campus in small town
▶ Interview required

General. Founded in 1969. Regionally accredited. **Enrollment:** 1,259 undergraduates. **Degrees:** 222 associate awarded. **Location:** 15 miles from Wheeling, West Virginia. **Calendar:** Quarter, limited summer session. **Full-time faculty:** 40 total. **Part-time faculty:** 131 total. **Class size:** 79% < 20, 20% 20-39, less than 1% 40-49, less than 1% 50-99.

Student profile.

Out-of-state:	15%	**25 or older:**	45%

Transfer out. Colleges most students transferred to 2015: Wheeling Jesuit University, Ohio University Eastern Campus, West Liberty State College.

Basis for selection. Open admission, but selective for some programs. Admission to registered nursing and LPN programs predicated on completion of remediation with grade of C or better and completion of selected general courses with C or better, based on ACCUPLACER placement test scores. Interview required for nursing and paramedic applicants after admission to program, recommended for all others. **Home schooled:** State high school equivalency certificate required.

2015-2016 Annual costs. Tuition/fees: $4,409; $7,508 out-of-state. Per-credit charge: $105 in-state; $209 out-of-state. Books/supplies: $910. Personal expenses: $1,800.

Financial aid. Need-based: Need-based aid available for part-time students. Work-study available nights, weekends and for part-time students. **Non-need-based:** Scholarships awarded for state residency.

Application procedures. Admission: No deadline. No application fee. Admission notification on a rolling basis. **Financial aid:** No deadline. FAFSA required. Applicants notified on a rolling basis starting 6/1; must reply within 2 week(s) of notification.

Academics. Special study options: Cross-registration, distance learning, double major, dual enrollment of high school students, internships, student-designed major, weekend college. **Credit/placement by examination:** AP, CLEP, institutional tests. **Support services:** GED test center, learning center, reduced course load, remedial instruction, study skills assistance, tutoring, writing center.

Majors. Business: General, accounting, business admin, entrepreneurial studies, office/clerical. **Computer sciences:** General, computer graphics, data entry, LAN/WAN management, programming, security, system admin, web page design. **Education:** Early childhood. **Engineering:** Civil, electrical. **Health services:** EMT paramedic, medical assistant, nursing (RN).

Most popular majors. Business/marketing 15%, computer/information sciences 11%, engineering/engineering technologies 18%, health sciences 10%, security/protective services 6%, social sciences 7%.

Technology on campus. Online library, wireless network available.

Student life. Freshman orientation: Available. Preregistration for classes offered. **Activities:** Phi Theta Kappa.

Athletics. Intercollegiate: Football (non-tackle).

Student services. Adult student services, career counseling, student employment services, financial aid counseling, on-campus daycare, personal counseling, placement for graduates, veterans' counselor. **Physically disabled:** Services for visually, hearing impaired. **Transfer:** Pre-admission transcript evaluation for new students. Transfer adviser, college fairs on campus for students transferring to 4-year colleges.

Contact. E-mail: info@belmontcollege.edu
Phone: (740) 695-9500 ext. 1563 Fax: (740) 699-3049
Michael Sterling, Director of Admissions, Belmont College, 120 Fox Shannon Place, St. Clairsville, OH 43950

Bowling Green State University: Firelands College
Huron, Ohio
www.firelands.bgsu.edu   CB code: 0749

▶ Public 2-year branch campus college
▶ Commuter campus in small town

General. Founded in 1967. Regionally accredited. **Enrollment:** 1,464 degree-seeking undergraduates; 796 non-degree-seeking students. **Degrees:** 203 associate awarded. **Location:** 50 miles from Cleveland, 60 miles from Toledo. **Calendar:** Semester, limited summer session. **Full-time faculty:** 50 total; 14% minority, 58% women. **Part-time faculty:** 76 total; 8% minority, 57% women. **Class size:** 46% < 20, 51% 20-39, 3% 40-49.

Student profile. Among degree-seeking undergraduates, 30% enrolled in a transfer program, 70% enrolled in a vocational program, 408 enrolled as first-time, first-year students.

Part-time:	35%	Hispanic/Latino:	6%
Women:	67%	Multi-racial, non-Hispanic:	4%
African American:	6%	25 or older:	34%

Basis for selection. Open admission. **Home schooled:** Statement describing home school structure and mission, transcript of courses and grades required. Home school program must be accredited.

High school preparation. College-preparatory program recommended. 16 units recommended. Recommended units include English 4, mathematics 3, social studies 3, science 3 (laboratory 2) and foreign language 2. One visual or performing arts recommended.

2015-2016 Annual costs. Tuition/fees: $4,946; $12,254 out-of-state. Per-credit charge: $196 in-state; $501 out-of-state. Books/supplies: $1,278. Personal expenses: $1,217.

Financial aid. All financial aid based on need. Need-based aid available for part-time students. Work-study available nights, weekends and for part-time students. **Additional information:** Scholarship application deadline May 1. Technology computer loan program available. Based on need, students may receive computer on semester by semester loan basis.

Application procedures. Admission: Closing date 8/12 (receipt date). $45 fee, may be waived for applicants with need. Admission notification on a rolling basis. **Financial aid:** Priority date 3/1; no closing date. FAFSA required. Applicants notified on a rolling basis starting 4/15; must reply within 2 week(s) of notification.

Academics. Nursing programs (RN, LPN, and RN-to-BSN) are available through affiliate agreements with Firelands Regional Medical Center, Lorain County Community College, and University of Toledo. Bachelor degree programs available in eight additional areas: Applied Health Science, Applied Health Science - Respiratory Care, Business Administration, Criminal Justice, Early Childhood Education, Liberal Studies, Social Work, and Visual Communication Technology. Fully online Associate of Arts degree. **Special study options:** Cross-registration, distance learning, dual enrollment of high school students, honors, independent study, internships, liberal arts/career combination, student-designed major, study abroad, teacher certification program. Satellite associate degree registered nurse program from Lorain County Community College and Firelands Regional Medical Center. Bachelor's degree programs available on campus. License preparation in nursing, radiology. **Credit/placement by examination:** AP, CLEP, institutional tests. 15 credit hours maximum toward associate degree. **Support services:** Learning center, reduced course load, remedial instruction, study skills assistance, tutoring, writing center.

Majors. Business: General, accounting, administrative services, business admin, operations. **Communications technology:** General. **Computer sciences:** Programming. **Engineering:** Electrical. **Health services:** Health information technology, medical radiologic technology/radiation therapy, nursing (RN), respiratory therapy technology, sonography. **Liberal arts:** Arts/sciences. **Protective services:** Criminal justice. **Social sciences:** General.

Most popular majors. Health sciences 14%, liberal arts 75%.

Technology on campus. 300 workstations in library, computer center. Commuter students can connect to campus network. Online course registration, online library, helpline, wireless network available.

Student life. Freshman orientation: Available. Preregistration for classes offered. **Activities:** Drama, Model UN, musical theater, student government, student newspaper, allied health club, Campus Fellowship, theater group, writing center, peace and justice club, virtual communication technology organization, women's resource group, HOPE Club.

Athletics. Intramural: Basketball, bowling, football (tackle) M, table tennis, volleyball. **Team name:** Falcons.

Student services. Adult student services, career counseling, student employment services, financial aid counseling, placement for graduates. **Physically disabled:** Services for visually, speech, hearing impaired. **Transfer:** Transfer adviser, college fairs on campus for students transferring to 4-year colleges.

Contact. E-mail: fireadm@bgsu.edu
Phone: (419) 433-5560 ext. 20607 Toll-free number: (800) 322-4787
Fax: (419) 372-0604
Debralee Divers, Director of Enrollment Mgmt & Student Retention Services, Bowling Green State University: Firelands College, One University Drive, Huron, OH 44839-9719

Bradford School
Columbus, Ohio
www.bradfordschoolcolumbus.edu   CB code: 3952

▶ For-profit 2-year business and technical college
▶ Commuter campus in very large city

General. Founded in 1911. Accredited by ACICS. **Enrollment:** 449 undergraduates. **Degrees:** 217 associate awarded. **Calendar:** Semester, extensive summer session.

Basis for selection. Open admission.

2015-2016 Annual costs. Diploma programs: $18,055-$21,840, books and supplies $1,872-$3,120, room and board $7,775-$9,330. Associate programs: $27,960-$32,020, books and supplies $1,960-$3,308, room and board $12,440-$13,995.

Financial aid. Need-based: Work-study available nights, weekends and for part-time students.

Application procedures. Admission: No deadline. $50 fee. Admission notification on a rolling basis. **Financial aid:** No deadline.

Academics. Credit/placement by examination: AP, CLEP.

Majors. Health services: Medical assistant, physical therapy assistant, veterinary technology/assistant. **Visual/performing arts:** Graphic design.

Student services. Career counseling, financial aid counseling, placement for graduates.

Contact. E-mail: bradfordcols@bradfordschoolcolumbus.edu
Phone: (614) 416-6200 Toll-free number: (800) 678-7981
Fax: (614) 416-6210
Bradford School, 2469 Stelzer Road, Columbus, OH 43219

Brown Mackie College: Akron
Akron, Ohio
www.brownmackie.edu   CB code: 3266

▶ For-profit 2-year business college
▶ Commuter campus in small city

General. Accredited by ACICS. **Enrollment:** 533 undergraduates. **Degrees:** 5 bachelor's, 149 associate awarded. **Calendar:** Quarter. **Full-time faculty:** 13 total. **Part-time faculty:** 60 total.

Basis for selection. Open admission.

2015-2016 Annual costs. Tuition/fees: $16,490. Per-credit charge: $327. Books/supplies: $1,500. Personal expenses: $2,664.

Financial aid. Need-based: Work-study available nights, weekends and for part-time students.

Application procedures. Admission: No deadline. No application fee. **Financial aid:** No deadline.

Academics. Credit/placement by examination: AP, CLEP. **Support services:** Tutoring.

Majors. Business: General, accounting, accounting technology, business admin, office management, office technology. **Computer sciences:** Data entry, networking, programming, support specialist. **Education:** Early childhood special. **Engineering:** Electrical. **Health services:** Medical assistant, occupational therapy assistant, office admin, pharmacy assistant, surgical technology, veterinary technology/assistant. **Protective services:** Criminal justice.

Technology on campus. 101 workstations in library, computer center.

Student services. Career counseling, financial aid counseling, personal counseling, placement for graduates.

Contact. Phone: (330) 733-8766 Fax: (330) 733-5853
Jackie Conte, Director of Admissions, Brown Mackie College: Akron, 755 White Pond Drive, Suite 101, Akron, OH 44320

Brown Mackie College: Cincinnati
Cincinnati, Ohio
www.brownmackie.edu

CB code: 3576

- For-profit 2-year business and nursing college
- Commuter campus in large city

General. Founded in 1927. Accredited by ACICS. 4 branch campuses in Akron, Cincinnati, Findlay, and Ft. Mitchell, Kentucky. **Enrollment:** 918 undergraduates. **Degrees:** 19 bachelor's, 152 associate awarded. **Location:** 10 miles from downtown. **Calendar:** Quarter, extensive summer session. **Full-time faculty:** 17 total. **Part-time faculty:** 71 total. **Class size:** 45% < 20, 55% 20-39.

Basis for selection. Open admission, but selective for some programs. Must have high school diploma or GED. Computer networking program admission based on previous college and/or work history. Students entering Computer Networking (MCSE) program who do not have associate degree required to have 21 ACT composite score or 1000 SAT composite score (exclusive of Writing). Interview required for some students.

2015-2016 Annual costs. Tuition/fees: $16,490. Per-credit charge: $327. Books/supplies: $1,500. Personal expenses: $2,700.

Financial aid. All financial aid based on need. Need-based aid available for part-time students. Work-study available nights, weekends and for part-time students.

Application procedures. Admission: No deadline. No application fee. Admission notification on a rolling basis. **Financial aid:** Priority date 3/15; no closing date. FAFSA, institutional form required. Applicants notified on a rolling basis.

Academics. Special study options: Cooperative education, independent study. Externship. **Credit/placement by examination:** AP, CLEP, institutional tests. 24 credit hours maximum toward associate degree. **Support services:** Learning center, remedial instruction, tutoring.

Majors. Business: Accounting, management science. **Computer sciences:** Computer science. **Health services:** Health care admin, medical assistant, optician, pharmacy assistant, surgical technology.

Most popular majors. Business/marketing 39%, computer/information sciences 21%, health sciences 16%.

Technology on campus. 142 workstations in library, computer center.

Student life. Freshman orientation: Mandatory. Preregistration for classes offered.

Student services. Career counseling, student employment services, financial aid counseling, personal counseling, placement for graduates, veterans' counselor. **Transfer:** Pre-admission transcript evaluation for new students. Transfer adviser for students transferring to 4-year colleges.

Contact. Phone: (513) 771-2424 Toll-free number: (800) 888-1445
Fax: (513) 771-3413
Jodi Marlow, Director of Admissions, Brown Mackie College: Cincinnati, 1011 Glendale-Milford Road, Cincinnati, OH 45215

Brown Mackie College: Findlay
Findlay, Ohio
www.brownmackie.edu

- For-profit 2-year business and junior college
- Commuter campus in small city
- Interview required

General. Accredited by ACICS. **Enrollment:** 448 undergraduates. **Degrees:** 16 bachelor's, 76 associate awarded. **Location:** 20 miles Bowling Green, 48 miles from Toledo. **Calendar:** Quarter, extensive summer session. **Full-time faculty:** 16 total. **Part-time faculty:** 58 total. **Class size:** 74% < 20, 26% 20-39.

Student profile.

Out-of-state: 31% **25 or older:** 72%

Basis for selection. Open admission. **Home schooled:** State high school equivalency certificate required.

2015-2016 Annual costs. Tuition/fees: $16,490. Per-credit charge: $327. Books/supplies: $1,500. Personal expenses: $2,700.

Financial aid. Need-based: Need-based aid available for part-time students. Work-study available nights, weekends and for part-time students. **Non-need-based:** Scholarships awarded for academics, state residency.

Application procedures. Admission: No deadline. No application fee. Admission notification on a rolling basis. **Financial aid:** No deadline. FAFSA required.

Academics. Special study options: License preparation in nursing. **Credit/placement by examination:** AP, CLEP, institutional tests. **Support services:** Learning center, remedial instruction, study skills assistance, tutoring.

Majors. Business: Accounting technology, business admin, office technology. **Health services:** Health care admin, medical assistant, pharmacy assistant, surgical technology. **Protective services:** Law enforcement admin.

Most popular majors. Business/marketing 23%, health sciences 58%, legal studies 11%, security/protective services 8%.

Technology on campus. 28 workstations in library. Commuter students can connect to campus network.

Student life. Freshman orientation: Mandatory. Preregistration for classes offered. **Activities:** Student newspaper.

Student services. Career counseling, student employment services, financial aid counseling, placement for graduates. **Physically disabled:** Services for visually impaired. **Transfer:** Re-entry adviser, pre-admission transcript evaluation for new students.

Contact. E-mail: syoakum@brownmackie.edu
Phone: (419) 423-2211 Toll-free number: (800) 842-3687
Fax: (419) 423-0725
Susan Yoakam, Admissions Director, Brown Mackie College: Findlay, 1700 Fostoria Avenue, Suite 100, Findlay, OH 45840

Brown Mackie College: North Canton
Canton, Ohio
www.brownmackie.edu

CB code: 3148

- For-profit 2-year career college
- Commuter campus in small city
- Interview required

General. Accredited by ACICS. **Enrollment:** 471 undergraduates. **Degrees:** 9 bachelor's, 94 associate awarded. **Calendar:** Differs by program. **Full-time faculty:** 12 total. **Part-time faculty:** 54 total.

Basis for selection. Open admission. **Adult students:** SAT/ACT scores not required. **Home schooled:** Transcript of courses and grades required.

2015-2016 Annual costs. Tuition/fees: $16,490. Per-credit charge: $327. Books/supplies: $1,250.

Financial aid. Need-based: Work-study available nights, weekends and for part-time students.

Application procedures. Admission: No deadline. No application fee. Admission notification on a rolling basis. **Financial aid:** FAFSA required.

Academics. Special study options: License preparation in nursing. **Credit/placement by examination:** AP, CLEP. **Support services:** Remedial instruction, tutoring.

Majors. Business: Accounting, business admin. **Computer sciences:** Networking. **Health services:** Health care admin, office assistant, surgical technology. **Protective services:** Criminal justice.

Most popular majors. Business/marketing 17%, computer/information sciences 8%, health sciences 32%, legal studies 19%.

Technology on campus. 25 workstations in library.

Student life. Freshman orientation: Mandatory. Preregistration for classes offered.

Student services. Physically disabled: Services for visually, speech, hearing impaired.

Contact. Phone: (330) 494-1214 Fax: (330) 494-8112
Brown Mackie College: North Canton, 4300 Munson Street Northwest, Canton, OH 44718-3674

Bryant & Stratton College: Cleveland
Cleveland, Ohio
www.bryantstratton.edu   CB code: 0814

◗ For-profit 2-year technical and career college
◗ Commuter campus in very large city
◗ Interview required

General. Founded in 1929. Regionally accredited. **Enrollment:** 291 degree-seeking undergraduates. **Degrees:** 15 bachelor's, 77 associate awarded. **Location:** Downtown. **Calendar:** Trimester, extensive summer session. **Full-time faculty:** 14 total. **Part-time faculty:** 50 total. **Class size:** 79% < 20, 21% 20-39.

Transfer out. Colleges most students transferred to 2015: ITT Technical Institute, Cuyahoga Community College, Myer University, Cleveland State University.

Basis for selection. Open admission, but selective for some programs. Institutional test scores and interview most important. Passing scores on entrance exams required. **Home schooled:** Transcript of courses and grades, interview required.

2015-2016 Annual costs. Tuition/fees: $17,190. Per-credit charge: $573. Books/supplies: $1,800. Personal expenses: $1,530. **Additional information:** Tuition and fees may vary by program.

Financial aid. Need-based: Need-based aid available for part-time students. Work-study available nights, weekends and for part-time students. **Non-need-based:** Scholarships awarded for academics.

Application procedures. Admission: Closing date 9/22. $35 fee. Admission notification on a rolling basis. **Financial aid:** Closing date 9/22. FAFSA, institutional form required. Applicants notified on a rolling basis starting 5/1; must reply within 2 week(s) of notification.

Academics. Special study options: Distance learning, double major, internships, liberal arts/career combination. Bachelor's degree programs available on campus. **Credit/placement by examination:** AP, CLEP, institutional tests. 26 credit hours maximum toward associate degree. **Support services:** GED preparation and test center, learning center, reduced course load, remedial instruction, study skills assistance, tutoring, writing center.

Majors. Business: General, administrative services. **Computer sciences:** Information technology.

Most popular majors. Computer/information sciences 60%, engineering/engineering technologies 40%.

Technology on campus. 106 workstations in dormitories, library, computer center. Online library, helpline, wireless network available.

Student life. Freshman orientation: Available. Preregistration for classes offered. Three-hour session 1 week prior to start of semester. **Housing:** Apartments available. **Activities:** Student government.

Athletics. Intramural: Softball. **Team name:** Bobcats.

Student services. Adult student services, alcohol/substance abuse counseling, career counseling, student employment services, financial aid counseling, personal counseling, placement for graduates. **Transfer:** Pre-admission transcript evaluation for new students. Transfer adviser, college fairs on campus for students transferring to 4-year colleges.

Contact. E-mail: bacassidy@bryantstratton.edu
Phone: (216) 771-1700 Fax: (216) 771-7787
William Cassidy, Director of Admissions, Bryant & Stratton College: Cleveland, 3121 Euclid Avenue, Cleveland, OH 44115

Central Ohio Technical College
Newark, Ohio
www.cotc.edu   CB code: 7321

◗ Public 2-year technical college
◗ Commuter campus in large town

General. Founded in 1971. Regionally accredited. Additional campuses at Coshocton, Knox, Pataskala, and Newark. Extensive course offerings available on-line. **Enrollment:** 2,721 degree-seeking undergraduates; 880 non-degree-seeking students. **Degrees:** 554 associate awarded. **Location:** 45 miles from Columbus. **Calendar:** Semester, limited summer session. **Full-time faculty:** 59 total. **Part-time faculty:** 158 total.

Student profile. Among degree-seeking undergraduates, 471 enrolled as first-time, first-year students.

Part-time:	66%	Hispanic/Latino:	2%
Out-of-state:	1%	Multi-racial, non-Hispanic:	3%
Women:	69%	25 or older:	33%
African American:	12%	Live on campus:	1%
Asian American:	1%		

Transfer out. Colleges most students transferred to 2015: Franklin University, Mount Vernon Nazarene, Ohio State University.

Basis for selection. Open admission, but selective for some programs.

High school preparation. Each selective admission program has separate high school course requirements.

2015-2016 Annual costs. Tuition/fees: $4,296; $7,056 out-of-state. Per-credit charge: $179 in-state; $294 out-of-state. Books/supplies: $1,320. Personal expenses: $2,208.

Financial aid. Need-based: Need-based aid available for part-time students. Work-study available nights, weekends and for part-time students. **Non-need-based:** Scholarships awarded for academics, state residency.

Application procedures. Admission: Priority date 6/17; no deadline. No application fee. Admission notification on a rolling basis. **Financial aid:** Priority date 2/15; no closing date. FAFSA required. Applicants notified on a rolling basis starting 5/1; must reply within 3 week(s) of notification.

Academics. Special study options: Cooperative education, distance learning, double major, dual enrollment of high school students, ESL, internships, weekend college. License preparation in nursing, paramedic, radiology. **Credit/placement by examination:** AP, CLEP, IB, institutional tests. 45 credit hours maximum toward associate degree. **Support services:** Learning center, reduced course load, remedial instruction, study skills assistance, tutoring.

Majors. Business: Accounting, business admin. **Communications:** Advertising. **Computer sciences:** Computer graphics, programming, support specialist, web page design. **Education:** Early childhood. **Health services:** EMT paramedic, nursing (RN), radiologic technology/medical imaging, sonography, surgical technology. **Liberal arts:** Arts/sciences. **Protective services:** Firefighting, forensics, law enforcement admin, police science.

Most popular majors. Business/marketing 14%, computer/information sciences 6%, health sciences 62%, security/protective services 6%.

Technology on campus. 177 workstations in library, computer center, student center. Commuter students can connect to campus network. Online course registration, helpline, wireless network available.

Student life. Freshman orientation: Mandatory. Preregistration for classes offered. Three-hour program. **Housing:** Apartments available. **Activities:** Choral groups, drama, music ensembles, student government, Phi Theta Kappa, theatre arts association, student nurses organization, criminal justice club, rad tech club, Habitat for Humanity College Chapter, ski club, Students in Free Enterprise.

Athletics. Intercollegiate: Volleyball W. **Intramural:** Badminton, basketball, soccer, table tennis, volleyball.

Student services. Career counseling, student employment services, financial aid counseling, minority student services, personal counseling, placement for graduates, veterans' counselor. **Physically disabled:** Services for visually, speech, hearing impaired. **Transfer:** Transfer adviser, college fairs on campus for students transferring to 4-year colleges.

Contact. E-mail: cotcgateway@cotc.edu
Phone: (740) 366-9222 Fax: (740) 366-5047
Brad Pulcini, Director of Gateway Operations, Central Ohio Technical College, 1179 University Drive, Newark, OH 43055

Chatfield College
Fayetteville, Ohio
www.chatfield.edu   CB code: 1143

♦ Private 2-year liberal arts college affiliated with the Roman Catholic Church
♦ Commuter campus in rural community

General. Founded in 1970. Regionally accredited. **Enrollment:** 261 degree-seeking undergraduates; 135 non-degree-seeking students. **Degrees:** 76 associate awarded. **Location:** 40 miles from Cincinnati. **Calendar:** Semester, limited summer session. **Full-time faculty:** 5 total; 20% women. **Part-time faculty:** 81 total; 9% have terminal degrees, 7% minority, 59% women. **Class size:** 96% < 20, 4% 20-39.

Student profile. Among degree-seeking undergraduates, 3% enrolled in a transfer program, 71 enrolled as first-time, first-year students, 3 transferred in from other institutions.

Part-time:	43%	Multi-racial, non-Hispanic:	1%
Women:	77%	25 or older:	52%
African American:	62%		

Transfer out. Colleges most students transferred to 2015: University of Cincinnati, Union Institute, Northern Kentucky University, Wilmington College, University of Mount Saint Joseph.

Basis for selection. Open admission. Interview recommended. **Home schooled:** Official documentation of home school program required. **Learning Disabled:** Students requesting classroom accommodations are to meet with the Dean prior to registration.

High school preparation. 16 units recommended. Recommended units include English 4, mathematics 3, social studies 3, science 3 and foreign language 2. Computer skills class recommended.

2015-2016 Annual costs. Tuition/fees: $9,645. Per-credit charge: $386. Books/supplies: $1,500.

Financial aid. Need-based: Need-based aid available for part-time students. Work-study available nights, weekends and for part-time students. **Non-need-based:** Scholarships awarded for academics, leadership. **Additional information:** Institutional grants/scholarships given primarily to first-year students to reduce debt load during initial year.

Application procedures. Admission: No deadline. $10 fee. Admission notification on a rolling basis. **Financial aid:** Priority date 5/1, closing date 8/3. FAFSA, institutional form required. Applicants notified on a rolling basis starting 4/1; must reply within 2 week(s) of notification.

Academics. Special study options: Cooperative education, cross-registration, dual enrollment of high school students, liberal arts/career combination. Cooperative programs leading to bachelor's in business and liberal studies with 2 local institutions. Third-year option: student can complete junior year at school through arrangements with several regional 4-year colleges. **Credit/placement by examination:** AP, CLEP, institutional tests. 15 credit hours maximum toward associate degree. Credits also awarded for CLEP, DSST, and ECE exams. Credit by examination may not count toward the 17 credits of residency hours required by the college. **Support services:** Remedial instruction, study skills assistance, tutoring.

Majors. Liberal arts: Arts/sciences.

Technology on campus. 58 workstations in library, computer center, student center. Online library, wireless network available.

Student life. Freshman orientation: Available. Preregistration for classes offered. **Activities:** Campus ministries, choral groups.

Student services. Adult student services, career counseling, financial aid counseling, personal counseling. **Transfer:** Transfer adviser, college fairs on campus for students transferring to 4-year colleges.

Contact. E-mail: admissions@chatfield.edu
Phone: (513) 875-3344 Fax: (513) 875-3912
John Penrose, Vice President of Enrollment, Chatfield College, 20918 State Route 251, St. Martin, OH 45118

Cincinnati College of Mortuary Science
Cincinnati, Ohio
https://www.ccms.edu   CB code: 0945

♦ Private 2-year school of mortuary science
♦ Commuter campus in very large city

General. Founded in 1882. Regionally accredited. **Enrollment:** 100 degree-seeking undergraduates. **Degrees:** 67 bachelor's, 94 associate awarded. **Location:** 5 miles from downtown. **Calendar:** Semester, extensive summer session. **Full-time faculty:** 4 total; 75% women. **Part-time faculty:** 6 total; 17% minority, 17% women. **Class size:** 30% <20, 70% 50-99.

Student profile. Among degree-seeking undergraduates, 100 transferred in from other institutions.

Out-of-state:	8%	25 or older:	40%
Women:	65%		

Basis for selection. 2.0 GPA and meeting the 30 semester prerequisite requirements for the AAS degree and 60 semester prerequisite requirements for the Bachelor of Mortuary Science Degree. **Home schooled:** Transcript of courses and grades, state high school equivalency certificate required. **Learning Disabled:** Documentation of the disability required.

High school preparation. College-preparatory program recommended.

2016-2017 Annual costs. Tuition/fees: $19,735. Per-credit charge: $375. Books/supplies: $1,000.

2014-2015 Financial aid. All financial aid based on need. Need-based aid available for part-time students. Work-study available nights, weekends and for part-time students.

Application procedures. Admission: Closing date 7/25 (postmark date). $50 fee, may be waived for applicants with need. Admission notification by 7/25. Admission notification on a rolling basis beginning on or about 1/16. **Financial aid:** No deadline. FAFSA required.

Academics. Special study options: Bachelor's degree programs available on campus. **Credit/placement by examination:** AP, CLEP. **Support services:** Remedial instruction, study skills assistance, tutoring.

Technology on campus. 12 workstations in library. Commuter students can connect to campus network. Online course registration, online library, wireless network available.

Student life. Freshman orientation: Mandatory. Preregistration for classes offered. Program held Thursday before first day of classes. **Housing:** Housing available in local funeral homes.

Student services. Financial aid counseling. **Transfer:** Pre-admission transcript evaluation for new students.

Contact. E-mail: bkabengele@ccms.edu
Phone: (513) 618-1926 Toll-free number: (888) 377-8433
Fax: (513) 761-3333
Blanche Kabengele, Admissions Director & Registrar, Cincinnati College of Mortuary Science, 645 West North Bend Road, Cincinnati, OH 45224-1428

Cincinnati State Technical and Community College
Cincinnati, Ohio
www.cincinnatistate.edu   CB code: 1984

♦ Public 2-year community and technical college
♦ Commuter campus in large city

General. Founded in 1966. Regionally accredited. **Enrollment:** 7,983 degree-seeking undergraduates; 1,647 non-degree-seeking students. **Degrees:** 1,238 associate awarded. **ROTC:** Army. **Location:** 5 miles from downtown. **Calendar:** Semester, extensive summer session. **Full-time faculty:** 196 total; 11% have terminal degrees, 19% minority, 57% women. **Part-time faculty:** 760 total; 15% minority, 49% women. **Class size:** 76% < 20, 24% 20-39. **Special facilities:** Aviation maintenance facility, culinary facility, television studio.

Student profile. Among degree-seeking undergraduates, 1,183 enrolled as first-time, first-year students.

Part-time:	65%	Hispanic/Latino:	2%
Out-of-state:	9%	Multi-racial, non-Hispanic:	3%
Women:	55%	International:	2%
African American:	26%	25 or older:	46%
Asian American:	2%		

Transfer out. Colleges most students transferred to 2015: University of Cincinnati, Northern Kentucky University, Wilmington College, College of Mount St. Joseph, Xavier University.

Basis for selection. Open admission, but selective for some programs. Health technology programs require biology and chemistry courses to have been taken in last 7 years. COMPASS test required for placement. **Home schooled:** Statement describing home school structure and mission, transcript of courses and grades required.

High school preparation. Specific course prerequisites for some programs.

2015-2016 Annual costs. Tuition/fees: $4,717; $9,177 out-of-state. Books/supplies: $1,176. Personal expenses: $2,220.

Financial aid. Need-based: Need-based aid available for part-time students. Work-study available nights, weekends and for part-time students. **Non-need-based:** Scholarships awarded for academics, athletics, state residency.

Application procedures. Admission: No deadline. No application fee. Admission notification on a rolling basis. **Financial aid:** Priority date 2/15; no closing date. FAFSA required. Applicants notified on a rolling basis starting 3/15; must reply within 4 week(s) of notification.

Academics. Special study options: Cooperative education, cross-registration, distance learning, double major, dual enrollment of high school students, ESL, honors, independent study, internships, student-designed major. Bachelor's degree programs available on campus. License preparation in aviation, nursing, occupational therapy, paramedic, real estate. **Credit/placement by examination:** AP, CLEP, IB, ACT, institutional tests. 55 credit hours maximum toward associate degree. **Support services:** GED preparation and test center, reduced course load, remedial instruction, study skills assistance, tutoring, writing center.

Majors. Biology: General. **Business:** Accounting, business admin, executive assistant, financial planning, hospitality admin, marketing, real estate. **Communications technology:** Desktop publishing. **Computer sciences:** General, applications programming, IT project management, support specialist, system admin, systems analysis. **Education:** Early childhood. **Foreign languages:** Sign language interpretation. **Health services:** Clinical lab technology, dietetics, EMT paramedic, health information technology, nuclear medical technology, nursing (RN), occupational therapy assistant, office assistant, sonography, surgical technology. **Liberal arts:** Arts/sciences. **Protective services:** Disaster management, firefighting. **Visual/performing arts:** Commercial/advertising art.

Most popular majors. Business/marketing 16%, engineering/engineering technologies 19%, health sciences 20%, liberal arts 19%, personal/culinary services 6%.

Technology on campus. 175 workstations in library, computer center, student center. Commuter students can connect to campus network. Online course registration, online library, helpline, repair service, wireless network available.

Student life. Freshman orientation: Available. Preregistration for classes offered. Day and evening sessions held for 2-3 hours before start of classes. **Activities:** Campus ministries, choral groups, international student organizations, student government, United African American Association, international students, Phi Theta Kappa, adult learners on campus, environmental club, students in free enterprise.

Athletics. NJCAA. **Intercollegiate:** Basketball, golf, soccer, volleyball W. **Team name:** Surge.

Student services. Adult student services, alcohol/substance abuse counseling, career counseling, services for economically disadvantaged, student employment services, financial aid counseling, on-campus daycare, personal counseling, veterans' counselor. **Physically disabled:** Services for visually, speech, hearing impaired. **Transfer:** Transfer center, transfer adviser, college fairs on campus for students transferring to 4-year colleges.

Contact. E-mail: adm@cincinnatistate.edu
Phone: (513) 861-7700 Fax: (513) 569-1562
Gabriele Boeckermann, Director of Admission, Cincinnati State Technical and Community College, 3520 Central Parkway, Cincinnati, OH 45223-2690

Clark State Community College
Springfield, Ohio
www.clarkstate.edu   CB code: 0777

▸ Public 2-year community college
▸ Commuter campus in small city

General. Founded in 1966. Regionally accredited. **Enrollment:** 4,843 degree-seeking undergraduates. **Degrees:** 416 associate awarded. **Location:** 30 miles from Dayton, 45 miles from Columbus. **Calendar:** Quarter, limited summer session. **Full-time faculty:** 76 total. **Part-time faculty:** 319 total. **Class size:** 58% < 20, 40% 20-39, 1% 40-49, less than 1% 50-99. **Special facilities:** Performing arts center.

Student profile.

| Out-of-state: | 1% | 25 or older: | 52% |

Transfer out. Colleges most students transferred to 2015: Wright State University.

Basis for selection. Open admission, but selective for some programs. Nursing and allied health applicants must have high school chemistry; allied health must also have algebra or equivalent with grade of 2.0 or better. Mathematics placement test with score of 12 or better required for nursing.

High school preparation. Chemistry required for nursing and medical technology. Algebra required for medical technology. 2 math units required for engineering programs.

2015-2016 Annual costs. Tuition/fees: $4,180; $7,820 out-of-state. Per-credit charge: $121 in-state; $243 out-of-state. Books/supplies: $1,008. Personal expenses: $550.

Financial aid. Need-based: Work-study available nights, weekends and for part-time students.

Application procedures. Admission: No deadline. $15 fee. Admission notification on a rolling basis. Early admission open to high school sophomores, juniors and seniors. Placement test, high school approval, and 3.0 GPA required. **Financial aid:** Priority date 6/15; no closing date. FAFSA required. Applicants notified on a rolling basis.

Academics. Special study options: Accelerated study, cooperative education, cross-registration, distance learning, double major, dual enrollment of high school students, honors, independent study, internships, liberal arts/career combination, study abroad. Bachelor's degree programs available on campus. License preparation in aviation, nursing, paramedic, physical therapy, real estate. **Credit/placement by examination:** AP, CLEP, institutional tests. 24 credit hours maximum toward associate degree. **Support services:** GED test center, learning center, reduced course load, remedial instruction, study skills assistance, tutoring.

Majors. Business: Accounting technology, business admin, human resources, logistics, marketing. **Computer sciences:** Applications programming, database management, information systems, networking. **Education:** General, early childhood, kindergarten/preschool. **Engineering:** Agricultural. **English:** English lit. **Health services:** Clinical lab technology, EMT paramedic, medical assistant, medical secretary, nursing (RN), physical therapy assistant. **Human services:** Social work. **Liberal arts:** Arts/sciences, library assistant. **Protective services:** Corrections, law enforcement admin. **Visual/performing arts:** Commercial/advertising art.

Most popular majors. Business/marketing 11%, computer/information sciences 7%, health sciences 43%, liberal arts 18%, security/protective services 8%.

Technology on campus. Commuter students can connect to campus network. Online course registration, online library, helpline, wireless network available.

Student life. Freshman orientation: Available. Preregistration for classes offered. Held prior to the beginning of each quarter. **Activities:** Campus ministries, choral groups, dance, drama, international student organizations, student government, student newspaper, professional and technological fraternities and sororities, minority student forum, Phi Theta Kappa, social work club.

Athletics. NJCAA. **Intercollegiate:** Baseball M, basketball, softball W, volleyball W. **Intramural:** Basketball, volleyball. **Team name:** Eagles.

Student services. Adult student services, chaplain/spiritual director, career counseling, services for economically disadvantaged, student employment services, financial aid counseling, health services, minority student services, on-campus daycare, personal counseling, placement for graduates, veterans' counselor. **Physically disabled:** Services for visually, speech, hearing impaired. **Transfer:** Pre-admission transcript evaluation for new students. Transfer adviser, college fairs on campus for students transferring to 4-year colleges.

Contact. E-mail: admissions@clarkstate.edu
Phone: (937) 328-6028 Fax: (937) 328-6133
Corey Holliday, Director of Admissions, Clark State Community College, Box 570, Springfield, OH 45501-0570

Cleveland Institute of Electronics
Cleveland, Ohio
www.cie-wc.edu   CB code: 0802

▶ For-profit 2-year technical college
▶ Very large city

General. Founded in 1934. Accredited by DETC. Curriculum completed entirely through distance learning. **Enrollment:** 800 undergraduates. **Calendar:** Differs by program. **Full-time faculty:** 3 total. **Part-time faculty:** 1 total.

Basis for selection. Open admission.

2015-2016 Annual costs. Tuition/fees: $4,945. Books/supplies: $600. **Additional information:** $4,945 Course 14B Electronics Technology with Digital Microprocessor Lab $4,340 Course 11 Electronics Technology with Advanced Troubleshooting $3,615 Course 6 Electronics Engineering $2,525 Course 1B Electronics Technology and Lab $2,525 Course 5B New Automation and Robotics Course $1,975 Course 1C Computer Programming - Java and C# $1,975 Course 1A Electronics Technology with FCC Prep $1,975 Course 2 Broadcast Engineering $1,975 Course 4 Wireless and Electronic Communications $1,975 Course 5 Industrial Electronics with PLC Lab $1,425 Course 2C CompTIA A+ Certification and PC Repair $1,425 Course 3C CompTIA Network+ Certification $1,425 Course 4C Intro to Computers and Microsoft Office $1,425 Course 5C Intro to Home Automation Installation $1,425 Course 6C Computer Security Specialist.

Financial aid. **Need-based:** Work-study available nights, weekends and for part-time students.

Application procedures. **Admission:** No deadline. No application fee. Admission notification on a rolling basis. High school students permitted to enroll with signed approval of parents and guidance counselors (if students are minors). **Financial aid:** No deadline.

Academics. **Special study options:** Accelerated study, distance learning, independent study. **Credit/placement by examination:** AP, CLEP.

Technology on campus. Online course registration available.

Student life. **Activities:** Student newspaper.

Student services. Student employment services, veterans' counselor.

Contact. E-mail: instruct@cie-wc.edu
Phone: (216) 781-9400 Toll-free number: (800) 243-6446
Fax: (216) 781-0331
Keith Conn, Dean of Instruction, Cleveland Institute of Electronics, 1776 East 17th Street, Cleveland, OH 44114-3679

Columbus State Community College
Columbus, Ohio   CB member
www.cscc.edu   CB code: 1148

▶ Public 2-year community and technical college
▶ Commuter campus in very large city

General. Founded in 1967. Regionally accredited. In addition to campuses in downtown Columbus and Delaware county, the College offers courses at 5 regional learning centers. **Enrollment:** 11,426 degree-seeking undergraduates; 13,718 non-degree-seeking students. **Degrees:** 2,335 associate awarded. **ROTC:** Army, Air Force. **Location:** 1 mile from downtown Columbus; a second campus is located in Delaware County. **Calendar:** Semester, extensive summer session. **Full-time faculty:** 328 total. **Part-time faculty:** 1,136 total. **Class size:** 47% < 20, 53% 20-39, less than 1% 40-49. **Special facilities:** The College operates the Aviation Maintenance Technology major at Bolton Field Airport,.

Student profile. Among degree-seeking undergraduates, 33% enrolled in a transfer program, 64% enrolled in a vocational program, 7% already have a bachelor's degree or higher, 1,909 enrolled as first-time, first-year students, 632 transferred in from other institutions.

Part-time:	64%	Hispanic/Latino:	5%
Out-of-state:	1%	Multi-racial, non-Hispanic:	4%
Women:	54%	International:	1%
African American:	22%	25 or older:	37%
Asian American:	3%		

Transfer out. **Colleges most students transferred to 2015:** Ohio State University, Franklin University, Ohio University, Capital University, Otterbein University.

Basis for selection. Open admission, but selective for some programs. Select applicant populations such as underage, international, felon, and dismissed transfer students may be required to submit documentation to determine admission status. Some career and technical programs have special admission requirements. ACT scores or College placement testing required for placement. English as a Second Language applicants required to complete ESL placement test. Placement testing required for all students who plan to take courses that have an English, math, and/or reading prerequisite if they do not have prior college credit. Interview required for chef apprenticeship and some health and human service technology programs. **Home schooled:** Some academic programs may require completion of GED. **Learning Disabled:** Students must provide documentation and register with Disability Services to receive services.

High school preparation. Algebra required for transfer programs and engineering, health, and business technology programs. Chemistry and biology required for health programs.

2015-2016 Annual costs. Tuition/fees: $4,128; $9,090 out-of-state. Books/supplies: $1,442. Personal expenses: $184.

2014-2015 Financial aid. **Need-based:** Average scholarship/grant was $4,945; average loan $3,802. 35% of total undergraduate aid awarded as scholarships/grants, 65% as loans/jobs. Need-based aid available for part-time students. Work-study available nights, weekends and for part-time students. **Non-need-based:** Scholarships awarded for academics, athletics, state residency.

Application procedures. **Admission:** Priority date 8/13; deadline 8/20 (receipt date). No application fee. Application must be submitted online. Admission notification on a rolling basis. Many health programs admit qualified students on space-available basis; students are advised to apply early. **Financial aid:** Priority date 6/1; no closing date. FAFSA required. Applicants notified on a rolling basis starting 4/1.

Academics. **Special study options:** Cooperative education, cross-registration, distance learning, double major, dual enrollment of high school students, ESL, honors, independent study, internships, liberal arts/career combination, student-designed major, study abroad, weekend college. License preparation in dental hygiene, nursing, paramedic, radiology, real estate. **Credit/placement by examination:** AP, CLEP, IB, institutional tests. **Support services:** GED preparation and test center, learning center, reduced course load, remedial instruction, study skills assistance, tutoring, writing center.

Majors. **Business:** Accounting technology, administrative services, business admin, entrepreneurial studies, hospitality admin, human resources, international, logistics, management information systems, marketing, purchasing, real estate, tourism/travel. **Communications technology:** Graphic/printing. **Computer sciences:** General, applications programming, information systems. **Foreign languages:** Sign language interpretation. **General:** Carpentry, maintenance. **Health services:** Clinical lab technology, dental hygiene, EMT paramedic, health information management, massage therapy, medical assistant, medical radiologic technology/radiation therapy, mental health services, nursing (RN), respiratory therapy technology, surgical technology, veterinary technology/assistant. **Liberal arts:** Arts/sciences. **Parks/recreation:** Exercise sciences, health/fitness, sports admin. **Protective services:** Firefighting, police science. **Visual/performing arts:** Commercial photography, game design. **Work/family studies:** Child care management.

Most popular majors. Business/marketing 12%, engineering/engineering technologies 7%, health sciences 19%, liberal arts 46%.

Technology on campus. Commuter students can connect to campus network. Online course registration, online library, helpline, wireless network available.

Student life. **Freshman orientation:** Available. Preregistration for classes offered. **Housing:** Students may live in residence halls of other local colleges if space is available. **Activities:** Bands, choral groups, dance, drama, international student organizations, music ensembles, Cougars in the Community, CSCC Pride, robotics club, numerous academic discipline organizations, Intervarsity Christian fellowship, Muslim Students Association.

Athletics. NJCAA. **Intercollegiate:** Basketball, golf, volleyball W. **Intramural:** Basketball, soccer, ultimate frisbee, volleyball. **Team name:** Cougars.

Student services. Adult student services, alcohol/substance abuse counseling, career counseling, services for economically disadvantaged, student employment services, financial aid counseling, minority student services, personal counseling, placement for graduates, veterans' counselor. **Physically disabled:** Services for visually, speech, hearing impaired. **Transfer:** Transfer adviser, college fairs on campus for students transferring to 4-year colleges.

Contact. E-mail: information@cscc.edu
Phone: (614) 287-5353 Toll-free number: (800) 621-6407 ext. 5353
Fax: (614) 287-6019
Gina Hiser, Director of Admissions, Columbus State Community College, 550 East Spring Street, Columbus, OH 43216-1609

Cuyahoga Community College
Cleveland, Ohio
www.tri-c.edu

CB member
CB code: 1159

- Public 2-year community college
- Commuter campus in very large city

General. Founded in 1963. Regionally accredited. Additional campuses in Brunswick, Highland Hills, Parma, Westlake and Westshore. **Enrollment:** 13,590 degree-seeking undergraduates. **Degrees:** 3,002 associate awarded. **ROTC:** Naval, Air Force. **Location:** Downtown. **Calendar:** Semester, limited summer session. **Full-time faculty:** 378 total; 20% have terminal degrees, 24% minority, 58% women. **Part-time faculty:** 1,312 total; 11% have terminal degrees, 21% minority, 57% women. **Class size:** 53% < 20, 45% 20-39, 2% 40-49, less than 1% 50-99. **Special facilities:** Technology center.

Transfer out. Colleges most students transferred to 2015: Cleveland State University, Baldwin-Wallace College, Kent State University, University of Akron.

Basis for selection. Open admission, but selective for some programs. Special requirements for some health technology programs (SAT or ACT required). English placement test required.

2015-2016 Annual costs. Tuition/fees: $3,172; $3,953 out-of-district; $7,468 out-of-state. Books/supplies: $1,700. Personal expenses: $1,105.

Financial aid. Need-based: Need-based aid available for part-time students. Work-study available nights, weekends and for part-time students. **Non-need-based:** Scholarships awarded for academics, art, athletics, leadership, minority status, music/drama.

Application procedures. Admission: No deadline. No application fee. Admission notification on a rolling basis. **Financial aid:** No deadline. FAFSA, institutional form required. Applicants notified on a rolling basis starting 5/15.

Academics. Special study options: Cooperative education, cross-registration, distance learning, dual enrollment of high school students, ESL, honors, independent study. **Credit/placement by examination:** AP, CLEP, institutional tests. 30 credit hours maximum toward associate degree. **Support services:** GED preparation and test center, learning center, reduced course load, remedial instruction, study skills assistance, tutoring, writing center.

Majors. Business: General, accounting, administrative services, business admin, entrepreneurial studies, hospitality admin, management information systems, real estate. **Communications technology:** General. **Computer sciences:** General. **Education:** Early childhood. **Foreign languages:** Sign language interpretation. **Health services:** Clinical lab technology, dental assistant, dental hygiene, dental lab technology, EMT paramedic, health information management, health information technology, medical assistant, nursing (RN), occupational therapy assistant, optician, pharmacy assistant, physical therapy assistant, surgical technology. **Liberal arts:** Arts/sciences. **Math:** General. **Protective services:** Corrections, fire safety technology, police science. **Visual/performing arts:** Commercial/advertising art, music, photography. **Work/family studies:** Child care management.

Most popular majors. Business/marketing 11%, health sciences 32%, liberal arts 39%.

Technology on campus. 2,000 workstations in library, computer center, student center. Online course registration, online library, helpline available.

Student life. Freshman orientation: Mandatory. Preregistration for classes offered. **Activities:** Bands, choral groups, dance, drama, musical theater, student government, student newspaper, Hillel, Afro-American society, veterans service fraternity, Young Socialist Alliance, Student Coalition Against Racism, National Education Association, Hispanic club, Phi Theta Kappa.

Athletics. NJCAA. **Intercollegiate:** Baseball M, basketball, cross-country, soccer, softball W, track and field, volleyball W, wrestling M. **Intramural:** Baseball M, basketball, bowling, gymnastics, handball, racquetball, softball, tennis, volleyball, weight lifting. **Team name:** Challengers.

Student services. Adult student services, alcohol/substance abuse counseling, career counseling, student employment services, financial aid counseling, health services, minority student services, on-campus daycare, personal counseling, placement for graduates, veterans' counselor, women's services. **Physically disabled:** Services for visually, speech, hearing impaired. **Transfer:** Transfer adviser, college fairs on campus for students transferring to 4-year colleges.

Contact. E-mail: customerservice@tri-c.edu
Phone: (216) 987-4200 Toll-free number: (800) 954-8742
Fax: (216) 696-2567
Rena Mason, Director of Admissions, Cuyahoga Community College, 2900 Community College Avenue, Cleveland, OH 44115-2878

Davis College
Toledo, Ohio
www.daviscollege.edu

CB code: 2155

- For-profit 2-year junior college
- Commuter campus in large city
- Interview required

General. Founded in 1858. Regionally accredited. **Enrollment:** 190 degree-seeking undergraduates; 3 non-degree-seeking students. **Degrees:** 39 associate awarded. **Location:** 6 miles from downtown, 45 miles from Detroit. **Calendar:** Quarter, limited summer session. **Full-time faculty:** 3 total; 100% women. **Part-time faculty:** 22 total; 73% women. **Class size:** 95% < 20, 5% 20-39.

Student profile. Among degree-seeking undergraduates, 19 enrolled as first-time, first-year students.

Part-time:	74%	Women:	82%
Out-of-state:	4%	25 or older:	66%

Transfer out. Colleges most students transferred to 2015: Lourdes College, Spring Arbor University, University of Toledo, Owens Community College, Monroe Community College.

Basis for selection. Character and personal qualities very important; Entrance Exam test scores, interview, talent and ability important. School and College Ability Tests (CPAt) required. Portfolio required for some graphic design degree programs. **Home schooled:** State high school equivalency certificate required.

2015-2016 Annual costs. Tuition/fees: $16,800. Per-credit charge: $350. Books/supplies: $1,500. Personal expenses: $2,691.

Financial aid. All financial aid based on need. Need-based aid available for part-time students. Work-study available nights, weekends and for part-time students.

Application procedures. Admission: Closing date 8/22 (receipt date). $30 fee. Admission notification on a rolling basis. **Financial aid:** No deadline. FAFSA required. Applicants notified on a rolling basis.

Academics. Special study options: Distance learning, internships, liberal arts/career combination. **Credit/placement by examination:** AP, CLEP, institutional tests. 16 credit hours maximum toward associate degree. **Support services:** GED preparation, learning center, reduced course load, remedial instruction, tutoring, writing center.

Majors. Business: Accounting technology, administrative services, business admin, human resources, marketing. **Computer sciences:** Networking. **Education:** Early childhood. **Health services:** Insurance coding, medical assistant, medical secretary. **Visual/performing arts:** Graphic design, interior design.

Most popular majors. Business/marketing 24%, computer/information sciences 7%, education 15%, health sciences 45%, visual/performing arts 9%.

Technology on campus. 90 workstations in library, computer center. Wireless network available.

Student life. Freshman orientation: Mandatory. Preregistration for classes offered.

Student services. Career counseling, student employment services, financial aid counseling, personal counseling, placement for graduates, veterans' counselor. **Transfer:** Pre-admission transcript evaluation for new students.

Contact. E-mail: dstern@daviscollege.edu
Phone: (419) 473-2700 Toll-free number: (800) 477-7021
Fax: (419) 473-2472
Dana Stern, Director of Admissions, Davis College, 4747 Monroe Street, Toledo, OH 43623

Daymar College: Chillicothe
Chillicothe, Ohio
www.daymarcollege.edu   CB code: 2468

◗ For-profit 2-year business college
◗ Commuter campus in large town
◗ Interview required

General. Founded in 1962. Regionally accredited; also accredited by ACICS. **Enrollment:** 38 undergraduates. **Degrees:** 15 associate awarded. **Location:** 45 miles from Columbus, 90 miles from Cincinnati. **Calendar:** Quarter, limited summer session. **Full-time faculty:** 7 total. **Part-time faculty:** 36 total.

Basis for selection. Open admission. Placement tests in English and math required.

2015-2016 Annual costs. Diploma programs: $17,000-$26,500. Associate programs: $33,000.

Financial aid. All financial aid based on need. Need-based aid available for part-time students. Work-study available nights, weekends and for part-time students.

Application procedures. Admission: $50 fee. Admission notification on a rolling basis. **Financial aid:** No deadline. FAFSA, institutional form required.

Academics. Credit/placement by examination: AP, CLEP. **Support services:** Remedial instruction, tutoring.

Majors. Business: Accounting, administrative services, business admin. **Computer sciences:** System admin. **Health services:** Medical secretary.

Technology on campus. 28 workstations in computer center.

Student life. Freshman orientation: Mandatory. Preregistration for classes offered.

Student services. Career counseling, financial aid counseling, placement for graduates.

Contact. E-mail: admissions@samuelstephencollege.edu
Phone: (740) 774-6300 Fax: (740) 774-6317
Admissions Representative, Daymar College: Chillicothe, 1410 Industrial Drive, Chillicothe, OH 45601

Eastern Gateway Community College
Steubenville, Ohio
www.egcc.edu   CB code: 2264

◗ Public 2-year community college
◗ Commuter campus in large town

General. Founded in 1966. Regionally accredited. **Enrollment:** 1,573 degree-seeking undergraduates. **Degrees:** 296 associate awarded. **Location:** 40 miles from Pittsburgh, PA. **Calendar:** Semester, limited summer session. **Full-time faculty:** 40 total. **Part-time faculty:** 236 total.

Transfer out. Colleges most students transferred to 2015: Franciscan University of Steubenville, Franklin University, West Liberty State College, Kent State University.

Basis for selection. Open admission, but selective for some programs. Special requirements for all allied health technologies programs. ACT required for admission to radiology, respiratory, practical nursing, medical laboratory, medical assisting, dental assisting technologies. **Home schooled:** Final transcript showing successful home school completion signed and dated by home school principal required.

2015-2016 Annual costs. Tuition/fees: $3,460; $3,640 out-of-district; $4,480 out-of-state. Per-credit charge: $111 in-district; $117 out-of-district; $145 out-of-state. Books/supplies: $1,500. Personal expenses: $500. **Additional information:** Residents of 5 neighboring West Virginia counties eligible for in-state, out-of-district tuition rates.

Financial aid. All financial aid based on need. Need-based aid available for part-time students. Work-study available nights, weekends and for part-time students.

Application procedures. Admission: No deadline. $20 fee. Admission notification on a rolling basis. **Financial aid:** Priority date 4/1; no closing date. FAFSA, institutional form required. Applicants notified on a rolling basis starting 6/15.

Academics. Special study options: Accelerated study, distance learning, dual enrollment of high school students, independent study, internships. Bachelor's degree programs available on campus. License preparation in nursing, paramedic, radiology, real estate. **Credit/placement by examination:** AP, CLEP, institutional tests. 42 credit hours maximum toward associate degree. **Support services:** GED preparation and test center, learning center, pre-admission summer program, remedial instruction, study skills assistance, tutoring, writing center.

Majors. Biology: General. **Business:** Accounting, administrative services, business admin, office management. **Computer sciences:** General. **Education:** General. **Engineering:** Construction, electrical, mechanical. **General:** Maintenance, power transmission. **Health services:** Clinical lab technology, dental assistant, EMT paramedic, licensed practical nurse, medical assistant, medical radiologic technology/radiation therapy, respiratory therapy technology. **Liberal arts:** Arts/sciences. **Protective services:** Police science, security services.

Technology on campus. 50 workstations in library, computer center. Online library, wireless network available.

Student life. Freshman orientation: Mandatory. Preregistration for classes offered. **Activities:** Student government, student newspaper.

Athletics. Intramural: Basketball M, football (non-tackle) M, softball. **Team name:** Gators.

Student services. Adult student services, career counseling, services for economically disadvantaged, student employment services, financial aid counseling, health services, on-campus daycare, veterans' counselor. **Physically disabled:** Services for visually, hearing impaired. **Transfer:** Re-entry adviser, pre-admission transcript evaluation for new students. Transfer center, transfer adviser, college fairs on campus for students transferring to 4-year colleges.

Contact. E-mail: admissions@egcc.edu
Phone: (740) 264-5591 ext. 212
Toll-free number: (800) 682-6553 ext. 212 Fax: (740) 266-2944
Ryan Ogrodnik, Director of Admissions, Eastern Gateway Community College, Eastern Gateway Community College- Jefferson County Campus, Steubenville, OH 43952

Edison State Community College
Piqua, Ohio
www.edisonohio.edu   CB code: 1191

◗ Public 2-year community college
◗ Commuter campus in large town

General. Founded in 1973. Regionally accredited. **Enrollment:** 1,773 degree-seeking undergraduates; 1,360 non-degree-seeking students. **Degrees:** 384 associate awarded. **Location:** 30 miles of Dayton. **Calendar:** Semester, extensive summer session. **Full-time faculty:** 52 total; 15% have terminal degrees, 8% minority, 60% women. **Part-time faculty:** 126 total; 12% have terminal degrees, 3% minority, 55% women. **Class size:** 83% < 20, 15% 20-39, less than 1% 40-49, 1% 50-99.

Student profile. Among degree-seeking undergraduates, 37% enrolled in a transfer program, 63% enrolled in a vocational program, 2% already have a bachelor's degree or higher, 404 enrolled as first-time, first-year students, 110 transferred in from other institutions.

Part-time:	68%	Asian American:	1%
Out-of-state:	1%	Hispanic/Latino:	1%
Women:	65%	Multi-racial, non-Hispanic:	1%
African American:	4%	25 or older:	36%

Transfer out. Colleges most students transferred to 2015: Wright State University, Ohio State University, Sinclair Community College, Franklin University, Bluffton University.

Basis for selection. Open admission, but selective for some programs. Special admissions requirements for nursing and other health care programs, early childhood education, and social services program. **Adult students:** Math and English placement with Compass. **Home schooled:** State high school equivalency certificate required. **Learning Disabled:** Students should begin the application process for services two to four months before the semester they wish to begin taking classes.

High school preparation. College-preparatory program recommended. Recommended units include English 4, mathematics 3, social studies 3, science 3 and foreign language 2. 1 fine arts recommended.

2015-2016 Annual costs. Tuition/fees: $4,234; $7,843 out-of-state. Per-credit charge: $120 in-state; $241 out-of-state. Books/supplies: $2,080. Personal expenses: $850.

2014-2015 Financial aid. Need-based: 98% of total undergraduate aid awarded as scholarships/grants, 2% as loans/jobs. Need-based aid available for part-time students. Work-study available nights, weekends and for part-time students. **Non-need-based:** Scholarships awarded for academics, alumni affiliation, art, athletics, job skills, leadership, minority status, state residency.

Application procedures. Admission: No deadline. No application fee. Admission notification on a rolling basis. **Financial aid:** Priority date 5/1; no closing date. FAFSA, institutional form required. Applicants notified on a rolling basis starting 5/15.

Academics. Special study options: Accelerated study, cooperative education, cross-registration, distance learning, double major, dual enrollment of high school students, ESL, independent study, internships, student-designed major. Bachelor's degree programs available on campus. License preparation in nursing, real estate. **Credit/placement by examination:** AP, CLEP, institutional tests. 30 credit hours maximum toward associate degree. DANTE, DSST and professional exams recommended by American Council on Education accepted. **Support services:** Learning center, pre-admission summer program, reduced course load, remedial instruction, study skills assistance, tutoring, writing center.

Majors. Biology: General. **Business:** General, accounting, business admin, executive assistant, human resources, marketing. **Communications:** Communications/speech/rhetoric. **Computer sciences:** General, networking, programming, security, web page design. **Education:** General. **English:** English lit. **Health services:** Clinical lab technology, medical assistant, medical secretary, nursing (RN), physical therapy assistant, prenursing. **History:** General. **Human services:** Social work. **Liberal arts:** Arts/sciences. **Math:** General. **Physical sciences:** Geology. **Protective services:** Police science. **Psychology:** General. **Social sciences:** Economics. **Visual/performing arts:** Art, dramatic.

Most popular majors. Business/marketing 12%, computer/information sciences 10%, health sciences 32%, liberal arts 32%.

Technology on campus. 67 workstations in library, computer center, student center. Commuter students can connect to campus network. Online course registration, online library, helpline, wireless network available.

Student life. Freshman orientation: Mandatory. Preregistration for classes offered. **Activities:** Campus ministries, drama, student government, student newspaper, Phi Theta Kappa, photo society, writers club, student ambassadors, StageLight Players, international club, digital media club, Arts League, Society of Human Resource Management, Campus Crusade for Christ.

Athletics. NJCAA. **Intercollegiate:** Baseball M, basketball, volleyball W. **Team name:** Chargers.

Student services. Adult student services, career counseling, student employment services, financial aid counseling, health services, on-campus daycare, placement for graduates, veterans' counselor. **Physically disabled:** Services for visually, speech, hearing impaired. **Transfer:** Pre-admission transcript evaluation for new students. Transfer adviser, college fairs on campus for students transferring to 4-year colleges.

Contact. E-mail: info@edisonohio.edu
Phone: (937) 778-7868 Fax: (937) 778-1920
Scott Burnam, VP of Student Affairs, Edison State Community College, 1973 Edison Drive, Piqua, OH 45356-9253

ETI Technical College of Niles
Niles, Ohio
www.eticollege.edu   CB code: 3149

▶ For-profit 2-year technical college
▶ Commuter campus in large town
▶ Interview required

General. Accredited by ACCSC. **Enrollment:** 37 degree-seeking undergraduates; 86 non-degree-seeking students. **Degrees:** 21 associate awarded. **Location:** 50 miles from Cleveland and Pittsburgh. **Calendar:** Semester, limited summer session. **Full-time faculty:** 9 total; 11% have terminal degrees, 11% minority, 56% women. **Part-time faculty:** 20 total; 65% women. **Class size:** 43% < 20, 57% 20-39.

Student profile. Among degree-seeking undergraduates, 100% enrolled in a vocational program, 2 enrolled as first-time, first-year students.

Women:	81%	African American:	27%

Basis for selection. Open admission, but selective for some programs. Practical Nursing students must pass an Evolve entrance exam to be considered for admission.

2015-2016 Annual costs. Tuition/fees: $9,386. Per-credit charge: $361. Books/supplies: $1,800. Personal expenses: $2,140.

2015-2016 Financial aid. Need-based: 2 full-time freshmen applied for aid; 2 deemed to have need; 2 received aid. Average scholarship/grant was $5,775; average loan $3,500. 61% of total undergraduate aid awarded as scholarships/grants, 39% as loans/jobs. Need-based aid available for part-time students. Work-study available nights, weekends and for part-time students.

Application procedures. Admission: No deadline. $50 fee. Admission notification on a rolling basis. **Financial aid:** No deadline. FAFSA required. Applicants notified on a rolling basis; must reply within 4 week(s) of notification.

Academics. Special study options: License preparation in nursing, real estate. **Credit/placement by examination:** AP, CLEP, institutional tests. **Support services:** GED preparation, tutoring.

Majors. Business: Accounting, administrative services. **Computer sciences:** Information technology, web page design. **Health services:** Insurance coding, medical assistant, medical secretary, medical transcription.

Most popular majors. Computer/information sciences 33%, engineering/engineering technologies 19%, health sciences 15%, legal studies 33%.

Technology on campus. 60 workstations in library, computer center. Online library available.

Student life. Freshman orientation: Mandatory. Preregistration for classes offered. **Activities:** Student government.

Student services. Career counseling, financial aid counseling, placement for graduates.

Contact. E-mail: dianemarsteller@eticollege.edu
Phone: (330) 652-9919 Fax: (330) 652-4399
Diane Marsteller, Director of Admissions, ETI Technical College of Niles, 2076 Youngstown Warren Road, Niles, OH 44446-4398

Fortis College: Centerville
Centerville, Ohio
www.fortis.edu   CB code: 1610

▶ For-profit 2-year junior and technical college
▶ Commuter campus in large town

General. Founded in 1953. Regionally accredited; also accredited by ACCSC. **Enrollment:** 887 degree-seeking undergraduates. **Degrees:** 4 bachelor's, 609 associate awarded. **Location:** 15 miles from Dayton. **Calendar:** Continuous, extensive summer session. **Full-time faculty:** 39 total. **Part-time faculty:** 123 total.

Basis for selection. Open admission. High school diploma or GED required for associate degree programs. Students without diploma or GED must pass Ability to Benefit test in order to enter diploma program. Students must have interview before submitting application for admission.

2015-2016 Annual costs. Books/supplies: $950. Personal expenses: $945. **Additional information:** Bachelor: 20841; associate degree programs: $27,615-44,402; certificates: $16,670-21,902. Books and supplies range $450-3,100 depending on program level and course of study. All costs are subject to change.

Financial aid. All financial aid based on need. Need-based aid available for part-time students. Work-study available nights, weekends and for part-time students.

Application procedures. Admission: No deadline. $100 fee, may be waived for applicants with need. Admission notification on a rolling basis. **Financial aid:** No deadline. FAFSA, institutional form required. Applicants notified on a rolling basis.

Academics. Special study options: Internships. **Credit/placement by examination:** AP, CLEP, institutional tests. 16 credit hours maximum toward associate degree. **Support services:** GED preparation, remedial instruction, tutoring.

Majors. Computer sciences: General, computer science. **Engineering:** Electrical. **Health services:** Medical assistant, nursing (RN).

Two-Year Colleges

Technology on campus. 176 workstations in library, computer center.

Student life. Freshman orientation: Mandatory. Preregistration for classes offered. Held first day of classes. **Activities:** Student government, student newspaper.

Student services. Adult student services, alcohol/substance abuse counseling, career counseling, student employment services, financial aid counseling, personal counseling, placement for graduates, veterans' counselor. **Transfer:** Pre-admission transcript evaluation for new students.

Contact. E-mail: twallace@fortiscollege.edu
Phone: (937) 433-3410 Toll-free number: (800) 837-7387
Sean Kuhn, Director, Fortis College: Centerville, 555 East Alex Bell
Road, Centerville, OH 45459-9627

Fortis College: Cuyahoga
Cuyahoga Falls, Ohio
www.fortis.edu

- For-profit 2-year nursing and technical college
- Commuter campus in small city
- Interview required

General. Regionally accredited; also accredited by ACCSC. **Enrollment:** 526 undergraduates. **Degrees:** 111 associate awarded. **Calendar:** Differs by program. **Full-time faculty:** 19 total. **Part-time faculty:** 55 total.

Basis for selection. Open admission. **Home schooled:** Transcript of courses and grades, state high school equivalency certificate required.

2015-2016 Annual costs. Associate degree programs: $26,162-$45,591; certificates:$10,397-16,550. Books and supplies range $150.00 to $2,777 depending on program level and course of study. All costs are subject to change.

Financial aid. Need-based: Work-study available nights, weekends and for part-time students.

Application procedures. Admission: No deadline. $55 fee.

Academics. Credit/placement by examination: AP, CLEP.

Majors. Business: Business admin. **Health services:** Medical assistant, office admin.

Contact. E-mail: LNelly@edaff.com
Phone: (330) 923-9959 ext. 4660 Fax: (330) 923-0886
Jeff Bucklew, Director of Admissions, Fortis College: Cuyahoga, 2545
Bailey Road, Cuyahoga Falls, OH 44221

Fortis College: Ravenna
Ravenna, Ohio
www.fortis.edu
CB code: 2195

- For-profit 2-year business college
- Large town

General. Regionally accredited; also accredited by ACCSC. **Enrollment:** 269 undergraduates. **Degrees:** 53 associate awarded. **Calendar:** Five 10-week sessions per calendar year. **Full-time faculty:** 12 total. **Part-time faculty:** 43 total.

Basis for selection. Test score on CPAt most important.

2015-2016 Annual costs. Associate degree programs: $26,625-30,720; certificates: $14,147-21,621 depending on program level and course of study. All costs are subject to change.

Financial aid. All financial aid based on need. Need-based aid available for part-time students. Work-study available nights, weekends and for part-time students.

Application procedures. Admission: No deadline. $100 fee. Admission notification on a rolling basis. **Financial aid:** FAFSA required. Applicants notified on a rolling basis.

Academics. Credit/placement by examination: AP, CLEP.

Majors. Business: Accounting, business admin. **Health services:** Health care admin.

Student life. Freshman orientation: Mandatory. Preregistration for classes offered. Held right before start of classes.

Contact. E-mail: sonyah@marcogrp.com
Phone: (330) 297-7319 Toll-free number: (800) 794-2856
Fax: (330) 296-2159
Stacy Gauding, Director of Admissions, Fortis College: Ravenna, 653
Enterprise Parkway, Ravenna, OH 44266

Gallipolis Career College
Gallipolis, Ohio
www.gallipoliscareercollege.com
CB code: 2469

- For-profit 2-year business and career college
- Commuter campus in small town
- Interview required

General. Accredited by ACICS. **Enrollment:** 90 degree-seeking undergraduates. **Degrees:** 27 associate awarded. **Location:** 45 miles from Huntington, West Virginia. **Calendar:** Quarter, extensive summer session. **Full-time faculty:** 1 total. **Part-time faculty:** 15 total. **Class size:** 89% < 20, 11% 20-39.

Student profile. Among degree-seeking undergraduates, 4 enrolled as first-time, first-year students.

Part-time:	50%	Women:	77%
Out-of-state:	3%	25 or older:	60%

Transfer out. Colleges most students transferred to 2015: University of Rio Grande.

Basis for selection. Open admission.

2016-2017 Annual costs. Tuition/fees (projected): $7,620. Per-credit charge: . Books/supplies: $1,400. Personal expenses: $4,000.

2014-2015 Financial aid. All financial aid based on need. 40% of total undergraduate aid awarded as scholarships/grants, 60% as loans/jobs. Need-based aid available for part-time students. Work-study available nights, weekends and for part-time students.

Application procedures. Admission: No deadline. $50 fee. Application must be submitted on paper. Admission notification on a rolling basis. **Financial aid:** No deadline. FAFSA required.

Academics. Special study options: Double major, independent study, internships. License preparation in real estate. **Credit/placement by examination:** AP, CLEP. 16 credit hours maximum toward associate degree. **Support services:** Remedial instruction, tutoring.

Majors. Business: Accounting, administrative services, business admin. **Computer sciences:** General. **Health services:** Medical secretary.

Most popular majors. Business/marketing 33%, computer/information sciences 17%.

Technology on campus. 36 workstations in library, computer center. Repair service available.

Student life. Freshman orientation: Available. Preregistration for classes offered. **Activities:** Student newspaper.

Student services. Career counseling, student employment services, financial aid counseling, placement for graduates. **Transfer:** Pre-admission transcript evaluation for new students.

Contact. E-mail: admissions@gallipoliscareercollege.edu
Phone: (740) 446-4367 ext. 12 Toll-free number: (800) 214-0452
Fax: (740) 446-4124
Bo Shirey, Director of Admissions, Gallipolis Career College, 1176
Jackson Pike, Suite 312, Gallipolis, OH 45631

Good Samaritan College of Nursing and Health Science
Cincinnati, Ohio
www.gscollege.edu
CB code: 1259

- Private 2-year nursing college affiliated with the Roman Catholic Church
- Commuter campus in very large city
- SAT or ACT (ACT writing optional) required

General. Hospital-based program. **Enrollment:** 358 undergraduates. **Degrees:** 2 bachelor's, 97 associate awarded. **Calendar:** Semester, limited summer session. **Full-time faculty:** 26 total. **Part-time faculty:** 9 total.

Basis for selection. Test scores very important. COMPASS and ATI critical thinking used for advising only. **Adult students:** SAT/ACT scores not required if out of high school 5 year(s) or more.

High school preparation. College-preparatory program recommended. 14 units required. Required and recommended units include English 4, mathematics 4, social studies 3, history 2, science 3, foreign language 2 and computer science 1.

2015-2016 Annual costs. Tuition/fees: $15,054. Per-credit charge: $512. Books/supplies: $1,650. Personal expenses: $1,000.

Financial aid. Need-based: Work-study available nights, weekends and for part-time students.

Application procedures. Admission: No deadline. $40 fee, may be waived for applicants with need. Admission notification on a rolling basis.

Academics. Special study options: Combined bachelor's/graduate degree. Bachelor's degree programs available on campus. **Credit/placement by examination:** AP, CLEP. **Support services:** Learning center, study skills assistance, tutoring.

Majors. Health services: Nursing (RN).

Technology on campus. Online course registration, wireless network available.

Student life. Freshman orientation: Mandatory. Preregistration for classes offered. **Activities:** Student newspaper.

Student services. Student employment services, financial aid counseling, health services, personal counseling.

Contact. E-mail: linda_hayes@trihealth.com
Phone: (513) 862-2743
Linda Hayes, Dean of Enrollment Management, Good Samaritan College of Nursing and Health Science, 375 Dixmyth Avenue, Cincinnati, OH 45220

Harrison College: Grove City
Grove City, Ohio
www.harrison.edu

◗ For-profit 2-year business and health science college
◗ Commuter campus in very large city

General. Regionally accredited; also accredited by ACICS. Additional campuses in Indiana and North Carolina. **Enrollment:** 273 undergraduates. **Degrees:** 1 bachelor's, 49 associate awarded. **Calendar:** Quarter, extensive summer session. **Full-time faculty:** 3 total. **Part-time faculty:** 11 total.

Basis for selection. Open admission, but selective for some programs.

2015-2016 Annual costs. Tuition varies by program. Per-credit-hour charges; $100-$475; program fees (including books); $275-$975. All costs are subject to change.

Financial aid. Need-based: Work-study available nights, weekends and for part-time students.

Application procedures. Admission: No deadline. No application fee. Admission notification on a rolling basis.

Academics. Special study options: Distance learning, double major, internships, weekend college. Bachelor's degree programs available on campus. **Credit/placement by examination:** AP, institutional tests. **Support services:** Learning center, reduced course load, study skills assistance, tutoring.

Majors. Business: Accounting, business admin, human resources, logistics. **Health services:** Insurance specialist, medical assistant. **Protective services:** Law enforcement admin.

Most popular majors. Business/marketing 24%, health sciences 61%, security/protective services 16%.

Technology on campus. Commuter students can connect to campus network. Online course registration, online library, helpline, wireless network available.

Student life. Freshman orientation: Available. Preregistration for classes offered.

Student services. Adult student services, career counseling, student employment services, financial aid counseling, legal services, personal counseling, placement for graduates. **Transfer:** Re-entry adviser for new students.

Contact. E-mail: admissions@harrison.edu
Toll-free number: (888) 544-4422
Jason Howanec, Director of Admissions, Harrison College: Grove City, 3880 Jackpot Road, Grove City, OH 43123

Herzing University
Akron, Ohio
www.herzing.edu   CB code: 7277

◗ For-profit 2-year career college
◗ Commuter campus in small city

General. Regionally accredited. **Enrollment:** 318 undergraduates. **Degrees:** 10 bachelor's, 65 associate awarded. **Calendar:** Semester, extensive summer session. **Full-time faculty:** 21 total. **Part-time faculty:** 14 total.

Basis for selection. Secondary school record very important, test scores recommended.

2015-2016 Annual costs. Diploma programs: $17,880-$26,180. Associate programs: $26,180-$53,640. Bachelor's programs: $61,515-$88,065.

Financial aid. Need-based: Work-study available nights, weekends and for part-time students.

Application procedures. Admission: No deadline.

Academics. Special study options: Accelerated study, internships. License preparation in aviation, nursing. **Credit/placement by examination:** AP, CLEP, institutional tests. **Support services:** Reduced course load, remedial instruction, study skills assistance, tutoring, writing center.

Majors. Business: Business admin. **Computer sciences:** Security. **Health services:** Dental assistant, health information management, insurance coding, insurance specialist, medical assistant, office admin. **Protective services:** Police science.

Technology on campus. 5 workstations in library. Online library, helpline, repair service, wireless network available.

Student life. Freshman orientation: Mandatory. Preregistration for classes offered. **Activities:** Student government.

Student services. Adult student services, career counseling, student employment services, financial aid counseling, placement for graduates.

Contact. E-mail: info@akr.herzing.edu
Phone: (330) 724-1600 Toll-free number: (800) 311-0512
Fax: (330) 724-9688
Maribeth Graham, Director of Admissions, Herzing University, 1600 South Arlington Street, Suite 100, Akron, OH 44306

Hocking College
Nelsonville, Ohio
www.hocking.edu   CB code: 1822

◗ Public 2-year technical college
◗ Commuter campus in small town

General. Founded in 1968. Regionally accredited. **Enrollment:** 3,130 degree-seeking undergraduates. **Degrees:** 707 associate awarded. **ROTC:** Army, Air Force. **Location:** 15 miles from Athens, 55 miles from Columbus. **Calendar:** Semester, extensive summer session. **Full-time faculty:** 155 total. **Part-time faculty:** 144 total. **Class size:** 61% < 20, 34% 20-39, 2% 40-49, 3% 50-99, less than 1% >100. **Special facilities:** Nature center, living history village, land lab, firing range, burn building, early learning center, fish hatchery.

Student profile.

Out-of-state:	2%	Live on campus:	16%
25 or older:	31%		

Transfer out. Colleges most students transferred to 2015: Ohio University, Rio Grande University, Franklin University, West Virginia University.

Basis for selection. Open admission, but selective for some programs. Special admissions requirements to nursing program (based on test scores), physical therapist assistant program (based on grades), and radiologic and surgical/operating room technology (based on test scores and grades). Some programs have additional admission requirements. Interview recommended. **Home schooled:** Applicants to health and public safety technology must have GED before classes begin. **Learning Disabled:** Documentation required for services in the Access Center - Office of Disability Services.

High school preparation. Recommended units include English 4, mathematics 3 and science 3. 1 algebra, 1 biology highly recommended for nursing, allied health, recreation/wildlife and forestry applicants.

2015-2016 Annual costs. Tuition/fees: $4,390; $8,780 out-of-state. Room/board: $3,830. Books/supplies: $1,350. Personal expenses: $1,300.

Financial aid. Need-based: Need-based aid available for part-time students. Work-study available nights, weekends and for part-time students. **Non-need-based:** Scholarships awarded for academics, minority status, state residency.

Application procedures. Admission: No deadline. $15 fee. Admission notification on a rolling basis. **Financial aid:** Priority date 2/28; no closing date. FAFSA, institutional form required. Applicants notified on a rolling basis starting 4/15.

Academics. Self paced online courses available. Enrollment possible any day college is in session. **Special study options:** Accelerated study, cooperative education, cross-registration, distance learning, double major, dual enrollment of high school students, ESL, honors, independent study, internships, student-designed major, study abroad. Bachelor's degree programs available on campus. License preparation in nursing, paramedic, physical therapy, radiology, real estate. **Credit/placement by examination:** AP, CLEP, institutional tests. 60 credit hours maximum toward associate degree. **Support services:** Learning center, pre-admission summer program, reduced course load, remedial instruction, study skills assistance, tutoring, writing center.

Majors. Business: General, accounting technology, administrative services, hotel/motel admin. **Communications technology:** Radio/TV. **Computer sciences:** Networking, programming. **Conservation:** General, fisheries, forest management, wildlife/wilderness. **Education:** Teacher assistance. **General:** Carpentry, electrician. **Health services:** EMT paramedic, health information technology, massage therapy, medical assistant, nursing (RN), optician, physical therapy assistant. **Liberal arts:** Arts/sciences. **Parks/recreation:** Sports admin. **Physical sciences:** Materials science. **Protective services:** Corrections, firefighting, police science. **Visual/performing arts:** Art, music.

Most popular majors. Agriculture 7%, business/marketing 15%, health sciences 31%, natural resources/environmental science 23%, personal/culinary services 6%, security/protective services 16%.

Technology on campus. 1 workstations in dormitories, library, computer center, student center. Dormitories wired for high-speed internet access and linked to campus network. Commuter students can connect to campus network. Online course registration, online library, helpline, wireless network available.

Student life. Freshman orientation: Mandatory, $20 fee. Preregistration for classes offered. **Policies:** All students have full use of student center. Clubs must be sanctioned by college. **Housing:** Coed dorms, single-sex dorms, wellness housing available. $200 partly refundable deposit. **Activities:** Campus ministries, choral groups, dance, drama, international student organizations, music ensembles, radio station, student government, Phi Theta Kappa, Kappa Beta Delta, SIFE, Unity Board, technology based clubs, Hocking Heights hall council.

Athletics. Intramural: Basketball, football (non-tackle), golf, soccer, softball, swimming, table tennis, tennis, ultimate frisbee, volleyball, weight lifting, wrestling.

Student services. Adult student services, alcohol/substance abuse counseling, career counseling, services for economically disadvantaged, student employment services, financial aid counseling, on-campus daycare, personal counseling, placement for graduates, veterans' counselor. **Physically disabled:** Services for visually, speech, hearing impaired. **Transfer:** Pre-admission transcript evaluation for new students. Transfer center, transfer adviser, college fairs on campus for students transferring to 4-year colleges.

Contact. E-mail: admissions@hocking.edu
Phone: (740) 753-7049 Toll-free number: (877) 462-5464
Fax: (740) 753-7065
Michael Belcher, Director of Strategic Enrollment, Hocking College, 3301 Hocking Parkway, Nelsonville, OH 45764-9704

Hondros College
Westerville, Ohio
www.nursing.hondros.edu   CB code: 3255

- For-profit 2-year nursing college
- Commuter campus in very large city
- Application essay, interview required

General. Accredited by ACICS. Additional campuses located in Columbus, Cincinnati, Dayton and Cleveland. **Enrollment:** 1,520 degree-seeking undergraduates. **Degrees:** 60 bachelor's, 324 associate awarded. **Location:** 10 miles from Columbus. **Calendar:** Quarter, extensive summer session.

Basis for selection. Special requirements for allied health related programs. **Adult students:** SAT/ACT scores not required. **Home schooled:** State high school equivalency certificate required.

2015-2016 Annual costs. Tuition/fees: $17,825.

Financial aid. Need-based: Need-based aid available for part-time students. Work-study available nights, weekends and for part-time students.

Application procedures. Admission: No deadline. $25 fee. Admission notification on a rolling basis. **Financial aid:** No deadline. FAFSA required.

Academics. Special study options: Combined bachelor's/graduate degree, distance learning. Bachelor's degree programs available on campus. License preparation in nursing. **Credit/placement by examination:** AP, CLEP. **Support services:** Remedial instruction, study skills assistance, tutoring.

Majors. Business: Real estate. **Health services:** Nursing (RN).

Technology on campus. PC or laptop required. 15 workstations in library, computer center, student center. Online course registration, online library, helpline, wireless network available.

Student life. Freshman orientation: Mandatory. Preregistration for classes offered. Held approximately one week prior to the quarter start. **Activities:** Student newspaper.

Student services. Career counseling, financial aid counseling, placement for graduates. **Transfer:** Re-entry adviser, pre-admission transcript evaluation for new students.

Contact. E-mail: admissions@hondros.edu
Toll-free number: (888) 466-3767 Fax: (614) 508-7280
Doug Banbury, Director of Admissions, Hondros College, 4140 Executive Parkway, Westerville, OH 43081-3855

International College of Broadcasting
Dayton, Ohio
www.icb.edu   CB code: 3047

- For-profit 2-year technical college
- Commuter campus in small city
- Interview required

General. Accredited by ACCSC. **Enrollment:** 82 degree-seeking undergraduates. **Degrees:** 26 associate awarded. **Location:** 50 miles from Cincinnati, 70 miles from Columbus. **Calendar:** Semester, limited summer session. **Full-time faculty:** 4 total. **Part-time faculty:** 9 total. **Class size:** 100% < 20.

Basis for selection. Open admission.

2015-2016 Annual costs. Tuition/fees: $31,950. Per-credit charge: $424.67. Personal expenses: $2,862.

2015-2016 Financial aid. Need-based: Need-based aid available for part-time students. Work-study available nights, weekends and for part-time students.

Application procedures. Admission: No deadline. $100 fee. **Financial aid:** No deadline. FAFSA required. Applicants notified on a rolling basis starting 11/1.

Academics. Credit/placement by examination: AP, CLEP. **Support services:** Reduced course load, remedial instruction, tutoring.

Majors. Communications: Communications/speech/rhetoric, radio/TV. **Visual/performing arts:** General.

Technology on campus. Wireless network available.

Contact. E-mail: admissions@icb.edu
Phone: (937) 258-8251 Fax: (937) 258-8714
James Stringfield, Director of Admissions, International College of
Broadcasting, 6 South Smithville Road, Dayton, OH 45431

ITT Technical Institute: Dayton
Dayton, Ohio
www.itt-tech.edu   CB code: 7312

- For-profit 2-year technical college
- Commuter campus in small city
- Interview required

General. Founded in 1935. Accredited by ACICS. **Enrollment:** 309 under-graduates. **Degrees:** 8 bachelor's, 93 associate awarded. **Location:** 5 miles from downtown. **Calendar:** Quarter, extensive summer session. **Full-time faculty:** 9 total. **Part-time faculty:** 24 total.

Basis for selection. Satisfactory scores from on-site tests in English and mathematics required.

2015-2016 Annual costs. Per-credit-hour charge, $493, will vary depending on program level and course of study. Academic fee, $200. Some programs require purchase of tools, which could cost an additional $100 to $655. All costs subject to change.

Financial aid. Need-based: Work-study available nights, weekends and for part-time students.

Application procedures. Admission: No deadline. No application fee. Admission notification on a rolling basis. **Financial aid:** No deadline. FAFSA, institutional form required. Applicants notified on a rolling basis.

Academics. Credit/placement by examination: AP, CLEP. **Support services:** Learning center, tutoring.

Majors. Business: Business admin. **Computer sciences:** Computer graphics, LAN/WAN management, networking, programming, web page design, webmaster. **Protective services:** Criminal justice. **Visual/performing arts:** Design.

Technology on campus. Online library available.

Student life. Freshman orientation: Available. Preregistration for classes offered.

Student services. Career counseling, student employment services, placement for graduates.

Contact. Phone: (937) 454-2267 Toll-free number: (800) 568-3241
Fax: (937) 454-2278
Joe Graham, Director of Recruitment, ITT Technical Institute: Dayton, 3325 Stop Eight Road, Dayton, OH 45414

ITT Technical Institute: Hilliard
Hilliard, Ohio
www.itt-tech.edu

- For-profit 2-year business and technical college
- Large town

General. Accredited by ACICS. **Enrollment:** 384 undergraduates. **Degrees:** 6 bachelor's, 77 associate awarded. **Calendar:** Quarter. **Full-time faculty:** 15 total. **Part-time faculty:** 42 total.

Basis for selection. Secondary school record very important.

2015-2016 Annual costs. Per-credit-hour charge, $493, will vary depending on program level and course of study. Academic fee, $200. Some programs require purchase of tools, which could cost an additional $100 to $655. All costs subject to change.

Financial aid. Need-based: Work-study available nights, weekends and for part-time students.

Academics. Credit/placement by examination: AP, CLEP.

Majors. Business: Business admin. **Computer sciences:** Networking, pro-gramming, web page design. **Protective services:** Criminal justice. **Visual/performing arts:** Design.

Contact. ITT Technical Institute: Hilliard, 3781 Park Mill Run Drive, Suite 1, Hilliard, OH 43026

ITT Technical Institute: Norwood
Norwood, Ohio
www.itt-tech.edu   CB code: 2739

- For-profit 2-year technical college
- Commuter campus in large town
- Interview required

General. Accredited by ACICS. **Enrollment:** 400 undergraduates. **Degrees:** 14 bachelor's, 72 associate awarded. **Calendar:** Quarter, extensive summer session. **Full-time faculty:** 8 total. **Part-time faculty:** 42 total.

Basis for selection. Satisfactory scores from on-site tests in English and mathematics required.

2015-2016 Annual costs. Per-credit-hour charge, $493, will vary depending on program level and course of study. Academic fee, $200. Some programs require purchase of tools, which could cost an additional $150 to $655. All costs subject to change.

Financial aid. Need-based: Work-study available nights, weekends and for part-time students.

Application procedures. Admission: No deadline. No application fee. Admission notification on a rolling basis. **Financial aid:** No deadline. FAFSA, institutional form required. Applicants notified on a rolling basis.

Academics. Credit/placement by examination: AP, CLEP. **Support services:** Learning center, tutoring.

Majors. Business: Accounting technology, business admin. **Computer sciences:** Computer graphics, networking, programming, web page design, webmaster. **Protective services:** Criminal justice. **Visual/performing arts:** Design.

Technology on campus. Online library available.

Student life. Freshman orientation: Available. Preregistration for classes offered.

Student services. Career counseling, student employment services, placement for graduates.

Contact. Phone: (513) 531-8300 Toll-free number: (800) 314-8324
Greg Hitt, Director of Recruitment, ITT Technical Institute: Norwood, 4750 Wesley Avenue, Norwood, OH 45212

ITT Technical Institute: Strongsville
Strongsville, Ohio
www.itt-tech.edu   CB code: 2773

- For-profit 2-year technical college
- Commuter campus in large town
- Interview required

General. Accredited by ACICS. **Enrollment:** 394 undergraduates. **Degrees:** 20 bachelor's, 99 associate awarded. **Calendar:** Quarter, extensive summer session. **Full-time faculty:** 11 total. **Part-time faculty:** 46 total.

Basis for selection. Satisfactory scores from on-site tests in English and mathematics required.

2015-2016 Annual costs. Per-credit-hour charge, $493, will vary depending on program level and course of study. Academic fee, $200. Some programs require purchase of tools, which could cost an additional $150 to $655. All costs subject to change.

Financial aid. Need-based: Work-study available nights, weekends and for part-time students.

Application procedures. Admission: No deadline. No application fee. Admission notification on a rolling basis. **Financial aid:** No deadline. FAFSA, institutional form required. Applicants notified on a rolling basis.

Academics. Credit/placement by examination: AP, CLEP. **Support services:** Learning center, tutoring.

Majors. Business: Accounting technology, business admin. **Computer sciences:** Computer graphics, LAN/WAN management, networking, programming, web page design, webmaster. **Protective services:** Criminal justice. **Visual/performing arts:** Design.

Technology on campus. Online library available.

Student life. Freshman orientation: Available. Preregistration for classes offered.

Student services. Career counseling, student employment services, placement for graduates.

Contact. Phone: (440) 234-9091 Toll-free number: (800) 331-1488 Fax: (440) 234-7568
Joanne Dyer, Director of Recruitment, ITT Technical Institute: Strongsville, 14955 Sprague Road, Strongsville, OH 44136

ITT Technical Institute: Youngstown
Youngstown, Ohio
www.itt-tech.edu

▶ For-profit 2-year technical college
▶ Commuter campus in small city
▶ Interview required

General. Founded in 1967. Accredited by ACICS. **Enrollment:** 511 undergraduates. **Degrees:** 22 bachelor's, 108 associate awarded. **Location:** 60 miles from Cleveland, 60 miles from Pittsburgh. **Calendar:** Quarter, extensive summer session. **Full-time faculty:** 15 total. **Part-time faculty:** 58 total.

Basis for selection. Satisfactory scores from on-site tests in English and mathematics required.

2015-2016 Annual costs. Per-credit-hour charge, $493, will vary depending on program level and course of study. Academic fee, $200. Some programs require purchase of tools, which could cost an additional $100 to $655. All costs subject to change.

Financial aid. Need-based: Work-study available nights, weekends and for part-time students.

Application procedures. Admission: No deadline. No application fee. Admission notification on a rolling basis. **Financial aid:** No deadline. FAFSA, institutional form required. Applicants notified on a rolling basis.

Academics. Credit/placement by examination: AP, CLEP. **Support services:** Learning center, tutoring.

Majors. Business: Business admin. **Computer sciences:** LAN/WAN management, networking, programming, web page design, webmaster. **Protective services:** Law enforcement admin. **Visual/performing arts:** Design.

Technology on campus. Online library available.

Student life. Freshman orientation: Available. Preregistration for classes offered.

Student services. Career counseling, student employment services, placement for graduates.

Contact. Phone: (330) 270-1600 Toll-free number: (800) 832-5001 Fax: (330) 270-8333
Tom Flynn, Director of Recruitment, ITT Technical Institute: Youngstown, 1030 North Meridian Road, Youngstown, OH 44509

James A. Rhodes State College
Lima, Ohio
www.rhodesstate.edu   **CB code: 0754**

▶ Public 2-year community and technical college
▶ Commuter campus in large town

General. Founded in 1971. Regionally accredited. **Enrollment:** 3,416 degree-seeking undergraduates. **Degrees:** 506 associate awarded. **Location:** 75 miles from Dayton, 75 miles from Toledo. **Calendar:** Semester, limited summer session. **Full-time faculty:** 87 total; 8% have terminal degrees, 5% minority, 62% women. **Part-time faculty:** 195 total; 7% have terminal degrees, 5% minority, 67% women. **Class size:** 67% < 20, 29% 20-39, 2% 40-49, 1% 50-99, less than 1% >100. **Special facilities:** RN to BSN completion

program; ambulance simulator; military friendly; police academy. **Partnerships:** Formal partnerships with Central Ohio Regional Healthcare Alliance, Tech Prep/PSEOP, Ford Training Center, Lima City High School, Allen County Health Partners, Agile Manufacturing, West Ohio Manufacturing Consortium.

Student profile.

Out-of-state:	1%	Live on campus:	1%
25 or older:	39%		

Transfer out. Colleges most students transferred to 2015: University of Findlay, Ohio State University, Franklin University, Bowling Green State University, Wright State University, Owens Community College, Northwest State Community College.

Basis for selection. Open admission, but selective for some programs. Open admissions for pre-Nursing and pre-Allied Health programs. Special requirements for nursing and health programs (ACT required); interview recommended. **Home schooled:** State high school equivalency certificate required. **Learning Disabled:** Students must self-disclose; accommodations are available.

High school preparation. Recommended units include English 4, mathematics 3, social studies 3 and science 3.

2015-2016 Annual costs. Tuition/fees: $4,806; $9,611 out-of-state. Per-credit charge: $160 in-state; $320 out-of-state. Books/supplies: $1,200. Personal expenses: $472.

Financial aid. Need-based: Need-based aid available for part-time students. Work-study available nights, weekends and for part-time students. **Non-need-based:** Scholarships awarded for academics.

Application procedures. Admission: No deadline. $25 fee ($25 out-of-state). Admission notification on a rolling basis. **Financial aid:** Priority date 2/15; no closing date. FAFSA required. Applicants notified on a rolling basis starting 5/1; must reply within 2 week(s) of notification.

Academics. Special study options: Cooperative education, cross-registration, distance learning, double major, dual enrollment of high school students, independent study, internships, liberal arts/career combination, student-designed major. Bachelor's degree programs available on campus. License preparation in dental hygiene, nursing, occupational therapy, paramedic, physical therapy, radiology, real estate. **Credit/placement by examination:** AP, CLEP, institutional tests. 10 credit hours maximum toward associate degree. **Support services:** Learning center, pre-admission summer program, reduced course load, remedial instruction, study skills assistance, tutoring, writing center.

Majors. Business: Accounting technology, administrative services, marketing. **Computer sciences:** General, LAN/WAN management, networking, programming, security, web page design. **Education:** Early childhood. **Engineering:** General. **Health services:** EMT paramedic, medical assistant, medical radiologic technology/radiation therapy, nursing (RN), occupational therapy assistant, physical therapy assistant, respiratory therapy technology. **Human services:** Social work. **Protective services:** Corrections, police science. **Work/family studies:** Child development.

Most popular majors. Business/marketing 18%, computer/information sciences 6%, engineering/engineering technologies 11%, health sciences 41%, public administration/social services 8%, security/protective services 6%.

Technology on campus. 332 workstations in library, computer center. Commuter students can connect to campus network. Online course registration, online library, helpline, repair service, wireless network available.

Student life. Freshman orientation: Mandatory. Preregistration for classes offered. Programs held before each quarter begins; specific dates and times mailed after application is made. **Activities:** Campus ministries, choral groups, drama, music ensembles, student government, academic area organizations, political party clubs, special interest clubs, fellowship and bible study.

Athletics. Intramural: Baseball M, basketball, golf M, volleyball W. **Team name:** Barons.

Student services. Adult student services, career counseling, student employment services, financial aid counseling, on-campus daycare, placement for graduates, veterans' counselor. **Physically disabled:** Services for visually, speech, hearing impaired. **Transfer:** Pre-admission transcript evaluation for new students. Transfer adviser, college fairs on campus for students transferring to 4-year colleges.

Contact. E-mail: admissions@rhodesstate.edu
Phone: (419) 995-8320 Fax: (419) 995-8098
Traci Cox, Director of Admissions, James A. Rhodes State College, 4240 Campus Drive, PS 148, Lima, OH 45804-3597

Kaplan College: Dayton
Dayton, Ohio
www.dayton.kaplancollege.com   CB code: 3380

- For-profit 2-year technical college
- Commuter campus in very large city
- Interview required

General. Founded in 1971. Accredited by ACCSC. **Enrollment:** 317 under-graduates. **Degrees:** 63 associate awarded. **Location:** 55 miles from Cincinnati, 80 miles from Columbus. **Calendar:** Quarter, extensive summer session. **Full-time faculty:** 36 total; 17% minority, 58% women. **Part-time faculty:** 32 total; 12% minority, 38% women. **Special facilities:** Photographic laboratories and computer laboratory for digital imaging, pharmacy technician laboratory, dental assisting laboratory and stick house for Electrical Technician program.

Student profile.

Out-of-state: 19%   25 or older: 33%

Basis for selection. Open admission, but selective for some programs. Entrance exam and interview required. Criminal Justice or Pharmacy Technician programs must also pass a background check. Essay and portfolio recommended.

2015-2016 Annual costs. Books/supplies: $1,350. Personal expenses: $1,701. **Additional information:** Associate of Applied Science in Nursing: $41,095. Dental Assistant: $16,814. Electrical Technician: $20,944. Heating, Ventilation, and Air Conditioning/Refrigeration: $20,845. Intravenous (IV) Therapy: $609. Medical Assistant: $15,925. Pharmacy Technician: $15,954. Phlebotomy Technician: $970. Photographic Technology: $46,862. State Tested Nursing Assistant: $1,005.

Financial aid. Need-based: Need-based aid available for part-time students. Work-study available nights, weekends and for part-time students.

Application procedures. Admission: No deadline. $10 fee. Admission notification on a rolling basis. **Financial aid:** No deadline. FAFSA, institutional form required. Applicants notified on a rolling basis starting 3/1.

Academics. Training directed toward technical and professional aspects of photography. **Special study options:** Double major, internships. **Credit/placement by examination:** AP, CLEP. **Support services:** GED preparation, tutoring.

Majors. Computer sciences: Networking. **Protective services:** Law enforcement admin. **Visual/performing arts:** Commercial photography, photography.

Technology on campus. 36 workstations in library. Online library available.

Student life. Freshman orientation: Available. Preregistration for classes offered. Held for 3 hours, prior to first day of classes.

Student services. Adult student services, career counseling, student employment services, financial aid counseling, placement for graduates. **Transfer:** Pre-admission transcript evaluation for new students. Transfer adviser for students transferring to 4-year colleges.

Contact. Phone: (937) 294-6155 Toll-free number: (800) 932-9698 Fax: (937) 294-2259
Curtis Kirby, Director of Admissions, Kaplan College: Dayton, 2800 East River Road, Dayton, OH 45439

Kent State University: Ashtabula
Ashtabula, Ohio
www.kent.edu/ashtabula   CB code: 1485

- Public 2-year branch campus college
- Commuter campus in large town

General. Founded in 1958. Regionally accredited. Off-site courses available. **Enrollment:** 2,095 degree-seeking undergraduates; 190 non-degree-seeking students. **Degrees:** 19 bachelor's, 395 associate awarded. **Location:** 50 miles from Cleveland, 50 miles from Erie, PA. **Calendar:** Semester, limited summer session. **Full-time faculty:** 48 total; 6% minority, 62% women. **Part-time faculty:** 58 total; 3% minority, 60% women. **Class size:** 81% < 20, 16% 20-39, 1% 40-49, 1% 50-99. **Special facilities:** Interactive television link with all county high schools.

Student profile. Among degree-seeking undergraduates, 252 enrolled as first-time, first-year students, 94 transferred in from other institutions.

Part-time:	46%	Asian American:	1%
Out-of-state:	4%	Hispanic/Latino:	3%
Women:	64%	Multi-racial, non-Hispanic:	2%
African American:	5%	25 or older:	44%

Basis for selection. Open admission, but selective for some programs. Special requirements for nursing, human services, physical therapy assisting programs. **Adult students:** SAT/ACT scores not required if applicant over 21 or out of high school 3 years or more. **Home schooled:** Transcript of courses and grades, state high school equivalency certificate required.

High school preparation. College-preparatory program recommended. 17 units recommended. Recommended units include English 4, mathematics 4, social studies 3, science 3 (laboratory 2), foreign language 2 and visual/performing arts 1.

2015-2016 Annual costs. Tuition/fees: $5,664; $13,864 out-of-state. Per-credit charge: $258 in-state; $620 out-of-state.

2015-2016 Financial aid. Need-based: 171 full-time freshmen applied for aid; 147 deemed to have need; 144 received aid. Average need met was 52%. Average scholarship/grant was $4,773; average loan $3,354. 53% of total undergraduate aid awarded as scholarships/grants, 47% as loans/jobs. Need-based aid available for part-time students. Work-study available nights, weekends and for part-time students. **Non-need-based:** Scholarships awarded for academics, alumni affiliation, art, athletics, leadership, minority status, music/drama, ROTC, state residency.

Application procedures. Admission: Closing date 8/15. $40 fee, may be waived for applicants with need. Admission notification on a rolling basis. **Financial aid:** Priority date 3/1; no closing date. FAFSA required. Applicants notified on a rolling basis starting 3/15; must reply within 2 week(s) of notification.

Academics. Special study options: Distance learning, double major, dual enrollment of high school students, internships, student-designed major, teacher certification program, weekend college. Bachelor's degree programs available on campus. License preparation in nursing, occupational therapy, physical therapy, radiology. **Credit/placement by examination:** AP, CLEP, IB, institutional tests. 15 credit hours maximum toward associate degree, 30 toward bachelor's. Certificate limit 50%. Limits are combined for CBE, CLEP, and AP. Students can petition college dean for a waiver of maximum limit. Credit must be completed by the semester preceding the semester in which a student plans to graduate. CBE credit does not fulfill the residency requirement. **Support services:** Learning center, remedial instruction, tutoring.

Majors. Business: General, accounting technology, administrative services. **Computer sciences:** Applications programming. **Engineering:** Aerospace. **Health services:** Medical radiologic technology/radiation therapy, nursing (RN), occupational therapy assistant, physical therapy assistant, respiratory therapy technology. **Protective services:** Criminal justice.

Most popular majors. Health sciences 50%, liberal arts 40%.

Technology on campus. Commuter students can connect to campus network. Online course registration, online library, helpline, student web hosting, wireless network available.

Student life. Freshman orientation: Available. Preregistration for classes offered. **Activities:** Campus ministries, student government.

Athletics. Team name: Golden Flashes.

Student services. Adult student services, career counseling, student employment services, financial aid counseling, personal counseling, placement for graduates, veterans' counselor. **Physically disabled:** Services for visually, speech, hearing impaired. **Transfer:** Pre-admission transcript evaluation for new students.

Contact. E-mail: kentadm@kent.edu
Phone: (440) 964-4217 Toll-free number: (800) 988-5368
Fax: (440) 964-4269
Kent State University: Ashtabula, 3300 Lake Road West, Ashtabula, OH 44004-2299

Kent State University: East Liverpool
East Liverpool, Ohio
www.kent.edu/columbiana   CB code: 0328

- Public 2-year branch campus college
- Commuter campus in large town

General. Founded in 1965. Regionally accredited. **Enrollment:** 1,168 degree-seeking undergraduates; 77 non-degree-seeking students. **Degrees:** 2 bachelor's, 140 associate awarded. **ROTC:** Army, Air Force. **Location:** 45 miles from Youngstown, 40 miles from Pittsburgh. **Calendar:** Semester, extensive summer session. **Full-time faculty:** 25 total; 12% minority, 52% women. **Part-time faculty:** 33 total; 48% women. **Class size:** 89% < 20, 9% 20-39, 1% 40-49.

Student profile. Among degree-seeking undergraduates, 77 enrolled as first-time, first-year students, 65 transferred in from other institutions.

Part-time:	42%	Asian American:	1%
Out-of-state:	8%	Hispanic/Latino:	3%
Women:	68%	Multi-racial, non-Hispanic:	3%
African American:	6%	25 or older:	39%

Basis for selection. Open admission, but selective for some programs. Special requirements for nursing, occupational therapy, and physical therapy applicants. Interview recommended. **Home schooled:** Transcript of courses and grades required.

High school preparation. College-preparatory program recommended. 17 units recommended. Recommended units include English 4, mathematics 4, science 3 (laboratory 2), foreign language 3 and visual/performing arts 1.

2015-2016 Annual costs. Tuition/fees: $5,664; $13,864 out-of-state. Per-credit charge: $258 in-state; $620 out-of-state.

2015-2016 Financial aid. Need-based: 55 full-time freshmen applied for aid; 48 deemed to have need; 48 received aid. Average need met was 47%. Average scholarship/grant was $4,992; average loan $3,409. 50% of total undergraduate aid awarded as scholarships/grants, 50% as loans/jobs. Need-based aid available for part-time students. Work-study available nights, weekends and for part-time students. **Non-need-based:** Scholarships awarded for academics, alumni affiliation, art, athletics, leadership, minority status, music/drama, ROTC, state residency.

Application procedures. Admission: Closing date 8/15. $40 fee, may be waived for applicants with need. Admission notification on a rolling basis. **Financial aid:** Priority date 3/1; no closing date. FAFSA required. Applicants notified by 3/15; must reply within 2 week(s) of notification.

Academics. Special study options: Accelerated study, distance learning, double major, dual enrollment of high school students, honors, independent study, internships, New York semester, student-designed major, Washington semester. Bachelor's degree programs available on campus. License preparation in nursing, occupational therapy, physical therapy. **Credit/placement by examination:** AP, CLEP, IB, institutional tests. 15 credit hours maximum toward associate degree, 30 toward bachelor's. Students can petition college dean for a waiver of maximum limit. Credit must be completed by the semester preceding the semester in which a student plans to graduate. CBE credit does not fulfill the residency requirement. **Support services:** Learning center, reduced course load, remedial instruction, study skills assistance, tutoring, writing center.

Honors college/program. Minimum high school GPA of 3.3 or higher, ACT composite of 23 and/or minimum 24 in English with a composite score of 22, 300 word essay, and letter of recommendation required. Various course offerings plus Freshman Year Colloquium to replace university composition requirement.

Majors. Business: General, accounting technology. **Computer sciences:** Applications programming. **Health services:** Nursing (RN), occupational therapy assistant, physical therapy assistant. **Protective services:** Criminal justice.

Most popular majors. Business/marketing 6%, health sciences 54%, liberal arts 36%.

Technology on campus. Commuter students can connect to campus network. Online course registration, online library, helpline, student web hosting, wireless network available.

Student life. Freshman orientation: Available. Preregistration for classes offered. **Activities:** Student government, ASL club, Harmony Alliance, environmental club.

Athletics. Team name: Golden Flashes.

Student services. Career counseling, student employment services, personal counseling, placement for graduates, veterans' counselor. **Physically disabled:** Services for visually, speech, hearing impaired. **Transfer:** College fairs on campus for students transferring to 4-year colleges.

Contact. E-mail: kentadm@kent.edu
Phone: (330) 382-7400 Toll-free number: (800) 988-5368
Fax: (330) 382-7562
Shelly Lingenfelter, Director, Enrollment Management, Kent State University: East Liverpool, 400 East Fourth Street, East Liverpool, OH 43920

Kent State University: Geauga
Burton, Ohio
www.kent.edu/geauga   CB code: 6979

- Public 2-year branch campus college
- Commuter campus in rural community

General. Regionally accredited. **Enrollment:** 2,284 degree-seeking undergraduates; 246 non-degree-seeking students. **Degrees:** 6 bachelor's, 359 associate awarded; master's offered. **Location:** 40 miles from Cleveland, 45 miles from Akron. **Calendar:** Semester. **Full-time faculty:** 41 total; 12% minority, 78% women. **Part-time faculty:** 104 total; 9% minority, 46% women. **Class size:** 74% < 20, 26% 20-39, less than 1% 40-49.

Student profile. Among degree-seeking undergraduates, 333 enrolled as first-time, first-year students, 152 transferred in from other institutions.

Part-time:	40%	Hispanic/Latino:	3%
Out-of-state:	2%	Multi-racial, non-Hispanic:	3%
Women:	63%	International:	1%
African American:	11%	25 or older:	31%
Asian American:	1%		

Basis for selection. Open admission, but selective for some programs. Special requirements for nursing programs. **Adult students:** SAT/ACT scores not required if applicant over 21 or out of high school 3 years or more. **Home schooled:** Transcript of courses and grades required.

High school preparation. College-preparatory program recommended. 17 units recommended. Recommended units include English 4, mathematics 4, science 3 (laboratory 2), foreign language 3 and visual/performing arts 1.

2015-2016 Annual costs. Tuition/fees: $5,664; $13,864 out-of-state. Per-credit charge: $258 in-state; $620 out-of-state.

2015-2016 Financial aid. Need-based: 202 full-time freshmen applied for aid; 162 deemed to have need; 155 received aid. Average need met was 52%. Average scholarship/grant was $4,616; average loan $3,298. 49% of total undergraduate aid awarded as scholarships/grants, 51% as loans/jobs. Need-based aid available for part-time students. Work-study available nights, weekends and for part-time students. **Non-need-based:** Scholarships awarded for academics, alumni affiliation, art, athletics, leadership, minority status, music/drama, ROTC, state residency.

Application procedures. Admission: Closing date 8/15. $40 fee, may be waived for applicants with need. Admission notification on a rolling basis. **Financial aid:** Priority date 3/1; no closing date. FAFSA required. Applicants notified by 3/15; must reply within 2 week(s) of notification.

Academics. Special study options: Distance learning, double major, dual enrollment of high school students, internships, New York semester, student-designed major, teacher certification program, Washington semester, weekend college. Bachelor's degree programs available on campus. License preparation in nursing. **Credit/placement by examination:** AP, CLEP, IB, institutional tests. 15 credit hours maximum toward associate degree, 30 toward bachelor's. Limits are combined for CBE, CLEP, and AP. Students can petition college dean for a waiver of maximum limit. Credit must be completed by the semester preceding the semester in which a student plans to graduate. CBE credit does not fulfill the residency requirement. **Support services:** Learning center, reduced course load, remedial instruction, study skills assistance, tutoring, writing center.

Majors. Business: General, accounting technology. **Computer sciences:** Applications programming. **Health services:** Nursing (RN).

Most popular majors. Health sciences 20%, liberal arts 77%.

Technology on campus. Commuter students can connect to campus network. Online course registration, online library, helpline, student web hosting available.

Student life. Freshman orientation: Available. Preregistration for classes offered. **Activities:** Campus ministries, student government, Students who are parents, student ambassadors, Gaia society, pride, veteran's group, Campus Crusade for Christ.

Athletics. Team name: Golden Flashes.

Student services. Financial aid counseling, personal counseling, placement for graduates, veterans' counselor. **Physically disabled:** Services for visually, speech, hearing impaired. **Transfer:** Pre-admission transcript evaluation for new students.

Contact. E-mail: geaugaadmissions@kent.edu
Phone: (440) 834-3716 Toll-free number: (800) 988-5368
Jennifer Sayre, Director, Enrollment Management, Kent State University: Geauga, Office of Admissions, Burton, OH 44021

Kent State University: Salem
Salem, Ohio
www.kent.edu/columbiana   CB code: 0683

▶ Public 2-year branch campus college
▶ Commuter campus in large town

General. Founded in 1962. Regionally accredited. **Enrollment:** 1,565 degree-seeking undergraduates; 173 non-degree-seeking students. **Degrees:** 50 bachelor's, 212 associate awarded. **ROTC:** Army, Air Force. **Location:** 25 miles from Youngstown, 35 miles from Canton. **Calendar:** Semester, limited summer session. **Full-time faculty:** 39 total; 5% minority, 62% women. **Part-time faculty:** 86 total; 2% minority, 71% women. **Class size:** 84% < 20, 16% 20-39.

Student profile. Among degree-seeking undergraduates, 180 enrolled as first-time, first-year students, 113 transferred in from other institutions.

Part-time:	28%	Hispanic/Latino:	2%
Out-of-state:	2%	Multi-racial, non-Hispanic:	2%
Women:	69%	International:	1%
African American:	4%	25 or older:	35%
Asian American:	1%		

Basis for selection. Open admission, but selective for some programs. Radiologic technology program requires 2.5 GPA, completion of certain courses, SAT/ACT. Nursing program requires 2.5 GPA, SAT/ACT. **Adult students:** SAT/ACT scores not required if applicant over 21 or out of high school 3 years or more. **Home schooled:** Transcript of courses and grades required.

High school preparation. College-preparatory program recommended. 17 units recommended. Recommended units include English 4, mathematics 4, science 3 (laboratory 2), foreign language 3 and visual/performing arts 1.

2015-2016 Annual costs. Tuition/fees: $5,664; $13,664 out-of-state. Per-credit charge: $258 in-state; $620 out-of-state.

2015-2016 Financial aid. Need-based: 145 full-time freshmen applied for aid; 135 deemed to have need; 133 received aid. Average need met was 50%. Average scholarship/grant was $4,853; average loan $3,331. 55% of total undergraduate aid awarded as scholarships/grants, 45% as loans/jobs. Need-based aid available for part-time students. Work-study available nights, weekends and for part-time students. **Non-need-based:** Scholarships awarded for academics, alumni affiliation, art, athletics, leadership, minority status, music/drama, ROTC, state residency.

Application procedures. Admission: Closing date 8/15 (receipt date). $40 fee, may be waived for applicants with need. Admission notification on a rolling basis. **Financial aid:** Priority date 3/1; no closing date. FAFSA required. Applicants notified by 3/15; must reply within 2 week(s) of notification.

Academics. Special study options: Accelerated study, cooperative education, cross-registration, distance learning, double major, dual enrollment of high school students, honors, independent study, internships, New York semester, student-designed major, teacher certification program, Washington semester. Bachelor's degree programs available on campus. License preparation in radiology. **Credit/placement by examination:** AP, CLEP, IB, institutional tests. 15 credit hours maximum toward associate degree, 30 toward bachelor's. Limits are combined for CBE, CLEP, and AP. Students can petition college dean for a waiver of maximum limit. Credit must be completed by the semester preceding the semester in which a student plans to graduate. CBE credit does not fulfill the residency requirement. **Support services:** Learning center, remedial instruction, study skills assistance, tutoring, writing center.

Majors. Business: General, accounting technology, administrative services. **Computer sciences:** Applications programming. **Health services:** Medical radiologic technology/radiation therapy. **Protective services:** Criminal justice.

Most popular majors. Business/marketing 6%, education 12%, health sciences 22%, liberal arts 53%.

Technology on campus. 118 workstations in library, computer center. Commuter students can connect to campus network. Online course registration, online library, helpline, student web hosting, wireless network available.

Student life. Freshman orientation: Available. Preregistration for classes offered. **Activities:** Student government, professional business and engineering clubs, art club, nontraditional student club, ski club, Women of Wonder, horticulture, criminal justice club, psychology club.

Athletics. Intramural: Basketball, racquetball, skiing, table tennis, tennis, volleyball. **Team name:** Golden Flashes.

Student services. Adult student services, career counseling, financial aid counseling, personal counseling, placement for graduates, veterans' counselor. **Physically disabled:** Services for visually, speech, hearing impaired. **Transfer:** Transfer adviser for students transferring to 4-year colleges.

Contact. E-mail: ask-us@salem.kent.edu
Phone: (330) 332-0361 Toll-free number: (800) 988-5368
Fax: (330) 332-9256
Michelle Lingenfelter, Director, Enrollment Management and Student Services, Kent State University: Salem, 2491 State Route 45 South, Salem, OH 44460

Kent State University: Stark
Canton, Ohio
www.kent.edu/stark   CB code: 0585

▶ Public 2-year branch campus college
▶ Commuter campus in large town

General. Founded in 1946. Regionally accredited. **Enrollment:** 4,332 degree-seeking undergraduates; 388 non-degree-seeking students. **Degrees:** 20 bachelor's, 793 associate awarded; master's offered. **ROTC:** Army, Air Force. **Location:** 5 miles from Canton, 20 miles from Akron. **Calendar:** Semester, limited summer session. **Full-time faculty:** 111 total; 10% minority, 55% women. **Part-time faculty:** 159 total; 6% minority, 54% women. **Class size:** 66% < 20, 30% 20-39, 3% 40-49, 1% 50-99.

Student profile. Among degree-seeking undergraduates, 611 enrolled as first-time, first-year students, 344 transferred in from other institutions.

Part-time:	30%	Asian American:	1%
Out-of-state:	2%	Hispanic/Latino:	2%
Women:	62%	Multi-racial, non-Hispanic:	3%
African American:	7%	25 or older:	28%

Basis for selection. Open admission, but selective for some programs. Special requirements for art, music, education, nursing, business. Essay required for honors college, early admission; audition required for music programs; portfolio required for art programs. **Adult students:** SAT/ACT scores not required if applicant over 21 or out of high school 3 years or more. **Home schooled:** Transcript of courses and grades, state high school equivalency certificate required.

High school preparation. College-preparatory program recommended. 17 units recommended. Recommended units include English 4, mathematics 4, science 3 (laboratory 2), foreign language 3 and visual/performing arts 1.

2015-2016 Annual costs. Tuition/fees: $5,664; $13,864 out-of-state. Per-credit charge: $258 in-state; $620 out-of-state.

2015-2016 Financial aid. Need-based: 457 full-time freshmen applied for aid; 375 deemed to have need; 368 received aid. Average need met was 57%. Average scholarship/grant was $4,456; average loan $3,247. 55% of total undergraduate aid awarded as scholarships/grants, 45% as loans/jobs. Need-based aid available for part-time students. Work-study available nights, weekends and for part-time students. **Non-need-based:** Scholarships awarded for academics, alumni affiliation, art, athletics, leadership, minority status, music/drama, ROTC, state residency.

Application procedures. Admission: Closing date 8/15 (receipt date). $40 fee, may be waived for applicants with need. Admission notification on a rolling basis. **Financial aid:** Priority date 3/1; no closing date. FAFSA required. Applicants notified by 3/15; must reply within 2 week(s) of notification.

Academics. Special study options: Cross-registration, distance learning, double major, dual enrollment of high school students, honors, independent study, internships, New York semester, student-designed major, study abroad, teacher certification program, Washington semester. Bachelor's degree programs available on campus. **Credit/placement by examination:** AP, CLEP, IB, institutional tests. 15 credit hours maximum toward associate degree, 30 toward bachelor's. Limits are combined for CBE, CLEP, and AP. Students can petition college dean for a waiver of maximum limit. Credit must be completed by the semester preceding the semester in which a student plans to graduate. CBE credit does not fulfill the residency requirement. **Support services:** Learning center, reduced course load, remedial instruction, study skills assistance, tutoring, writing center.

Honors college/program. 3.3 GPA, essay, 25 ACT required; 3.5 GPA, 27 ACT for scholarship consideration.

Majors. Protective services: Criminal justice.

Most popular majors. Liberal arts 99%.

Technology on campus. 145 workstations in library, computer center, student center. Commuter students can connect to campus network. Online course registration, online library, helpline, student web hosting, wireless network available.

Student life. Freshman orientation: Mandatory. Preregistration for classes offered. **Activities:** Concert band, campus ministries, choral groups, drama, literary magazine, music ensembles, musical theater, student government, Rooted in Faith, student education association, Pan African student alliance, SPECTRUM, Take Action Spread Knowlege.

Athletics. Intramural: Basketball, football (non-tackle), golf, softball. **Team name:** Golden Flashes.

Student services. Adult student services, chaplain/spiritual director, career counseling, student employment services, financial aid counseling, minority student services, personal counseling, veterans' counselor. **Physically disabled:** Services for visually, speech, hearing impaired. **Transfer:** Transfer adviser for students transferring to 4-year colleges.

Contact. E-mail: starkadmissions@kent.edu
Phone; (330) 244-3251 Toll-free number: (800) 988-5368
Fax: (330) 494-0301
Deborah Phillipp, Director, Enrollment Management, Kent State University: Stark, 6000 Frank Avenue NW, Canton, OH 44720-7599

Kent State University: Trumbull
Warren, Ohio
www.kent.edu/trumbull   **CB code: 0593**

▶ Public 2-year branch campus college
▶ Commuter campus in small city

General. Founded in 1954. Regionally accredited. **Enrollment:** 2,485 degree-seeking undergraduates; 94 non-degree-seeking students. **Degrees:** 15 bachelor's, 259 associate awarded; master's offered. **ROTC:** Army, Air Force. **Location:** 3 miles from downtown, 20 miles from Youngstown. **Calendar:** Semester, limited summer session. **Full-time faculty:** 52 total; 14% minority, 52% women. **Part-time faculty:** 55 total; 4% minority, 38% women. **Class size:** 78% < 20, 18% 20-39, 4% 40-49, less than 1% 50-99.

Student profile. Among degree-seeking undergraduates, 277 enrolled as first-time, first-year students, 201 transferred in from other institutions.

Part-time:	34%	Hispanic/Latino:	3%
Out-of-state:	2%	Multi-racial, non-Hispanic:	2%
Women:	60%	International:	1%
African American:	9%	25 or older:	40%
Asian American:	1%		

Basis for selection. Open admission, but selective for some programs. **Adult students:** SAT/ACT scores not required if applicant over 21 or out of high school 3 years or more. **Home schooled:** Transcript of courses and grades required.

High school preparation. College-preparatory program recommended. 17 units recommended. Recommended units include English 4, mathematics 4, science 3 (laboratory 2), foreign language 3 and visual/performing arts 1.

2015-2016 Annual costs. Tuition/fees: $5,664; $13,864 out-of-state. Per-credit charge: $258 in-state; $620 out-of-state.

2015-2016 Financial aid. Need-based: 210 full-time freshmen applied for aid; 182 deemed to have need; 175 received aid. Average need met was 52%. Average scholarship/grant was $4,702; average loan $3,351. 54% of total undergraduate aid awarded as scholarships/grants, 46% as loans/jobs. Need-based aid available for part-time students. Work-study available nights, weekends and for part-time students. **Non-need-based:** Scholarships awarded for academics, alumni affiliation, art, athletics, leadership, minority status, music/drama, ROTC, state residency.

Application procedures. Admission: Closing date 8/15 (receipt date). $40 fee, may be waived for applicants with need. Admission notification on

a rolling basis. **Financial aid:** Priority date 3/1; no closing date. FAFSA required. Applicants notified by 3/15; must reply within 2 week(s) of notification.

Academics. Special study options: Cross-registration, distance learning, double major, dual enrollment of high school students, honors, independent study, internships, New York semester, student-designed major, Washington semester. Bachelor's degree programs available on campus. License preparation in nursing. **Credit/placement by examination:** AP, CLEP, IB, institutional tests. 15 credit hours maximum toward associate degree, 30 toward bachelor's. Limits are combined for CBE, CLEP, and AP. Students can petition college dean for a waiver of maximum limit. Credit must be completed by the semester preceding the semester in which a student plans to graduate. CBE credit does not fulfill the residency requirement. **Support services:** Learning center, pre-admission summer program, reduced course load, remedial instruction, tutoring.

Honors college/program. ACT cumulative score of 25 and high school GPA of 3.5 required.

Majors. Business: General, accounting technology, administrative services. **Computer sciences:** Applications programming. **Conservation:** Urban forestry. **Health services:** EMT paramedic, health care admin. **Protective services:** Criminal justice.

Most popular majors. Business/marketing 9%, computer/information sciences 8%, liberal arts 74%.

Technology on campus. 265 workstations in library, computer center. Commuter students can connect to campus network. Online course registration, online library, helpline, repair service, student web hosting, wireless network available.

Student life. Freshman orientation: Available. Preregistration for classes offered. **Activities:** Drama, film society, musical theater, nontraditional student and minority student organizations, independent black/minority coalition, Christian Fellowship, environmental council, alcohol, drugs and AIDS awareness programs.

Athletics. NJCAA. **Team name:** Golden Flashes.

Student services. Adult student services, career counseling, student employment services, health services, personal counseling, placement for graduates, veterans' counselor. **Physically disabled:** Services for visually, speech, hearing impaired. **Transfer:** Transfer adviser, college fairs on campus for students transferring to 4-year colleges.

Contact. E-mail: admissions@kent.edu
Phone: (330) 847-0571 Toll-free number: (800) 988-5368
Fax: (330) 847-6571
James Ritter, Director, Kent State University: Trumbull, 4314 Mahoning Avenue, NW, Warren, OH 44483-1998

Kent State University: Tuscarawas
New Philadelphia, Ohio
www.kent.edu/tusc   **CB code: 1434**

▶ Public 2-year branch campus college
▶ Commuter campus in large town

General. Founded in 1962. Regionally accredited. **Enrollment:** 1,861 degree-seeking undergraduates; 285 non-degree-seeking students. **Degrees:** 33 bachelor's, 334 associate awarded. **ROTC:** Army, Air Force. **Location:** 30 miles from Canton; 55 miles from Wheeling, WV. **Calendar:** Semester, limited summer session. **Full-time faculty:** 47 total; 11% minority, 47% women. **Part-time faculty:** 60 total; 3% minority, 47% women. **Class size:** 67% < 20, 26% 20-39, 4% 40-49, 3% 50-99. **Partnerships:** Formal partnership with Buckeye Career Center engaged in Tech Prep program.

Student profile. Among degree-seeking undergraduates, 244 enrolled as first-time, first-year students, 103 transferred in from other institutions.

Part-time:	34%	Hispanic/Latino:	1%
Out-of-state:	2%	Multi-racial, non-Hispanic:	2%
Women:	59%	International:	1%
African American:	3%	25 or older:	34%
Asian American:	1%		

Basis for selection. Open admission, but selective for some programs and for out-of-state students. Special requirements for nursing program. **Adult students:** SAT/ACT scores not required if applicant over 21 or out of high school 3 years or more. **Home schooled:** Transcript of courses and grades required.

High school preparation. College-preparatory program recommended. 17 units recommended. Recommended units include English 4, mathematics 4, science 3 (laboratory 2), foreign language 3 and visual/performing arts 1.

2015-2016 Annual costs. Tuition/fees: $5,664; $13,864 out-of-state. Per-credit charge: $258 in-state; $620 out-of-state. Books/supplies: $1,400.

2015-2016 Financial aid. Need-based: 170 full-time freshmen applied for aid; 142 deemed to have need; 136 received aid. Average need met was 51%. Average scholarship/grant was $4,242; average loan $3,356. 54% of total undergraduate aid awarded as scholarships/grants, 46% as loans/jobs. Need-based aid available for part-time students. Work-study available nights, weekends and for part-time students. **Non-need-based:** Scholarships awarded for academics, alumni affiliation, art, athletics, leadership, minority status, music/drama, ROTC, state residency.

Application procedures. Admission: Closing date 8/15 (receipt date). $40 fee, may be waived for applicants with need. Admission notification on a rolling basis. **Financial aid:** Priority date 3/1; no closing date. FAFSA required. Applicants notified by 3/15; must reply within 2 week(s) of notification.

Academics. Special study options: Accelerated study, distance learning, double major, dual enrollment of high school students, honors, independent study, internships, New York semester, student-designed major, Washington semester. Bachelor's degree programs available on campus. License preparation in nursing. **Credit/placement by examination:** AP, CLEP, IB, institutional tests. 15 credit hours maximum toward associate degree, 30 toward bachelor's. Limits are combined for CBE, CLEP, and AP. Students can petition college dean for a waiver of maximum limit. Credit must be completed by the semester preceding the semester in which a student plans to graduate. CBE credit does not fulfill the residency requirement. **Support services:** Learning center, reduced course load, remedial instruction, study skills assistance, tutoring, writing center.

Majors. Business: General, accounting technology, administrative services. **Computer sciences:** Applications programming. **Health services:** Nursing (RN), veterinary technology/assistant. **Protective services:** Criminal justice.

Most popular majors. Business/marketing 6%, engineering/engineering technologies 14%, health sciences 28%, liberal arts 42%.

Technology on campus. 300 workstations in library, computer center. Commuter students can connect to campus network. Online course registration, online library, helpline, student web hosting, wireless network available.

Student life. Freshman orientation: Mandatory. Preregistration for classes offered. **Activities:** Drama, literary magazine, musical theater, student government, Pride Tuscarawas, Current Issues and Interdisciplinary Perspectives, Veteran's club.

Athletics. Intramural: Basketball M, volleyball. **Team name:** Golden Flashes.

Student services. Career counseling, student employment services, on-campus daycare. **Physically disabled:** Services for visually, hearing impaired. **Transfer:** Transfer adviser for students transferring to 4-year colleges.

Contact. E-mail: infotusc@kent.edu
Phone: (330) 339-3391 Toll-free number: (800) 988-5368
Fax: (330) 339-3321
Laurie Donley, Director of Enrollment Management, Kent State University: Tuscarawas, 330 University Drive NE, New Philadelphia, OH 44663-9403

Lakeland Community College
Kirtland, Ohio   CB member
www.lakelandcc.edu   CB code: 1422

- Public 2-year community and technical college
- Commuter campus in large town

General. Founded in 1967. Regionally accredited. **Enrollment:** 5,726 degree-seeking undergraduates. **Degrees:** 1,009 associate awarded. **Location:** 15 miles from Cleveland. **Calendar:** Semester, extensive summer session. **Full-time faculty:** 120 total. **Part-time faculty:** 553 total. **Special facilities:** Planetarium, observatory, licensed preschool program, laboratory.

Student profile. Among degree-seeking undergraduates, 45% enrolled in a transfer program, 48% enrolled in a vocational program.

Out-of-state: 1% **25 or older:**   41%

Transfer out. Colleges most students transferred to 2015: Cleveland State University, University of Akron, Kent State University, Ohio State University, John Carroll University.

Basis for selection. Open admission, but selective for some programs. Admissions to health technology programs based on test scores and successful completion of prerequisite coursework. **Home schooled:** Must submit college ready ACT or SAT scores or complete the Compass exam. **Learning Disabled:** Placement testing required.

High school preparation. College-preparatory program recommended. Recommended units include English 4, mathematics 4, social studies 3, science 3 and foreign language 2. Health technology programs require algebra, biology, chemistry.

2015-2016 Annual costs. Tuition/fees: $3,287; $4,136 out-of-district; $9,176 out-of-state. Per-credit charge: $98 in-district; $126 out-of-district; $294 out-of-state. Books/supplies: $1,200. Personal expenses: $1,441.

Financial aid. Need-based: Need-based aid available for part-time students. Work-study available nights, weekends and for part-time students. **Non-need-based:** Scholarships awarded for academics, art, athletics, job skills, leadership, minority status, music/drama, state residency. **Additional information:** Loans available for tuition and books.

Application procedures. Admission: Closing date 8/16. $15 fee, may be waived for applicants with need. Admission notification on a rolling basis. **Financial aid:** Closing date 3/1. FAFSA, institutional form required. Applicants notified on a rolling basis starting 5/1.

Academics. Special study options: Accelerated study, combined bachelor's/graduate degree, cooperative education, cross-registration, distance learning, dual enrollment of high school students, ESL, independent study, internships, liberal arts/career combination, weekend college. Bachelor's degree programs available on campus. License preparation in dental hygiene, nursing, paramedic, radiology, real estate. **Credit/placement by examination:** AP, CLEP, institutional tests. 44 credit hours maximum toward associate degree. **Support services:** GED preparation and test center, learning center, reduced course load, remedial instruction, study skills assistance, tutoring, writing center.

Majors. Biology: Biotechnology. **Business:** Accounting, administrative services, business admin, e-commerce, hospitality admin, management information systems, small business admin, tourism promotion, tourism/travel. **Computer sciences:** Information systems, LAN/WAN management, programming, web page design. **Education:** Early childhood. **Health services:** Clinical lab technology, dental hygiene, histologic technology, medical radiologic technology/radiation therapy, nursing (RN), ophthalmic lab technology, optician, respiratory therapy technology, surgical technology. **Liberal arts:** Arts/sciences. **Protective services:** Corrections, firefighting, police science, security services. **Visual/performing arts:** Commercial/advertising art. **Work/family studies:** Child care management.

Most popular majors. Business/marketing 9%, health sciences 25%, liberal arts 47%, security/protective services 6%.

Technology on campus. 500 workstations in library, computer center, student center. Commuter students can connect to campus network. Online course registration, online library, helpline, repair service, wireless network available.

Student life. Freshman orientation: Mandatory. Preregistration for classes offered. **Activities:** Bands, choral groups, drama, international student organizations, music ensembles, Model UN, radio station, student government, student newspaper, TV station, Access Unlimited, minority student union, Newman Catholic student association, La Tertulia.

Athletics. NJCAA. **Intercollegiate:** Baseball M, basketball, golf M, soccer M, softball W, volleyball W. **Team name:** Lakers.

Student services. Adult student services, career counseling, student employment services, financial aid counseling, health services, on-campus daycare, personal counseling, placement for graduates, veterans' counselor, women's services. **Physically disabled:** Services for visually, speech, hearing impaired. **Transfer:** Transfer center, transfer adviser, college fairs on campus for students transferring to 4-year colleges.

Contact. E-mail: tcooper@lakelandcc.edu
Phone: (440) 525-7100 Toll-free number: (800) 589-8520
Fax: (440) 525-7651
Tracey Cooper, Director of Admissions/Registrar, Lakeland Community College, 7700 Clocktower Drive, Kirtland, OH 44094-5198

Two-Year Colleges

Lincoln College of Technology: Dayton

Dayton, Ohio

www.swcollege.net

CB code: 2483

- For-profit 2-year business college
- Commuter campus in small city

General. Accredited by ACICS. **Enrollment:** 340 undergraduates. **Degrees:** 34 associate awarded. **Calendar:** Quarter, extensive summer session. **Full-time faculty:** 19 total. **Part-time faculty:** 4 total. **Class size:** 76% < 20, 24% 20-39.

Basis for selection. Open admission. Applicants not holding high school diploma or GED must take Wonderlic exam.

2015-2016 Annual costs. Books/supplies: $825. **Additional information:** Certificate programs: $10,255. Diploma programs: $15,320 to $26,705. Associate programs: $30,515 to $33,048. Costs include total tuition, materials, tool fees, and registration fee.

Financial aid. All financial aid based on need. Need-based aid available for part-time students. Work-study available nights, weekends and for part-time students.

Application procedures. Admission: No deadline. $125 fee. Admission notification on a rolling basis. **Financial aid:** No deadline. FAFSA required.

Academics. Special study options: Liberal arts/career combination. **Credit/placement by examination:** AP, CLEP. **Support services:** GED preparation, tutoring.

Majors. Business: Business admin. **Computer sciences:** General. **Health services:** Medical secretary. **Protective services:** Law enforcement admin.

Technology on campus. 44 workstations in library, computer center.

Student life. Freshman orientation: Mandatory. Preregistration for classes offered.

Student services. Career counseling, financial aid counseling, on-campus daycare, personal counseling, placement for graduates.

Contact. Phone: (937) 224-0061
Bill Furlong, Director, Lincoln College of Technology: Dayton, 111 West 1st Street, Dayton, OH 45402

Lorain County Community College

Elyria, Ohio

www.lorainccc.edu

CB code: 1417

- Public 2-year community college
- Commuter campus in small city

General. Founded in 1963. Regionally accredited. **Enrollment:** 8,907 degree-seeking undergraduates; 2,700 non-degree-seeking students. **Degrees:** 1,315 associate awarded. **Location:** 26 miles of Cleveland. **Calendar:** Semester, extensive summer session. **Full-time faculty:** 123 total. **Part-time faculty:** 577 total. **Special facilities:** Performing arts center, advanced technologies center, technology park, conference center, entrepreneurial incubator, culinary arts center.

Student profile. Among degree-seeking undergraduates, 1,666 enrolled as first-time, first-year students.

Part-time:	65%	Women:	63%
Out-of-state:	1%	25 or older:	44%

Basis for selection. Open admission. **Home schooled:** GED required.

2015-2016 Annual costs. Tuition/fees: $3,077; $3,679 out-of-district; $7,302 out-of-state. Per-credit charge: $118.34 in-district; $141.39 out-of-district; $280.84 out-of-state. Books/supplies: $1,404. Personal expenses: $1,108.

2014-2015 Financial aid. Need-based: 67% of total undergraduate aid awarded as scholarships/grants, 33% as loans/jobs. Need-based aid available for part-time students. Work-study available nights, weekends and for part-time students. **Non-need-based:** Scholarships awarded for academics.

Application procedures. Admission: No deadline. No application fee. Admission notification on a rolling basis beginning on or about 4/15. **Financial aid:** Priority date 8/15; no closing date. FAFSA required. Applicants

notified on a rolling basis starting 7/1; must reply within 3 week(s) of notification.

Academics. Special study options: Cooperative education, cross-registration, distance learning, dual enrollment of high school students, ESL, independent study, liberal arts/career combination, study abroad, teacher certification program, weekend college. Bachelor's degree programs available on campus. License preparation in dental hygiene, nursing, paramedic, physical therapy, radiology. **Credit/placement by examination:** AP, CLEP, institutional tests. 30 credit hours maximum toward associate degree. **Support services:** GED preparation and test center, learning center, pre-admission summer program, reduced course load, remedial instruction, study skills assistance, tutoring.

Majors. Biology: General. **Business:** General, accounting, administrative services, banking/financial services, business admin, entrepreneurial studies, hotel/motel admin, human resources, tourism/travel. **Computer sciences:** General, information technology, networking, web page design. **Education:** Early childhood, multi-level teacher. **Engineering:** General, electrical, industrial. **Health services:** Athletic training, clinical lab technology, dental hygiene, medical assistant, medical radiologic technology/radiation therapy, medical secretary, nuclear medical technology, nursing (RN), physical therapy assistant, sonography, surgical technology. **Human services:** General, social work. **Liberal arts:** Arts/sciences. **Math:** General. **Parks/recreation:** Sports admin. **Protective services:** Corrections, firefighting, police science. **Social sciences:** General.

Most popular majors. Business/marketing 14%, engineering/engineering technologies 8%, health sciences 27%, liberal arts 39%.

Technology on campus. 250 workstations in library, computer center. Online course registration, online library, helpline, wireless network available.

Student life. Freshman orientation: Mandatory. Preregistration for classes offered. All students enrolled in 12 or fewer credits must take College Experience course. **Activities:** Bands, choral groups, drama, film society, music ensembles, musical theater, radio station, student government, student newspaper, symphony orchestra, TV station, Black Progressives, Los Unidos, student nurses association, Phi Theta Kappa, campus Baptist ministries, Campus Crusades for Christ, student dental hygienist club, early childhood education club.

Athletics. Intramural: Archery, badminton, basketball, bowling, cross-country, golf, racquetball, rifle, soccer, softball, tennis, volleyball. **Team name:** Commodores.

Student services. Adult student services, alcohol/substance abuse counseling, chaplain/spiritual director, career counseling, services for economically disadvantaged, student employment services, financial aid counseling, health services, on-campus daycare, personal counseling, placement for graduates, veterans' counselor, women's services. **Physically disabled:** Services for visually, hearing impaired. **Transfer:** Transfer center, transfer adviser, college fairs on campus for students transferring to 4-year colleges.

Contact. Phone: (440) 366-4032 Toll-free number: (800) 995-5222 Fax: (440) 366-4167
Stephanie Sutton, Dean of Enrollment & Financial Services, Lorain County Community College, 1005 Abbe Road North, Elyria, OH 44035-1691

Marion Technical College

Marion, Ohio

www.mtc.edu

CB code: 0699

- Public 2-year community and technical college
- Commuter campus in large town

General. Founded in 1971. Regionally accredited. **Enrollment:** 1,681 degree-seeking undergraduates; 762 non-degree-seeking students. **Degrees:** 284 associate awarded. **Location:** 45 miles from Columbus. **Calendar:** Semester, limited summer session. **Full-time faculty:** 52 total. **Part-time faculty:** 97 total.

Student profile. Among degree-seeking undergraduates, 5% already have a bachelor's degree or higher, 371 enrolled as first-time, first-year students, 254 transferred in from other institutions.

Part-time:	70%	Women:	63%
Out-of-state:	1%	25 or older:	40%

Basis for selection. Open admission, but selective for some programs. Additional application required for limited enrollment programs. Interview required for health technologies, human and social services, law enforcement academy. **Adult students:** ACT may be required for limited enrollment programs. **Home schooled:** Transcript of courses and grades required. Appropriate standardized test or other documentation as defined by policy. **Learning Disabled:** Students must meet with Student Resource Center for assessment.

High school preparation. College-preparatory program recommended. Recommended units include English 4, mathematics 2, social studies 1, science 2 and foreign language 2. Algebra, biology, and chemistry required for health technology applicants. Algebra and physics recommended for engineering applicants.

2015-2016 Annual costs. Tuition/fees: $4,782; $6,702 out-of-state. Per-credit charge: $170 in-state; $220 out-of-state. Books/supplies: $1,200. Personal expenses: $900.

2014-2015 Financial aid. All financial aid based on need. 59% of total undergraduate aid awarded as scholarships/grants, 41% as loans/jobs. Need-based aid available for part-time students. Work-study available nights, weekends and for part-time students.

Application procedures. **Admission:** Priority date 5/1; no deadline. $20 fee, may be waived for applicants with need. Admission notification on a rolling basis. **Financial aid:** Closing date 5/1. FAFSA, institutional form required. Applicants notified on a rolling basis.

Academics. **Special study options:** Accelerated study, combined bachelor's/graduate degree, cooperative education, cross-registration, distance learning, double major, dual enrollment of high school students, external degree, independent study, internships, liberal arts/career combination, student-designed major. License preparation in nursing, occupational therapy, physical therapy, radiology, real estate. **Credit/placement by examination:** AP, CLEP, institutional tests. 48 credit hours maximum toward associate degree. Maximum of 48 quarter hours of credit may be earned through exam, life experience or combination. **Support services:** GED preparation and test center, learning center, reduced course load, remedial instruction, study skills assistance, tutoring.

Majors. **Business:** Accounting, administrative services, business admin, human resources, marketing. **Computer sciences:** General, applications programming, information technology, LAN/WAN management, networking, programming, vendor certification, web page design, webmaster. **Health services:** Clinical lab technology, medical assistant, medical radiologic technology/radiation therapy, nursing (RN), occupational therapy assistant, pharmacy assistant, physical therapy assistant. **Protective services:** Law enforcement admin.

Most popular majors. Business/marketing 64%, engineering/engineering technologies 6%, health sciences 15%.

Technology on campus. 229 workstations in library, computer center, student center. Commuter students can connect to campus network. Online course registration, online library, helpline, wireless network available.

Student life. **Freshman orientation:** Available. Preregistration for classes offered. Held 1-2 weeks before classes begin. **Activities:** Campus ministries, choral groups, drama, literary magazine, student government, joint activities committee, Campus Christian Fellowship, program of outdoor pursuits club, cultural arts program, student organized clubs/organizations, Beta Nu Pi honorary society (Phi Theta Kappa local chapter); Student Society of Leadership and Success.

Athletics. USCAA. **Intercollegiate:** Golf, volleyball W. **Intramural:** Badminton, basketball, cross-country, football (non-tackle), racquetball, skiing, softball, table tennis, tennis, volleyball.

Student services. Adult student services, career counseling, student employment services, financial aid counseling, personal counseling, placement for graduates, veterans' counselor. **Physically disabled:** Services for visually, speech, hearing impaired. **Transfer:** Pre-admission transcript evaluation for new students. College fairs on campus for students transferring to 4-year colleges.

Contact. E-mail: enroll@mtc.edu
Phone: (740) 389-4636 ext. 334 Fax: (740) 389-6136
Joel Liles, Dean of Enrollment Services, Marion Technical College, 1467 Mt. Vernon Avenue, Marion, OH 43302-5694

Miami University: Hamilton
Hamilton, Ohio
www.ham.muohio.edu   CB code: 1526

♦ Public 2-year branch campus college
♦ Commuter campus in small city

General. Founded in 1968. Regionally accredited. Degrees earned on Hamilton campus conferred by main (Oxford) campus. **Enrollment:** 3,386 undergraduates. **Degrees:** 204 bachelor's, 116 associate awarded. **ROTC:** Naval, Air Force. **Location:** 25 miles from Cincinnati. **Calendar:** Semester, limited summer session. **Full-time faculty:** 84 total. **Part-time faculty:** 140 total. **Class size:** 67% < 20, 24% 20-39, 6% 40-49, 3% 50-99. **Special facilities:** Botanical conservatory.

Basis for selection. Open admission, but selective for some programs. Additional application required for competitive nursing program. **Home schooled:** Applicants must present GED scores or credentials that demonstrate equivalent levels of academic achievement, ability and performance to that of state-chartered diploma at least 8 weeks before classes begin.

High school preparation. 16 units recommended. Recommended units include English 4, mathematics 3, social studies 2, history 1, science 3, foreign language 2 and visual/performing arts 1.

2015-2016 Annual costs. Tuition/fees: $5,413; $14,689 out-of-state. Books/supplies: $730. Personal expenses: $2,025.

Financial aid. **Need-based:** Need-based aid available for part-time students. Work-study available nights, weekends and for part-time students. **Non-need-based:** Scholarships awarded for academics, athletics, leadership, minority status, state residency. **Additional information:** Special gift funds for needy, multicultural students who enter with appropriate academic record. Separate application required for scholarships; closing date January 31.

Application procedures. **Admission:** No deadline. $30 fee, may be waived for applicants with need. Admission notification on a rolling basis. Nursing application deadline for Fall admission 2/1. **Financial aid:** Priority date 2/15; no closing date. FAFSA required. Applicants notified on a rolling basis starting 4/1.

Academics. Some graduate coursework available. **Special study options:** Cooperative education, cross-registration, distance learning, double major, dual enrollment of high school students, ESL, honors, independent study, internships, liberal arts/career combination, student-designed major, study abroad, teacher certification program. Bachelor's degree programs available on campus. License preparation in nursing, real estate. **Credit/placement by examination:** AP, CLEP, IB, institutional tests. 32 credit hours maximum toward associate degree, 32 toward bachelor's. **Support services:** Learning center, reduced course load, remedial instruction, study skills assistance, tutoring, writing center.

Majors. **Business:** Accounting technology, business admin, marketing, office management, real estate. **Computer sciences:** General, networking, support specialist. **Education:** Kindergarten/preschool. **Health services:** Nursing (RN). **Protective services:** Law enforcement admin.

Technology on campus. 300 workstations in library, computer center, student center. Commuter students can connect to campus network. Online course registration, online library, helpline, wireless network available.

Student life. **Freshman orientation:** Available. Preregistration for classes offered. **Activities:** Choral groups, drama, musical theater, student government, campus activities committee, student nursing association, minority action committee, Campus Crusade for Christ, athletic club, Organization for Wiser and Worldwide Learners.

Athletics. **Intramural:** Basketball, bowling, skiing, soccer, softball, table tennis, tennis, volleyball, weight lifting. **Team name:** Harriers.

Student services. Career counseling, student employment services, financial aid counseling, minority student services, on-campus daycare, personal counseling, placement for graduates, veterans' counselor. **Physically disabled:** Services for visually, speech, hearing impaired. **Transfer:** Pre-admission transcript evaluation for new students.

Contact. Phone: (513) 785-3111 Fax: (513) 785-1807
Archie Nelson, Director of Admission and Financial Aid, Miami University: Hamilton, 1601 University Boulevard, Hamilton, OH 45011-3399

Miami University: Middletown
Middletown, Ohio
www.mid.muohio.edu   CB code: 1509

♦ Public 2-year branch campus and community college
♦ Commuter campus in large town

General. Founded in 1963. Regionally accredited. Degrees earned on Middletown campus conferred by main (Oxford) campus. **Enrollment:** 2,034 degree-seeking undergraduates. **Degrees:** 115 bachelor's, 63 associate awarded. **ROTC:** Naval, Air Force. **Location:** 30 miles from Cincinnati, 20 miles from Dayton. **Calendar:** Semester, extensive summer session. **Full-time faculty:** 60 total. **Special facilities:** Nature trail.

Student profile.

Out-of-state: 1% **25 or older:** 28%

Basis for selection. Open admission, but selective for some programs. Special requirements for allied health programs. Interview recommended for nursing program. **Home schooled:** Submit curriculum and description of resources used during last 4 years.

High school preparation. 16 units recommended. Recommended units include English 4, mathematics 3, social studies 3, science 3, foreign language 2 and academic electives 1. One fine arts also recommended.

2015-2016 Annual costs. Tuition/fees: $5,413; $14,689 out-of-state. Per-credit charge: $216 in-state; $602 out-of-state. Books/supplies: $1,195. Personal expenses: $4,088.

Financial aid. All financial aid based on need. Need-based aid available for part-time students. Work-study available nights, weekends and for part-time students.

Application procedures. Admission: Priority date 8/1; no deadline. $35 fee, may be waived for applicants with need. Admission notification on a rolling basis beginning on or about 3/1. **Financial aid:** Priority date 2/15; no closing date. FAFSA required. Applicants notified on a rolling basis.

Academics. Special study options: Cooperative education, cross-registration, distance learning, double major, dual enrollment of high school students, independent study, internships, liberal arts/career combination, student-designed major, study abroad, teacher certification program. Bachelor's degree programs available on campus. License preparation in nursing. **Credit/placement by examination:** AP, CLEP, IB, institutional tests. 30 credit hours maximum toward bachelor's degree. **Support services:** Learning center, pre-admission summer program, reduced course load, remedial instruction, study skills assistance, tutoring, writing center.

Majors. Biology: Molecular, zoology. **Business:** General, accounting, administrative services, business admin, finance, office management, office/clerical. **Communications:** Communications/speech/rhetoric. **Computer sciences:** General, applications programming, systems analysis. **English:** English lit. **Foreign languages:** Spanish. **Health services:** Nursing (RN). **History:** General. **Liberal arts:** Arts/sciences, humanities. **Math:** General. **Philosophy/religion:** Philosophy. **Physical sciences:** Chemistry, physics. **Psychology:** General. **Social sciences:** Anthropology, geography, political science, sociology.

Technology on campus. 170 workstations in library, computer center. Commuter students can connect to campus network. Online course registration, online library, helpline, student web hosting available.

Student life. Freshman orientation: Mandatory. Preregistration for classes offered. Full-day program, choice of 5 days ranging from June 4 through August 11. **Activities:** Drama, literary magazine, student government, student newspaper.

Athletics. Intercollegiate: Baseball M, basketball, golf, tennis, volleyball W. **Intramural:** Basketball, golf, racquetball, soccer, softball, table tennis, tennis, volleyball. **Team name:** Thunder Hawks.

Student services. Adult student services, career counseling, student employment services, financial aid counseling, minority student services, on-campus daycare, personal counseling, placement for graduates, veterans' counselor. **Physically disabled:** Services for visually, speech, hearing impaired. **Transfer:** College fairs on campus for students transferring to 4-year colleges.

Contact. E-mail: mlflynn@muohio.edu
Phone: (513) 727-3216 Fax: (513) 727-3223
Archie Nelson, Director of Admission and Financial Aid, Miami University: Middletown, 4200 East University Boulevard, Middletown, OH 45042

Miami-Jacobs Career College: Columbus
Columbus, Ohio
www.miamijacobs.edu   **CB code: 3344**

- For-profit 2-year junior college
- Commuter campus in very large city
- Application essay, interview required

General. Accredited by ACICS. **Enrollment:** 366 undergraduates. **Degrees:** 21 associate awarded. **Calendar:** Differs by program. **Full-time faculty:** 9 total. **Part-time faculty:** 31 total.

Basis for selection. 2 references required.

2015-2016 Annual costs. Books/supplies: $1,500. **Additional information:** Certificate programs: Dental Assisting $23,092, Massage Therapy $10,600, Medical Billing and Coding $23,495. Books and supplies $1,258-$3,600. Associate programs: Accounting $31,603, Business Administration $31,891, Criminal Justice $31,891, Electronic Health Records $31,699, Medical Assisting $31,891, Paralegal $31,891. Books and supplies $4,800.

Financial aid. Need-based: Work-study available nights, weekends and for part-time students.

Application procedures. Admission: No deadline. $100 fee, may be waived for applicants with need. Admission notification on a rolling basis. **Financial aid:** FAFSA required.

Academics. Special study options: Bachelor's degree programs available on campus. **Credit/placement by examination:** AP, CLEP.

Majors. Health services: Dental assistant, health information technology, massage therapy, medical assistant, surgical technology.

Student life. Freshman orientation: Mandatory. Preregistration for classes offered.

Student services. Adult student services, career counseling, financial aid counseling, placement for graduates, veterans' counselor. **Physically disabled:** Services for visually impaired.

Contact. Phone: (614) 221-7770 Fax: (614) 221-8429
Ann Contingulia, Director of Admissions, Miami-Jacobs Career College: Columbus, 150 East Gay Street, 15th Floor, Columbus, OH 43215

Miami-Jacobs Career College: Dayton
Dayton, Ohio
www.miamijacobs.edu   **CB code: 1528**

- For-profit 2-year career college
- Commuter campus in small city
- Application essay, interview required

General. Founded in 1860. Accredited by ACICS. **Enrollment:** 159 undergraduates. **Degrees:** 22 associate awarded. **Location:** Downtown. **Calendar:** Quarter, extensive summer session. **Full-time faculty:** 4 total. **Part-time faculty:** 31 total.

Basis for selection. Interview, essay, recommendations most important. Wonderlic exam required.

2015-2016 Annual costs. Personal expenses: $2,500. **Additional information:** Certificate programs: Massage Therapy $10,600, Medical Billing and Coding $23,495. Books and supplies $1,900-$3,600. Associate programs: Business Administration $31,891, Criminal Justice $31,891, Electronic Health Records $31,699, Medical Assisting $31,891. Books and supplies $4,800.

Financial aid. All financial aid based on need. Need-based aid available for part-time students. Work-study available nights, weekends and for part-time students.

Application procedures. Admission: No deadline. $40 fee. Admission notification on a rolling basis. **Financial aid:** No deadline. FAFSA, institutional form required. Applicants notified on a rolling basis.

Academics. College has dress code and attendance policy establishing patterns and habits to be carried over into employment setting. **Special study options:** Accelerated study, cross-registration, distance learning, double major, dual enrollment of high school students, independent study, internships, weekend college. **Credit/placement by examination:** AP, CLEP, institutional tests. 45 credit hours maximum toward associate degree. **Support services:** Pre-admission summer program, reduced course load, remedial instruction, tutoring.

Majors. Business: Accounting, administrative services, office management, office technology, office/clerical. **Computer sciences:** General, applications programming, data processing, information systems, information technology, networking, programming. **Engineering:** Software. **Health services:** Health information technology, massage therapy, medical assistant, medical secretary, medical transcription, respiratory therapy technology, surgical technology. **Protective services:** Law enforcement admin.

Technology on campus. 180 workstations in computer center.

Student life. Freshman orientation: Mandatory. Preregistration for classes offered.

Student services. Adult student services, career counseling, student employment services, financial aid counseling, personal counseling, placement for graduates, veterans' counselor. **Transfer:** Transfer adviser for students transferring to 4-year colleges.

Contact. Phone: (937) 222-7337
Beth Wilson, Director of Admissions, Miami-Jacobs Career College: Dayton, 110 North Patterson Boulevard, Dayton, OH 45402

Miami-Jacobs Career College: Sharonville
Sharonville, Ohio
www.miamijacobs.edu

▶ For-profit 2-year business college
▶ Large city

General. Accredited by ACICS. **Enrollment:** 69 undergraduates. **Degrees:** 27 associate awarded. **Calendar:** Quarter. **Full-time faculty:** 2 total. **Part-time faculty:** 22 total.

Basis for selection. Open admission, but selective for some programs.

2015-2016 Annual costs. Books/supplies: $1,500. **Additional information:** Associate programs: Dental Assisting $31,303, Management $31,603, Medical Assisting $31,891. Books and supplies $4,200-$4,800.

Financial aid. Need-based: Work-study available nights, weekends and for part-time students.

Application procedures. Admission: No deadline. $40 fee.

Academics. Credit/placement by examination: AP, CLEP.

Majors. Health services: Dental assistant, health information technology, massage therapy, medical assistant, surgical technology.

Contact. Phone: (513) 723-0520
Sheila Woods, Director of Admissions, Miami-Jacobs Career College: Sharonville, Two Crowne Point Court, Suite 100, Sharonville, OH 45241

National College: Canton
Canton, Ohio
www.national-college.edu

▶ For-profit 2-year branch campus college
▶ Large city

General. Regionally accredited; also accredited by ACICS. **Enrollment:** 46 degree-seeking undergraduates. **Degrees:** 16 associate awarded. **Calendar:** Quarter. **Full-time faculty:** 1 total. **Part-time faculty:** 12 total.

Basis for selection. Open admission.

2016-2017 Annual costs. Tuition/fees: $14,460. Per-credit charge: $317.

Financial aid. Need-based: Work-study available nights, weekends and for part-time students.

Application procedures. Admission: $50 fee.

Academics. Credit/placement by examination: AP.

Majors. Business: Accounting technology, business admin. **Computer sciences:** System admin. **Health services:** Medical assistant, pharmacy assistant.

Contact. Phone: (330) 492-5300
Trent Ramey, Director of Admissions, National College: Canton, 4736 Dressler Road NW, Canton, OH 44718

National College: Cincinnati
Cincinnati, Ohio
www.national-college.edu

▶ For-profit 2-year branch campus college
▶ Large city

General. Regionally accredited; also accredited by ACICS. **Enrollment:** 96 degree-seeking undergraduates. **Degrees:** 18 associate awarded. **Calendar:** Quarter. **Full-time faculty:** 2 total. **Part-time faculty:** 13 total.

Basis for selection. Open admission.

2016-2017 Annual costs. Tuition/fees: $14,460. Per-credit charge: $317. Books/supplies: $1,980.

Financial aid. Need-based: Work-study available nights, weekends and for part-time students.

Application procedures. Admission: No deadline. $50 fee.

Academics. Credit/placement by examination: AP, CLEP.

Majors. Business: Accounting/business management, administrative services, business admin. **Health services:** Pharmacy assistant, surgical technology.

Contact. Phone: (513) 761-1291
Bryan Evans, Director of Admissions, National College: Cincinnati, 6871 Steger Drive, Cincinnati, OH 45237

National College: Columbus
Columbus, Ohio
www.ncbt.edu

▶ For-profit 2-year branch campus college
▶ Very large city

General. Regionally accredited; also accredited by ACICS. **Enrollment:** 52 degree-seeking undergraduates. **Degrees:** 30 associate awarded. **Calendar:** Quarter. **Full-time faculty:** 4 total. **Part-time faculty:** 11 total.

Basis for selection. Open admission.

2016-2017 Annual costs. Tuition/fees: $14,460. Per-credit charge: $317.

Financial aid. Need-based: Work-study available nights, weekends and for part-time students.

Application procedures. Admission: No deadline. $50 fee.

Academics. Credit/placement by examination: AP, CLEP.

Majors. Health services: Office assistant.

Contact. Phone: (614) 282-2800
Trent Ramey, Director of Admissions, National College: Columbus, 5665 Forest Hills Boulevard, Columbus, OH 43231

National College: Kettering
Kettering, Ohio
www.national-college.edu

▶ For-profit 2-year business and technical college
▶ Large city

General. Accredited by ACICS. **Enrollment:** 112 degree-seeking undergraduates. **Degrees:** 45 associate awarded. **Calendar:** Quarter. **Full-time faculty:** 9 total. **Part-time faculty:** 11 total.

Basis for selection. Open admission.

2016-2017 Annual costs. Tuition/fees: $14,460. Per-credit charge: $317.

Financial aid. Need-based: Work-study available nights, weekends and for part-time students.

Application procedures. Admission: No deadline. $50 fee. **Financial aid:** No deadline.

Academics. Credit/placement by examination: AP, CLEP.

Majors. Business: Business admin. **Computer sciences:** General.

Contact. Phone: (937) 299-9450
Linda Clemons, Director of Admissions, National College: Kettering, 1837 Woodman Center Drive, Kettering, OH 45420

National College: Stow
Stow, Ohio
www.national-college.edu

⬧ For-profit 2-year branch campus college
⬧ Large town

General. Regionally accredited; also accredited by ACICS. **Enrollment:** 58 degree-seeking undergraduates. **Degrees:** 14 associate awarded. **Calendar:** Quarter. **Full-time faculty:** 3 total. **Part-time faculty:** 12 total.

Basis for selection. Open admission.

2016-2017 Annual costs. Tuition/fees: $14,460. Per-credit charge: $317. Books/supplies: $1,980.

Financial aid. Need-based: Work-study available nights, weekends and for part-time students.

Application procedures. Admission: No deadline. $50 fee.

Academics. Credit/placement by examination: AP, CLEP.

Majors. Business: Accounting/business management, administrative services, business admin. **Health services:** Health information technology, medical assistant, pharmacy assistant.

Contact. Phone: (330) 676-1351
Selinda McCumbers, Director of Admissions, National College: Stow, 3855 Fishercreek Road, Stow, OH 44224

National College: Willoughby Hills
Willoughby Hills, Ohio
www.national-college.edu

⬧ For-profit 2-year career college
⬧ Small town

General. Accredited by ACICS. **Enrollment:** 42 degree-seeking undergraduates. **Degrees:** 15 associate awarded. **Calendar:** Quarter. **Full-time faculty:** 4 total. **Part-time faculty:** 9 total.

Basis for selection. Open admission.

2016-2017 Annual costs. Tuition/fees: $14,460. Per-credit charge: $317.

Financial aid. Need-based: Work-study available nights, weekends and for part-time students.

Application procedures. Admission: No deadline. $50 fee.

Academics. Credit/placement by examination: AP, CLEP.

Majors. Business: Accounting. **Computer sciences:** System admin. **Health services:** Health information technology, medical assistant, pharmacy assistant.

Contact. Phone: (440) 944-0825
Trent Ramey, Regional Director of Admissions, National College: Willoughby Hills, 27557 Chardon Road, Willoughby Hills, OH 44092

National College: Youngstown
Youngstown, Ohio
www.national-college.edu

⬧ For-profit 2-year branch campus college
⬧ Small city

General. Regionally accredited; also accredited by ACICS. **Enrollment:** 80 degree-seeking undergraduates. **Degrees:** 41 associate awarded. **Calendar:** Quarter. **Full-time faculty:** 5 total. **Part-time faculty:** 13 total.

Basis for selection. Open admission.

2016-2017 Annual costs. Tuition/fees: $14,460. Per-credit charge: $317.

Financial aid. Need-based: Work-study available nights, weekends and for part-time students.

Application procedures. Admission: No deadline. $50 fee. **Financial aid:** No deadline.

Academics. Credit/placement by examination: AP, CLEP.

Majors. Business: Business admin. **Health services:** Health information technology, office assistant, physical therapy assistant.

Contact. Phone: (330) 759-0205
Trent Ramey, Regional Director of Admissions, National College: Youngstown, 3487 Belmont Avenue, Youngstown, OH 44505

North Central State College
Mansfield, Ohio
www.ncstatecollege.edu   **CB code: 0721**

⬧ Public 2-year community and technical college
⬧ Commuter campus in small city

General. Founded in 1961. Regionally accredited. **Enrollment:** 1,974 degree-seeking undergraduates; 978 non-degree-seeking students. **Degrees:** 360 associate awarded. **Location:** 70 miles from Cleveland and Columbus. **Calendar:** Semester, limited summer session. **Full-time faculty:** 48 total. **Part-time faculty:** 138 total. **Partnerships:** Formal on-campus internship program partnering with various businesses.

Student profile. Among degree-seeking undergraduates, 11% enrolled in a transfer program, 89% enrolled in a vocational program, 4% already have a bachelor's degree or higher, 444 enrolled as first-time, first-year students, 494 transferred in from other institutions.

Part-time:	67%	Hispanic/Latino:	1%
Out-of-state:	1%	Multi-racial, non-Hispanic:	2%
Women:	62%	25 or older:	30%
African American:	5%	Live on campus:	1%
Asian American:	1%		

Transfer out. 19% of students enrolled in the transfer program go on to 4-year colleges. **Colleges most students transferred to 2015:** Ashland University, Mount Vernon Nazarene College, Ohio State University, Franklin University, Miami University of Ohio.

Basis for selection. Open admission, but selective for some programs. Nursing and certain allied health programs have an application process, including the TEAS V assessment. Interview recommended for all health and public service programs.

High school preparation. College-preparatory program recommended. One algebra and 1 chemistry required for nursing, physical therapist assistant, respiratory therapy, radiologic technology and pharmacy technology programs.

2015-2016 Annual costs. Tuition/fees: $4,488; $8,976 out-of-state. Per-credit charge: $126 in-state; $251 out-of-state. Books/supplies: $1,500. Personal expenses: $501.

Financial aid. All financial aid based on need. Need-based aid available for part-time students. Work-study available nights, weekends and for part-time students.

Application procedures. Admission: No deadline. No application fee. Admission notification on a rolling basis. **Financial aid:** Priority date 4/1; no closing date. FAFSA required. Applicants notified on a rolling basis starting 5/30; must reply within 1 week(s) of notification.

Academics. Special study options: Accelerated study, combined bachelor's/graduate degree, distance learning, double major, dual enrollment of high school students, ESL, honors, independent study, internships, student-designed major. Evening cohort program in business management. Bachelor's degree programs available on campus. License preparation in nursing, paramedic, radiology, real estate. **Credit/placement by examination:** AP, CLEP, IB, institutional tests. **Support services:** Learning center, pre-admission summer program, reduced course load, remedial instruction, study skills assistance, tutoring, writing center. Extensive academic advising services for dual credit, entering and continuing students.

Majors. Biology: Biotechnology. **Business:** General, accounting technology, business admin, marketing. **Communications:** Communications/speech/rhetoric. **Communications technology:** Animation/special effects, radio/TV. **Computer sciences:** LAN/WAN management, web page design. **Education:** General, early childhood. **English:** English lit. **Health services:** Nursing (RN), occupational therapy assistant, physical therapy assistant, radiologic technology/medical imaging, respiratory therapy technology. **Human services:** Social work. **Math:** General. **Philosophy/religion:** Philosophy. **Protective services:** Corrections, police science. **Psychology:** General. **Social sciences:** Sociology.

Most popular majors. Business/marketing 17%, computer/information sciences 7%, engineering/engineering technologies 7%, health sciences 42%, public administration/social services 8%.

Technology on campus. 144 workstations in library, computer center, student center. Commuter students can connect to campus network. Online course registration, online library, helpline, wireless network available.

Student life. Freshman orientation: Mandatory. Preregistration for classes offered. Two- or three-hour evening program held prior to beginning of each quarter. **Housing:** Apartments available. **Activities:** Campus ministries, choral groups, drama, international student organizations, student government, campus activities board; Catholic Young Adults; international club; National Society for Leadership and Success; outdoor adventure club; Outloud; Phi Theta Kappa; Student Veterans Association; Student Nurses Association.

Athletics. Intramural: Basketball, football (non-tackle), soccer, softball, table tennis, tennis, volleyball. **Team name:** Mavericks.

Student services. Career counseling, services for economically disadvantaged, student employment services, financial aid counseling, on-campus daycare, personal counseling, placement for graduates, veterans' counselor. **Physically disabled:** Services for visually, speech, hearing impaired. **Transfer:** Pre-admission transcript evaluation for new students. Transfer adviser, college fairs on campus for students transferring to 4-year colleges.

Contact. E-mail: Admissionsgroup@ncstatecollege.edu
Phone: (419) 755-4761 Toll-free number: (888) 755-4899
Fax: (419) 755-4757
Thomas Mansperger, Director of Gateway Services, North Central State College, 2441 Kenwood Circle, PO Box 698, Mansfield, OH 44901-0698

Northwest State Community College
Archbold, Ohio
www.northweststate.edu   CB code: 1235

▸ Public 2-year community and technical college
▸ Commuter campus in small town

General. Founded in 1968. Regionally accredited. **Enrollment:** 1,443 degree-seeking undergraduates; 2,174 non-degree-seeking students. **Degrees:** 273 associate awarded. **Location:** 45 miles from Toledo. **Calendar:** Semester, limited summer session. **Full-time faculty:** 55 total; 9% have terminal degrees, 47% women. **Part-time faculty:** 100 total; 5% have terminal degrees, 3% minority, 61% women. **Class size:** 85% < 20, 13% 20-39, less than 1% 40-49, less than 1% 50-99, less than 1% >100. **Special facilities:** Childcare center.

Student profile. Among degree-seeking undergraduates, 15% enrolled in a transfer program, 2% already have a bachelor's degree or higher, 263 enrolled as first-time, first-year students, 56 transferred in from other institutions.

Part-time:	65%	Hispanic/Latino:	9%
Out-of-state:	4%	Multi-racial, non-Hispanic:	1%
Women:	64%	25 or older:	41%
African American:	2%		

Transfer out. Colleges most students transferred to 2015: University of Toledo, Bowling Green State University, Wright State University, Defiance College, Bluffton University.

Basis for selection. Open admission, but selective for some programs. Special requirements for nursing program; interview required. **Adult students:** SAT/ACT scores not required. COMPASS test administered on-site.

High school preparation. Recommended units include English 4, mathematics 3, social studies 3 and science 3. College-preparatory program preferred.

2015-2016 Annual costs. Tuition/fees: $4,780; $9,310 out-of-state. Per-credit charge: $157 in-state; $308 out-of-state. Books/supplies: $1,200. Personal expenses: $4,100.

Financial aid. Need-based: Need-based aid available for part-time students. Work-study available nights, weekends and for part-time students. **Non-need-based:** Scholarships awarded for academics.

Application procedures. Admission: No deadline. No application fee. Admission notification on a rolling basis. **Financial aid:** Priority date 6/1;

no closing date. FAFSA, institutional form required. Applicants notified on a rolling basis starting 4/1.

Academics. Special study options: Cooperative education, distance learning, dual enrollment of high school students, independent study, internships, student-designed major, weekend college. Bachelor's degree programs available on campus. License preparation in nursing, real estate. **Credit/placement by examination:** AP, CLEP, institutional tests. 40 credit hours maximum toward associate degree. **Support services:** Learning center, remedial instruction, tutoring.

Majors. Business: Accounting, administrative services, banking/financial services, business admin, entrepreneurial studies, executive assistant, international, logistics, marketing, nonprofit/public, office management. **Computer sciences:** Data entry, programming, security, system admin, web page design. **Education:** Kindergarten/preschool, teacher assistance. **Engineering:** Computer. **Health services:** Medical assistant, medical secretary, nursing (RN). **History:** General. **Human services:** Social work. **Liberal arts:** Arts/sciences. **Protective services:** Corrections, criminal justice, law enforcement admin, police science. **Visual/performing arts:** Design. **Work/family studies:** Child care management.

Most popular majors. Business/marketing 27%, computer/information sciences 11%, engineering/engineering technologies 9%, health sciences 26%, liberal arts 8%, security/protective services 10%.

Technology on campus. 450 workstations in library, computer center. Online course registration, online library, helpline, wireless network available.

Student life. Freshman orientation: Mandatory. Preregistration for classes offered. Held numerous times prior to each semester. Available in an on-line format. **Activities:** Campus ministries, international student organizations, student government, Student Nurses Association, Phi Theta Kappa, Campus Crusade for Christ, Student Body Organization, Students for Community Outreach & Awareness, Kappa Beta Delta.

Athletics. Intramural: Basketball, bowling, football (non-tackle), softball, table tennis, volleyball. **Team name:** Pacers.

Student services. Adult student services, career counseling, student employment services, financial aid counseling, on-campus daycare, personal counseling, placement for graduates, veterans' counselor. **Physically disabled:** Services for visually, hearing impaired. **Transfer:** Transfer adviser, college fairs on campus for students transferring to 4-year colleges.

Contact. E-mail: admissions@northweststate.edu
Phone: (419) 267-1320 Toll-free number: (855) 267-5511
Fax: (419) 267-5604
Amanda Potts, Director of Admissions, Northwest State Community College, 22600 State Route 34, Archbold, OH 43502-9517

Ohio Business College: Hilliard
Hilliard, Ohio
www.ohiobusinesscollege.edu

▸ For-profit 2-year business and health science college
▸ Very large city
▸ Interview required

General. Accredited by ACICS. **Enrollment:** 150 degree-seeking undergraduates. **Degrees:** 12 associate awarded. **Calendar:** Differs by program. **Full-time faculty:** 6 total. **Part-time faculty:** 13 total.

Basis for selection. Open admission.

2015-2016 Annual costs. Books/supplies: $1,160. **Additional information:** Certificate programs: $3,255-$12,375, books and supplies $561-$3,240. Associate programs: $21,620-$25,380, books and supplies $5,820-$6,775.

Financial aid. Need-based: Work-study available nights, weekends and for part-time students.

Application procedures. Admission: No deadline. $25 fee.

Academics. Credit/placement by examination: AP, CLEP. **Support services:** Remedial instruction, study skills assistance, tutoring.

Majors. Health services: Massage therapy, medical assistant.

Contact. Phone: (614) 891-5030 Toll-free number: (800) 954-4274
Chris Brown, Admissions Director, Ohio Business College: Hilliard, 4525 Trueman Boulevard, Hilliard, OH 43026

Ohio Business College: Sandusky
Sandusky, Ohio
www.ohiobusinesscollege.edu   CB code: 3260

- For-profit 2-year business college
- Commuter campus in small city
- Interview required

General. Accredited by ACICS. **Enrollment:** 265 degree-seeking undergraduates. **Degrees:** 86 associate awarded. **Location:** 60 miles from Cleveland and Toledo. **Calendar:** Quarter, limited summer session. **Full-time faculty:** 6 total. **Part-time faculty:** 26 total.

Student profile. Among degree-seeking undergraduates, 29 enrolled as first-time, first-year students.

Part-time:	36%	25 or older:	60%
Women:	74%		

Transfer out. Colleges most students transferred to 2015: DeVry University, Franklin University, Kaplan University, National American University, Strayer University, Tiffin University.

Basis for selection. Open admission.

2015-2016 Annual costs. Certificate programs: $3,255-$12,375, books and supplies $561-$3,240. Associate programs: $21,620-$25,380, books and supplies $5,820-$6,775.

Financial aid. Need-based: Need-based aid available for part-time students. Work-study available nights, weekends and for part-time students.

Application procedures. Admission: No deadline. $25 fee. Application must be submitted on paper. Admission notification on a rolling basis. **Financial aid:** No deadline. FAFSA required.

Academics. Special study options: Independent study. Externships. License preparation in real estate. **Credit/placement by examination:** AP, CLEP, institutional tests. **Support services:** Remedial instruction, tutoring.

Majors. Business: Accounting, administrative services, banking/financial services, business admin, human resources. **Computer sciences:** Data entry, programming, web page design. **Engineering:** Software. **Health services:** Health information management, medical secretary.

Technology on campus. Wireless network available.

Student life. Freshman orientation: Mandatory. Preregistration for classes offered.

Contact. E-mail: sandusky@ohiobusinesscollege.edu
Phone: (419) 627-8345 Toll-free number: (888) 627-8345
Fax: (419) 627-1958
Brock Morgan, Director of Admissions, Ohio Business College: Sandusky, 5202 Timber Commons Drive, Sandusky, OH 44870

Ohio Business College: Sheffield
Sheffield Village, Ohio
www.ohiobusinesscollege.edu   CB code: 2470

- For-profit 2-year branch campus and business college
- Commuter campus in small city

General. Founded in 1903. Accredited by ACICS. **Enrollment:** 410 degree-seeking undergraduates. **Degrees:** 103 associate awarded. **Location:** 35 miles from Cleveland. **Calendar:** Quarter, extensive summer session. **Full-time faculty:** 6 total. **Part-time faculty:** 23 total.

Basis for selection. Open admission. Entrance examinations required of all applicants for placement purposes.

2015-2016 Annual costs. Books/supplies: $2,640. **Additional information:** Certificate programs: $3,255-$12,375, books and supplies $561-$3,240. Associate programs: $21,620-$25,380, books and supplies $5,820-$6,775.

Financial aid. Need-based: Need-based aid available for part-time students. Work-study available nights, weekends and for part-time students.

Application procedures. Admission: No deadline. $25 fee. Admission notification on a rolling basis. **Financial aid:** No deadline. FAFSA required. Applicants notified on a rolling basis.

Academics. All students exposed to extensive computer usage regardless of major. **Special study options:** Double major, independent study, internships. **Credit/placement by examination:** AP, CLEP, institutional tests. 80 credit hours maximum toward associate degree. **Support services:** Remedial instruction, tutoring.

Majors. Business: Accounting, administrative services, business admin, office technology. **Health services:** Medical secretary.

Technology on campus. 55 workstations in computer center.

Student life. Freshman orientation: Available. Preregistration for classes offered. **Activities:** Student government, student newspaper, Business Professionals of America.

Student services. Adult student services, career counseling, student employment services, placement for graduates, veterans' counselor. **Physically disabled:** Services for visually, hearing impaired. **Transfer:** Transfer adviser for students transferring to 4-year colleges.

Contact. E-mail: lorain@ohiobusinesscollege.edu
Phone: (440) 277-0021 Toll-free number: (888) 514-3126
Fax: (440) 277-7989
John Tobin, Admissions Manager, Ohio Business College: Sheffield, 5095 Waterford Drive, Sheffield Village, OH 44055

Ohio College of Massotherapy
Akron, Ohio
www.ocm.edu   CB code: 2985

- Private 2-year health science college
- Commuter campus in very large city

General. Accredited by ACCSC. **Enrollment:** 150 undergraduates. **Degrees:** 9 associate awarded. **Calendar:** Differs by program. **Part-time faculty:** 16 total. **Special facilities:** Massage and spa clinic.

Basis for selection. Open admission. **Home schooled:** State high school equivalency certificate required.

2015-2016 Annual costs. Associate program: Massage therapy tuition and fees $16,333, books and materials $395; Diploma program: Massage therapy tuition and fees $9988, books and materials $268.

Financial aid. Need-based: Work-study available nights, weekends and for part-time students.

Application procedures. Admission: Closing date 8/21. $25 fee. **Financial aid:** Priority date 10/1; no closing date.

Academics. Special study options: Distance learning. **Credit/placement by examination:** AP, CLEP. **Support services:** Reduced course load, tutoring.

Majors. Health services: Massage therapy.

Technology on campus. 4 workstations in computer center.

Student life. Freshman orientation: Mandatory. Preregistration for classes offered.

Contact. E-mail: admissions@ocm.edu
Phone: (330) 665-1084 Fax: (330) 665-5021
Margie Martens, Admissions/Marketing Manager, Ohio College of Massotherapy, 225 Heritage Woods Drive, Akron, OH 44321

Ohio State University Agricultural Technical Institute
Wooster, Ohio
www.ati.osu.edu   CB code: 1009

- Public 2-year agricultural and branch campus college
- Residential campus in large town

General. Founded in 1971. Regionally accredited. Additional campuses in Lima, Marion, Columbus, Newark, Mansfield. **Enrollment:** 722 degree-seeking undergraduates; 29 non-degree-seeking students. **Degrees:** 140 associate awarded. **ROTC:** Army, Naval, Air Force. **Location:** 30 miles from Akron, 60 miles from Cleveland. **Calendar:** Semester, limited summer session. **Full-time faculty:** 24 total; 17% minority, 29% women. **Part-time faculty:** 53 total; 9% minority, 36% women. **Class size:** 54% < 20, 37%

20-39, 4% 40-49, 5% 50-99. **Special facilities:** Arboretum, greenhouse conservatory, golf course, Grace Drake Learning Laboratory (working beef, sheep, swine, and crop facilities), equine facility. **Partnerships:** Formal partnerships with GM, Honda, GE, Goodyear, Honeywell, Dow Chemical.

Student profile. Among degree-seeking undergraduates, 331 enrolled as first-time, first-year students, 30 transferred in from other institutions.

Part-time:	9%	Hispanic/Latino:	1%
Out-of-state:	2%	Multi-racial, non-Hispanic:	1%
Women:	49%	25 or older:	6%
Asian American:	1%	Live on campus:	61%

Basis for selection. Open admission, but selective for out-of-state students. Out-of-state applicants evaluated on the basis of secondary school record, class rank, test scores. **Adult students:** SAT/ACT scores not required if out of high school 2 year(s) or more. **Home schooled:** May be required to provide GED.

High school preparation. College-preparatory program recommended. 19 units required; 22 recommended. Required and recommended units include English 4, mathematics 3-4, social studies 2-3, science 3 (laboratory 3), foreign language 2-3, computer science 1 and academic electives 1.

2015-2016 Annual costs. Tuition/fees: $7,104; $24,432 out-of-state. Room/board: $8,130. Books/supplies: $1,234. Personal expenses: $2,272.

2015-2016 Financial aid. All financial aid based on need. 300 full-time freshmen applied for aid; 222 deemed to have need; 218 received aid. Average need met was 51%. Average scholarship/grant was $4,856; average loan $3,912. 36% of total undergraduate aid awarded as scholarships/grants, 64% as loans/jobs. Need-based aid available for part-time students. Work-study available nights, weekends and for part-time students.

Application procedures. Admission: Closing date 6/1 (receipt date). $60 fee, may be waived for applicants with need. Admission notification on a rolling basis beginning on or about 11/15. Must reply by May 1 or within 3 week(s) if notified thereafter. **Financial aid:** Priority date 2/15; no closing date. FAFSA required. Applicants notified by 3/15; must reply by 5/1 or within 4 week(s) of notification.

Academics. Students often complete bachelor's degree on Columbus campus. **Special study options:** Cross-registration, double major, ESL, independent study, internships, student-designed major, study abroad. **Credit/placement by examination:** AP, CLEP, IB, institutional tests. 30 credit hours maximum toward associate degree. **Support services:** Learning center, reduced course load, remedial instruction, study skills assistance, tutoring, writing center.

Majors. Business: Business admin, restaurant/food services. **Conservation:** General, environmental science, environmental studies. **Education:** Agricultural. **General:** Power transmission.

Most popular majors. Agriculture 84%, engineering/engineering technologies 7%.

Technology on campus. 85 workstations in dormitories, library, computer center. Dormitories wired for high-speed internet access and linked to campus network. Commuter students can connect to campus network. Online course registration, online library, helpline, wireless network available.

Student life. Freshman orientation: Mandatory, $50 fee. Preregistration for classes offered. 1-day programs throughout the summer prior to enrollment. **Policies:** All first-time, first-year students must live on campus unless they live within a 25 mile radius of campus or meet one of the following exemptions: are married, have a child, or enroll with 30+ credits from a previous institution. **Housing:** Guaranteed on-campus for freshmen. Single-sex dorms, special housing for disabled, apartments, wellness housing available. $350 nonrefundable deposit, deadline 6/1. 2 or 3 bedroom apartments by gender. **Activities:** Campus Crusade for Christ.

Athletics. Intramural: Basketball, football (tackle), racquetball, softball, volleyball.

Student services. Adult student services, services for economically disadvantaged, financial aid counseling, health services, personal counseling. **Physically disabled:** Services for visually, speech, hearing impaired.

Contact. E-mail: askabuckeye@osu.edu
Phone: (330) 287-1327 Toll-free number: (800) 647-8283
Fax: (330) 287-1333
Ohio State University Agricultural Technical Institute, 1328 Dover Road, Wooster, OH 44691

Ohio Technical College
Cleveland, Ohio
www.ohiotech.edu   CB code: 2999

- For-profit 2-year technical and career college
- Commuter campus in large city

General. Accredited by ACCSC. **Enrollment:** 225 degree-seeking undergraduates. **Degrees:** 156 associate awarded. **Location:** 2 miles from downtown. **Calendar:** Continuous, extensive summer session. **Full-time faculty:** 70 total. **Part-time faculty:** 16 total. **Class size:** 100% 20-39.

Basis for selection. Open admission, but selective for some programs. Applicants must pass Wonderlic test to be admitted. High Performance & Racing Program also requires a personal interview with the department head. **Home schooled:** State high school equivalency certificate required.

2015-2016 Annual costs. Personal expenses: $1,837. **Additional information:** Diploma programs: range from $20,900- $29,700; Associates programs: range from $31,620-$33,420. Books, supplies, fees range depending on program level and course of study. All costs are subject to change.

Financial aid. Need-based: Work-study available nights, weekends and for part-time students.

Application procedures. Admission: No deadline. $100 fee. Admission notification on a rolling basis. **Financial aid:** No deadline.

Academics. Credit/placement by examination: AP, CLEP. **Support services:** Learning center, study skills assistance.

Technology on campus. 25 workstations in library, computer center.

Student life. Freshman orientation: Mandatory. Preregistration for classes offered. Campus visitations are held twice a month. These are usually for enrolled students, but are also open to those students looking for information on the programs offered. **Activities:** Student newspaper.

Athletics. Team name: Top Techs.

Student services. Student employment services, personal counseling, placement for graduates.

Contact. E-mail: info@ohiotechnicalcollege.com
Phone: (216) 881-1700 Toll-free number: (800) 322-7000
Fax: (216) 881-9145
Tom King, Admissions Director, Ohio Technical College, 1374 East 51st Street, Cleveland, OH 44103-1269

Ohio Valley College of Technology
East Liverpool, Ohio
www.ovct.edu   CB code: 5852

- For-profit 2-year junior and technical college
- Commuter campus in large town

General. Founded in 1886. Accredited by ACICS. **Enrollment:** 146 undergraduates. **Degrees:** 80 associate awarded. **Location:** 30 miles from Youngstown, 35 miles from Pittsburgh. **Calendar:** Semester, extensive summer session. **Full-time faculty:** 5 total. **Part-time faculty:** 16 total. **Class size:** 60% < 20, 40% 20-39.

Student profile.

Out-of-state:	13%	25 or older:	75%

Basis for selection. Class rank, GPA considered, entrance exam for Nursing Program.

2015-2016 Annual costs. Tuition/fees: $27,360.

Financial aid. All financial aid based on need. Need-based aid available for part-time students. Work-study available nights, weekends and for part-time students.

Application procedures. Admission: No deadline. $25 fee. Admission notification on a rolling basis. **Financial aid:** No deadline. FAFSA required. Applicants notified on a rolling basis; must reply within 6 week(s) of notification.

Academics. Special study options: Internships. License preparation in nursing. **Credit/placement by examination:** AP, CLEP, institutional tests. **Support services:** Reduced course load, study skills assistance, tutoring.

Majors. **Business:** Business admin. **Computer sciences:** Information technology. **Health services:** Dental assistant, medical secretary, nursing (RN), office assistant, pharmacy assistant.

Most popular majors. Business/marketing 9%, computer/information sciences 18%, health sciences 80%.

Technology on campus. 20 workstations in computer center. Wireless network available.

Student life. Freshman orientation: Mandatory. Preregistration for classes offered. **Activities:** Student newspaper.

Student services. Career counseling, student employment services, financial aid counseling, placement for graduates. **Transfer:** Transfer adviser for students transferring to 4-year colleges.

Contact. E-mail: info@ovct.edu
Phone: (330) 385-1070 Fax: (330) 385-4606
Chad Baker, Senior Admissions Representative, Ohio Valley College of Technology, 15258 State Route 170, East Liverpool, OH 43920-9585

Owens Community College
Toledo, Ohio
www.owens.edu   **CB code: 1643**

▶ Public 2-year community college
▶ Commuter campus in large city

General. Founded in 1966. Regionally accredited. Branch campus in Findlay. Learning Center in Downtown Toledo. **Enrollment:** 8,218 degree-seeking undergraduates; 1,120 non-degree-seeking students. **Degrees:** 1,345 associate awarded. **Location:** 6 miles from downtown Toledo. **Calendar:** Semester, limited summer session. **Full-time faculty:** 189 total; 21% have terminal degrees, 5% minority, 54% women. **Part-time faculty:** 1,070 total; 8% have terminal degrees, 7% minority, 52% women. **Class size:** 80% < 20, 20% 20-39, less than 1% 40-49. **Special facilities:** Center for Emergency Preparedness. **Partnerships:** Formal partnerships with John Deere, Caterpillar, General Motors Corporation.

Student profile. Among degree-seeking undergraduates, 1,652 enrolled as first-time, first-year students.

Part-time:	60%	Hispanic/Latino:	8%
Out-of-state:	3%	Multi-racial, non-Hispanic:	3%
Women:	59%	International:	1%
African American:	14%	25 or older:	32%
Asian American:	1%		

Transfer out. Colleges most students transferred to 2015: Bowling Green State University, Lourdes College, University of Findlay, University of Toledo.

Basis for selection. Open admission, but selective for some programs. Admission to health technologies, Peace Officer Academy, and early childhood education requires high school transcripts and test scores.

High school preparation. 20 units recommended. Recommended units include English 4, mathematics 4, social studies 2, history 1, science 3 (laboratory 1), computer science 1 and academic electives 4.

2015-2016 Annual costs. Tuition/fees: $4,414; $8,698 out-of-state. Per-credit charge: $153 in-state; $306 out-of-state. Books/supplies: $1,400. Personal expenses: $1,080.

Financial aid. Need-based: Need-based aid available for part-time students. Work-study available nights, weekends and for part-time students. **Non-need-based:** Scholarships awarded for academics, athletics, job skills, state residency. **Additional information:** Other types of financial aid available: federal family education loan program, private foundation loan (SCHELL).

Application procedures. Admission: No deadline. $20 fee. Admission notification on a rolling basis beginning on or about 8/15. February 1 application deadline for dental hygiene and physical therapist assistant programs. **Financial aid:** Priority date 3/31; no closing date. FAFSA required.

Academics. Special study options: Accelerated study, cooperative education, distance learning, double major, dual enrollment of high school students, ESL, honors, independent study, internships, study abroad, weekend college. License preparation in dental hygiene, nursing, paramedic, radiology, real estate. **Credit/placement by examination:** AP, CLEP, institutional tests. No limit placed upon number of credit hours student may obtain via proficiency exams as long as student has met graduation residency requirement. **Support services:** GED preparation and test center, learning center, pre-admission summer program, reduced course load, remedial instruction, study skills assistance, tutoring, writing center.

Majors. Business: General, accounting technology, executive assistant, logistics, office management, restaurant/food services, sales/distribution. **Computer sciences:** Applications programming, information technology, security. **Education:** Early childhood. **Health services:** Dental hygiene, dietetics, health information technology, management/clinical assistant, massage therapy, medical radiologic technology/radiation therapy, medical secretary, MRI technology, nuclear medical technology, nursing (RN), occupational therapy assistant, physical therapy assistant, sonography, surgical technology. **Protective services:** Law enforcement admin, police science. **Visual/performing arts:** Commercial photography, commercial/advertising art, music technology.

Most popular majors. Business/marketing 19%, engineering/engineering technologies 12%, health sciences 29%, liberal arts 15%, security/protective services 6%.

Technology on campus. 264 workstations in library, computer center. Commuter students can connect to campus network. Online course registration, online library, helpline, wireless network available.

Student life. Freshman orientation: Mandatory, $65 fee. Preregistration for classes offered. Three-hour session scheduled prior to start of semester. **Policies:** Code of Student Conduct provides guidelines for acceptable behavior. **Activities:** Bands, choral groups, dance, drama, international student organizations, literary magazine, music ensembles, musical theater, student government, student newspaper, Campus Activities Board, Global Connections, OCC Gay/Straight Alliance, Rotaract Club.

Athletics. NJCAA. **Intercollegiate:** Baseball M, basketball, golf M, soccer, softball W, volleyball W. **Intramural:** Basketball, bowling, football (non-tackle), golf, skiing, softball, table tennis, tennis, volleyball, weight lifting. **Team name:** Express.

Student services. Adult student services, career counseling, services for economically disadvantaged, student employment services, financial aid counseling, on-campus daycare, placement for graduates, veterans' counselor. **Physically disabled:** Services for visually, hearing impaired. **Transfer:** Pre-admission transcript evaluation for new students. Transfer adviser, college fairs on campus for students transferring to 4-year colleges.

Contact. Phone: (567) 661-7777 Toll-free number: (800) 466-9367 Fax: (567) 661-7418
Meghan Schmidbauer, Director, Admissions, Owens Community College, 30335 Oregon Road, Toledo, OH 43699-1947

PowerSport Institute
North Randall, Ohio
www.psi-now.com

▶ For-profit 2-year technical college
▶ Commuter campus in very large city
▶ Interview required

General. Regionally accredited; also accredited by ACCSC. **Enrollment:** 75 degree-seeking undergraduates; 106 non-degree-seeking students. **Degrees:** 31 associate awarded. **Location:** Located in Cleveland, Ohio. **Calendar:** Quarter. **Full-time faculty:** 16 total. **Class size:** 100% < 20.

Student profile. Among degree-seeking undergraduates, 100% enrolled in a vocational program.

Transfer out. 2% of students enrolled in the transfer program go on to 4-year colleges.

Basis for selection. Open admission. **Home schooled:** Transcript of courses and grades required.

2016-2017 Annual costs. Tuition/fees (projected): $27,000.

2015-2016 Financial aid. Need-based: Average need met was 100%. Average scholarship/grant was $2,205. 56% of total undergraduate aid awarded as scholarships/grants, 44% as loans/jobs. Work-study available nights, weekends and for part-time students. **Non-need-based:** Scholarships awarded for academics.

Application procedures. Admission: No deadline. $50 fee. Application must be submitted on paper. Admission notification on a rolling basis. **Financial aid:** No deadline. FAFSA, institutional form required. Applicants notified on a rolling basis starting 1/15.

Academics. Credit/placement by examination: AP, CLEP, institutional tests. **Support services:** Study skills assistance, tutoring.

Technology on campus. 3 workstations in library, computer center.

Student life. Freshman orientation: Mandatory. Preregistration for classes offered. **Housing:** Apartments available. $250 nonrefundable deposit. Collegiate Housing Services at apartments in surrounding suburbs. **Activities:** Student government.

Student services. Career counseling, student employment services, financial aid counseling, personal counseling, placement for graduates. **Transfer:** Pre-admission transcript evaluation for new students.

Contact. E-mail: tking@ohiotech.edu
Phone: (216) 881-1700 Toll-free number: (800) 322-7000
Fax: (216) 881-9145
Tom King, Director of Admissions, PowerSport Institute, 21210 Emery Road, North Randall, OH 44128

Remington College: Cleveland
Cleveland, Ohio
http://cleveland.remingtoncollege.edu   CB code: 3154

- Private 2-year technical and career college
- Very large city
- Interview required

General. Accredited by ACCSC. **Enrollment:** 911 undergraduates. **Degrees:** 32 associate awarded. **Location:** 8 miles from Cleveland. **Calendar:** Differs by program. **Full-time faculty:** 23 total. **Part-time faculty:** 17 total.

Basis for selection. Wonderlic SLE exam required for some programs. The Wonderlic SLE exam will be used as the sole acceptable entrance exam for all applicants seeking admission. The required passing score for the Wonderlic exam will be 17 or higher for the Computer and Network Administration associate degree program, 13 or higher for all other associate degrees, and 12 or higher for all diploma programs. Applicants will be allowed to take the entrance exam a maximum of three times.

2015-2016 Annual costs. Diploma programs: $15,995-$21,700. Associate programs: business administration $33,900; criminal justice $33,900; physical therapist assistant $42,900.

Financial aid. Need-based: Work-study available nights, weekends and for part-time students.

Application procedures. Admission: No deadline. $50 fee. **Financial aid:** No deadline.

Academics. Special study options: Independent study. Externships. **Credit/placement by examination:** AP, CLEP. **Support services:** Learning center.

Majors. Business: Business admin. **Computer sciences:** Networking.

Technology on campus. Online library available.

Student services. Career counseling, financial aid counseling, placement for graduates.

Contact. E-mail: admissions@remingtoncollege.edu
Phone: (216) 502-3035
Patrick Resetar, Campus President, Remington College: Cleveland, 14445 Broadway Avenue, Cleveland, OH 44125

Rosedale Bible College
Irwin, Ohio
www.rosedale.edu   CB code: 3936

- Private 2-year Bible and junior college affiliated with the Mennonite Church
- Residential campus in rural community

General. Accredited by ABHE. **Enrollment:** 56 degree-seeking undergraduates. **Degrees:** 13 associate awarded. **Location:** 20 miles from Columbus. **Calendar:** Semester. **Full-time faculty:** 1 total. **Part-time faculty:** 7 total; 43% women. **Class size:** 62% < 20, 38% 20-39.

Student profile. Among degree-seeking undergraduates, 11 transferred in from other institutions.

Basis for selection. Open admission. **Home schooled:** Transcript of courses and grades required.

2015-2016 Annual costs. Tuition/fees: $8,311. Per-credit charge: $266. Room/board: $5,650.

Financial aid. Need-based: Need-based aid available for part-time students. Work-study available nights, weekends and for part-time students. **Non-need-based:** Scholarships awarded for academics, leadership, religious affiliation.

Application procedures. Admission: No deadline. $50 fee. Admission notification on a rolling basis. **Financial aid:** No deadline. FAFSA, institutional form required. Applicants notified on a rolling basis.

Academics. Special study options: Double major, dual enrollment of high school students, independent study, study abroad. **Credit/placement by examination:** AP, CLEP. **Support services:** Reduced course load, tutoring.

Majors. Theology: Bible.

Technology on campus. 8 workstations in library, computer center. Wireless network available.

Student life. Freshman orientation: Mandatory. Preregistration for classes offered. **Policies:** Religious observance required. **Housing:** Guaranteed on-campus for all undergraduates. Single-sex dorms, apartments available. **Activities:** Campus ministries, choral groups, drama, music ensembles, student government.

Athletics. Intramural: Basketball M, ultimate frisbee, volleyball.

Student services. Chaplain/spiritual director, financial aid counseling, health services. **Transfer:** Pre-admission transcript evaluation for new students.

Contact. E-mail: admissions@rosedale.edu
Phone: (740) 857-1311 Fax: (877) 857-1312
Darnell Brenneman, Enrollment Services Coordinator, Rosedale Bible College, 2270 Rosedale Road, Irwin, OH 43029

School of Advertising Art
Kettering, Ohio
www.saa.edu   CB code: 5953

- For-profit 2-year graphic design art college.
- Commuter campus in small city
- Interview required

General. Accredited by ACCSC. **Enrollment:** 173 undergraduates. **Degrees:** 56 associate awarded. **Location:** 5 miles from Dayton. **Calendar:** Semester. **Full-time faculty:** 8 total; 38% minority, 25% women. **Part-time faculty:** 5 total. **Class size:** 100% 20-39. **Special facilities:** Memberships to the local YMCA and the Dayton Art Museum.

Student profile.

Out-of-state:	4%	25 or older:	4%

Transfer out. Colleges most students transferred to 2015: Art Institute of Pittsburgh, Art Institute of Atlanta, Columbus College of Art and Design, American Inter-Continental University of London, Art Institute of San Francisco.

Basis for selection. Portfolio and creative potential most important with acceptable GPA. SAT or ACT recommended. Portfolio of 8 to 12 pieces of own artwork required. Depending on GPA and attendance, personal essay and 2 letters of recommendation may be required. **Home schooled:** State high school equivalency certificate required. Proof of completion of high school requirements required.

High school preparation. Recommended units include English 4 and visual/performing arts 3. 3 art units recommended.

2016-2017 Annual costs. Tuition/fees (projected): $31,311. Books/supplies: $565.

Financial aid. Need-based: Work-study available nights, weekends and for part-time students. **Non-need-based:** Scholarships awarded for academics, art, leadership, minority status.

Application procedures. Admission: No deadline. $100 fee, may be waived for applicants with need. Admission notification on a rolling basis. Students may pay discounted enrollment fee of $50 (normal fee is $100) if they elect to enroll by January 1. **Financial aid:** Priority date 7/1; no closing date. FAFSA required. Applicants notified on a rolling basis starting 4/1; must reply by 7/1 or within 1 week(s) of notification.

Academics. Special study options: Internships. **Credit/placement by examination:** AP, CLEP. **Support services:** Tutoring.

Majors. Communications: Advertising. **Computer sciences:** Computer graphics. **Visual/performing arts:** Commercial/advertising art.

Technology on campus. PC or laptop required. Repair service, student web hosting, wireless network available.

Student life. Freshman orientation: Available. Preregistration for classes offered. Four-hour session held on a Saturday in the summer. **Activities:** Student government.

Student services. Career counseling, financial aid counseling, personal counseling, placement for graduates. **Transfer:** Re-entry adviser, pre-admission transcript evaluation for new students. Transfer adviser for students transferring to 4-year colleges.

Contact. E-mail: admissions@saa.edu
Phone: (937) 294-0592 Toll-free number: (877) 300-9866
Fax: (937) 294-5869
Mariesa Bloom, Director of Admissions, School of Advertising Art, 1725 East David Road, Kettering, OH 45440-1612

Sinclair Community College
Dayton, Ohio — CB member
www.sinclair.edu — CB code: 1720

- Public 2-year community college
- Commuter campus in small city

General. Founded in 1887. Regionally accredited. **Enrollment:** 16,275 degree-seeking undergraduates; 1,965 non-degree-seeking students. **Degrees:** 1,658 associate awarded. **ROTC:** Army, Air Force. **Location:** 50 miles from Cincinnati, 70 miles from Columbus. **Calendar:** Semester, extensive summer session. **Full-time faculty:** 356 total; 87% have terminal degrees, 18% minority, 56% women. **Part-time faculty:** 975 total; 77% have terminal degrees, 12% minority, 57% women. **Class size:** 61% < 20, 39% 20-39, less than 1% 40-49, less than 1% 50-99. **Special facilities:** Art galleries, theater, unmanned aerial systems research center. **Partnerships:** Formal partnerships with eight area high schools.

Student profile. Among degree-seeking undergraduates, 32% enrolled in a transfer program, 53% enrolled in a vocational program, 4,585 enrolled as first-time, first-year students.

Part-time:	64%	Hispanic/Latino:	3%
Out-of-state:	2%	Native American:	1%
Women:	57%	Multi-racial, non-Hispanic:	3%
African American:	13%	International:	2%
Asian American:	1%	25 or older:	53%

Transfer out. Colleges most students transferred to 2015: Wright State University, University of Cincinnati, University of Dayton, Ohio State University, Miami University.

Basis for selection. Open admission, but selective for some programs. Admission to allied health programs, paralegal program, tooling and machining program, early childhood education all based on placement test scores and/or high school grades and specific program criteria. Interview required for some allied health programs. **Adult students:** Accuplacer placement required, if student does not have valid transfer credit, ACT, SAT, or COMPASS scores.

2015-2016 Annual costs. Tuition/fees: $2,971; $4,388 out-of-district; $8,472 out-of-state. Per-credit charge: $99 in-district; $146 out-of-district; $282 out-of-state. Books/supplies: $1,140. Personal expenses: $1,350.

Financial aid. Need-based: Need-based aid available for part-time students. Work-study available nights, weekends and for part-time students. **Non-need-based:** Scholarships awarded for academics, alumni affiliation, art, athletics, leadership, minority status, music/drama, state residency.

Application procedures. Admission: No deadline. No application fee. Admission notification on a rolling basis. **Financial aid:** Priority date 5/1; no closing date. FAFSA required. Applicants notified on a rolling basis starting 4/1.

Academics. Special study options: Accelerated study, cooperative education, cross-registration, distance learning, dual enrollment of high school students, ESL, honors, independent study, internships, liberal arts/career combination, student-designed major. License preparation in aviation, dental hygiene, nursing, occupational therapy, paramedic, physical therapy, radiology, real estate. **Credit/placement by examination:** AP, CLEP, institutional tests. **Support services:** Learning center, pre-admission summer program, reduced course load, remedial instruction, study skills assistance, tutoring, writing center.

Majors. Biology: General. **Business:** Accounting, business admin, entrepreneurial studies, event planning, hotel/motel admin, logistics, office technology, real estate, tourism/travel. **Communications:** Advertising, communications/speech/rhetoric, digital media. **Computer sciences:** Networking, programming, security, support specialist, web page design. **Education:** Kindergarten/preschool, physical. **Engineering:** General, industrial. **English:** Creative writing, English lit. **Foreign languages:** General, sign language interpretation. **General:** Electrician. **Health services:** Clinical lab technology, dental hygiene, dietetics, EMT paramedic, health care admin, health information management, health information technology, medical assistant, mental health services, nursing (RN), occupational therapy assistant, physical therapy assistant, radiologic technology/medical imaging, respiratory therapy technology, substance abuse counseling, surgical technology, veterinary technology/assistant. **History:** General. **Human services:** Social work. **Liberal arts:** Arts/sciences. **Math:** General. **Parks/recreation:** Exercise sciences. **Physical sciences:** Chemistry. **Protective services:** Computer forensics, corrections, fire safety technology, fire services admin, police science. **Psychology:** General. **Social sciences:** Geography, political science, sociology. **Visual/performing arts:** Art, commercial/advertising art, dramatic, interior design, music theory/composition, theater design.

Most popular majors. Business/marketing 12%, computer/information sciences 6%, engineering/engineering technologies 9%, health sciences 31%, liberal arts 11%, visual/performing arts 6%.

Technology on campus. 1,000 workstations in library, computer center, student center. Commuter students can connect to campus network. Online course registration, online library, helpline, repair service, wireless network available.

Student life. Freshman orientation: Available. Preregistration for classes offered. Required for degree- and certificate-seeking students. **Activities:** Bands, campus ministries, choral groups, dance, drama, international student organizations, music ensembles, Model UN, musical theater, opera, student government, student newspaper, African American cultural club, Native American cultural club, Appalachian club, College Democrats, College Republicans, Campus Bible Fellowship, Muslim student association, Phi Theta Kappa (honorary club), global awareness and action club.

Athletics. NJCAA. **Intercollegiate:** Baseball M, basketball, softball W, volleyball W. **Intramural:** Basketball, football (non-tackle), soccer, volleyball. **Team name:** Tartan Pride.

Student services. Adult student services, alcohol/substance abuse counseling, chaplain/spiritual director, career counseling, services for economically disadvantaged, student employment services, financial aid counseling, minority student services, on-campus daycare, personal counseling, placement for graduates, veterans' counselor, women's services. **Physically disabled:** Services for visually, speech, hearing impaired. **Transfer:** Pre-admission transcript evaluation for new students. Transfer adviser, college fairs on campus for students transferring to 4-year colleges.

Contact. E-mail: newstudentenrollment@sinclair.edu
Phone: (937) 512-3000 Toll-free number: (800) 315-3000
Fax: (937) 512-4320
Janet Schmitt, Director of Strategic Enrollment Management, Sinclair Community College, 444 West Third Street, Dayton, OH 45402-1460

Southern State Community College
Hillsboro, Ohio
www.sscc.edu — CB code: 1752

- Public 2-year community college
- Commuter campus in small town

General. Founded in 1975. Regionally accredited. **Enrollment:** 2,218 degree-seeking undergraduates. **Degrees:** 330 associate awarded. **Location:** 60 miles from Cincinnati, 55 miles from Columbus. **Calendar:** Semester, limited summer session. **Full-time faculty:** 58 total; 17% have terminal degrees, 2% minority, 45% women. **Part-time faculty:** 121 total; 11% have terminal degrees, 2% minority, 47% women. **Class size:** 79% < 20, 21% 20-39, less than 1% 40-49.

Basis for selection. Open admission, but selective for some programs. Special requirements for nursing, respiratory therapy, Allied health programs. Interview required for nursing program. **Learning Disabled:** If modifications requested, appointment with Disabilities Service Coordinator required.

2015-2016 Annual costs. Tuition/fees: $4,364; $7,938 out-of-state. Per-credit charge: $162 in-state; $306 out-of-state. Books/supplies: $2,067.

Financial aid. Need-based: Need-based aid available for part-time students. Work-study available nights, weekends and for part-time students. **Non-need-based:** Scholarships awarded for academics, art, athletics, music/drama.

Application procedures. Admission: No deadline. No application fee. Admission notification on a rolling basis. **Financial aid:** Priority date 7/1, closing date 9/1. FAFSA, institutional form required. Applicants notified by 4/15; must reply within 2 week(s) of notification.

Academics. Special study options: Cross-registration, distance learning, dual enrollment of high school students, internships, liberal arts/career combination, student-designed major. License preparation in nursing, real estate. **Credit/placement by examination:** AP, CLEP, institutional tests. 30 credit hours maximum toward associate degree. **Support services:** GED preparation and test center, learning center, remedial instruction, study skills assistance, tutoring.

Majors. Business: General, accounting technology, administrative services, business admin, entrepreneurial studies, real estate. **Computer sciences:** Applications programming, programming, systems analysis. **Education:** Early childhood, teacher assistance. **Health services:** Medical assistant, nursing (RN), respiratory therapy technology, substance abuse counseling. **Liberal arts:** Arts/sciences. **Protective services:** Corrections, police science.

Most popular majors. Business/marketing 12%, computer/information sciences 8%, health sciences 33%, liberal arts 33%.

Technology on campus. 452 workstations in library, computer center. Commuter students can connect to campus network. Online course registration, online library, helpline, wireless network available.

Student life. Freshman orientation: Mandatory. Preregistration for classes offered. **Activities:** Bands, choral groups, drama.

Athletics. USCAA. **Intercollegiate:** Basketball, soccer M, softball W, volleyball W. **Team name:** Patriots.

Student services. Career counseling, student employment services, financial aid counseling, on-campus daycare, personal counseling, placement for graduates. **Physically disabled:** Services for visually, speech, hearing impaired. **Transfer:** Transfer adviser, college fairs on campus for students transferring to 4-year colleges.

Contact. E-mail: info@sscc.edu
Phone: (937) 393-3431 ext. 2607 Fax: (937) 393-6682
Wendy Johnson, Director of Admissions, Southern State Community College, 100 Hobart Drive, Hillsboro, OH 45133

Stark State College
North Canton, Ohio
www.starkstate.edu
CB code: 1688

❧ Public 2-year community college
❧ Commuter campus in small city

General. Founded in 1970. Regionally accredited. **Enrollment:** 8,959 degree-seeking undergraduates; 3,686 non-degree-seeking students. **Degrees:** 1,195 associate awarded. **Location:** 50 miles from Cleveland. **Calendar:** Semester, extensive summer session. **Full-time faculty:** 204 total. **Part-time faculty:** 404 total. **Special facilities:** LG fuel cell systems.

Student profile. Among degree-seeking undergraduates, 1,559 enrolled as first-time, first-year students.

Part-time:	64%	Asian American:	2%
Out-of-state:	1%	Hispanic/Latino:	1%
Women:	60%	Multi-racial, non-Hispanic:	3%
African American:	14%	25 or older:	38%

Basis for selection. Open admission, but selective for some programs. Special requirements for allied health programs. **Home schooled:** Transcript of courses and grades, state high school equivalency certificate required. Completion of ACT or COMPASS testing. **Learning Disabled:** All students should meet with disability services coordinator.

High school preparation. College-preparatory program recommended. Recommended units include English 4, mathematics 4, social studies 3, science 3 and foreign language 1.

2015-2016 Annual costs. Tuition/fees: $4,608; $7,338 out-of-state. Per-credit charge: $117 in-state; $208 out-of-state. Books/supplies: $1,100. Personal expenses: $2,874.

2014-2015 Financial aid. All financial aid based on need. 41% of total undergraduate aid awarded as scholarships/grants, 59% as loans/jobs. Need-based aid available for part-time students. Work-study available nights, weekends and for part-time students.

Application procedures. Admission: Priority date 6/1; no deadline. $95 fee. Admission notification on a rolling basis. **Financial aid:** Priority date 5/1; no closing date. FAFSA, institutional form required. Applicants notified on a rolling basis starting 4/1; must reply within 4 week(s) of notification.

Academics. Special study options: Accelerated study, cooperative education, cross-registration, distance learning, double major, dual enrollment of high school students, independent study, internships, liberal arts/career combination, student-designed major, weekend college. License preparation in dental hygiene, nursing, occupational therapy, paramedic, physical therapy. **Credit/placement by examination:** AP, CLEP, institutional tests. 12 credit hours maximum toward associate degree. **Support services:** Learning center, pre-admission summer program, reduced course load, remedial instruction, study skills assistance, tutoring, writing center.

Majors. Architecture: Environmental design, urban/community planning. **Business:** General, accounting, accounting technology, accounting/business management, accounting/finance, administrative services, business admin, communications, construction management, e-commerce, executive assistant, hospitality admin, international, logistics, management information systems, market research, marketing, office management, office technology, operations, sales/distribution, taxation. **Computer sciences:** General, applications programming, computer graphics, computer science, data entry, data processing, database management, information systems, information technology, networking, programming, security, systems analysis, web page design, webmaster, word processing. **Conservation:** Environmental studies. **Education:** Early childhood. **Engineering:** Architectural, civil, electrical, environmental, software. **Health services:** Clinical lab assistant, clinical lab technology, dental hygiene, health information technology, massage therapy, medical assistant, nursing (RN), occupational therapy assistant, office assistant, physical therapy assistant, respiratory therapy assistant, respiratory therapy technology. **Liberal arts:** Arts/sciences. **Math:** General. **Protective services:** Firefighting. **Social sciences:** General. **Work/family studies:** Aging, child care service.

Most popular majors. Business/marketing 13%, computer/information sciences 7%, engineering/engineering technologies 11%, English 11%, health sciences 27%, liberal arts 15%, public administration/social services 6%.

Technology on campus. 1,875 workstations in computer center, student center. Commuter students can connect to campus network. Online course registration, online library, helpline, wireless network available.

Student life. Freshman orientation: Mandatory. Preregistration for classes offered. Half-day prior to all semesters. Evening sessions are 2 hours. **Activities:** Campus ministries, literary magazine, student newspaper, Bible study group, Minority Awareness Association, Phi Theta Kappa.

Athletics. Team name: Spartans.

Student services. Adult student services, chaplain/spiritual director, career counseling, services for economically disadvantaged, student employment services, financial aid counseling, minority student services, on-campus daycare, personal counseling, placement for graduates, veterans' counselor. **Physically disabled:** Services for visually, speech, hearing impaired. **Transfer:** Pre-admission transcript evaluation for new students. Transfer adviser, college fairs on campus for students transferring to 4-year colleges.

Contact. E-mail: info@starkstate.edu
Phone: (330) 494-6170 ext. 4228 Toll-free number: (800) 797-8275
Fax: (330) 497-6313
J. P. Cooney, Executive Director, Stark State College, 6200 Frank Avenue NW, North Canton, OH 44720

Stautzenberger College
Maumee, Ohio
www.sctoday.edu
CB code: 2487

❧ For-profit 2-year technical and career college
❧ Commuter campus in large town
❧ Interview required

General. Founded in 1928. Accredited by ACICS. **Enrollment:** 708 undergraduates. **Degrees:** 93 associate awarded. **Location:** Suburb of Toledo, 50 miles from Detroit, 120 miles from Cleveland. **Calendar:** Quarter, extensive summer session. **Full-time faculty:** 12 total. **Part-time faculty:** 80 total. **Class size:** 85% < 20, 15% 20-39. **Special facilities:** Veterinary technician labs, medical assisting labs, practical nursing labs, massage therapy clinic. **Partnerships:** Formal partnership with Microsoft IT Academy.

Basis for selection. Open admission, but selective for some programs. Campus visit and completion of program questionnaire required. **Learning Disabled:** Any special accommodations must be requested in writing with appropriate documentation. Approval needed before acceptance.

2015-2016 Annual costs. Tuition/fees: $5,850; $10,350 out-of-state. Per-credit charge: . Books/supplies: $300. Personal expenses: $2,619.

Financial aid. All financial aid based on need. Need-based aid available for part-time students. Work-study available nights, weekends and for part-time students.

Application procedures. Admission: No deadline. $25 fee. Application must be submitted on paper. Admission notification on a rolling basis. **Financial aid:** No deadline. FAFSA required. Applicants notified on a rolling basis.

Academics. Special study options: Distance learning, double major, internships, weekend college. License preparation in real estate. **Credit/placement by examination:** AP, CLEP. **Support services:** Learning center, study skills assistance, tutoring.

Majors. Business: Accounting, accounting technology, banking/financial services, business admin, entrepreneurial studies, office technology. **Computer sciences:** Data entry, LAN/WAN management, networking, web page design. **Health services:** Insurance coding, massage therapy, medical assistant, medical secretary, medical transcription, receptionist, veterinary technology/assistant.

Technology on campus. 200 workstations in library, computer center.

Student life. Freshman orientation: Available. Preregistration for classes offered.

Student services. Financial aid counseling, placement for graduates, veterans' counselor. **Transfer:** Pre-admission transcript evaluation for new students.

Contact. E-mail: admissions@stautzenberger.com
Phone: (419) 866-0261 Toll-free number: (800) 552-5099
Fax: (419) 867-9821
Amanda Boyd, Director of Admission, Stautzenberger College, 1796 Indian Wood Circle, Maumee, OH 43537-4007

Stautzenberger College: Brecksville
Brecksville, Ohio
www.sctoday.edu

▶ For-profit 2-year career college
▶ Commuter campus in large town
▶ Interview required

General. Accredited by ACICS. **Enrollment:** 335 undergraduates. **Degrees:** 67 associate awarded. **Location:** 15 miles from Cleveland. **Calendar:** Quarter, extensive summer session. **Full-time faculty:** 11 total; 36% have terminal degrees, 82% women. **Part-time faculty:** 47 total; 26% have terminal degrees. **Class size:** 85% < 20, 15% 20-39.

Transfer out. Colleges most students transferred to 2015: Cuyahoga Community College, Stautzenberger College Toledo, Lorain County Community College, Kent State University.

Basis for selection. Open admission. **Home schooled:** Interview required.

High school preparation. College-preparatory program recommended.

2015-2016 Annual costs. Tuition/fees: $11,070. Books/supplies: $1,950. Personal expenses: $4,086.

Financial aid. All financial aid based on need. Need-based aid available for part-time students. Work-study available nights, weekends and for part-time students.

Application procedures. Admission: No deadline. $35 fee. Admission notification on a rolling basis. **Financial aid:** No deadline. FAFSA required. Applicants notified on a rolling basis.

Academics. Special study options: Distance learning, internships. **Credit/placement by examination:** AP, CLEP, institutional tests. **Support services:** Reduced course load, remedial instruction, study skills assistance, tutoring, writing center.

Majors. Health services: Clinical lab technology, office admin, sonography, surgical technology, veterinary technology/assistant.

Most popular majors. Health sciences 87%, legal studies 10%.

Technology on campus. PC or laptop required. 45 workstations in library, computer center. Commuter students can connect to campus network. Online course registration, online library, helpline, wireless network available.

Student life. Freshman orientation: Mandatory. Preregistration for classes offered. **Activities:** Student government.

Student services. Adult student services, career counseling, student employment services, financial aid counseling, personal counseling, placement for graduates. **Physically disabled:** Services for visually, speech, hearing impaired. **Transfer:** Pre-admission transcript evaluation for new students.

Contact. E-mail: carvay@stautzenberger.com
Phone: (440) 838-1999 Fax: (440) 838-0960
John Girard, Director, Stautzenberger College: Brecksville, 8001 Katherine Boulevard, Brecksville, OH 44141

Terra State Community College
Fremont, Ohio   **CB member**
www.terra.edu   **CB code: 0365**

▶ Public 2-year community and technical college
▶ Commuter campus in large town

General. Founded in 1968. Regionally accredited. **Enrollment:** 2,901 undergraduates. **Degrees:** 281 associate awarded. **Location:** 33 miles from Toledo, 86 miles from Columbus. **Calendar:** Semester, limited summer session.

Transfer out. Colleges most students transferred to 2015: Bowling Green State University, University of Toledo, Owens Community College, Ohio State University, Tiffin University.

Basis for selection. Open admission.

High school preparation. Recommended units include English 4, mathematics 3, social studies 3 and science 3. Algebra recommended for engineering and computer programming applicants.

2015-2016 Annual costs. Tuition/fees: $4,284; $8,568 out-of-state. Per-credit charge: $133 in-state; $217 out-of-state. Books/supplies: $1,350. Personal expenses: $150.

Financial aid. Need-based: Need-based aid available for part-time students. Work-study available nights, weekends and for part-time students. **Non-need-based:** Scholarships awarded for academics.

Application procedures. Admission: No deadline. No application fee. Admission notification on a rolling basis. **Financial aid:** Priority date 5/1; no closing date. FAFSA, institutional form required. Applicants notified on a rolling basis starting 5/15.

Academics. Special study options: Accelerated study, cooperative education, distance learning, double major, dual enrollment of high school students, honors, independent study, internships, student-designed major, weekend college. Bachelor's degree programs available on campus. License preparation in real estate. **Credit/placement by examination:** AP, CLEP, institutional tests. **Support services:** Learning center, reduced course load, remedial instruction, study skills assistance, tutoring, writing center.

Majors. Biology: General. **Business:** General, accounting, banking/financial services, business admin, executive assistant, hospitality admin, marketing, operations, real estate. **Communications technology:** Animation/special effects, desktop publishing. **Computer sciences:** Data processing, networking, programming, web page design. **Education:** General, kindergarten/preschool. **Engineering:** General. **English:** English lit. **Foreign languages:** Translation. **Health services:** Health care admin, health information management, health information technology, insurance coding, management/clinical assistant, medical assistant, medical secretary, nursing (RN), office assistant. **History:** General. **Human services:** Social work. **Liberal arts:** Arts/sciences, humanities. **Math:** General. **Physical sciences:** Chemistry, physics. **Protective services:** Police science. **Psychology:** General. **Social sciences:** Economics. **Visual/performing arts:** Art history/conservation, jazz, music, music management, music performance, music technology, studio arts.

Most popular majors. Business/marketing 14%, computer/information sciences 10%, engineering/engineering technologies 21%, health sciences 25%, liberal arts 6%, security/protective services 6%.

Technology on campus. 299 workstations in library, computer center. Commuter students can connect to campus network. Online course registration, online library, helpline, wireless network available.

Student life. Freshman orientation: Mandatory. Preregistration for classes offered. **Activities:** Bands, choral groups, music ensembles, student government, Phi Theta Kappa, Koinonia, Society of Plastic Engineers.

Athletics. NJCAA. **Team name:** ThunderCats.

Student services. Career counseling, student employment services, personal counseling, placement for graduates, veterans' counselor. **Physically disabled:** Services for visually, speech, hearing impaired. **Transfer:** Re-entry adviser, pre-admission transcript evaluation for new students. Transfer center, transfer adviser, college fairs on campus for students transferring to 4-year colleges.

Contact. E-mail: admissions@terra.edu
Phone: (419) 559-2349 Toll-free number: (866) 288-3772 ext. 2349
Fax: (419) 334-9035
Kristen Taylor, Admissions Director, Terra State Community College, 2830 Napoleon Road, Fremont, OH 43420-9600

Trumbull Business College
Warren, Ohio
www.trumbull.edu
CB code: 3270

- For-profit 2-year business college
- Commuter campus in large town

General. Accredited by ACICS. **Enrollment:** 158 degree-seeking undergraduates. **Degrees:** 69 associate awarded. **Calendar:** Quarter.

Basis for selection. Open admission. **Home schooled:** Transcript of courses and grades required.

2015-2016 Annual costs. Tuition/fees: $11,340. Per-credit charge: $252. Books/supplies: $1,750.

Financial aid. Need-based: Need-based aid available for part-time students. Work-study available nights, weekends and for part-time students.

Application procedures. Admission: No deadline. $75 fee. Admission notification on a rolling basis. **Financial aid:** FAFSA required.

Academics. Special study options: Distance learning. **Credit/placement by examination:** AP, CLEP. **Support services:** Tutoring.

Majors. Business: Accounting, administrative services, business admin, office technology. **Health services:** Health information technology, medical assistant. **Visual/performing arts:** Digital arts.

Technology on campus. 100 workstations in library, computer center. Online library, wireless network available.

Student life. Freshman orientation: Mandatory. Preregistration for classes offered.

Student services. Career counseling, financial aid counseling, placement for graduates.

Contact. E-mail: info@trumbull.edu
Phone: (330) 369-3200
Trumbull Business College, 3200 Ridge Road, Warren, OH 44484

University of Akron: Wayne College
Orrville, Ohio
www.wayne.uakron.edu
CB code: 1892

- Public 2-year branch campus and junior college
- Commuter campus in small town

General. Founded in 1972. Regionally accredited. **Enrollment:** 2,604 undergraduates. **Degrees:** 65 associate awarded. **ROTC:** Army, Air Force. **Location:** 35 miles from Akron. **Calendar:** Semester, limited summer session. **Full-time faculty:** 24 total; 62% have terminal degrees, 8% minority, 54% women. **Part-time faculty:** 162 total; 17% have terminal degrees, 7%

minority, 48% women. **Class size:** 64% < 20, 33% 20-39, 2% 40-49, less than 1% 50-99. **Special facilities:** Nature trail, arboretum, wetlands, distance learning room, farmhouse.

Transfer out. Colleges most students transferred to 2015: Ashland University, Kent State, Cleveland State, Ohio State, Ohio University.

Basis for selection. Open admission. **Adult students:** SAT/ACT scores not required if applicant over 24. **Home schooled:** Recommend completion of GED.

High school preparation. Recommended units include English 4, mathematics 3, social studies 3, science 3 and foreign language 2.

2015-2016 Annual costs. Tuition/fees: $6,116; $13,542 out-of-state. Per-credit charge: $248 in-state; $526 out-of-state. Books/supplies: $900. Personal expenses: $3,066.

Financial aid. Need-based: Need-based aid available for part-time students. Work-study available nights, weekends and for part-time students. **Non-need-based:** Scholarships awarded for academics, art, athletics, leadership, minority status, music/drama, state residency. **Additional information:** All financial aid processed through University of Akron.

Application procedures. Admission: $45 fee, may be waived for applicants with need. Admission notification on a rolling basis. **Financial aid:** Closing date 3/15. FAFSA, institutional form required. Applicants notified on a rolling basis starting 4/15.

Academics. First 2 years of general bachelor's degree classes available for students who plan to continue at University of Akron or other colleges and universities. Paraprofessional and technical programs (associates and certificates) available in business, industry, public services occupation areas. **Special study options:** Cooperative education, cross-registration, distance learning, dual enrollment of high school students, honors, independent study, internships, liberal arts/career combination, student-designed major, weekend college. Bachelor's degree programs available on campus. **Credit/placement by examination:** AP, CLEP, institutional tests. **Support services:** Learning center, remedial instruction, study skills assistance, tutoring, writing center.

Majors. Business: General, accounting, administrative services, business admin, management information systems, marketing, office management, office technology. **Computer sciences:** Applications programming, data processing, networking. **Health services:** Health care admin, medical assistant, medical radiologic technology/radiation therapy, medical secretary, respiratory therapy technology, surgical technology. **Liberal arts:** Arts/sciences.

Most popular majors. Business/marketing 7%, communications/journalism 34%, health sciences 31%, liberal arts 11%, science technologies 18%.

Technology on campus. 276 workstations in library, computer center, student center. Commuter students can connect to campus network. Online course registration, helpline, wireless network available.

Student life. Freshman orientation: Mandatory. Preregistration for classes offered. **Activities:** Literary magazine, student government, student newspaper.

Athletics. NJCAA. **Intercollegiate:** Basketball; cheerleading W, golf M, volleyball W. **Intramural:** Basketball, racquetball, volleyball W. **Team name:** Warriors.

Student services. Adult student services, career counseling, student employment services, financial aid counseling, personal counseling, placement for graduates, veterans' counselor. **Physically disabled:** Services for visually, speech, hearing impaired. **Transfer:** Pre-admission transcript evaluation for new students. Transfer adviser, college fairs on campus for students transferring to 4-year colleges.

Contact. E-mail: wayneadmissions@uakron.edu
Phone: (330) 683-2010 Toll-free number: (800) 221-8308 ext. 8900
Fax: (330) 684-8989
Alicia Broadus, Coordinator of Admissions, University of Akron: Wayne College, 1901 Smucker Road, Orrville, OH 44667-9758

University of Cincinnati: Blue Ash College
Cincinnati, Ohio
www.rwc.uc.edu
CB code: 0354

- Public 2-year branch campus college
- Commuter campus in large city

General. Founded in 1967. Regionally accredited. **Enrollment:** 4,790 degree-seeking undergraduates. **Degrees:** 40 bachelor's, 529 associate awarded. **ROTC:** Army, Naval, Air Force. **Location:** 15 miles from downtown. **Calendar:** Quarter, limited summer session. **Full-time faculty:** 182 total. **Part-time faculty:** 166 total. **Class size:** 41% < 20, 58% 20-39, less than 1% 40-49, less than 1% 50-99. **Partnerships:** Formal partnerships with GEAE Sharonville, Ford, GM, Ethicon Blue Ash, Soft Skills & IT Training, Ford, Sara Lee, 30 small companies.

Transfer out. Colleges most students transferred to 2015: University of Cincinnati, Xavier University, Northern Kentucky University, College of Mount St. Joseph.

Basis for selection. Open admission, but selective for some programs. TOEFL or ability to benefit test required of non-native English speakers for placement. **Home schooled:** Students should have 17 ACT or 870 SAT (exclusive of Writing), copy of curriculum, and high school transcript.

High school preparation. Recommended units include English 4, mathematics 3, social studies 2, history 2, science 2 and foreign language 2.

2015-2016 Annual costs. Tuition/fees: $6,024; $14,808 out-of-state. Per-credit charge: $251 in-state; $617 out-of-state. Books/supplies: $700.

Financial aid. All financial aid based on need. Need-based aid available for part-time students. Work-study available nights, weekends and for part-time students. **Additional information:** All financial aid applications and awards administered through main campus.

Application procedures. Admission: No deadline. $50 fee, may be waived for applicants with need. Admission notification on a rolling basis. **Financial aid:** Priority date 3/15; no closing date. FAFSA required. Applicants notified on a rolling basis starting 3/15; must reply within 2 week(s) of notification.

Academics. Special study options: Accelerated study, cooperative education, cross-registration, distance learning, double major, dual enrollment of high school students, independent study, internships, liberal arts/career combination, student-designed major, study abroad, teacher certification program, weekend college. Bachelor's degree programs available on campus. License preparation in dental hygiene, nursing, paramedic, radiology, real estate. **Credit/placement by examination:** AP, CLEP, IB, institutional tests. Students must complete at least 45 credits at school to receive degree. CLEP credit by evaluation and credit by portfolio may be available. **Support services:** Learning center, pre-admission summer program, reduced course load, remedial instruction, study skills assistance, tutoring, writing center.

Majors. Biology: General. **Business:** General, accounting technology, administrative services, business admin, executive assistant, financial planning, office/clerical, real estate, sales/distribution. **Communications:** Communications/speech/rhetoric, digital media. **Communications technology:** Graphics. **Computer sciences:** General, computer graphics, information technology, web page design, webmaster. **Education:** General, early childhood, elementary, middle, secondary. **Health services:** Clinical nutrition, community health, dental hygiene, dietetics, EMT paramedic, insurance specialist, medical radiologic technology/radiation therapy, medical secretary, medical transcription, nuclear medical technology, nursing (RN), office assistant, predental, premedicine, prepharmacy, preveterinary, radiation protection, radiologic technology/medical imaging, veterinary technology/assistant, vocational rehab counseling. **Human services:** Social work. **Liberal arts:** Arts/sciences. **Physical sciences:** Chemistry. **Protective services:** Criminal justice. **Social sciences:** Economics, urban studies. **Visual/performing arts:** Design, graphic design. **Work/family studies:** Food/nutrition.

Most popular majors. Business/marketing 18%, computer/information sciences 16%, education 6%, health sciences 39%.

Technology on campus. 275 workstations in computer center. Commuter students can connect to campus network. Online course registration, online library, helpline available.

Student life. Freshman orientation: Available. Preregistration for classes offered. One-day program. **Policies:** Student organization members must be in good academic standing. **Activities:** Student government, student newspaper, campus ministry, international student club.

Athletics. Intramural: Golf.

Student services. Adult student services, career counseling, student employment services, financial aid counseling, minority student services, on-campus daycare, placement for graduates. **Physically disabled:** Services for visually, hearing impaired. **Transfer:** Pre-admission transcript evaluation for new students. College fairs on campus for students transferring to 4-year colleges.

Contact. Phone: (513) 745-5700 Fax: (513) 745-5768
Chris Powers, Director, Enrollment Services, University of Cincinnati: Blue Ash College, 9555 Plainfield Road, Cincinnati, OH 45236-1096

University of Cincinnati: Clermont College
Batavia, Ohio
www.ucclermont.edu   **CB code: 3073**

- Public 2-year branch campus college
- Commuter campus in small town

General. Founded in 1972. Regionally accredited. College serves Clermont, Brown, and eastern Hamilton counties. One of 2 open-access regional colleges of the University of Cincinnati. **Enrollment:** 2,590 degree-seeking undergraduates; 509 non-degree-seeking students. **Degrees:** 60 bachelor's, 411 associate awarded. **ROTC:** Army. **Location:** 17 miles from Cincinnati. **Calendar:** Semester, limited summer session. **Full-time faculty:** 96 total. **Part-time faculty:** 186 total. **Partnerships:** Formal partnership with Sporty's Academy, Inc. for Aviation Technology program flight instruction and ground services.

Student profile. Among degree-seeking undergraduates, 41% enrolled in a transfer program, 59% enrolled in a vocational program, 608 enrolled as first-time, first-year students.

Part-time:	36%	Hispanic/Latino:	2%
Women:	55%	Multi-racial, non-Hispanic:	2%
African American:	3%	International:	1%
Asian American:	1%	25 or older:	28%

Transfer out. Colleges most students transferred to 2015: Northern Kentucky University, University of Cincinnati, Wilmington College.

Basis for selection. Open admission, but selective for some programs. Special requirements for allied health, police academy and technical baccalaureate programs. **Home schooled:** Transcript of courses and grades required. All existing school records and formal documentation of high school curriculum required. Course content descriptions, copy of superintendent release form, notarized statement from parent, and precollege curriculum form completed and signed by parent may also be required. Appointment involving student, teacher, and admissions representative may be encouraged.

High school preparation. College-preparatory program recommended. 16 units recommended. Recommended units include English 4, mathematics 3, social studies 2, science 2, foreign language 2 and academic electives 2. 1 fine arts recommended.

2015-2016 Annual costs. Tuition/fees: $5,316; $12,550 out-of-state. Per-credit charge: $222 in-state; $523 out-of-state. Books/supplies: $1,308. Personal expenses: $3,816.

Financial aid. Need-based: Need-based aid available for part-time students. Work-study available nights, weekends and for part-time students. **Non-need-based:** Scholarships awarded for academics, leadership, minority status, state residency. **Additional information:** All financial aid applications and awards administered through Uptown campus except in-house loans and scholarships.

Application procedures. Admission: Priority date 1/31; deadline 7/11 (receipt date). $50 fee, may be waived for applicants with need. Application must be submitted online. Admission notification on a rolling basis. **Financial aid:** No deadline. FAFSA required. Applicants notified on a rolling basis.

Academics. Special study options: Cooperative education, cross-registration, distance learning, double major, dual enrollment of high school students, ESL, honors, independent study, internships, student-designed major, study abroad. Bachelor's degree programs available on campus. License preparation in aviation, nursing, paramedic, physical therapy, real estate. **Credit/placement by examination:** AP, CLEP, IB, institutional tests. 50% of hours needed for degree may be earned by examination. **Support services:** GED test center, learning center, reduced course load, remedial instruction, study skills assistance, tutoring, writing center. College Success Program and Achievement Coach services available to students who place into 2 or more developmental courses based on placement test.

Majors. Biology: General. **Business:** General, accounting technology, administrative services, business admin, marketing, office management, office technology. **Communications:** Communications/speech/rhetoric. **Computer sciences:** General, applications programming, data entry, data processing, information technology, networking, programming, vendor certification. **Conservation:** Environmental science. **Education:** Early childhood, elementary, kindergarten/preschool, middle, secondary. **English:** English lit. **Health services:** EMT ambulance attendant, EMT paramedic, health information technology, medical assistant, office assistant, physical therapy assistant, predental, premedicine, prenursing, prepharmacy, preveterinary, respiratory therapy technology, surgical technology. **Human services:** Social work. **Liberal arts:** Arts/sciences. **Parks/recreation:** Sports admin. **Physical sciences:** Chemistry. **Protective services:** Corrections, criminal justice, forensics, law enforcement admin, security services. **Psychology:** General. **Work/family studies:** General.

Technology on campus. 104 workstations in library, computer center, student center. Commuter students can connect to campus network. Online course registration, online library, helpline, wireless network available.

Student life. Freshman orientation: Mandatory. Preregistration for classes offered. Held prior to the beginning of each term for 2-3 hours. **Housing:** Students are eligible for university-housing at main campus. **Activities:** Campus ministries, dance, literary magazine, student government, student newspaper, College Young Democrats, Active Minds, psychology club, UC Clermont Advocates Network, Phi Theta Kappa, UC Clermont Association of Paralegal Students, Student Veterans Organization, UC IT Professionals, Professionalism Academics Character Experiences.

Athletics. USCAA. **Intercollegiate:** Baseball M, basketball, soccer, softball W, volleyball W. **Team name:** Cougars.

Student services. Adult student services, alcohol/substance abuse counseling, career counseling, services for economically disadvantaged, student employment services, financial aid counseling, personal counseling, placement for graduates, veterans' counselor. **Physically disabled:** Services for visually, speech, hearing impaired. **Transfer:** Transfer adviser, college fairs on campus for students transferring to 4-year colleges.

Contact. E-mail: clc.admissions@uc.edu
Phone: (513) 556-1100 Toll-free number: (866) 446-2822
Fax: (513) 732-5303
Blaine Kelley, Director of Student Recruitment, University of Cincinnati: Clermont College, 4200 Clermont College Drive, Batavia, OH 45103

University of Northwestern Ohio
Lima, Ohio
www.unoh.edu   CB code: 0816

▶ Private 2-year business and technical college
▶ Residential campus in large town

General. Founded in 1920. Regionally accredited. **Enrollment:** 3,628 full-time, degree-seeking students. **Degrees:** 141 bachelor's, 1,341 associate awarded; master's offered. **ROTC:** Army. **Location:** 75 miles from Toledo, 90 miles from Columbus. **Calendar:** Continuous, extensive summer session. **Full-time faculty:** 112 total. **Part-time faculty:** 60 total.

Student profile.

Out-of-state:	21%	Live on campus:	65%
25 or older:	18%		

Transfer out. Colleges most students transferred to 2015: Rhodes State College, Ohio State University.

Basis for selection. Students with 1.5 GPA or lower admitted conditionally. **Home schooled:** Statement describing home school structure and mission required. **Learning Disabled:** Students must self-disclose personal needs and provide IEP.

2015-2016 Annual costs. Books/supplies: $1,798. Personal expenses: $1,818. **Additional information:** College of Applied Technologies: $11,800; College of Business, Health Professions, and Occupational Professions: $12,300. Books, supplies, fees range depending on program level and course of study. All costs are subject to change.

Financial aid. Need-based: Need-based aid available for part-time students. Work-study available nights, weekends and for part-time students. **Non-need-based:** Scholarships awarded for academics, job skills, minority status.

Application procedures. Admission: No deadline. $20 fee. Admission notification on a rolling basis. **Financial aid:** Priority date 4/1; no closing date. FAFSA required. Applicants notified on a rolling basis starting 4/30; must reply within 2 week(s) of notification.

Academics. Students wanting credit for life experience must register for 1-hour course in portfolio development. **Special study options:** Accelerated study, distance learning, dual enrollment of high school students, independent study, internships. Bachelor's degree programs available on campus. **Credit/placement by examination:** AP, CLEP, SAT, ACT, institutional tests. 25 credit hours maximum toward associate degree. **Support services:** Learning center, remedial instruction, study skills assistance, tutoring, writing center.

Majors. Business: Accounting, administrative services, business admin, marketing, office technology, tourism/travel. **Computer sciences:** General, applications programming. **Health services:** Medical assistant, medical secretary.

Most popular majors. Business/marketing 6%, trade and industry 73%.

Technology on campus. 212 workstations in library, computer center, student center. Commuter students can connect to campus network. Online course registration available.

Student life. Freshman orientation: Available. Preregistration for classes offered. Held 4 to 6 weeks before quarter or session begins. **Housing:** Guaranteed on-campus for all undergraduates. Single-sex dorms, special housing for disabled, apartments, wellness housing available. $100 deposit.

Athletics. NAIA. **Intercollegiate:** Baseball M, basketball, bowling, golf, soccer, tennis, volleyball M. **Intramural:** Basketball, cheerleading W, soccer, volleyball. **Team name:** Racers.

Student services. Adult student services, career counseling, student employment services, financial aid counseling, minority student services, personal counseling, placement for graduates, veterans' counselor. **Physically disabled:** Services for visually, hearing impaired. **Transfer:** Pre-admission transcript evaluation for new students.

Contact. E-mail: info@unoh.edu
Phone: (419) 998-3120 Fax: (419) 229-6926
Tony Azzarello, Director of Admissions, University of Northwestern Ohio, 1441 North Cable Road, Lima, OH 45805

Vatterott College: Cleveland
Broadview Heights, Ohio
www.vatterott-college.edu

▶ For-profit 2-year technical college
▶ Commuter campus in large town

General. Accredited by ACCSC. **Enrollment:** 218 undergraduates. **Degrees:** 40 associate awarded. **Calendar:** Semester. **Full-time faculty:** 13 total. **Part-time faculty:** 7 total.

Basis for selection. Open admission.

2015-2016 Annual costs. Books/supplies: $1,877. **Additional information:** Diploma programs: (40 weeks) $18,500-$18,832; (60 weeks) $27,872-$29,264. Associate programs: (90 weeks) $42,106-$42,506. Costs include fees, books and supplies.

Financial aid. Need-based: Work-study available nights, weekends and for part-time students.

Application procedures. Admission: No deadline. No application fee. **Financial aid:** No deadline.

Academics. Credit/placement by examination: AP, CLEP.

Majors. Computer sciences: System admin. **General:** Building inspection.

Contact. E-mail: cleveland@vatterott-college.edu
Phone: (440) 526-1660 Toll-free number: (800) 864-5644
Fax: (440) 526-1933
Karen Fisher, Director of Admissions, Vatterott College: Cleveland, 5025 East Royalton Road, Broadview Heights, OH 44147

Virginia Marti College of Art and Design
Lakewood, Ohio
www.vmcad.edu   CB code: 0396

▶ For-profit 2-year visual arts and business college
▶ Commuter campus in large city
▶ Application essay, interview required

General. Founded in 1966. Accredited by ACCSC. **Enrollment:** 160 undergraduates. **Degrees:** 38 associate awarded. **Location:** 7 miles from Cleveland. **Calendar:** Quarter, extensive summer session. **Full-time faculty:** 5 total. **Part-time faculty:** 53 total.

Basis for selection. School achievement record, admission test scores and interview considered. Essay questions and letter of recommendation reviewed. Career Ability Placement Survey (CAPS) required for admission. Portfolio recommended but not required for graphic design, interior design, and fashion design majors; in lieu of portfolio, preliminary art courses required in first quarter. **Home schooled:** Transcript of courses and grades required. **Learning Disabled:** Provide high school IEP for review of special needs.

2015-2016 Annual costs. Books/supplies: $1,800. Personal expenses: $1,746. **Additional information:** Bachelor degree programs: range from

$21,060 -$21,450; Associates programs: $9,600. Books, supplies, fees range depending on program level and course of study. All costs are subject to change.

Financial aid. All financial aid based on need. Work-study available nights, weekends and for part-time students.

Application procedures. Admission: No deadline. No application fee. Admission notification on a rolling basis. **Financial aid:** No deadline. FAFSA required. Applicants notified on a rolling basis.

Academics. Special study options: Dual enrollment of high school students, independent study, internships, study abroad. **Credit/placement by examination:** AP, CLEP, institutional tests. **Support services:** Remedial instruction, study skills assistance, tutoring.

Majors. Business: Fashion. **Communications:** Digital media. **Computer sciences:** Computer science. **Visual/performing arts:** Art, art history/conservation, commercial/advertising art, design, fashion design, illustration, interior design, photography.

Technology on campus. 28 workstations in library, computer center. Commuter students can connect to campus network. Online course registration, wireless network available.

Student life. Freshman orientation: Mandatory. Preregistration for classes offered. Two-four hour program held 1 week prior to start of classes. **Policies:** Students participate in yearly fashion shows; competitions; trips to New York, France, and Italy. **Activities:** Student government, student chapters of American Institute of Graphic Artists, Fashion Group International, American Society of Interior Designers.

Student services. Career counseling, student employment services, placement for graduates, veterans' counselor. **Transfer:** Pre-admission transcript evaluation for new students. Transfer adviser for students transferring to 4-year colleges.

Contact. E-mail: qmarti@vmcad.edu
Phone: (216) 221-8584 ext. 106 Toll-free number: (800) 473-4350
Quinn Marti, Director of Admissions, Virginia Marti College of Art and Design, 11724 Detroit Avenue, Lakewood, OH 44107

Washington State Community College
Marietta, Ohio
www.wscc.edu   CB code: 0381

▶ Public 2-year community college
▶ Commuter campus in large town

General. Founded in 1971. Regionally accredited. **Enrollment:** 1,136 degree-seeking undergraduates. **Degrees:** 291 associate awarded. **Location:** 112 miles from Columbus. **Calendar:** Semester, limited summer session. **Full-time faculty:** 64 total. **Part-time faculty:** 107 total.

Student profile.

Out-of-state: 12%   25 or older: 46%

Basis for selection. Open admission, but selective for some programs. Special requirements for medical laboratory technology, nursing, physical therapist assistant, radiology, respiratory therapy programs. ACT required for nursing, radiologic technology, physical therapist assistant programs. Interview required for programs with selective admission.

2015-2016 Annual costs. Tuition/fees: $4,410; $8,580 out-of-state. Per-credit charge: $139 in-state; $278 out-of-state. Books/supplies: $1,900. Personal expenses: $1,573.

2014-2015 Financial aid. Need-based: 40% of total undergraduate aid awarded as scholarships/grants, 60% as loans/jobs. Work-study available nights, weekends and for part-time students.

Application procedures. Admission: No deadline. No application fee. Admission notification on a rolling basis. **Financial aid:** No deadline. FAFSA, institutional form required. Applicants notified on a rolling basis starting 5/15; must reply within 2 week(s) of notification.

Academics. Special study options: Distance learning, double major, dual enrollment of high school students, honors, independent study, internships, student-designed major. License preparation in nursing, physical therapy, radiology. **Credit/placement by examination:** AP, CLEP, institutional tests. 60 credit hours maximum toward associate degree. **Support services:** Learning center, pre-admission summer program, reduced course load, remedial instruction, study skills assistance, tutoring.

Honors college/program. Students must have a 3.0 GPA and an ACT composite score of 18. The honors program involves special sections of particular courses as well as service learning and special lectures.

Majors. Business: General, accounting, business admin. **Communications:** Broadcast journalism, media studies. **Communications technology:** Animation/special effects. **Computer sciences:** Computer graphics, data processing, programming. **Education:** General, elementary, multi-level teacher, secondary. **Engineering:** General, electrical. **Health services:** General, clinical lab assistant, medical radiologic technology/radiation therapy, medical secretary, nursing (RN), physical therapy assistant, respiratory therapy technology. **Liberal arts:** Arts/sciences. **Math:** General. **Protective services:** Corrections, law enforcement admin. **Visual/performing arts:** Graphic design, studio arts.

Technology on campus. Helpline, wireless network available.

Student life. Freshman orientation: Mandatory. Preregistration for classes offered. Held 2-3 times prior to each academic term. **Policies:** All student life policies are available in the student handbook. **Activities:** Student government, Military Veterans Club, Phi Theta Kappa, Circle K, Branches (social services club).

Student services. Adult student services, career counseling, student employment services, financial aid counseling, veterans' counselor. **Physically disabled:** Services for visually, hearing impaired. **Transfer:** Transfer adviser, college fairs on campus for students transferring to 4-year colleges.

Contact. E-mail: admissions@wscc.edu
Phone: (740) 568-1900 Fax: (740) 373-7496
Carrie Thrash, Director of Admissions, Washington State Community College, 710 Colegate Drive, Marietta, OH 45750

Wright State University: Lake Campus
Celina, Ohio
http://lake.wright.edu/   CB code: 1947

▶ Public 2-year branch campus college
▶ Commuter campus in large town

General. Founded in 1969. Regionally accredited. Located on 173 scenic acres on the north shore of Grand Lake St. Marys between Celina and St. Marys, Ohio. **Enrollment:** 992 degree-seeking undergraduates; 166 non-degree-seeking students. **Degrees:** 88 bachelor's, 68 associate awarded; master's offered. **Location:** 65 miles from Dayton. **Calendar:** Semester, limited summer session. **Full-time faculty:** 31 total; 3% minority, 36% women. **Class size:** 67% < 20, 28% 20-39, 5% 40-49.

Student profile. Among degree-seeking undergraduates, 2% already have a bachelor's degree or higher, 265 enrolled as first-time, first-year students, 60 transferred in from other institutions.

Part-time:	18%	Hispanic/Latino:	2%
Out-of-state:	1%	Multi-racial, non-Hispanic:	2%
Women:	50%	International:	1%
African American:	4%	25 or older:	19%
Asian American:	1%	Live on campus:	7%

Basis for selection. Open admission, but selective for some programs. Special requirements for engineering and education programs. SAT/ACT required for all students but only used for placement in selective programs. **Adult students:** SAT/ACT scores not required if out of high school 1 year(s) or more. **Home schooled:** Statement describing home school structure and mission required. Each applicant should clearly articulate all secondary coursework completed while providing written verification from the appropriate school district excusing the student from compulsory attendance.

High school preparation. College-preparatory program recommended. 16 units recommended. Recommended units include English 4, mathematics 3, social studies 3, science 3 (laboratory 3), foreign language 2 and visual/performing arts 1. Math requirement includes 2 algebra. Art, music or theater recommended.

2015-2016 Annual costs. Tuition/fees: $5,842; $14,022 out-of-state. Per-credit charge: $265 in-state; $650 out-of-state.

Financial aid. Need-based: Need-based aid available for part-time students. Work-study available nights, weekends and for part-time students. **Non-need-based:** Scholarships awarded for academics, alumni affiliation, art, athletics, leadership, minority status, music/drama, ROTC, state residency.

Application procedures. Admission: No deadline. $30 fee. Admission notification on a rolling basis. **Financial aid:** Priority date 3/1; no closing date. FAFSA required. Applicants notified on a rolling basis starting 3/15.

Academics. Special study options: Cooperative education, cross-registration, distance learning, double major, dual enrollment of high school students, honors, independent study, internships, semester at sea, student-designed major, study abroad. Bachelor's degree programs available on campus. **Credit/placement by examination:** AP, CLEP, IB, institutional tests. **Support services:** Learning center, pre-admission summer program, reduced course load, remedial instruction, tutoring, writing center.

Honors college/program. First-year students direct from high school should meet at least two of the following criteria: 1) GPA of 3.25 or better in high school. 2) Rank in top 10 percent of the graduating class. 3) Score at 90th percentile on the ACT (approximately 27 Composite) or the SAT (approximately 1210 Critical Reading and Math).

Majors. Biology: General. **Business:** General, business admin, management information systems. **Communications:** Communications/speech/rhetoric. **History:** General. **Human services:** Social work. **Liberal arts:** Arts/sciences. **Physical sciences:** Chemistry, geology. **Psychology:** General. **Social sciences:** Sociology. **Visual/performing arts:** Graphic design. **Work/family studies:** Institutional food production.

Most popular majors. Business/marketing 62%, engineering/engineering technologies 9%, visual/performing arts 12%.

Technology on campus. 130 workstations in library, computer center. Dormitories wired for high-speed internet access. Commuter students can connect to campus network. Online course registration, online library, help-line, repair service, wireless network available.

Student life. Freshman orientation: Mandatory. Preregistration for classes offered. **Housing:** Apartments available. $150 fully refundable deposit. **Activities:** Drama, student government, student newspaper, Business Professionals of America, Student Manufacturing Engineers, Circle K.

Athletics. NCAA. **Intercollegiate:** Baseball M, basketball, volleyball W. **Team name:** Lakers.

Student services. Adult student services, career counseling, student employment services, financial aid counseling, health services, legal services, on-campus daycare, personal counseling, placement for graduates, veterans' counselor. **Physically disabled:** Services for visually, hearing impaired. **Transfer:** Transfer center for students transferring to 4-year colleges.

Contact. E-mail: discoverlakecampus@wright.edu
Phone: (419) 586-0300 Toll-free number: (800) 237-1477
Fax: (419) 586-0358
Jill Puthoff, Coordinator of Admission, Wright State University: Lake Campus, 7600 Lake Campus Drive, State Route 703, Celina, OH 45822-2952

Zane State College
Zanesville, Ohio
www.zanestate.edu　　　　　**CB code: 1535**

▶ Public 2-year community and technical college
▶ Commuter campus in large town

General. Founded in 1969. Regionally accredited. **Enrollment:** 2,607 degree-seeking undergraduates. **Degrees:** 377 associate awarded. **Location:** 60 miles from Columbus. **Calendar:** Semester, limited summer session. **Full-time faculty:** 62 total. **Part-time faculty:** 186 total. **Special facilities:** Natural resource center.

Transfer out. Colleges most students transferred to 2015: Ohio University, Ohio State University, Muskingum University, Franklin University, Miami University.

Basis for selection. Open admission, but selective for some programs. Special requirements for allied health programs. **Home schooled:** Transcript of courses and grades, state high school equivalency certificate required. **Learning Disabled:** Valid documentation needs to be provided to Student Services for accomodations to be provided to the student for each course he/she is enrolled.

High school preparation. 15 units recommended. Recommended units include English 4, mathematics 3, social studies 4 and science 4.

2015-2016 Annual costs. Tuition/fees: $4,560; $9,120 out-of-state. Per-credit charge: $152 in-state; $304 out-of-state. Books/supplies: $1,500.

Financial aid. Need-based: Need-based aid available for part-time students. Work-study available nights, weekends and for part-time students.

Application procedures. Admission: No deadline. No application fee. Admission notification on a rolling basis. **Financial aid:** Priority date 5/1, closing date 6/30. FAFSA required. Must reply by 9/1.

Academics. Special study options: Accelerated study, combined bachelor's/graduate degree, cross-registration, distance learning, double major, dual enrollment of high school students, internships, liberal arts/career combination, student-designed major, weekend college. Bachelor's degree programs available on campus. License preparation in occupational therapy, physical therapy, radiology, real estate. **Credit/placement by examination:** AP, CLEP, institutional tests. All new freshmen must take assessment tests for English and math. **Support services:** Learning center, reduced course load, remedial instruction, study skills assistance, tutoring, writing center.

Majors. Business: Accounting, administrative services, business admin, marketing, sales/distribution. **Computer sciences:** General, computer science, information systems. **Conservation:** Management/policy. **Health services:** Clinical lab technology, medical assistant, medical radiologic technology/radiation therapy, occupational therapy assistant, physical therapy assistant. **Human services:** Social work. **Work/family studies:** Child care management.

Most popular majors. Business/marketing 40%, computer/information sciences 19%, engineering/engineering technologies 9%, health sciences 29%, parks/recreation 7%.

Technology on campus. Online course registration, online library, help-line, wireless network available.

Student life. Freshman orientation: Mandatory. Preregistration for classes offered. **Activities:** Campus ministries, student government.

Athletics. NAIA. **Intercollegiate:** Baseball M, basketball, volleyball W.

Student services. Adult student services, career counseling, student employment services, financial aid counseling, minority student services, personal counseling, placement for graduates, veterans' counselor. **Physically disabled:** Services for visually, speech, hearing impaired. **Transfer:** Pre-admission transcript evaluation for new students. Transfer adviser, college fairs on campus for students transferring to 4-year colleges.

Contact. E-mail: pyoung@zanestate.edu
Phone: (740) 454-2501 ext. 1225
Toll-free number: (800) 686-8324 ext. 1226 Fax: (740) 454-0035
Paul Young, Director of Admissions, Zane State College, 1555 Newark Road, Zanesville, OH 43701-2626

Oklahoma

Carl Albert State College
Poteau, Oklahoma
www.carlalbert.edu   **CB code: 1474**

▶ Public 2-year community and junior college
▶ Commuter campus in large town

General. Founded in 1932. Regionally accredited. **Enrollment:** 2,856 undergraduates. **Degrees:** 505 associate awarded. **Location:** 35 miles from Fort Smith, Arkansas. **Calendar:** Semester, limited summer session. **Full-time faculty:** 54 total. **Part-time faculty:** 61 total.

Transfer out. Colleges most students transferred to 2015: Northeastern State University, University of Arkansas, Southeastern State University, University of Central Oklahoma.

Basis for selection. Open admission, but selective for some programs. Nursing and physical therapy assistant programs employ selective enrollment.

High school preparation. 15 units recommended. Recommended units include English 4, mathematics 3, social studies 1, history 2, science 2 (laboratory 2) and academic electives 1. One social science unit should be in American history.

2015-2016 Annual costs. Tuition/fees: $3,151; $6,519 out-of-state. Per-credit charge: $73 in-state; $185 out-of-state. Room/board: $4,222. Books/supplies: $1,600. Personal expenses: $1,875.

Financial aid. All financial aid based on need. Need-based aid available for part-time students. Work-study available nights, weekends and for part-time students.

Application procedures. Admission: No deadline. No application fee. Admission notification on a rolling basis. **Financial aid:** No deadline. FAFSA, institutional form required. Applicants notified on a rolling basis.

Academics. Special study options: Distance learning, dual enrollment of high school students, honors, independent study, liberal arts/career combination. License preparation in nursing, physical therapy, radiology. **Credit/placement by examination:** AP, CLEP, institutional tests. 18 credit hours maximum toward associate degree. **Support services:** GED test center, learning center, remedial instruction, study skills assistance, tutoring.

Majors. Biology: General, zoology. **Business:** General, accounting, administrative services, business admin. **Communications:** Journalism. **Computer sciences:** Computer science. **Education:** Elementary, secondary. **English:** English lit, rhetoric/composition. **Health services:** Nursing (RN), physical therapy assistant, premedicine, prepharmacy, preveterinary. **Math:** General. **Parks/recreation:** Health/fitness. **Protective services:** Criminal justice. **Psychology:** General. **Social sciences:** General, sociology. **Visual/performing arts:** Art, dramatic, music.

Most popular majors. Business/marketing 13%, education 8%, family/consumer sciences 10%, health sciences 37%, liberal arts 12%, social sciences 10%.

Technology on campus. 50 workstations in library, computer center. Dormitories wired for high-speed internet access. Commuter students can connect to campus network. Online library available.

Student life. Freshman orientation: Mandatory. Preregistration for classes offered. One-day session held at beginning of semester offered online. **Housing:** Single-sex dorms available. $100 deposit. Scholar's housing available. **Activities:** Choral groups, dance, drama, music ensembles, musical theater, radio station, student government, student newspaper, African-American awareness, American Indian student association, Young Democrats, Young Republicans.

Athletics. NJCAA. **Intercollegiate:** Baseball M, basketball M, cheerleading W. **Team name:** Vikings.

Student services. Chaplain/spiritual director, career counseling, services for economically disadvantaged, financial aid counseling, on-campus daycare, veterans' counselor. **Physically disabled:** Services for hearing impaired. **Transfer:** Pre-admission transcript evaluation for new students. Transfer adviser, college fairs on campus for students transferring to 4-year colleges.

Contact. E-mail: admissions@carlalbert.edu
Phone: (918) 647-1300 Fax: (918) 647-1306
Dee Ann Dickerson, Registrar, Carl Albert State College, 1507 South McKenna, Poteau, OK 74953-5208

College of the Muscogee Nation
Okmulgee, Oklahoma
www.mvsktc.org

▶ Public 2-year junior college
▶ Large town

General. Candidate for regional accreditation. **Enrollment:** 186 degree-seeking undergraduates. **Degrees:** 25 associate awarded. **Calendar:** Trimester. **Full-time faculty:** 7 total. **Part-time faculty:** 11 total.

Basis for selection. Open admission.

2015-2016 Annual costs. Tuition/fees: $6,600; $6,600 out-of-state. Per-credit charge: $147. Room/board: $9,100. Books/supplies: $1,600. Personal expenses: $2,000.

Financial aid. Need-based: Work-study available nights, weekends and for part-time students.

Application procedures. Admission: No deadline. No application fee. **Financial aid:** No deadline.

Academics. Credit/placement by examination: AP.

Majors. Area/ethnic studies: Native American.

Contact. E-mail: emccormack@mcn-nsn.gov
Phone: (918) 549-2808
Kathy McCormack, Director of Admissions, College of the Muscogee Nation, 2170 Raven Circle, Okmulgee, OK 74447

Connors State College
Warner, Oklahoma
www.connorsstate.edu   **CB code: 6117**

▶ Public 2-year community and junior college
▶ Commuter campus in rural community

General. Founded in 1908. Regionally accredited. Main campus in Warner. Branch campus in Muskogee. **Enrollment:** 2,600 undergraduates. **Degrees:** 383 associate awarded. **Location:** 20 miles from Muskogee, 65 miles from Tulsa. **Calendar:** Semester, extensive summer session. **Full-time faculty:** 67 total. **Class size:** 64% < 20, 32% 20-39, 3% 40-49, 1% 50-99. **Special facilities:** 1,300 acre wetlands and nature preserve.

Student profile.

Out-of-state:	4%	Live on campus:	10%
25 or older:	42%		

Transfer out. Colleges most students transferred to 2015: Northeastern State University, Oklahoma State University.

Basis for selection. Open admission, but selective for some programs. Special requirements for nursing and equine programs; interview required. **Adult students:** Must complete secondary assessment. **Home schooled:** Transcript of courses and grades required. Student's equivalent public high school class must have graduated; must take ACT; proficiency in subject area curricula required. **Learning Disabled:** Students with documented disabilities must complete designated paperwork in the office of the Vice President for Student Services.

High school preparation. College-preparatory program recommended.

2015-2016 Annual costs. Tuition/fees: $3,798; $8,500 out-of-state. Per-credit charge: $84 in-state; $241 out-of-state. Room/board: $5,690. Books/supplies: $1,400.

Financial aid. Need-based: Need-based aid available for part-time students. Work-study available nights, weekends and for part-time students. **Non-need-based:** Scholarships awarded for academics, alumni affiliation, athletics, leadership, state residency.

Application procedures. Admission: No deadline. No application fee. Admission notification on a rolling basis. High school diploma required of applicants younger than 18. **Financial aid:** Closing date 3/1. FAFSA, institutional form required. Applicants notified on a rolling basis starting 4/1; must reply within 2 week(s) of notification.

Academics. Special study options: Distance learning, dual enrollment of high school students, internships, liberal arts/career combination. License preparation in nursing. **Credit/placement by examination:** AP, CLEP, institutional tests. 18 credit hours maximum toward associate degree. **Support services:** Learning center, remedial instruction, tutoring.

Majors. Biology: General. **Business:** General, accounting, business admin. **Communications:** Communications/speech/rhetoric, journalism. **Computer sciences:** General, data processing. **Education:** Early childhood, elementary, physical. **English:** English lit, rhetoric/composition. **Health services:** Nursing (RN), premedicine, preveterinary. **History:** General. **Human services:** Social work. **Liberal arts:** Arts/sciences. **Math:** General. **Physical sciences:** Chemistry, physics. **Protective services:** Police science. **Psychology:** General. **Social sciences:** General, sociology. **Visual/performing arts:** Art. **Work/family studies:** General, business, child care management.

Technology on campus. 217 workstations in dormitories, library, computer center. Dormitories wired for high-speed internet access and linked to campus network. Online library, wireless network available.

Student life. Housing: Single-sex dorms, apartments, wellness housing available. $55 nonrefundable deposit. **Activities:** Campus ministries, drama, student government, student newspaper, Phi Theta Kappa, Aggie club, math and science club, Baptist Collegiate Ministries, behavioral science club, Phi Beta Lambda, President's leadership class.

Athletics. NJCAA. **Intercollegiate:** Baseball M, basketball, cheerleading, rodeo, softball W. **Team name:** Cowboys.

Student services. Adult student services, career counseling, services for economically disadvantaged, student employment services, financial aid counseling, health services, minority student services, veterans' counselor. **Physically disabled:** Services for visually, hearing impaired. **Transfer:** Pre-admission transcript evaluation for new students. College fairs on campus for students transferring to 4-year colleges.

Contact. E-mail: cscenroll@connorsstate.edu
Phone: (918) 463-2931 ext. 6300 Fax: (918) 463-6327
Sonya Baker, Registrar, Connors State College, RR 1, Box 1000, Warner, OK 74469-9700

Eastern Oklahoma State College
Wilburton, Oklahoma **CB member**
www.eosc.edu **CB code: 6189**

▶ Public 2-year community college
▶ Commuter campus in rural community

General. Founded in 1908. Regionally accredited. **Enrollment:** 1,317 degree-seeking undergraduates; 322 non-degree-seeking students. **Degrees:** 305 associate awarded. **Location:** 90 miles from Tulsa. **Calendar:** Semester, limited summer session. **Full-time faculty:** 45 total; 27% have terminal degrees, 4% minority, 67% women. **Part-time faculty:** 47 total; 4% minority, 66% women. **Class size:** 22% < 20, 61% 20-39, 16% 40-49, less than 1% 50-99, less than 1% >100. **Special facilities:** Miner training institute, center for correction officer studies.

Student profile. Among degree-seeking undergraduates, 461 enrolled as first-time, first-year students.

Part-time:	32%	25 or older:	65%
Out-of-state:	2%	Live on campus:	20%
Women:	67%		

Transfer out. Colleges most students transferred to 2015: East Central State University, Northeastern State University, Southeastern Oklahoma State University.

Basis for selection. Open admission, but selective for some programs. Special requirements for nursing program; interview required.

High school preparation. 12 units recommended. Recommended units include English 4, mathematics 3, social studies 2 and science 2. 1 citizenship or government.

2015-2016 Annual costs. Tuition/fees: $3,947; $7,564 out-of-state. Per-credit charge: $95.44 in-state; $216 out-of-state. Room/board: $5,370. Books/supplies: $614. Personal expenses: $500.

2014-2015 Financial aid. All financial aid based on need. 899 full-time freshmen applied for aid; 660 deemed to have need; 642 received aid. Average need met was 55%. Average scholarship/grant was $2,124; average loan

$3,290. 61% of total undergraduate aid awarded as scholarships/grants, 39% as loans/jobs. Need-based aid available for part-time students. Work-study available nights, weekends and for part-time students.

Application procedures. Admission: No deadline. $15 fee. Admission notification on a rolling basis. **Financial aid:** Priority date 3/1, closing date 6/30. FAFSA, institutional form required. Applicants notified on a rolling basis starting 5/1; must reply within 2 week(s) of notification.

Academics. Special study options: Cooperative education, distance learning, dual enrollment of high school students, honors, internships. License preparation in nursing. **Credit/placement by examination:** AP, CLEP, institutional tests. 30 credit hours maximum toward associate degree. **Support services:** Learning center, remedial instruction, study skills assistance, tutoring.

Majors. Biology: General, bacteriology, entomology. **Business:** General, accounting, administrative services, business admin, management information systems, office/clerical. **Communications:** Media studies. **Computer sciences:** General, computer science, programming, systems analysis. **Conservation:** General, environmental studies, forestry, wildlife/wilderness. **Education:** Agricultural, art, biology, business, chemistry, computer, drama/dance, elementary, health, history, mathematics, music, physical, physics, science, secondary, social science, social studies, speech. **Engineering:** General. **English:** English lit. **Health services:** Medical secretary, nursing (RN), predental, premedicine, prenursing, prepharmacy, preveterinary. **History:** General. **Math:** General. **Parks/recreation:** Facilities management, health/fitness. **Physical sciences:** Chemistry, physics. **Protective services:** Criminal justice, law enforcement admin. **Psychology:** General. **Social sciences:** General, sociology. **Visual/performing arts:** Dramatic, music. **Work/family studies:** Child care management.

Most popular majors. Biological/life sciences 6%, business/marketing 9%, education 31%, health sciences 28%, psychology 6%.

Technology on campus. 250 workstations in dormitories, library, computer center. Dormitories linked to campus network. Commuter students can connect to campus network. Online library, helpline, wireless network available.

Student life. Freshman orientation: Mandatory. Preregistration for classes offered. **Housing:** Coed dorms, single-sex dorms, apartments available. $50 deposit, deadline 8/15. **Activities:** Pep band, choral groups, drama, music ensembles, musical theater, radio station, student government, student newspaper, campus religious organizations, Afro-American and Native American clubs, professional clubs.

Athletics. NJCAA. **Intercollegiate:** Baseball M, basketball, cheerleading, soccer, softball W. **Intramural:** Basketball, handball, racquetball, softball, swimming, table tennis, tennis, volleyball. **Team name:** Mountaineers.

Student services. Adult student services, career counseling, student employment services, financial aid counseling, health services, personal counseling, placement for graduates, veterans' counselor. **Physically disabled:** Services for visually, speech, hearing impaired. **Transfer:** Pre-admission transcript evaluation for new students. Transfer adviser, college fairs on campus for students transferring to 4-year colleges.

Contact. Phone: (918) 465-2361 Fax: (918) 465-2431
Jennifer Labor, Registrar, Eastern Oklahoma State College, 1301 West Main Street, Wilburton, OK 74578-4999

Murray State College
Tishomingo, Oklahoma
www.mscok.edu **CB code: 6421**

▶ Public 2-year junior college
▶ Commuter campus in small town

General. Founded in 1908. Regionally accredited. **Enrollment:** 3,124 undergraduates. **Degrees:** 402 associate awarded. **Location:** 120 miles from Oklahoma City, 120 miles from Dallas. **Calendar:** Semester, limited summer session. **Full-time faculty:** 42 total; 57% women. **Part-time faculty:** 94 total; 48% women.

Student profile.

Out-of-state:	2%	Live on campus:	12%

Basis for selection. Open admission, but selective for some programs. Special requirements for nursing, gunsmithing, OTA, PTA, and veterinary technology programs. **Home schooled:** Transcript of courses and grades required.

High school preparation. 15 units recommended. Recommended units include English 4, mathematics 3, social studies 1, history 2, science 2 (laboratory 2) and academic electives 3. Recommend 1 unit in citizenship.

2015-2016 Annual costs. Tuition/fees: $4,070; $9,620 out-of-state. Per-credit charge: $116 in-state; $301 out-of-state. Room/board: $6,600. Books/supplies: $1,400. Personal expenses: $1,640.

Financial aid. Need-based: Work-study available nights, weekends and for part-time students.

Application procedures. Admission: No deadline. No application fee. Admission notification on a rolling basis beginning on or about 4/15. **Financial aid:** Priority date 4/15, closing date 6/30. Applicants notified on a rolling basis starting 5/1.

Academics. Special study options: Cooperative education, distance learning, dual enrollment of high school students. License preparation in nursing, occupational therapy, physical therapy. **Credit/placement by examination:** AP, CLEP. **Support services:** Learning center, remedial instruction, tutoring.

Majors. Business: Administrative services, business admin. **Computer sciences:** General, computer science. **Conservation:** General. **Education:** Elementary. **English:** English lit. **Health services:** Preveterinary. **History:** General. **Liberal arts:** Arts/sciences. **Math:** General. **Protective services:** Law enforcement admin, police science. **Psychology:** General. **Social sciences:** Criminology, sociology. **Visual/performing arts:** General. **Work/family studies:** Child care management.

Most popular majors. Business/marketing 12%, health sciences 16%, liberal arts 33%.

Technology on campus. Dormitories wired for high-speed internet access. Commuter students can connect to campus network. Helpline, wireless network available.

Student life. Freshman orientation: Mandatory. Preregistration for classes offered. **Housing:** Coed dorms available. $50 deposit. **Activities:** Campus ministries, choral groups, drama, music ensembles, musical theater, student government.

Athletics. NJCAA. **Intercollegiate:** Baseball M, basketball, golf. **Intramural:** Baseball M, basketball. **Team name:** Aggies.

Student services. Career counseling, services for economically disadvantaged, financial aid counseling, veterans' counselor. **Transfer:** College fairs on campus for students transferring to 4-year colleges.

Contact. E-mail: registrar@mscok.edu
Phone: (580) 387-7234 Fax: (580) 371-0529
Pam, Registrar, Murray State College, One Murray Campus, Tishomingo, OK 73460

Northeastern Oklahoma Agricultural and Mechanical College

Miami, Oklahoma   **CB member**
www.neo.edu   **CB code: 6484**

▸ Public 2-year community and junior college
▸ Commuter campus in large town

General. Founded in 1919. Regionally accredited. **Enrollment:** 2,029 degree-seeking undergraduates. **Degrees:** 424 associate awarded. **ROTC:** Air Force. **Location:** 76 miles from Tulsa, 45 miles from Joplin. **Calendar:** Semester, extensive summer session. **Full-time faculty:** 71 total; 11% have terminal degrees, 11% minority, 56% women. **Part-time faculty:** 47 total; 15% minority, 53% women. **Class size:** 56% < 20, 42% 20-39, less than 1% 40-49, less than 1% 50-99. **Special facilities:** College farm, equine center, music hall, activity center, athletic training facility, arts and cultural center, American Indian Center for Excellence.

Student profile.

Out-of-state:	17% **Live on campus:**	31%

Transfer out. Colleges most students transferred to 2015: Oklahoma State University, Northeastern State University, University of Central Oklahoma, Missouri Southern State University, Pittsburg State University.

Basis for selection. Open admission. **Adult students:** Students over the age of 21 must complete placement testing before enrolling in college level classes. **Home schooled:** Transcript of courses and grades required. **Learning Disabled:** Applicants should contact director of disabilities services.

High school preparation. College-preparatory program recommended.

2015-2016 Annual costs. Tuition/fees: $3,833; $9,173 out-of-state. Per-credit charge: $78 in-state; $256 out-of-state. Room/board: $5,768. Books/supplies: $850. Personal expenses: $1,000.

Financial aid. Need-based: Need-based aid available for part-time students. Work-study available nights, weekends and for part-time students. **Non-need-based:** Scholarships awarded for academics, athletics, leadership, music/drama, state residency.

Application procedures. Admission: No deadline. No application fee. Admission notification on a rolling basis. **Financial aid:** Priority date 4/1; no closing date. FAFSA required. Applicants notified on a rolling basis starting 4/1; must reply by 8/30 or within 2 week(s) of notification.

Academics. Extension courses offered in neighboring towns and online, Reach Higher program for adult students, bachelor's programs offered on campus through other institutions. **Special study options:** Distance learning, double major, dual enrollment of high school students, independent study, internships. Bachelor's degree programs available on campus. License preparation in nursing, physical therapy. **Credit/placement by examination:** AP, CLEP, institutional tests. 36 credit hours maximum toward associate degree. **Support services:** GED preparation and test center, learning center, reduced course load, remedial instruction, study skills assistance, tutoring, writing center.

Majors. Area/ethnic studies: Native American. **Biology:** General. **Business:** Accounting, administrative services, business admin, marketing. **Communications:** Radio/TV. **Computer sciences:** General, programming. **Conservation:** Forestry. **Education:** Early childhood. **English:** English lit. **Health services:** Athletic training, clinical lab technology, medical secretary, nursing (RN), physical therapy assistant, predental, premedicine, prenursing, prepharmacy, preveterinary. **Math:** General. **Parks/recreation:** Health/fitness, sports admin. **Physical sciences:** General. **Protective services:** Criminal justice. **Psychology:** General. **Social sciences:** General. **Visual/performing arts:** Art, dramatic, music.

Most popular majors. Business/marketing 10%, education 9%, health sciences 36%, liberal arts 16%, natural resources/environmental science 11%, psychology 7%.

Technology on campus. 105 workstations in dormitories, library, computer center, student center. Dormitories linked to campus network. Commuter students can connect to campus network. Online library, helpline, wireless network available.

Student life. Freshman orientation: Mandatory, $88 fee. Preregistration for classes offered. **Policies:** Single students under the age of 21 who reside more than 50 miles away are required to live on-campus. **Housing:** Guaranteed on-campus for all undergraduates. Single-sex dorms, special housing for disabled, wellness housing available. $75 fully refundable deposit. **Activities:** Bands, campus ministries, choral groups, dance, drama, music ensembles, musical theater, student government, TV station, Ministerial Alliance, Baptist student union, Aggie Society, Collegiates for Christ, Young Democrats, Young Republicans, Phi Theta Kappa, Afro-American Society, Native American student association, Masquers.

Athletics. NJCAA. **Intercollegiate:** Baseball M, basketball, football (tackle) M, rodeo, soccer, softball W, volleyball W, wrestling M. **Intramural:** Baseball, basketball, bowling, football (tackle) M, soccer, softball, swimming, volleyball. **Team name:** Norsemen.

Student services. Adult student services, alcohol/substance abuse counseling, career counseling, services for economically disadvantaged, financial aid counseling, health services, minority student services, personal counseling, veterans' counselor. **Physically disabled:** Services for visually, speech, hearing impaired. **Transfer:** Re-entry adviser, pre-admission transcript evaluation for new students. Transfer adviser, college fairs on campus for students transferring to 4-year colleges.

Contact. E-mail: neoadmission@neo.edu
Phone: (918) 540-6399 Toll-free number: (888) 464-6636
Fax: (918) 540-6946
Michelle Shackelford, Registrar, Northeastern Oklahoma Agricultural and Mechanical College, 200 I Street Northeast, Miami, OK 74354-6497

Northern Oklahoma College

Tonkawa, Oklahoma   **CB member**
www.noc.edu   **CB code: 6486**

▸ Public 2-year community college
▸ Commuter campus in small town

General. Founded in 1901. Regionally accredited. **Enrollment:** 5,023 degree-seeking undergraduates. **Degrees:** 852 associate awarded. **Location:** 90 miles from Oklahoma City; 70 miles from Wichita, KS. **Calendar:** Semester, limited summer session. **Full-time faculty:** 65 total. **Part-time faculty:** 98 total. **Special facilities:** Museum of science and history, observatory, arboretum.

Student profile.

Out-of-state: 1% Live on campus: 17%

Transfer out. Colleges most students transferred to 2015: Oklahoma State University, Northwestern Oklahoma State University, Oklahoma University, University of Central Oklahoma.

Basis for selection. Open admission, but selective for out-of-state students. Out-of-state applicants must have high school diploma and rank in top half of class or have 19 ACT. ACT required for students under 21 years old for placement. Students with below 19 ACT in English, math, and reading must take placement tests. **Adult students:** Placement testing required.

High school preparation. High school units mandated by state law may vary with program.

2015-2016 Annual costs. Tuition/fees: $3,249; $8,409 out-of-state. Per-credit charge: $78 in-state; $250 out-of-state. Room/board: $5,770. Books/supplies: $600. Personal expenses: $1,200.

Financial aid. Need-based: Need-based aid available for part-time students. Work-study available nights, weekends and for part-time students. **Non-need-based:** Scholarships awarded for academics, art, athletics, music/drama.

Application procedures. Admission: No deadline. No application fee. Admission notification on a rolling basis. **Financial aid:** Priority date 6/1; no closing date. FAFSA, institutional form required. Applicants notified on a rolling basis starting 4/1.

Academics. Special study options: Distance learning, dual enrollment of high school students, honors, independent study, internships, liberal arts/career combination, study abroad. License preparation in nursing, radiology. **Credit/placement by examination:** AP, CLEP, institutional tests. 30 credit hours maximum toward associate degree. **Support services:** Learning center, remedial instruction, tutoring.

Majors. Area/ethnic studies: Native American. **Biology:** General, zoology. **Business:** General, accounting, business admin, office management. **Communications:** Broadcast journalism, journalism, public relations. **Computer sciences:** General, web page design. **Education:** Elementary, physical, secondary. **English:** English lit. **Health services:** Medical radiologic technology/radiation therapy, nursing (RN), premedicine, prepharmacy, respiratory therapy technology, surgical technology. **Liberal arts:** Arts/sciences. **Math:** General. **Physical sciences:** Chemistry, physics. **Protective services:** Law enforcement admin. **Social sciences:** General. **Visual/performing arts:** Art, music management.

Technology on campus. 200 workstations in dormitories, library, computer center. Dormitories wired for high-speed internet access and linked to campus network. Commuter students can connect to campus network. Online course registration, online library, student web hosting, wireless network available.

Student life. Freshman orientation: Mandatory. Preregistration for classes offered. **Housing:** Single-sex dorms, apartments available. $60 deposit. **Activities:** Bands, choral groups, drama, literary magazine, music ensembles, musical theater, opera, radio station, student government, student newspaper, symphony orchestra, TV station.

Athletics. NJCAA. **Intercollegiate:** Baseball M, basketball, cheerleading, soccer, softball W. **Intramural:** Basketball, racquetball, softball, tennis, volleyball. **Team name:** Mavericks.

Student services. Career counseling, financial aid counseling, health services, personal counseling, veterans' counselor. **Physically disabled:** Services for visually, speech, hearing impaired. **Transfer:** College fairs on campus for students transferring to 4-year colleges.

Contact. E-mail: rick.edgington@noc.edu
Phone: (580) 628-6221 Toll-free number: (888) 429-5715
Fax: (580) 628-6371
Rick Edgington, Vice President for Enrollment Mgmt, Northern Oklahoma College, Box 310, Tonkawa, OK 74653-0310

Oklahoma City Community College
Oklahoma City, Oklahoma **CB member**
www.occc.edu **CB code: 0270**

‣ Public 2-year community and technical college
‣ Commuter campus in very large city

General. Founded in 1969. Regionally accredited. **Enrollment:** 13,000 degree-seeking undergraduates. **Degrees:** 1,860 associate awarded. **Calendar:** Semester, extensive summer session. **Full-time faculty:** 148 total; 20% minority, 51% women. **Part-time faculty:** 382 total; 18% minority, 57% women. **Class size:** 54% < 20, 45% 20-39, less than 1% 40-49, less than 1% 50-99. **Special facilities:** Olympic-size swimming pool, diving well.

Student profile.

Out-of-state: 2% 25 or older: 46%

Transfer out. Colleges most students transferred to 2015: University of Central Oklahoma, University of Oklahoma-OU Health Science Center, Oklahoma State University, University of Oklahoma, Oklahoma City University.

Basis for selection. Open admission, but selective for some programs. Special requirements for nursing, speech language pathology, occupational therapy and physical therapy programs; reading test required. **Home schooled:** If under the age of 21, official high school transcript and ACT required.

High school preparation. 15 units required. Required and recommended units include English 4, mathematics 3, social studies 1, history 2, science 3 (laboratory 1-2) and academic electives 1. History recommendation includes 1 unit of American history and 2 units of citizenship skills or other history. Math must include one semester of Algebra II.

2015-2016 Annual costs. Tuition/fees: $3,391; $8,425 out-of-state. Per-credit charge: $88 in-state; $255 out-of-state. Books/supplies: $1,000. Personal expenses: $1,252.

Financial aid. Need-based: Need-based aid available for part-time students. Work-study available nights, weekends and for part-time students. **Non-need-based:** Scholarships awarded for academics, alumni affiliation, art, leadership, music/drama, state residency.

Application procedures. Admission: No deadline. $25 fee. Admission notification on a rolling basis. **Financial aid:** Priority date 4/15; no closing date. FAFSA required. Applicants notified on a rolling basis starting 2/15.

Academics. Special study options: Accelerated study, cooperative education, distance learning, double major, dual enrollment of high school students, ESL, honors, independent study, internships, liberal arts/career combination, student-designed major, weekend college. License preparation in nursing, occupational therapy, paramedic, physical therapy, real estate. **Credit/placement by examination:** AP, CLEP, IB, institutional tests. 45 credit hours maximum toward associate degree. Credit will not be transcripted until 12 resident hours have been completed. **Support services:** GED preparation and test center, learning center, reduced course load, remedial instruction, study skills assistance, tutoring, writing center.

Majors. Biology: General, bioinformatics, biotechnology. **Business:** General, finance, office/clerical, real estate, tourism promotion, tourism/travel. **Communications:** Broadcast journalism, journalism. **Communications technology:** Desktop publishing, graphics, photo/film/video. **Computer sciences:** General, computer science, data processing, programming, security, systems analysis, web page design. **Education:** General, multi-level teacher, secondary. **Engineering:** General. **Foreign languages:** French, Spanish, translation. **Health services:** EMT paramedic, nursing (RN), occupational therapy assistant, physical therapy assistant. **History:** General. **Liberal arts:** Arts/sciences. **Math:** General. **Physical sciences:** Chemistry, physics. **Psychology:** General. **Social sciences:** Sociology. **Visual/performing arts:** Commercial/advertising art, music, studio arts, theater design. **Work/family studies:** Child care management.

Technology on campus. 2,000 workstations in library, computer center, student center. Commuter students can connect to campus network. Online course registration, online library, helpline, wireless network available.

Student life. Freshman orientation: Available. Preregistration for classes offered. Held continuously for 3 hours on days, evenings and weekends. **Activities:** Jazz band, campus ministries, choral groups, drama, international student organizations, literary magazine, music ensembles, musical theater, student government, student newspaper, Phi Theta Kappa, Chi Alpha, Christians on Campus, African-American student association, Asian cultural exchange, Native American cultural awareness organization, Young Democrats, deaf student association.

Two-Year Colleges

Athletics. Intramural: Baseball M, basketball, golf, soccer, softball, volleyball.

Student services. Career counseling, student employment services, financial aid counseling, on-campus daycare, personal counseling, placement for graduates, veterans' counselor. **Physically disabled:** Services for visually, speech, hearing impaired. **Transfer:** Transfer center, transfer adviser, college fairs on campus for students transferring to 4-year colleges.

Contact. E-mail: admissions@occc.edu
Phone: (405) 682-6222 Fax: (405) 682-7817
Jon Horinek, Director of Recruitment and Admissions, Oklahoma City Community College, 7777 South May Avenue, Oklahoma City, OK 73159

Oklahoma State University Institute of Technology: Okmulgee

Okmulgee, Oklahoma   **CB member**
www.osuit.edu   **CB code: 3382**

▸ Public 2-year branch campus and technical college
▸ Commuter campus in large town

General. Founded in 1946. Regionally accredited. **Enrollment:** 2,167 degree-seeking undergraduates; 309 non-degree-seeking students. **Degrees:** 65 bachelor's, 673 associate awarded. **Location:** 35 miles from Tulsa. **Calendar:** Trimester, extensive summer session. **Full-time faculty:** 122 total; 6% have terminal degrees, 20% minority, 31% women. **Part-time faculty:** 60 total; 3% have terminal degrees, 33% minority, 57% women. **Class size:** 81% < 20, 19% 20-39. **Special facilities:** Chesapeake Energy Natural Gas Compression Training Center, School of Watchmaking. **Partnerships:** Formal agreements with our schools to establish program requirements, provide internships, and provide sponsorships for our technical programs.

Student profile. Among degree-seeking undergraduates, 21% enrolled in a transfer program, 79% enrolled in a vocational program, 1% already have a bachelor's degree or higher, 508 enrolled as first-time, first-year students, 196 transferred in from other institutions.

Part-time:	22%	Native American:	14%
Out-of-state:	10%	Multi-racial, non-Hispanic:	9%
Women:	32%	International:	1%
African American:	5%	25 or older:	29%
Asian American:	1%	Live on campus:	29%
Hispanic/Latino:	5%		

Transfer out. Colleges most students transferred to 2015: Northeastern State University, Tulsa Community College, Oklahoma State University.

Basis for selection. Open admission, but selective for some programs. Special requirements for bachelors and some AAS programs.

High school preparation. College-preparatory program recommended. 15 units required. Required units include English 4, mathematics 3, history 3, science 3 (laboratory 3) and academic electives 2.

2015-2016 Annual costs. Tuition/fees: $4,860; $10,470 out-of-state. Per-credit charge: $124 in-state; $311 out-of-state. Room/board: $6,008. Books/supplies: $1,650. Personal expenses: $1,851.

2015-2016 Financial aid. Need-based: Average need met was 75%. Average scholarship/grant was $7,145; average loan $3,100. 47% of total undergraduate aid awarded as scholarships/grants, 53% as loans/jobs. Need-based aid available for part-time students. Work-study available nights, weekends and for part-time students. **Non-need-based:** Scholarships awarded for academics, alumni affiliation, job skills, leadership, minority status, state residency. **Additional information:** OSUIT Foundation Scholarship application due March 1.

Application procedures. Admission: No deadline. No application fee. Admission notification on a rolling basis. **Financial aid:** Priority date 3/1; no closing date. FAFSA required. Must reply within 4 week(s) of notification.

Academics. Special study options: Cooperative education, distance learning, double major, dual enrollment of high school students, independent study, internships. Bachelor's degree programs available on campus. License preparation in nursing. **Credit/placement by examination:** AP, CLEP, IB, institutional tests. 15 credit hours maximum toward associate degree, 15 toward bachelor's. **Support services:** GED preparation and test center, learning center, remedial instruction, study skills assistance, tutoring.

Majors. Business: General. **Computer sciences:** Information technology. **Education:** Multi-level teacher. **Health services:** Nursing (RN), orthotics/prosthetics. **Visual/performing arts:** Graphic design, multimedia, photography.

Most popular majors. Business/marketing 6%, computer/information sciences 7%, education 8%, engineering/engineering technologies 30%, health sciences 14%, trade and industry 25%.

Technology on campus. 50 workstations in dormitories, library, student center. Dormitories wired for high-speed internet access and linked to campus network. Commuter students can connect to campus network. Online library, helpline, wireless network available.

Student life. Freshman orientation: Available. Preregistration for classes offered. **Housing:** Coed dorms, single-sex dorms, special housing for disabled, apartments available. $150 fully refundable deposit. Housing for parents with dependent children available. **Activities:** Campus ministries, international student organizations, student government, Baptist Collegiate Ministries, Multicultural and International Student Association, Native American Student Association, Phi Theta Kappa, Student Abassadors, Government Association.

Athletics. Intramural: Basketball, football (non-tackle), racquetball, soccer, softball, table tennis, volleyball. **Team name:** Cowboys.

Student services. Alcohol/substance abuse counseling, career counseling, financial aid counseling, health services, on-campus daycare, personal counseling, veterans' counselor. **Physically disabled:** Services for visually, speech, hearing impaired. **Transfer:** Pre-admission transcript evaluation for new students. College fairs on campus for students transferring to 4-year colleges.

Contact. E-mail: admissions@okstate.edu
Phone: (918) 293-4680 Toll-free number: (800) 722-4471 ext. 4680
Fax: (918) 293-4643
Crystal Bowles, Registrar, Oklahoma State University Institute of Technology: Okmulgee, 1801 East Fourth Street, Okmulgee, OK 74447-3901

Oklahoma State University: Oklahoma City

Oklahoma City, Oklahoma
www.osuokc.edu/home   **CB code: 1436**

▸ Public 2-year branch campus and technical college
▸ Commuter campus in very large city

General. Founded in 1961. Regionally accredited. **Enrollment:** 5,537 degree-seeking undergraduates; 426 non-degree-seeking students. **Degrees:** 31 bachelor's, 937 associate awarded. **Location:** 10 miles from downtown. **Calendar:** Semester, extensive summer session. **Full-time faculty:** 85 total. **Part-time faculty:** 329 total. **Special facilities:** Horticulture center, precision driving training center, child development center, golf maintenance training facility, learning resource center, power transmission distribution pole yard.

Student profile. Among degree-seeking undergraduates, 13% enrolled in a transfer program, 795 enrolled as first-time, first-year students, 793 transferred in from other institutions.

Part-time:	66%	Hispanic/Latino:	11%
Women:	60%	Native American:	4%
African American:	14%	Multi-racial, non-Hispanic:	12%
Asian American:	3%	25 or older:	49%

Transfer out. Colleges most students transferred to 2015: University of Central Oklahoma, Oklahoma State University: Stillwater, University of Oklahoma.

Basis for selection. Open admission, but selective for some programs. Special requirements for nursing program, radiologic technology and emergency responder bachelor program. Interviews required for nursing program.

High school preparation. 15 units required. Required units include English 4, mathematics 3, social studies 1, history 2, science 2 (laboratory 2) and academic electives 3. Additional units of subjects above, from computer science and/or foreign language.

2015-2016 Annual costs. Tuition/fees: $3,634; $9,922 out-of-state. Per-credit charge: $95 in-state; $305 out-of-state. Books/supplies: $1,440.

Financial aid. All financial aid based on need. Need-based aid available for part-time students. Work-study available nights, weekends and for part-time students.

Application procedures. Admission: No deadline. No application fee. Admission notification on a rolling basis. **Financial aid:** Priority date 7/19; no closing date. FAFSA required. Applicants notified on a rolling basis starting 8/1; must reply within 2 week(s) of notification.

Academics. Special study options: Distance learning, double major, dual enrollment of high school students, honors, independent study, internships, liberal arts/career combination, weekend college. Fire/police/EMS training available. Bachelor's degree programs available on campus. License preparation in nursing, paramedic, radiology. **Credit/placement by examination:** AP, CLEP, institutional tests. 45 credit hours maximum toward associate degree. Credit granted for Fundamentals of Nursing (6 hours), Adult Nursing (8 hours). **Support services:** GED preparation and test center, learning center, remedial instruction, study skills assistance, tutoring, writing center.

Majors. Business: Accounting technology, accounting/finance, business admin, construction management, management science, office technology. **Computer sciences:** General, computer graphics, information technology. **Foreign languages:** Sign language interpretation, sign language linguistics, translation. **General:** Power transmission. **Health services:** Cardiovascular technology, dietetic technician, EMT paramedic, environmental health, health care admin, radiologic technology/medical imaging, sonography, substance abuse counseling, veterinary technology/assistant. **Protective services:** Fire safety technology, police science. **Work/family studies:** Child care management.

Technology on campus. 127 workstations in library, computer center, student center. Commuter students can connect to campus network. Online course registration, online library, repair service, wireless network available.

Student life. Freshman orientation: Mandatory. Preregistration for classes offered. **Activities:** Student government, student newspaper, Oklahoma Intercollegiate Legislature, OSU-Oklahoma City Chapter of the Emergency Medical Technician Student Association, Go Green, Mission Dance, Native American Student Association, Hispanic Student Association, martial arts club, Black Student Association, Wind Energy Student Association.

Athletics. Team name: Cowboys.

Student services. Adult student services, career counseling, student employment services, financial aid counseling, on-campus daycare, personal counseling, placement for graduates, veterans' counselor. **Physically disabled:** Services for visually, speech, hearing impaired. **Transfer:** Transfer center, transfer adviser, college fairs on campus for students transferring to 4-year colleges.

Contact. E-mail: admissions@osuokc.edu
Phone: (405) 945-3224 Toll-free number: (800) 560-4099
Fax: (405) 945-3277
Kyle Williams, Director of Enrollment Management, Oklahoma State University: Oklahoma City, 900 North Portland Avenue, Oklahoma City, OK 73107-6195

Platt College: Moore
Moore, Oklahoma
www.plattcolleges.edu

- For-profit 2-year culinary school and health science college
- Large city

General. Regionally accredited; also accredited by ACCSC. **Enrollment:** 172 undergraduates. **Degrees:** 52 associate awarded. **Calendar:** Quarter. **Full-time faculty:** 13 total. **Part-time faculty:** 8 total.

Basis for selection. Open admission, but selective for some programs.

2015-2016 Annual costs. Certificate programs: Dental Assistant $15,420; Medical Assistant $15,420; Surgical Technologist $23,720; Pastry Arts (Morning) $22,520. Associate programs: Practical Nursing $28,200; Respiratory Care $30,020.

Financial aid. Need-based: Work-study available nights, weekends and for part-time students.

Application procedures. Admission: No deadline. $25 fee.

Academics. Credit/placement by examination: AP, CLEP.

Majors. Health services: Clinical lab technology, licensed practical nurse, respiratory therapy technology.

Contact. Phone: (405) 912-3260
David Haynes, Director of Admissions, Platt College: Moore, 201 North Eastern, Moore, OK 73160

Platt College: Oklahoma City Central
Oklahoma City, Oklahoma
www.plattcolleges.edu

- For-profit 2-year branch campus and career college
- Small city
- Interview required

General. Accredited by ACCSC. **Enrollment:** 200 undergraduates. **Degrees:** 11 associate awarded. **Calendar:** Semester. **Full-time faculty:** 14 total. **Part-time faculty:** 12 total.

Basis for selection. Open admission, but selective for some programs. Entrance exam required for placement. **Home schooled:** Transcript of courses and grades required.

2015-2016 Annual costs. Certificate programs: Dental Assistant $15,420; Medical Assistant $15,420. Associate programs: Practical Nursing $28,200; Nursing $36,020; Culinary Arts (Morning) $31,720. Bachelor's programs: Nursing $46,120; Hospitality and Restaurant Management $46,020.

Financial aid. Need-based: Work-study available nights, weekends and for part-time students.

Application procedures. Admission: No deadline. $25 fee. Admission notification on a rolling basis. **Financial aid:** No deadline. FAFSA required.

Academics. Special study options: License preparation in nursing. **Credit/placement by examination:** AP, CLEP. **Support services:** GED preparation, study skills assistance, tutoring.

Majors. Health services: Licensed practical nurse.

Student life. Freshman orientation: Mandatory. Preregistration for classes offered.

Student services. Adult student services, alcohol/substance abuse counseling, career counseling, financial aid counseling, personal counseling, placement for graduates.

Contact. E-mail: klamb@plattcollege.org
Phone: (405) 946-7799 Fax: (405) 943-2150
Kim Lamb, Director of Admissions, Platt College: Oklahoma City Central, 309 South Ann Arbor, Oklahoma City, OK 73128

Platt College: Tulsa
Tulsa, Oklahoma
www.plattcolleges.edu

- For-profit 2-year culinary school and health science college
- Commuter campus in large city
- Interview required

General. Accredited by ACCSC. **Enrollment:** 360 undergraduates. **Degrees:** 2 bachelor's, 87 associate awarded. **Calendar:** Differs by program. **Full-time faculty:** 30 total. **Part-time faculty:** 30 total. **Class size:** 100% < 20.

Basis for selection. Open admission, but selective for some programs. High school diploma or GED required for some programs. Others require successful completion of entrance exams. Nursing programs require additional interview with Director of Nursing. **Home schooled:** State high school equivalency certificate required.

2015-2016 Annual costs. Certificate programs: Dental Assistant $15,420; Medical Assistant $15,420; Pharmacy Technician $12,500; Pastry Arts (Morning) $22,520. Associate programs: Practical Nursing $28,200; Nursing $36,020; Culinary Arts (Morning) $31,720. Bachelor's programs: Nursing $46,120; Hospitality and Restaurant Management $46,020.

Financial aid. All financial aid based on need. Need-based aid available for part-time students. Work-study available nights, weekends and for part-time students.

Application procedures. Admission: No deadline. $100 fee. **Financial aid:** No deadline. FAFSA required.

Academics. Special study options: Liberal arts/career combination. Bachelor's degree programs available on campus. License preparation in nursing. **Credit/placement by examination:** AP, CLEP. **Support services:** Remedial instruction, tutoring.

Majors. Computer sciences: Security. **Health services:** Licensed practical nurse, nursing (RN), respiratory therapy technology.

Technology on campus. 35 workstations in library, computer center. Online library, wireless network available.

Student life. Freshman orientation: Mandatory. Preregistration for classes offered. Held for 5 hours on first day of classes.

Student services. Student employment services, financial aid counseling, placement for graduates. **Transfer:** Pre-admission transcript evaluation for new students.

Contact. E-mail: stephanieh@plattcollege.org
Phone: (918) 663-9000 Fax: (918) 622-1240
Richard Dixon, Admission Director, Platt College: Tulsa, 3801 South Sheridan, Tulsa, OK 74145-1132

Redlands Community College
El Reno, Oklahoma
www.redlandscc.edu   CB code: 7324

- Public 2-year community college
- Commuter campus in large town

General. Founded in 1938. Regionally accredited. **Enrollment:** 2,500 undergraduates. **Degrees:** 224 associate awarded. **Location:** 25 miles from Oklahoma City. **Calendar:** Semester, limited summer session. **Full-time faculty:** 46 total. **Part-time faculty:** 88 total. **Class size:** 56% < 20, 41% 20-39, 2% 40-49, less than 1% 50-99, less than 1% >100. **Special facilities:** Applied agricultural research center, ranch, working farm and equine centers, viticulture and enology programs.

Student profile.

Out-of-state:	97%	Live on campus:	10%
25 or older:	29%		

Transfer out. Colleges most students transferred to 2015: University of Central Oklahoma, Southwestern Oklahoma State University, Oklahoma State University, University of Oklahoma, University of Science and Arts of Oklahoma.

Basis for selection. Open admission, but selective for some programs. All applicants who have high school diploma or GED are admitted and may be required to take ACT or COMPASS tests. Students without high school diploma or GED must take COMPASS tests. Competitive admissions to nursing and honors programs. Students without ACT or with ACT below 19 required to take COMPASS placement tests offered on campus. SAT or ACT recommended.

High school preparation. College-preparatory program recommended. Recommended units include English 4, mathematics 3, social studies 2, science 2 and foreign language 1.

2015-2016 Annual costs. Tuition/fees: $3,882; $6,026 out-of-state. Per-credit charge: $129 in-state; $201 out-of-state. Room/board: $7,468. Books/supplies: $960.

Financial aid. Need-based: Need-based aid available for part-time students. Work-study available nights, weekends and for part-time students. **Non-need-based:** Scholarships awarded for academics, athletics, leadership.

Application procedures. Admission: No deadline. $25 fee, may be waived for applicants with need. Admission notification on a rolling basis. **Financial aid:** Priority date 8/1; no closing date. FAFSA required. Applicants notified on a rolling basis starting 6/1; must reply within 6 week(s) of notification.

Academics. Special study options: Accelerated study, cooperative education, cross-registration, distance learning, double major, dual enrollment of high school students, external degree, honors, independent study, internships, liberal arts/career combination. License preparation in nursing, paramedic. **Credit/placement by examination:** AP, CLEP, institutional tests. 32 credit hours maximum toward associate degree. **Support services:** Learning center, reduced course load, remedial instruction, study skills assistance, tutoring.

Majors. Business: Business admin. **Computer sciences:** General. **Education:** General. **English:** English lit, rhetoric/composition. **Health services:** EMT paramedic, nursing (RN), veterinary technology/assistant. **Math:** General. **Parks/recreation:** Exercise sciences, health/fitness. **Physical sciences:** General. **Protective services:** Police science. **Psychology:** General. **Social sciences:** General. **Visual/performing arts:** Art. **Work/family studies:** Child care management, child development.

Most popular majors. Agriculture 7%, business/marketing 14%, family/consumer sciences 6%, health sciences 19%, liberal arts 30%, security/protective services 9%.

Technology on campus. 300 workstations in dormitories, library, computer center. Dormitories wired for high-speed internet access. Commuter students can connect to campus network. Online course registration, online library, helpline, wireless network available.

Student life. Freshman orientation: Available. Preregistration for classes offered. Class held Thursday and Friday prior to start of Fall semester; charge associated with class is standard tuition rate for one credit hour. **Policies:** Students must abide by policies, regulations, and requirements specified in Student Handbook. **Housing:** Apartments, wellness housing available. $200 partly refundable deposit. Limited housing for agriculture students at working ranch available. **Activities:** Campus ministries, choral groups, Model UN, student government, student nursing association, Aggie club, Phi Theta Kappa, Young Democrats, College Republicans, art club, Students in Free Enterprise, fencing club, photography club.

Athletics. NJCAA. **Intercollegiate:** Baseball M, basketball, golf W, volleyball W. **Intramural:** Basketball, racquetball, swimming, weight lifting. **Team name:** Cougars.

Student services. Adult student services, career counseling, services for economically disadvantaged, student employment services, financial aid counseling, placement for graduates, veterans' counselor. **Transfer:** Transfer adviser, college fairs on campus for students transferring to 4-year colleges.

Contact. E-mail: studentservices@redlandscc.edu
Phone: (405) 262-2552 ext. 1417
Toll-free number: (866) 415-6367 ext. 1417 Fax: (405) 422-1239
Tricia Hobson, Director of Enrollment Management, Redlands Community College, 1300 South Country Club Road, El Reno, OK 73036

Rose State College
Midwest City, Oklahoma
www.rose.edu   CB code: 1462

- Public 2-year community college
- Commuter campus in small city

General. Founded in 1968. Regionally accredited. On-campus student housing available beginning with the fall 2015 semester. **Enrollment:** 5,998 degree-seeking undergraduates; 571 non-degree-seeking students. **Degrees:** 1,032 associate awarded. **ROTC:** Air Force. **Location:** 5 miles from Oklahoma City. **Calendar:** Semester, extensive summer session. **Full-time faculty:** 114 total; 17% have terminal degrees, 13% minority, 65% women. **Part-time faculty:** 233 total; 16% have terminal degrees, 20% minority, 49% women. **Class size:** 59% < 20, 40% 20-39, less than 1% 40-49, less than 1% 50-99. **Special facilities:** Regional history center, 1400-seat performing arts theater, wetlands project, fabrication lab (FAB LAB).

Student profile. Among degree-seeking undergraduates, 66% enrolled in a transfer program, 34% enrolled in a vocational program, 1,372 enrolled as first-time, first-year students, 695 transferred in from other institutions.

Part-time:	55%	Hispanic/Latino:	6%
Out-of-state:	1%	Native American:	5%
Women:	62%	Multi-racial, non-Hispanic:	10%
African American:	17%	25 or older:	44%
Asian American:	2%	Live on campus:	2%

Transfer out. Colleges most students transferred to 2015: Oklahoma State University, Southwestern Oklahoma State University, University of Oklahoma, University of Central Oklahoma.

Basis for selection. Open admission, but selective for some programs. Interview required for health science programs and possibly for entry into specialized programs. **Adult students:** COMPASS Placement test required. **Home schooled:** Transcript of courses and grades required. Peer class must have graduated.

High school preparation. 15 units required. Required units include English 4, mathematics 3, social studies 1, history 2, science 3 (laboratory 3) and academic electives 2. Electives may include English, lab science, math, history/citizenship skills, computer science or foreign language.

2015-2016 Annual costs. Tuition/fees: $3,375; $9,752 out-of-state. Per-credit charge: $92 in-state; $304 out-of-state. Room only: $6,000. Books/supplies: $1,000.

2014-2015 Financial aid. Need-based: 59% of total undergraduate aid awarded as scholarships/grants, 41% as loans/jobs. Need-based aid available

for part-time students. Work-study available nights, weekends and for part-time students. **Non-need-based:** Scholarships awarded for academics, athletics, leadership. **Additional information:** Ticket to Rose grant available to students from Midwest City/Choctaw high schools to cover unmet need in tuition/fees.

Application procedures. Admission: No deadline. No application fee. Admission notification on a rolling basis. **Financial aid:** Priority date 6/1; no closing date. FAFSA required. Applicants notified on a rolling basis starting 3/1; must reply within 4 week(s) of notification.

Academics. Student Success Center available for academic planning. **Special study options:** Accelerated study, cooperative education, distance learning, double major, ESL, honors, internships, liberal arts/career combination, study abroad. License preparation in dental hygiene, nursing, radiology. **Credit/placement by examination:** AP, CLEP, IB, institutional tests. 47 credit hours maximum toward associate degree. **Support services:** Learning center, pre-admission summer program, reduced course load, remedial instruction, study skills assistance, tutoring, writing center. Student Success Workshops, one-on-one time with students, resource referral, TriO program, personal counseling services available through Student Success Center, ESL tutoring.

Majors. Area/ethnic studies: Native American. **Biology:** General. **Business:** General, accounting technology, business admin, operations. **Communications:** Broadcast journalism, journalism, photojournalism. **Computer sciences:** General, LAN/WAN management, networking, programming. **Conservation:** Environmental science. **Education:** Multi-level teacher. **Engineering:** General. **English:** English lit. **Foreign languages:** General. **Health services:** Clinical lab assistant, dental assistant, dental hygiene, health information technology, nursing (RN), predental, premedicine, prenursing, prepharmacy, radiologic technology/medical imaging, respiratory therapy assistant, respiratory therapy technology. **History:** General. **Human services:** Social work. **Liberal arts:** Arts/sciences, library assistant. **Math:** General. **Parks/recreation:** Health/fitness. **Physical sciences:** Chemistry, geology, physics. **Protective services:** Homeland security, police science. **Psychology:** General. **Social sciences:** General, political science, sociology. **Visual/performing arts:** Multimedia, theater arts management. **Work/family studies:** Child care management, child development.

Most popular majors. Business/marketing 9%, health sciences 21%, liberal arts 27%, psychology 7%, social sciences 13%.

Technology on campus. 600 workstations in library, computer center, student center. Dormitories wired for high-speed internet access. Commuter students can connect to campus network. Online course registration, online library, helpline, student web hosting, wireless network available.

Student life. Freshman orientation: Available, $113 fee. Preregistration for classes offered. First year course offered throughout August in various formats including on-line, 8 week and 16 week. **Housing:** Apartments available. College housing available. **Activities:** Jazz band, choral groups, dance, drama, literary magazine, music ensembles, musical theater, student government, student newspaper, Phi Theta Kappa, criminal justice club, Black Student Association, Broadcasting Club, drama club, Oklahoma Intercollegiate Legislature, American Indian association.

Athletics. NJCAA. **Intercollegiate:** Baseball M, soccer, softball W. **Intramural:** Bowling, volleyball. **Team name:** Raiders.

Student services. Adult student services, alcohol/substance abuse counseling, career counseling, services for economically disadvantaged, student employment services, financial aid counseling, personal counseling, placement for graduates, veterans' counselor. **Physically disabled:** Services for visually, speech, hearing impaired. **Transfer:** Pre-admission transcript evaluation for new students. College fairs on campus for students transferring to 4-year colleges.

Contact. Phone: (405) 733-7308 Toll-free number: (866) 621-0987 Fax: (405) 736-0309
Mechelle Aitson-Roessler, Registrar/Director of Admissions, Rose State College, 6420 SE 15th Street, Midwest City, OK 73110-2799

Seminole State College
Seminole, Oklahoma
www.sscok.edu
CB code: 0316

♦ Public 2-year community and junior college
♦ Commuter campus in small town

General. Founded in 1931. Regionally accredited. **Enrollment:** 1,399 degree-seeking undergraduates; 428 non-degree-seeking students. **Degrees:** 316 associate awarded. **Location:** 55 miles from Oklahoma City. **Calendar:** Semester, extensive summer session. **Full-time faculty:** 37 total; 8% have

terminal degrees, 19% minority, 62% women. **Part-time faculty:** 63 total; 8% minority, 67% women.

Student profile. Among degree-seeking undergraduates, 415 enrolled as first-time, first-year students, 905 transferred in from other institutions.

Part-time:	36%	Hispanic/Latino:	5%
Out-of-state:	2%	Native American:	26%
Women:	65%	International:	2%
African American:	8%	25 or older:	43%
Asian American:	1%	Live on campus:	8%

Transfer out. Colleges most students transferred to 2015: East Central University, University of Central Oklahoma, Oklahoma State University, Oklahoma University, Oklahoma Baptist University.

Basis for selection. Open admission, but selective for some programs. Additional requirements for admission to A.D. Nursing Program and MLT Program include 19 ACT, score of 15 on Nelson Denny Reading Test, and a college GPA of 3.0. **Home schooled:** Transcript of courses and grades required. **Learning Disabled:** Documentation from high school, such as IEP or any documentation from physician required.

High school preparation. 15 units recommended. Recommended units include English 4, mathematics 3, social studies 2, history 3, science 2 and academic electives 2. 3 Foreign Language or Computer Science.

2015-2016 Annual costs. Tuition/fees: $3,809; $8,969 out-of-state. Per-credit charge: $83 in-state; $255 out-of-state. Room/board: $7,070. Books/supplies: $1,109. Personal expenses: $900.

Financial aid. Need-based: Need-based aid available for part-time students. Work-study available nights, weekends and for part-time students. **Non-need-based:** Scholarships awarded for academics, art, athletics, leadership, music/drama, state residency.

Application procedures. Admission: No deadline. $15 fee. Application must be submitted on paper. Admission notification on a rolling basis. **Financial aid:** Priority date 3/1; no closing date. FAFSA, institutional form required. Applicants notified on a rolling basis starting 3/1; must reply within 4 week(s) of notification.

Academics. Special study options: Cooperative education, distance learning, double major, dual enrollment of high school students, ESL, independent study, study abroad, weekend college. License preparation in nursing. **Credit/placement by examination:** AP, CLEP, institutional tests. 30 credit hours maximum toward associate degree. **Support services:** Learning center, reduced course load, remedial instruction, study skills assistance, tutoring, writing center.

Majors. Business: Business admin, office management, office/clerical. **Computer sciences:** Computer science. **Education:** General, elementary. **Health services:** Clinical lab technology, nursing (RN). **Liberal arts:** Arts/sciences. **Math:** General. **Parks/recreation:** Health/fitness. **Social sciences:** General. **Visual/performing arts:** Art.

Most popular majors. Business/marketing 20%, computer/information sciences 10%, health sciences 10%, liberal arts 60%.

Technology on campus. 100 workstations in dormitories, library, computer center, student center. Dormitories wired for high-speed internet access and linked to campus network. Commuter students can connect to campus network. Online library, wireless network available.

Student life. Freshman orientation: Mandatory. Preregistration for classes offered. **Housing:** Coed dorms available. $100 fully refundable deposit. **Activities:** Campus ministries, international student organizations, music ensembles, student government, Native American Student Association, Baptist Student Union, Phi Theta Kappa, Psi Beta Honor Society, National English Honor Society, Student Nurses Association.

Athletics. NJCAA. **Intercollegiate:** Baseball M, basketball, golf, softball W, tennis, volleyball W. **Team name:** Trojans.

Student services. Adult student services, career counseling, services for economically disadvantaged, financial aid counseling, personal counseling, veterans' counselor. **Physically disabled:** Services for visually, speech, hearing impaired. **Transfer:** Pre-admission transcript evaluation for new students. Transfer adviser, college fairs on campus for students transferring to 4-year colleges.

Contact. E-mail: admissions@sscok.edu
Phone: (405) 382-9230 Fax: (405) 382-9524
Corey Quiett, Registrar, Seminole State College, PO Box 351, Seminole, OK 74818-0351

Tulsa Community College
Tulsa, Oklahoma — **CB member**
www.tulsacc.edu — **CB code: 6839**

- Public 2-year community college
- Commuter campus in large city

General. Founded in 1968. Regionally accredited. 4 branch campuses located in Tulsa. **Enrollment:** 14,069 degree-seeking undergraduates; 2,639 non-degree-seeking students. **Degrees:** 2,136 associate awarded. **Calendar:** Semester, extensive summer session. **Full-time faculty:** 301 total; 24% have terminal degrees, 18% minority, 60% women. **Part-time faculty:** 566 total; 19% minority, 59% women. **Class size:** 98% < 20, 2% 20-39.

Student profile. Among degree-seeking undergraduates, 3,734 enrolled as first-time, first-year students, 511 transferred in from other institutions.

Part-time:	61%	Hispanic/Latino:	8%
Out-of-state:	1%	Native American:	8%
Women:	60%	Multi-racial, non-Hispanic:	9%
African American:	9%	International:	2%
Asian American:	4%	25 or older:	41%

Transfer out. Colleges most students transferred to 2015: University of Oklahoma, Oklahoma State University, Northeastern Oklahoma State University, Tulsa University, University of Central Oklahoma.

Basis for selection. Open admission, but selective for some programs. Special requirements for health-related, legal assistant, and management programs. Interview required for health, legal assistant, and nursing programs. **Adult students:** ACT or Accuplacer CPT required for placement.

High school preparation. College-preparatory program recommended. 16 units required; 20 recommended. Required and recommended units include English 4, mathematics 3-4, history 3, science 3-4 (laboratory 3-4) and visual/performing arts 2.

2015-2016 Annual costs. Tuition/fees: $3,623; $9,803 out-of-state. Per-credit charge: $91 in-state; $297 out-of-state. Books/supplies: $1,500. Personal expenses: $1,315.

2015-2016 Financial aid. Need-based: Average need met was 70%. Average scholarship/grant was $2,828; average loan $1,576. 70% of total undergraduate aid awarded as scholarships/grants, 30% as loans/jobs. Need-based aid available for part-time students. **Non-need-based:** Scholarships awarded for academics, art, job skills, leadership, minority status, state residency.

Application procedures. Admission: No deadline. $20 fee. Admission notification on a rolling basis. **Financial aid:** Priority date 6/1; no closing date. FAFSA required. Applicants notified on a rolling basis starting 2/1.

Academics. Many short-period intensive courses within conventional semesters. **Special study options:** Accelerated study, cooperative education, cross-registration, distance learning, dual enrollment of high school students, ESL, honors, independent study, internships, liberal arts/career combination, study abroad, weekend college. **Credit/placement by examination:** AP, CLEP, IB, institutional tests. 30 credit hours maximum toward associate degree. **Support services:** Learning center, remedial instruction, study skills assistance, tutoring, writing center.

Majors. Biology: Biotechnology. **Business:** General, accounting, administrative services, business admin, fashion, finance, hospitality admin, hospitality/recreation, human resources, insurance, management information systems, managerial economics, office technology, real estate, tourism/travel. **Communications:** Journalism. **Communications technology:** General. **Computer sciences:** General, applications programming, programming. **Education:** General, physical. **Engineering:** General. **English:** English lit, rhetoric/composition. **Foreign languages:** French, German, Italian, Japanese, Russian, sign language interpretation, Spanish. **Health services:** Clinical lab assistant, clinical lab technology, dental hygiene, medical assistant, medical radiologic technology/radiation therapy, medical secretary, occupational therapy assistant, physical therapy assistant, respiratory therapy technology. **History:** General. **Human services:** Social work. **Liberal arts:** Library assistant. **Math:** General. **Parks/recreation:** Sports admin. **Philosophy/religion:** Philosophy. **Physical sciences:** Astronomy, chemistry, geology, physics. **Protective services:** Criminal justice, fire safety technology, police science. **Psychology:** General. **Social sciences:** General, economics, geography, political science, sociology. **Visual/performing arts:** Dramatic, interior design, music. **Work/family studies:** Child care management.

Most popular majors. Business/marketing 22%, engineering/engineering technologies 6%, health sciences 26%, interdisciplinary studies 7%, liberal arts 6%, social sciences 10%.

Technology on campus. 2,306 workstations in library, computer center. Online course registration, online library available.

Student life. Freshman orientation: Available. Preregistration for classes offered. **Activities:** Bands, campus ministries, choral groups, dance, drama, film society, international student organizations, literary magazine, music ensembles, musical theater, opera, radio station, student government, student newspaper, symphony orchestra, TV station.

Athletics. Intramural: Basketball, soccer, softball, table tennis, tennis, volleyball.

Student services. Career counseling, student employment services, health services, on-campus daycare, personal counseling, placement for graduates, veterans' counselor. **Physically disabled:** Services for visually, hearing impaired. **Transfer:** College fairs on campus for students transferring to 4-year colleges.

Contact. E-mail: admissions@tulsacc.edu
Phone: (918) 595-2010 Fax: (918) 595-3414
Traci Heck, Dean of Admissions and Records, Tulsa Community College, 6111 East Skelly Drive, Tulsa, OK 74135-6198

Tulsa Welding School
Tulsa, Oklahoma
www.weldingschool.com — **CB code: 2958**

- For-profit 2-year technical college
- Commuter campus in very large city
- Interview required

General. Accredited by ACCSC. **Enrollment:** 1,783 degree-seeking undergraduates. **Degrees:** 21 associate awarded. **Calendar:** Differs by program. **Full-time faculty:** 31 total.

Student profile.

Out-of-state:	60%	25 or older:	37%
Women:	5%		

Basis for selection. Open admission. **Home schooled:** Applicants must pass ATB test.

2015-2016 Annual costs. Program tuition varies from $14,300 to $38,957.

2014-2015 Financial aid. All financial aid based on need. 42% of total undergraduate aid awarded as scholarships/grants, 58% as loans/jobs. Work-study available nights, weekends and for part-time students.

Application procedures. Admission: No deadline. No application fee. Admission notification on a rolling basis. Must have high school diploma or GED or pass Ability To Benefit test. **Financial aid:** No deadline. FAFSA required.

Academics. Credit/placement by examination: AP, CLEP. **Support services:** GED preparation.

Technology on campus. 3 workstations in library.

Student life. Freshman orientation: Mandatory. Preregistration for classes offered.

Student services. Adult student services, student employment services, financial aid counseling. **Physically disabled:** Services for hearing impaired.

Contact. E-mail: tulsainfo@twsweld.com
Phone: (918) 587-6789 ext. 240
Toll-free number: (800) 331-2934 ext. 221 Fax: (918) 295-6821
Joe McKinney, Senior Director of High School Admissions, Tulsa Welding School, 2545 East 11th Street, Tulsa, OK 74104-3909

Vatterott College: Oklahoma City
Oklahoma City, Oklahoma
www.vatterott.edu — **CB code: 2899**

- For-profit 2-year technical and career college
- Residential campus in very large city

General. Accredited by ACCSC. **Enrollment:** 280 undergraduates. **Degrees:** 74 associate awarded. **Calendar:** Differs by program. **Full-time faculty:** 7 total. **Part-time faculty:** 14 total. **Class size:** 75% < 20, 25% 20-39.

Basis for selection. Open admission.

2015-2016 Annual costs. Diploma programs: (40 weeks) $18,884; (60 weeks) $28,034-$28,480. Associate programs: (70 weeks) $30,559-$37,450; (90 weeks) $39,114-$41,822. Costs include fees, books and supplies.

Financial aid. All financial aid based on need. Work-study available nights, weekends and for part-time students.

Application procedures. Admission: No deadline. No application fee. **Financial aid:** No deadline. FAFSA required.

Academics. Credit/placement by examination: AP, CLEP. **Support services:** Learning center, remedial instruction, study skills assistance, tutoring.

Majors. Computer sciences: General, information technology, LAN/WAN management, programming.

Technology on campus. 125 workstations in library, computer center.

Student life. Freshman orientation: Mandatory. Preregistration for classes offered.

Student services. Career counseling, financial aid counseling.

Contact. Phone: (405) 945-0088 Toll-free number: (888) 553-6627 Fax: (405) 945-0788
Jesse Hardiman, Director of Admissions, Vatterott College: Oklahoma City, 5537 Northwest Expressway, Oklahoma City, OK 73132

Vatterott College: Tulsa
Tulsa, Oklahoma
www.vatterott.edu   CB code: 3637

- For-profit 2-year branch campus and technical college
- Commuter campus in large city
- Interview required

General. Accredited by ACCSC. **Enrollment:** 164 undergraduates. **Degrees:** 36 associate awarded. **Calendar:** Differs by program. **Full-time faculty:** 16 total; 19% women. **Part-time faculty:** 1 total; 100% women. **Special facilities:** Extensive HVAC lab.

Basis for selection. High school diploma or GED required.

2015-2016 Annual costs. Diploma programs: (60 weeks) $26,076-$29,140. Associate programs: (70 weeks) $30,559-$34,180; (90 weeks) $39,984-$41,838. Costs include fees, books and supplies.

Financial aid. Need-based: Work-study available nights, weekends and for part-time students.

Application procedures. Admission: No deadline. No application fee.

Academics. Credit/placement by examination: AP, CLEP, institutional tests. **Support services:** Study skills assistance, tutoring.

Majors. Computer sciences: LAN/WAN management, web page design. **Health services:** Office assistant.

Technology on campus. 20 workstations in library, computer center.

Student life. Freshman orientation: Available. Preregistration for classes offered. **Activities:** Student newspaper.

Student services. Transfer: Pre-admission transcript evaluation for new students. College fairs on campus for students transferring to 4-year colleges.

Contact. E-mail: tulsa@vatterott-college.edu
Phone: (918) 835-8288 Toll-free number: (888) 857-4016
Fax: (918) 835-9698
Director of Admissions, Vatterott College: Tulsa, 4343 South 118th East Avenue, Tulsa, OK 74146

Virginia College in Tulsa
Tulsa, Oklahoma
www.vc.edu/college/tulsa-oklahoma-colleges.cfm

- For-profit 2-year health science and career college
- Large city

General. Regionally accredited; also accredited by ACICS. **Enrollment:** 121 undergraduates. **Degrees:** 20 associate awarded. **Calendar:** Quarter.

Basis for selection. Open admission.

2015-2016 Annual costs. Certificate programs: $12,816-$20,100. Associate programs: $32,160-$35,600. Bachelor's programs: $60,300-$64,080. Clock hour certificate program: $21,225.

Financial aid. Need-based: Work-study available nights, weekends and for part-time students.

Application procedures. Admission: $100 fee.

Academics. Credit/placement by examination: AP, CLEP.

Majors. Business: Business admin. **Computer sciences:** System admin. **Health services:** Health information management, insurance coding, medical assistant, office assistant.

Contact. E-mail: tulsa.info@vc.edu
Deanna Giles, Director of Admissions, Virginia College in Tulsa, 5124 South Peoria Avenue, Tulsa, OK 74105

Western Oklahoma State College
Altus, Oklahoma
www.wosc.edu   CB code: 6020

- Public 2-year community college
- Commuter campus in large town

General. Founded in 1926. Regionally accredited. **Enrollment:** 1,178 degree-seeking undergraduates. **Degrees:** 260 associate awarded. **Location:** 55 miles from Lawton, 140 miles from Oklahoma City. **Calendar:** Semester, limited summer session. **Full-time faculty:** 44 total. **Part-time faculty:** 35 total. **Class size:** 78% < 20, 20% 20-39, less than 1% 40-49, 1% 50-99.

Transfer out. Colleges most students transferred to 2015: Southwestern Oklahoma State University, Cameron University, Oklahoma State University, University of Central Oklahoma, University of Oklahoma.

Basis for selection. Open admission, but selective for some programs. SAT or ACT required for applicants under 21 for placement; no minimum score required. **Adult students:** COMPASS or ACT required for adults who don't have high school diploma or GED. Must demonstrate proficiency in English, math, science, and reading through COMPASS or ACT subtest scores. **Home schooled:** Transcript of courses and grades required. Must have ACT or SAT. High school class must have graduated and must satisfy curricular requirements.

2015-2016 Annual costs. Tuition/fees: $3,299; $7,654 out-of-state. Per-credit charge: $71 in-state; $216 out-of-state. Room/board: $4,250. Books/supplies: $1,300. Personal expenses: $1,200.

2014-2015 Financial aid. Need-based: Need-based aid available for part-time students. Work-study available nights, weekends and for part-time students. **Non-need-based:** Scholarships awarded for academics, alumni affiliation, art, athletics, leadership, music/drama, state residency.

Application procedures. Admission: No deadline. $15 fee. Application must be submitted online. Admission notification on a rolling basis. **Financial aid:** Closing date 3/1. FAFSA, institutional form required. Applicants notified on a rolling basis; must reply within 3 week(s) of notification.

Academics. Special study options: Cooperative education, distance learning, dual enrollment of high school students, liberal arts/career combination. Cooperative agreements with local technology centers; students may dual-enroll and earn college credits for career tech courses. License preparation in aviation, nursing, radiology. **Credit/placement by examination:** AP, CLEP, IB, institutional tests. 30 credit hours maximum toward associate degree. **Support services:** GED test center, learning center, remedial instruction, study skills assistance, tutoring.

Majors. Biology: General. **Business:** Administrative services, business admin, office/clerical. **Computer sciences:** General, computer science, information systems, programming. **Education:** Physical. **Engineering:** Engineering science. **English:** English lit. **Health services:** Health information management, medical radiologic technology/radiation therapy, medical secretary, nursing (RN). **Liberal arts:** Arts/sciences. **Math:** General. **Parks/recreation:** Health/fitness. **Philosophy/religion:** Religion. **Protective services:** Corrections, firefighting, police science. **Social sciences:** General. **Visual/performing arts:** Art, music. **Work/family studies:** Child care management, child development.

Most popular majors. Business/marketing 10%, health sciences 28%, liberal arts 32%, psychology 6%.

Technology on campus. 50 workstations in library. Dormitories wired for high-speed internet access and linked to campus network. Commuter students can connect to campus network. Online course registration, online library, helpline, wireless network available.

Student life. Freshman orientation: Mandatory. Preregistration for classes offered. **Housing:** Coed dorms available. $50 fully refundable deposit. **Activities:** Bands, choral groups, drama, music ensembles, musical theater, student government, student newspaper, Baptist student union, Wesley Foundation, tutoring club, College Democrats, College Republicans, Fellowship of Christian Athletes.

Athletics. NJCAA. **Intercollegiate:** Baseball M, basketball, softball W. **Intramural:** Basketball, volleyball. **Team name:** Pioneers.

Student services. Career counseling, financial aid counseling, health services, personal counseling, veterans' counselor. **Physically disabled:** Services for visually, hearing impaired. **Transfer:** College fairs on campus for students transferring to 4-year colleges.

Contact. E-mail: lana.scott@wosc.edu
Phone: (580) 477-7717 Fax: (580) 477-7723
Lana Scott, Director of Admissions and Registrar, Western Oklahoma State College, 2801 North Main Street, Altus, OK 73521

Wright Career College: Oklahoma City
Oklahoma City, Oklahoma
www.wrightcc.edu

▶ Private 2-year career college
▶ Large city

General. Regionally accredited; also accredited by ACICS. **Enrollment:** 104 undergraduates. **Degrees:** 78 associate awarded. **Calendar:** Continuous.

Basis for selection. Open admission.

Financial aid. Need-based: Work-study available nights, weekends and for part-time students.

Application procedures. Admission: No deadline. No application fee.

Academics. Credit/placement by examination: AP.

Majors. Business: Business admin. **Computer sciences:** Security, system admin. **Health services:** Insurance coding. **Parks/recreation:** Physical fitness technician.

Contact. Phone: (405) 681-2300
Wright Career College: Oklahoma City, 2219 West Interstate 240 Service Road, Oklahoma City, OK 73159

Wright Career College: Tulsa
Tulsa, Oklahoma
www.wrightcc.edu

▶ Private 2-year career college
▶ Large city

General. Regionally accredited; also accredited by ACICS. **Enrollment:** 140 undergraduates. **Degrees:** 36 associate awarded. **Calendar:** Continuous.

Basis for selection. Open admission.

Financial aid. Need-based: Work-study available nights, weekends and for part-time students.

Application procedures. Admission: No application fee.

Academics. Credit/placement by examination: AP.

Majors. Business: Business admin. **Computer sciences:** Security. **Health services:** Insurance coding.

Contact. Phone: (918) 628-7700
Wright Career College: Tulsa, 1625 W. Fountainhead Pkwy, Tempe, AZ 85282

Oregon

Blue Mountain Community College
Pendleton, Oregon
www.bluecc.edu
CB code: 4025

- Public 2-year community college
- Commuter campus in large town
- Application essay required

General. Founded in 1962. Regionally accredited. Located in agricultural area. **Enrollment:** 591 degree-seeking undergraduates. **Degrees:** 376 associate awarded. **Location:** 200 miles from Portland; 200 miles from Boise, Idaho. **Calendar:** Quarter, limited summer session. **Full-time faculty:** 55 total. **Part-time faculty:** 184 total. **Class size:** 74% < 20, 25% 20-39, less than 1% 40-49, less than 1% 50-99. **Special facilities:** Betty Feves Art Gallery.

Transfer out. Colleges most students transferred to 2015: Eastern Oregon University, Oregon State University, University of Oregon.

Basis for selection. Open admission, but selective for some programs. Admission to nursing program based on prerequisite course work, GPA, criminal background check, and point system. Dental Assisting students admitted based on prerequisites, GPA and criminal background check.

High school preparation. College-preparatory program required.

2015-2016 Annual costs. Tuition/fees: $4,756; $13,216 out-of-state. Per-credit charge: $94 in-state; $282 out-of-state. Books/supplies: $1,364. Personal expenses: $1,398. **Additional information:** Students in limited entry programs such as dental and nursing and some academic programs such as agriculture, diesel, music and art pay additional program and/or course fees. Washington state, Idaho, Nevada, California and Montana residents all pay in-state rates.

Financial aid. Need-based: Need-based aid available for part-time students. Work-study available nights, weekends and for part-time students. **Non-need-based:** Scholarships awarded for athletics, music/drama.

Application procedures. Admission: No deadline. $25 fee. Admission notification on a rolling basis. **Financial aid:** Priority date 3/30; no closing date. FAFSA required. Applicants notified on a rolling basis starting 4/1; must reply within 2 week(s) of notification.

Academics. Special study options: Cooperative education, cross-registration, distance learning, dual enrollment of high school students, ESL, liberal arts/career combination. Bachelor's degree programs available on campus. License preparation in nursing, occupational therapy. **Credit/placement by examination:** AP, CLEP, institutional tests. 22 credit hours maximum toward associate degree. **Support services:** GED preparation and test center, learning center, reduced course load, remedial instruction, study skills assistance, tutoring.

Majors. Business: Accounting technology, administrative services, business admin, marketing. **Education:** Early childhood, teacher assistance. **Health services:** Medical secretary, nursing (RN). **Liberal arts:** Arts/sciences.

Most popular majors. Business/marketing 8%, health sciences 10%, liberal arts 57%.

Technology on campus. 200 workstations in library, computer center, student center. Commuter students can connect to campus network. Online course registration, online library, wireless network available.

Student life. Freshman orientation: Mandatory, $80 fee. Preregistration for classes offered. Half-day session held prior to start of classes; online session available. **Activities:** Choral groups, drama, music ensembles, musical theater, student government, multicultural club, MECHA, Native American club, Phi Theta Kappa.

Athletics. NAIA. **Intercollegiate:** Baseball M, basketball, rodeo, softball W, volleyball W. **Team name:** Timberwolves.

Student services. Career counseling, services for economically disadvantaged, financial aid counseling, veterans' counselor. **Physically disabled:** Services for visually, speech, hearing impaired. **Transfer:** Pre-admission transcript evaluation for new students. Transfer center, transfer adviser, college fairs on campus for students transferring to 4-year colleges.

Contact. E-mail: getinfo@bluecc.edu
Phone: (541) 278-5759 Fax: (541) 278-5871
Theresa Bosworth, Director of Admissions, Records and Testing/Registrar, Blue Mountain Community College, 2411 NW Carden Avenue, Pendleton, OR 97801

Central Oregon Community College
Bend, Oregon
www.cocc.edu
CB code: 4090

- Public 2-year community college
- Commuter campus in small city

General. Founded in 1949. Regionally accredited. **Enrollment:** 5,321 degree-seeking undergraduates; 752 non-degree-seeking students. **Degrees:** 909 associate awarded. **ROTC:** Army. **Location:** 150 miles from Portland, 120 miles from Salem. **Calendar:** Quarter, limited summer session. **Full-time faculty:** 128 total; 40% have terminal degrees. **Part-time faculty:** 201 total. **Class size:** 53% < 20, 46% 20-39, 1% 40-49, less than 1% 50-99. **Special facilities:** Exercise physiology laboratory, dental clinic, math SMART Lab, unmanned aerial system lab and simulator, level 5 helicopter simulator.

Student profile. Among degree-seeking undergraduates, 39% enrolled in a transfer program, 35% enrolled in a vocational program, 809 enrolled as first-time, first-year students, 564 transferred in from other institutions.

Part-time:	54%	Hispanic/Latino:	10%
Out-of-state:	6%	Native American:	2%
Women:	54%	Multi-racial, non-Hispanic:	4%
African American:	1%	25 or older:	43%
Asian American:	1%	Live on campus:	4%

Transfer out. Colleges most students transferred to 2015: Oregon State University, University of Oregon, Southern Oregon University, Portland State University.

Basis for selection. Open admission, but selective for some programs. Special requirements for nursing, emergency medical services. Limited enrollment (first-come first-served basis, with fall term only start date) for medical assistant, dental assistant, and massage therapy. **Home schooled:** High school diploma or GED not required if student is 18 or older.

2015-2016 Annual costs. Tuition/fees: $4,444; $5,749 out-of-district; $11,419 out-of-state. Per-credit charge: $91 in-district; $120 out-of-district; $246 out-of-state. Room/board: $10,550. Books/supplies: $1,800. Personal expenses: $1,257.

2015-2016 Financial aid. Need-based: 320 full-time freshmen applied for aid; 273 deemed to have need; 272 received aid. Average need met was 70%. Average scholarship/grant was $5,978; average loan $3,205. 39% of total undergraduate aid awarded as scholarships/grants, 61% as loans/jobs. Need-based aid available for part-time students. Work-study available nights, weekends and for part-time students. **Non-need-based:** Awarded to 16 full-time undergraduates, including 7 freshmen. Scholarships awarded for academics, leadership, state residency. **Additional information:** Institution-sponsored short-term loans. Extensive part-time student employment.

Application procedures. Admission: Priority date 6/15; no deadline. $25 fee, may be waived for applicants with need. Admission notification on a rolling basis. **Financial aid:** No deadline. FAFSA required. Applicants notified on a rolling basis starting 4/1; must reply within 4 week(s) of notification.

Academics. Special study options: Cooperative education, distance learning, double major, dual enrollment of high school students, ESL, independent study, internships, study abroad. License preparation in aviation, nursing, paramedic, physical therapy, radiology. **Credit/placement by examination:** AP, CLEP, IB, institutional tests. Credit for prior training or certification varies by program. **Support services:** GED preparation, learning center, pre-admission summer program, reduced course load, remedial instruction, study skills assistance, tutoring, writing center.

Majors. Architecture: Landscape. **Biology:** General. **Business:** Accounting, business admin, customer service, franchise operations, hotel/motel admin, management information systems, marketing. **Communications:** Communications/speech/rhetoric. **Computer sciences:** General, computer science, networking. **Conservation:** General, forest technology. **Education:** General. **Engineering:** General. **English:** English lit. **Foreign languages:** General. **Health services:** EMT paramedic, health information technology, licensed practical nurse, massage therapy, nursing (RN), physical therapy, premedicine, prepharmacy, radiologic technology/medical imaging, substance abuse counseling, veterinary technology/assistant. **History:** General. **Liberal arts:** Arts/sciences, humanities. **Math:** General. **Parks/recreation:** General, health/fitness. **Physical sciences:** General. **Protective services:**

Criminal justice, firefighting, forest/wildland firefighting. **Social sciences:** General. **Visual/performing arts:** Studio arts.

Most popular majors. Health sciences 12%, liberal arts 68%.

Technology on campus. 230 workstations in dormitories, library, computer center, student center. Dormitories wired for high-speed internet access and linked to campus network. Commuter students can connect to campus network. Online course registration, online library, helpline, wireless network available.

Student life. Freshman orientation: Available. Preregistration for classes offered. **Housing:** Coed dorms, special housing for disabled available. $250 nonrefundable deposit. **Activities:** Bands, campus ministries, choral groups, drama, music ensembles, opera, radio station, student government, student newspaper, symphony orchestra.

Athletics. Intramural: Basketball, cross-country, football (non-tackle), golf, soccer, softball, table tennis, track and field, volleyball, weight lifting. **Team name:** Bobcats.

Student services. Adult student services, alcohol/substance abuse counseling, career counseling, services for economically disadvantaged, student employment services, financial aid counseling, health services, minority student services, personal counseling, placement for graduates, veterans' counselor, women's services. **Physically disabled:** Services for visually, speech, hearing impaired. **Transfer:** Pre-admission transcript evaluation for new students. Transfer adviser, college fairs on campus for students transferring to 4-year colleges.

Contact. E-mail: welcome@cocc.edu
Phone: (541) 383-7500 Fax: (541) 383-7506
Courtney Whetstine, Director, Admissions and Records, Central Oregon Community College, 2600 Northwest College Way, Bend, OR 97703

Chemeketa Community College
Salem, Oregon
www.chemeketa.edu   **CB code: 4745**

 Public 2-year community and junior college
 Commuter campus in small city

General. Founded in 1962. Regionally accredited. **Enrollment:** 9,563 degree-seeking undergraduates. **Degrees:** 1,791 associate awarded. **Location:** 45 miles from Portland. **Calendar:** Quarter, extensive summer session. **Full-time faculty:** 191 total. **Part-time faculty:** 527 total. **Class size:** 54% < 20, 44% 20-39, 1% 40-49, less than 1% 50-99. **Special facilities:** Planetarium, vineyard and winemaking facility. **Partnerships:** Formal partnerships with local high schools.

Student profile.

Out-of-state:	5% **25 or older:**	43%

Transfer out. Colleges most students transferred to 2015: University of Oregon, Oregon State University, Western Oregon University, Eastern Oregon University, Portland State University.

Basis for selection. Open admission, but selective for some programs. Limited-enrollment programs may charge admission fee, have application deadlines and require interview; preparatory courses may also be required.

2015-2016 Annual costs. Tuition/fees: $4,230; $11,520 out-of-state. Per-credit charge: $80 in-state; $242 out-of-state. Books/supplies: $1,350. Personal expenses: $1,125.

Financial aid. All financial aid based on need. Need-based aid available for part-time students. Work-study available nights, weekends and for part-time students.

Application procedures. Admission: No deadline. No application fee. Admission notification on a rolling basis. **Financial aid:** Priority date 4/1; no closing date. FAFSA required. Applicants notified on a rolling basis starting 6/30; must reply within 2 week(s) of notification.

Academics. Special study options: Accelerated study, cooperative education, distance learning, double major, dual enrollment of high school students, ESL, independent study, internships, study abroad, teacher certification program, weekend college. License preparation in dental hygiene, nursing, paramedic. **Credit/placement by examination:** AP, CLEP, IB, institutional tests. 12 credit hours maximum toward associate degree. **Support services:** GED preparation and test center, learning center, pre-admission summer program, remedial instruction, study skills assistance, tutoring, writing center.

Majors. Business: Accounting, accounting technology, administrative services, business admin, executive assistant, hospitality admin, tourism/travel. **Communications technology:** Graphic/printing. **Computer sciences:** General, applications programming, web page design. **Education:** Speech impaired. **Engineering:** Electrical. **General:** Building inspection, power transmission. **Health services:** Dental assistant, EMT paramedic, medical informatics, medical secretary, medical transcription, nursing (RN), office admin, pharmacy assistant, prenursing, speech-language pathology assistant, substance abuse counseling. **Human services:** Social work. **Liberal arts:** Arts/sciences. **Protective services:** Criminal justice, fire safety technology, firefighting, juvenile corrections, police science. **Visual/performing arts:** Design, graphic design. **Work/family studies:** Child care management.

Most popular majors. Health sciences 8%, liberal arts 69%, security/protective services 7%.

Technology on campus. 1,000 workstations in library, computer center. Commuter students can connect to campus network. Online course registration, online library, helpline, wireless network available.

Student life. Freshman orientation: Mandatory. Preregistration for classes offered. **Activities:** Choral groups, dance, literary magazine, student government, student newspaper, sexual minority students organization, Christian student organization, LDS club, College Republicans, Democratic students, Phi Theta Kappa, Latino development network.

Athletics. Intercollegiate: Baseball M, basketball, soccer M, softball W, volleyball W. **Intramural:** Soccer M, softball W. **Team name:** The Storm.

Student services. Adult student services, alcohol/substance abuse counseling, career counseling, student employment services, financial aid counseling, minority student services, on-campus daycare, placement for graduates, veterans' counselor. **Physically disabled:** Services for visually, speech, hearing impaired. **Transfer:** Pre-admission transcript evaluation for new students. Transfer adviser, college fairs on campus for students transferring to 4-year colleges.

Contact. E-mail: admissions@chemeketa.edu
Phone: (503) 399-5006 Fax: (503) 399-3918
Melissa Frey, Enrollment Services Coordinator, Chemeketa Community College, Admissions Office, Salem, OR 97309-7070

Clackamas Community College
Oregon City, Oregon
www.clackamas.edu   **CB code: 4111**

 Public 2-year community college
 Commuter campus in large town

General. Founded in 1966. Regionally accredited. **Enrollment:** 6,100 degree-seeking undergraduates; 1,202 non-degree-seeking students. **Degrees:** 839 associate awarded. **Location:** 15 miles from Portland. **Calendar:** Quarter, extensive summer session. **Full-time faculty:** 119 total; 9% minority, 46% women. **Part-time faculty:** 299 total; 9% minority, 50% women. **Special facilities:** Environmental learning center, observatory, professional summer theater. **Partnerships:** Formal partnerships with Intel Microelectronics, Portland General Electric/Pacificorps.

Student profile. Among degree-seeking undergraduates, 1,494 enrolled as first-time, first-year students, 319 transferred in from other institutions.

Part-time:	57%	Hispanic/Latino:	9%
Out-of-state:	1%	Native American:	1%
Women:	49%	Multi-racial, non-Hispanic:	5%
African American:	2%	25 or older:	43%
Asian American:	3%		

Transfer out. Colleges most students transferred to 2015: Portland State University, Oregon State University, University of Oregon.

Basis for selection. Open admission, but selective for some programs. Special prerequisite requirements for Allied Health and Nursing and water quality programs. Special admission process for accelerated degree programs and degree partnership programs.

2016-2017 Annual costs. Tuition/fees (projected): $4,623; $11,559 out-of-state. Per-credit charge: $87 in-state; $249 out-of-state. Books/supplies: $1,800. Personal expenses: $900.

Financial aid. Need-based: Need-based aid available for part-time students. Work-study available nights, weekends and for part-time students. **Non-need-based:** Scholarships awarded for academics, art, athletics, leadership, music/drama. **Additional information:** Institutional tuition rebate guarantee. Frozen tuition rates for new fall students who graduate within 3 years.

Any tuition increase levied by college during those 3 years will be refunded to student upon graduation.

Application procedures. Admission: No deadline. No application fee. Admission notification on a rolling basis. **Financial aid:** No deadline. FAFSA, institutional form required. Applicants notified on a rolling basis starting 3/15; must reply within 3 week(s) of notification.

Academics. Some occupational technologies offered as self-paced programs. **Special study options:** Accelerated study, cooperative education, distance learning, double major, dual enrollment of high school students, ESL, independent study, internships, study abroad. License preparation in nursing. **Credit/placement by examination:** AP, CLEP, IB, institutional tests. 24 credit hours maximum toward associate degree. Hours of credit by examination may be counted toward a certificate: 12. The credits do not count toward residence requirements for a degree. **Support services:** GED preparation and test center, learning center, reduced course load, remedial instruction, study skills assistance, tutoring, writing center.

Majors. Biology: General. **Business:** Accounting, administrative services, business admin, marketing, operations, retailing. **Communications:** Digital media. **Communications technology:** Recording arts. **Computer sciences:** Applications programming, computer science, networking, webmaster. **Engineering:** General, industrial. **Foreign languages:** Comparative lit. **General:** Power transmission. **Health services:** EMT paramedic, medical informatics, nursing (RN). **Human services:** Community org/advocacy, social work. **Liberal arts:** Arts/sciences. **Physical sciences:** Geology. **Protective services:** Corrections, firefighting, police science. **Work/family studies:** Child care management.

Most popular majors. Business/marketing 9%, engineering/engineering technologies 7%, liberal arts 64%.

Technology on campus. 500 workstations in library, computer center. Commuter students can connect to campus network. Online course registration, online library, helpline, wireless network available.

Student life. Freshman orientation: Available. Preregistration for classes offered. Held for one day during the week before classes begin. **Activities:** Bands, choral groups, drama, music ensembles, student government, student newspaper, Phi Theta Kappa, dance club, STEM club, Student Nurses Association, Northwest Collegiate Ministries.

Athletics. NJCAA. **Intercollegiate:** Baseball M, basketball, cross-country, soccer W, softball W, track and field, volleyball W, wrestling M. **Intramural:** Basketball, football (non-tackle) M, soccer, ultimate frisbee, volleyball. **Team name:** Cougar.

Student services. Adult student services, alcohol/substance abuse counseling, career counseling, student employment services, financial aid counseling, minority student services, on-campus daycare, personal counseling, placement for graduates, veterans' counselor, women's services. **Physically disabled:** Services for visually, speech, hearing impaired. **Transfer:** Transfer adviser, college fairs on campus for students transferring to 4-year colleges.

Contact. E-mail: admissions@clackamas.edu
Phone: (503) 594-6100 Fax: (503) 722-5864
Chris Sweet, Registrar/Enrollment Services Operations Manager, Clackamas Community College, 19600 Molalla Avenue, Oregon City, OR 97045

Clatsop Community College
Astoria, Oregon
www.clatsopcc.edu · · · · · **CB code: 4089**

▸ Public 2-year community and maritime college
▸ Commuter campus in large town

General. Founded in 1958. Regionally accredited. USCG licensing training. **Enrollment:** 619 degree-seeking undergraduates. **Degrees:** 101 associate awarded. **Location:** 90 miles from Portland. **Calendar:** Quarter, limited summer session. **Full-time faculty:** 26 total; 15% have terminal degrees, 50% women. **Part-time faculty:** 50 total; 8% have terminal degrees, 4% minority, 46% women. **Class size:** 73% < 20, 24% 20-39, 1% 40-49, 2% 50-99. **Special facilities:** Maritime and environmental research training station (MERTS) campus, including a 51-foot research and training vessel, RV Forerunner, waste treatment laboratory, maritime fire suppression live-fire facility.

Transfer out. Colleges most students transferred to 2015: Portland State University, Oregon State University, Western Oregon University, Eastern Oregon University.

Basis for selection. Open admission, but selective for some programs. Special admissions requirements for nursing program applicants and international students.

High school preparation. College-preparatory program recommended.

2015-2016 Annual costs. Tuition/fees: $4,995; $9,450 out-of-state. Per-credit charge: $99 in-state; $198 out-of-state. Books/supplies: $1,404. Personal expenses: $2,271.

Financial aid. Need-based: Need-based aid available for part-time students. Work-study available nights, weekends and for part-time students. **Non-need-based:** Scholarships awarded for academics, art, leadership, minority status, state residency.

Application procedures. Admission: No deadline. $15 fee. Admission notification on a rolling basis. **Financial aid:** Priority date 5/1; no closing date. FAFSA, institutional form required. Applicants notified on a rolling basis starting 2/1.

Academics. Special study options: Cooperative education, distance learning, double major, dual enrollment of high school students, ESL, independent study, student-designed major. License preparation in nursing. **Credit/placement by examination:** AP, CLEP, IB, institutional tests. 24 credit hours maximum toward associate degree. **Support services:** GED preparation and test center, learning center, reduced course load, remedial instruction, study skills assistance, tutoring, writing center.

Majors. Business: Accounting, business admin. **Education:** Early childhood. **Health services:** Nursing (RN). **Liberal arts:** Arts/sciences. **Protective services:** Firefighting.

Most popular majors. Business/marketing 6%, health sciences 12%, liberal arts 63%, security/protective services 7%, trade and industry 6%.

Technology on campus. 80 workstations in library, computer center, student center. Online course registration, online library, wireless network available.

Student life. Freshman orientation: Available. Preregistration for classes offered. One day session held the week prior to start of fall classes. **Activities:** Concert band, choral groups, literary magazine, student government, student newspaper, Phi Theta Kappa.

Student services. Career counseling, services for economically disadvantaged, student employment services, financial aid counseling, personal counseling, placement for graduates, veterans' counselor. **Physically disabled:** Services for visually, speech, hearing impaired. **Transfer:** Pre-admission transcript evaluation for new students. Transfer center, transfer adviser, college fairs on campus for students transferring to 4-year colleges.

Contact. E-mail: admissions@clatsopcc.edu
Phone: (503) 338-2411 Toll-free number: (866) 252-8768
Fax: (503) 325-5738
Monica Van Steenberg, Admissions, Clatsop Community College, 1651 Lexington, Astoria, OR 97103

Klamath Community College
Klamath Falls, Oregon
www.klamathcc.edu · · · · · **CB code: 4127**

▸ Public 2-year community college
▸ Commuter campus in small city

General. Regionally accredited. **Enrollment:** 1,227 degree-seeking undergraduates; 391 non-degree-seeking students. **Degrees:** 144 associate awarded. **Calendar:** Quarter, limited summer session. **Full-time faculty:** 31 total. **Part-time faculty:** 85 total.

Student profile. Among degree-seeking undergraduates, 178 enrolled as first-time, first-year students.

Part-time:	58%	Women:	54%
Out-of-state:	4%	25 or older:	46%

Transfer out. Colleges most students transferred to 2015: Oregon Institute of Technology, Southern Oregon University, Oregon State University.

Basis for selection. Open admission.

High school preparation. Recommended units include English 4, mathematics 3, science 3 (laboratory 3).

Two-Year Colleges

2015-2016 Annual costs. Tuition/fees: $4,606; $7,823 out-of-state. Per-credit charge: $90 in-state; $161 out-of-state. Books/supplies: $1,320. Personal expenses: $2,100.

Financial aid. Need-based: Need-based aid available for part-time students. Work-study available nights, weekends and for part-time students.

Application procedures. Admission: No deadline. No application fee. Admission notification on a rolling basis beginning on or about 6/13. **Financial aid:** No deadline. FAFSA required.

Academics. Special study options: Accelerated study, combined bachelor's/graduate degree, cooperative education, cross-registration, distance learning, double major, dual enrollment of high school students, independent study. License preparation in aviation, dental hygiene, nursing, paramedic. **Credit/placement by examination:** AP, CLEP, IB, institutional tests. Varies by Degree/Certificate. **Support services:** GED preparation and test center, learning center, reduced course load, remedial instruction, study skills assistance, tutoring.

Majors. Business: Accounting technology, business admin, marketing. **Computer sciences:** Computer science, webmaster. **Conservation:** Environmental science. **Education:** Early childhood, teacher assistance. **Liberal arts:** Arts/sciences. **Protective services:** Law enforcement admin.

Most popular majors. Business/marketing 31%, education 7%, liberal arts 45%, security/protective services 9%, trade and industry 6%.

Technology on campus. 291 workstations in library, computer center, student center. Commuter students can connect to campus network. Online course registration, online library, wireless network available.

Student life. Freshman orientation: Mandatory. Preregistration for classes offered. **Activities:** Student government.

Athletics. Team name: Badgers.

Student services. Alcohol/substance abuse counseling, career counseling, student employment services, financial aid counseling, personal counseling, veterans' counselor. **Physically disabled:** Services for visually, speech, hearing impaired. **Transfer:** Pre-admission transcript evaluation for new students. College fairs on campus for students transferring to 4-year colleges.

Contact. E-mail: admissions@klamathcc.edu
Phone: (541) 880-2212 Fax: (541) 885-7758
Jared Dill, Admissions Recruitment and Support Manager, Klamath Community College, 7390 South 6th Street, Klamath Falls, OR 97603

Lane Community College
Eugene, Oregon
www.lanecc.edu
CB member
CB code: 4407

- Public 2-year community college
- Commuter campus in small city

General. Founded in 1964. Regionally accredited. Outreach centers in downtown Eugene, Cottage Grove, and Florence. **Enrollment:** 8,370 degree-seeking undergraduates; 866 non-degree-seeking students. **Degrees:** 1,166 associate awarded. **Location:** 110 miles from Portland. **Calendar:** Quarter, extensive summer session. **Full-time faculty:** 247 total; 11% minority, 57% women. **Part-time faculty:** 312 total; 10% minority, 59% women. **Class size:** 28% < 20, 68% 20-39, 3% 40-49, less than 1% 50-99, less than 1% >100. **Partnerships:** Formal partnerships with professional technical advisory groups.

Student profile. Among degree-seeking undergraduates, 1,026 enrolled as first-time, first-year students.

Part-time:	54%	Native American:	2%
Out-of-state:	3%	Native Hawaiian/Pacific islander:	1%
Women:	52%	Multi-racial, non-Hispanic:	5%
African American:	2%	International:	1%
Asian American:	2%	25 or older:	58%
Hispanic/Latino:	10%		

Transfer out. Colleges most students transferred to 2015: University of Oregon, Oregon State University.

Basis for selection. Open admission, but selective for some programs. Special requirements for certain allied health, culinary arts, and flight technology programs.

2015-2016 Annual costs. Tuition/fees: $4,869; $11,214 out-of-state. Per-credit charge: $98 in-state; $239 out-of-state. Books/supplies: $1,086. Personal expenses: $1,035.

Financial aid. Need-based: Need-based aid available for part-time students. Work-study available nights, weekends and for part-time students. **Non-need-based:** Scholarships awarded for art, athletics, minority status, music/drama.

Application procedures. Admission: No deadline. No application fee. Admission notification on a rolling basis. **Financial aid:** Closing date 2/15. FAFSA required. Applicants notified on a rolling basis starting 6/1; must reply within 2 week(s) of notification.

Academics. Special study options: Accelerated study, cooperative education, cross-registration, distance learning, double major, dual enrollment of high school students, ESL, honors, independent study, internships, liberal arts/career combination, study abroad, weekend college. License preparation in aviation, dental hygiene, nursing, paramedic, physical therapy. **Credit/placement by examination:** AP, CLEP, IB, institutional tests. Only 25% of degree or certificate requirements may be met using credit by exam/assessment. **Support services:** GED preparation and test center, learning center, pre-admission summer program, reduced course load, remedial instruction, study skills assistance, tutoring, writing center.

Majors. Business: General, accounting technology, hotel/motel admin, office management, office/clerical, retailing. **Communications:** Broadcast journalism, digital media. **Communications technology:** Animation/special effects. **Computer sciences:** Networking, programming. **Conservation:** Environmental studies, water/wetlands/marine. **General:** Electrician. **Health services:** Dental hygiene, EMT paramedic, nursing (RN), physical therapy assistant, respiratory therapy technology. **Human services:** Community org/advocacy. **Liberal arts:** Arts/sciences. **Parks/recreation:** Sports admin. **Protective services:** Criminal justice. **Visual/performing arts:** Commercial/advertising art. **Work/family studies:** Child care service.

Most popular majors. Business/marketing 7%, health sciences 14%, liberal arts 56%.

Technology on campus. 800 workstations in library, computer center. Dormitories wired for high-speed internet access. Commuter students can connect to campus network. Online course registration, online library, helpline, wireless network available.

Student life. Freshman orientation: Mandatory. Preregistration for classes offered. **Housing:** Coed dorms available. LEED certified downtown student housing center available. **Activities:** Bands, choral groups, dance, drama, international student organizations, literary magazine, music ensembles, musical theater, radio station, student government, student newspaper, symphony orchestra, TV station, Women's Center, Associated Students of Lane Community College, multi-cultural center, Movimiento Estudiantil Chicano de Aztlán, The Black Student Union, Native American Student Association.

Athletics. Intercollegiate: Baseball M, basketball, cross-country, soccer, track and field. **Intramural:** Badminton, basketball, soccer, volleyball. **Team name:** Titans.

Student services. Adult student services, alcohol/substance abuse counseling, career counseling, services for economically disadvantaged, student employment services, financial aid counseling, health services, legal services, minority student services, on-campus daycare, personal counseling, placement for graduates, veterans' counselor, women's services. **Physically disabled:** Services for visually, speech, hearing impaired. **Transfer:** Pre-admission transcript evaluation for new students. Transfer adviser, college fairs on campus for students transferring to 4-year colleges.

Contact. Phone: (541) 463-3100 Fax: (541) 463-3995
Helen Garrett, Director of Admissions, Lane Community College, 4000 East 30th Avenue, Eugene, OR 97405

Le Cordon Bleu College of Culinary Arts: Portland
Portland, Oregon
www.chefs.edu/portland

- For-profit 2-year culinary school
- Commuter campus in very large city

General. Regionally accredited; also accredited by ACCSC. **Enrollment:** 452 undergraduates. **Degrees:** 107 associate awarded. **Calendar:** Differs by program. **Full-time faculty:** 17 total. **Part-time faculty:** 1 total.

Basis for selection. Open admission.

2015-2016 Annual costs. Certificate programs: $19,500. Associate programs: $40,000. Books and supplies are included.

Financial aid. Need-based: Work-study available nights, weekends and for part-time students.

Application procedures. Admission: No deadline. $50 fee. Admission notification on a rolling basis. **Financial aid:** No deadline.

Academics. Credit/placement by examination: AP, CLEP.

Majors. Business: Hospitality admin.

Contact. Phone: (888) 848-3202 Toll-free number: (888) 848-3202 Sara Baisch, Admissions Services Coordinator, Le Cordon Bleu College of Culinary Arts: Portland, 600 SW 10th Avenue, Suite #500, Portland, OR 97205

Linn-Benton Community College
Albany, Oregon   **CB member**
www.linnbenton.edu   **CB code: 4413**

- Public 2-year community college
- Commuter campus in small city

General. Founded in 1966. Regionally accredited. Courses available at off-campus centers in Corvallis, Lebanon, and Sweet Home. **Enrollment:** 5,635 degree-seeking undergraduates; 86 non-degree-seeking students. **Degrees:** 680 associate awarded. **ROTC:** Army, Naval, Air Force. **Location:** 70 miles from Portland, 45 miles from Eugene. **Calendar:** Quarter, limited summer session. **Class size:** 55% < 20, 44% 20-39, less than 1% 40-49, less than 1% 50-99.

Student profile. Among degree-seeking undergraduates, 1,367 enrolled as first-time, first-year students, 231 transferred in from other institutions.

Part-time:	52%	Hispanic/Latino:	10%
Out-of-state:	1%	Native American:	1%
Women:	51%	Multi-racial, non-Hispanic:	4%
African American:	2%	International:	3%
Asian American:	3%	25 or older:	29%

Transfer out. Colleges most students transferred to 2015: Oregon State University, Western Oregon University, University of Oregon, Portland State University, and Southern Oregon University.

Basis for selection. Open admission, but selective for some programs. Special requirements for various healthcare programs as well as high school diploma or GED required of applicants under 18.

High school preparation. College-preparatory program required.

2015-2016 Annual costs. Tuition/fees: $4,694; $9,977 out-of-state. Per-credit charge: $96.61 in-state; $225.43 out-of-state. Books/supplies: $1,602. Personal expenses: $1,431.

2014-2015 Financial aid. Need-based: 490 full-time freshmen applied for aid; 430 deemed to have need; 412 received aid. Average need met was 57%. Average scholarship/grant was $4,943; average loan $2,755. 51% of total undergraduate aid awarded as scholarships/grants, 49% as loans/jobs. Need-based aid available for part-time students. Work-study available nights, weekends and for part-time students. **Non-need-based:** Awarded to 228 full-time undergraduates, including 72 freshmen. Scholarships awarded for academics, alumni affiliation, art, athletics, leadership, music/drama.

Application procedures. Admission: No application fee. Admission notification on a rolling basis. **Financial aid:** No deadline. FAFSA required. Applicants notified on a rolling basis starting 3/30; must reply within 4 week(s) of notification.

Academics. Special study options: Accelerated study, cooperative education, distance learning, dual enrollment of high school students, ESL, independent study, internships. License preparation in nursing, occupational therapy, radiology. **Credit/placement by examination:** AP, CLEP, IB, institutional tests. 24 credit hours maximum toward associate degree. **Support services:** GED preparation and test center, learning center, remedial instruction, study skills assistance, tutoring, writing center.

Majors. Biology: General. **Business:** Accounting technology, business admin, office management. **Communications:** Journalism. **Computer sciences:** General. **Conservation:** Environmental science. **Education:** Early childhood, elementary, physical. **Engineering:** General. **English:** English lit, rhetoric/composition. **Foreign languages:** General. **General:** Lineworker, power transmission. **Health services:** Health services admin, medical assistant, medical informatics, medical secretary, nursing (RN), occupational therapy assistant, public health ed, radiologic technology/medical imaging. **History:** General. **Human services:** Social work. **Liberal arts:** Arts/sciences.

Math: General. **Philosophy/religion:** Religion. **Physical sciences:** Chemistry, geology, physics. **Protective services:** Criminal justice. **Psychology:** General. **Social sciences:** Anthropology, economics, political science, sociology. **Visual/performing arts:** Art, dramatic, music. **Work/family studies:** Merchandising.

Most popular majors. Business/marketing 8%, health sciences 17%, liberal arts 36%, trade and industry 11%.

Technology on campus. 500 workstations in library, computer center, student center. Commuter students can connect to campus network. Online course registration, online library, helpline, wireless network available.

Student life. Freshman orientation: Mandatory. Preregistration for classes offered. **Activities:** Concert band, choral groups, dance, drama, music ensembles, student government, student newspaper, symphony orchestra.

Athletics. Intercollegiate: Baseball M, basketball, volleyball W. **Team name:** Roadrunners.

Student services. Adult student services, career counseling, services for economically disadvantaged, student employment services, financial aid counseling, minority student services, personal counseling, placement for graduates, veterans' counselor. **Physically disabled:** Services for visually, speech, hearing impaired. **Transfer:** Transfer center, transfer adviser, college fairs on campus for students transferring to 4-year colleges.

Contact. E-mail: admissions@linnbenton.edu
Phone: (541) 917-4811 Fax: (541) 917-4868
Danny Aynes, Director, Enrollment Services/Registrar, Linn-Benton Community College, 6500 Pacific Blvd SW, Albany, OR 97321

Mt. Hood Community College
Gresham, Oregon   **CB member**
www.mhcc.edu   **CB code: 4508**

- Public 2-year community college
- Commuter campus in small city

General. Founded in 1965. Regionally accredited. **Enrollment:** 7,597 degree-seeking undergraduates. **Degrees:** 1,243 associate awarded. **Location:** 12 miles from Portland. **Calendar:** Quarter, extensive summer session. **Full-time faculty:** 156 total; 14% have terminal degrees, 11% minority, 53% women. **Part-time faculty:** 386 total; 9% minority, 58% women. **Class size:** 52% < 20, 44% 20-39, 3% 40-49, 1% 50-99, less than 1% >100. **Special facilities:** Planetarium, solar observatory, aquatic center. **Partnerships:** Formal partnerships with WorkSource Portland Metro East, Business and Industry Workforce Training-Boeing, Tri-Met, additional small to medium firms, select BOLI-Apprenticeship Training Centers.

Student profile.

Out-of-state:	5%	25 or older:	39%

Transfer out. Colleges most students transferred to 2015: Portland State University, Oregon State University, University of Oregon, Concordia University, Eastern Oregon University.

Basis for selection. Open admission, but selective for some programs. Special requirements for allied health, graphic design. **Learning Disabled:** Individuals are required to submit documentation to verify eligibility under Sections 504 of the Rehabilitation Act of 1973 and the Americans with Disabilities Act of 1990.

2015-2016 Annual costs. Tuition/fees: $4,669; $9,776 out-of-state. Per-credit charge: $95.5 in-state; $209 out-of-state. Books/supplies: $1,560. Personal expenses: $1,035.

Financial aid. Need-based: Need-based aid available for part-time students. Work-study available nights, weekends and for part-time students. **Non-need-based:** Scholarships awarded for academics.

Application procedures. Admission: No deadline. No application fee. Admission notification on a rolling basis. **Financial aid:** Closing date 4/1. FAFSA, institutional form required. Applicants notified on a rolling basis starting 4/1; must reply within 2 week(s) of notification.

Academics. Special study options: Accelerated study, cooperative education, cross-registration, distance learning, dual enrollment of high school students, ESL, external degree, independent study, internships, liberal arts/career combination, study abroad, weekend college. Bachelor's degree programs available on campus. License preparation in dental hygiene, nursing, physical therapy. **Credit/placement by examination:** AP, CLEP, IB, institutional tests. 45 credit hours maximum toward associate degree. **Support services:** GED preparation and test center, learning center, pre-admission summer program, reduced course load, remedial instruction, study skills assistance, tutoring.

Majors. Biology: General, biochemistry. **Business:** Accounting technology, business admin, entrepreneurial studies, executive assistant, hospitality admin, resort management, tourism/travel. **Communications:** Radio/TV. **Communications technology:** Radio/TV. **Computer sciences:** General, database management, information technology, networking, web page design. **Conservation:** General, fisheries, forest technology. **Education:** Early childhood. **English:** English lit. **General:** Power transmission. **Health services:** Dental hygiene, EMT paramedic, health information management, medical assistant, medical informatics, medical secretary, medical transcription, mental health counseling, nursing (RN), office assistant, physical therapy assistant, prechiropractic, prepharmacy, preveterinary, respiratory therapy technology, surgical technology. **History:** General. **Liberal arts:** Arts/sciences. **Math:** General. **Parks/recreation:** Outdoor education. **Philosophy/religion:** Philosophy. **Physical sciences:** Chemistry, geology, physics. **Psychology:** General. **Social sciences:** General, economics, geography, political science, sociology. **Visual/performing arts:** Art, art history/conservation, ceramics, commercial photography, design, digital arts, dramatic, drawing, game design, graphic design, painting, printmaking, sculpture, studio arts.

Most popular majors. Business/marketing 8%, health sciences 14%, liberal arts 62%.

Technology on campus. 210 workstations in library, computer center, student center. Commuter students can connect to campus network. Online course registration, online library, helpline, wireless network available.

Student life. Freshman orientation: Available. Preregistration for classes offered. **Activities:** Bands, choral groups, drama, international student organizations, literary magazine, music ensembles, musical theater, radio station, student government, student newspaper, symphony orchestra, TV station, science club, campus ambassadors, hotel/tourism/restaurant club, MECHA, veterans association, Rho Theta, student activities board, Japanese club, English conversation club, student nurses association, mental health and human services club, Wildside outdoor activity club, Student Success Teams, gamers club, Student Diversity Council.

Athletics. Intercollegiate: Baseball M, basketball, cross-country, track and field, volleyball W. **Intramural:** Basketball, softball W, volleyball. **Team name:** Saints.

Student services. Adult student services, career counseling, services for economically disadvantaged, student employment services, financial aid counseling, minority student services, on-campus daycare, personal counseling, placement for graduates, veterans' counselor. **Physically disabled:** Services for visually, speech, hearing impaired. **Transfer:** Transfer adviser, college fairs on campus for students transferring to 4-year colleges.

Contact. E-mail: admweb@mhcc.edu
Phone: (503) 491-7393 Fax: (503) 491-7388
John Hamblin, Manager, Admissions, Records and Registration, Mt. Hood Community College, 26000 SE Stark Street, Gresham, OR 97030

Pioneer Pacific College
Wilsonville, Oregon
www.pioneerpacific.edu
CB member
CB code: 0492

⬧ For-profit 2-year career college
⬧ Commuter campus in large town
⬧ Interview required

General. Accredited by ACICS. Additional campuses include the Health Career Institute in Wilsonville, learning site in Clackamas, branch campus in Springfield. **Enrollment:** 1,195 undergraduates. **Degrees:** 27 bachelor's, 261 associate awarded. **Location:** 20 miles from Portland. **Calendar:** Differs by program, extensive summer session. **Full-time faculty:** 70 total. **Part-time faculty:** 78 total. **Class size:** 94% < 20, 6% 20-39.

Student profile.

Out-of-state:	1%	**25 or older:** 67%

Transfer out. Colleges most students transferred to 2015: University of Phoenix, Clackamas Community College.

Basis for selection. Open admission, but selective for some programs. Selective admissions to practical nursing program.

2015-2016 Annual costs. Personal expenses: $3,619.

Financial aid. All financial aid based on need. Need-based aid available for part-time students. Work-study available nights, weekends and for part-time students.

Application procedures. Admission: No deadline. $50 fee. Application must be submitted on paper. Admission notification on a rolling basis. **Financial aid:** No deadline. FAFSA required. Applicants notified on a rolling basis starting 2/27.

Academics. Special study options: Accelerated study, honors, internships, liberal arts/career combination. Externships. Bachelor's degree programs available on campus. **Credit/placement by examination:** AP, CLEP, institutional tests. **Support services:** Study skills assistance, tutoring.

Majors. Business: Accounting, business admin, marketing. **Computer sciences:** Information systems, webmaster. **Health services:** Health care admin, medical assistant. **Protective services:** Criminal justice.

Most popular majors. Business/marketing 23%, computer/information sciences 13%, health sciences 43%, security/protective services 15%.

Technology on campus. 250 workstations in library, computer center. Online library, wireless network available.

Student life. Freshman orientation: Mandatory. Preregistration for classes offered.

Student services. Career counseling, student employment services, financial aid counseling, placement for graduates. **Transfer:** Pre-admission transcript evaluation for new students.

Contact. E-mail: inquiries@pioneerpacific.edu
Phone: (503) 682-3903 Toll-free number: (866) 772-4636
Fax: (503) 682-1514
Vickie Church, Director of Admissions, Pioneer Pacific College, 27501 Southwest Parkway Avenue, Wilsonville, OR 97070

Pioneer Pacific College: Springfield
Springfield, Oregon
www.pioneerpacific.edu

⬧ For-profit 2-year branch campus, business, health science, nursing, pharmacy and career college
⬧ Commuter campus in small city

General. Accredited by ACICS. **Location:** 10 miles from Eugene. **Calendar:** Differs by program.

Annual costs/financial aid. Personal expenses: $3,619.

Contact. Phone: (541) 684-4644
Director of Admissions, 3800 Sports Way, Springfield, OR 97477

Portland Community College
Portland, Oregon
www.pcc.edu
CB member
CB code: 4617

⬧ Public 2-year community college
⬧ Commuter campus in very large city

General. Founded in 1961. Regionally accredited. 4 comprehensive campuses; classes offered at several centers throughout district. **Enrollment:** 27,946 degree-seeking undergraduates. **Degrees:** 3,617 associate awarded. **Location:** 5 miles from downtown. **Calendar:** Quarter, extensive summer session. **Full-time faculty:** 493 total; 18% minority, 57% women. **Part-time faculty:** 1,617 total; 21% minority, 57% women.

Transfer out. Colleges most students transferred to 2015: Portland State University, University of Oregon, Oregon State University.

Basis for selection. Open admission, but selective for some programs. Enrollment in certain programs or courses may require prerequisite course work or permission by a department representative.

High school preparation. High school diploma required for some allied health programs.

2015-2016 Annual costs. Tuition/fees: $4,690; $10,450 out-of-state. Per-credit charge: $96 in-state; $224 out-of-state. Books/supplies: $1,632.

Financial aid. All financial aid based on need. Need-based aid available for part-time students. Work-study available nights, weekends and for part-time students.

Application procedures. Admission: No deadline. No application fee. **Financial aid:** Priority date 3/1; no closing date. FAFSA required. Applicants notified on a rolling basis starting 6/1; must reply within 3 week(s) of notification.

Academics. Special study options: Cooperative education, distance learning, double major, dual enrollment of high school students, ESL, honors, internships, study abroad, weekend college. License preparation in aviation, dental hygiene, nursing, paramedic, radiology, real estate. **Credit/placement by examination:** AP, CLEP, institutional tests. 45 credit hours maximum toward associate degree. **Support services:** GED preparation and test center, learning center, reduced course load, remedial instruction, study skills assistance, tutoring, writing center.

Majors. Biology: Biotechnology. **Business:** General, accounting technology, administrative services, business admin, management information systems, marketing, office management, retailing. **Computer sciences:** Applications programming, system admin, web page design. **Education:** Early childhood, teacher assistance. **Foreign languages:** American Sign Language, sign language interpretation. **General:** Building inspection, power transmission, site management. **Health services:** Clinical lab technology, dental hygiene, dental lab technology, EMT paramedic, health information technology, medical radiologic technology/radiation therapy, ophthalmic technology, substance abuse counseling, veterinary technology/assistant. **Human services:** General. **Liberal arts:** Arts/sciences. **Parks/recreation:** Health/fitness. **Protective services:** Criminal justice, firefighting. **Visual/performing arts:** Commercial/advertising art, design, interior design. **Work/family studies:** Child care management.

Most popular majors. Business/marketing 10%, health sciences 11%, liberal arts 63%.

Technology on campus. 3,043 workstations in library, computer center, student center. Commuter students can connect to campus network. Online course registration, online library, helpline, wireless network available.

Student life. Freshman orientation: Mandatory. Preregistration for classes offered. Online orientation available. **Activities:** Bands, choral groups, dance, drama, international student organizations, literary magazine, music ensembles, musical theater, student government.

Athletics. NJCAA. **Intercollegiate:** Basketball. **Intramural:** Basketball, bowling, cross-country, racquetball, soccer, softball, swimming, tennis, volleyball. **Team name:** Panthers.

Student services. Adult student services, career counseling, services for economically disadvantaged, student employment services, financial aid counseling, minority student services, on-campus daycare, personal counseling, placement for graduates, veterans' counselor, women's services. **Physically disabled:** Services for visually, speech, hearing impaired. **Transfer:** Pre-admission transcript evaluation for new students. Transfer center, transfer adviser, college fairs on campus for students transferring to 4-year colleges.

Contact. Phone: (971) 722-8888 Fax: (971) 722-4988
Veronica Garcia, Dean of Enrollment Services, Portland Community College, 12000 SW 49th Avenue, Portland, OR 97219-7132

Rogue Community College
Grants Pass, Oregon
www.roguecc.edu

CB member
CB code: 4653

▶ Public 2-year community college
▶ Commuter campus in large town

General. Founded in 1970. Regionally accredited. Branch campuses in Medford and White City, learning centers in Medford and Cave Junction. **Enrollment:** 4,216 degree-seeking undergraduates; 738 non-degree-seeking students. **Degrees:** 624 associate awarded. **Location:** 30 miles from Medford, 240 miles from Portland. **Calendar:** Quarter, limited summer session. **Full-time faculty:** 75 total; 7% minority, 52% women. **Part-time faculty:** 365 total; 5% minority, 44% women. **Class size:** 56% < 20, 41% 20-39, 2% 40-49, 1% 50-99. **Special facilities:** Outdoor concert bowl.

Student profile. Among degree-seeking undergraduates, 83% enrolled in a transfer program, 17% enrolled in a vocational program, 3% already have a bachelor's degree or higher, 837 enrolled as first-time, first-year students, 48 transferred in from other institutions.

Part-time:	59%	Hispanic/Latino:	15%
Out-of-state:	3%	Native American:	1%
Women:	59%	Multi-racial, non-Hispanic:	4%
African American:	1%	25 or older:	50%
Asian American:	1%		

Transfer out. 25% of students enrolled in the transfer program go on to 4-year colleges. **Colleges most students transferred to 2015:** Southern Oregon University, Oregon State University, University of Oregon, Portland State University, Oregon Institute of Technology.

Basis for selection. Open admission, but selective for some programs. Special requirements for apprenticeship, dental assistant, nursing, practical nursing, massage therapy, emergency medical technology, human services, paramedicine, and occupational skills training. Interview recommended for allied health, nursing programs.

2015-2016 Annual costs. Tuition/fees: $4,905; $5,850 out-of-state. Per-credit charge: $95 in-state; $116 out-of-state. Books/supplies: $1,200. Personal expenses: $1,431.

2014-2015 Financial aid. Need-based: 304 full-time freshmen applied for aid; 268 deemed to have need; 268 received aid. Average need met was 65%. Average scholarship/grant was $4,736; average loan $2,881. 72% of total undergraduate aid awarded as scholarships/grants, 28% as loans/jobs. Need-based aid available for part-time students. Work-study available nights, weekends and for part-time students. **Non-need-based:** Awarded to 206 full-time undergraduates, including 52 freshmen. Scholarships awarded for academics.

Application procedures. Admission: No deadline. No application fee. Application must be submitted online. Admission notification on a rolling basis. **Financial aid:** Priority date 5/1; no closing date. FAFSA, institutional form required. Applicants notified on a rolling basis; must reply within 2 week(s) of notification.

Academics. Special study options: Cooperative education, distance learning, double major, dual enrollment of high school students, ESL, independent study, liberal arts/career combination, study abroad. License preparation in nursing, paramedic. **Credit/placement by examination:** AP, CLEP, institutional tests. 48 credit hours maximum toward associate degree. **Support services:** GED preparation and test center, learning center, remedial instruction, study skills assistance, tutoring, writing center.

Majors. Business: General, accounting technology, business admin, marketing. **Computer sciences:** General, computer science. **General:** Power transmission. **Health services:** EMT paramedic, nursing (RN), office computer specialist. **Human services:** Social work. **Liberal arts:** Arts/sciences. **Protective services:** Fire safety technology, police science. **Visual/performing arts:** General. **Work/family studies:** Child care management, family/community services.

Most popular majors. Business/marketing 7%, health sciences 8%, liberal arts 67%.

Technology on campus. 700 workstations in library, computer center. Commuter students can connect to campus network. Online course registration, wireless network available.

Student life. Freshman orientation: Mandatory. Preregistration for classes offered. **Activities:** Bands, choral groups, drama, musical theater, student government, student newspaper, Latino club.

Athletics. Intercollegiate: Cross-country, soccer. **Intramural:** Basketball, soccer, volleyball. **Team name:** Ospreys.

Student services. Career counseling, services for economically disadvantaged, student employment services, financial aid counseling, on-campus daycare, personal counseling, placement for graduates, veterans' counselor. **Physically disabled:** Services for visually, speech, hearing impaired. **Transfer:** Pre-admission transcript evaluation for new students. Transfer adviser, college fairs on campus for students transferring to 4-year colleges.

Contact. E-mail: jduarte@roguecc.edu
Phone: (541) 956-7427
John Duarte, Director of Enrollment Services, Rogue Community College, 3345 Redwood Highway, Grants Pass, OR 97527

Southwestern Oregon Community College
Coos Bay, Oregon
www.socc.edu

CB code: 4729

▶ Public 2-year culinary school and community college
▶ Commuter campus in large town

General. Founded in 1961. Regionally accredited. **Enrollment:** 2,306 degree-seeking undergraduates. **Degrees:** 399 associate awarded. **Location:** 125 miles from Eugene, 225 miles from Portland. **Calendar:** Quarter, limited summer session. **Full-time faculty:** 55 total. **Part-time faculty:** 143 total.

Special facilities: Culinary institute, small business development center, university center.

Student profile.

Out-of-state:	17%	Live on campus:	17%
25 or older:	34%		

Transfer out. Colleges most students transferred to 2015: Oregon State University, Southern Oregon University, University of Oregon, Linfield College, Eastern Oregon University.

Basis for selection. Open admission, but selective for some programs. Special requirements for some programs, for example, nursing, medical assisting, culinary, phlebotomy, etc. Background check required for emergency response and EMTs.

2015-2016 Annual costs. Tuition/fees: $5,595; $5,595 out-of-state. Room/board: $7,400. Books/supplies: $1,500. Personal expenses: $540.

Financial aid. Need-based: Need-based aid available for part-time students. Work-study available nights, weekends and for part-time students. **Non-need-based:** Scholarships awarded for art, athletics, leadership, music/drama.

Application procedures. Admission: No deadline. $40 fee, may be waived for applicants with need. Admission notification on a rolling basis. **Financial aid:** Closing date 3/1. FAFSA required. Applicants notified on a rolling basis starting 5/1; must reply within 3 week(s) of notification.

Academics. Special study options: Cooperative education, distance learning, double major, dual enrollment of high school students, ESL, honors, independent study, internships, liberal arts/career combination. Bachelor's degree programs available on campus. License preparation in nursing. **Credit/placement by examination:** AP, CLEP, institutional tests. **Support services:** GED preparation and test center, learning center, reduced course load, remedial instruction, study skills assistance, tutoring, writing center.

Majors. Business: Accounting technology, administrative services, banking/financial services, business admin, entrepreneurial studies, management information systems, office management, sales/distribution. **Computer sciences:** Applications programming, computer science, information systems, webmaster. **Conservation:** Environmental studies. **Education:** Teacher assistance. **Engineering:** General. **Health services:** Licensed practical nurse, medical assistant, substance abuse counseling. **Human services:** Social work. **Liberal arts:** Arts/sciences. **Math:** General. **Protective services:** Corrections, criminal justice, firefighting, police science. **Work/family studies:** Child care management, family studies.

Most popular majors. Business/marketing 10%, health sciences 8%, liberal arts 58%, security/protective services 8%.

Technology on campus. 338 workstations in dormitories, library, computer center. Dormitories wired for high-speed internet access and linked to campus network. Commuter students can connect to campus network. Online course registration, online library, helpline, wireless network available.

Student life. Freshman orientation: Available. Preregistration for classes offered. **Housing:** Guaranteed on-campus for freshmen. Single-sex dorms, special housing for disabled, apartments, themed housing, wellness housing available. $250 partly refundable deposit. **Activities:** Bands, choral groups, drama, literary magazine, music ensembles, student government, student newspaper, Rotaract, Phi Theta Kappa, student ambassadors.

Athletics. NJCAA. **Intercollegiate:** Baseball M, basketball, cross-country, golf, soccer, softball W, track and field, volleyball W, wrestling M. **Intramural:** Basketball. **Team name:** Lakers.

Student services. Adult student services, alcohol/substance abuse counseling, career counseling, services for economically disadvantaged, student employment services, financial aid counseling, health services, on-campus daycare, personal counseling, placement for graduates, veterans' counselor. **Physically disabled:** Services for visually, speech, hearing impaired. **Transfer:** Transfer center, college fairs on campus for students transferring to 4-year colleges.

Contact. E-mail: admissions@socc.edu
Phone: (541) 888-7636 Toll-free number: (800) 962-2838 ext. 7636
Fax: (541) 888-7247
Tom Nicholls, Director of Enrollment Management, Southwestern Oregon Community College, 1988 Newmark Avenue, Coos Bay, OR 97420-2956

Tillamook Bay Community College
Tillamook, Oregon
www.tbcc.cc.or.us
CB code: 7470

- Public 2-year community college
- Small town

General. Candidate for regional accreditation. **Enrollment:** 392 degree-seeking undergraduates. **Degrees:** 58 associate awarded. **Calendar:** Quarter. **Full-time faculty:** 8 total. **Part-time faculty:** 32 total.

Basis for selection. Open admission.

2015-2016 Annual costs. Tuition/fees: $4,906; $5,356 out-of-state. Room/board: $3,663.

Financial aid. Need-based: Work-study available nights, weekends and for part-time students.

Application procedures. Admission: No deadline. No application fee. **Financial aid:** No deadline.

Academics. Credit/placement by examination: AP.

Majors. Business: Accounting, business admin, hospitality admin, retail management. **Liberal arts:** Arts/sciences.

Student life. Freshman orientation: Available. Preregistration for classes offered.

Contact. E-mail: StudentServices@tillamookbay.cc
Phone: (503) 842-8222 ext. 1100
Michele Burton, Director of Student Services, Tillamook Bay Community College, 4301 Third Street, Tillamook, OR 97141

Treasure Valley Community College
Ontario, Oregon
www.tvcc.cc
CB code: 4825

- Public 2-year community college
- Commuter campus in large town

General. Founded in 1961. Regionally accredited. **Enrollment:** 1,838 degree-seeking undergraduates; 332 non-degree-seeking students. **Degrees:** 325 associate awarded. **Location:** 52 miles from Boise, ID. **Calendar:** Quarter, extensive summer session. **Full-time faculty:** 47 total; 89% have terminal degrees, 2% minority, 51% women. **Part-time faculty:** 39 total; 67% have terminal degrees, 10% minority, 54% women. **Class size:** 53% < 20, 45% 20-39, 2% 40-49, less than 1% 50-99. **Partnerships:** Formal partnership with Silverhawk Aviation, an FAA certified flight school.

Student profile. Among degree-seeking undergraduates, 67% enrolled in a transfer program, 33% enrolled in a vocational program, 1% already have a bachelor's degree or higher, 455 enrolled as first-time, first-year students, 118 transferred in from other institutions.

Part-time:	48%	Hispanic/Latino:	25%
Out-of-state:	67%	Native American:	1%
Women:	59%	Multi-racial, non-Hispanic:	3%
African American:	2%	25 or older:	46%
Asian American:	1%	Live on campus:	6%

Transfer out. Colleges most students transferred to 2015: Eastern Oregon University, Boise State University, Oregon State University, University of Oregon, University of Idaho.

Basis for selection. Open admission, but selective for some programs. Special requirements for nursing program. **Home schooled:** Transcript of courses and grades, state high school equivalency certificate required.

High school preparation. College-preparatory program recommended.

2016-2017 Annual costs. Tuition/fees (projected): $5,310; $5,760 out-of-state. Room/board: $7,069. Books/supplies: $2,725. Personal expenses: $1,760.

2015-2016 Financial aid. Need-based: 304 full-time freshmen applied for aid; 290 deemed to have need; 287 received aid. Average need met was 43%. Average scholarship/grant was $5,556; average loan $3,058. 40% of total undergraduate aid awarded as scholarships/grants, 60% as loans/jobs. Need-based aid available for part-time students. Work-study available nights, weekends and for part-time students. **Non-need-based:** Awarded to 67 full-time undergraduates, including 52 freshmen. Scholarships awarded for academics, athletics, leadership, music/drama.

Application procedures. Admission: No deadline. No application fee. Application must be submitted online. Admission notification on a rolling basis. **Financial aid:** No deadline. FAFSA required. Applicants notified on a rolling basis starting 5/1.

Academics. Special study options: Combined bachelor's/graduate degree, cooperative education, distance learning, dual enrollment of high school students, ESL, independent study, internships. Education program with Eastern Oregon University and nursing program with Oregon Health & Science University. License preparation in aviation, nursing, paramedic. **Credit/ placement by examination:** AP, CLEP, institutional tests. 45 credit hours maximum toward associate degree. **Support services:** GED preparation and test center, learning center, pre-admission summer program, reduced course load, remedial instruction, study skills assistance, tutoring, writing center.

Majors. Biology: General. **Business:** General, management information systems, office management. **Communications:** Communications/speech/ rhetoric. **Computer sciences:** General. **Conservation:** General, wildlife/wilderness. **Education:** Elementary, physical, teacher assistance. **Engineering:** General. **English:** English lit. **Foreign languages:** General. **General:** Carpentry. **Health services:** Dental hygiene, medical secretary, medical transcription, nursing (RN), physical therapy, prechiropractic, predental, premedicine, prepharmacy, preveterinary. **History:** General. **Human services:** Social work. **Liberal arts:** Arts/sciences. **Math:** General. **Physical sciences:** Chemistry, geology, physics. **Protective services:** Criminal justice, fire safety technology, firefighting, police science. **Psychology:** General. **Social sciences:** General, political science. **Visual/performing arts:** Art, music.

Most popular majors. Business/marketing 15%, health sciences 19%, liberal arts 24%.

Technology on campus. 250 workstations in library, computer center, student center. Dormitories linked to campus network. Commuter students can connect to campus network. Online course registration, online library, helpline, wireless network available.

Student life. Freshman orientation: Available. Preregistration for classes offered. New student orientation sessions held prior to the start of the quarter as well as college orientation short duration classes available. **Housing:** Coed dorms, special housing for disabled, wellness housing available. $250 fully refundable deposit. 2 ADA-compliant suites available. **Activities:** Bands, campus ministries, choral groups, music ensembles, student government, Young Republicans, LDS student association.

Athletics. Intercollegiate: Baseball M, basketball, cross-country, rodeo, soccer, softball W, tennis, track and field, volleyball W. **Intramural:** Basketball, soccer, softball, table tennis, volleyball. **Team name:** Chukars.

Student services. Career counseling, student employment services, financial aid counseling. **Physically disabled:** Services for visually, speech, hearing impaired. **Transfer:** Pre-admission transcript evaluation for new students. Transfer adviser, college fairs on campus for students transferring to 4-year colleges.

Contact. E-mail: admissions@tvcc.cc
Phone: (541) 881-5822 Fax: (541) 881-5520
Michelle McKay, Associate Vice President of Student Services, Treasure Valley Community College, 650 College Boulevard, Ontario, OR 97914-3423

Umpqua Community College
Roseburg, Oregon
www.umpqua.edu   CB code: 4862

▶ Public 2-year community college
▶ Commuter campus in large town

General. Founded in 1964. Regionally accredited. **Enrollment:** 1,146 degree-seeking undergraduates; 1,114 non-degree-seeking students. **Degrees:** 275 associate awarded. **Location:** 70 miles from Eugene. **Calendar:** Quarter, limited summer session. **Full-time faculty:** 57 total; 9% have terminal degrees, 9% minority, 51% women. **Part-time faculty:** 103 total; 2% have terminal degrees, 6% minority, 50% women. **Class size:** 63% < 20, 35% 20-39, 1% 40-49, less than 1% 50-99, less than 1% >100. **Special facilities:** Observatory.

Student profile. Among degree-seeking undergraduates, 4% enrolled in a transfer program, 2% enrolled in a vocational program, 2% already have a bachelor's degree or higher, 218 enrolled as first-time, first-year students.

Part-time:	63%	**Women:**	58%
Out-of-state:	1%	**25 or older:**	57%

Transfer out. Colleges most students transferred to 2015: Oregon State University, University of Oregon, Northwest Christian College, Western Oregon University, Southern Oregon University.

Basis for selection. Open admission, but selective for some programs. Special requirements for nursing program. COMPASS placement test and/ or ACT ASSET test used for placement only. **Home schooled:** High school release required.

2015-2016 Annual costs. Tuition/fees: $5,325; $10,545 out-of-state. Per-credit charge: $105 in-state; $221 out-of-state. Books/supplies: $1,800. Personal expenses: $1,200.

2014-2015 Financial aid. Need-based: 182 full-time freshmen applied for aid; 74 deemed to have need; 68 received aid. Average need met was 84%. Average scholarship/grant was $6,148. 82% of total undergraduate aid awarded as scholarships/grants, 18% as loans/jobs. Need-based aid available for part-time students. Work-study available nights, weekends and for part-time students. **Non-need-based:** Awarded to 96 full-time undergraduates, including 23 freshmen. Scholarships awarded for academics, athletics.

Application procedures. Admission: No deadline. $25 fee. Admission notification on a rolling basis. **Financial aid:** Priority date 3/10; no closing date. FAFSA, institutional form required. Applicants notified on a rolling basis starting 2/9; must reply within 2 week(s) of notification.

Academics. Special study options: Cooperative education, distance learning, dual enrollment of high school students, ESL, honors, independent study, internships, student-designed major. Bachelor's degree programs available on campus. License preparation in nursing, paramedic, real estate. **Credit/ placement by examination:** AP, CLEP, institutional tests. 45 credit hours maximum toward associate degree. 24 hours of credit by exam may be counted toward 1-year certificate program. **Support services:** GED preparation and test center, learning center, remedial instruction, study skills assistance, tutoring.

Majors. Business: General, accounting, accounting technology, administrative services, business admin, executive assistant, management information systems, marketing. **Computer sciences:** Information systems. **Education:** General, early childhood. **Health services:** EMT paramedic, medical secretary, nursing (RN), staff services technology. **Liberal arts:** Arts/sciences. **Protective services:** Firefighting, police science. **Work/family studies:** Child care management.

Most popular majors. Computer/information sciences 6%, health sciences 39%, legal studies 10%, liberal arts 19%, public administration/social services 6%, trade and industry 6%.

Technology on campus. 400 workstations in library, computer center, student center. Commuter students can connect to campus network. Online course registration, helpline, wireless network available.

Student life. Freshman orientation: Mandatory. Preregistration for classes offered. Held the Thursday or Friday prior to beginning of term. **Activities:** Bands, choral groups, drama, music ensembles, musical theater, student government, student newspaper.

Athletics. Intercollegiate: Basketball, volleyball W. **Team name:** River Hawks.

Student services. Adult student services, career counseling, services for economically disadvantaged, student employment services, financial aid counseling, on-campus daycare, personal counseling, placement for graduates, veterans' counselor. **Physically disabled:** Services for visually, hearing impaired. **Transfer:** Transfer center, transfer adviser, college fairs on campus for students transferring to 4-year colleges.

Contact. E-mail: lavera.noland@umpqua.edu
Phone: (541) 440-7743 Toll-free number: (800) 820-5161
Fax: (541) 440-4612
David Farrington, Director of Enrollment Services, Umpqua Community College, 1140 Umpqua College Road, Roseburg, OR 97470-0226

Pennsylvania

Antonelli Institute of Art and Photography
Erdenheim, Pennsylvania
www.antonelli.edu   CB code: 0971

- For-profit 2-year visual arts and junior college
- Commuter campus in large town
- Interview required

General. Founded in 1938. Accredited by ACCSC. **Enrollment:** 189 degree-seeking undergraduates. **Degrees:** 83 associate awarded. **Location:** 1 mile from Philadelphia. **Calendar:** Semester, limited summer session. **Class size:** 100% < 20. **Special facilities:** Wet black and white darkroom, computer graphics labs, digital photo labs.

Student profile.

Out-of-state: 21%   Live on campus: 48%
25 or older: 4%

Transfer out. Colleges most students transferred to 2015: Brooks Institute, Arcadia University, Chestnut Hill College.

Basis for selection. Emphasis placed on interview, recommendations, and samples of art and photography. Although not required, student portfolios will be evaluated. **Home schooled:** Transcript of courses and grades, interview required. Documentation of high school graduation/equivalency from local school district, state department of education or recognized home school organization required. If these items are not available, a GED will be required.

2015-2016 Annual costs. Tuition/fees: $20,920. Books/supplies: $5,900. Personal expenses: $2,210. **Additional information:** Tuition quoted is for the photography degree program; annual tuition for the graphic design degree program is $18,820. Estimated kit and supply costs vary depending on degree program. All costs are subject to change.

Financial aid. All financial aid based on need. Need-based aid available for part-time students. Work-study available nights, weekends and for part-time students.

Application procedures. Admission: No deadline. $50 fee, may be waived for applicants with need. Admission notification on a rolling basis. **Financial aid:** No deadline. FAFSA required. Applicants notified on a rolling basis; must reply within 2 week(s) of notification.

Academics. Credit/placement by examination: AP, CLEP.

Majors. Visual/performing arts: Graphic design, photography.

Technology on campus. 60 workstations in library, computer center. Online library, wireless network available.

Student life. Freshman orientation: Mandatory. Preregistration for classes offered. **Housing:** $375 fully refundable deposit. Residences available from local apartments.

Student services. Career counseling, student employment services, financial aid counseling, personal counseling, placement for graduates. **Transfer:** Pre-admission transcript evaluation for new students. Transfer adviser for students transferring to 4-year colleges.

Contact. E-mail: admissions@antonelli.edu
Phone: (215) 836-2222 Toll-free number: (800) 722-7871
Fax: (215) 836-2794
Director of Admissions, Antonelli Institute of Art and Photography, 300 Montgomery Avenue, Erdenheim, PA 19038-8242

Berks Technical Institute
Wyomissing, Pennsylvania
www.berks.edu   CB code: 3198

- For-profit 2-year business and technical college
- Commuter campus in small city

General. Accredited by ACCSC. **Enrollment:** 1,140 undergraduates. **Degrees:** 356 associate awarded. **Location:** 64 miles from Philadelphia. **Calendar:** Quarter. **Full-time faculty:** 34 total. **Part-time faculty:** 49 total. **Class size:** 89% < 20, 11% 20-39.

Basis for selection. Test scores very important; interview and school record important. **Learning Disabled:** Meeting with dean of education and department head if deemed necessary by dean of education.

2015-2016 Annual costs. Books/supplies: $992. **Additional information:** Tuition varies by program; total program tuition and fees range from $27,849 to $32,455. Massage Therapy diploma program, $10,600. Books and supplies vary depending on program and level. All costs are subject to change.

Financial aid. All financial aid based on need. Need-based aid available for part-time students. Work-study available nights, weekends and for part-time students.

Application procedures. Admission: No deadline. $50 fee. Admission notification on a rolling basis. **Financial aid:** No deadline. FAFSA required. Applicants notified on a rolling basis; must reply within 2 week(s) of notification.

Academics. Special study options: Internships. **Credit/placement by examination:** AP, CLEP. **Support services:** Learning center, reduced course load, remedial instruction, study skills assistance, tutoring, writing center.

Majors. Business: Accounting, business admin. **Computer sciences:** General, computer graphics, computer science, networking, programming. **Health services:** Medical assistant, medical secretary. **Protective services:** Law enforcement admin. **Visual/performing arts:** Commercial/advertising art.

Technology on campus. 200 workstations in library, computer center. Repair service available.

Student life. Freshman orientation: Mandatory. Preregistration for classes offered.

Student services. Financial aid counseling, placement for graduates. **Transfer:** Pre-admission transcript evaluation for new students. Transfer adviser for students transferring to 4-year colleges.

Contact. E-mail: platham@berks.edu
Phone: (610) 372-1722 Toll-free number: (866) 591-8384
Carol Jones, Director of Admissions, Berks Technical Institute, 2205 Ridgewood Road, Wyomissing, PA 19610

Bidwell Training Center
Pittsburgh, Pennsylvania
www.bidwell-training.org   CB code: 3199

- Private 1-year business and health science college
- Commuter campus in large city
- Interview required

General. Accredited by ACCSC. **Enrollment:** 150 undergraduates. **Degrees:** 23 associate awarded. **Calendar:** Differs by program. **Full-time faculty:** 16 total. **Part-time faculty:** 1 total.

Basis for selection. Interview and test scores very important. **Learning Disabled:** Academic support available.

2015-2016 Annual costs. Tuition/fees: $14,000. **Additional information:** Cost quoted is for the chemical laboratory technician program. Tuition for other programs varies by program. All costs are subject to change.

Financial aid. All financial aid based on need. Work-study available nights, weekends and for part-time students.

Application procedures. Admission: No deadline. No application fee. Admission notification on a rolling basis. **Financial aid:** No deadline. FAFSA required. Applicants notified on a rolling basis.

Academics. Special study options: Internships. **Credit/placement by examination:** AP, CLEP, institutional tests. **Support services:** GED preparation, remedial instruction, study skills assistance, tutoring.

Technology on campus. 85 workstations in library, computer center.

Student life. Freshman orientation: Mandatory. Preregistration for classes offered.

Student services. Adult student services, career counseling, student employment services, financial aid counseling, personal counseling, placement for graduates.

Contact. E-mail: dfarah@mcg-btc.org
Phone: (412) 323-4000 ext. 156
Toll-free number: (800) 516-1800 ext. 150 Fax: (412) 321-2120
Ken Huselton, Senior Director of Operations, Bidwell Training Center, 1815 Metropolitan Street, Pittsburgh, PA 15233

Bradford School: Pittsburgh
Pittsburgh, Pennsylvania
www.bradfordpittsburgh.edu   **CB code: 2206**

- For-profit 2-year junior college
- Commuter campus in very large city
- Interview required

General. Accredited by ACICS. **Enrollment:** 439 full-time, degree-seeking students. **Degrees:** 158 associate awarded. **Calendar:** Semester. **Full-time faculty:** 10 total. **Part-time faculty:** 9 total.

Basis for selection. High school record, class rank, recommendations, interview most important.

2015-2016 Annual costs. Tuition/fees: $15,340. Room/board: $6,960. **Additional information:** Estimated cost of books and supplies range from $1,180 to $1,800 depending on degree program. All costs are subject to change.

Financial aid. Need-based: Work-study available nights, weekends and for part-time students.

Application procedures. Admission: No deadline. $50 fee. Admission notification on a rolling basis. **Financial aid:** FAFSA required.

Academics. Credit/placement by examination: AP, CLEP.

Majors. Business: Accounting technology, administrative services, hotel/motel admin, retailing. **Computer sciences:** Networking, programming. **Health services:** Dental assistant, medical assistant. **Visual/performing arts:** Graphic design.

Most popular majors. Business/marketing 35%, health sciences 38%, legal studies 6%, visual/performing arts 18%.

Technology on campus. 150 workstations in library.

Student life. Housing: Coed dorms available. $100 nonrefundable deposit.

Student services. Financial aid counseling, placement for graduates.

Contact. Phone: (412) 391-6710 Toll-free number: (800) 391-6810 Fax: (412) 471-6714
Bradford School: Pittsburgh, 125 West Station Square Drive, Pittsburgh, PA 15219

Bucks County Community College
Newtown, Pennsylvania   **CB member**
www.bucks.edu   **CB code: 2066**

- Public 2-year community college
- Commuter campus in large town

General. Founded in 1964. Regionally accredited. While our main campus is located in Newtown, we have a campus at the southern part of Bucks County, near Bristol; another campus toward the northern end of the county, near Perkasie; and we have a Virtual Campus, providing online courses and services. **Enrollment:** 8,532 degree-seeking undergraduates; 447 non-degree-seeking students. **Degrees:** 860 associate awarded. **Location:** 35 miles from Philadelphia. **Calendar:** Semester, limited summer session. **Full-time faculty:** 151 total; 39% have terminal degrees, 7% minority, 60% women. **Part-time faculty:** 540 total; 19% have terminal degrees, 6% minority, 56% women. **Partnerships:** Formal partnerships with Bucks County Technical High School, Eastern Center for Arts and Technology, Middle Bucks Institute of Technology, Northern Montgomery County Technical Career Center, Upper Bucks County Area Vocational Technical High School, Western Center for Technical Studies.

Student profile. Among degree-seeking undergraduates, 80% enrolled in a transfer program, 3% enrolled in a vocational program, 2,151 enrolled as first-time, first-year students.

Part-time:	65%	Hispanic/Latino:	6%
Out-of-state:	1%	Native American:	1%
Women:	55%	Multi-racial, non-Hispanic:	2%
African American:	5%	25 or older:	30%
Asian American:	3%		

Transfer out. Colleges most students transferred to 2015: Temple University, Pennsylvania State University, West Chester University, Gwynedd Mercy University, Drexel University.

Basis for selection. Open admission, but selective for some programs. Admission to nursing, fine arts, chef apprenticeship and fine woodworking programs based on satisfaction of prerequisites. Placement test administered after admission. Admission to paralegal certificate program is restricted. Proof of specific previous college study is required. Interview required for chef apprentice, fine arts, fine woodworking, and nursing programs. Audition required for music program; portfolio required for art, fine woodworking programs; essay required for chef apprentice program. **Adult students:** Students over 65 exempt from placement tests, except in mathematics for proper placement. **Home schooled:** Final official transcript certified by state required. **Learning Disabled:** Special testing accommodations for the entrance assessment test for students with learning disabilities.

High school preparation. College-preparatory program recommended.

2015-2016 Annual costs. Tuition/fees: $5,210; $9,260 out-of-district; $13,310 out-of-state. Per-credit charge: $135 in-district; $270 out-of-district; $405 out-of-state. Books/supplies: $1,700. Personal expenses: $1,350.

Financial aid. Need-based: Need-based aid available for part-time students. Work-study available nights, weekends and for part-time students. **Non-need-based:** Scholarships awarded for academics, art, music/drama. **Additional information:** Files are processed in order of receipt and completion date.

Application procedures. Admission: No deadline. No application fee. Admission notification on a rolling basis. **Financial aid:** Closing date 5/1. FAFSA required. Applicants notified on a rolling basis starting 6/1; must reply within 2 week(s) of notification.

Academics. Special study options: Cooperative education, distance learning, dual enrollment of high school students, ESL, external degree, honors, independent study, internships, student-designed major, weekend college. License preparation in nursing, occupational therapy, physical therapy, radiology, real estate. **Credit/placement by examination:** AP, CLEP, institutional tests. 30 credit hours maximum toward associate degree. **Support services:** GED preparation and test center, learning center, reduced course load, remedial instruction, study skills assistance, tutoring, writing center.

Majors. Area/ethnic studies: American, women's. **Biology:** Neuroscience. **Business:** General, accounting technology, business admin, retailing, small business admin, tourism/travel. **Communications:** Communications/speech/rhetoric, journalism. **Computer sciences:** General, applications programming, information systems, networking, system admin, web page design. **Conservation:** Environmental science. **Education:** Biology, chemistry, early childhood, history, mathematics, physical. **English:** English lit. **General:** Building inspection. **Health services:** Insurance coding, medical assistant, nursing (RN). **History:** General. **Liberal arts:** Arts/sciences, humanities. **Math:** General. **Parks/recreation:** Exercise sciences, sports admin. **Protective services:** Criminal justice. **Psychology:** General. **Visual/performing arts:** General, cinematography, commercial photography, commercial/advertising art, dramatic, music. **Work/family studies:** Child care service, family studies, institutional food production.

Most popular majors. Business/marketing 23%, education 9%, health sciences 12%, liberal arts 13%, psychology 6%, security/protective services 6%.

Technology on campus. 750 workstations in library, computer center. Commuter students can connect to campus network. Online course registration, online library, helpline, wireless network available.

Student life. Freshman orientation: Mandatory. Preregistration for classes offered. **Activities:** Bands, choral groups, dance, drama, film society, literary magazine, music ensembles, radio station, student government, student newspaper, Variety of service, social, and recreational programs, including Phi Theta Kappa, Inter-Varsity Christian Fellowship, Catholic club, Hillel, Habitat for Humanity, Future Teacher's Organization, Eco club, Black & Latino Association, Community Volunteer Corps.

Athletics. NJCAA. **Intercollegiate:** Baseball M, basketball, equestrian, golf M, soccer, tennis, volleyball W. **Intramural:** Baseball M, basketball M, equestrian, football (tackle) M, skiing, softball, table tennis, tennis, ultimate frisbee, volleyball W. **Team name:** Centurions.

Student services. Adult student services, alcohol/substance abuse counseling, career counseling, services for economically disadvantaged, student employment services, financial aid counseling, minority student services, on-campus daycare, personal counseling, veterans' counselor, women's services. **Physically disabled:** Services for visually, speech, hearing impaired. **Transfer:** Pre-admission transcript evaluation for new students. Transfer center, transfer adviser, college fairs on campus for students transferring to 4-year colleges.

Contact. E-mail: admissions@bucks.edu
Phone: (215) 968-8100 Fax: (215) 968-8110
Marlene Barlow, Director of Admissions, Bucks County Community College, 275 Swamp Road, Newtown, PA 18940

Butler County Community College
Butler, Pennsylvania
www.bc3.edu   **CB code: 2069**

▶ Public 2-year community college
▶ Commuter campus in small city

General. Founded in 1965. Regionally accredited. Classes offered in Cranberry township, Mercer, and Lawrence and Jefferson counties. **Enrollment:** 3,686 undergraduates. **Degrees:** 467 associate awarded. **Location:** 35 miles from Pittsburgh. **Calendar:** Semester, limited summer session. **Full-time faculty:** 63 total. **Part-time faculty:** 296 total. **Class size:** 76% < 20, 24% 20-39. **Special facilities:** Cultural center/theater, meteorology lab, computer forensics lab. **Partnerships:** Formal partnerships with American Management Association, Workforce & Economic Development Network of PA, Backflow Management, Inc., Carnegie Mellon University, 13 regional fire schools, 12 local high schools.

Student profile.

Out-of-state:	1%	**25 or older:** 37%

Transfer out. Colleges most students transferred to 2015: Slippery Rock University of Pennsylvania, Clarion University of Pennsylvania, Indiana University of Pennsylvania.

Basis for selection. Open admission, but selective for some programs. Admission to nursing, medical assistant, physical therapist assistant, massage therapy, and metrology programs based on high school record.

2015-2016 Annual costs. Tuition/fees: $4,230; $7,230 out-of-district; $10,230 out-of-state. Books/supplies: $1,000.

Financial aid. Need-based: Need-based aid available for part-time students. Work-study available nights, weekends and for part-time students. **Non-need-based:** Scholarships awarded for academics, state residency.

Application procedures. Admission: No deadline. $25 fee, may be waived for applicants with need. Admission notification on a rolling basis. **Financial aid:** Priority date 4/15; no closing date. FAFSA required. Applicants notified on a rolling basis starting 5/1; must reply within 2 week(s) of notification.

Academics. Special study options: Cooperative education, distance learning, independent study, internships. License preparation in nursing, physical therapy. **Credit/placement by examination:** AP, CLEP, institutional tests. 45 credit hours maximum toward associate degree. **Support services:** GED preparation, learning center, pre-admission summer program, reduced course load, remedial instruction, study skills assistance, tutoring, writing center.

Majors. Biology: General. **Business:** Accounting technology, administrative services, business admin, human resources, selling. **Communications:** Digital media, organizational. **Computer sciences:** General, applications programming, security, system admin, web page design. **Education:** General, elementary, kindergarten/preschool. **Engineering:** General. **English:** English lit. **Health services:** Health care admin, massage therapy, nursing (RN), office assistant, physical therapy assistant, radiologic technology/medical imaging. **Math:** General. **Parks/recreation:** General, sports admin. **Physical sciences:** General. **Protective services:** Homeland security, law enforcement admin, police science. **Psychology:** General. **Visual/performing arts:** Photography. **Work/family studies:** Institutional food production.

Most popular majors. Business/marketing 25%, computer/information sciences 9%, education 6%, engineering/engineering technologies 7%, health sciences 21%, liberal arts 7%, psychology 6%, security/protective services 6%.

Technology on campus. 108 workstations in library, computer center. Online course registration, helpline, wireless network available.

Student life. Freshman orientation: Available. Preregistration for classes offered. **Activities:** Drama, literary magazine, student government, student newspaper, Christian outreach organization.

Athletics. NJCAA. **Intercollegiate:** Baseball M, basketball, golf M, softball W, volleyball W. **Intramural:** Basketball, table tennis, volleyball. **Team name:** Pioneers.

Student services. Adult student services, career counseling, services for economically disadvantaged, student employment services, financial aid counseling, on-campus daycare, personal counseling, placement for graduates, veterans' counselor. **Physically disabled:** Services for visually, speech, hearing impaired. **Transfer:** Pre-admission transcript evaluation for new students. Transfer adviser, college fairs on campus for students transferring to 4-year colleges.

Contact. E-mail: admissions@bc3.edu
Phone: (724) 287-8711 ext. 8346 Toll-free number: (888) 826-2829
Fax: (724) 287-3460
Pattie Bajuszik, Director of Admissions, Butler County Community College, PO Box 1203, Butler, PA 16003-1203

Cambria-Rowe Business College
Johnstown, Pennsylvania
www.crbc.net   **CB code: 2210**

▶ For-profit 2-year business and career college
▶ Commuter campus in small city

General. Founded in 1891. Accredited by ACICS. **Enrollment:** 136 degree-seeking undergraduates. **Degrees:** 80 associate awarded. **Location:** 60 miles from Pittsburgh. **Calendar:** Quarter, limited summer session. **Full-time faculty:** 10 total. **Part-time faculty:** 1 total.

Student profile. Among degree-seeking undergraduates, 34 enrolled as first-time, first-year students.

Part-time:	1%	**25 or older:**	45%
Women:	82%		

Transfer out. Colleges most students transferred to 2015: Saint Francis University, Mount Aloysius College.

Basis for selection. Open admission. Interview recommended. **Home schooled:** Transcript of courses and grades required.

2015-2016 Annual costs. Tuition/fees: $14,830. Per-credit charge: $260.

Financial aid. Need-based: Need-based aid available for part-time students. Work-study available nights, weekends and for part-time students. **Non-need-based:** Scholarships awarded for academics, leadership.

Application procedures. Admission: No deadline. $30 fee. Students notified within 2 weeks of receipt of application. **Financial aid:** No deadline. FAFSA required. Applicants notified on a rolling basis.

Academics. Special study options: Accelerated study. **Credit/placement by examination:** AP, CLEP, institutional tests. **Support services:** Tutoring.

Majors. Business: General, accounting, administrative services, business admin. **Computer sciences:** Support specialist. **Health services:** Medical secretary, medical transcription.

Most popular majors. Business/marketing 50%, computer/information sciences 7%, health sciences 43%.

Technology on campus. PC or laptop required. Online library, repair service, wireless network available.

Student life. Freshman orientation: Mandatory. Preregistration for classes offered. Usually held 3 weeks prior to start date.

Student services. Adult student services, career counseling, student employment services, financial aid counseling, personal counseling, placement for graduates.

Contact. E-mail: admissions@crbc.net
Phone: (814) 536-5168 Toll-free number: (800) 639-2273
Fax: (814) 536-5160
Amy Horwath, Campus Director, Cambria-Rowe Business College, 221 Central Avenue, Johnstown, PA 15902

Cambria-Rowe Business College: Indiana
Indiana, Pennsylvania
www.crbc.net   CB code: 3274

- For-profit 2-year business and career college
- Commuter campus in small town
- Interview required

General. Accredited by ACICS. **Enrollment:** 105 degree-seeking undergraduates. **Degrees:** 58 associate awarded. **Calendar:** Quarter. **Full-time faculty:** 8 total; 25% have terminal degrees, 88% women. **Part-time faculty:** 1 total; 100% women.

Basis for selection. High school transcript or GED scores and Wonderlic Test required.

2015-2016 Annual costs. Tuition/fees: $14,830. Per-credit charge: $260.

Financial aid. Need-based: Need-based aid available for part-time students. Work-study available nights, weekends and for part-time students. **Non-need-based:** Scholarships awarded for academics, leadership.

Application procedures. Admission: No deadline. $30 fee. Admission notification on a rolling basis. **Financial aid:** No deadline. FAFSA required. Applicants notified on a rolling basis.

Academics. Credit/placement by examination: AP, CLEP, institutional tests. **Support services:** Tutoring.

Majors. Business: Accounting, administrative services, business admin, management information systems. **Computer sciences:** Support specialist. **Health services:** Medical secretary.

Most popular majors. Business/marketing 40%, computer/information sciences 13%, health sciences 47%.

Technology on campus. PC or laptop required. Online library, repair service, wireless network available.

Student life. Freshman orientation: Mandatory. Preregistration for classes offered.

Student services. Adult student services, career counseling, financial aid counseling, personal counseling, placement for graduates. **Transfer:** Pre-admission transcript evaluation for new students.

Contact. E-mail: sbell-leger@crbc.net
Phone: (724) 463-0222 Toll-free number: (800) 639-2273
Stacey Bell-Leger, Admissions Representative, Cambria-Rowe Business College: Indiana, 422 South 13th Street, Indiana, PA 15701

Career Training Academy
New Kensington, Pennsylvania
www.careerta.edu   CB code: 3205

- For-profit 2-year career college
- Commuter campus in small town
- Application essay, interview required

General. Accredited by ACCSC. **Enrollment:** 171 undergraduates. **Degrees:** 36 associate awarded. **Location:** 18 miles from Pittsburgh. **Calendar:** Differs by program, extensive summer session. **Full-time faculty:** 1 total. **Part-time faculty:** 13 total. **Special facilities:** Day care center. **Partnerships:** Formal partnership with Children's Community Pediatrics for the Medical Assistant Comprehensive and Advanced Medical Coder/Biller programs.

Basis for selection. Open admission, but selective for some programs. All programs require interview, essay, 1.5 GPA or 235 GED, and health form.

2015-2016 Annual costs. Tuition and fees for entire programs (diploma or associate degree) range from $10,200 to $23,053; programs vary from 6 to 18 months in duration. Additional expenses include books and supplies, which range from $1,183 to $3,952 depending upon program of study.

Financial aid. All financial aid based on need. Work-study available nights, weekends and for part-time students. **Additional information:** Work study available after class day.

Application procedures. Admission: No deadline. $30 fee. Application must be submitted on paper. Admission notification on a rolling basis. **Financial aid:** No deadline. FAFSA, institutional form required.

Academics. Mentor program available to all students. **Special study options:** Internships. Externships. **Credit/placement by examination:** AP, CLEP. **Support services:** Tutoring.

Majors. Health services: Massage therapy, medical assistant.

Technology on campus. Wireless network available.

Student life. Freshman orientation: Mandatory. Preregistration for classes offered.

Student services. Adult student services, alcohol/substance abuse counseling, career counseling, services for economically disadvantaged, student employment services, financial aid counseling, on-campus daycare, personal counseling, placement for graduates, veterans' counselor, women's services. **Transfer:** Pre-admission transcript evaluation for new students.

Contact. E-mail: admissions@careerta.edu
Phone: (724) 337-1000 Fax: (724) 335-7140
Tyna Putignano, Director of Admissions, Career Training Academy, 950 Fifth Avenue, New Kensington, PA 15068

Career Training Academy: Monroeville
Monroeville, Pennsylvania
www.careerta.edu   CB code: 3207

- For-profit 2-year branch campus college
- Commuter campus in small city
- Application essay required

General. Accredited by ACCSC. **Enrollment:** 115 undergraduates. **Degrees:** 29 associate awarded. **Location:** 10 miles from Pittsburgh. **Calendar:** Differs by program. **Full-time faculty:** 1 total. **Part-time faculty:** 7 total.

Basis for selection. Open admission, but selective for some programs. High school diploma/GED and transcript or TABE scores required.

2015-2016 Annual costs. Personal expenses: $2,889. **Additional information:** Tuition and fees for entire programs (diploma or associate degree) range from $10,200 to $23,053; programs vary from 6 to 18 months in duration. Additional expenses include books and supplies, which range from $1,183 to $3,952 depending upon program of study.

Financial aid. All financial aid based on need. Need-based aid available for part-time students. Work-study available nights, weekends and for part-time students.

Application procedures. Admission: No deadline. $30 fee. **Financial aid:** No deadline. FAFSA, institutional form required.

Academics. Special study options: Internships. **Credit/placement by examination:** AP, CLEP. **Support services:** Remedial instruction, study skills assistance, tutoring.

Majors. Health services: Medical assistant, ward clerk.

Student life. Freshman orientation: Mandatory. Preregistration for classes offered.

Student services. Career counseling, student employment services, financial aid counseling, placement for graduates.

Contact. E-mail: admissions2@careerta.edu
Phone: (412) 372-3900 Toll-free number: (888) 515-8754
Tyna Putignano, Director of Admissions, Career Training Academy: Monroeville, 4314 Old William Penn Highway #103, Monroeville, PA 15146

Career Training Academy: Pittsburgh
Pittsburgh, Pennsylvania
www.careerta.edu

- For-profit 2-year branch campus college
- Commuter campus in small city
- Application essay, interview required

General. Regionally accredited; also accredited by ACCSC. **Enrollment:** 83 undergraduates. **Degrees:** 27 associate awarded. **Calendar:** Differs by program. **Full-time faculty:** 2 total. **Part-time faculty:** 9 total.

Basis for selection. Open admission, but selective for some programs. Interview and essay or personal statement, high school diploma or GED, and transcript or TABE scores required.

2015-2016 Annual costs. Tuition and fees for entire programs (diploma or associate degree) range from $10,200 to $23,053; programs vary from 6 to 18 months in duration. Additional expenses include books and supplies, which range from $1,183 to $3,952 depending upon program of study.

Financial aid. Need-based: Work-study available nights, weekends and for part-time students.

Application procedures. Admission: No deadline. $30 fee. **Financial aid:** No deadline.

Academics. Credit/placement by examination: AP, CLEP. **Support services:** Learning center, tutoring.

Majors. Health services: Insurance specialist, massage therapy, medical assistant.

Technology on campus. Wireless network available.

Student life. Freshman orientation: Mandatory. Preregistration for classes offered.

Student services. Alcohol/substance abuse counseling, career counseling, services for economically disadvantaged, financial aid counseling, personal counseling, placement for graduates.

Contact. E-mail: admissions3@careerta.edu
Phone: (412) 367-4000 Fax: (412) 369-7223
Tyna Putignano, Admissions, Career Training Academy: Pittsburgh, 1500 Shoppes at Northway, Pittsburgh, PA 15237

Commonwealth Technical Institute
Johnstown, Pennsylvania
www.hgac.org   CB code: 3125

- Private 2-year technical college
- Residential campus in small city

General. Accredited by ACCSC. Specially geared toward students with disabilities. **Enrollment:** 177 degree-seeking undergraduates. **Degrees:** 35 associate awarded. **Calendar:** Semester. **Full-time faculty:** 26 total.

Student profile.

25 or older: 85%   Live on campus: 90%

Transfer out. Colleges most students transferred to 2015: Cambria County Area Community College.

Basis for selection. Open admission. **Home schooled:** Transcript of courses and grades, state high school equivalency certificate required.

2015-2016 Annual costs. Tuition/fees: $11,152. Room/board: $11,152.

Financial aid. All financial aid based on need. Need-based aid available for part-time students. Work-study available nights, weekends and for part-time students.

Application procedures. Admission: No deadline. No application fee. Admission notification on a rolling basis. **Financial aid:** No deadline. FAFSA required. Applicants notified on a rolling basis.

Academics. Credit/placement by examination: AP, CLEP. **Support services:** GED preparation and test center, remedial instruction, tutoring.

Majors. Health services: Dental lab technology, medical secretary.

Technology on campus. Dormitories wired for high-speed internet access.

Student life. Freshman orientation: Mandatory. Preregistration for classes offered. **Housing:** Single-sex dorms, special housing for disabled, wellness housing available. **Activities:** Choral groups, student government.

Athletics. Intramural: Basketball, volleyball.

Student services. Alcohol/substance abuse counseling, financial aid counseling, health services, personal counseling, veterans' counselor. **Physically disabled:** Services for visually, speech, hearing impaired.

Contact. Phone: (814) 255-8237 Toll-free number: (800) 762-4211
Fax: (814) 255-8283
Ann Yurcisin, Director of Admissions, Commonwealth Technical Institute, 727 Goucher Street, Johnstown, PA 15905-3902

Community College of Allegheny County
Pittsburgh, Pennsylvania   CB member
www.ccac.edu   CB code: 2156

- Public 2-year community college
- Commuter campus in very large city

General. Founded in 1966. Regionally accredited. Campuses located in and around Pittsburgh. **Enrollment:** 15,335 degree-seeking undergraduates; 650 non-degree-seeking students. **Degrees:** 1,970 associate awarded. **Calendar:** Semester, extensive summer session. **Full-time faculty:** 260 total. **Part-time faculty:** 928 total.

Student profile. Among degree-seeking undergraduates, 3,464 enrolled as first-time, first-year students.

Part-time: 64%   Women: 57%
Out-of-state: 2%   25 or older: 44%

Transfer out. Colleges most students transferred to 2015: University of Pittsburgh, Robert Morris University, Duquesne University, Point Park University, Carlow College.

Basis for selection. Open admission. Audition recommended for music program.

2015-2016 Annual costs. Tuition/fees: $4,064; $7,206 out-of-district; $10,349 out-of-state. Per-credit charge: $104.75 in-district; $209.5 out-of-district; $314.25 out-of-state. Books/supplies: $1,000. Personal expenses: $6,294.

Financial aid. Need-based: Work-study available nights, weekends and for part-time students. **Non-need-based:** Scholarships awarded for academics, minority status.

Application procedures. Admission: No deadline. No application fee. Admission notification on a rolling basis. **Financial aid:** No deadline. FAFSA required. Applicants notified on a rolling basis starting 6/1.

Academics. Special study options: Accelerated study, cooperative education, cross-registration, distance learning, dual enrollment of high school students, ESL, external degree, honors, independent study, weekend college. License preparation in nursing. **Credit/placement by examination:** AP, CLEP, SAT, ACT, institutional tests. 30 credit hours maximum toward associate degree. **Support services:** GED preparation and test center, learning center, reduced course load, remedial instruction, study skills assistance, tutoring, writing center.

Majors. Biology: General. **Business:** Accounting technology, administrative services, banking/financial services, business admin, entrepreneurial studies, human resources, management information systems, marketing. **Communications:** Journalism. **Education:** Elementary, teacher assistance. **Foreign languages:** General. **General:** Electrician, maintenance, painting, power transmission. **Health services:** Cardiovascular technology, clinical lab technology, health information technology, medical assistant, medical radiologic technology/radiation therapy, mental health services, nuclear medical technology, nursing (RN), occupational therapy assistant, pharmacy assistant, physical therapy assistant, respiratory therapy technology, sonography, surgical technology. **Human services:** Social work. **Liberal arts:** Arts/sciences, humanities. **Math:** General. **Parks/recreation:** Health/fitness. **Physical sciences:** Chemistry, physics. **Protective services:** Corrections, fire safety technology, police science. **Psychology:** General. **Social sciences:** General, sociology. **Visual/performing arts:** Art, commercial/advertising art, music. **Work/family studies:** Child development.

Most popular majors. Business/marketing 16%, health sciences 25%, liberal arts 32%, trade and industry 6%.

Technology on campus. 3,700 workstations in library, computer center. Commuter students can connect to campus network. Helpline available.

Student life. Freshman orientation: Available. Preregistration for classes offered. **Activities:** Choral groups, dance, drama, international student organizations, music ensembles, musical theater, radio station, student government, student newspaper.

Athletics. NJCAA. **Intercollegiate:** Baseball M, basketball, bowling, golf, ice hockey M, softball W, tennis, volleyball W.

Student services. Adult student services, career counseling, student employment services, health services, on-campus daycare, personal counseling, placement for graduates, veterans' counselor. **Physically disabled:** Services for visually, speech, hearing impaired. **Transfer:** Transfer adviser for students transferring to 4-year colleges.

Contact. E-mail: admissions@ccac.edu
Phone: (412) 237-2511 Fax: (412) 237-4581
Mary Lou Kennedy, Director of Admissions, Community College of Allegheny County, 808 Ridge Avenue, Pittsburgh, PA 15212

Community College of Beaver County
Monaca, Pennsylvania   CB member
www.ccbc.edu   CB code: 2126

▶ Public 2-year community college
▶ Commuter campus in small town

General. Founded in 1966. Regionally accredited. **Enrollment:** 2,255 undergraduates. **Degrees:** 378 associate awarded. **Location:** 30 miles from Pittsburgh. **Calendar:** Semester, limited summer session. **Full-time faculty:** 63 total. **Part-time faculty:** 139 total. **Class size:** 58% < 20, 41% 20-39, less than 1% 40-49. **Special facilities:** Student-monitored control tower for aviation, computerized mannequins/patient simulators for nursing, casino dealer training classroom at Washington County Center.

Student profile.

Out-of-state:	5%	25 or older: 31%

Transfer out. Colleges most students transferred to 2015: Slippery Rock State University, Geneva College, Robert Morris College, Edinboro State University.

Basis for selection. Open admission, but selective for some programs. NLN Pre-Admission PN test given for admission into nursing program. Interview recommended.

2015-2016 Annual costs. Tuition/fees: $5,460; $10,320 out-of-district; $15,180 out-of-state. Per-credit charge: $142 in-district; $284 out-of-district; $426 out-of-state. Books/supplies: $1,200. Personal expenses: $1,200.

Financial aid. Need-based: Need-based aid available for part-time students. Work-study available nights, weekends and for part-time students. **Non-need-based:** Scholarships awarded for academics, athletics, state residency.

Application procedures. Admission: Priority date 6/1; no deadline. No application fee. Application must be submitted on paper. Admission notification on a rolling basis. Application deadline January 20 for nursing, must reply within 3 weeks of notification. **Financial aid:** Priority date 5/1, closing date 7/1. FAFSA, institutional form required. Applicants notified on a rolling basis starting 8/5; must reply within 2 week(s) of notification.

Academics. Special study options: Cross-registration, distance learning, double major, dual enrollment of high school students, independent study, internships, liberal arts/career combination. License preparation in aviation, nursing, radiology. **Credit/placement by examination:** AP, CLEP, institutional tests. 45 credit hours maximum toward associate degree. **Support services:** GED preparation and test center, learning center, reduced course load, remedial instruction, study skills assistance, tutoring, writing center.

Majors. Biology: General. **Business:** Accounting technology, business admin, human resources, management information systems, marketing. **Communications:** Digital media. **Communications technology:** General. **Computer sciences:** Applications programming, networking. **Education:** General, teacher assistance. **Engineering:** Materials. **English:** English lit. **Health services:** Health aide, medical secretary, nursing (RN). **History:** General. **Liberal arts:** Arts/sciences, humanities. **Protective services:** Police science. **Psychology:** General. **Social sciences:** General. **Visual/performing arts:** Studio arts.

Most popular majors. Business/marketing 13%, health sciences 19%, liberal arts 10%, security/protective services 17%, trade and industry 28%.

Technology on campus. 220 workstations in library, computer center, student center. Online library, helpline, wireless network available.

Student life. Freshman orientation: Mandatory. Preregistration for classes offered. Daylong event takes place the Friday before start of the fall semester. Online version also available. **Activities:** Literary magazine, student government, student newspaper.

Athletics. NJCAA. **Intercollegiate:** Basketball M, softball W, volleyball W. **Intramural:** Basketball M, golf. **Team name:** Titans.

Student services. Adult student services, career counseling, services for economically disadvantaged, student employment services, financial aid counseling, personal counseling, placement for graduates. **Physically disabled:** Services for visually, speech, hearing impaired. **Transfer:** Pre-admission transcript evaluation for new students. Transfer adviser, college fairs on campus for students transferring to 4-year colleges.

Contact. E-mail: admissions@ccbc.edu
Phone: (724) 480-3500 Toll-free number: (800) 335-0222
Angela Vedro, Director of Enrollment Services, Community College of Beaver County, One Campus Drive, Monaca, PA 15061-2588

Community College of Philadelphia
Philadelphia, Pennsylvania   CB member
www.ccp.edu   CB code: 2682

▶ Public 2-year community college
▶ Commuter campus in very large city

General. Founded in 1965. Regionally accredited. Regional centers located in northeast, northwest, and west Philadelphia. Many additional temporary facilities located throughout city. **Enrollment:** 17,948 degree-seeking undergraduates; 1,023 non-degree-seeking students. **Degrees:** 1,920 associate awarded. **ROTC:** Army. **Calendar:** Semester, extensive summer session. **Full-time faculty:** 395 total; 25% minority, 52% women. **Part-time faculty:** 635 total; 34% minority, 51% women. **Class size:** 29% < 20, 70% 20-39, less than 1% 40-49.

Student profile. Among degree-seeking undergraduates, 75% enrolled in a transfer program, 25% enrolled in a vocational program, 4,361 enrolled as first-time, first-year students, 603 transferred in from other institutions.

Part-time:	71%	Hispanic/Latino:	12%
Out-of-state:	3%	Multi-racial, non-Hispanic:	3%
Women:	62%	International:	12%
African American:	44%	25 or older:	50%
Asian American:	5%		

Transfer out. Colleges most students transferred to 2015: Temple University, Drexel University, University of Phoenix, Delaware County Community College, Penn State University.

Basis for selection. Open admission, but selective for some programs. Special requirements for health, music, art and some technical programs. Audition required for music program; portfolio required for art program.

High school preparation. One chemistry, 2 math required of health program applicants.

2015-2016 Annual costs. Tuition/fees: $5,550; $10,140 out-of-district; $14,730 out-of-state. Books/supplies: $1,100. Personal expenses: $856. **Additional information:** In-state, out-of-district students pay an additional $10 nonresident capital fee per credit; out-of-state students pay an additional $20 nonresident capital fee per credit.

2014-2015 Financial aid. All financial aid based on need. Need-based aid available for part-time students. Work-study available nights, weekends and for part-time students.

Application procedures. Admission: No deadline. $20 fee. Admission notification on a rolling basis. **Financial aid:** Closing date 5/1. FAFSA, institutional form required. Applicants notified on a rolling basis.

Academics. Special study options: Accelerated study, distance learning, dual enrollment of high school students, ESL, honors, internships, study abroad, weekend college. License preparation in dental hygiene, nursing, radiology, real estate. **Credit/placement by examination:** AP, CLEP, institutional tests. 30 credit hours maximum toward associate degree. **Support services:** GED preparation and test center, learning center, pre-admission summer program, reduced course load, remedial instruction, tutoring.

Majors. Area/ethnic studies: Women's. **Business:** General, accounting, administrative services, banking/financial services, business admin, fashion, international marketing, logistics, office/clerical, operations, real estate, sales/distribution. **Communications technology:** Recording arts. **Computer sciences:** General, applications programming, data processing, networking, programming, security, system admin, webmaster. **Education:** General, business, secondary. **Engineering:** General. **English:** Rhetoric/composition. **Foreign languages:** Sign language interpretation. **General:** Site management. **Health services:** Clinical lab technology, dental hygiene, health information technology, health services admin, medical assistant, medical radiologic technology/radiation therapy, mental health services, nursing (RN), physical therapy assistant, respiratory therapy technology. **Liberal arts:** Arts/sciences. **Math:** General. **Physical sciences:** General. **Protective services:** Fire safety technology, forensics, police science. **Social sciences:** Geography.

Visual/performing arts: Art, commercial photography, commercial/advertising art, dramatic, music, music performance. **Work/family studies:** Child care management, institutional food production.

Most popular majors. Business/marketing 13%, health sciences 12%, liberal arts 41%.

Technology on campus. 994 workstations in library, student center. Commuter students can connect to campus network. Online course registration, helpline, wireless network available.

Student life. Freshman orientation: Available. Preregistration for classes offered. **Activities:** Jazz band, choral groups, dance, drama, film society, music ensembles, radio station, student government, student newspaper, TV station, Christian Coalition, Newman club, Black Student Congress, Latin American student organization, Phi Theta Kappa, Muslim student association, Vietnamese student organization, Asian-American association.

Athletics. NJCAA. **Intercollegiate:** Baseball M, basketball, cross-country, soccer M, softball W, volleyball W. **Intramural:** Basketball, soccer, softball, tennis, track and field, volleyball. **Team name:** Colonials.

Student services. Adult student services, career counseling, student employment services, financial aid counseling, health services, on-campus daycare, personal counseling, placement for graduates, veterans' counselor, women's services. **Physically disabled:** Services for visually, speech, hearing impaired. **Transfer:** Transfer adviser, college fairs on campus for students transferring to 4-year colleges.

Contact. E-mail: admissions@ccp.edu
Phone: (215) 751-8010
Jason Hand, Director of Admissions and Enrollment Management, Community College of Philadelphia, 1700 Spring Garden Street, Philadelphia, PA 19130-3991

Consolidated School of Business: Lancaster
Lancaster, Pennsylvania
www.csb.edu   CB code: 2240

- For-profit 2-year career college
- Commuter campus in small city
- Interview required

General. Founded in 1986. Accredited by ACICS. Additional campus in York. **Enrollment:** 99 undergraduates. **Degrees:** 42 associate awarded. **Location:** 85 miles from Philadelphia, 35 miles from Harrisburg. **Calendar:** Differs by program. **Full-time faculty:** 7 total. **Part-time faculty:** 3 total.

Basis for selection. Open admission.

High school preparation. Recommended computer application coursework for accelerated or advanced placement.

2015-2016 Annual costs. Books/supplies: $1,550. **Additional information:** Associate degree programs: $28,200-$28,500; certificates: $14,600. Books and supplies range $1,450-$3,100 depending on program level and course of study. All costs are subject to change.

Financial aid. Need-based: Need-based aid available for part-time students. Work-study available nights, weekends and for part-time students. **Non-need-based:** Scholarships awarded for academics, leadership.

Application procedures. Admission: No deadline. No application fee. Admission notification on a rolling basis. **Financial aid:** No deadline. FAFSA required. Applicants notified on a rolling basis.

Academics. Programs consist of 3 core elements: business English, computer applications and approximately 34 credit hours of specialty courses. Curriculum developed with area employer's input to maximize job placement. **Special study options:** Accelerated study, dual enrollment of high school students, internships. **Credit/placement by examination:** AP, CLEP. **Support services:** Study skills assistance, tutoring.

Majors. Business: Accounting, accounting technology, administrative services, business admin, executive assistant, office technology. **Computer sciences:** Data entry, data processing, web page design, webmaster, word processing. **Health services:** Health information management, insurance coding, insurance specialist, management/clinical assistant, medical secretary, medical transcription, office admin, office assistant, office computer specialist, receptionist.

Technology on campus. PC or laptop required. Wireless network available.

Student life. Freshman orientation: Mandatory. Preregistration for classes offered. **Activities:** Student newspaper.

Student services. Adult student services, career counseling, student employment services, financial aid counseling, placement for graduates. **Physically disabled:** Services for speech, hearing impaired. **Transfer:** Pre-admission transcript evaluation for new students.

Contact. E-mail: admissions@csb.edu
Phone: (717) 394-6211 Toll-free number: (800) 541-8298
Fax: (717) 394-6213
Director of Admissions, Consolidated School of Business: Lancaster, 2124 Ambassador Circle, Lancaster, PA 17603

Consolidated School of Business: York
York, Pennsylvania
www.csb.edu   CB code: 2242

- For-profit 2-year career college
- Commuter campus in small city
- Interview required

General. Founded in 1986. Accredited by ACICS. Additional campus in Lancaster. **Enrollment:** 107 undergraduates. **Degrees:** 38 associate awarded. **Location:** 28 miles from Harrisburg, 33 miles from Baltimore. **Calendar:** Differs by program, extensive summer session. **Full-time faculty:** 7 total. **Part-time faculty:** 3 total.

Basis for selection. Open admission. Interview and tour must be completed before acceptance issued. All financial aid matters must be satisfied before classes begin.

2015-2016 Annual costs. Books/supplies: $1,550. **Additional information:** Associate degree programs: $28,200-$28,500; certificates: $14,600. Books and supplies range $1,450-$3,100 depending on program level and course of study. All costs are subject to change.

Financial aid. Need-based: Need-based aid available for part-time students. Work-study available nights, weekends and for part-time students. **Non-need-based:** Scholarships awarded for academics.

Application procedures. Admission: No deadline. No application fee. Admission notification on a rolling basis. **Financial aid:** No deadline. FAFSA required. Applicants notified on a rolling basis.

Academics. Programs consist of 3 core elements: business English, computer applications and approximately 34 credit hours of specialty courses. Curriculum developed with area employers' input to maximize job placement. **Special study options:** Accelerated study, dual enrollment of high school students, internships. **Credit/placement by examination:** AP, CLEP. **Support services:** Study skills assistance, tutoring.

Majors. Business: Accounting, accounting technology, administrative services, business admin, executive assistant, office technology. **Computer sciences:** Data processing, LAN/WAN management, web page design, webmaster, word processing. **Health services:** Insurance coding, insurance specialist, management/clinical assistant, medical secretary, medical transcription, office computer specialist, receptionist.

Technology on campus. PC or laptop required. Wireless network available.

Student life. Freshman orientation: Mandatory. Preregistration for classes offered. **Activities:** Student newspaper.

Student services. Adult student services, career counseling, student employment services, financial aid counseling, placement for graduates. **Transfer:** Pre-admission transcript evaluation for new students.

Contact. E-mail: admissions@csb.edu
Phone: (717) 764-9550 Toll-free number: (800) 520-0691
Director of Admissions, Consolidated School of Business: York, York City Business and Industry Park, York, PA 17404

Dean Institute of Technology
Pittsburgh, Pennsylvania
www.deantech.edu   CB code: 2199

- For-profit 2-year technical college
- Commuter campus in large city
- Interview required

General. Founded in 1948. Accredited by ACCSC. **Enrollment:** 166 under-graduates. **Degrees:** 46 associate awarded. **Location:** 2 miles from downtown. **Calendar:** Quarter, extensive summer session. **Full-time faculty:** 12 total. **Part-time faculty:** 11 total.

Transfer out. **Colleges most students transferred to 2015:** Point Park College.

Basis for selection. Open admission.

2015-2016 Annual costs. Books/supplies: $709. Personal expenses: $1,440. **Additional information:** Tuition varies by program and level. Associate's degrees: $22,700; Diplomas: $9,950-$10,500; Certificates: $3,000-$5,250. All costs are subject to change.

Financial aid. **Need-based:** Need-based aid available for part-time students. Work-study available nights, weekends and for part-time students.

Application procedures. **Admission:** No deadline. $50 fee. Admission notification on a rolling basis. Must reply by May 1 or within 3 week(s) if notified thereafter. **Financial aid:** Closing date 8/1. FAFSA required. Applicants notified on a rolling basis; must reply within 8 week(s) of notification.

Academics. **Special study options:** Cooperative education. **Credit/placement by examination:** AP, CLEP, institutional tests. 12 credit hours maximum toward associate degree. **Support services:** Tutoring.

Majors. **General:** Electrician.

Most popular majors. Engineering/engineering technologies 47%, trade and industry 53%.

Technology on campus. 30 workstations in computer center.

Student services. Career counseling, personal counseling, placement for graduates, veterans' counselor. **Transfer:** Transfer adviser for students transferring to 4-year colleges.

Contact. E-mail: info@deantech.edu
Phone: (412) 531-4433 Fax: (412) 531-4435
Richard Ali, Director of Education/Admissions, Dean Institute of Technology, 1501 West Liberty Avenue, Pittsburgh, PA 15226

Delaware County Community College
Media, Pennsylvania   **CB member**
www.dccc.edu   **CB code: 2125**

▶ Public 2-year community college
▶ Commuter campus in large town

General. Founded in 1967. Regionally accredited. **Enrollment:** 11,742 degree-seeking undergraduates. **Degrees:** 1,236 associate awarded. **Location:** 20 miles from Philadelphia. **Calendar:** Semester, limited summer session. **Full-time faculty:** 141 total; 9% minority, 58% women. **Part-time faculty:** 731 total; 6% minority, 52% women. **Special facilities:** Fitness center, advanced technology center, science, technology, education and mathematics complex. **Partnerships:** Formal partnerships with many local businesses.

Student profile.

Out-of-state: 1%   25 or older: 38%

Basis for selection. Open admission, but selective for some programs. The following students, programs have special admissions requirements: non-high school graduates over the age of 19, nursing, paramedic, plumbing apprenticeship, police academy, respiratory therapy, surgical technology. **Home schooled:** Placement testing is done for most first-time students.

2015-2016 Annual costs. Tuition/fees: $4,950; $9,900 out-of-district; $14,850 out-of-state. Per-credit charge: $110 in-district; $220 out-of-district; $330 out-of-state. Books/supplies: $2,000. Personal expenses: $5,735.

2014-2015 Financial aid. **Need-based:** 838 full-time freshmen applied for aid; 629 deemed to have need; 629 received aid. Average need met was 90%. Average scholarship/grant was $3,048; average loan $3,500. 67% of total undergraduate aid awarded as scholarships/grants, 33% as loans/jobs. Need-based aid available for part-time students. Work-study available nights, weekends and for part-time students. **Non-need-based:** Awarded to 2,116 full-time undergraduates, including 629 freshmen. Scholarships awarded for academics, job skills. **Additional information:** DCCC provides federal, college-funded and international work study.

Application procedures. **Admission:** No deadline. $25 fee, may be waived for applicants with need. Admission notification on a rolling basis.

Financial aid: Closing date 7/1. FAFSA required. Applicants notified on a rolling basis.

Academics. Special student support and tutoring programs offered if the students meet particular criteria for admission to the support programs. **Special study options:** Accelerated study, cooperative education, distance learning, double major, dual enrollment of high school students, ESL, independent study, internships, student-designed major, study abroad. License preparation in nursing, physical therapy. **Credit/placement by examination:** AP, CLEP, institutional tests. 16 credit hours maximum toward associate degree. **Support services:** GED preparation and test center, learning center, pre-admission summer program, reduced course load, remedial instruction, study skills assistance, tutoring, writing center.

Majors. **Business:** Accounting technology, business admin, construction management, e-commerce, entrepreneurial studies, hotel/motel admin, management information systems, office management. **Communications:** Communications/speech/rhetoric, journalism. **Communications technology:** Animation/special effects. **Computer sciences:** General, applications programming, data entry, information systems, networking, web page design, webmaster. **Education:** Early childhood, multi-level teacher, teacher assistance. **Engineering:** General. **General:** Maintenance, power transmission. **Health services:** EMT paramedic, health care admin, insurance specialist, medical assistant, nursing (RN), respiratory therapy technology, surgical technology, ward supervisor. **History:** General. **Liberal arts:** Arts/sciences. **Protective services:** Police science. **Psychology:** General. **Social sciences:** Anthropology, sociology. **Visual/performing arts:** Commercial/advertising art, studio arts.

Most popular majors. Business/marketing 18%, education 16%, health sciences 8%, interdisciplinary studies 7%, liberal arts 25%.

Technology on campus. 1,400 workstations in library, computer center, student center. Online course registration, online library, helpline, repair service, wireless network available.

Student life. **Freshman orientation:** Available. Preregistration for classes offered. Held at the beginning of each semester. **Housing:** Host family housing available. **Activities:** Drama, literary magazine, radio station, student government, student newspaper, art and design clubs, Campus Bible Fellowship, criminal justice club, engineering club, Future Financial Professionals, Gay Straight Alliance, hotel/restaurant management club, literature club, multicultural club, political science club.

Athletics. **Intercollegiate:** Baseball M, basketball, golf, soccer M, softball W, tennis, volleyball W. **Intramural:** Basketball, volleyball. **Team name:** Phantoms.

Student services. Adult student services, alcohol/substance abuse counseling, career counseling, services for economically disadvantaged, student employment services, financial aid counseling, health services, minority student services, personal counseling, placement for graduates, veterans' counselor, women's services. **Physically disabled:** Services for visually, speech, hearing impaired. **Transfer:** Transfer center, transfer adviser, college fairs on campus for students transferring to 4-year colleges.

Contact. E-mail: admiss@dccc.edu
Phone: (610) 359-5050 Fax: (610) 723-1530
Hope Diehl, Director of Admissions and Enrollment Services, Delaware County Community College, 901 South Media Line Road, Media, PA 19063

Douglas Education Center
Monessen, Pennsylvania
www.dec.edu   **CB code: 3288**

▶ For-profit 2-year visual arts and business college
▶ Residential campus in small town
▶ Interview required

General. Accredited by ACICS. **Enrollment:** 267 undergraduates. **Degrees:** 111 associate awarded. **Location:** 30 miles from Pittsburgh. **Calendar:** Semester. **Full-time faculty:** 6 total. **Part-time faculty:** 28 total.

Basis for selection. Open admission. Successful completion of the Wonderlic Scholastic Level Examination. Portfolios recommended. **Adult students:** SAT/ACT scores not required.

2015-2016 Annual costs. Books/supplies: $3,000. **Additional information:** Tuition and fees vary depending on program. Examples of Associate's degree programs: Medical Assistant Program, $20,800; The Factory Digital Film-making Program, $33,500. Certificate programs: Cosmetology Program, $15,850; Esthetician and Nail Technologist Program, $4,675. Costs listed included tuition and fees; books, supplies, and additional costs vary by program. All costs are subject to change.

Financial aid. All financial aid based on need. Need-based aid available for part-time students. Work-study available nights, weekends and for part-time students.

Application procedures. Admission: No deadline. $50 fee. Application must be submitted on paper. Admission notification on a rolling basis. **Financial aid:** No deadline. FAFSA required. Applicants notified on a rolling basis.

Academics. Credit/placement by examination: AP, CLEP. **Support services:** Learning center, remedial instruction, tutoring.

Majors. Business: Business admin, office technology. **Health services:** Health information management, medical assistant, medical secretary, office admin. **Visual/performing arts:** Cinematography, commercial/advertising art, graphic design, illustration.

Most popular majors. Health sciences 11%, visual/performing arts 82%.

Technology on campus. Commuter students can connect to campus network. Wireless network available.

Student life. Freshman orientation: Mandatory. Preregistration for classes offered. **Housing:** Apartments available.

Student services. Adult student services, career counseling, student employment services, financial aid counseling, placement for graduates. **Transfer:** Pre-admission transcript evaluation for new students.

Contact. E-mail: dec@dec.edu
Phone: (724) 684-3684 ext. 100
Toll-free number: (800) 413-6013 ext. 100
Tony Baez-Milan, Director of Admissions, Douglas Education Center, 130 Seventh Street, Monessen, PA 15062

DuBois Business College
DuBois, Pennsylvania
www.dbcollege.edu
CB code: 3886

- For-profit 2-year business and technical college
- Commuter campus in large town
- Interview required

General. Founded in 1885. Accredited by ACICS. **Enrollment:** 90 undergraduates. **Degrees:** 44 associate awarded. **Location:** 100 miles from Pittsburgh. **Calendar:** Quarter, extensive summer session. **Full-time faculty:** 11 total. **Part-time faculty:** 3 total. **Partnerships:** Formal partnerships with 32 Tech Prep high schools.

Student profile.

Out-of-state:	1%	Live on campus:	40%
25 or older:	40%		

Basis for selection. Open admission. Each candidate for admission considered individually on merit and potential. High school graduation or its equivalent or GED is the basic requirement for admission. Other factors, such as high school transcripts, rank in class, attendance, and personal evaluations, are carefully considered. All students required to take and to pass an entrance assessment. In addition, students wishing to enter the Clinical Medical Assistant program must successfully complete a physical examination, have adequate immunizations, and pass a criminal record background check.

High school preparation. Courses in shorthand, accounting, computer, typing, law, psychology, and speech recommended.

2015-2016 Annual costs. Books/supplies: $2,500. **Additional information:** Diploma programs 9-12 months: $11,280-$15,040, lab fee $600-$800, books and supplies $3,368-$6,237. Associate programs 18-21 months: $22,560-$26,320, lab fee $1,200-$1,400, books and supplies $4,582-$7,882.

Financial aid. Need-based: Work-study available nights, weekends and for part-time students.

Application procedures. Admission: No deadline. $25 fee, may be waived for applicants with need. Admission notification on a rolling basis. Must reply by May 1 or within 5 week(s) if notified thereafter. **Financial aid:** Closing date 8/1. FAFSA required. Applicants notified on a rolling basis.

Academics. Special study options: Cooperative education, double major, internships, liberal arts/career combination, study abroad. **Credit/placement**

by examination: AP, CLEP, institutional tests. **Support services:** Reduced course load, remedial instruction, tutoring.

Majors. Business: Accounting/business management, business admin, executive assistant. **Computer sciences:** Support specialist, webmaster. **Health services:** Medical assistant, medical secretary.

Technology on campus. 100 workstations in library, computer center.

Student life. Freshman orientation: Mandatory. Preregistration for classes offered. **Housing:** $225 deposit. **Activities:** Student government, student newspaper, student association.

Athletics. Intercollegiate: Volleyball. **Intramural:** Volleyball.

Student services. Adult student services, career counseling, student employment services, financial aid counseling, personal counseling, placement for graduates, veterans' counselor. **Physically disabled:** Services for visually, speech, hearing impaired. **Transfer:** Transfer adviser for students transferring to 4-year colleges.

Contact. E-mail: admissions@dbcollege.edu
Phone: (814) 371-6920 Toll-free number: (800) 692-6213
Fax: (814) 371-3974
Terry Khoury, Director of Admissions, DuBois Business College, One Beaver Drive, DuBois, PA 15801

DuBois Business College: Huntingdon
Huntingdon, Pennsylvania
www.dbcollege.edu
CB code: 3290

- For-profit 2-year business college
- Small town

General. Accredited by ACICS. **Enrollment:** 80 undergraduates. **Degrees:** 36 associate awarded. **Calendar:** Differs by program. **Full-time faculty:** 6 total. **Part-time faculty:** 2 total.

Basis for selection. Open admission.

2015-2016 Annual costs. Diploma programs 9-12 months: $11,280-$15,040, lab fee $600-$800, books and supplies $3,368-$6,237. Associate programs 8-21 months: $22,560-$26,320, lab fee $1,200-$1,400, books and supplies $4,582-$7,882.

Financial aid. Need-based: Work-study available nights, weekends and for part-time students.

Application procedures. Admission: No deadline. $25 fee. Admission notification on a rolling basis. **Financial aid:** Closing date 8/1.

Academics. Credit/placement by examination: AP, CLEP.

Majors. Business: Accounting/business management, business admin, executive assistant. **Computer sciences:** Support specialist, webmaster. **Health services:** Medical assistant, medical secretary.

Most popular majors. Business/marketing 35%, health sciences 11%, legal studies 54%.

Contact. E-mail: hcc@dbcollege.edu
Phone: (814) 641-0440 Toll-free number: (800) 692-6213
Fax: (814) 641-0205
Terry Khoury, Director of Admission, DuBois Business College: Huntingdon, 1001 Moore Street, Huntingdon, PA 16652

DuBois Business College: Oil City
Oil City, Pennsylvania
www.dbcollege.edu
CB code: 3292

- For-profit 2-year branch campus and business college
- Large town

General. Accredited by ACICS. **Enrollment:** 29 undergraduates. **Degrees:** 9 associate awarded. **Location:** 90 miles from Pittsburgh. **Calendar:** Quarter. **Full-time faculty:** 5 total. **Part-time faculty:** 1 total.

Basis for selection. Open admission.

2015-2016 Annual costs. Books/supplies: $2,500. **Additional information:** Diploma programs 9-12 months: $11,280-$15,040, lab fee $600-$800, books and supplies $3,368-$6,237. Associate programs 18-21 months: $22,560-$26,320, lab fee $1,200-$1,400, books and supplies $4,582-$7,882.

Financial aid. Need-based: Work-study available nights, weekends and for part-time students.

Application procedures. Admission: No deadline. $25 fee. Admission notification on a rolling basis. **Financial aid:** FAFSA required.

Academics. Credit/placement by examination: AP, CLEP.

Majors. Business: Accounting/business management, business admin, executive assistant. **Computer sciences:** IT project management, support specialist. **Health services:** Medical assistant, office admin.

Contact. E-mail: occ@dbcollege.edu
Phone: (814) 677-1322 Fax: (814) 677-8237
Terry Khoury, Director of Admissions, DuBois Business College: Oil City, 701 East Third Street, Oil City, PA 16301

Erie Institute of Technology
Erie, Pennsylvania
www.erieit.edu   CB code: 2284

- For-profit 2-year technical college
- Small city

General. Accredited by ACCSC. **Enrollment:** 232 undergraduates. **Degrees:** 40 associate awarded. **Calendar:** Semester. **Full-time faculty:** 21 total.

Basis for selection. Open admission, but selective for some programs. Math requirement for some programs.

2015-2016 Annual costs. Books/supplies: $3,000. Personal expenses: $30. **Additional information:** Tuition and fees vary depending on program. Cost of certificate programs: $15,030-$24,600. Associate's degrees: $28,395-$37,170. Books and supplies vary by program. All costs are subject to change.

Financial aid. Need-based: Work-study available nights, weekends and for part-time students.

Application procedures. Admission: No deadline. $25 fee. Admission notification on a rolling basis.

Academics. Credit/placement by examination: AP, CLEP.

Majors. Computer sciences: General.

Most popular majors. Computer/information sciences 59%, engineering/engineering technologies 41%.

Contact. Phone: (814) 868-9900 Toll-free number: (866) 868-3743 Fax: (814) 868-9977
Brian Boyce, Director of Admissions, Erie Institute of Technology, 940 Millcreek Mall, Erie, PA 16565

Fortis Institute: Erie
Erie, Pennsylvania
www.fortis.edu   CB code: 2502

- For-profit 2-year health science and career college
- Commuter campus in small city

General. Accredited by ACICS. **Enrollment:** 404 undergraduates. **Degrees:** 187 associate awarded. **Location:** 93 miles from Buffalo, NY; 102 miles from Cleveland; 128 miles from Pittsburgh. **Calendar:** Quarter, limited summer session.

Basis for selection. Open admission, but selective for some programs. Specific admission requirements for medical programs.

2015-2016 Annual costs. Tuition and fees vary by program. Associate's degree programs range $20,668-$36,993. Diploma/certificate programs range $11,874-$18,828. Books and supplies range $166-$3,600 depending on program level and course of study.

Financial aid. Need-based: Work-study available nights, weekends and for part-time students.

Application procedures. Admission: No deadline. $25 fee. Admission notification on a rolling basis.

Academics. Diploma and degree programs are offered in the following disciplines: Nursing, Dental Hygiene, Dental Assisting, Medical Assisting, Health Information Technology, Welding, HVAC, Construction Management, Barbering, Cosmetology, Computer Information Systems, Criminal Justice, and Business. **Special study options:** Internships, liberal arts/career combination. License preparation in dental hygiene, nursing. **Credit/placement by examination:** AP, CLEP. **Support services:** GED preparation and test center, learning center, remedial instruction, tutoring.

Technology on campus. Commuter students can connect to campus network. Online library, wireless network available.

Student life. Freshman orientation: Mandatory. Preregistration for classes offered.

Student services. Career counseling, student employment services, financial aid counseling, placement for graduates. **Transfer:** Re-entry adviser, pre-admission transcript evaluation for new students. Transfer adviser for students transferring to 4-year colleges.

Contact. E-mail: bborgeson@fortisinstitute.edu
Phone: (814) 838-7673 Fax: (814) 838-8642
Michael Murray, Director of Admissions, Fortis Institute: Erie, 5757 West Twenty-Sixth Street, Erie, PA 16506

Fortis Institute: Forty Fort
Forty Fort, Pennsylvania
www.fortis.edu   CB code: 3190

- For-profit 2-year technical college
- Commuter campus in small town

General. Regionally accredited; also accredited by ACCSC. **Enrollment:** 186 undergraduates. **Degrees:** 25 associate awarded. **Calendar:** Differs by program. **Full-time faculty:** 5 total. **Part-time faculty:** 21 total.

Basis for selection. Admissions based on secondary school record and institutional entrance exam.

2015-2016 Annual costs. Tuition and fees vary depending on program. Associate's degree; Medical Assistant Technician $26,240. Diploma/certificate programs range $10,105-$25,840. Books and supplies range $235-$2,000 depending on program level and course of study.

Financial aid. Need-based: Work-study available nights, weekends and for part-time students.

Application procedures. Admission: No deadline. $25 fee.

Academics. Credit/placement by examination: AP, CLEP.

Majors. Health services: Office assistant.

Contact. Phone: (570) 288-8400
Heather Contardi, Admissions Director, Fortis Institute: Forty Fort, 166 Slocum Street, Forty Fort, PA 18704-2936

Harcum College
Bryn Mawr, Pennsylvania   CB member
www.harcum.edu   CB code: 2287

- Private 2-year junior college
- Commuter campus in large town
- Application essay required

General. Founded in 1915. Regionally accredited. **Enrollment:** 1,663 undergraduates. **Degrees:** 395 associate awarded. **Location:** 10 miles from Philadelphia. **Calendar:** Semester, limited summer session. **Full-time faculty:** 55 total. **Part-time faculty:** 415 total. **Class size:** 87% < 20, 12% 20-39, less than 1% 40-49. **Special facilities:** Veterinary services building, physical therapist assistant lab, dental clinic, nursing lab, radiology lab.

Student profile.

Out-of-state:	10%	Live on campus:	17%
25 or older:	40%		

Transfer out. Colleges most students transferred to 2015: Cabrini College, West Chester University, Temple University, Rosemont College, Widener University.

Basis for selection. School record of primary importance. Writing sample required. 750 SAT (exclusive of Writing) and/or 2.0 GPA required. Nursing, dental hygiene, physical therapy assistant, veterinary technology require 900 SAT (exclusive of Writing) and 2.5 GPA. ACCUPLACER exam used for placement. Interview required of dental hygiene, radiology technician, nursing and neurodiognostic technician programs; recommended for all others. **Adult students:** SAT/ACT scores not required if out of high school 3 year(s) or more. **Learning Disabled:** Must provide documentation of disability to ensure proper accommodations are made.

High school preparation. Recommended units include English 4, mathematics 2, social studies 2, history 2, science 2 and academic electives 2. Required units for veterinary technology, dental hygiene, and physical therapy assistant programs include 2 algebra, geometry, biology, chemistry. 1 unit biology and algebra required for dental assisting program. 2 algebra, biology, and chemistry required for medical laboratory technology.

2015-2016 Annual costs. Tuition/fees: $22,060. Per-credit charge: $695. Room/board: $9,100. Books/supplies: $1,500. Personal expenses: $1,795.

Financial aid. Need-based: Need-based aid available for part-time students. Work-study available nights, weekends and for part-time students. **Non-need-based:** Scholarships awarded for academics, alumni affiliation, athletics, leadership.

Application procedures. Admission: Closing date 2/15. $50 fee, may be waived for applicants with need. Admission notification on a rolling basis. **Financial aid:** Priority date 4/15, closing date 5/1. FAFSA required. Applicants notified on a rolling basis starting 3/1; must reply within 3 week(s) of notification.

Academics. 86% of academic programs offered have internship/practicum component. **Special study options:** Accelerated study, cooperative education, distance learning, double major, dual enrollment of high school students, ESL, independent study, internships, liberal arts/career combination. License preparation in dental hygiene, nursing, occupational therapy, physical therapy, radiology. **Credit/placement by examination:** AP, CLEP, institutional tests. 30 credit hours maximum toward associate degree. Maximum of 30 credits total for transfer credits, life experience, challenge examination, and CLEP. **Support services:** Learning center, pre-admission summer program, reduced course load, remedial instruction, study skills assistance, tutoring, writing center.

Majors. Business: General, business admin, fashion, sales/distribution. **Education:** Early childhood. **Health services:** Clinical lab technology, dental assistant, dental hygiene, histologic assistant, nursing (RN), occupational therapy assistant, physical therapy, physical therapy assistant, radiologic technology/medical imaging, veterinary technology/assistant. **Parks/recreation:** Sports admin. **Protective services:** Law enforcement admin. **Psychology:** General. **Visual/performing arts:** Fashion design, interior design. **Work/family studies:** Child care service.

Most popular majors. Business/marketing 8%, education 9%, health sciences 63%, visual/performing arts 14%.

Technology on campus. 86 workstations in dormitories, library, computer center, student center. Dormitories wired for high-speed internet access. Commuter students can connect to campus network. Online course registration, online library, helpline, repair service, wireless network available.

Student life. Freshman orientation: Available. Preregistration for classes offered. One-day introduction to campus services, separate evening orientation for Lifelong Learners. **Housing:** Guaranteed on-campus for all undergraduates. Coed dorms, special housing for disabled available. $200 deposit. **Activities:** International student organizations, literary magazine, student government, student newspaper, Ebony Club, Campus Ambassadors, animal technician student organization, Phi Theta Kappa, peer mentors, community service club, dental assisting club, Association for the Education of Young Children, physical therapy assistant club.

Athletics. NJCAA. **Intercollegiate:** Basketball, soccer, track and field, volleyball W. **Team name:** Bears.

Student services. Adult student services, alcohol/substance abuse counseling, career counseling, services for economically disadvantaged, student employment services, financial aid counseling, health services, minority student services, on-campus daycare, personal counseling, placement for graduates, veterans' counselor, women's services. **Physically disabled:** Services for visually, speech, hearing impaired. **Transfer:** Re-entry adviser, pre-admission transcript evaluation for new students. Transfer center, transfer adviser, college fairs on campus for students transferring to 4-year colleges.

Contact. E-mail: enroll@harcum.edu
Phone: (610) 526-6050 Toll-free number: (800) 345-2600
Fax: (610) 526-6147
Rachel Bowen, Executive Director of Enrollment Mgt, Harcum College, 750 Montgomery Avenue, Bryn Mawr, PA 19010-3476

Harrisburg Area Community College
Harrisburg, Pennsylvania — **CB member**
www.hacc.edu — **CB code: 2309**

- Public 2-year community college
- Commuter campus in small city

General. Founded in 1964. Regionally accredited. County high schools utilized for credit-course offerings. Availability varies by semester. **Enrollment:** 14,830 degree-seeking undergraduates; 4,291 non-degree-seeking students. **Degrees:** 1,887 associate awarded. **ROTC:** Army. **Location:** 90 miles from Philadelphia, 180 miles from New York City. **Calendar:** Semester, limited summer session. **Full-time faculty:** 335 total; 69% have terminal degrees, 19% minority, 63% women. **Part-time faculty:** 756 total; 36% have terminal degrees, 14% minority, 60% women. **Class size:** 66% < 20, 34% 20-39, less than 1% 40-49.

Student profile. Among degree-seeking undergraduates, 2,561 enrolled as first-time, first-year students, 1,417 transferred in from other institutions.

Part-time:	69%	Hispanic/Latino:	10%
Out-of-state:	2%	Multi-racial, non-Hispanic:	3%
Women:	65%	International:	2%
African American:	12%	25 or older:	41%
Asian American:	3%		

Transfer out. Colleges most students transferred to 2015: Penn State University, Shippensburg University, Millersville University, Elizabethtown College, York College.

Basis for selection. Open admission, but selective for some programs. Special requirements for allied health programs and chef apprenticeship. ACT required for allied health programs, score report by February 1. Interview required for allied health, and chef apprenticeship programs; essay required for chef apprenticeship program. **Home schooled:** Statement describing home school structure and mission, transcript of courses and grades, letter of recommendation (nonparent) required.

2015-2016 Annual costs. Tuition/fees: $6,165; $7,500 out-of-district; $8,790 out-of-state. Per-credit charge: $162.5 in-district; $207 out-of-district; $250 out-of-state. Books/supplies: $1,728. Personal expenses: $1,600. **Additional information:** Required fees are $1,140 for sponsored In-State, $1,290 for Non-Sponsored In-State, and $1,440 for Out-Of-State.

2015-2016 Financial aid. Need-based: 99% of total undergraduate aid awarded as scholarships/grants, 1% as loans/jobs. Need-based aid available for part-time students. Work-study available nights, weekends and for part-time students. **Non-need-based:** Scholarships awarded for academics, art, leadership, music/drama, religious affiliation, state residency. **Additional information:** Federal work study community service positions available.

Application procedures. Admission: No deadline. $35 fee, may be waived for applicants with need. Admission notification on a rolling basis. Must reply by May 1 or within 6 week(s) if notified thereafter. **Financial aid:** Priority date 4/15; no closing date. FAFSA, institutional form required. Applicants notified on a rolling basis starting 4/30.

Academics. Special study options: Distance learning, double major, dual enrollment of high school students, ESL, honors, independent study, internships, study abroad. Albright College (Reading Campus and Harrisburg Campus), Drexel University (Behavioral & Addictions Counseling Sciences Programs only), Eastern University (St. Davids campus and Central PA campus), Elizabethtown College, Elizabethtown College Accelerated Program, Lebanon Valley College, Millersville University, Penn State Harrisburg, Peirce College (Paralegal Studies only), Shippensburg University, Susquehanna University, Temple University, Wilson College. License preparation in dental hygiene, nursing, paramedic, radiology, real estate. **Credit/placement by examination:** AP, CLEP, IB, institutional tests. 30 credit hours maximum toward associate degree. **Support services:** GED preparation and test center, learning center, remedial instruction, study skills assistance, tutoring, writing center.

Majors. Architecture: Architecture. **Biology:** General. **Business:** General, accounting technology, accounting/business management, administrative services, banking/financial services, business admin, hospitality admin, hotel/motel admin, real estate, sales/distribution, small business admin, tourism/

travel. **Communications:** Media studies. **Computer sciences:** General, computer science, networking, security, web page design. **Conservation:** Environmental science, environmental studies. **Education:** Early childhood, secondary. **Engineering:** General, robotics. **General:** Building inspection, electrician, lineworker. **Health services:** Cardiovascular technology, clinical lab technology, dental hygiene, dietetics, EMT paramedic, health care admin, health services admin, medical assistant, nuclear medical technology, nursing (RN), radiologic technology/medical imaging, respiratory therapy technology, sonography, surgical technology. **Human services:** Social work. **Math:** General. **Philosophy/religion:** Philosophy. **Physical sciences:** General, chemistry. **Protective services:** Criminalistics, firefighting, law enforcement admin, police science. **Psychology:** General. **Social sciences:** General, GIS/cartography, international relations. **Visual/performing arts:** General, art, crafts, design, dramatic, graphic design, music management, photography. **Work/family studies:** Institutional food production.

Most popular majors. Business/marketing 21%, health sciences 26%, liberal arts 13%, security/protective services 6%.

Technology on campus. 350 workstations in library, computer center, student center. Online course registration, helpline, wireless network available.

Student life. Freshman orientation: Mandatory. Preregistration for classes offered. Varies by campus. **Activities:** Choral groups, drama, international student organizations, literary magazine, student government, student newspaper, Allies, African American Student Association, Christian Student Fellowship, International Awareness, Student Environmental Action Coalition, Phi Beta Lambda, psychology club, Mosaico club, bilingual club.

Athletics. Intercollegiate: Basketball, golf M, soccer M, tennis, volleyball. **Intramural:** Football (non-tackle) M, ultimate frisbee M.

Student services. Career counseling, student employment services, financial aid counseling, minority student services, veterans' counselor. **Physically disabled:** Services for visually, hearing impaired. **Transfer:** Pre-admission transcript evaluation for new students. Transfer adviser, college fairs on campus for students transferring to 4-year colleges.

Contact. E-mail: admit@hacc.edu
Phone: (717) 780-2400 Toll-free number: (800) 222-4222
Fax: (717) 236-7674
Tisa Riley, Director of Enrollment Services, Harrisburg Area Community College, One HACC Drive, Cooper 206, Harrisburg, PA 17110-2999

Hussian College, School of Art
Philadelphia, Pennsylvania
www.hussianart.edu   CB code: 7309

- For-profit 2-year visual arts college
- Commuter campus in very large city
- Interview required

General. Founded in 1946. Accredited by ACCSC. Hussian is located in Old City, Philadelphia just steps away from the Market-Frankford Line. It is also within walking distance of many bus routes as well as PATCO and Regional Rail. **Enrollment:** 79 degree-seeking undergraduates. **Degrees:** 12 bachelor's, 18 associate awarded. **Calendar:** Semester, limited summer session. **Part-time faculty:** 23 total. **Class size:** 31% < 20, 69% 20-39. **Partnerships:** The school offers credit to approved technical high school programs who provide training in commercial art.

Student profile.

Out-of-state: 14% **25 or older:**   2%

Basis for selection. Personal interview and portfolio review required for acceptance; talent, ability, communication skills and potential most important. Portfolio development and creative assessments are also available. Demonstration of creative aptitude required through portfolio review, creative assessment activity, or workshop participation. Special emphasis is placed on discerning if a student is able to do observational drawing.

2015-2016 Annual costs. Tuition/fees: $18,050. Books/supplies: $900. Personal expenses: $3,563.

Financial aid. Need-based: Work-study available nights, weekends and for part-time students.

Application procedures. Admission: No deadline. No application fee. Admission notification on a rolling basis. **Financial aid:** No deadline. FAFSA, institutional form required. Applicants notified on a rolling basis starting 2/15; must reply within 3 week(s) of notification.

Academics. Second-semester freshmen must earn GPA of 2.0 or above to continue in good standing. **Special study options:** Internships. Bachelor's degree programs available on campus. **Credit/placement by examination:** AP, CLEP, IB, institutional tests. Proficiency credit for special aptitude/experience on an individualized basis. **Support services:** Reduced course load, remedial instruction, study skills assistance, tutoring.

Majors. Visual/performing arts: Commercial/advertising art.

Technology on campus. PC or laptop required. 60 workstations in computer center. Online library, wireless network available.

Student life. Freshman orientation: Mandatory. Preregistration for classes offered. Held prior to official start of classes. **Housing:** No housing offered. Suggestions available for local housing options.

Student services. Alcohol/substance abuse counseling, career counseling, financial aid counseling, legal services, personal counseling, placement for graduates, veterans' counselor. **Transfer:** Pre-admission transcript evaluation for new students.

Contact. E-mail: info@hussianart.edu
Mark Cernero, Director of Admissions, Hussian College, School of Art, The Bourse, Suite 300, Philadelphia, PA 19106

ITT Technical Institute: Pittsburgh
Pittsburgh, Pennsylvania
www.itt-tech.edu   CB code: 2745

- For-profit 2-year technical college
- Commuter campus in large city
- Interview required

General. Accredited by ACICS. **Enrollment:** 179 undergraduates. **Degrees:** 84 associate awarded. **Calendar:** Quarter, extensive summer session. **Full-time faculty:** 4 total. **Part-time faculty:** 24 total.

Basis for selection. Satisfactory scores from on-site tests in English and mathematics required.

2015-2016 Annual costs. Per-credit-hour charge, $493; academic fee, $200. Some programs require purchase of tools, which could cost an additional $500. All costs subject to change.

Financial aid. Need-based: Work-study available nights, weekends and for part-time students.

Application procedures. Admission: No deadline. No application fee. Admission notification on a rolling basis. **Financial aid:** No deadline. FAFSA, institutional form required. Applicants notified on a rolling basis.

Academics. Credit/placement by examination: AP, CLEP. **Support services:** Learning center, tutoring.

Majors. Computer sciences: Networking, web page design. **Protective services:** Law enforcement admin. **Visual/performing arts:** Design.

Most popular majors. Computer/information sciences 47%, engineering/engineering technologies 37%, security/protective services 16%.

Technology on campus. Online library available.

Student life. Freshman orientation: Available. Preregistration for classes offered.

Student services. Career counseling, student employment services, placement for graduates.

Contact. Toll-free number: (800) 353-8324
Robert Burnfield, Director of Recruitment, ITT Technical Institute: Pittsburgh, 5460 Campbells Run Road, Pittsburgh, PA 15205

ITT Technical Institute: Plymouth Meeting
Plymouth Meeting, Pennsylvania
www.itt-tech.edu

- For-profit 2-year visual arts and technical college
- Commuter campus in large town

General. Accredited by ACICS. **Enrollment:** 273 undergraduates. **Degrees:** 73 associate awarded. **Calendar:** Quarter. **Full-time faculty:** 5 total. **Part-time faculty:** 35 total.

Basis for selection. Must pass admissions test or have scored, within previous five years, minimum of 17 ACT or 800 SAT (exclusive of Writing), or have earned either 36 quarter credit hours (or 24 semester or trimester credit hours) with overall cumulative GPA of 2.0 from accredited institution. Meeting with a representative of ITT Tech and arranging a time to tour the school is required.

2015-2016 Annual costs. Per-credit-hour charge, $493; academic fee, $200. Some programs require purchase of tools, which could cost an additional $100 to $500. All costs subject to change.

Financial aid. **Need-based:** Work-study available nights, weekends and for part-time students.

Application procedures. **Admission:** No application fee.

Academics. **Credit/placement by examination:** AP, CLEP.

Majors. **Computer sciences:** Networking, web page design. **Protective services:** Law enforcement admin. **Visual/performing arts:** Design.

Student services. Career counseling, student employment services, placement for graduates.

Contact. Toll-free number: (866) 902-8324 Fax: (610) 491-9047 ITT Technical Institute: Plymouth Meeting, 220 West Germantown Pike, Suite 100, Plymouth Meeting, PA 19462

JNA Institute of Culinary Arts
Philadelphia, Pennsylvania
www.culinaryarts.edu
CB code: 3049

- For-profit 2-year technical college
- Commuter campus in very large city
- Interview required

General. Accredited by ACCSC. **Enrollment:** 59 undergraduates. **Degrees:** 22 associate awarded. **Calendar:** Quarter, extensive summer session. **Full-time faculty:** 5 total. **Part-time faculty:** 3 total. **Special facilities:** Student-operated restaurant and catering services.

Student profile.

Out-of-state:	12%	25 or older:	38%

Basis for selection. Open admission.

2015-2016 Annual costs. Tuition/fees: $12,725. Books/supplies: $215. **Additional information:** Tuition listed is for the Food Service Diploma Program. Culinary Arts/Restaurant Management Associate Program is $25,300 with a $75 registration fee. All costs are subject to change.

Financial aid. **Need-based:** Work-study available nights, weekends and for part-time students.

Application procedures. **Admission:** No deadline. No application fee. **Financial aid:** No deadline. FAFSA required.

Academics. We have four starts for new students per year: February, May, August, and November. **Special study options:** Internships. **Credit/placement by examination:** AP, CLEP.

Student life. **Freshman orientation:** Mandatory. Preregistration for classes offered. **Housing:** Nearby apartments available. **Activities:** Culinary clubs.

Student services. Career counseling, student employment services, financial aid counseling, legal services, placement for graduates.

Contact. E-mail: admissions@culinaryarts.edu
Phone: (215) 468-8800 Toll-free number: (877) 872-3197
Cheryl Cohen Freedman, Director of Admissions, JNA Institute of Culinary Arts, 1212 South Broad Street, Philadelphia, PA 19146

Johnson College
Scranton, Pennsylvania
www.johnson.edu
CB member
CB code: 1542

- Private 2-year technical college
- Commuter campus in small city
- Application essay required

General. Founded in 1912. Accredited by ACCSC. **Enrollment:** 430 degree-seeking undergraduates; 39 non-degree-seeking students. **Degrees:** 151 associate awarded. **Location:** 117 miles from Philadelphia, 125 miles from New York City. **Calendar:** Semester, limited summer session. **Full-time faculty:** 25 total. **Part-time faculty:** 5 total. **Class size:** 44% < 20, 56% 20-39. **Special facilities:** Materials test laboratory, veterinary hospital. **Partnerships:** Formal partnerships with tech prep programs.

Student profile. Among degree-seeking undergraduates, 100% enrolled in a vocational program, 3% already have a bachelor's degree or higher, 147 enrolled as first-time, first-year students.

Part-time:	10%	Hispanic/Latino:	5%
Women:	29%	Multi-racial, non-Hispanic:	2%
African American:	3%	25 or older:	16%
Asian American:	2%	Live on campus:	23%

Transfer out. **Colleges most students transferred to 2015:** State University of New York Utica/Rome.

Basis for selection. Students in all programs are required to meet minimal admission requirements in order to be accepted. **Home schooled:** Transcript of courses and grades, state high school equivalency certificate required.

High school preparation. College-preparatory program required. 3 units required. Required units include English 2 and mathematics 1. One year chemistry and biology with C or higher required for veterinary science technology majors. One year chemistry or biology and one year algebra II or geometry with C or higher required for radiologic technology.

2015-2016 Annual costs. Tuition/fees: $17,684. Per-credit charge: $510. Room/board: $5,010. Books/supplies: $2,000. Personal expenses: $500. **Additional information:** Required fees for Radiologic & Physical Therapist Assistant are $1950, Carpentry & HVAC fees are $1500, welding fees are $2050. Other expenses include book, tools and supplies and are estimated at $2000 per semester.

2014-2015 Financial aid. **Need-based:** 149 full-time freshmen applied for aid; 142 deemed to have need; 136 received aid. Average need met was 41%. Average scholarship/grant was $6,782; average loan $2,967. 47% of total undergraduate aid awarded as scholarships/grants, 53% as loans/jobs. Need-based aid available for part-time students. Work-study available nights, weekends and for part-time students. **Non-need-based:** Awarded to 17 full-time undergraduates, including 6 freshmen. Scholarships awarded for academics.

Application procedures. **Admission:** Priority date 5/1; deadline 8/1 (receipt date). No application fee. Admission notification on a rolling basis. Must reply within 30 days. **Financial aid:** Priority date 4/28; no closing date. FAFSA required. Applicants notified on a rolling basis starting 3/15; must reply within 2 week(s) of notification.

Academics. Extensive shop and laboratory facilities. **Special study options:** Cooperative education, dual enrollment of high school students, internships. License preparation in physical therapy, radiology. **Credit/placement by examination:** AP, CLEP, institutional tests. 9 credit hours maximum toward associate degree. **Support services:** Learning center, pre-admission summer program, reduced course load, remedial instruction, study skills assistance, tutoring.

Majors. **Business:** Logistics. **Computer sciences:** Networking. **General:** Carpentry. **Health services:** Radiologic technology/medical imaging, veterinary technology/assistant.

Most popular majors. Computer/information sciences 11%, engineering/engineering technologies 22%, health sciences 27%, trade and industry 40%.

Technology on campus. 52 workstations in library, computer center. Online library, repair service, wireless network available.

Student life. **Freshman orientation:** Mandatory, $100 fee. Preregistration for classes offered. **Housing:** Special housing for disabled, apartments available. $250 fully refundable deposit, deadline 6/1. **Activities:** Student government, Social Force.

Student services. Career counseling, student employment services, placement for graduates.

Athletics. NJCAA. **Intercollegiate:** Basketball, bowling, cheerleading W, cross-country. **Intramural:** Basketball, table tennis, volleyball. **Team name:** Jaguars.

Student services. Career counseling, services for economically disadvantaged, student employment services, financial aid counseling, personal counseling, placement for graduates, veterans' counselor. **Physically disabled:** Services for visually impaired. **Transfer:** Pre-admission transcript evaluation for new students. Transfer adviser, college fairs on campus for students transferring to 4-year colleges.

Contact. E-mail: admit@johnson.edu
Phone: (570) 702-8900 Toll-free number: (800) 293-9675
Fax: (570) 348-2181
Rita Lapera, Director of Enrollment Services, Johnson College, 3427 North Main Avenue, Scranton, PA 18508

Kaplan Career Institute: Broomall
Broomall, Pennsylvania
www.kaplancareerinstitute.com   CB code: 3398

- For-profit 2-year career college
- Commuter campus in large town
- Application essay, interview required

General. Accredited by ACCSC. Dental assistant, electrical technician, heating/ventilation/air conditioning/regfrigeration, medical assistant, and pharmacy technician diploma programs available. **Enrollment:** 560 degree-seeking undergraduates. **Degrees:** 19 associate awarded. **Location:** 7 miles from Philadelphia. **Calendar:** Quarter, extensive summer session. **Full-time faculty:** 5 total. **Part-time faculty:** 26 total.

Basis for selection. Open admission.

2015-2016 Annual costs. Associate degree program: Medical assisting $29,615. Diploma programs range from $15,464 to $18,965. Fees, books and supplies included. All fees subject to change.

Financial aid. Need-based: Need-based aid available for part-time students. Work-study available nights, weekends and for part-time students.

Application procedures. Admission: No deadline. $10 fee. Admission notification on a rolling basis. **Financial aid:** No deadline. FAFSA required. Applicants notified on a rolling basis.

Academics. Credit/placement by examination: AP, CLEP. **Support services:** Remedial instruction, tutoring.

Majors. Health services: Medical assistant.

Student life. Freshman orientation: Mandatory. Preregistration for classes offered.

Student services. Adult student services, career counseling, student employment services, personal counseling, placement for graduates, veterans' counselor.

Contact. Phone: (610) 353-7630 Toll-free number: (800) 935-1857
Fax: (610) 359-1370
Bill Schnell, Director of Admissions, Kaplan Career Institute: Broomall, 1991 Sproul Road, Suite 42, Broomall, PA 19008

Kaplan Career Institute: Franklin Mills
Philadelphia, Pennsylvania
www.kaplancareerinstitute.com   CB code: 3386

- For-profit 2-year technical and career college
- Commuter campus in large town
- Interview required

General. Founded in 1981. Accredited by ACCSC. **Enrollment:** 640 undergraduates. **Degrees:** 115 associate awarded. **Location:** 5 miles from Philadelphia. **Calendar:** Differs by program, extensive summer session. **Full-time faculty:** 20 total. **Part-time faculty:** 19 total.

Basis for selection. Open admission.

2015-2016 Annual costs. Computer Networking Technology: $33,264. Electrical Technician: $18,965. Medical Assistant: $16,315. Medical Billing and Coding: $16,315. Pharmacy Technician: $15,464. Respiratory Care: $42,465.

Financial aid. Need-based: Work-study available nights, weekends and for part-time students. **Additional information:** Scholarships for graduating

seniors. Awards based on institutional scholarship aptitude test and interview with independent committee. Parental income not considered.

Application procedures. Admission: No deadline. $10 fee. Admission notification on a rolling basis. **Financial aid:** Closing date 9/20. Applicants notified on a rolling basis.

Academics. Special study options: Internships. **Credit/placement by examination:** AP, CLEP.

Majors. Computer sciences: Programming. **Health services:** Respiratory therapy assistant. **Protective services:** Criminal justice.

Most popular majors. Computer/information sciences 53%, health sciences 47%.

Student services. Career counseling, student employment services, placement for graduates.

Contact. Phone: (215) 612-6600 Toll-free number: (800) 989-1014
Fax: (215) 612-6695
Dan Watkins, Director of Admissions, Kaplan Career Institute: Franklin Mills, 177 Franklin Mills Boulevard, Philadelphia, PA 19154

Kaplan Career Institute: Harrisburg
Harrisburg, Pennsylvania
www.kaplancareerinstitute.com   CB code: 3212

- For-profit 2-year health science and technical college
- Commuter campus in small city
- Application essay, interview required

General. Accredited by ACICS. Formerly known as Thompson Institute. **Enrollment:** 217 undergraduates. **Degrees:** 46 associate awarded. **Calendar:** Continuous, extensive summer session. **Full-time faculty:** 8 total. **Part-time faculty:** 13 total.

Student profile.

25 or older:	45% **Live on campus:**	10%

Basis for selection. Open admission, but selective for some programs. Students must achieve passing score on assessment exam. Criminal Justice entrants must undergo criminal background check. **Home schooled:** Interview required. Must have Commonwealth diploma.

2015-2016 Annual costs. Personal expenses: $2,862. **Additional information:** Associate degree programs: Computer networking technology $36,089; criminal justice $28,985. Diploma programs: Medical assistant $15,365; medical billing and coding $15,315. Fees, books and supplies included. All costs are subject to change.

Financial aid. Need-based: Need-based aid available for part-time students. Work-study available nights, weekends and for part-time students.

Application procedures. Admission: No deadline. $10 fee. Application must be submitted on paper. Admission notification on a rolling basis. **Financial aid:** No deadline. FAFSA, institutional form required.

Academics. Special study options: Internships. **Credit/placement by examination:** AP, CLEP. Credits in any combination (CLEP, experiential, examination, transfer) may not exceed 50% of the program. **Support services:** Study skills assistance, tutoring.

Majors. Business: Business admin. **Computer sciences:** LAN/WAN management, networking, web page design, webmaster. **Health services:** Medical assistant. **Protective services:** Corrections, criminal justice, law enforcement admin.

Technology on campus. 30 workstations in library, computer center. Commuter students can connect to campus network. Online library, helpline, student web hosting available.

Student life. Freshman orientation: Mandatory. Preregistration for classes offered. **Housing:** Apartments available.

Student services. Adult student services, career counseling, services for economically disadvantaged, student employment services, financial aid counseling, placement for graduates.

Contact. E-mail: mhale@kaplan.edu
Phone: (717) 558-1300 Toll-free number: (800) 935-1857
Fax: (717) 558-1342
Mark Hale, Director of Admissions, Kaplan Career Institute: Harrisburg, 5650 Derry Street, Harrisburg, PA 17111-4112

Kaplan Career Institute: Pittsburgh
Pittsburgh, Pennsylvania
www.kaplancareerinstitute.com   **CB code: 3823**

- For-profit 2-year business and health science college
- Commuter campus in large city
- Application essay, interview required

General. Accredited by ACICS. **Enrollment:** 444 undergraduates. **Degrees:** 118 associate awarded. **Calendar:** Quarter, extensive summer session. **Full-time faculty:** 17 total. **Part-time faculty:** 31 total. **Special facilities:** Firearms training simulator.

Basis for selection. Wonderlic required. Students are required to achieve a minimum score on an independently developed entrance examination and, under the Kaplan Commitment undergraduate students must show a minimum level of academic performance in their initial classes before they will be fully accepted into their programs.

2015-2016 Annual costs. Accounting Management: $31,809. Business Administration/Management: $31,837. Computer Numerical Control Machinist: $9,500. Criminal Justice: $31,775. Electrical Technician: $18,064. Federal, State and Local Payroll Tax Workshop: $510. Heating, Ventilation, Air Conditioning and Refrigeration: $17,104. Medical Assistant: $16,471. Medical Assisting: $31,789. Medical Billing and Coding: $13,536. Medical Office Assistant: $13,536. Occupational Therapy Assistant: $34,904. Practical Nursing: $29,806.

Financial aid. All financial aid based on need. Need-based aid available for part-time students. Work-study available nights, weekends and for part-time students.

Application procedures. Admission: No deadline. $10 fee, may be waived for applicants with need. Admission notification on a rolling basis. **Financial aid:** Closing date 4/30. FAFSA, institutional form required. Applicants notified on a rolling basis.

Academics. Special study options: Double major, internships. License preparation in occupational therapy. **Credit/placement by examination:** AP, CLEP. 11 credit hours maximum toward associate degree. **Support services:** Reduced course load, study skills assistance, tutoring.

Majors. Business: Accounting, administrative services, business admin, fashion. **Computer sciences:** General, applications programming, information technology, LAN/WAN management, programming, security, systems analysis, webmaster. **Engineering:** Computer. **Health services:** Medical assistant, medical secretary, occupational therapy assistant. **Protective services:** Corrections, criminal justice, law enforcement admin, police science, security services.

Technology on campus. 225 workstations in library, computer center. Online library, helpline, repair service available.

Student life. Freshman orientation: Mandatory, $20 fee. Preregistration for classes offered.

Student services. Career counseling, student employment services, financial aid counseling, personal counseling, placement for graduates.

Contact. E-mail: lglaser@kaplan.edu
Phone: (412) 338-4770 Toll-free number: (800) 935-1857
Fax: (412) 261-0998
Kaplan Career Institute: Pittsburgh, 933 Penn Avenue, Pittsburgh, PA 15222

Keystone Technical Institute
Harrisburg, Pennsylvania
www.kti.edu   **CB code: 3188**

- For-profit 2-year culinary school and technical college
- Commuter campus in small city
- Interview required

General. Accredited by ACCSC. **Enrollment:** 341 undergraduates. **Degrees:** 88 associate awarded. **Location:** 206 miles from Philadelphia, 200 miles from Washington, DC. **Calendar:** Differs by program. **Full-time faculty:** 25 total. **Part-time faculty:** 13 total.

Basis for selection. Open admission. **Home schooled:** Transcript of courses and grades required. For state grants, applicants must submit either accredited diploma or certification from local superintendent of compliance with Home Education Act. **Learning Disabled:** Provide copy of independent educational program.

2015-2016 Annual costs. Books/supplies: $2,800. Personal expenses: $1,200. **Additional information:** Tuition and fees vary by program. Associate's degrees: $23,141-$31,843; Certificate's: $2,941-$28,326. Books and supplies vary depending on program level and course of study. All costs are subject to change.

Financial aid. All financial aid based on need. Need-based aid available for part-time students. Work-study available nights, weekends and for part-time students.

Application procedures. Admission: No deadline. $20 fee. Admission notification on a rolling basis. **Financial aid:** Closing date 8/1. FAFSA required. Applicants notified on a rolling basis.

Academics. Special study options: Internships. License preparation in radiology. **Credit/placement by examination:** AP, CLEP. **Support services:** Study skills assistance, tutoring.

Majors. Business: Administrative services. **Computer sciences:** Support specialist. **Health services:** Dental assistant, massage therapy, medical assistant, medical secretary. **Work/family studies:** Child care service.

Most popular majors. Health sciences 76%, legal studies 15%.

Technology on campus. 65 workstations in library. Online library, helpline, repair service available.

Student life. Freshman orientation: Mandatory. Preregistration for classes offered. Held first day of class for all new students.

Student services. Adult student services, alcohol/substance abuse counseling, career counseling, services for economically disadvantaged, student employment services, financial aid counseling, on-campus daycare, placement for graduates. **Transfer:** Re-entry adviser, pre-admission transcript evaluation for new students. Transfer adviser, college fairs on campus for students transferring to 4-year colleges.

Contact. E-mail: info@kti.edu
Phone: (717) 545-4747 Toll-free number: (888) 530-4772
Todd Harlow, Admissions Director, Keystone Technical Institute, 2301 Academy Drive, Harrisburg, PA 17112-1012

Lackawanna College
Scranton, Pennsylvania
www.lackawanna.edu   **CB code: 2373**

- Private 2-year junior college
- Commuter campus in small city
- Interview required

General. Founded in 1894. Regionally accredited. **Enrollment:** 1,420 degree-seeking undergraduates. **Degrees:** 326 associate awarded. **ROTC:** Army. **Location:** 125 miles from New York City, 125 miles from Philadelphia. **Calendar:** Semester, limited summer session. **Full-time faculty:** 30 total; 13% have terminal degrees, 53% women. **Part-time faculty:** 143 total; 60% women. **Class size:** 74% < 20, 26% 20-39, less than 1% 40-49. **Special facilities:** Environmental institute, police academy. **Partnerships:** Formal partnerships with Tobyhanna Army Depot and Cinram Corporation; IT Security Pipeline Program and Misericordia University.

Student profile.

Out-of-state:	13%	Live on campus:	21%
25 or older:	21%		

Transfer out. Colleges most students transferred to 2015: Keystone College, Misericordia University, Pennsylvania State University, Marywood University, East Stroudsburg University.

Basis for selection. Open admission. **Adult students:** SAT/ACT scores not required. **Home schooled:** Transcript of courses and grades, state high school equivalency certificate, interview required. **Learning Disabled:** Submit current documentation of disability for arrangement of accommodations.

High school preparation. 11 units recommended. Recommended units include English 4, mathematics 3, social studies 1 and science 3.

2015-2016 Annual costs. Tuition/fees: $14,210. Per-credit charge: $465. Room/board: $8,300. Books/supplies: $1,500. Personal expenses: $1,560.

2014-2015 Financial aid. Need-based: 1,337 full-time freshmen applied for aid; 1,206 deemed to have need; 388 received aid. Average need met was 14%. Average scholarship/grant was $7,123; average loan $3,060. 46% of total undergraduate aid awarded as scholarships/grants, 54% as loans/jobs. Need-based aid available for part-time students. Work-study available nights, weekends and for part-time students. **Non-need-based:** Awarded to 48 full-time undergraduates, including 19 freshmen. Scholarships awarded for academics, athletics.

Application procedures. Admission: No deadline. $35 fee, may be waived for applicants with need. Admission notification on a rolling basis. Must reply by May 1 or within 4 week(s) if notified thereafter. **Financial aid:** Priority date 5/1; no closing date. FAFSA, institutional form required. Applicants notified on a rolling basis starting 5/1.

Academics. Peer and professional tutoring available upon request, in addition to online tutoring, evenings and weekends. **Special study options:** Cooperative education, distance learning, double major, dual enrollment of high school students, honors, independent study, internships. License preparation in nursing, paramedic, real estate. **Credit/placement by examination:** AP, CLEP, institutional tests. 30 credit hours maximum toward associate degree. **Support services:** GED preparation and test center, learning center, pre-admission summer program, reduced course load, remedial instruction, tutoring, writing center.

Majors. Biology: General. **Business:** General, accounting, administrative services, banking/financial services, business admin, management information systems. **Computer sciences:** Security. **Conservation:** Environmental science, environmental studies. **Education:** General. **Health services:** Medical secretary, sonography, surgical technology. **Liberal arts:** Arts/sciences. **Protective services:** Criminal justice, police science. **Social sciences:** General. **Work/family studies:** Child care service.

Most popular majors. Business/marketing 24%, engineering/engineering technologies 7%, health sciences 24%, liberal arts 15%, security/protective services 17%.

Technology on campus. 261 workstations in dormitories, library, computer center. Dormitories wired for high-speed internet access and linked to campus network. Commuter students can connect to campus network. Online course registration, online library, helpline, wireless network available.

Student life. Freshman orientation: Mandatory. Preregistration for classes offered. Two day program, scheduled the weekend before the start of classes. **Housing:** Guaranteed on-campus for freshmen. Coed dorms, single-sex dorms available. $375 fully refundable deposit. **Activities:** Drama, literary magazine, student government, student newspaper, spiritual study group, student government association, diversity club and social justice center.

Athletics. NJCAA. **Intercollegiate:** Baseball M, basketball, cheerleading, cross-country, football (tackle) M, golf M, soccer W, softball W, volleyball W. **Team name:** Falcons.

Student services. Adult student services, career counseling, services for economically disadvantaged, student employment services, financial aid counseling, health services, personal counseling, placement for graduates, veterans' counselor. **Transfer:** Re-entry adviser, pre-admission transcript evaluation for new students. Transfer adviser, college fairs on campus for students transferring to 4-year colleges.

Contact. E-mail: findyourfuture@lackawanna.edu
Phone: (570) 961-7814 Toll-free number: (877) 346-3552
Fax: (570) 961-7843
Brian Costanzo, Dean of Enrollment Management, Lackawanna College, 501 Vine Street, Scranton, PA 18509

Lansdale School of Business
North Wales, Pennsylvania
www.lsb.edu   CB code: 5853

- For-profit 2-year career college
- Commuter campus in small town
- Interview required

General. Accredited by ACICS. Additional locations in Phoenixville and Warminster, PA. **Enrollment:** 344 undergraduates. **Degrees:** 80 associate awarded. **Location:** 25 miles from Philadelphia. **Calendar:** Semester, extensive summer session. **Full-time faculty:** 6 total. **Part-time faculty:** 37 total.

Transfer out. Colleges most students transferred to 2015: Eastern College, Delaware Valley College.

Basis for selection. Open admission.

2015-2016 Annual costs. Tuition/fees: $21,700. **Additional information:** Cost quoted is for the allied-health medical assistant program. Cost for other programs varies by program. All costs are subject to change.

Financial aid. Need-based: Work-study available nights, weekends and for part-time students.

Application procedures. Admission: No deadline. $40 fee. Admission notification on a rolling basis. **Financial aid:** Priority date 7/1, closing date 8/16. FAFSA required.

Academics. Special study options: Double major, internships. Bachelor's degree programs available on campus. **Credit/placement by examination:** AP, CLEP, institutional tests. 30 credit hours maximum toward associate degree. **Support services:** Reduced course load.

Majors. Business: Accounting, marketing, office technology. **Computer sciences:** Computer graphics, data entry, system admin, web page design, webmaster. **Health services:** Medical assistant.

Most popular majors. Business/marketing 34%, computer/information sciences 18%, health sciences 33%, legal studies 15%.

Technology on campus. 64 workstations in library, computer center.

Student life. Freshman orientation: Mandatory. Preregistration for classes offered. **Activities:** Student government.

Contact. E-mail: mjohnson@lsb.edu
Phone: (215) 699-5700 Toll-free number: (800) 219-0486
Fax: (215) 699-8770
Marianne Johnson, Director of Admissions, Lansdale School of Business, 290 Wissahickon Avenue, North Wales, PA 19454-4114

Laurel Business Institute
Uniontown, Pennsylvania
www.laurel.edu   CB code: 2329

- For-profit 2-year technical and career college
- Commuter campus in large town
- Application essay, interview required

General. Founded in 1985. Accredited by ACICS. **Enrollment:** 233 undergraduates. **Degrees:** 60 associate awarded. **Location:** 50 miles from Pittsburgh. **Calendar:** Trimester, extensive summer session. **Full-time faculty:** 20 total. **Part-time faculty:** 6 total. **Class size:** 95% < 20, 5% 20-39. **Special facilities:** Microsoft testing center, Prometric testing site. **Partnerships:** Formal partnership with Nemacolin Woodlands resort.

Student profile.

Out-of-state:	1%	**25 or older:** 85%

Transfer out. Colleges most students transferred to 2015: University of Phoenix, Central Penn.

Basis for selection. Must be high school graduate or must have GED and must also achieve a minimum score on an entrance exam administered by the admission department. This minimum score varies by program. Some programs also require job shadowing and acceptance into the program by the program director.

2015-2016 Annual costs. Tuition/fees: $9,694. Per-credit charge: $295. Books/supplies: $1,410. Personal expenses: $1,280. **Additional information:** Annual tuition varies by program and ranges from $4,397 to $6,274 per term; per-credit-hour charges range from $295 to $350.

Financial aid. All financial aid based on need. Need-based aid available for part-time students. Work-study available nights, weekends and for part-time students.

Application procedures. Admission: No deadline. $50 fee. Application must be submitted on paper. Admission notification on a rolling basis. **Financial aid:** No deadline. FAFSA, institutional form required. Applicants notified on a rolling basis; must reply within 4 week(s) of notification.

Academics. Special study options: Accelerated study, double major, dual enrollment of high school students, honors, internships. **Credit/placement by examination:** AP, CLEP, institutional tests. 24 credit hours maximum toward associate degree. **Support services:** Reduced course load, tutoring.

Majors. Business: Accounting, business admin, executive assistant. **Education:** Early childhood. **Health services:** Insurance specialist, massage therapy, office assistant, respiratory therapy technology. **Work/family studies:** Child care management.

Most popular majors. Business/marketing 23%, computer/information sciences 14%, education 12%, family/consumer sciences 6%, health sciences 28%, personal/culinary services 19%.

Technology on campus. 50 workstations in library, computer center. Online library available.

Student life. Freshman orientation: Mandatory. Preregistration for classes offered. Orientation takes place prior to the first day of each term. **Policies:** Attendance required in all classes. Excessive absences will result in points being deducted from final grade. **Activities:** Student newspaper, Phi Beta Lambda.

Student services. Student employment services, placement for graduates. **Physically disabled:** Services for visually, speech impaired. **Transfer:** Pre-admission transcript evaluation for new students.

Contact. E-mail: admission@laurel.edu
Phone: (724) 439-4900 Fax: (724) 439-3607
Maria Clyde, Director of Admission, Laurel Business Institute, 11 East Penn Street, Uniontown, PA 15401

Laurel Technical Institute
Sharon, Pennsylvania
www.laurel.edu   CB code: 2466

▶ For-profit 2-year technical and career college
▶ Commuter campus in large town
▶ Interview required

General. Accredited by ACICS. Campuses are located in Meadville, Sharon and Uniontown. Newest addition is the LBI School of Cosmetology in Morgantown, WV. **Enrollment:** 171 degree-seeking undergraduates. **Degrees:** 58 associate awarded. **Location:** 50 miles from Pittsburgh; 15 miles from Youngstown, Ohio. **Calendar:** Trimester, extensive summer session. **Full-time faculty:** 20 total. **Part-time faculty:** 10 total.

Student profile. Among degree-seeking undergraduates, 70 enrolled as first-time, first-year students.

Part-time:	18%	Women:	70%

Basis for selection. All applicants must take Wonderlic SLE assessment and pass with appropriate score pending program requirements. Respiratory Therapy and Medical Lab Tech prospects must job shadow and write essay. **Learning Disabled:** ADA compliant.

High school preparation. Recommended units include English 3, mathematics 3 and science 2. Accounting, business, computer and English preferred.

2015-2016 Annual costs. Tuition varies by program and level. Certificates: $9,102-$20,269; Associate's: $21,985-$35,782. Book and supplies vary. All costs are subject to change.

Financial aid. Need-based: Work-study available nights, weekends and for part-time students. **Non-need-based:** Scholarships awarded for academics.

Application procedures. Admission: No deadline. $50 fee. Admission notification on a rolling basis. **Financial aid:** No deadline. Institutional form required.

Academics. Special study options: Internships. High school dual enrollment for qualified juniors and seniors. **Credit/placement by examination:** AP, CLEP, institutional tests. 15 credit hours maximum toward associate degree. **Support services:** Study skills assistance, tutoring.

Majors. Business: Business admin. **Education:** Early childhood. **Health services:** Health information technology, respiratory therapy assistant.

Technology on campus. 35 workstations in library, computer center.

Student life. Freshman orientation: Mandatory. Preregistration for classes offered. Orientation takes place prior to the first day of each semester. **Activities:** Student government, student newspaper, HOSA chapter, PBL chapter.

Student services. Career counseling, financial aid counseling, placement for graduates. **Transfer:** Pre-admission transcript evaluation for new students.

Contact. E-mail: lti.admission@laurel.edu
Phone: (724) 983-0700 Fax: (724) 983-8355
Maria Clyde, Director of Admission, Laurel Technical Institute, 200 Sterling Avenue, Sharon, PA 16146

Lehigh Carbon Community College
Schnecksville, Pennsylvania
www.lccc.edu   CB code: 2381

▶ Public 2-year community college
▶ Commuter campus in small town

General. Founded in 1966. Regionally accredited. 3 campuses serve both rural and urban students. **Enrollment:** 5,801 degree-seeking undergraduates; 937 non-degree-seeking students. **Degrees:** 690 associate awarded. **ROTC:** Army. **Location:** 8 miles from Allentown, 70 miles from Philadelphia. **Calendar:** Semester, limited summer session. **Full-time faculty:** 88 total; 19% have terminal degrees, 3% minority, 61% women. **Part-time faculty:** 355 total; less than 1% have terminal degrees, 5% minority, 50% women. **Class size:** 57% < 20, 43% 20-39, less than 1% 50-99.

Student profile. Among degree-seeking undergraduates, 68% enrolled in a transfer program, 32% enrolled in a vocational program, 1% already have a bachelor's degree or higher, 1,405 enrolled as first-time, first-year students, 1,024 transferred in from other institutions.

Part-time:	56%	25 or older:	31%
Women:	60%		

Transfer out. Colleges most students transferred to 2015: Kutztown University, Bloomsburg University, Penn State University, Temple University, West Chester University.

Basis for selection. Open admission, but selective for some programs. Special requirements for aviation, allied health, nursing and veterinary technician programs. COMPASS used for course placement. High school diploma or GED required of applicants to allied health and professional pilot programs, and applicants under the age of 18. Interview required for allied health, aviation, medical assistant, veterinary technician programs. **Home schooled:** Personal interview encouraged.

High school preparation. Special requirements for allied health programs and nursing.

2015-2016 Annual costs. Tuition/fees: $3,800; $7,070 out-of-district; $10,340 out-of-state. Per-credit charge: $100 in-district; $209 out-of-district; $318 out-of-state. Books/supplies: $2,000. Personal expenses: $1,200.

2014-2015 Financial aid. Need-based: 874 full-time freshmen applied for aid; 618 deemed to have need; 618 received aid. Average need met was 100%. Average scholarship/grant was $4,342; average loan $2,898. 67% of total undergraduate aid awarded as scholarships/grants, 33% as loans/jobs. Need-based aid available for part-time students. Work-study available nights, weekends and for part-time students. **Non-need-based:** Awarded to 116 full-time undergraduates, including 55 freshmen. Scholarships awarded for academics, job skills.

Application procedures. Admission: No deadline. No application fee. Admission notification on a rolling basis. **Financial aid:** Priority date 5/1; no closing date. FAFSA required. Applicants notified on a rolling basis starting 1/1; must reply within 2 week(s) of notification.

Academics. Special study options: Cooperative education, cross-registration, distance learning, dual enrollment of high school students, ESL, external degree, honors, independent study, internships, study abroad. Bachelor's degree programs available on campus. License preparation in aviation, nursing, occupational therapy, physical therapy. **Credit/placement by examination:** AP, CLEP, institutional tests. 26 credit hours maximum toward associate degree. **Support services:** GED preparation and test center, learning center, pre-admission summer program, reduced course load, remedial instruction, study skills assistance, tutoring, writing center.

Honors college/program. Top 10% of sponsoring school district, with 1200 SAT (exclusive of Writing), skills assessment score of 90 or above in reading and writing, and 70 or above in algebra required.

Majors. Biology: General, biotechnology. **Business:** General, accounting technology, business admin, human resources, resort management. **Communications:** Communications/speech/rhetoric. **Communications technology:** Animation/special effects, radio/TV, recording arts. **Computer sciences:** General, applications programming, networking, programming, security, web page design. **Conservation:** Environmental science. **Education:** General, early childhood, special ed, teacher assistance. **Engineering:** General. **General:** Site management. **Health services:** Health information technology, medical assistant, nursing (RN), occupational therapy assistant, physical therapy assistant, veterinary technology/assistant. **Human services:** General, social work. **Liberal arts:** Arts/sciences. **Math:** General. **Parks/recreation:** Exercise sciences, sports admin. **Physical sciences:** General, chemistry. **Protective services:** Criminal justice, law enforcement admin. **Psychology:** General. **Social sciences:** GIS/cartography. **Visual/performing arts:** Art, fashion design, game design, graphic design, interior design.

Most popular majors. Business/marketing 13%, education 8%, health sciences 27%, liberal arts 15%, security/protective services 6%.

Technology on campus. 1,100 workstations in library, computer center. Commuter students can connect to campus network. Online course registration, online library, wireless network available.

Student life. Freshman orientation: Available. Preregistration for classes offered. Takes place in June and July for durations of approximately 5 hours; all new students expected to attend. **Policies:** Must follow student bill of rights and responsibilities. **Activities:** Choral groups, drama, international student organizations, radio station, student government, student newspaper, ANIME club, Justice Society, Kappa Delta Pi, veterans club, Literary Magazine, Psi Beta, Student Government Association, science technology mathematics and engineering club, Teacher Education Association.

Athletics. NJCAA. **Intercollegiate:** Baseball M, basketball, cheerleading, golf, soccer M, softball W, volleyball W. **Intramural:** Basketball, football (non-tackle) M, table tennis, tennis, ultimate frisbee, volleyball. **Team name:** Cougars.

Student services. Adult student services, career counseling, student employment services, financial aid counseling, minority student services, on-campus daycare, personal counseling, placement for graduates, veterans' counselor. **Physically disabled:** Services for visually, speech, hearing impaired. **Transfer:** Pre-admission transcript evaluation for new students. Transfer adviser, college fairs on campus for students transferring to 4-year colleges.

Contact. E-mail: admissions@lccc.edu
Phone: (610) 799-1575 Fax: (610) 799-1629
Louis Hegyes, Director of Recruitment/Admissions, Lehigh Carbon Community College, 4525 Education Park Drive, Schnecksville, PA 18078-2502

Lincoln Technical Institute: Allentown
Allentown, Pennsylvania
www.lincolntech.com   CB code: 2741

▸ For-profit 2-year technical college
▸ Commuter campus in small city
▸ Interview required

General. Founded in 1946. Accredited by ACCSC. **Enrollment:** 540 undergraduates. **Degrees:** 67 associate awarded. **Location:** 60 miles from Philadelphia. **Calendar:** Differs by program. **Full-time faculty:** 19 total. **Part-time faculty:** 3 total.

Basis for selection. Open admission.

2015-2016 Annual costs. Diploma programs: $13,900-$28,700 for tuition and books. Associate degree programs: $28,200-$31,800 for tuition and books. Additional fees may apply and vary by program and level. All costs are subject to change.

Financial aid. Need-based: Work-study available nights, weekends and for part-time students.

Application procedures. Admission: No deadline. $150 fee, may be waived for applicants with need. **Financial aid:** No deadline.

Academics. Credit/placement by examination: AP, CLEP.

Majors. Health services: Medical assistant.

Most popular majors. Computer/information sciences 29%, health sciences 13%, trade and industry 58%.

Student life. Freshman orientation: Mandatory. Preregistration for classes offered. **Housing:** Wellness housing available. **Activities:** TV station.

Contact. Phone: (610) 398-5300 Toll-free number: (800) 201-1445
Fax: (610) 395-2706
Mark Garner, Director of Admissions, Lincoln Technical Institute: Allentown, 5151 Tilghman Street, Allentown, PA 18104

Lincoln Technical Institute: Northeast Philadelphia
Philadelphia, Pennsylvania
www.lincolntech.com

▸ For-profit 2-year technical college
▸ Very large city

General. Accredited by ACICS. **Enrollment:** 310 undergraduates. **Degrees:** 24 associate awarded. **Calendar:** Differs by program. **Full-time faculty:** 15 total. **Part-time faculty:** 6 total.

Basis for selection. Open admission.

2015-2016 Annual costs. Diploma programs range from $14,604 to $29,082. Associate's Degree in Medical Assisting Technology costs $28,572. Additional fees may apply and vary by program and level. All costs are subject to change.

Financial aid. Need-based: Work-study available nights, weekends and for part-time students.

Application procedures. Admission: No deadline. $150 fee.

Academics. Credit/placement by examination: AP, CLEP. **Support services:** Tutoring.

Majors. Health services: Medical assistant, medical secretary, office assistant.

Technology on campus. Online library available.

Student life. Freshman orientation: Mandatory. Preregistration for classes offered.

Contact. Phone: (215) 969-0869 Toll-free number: (800) 201-1445
Fax: (215) 969-3457
Paula Little, Director of Admissions, Lincoln Technical Institute: Northeast Philadelphia, 2180 Hornig Road, Philadelphia, PA 19116

Lincoln Technical Institute: Philadelphia
Philadelphia, Pennsylvania
www.lincolntech.com   CB code: 9010

▸ For-profit 2-year technical college
▸ Commuter campus in very large city

General. Accredited by ACCSC. **Enrollment:** 360 undergraduates. **Degrees:** 28 associate awarded. **Calendar:** Quarter. **Full-time faculty:** 17 total.

Basis for selection. Open admission.

2015-2016 Annual costs. Automotive Technology diploma program, $28,747; Automotive Service Management associate degree program, $35,227. Cost of books and supplies included in tuition. Other fees may apply and will vary depending on program level. All costs are subject to change.

Financial aid. Need-based: Work-study available nights, weekends and for part-time students.

Application procedures. Admission: No deadline. $150 fee. Admission notification on a rolling basis.

Academics. Credit/placement by examination: AP, CLEP.

Contact. E-mail: dcunningham@lincolntech.com
Phone: (215) 335-0800 Toll-free number: (800) 201-1445
Fax: (215) 335-1443
Pat Fittipaldi, Director of Admissions, Lincoln Technical Institute: Philadelphia, 9191 Torresdale Avenue, Philadelphia, PA 19136

Luzerne County Community College
Nanticoke, Pennsylvania
www.luzerne.edu   CB code: 2382

▸ Public 2-year community college
▸ Commuter campus in large town

General. Founded in 1966. Regionally accredited. **Enrollment:** 5,227 degree-seeking undergraduates; 561 non-degree-seeking students. **Degrees:** 77 associate awarded. **Location:** 8 miles from Wilkes-Barre. **Calendar:** Semester, extensive summer session. **Full-time faculty:** 112 total; 51% women. **Part-time faculty:** 374 total; 53% women. **Class size:** 64% < 20, 36% 20-39, less than 1% 40-49.

Student profile. Among degree-seeking undergraduates, 1,286 enrolled as first-time, first-year students.

Part-time:	50%	Hispanic/Latino:	11%
Women:	60%	Multi-racial, non-Hispanic:	1%
African American:	5%	25 or older:	36%
Asian American:	2%		

Transfer out. Colleges most students transferred to 2015: Bloomsburg University, Wilkes University, King's College, College Misericordia.

Basis for selection. Open admission, but selective for some programs. High school record, college record, test scores considered for admission to health sciences programs. Diagnostic Entrance Test required of nursing applicants. Interview recommended for health sciences program. **Home schooled:** Transcript of courses and grades, state high school equivalency certificate required. **Learning Disabled:** Comprehensive services for special needs students at no cost providing the students present the required documentation.

High school preparation. 1 algebra, 1 chemistry, 1 biology required of nursing, respiratory therapy, surgical technology, and dental hygiene applicants.

2015-2016 Annual costs. Tuition/fees: $4,770; $8,370 out-of-district; $11,970 out-of-state. Per-credit charge: $120 in-district; $240 out-of-district; $360 out-of-state. Books/supplies: $2,000. Personal expenses: $1,400.

Financial aid. Need-based: Need-based aid available for part-time students. Work-study available nights, weekends and for part-time students.

Application procedures. Admission: No deadline. No application fee. Admission notification on a rolling basis. **Financial aid:** Priority date 4/15; no closing date. FAFSA, institutional form required. Applicants notified on a rolling basis starting 7/1.

Academics. Special study options: Distance learning, dual enrollment of high school students, ESL, internships, liberal arts/career combination, student-designed major. **Credit/placement by examination:** AP, CLEP, institutional tests. 30 credit hours maximum toward associate degree. **Support services:** GED preparation and test center, learning center, pre-admission summer program, reduced course load, remedial instruction, study skills assistance, tutoring, writing center.

Majors. Business: General, accounting, accounting technology, administrative services, banking/financial services, business admin, management information systems, real estate. **Communications:** Advertising, journalism. **Communications technology:** Recording arts. **Computer sciences:** General, applications programming, computer graphics, security, web page design. **Education:** General, teacher assistance. **General:** Electrician, maintenance. **Health services:** Dental assistant, dental hygiene, EMT paramedic, insurance specialist, medical transcription, nursing (RN), prechiropractic, preoptometry, prepharmacy, respiratory therapy technology, surgical technology. **Liberal arts:** Arts/sciences, humanities. **Math:** General. **Parks/recreation:** Health/fitness. **Protective services:** Criminal justice, fire safety technology. **Social sciences:** General. **Visual/performing arts:** Graphic design, illustration, photography. **Work/family studies:** Institutional food production.

Most popular majors. Computer/information sciences 6%, family/consumer sciences 14%, health sciences 46%, personal/culinary services 8%, trade and industry 16%.

Technology on campus. 150 workstations in library, computer center, student center. Commuter students can connect to campus network. Online course registration, online library, helpline, student web hosting, wireless network available.

Student life. Freshman orientation: Mandatory. Preregistration for classes offered. **Activities:** Campus ministries, choral groups, drama, radio station, student government, TV station, Circle K, Brothers and Sisters in Christ, ACLU, NAACP, Amnesty International, NOW, GLBTA.

Athletics. Intercollegiate: Baseball M, basketball, cross-country, golf, softball W, volleyball W. **Intramural:** Badminton, basketball, football (non-tackle), volleyball. **Team name:** Trailblazers.

Student services. Adult student services, career counseling, student employment services, health services, personal counseling, placement for graduates, veterans' counselor. **Physically disabled:** Services for visually, hearing impaired. **Transfer:** Pre-admission transcript evaluation for new students. Transfer adviser, college fairs on campus for students transferring to 4-year colleges.

Contact. E-mail: admissions@luzerne.edu
Phone: (570) 740-0337 Toll-free number: (800) 377-5222 ext. 337
Fax: (570) 740-0238
Francis Curry, Director of Admissions, Luzerne County Community College, 1333 South Prospect Street, Nanticoke, PA 18634-3899

Manor College
Jenkintown, Pennsylvania
www.manor.edu   CB code: 2260

- Private 2-year junior college affiliated with the Ukrainian Catholic Church
- Commuter campus in small town

General. Founded in 1947. Regionally accredited. **Enrollment:** 678 degree-seeking undergraduates; 19 non-degree-seeking students. **Degrees:** 142 associate awarded. **Location:** 12 miles from Philadelphia. **Calendar:** Semester, limited summer session. **Full-time faculty:** 26 total; 46% have terminal degrees, 8% minority, 69% women. **Part-time faculty:** 112 total; 31% have terminal degrees, 12% minority, 59% women. **Class size:** 86% < 20, 14% 20-39. **Special facilities:** Ukrainian heritage studies center and museum, dental health center, law library, veterinary technology radiology lab and surgical suite, Civil War library.

Student profile. Among degree-seeking undergraduates, 80% enrolled in a transfer program, 20% enrolled in a vocational program, 2% already have a bachelor's degree or higher, 169 enrolled as first-time, first-year students.

Part-time:	37%	Hispanic/Latino:	9%
Out-of-state:	4%	Native American:	1%
Women:	73%	Multi-racial, non-Hispanic:	4%
African American:	40%	25 or older:	28%
Asian American:	2%	Live on campus:	12%

Transfer out. 60% of students enrolled in the transfer program go on to 4-year colleges. **Colleges most students transferred to 2015:** Holy Family University, LaSalle University, Temple University, Drexel University, Community College of Philadelphia.

Basis for selection. GPA, course selection; institutional placement test required of all applicants except those holding bachelor's degree. SAT or ACT scores are particularly considered in Allied Health and Veterinary Technician programs. SAT or ACT recommended. SAT or ACT Verbal and Math subtests required for students intending to major in Allied Health, Dental Hygiene, and Veterinary Technology programs. These tests are optional for students intending to go into all other programs. **Adult students:** SAT/ACT scores not required if applicant over 21. **Home schooled:** Statement describing home school structure and mission required. **Learning Disabled:** IEP required of all with diagnosed disability.

High school preparation. 16 units required. Required units include English 4, mathematics 3, social studies 2, history 2, science 3 (laboratory 2). Biology with laboratory; chemistry with laboratory; three math courses required of all Allied Health Science applicants.

2015-2016 Annual costs. Tuition/fees: $16,550. Room/board: $7,500. Books/supplies: $1,250. Personal expenses: $3,100. **Additional information:** Full-time tuition for Dental Hygiene, Expanded Dental Functions Assisting, and Veterinary Technology is $16,700. Part-time tuition for these programs is $699 per credit.

2015-2016 Financial aid. All financial aid based on need. 133 full-time freshmen applied for aid; 130 deemed to have need; 126 received aid. Average need met was 65%. Average scholarship/grant was $17,315; average loan $6,355. 45% of total undergraduate aid awarded as scholarships/grants, 55% as loans/jobs. Need-based aid available for part-time students. Work-study available nights, weekends and for part-time students.

Application procedures. Admission: Closing date 9/1 (receipt date). No application fee. Application must be submitted online. Admission notification on a rolling basis. **Financial aid:** Priority date 3/1; no closing date. FAFSA, institutional form required. Applicants notified on a rolling basis; must reply within 1 week(s) of notification.

Academics. Special study options: Accelerated study, distance learning, double major, dual enrollment of high school students, honors, independent study, internships. License preparation in dental hygiene, real estate. **Credit/placement by examination:** AP, CLEP, institutional tests. 30 credit hours maximum toward associate degree. **Support services:** Learning center, reduced course load, remedial instruction, study skills assistance, tutoring, writing center.

Majors. Business: Accounting, business admin, international, marketing. **Communications:** Communications/speech/rhetoric. **Computer sciences:** Applications programming. **Education:** Early childhood, elementary. **Health services:** Dental assistant, dental hygiene, prenursing, preveterinary, veterinary technology/assistant. **Liberal arts:** Arts/sciences. **Psychology:** General.

Most popular majors. Business/marketing 17%, health sciences 44%, legal studies 7%, liberal arts 21%, psychology 6%.

Technology on campus. 125 workstations in dormitories, library, computer center. Dormitories wired for high-speed internet access and linked to campus network. Commuter students can connect to campus network. Online library, helpline, wireless network available.

Student life. Freshman orientation: Mandatory, $35 fee. Preregistration for classes offered. Three 1-day orientations in January and August. **Policies:** Alcohol and drug policy strictly enforced; mandatory meningitis vaccines and completed health record forms to live in residence hall. **Housing:** Coed dorms available. $100 fully refundable deposit, deadline 9/1. **Activities:** Campus ministries, choral groups, international student organizations, music ensembles, Model UN, student government, Rotaract, Music Ministry, Admissions Ambassadors, Orientation Leaders, Student Senate.

Athletics. NJCAA. **Intercollegiate:** Basketball, soccer, volleyball W. **Team name:** Blue Jays.

Student services. Adult student services, alcohol/substance abuse counseling, chaplain/spiritual director, career counseling, services for economically disadvantaged, student employment services, financial aid counseling, health services, personal counseling, placement for graduates. **Physically disabled:** Services for visually impaired. **Transfer:** Pre-admission transcript evaluation for new students. Transfer center, transfer adviser, college fairs on campus for students transferring to 4-year colleges.

Contact. E-mail: enroll@manor.edu
Phone: (215) 884-2216 Fax: (215) 576-6564
John Dempster, Director of Admissions, Manor College, 700 Fox Chase Road, Jenkintown, PA 19046-3319

McCann School of Business and Technology: Dickson City
Dickson City, Pennsylvania
www.mccann.edu

- For-profit 2-year business and technical college
- Commuter campus in small city

General. Accredited by ACICS. **Calendar:** Quarter.

Annual costs/financial aid. Tuition and fees vary depending on program and level. Examples of Associate's degree programs: Business Administration $27,477; Criminal Justice $27,893. Examples of Certificate programs: Accounting Assistant $17,448; Medical Billing and Coding $18,835. All costs are subject to change.

Contact. Phone: (570) 307-2000
Director of Admissions, 2227 Scranton Carbondale Highway, Dickson City, PA 18519

McCann School of Business and Technology: Hazleton
Hazle Township, Pennsylvania
www.mccann.edu   CB code: 3887

- For-profit 2-year business and technical college
- Commuter campus in large town
- Interview required

General. Founded in 1897. Accredited by ACICS. **Enrollment:** 301 degree-seeking undergraduates. **Degrees:** 109 associate awarded. **Location:** 35 miles from Wilkes Barre. **Calendar:** Quarter, extensive summer session. **Full-time faculty:** 12 total. **Part-time faculty:** 48 total.

Basis for selection. Open admission. **Home schooled:** Transcript of courses and grades required.

2015-2016 Annual costs. Books/supplies: $1,950. Personal expenses: $1,600. **Additional information:** Tuition and fees vary depending on program and level. Examples of Associate's degree programs: Business Administration $27,477; Criminal Justice $27,893. Examples of Certificate programs: Medical Assisting $27,345; Medical Billing and Coding $19,485. All costs are subject to change.

Financial aid. Need-based: Work-study available nights, weekends and for part-time students.

Application procedures. Admission: No deadline. $40 fee, may be waived for applicants with need. Application must be submitted on paper.

Admission notification on a rolling basis. **Financial aid:** No deadline. FAFSA required. Applicants notified on a rolling basis.

Academics. Special study options: Internships. License preparation in paramedic. **Credit/placement by examination:** AP, CLEP. **Support services:** Reduced course load, remedial instruction, tutoring.

Majors. Business: Accounting, administrative services, business admin, hospitality/recreation, marketing, office/clerical. **Computer sciences:** General, applications programming, LAN/WAN management, support specialist. **Education:** Early childhood, teacher assistance. **Health services:** Medical secretary.

Technology on campus. 80 workstations in library, computer center.

Student life. Freshman orientation: Mandatory. Preregistration for classes offered. **Activities:** Student government, student newspaper, Circle-K.

Student services. Adult student services, career counseling, student employment services, financial aid counseling, placement for graduates, veterans' counselor. **Transfer:** Transfer adviser for students transferring to 4-year colleges.

Contact. E-mail: info@mccann.edu
Phone: (570) 454-6172 Toll-free number: (888) 790-1096
Fax: (570) 454-6286
Michael Mazalusky, Director of Admissions, McCann School of Business and Technology: Hazleton, 370 Maplewood Drive, Hazle Township, PA 18202

McCann School of Business and Technology: Pottsville
Pottsville, Pennsylvania
www.mccann.edu   CB code: 3296

- For-profit 2-year branch campus and technical college
- Commuter campus in small town
- Interview required

General. Accredited by ACICS. **Enrollment:** 240 degree-seeking undergraduates. **Degrees:** 847 associate awarded. **Location:** One hour from Harrisburg. **Calendar:** Quarter, extensive summer session. **Full-time faculty:** 5 total. **Part-time faculty:** 40 total. **Special facilities:** On-site massage therapy training center.

Basis for selection. Open admission. Students must achieve a score of 13 on the Wonderlic Basic Skills Assessment, must possess a GED or high school diploma. **Home schooled:** State high school equivalency certificate required.

2015-2016 Annual costs. Books/supplies: $1,950. **Additional information:** Tuition and fees vary depending on program and level. Examples of Associate's degree programs: Business Administration with Marketing Option $27,627; Criminal Justice $27,893. Examples of Certificate programs: Clinical Medical Assistant $17,572; Phlebotomist $13,284. All costs are subject to change.

Financial aid. Need-based: Work-study available nights, weekends and for part-time students.

Application procedures. Admission: No deadline. $40 fee.

Academics. Special study options: Distance learning, internships. **Credit/placement by examination:** AP, CLEP. **Support services:** Reduced course load, remedial instruction, tutoring.

Majors. Business: Accounting, administrative services, business admin. **Computer sciences:** General. **Education:** Early childhood. **General:** Electrician. **Health services:** Clinical lab assistant, health information management, medical transcription, office admin, office assistant, office computer specialist, receptionist. **Protective services:** Criminal justice, police science.

Technology on campus. 125 workstations in library, computer center. Commuter students can connect to campus network. Online library, helpline, repair service, wireless network available.

Student life. Freshman orientation: Mandatory. Preregistration for classes offered. **Activities:** Student government.

Student services. Adult student services, career counseling, student employment services, financial aid counseling, placement for graduates.

Contact. Phone: (570) 622-7622 Toll-free number: (888) 781-3025 Fax: (570) 622-7770
Amelia Hopkins, Director of Admissions, McCann School of Business and Technology: Pottsville, 2650 Woodglen Road, Pottsville, PA 17901

McCann School of Business and Technology: Sunbury

Sunbury, Pennsylvania
www.mccann.edu   **CB code: 3298**

- For-profit 2-year branch campus and technical college
- Commuter campus in small town

General. Accredited by ACICS. **Calendar:** Quarter.

Annual costs/financial aid. Tuition and fees vary depending on program and level. Examples of Associate's degree programs: Business Administration-Marketing Option $27,552; Criminal Justice $27,968. Examples of Certificate programs: Massage Therapy $10,600; Medical Billing and Coding $18,910. All costs are subject to change. Books/supplies: $1,950.

Contact. Phone: (570) 286-3058
Director of Admissions, 1147 North 4th Street, Sunbury, PA 17801

Metropolitan Career Center Computer Technology Institute

Philadelphia, Pennsylvania
www.cti-careers.org

- Private 2-year technical and career college
- Very large city

General. Accredited by ACCSC. Medical insurance specialist/medical biller diploma available. **Enrollment:** 34 degree-seeking undergraduates. **Degrees:** 22 associate awarded. **Calendar:** Differs by program. **Full-time faculty:** 2 total; 50% minority, 50% women. **Part-time faculty:** 4 total; 25% minority. **Class size:** 100% < 20.

Basis for selection. Must score at least 12 on entrance exam.

2015-2016 Annual costs. Tuition/fees: $12,147. Per-credit charge: $387. Books/supplies: $1,600. Personal expenses: $2,102. **Additional information:** Full program cost is $23,994; does not include all fees and supplies.

Financial aid. All financial aid based on need. Need-based aid available for part-time students. Work-study available nights, weekends and for part-time students.

Application procedures. Admission: No deadline. $50 fee. Admission notification on a rolling basis. **Financial aid:** No deadline. FAFSA required. Applicants notified on a rolling basis starting 1/1; must reply within 2 week(s) of notification.

Academics. Credit/placement by examination: AP, CLEP. **Support services:** Remedial instruction.

Student services. Career counseling, student employment services, placement for graduates. **Transfer:** Re-entry adviser, pre-admission transcript evaluation for new students. Transfer adviser for students transferring to 4-year colleges.

Contact. Phone: (215) 568-9215 Fax: (215) 568-3511
Veronica Phillips, Director of Admissions, Metropolitan Career Center Computer Technology Institute, 100 South Broad Street, Suite 830, Philadelphia, PA 19110

Montgomery County Community College

Blue Bell, Pennsylvania   **CB member**
www.mc3.edu   **CB code: 2445**

- Public 2-year community college
- Commuter campus in large town

General. Founded in 1964. Regionally accredited. Campus in Pottstown serves students in western part of the county. Culinary Arts Institute. Montgomery County Public Safety Training Campus. **Enrollment:** 10,482 degree-seeking undergraduates; 1,890 non-degree-seeking students. **Degrees:** 1,307

associate awarded. **Location:** 20 miles from Philadelphia. **Calendar:** Semester, extensive summer session. **Full-time faculty:** 176 total; 13% minority, 61% women. **Part-time faculty:** 547 total; 9% minority, 54% women. **Class size:** 57% < 20, 43% 20-39. **Special facilities:** Dental hygiene clinic; observatory and observational deck.

Student profile. Among degree-seeking undergraduates, 62% enrolled in a transfer program, 38% enrolled in a vocational program, 2,771 enrolled as first-time, first-year students.

Part-time:	64%	Hispanic/Latino:	6%
Out-of-state:	1%	Multi-racial, non-Hispanic:	3%
Women:	56%	International:	2%
African American:	15%	25 or older:	36%
Asian American:	6%		

Transfer out. 60% of students enrolled in the transfer program go on to 4-year colleges. **Colleges most students transferred to 2015:** Temple University, Drexel, West Chester University, Penn State, Kutztown University.

Basis for selection. Open admission, but selective for some programs. Special requirements for health sciences programs. **Home schooled:** Transcript of courses and grades required. Must provide approved curriculum and portfolio. **Learning Disabled:** Recommend meeting with Director of Services for Students with Disabilities. Require current documentation from students of accommodations needed.

High school preparation. Biology, chemistry, and algebra required of nursing and medical laboratory technician applicants, chemistry of dental hygiene applicants.

2015-2016 Annual costs. Tuition/fees: $4,920; $9,240 out-of-district; $13,560 out-of-state. Per-credit charge: $134 in-district; $268 out-of-district; $402 out-of-state. Books/supplies: $1,300. Personal expenses: $1,640. **Additional information:** Additional fees for Culinary Courses may apply.

2014-2015 Financial aid. **Need-based:** 1,002 full-time freshmen applied for aid; 856 deemed to have need; 760 received aid. Average need met was 21%. Average scholarship/grant was $2,915; average loan $1,621. 65% of total undergraduate aid awarded as scholarships/grants, 35% as loans/jobs. Need-based aid available for part-time students. Work-study available nights, weekends and for part-time students. **Non-need-based:** Awarded to 1,166 full-time undergraduates, including 473 freshmen. Scholarships awarded for academics.

Application procedures. Admission: No deadline. No application fee. Admission notification on a rolling basis. **Financial aid:** Priority date 5/1; no closing date. FAFSA required. Applicants notified on a rolling basis starting 2/1.

Academics. Special study options: Accelerated study, cooperative education, distance learning, dual enrollment of high school students, ESL, honors, independent study, internships, student-designed major, study abroad, teacher certification program, weekend college. Bachelor's degree programs available on campus. License preparation in dental hygiene, nursing, radiology, real estate. **Credit/placement by examination:** AP, CLEP, institutional tests. 30 credit hours maximum toward associate degree. **Support services:** GED preparation and test center, learning center, pre-admission summer program, reduced course load, remedial instruction, study skills assistance, tutoring.

Majors. Biology: Biotechnology. **Business:** General, accounting technology, administrative services, business admin, communications, hospitality/recreation, real estate, sales/distribution, travel services. **Communications:** Communications/speech/rhetoric, digital media. **Communications technology:** Recording arts. **Computer sciences:** Computer science, information systems, information technology, system admin, web page design, webmaster. **Conservation:** Environmental studies. **Education:** Elementary, music, physical, secondary, teacher assistance. **Engineering:** Engineering science, software. **Health services:** Clinical lab technology, dental hygiene, mental health services, nursing (RN), office admin, radiologic technology/medical imaging, substance abuse counseling, surgical technology. **Liberal arts:** Arts/sciences, humanities. **Math:** General. **Parks/recreation:** Health/fitness. **Physical sciences:** General. **Protective services:** Fire safety technology, police science, security management. **Psychology:** Behavior analysis. **Social sciences:** General. **Visual/performing arts:** Acting, art, dance, graphic design. **Work/family studies:** Child care management.

Most popular majors. Business/marketing 13%, family/consumer sciences 6%, health sciences 17%, liberal arts 39%.

Technology on campus. 1,028 workstations in library, student center. Commuter students can connect to campus network. Online course registration, online library, helpline, wireless network available.

Student life. Freshman orientation: Mandatory. Preregistration for classes offered. Two hour session; required for first time college students. **Activities:** Jazz band, choral groups, dance, drama, film society, international student organizations, literary magazine, music ensembles, radio station, student government, student newspaper, TV station, African-American club, Christian fellowship club, Gender Sexuality Alliance, Japanese Culture, Muslim student association, Rotaract - community service, Asian club, international club, Mentoring service club, veterans organization.

Athletics. NJCAA. **Intercollegiate:** Baseball M, basketball, soccer, softball W, volleyball W. **Intramural:** Badminton, basketball, bowling, cross-country, football (non-tackle) M, racquetball, soccer, table tennis, tennis, volleyball, weight lifting. **Team name:** Mustangs.

Student services. Adult student services, career counseling, services for economically disadvantaged, student employment services, financial aid counseling, health services, minority student services, on-campus daycare, personal counseling, placement for graduates, veterans' counselor, women's services. **Physically disabled:** Services for visually, speech, hearing impaired. **Transfer:** Pre-admission transcript evaluation for new students. Transfer center, transfer adviser, college fairs on campus for students transferring to 4-year colleges.

Contact. E-mail: admissionsregistration@mc3.edu
Phone: (215) 641-6551 Fax: (215) 641-6681
Joyce Wheatley, Director of Student Recruitment, Montgomery County Community College, 340 DeKalb Pike, Blue Bell, PA 19422

New Castle School of Trades
New Castle, Pennsylvania
www.ncstrades.edu   CB code: 2404

- For-profit 2-year technical college
- Commuter campus in large town
- Interview required

General. Accredited by ACCSC. **Enrollment:** 825 undergraduates. **Degrees:** 274 associate awarded. **Location:** 10 miles from Youngstown, Ohio. **Calendar:** Continuous. **Full-time faculty:** 25 total. **Part-time faculty:** 25 total.

Basis for selection. Secondary school record and Wonderlic test scores. Most important is the one-on-one interview to determine admission. Wonderlic exam used for admission.

2015-2016 Annual costs. Books/supplies: $2,700. **Additional information:** Tuition varies by program; $5,970 to $19,650. Books and tool expenses also vary by program. All costs are subject to change.

Financial aid. Need-based: Need-based aid available for part-time students. Work-study available nights, weekends and for part-time students.

Application procedures. Admission: No deadline. $25 fee. Admission notification on a rolling basis.

Academics. Credit/placement by examination: AP, CLEP. **Support services:** Learning center, study skills assistance, tutoring.

Majors. General: Building construction, electrician.

Technology on campus. 35 workstations in library, computer center.

Student life. Freshman orientation: Available. Preregistration for classes offered.

Student services. Career counseling, student employment services, financial aid counseling, personal counseling, placement for graduates, veterans' counselor.

Contact. E-mail: ncstrades@aol.com
Phone: (724) 964-8811 Toll-free number: (800) 837-8299
Fax: (724) 964-8177
Jim Catheline, Director of Admissions, New Castle School of Trades, 4117 Pulaski Road, New Castle, PA 16101

Northampton Community College
Bethlehem, Pennsylvania   CB member
www.northampton.edu   CB code: 2573

- Public 2-year community college
- Commuter campus in small city

General. Founded in 1966. Regionally accredited. Branch campus at Monroe County. Off-campus site in southside Bethlehem. Individualized transfer study program. **Enrollment:** 9,727 degree-seeking undergraduates; 542 non-degree-seeking students. **Degrees:** 1,293 associate awarded. **Location:** 60 miles from Philadelphia, 90 miles from New York City. **Calendar:** Semester, limited summer session. **Full-time faculty:** 122 total; 31% have terminal degrees, 15% minority, 59% women. **Part-time faculty:** 585 total; 10% have terminal degrees, 11% minority, 56% women. **Special facilities:** ISO Class 7 clean room facility, electrotechnology applications center, kindergarten, student-run restaurant, innovation lab, fab lab, Center for Civic & Community Engagement, STEM Learning Center. **Partnerships:** Formal partnerships with General Motors and Chrysler.

Student profile. Among degree-seeking undergraduates, 60% enrolled in a transfer program, 40% enrolled in a vocational program, 7% already have a bachelor's degree or higher, 2,085 enrolled as first-time, first-year students, 905 transferred in from other institutions.

Part-time:	53%	Hispanic/Latino:	20%
Out-of-state:	2%	Multi-racial, non-Hispanic:	3%
Women:	59%	International:	1%
African American:	13%	25 or older:	33%
Asian American:	2%	Live on campus:	6%

Transfer out. 70% of students enrolled in the transfer program go on to 4-year colleges. **Colleges most students transferred to 2015:** East Stroudsburg University, Kutztown University, Cedar Crest College, DeSales University, Temple University.

Basis for selection. Open admission, but selective for some programs. Special requirements for allied health, veterinary technician, and culinary arts programs. Interview required for radiography, veterinary technology, and diagnostic medical sonography programs; audition required for theater program.

High school preparation. Biology, chemistry, and algebra requirements for allied health programs.

2015-2016 Annual costs. Tuition/fees: $3,990; $8,700 out-of-district; $12,840 out-of-state. Per-credit charge: $94 in-district; $188 out-of-district; $282 out-of-state. Room/board: $8,092. Books/supplies: $1,600. Personal expenses: $1,500.

2015-2016 Financial aid. Need-based: 73% of total undergraduate aid awarded as scholarships/grants, 27% as loans/jobs. Need-based aid available for part-time students. Work-study available nights, weekends and for part-time students. **Non-need-based:** Scholarships awarded for academics, alumni affiliation, art, leadership, minority status, music/drama, state residency.

Application procedures. Admission: No deadline. $25 fee, may be waived for applicants with need. Admission notification on a rolling basis. **Financial aid:** Priority date 3/31; no closing date. FAFSA required. Applicants notified on a rolling basis starting 4/1.

Academics. Special study options: Distance learning, dual enrollment of high school students, ESL, exchange student, honors, independent study, internships, student-designed major, study abroad, teacher certification program. Bachelor's degree programs available on campus. License preparation in dental hygiene, nursing, radiology, real estate. **Credit/placement by examination:** AP, CLEP, institutional tests. 30 credit hours maximum toward associate degree. **Support services:** GED preparation and test center, learning center, reduced course load, remedial instruction, study skills assistance, tutoring, writing center.

Majors. Biology: General, biotechnology. **Business:** General, accounting technology, administrative services, business admin, construction management, event planning, hotel/motel admin, marketing, restaurant/food services. **Communications:** Communications/speech/rhetoric, journalism. **Communications technology:** Radio/TV. **Computer sciences:** Computer science, networking, programming, security, web page design. **Conservation:** Environmental science. **Education:** Early childhood, middle, secondary, teacher assistance. **Engineering:** General. **General:** Electrician. **Health services:** Athletic training, dental hygiene, medical secretary, nursing (RN), public health ed, radiologic technology/medical imaging, sonography, veterinary technology/assistant. **Human services:** Social work. **Liberal arts:** Arts/sciences. **Math:** General. **Parks/recreation:** Sports admin. **Physical sciences:** Chemistry, physics. **Protective services:** Criminal justice, fire services admin, firefighting. **Psychology:** Applied. **Visual/performing arts:** Acting, graphic design, interior design, studio arts.

Most popular majors. Business/marketing 18%, health sciences 13%, liberal arts 21%, security/protective services 8%.

Technology on campus. 1,600 workstations in dormitories, library, computer center, student center. Dormitories wired for high-speed internet access and linked to campus network. Commuter students can connect to campus network. Online course registration, online library, helpline, student web hosting, wireless network available.

Student life. Freshman orientation: Mandatory. Preregistration for classes offered. Half day program offered throughout the summer. **Housing:** Coed dorms, apartments available. $150 deposit. **Activities:** Campus ministries, choral groups, dance, film society, international student organizations, literary magazine, music ensembles, radio station, student government, student newspaper, Christian fellowship club, Hispanic American cultural club, International Student Organization, Muslim student association, Phi Theta Kappa, political science club, student senate, multi-cultural club, Pan African student caucus, social work club, and women's club.

Athletics. NJCAA. **Intercollegiate:** Baseball M, basketball, cross-country, golf M, lacrosse M, soccer, softball W, tennis W, volleyball W. **Intramural:** Basketball, football (non-tackle), soccer, volleyball. **Team name:** Spartans.

Student services. Adult student services, alcohol/substance abuse counseling, career counseling, services for economically disadvantaged, student employment services, financial aid counseling, health services, minority student services, on-campus daycare, personal counseling, placement for graduates, veterans' counselor. **Physically disabled:** Services for visually, speech, hearing impaired. **Transfer:** Pre-admission transcript evaluation for new students. Transfer center, transfer adviser, college fairs on campus for students transferring to 4-year colleges.

Contact. E-mail: adminfo@northampton.edu
Phone: (610) 861-5500 Fax: (610) 861-4560
James McCarthy, Director of Admissions, Northampton Community College, 3835 Green Pond Road, Bethlehem, PA 18020-7599

Orleans Technical Institute
Philadelphia, Pennsylvania
www.orleanstech.edu — CB code: 3127

- Private 2-year technical and career college
- Commuter campus in very large city
- Application essay, interview required

General. Regionally accredited; also accredited by ACCSC. **Enrollment:** 548 degree-seeking undergraduates. **Degrees:** 16 associate awarded. **Calendar:** Differs by program, limited summer session. **Full-time faculty:** 19 total. **Part-time faculty:** 17 total. **Class size:** 53% < 20, 47% 20-39.

Student profile.

Out-of-state: 5% 25 or older: 69%

Transfer out. Colleges most students transferred to 2015: Community College of Philadelphia.

Basis for selection. Applicants for our Building Trades Programs without a high school diploma or GED may be eligible. Must achieve required scores on the Career Programs Assessment Test. Applicants must pass an entrance test. **Home schooled:** State high school equivalency certificate required.

2015-2016 Annual costs. Books/supplies: $810. Personal expenses: $1,320. **Additional information:** Tuition and required fees vary by program and range from $12,990 to $13,791. Books and supplies range from $526 to $1,415. All costs are subject to change.

Financial aid. Need-based: Need-based aid available for part-time students. Work-study available nights, weekends and for part-time students. **Non-need-based:** Scholarships awarded for academics.

Application procedures. Admission: No deadline. $125 fee. Admission notification on a rolling basis. **Financial aid:** No deadline. FAFSA, institutional form required. Applicants notified on a rolling basis.

Academics. Credit/placement by examination: AP, CLEP, institutional tests. **Support services:** Tutoring.

Technology on campus. PC or laptop required.

Student life. Freshman orientation: Mandatory. Preregistration for classes offered.

Student services. Adult student services, career counseling, financial aid counseling, personal counseling, placement for graduates. **Physically disabled:** Services for visually impaired. **Transfer:** Re-entry adviser, pre-admission transcript evaluation for new students.

Contact. E-mail: gettingstarted@jevs.org
Phone: (215) 728-4426 Fax: (215) 745-1689
Debbie Bello, Director of Admissions, Orleans Technical Institute, 2770 Red Lion Road, Philadelphia, PA 19114

Penn Commercial Business and Technical School
Washington, Pennsylvania
www.penncommercial.edu — CB code: 3300

- For-profit 2-year business and technical college
- Commuter campus in small city

General. Accredited by ACICS. **Enrollment:** 307 undergraduates. **Degrees:** 102 associate awarded. **Location:** 30 miles from Pittsburgh. **Calendar:** Quarter, limited summer session. **Full-time faculty:** 24 total; 54% women. **Part-time faculty:** 16 total; 62% women. **Special facilities:** Beauty salon, massage and spa parlor, daycare facility, Carmella's Pizza.

Transfer out. Colleges most students transferred to 2015: Waynesburg University, California University of Pennsylvania, Westmoreland County Community College, Community College of Allegheny County.

Basis for selection. Open admission, but selective for some programs. **Home schooled:** Interview required.

2015-2016 Annual costs. Per-credit charge: $197. Books/supplies: $945. Personal expenses: $2,438. **Additional information:** Tuition and fees vary by program; $1,485-$21,769. All costs are subject to change.

Financial aid. Need-based: Work-study available nights, weekends and for part-time students.

Application procedures. Admission: No deadline. $25 fee. Admission notification on a rolling basis. **Financial aid:** Closing date 5/15.

Academics. Special study options: Independent study. License preparation in nursing. **Credit/placement by examination:** AP, CLEP, institutional tests. **Support services:** GED preparation and test center, learning center, reduced course load, remedial instruction, study skills assistance, tutoring, writing center.

Majors. Business: General, administrative services, business admin. **Computer sciences:** Information technology, networking. **Health services:** Medical secretary, office assistant.

Technology on campus. 280 workstations in library, computer center. Online library, repair service, wireless network available.

Student life. Freshman orientation: Mandatory. Preregistration for classes offered. **Activities:** Student newspaper.

Student services. Adult student services, alcohol/substance abuse counseling, career counseling, services for economically disadvantaged, student employment services, financial aid counseling, health services, on-campus daycare, personal counseling, placement for graduates, veterans' counselor, women's services. **Physically disabled:** Services for visually, speech, hearing impaired. **Transfer:** Re-entry adviser, pre-admission transcript evaluation for new students. College fairs on campus for students transferring to 4-year colleges.

Contact. E-mail: pcadmissions@penncommercial.edu
Phone: (724) 222-5330 ext. 1 Fax: (724) 225-3561
Darlene Gibson, Director of Admissions, Penn Commercial Business and Technical School, 242 Oak Spring Road, Washington, PA 15301

Pennco Tech
Bristol, Pennsylvania
www.penncotech.edu — CB code: 0380

- For-profit 2-year technical college
- Commuter campus in large town

General. Founded in 1973. Accredited by ACCSC. Branch campus in Blackwood, New Jersey. **Enrollment:** 500 undergraduates. **Degrees:** 56 associate awarded. **Location:** 18 miles from Philadelphia. **Calendar:** Modular, year-round calendar. Limited summer session. **Full-time faculty:** 25 total. **Part-time faculty:** 16 total.

Basis for selection. Open admission.

2015-2016 Annual costs. Books/supplies: $850. **Additional information:** Tuition varies by program and level. Undergraduate Certificate Programs (Day): $7,166-$20,995; Undergraduate Certificate Programs (Evening): $12,950-$20,995; Associate's degrees (Day): $31,850. Books and supplies vary depending on program. All costs are subject to change.

Financial aid. Need-based: Work-study available nights, weekends and for part-time students.

Application procedures. Admission: No deadline. $100 fee. Admission notification on a rolling basis. **Financial aid:** No deadline. Applicants notified on a rolling basis.

Academics. Credit/placement by examination: AP, CLEP, institutional tests. 30 credit hours maximum toward associate degree. **Support services:** Tutoring.

Student life. Activities: Choral groups, TV station.

Student services. Career counseling, student employment services, on-campus daycare, personal counseling, placement for graduates.

Contact. E-mail: admissions@penncotech.com
Phone: (215) 824-3200 Toll-free number: (800) 575-9399
John Keenan, Director of Admissions, Pennco Tech, 3815 Otter Street, Bristol, PA 19007

Pennsylvania Highlands Community College
Johnstown, Pennsylvania
www.pennhighlands.edu
CB code: 2484

- Public 2-year community college
- Commuter campus in large town

General. Regionally accredited. **Enrollment:** 1,295 degree-seeking undergraduates; 1,161 non-degree-seeking students. **Degrees:** 232 associate awarded. **Location:** 70 miles from Pittsburgh. **Calendar:** Semester, limited summer session. **Full-time faculty:** 26 total. **Part-time faculty:** 82 total.

Student profile. Among degree-seeking undergraduates, 64% enrolled in a transfer program, 4% enrolled in a vocational program, 332 enrolled as first-time, first-year students.

Part-time:	36%	Asian American:	1%
Out-of-state:	1%	Hispanic/Latino:	2%
Women:	57%	Multi-racial, non-Hispanic:	2%
African American:	5%	25 or older:	29%

Transfer out. Colleges most students transferred to 2015: University of Pittsburgh at Johnstown, Indiana University of Pennsylvania, Mount Aloysius College, Penn State University, Saint Francis University.

Basis for selection. Open admission. **Adult students:** SAT/ACT scores not required. **Home schooled:** Transcript of courses and grades required.

High school preparation. College-preparatory program recommended.

2015-2016 Annual costs. Tuition/fees: $5,670; $7,710 out-of-district; $10,650 out-of-state. Per-credit charge: $127 in-district; $195 out-of-district; $293 out-of-state. Books/supplies: $1,200. Personal expenses: $500. **Additional information:** Lab/Material Fees for specific courses depending on consumable supplies and materials required: $10-$950.

2015-2016 Financial aid. Need-based: 52% of total undergraduate aid awarded as scholarships/grants, 48% as loans/jobs. Need-based aid available for part-time students. Work-study available nights, weekends and for part-time students. **Non-need-based:** Scholarships awarded for academics, state residency.

Application procedures. Admission: No deadline. $20 fee, may be waived for applicants with need. Admission notification on a rolling basis. **Financial aid:** Closing date 4/1. FAFSA required. Applicants notified on a rolling basis; must reply by 8/1.

Academics. Special study options: Cooperative education, distance learning, dual enrollment of high school students, honors, independent study, internships. **Credit/placement by examination:** AP, CLEP, institutional tests. **Support services:** GED test center, learning center, reduced course load, remedial instruction, study skills assistance, tutoring.

Majors. Business: General, accounting, operations. **Computer sciences:** General, computer science. **Conservation:** Environmental science. **Education:** General, early childhood. **General:** Lineworker. **Health services:** EMT paramedic, health information technology, histologic assistant, medical assistant, radiologic technology/medical imaging. **Protective services:** Corrections, law enforcement admin. **Psychology:** General. **Work/family studies:** Child care management.

Most popular majors. Business/marketing 22%, computer/information sciences 6%, health sciences 16%, liberal arts 27%, security/protective services 8%.

Technology on campus. 250 workstations in library, computer center, student center. Commuter students can connect to campus network. Online course registration, online library, helpline, wireless network available.

Student life. Freshman orientation: Available. Preregistration for classes offered. **Activities:** Student government.

Athletics. NJCAA. **Intercollegiate:** Basketball M, bowling, cross-country, volleyball W. **Intramural:** Basketball, table tennis, volleyball. **Team name:** Black Bears.

Student services. Career counseling, services for economically disadvantaged, student employment services, financial aid counseling, placement for graduates, veterans' counselor. **Physically disabled:** Services for visually, speech, hearing impaired. **Transfer:** Pre-admission transcript evaluation for new students. College fairs on campus for students transferring to 4-year colleges.

Contact. E-mail: jmaul@pennhighlands.edu
Phone: (814) 262-6446 Toll-free number: (888) 385-7325
Fax: (814) 262-6420
Jeff Maul, Director of Admissions, Pennsylvania Highlands Community College, 101 Community College Way, Johnstown, PA 15904

Pennsylvania Institute of Health and Technology
Mount Braddock, Pennsylvania
www.piht.edu
CB code: 3214

- For-profit 2-year business college
- Commuter campus in small town
- Interview required

General. Accredited by ACICS. **Enrollment:** 100 degree-seeking undergraduates. **Degrees:** 48 associate awarded. **Calendar:** Differs by program. **Full-time faculty:** 2 total. **Part-time faculty:** 10 total.

Basis for selection. Open admission.

2015-2016 Annual costs. Tuition per-term for associate degree programs in Medical Assisting and Medical Office Administration: $3,750; fees are $475 a term with a $25 first-term enrollment fee. Practical Nursing diploma program for first term: $5,050; fees are $522. All costs are subject to change.

Financial aid. Need-based: Work-study available nights, weekends and for part-time students.

Application procedures. Admission: No deadline. $25 fee.

Academics. Credit/placement by examination: AP, CLEP.

Majors. Business: General, administrative services. **Computer sciences:** Information technology. **Health services:** Medical secretary, office assistant.

Contact. E-mail: admissions@piht.edu
Phone: (724) 437-4600 Fax: (724) 437-6053
Mary Jo Barnhart, Director of Student Services, Pennsylvania Institute of Health and Technology, Route 119 North and Mount Braddock Road, Mount Braddock, PA 15465

Pennsylvania Institute of Technology
Media, Pennsylvania
www.pit.edu
CB code: 2675

- Private 2-year junior and technical college
- Commuter campus in small town
- Application essay, interview required

General. Founded in 1953. Regionally accredited. There is an additional location in center city Philadelphia. **Enrollment:** 595 degree-seeking undergraduates; 1 non-degree-seeking students. **Degrees:** 111 associate awarded. **Location:** 13 miles from Philadelphia, 15 miles from Wilmington, Delaware. **Calendar:** Semester, extensive summer session. **Class size:** 91% < 20, 9% 20-39.

Student profile. Among degree-seeking undergraduates, 299 enrolled as first-time, first-year students.

Part-time:	49%	25 or older:	40%
Women:	75%		

Basis for selection. Open admission, but selective for some programs. Selective admission to Practical Nursing and Physical Therapist Assistant programs. Interview and essay used for placement purposes only.

2015-2016 Annual costs. Tuition/fees: $13,200. Books/supplies: $900. **Additional information:** Tuition varies by program. School of Professional Programs certificates tuition is $15,450; Practical nursing program tuition is $21,500.

Financial aid. Need-based: Need-based aid available for part-time students. Work-study available nights, weekends and for part-time students. **Non-need-based:** Scholarships awarded for academics, leadership. **Additional information:** Application deadline of May 1 for PHEAA and Philadelphia State Grant aid.

Application procedures. Admission: No deadline. $25 fee, may be waived for applicants with need. Admission notification on a rolling basis. **Financial aid:** No deadline. FAFSA, institutional form required. Applicants notified on a rolling basis starting 7/1.

Academics. Curricula designed to prepare students for positions in industry through combination of general education and job specific courses, or to transfer to a four-year institution. **Special study options:** Cooperative education, double major, dual enrollment of high school students, independent study, internships. Blended learning. **Credit/placement by examination:** AP, CLEP, institutional tests. 60 credit hours maximum toward associate degree. **Support services:** Learning center, pre-admission summer program, reduced course load, remedial instruction, tutoring.

Majors. Business: Business admin. **Communications:** General. **Computer sciences:** Computer science, networking. **Health services:** Health care admin, health information technology, medical assistant, office admin, pharmacy assistant, physical therapy assistant.

Most popular majors. Computer/information sciences 14%, engineering/ engineering technologies 11%, health sciences 73%.

Technology on campus. 80 workstations in library, computer center, student center. Commuter students can connect to campus network. Online course registration, online library, wireless network available.

Student life. Freshman orientation: Mandatory. Preregistration for classes offered. Held 1 week before start of classes. **Activities:** Student government, amateur radio club.

Student services. Adult student services, career counseling, student employment services, financial aid counseling, personal counseling, placement for graduates, veterans' counselor. **Physically disabled:** Services for speech, hearing impaired. **Transfer:** Transfer adviser, college fairs on campus for students transferring to 4-year colleges.

Contact. E-mail: info@pit.edu
Phone: (610) 565-7900 Toll-free number: (800) 422-0025
Fax: (610) 892-1510
John DeTurris, Director of Admissions, Pennsylvania Institute of Technology, 800 Manchester Avenue, Media, PA 19063-4098

Pittsburgh Institute of Aeronautics
Pittsburgh, Pennsylvania
www.pia.edu   CB code: 0652

▶   Private 2-year technical college
▶   Commuter campus in large city

General. Founded in 1929. Regionally accredited; also accredited by ACCSC. All locations are located in active airports. **Enrollment:** 176 degree-seeking undergraduates; 201 non-degree-seeking students. **Degrees:** 68 associate awarded. **Location:** 8 miles from Pittsburgh. **Calendar:** Quarter, extensive summer session. **Full-time faculty:** 20 total; 10% minority, 10% women. **Part-time faculty:** 2 total. **Special facilities:** Fleet of over 12 aircraft, large multitudes of training aids, aviation electronics shops and labs.

Student profile. Among degree-seeking undergraduates, 17% enrolled in a transfer program, 49 enrolled as first-time, first-year students.

Out-of-state: 38%   Women: 5%

Basis for selection. Open admission. School visit required before classes begin. **Adult students:** SAT/ACT scores not required.

2015-2016 Annual costs. Tuition/fees: $15,600. Books/supplies: $1,341. Personal expenses: $5,805.

Financial aid. Need-based: Work-study available nights, weekends and for part-time students.

Application procedures. Admission: No deadline. $150 fee. Admission notification on a rolling basis. **Financial aid:** Priority date 5/1; no closing date. FAFSA required. Applicants notified on a rolling basis.

Academics. Special study options: License preparation in aviation. **Credit/placement by examination:** AP, CLEP, institutional tests. **Support services:** Learning center, remedial instruction, tutoring.

Technology on campus. 35 workstations in library, computer center. Commuter students can connect to campus network. Wireless network available.

Student life. Housing: Referral housing available. **Activities:** Student government, student newspaper.

Student services. Adult student services, alcohol/substance abuse counseling, career counseling, student employment services, financial aid counseling, personal counseling, placement for graduates, veterans' counselor. **Transfer:** Pre-admission transcript evaluation for new students.

Contact. E-mail: admissions@pia.edu
Phone: (412) 346-2100 Toll-free number: (800) 444-1440
Fax: (412) 466-0513
Steven Sabold, Director of Admissions, Pittsburgh Institute of Aeronautics, PO Box 10897, Pittsburgh, PA 15236-0897

Pittsburgh Institute of Mortuary Science
Pittsburgh, Pennsylvania
www.pims.edu   CB code: 7030

▶   Private 2-year technical college
▶   Commuter campus in large city
▶   Application essay required

General. Founded in 1939. Accredited by American Board of Funeral Services Education, Inc. **Enrollment:** 248 undergraduates. **Degrees:** 76 associate awarded. **Calendar:** Trimester, extensive summer session. **Full-time faculty:** 2 total; 100% have terminal degrees. **Part-time faculty:** 26 total; 12% have terminal degrees, 27% women. **Special facilities:** Preparation center, specialized library.

Transfer out. Colleges most students transferred to 2015: Point Park University.

Basis for selection. Rolling admissions based on combination of requisite high school grade point average, 300 word essay, and receipt of all required documents. **Home schooled:** Transcript of courses and grades, state high school equivalency certificate, letter of recommendation (nonparent) required. 300 word essay required. High School grade point average minimum of 2.0 out of 4. **Learning Disabled:** Diagnosis documentation within 3 years of enrollment required.

High school preparation. College-preparatory program recommended.

2015-2016 Annual costs. Tuition/fees: $14,125. Per-credit charge: $290. Books/supplies: $1,400. Personal expenses: $4,164.

Financial aid. Need-based: Need-based aid available for part-time students. Work-study available nights, weekends and for part-time students.

Application procedures. Admission: Priority date 9/1; no deadline. $50 fee. Admission notification on a rolling basis. **Financial aid:** No deadline. FAFSA required. Applicants notified on a rolling basis.

Academics. Four-pronged approach to funeral service management via natural sciences, social sciences, mortuary sciences, and business studies. Students with previous associate degrees will earn diploma or another associate degree in embalming and funeral directing. **Special study options:** Distance learning. **Credit/placement by examination:** AP, CLEP, institutional tests. 49 credit hours maximum toward associate degree. Credits accepted from 30 to 40 determined by program of study. **Support services:** Reduced course load, tutoring.

Technology on campus. 10 workstations in library, computer center.

Student life. Freshman orientation: Mandatory. Preregistration for classes offered. Generally held week before start of classes. **Housing:** Housing available at local funeral homes. **Activities:** Student government.

Student services. Alcohol/substance abuse counseling, career counseling, student employment services, financial aid counseling, personal counseling, placement for graduates, veterans' counselor. **Transfer:** Pre-admission transcript evaluation for new students. Transfer adviser for students transferring to 4-year colleges.

Contact. E-mail: pims5808@aol.com
Phone: (412) 362-8500 Toll-free number: (800) 933-5808
Fax: (412) 362-1684
Karen Rocco, Registrar, Pittsburgh Institute of Mortuary Science, 5808
Baum Boulevard, Pittsburgh, PA 15206-3706

Reading Area Community College
Reading, Pennsylvania
CB member
www.racc.edu   **CB code: 2743**

- Public 2-year community college
- Commuter campus in small city

General. Founded in 1971. Regionally accredited. **Enrollment:** 3,672
degree-seeking undergraduates. **Degrees:** 393 associate awarded. **Location:**
55 miles from Philadelphia. **Calendar:** Semester, limited summer session.
Full-time faculty: 64 total. **Part-time faculty:** 189 total. **Class size:** 44%
< 20, 56% 20-39, less than 1% 40-49, less than 1% 50-99. **Special facilities:**
Performing arts center, training and technology center.

Student profile.

Out-of-state: 1%   **25 or older:**   47%

Transfer out. Colleges most students transferred to 2015: Albright College, Kutztown University, Alvernia College, West Chester University, Penn
State-Berks.

Basis for selection. Open admission, but selective for some programs.
Special admissions criteria for culinary arts, electric utility technology, medical laboratory technician, nursing, practical nursing, respiratory care programs. Interview suggested. **Home schooled:** Transcript of courses and
grades, state high school equivalency certificate required. **Learning Disabled:** Students must submit necessary documentation prior to accommodations being made.

High school preparation. 16 units required for nursing program, including 4 English, 3 social studies, 2 math (1 must be algebra), and 2 science
with related laboratory or equivalent.

2015-2016 Annual costs. Tuition/fees: $5,130; $8,850 out-of-district;
$12,510 out-of-state. Books/supplies: $1,800. Personal expenses: $1,200.

Financial aid. Need-based: Work-study available nights, weekends and
for part-time students.

Application procedures. Admission: Closing date 9/16. No application
fee. Admission notification on a rolling basis. **Financial aid:** No deadline.
FAFSA, institutional form required. Applicants notified on a rolling basis
starting 4/15; must reply within 2 week(s) of notification.

Academics. Special study options: Cooperative education, cross-
registration, distance learning, dual enrollment of high school students, ESL,
honors, independent study, internships, student-designed major. License preparation in nursing. **Credit/placement by examination:** AP, CLEP, institutional tests. 45 credit hours maximum toward associate degree. **Support
services:** GED preparation and test center, learning center, pre-admission
summer program, reduced course load, remedial instruction, study skills
assistance, tutoring.

Majors. Biology: General. **Business:** General, accounting, administrative
services, business admin, office management, office technology, office/cleri-
cal, operations. **Communications:** General. **Computer sciences:** Data processing, networking, programming, web page design, webmaster. **Education:**
General, business, early childhood, elementary, middle, secondary. **Engineering:** General, electrical. **Health services:** Clinical lab science, medical secretary, nursing (RN), predental, premedicine, prepharmacy, respiratory therapy
technology. **Human services:** Social work. **Liberal arts:** Arts/sciences. **Protective services:** Law enforcement admin, police science. **Psychology:** General. **Social sciences:** General, criminology. **Work/family studies:** Child
care management.

Most popular majors. Business/marketing 16%, education 6%, health
sciences 25%, liberal arts 23%, security/protective services 7%, trade and
industry 7%.

Technology on campus. 90 workstations in library, computer center.
Online course registration, online library, helpline, wireless network available.

Student life. Freshman orientation: Mandatory. Preregistration for
classes offered. Half-day program designed to introduce new students to
important policies and procedures, campus resources, college success skills.
Activities: Choral groups, dance, international student organizations, literary
magazine, student government, student newspaper.

Athletics. Team name: Ravens.

Student services. Career counseling, services for economically disadvantaged, student employment services, on-campus daycare, personal counseling,
placement for graduates, veterans' counselor. **Physically disabled:** Services
for visually, hearing impaired. **Transfer:** Transfer center, transfer adviser,
college fairs on campus for students transferring to 4-year colleges.

Contact. E-mail: admissions@racc.edu
Phone: (610) 607-6224 Toll-free number: (800) 626-1665
Fax: (610) 607-6238
Mickey Baines, Director of Admissions & Enrollment Services, Reading
Area Community College, 10 South Second Street, Reading, PA
19603-1706

Rosedale Technical Institute
Pittsburgh, Pennsylvania
www.rosedaletech.org   **CB code: 3025**

- Private 2-year technical and career college
- Commuter campus in large city
- Interview required

General. Accredited by ACCSC. **Enrollment:** 330 full-time, degree-
seeking students. **Degrees:** 158 associate awarded. **Calendar:** Differs by
program, extensive summer session. **Full-time faculty:** 31 total. **Part-time
faculty:** 4 total.

Basis for selection. Open admission, but selective for some programs.
High school diploma or equivalency required. General knowledge test used
in admissions process, and interview is required. Applicants to automotive and
diesel programs must be eligible for valid driver's license prior to graduation.
Wonderlic exam required for admissions.

2015-2016 Annual costs. Tuition/fees: $14,530. Books/supplies: $1,000.

Financial aid. Need-based: Work-study available nights, weekends and
for part-time students.

Application procedures. Admission: No deadline. $20 fee. Admission
notification on a rolling basis. **Financial aid:** Closing date 8/1. FAFSA
required.

Academics. Credit/placement by examination: AP, CLEP. **Support services:** Learning center, study skills assistance, tutoring.

Majors. General: Electrician.

Technology on campus. 60 workstations in library, computer center.
Online library, wireless network available.

Student life. Freshman orientation: Mandatory. Preregistration for
classes offered. Held 2 weeks prior to start of classes. **Activities:** Student
newspaper.

Student services. Career counseling, student employment services, financial aid counseling, legal services, personal counseling, placement for graduates.

Contact. E-mail: admissions@rosedaletech.org
Phone: (412) 521-6200 Toll-free number: (800) 521-6262
Fax: (412) 521-2520
Debbie Bier, Director of Admissions, Rosedale Technical Institute, 215
Beecham Drive, Pittsburgh, PA 15205-9791

South Hills School of Business & Technology
State College, Pennsylvania
www.southhills.edu   **CB code: 2467**

- For-profit 2-year business and technical college
- Commuter campus in large town
- Interview required

General. Founded in 1970. Regionally accredited; also accredited by
ACICS. Free brush-up classes and career services for graduates. Branch
campuses in Altoona, Lewistown, and Philipsburg. **Enrollment:** 630 undergraduates. **Degrees:** 191 associate awarded. **Location:** 125 miles from Pittsburgh, 200 miles from Philadelphia. **Calendar:** Quarter, limited summer
session. **Full-time faculty:** 47 total; 6% have terminal degrees, 66% women.
Part-time faculty: 23 total.

Student profile.

Out-of-state:	1%	25 or older:	26%

Transfer out. Colleges most students transferred to 2015: St. Francis University, Lock Haven University, Mount Aloysius, Pennsylvania State University.

Basis for selection. Open admission, but selective for some programs. Diagnostic medical sonography program requires resume, faculty interview, 2 letters of recommendation, criminal background/child abuse clearances; all medical and legal programs require criminal background/child abuse clearances. Graphic arts program requires submission of artwork portfolio. **Adult students:** SAT tests recommended for all students applying for the Diagnostic Medical Sonography program only. **Home schooled:** Transcript of courses and grades required.

High school preparation. Recommended units include English 4, mathematics 3, social studies 4 and science 3.

2015-2016 Annual costs. Books/supplies: $1,800. **Additional information:** Tuition varies by program. Associate's programs: $33,042-$54,846. Books and supplies also vary by program. All costs are subject to change.

Financial aid. All financial aid based on need. Need-based aid available for part-time students. Work-study available nights, weekends and for part-time students.

Application procedures. Admission: No deadline. No application fee. Admission notification on a rolling basis. **Financial aid:** Closing date 6/30. FAFSA required. Applicants notified on a rolling basis starting 7/5.

Academics. Special study options: Double major, internships. Technical preparatory program. **Credit/placement by examination:** AP, CLEP. 9 credit hours maximum toward associate degree. **Support services:** Pre-admission summer program, study skills assistance, tutoring.

Majors. Business: Accounting, marketing. **Computer sciences:** Computer science. **Health services:** Health information technology, medical assistant, medical secretary, sonography. **Protective services:** Criminal justice. **Visual/performing arts:** Graphic design.

Most popular majors. Business/marketing 23%, computer/information sciences 24%, health sciences 31%, security/protective services 9%, visual/performing arts 11%.

Technology on campus. 415 workstations in library, computer center, student center. Commuter students can connect to campus network. Online library, wireless network available.

Student life. Freshman orientation: Mandatory. Preregistration for classes offered. One-day program. **Activities:** Student government, student newspaper.

Student services. Career counseling, student employment services, financial aid counseling, placement for graduates. **Transfer:** Pre-admission transcript evaluation for new students. Transfer adviser, college fairs on campus for students transferring to 4-year colleges.

Contact. E-mail: admissions@southhills.edu
Phone: (814) 234-7755 Toll-free number: (888) 282-7427
Fax: (814) 234-0926
Vickey Warshaw, Director of Admissions, South Hills School of Business & Technology, 480 Waupelani Drive, State College, PA 16801-4516

Thaddeus Stevens College of Technology
Lancaster, Pennsylvania
www.stevenscollege.edu

CB code: 0560

▶ Public 2-year technical and career college
▶ Residential campus in small city

General. Founded in 1905. Regionally accredited. **Enrollment:** 800 degree-seeking undergraduates. **Degrees:** 254 associate awarded. **Location:** 60 miles from Philadelphia, 30 miles from Harrisburg. **Calendar:** Semester, limited summer session. **Full-time faculty:** 49 total. **Part-time faculty:** 23 total.

Student profile.

25 or older:	8%	Live on campus:	50%

Basis for selection. Priority given to orphans and financially needy students. Admission based on school achievement record and institutional placement examination (COMPASS). SAT and ACT scores can also be submitted for consideration. Students must score proficient or higher on the PSSA exams administered in their junior year of high school. Interview recommended for associate of specialized technology program. **Home schooled:** Transcript of courses and grades required.

High school preparation. 14 units required. Required and recommended units include English 4, mathematics 2-4 and science 2-6. Algebra required for entry to some associate degree programs.

2015-2016 Annual costs. Tuition/fees: $7,430; $7,430 out-of-state. Room/board: $8,620. Books/supplies: $500.

Financial aid. Need-based: Work-study available nights, weekends and for part-time students. **Additional information:** Tuition and room and board costs waived for students with adjusted family income of $18,500 or less. Tuition and other costs also waived for orphans.

Application procedures. Admission: Priority date 1/1; deadline 7/30 (postmark date). $25 fee, may be waived for applicants with need. Admission notification on a rolling basis beginning on or about 9/1. Must reply by May 1 or within 4 week(s) if notified thereafter. Applicant must reply within 30 days of receiving notification of decision. **Financial aid:** Priority date 3/15; no closing date. Applicants notified on a rolling basis starting 7/15.

Academics. Special study options: Cooperative education, dual enrollment of high school students, internships. **Credit/placement by examination:** AP, CLEP, ACT, institutional tests. **Support services:** Learning center, pre-admission summer program, reduced course load, remedial instruction, study skills assistance, tutoring.

Majors. Architecture: Technology. **Business:** Business admin. **Communications technology:** Graphic/printing. **Computer sciences:** Networking. **Engineering:** Mechanical. **General:** Carpentry, masonry, plumbing, power transmission.

Most popular majors. Communication technologies 7%, computer/information sciences 6%, engineering/engineering technologies 10%, trade and industry 64%.

Technology on campus. 32 workstations in library, computer center. Dormitories linked to campus network. Helpline, wireless network available.

Student life. Freshman orientation: Mandatory. Preregistration for classes offered. **Housing:** Single-sex dorms available. **Activities:** Campus ministries, student government, Power Source, Latino Scholars Alliance, Tech Phi Tech, Women in Trades and Technology.

Athletics. NJCAA. **Intercollegiate:** Basketball M, cross-country, football (tackle) M, track and field, wrestling M. **Intramural:** Basketball, boxing M, volleyball. **Team name:** Bulldogs.

Student services. Adult student services, alcohol/substance abuse counseling, career counseling, services for economically disadvantaged, student employment services, financial aid counseling, health services, minority student services, personal counseling, placement for graduates, women's services. **Transfer:** Transfer adviser for students transferring to 4-year colleges.

Contact. E-mail: admissions@stevenscollege.edu
Phone: (717) 299-7701 Toll-free number: (800) 842-3832
Fax: (717) 391-6929
Erin Nelsen, Director of Enrollment Services, Thaddeus Stevens College of Technology, 750 East King Street, Lancaster, PA 17602

Triangle Tech: Bethlehem
Bethlehem, Pennsylvania
www.triangle-tech.edu

▶ For-profit 2-year branch campus and technical college
▶ Commuter campus in small city
▶ Interview required

General. Regionally accredited; also accredited by ACCSC. **Enrollment:** 120 degree-seeking undergraduates. **Degrees:** 68 associate awarded. **Calendar:** Semester, extensive summer session. **Full-time faculty:** 11 total. **Class size:** 100% < 20.

Student profile. Among degree-seeking undergraduates, 100% enrolled in a vocational program, 45 enrolled as first-time, first-year students.

Out-of-state:	15%	Hispanic/Latino:	18%
Women:	2%	Multi-racial, non-Hispanic:	1%
African American:	7%	25 or older:	35%
Asian American:	2%		

Basis for selection. Open admission. School tour required. **Home schooled:** State high school equivalency certificate required.

High school preparation. Recommended units include mathematics 3.

2016-2017 Annual costs. Tuition/fees: $16,779. **Additional information:** Fees will vary depending on program.

2014-2015 Financial aid. Need-based: 49 full-time freshmen applied for aid; 48 deemed to have need; 48 received aid. Average need met was 72%. Average scholarship/grant was $3,852; average loan $2,686. 39% of total undergraduate aid awarded as scholarships/grants, 61% as loans/jobs. Need-based aid available for part-time students. Work-study available nights, weekends and for part-time students. **Non-need-based:** Awarded to 13 full-time undergraduates, including 8 freshmen. Scholarships awarded for academics.

Application procedures. Admission: No deadline. No application fee. Admission notification on a rolling basis. **Financial aid:** No deadline. FAFSA required. Applicants notified on a rolling basis.

Academics. Credit/placement by examination: AP, CLEP, institutional tests. **Support services:** Learning center, remedial instruction, study skills assistance, tutoring.

Majors. General: Carpentry, electrician.

Technology on campus. 55 workstations in library, computer center.

Student life. Freshman orientation: Mandatory. Preregistration for classes offered.

Student services. Career counseling, financial aid counseling. **Transfer:** Re-entry adviser, pre-admission transcript evaluation for new students. Transfer center, transfer adviser, college fairs on campus for students transferring to 4-year colleges.

Contact. Phone: (610) 266-2910 Toll-free number: (800) 874-8324
Fax: (610) 266-2911
Terry Kucic, Executive Director of Admissions, Triangle Tech: Bethlehem, 3184 Airport Road, Bethlehem, PA 18017

Triangle Tech: DuBois
Falls Creek, Pennsylvania
www.triangle-tech.edu   CB code: 7133

- For-profit 2-year technical college
- Commuter campus in large town
- Interview required

General. Accredited by ACCSC. **Enrollment:** 133 degree-seeking undergraduates. **Degrees:** 96 associate awarded. **Location:** 145 miles from Pittsburgh. **Calendar:** Semester, extensive summer session. **Full-time faculty:** 11 total; 18% women. **Class size:** 70% < 20, 30% 20-39.

Student profile. Among degree-seeking undergraduates, 100% enrolled in a vocational program, 71 enrolled as first-time, first-year students.

Women:	6%	Multi-racial, non-Hispanic:	2%
Hispanic/Latino:	3%	25 or older:	40%
Native American:	2%		

Basis for selection. Open admission. **Home schooled:** State high school equivalency certificate required.

High school preparation. Recommended units include English 4 and mathematics 4.

2015-2016 Annual costs. Tuition/fees: $16,542. Books/supplies: $1,057. Personal expenses: $1,440. **Additional information:** Fees will vary depending on program.

2014-2015 Financial aid. All financial aid based on need. 65 full-time freshmen applied for aid; 61 deemed to have need; 61 received aid. Average need met was 31%. Average scholarship/grant was $6,607; average loan $3,333. 59% of total undergraduate aid awarded as scholarships/grants, 41% as loans/jobs. Need-based aid available for part-time students. Work-study available nights, weekends and for part-time students.

Application procedures. Admission: No deadline. No application fee. Admission notification on a rolling basis. **Financial aid:** No deadline. FAFSA, institutional form required. Applicants notified on a rolling basis.

Academics. Special study options: Dual enrollment of high school students. **Credit/placement by examination:** AP, CLEP, institutional tests.

Support services: Learning center, remedial instruction, study skills assistance, tutoring.

Majors. General: Electrician.

Most popular majors. Engineering/engineering technologies 6%, trade and industry 90%.

Technology on campus. 55 workstations in library, computer center.

Student life. Freshman orientation: Mandatory. Preregistration for classes offered. Held the Thursday before classes begin, approximately 1-1/2 hours. **Activities:** Student government.

Student services. Career counseling, student employment services, financial aid counseling, placement for graduates. **Transfer:** Pre-admission transcript evaluation for new students.

Contact. E-mail: scraig@triangle-tech.edu
Phone: (814) 371-2090 Toll-free number: (800) 874-8324
Fax: (814) 371-9227
Terry Kucic, Executive Director of Admissions, Triangle Tech: DuBois, 225 Tannery Row Road, Falls Creek, PA 15840-3333

Triangle Tech: Erie
Erie, Pennsylvania
www.triangle-tech.edu   CB code: 1572

- For-profit 2-year technical and career college
- Commuter campus in small city
- Interview required

General. Founded in 1976. Accredited by ACCSC. **Enrollment:** 30 degree-seeking undergraduates. **Degrees:** 21 associate awarded. **Location:** 127 miles from Pittsburgh, PA. **Calendar:** Semester, extensive summer session. **Full-time faculty:** 6 total; 17% minority. **Class size:** 100% < 20.

Student profile. Among degree-seeking undergraduates, 100% enrolled in a vocational program, 20 enrolled as first-time, first-year students.

Women:	10%	Hispanic/Latino:	6%
African American:	3%	Native American:	3%
Asian American:	3%	25 or older:	23%

Basis for selection. Open admission. **Home schooled:** State high school equivalency certificate required.

2015-2016 Annual costs. Tuition/fees: $16,409. Books/supplies: $1,100. Personal expenses: $1,440. **Additional information:** Fees will vary depending on program.

2014-2015 Financial aid. All financial aid based on need. 26 full-time freshmen applied for aid; 25 deemed to have need; 25 received aid. Average need met was 84%. Average scholarship/grant was $5,370; average loan $2,811. 50% of total undergraduate aid awarded as scholarships/grants, 50% as loans/jobs. Need-based aid available for part-time students. Work-study available nights, weekends and for part-time students.

Application procedures. Admission: No deadline. No application fee. Admission notification on a rolling basis. **Financial aid:** No deadline. FAFSA required. Applicants notified on a rolling basis.

Academics. Credit/placement by examination: AP, CLEP, institutional tests. 36 credit hours maximum toward associate degree. **Support services:** Remedial instruction, study skills assistance, tutoring.

Majors. General: Electrician.

Most popular majors. Engineering/engineering technologies 18%, trade and industry 82%.

Technology on campus. 53 workstations in library, computer center.

Student life. Freshman orientation: Mandatory. Preregistration for classes offered. **Activities:** Student government.

Student services. Career counseling, student employment services, financial aid counseling, personal counseling, placement for graduates. **Transfer:** Re-entry adviser, pre-admission transcript evaluation for new students. Transfer adviser for students transferring to 4-year colleges.

Contact. Phone: (814) 453-6016 Fax: (814) 454-2818
Terry Kucic, Executive Director of Admissions, Triangle Tech: Erie, 2000 Liberty Street, Erie, PA 16502-2594

Triangle Tech: Greensburg
Greensburg, Pennsylvania
www.triangle-tech.edu   CB code: 0658

- For-profit 2-year technical college
- Commuter campus in large town
- Interview required

General. Founded in 1944. Accredited by ACCSC. **Enrollment:** 163 degree-seeking undergraduates. **Degrees:** 122 associate awarded. **Location:** 40 miles from Pittsburgh. **Calendar:** Semester, extensive summer session. **Full-time faculty:** 16 total; 6% women. **Class size:** 100% < 20.

Student profile. Among degree-seeking undergraduates, 100% enrolled in a vocational program, 59 enrolled as first-time, first-year students.

Women:	2%	Multi-racial, non-Hispanic:	1%
African American:	6%	25 or older:	47%

Basis for selection. Open admission. **Home schooled:** State high school equivalency certificate required.

2015-2016 Annual costs. Tuition/fees: $16,530. Books/supplies: $1,176. Personal expenses: $1,608. **Additional information:** Fees will vary depending on program.

2014-2015 Financial aid. **Need-based:** 82 full-time freshmen applied for aid; 82 deemed to have need; 82 received aid. Average need met was 41%. Average scholarship/grant was $6,355; average loan $2,873. 67% of total undergraduate aid awarded as scholarships/grants, 33% as loans/jobs. Need-based aid available for part-time students. Work-study available nights, weekends and for part-time students. **Non-need-based:** Awarded to 5 full-time undergraduates, including 4 freshmen.

Application procedures. **Admission:** No deadline. No application fee. Admission notification on a rolling basis. **Financial aid:** No deadline. FAFSA, institutional form required. Applicants notified on a rolling basis starting 1/1.

Academics. **Credit/placement by examination:** AP, CLEP, institutional tests. **Support services:** Learning center, remedial instruction, study skills assistance, tutoring.

Majors. **General:** Electrician.

Most popular majors. Engineering/engineering technologies 25%, trade and industry 75%.

Technology on campus. 52 workstations in library, computer center.

Student life. **Freshman orientation:** Mandatory. Preregistration for classes offered. **Activities:** Student government.

Student services. Career counseling, student employment services, financial aid counseling, personal counseling, placement for graduates, veterans' counselor. **Transfer:** Re-entry adviser, pre-admission transcript evaluation for new students. Transfer adviser for students transferring to 4-year colleges.

Contact. Phone: (724) 832-1050 Toll-free number: (800) 874-8324
Fax: (724) 834-0325
Terry Kucic, Executive Director of Admissions, Triangle Tech: Greensburg, 222 East Pittsburgh Street, Suite A, Greensburg, PA 15601-3304

Triangle Tech: Pittsburgh
Pittsburgh, Pennsylvania
www.triangle-tech.edu   CB code: 0734

- For-profit 2-year technical college
- Commuter campus in large city
- Interview required

General. Founded in 1944. Accredited by ACCSC. **Enrollment:** 169 degree-seeking undergraduates. **Degrees:** 132 associate awarded. **Location:** 5 miles from downtown. **Calendar:** Semester, extensive summer session. **Full-time faculty:** 18 total; 6% women. **Class size:** 90% < 20, 10% 20-39.

Student profile. Among degree-seeking undergraduates, 38 enrolled as first-time, first-year students.

Out-of-state:	1%	25 or older:	44%
Women:	5%		

Transfer out. Colleges most students transferred to 2015: Point Park University, Robert Morris University, Edinboro University, Slippery Rock University, University of Pittsburgh.

Basis for selection. Open admission, but selective for some programs. Must have high school diploma or GED. Applicants must take TABE test for placement. **Home schooled:** Transcript of courses and grades, state high school equivalency certificate required.

2016-2017 Annual costs. Tuition/fees: $16,586. Books/supplies: $1,157. Personal expenses: $1,608. **Additional information:** Fees will vary depending on program.

2014-2015 Financial aid. **Need-based:** 89 full-time freshmen applied for aid; 89 deemed to have need; 89 received aid. Average need met was 15%. Average scholarship/grant was $5,637; average loan $2,809. 52% of total undergraduate aid awarded as scholarships/grants, 48% as loans/jobs. Need-based aid available for part-time students. Work-study available nights, weekends and for part-time students. **Non-need-based:** Awarded to 1 full-time undergraduates, including 3 freshmen. Scholarships awarded for academics, state residency.

Application procedures. **Admission:** No deadline. $75 fee. Admission notification on a rolling basis. **Financial aid:** No deadline. FAFSA, institutional form required. Applicants notified on a rolling basis.

Academics. **Credit/placement by examination:** AP, CLEP, institutional tests. 36 credit hours maximum toward associate degree. **Support services:** Learning center, remedial instruction, study skills assistance, tutoring.

Majors. **General:** Carpentry, electrician, power transmission.

Most popular majors. Trade and industry 95%.

Technology on campus. 46 workstations in library, computer center. Online library available.

Student life. **Freshman orientation:** Mandatory. Preregistration for classes offered. Held approximately 5 days prior to start; about 2-1/2 hours long. **Activities:** Student government.

Student services. Career counseling, student employment services, financial aid counseling, personal counseling, placement for graduates. **Transfer:** Pre-admission transcript evaluation for new students. College fairs on campus for students transferring to 4-year colleges.

Contact. E-mail: info@triangle-tech.edu
Phone: (412) 359-1000 Toll-free number: (800) 874-8324
Fax: (412) 359-1012
Terry Kucic, Executive Director of Admissions, Triangle Tech: Pittsburgh, 1940 Perrysville Avenue, Pittsburgh, PA 15214-3897

Triangle Tech: Sunbury
Sunbury, Pennsylvania
www.triangle-tech.edu

- For-profit 2-year technical college
- Commuter campus in large town
- Interview required

General. Accredited by ACCSC. **Enrollment:** 111 degree-seeking undergraduates. **Degrees:** 65 associate awarded. **Calendar:** Semester. **Full-time faculty:** 11 total; 9% women. **Class size:** 100% < 20.

Student profile. Among degree-seeking undergraduates, 100% enrolled in a vocational program, 1% already have a bachelor's degree or higher, 66 enrolled as first-time, first-year students.

Women:	5%	25 or older:	21%

Basis for selection. Open admission.

High school preparation. Recommended units include English 4 and mathematics 4.

2016-2017 Annual costs. Tuition/fees (projected): $16,692. Books/supplies: $1,026. Personal expenses: $1,440. **Additional information:** Fees will vary by program.

2014-2015 Financial aid. **Need-based:** 62 full-time freshmen applied for aid; 62 deemed to have need; 58 received aid. Average need met was 97%. Average scholarship/grant was $6,564; average loan $3,155. 47% of total undergraduate aid awarded as scholarships/grants, 53% as loans/jobs. Need-based aid available for part-time students. Work-study available nights, weekends and for part-time students. **Non-need-based:** Awarded to 3 full-time undergraduates, including 3 freshmen.

Application procedures. Admission: No deadline. No application fee. Admission notification on a rolling basis. **Financial aid:** No deadline. FAFSA, institutional form required. Applicants notified on a rolling basis.

Academics. Credit/placement by examination: AP, CLEP, institutional tests. **Support services:** Study skills assistance, tutoring.

Majors. General: Carpentry.

Technology on campus. 27 workstations in library, computer center.

Student life. Freshman orientation: Mandatory. Preregistration for classes offered. **Activities:** Student government.

Student services. Adult student services, career counseling, student employment services, financial aid counseling, placement for graduates. **Transfer:** Pre-admission transcript evaluation for new students.

Contact. E-mail: tkucic@triangle-tech.edu
Phone: (570) 988-0700 Toll-free number: (800) 874-8324
Fax: (570) 988-4641
Terry Kucic, Executive Director of Admissions, Triangle Tech: Sunbury, 191 Performance Road, Sunbury, PA 17801

University of Pittsburgh at Titusville
Titusville, Pennsylvania
www.upt.pitt.edu   CB code: 2937

> Public 2-year branch campus and liberal arts college
> Residential campus in small town

General. Founded in 1963. Regionally accredited. **Enrollment:** 342 degree-seeking undergraduates; 4 non-degree-seeking students. **Degrees:** 56 associate awarded. **Location:** 100 miles from Pittsburgh, 50 miles from Erie. **Calendar:** Semester, limited summer session. **Full-time faculty:** 24 total. **Part-time faculty:** 30 total. **Class size:** 76% < 20, 23% 20-39, less than 1% 40-49.

Student profile. Among degree-seeking undergraduates, 142 enrolled as first-time, first-year students, 21 transferred in from other institutions.

Part-time:	15%	Hispanic/Latino:	4%
Out-of-state:	6%	Multi-racial, non-Hispanic:	4%
Women:	66%	25 or older:	17%
African American:	23%	Live on campus:	69%
Asian American:	1%		

Transfer out. Colleges most students transferred to 2015: Clarion University, Edinboro University, Indiana University of Pennsylvania, Penn State University, Slippery Rock University of Pennsylvania.

Basis for selection. Decisions based on academic performance. Applicants deserving additional consideration referred to Admissions Committee. SAT recommended. Essay, interview recommended. **Adult students:** SAT/ACT scores not required if out of high school 1 year(s) or more. **Home schooled:** Math/English placement tests required. **Learning Disabled:** Students with disabilities asked to provide comprehensive documentation to Disability Resources and Services representative to establish eligibility for accommodations.

High school preparation. College-preparatory program recommended. 15 units required. Required and recommended units include English 4, mathematics 2, science 1 (laboratory 1), foreign language 2 and academic electives 7. One unit lab science required.

2015-2016 Annual costs. Tuition/fees: $11,584; $21,146 out-of-state. Per-credit charge: $448 in-state; $846 out-of-state. Room/board: $10,224. Books/supplies: $1,217. Personal expenses: $1,217.

2014-2015 Financial aid. Need-based: 150 full-time freshmen applied for aid; 141 deemed to have need; 141 received aid. Average need met was 68%. Average scholarship/grant was $8,018; average loan $6,153. 46% of total undergraduate aid awarded as scholarships/grants, 54% as loans/jobs. Need-based aid available for part-time students. Work-study available nights, weekends and for part-time students. **Non-need-based:** Awarded to 20 full-time undergraduates, including 10 freshmen. Scholarships awarded for academics, state residency.

Application procedures. Admission: Priority date 5/1; deadline 8/24. $45 fee, may be waived for applicants with need. Admission notification on

a rolling basis beginning on or about 10/1. Must reply by May 1 or within 2 week(s) if notified thereafter. **Financial aid:** Priority date 3/1; no closing date. FAFSA required. Applicants notified on a rolling basis starting 3/1; must reply within 2 week(s) of notification.

Academics. Special study options: Cross-registration, distance learning, double major, dual major, dual enrollment of high school students, independent study, internships, liberal arts/career combination. Bachelor's degree programs available on campus. License preparation in nursing. **Credit/placement by examination:** AP, CLEP, SAT, ACT, institutional tests. 6 credit hours maximum toward associate degree. **Support services:** Learning center, reduced course load, remedial instruction, study skills assistance, tutoring.

Majors. Business: General, accounting, management information systems. **Health services:** Nursing (RN), physical therapy assistant. **Liberal arts:** Arts/sciences. **Work/family studies:** General.

Most popular majors. Business/marketing 14%, health sciences 45%, liberal arts 9%, psychology 11%, security/protective services 9%.

Technology on campus. 62 workstations in dormitories, library, computer center, student center. Dormitories wired for high-speed internet access and linked to campus network. Commuter students can connect to campus network. Online course registration, online library, helpline, student web hosting, wireless network available.

Student life. Freshman orientation: Mandatory, $60 fee. Preregistration for classes offered. Held weekend (Thursday through Sunday) prior to start of fall semester; includes freshman services, projects, activities. **Policies:** Organizations must complete 1 community service and fundraising activity per year to receive student activity funding. **Housing:** Guaranteed on-campus for all undergraduates. Coed dorms available. $100 nonrefundable deposit, deadline 8/1. Townhouse apartments without cooking facilities available. **Activities:** Campus ministries, student government, diversity club, Students in Free Enterprise, commuter student association, Alpha Omega Christian fellowship, Phi Theta Kappa, student activities board, chemistry club, student physical therapy association, College Republicans.

Athletics. USCAA. **Intercollegiate:** Basketball. **Intramural:** Basketball, bowling, football (tackle), golf, racquetball, skiing, soccer, softball, table tennis, tennis, volleyball. **Team name:** Panthers.

Student services. Adult student services, alcohol/substance abuse counseling, career counseling, student employment services, financial aid counseling, health services, minority student services, personal counseling, placement for graduates, veterans' counselor. **Physically disabled:** Services for visually impaired. **Transfer:** Pre-admission transcript evaluation for new students. Transfer adviser, college fairs on campus for students transferring to 4-year colleges.

Contact. E-mail: uptadm@pitt.edu
Phone: (814) 827-4509 Toll-free number: (888) 878-0462
Fax: (814) 827-4519
Robert Wyant, Director of Admissions, University of Pittsburgh at Titusville, UPT Admissions Office, Titusville, PA 16354-0287

Valley Forge Military College
Wayne, Pennsylvania   CB member
www.vfmac.edu   CB code: 2955

> Private 2-year junior and military college
> Residential campus in small city
> SAT or ACT (ACT writing optional) required

General. Founded in 1928. Regionally accredited. Received "Military Friendly" Designation for 2013-2014, one of only 5 military junior colleges in nation offering Army ROTC early commissioning program leading to commission as second lieutenant in U.S. Army Reserve at end of second year. **Enrollment:** 347 degree-seeking undergraduates. **Degrees:** 62 associate awarded. **ROTC:** Army, Air Force. **Location:** 15 miles from Philadelphia. **Calendar:** Semester, limited summer session. **Full-time faculty:** 19 total; 32% have terminal degrees, 21% minority, 42% women. **Part-time faculty:** 6 total; 17% minority, 83% women. **Special facilities:** Motorized artillery unit, mounted cavalry troop, aviation training.

Student profile. Among degree-seeking undergraduates, 100% enrolled in a transfer program, 177 enrolled as first-time, first-year students.

Out-of-state:	47%	Women:	13%

Transfer out. Colleges most students transferred to 2015: Temple University, Drexel University, Cabrini.

Basis for selection. School achievement record, test scores, minimum 2.0 GPA and SAT combined score of 800 (Math and Verbal) or higher, or

ACT score of 17 or higher required for admission. TOEFL score accepted in lieu of SAT or ACT scores for international students. Interview recommended. **Home schooled:** Statement describing home school structure and mission, transcript of courses and grades, state high school equivalency certificate, interview, letter of recommendation (nonparent) required. **Learning Disabled:** Specialist testing, academic support, ADA accommodations discussed and offered.

High school preparation. College-preparatory program recommended. Required and recommended units include English 4, mathematics 3, science 3 and foreign language 2.

2015-2016 Annual costs. Tuition/fees: $29,975. Room/board: $14,700. Books/supplies: $1,000. Personal expenses: $5,000.

2014-2015 Financial aid. All financial aid based on need. 147 full-time freshmen applied for aid; 147 deemed to have need; 122 received aid. Average need met was 72%. Average scholarship/grant was $22,000. 64% of total undergraduate aid awarded as scholarships/grants, 36% as loans/jobs. Work-study available nights, weekends and for part-time students. **Additional information:** Students enrolled in advanced military science program can receive up to $5,000 from the Army. In addition, competitively awarded ROTC scholarships pay average of another $14,100 per school year for direct educational expenses.

Application procedures. Admission: No deadline. $25 fee, may be waived for applicants with need. Admission notification on a rolling basis. Must reply by May 1 or within 2 week(s) if notified thereafter. **Financial aid:** Priority date 5/1, closing date 5/1. FAFSA required. Applicants notified on a rolling basis starting 5/15; must reply by 5/1 or within 2 week(s) of notification.

Academics. Special study options: Distance learning, dual enrollment of high school students, ESL. **Credit/placement by examination:** AP, CLEP, SAT, ACT, institutional tests. 15 credit hours maximum toward associate degree. **Support services:** Learning center, reduced course load, remedial instruction, study skills assistance, tutoring, writing center.

Majors. Biology: General. **Business:** General. **Engineering:** General, engineering science. **Liberal arts:** Arts/sciences. **Physical sciences:** General. **Protective services:** Criminal justice.

Technology on campus. 60 workstations in library, computer center. Dormitories wired for high-speed internet access and linked to campus network. Online library, helpline, repair service, wireless network available.

Student life. Freshman orientation: Mandatory. Preregistration for classes offered. 3-day orientation with placement testing. **Policies:** Religious observance required. **Housing:** Guaranteed on-campus for all undergraduates. Single-sex dorms, wellness housing available. $500 partly refundable deposit, deadline 5/1. **Activities:** Bands, campus ministries, choral groups, Model UN, student government, Catholic Fellowship, Jewish Fellowship, Christian Fellowship, Muslim Fellowship, Young Republicans, regimental marching band, drum and bugle corps, regimental choir.

Athletics. NAIA. **Intercollegiate:** Basketball M, cross-country, football (tackle) M, lacrosse M, rifle M, soccer, track and field, wrestling M. **Intramural:** Baseball M, basketball, fencing M, golf M, judo M, rugby M, soccer, softball W, volleyball W, water polo M, weight lifting M. **Team name:** Trojans.

Student services. Alcohol/substance abuse counseling, chaplain/spiritual director, career counseling, services for economically disadvantaged, financial aid counseling, health services, minority student services, personal counseling, placement for graduates, veterans' counselor. **Physically disabled:** Services for visually, speech, hearing impaired. **Transfer:** Pre-admission transcript evaluation for new students. Transfer center, transfer adviser, college fairs on campus for students transferring to 4-year colleges.

Contact. E-mail: admissions_college@vfmac.edu
Phone: (610) 989-1300 Toll-free number: (800) 234-8362
Fax: (610) 688-1545
Kristen Rose, Director of Admissions, Valley Forge Military College, 1001 Eagle Road, Wayne, PA 19087

Vet Tech Institute
Pittsburgh, Pennsylvania
www.vettechinstitute.edu   CB code: 7134

▶ For-profit 2-year health science and technical college
▶ Commuter campus in large city

General. Accredited by ACCSC. Veterinary technician AVMA accredited. **Enrollment:** 385 degree-seeking undergraduates. **Degrees:** 184 associate awarded. **Calendar:** Semester. **Full-time faculty:** 9 total. **Part-time faculty:** 5 total. **Special facilities:** Animal tech rooms, on-site kennel.

Transfer out. Colleges most students transferred to 2015: Point Park College.

Basis for selection. Satisfactory performance on school admission test required. Essay, interview recommended.

2015-2016 Annual costs. Tuition/fees: $14,680. Books/supplies: $875.

Financial aid. Need-based: Work-study available nights, weekends and for part-time students. **Non-need-based:** Scholarships awarded for academics.

Application procedures. Admission: No deadline. $50 fee. Admission notification on a rolling basis. **Financial aid:** No deadline. FAFSA required. Applicants notified on a rolling basis.

Academics. Special study options: Internships. **Credit/placement by examination:** AP, CLEP. **Support services:** Tutoring.

Majors. Health services: Veterinary technology/assistant.

Technology on campus. 38 workstations in library, computer center.

Student life. Freshman orientation: Mandatory. Preregistration for classes offered.

Student services. Career counseling, student employment services, financial aid counseling, placement for graduates.

Contact. E-mail: admissions@vettechinstitute.edu
Phone: (412) 391-7021 Toll-free number: (800) 570-0693
Fax: (412) 232-4348
Vet Tech Institute, 125 Seventh Street, Pittsburgh, PA 15222-3400

Westmoreland County Community College
Youngwood, Pennsylvania
www.wccc.edu   CB code: 2968

▶ Public 2-year community college
▶ Commuter campus in small town

General. Founded in 1970. Regionally accredited. **Enrollment:** 4,694 degree-seeking undergraduates; 823 non-degree-seeking students. **Degrees:** 586 associate awarded. **Location:** 30 miles from Pittsburgh. **Calendar:** Semester, limited summer session. **Full-time faculty:** 83 total; 2% minority, 48% women. **Part-time faculty:** 357 total; 7% minority, 59% women. **Class size:** 75% < 20, 25% 20-39. **Special facilities:** Culinary arts kitchens, greenhouse, student lounges, theater.

Student profile. Among degree-seeking undergraduates, 21% enrolled in a transfer program, 79% enrolled in a vocational program, 1,302 enrolled as first-time, first-year students.

Part-time:	47%	Hispanic/Latino:	2%
Women:	61%	Multi-racial, non-Hispanic:	3%
African American:	3%	25 or older:	34%

Transfer out. Colleges most students transferred to 2015: University of Pittsburgh, Indiana University of Pennsylvania, California University of Pennsylvania, Seton Hill University, St. Vincent College.

Basis for selection. Open admission, but selective for some programs. Allied Health program applicants required to take Comparative Guidance and Placement test, submit application by 11/30 of the year prior to enrollment, and satisfactory results from pre-entrance physicals. Interview recommended.

2016-2017 Annual costs. Tuition/fees (projected): $5,070; $8,730 out-of-district; $12,390 out-of-state. Per-credit charge: $122 in-district; $244 out-of-district; $366 out-of-state. Books/supplies: $1,200. Personal expenses: $1,000.

Financial aid. Need-based: Need-based aid available for part-time students. Work-study available nights, weekends and for part-time students. **Non-need-based:** Scholarships awarded for academics.

Application procedures. Admission: No deadline. No application fee. Admission notification on a rolling basis. **Financial aid:** No deadline. FAFSA, institutional form required. Applicants notified on a rolling basis starting 5/1.

Academics. Special study options: Accelerated study, cooperative education, cross-registration, distance learning, double major, dual enrollment of high school students, honors, independent study, internships, student-designed major, study abroad. License preparation in dental hygiene, nursing, radiology, real estate. **Credit/placement by examination:** AP, CLEP, institutional tests. 30 credit hours maximum toward associate degree. **Support services:** Learning center, remedial instruction, study skills assistance, tutoring, writing center.

Majors. Business: General, accounting technology, administrative services, banking/financial services, business admin, human resources, sales/distribution, tourism/travel. **Communications technology:** Radio/TV. **Computer sciences:** Networking, programming, security, support specialist, web page design. **Education:** Early childhood. **Engineering:** Pre-engineering, robotics. **General:** Power transmission. **Health services:** Dental hygiene, dietetic technician, nursing (RN), radiologic technology/medical imaging, sonography. **Liberal arts:** Arts/sciences. **Protective services:** Criminal justice, fire safety technology, forensics.

Most popular majors. Business/marketing 14%, computer/information sciences 8%, health sciences 35%, liberal arts 16%, security/protective services 6%, trade and industry 6%.

Technology on campus. 620 workstations in library, computer center. Commuter students can connect to campus network. Online course registration, online library, helpline, student web hosting, wireless network available.

Student life. Freshman orientation: Available. Preregistration for classes offered. **Policies:** All clubs required to complete 10 hours of community service per semester and send two representatives to each student government meeting twice monthly. **Activities:** Bands, choral groups, drama, literary magazine, music ensembles, musical theater, student government, student newspaper, symphony orchestra, Black Awareness Committee, ReachOut Christian Club, Veteran's Club, Cultural Programming Committee, Political Science Club.

Athletics. NJCAA. **Intercollegiate:** Baseball M, basketball, bowling, cross-country, golf, soccer, softball W, volleyball W. **Intramural:** Baseball M, basketball, bowling, golf, skiing, soccer, softball, volleyball. **Team name:** Wolfpack.

Student services. Career counseling, services for economically disadvantaged, student employment services, financial aid counseling, on-campus daycare, personal counseling, placement for graduates, veterans' counselor. **Physically disabled:** Services for visually, speech, hearing impaired. **Transfer:** Pre-admission transcript evaluation for new students. Transfer adviser, college fairs on campus for students transferring to 4-year colleges.

Contact. E-mail: admissions@wccc.edu
Phone: (724) 925-4077 Toll-free number: (800) 262-2103 ext. 4077
Fax: (724) 925-4292
Janice Grabowski, Director of Admissions, Westmoreland County Community College, 145 Pavilion Lane, Youngwood, PA 15697

Williamson College of the Trades
Media, Pennsylvania
www.williamson.edu
CB code: 0765

▶ Private 2-year technical college for men affiliated with the nondenominational tradition
▶ Residential campus in large town
▶ Application essay, interview required

General. Founded in 1888. Accredited by ACCSC. Discipline-oriented post-secondary school that prepares students to be tradesmen through academic instruction and hands-on training in a structured environment; scholarship-only students. **Enrollment:** 265 degree-seeking undergraduates. **Degrees:** 67 associate awarded. **Location:** 14 miles from Philadelphia, 14 miles from Wilmington, Delaware. **Calendar:** Semester. **Full-time faculty:** 18 total. **Part-time faculty:** 15 total. **Class size:** 100% < 20. **Special facilities:** Natural arboretum.

Student profile. Among degree-seeking undergraduates, 100% enrolled in a vocational program, 100 enrolled as first-time, first-year students.

Out-of-state: 25% **Live on campus:** 100%

Basis for selection. Family financial need, average or better performance on entrance exam, and exceptional interview score. Applicants must be male legal residents of the United States and may not turn 20 years old prior to June 1 of year of admission. Additionally, eligible applicants may not be married or have children of their own. Finally, eligible applicants must be able to pass a pre-admission drug screen and should be of good moral character. Armed Services Vocational Aptitude Battery (ASVAB) required by application deadline. Essay is completed on campus in the form of a writing sample as part of a Testing Day Session. **Learning Disabled:** There

are no special requirements or procedures for students with learning disabilities.

2015-2016 Annual costs. Required fees for personal clothing and tools for the freshman year average $1,330.

2014-2015 Financial aid. All financial aid based on need. 100 full-time freshmen applied for aid; 100 deemed to have need; 100 received aid. Average need met was 100%. Average scholarship/grant was $27,000. Work-study available nights, weekends and for part-time students. **Additional information:** Each enrolled student receives a full scholarship covering tuition, room and board, and textbooks for the three-year program.

Application procedures. Admission: Closing date 2/24 (postmark date). No application fee. Admission notification by 5/1. Must reply by 5/15. **Financial aid:** Closing date 2/22. Applicants notified by 5/1; must reply by 5/15.

Academics. Special study options: Cooperative education, internships. **Credit/placement by examination:** AP, CLEP. **Support services:** Pre-admission summer program, tutoring.

Majors. General: Carpentry, masonry.

Most popular majors. Agriculture 22%, trade and industry 78%.

Technology on campus. 165 workstations in dormitories, library, computer center. Wireless network available.

Student life. Freshman orientation: Mandatory. Preregistration for classes offered. Takes place during the first 4 days of school and includes shop orientation, rules/regulations, activities/student services orientation, and classroom schedules. **Policies:** Student life is carefully structured, including a standard daily schedule, dress code, required chapel, and clearly defined student responsibilities. Freshmen not permitted cars on campus. **Housing:** Guaranteed on-campus for all undergraduates. **Activities:** Jazz band, campus ministries, choral groups, student government, student newspaper, Fellowship of Christian Athletes, Campus Crusade for Christ, Bible study groups.

Athletics. NJCAA, USCAA. **Intercollegiate:** Baseball M, basketball M, cross-country M, football (tackle) M, lacrosse M, soccer M, tennis M, wrestling M. **Intramural:** Archery M. **Team name:** Mechanics.

Student services. Alcohol/substance abuse counseling, chaplain/spiritual director, career counseling, services for economically disadvantaged, student employment services, health services, personal counseling, placement for graduates.

Contact. E-mail: jmerillat@williamson.edu
Phone: (610) 566-1776 ext. 235 Fax: (610) 566-6502
Jay Merillat, Dean of Enrollments, Williamson College of the Trades, 106 S. New Middletown Rd., Media, PA 19063

YTI Career Institute: Altoona
Altoona, Pennsylvania
www.yti.edu

▶ For-profit 2-year technical and career college
▶ Commuter campus in small city

General. Regionally accredited; also accredited by ACCSC. **Enrollment:** 334 undergraduates. **Degrees:** 90 associate awarded. **Calendar:** Quarter. **Full-time faculty:** 27 total. **Special facilities:** Dental lab, medical assistant lab, pharmacy technician lab, respiratory lab, computer system tech lab. **Partnerships:** Formal partnerships with local businesses to participate in a 12-week externship and/or a 4-5 week externship.

Basis for selection. Open admission, but selective for some programs. **Home schooled:** Transcript of courses and grades required.

2015-2016 Annual costs. Total tuition for diploma programs range from $14,150 to $14,620; associate degree programs range from $22,070 to $32,300. Books and supplies range from $2,100 to $4,300, depending on program.

Financial aid. Need-based: Work-study available nights, weekends and for part-time students.

Application procedures. Admission: No deadline. $50 fee. Application must be submitted on paper.

Academics. Credit/placement by examination: AP, CLEP.

Majors. Business: Business admin. **Health services:** Medical assistant. **Protective services:** Criminal justice.

Most popular majors. Health sciences 53%, security/protective services 47%.

Contact. E-mail: altoonaadmission@yti.edu
Phone: (814) 944-5643 Toll-free number: (800) 795-0971
Fax: (814) 944-5309
Tanya McCormick, Director of Admissions, YTI Career Institute: Altoona, 2900 Fairway Drive, Altoona, PA 16602

YTI Career Institute: Lancaster
Lancaster, Pennsylvania
www.yti.edu

- For-profit 2-year technical and career college
- Commuter campus in small city
- Interview required

General. Accredited by ACCSC. **Enrollment:** 421 degree-seeking undergraduates; 228 non-degree-seeking students. **Degrees:** 89 associate awarded. **Calendar:** Quarter. **Full-time faculty:** 40 total. **Part-time faculty:** 35 total. **Class size:** 77% < 20, 23% 20-39.

Student profile. Among degree-seeking undergraduates, 145 enrolled as first-time, first-year students.

Basis for selection. Open admission, but selective for some programs. Medical Assistant program requires criminal background check and immunization form completed by a certified physician to include documentation for Hepatitis B and TB. Dental Assisting program requires verification of steps 1 and 2 of the Hepatitis B vaccination. Criminal Justice and First Response programs require background record check, valid driver's license, and applicants must be at least 18 years of age at time of matriculation. COMPASS used for placement.

2015-2016 Annual costs. Personal expenses: $899. **Additional information:** Diploma program costs range from $3,000 to $20,100; associate degree programs range from $26,270 to $35,900. Books and supplies range from $450 to $4,500, depending on program.

Financial aid. All financial aid based on need. Need-based aid available for part-time students. Work-study available nights, weekends and for part-time students.

Application procedures. Admission: No deadline. $50 fee. **Financial aid:** No deadline. FAFSA required. Applicants notified on a rolling basis; must reply within 4 week(s) of notification.

Academics. Special study options: Internships. License preparation in radiology. **Credit/placement by examination:** AP, CLEP. **Support services:** Learning center, study skills assistance, tutoring.

Majors. Health services: Medical assistant. **Protective services:** Law enforcement admin.

Technology on campus. Commuter students can connect to campus network. Online library, helpline, wireless network available.

Contact. Phone: (717) 295-1100 Toll-free number: (866) 984-5262
Fax: (717) 295-1135
Joseph Fotunato, VP of Admissions, YTI Career Institute: Lancaster, 3050 Hempland Road, Lancaster, PA 17601

YTI Career Institute: York
York, Pennsylvania
www.yti.edu   **CB code: 2943**

- For-profit 2-year technical and career college
- Commuter campus in small city
- Interview required

General. Regionally accredited; also accredited by ACCSC. **Enrollment:** 698 degree-seeking undergraduates. **Degrees:** 482 associate awarded. **Calendar:** Quarter. **Full-time faculty:** 37 total. **Part-time faculty:** 29 total.

Basis for selection. Open admission, but selective for some programs. Medical Assistant programs require criminal background check and a health information form completed by a certified physician to include documentation for Hepatitis B and TB immunizations. Dental Assisting programs require a health information form completed by a certified physician to include documentation for Hepatitis B immunizations. Veterinary Technician programs require health immunization forms completed by a certified physician to include Hepatitis A, B, and Tetanus immunizations. Computer Systems Specialist Program applicants must pass a preliminary criminal background check. Heating, Air Conditioning & Refrigeration Technology and Electrical Technology programs must pass a preliminary criminal background check and possess a valid driver's license. Motorsports Technology program must have a valid motorcycle license or permit. COMPASS used for placement.

2015-2016 Annual costs. Personal expenses: $2,097. **Additional information:** Total diploma program costs range from $13,500 to $17,500; associate degree programs range from $27,730 to $36,770. Books and supplies range from $2,700 to $4,600 depending on program.

Financial aid. Need-based: Work-study available nights, weekends and for part-time students.

Application procedures. Admission: No deadline. $50 fee. Admission notification on a rolling basis.

Academics. Special study options: Internships. **Credit/placement by examination:** AP, CLEP, institutional tests. **Support services:** Learning center, study skills assistance, tutoring.

Majors. Business: Business admin. **Computer sciences:** Systems analysis. **Health services:** Medical assistant, veterinary technology/assistant.

Most popular majors. Business/marketing 9%, computer/information sciences 13%, engineering/engineering technologies 15%, health sciences 31%, personal/culinary services 18%, security/protective services 11%.

Technology on campus. 250 workstations in library, computer center. Commuter students can connect to campus network. Helpline, wireless network available.

Student life. Freshman orientation: Mandatory. Preregistration for classes offered.

Student services. Career counseling, student employment services, financial aid counseling. **Transfer:** Re-entry adviser, pre-admission transcript evaluation for new students. Transfer adviser for students transferring to 4-year colleges.

Contact. E-mail: daniel.dimeglio@yti.edu
Phone: (717) 757-1100 Toll-free number: (800) 227-9675
Fax: (717) 757-4964
Daniel Dimeglio, Director of Admissions, YTI Career Institute: York, 1405 Williams Road, York, PA 17402

Puerto Rico

Centro de Estudios Multidisciplinarios
San Juan, Puerto Rico
www.cempr.edu

- Private 2-year health science college
- Large city

General. Accredited by ACCSC. **Enrollment:** 987 undergraduates. **Degrees:** 134 bachelor's, 240 associate awarded. **Calendar:** Quarter. **Full-time faculty:** 3 total. **Part-time faculty:** 90 total.

Basis for selection. Open admission.

Financial aid. Need-based: Work-study available nights, weekends and for part-time students.

Application procedures. Admission: No deadline. $30 fee.

Academics. Special study options: Bachelor's degree programs available on campus. **Credit/placement by examination:** AP, CLEP.

Majors. Health services: Nursing (RN), pharmacy assistant, respiratory therapy technology.

Contact. E-mail: jmrestotorres@yahoo.com
Phone: (787) 765-4210 Toll-free number: (877) 779-2236
Fax: (787) 765-4277
Juan Resto, Director of Admissions, Centro de Estudios Multidisciplinarios, PO Box 191317, San Juan, PR 00919-1317

Colegio de Cinematograflf8a, Artes y Televisión
San Juan, Puerto Rico
www.ccat.edu

- Private 2-year liberal arts and technical college
- Commuter campus in small city

General. Accredited by ACCSC. **Enrollment:** 720 undergraduates. **Degrees:** 90 associate awarded. **Location:** 5 miles from San Juan. **Calendar:** Semester, limited summer session. **Full-time faculty:** 2 total. **Part-time faculty:** 28 total. **Class size:** 27% < 20, 73% 20-39.

Transfer out. Colleges most students transferred to 2015: University of the Sacred Heart, University of Puerto Rico.

Basis for selection. Open admission. **Home schooled:** Statement describing home school structure and mission required. College Board results required.

2015-2016 Annual costs. Books/supplies: $360.

Financial aid. Need-based: Work-study available nights, weekends and for part-time students. **Non-need-based:** Scholarships awarded for alumni affiliation, art, athletics, job skills, leadership, minority status, music/drama, religious affiliation, ROTC, state residency.

Application procedures. Admission: Closing date 9/3 (receipt date). $25 fee, may be waived for applicants with need. Admission notification on a rolling basis. **Financial aid:** No deadline. FAFSA required. Applicants notified on a rolling basis.

Academics. Special study options: Internships. **Credit/placement by examination:** AP, CLEP. **Support services:** Reduced course load, study skills assistance, tutoring.

Majors. Communications: Radio/TV. **Communications technology:** Recording arts. **Visual/performing arts:** Cinematography.

Technology on campus. 50 workstations in library, computer center. Commuter students can connect to campus network.

Student life. Freshman orientation: Available. Preregistration for classes offered.

Student services. Career counseling, financial aid counseling.

Contact. E-mail: admissions@ccat.edu
Phone: (787) 779-2500 Fax: (787) 995-2525
Nydia Alvaranza, Admissions Officer, Colegio de Cinematografía, Artes y Televisión, PO Box 10774, San Juan, PR 00922

Columbia Central University: Yauco
Yauco, Puerto Rico
www.columbiacentral.edu   CB code: 3215

- For-profit 2-year business and health science college
- Commuter campus in large town

General. Regionally accredited. **Enrollment:** 626 degree-seeking undergraduates. **Degrees:** 56 bachelor's, 65 associate awarded. **Calendar:** Differs by program. **Full-time faculty:** 7 total; 43% have terminal degrees, 100% minority, 71% women. **Part-time faculty:** 34 total; 9% have terminal degrees, 100% minority, 59% women. **Class size:** 82% < 20, 18% 20-39.

Student profile. Among degree-seeking undergraduates, 6% enrolled in a vocational program, 64 enrolled as first-time, first-year students, 81 transferred in from other institutions.

Part-time:	50%	Hispanic/Latino:	100%
Women:	70%	25 or older:	32%

Transfer out. Colleges most students transferred to 2015: Inter American University of Puerto Rico, Universidad del Este, Ponce Paramedical College.

Basis for selection. Open admission, but selective for some programs. Neither interviews nor personal statements are required. **Home schooled:** Transcript of courses and grades, state high school equivalency certificate required.

2015-2016 Annual costs. Tuition/fees: $6,290. Books/supplies: $862. Personal expenses: $150. **Additional information:** Additional fees may apply.

2014-2015 Financial aid. All financial aid based on need. 71 full-time freshmen applied for aid; 71 deemed to have need; 71 received aid. 99% of total undergraduate aid awarded as scholarships/grants, 1% as loans/jobs. Need-based aid available for part-time students. Work-study available nights, weekends and for part-time students.

Application procedures. Admission: No deadline. $50 fee. Admission notification on a rolling basis. **Financial aid:** No deadline. FAFSA, institutional form required.

Academics. Special study options: Distance learning, independent study. Bachelor's degree programs available on campus. License preparation in nursing. **Credit/placement by examination:** AP, CLEP. **Support services:** Reduced course load, study skills assistance, tutoring.

Majors. Business: Business admin, office technology. **Computer sciences:** Programming. **Health services:** Nursing (RN).

Most popular majors. Business/marketing 7%, health sciences 93%.

Technology on campus. 33 workstations in library, computer center, student center. Commuter students can connect to campus network. Online course registration, online library, repair service, wireless network available.

Student life. Freshman orientation: Mandatory. Preregistration for classes offered. **Activities:** Student government.

Student services. Alcohol/substance abuse counseling, career counseling, student employment services, financial aid counseling, personal counseling, placement for graduates. **Transfer:** Re-entry adviser, pre-admission transcript evaluation for new students. Transfer adviser for students transferring to 4-year colleges.

Contact. E-mail: info@columbiacentral.edu
Phone: (787) 856-0945 ext. 117 Fax: (787) 267-0994
Carmen Pabon, Admissions Coordinator, Columbia Central University: Yauco, PO Box 3062, Yauco, PR 00698-3062

EDIC College
Caguas, Puerto Rico
www.ediccollege.com

- For-profit 2-year health science and technical college
- Large city
- Interview required

General. Regionally accredited; also accredited by ACICS. **Enrollment:** 880 full-time, degree-seeking students. **Degrees:** 225 associate awarded. **Location:** 45 miles from San Juan. **Calendar:** Semester. **Full-time faculty:** 15 total. **Part-time faculty:** 108 total.

Basis for selection. Open admission, but selective for some programs. For associate degree program, 2.3 GPA required. **Home schooled:** Transcript of courses and grades required.

2015-2016 Annual costs. Tuition/fees: $6,625. Per-credit charge: $275. Books/supplies: $150. Personal expenses: $1,500.

Financial aid. All financial aid based on need. Need-based aid available for part-time students. Work-study available nights, weekends and for part-time students.

Application procedures. Admission: Closing date 9/14 (receipt date). $25 fee. Application must be submitted on paper. Admission notification by 9/13. Admission notification on a rolling basis beginning on or about 1/13. Must reply by 9/13. **Financial aid:** No deadline. FAFSA, institutional form required. Applicants notified on a rolling basis.

Academics. Special study options: Distance learning. License preparation in nursing, paramedic, radiology. **Credit/placement by examination:** AP, CLEP. **Support services:** Learning center, tutoring.

Majors. Health services: Radiologic technology/medical imaging, sonography. **Physical sciences:** Optics.

Technology on campus. 1 workstations in library. Commuter students can connect to campus network. Online course registration, online library, wireless network available.

Student life. Freshman orientation: Mandatory. Preregistration for classes offered.

Student services. Adult student services, financial aid counseling, placement for graduates, veterans' counselor. **Transfer:** Pre-admission transcript evaluation for new students.

Contact. E-mail: admisiones@ediccollege.edu
Phone: (787) 744-8519 ext. 229 Fax: (787) 258-6300
Virginia Cartagena, Admissions Director, EDIC College, Box 9120, Caguas, PR 00726-9120

Huertas College
Caguas, Puerto Rico
www.huertas.edu

CB member
CB code: 3406

▶ For-profit 2-year junior and technical college
▶ Commuter campus in large city
▶ Interview required

General. Founded in 1945. **Enrollment:** 1,280 degree-seeking undergraduates; 1 non-degree-seeking students. **Degrees:** 310 associate awarded. **Location:** 25 miles from San Juan, 32 miles from Naranjito. **Calendar:** Semester, extensive summer session. **Full-time faculty:** 12 total; 8% have terminal degrees, 100% minority, 75% women. **Part-time faculty:** 103 total; 12% have terminal degrees, 100% minority, 64% women. **Special facilities:** Simulation clinic for health-related programs, 3-D room.

Student profile. Among degree-seeking undergraduates, 248 enrolled as first-time, first-year students.

Part-time:	12%	Hispanic/Latino:	100%
Women:	58%	25 or older:	40%

Transfer out. Colleges most students transferred to 2015: Columbia Centro Universitario, EDIC College, National University.

Basis for selection. Open admission. **Learning Disabled:** Students with learning disabilities referred to counseling office for assistance.

High school preparation. Students with work experience present a letter from their employer indicating domain of knowledge and skills related to program.

2015-2016 Annual costs. Tuition/fees: $6,550. Per-credit charge: $218. Books/supplies: $800.

2015-2016 Financial aid. All financial aid based on need. 225 full-time freshmen applied for aid; 225 deemed to have need; 225 received aid. 98% of total undergraduate aid awarded as scholarships/grants, 2% as loans/jobs.

Need-based aid available for part-time students. Work-study available nights, weekends and for part-time students.

Application procedures. Admission: No deadline. $10 fee, may be waived for applicants with need. Admission notification on a rolling basis. **Financial aid:** No deadline. FAFSA, institutional form required. Applicants notified on a rolling basis.

Academics. Special study options: Accelerated study. Bachelor's degree programs available on campus. **Credit/placement by examination:** AP, CLEP, institutional tests. **Support services:** Learning center, study skills assistance, tutoring.

Majors. Business: Accounting, administrative services, business admin. **Computer sciences:** Computer science. **Health services:** Dental assistant, health information technology, pharmacy assistant, respiratory therapy technology.

Most popular majors. Business/marketing 9%, engineering/engineering technologies 10%, health sciences 67%.

Technology on campus. 50 workstations in library, computer center. Wireless network available.

Student life. Freshman orientation: Mandatory. Preregistration for classes offered. Program held in first 2 weeks of classes.

Student services. Career counseling, student employment services, health services, personal counseling, placement for graduates, veterans' counselor. **Transfer:** Pre-admission transcript evaluation for new students. Transfer adviser for students transferring to 4-year colleges.

Contact. E-mail: admisiones@huertas.edu
Phone: (787) 746-1400 ext. 1101 Fax: (787) 747-0170
Hector Morales, Admissions Coordinator, Huertas College, PO Box 8429, Caguas, PR 00726

Humacao Community College
Humacao, Puerto Rico
www.hccpr.edu

CB code: 2313

▶ Private 2-year business and community college
▶ Commuter campus in small city

General. Founded in 1956. Accredited by ACICS. **Enrollment:** 506 degree-seeking undergraduates; 48 non-degree-seeking students. **Degrees:** 15 bachelor's, 161 associate awarded. **Location:** 42 miles from San Juan. **Calendar:** Trimester, extensive summer session. **Full-time faculty:** 14 total; 7% have terminal degrees, 79% women. **Part-time faculty:** 20 total; 5% have terminal degrees, 35% women. **Class size:** 80% < 20, 19% 20-39, 1% 40-49.

Student profile. Among degree-seeking undergraduates, 108 enrolled as first-time, first-year students.

Part-time:	20%	Hispanic/Latino:	100%
Women:	67%	25 or older:	32%

Transfer out. Colleges most students transferred to 2015: Turabo University, University of Puerto Rico (all campuses), Inter American University of Puerto Rico (all campuses), Huertas Junior College.

Basis for selection. Open admission. **Home schooled:** Transcript of courses and grades, state high school equivalency certificate required.

High school preparation. 15 units recommended. Recommended units include English 3, mathematics 3, social studies 3, science 3 and academic electives 3.

2016-2017 Annual costs. Tuition/fees: $5,382. Books/supplies: $2,644. Personal expenses: $4,018.

2014-2015 Financial aid. All financial aid based on need. 114 full-time freshmen applied for aid; 114 deemed to have need; 114 received aid. Average need met was 100%. Average scholarship/grant was $5,765. 99% of total undergraduate aid awarded as scholarships/grants, 1% as loans/jobs. Need-based aid available for part-time students. Work-study available nights, weekends and for part-time students.

Application procedures. Admission: No deadline. $15 fee. Application must be submitted on paper. Admission notification on a rolling basis. **Financial aid:** Priority date 1/1, closing date 6/30. FAFSA, institutional form required. Applicants notified on a rolling basis starting 3/4; must reply within 2 week(s) of notification.

Academics. **Special study options:** Distance learning. License preparation in dental hygiene. **Credit/placement by examination:** AP, CLEP. 9 credit hours maximum toward associate degree. **Support services:** Learning center, tutoring.

Majors. **Business:** Administrative services, business admin. **Computer sciences:** Information systems. **Health services:** Dental assistant, health information technology, medical secretary, pharmacy assistant.

Most popular majors. Biological/life sciences 9%, business/marketing 45%, computer/information sciences 12%, engineering/engineering technologies 14%, health sciences 20%.

Technology on campus. 242 workstations in library, computer center, student center. Online library, wireless network available.

Student life. **Freshman orientation:** Mandatory. Preregistration for classes offered. **Activities:** Student government.

Student services. Adult student services, alcohol/substance abuse counseling, career counseling, financial aid counseling, personal counseling, placement for graduates, veterans' counselor. **Transfer:** Re-entry adviser, pre-admission transcript evaluation for new students. Transfer adviser for students transferring to 4-year colleges.

Contact. Phone: (787) 285-2525 Fax: (787) 850-1577
Loalis Quiñones, Admissions Official, Humacao Community College, PO Box 9139, Humacao, PR 00792-9139

ICPR Junior College
San Juan, Puerto Rico
www.icprjc.edu

CB member
CB code: 7315

- For-profit 2-year business, junior and career college
- Commuter campus in large city

General. Founded in 1946. Regionally accredited. Multicampus institution with main campus in Hato Rey, extension campus in Bayamón, branch campuses in Arecibo, Mayagüez, and Manatí. **Enrollment:** 2,554 degree-seeking undergraduates. **Degrees:** 69 associate awarded. **Calendar:** Semester, extensive summer session. **Full-time faculty:** 61 total; 75% women. **Part-time faculty:** 5,988 total; 1% women. **Class size:** 80% < 20, 19% 20-39, less than 1% 40-49.

Basis for selection. Open admission. Paper application required. **Home schooled:** Statement describing home school structure and mission, transcript of courses and grades, state high school equivalency certificate required.

High school preparation. Recommended units include English 4, mathematics 4, social studies 4, history 4, science 4 (laboratory 4), foreign language 4, computer science 4, visual/performing arts 4 and academic electives 4.

2015-2016 Annual costs. Books/supplies: $1,956. Personal expenses: $600. **Additional information:** Tuition for Nursing Program, Medical Sonography, Culinary Arts, and Pharmacy is $6,809. Tuition for other programs is $6,450.

2015-2016 Financial aid. **Need-based:** 75% of total undergraduate aid awarded as scholarships/grants, 25% as loans/jobs. Need-based aid available for part-time students. Work-study available nights, weekends and for part-time students. **Non-need-based:** Scholarships awarded for academics, state residency.

Application procedures. **Admission:** No deadline. No application fee. Application must be submitted on paper. Admission notification on a rolling basis. **Financial aid:** Closing date 6/14. FAFSA, institutional form required. Applicants notified on a rolling basis starting 11/15.

Academics. **Special study options:** Independent study. **Credit/placement by examination:** AP, CLEP. **Support services:** Tutoring.

Majors. **Business:** Accounting, administrative services, business admin, hotel/motel admin, management information systems, marketing, office technology, tourism/travel. **Computer sciences:** General, applications programming. **Health services:** Medical secretary, nursing (RN), sonography. **Protective services:** Forensics.

Most popular majors. Computer/information sciences 34%, health sciences 34%.

Technology on campus. 500 workstations in library, computer center, student center. Wireless network available.

Student life. **Freshman orientation:** Available. Preregistration for classes offered.

Student services. Alcohol/substance abuse counseling, career counseling, services for economically disadvantaged, student employment services, financial aid counseling, personal counseling, placement for graduates, veterans' counselor. **Physically disabled:** Services for hearing impaired. **Transfer:** Re-entry adviser, pre-admission transcript evaluation for new students.

Contact. E-mail: kgutierrez@icprjc.edu
Phone: (787) 753-6335 ext. 4101 Toll-free number: (787) 751-4277
Fax: (787) 763-7249
Katiria Gutierrez, Marketing Manager, ICPR Junior College, PO Box 190304, San Juan, PR 00919-0304

Ponce Paramedical College
Coto Laurel, Puerto Rico
www.popac.edu

- For-profit 2-year health science and career college
- Small city

General. Accredited by ACCSC. **Enrollment:** 2,607 undergraduates. **Degrees:** 277 associate awarded. **Calendar:** Continuous, extensive summer session. **Full-time faculty:** 70 total. **Part-time faculty:** 168 total.

Basis for selection. Open admission. **Home schooled:** Transcript of courses and grades, state high school equivalency certificate, interview required.

Financial aid. **Need-based:** Work-study available nights, weekends and for part-time students.

Application procedures. **Admission:** No deadline. $25 fee. Admission notification on a rolling basis. **Financial aid:** No deadline.

Academics. **Credit/placement by examination:** AP, CLEP. **Support services:** Tutoring.

Majors. **Health services:** Nursing (RN), respiratory therapy technology.

Technology on campus. Online library available.

Student life. **Freshman orientation:** Available. Preregistration for classes offered. **Activities:** Student newspaper.

Athletics. **Team name:** POPAC.

Student services. Financial aid counseling, health services, personal counseling, placement for graduates.

Contact. E-mail: admisiones@popac.edu
Phone: (787) 848-1589 ext. 413 Toll-free number: (800) 981-7184
Carlos Torres, Director of Admissions, Ponce Paramedical College, Calle Acacia 1213, Urb. Villa Flores, Ponce, PR 00780-0106

Universal Technology College of Puerto Rico
Aguadilla, Puerto Rico
www.unitecpr.edu

- Private 2-year health science and career college
- Commuter campus in small city

General. Accredited by ACCSC. **Enrollment:** 1,260 undergraduates. **Degrees:** 60 bachelor's, 169 associate awarded. **Calendar:** Semester, limited summer session. **Full-time faculty:** 22 total. **Part-time faculty:** 57 total. **Class size:** 10% < 20, 90% 20-39. **Special facilities:** Art gallery, peace gallery (commemorating winners of Nobel Prize).

Basis for selection. Open admission. **Home schooled:** State high school equivalency certificate required.

2015-2016 Annual costs. Books/supplies: $450. Personal expenses: $250.

Financial aid. All financial aid based on need. Need-based aid available for part-time students. Work-study available nights, weekends and for part-time students.

Application procedures. Admission: No deadline. $20 fee. Application must be submitted on paper. Admission notification on a rolling basis. **Financial aid:** Priority date 4/30, closing date 6/30. FAFSA, institutional form required. Applicants notified on a rolling basis starting 2/1; must reply by 6/30.

Academics. Special study options: Weekend college. License preparation in nursing, paramedic. **Credit/placement by examination:** AP, CLEP. **Support services:** Reduced course load, study skills assistance, tutoring.

Majors. Business: Administrative services. **Computer sciences:** Programming. **Health services:** Nursing (RN).

Most popular majors. Business/marketing 30%, health sciences 70%.

Student life. Freshman orientation: Mandatory. Preregistration for classes offered. **Activities:** Student newspaper.

Athletics. Team name: Delfines.

Student services. Financial aid counseling, on-campus daycare, placement for graduates, veterans' counselor. **Transfer:** Re-entry adviser, pre-admission transcript evaluation for new students.

Contact. E-mail: admisiones@unitecpr.net
Phone: (787) 882-2065 ext. 308
Toll-free number: (188) 864-8322 ext. 308 Fax: (787) 891-2370
Teresita Rivera, Admissions Coordinator, Universal Technology College of Puerto Rico, Apartado 1955, Victoria Station, Aguadilla, PR 00605

Rhode Island

Community College of Rhode Island
Warwick, Rhode Island   **CB member**
www.ccri.edu   **CB code: 3733**

▸ Public 2-year community college
▸ Commuter campus in small city

General. Founded in 1964. Regionally accredited. Additional campuses in Lincoln, Providence, and Newport. Several satellite locations. **Enrollment:** 15,255 degree-seeking undergraduates; 940 non-degree-seeking students. **Degrees:** 1,645 associate awarded. **ROTC:** Army. **Location:** 10 miles from Providence. **Calendar:** Semester, extensive summer session. **Full-time faculty:** 327 total. **Part-time faculty:** 496 total. **Class size:** 49% < 20, 51% 20-39, less than 1% 50-99. **Special facilities:** Observatory.

Student profile. Among degree-seeking undergraduates, 2,941 enrolled as first-time, first-year students, 475 transferred in from other institutions.

Part-time:	69%	Asian American:	3%
Out-of-state:	4%	Hispanic/Latino:	20%
Women:	59%	Multi-racial, non-Hispanic:	5%
African American:	9%	25 or older:	38%

Transfer out. Colleges most students transferred to 2015: Rhode Island College, University of Rhode Island, New England Institute of Technology, Johnson and Wales University, Roger Williams University, Bryant University.

Basis for selection. Open admission, but selective for some programs. Placement testing in mathematics and English required; testing in chemistry may be required for programs with limited enrollment. **Adult students:** SAT/ACT scores not required.

High school preparation. College-preparatory program required. Some programs may require mathematics and science background. Special considerations for nursing and allied health applicants.

2015-2016 Annual costs. Tuition/fees: $4,266; $11,496 out-of-state. Per-credit charge: $180 in-state; $534 out-of-state. Books/supplies: $1,200. Personal expenses: $3,070.

Financial aid. Need-based: Need-based aid available for part-time students. Work-study available nights, weekends and for part-time students. **Non-need-based:** Scholarships awarded for athletics.

Application procedures. Admission: No deadline. $20 fee, may be waived for applicants with need, free for online applicants. Admission notification on a rolling basis beginning on or about 1/1. Application closing date and admitted student reply deadline is the first week of fall semester in September and first week of spring semester in January. After the first week of each semester, applicants are processed for the following semester. **Financial aid:** Priority date 3/1, closing date 7/1. FAFSA, institutional form required. Applicants notified on a rolling basis starting 5/1; must reply within 2 week(s) of notification.

Academics. Special study options: Cooperative education, cross-registration, distance learning, double major, dual enrollment of high school students, ESL, honors, independent study, internships, study abroad, weekend college. License preparation in dental hygiene, nursing, occupational therapy, physical therapy, radiology, real estate. **Credit/placement by examination:** AP, CLEP. 30 credit hours maximum toward associate degree. **Support services:** GED preparation and test center, learning center, reduced course load, remedial instruction, study skills assistance, tutoring, writing center.

Majors. Business: General, accounting, administrative services, banking/financial services, business admin, marketing. **Computer sciences:** General, applications programming, networking, support specialist, webmaster. **Education:** Kindergarten/preschool, special ed. **Engineering:** General, mechanical, surveying. **Health services:** Clinical lab technology, dental hygiene, histologic assistant, massage therapy, medical secretary, mental health counseling, nursing (RN), occupational therapy assistant, optician, physical therapy assistant, radiologic technology/medical imaging, respiratory therapy technology, sonography, substance abuse counseling. **Human services:** Social work. **Liberal arts:** Arts/sciences. **Protective services:** Disaster management, firefighting, police science. **Visual/performing arts:** Art, dramatic, jazz, music. **Work/family studies:** Aging.

Most popular majors. Business/marketing 10%, health sciences 25%, liberal arts 47%, security/protective services 6%.

Technology on campus. 1,200 workstations in library, computer center, student center. Commuter students can connect to campus network. Online course registration, online library, helpline, wireless network available.

Student life. Freshman orientation: Mandatory. Preregistration for classes offered. **Activities:** Bands, choral groups, dance, drama, international student organizations, music ensembles, student government, student newspaper, TV station, Black American student association, Latin American student organization, Spanish club, Asian club, Christian club, American Sign Language club & deaf students union, Bible study club, cultural alliance club, Muslim student association, Students for Environmental Action.

Athletics. NJCAA. **Intercollegiate:** Baseball M, basketball, cross-country, golf, soccer, softball W, tennis, track and field, volleyball W. **Intramural:** Table tennis. **Team name:** Knights.

Student services. Adult student services, alcohol/substance abuse counseling, career counseling, services for economically disadvantaged, student employment services, financial aid counseling, health services, minority student services, on-campus daycare, personal counseling, placement for graduates, veterans' counselor, women's services. **Physically disabled:** Services for visually, speech, hearing impaired. **Transfer:** Re-entry adviser, pre-admission transcript evaluation for new students. Transfer adviser, college fairs on campus for students transferring to 4-year colleges.

Contact. E-mail: webadmission@ccri.edu
Phone: (401) 825-2003 Fax: (401) 825-2394
Terri Kless, Director of Admissions, Community College of Rhode Island, 400 East Avenue, Warwick, RI 02886-1807

South Carolina

Two-Year Colleges

Aiken Technical College
Aiken, South Carolina
www.atc.edu   CB code: 5037

▸ Public 2-year community and technical college
▸ Commuter campus in small city

General. Founded in 1972. Regionally accredited. **Enrollment:** 2,259 degree-seeking undergraduates. **Degrees:** 249 associate awarded. **Location:** 9 miles from Aiken, 12 miles from Augusta, Georgia. **Calendar:** Semester, extensive summer session. **Full-time faculty:** 57 total. **Part-time faculty:** 143 total. **Class size:** 71% < 20, 28% 20-39, less than 1% 40-49. **Special facilities:** Center for energy and advanced manufacturing, manufacturing and technology training center.

Student profile. Among degree-seeking undergraduates, 169 transferred in from other institutions.

Out-of-state: 14%   **25 or older:**   41%

Transfer out. Colleges most students transferred to 2015: Augusta State University, Lander University, University of South Carolina.

Basis for selection. Open admission, but selective for some programs. Test scores considered if submitted. Special requirements for all health programs. **Adult students:** SAT/ACT scores not required. COMPASS is Required, no SAT or ACT required.

2015-2016 Annual costs. Tuition/fees: $5,246; $5,696 out-of-district; $8,020 out-of-state. Per-credit charge: $164 in-district; $179 out-of-district; $254 out-of-state. Books/supplies: $1,000. Personal expenses: $3,000.

Financial aid. Need-based: Need-based aid available for part-time students. Work-study available nights, weekends and for part-time students. **Non-need-based:** Scholarships awarded for academics, leadership, minority status, state residency.

Application procedures. Admission: Priority date 7/1; no deadline. No application fee. Admission notification on a rolling basis. **Financial aid:** Priority date 6/1, closing date 7/1. FAFSA required. Applicants notified on a rolling basis starting 4/1; must reply within 2 week(s) of notification.

Academics. Special study options: Accelerated study, cooperative education, cross-registration, distance learning, double major, dual enrollment of high school students, independent study, internships, liberal arts/career combination. License preparation in nursing, radiology. **Credit/placement by examination:** AP, CLEP, institutional tests. **Support services:** Learning center, pre-admission summer program, reduced course load, remedial instruction, study skills assistance, tutoring, writing center. Tutorial assistance to students through open labs, individual and group tutoring, and software programs.

Majors. Business: Accounting, administrative services, business admin, sales/distribution. **Computer sciences:** Data processing, system admin. **Engineering:** Computer, electrical. **Health services:** Medical radiologic technology/radiation therapy, nursing (RN). **Liberal arts:** Arts/sciences. **Protective services:** Criminal justice. **Work/family studies:** Child care management.

Most popular majors. Business/marketing 10%, computer/information sciences 7%, health sciences 33%, interdisciplinary studies 10%, liberal arts 22%, security/protective services 6%, trade and industry 6%.

Technology on campus. 879 workstations in library, computer center, student center. Online course registration, online library, helpline, repair service, wireless network available.

Student life. Freshman orientation: Available. Preregistration for classes offered. Online orientation available. **Policies:** Student Honor Code represents a standard of conduct to which each student should aspire. **Activities:** Campus ministries, student government, Phi Theta Kappa Honor Society.

Student services. Adult student services, career counseling, services for economically disadvantaged, student employment services, financial aid counseling, minority student services, personal counseling, placement for graduates, veterans' counselor. **Physically disabled:** Services for visually, speech, hearing impaired. **Transfer:** Pre-admission transcript evaluation for new students. Transfer adviser, college fairs on campus for students transferring to 4-year colleges.

Contact. Phone: (803) 593-9954 ext. 1247 Fax: (803) 593-6526 Jessica Moon, Director of Admissions and Records, Aiken Technical College, PO Drawer 696, Aiken, SC 29802

Central Carolina Technical College
Sumter, South Carolina
www.cctech.edu   CB code: 5665

▸ Public 2-year community and technical college
▸ Commuter campus in large town

General. Founded in 1963. Regionally accredited. Branch campuses in Clarendon, Kershaw, and Lee Counties. Additional facility located at Shaw Air Force Base. **Enrollment:** 4,300 degree-seeking undergraduates. **Degrees:** 351 associate awarded. **Location:** 45 miles from Columbia. **Calendar:** Semester, extensive summer session. **Full-time faculty:** 100 total. **Part-time faculty:** 136 total. **Special facilities:** South Carolina Environmental Training Center.

Transfer out. Colleges most students transferred to 2015: University of South Carolina, Clemson University, Lander University, Limestone College, Francis Marion University.

Basis for selection. Open admission, but selective for some programs. Test scores required for placement. Associate degree nursing program: 74 TEAS. LPN program: 67 TEAS. Interview required for nursing program.

High school preparation. Required units include English 4, mathematics 4, social studies 1, history 1, science 3, foreign language 1, computer science 1 and academic electives 7. Economics .5, US Government .5.

2015-2016 Annual costs. Tuition/fees: $4,950; $5,790 out-of-district; $8,460 out-of-state. Per-credit charge: $165 in-district; $193 out-of-district; $282 out-of-state. Books/supplies: $1,100. Personal expenses: $1,030.

Financial aid. Need-based: Need-based aid available for part-time students. Work-study available nights, weekends and for part-time students.

Application procedures. Admission: No deadline. No application fee. Admission notification on a rolling basis. **Financial aid:** No deadline. FAFSA required. Applicants notified on a rolling basis starting 4/11; must reply within 2 week(s) of notification.

Academics. Special study options: Distance learning, dual enrollment of high school students, weekend college. License preparation in nursing, paramedic. **Credit/placement by examination:** AP, CLEP, IB, institutional tests. **Support services:** Remedial instruction, study skills assistance, tutoring, writing center.

Majors. Business: Accounting, administrative services, management science. **Computer sciences:** Programming. **Conservation:** Management/policy. **Health services:** Nursing (RN), surgical technology. **Liberal arts:** Arts/sciences.

Most popular majors. Business/marketing 22%, computer/information sciences 7%, family/consumer sciences 8%, health sciences 28%, liberal arts 14%, security/protective services 6%.

Technology on campus. 125 workstations in library, computer center. Commuter students can connect to campus network. Online course registration, online library, helpline available.

Student life. Freshman orientation: Available. Preregistration for classes offered. **Activities:** Phi Theta Kappa, Earth club, computer club.

Student services. Career counseling, services for economically disadvantaged, student employment services, financial aid counseling, personal counseling, placement for graduates, veterans' counselor, women's services. **Physically disabled:** Services for visually, speech, hearing impaired. **Transfer:** Pre-admission transcript evaluation for new students. College fairs on campus for students transferring to 4-year colleges.

Contact. E-mail: admissions@cctech.edu
Phone: (803) 778-6605 Toll-free number: (800) 221-8711 ext. 205
Fax: (803) 778-6696
Barbara Wright, Director of Admissions and Student Services, Central Carolina Technical College, 506 North Guignard Drive, Sumter, SC 29150-2499

Clinton College
Rock Hill, South Carolina
https://clintoncollege.edu/

CB code: 5743

♦ Private 2-year junior and liberal arts college
♦ Residential campus in small city

General. Regionally accredited; also accredited by TRACS. **Enrollment:** 184 degree-seeking undergraduates. **Degrees:** 2 bachelor's, 22 associate awarded. **Calendar:** Semester. **Full-time faculty:** 9 total. **Part-time faculty:** 30 total.

Student profile.

Out-of-state:	10%	Live on campus:	90%
25 or older:	4%		

Basis for selection. Open admission. **Home schooled:** Statement describing home school structure and mission, transcript of courses and grades required.

2015-2016 Annual costs. Tuition/fees: $6,751. Per-credit charge: $400. Room/board: $9,551. Books/supplies: $1,200. **Additional information:** Off-campus residents pay $400 less in fees.

Financial aid. All financial aid based on need. Need-based aid available for part-time students. Work-study available nights, weekends and for part-time students.

Application procedures. Admission: No deadline. $25 fee. Institutional placement test given after enrollment. **Financial aid:** No deadline. FAFSA required.

Academics. Credit/placement by examination: AP, CLEP.

Majors. Business: General. **Education:** Early childhood. **Liberal arts:** Arts/sciences. **Physical sciences:** General. **Theology:** Bible.

Student life. Activities: Choral groups, student government.

Athletics. NJCAA. **Intercollegiate:** Basketball M. **Team name:** Golden Bulls.

Contact. E-mail: rcopeland@clintonjuniorcollege.edu
Phone: (803) 327-7402 ext. 242
Robert Copeland, Vice President for Student Affairs, Clinton College, 1029 Crawford Road, Rock Hill, SC 29730

Denmark Technical College
Denmark, South Carolina
www.denmarktech.edu

CB code: 5744

♦ Public 2-year technical college
♦ Residential campus in small town

General. Founded in 1948. Regionally accredited. **Enrollment:** 988 degree-seeking undergraduates. **Degrees:** 90 associate awarded. **Location:** 55 miles from Columbia. **Calendar:** Semester, extensive summer session. **Full-time faculty:** 35 total. **Part-time faculty:** 15 total.

Student profile.

Out-of-state:	4%	Hispanic/Latino:	1%
African American:	92%	Live on campus:	33%

Basis for selection. Open admission. Interview recommended.

High school preparation. Recommended units include English 4, mathematics 4, social studies 2, science 2 and foreign language 2. College preparatory program required for AA and AS transfer college programs.

2015-2016 Annual costs. Tuition/fees: $3,486; $6,756 out-of-state. Room/board: $3,858. Books/supplies: $1,100.

Financial aid. Need-based: Need-based aid available for part-time students. Work-study available nights, weekends and for part-time students.

Application procedures. Admission: No deadline. $10 fee, may be waived for applicants with need. Admission notification on a rolling basis. **Financial aid:** No deadline. FAFSA required. Applicants notified on a rolling basis starting 6/1; must reply within 2 week(s) of notification.

Academics. Special study options: Cooperative education, cross-registration, independent study, internships. License preparation in nursing.

Credit/placement by examination: AP, CLEP, institutional tests. **Support services:** GED preparation, learning center, reduced course load, remedial instruction, tutoring.

Majors. Business: General. **Liberal arts:** Arts/sciences.

Technology on campus. 85 workstations in library, computer center. Dormitories wired for high-speed internet access and linked to campus network. Commuter students can connect to campus network. Wireless network available.

Student life. Freshman orientation: Mandatory. Preregistration for classes offered. **Housing:** Single-sex dorms available. **Activities:** Choral groups, student government, student newspaper, Student Christian Association.

Athletics. Intercollegiate: Basketball. **Intramural:** Basketball. **Team name:** Panthers, Lady Panthers.

Student services. Career counseling, student employment services, health services, personal counseling, placement for graduates, veterans' counselor. **Transfer:** College fairs on campus for students transferring to 4-year colleges.

Contact. E-mail: braileyc@denmarktech.edu
Phone: (803) 793-5176 Fax: (803) 793-5290
Crystal Brailey, Director of Admissions, Denmark Technical College, 1126 Solomon Blatt Boulevard, Denmark, SC 29042

Florence-Darlington Technical College
Florence, South Carolina
www.fdtc.edu

CB code: 5207

♦ Public 2-year community and technical college
♦ Commuter campus in small city

General. Founded in 1964. Regionally accredited. Campus houses Southeastern Institute of Manufacturing and Technology, which provides engineering/CAD/CAM, rapid prototyping, and 3D/virtual reality services as well as manufacturing workforce development and business process training. **Enrollment:** 6,214 degree-seeking undergraduates. **Degrees:** 499 associate awarded. **Location:** 80 miles from Columbia, 50 miles from Myrtle Beach. **Calendar:** Semester, extensive summer session. **Full-time faculty:** 244 total. **Part-time faculty:** 239 total. **Partnerships:** Formal partnerships with local, regional, and national corporations which enhance student opportunities for training.

Transfer out. Colleges most students transferred to 2015: Francis Marion University, Clemson University, University of South Carolina.

Basis for selection. Open admission, but selective for some programs. Computerized Placement Test administered as alternative to SAT/ACT for placement for most programs. NLN, HOAE or HOBET required for some allied health programs. **Home schooled:** GED may be required.

High school preparation. Algebra I, algebra II, biology, and chemistry required for most health programs.

2015-2016 Annual costs. Tuition/fees: $5,060; $5,390 out-of-district; $7,670 out-of-state. Per-credit charge: $163 in-district; $174 out-of-district; $250 out-of-state. Books/supplies: $900. Personal expenses: $2,338.

Financial aid. Need-based: Need-based aid available for part-time students. Work-study available nights, weekends and for part-time students. **Non-need-based:** Scholarships awarded for academics.

Application procedures. Admission: Priority date 7/15; no deadline. No application fee. Admission notification on a rolling basis beginning on or about 1/1. **Financial aid:** Priority date 5/1; no closing date. FAFSA required. Applicants notified on a rolling basis starting 7/1; must reply within 2 week(s) of notification.

Academics. Special study options: Cooperative education, cross-registration, distance learning, double major, dual enrollment of high school students, independent study, internships, liberal arts/career combination. Cooperative program with Greenville Technical College for physical therapy, Fayetteville Technical College for funeral services. License preparation in dental hygiene, nursing, physical therapy. **Credit/placement by examination:** AP, CLEP, IB, institutional tests. Student may receive credit for up to 50% of the course work required by his or her major. **Support services:** GED preparation, learning center, pre-admission summer program, reduced course load, remedial instruction, study skills assistance, tutoring, writing center.

Majors. Business: Accounting, administrative services, entrepreneurial studies, sales/distribution. **Computer sciences:** Data processing. **Education:** Voc/tech. **Health services:** Clinical lab technology, dental hygiene, health information technology, medical radiologic technology/radiation therapy, nursing (RN), physical therapy assistant, respiratory therapy technology. **Human services:** Social work. **Liberal arts:** Arts/sciences. **Physical sciences:** General. **Protective services:** Criminal justice.

Technology on campus. 128 workstations in library, computer center. Commuter students can connect to campus network. Online course registration, wireless network available.

Student life. Freshman orientation: Available. Preregistration for classes offered. **Activities:** Campus ministries, music ensembles, student government, student newspaper.

Athletics. NJCAA. **Intercollegiate:** Baseball M, softball W. **Team name:** Stingers.

Student services. Career counseling, services for economically disadvantaged, student employment services, financial aid counseling, on-campus daycare, personal counseling, placement for graduates, veterans' counselor. **Physically disabled:** Services for hearing impaired. **Transfer:** Transfer adviser for students transferring to 4-year colleges.

Contact. E-mail: admissions@fdtc.edu
Phone: (843) 661-8324 Toll-free number: (800) 228-5745
Fax: (843) 661-8041
Maggie Gause, Director of Admissions, Florence-Darlington Technical College, PO Box 100548, Florence, SC 29501-0548

Forrest Junior College
Anderson, South Carolina
www.forrestcollege.edu
CB code: 7138

- For-profit 2-year business college
- Commuter campus in large town
- Application essay, interview required

General. Accredited by ACICS. Majority of students are working adults with children. Free child care provided. **Enrollment:** 86 degree-seeking undergraduates. **Degrees:** 28 associate awarded. **Location:** 30 miles from Greenville. **Calendar:** Quarter, extensive summer session. **Full-time faculty:** 6 total; 50% minority, 50% women. **Part-time faculty:** 24 total; 4% have terminal degrees, 42% minority, 50% women. **Class size:** 91% < 20, 9% 20-39.

Student profile. Among degree-seeking undergraduates, 10 transferred in from other institutions.

Transfer out. Colleges most students transferred to 2015: Greenville Technical College, Piedmont Technical College, Lander University, Strayer University, Webster University.

Basis for selection. Open admission, but selective for some programs. Special program requirements will vary depending upon the area of study. Each applicant is given individual consideration for admission. Audition, portfolio recommended. **Home schooled:** Transcript of courses and grades, state high school equivalency certificate required.

High school preparation. College-preparatory program required. Just need a high school diploma and GED from accredited high school.

2016-2017 Annual costs. Tuition/fees (projected): $9,195. Per-credit charge: $245. Books/supplies: $1,575. Personal expenses: $2,187.

2014-2015 Financial aid. All financial aid based on need. 16 full-time freshmen applied for aid; 16 deemed to have need; 16 received aid. Average need met was 90%. Average loan was $3,500. Need-based aid available for part-time students. Work-study available nights, weekends and for part-time students.

Application procedures. Admission: No deadline. $50 fee. Admission notification on a rolling basis. **Financial aid:** No deadline. FAFSA required. Applicants notified on a rolling basis starting 4/30; must reply by 5/31 or within 4 week(s) of notification.

Academics. Special study options: Double major, independent study, internships, liberal arts/career combination, weekend college. **Credit/placement by examination:** AP, CLEP, institutional tests. **Support services:** GED preparation, reduced course load, remedial instruction, study skills assistance, tutoring.

Majors. Business: General, accounting, administrative services, business admin, communications, human resources, managerial economics, marketing, office management, office technology, office/clerical. **Computer sciences:** General, information systems. **Education:** Early childhood, sales/marketing, teacher assistance. **Health services:** Clinical lab assistant, clinical lab technology, health information management, health information technology, medical assistant, medical secretary, medical transcription. **Work/family studies:** Child care management.

Most popular majors. Business/marketing 11%, health sciences 79%, security/protective services 11%.

Technology on campus. PC or laptop required. 52 workstations in library, computer center. Online library, repair service available.

Student life. Freshman orientation: Mandatory. Preregistration for classes offered. **Activities:** Literary magazine, student government, student newspaper.

Student services. Adult student services, career counseling, student employment services, financial aid counseling, on-campus daycare, placement for graduates. **Transfer:** Pre-admission transcript evaluation for new students.

Contact. E-mail: candacebentley@forrestcollege.edu
Phone: (864) 225-7653 ext. 2201 Fax: (864) 261-7471
Janie Turmon, Admissions Officer, Forrest Junior College, 601 East River Street, Anderson, SC 29624

Golf Academy of America: Myrtle Beach
Myrtle Beach, South Carolina
www.golfacademy.edu
CB code: 3223

- For-profit 2-year golf academy
- Large town

General. Accredited by ACICS. **Enrollment:** 130 degree-seeking undergraduates. **Degrees:** 180 associate awarded. **Calendar:** Differs by program. **Full-time faculty:** 10 total. **Part-time faculty:** 7 total.

Basis for selection. Open admission.

2015-2016 Annual costs. Tuition/fees: $17,150. Personal expenses: $1,552.

Financial aid. Need-based: Work-study available nights, weekends and for part-time students.

Application procedures. Admission: No deadline. $50 fee.

Academics. Credit/placement by examination: AP, CLEP.

Majors. Parks/recreation: Golf management.

Contact. E-mail: myrtlebeach.info@golfacademy.edu
Phone: (480) 236-0481 Toll-free number: (800) 342-7342
Fax: (480) 905-8705
Valerie Pimentel, Admissions Director, Golf Academy of America: Myrtle Beach, 7373 North Scottsdale Road, Suite B-100, Scottsdale, AZ 82253

Greenville Technical College
Greenville, South Carolina
www.gvltec.edu
CB code: 5278

- Public 2-year community and technical college
- Commuter campus in large city

General. Founded in 1962. Regionally accredited. Classes and some programs offered at satellite campuses in Greenville County. **Enrollment:** 10,929 degree-seeking undergraduates; 1,351 non-degree-seeking students. **Degrees:** 1,214 associate awarded. **ROTC:** Army. **Calendar:** Semester, extensive summer session. **Full-time faculty:** 341 total; 11% have terminal degrees, 14% minority, 61% women. **Part-time faculty:** 476 total; 9% have terminal degrees, 16% minority, 61% women.

Student profile. Among degree-seeking undergraduates, 2,241 enrolled as first-time, first-year students.

| Part-time: | 56% | Women: | 59% |
| Out-of-state: | 1% | Live on campus: | 3% |

Transfer out. 75% of students enrolled in the transfer program go on to 4-year colleges.

Basis for selection. Open admission, but selective for some programs. Weighted admissions requirements for registered nursing, licensed practical nursing, certain allied health programs. Interview required for allied health sciences, nursing, photography, and aircraft mechanic applicants and recommended for all others. Portfolio required for visual arts program. **Home schooled:** Applicants who are members of a South Carolina Home School Association must provide a current copy of membership card. **Learning Disabled:** Contact Student Disability Services early in admission process for appropriate accommodations. Self-identification and documentation required.

High school preparation. College-preparatory program recommended. Algebra, biology, and chemistry are required for most health care program applicants.

2015-2016 Annual costs. Tuition/fees: $5,220; $5,670 out-of-district; $10,500 out-of-state. Books/supplies: $1,110. Personal expenses: $745.

2014-2015 Financial aid. **Need-based:** 53% of total undergraduate aid awarded as scholarships/grants, 47% as loans/jobs. Need-based aid available for part-time students. Work-study available nights, weekends and for part-time students. **Non-need-based:** Scholarships awarded for academics, state residency.

Application procedures. **Admission:** Closing date 8/1. $35 fee. Admission notification on a rolling basis. **Financial aid:** Priority date 5/1; no closing date. FAFSA required. Applicants notified on a rolling basis starting 5/1; must reply within 2 week(s) of notification.

Academics. **Special study options:** Accelerated study, cooperative education, distance learning, dual enrollment of high school students, ESL, honors, independent study, internships, liberal arts/career combination, teacher certification program, weekend college. License preparation in aviation, dental hygiene, nursing, occupational therapy, paramedic, physical therapy, radiology, real estate. **Credit/placement by examination:** AP, CLEP, IB, institutional tests. Department heads require portfolio for prior learning through work experience. **Support services:** Learning center, reduced course load, remedial instruction, study skills assistance, tutoring, writing center.

Honors college/program. Require 3.5 GPA and interview with head of department.

Majors. **Business:** Accounting, administrative services, business admin, purchasing, sales/distribution. **Computer sciences:** Data processing. **Health services:** Clinical lab technology, dental hygiene, EMT paramedic, health information technology, medical radiologic technology/radiation therapy, nursing (RN), occupational therapy assistant, physical therapy assistant, respiratory therapy technology, sonography. **Liberal arts:** Arts/sciences. **Protective services:** Criminal justice, firefighting. **Work/family studies:** Child care management.

Most popular majors. Business/marketing 13%, computer/information sciences 6%, engineering/engineering technologies 7%, health sciences 26%, liberal arts 26%.

Technology on campus. 856 workstations in library, computer center. Dormitories wired for high-speed internet access. Commuter students can connect to campus network. Online course registration, online library, helpline, wireless network available.

Student life. Freshman orientation: Mandatory. Preregistration for classes offered. **Housing:** Coed dorms, special housing for disabled available. $150 nonrefundable deposit. College-affiliated housing available on Barton campus. **Activities:** Campus ministries, choral groups, drama, international student organizations, student government, student newspaper, Baptist collegiate ministry, human services organization, Spanish club, National Technical Honor Society, Phi Theta Kappa, ROTARACT, Tech Warriors, Associated General Contractors, International Association of Administrative Professionals.

Athletics. Intramural: Badminton, basketball, bowling, football (nontackle), softball, table tennis, tennis, volleyball.

Student services. Adult student services, alcohol/substance abuse counseling, chaplain/spiritual director, career counseling, services for economically disadvantaged, student employment services, financial aid counseling, on-campus daycare, personal counseling, placement for graduates, veterans' counselor. **Physically disabled:** Services for visually, speech, hearing impaired. **Transfer:** Re-entry adviser, pre-admission transcript evaluation for new students. Transfer adviser for students transferring to 4-year colleges.

Contact. E-mail: greenvilletech@gvltec.edu
Phone: (864) 250-8000 Toll-free number: (800) 922-1183
Fax: (864) 250-8534
Carolyn Watkins, Dean of Admissions, Greenville Technical College, PO Box 5616, Greenville, SC 29606-5616

Horry-Georgetown Technical College
Conway, South Carolina
www.hgtc.edu   CB code: 5305

▸ Public 2-year community and technical college
▸ Commuter campus in large town

General. Founded in 1965. Regionally accredited. **Enrollment:** 6,354 degree-seeking undergraduates; 743 non-degree-seeking students. **Degrees:** 1,141 associate awarded. **Location:** 4 miles from Conway, 8 miles from Myrtle Beach. **Calendar:** Semester, extensive summer session. **Full-time faculty:** 155 total. **Part-time faculty:** 312 total. **Special facilities:** Golf course, culinary arts center, wildlife pavilion.

Student profile. Among degree-seeking undergraduates, 1,035 enrolled as first-time, first-year students.

Part-time:	53%	Women:	64%
Out-of-state:	4%	25 or older:	46%

Transfer out. Colleges most students transferred to 2015: Coastal Carolina University, Francis Marion University, University of South Carolina.

Basis for selection. Open admission, but selective for some programs. Special requirements and background checks for engineering technology, all health science programs, early care and education, human services, cosmetology, aesthetics, massage therapy, and nail technician. **Adult students:** COMPASS Placement test for any student who has not had college level English and/or math, and does not have current SAT/ACT. **Home schooled:** Homeschooled Students must have written permission from the state affiliation or local school district.

2015-2016 Annual costs. Tuition/fees: $3,960; $4,902 out-of-district; $6,918 out-of-state. Per-credit charge: $154 in-district; $193 out-of-district; $278 out-of-state. Books/supplies: $1,600. Personal expenses: $1,615.

2014-2015 Financial aid. **Need-based:** 61% of total undergraduate aid awarded as scholarships/grants, 39% as loans/jobs. Need-based aid available for part-time students. Work-study available nights, weekends and for part-time students. **Non-need-based:** Scholarships awarded for academics, state residency. **Additional information:** Participates in South Carolina lottery tuition assistance program. Full-time technical college students who are state residents receive assistance for tuition not covered by federal or need-based grants.

Application procedures. **Admission:** No deadline. $30 fee ($30 out-of-state), may be waived for applicants with need. Admission notification on a rolling basis. **Financial aid:** Priority date 4/1, closing date 6/30. FAFSA required. Applicants notified on a rolling basis starting 4/1.

Academics. **Special study options:** Accelerated study, distance learning, double major, dual enrollment of high school students, exchange student, independent study, internships. License preparation in dental hygiene, nursing, paramedic, radiology, real estate. **Credit/placement by examination:** AP, CLEP, IB, institutional tests. **Support services:** Learning center, reduced course load, remedial instruction, study skills assistance, tutoring, writing center.

Majors. **Business:** General, accounting, administrative services, hotel/motel admin. **Computer sciences:** Data processing. **Conservation:** Forest technology. **Education:** Voc/tech. **Engineering:** Electrical. **Health services:** Dental hygiene, EMT paramedic, medical radiologic technology/radiation therapy, nursing (RN), pharmacy assistant. **Human services:** Social work. **Liberal arts:** Arts/sciences. **Parks/recreation:** Golf management. **Protective services:** Criminal justice. **Visual/performing arts:** Design. **Work/family studies:** Child care management.

Most popular majors. Business/marketing 16%, engineering/engineering technologies 6%, family/consumer sciences 11%, health sciences 26%, liberal arts 17%, security/protective services 6%.

Technology on campus. 1,000 workstations in library, computer center, student center. Commuter students can connect to campus network. Online course registration, online library, helpline, wireless network available.

Student life. Freshman orientation: Available. Preregistration for classes offered. **Activities:** Choral groups.

Student services. Career counseling, student employment services, financial aid counseling, on-campus daycare, personal counseling, placement for graduates, veterans' counselor. **Transfer:** Transfer adviser for students transferring to 4-year colleges.

Contact. E-mail: admissions@hgtc.edu
Phone: (843) 349-5277 ext. 5277 Fax: (843) 349-7501
Thyssene Frederick, Director of Student Recruitment and Admissions, Horry-Georgetown Technical College, PO Box 261966, Conway, SC 29528-6066

Midlands Technical College
Columbia, South Carolina
www.midlandstech.edu

CB member
CB code: 5584

- Public 2-year community and technical college
- Commuter campus in large city

General. Founded in 1974. Regionally accredited. Campuses include Airport Campus, Beltline Campus, Batesburg-Leesville Center, Northeast/Enterprise Campus, Fort Jackson, and Harbison Campus. Courses taught at other locations on a class by class basis. Extensive business incubator program emphasizing advanced manufacturing. **Enrollment:** 10,946 degree-seeking undergraduates. **Degrees:** 993 associate awarded. **Calendar:** Semester, limited summer session. **Full-time faculty:** 269 total; 18% minority, 63% women. **Part-time faculty:** 424 total; 20% minority, 61% women. **Class size:** 67% < 20, 33% 20-39, less than 1% 40-49. **Special facilities:** Business accelerator at the Northeast Campus. **Partnerships:** Formal partnerships with middle schools.

Student profile. Among degree-seeking undergraduates, 30% enrolled in a transfer program, 70% enrolled in a vocational program, 9% already have a bachelor's degree or higher.

Out-of-state: 1% **25 or older:** 45%

Transfer out. Colleges most students transferred to 2015: University of South Carolina.

Basis for selection. Open admission, but selective for some programs. High school record, SAT/ACT or college placement test scores, and interviews considered for nursing/health science applicants. National League for Nursing Test required of nursing applicants. Admission cut-off scores established for full admission into each program. Students falling below cut-off scores may enter in developmental studies. Interview, orientation required for health science and nursing programs. **Home schooled:** Must be an approved Home School Association in South Carolina. If student is applying for concurrent admission they must have a letter of permission from the home school association and a letter of permission from their parent/guardian.

2015-2016 Annual costs. Tuition/fees: $4,930; $6,100 out-of-district; $14,350 out-of-state. Books/supplies: $1,982. Personal expenses: $2,041. **Additional information:** General education courses require additional $27 per-credit-hour fee, technical courses require additional $12 per-credit-hour fee.

Financial aid. All financial aid based on need. Need-based aid available for part-time students. Work-study available nights, weekends and for part-time students.

Application procedures. Admission: Priority date 7/20; no deadline. $35 fee. Admission notification on a rolling basis. **Financial aid:** Priority date 4/15; no closing date. FAFSA required. Applicants notified on a rolling basis; must reply within 2 week(s) of notification.

Academics. Special study options: Cooperative education, distance learning, dual enrollment of high school students, ESL, liberal arts/career combination. License preparation in dental hygiene, nursing, physical therapy, radiology. **Credit/placement by examination:** AP, CLEP, institutional tests. **Support services:** GED preparation, learning center, remedial instruction, study skills assistance, tutoring, writing center.

Majors. Business: Accounting, administrative services, business admin. **Communications technology:** Graphic/printing. **Computer sciences:** Computer science, data processing, information systems. **Health services:** Clinical lab technology, dental assistant, dental hygiene, health information technology, medical radiologic technology/radiation therapy, nuclear medical technology, nursing (RN), pharmacy assistant, physical therapy assistant, respiratory therapy assistant, respiratory therapy technology. **Liberal arts:** Arts/sciences. **Protective services:** Criminal justice. **Visual/performing arts:** Commercial/advertising art. **Work/family studies:** Child development.

Most popular majors. Business/marketing 10%, computer/information sciences 6%, health sciences 18%, interdisciplinary studies 6%, liberal arts 35%.

Technology on campus. Commuter students can connect to campus network. Online course registration, online library, helpline, wireless network available.

Student life. Freshman orientation: Available. Preregistration for classes offered. **Activities:** Drama, international student organizations, literary magazine, student government, student newspaper.

Student services. Adult student services, career counseling, services for economically disadvantaged, student employment services, financial aid counseling, placement for graduates, veterans' counselor. **Physically disabled:** Services for visually, speech, hearing impaired. **Transfer:** Re-entry adviser, pre-admission transcript evaluation for new students. Transfer adviser, college fairs on campus for students transferring to 4-year colleges.

Contact. E-mail: mtcinfo@midlandstech.edu
Phone: (803) 738-8324 Toll-free number: (800) 922-8038
Fax: (803) 738-7784
Derrah Cassidy, Director of Admissions, Midlands Technical College, PO Box 2408, Columbia, SC 29202

Miller-Motte Technical College
North Charleston, South Carolina
www.miller-motte.edu

- For-profit 2-year branch campus and technical college
- Small city

General. Accredited by ACICS. **Enrollment:** 635 undergraduates. **Degrees:** 179 associate awarded. **Calendar:** Quarter, extensive summer session. **Full-time faculty:** 5 total. **Part-time faculty:** 39 total. **Special facilities:** Atrium day spa for massage and esthetics students.

Basis for selection. Open admission. Must score 13 or higher on Wonderlic entrance exam, pass a background check, and be selected by admissions representative as good candidate for potential program. **Adult students:** SAT/ACT scores not required. **Home schooled:** Transcript of courses and grades, interview required.

2015-2016 Annual costs. Management-International Trade: $25,560; books and supplies $5,600. Medical Assisting: $27,960; books and supplies $5,600. Surgical Technology: $27,380; books and supplies $4,200. Paralegal: $27,960; books and supplies $5,600. Criminal justice: $25,560; books and supplies $5,600. Medical Billing and Coding: $20,420; books and supplies $4,200. Clinical Office Assistant: $19,840; books and supplies $4,200. Esthetics Technology: $10,560; books and supplies $410. Electronic Health Records: $27,960; books and supplies $5,600. Massage Therapy: $10,600; books and supplies $1,900. Cosmetology: $20,788; books and supplies $1,050. Figures are for total program cost.

Financial aid. Need-based: Work-study available nights, weekends and for part-time students.

Application procedures. Admission: No deadline. $40 fee. **Financial aid:** FAFSA, institutional form required. Applicants notified on a rolling basis.

Academics. Credit/placement by examination: AP, CLEP. **Support services:** Tutoring.

Majors. Business: Accounting/business management, business admin. **Health services:** Massage therapy, medical assistant, surgical technology.

Contact. Phone: (843) 574-0101 Toll-free number: (877) 617-4740
Fax: (843) 329-4992
Ulitza Kronemeyer, Director of Admissions, Miller-Motte Technical College, 8085 Rivers Avenue, Suite E, North Charleston, SC 29406

Miller-Motte Technical College: Conway
Conway, South Carolina
www.miller-motte.edu

- For-profit 2-year health science and career college
- Small city

General. Regionally accredited; also accredited by ACICS. **Enrollment:** 622 undergraduates. **Degrees:** 102 associate awarded. **Calendar:** Quarter. **Full-time faculty:** 6 total. **Part-time faculty:** 34 total.

Basis for selection. Open admission.

2015-2016 Annual costs. Medical Assisting: $28,099; books and supplies $4,000. Medical Clinical Assistant: $19,104; books and supplies $3,000. Medical Office Assistant: $18,937; books and supplies $2,500. Esthetics Technology: $10,560; books and supplies $410. Medical Billing and Coding

Specialist: $20,545; books and supplies $3,000. Cosmetology: $20,788; books and supplies $1,050. Massage Therapy: $10,600; books and supplies $1,900. Figures are for total program cost.

Financial aid. Need-based: Work-study available nights, weekends and for part-time students.

Application procedures. Admission: No deadline. $40 fee. **Financial aid:** No deadline.

Academics. Credit/placement by examination: AP, CLEP.

Majors. Health services: Massage therapy, medical assistant.

Contact. E-mail: jill.miskelly@miller-motte.edu
Phone: (843) 591-1102
Jill Roth, Director of Admissions, Miller-Motte Technical College: Conway, 2451 Highway 501 East, Conway, SC 29526

Northeastern Technical College
Cheraw, South Carolina
www.netc.edu   CB code: 5095

- Public 2-year community and technical college
- Commuter campus in small town

General. Founded in 1969. Regionally accredited. **Enrollment:** 705 degree-seeking undergraduates. **Degrees:** 155 associate awarded. **Location:** 89 miles from Columbia. **Calendar:** Semester, extensive summer session. **Full-time faculty:** 30 total; 7% have terminal degrees, 13% minority, 57% women. **Part-time faculty:** 100 total; 3% have terminal degrees, 20% minority, 53% women.

Student profile.

Out-of-state: 1%   25 or older: 87%

Transfer out. Colleges most students transferred to 2015: Francis Marion University, Clemson University, Coastal Carolina University, Florence-Darlington Technical College, University of South Carolina.

Basis for selection. Open admission, but selective for some programs. Special requirements for nursing program, including high school math and science courses and 960 SAT (exclusive of Writing). Interview recommended. **Home schooled:** Must be under auspices of school district or an approved homeschool agency.

High school preparation. Algebra I and II, chemistry with laboratory required for nursing applicants.

2015-2016 Annual costs. Tuition/fees: $4,800; $5,070 out-of-district; $8,070 out-of-state. Per-credit charge: $159 in-district; $168 out-of-district; $268 out-of-state. Books/supplies: $1,500. Personal expenses: $1,800.

Financial aid. Need-based: Work-study available nights, weekends and for part-time students.

Application procedures. Admission: Priority date 6/30; deadline 7/31 (receipt date). $30 fee, may be waived for applicants with need. Application must be submitted online. Admission notification on a rolling basis. **Financial aid:** No deadline. FAFSA required. Applicants notified on a rolling basis; must reply within 8 week(s) of notification.

Academics. Special study options: Cross-registration, distance learning, dual enrollment of high school students, independent study, liberal arts/career combination. **Credit/placement by examination:** AP, CLEP, IB, institutional tests. Credit by examination limited to 50% of semester hours required for degree. ASSET and English language proficiency required for placement. **Support services:** Remedial instruction, tutoring, writing center.

Majors. Business: Accounting, administrative services, business admin, office technology, office/clerical. **Computer sciences:** Data processing. **Education:** General. **Health services:** Licensed practical nurse, nursing (RN). **Liberal arts:** Arts/sciences.

Most popular majors. Business/marketing 30%, engineering/engineering technologies 11%, liberal arts 30%, public administration/social services 7%, trade and industry 27%.

Technology on campus. 125 workstations in library, computer center. Online library, wireless network available.

Student life. Freshman orientation: Available. Preregistration for classes offered. Four early orientations held in the summer. **Activities:** Student government, student newspaper, service-leadership organization.

Student services. Career counseling, student employment services, personal counseling, placement for graduates, veterans' counselor. **Transfer:** Transfer adviser for students transferring to 4-year colleges.

Contact. E-mail: admissions@netc.edu
Phone: (843) 921-6900 Fax: (843) 921-1476
Danielle Pace, Director of Enrollment Management, Northeastern Technical College, Drawer 1007, Cheraw, SC 29520

Orangeburg-Calhoun Technical College
Orangeburg, South Carolina
www.octech.edu   CB code: 5527

- Public 2-year community and technical college
- Commuter campus in large town

General. Founded in 1968. Regionally accredited. **Enrollment:** 2,399 degree-seeking undergraduates. **Degrees:** 195 associate awarded. **ROTC:** Army. **Location:** 75 miles from Charleston, 45 miles from Columbia. **Calendar:** Semester, extensive summer session. **Full-time faculty:** 76 total. **Part-time faculty:** 89 total.

Basis for selection. Open admission, but selective for some programs. COMPASS and ASSET used for placement. SAT/ACT may be submitted in place of ASSET or COMPASS. Admission to nursing and allied health programs based on school achievement record and test scores. **Adult students:** ACT and SAT test scores are only valid for us for 5 years. Students may also take the COMPASS placement test if they do not have ACT or SAT scores or if their scores do not meet admissions criteria.

High school preparation. 24 units recommended. Recommended units include English 4, mathematics 4, social studies 3, history 1, science 3, foreign language 1, computer science 1 and academic electives 7.

2015-2016 Annual costs. Tuition/fees: $4,970; $5,930 out-of-district; $7,706 out-of-state. Per-credit charge: $160 in-district; $200 out-of-district; $274 out-of-state. Books/supplies: $800. Personal expenses: $2,123.

Financial aid. All financial aid based on need. Need-based aid available for part-time students. Work-study available nights, weekends and for part-time students.

Application procedures. Admission: No deadline. $25 fee, may be waived for applicants with need. Admission notification on a rolling basis beginning on or about 1/1. **Financial aid:** Priority date 6/4; no closing date. FAFSA, institutional form required. Applicants notified on a rolling basis starting 5/1; must reply within 2 week(s) of notification.

Academics. Special study options: Cooperative education, cross-registration, distance learning, double major, dual enrollment of high school students, independent study, liberal arts/career combination. License preparation in nursing, radiology, real estate. **Credit/placement by examination:** AP, CLEP, institutional tests. 60% of hours needed for degree may be earned by examination. **Support services:** GED preparation and test center, learning center, pre-admission summer program, reduced course load, remedial instruction, study skills assistance, tutoring, writing center.

Majors. Business: General, accounting, administrative services. **Computer sciences:** Data processing, programming. **Conservation:** Forest resources. **Health services:** Clinical lab assistant, clinical lab technology, medical radiologic technology/radiation therapy, nursing (RN). **Liberal arts:** Arts/sciences. **Protective services:** Criminal justice.

Technology on campus. 100 workstations in library, computer center, student center. Commuter students can connect to campus network. Online course registration, online library, helpline, repair service, wireless network available.

Student life. Freshman orientation: Available. Preregistration for classes offered. **Activities:** Student government, honor fraternities, curriculum clubs.

Athletics. Intramural: Basketball M, cheerleading M, football (tackle) M.

Student services. Adult student services, career counseling, services for economically disadvantaged, student employment services, financial aid counseling, minority student services, personal counseling, placement for graduates, veterans' counselor. **Physically disabled:** Services for visually, speech, hearing impaired. **Transfer:** Pre-admission transcript evaluation for new students. Transfer adviser, college fairs on campus for students transferring to 4-year colleges.

Contact. E-mail: askme@octech.edu
Phone: (803) 535-1224 Fax: (803) 535-1388
Sernetta Quick, Director of Admissions and Recruitment, Orangeburg-Calhoun Technical College, 3250 St. Matthews Road, Orangeburg, SC 29118-8222

Piedmont Technical College
Greenwood, South Carolina
www.ptc.edu   CB code: 5550

- Public 2-year community and technical college
- Commuter campus in small city

General. Founded in 1966. Regionally accredited. Serves 7-county region of the state (satellite campus in each county offering Internet classes, traditional classes and interactive televised classes with main campus). **Enrollment:** 4,369 degree-seeking undergraduates; 836 non-degree-seeking students. **Degrees:** 648 associate awarded. **Location:** 75 miles from Columbia, 50 miles from Greenville. **Calendar:** Semester, extensive summer session. **Special facilities:** Engineering lab, South Carolina Center for Funeral Service Education, technologically advanced nursing labs equipped with SIMS man Bruce, Center for Advanced Manufacturing, Mechatronics.

Student profile. Among degree-seeking undergraduates, 11% enrolled in a transfer program, 9% enrolled in a vocational program, 1,111 enrolled as first-time, first-year students.

Part-time:	59%	Women:	67%
Out-of-state:	5%		

Transfer out. Colleges most students transferred to 2015: Lander University, Clemson University, University of South Carolina, South Carolina State University.

Basis for selection. Open admission, but selective for some programs. Students with a composite SAT score of at least 960 with a minimum of 480 on Critical Reading and 480 on Math do not need to take the institutional placement test. Students with a composite ACT score of at least 20 waives the Writing and Reading portion of the placement test and an ACT Math score of at least 19 waives the Math portion of the placement test.

2015-2016 Annual costs. Tuition/fees: $4,955; $5,645 out-of-district; $7,145 out-of-state. Per-credit charge: $159 in-district; $182 out-of-district; $232 out-of-state. Books/supplies: $2,000. Personal expenses: $250.

2014-2015 Financial aid. All financial aid based on need. 99% of total undergraduate aid awarded as scholarships/grants, 1% as loans/jobs. Need-based aid available for part-time students. Work-study available nights, weekends and for part-time students.

Application procedures. Admission: No deadline. No application fee. Admission notification on a rolling basis. **Financial aid:** Priority date 5/1; no closing date. FAFSA required. Applicants notified on a rolling basis starting 6/1; must reply within 2 week(s) of notification.

Academics. Special study options: Cooperative education, distance learning, double major, dual enrollment of high school students, independent study, internships, liberal arts/career combination. Bachelor's degree programs available on campus. License preparation in nursing, real estate. **Credit/placement by examination:** AP, CLEP, IB, institutional tests. 24 credit hours maximum toward associate degree. **Support services:** GED preparation, learning center, pre-admission summer program, reduced course load, remedial instruction, study skills assistance, tutoring, writing center.

Majors. Business: General, administrative services. **Computer sciences:** Data processing. **General:** Building construction. **Health services:** Cardiovascular technology, medical radiologic technology/radiation therapy, nursing (RN), respiratory therapy technology, veterinary technology/assistant. **Liberal arts:** Arts/sciences. **Protective services:** Criminal justice. **Work/family studies:** Child care management.

Most popular majors. Business/marketing 22%, computer/information sciences 6%, engineering/engineering technologies 11%, health sciences 15%, liberal arts 14%, public administration/social services 6%, trade and industry 10%.

Technology on campus. 250 workstations in computer center, student center. Commuter students can connect to campus network. Online library, helpline available.

Student life. Freshman orientation: Available. Preregistration for classes offered. **Activities:** Alpha Delta Omega, Christian student union, computer club, horticulture club, Kappa Beta Delta, Lambda Chi Nu, Phi Theta Kappa, psychology club, rad tech club, student nurses association.

Student services. Adult student services, career counseling, services for economically disadvantaged, student employment services, financial aid counseling, minority student services, personal counseling, placement for graduates, veterans' counselor. **Transfer:** Pre-admission transcript evaluation for new students. Transfer adviser, college fairs on campus for students transferring to 4-year colleges.

Contact. E-mail: Frazier.r@ptc.edu
Phone: (864) 941-8369 Toll-free number: (800) 868-5528
Fax: (864) 941-8555
Renae Frazier, Dean of Enrollment Management, Piedmont Technical College, 620 North Emerald Road, Greenwood, SC 29646

Spartanburg Community College
Spartanburg, South Carolina
www.sccsc.edu   CB code: 5668

- Public 2-year community and technical college
- Commuter campus in small city

General. Founded in 1961. Regionally accredited. Satellite campuses located in Greer, Gaffney and downtown Spartanburg. Limited courses available on-site in Union. **Enrollment:** 4,163 degree-seeking undergraduates; 765 non-degree-seeking students. **Degrees:** 532 associate awarded. **Location:** 4 miles from downtown. **Calendar:** Semester, limited summer session. **Full-time faculty:** 120 total. **Part-time faculty:** 321 total. **Class size:** 64% < 20, 36% 20-39. **Special facilities:** Horticultural arboretum. **Partnerships:** Formal partnership with Ford Asset Program (auto mechanic training program).

Student profile. Among degree-seeking undergraduates, 41% enrolled in a transfer program, 59% enrolled in a vocational program, 961 enrolled as first-time, first-year students.

Part-time:	47%	Asian American:	4%
Out-of-state:	2%	Hispanic/Latino:	7%
Women:	57%	Multi-racial, non-Hispanic:	2%
African American:	23%	25 or older:	38%

Transfer out. Colleges most students transferred to 2015: Clemson University, University of South Carolina Upstate, University of South Carolina at Columbia, Wofford College, Spartanburg Methodist College.

Basis for selection. Open admission, but selective for some programs. Test of Adult Basic Education required for admission. Programmer's Aptitude Test required for computer programming and data processing. Admission to some health science programs limited based on size of class. Interviews preferred and essays recommended, but neither is required. **Home schooled:** Transcript of courses and grades required. State Department approval of the applicable home school association.

High school preparation. College-preparatory program recommended. 21 units required. Required units include English 4, mathematics 2, social studies 2, history 2, science 2 (laboratory 2), foreign language 1 and academic electives 6. One biology and/or chemistry and 1 algebra required for most health programs. Algebra required for all engineering and computer programs.

2015-2016 Annual costs. Tuition/fees: $4,092; $5,110 out-of-district; $8,372 out-of-state. Per-credit charge: $171 in-district; $213 out-of-district; $349 out-of-state. Books/supplies: $1,200. Personal expenses: $2,907.

Financial aid. Need-based: Need-based aid available for part-time students. Work-study available nights, weekends and for part-time students. **Non-need-based:** Scholarships awarded for academics. **Additional information:** Participates in South Carolina lottery tuition assistance program. Full-time technical college students who are state residents receive assistance for tuition not covered by federal or need-based grants.

Application procedures. Admission: No deadline. $25 fee. Admission notification on a rolling basis. **Financial aid:** Priority date 2/28, closing date 5/1. FAFSA required. Applicants notified on a rolling basis starting 5/1.

Academics. Special study options: Cooperative education, distance learning, double major, dual enrollment of high school students, independent study. License preparation in dental hygiene, nursing, occupational therapy, physical therapy, radiology. **Credit/placement by examination:** AP, CLEP, IB, institutional tests. Students must complete 25% of core courses in their program of study through instruction offered by the college. **Support services:** GED preparation and test center, learning center, remedial instruction, study skills assistance, tutoring, writing center.

Majors. Business: Accounting, administrative services, business admin, hospitality admin, hotel/motel admin, marketing, restaurant/food services.

Computer sciences: Data processing. **Education:** Voc/tech. **Health services:** Clinical lab technology, medical radiologic technology/radiation therapy, nursing (RN), predental, respiratory therapy technology. **Liberal arts:** Arts/sciences.

Technology on campus. 2,000 workstations in library, computer center, student center. Commuter students can connect to campus network. Online course registration, helpline, repair service, wireless network available.

Student life. Freshman orientation: Mandatory. Preregistration for classes offered. Two-hour session held on campus prior to start of semester. **Activities:** Campus ministries, drama, student government, Campus Crusade for Christ.

Student services. Adult student services, career counseling, services for economically disadvantaged, student employment services, financial aid counseling, personal counseling, placement for graduates, veterans' counselor, women's services. **Physically disabled:** Services for visually, speech, hearing impaired. **Transfer:** Transfer adviser, college fairs on campus for students transferring to 4-year colleges.

Contact. E-mail: admissions@sccsc.edu
Phone: (864) 592-4800 Toll-free number: (866) 592-4700
Fax: (864) 592-4642
Lynn Dale, Director of Enrollment Services, Spartanburg Community College, Box 4386, Spartanburg, SC 29305-4386

Spartanburg Methodist College
Spartanburg, South Carolina **CB member**
www.smcsc.edu **CB code: 5627**

⬧ Private 2-year junior and liberal arts college affiliated with the United Methodist Church
⬧ Residential campus in small city
⬧ SAT or ACT (ACT writing optional) required

General. Founded in 1911. Regionally accredited. **Enrollment:** 769 degree-seeking undergraduates; 2 non-degree-seeking students. **Degrees:** 198 associate awarded. **ROTC:** Army. **Location:** 30 miles from Greenville, 60 miles from Charlotte. **Calendar:** Semester, limited summer session. **Full-time faculty:** 28 total; 61% have terminal degrees, 14% minority, 43% women. **Part-time faculty:** 40 total; 20% have terminal degrees, 12% minority, 60% women. **Class size:** 34% < 20, 66% 20-39.

Student profile. Among degree-seeking undergraduates, 100% enrolled in a transfer program, 440 enrolled as first-time, first-year students, 27 transferred in from other institutions.

Part-time:	1%	Hispanic/Latino:	7%
Out-of-state:	5%	Multi-racial, non-Hispanic:	2%
Women:	46%	International:	1%
African American:	33%	Live on campus:	65%
Asian American:	1%		

Transfer out. 72% of students enrolled in the transfer program go on to 4-year colleges. **Colleges most students transferred to 2015:** University of South Carolina Upstate, Clemson University, University of South Carolina, Lander University, College of Charleston.

Basis for selection. GPA, SAT/ACT, and class rank used. Audition, essay, interview recommended. **Adult students:** SAT/ACT scores not required if applicant over 21. **Home schooled:** Applicants need complete high school academic transcript. Recommend students be supervised through accredited home school association to provide curriculum and academic oversight throughout high school program.

High school preparation. College-preparatory program recommended. 24 units recommended. Recommended units include English 4, mathematics 4, social studies 2, history 1, science 3, foreign language 1, computer science 1 and academic electives 7. 1 unit of physical education or Junior ROTC recommended.

2016-2017 Annual costs. Tuition/fees (projected): $17,500. Room/board: $9,100. Books/supplies: $1,450. Personal expenses: $2,300.

Financial aid. Need-based: Need-based aid available for part-time students. Work-study available nights, weekends and for part-time students. **Non-need-based:** Scholarships awarded for academics, athletics, religious affiliation.

Application procedures. Admission: No deadline. $25 fee, may be waived for applicants with need. Admission notification on a rolling basis beginning on or about 9/1. Housing deposit refundable until June 1. Applicant notified of decision within a week. **Financial aid:** Priority date 6/30, closing date 8/22. FAFSA required. Applicants notified on a rolling basis starting 3/1; must reply within 2 week(s) of notification.

Academics. Special study options: Dual enrollment of high school students, ESL, honors, independent study, liberal arts/career combination, study abroad. **Credit/placement by examination:** AP, CLEP, SAT, ACT, institutional tests. 15 credit hours maximum toward associate degree. **Support services:** Learning center, pre-admission summer program, reduced course load, remedial instruction, study skills assistance, tutoring, writing center.

Majors. Business: Business admin. **Liberal arts:** Arts/sciences. **Protective services:** Law enforcement admin. **Visual/performing arts:** General.

Most popular majors. Business/marketing 11%, liberal arts 75%, security/protective services 9%.

Technology on campus. 45 workstations in dormitories, library, computer center, student center. Dormitories wired for high-speed internet access and linked to campus network. Commuter students can connect to campus network. Online library, helpline, wireless network available.

Student life. Freshman orientation: Mandatory, $25 fee. Preregistration for classes offered. One session in mid-July, one session in early August, one session during move-in weekend (mid-August). **Policies:** No alcohol, drugs, or firearms allowed on campus. Campus is tobacco free. **Housing:** Guaranteed on-campus for all undergraduates. Single-sex dorms, special housing for disabled, wellness housing available. $100 fully refundable deposit, deadline 11/30. **Activities:** Jazz band, campus ministries, choral groups, dance, drama, literary magazine, music ensembles, student government, student newspaper, computer programming club, Psi Omega Theatre Fraternity, People Organizing People Successfully, Presbyterian student association, Wesley Fellowship, Campus Crusade for Christ, Sigma Kappa Delta, Phi Theta Kappa, Psi Beta.

Athletics. NJCAA. **Intercollegiate:** Baseball M, basketball, cheerleading, cross-country, golf, soccer, softball W, tennis, volleyball W, wrestling M. **Intramural:** Basketball, football (non-tackle) M, softball, table tennis, tennis, volleyball. **Team name:** Pioneers.

Student services. Adult student services, alcohol/substance abuse counseling, chaplain/spiritual director, career counseling, services for economically disadvantaged, student employment services, financial aid counseling, health services, personal counseling, placement for graduates, veterans' counselor. **Transfer:** Pre-admission transcript evaluation for new students. Transfer center, transfer adviser, college fairs on campus for students transferring to 4-year colleges.

Contact. E-mail: admiss@smcsc.edu
Phone: (864) 587-4213 Toll-free number: (800) 772-7286
Fax: (864) 587-4355
Wells Shepard, Director of Admissions, Spartanburg Methodist College, 1000 Powell Mill Road, Spartanburg, SC 29301-5899

Technical College of the Lowcountry
Beaufort, South Carolina
www.tcl.edu **CB code: 5047**

⬧ Public 2-year community and technical college
⬧ Commuter campus in small city

General. Founded in 1972. Regionally accredited. **Enrollment:** 2,332 degree-seeking undergraduates. **Degrees:** 231 associate awarded. **Location:** 45 miles from Savannah, GA. **Calendar:** Semester, extensive summer session.

Basis for selection. Open admission, but selective for some programs. SAT/ACT required for placement and counseling. Nursing students encouraged to have personal interview and must submit NET test results. Interview recommended for nursing program. **Adult students:** After admission all students take either COMPASS or ASSET for placement.

2015-2016 Annual costs. Tuition/fees: $5,200; $5,950 out-of-district; $11,320 out-of-state. Per-credit charge: $166 in-district; $191 out-of-district; $370 out-of-state.

Financial aid. All financial aid based on need. Need-based aid available for part-time students. Work-study available nights, weekends and for part-time students. **Additional information:** State lottery aid may be available to South Carolina residents who take 6 credit hours or more.

Application procedures. Admission: No deadline. $25 fee. Admission notification on a rolling basis. **Financial aid:** No deadline. FAFSA required.

Academics. Special study options: Cooperative education, cross-registration, distance learning, double major, dual enrollment of high school students, ESL, independent study, internships. **Credit/placement by examination:** AP, CLEP, institutional tests. **Support services:** GED preparation and test center, learning center, pre-admission summer program, reduced course load, remedial instruction, study skills assistance, tutoring, writing center.

Majors. Business: General, administrative services. **Computer sciences:** Data processing. **Health services:** Medical radiologic technology/radiation therapy, nursing (RN), physical therapy assistant. **Liberal arts:** Arts/sciences. **Protective services:** Criminal justice. **Work/family studies:** Child care service.

Technology on campus. 400 workstations in library, computer center, student center. Online library, helpline available.

Student life. Freshman orientation: Available. Preregistration for classes offered. One-day session at start of fall semester. **Activities:** Student government, Phi Theta Kappa, Rotaract Club, professional societies.

Student services. Career counseling, student employment services, financial aid counseling, personal counseling, placement for graduates, veterans' counselor.

Contact. E-mail: afaubion@tcl.edu
Phone: (843) 525-8208 Toll-free number: (800) 768-8252
Fax: (843) 525-8285
Ashley Faubion, Admissions Manager, Technical College of the Lowcountry, 921 South Ribaut Road, Beaufort, SC 29901-1288

Tri-County Technical College
Pendleton, South Carolina
www.tctc.edu   CB code: 5789

- Public 2-year community and technical college
- Commuter campus in small town

General. Founded in 1962. Regionally accredited. **Enrollment:** 5,322 degree-seeking undergraduates. **Degrees:** 867 associate awarded. **ROTC:** Army, Air Force. **Location:** 5 miles from Clemson. **Calendar:** Semester, limited summer session. **Full-time faculty:** 131 total. **Part-time faculty:** 305 total.

Student profile.

Out-of-state: 2%   25 or older: 85%

Transfer out. Colleges most students transferred to 2015: Clemson University, University of South Carolina, Lander University, Anderson University, Southern Wesleyan University.

Basis for selection. Open admission, but selective for some programs. **Home schooled:** Documentation of home-schooled diploma can be supplied by a state department of education or a regional accrediting organization.

2015-2016 Annual costs. Tuition/fees: $4,959; $6,459 out-of-district; $11,019 out-of-state. Per-credit charge: $165 in-district; $215 out-of-district; $367 out-of-state. Books/supplies: $900. Personal expenses: $1,920.

Financial aid. Need-based: Need-based aid available for part-time students. Work-study available nights, weekends and for part-time students. **Non-need-based:** Scholarships awarded for academics, state residency. **Additional information:** Deadline for application to institutional scholarships 4/2.

Application procedures. Admission: Closing date 7/30 (postmark date). $30 fee. Admission notification on a rolling basis. **Financial aid:** Priority date 4/1, closing date 7/30. FAFSA required. Applicants notified on a rolling basis starting 6/15; must reply within 2 week(s) of notification.

Academics. Special study options: Cooperative education, distance learning, dual enrollment of high school students, internships, liberal arts/career combination. License preparation in nursing, real estate. **Credit/placement by examination:** AP, CLEP, IB, institutional tests. Credit available from documented work experience, course waiver, noncollective organization training programs, technical advanced placement. **Support services:** Learning center, reduced course load, remedial instruction, study skills assistance, tutoring, writing center.

Majors. Business: Accounting, administrative services, business admin. **Communications technology:** Radio/TV. **Computer sciences:** Data processing. **Health services:** Clinical lab technology, nursing (RN), veterinary technology/assistant. **Liberal arts:** Arts/sciences. **Protective services:** Criminal justice. **Work/family studies:** Child care service, clothing/textiles.

Technology on campus. 800 workstations in library, computer center. Commuter students can connect to campus network. Online course registration, online library, helpline, wireless network available.

Student life. Freshman orientation: Mandatory. Preregistration for classes offered. **Activities:** Choral groups, drama, international student organizations, student government, minority student association, criminal justice club, Tri-County Voices (chorus), student veterinary technician association, student nurses association, future lab professionals, environmental club, international student association, Spanish club, book discussion group.

Athletics. Team name: Hawks.

Student services. Career counseling, services for economically disadvantaged, student employment services, financial aid counseling, minority student services, placement for graduates, veterans' counselor. **Physically disabled:** Services for visually, speech, hearing impaired. **Transfer:** Pre-admission transcript evaluation for new students. Transfer adviser, college fairs on campus for students transferring to 4-year colleges.

Contact. E-mail: info@tctc.edu
Phone: (864) 646-1550 Fax: (864) 646-5080
Renae Frazier, Director of Recruitment & Admissions, Tri-County Technical College, PO Box 587, Pendleton, SC 29670

Trident Technical College
Charleston, South Carolina   CB member
www.tridenttech.edu   CB code: 5049

- Public 2-year community and technical college
- Commuter campus in large city

General. Founded in 1964. Regionally accredited. 4 campuses: Palmer Campus in downtown Charleston, Main Campus in North Charleston, Mount Pleasant Campus in Mount Pleasant and Berkeley Campus in Moncks Corner. **Enrollment:** 12,892 degree-seeking undergraduates. **Degrees:** 1,717 associate awarded. **Location:** 15 miles from downtown. **Calendar:** Semester, extensive summer session. **Full-time faculty:** 339 total; 15% have terminal degrees, 17% minority, 55% women. **Part-time faculty:** 781 total; 17% minority, 59% women. **Class size:** 56% < 20, 43% 20-39, less than 1% 40-49, less than 1% 50-99, less than 1% >100.

Student profile.

Out-of-state: 2%   25 or older: 49%

Basis for selection. Open admission, but selective for some programs. Special requirements for nursing students. **Adult students:** SAT/ACT scores not required. **Learning Disabled:** Student should provide current medical, psychological, and/or psychiatric documentation providing a diagnosis and describing how his/her disability affects his/her ability to function in a collegiate, adult learning environment. Documentation indicating what accommodations the student received in high school and/or at another college may also be helpful.

2015-2016 Annual costs. Tuition/fees: $4,070; $4,512 out-of-district; $7,676 out-of-state. Per-credit charge: $168 in-district; $187 out-of-district; $319 out-of-state. Books/supplies: $2,000. Personal expenses: $2,646.

Financial aid. Need-based: Need-based aid available for part-time students. Work-study available nights, weekends and for part-time students. **Non-need-based:** Scholarships awarded for academics, alumni affiliation, state residency.

Application procedures. Admission: Closing date 8/6 (postmark date). $30 fee. Admission notification on a rolling basis. Applicants to early admissions program must rank in upper half of high school class and must have combined SAT score (exclusive of Writing) of 800 or ACT composite score of 17. **Financial aid:** No deadline. FAFSA required. Applicants notified on a rolling basis; must reply within 6 week(s) of notification.

Academics. Special study options: Accelerated study, cooperative education, cross-registration, distance learning, double major, dual enrollment of high school students, ESL, independent study, internships, study abroad, weekend college. License preparation in aviation, dental hygiene, nursing, occupational therapy, paramedic, physical therapy, radiology, real estate. **Credit/placement by examination:** AP, CLEP, IB, institutional tests. 16 credit hours maximum toward associate degree. **Support services:** Learning center, reduced course load, remedial instruction, study skills assistance, tutoring, writing center.

Majors. Business: General, accounting, administrative services, business admin, logistics. **Communications:** Broadcast journalism. **Communications technology:** Radio/TV. **Computer sciences:** Data processing, networking. **Health services:** Clinical lab technology, dental hygiene, EMT paramedic, medical radiologic technology/radiation therapy, nursing (RN), occupational therapy assistant, physical therapy assistant, respiratory therapy technology. **Liberal arts:** Arts/sciences. **Protective services:** Fire services admin, homeland security, law enforcement admin. **Visual/performing arts:** Commercial/advertising art. **Work/family studies:** Child care management.

Most popular majors. Business/marketing 11%, health sciences 25%, interdisciplinary studies 7%, liberal arts 30%.

Technology on campus. 3,000 workstations in library, computer center, student center. Online library, helpline, wireless network available.

Student life. Freshman orientation: Available. Preregistration for classes offered. Forty-five minute ongoing service. **Activities:** Choral groups, drama, international student organizations, Model UN, radio station, student government, student newspaper, Phi Theta Kappa international honor society, Alpha Mu Gamma, Asian Studies, Black Student Association, Campus Crusade for Christ, La Sociedad Hispanoamericana, Society of Student Leaders.

Student services. Adult student services, alcohol/substance abuse counseling, career counseling, services for economically disadvantaged, student employment services, financial aid counseling, personal counseling, placement for graduates, veterans' counselor. **Physically disabled:** Services for visually, hearing impaired. **Transfer:** Pre-admission transcript evaluation for new students. Transfer center, transfer adviser, college fairs on campus for students transferring to 4-year colleges.

Contact. E-mail: admissions@tridenttech.edu
Phone: (843) 574-6125 Toll-free number: (877) 349-7184
Fax: (843) 574-6483
Clara Martin, Director of Admissions, Trident Technical College, PO.Box 118067, AM-M, Charleston, SC 29423-8067

University of South Carolina: Lancaster
Lancaster, South Carolina
usclancaster.sc.edu   CB code: 5849

▸ Public 2-year branch campus and junior college
▸ Commuter campus in large town

General. Founded in 1959. Regionally accredited. **Enrollment:** 1,722 undergraduates. **Degrees:** 152 associate awarded. **ROTC:** Army. **Location:** 50 miles from Columbia, 40 miles from Charlotte, NC. **Calendar:** Semester, limited summer session. **Full-time faculty:** 63 total. **Part-time faculty:** 31 total. **Special facilities:** Health sciences facilities, diabetic education center.

Student profile.

Out-of-state: 2%   **25 or older:**   19%

Transfer out. Colleges most students transferred to 2015: University of South Carolina-Columbia, Winthrop University, Clemson University, York Technical College.

Basis for selection. Open admission. SAT/ACT required but applicants with scores below required levels may be admitted provisionally. **Adult students:** SAT/ACT scores not required if applicant over 21. **Home schooled:** Transcript of courses and grades required.

High school preparation. College-preparatory program recommended. 23 units recommended. Recommended units include English 4, mathematics 3, social studies 3, history 1, science 3 (laboratory 3), foreign language 2 and academic electives 4. One unit physical education/ ROTC required.

2015-2016 Annual costs. Tuition/fees: $6,886; $16,606 out-of-state. Per-credit charge: $262 in-state; $656 out-of-state. Books/supplies: $1,036. Personal expenses: $950.

Financial aid. Need-based: Work-study available nights, weekends and for part-time students.

Application procedures. Admission: Priority date 7/30; no deadline. $40 fee, may be waived for applicants with need. Admission notification on a rolling basis. **Financial aid:** Priority date 4/15; no closing date. FAFSA required. Applicants notified on a rolling basis starting 6/1; must reply within 2 week(s) of notification.

Academics. Special study options: Accelerated study, cross-registration, distance learning, dual enrollment of high school students, honors, independent study, internships, liberal arts/career combination, study abroad. Bachelor's degree programs available on campus. License preparation in nursing. **Credit/placement by examination:** AP, CLEP, IB, institutional tests. 30 credit hours maximum toward associate degree. **Support services:** Learning center, study skills assistance, tutoring, writing center.

Majors. Business: Administrative services, business admin. **Health services:** Nursing (RN). **Liberal arts:** Arts/sciences. **Protective services:** Criminal justice. **Visual/performing arts:** Art.

Technology on campus. 110 workstations in library, computer center, student center. Commuter students can connect to campus network. Online course registration, repair service, wireless network available.

Student life. Freshman orientation: Mandatory, $35 fee. Preregistration for classes offered. Two-day program. **Activities:** Campus ministries, drama, literary magazine, student government, student newspaper, black awareness group, adult group for education, Campus Crusade for Christ.

Athletics. NJCAA. **Intercollegiate:** Baseball M, golf M, soccer W, tennis. **Intramural:** Basketball, table tennis, volleyball. **Team name:** Lancers.

Student services. Adult student services, career counseling, student employment services, financial aid counseling, health services, personal counseling, veterans' counselor. **Transfer:** Pre-admission transcript evaluation for new students. College fairs on campus for students transferring to 4-year colleges.

Contact. E-mail: uscladms@mailbox.sc.edu
Phone: (803) 313-7073 Fax: (803) 313-7116
John Jones, Director of Enrollment Management, University of South Carolina: Lancaster, PO Box 889, Lancaster, SC 29721

University of South Carolina: Salkehatchie
Allendale, South Carolina
uscsalkehatchie.sc.edu   CB code: 5847

▸ Public 2-year branch campus college
▸ Commuter campus in rural community
▸ SAT or ACT required

General. Founded in 1965. Regionally accredited. **Enrollment:** 730 full-time, degree-seeking students. **Degrees:** 222 associate awarded. **ROTC:** Army, Naval, Air Force. **Location:** 75 miles from Columbia, 75 miles from Charleston. **Calendar:** Semester, limited summer session. **Full-time faculty:** 18 total. **Part-time faculty:** 44 total.

Student profile.

Out-of-state: 1%   **25 or older:**   26%

Transfer out. Colleges most students transferred to 2015: University of South Carolina-Columbia, University of South Carolina-Aiken.

Basis for selection. Secondary school record and class rank most important. Standardized test scores also important. **Adult students:** SAT/ACT scores not required if applicant over 25.

High school preparation. College-preparatory program required. Required units include English 4, mathematics 3, social studies 3, history 1, science 2 (laboratory 2), foreign language 2 and academic electives 2.

2015-2016 Annual costs. Tuition/fees: $6,878; $9,980 out-of-state. Per-credit charge: $270 in-state; $400 out-of-state. Books/supplies: $1,036. Personal expenses: $1,746.

Financial aid. Need-based: Need-based aid available for part-time students. Work-study available nights, weekends and for part-time students. **Non-need-based:** Scholarships awarded for academics.

Application procedures. Admission: Priority date 8/19; no deadline. $40 fee, may be waived for applicants with need. Admission notification on a rolling basis. **Financial aid:** Priority date 4/30; no closing date. FAFSA required. Applicants notified on a rolling basis starting 6/1.

Academics. Special study options: Cross-registration, dual enrollment of high school students, independent study, student-designed major, study abroad. Bachelor's degree programs available on campus. **Credit/placement by examination:** AP, CLEP, IB, institutional tests. 15 credit hours maximum toward associate degree. **Support services:** Learning center, pre-admission summer program, reduced course load, tutoring.

Majors. Liberal arts: Arts/sciences.

Technology on campus. 102 workstations in library, computer center.

Student life. Freshman orientation: Mandatory. Preregistration for classes offered. **Activities:** Student government, minority student organization:

Athletics. NJCAA. **Intercollegiate:** Baseball M, basketball M, soccer, softball W. **Team name:** Indians.

Student services. Career counseling, financial aid counseling, personal counseling, veterans' counselor. **Physically disabled:** Services for visually, hearing impaired.

Contact. Phone: (803) 584-3446 Toll-free number: (800) 922-5500
Fax: (803) 584-3884
Jane Brewer, Dean for Student Services, University of South Carolina: Salkehatchie, PO Box 617, Allendale, SC 29810

University of South Carolina: Sumter
Sumter, South Carolina
www.uscsumter.edu   CB code: 5821

- Public 2-year branch campus college
- Commuter campus in small city
- SAT or ACT (ACT writing optional) required

General. Founded in 1966. Regionally accredited. **Enrollment:** 650 degree-seeking undergraduates. **Degrees:** 92 associate awarded. **ROTC:** Army. **Location:** 40 miles from Columbia, 98 miles from Charleston. **Calendar:** Semester, limited summer session. **Full-time faculty:** 33 total. **Part-time faculty:** 28 total. **Class size:** 68% < 20, 30% 20-39, 2% 40-49. **Partnerships:** Formal partnerships with high schools (college-level courses for eligible high school students.).

Student profile.

Out-of-state: 1% **25 or older:**   20%

Transfer out. Colleges most students transferred to 2015: Central Carolina Technical College, College of Charleston, Midlands Technical College.

Basis for selection. Entering freshmen must have 2.25 GPA. Class rank and test scores also important. All freshmen required to take foreign language tests. Placement in mathematics may require additional testing. Interview required for academically marginal. **Adult students:** SAT/ACT scores not required if applicant over 23. **Home schooled:** Official transcripts, SAT/ACT and a GPR converted to the South Carolina Uniform grading scale if home schooled in South Carolina. **Learning Disabled:** Must submit recent documentation.

High school preparation. College-preparatory program required. 20 units required. Required and recommended units include English 4, mathematics 3-4, social studies 3, history 2, science 3 (laboratory 3), foreign language 2-3 and academic electives 4. 1 physical education required, 1 computer science recommended.

2015-2016 Annual costs. Tuition/fees: $6,886; $16,606 out-of-state. Per-credit charge: $262 in-state; $656 out-of-state. Books/supplies: $932. Personal expenses: $2,053.

Financial aid. All financial aid based on need. Need-based aid available for part-time students. Work-study available nights, weekends and for part-time students.

Application procedures. Admission: Priority date 8/1; no deadline. $50 fee, may be waived for applicants with need. Admission notification on a rolling basis. **Financial aid:** Priority date 4/15; no closing date. FAFSA required. Applicants notified on a rolling basis starting 4/16; must reply within 2 week(s) of notification.

Academics. Special study options: Cross-registration, distance learning, dual enrollment of high school students, independent study, liberal arts/career combination, student-designed major, teacher certification program. Bachelor's degree programs available on campus. **Credit/placement by examination:** AP, CLEP, institutional tests. 30 credit hours maximum toward associate degree. **Support services:** Learning center, remedial instruction, study skills assistance, tutoring, writing center.

Majors. Liberal arts: Arts/sciences.

Technology on campus. 195 workstations in library, computer center, student center. Commuter students can connect to campus network. Online course registration, online library, student web hosting, wireless network available.

Student life. Freshman orientation: Mandatory. Preregistration for classes offered. **Activities:** Choral groups, drama, literary magazine, music ensembles, student government, student newspaper, African-American club, Baptist student clubs, campus activities board, Circle K, student art guild,

student education association, student nursing organization, environmental club.

Athletics. NJCAA. **Intercollegiate:** Baseball M, soccer, softball W. **Intramural:** Baseball M, basketball, bowling, football (non-tackle), golf, handball, racquetball, soccer M, softball, table tennis, tennis, volleyball, weight lifting. **Team name:** Fire Ants.

Student services. Adult student services, chaplain/spiritual director, career counseling, services for economically disadvantaged, student employment services, financial aid counseling, personal counseling, placement for graduates, veterans' counselor. **Physically disabled:** Services for visually, speech, hearing impaired.

Contact. E-mail: kbritton@uscsumter.edu
Phone: (803) 938-3762 Fax: (803) 938-3901
Keith Britton, Director of Admissions, University of South Carolina: Sumter, 200 Miller Road, Sumter, SC 29150-2498

University of South Carolina: Union
Union, South Carolina
uscunion.sc.edu   CB code: 5846

- Public 2-year branch campus and liberal arts college
- Commuter campus in small town
- SAT or ACT (ACT writing optional) required

General. Founded in 1965. Regionally accredited. Off-campus site at Laurens offers full range of courses. **Enrollment:** 430 full-time, degree-seeking students. **Degrees:** 52 associate awarded. **Location:** 30 miles from Spartanburg, 60 miles from Columbia. **Calendar:** Semester, limited summer session. **Full-time faculty:** 13 total. **Part-time faculty:** 21 total.

Student profile.

Out-of-state: 1% **25 or older:**   40%

Basis for selection. Secondary school record most important. Standardized test scores and class rank also important. Students with high school diploma or GED but without required high school curriculum units may be admitted into Opportunity Program based on school achievement record and SAT/ACT. Institutional placement tests in mathematics and writing required of all freshmen. **Adult students:** SAT/ACT scores not required.

High school preparation. College-preparatory program required. 20 units required. Required units include English 4, mathematics 3, social studies 3, science 3 (laboratory 3), foreign language 2 and academic electives 4.

2015-2016 Annual costs. Tuition/fees: $6,886; $16,606 out-of-state. Per-credit charge: $262 in-state; $656 out-of-state. Books/supplies: $744. Personal expenses: $1,307.

Financial aid. All financial aid based on need. Work-study available nights, weekends and for part-time students.

Application procedures. Admission: No deadline. $40 fee, may be waived for applicants with need. Admission notification on a rolling basis beginning on or about 6/1. **Financial aid:** Priority date 4/15; no closing date. FAFSA required. Applicants notified on a rolling basis starting 7/15; must reply within 2 week(s) of notification.

Academics. Upper division courses leading to bachelor's degree in interdisciplinary studies available. Degree awarded by Columbia campus. **Special study options:** Cross-registration, distance learning, dual enrollment of high school students, independent study, internships, student-designed major. Bachelor's degree programs available on campus. **Credit/placement by examination:** AP, CLEP, institutional tests. **Support services:** Pre-admission summer program, reduced course load, remedial instruction, tutoring, writing center.

Majors. Liberal arts: Arts/sciences.

Technology on campus. PC or laptop required. Wireless network available.

Student life. Freshman orientation: Mandatory. Preregistration for classes offered. **Activities:** Drama, literary magazine, student government, student newspaper, Afro-American and political groups, student media association, computer club, history club, art club, travel club, music club, biology club.

Athletics. Intramural: Baseball M, basketball, racquetball, softball, table tennis, tennis, volleyball. **Team name:** Bantams.

Student services. Adult student services, career counseling, student employment services, financial aid counseling. **Transfer:** College fairs on campus for students transferring to 4-year colleges.

Contact. Phone: (864) 429-8728 Fax: (864) 424-8085
Brad Greer, Director of Enrollment Services, University of South Carolina: Union, PO Drawer 729, Union, SC 29379

Virginia College in Charleston
North Charleston, South Carolina
www.vc.edu/college/charleston-colleges.cfm

- For-profit 2-year health science and career college
- Large city

General. Regionally accredited; also accredited by ACICS. **Enrollment:** 414 undergraduates. **Degrees:** 3 bachelor's, 74 associate awarded. **Calendar:** Quarter. **Full-time faculty:** 14 total. **Part-time faculty:** 55 total.

Basis for selection. Open admission.

2015-2016 Annual costs. Diploma programs $14,652-$23,220. Associate degree programs $37,152-$39,072. Bachelor's program: $72,756.

Financial aid. Need-based: Work-study available nights, weekends and for part-time students.

Application procedures. Admission: $100 fee.

Academics. Credit/placement by examination: AP, CLEP.

Majors. Business: Business admin. **Health services:** Health information management, surgical technology.

Contact. E-mail: charleston.info@vc.edu
Phone: (843) 614-4300
Makina Wallace, Director of Admissions, Virginia College in Charleston, 6185 Rivers Avenue, North Charleston, SC 29406

Virginia College in Columbia
Columbia, South Carolina
www.vc.edu/college/columbia-colleges.cfm

- For-profit 2-year health science and career college
- Large city

General. Regionally accredited; also accredited by ACICS. **Enrollment:** 589 undergraduates. **Degrees:** 81 associate awarded. **Calendar:** Quarter. **Full-time faculty:** 10 total. **Part-time faculty:** 77 total.

Basis for selection. Open admission.

2015-2016 Annual costs. Total program tuition costs: Certificate programs range from $14,652 to $23,220; Associate degree programs range from $37,152 to $43,956.

Financial aid. Need-based: Work-study available nights, weekends and for part-time students.

Application procedures. Admission: $100 fee.

Academics. Credit/placement by examination: AP, CLEP.

Majors. Business: Business admin. **Health services:** Health information management, surgical technology.

Contact. E-mail: columbia.info@vc.edu
Phone: (803) 509-7100
Virginia College in Columbia, 7201 Two Notch Road, Columbia, SC 29223

Virginia College in Florence
Florence, South Carolina
www.vc.edu/florence

- For-profit 2-year career college
- Large town

General. Regionally accredited; also accredited by ACICS. **Enrollment:** 414 undergraduates. **Degrees:** 60 associate awarded. **Calendar:** Quarter. **Full-time faculty:** 2 total. **Part-time faculty:** 19 total.

Basis for selection. Open admission.

2015-2016 Annual costs. Diploma programs $23,220. Associate degree programs $37,152.

Financial aid. Need-based: Work-study available nights, weekends and for part-time students.

Academics. Credit/placement by examination: AP.

Majors. Health services: Medical assistant.

Contact. E-mail: florence.info@vc.edu
Phone: (843) 407-2200
Shannon Schwartz, Director of Admissions, Virginia College in Florence, 2400 David H. McLeod Blvd., Florence, SC 29501

Virginia College in Greenville
Greenville, South Carolina
www.vc.edu/campus/greenville-south-carolina-college.cfm

- For-profit 2-year business and career college
- Very large city

General. Regionally accredited; also accredited by ACICS. **Enrollment:** 453 undergraduates. **Degrees:** 48 associate awarded. **Calendar:** Quarter. **Full-time faculty:** 18 total. **Part-time faculty:** 30 total.

Basis for selection. Open admission.

2015-2016 Annual costs. Certificate programs $14,652-$23,220. Associate degree programs $37,152-$39,072.

Financial aid. Need-based: Work-study available nights, weekends and for part-time students.

Application procedures. Admission: $100 fee.

Academics. Credit/placement by examination: AP, CLEP.

Majors. Business: Business admin. **Health services:** Health information management, surgical technology.

Contact. E-mail: greenville.info@vc.edu
Phone: (864) 679-4900
Wayne McLaws, Director of Admissions, Virginia College in Greenville, 78 Global Drive, Greenville, SC 29607

Virginia College in Spartanburg
Spartanburg, South Carolina
www.spartanburg.vc.edu

- For-profit 2-year technical and career college
- Large city

General. Regionally accredited; also accredited by ACICS. **Enrollment:** 413 undergraduates. **Degrees:** 82 associate awarded. **Calendar:** Quarter. **Full-time faculty:** 8 total. **Part-time faculty:** 56 total.

Basis for selection. Open admission.

2015-2016 Annual costs. Certificate programs range from $14,652-$23,220. Associate degree programs $37,152-$43,956. Bachelor's program $71,208.

Financial aid. Need-based: Work-study available nights, weekends and for part-time students.

Application procedures. Admission: $100 fee.

Academics. Credit/placement by examination: AP, CLEP.

Majors. Business: Business admin. **Health services:** Health information management, surgical technology.

Contact. E-mail: spartanburg.info@vc.edu
Phone: (864) 504-3200
Virginia College in Spartanburg, 8150 Warren H. Abernathy Highway, Spartanburg, SC 29301

Williamsburg Technical College
Kingstree, South Carolina
www.wiltech.edu CB code: 5892

▶ Public 2-year community and technical college
▶ Commuter campus in small town

General. Founded in 1969. Regionally accredited. **Enrollment:** 686 degree-seeking undergraduates; 7 non-degree-seeking students. **Degrees:** 64 associate awarded. **Location:** 75 miles from Charleston, 40 miles from Florence. **Calendar:** Semester, extensive summer session.

Student profile. Among degree-seeking undergraduates, 254 enrolled as first-time, first-year students, 26 transferred in from other institutions.

Part-time: 71% **Women:** 57%

Transfer out. Colleges most students transferred to 2015: Francis Marion University, Coker College, Limestone College, University of South Carolina, Coastal Carolina University.

Basis for selection. Open admission. Academically weak students must enroll in Applied Studies Program.

High school preparation. 25 units recommended. Recommended units include English 4, mathematics 4, social studies 3, history 1, science 3, foreign language 1 and academic electives 7. Recommend 1 unit computer technology, 6 or more units in occupational area will substitute for one science.

2015-2016 Annual costs. Tuition/fees: $4,008; $4,128 out-of-district; $7,608 out-of-state. Books/supplies: $1,125. Personal expenses: $2,205.

2014-2015 Financial aid. Need-based: Need-based aid available for part-time students. Work-study available nights, weekends and for part-time students. **Non-need-based:** Scholarships awarded for academics, leadership, minority status, state residency. **Additional information:** Tuition waivers for children of war veterans.

Application procedures. Admission: No deadline. No application fee. Admission notification on a rolling basis. **Financial aid:** No deadline. FAFSA required. Applicants notified on a rolling basis starting 7/1; must reply within 4 week(s) of notification.

Academics. Special study options: Distance learning, double major, dual enrollment of high school students, honors, independent study, internships, liberal arts/career combination, student-designed major. Bachelor's degree programs available on campus. License preparation in nursing. **Credit/placement by examination:** AP, CLEP, institutional tests. 18 credit hours maximum toward associate degree. **Support services:** Learning center, pre-admission summer program, remedial instruction, study skills assistance, tutoring.

Majors. Business: General, administrative services, information resources management, office management. **Computer sciences:** General. **Education:** Early childhood, teacher assistance. **Engineering:** Electrical. **Liberal arts:** Arts/sciences.

Technology on campus. 60 workstations in library, computer center. Commuter students can connect to campus network. Online library, wireless network available.

Student life. Freshman orientation: Mandatory. Preregistration for classes offered. **Activities:** Student government, Phi Theta Kappa Honor Society.

Student services. Career counseling, services for economically disadvantaged, financial aid counseling, personal counseling, placement for graduates, veterans' counselor. **Physically disabled:** Services for hearing impaired. **Transfer:** Pre-admission transcript evaluation for new students. College fairs on campus for students transferring to 4-year colleges.

Contact. E-mail: dubosec@wiltech.edu
Phone: (843) 355-4165 Toll-free number: (800) 768-2021
Fax: (843) 355-4289
Alexis DuBose, Registrar, Williamsburg Technical College, 601 Martin Luther King Avenue, Kingstree, SC 29556-4197

York Technical College
Rock Hill, South Carolina
www.yorktech.edu CB code: 5989

▶ Public 2-year community and technical college
▶ Commuter campus in large town

General. Founded in 1962. Regionally accredited. Member of Charlotte Area Consortium of Colleges and Universities. **Enrollment:** 4,416 degree-seeking undergraduates. **Degrees:** 517 associate awarded. **Location:** 70 miles from Columbia; 14 miles from Charlotte, NC. **Calendar:** Semester, extensive summer session. **Full-time faculty:** 127 total. **Part-time faculty:** 225 total. **Partnerships:** Formal partnerships with 3D Systems, Okuma Corporation.

Student profile.

Out-of-state: 5% **25 or older:** 65%

Transfer out. Colleges most students transferred to 2015: Winthrop University, Clemson University, University of South Carolina.

Basis for selection. Open admission, but selective for some programs. COMPASS, SAT, or ACT scores may be used for admission and placement. Additional qualification criteria required for admission to limited enrollment Health Science programs. **Home schooled:** Applicants must have graduated from approved South Carolina homeschool association or a homeschool recognized by the Department of Education in its home state to be classified as a high school graduate. **Learning Disabled:** Students with disabilities who wish to receive special testing accommodations should contact Special Resources Office in Student Services.

High school preparation. College prep chemistry required for dental hygiene and nursing (RN) program.

2015-2016 Annual costs. Tuition/fees: $5,020; $5,470 out-of-district; $11,350 out-of-state. Per-credit charge: $161 in-district; $176 out-of-district; $372 out-of-state. Books/supplies: $1,200.

Financial aid. Need-based: Need-based aid available for part-time students. Work-study available nights, weekends and for part-time students. **Non-need-based:** Scholarships awarded for academics, leadership, state residency.

Application procedures. Admission: No deadline. No application fee. Application must be submitted online. Admission notification on a rolling basis. **Financial aid:** Priority date 6/1; no closing date. FAFSA required. Applicants notified on a rolling basis starting 4/1; must reply within 2 week(s) of notification.

Academics. Special study options: Cooperative education, distance learning, dual enrollment of high school students, liberal arts/career combination. License preparation in dental hygiene, nursing, paramedic, radiology, real estate. **Credit/placement by examination:** AP, CLEP, institutional tests. At least 25% of semester credit hours required for program completion must be earned through instruction at York Technical College. **Support services:** Learning center, reduced course load, remedial instruction, study skills assistance, tutoring, writing center.

Majors. Business: General, accounting, administrative services, business admin, human resources, logistics. **Computer sciences:** Applications programming, LAN/WAN management, programming. **Education:** Early childhood. **Health services:** Clinical lab technology, dental hygiene, medical radiologic technology/radiation therapy, nursing (RN), radiologic technology/medical imaging. **Liberal arts:** Arts/sciences. **Protective services:** Fire services admin, police science.

Most popular majors. Business/marketing 34%, engineering/engineering technologies 10%, family/consumer sciences 9%, health sciences 16%, liberal arts 15%.

Technology on campus. 180 workstations in library, computer center. Commuter students can connect to campus network. Online library, helpline, wireless network available.

Student life. Freshman orientation: Mandatory. Preregistration for classes offered. Held by department of study before classes begin. **Activities:** Jacobin Society, Phi Theta Kappa, Christian Fellowship, Students With Vision.

Student services. Career counseling, student employment services, financial aid counseling, on-campus daycare, personal counseling, placement for graduates, veterans' counselor. **Physically disabled:** Services for visually, hearing impaired. **Transfer:** Transfer adviser, college fairs on campus for students transferring to 4-year colleges.

Two-Year Colleges

Contact. E-mail: admissionsoffice@yorktech.com
Phone: (803) 327-8008 Toll-free number: (800) 922-8324
Fax: (803) 981-7237
Kenny Aldridge, Admissions Department Manager, York Technical
College, 452 South Anderson Road, Rock Hill, SC 29730

Two-Year Colleges

South Dakota

Globe University: Sioux Falls
Sioux Falls, South Dakota
www.globeuniversity.edu

- For-profit 2-year career college
- Commuter campus in small city
- Interview required

General. Regionally accredited; also accredited by ACICS. **Enrollment:** 138 undergraduates. **Degrees:** 3 bachelor's, 37 associate awarded. **Calendar:** Quarter, extensive summer session. **Partnerships:** Agreements with Microsoft Developers Network Academic Alliance.

Basis for selection. Open admission.

2015-2016 Annual costs. Tuition/fees: $18,702. Per-credit charge: $390. Books/supplies: $1,260.

Financial aid. Need-based: Need-based aid available for part-time students. Work-study available nights, weekends and for part-time students.

Application procedures. Admission: No deadline. $50 fee. Admission notification on a rolling basis. **Financial aid:** No deadline. FAFSA, institutional form required. Applicants notified on a rolling basis starting 7/1; must reply within 2 week(s) of notification.

Academics. Special study options: Distance learning, independent study, internships, liberal arts/career combination. **Credit/placement by examination:** AP, CLEP. **Support services:** Remedial instruction, study skills assistance, tutoring, writing center.

Majors. Business: Accounting, business admin, marketing. **Health services:** Massage therapy, medical assistant, medical secretary, veterinary technology/assistant. **Protective services:** Law enforcement admin.

Most popular majors. Business/marketing 21%, health sciences 69%, legal studies 9%.

Technology on campus. 60 workstations in library, computer center, student center. Commuter students can connect to campus network. Online library, helpline, student web hosting, wireless network available.

Student life. Freshman orientation: Mandatory. Preregistration for classes offered. Day and evening sessions available the week prior to classes starting. **Activities:** Literary magazine.

Student services. Career counseling, student employment services, financial aid counseling, placement for graduates. **Transfer:** Re-entry adviser for new students.

Contact. Toll-free number: (866) 437-0705
Charlie Buehler, Director of Admissions, Globe University: Sioux Falls, 5101 South Broadband Lane, Sioux Falls, SD 57108

Kilian Community College
Sioux Falls, South Dakota
www.kilian.edu   CB code: 6149

- Private 2-year community college
- Commuter campus in small city

General. Founded in 1976. Regionally accredited. **Enrollment:** 145 degree-seeking undergraduates; 25 non-degree-seeking students. **Degrees:** 56 associate awarded. **Location:** 180 miles from Omaha, NE; 240 miles from Minneapolis-St. Paul. **Calendar:** Trimester, limited summer session. **Full-time faculty:** 4 total; 50% have terminal degrees, 75% women. **Part-time faculty:** 19 total; 21% have terminal degrees, 10% minority, 47% women. **Class size:** 100% < 20.

Student profile. Among degree-seeking undergraduates, 53% enrolled in a transfer program, 33% enrolled in a vocational program, 1% already have a bachelor's degree or higher, 26 enrolled as first-time, first-year students, 25 transferred in from other institutions.

Part-time:	90%	Asian American:	3%
Out-of-state:	2%	Hispanic/Latino:	1%
Women:	68%	Native American:	8%
African American:	18%	25 or older:	45%

Transfer out. 60% of students enrolled in the transfer program go on to 4-year colleges. **Colleges most students transferred to 2015:** University of Sioux Falls, University of South Dakota, South Dakota State University, National American University.

Basis for selection. Open admission. **Learning Disabled:** Students must provide documentation to Dean of Student Services/Counselor prior to enrolling.

2015-2016 Annual costs. Tuition/fees: $10,650. Per-credit charge: $355. Books/supplies: $1,800. Personal expenses: $4,113.

Financial aid. Need-based: Need-based aid available for part-time students. Work-study available nights, weekends and for part-time students. **Non-need-based:** Scholarships awarded for academics, leadership.

Application procedures. Admission: No deadline. No application fee. Admission notification on a rolling basis. **Financial aid:** No deadline. FAFSA, institutional form required. Applicants notified on a rolling basis starting 7/1; must reply within 2 week(s) of notification.

Academics. Special study options: Cross-registration, double major, dual enrollment of high school students, ESL, independent study, internships. **Credit/placement by examination:** AP, CLEP, institutional tests. 31 credit hours maximum toward associate degree. **Support services:** Learning center, reduced course load, remedial instruction, study skills assistance, tutoring, writing center.

Majors. Business: Accounting, business admin. **Computer sciences:** General. **Education:** Early childhood. **Health services:** Medical secretary, substance abuse counseling. **History:** General. **Human services:** Social work. **Liberal arts:** Arts/sciences. **Protective services:** Criminal justice. **Psychology:** General. **Social sciences:** Sociology.

Most popular majors. Business/marketing 9%, education 9%, health sciences 11%, liberal arts 32%, public administration/social services 16%, security/protective services 11%.

Technology on campus. 48 workstations in computer center, student center. Online library, wireless network available.

Student life. Freshman orientation: Available. Preregistration for classes offered. Two-three hour program held the week before classes begin.

Student services. Adult student services, financial aid counseling, personal counseling. **Transfer:** Pre-admission transcript evaluation for new students. Transfer adviser, college fairs on campus for students transferring to 4-year colleges.

Contact. E-mail: wthorson@kilian.edu
Phone: (605) 221-3100 Toll-free number: (800) 888-1147
Fax: (605) 336-2606
Wendy Thorson, Director of Admissions, Kilian Community College, 300 East 6th Street, Sioux Falls, SD 57103-7020

Lake Area Technical Institute
Watertown, South Dakota
www.lakeareatech.edu   CB code: 0717

- Public 2-year technical college
- Commuter campus in large town

General. Founded in 1965. Regionally accredited. **Enrollment:** 1,691 degree-seeking undergraduates; 155 non-degree-seeking students. **Degrees:** 491 associate awarded. **Location:** 90 miles from Sioux Falls. **Calendar:** Semester, limited summer session. **Full-time faculty:** 102 total; 43% women. **Part-time faculty:** 68 total; 50% women. **Special facilities:** Anatomy lab, interdisciplinary health simulation lab, 3D printer lab/maker space.

Student profile. Among degree-seeking undergraduates, 100% enrolled in a vocational program, 1,236 enrolled as first-time, first-year students.

Part-time:	9%	Hispanic/Latino:	1%
Women:	45%	Native American:	2%
Asian American:	1%		

Basis for selection. Open admission, but selective for some programs. Testing requirements vary by program. Entrance exam required for Nursing. Writing sample required for Occupational Therapy Assistant, and Physical Therapist Assistant programs. Photography requires a portfolio including digital image photography, and an essay. **Home schooled:** State high school equivalency certificate required.

High school preparation. 3 units math/science recommended.

2015-2016 Annual costs. Tuition/fees: $6,089; $6,089 out-of-state. Per-credit charge: $109. Books/supplies: $1,300. Personal expenses: $1,300.

2014-2015 Financial aid. All financial aid based on need. 463 full-time freshmen applied for aid; 380 deemed to have need; 378 received aid. Average need met was 54%. Average scholarship/grant was $4,383; average loan $4,024. 33% of total undergraduate aid awarded as scholarships/grants, 67% as loans/jobs. Need-based aid available for part-time students. Work-study available nights, weekends and for part-time students.

Application procedures. Admission: No deadline. $25 fee. Admission notification on a rolling basis. **Financial aid:** Priority date 4/1; no closing date. FAFSA required. Applicants notified on a rolling basis starting 5/1.

Academics. Special study options: Distance learning, dual enrollment of high school students, internships. License preparation in aviation, nursing, paramedic. **Credit/placement by examination:** AP, CLEP, institutional tests. **Support services:** GED preparation and test center, learning center, reduced course load, remedial instruction, study skills assistance, tutoring.

Majors. Business: Banking/financial services, marketing. **Computer sciences:** Computer science. **Conservation:** Environmental science. **General:** Building construction. **Health services:** Clinical lab technology, dental assistant, EMT paramedic, medical assistant, occupational therapy assistant, physical therapy assistant. **Protective services:** Police science.

Most popular majors. Agriculture 23%, business/marketing 12%, engineering/engineering technologies 7%, health sciences 17%, public administration/social services 6%, trade and industry 32%.

Technology on campus. 70 workstations in library, computer center, student center. Online library, helpline, wireless network available.

Student life. Freshman orientation: Mandatory. Preregistration for classes offered. **Activities:** Campus ministries, student government.

Athletics. Intercollegiate: Rodeo. **Intramural:** Basketball, bowling, softball, volleyball.

Student services. Alcohol/substance abuse counseling, career counseling, student employment services, financial aid counseling, health services, minority student services, on-campus daycare, personal counseling, placement for graduates, veterans' counselor. **Transfer:** Transfer adviser for students transferring to 4-year colleges.

Contact. Phone: (605) 882-5284 Toll-free number: (800) 657-4344 Fax: (605) 882-6299
LuAnn Strait, Director of Institutional Relations, Lake Area Technical Institute, PO Box 730, Watertown, SD 57201

Mitchell Technical Institute
Mitchell, South Dakota
www.mitchelltech.edu   **CB code: 7038**

◆ Public 2-year technical college
◆ Commuter campus in large town

General. Founded in 1968. Regionally accredited. **Enrollment:** 1,096 degree-seeking undergraduates; 165 non-degree-seeking students. **Degrees:** 349 associate awarded. **Location:** 70 miles from Sioux Falls. **Calendar:** Semester, limited summer session. **Full-time faculty:** 80 total; 1% have terminal degrees, 1% minority, 42% women. **Part-time faculty:** 13 total; 62% women. **Class size:** 72% < 20, 24% 20-39, 4% 40-49. **Special facilities:** Satellite communications earth station, indoor utilities field, wind turbine, high fidelity medical simulation lab. **Partnerships:** Formal partnerships with AGCO Dealer Service and Workforce Recruitment Program.

Student profile. Among degree-seeking undergraduates, 100% enrolled in a vocational program, 3% already have a bachelor's degree or higher, 377 enrolled as first-time, first-year students, 110 transferred in from other institutions.

Part-time:	23%	Hispanic/Latino:	2%
Out-of-state:	9%	Native American:	3%
Women:	33%	Multi-racial, non-Hispanic:	1%
Asian American:	1%	25 or older:	27%

Transfer out. 4% of students enrolled in the transfer program go on to 4-year colleges. **Colleges most students transferred to 2015:** South Dakota State University, Dakota Wesleyan University, University of South Dakota, Black Hills State University, Dakota State University.

Basis for selection. Additional application, job shadow essay, interviews, and weighting of GPA and ACT required for radiologic technology and radiation therapy. Accuplacer is used for students without an ACT test. Interviews required for selected programs. **Adult students:** ACCUPLACER scores in place of the ACT. **Home schooled:** Statement describing home school structure and mission, transcript of courses and grades required.

2015-2016 Annual costs. Tuition/fees: $5,880; $5,880 out-of-state. Per-credit charge: $109. Books/supplies: $758. Personal expenses: $2,300.

2015-2016 Financial aid. Need-based: Average need met was 52%. Average scholarship/grant was $4,463; average loan $2,965. 63% of total undergraduate aid awarded as scholarships/grants, 37% as loans/jobs. Need-based aid available for part-time students. Work-study available nights, weekends and for part-time students. **Non-need-based:** Scholarships awarded for academics, alumni affiliation, job skills.

Application procedures. Admission: Closing date 9/1. No application fee. Admission notification on a rolling basis. **Financial aid:** No deadline. FAFSA required. Applicants notified on a rolling basis; must reply within 3 week(s) of notification.

Academics. Special study options: Distance learning, double major, dual enrollment of high school students, internships. License preparation in radiology. **Credit/placement by examination:** AP, CLEP, ACT, institutional tests. 12 credit hours maximum toward associate degree. **Support services:** Learning center, reduced course load, remedial instruction, study skills assistance, tutoring.

Majors. Business: Accounting/business management. **Computer sciences:** Support specialist, system admin. **General:** Building construction, electrician, lineworker. **Health services:** Clinical lab technology, medical assistant, medical radiologic technology/radiation therapy, office assistant, radiologic technology/medical imaging, speech-language pathology assistant. **Social sciences:** GIS/cartography.

Most popular majors. Agriculture 17%, business/marketing 6%, communications/journalism 6%, computer/information sciences 7%, engineering/engineering technologies 11%, health sciences 21%, trade and industry 29%.

Technology on campus. PC or laptop required. 100 workstations in library, computer center. Online library, helpline, repair service, wireless network available.

Student life. Freshman orientation: Mandatory. Preregistration for classes offered. **Activities:** Student government.

Athletics. Intercollegiate: Rodeo. **Intramural:** Basketball, bowling, volleyball. **Team name:** Mavericks.

Student services. Adult student services, career counseling, services for economically disadvantaged, student employment services, financial aid counseling, personal counseling, placement for graduates. **Physically disabled:** Services for visually, speech, hearing impaired. **Transfer:** Transfer adviser for students transferring to 4-year colleges.

Contact. E-mail: questions@mitchelltech.edu
Phone: (605) 995-3025 Toll-free number: (800) 684-1969
Fax: (605) 996-3299
Clayton Deuter, Director of Admission, Mitchell Technical Institute, 1800 E Spruce Street, Mitchell, SD 57301

Sisseton Wahpeton College
Sisseton, South Dakota
www.swc.tc   **CB code: 3403**

◆ Public 2-year technical college
◆ Commuter campus in large town

General. Founded in 1979. Regionally accredited. Member of American Indian Higher Education Consortium. Dakota language and culture resource. **Enrollment:** 127 degree-seeking undergraduates; 5 non-degree-seeking students. **Degrees:** 13 associate awarded. **Location:** 48 miles from Watertown; 85 miles from Fargo, ND. **Calendar:** Semester, limited summer session. **Full-time faculty:** 10 total; 20% minority, 50% women. **Part-time faculty:** 13 total; 8% have terminal degrees, 62% minority, 54% women. **Special facilities:** Indians in North America book collection, Song to the Great Spirit building, Institute for Excellence in Dakota language.

Student profile. Among degree-seeking undergraduates, 27 enrolled as first-time, first-year students.

Part-time:	35%	**Women:**	68%
Out-of-state:	1%		

Transfer out. Colleges most students transferred to 2015: University of Minnesota, North Dakota State University, University of North Dakota, South Dakota State University, University of South Dakota.

Basis for selection. Open admission. If student is member of recognized Native American tribe, must submit certification of tribal membership. **Adult students:** Compass Test. **Home schooled:** State high school equivalency certificate required.

High school preparation. College-preparatory program recommended.

2015-2016 Annual costs. Tuition/fees: $3,940. Per-credit charge: $115. Books/supplies: $600. Personal expenses: $1,680. **Additional information:** Non-ISC funded students pay $125 per-credit-hour.

Financial aid. Need-based: Need-based aid available for part-time students. Work-study available nights, weekends and for part-time students.

Application procedures. Admission: Closing date 7/1. No application fee. Admission notification on a rolling basis. **Financial aid:** Priority date 12/15; no closing date. FAFSA required. Applicants notified on a rolling basis.

Academics. Special study options: Double major, dual enrollment of high school students, independent study, internships, liberal arts/career combination. **Credit/placement by examination:** AP, CLEP, institutional tests. **Support services:** GED preparation and test center, learning center, remedial instruction, tutoring.

Majors. Area/ethnic studies: Native American. **Business:** Accounting, business admin. **Computer sciences:** General. **Education:** Early childhood. **General:** Carpentry. **Health services:** Substance abuse counseling. **Liberal arts:** Arts/sciences. **Physical sciences:** Environmental chemistry.

Most popular majors. Business/marketing 11%, computer/information sciences 20%, health sciences 27%, interdisciplinary studies 7%, liberal arts 15%.

Technology on campus. 148 workstations in library, computer center, student center. Wireless network available.

Student life. Freshman orientation: Mandatory. Preregistration for classes offered. Two-day program. **Activities:** Student government.

Student services. Career counseling, financial aid counseling, personal counseling. **Transfer:** Transfer adviser for students transferring to 4-year colleges.

Contact. E-mail: dredday@swc.tc
Phone: (605) 698-3966 ext. 1101 Fax: (605) 698-3132
Darlene Redday, Admissions Officer/Registrar, Sisseton Wahpeton College, BIA 700, Box 689, Sisseton, SD 57262-0689

Southeast Technical Institute
Sioux Falls, South Dakota
www.southeasttech.edu   CB code: 7054

♦ Public 2-year technical college
♦ Commuter campus in small city

General. Founded in 1969. Regionally accredited. **Enrollment:** 1,899 degree-seeking undergraduates; 148 non-degree-seeking students. **Degrees:** 689 associate awarded. **Location:** 220 miles from Minneapolis-St. Paul; 200 miles from Omaha, NE. **Calendar:** Semester, limited summer session. **Full-time faculty:** 84 total. **Part-time faculty:** 82 total.

Student profile. Among degree-seeking undergraduates, 100% enrolled in a vocational program, 5% already have a bachelor's degree or higher, 416 enrolled as first-time, first-year students.

Part-time:	32%	**25 or older:**	27%
Out-of-state:	9%	**Live on campus:**	2%
Women:	52%		

Transfer out. Colleges most students transferred to 2015: University of Sioux Falls, Bellevue University, Colorado Technical University, South Dakota State University, University of South Dakota.

Basis for selection. Open admission, but selective for some programs. Additional testing and background checks required for all health and human

services programs. ACT recommended for all, but only required for health students. **Home schooled:** Statement describing home school structure and mission, transcript of courses and grades, interview required. ACT and institutional entrance exam required.

High school preparation. 22 units recommended. Recommended units include English 4, mathematics 3, social studies 3, science 3, computer science 1, visual/performing arts 1 and academic electives 6. Physical education .5, economics or personal finance .5.

2015-2016 Annual costs. Tuition/fees: $6,600; $6,600 out-of-state. Per-credit charge: $109. Books/supplies: $1,400. Personal expenses: $1,800.

Financial aid. All financial aid based on need. Need-based aid available for part-time students. Work-study available nights, weekends and for part-time students.

Application procedures. Admission: No deadline. No application fee. Admission notification on a rolling basis. Must reply by May 1 or within 4 week(s) if notified thereafter. **Financial aid:** Priority date 5/1; no closing date. FAFSA required. Applicants notified on a rolling basis starting 5/1; must reply within 3 week(s) of notification.

Academics. Special study options: Double major, dual enrollment of high school students, independent study. Bachelor's degree programs available on campus. License preparation in nursing, real estate. **Credit/placement by examination:** AP, CLEP, IB, institutional tests. 30 credit hours maximum toward associate degree. **Support services:** GED preparation and test center, learning center, reduced course load, remedial instruction, study skills assistance, tutoring.

Majors. Architecture: Technology. **Biology:** Biomedical sciences. **Business:** Accounting, banking/financial services, business admin, construction management, entrepreneurial studies, human resources, insurance, marketing. **Communications:** Advertising. **Communications technology:** Animation/special effects, graphic/printing. **Computer sciences:** General, applications programming, LAN/WAN management, networking, programming. **General:** Site management. **Health services:** Cardiovascular technology, electroencephalograph technology, nuclear medical technology, nursing (RN), sonography, ward clerk. **Protective services:** Law enforcement admin. **Visual/performing arts:** Commercial/advertising art. **Work/family studies:** Child care management.

Most popular majors. Business/marketing 40%, health sciences 25%, trade and industry 23%.

Technology on campus. PC or laptop required. 88 workstations in library, computer center, student center. Commuter students can connect to campus network. Online course registration, online library, helpline, repair service, student web hosting, wireless network available.

Student life. Freshman orientation: Available. Preregistration for classes offered. Held 8 times throughout the summer, about 4 hours. **Housing:** Apartments available. $100 fully refundable deposit, deadline 7/1. **Activities:** Student government.

Student services. Career counseling, student employment services, financial aid counseling, on-campus daycare, personal counseling, placement for graduates. **Physically disabled:** Services for visually, speech, hearing impaired. **Transfer:** Pre-admission transcript evaluation for new students. College fairs on campus for students transferring to 4-year colleges.

Contact. E-mail: admissions@southeasttech.edu
Phone: (605) 367-6040 Toll-free number: (800) 247-0789
Fax: (605) 367-8305
Jim Rokusek, Director of Student Services, Southeast Technical Institute, 2320 North Career Avenue, Sioux Falls, SD 57107

Western Dakota Technical Institute
Rapid City, South Dakota
www.wdt.edu   CB code: 6393

♦ Public 2-year technical college
♦ Commuter campus in small city

General. Founded in 1978. Regionally accredited. **Enrollment:** 810 degree-seeking undergraduates. **Degrees:** 203 associate awarded. **Location:** 3 miles from downtown. **Calendar:** Semester, limited summer session. **Full-time faculty:** 41 total. **Part-time faculty:** 36 total. **Class size:** 69% < 20, 31% 20-39.

Student profile.

Out-of-state:	3%	**25 or older:**	44%

Transfer out. Colleges most students transferred to 2015: Black Hills State University.

Basis for selection. Open admission, but selective for some programs. Special requirements for nursing, law enforcement, surgical technology, phlebotomy and paralegal programs. Applicants may be placed on waiting lists for programs reaching capacity. Interview, recommendations required for law enforcement, practical nursing, surgical technology and phlebotomy programs.

High school preparation. Recommended units include English 4 and mathematics 2.

2015-2016 Annual costs. Tuition/fees: $5,850; $5,850 out-of-state. Per-credit charge: $109. Books/supplies: $2,119. Personal expenses: $1,906.

Financial aid. Need-based: Need-based aid available for part-time students. Work-study available nights, weekends and for part-time students.

Application procedures. Admission: Closing date 8/1 (postmark date). $20 fee. Admission notification on a rolling basis. **Financial aid:** Priority date 4/20; no closing date. FAFSA required. Applicants notified on a rolling basis starting 4/30; must reply within 2 week(s) of notification.

Academics. Special study options: Distance learning, dual enrollment of high school students, internships. License preparation in nursing, paramedic. **Credit/placement by examination:** AP, CLEP, institutional tests. 35 credit hours maximum toward associate degree. **Support services:** Learning center, pre-admission summer program, reduced course load, remedial instruction, study skills assistance, tutoring.

Majors. Business: Accounting, business admin, marketing. **Computer sciences:** Networking. **General:** Electrician. **Health services:** EMT paramedic, medical assistant, medical transcription, pharmacy assistant, surgical technology. **Liberal arts:** Library assistant. **Protective services:** Criminal justice, firefighting, police science.

Most popular majors. Business/marketing 15%, computer/information sciences 7%, engineering/engineering technologies 13%, health sciences 23%, security/protective services 12%, trade and industry 27%.

Technology on campus. PC or laptop required. 32 workstations in library, computer center. Commuter students can connect to campus network. Online course registration, online library, helpline, repair service, wireless network available.

Student life. Freshman orientation: Mandatory. Preregistration for classes offered. One-day session held prior to start of classes. **Policies:** Regular attendance required. Must make commitment to attend classes/labs 5 days a week from 8AM to 3PM. **Activities:** Student government, student newspaper, minority club, single-parent club.

Student services. Adult student services, alcohol/substance abuse counseling, career counseling, services for economically disadvantaged, student employment services, financial aid counseling, minority student services, personal counseling, placement for graduates, veterans' counselor, women's services. **Physically disabled:** Services for visually, speech, hearing impaired. **Transfer:** Pre-admission transcript evaluation for new students. Transfer adviser for students transferring to 4-year colleges.

Contact. E-mail: admissions@wdt.edu
Phone: (605) 718-2411 Toll-free number: (800) 544-8765
Fax: (605) 394-2204
Jill Elder, Admissions Coordinator, Western Dakota Technical Institute, 800 Mickelson Drive, Rapid City, SD 57703

Tennessee

Chattanooga College
Chattanooga, Tennessee
www.chattanoogacollege.edu
CB code: 2267

◆ For-profit 2-year technical college
◆ Large city

General. Regionally accredited; also accredited by ACCSC. **Enrollment:** 340 undergraduates. **Degrees:** 68 associate awarded. **Calendar:** Quarter. **Full-time faculty:** 14 total. **Part-time faculty:** 7 total.

Basis for selection. Comprehensive Career Program Assessment Test (CPAT) required. 145 minimum level to enter diploma program. Interview required with emphasis on attitude.

Financial aid. Need-based: Work-study available nights, weekends and for part-time students.

Application procedures. Admission: No deadline. $25 fee. Admission notification on a rolling basis. **Financial aid:** No deadline. Institutional form required.

Academics. Credit transfer available for a grade of B or above. **Credit/placement by examination:** AP, CLEP.

Majors. Business: Tourism/travel. **Computer sciences:** Programming. **Health services:** Dental assistant, health information technology, medical assistant, office admin. **Protective services:** Criminal justice.

Contact. E-mail: tonym@ecpconline.com
Phone: (423) 624-0077
Tony McFadden, Director of Admissions, Chattanooga College, 3805 Brainerd Road, Chattanooga, TN 37411

Chattanooga State Community College
Chattanooga, Tennessee
www.chattanoogastate.edu
CB code: 1084

◆ Public 2-year community and technical college
◆ Commuter campus in small city

General. Founded in 1963. Regionally accredited. Credit-bearing courses offered at various off-campus locations. **Enrollment:** 9,374 degree-seeking undergraduates. **Degrees:** 934 associate awarded. **Location:** 129 miles from Nashville. **Calendar:** Semester, limited summer session. **Full-time faculty:** 203 total. **Part-time faculty:** 389 total.

Student profile.

Out-of-state: 9% 25 or older: 41%

Transfer out. Colleges most students transferred to 2015: Austin Peay State University, East Tennessee State University, Middle Tennessee State University, Tennessee Tech University, University of Tennessee at Chattanooga.

Basis for selection. Open admission, but selective for some programs. Special requirements for allied health program. National standardized dental assisting and dental hygiene tests required of applicants to these programs. Interview required for allied health, nursing programs. **Adult students:** Placement test required. **Home schooled:** Transcript of courses and grades required. Students must register with local department/board of education or present affiliation with accredited homeschool agency.

High school preparation. 19 units recommended. Recommended units include English 4, mathematics 3, social studies 1, history 1, science 2 (laboratory 1), foreign language 2 and visual/performing arts 1. College preparatory program required for students choosing transfer majors.

2015-2016 Annual costs. Tuition/fees: $4,153; $16,123 out-of-state. Books/supplies: $1,800.

Financial aid. Need-based: Need-based aid available for part-time students. Work-study available nights, weekends and for part-time students. **Non-need-based:** Scholarships awarded for state residency.

Application procedures. Admission: Priority date 8/16; no deadline. No application fee. Admission notification on a rolling basis. High school students may enroll in college classes during their high school years, but are not admitted as a first-year freshman. **Financial aid:** Priority date 6/1; no closing date. FAFSA required. Applicants notified on a rolling basis starting 4/1; must reply within 2 week(s) of notification.

Academics. Special study options: Accelerated study, cooperative education, cross-registration, distance learning, double major, dual enrollment of high school students, honors, independent study, internships, student-designed major, teacher certification program. Bachelor's degree programs available on campus. License preparation in dental hygiene, nursing, occupational therapy, paramedic, physical therapy, radiology, real estate. **Credit/placement by examination:** AP, CLEP, IB, institutional tests. Final 20 hours must be taken in residency; maximum of 40 hours may be awarded by combination of credit by exam and credit for experience. **Support services:** GED preparation and test center, learning center, pre-admission summer program, reduced course load, remedial instruction, study skills assistance, tutoring, writing center.

Honors college/program. 25 ACT/1130-1160 SAT and 3.5 GPA required.

Majors. Business: Accounting technology, administrative services, business admin, management information systems, office/clerical. **Communications:** Advertising. **Computer sciences:** Web page design. **Education:** General. **Engineering:** Pre-engineering. **English:** Technical writing. **Foreign languages:** Sign language interpretation. **Health services:** Dental hygiene, environmental health, health information technology, medical radiologic technology/radiation therapy, nursing (RN), physical therapy assistant, respiratory therapy technology, veterinary technology/assistant. **Human services:** Community org/advocacy. **Liberal arts:** Arts/sciences. **Protective services:** Firefighting. **Visual/performing arts:** Commercial/advertising art. **Work/family studies:** Food/nutrition.

Most popular majors. Business/marketing 6%, engineering/engineering technologies 18%, health sciences 29%, liberal arts 37%.

Technology on campus. 1,200 workstations in library, computer center, student center. Commuter students can connect to campus network. Online course registration, online library, helpline, wireless network available.

Student life. Freshman orientation: Mandatory. Preregistration for classes offered. 5-hour sessions held July-August. **Activities:** Jazz band, choral groups, drama, music ensembles, radio station, student government, student newspaper, TV station, Baptist student union.

Athletics. NJCAA. **Intercollegiate:** Baseball M, basketball. **Intramural:** Racquetball, soccer, softball, table tennis, tennis. **Team name:** Tigers.

Student services. Adult student services, alcohol/substance abuse counseling, career counseling, services for economically disadvantaged, student employment services, financial aid counseling, minority student services, on-campus daycare, personal counseling, placement for graduates, veterans' counselor. **Physically disabled:** Services for visually, speech, hearing impaired. **Transfer:** Transfer adviser, college fairs on campus for students transferring to 4-year colleges.

Contact. Phone: (423) 697-4401 Fax: (423) 697-4709
Gail Campbell, Director Admissions and Records, Chattanooga State Community College, 4501 Amnicola Highway, Chattanooga, TN 37406

Cleveland State Community College
Cleveland, Tennessee
www.clevelandstatecc.edu
CB code: 2848

◆ Public 2-year community college
◆ Commuter campus in small city

General. Founded in 1967. Regionally accredited. **Enrollment:** 2,387 degree-seeking undergraduates; 1,122 non-degree-seeking students. **Degrees:** 369 associate awarded. **Location:** 30 miles from Chattanooga, 80 miles from Knoxville. **Calendar:** Semester, limited summer session. **Full-time faculty:** 76 total; 17% have terminal degrees, 12% minority, 58% women. **Part-time faculty:** 144 total; 10% have terminal degrees, 5% minority, 59% women. **Class size:** 58% < 20, 40% 20-39, 2% 40-49, less than 1% 50-99. **Special facilities:** Nature trail.

Student profile. Among degree-seeking undergraduates, 35% enrolled in a transfer program, 40% enrolled in a vocational program, 835 enrolled as first-time, first-year students, 163 transferred in from other institutions.

Part-time:	34%	**Women:**	61%
Out-of-state:	1%	**25 or older:**	26%

Transfer out. Colleges most students transferred to 2015: University of Tennessee-Chattanooga, University of Tennessee-Knoxville, Tennessee Technological University, Lee University.

Basis for selection. Open admission, but selective for some programs. Program admission required for nursing and medical office assistant. **Home schooled:** Transcript of courses and grades required.

High school preparation. 22 units required. Required units include English 4, mathematics 4, social studies 3, history 1, science 3 (laboratory 1), foreign language 2, visual/performing arts 1 and academic electives 3. 1.5 physical education, .5 personal finance.

2015-2016 Annual costs. Tuition/fees: $4,127; $15,917 out-of-state. Per-credit charge: $152 in-state; $627 out-of-state. Books/supplies: $650. Personal expenses: $3,237.

2015-2016 Financial aid. Need-based: 532 full-time freshmen applied for aid; 361 deemed to have need; 361 received aid. Average need met was 63%. Average scholarship/grant was $2,498; average loan $1,479. 79% of total undergraduate aid awarded as scholarships/grants, 21% as loans/jobs. Need-based aid available for part-time students. Work-study available nights, weekends and for part-time students. **Non-need-based:** Scholarships awarded for athletics, minority status.

Application procedures. Admission: No deadline. No application fee. Admission notification on a rolling basis. **Financial aid:** Priority date 5/15; no closing date. FAFSA, institutional form required. Applicants notified on a rolling basis starting 7/1; must reply within 2 week(s) of notification.

Academics. Special study options: Cooperative education, cross-registration, distance learning, double major, dual enrollment of high school students, honors, independent study, internships, study abroad. License preparation in nursing. **Credit/placement by examination:** AP, CLEP, institutional tests. 15 credit hours maximum toward associate degree. Students scoring above 32 on the English portion of the enhanced ACT receive 6 credits of English composition. AP credit awarded is determined on an individual basis by the relevant department for grades of 3 or higher. **Support services:** GED test center, learning center, reduced course load, remedial instruction, study skills assistance, tutoring.

Majors. Business: Administrative services, business admin. **Computer sciences:** Web page design. **Education:** General. **Health services:** Nursing (RN). **Human services:** General. **Liberal arts:** Arts/sciences. **Visual/performing arts:** Music performance. **Work/family studies:** Child development.

Most popular majors. Business/marketing 12%, health sciences 7%, liberal arts 73%.

Technology on campus. 850 workstations in library, computer center, student center. Commuter students can connect to campus network. Online course registration, online library, helpline, repair service, wireless network available.

Student life. Freshman orientation: Mandatory. Preregistration for classes offered. Half-day program includes campus tour, career and academic counseling, placement assessment, and registration. **Activities:** Campus ministries, choral groups, literary magazine, student government, student newspaper, Baptist Student Union, Circle-K, Phi Theta Kappa, Professional Secretaries International, Adult Student League.

Athletics. NJCAA. **Intercollegiate:** Baseball M, basketball, softball W. **Intramural:** Badminton, bowling, golf, table tennis, tennis, volleyball. **Team name:** Cougars.

Student services. Adult student services, career counseling, student employment services, financial aid counseling, minority student services, personal counseling, placement for graduates, veterans' counselor. **Physically disabled:** Services for visually, speech, hearing impaired. **Transfer:** Re-entry adviser, pre-admission transcript evaluation for new students. Transfer adviser for students transferring to 4-year colleges.

Contact. E-mail: SBayne@clevelandstatecc.edu
Phone: (423) 472-7141 ext. 454 Toll-free number: (800) 604-2722
Fax: (423) 614-8711
Suzanne Bayne, Assistant Director, Enrollment Services, Admissions, & Recruitment, Cleveland State Community College, 3535 Adkisson Drive, Cleveland, TN 37320-3570

Columbia State Community College
Columbia, Tennessee
www.columbiastate.edu   CB code: 1081

▸ Public 2-year community college
▸ Commuter campus in large town

General. Founded in 1966. Regionally accredited. **Enrollment:** 4,271 degree-seeking undergraduates. **Degrees:** 687 associate awarded. **Location:** 40 miles from Nashville. **Calendar:** Semester, limited summer session. **Full-time faculty:** 99 total. **Part-time faculty:** 202 total. **Class size:** 34% < 20, 21% 20-39, 9% 40-49, 16% 50-99, 20% >100.

Basis for selection. Open admission, but selective for some programs. Special requirements for allied health sciences.

High school preparation. Recommended units include English 4, mathematics 3, social studies 1, history 1, science 2 (laboratory 1) and foreign language 2. One visual and performing arts recommended.

2015-2016 Annual costs. Tuition/fees: $4,099; $16,069 out-of-state. Books/supplies: $1,200. Personal expenses: $1,586.

2014-2015 Financial aid. Need-based: 75% of total undergraduate aid awarded as scholarships/grants, 25% as loans/jobs. Need-based aid available for part-time students. Work-study available nights, weekends and for part-time students. **Non-need-based:** Scholarships awarded for academics, athletics, state residency.

Application procedures. Admission: Closing date 8/9. $10 fee. Admission notification on a rolling basis. **Financial aid:** Priority date 3/15, closing date 7/31. FAFSA, institutional form required. Applicants notified on a rolling basis starting 5/15; must reply within 2 week(s) of notification.

Academics. Special study options: Cooperative education, distance learning, dual enrollment of high school students, study abroad. License preparation in nursing, radiology. **Credit/placement by examination:** AP, CLEP, institutional tests. 42 credit hours maximum toward associate degree. **Support services:** GED test center, learning center, remedial instruction, study skills assistance, tutoring.

Majors. Business: Business admin, management information systems. **Computer sciences:** Web page design. **Education:** General. **Health services:** Medical radiologic technology/radiation therapy, nursing (RN), respiratory therapy technology, veterinary technology/assistant. **Liberal arts:** Arts/sciences. **Math:** General. **Protective services:** Police science.

Technology on campus. 60 workstations in library, computer center. Commuter students can connect to campus network. Online course registration, online library, helpline, wireless network available.

Student life. Freshman orientation: Available. Preregistration for classes offered. **Activities:** Choral groups, drama, international student organizations, literary magazine, student government, student newspaper, Phi Theta Kappa, Student Nursing Association, Student Tennessee Education Association, student radiographer organization, North American Veterinary Technician Association, Pulmonary Pit Club.

Athletics. NJCAA. **Intercollegiate:** Baseball M, basketball, softball W. **Intramural:** Basketball, softball M. **Team name:** Chargers, Lady Chargers.

Student services. Career counseling, student employment services, financial aid counseling, minority student services, personal counseling, placement for graduates, veterans' counselor. **Physically disabled:** Services for visually, hearing impaired. **Transfer:** College fairs on campus for students transferring to 4-year colleges.

Contact. E-mail: admissions@columbiastate.edu
Phone: (931) 540-2790 Fax: (931) 560-4125
David Ogden, Director of Admissions and Registrar, Columbia State Community College, 1665 Hampshire Pike, Columbia, TN 38401

Daymar Institute: Clarksville
Clarksville, Tennessee
www.daymarinstitute.edu   CB code: 3225

▸ For-profit 2-year business and career college
▸ Small city

General. Regionally accredited; also accredited by ACICS. **Enrollment:** 513 undergraduates. **Degrees:** 26 bachelor's, 173 associate awarded. **Calendar:** Differs by program. **Full-time faculty:** 22 total. **Part-time faculty:** 17 total.

Basis for selection. Open admission.

2015-2016 Annual costs. Books/supplies: $2,250. **Additional information:** Diploma programs: $22,000-$26,500. Associate programs: $33,000.

Financial aid. **Need-based:** Work-study available nights, weekends and for part-time students.

Application procedures. **Admission:** No deadline. $20 fee.

Academics. **Credit/placement by examination:** AP, CLEP.

Majors. **Business:** Accounting, administrative services, business admin. **Computer sciences:** General. **Health services:** Health information technology, medical assistant. **Protective services:** Law enforcement admin.

Contact. E-mail: chays@draughons.edu
Phone: (931) 552-7600 Toll-free number: (877) 258-7796
Amy Melton, Campus Director, Daymar Institute: Clarksville, 1860 Wilma Rudolph Boulevard, Clarksville, TN 37040

Daymar Institute: Murfreesboro
Murfreesboro, Tennessee
www.daymarinstitute.edu

- For-profit 2-year career college
- Commuter campus in very large city

General. Regionally accredited; also accredited by ACICS. **Enrollment:** 131 undergraduates. **Degrees:** 8 bachelor's, 44 associate awarded. **Location:** 25 miles from Nashville. **Calendar:** Quarter, extensive summer session. **Full-time faculty:** 9 total. **Part-time faculty:** 23 total.

Basis for selection. Open admission, but selective for some programs. All applicants must take an assessment, with the exception of those who have transfer credits in English and mathematics or a composite score of 18 on the ACT or 870 on the SAT. Some programs may have additional requirements. Must provide proof of immunizations.

2015-2016 Annual costs. Diploma programs: $22,000-$26,500. Associate programs: $33,000.

Financial aid. **Need-based:** Work-study available nights, weekends and for part-time students.

Application procedures. **Admission:** No deadline. No application fee. **Financial aid:** No deadline.

Academics. **Special study options:** Distance learning, dual enrollment of high school students. Bachelor's degree programs available on campus. **Credit/placement by examination:** AP, CLEP. **Support services:** Tutoring.

Majors. **Business:** Accounting, accounting/business management. **Computer sciences:** General. **Health services:** Dental assistant, medical assistant, pharmacy assistant. **Protective services:** Corrections.

Most popular majors. Business/marketing 17%, health sciences 63%, security/protective services 11%.

Technology on campus. Commuter students can connect to campus network.

Student life. **Freshman orientation:** Mandatory. Preregistration for classes offered. **Activities:** Student newspaper.

Athletics. **Team name:** N/A.

Student services. Career counseling, financial aid counseling.

Contact. E-mail: jviola@daymarinstitute.edu
Phone: (615) 217-9347 Toll-free number: (877) 258-7796
Jennifer Viola, Director of Admissions, Daymar Institute: Murfreesboro, 415 Golden Bear Court, Murfreesboro, TN 37128

Daymar Institute: Nashville
Nashville, Tennessee
www.daymarinstitute.edu   **CB code: 7325**

- For-profit 2-year career college
- Commuter campus in very large city
- Interview required

General. Founded in 1884. Regionally accredited; also accredited by ACICS. Branch campuses in Clarksville, Murfreesboro, Bowling Green, Kentucky. **Enrollment:** 410 undergraduates. **Degrees:** 9 bachelor's, 31 associate awarded. **Location:** 2 miles from downtown. **Calendar:** Quarter, extensive summer session. **Full-time faculty:** 14 total. **Part-time faculty:** 39 total. **Class size:** 30% < 20, 15% 20-39, 21% 40-49, 34% 50-99, less than 1% >100.

Student profile.

Out-of-state:	5%	25 or older:	75%

Transfer out. **Colleges most students transferred to 2015:** Middle Tennessee State University, Tennessee State University, Western Kentucky University, David Lipscomb University, Fisk University.

Basis for selection. Open admission, but selective for some programs. Selective to allied health programs.

2015-2016 Annual costs. Books/supplies: $2,500. **Additional information:** Diploma programs: $22,000-$26,500. Associate programs: $33,000.

Financial aid. All financial aid based on need. Need-based aid available for part-time students. Work-study available nights, weekends and for part-time students. **Additional information:** Financial aid form for in-state applicants must be filed before 5/1.

Application procedures. **Admission:** No deadline. No application fee. Admission notification on a rolling basis. **Financial aid:** No deadline. FAFSA required. Applicants notified on a rolling basis.

Academics. **Special study options:** Distance learning, independent study, internships, liberal arts/career combination, weekend college. Bachelor's degree programs available on campus. **Credit/placement by examination:** AP, CLEP, institutional tests. 15 credit hours maximum toward associate degree, 15 toward bachelor's. **Support services:** GED preparation, reduced course load, study skills assistance, tutoring.

Majors. **Business:** Accounting, accounting technology, business admin, human resources. **Computer sciences:** Networking, web page design. **Health services:** Dental assistant, health information management, insurance coding, medical assistant, pharmacy assistant. **Protective services:** Criminal justice.

Most popular majors. Business/marketing 21%, computer/information sciences 17%, health sciences 37%, legal studies 25%.

Technology on campus. 75 workstations in library, computer center. Online library available.

Student life. **Freshman orientation:** Mandatory. Preregistration for classes offered. **Activities:** Student government, student newspaper.

Student services. Adult student services, career counseling, financial aid counseling, personal counseling, placement for graduates. **Transfer:** Pre-admission transcript evaluation for new students.

Contact. E-mail: ecollier@daymarinstitute.edu
Phone: (615) 361-7555 Toll-free number: (877) 258-7796
Elizabeth Collier, Director of Admissions, Daymar Institute: Nashville, 340 & 283 Plus Park at Pavilion Boulevard, Nashville, TN 37217

Dyersburg State Community College
Dyersburg, Tennessee
www.dscc.edu   **CB code: 7323**

- Public 2-year community college
- Commuter campus in large town

General. Founded in 1967. Regionally accredited. **Enrollment:** 1,930 degree-seeking undergraduates; 927 non-degree-seeking students. **Degrees:** 275 associate awarded. **Location:** 78 miles from Memphis. **Calendar:** Semester, limited summer session. **Full-time faculty:** 53 total; 17% minority, 57% women. **Part-time faculty:** 121 total; 5% minority, 68% women. **Class size:** 50% < 20, 46% 20-39, 2% 40-49, 2% 50-99.

Student profile. Among degree-seeking undergraduates, 44% enrolled in a transfer program, 617 enrolled as first-time, first-year students, 176 transferred in from other institutions.

Part-time:	37%	Asian American:	1%
Out-of-state:	1%	Hispanic/Latino:	2%
Women:	67%	Multi-racial, non-Hispanic:	2%
African American:	23%	25 or older:	32%

Transfer out. Colleges most students transferred to 2015: University of Tennessee-Martin, University of Memphis, Middle Tennessee State University.

Basis for selection. Open admission, but selective for some programs. Admission into nursing program based on point system that includes preadmission examination test score, GPA, science courses taken with grade of "B" or above, and prior health care experience. High school students who meet specific admission requirements may enroll as first time freshmen. **Learning Disabled:** Students with disabilities encouraged to inform the college of any needed assistance during application process.

High school preparation. College-preparatory program recommended. 22 units required. Required and recommended units include English 4, mathematics 4, social studies 3, history 1, science 3, foreign language 2, visual/performing arts 1 and academic electives 3. Physical education and wellness 1.5 units, personal finance .5 units.

2015-2016 Annual costs. Tuition/fees: $4,127; $16,097 out-of-state. Per-credit charge: $152 in-state; $627 out-of-state. Books/supplies: $1,200. Personal expenses: $1,080.

2014-2015 Financial aid. Need-based: 76% of total undergraduate aid awarded as scholarships/grants, 24% as loans/jobs. Need-based aid available for part-time students. Work-study available nights, weekends and for part-time students. **Non-need-based:** Scholarships awarded for academics, alumni affiliation, athletics, job skills, leadership, minority status, music/drama, state residency.

Application procedures. Admission: No application fee. Admission notification on a rolling basis. **Financial aid:** Priority date 3/1; no closing date. FAFSA required. Applicants notified on a rolling basis starting 3/1; must reply within 2 week(s) of notification.

Academics. Special study options: Accelerated study, cooperative education, distance learning, dual enrollment of high school students, honors, independent study, internships, study abroad. License preparation in nursing, paramedic. **Credit/placement by examination:** AP, CLEP, institutional tests. 24 credit hours maximum toward associate degree. **Support services:** GED preparation and test center, learning center, pre-admission summer program, reduced course load, remedial instruction, study skills assistance, tutoring, writing center.

Majors. Business: Business admin. **Computer sciences:** Information systems, web page design. **Education:** General. **Health services:** EMT paramedic, health information technology, medical informatics, nursing (RN). **Liberal arts:** Arts/sciences. **Protective services:** Criminal justice, police science. **Visual/performing arts:** Music performance. **Work/family studies:** Child development.

Most popular majors. Business/marketing 11%, education 6%, health sciences 37%, liberal arts 27%, social sciences 9%.

Technology on campus. 1,058 workstations in library, computer center, student center. Commuter students can connect to campus network. Online course registration, online library, helpline, wireless network available.

Student life. Freshman orientation: Available. Preregistration for classes offered. **Activities:** Campus ministries, choral groups, drama, international student organizations, music ensembles, musical theater, student government, TV station, American Chemical Society Affiliates, business and office systems association, student nurses association, Minority Association for Successful Students, astronomy club, advanced technology association, music club, Phi Theta Kappa, psychology club.

Athletics. NJCAA. **Intercollegiate:** Baseball M, basketball, cheerleading, softball W. **Intramural:** Basketball, sand volleyball. **Team name:** Eagles.

Student services. Adult student services, alcohol/substance abuse counseling, chaplain/spiritual director, career counseling, services for economically disadvantaged, student employment services, financial aid counseling, minority student services, personal counseling, placement for graduates, veterans' counselor, women's services. **Physically disabled:** Services for visually, speech, hearing impaired. **Transfer:** Pre-admission transcript evaluation for new students. Transfer adviser, college fairs on campus for students transferring to 4-year colleges.

Contact. E-mail: enroll@dscc.edu
Phone: (731) 286-3330 Toll-free number: (855) 372-2669
Fax: (731) 286-3325
Margaret Jones, Assistant Director Of Admissions, Dyersburg State Community College, 1510 Lake Road, Dyersburg, TN 38024

Fountainhead College of Technology
Knoxville, Tennessee
www.fountainheadcollege.edu   **CB code: 0446**

- For-profit 2-year technical and career college
- Commuter campus in large city
- Interview required

General. Founded in 1947. Accredited by ACCSC. **Enrollment:** 230 undergraduates. **Degrees:** 26 bachelor's, 50 associate awarded. **Location:** 200 miles from Nashville, 200 miles from Atlanta. **Calendar:** Semester, extensive summer session. **Full-time faculty:** 5 total. **Part-time faculty:** 4 total.

Basis for selection. Open admission, but selective for some programs. Institutional aptitude test required for placement.

2015-2016 Annual costs. Tuition/fees: $14,750. Per-credit charge: $485. Books/supplies: $1,250. Personal expenses: $2,007.

Financial aid. All financial aid based on need. Work-study available nights, weekends and for part-time students.

Application procedures. Admission: No deadline. $100 fee. Admission notification on a rolling basis. **Financial aid:** No deadline. FAFSA required. Applicants notified on a rolling basis.

Academics. Special study options: Bachelor's degree programs available on campus. **Credit/placement by examination:** AP, CLEP, institutional tests. 27 credit hours maximum toward associate degree. **Support services:** Tutoring.

Majors. Computer sciences: Programming, system admin. **Health services:** Health information technology, insurance specialist.

Technology on campus. PC or laptop required. 200 workstations in computer center. Online library, wireless network available.

Student life. Freshman orientation: Mandatory. Preregistration for classes offered.

Student services. Career counseling, student employment services, financial aid counseling, personal counseling, placement for graduates.

Contact. E-mail: info@fountainheadcollege.edu
Phone: (865) 688-9422 Toll-free number: (888) 218-7335
Fax: (865) 688-2419
Teresa Trusler, Admissions Representative, Fountainhead College of Technology, 3203 Tazewell Pike, Knoxville, TN 37918

Hiwassee College
Madisonville, Tennessee
www.hiwassee.edu   **CB code: 1298**

- Private 2-year junior and liberal arts college affiliated with the United Methodist Church
- Residential campus in small town
- SAT or ACT (ACT writing optional) required

General. Founded in 1849. Regionally accredited; also accredited by TRACS. Christian principles emphasized; involvement in total campus life encouraged. **Enrollment:** 269 degree-seeking undergraduates. **Degrees:** 19 bachelor's, 42 associate awarded. **Location:** 50 miles from Knoxville, 75 miles from Chattanooga. **Calendar:** Semester, limited summer session.

Basis for selection. ACT of 18 and a GPA of 2.5. **Adult students:** SAT/ACT scores not required.

High school preparation. Required and recommended units include English 4, mathematics 3, social studies 3, history 1, science 3 (laboratory 2), foreign language 2 and academic electives 4.

2015-2016 Annual costs. Tuition/fees: $15,543. Room/board: $6,784.

Financial aid. Need-based: Work-study available nights, weekends and for part-time students.

Application procedures. Admission: Closing date 8/1. $25 fee. Admission notification on a rolling basis. **Financial aid:** Closing date 8/15.

Academics. Special study options: Distance learning, dual enrollment of high school students, ESL, independent study, internships, student-designed major, study abroad. License preparation in dental hygiene. **Credit/placement by examination:** AP, CLEP, IB, institutional tests. **Support services:** Learning center, reduced course load, remedial instruction, study skills assistance, tutoring.

Majors. Conservation: Forest technology. **Health services:** Dental hygiene. **Liberal arts:** Arts/sciences.

Technology on campus. Dormitories wired for high-speed internet access and linked to campus network. Commuter students can connect to campus network. Online library, helpline, repair service, wireless network available.

Student life. Freshman orientation: Mandatory. Preregistration for classes offered. **Policies:** Religious observance required. **Housing:** $50 deposit, deadline 8/1. **Activities:** Campus ministries, choral groups, dance, drama, literary magazine, music ensembles, musical theater, student government, student newspaper.

Athletics. NCCAA. **Intercollegiate:** Baseball M, basketball, cheerleading, cross-country, golf, soccer, softball W, volleyball W. **Intramural:** Basketball, football (non-tackle), volleyball. **Team name:** Tigers.

Student services. Adult student services, alcohol/substance abuse counseling, chaplain/spiritual director, career counseling, services for economically disadvantaged, financial aid counseling. **Transfer:** Pre-admission transcript evaluation for new students. Transfer adviser, college fairs on campus for students transferring to 4-year colleges.

Contact. E-mail: enroll@hiwassee.edu
Phone: (423) 420-1212 Toll-free number: (800) 356-2187
Fax: (423) 442-3520
Bethany Brady, Assistant Director of Admissions, Hiwassee College, 225 Hiwassee College Drive, Madisonville, TN 37354-6099

Huntington College of Health Sciences
Knoxville, Tennessee
www.hchs.edu   **CB code: 3945**

▶ For-profit 2-year virtual health science college
▶ Small city

General. Accredited by DETC. **Calendar:** Differs by program.

Annual costs/financial aid. Tuition/fees (2015-2016): $7,350. Diploma programs: $4,410; Associates programs: $3,920. Books, supplies, fees range depending on program level and course of study. All costs are subject to change. Books/supplies: $1,350.

Contact. Phone: (865) 524-8079 ext. 1
Director of Administration, 1204-D Kenesaw Avenue, Knoxville, TN 37919-7736

Jackson State Community College
Jackson, Tennessee
www.jscc.edu   **CB code: 2266**

▶ Public 2-year community college
▶ Commuter campus in small city

General. Founded in 1965. Regionally accredited. **Enrollment:** 3,243 degree-seeking undergraduates. **Degrees:** 468 associate awarded. **ROTC:** Army. **Location:** 80 miles from Memphis, 130 miles from Nashville. **Calendar:** Semester, limited summer session. **Full-time faculty:** 95 total; 17% have terminal degrees, 6% minority, 67% women. **Part-time faculty:** 179 total. **Class size:** 25% < 20, 70% 20-39, 4% 40-49, less than 1% 50-99.

Transfer out. Colleges most students transferred to 2015: Union University, University of Memphis, University of Tennessee at Martin, Middle Tennessee State University.

Basis for selection. Open admission, but selective for some programs. Special requirements for nursing, medical laboratory technology, radiology, physical therapy assistant, and emergency medical technician programs. Interview required for allied health, nursing programs. **Adult students:** Students 21 years or older take COMPASS placement test. **Home schooled:** Transcript of courses and grades required. **Learning Disabled:** Students wtih documented disabilities are encouraged to register with the Disability Resource Center after admission to the College.

High school preparation. 22 units recommended. Recommended units include English 4, mathematics 4, social studies 3, science 3, foreign language 2, visual/performing arts 1 and academic electives 3. 2 units wellness studies.

2015-2016 Annual costs. Tuition/fees: $4,398; $16,368 out-of-state. Per-credit charge: $152 in-state; $475 out-of-state. Books/supplies: $1,200. Personal expenses: $4,544.

Financial aid. Need-based: Need-based aid available for part-time students. Work-study available nights, weekends and for part-time students. **Non-need-based:** Scholarships awarded for academics, art, athletics, job skills, leadership, minority status, music/drama.

Application procedures. Admission: No deadline. No application fee. Admission notification on a rolling basis. Students are given Early Admission status once JSCC has received a 7th semester high school transcript, application, and shot records. The final transcript must be sent before students can be fully admitted. **Financial aid:** Priority date 3/15; no closing date. FAFSA, institutional form required. Applicants notified on a rolling basis starting 5/15; must reply within 2 week(s) of notification.

Academics. Special study options: Accelerated study, cooperative education, distance learning, double major, dual enrollment of high school students, honors, internships, liberal arts/career combination, study abroad, weekend college. License preparation in nursing, paramedic, physical therapy, radiology. **Credit/placement by examination:** AP, CLEP, institutional tests. 21 credit hours maximum toward associate degree. Must complete additional 15 college credit hours before credit by examination is awarded. **Support services:** GED test center, learning center, reduced course load, remedial instruction, study skills assistance, tutoring, writing center.

Majors. Biology: General. **Business:** Accounting, business admin, management information systems. **Communications:** Communications/speech/rhetoric. **Computer sciences:** General. **Education:** General. **Engineering:** General. **English:** English lit. **Health services:** Clinical lab technology, medical radiologic technology/radiation therapy, nursing (RN), physical therapy assistant, premedicine, prenursing. **History:** General. **Human services:** General, social work. **Liberal arts:** Arts/sciences. **Math:** General. **Parks/recreation:** Health/fitness. **Philosophy/religion:** Philosophy. **Physical sciences:** General, chemistry. **Protective services:** Police science. **Psychology:** General. **Social sciences:** Political science, sociology. **Visual/performing arts:** Art. **Work/family studies:** Child development.

Most popular majors. Business/marketing 8%, computer/information sciences 7%, health sciences 38%, liberal arts 23%.

Technology on campus. 1,000 workstations in library, computer center, student center. Commuter students can connect to campus network. Online course registration, online library, helpline, wireless network available.

Student life. Freshman orientation: Mandatory. Preregistration for classes offered. Three-hour orientation-registration session held before classes begin. **Activities:** Choral groups, international student organizations, literary magazine, student government, Baptist Collegiate Ministries, Phi Theta Kappa, Science Ambassadors, student veteran's association, human rights club, biology club, Black Student Association, art club, sociology club.

Athletics. NJCAA. **Intercollegiate:** Baseball M, basketball, softball W. **Team name:** Generals.

Student services. Career counseling, student employment services, financial aid counseling, personal counseling, placement for graduates, veterans' counselor. **Physically disabled:** Services for visually, speech, hearing impaired. **Transfer:** College fairs on campus for students transferring to 4-year colleges.

Contact. E-mail: admissions2@jscc.edu
Phone: (731) 425-8844 Toll-free number: (800) 355-5722 ext. 58844
Fax: (731) 425-2653
Robin Marek, Director of Admissions and Records, Jackson State Community College, 2046 North Parkway, Jackson, TN 38301-3797

John A. Gupton College
Nashville, Tennessee
www.guptoncollege.edu   **CB code: 0539**

▶ Private 2-year school of mortuary science
▶ Commuter campus in large city

General. Founded in 1946. Regionally accredited. **Enrollment:** 119 degree-seeking undergraduates. **Degrees:** 40 associate awarded. **Calendar:** Semester, limited summer session. **Full-time faculty:** 5 total; 40% women. **Part-time faculty:** 8 total; 62% have terminal degrees, 25% minority, 25% women. **Class size:** 42% 20-39, 58% 50-99.

Transfer out. Colleges most students transferred to 2015: Middle Tennessee State University, Western Kentucky University, Jackson State Community College.

Basis for selection. Open admission, but selective for some programs. Two letters of recommendation are needed. **Home schooled:** Transcript of courses and grades, state high school equivalency certificate, letter of recommendation (nonparent) required.

High school preparation. 10 units recommended. Recommended units include English 4, mathematics 3 and science 3.

2016-2017 Annual costs. Tuition/fees (projected): $10,040. Per-credit charge: $310. Room only: $3,600. Personal expenses: $1,500.

Financial aid. All financial aid based on need. Need-based aid available for part-time students. Work-study available nights, weekends and for part-time students.

Application procedures. Admission: No deadline. $50 fee. Admission notification on a rolling basis. **Financial aid:** No deadline. FAFSA required. Applicants notified on a rolling basis; must reply within 2 week(s) of notification.

Academics. Credit/placement by examination: AP, CLEP. **Support services:** Reduced course load, tutoring.

Technology on campus. 12 workstations in library, computer center. Wireless network available.

Student life. Freshman orientation: Mandatory. Preregistration for classes offered. **Housing:** Apartments, wellness housing available. $450 fully refundable deposit.

Student services. Career counseling. **Transfer:** Pre-admission transcript evaluation for new students.

Contact. E-mail: purcell@guptoncollege.edu
Phone: (615) 327-3927 Fax: (615) 321-4518
Terri Purcell, Director of Admissions, John A. Gupton College, 1616 Church Street, Nashville, TN 37203-2920

Lincoln College of Technology: Nashville
Nashville, Tennessee
www.nadcedu.com   CB code: 3098

▶ For-profit 1-year technical college
▶ Commuter campus in large city
▶ Interview required

General. Accredited by ACCSC. **Enrollment:** 1,782 undergraduates. **Degrees:** 60 associate awarded. **Calendar:** Differs by program, extensive summer session. **Full-time faculty:** 67 total. **Class size:** 100% 20-39.

Student profile.

Out-of-state: 90%   **Live on campus:**   30%
25 or older: 1%

Basis for selection. Secondary school record, interview, test scores most important. State proficiency tests used in admission decisions.

2015-2016 Annual costs. Books/supplies: $987. **Additional information:** Certificate programs: $14,754. Diploma programs: $29,867 to $36,344. Associate programs: $35,817. Costs include total tuition, materials, tool fees, and registration fee.

Financial aid. All financial aid based on need. Work-study available nights, weekends and for part-time students.

Application procedures. Admission: No deadline. $100 fee. Admission notification on a rolling basis. **Financial aid:** No deadline. FAFSA required. Applicants notified on a rolling basis.

Academics. Credit/placement by examination: AP, CLEP, institutional tests. **Support services:** Study skills assistance, tutoring.

Technology on campus. 46 workstations in library, computer center. Dormitories wired for high-speed internet access. Online library available.

Student life. Freshman orientation: Mandatory. Preregistration for classes offered. **Housing:** Single-sex dorms available. $200 deposit.

Student services. Career counseling, student employment services, financial aid counseling, placement for graduates, veterans' counselor. **Physically disabled:** Services for visually impaired.

Contact. E-mail: admissions@nadcedu.com
Phone: (615) 226-3990 Toll-free number: (800) 228-6232
Fax: (615) 262-8466
Shayne Pulver, Director of Admissions, Lincoln College of Technology: Nashville, 1524 Gallatin Road, Nashville, TN 37206

Miller-Motte Technical College: Chattanooga
Chattanooga, Tennessee
www.miller-motte.edu

▶ For-profit 2-year technical college
▶ Commuter campus in large city

General. Accredited by ACICS. **Enrollment:** 348 undergraduates. **Degrees:** 72 associate awarded. **Calendar:** Quarter. **Full-time faculty:** 5 total. **Part-time faculty:** 33 total.

Basis for selection. Open admission.

2015-2016 Annual costs. Certificate programs: $8,090-$20,936, books and supplies $290-$3,600. Associate programs: $28,858-$29,452, books and supplies $4,800.

Financial aid. Need-based: Work-study available nights, weekends and for part-time students.

Application procedures. Admission: $40 fee.

Academics. Credit/placement by examination: AP, CLEP.

Majors. Health services: Dental assistant, health information technology, massage therapy, medical assistant, surgical technology.

Contact. E-mail: gwheelous@miller-motte.com
Phone: (423) 510-9675 Toll-free number: (888) 794-9357
Fax: (423) 510-1985
George Wheelous, Director of Admissions, Miller-Motte Technical College: Chattanooga, 6020 Shallowford Road, Suite 100, Chattanooga, TN 37421

Miller-Motte Technical College: Clarksville
Clarksville, Tennessee
www.miller-motte.edu   CB code: 3228

▶ For-profit 2-year business and health science college
▶ Commuter campus in small city
▶ Interview required

General. Accredited by ACICS. **Enrollment:** 404 undergraduates. **Degrees:** 83 associate awarded. **Location:** 45 miles from Nashville. **Calendar:** Quarter, extensive summer session. **Full-time faculty:** 13 total. **Part-time faculty:** 41 total. **Special facilities:** Simulated operating rooms, medical laboratories, simulated doctor's exam room.

Student profile.

Out-of-state: 50%   **25 or older:**   60%

Transfer out. Colleges most students transferred to 2015: Austin Peay University, Hopkinsville Community College.

Basis for selection. Open admission, but selective for some programs. 2 years experience or 2-year/4-year degree and interview with department head required for entrance into network administration certificate program. **Learning Disabled:** Letter of request for any accommodation required.

2015-2016 Annual costs. Books/supplies: $1,200. Personal expenses: $1,350. **Additional information:** Certificate programs: $10,200-$20,788, books and supplies $400-$3,000. Associate programs: $25,080-$33,180, books and supplies $3,600-$4,800.

Financial aid. All financial aid based on need. Need-based aid available for part-time students. Work-study available nights, weekends and for part-time students.

Application procedures. Admission: No deadline. $40 fee. Application must be submitted on paper. Admission notification on a rolling basis. **Financial aid:** No deadline. FAFSA, institutional form required. Applicants notified on a rolling basis.

Academics. Special study options: Weekend college. **Credit/placement by examination:** AP, CLEP, institutional tests. 40 credit hours maximum toward associate degree. No more than 50% of required credit hours in a major and/or entire program. **Support services:** Reduced course load, remedial instruction, study skills assistance, tutoring.

Majors. Business: Accounting, business admin. **Computer sciences:** General. **Health services:** Massage therapy, medical assistant, phlebotomy, surgical technology.

Most popular majors. Business/marketing 7%, computer/information sciences 22%, engineering/engineering technologies 6%, health sciences 46%, legal studies 15%.

Technology on campus. 75 workstations in library, computer center. Online library available.

Student life. Freshman orientation: Mandatory. Preregistration for classes offered. **Activities:** Student government.

Student services. Adult student services, career counseling, student employment services, financial aid counseling, placement for graduates, veterans' counselor. **Transfer:** Re-entry adviser, pre-admission transcript evaluation for new students.

Contact. E-mail: gayle.kilgore@miller-motte.edu
Phone: (931) 553-0071 Toll-free number: (800) 558-0071
Kayle Kilgore, Director of Admissions, Miller-Motte Technical College: Clarksville, 1820 Business Park Drive, Clarksville, TN 37040

Motlow State Community College
Lynchburg, Tennessee
www.mscc.edu   **CB code: 1543**

- Public 2-year community college
- Commuter campus in rural community

General. Founded in 1969. Regionally accredited. **Enrollment:** 5,065 degree-seeking undergraduates. **Degrees:** 728 associate awarded. **Location:** 65 miles from Nashville. **Calendar:** Semester, limited summer session. **Full-time faculty:** 137 total. **Part-time faculty:** 190 total.

Student profile. Among degree-seeking undergraduates, 1,880 enrolled as first-time, first-year students, 213 transferred in from other institutions.

Part-time:	47%	**Women:**	58%
Out-of-state:	1%		

Transfer out. Colleges most students transferred to 2015: Middle Tennessee State University, Tennessee Technological University.

Basis for selection. Open admission, but selective for some programs. Separate admissions criteria for nursing program. **Home schooled:** Transcript of courses and grades required.

High school preparation. 16 units recommended. Recommended units include English 4, mathematics 3, social studies 2, history 1, science 2 (laboratory 1) and foreign language 2.

2015-2016 Annual costs. Tuition/fees: $4,129; $16,099 out-of-state. Books/supplies: $1,200. Personal expenses: $1,000.

Financial aid. Need-based: Need-based aid available for part-time students. Work-study available nights, weekends and for part-time students. **Non-need-based:** Scholarships awarded for academics, alumni affiliation, art, athletics, leadership, music/drama.

Application procedures. Admission: Priority date 7/25; deadline 8/15 (receipt date). No application fee. Application must be submitted online. Admission notification on a rolling basis. **Financial aid:** Closing date 2/15. FAFSA, institutional form required. Applicants notified on a rolling basis starting 3/15.

Academics. Special study options: Accelerated study, cooperative education, distance learning, double major, dual enrollment of high school students, honors, independent study, internships, study abroad, weekend college. License preparation in nursing, paramedic. **Credit/placement by examination:** AP, CLEP, institutional tests. Maximum number of credits by examination that may be earned is limited to 25% of total number of credits needed

for graduation. **Support services:** GED test center, reduced course load, remedial instruction, study skills assistance, tutoring, writing center.

Majors. Business: Business admin. **Education:** General, elementary, secondary. **Health services:** Nursing (RN). **Liberal arts:** Arts/sciences.

Technology on campus. 250 workstations in library, computer center. Commuter students can connect to campus network. Online course registration, online library, helpline, repair service, wireless network available.

Student life. Freshman orientation: Mandatory. Preregistration for classes offered. **Activities:** Campus ministries, choral groups, drama, international student organizations, music ensembles, student government, Baptist student union, African American student association, outing club, communications club, law and government club, literary club, Phi Theta Kappa, psychology club, Tennessee Association of Student Nurses.

Athletics. NJCAA. **Intercollegiate:** Baseball M, basketball, softball W. **Intramural:** Baseball M, basketball, bowling, softball. **Team name:** Bucks.

Student services. Adult student services, career counseling, student employment services, financial aid counseling, veterans' counselor. **Physically disabled:** Services for visually impaired. **Transfer:** Pre-admission transcript evaluation for new students. College fairs on campus for students transferring to 4-year colleges.

Contact. E-mail: galsup@mscc.edu
Phone: (931) 393-1529 Toll-free number: (800) 654-4877
Fax: (931) 393-1971
Greer Alsup, Director of Admissions and Records, Motlow State Community College, Box 8500, Lynchburg, TN 37352-8500

Nashville State Community College
Nashville, Tennessee
www.nscc.edu   **CB code: 0850**

- Public 2-year community and technical college
- Commuter campus in very large city

General. Founded in 1969. Regionally accredited. **Enrollment:** 7,979 degree-seeking undergraduates; 2,213 non-degree-seeking students. **Degrees:** 714 associate awarded. **Location:** 6 miles from downtown Nashville. **Calendar:** Semester, limited summer session. **Full-time faculty:** 165 total. **Part-time faculty:** 369 total. **Class size:** 51% < 20, 49% 20-39, less than 1% 40-49. **Special facilities:** Television production studio.

Student profile. Among degree-seeking undergraduates, 54% enrolled in a transfer program, 46% enrolled in a vocational program, 2,101 enrolled as first-time, first-year students, 664 transferred in from other institutions.

Part-time:	48%	**Women:**	59%
Out-of-state:	4%	**25 or older:**	39%

Transfer out. Colleges most students transferred to 2015: Middle Tennessee University, Tennessee State University, Tennessee Technical University.

Basis for selection. Open admission, but selective for some programs. Test scores used for placement. Interview required for occupational therapy assistant, surgical technology and nursing programs. **Adult students:** Degree-seeking students over 21 with no previous college-level English and/or math required to take COMPASS placement exam. **Home schooled:** Transcript should be official copy from organization as defined by state law and must have certification of registration with superintendent of local education agency where student would have attended.

High school preparation. Recommended units include English 4, mathematics 3, social studies 2, history 2, science 2 (laboratory 1), foreign language 2 and visual/performing arts 1. 1 visual/performing art recommended. Business technologies majors: 1 unit bookkeeping or accounting recommended. Engineering technologies majors: additional math and science recommended.

2015-2016 Annual costs. Tuition/fees: $4,053; $16,023 out-of-state. Per-credit charge: $152 in-state; $627 out-of-state. Books/supplies: $1,500. Personal expenses: $502.

2014-2015 Financial aid. Need-based: Need-based aid available for part-time students. Work-study available nights, weekends and for part-time students. **Non-need-based:** Scholarships awarded for academics, minority status.

Application procedures. Admission: No deadline. $20 fee. **Financial aid:** Priority date 3/1, closing date 7/1. FAFSA required. Applicants notified on a rolling basis starting 6/1; must reply within 2 week(s) of notification.

Academics.
Special study options: Cooperative education, distance learning, double major, dual enrollment of high school students, ESL, honors, internships, student-designed major, study abroad. License preparation in nursing, occupational therapy. **Credit/placement by examination:** AP, CLEP, institutional tests. 20 credit hours maximum toward associate degree. **Support services:** Learning center, reduced course load, remedial instruction, study skills assistance, tutoring, writing center.

Majors. Business: Accounting technology, administrative services, business admin. **Computer sciences:** General, networking, web page design. **Education:** General. **Health services:** Health care admin, medical informatics, nursing (RN), occupational therapy assistant. **Human services:** Community org/advocacy. **Liberal arts:** Arts/sciences. **Protective services:** Criminal justice, police science. **Visual/performing arts:** Commercial/advertising art, music performance. **Work/family studies:** Child development.

Technology on campus. 518 workstations in library, computer center. Commuter students can connect to campus network. Online course registration, online library, helpline, wireless network available.

Student life. Freshman orientation: Available. Preregistration for classes offered. **Activities:** International student organizations, literary magazine, student government, student newspaper, black student organization.

Student services. Adult student services, career counseling, student employment services, personal counseling, placement for graduates, veterans' counselor. **Physically disabled:** Services for visually, hearing impaired. **Transfer:** Pre-admission transcript evaluation for new students. College fairs on campus for students transferring to 4-year colleges.

Contact. E-mail: admissions@nscc.edu
Phone: (615) 353-3215 Toll-free number: (800) 272-7363
Fax: (615) 353-3243
Laura Moran, Director of Admissions, Nashville State Community College, 120 White Bridge Road, Nashville, TN 37209-4515

National College: Bartlett
Bartlett, Tennessee
www.ncbt.edu

‣ For-profit 2-year branch campus college
‣ Large town

General. Regionally accredited; also accredited by ACICS. **Enrollment:** 120 degree-seeking undergraduates. **Degrees:** 34 associate awarded. **Calendar:** Quarter. **Full-time faculty:** 2 total. **Part-time faculty:** 19 total.

Basis for selection. Open admission.

2016-2017 Annual costs. Tuition/fees: $14,460. Per-credit charge: $317.

Financial aid. Need-based: Work-study available nights, weekends and for part-time students.

Application procedures. Admission: No deadline. $50 fee. **Financial aid:** No deadline.

Academics. Credit/placement by examination: AP, CLEP.

Majors. Business: Accounting/business management, administrative services, business admin. **Health services:** Health information technology, medical assistant, pharmacy assistant.

Contact. Phone: (901) 213-1681
Larry Steele, Director of Admissions, National College: Bartlett, 5760 Stage Road, Bartlett, TN 38134

National College: Bristol
Bristol, Tennessee
www.national-college.edu   CB code: 3247

‣ For-profit 2-year business college
‣ Commuter campus in large town

General. Accredited by ACICS. Eight campuses in Virginia. **Enrollment:** 92 degree-seeking undergraduates. **Degrees:** 4 bachelor's, 44 associate awarded. **Calendar:** Quarter, limited summer session. **Full-time faculty:** 2 total. **Part-time faculty:** 9 total.

Basis for selection. Open admission. Interview recommended.

2016-2017 Annual costs. Tuition/fees: $14,460. Per-credit charge: $317. Books/supplies: $1,200.

Financial aid. All financial aid based on need. Need-based aid available for part-time students. Work-study available nights, weekends and for part-time students.

Application procedures. Admission: No deadline. $50 fee, may be waived for applicants with need. Admission notification on a rolling basis. **Financial aid:** No deadline. FAFSA required. Applicants notified on a rolling basis starting 9/1.

Academics. Special study options: Double major, internships. **Credit/placement by examination:** AP, CLEP, institutional tests. **Support services:** Tutoring.

Majors. Business: Accounting, administrative services, business admin, office management. **Computer sciences:** Computer science. **Health services:** Medical assistant.

Technology on campus. 35 workstations in library, computer center.

Student life. Freshman orientation: Mandatory. Preregistration for classes offered.

Student services. Career counseling, personal counseling.

Contact. E-mail: market@educorp.edu
Phone: (423) 878-4440
Larry Steele, Regional Director of Admissions, National College: Bristol, 1328 Highway 11W, Bristol, TN 37620

National College: Knoxville
Knoxville, Tennessee
www.ncbt.edu

‣ For-profit 2-year business and technical college
‣ Large city

General. Accredited by ACICS. **Enrollment:** 64 degree-seeking undergraduates. **Degrees:** 19 associate awarded. **Calendar:** Quarter. **Full-time faculty:** 3 total. **Part-time faculty:** 15 total.

Basis for selection. Open admission. Interview recommended.

2016-2017 Annual costs. Tuition/fees: $14,460. Per-credit charge: $317.

Financial aid. Need-based: Work-study available nights, weekends and for part-time students.

Application procedures. Admission: No deadline. $50 fee. **Financial aid:** No deadline.

Academics. Credit/placement by examination: AP, CLEP.

Majors. Business: Accounting, administrative services, business admin. **Health services:** Health information management, medical assistant, pharmacy assistant, surgical technology.

Contact. Phone: (865) 539-2011
Larry Steele, Regional Director of Admissions, National College: Knoxville, 8415 Kingston Pike, Knoxville, TN 37919

National College: Madison
Madison, Tennessee
www.national-college.edu

‣ For-profit 2-year branch campus college
‣ Large town

General. Regionally accredited; also accredited by ACICS. **Enrollment:** 94 degree-seeking undergraduates. **Degrees:** 33 associate awarded. **Calendar:** Quarter. **Full-time faculty:** 2 total. **Part-time faculty:** 20 total.

Basis for selection. Open admission.

2016-2017 Annual costs. Tuition/fees: $14,460. Per-credit charge: $317.

Financial aid. Need-based: Work-study available nights, weekends and for part-time students.

Application procedures. Admission: No deadline. $50 fee. **Financial aid:** No deadline.

Academics. Credit/placement by examination: AP, CLEP.

Majors. Business: Accounting/business management, administrative services, business admin, hospitality admin, tourism/travel. **Health services:** Health information technology, medical assistant, pharmacy assistant.

Contact. Phone: (615) 612-3015
Larry Steele, Regional Director of Admissions, National College: Madison, 900 Madison Square, Madison, TN 37115

National College: Memphis
Memphis, Tennessee
www.ncbt.edu

▶ For-profit 2-year branch campus college
▶ Very large city

General. Regionally accredited; also accredited by ACICS. **Enrollment:** 195 degree-seeking undergraduates. **Degrees:** 62 associate awarded. **Calendar:** Quarter. **Full-time faculty:** 3 total. **Part-time faculty:** 29 total.

Basis for selection. Open admission.

2016-2017 Annual costs. Tuition/fees: $14,460. Per-credit charge: $317. Books/supplies: $1,980.

Financial aid. Need-based: Work-study available nights, weekends and for part-time students.

Application procedures. Admission: No deadline. $50 fee. **Financial aid:** No deadline.

Academics. Credit/placement by examination: AP, CLEP.

Majors. Business: Accounting/business management, administrative services, business admin. **Health services:** Health information technology, medical assistant, pharmacy assistant, surgical technology.

Contact. Phone: (901) 363-9046
Shelly Burrow, Director of Admissions, National College: Memphis, 3545 Lamar Avenue, Suite 1, Memphis, TN 38118

National College: Nashville
Nashville, Tennessee
www.ncbt.edu   **CB code: 3227**

▶ For-profit 2-year business and technical college
▶ Commuter campus in large city

General. Accredited by ACICS. **Enrollment:** 102 degree-seeking undergraduates. **Degrees:** 23 associate awarded. **Calendar:** Quarter. **Full-time faculty:** 2 total. **Part-time faculty:** 22 total.

Basis for selection. Open admission. Interview recommended.

2016-2017 Annual costs. Tuition/fees: $14,460. Per-credit charge: $317. Books/supplies: $900. Personal expenses: $3,259.

Financial aid. All financial aid based on need. Need-based aid available for part-time students. Work-study available nights, weekends and for part-time students.

Application procedures. Admission: No deadline. $50 fee. **Financial aid:** No deadline. FAFSA required.

Academics. Special study options: Liberal arts/career combination. **Credit/placement by examination:** AP, CLEP.

Majors. Business: Accounting, administrative services, business admin. **Computer sciences:** General. **Health services:** Medical assistant, medical secretary.

Student life. Freshman orientation: Mandatory. Preregistration for classes offered.

Contact. E-mail: market@educorp.edu
Phone: (615) 333-3344
Larry Steele, Regional Director of Admissions, National College: Nashville, 1638 Bell Road, Nashville, TN 37211

Northeast State Community College
Blountville, Tennessee
www.NortheastState.edu   **CB code: 0453**

▶ Public 2-year community and technical college
▶ Commuter campus in small city

General. Founded in 1965. Regionally accredited. **Enrollment:** 6,084 degree-seeking undergraduates. **Degrees:** 828 associate awarded. **Location:** 12 miles from Johnson City, 10 miles from Kingsport. **Calendar:** Semester, limited summer session. **Full-time faculty:** 122 total. **Part-time faculty:** 216 total.

Transfer out. Colleges most students transferred to 2015: East Tennessee State University, Milligan College, Tennessee Tech, University of Tennessee.

Basis for selection. Open admission, but selective for some programs. Special requirements for health professions. **Adult students:** COMPASS placement test required for applicants 21 and older without math or English transfer credit.

High school preparation. Recommended units include English 4, mathematics 3, social studies 1, history 1, science 2, foreign language 2 and visual/performing arts 1.

2015-2016 Annual costs. Tuition/fees: $4,115; $16,085 out-of-state. Books/supplies: $1,500.

Financial aid. Need-based: Need-based aid available for part-time students. Work-study available nights, weekends and for part-time students. **Non-need-based:** Scholarships awarded for academics, alumni affiliation, art, job skills, leadership, minority status, music/drama, religious affiliation.

Application procedures. Admission: No deadline. $10 fee. Admission notification on a rolling basis beginning on or about 6/1. **Financial aid:** Priority date 3/31; no closing date. FAFSA required. Applicants notified on a rolling basis starting 3/1; must reply within 3 week(s) of notification.

Academics. Special study options: Accelerated study, cooperative education, distance learning, double major, dual enrollment of high school students, honors, independent study, study abroad, weekend college. License preparation in paramedic. **Credit/placement by examination:** AP, CLEP, institutional tests. 15 credit hours maximum toward associate degree. **Support services:** GED test center, reduced course load, remedial instruction, tutoring.

Majors. Business: Administrative services, business admin. **Computer sciences:** General, webmaster. **General:** Electrician, power transmission. **Health services:** Cardiovascular technology, clinical lab assistant, dental lab technology, medical assistant. **Liberal arts:** Arts/sciences. **Protective services:** Criminal justice, forensics, police science. **Social sciences:** General. **Work/family studies:** Child development, family studies.

Most popular majors. Business/marketing 9%, engineering/engineering technologies 12%, health sciences 12%, liberal arts 49%, trade and industry 9%.

Technology on campus. 900 workstations in library, computer center. Commuter students can connect to campus network. Online library, wireless network available.

Student life. Freshman orientation: Mandatory. Preregistration for classes offered. Offered online; takes place prior to registration. **Activities:** Drama, literary magazine, student government.

Athletics. Team name: Bears.

Student services. Career counseling, services for economically disadvantaged, student employment services, financial aid counseling, health services, minority student services, personal counseling, placement for graduates, veterans' counselor. **Physically disabled:** Services for visually, speech, hearing impaired. **Transfer:** Transfer adviser, college fairs on campus for students transferring to 4-year colleges.

Contact. E-mail: jgstarling@northeaststate.edu
Phone: (423) 323-0253 Toll-free number: (800) 836-7822
Fax: (423) 323-0215
Jennifer Starling, Dean of Enrollment Management, Northeast State Community College, Box 246, Blountville, TN 37617-0246

Two-Year Colleges

Nossi College of Art
Nashville, Tennessee
www.nossi.edu   **CB code: 3118**

- For-profit 2-year visual arts and technical college
- Commuter campus in large town
- Application essay, interview required

General. Accredited by ACCSC. **Enrollment:** 268 degree-seeking undergraduates. **Degrees:** 9 bachelor's, 28 associate awarded. **Location:** 5 miles from Nashville. **Calendar:** Semester, extensive summer session. **Full-time faculty:** 3 total. **Part-time faculty:** 30 total; 30% minority, 30% women.

Student profile. Among degree-seeking undergraduates, 1% already have a bachelor's degree or higher, 62 enrolled as first-time, first-year students.

Out-of-state:	20%	**25 or older:** 70%
Women:	60%	

Basis for selection. Prospects must show examples of their work in the area they are applying for. Portfolio required for commercial art program. **Home schooled:** Transcript of courses and grades required.

2016-2017 Annual costs. Tuition/fees (projected): $17,700. Books/supplies: $700.

Financial aid. **Need-based:** Need-based aid available for part-time students. Work-study available nights, weekends and for part-time students.

Application procedures. **Admission:** No deadline. $100 fee.

Academics. **Special study options:** Independent study, internships. **Credit/placement by examination:** AP, CLEP. **Support services:** Tutoring.

Majors. **Visual/performing arts:** General, commercial photography, commercial/advertising art, graphic design.

Technology on campus. PC or laptop required. 40 workstations in library, computer center. Wireless network available.

Student life. **Freshman orientation:** Mandatory. Preregistration for classes offered. **Housing:** Apartment housing available.

Student services. Adult student services, alcohol/substance abuse counseling, career counseling, student employment services, financial aid counseling, personal counseling, placement for graduates. **Transfer:** Pre-admission transcript evaluation for new students.

Contact. E-mail: admissions@nossi.edu
Phone: (615) 514-2787 ext. 17 Toll-free number: (887) 860-1601
Fax: (615) 514-2788
Mary Alexander, Director of Admissions, Nossi College of Art, 590 Cheron Road, Nashville, TN 37115

Pellissippi State Community College
Knoxville, Tennessee
www.pstcc.edu   **CB code: 0319**

- Public 2-year community and technical college
- Commuter campus in small city

General. Founded in 1974. Regionally accredited. **Enrollment:** 10,325 degree-seeking undergraduates. **Degrees:** 1,598 associate awarded. **ROTC:** Army. **Location:** 178 miles from Nashville, 388 miles from Memphis. **Calendar:** Semester, extensive summer session. **Full-time faculty:** 231 total. **Part-time faculty:** 342 total. **Class size:** 46% < 20, 52% 20-39, 2% 40-49, less than 1% 50-99, less than 1% >100.

Student profile.

Out-of-state:	1%	**25 or older:** 40%

Transfer out. **Colleges most students transferred to 2015:** University of Tennessee in Knoxville, East Tennessee State University, Tennessee Technological University, Maryville College, Middle Tennessee State University.

Basis for selection. Open admission. **Adult students:** Institutional placement test required of students 21 and older who have not had college-level math or English. **Learning Disabled:** Accommodations for testing/programs provided on case-by-case basis with supporting documentation.

High school preparation. 14 units recommended. Recommended units include English 4, mathematics 3, social studies 1, history 1, science 1 (laboratory 1) and foreign language 2. 1 U.S. history and one visual and performing arts required.

2015-2016 Annual costs. Tuition/fees: $4,168; $15,728 out-of-state. Books/supplies: $1,300. Personal expenses: $1,500.

Financial aid. **Need-based:** Need-based aid available for part-time students. Work-study available nights, weekends and for part-time students. **Non-need-based:** Scholarships awarded for academics, art, minority status, music/drama.

Application procedures. **Admission:** Closing date 8/20 (postmark date). $20 fee, may be waived for applicants with need. Admission notification on a rolling basis beginning on or about 9/1. **Financial aid:** Priority date 5/1; no closing date. FAFSA required. Applicants notified on a rolling basis starting 7/15; must reply within 2 week(s) of notification.

Academics. **Special study options:** Cooperative education, distance learning, double major, dual enrollment of high school students, ESL, honors, independent study, internships, liberal arts/career combination, weekend college. **Credit/placement by examination:** AP, CLEP, IB, institutional tests. 36 credit hours maximum toward associate degree. **Support services:** GED preparation and test center, learning center, pre-admission summer program, reduced course load, remedial instruction, study skills assistance, tutoring, writing center.

Majors. **Business:** Accounting technology, administrative services, business admin, e-commerce. **Computer sciences:** Computer science, information systems, web page design. **Human services:** Community org/advocacy. **Liberal arts:** Arts/sciences. **Social sciences:** GIS/cartography. **Visual/performing arts:** Cinematography, commercial/advertising art, interior design. **Work/family studies:** Child development.

Most popular majors. Business/marketing 9%, liberal arts 59%, visual/performing arts 9%.

Technology on campus. 1,290 workstations in library, computer center, student center. Commuter students can connect to campus network. Online course registration, online library, helpline, repair service, wireless network available.

Student life. **Freshman orientation:** Available. Preregistration for classes offered. **Activities:** Jazz band, campus ministries, choral groups, drama, international student organizations, literary magazine, music ensembles, musical theater, student government, student newspaper, Association of Information Technology Professionals, Institute of Electrical and Electronics Engineers, paralegal association, Active Black Students Association, Students In Free Enterprise, Phi Theta Kappa.

Athletics. **Intramural:** Archery, basketball, football (non-tackle), golf, soccer, softball, tennis, volleyball.

Student services. Career counseling, student employment services, personal counseling, placement for graduates, veterans' counselor. **Physically disabled:** Services for visually, speech, hearing impaired. **Transfer:** Transfer adviser, college fairs on campus for students transferring to 4-year colleges.

Contact. E-mail: latouzeau@pstcc.edu
Phone: (865) 694-6570 Fax: (865) 539-7217
Leigh Anne Touzeau, Assistant Vice President, Enrollment Services, Pellissippi State Community College, Box 22990, Knoxville, TN 37933-0990

Remington College: Memphis
Memphis, Tennessee
http://memphis.remingtoncollege.edu   **CB code: 3159**

- Private 2-year business and technical college
- Commuter campus in very large city
- Interview required

General. Accredited by ACCSC. **Enrollment:** 1,361 undergraduates. **Degrees:** 79 associate awarded. **Calendar:** Quarter, extensive summer session. **Full-time faculty:** 32 total. **Part-time faculty:** 5 total. **Class size:** 81% < 20, 19% 20-39.

Basis for selection. All applicants must pass college administered entrance exam prior to acceptance.

2015-2016 Annual costs. Diploma programs: ventilation and air conditioning $20,995; medical assisting $19,990; medical billing and coding

$15,995; pharmacy technician $19,990. Associate programs: business administration $33,900; business office management $33,900; computer and network administration $33,900; criminal justice $33,900; electronics and computer technology $33,900. Bachelor's program: criminal justice $24,700.

Financial aid. All financial aid based on need. Need-based aid available for part-time students. Work-study available nights, weekends and for part-time students.

Application procedures. Admission: No deadline. $50 fee. Admission notification on a rolling basis. **Financial aid:** No deadline. FAFSA, institutional form required. Applicants notified on a rolling basis; must reply within 2 week(s) of notification.

Academics. Special study options: Cooperative education, independent study, liberal arts/career combination. Bachelor's degree programs available on campus. **Credit/placement by examination:** AP, CLEP, institutional tests. 48 credit hours maximum toward associate degree, 96 toward bachelor's. **Support services:** Tutoring.

Majors. Business: Office technology. **Computer sciences:** LAN/WAN management. **Protective services:** Criminal justice.

Technology on campus. Commuter students can connect to campus network. Helpline, repair service, wireless network available.

Student life. Freshman orientation: Mandatory. Preregistration for classes offered. Three hour session held Saturday two weeks before quarter begins. **Activities:** Student newspaper.

Student services. Adult student services, career counseling, student employment services, financial aid counseling, placement for graduates. **Transfer:** Pre-admission transcript evaluation for new students.

Contact. E-mail: admissions@remingtoncollege.edu
Phone: (901) 389-5302
Marc Wright, Director of Admissions, Remington College: Memphis, 2710 Nonconnah Boulevard, Memphis, TN 38132

Remington College: Nashville
Nashville, Tennessee
http://nashville.remingtoncollege.edu

▸ Private 2-year technical and career college
▸ Very large city

General. Accredited by ACCSC. **Enrollment:** 597 undergraduates. **Degrees:** 42 associate awarded. **Calendar:** Quarter, extensive summer session. **Full-time faculty:** 16 total. **Part-time faculty:** 15 total. **Special facilities:** Forensics lab, crime scene lab, courtroom, laser shot range, 3 medical office labs, dental lab, salon.

Basis for selection. Open admission, but selective for some programs. Selective admissions to allied health programs.

2015-2016 Annual costs. Diploma programs: dental assisting $15,995; medical assisting (12 months) $19,990; pharmacy technician $19,990. Associate programs: criminal justice $33,900; dental hygiene $48,000.

Financial aid. Need-based: Work-study available nights, weekends and for part-time students.

Application procedures. Admission: No deadline. $50 fee. **Financial aid:** No deadline.

Academics. Credit/placement by examination: AP, CLEP.

Majors. Protective services: Law enforcement admin.

Contact. E-mail: admissions@remingtoncollege.edu
Phone: (615) 229-6057
Larry Collins, Campus President, Remington College: Nashville, 441 Donelson Pike, Suite 150, Nashville, TN 37214

Roane State Community College
Harriman, Tennessee
www.roanestate.edu   CB code: 1656

▸ Public 2-year community and junior college
▸ Commuter campus in small town

General. Founded in 1971. Regionally accredited. **Enrollment:** 4,421 degree-seeking undergraduates. **Degrees:** 817 associate awarded. **Location:** 40 miles from Knoxville. **Calendar:** Semester, limited summer session. **Full-time faculty:** 124 total; 15% minority, 52% women. **Part-time faculty:** 254 total; 5% minority, 58% women. **Class size:** 55% < 20, 44% 20-39, less than 1% 40-49, less than 1% 50-99. **Special facilities:** Observatory, agricultural exposition center.

Student profile.

Out-of-state: 1% 25 or older: 39%

Transfer out. Colleges most students transferred to 2015: University of Tennessee-Knoxville, Tennessee Technological University, Middle Tennessee State University, East Tennessee State University.

Basis for selection. Open admission, but selective for some programs. All health science programs require 20 ACT and 2.5 GPA for 9 hours general course work. Additional requirements for nursing program. Interview required for some health programs; audition required for some music programs. **Adult students:** Placement assessment may be required. **Home schooled:** State high school equivalency certificate required.

High school preparation. 16 units required. Required units include English 4, mathematics 4, history 2, science 3, foreign language 2 and visual/performing arts 1.

2015-2016 Annual costs. Tuition/fees: $4,131; $16,101 out-of-state. Per-credit charge: $152 in-state; $627 out-of-state. Books/supplies: $1,500.

Financial aid. Need-based: Need-based aid available for part-time students. Work-study available nights, weekends and for part-time students. **Non-need-based:** Scholarships awarded for academics, art, athletics, leadership, music/drama, state residency.

Application procedures. Admission: No deadline. $20 fee. Admission notification on a rolling basis. **Financial aid:** Priority date 4/1; no closing date. FAFSA, institutional form required. Applicants notified on a rolling basis starting 5/1.

Academics. Online academic support services available evenings and weekends. **Special study options:** Accelerated study, cooperative education, distance learning, double major, dual enrollment of high school students, ESL, honors, independent study, internships, liberal arts/career combination, study abroad, teacher certification program, weekend college. Bachelor's degree programs available on campus. License preparation in dental hygiene, nursing, occupational therapy, paramedic, physical therapy, radiology. **Credit/placement by examination:** AP, CLEP, IB, institutional tests. 18 credit hours maximum toward associate degree. **Support services:** GED preparation and test center, learning center, remedial instruction, study skills assistance, tutoring, writing center.

Majors. Business: Business admin, management science. **Computer sciences:** Web page design. **Education:** General, early childhood. **Health services:** Dental hygiene, environmental health, health information technology, medical radiologic technology/radiation therapy, nursing (RN), occupational therapy assistant, optician, physical therapy assistant, respiratory therapy technology. **Liberal arts:** Arts/sciences. **Protective services:** Criminal justice, police science. **Social sciences:** GIS/cartography.

Most popular majors. Business/marketing 8%, education 7%, health sciences 32%, liberal arts 40%, science technologies 9%.

Technology on campus. 600 workstations in library, computer center, student center. Commuter students can connect to campus network. Online course registration, online library, helpline, wireless network available.

Student life. Freshman orientation: Mandatory. Preregistration for classes offered. One half-day orientation. **Activities:** Jazz band, campus ministries, choral groups, dance, drama, international student organizations, music ensembles, musical theater, student government, American Chemical Society, Baptist collegiate ministry, International Association of Administrative Professionals, Oak Ridge Institute for Continued Learning, occupational therapy student club, Phi Theta Kappa, physical therapy student association, Playmakers, psychology and sociology club, respiratory therapy student association.

Athletics. NJCAA. **Intercollegiate:** Baseball M, basketball, softball W. **Intramural:** Basketball, softball. **Team name:** Raiders.

Student services. Career counseling, student employment services, financial aid counseling, minority student services, personal counseling, placement for graduates, veterans' counselor. **Physically disabled:** Services for visually, speech, hearing impaired. **Transfer:** Transfer adviser, college fairs on campus for students transferring to 4-year colleges.

Contact. E-mail: admissions@roanestate.edu
Phone: (865) 882-4523 Toll-free number: (866) 462-7722 ext. 4523
Fax: (865) 882-4527
Brenda Rector, Director of Admissions and Records, Roane State
Community College, 276 Patton Lane, Harriman, TN 37748

Southwest Tennessee Community College
Memphis, Tennessee
www.southwest.tn.edu   CB code: 0274

▶ Public 2-year community college
▶ Commuter campus in very large city

General. Founded in 1970. Regionally accredited. **Enrollment:** 8,402
degree-seeking undergraduates. **Degrees:** 751 associate awarded. **ROTC:**
Army, Air Force. **Calendar:** Semester, extensive summer session. **Full-time
faculty:** 220 total. **Part-time faculty:** 450 total. **Class size:** 45% < 20, 55%
20-39, less than 1% 40-49.

Transfer out. Colleges most students transferred to 2015: University of
Memphis, Middle Tennessee State University, Tennessee State University,
University of Tennessee at Martin.

Basis for selection. Open admission, but selective for some programs.
Special requirements for admission to nursing, dietetic technician, laboratory
phlebotomy, medical assistant, medical laboratory technician, physical therapist assistant, radiologic technology, paramedic programs. **Adult students:**
ACT COMPASS exam required for placement. **Learning Disabled:** Require
documentation of disability to be shown to disability counselor.

High school preparation. 15 units required. Required units include
English 4, mathematics 3, social studies 1, history 1, science 2 (laboratory
1), foreign language 2 and visual/performing arts 1.

2015-2016 Annual costs. Tuition/fees: $3,963; $15,363 out-of-state. Per-
credit charge: $152 in-state; $627 out-of-state. Books/supplies: $1,200. Per-
sonal expenses: $1,500.

Financial aid. Need-based: Need-based aid available for part-time students. Work-study available nights, weekends and for part-time students.
Non-need-based: Scholarships awarded for academics, athletics, minority
status, music/drama, state residency. **Additional information:** State grants
available to eligible students who apply by 4/1.

Application procedures. Admission: No deadline. $10 fee. Admission
notification on a rolling basis. **Financial aid:** Closing date 3/15. FAFSA
required. Applicants notified on a rolling basis starting 6/1; must reply within
4 week(s) of notification.

Academics. Special study options: Cooperative education, distance learning, double major, dual enrollment of high school students, ESL, honors,
independent study, internships, liberal arts/career combination, student-
designed major, study abroad, weekend college. On-site extension courses
at business, industry and government installations. License preparation in
nursing, paramedic, physical therapy, radiology, real estate. **Credit/place-
ment by examination:** AP, CLEP, institutional tests. **Support services:**
GED preparation and test center, learning center, pre-admission summer
program, reduced course load, remedial instruction, study skills assistance,
tutoring.

Majors. Biology: Biotechnology. **Business:** General, accounting technology, administrative services, business admin, hotel/motel admin, management
information systems. **Computer sciences:** General, web page design. **Education:** General. **Health services:** Clinical lab technology, dietician assistant,
EMT paramedic, medical radiologic technology/radiation therapy, nursing
(RN), physical therapy assistant. **Liberal arts:** Arts/sciences. **Protective
services:** Police science. **Visual/performing arts:** Commercial/advertising
art. **Work/family studies:** Child development.

Most popular majors. Business/marketing 14%, engineering/engineering
technologies 6%, health sciences 19%, liberal arts 42%.

Technology on campus. 500 workstations in library, computer center.
Commuter students can connect to campus network. Online course registration, online library, helpline, wireless network available.

Student life. Freshman orientation: Available. Preregistration for classes
offered. **Activities:** Bands, choral groups, drama, music ensembles, student
government, student newspaper, NAACP, Baptist student union, Human
Key Society, National Student Support Council for Africa, black student
association, Phi Theta Kappa honor society, police science association, science club, radiologic technology student association, Collegiate Secretaries.

Athletics. NJCAA. **Intercollegiate:** Baseball M, basketball, softball W.
Team name: Saluqis.

Student services. Adult student services, career counseling, services for
economically disadvantaged, student employment services, financial aid
counseling, on-campus daycare, personal counseling, placement for graduates, veterans' counselor. **Physically disabled:** Services for visually, speech,
hearing impaired. **Transfer:** Re-entry adviser, pre-admission transcript evaluation for new students. Transfer center, transfer adviser, college fairs on
campus for students transferring to 4-year colleges.

Contact. E-mail: admissions@southwest.tn.edu
Phone: (901) 333-5924 Toll-free number: (877) 717-7822
Fax: (901) 333-4473
Tina Studaway, Director, Southwest Tennessee Community College, PO
Box 780, Memphis, TN 38101-0780

Vatterott College: Memphis
Memphis, Tennessee
www.vatterott.edu

▶ For-profit 2-year technical college
▶ Commuter campus in large city

General. Accredited by ACCSC. **Enrollment:** 1,020 undergraduates.
Degrees: 194 associate awarded. **Calendar:** Differs by program. **Full-time
faculty:** 9 total. **Part-time faculty:** 26 total.

Basis for selection. Open admission.

2015-2016 Annual costs. Books/supplies: $1,050. **Additional informa-
tion:** Diploma programs: (60 weeks) $28,000-$28,034. Associate programs:
(70 weeks) $34,900-$35,386; (90 weeks) $40,650-$41,450. Costs include
fees, books and supplies.

Financial aid. Need-based: Work-study available nights, weekends and
for part-time students.

Application procedures. Admission: No deadline. No application fee.

Academics. Credit/placement by examination: AP, CLEP, institutional
tests. **Support services:** Learning center.

Majors. Computer sciences: System admin.

Technology on campus. 20 workstations in library.

Contact. E-mail: paulette.thomas@vatterott-college.edu
Phone: (901) 761-5730 Toll-free number: (888) 553-6627
Fax: (901) 763-2897
Paulette Thomas, Director of Admissions, Vatterott College: Memphis,
2655 Dividend Drive, Memphis, TN 38132

Virginia College School of Business and Health in Chattanooga
Chattanooga, Tennessee
www.chattanooga.vc.edu

▶ For-profit 2-year business and career college
▶ Large city

General. Regionally accredited; also accredited by ACICS. **Enrollment:**
345 undergraduates. **Degrees:** 41 associate awarded. **Calendar:** Quarter.
Full-time faculty: 12 total. **Part-time faculty:** 77 total.

Basis for selection. Open admission.

2015-2016 Annual costs. Diploma programs: $14,652-$22,560. Associate programs: $36,096. Clock hour diploma program: Cosmetology $20,520.

Financial aid. Need-based: Work-study available nights, weekends and
for part-time students.

Application procedures. Admission: $100 fee.

Academics. Credit/placement by examination: AP, CLEP.

Majors. Business: Administrative services, business admin. **Health services:** Health information management, insurance coding, medical assistant,
surgical technology.

Contact. E-mail: chattanooga.info@vc.edu
Virginia College School of Business and Health in Chattanooga, 721
Eastgate Loop, Chattanooga, TN 37411

Volunteer State Community College
Gallatin, Tennessee
www.volstate.edu   **CB code: 1881**

- Public 2-year community and junior college
- Commuter campus in large town

General. Founded in 1970. Regionally accredited. **Enrollment:** 6,536
degree-seeking undergraduates; 1,532 non-degree-seeking students. **Degrees:**
885 associate awarded. **Location:** 25 miles from Nashville. **Calendar:**
Semester, limited summer session. **Full-time faculty:** 169 total; 21% have
terminal degrees, 18% minority, 54% women. **Part-time faculty:** 242 total;
8% have terminal degrees, 7% minority, 57% women. **Class size:** 63% < 20,
36% 20-39, 1% 40-49, less than 1% 50-99. **Special facilities:** Community
garden.

Student profile. Among degree-seeking undergraduates, 63% enrolled in
a transfer program, 37% enrolled in a vocational program, 2,345 enrolled as
first-time, first-year students, 384 transferred in from other institutions.

Part-time:	36%	Asian American:	1%
Out-of-state:	2%	Hispanic/Latino:	5%
Women:	59%	Multi-racial, non-Hispanic:	3%
African American:	11%	25 or older:	40%

Transfer out. Colleges most students transferred to 2015: Middle Tennessee State University, Austin Peay State University, Tennessee State University, Tennessee Technical University.

Basis for selection. Open admission, but selective for some programs.
Allied Health students admitted based on GPA and interview after completing
designated amount of college coursework. Test scores, when required in
selective programs, must be received by 8/30. Interview required for allied
health program. **Adult students:** Unless exempt by ACT, ASSET placement
test required. **Home schooled:** Transcript must be official copy from affiliated
organization as defined by state law or be accompanied by certification of
registration with superintendent of local education agency where student
would otherwise attend.

High school preparation. 16 units required. Required units include
English 4, mathematics 4, social studies 1, history 1, science 3 (laboratory
1), foreign language 2 and visual/performing arts 1.

2015-2016 Annual costs. Tuition/fees: $3,925; $15,325 out-of-state.
Books/supplies: $1,200. Personal expenses: $400.

2014-2015 Financial aid. Need-based: 1,054 full-time freshmen applied
for aid; 785 deemed to have need; 785 received aid. Average need met was
57%. Average scholarship/grant was $4,553; average loan $2,550. 75% of
total undergraduate aid awarded as scholarships/grants, 25% as loans/jobs.
Need-based aid available for part-time students. Work-study available nights,
weekends and for part-time students. **Non-need-based:** Awarded to 900
full-time undergraduates, including 493 freshmen. Scholarships awarded for
academics, art, athletics, leadership, minority status, music/drama, state residency.

Application procedures. Admission: Priority date 7/31; deadline 8/25
(receipt date). $20 fee. Admission notification on a rolling basis. **Financial
aid:** Priority date 4/15; no closing date. FAFSA, institutional form required.
Applicants notified on a rolling basis; must reply within 2 week(s) of notification.

Academics. Special study options: Accelerated study, cooperative education, distance learning, double major, dual enrollment of high school students,
ESL, honors, independent study, internships, study abroad. Bachelor's degree
programs available on campus. License preparation in dental hygiene, paramedic, physical therapy, radiology, real estate. **Credit/placement by examination:** AP, CLEP, institutional tests. 15 credit hours maximum toward
associate degree. Maximum 12 hours of credit by examination in specific
allied health programs. **Support services:** GED test center, learning center,
pre-admission summer program, reduced course load, remedial instruction,
study skills assistance, tutoring, writing center.

Majors. Business: Business admin. **Education:** General. **Health services:**
Clinical lab technology, health information technology, medical radiologic
technology/radiation therapy, ophthalmic technology, physical therapy assistant, respiratory therapy technology, veterinary technology/assistant. **Liberal
arts:** Arts/sciences. **Protective services:** Firefighting, police science. **Work/
family studies:** Child development.

Most popular majors. Business/marketing 7%, health sciences 21%, liberal arts 62%.

Technology on campus. 700 workstations in library, computer center.
Commuter students can connect to campus network. Online course registration, online library, helpline, wireless network available.

Student life. Freshman orientation: Mandatory. Preregistration for
classes offered. One-day program held multiple times prior to registration
both on campus and online. **Activities:** Campus ministries, choral groups,
dance, drama, international student organizations, literary magazine, music
ensembles, radio station, student government, student newspaper, African-
American student union, returning women's organization, College Democrats,
College Republicans.

Athletics. NJCAA. **Intercollegiate:** Baseball M, basketball, softball W.
Team name: Pioneers.

Student services. Adult student services, career counseling, services for
economically disadvantaged, student employment services, financial aid
counseling, health services, minority student services, personal counseling,
placement for graduates, veterans' counselor. **Physically disabled:** Services
for visually, speech, hearing impaired. **Transfer:** Pre-admission transcript
evaluation for new students. Transfer adviser, college fairs on campus for
students transferring to 4-year colleges.

Contact. E-mail: admissions@volstate.edu
Phone: (615) 452-8600 ext. 3688
Toll-free number: (888) 335-8722 ext. 3688 Fax: (615) 230-4875
Tim Amyx, Director of Admissions & Registration, Volunteer State
Community College, 1480 Nashville Pike, Gallatin, TN 37066-3188

Walters State Community College
Morristown, Tennessee
www.ws.edu   **CB code: 1893**

- Public 2-year culinary school and community college
- Commuter campus in small city

General. Founded in 1970. Regionally accredited. Degree programs and
courses held at sites throughout 10-county service delivery area; campus
facilities located in Morristown, Greeneville, Sevierville, and Tazewell.
Enrollment: 4,553 degree-seeking undergraduates; 1,394 non-degree-
seeking students. **Degrees:** 811 associate awarded. **ROTC:** Army. **Location:**
45 miles from Knoxville. **Calendar:** Semester, limited summer session. **Full-
time faculty:** 164 total; 32% have terminal degrees, 4% minority, 57%
women. **Part-time faculty:** 208 total; 21% have terminal degrees, 58%
women. **Class size:** 43% < 20, 57% 20-39, less than 1% 40-49, less than
1% 50-99. **Special facilities:** Observatory, training restaurant, exposition
center, industrial technology manufacturing laboratory with complete computer integrated manufacturing (CIM), work center and coordinate measuring
machine, public safety law enforcement training center, greenhouse, production horticulture lab, arboretum, center for workforce education, clean energy
laboratory, fire science/EMT training.

Student profile. Among degree-seeking undergraduates, 1,622 enrolled as
first-time, first-year students, 171 transferred in from other institutions.

Part-time:	30%	Hispanic/Latino:	3%
Women:	60%	Multi-racial, non-Hispanic:	2%
African American:	3%	International:	1%
Asian American:	1%	25 or older:	18%

Transfer out. Colleges most students transferred to 2015: University
of Tennessee-Knoxville, East Tennessee State University, Carson Newman
College, Tusculum College, Lincoln Memorial University.

Basis for selection. Open admission, but selective for some programs.
Special requirements for education, allied health and public safety programs.
Adult students: Placement assessment required.

High school preparation. College-preparatory program recommended.
14 units required. Required units include English 4, mathematics 3, social
studies 1, history 1, science 2 (laboratory 1), foreign language 2 and visual/
performing arts 1. College-preparatory program required for 2-year transfer
program: 1 unit biological science, 4 English, 2 foreign language, 3 mathematics, 1 physical science, 2 social science, 1 visual or performing arts. Same
preparation recommended for all students.

2015-2016 Annual costs. Tuition/fees: $4,116; $16,086 out-of-state.
Books/supplies: $1,200. Personal expenses: $1,400.

2014-2015 Financial aid. Need-based: 937 full-time freshmen applied
for aid; 755 deemed to have need; 753 received aid. Average need met was
58%. Average scholarship/grant was $4,713. 99% of total undergraduate aid

awarded as scholarships/grants, 1% as loans/jobs. Need-based aid available for part-time students. Work-study available nights, weekends and for part-time students. **Non-need-based:** Awarded to 1,890 full-time undergraduates, including 692 freshmen. Scholarships awarded for academics, athletics, minority status, music/drama, state residency.

Application procedures. Admission: No deadline. No application fee. Admission notification on a rolling basis. **Financial aid:** Priority date 6/30; no closing date. FAFSA required. Applicants notified by 5/10; Applicants notified on a rolling basis.

Academics. Instructional alternatives include interactive television, web-based, video streaming, telecourses, and mobilized campus. **Special study options:** Accelerated study, cooperative education, distance learning, dual enrollment of high school students, ESL, external degree, honors, independent study, internships, liberal arts/career combination, study abroad. Bachelor's degree programs available on campus. License preparation in nursing, paramedic, physical therapy. **Credit/placement by examination:** AP, CLEP, institutional tests. 42 credit hours maximum toward associate degree. **Support services:** GED test center, learning center, reduced course load, remedial instruction, study skills assistance, tutoring, writing center.

Honors college/program. 24 ACT and completion of honors core program required. Students over 21 without required ACT score must submit scores of 68 on writing portion and 50 on algebra portion of COMPASS.

Majors. Business: Business admin, management information systems. **Computer sciences:** Web page design. **Education:** General. **Health services:** EMT paramedic, health information technology, nursing (RN), physical therapy assistant, respiratory therapy technology. **Liberal arts:** Arts/sciences. **Protective services:** Police science. **Work/family studies:** Child development.

Most popular majors. Business/marketing 9%, health sciences 19%, liberal arts 61%.

Technology on campus. 1,405 workstations in library, computer center, student center. Commuter students can connect to campus network. Online course registration, online library, helpline, wireless network available.

Student life. Freshman orientation: Mandatory. Preregistration for classes offered. **Activities:** Campus ministries, choral groups, drama, international student organizations, literary magazine, musical theater, student government, Baptist collegiate ministry, Methodist student group, international club, Sevierville Collegiate Ministry, Service Learners of WSGC, Sevier County Ambassadors, Senators Pages, Phi Theta Kappa.

Athletics. NJCAA. **Intercollegiate:** Baseball M, basketball, cheerleading, golf, softball W, volleyball W. **Intramural:** Basketball, football (tackle), soccer, softball. **Team name:** Senators.

Student services. Adult student services, alcohol/substance abuse counseling, chaplain/spiritual director, career counseling, student employment services, financial aid counseling, health services, minority student services, personal counseling, placement for graduates, veterans' counselor. **Physically disabled:** Services for visually, speech, hearing impaired. **Transfer:** Reentry adviser for new students. Transfer center, transfer adviser, college fairs on campus for students transferring to 4-year colleges.

Contact. E-mail: mike.campbell@ws.edu
Phone: (423) 585-2685 Toll-free number: (800) 225-4770
Fax: (423) 585-6786
Mike Campbell, Assistant Vice President for Student Affairs, Walters State Community College, 500 South Davy Crockett Parkway, Morristown, TN 37813-6899

West Tennessee Business College
Jackson, Tennessee
www.wtbc.edu

▶ For-profit 2-year career college
▶ Commuter campus in small city
▶ Interview required

General. Accredited by ACICS. **Enrollment:** 211 undergraduates. **Degrees:** 12 associate awarded. **Location:** 80 miles from Memphis. **Calendar:** Differs by program. **Full-time faculty:** 13 total. **Part-time faculty:** 3 total.

Basis for selection. Applicants required to take the CPAt in-house test by ACT.

2015-2016 Annual costs. Diploma programs range from $13,775-$15,605. Books, supplies, fees range depending on program level and course of study. All costs are subject to change.

Financial aid. Need-based: Work-study available nights, weekends and for part-time students.

Application procedures. Admission: No deadline. $50 fee. Admission notification on a rolling basis. **Financial aid:** No deadline.

Academics. Credit/placement by examination: AP, CLEP.

Majors. Business: Administrative services, business admin. **Health services:** Medical secretary.

Technology on campus. 130 workstations in computer center, student center. Online library, wireless network available.

Student life. Freshman orientation: Mandatory. Preregistration for classes offered.

Student services. Career counseling, student employment services, financial aid counseling, placement for graduates.

Contact. E-mail: ann.record@wtbc.edu
Phone: (731) 668-7240 Toll-free number: (800) 737-9822
Ann Record, Admissions Director, West Tennessee Business College, 1186 Highway 45 Bypass, Jackson, TN 38301

Texas

Alvin Community College
Alvin, Texas
www.alvincollege.edu   CB code: 6005

- Public 2-year community and liberal arts college
- Commuter campus in large town

General. Founded in 1948. Regionally accredited. **Enrollment:** 5,116 undergraduates. **Degrees:** 732 associate awarded. **ROTC:** Air Force. **Location:** 32 miles from Houston. **Calendar:** Semester, extensive summer session. **Full-time faculty:** 111 total; 20% have terminal degrees, 13% minority, 59% women. **Part-time faculty:** 156 total; 8% have terminal degrees, 18% minority, 64% women. **Special facilities:** Radio station, recording studio, indoor firing range for law enforcement program, Nolan Ryan exhibit.

Transfer out. Colleges most students transferred to 2015: University of Houston-Clear Lake, University of Houston, Texas A&M, Sam Houston State University, Southwest Texas State University.

Basis for selection. Open admission, but selective for some programs. Texas Academic Skills Program test required by Texas law. Special requirements for nursing, respiratory therapy, criminal justice, court reporting, musical theater, Intraoperative Neurophysiologic Monitoring Program, EMT, nursing programs, human services substance abuse counseling program, diagnostic cardiovascular sonography programs, honors programs. Interview required for court reporting, medical laboratory technology, nursing, respiratory therapy programs; audition required for music, musical theater programs.

High school preparation. 25 units recommended. Recommended units include English 4, mathematics 4, social studies 4, science 3, foreign language 3 and academic electives 7.

2015-2016 Annual costs. Tuition/fees: $1,814; $3,164 out-of-district; $4,664 out-of-state. Per-credit charge: $45 in-district; $90 out-of-district; $140 out-of-state. Books/supplies: $1,775.

2014-2015 Financial aid. All financial aid based on need. 94% of total undergraduate aid awarded as scholarships/grants, 6% as loans/jobs. Need-based aid available for part-time students. Work-study available nights, weekends and for part-time students.

Application procedures. Admission: No deadline. No application fee. Admission notification on a rolling basis. **Financial aid:** No deadline. FAFSA required. Applicants notified on a rolling basis; must reply within 2 week(s) of notification.

Academics. Special study options: Cooperative education, cross-registration, distance learning, dual enrollment of high school students, ESL, honors, internships, liberal arts/career combination, study abroad. License preparation in nursing, paramedic. **Credit/placement by examination:** AP, CLEP, institutional tests. **Support services:** GED preparation and test center, learning center, reduced course load, remedial instruction, study skills assistance, tutoring, writing center.

Majors. Biology: General. **Business:** General, business admin, executive assistant. **Communications:** Radio/TV. **Computer sciences:** General, programming. **Education:** Early childhood, middle, physical, secondary. **Health services:** Cardiovascular technology, electroencephalograph technology, EMT paramedic, mental health services, nursing (RN), respiratory therapy technology, sonography. **History:** General. **Liberal arts:** Arts/sciences. **Math:** General. **Parks/recreation:** Health/fitness. **Physical sciences:** General. **Protective services:** Corrections, criminal justice, police science. **Psychology:** General. **Social sciences:** Sociology. **Visual/performing arts:** Art, dramatic, music performance. **Work/family studies:** Child development.

Most popular majors. Business/marketing 8%, health sciences 21%, liberal arts 44%, science technologies 9%.

Technology on campus. 600 workstations in library, computer center. Online course registration, online library, wireless network available.

Student life. Freshman orientation: Mandatory. Preregistration for classes offered. **Housing:** Housing provided for scholarship athletes. **Activities:** Bands, choral groups, dance, drama, literary magazine, music ensembles, musical theater, radio station, student government, TV station, Newman

Association, Phi Theta Kappa, Pan American College Forum, Baptist student union.

Athletics. NJCAA. **Intercollegiate:** Baseball M, softball W. **Team name:** Dolphins.

Student services. Career counseling, student employment services, financial aid counseling, on-campus daycare, personal counseling, placement for graduates, veterans' counselor. **Physically disabled:** Services for visually, speech, hearing impaired. **Transfer:** Transfer adviser, college fairs on campus for students transferring to 4-year colleges.

Contact. E-mail: info@alvincollege.edu
Phone: (281) 756-3531 Fax: (281) 756-3843
Stephanie Stockstill, Director of Admissions/Academic Advising, Alvin Community College, 3110 Mustang Road, Alvin, TX 77511-4898

Amarillo College
Amarillo, Texas
www.actx.edu   CB code: 6006

- Public 2-year community college
- Commuter campus in small city

General. Founded in 1929. Regionally accredited. In addition to traditional population pursuing courses for credit, institution serves 12,000 workforce development and leisure studies students. **Enrollment:** 7,869 degree-seeking undergraduates. **Degrees:** 1,014 associate awarded. **Location:** 300 miles from Dallas, 300 miles from Denver. **Calendar:** Semester, extensive summer session. **Full-time faculty:** 221 total. **Part-time faculty:** 204 total. **Class size:** 53% < 20, 38% 20-39, 4% 40-49, 4% 50-99, less than 1% >100. **Special facilities:** Art museum, natural science museum, children's theater.

Student profile.

Out-of-state: 1% **Live on campus:** 1%

Transfer out. Colleges most students transferred to 2015: West Texas A&M University, Texas Tech University.

Basis for selection. Open admission.

High school preparation. 18 units recommended. Recommended units include English 4, mathematics 2, social studies 2, history 2, science 2, foreign language 3 and academic electives 3.

2015-2016 Annual costs. Tuition/fees: $2,512; $3,802 out-of-district; $5,722 out-of-state. Books/supplies: $996. Personal expenses: $1,302.

Financial aid. Need-based: Work-study available nights, weekends and for part-time students. **Non-need-based:** Scholarships awarded for academics, state residency.

Application procedures. Admission: Priority date 8/1; no deadline. No application fee. Admission notification on a rolling basis. **Financial aid:** Priority date 6/15; no closing date. FAFSA, institutional form required. Applicants notified on a rolling basis starting 6/15; must reply within 2 week(s) of notification.

Academics. Special study options: Accelerated study, cooperative education, distance learning, dual enrollment of high school students, ESL, honors, internships, weekend college. License preparation in nursing, real estate. **Credit/placement by examination:** AP, CLEP, institutional tests. 15 credit hours maximum toward associate degree. **Support services:** GED preparation and test center, learning center, remedial instruction, study skills assistance, tutoring, writing center.

Majors. Biology: General. **Business:** General, accounting, administrative services, finance, office/clerical, real estate, tourism promotion. **Communications:** Advertising, broadcast journalism, communications/speech/rhetoric, journalism. **Communications technology:** General. **Computer sciences:** General, computer graphics, information systems, programming. **Education:** General, elementary, music, physical. **Engineering:** General, computer. **English:** English lit, rhetoric/composition. **General:** Power transmission. **Health services:** Clinical lab science, clinical lab technology, dental hygiene, EMT paramedic, health information technology, medical radiologic technology/radiation therapy, nuclear medical technology, nursing (RN), occupational therapy assistant, physical therapy assistant, predental, premedicine, prepharmacy, preveterinary, respiratory therapy technology, substance abuse counseling, surgical technology. **Human services:** Social work. **Liberal arts:** Arts/sciences. **Math:** General. **Parks/recreation:** Health/fitness. **Philosophy/religion:** Religion. **Physical sciences:** General, chemistry, geology, physics. **Protective services:** Corrections, fire safety technology, police science. **Psychology:** General. **Social sciences:** General. **Visual/performing**

arts: Art, commercial photography, commercial/advertising art, design, dramatic, interior design, music, photography. **Work/family studies:** Child care management.

Technology on campus. Online course registration, online library, helpline available.

Student life. Freshman orientation: Mandatory. Preregistration for classes offered. **Housing:** Apartments available. **Activities:** Bands, choral groups, dance, drama, literary magazine, music ensembles, musical theater, opera, radio station, student government, student newspaper, TV station.

Athletics. Intramural: Basketball, tennis, volleyball.

Student services. Adult student services, career counseling, student employment services, on-campus daycare, personal counseling, placement for graduates, veterans' counselor. **Physically disabled:** Services for visually, speech, hearing impaired. **Transfer:** Transfer adviser, college fairs on campus for students transferring to 4-year colleges.

Contact. E-mail: AskAC@actx.edu
Phone: (806) 371-5030 Fax: (806) 371-5066
Diane Brice, Registrar and Director of Admissions, Amarillo College, Box 447, Amarillo, TX 79178

Angelina College
Lufkin, Texas
www.angelina.edu   CB code: 6025

▶ Public 2-year community college
▶ Commuter campus in large town

General. Founded in 1966. Regionally accredited. Teaching centers located in 5 contiguous counties. Branch campuses located in Jasper, Crockett, Livingston and Nacogdoches. **Enrollment:** 5,236 degree-seeking undergraduates. **Degrees:** 325 associate awarded. **ROTC:** Army. **Location:** 120 miles from Houston, 112 miles from Shreveport, LA. **Calendar:** Semester, extensive summer session. **Full-time faculty:** 87 total; 7% have terminal degrees, 9% minority, 58% women. **Part-time faculty:** 218 total; 8% have terminal degrees, 11% minority, 62% women. **Class size:** 80% < 20, 20% 20-39, less than 1% 40-49. **Special facilities:** Computer-aided design laboratory, performing arts center, health occupations laboratory.

Student profile. Among degree-seeking undergraduates, 1,604 enrolled as first-time, first-year students, 263 transferred in from other institutions.

Part-time:	74%	Hispanic/Latino:	22%
Women:	63%	Native American:	1%
African American:	13%	Multi-racial, non-Hispanic:	3%
Asian American:	1%		

Transfer out. Colleges most students transferred to 2015: Stephen F. Austin State University, Sam Houston State University.

Basis for selection. Open admission, but selective for some programs. Special requirements for nursing, respiratory care, EMS, pharmacy, surgery technology, diagnostic medical sonography and radiologic technology programs; interview required. General Aptitude Test Battery required of nursing applicants. All students must take Texas Higher Education Assessment Test or ACCUPLACER before enrolling. **Adult students:** Physical education requirements waived for veterans. **Home schooled:** Transcript of courses and grades required. Transcript must be signed by the School Principal and notarized. **Learning Disabled:** May have to take different test based on disability.

2015-2016 Annual costs. Tuition/fees: $2,220; $3,480 out-of-district; $4,860 out-of-state. Per-credit charge: $62 in-district; $104 out-of-district; $150 out-of-state. Room/board: $5,600. Books/supplies: $1,500. Personal expenses: $2,200.

Financial aid. Need-based: Need-based aid available for part-time students. Work-study available nights, weekends and for part-time students. **Non-need-based:** Scholarships awarded for academics, art, athletics, job skills, leadership, music/drama, state residency.

Application procedures. Admission: No deadline. No application fee. Admission notification on a rolling basis. **Financial aid:** Priority date 7/15; no closing date. FAFSA required. Applicants notified on a rolling basis starting 3/15.

Academics. Special study options: Accelerated study, cooperative education, distance learning, dual enrollment of high school students, internships, liberal arts/career combination. License preparation in nursing, paramedic, radiology, real estate. **Credit/placement by examination:** AP, CLEP, IB; institutional tests. 24 credit hours maximum toward associate degree. **Support**

---

services: GED preparation and test center, learning center, reduced course load, remedial instruction, study skills assistance, tutoring.

Majors. Biology: General. **Business:** General, accounting, administrative services, business admin. **Communications:** Communications/speech/rhetoric. **Communications technology:** Recording arts. **Computer sciences:** General, data processing, networking. **Education:** Multi-level teacher. **Engineering:** General. **English:** Rhetoric/composition. **Health services:** EMT paramedic, nursing (RN), predental, premedicine, prepharmacy, prephysical therapy, preveterinary, radiologic technology/medical imaging, respiratory therapy technology, sonography. **Math:** General. **Parks/recreation:** Health/fitness. **Physical sciences:** Physics. **Protective services:** Criminal justice. **Visual/performing arts:** Art, design, dramatic, music. **Work/family studies:** Child development.

Most popular majors. Business/marketing 13%, education 6%, engineering/engineering technologies 6%, health sciences 29%, liberal arts 15%, visual/performing arts 6%.

Technology on campus. 60 workstations in library, student center. Commuter students can connect to campus network. Online course registration, online library, helpline, wireless network available.

Student life. Freshman orientation: Mandatory. Preregistration for classes offered. **Housing:** Coed dorms, wellness housing available. $100 fully refundable deposit, deadline 7/15. Apartments for single parents available. **Activities:** Bands, campus ministries, choral groups, dance, drama, music ensembles, musical theater, student government, student newspaper, Baptist Student Ministry, Campus Crusade for Christ, Young Democrats Society, Young Republican Society.

Athletics. NJCAA. Intercollegiate: Baseball M, basketball, cheerleading, softball W. **Intramural:** Golf, volleyball. **Team name:** Roadrunners.

Student services. Adult student services, career counseling, services for economically disadvantaged, student employment services, financial aid counseling, placement for graduates, veterans' counselor. **Physically disabled:** Services for visually, speech, hearing impaired. **Transfer:** Pre-admission transcript evaluation for new students. Transfer adviser, college fairs on campus for students transferring to 4-year colleges.

Contact. E-mail: registrar@angelina.edu
Phone: (936) 639-5210 Fax: (936) 633-3206
Sandra Cox, Registrar, Angelina College, PO Box 1768, Lufkin, TX 75902-1768

Austin Community College
Austin, Texas   CB member
www.austincc.edu   CB code: 6759

▶ Public 2-year community college
▶ Commuter campus in very large city

General. Founded in 1972. Regionally accredited. Eleven campuses serving the greater Austin area, 6 instructional centers in surrounding towns. **Enrollment:** 41,574 undergraduates. **Degrees:** 2,154 associate awarded. **ROTC:** Army, Air Force. **Location:** 85 miles from San Antonio. **Calendar:** Semester, extensive summer session. **Full-time faculty:** 536 total; 29% have terminal degrees, 26% minority, 55% women. **Part-time faculty:** 1,332 total; 20% have terminal degrees, 23% minority, 49% women. **Class size:** 43% < 20, 57% 20-39, less than 1% 40-49. **Special facilities:** Water-quality monitoring well. **Partnerships:** Formal partnerships with Sustainability Project, Semiconductor Manufacturing Program, Seton Health.

Student profile. 79% enrolled in a transfer program, 21% enrolled in a vocational program, 7% already have a bachelor's degree or higher.

Transfer out. Colleges most students transferred to 2015: University of Texas at Austin, Texas State University, Virginia College at Austin, University of Texas at San Antonio, and Concordia.

Basis for selection. Open admission, but selective for some programs. Special requirements for health sciences programs. Students may submit SAT or ACT test scores for exemption from Texas Success Initiative (TSI). **Adult students:** SAT/ACT scores not required. Texas Success Initiative test may be required.

2015-2016 Annual costs. Tuition/fees: $2,550; $9,210 out-of-district; $11,340 out-of-state. Per-credit charge: $67 in-district; $289 out-of-district; $360 out-of-state. Books/supplies: $1,200. Personal expenses: $2,208. **Additional information:** In-district and Out-of-district students pay the same tuition, but there is an additional Out-of-district fee that is charged to Out-of-district students.

2014-2015 Financial aid. **Need-based:** 1,323 full-time freshmen applied for aid; 1,012 deemed to have need; 855 received aid. 52% of total undergraduate aid awarded as scholarships/grants, 48% as loans/jobs. Need-based aid available for part-time students. Work-study available nights, weekends and for part-time students.

Application procedures. **Admission:** No deadline. No application fee. Applications accepted at all times for any future semester enrollment. **Financial aid:** Priority date 4/1, closing date 6/1. FAFSA required. Applicants notified on a rolling basis starting 3/30; must reply within 2 week(s) of notification.

Academics. **Special study options:** Accelerated study, distance learning, dual enrollment of high school students, ESL, honors, independent study, internships, study abroad, teacher certification program, weekend college. License preparation in dental hygiene, nursing, occupational therapy, paramedic, physical therapy, radiology, real estate. **Credit/placement by examination:** AP, CLEP, IB, institutional tests. 30 credit hours maximum toward associate degree. **Support services:** GED preparation and test center, learning center, reduced course load, remedial instruction, study skills assistance, tutoring.

Majors. **Biology:** General. **Business:** General, accounting technology, administrative services, business admin, hospitality admin, international, marketing, real estate, tourism/travel. **Communications:** Journalism, radio/TV. **Communications technology:** Animation/special effects. **Computer sciences:** General, networking, programming. **Education:** Early childhood, health, middle, secondary. **Engineering:** General. **English:** Creative writing, rhetoric/composition, technical writing, writing. **Foreign languages:** Arabic, Chinese, French, German, Japanese, Latin, Russian, sign language interpretation, Spanish. **General:** Carpentry. **Health services:** Clinical lab technology, dental hygiene, EMT paramedic, health information technology, nursing (RN), occupational therapy assistant, pharmacy assistant, physical therapy assistant, predental, premedicine, prepharmacy, preveterinary, radiologic technology/medical imaging, recreational therapy, sonography, substance abuse counseling, surgical technology, veterinary technology/assistant. **History:** General. **Human services:** Social work. **Math:** General. **Parks/recreation:** Health/fitness. **Philosophy/religion:** Philosophy. **Physical sciences:** General, chemistry, geology, physics. **Protective services:** Corrections, fire safety technology, police science. **Psychology:** General. **Social sciences:** Anthropology, economics, geography, GIS/cartography, political science, sociology. **Visual/performing arts:** Art, commercial photography, commercial/advertising art, dance, dramatic, music, music management. **Work/family studies:** Child development.

Most popular majors. Business/marketing 15%, engineering/engineering technologies 7%, health sciences 22%, liberal arts 8%, security/protective services 6%, visual/performing arts 7%.

Technology on campus. 1,775 workstations in library, computer center. Commuter students can connect to campus network. Online course registration, online library, helpline, wireless network available.

Student life. **Freshman orientation:** Mandatory. Preregistration for classes offered. **Policies:** No alcohol, no drugs, no hazing. **Activities:** Jazz band, dance, drama, international student organizations, literary magazine, music ensembles, student government, student newspaper, Phi Theta Kappa, Center for Student Political Studies, Gay-Straight Alliance, Men of Power, Physical Therapist Assistant club, Social and Human Services, Women of Influence, Student Vocational Nursing Association, Society of Students for Deaf Inclusion.

Athletics. **Intramural:** Basketball, soccer, volleyball W.

Student services. Alcohol/substance abuse counseling, career counseling, services for economically disadvantaged, student employment services, financial aid counseling, minority student services, on-campus daycare, placement for graduates, veterans' counselor. **Physically disabled:** Services for visually, speech, hearing impaired. **Transfer:** Transfer center, transfer adviser, college fairs on campus for students transferring to 4-year colleges.

Contact. E-mail: admission@austincc.edu
Phone: (512) 223-7503 Fax: (512) 223-7125
Linda Kluck, Executive Director of Admissions and Records, Austin Community College, PO Box 15306, Austin, TX 78761-5306

Blinn College
Brenham, Texas
www.blinn.edu

CB code: 6043

- Public 2-year community college
- Commuter campus in large town

General. Founded in 1883. Regionally accredited. Campuses located at Brenham, Bryan, Sealy, and Schulenburg. **Enrollment:** 18,021 degree-seeking undergraduates; 1,755 non-degree-seeking students. **Degrees:** 1,426 associate awarded. **Location:** 79 miles from Houston, 90 miles from Austin. **Calendar:** Semester, extensive summer session. **Full-time faculty:** 398 total; 8% minority, 52% women. **Part-time faculty:** 250 total; 18% minority, 55% women. **Special facilities:** College-operated museum, state park, city-operated historical museums, observatory, ice cream factory, George Bush library, children's museum, natural science center, art museums.

Student profile. Among degree-seeking undergraduates, 8,378 enrolled as first-time, first-year students.

Part-time:	43%	Hispanic/Latino:	19%
Out-of-state:	1%	Multi-racial, non-Hispanic:	3%
Women:	50%	International:	1%
African American:	10%	25 or older:	14%
Asian American:	2%	Live on campus:	10%

Transfer out. **Colleges most students transferred to 2015:** Texas A&M-College Station, Sam Houston State University, Texas State University, University of Texas at Austin, University of Houston.

Basis for selection. Open admission, but selective for some programs. Special requirements for ADN Health Science programs and some technology-based programs. The TSIA (Texas Success Initiative Assessment) test is required for all per state law. **Home schooled:** Transcript of courses and grades required.

2015-2016 Annual costs. Tuition/fees: $2,820; $4,890 out-of-district; $7,380 out-of-state. Per-credit charge: $48 in-district; $117 out-of-district; $200 out-of-state. Room/board: $6,100. Books/supplies: $1,000. Personal expenses: $1,350.

Financial aid. **Need-based:** Need-based aid available for part-time students. Work-study available nights, weekends and for part-time students.

Application procedures. **Admission:** Closing date 8/20 (receipt date). No application fee. Application must be submitted online. Admission notification on a rolling basis. **Financial aid:** Priority date 6/1; no closing date. FAFSA, institutional form required. Applicants notified on a rolling basis starting 7/1.

Academics. All campuses offer academic support services. **Special study options:** Cross-registration, distance learning, dual enrollment of high school students, ESL, liberal arts/career combination, study abroad. License preparation in dental hygiene, nursing, paramedic, physical therapy, radiology, real estate. **Credit/placement by examination:** AP, CLEP, IB, institutional tests. 12 credit hours maximum toward associate degree. TSIA (Texas Success Initiative Assessment) test used for placement. Students submitting sufficient score on Exit Level TAKS, SAT, or ACT are exempt from TSIA. **Support services:** GED preparation and test center, learning center, pre-admission summer program, reduced course load, remedial instruction, study skills assistance, tutoring, writing center.

Majors. **Biology:** General. **Business:** Accounting, office/clerical, small business admin. **Computer sciences:** System admin. **Education:** Multi-level teacher. **English:** English lit, rhetoric/composition. **Foreign languages:** General, French, German, sign language interpretation, Spanish. **Health services:** Medical radiologic technology/radiation therapy, nursing (RN). **History:** General. **Liberal arts:** Arts/sciences. **Math:** General. **Parks/recreation:** Exercise sciences. **Philosophy/religion:** Philosophy. **Physical sciences:** Chemistry, physics. **Protective services:** Criminal justice, firefighting. **Psychology:** General. **Social sciences:** General. **Visual/performing arts:** Design, dramatic, music. **Work/family studies:** Child care management.

Most popular majors. Biological/life sciences 10%, business/marketing 20%, English 7%, health sciences 15%, liberal arts 7%, security/protective services 7%.

Technology on campus. 500 workstations in library, computer center. Dormitories wired for high-speed internet access and linked to campus network. Commuter students can connect to campus network. Online course registration, online library, helpline, wireless network available.

Student life. **Freshman orientation:** Available, $25 fee. Preregistration for classes offered. New Student Orientation is held at various times during summer, up to 3 guests are welcome (fee is $10.00 per guest). **Policies:** Student classroom attendance policy, full-time student status for residence halls. **Housing:** Coed dorms, single-sex dorms, special housing for disabled, apartments, wellness housing available. $125 nonrefundable deposit. **Activities:** Bands, campus ministries, choral groups, dance, drama, international student organizations, music ensembles, musical theater, student government, student newspaper, College Republicans, Young Democrats, Bahai Club, Baptist Student Ministries, Catholic Student Organization, Wesley Foundation, Blinn College Lion's Club, Ebony and Ivory, Hispanic Organization, Kappa Kappa Psi, Chi Alpha.

Athletics. NJCAA. **Intercollegiate:** Baseball M, basketball, cheerleading, football (tackle) M, softball W, volleyball W. **Intramural:** Basketball, softball, volleyball. **Team name:** Buccaneers.

Student services. Career counseling, financial aid counseling, personal counseling, veterans' counselor. **Physically disabled:** Services for visually, speech, hearing impaired. **Transfer:** Transfer adviser, college fairs on campus for students transferring to 4-year colleges.

Contact. E-mail: admissions@blinn.edu
Phone: (979) 830-4000 Fax: (979) 830-4110
Kristi Urban, Director Admissions & Records, Blinn College, 902 College Avenue, Brenham, TX 77833

Brazosport College
Lake Jackson, Texas
www.brazosport.edu
CB code: 6054

- Public 2-year community college
- Commuter campus in large town

General. Founded in 1948. Regionally accredited. **Enrollment:** 4,173 degree-seeking undergraduates. **Degrees:** 38 bachelor's, 416 associate awarded. **Location:** 50 miles from Houston. **Calendar:** Semester, extensive summer session. **Full-time faculty:** 87 total. **Part-time faculty:** 167 total. **Class size:** 53% < 20, 46% 20-39, less than 1% 40-49, less than 1% 50-99. **Special facilities:** Chemical unit operations laboratory, music performance hall, child care center, center for business and industry training.

Student profile. Among degree-seeking undergraduates, 60% enrolled in a transfer program, 40% enrolled in a vocational program, 597 enrolled as first-time, first-year students.

Part-time:	81%	Asian American:	1%
Out-of-state:	1%	Hispanic/Latino:	37%
Women:	49%	25 or older:	30%
African American:	8%		

Transfer out. Colleges most students transferred to 2015: University of Houston, Sam Houston State University, Texas A&M University, Stephen F. Austin State University, University of Texas.

Basis for selection. Open admission, but selective for some programs. Special requirements for nursing and applied technology programs. **Home schooled:** Transcript of courses and grades required.

2015-2016 Annual costs. Tuition/fees: $2,505; $3,525 out-of-district; $5,145 out-of-state. Per-credit charge: $62 in-district; $96 out-of-district; $150 out-of-state. Books/supplies: $1,500. Personal expenses: $2,864.

Financial aid. Need-based: Need-based aid available for part-time students. Work-study available nights, weekends and for part-time students. **Non-need-based:** Scholarships awarded for academics, art, job skills, leadership, music/drama, state residency.

Application procedures. Admission: Closing date 8/28 (receipt date). No application fee. Admission notification on a rolling basis. **Financial aid:** Priority date 7/1; no closing date. FAFSA, institutional form required. Applicants notified on a rolling basis starting 5/1.

Academics. Special study options: Cooperative education, distance learning, dual enrollment of high school students, ESL, honors, internships. Bachelor's degree programs available on campus. License preparation in nursing, paramedic. **Credit/placement by examination:** AP, CLEP, institutional tests. 24 credit hours maximum toward associate degree. Minimum of 6 semester credit hours must be earned in residence before credit posted on transcript. **Support services:** GED preparation and test center, learning center, remedial instruction, study skills assistance, tutoring.

Majors. Biology: General. **Business:** General, accounting, administrative services, business admin, finance, purchasing. **Communications:** Communications/speech/rhetoric. **Computer sciences:** General, programming. **Education:** General, elementary, health, secondary. **Engineering:** General. **English:** English lit, rhetoric/composition. **Foreign languages:** General. **General:** Electrician, pipefitting. **Health services:** Nursing (RN). **History:** General. **Human services:** General. **Liberal arts:** Arts/sciences, library assistant. **Math:** General. **Physical sciences:** General, chemistry, physics, planetary. **Protective services:** Police science. **Psychology:** General. **Social sciences:** Economics, political science, sociology. **Theology:** Theology. **Visual/performing arts:** Art, dramatic, music. **Work/family studies:** General, child care management.

Most popular majors. Business/marketing 6%, engineering/engineering technologies 13%, health sciences 7%, liberal arts 54%, science technologies 9%.

Technology on campus. 40 workstations in library, computer center. Online course registration, wireless network available.

Student life. Freshman orientation: Mandatory. Preregistration for classes offered. **Activities:** Bands, choral groups, drama, music ensembles, student government, student newspaper, Baptist student ministry, Phi Theta Kappa.

Athletics. Intramural: Archery, basketball, bowling, fencing, football (non-tackle), golf, soccer, softball, table tennis, tennis, volleyball.

Student services. Career counseling, student employment services, financial aid counseling, on-campus daycare, personal counseling, placement for graduates, veterans' counselor. **Physically disabled:** Services for visually impaired. **Transfer:** Transfer adviser, college fairs on campus for students transferring to 4-year colleges.

Contact. Phone: (979) 230-3216 Fax: (979) 230-3376
Priscilla Sanchez, Student Admissions and Registrar, Brazosport College, 500 College Drive, Lake Jackson, TX 77566

Brookhaven College
Farmers Branch, Texas
www.brookhavencollege.edu
CB code: 6070

- Public 2-year community college
- Commuter campus in large town

General. Founded in 1965. Regionally accredited. **Enrollment:** 10,160 degree-seeking undergraduates; 2,243 non-degree-seeking students. **Degrees:** 926 associate awarded. **Location:** 12 miles from downtown Dallas. **Calendar:** Semester, limited summer session. **Full-time faculty:** 133 total; 35% minority, 58% women. **Part-time faculty:** 449 total; 30% minority, 54% women. **Special facilities:** Jogging/exercise trail, fine arts facilities including gallery, performance hall, ceramics/kiln yard, Macintosh computer lab; athletic facilities include soccer, baseball, softball fields, tennis courts.

Student profile. Among degree-seeking undergraduates, 22% enrolled in a transfer program, 25% enrolled in a vocational program, 5% already have a bachelor's degree or higher, 1,294 enrolled as first-time, first-year students, 3,656 transferred in from other institutions.

Part-time:	81%	Women:	59%

Transfer out. Colleges most students transferred to 2015: Universtiy of Texas at Dallas, University of North Texas, University of Texas at Arlington, Texas A&M-Commerce.

Basis for selection. Open admission, but selective for some programs. Observes TASP guidelines. Admission to nursing program based on a point system consisting of three parts: HESI score, GPA of prerequisite courses, and completion of support courses. **Learning Disabled:** Accommodations can only be obtained by providing documentation to the Disability Services office.

2015-2016 Annual costs. Tuition/fees: $1,770; $3,330 out-of-district; $5,220 out-of-state. Per-credit charge: $59 in-district; $111 out-of-district; $200 out-of-state. Books/supplies: $2,000. Personal expenses: $1,170.

Financial aid. Need-based: Work-study available nights, weekends and for part-time students. **Non-need-based:** Scholarships awarded for academics, leadership, music/drama. **Additional information:** Some tuition waivers available based upon state residency and veteran status.

Application procedures. Admission: No deadline. No application fee. Admission notification on a rolling basis. **Financial aid:** Priority date 6/1; no closing date. FAFSA required. Applicants notified on a rolling basis.

Academics. Special study options: Cooperative education, distance learning, dual enrollment of high school students, ESL, honors, internships, study abroad, weekend college. License preparation in nursing, paramedic, radiology. **Credit/placement by examination:** AP, CLEP, IB, institutional tests. At least 25% of credit hours required for graduation must be taken by instruction and not by credit-by-exam. **Support services:** GED preparation, learning center, remedial instruction, study skills assistance, tutoring, writing center.

Majors. Business: General, accounting, business admin, e-commerce, executive assistant, marketing, office management. **Communications:** Communications/speech/rhetoric. **Computer sciences:** Information systems, programming. **Education:** Early childhood, multi-level teacher, secondary. **Health services:** EMT paramedic, nursing (RN), radiologic technology/medical imaging. **Liberal arts:** Arts/sciences, humanities. **Social sciences:** GIS/cartography. **Visual/performing arts:** Design, graphic design, music. **Work/family studies:** Child development.

Most popular majors. Health sciences 10%, liberal arts 30%, mathematics 45%.

Technology on campus. Commuter students can connect to campus network. Online library, helpline, wireless network available.

Student life. Freshman orientation: Mandatory. Preregistration for classes offered. **Activities:** Jazz band, campus ministries, choral groups, dance, drama, film society, international student organizations, music ensembles, Model UN, musical theater, student government, student newspaper, Phi Theta Kappa, SERVE, International Movement for Peace Among People.

Athletics. NJCAA. **Intercollegiate:** Baseball M, basketball M, soccer W, volleyball W. **Team name:** Bears.

Student services. Adult student services, career counseling, student employment services, health services, personal counseling, placement for graduates, veterans' counselor. **Physically disabled:** Services for visually, speech, hearing impaired. **Transfer:** College fairs on campus for students transferring to 4-year colleges.

Contact. E-mail: bhcAdmissions@dcccd.edu
Phone: (972) 860-4883 Fax: (972) 860-4886
Thoa Vo, Director of Admissions, Brookhaven College, 3939 Valley View Lane, Farmers Branch, TX 75244-4997

Cedar Valley College
Lancaster, Texas
www.cedarvalleycollege.edu   CB code: 6148

▶ Public 2-year community college
▶ Commuter campus in large town
▶ Interview required

General. Founded in 1974. Regionally accredited. One of seven colleges in the Dallas County Community College District (DCCCD). **Enrollment:** 4,954 degree-seeking undergraduates; 6,685 non-degree-seeking students. **Degrees:** 473 associate awarded. **Location:** 10 miles from Dallas. **Calendar:** Semester, limited summer session. **Full-time faculty:** 66 total. **Part-time faculty:** 183 total. **Special facilities:** Two LEEDS certified buildings that house the veterinary technology and industrial technology programs. **Partnerships:** Formal partnerships with IBM, Texas A&M University, University of North Texas.

Student profile. Among degree-seeking undergraduates, 864 transferred in from other institutions.

Transfer out. Colleges most students transferred to 2015: University of Texas at Arlington, Texas A&M at Commerce, University of North Texas, Stephen F. Austin State University, Texas State University.

Basis for selection. Open admission. Student must be a graduate of an accredited high school, or at least 18 years of age, or be admitted by individual approval. **Home schooled:** Interview required.

High school preparation. College-preparatory program required.

2015-2016 Annual costs. Tuition/fees: $1,770; $3,330 out-of-district; $5,220 out-of-state. Per-credit charge: $59 in-district; $111 out-of-district; $174 out-of-state. Books/supplies: $800. Personal expenses: $1,045.

2014-2015 Financial aid. Need-based: 399 full-time freshmen applied for aid; 273 deemed to have need; 273 received aid. Average scholarship/grant was $4,408. 72% of total undergraduate aid awarded as scholarships/grants, 28% as loans/jobs. Work-study available nights, weekends and for part-time students.

Application procedures. Admission: No deadline. No application fee. Application must be submitted on paper. Admission notification on a rolling basis. **Financial aid:** Priority date 5/1; no closing date. FAFSA required. Applicants notified on a rolling basis.

Academics. Special study options: Accelerated study, cooperative education, distance learning, dual enrollment of high school students, ESL, honors, liberal arts/career combination, student-designed major, study abroad, weekend college. License preparation in real estate. **Credit/placement by examination:** AP, CLEP, institutional tests. 45 credit hours maximum toward associate degree. **Support services:** GED preparation and test center, learning center, pre-admission summer program, reduced course load, remedial instruction, study skills assistance, tutoring, writing center.

Majors. Business: Accounting/business management, administrative services, business admin, management information systems, marketing, office management, office technology, real estate. **Communications technology:**

Recording arts. **Computer sciences:** Data processing, networking, programming. **General:** Building construction. **Health services:** Veterinary technology/assistant. **Protective services:** Law enforcement admin. **Visual/performing arts:** Design, music performance.

Technology on campus. 400 workstations in library, computer center, student center. Commuter students can connect to campus network. Online course registration, online library, helpline, repair service, wireless network available.

Student life. Freshman orientation: Mandatory. Preregistration for classes offered. One day program includes assessment testing. **Activities:** Bands, campus ministries, choral groups, drama, literary magazine, music ensembles, musical theater, student government, student newspaper, Sierra club, Christian student union, Latin American student organization, Phi Theta Kappa, student ambassadors, pre-professional club, art club, veterinary technology club, sustainability.

Athletics. NJCAA. **Intercollegiate:** Baseball M, basketball, soccer W, volleyball W. **Intramural:** Soccer W, volleyball W. **Team name:** Suns.

Student services. Adult student services, career counseling, services for economically disadvantaged, student employment services, financial aid counseling, health services, personal counseling, veterans' counselor. **Physically disabled:** Services for visually, speech, hearing impaired. **Transfer:** Pre-admission transcript evaluation for new students. College fairs on campus for students transferring to 4-year colleges.

Contact. E-mail: ljohnson@dcccd.edu
Phone: (972) 860-8201 Fax: (972) 860-8001
Lucia Johnson, Director of Admissions and Registrar, Cedar Valley College, 3030 North Dallas Avenue, Lancaster, TX 75134

Central Texas College
Killeen, Texas
www.ctcd.edu   CB code: 6130

▶ Public 2-year community college
▶ Commuter campus in small city

General. Founded in 1965. Regionally accredited. **Enrollment:** 11,442 degree-seeking undergraduates; 5,377 non-degree-seeking students. **Degrees:** 3,186 associate awarded. **ROTC:** Army. **Location:** 60 miles from Austin. **Calendar:** Semester, extensive summer session. **Special facilities:** Planetarium, space theater. **Partnerships:** Formal partnerships with Killeen and Copperas Cove ISDs (school to career facilitator program).

Student profile. Among degree-seeking undergraduates, 63% enrolled in a transfer program, 37% enrolled in a vocational program, 2,211 enrolled as first-time, first-year students.

Part-time:	80%	Hispanic/Latino:	21%
Women:	46%	Native American:	2%
African American:	30%	Native Hawaiian/Pacific islander:	2%
Asian American:	4%	Live on campus:	1%

Transfer out. Colleges most students transferred to 2015: University of Mary Hardin-Baylor, Texas A&M Central Texas, Texas State University, University of North Texas, Texas Tech University.

Basis for selection. Open admission, but selective for some programs. Special admission requirements for nursing, paramedic, emergency medical, medical laboratory, mental health services, and aviation science programs. Interview required for medical laboratory technician, nursing programs; audition recommended for music; portfolio recommended for art.

High school preparation. College-preparatory program recommended. 22 units recommended. Recommended units include English 4, mathematics 3, social studies 1.5, history 1, science 2 (laboratory 1), computer science 1, visual/performing arts 1 and academic electives 1. Economics .5, speech .5, electives 4.5, health .5, physical education 1.5.

2015-2016 Annual costs. Tuition/fees: $2,280; $2,940 out-of-district; $6,420 out-of-state. Per-credit charge: $76 in-district; $98 out-of-district; $214 out-of-state. Room/board: $4,800. Books/supplies: $1,500. Personal expenses: $500.

Financial aid. All financial aid based on need. Need-based aid available for part-time students. Work-study available nights, weekends and for part-time students.

Application procedures. Admission: No deadline. No application fee. Admission notification on a rolling basis. **Financial aid:** Closing date 6/1. FAFSA, institutional form required. Applicants notified on a rolling basis starting 3/1; must reply within 4 week(s) of notification.

Academics. Special study options: Accelerated study, cross-registration, distance learning, dual enrollment of high school students, ESL, independent study, internships, liberal arts/career combination, weekend college. License preparation in aviation, nursing, paramedic, real estate. **Credit/placement by examination:** AP, CLEP, IB, institutional tests. 45 credit hours maximum toward associate degree. **Support services:** GED preparation and test center, learning center, reduced course load, remedial instruction, study skills assistance, tutoring.

Majors. Biology: General. **Business:** Administrative services, business admin, hospitality admin, office management, real estate. **Communications:** Broadcast journalism, radio/TV. **Communications technology:** Graphic/printing. **Computer sciences:** General, information technology, networking, programming, security, system admin. **Conservation:** Environmental science. **Education:** General. **Engineering:** General. **Foreign languages:** General. **Health services:** Clinical lab assistant, clinical lab technology, nursing (RN), premedicine, substance abuse counseling. **Human services:** Social work. **Liberal arts:** Arts/sciences. **Math:** General. **Physical sciences:** Chemistry, geology, physics. **Protective services:** Corrections, homeland security, law enforcement admin, police science. **Social sciences:** General. **Visual/performing arts:** Art, music. **Work/family studies:** Child care management.

Technology on campus. 600 workstations in library, computer center. Dormitories linked to campus network. Online course registration, online library, wireless network available.

Student life. Freshman orientation: Available. Preregistration for classes offered. **Housing:** Coed dorms available. $100 nonrefundable deposit, deadline 8/1. **Activities:** Jazz band, choral groups, drama, international student organizations, radio station, student government, TV station.

Athletics. Intramural: Basketball, soccer, softball, volleyball.

Student services. Adult student services, alcohol/substance abuse counseling, career counseling, services for economically disadvantaged, student employment services, financial aid counseling, on-campus daycare, personal counseling, placement for graduates, veterans' counselor. **Physically disabled:** Services for visually, speech, hearing impaired. **Transfer:** Re-entry adviser, pre-admission transcript evaluation for new students. Transfer center, transfer adviser, college fairs on campus for students transferring to 4-year colleges.

Contact. E-mail: admissions@ctcd.edu
Phone: (254) 526-1696 Toll-free number: (800) 792-3348 ext. 1696
Fax: (254) 526-1481
Shannon Bralley, Director, Admissions and Recruitment, Central Texas College, Central Texas College, Killeen, TX 76540-1800

Application procedures. Admission: No deadline. No application fee. Admission notification on a rolling basis. **Financial aid:** Closing date 7/1. FAFSA required. Applicants notified on a rolling basis starting 8/15.

Academics. Special study options: Distance learning, dual enrollment of high school students. Bachelor's degree programs available on campus. License preparation in nursing, real estate. **Credit/placement by examination:** AP, CLEP, IB. 22 credit hours maximum toward associate degree. **Support services:** GED preparation and test center, remedial instruction, tutoring.

Majors. Biology: General, biotechnology. **Business:** General, accounting, accounting technology, administrative services. **Communications:** General, journalism. **Computer sciences:** General. **Education:** General, elementary, secondary. **Engineering:** Pre-engineering. **English:** English lit. **Health services:** Medical assistant, nursing (RN), predental, premedicine, prenursing, prepharmacy, preveterinary, respiratory therapy assistant. **Human services:** Social work. **Math:** General. **Parks/recreation:** Exercise sciences. **Physical sciences:** General, chemistry, physics. **Protective services:** Criminal justice. **Psychology:** General. **Visual/performing arts:** Art, dramatic, music, photography. **Work/family studies:** Child care service.

Most popular majors. Family/consumer sciences 8%, health sciences 9%, liberal arts 74%.

Technology on campus. Wireless network available.

Student life. Freshman orientation: Mandatory. Preregistration for classes offered. **Housing:** Single-sex dorms available. $100 nonrefundable deposit. **Activities:** Bands, choral groups, dance, drama, music ensembles, student government, student newspaper, Blue Jackets, Phi Theta Kappa, agriculture club, art club, photography club, auto tech club, psychology club, science club, creative writing club.

Athletics. NJCAA. **Intercollegiate:** Baseball M, basketball, cheerleading, football (tackle) M, rodeo, soccer, softball W, volleyball W. **Team name:** Wranglers.

Student services. Adult student services, career counseling, services for economically disadvantaged, financial aid counseling, personal counseling. **Transfer:** Pre-admission transcript evaluation for new students. Transfer adviser, college fairs on campus for students transferring to 4-year colleges.

Contact. E-mail: admissions@cisco.edu
Phone: (254) 442-5000 Fax: (254) 442-5000
Shirley Dove, Director of Admissions, Cisco College, 101 College Heights, Cisco, TX 76437

Cisco College
Cisco, Texas
www.cisco.edu CB code: 6096

- Public 2-year community college
- Commuter campus in small town

General. Founded in 1940. Regionally accredited. Cisco College operates from 2 campuses, one in Cisco and the other in Abilene. **Enrollment:** 3,480 degree-seeking undergraduates. **Degrees:** 312 associate awarded. **Location:** 100 miles from Fort Worth. **Calendar:** Semester, limited summer session. **Full-time faculty:** 85 total. **Part-time faculty:** 122 total. **Class size:** 59% < 20, 38% 20-39, 2% 40-49, 1% 50-99.

Student profile.

Out-of-state:	3%	Live on campus:	22%
25 or older:	30%		

Transfer out. Colleges most students transferred to 2015: Texas State University, Tarleton State University, University of Texas-Arlington, Angelo State University, Texas Tech University.

Basis for selection. Open admission.

2016-2017 Annual costs. Tuition/fees (projected): $2,790; $3,540 out-of-district; $4,620 out-of-state. Per-credit charge: $93 in-district; $118 out-of-district; $154 out-of-state. Room/board: $4,152. Books/supplies: $1,600. Personal expenses: $3,391.

2014-2015 Financial aid. Need-based: 59% of total undergraduate aid awarded as scholarships/grants, 41% as loans/jobs. Work-study available nights, weekends and for part-time students. **Non-need-based:** Scholarships awarded for athletics, music/drama. **Additional information:** Financial aid application deadline July 1 for Fall semester, November 1 for Spring semester.

Clarendon College
Clarendon, Texas
www.clarendoncollege.edu CB code: 6097

- Public 2-year community college
- Residential campus in rural community

General. Founded in 1898. Regionally accredited. **Enrollment:** 1,350 degree-seeking undergraduates. **Degrees:** 116 associate awarded. **Location:** 60 miles from Amarillo. **Calendar:** Semester, limited summer session. **Full-time faculty:** 40 total. **Part-time faculty:** 36 total. **Class size:** 73% < 20, 24% 20-39, 1% 40-49, 1% 50-99, less than 1% >100. **Partnerships:** Formal partnership with Tech Prep.

Student profile.

Out-of-state:	8%	Live on campus:	24%

Transfer out. Colleges most students transferred to 2015: West Texas A&M University, Texas Tech University, Texas A&M University, Tarleton State University, Midwestern State University.

Basis for selection. Open admission, but selective for some programs. Special requirements for certain technical programs. Interview before May 1 required for ranch and feedlot operations program. 3 personal references, interview required for vocational nursing program. **Home schooled:** Transcript of courses and grades required.

High school preparation. 24 units recommended. Recommended units include English 4, mathematics 4, social studies 2, history 2, science 4, foreign language 2, academic electives 3.5. 0.5 health, 0.5 economics, 1 computer, 0.5 speech recommended.

2015-2016 Annual costs. Tuition/fees: $3,030; $3,720 out-of-district; $4,650 out-of-state. Room/board: $4,176. Books/supplies: $1,000. Personal expenses: $3,894.

Financial aid. Need-based: Need-based aid available for part-time students. Work-study available nights, weekends and for part-time students. **Non-need-based:** Scholarships awarded for academics, art, athletics, leadership, music/drama, state residency.

Application procedures. Admission: Priority date 8/15; no deadline. No application fee. Application must be submitted online. Admission notification on a rolling basis. **Financial aid:** Priority date 8/1; no closing date. FAFSA, institutional form required. Applicants notified on a rolling basis starting 5/15; must reply by 8/15 or within 2 week(s) of notification.

Academics. Special study options: Cross-registration, distance learning, dual enrollment of high school students, ESL, internships, liberal arts/career combination, student-designed major. License preparation in nursing. **Credit/placement by examination:** AP, CLEP. 30 credit hours maximum toward associate degree. **Support services:** GED test center, learning center, remedial instruction, tutoring.

Majors. Biology: General. **Business:** General, accounting, finance, management science, marketing. **Communications:** Communications/speech/rhetoric. **Computer sciences:** General. **Conservation:** Environmental science. **Education:** General. **Engineering:** General. **English:** English lit, rhetoric/composition. **Foreign languages:** General. **Health services:** Nursing (RN). **History:** General. **Liberal arts:** Arts/sciences. **Math:** General. **Parks/recreation:** General, exercise sciences, health/fitness. **Physical sciences:** Chemistry, geology, physics. **Protective services:** Criminal justice. **Psychology:** General. **Social sciences:** Economics, political science, sociology. **Visual/performing arts:** Art, commercial/advertising art, dramatic, music.

Most popular majors. Agriculture 10%, health sciences 31%, liberal arts 40%, parks/recreation 7%.

Technology on campus. 221 workstations in library, computer center. Dormitories wired for high-speed internet access. Commuter students can connect to campus network. Online course registration, online library, wireless network available.

Student life. Freshman orientation: Mandatory. Preregistration for classes offered. Eight week course that meets two times a week during the 8 week session for the on-campus setting. Online option is available. This course is full semester in length. **Housing:** Guaranteed on-campus for freshmen. Coed dorms, single-sex dorms, special housing for disabled available. $150 partly refundable deposit. **Activities:** Jazz band, choral groups, drama, music ensembles, student government, multicultural club, student ambassadors, Block & Bridle, rodeo club.

Athletics. NJCAA. **Intercollegiate:** Baseball M, basketball, cheerleading, cross-country, rodeo, softball W, volleyball W. **Intramural:** Basketball, football (non-tackle), golf, rodeo, table tennis, volleyball. **Team name:** Bulldogs.

Student services. Career counseling, financial aid counseling. **Physically disabled:** Services for visually, speech, hearing impaired. **Transfer:** College fairs on campus for students transferring to 4-year colleges.

Contact. E-mail: admissions@clarendoncollege.edu
Phone: (806) 874-3571 Toll-free number: (800) 687-9737
Fax: (806) 874-5080
Martha Smith, Director of Admissions, Clarendon College, PO Box 968, Clarendon, TX 79226

Coastal Bend College
Beeville, Texas
www.coastalbend.edu   **CB code: 6055**

▶ Public 2-year community college
▶ Commuter campus in large town

General. Founded in 1965. Regionally accredited. In addition to main campus in Beeville, there are campuses in Alice, Kingsville, and Pleasanton. **Enrollment:** 2,382 degree-seeking undergraduates. **Degrees:** 311 associate awarded. **Location:** 60 miles from Corpus Christi, 90 miles from San Antonio. **Calendar:** Semester, limited summer session. **Full-time faculty:** 96 total. **Part-time faculty:** 123 total. **Partnerships:** Formal partnerships with national corporations to provide truck driver training, with local businesses to provide training for employees, and with high schools and tech prep programs.

Student profile.

Out-of-state:	1%	Live on campus:	5%
25 or older:	60%		

Transfer out. Colleges most students transferred to 2015: Texas A&M-Corpus Christi, Texas A&M-Kingsville, Southwest Texas State University, Texas A&M-College Station, University of Texas.

Basis for selection. Open admission, but selective for some programs. Texas requires that all students satisfy Texas THEA test requirements before being enrolled in college-level courses in public college or university. Scores not used in admission decisions. Special requirements for dental hygiene and vocational nursing programs. **Adult students:** SAT/ACT scores not required. **Home schooled:** Transcript of courses and grades required. Transcript must be notarized.

2015-2016 Annual costs. Tuition/fees: $2,646; $4,506 out-of-district; $4,956 out-of-state. Per-credit charge: $70 in-district; $132 out-of-district; $147 out-of-state. Room/board: $5,200. Books/supplies: $2,000. Personal expenses: $1,500.

Financial aid. Need-based: Need-based aid available for part-time students. Work-study available nights, weekends and for part-time students. **Non-need-based:** Scholarships awarded for academics, leadership.

Application procedures. Admission: No deadline. No application fee. Admission notification on a rolling basis. **Financial aid:** Priority date 4/1; no closing date. FAFSA, institutional form required. Applicants notified on a rolling basis starting 5/1; must reply within 2 week(s) of notification.

Academics. Special study options: Cooperative education, cross-registration, distance learning, dual enrollment of high school students, independent study, internships, liberal arts/career combination, weekend college. License preparation in dental hygiene, nursing, radiology. **Credit/placement by examination:** AP, CLEP, institutional tests. 30 credit hours maximum toward associate degree. ACCUPLACER, ASSET, COMPASS, MAPS tests may be used instead of THEA. **Support services:** GED preparation and test center, learning center, remedial instruction, study skills assistance, tutoring.

Majors. Biology: General. **Business:** General, accounting, administrative services, business admin, office technology, office/clerical. **Communications:** Communications/speech/rhetoric. **Computer sciences:** General, computer science, data processing, programming. **Conservation:** General. **Education:** General, elementary, secondary. **Engineering:** General. **English:** English lit, rhetoric/composition. **Foreign languages:** Spanish. **Health services:** Dental hygiene, health information technology, medical secretary, nursing (RN), predental, premedicine, prepharmacy, preveterinary. **History:** General. **Liberal arts:** Arts/sciences. **Math:** General. **Physical sciences:** Chemistry, geology, physics. **Protective services:** Corrections, criminal justice, police science. **Psychology:** General. **Social sciences:** Political science, sociology. **Visual/performing arts:** General, commercial/advertising art, music, studio arts. **Work/family studies:** General, child care management.

Technology on campus. 700 workstations in library, computer center. Dormitories wired for high-speed internet access and linked to campus network. Commuter students can connect to campus network. Online course registration, online library, helpline, wireless network available.

Student life. Freshman orientation: Mandatory. Preregistration for classes offered. Half-day program, parents welcome. **Housing:** Single-sex dorms, apartments available. $250 partly refundable deposit, deadline 8/15. **Activities:** Student government, Baptist student union, Newman Club.

Athletics. NJCAA. **Intercollegiate:** Basketball, volleyball W. **Intramural:** Archery, badminton, basketball, bowling, cross-country, golf, soccer, softball, swimming, table tennis, tennis, track and field, volleyball, weight lifting. **Team name:** Cougars.

Student services. Career counseling, services for economically disadvantaged, student employment services, financial aid counseling, on-campus daycare, personal counseling, placement for graduates, veterans' counselor. **Physically disabled:** Services for visually, speech, hearing impaired. **Transfer:** Pre-admission transcript evaluation for new students. Transfer adviser, college fairs on campus for students transferring to 4-year colleges.

Contact. E-mail: register@coastalbend.edu
Phone: (361) 354-2254 Toll-free number: (800) 722-2838 ext. 2254
Fax: (361) 354-2554
Alicia Ulloa, Registrar and Director Admissions, Coastal Bend College, 3800 Charco Road, Beeville, TX 78102

College of the Mainland
Texas City, Texas
www.com.edu   **CB code: 6133**

▶ Public 2-year community and technical college
▶ Commuter campus in large town

General. Founded in 1966. Regionally accredited. **Enrollment:** 4,013 degree-seeking undergraduates. **Degrees:** 357 associate awarded. **ROTC:** Air Force. **Location:** 25 miles from Houston. **Calendar:** Semester, extensive summer session. **Full-time faculty:** 104 total; 20% have terminal degrees,

25% minority, 50% women. **Part-time faculty:** 150 total; 3% have terminal degrees, 28% minority, 56% women.

Student profile. Among degree-seeking undergraduates, 420 enrolled as first-time, first-year students.

Part-time:	78%	Asian American:	3%
Women:	58%	Hispanic/Latino:	27%
African American:	17%	25 or older:	29%

Transfer out. Colleges most students transferred to 2015: University of Houston-Clear Lake.

Basis for selection. Open admission, but selective for some programs. Special requirements for nursing program.

2015-2016 Annual costs. Tuition/fees: $1,773; $2,973 out-of-district; $3,873 out-of-state. Books/supplies: $1,600. Personal expenses: $1,132.

Financial aid. All financial aid based on need. Need-based aid available for part-time students. Work-study available nights, weekends and for part-time students.

Application procedures. Admission: Closing date 8/13. No application fee. Admission notification on a rolling basis. **Financial aid:** Priority date 6/1; no closing date. FAFSA required. Applicants notified on a rolling basis starting 5/1; must reply within 4 week(s) of notification.

Academics. Special study options: Cooperative education, distance learning, dual enrollment of high school students, ESL, honors, internships, study abroad, teacher certification program, weekend college. License preparation in nursing, paramedic, real estate. **Credit/placement by examination:** AP, CLEP, institutional tests. 24 credit hours maximum toward associate degree. **Support services:** GED preparation and test center, learning center, remedial instruction, study skills assistance, tutoring, writing center.

Majors. Biology: General. **Business:** General, accounting, administrative services, banking/financial services, business admin, labor relations, marketing, office management, office technology, office/clerical, real estate. **Communications:** Journalism. **Computer sciences:** General, programming. **Education:** Elementary, secondary. **Engineering:** General. **Health services:** Licensed practical nurse. **History:** General. **Human services:** General, social work. **Liberal arts:** Arts/sciences. **Math:** General. **Physical sciences:** Chemistry, planetary. **Protective services:** Fire safety technology, police science. **Psychology:** General. **Social sciences:** General, economics, political science, sociology. **Visual/performing arts:** General, dramatic, music, studio arts. **Work/family studies:** Child care management.

Most popular majors. Health sciences 13%, liberal arts 42%, science technologies 22%.

Technology on campus. 100 workstations in library, computer center. Online course registration, online library, helpline, wireless network available.

Student life. Freshman orientation: Mandatory. Preregistration for classes offered. **Activities:** Concert band, campus ministries, choral groups, drama, international student organizations, music ensembles, student government, Phi Beta Kappa, Students for Christ, COM Amigos, Organization of African-American Culture, biology club.

Athletics. Intramural: Basketball, football (non-tackle) M, racquetball, soccer, softball, tennis, volleyball. **Team name:** Ducks.

Student services. Career counseling, student employment services, financial aid counseling, on-campus daycare, personal counseling, placement for graduates, veterans' counselor. **Physically disabled:** Services for visually, speech, hearing impaired. **Transfer:** Transfer adviser, college fairs on campus for students transferring to 4-year colleges.

Contact. E-mail: kmusik@com.edu
Phone: (409) 933-8264 Toll-free number: (888) 258-8859 ext. 8264
Fax: (409) 938-3126
Kelly Musick, Director of Admissions and Records, College of the Mainland, 1200 Amburn Road, Texas City, TX 77591

Collin County Community College District
McKinney, Texas
www.collin.edu   CB code: 1951

▶ Public 2-year community college
▶ Commuter campus in large city

General. Founded in 1985. Regionally accredited. **Enrollment:** 24,185 degree-seeking undergraduates; 4,002 non-degree-seeking students. **Degrees:** 2,342 associate awarded. **ROTC:** Air Force. **Location:** 25 miles from Dallas.

Calendar: Semester, extensive summer session. **Full-time faculty:** 420 total; 37% have terminal degrees, 19% minority, 59% women. **Part-time faculty:** 797 total; 16% have terminal degrees, 22% minority, 56% women. **Class size:** 29% < 20, 70% 20-39, less than 1% 40-49, less than 1% 50-99. **Special facilities:** Regional fire training facility. **Partnerships:** Formal partnership with Cisco to provide Certified Network Professional Certification.

Student profile. Among degree-seeking undergraduates, 5,278 enrolled as first-time, first-year students, 1,992 transferred in from other institutions.

Part-time:	61%	Native American:	1%
Women:	54%	International:	4%
African American:	12%	25 or older:	27%

Transfer out. Colleges most students transferred to 2015: University of Texas at Dallas, University of North Texas, Texas A&M University, University of Texas at Austin, Texas Woman's University.

Basis for selection. Open admission, but selective for some programs. Special requirements for specific programs: nursing, dental hygiene, emergency medical services, fire science, respiratory care, interpreter prep program, honors Institute, center for advanced study In mathematics and natural sciences. **Home schooled:** If under 18 years of age, must provide written parental/guardian permission.

High school preparation. 17 units recommended. Recommended units include English 4, mathematics 3, social studies 2, history 2, science 2 (laboratory 2) and foreign language 2.

2016-2017 Annual costs. Tuition/fees (projected): $1,434; $2,344 out-of-district; $4,144 out-of-state. Per-credit charge: $39 in-district; $78 out-of-district; $138 out-of-state. Books/supplies: $1,500. Personal expenses: $1,926.

2014-2015 Financial aid. Need-based: 68% of total undergraduate aid awarded as scholarships/grants, 32% as loans/jobs. Need-based aid available for part-time students. Work-study available nights, weekends and for part-time students. **Non-need-based:** Scholarships awarded for academics, art, athletics, job skills, leadership, minority status, music/drama, state residency.

Application procedures. Admission: No deadline. No application fee. Admission notification on a rolling basis. **Financial aid:** Priority date 6/1; no closing date. FAFSA, institutional form required. Applicants notified on a rolling basis starting 5/1; must reply within 2 week(s) of notification.

Academics. Special study options: Cooperative education, distance learning, dual enrollment of high school students, ESL, honors, internships, weekend college. Learning communities, service learning opportunities. License preparation in dental hygiene, nursing, paramedic. **Credit/placement by examination:** AP, CLEP, IB, institutional tests. 18 credit hours maximum toward associate degree. 6 hours traditional credit must be completed in residence before examination credit awarded. **Support services:** Learning center, remedial instruction, study skills assistance, tutoring, writing center.

Honors college/program. Students with GPA of 3.5 or over admitted.

Majors. Business: General, administrative services, business admin, hospitality admin, real estate, retail management. **Communications:** Communications/speech/rhetoric. **Computer sciences:** General, LAN/WAN management, security, system admin, web page design. **Education:** Early childhood, middle, secondary. **Engineering:** General. **Foreign languages:** Sign language interpretation. **Health services:** Dental hygiene, electroencephalograph technology, EMT paramedic, health information technology, insurance coding, nursing (RN), respiratory therapy technology, surgical technology. **Liberal arts:** Arts/sciences. **Protective services:** Fire safety technology. **Social sciences:** GIS/cartography. **Visual/performing arts:** Commercial/advertising art, game design, graphic design, illustration, interior design, music, music management. **Work/family studies:** Child care service.

Most popular majors. Business/marketing 6%, health sciences 8%, liberal arts 72%.

Technology on campus. 2,000 workstations in library, computer center. Online course registration, online library, helpline, wireless network available.

Student life. Freshman orientation: Available. Preregistration for classes offered. One-day program; online section available for distance learning students. **Activities:** Jazz band, campus ministries, choral groups, dance, drama, international student organizations, literary magazine, music ensembles, Model UN, musical theater, student government, Baptist Student Ministry, Middle Eastern Student Association, Muslim Student Association, Latter Day Saint Student Association, UNITEWOMEN.org, Society of Women Engineers, LULAC, Student Veterans of America,.

Athletics. NJCAA. **Intercollegiate:** Basketball, tennis. **Team name:** Cougars.

Student services. Adult student services, alcohol/substance abuse counseling, career counseling, student employment services, financial aid counseling, on-campus daycare, personal counseling, placement for graduates, veterans' counselor. **Physically disabled:** Services for visually, speech, hearing impaired. **Transfer:** Transfer adviser, college fairs on campus for students transferring to 4-year colleges.

Contact. E-mail: tfields@collin.edu
Phone: (972) 881-5710 Fax: (972) 881-5175
Todd Fields, Registrar/ Director of Admissions, Collin County Community College District, 2800 East Spring Creek Parkway, Plano, TX 75074

Commonwealth Institute of Funeral Service
Houston, Texas
www.commonwealthinst.org   CB code: 7031

- Private 2-year school of mortuary science
- Commuter campus in very large city

General. Founded in 1988. Accredited by American Board of Funeral Service Education, Inc. **Enrollment:** 226 degree-seeking undergraduates. **Degrees:** 74 associate awarded. **Location:** 15 miles from downtown. **Calendar:** Quarter. **Full-time faculty:** 2 total. **Part-time faculty:** 11 total. **Class size:** 50% < 20, 50% 50-99.

Student profile.

Out-of-state: 20% **25 or older:**   49%

Basis for selection. Class rank and standardized test scores most important. SAT or ACT recommended. TASP required.

2015-2016 Annual costs. Personal expenses: $1,102.

Financial aid. All financial aid based on need. Need-based aid available for part-time students. Work-study available nights, weekends and for part-time students.

Application procedures. Admission: No deadline. $50 fee. Admission notification on a rolling basis beginning on or about 8/28. Application deadline is within 72 hours of enrollment deadline. Student must be accepted into program 30 days before enrollment. **Financial aid:** Priority date 8/31; no closing date. FAFSA required. Applicants notified on a rolling basis starting 7/12.

Academics. Credit/placement by examination: AP, CLEP. **Support services:** Tutoring.

Technology on campus. 15 workstations in library, computer center.

Student life. Housing: Some local funeral homes provide student employees accommodations while attending college. **Activities:** Student government.

Student services. Career counseling, student employment services, financial aid counseling, personal counseling, placement for graduates, veterans' counselor. **Transfer:** Re-entry adviser, pre-admission transcript evaluation for new students. Transfer adviser for students transferring to 4-year colleges.

Contact. Phone: (281) 873-0262 Fax: (281) 873-5232
Patricia Moreno, Registrar, Commonwealth Institute of Funeral Service, 415 Barren Springs Drive, Houston, TX 77090-5913

Court Reporting Institute of Dallas
Dallas, Texas
www.crid.com   CB code: 3231

- For-profit 2-year technical and career college
- Very large city

General. Accredited by ACICS. **Enrollment:** 38 undergraduates. **Degrees:** 6 associate awarded. **Calendar:** Quarter. **Full-time faculty:** 9 total. **Part-time faculty:** 4 total.

Basis for selection. Open admission. **Adult students:** SAT/ACT scores not required.

2015-2016 Annual costs. Books/supplies: $700. **Additional information:** Court Reporting Day(full-time): $3,200. Court Reporting Night (part-time): $2,000. Court Reporting Online (full-time): $3,200. Court Reporting Online (part-time): $2,000. Technology fee per quarter: $200.

Financial aid. Need-based: Work-study available nights, weekends and for part-time students.

Application procedures. Admission: No deadline. $100 fee. **Financial aid:** No deadline.

Academics. Credit/placement by examination: AP, CLEP.

Student life. Activities: Student newspaper.

Contact. E-mail: dcortinas@crid.com
Phone: (214) 350-9722 Toll-free number: (866) 382-1284
Lucy Minda, Director, Court Reporting Institute of Dallas, 1341 West Mockingbird Lane, Suite 200E, Dallas, TX 75247

Culinary Institute LeNotre
Houston, Texas
www.culinaryinstitute.edu

- For-profit 2-year culinary school and technical college
- Commuter campus in very large city
- Application essay required

General. Regionally accredited; also accredited by ACCSC. Classic and innovative training from internationally experienced chef-instructors. **Enrollment:** 187 degree-seeking undergraduates; 49 non-degree-seeking students. **Degrees:** 85 associate awarded. **Calendar:** Differs by program, extensive summer session. **Full-time faculty:** 12 total; 17% women. **Part-time faculty:** 15 total; 33% minority, 73% women. **Special facilities:** College operated fine dining restaurant.

Student profile. Among degree-seeking undergraduates, 187 enrolled as first-time, first-year students.

Out-of-state: 10% **Women:**   55%

Basis for selection. Open admission. **Home schooled:** State high school equivalency certificate required.

2015-2016 Financial aid. Need-based: Work-study available nights, weekends and for part-time students.

Application procedures. Admission: No deadline. $50 fee. Application must be submitted on paper. Admission notification on a rolling basis. **Financial aid:** No deadline.

Academics. Special study options: Accelerated study, ESL, independent study, internships, study abroad. **Credit/placement by examination:** AP, CLEP. **Support services:** Learning center, reduced course load, remedial instruction, tutoring.

Majors. Business: Hospitality admin, restaurant/food services.

Technology on campus. 25 workstations in library, computer center. Online library, wireless network available.

Student life. Freshman orientation: Mandatory. Preregistration for classes offered.

Student services. Career counseling, student employment services, financial aid counseling, placement for graduates, veterans' counselor. **Transfer:** Re-entry adviser, pre-admission transcript evaluation for new students. Transfer adviser for students transferring to 4-year colleges.

Contact. E-mail: ehogaboom@ciaml.com
Phone: (713) 692-0077 Toll-free number: (888) 536-6873
Fax: (713) 692-7399
Ellen Hogaboom, Manager of Admissions, Culinary Institute LeNotre, 7070 Allensby Street, Houston, TX 77022

Dallas Institute of Funeral Service
Dallas, Texas
www.dallasinstitute.edu   CB code: 7032

- Private 2-year school of mortuary science
- Commuter campus in very large city

General. Regionally accredited. 15-month AAS in funeral service program and 6-month funeral director's program (Texas, Louisiana, and Missouri students only). **Enrollment:** 114 degree-seeking undergraduates. **Degrees:** 69 associate awarded. **Calendar:** Quarter, limited summer session. **Full-time**

faculty: 6 total. **Part-time faculty:** 3 total. **Special facilities:** On-campus embalming facilities.

Student profile. Among degree-seeking undergraduates, 25 enrolled as first-time, first-year students.

Basis for selection. Open admission. **Home schooled:** Transcript of courses and grades required. **Learning Disabled:** Student with learning disabilities must provide appropriate documentation.

2015-2016 Annual costs. Books/supplies: $2,000. Personal expenses: $1,190.

Financial aid. **Need-based:** Work-study available nights, weekends and for part-time students.

Application procedures. **Admission:** $50 fee. Admission notification on a rolling basis. Application deadline is 30 days prior to enrollment. **Financial aid:** No deadline. Applicants notified on a rolling basis.

Academics. **Special study options:** Distance learning. **Credit/placement by examination:** AP, CLEP. **Support services:** Study skills assistance, tutoring.

Technology on campus. 24 workstations in library, computer center. Wireless network available.

Student life. **Freshman orientation:** Mandatory. Preregistration for classes offered.

Student services. **Physically disabled:** Services for visually, hearing impaired.

Contact. Phone: (214) 388-5466 Toll-free number: (800) 235-5444
Fax: (214) 388-0316
Terry Parrish, Director of Admissions, Dallas Institute of Funeral Service, 3909 South Buckner Boulevard, Dallas, TX 75227-4314

Del Mar College
Corpus Christi, Texas
www.delmar.edu
CB code: 6160

▸ Public 2-year community college
▸ Commuter campus in large city

General. Founded in 1935. Regionally accredited. Courses taught at multiple off-campus sites in the Coastal Bend Region. Center for Early Learning provides day-care on campus. Collegiate High School operated on-campus in cooperation with Corpus Christi Independent School District. **Enrollment:** 10,159 degree-seeking undergraduates; 693 non-degree-seeking students. **Degrees:** 927 associate awarded. **ROTC:** Army. **Location:** 155 miles from San Antonio. **Calendar:** Semester, extensive summer session. **Full-time faculty:** 283 total. **Part-time faculty:** 540 total. **Partnerships:** Formal partnerships with Corpus Christi Army Depot, University of the Incarnate Word.

Student profile. Among degree-seeking undergraduates, 12% enrolled in a vocational program, 2% already have a bachelor's degree or higher, 1,142 enrolled as first-time, first-year students.

Part-time:	74%	Asian American:	2%
Out-of-state:	1%	Hispanic/Latino:	66%
Women:	57%	Multi-racial, non-Hispanic:	3%
African American:	3%	25 or older:	38%

Transfer out. **Colleges most students transferred to 2015:** Texas A&M University (College Station, Corpus Christi, Kingsville); University of Texas (Austin, San Antonio).

Basis for selection. Open admission, but selective for some programs. Admissions criteria for health science programs vary by program. Interview required for health science programs. **Home schooled:** Transcript of courses and grades required. Must provide notarized transcript with date of graduation.

High school preparation. 24 units recommended. Recommended units include English 4, mathematics 3, social studies 1, history 2, science 2, foreign language 2 and academic electives 10.

2015-2016 Annual costs. Tuition/fees: $2,914; $4,414 out-of-district; $5,524 out-of-state. Per-credit charge: $56 in-district; $106 out-of-district; $143 out-of-state. Books/supplies: $1,215. Personal expenses: $1,044.

Financial aid. **Need-based:** Need-based aid available for part-time students. Work-study available nights, weekends and for part-time students.

Application procedures. **Admission:** No deadline. No application fee. Admission notification on a rolling basis. **Financial aid:** Priority date 5/1; no closing date. FAFSA, institutional form required. Applicants notified on a rolling basis starting 7/1; must reply within 2 week(s) of notification.

Academics. Short semester courses, accelerated associate degree program. **Special study options:** Accelerated study, cooperative education, distance learning, double major, dual enrollment of high school students, ESL, honors, independent study, internships, teacher certification program, weekend college. License preparation in aviation, dental hygiene, nursing, occupational therapy, paramedic, physical therapy, radiology, real estate. **Credit/placement by examination:** AP, CLEP, IB, institutional tests. 30 credit hours maximum toward associate degree. Credit may not be earned by examination for most performance-oriented courses. **Support services:** GED preparation and test center, learning center, remedial instruction, study skills assistance, tutoring, writing center.

Majors. **Biology:** General. **Business:** General, accounting technology, administrative services, business admin, finance, hotel/motel admin, logistics, management information systems, marketing. **Communications:** Advertising, journalism, radio/TV. **Communications technology:** Desktop publishing, photo/film/video, recording arts. **Computer sciences:** Applications programming, security. **Education:** Art, bilingual, Deaf/hearing impaired, developmentally delayed, early childhood, early childhood special, elementary, English, foreign languages, health, history, mathematics, middle, music, secondary, social studies, special ed. **Engineering:** Electrical. **English:** English lit, rhetoric/composition. **Foreign languages:** General, sign language interpretation. **General:** Maintenance. **Health services:** Clinical lab technology, dental assistant, dental hygiene, EMT paramedic, health information technology, marriage/family therapy, medical secretary, mental health services, nuclear medical technology, nursing (RN), occupational therapy assistant, pharmacy assistant, physical therapy assistant, prenursing, prepharmacy, radiologic technology/medical imaging, respiratory therapy technology, sonography, substance abuse counseling, surgical technology. **History:** General. **Human services:** Social work. **Liberal arts:** Arts/sciences. **Math:** General. **Parks/recreation:** Health/fitness. **Physical sciences:** Chemistry, geology, physics. **Protective services:** Corrections, criminal justice, fire safety technology, firefighting, police science. **Psychology:** General. **Social sciences:** Political science, sociology. **Visual/performing arts:** Art, dramatic, music performance, music theory/composition. **Work/family studies:** Child care management, child development.

Most popular majors. Business/marketing 9%, education 16%, health sciences 19%, trade and industry 9%.

Technology on campus. 2,570 workstations in library, computer center, student center. Commuter students can connect to campus network. Online course registration, online library, helpline, wireless network available.

Student life. **Freshman orientation:** Available. Preregistration for classes offered. Held at a two hour session 6 weeks prior to scheduled registration. **Activities:** Bands, campus ministries, choral groups, dance, drama, international student organizations, literary magazine, music ensembles, opera, student government, student newspaper, Catholic Newman association, Latter-day Saints student association, Baptist student ministry, LULAC, student veteran's association, College Republicans, black student union.

Athletics. **Intramural:** Badminton, basketball, bowling, cross-country, football (non-tackle), golf, racquetball, swimming, table tennis, tennis, volleyball. **Team name:** Vikings.

Student services. Adult student services, career counseling, student employment services, financial aid counseling, on-campus daycare, personal counseling, placement for graduates, veterans' counselor. **Physically disabled:** Services for visually, speech, hearing impaired. **Transfer:** College fairs on campus for students transferring to 4-year colleges.

Contact. E-mail: reginfo@delmar.edu
Phone: (361) 698-1255 Toll-free number: (800) 652-3357
Fax: (361) 698-1595
Graciela Martinez, Director of Admissions, Del Mar College, 101 Baldwin Boulevard, Corpus Christi, TX 78404-3897

Eastfield College
Mesquite, Texas
www.efc.dcccd.edu
CB code: 6201

▸ Public 2-year community and liberal arts college
▸ Commuter campus in small city

General. Founded in 1970. Regionally accredited. **Enrollment:** 10,890 degree-seeking undergraduates; 3,356 non-degree-seeking students. **Degrees:** 1,086 associate awarded. **Location:** 1 mile from Dallas. **Calendar:** Semester, limited summer session. **Full-time faculty:** 123 total. **Part-time faculty:**

Two-Year Colleges

351 total. **Class size:** 79% < 20, 20% 20-39, less than 1% 40-49, less than 1% 50-99, less than 1% >100. **Special facilities:** Automotive diagnostics and restoration, Child Development Center.

Student profile. Among degree-seeking undergraduates, 18% enrolled in a vocational program, 1,601 enrolled as first-time, first-year students.

Part-time:	73%	Asian American:	4%
Out-of-state:	1%	Hispanic/Latino:	46%
Women:	61%	25 or older:	37%
African American:	23%		

Transfer out. Colleges most students transferred to 2015: University of Texas-Arlington, University of Texas-Dallas, University of North Texas, Texas A&M-Commerce, Southern Methodist University.

Basis for selection. Open admission. Interview recommended for international students.

High school preparation. 22 units recommended. Recommended units include English 4, mathematics 3, social studies 1, history 1, science 2, academic electives 5.5. 0.5 health education; 0.5 speech; 1 history, geography or science; 1 technical applications; 1 history or geography recommended.

2015-2016 Annual costs. Tuition/fees: $1,770; $3,330 out-of-district; $5,220 out-of-state. Per-credit charge: $59 in-district; $111 out-of-district; $174 out-of-state. Books/supplies: $400. Personal expenses: $935.

Financial aid. Need-based: Need-based aid available for part-time students. Work-study available nights, weekends and for part-time students.

Application procedures. Admission: No deadline. No application fee. Admission notification on a rolling basis. **Financial aid:** Priority date 5/1; no closing date. FAFSA, institutional form required. Applicants notified on a rolling basis starting 4/15.

Academics. Special study options: Cooperative education, distance learning, dual enrollment of high school students, ESL, honors, independent study, weekend college. **Credit/placement by examination:** AP, CLEP, IB, institutional tests. 15 credit hours maximum toward associate degree. **Support services:** GED preparation, learning center, pre-admission summer program, remedial instruction, study skills assistance, tutoring.

Majors. Business: Accounting, business admin, e-commerce, executive assistant, office management, office technology. **Communications technology:** Graphic/printing. **Computer sciences:** General, applications programming, computer science, data processing, networking, programming. **Health services:** Substance abuse counseling. **Human services:** Social work. **Liberal arts:** Arts/sciences. **Protective services:** Criminal justice. **Work/family studies:** Child development.

Most popular majors. Business/marketing 11%, liberal arts 68%, trade and industry 6%.

Technology on campus. 152 workstations in library, computer center. Online library available.

Student life. Freshman orientation: Available. Preregistration for classes offered. Online and on-campus orientations offered. **Policies:** Student code of conduct in effect. **Activities:** Bands, choral groups, dance, drama, literary magazine, music ensembles, student government, student newspaper, Fellowship of Christian Athletes, Latter-day Saint student association, multicultural club, Vital Signers, piano club, poetry club, automotive club, jazz dance club.

Athletics. NJCAA. **Intercollegiate:** Baseball M, basketball M, golf M, soccer W, volleyball W. **Intramural:** Basketball M, bowling, golf M, gymnastics, tennis, volleyball. **Team name:** Harvesters.

Student services. Career counseling, student employment services, health services, on-campus daycare, personal counseling, placement for graduates, veterans' counselor. **Physically disabled:** Services for visually, speech, hearing impaired. **Transfer:** College fairs on campus for students transferring to 4-year colleges.

Contact. E-mail: efc@dcccd.edu
Phone: (972) 860-7100 Fax: (972) 860-8306
Kimberly Lowry, Executive Dean, Student and Enrollment Services, Eastfield College, 3737 Motley Drive, Mesquite, TX 75150

El Centro College
Dallas, Texas   **CB member**
www.elcentrocollege.edu   **CB code:** 6199

- Public 2-year community college
- Commuter campus in very large city

General. Founded in 1966. Regionally accredited. Three campuses: El Centro downtown campus, Bill J. Priest campus and West Dallas Campus. **Enrollment:** 8,212 degree-seeking undergraduates; 2,216 non-degree-seeking students. **Degrees:** 967 associate awarded. **ROTC:** Army. **Calendar:** Semester, limited summer session. **Full-time faculty:** 83 total; 12% have terminal degrees, 47% minority, 31% women. **Part-time faculty:** 220 total; 12% have terminal degrees, 62% minority, 44% women. **Class size:** 62% < 20, 37% 20-39, less than 1% 40-49, less than 1% 50-99. **Special facilities:** Outdoor amphitheater, art gallery and studios, interior design and fashion design studios, allied health laboratories, culinary labs. **Partnerships:** Formal partnerships with regional CISCO training center, many local businesses, and area high schools.

Student profile. Among degree-seeking undergraduates, 822 enrolled as first-time, first-year students.

Part-time:	85%	Asian American:	5%
Out-of-state:	1%	Hispanic/Latino:	41%
Women:	69%	Multi-racial, non-Hispanic:	1%
African American:	28%	25 or older:	49%

Transfer out. Colleges most students transferred to 2015: University of Texas at Arlington, University of North Texas, University of Texas at Dallas, Southern Methodist University.

Basis for selection. Open admission, but selective for some programs. Specific application requirements for nursing, some allied health, and food and hospitality programs. Interview recommended for international students.

2015-2016 Annual costs. Tuition/fees: $1,770; $3,330 out-of-district; $5,220 out-of-state. Per-credit charge: $59 in-district; $111 out-of-district; $200 out-of-state. Books/supplies: $1,400. Personal expenses: $1,758.

Financial aid. Need-based: Need-based aid available for part-time students. Work-study available nights, weekends and for part-time students. **Additional information:** Interview required for financial aid applicants.

Application procedures. Admission: No deadline. No application fee. Admission notification on a rolling basis beginning on or about 6/1. **Financial aid:** Priority date 5/1; no closing date. FAFSA required. Applicants notified on a rolling basis; must reply within 2 week(s) of notification.

Academics. Special study options: Accelerated study, cooperative education, cross-registration, distance learning, double major, dual enrollment of high school students, ESL, external degree, honors, internships, liberal arts/career combination, teacher certification program. License preparation in nursing, paramedic, radiology. **Credit/placement by examination:** AP, CLEP, IB, institutional tests. 45 credit hours maximum toward associate degree. **Support services:** GED preparation, learning center, reduced course load, remedial instruction, study skills assistance, tutoring.

Majors. Business: Accounting, business admin, executive assistant, management information systems. **Computer sciences:** Data processing, information systems, programming. **Education:** Teacher assistance. **Health services:** Cardiovascular technology, clinical lab technology, health information management, health information technology, medical radiologic technology/radiation therapy, nursing (RN), respiratory therapy technology, sonography. **Liberal arts:** Arts/sciences. **Visual/performing arts:** Fashion design, interior design.

Most popular majors. Health sciences 55%, legal studies 8%, liberal arts 24%.

Technology on campus. 832 workstations in library, computer center, student center. Commuter students can connect to campus network. Online course registration, online library, helpline, wireless network available.

Student life. Freshman orientation: Mandatory. Preregistration for classes offered. **Activities:** Choral groups, drama, music ensembles, musical theater, student government, Phi Theta Kappa, organization of Latin American students, El Centro computer society, international college association, Disabled and Realizing Excellence, teacher education preparatory program, Circle-K, association of black college students.

Student services. Adult student services, career counseling, services for economically disadvantaged, student employment services, financial aid counseling, health services, minority student services, personal counseling, placement for graduates, veterans' counselor. **Physically disabled:** Services for visually, hearing impaired. **Transfer:** Transfer adviser, college fairs on campus for students transferring to 4-year colleges.

Contact. E-mail: rgarza@dcccd.edu
Phone: (214) 860-2311 Fax: (214) 860-2233
Rebecca Garza, Director of Admissions/Registrar, El Centro College, 801 Main Street, Dallas, TX 75202

El Paso Community College
El Paso, Texas
www.epcc.edu

CB member
CB code: 6203

- Public 2-year community college
- Commuter campus in very large city

General. Founded in 1969. Regionally accredited. Comprised of five campuses in greater El Paso. **Enrollment:** 27,488 degree-seeking undergraduates. **Degrees:** 3,214 associate awarded. **ROTC:** Army. **Location:** 240 miles from Albuquerque, New Mexico. **Calendar:** Semester, extensive summer session. **Full-time faculty:** 472 total. **Part-time faculty:** 921 total. **Special facilities:** Advanced technology center. **Partnerships:** Formal partnerships with local high schools for Tech Prep programs and with hospitals for health programs.

Transfer out. Colleges most students transferred to 2015: University of Texas at El Paso, New Mexico State University.

Basis for selection. Open admission, but selective for some programs. Observes TASP requirements. Nelson-Denny Reading Test, institutional math test and minimum GPA required for admission to health programs.

2015-2016 Annual costs. Tuition/fees: $2,970; $5,040 out-of-state. Per-credit charge: $84 in-state; $153 out-of-state. Books/supplies: $1,026. Personal expenses: $1,841. **Additional information:** Out of state student per credit hour rate is $200 for 1st credit hour, $306 for 2 credit hours, $459 for 3 credit hours. Each additional credit hour is $153.

Financial aid. Need-based: Work-study available nights, weekends and for part-time students. **Non-need-based:** Scholarships awarded for academics, athletics.

Application procedures. Admission: No deadline. No application fee. Admission notification on a rolling basis. **Financial aid:** Priority date 5/1; no closing date. FAFSA, institutional form required. Applicants notified on a rolling basis starting 7/1; must reply within 2 week(s) of notification.

Academics. Special study options: Cooperative education, cross-registration, distance learning, double major, dual enrollment of high school students, ESL, honors, independent study, internships, teacher certification program, weekend college. License preparation in dental hygiene, nursing, physical therapy, radiology. **Credit/placement by examination:** AP, CLEP, IB, institutional tests. 45 credit hours maximum toward associate degree. **Support services:** GED preparation and test center, learning center, remedial instruction, study skills assistance, tutoring, writing center.

Majors. Area/ethnic studies: Women's. **Biology:** General. **Business:** General, accounting, administrative services, business admin, fashion, finance, hospitality/recreation, international, management science, office/clerical, operations, real estate, tourism promotion, tourism/travel. **Communications:** Communications/speech/rhetoric, journalism. **Communications technology:** General. **Computer sciences:** General, computer science, information systems, programming, systems analysis. **Education:** Elementary, physical, secondary, special ed, technology/industrial arts. **Engineering:** General. **English:** English lit, rhetoric/composition. **Foreign languages:** General, sign language interpretation. **Health services:** Clinical lab technology, dental assistant, dental hygiene, dietetics, health information technology, medical assistant, medical radiologic technology/radiation therapy, mental health services, nursing (RN), optician, physical therapy assistant, predental, premedicine, prepharmacy, preveterinary, respiratory therapy technology, substance abuse counseling, surgical technology. **History:** General. **Liberal arts:** Arts/sciences. **Math:** General. **Parks/recreation:** Health/fitness. **Physical sciences:** Chemistry, geology, physics. **Protective services:** Corrections, criminal justice, fire safety technology. **Psychology:** General. **Social sciences:** General, political science, sociology. **Visual/performing arts:** Art, cinematography, commercial photography, commercial/advertising art, dramatic, fashion design, interior design, music, photography. **Work/family studies:** Child care management, family studies, institutional food production.

Technology on campus. 2,000 workstations in library, computer center. Wireless network available.

Student life. Freshman orientation: Mandatory. Preregistration for classes offered. **Activities:** Jazz band, choral groups, dance, drama, film society, literary magazine, music ensembles, radio station, student government, student newspaper, TV station, Phi Theta Kappa, African-American coalition, art student society, architecture club, social science club.

Athletics. NJCAA. **Intercollegiate:** Baseball M, softball W. **Intramural:** Basketball, bowling, cross-country, soccer, softball, table tennis, tennis, track and field, volleyball, weight lifting. **Team name:** Tejanos/Tejanas.

Student services. Career counseling, student employment services, health services, personal counseling, placement for graduates, veterans' counselor, women's services. **Physically disabled:** Services for visually, speech, hearing impaired. **Transfer:** Transfer adviser, college fairs on campus for students transferring to 4-year colleges.

Contact. Phone: (915) 831-2580 Fax: (915) 831-2161
Linda Gonzalez, VP of Student Services, El Paso Community College, Box 20500, El Paso, TX 79998

Frank Phillips College
Borger, Texas
www.fpctx.edu

CB code: 6222

- Public 2-year community and junior college
- Commuter campus in large town

General. Founded in 1948. Regionally accredited. Guaranteed transfer program. Contract training provided on site or at on-campus location for Occupational Safety and Health Administration mandated certification. **Enrollment:** 569 degree-seeking undergraduates. **Degrees:** 66 associate awarded. **Location:** 60 miles from Amarillo. **Calendar:** Semester, extensive summer session. **Full-time faculty:** 34 total. **Part-time faculty:** 36 total. **Class size:** 31% < 20, 68% 20-39, 1% 40-49.

Student profile.

Out-of-state:	5%	Live on campus:	20%
25 or older:	22%		

Transfer out. Colleges most students transferred to 2015: West Texas A&M University, Texas A&M University, Texas Tech University.

Basis for selection. Open admission. SAT/ACT. TSI test is used for placement. Veterans receive preferential admission. Texas Success Initiative guidelines followed. **Home schooled:** Transcript of courses and grades required.

2015-2016 Annual costs. Tuition/fees: $2,755; $3,445 out-of-district; $3,743 out-of-state. Room/board: $4,670. Books/supplies: $605. Personal expenses: $985.

Financial aid. Need-based: Need-based aid available for part-time students. Work-study available nights, weekends and for part-time students. **Non-need-based:** Scholarships awarded for academics, athletics, music/drama, state residency. **Additional information:** Some Texas fire department and police department personnel, active duty military personnel, children of military missing in action may qualify for reduced or waived tuition. Out-of-state tuition waived for students living in Oklahoma counties adjacent to Texas.

Application procedures. Admission: No deadline. No application fee. Admission notification on a rolling basis. **Financial aid:** Closing date 7/1. FAFSA, institutional form required. Applicants notified on a rolling basis; must reply within 2 week(s) of notification.

Academics. Special study options: Cooperative education, distance learning, dual enrollment of high school students, internships, liberal arts/career combination. License preparation in nursing. **Credit/placement by examination:** AP, CLEP, IB, institutional tests. 24 credit hours maximum toward associate degree. **Support services:** GED preparation and test center, learning center, pre-admission summer program, reduced course load, remedial instruction, study skills assistance, tutoring, writing center.

Majors. Biology: General. **Business:** General, accounting, administrative services, business admin. **Computer sciences:** General. **Education:** General, elementary, secondary. **English:** English lit. **General:** Pipefitting, power transmission. **Health services:** Medical secretary. **History:** General. **Liberal arts:** Arts/sciences. **Math:** General. **Philosophy/religion:** Philosophy. **Physical sciences:** Chemistry, physics. **Psychology:** General. **Social sciences:** General, political science, sociology. **Visual/performing arts:** Music.

Most popular majors. Engineering/engineering technologies 24%, liberal arts 57%.

Technology on campus. 59 workstations in dormitories, library, student center. Dormitories wired for high-speed internet access. Online course registration, wireless network available.

Student life. Freshman orientation: Mandatory. Preregistration for classes offered. Session available at start of and during semester. **Housing:** Single-sex dorms, apartments, wellness housing available. $150 fully refundable deposit, deadline 8/1. **Activities:** Choral groups, drama, music ensembles, student government, rodeo club, agriculture club, Phi Theta Kappa, cosmetology club, licensed vocational nursing club, Circle K, business club, art club, computer club, Future Educators Association.

Athletics. NJCAA. **Intercollegiate:** Baseball M, basketball, softball W, volleyball W. **Intramural:** Basketball, bowling, cheerleading, racquetball, softball, table tennis, tennis, volleyball. **Team name:** Plainsmen.

Student services. Adult student services, alcohol/substance abuse counseling, career counseling, services for economically disadvantaged, student employment services, financial aid counseling, personal counseling, placement for graduates, veterans' counselor. **Transfer:** Re-entry adviser, pre-admission transcript evaluation for new students. Transfer adviser, college fairs on campus for students transferring to 4-year colleges.

Contact. E-mail: admissions@fpctx.edu
Phone: (806) 457-4200 ext. 707 Fax: (806) 457-4225
Michele Stevens, Director of Enrollment Management, Frank Phillips College, Box 5118, Borger, TX 79008-5118

Galveston College
Galveston, Texas
www.gc.edu   CB code: 6255

▶ Public 2-year community college
▶ Commuter campus in small city

General. Founded in 1967. Regionally accredited. **Enrollment:** 1,751 degree-seeking undergraduates; 320 non-degree-seeking students. **Degrees:** 228 associate awarded. **Location:** 50 miles from Houston. **Calendar:** Semester, limited summer session. **Full-time faculty:** 56 total. **Part-time faculty:** 41 total. **Class size:** 56% < 20, 42% 20-39, 2% 40-49. **Special facilities:** Center for health related technology. **Partnerships:** Formal partnership with UTMB in health career profession.

Student profile. Among degree-seeking undergraduates, 238 enrolled as first-time, first-year students.

Part-time:	72%	Women:	61%
Out-of-state:	5%	25 or older:	38%

Transfer out. Colleges most students transferred to 2015: University of Houston at Clear Lake, University of Texas Medical Branch at Galveston, Texas A&M University at Galveston.

Basis for selection. Open admission, but selective for some programs. Health occupations majors have special admission requirements.

2015-2016 Annual costs. Tuition/fees: $1,900; $2,260 out-of-district; $4,150 out-of-state. Per-credit charge: $37 in-district; $49 out-of-district; $112 out-of-state. Books/supplies: $878. Personal expenses: $1,560.

Financial aid. All financial aid based on need. Need-based aid available for part-time students. Work-study available nights, weekends and for part-time students.

Application procedures. Admission: No deadline. $30 fee. Application must be submitted on paper. Admission notification on a rolling basis. **Financial aid:** Priority date 6/7; no closing date. FAFSA required. Applicants notified on a rolling basis starting 6/1.

Academics. Special study options: Cooperative education, distance learning, dual enrollment of high school students, independent study, internships. License preparation in dental hygiene, nursing, paramedic, radiology, real estate. **Credit/placement by examination:** AP, CLEP. 24 credit hours maximum toward associate degree. **Support services:** GED test center, learning center, remedial instruction, tutoring.

Majors. Biology: General, marine. **Business:** Accounting, administrative services, business admin. **Computer sciences:** General, computer science, information systems, programming. **Education:** Elementary, physical. **Engineering:** General. **English:** English lit, rhetoric/composition. **Foreign languages:** Spanish. **General:** Power transmission. **Health services:** EMT paramedic, health care admin, health information technology, medical radiologic technology/radiation therapy, medical secretary, nuclear medical technology, nursing (RN). **History:** General. **Human services:** Social work. **Liberal arts:** Arts/sciences. **Math:** General. **Physical sciences:** Chemistry, geology, physics. **Protective services:** Criminal justice. **Psychology:** General. **Social sciences:** Anthropology, economics, geography, political science, sociology. **Visual/performing arts:** Art, ceramics, dramatic, music. **Work/family studies:** Family studies.

Most popular majors. Health sciences 36%, liberal arts 49%.

Technology on campus. 170 workstations in library, computer center, student center. Commuter students can connect to campus network. Online library, helpline, wireless network available.

Student life. Freshman orientation: Mandatory. Preregistration for classes offered. **Housing:** Special housing for scholarship athletes available. **Activities:** Choral groups, drama, music ensembles, student government, student newspaper, Student Government Association, African American club, criminal justice club, film club, Hispanic Student Organization, HVAC-R club, international culture club, nuclear medicine club, welding club, Island Potters guild, Phi Theta Kappa Honors Society, radiography club, sports activity club, STEM Club, Student Nurses Association, veterans club.

Athletics. NJCAA. **Intercollegiate:** Baseball M, softball W, volleyball W. **Intramural:** Basketball, bowling, golf, soccer, volleyball. **Team name:** Whitecaps.

Student services. Career counseling, student employment services, financial aid counseling, personal counseling, placement for graduates, veterans' counselor. **Physically disabled:** Services for visually, speech, hearing impaired. **Transfer:** Transfer adviser, college fairs on campus for students transferring to 4-year colleges.

Contact. E-mail: adm@gc.edu
Phone: (409) 944-1230 Fax: (409) 944-1501
Scott Branum, Director of Admissions/Registrar, Galveston College, 4015 Avenue Q, Galveston, TX 77550-7447

Golf Academy of America: Dallas
Farmers Branch, Texas
www.golfacademy.edu/dallas

▶ For-profit 2-year golf academy
▶ Large town

General. Regionally accredited; also accredited by ACICS. **Enrollment:** 80 undergraduates. **Degrees:** 97 associate awarded. **Calendar:** Differs by program. **Full-time faculty:** 3 total. **Part-time faculty:** 8 total.

Basis for selection. Open admission.

2015-2016 Annual costs. Tuition and fees for associate degree program in Golf Complex Operations and Management for North American Residents, $34,350; International Students $35,780. May vary by campus.

Financial aid. Need-based: Work-study available nights, weekends and for part-time students.

Application procedures. Financial aid: No deadline.

Academics. Credit/placement by examination: AP.

Majors. Parks/recreation: Facilities management.

Contact. E-mail: dallas.info@golfacademy.edu
Toll-free number: (800) 342-7342
John Keriazakos, Director of Admissions, Golf Academy of America: Dallas, 1861 Valley View Lane, Suite 100, Farmers Branch, TX 75234

Grayson College
Denison, Texas   CB member
www.grayson.edu   CB code: 6254

▶ Public 2-year community and technical college
▶ Commuter campus in large town

General. Founded in 1963. Regionally accredited. **Enrollment:** 4,500 undergraduates. **Degrees:** 554 associate awarded. **Location:** 7 miles from Sherman, 75 miles from Dallas. **Calendar:** Semester, limited summer session. **Full-time faculty:** 102 total. **Part-time faculty:** 139 total. **Special facilities:** Vineyard.

Student profile.

Out-of-state:	2%	Live on campus:	6%

Basis for selection. Open admission, but selective for some programs. Special requirements for nursing, radiology, medical lab tech, vocational nursing certificate, EMT/paramedic programs. Observes TASP requirements. **Home schooled:** Transcript of courses and grades required.

2015-2016 Annual costs. Tuition/fees: $2,310; $3,450 out-of-district; $4,830 out-of-state. Per-credit charge: $49 in-district; $87 out-of-district; $133 out-of-state. Room/board: $5,340. Books/supplies: $1,400. Personal expenses: $2,295.

Financial aid. Need-based: Need-based aid available for part-time students. Work-study available nights, weekends and for part-time students. **Additional information:** Short term loans available.

Application procedures. Admission: No deadline. No application fee. Application must be submitted online. Admission notification on a rolling basis. Priority date for receipt of applications vary. Dates are published in the schedule of classes. **Financial aid:** Priority date 6/1; no closing date. FAFSA required. Applicants notified on a rolling basis; must reply within 5 week(s) of notification.

Academics. Special study options: Distance learning, dual enrollment of high school students, ESL, honors. License preparation in nursing, paramedic, radiology. **Credit/placement by examination:** AP, CLEP, institutional tests. 24 credit hours maximum toward associate degree. **Support services:** GED preparation and test center, learning center, reduced course load, remedial instruction, study skills assistance, tutoring.

Majors. Biology: General. **Business:** General, accounting, administrative services, office management, office technology, office/clerical. **Computer sciences:** General, programming. **Education:** General, elementary, secondary. **Engineering:** General. **English:** Rhetoric/composition. **Health services:** Clinical lab science, EMT paramedic, nursing (RN), substance abuse counseling. **Liberal arts:** Arts/sciences. **Math:** General. **Physical sciences:** Chemistry, geology, physics. **Protective services:** Law enforcement admin, police science. **Psychology:** General. **Social sciences:** Sociology. **Visual/performing arts:** Art, commercial/advertising art, dramatic, music.

Technology on campus. 150 workstations in library, computer center. Dormitories wired for high-speed internet access and linked to campus network. Online course registration, online library, helpline, wireless network available.

Student life. Freshman orientation: Mandatory. Preregistration for classes offered. Web-based program. Dates vary. **Housing:** Coed dorms, special housing for disabled, wellness housing available. $175 fully refundable deposit. **Activities:** Bands, campus ministries, choral groups, drama, international student organizations, music ensembles, Model UN, student government.

Athletics. NJCAA. **Intercollegiate:** Baseball M, softball W. **Intramural:** Baseball M, softball W. **Team name:** Vikings.

Student services. Adult student services, career counseling, services for economically disadvantaged, financial aid counseling, personal counseling, veterans' counselor. **Physically disabled:** Services for visually, speech, hearing impaired. **Transfer:** College fairs on campus for students transferring to 4-year colleges.

Contact. E-mail: admissions@grayson.edu
Phone: (903) 465-8604 Fax: (903) 463-8758
Christy KIemiuk, Director of Admissions and Records, Grayson College, 6101 Grayson Drive, Denison, TX 75020

Hallmark University
San Antonio, Texas
http://hallmarkuniversity.edu/ CB code: 2307

▶ Private 2-year business and health science college
▶ Commuter campus in very large city
▶ Interview required

General. Founded in 1969. Accredited by ACCSC. Additional satellite campus focusing on aeronautics (Hallmark University, College of Aeronautics) located on the property of San Antonio International Airport. Offers day/evening certificate/degree programs in aviation maintenance: airframe and powerplant technology. **Enrollment:** 582 degree-seeking undergraduates. **Degrees:** 44 bachelor's, 249 associate awarded; master's offered. **Location:** We are located in the city of San Antonio and about 80 miles from Austin, Texas. **Calendar:** Differs by program, extensive summer session. **Full-time faculty:** 31 total; 16% have terminal degrees, 19% minority, 36% women. **Part-time faculty:** 29 total; 14% have terminal degrees, 55% minority, 31% women. **Class size:** 95% < 20, 5% 20-39. **Special facilities:** Mega-computer laboratory, virtual library.

Student profile. Among degree-seeking undergraduates, 124 enrolled as first-time, first-year students, 15 transferred in from other institutions.

Transfer out. Colleges most students transferred to 2015: University of Phoenix, UTSA, Alamo Community College District, DeVry University.

Basis for selection. Main Campus: High school diploma or GED required. Hybrid Readiness Assessment, interview, tour, pass entrance test for certificate, diploma, associate applied science degree programs only. Special admission requirements for B.S. degree, the A.A.S. in Nursing and the MBA program. Satellite Campus: High school diploma or GED required, interview, tour, and pass Entrance Assessment. Applicant must be able to clear the FAA requirement within thirty days of his/her enrollment date. ACT/SAT used only for admission to bachelor's and master's program. Test scores must be within 12 years of the time of application. Student exempt from the ACT/SAT requirement if one of following requirements is met: student holds associate degree from accredited college/university; student has completed minimum of 30 college credits earning cumulative GPA of 2.5 on 4.0 scale and is determined to be college ready; student has passed the ACCUPLACER. Essay/personal statement required for bachelor's degree program and AS in Business Administration, MBA interview and essay required. **Home schooled:** Transcript of courses and grades, interview required. Student must be approved by the Acceptance Committee for admissions after meeting all entrance requirements including Hybrid Readiness Assessment, tour, interview, meeting entrance requirements for each diploma, certificate, associates, bachelors, or MBA program. Special requirements for admission into some programs. **Learning Disabled:** Request for accommodations evaluated on a case-by-case basis by the Director of Student Affairs, Dean of Academics or the Senior Vice President of Operations. Committed to providing reasonable accommodations and individual attention to qualified disabled students.

2016-2017 Annual costs. Tuition and fees vary by program.

2015-2016 Financial aid. Need-based: 25% of total undergraduate aid awarded as scholarships/grants, 75% as loans/jobs. Work-study available nights, weekends and for part-time students.

Application procedures. Admission: No deadline. $110 fee. Application must be submitted on paper. Admission notification on a rolling basis. Registration Fee for all programs at the Main Campus is $60 except for the School of Nursing, it is $25. Registration Fee for all applicants at the Satellite Campus is $110. Registration fee for the Main Campus is $60 except for the nursing program and the fee is $25. The Registration fee for the Satellite Campus is $110. A Security Fee is also required in the amount of $150. Application process/documentation must be received by the University prior to enrollment and final acceptance of the applicant. **Financial aid:** No deadline. FAFSA, institutional form required. Applicants notified on a rolling basis.

Academics. Special study options: Accelerated study, distance learning. Bachelor's degree programs available on campus. License preparation in aviation, nursing. **Credit/placement by examination:** AP, CLEP, SAT, ACT, institutional tests. Varies by program/campus. **Support services:** Remedial instruction, study skills assistance, tutoring. Student Affairs Office may refer students to outside sources for assistance and/or assistance may be available on campus, but must be requested by the student.

Majors. Business: Office technology. **Computer sciences:** Information technology, networking. **Health services:** Medical assistant, nursing (RN).

Most popular majors. Computer/information sciences 16%, health sciences 18%.

Technology on campus. 200 workstations in computer center. Commuter students can connect to campus network. Online library, helpline, wireless network available.

Student life. Freshman orientation: Mandatory. Preregistration for classes offered. Held for incoming students for our day and evening programs, generally held the first day of the term for approximately six hours. Student schedules are set by program.

Athletics. Team name: Eagles.

Student services. Alcohol/substance abuse counseling, career counseling, student employment services, financial aid counseling, health services, legal services, minority student services, placement for graduates. **Transfer:** Preadmission transcript evaluation for new students.

Contact. E-mail: slross@hallmarkuniversity.edu
Phone: (210) 690-9000 ext. 214 Toll-free number: (800) 880-6600
Fax: (210) 697-8225
Slava Ross, Vice President of Admissions, Hallmark University, Hallmark University, San Antonio, TX 78230-1736

Hill College
Hillsboro, Texas
www.hillcollege.edu CB code: 6285

▶ Public 2-year community college
▶ Commuter campus in small town

General. Founded in 1923. Regionally accredited. **Enrollment:** 4,098 undergraduates. **Degrees:** 310 associate awarded. **Location:** 32 miles from Waco, 64 miles from Dallas. **Calendar:** Semester, limited summer session. **Full-time faculty:** 87 total. **Part-time faculty:** 138 total. **Special facilities:** Texas Heritage Museum.

Transfer out. Colleges most students transferred to 2015: Tarleton State University, University of Texas at Arlington, University of North Texas.

Basis for selection. Open admission, but selective for some programs. Observes TSI guidelines. State test required for academic students unless exempted by state. Special requirements for nursing program. **Home schooled:** Transcript of courses and grades required.

2015-2016 Annual costs. Tuition/fees: $2,370; $3,120 out-of-district; $3,520 out-of-state. Room/board: $3,650. Books/supplies: $2,443. Personal expenses: $1,763. **Additional information:** Cost 1516: t&f confirmed via website - http://www.hillcollege.edu/Admissions_and_Aid/FinAid/fees.html. et 9/9.

Financial aid. Need-based: Need-based aid available for part-time students. Work-study available nights, weekends and for part-time students. **Non-need-based:** Scholarships awarded for academics, athletics, music/drama.

Application procedures. Admission: No deadline. No application fee. Application must be submitted online. Admission notification on a rolling basis. **Financial aid:** Closing date 7/31. FAFSA, institutional form required. Applicants notified on a rolling basis.

Academics. Special study options: Cooperative education, distance learning, dual enrollment of high school students, honors, independent study, internships, liberal arts/career combination. **Credit/placement by examination:** AP, CLEP. 24 credit hours maximum toward associate degree. **Support services:** GED test center, learning center, reduced course load, remedial instruction, study skills assistance, tutoring.

Majors. Biology: General. **Business:** Business admin. **Computer sciences:** General, applications programming, computer science, data processing, programming. **Education:** General. **Engineering:** General. **English:** English lit, rhetoric/composition. **Foreign languages:** General. **Health services:** EMT paramedic, nursing (RN), premedicine, sonography. **History:** General. **Liberal arts:** Arts/sciences. **Math:** General. **Parks/recreation:** Health/fitness. **Physical sciences:** Chemistry. **Protective services:** Corrections, law enforcement admin. **Social sciences:** Sociology. **Visual/performing arts:** Dramatic, music, studio arts.

Technology on campus. Dormitories wired for high-speed internet access. Commuter students can connect to campus network. Online course registration, online library, helpline, wireless network available.

Student life. Freshman orientation: Mandatory. Preregistration for classes offered. **Housing:** Single-sex dorms, wellness housing available. $300 partly refundable deposit. **Activities:** Bands, choral groups, drama, music ensembles, student government, Young Democrats, Young Republicans, Baptist student union, student government association, Rebels with a Cause.

Athletics. NJCAA. **Intercollegiate:** Baseball M, basketball, rodeo, soccer, softball W, volleyball W. **Intramural:** Volleyball. **Team name:** Rebels.

Student services. Adult student services, chaplain/spiritual director, career counseling, services for economically disadvantaged, student employment services, financial aid counseling, personal counseling, placement for graduates, veterans' counselor. **Physically disabled:** Services for visually, speech, hearing impaired. **Transfer:** Transfer adviser, college fairs on campus for students transferring to 4-year colleges.

Contact. E-mail: enrollmentinfo@hillcollege.edu
Phone: (254) 659-7600 Fax: (254) 582-7591
Sherry Davis, Director of Student Records and Registration, Hill College, 112 Lamar Drive, Hillsboro, TX 76645

Houston Community College System

Houston, Texas   **CB member**
www.hccs.edu   **CB code: 0929**

▶ Public 2-year community college
▶ Commuter campus in very large city

General. Founded in 1971. Regionally accredited. HCC is a multi-campus college enrolling a large number of international students. Students may attend the campus of their choice. The college has partnerships to facilitate earning engineering degrees at the University of Texas and Texas A&M

Universities. **Enrollment:** 56,359 degree-seeking undergraduates; 163 non-degree-seeking students. **Degrees:** 5,953 associate awarded. **ROTC:** Army, Air Force. **Location:** 50 miles from Galveston, 86 miles from Beaumont, 243 miles from Dallas, 206 miles from San Antonio. **Calendar:** Semester, extensive summer session. **Full-time faculty:** 759 total; 42% minority, 51% women. **Part-time faculty:** 1,742 total; 53% minority, 54% women. **Special facilities:** Public Safety Institute, West Houston Center For Science and Engineering. **Partnerships:** Formal partnerships with local high schools for tech-prep and school-to-work programs; contract training agreements with industry.

Student profile. Among degree-seeking undergraduates, 74% enrolled in a transfer program, 26% enrolled in a vocational program, 6% already have a bachelor's degree or higher, 7,967 enrolled as first-time, first-year students, 4,369 transferred in from other institutions.

Part-time:	70%	Hispanic/Latino:	33%
Out-of-state:	7%	Multi-racial, non-Hispanic:	2%
Women:	58%	International:	10%
African American:	30%	25 or older:	44%
Asian American:	9%		

Transfer out. Colleges most students transferred to 2015: University of Houston (Central, Downtown), University of Texas Austin, Texas A&M University, Texas Southern University, Prairie View A&M University.

Basis for selection. Open admission, but selective for some programs. The health science programs admit applicants through a competitive and selective process. The number of students admitted into each program is limited. **Adult students:** Unless exempted, must take the Texas Success Initiative (TSI) Assessment Test. A pre-assessment activity must be completed before taking the test. Performance on the test will determine college-readiness status and possible referral to developmental course work.

2016-2017 Annual costs. Tuition/fees (projected): $2,031; $4,191 out-of-district; $4,686 out-of-state. Books/supplies: $3,000. Personal expenses: $4,000. **Additional information:** All required fees are included in the tuition figures.

2015-2016 Financial aid. Need-based: 2,361 full-time freshmen applied for aid; 2,046 deemed to have need; 2,046 received aid. Average need met was 78%. Average loan was $2,600. 64% of total undergraduate aid awarded as scholarships/grants, 36% as loans/jobs. Need-based aid available for part-time students. Work-study available nights, weekends and for part-time students. **Non-need-based:** Scholarships awarded for academics, state residency. **Additional information:** Although financial aid applications can be submitted at any time during the academic year, FAFSA's received after priority filing date of April 15 will be considered for funding only after all on-time filers have been awarded and then only if funds are available.

Application procedures. Admission: No deadline. No application fee. Application must be submitted online. Admission notification on a rolling basis. There is a non-refundable application fee of $75 for international students. **Financial aid:** Priority date 4/15, closing date 6/30. FAFSA required. Applicants notified by 3/15; Applicants notified on a rolling basis starting 3/15.

Academics. Special study options: Cooperative education, distance learning, dual enrollment of high school students, ESL, honors, independent study, internships, study abroad, teacher certification program, weekend college. License preparation in dental hygiene, nursing, occupational therapy, paramedic, physical therapy, radiology, real estate. **Credit/placement by examination:** AP, CLEP, IB, institutional tests. 24 credit hours maximum toward associate degree. **Support services:** GED preparation and test center, learning center, remedial instruction, tutoring, writing center. Non-course based remedial programs are available.

Honors college/program. Applicants must meet established criteria and submit proof of the following: a 3.5 GPA and college-level placement on the TSI or a combined SAT score of 1100 (math and critical reading) or a composite ACT score of 26; an essay on an assigned topic; two letters of recommendation, one each from a counselor, teacher, and a community leader or supervisor; official high school transcripts.

Majors. Business: Accounting, banking/financial services, business admin, communications, fashion, hotel/motel admin, international, logistics, marketing, office technology, real estate, restaurant/food services, tourism/travel. **Communications technology:** Animation/special effects, graphic/printing, radio/TV. **Computer sciences:** Applications programming, networking, programming, system admin. **Education:** General, elementary, secondary. **Engineering:** Engineering science. **Foreign languages:** Sign language interpretation. **Health services:** Cardiovascular technology, clinical lab technology, dental hygiene, EMT paramedic, health information technology, histologic assistant, mental health services, nuclear medical technology, nursing (RN), occupational therapy assistant, radiologic technology/medical imaging, respiratory therapy technology. **Parks/recreation:** Health/fitness. **Protective services:** Fire investigation/protection, fire safety technology, police science. **Social sciences:** Anthropology. **Visual/performing arts:** Cinematography, fashion design, interior design, music management, music performance, music theory/composition. **Work/family studies:** Child development.

Most popular majors. Business/marketing 6.5%, health sciences 8.8%, liberal arts 73.6%.

Technology on campus. 4,121 workstations in library, computer center. Online course registration, online library, helpline, wireless network available.

Student life. Freshman orientation: Mandatory. Preregistration for classes offered. All first-time college or transfer student with less than 12 college level hours who are enrolling in HCC credit courses is required to complete a new student pre-enrollment session at one of the campuses. **Activities:** Bands, campus ministries, choral groups, drama, international student organizations, music ensembles, musical theater, student government, student newspaper, International Student Chamber of Commerce , National Society of Collegiate Scholars, Vietnamese Student Association, Phi Theta Kappa, Men of Honor, Rotaract Club, Veterans Student Organization, Student Association, logistics and supply club.

Athletics. Intramural: Basketball, football (non-tackle), golf, soccer, softball, tennis, volleyball.

Student services. Alcohol/substance abuse counseling, career counseling, services for economically disadvantaged, student employment services, financial aid counseling, minority student services, on-campus daycare, personal counseling, placement for graduates, veterans' counselor, women's services. **Physically disabled:** Services for visually, speech, hearing impaired. **Transfer:** College fairs on campus for students transferring to 4-year colleges.

Contact. E-mail: admissions@hccs.edu
Phone: (713) 718-8500
Mary Lemburg, Registrar, Houston Community College System, PO Box 667517, MC 1136, Houston, TX 77266-7517

Howard College
Big Spring, Texas
www.howardcollege.edu
CB code: 6277

- Public 2-year community college
- Commuter campus in large town

General. Founded in 1945. Regionally accredited. **Enrollment:** 4,360 degree-seeking undergraduates. **Degrees:** 314 associate awarded. **Location:** 105 miles from Lubbock, 40 miles from Midland. **Calendar:** Semester, limited summer session. **Full-time faculty:** 133 total. **Part-time faculty:** 81 total. **Special facilities:** Rodeo arena, performing arts center, coliseum.

Student profile. Among degree-seeking undergraduates, 65% enrolled in a transfer program, 37% enrolled in a vocational program, 1% already have a bachelor's degree or higher, 592 enrolled as first-time, first-year students.

Part-time:	78%	Hispanic/Latino:	46%
Out-of-state:	8%	Multi-racial, non-Hispanic:	2%
Women:	59%	International:	1%
African American:	4%	25 or older:	28%
Asian American:	1%	Live on campus:	8%

Transfer out. 17% of students enrolled in the transfer program go on to 4-year colleges. **Colleges most students transferred to 2015:** Texas Tech University, Angelo State University, Tarleton State University, University of Texas-Permian Basin, Texas A&M University.

Basis for selection. Open admission, but selective for some programs. Special requirements for health, cosmetology programs. Interview required for dental hygiene, degree and licensed vocational nursing, cosmetology programs. **Home schooled:** Transcript of courses and grades required.

2015-2016 Annual costs. Tuition/fees: $2,542; $3,772 out-of-district; $5,402 out-of-state. Per-credit charge: $67 in-district; $106 out-of-district; $159 out-of-state. Room/board: $4,530. Books/supplies: $1,217. Personal expenses: $1,472.

Financial aid. Need-based: Need-based aid available for part-time students. Work-study available nights, weekends and for part-time students. **Non-need-based:** Scholarships awarded for academics, art, athletics, leadership, music/drama.

Application procedures. Admission: No deadline. No application fee. Admission notification on a rolling basis. **Financial aid:** Priority date 4/1; no closing date. FAFSA, institutional form required. Applicants notified on a rolling basis starting 7/15; must reply within 2 week(s) of notification.

Academics. Special study options: Cooperative education, cross-registration, distance learning, dual enrollment of high school students, ESL,

---

internships, liberal arts/career combination, weekend college. License preparation in dental hygiene, nursing, occupational therapy, paramedic, radiology. **Credit/placement by examination:** AP, CLEP, institutional tests. 18 credit hours maximum toward associate degree. **Support services:** GED preparation and test center, learning center, pre-admission summer program, reduced course load, remedial instruction, study skills assistance, tutoring, writing center.

Majors. Biology: General. **Business:** General, accounting, office/clerical. **Communications:** General. **Computer sciences:** General. **Education:** General. **English:** English lit. **Foreign languages:** General, sign language interpretation. **Health services:** Athletic training, dental hygiene, dental lab technology, EMT ambulance attendant, health information management, health information technology, medical assistant, nursing (RN), physical therapy assistant, predental, premedicine, respiratory therapy technology, substance abuse counseling. **Liberal arts:** Arts/sciences. **Math:** General. **Parks/recreation:** Health/fitness. **Physical sciences:** Chemistry, physics. **Protective services:** Corrections, forensics, law enforcement admin. **Psychology:** General. **Social sciences:** General. **Visual/performing arts:** General, art, dramatic, music. **Work/family studies:** Child care management.

Most popular majors. Business/marketing 19%, computer/information sciences 7%, health sciences 21%, liberal arts 43%, security/protective services 6%.

Technology on campus. 100 workstations in dormitories, library, computer center, student center. Dormitories wired for high-speed internet access and linked to campus network. Commuter students can connect to campus network. Online course registration, online library, helpline, repair service, wireless network available.

Student life. Freshman orientation: Available. Preregistration for classes offered. **Housing:** Single-sex dorms, wellness housing available. **Activities:** Bands, choral groups, dance, drama, music ensembles, musical theater, student government.

Athletics. NJCAA. Intercollegiate: Baseball M, basketball, cheerleading, rodeo, softball W. **Intramural:** Basketball, bowling, golf, handball, racquetball, softball, table tennis, tennis, volleyball. **Team name:** Hawks.

Student services. Adult student services, alcohol/substance abuse counseling, career counseling, services for economically disadvantaged, student employment services, financial aid counseling, health services, on-campus daycare, personal counseling, placement for graduates, veterans' counselor. **Physically disabled:** Services for hearing impaired. **Transfer:** Transfer adviser, college fairs on campus for students transferring to 4-year colleges.

Contact. E-mail: REGISTRAR@howardcollege.edu
Phone: (432) 264-5000 Fax: (432) 264-5072
TaNeal Richardson, Registrar, Howard College, 1001 Birdwell Lane, Big Spring, TX 79720

International Academy of Design and Technology: San Antonio
San Antonio, Texas
www.iadt.edu

- For-profit 2-year technical college
- Very large city

General. Regionally accredited; also accredited by ACICS. **Enrollment:** 450 undergraduates. **Degrees:** 60 bachelor's, 88 associate awarded. **Calendar:** Quarter. **Full-time faculty:** 6 total. **Part-time faculty:** 47 total.

Basis for selection. Open admission.

2015-2016 Annual costs. Allied health program costs vary by program ranging from $2,200 to $37,775. Tuition rate for 15 credits including books is $400 per credit. AA tuition $32,800; BA tuition $64,800; Certificate tuition: $15,050.

Financial aid. Need-based: Work-study available nights, weekends and for part-time students.

Application procedures. Admission: No deadline. $50 fee. **Financial aid:** No deadline.

Academics. Special study options: Bachelor's degree programs available on campus. **Credit/placement by examination:** AP, CLEP.

Majors. Business: Fashion, merchandising. **Visual/performing arts:** Graphic design.

Contact. E-mail: ngarcia@iadtsanantonio.com
Phone: (210) 530-9449
International Academy of Design and Technology: San Antonio, 4511
Horizon Hill Boulevard, San Antonio, TX 78229

ITT Technical Institute: Arlington
Arlington, Texas
www.itt-tech.edu   CB code: 3572

- For-profit 2-year technical college
- Commuter campus in large city
- Interview required

General. Founded in 1982. Accredited by ACICS. **Enrollment:** 595 undergraduates. **Degrees:** 50 bachelor's, 107 associate awarded. **Location:** 11 miles from Fort Worth, 18 miles from Dallas. **Calendar:** Quarter, extensive summer session. **Full-time faculty:** 9 total. **Part-time faculty:** 75 total.

Basis for selection. Satisfactory score from on-site English and mathematics tests required.

2015-2016 Annual costs. Per-credit-hour charge, $493. Academic fee, $200. Some programs require purchase of tools, which could cost an additional $500. All costs subject to change.

Financial aid. Need-based: Work-study available nights, weekends and for part-time students.

Application procedures. Admission: No deadline. No application fee. Admission notification on a rolling basis. **Financial aid:** No deadline. FAFSA, institutional form required. Applicants notified on a rolling basis.

Academics. Credit/placement by examination: AP, CLEP. **Support services:** Learning center, tutoring.

Majors. Business: General. **Computer sciences:** LAN/WAN management, networking, programming, web page design. **Visual/performing arts:** Design, graphic design.

Technology on campus. Online library available.

Student life. Freshman orientation: Available. Preregistration for classes offered.

Student services. Career counseling, student employment services, placement for graduates.

Contact. Phone: (817) 794-5100 Toll-free number: (888) 288-4950
Fax: (817) 275-8446
Ed Leal, Director of Recruitment, ITT Technical Institute: Arlington, 551 Ryan Plaza Drive, Arlington, TX 76011

ITT Technical Institute: Austin
Austin, Texas
www.itt-tech.edu   CB code: 2692

- For-profit 2-year technical college
- Commuter campus in large city
- Interview required

General. Accredited by ACICS. **Enrollment:** 438 undergraduates. **Degrees:** 10 bachelor's, 106 associate awarded. **Calendar:** Quarter, extensive summer session. **Full-time faculty:** 7 total. **Part-time faculty:** 49 total.

Basis for selection. Satisfactory scores from on-site tests in English and mathematics required.

2015-2016 Annual costs. Per-credit-hour charge, $493. Academic fee, $200. Some programs require purchase of tools, which could cost an additional $500. All costs subject to change.

Financial aid. Need-based: Work-study available nights, weekends and for part-time students.

Application procedures. Admission: No deadline. No application fee. Admission notification on a rolling basis. **Financial aid:** No deadline. FAFSA, institutional form required. Applicants notified on a rolling basis.

Academics. Credit/placement by examination: AP, CLEP. **Support services:** Learning center, tutoring.

Majors. Business: Accounting technology. **Computer sciences:** Networking, programming, web page design. **Visual/performing arts:** Design.

Technology on campus. Online library available.

Student life. Freshman orientation: Available. Preregistration for classes offered.

Student services. Career counseling, student employment services, placement for graduates.

Contact. Phone: (512) 467-6800 Toll-free number: (800) 431-0677
Fax: (512) 467-6677
Jim Branham, Director of Recruitment, ITT Technical Institute: Austin, 6330 Highway 290 East, Suite 150, Austin, TX 78723

ITT Technical Institute: Houston North
Houston, Texas
www.itt-tech.edu   CB code: 2712

- For-profit 2-year technical college
- Commuter campus in very large city
- Interview required

General. Accredited by ACICS. **Enrollment:** 645 undergraduates. **Degrees:** 65 bachelor's, 213 associate awarded. **Calendar:** Quarter, extensive summer session. **Full-time faculty:** 10 total. **Part-time faculty:** 48 total.

Basis for selection. Satisfactory scores from on-site tests in English and mathematics required.

2015-2016 Annual costs. Per-credit-hour charge, $493. Academic fee, $200. Some programs require purchase of tools, which could cost an additional $500. All costs subject to change.

Financial aid. Need-based: Work-study available nights, weekends and for part-time students.

Application procedures. Admission: No deadline. Admission notification on a rolling basis. **Financial aid:** No deadline. FAFSA, institutional form required. Applicants notified on a rolling basis.

Academics. Credit/placement by examination: AP, CLEP. **Support services:** Learning center, tutoring.

Majors. Computer sciences: Networking, programming. **Visual/performing arts:** Design.

Technology on campus. Online library available.

Student services. Career counseling, student employment services, placement for graduates.

Contact. Phone: (281) 873-0512 Toll-free number: (800) 879-6486
Benjamin Moore, Director of Recruitment, ITT Technical Institute: Houston North, 15651 North Freeway, Houston, TX 77090

ITT Technical Institute: Houston West
Houston, Texas
www.itt-tech.edu   CB code: 3573

- For-profit 2-year technical college
- Commuter campus in very large city
- Interview required

General. Founded in 1983. Accredited by ACICS. **Enrollment:** 615 undergraduates. **Degrees:** 58 bachelor's, 217 associate awarded. **Calendar:** Quarter, extensive summer session. **Full-time faculty:** 6 total. **Part-time faculty:** 30 total.

Basis for selection. Satisfactory score from on-site English and mathematics tests required.

2015-2016 Annual costs. Per-credit-hour charge, $493. Academic fee, $200. Some programs require purchase of tools, which could cost an additional $500. All costs subject to change.

Financial aid. Need-based: Work-study available nights, weekends and for part-time students.

Application procedures. Admission: No deadline. Admission notification on a rolling basis. **Financial aid:** No deadline. FAFSA, institutional form required. Applicants notified on a rolling basis.

Academics. Credit/placement by examination: AP, CLEP. **Support services:** Learning center, tutoring.

Majors. Business: General. **Computer sciences:** LAN/WAN management, networking, programming. **Visual/performing arts:** Design, graphic design.

Technology on campus. Online library available.

Student life. Freshman orientation: Available. Preregistration for classes offered.

Student services. Career counseling, student employment services, placement for graduates.

Contact. Phone: (713) 952-2294 Toll-free number: (800) 235-4787 Fax: (713) 952-2393
Johnny Jackson, Director of Recruitment, ITT Technical Institute: Houston West, 2950 South Gessner, Houston, TX 77063-3751

ITT Technical Institute: Richardson
Richardson, Texas
www.itt-tech.edu   CB code: 2747

- For-profit 2-year technical college
- Commuter campus in small city
- Interview required

General. Accredited by ACICS. **Enrollment:** 708 undergraduates. **Degrees:** 40 bachelor's, 169 associate awarded. **Location:** 12 miles from Dallas. **Calendar:** Quarter, extensive summer session. **Full-time faculty:** 11 total. **Part-time faculty:** 48 total.

Basis for selection. Satisfactory scores from on-site tests in English and mathematics required.

2015-2016 Annual costs. Per-credit-hour charge, $493. Academic fee, $200. Some programs require purchase of tools, which could cost an additional $500 to $655. All costs subject to change.

Financial aid. Need-based: Work-study available nights, weekends and for part-time students.

Application procedures. Admission: No deadline. Admission notification on a rolling basis. **Financial aid:** No deadline. FAFSA, institutional form required. Applicants notified on a rolling basis.

Academics. Credit/placement by examination: AP, CLEP. **Support services:** Learning center, tutoring.

Majors. Business: General, accounting technology. **Computer sciences:** LAN/WAN management, networking, programming. **Health services:** Nursing (RN). **Visual/performing arts:** Design.

Student services. Career counseling, student employment services, placement for graduates.

Contact. Phone: (972) 690-9100 Toll-free number: (888) 488-5761 Fax: (972) 690-0853
Nate Wallace, Director of Recruitment, ITT Technical Institute: Richardson, 2101 Waterview Parkway, Richardson, TX 75080

ITT Technical Institute: San Antonio
San Antonio, Texas
www.itt-tech.edu   CB code: 2328

- For-profit 2-year technical college
- Commuter campus in very large city
- Interview required

General. Founded in 1988. Accredited by ACICS. **Enrollment:** 502 undergraduates. **Degrees:** 44 bachelor's, 117 associate awarded. **Location:** 200 miles from Houston, 75 miles from Austin. **Calendar:** Quarter, extensive summer session. **Full-time faculty:** 10 total. **Part-time faculty:** 82 total.

Basis for selection. Satisfactory scores from on-site tests in English and mathematics required.

2015-2016 Annual costs. Per-credit-hour charge, $493. Academic fee, $200. Some programs require purchase of tools, which could cost an additional $100 to $500. All costs subject to change.

Financial aid. Need-based: Work-study available nights, weekends and for part-time students.

Application procedures. Admission: No deadline. Admission notification on a rolling basis. **Financial aid:** No deadline. FAFSA, institutional form required. Applicants notified on a rolling basis.

Academics. Credit/placement by examination: AP, CLEP. **Support services:** Learning center, tutoring.

Majors. Business: General, accounting technology. **Computer sciences:** Networking, programming, web page design. **Visual/performing arts:** Design, graphic design.

Technology on campus. Online library available.

Student life. Freshman orientation: Available. Preregistration for classes offered.

Student services. Career counseling, student employment services, placement for graduates.

Contact. Phone: (210) 694-4612 Toll-free number: (800) 880-0570 Fax: (210) 694-4651
Michell "Buddy" Hoyt, Director of Recruitment, ITT Technical Institute: San Antonio, 5700 Northwest Parkway, San Antonio, TX 78249-3303

ITT Technical Institute: Webster
Webster, Texas
www.itt-tech.edu   CB code: 2715

- For-profit 2-year technical college
- Commuter campus in very large city
- Interview required

General. Accredited by ACICS. **Enrollment:** 378 undergraduates. **Degrees:** 36 bachelor's, 107 associate awarded. **Calendar:** Quarter, extensive summer session. **Full-time faculty:** 6 total. **Part-time faculty:** 33 total.

Basis for selection. Satisfactory scores from on-site tests in English and mathematics required.

2015-2016 Annual costs. Per-credit-hour charge, $493. Academic fee, $200. Some programs require purchase of tools, which could cost an additional $100 to $500. All costs subject to change.

Financial aid. Need-based: Work-study available nights, weekends and for part-time students.

Application procedures. Admission: No deadline. Admission notification on a rolling basis. **Financial aid:** No deadline. Institutional form required. Applicants notified on a rolling basis.

Academics. Credit/placement by examination: AP, CLEP. **Support services:** Learning center, tutoring.

Majors. Computer sciences: LAN/WAN management, programming. **Visual/performing arts:** Design.

Technology on campus. Online library available.

Student life. Freshman orientation: Available. Preregistration for classes offered.

Student services. Career counseling, student employment services, placement for graduates.

Contact. Toll-free number: (888) 488-9347
Derric Sutton, Director of Recruitment, ITT Technical Institute: Webster, 1001 Magnolia Avenue, Webster, TX 77598

Jacksonville College
Jacksonville, Texas
www.jacksonville-college.edu   CB code: 6317

- Private 2-year junior and liberal arts college affiliated with the Baptist faith
- Residential campus in large town

General. Founded in 1899. Regionally accredited. Owned and operated by the Baptist Missionary Association of Texas and affiliated with the Southern Baptists of Texas Convention. **Enrollment:** 304 degree-seeking undergraduates. **Degrees:** 75 associate awarded. **Location:** 120 miles from Dallas, 25 miles from Tyler. **Calendar:** Semester, limited summer session. **Full-time faculty:** 23 total. **Part-time faculty:** 14 total. **Class size:** 67% < 20, 32% 20-39, 1% >100.

Student profile.

Out-of-state:	6%	Live on campus:	57%

Transfer out. Colleges most students transferred to 2015: University of Texas at Tyler, Stephen F. Austin State University, Dallas Baptist University, East Texas Baptist University, Texas A&M University.

Basis for selection. Open admission. High school graduates must have a combination of high school diploma AND either successful completion of Texas exit criteria OR satisfactory ACT or SAT scores. GED is acceptable on its own merit. Interview recommended. **Home schooled:** Transcript of courses and grades required. Must take ACT, SAT, or THEA due to no Texas Assessment of Knowledge and Skills (TAKS) testing.

2015-2016 Annual costs. Tuition/fees: $7,700. Per-credit charge: $210. Room/board: $6,000. Books/supplies: $1,000. Personal expenses: $1,310.

Financial aid. Need-based: Need-based aid available for part-time students. Work-study available nights, weekends and for part-time students. **Non-need-based:** Scholarships awarded for academics, athletics, leadership, music/drama, religious affiliation, state residency.

Application procedures. Admission: Priority date 8/15; no deadline. $15 fee. Application must be submitted on paper. Admission notification on a rolling basis beginning on or about 1/15. **Financial aid:** Priority date 8/1; no closing date. FAFSA, institutional form required. Applicants notified on a rolling basis.

Academics. Special study options: Dual enrollment of high school students, honors. **Credit/placement by examination:** AP, CLEP, institutional tests. **Support services:** Learning center, reduced course load, remedial instruction, tutoring, writing center.

Majors. Liberal arts: Arts/sciences.

Technology on campus. 45 workstations in dormitories, library, computer center. Dormitories wired for high-speed internet access and linked to campus network. Commuter students can connect to campus network. Helpline, wireless network available.

Student life. Freshman orientation: Available. Preregistration for classes offered. **Policies:** Religious observance required. **Housing:** Guaranteed on-campus for freshmen. Single-sex dorms, apartments available. $80 deposit. **Activities:** Bands, campus ministries, choral groups, drama, music ensembles, student government, ministerial alliance, mission band.

Athletics. NJCAA. **Intercollegiate:** Basketball, golf, soccer, tennis. **Intramural:** Football (non-tackle), sand volleyball, softball, table tennis. **Team name:** Jaguars.

Student services. Chaplain/spiritual director, career counseling, financial aid counseling, personal counseling. **Transfer:** Transfer adviser, college fairs on campus for students transferring to 4-year colleges.

Contact. E-mail: admissions@jacksonville-college.edu
Phone: (903) 586-2518 Toll-free number: (800) 256-8522
Fax: (903) 586-0743
Sandra Clay, Director of Admissions, Jacksonville College, 105 B.J. Albritton Drive, Jacksonville, TX 75766-4759

Kilgore College
Kilgore, Texas
www.kilgore.edu

CB member
CB code: 6341

▶ Public 2-year community college
▶ Commuter campus in large town

General. Founded in 1935. Regionally accredited. **Enrollment:** 5,630 degree-seeking undergraduates; 36 non-degree-seeking students. **Degrees:** 782 associate awarded. **Location:** 60 miles from Shreveport, Louisiana, 120 miles from Dallas. **Calendar:** Semester, extensive summer session. **Full-time faculty:** 173 total; 8% have terminal degrees, 11% minority, 58% women. **Part-time faculty:** 104 total; 8% have terminal degrees, 14% minority, 62% women. **Class size:** 66% < 20, 32% 20-39, 1% 40-49, less than 1% 50-99. **Special facilities:** East Texas Oil Museum.

Student profile. Among degree-seeking undergraduates, 992 enrolled as first-time, first-year students.

Part-time:	60%	25 or older:	28%
Out-of-state:	1%	Live on campus:	7%
Women:	58%		

Transfer out. Colleges most students transferred to 2015: University of Texas at Tyler, University of North Texas, Stephen F. Austin State University, Texas A&M University, University of Texas at Austin.

Basis for selection. Open admission, but selective for some programs. For health occupation programs and some public service programs, standardized test scores, secondary school record, essay used as admissions criteria.

2015-2016 Annual costs. Tuition/fees: $1,830; $3,900 out-of-district; $5,400 out-of-state. Per-credit charge: $32 in-district; $101 out-of-district; $151 out-of-state. Room/board: $4,640. Books/supplies: $2,303. Personal expenses: $1,640.

Financial aid. Need-based: Need-based aid available for part-time students. Work-study available nights, weekends and for part-time students. **Non-need-based:** Scholarships awarded for academics, alumni affiliation, art, athletics, job skills, leadership, music/drama, state residency. **Additional information:** State of Texas grants and loans available for honor graduates with unmet needs and for non-traditional students.

Application procedures. Admission: Priority date 8/15; no deadline. No application fee. Admission notification on a rolling basis. **Financial aid:** Priority date 6/1, closing date 7/1. FAFSA, institutional form required. Applicants notified on a rolling basis starting 3/1; must reply within 2 week(s) of notification.

Academics. Special study options: Cooperative education, distance learning, dual enrollment of high school students, ESL, internships. License preparation in nursing. **Credit/placement by examination:** AP, CLEP, institutional tests. 14 credit hours maximum toward associate degree. **Support services:** GED preparation and test center, learning center, pre-admission summer program, reduced course load, remedial instruction, study skills assistance, tutoring, writing center.

Majors. Biology: General. **Business:** General, accounting, business admin, e-commerce, executive assistant, management information systems, operations. **Communications:** Communications/speech/rhetoric, journalism. **Computer sciences:** General, programming, systems analysis. **Education:** General, art, biology, chemistry, health, health occupations, history, physical, social science. **Engineering:** General, chemical, civil. **English:** English lit. **Foreign languages:** Spanish. **Health services:** Athletic training, clinical lab technology, EMT paramedic, medical radiologic technology/radiation therapy, nursing (RN), physical therapy assistant, surgical technology. **History:** General. **Liberal arts:** Arts/sciences. **Math:** General. **Parks/recreation:** Health/fitness. **Physical sciences:** Chemistry, physics. **Protective services:** Criminal justice, law enforcement admin, police science. **Psychology:** General. **Social sciences:** Sociology. **Visual/performing arts:** Art, commercial photography, commercial/advertising art, dance, dramatic, music. **Work/family studies:** Child care management.

Most popular majors. Business/marketing 10%, education 8%, engineering/engineering technologies 10%, health sciences 30%, liberal arts 16%, science technologies 7%.

Technology on campus. 350 workstations in library, computer center, student center. Dormitories wired for high-speed internet access and linked to campus network. Commuter students can connect to campus network. Online course registration, online library, helpline, wireless network available.

Student life. Freshman orientation: Mandatory, $40 fee. Preregistration for classes offered. **Housing:** Single-sex dorms available. $210 partly refundable deposit, deadline 8/15. **Activities:** Bands, campus ministries, choral groups, dance, drama, international student organizations, literary magazine, music ensembles, musical theater, radio station, student government, student newspaper, TV station, church organizations, physical therapy club.

Athletics. NJCAA. **Intercollegiate:** Basketball, football (tackle) M, softball W. **Intramural:** Badminton, bowling, handball, racquetball, softball, swimming, tennis, volleyball. **Team name:** Rangers.

Student services. Career counseling, student employment services, financial aid counseling, health services, on-campus daycare, personal counseling, placement for graduates, veterans' counselor. **Physically disabled:** Services for visually, speech, hearing impaired. **Transfer:** Pre-admission transcript evaluation for new students. College fairs on campus for students transferring to 4-year colleges.

Contact. E-mail: aknox@kilgore.edu
Phone: (903) 983-8209 Fax: (903) 983-8607
Chris Gore, Director of Admissions and Registrar, Kilgore College, 1100 Broadway, Kilgore, TX 75662-3299

Lamar Institute of Technology
Beaumont, Texas
www.lit.edu   CB code: 4239

- Public 2-year technical college
- Commuter campus in small city

General. Enrollment: 2,351 degree-seeking undergraduates. **Degrees:** 385 associate awarded. **Location:** 80 miles from Houston. **Calendar:** Semester, limited summer session. **Full-time faculty:** 74 total. **Part-time faculty:** 57 total. **Class size:** 63% < 20, 35% 20-39, 1% 40-49, less than 1% 50-99. **Special facilities:** Stand-alone Process Distillation Unit for petro-chemical majors.

Student profile.

Out-of-state: 2% **Live on campus:**   3%
25 or older: 35%

Basis for selection. Open admission, but selective for some programs. Special requirements for various allied health programs (dental hygiene, sonography, health information technology, radiology, respiratory care).

2015-2016 Annual costs. Tuition/fees: $5,274; $15,804 out-of-state. Per-credit charge: $127.47 in-state; $478.47 out-of-state. Books/supplies: $780.

Financial aid. Need-based: Work-study available nights, weekends and for part-time students.

Application procedures. Admission: No deadline. No application fee. Admission notification on a rolling basis. **Financial aid:** Priority date 4/1; no closing date.

Academics. Credit/placement by examination: AP, CLEP, IB, SAT, ACT, institutional tests.

Majors. Business: Accounting technology, administrative services, business admin, real estate. **Computer sciences:** General, web page design. **Health services:** Dental hygiene, EMT paramedic, health information technology, medical radiologic technology/radiation therapy, respiratory therapy technology, sonography. **Human services:** General. **Protective services:** Fire safety technology, forensics. **Social sciences:** GIS/cartography. **Work/family studies:** Child care service.

Most popular majors. Business/marketing 17%, computer/information sciences 6%, engineering/engineering technologies 26%, health sciences 26%, science technologies 13%.

Technology on campus. 150 workstations in library, computer center. Dormitories wired for high-speed internet access and linked to campus network. Online course registration, online library, wireless network available.

Student life. Freshman orientation: Available. Preregistration for classes offered. **Housing:** Single-sex dorms, wellness housing available. Access to dormitories located on Lamar University campus.

Student services. Alcohol/substance abuse counseling, career counseling, services for economically disadvantaged, student employment services, financial aid counseling, health services, placement for graduates, veterans' counselor. **Physically disabled:** Services for visually, hearing impaired.

Contact. Phone: (409) 880-8321 Toll-free number: (800) 950-6989 Fax: (409) 880-1711
Vivian Jefferson, Vice President for Student Services, Lamar Institute of Technology, PO Box 10043, Beaumont, TX 77705

Lamar State College at Orange
Orange, Texas
www.lsco.edu   CB code: 1694

- Public 2-year junior and liberal arts college
- Commuter campus in small city

General. Regionally accredited. **Enrollment:** 1,841 degree-seeking undergraduates. **Degrees:** 189 associate awarded. **Location:** 92 miles from Houston. **Calendar:** Semester, limited summer session. **Full-time faculty:** 48 total; 17% have terminal degrees, 10% minority, 60% women. **Part-time faculty:** 66 total; 14% have terminal degrees, 3% minority, 58% women. **Partnerships:** Formal partnership with CISCO.

Student profile.

Out-of-state: 11% **25 or older:**   33%

Basis for selection. Open admission, but selective for some programs. Nursing program competitive; high school record and test scores may be evaluated for admission. Interview required for students without high school diploma or GED, to determine if applicant can benefit from available educational programs.

High school preparation. 12 units recommended. Recommended units include English 4, mathematics 3, history 2 and science 3.

2015-2016 Annual costs. Tuition/fees: $4,807; $16,507 out-of-state. Per-credit charge: $125 in-state; $515 out-of-state. Books/supplies: $800. Personal expenses: $1,950.

Financial aid. All financial aid based on need. Need-based aid available for part-time students. Work-study available nights, weekends and for part-time students.

Application procedures. Admission: No deadline. No application fee. Admission notification on a rolling basis. **Financial aid:** Priority date 4/1; no closing date. FAFSA, institutional form required. Applicants notified on a rolling basis starting 5/15; must reply within 2 week(s) of notification.

Academics. Special study options: Cooperative education, distance learning, dual enrollment of high school students, internships, liberal arts/career combination. License preparation in nursing, paramedic. **Credit/placement by examination:** AP, CLEP. 15 credit hours maximum toward associate degree. **Support services:** GED test center, learning center, remedial instruction, study skills assistance, tutoring.

Majors. Biology: General. **Business:** General, accounting technology, administrative services, business admin. **Computer sciences:** General. **Education:** General. **English:** Rhetoric/composition. **Health services:** Clinical lab technology, EMT paramedic, medical secretary, nursing (RN). **Liberal arts:** Arts/sciences. **Protective services:** Corrections, criminal justice. **Social sciences:** Sociology.

Most popular majors. Business/marketing 13%, education 10%, health sciences 35%, liberal arts 19%, science technologies 8%.

Technology on campus. 150 workstations in library, computer center, student center. Commuter students can connect to campus network. Online library, helpline, wireless network available.

Student life. Freshman orientation: Available. Preregistration for classes offered. **Activities:** Student government.

Student services. Career counseling, financial aid counseling, placement for graduates, veterans' counselor. **Physically disabled:** Services for visually, hearing impaired.

Contact. Phone: (409) 882-3364 Fax: (409) 882-3055
Becky McAnelley, Director of Admissions, Lamar State College at Orange, 410 Front Street, Orange, TX 77630

Lamar State College at Port Arthur
Port Arthur, Texas
www.lamarpa.edu   CB code: 6589

- Public 2-year community and technical college
- Commuter campus in small city

General. Regionally accredited. **Enrollment:** 1,802 degree-seeking undergraduates. **Degrees:** 421 associate awarded. **Location:** 90 miles from Houston. **Calendar:** Semester, limited summer session. **Partnerships:** Formal partnerships with Microsoft and Novell (authorized training center).

Student profile. Among degree-seeking undergraduates, 5% enrolled in a transfer program, 31% enrolled in a vocational program, 1% already have a bachelor's degree or higher.

Transfer out. Colleges most students transferred to 2015: Lamar University.

Basis for selection. Open admission. **Adult students:** SAT/ACT scores not required. **Home schooled:** Transcript of courses and grades required.

2015-2016 Annual costs. Tuition/fees: $5,553; $16,393 out-of-state. Per-credit charge: $128 in-state; $518 out-of-state. Books/supplies: $1,000. Personal expenses: $2,457.

Financial aid. All financial aid based on need. Need-based aid available for part-time students. Work-study available nights, weekends and for part-time students.

Application procedures. Admission: No deadline. No application fee. Admission notification on a rolling basis. **Financial aid:** Priority date 4/1; no closing date. FAFSA, institutional form required. Applicants notified on a rolling basis starting 4/15; must reply within 2 week(s) of notification.

Academics. Special study options: Distance learning, dual enrollment of high school students, internships, liberal arts/career combination. License preparation in nursing. **Credit/placement by examination:** AP, CLEP. SAT used for math placement if submitted. **Support services:** Learning center, remedial instruction, study skills assistance, tutoring.

Majors. Business: Accounting technology, administrative services, business admin. **Communications:** Radio/TV. **Computer sciences:** Networking, programming, web page design. **Education:** Multi-level teacher. **Health services:** Insurance coding, medical secretary, nursing (RN), substance abuse counseling, surgical technology. **Parks/recreation:** Exercise sciences. **Protective services:** Criminal justice. **Visual/performing arts:** Dramatic, music, music performance, studio arts.

Technology on campus. 48 workstations in library, student center. Commuter students can connect to campus network. Online course registration, online library, wireless network available.

Student life. Freshman orientation: Available. Preregistration for classes offered. Held 1 day in July and 1 in August. **Activities:** Choral groups, drama, music ensembles, musical theater, student government, Professional Cosmetology Association, Alpha Beta Gamma, Alpha Lambda Rho, Art Club, Seahawk Records, Baptist student ministry, Chi Alpha, history club, Instrument Society of Automation, Sigma Kappa Delta.

Athletics. NJCAA. **Intercollegiate:** Basketball M, softball W. **Team name:** Seahawks.

Student services. Career counseling, services for economically disadvantaged, student employment services, financial aid counseling, personal counseling, placement for graduates, veterans' counselor. **Physically disabled:** Services for visually, speech, hearing impaired. **Transfer:** Pre-admission transcript evaluation for new students. College fairs on campus for students transferring to 4-year colleges.

Contact. E-mail: Nichoca@lamarpa.edu
Phone: (409) 984-6168 Toll-free number: (800) 477-5872 ext. 6168
Fax: (409) 984-6025
Connie Nicholas, Registrar, Lamar State College at Port Arthur, Box 310, Port Arthur, TX 77641-0310

Laredo Community College
Laredo, Texas
www.laredo.edu　　　　　　　　　**CB code: 6362**

- Public 2-year community college
- Commuter campus in large city

General. Founded in 1946. Regionally accredited. Two-campus institution. **Enrollment:** 7,585 degree-seeking undergraduates. **Degrees:** 938 associate awarded. **ROTC:** Army. **Location:** 150 miles from San Antonio, 140 miles from Corpus Christi. **Calendar:** Semester, extensive summer session. **Full-time faculty:** 200 total. **Part-time faculty:** 160 total. **Special facilities:** Environmental science center, special collections relating to regional history.

Student profile.

Out-of-state:	8%	Live on campus:	2%
25 or older:	30%		

Transfer out. Colleges most students transferred to 2015: Texas A&M International University, University of Texas at San Antonio.

Basis for selection. Open admission, but selective for some programs. Special requirements for nursing and allied health programs.

2015-2016 Annual costs. Tuition/fees: $4,080; $5,580 out-of-district; $7,140 out-of-state. Per-credit charge: $50 in-district; $100 out-of-district; $200 out-of-state. Books/supplies: $1,250. Personal expenses: $1,288.

Financial aid. Need-based: Work-study available nights, weekends and for part-time students.

Application procedures. Admission: No deadline. No application fee. Admission notification on a rolling basis. **Financial aid:** Priority date 5/1; no closing date. FAFSA, institutional form required. Applicants notified on a rolling basis.

Academics. Mandatory assessment program provides effective educational services for students. **Special study options:** Accelerated study, cooperative

---

education, cross-registration, distance learning, dual enrollment of high school students, ESL, exchange student, honors, liberal arts/career combination, teacher certification program, weekend college. License preparation in nursing, occupational therapy, paramedic, physical therapy, radiology, real estate. **Credit/placement by examination:** AP, CLEP, institutional tests. 30 credit hours maximum toward associate degree. **Support services:** GED preparation and test center, learning center, remedial instruction, tutoring.

Majors. Biology: General, bacteriology, botany, marine. **Business:** General, accounting, administrative services, fashion, finance, marketing, office management, office technology, office/clerical, real estate, sales/distribution. **Communications:** Broadcast journalism, communications/speech/rhetoric. **Computer sciences:** General, computer science, information systems, programming. **Education:** General, agricultural, art, bilingual, biology, business, chemistry, computer, early childhood, elementary, English, family/consumer sciences, foreign languages, health, history, mathematics, music, physical, physics, reading, Spanish, special ed, speech. **Engineering:** General, agricultural, architectural, electrical, petroleum. **English:** English lit. **Foreign languages:** General, Spanish. **General:** Power transmission. **Health services:** Clinical lab technology, EMT paramedic, medical assistant, medical radiologic technology/radiation therapy, medical secretary, mental health services, nursing (RN), occupational health, occupational therapy assistant, physical therapy assistant, predental, premedicine, prepharmacy, preveterinary. **History:** General. **Human services:** Social work. **Liberal arts:** Arts/sciences. **Math:** General. **Philosophy/religion:** Philosophy. **Physical sciences:** Chemistry, geology, physics. **Protective services:** Criminal justice, fire safety technology. **Psychology:** General. **Social sciences:** General, economics, political science, sociology. **Visual/performing arts:** Art, dramatic, music. **Work/family studies:** General, child care management.

Technology on campus. 514 workstations in library, computer center. Dormitories wired for high-speed internet access. Online course registration, online library, repair service available.

Student life. Freshman orientation: Available. Preregistration for classes offered. **Housing:** Coed dorms available. $100 fully refundable deposit. **Activities:** Bands, choral groups, dance, drama, literary magazine, music ensembles, musical theater, opera, student government, student newspaper, symphony orchestra, TV station.

Athletics. NJCAA. **Intercollegiate:** Baseball M, tennis, volleyball W. **Intramural:** Baseball M, basketball, bowling, football (tackle) M, golf, handball, racquetball, softball, tennis, volleyball. **Team name:** Palominos.

Student services. Alcohol/substance abuse counseling, chaplain/spiritual director, career counseling, services for economically disadvantaged, student employment services, financial aid counseling, health services, on-campus daycare, personal counseling, placement for graduates, veterans' counselor. **Physically disabled:** Services for visually, speech, hearing impaired. **Transfer:** Transfer adviser, college fairs on campus for students transferring to 4-year colleges.

Contact. E-mail: admissions@laredo.edu
Phone: (956) 721-5117 Fax: (956) 721-5493
Felix Gamez, Director of Admissions and Records, Laredo Community College, West End Washington Street, Laredo, TX 78040-4395

Le Cordon Bleu College of Culinary Arts: Austin
Austin, Texas
www.chefs.edu/austin　　　　　　　　**CB code: 4188**

- For-profit 2-year culinary school
- Very large city

General. Regionally accredited; also accredited by ACICS. **Enrollment:** 643 undergraduates. **Degrees:** 135 associate awarded. **Calendar:** Quarter. **Full-time faculty:** 20 total. **Part-time faculty:** 2 total.

Basis for selection. Open admission, but selective for some programs.

2015-2016 Annual costs. Certificate programs: $19,500. Associate programs: $40,000. Books and supplies are included.

Financial aid. Need-based: Work-study available nights, weekends and for part-time students.

Application procedures. Admission: No deadline. $50 fee. **Financial aid:** No deadline.

Academics. Credit/placement by examination: AP, CLEP. **Support services:** Learning center, tutoring.

Contact. E-mail: info@austin.chefs.edu
Phone: (512) 837-2665 Toll-free number: (888) 553-3433
Mark Lopez, Director of Admissions, Le Cordon Bleu College of
Culinary Arts: Austin, 3110 Esperanza Crossing, Suite 100, Austin, TX
78758-3641

Lee College
Baytown, Texas
www.lee.edu
CB member
CB code: 6363

- Public 2-year community college
- Commuter campus in small city

General. Founded in 1934. Regionally accredited. **Enrollment:** 6,817
degree-seeking undergraduates. **Degrees:** 736 associate awarded. **Location:**
25 miles from Houston. **Calendar:** Semester, limited summer session. **Full-
time faculty:** 141 total. **Part-time faculty:** 140 total. **Special facilities:** Pilot
plant for process technology students.

Basis for selection. Open admission, but selective for some programs.
TSI guidelines observed. Special requirements for allied health programs.
Home schooled: Transcript of courses and grades required.

2015-2016 Annual costs. Tuition/fees: $2,058; $2,958 out-of-district;
$4,368 out-of-state. Per-credit charge: $50 in-district; $80 out-of-district;
$127 out-of-state. Books/supplies: $1,500. Personal expenses: $1,696.

Financial aid. Need-based: Need-based aid available for part-time students. Work-study available nights, weekends and for part-time students.
Non-need-based: Scholarships awarded for academics, art, athletics, job
skills, leadership, music/drama.

Application procedures. Admission: No deadline. No application fee.
Admission notification on a rolling basis. **Financial aid:** Priority date 4/1;
no closing date. FAFSA required. Applicants notified on a rolling basis
starting 6/1.

Academics. Special study options: Cooperative education, distance learning, dual enrollment of high school students, honors, independent study,
internships, weekend college. **Credit/placement by examination:** AP,
CLEP, institutional tests. 30 credit hours maximum toward associate degree.
Support services: GED preparation and test center, learning center, remedial
instruction, tutoring, writing center.

Majors. Business: Accounting, administrative services, business admin,
office/clerical. **Communications technology:** Graphic/printing. **Computer
sciences:** General, data processing, information systems, programming.
English: English lit, technical writing. **Foreign languages:** General. **General:** Pipefitting. **Health services:** Health information technology, physical
therapy assistant, substance abuse counseling. **Liberal arts:** Arts/sciences.
Math: General. **Parks/recreation:** Health/fitness. **Physical sciences:** General. **Protective services:** Police science. **Social sciences:** General. **Visual/
performing arts:** Dramatic, music.

Technology on campus. 500 workstations in library, computer center,
student center. Online course registration, online library, helpline, wireless
network available.

Student life. Freshman orientation: Mandatory. Preregistration for
classes offered. **Activities:** Bands, choral groups, drama, international student
organizations, literary magazine, music ensembles, student government, Baptist student union, awareness club, Phi Theta Kappa, nursing students association, environmental science club, cosmetology club, digital information society, student honors council.

Athletics. NJCAA. **Intercollegiate:** Basketball M, volleyball W. **Intramural:** Basketball, bowling, football (non-tackle), softball, table tennis, volleyball. **Team name:** Rebels.

Student services. Adult student services, career counseling, student
employment services, financial aid counseling, personal counseling, placement for graduates, veterans' counselor. **Physically disabled:** Services for
hearing impaired. **Transfer:** Transfer adviser for students transferring to 4-
year colleges.

Contact. E-mail: admissions@lee.edu
Phone: (281) 425-6393 Fax: (281) 425-6831
Lee College, Box 818, Baytown, TX 77522-0818

Lincoln College of Technology: Grand Prairie
Grand Prairie, Texas
www.lincolntech.com
CB code: 3059

- For-profit 2-year technical college
- Large city

General. Regionally accredited; also accredited by ACCSC. **Enrollment:**
947 undergraduates. **Degrees:** 8 associate awarded. **Calendar:** Semester.
Full-time faculty: 53 total. **Part-time faculty:** 2 total.

Basis for selection. Open admission.

2015-2016 Annual costs. Certificate programs: $7,750 to $13,053.
Diploma programs: $18,270 to $36,207. Associate programs: $31,688. Costs
include total tuition, materials, tool fees, and registration fee.

Financial aid. Need-based: Work-study available nights, weekends and
for part-time students.

Application procedures. Admission: No deadline. $100 fee. **Financial
aid:** No deadline.

Academics. Credit/placement by examination: AP, CLEP.

Contact. Toll-free number: (877) 533-2598
Joe Hernandez, Director of Admissions, Lincoln College of Technology:
Grand Prairie, 2915 Alouette Drive, Grand Prairie, TX 75052

Lone Star College System
The Woodlands, Texas
www.lonestar.edu
CB code: 6508

- Public 2-year community college
- Commuter campus in very large city

General. Founded in 1972. Regionally accredited. Includes 6 colleges: LSC-
CyFair, LSC-Kingwood, LSC-North Harris, LSC-Montgomery, LSC-
Tomball, LSC-University Park. **Enrollment:** 83,932 degree-seeking undergraduates. **Degrees:** 5,578 associate awarded. **ROTC:** Army, Air Force.
Location: 40 miles from Houston. **Calendar:** Semester, extensive summer
session. **Full-time faculty:** 869 total; 29% have terminal degrees, 27% minority, 56% women. **Part-time faculty:** 3,471 total; 17% have terminal degrees,
36% minority, 58% women. **Class size:** 34% < 20, 64% 20-39, less than 1%
40-49, less than 1% 50-99, less than 1% >100.

Student profile. Among degree-seeking undergraduates, 12,209 enrolled
as first-time, first-year students, 14,753 transferred in from other institutions.

Part-time:	71%	25 or older:	29%
Women:	60%		

Transfer out. Colleges most students transferred to 2015: University
of Houston, Sam Houston State University, Texas A&M-College Station,
University of Texas-Austin, University of Houston-Downtown.

Basis for selection. Open admission, but selective for some programs.
Placement testing required in reading, writing, and math. Special requirements
for nursing, respiratory therapy, occupational therapy, physical therapist
assistant program, veterinary technician, diagnostic medical imagery, cosmetology.

High school preparation. College-preparatory program recommended.

2016-2017 Annual costs. Tuition/fees: $1,864; $3,964 out-of-district;
$4,414 out-of-state. Per-credit charge: $42 in-district; $112 out-of-district;
$127 out-of-state. Books/supplies: $600. Personal expenses: $1,692.

2014-2015 Financial aid. Need-based: 1,484 full-time freshmen applied
for aid; 1,266 deemed to have need; 922 received aid. Average need met
was 42%. Average scholarship/grant was $2,245; average loan $1,353. 62%
of total undergraduate aid awarded as scholarships/grants, 38% as loans/jobs.
Need-based aid available for part-time students. Work-study available nights,
weekends and for part-time students. **Non-need-based:** Awarded to 576 full-
time undergraduates, including 143 freshmen. Scholarships awarded for academics.

Application procedures. Admission: No deadline. No application fee.
Admission notification on a rolling basis. **Financial aid:** Priority date 5/10;
no closing date. FAFSA required. Applicants notified on a rolling basis
starting 4/1.

Two-Year Colleges

Academics. Special study options: Accelerated study, cooperative education, cross-registration, distance learning, dual enrollment of high school students, ESL, external degree, honors, independent study, internships, study abroad, teacher certification program, weekend college. Bachelor's degree programs available on campus. License preparation in dental hygiene, nursing, occupational therapy, paramedic, physical therapy, radiology, real estate. **Credit/placement by examination:** AP, CLEP, IB, institutional tests. 42 credit hours maximum toward associate degree. **Support services:** GED preparation, learning center, pre-admission summer program, reduced course load, remedial instruction, study skills assistance, tutoring, writing center.

Majors. Area/ethnic studies: Chicano/Hispanic-American/Latino. **Biology:** General. **Business:** Accounting, administrative services, business admin, hospitality admin, logistics. **Communications:** Communications/speech/rhetoric, radio/TV. **Computer sciences:** General. **Education:** Multi-level teacher. **Engineering:** Mechanical. **General:** Power transmission. **Health services:** Dental hygiene, electroencephalograph technology, EMT paramedic, health information technology, medical radiologic technology/radiation therapy, medical secretary, mental health services, nursing (RN), occupational therapy assistant, pharmacy assistant, physical therapy assistant, respiratory therapy technology, sonography, surgical technology, veterinary technology/assistant. **Liberal arts:** Arts/sciences. **Protective services:** Criminal justice, firefighting. **Social sciences:** GIS/cartography. **Visual/performing arts:** Music.

Most popular majors. Engineering/engineering technologies 16%, health sciences 10%, liberal arts 62%.

Technology on campus. 500 workstations in library, computer center, student center. Commuter students can connect to campus network. Online course registration, online library, helpline, wireless network available.

Student life. Freshman orientation: Mandatory. Preregistration for classes offered. Held on campus and online. Dates vary by campus. **Activities:** Bands, campus ministries, choral groups, dance, drama, film society, international student organizations, music ensembles, musical theater, opera, student government, symphony orchestra, Phi Theta Kappa, honors student association, student nurses association, African American society, Latin American student association, Asian student association, Campus Crusade for Christ, Muslim student organization, Show of Hands (deaf students).

Athletics. Intercollegiate: Baseball M. **Intramural:** Badminton, basketball, bowling, football (non-tackle), golf, soccer, table tennis, tennis, volleyball W.

Student services. Adult student services, alcohol/substance abuse counseling, career counseling, services for economically disadvantaged, student employment services, financial aid counseling, minority student services, on-campus daycare, personal counseling, placement for graduates, veterans' counselor, women's services. **Physically disabled:** Services for visually, speech, hearing impaired. **Transfer:** Transfer adviser, college fairs on campus for students transferring to 4-year colleges.

Contact. Phone: (832) 813-6500
Connie Garrick, Executive Director - Student Info Services, Lone Star College System, 5000 Research Forest Drive, The Woodlands, TX 77381-4356

McLennan Community College
Waco, Texas
www.mclennan.edu

CB member
CB code: 6429

◗ Public 2-year community and junior college
◗ Commuter campus in small city

General. Founded in 1965. Regionally accredited. **Enrollment:** 8,305 degree-seeking undergraduates. **Degrees:** 1,174 associate awarded. **ROTC:** Air Force. **Location:** 100 miles from Dallas and Austin. **Calendar:** Semester, extensive summer session. **Full-time faculty:** 203 total. **Part-time faculty:** 256 total. **Class size:** 43% < 20, 51% 20-39, 4% 40-49, 2% 50-99, less than 1% >100.

Student profile. Among degree-seeking undergraduates, 75% enrolled in a transfer program, 25% enrolled in a vocational program, 2% already have a bachelor's degree or higher, 1,226 enrolled as first-time, first-year students.

Part-time:	58%	Asian American:	1%
Women:	65%	Hispanic/Latino:	28%
African American:	13%	Multi-racial, non-Hispanic:	3%

Basis for selection. Open admission, but selective for some programs. Observes TSI guidelines in testing for placement. Admission to health careers programs is competitive. **Adult students:** SAT/ACT scores not required. **Home schooled:** Transcript of courses and grades, state high school equivalency certificate required.

High school preparation. College-preparatory program recommended.

2015-2016 Annual costs. Tuition/fees: $3,450; $3,990 out-of-district; $5,700 out-of-state. Per-credit charge: $106 in-district; $124 out-of-district; $181 out-of-state. Books/supplies: $2,200. Personal expenses: $1,962.

Financial aid. Need-based: Need-based aid available for part-time students. Work-study available nights, weekends and for part-time students. **Non-need-based:** Scholarships awarded for athletics.

Application procedures. Admission: No deadline. No application fee. Admission notification on a rolling basis. **Financial aid:** Closing date 6/1. FAFSA required. Applicants notified on a rolling basis starting 5/1.

Academics. Special study options: Distance learning, dual enrollment of high school students, honors, internships, study abroad, teacher certification program. Bachelor's degree programs available on campus. License preparation in nursing, paramedic, physical therapy, radiology, real estate. **Credit/placement by examination:** AP, CLEP, institutional tests. 24 credit hours maximum toward associate degree. **Support services:** Learning center, reduced course load, remedial instruction, tutoring, writing center.

Majors. Business: General, accounting, office technology, real estate. **Communications:** Communications/speech/rhetoric. **Computer sciences:** General, data processing, programming. **Foreign languages:** Sign language interpretation. **Health services:** Clinical lab technology, EMT paramedic, health information technology, medical radiologic technology/radiation therapy, medical secretary, mental health services, respiratory therapy technology, substance abuse counseling. **Protective services:** Law enforcement admin. **Work/family studies:** Child care management.

Technology on campus. 900 workstations in library, computer center, student center. Commuter students can connect to campus network. Online library, helpline, wireless network available.

Student life. Freshman orientation: Mandatory. Preregistration for classes offered. **Activities:** Concert band, campus ministries, choral groups, dance, drama, international student organizations, literary magazine, music ensembles, musical theater, student government.

Athletics. NJCAA. **Intercollegiate:** Baseball M, basketball, golf M, softball W. **Team name:** Highlanders/Highlassies.

Student services. Adult student services, career counseling, student employment services, financial aid counseling, health services, on-campus daycare, personal counseling, placement for graduates, veterans' counselor. **Physically disabled:** Services for visually, hearing impaired. **Transfer:** Transfer adviser, college fairs on campus for students transferring to 4-year colleges.

Contact. Phone: (254) 299-8628 Fax: (254) 299-8622
Karen Clark, Director of Admissions, McLennan Community College, 1400 College Drive, Waco, TX 76708

Midland College
Midland, Texas
www.midland.edu

CB code: 6459

◗ Public 2-year community college
◗ Commuter campus in small city

General. Founded in 1969. Regionally accredited. The Williams Regional Technical Training Center (WRTTC) is a full service extension campus in Fort Stockton. **Enrollment:** 5,430 undergraduates. **Degrees:** 19 bachelor's, 452 associate awarded. **Location:** 300 miles from El Paso and Fort Worth. **Calendar:** Semester, extensive summer session. **Full-time faculty:** 121 total. **Part-time faculty:** 163 total. **Class size:** 67% < 20, 32% 20-39, less than 1% 40-49, 1% 50-99.

Student profile.

Out-of-state:	1%	Live on campus:	5%
25 or older:	21%		

Transfer out. Colleges most students transferred to 2015: University of Texas of the Permian Basin, Texas A&M University, Angelo State University, Sul Ross State University, Texas Tech University.

Basis for selection. Open admission, but selective for some programs. Programs in the Health Sciences Division require an additional application, and may require entrance exams.

2015-2016 Annual costs. Tuition/fees: $2,460; $3,960 out-of-district; $5,160 out-of-state. Per-credit charge: $154 in-district; $204 out-of-district;

$392 out-of-state. Room/board: $4,700. Books/supplies: $1,416. Personal expenses: $1,995.

Financial aid. Need-based: Need-based aid available for part-time students. Work-study available nights, weekends and for part-time students. **Non-need-based:** Scholarships awarded for academics, athletics, minority status, music/drama, state residency.

Application procedures. Admission: No deadline. No application fee. Admission notification on a rolling basis. **Financial aid:** Priority date 4/2, closing date 6/1. FAFSA required. Applicants notified on a rolling basis starting 5/15; must reply within 2 week(s) of notification.

Academics. Special study options: Cooperative education, cross-registration, distance learning, dual enrollment of high school students, ESL, honors, internships. Bachelor's degree programs available on campus. License preparation in nursing, paramedic, radiology, real estate. **Credit/placement by examination:** AP, CLEP, IB, institutional tests. 12 credit hours maximum toward associate degree. **Support services:** GED preparation and test center, learning center, reduced course load, remedial instruction, study skills assistance, tutoring, writing center.

Majors. Biology: General. **Business:** General, office/clerical. **Computer sciences:** General, computer graphics, data processing, programming. **Education:** Early childhood, multi-level teacher, physical, secondary, teacher assistance. **Engineering:** Petroleum. **Foreign languages:** General. **Health services:** EMT paramedic, health information technology, nursing (RN), respiratory therapy technology, sonography, substance abuse counseling. **Protective services:** Firefighting, police science. **Work/family studies:** Child development.

Most popular majors. Business/marketing 8%, engineering/engineering technologies 7%, liberal arts 66%.

Technology on campus. 50 workstations in library, student center. Dormitories wired for high-speed internet access. Commuter students can connect to campus network. Online course registration, online library, wireless network available.

Student life. Freshman orientation: Available. Preregistration for classes offered. **Housing:** Coed dorms, single-sex dorms, apartments available. $100 fully refundable deposit, deadline 7/1. **Activities:** Bands, choral groups, drama, international student organizations, literary magazine, music ensembles, student government, student newspaper, symphony orchestra.

Athletics. NJCAA. **Intercollegiate:** Baseball M, basketball, golf M, softball W, volleyball W. **Intramural:** Basketball, football (non-tackle), tennis, volleyball. **Team name:** Chaparrals.

Student services. Career counseling, student employment services, financial aid counseling, on-campus daycare, personal counseling, veterans' counselor. **Physically disabled:** Services for visually, speech, hearing impaired. **Transfer:** College fairs on campus for students transferring to 4-year colleges.

Contact. E-mail: enroll@midland.edu
Phone: (432) 685-4501 Fax: (432) 685-6887
Jeremy Martinez, Director of Enrollment Services and Recruiting, Midland College, 3600 North Garfield, Midland, TX 79705

Mountain View College
Dallas, Texas
www.mvc.dcccd.edu   CB code: 6438

- Public 2-year community college
- Commuter campus in very large city

General. Founded in 1970. Regionally accredited. College campus designated as Urban Wildlife Sanctuary by the Humane Society of the United States. **Enrollment:** 7,300 degree-seeking undergraduates; 1,650 non-degree-seeking students. **Degrees:** 798 associate awarded. **Location:** 8 miles from downtown Dallas. **Calendar:** Semester, extensive summer session. **Full-time faculty:** 86 total. **Part-time faculty:** 212 total. **Partnerships:** Formal partnerships with many local businesses and local offices of national/international corporations.

Student profile. Among degree-seeking undergraduates, 1,137 enrolled as first-time, first-year students.

Part-time:	76%	Women:	59%
Out-of-state:	1%	25 or older:	38%

Transfer out. Colleges most students transferred to 2015: University of Texas at Arlington, University of North Texas, Texas A&M University.

Basis for selection. Open admission, but selective for some programs. Texas TSI guidelines observed. Students may be tested and placed in pre-college-level coursework. Certain programs are applied for separately and have admission requirements. A placement exam may be required. ACT, SAT, and end-of-course exams may negate the need for a placement exam. **Home schooled:** Transcript of courses and grades required. Texas law states that home-schooled students are considered private-school students and the same rules apply.

2015-2016 Annual costs. Tuition/fees: $1,770; $3,330 out-of-district; $5,220 out-of-state. Per-credit charge: $59 in-district; $111 out-of-district; $200 out-of-state. Books/supplies: $1,200. Personal expenses: $1,664.

Financial aid. Need-based: Need-based aid available for part-time students. Work-study available nights, weekends and for part-time students.

Application procedures. Admission: No deadline. No application fee. Admission notification on a rolling basis. **Financial aid:** Priority date 5/1; no closing date. FAFSA, institutional form required. Applicants notified on a rolling basis starting 6/1.

Academics. Special study options: Accelerated study, distance learning, dual enrollment of high school students, ESL, honors, liberal arts/career combination, teacher certification program, weekend college. License preparation in aviation, nursing. **Credit/placement by examination:** AP, CLEP, IB, institutional tests. 45 credit hours maximum toward associate degree. Test scores or local assessment must show ability to enroll in college level classes. **Support services:** Learning center, reduced course load, remedial instruction, study skills assistance, tutoring, writing center.

Majors. Business: General, accounting, business admin. **Computer sciences:** Computer science, data processing, LAN/WAN management, networking, programming, web page design. **Education:** Early childhood, kindergarten/preschool, middle. **Health services:** Nursing (RN). **Liberal arts:** Arts/sciences. **Math:** General. **Protective services:** Criminal justice. **Visual/performing arts:** Music, studio arts.

Most popular majors. Business/marketing 9%, education 9%, liberal arts 75%.

Technology on campus. 700 workstations in library, computer center, student center. Commuter students can connect to campus network. Online course registration, online library, helpline, wireless network available.

Student life. Freshman orientation: Available. Preregistration for classes offered. **Activities:** Concert band, campus ministries, choral groups, dance, drama, international student organizations, music ensembles, musical theater, student government, LULAC, Black student club, Campus Crusade for Christ.

Athletics. NJCAA. **Intercollegiate:** Baseball M, basketball, soccer, softball W, volleyball W. **Intramural:** Basketball, soccer, volleyball. **Team name:** Lions.

Student services. Adult student services, career counseling, services for economically disadvantaged, student employment services, financial aid counseling, health services, minority student services, personal counseling, placement for graduates, veterans' counselor. **Physically disabled:** Services for visually, speech, hearing impaired. **Transfer:** Transfer center, transfer adviser, college fairs on campus for students transferring to 4-year colleges.

Contact. E-mail: mvcadmissions@dcccd.edu
Phone: (214) 860-8600 Fax: (972) 698-3074
Glenda Hall, Director of Admissions, Mountain View College, Attn: Admissions, Dallas, TX 75211-6599

Navarro College
Corsicana, Texas
www.navarrocollege.edu   CB code: 6465

- Public 2-year community and junior college
- Commuter campus in large town

General. Founded in 1946. Regionally accredited. **Enrollment:** 9,478 degree-seeking undergraduates. **Degrees:** 858 associate awarded. **Location:** 50 miles from Dallas. **Calendar:** Semester, extensive summer session. **Full-time faculty:** 132 total. **Part-time faculty:** 470 total. **Special facilities:** Arts, science and technology center; IMAX theater.

Student profile. Among degree-seeking undergraduates, 71% enrolled in a transfer program, 29% enrolled in a vocational program, 1,579 enrolled as first-time, first-year students.

Part-time:	62%	Women:	59%
Out-of-state:	1%	Live on campus:	8%

Basis for selection. Open admission, but selective for some programs. Special requirements for health professions programs. Portfolio required for art.

2016-2017 Annual costs. Tuition/fees (projected): $2,188; $3,388 out-of-district; $4,888 out-of-state. Room/board: $5,504. Books/supplies: $1,581. Personal expenses: $2,558.

2014-2015 Financial aid. Need-based: 66% of total undergraduate aid awarded as scholarships/grants, 34% as loans/jobs. Work-study available nights, weekends and for part-time students.

Application procedures. Admission: No deadline. No application fee. Admission notification on a rolling basis. **Financial aid:** Priority date 6/1; no closing date. FAFSA required. Applicants notified on a rolling basis starting 7/1; must reply within 2 week(s) of notification.

Academics. Special study options: Distance learning, dual enrollment of high school students, ESL, honors, independent study, internships, liberal arts/career combination, weekend college. Bachelor's degree programs available on campus. License preparation in nursing, occupational therapy, paramedic, physical therapy. **Credit/placement by examination:** AP, CLEP, institutional tests. 30 credit hours maximum toward associate degree. CLEP credit awarded only after successful completion of 12 credit hours in residence. **Support services:** GED preparation and test center, learning center, reduced course load, remedial instruction, tutoring.

Majors. Biology: General. **Business:** General, accounting, administrative services, business admin, office technology. **Communications:** Communications/speech/rhetoric. **Communications technology:** Graphic/printing. **Computer sciences:** General. **Education:** General, elementary, physical, secondary. **Engineering:** General. **English:** English lit, rhetoric/composition. **Foreign languages:** Linguistics. **Health services:** Licensed practical nurse, predental, premedicine, prepharmacy, preveterinary. **Liberal arts:** Arts/sciences. **Math:** General. **Physical sciences:** Chemistry, physics. **Protective services:** Criminal justice, fire safety technology, police science. **Psychology:** General. **Social sciences:** General. **Visual/performing arts:** Art, commercial/advertising art, dramatic, music, music performance, voice/opera. **Work/family studies:** Child care management.

Technology on campus. Dormitories wired for high-speed internet access and linked to campus network. Commuter students can connect to campus network. Online course registration, online library, wireless network available.

Student life. Freshman orientation: Mandatory. Preregistration for classes offered. **Housing:** Single-sex dorms available. $210 deposit. **Activities:** Bands, choral groups, drama, international student organizations, music ensembles, student government, religious organizations, honorary and special interest clubs.

Athletics. NJCAA. **Intercollegiate:** Baseball M, basketball M, cheerleading, football (tackle) M, soccer W, softball W, volleyball W. **Intramural:** Softball. **Team name:** Bulldogs.

Student services. Career counseling, student employment services, personal counseling, placement for graduates, veterans' counselor. **Transfer:** Pre-admission transcript evaluation for new students. Transfer adviser, college fairs on campus for students transferring to 4-year colleges.

Contact. E-mail: admissions@navarrocollege.edu
Phone: (903) 875-7348 Toll-free number: (800) 628-2776
Fax: (903) 875-7353
Tammy Adams, Registrar, Navarro College, 3200 West Seventh Avenue, Corsicana, TX 75110

Student profile. Among degree-seeking undergraduates, 3,313 enrolled as first-time, first-year students.

Part-time:	68%	25 or older:	25%
Out-of-state:	1%	Live on campus:	2%
Women:	56%		

Basis for selection. Open admission, but selective for some programs. Observes TASP guidelines. Special requirements for some health professions programs.

High school preparation. 16 units recommended. Recommended units include English 4, mathematics 2, social studies 2 and science 2.

2015-2016 Annual costs. Tuition/fees: $2,280; $3,540 out-of-district; $6,000 out-of-state. Per-credit charge: $50 in-district; $92 out-of-district; $174 out-of-state. Room/board: $3,888. Books/supplies: $1,500. Personal expenses: $1,828.

Financial aid. All financial aid based on need. Need-based aid available for part-time students. Work-study available nights, weekends and for part-time students.

Application procedures. Admission: No deadline. No application fee. Admission notification on a rolling basis. High school transcript, proof of state residency, pre-TASP placement required for certain courses of study. **Financial aid:** Priority date 5/1, closing date 6/1. FAFSA required. Applicants notified on a rolling basis starting 6/1; must reply within 4 week(s) of notification.

Academics. Special study options: Cross-registration, distance learning, dual enrollment of high school students. **Credit/placement by examination:** AP, CLEP, institutional tests. 18 credit hours maximum toward associate degree. **Support services:** GED preparation and test center, learning center, remedial instruction, study skills assistance, tutoring, writing center.

Majors. Business: General, administrative services, office technology, office/clerical. **Computer sciences:** General, data processing. **Health services:** EMT paramedic, nursing (RN), occupational health, occupational therapy assistant. **Protective services:** Criminal justice, police science. **Social sciences:** Criminology. **Visual/performing arts:** Commercial photography.

Technology on campus. 60 workstations in dormitories, library, computer center, student center. Dormitories linked to campus network. Commuter students can connect to campus network. Online course registration, online library, helpline available.

Student life. Freshman orientation: Mandatory. Preregistration for classes offered. Held one day throughout summer and when classes commence. **Housing:** Coed dorms, special housing for disabled, wellness housing available. $150 deposit. **Activities:** Choral groups, dance, drama, literary magazine, music ensembles, student government, Baptist student union, Future Farmers of America, honor society, Young Republicans, nursing student association, criminal justice club, Methodist student organization, computer club.

Athletics. NJCAA. **Intercollegiate:** Baseball M, rodeo, tennis W, volleyball W. **Intramural:** Badminton, basketball, bowling, equestrian, golf, racquetball, softball, table tennis, tennis, track and field, volleyball. **Team name:** Lions.

Student services. Adult student services, career counseling, student employment services, personal counseling, veterans' counselor, women's services. **Transfer:** Transfer adviser for students transferring to 4-year colleges.

Contact. E-mail: admissions@nctc.edu
Phone: (940) 668-4222 ext. 222 Fax: (940) 668-6049
Melinda Carroll, Director of Admissions, North Central Texas College, 1525 West California Street, Gainesville, TX 76240

North Central Texas College
Gainesville, Texas
www.nctc.edu
CB code: 6245

▶ Public 2-year community college
▶ Commuter campus in large city

General. Founded in 1924. Regionally accredited. **Enrollment:** 9,427 degree-seeking undergraduates; 191 non-degree-seeking students. **Degrees:** 816 associate awarded. **ROTC:** Air Force. **Location:** 70 miles from main campus to Dallas. 35 miles from largest campus to Dallas. **Calendar:** Semester, extensive summer session. **Full-time faculty:** 152 total. **Part-time faculty:** 251 total. **Special facilities:** Planetarium, experimental farm, cattle center, horse arena.

North Lake College
Irving, Texas
www.northlakecollege.edu
CB code: 6519

▶ Public 2-year community and liberal arts college
▶ Commuter campus in large city

General. Founded in 1977. Regionally accredited. **Enrollment:** 7,793 degree-seeking undergraduates. **Degrees:** 897 associate awarded. **Location:** 15 miles from Dallas. **Calendar:** Semester, limited summer session. **Full-time faculty:** 115 total. **Part-time faculty:** 348 total. **Class size:** 59% < 20, 36% 20-39, 3% 40-49, less than 1% 50-99, less than 1% >100. **Special facilities:** Natatorium, pool.

Student profile.

Out-of-state: 3% **25 or older:** 40%

Transfer out. Colleges most students transferred to 2015: University of Texas at Arlington, University of North Texas, University of Texas at Dallas.

Basis for selection. Open admission. **Home schooled:** Transcript of courses and grades, interview required. Must take placement test.

High school preparation. College-preparatory program recommended.

2015-2016 Annual costs. Tuition/fees: $1,770; $3,330 out-of-district; $5,220 out-of-state. Per-credit charge: $59 in-district; $111 out-of-district; $200 out-of-state. Books/supplies: $600.

Financial aid. Need-based: Need-based aid available for part-time students. Work-study available nights, weekends and for part-time students. **Non-need-based:** Scholarships awarded for academics, minority status, state residency.

Application procedures. Admission: No deadline. No application fee. Admission notification on a rolling basis. **Financial aid:** Priority date 3/1, closing date 5/1. FAFSA required. Applicants notified on a rolling basis starting 7/1.

Academics. Special study options: Accelerated study, cooperative education, cross-registration, distance learning, double major, dual enrollment of high school students, ESL, honors, independent study, internships, liberal arts/career combination, study abroad, teacher certification program. License preparation in nursing, real estate. **Credit/placement by examination:** AP, CLEP, institutional tests. 15 credit hours maximum toward associate degree. **Support services:** GED preparation and test center, learning center, pre-admission summer program, reduced course load, remedial instruction, study skills assistance, tutoring, writing center.

Majors. Architecture: Technology. **Business:** Accounting, administrative services, business admin, management science, office management, office technology, real estate. **Communications:** Communications/speech/rhetoric. **Communications technology:** Graphics, photo/film/video. **Computer sciences:** General, applications programming, computer science, information systems, information technology, networking, programming, security, systems analysis, web page design. **Education:** Elementary, ESL, kindergarten/preschool, music, teacher assistance. **English:** American lit, English lit. **General:** Carpentry, power transmission. **Liberal arts:** Arts/sciences. **Math:** General, computational, statistics. **Psychology:** General. **Visual/performing arts:** Cinematography.

Technology on campus. 1,200 workstations in library, computer center, student center. Online course registration, online library, helpline, wireless network available.

Student life. Freshman orientation: Mandatory. Preregistration for classes offered. **Activities:** Bands, choral groups, dance, drama, film society, international student organizations, literary magazine, music ensembles, musical theater, opera, student government, student newspaper, association of black collegians, environmental club, Christians on Campus, Phi Theta Kappa, single parents association, Estamos Unidos, South Asian student organization, student ambassadors, anime club.

Athletics. NJCAA. **Intercollegiate:** Baseball, basketball, cheerleading W, gymnastics, swimming, volleyball, weight lifting. **Intramural:** Baseball, basketball, cheerleading W, soccer, swimming. **Team name:** Blazers.

Student services. Adult student services, alcohol/substance abuse counseling, career counseling, services for economically disadvantaged, student employment services, financial aid counseling, health services, minority student services, personal counseling, placement for graduates, veterans' counselor. **Physically disabled:** Services for visually, hearing impaired. **Transfer:** Pre-admission transcript evaluation for new students. Transfer center, transfer adviser, college fairs on campus for students transferring to 4-year colleges.

Contact. Phone: (972) 273-3183 Fax: (972) 273-3112
Francyenne Maynard, Dean, Student Support Services, North Lake College, 5001 North MacArthur Boulevard, Irving, TX 75038-3899

Northeast Texas Community College
Mount Pleasant, Texas
www.ntcc.edu   CB code: 6531

- Public 2-year community college
- Commuter campus in large town

General. Founded in 1984. Regionally accredited. **Enrollment:** 3,037 undergraduates. **Degrees:** 353 associate awarded. **Location:** 60 miles from Texarkana, 118 miles from Dallas. **Calendar:** Semester, extensive summer session. **Full-time faculty:** 66 total. **Part-time faculty:** 116 total.

Basis for selection. Open admission, but selective for some programs. The following specialized programs are selective: health science programs, cosmetology, automotive technology, and some criminal justice programs. **Home schooled:** Statement describing home school structure and mission, transcript of courses and grades, state high school equivalency certificate, letter of recommendation (nonparent) required.

High school preparation. 0.5 fine arts recommended.

2015-2016 Annual costs. Tuition/fees: $2,506; $4,276 out-of-district; $5,696 out-of-state. Room/board: $5,800. Books/supplies: $1,273. Personal expenses: $2,394.

Financial aid. Need-based: Need-based aid available for part-time students. Work-study available nights, weekends and for part-time students.

Application procedures. Admission: No deadline. No application fee. Application must be submitted online. Admission notification on a rolling basis. **Financial aid:** Priority date 6/1; no closing date. FAFSA, institutional form required. Applicants notified on a rolling basis starting 6/1.

Academics. Special study options: Cooperative education, distance learning, dual enrollment of high school students, ESL, honors, internships, liberal arts/career combination. License preparation in nursing, paramedic, physical therapy. **Credit/placement by examination:** AP, CLEP, institutional tests. 15 credit hours maximum toward associate degree. **Support services:** GED preparation and test center, learning center, remedial instruction, study skills assistance, tutoring, writing center.

Majors. Biology: General, biomedical sciences. **Business:** Accounting, accounting/business management, administrative services, business admin, office technology. **Communications:** General. **Computer sciences:** General, data entry, networking. **Conservation:** Environmental science. **Education:** Multi-level teacher. **Engineering:** Civil, electrical, industrial, mechanical. **English:** English lit. **Foreign languages:** Spanish. **Health services:** Clinical lab technology, EMT paramedic, medical assistant, medical secretary, nursing (RN), physical therapy assistant. **History:** General. **Human services:** Social work. **Liberal arts:** Arts/sciences. **Math:** General. **Parks/recreation:** Health/fitness. **Physical sciences:** Chemistry, physics. **Protective services:** Corrections, law enforcement admin, police science. **Psychology:** General. **Social sciences:** Political science, sociology. **Visual/performing arts:** Art, dramatic, music.

Most popular majors. Business/marketing 12%, health sciences 26%, liberal arts 30%.

Technology on campus. 150 workstations in dormitories, library, computer center. Dormitories wired for high-speed internet access. Commuter students can connect to campus network. Online course registration, online library, wireless network available.

Student life. Freshman orientation: Mandatory, $30 fee. Preregistration for classes offered. On campus and online orientation programs offered. **Housing:** Single-sex dorms available. $200 fully refundable deposit. **Activities:** Jazz band, choral groups, drama, literary magazine, music ensembles, musical theater, student government, student newspaper.

Athletics. NJCAA. **Intercollegiate:** Baseball M, rodeo, soccer, softball W. **Intramural:** Basketball M, softball, tennis, volleyball. **Team name:** Eagles.

Student services. Career counseling, services for economically disadvantaged, student employment services, financial aid counseling, minority student services, veterans' counselor. **Physically disabled:** Services for visually, speech, hearing impaired. **Transfer:** Pre-admission transcript evaluation for new students. College fairs on campus for students transferring to 4-year colleges.

Contact. E-mail: admrec@ntcc.edu
Phone: (903) 434-8122 Toll-free number: (800) 870-0142 ext. 8122
Fax: (903) 572-6712
Troy White, Admissions Coordinator, Northeast Texas Community College, 2886 FM 1735, Mount Pleasant, TX 75455

Northwest Vista College
San Antonio, Texas
www.alamo.edu/nvc   CB code: 6517

- Public 2-year community college
- Commuter campus in very large city

General. Regionally accredited. **Enrollment:** 13,505 degree-seeking undergraduates. **Degrees:** 2,768 associate awarded. **ROTC:** Army. **Location:** 16 miles from downtown. **Calendar:** Semester, extensive summer session. **Full-time faculty:** 159 total. **Part-time faculty:** 729 total.

Student profile. Among degree-seeking undergraduates, 2,660 enrolled as first-time, first-year students.

Part-time:	69%	Asian American:	2%
Women:	54%	Hispanic/Latino:	64%
African American:	6%	Multi-racial, non-Hispanic:	4%

Transfer out. Colleges most students transferred to 2015: University of Texas at San Antonio, Texas State University, Palo Alto College, San Antonio College, St. Philip's College.

Basis for selection. Open admission. **Home schooled:** Transcript of courses and grades required.

High school preparation. 22 units recommended. Recommended units include English 4, mathematics 3, social studies 5, history 1, science 3, foreign language 2 and academic electives 3.

2015-2016 Annual costs. Tuition/fees: $2,088; $5,550 out-of-district; $10,740 out-of-state. Books/supplies: $1,996.

Financial aid. Need-based: Need-based aid available for part-time students. Work-study available nights, weekends and for part-time students. **Non-need-based:** Scholarships awarded for academics, leadership.

Application procedures. Admission: Priority date 4/23; deadline 8/19. No application fee. **Financial aid:** Priority date 4/1; no closing date. FAFSA required. Applicants notified on a rolling basis starting 5/15; must reply within 2 week(s) of notification.

Academics. Special study options: Cross-registration, distance learning, dual enrollment of high school students, ESL, internships, liberal arts/career combination, teacher certification program, weekend college. **Credit/placement by examination:** AP, CLEP, institutional tests. 32 credit hours maximum toward associate degree. **Support services:** Learning center, remedial instruction, study skills assistance, tutoring, writing center.

Majors. Biology: General. **Business:** Business admin. **Communications:** Communications/speech/rhetoric, journalism, media studies. **Communications technology:** General. **Computer sciences:** General, computer science, networking, programming, security, system admin. **Education:** General. **English:** English lit, rhetoric/composition. **Foreign languages:** General. **History:** General. **Human services:** Social work. **Liberal arts:** Arts/sciences. **Math:** General. **Parks/recreation:** Exercise sciences, health/fitness. **Physical sciences:** Chemistry. **Protective services:** Law enforcement admin. **Psychology:** General. **Social sciences:** General, economics, political science, sociology. **Visual/performing arts:** Art, dance, dramatic, music.

Technology on campus. 3,500 workstations in library, computer center, student center. Commuter students can connect to campus network. Online course registration, online library, helpline, wireless network available.

Student life. Freshman orientation: Mandatory. Preregistration for classes offered. **Activities:** Campus ministries, dance, drama, film society, literary magazine, musical theater, student government, student newspaper.

Athletics. Team name: Wildcats.

Student services. Career counseling, student employment services, financial aid counseling, health services, personal counseling, placement for graduates, veterans' counselor. **Physically disabled:** Services for visually, speech, hearing impaired. **Transfer:** Pre-admission transcript evaluation for new students. Transfer center, transfer adviser, college fairs on campus for students transferring to 4-year colleges.

Contact. E-mail: nvc-admissions@alamo.edu
Phone: (210) 486-4700 Fax: (210) 486-9091
Robin Sandberg, Director of Enrollment Management, Northwest Vista College, 3535 North Ellison Drive, San Antonio, TX 78251-4217

Odessa College
Odessa, Texas
www.odessa.edu

CB code: 6540

▶ Public 2-year community college
▶ Commuter campus in small city

General. Founded in 1946. Regionally accredited. Extension centers in Pecos, Monahans, Andrews, Crane, Kermit, McCamey, Seminole. **Enrollment:** 5,569 degree-seeking undergraduates. **Degrees:** 528 associate awarded. **Location:** 140 miles from Lubbock, 290 miles from El Paso. **Calendar:** Semester, extensive summer session. **Full-time faculty:** 130 total; 15% have terminal degrees, 32% minority, 52% women. **Part-time faculty:** 60 total; 38% minority, 55% women. **Class size:** 83% < 20, 17% 20-39.

Student profile. Among degree-seeking undergraduates, 41% enrolled in a vocational program, 691 enrolled as first-time, first-year students, 146 transferred in from other institutions.

Part-time:	68%	Native American:	1%
Out-of-state:	4%	Native Hawaiian/Pacific islander:	2%
Women:	60%	25 or older:	24%
African American:	5%	Live on campus:	4%
Hispanic/Latino:	60%		

Basis for selection. Open admission, but selective for some programs. Allied health programs require successful completion of placement exams, supporting applications, and interviews. Requirements for other selective programs vary. **Home schooled:** Transcript of courses and grades required.

2015-2016 Annual costs. Tuition/fees: $2,580; $3,900 out-of-district; $5,160 out-of-state. Room/board: $5,200. Books/supplies: $1,400. Personal expenses: $1,234.

2015-2016 Financial aid. Need-based: Need-based aid available for part-time students. Work-study available nights, weekends and for part-time students. **Non-need-based:** Scholarships awarded for academics, athletics, music/drama.

Application procedures. Admission: No deadline. No application fee. Admission notification on a rolling basis. **Financial aid:** Priority date 5/1; no closing date. FAFSA required. Applicants notified on a rolling basis starting 6/1.

Academics. Special study options: Cooperative education, cross-registration, distance learning, dual enrollment of high school students, ESL, independent study, internships, liberal arts/career combination. License preparation in nursing, paramedic, physical therapy, radiology. **Credit/placement by examination:** AP, CLEP, institutional tests. 30 credit hours maximum toward associate degree. **Support services:** GED preparation and test center, learning center, reduced course load, remedial instruction, study skills assistance, tutoring, writing center.

Majors. Biology: General. **Business:** General, administrative services, business admin. **Communications:** Broadcast journalism, media studies. **Computer sciences:** Computer science, information systems, programming. **Education:** General, teacher assistance. **Foreign languages:** General. **General:** Carpentry, maintenance. **Health services:** Clinical lab science, EMT paramedic, medical radiologic technology/radiation therapy, medical secretary, nursing (RN), physical therapy assistant, respiratory therapy technology, substance abuse counseling, surgical technology. **Liberal arts:** Arts/sciences. **Math:** General. **Physical sciences:** Chemistry, geology. **Protective services:** Fire safety technology, firefighting, police science. **Psychology:** General. **Social sciences:** General, sociology. **Visual/performing arts:** Art, commercial photography, music. **Work/family studies:** Child care management, child development.

Most popular majors. Business/marketing 11%, education 6%, health sciences 18%, liberal arts 38%.

Technology on campus. 775 workstations in dormitories, library, computer center, student center. Dormitories wired for high-speed internet access and linked to campus network. Commuter students can connect to campus network. Online course registration, online library, helpline, student web hosting, wireless network available.

Student life. Freshman orientation: Mandatory. Preregistration for classes offered. **Housing:** Apartments available. $250 partly refundable deposit. **Activities:** Bands, choral groups, dance, drama, music ensembles, opera, radio station, student government, Baptist student union, veterans organization, Black organization of successful students, student alliance of Latinos succeeding academically.

Athletics. NJCAA. **Intercollegiate:** Baseball M, basketball, cheerleading, cross-country, golf M, rodeo, softball W, volleyball W. **Intramural:** Basketball, football (non-tackle) M, racquetball, softball, table tennis, tennis, ultimate frisbee, volleyball. **Team name:** Wranglers.

Student services. Career counseling, student employment services, financial aid counseling, on-campus daycare, personal counseling, placement for graduates, veterans' counselor. **Physically disabled:** Services for visually, hearing impaired. **Transfer:** Pre-admission transcript evaluation for new students. Transfer adviser, college fairs on campus for students transferring to 4-year colleges.

Contact. E-mail: admissions@odessa.edu
Phone: (432) 335-6432 Fax: (432) 335-6636
Odessa College, 201 West University, Odessa, TX 79764-7127

Palo Alto College

San Antonio, Texas
www.alamo.edu/pac

CB member
CB code: 3730

▶ Public 2-year community college
▶ Commuter campus in very large city

General. Founded in 1987. Regionally accredited. **Enrollment:** 8,376 undergraduates. **Degrees:** 771 associate awarded. **ROTC:** Army. **Calendar:** Semester, limited summer session. **Full-time faculty:** 107 total. **Part-time faculty:** 126 total. **Special facilities:** Stinson Airport FAA aviation education resource center, veterinary computer and clinical labs, outdoor animal pen.

Transfer out. Colleges most students transferred to 2015: Texas A&M San Antonio, University of Texas at San Antonio, St. Mary's University, Our Lady of the Lake University, Texas State University.

Basis for selection. Open admission.

2015-2016 Annual costs. Tuition/fees: $2,088; $5,550 out-of-district; $10,740 out-of-state. Books/supplies: $1,900.

Financial aid. All financial aid based on need. Need-based aid available for part-time students. Work-study available nights, weekends and for part-time students.

Application procedures. Admission: No deadline. No application fee. Application must be submitted online. Admission notification on a rolling basis. **Financial aid:** Priority date 4/1, closing date 5/1. FAFSA required. Applicants notified on a rolling basis starting 5/31.

Academics. Special study options: Accelerated study, distance learning, dual enrollment of high school students, ESL, internships, liberal arts/career combination, study abroad, weekend college. License preparation in aviation. **Credit/placement by examination:** AP, CLEP, institutional tests. 32 credit hours maximum toward associate degree. **Support services:** GED preparation, learning center, remedial instruction, study skills assistance, tutoring, writing center.

Majors. Area/ethnic studies: Chicano/Hispanic-American/Latino. **Biology:** General. **Business:** Administrative services, business admin, logistics. **Communications:** Communications/speech/rhetoric, journalism, radio/TV. **Computer sciences:** General, computer science, information systems. **Education:** Multi-level teacher. **Engineering:** Civil. **English:** English lit. **Foreign languages:** Spanish. **Health services:** Prenursing, veterinary technology/assistant. **History:** General. **Human services:** Social work. **Liberal arts:** Arts/sciences, humanities. **Math:** General. **Parks/recreation:** Health/fitness. **Physical sciences:** Chemistry, geology. **Protective services:** Criminal justice. **Psychology:** General. **Social sciences:** Economics, political science, sociology. **Visual/performing arts:** Dance, dramatic, music, studio arts.

Technology on campus. Commuter students can connect to campus network. Online course registration, online library, wireless network available.

Student life. Freshman orientation: Mandatory. Preregistration for classes offered. **Activities:** Jazz band, campus ministries, choral groups, dance, drama, music ensembles, student government, student newspaper, Chi Alpha Epsilon, Delta Sigma Omicon, Phi Theta Kappa, Sigma Lambda, Tri-Beta Biological Honor Society (Delta Pi), Destinos.

Athletics. Intramural: Basketball, football (non-tackle). **Team name:** Palominos.

Student services. Adult student services, alcohol/substance abuse counseling, career counseling, services for economically disadvantaged, student employment services, financial aid counseling, health services, minority student services, on-campus daycare, personal counseling, veterans' counselor. **Physically disabled:** Services for visually, speech, hearing impaired. **Transfer:** Transfer center, transfer adviser, college fairs on campus for students transferring to 4-year colleges.

Contact. Phone: (210) 486-3700
Elizabeth Villarreal, Director of Enrollment Management, Palo Alto College, 1400 West Villaret Boulevard, San Antonio, TX 78224-2499

Panola College

Carthage, Texas
www.panola.edu

CB code: 6572

▶ Public 2-year community and junior college
▶ Commuter campus in small town

General. Founded in 1947. Regionally accredited. Additional campuses in Marshall and Center, Texas. **Enrollment:** 2,674 degree-seeking undergraduates; 1 non-degree-seeking students. **Degrees:** 278 associate awarded. **Location:** 40 miles from Shreveport, Louisiana; 150 miles from Dallas. **Calendar:** Semester, limited summer session. **Full-time faculty:** 69 total; 7% have terminal degrees, 9% minority, 62% women. **Part-time faculty:** 78 total; 4% have terminal degrees, 12% minority, 63% women. **Class size:** 72% < 20, 24% 20-39, 3% 40-49, less than 1% 50-99.

Student profile. Among degree-seeking undergraduates, 67% enrolled in a transfer program, 32% enrolled in a vocational program, 2% already have a bachelor's degree or higher, 435 enrolled as first-time, first-year students, 338 transferred in from other institutions.

Part-time:	50%	Hispanic/Latino:	13%
Out-of-state:	6%	Multi-racial, non-Hispanic:	1%
Women:	68%	International:	1%
African American:	21%	25 or older:	11%

Transfer out. Colleges most students transferred to 2015: Stephen F. Austin State University, University of Texas at Tyler, Texas A&M Commerce, East Texas Baptist University.

Basis for selection. Open admission, but selective for some programs. Institution observes Texas Success Initiative guidelines. Departmental admission required prior to registration for some occupational/vocational programs of study. Dual credit/early admissions high school enrollment offers high school students an opportunity to earn credits toward a college degree while completing requirements for high school graduation. Interview required for some health program applicants. Auditions required for some fine arts scholarships. **Home schooled:** Transcript of courses and grades required.

High school preparation. 26 units recommended. Recommended units include English 4, mathematics 4, social studies 4, science 4, foreign language 2, visual/performing arts 1.5.

2015-2016 Annual costs. Tuition/fees: $2,190; $3,630 out-of-district; $4,560 out-of-state. Per-credit charge: $60 in-state; $200 out-of-state. Room/board: $4,600. Books/supplies: $1,961. Personal expenses: $3,432.

2014-2015 Financial aid. Need-based: 61% of total undergraduate aid awarded as scholarships/grants, 39% as loans/jobs. Need-based aid available for part-time students. Work-study available nights, weekends and for part-time students. **Non-need-based:** Scholarships awarded for academics, alumni affiliation, art, athletics, leadership, music/drama.

Application procedures. Admission: No deadline. No application fee. **Financial aid:** Priority date 6/1; no closing date. FAFSA, institutional form required. Applicants notified on a rolling basis starting 6/1.

Academics. Panola offers a variety of online and interactive television classes on its campuses as well as at area high schools and an on campus early college high school. **Special study options:** Combined bachelor's/graduate degree, distance learning, dual enrollment of high school students, liberal arts/career combination. License preparation in nursing, occupational therapy, paramedic. **Credit/placement by examination:** AP, CLEP. 12 credit hours maximum toward associate degree. **Support services:** GED preparation and test center, learning center, remedial instruction, study skills assistance, tutoring.

Majors. Business: General, office management. **Computer sciences:** General. **Education:** General. **Health services:** Clinical lab technology, health information technology, medical assistant, nursing (RN), occupational therapy assistant, office admin. **Liberal arts:** Arts/sciences.

Most popular majors. Education 7%, engineering/engineering technologies 20%, health sciences 26%, liberal arts 40%.

Technology on campus. 509 workstations in dormitories, library, computer center, student center. Dormitories wired for high-speed internet access and linked to campus network. Commuter students can connect to campus network. Online course registration, online library, helpline, wireless network available.

Student life. Freshman orientation: Available. Preregistration for classes offered. **Housing:** Coed dorms, single-sex dorms, apartments, wellness housing available. $200 partly refundable deposit, deadline 7/15. **Activities:** Bands, campus ministries, choral groups, drama, music ensembles, musical theater, student government, student newspaper, Student Government Association, forensic/drama club, chemistry club, Phi Theta Kappa, nursing club, health technology club, occupational therapy assistant club, Green Jackets service club, Caddo club.

Athletics. NJCAA. **Intercollegiate:** Baseball M, basketball, rodeo, volleyball W. **Intramural:** Basketball, football (non-tackle), sand volleyball, table tennis, volleyball, weight lifting. **Team name:** Ponies and Fillies.

Student services. Alcohol/substance abuse counseling, career counseling, services for economically disadvantaged, financial aid counseling, personal counseling, veterans' counselor. **Physically disabled:** Services for visually, speech, hearing impaired. **Transfer:** Pre-admission transcript evaluation for new students. College fairs on campus for students transferring to 4-year colleges.

Contact. E-mail: jdorman@panola.edu
Phone: (903) 693-2038 Fax: (903) 693-2031
Jeremy Dorman, Registrar/Director of Admissions, Panola College, 1109 West Panola Street, Carthage, TX 75633

Paris Junior College
Paris, Texas
www.parisjc.edu

CB member
CB code: 6573

♦ Public 2-year community and junior college
♦ Commuter campus in large town

General. Founded in 1924. Regionally accredited. **Enrollment:** 4,998 degree-seeking undergraduates. **Degrees:** 654 associate awarded. **Location:** 110 miles from Dallas. **Calendar:** Semester, limited summer session. **Full-time faculty:** 92 total. **Part-time faculty:** 159 total. **Class size:** 65% < 20, 30% 20-39, 3% 40-49, 1% 50-99. **Special facilities:** Collection of historical documents and artifacts of region.

Basis for selection. Open admission, but selective for some programs. Special admission to nursing program; interview required.

2015-2016 Annual costs. Tuition/fees: $1,890; $2,970 out-of-district; $4,380 out-of-state. Per-credit charge: $50 in-district; $86 out-of-district; $133 out-of-state. Room/board: $5,442. Books/supplies: $2,438.

Financial aid. **Need-based:** Need-based aid available for part-time students. Work-study available nights, weekends and for part-time students. **Non-need-based:** Scholarships awarded for athletics, music/drama.

Application procedures. **Admission:** No deadline. No application fee. Admission notification on a rolling basis. **Financial aid:** No deadline. FAFSA required. Applicants notified on a rolling basis starting 6/1.

Academics. **Special study options:** Accelerated study, distance learning, dual enrollment of high school students, internships. License preparation in nursing, paramedic, radiology. **Credit/placement by examination:** AP, CLEP, institutional tests. **Support services:** GED preparation and test center, learning center, reduced course load, remedial instruction, study skills assistance, tutoring, writing center.

Majors. **Biology:** General. **Business:** General, accounting, administrative services, business admin, office management, office technology. **Communications:** Journalism. **Computer sciences:** General, LAN/WAN management. **Education:** General, early childhood, multi-level teacher, secondary. **Engineering:** General. **English:** English lit. **Foreign languages:** General, French, German, Spanish. **Health services:** EMT paramedic, nursing (RN), predental, premedicine, prenursing, prepharmacy, preveterinary, radiologic technology/medical imaging. **History:** General. **Human services:** Social work. **Liberal arts:** Arts/sciences. **Math:** General. **Parks/recreation:** Health/fitness. **Physical sciences:** General, chemistry, physics. **Protective services:** Criminal justice. **Psychology:** General. **Social sciences:** General, criminology, political science, sociology. **Visual/performing arts:** Art, dramatic, metal/jewelry, music, studio arts.

Technology on campus. Dormitories wired for high-speed internet access and linked to campus network. Commuter students can connect to campus network. Helpline available.

Student life. **Freshman orientation:** Mandatory. Preregistration for classes offered. **Housing:** Single-sex dorms available. **Activities:** Jazz band, campus ministries, choral groups, drama, music ensembles, musical theater, student government, student newspaper, Baptist student union, Afro-American club, honorary business fraternity, honorary scholastic fraternity.

Athletics. NJCAA. **Intercollegiate:** Baseball M, basketball, golf M, soccer, softball W, volleyball W. **Team name:** Dragons.

Student services. Adult student services, alcohol/substance abuse counseling, career counseling, services for economically disadvantaged, student employment services, financial aid counseling, health services, personal counseling, placement for graduates, veterans' counselor. **Physically disabled:** Services for visually, hearing impaired.

Contact. E-mail: admissions@parisjc.edu
Phone: (903) 782-0425 Toll-free number: (800) 232-5804
Fax: (903) 782-0427
Amie Cato, Director of Admissions, Paris Junior College, 2400 Clarksville Street, Paris, TX 75460

Ranger College
Ranger, Texas
www.rangercollege.edu

CB code: 6608

♦ Public 2-year junior college
♦ Rural community

General. Founded in 1926. Regionally accredited. **Enrollment:** 1,856 degree-seeking undergraduates. **Degrees:** 111 associate awarded. **Location:** 85 miles from Fort Worth, 65 miles from Abilene. **Calendar:** Semester, limited summer session. **Full-time faculty:** 29 total. **Part-time faculty:** 89 total.

Basis for selection. Open admission, but selective for some programs. Observe all TSI guidelines. Special requirements for vocational nursing program candidates include additional applications and testing.

2015-2016 Annual costs. Books/supplies: $1,395. Personal expenses: $1,405.

2014-2015 Financial aid. All financial aid based on need. 71% of total undergraduate aid awarded as scholarships/grants, 29% as loans/jobs. Need-based aid available for part-time students. Work-study available nights, weekends and for part-time students.

Application procedures. **Admission:** No deadline. No application fee. Application must be submitted on paper. Candidates accepted into the vocational nursing program will receive notification and must reply by the date indicated. **Financial aid:** Priority date 7/28; no closing date. FAFSA required. Applicants notified on a rolling basis; must reply within 2 week(s) of notification.

Academics. **Special study options:** Distance learning, dual enrollment of high school students, honors. 2-2 programs in education, business administration, computer systems, and information sciences with Tarleton State University. License preparation in nursing. **Credit/placement by examination:** AP, CLEP, institutional tests. 12 credit hours maximum toward associate degree. **Support services:** GED test center, learning center, reduced course load, remedial instruction.

Majors. **Business:** Administrative services. **Computer sciences:** General. **Liberal arts:** Arts/sciences.

Technology on campus. 30 workstations in library, computer center.

Student life. **Freshman orientation:** Mandatory. Preregistration for classes offered. **Housing:** Single-sex dorms available. **Activities:** Bands, dance, music ensembles, student government, student newspaper.

Athletics. NJCAA. **Intercollegiate:** Baseball M, basketball, cheerleading, golf, rodeo, soccer, softball W, volleyball W. **Team name:** Rangers.

Student services. Career counseling, student employment services, health services, personal counseling, placement for graduates, veterans' counselor. **Transfer:** Transfer adviser for students transferring to 4-year colleges.

Contact. Phone: (254) 647-3234 ext. 215 Fax: (254) 647-3739
John Slaughter, Registrar, Ranger College, 1100 College Circle, Ranger, TX 76470

Remington College: Dallas
Garland, Texas
www.remingtoncollege.edu/dallas

CB code: 3232

♦ Private 2-year junior and technical college
♦ Small city

General. Regionally accredited; also accredited by ACCSC. **Enrollment:** 1,561 undergraduates. **Degrees:** 8 bachelor's, 103 associate awarded. **Calendar:** Differs by program. **Full-time faculty:** 36 total. **Part-time faculty:** 5 total.

Basis for selection. Open admission.

2015-2016 Annual costs. Personal expenses: $3,360. **Additional information:** Cost of diploma programs in Medical Billing and Coding, Pastry Arts: $15,995. Cost of diploma program in Cosmetology, $21,700. Cost of diploma programs in Medical Assisting (with or without X-Ray tech), Pharmacy Technician, $19,990. Associate degree programs in Business Administration, Computer and Network Administration, Criminal Justice, Culinary Arts, $33,900. Bachelor's in Criminal Justice, $24,700.Includes books, equipment, lab fees, and uniforms (if necessary).

Financial aid. Need-based: Work-study available nights, weekends and for part-time students.

Application procedures. Admission: No deadline. $50 fee. **Financial aid:** No deadline.

Academics. Credit/placement by examination: AP, CLEP.

Majors. Business: Business admin. **Computer sciences:** Networking. **Health services:** Medical assistant. **Protective services:** Law enforcement admin.

Contact. E-mail: admissions@remingtoncollege.edu
Phone: (972) 268-6506
Marc Wright, Director of Admissions, Remington College: Dallas, 1800 Eastgate Drive, Garland, TX 75041

Remington College: Fort Worth
Fort Worth, Texas
http://fort-worth.remingtoncollege.edu   CB code: 3151

- Private 2-year technical and career college
- Commuter campus in large city
- Interview required

General. Accredited by ACCSC. **Enrollment:** 746 undergraduates. **Degrees:** 43 associate awarded. **Location:** 7 miles from downtown. **Calendar:** Differs by program. **Full-time faculty:** 18 total. **Part-time faculty:** 16 total.

Basis for selection. Open admission. **Home schooled:** Transcript of courses and grades required.

2015-2016 Annual costs. Cost of diploma programs in Medical Billing and Coding, Dental Assisting: $15,995; Pharmacy Technician, Medical Assisting, $19,990; HVAC, $20,995; Medical Assisting with X-Ray Tech and EKG, $22,600. Associate degree programs in Computer and Network Administration, Criminal Justice, Digital Graphic Art, $33,900. Includes books, equipment, lab fees, and uniforms (if necessary).

Financial aid. Need-based: Work-study available nights, weekends and for part-time students.

Application procedures. Admission: No deadline. $50 fee. **Financial aid:** No deadline.

Academics. Credit/placement by examination: AP, CLEP.

Majors. Business: Business admin. **Computer sciences:** Computer graphics, networking. **Protective services:** Criminal justice.

Student services. Career counseling, financial aid counseling, placement for graduates.

Contact. E-mail: admissions@remingtoncollege.edu
Phone: (817) 522-4500
Ty Vaughn, Director of Admissions, Remington College: Fort Worth, 300 East Loop 820, Fort Worth, TX 76112

Remington College: Greenspoint Campus
Houston, Texas
http://greenspoint.remingtoncollege.edu

- Private 2-year health science and technical college
- Commuter campus in very large city

General. Accredited by ACCSC. **Enrollment:** 868 undergraduates. **Degrees:** 45 associate awarded. **Calendar:** Quarter. **Full-time faculty:** 25 total. **Part-time faculty:** 7 total.

Basis for selection. Open admission.

2015-2016 Annual costs. Cost of diploma programs in Medical Billing and Coding, Dental Assisting: $15,995; Cosmetology, $21,700; Cost of diploma programs in Medical Assisting (with or without X-Ray tech), Pharmacy Technician, $19,990. Medical Assisting with X-Ray Tech and EKG, $22,600. Associate degree programs in Business Office Management, Criminal Justice, $33,900. Includes books, equipment, lab fees, and uniforms (if necessary).

Financial aid. Need-based: Work-study available nights, weekends and for part-time students.

Application procedures. Admission: No deadline. $50 fee. Admission notification on a rolling basis. **Financial aid:** No deadline.

Academics. Credit/placement by examination: AP, CLEP.

Majors. Business: Business admin. **Health services:** Insurance coding, medical assistant, pharmacy assistant. **Protective services:** Law enforcement admin.

Contact. E-mail: admissions@remingtoncollege.edu
Phone: (832) 699-2221
Edmund Flores, Director of Admissions, Remington College: Greenspoint Campus, 11310 Greens Crossing, Suite 300, Houston, TX 77067

Remington College: Webster Campus
Webster, Texas
http://webster.remingtoncollege.edu

- Private 2-year career college
- Large town

General. Regionally accredited; also accredited by ACCSC. **Enrollment:** 509 undergraduates. **Calendar:** Semester. **Full-time faculty:** 16 total. **Part-time faculty:** 5 total.

Basis for selection. Open admission, but selective for out-of-state students.

2015-2016 Annual costs. Cost of diploma programs in Medical Assisting, Medical Billing and Coding, Dental Assisting: $15,995; Cosmetology, $21,700; Medical Assisting with X-Ray Tech and EKG, $22,600. Associate degree program in Business Office Management, $33,900. Includes books, equipment, lab fees, and uniforms (if necessary).

Financial aid. Need-based: Work-study available nights, weekends and for part-time students.

Application procedures. Admission: No deadline. $50 fee.

Academics. Credit/placement by examination: AP, CLEP.

Majors. Business: Business admin. **Computer sciences:** Networking.

Contact. Phone: (713) 581-9000
Robert Mauk, Campus President, Remington College: Webster Campus, 20985 Interstate 45 South, Webster, TX 77598

Remington College: Westchase Campus
Houston, Texas
http://houston.remingtoncollege.edu   CB code: 3152

- Private 2-year technical college
- Commuter campus in very large city

General. Accredited by ACCSC. **Enrollment:** 609 undergraduates. **Degrees:** 17 associate awarded. **Calendar:** Quarter. **Full-time faculty:** 21 total. **Part-time faculty:** 8 total.

Basis for selection. Open admission. ASSET used as admissions exams for degree programs.

2015-2016 Annual costs. Personal expenses: $1,764. **Additional information:** Cost of diploma programs in Medical Assisting, Medical Billing and Coding, Pharmacy Technician: $15,995; Electronic Technology, $20,995; Cosmetology, $21,700; Medical Assisting (with or without X-Ray Tech), $19,990; Associate degree programs in Business Office Management, Criminal Justice, $33,900. Includes books, equipment, lab fees, and uniforms (if necessary).

Financial aid. Need-based: Need-based aid available for part-time students. Work-study available nights, weekends and for part-time students. **Non-need-based:** Scholarships awarded for state residency.

Application procedures. Admission: No deadline. $50 fee. Application must be submitted on paper. Admission notification on a rolling basis. **Financial aid:** No deadline. FAFSA, institutional form required. Applicants notified on a rolling basis.

Academics. Special study options: Internships. **Credit/placement by examination:** AP, CLEP. **Support services:** Tutoring.

Majors. Computer sciences: General, applications programming, networking, programming, systems analysis. **Engineering:** Electrical, software.

Technology on campus. 200 workstations in library, computer center. Online library, helpline, repair service available.

Student services. Adult student services, career counseling, student employment services, financial aid counseling. **Transfer:** Pre-admission transcript evaluation for new students.

Contact. Phone: (281) 712-8114
Mark Donahue, Director of Admissions, Remington College: Westchase Campus, 3110 Hayes Road, Suite 380, Houston, TX 77082

Richland College
Dallas, Texas
www.rlc.dcccd.edu   **CB code: 6607**

▶ Public 2-year community college
▶ Commuter campus in very large city

General. Founded in 1972. Regionally accredited. **Enrollment:** 12,762 degree-seeking undergraduates. **Degrees:** 1,764 associate awarded. **Location:** 15 miles from downtown. **Calendar:** Semester, extensive summer session. **Full-time faculty:** 144 total. **Part-time faculty:** 632 total. **Special facilities:** Planetarium, laser light theater, horticulture demonstration garden, meditation labyrinth.

Student profile.

Out-of-state:	2%	25 or older:	39%

Basis for selection. Open admission. Students required by legislative mandate to take TASP test or alternative assessment before enrolling in college-level courses. **Home schooled:** Require completed application, concurrent enrollment permission form, student information profile sheet, student health history form, authorization to release test scores, official home school transcripts.

2015-2016 Annual costs. Tuition/fees: $1,770; $3,330 out-of-district; $5,220 out-of-state. Per-credit charge: $59 in-district; $111 out-of-district; $200 out-of-state. Books/supplies: $350. Personal expenses: $935.

Financial aid. Need-based: Need-based aid available for part-time students. Work-study available nights, weekends and for part-time students. **Non-need-based:** Scholarships awarded for art, leadership, music/drama.

Application procedures. Admission: No deadline. No application fee. Admission notification on a rolling basis. **Financial aid:** Priority date 5/11; no closing date. FAFSA required. Applicants notified on a rolling basis starting 6/1; must reply within 2 week(s) of notification.

Academics. Special study options: Cooperative education, cross-registration, distance learning, dual enrollment of high school students, ESL, honors, independent study, internships, study abroad, teacher certification program, weekend college. License preparation in real estate. **Credit/placement by examination:** AP, CLEP, institutional tests. 45 credit hours maximum toward associate degree. **Support services:** Learning center, remedial instruction, study skills assistance, tutoring.

Majors. Business: Accounting, administrative services, business admin, entrepreneurial studies, management information systems, real estate, tourism/travel. **Communications technology:** General. **Computer sciences:** General, applications programming. **Education:** Bilingual, teacher assistance. **Health services:** Health information technology, insurance coding, medical informatics. **Liberal arts:** Arts/sciences.

Technology on campus. 210 workstations in library, computer center. Commuter students can connect to campus network. Online course registration, online library, wireless network available.

Student life. Freshman orientation: Mandatory. Preregistration for classes offered. Sessions held online with alternative optional on-campus

orientation. **Activities:** Bands, campus ministries, choral groups, dance, drama, music ensembles, musical theater, student government, student newspaper, TV station, Spanish heritage association, arts club, Educators of America, Sierra Student Coalition, German film club.

Athletics. NJCAA. **Intercollegiate:** Baseball M, basketball M, soccer, volleyball W. **Intramural:** Basketball, bowling, cross-country, football (nontackle), golf, soccer, softball, tennis, volleyball. **Team name:** Thunder Ducks.

Student services. Adult student services, career counseling, services for economically disadvantaged, student employment services, financial aid counseling, health services, minority student services, personal counseling, placement for graduates, veterans' counselor, women's services. **Physically disabled:** Services for visually, speech, hearing impaired. **Transfer:** Transfer adviser, college fairs on campus for students transferring to 4-year colleges.

Contact. Phone: (972) 238-6106 Fax: (972) 238-6346
Rebecca Witherspoon, Director of Admissions, Richland College, 12800 Abrams Road, Dallas, TX 75243-2199

San Antonio College
San Antonio, Texas   **CB member**
www.alamo.edu/sac   **CB code: 6645**

▶ Public 2-year community college
▶ Commuter campus in very large city

General. Founded in 1925. Regionally accredited. **Enrollment:** 19,523 degree-seeking undergraduates. **Degrees:** 2,672 associate awarded. **ROTC:** Army, Air Force. **Location:** Downtown. **Calendar:** Semester, extensive summer session. **Full-time faculty:** 369 total. **Part-time faculty:** 1,192 total. **Special facilities:** Planetarium.

Transfer out. Colleges most students transferred to 2015: University of Texas at San Antonio.

Basis for selection. Open admission, but selective for some programs. Nursing requires 2.5 GPA, satisfactory completion of human anatomy/physiology and ethics. Mortuary science program requires admissions interview, proof of complete hepatitis B vaccination series (or submit a waiver/declination form), and counseling card. Dental assisting requires complete dental assisting technology program application, proof of advisement, formal admission to college, and counseling card. **Home schooled:** Transcript of courses and grades required.

2015-2016 Annual costs. Tuition/fees: $2,088; $5,550 out-of-district; $10,740 out-of-state. Books/supplies: $1,200. Personal expenses: $2,571.

Financial aid. All financial aid based on need. Need-based aid available for part-time students. Work-study available nights, weekends and for part-time students. **Additional information:** Leveraging Educational Assistance Partnership, public student incentive grant, towards excellence access and success grants (Texas and Texas II grants) available.

Application procedures. Admission: No application fee. Application must be submitted online. Admission notification on a rolling basis. Nursing applicants must apply by January 15. **Financial aid:** Priority date 3/1, closing date 5/1. FAFSA required.

Academics. Special study options: Cooperative education, cross-registration, distance learning, dual enrollment of high school students, ESL, honors, internships, liberal arts/career combination, study abroad, teacher certification program, weekend college. License preparation in dental hygiene, nursing, paramedic, real estate. **Credit/placement by examination:** AP, CLEP, IB, institutional tests. 32 credit hours maximum toward associate degree. Student must earn 6 credits at college before credit by examination may be posted on transcript. No credit by examination may be earned for course already completed in classroom. **Support services:** GED preparation and test center, learning center, reduced course load, remedial instruction, study skills assistance, tutoring, writing center.

Majors. Business: Accounting technology, business admin. **Communications:** Journalism, radio/TV. **Computer sciences:** Programming, security. **Education:** Teacher assistance. **Engineering:** General. **Foreign languages:** Sign language interpretation. **Health services:** Medical assistant, nursing (RN), substance abuse counseling. **Human services:** General. **Math:** General. **Protective services:** Corrections, criminal justice, fire safety technology, police science, security management. **Psychology:** General. **Visual/performing arts:** Graphic design. **Work/family studies:** Child development.

Technology on campus. 325 workstations in library, computer center, student center. Commuter students can connect to campus network. Online course registration, online library, helpline, wireless network available.

Student life. Freshman orientation: Mandatory. Preregistration for classes offered. **Activities:** Bands, choral groups, dance, drama, film society, international student organizations, literary magazine, music ensembles, musical theater, radio station, student government, student newspaper, symphony orchestra, TV station, Baptist student center, Catholic student center, Methodist student center, Church of Christ student center, black student alliance, United Mexican-American Students, College Republicans, Young Democrats, Young Socialist Alliance.

Athletics. Intramural: Basketball, bowling, cheerleading, cross-country, fencing, golf, racquetball, soccer, softball, swimming, table tennis, tennis, triathlon, volleyball, water polo.

Student services. Adult student services, alcohol/substance abuse counseling, chaplain/spiritual director, career counseling, services for economically disadvantaged, student employment services, financial aid counseling, health services, on-campus daycare, personal counseling, placement for graduates, veterans' counselor, women's services. **Physically disabled:** Services for visually, speech, hearing impaired. **Transfer:** Pre-admission transcript evaluation for new students. Transfer center, transfer adviser, college fairs on campus for students transferring to 4-year colleges.

Contact. E-mail: sac-ar@mail.accd.edu
Phone: (210) 486-0200 Fax: (210) 486-9229
J. Martin Ortega, Director of Enrollment Management, San Antonio College, 1300 San Pedro Avenue, San Antonio, TX 78212-4299

San Jacinto College
Pasadena, Texas
www.sanjac.edu   CB code: 6694

▶ Public 2-year community and technical college
▶ Commuter campus in very large city

General. Founded in 1960. Regionally accredited. Campuses in Houston and Pasadena and multiple extension centers. Aerospace and Biotechnology Academy (NASA-Johnson Space Center). **Enrollment:** 23,870 degree-seeking undergraduates; 4,456 non-degree-seeking students. **Degrees:** 3,756 associate awarded. **ROTC:** Army, Air Force. **Location:** 20 miles from Houston. **Calendar:** Semester, limited summer session. **Full-time faculty:** 490 total; 17% have terminal degrees, 27% minority, 53% women. **Part-time faculty:** 703 total; 12% have terminal degrees, 38% minority, 55% women. **Class size:** 38% < 20, 61% 20-39, less than 1% 40-49, less than 1% 50-99. **Special facilities:** Nature preserve (North Campus). **Partnerships:** Formal partnerships with NASA Space Center Houston, Partnership for Innovation in Biotechnology and Life Sciences, Boeing for Reduced Gravity Student Flight Program, University of Houston-College of Engineering for Aerospace Workforce Innovation Network.

Student profile. Among degree-seeking undergraduates, 39% enrolled in a transfer program, 31% enrolled in a vocational program, 3% already have a bachelor's degree or higher, 5,574 enrolled as first-time, first-year students, 1,528 transferred in from other institutions.

Part-time:	75%	Hispanic/Latino:	53%
Out-of-state:	1%	Multi-racial, non-Hispanic:	2%
Women:	56%	International:	2%
African American:	10%	25 or older:	29%
Asian American:	5%		

Transfer out. 44% of students enrolled in the transfer program go on to 4-year colleges. **Colleges most students transferred to 2015:** University of Houston, University of Houston-Clear Lake, Houston Community College, Texas A&M University, University of Houston-Downtown.

Basis for selection. Open admission, but selective for some programs. Special requirements for health science program. Psychological Services Bureau test and interview required of nursing applicants. SAT or ACT score used for nursing, medical laboratory technology, radiography, and respiratory programs. In some selective programs, specific courses taken successfully within San Jacinto district may obviate need for qualifying SAT/ACT scores. Interview recommended for nursing program, and EMT programs. **Home schooled:** State high school equivalency certificate required. **Learning Disabled:** Student must complete the Disability Service Application and provide documentation of a disability.

High school preparation. College-preparatory program recommended. 11 units recommended. Recommended units include English 4, mathematics 3, (laboratory 2) and foreign language 2.

2015-2016 Annual costs. Tuition/fees: $1,690; $2,950 out-of-district; $4,750 out-of-state. Per-credit charge: $47 in-district; $89 out-of-district; $149 out-of-state. Books/supplies: $1,400.

2014-2015 Financial aid. All financial aid based on need. 1,617 full-time freshmen applied for aid; 1,426 deemed to have need; 1,017 received aid. Average need met was 26%. Average scholarship/grant was $5,003; average loan $3,328. 81% of total undergraduate aid awarded as scholarships/grants, 19% as loans/jobs. Need-based aid available for part-time students. Work-study available nights, weekends and for part-time students.

Application procedures. Admission: No deadline. No application fee. Application must be submitted online. Admission notification on a rolling basis. **Financial aid:** Priority date 6/30; no closing date. FAFSA required. Applicants notified on a rolling basis starting 5/1; must reply within 4 week(s) of notification.

Academics. Special study options: Accelerated study, cooperative education, cross-registration, distance learning, double major, dual enrollment of high school students, ESL, honors, internships, teacher certification program, weekend college. License preparation in aviation, dental hygiene, nursing, paramedic, radiology, real estate. **Credit/placement by examination:** AP, CLEP, IB, institutional tests. 30 credit hours maximum toward associate degree. A student must have earned at least three credit hours of course work at San Jacinto College before the College will post credit for CLEP, AP, IB, or departmental examinations to the student's transcript. Freshman College Composition CLEP subject examination must be accompanied by essay. **Support services:** GED preparation and test center, learning center, pre-admission summer program, remedial instruction, study skills assistance, tutoring, writing center.

Majors. Area/ethnic studies: Chicano/Hispanic-American/Latino. **Biology:** General. **Business:** General, accounting, administrative services, business admin, international, management information systems, real estate. **Communications:** Digital media, journalism. **Communications technology:** Radio/TV. **Computer sciences:** General. **Conservation:** Environmental science. **Education:** Science, secondary. **Engineering:** General. **English:** English lit, rhetoric/composition. **Foreign languages:** General. **General:** Power transmission. **Health services:** Clinical lab technology, EMT paramedic, health information technology, mental health services, nursing (RN), optometric assistant, physical therapy assistant, radiologic technology/medical imaging, respiratory therapy technology, sonography, surgical technology. **History:** General. **Math:** General. **Parks/recreation:** Health/fitness. **Philosophy/religion:** Philosophy. **Physical sciences:** General, chemistry, geology, physics. **Protective services:** Firefighting, police science. **Psychology:** General. **Social sciences:** General, political science, sociology. **Visual/performing arts:** Art, commercial/advertising art, dance, dramatic, interior design, music. **Work/family studies:** Child development.

Most popular majors. Business/marketing 12%, health sciences 13%, interdisciplinary studies 7%, liberal arts 34%, military 7%.

Technology on campus. 772 workstations in library, computer center, student center. Online course registration, helpline, repair service, wireless network available.

Student life. Freshman orientation: Mandatory. Preregistration for classes offered. Choice of on-campus or online orientation. 4-hour sessions scheduled several times prior to beginning of semester. **Policies:** Student conduct code. **Activities:** Jazz band, choral groups, dance, drama, literary magazine, music ensembles, musical theater, student government, student newspaper, Phi Theta Kappa honor society, Latin American student organization, College Republicans, College Democrats, Phi Beta Lambda, Texas student education association, student government association, nurses association, ABG Radiography.

Athletics. NJCAA. **Intercollegiate:** Baseball M, basketball, soccer M, softball W, volleyball W. **Intramural:** Basketball, football (non-tackle), golf, soccer, softball, table tennis, tennis, volleyball, weight lifting. **Team name:** Ravens / Gators / Coyotes.

Student services. Adult student services, alcohol/substance abuse counseling, career counseling, student employment services, financial aid counseling, on-campus daycare, personal counseling, placement for graduates, veterans' counselor. **Transfer:** Transfer adviser, college fairs on campus for students transferring to 4-year colleges.

Contact. E-mail: information@sjcd.edu
Phone: (281) 998-6150 Fax: (281) 478-2720
Wanda Munson, Dean of Enrollment Management & College Registrar, San Jacinto College, 8060 Spencer Highway, Pasadena, TX 77505-5999

South Plains College
Levelland, Texas
www.southplainscollege.edu   CB code: 6695

▶ Public 2-year community and junior college
▶ Commuter campus in large town

General. Founded in 1957. Regionally accredited. **Enrollment:** 7,863 degree-seeking undergraduates; 1,523 non-degree-seeking students. **Degrees:** 850 associate awarded. **Location:** 30 miles from Lubbock. **Calendar:** Semester, extensive summer session. **Full-time faculty:** 303 total; 51% women. **Part-time faculty:** 175 total; 58% women. **Special facilities:** Audio/video recording studio, fine art gallery.

Student profile. Among degree-seeking undergraduates, 2,190 enrolled as first-time, first-year students, 3,314 transferred in from other institutions.

Part-time:	41%	Women:	54%
Out-of-state:	1%	Live on campus:	11%

Transfer out. Colleges most students transferred to 2015: Texas Tech University, Angelo State University, West Texas A&M University, Eastern New Mexico State University, Lubbock Christian University.

Basis for selection. Open admission, but selective for some programs. State law requires TSI exam before student may enroll in college-level course work. Special requirements for allied health, cosmetology, law enforcement academy programs. Interview required for health care.

2016-2017 Annual costs. Tuition/fees (projected): $3,784; $4,720 out-of-district; $5,104 out-of-state. Per-credit charge: $29 in-district; $68 out-of-district; $84 out-of-state. Room/board: $3,900. Books/supplies: $1,250. Personal expenses: $2,000.

2014-2015 Financial aid. Need-based: 76% of total undergraduate aid awarded as scholarships/grants, 24% as loans/jobs. Need-based aid available for part-time students. Work-study available nights, weekends and for part-time students. **Non-need-based:** Scholarships awarded for academics, art, athletics, leadership, music/drama, state residency.

Application procedures. Admission: No deadline. No application fee. Admission notification on a rolling basis. **Financial aid:** Priority date 6/1; no closing date. FAFSA required. Applicants notified on a rolling basis starting 6/30; must reply within 2 week(s) of notification.

Academics. Special study options: Distance learning, dual enrollment of high school students, internships. License preparation in nursing, occupational therapy, paramedic, physical therapy, radiology, real estate. **Credit/placement by examination:** AP, CLEP, institutional tests. 15 credit hours maximum toward associate degree. **Support services:** GED preparation, learning center, remedial instruction, study skills assistance, tutoring.

Majors. Biology: General. **Business:** General, accounting, administrative services, business admin, office management, real estate. **Communications:** Advertising, broadcast journalism, communications/speech/rhetoric, journalism, organizational, persuasive communications, photojournalism, radio/TV, sports. **Communications technology:** Graphic/printing. **Computer sciences:** General, computer science, data processing. **Education:** General. **Engineering:** General. **English:** English lit. **Foreign languages:** General. **General:** Power transmission. **Health services:** EMT paramedic, health information technology, medical radiologic technology/radiation therapy, nursing (RN), physical therapy assistant, predental, premedicine, prenursing, preop/surgical nursing, prepharmacy, preveterinary, respiratory therapy technology, surgical technology. **History:** General. **Liberal arts:** Arts/sciences. **Math:** General. **Parks/recreation:** Health/fitness. **Physical sciences:** Chemistry, geology, physics. **Protective services:** Fire safety technology, firefighting, law enforcement admin. **Psychology:** General. **Social sciences:** Political science, sociology. **Visual/performing arts:** Commercial/advertising art, design, dramatic, graphic design, music. **Work/family studies:** General, child care management.

Technology on campus. 2,000 workstations in dormitories, library, computer center, student center. Dormitories linked to campus network. Commuter students can connect to campus network. Online course registration, online library, wireless network available.

Student life. Freshman orientation: Available, $25 fee. Preregistration for classes offered. **Housing:** Single-sex dorms, special housing for disabled, apartments available. $100 deposit. **Activities:** Bands, campus ministries, choral groups, dance, drama, international student organizations, literary magazine, music ensembles, musical theater, opera, radio station, student government, student newspaper, symphony orchestra, TV station.

Athletics. NJCAA. **Intercollegiate:** Basketball, cheerleading, cross-country, rodeo, track and field. **Intramural:** Basketball, football (non-tackle), golf, racquetball, soccer, softball, table tennis, tennis, volleyball. **Team name:** Texans/Lady Texans.

Student services. Career counseling, student employment services, financial aid counseling, health services, minority student services, personal counseling, placement for graduates, veterans' counselor. **Physically disabled:** Services for visually, hearing impaired. **Transfer:** Transfer adviser, college fairs on campus for students transferring to 4-year colleges.

Contact. E-mail: arangel@southplainscollege.edu
Phone: (806) 894-9611 ext. 2373 Fax: (806) 897-3167
Andrea Rangel, Dean of Admissions and Records, South Plains College, 1401 South College Avenue, Levelland, TX 79336

South Texas College
McAllen, Texas
www.southtexascollege.edu — CB code: 6654

▸ Public 2-year community and technical college
▸ Commuter campus in very large city

General. Regionally accredited. Virtual campus with full online student services and student learning support. **Enrollment:** 31,143 degree-seeking undergraduates. **Degrees:** 201 bachelor's, 3,179 associate awarded. **Location:** 250 miles from San Antonio. **Calendar:** Semester, extensive summer session. **Full-time faculty:** 572 total; 19% have terminal degrees, 66% minority, 41% women. **Part-time faculty:** 400 total; 6% have terminal degrees, 76% minority, 54% women. **Class size:** 55% < 20, 43% 20-39, less than 1% 40-49, less than 1% 50-99. **Special facilities:** Center for performing arts.

Student profile.

Out-of-state:	4%	25 or older:	17%

Transfer out. Colleges most students transferred to 2015: University of Texas-Pan American, University of Texas-Brownsville, Texas A&M University Kingsville, University of Texas-San Antonio, Texas A&M University.

Basis for selection. Open admission, but selective for some programs. Nursing and allied health programs determine admissions based on an internal ranking system which factors GPA for all coursework including prerequisite courses, GPA for all non-native coursework, and test scores including college entrance exams and college placement tests. **Home schooled:** Transcript of courses and grades required. **Learning Disabled:** Accommodations made for ADA students upon request and documentation of services needed. No special admission requirements.

2015-2016 Annual costs. Tuition/fees: $3,480; $3,753 out-of-district; $4,470 out-of-state. Books/supplies: $1,200. Personal expenses: $1,400.

Financial aid. Need-based: Need-based aid available for part-time students. Work-study available nights, weekends and for part-time students. **Non-need-based:** Scholarships awarded for academics.

Application procedures. Admission: No deadline. No application fee. Admission notification on a rolling basis. **Financial aid:** Priority date 3/15; no closing date. FAFSA required. Applicants notified on a rolling basis starting 4/15.

Academics. Special study options: Accelerated study, cooperative education, distance learning, double major, dual enrollment of high school students, ESL, honors, independent study, internships, study abroad, weekend college. Bachelor's degree programs available on campus. License preparation in nursing, occupational therapy, paramedic, physical therapy, radiology, real estate. **Credit/placement by examination:** AP, CLEP, IB, institutional tests. **Support services:** GED test center, learning center, remedial instruction, study skills assistance, tutoring, writing center.

Majors. Architecture: Technology. **Area/ethnic studies:** Chicano/Hispanic-American/Latino. **Biology:** General. **Business:** Accounting, banking/financial services, business admin, logistics, marketing, office management. **Computer sciences:** General, applications programming, computer science, networking, security, support specialist, web page design, webmaster. **Education:** Early childhood, elementary, middle, secondary. **Engineering:** General. **English:** English lit. **Foreign languages:** Sign language interpretation, Spanish. **Health services:** EMT paramedic, health information technology, nursing assistant, occupational therapy assistant, office assistant, pharmacy assistant, physical therapy assistant, radiologic technology/medical imaging. **History:** General. **Liberal arts:** Arts/sciences. **Math:** General. **Parks/recreation:** Exercise sciences. **Philosophy/religion:** Philosophy. **Physical sciences:** Chemistry, physics. **Protective services:** Law enforcement admin. **Psychology:** General. **Social sciences:** General, political science. **Visual/performing arts:** General, music, studio arts. **Work/family studies:** Child development.

Most popular majors. Biological/life sciences 6%, business/marketing 10%, education 11%, health sciences 12%, liberal arts 21%, psychology 6%, security/protective services 10%.

Technology on campus. Online course registration, online library, helpline, wireless network available.

Student life. Freshman orientation: Available. Preregistration for classes offered. **Activities:** Bands, campus ministries, choral groups, dance, drama, film society, international student organizations, literary magazine, music ensembles, musical theater, student government.

Athletics. Intramural: Basketball, football (non-tackle), football (tackle), softball, volleyball. **Team name:** Jaguars.

Student services. Adult student services, alcohol/substance abuse counseling, career counseling, services for economically disadvantaged, student employment services, financial aid counseling, minority student services, on-campus daycare, personal counseling, placement for graduates, veterans' counselor, women's services. **Physically disabled:** Services for visually, speech, hearing impaired. **Transfer:** Pre-admission transcript evaluation for new students. Transfer center, transfer adviser, college fairs on campus for students transferring to 4-year colleges.

Contact. E-mail: admissions@southtexascollege.edu
Phone: (956) 872-8311 Toll-free number: (800) 742-7822
Fax: (956) 872-8321
Lazaro Barroso, Director of College Connections and Admisions, South Texas College, 3201 West Pecan Boulevard, McAllen, TX 78502

Southwest Texas Junior College
Uvalde, Texas
www.swtjc.edu   CB code: 6666

▶ Public 2-year community and junior college
▶ Commuter campus in large town

General. Founded in 1946. Regionally accredited. **Enrollment:** 5,608 degree-seeking undergraduates. **Degrees:** 568 associate awarded. **Location:** 80 miles from San Antonio, 70 miles from Del Rio. **Calendar:** Semester, limited summer session. **Full-time faculty:** 112 total. **Part-time faculty:** 62 total.

Student profile.

Part-time:	66%	25 or older:	18%
Out-of-state:	1%	Live on campus:	9%
Women:	58%		

Basis for selection. Open admission.

2015-2016 Annual costs. Tuition/fees: $2,617; $4,207 out-of-district; $5,107 out-of-state. Per-credit charge: $57 in-district; $110 out-of-district; $140 out-of-state. Room/board: $3,600. Books/supplies: $1,835. Personal expenses: $2,621.

Financial aid. Need-based: Need-based aid available for part-time students. Work-study available nights, weekends and for part-time students.

Application procedures. Admission: No deadline. No application fee. Admission notification on a rolling basis. **Financial aid:** Priority date 6/15; no closing date. FAFSA required. Applicants notified on a rolling basis starting 5/1; must reply within 2 week(s) of notification.

Academics. Special study options: Dual enrollment of high school students. License preparation in nursing, radiology. **Credit/placement by examination:** AP, CLEP. TASP required of all students for placement and counseling. **Support services:** GED preparation and test center, learning center, remedial instruction, study skills assistance, tutoring, writing center.

Majors. Business: Administrative services, management information systems, office technology. **Computer sciences:** General, data processing. **Education:** General. **Health services:** Licensed practical nurse, nursing (RN). **Liberal arts:** Arts/sciences.

Technology on campus. 150 workstations in dormitories, library, computer center. Dormitories wired for high-speed internet access and linked to campus network. Commuter students can connect to campus network. Online library, helpline available.

Student life. Freshman orientation: Mandatory. Preregistration for classes offered. **Housing:** Coed dorms, single-sex dorms available. **Activities:** Drama, literary magazine, music ensembles, student government, student newspaper.

Athletics. Intercollegiate: Basketball, rodeo. **Intramural:** Baseball M, basketball, golf, racquetball, softball, swimming, tennis, volleyball. **Team name:** Cowboys.

Student services. Adult student services, chaplain/spiritual director, career counseling, services for economically disadvantaged, student employment services, financial aid counseling, health services, minority student services, on-campus daycare, personal counseling, placement for graduates, veterans' counselor. **Physically disabled:** Services for visually, hearing

impaired. **Transfer:** Pre-admission transcript evaluation for new students. Transfer adviser, college fairs on campus for students transferring to 4-year colleges.

Contact. E-mail: admoffice@swtjc.edu
Phone: (830) 278-4401 ext. 7255 Fax: (830) 591-7396
Luis Fernandez, Registrar, Southwest Texas Junior College, 2401 Garner Field Road, Uvalde, TX 78801

St. Philip's College
San Antonio, Texas
www.alamo.edu/spc   CB code: 6642

▶ Public 2-year community college
▶ Commuter campus in very large city

General. Founded in 1898. Regionally accredited. Some courses held at off-campus sites throughout San Antonio. **Enrollment:** 10,739 degree-seeking undergraduates. **Degrees:** 931 associate awarded. **ROTC:** Army. **Location:** 1 mile from downtown San Antonio. **Calendar:** Semester, extensive summer session. **Full-time faculty:** 168 total; 12% have terminal degrees, 45% minority, 46% women. **Part-time faculty:** 230 total; 9% have terminal degrees, 43% minority, 50% women. **Class size:** 55% < 20, 41% 20-39, 4% 40-49, less than 1% 50-99. **Special facilities:** Restaurant on campus run by hospitality students, human patient simulator, diesel lab. **Partnerships:** Formal partnerships with Boeing and Dee Howard for aircraft technology training.

Student profile. Among degree-seeking undergraduates, 35% enrolled in a transfer program, 65% enrolled in a vocational program.

Out-of-state:	1%	25 or older:	37%

Transfer out. Colleges most students transferred to 2015: University of Texas at San Antonio, Texas State University.

Basis for selection. Open admission, but selective for some programs. Special requirements for nursing and certain allied health programs. **Adult students:** Students age 65 and older do not have to test if they are auditing classes. **Home schooled:** Transcript of courses and grades required.

2015-2016 Annual costs. Tuition/fees: $2,088; $5,550 out-of-district; $10,740 out-of-state. Books/supplies: $2,200. Personal expenses: $2,998.

2014-2015 Financial aid. All financial aid based on need. 74% of total undergraduate aid awarded as scholarships/grants, 26% as loans/jobs. Need-based aid available for part-time students. Work-study available nights, weekends and for part-time students.

Application procedures. Admission: No deadline. No application fee. **Financial aid:** No deadline. FAFSA required.

Academics. Special study options: Accelerated study, cooperative education, cross-registration, distance learning, double major, dual enrollment of high school students, ESL, honors, independent study, internships, study abroad, weekend college. License preparation in aviation, nursing, occupational therapy, physical therapy, radiology, real estate. **Credit/placement by examination:** AP, CLEP, institutional tests. 32 credit hours maximum toward associate degree. **Support services:** GED preparation and test center, learning center, pre-admission summer program, reduced course load, remedial instruction, study skills assistance, tutoring, writing center.

Majors. Biology: General. **Business:** General, accounting, accounting technology, administrative services, business admin, hotel/motel admin, office technology, office/clerical, tourism/travel. **Communications:** General, communications/speech/rhetoric, journalism, media studies. **Communications technology:** Animation/special effects. **Computer sciences:** General, computer science, data entry, information systems, LAN/WAN management, networking, programming, security, system admin, web page design, webmaster. **Conservation:** Environmental science. **Education:** General, early childhood, multi-level teacher, secondary. **Engineering:** Mechanical. **English:** English lit, rhetoric/composition. **Foreign languages:** General, Spanish. **General:** Carpentry, electrician. **Health services:** General, clinical lab technology, facilities admin, health information technology, histologic assistant, medical assistant, medical secretary, nursing (RN), occupational therapy assistant, physical therapy assistant, predental, premedicine, prenursing, prepharmacy, radiologic technology/medical imaging, respiratory therapy technology, sonography. **History:** General. **Human services:** Social work. **Liberal arts:** Arts/sciences, humanities. **Math:** General, statistics. **Parks/recreation:** Exercise sciences, health/fitness. **Philosophy/religion:** Philosophy. **Physical sciences:** General, chemistry, geology, physics. **Protective services:** Criminal justice, police science. **Psychology:** General. **Social sciences:** Economics, political science, sociology, urban studies. **Visual/performing arts:** Art, dance, design, dramatic, illustration, music, studio arts. **Work/family studies:** Child development.

Most popular majors. Business/marketing 7%, engineering/engineering technologies 6%, health sciences 24%, liberal arts 24%, personal/culinary services 9%, trade and industry 14%.

Technology on campus. 2,994 workstations in library, computer center. Commuter students can connect to campus network. Online course registration, online library, helpline, repair service available.

Student life. Freshman orientation: Mandatory. Preregistration for classes offered. **Activities:** Jazz band, campus ministries, choral groups, dance, drama, international student organizations, literary magazine, music ensembles, musical theater, student government, African-American Men on the Move, Student Government Association, Phi Theta Kappa, Future United Latino Leaders of Change.

Athletics. Intercollegiate: Basketball. **Intramural:** Basketball, volleyball. **Team name:** Tigers.

Student services. Adult student services, chaplain/spiritual director, career counseling, services for economically disadvantaged, student employment services, financial aid counseling, health services, on-campus daycare, personal counseling, placement for graduates, veterans' counselor. **Physically disabled:** Services for visually, hearing impaired. **Transfer:** Transfer center, transfer adviser, college fairs on campus for students transferring to 4-year colleges.

Contact. E-mail: bbutler@alamo.edu
Phone: (210) 486-2300 Fax: (210) 486-2836
Beautrice Butler, Director of Enrollment Management, St. Philip's College, 1801 Martin Luther King Drive, San Antonio, TX 78203

Tarrant County College
Fort Worth, Texas
www.tccd.edu

CB member
CB code: 6834

- Public 2-year community college
- Commuter campus in very large city

General. Founded in 1965. Regionally accredited. Five campuses located within Tarrant County: South, Northwest, and Trinity River Campuses in Fort Worth; Northeast Campus in Hurst; and Southeast Campus in Arlington. **Enrollment:** 52,613 degree-seeking undergraduates. **Degrees:** 5,323 associate awarded. **ROTC:** Army, Air Force. **Calendar:** Semester, extensive summer session. **Full-time faculty:** 663 total; 29% minority, 56% women. **Part-time faculty:** 1,508 total; 28% minority, 53% women.

Student profile.

Out-of-state: 1% **25 or older:**   35%

Transfer out. Colleges most students transferred to 2015: University of Texas at Arlington, University of North Texas, Texas Woman's University, Texas Tech University, Texas State University.

Basis for selection. Open admission, but selective for some programs. Special requirements for nursing and allied health programs, and certain automotive programs; must submit separate application and meet highly selective admission criteria. All new-to-college students are required to take a placement test to determine college readiness in reading, writing, and mathematics before enrolling in restricted courses. Interview and essay may be required for selective admission programs.

2016-2017 Annual costs. Tuition/fees: $1,770; $3,180 out-of-district; $7,650 out-of-state. Per-credit charge: $59 in-district; $106 out-of-district; $255 out-of-state. Books/supplies: $1,559. Personal expenses: $2,015.

2014-2015 Financial aid. Need-based: 71% of total undergraduate aid awarded as scholarships/grants, 29% as loans/jobs. Need-based aid available for part-time students. Work-study available nights, weekends and for part-time students. **Non-need-based:** Scholarships awarded for academics.

Application procedures. Admission: Closing date 8/15 (receipt date). No application fee. Admission notification on a rolling basis. There is a deadline for International applicants. Applicants 18 years of age or older without high school diploma may be admitted on individual basis. **Financial aid:** Priority date 5/1; no closing date. FAFSA, institutional form required. Applicants notified on a rolling basis starting 5/1; must reply within 2 week(s) of notification.

Academics. Core curriculum guaranteed to transfer to any Texas public university. **Special study options:** Distance learning, double major, dual enrollment of high school students, ESL, honors, liberal arts/career combination, weekend college. Saturday classes available. License preparation in aviation, dental hygiene, nursing, paramedic, physical therapy, radiology, real estate. **Credit/placement by examination:** AP, CLEP, institutional tests.

18 credit hours maximum toward associate degree. **Support services:** GED preparation and test center, learning center, pre-admission summer program, reduced course load, remedial instruction, study skills assistance, tutoring, writing center.

Majors. Business: General, accounting technology, administrative services, business admin, hospitality admin, logistics, operations, real estate, tourism/travel, transportation. **Communications technology:** Radio/TV. **Computer sciences:** General, networking. **Education:** Early childhood, middle, secondary. **Engineering:** General. **Foreign languages:** Sign language interpretation. **Health services:** Dental hygiene, dietetic technician, dietician assistant, EMT paramedic, health information technology, mental health services, nursing (RN), physical therapy assistant, radiologic technology/medical imaging, respiratory therapy technology. **Liberal arts:** Library assistant. **Protective services:** Criminal justice, fire safety technology. **Social sciences:** GIS/cartography. **Visual/performing arts:** Commercial/advertising art. **Work/family studies:** Child development.

Most popular majors. Health sciences 7%, liberal arts 77%.

Technology on campus. 6,600 workstations in library, computer center, student center. Commuter students can connect to campus network. Online course registration, online library, wireless network available.

Student life. Freshman orientation: Mandatory. Preregistration for classes offered. 1-2 hours, held intermittently. **Activities:** Bands, choral groups, dance, drama, international student organizations, literary magazine, music ensembles, student government, student newspaper.

Athletics. Intramural: Basketball M, table tennis.

Student services. Adult student services, career counseling, services for economically disadvantaged, student employment services, financial aid counseling, health services, minority student services, personal counseling, placement for graduates, veterans' counselor. **Physically disabled:** Services for visually, speech, hearing impaired. **Transfer:** College fairs on campus for students transferring to 4-year colleges.

Contact. E-mail: online.admissions@tccd.edu
Phone: (817) 515-1580 Fax: (817) 515-0624
Nichole Mancone, District Director of Admissions & Records, Tarrant County College, 300 Trinity Campus Circle, Fort Worth, TX 76102-1964

Temple College
Temple, Texas
www.templejc.edu

CB code: 6818

- Public 2-year community college
- Commuter campus in small city

General. Founded in 1926. Regionally accredited. **Enrollment:** 4,874 degree-seeking undergraduates. **Degrees:** 500 associate awarded. **Location:** 65 miles from Austin. **Calendar:** Semester, limited summer session. **Full-time faculty:** 121 total. **Part-time faculty:** 173 total. **Class size:** 51% < 20, 48% 20-39, less than 1% 40-49, 1% 50-99. **Special facilities:** Health sciences simulation center. **Partnerships:** Formal partnerships with area high schools for tech prep programs.

Student profile.

Out-of-state: 1% **25 or older:**   38%

Transfer out. Colleges most students transferred to 2015: Texas A&M University, Texas A&M - Central Texas, Tarleton State University, Texas State University, University of Texas at Austin, University of Mary Hardin-Baylor.

Basis for selection. Open admission, but selective for some programs. Limited enrollment in allied health programs; interview required. **Home schooled:** Transcript of courses and grades required.

High school preparation. College-preparatory program required. 23 units recommended. Recommended units include English 4, mathematics 3, social studies 2, history 2, science 3, foreign language 2 and academic electives 7.

2015-2016 Annual costs. Tuition/fees: $2,670; $4,770 out-of-district; $7,170 out-of-state. Per-credit charge: $89 in-district; $159 out-of-district; $239 out-of-state. Books/supplies: $1,329. Personal expenses: $1,658.

Financial aid. All financial aid based on need. Need-based aid available for part-time students. Work-study available nights, weekends and for part-time students.

Application procedures. Admission: No deadline. No application fee. Admission notification on a rolling basis. **Financial aid:** Priority date 6/1;

no closing date. FAFSA required. Applicants notified on a rolling basis starting 5/1; must reply within 4 week(s) of notification.

Academics. Special study options: Accelerated study, cooperative education, distance learning, dual enrollment of high school students, honors, internships. License preparation in dental hygiene, nursing, paramedic. **Credit/placement by examination:** AP, CLEP, IB, institutional tests. 32 credit hours maximum toward associate degree. Last 18 hours or total 32 hours earned in residence may not be earned through credit by examination. **Support services:** GED preparation, learning center, remedial instruction, study skills assistance, tutoring, writing center.

Majors. Biology: General. **Business:** General, office management. **Computer sciences:** General, data entry, LAN/WAN management, programming, system admin, webmaster. **Education:** Elementary, teacher assistance. **Engineering:** General. **Health services:** Dental hygiene, EMT paramedic, nursing (RN), respiratory therapy technology, sonography. **Human services:** Social work. **Liberal arts:** Arts/sciences. **Math:** General. **Protective services:** Criminal justice. **Social sciences:** GIS/cartography. **Visual/performing arts:** Art, music. **Work/family studies:** Child development.

Most popular majors. Business/marketing 14%, health sciences 26%, liberal arts 39%.

Technology on campus. 150 workstations in dormitories, library, computer center, student center. Dormitories wired for high-speed internet access and linked to campus network. Commuter students can connect to campus network. Online library, helpline, repair service, wireless network available.

Student life. Freshman orientation: Available. Preregistration for classes offered. Held prior to fall semester; 4 hours over 2 days. **Housing:** Apartments available. Privately run student apartments on campus. **Activities:** Bands, campus ministries, choral groups, dance, drama, literary magazine, music ensembles, musical theater, student government, symphony orchestra, Black American Cultural Club, Society of Latin American Cultures, College Republicans, Young Democrats, Literary Club, Baptist Student Ministries.

Athletics. NJCAA. **Intercollegiate:** Baseball M, basketball, softball W, tennis, volleyball W. **Intramural:** Basketball, bowling, football (non-tackle), golf, racquetball, soccer, softball, swimming, table tennis, tennis, volleyball. **Team name:** Leopards.

Student services. Adult student services, career counseling, services for economically disadvantaged, student employment services, financial aid counseling, personal counseling, placement for graduates, veterans' counselor. **Physically disabled:** Services for visually, hearing impaired. **Transfer:** Pre-admission transcript evaluation for new students. Transfer adviser, college fairs on campus for students transferring to 4-year colleges.

Contact. E-mail: carey.rose@templejc.edu
Phone: (254) 298-8300 Toll-free number: (800) 460-4636
Fax: (254) 298-8288
Carey Rose, Director of Admission and Records, Temple College, 2600 South First Street, Temple, TX 76504-7435

Texarkana College
Texarkana, Texas
www.texarkanacollege.edu
CB code: 6819

- Public 2-year community college
- Commuter campus in small city

General. Founded in 1927. Regionally accredited. **Enrollment:** 1,386 full-time, degree-seeking students. **Degrees:** 383 associate awarded. **Location:** 80 miles from Shreveport, Louisiana; 120 miles from Little Rock, Arkansas; 180 miles from Dallas. **Calendar:** Semester, extensive summer session. **Full-time faculty:** 89 total. **Part-time faculty:** 94 total. **Special facilities:** Campus wetlands, outdoor classroom.

Student profile. Among full-time, degree-seeking students, 78% enrolled in a transfer program, 22% enrolled in a vocational program.

Out-of-state:	20%	Live on campus:	1%
25 or older:	38%		

Transfer out. Colleges most students transferred to 2015: Texas A&M at Texarkana, Southern Arkansas University.

Basis for selection. Open admission. Interview recommended for nursing program. **Adult students:** Placement testing through the Texas Success Initiative (TSI) Assessment unless eligible for an exemption or waiver.

2015-2016 Annual costs. Tuition/fees: $2,420; $3,890 out-of-district; $5,300 out-of-state. Per-credit charge: $48 in-district; $97 out-of-district; $144 out-of-state. Books/supplies: $1,205. Personal expenses: $1,952.

2014-2015 Financial aid. Need-based: 70% of total undergraduate aid awarded as scholarships/grants, 30% as loans/jobs. Need-based aid available for part-time students. Work-study available nights, weekends and for part-time students. **Non-need-based:** Scholarships awarded for academics, art, music/drama.

Application procedures. Admission: No deadline. No application fee. Admission notification on a rolling basis. **Financial aid:** Priority date 7/24; no closing date. FAFSA, institutional form required. Applicants notified on a rolling basis starting 3/1.

Academics. Special study options: Cooperative education, cross-registration, distance learning, dual enrollment of high school students, honors, internships, liberal arts/career combination. License preparation in nursing, paramedic. **Credit/placement by examination:** AP, CLEP, IB. 14 credit hours maximum toward associate degree. **Support services:** GED test center, learning center, pre-admission summer program, remedial instruction, study skills assistance, tutoring.

Majors. Biology: General. **Business:** General, administrative services, business admin, marketing. **Communications:** Journalism. **Computer sciences:** General. **Engineering:** General. **Foreign languages:** General. **Health services:** EMT paramedic, nursing (RN), substance abuse counseling. **History:** General. **Liberal arts:** Humanities. **Math:** General. **Physical sciences:** Chemistry, physics. **Protective services:** Criminal justice, law enforcement admin. **Social sciences:** General, political science. **Visual/performing arts:** Art, dramatic, music. **Work/family studies:** Child development.

Most popular majors. Health sciences 13%, liberal arts 53%.

Technology on campus. 500 workstations in library, computer center. Commuter students can connect to campus network. Online course registration, online library, helpline, wireless network available.

Student life. Freshman orientation: Mandatory, $20 fee. Preregistration for classes offered. **Housing:** Apartments available. $150 fully refundable deposit, deadline 5/1. **Activities:** Concert band, campus ministries, choral groups, drama, musical theater, radio station, student government, student newspaper, Baptist student union, Black student association, 21st century Democrats, Young Republicans, Earth club.

Athletics. NJCAA. **Intramural:** Basketball, football (non-tackle), racquetball, soccer, tennis, volleyball. **Team name:** Bulldogs.

Student services. Career counseling, student employment services, financial aid counseling, personal counseling, veterans' counselor. **Physically disabled:** Services for visually, speech, hearing impaired. **Transfer:** Transfer center, transfer adviser, college fairs on campus for students transferring to 4-year colleges.

Contact. E-mail: admissions@texarkanacollege.edu
Phone: (903) 823-3012 Fax: (903) 823-3451
Lee Williams, Director of Admissions, Texarkana College, 2500 North Robison Road, Texarkana, TX 75599

Texas State Technical College
Waco, Texas
www.tstc.edu
CB code: 6328

- Public 2-year technical college
- Residential campus in small city

General. Founded in 1965. Regionally accredited. **Enrollment:** 8,160 degree-seeking undergraduates; 3,156 non-degree-seeking students. **Degrees:** 1,634 associate awarded. **Location:** 90 miles from Dallas, 99 miles from Austin. **Calendar:** Semester, extensive summer session. **Full-time faculty:** 523 total. **Part-time faculty:** 135 total. **Special facilities:** Advanced manufacturing center, 8,600-foot dual runway at TSTC-Waco airport, challenger learning centers, planetarium.

Student profile. Among degree-seeking undergraduates, 85% enrolled in a vocational program, 1% already have a bachelor's degree or higher, 1,625 enrolled as first-time, first-year students.

Part-time:	54%	Asian American:	1%
Women:	34%	Hispanic/Latino:	50%
African American:	7%		

Basis for selection. Open admission. Aircraft pilot training, dental assistant technology, and pharmacy technician students must provide updated immunization data to be admitted and to register. Aircraft pilot training students must provide a current Class II Medical certificate to be eligible to register; fall start only. ACCUPLACER or THEA test required prior to enrollment; used for placement purposes only. Interview required for students who indicate felony charges. **Home schooled:** Transcript of courses and grades required.

2015-2016 Annual costs. Tuition/fees: $4,434; $9,660 out-of-state. Room/board: $5,370.

Financial aid. All financial aid based on need. Need-based aid available for part-time students. Work-study available nights, weekends and for part-time students.

Application procedures. Admission: No deadline. No application fee. Admission notification on a rolling basis. **Financial aid:** Priority date 6/1; no closing date. FAFSA required. Applicants notified on a rolling basis starting 5/15.

Academics. Special study options: Cooperative education, distance learning, double major, dual enrollment of high school students. License preparation in aviation, dental hygiene, nursing, paramedic. **Credit/placement by examination:** AP, CLEP, IB, institutional tests. 24 credit hours maximum toward associate degree. **Support services:** GED test center, learning center, remedial instruction, study skills assistance, tutoring.

Majors. Communications technology: Animation/special effects. **Computer sciences:** LAN/WAN management, programming, security, system admin, web page design. **Visual/performing arts:** Commercial/advertising art, game design, graphic design.

Technology on campus. 1,000 workstations in library, computer center, student center. Dormitories wired for high-speed internet access and linked to campus network. Commuter students can connect to campus network. Online course registration, online library, helpline, repair service, student web hosting, wireless network available.

Student life. Freshman orientation: Mandatory. Preregistration for classes offered. Held prior to semester. **Housing:** Coed dorms, special housing for disabled, apartments, wellness housing available. $150 fully refundable deposit. Duplexes and houses available to married students or students with families. **Activities:** Campus ministries, student government, student newspaper.

Athletics. Intramural: Basketball, football (non-tackle), golf, racquetball, softball, volleyball. **Team name:** Tornadoes.

Student services. Adult student services, career counseling, student employment services, financial aid counseling, health services, personal counseling, placement for graduates, veterans' counselor, women's services. **Physically disabled:** Services for visually, speech, hearing impaired. **Transfer:** Pre-admission transcript evaluation for new students. Transfer adviser for students transferring to 4-year colleges.

Contact. Phone: (254) 867-2361
Toll-free number: (800) 792-8784 ext. 2361 Fax: (254) 867-2250
Mary Daniel, Director of Admissions and Records/Registrar, Texas State Technical College, 3801 Campus Drive, Waco, TX 76705

Texas State Technical College: Harlingen
Harlingen, Texas
www.tstc.edu/
CB code: 6843

‣ Public 2-year technical college
‣ Commuter campus in small city

General. Founded in 1969. Regionally accredited. **Enrollment:** 3,022 degree-seeking undergraduates; 1,767 non-degree-seeking students. **Degrees:** 515 associate awarded. **Location:** 25 miles from Brownsville, 30 miles from South Padre Island. **Calendar:** Semester, extensive summer session. **Full-time faculty:** 160 total; 7% have terminal degrees, 69% minority, 39% women. **Part-time faculty:** 32 total; 16% have terminal degrees, 50% minority, 59% women. **Class size:** 44% < 20, 50% 20-39, 2% 40-49, 3% 50-99, less than 1% >100. **Special facilities:** Motors lab for aviation technology, aviation hangars, agricultural pavilion, industrial labs, challenger learning center.

Student profile. Among degree-seeking undergraduates, 10% enrolled in a transfer program, 70% enrolled in a vocational program, 1% already have a bachelor's degree or higher, 559 enrolled as first-time, first-year students.

Part-time:	62%	African American:	1%
Out-of-state:	1%	Hispanic/Latino:	89%
Women:	51%		

Transfer out. Colleges most students transferred to 2015: UTRGV Brownsville, UTRGV Edinburg, South Texas College, Texas Southmost College, University of Texas-San Antonio.

Basis for selection. Open admission, but selective for some programs. Competitive admissions for dental assisting, surgical technology, dental hygiene, and health information technology programs. Associate degree candidates required to take state-mandated Texas Academic Skills Program. Results used only for placement. SAT/ACT scores may be substituted. **Home schooled:** Statement describing home school structure and mission required.

2015-2016 Annual costs. Tuition/fees: $4,434; $9,660 out-of-state. Room/board: $4,270. Books/supplies: $1,009. Personal expenses: $1,839.

2015-2016 Financial aid. Need-based: 86% of total undergraduate aid awarded as scholarships/grants, 14% as loans/jobs. Need-based aid available for part-time students. Work-study available nights, weekends and for part-time students.

Application procedures. Admission: No deadline. No application fee. Admission notification on a rolling basis. **Financial aid:** Priority date 3/1; no closing date. FAFSA, institutional form required. Applicants notified on a rolling basis.

Academics. Special study options: Cooperative education, distance learning, dual enrollment of high school students, ESL, honors, internships, liberal arts/career combination, teacher certification program, weekend college. License preparation in aviation, dental hygiene, nursing. **Credit/placement by examination:** AP, CLEP, institutional tests. **Support services:** GED preparation and test center, learning center, remedial instruction, study skills assistance, tutoring.

Majors. Biology: General. **Business:** Administrative services, executive assistant. **Computer sciences:** Information technology, networking, programming. **Education:** Teacher assistance. **Engineering:** General. **Health services:** Dental hygiene, dental lab technology, health information technology, medical assistant, surgical technology. **Math:** General. **Physical sciences:** Physics. **Visual/performing arts:** Commercial/advertising art.

Most popular majors. Biological/life sciences 12%, business/marketing 7%, education 8%, engineering/engineering technologies 23%, health sciences 20%, personal/culinary services 6%, trade and industry 12%.

Technology on campus. 1,850 workstations in library, computer center, student center. Online library, helpline available.

Student life. Freshman orientation: Mandatory. Preregistration for classes offered. **Housing:** Guaranteed on-campus for all undergraduates. Special housing for disabled, apartments available. $100 deposit. **Activities:** Campus ministries, dance, student government.

Athletics. Intramural: Basketball, football (non-tackle), racquetball, soccer, softball, table tennis, volleyball. **Team name:** Mustangs.

Student services. Alcohol/substance abuse counseling, career counseling, student employment services, financial aid counseling, health services, on-campus daycare, personal counseling, placement for graduates, veterans' counselor, women's services. **Physically disabled:** Services for visually, speech, hearing impaired. **Transfer:** Pre-admission transcript evaluation for new students. Transfer adviser for students transferring to 4-year colleges.

Contact. E-mail: lenora.yanez@harlingen.tstc.edu
Phone: (956) 364-4101 Toll-free number: (800) 852-8784
Fax: (956) 364-5117
Lenora Yanez, Registrar, Texas State Technical College: Harlingen, 1902 North Loop 499, Harlingen, TX 78550-3697

Texas State Technical College: Marshall
Marshall, Texas
www.marshall.tstc.edu

‣ Public 2-year technical college
‣ Large town

General. Regionally accredited. **Enrollment:** 492 degree-seeking undergraduates. **Degrees:** 1,638 associate awarded. **Location:** 150 miles from Dallas, 230 miles from Houston. **Calendar:** Semester, extensive summer session. **Full-time faculty:** 30 total. **Part-time faculty:** 17 total.

Basis for selection. Open admission. Admission tests used only for placement.

2015-2016 Annual costs. Tuition/fees: $4,434; $9,660 out-of-state. Room only: $2,410.

Financial aid. Need-based: Work-study available nights, weekends and for part-time students.

Two-Year Colleges

Application procedures. Admission: Closing date 8/2. No application fee. Admission notification on a rolling basis. **Financial aid:** Priority date 6/1; no closing date. FAFSA required.

Academics. Credit/placement by examination: AP, CLEP.

Majors. Business: E-commerce. **Communications technology:** General. **Computer sciences:** Artificial intelligence, LAN/WAN management, networking. **Health services:** Environmental health.

Student life. Freshman orientation: Mandatory, $15 fee. Preregistration for classes offered. **Activities:** Student newspaper.

Contact. Phone: (903) 935-1010
Patricia Robbins, Director of Admissions, Texas State Technical College: Marshall, 2650 East End Boulevard South, Marshall, TX 75672

Texas State Technical College: West Texas
Sweetwater, Texas
www.westtexas.tstc.edu   CB code: 3137

- Public 2-year technical college
- Commuter campus in large town

General. Founded in 1970. Regionally accredited. Additional campuses in Sweetwater, Abilene, Breckenridge, Brownwood. **Enrollment:** 897 degree-seeking undergraduates. **Degrees:** 203 associate awarded. **Location:** 50 miles from Abilene. **Calendar:** Trimester, limited summer session. **Full-time faculty:** 65 total. **Part-time faculty:** 14 total. **Special facilities:** Aero engineering facility at regional airport, ambulance simulator, robotics lab, wind tower. **Partnerships:** Formal partnership with Florida Power & Light Energy for development of TSTC West Texas' Wind Energy Technology Program.

Student profile.

Out-of-state:	1%	Live on campus:	16%
25 or older:	44%		

Basis for selection. Open admission, but selective for some programs. Certain programs may require background checks, driving records, physicals, etc.

2015-2016 Annual costs. Tuition/fees: $4,434; $9,660 out-of-state. Room/board: $5,280. Books/supplies: $1,100. Personal expenses: $650.

Financial aid. Need-based: Need-based aid available for part-time students. Work-study available nights, weekends and for part-time students. **Non-need-based:** Scholarships awarded for academics, leadership.

Application procedures. Admission: Priority date 8/1; no deadline. No application fee. Admission notification on a rolling basis. Application deadline is 45 days prior to start of semester. **Financial aid:** Priority date 5/1, closing date 7/1. FAFSA, institutional form required. Applicants notified on a rolling basis starting 7/1.

Academics. Special study options: Cooperative education, cross-registration, distance learning, dual enrollment of high school students, internships, liberal arts/career combination. 1-1 and 1-1-2 electronics technology programs with numerous area institutions. License preparation in aviation, nursing, paramedic. **Credit/placement by examination:** AP, CLEP, institutional tests. Varies per program and individual student. **Support services:** Learning center, reduced course load, remedial instruction, study skills assistance, tutoring.

Majors. Business: Management information systems. **Communications technology:** General. **Computer sciences:** Networking, programming, web page design. **Conservation:** Environmental science. **Health services:** EMT paramedic, health information technology, licensed practical nurse, substance abuse counseling. **Visual/performing arts:** Design.

Technology on campus. 50 workstations in library, student center. Dormitories wired for high-speed internet access. Commuter students can connect to campus network. Online library, helpline, wireless network available.

Student life. Freshman orientation: Mandatory. Preregistration for classes offered. Held day before start of classes. **Housing:** Coed dorms, special housing for disabled, apartments, wellness housing available. $150 deposit. **Activities:** Student government, Baptist student union, SGA, SkillsUSA, PTK, AutoTech, welding club, diesel club.

Athletics. Intramural: Basketball, bowling, golf, softball, swimming, table tennis, tennis, volleyball.

Student services. Alcohol/substance abuse counseling, career counseling, services for economically disadvantaged, student employment services, financial aid counseling, health services, personal counseling, placement for graduates, veterans' counselor, women's services. **Physically disabled:** Services for hearing impaired. **Transfer:** Transfer adviser, college fairs on campus for students transferring to 4-year colleges.

Contact. E-mail: marisol.solis@tstc.edu
Phone: (325) 235-7300 Fax: (325) 235-7416
Janyth Ussery, Director of Admissions & Records, Texas State Technical College: West Texas, 300 Homer K Taylor Drive, Sweetwater, TX 79556

Trinity Valley Community College
Athens, Texas
www.tvcc.edu   CB code: 6271

- Public 2-year community college
- Commuter campus in large town

General. Founded in 1946. Regionally accredited. 3 extension centers in state. **Enrollment:** 6,254 degree-seeking undergraduates; 607 non-degree-seeking students. **Degrees:** 984 associate awarded. **Location:** 70 miles from Dallas. **Calendar:** Semester, limited summer session. **Special facilities:** 2 operating ranches with more than 500 acres.

Student profile. Among degree-seeking undergraduates, 690 enrolled as first-time, first-year students.

Part-time:	69%	Women:	59%

Basis for selection. Open admission, but selective for some programs. Institution observes all TASP requirements. Special requirements for nursing program.

High school preparation. College-preparatory program recommended.

2015-2016 Annual costs. Tuition/fees: $2,340; $4,110 out-of-district; $4,680 out-of-state. Per-credit charge: $34 in-district; $93 out-of-district; $112 out-of-state. Room/board: $5,580.

Financial aid. Need-based: Need-based aid available for part-time students. Work-study available nights, weekends and for part-time students. **Non-need-based:** Scholarships awarded for academics, athletics.

Application procedures. Admission: No deadline. No application fee. Admission notification on a rolling basis. **Financial aid:** Closing date 7/1. FAFSA, institutional form required. Applicants notified on a rolling basis starting 7/1; must reply within 2 week(s) of notification.

Academics. Special study options: Distance learning, dual enrollment of high school students, honors, internships, liberal arts/career combination. **Credit/placement by examination:** AP, CLEP. 18 credit hours maximum toward associate degree. **Support services:** GED preparation and test center, learning center, remedial instruction, tutoring.

Majors. Biology: General. **Business:** Accounting, administrative services, business admin, office technology. **Communications:** Communications/speech/rhetoric, journalism. **Computer sciences:** General, computer graphics, data processing, programming. **Education:** General, early childhood, elementary, middle. **Engineering:** General, polymer. **English:** English lit, rhetoric/composition. **Foreign languages:** Spanish. **Health services:** Nursing (RN), predental, premedicine, prenursing, prepharmacy, preveterinary. **Liberal arts:** Arts/sciences. **Math:** General. **Parks/recreation:** Health/fitness. **Physical sciences:** Chemistry, physics. **Protective services:** Firefighting, law enforcement admin. **Psychology:** General. **Social sciences:** General, sociology. **Visual/performing arts:** General, art, dramatic, music. **Work/family studies:** Child care management.

Student life. Freshman orientation: Available, $20 fee. Preregistration for classes offered. **Housing:** Single-sex dorms available. **Activities:** Bands, campus ministries, choral groups, dance, drama, international student organizations, music ensembles, student government, student newspaper, Baptist student union, nontraditional student organization, Phi Beta Kappa, criminal justice fraternity.

Athletics. NJCAA. **Intercollegiate:** Basketball, football (tackle) M. **Intramural:** Basketball, bowling, handball M, racquetball, soccer M, softball, table tennis, tennis, volleyball. **Team name:** Cardinals.

Student services. Career counseling, student employment services, personal counseling, placement for graduates, veterans' counselor. **Physically disabled:** Services for speech impaired. **Transfer:** Pre-admission transcript evaluation for new students. Transfer adviser, college fairs on campus for students transferring to 4-year colleges.

Two-Year Colleges

Contact. Phone: (903) 675-6357 Fax: (903) 675-6209
Colette Hilliard, Dean of Enrollment, Trinity Valley Community College, 100 Cardinal Drive, Athens, TX 75751

Tyler Junior College
Tyler, Texas
www.tjc.edu   **CB code: 6833**

- Public 2-year community and junior college
- Commuter campus in small city

General. Founded in 1926. Regionally accredited. **Enrollment:** 10,887 degree-seeking undergraduates; 47 non-degree-seeking students. **Degrees:** 1,438 associate awarded. **Location:** 85 miles from Dallas, 85 miles from Shreveport, Louisiana. **Calendar:** Semester, extensive summer session. **Full-time faculty:** 303 total; 14% have terminal degrees, 10% minority, 57% women. **Part-time faculty:** 250 total; 11% have terminal degrees, 13% minority, 64% women. **Class size:** 49% < 20, 45% 20-39, 5% 40-49, 2% 50-99, less than 1% >100. **Special facilities:** Planetarium, conservatory.

Student profile. Among degree-seeking undergraduates, 2,891 enrolled as first-time, first-year students, 716 transferred in from other institutions.

Part-time:	45%	Hispanic/Latino:	18%
Out-of-state:	2%	Multi-racial, non-Hispanic:	3%
Women:	59%	International:	1%
African American:	22%	25 or older:	25%
Asian American:	1%	Live on campus:	10%

Transfer out. Colleges most students transferred to 2015: Stephen F. Austin State University, Texas A&M University, University of Texas at Tyler.

Basis for selection. Open admission, but selective for some programs. Special requirements for allied health programs. Texas Higher Education Assessment (THEA) required by Texas law for all incoming students. Interview required for some allied health programs, recommended for others. **Home schooled:** Must complete equivalent of accepted high school diploma.

High school preparation. College-preparatory program recommended.

2015-2016 Annual costs. Tuition/fees: $2,352; $3,762 out-of-district; $4,362 out-of-state. Per-credit charge: $30 in-district; $77 out-of-district; $97 out-of-state. Room/board: $7,022. Books/supplies: $1,800. Personal expenses: $2,124.

2014-2015 Financial aid. Need-based: 2,089 full-time freshmen applied for aid; 1,612 deemed to have need; 1,597 received aid. Average need met was 57%. Average scholarship/grant was $4,042; average loan $2,003. 66% of total undergraduate aid awarded as scholarships/grants, 34% as loans/jobs. Need-based aid available for part-time students. Work-study available nights, weekends and for part-time students. **Non-need-based:** Awarded to 723 full-time undergraduates, including 452 freshmen. Scholarships awarded for academics, alumni affiliation, art, athletics, music/drama.

Application procedures. Admission: No deadline. No application fee. Admission notification on a rolling basis. When a room assignment is made, the room and meal plan charges are placed on the student's account. Charges are on a per semester basis. Before a student can move into a Residence Hall the charges must be paid or arrangements to pay must be made. **Financial aid:** Priority date 4/1, closing date 6/1. FAFSA, institutional form required. Applicants notified on a rolling basis starting 4/1; must reply within 2 week(s) of notification.

Academics. Special study options: Distance learning, honors, study abroad, teacher certification program. License preparation in dental hygiene, nursing, paramedic, radiology, real estate. **Credit/placement by examination:** AP, CLEP, IB, SAT, ACT, institutional tests. **Support services:** GED preparation and test center, learning center, remedial instruction, study skills assistance, tutoring.

Honors college/program. SAT 1070 (exclusive of Writing), minimum 500 Math and Verbal; ACT 23, minimum 19 in each area.

Majors. Biology: General. **Business:** General, accounting technology, administrative services, business admin, managerial economics, marketing, office management. **Communications:** Journalism. **Communications technology:** Graphic/printing. **Computer sciences:** General, applications programming, information systems, web page design. **Conservation:** Environmental science. **Education:** General, early childhood, special ed. **Engineering:** General. **English:** Rhetoric/composition. **Foreign languages:** General, sign language interpretation. **Health services:** Clinical lab assistant, dental hygiene, EMT ambulance attendant, EMT paramedic, health information technology, medical radiologic technology/radiation therapy, medical secretary, nursing (RN), office admin, ophthalmic lab technology, predental, premedicine, prenursing, prepharmacy, preveterinary, radiologic technology/

medical imaging, respiratory therapy technology, sonography, substance abuse counseling, surgical technology. **History:** General. **Human services:** General, social work. **Liberal arts:** Arts/sciences. **Math:** General. **Parks/recreation:** Exercise sciences, health/fitness. **Physical sciences:** Chemistry, geology, physics. **Protective services:** Criminal justice, fire safety technology, police science. **Psychology:** General. **Social sciences:** Sociology. **Visual/performing arts:** General, art, commercial/advertising art, dance, dramatic, music, music performance, studio arts. **Work/family studies:** Child care management.

Most popular majors. Business/marketing 7%, health sciences 24%, liberal arts 28%, security/protective services 6%.

Technology on campus. 95 workstations in library, computer center, student center. Dormitories wired for high-speed internet access. Commuter students can connect to campus network. Online course registration, online library, helpline, repair service, student web hosting, wireless network available.

Student life. Freshman orientation: Mandatory, $50 fee. Preregistration for classes offered. Held over 2 days in the summer. **Housing:** Coed dorms, single-sex dorms available. $100 nonrefundable deposit. **Activities:** Bands, campus ministries, choral groups, dance, drama, film society, international student organizations, literary magazine, music ensembles, musical theater, student government, student newspaper, symphony orchestra, TV station, Wesleyan Ministries, Phi Theta Kappa, Hispanic student organization.

Athletics. NAIA, NJCAA. **Intercollegiate:** Baseball M, basketball, cheerleading, football (tackle) M, golf, soccer, tennis, volleyball W. **Intramural:** Badminton, basketball, football (tackle) M, handball, racquetball, softball, table tennis, tennis, volleyball M. **Team name:** Apaches.

Student services. Adult student services, alcohol/substance abuse counseling, chaplain/spiritual director, career counseling, services for economically disadvantaged, student employment services, financial aid counseling, health services, personal counseling, placement for graduates, veterans' counselor, women's services. **Physically disabled:** Services for visually, speech, hearing impaired. **Transfer:** College fairs on campus for students transferring to 4-year colleges.

Contact. E-mail: admissions@tjc.edu
Phone: (903) 510-2523 Toll-free number: (800) 687-5680 ext. 2523
Nidia Hassan, Director of Admissions, Tyler Junior College, Box 9020, Tyler, TX 75711-9020

Vernon College
Vernon, Texas
www.vernoncollege.edu   **CB code: 6913**

- Public 2-year community and junior college
- Commuter campus in large town

General. Founded in 1970. Regionally accredited. **Enrollment:** 2,367 degree-seeking undergraduates. **Degrees:** 258 associate awarded. **Location:** 50 miles from Wichita Falls. **Calendar:** Semester, extensive summer session. **Full-time faculty:** 88 total. **Part-time faculty:** 65 total.

Student profile.

Out-of-state:	5%	Live on campus:	6%
25 or older:	49%		

Basis for selection. Open admission, but selective for some programs. Additional requirements for nursing and cosmetology applicants.

2015-2016 Annual costs. Tuition/fees: $2,640; $4,050 out-of-district; $6,000 out-of-state. Per-credit charge: $48 in-district; $95 out-of-district; $200 out-of-state. Room/board: $3,912. Books/supplies: $1,600. Personal expenses: $1,238.

2015-2016 Financial aid. All financial aid based on need. 65% of total undergraduate aid awarded as scholarships/grants, 35% as loans/jobs. Need-based aid available for part-time students. Work-study available nights, weekends and for part-time students.

Application procedures. Admission: No deadline. $10 fee. Admission notification on a rolling basis. **Financial aid:** Priority date 7/1; no closing date. FAFSA required. Applicants notified on a rolling basis starting 4/1.

Academics. Special study options: Cooperative education, distance learning, dual enrollment of high school students, internships. License preparation in aviation, nursing, paramedic, real estate. **Credit/placement by examination:** AP, CLEP, IB, institutional tests. **Support services:** GED test center, learning center, reduced course load, remedial instruction, study skills assistance, tutoring, writing center.

Majors. Business: General, accounting, administrative services, human resources, marketing, office technology. **Computer sciences:** Data processing. **Health services:** Nursing (RN). **Liberal arts:** Arts/sciences. **Protective services:** Criminal justice.

Technology on campus. 60 workstations in library, computer center. Dormitories wired for high-speed internet access. Online course registration available.

Student life. Freshman orientation: Available. Preregistration for classes offered. **Housing:** Single-sex dorms available. **Activities:** Choral groups, drama, music ensembles, musical theater, student government.

Athletics. NJCAA. **Intercollegiate:** Baseball M, rodeo, softball W, volleyball W. **Intramural:** Archery, badminton, baseball M, basketball, football (non-tackle), golf, handball, racquetball, softball, swimming, table tennis, tennis, track and field, volleyball. **Team name:** Chaparral.

Student services. Adult student services, career counseling, services for economically disadvantaged, student employment services, financial aid counseling, health services, personal counseling, placement for graduates, veterans' counselor. **Physically disabled:** Services for visually, speech, hearing impaired. **Transfer:** Transfer adviser for students transferring to 4-year colleges.

Contact. E-mail: sdavenport@vernoncollege.edu
Phone: (940) 552-6291 Fax: (940) 553-1753
Joe Hite, Dean of Admissions and Financial Aid/Registrar, Vernon College, 4400 College Drive, Vernon, TX 76384-4092

Vet Tech Institute of Houston
Houston, Texas
www.bradfordschools.com

- For-profit 2-year technical college
- Very large city
- Interview required

General. Regionally accredited; also accredited by ACICS. **Enrollment:** 260 degree-seeking undergraduates. **Degrees:** 134 associate awarded. **Calendar:** Semester. **Full-time faculty:** 10 total. **Part-time faculty:** 5 total.

Basis for selection. Interviews required.

2015-2016 Annual costs. Cost for full-time students entering Fall 2015, $6,780 per semester; Spring 2016, $6,780 per semester. Books and supplies vary from semester to semester, ranging from $100 to $1,500.

Financial aid. Need-based: Work-study available nights, weekends and for part-time students.

Application procedures. Admission: No deadline. $50 fee. **Financial aid:** No deadline.

Academics. Credit/placement by examination: AP, CLEP. **Support services:** Learning center, tutoring.

Majors. Health services: Veterinary technology/assistant.

Contact. E-mail: mortiz@bradfordschoolhouston.edu
Phone: (713) 629-1500
Mike SanFilipo, Director of Admissions, Vet Tech Institute of Houston, 4669 Southwest Freeway, Houston, TX 77027

Victoria College
Victoria, Texas
www.victoriacollege.edu   CB code: 6915

- Public 2-year community college
- Commuter campus in small city

General. Founded in 1925. Regionally accredited. **Enrollment:** 3,410 degree-seeking undergraduates; 641 non-degree-seeking students. **Degrees:** 464 associate awarded. **Location:** 110 miles from San Antonio, 125 miles from Austin. **Calendar:** Semester, limited summer session. **Full-time faculty:** 112 total; 13% minority, 64% women. **Part-time faculty:** 128 total; 20% minority, 62% women. **Special facilities:** Museum, performing arts center.

Student profile. Among degree-seeking undergraduates, 75% enrolled in a transfer program, 25% enrolled in a vocational program, 1% already have a bachelor's degree or higher, 703 enrolled as first-time, first-year students, 260 transferred in from other institutions.

Part-time:	67%	Hispanic/Latino:	48%
Women:	66%	Multi-racial, non-Hispanic:	1%
African American:	6%	25 or older:	29%
Asian American:	2%		

Transfer out. Colleges most students transferred to 2015: University of Houston - Victoria, Texas State University - San Marcos, Texas A&M University, University of Texas at Austin, Texas A&M University - Corpus Christi.

Basis for selection. Open admission, but selective for some programs. Special requirements for allied health programs; interview required.

High school preparation. 24 units recommended. Recommended units include English 4, mathematics 3, social studies 2.5, history 1, science 3, foreign language 2, academic electives 3.5. 0.5 economics, 1 fine arts, 0.5 speech, 1 technical applications recommended.

2015-2016 Annual costs. Tuition/fees: $2,640; $4,050 out-of-district; $4,650 out-of-state. Per-credit charge: $46 in-district; $93 out-of-district; $200 out-of-state. Books/supplies: $1,600. Personal expenses: $1,356.

2014-2015 Financial aid. Need-based: 69% of total undergraduate aid awarded as scholarships/grants, 31% as loans/jobs. Work-study available nights, weekends and for part-time students. **Non-need-based:** Scholarships awarded for academics, art, minority status, music/drama.

Application procedures. Admission: No deadline. No application fee. Admission notification on a rolling basis beginning on or about 7/1. **Financial aid:** Priority date 4/15; no closing date. FAFSA, institutional form required. Applicants notified on a rolling basis.

Academics. Special study options: Distance learning, dual enrollment of high school students. 2+2 plans with University of Texas-San Antonio, University of Houston-Victoria, Texas A&M-Corpus Christi, University of Texas-Brownsville. License preparation in nursing, paramedic, physical therapy. **Credit/placement by examination:** AP, CLEP, IB, institutional tests. **Support services:** GED preparation and test center, learning center, remedial instruction, tutoring.

Majors. Business: Administrative services, business admin. **Health services:** Clinical lab technology, EMT paramedic, nursing (RN), physical therapy assistant, respiratory therapy technology. **Protective services:** Firefighting, police science.

Most popular majors. Business/marketing 7%, engineering/engineering technologies 6%, health sciences 22%, liberal arts 61%.

Technology on campus. 500 workstations in library, computer center, student center. Commuter students can connect to campus network. Online course registration, online library, helpline, wireless network available.

Student life. Freshman orientation: Mandatory. Preregistration for classes offered. Students required to enroll in EDUC 1300 class. **Activities:** Bands, campus ministries, choral groups, music ensembles, student government.

Athletics. NJCAA. **Intramural:** Baseball M, basketball, tennis, volleyball. **Team name:** Pirates.

Student services. Career counseling, services for economically disadvantaged, financial aid counseling, personal counseling, veterans' counselor. **Physically disabled:** Services for visually impaired. **Transfer:** College fairs on campus for students transferring to 4-year colleges.

Contact. E-mail: registrar@victoriacollege.edu
Phone: (361) 572-6408 Fax: (361) 582-2525
Missy Klimitchek, Registrar, Victoria College, 2200 East Red River, Victoria, TX 77901

Virginia College in Austin
Austin, Texas
www.vc.edu/campus/austin-texas-college.cfm

- For-profit 2-year business and health science college
- Commuter campus in very large city

General. Accredited by ACICS. **Enrollment:** 569 undergraduates. **Degrees:** 96 associate awarded. **Calendar:** Differs by program. **Full-time faculty:** 18 total. **Part-time faculty:** 33 total.

Basis for selection. Open admission, but selective for some programs.

2015-2016 Annual costs. Reported costs are for the entire associate degree program and include tuition, fees, books and supplies. Business Administration, Medical Office Management, Office Administration, Paralegal Studies, $37,252. Surgical Technology, $39,172. Respiratory Care, $44,612. Diagnostic Medical Sonography, $48,772.

Financial aid. **Need-based:** Work-study available nights, weekends and for part-time students.

Application procedures. **Admission:** No deadline. $100 fee.

Academics. **Credit/placement by examination:** AP, CLEP.

Majors. Business: Executive assistant, office management. **Health services:** Office assistant, respiratory therapy technology, surgical technology.

Contact. Phone: (512) 371-3500 Fax: (512) 371-3502
Tyka Booker, Director of Admissions, Virginia College in Austin, 6301 E. Highway 290, Austin, TX 78723

Wade College
Dallas, Texas
www.wadecollege.edu   CB code: 1537

- For-profit 2-year business and career college
- Commuter campus in very large city
- Application essay, interview required

General. Founded in 1965. Regionally accredited. **Enrollment:** 250 undergraduates. **Degrees:** 21 bachelor's, 82 associate awarded. **Location:** 2 miles from downtown Dallas. **Calendar:** Trimester, extensive summer session. **Full-time faculty:** 7 total. **Part-time faculty:** 16 total. **Class size:** 81% < 20, 19% 20-39.

Basis for selection. Open admission, but selective for some programs. Special requirements for students seeking BA degree in Merchandising and Design. **Adult students:** SAT/ACT scores not required.

High school preparation. College-preparatory program required.

2015-2016 Annual costs. Tuition/fees: $15,575. Per-credit charge: $515. **Additional information:** Books/Supplies $0 (all inclusive tuition/books/fees). Tuition shown for the Associate of Arts degree in Merchandising and Design. Bachelor of Arts per credit-hour charge of $585.

Financial aid. All financial aid based on need. Need-based aid available for part-time students. Work-study available nights, weekends and for part-time students.

Application procedures. **Admission:** No deadline. $25 fee. Application must be submitted on paper. Admission notification on a rolling basis. **Financial aid:** No deadline. FAFSA required. Applicants notified on a rolling basis; must reply within 4 week(s) of notification.

Academics. **Special study options:** Accelerated study, double major, internships, liberal arts/career combination. Weekend classes offered but cannot complete degree attending weekends only. Bachelor's degree programs available on campus. **Credit/placement by examination:** AP, CLEP, IB, institutional tests. **Support services:** Pre-admission summer program, reduced course load, remedial instruction, study skills assistance, tutoring, writing center.

Majors. Business: Sales/distribution. **Visual/performing arts:** Design.

Most popular majors. Business/marketing 50%, visual/performing arts 50%.

Technology on campus. 80 workstations in library, computer center. Commuter students can connect to campus network. Online library, wireless network available.

Student life. Freshman orientation: Mandatory. Preregistration for classes offered. Held on the first day of classes. **Activities:** Student newspaper, Phi Theta Kappa, Mu Kappa Tau, concentration-specific clubs in graphic design, interior design, fashion design, merchandising and design.

Student services. Adult student services, career counseling, student employment services, financial aid counseling, placement for graduates, veterans' counselor. **Transfer:** Re-entry adviser, pre-admission transcript evaluation for new students. Transfer adviser for students transferring to 4-year colleges.

Contact. E-mail: admissions@wadecollege.edu
Phone: (214) 658-8800 Toll-free number: (800) 624-4850
Fax: (214) 637-0827
John Conte, Executive Vice President, Wade College, 1950 North Stemmons Freeway, Suite 4080, Dallas, TX 75207

Weatherford College
Weatherford, Texas
www.wc.edu   CB code: 6931

- Public 2-year community college
- Commuter campus in large town

General. Founded in 1869. Regionally accredited. Off-campus courses held in Aledo, Bridgeport, Jacksboro, Springtown, Azle. Satellite campus in Mineral Wells, Granbury and Decatur. **Enrollment:** 5,316 degree-seeking undergraduates. **Degrees:** 780 associate awarded. **ROTC:** Air Force. **Location:** 25 miles from Fort Worth. **Calendar:** Semester, extensive summer session. **Full-time faculty:** 98 total. **Part-time faculty:** 104 total. **Special facilities:** 300-acre college farm. **Partnerships:** Dual credit articulation agreements.

Student profile.

Out-of-state:	3%	Live on campus:	5%
25 or older:	50%		

Transfer out. Colleges most students transferred to 2015: Tarleton State University, University of North Texas, University of Texas at Arlington, Texas Tech University.

Basis for selection. Open admission, but selective for some programs. Nursing school, fire science requires entrance examination. Peace officer requires physical, drug testing, background check.

2015-2016 Annual costs. Tuition/fees: $2,400; $3,720 out-of-district; $5,280 out-of-state. Room/board: $7,430. Books/supplies: $1,200. Personal expenses: $1,464.

Financial aid. All financial aid based on need. Work-study available nights, weekends and for part-time students.

Application procedures. **Admission:** No deadline. No application fee. Admission notification on a rolling basis. **Financial aid:** Priority date 7/3; no closing date. FAFSA required. Applicants notified on a rolling basis; must reply within 2 week(s) of notification.

Academics. **Special study options:** Cooperative education, distance learning, dual enrollment of high school students, ESL, honors, internships, liberal arts/career combination, teacher certification program, weekend college. License preparation in dental hygiene, nursing, occupational therapy, paramedic, physical therapy, radiology, real estate. **Credit/placement by examination:** AP, CLEP, institutional tests. 30 credit hours maximum toward associate degree. Credit earned by examination does not reduce resident requirement of 15 semester hours of class completed at college. **Support services:** GED preparation and test center, learning center, remedial instruction, study skills assistance, tutoring.

Majors. Business: General, accounting, administrative services, human resources, marketing, office/clerical, operations. **Communications:** Communications/speech/rhetoric. **Computer sciences:** General, data processing, programming. **Health services:** EMT paramedic, licensed practical nurse, medical radiologic technology/radiation therapy, occupational therapy assistant, pharmacy assistant, predental, premedicine, prenursing, prepharmacy, radiologic technology/medical imaging, radiologist assistant, respiratory therapy assistant, respiratory therapy technology, sonography, veterinary technology/assistant. **Liberal arts:** Arts/sciences. **Protective services:** Corrections, firefighting, law enforcement admin, police science. **Social sciences:** Sociology. **Work/family studies:** Child care service.

Technology on campus. 300 workstations in dormitories, library, computer center. Dormitories wired for high-speed internet access and linked to campus network. Commuter students can connect to campus network. Online course registration, wireless network available.

Student life. Freshman orientation: Mandatory. Preregistration for classes offered. Half-day sessions held before registration. **Housing:** Special housing for disabled, apartments, wellness housing available. $250 deposit, deadline 8/15. **Activities:** Jazz band, choral groups, dance, drama, music ensembles, musical theater, student government, black awareness student organization, Hispanic student organization, Baptist student union, international student organization, Wesleyan foundation, Baptist student ministries, A Better Life Through Education, disabled club.

Athletics. NJCAA. **Intercollegiate:** Baseball M, basketball, cheerleading, rodeo, softball W. **Intramural:** Basketball, softball, tennis, volleyball. **Team name:** Coyotes.

Student services. Adult student services, career counseling, services for economically disadvantaged, student employment services, financial aid counseling, personal counseling, placement for graduates, veterans' counselor. **Physically disabled:** Services for visually, speech, hearing impaired. **Transfer:** Pre-admission transcript evaluation for new students. Transfer adviser, college fairs on campus for students transferring to 4-year colleges.

Contact. Phone: (817) 598-6241 Toll-free number: (800) 287-5471 Fax: (817) 598-6205
Ralph Willingham, Director of Admissions, Weatherford College, 225 College Park Drive, Weatherford, TX 76086

Western Technical College
El Paso, Texas
www.westerntech.edu   CB code: 2941

- For-profit 2-year technical college
- Commuter campus in very large city

General. Accredited by ACCSC. Two campuses: main campus East, branch campus in NE section. **Enrollment:** 773 degree-seeking undergraduates. **Degrees:** 197 associate awarded. **Calendar:** Differs by program. **Full-time faculty:** 41 total; 2% have terminal degrees, 80% minority, 12% women. **Part-time faculty:** 19 total; 5% have terminal degrees, 68% minority, 32% women.

Student profile. Among degree-seeking undergraduates, 100% enrolled in a vocational program.

Basis for selection. Open admission, but selective for some programs. Some programs require Wonderlic or other entrance requirements. **Home schooled:** State high school equivalency certificate required.

2015-2016 Annual costs. Tuition/fees: $13,989. Room/board: $10,185. Books/supplies: $1,193.

2014-2015 Financial aid. All financial aid based on need. 40% of total undergraduate aid awarded as scholarships/grants, 60% as loans/jobs. Need-based aid available for part-time students. Work-study available nights, weekends and for part-time students.

Application procedures. Admission: No deadline. $100 fee. **Financial aid:** No deadline. FAFSA required. Applicants notified on a rolling basis.

Academics. Credit/placement by examination: AP, CLEP. 12 credit hours maximum toward associate degree. **Support services:** GED preparation and test center, remedial instruction, tutoring.

Majors. Business: Business admin.

Technology on campus. 200 workstations in library, computer center, student center. Online library, wireless network available.

Student life. Freshman orientation: Mandatory. Preregistration for classes offered.

Student services. Financial aid counseling, on-campus daycare, placement for graduates.

Contact. Phone: (915) 532-3737 Toll-free number: (800) 225-5984 Fax: (915) 532-6946
Lynda Cervantes, Director of Admissions, Western Technical College, 9624 Plaza Circle, El Paso, TX 79927

Western Technical College: Diana Drive
El Paso, Texas
www.westerntech.edu

- For-profit 2-year branch campus and technical college
- Commuter campus in very large city
- Interview required

General. Accredited by ACCSC. **Enrollment:** 482 degree-seeking undergraduates. **Degrees:** 97 associate awarded. **Calendar:** Differs by program. **Full-time faculty:** 27 total; 41% have terminal degrees, 100% minority, 30% women. **Part-time faculty:** 13 total; 92% have terminal degrees, 100% minority, 38% women.

Student profile. Among degree-seeking undergraduates, 100% enrolled in a vocational program.

Basis for selection. Open admission, but selective for some programs. Assessment test and various minimum scores required for following programs: medical clinical assistant, health information technology, massage therapy, and physical therapist assistant. **Home schooled:** State high school equivalency certificate required.

2014-2015 Financial aid. Need-based: 42% of total undergraduate aid awarded as scholarships/grants, 58% as loans/jobs. Work-study available nights, weekends and for part-time students.

Application procedures. Admission: No deadline. $100 fee. **Financial aid:** No deadline.

Academics. Credit/placement by examination: AP, CLEP. 12 credit hours maximum toward associate degree. **Support services:** GED preparation and test center, remedial instruction, tutoring.

Majors. Business: Business admin. **Computer sciences:** General. **Health services:** Physical therapy assistant.

Technology on campus. Online library, wireless network available.

Student life. Freshman orientation: Mandatory. Preregistration for classes offered.

Student services. Financial aid counseling, placement for graduates.

Contact. Phone: (915) 566-9621 Toll-free number: (800) 522-2072 Fax: (915) 565-9903
Lynda Cervantes, Director of Admissions, Western Technical College: Diana Drive, 9451 Diana Drive, El Paso, TX 79924

Western Texas College
Snyder, Texas
www.wtc.edu   CB code: 6951

- Public 2-year community and junior college
- Commuter campus in large town

General. Founded in 1969. Regionally accredited. **Enrollment:** 1,491 degree-seeking undergraduates. **Degrees:** 185 associate awarded. **Location:** 80 miles from Lubbock. **Calendar:** Semester, extensive summer session. **Full-time faculty:** 47 total. **Part-time faculty:** 56 total. **Class size:** 80% < 20, 19% 20-39, less than 1% 40-49, less than 1% 50-99.

Student profile.

Out-of-state:	3%	Live on campus:	10%
25 or older:	32%		

Transfer out. Colleges most students transferred to 2015: Texas Tech University, Angelo State University, University of Texas, Texas A&M University.

Basis for selection. Open admission, but selective for some programs. Institutional placement tests may be submitted in place of SAT/ACT. Special requirements for nursing program. Interview recommended. **Home schooled:** Transcript of courses and grades required.

2015-2016 Annual costs. Tuition/fees: $2,460; $3,510 out-of-district; $4,620 out-of-state. Room/board: $5,100. Books/supplies: $600. Personal expenses: $900.

Financial aid. Need-based: Need-based aid available for part-time students. Work-study available nights, weekends and for part-time students. **Non-need-based:** Scholarships awarded for academics, art, athletics, leadership, music/drama, state residency.

Application procedures. Admission: No deadline. No application fee. Application must be submitted on paper. Admission notification on a rolling basis beginning on or about 11/5. **Financial aid:** Priority date 5/1; no closing date. FAFSA, institutional form required. Applicants notified on a rolling basis starting 5/1; must reply within 2 week(s) of notification.

Academics. Special study options: Distance learning, dual enrollment of high school students, honors, internships. License preparation in nursing, paramedic. **Credit/placement by examination:** AP, CLEP, institutional tests. 12 credit hours maximum toward associate degree. **Support services:** GED preparation and test center, learning center, pre-admission summer program, reduced course load, remedial instruction, tutoring.

Two-Year Colleges

Majors. Biology: General. **Business:** General, accounting, administrative services, business admin. **Communications:** Journalism. **Communications technology:** Radio/TV. **Computer sciences:** General, computer science, data processing, LAN/WAN management, programming. **Education:** General, early childhood. **Engineering:** General. **English:** English lit. **Foreign languages:** General. **General:** Power transmission. **Health services:** EMT paramedic, predental, premedicine, prenursing, prepharmacy, preveterinary. **History:** General. **Liberal arts:** Arts/sciences. **Math:** General. **Parks/recreation:** Facilities management, health/fitness. **Philosophy/religion:** Philosophy. **Physical sciences:** Chemistry, geology, physics. **Psychology:** General. **Social sciences:** General, economics, geography, international relations, political science, sociology. **Visual/performing arts:** Art, ceramics, dramatic, drawing, metal/jewelry, painting, photography, sculpture.

Technology on campus. 70 workstations in dormitories, library, computer center, student center. Dormitories wired for high-speed internet access and linked to campus network. Online course registration, online library available.

Student life. Freshman orientation: Available. Preregistration for classes offered. **Housing:** Guaranteed on-campus for all undergraduates. Single-sex dorms, apartments available. $50 deposit. **Activities:** Drama, literary magazine, musical theater, student government, TV station, Baptist student union, Phi Theta Kappa.

Athletics. NJCAA. **Intercollegiate:** Baseball M, basketball, cross-country, golf, rodeo, soccer, softball W, track and field, volleyball W. **Intramural:** Basketball, cheerleading W, golf, handball, racquetball, volleyball, weight lifting. **Team name:** Westerners.

Student services. Adult student services, alcohol/substance abuse counseling, career counseling, services for economically disadvantaged, student employment services, financial aid counseling, personal counseling, placement for graduates, veterans' counselor. **Transfer:** Pre-admission transcript evaluation for new students. Transfer adviser, college fairs on campus for students transferring to 4-year colleges.

Contact. E-mail: rferguson@wtc.edu
Phone: (325) 574-7918 Toll-free number: (888) 468-6982
Fax: (325) 573-9321
Kristy Lloyd, Director of Admissions, Western Texas College, 6200 College Avenue, Snyder, TX 79549

Wharton County Junior College
Wharton, Texas
www.wcjc.edu   CB code: 6939

▶ Public 2-year community and junior college
▶ Commuter campus in small town

General. Founded in 1946. Regionally accredited. **Enrollment:** 7,416 degree-seeking undergraduates. **Degrees:** 499 associate awarded. **Location:** 60 miles from Houston. **Calendar:** Semester, limited summer session. **Full-time faculty:** 168 total; 14% have terminal degrees, 22% minority, 61% women. **Part-time faculty:** 116 total; 7% have terminal degrees, 36% minority, 48% women. **Class size:** 39% < 20, 59% 20-39, less than 1% 40-49, less than 1% 50-99.

Student profile. Among degree-seeking undergraduates, 70% enrolled in a transfer program, 30% enrolled in a vocational program, 1% already have a bachelor's degree or higher, 1,684 enrolled as first-time, first-year students, 503 transferred in from other institutions.

Part-time:	61%	Hispanic/Latino:	37%
Women:	55%	Multi-racial, non-Hispanic:	1%
African American:	12%	25 or older:	17%
Asian American:	12%	Live on campus:	2%

Transfer out. Colleges most students transferred to 2015: Texas A&M University, University of Houston, Sam Houston State University, Texas State University, University of Texas.

Basis for selection. Open admission, but selective for some programs. Test scores and school achievement record important factors for admission into nursing, dental hygiene, physical therapy, and radiology programs. Audition required for music scholarship applicants.

High school preparation. College-preparatory program recommended. Recommended units include English 4, mathematics 3, science 3 and foreign language 2.

2015-2016 Annual costs. Tuition/fees: $2,640; $5,130 out-of-state. Per-credit charge: $32 in-state; $64 out-of-state. Room/board: $4,100. Books/supplies: $1,240. Personal expenses: $1,920.

2014-2015 Financial aid. Need-based: 68% of total undergraduate aid awarded as scholarships/grants, 32% as loans/jobs. Need-based aid available for part-time students. Work study available nights, weekends and for part-time students. **Non-need-based:** Scholarships awarded for academics, athletics, music/drama.

Application procedures. Admission: Priority date 7/1; no deadline. No application fee. Admission notification on a rolling basis beginning on or about 2/1. **Financial aid:** Closing date 6/1. FAFSA, institutional form required. Applicants notified on a rolling basis starting 3/1; must reply within 8 week(s) of notification.

Academics. Special study options: Cooperative education, cross-registration, distance learning, dual enrollment of high school students, internships, teacher certification program. License preparation in dental hygiene, nursing, paramedic, physical therapy, radiology. **Credit/placement by examination:** AP, CLEP, institutional tests. 16 credit hours maximum toward associate degree. **Support services:** GED preparation and test center, learning center, remedial instruction, tutoring.

Majors. Biology: General. **Business:** Business admin. **Communications technology:** Animation/special effects. **Computer sciences:** General, networking, web page design. **Education:** Early childhood, elementary. **English:** English lit. **Health services:** Dental hygiene, EMT paramedic, health information technology, nursing (RN), physical therapy assistant, radiologic technology/medical imaging. **History:** General. **Liberal arts:** Arts/sciences. **Math:** General. **Parks/recreation:** Exercise sciences. **Physical sciences:** Chemistry, physics. **Protective services:** Police science. **Psychology:** General. **Social sciences:** Criminology, sociology. **Visual/performing arts:** Art, dramatic, music. **Work/family studies:** Child development.

Most popular majors. Business/marketing 11%, engineering/engineering technologies 7%, health sciences 24%, liberal arts 40%, science technologies 9%.

Technology on campus. 500 workstations in library, computer center, student center. Commuter students can connect to campus network. Online course registration, online library, wireless network available.

Student life. Freshman orientation: Available. Preregistration for classes offered. **Housing:** Single-sex dorms available. $100 deposit, deadline 7/1. **Activities:** Bands, choral groups, drama, music ensembles, musical theater, student government.

Athletics. NJCAA. **Intercollegiate:** Baseball M, rodeo, volleyball W. **Team name:** Pioneers.

Student services. Career counseling, services for economically disadvantaged, financial aid counseling, personal counseling, veterans' counselor. **Physically disabled:** Services for visually, speech, hearing impaired. **Transfer:** Transfer adviser, college fairs on campus for students transferring to 4-year colleges.

Contact. E-mail: registrar@wcjc.edu
Phone: (979) 532-4560 ext. 6303 Toll-free number: (800) 561-9252
Fax: (979) 532-6494
Karen Preisler, Director of Admissions and Registration, Wharton County Junior College, 911 Boling Highway, Wharton, TX 77488-0080

Utah

Broadview Entertainment Arts University
Salt Lake City, Utah
www.broadviewuniversity.edu

‣ For-profit 2-year university and visual arts college
‣ Commuter campus in small city
‣ Interview required

General. Regionally accredited; also accredited by ACICS. **Enrollment:** 151 undergraduates. **Degrees:** 9 bachelor's, 7 associate awarded. **Calendar:** Quarter, extensive summer session.

Basis for selection. Open admission. **Adult students:** SAT/ACT scores not required.

2015-2016 Annual costs. Tuition/fees: $18,027. Per-credit charge: $375. Books/supplies: $1,260. **Additional information:** Per-credit-hour charge for 1-11 hours, $435; for 12-16 hours, $375. Course fees: $100 to $650 per course.

Financial aid. Need-based: Need-based aid available for part-time students. Work-study available nights, weekends and for part-time students.

Application procedures. Admission: No deadline. $50 fee. Admission notification on a rolling basis. **Financial aid:** No deadline. FAFSA, institutional form required. Applicants notified on a rolling basis starting 7/1; must reply within 2 week(s) of notification.

Academics. Special study options: Distance learning, independent study, internships, liberal arts/career combination. **Credit/placement by examination:** AP, CLEP. **Support services:** Remedial instruction, study skills assistance, tutoring, writing center.

Majors. Communications technology: Animation/special effects, recording arts. **Visual/performing arts:** Music management.

Technology on campus. 60 workstations in library, computer center, student center. Commuter students can connect to campus network. Online library, helpline, student web hosting, wireless network available.

Student life. Freshman orientation: Mandatory. Preregistration for classes offered. Day and evening sessions available the week prior to classes starting. **Activities:** Literary magazine.

Student services. Career counseling, student employment services, financial aid counseling, placement for graduates. **Transfer:** Re-entry adviser for new students.

Contact. Phone: (801) 300-4300 Toll-free number: (877) 801-8889 Mikel Gregory, Director of Admissions, Broadview Entertainment Arts University, 240 East Morris Avenue, Salt Lake City, UT 84115

Broadview University: Layton
Layton, Utah
www.broadviewuniversity.edu

‣ For-profit 2-year university and career college
‣ Commuter campus in small city
‣ Interview required

General. Regionally accredited; also accredited by ACICS. **Enrollment:** 163 undergraduates. **Degrees:** 9 bachelor's, 52 associate awarded. **Calendar:** Quarter, extensive summer session.

Basis for selection. Open admission. **Adult students:** SAT/ACT scores not required. An applicant must achieve minimum score on the Accuplacer as indicated for the selected program. Based on scores achieved, student may be placed in math and/or writing foundations courses; provide documentation of a bachelor's degree granted by an approved institution; provide documentation of a minimum composite score of 21 on the ACT; provide documentation of a minimum composite SAT score of 1485 or 990 if SAT was taken prior to March 2006.

2015-2016 Annual costs. Tuition/fees: $18,027. Per-credit charge: $375. Books/supplies: $1,260. **Additional information:** Per-credit-hour charge for 1-11 hours, $435; for 12-16 hours, $375. Course fees: $100 to $650 per course.

Financial aid. Need-based: Need-based aid available for part-time students. Work-study available nights, weekends and for part-time students.

Application procedures. Admission: No deadline. $50 fee. Admission notification on a rolling basis. **Financial aid:** No deadline. FAFSA, institutional form required. Applicants notified on a rolling basis starting 7/1; must reply within 2 week(s) of notification.

Academics. Special study options: Distance learning, independent study, internships, liberal arts/career combination. **Credit/placement by examination:** AP, CLEP. **Support services:** Remedial instruction, study skills assistance, tutoring, writing center.

Majors. Business: Accounting, business admin. **Computer sciences:** Networking. **Health services:** Massage therapy, medical assistant, medical secretary, veterinary technology/assistant. **Protective services:** Law enforcement admin.

Most popular majors. Business/marketing 16%, computer/information sciences 9%, health sciences 60%, legal studies 9%, security/protective services 7%.

Technology on campus. 60 workstations in library, computer center, student center. Commuter students can connect to campus network. Online library, helpline, student web hosting, wireless network available.

Student life. Freshman orientation: Mandatory. Preregistration for classes offered. Day and evening sessions available the week prior to classes starting. **Activities:** Literary magazine.

Student services. Career counseling, student employment services, financial aid counseling, placement for graduates. **Transfer:** Re-entry adviser for new students.

Contact. Phone: (801) 660-6000 Toll-free number: (866) 253-7744 Shae Erhart, Director of Admissions, Broadview University: Layton, 869 West Hill Field Road, Layton, UT 84041

Broadview University: West Jordan
West Jordan, Utah
www.broadviewuniversity.edu **CB code: 2892**

‣ For-profit 2-year technical and career college
‣ Commuter campus in small city
‣ Interview required

General. Regionally accredited; also accredited by ACICS. **Enrollment:** 237 undergraduates. **Degrees:** 11 bachelor's, 44 associate awarded; master's offered. **Location:** 8 miles from Salt Lake City. **Calendar:** Quarter, extensive summer session.

Basis for selection. Open admission, but selective for some programs.

2015-2016 Annual costs. Tuition/fees: $18,027. Per-credit charge: $375. Books/supplies: $1,260. **Additional information:** Per-credit-hour charge for 1-11 hours, $435; for 12-16 hours, $375. Course fees: $100 to $650 per course.

Financial aid. Need-based: Need-based aid available for part-time students. Work-study available nights, weekends and for part-time students.

Application procedures. Admission: No deadline. $50 fee. Admission notification on a rolling basis. **Financial aid:** No deadline. FAFSA, institutional form required. Applicants notified on a rolling basis starting 7/1; must reply within 2 week(s) of notification.

Academics. Special study options: Distance learning, independent study, internships, liberal arts/career combination. Bachelor's degree programs available on campus. **Credit/placement by examination:** AP, CLEP. **Support services:** Remedial instruction, study skills assistance, tutoring, writing center.

Majors. Business: Accounting, business admin, marketing. **Computer sciences:** Networking. **Health services:** Massage therapy, medical assistant, veterinary technology/assistant. **Parks/recreation:** Physical fitness technician. **Protective services:** Law enforcement admin.

Most popular majors. Business/marketing 7%, health sciences 68%, legal studies 15%.

Technology on campus. 90 workstations in library, computer center, student center. Commuter students can connect to campus network. Online library, helpline, student web hosting, wireless network available.

Student life. Freshman orientation: Mandatory. Preregistration for classes offered. Day and evening sessions available the week prior to classes starting. **Policies:** Drug and alcohol-free campus. **Activities:** Literary magazine.

Student services. Career counseling, student employment services, financial aid counseling, placement for graduates. **Transfer:** Re-entry adviser for new students.

Contact. Phone: (801) 304-4224 Toll-free number: (866) 304-4224
Fax: (801) 304-4229
Aaron Escher, Director of Admissions, Broadview University: West Jordan, 1902 West 7800 South, West Jordan, UT 84088

Careers Unlimited
Orem, Utah
www.ucdh.edu

▶ For-profit 2-year health science college
▶ Commuter campus in large city
▶ Interview required

General. Accredited by ACCSC. On site dental clinic. **Enrollment:** 118 undergraduates. **Degrees:** 58 bachelor's awarded. **Location:** 45 miles from Salt Lake City. **Calendar:** Trimester, limited summer session. **Full-time faculty:** 8 total; 62% women. **Part-time faculty:** 14 total. **Class size:** 100% 50-99. **Special facilities:** 72 Dental operatories, 18 X-Ray bays.

Basis for selection. 33 credit hours of prerequisite and general education coursework required for admissions.

Financial aid. Need-based: Work-study available nights, weekends and for part-time students.

Application procedures. Admission: No deadline. $50 fee. Application must be submitted on paper. Admission notification on a rolling basis. **Financial aid:** No deadline.

Academics. Special study options: Accelerated study. Bachelor's degree programs available on campus. License preparation in dental hygiene. **Credit/placement by examination:** AP, CLEP.

Student life. Freshman orientation: Mandatory. Preregistration for classes offered.

Contact. E-mail: admissions@ucdh.edu
Phone: (801) 426-8234 Fax: (801) 224-5437
Hannah Vance, Director of Admissions, Careers Unlimited, 1176 South 1480 West, Orem, UT 84058

Eagle Gate College: Layton
Layton, Utah
www.eaglegatecollege.edu

▶ For-profit 2-year career college
▶ Commuter campus in small city

General. Accredited by ACICS. **Enrollment:** 241 undergraduates. **Degrees:** 20 bachelor's, 110 associate awarded. **Location:** 20 miles from Salt Lake City, 10 miles from Ogden. **Calendar:** Quarter, extensive summer session. **Full-time faculty:** 17 total. **Part-time faculty:** 31 total. **Class size:** 90% < 20, 10% 20-39.

Basis for selection. Open admission. **Home schooled:** Statement describing home school structure and mission, state high school equivalency certificate required.

2015-2016 Annual costs. Medical Assisting: diploma $17,650; associate $34,200. Nursing: associate $52,300; bachelor's $70,300. Additional fees may apply.

Financial aid. Need-based: Work-study available nights, weekends and for part-time students.

Application procedures. Admission: No deadline. No application fee. **Financial aid:** No deadline.

Academics. Special study options: Accelerated study, distance learning. Bachelor's degree programs available on campus. **Credit/placement by examination:** AP, CLEP. 45 credit hours maximum toward associate degree, 90 toward bachelor's. **Support services:** Learning center, reduced course load, tutoring, writing center.

Majors. Business: Accounting, business admin. **Computer sciences:** Web page design. **Health services:** Insurance coding, medical assistant, pharmacy assistant. **Protective services:** Law enforcement admin. **Visual/performing arts:** Graphic design.

Most popular majors. Business/marketing 20%, computer/information sciences 8%, health sciences 28%, legal studies 11%, security/protective services 22%, visual/performing arts 14%.

Technology on campus. 54 workstations in library, computer center. Commuter students can connect to campus network. Wireless network available.

Student life. Freshman orientation: Mandatory. Preregistration for classes offered.

Student services. Adult student services, career counseling, student employment services, financial aid counseling, placement for graduates.

Contact. E-mail: admissions@eaglegatecollege.edu
Phone: (801) 546-7500 ext. 7512 Toll-free number: (800) 429-4513
Fax: (801) 593-6654
Lacei Torgerson, Director of Admissions, Eagle Gate College: Layton, 915 North 400 West Layton, Layton, UT 84041

Eagle Gate College: Murray
Murray, Utah
www.eaglegatecollege.edu

▶ For-profit 2-year business and technical college
▶ Large town

General. Regionally accredited; also accredited by ACICS. **Enrollment:** 290 undergraduates. **Degrees:** 18 bachelor's, 83 associate awarded. **Calendar:** Five ten-week terms. **Full-time faculty:** 9 total. **Part-time faculty:** 34 total.

Basis for selection. Open admission.

2015-2016 Annual costs. Medical Assisting: diploma $17,650; associate $34,200. Nursing: associate $52,300; bachelor's $70,300. Additional fees may apply.

Financial aid. Need-based: Work-study available nights, weekends and for part-time students.

Application procedures. Admission: No deadline. No application fee. Admission notification on a rolling basis. **Financial aid:** No deadline.

Academics. Special study options: Bachelor's degree programs available on campus. **Credit/placement by examination:** AP, CLEP.

Majors. Business: Accounting/finance, business admin. **Computer sciences:** General. **Health services:** Dental assistant, insurance coding, medical assistant, pharmacy assistant. **Protective services:** Law enforcement admin. **Visual/performing arts:** Graphic design.

Most popular majors. Business/marketing 30%, computer/information sciences 17%, health sciences 14%, security/protective services 30%, visual/performing arts 10%.

Contact. Phone: (801) 281-7700 Toll-free number: (866) 284-8680
Lacei Torgerson, Director of Admissions, Eagle Gate College: Murray, 5588 South Green Street, Murray, UT 84123

LDS Business College
Salt Lake City, Utah
www.ldsbc.edu　　　　　　　　　　　**CB code: 4412**

▶ Private 2-year business and career college affiliated with the Church of Jesus Christ of Latter-day Saints
▶ Commuter campus in large city
▶ Interview required

General. Founded in 1886. Regionally accredited. **Enrollment:** 2,168 degree-seeking undergraduates. **Degrees:** 379 associate awarded. **ROTC:**

Two-Year Colleges

Army, Air Force. **Calendar:** Semester, limited summer session. **Full-time faculty:** 31 total; 48% have terminal degrees. **Part-time faculty:** 147 total; 70% have terminal degrees. **Class size:** 38% < 20, 58% 20-39, 3% 40-49, less than 1% >100.

Student profile.

Out-of-state:	35%	25 or older:	21%

Transfer out. Colleges most students transferred to 2015: Brigham Young University, University of Utah, Utah State University.

Basis for selection. Open admission, but selective for some programs. Students in interior design program must submit color board. Non-native speakers must pass an English proficiency test. SAT/ACT recommended for counseling; used as pre-test and placement in English or math. **Adult students:** Students who have not taken ACT or SAT must take COMPASS for placement in English and math. **Home schooled:** Students must submit ACT or GED if not from accredited program. Students qualify for admission after reaching age 17. **Learning Disabled:** Must submit documentation under ADA.

2015-2016 Annual costs. Tuition/fees: $3,160. Room/board: $5,582. Books/supplies: $650.

Financial aid. Need-based: Need-based aid available for part-time students. Work-study available nights, weekends and for part-time students. **Non-need-based:** Scholarships awarded for academics, leadership.

Application procedures. Admission: Closing date 9/1 (receipt date). $35 fee. Application must be submitted online. Admission notification on a rolling basis beginning on or about 10/15. **Financial aid:** Priority date 7/1; no closing date. FAFSA required. Applicants notified on a rolling basis starting 3/1; must reply by 7/1 or within 3 week(s) of notification.

Academics. Special study options: Dual enrollment of high school students, internships. **Credit/placement by examination:** AP, CLEP, IB, institutional tests. 30 credit hours maximum toward associate degree. **Support services:** Learning center, reduced course load, study skills assistance, tutoring, writing center.

Majors. Business: General, accounting, business admin, entrepreneurial studies, executive assistant, office management, selling. **Computer sciences:** General, LAN/WAN management. **Health services:** Health information management, medical secretary, office admin, office assistant. **Visual/performing arts:** Interior design, photography.

Most popular majors. Business/marketing 53%, health sciences 6%, liberal arts 26%, visual/performing arts 8%.

Technology on campus. 350 workstations in library, computer center. Commuter students can connect to campus network. Online course registration, helpline, wireless network available.

Student life. Freshman orientation: Available. Preregistration for classes offered. Full-day Monday and half-day Tuesday session held before start of classes. **Policies:** Religious observance required. **Activities:** Choral groups, drama, student government.

Athletics. Team name: Lions.

Student services. Career counseling, student employment services, financial aid counseling, personal counseling, placement for graduates. **Transfer:** Transfer adviser, college fairs on campus for students transferring to 4-year colleges.

Contact. E-mail: admissions@ldsbc.edu
Phone: (801) 524-8145 Toll-free number: (800) 999-5767
Fax: (801) 524-1900
Dawn Fellows, Assistant Director of Admission, LDS Business College, 95 North 300 West, Salt Lake City, UT 84101-3500

Provo College
Provo, Utah
www.provocollege.edu   CB code: 3021

- For-profit 2-year junior college
- Small city

General. Regionally accredited; also accredited by ACICS. **Enrollment:** 372 undergraduates. **Degrees:** 140 associate awarded. **Calendar:** Quarter, extensive summer session. **Full-time faculty:** 17 total. **Part-time faculty:** 33 total.

Basis for selection. Open admission, but selective for some programs.

2015-2016 Annual costs. Books/supplies: $600. Personal expenses: $2,088.

Financial aid. Need-based: Work-study available nights, weekends and for part-time students.

Application procedures. Admission: No deadline. No application fee. Admission notification on a rolling basis. **Financial aid:** No deadline.

Academics. Credit/placement by examination: AP, CLEP. **Support services:** Learning center, tutoring.

Majors. Business: Accounting, administrative services, business admin, hospitality/recreation. **Computer sciences:** General, programming. **Health services:** Dental assistant, medical secretary, physical therapy assistant. **Protective services:** Law enforcement admin. **Visual/performing arts:** General, commercial/advertising art.

Most popular majors. Business/marketing 7%, health sciences 61%, security/protective services 16%, visual/performing arts 16%.

Contact. E-mail: admissions@provocollege.edu
Phone: (801) 375-1861 Toll-free number: (800) 748-4834
Fax: (801) 375-9728
Josh Martin, Director of Admissions, Provo College, 1450 West 820 North, Provo, UT 84601

Salt Lake Community College
Salt Lake City, Utah   CB member
www.slcc.edu   CB code: 4864

- Public 2-year community and technical college
- Commuter campus in very large city

General. Founded in 1948. Regionally accredited. 5 campus locations, 8 teaching centers. **Enrollment:** 22,326 degree-seeking undergraduates; 6,488 non-degree-seeking students. **Degrees:** 3,382 associate awarded. **ROTC:** Army, Air Force. **Location:** 5 miles from downtown. **Calendar:** Semester, extensive summer session. **Full-time faculty:** 339 total; 45% women. **Part-time faculty:** 1,155 total; 40% women. **Class size:** 48% < 20, 52% 20-39, less than 1% 40-49, less than 1% 50-99.

Student profile. Among degree-seeking undergraduates, 2,992 enrolled as first-time, first-year students.

Part-time:	67%	Native American:	1%
Out-of-state:	5%	Native Hawaiian/Pacific islander:	1%
Women:	50%	Multi-racial, non-Hispanic:	2%
African American:	2%	International:	2%
Asian American:	4%	25 or older:	47%
Hispanic/Latino:	17%		

Transfer out. Colleges most students transferred to 2015: University of Utah, Utah State University, Weber State University, Westminster College.

Basis for selection. Open admission, but selective for some programs. Admission for flight technology programs based on testing; admissions for health sciences based on school records, testing and prerequisite courses.

High school preparation. 27 units recommended. Recommended units include English 4, mathematics 2, social studies 3, science 2 and academic electives 11. Biological science recommended for health science programs. Algebra recommended for preengineering and electronics.

2015-2016 Annual costs. Tuition/fees: $3,568; $11,336 out-of-state. Books/supplies: $1,680. Personal expenses: $2,970.

Financial aid. Need-based: Need-based aid available for part-time students. Work-study available nights, weekends and for part-time students. **Non-need-based:** Scholarships awarded for academics, alumni affiliation, art, athletics, leadership, minority status, music/drama.

Application procedures. Admission: No deadline. $40 fee. Admission notification on a rolling basis. **Financial aid:** Priority date 5/1; no closing date. FAFSA, institutional form required. Applicants notified on a rolling basis starting 5/1; must reply within 4 week(s) of notification.

Academics. Special study options: Cooperative education, distance learning, dual enrollment of high school students, ESL, exchange student, study abroad. Bachelor's degree programs available on campus. License preparation in aviation, dental hygiene, nursing. **Credit/placement by examination:** AP, CLEP, IB, SAT, ACT, institutional tests. 50 credit hours maximum toward associate degree. **Support services:** GED preparation and test center, learning center, pre-admission summer program, reduced course load, remedial instruction, study skills assistance, tutoring, writing center.

Majors. **Biology:** General. **Business:** General, accounting technology, business admin, finance, marketing, restaurant/food services. **Communications:** Communications/speech/rhetoric, digital media. **Communications technology:** Animation/special effects, photo/film/video, radio/TV. **Computer sciences:** General, computer science. **Education:** Early childhood special, kindergarten/preschool. **Engineering:** Electrical, manufacturing, materials, mechanical. **English:** English lit. **Foreign languages:** Sign language interpretation. **General:** Carpentry, electrician, maintenance, pipefitting, plumbing, site management. **Health services:** Dental hygiene, medical radiologic technology/radiation therapy, nursing (RN), occupational therapy assistant, physical therapy assistant. **History:** General. **Human services:** Social work. **Liberal arts:** Humanities. **Math:** General. **Parks/recreation:** Sports admin. **Physical sciences:** Chemistry, geology, physics. **Protective services:** Criminal justice. **Psychology:** General. **Social sciences:** Economics, geography, political science, sociology. **Visual/performing arts:** Design, music, photography, theater design. **Work/family studies:** Family studies.

Most popular majors. Business/marketing 7%, health sciences 11%, liberal arts 56%.

Technology on campus. 2,400 workstations in library, computer center, student center. Commuter students can connect to campus network. Online course registration, helpline, wireless network available.

Student life. **Freshman orientation:** Available. Preregistration for classes offered. One-day program. **Activities:** Bands, choral groups, dance, drama, literary magazine, radio station, student government, student newspaper, TV station, Circle-K, Latter-Day Saints student association, Hispanos Unidos, African-American student association, American Indian club, Asian club, Polynesian club, American Sign Language club, professional societies.

Athletics. NJCAA. **Intercollegiate:** Baseball M, basketball, softball W, volleyball W. **Team name:** Bruins.

Student services. Alcohol/substance abuse counseling, career counseling, services for economically disadvantaged, student employment services, financial aid counseling, health services, minority student services, on-campus daycare, personal counseling, placement for graduates, veterans' counselor. **Physically disabled:** Services for visually, speech, hearing impaired. **Transfer:** Transfer center, transfer adviser, college fairs on campus for students transferring to 4-year colleges.

Contact. E-mail: futurestudents@slcc.edu
Phone: (801) 957-4298 Fax: (801) 957-4961
Eric Weber, Dean of Student Enrollment Services, Salt Lake Community College, 4600 South Redwood Road, Salt Lake City, UT 84130-0808

Snow College
Ephraim, Utah
www.snow.edu
CB code: 4727

- Public 2-year junior college
- Residential campus in small town

General. Founded in 1888. Regionally accredited. Collaborative program with Julliard in music, theater arts, and dance. Classes, conferences, and workshops hosted by Great Basin Environmental Education Center, offering students outdoor and environmental-service friendly education. **Enrollment:** 4,605 degree-seeking undergraduates. **Degrees:** 8 bachelor's, 801 associate awarded. **Location:** 120 miles from Salt Lake City, 70 miles from Provo. **Calendar:** Semester, limited summer session. **Full-time faculty:** 116 total; 3% minority, 32% women. **Part-time faculty:** 136 total. **Class size:** 62% < 20, 31% 20-39, 4% 40-49, 2% 50-99, less than 1% >100.

Student profile.

Out-of-state:	4%	Live on campus:	5%
25 or older:	11%		

Transfer out. **Colleges most students transferred to 2015:** Utah State University, Salt Lake Community College, Utah Valley State College, Southern Utah University.

Basis for selection. Open admission. Auditions recommended for fine arts. **Home schooled:** State high school equivalency certificate required.

High school preparation. College-preparatory program recommended. 15 units recommended. Recommended units include English 4, mathematics 2, social studies 3, science 3 (laboratory 3).

2015-2016 Annual costs. Tuition/fees: $3,484; $11,676 out-of-state. Per-credit charge: $137 in-state; $497 out-of-state. Room only: $1,750. Books/supplies: $750. Personal expenses: $900.

Financial aid. **Need-based:** Work-study available nights, weekends and for part-time students. **Non-need-based:** Scholarships awarded for academics, alumni affiliation, athletics, leadership, music/drama, state residency.

Application procedures. **Admission:** Priority date 6/1; no deadline. $30 fee. Admission notification on a rolling basis beginning on or about 12/1. Applications received after 5/15 will be on a space-available basis. **Financial aid:** Priority date 3/1, closing date 6/1. FAFSA, institutional form required. Applicants notified on a rolling basis starting 8/1; must reply within 1 week(s) of notification.

Academics. **Special study options:** Cooperative education, distance learning, dual enrollment of high school students, ESL, honors, independent study. **Credit/placement by examination:** AP, CLEP, institutional tests. 45 credit hours maximum toward associate degree. **Support services:** GED test center, learning center, reduced course load, remedial instruction, study skills assistance, tutoring, writing center.

Majors. **Biology:** General, bacteriology, botany, physiology, zoology. **Business:** General, accounting, business admin, managerial economics. **Communications:** Journalism. **Computer sciences:** General, computer science, information systems. **Conservation:** General, forestry, wildlife/wilderness. **Education:** General, business, early childhood, elementary, ESL, family/consumer sciences, health, physical, secondary, special ed. **Engineering:** General. **English:** English lit, writing. **Foreign languages:** General, French, Japanese, Spanish. **Health services:** Clinical lab science, EMT paramedic, licensed practical nurse, pharmacy assistant, predental, premedicine, prenursing, prepharmacy, preveterinary, veterinary technology/assistant. **History:** General. **Human services:** Social work. **Math:** General, statistics. **Parks/recreation:** General, health/fitness, outdoor education. **Philosophy/religion:** Philosophy. **Physical sciences:** Chemistry, geology, physics. **Protective services:** Law enforcement admin. **Psychology:** General. **Social sciences:** General, anthropology, economics, geography, political science, sociology. **Visual/performing arts:** General, art, dance, music. **Work/family studies:** General, child care management, clothing/textiles, family/community services, food/nutrition.

Most popular majors. Business/marketing 6%, education 11%, health sciences 14%, liberal arts 37%, visual/performing arts 7%.

Technology on campus. 450 workstations in library, computer center, student center. Dormitories wired for high-speed internet access and linked to campus network. Online course registration, online library, helpline, wireless network available.

Student life. **Freshman orientation:** Available. Preregistration for classes offered. Begins 2 days prior to fall semester. **Housing:** Coed dorms, single-sex dorms, apartments available. $200 partly refundable deposit, deadline 6/1. **Activities:** Bands, choral groups, dance, drama, international student organizations, literary magazine, music ensembles, musical theater, radio station, student government, student newspaper, symphony orchestra, TV station, Latter-Day Saints student association, associated women students, associated men students, Badgers Against Alcohol & Drugs, Polynesian club, ski club, Spanish club, international club.

Athletics. NJCAA. **Intercollegiate:** Basketball, football (tackle) M, softball W, volleyball W. **Intramural:** Basketball, bowling, football (non-tackle) M, golf, racquetball, rugby M, soccer, softball, tennis, ultimate frisbee, volleyball, water polo. **Team name:** Badgers.

Student services. Adult student services, alcohol/substance abuse counseling, career counseling, services for economically disadvantaged, financial aid counseling, health services, on-campus daycare, personal counseling, veterans' counselor. **Physically disabled:** Services for visually, hearing impaired. **Transfer:** Pre-admission transcript evaluation for new students. Transfer adviser, college fairs on campus for students transferring to 4-year colleges.

Contact. E-mail: hsrelations@snow.edu
Phone: (435) 283-7150 Toll-free number: (800) 848-3399
Fax: (435) 283-6879
Brandon Wright, Director of Admissions, Snow College, 150 East College Avenue, Ephraim, UT 84627

Vista College: Online
Clearfield, Utah
www.vistacollege.edu

- For-profit 2-year career college
- Small city

General. Regionally accredited; also accredited by ACCSC. **Enrollment:** 207 undergraduates. **Degrees:** 58 associate awarded. **Calendar:** Quarter. **Full-time faculty:** 4 total. **Part-time faculty:** 4 total.

Basis for selection. Open admission.

Financial aid. Need-based: Work-study available nights, weekends and for part-time students.

Application procedures. Admission: $100 fee.

Academics. Credit/placement by examination: AP, CLEP.

Majors. Business: Business admin. **Computer sciences:** System admin. **Health services:** Office assistant. **Protective services:** Criminal justice.

Contact. E-mail: admissions@vistacollege.edu
Phone: (801) 774-9900 Toll-free number: (866) 442-4197
Vista College: Online, 1785 E. 1450 S. Suite 300, Clearfield, UT 84015

Vermont

Community College of Vermont
Montpelier, Vermont
www.ccv.edu

CB member
CB code: 3286

◗ Public 2-year community and liberal arts college
◗ Commuter campus in small town

General. Founded in 1970. Regionally accredited. **Enrollment:** 3,883 degree-seeking undergraduates. **Degrees:** 517 associate awarded. **Calendar:** Semester, extensive summer session. **Part-time faculty:** 729 total; 11% have terminal degrees, 60% women.

Transfer out. Colleges most students transferred to 2015: University of Vermont, Johnson State College, Champlain College, Vermont Technical College.

Basis for selection. Open admission. **Learning Disabled:** Students must meet with Americans with Disabilities coordinator and bring appropriate documentation.

2015-2016 Annual costs. Tuition/fees: $7,530; $14,910 out-of-state. Per-credit charge: $246 in-state; $492 out-of-state. Books/supplies: $1,000. **Additional information:** New England Board of Higher Education rate for students from other New England states: 150% of Vermont resident tuition. Available to degree candidates in academic areas not offered by educational institutions in their home states.

Financial aid. All financial aid based on need. Need-based aid available for part-time students. Work-study available nights, weekends and for part-time students.

Application procedures. Admission: No deadline. No application fee. Admission notification on a rolling basis. **Financial aid:** No deadline. FAFSA, institutional form required. Applicants notified on a rolling basis starting 9/1; must reply within 3 week(s) of notification.

Academics. Special study options: Cross-registration, distance learning, double major, dual enrollment of high school students, external degree, independent study, internships, liberal arts/career combination, student-designed major, study abroad. **Credit/placement by examination:** AP, CLEP, IB, institutional tests. 45 credit hours maximum toward associate degree. **Support services:** Learning center, reduced course load, remedial instruction, study skills assistance, tutoring, writing center.

Majors. Business: General, accounting, hospitality admin, office management, tourism/travel. **Communications:** Media studies. **Computer sciences:** General, system admin. **Conservation:** Environmental science. **Education:** General, early childhood. **Health services:** Office assistant. **Liberal arts:** Arts/sciences. **Protective services:** Criminal justice, disaster management. **Visual/performing arts:** General, graphic design.

Most popular majors. Business/marketing 25%, education 7%, liberal arts 41%, public administration/social services 9%.

Technology on campus. 880 workstations in library, computer center. Commuter students can connect to campus network. Online course registration, online library, helpline, wireless network available.

Student life. Freshman orientation: Available. Preregistration for classes offered. **Activities:** Choral groups, student government.

Student services. Adult student services, career counseling, services for economically disadvantaged, financial aid counseling, placement for graduates, veterans' counselor. **Physically disabled:** Services for visually, speech, hearing impaired. **Transfer:** Transfer adviser, college fairs on campus for students transferring to 4-year colleges.

Contact. E-mail: inquire@ccv.edu
Phone: (802) 828-2800 Toll-free number: (800) 228-6686
Fax: (802) 828-2805
Adam Warrington, Director of Admissions, Community College of Vermont, PO Box 489, Montpelier, VT 05601

Landmark College
Putney, Vermont
www.landmark.edu

CB code: 0081

◗ Private 2-year liberal arts college
◗ Residential campus in small town
◗ Application essay, interview required

General. Founded in 1983. Regionally accredited. College exclusively for bright students diagnosed with dyslexia, attention disorders, autism spectrum disorders, specific learning disabilities, and other learning-related mental health disorders. **Enrollment:** 452 degree-seeking undergraduates. **Degrees:** 99 associate awarded. **Location:** 8 miles from Brattleboro; 23 miles from Keene, NH. **Calendar:** Semester, limited summer session. **Full-time faculty:** 78 total; 31% have terminal degrees, 4% minority, 62% women. **Part-time faculty:** 11 total; 46% women. **Class size:** 99% < 20, less than 1% 20-39.

Student profile.

Out-of-state:	95%	Live on campus:	95%
25 or older:	4%		

Basis for selection. Successful applicants are highly motivated, have average-to-superior intellectual ability and diagnosis of dyslexia, attentional disorder (ADHD), or specific learning disability. Serves exclusively students with diagnosed learning disorders, ADHD, autism spectrum disorders, or other diagnosed psychological disorders that impede learning. For this reason, a current diagnosis by a professional is required of all students attending Landmark College; this diagnosis must have been made or confirmed within the last three years. One of the following cognitive ability tests required: WAIS, WISC, or Woodcock-Johnson Cognitive Scale. One of the following reading achievement tests required: Wechsler Individual Achievement Test, Woodcock-Johnson Achievement Test, Nelson Denny Reading Test, or Gray Oral Reading test. **Home schooled:** Transcript of courses and grades, state high school equivalency certificate required. If student does not have either official transcript from diploma-granting organization or from approving school district or GED/HSED and statistical information, portfolio of student's work indicative of his or her academic achievement required. **Learning Disabled:** Diagnosis of a learning disability, ADHD, or ASD required for admission. Students must provide psycho-educational testing results and documentation of diagnosis.

High school preparation. College-preparatory program recommended. Recommended units include English 4, mathematics 3, social studies 3, history 3, science 3, foreign language 1, visual/performing arts 1 and academic electives 1.

2015-2016 Annual costs. Tuition/fees: $52,792. Room/board: $10,710. Books/supplies: $1,500. Personal expenses: $2,000. **Additional information:** Required fees include laptop computer, protective sleeve, warranty, and Office software. Students who already own a Tablet/PC with Windows 8 can apply for an exception.

Financial aid. Need-based: Need-based aid available for part-time students. Work-study available nights, weekends and for part-time students. **Non-need-based:** Scholarships awarded for academics, art, leadership, minority status, music/drama. **Additional information:** Students encouraged to apply to state departments of vocational rehabilitation for additional financial assistance.

Application procedures. Admission: Priority date 12/1; no deadline. $75 fee, may be waived for applicants with need. Admission notification on a rolling basis beginning on or about 12/1. **Financial aid:** Priority date 2/15; no closing date. FAFSA required. Applicants notified on a rolling basis starting 3/15; must reply within 2 week(s) of notification.

Academics. All academic offerings and policies are designed to promote academic success among students diagnosed with ADHD, ASD, or other learning disabilities. **Special study options:** Independent study, internships, student-designed major, study abroad. Bachelor's degree programs available on campus. **Credit/placement by examination:** AP, CLEP, SAT, ACT, institutional tests. **Support services:** Learning center, pre-admission summer program, reduced course load, remedial instruction, study skills assistance, tutoring, writing center. Personal success coaching provided by certified coaches.

Majors. Business: Business admin. **Liberal arts:** Arts/sciences.

Most popular majors. Liberal arts 92%.

Technology on campus. PC or laptop required. 50 workstations in dormitories, library, student center. Dormitories wired for high-speed internet access and linked to campus network. Commuter students can connect to campus network. Online library, helpline, repair service, wireless network available.

Student life. Freshman orientation: Mandatory. Preregistration for classes offered. Held the 5 days prior to start of term. Separate 3-day early orientation session available to students with ASD; $500 fee. **Policies:** Alcohol not permitted on-campus. All new students must live on-campus. **Housing:** Guaranteed on-campus for all undergraduates. Coed dorms, special housing for disabled, wellness housing available. **Activities:** Jazz band, choral groups, dance, drama, literary magazine, music ensembles, radio station, student government, student newspaper, Phi Theta Kappa honor society, community service club, GLBTQA, community outreach group, peer educators, Hillel, student government association.

Athletics. Intercollegiate: Baseball M, basketball, cross-country, equestrian, soccer. **Intramural:** Basketball, football (non-tackle), softball. **Team name:** Sharks.

Student services. Adult student services, alcohol/substance abuse counseling, chaplain/spiritual director, career counseling, student employment services, financial aid counseling, health services, personal counseling, placement for graduates, women's services. **Physically disabled:** Services for visually, speech, hearing impaired. **Transfer:** Transfer center, transfer adviser, college fairs on campus for students transferring to 4-year colleges.

Contact. E-mail: admissions@landmark.edu
Phone: (802) 387-6718 Fax: (802) 387-6868
Gregory Matthews, Vice President for Enrollment Management, Landmark College, 19 River Road South, Putney, VT 05346

New England Culinary Institute
Montpelier, Vermont
www.neci.edu
CB code: 3405

▶ For-profit 2-year culinary school
▶ Residential campus in small town
▶ Application essay required

General. Founded in 1980. Accredited by ACCSC. All students required to complete paid internship; more than 500 signed internship agreements with restaurants and culinary outlets nationwide. **Enrollment:** 462 degree-seeking undergraduates. **Degrees:** 62 bachelor's, 78 associate awarded. **Location:** 39 miles from Burlington. **Calendar:** Continuous, extensive summer session. **Full-time faculty:** 23 total. **Part-time faculty:** 21 total. **Special facilities:** Gourmet restaurant, bakeshop, cafeteria, catering business, American cuisine restaurant, meat fabrication lab.

Student profile.

Out-of-state:	79%	Live on campus:	45%
25 or older:	30%		

Basis for selection. Academic transcripts, test scores, letters of reference, essay or personal statement, and industry experience considered. SAT or ACT recommended. Advanced standing available to students through school testing. Interview may be required, tour recommended. **Home schooled:** Transcript of courses and grades required. Personal interview may be required. **Learning Disabled:** Shadow experience recommended if there is question regarding ability to succeed.

High school preparation. College-preparatory program recommended. Transcript must demonstrate proficiency in English and math. Foreign language and culinary arts training highly desirable.

2015-2016 Annual costs. Tuition/fees: $31,390. Room/board: $8,000. Books/supplies: $1,375. Personal expenses: $3,204.

Financial aid. Need-based: Work-study available nights, weekends and for part-time students. **Non-need-based:** Scholarships awarded for academics, alumni affiliation, job skills, leadership.

Application procedures. Admission: No deadline. No application fee. Admission notification on a rolling basis. **Financial aid:** No deadline. FAFSA required. Applicants notified on a rolling basis.

Academics. Upper level of bachelor's programs offered both on-ground and fully online. Students engage in significant industry internships in all on-ground certificate and degree programs. **Special study options:** Accelerated study, distance learning; dual enrollment of high school students, internships. Bachelor's degree programs available on campus. **Credit/placement by examination:** AP, CLEP, institutional tests. Credit by examination considered form of transfer credit. Maximum credit earned by transfer, prior learning, or examination will not be more than 60% of program total. **Support services:** Learning center, remedial instruction, study skills assistance, tutoring.

Majors. Business: Hospitality admin, restaurant/food services.

Most popular majors. Personal/culinary services 98%.

Technology on campus. PC or laptop required. 10 workstations in library, student center. Dormitories wired for high-speed internet access. Commuter students can connect to campus network. Online library, helpline, wireless network available.

Student life. Freshman orientation: Mandatory. Preregistration for classes offered. Held 2-3 days prior to first day of classes. **Housing:** Guaranteed on-campus for freshmen. Coed dorms, single-sex dorms available. **Activities:** Student government, student newspaper.

Student services. Career counseling, student employment services, financial aid counseling, placement for graduates, veterans' counselor. **Transfer:** Pre-admission transcript evaluation for new students.

Contact. E-mail: admissions@neci.edu
Phone: (802) 223-6324 Toll-free number: (877) 223-6324
Fax: (802) 225-3280
Dwight Cross, Director of Admissions, New England Culinary Institute, 56 College Street, Montpelier, VT 05602

Virginia

Advanced Technology Institute
Virginia Beach, Virginia
www.auto.edu

- For-profit 2-year technical college
- Commuter campus in large city
- Interview required

General. Accredited by ACCSC. **Enrollment:** 717 undergraduates. **Degrees:** 90 associate awarded. **Calendar:** Semester, limited summer session.

Basis for selection. Written application and interview, followed by tour of the school prior to starting class.

2015-2016 Annual costs. Tuition/fees: $12,700. Personal expenses: $1,950.

Financial aid. Need-based: Work-study available nights, weekends and for part-time students.

Application procedures. Admission: No deadline. $45 fee. Admission notification on a rolling basis. **Financial aid:** No deadline.

Academics. Credit/placement by examination: AP, CLEP.

Technology on campus. Commuter students can connect to campus network.

Student life. Freshman orientation: Mandatory. Preregistration for classes offered.

Student services. Adult student services, career counseling, student employment services, financial aid counseling, veterans' counselor.

Contact. Phone: (757) 490-1241 Toll-free number: (800) 468-1093 Fax: (757) 499-5929
Mike Corcoran, Director of Admissions, Advanced Technology Institute, 5700 Southern Boulevard, Virginia Beach, VA 23462

American National University: Charlottesville
Charlottesville, Virginia
www.an.edu   CB code: 3248

- For-profit 2-year business college
- Commuter campus in small city
- Interview required

General. Accredited by ACICS. **Enrollment:** 115 degree-seeking undergraduates. **Degrees:** 21 associate awarded. **Calendar:** Quarter, limited summer session. **Full-time faculty:** 2 total. **Part-time faculty:** 9 total.

Basis for selection. Open admission.

2016-2017 Annual costs. Tuition/fees: $14,460. Per-credit charge: $317. Books/supplies: $1,200.

Financial aid. All financial aid based on need. Need-based aid available for part-time students. Work-study available nights, weekends and for part-time students.

Application procedures. Admission: No deadline. $50 fee, may be waived for applicants with need. Admission notification on a rolling basis. **Financial aid:** No deadline. FAFSA required. Applicants notified on a rolling basis.

Academics. Special study options: Double major, internships, liberal arts/career combination. **Credit/placement by examination:** AP, CLEP, institutional tests. **Support services:** Tutoring.

Majors. Business: Accounting, administrative services, business admin. **Computer sciences:** Computer science. **Health services:** Medical assistant.

Technology on campus. 35 workstations in library, computer center.

Student life. Freshman orientation: Mandatory. Preregistration for classes offered.

Contact. Phone: (804) 295-0136 Toll-free number: (800) 664-1886 Fax: (804) 979-8061
Crystal Souder, Director of Admissions, American National University: Charlottesville, 3926 Seminole Trail, Charlottesville, VA 22903

American National University: Danville
Danville, Virginia
www.an.edu   CB code: 3249

- For-profit 2-year branch campus and business college
- Commuter campus in small city

General. Accredited by ACICS. **Enrollment:** 123 degree-seeking undergraduates. **Degrees:** 6 bachelor's, 31 associate awarded. **Calendar:** Quarter, limited summer session. **Full-time faculty:** 1 total. **Part-time faculty:** 15 total.

Basis for selection. Open admission. Interview recommended.

2016-2017 Annual costs. Tuition/fees: $14,460. Per-credit charge: $317. Books/supplies: $2,817.

Financial aid. All financial aid based on need. Need-based aid available for part-time students. Work-study available nights, weekends and for part-time students.

Application procedures. Admission: No deadline. $50 fee, may be waived for applicants with need. Admission notification on a rolling basis. **Financial aid:** No deadline. FAFSA required. Applicants notified on a rolling basis starting 9/1.

Academics. Special study options: Double major, internships. **Credit/placement by examination:** AP, CLEP, institutional tests. **Support services:** Tutoring.

Majors. Business: Accounting, administrative services, business admin. **Computer sciences:** Computer science. **Health services:** Medical assistant.

Technology on campus. 35 workstations in library, computer center.

Student life. Freshman orientation: Mandatory. Preregistration for classes offered.

Student services. Career counseling, student employment services, personal counseling, placement for graduates.

Contact. E-mail: info@an.edu
Phone: (434) 793-6822
Jeff Moore, Director of Admissions, American National University: Danville, 336 Old Riverside Drive, Danville, VA 24541

American National University: Harrisonburg
Harrisonburg, Virginia
www.an.edu   CB code: 3173

- For-profit 2-year business college
- Commuter campus in large town

General. Accredited by ACICS. **Enrollment:** 95 degree-seeking undergraduates. **Degrees:** 2 bachelor's, 37 associate awarded. **Calendar:** Quarter, limited summer session. **Full-time faculty:** 8 total. **Part-time faculty:** 12 total.

Basis for selection. Open admission, but selective for some programs. Interview recommended.

2016-2017 Annual costs. Tuition/fees: $14,460. Per-credit charge: $317. Books/supplies: $1,200.

Financial aid. All financial aid based on need. Need-based aid available for part-time students. Work-study available nights, weekends and for part-time students.

Application procedures. Admission: No deadline. $50 fee, may be waived for applicants with need. Admission notification on a rolling basis. **Financial aid:** No deadline. FAFSA required. Applicants notified on a rolling basis starting 9/1.

Academics. Special study options: Double major, internships. **Credit/placement by examination:** AP, CLEP, institutional tests. **Support services:** Tutoring.

Majors. Business: Accounting, administrative services, business admin, office management. **Computer sciences:** Computer science. **Health services:** Medical assistant.

Technology on campus. 35 workstations in library, computer center.

Student life. Freshman orientation: Mandatory. Preregistration for classes offered.

Student services. Career counseling, personal counseling.

Contact. E-mail: market@national-college.edu
Phone: (540) 432-0943 Fax: (540) 432-1133
Stephanie Bell, Director of Admissions, American National University: Harrisonburg, 1515 Country Club Road, Harrisonburg, VA 22802

American National University: Lynchburg
Lynchburg, Virginia
www.an.edu
CB code: 3172

- For-profit 2-year business college
- Commuter campus in small city

General. Accredited by ACICS. **Enrollment:** 118 degree-seeking undergraduates. **Degrees:** 32 associate awarded. **Calendar:** Quarter, limited summer session. **Full-time faculty:** 2 total. **Part-time faculty:** 14 total.

Basis for selection. Open admission. Interview recommended.

2016-2017 Annual costs. Tuition/fees: $14,460. Per-credit charge: $317. Books/supplies: $1,200.

Financial aid. All financial aid based on need. Need-based aid available for part-time students. Work-study available nights, weekends and for part-time students.

Application procedures. Admission: No deadline. $50 fee, may be waived for applicants with need. Admission notification on a rolling basis. **Financial aid:** No deadline. FAFSA required. Applicants notified on a rolling basis starting 9/1.

Academics. Special study options: Double major, internships. **Credit/placement by examination:** AP, CLEP, institutional tests. **Support services:** Tutoring.

Majors. Business: Accounting, administrative services, business admin. **Computer sciences:** General, computer science. **Health services:** Medical assistant.

Technology on campus. 35 workstations in library, computer center.

Student life. Freshman orientation: Mandatory. Preregistration for classes offered.

Student services. Career counseling, student employment services, financial aid counseling, personal counseling, placement for graduates, veterans' counselor.

Contact. E-mail: market@national-college.edu
Phone: (804) 239-3500 Toll-free number: (800) 664-1886
Nancy Wilcox, Director of Admissions, American National University: Lynchburg, 104 Candlewood Court, Lynchburg, VA 24502

American National University: Martinsville
Martinsville, Virginia
www.an.edu
CB code: 3171

- For-profit 2-year business and junior college
- Commuter campus in small city

General. Accredited by ACICS. **Enrollment:** 91 degree-seeking undergraduates. **Degrees:** 36 associate awarded. **Calendar:** Quarter, limited summer session. **Full-time faculty:** 5 total. **Part-time faculty:** 14 total.

Basis for selection. Open admission.

2016-2017 Annual costs. Tuition/fees: $14,460. Per-credit charge: $317. Books/supplies: $1,200.

Financial aid. All financial aid based on need. Need-based aid available for part-time students. Work-study available nights, weekends and for part-time students.

Application procedures. Admission: No deadline. $50 fee, may be waived for applicants with need. Admission notification on a rolling basis. **Financial aid:** No deadline. FAFSA required. Applicants notified on a rolling basis.

Academics. Special study options: Double major, internships. **Credit/placement by examination:** AP, CLEP, institutional tests. **Support services:** Tutoring.

Majors. Business: Accounting, administrative services, business admin. **Computer sciences:** Computer science.

Technology on campus. 35 workstations in library, computer center.

Student life. Freshman orientation: Mandatory. Preregistration for classes offered.

Student services. Career counseling, student employment services, personal counseling.

Contact. Phone: (540) 632-5621
Barbara Rakes, Director of Admissions, American National University: Martinsville, 905 North Memorial Boulevard, Martinsville, VA 24112

Blue Ridge Community College
Weyers Cave, Virginia
www.brcc.edu
CB code: 5083

- Public 2-year community college
- Commuter campus in large town

General. Founded in 1965. Regionally accredited. **Enrollment:** 4,388 degree-seeking undergraduates. **Degrees:** 611 associate awarded. **Location:** 12 miles from Harrisonburg, 15 miles from Staunton. **Calendar:** Semester, limited summer session. **Full-time faculty:** 95 total. **Part-time faculty:** 258 total. **Special facilities:** Arboretum, fine arts center. **Partnerships:** Formal partnership with Tech Prep Consortium.

Student profile.

Out-of-state:	2%	25 or older:	24%

Transfer out. Colleges most students transferred to 2015: James Madison University, Mary Baldwin College, Old Dominion University, Eastern Mennonite University, Bridgewater College.

Basis for selection. Open admission, but selective for some programs. Special requirements for commercial driving, veterinary assistant technology and nursing programs (also has residency requirement); interview required.

High school preparation. College-preparatory program recommended. 8 units recommended. Recommended units include English 4, mathematics 2, social studies 1 and science 1.

2015-2016 Annual costs. Tuition/fees: $5,019; $10,317 out-of-state. Per-credit charge: $138 in-state; $315 out-of-state. Books/supplies: $600. Personal expenses: $900. **Additional information:** Out-of-state students pay an additional $540 capital outlay fee.

Financial aid. Need-based: Need-based aid available for part-time students. Work-study available nights, weekends and for part-time students. **Non-need-based:** Scholarships awarded for academics, job skills, leadership, minority status.

Application procedures. Admission: No deadline. No application fee. Admission notification on a rolling basis. Closing date for veterinary assistant technology is January 1. Nursing clinical component application deadline is January 31. **Financial aid:** Priority date 5/1; no closing date. FAFSA, institutional form required. Applicants notified on a rolling basis starting 5/30; must reply within 2 week(s) of notification.

Academics. Special study options: Accelerated study, cross-registration, distance learning, double major, dual enrollment of high school students, honors, independent study, internships, study abroad, teacher certification program. Bachelor's degree programs available on campus. License preparation in nursing, real estate. **Credit/placement by examination:** AP, CLEP, IB, institutional tests. 25 credit hours maximum toward associate degree. Credit cannot duplicate earned course credits, nor courses audited or failed.

Support services: Learning center, remedial instruction, study skills assistance, tutoring, writing center.

Majors. Business: Accounting, administrative services, business admin. **Computer sciences:** General, information systems, programming, systems analysis. **Health services:** Nursing (RN), veterinary technology/assistant. **Liberal arts:** Arts/sciences.

Technology on campus. 285 workstations in library, computer center, student center. Commuter students can connect to campus network. Online course registration, online library, helpline, wireless network available.

Student life. Freshman orientation: Available. Preregistration for classes offered. Held week before classes begin, open to parents. **Activities:** Drama, international student organizations, student government, Phi Theta Kappa, Christian Fellowship, Students in Free Enterprise, Vet Tech Club, Alpha Beta Gamma, Buddies Club, Collegiate FFA, Environmental Awareness, SPECTRUM Multicultural.

Athletics. Intramural: Basketball M.

Student services. Adult student services, career counseling, services for economically disadvantaged, student employment services, financial aid counseling, minority student services, placement for graduates, veterans' counselor, women's services. **Physically disabled:** Services for visually, speech, hearing impaired. **Transfer:** Pre-admission transcript evaluation for new students. Transfer adviser, college fairs on campus for students transferring to 4-year colleges.

Contact. Phone: (540) 453-2287
Toll-free number: (888) 750-2722 ext. 2287 Fax: (540) 453-2437
Dean of Academic Support Services, Blue Ridge Community College, Box 80, Weyers Cave, VA 24486-9989

Bryant & Stratton College: Richmond
Richmond, Virginia
www.bryantstratton.edu   CB code: 4762

- For-profit 2-year career college
- Commuter campus in small city

General. Enrollment: 626 degree-seeking undergraduates. **Degrees:** 29 bachelor's, 157 associate awarded. **Calendar:** Trimester, extensive summer session. **Full-time faculty:** 19 total. **Part-time faculty:** 50 total. **Class size:** 100% 20-39.

Basis for selection. Open admission, but selective for some programs. **Adult students:** SAT/ACT scores not required. **Home schooled:** Interview required.

2015-2016 Annual costs. Tuition/fees: $17,190. Per-credit charge: $573. Books/supplies: $1,000. Personal expenses: $2,610. **Additional information:** Tuition and fees may vary by program.

Financial aid. All financial aid based on need. Need-based aid available for part-time students. Work-study available nights, weekends and for part-time students.

Application procedures. Admission: No deadline. $35 fee. Application must be submitted on paper. Admission notification on a rolling basis. **Financial aid:** Closing date 9/17. FAFSA required.

Academics. Special study options: Distance learning, double major, independent study, internships. Bachelor's degree programs available on campus. License preparation in nursing. **Credit/placement by examination:** AP, CLEP, institutional tests. 30 credit hours maximum toward associate degree, 60 toward bachelor's. Up to 50% of total credit hours required for graduation, including 50% of the total required hours in major study areas, may be earned through combination of transfer credits and proficiency evaluations. **Support services:** Learning center, study skills assistance, tutoring.

Majors. Business: Accounting, administrative services, business admin, human resources. **Computer sciences:** Information technology. **Health services:** Medical assistant, medical secretary. **Protective services:** Criminal justice.

Technology on campus. 250 workstations in library, computer center. Commuter students can connect to campus network. Online course registration, online library, helpline, wireless network available.

Student life. Freshman orientation: Mandatory. Preregistration for classes offered. Day and evening sessions held the day before classes begin. **Activities:** Student government.

Student services. Career counseling, student employment services, financial aid counseling, placement for graduates, veterans' counselor. **Physically disabled:** Services for hearing impaired.

Contact. Phone: (804) 745-2444 Toll-free number: (800) 735-2420
Fax: (804) 745-6884
Paul Dhaliwal, Director of Admissions, Bryant & Stratton College: Richmond, 8141 Hull Street Road, Richmond, VA 23235

Bryant & Stratton College: Virginia Beach
Virginia Beach, Virginia
www.bryantstratton.edu   CB code: 4761

- For-profit 2-year business and junior college
- Commuter campus in large city
- Interview required

General. Founded in 1952. Regionally accredited. **Enrollment:** 585 degree-seeking undergraduates. **Degrees:** 41 bachelor's, 143 associate awarded. **Location:** 10 miles from Norfolk. **Calendar:** Semester, extensive summer session. **Full-time faculty:** 17 total. **Part-time faculty:** 49 total. **Class size:** 89% < 20, 11% 20-39.

Transfer out. Colleges most students transferred to 2015: Tidewater Community College, Strayer University, University of Phoenix.

Basis for selection. Open admission, but selective for some programs. Personal interview most important. TOEFL used for non-native English speakers.

High school preparation. Recommended units include English 4, mathematics 2, social studies 3, science 2, foreign language 2 and academic electives 1.

2015-2016 Annual costs. Tuition/fees: $17,190. Per-credit charge: $573. Books/supplies: $1,600. Personal expenses: $2,785. **Additional information:** Tuition and fees may vary by program.

Financial aid. Need-based: Need-based aid available for part-time students. Work-study available nights, weekends and for part-time students.

Application procedures. Admission: No deadline. $35 fee, may be waived for applicants with need. Admission notification on a rolling basis. **Financial aid:** Closing date 9/17. FAFSA required. Applicants notified on a rolling basis.

Academics. Free tutoring and extensive academic advising available. Portfolio projects in all classes. **Special study options:** Cooperative education, double major, independent study, internships, liberal arts/career combination, weekend college. **Credit/placement by examination:** AP, CLEP, institutional tests. 30 credit hours maximum toward associate degree, 60 toward bachelor's. **Support services:** Learning center, reduced course load, remedial instruction, study skills assistance, tutoring, writing center.

Majors. Business: Accounting, administrative services, business admin, human resources. **Computer sciences:** General. **Health services:** Medical assistant, office assistant. **Protective services:** Law enforcement admin.

Most popular majors. Business/marketing 44%, computer/information sciences 9%, health sciences 13%, legal studies 20%, security/protective services 14%.

Technology on campus. 150 workstations in library, computer center. Online library, wireless network available.

Student life. Freshman orientation: Mandatory. Preregistration for classes offered. Held week classes start, 2 to 3 hours. **Activities:** Student government, student newspaper, Alpha Beta Gamma, Phi Beta Lambda, law society, medical club, computer club, Society for the Advancement of Management.

Student services. Adult student services, career counseling, student employment services, on-campus daycare, personal counseling, placement for graduates, veterans' counselor. **Transfer:** Pre-admission transcript evaluation for new students.

Contact. E-mail: dmsoutherland@bryantstratton.edu
Phone: (757) 499-7900 Fax: (757) 499-9977
Monique Griffin, Director of Admissions, Bryant & Stratton College: Virginia Beach, 301 Centre Pointe Drive, Virginia Beach, VA 23462-4417

Central Virginia Community College
Lynchburg, Virginia
www.cvcc.vccs.edu

CB member
CB code: 5141

▶ Public 2-year community college
▶ Commuter campus in small city

General. Founded in 1966. Regionally accredited. **Enrollment:** 2,737 degree-seeking undergraduates. **Degrees:** 450 associate awarded. **Location:** 120 miles from Richmond. **Calendar:** Semester, limited summer session. **Full-time faculty:** 64 total. **Part-time faculty:** 312 total. **Class size:** 77% < 20, 23% 20-39, less than 1% 40-49. **Special facilities:** Fitness center, nature trail.

Student profile. Among degree-seeking undergraduates, 118 transferred in from other institutions.

Out-of-state: 2% **25 or older:** 25%

Transfer out. Colleges most students transferred to 2015: Lynchburg College, Virginia Polytechnic Institute and State University, Longwood College, Old Dominion University, Liberty University.

Basis for selection. Open admission, but selective for some programs. Allied health program applicants must have 2 interviews with program head and meet specific criteria. Only 15 applicants accepted into each program each year. Interview required for health program. **Adult students:** SAT/ACT scores not required.

High school preparation. College-preparatory program required.

2015-2016 Annual costs. Tuition/fees: $4,470; $9,768 out-of-state. Per-credit charge: $134 in-state; $310.6 out-of-state. Books/supplies: $957. Personal expenses: $1,584. **Additional information:** Out-of-state students pay an additional $540 capital outlay fee.

Financial aid. Need-based: Work-study available nights, weekends and for part-time students. **Non-need-based:** Scholarships awarded for academics, alumni affiliation. **Additional information:** Payment plan available.

Application procedures. Admission: Priority date 8/18; no deadline. No application fee. Admission notification on a rolling basis. **Financial aid:** Priority date 3/15; no closing date. FAFSA required. Applicants notified on a rolling basis starting 5/1; must reply within 2 week(s) of notification.

Academics. GPA of 2.0 required to graduate. System-wide core curriculum to ensure ease of transfer. **Special study options:** Cooperative education, distance learning, dual enrollment of high school students, independent study, internships, study abroad. Bachelor's degree programs available on campus. License preparation in paramedic, radiology, real estate. **Credit/placement by examination:** AP, CLEP, IB, institutional tests. 45 credit hours maximum toward associate degree. **Support services:** Learning center, reduced course load, remedial instruction, study skills assistance, tutoring, writing center.

Majors. Biology: General. **Business:** General, accounting, administrative services, business admin, finance, management information systems. **Computer sciences:** Information systems. **Education:** General. **Engineering:** General. **Health services:** Clinical lab technology, physics/radiologic health. **Liberal arts:** Arts/sciences. **Physical sciences:** General. **Protective services:** Law enforcement admin. **Visual/performing arts:** Commercial/advertising art.

Technology on campus. 230 workstations in library, computer center. Commuter students can connect to campus network. Online library, wireless network available.

Student life. Freshman orientation: Available. Preregistration for classes offered. **Activities:** Drama, literary magazine, student government, Black Student Alliance, art club, Phi Theta Kappa, Spanish club, medical lab club, respiratory club, environmental science club, radiology club, police science club, student veterans organization.

Athletics. Team name: Cougars.

Student services. Career counseling, student employment services, financial aid counseling, personal counseling, placement for graduates, veterans' counselor. **Physically disabled:** Services for visually, speech, hearing impaired. **Transfer:** Transfer adviser, college fairs on campus for students transferring to 4-year colleges.

Contact. E-mail: studentservices@cvcc.vccs.edu
Phone: (434) 832-7633 Toll-free number: (800) 562-3060
Fax: (434) 832-7793
Michael Farris, Dean of Enrollment Management, Central Virginia Community College, 3506 Wards Road, Lynchburg, VA 24502-2498

Dabney S. Lancaster Community College
Clifton Forge, Virginia
www.dslcc.edu

CB code: 5139

▶ Public 2-year community and technical college
▶ Commuter campus in small town

General. Founded in 1967. Regionally accredited. Virginia Governor's School on campus. Shared facilities with Virginia Army National Guard. **Enrollment:** 667 degree-seeking undergraduates. **Degrees:** 109 associate awarded. **Location:** 55 miles from Roanoke. **Calendar:** Semester, extensive summer session. **Full-time faculty:** 20 total. **Part-time faculty:** 90 total. **Class size:** 88% < 20, 11% 20-39, less than 1% 40-49. **Special facilities:** Wood harvesting lab, forestry lab, wind turbine service technician lab, EMS lab, nursing simulation lab, culinary arts lab.

Basis for selection. Open admission, but selective for some programs. Special requirements for ADN, LPN, PN Transitions, and EMS programs. High school diploma or GED required of applicants under 18. Interview required for ADN and LPN programs. **Adult students:** Placement testing may be required in English and Math.

High school preparation. Course recommendations vary according to planned curriculum.

2015-2016 Annual costs. Tuition/fees: $4,365; $9,663 out-of-state. Per-credit charge: $134 in-state; $311 out-of-state. Books/supplies: $580. Personal expenses: $1,680.

Financial aid. All financial aid based on need. Need-based aid available for part-time students. Work-study available nights, weekends and for part-time students.

Application procedures. Admission: No deadline. No application fee. Admission notification on a rolling basis beginning on or about 2/1. **Financial aid:** Priority date 3/1, closing date 6/30. FAFSA required. Applicants notified on a rolling basis starting 4/15; must reply within 2 week(s) of notification.

Academics. Special study options: Cooperative education, distance learning, double major, dual enrollment of high school students, independent study, internships. License preparation in nursing. **Credit/placement by examination:** AP, CLEP, institutional tests. **Support services:** GED preparation, learning center, pre-admission summer program, reduced course load, remedial instruction, study skills assistance, tutoring, writing center.

Majors. Business: Administrative services, business admin, communications, office management, office/clerical. **Communications technology:** Graphic/printing. **Computer sciences:** General. **Conservation:** Forestry. **Liberal arts:** Arts/sciences. **Protective services:** Criminal justice, police science.

Most popular majors. Education 11%, health sciences 43%, liberal arts 14%, natural resources/environmental science 18%, science technologies 6%, security/protective services 6%.

Technology on campus. 60 workstations in library, computer center, student center. Commuter students can connect to campus network. Online library, helpline, wireless network available.

Student life. Freshman orientation: Mandatory. Preregistration for classes offered. **Activities:** Literary magazine, student government, student newspaper, various social/religious/service clubs available.

Athletics. Intramural: Basketball, bowling, football (non-tackle), softball, table tennis, tennis, volleyball, weight lifting. **Team name:** Roadrunners.

Student services. Adult student services, alcohol/substance abuse counseling, career counseling, services for economically disadvantaged, student employment services, financial aid counseling, personal counseling, placement for graduates, veterans' counselor. **Physically disabled:** Services for visually, speech, hearing impaired. **Transfer:** Re-entry adviser for new students. Transfer adviser, college fairs on campus for students transferring to 4-year colleges.

Contact. Phone: (540) 863-2820 Toll-free number: (877) 133-7522
Fax: (540) 863-2915
Matt McGraw, Director of Student Services, Dabney S. Lancaster Community College, 1000 Dabney Drive, Clifton Forge, VA 24422

Danville Community College
Danville, Virginia
www.dcc.vccs.edu

CB code: 5163

▶ Public 2-year community college
▶ Commuter campus in small city

General. Founded in 1967. Regionally accredited. **Enrollment:** 1,972 degree-seeking undergraduates. **Degrees:** 305 associate awarded. **Location:** 45 miles from Greensboro, NC. **Calendar:** Semester, limited summer session. **Full-time faculty:** 66 total. **Part-time faculty:** 213 total. **Class size:** 71% < 20, 28% 20-39, 1% 50-99.

Student profile.

Out-of-state:	2%	25 or older: 52%

Transfer out. Colleges most students transferred to 2015: Averett University, Virginia Polytechnic Institute, Radford University.

Basis for selection. Open admission, but selective for some programs. Special requirements for nursing program.

High school preparation. Recommended units include English 4 and mathematics 1.

2015-2016 Annual costs. Tuition/fees: $4,350; $9,648 out-of-state. Per-credit charge: $134 in-state; $311 out-of-state. Books/supplies: $700. Personal expenses: $1,328. **Additional information:** Out-of-state students pay an additional $540 capital outlay fee.

Financial aid. All financial aid based on need. Need-based aid available for part-time students. Work-study available nights, weekends and for part-time students.

Application procedures. Admission: Priority date 8/20; no deadline. No application fee. Admission notification on a rolling basis beginning on or about 1/15. **Financial aid:** Priority date 6/1; no closing date. FAFSA required. Applicants notified on a rolling basis starting 5/1; must reply within 2 week(s) of notification.

Academics. System-wide core curriculum to ensure ease of transfer. **Special study options:** Accelerated study, cooperative education, distance learning, double major, dual enrollment of high school students, honors, independent study, internships. Bachelor's degree programs available on campus. License preparation in dental hygiene, nursing, real estate. **Credit/placement by examination:** AP, CLEP, institutional tests. **Support services:** GED preparation and test center, learning center, pre-admission summer program, reduced course load, remedial instruction, study skills assistance, tutoring.

Majors. Business: General, accounting, administrative services, business admin, executive assistant, receptionist. **Communications technology:** Graphic/printing. **Computer sciences:** General, computer science, programming. **Engineering:** General. **Health services:** Dental hygiene, medical secretary, office assistant, respiratory therapy assistant. **Liberal arts:** Arts/sciences, humanities. **Protective services:** Law enforcement admin. **Work/family studies:** Child development.

Most popular majors. Business/marketing 41%, education 15%, liberal arts 33%, security/protective services 10%.

Technology on campus. 425 workstations in library, computer center. Online course registration, online library available.

Student life. Freshman orientation: Mandatory. Preregistration for classes offered. Two 1-day summer sessions to choose from. **Activities:** Choral groups, student government, African-American culture club, Christian Students Fellowship, graphics club, International Association of Administrative Professionals, Phi Theta Kappa, National Vocational-Technical Honor Society, gospel club, Lambda Alpha Epsilon.

Athletics. Team name: Knights.

Student services. Adult student services, chaplain/spiritual director, career counseling, student employment services, financial aid counseling, on-campus daycare, personal counseling, placement for graduates, veterans' counselor, women's services. **Physically disabled:** Services for visually, speech, hearing impaired. **Transfer:** College fairs on campus for students transferring to 4-year colleges.

Contact. E-mail: ethornton@dcc.vccs.edu
Phone: (434) 797-8467 Toll-free number: (800) 560-4291
Fax: (434) 797-8451
Cheryl Terry, Dean of Student Success and Academic Advancement, Danville Community College, 1008 South Main Street, Danville, VA 24541

Eastern Shore Community College
Melfa, Virginia
www.es.vccs.edu   CB code: 5844

- Public 2-year community college
- Commuter campus in rural community

General. Founded in 1971. Regionally accredited. **Enrollment:** 503 degree-seeking undergraduates. **Degrees:** 66 associate awarded. **Location:** 70 miles from Norfolk, 60 miles from Salisbury, MD. **Calendar:** Semester, limited summer session. **Full-time faculty:** 68 total; 10% minority, 52% women. **Part-time faculty:** 46 total; 9% minority, 50% women.

Transfer out. Colleges most students transferred to 2015: Old Dominion University, University of Maryland, Eastern Shore, Virginia Polytechnic Institute.

Basis for selection. Open admission, but selective for some programs. Practical Nursing program has prerequisites for admission; must take PSB nursing aptitude test and meet state requirements for screening. Additionally, all students must take a placement test prior to enrolling in any program. **Adult students:** All applicants must take College placement test in English and Math prior to enrolling in courses. **Learning Disabled:** ESCC honors all reasonable, documented requests for accommodations. In order to obtain special accommodations, a student must meet with a counselor prior to classes.

High school preparation. College-preparatory program recommended. 18 units recommended. Recommended units include English 4, mathematics 3, social studies 2, history 1 and science 2.

2015-2016 Annual costs. Tuition/fees: $4,395; $9,693 out-of-state. Per-credit charge: $134 in-state; $311 out-of-state. Books/supplies: $900. Personal expenses: $1,500. **Additional information:** Out-of-state students pay an additional $18 per credit hour for a Capital Fee.

Financial aid. All financial aid based on need. Need-based aid available for part-time students. Work-study available nights, weekends and for part-time students. **Additional information:** ESCC is a member of the Servicemembers Opportunity Colleges program.

Application procedures. Admission: No deadline. No application fee. Admission notification on a rolling basis. **Financial aid:** Priority date 5/1; no closing date. FAFSA required. Applicants notified on a rolling basis starting 6/1; must reply within 2 week(s) of notification.

Academics. Special study options: Cross-registration, distance learning, dual enrollment of high school students, internships. License preparation in nursing. **Credit/placement by examination:** AP, CLEP, institutional tests. 30 credit hours maximum toward associate degree. Students who do not achieve minimum scores on institutional placement tests must enroll in developmental courses. **Support services:** GED preparation and test center, learning center, reduced course load, remedial instruction, study skills assistance, tutoring, writing center.

Majors. Business: Business admin, office/clerical. **Computer sciences:** General. **Education:** General, science. **Engineering:** Electrical. **Liberal arts:** Arts/sciences.

Technology on campus. 60 workstations in library, computer center. Online course registration, online library, helpline, wireless network available.

Student life. Freshman orientation: Available. Preregistration for classes offered. **Activities:** Campus ministries, literary magazine, student government, Phi Theta Kappa, Phi Beta Lambda, ACTS, photography club, chess club.

Student services. Adult student services, career counseling, student employment services, financial aid counseling, personal counseling, placement for graduates, veterans' counselor. **Physically disabled:** Services for visually, hearing impaired. **Transfer:** Transfer adviser, college fairs on campus for students transferring to 4-year colleges.

Contact. E-mail: jbaggett@es.vccs.edu
Phone: (757) 789-1731 Fax: (757) 789-1737
Eastern Shore Community College, 29300 Lankford Highway, Melfa, VA 23410-9755

Germanna Community College
Locust Grove, Virginia
www.germanna.edu   CB code: 5276

- Public 2-year community college
- Commuter campus in rural community

General. Founded in 1969. Regionally accredited. Off-campus sites in high schools; dual enrollment courses offered at area high schools. **Enrollment:** 7,379 degree-seeking undergraduates. **Degrees:** 789 associate awarded. **Location:** 15 miles from Culpeper, 18 miles from Fredericksburg. **Calendar:** Semester, limited summer session. **Full-time faculty:** 103 total. **Part-time faculty:** 321 total. **Class size:** 40% < 20, 60% 20-39, less than 1% 50-99. **Special facilities:** Art exhibits, local history collection.

Student profile.

Out-of-state:	1%	25 or older:	29%

Transfer out. Colleges most students transferred to 2015: University of Mary Washington, Old Dominion University, Radford University, Virginia Commonwealth University, Virginia Tech.

Basis for selection. Open admission, but selective for some programs. Special requirements for nursing program with local applicants given preference. **Adult students:** SAT, GCC placement tests, or proof of college transcripts required. **Home schooled:** Transcript of courses and grades required. Provide current copy of signed home school agreement between appropriate school system and authorizing parent or guardian. Provide written recommendation from home school teacher or tutor.

2015-2016 Annual costs. Tuition/fees: $4,575; $9,873 out-of-state. Per-credit charge: $135 in-state; $312 out-of-state. Books/supplies: $800. Personal expenses: $2,770. **Additional information:** Out-of-state students pay an additional $540 capital outlay fee.

Financial aid. Need-based: Need-based aid available for part-time students. Work-study available nights, weekends and for part-time students. **Non-need-based:** Scholarships awarded for academics.

Application procedures. Admission: No deadline. No application fee. Admission notification on a rolling basis. Nursing program applications must be completed by February 1. **Financial aid:** Priority date 4/1; no closing date. FAFSA required. Applicants notified on a rolling basis starting 5/15; must reply within 2 week(s) of notification.

Academics. System-wide core curriculum to ensure ease of transfer. **Special study options:** Accelerated study, distance learning, double major, dual enrollment of high school students, ESL, independent study, internships, liberal arts/career combination. Bachelor's degree programs available on campus. License preparation in dental hygiene, nursing. **Credit/placement by examination:** AP, CLEP, institutional tests. 8 credit hours maximum toward associate degree. **Support services:** GED test center, reduced course load, remedial instruction, study skills assistance, tutoring.

Majors. Biology: General. **Business:** General, business admin. **Computer sciences:** Information technology. **Education:** General, elementary. **Health services:** Dental hygiene, nursing (RN), radiologic technology/medical imaging. **Liberal arts:** Arts/sciences. **Protective services:** Police science. **Psychology:** General.

Most popular majors. Biological/life sciences 10%, business/marketing 22%, education 7%, health sciences 16%, liberal arts 41%.

Technology on campus. 90 workstations in library, computer center. Online course registration, online library, helpline, wireless network available.

Student life. Freshman orientation: Mandatory. Preregistration for classes offered. **Activities:** Student government, black studies, student Christian associations.

Athletics. Team name: Grizzly Bears.

Student services. Career counseling, student employment services, financial aid counseling, personal counseling, placement for graduates, veterans' counselor. **Physically disabled:** Services for visually, hearing impaired. **Transfer:** Transfer adviser, college fairs on campus for students transferring to 4-year colleges.

Contact. Phone: (540) 423-9122 Fax: (540) 423-9158
Rita Dunston, Registrar, Germanna Community College, 2130 Germanna Highway, Locust Grove, VA 22508-2102

J. Sargeant Reynolds Community College
Richmond, Virginia
www.reynolds.edu   CB code: 5340

- Public 2-year community college
- Commuter campus in very large city

General. Founded in 1972. Regionally accredited. **Enrollment:** 9,152 degree-seeking undergraduates; 1,735 non-degree-seeking students. **Degrees:** 702 associate awarded. **Location:** Downtown and suburban campi. **Calendar:** Semester, extensive summer session. **Full-time faculty:** 140 total; 21% minority, 54% women. **Part-time faculty:** 505 total; 35% minority, 59% women. **Class size:** 69% < 20, 31% 20-39. **Special facilities:** Distance education center. **Partnerships:** Formal partnerships with local medical facilities, Ford, General Motors.

Student profile. Among degree-seeking undergraduates, 1,495 enrolled as first-time, first-year students, 1,121 transferred in from other institutions.

Part-time:	67%	Hispanic/Latino:	3%
Out-of-state:	1%	Native American:	1%
Women:	60%	Multi-racial, non-Hispanic:	7%
African American:	36%	25 or older:	40%
Asian American:	6%		

Transfer out. Colleges most students transferred to 2015: Virginia Commonwealth University, Old Dominion University.

Basis for selection. Open admission, but selective for some programs. Special requirements for nursing, health technology, engineering, legal assisting programs; interview recommended. **Home schooled:** State high school equivalency certificate required.

High school preparation. College preparatory units recommended for applicants to college transfer programs. Recommended units vary per program of study and include up to 4 English, 4 math, 2 lab science, 2 foreign language, 2 social studies.

2015-2016 Annual costs. Tuition/fees: $4,653; $9,951 out-of-state. Per-credit charge: $138 in-state; $313 out-of-state. Books/supplies: $1,700. **Additional information:** Out-of-state students pay an additional $540 capital outlay fee.

2014-2015 Financial aid. Need-based: 545 full-time freshmen applied for aid; 541 deemed to have need; 541 received aid. 72% of total undergraduate aid awarded as scholarships/grants, 28% as loans/jobs. Need-based aid available for part-time students. Work-study available nights, weekends and for part-time students. **Non-need-based:** Awarded to 851 full-time undergraduates, including 148 freshmen. Scholarships awarded for academics.

Application procedures. Admission: No deadline. No application fee. Admission notification on a rolling basis beginning on or about 1/15. **Financial aid:** Closing date 4/15. FAFSA required. Applicants notified on a rolling basis starting 7/15; must reply within 2 week(s) of notification.

Academics. Special study options: Cooperative education, distance learning, double major, dual enrollment of high school students, ESL, independent study, internships, weekend college. License preparation in nursing, paramedic, real estate. **Credit/placement by examination:** AP, CLEP, IB, institutional tests. 50 credit hours maximum toward associate degree. Essay required for CLEP exams. **Support services:** GED preparation, learning center, pre-admission summer program, reduced course load, remedial instruction, study skills assistance, tutoring, writing center. Student Assistance and Intervention for Learning Strategies (SAILS) flags students who may be having difficulty. Coaching is offered to these students.

Majors. Architecture: Building sciences. **Business:** Business admin, small business admin. **Computer sciences:** Computer science, data entry, networking, programming, web page design. **Engineering:** General. **Foreign languages:** Sign language interpretation. **General:** Site management. **Health services:** Clinical lab technology, dental lab technology, nursing (RN), optician, respiratory therapy technology. **Liberal arts:** Arts/sciences. **Protective services:** Firefighting, law enforcement admin. **Social sciences:** General. **Work/family studies:** Child development, merchandising.

Most popular majors. Business/marketing 18%, health sciences 24%, interdisciplinary studies 13%, security/protective services 13%, social sciences 16%.

Technology on campus. 300 workstations in library, computer center, student center. Commuter students can connect to campus network. Online course registration, online library, helpline, wireless network available.

Student life. Freshman orientation: Available. Preregistration for classes offered. **Activities:** Campus ministries, film society, international student organizations, student government, horticultural club, PAVE club, Phi Beta Lambda, Phi Theta Kappa, anime club, Spectrum LGBT, Muslim Student Association, Student Nurses of America, Teachers of Tomorrow, video games club, writing Club, history club.

Student services. Career counseling, financial aid counseling, veterans' counselor. **Physically disabled:** Services for visually, speech, hearing impaired. **Transfer:** Transfer adviser, college fairs on campus for students transferring to 4-year colleges.

Contact. E-mail: kpettis-walden@reynolds.edu
Phone: (804) 523-5029 Fax: (804) 371-3650
Karen Pettis-Walden, Director of Admissions and Records, J. Sargeant Reynolds Community College, PO Box 85622, Richmond, VA 23285-5622

John Tyler Community College
Chester, Virginia   **CB member**
www.jtcc.edu   **CB code: 5342**

- Public 2-year community college
- Commuter campus in small city

General. Founded in 1965. Regionally accredited. **Enrollment:** 6,220 degree-seeking undergraduates; 3,815 non-degree-seeking students. **Degrees:** 764 associate awarded. **ROTC:** Army. **Location:** 16 miles from Richmond. **Calendar:** Semester, extensive summer session. **Full-time faculty:** 124 total. **Part-time faculty:** 450 total. **Class size:** 65% < 20, 35% 20-39.

Student profile. Among degree-seeking undergraduates, 1,328 enrolled as first-time, first-year students.

Part-time:	61%	Hispanic/Latino:	9%
Out-of-state:	4%	Native American:	1%
Women:	59%	Multi-racial, non-Hispanic:	4%
African American:	28%	25 or older:	35%
Asian American:	3%		

Basis for selection. Open admission, but selective for some programs. Special requirements for nursing, funeral services and police science programs. **Home schooled:** Parents of students must provide written permission to enroll their children and meet with the dean of student services prior to applying. Placement tests required.

High school preparation. Required units include English 4 and mathematics 4. Biology and/or chemistry required for allied health programs.

2015-2016 Annual costs. Tuition/fees: $4,345; $9,643 out-of-state. Per-credit charge: $134 in-state; $311 out-of-state. Books/supplies: $1,328. Personal expenses: $2,210. **Additional information:** Out-of-state students pay an additional $540 capital outlay fee.

Financial aid. **Need-based:** Need-based aid available for part-time students. Work-study available nights, weekends and for part-time students. **Non-need-based:** Scholarships awarded for academics, state residency.

Application procedures. **Admission:** Priority date 8/1; no deadline. No application fee. Admission notification on a rolling basis. High school students may attend with written approval of school principal. **Financial aid:** Priority date 4/1; no closing date. FAFSA required. Applicants notified on a rolling basis starting 5/30.

Academics. Students seeking associate degree must complete 25 percent of core courses at college. **Special study options:** Cooperative education, distance learning, dual enrollment of high school students, internships, weekend college. 2-2 transfer programs in various engineering technology disciplines and business education; 1-3 transfer certificate in art. License preparation in nursing. **Credit/placement by examination:** AP, CLEP, IB, institutional tests. **Support services:** Learning center, remedial instruction, study skills assistance, tutoring, writing center.

Majors. **Architecture:** Technology. **Business:** Business admin. **Computer sciences:** General, information technology. **Engineering:** General. **Health services:** Nursing (RN). **Liberal arts:** Humanities. **Protective services:** Law enforcement admin. **Work/family studies:** Child care service.

Most popular majors. Business/marketing 16%, engineering/engineering technologies 6%, health sciences 18%, liberal arts 46%.

Technology on campus. 2,115 workstations in library, student center. Commuter students can connect to campus network. Online course registration, online library, wireless network available.

Student life. **Freshman orientation:** Mandatory. Preregistration for classes offered. **Activities:** Drama, student government, Nursing Students Association, human services club, funeral services club, biology club, art club, Elements of Life club, chemistry club, Future Teachers club, Phi Theta Kappa, Disciples of Christ club.

Athletics. **Team name:** Trailblazers.

Student services. Adult student services, alcohol/substance abuse counseling, career counseling, financial aid counseling, personal counseling, veterans' counselor. **Physically disabled:** Services for visually, speech, hearing impaired. **Transfer:** Transfer adviser, college fairs on campus for students transferring to 4-year colleges.

Contact. E-mail: admissionsandrecords@jtcc.edu
Phone: (804) 706-5211 Toll-free number: (800) 552-3490
Fax: (804) 796-4362
Joy James, Director of Admissions & Records/Veteran Affairs and Registrar, John Tyler Community College, 13101 Jefferson Davis Highway, Chester, VA 23831-5316

Lord Fairfax Community College
Middletown, Virginia
www.lfcc.edu   **CB code: 5381**

- Public 2-year community college
- Commuter campus in small town

General. Founded in 1969. Regionally accredited. Locations in Fauquier, Middletown and the Luray-Page County Center. **Enrollment:** 4,262 degree-seeking undergraduates. **Degrees:** 647 associate awarded. **Calendar:** Semester, limited summer session. **Full-time faculty:** 83 total. **Part-time faculty:** 382 total.

Transfer out. **Colleges most students transferred to 2015:** George Mason University, James Madison University, Old Dominion University, Shenandoah University, University of Mary Washington.

Basis for selection. Open admission, but selective for some programs. Selective admission for health profession. **Adult students:** SAT/ACT scores not required.

2015-2016 Annual costs. Tuition/fees: $4,424; $9,722 out-of-state. Per-credit charge: $135 in-state; $312 out-of-state. Books/supplies: $800. **Additional information:** Out-of-state students pay an additional $540 capital outlay fee.

Financial aid. All financial aid based on need. Need-based aid available for part-time students. Work-study available nights, weekends and for part-time students.

Application procedures. **Admission:** No deadline. No application fee. Admission notification on a rolling basis. **Financial aid:** Priority date 5/1; no closing date. FAFSA required. Applicants notified on a rolling basis starting 6/1.

Academics. **Special study options:** Distance learning, double major, dual enrollment of high school students, ESL, honors, independent study. Bachelor's degree programs available on campus. License preparation in dental hygiene, nursing, paramedic, real estate. **Credit/placement by examination:** AP, CLEP, institutional tests. **Support services:** GED test center, learning center, reduced course load, remedial instruction, study skills assistance, tutoring.

Majors. **Business:** Accounting, administrative services, business admin, management information systems, marketing, office management. **Communications:** Communications/speech/rhetoric. **Computer sciences:** General, database management, networking, webmaster. **Education:** General. **Engineering:** General, civil, electrical, mechanical. **Health services:** Dental hygiene, nursing (RN). **Liberal arts:** Arts/sciences. **Philosophy/religion:** Philosophy, religion.

Technology on campus. Online course registration, online library available.

Student life. **Freshman orientation:** Mandatory. Preregistration for classes offered. **Activities:** Dance, drama, international student organizations, musical theater, student government, student newspaper, special interest and program-related organizations, ambassadors club, honor society.

Athletics. **Intercollegiate:** Basketball, soccer. **Team name:** Cannons.

Student services. Adult student services, career counseling, services for economically disadvantaged, financial aid counseling, veterans' counselor. **Physically disabled:** Services for visually, speech, hearing impaired. **Transfer:** Transfer center, transfer adviser, college fairs on campus for students transferring to 4-year colleges.

Contact. E-mail: admissions@lfcc.edu
Toll-free number: (800) 906-5322 Fax: (540) 868-7005
Karen Bucher, Dean of Students, Lord Fairfax Community College, 173 Skirmisher Lane, Middletown, VA 22645

Miller-Motte Technical College: Lynchburg
Lynchburg, Virginia
www.miller-motte.edu

- For-profit 2-year technical college
- Commuter campus in small city
- Interview required

General. Accredited by ACICS. **Enrollment:** 409 undergraduates. **Degrees:** 106 associate awarded. **Location:** 60 miles from Charlottesville,

180 miles from Richmond. **Calendar:** Quarter. **Full-time faculty:** 2 total. **Part-time faculty:** 35 total. **Special facilities:** College-operated massage therapy clinic, aesthetics clinic.

Basis for selection. Open admission. **Home schooled:** Statement describing home school structure and mission required.

2015-2016 Annual costs. Management: $25,563; books and supplies $3,200. Medical Assisting: $27,963; books and supplies $3,200. Surgical Technology: $27,232; books and supplies $2,400. Criminal Justice: $25,563; books and supplies $3,200. Healthcare Technology: $27,963; books and supplies $3,200. Electronic Health Records: $27,963; books and supplies $3,200. Network Administration and Security: $27,483; books and supplies $3,200. Massage Therapy: $10,600; books and supplies $1,900. Figures are for total program cost.

Financial aid. All financial aid based on need. Need-based aid available for part-time students. Work-study available nights, weekends and for part-time students.

Application procedures. Admission: No deadline. $35 fee. Application must be submitted on paper. Admission notification on a rolling basis. **Financial aid:** No deadline. FAFSA required. Applicants notified on a rolling basis.

Academics. Special study options: Cooperative education, dual enrollment of high school students. **Credit/placement by examination:** AP, CLEP, institutional tests. Students are encouraged to test out of introductory classes if they feel they have the necessary experience. There is a $100 non-refundable examination fee. Students are not encouraged to test out of advanced classes leading to the associate degree. **Support services:** Learning center, study skills assistance, tutoring.

Majors. Business: Management science. **Computer sciences:** General. **Health services:** Clinical lab assistant, health information technology, massage therapy, medical assistant, office assistant, pharmacy assistant, phlebotomy, surgical technology. **Protective services:** Corrections.

Technology on campus. 75 workstations in library, computer center.

Student life. Freshman orientation: Available. Preregistration for classes offered.

Student services. Student employment services, financial aid counseling.

Contact. Phone: (434) 239-5222 Toll-free number: (877) 333-6622 Fax: (434) 239-1069
Valerie Wall, Director of Admissions, Miller-Motte Technical College: Lynchburg, 1011 Creekside Lane, Lynchburg, VA 24502

Mountain Empire Community College
Big Stone Gap, Virginia
www.mecc.edu   CB code: 5451

- Public 2-year community college
- Commuter campus in small town

General. Founded in 1970. Regionally accredited. **Enrollment:** 2,924 undergraduates. **Degrees:** 239 associate awarded. **Location:** 40 miles from Bristol. **Calendar:** Semester, limited summer session. **Full-time faculty:** 56 total. **Part-time faculty:** 127 total.

Student profile.

Out-of-state: 4% **25 or older:**   40%

Transfer out. Colleges most students transferred to 2015: University of Virginia's College at Wise, Radford University, Virginia Polytechnic Institute and State University, East Tennessee State University.

Basis for selection. Open admission, but selective for some programs. Nursing students must meet admission test score, plus biology, chemistry and algebra I required. Respiratory therapy students must meet admission test score, plus algebra I and biology required. High school diploma or GED required for practical nursing, nursing and respiratory care programs.

High school preparation. College-preparatory program recommended. 1 algebra, 1 biology, 1 chemistry required for nursing program; 1 algebra, 1 biology required for respiratory care program.

2015-2016 Annual costs. Tuition/fees: $4,365; $9,663 out-of-state. Per-credit charge: $134 in-state; $311 out-of-state. Books/supplies: $860. **Additional information:** Out-of-state students pay an additional $540 capital outlay fee.

Financial aid. Need-based: Need-based aid available for part-time students. Work-study available nights, weekends and for part-time students. **Non-need-based:** Scholarships awarded for academics, state residency. **Additional information:** The college does not participate in loan programs. All financial aid is in form of grants, scholarships, or work study.

Application procedures. Admission: No deadline. No application fee. Admission notification on a rolling basis beginning on or about 1/1. **Financial aid:** Priority date 5/1; no closing date. FAFSA required. Applicants notified on a rolling basis starting 1/1.

Academics. System-wide core curriculum to ensure ease of transfer. **Special study options:** Accelerated study, distance learning, double major, dual enrollment of high school students, independent study, internships, liberal arts/career combination, student-designed major. Bachelor's degree programs available on campus. License preparation in nursing, real estate. **Credit/placement by examination:** AP, CLEP, IB, institutional tests. 16 credit hours maximum toward associate degree. Maximum 25% of credits awarded for work and/or life experience. **Support services:** Learning center, preadmission summer program, reduced course load, remedial instruction, tutoring.

Majors. Biology: General. **Business:** General, accounting, business admin, office management, office/clerical. **Computer sciences:** General, information systems, information technology, networking, word processing. **Conservation:** General, environmental science, forestry. **Education:** General. **Engineering:** Electrical, manufacturing. **Health services:** EMT paramedic, medical secretary, medical transcription, nursing (RN), respiratory therapy technology. **Human services:** Social work. **Liberal arts:** Arts/sciences. **Math:** General. **Protective services:** Corrections, criminal justice, law enforcement admin.

Most popular majors. Business/marketing 17%, computer/information sciences 16%, education 12%, health sciences 10%, legal studies 6%, liberal arts 26%.

Technology on campus. 400 workstations in library, computer center. Wireless network available.

Student life. Freshman orientation: Mandatory. Preregistration for classes offered. **Activities:** Campus ministries, drama, music ensembles, student government, student newspaper, service, business, nursing organizations available.

Athletics. Intramural: Archery, badminton, basketball, bowling, softball, table tennis, tennis, volleyball. **Team name:** Red Fox Fliers.

Student services. Career counseling, student employment services, financial aid counseling, health services, personal counseling, placement for graduates, veterans' counselor. **Transfer:** Pre-admission transcript evaluation for new students. Transfer adviser for students transferring to 4-year colleges.

Contact. E-mail: khall@me.vccs.edu
Phone: (276) 523-2400 Fax: (276) 523-8297
Kristy Hall, Director of Enrollment Services, Mountain Empire Community College, 3441 Mountain Empire Road, Big Stone Gap, VA 24219

New River Community College
Dublin, Virginia
www.nr.edu   CB code: 5513

- Public 2-year community college
- Commuter campus in rural community

General. Founded in 1966. Regionally accredited. **Enrollment:** 4,200 undergraduates. **Degrees:** 420 associate awarded. **Location:** 50 miles from Roanoke. **Calendar:** Semester, limited summer session. **Full-time faculty:** 56 total. **Part-time faculty:** 166 total.

Transfer out. Colleges most students transferred to 2015: Radford University, Virginia Tech, Old Dominion University.

Basis for selection. Open admission. Interview required for nursing program.

2015-2016 Annual costs. Tuition/fees: $4,352; $9,650 out-of-state. Per-credit charge: $134 in-state; $311 out-of-state. Books/supplies: $700. Personal expenses: $1,200.

Financial aid. Need-based: Need-based aid available for part-time students. Work-study available nights, weekends and for part-time students.

Application procedures. Admission: No deadline. No application fee. Admission notification on a rolling basis. **Financial aid:** Closing date 4/15. FAFSA, institutional form required. Applicants notified on a rolling basis.

Academics. Special study options: Cooperative education, distance learning, dual enrollment of high school students, teacher certification program. **Credit/placement by examination:** AP, CLEP, IB, institutional tests. **Support services:** GED preparation and test center, learning center, remedial instruction, study skills assistance, tutoring, writing center.

Majors. Business: Accounting, administrative services, business admin, logistics, office technology. **Computer sciences:** Computer graphics, information technology, programming. **Education:** General, early childhood. **Engineering:** General, computer. **Health services:** Medical secretary. **Liberal arts:** Arts/sciences. **Protective services:** Forensics, law enforcement admin. **Visual/performing arts:** Game design.

Technology on campus. Commuter students can connect to campus network. Online course registration, online library, repair service, wireless network available.

Student life. Freshman orientation: Available. Preregistration for classes offered. **Activities:** Music ensembles, student government, Black Awareness Association, Phi Beta Lambda, Phi Theta Kappa.

Athletics. Intramural: Baseball M, basketball, soccer, softball, table tennis.

Student services. Career counseling, student employment services, financial aid counseling, on-campus daycare, personal counseling, placement for graduates, veterans' counselor. **Physically disabled:** Services for visually, speech, hearing impaired. **Transfer:** Transfer adviser, college fairs on campus for students transferring to 4-year colleges.

Contact. E-mail: admissions@nr.edu
Phone: (540) 674-3603 Toll-free number: (866) 462-6722
Fax: (540) 674-3644
Tammy Smith, Coordinator of Admissions and Records, New River Community College, 5251 College Dr, Dublin, VA 24084

Northern Virginia Community College
Annandale, Virginia   **CB member**
www.nvcc.edu   **CB code: 5515**

◗ Public 2-year community college
◗ Commuter campus in small city

General. Founded in 1965. Regionally accredited. 6 campuses in Alexandria, Annandale, Loudoun County, Manassas, Springfield (medical education), Woodbridge. **Enrollment:** 43,871 degree-seeking undergraduates. **Degrees:** 5,643 associate awarded. **Location:** 12 miles from Washington, DC. **Calendar:** Semester, limited summer session. **Full-time faculty:** 954 total. **Part-time faculty:** 1,864 total.

Transfer out. Colleges most students transferred to 2015: George Mason University.

Basis for selection. Open admission, but selective for some programs. Admission to health and veterinary technology programs based on academic prerequisites, placement tests, and space availability. Interview recommended for allied health, animal science, dental hygiene, nursing programs.

2015-2016 Annual costs. Tuition/fees: $5,138; $10,515 out-of-state. Per-credit charge: $158.15 in-state; $337.4 out-of-state. Books/supplies: $900. Personal expenses: $2,435. **Additional information:** Out-of-state students pay an additional $540 capital outlay fee.

Financial aid. Need-based: Work-study available nights, weekends and for part-time students. **Non-need-based:** Scholarships awarded for academics, state residency.

Application procedures. Admission: No deadline. No application fee. Admission notification on a rolling basis. **Financial aid:** Priority date 3/1; no closing date. FAFSA, institutional form required. Applicants notified on a rolling basis starting 5/15; must reply within 2 week(s) of notification.

Academics. System-wide core curriculum to ensure ease of transfer. **Special study options:** Cooperative education, distance learning, double major, dual enrollment of high school students, ESL, honors, independent study, internships, liberal arts/career combination, student-designed major, study abroad, weekend college. Old Dominion University Teletechnet degree programs. **Credit/placement by examination:** AP, CLEP, IB, institutional tests. Maximum of 75% of credit hours required for program may be awarded

through CLEP. 25% of requirements must be completed at institution. **Support services:** Learning center, reduced course load, remedial instruction, tutoring, writing center.

Majors. Business: Accounting, business admin, international, management information systems, office management, purchasing, real estate, tourism/travel. **Communications:** Communications/speech/rhetoric. **Computer sciences:** General, computer science, programming. **Education:** Art, early childhood. **Engineering:** Civil. **Health services:** Clinical lab assistant, clinical lab technology, dental hygiene, EMT paramedic, health information technology, medical radiologic technology/radiation therapy, physical therapy assistant, respiratory therapy technology, substance abuse counseling, veterinary technology/assistant. **Liberal arts:** Arts/sciences. **Math:** General. **Parks/recreation:** Facilities management. **Protective services:** Fire safety technology, fire services admin, law enforcement admin, security services. **Psychology:** General. **Visual/performing arts:** Commercial photography, commercial/advertising art, interior design, music, photography, studio arts. **Work/family studies:** Institutional food production.

Technology on campus. 2,000 workstations in library, computer center.

Student life. Activities: Bands, choral groups, dance, drama, international student organizations, music ensembles, musical theater, student government, student newspaper, symphony orchestra, TV station, honor societies, African American student organizations, religious groups, Korean and Vietnamese student organizations, data processing management club, art association, physical therapist assistants club, Omega Engineering Students.

Athletics. Intramural: Basketball, football (tackle), soccer, volleyball.

Student services. Career counseling, veterans' counselor. **Physically disabled:** Services for visually, hearing impaired. **Transfer:** Transfer adviser, college fairs on campus for students transferring to 4-year colleges.

Contact. Phone: (703) 323-3000
Northern Virginia Community College, 8333 Little River Turnpike, Annandale, VA 22003-3796

Patrick Henry Community College
Martinsville, Virginia
www.ph.vccs.edu   **CB code: 5549**

◗ Public 2-year community college
◗ Commuter campus in large town

General. Founded in 1962. Regionally accredited. **Enrollment:** 2,200 degree-seeking undergraduates. **Degrees:** 400 associate awarded. **Location:** 50 miles from Roanoke, 50 miles from Greensboro, NC. **Calendar:** Semester, limited summer session. **Full-time faculty:** 50 total. **Part-time faculty:** 115 total. **Special facilities:** Southern history collection, Virginia literature collection, fine arts theater.

Basis for selection. Open admission. High school diploma or GED required for some programs.

2015-2016 Annual costs. Tuition/fees: $4,360; $9,658 out-of-state. Per-credit charge: $134 in-state; $311 out-of-state. Books/supplies: $500. Personal expenses: $840. **Additional information:** Out-of-state students pay an additional $540 capital outlay fee.

Financial aid. Need-based: Need-based aid available for part-time students. Work-study available nights, weekends and for part-time students.

Application procedures. Admission: Priority date 8/1; no deadline. No application fee. Admission notification on a rolling basis beginning on or about 2/1. Deadline for nursing applicants 3/1. **Financial aid:** Priority date 6/1; no closing date. FAFSA required. Applicants notified on a rolling basis starting 6/15.

Academics. System-wide core curriculum to ensure ease of transfer. **Special study options:** Cooperative education, distance learning, double major, dual enrollment of high school students, independent study, internships, teacher certification program, weekend college. Bachelor's degree programs available on campus. License preparation in nursing. **Credit/placement by examination:** AP, CLEP, institutional tests. 12 credit hours maximum toward associate degree. **Support services:** Learning center, pre-admission summer program, reduced course load, remedial instruction, study skills assistance, tutoring, writing center.

Majors. Business: Accounting, business admin. **Computer sciences:** General, programming. **Liberal arts:** Arts/sciences.

Technology on campus. 500 workstations in library, computer center, student center. Commuter students can connect to campus network. Online library, helpline, repair service, wireless network available.

Student life. Freshman orientation: Available. Preregistration for classes offered. **Activities:** Bands, choral groups, drama, musical theater, student government, student newspaper, TV station, black student association, Phi Theta Kappa, campus awareness network, nurses association.

Athletics. NJCAA. **Intercollegiate:** Baseball M, basketball, cheerleading, golf M, soccer, softball. **Intramural:** Basketball, soccer, softball, table tennis, tennis, volleyball. **Team name:** Patriots.

Student services. Adult student services, career counseling, financial aid counseling, personal counseling, placement for graduates, veterans' counselor. **Physically disabled:** Services for visually, speech, hearing impaired. **Transfer:** Transfer adviser, college fairs on campus for students transferring to 4-year colleges.

Contact. E-mail: meggleson@patrickhenry.edu
Phone: (276) 656-0325 Toll-free number: (800) 232-7997
Fax: (276) 632-0183
Meghan Eggleston, Coordinator of Admissions, Patrick Henry Community College, 645 Patriot Avenue, Martinsville, VA 24112

Paul D. Camp Community College
Franklin, Virginia
www.pdc.edu   CB code: 5557

- Public 2-year community college
- Commuter campus in small town

General. Founded in 1970. Regionally accredited. Campuses in Franklin and Suffolk, site in Smithsfield. **Enrollment:** 789 degree-seeking undergraduates. **Degrees:** 185 associate awarded. **Location:** 50 miles from Norfolk. **Calendar:** Semester, limited summer session. **Full-time faculty:** 19 total; 10% have terminal degrees, 42% minority, 58% women. **Part-time faculty:** 60 total. **Class size:** 87% < 20, 11% 20-39, 2% 40-49.

Transfer out. Colleges most students transferred to 2015: Old Dominion University, Christopher Newport University, Norfolk State University.

Basis for selection. Open admission, but selective for some programs. Limited enrollment to select nursing and allied health programs. **Home schooled:** Letter of recommendation (nonparent) required. Student must provide Admissions and Records Office current copy of signed home school agreement between appropriate school system and authorizing parent or guardian.

2015-2016 Annual costs. Tuition/fees: $4,340; $10,178 out-of-state. Per-credit charge: $134 in-state; $329 out-of-state. Books/supplies: $1,844.

2014-2015 Financial aid. All financial aid based on need. Need-based aid available for part-time students. Work-study available nights, weekends and for part-time students.

Application procedures. Admission: Priority date 8/1; no deadline. No application fee. Admission notification on a rolling basis. **Financial aid:** Priority date 5/15; no closing date. FAFSA required. Applicants notified on a rolling basis starting 8/1; must reply within 2 week(s) of notification.

Academics. Special study options: Cross-registration, distance learning, dual enrollment of high school students, honors, independent study, internships. License preparation in nursing. **Credit/placement by examination:** AP, CLEP, institutional tests. 52 credit hours maximum toward associate degree. **Support services:** GED preparation, learning center, pre-admission summer program, reduced course load, remedial instruction, study skills assistance, tutoring.

Majors. Business: Administrative services, business admin, office management. **Computer sciences:** General. **Education:** General. **Health services:** Nursing (RN). **Protective services:** Police science.

Technology on campus. 100 workstations in library, computer center. Online course registration, online library available.

Student life. Freshman orientation: Mandatory. Preregistration for classes offered. **Activities:** Campus ministries, literary magazine, student government, student newspaper, honor societies.

Student services. Adult student services, career counseling, services for economically disadvantaged, student employment services, financial aid counseling, personal counseling, placement for graduates, veterans' counselor.

Transfer: Pre-admission transcript evaluation for new students. College fairs on campus for students transferring to 4-year colleges.

Contact. Phone: (757) 569-6700 Fax: (757) 569-6795
Trina Jones, Dean Student Services, Paul D. Camp Community College, 100 North College Drive, Franklin, VA 23851-0737

Piedmont Virginia Community College
Charlottesville, Virginia
www.pvcc.edu   CB code: 5561

- Public 2-year community college
- Commuter campus in large town

General. Founded in 1969. Regionally accredited. **Enrollment:** 3,502 degree-seeking undergraduates. **Degrees:** 502 associate awarded. **ROTC:** Army, Air Force. **Location:** 70 miles from Richmond. **Calendar:** Semester, limited summer session. **Full-time faculty:** 78 total. **Part-time faculty:** 213 total. **Class size:** 49% < 20, 49% 20-39, 1% 40-49, less than 1% 50-99. **Partnerships:** Formal partnerships with local businesses, including nursing/retirement home and hospitals.

Student profile.

Out-of-state:	1%	25 or older:	34%

Transfer out. Colleges most students transferred to 2015: University of Virginia, Virginia Commonwealth University, James Madison University, Virginia Tech, Old Dominion University.

Basis for selection. Open admission, but selective for some programs. Special requirements for nursing, radiography, sonography, surgical technology, EMS, and LPN programs; interview recommended. **Home schooled:** Students must meet with counselor prior to enrolling and test into college level courses.

2015-2016 Annual costs. Tuition/fees: $4,445; $9,743 out-of-state. Per-credit charge: $135 in-state; $311.6 out-of-state. Books/supplies: $1,077. Personal expenses: $1,908. **Additional information:** Out-of-state students pay an additional $540 capital outlay fee.

Financial aid. Need-based: Need-based aid available for part-time students. Work-study available nights, weekends and for part-time students. **Non-need-based:** Scholarships awarded for academics.

Application procedures. Admission: No deadline. No application fee. Application must be submitted online. Admission notification on a rolling basis. Accepted applicants to nursing program must reply within 10 days. **Financial aid:** No deadline. FAFSA required. Applicants notified on a rolling basis starting 4/1.

Academics. System-wide core curriculum to ensure ease of transfer. **Special study options:** Accelerated study, cooperative education, distance learning, dual enrollment of high school students, ESL, honors, independent study, internships, weekend college. License preparation in nursing, paramedic, radiology. **Credit/placement by examination:** AP, CLEP, institutional tests. Must obtain 25% of degree requirement credits at PVCC. **Support services:** Learning center, pre-admission summer program, reduced course load, remedial instruction, study skills assistance, tutoring, writing center.

Majors. Business: Accounting technology, business admin. **Computer sciences:** General. **Education:** General. **Engineering:** General. **Health services:** EMT paramedic, nursing (RN), radiologic technology/medical imaging, sonography. **Liberal arts:** Arts/sciences. **Protective services:** Police science. **Visual/performing arts:** General.

Most popular majors. Business/marketing 20%, health sciences 20%, liberal arts 35%.

Technology on campus. 306 workstations in library, computer center. Online course registration, online library, helpline, wireless network available.

Student life. Freshman orientation: Mandatory. Preregistration for classes offered. **Activities:** Choral groups, dance, drama, international student organizations, literary magazine, music ensembles, student government, student newspaper, black student alliance, Phi Theta Kappa, Christian Fellowship, investment club, engineering club, Masquers club, volunteer club, student ambassadors.

Athletics. Intramural: Basketball, golf, lacrosse W, soccer, table tennis, tennis, ultimate frisbee, volleyball, weight lifting.

Student services. Adult student services, career counseling, services for economically disadvantaged, student employment services, financial aid counseling, personal counseling, placement for graduates, veterans' counselor.

Physically disabled: Services for visually, speech, hearing impaired. **Transfer:** Pre-admission transcript evaluation for new students. Transfer center, transfer adviser, college fairs on campus for students transferring to 4-year colleges.

Contact. E-mail: admissions@pvcc.edu
Phone: (434) 961-6551 Fax: (434) 961-5425
Mary Lee Walsh, Dean of Student Services, Piedmont Virginia Community College, 501 College Drive, Charlottesville, VA 22902-7589

Rappahannock Community College
Glenns, Virginia
www.rappahannock.edu   CB code: 5590

- Public 2-year community college
- Commuter campus in rural community

General. Founded in 1970. Regionally accredited. **Enrollment:** 1,791 degree-seeking undergraduates. **Degrees:** 246 associate awarded. **Location:** 50 miles from Richmond. **Calendar:** Semester, limited summer session. **Full-time faculty:** 28 total. **Part-time faculty:** 196 total.

Transfer out. Colleges most students transferred to 2015: Old Dominion University, Virginia Commonwealth University.

Basis for selection. Open admission, but selective for some programs. Placement test in reading/writing and one in math required. There is an application process for ADN, PN, and EMS programs.

2015-2016 Annual costs. Tuition/fees: $4,460; $9,758 out-of-state. Per-credit charge: $134 in-state; $311 out-of-state. Books/supplies: $1,360. Personal expenses: $4,630. **Additional information:** Out-of-state students pay an additional $540 capital outlay fee.

Financial aid. Need-based: Need-based aid available for part-time students. Work-study available nights, weekends and for part-time students.

Application procedures. Admission: No deadline. No application fee. Admission notification on a rolling basis. **Financial aid:** Priority date 4/15; no closing date. FAFSA, institutional form required. Applicants notified on a rolling basis starting 6/30.

Academics. Special study options: Cooperative education, cross-registration, distance learning, double major, dual enrollment of high school students, honors, independent study, internships, liberal arts/career combination, teacher certification program. License preparation in nursing. **Credit/placement by examination:** AP, CLEP, institutional tests. **Support services:** GED preparation and test center, learning center, reduced course load, remedial instruction, study skills assistance, tutoring.

Majors. Business: Business admin. **Health services:** Licensed practical nurse, nursing (RN). **Liberal arts:** Arts/sciences. **Protective services:** Law enforcement admin.

Technology on campus. 60 workstations in library, computer center. Online course registration, online library, helpline, wireless network available.

Student life. Freshman orientation: Available. Preregistration for classes offered. **Activities:** Phi Theta Kappa Honors Society.

Athletics. Intramural: Softball W. **Team name:** Gulls.

Student services. Adult student services, career counseling, services for economically disadvantaged, financial aid counseling, personal counseling, veterans' counselor. **Physically disabled:** Services for visually, speech, hearing impaired. **Transfer:** Transfer adviser, college fairs on campus for students transferring to 4-year colleges.

Contact. Phone: (804) 758-6700 Fax: (804) 758-3852
Felicia Packett, Registrar, Rappahannock Community College, 12745 College Drive, Glenns, VA 23149-2616

Richard Bland College
Petersburg, Virginia   CB member
www.rbc.edu   CB code: 5574

- Public 2-year junior and liberal arts college
- Commuter campus in small city
- SAT or ACT, application essay required

General. Founded in 1960. Regionally accredited. Affiliated with The College of William and Mary. Only two-year residential college in Virginia. **Enrollment:** 1,528 degree-seeking undergraduates. **Degrees:** 219 associate awarded. **ROTC:** Army. **Location:** 3 miles from Petersburg, 25 miles from Richmond. **Calendar:** Semester, limited summer session. **Full-time faculty:** 33 total. **Part-time faculty:** 23 total. **Class size:** 32% < 20, 52% 20-39, 8% 40-49, 8% 50-99. **Special facilities:** Nature trail, Civil War sites.

Student profile. Among degree-seeking undergraduates, 1,528 enrolled as first-time, first-year students.

Out-of-state:	5%	Live on campus:	15%
25 or older:	9%		

Transfer out. Colleges most students transferred to 2015: Virginia Commonwealth University, College of William and Mary, James Madison University, Longwood University, Virginia Tech.

Basis for selection. Academic record most important; test scores, essay also important; recommendations, extracurricular activities, interview considered. 2.0 GPA required for all commuter students, 2.5 GPA for residential students. Interview recommended depending on GPA. **Home schooled:** Transcript of courses and grades required. GED or SAT required. SAT scores must be equal to or greater than the mean score for current students. **Learning Disabled:** Students eligible for ADA should contact the Division of Student Affairs one month prior to the start of classes to request services.

High school preparation. 13 units required. Required and recommended units include English 4, mathematics 3-4, history 2-3, science 2-3 and foreign language 2.

2015-2016 Annual costs. Tuition/fees: $5,493; $15,236 out-of-state. Per-credit charge: $245 in-state; $652 out-of-state. Room/board: $10,572. Books/supplies: $1,200. Personal expenses: $1,996.

Financial aid. Need-based: Need-based aid available for part-time students. Work-study available nights, weekends and for part-time students. **Non-need-based:** Scholarships awarded for academics.

Application procedures. Admission: Priority date 3/1; no deadline. $25 fee, may be waived for applicants with need. Application must be submitted on paper. Admission notification on a rolling basis beginning on or about 10/1. Must reply by May 1 or within 2 week(s) if notified thereafter. **Financial aid:** Priority date 3/1; no closing date. FAFSA required. Must reply by 5/1 or within 2 week(s) of notification.

Academics. Special study options: Dual enrollment of high school students, honors. Educational trips abroad during spring break and summer session for academic credit. **Credit/placement by examination:** AP, CLEP, institutional tests. 30 credit hours maximum toward associate degree. **Support services:** Reduced course load, remedial instruction, study skills assistance, tutoring, writing center.

Majors. Liberal arts: Arts/sciences.

Technology on campus. 100 workstations in dormitories, library, student center. Dormitories wired for high-speed internet access and linked to campus network. Commuter students can connect to campus network. Online library, wireless network available.

Student life. Freshman orientation: Available. Preregistration for classes offered. Half day program to include a separate orientation for parents and meetings with advisors. **Policies:** Campus-wide honor code observed. **Housing:** Coed dorms available. **Activities:** Choral groups, dance, drama, film society, international student organizations, literary magazine, student government, Spanish club, Gay Lesbian Bisexual Transgender Alliance, Student Ambassadors, wellness club, biology club, dance club.

Athletics. Intramural: Basketball, bowling, cheerleading W, cross-country, football (non-tackle), golf, soccer, tennis. **Team name:** Statesman.

Student services. Career counseling, financial aid counseling. **Physically disabled:** Services for visually, speech, hearing impaired. **Transfer:** Pre-admission transcript evaluation for new students. Transfer adviser, college fairs on campus for students transferring to 4-year colleges.

Contact. E-mail: admit@rbc.edu
Phone: (804) 862-6249 Fax: (804) 862-6490
James Hart, Dean of Enrollment Services, Richard Bland College, 8311 Halifax Road, Petersburg, VA 23805

Southside Virginia Community College
Alberta, Virginia
www.southside.edu   CB code: 5660

▶ Public 2-year community college
▶ Commuter campus in rural community
▶ Interview required

General. Founded in 1970. Regionally accredited. Additional campuses in Keysville and Emporia. **Enrollment:** 2,509 degree-seeking undergraduates; 1,930 non-degree-seeking students. **Degrees:** 583 associate awarded. **ROTC:** Army. **Location:** 70 miles from Richmond. **Calendar:** Semester, limited summer session. **Full-time faculty:** 70 total. **Part-time faculty:** 151 total. **Special facilities:** Nature trail, fitness trail.

Student profile. Among degree-seeking undergraduates, 46% enrolled in a transfer program, 54% enrolled in a vocational program, 267 enrolled as first-time, first-year students.

Part-time:	55%	**Women:**	67%
Out-of-state:	1%	**25 or older:**	25%

Transfer out. Colleges most students transferred to 2015: Longwood University, Old Dominion University, Virginia Commonwealth University.

Basis for selection. Open admission, but selective for some programs. National League for Nursing Pre-Admissions Examination required for nursing applicants. Psychological Services Bureau Revised Aptitude for Practical Nursing Examination required for practical nursing applicants. **Home schooled:** If not enrolled in program leading to completion credential, student should obtain GED.

2015-2016 Annual costs. Tuition/fees: $4,350; $9,648 out-of-state. Per-credit charge: $134 in-state; $310.6 out-of-state.

Financial aid. Need-based: Need-based aid available for part-time students. Work-study available nights, weekends and for part-time students. **Non-need-based:** Scholarships awarded for academics.

Application procedures. Admission: No deadline. No application fee. Admission notification on a rolling basis. **Financial aid:** Priority date 6/1, closing date 8/1. FAFSA required. Applicants notified on a rolling basis starting 6/15.

Academics. System-wide core curriculum to ensure ease of transfer. **Special study options:** Cross-registration, distance learning, dual enrollment of high school students, honors, internships, study abroad. Cooperative programs in respiratory therapy with J. Sargeant Reynolds Community College, medical laboratory program with Central Virginia Community College. Bachelor's degree programs available on campus. License preparation in nursing. **Credit/placement by examination:** AP, CLEP, institutional tests. 45 credit hours maximum toward associate degree. **Support services:** GED preparation and test center, reduced course load, remedial instruction, study skills assistance, tutoring.

Majors. Business: Administrative services, business admin, management science. **Computer sciences:** General. **Education:** General. **Health services:** Clinical lab technology, nursing (RN), respiratory therapy technology. **Liberal arts:** Arts/sciences. **Protective services:** Police science.

Technology on campus. 200 workstations in library, computer center. Online course registration, helpline, wireless network available.

Student life. Freshman orientation: Available. Preregistration for classes offered. **Activities:** Choral groups, drama, music ensembles, student government, Phi Theta Kappa, Criminal Justice Organization, Phi Beta Lambda, Lambda Alpha Epsilon, Alpha Delta Omega.

Athletics. Intramural: Baseball M, basketball, softball, table tennis, tennis, volleyball. **Team name:** Panthers.

Student services. Career counseling, financial aid counseling, personal counseling, veterans' counselor. **Transfer:** Pre-admission transcript evaluation for new students. College fairs on campus for students transferring to 4-year colleges.

Contact. E-mail: rhina.jones@southside.edu
Phone: (434) 949-1000 Fax: (434) 949-7863
Dorothea Sizemore, Director of Admissions, Southside Virginia Community College, 109 Campus Drive, Alberta, VA 23821

Southwest Virginia Community College
Richlands, Virginia
www.sw.edu   CB code: 5659

▶ Public 2-year community college
▶ Commuter campus in small town

General. Founded in 1967. Regionally accredited. **Enrollment:** 1,838 degree-seeking undergraduates. **Degrees:** 259 associate awarded. **Location:** 45 miles from Bluefield and Bristol. **Calendar:** Semester, extensive summer session. **Full-time faculty:** 50 total. **Part-time faculty:** 124 total. **Class size:** 75% < 20, 21% 20-39, 2% 40-49, 1% 50-99. **Special facilities:** Community center, arts center.

Student profile. Among degree-seeking undergraduates, 42% enrolled in a transfer program, 58% enrolled in a vocational program.

Out-of-state:	3%	**Native American:**	1%
African American:	1%	**Multi-racial, non-Hispanic:**	1%
Hispanic/Latino:	1%	**25 or older:**	40%

Transfer out. Colleges most students transferred to 2015: Virginia Tech, Radford University, University of Virginia at Wise, East Tennessee State University.

Basis for selection. Open admission, but selective for some programs. Special requirements for engineering and health programs. Students required to take COMPASS, ASSET or some other placement test with the scores used to determine if students will need to take developmental English, math or reading. Interview required for full-time.

High school preparation. Subject and unit requirements vary with degree programs.

2015-2016 Annual costs. Tuition/fees: $4,335; $9,633 out-of-state. Per-credit charge: $134 in-state; $310 out-of-state. Books/supplies: $1,000. Personal expenses: $1,700. **Additional information:** Out-of-state students pay an additional $540 capital outlay fee.

2014-2015 Financial aid. All financial aid based on need. Need-based aid available for part-time students. Work-study available nights, weekends and for part-time students.

Application procedures. Admission: No deadline. No application fee. Admission notification on a rolling basis. Applicants for nursing and allied health programs must apply by 1/15 and reply within 2 weeks of acceptance. No deferred admission for these programs. **Financial aid:** Priority date 5/30; no closing date. FAFSA, institutional form required. Applicants notified on a rolling basis starting 7/1.

Academics. Special study options: Accelerated study, cooperative education, distance learning, double major, dual enrollment of high school students, honors, independent study, internships. Bachelor's degree programs available on campus. **Credit/placement by examination:** AP, CLEP. **Support services:** Learning center, pre-admission summer program, reduced course load, remedial instruction, study skills assistance, tutoring, writing center.

Majors. Business: General, accounting, administrative services, business admin, managerial economics. **Computer sciences:** General, LAN/WAN management. **Conservation:** Environmental studies. **Education:** General, early childhood. **Engineering:** General, electrical. **Health services:** EMT paramedic, medical secretary, nursing (RN), occupational therapy assistant, radiologic technology/medical imaging. **Liberal arts:** Arts/sciences. **Protective services:** Corrections, police science.

Most popular majors. Business/marketing 8%, health sciences 30%, liberal arts 45%, security/protective services 8%.

Technology on campus. 150 workstations in library, computer center. Commuter students can connect to campus network. Online course registration, online library, helpline, wireless network available.

Student life. Freshman orientation: Available, $130 fee. Preregistration for classes offered. **Activities:** Jazz band, choral groups, international student organizations, literary magazine, music ensembles, student government, Intervoice Club, Black Student Union, Phi Theta Kappa, Phi Beta Lambda, Lambda Alpha Epsilon, Helping Minds, Campus Crusade for Christ, Campus Republicans, art club, Project ACHIEVE.

Athletics. Intramural: Basketball M, football (non-tackle) M. **Team name:** Eagles.

Student services. Adult student services, career counseling, services for economically disadvantaged, student employment services, financial aid counseling, health services, minority student services, personal counseling, placement for graduates, veterans' counselor. **Physically disabled:** Services for visually, speech, hearing impaired. **Transfer:** Transfer adviser, college fairs on campus for students transferring to 4-year colleges.

Contact. E-mail: admissions@sw.edu
Phone: (276) 964-7238 Toll-free number: (800) 822-7822
Fax: (276) 964-7716
Dionne Cook, Admissions Counselor, Southwest Virginia Community College, PO Box SVCC, Richlands, VA 24641-1101

Thomas Nelson Community College
Hampton, Virginia
www.tncc.edu   CB code: 5793

◗ Public 2-year community college
◗ Commuter campus in small city

General. Founded in 1967. Regionally accredited. **Enrollment:** 7,970 degree-seeking undergraduates. **Degrees:** 903 associate awarded. **Location:** 20 miles from Norfolk, 35 miles from Virginia Beach. **Calendar:** Semester, limited summer session. **Full-time faculty:** 110 total. **Part-time faculty:** 495 total.

Transfer out. Colleges most students transferred to 2015: Old Dominion University, Virginia Commonwealth University, Christopher Newport University, College of William and Mary, Virginia Tech.

Basis for selection. Open admission, but selective for some programs. Special requirements for nursing program and dental hygiene program. SAT Critical Reading or ACT English Reading and Math may be substituted for institutional placement examinations if scores high enough. **Adult students:** SAT/ACT scores not required. **Home schooled:** Transcript of courses and grades required. Must be 18 or have GED.

High school preparation. Nursing program requires specific high school units.

2015-2016 Annual costs. Tuition/fees: $4,416; $9,714 out-of-state. Per-credit charge: $136 in-state; $313 out-of-state. Books/supplies: $1,300. Personal expenses: $2,100. **Additional information:** Out-of-state students pay an additional $540 capital outlay fee.

Financial aid. Need-based: Need-based aid available for part-time students. Work-study available nights, weekends and for part-time students.

Application procedures. Admission: No deadline. No application fee. Application must be submitted online. Admission notification on a rolling basis. **Financial aid:** Priority date 5/1; no closing date. FAFSA, institutional form required. Applicants notified on a rolling basis starting 6/1; must reply within 2 week(s) of notification.

Academics. System-wide core curriculum to ensure ease of transfer, 2+2 program available. **Special study options:** Accelerated study, cooperative education, cross-registration, distance learning, dual enrollment of high school students, ESL, honors, independent study, internships. License preparation in dental hygiene, nursing, paramedic, real estate. **Credit/placement by examination:** AP, CLEP, institutional tests. **Support services:** Learning center, remedial instruction, study skills assistance, tutoring, writing center.

Majors. Business: Accounting, business admin, management science, office management. **Computer sciences:** General, computer graphics, computer science, information systems, networking, programming. **Education:** Early childhood. **Engineering:** General, electrical. **Health services:** Licensed practical nurse. **Human services:** General, social work. **Liberal arts:** Arts/sciences. **Protective services:** Fire services admin, law enforcement admin. **Social sciences:** General. **Visual/performing arts:** Commercial/advertising art, photography, studio arts.

Technology on campus. 169 workstations in library, computer center. Online course registration, online library, helpline, wireless network available.

Student life. Freshman orientation: Mandatory. Preregistration for classes offered. **Activities:** Choral groups, drama, international student organizations, student government, Phi Theta Kappa, African American history and culture club, American Dental Hygienists' Association, Student Nurses Association, Student Veterans of America, LGBT support group, The American Red Cross Club of TNCC, Christian clubs, video production club.

Athletics. Intramural: Basketball, football (tackle), soccer. **Team name:** Gators.

Student services. Career counseling, student employment services, financial aid counseling, personal counseling, veterans' counselor. **Physically disabled:** Services for visually, speech, hearing impaired. **Transfer:** Transfer

---

center, transfer adviser, college fairs on campus for students transferring to 4-year colleges.

Contact. E-mail: admissions@tncc.edu
Phone: (757) 825-2800 Fax: (757) 825-2763
Vicki Richmond, Associate Vice President for Enrollment Services, Thomas Nelson Community College, PO Box 9407, Hampton, VA 23670

Tidewater Community College
Norfolk, Virginia   CB member
www.tcc.edu   CB code: 5032

◗ Public 2-year community college
◗ Commuter campus in large city

General. Founded in 1968. Regionally accredited. Multi-location institution with campuses at Portsmouth, Virginia Beach, Chesapeake, and Norfolk. **Enrollment:** 24,631 degree-seeking undergraduates. **Degrees:** 2,894 associate awarded. **ROTC:** Army, Naval. **Calendar:** Semester, extensive summer session. **Full-time faculty:** 364 total. **Part-time faculty:** 1,277 total. **Class size:** 36% < 20, 63% 20-39, less than 1% 40-49, less than 1% 50-99. **Special facilities:** Regional health professions center, performing arts center, visual arts center, regional automotive center.

Student profile.

Out-of-state: 10%   **25 or older:**   53%

Transfer out. Colleges most students transferred to 2015: Old Dominion University, Norfolk State University, Virginia Wesleyan College, Christopher Newport University.

Basis for selection. Open admission, but selective for some programs. Special requirements for health professions programs. Placement testing required for English or mathematics courses. Interview required for medical technologies and other limited enrollment programs.

2015-2016 Annual costs. Tuition/fees: $5,171; $10,469 out-of-state. Per-credit charge: $136 in-state; $313 out-of-state. Books/supplies: $1,500. Personal expenses: $2,500. **Additional information:** Out-of-state students pay an additional $540 capital outlay fee.

Financial aid. Need-based: Need-based aid available for part-time students. Work-study available nights, weekends and for part-time students.

Application procedures. Admission: No deadline. No application fee. Admission notification on a rolling basis. **Financial aid:** Priority date 4/1; no closing date. FAFSA required. Applicants notified on a rolling basis starting 4/1.

Academics. System-wide core curriculum to ensure ease of transfer. **Special study options:** Cooperative education, cross-registration, distance learning, double major, dual enrollment of high school students, ESL, honors, independent study, internships, study abroad. Member Virginia Tidewater Consortium of Higher Education. License preparation in nursing, occupational therapy, paramedic, physical therapy, radiology, real estate. **Credit/placement by examination:** AP, CLEP, institutional tests. **Support services:** Learning center, reduced course load, remedial instruction, study skills assistance, tutoring, writing center.

Majors. Business: Accounting, administrative services, banking/financial services, business admin, hospitality admin, real estate, sales/distribution. **Computer sciences:** General, networking, systems analysis. **Conservation:** Environmental studies. **Education:** General, early childhood, teacher assistance. **Engineering:** General, industrial. **Foreign languages:** American Sign Language. **Health services:** EMT paramedic, health information technology, medical radiologic technology/radiation therapy, nursing (RN), occupational therapy assistant, physical therapy assistant, respiratory therapy technology. **Human services:** General. **Liberal arts:** Arts/sciences. **Parks/recreation:** General, facilities management. **Protective services:** Firefighting. **Social sciences:** General. **Visual/performing arts:** Commercial/advertising art, graphic design, interior design, multimedia, photography, studio arts.

Most popular majors. Biological/life sciences 8%, business/marketing 21%, engineering/engineering technologies 8%, health sciences 11%, liberal arts 22%, social sciences 14%.

Technology on campus. Commuter students can connect to campus network. Online course registration, online library, helpline, repair service, wireless network available.

Student life. Freshman orientation: Mandatory. Preregistration for classes offered. **Activities:** Concert band, campus ministries, choral groups, dance, drama, international student organizations, literary magazine, music ensembles, student government, student newspaper, Phi Theta Kappa, black student union, Christian Fellowship, business club, science fiction and astronomy club, student nurses association, military and veterans student association, computer club.

Athletics. Intercollegiate: Basketball, soccer M. **Team name:** Storm.

Student services. Adult student services, career counseling, student employment services, financial aid counseling, on-campus daycare, personal counseling, placement for graduates, veterans' counselor, women's services. **Physically disabled:** Services for visually, speech, hearing impaired. **Transfer:** Transfer adviser, college fairs on campus for students transferring to 4-year colleges.

Contact. E-mail: info@tcc.edu
Phone: (757) 822-1100 Toll-free number: (800) 371-0898
Daniel DeMarte, Vice President for Student Learning and Chief Academic Officer, Tidewater Community College, 300 Granby Street, Norfolk, VA 23510

Virginia College in Richmond
Richmond, Virginia
www.richmond.vc.edu

- For-profit 2-year culinary school and career college
- Very large city

General. Regionally accredited; also accredited by ACICS. Richmond campus includes Culinard: The Culinary Institute of Virginia College, which offers 36-week programs in pastry and culinary arts. **Enrollment:** 446 undergraduates. **Degrees:** 56 associate awarded. **Calendar:** Quarter. **Full-time faculty:** 17 total. **Part-time faculty:** 54 total.

Basis for selection. Open admission.

2015-2016 Annual costs. Certificate programs: $13,932-$23,220. Associate programs: $37,152-$40,700. Clock hour certificate program: Cosmetology $21,225.

Financial aid. Need-based: Work-study available nights, weekends and for part-time students.

Application procedures. Admission: $100 fee.

Academics. Credit/placement by examination: AP, CLEP.

Majors. Business: Business admin. **Health services:** Health information management, surgical technology.

Contact. E-mail: richmond.info@vc.edu
Phone: (804) 977-5100
Virginia College in Richmond, 7200 Midlothian Turnpike, Richmond, VA 23225

Virginia Highlands Community College
Abingdon, Virginia
www.vhcc.edu   CB code: 5927

- Public 2-year community college
- Commuter campus in small town

General. Founded in 1967. Regionally accredited. **Enrollment:** 2,363 degree-seeking undergraduates. **Degrees:** 312 associate awarded. **Location:** 120 miles from Roanoke. **Calendar:** Semester, extensive summer session. **Full-time faculty:** 62 total. **Part-time faculty:** 160 total. **Special facilities:** Greenhouse, regional artisan center.

Student profile.

Out-of-state:	11%	25 or older:	36%

Transfer out. Colleges most students transferred to 2015: East Tennessee State University, Virginia Tech, Radford University, Old Dominion University, University of Virginia at Wise.

Basis for selection. Open admission, but selective for some programs. COMPASS required for placement. Paramedic, nursing, radiography, physical therapy, dental hygiene, and medical laboratory technology programs have special requirements. **Learning Disabled:** Developmental courses required of students who test below set standards on COMPASS and/or ASSET test.

2015-2016 Annual costs. Tuition/fees: $4,335; $9,633 out-of-state. Per-credit charge: $134 in-state; $311 out-of-state. Books/supplies: $750. Personal expenses: $1,272. **Additional information:** Out-of-state students pay an additional $540 capital outlay fee.

Financial aid. Need-based: Work-study available nights, weekends and for part-time students.

Application procedures. Admission: No deadline. No application fee. Admission notification on a rolling basis. **Financial aid:** No deadline. FAFSA, institutional form required. Applicants notified on a rolling basis starting 5/1.

Academics. Special study options: Cooperative education, distance learning, double major, dual enrollment of high school students, independent study, internships, liberal arts/career combination. License preparation in nursing, paramedic, real estate. **Credit/placement by examination:** AP, CLEP, institutional tests. 45 credit hours maximum toward associate degree. **Support services:** Learning center, pre-admission summer program, reduced course load, remedial instruction, tutoring.

Majors. Business: Accounting, administrative services, business admin, office management. **Computer sciences:** General, data processing. **Education:** General, drama/dance. **Health services:** Clinical lab assistant, dental hygiene, medical radiologic technology/radiation therapy, nursing (RN), physical therapy assistant. **Human services:** Social work. **Liberal arts:** Arts/sciences. **Protective services:** Police science.

Technology on campus. 230 workstations in library, computer center, student center. Online course registration, wireless network available.

Student life. Freshman orientation: Mandatory, $68 fee. Preregistration for classes offered. **Activities:** Choral groups, drama, music ensembles, musical theater, student government, IMPACT club, law enforcement club, Roteract club, College Republicans, College Democrats, Aanglers' club, VATNP (nursing) club, National Honors Society, Christian club, SIFE.

Athletics. Intramural: Basketball. **Team name:** Wolves.

Student services. Career counseling, services for economically disadvantaged, student employment services, financial aid counseling, personal counseling, placement for graduates, veterans' counselor. **Physically disabled:** Services for visually, speech, hearing impaired. **Transfer:** Transfer adviser, college fairs on campus for students transferring to 4-year colleges.

Contact. E-mail: dbarrett@vhcc.edu
Phone: (276) 739-2460 Fax: (276) 739-2591
Karen Cheers, Director of Admissions, Records and Financial Aid, Virginia Highlands Community College, PO Box 828, Abingdon, VA 24212-0828

Virginia Western Community College
Roanoke, Virginia
www.virginiawestern.edu   CB code: 5868

- Public 2-year community college
- Commuter campus in small city

General. Founded in 1966. Regionally accredited. **Enrollment:** 5,264 degree-seeking undergraduates; 3,368 non-degree-seeking students. **Degrees:** 665 associate awarded. **Location:** 3 miles from downtown. **Calendar:** Semester, extensive summer session. **Full-time faculty:** 92 total; 8% minority, 62% women. **Part-time faculty:** 266 total; 7% minority, 54% women. **Class size:** 59% < 20, 40% 20-39; less than 1% 40-49. **Special facilities:** Community arboretum, public dental hygiene clinic, center for science and health professions.

Student profile. Among degree-seeking undergraduates, 60% enrolled in a transfer program, 40% enrolled in a vocational program, 2% already have a bachelor's degree or higher, 1,376 enrolled as first-time, first-year students, 266 transferred in from other institutions.

Part-time:	54%	Asian American:	3%
Out-of-state:	2%	Hispanic/Latino:	3%
Women:	56%	Multi-racial, non-Hispanic:	3%
African American:	15%	25 or older:	32%

Transfer out. Colleges most students transferred to 2015: Virginia Tech, Radford University, Old Dominion University, Roanoke College, Hollins University.

Basis for selection. Open admission, but selective for some programs. Special requirements for health programs and communication design program. Interview required for health technologies. **Learning Disabled:** Student Support Services/REACH program provides accommodations for students with learning disabilities.

Two-Year Colleges

2015-2016 Annual costs. Tuition/fees: $4,713; $10,551 out-of-state. Per-credit charge: $136 in-state; $313 out-of-state. Books/supplies: $1,500. **Additional information:** Out-of-state students pay an additional $540 capital outlay fee.

Financial aid. Need-based: Need-based aid available for part-time students. Work-study available nights, weekends and for part-time students. **Non-need-based:** Scholarships awarded for academics, state residency.

Application procedures. Admission: No deadline. No application fee. Application must be submitted online. Admission notification on a rolling basis. **Financial aid:** No deadline. FAFSA required. Applicants notified on a rolling basis starting 4/1.

Academics. Special study options: Cooperative education, distance learning, double major, dual enrollment of high school students, ESL, independent study, internships, liberal arts/career combination, study abroad, weekend college. License preparation in dental hygiene, nursing, radiology. **Credit/placement by examination:** AP, CLEP, IB, institutional tests. **Support services:** Learning center, pre-admission summer program, reduced course load, remedial instruction, study skills assistance, tutoring, writing center.

Majors. Biology: Biotechnology. **Business:** General, accounting, administrative services, business admin, management information systems, office technology. **Communications technology:** General. **Computer sciences:** General. **Education:** General, early childhood, social science. **Engineering:** General, surveying. **Health services:** Dental hygiene, mental health services, nursing (RN), radiologic technology/medical imaging. **Liberal arts:** Arts/sciences, humanities. **Math:** General. **Protective services:** Criminal justice, police science. **Social sciences:** General. **Visual/performing arts:** Commercial/advertising art, studio arts. **Work/family studies:** Child care management.

Most popular majors. Business/marketing 14%, engineering/engineering technologies 8%, health sciences 23%, interdisciplinary studies 11%, liberal arts 17%, social sciences 11%.

Technology on campus. 100 workstations in library, computer center, student center. Online course registration, online library, helpline, wireless network available.

Student life. Freshman orientation: Mandatory. Preregistration for classes offered. **Activities:** Campus ministries, international student organizations, literary magazine, student government, student newspaper, Armed Forces student association, audio visual production club, Campus Body of Christ, College Democrats, gaming club, Sister Circle, community action network, Latin Movement, outdoors club.

Athletics. Intramural: Basketball, cheerleading W, softball, tennis. **Team name:** Rapids.

Student services. Adult student services, alcohol/substance abuse counseling, career counseling, services for economically disadvantaged, student employment services, financial aid counseling, minority student services, personal counseling, veterans' counselor. **Physically disabled:** Services for visually, speech, hearing impaired. **Transfer:** Re-entry adviser for new students. Transfer center, transfer adviser, college fairs on campus for students transferring to 4-year colleges.

Contact. E-mail: infocenter@virginiawestern.edu
Phone: (540) 857-7231 Fax: (540) 857-6163
Lorraine Conklin, Registrar, Virginia Western Community College, 3094 Colonial Avenue, Roanoke, VA 24013

Wytheville Community College
Wytheville, Virginia
www.wcc.vccs.edu   CB code: 5917

◗ Public 2-year community college
◗ Commuter campus in small town

General. Founded in 1962. Regionally accredited. **Enrollment:** 1,733 degree-seeking undergraduates. **Degrees:** 467 associate awarded. **Location:** 74 miles from Roanoke. **Calendar:** Semester, limited summer session. **Full-time faculty:** 45 total. **Part-time faculty:** 87 total.

Student profile. Among degree-seeking undergraduates, 33% enrolled in a transfer program, 38% enrolled in a vocational program.

Out-of-state: 5% **25 or older:**   32%

Transfer out. Colleges most students transferred to 2015: Radford University, Old Dominion University, Virginia Tech, James Madison University, Liberty University.

Basis for selection. Open admission, but selective for some programs. Limited admissions to allied health programs. High school transcripts required of all allied health applicants. High school students can enroll in college classes through the dual enrollment program. Interview required for allied health, police science. **Home schooled:** Statement describing home school structure and mission required.

High school preparation. College-preparatory program recommended.

2015-2016 Annual costs. Tuition/fees: $4,380; $9,678 out-of-state. Per-credit charge: $134 in-state; $311 out-of-state. Books/supplies: $840. Personal expenses: $250. **Additional information:** Out-of-state students pay an additional $540 capital outlay fee.

Financial aid. All financial aid based on need. Need-based aid available for part-time students. Work-study available nights, weekends and for part-time students.

Application procedures. Admission: No deadline. No application fee. Admission notification on a rolling basis. **Financial aid:** Priority date 4/1; no closing date. FAFSA, institutional form required. Applicants notified on a rolling basis starting 5/1; must reply within 4 week(s) of notification.

Academics. Special study options: Distance learning, dual enrollment of high school students, honors, independent study, internships. Bachelor's degree programs available on campus. License preparation in dental hygiene, nursing, physical therapy, radiology. **Credit/placement by examination:** AP, CLEP, institutional tests. **Support services:** Remedial instruction, tutoring, writing center.

Majors. Business: Accounting, administrative services, business admin, managerial economics. **Computer sciences:** Information systems. **Education:** General. **General:** Carpentry, electrician. **Health services:** Clinical lab technology, dental hygiene, nursing (RN), physical therapy assistant, radiologic technology/medical imaging, respiratory therapy technology. **Liberal arts:** Arts/sciences. **Protective services:** Police science. **Work/family studies:** Child care management.

Most popular majors. Health sciences 34%, liberal arts 13%, physical sciences 9%, security/protective services 6%.

Technology on campus. 133 workstations in library, computer center, student center. Commuter students can connect to campus network. Online course registration, helpline, wireless network available.

Student life. Freshman orientation: Available. Preregistration for classes offered. **Activities:** Bands, drama, music ensembles, student government, student newspaper.

Athletics. Intercollegiate: Volleyball W. **Intramural:** Basketball, volleyball. **Team name:** Wildcats.

Student services. Career counseling, services for economically disadvantaged, student employment services, financial aid counseling, personal counseling, placement for graduates, veterans' counselor. **Physically disabled:** Services for visually, hearing impaired. **Transfer:** College fairs on campus for students transferring to 4-year colleges.

Contact. E-mail: kalexander@wcc.vccs.edu
Phone: (276) 223-4701 Toll-free number: (800) 468-1195
Fax: (276) 223-4860
Karen Alexander, Registrar, Wytheville Community College, 1000 East Main Street, Wytheville, VA 24382

Two-Year Colleges

Washington

Bates Technical College
Tacoma, Washington
www.bates.ctc.edu   CB code: 4152

▶ Public 2-year technical college
▶ Commuter campus in small city

General. Bates Technical College offers courses on three different campuses located in Tacoma. **Enrollment:** 995 degree-seeking undergraduates. **Degrees:** 332 associate awarded. **Location:** Within a half mile of downtown. **Calendar:** Quarter, extensive summer session. **Full-time faculty:** 113 total; less than 1% have terminal degrees, 7% minority, 43% women. **Part-time faculty:** 36 total; 19% minority, 58% women.

Transfer out. Colleges most students transferred to 2015: University of Washington.

Basis for selection. Open admission, but selective for some programs. A few programs have additional prerequisites for formal acceptance into training program. COMPASS test required for admission. **Adult students:** SAT/ACT scores not required.

2015-2016 Annual costs. Tuition/fees: $4,703; $10,106 out-of-state. Per-credit charge: $84 in-state; $204 out-of-state.

Financial aid. All financial aid based on need. Need-based aid available for part-time students. Work-study available nights, weekends and for part-time students.

Application procedures. Admission: No deadline. $50 fee. **Financial aid:** No deadline. FAFSA, institutional form required. Applicants notified on a rolling basis starting 9/7.

Academics. Special study options: Cooperative education, distance learning, dual enrollment of high school students, ESL, independent study, internships, teacher certification program. License preparation in dental hygiene, nursing, occupational therapy. **Credit/placement by examination:** AP, CLEP, IB. Normally a maximum of 25 percent of program credits accepted. **Support services:** GED preparation and test center, learning center, reduced course load, remedial instruction, study skills assistance, tutoring. Veterans Center and Diversity Center available on campus to support students. Support for students with disabilities are available through Student Services.

Majors. Business: Administrative services, marketing. **Communications technology:** Radio/TV. **Computer sciences:** Database management, networking, programming, web page design, webmaster. **General:** Carpentry, electrician, maintenance. **Health services:** Dental assistant, dental lab technology, hearing instrument specialist, licensed practical nurse, occupational therapy assistant. **Protective services:** Fire systems technology, firefighting. **Work/family studies:** Child care service.

Most popular majors. Computer/information sciences 6%, health sciences 36%, security/protective services 6%, trade and industry 30%.

Technology on campus. 80 workstations in library, computer center, student center. Commuter students can connect to campus network. Online course registration, online library, repair service, wireless network available.

Student life. Freshman orientation: Available. Preregistration for classes offered. **Activities:** International student organizations, student government, TV station.

Athletics. Team name: Bobcats.

Student services. Adult student services, career counseling, services for economically disadvantaged, student employment services, financial aid counseling, minority student services, on-campus daycare, placement for graduates, veterans' counselor. **Physically disabled:** Services for visually, speech, hearing impaired. **Transfer:** Pre-admission transcript evaluation for new students.

Contact. E-mail: registration@bates.ctc.edu
Phone: (253) 680-7002
Bates Technical College, 1101 South Yakima Avenue, Tacoma, WA 98405

Bellevue College
Bellevue, Washington
www.bellevuecollege.edu   CB code: 4029

▶ Public 2-year community college
▶ Commuter campus in small city

General. Founded in 1965. Regionally accredited. **Enrollment:** 13,469 undergraduates. **Degrees:** 62 bachelor's, 2,023 associate awarded. **Location:** 12 miles from Seattle. **Calendar:** Quarter, limited summer session. **Full-time faculty:** 166 total. **Part-time faculty:** 533 total. **Special facilities:** Planetarium, National Workforce Center for Emerging Technologies, greenhouses, observatory, scanning electron microscope.

Transfer out. Colleges most students transferred to 2015: University of Washington, Washington State University, Central Washington University, Seattle University, Western Washington University.

Basis for selection. Open admission, but selective for some programs. Interview, essay, 2 letters of recommendation, transcripts required of applicants to allied health programs, including radiologic technology, diagnostic ultrasound, radiation therapy. **Home schooled:** Must be at least 18 years old. **Learning Disabled:** Student may request reasonable classroom accommodations through Disability Support Services Office. Student must provide documentation from appropriate professional.

High school preparation. Allied health programs have special requirements.

2015-2016 Annual costs. Tuition/fees: $4,077; $9,480 out-of-state. Per-credit charge: $85 in-state; $206 out-of-state. Books/supplies: $924. Personal expenses: $1,968.

Financial aid. Need-based: Need-based aid available for part-time students. Work-study available nights, weekends and for part-time students. **Non-need-based:** Scholarships awarded for academics, athletics.

Application procedures. Admission: No deadline. $34 fee. Admission notification on a rolling basis. **Financial aid:** Priority date 4/16; no closing date. FAFSA, institutional form required. Applicants notified on a rolling basis starting 8/1.

Academics. Special study options: Distance learning, dual enrollment of high school students, ESL, honors, independent study, internships, study abroad. Bachelor's degree programs available on campus. **Credit/placement by examination:** AP, CLEP, institutional tests. 15 credit hours maximum toward associate degree. **Support services:** GED preparation and test center, learning center, remedial instruction, tutoring, writing center.

Majors. Business: General, accounting technology, administrative services, business admin, marketing, office management, real estate. **Communications technology:** Photo/film/video. **Computer sciences:** General, computer graphics, database management, networking, programming, security, support specialist, web page design. **Education:** Early childhood, elementary, mathematics. **Engineering:** Chemical, electrical, mechanical. **Health services:** Medical radiologic technology/radiation therapy, nuclear medical technology, nursing (RN), sonography. **Liberal arts:** Arts/sciences. **Physical sciences:** General. **Protective services:** Fire services admin, firefighting, law enforcement admin. **Visual/performing arts:** Interior design.

Most popular majors. Business/marketing 11%, health sciences 7%, liberal arts 69%.

Technology on campus. 244 workstations in library, computer center. Commuter students can connect to campus network. Online course registration, online library, helpline, student web hosting, wireless network available.

Student life. Freshman orientation: Available. Preregistration for classes offered. Quarterly, prior to start of term. **Activities:** Jazz band, choral groups, dance, drama, literary magazine, music ensembles, musical theater, radio station, student government, student newspaper, TV station.

Athletics. NAIA, NJCAA. **Intercollegiate:** Baseball M, basketball, cross-country, golf M, soccer, softball W, tennis, track and field, volleyball W. **Intramural:** Badminton, basketball, racquetball, soccer W, softball W, table tennis, tennis, volleyball. **Team name:** Bulldogs.

Student services. Career counseling, services for economically disadvantaged, student employment services, financial aid counseling, health services, minority student services, on-campus daycare, personal counseling, placement for graduates, veterans' counselor, women's services. **Physically disabled:** Services for visually, speech, hearing impaired. **Transfer:** Transfer center, transfer adviser, college fairs on campus for students transferring to 4-year colleges.

Contact. E-mail: admissions@bellevuecollege.edu
Phone: (425) 564-2222 Fax: (425) 564-4065
Catherine Kwong, Director, Registrar Services & Evaluations, Bellevue College, 3000 Landerholm Circle SE, Bellevue, WA 98007-6484

Bellingham Technical College
Bellingham, Washington
www.btc.edu

CB member
CB code: 3499

- Public 2-year technical college
- Commuter campus in small city

General. Regionally accredited. **Enrollment:** 2,112 degree-seeking undergraduates. **Degrees:** 403 associate awarded. **Location:** 90 miles from Seattle, 52 miles from Vancouver, B.C. **Calendar:** Quarter, limited summer session. **Full-time faculty:** 62 total. **Part-time faculty:** 113 total. **Special facilities:** 1,200 (includes computer labs) college owned computers for student use.

Basis for selection. Open admission, but selective for some programs. Most programs admit students on a first-come, first-served, space available basis. Must complete assessment tests in reading and mathematics. Admission to the Dental Hygiene program is selective. Admission to the Nursing program is by lottery selection. Specific admission criteria, such as completion of prerequisites, are required for other programs.

2015-2016 Annual costs. Tuition/fees: $3,775; $9,178 out-of-state. Per-credit charge: $81 in-state; $201 out-of-state. Books/supplies: $1,080. Personal expenses: $1,680.

2014-2015 Financial aid. All financial aid based on need. 60% of total undergraduate aid awarded as scholarships/grants, 40% as loans/jobs. Need-based aid available for part-time students. Work-study available nights, weekends and for part-time students.

Application procedures. Admission: No deadline. No application fee. Application must be submitted online. Admission notification on a rolling basis. **Financial aid:** Priority date 3/1; no closing date. FAFSA, institutional form required. Applicants notified on a rolling basis starting 7/1; must reply within 2 week(s) of notification.

Academics. Special study options: Distance learning, dual enrollment of high school students, ESL, internships. License preparation in dental hygiene, nursing, paramedic, radiology, real estate. **Credit/placement by examination:** AP, CLEP, IB, institutional tests. **Support services:** GED preparation and test center, learning center, remedial instruction, study skills assistance, tutoring.

Majors. Business: Accounting technology, executive assistant, human resources, marketing. **Computer sciences:** Data entry, networking. **Conservation:** Fisheries. **Education:** Voc/tech. **General:** Electrician, maintenance. **Health services:** Dental assistant, dental hygiene, EMT paramedic, insurance coding, medical radiologic technology/radiation therapy, nursing (RN), radiologic technology/medical imaging, surgical technology, veterinary technology/assistant.

Technology on campus. 90 workstations in library. Commuter students can connect to campus network. Online course registration, online library, wireless network available.

Student life. Freshman orientation: Mandatory. Preregistration for classes offered. 3 hour new student event the day before the quarter starts. **Activities:** Student government.

Student services. Adult student services, career counseling, services for economically disadvantaged, financial aid counseling, minority student services, veterans' counselor. **Physically disabled:** Services for visually, speech, hearing impaired. **Transfer:** Pre-admission transcript evaluation for new students.

Contact. E-mail: admissions@btc.edu
Phone: (360) 752-8345 Fax: (360) 676-2798
Karen Bade, Director of Admissions, Bellingham Technical College, 3028 Lindbergh Avenue, Bellingham, WA 98225-1599

Big Bend Community College
Moses Lake, Washington
www.bigbend.edu

CB code: 4024

- Public 2-year community college
- Commuter campus in large town

General. Founded in 1962. Regionally accredited. **Enrollment:** 1,614 degree-seeking undergraduates; 402 non-degree-seeking students. **Degrees:** 422 associate awarded. **Location:** 107 miles from Spokane, 170 miles from Seattle. **Calendar:** Quarter, limited summer session. **Full-time faculty:** 46 total; 6% minority, 33% women. **Part-time faculty:** 58 total; 16% minority, 57% women. **Partnerships:** Formal partnership with high schools for Tech Prep programs.

Student profile. Among degree-seeking undergraduates, 45% enrolled in a transfer program, 31% enrolled in a vocational program, 364 enrolled as first-time, first-year students, 363 transferred in from other institutions.

Part-time:	23%	Hispanic/Latino:	35%
Out-of-state:	3%	Native American:	1%
Women:	52%	Multi-racial, non-Hispanic:	2%
African American:	1%	25 or older:	12%
Asian American:	2%	Live on campus:	8%

Transfer out. Colleges most students transferred to 2015: Central Washington University, Eastern Washington University, Washington State University.

Basis for selection. Open admission, but selective for some programs. Special admission criteria for aviation and nursing programs.

2015-2016 Annual costs. Tuition/fees: $4,071; $9,474 out-of-state. Per-credit charge: $85 in-state; $206 out-of-state. Books/supplies: $1,050. Personal expenses: $1,680. **Additional information:** Room charge is $2,790 for single and $3,330 for double occupancy.

2014-2015 Financial aid. All financial aid based on need. 71% of total undergraduate aid awarded as scholarships/grants, 29% as loans/jobs. Need-based aid available for part-time students. Work-study available nights, weekends and for part-time students.

Application procedures. Admission: No deadline. $30 fee. Admission notification on a rolling basis. **Financial aid:** Priority date 4/15; no closing date. FAFSA, institutional form required. Applicants notified on a rolling basis starting 5/15; must reply within 2 week(s) of notification.

Academics. Special study options: Distance learning, dual enrollment of high school students, ESL, liberal arts/career combination. License preparation in aviation, nursing. **Credit/placement by examination:** AP, CLEP, institutional tests. 45 credit hours maximum toward associate degree. **Support services:** GED preparation and test center, learning center, reduced course load, remedial instruction, study skills assistance, tutoring, writing center. Disability support services.

Majors. Business: General, accounting technology, office management. **Computer sciences:** Vendor certification. **Education:** Early childhood. **Engineering:** General. **English:** English lit. **Foreign languages:** General. **General:** Electrician. **Health services:** Medical assistant, nursing (RN), office admin. **History:** General. **Liberal arts:** Arts/sciences. **Math:** General. **Philosophy/religion:** General. **Physical sciences:** General. **Protective services:** Disaster management. **Psychology:** General. **Social sciences:** Anthropology, political science, sociology.

Most popular majors. Health sciences 10%, liberal arts 71%, trade and industry 10%.

Technology on campus. 765 workstations in library, computer center, student center. Dormitories wired for high-speed internet access and linked to campus network. Commuter students can connect to campus network. Online course registration, online library, helpline, student web hosting, wireless network available.

Student life. Freshman orientation: Available. Preregistration for classes offered. Half-day fall student advising and registration sessions held throughout the summer. Full-day student orientation held in September. **Housing:** Coed dorms, wellness housing available. $200 fully refundable deposit. **Activities:** Choral groups, music ensembles, student government.

Athletics. Intercollegiate: Baseball M, basketball, softball W, volleyball W. **Team name:** Vikings.

Student services. Career counseling, services for economically disadvantaged, student employment services, financial aid counseling, minority student services, on-campus daycare, personal counseling, placement for graduates, veterans' counselor. **Physically disabled:** Services for visually, speech, hearing impaired. **Transfer:** Transfer adviser, college fairs on campus for students transferring to 4-year colleges.

Contact. E-mail: admissions@bigbend.edu
Phone: (509) 793-2061 Toll-free number: (877) 745-1212
Fax: (509) 762-6243
Candy Lacher, Associate Vice President of Student Services, Big Bend Community College, 7662 Chanute Street NE, Moses Lake, WA 98837-3299

Carrington College: Spokane
Spokane, Washington
www.carrington.edu

- For-profit 2-year career college
- Very large city

General. Regionally accredited; also accredited by ACICS. **Enrollment:** 511 degree-seeking undergraduates. **Degrees:** 23 associate awarded. **Calendar:** Differs by program. **Full-time faculty:** 10 total. **Part-time faculty:** 22 total.

Basis for selection. Applicants must be at least 18 in Washington by the first day of classes, have a high school diploma or its equivalent, interview with an Enrollment Services Representative, complete admission testing, and fulfill additional program-specific requirements.

2015-2016 Annual costs. Tuition costs vary by program. Total program cost for the largest program (Medical Assisting-Cert.) is $16,317.

Financial aid. Need-based: Work-study available nights, weekends and for part-time students.

Application procedures. Admission: No deadline. No application fee. **Financial aid:** No deadline.

Academics. Credit/placement by examination: AP, CLEP.

Majors. Health services: Medical radiologic technology/radiation therapy, office admin.

Contact. Phone: (888) 720-5014
Carrington College: Spokane, 10102 East Knox Avenue, Spokane, WA 99206-4187

Cascadia College
Bothell, Washington
www.cascadia.edu   CB code: 2859

- Public 2-year community college
- Commuter campus in large town

General. Enrollment: 2,327 degree-seeking undergraduates; 1,094 non-degree-seeking students. **Degrees:** 487 associate awarded. **Location:** 15 miles from Seattle. **Calendar:** Quarter, extensive summer session. **Full-time faculty:** 41 total. **Part-time faculty:** 107 total. **Special facilities:** Shared research library and activity/recreation facilities with the University of Washington Bothell.

Student profile. Among degree-seeking undergraduates, 82% enrolled in a transfer program, 14% enrolled in a vocational program, 5% already have a bachelor's degree or higher, 613 enrolled as first-time, first-year students, 1,040 transferred in from other institutions.

Part-time:	43%	Asian American:	10%
Out-of-state:	10%	Hispanic/Latino:	9%
Women:	50%	Multi-racial, non-Hispanic:	9%
African American:	1%	International:	9%

Basis for selection. Open admission. All students taking college-level credit classes required to assess their current skill levels in English and Math with the COMPASS placement test.

2015-2016 Annual costs. Tuition/fees: $3,947; $9,350 out-of-state. Per-credit charge: $83 in-state; $203 out-of-state. Books/supplies: $1,026.

Financial aid. Need-based: Work-study available nights, weekends and for part-time students.

Application procedures. Admission: No deadline. $35 fee, may be waived for applicants with need. **Financial aid:** Priority date 4/15; no closing date. FAFSA, institutional form required.

Academics. Special study options: Distance learning, dual enrollment of high school students, ESL, independent study, internships, study abroad. Bachelor's degree programs available on campus. **Credit/placement by examination:** AP, CLEP, IB, institutional tests. 45 credit hours maximum toward associate degree. **Support services:** GED preparation, learning center, remedial instruction, study skills assistance, tutoring, writing center.

Majors. Biology: General. **Computer sciences:** General. **Conservation:** Environmental science. **Education:** Elementary. **Physical sciences:** Chemistry, geology, physics.

Most popular majors. Business/marketing 15%, interdisciplinary studies 66%.

Technology on campus. Commuter students can connect to campus network. Online library, helpline, wireless network available.

Student life. Freshman orientation: Mandatory. Preregistration for classes offered. Orientation, advising, and registration sessions last approximately two hours and are offered several times before each quarter begins. Students given assistance in selecting courses, building schedules, registering for classes, and are also introduced to web registration as well as other online services. **Activities:** Film society, international student organizations, literary magazine, music ensembles, student government, student newspaper, Students in Service, Campus Crusade for Christ, Access Futures.

Athletics. Team name: Kodiaks.

Student services. Adult student services, career counseling, services for economically disadvantaged, student employment services, financial aid counseling, personal counseling, veterans' counselor. **Physically disabled:** Services for visually, speech, hearing impaired. **Transfer:** Pre-admission transcript evaluation for new students. Transfer center, transfer adviser, college fairs on campus for students transferring to 4-year colleges.

Contact. E-mail: admissions@cascadia.edu
Phone: (425) 352-8860 Fax: (425) 352-8137
Shawn Miller, Associate Dean for Admissions and Retention, Cascadia College, 18345 Campus Way, NE, Bothell, WA 98011

Centralia College
Centralia, Washington
www.centralia.edu   CB code: 4045

- Public 2-year community college
- Commuter campus in large town

General. Founded in 1925. Regionally accredited. Home to the Pacific Northwest Center of Excellence for Clean Energy. **Enrollment:** 2,097 degree-seeking undergraduates. **Degrees:** 28 bachelor's, 501 associate awarded. **Location:** 90 miles from Seattle, 90 miles from Portland, Oregon. **Calendar:** Quarter, extensive summer session. **Full-time faculty:** 62 total; 3% minority, 55% women. **Part-time faculty:** 153 total; 5% minority, 53% women. **Class size:** 50% < 20, 43% 20-39, 5% 40-49, 2% 50-99. **Special facilities:** Kiser Natural Outdoor Learning Lab, River Heights Nature Preserve.

Student profile.

Out-of-state:	1%	25 or older:	46%

Transfer out. Colleges most students transferred to 2015: Western Washington University, Washington State University, The Evergreen State College, Saint Martin's College, Central Washington University.

Basis for selection. Open admission, but selective for some programs. Special requirements for nursing program, includes prerequisites and grade point average criteria. Bachelor's program requires screening by an admissions committee. **Home schooled:** Transcript of courses and grades required. **Learning Disabled:** Students with learning disabilities must register with Disability Services to receive special accommodations.

High school preparation. College-preparatory program recommended. 16 units recommended. Recommended units include English 4, mathematics 3, social studies 2, history 1, science 2 (laboratory 1), foreign language 2 and academic electives 1.

2015-2016 Annual costs. Tuition/fees: $4,211; $9,204 out-of-state. Per-credit charge: $85 in-state; $196 out-of-state. Books/supplies: $1,002. Personal expenses: $3,030.

Financial aid. Need-based: Need-based aid available for part-time students. Work-study available nights, weekends and for part-time students. **Non-need-based:** Scholarships awarded for academics, alumni affiliation, art, athletics, leadership, minority status, music/drama.

Application procedures. Admission: Priority date 9/1; no deadline. No application fee. Admission notification on a rolling basis beginning on or about 12/1. **Financial aid:** Priority date 5/1, closing date 9/1. FAFSA, institutional form required. Applicants notified on a rolling basis starting 7/10; must reply within 2 week(s) of notification.

Academics. Online tutoring available 24/7. **Special study options:** Cooperative education, cross-registration, distance learning, double major, dual enrollment of high school students, ESL, honors, independent study, internships, liberal arts/career combination, student-designed major, study abroad, teacher certification program, weekend college. Bachelor's degree programs available on campus. License preparation in nursing, paramedic, real estate. **Credit/placement by examination:** AP, CLEP, IB, institutional tests. 45 credit hours maximum toward associate degree. **Support services:** GED preparation and test center, learning center, reduced course load, remedial instruction, study skills assistance, tutoring, writing center.

Honors college/program. Selective application process after completion of 30 college credits. Limited to 20 students per year.

Majors. Biology: General, botany. **Business:** General, accounting, business admin, marketing, office technology, office/clerical, receptionist, sales/distribution. **Communications:** Broadcast journalism, journalism, radio/TV. **Communications technology:** Graphics, radio/TV. **Computer sciences:** General, computer science, data processing, information systems, LAN/WAN management, networking, programming. **Conservation:** Wildlife/wilderness. **Education:** General, early childhood, teacher assistance. **Engineering:** General. **English:** English lit. **Foreign languages:** General, French, German, Spanish. **General:** Building inspection, maintenance, site management. **Health services:** Nursing (RN), polarity therapy, sonography. **History:** General. **Liberal arts:** Arts/sciences. **Math:** General. **Parks/recreation:** Health/fitness. **Physical sciences:** General, chemistry, geology, physics, planetary. **Protective services:** Forensics, law enforcement admin, police science. **Psychology:** General. **Social sciences:** General, anthropology, economics, political science, sociology. **Visual/performing arts:** General, art, commercial/advertising art, dramatic, graphic design, music, music theory/composition, studio arts. **Work/family studies:** Child care service.

Most popular majors. Business/marketing 7%, engineering/engineering technologies 6%, health sciences 11%, liberal arts 59%.

Technology on campus. 160 workstations in library, computer center, student center. Online course registration, online library, helpline, wireless network available.

Student life. Freshman orientation: Available, $20 fee. Preregistration for classes offered. Held 2 days prior to fall quarter. **Activities:** Bands, choral groups, drama, international student organizations, literary magazine, music ensembles, musical theater, radio station, student government, student newspaper, TV station, honors club, international student club, Rotaract.

Athletics. Intercollegiate: Baseball M, basketball, golf W, softball W, volleyball W. **Team name:** Trailblazers.

Student services. Adult student services, career counseling, services for economically disadvantaged, student employment services, financial aid counseling, minority student services, on-campus daycare, personal counseling, placement for graduates, veterans' counselor. **Physically disabled:** Services for visually, speech, hearing impaired. **Transfer:** Re-entry adviser, preadmission transcript evaluation for new students. Transfer center, transfer adviser, college fairs on campus for students transferring to 4-year colleges.

Contact. E-mail: admissions@centralia.edu
Phone: (360) 736-9391 ext. 221 Fax: (360) 330-7503
Qy-Ana Manning, Registrar, Centralia College, 600 Centralia College Boulevard, Centralia, WA 98531

Clark College
Vancouver, Washington
www.clark.edu
CB code: 4055

- Public 2-year community college
- Commuter campus in small city

General. Founded in 1933. Regionally accredited. **Enrollment:** 8,234 degree-seeking undergraduates; 2,243 non-degree-seeking students. **Degrees:** 1,894 associate awarded. **ROTC:** Army, Air Force. **Location:** 8 miles from Portland, Oregon. **Calendar:** Quarter, extensive summer session. **Full-time faculty:** 192 total; 19% have terminal degrees, 12% minority, 62% women. **Part-time faculty:** 382 total; 11% have terminal degrees, 9% minority, 58% women. **Class size:** 61% < 20, 36% 20-39, 2% 40-49, less than 1% 50-99. **Special facilities:** Environmental education center, arboretum. **Partnerships:** Formal partnerships with Toyota T-10 and Cisco; industry partnerships to train students in specific equipment use.

Student profile. Among degree-seeking undergraduates, 1,215 enrolled as first-time, first-year students, 345 transferred in from other institutions.

Part-time:	48%	Hispanic/Latino:	9%
Out-of-state:	4%	Native American:	1%
Women:	58%	Multi-racial, non-Hispanic:	8%
African American:	2%	International:	1%
Asian American:	4%	25 or older:	34%

Transfer out. Colleges most students transferred to 2015: Washington State University-Vancouver, Portland State University, University of Washington, Western Washington University, Central Washington.

Basis for selection. Open admission, but selective for some programs. GPA requirements vary by program. COMPASS required for placement in math and English. Interview required for dental hygiene, nursing, and pharmacy technician applicants.

2015-2016 Annual costs. Tuition/fees: $3,930; $9,333 out-of-state. Per-credit charge: $82 in-state; $203 out-of-state. Books/supplies: $1,050. Personal expenses: $1,680.

2014-2015 Financial aid. Need-based: 77% of total undergraduate aid awarded as scholarships/grants, 23% as loans/jobs. Need-based aid available for part-time students. Work-study available nights, weekends and for part-time students. **Non-need-based:** Scholarships awarded for academics, alumni affiliation, art, athletics, leadership, minority status, music/drama, state residency.

Application procedures. Admission: Closing date 9/2. $25 fee. Admission notification on a rolling basis. **Financial aid:** Priority date 5/18; no closing date. FAFSA required. Applicants notified on a rolling basis starting 6/1; must reply within 2 week(s) of notification.

Academics. Special study options: Accelerated study, cooperative education, distance learning, dual enrollment of high school students, ESL, honors, independent study, internships, liberal arts/career combination, study abroad, weekend college. Bachelor's degree programs available on campus. License preparation in dental hygiene, nursing, radiology. **Credit/placement by examination:** AP, CLEP, IB, institutional tests. 30 credit hours maximum toward associate degree. **Support services:** GED preparation and test center, learning center, reduced course load, remedial instruction, study skills assistance, tutoring, writing center.

Majors. Business: Accounting technology, business admin, executive assistant, human resources, office technology. **Communications technology:** Graphics. **Computer sciences:** Data entry, networking, programming, webmaster. **Education:** Early childhood. **Health services:** Dental hygiene, EMT paramedic, medical assistant, medical secretary, nursing (RN), radiologic technology/medical imaging, substance abuse counseling. **Liberal arts:** Arts/sciences. **Parks/recreation:** Sports admin.

Most popular majors. Business/marketing 10%, health sciences 13%, liberal arts 56%.

Technology on campus. 923 workstations in library, computer center, student center. Online course registration, online library, helpline, wireless network available.

Student life. Freshman orientation: Available. Preregistration for classes offered. Sessions held during quarterly registration period. Online orientation option available. **Activities:** Bands, choral groups, drama, international student organizations, literary magazine, Model UN, musical theater, student government, student newspaper, symphony orchestra, American Sign Language, Clark College Feminists, manga anime club, club for social action, Generation for Truth prayer club, international club, Japanese language club, Queer Penguins and Allies, multicultural student union, Students for Political Action Now.

Athletics. Intercollegiate: Basketball, cross-country, soccer, track and field, volleyball W. **Intramural:** Basketball, fencing, football (non-tackle), soccer, softball, table tennis, volleyball. **Team name:** Penguins.

Student services. Adult student services, alcohol/substance abuse counseling, career counseling, services for economically disadvantaged, student employment services, financial aid counseling, health services, legal services, minority student services, on-campus daycare, personal counseling, placement for graduates, veterans' counselor. **Physically disabled:** Services for visually, speech, hearing impaired. **Transfer:** Transfer adviser, college fairs on campus for students transferring to 4-year colleges.

Contact. E-mail: admissions@clark.edu
Phone: (360) 992-2107 Fax: (360) 992-2879
Miranda Saari, Associate Director of Admissions and Assessment, Clark College, Welcome Center, MS PUB002, Vancouver, WA 98663

Clover Park Technical College
Lakewood, Washington
www.cptc.edu
CB code: 3971

- Public 2-year technical college
- Commuter campus in small city

General. Regionally accredited. **Enrollment:** 4,509 undergraduates. **Degrees:** 459 associate awarded. **Location:** 10 miles from Tacoma, 40 miles from Seattle. **Calendar:** Quarter, extensive summer session. **Full-time faculty:** 91 total. **Part-time faculty:** 66 total. **Class size:** 70% < 20, 27% 20-39, 2% 40-49, 1% 50-99.

Basis for selection. Open admission, but selective for some programs. Some programs have test score minimums and/or course prerequisite requirements.

2015-2016 Annual costs. Tuition/fees: $3,886; $9,289 out-of-state. Per-credit charge: $82 in-state; $202 out-of-state. Books/supplies: $1,333. Personal expenses: $1,950.

Financial aid. All financial aid based on need. Need-based aid available for part-time students. Work-study available nights, weekends and for part-time students.

Application procedures. **Admission:** No deadline. $50 fee. Application must be submitted on paper. Admission notification on a rolling basis. **Financial aid:** Closing date 4/12. FAFSA, institutional form required. Applicants notified on a rolling basis starting 5/1.

Academics. **Special study options:** Distance learning, dual enrollment of high school students, ESL, internships. License preparation in aviation, nursing. **Credit/placement by examination:** AP, CLEP, institutional tests. 15 credit hours maximum toward associate degree. 25 percent of total approved hours may be awarded for prior work and/or life experience. **Support services:** GED preparation and test center, tutoring.

Majors. **Business:** Accounting technology, marketing, office management. **Communications technology:** Desktop publishing. **Computer sciences:** Networking, programming, security, web page design. **Education:** Early childhood. **Health services:** Clinical lab assistant, dental assistant, histologic assistant, licensed practical nurse, massage therapy, nursing (RN), pharmacy assistant, surgical technology. **Protective services:** Disaster management, fire systems technology. **Visual/performing arts:** Interior design.

Most popular majors. Business/marketing 7%, computer/information sciences 19%, engineering/engineering technologies 8%, health sciences 34%, personal/culinary services 6%, trade and industry 19%.

Technology on campus. 94 workstations in library. Online library, wireless network available.

Student life. **Freshman orientation:** Available. Preregistration for classes offered. **Activities:** International student organizations, student government.

Student services. Adult student services, career counseling, services for economically disadvantaged, student employment services, financial aid counseling, minority student services, on-campus daycare, veterans' counselor. **Physically disabled:** Services for visually, speech, hearing impaired.

Contact. Phone: (253) 589-5678 Fax: (253) 589-5852
Cindy Mowry, Director of Enrollment Services, Clover Park Technical College, 4500 Steilacoom Boulevard, SW, Lakewood, WA 98499-4098

Columbia Basin College
Pasco, Washington
www.columbiabasin.edu   CB code: 4077

▸ Public 2-year community college
▸ Commuter campus in small city

General. Founded in 1955. Regionally accredited. **Enrollment:** 1,595 degree-seeking undergraduates. **Degrees:** 57 bachelor's, 1,077 associate awarded. **Location:** 135 miles from Spokane, 225 miles from Seattle. **Calendar:** Quarter, limited summer session. **Full-time faculty:** 256 total. **Part-time faculty:** 24 total. **Special facilities:** Performing arts theater, health science center, observatory, math and science working atrium, regional medical library, tutor and writing center, research farm, center for career & technical education.

Student profile.

Out-of-state: 1% **25 or older:**   58%

Transfer out. Colleges most students transferred to 2015: Washington State University.

Basis for selection. Open admission, but selective for some programs. Special application process and requirements for nursing, dental hygiene, radiologic technology, paramedic, medical assistant, automotive technology,

nuclear technology, and surgical technician programs. Applicants not graduates of regionally accredited high schools or those without a GED must submit Washington Pre-College Test, SAT, or ACT scores.

High school preparation. College-preparatory program required. 11 units recommended. Recommended units include English 3, mathematics 2, social studies 3, science 2 and foreign language 1.

2015-2016 Annual costs. Tuition/fees: $4,241; $9,644 out-of-state. Per-credit charge: $82 in-state; $202 out-of-state. Books/supplies: $1,026. Personal expenses: $1,614.

Financial aid. **Need-based:** Need-based aid available for part-time students. Work-study available nights, weekends and for part-time students. **Non-need-based:** Scholarships awarded for academics, athletics, state residency.

Application procedures. **Admission:** $29 fee, may be waived for applicants with need. Application must be submitted on paper. Admission notification on a rolling basis. **Financial aid:** Closing date 4/15. FAFSA, institutional form required. Applicants notified on a rolling basis starting 6/15; must reply within 2 week(s) of notification.

Academics. **Special study options:** Cross-registration, distance learning, dual enrollment of high school students, ESL, internships, liberal arts/career combination, weekend college. Bachelor's degree programs available on campus. License preparation in dental hygiene, nursing, paramedic, radiology. **Credit/placement by examination:** AP, CLEP, IB, institutional tests. 30 credit hours maximum toward associate degree. **Support services:** GED preparation and test center, learning center, reduced course load, remedial instruction, study skills assistance, tutoring, writing center.

Majors. **Business:** General, accounting technology, business admin, office management, purchasing. **Computer sciences:** General, data processing, networking, programming, support specialist, webmaster. **Education:** Early childhood. **Health services:** Clinical lab technology, dental hygiene, EMT ambulance attendant, EMT paramedic, health information management, licensed practical nurse, medical transcription, nursing (RN), sonography, surgical technology. **Liberal arts:** Arts/sciences. **Physical sciences:** General. **Protective services:** Firefighting, law enforcement admin, police science.

Most popular majors. Health sciences 7%, liberal arts 77%.

Technology on campus. 680 workstations in library, computer center. Online course registration, online library, wireless network available.

Student life. **Freshman orientation:** Mandatory. Preregistration for classes offered. **Activities:** Bands, choral groups, drama, music ensembles, musical theater, student government, student newspaper.

Athletics. NJCAA. **Intercollegiate:** Baseball M, basketball, golf, soccer, softball W, volleyball W. **Intramural:** Basketball, bowling, soccer M, softball, volleyball. **Team name:** Hawks.

Student services. Adult student services, career counseling, student employment services, minority student services, personal counseling, placement for graduates, veterans' counselor, women's services. **Physically disabled:** Services for visually, speech, hearing impaired. **Transfer:** Transfer adviser, college fairs on campus for students transferring to 4-year colleges.

Contact. E-mail: admissions@columbiabasin.edu
Phone: (509) 547-0511 Fax: (509) 546-0401
Patricia Campbell, Director of Admissions and Registration, Columbia Basin College, 2600 North 20th Avenue, Pasco, WA 99301

Edmonds Community College
Lynnwood, Washington   CB member
www.edcc.edu   CB code: 4307

▸ Public 2-year community college
▸ Commuter campus in small city

General. Founded in 1967. Regionally accredited. **Enrollment:** 9,540 undergraduates. **Degrees:** 1,040 associate awarded. **Location:** 15 miles from Seattle. **Calendar:** Quarter, extensive summer session. **Full-time faculty:** 129 total. **Part-time faculty:** 306 total. **Special facilities:** Center for Business and Employment Development, golf course.

Transfer out. Colleges most students transferred to 2015: University of Washington, Central Washington University, Western Washington University, Washington State University.

Basis for selection. Open admission, but selective for some programs. Interview recommended for international studies, travel tourism majors; audition required for music performance majors. **Learning Disabled:** SSD is available to provide appropriate accommodation.

2015-2016 Annual costs. Tuition/fees: $4,308; $9,711 out-of-state. Per-credit charge: $85 in-state; $206 out-of-state. Books/supplies: $900. Personal expenses: $1,824. **Additional information:** Room fee ranges $2,085-$3,375 depending on unit.

Financial aid. Need-based: Need-based aid available for part-time students. Work-study available nights, weekends and for part-time students. **Non-need-based:** Scholarships awarded for athletics.

Application procedures. Admission: No deadline. $32 fee, may be waived for applicants with need. Admission notification on a rolling basis. TOEFL optional for students whose first language is not English. **Financial aid:** Priority date 5/1; no closing date. FAFSA, institutional form required. Applicants notified on a rolling basis starting 6/1; must reply within 4 week(s) of notification.

Academics. Special study options: Cooperative education, cross-registration, distance learning, dual enrollment of high school students, ESL, exchange student, honors, independent study, internships, study abroad, weekend college. **Credit/placement by examination:** AP, CLEP, institutional tests. 15 credit hours maximum toward associate degree. **Support services:** GED preparation and test center, learning center, remedial instruction, tutoring, writing center.

Majors. Biology: General. **Business:** General, accounting technology, business admin, construction management, e-commerce, hospitality admin, international, office management, office/clerical, travel services. **Computer sciences:** Computer graphics, data processing, database management, networking, security, web page design, webmaster. **Education:** Early childhood, elementary. **Engineering:** Chemical, electrical, mechanical. **Health services:** Community health services, health information technology, medical radiologic technology/radiation therapy, mental health services, nursing (RN), substance abuse counseling, vocational rehab counseling. **Liberal arts:** Arts/sciences. **Physical sciences:** General. **Protective services:** Disaster management, fire services admin. **Visual/performing arts:** Commercial photography.

Most popular majors. Business/marketing 25%, computer/information sciences 9%, health sciences 7%, legal studies 6%, liberal arts 41%.

Technology on campus. 1,129 workstations in library, computer center. Commuter students can connect to campus network. Online course registration available.

Student life. Freshman orientation: Available. Preregistration for classes offered. Students receive brief orientation prior to placement test. **Housing:** Host families available for international students. **Activities:** Jazz band, choral groups, dance, drama, international student organizations, literary magazine, music ensembles, student government, student newspaper, Phi Theta Kappa, Design and Invention Club, I-Hope Club, DESI Club, Baptist Collegiate Ministry, Black Student Association, American Indian Student Association, Gay and Lesbian Alliance, Digital Production Club.

Athletics. Intercollegiate: Baseball M, basketball, golf, soccer, softball W, volleyball W. **Intramural:** Basketball M, bowling, golf, table tennis, volleyball. **Team name:** Tritons.

Student services. Adult student services, career counseling, student employment services, financial aid counseling, minority student services, on-campus daycare, personal counseling, placement for graduates, women's services. **Physically disabled:** Services for visually, speech, hearing impaired. **Transfer:** Transfer center, transfer adviser, college fairs on campus for students transferring to 4-year colleges.

Contact. E-mail: admissions@edcc.edu
Phone: (425) 640-1459 Fax: (425) 640-1159
Nanci Froemming, Office Manager, Enrollment Services, Edmonds Community College, 20000 68th Avenue West, Lynnwood, WA 98036-5912

Everett Community College
Everett, Washington
www.everettcc.edu   CB code: 4303

- Public 2-year community college
- Commuter campus in small city

General. Founded in 1941. Regionally accredited. **Enrollment:** 6,990 undergraduates. **Degrees:** 1,199 associate awarded. **Location:** 30 miles from Seattle. **Calendar:** Quarter, limited summer session. **Full-time faculty:** 108 total. **Part-time faculty:** 231 total. **Class size:** 37% < 20, 60% 20-39, 3% 40-49, less than 1% 50-99. **Partnerships:** Formal partnership with Boeing.

Student profile.

Out-of-state:	2%	**25 or older:** 41%

Transfer out. Colleges most students transferred to 2015: Western Washington University, University of Washington, Central Washington University, Washington State University.

Basis for selection. Open admission, but selective for some programs. Special requirements for nursing, fire science, and criminal justice. Interview recommended for nursing.

High school preparation. College-preparatory program recommended. 16 units recommended. Recommended units include English 4, mathematics 3, social studies 3, history 2, science 2 and foreign language 2.

2015-2016 Annual costs. Tuition/fees: $4,101; $9,504 out-of-state. Per-credit charge: $85 in-state; $206 out-of-state. Books/supplies: $924. Personal expenses: $1,590. **Additional information:** Room ranges $5,100-$6,495 depending on unit.

Financial aid. Need-based: Need-based aid available for part-time students. Work-study available nights, weekends and for part-time students. **Non-need-based:** Scholarships awarded for academics, alumni affiliation, art, athletics, job skills, leadership, minority status, music/drama, state residency.

Application procedures. Admission: No deadline. No application fee. Admission notification on a rolling basis. **Financial aid:** Priority date 5/5; no closing date. FAFSA, institutional form required. Applicants notified on a rolling basis starting 4/15; must reply within 4 week(s) of notification.

Academics. Offers direct-transfer associate degrees that assure full transfer to most Washington and Oregon universities. Transfer degrees for specific majors at designated universities can be designed by the student and faculty advisor. **Special study options:** Cooperative education, distance learning, dual enrollment of high school students, ESL, independent study, internships, study abroad. Bachelor's degree programs available on campus. License preparation in aviation, nursing, paramedic. **Credit/placement by examination:** AP, CLEP, IB, institutional tests. 45 credit hours maximum toward associate degree. **Support services:** GED preparation and test center, learning center, reduced course load, remedial instruction, study skills assistance, tutoring, writing center.

Majors. Business: General, accounting, administrative services, business admin, management information systems, office/clerical. **Computer sciences:** Data processing, web page design. **Education:** Early childhood, teacher assistance. **Health services:** Dental hygiene, medical assistant, nursing (RN), predental, premedicine, prepharmacy, preveterinary. **History:** General. **Liberal arts:** Arts/sciences. **Philosophy/religion:** Philosophy. **Physical sciences:** General. **Protective services:** Firefighting, police science. **Psychology:** General.

Most popular majors. Business/marketing 17%, health sciences 14%, liberal arts 57%.

Technology on campus. 900 workstations in library, computer center, student center. Online course registration, wireless network available.

Student life. Freshman orientation: Mandatory. Preregistration for classes offered. One-day program of placement testing, orientation and advising sessions. **Housing:** Housing in private homes available for foreign students. **Activities:** Choral groups, drama, literary magazine, music ensembles, musical theater, student government, student newspaper, 25 student clubs.

Athletics. Intercollegiate: Baseball M, basketball, cross-country, soccer, softball W, volleyball W. **Intramural:** Basketball, bowling, golf, soccer, softball, tennis, volleyball, weight lifting. **Team name:** Trojans.

Student services. Adult student services, career counseling, services for economically disadvantaged, student employment services, financial aid counseling, minority student services, on-campus daycare, personal counseling, placement for graduates, veterans' counselor, women's services. **Physically disabled:** Services for visually, speech, hearing impaired. **Transfer:** Transfer adviser, college fairs on campus for students transferring to 4-year colleges.

Contact. E-mail: admissions@everettcc.edu
Phone: (425) 388-9219 Fax: (425) 388-9173
Laurie Franklin, Dean of Enrollment/Student Financial Services, Everett Community College, 2000 Tower Street, Everett, WA 98201-1352

Grays Harbor College
Aberdeen, Washington
www.ghc.edu

CB code: 4332

▶ Public 2-year community college
▶ Commuter campus in large town

General. Founded in 1930. Regionally accredited. **Enrollment:** 1,970 undergraduates. **Degrees:** 331 associate awarded. **Location:** 100 miles from Seattle. **Calendar:** Quarter, limited summer session. **Full-time faculty:** 68 total. **Part-time faculty:** 52 total. **Class size:** 77% < 20, 22% 20-39, less than 1% 40-49, less than 1% 50-99. **Special facilities:** 4-acre lake linked to Grays Harbor estuary, fish hatcheries, theater. **Partnerships:** Formal partnerships with local businesses for internships and short-term training.

Transfer out. Colleges most students transferred to 2015: Washington State University, Evergreen State College, Western Washington University, Central Washington University, Eastern Washington University.

Basis for selection. Open admission, but selective for some programs. High school diploma or GED required of applicants under 18 years of age. Limited admission to nursing program.

2015-2016 Annual costs. Tuition/fees: $4,041; $9,444 out-of-state. Per-credit charge: $85 in-state; $206 out-of-state. Books/supplies: $1,026. Personal expenses: $1,932.

Financial aid. Need-based: Need-based aid available for part-time students. Work-study available nights, weekends and for part-time students. **Non-need-based:** Scholarships awarded for academics, art, athletics, music/drama.

Application procedures. Admission: Priority date 9/1; no deadline. No application fee. Admission notification on a rolling basis. **Financial aid:** Closing date 5/1. FAFSA, institutional form required. Applicants notified on a rolling basis starting 5/15.

Academics. Special study options: Accelerated study, cooperative education, distance learning, double major, dual enrollment of high school students, ESL, independent study, internships, study abroad. Bachelor's degree programs available on campus. License preparation in nursing. **Credit/placement by examination:** AP, CLEP, institutional tests. 45 credit hours maximum toward associate degree. **Support services:** GED preparation and test center, learning center, reduced course load, remedial instruction, study skills assistance, tutoring, writing center.

Majors. Business: General, accounting technology, business admin, entrepreneurial studies, office management. **Conservation:** Forestry. **General:** Carpentry. **Health services:** Nursing (RN). **Liberal arts:** Arts/sciences. **Physical sciences:** General. **Protective services:** Police science.

Technology on campus. 382 workstations in library, computer center, student center. Online course registration, online library, student web hosting, wireless network available.

Student life. Freshman orientation: Mandatory. Preregistration for classes offered. Offered online or face to face. **Activities:** Bands, campus ministries, choral groups, drama, music ensembles, musical theater, student government, student newspaper, symphony orchestra, Native American student association, Tyee honorary service club, human services student association, Hispanic/Latino club, student nurses association, non-traditional students community, natural resources club, gay, lesbian, bisexual, transgender and straight students club.

Athletics. Intercollegiate: Baseball M, basketball, golf, softball W, volleyball W. **Team name:** Chokers.

Student services. Adult student services, career counseling, services for economically disadvantaged, student employment services, financial aid counseling, minority student services, on-campus daycare, personal counseling, placement for graduates, veterans' counselor. **Physically disabled:** Services for visually, speech, hearing impaired. **Transfer:** Pre-admission transcript evaluation for new students. Transfer adviser, college fairs on campus for students transferring to 4-year colleges.

Contact. E-mail: admissions@ghc.edu
Phone: (360) 538-4026 Toll-free number: (800) 562-4830
Fax: (360) 538-4293
Nancy DeVerse, Associate Dean for Student Services/Registrar, Grays Harbor College, 1620 Edward P Smith Drive, Aberdeen, WA 98520

Green River Community College
Auburn, Washington
www.greenriver.edu

CB code: 4337

▶ Public 2-year community college
▶ Commuter campus in large town

General. Founded in 1965. Regionally accredited. **Enrollment:** 5,463 degree-seeking undergraduates. **Degrees:** 1,410 associate awarded. **Location:** 35 miles from Seattle. **Calendar:** Quarter, limited summer session. **Full-time faculty:** 154 total. **Part-time faculty:** 333 total. **Class size:** 17% < 20, 80% 20-39, 4% 40-49.

Basis for selection. Open admission, but selective for some programs. Special requirements for health occupation programs. Interview required for occupational therapy.

2015-2016 Annual costs. Tuition/fees: $4,341; $9,744 out-of-state. Per-credit charge: $85 in-state; $206 out-of-state. Books/supplies: $1,200. Personal expenses: $1,170.

Financial aid. All financial aid based on need. Need-based aid available for part-time students. Work-study available nights, weekends and for part-time students.

Application procedures. Admission: No deadline. $20 fee. Admission notification on a rolling basis. **Financial aid:** Closing date 4/15. FAFSA, institutional form required. Applicants notified on a rolling basis starting 6/30; must reply within 2 week(s) of notification.

Academics. Special study options: Cooperative education, cross-registration, distance learning, dual enrollment of high school students, ESL, independent study, internships, study abroad. **Credit/placement by examination:** AP, CLEP, institutional tests. **Support services:** GED preparation and test center, learning center, reduced course load, remedial instruction, tutoring, writing center.

Majors. Business: Accounting, marketing, office technology, office/clerical, real estate. **Computer sciences:** Database management, networking, security, system admin. **Conservation:** Water/wetlands/marine. **Education:** Early childhood, teacher assistance. **General:** Carpentry. **Health services:** Medical secretary, occupational therapy assistant, physical therapy assistant. **Liberal arts:** Arts/sciences. **Protective services:** Police science. **Visual/performing arts:** General.

Most popular majors. Business/marketing 16%, health sciences 6%, liberal arts 52%, trade and industry 13%.

Technology on campus. 210 workstations in library, computer center.

Student life. Freshman orientation: Available. Preregistration for classes offered. **Housing:** Apartments available. **Activities:** Jazz band, choral groups, dance, drama, music ensembles, radio station, student government, student newspaper, Asian Student Union, Black Student Union, Native American Student Association, Los Latinos Unidos, Phi Theta Kappa, Teachers of Tomorrow, Skills USA, forestry club, court reporting club, American Society of Mechanical Engineers.

Athletics. NJCAA. **Intercollegiate:** Baseball M, basketball, golf, soccer, softball W, tennis, volleyball W. **Intramural:** Badminton, baseball M, basketball, soccer, softball, tennis, volleyball. **Team name:** Gators.

Student services. Career counseling, services for economically disadvantaged, student employment services, financial aid counseling, health services, minority student services, on-campus daycare, personal counseling, placement for graduates, veterans' counselor, women's services. **Physically disabled:** Services for visually, hearing impaired. **Transfer:** Transfer center, transfer adviser, college fairs on campus for students transferring to 4-year colleges.

Contact. E-mail: EnrollmentServices@greenriver.edu
Phone: (253) 833-9111 ext. 2500 Fax: (253) 288-3454
Denise Bennatts, Registrar, Green River Community College, 12401 SE 320th Street, Auburn, WA 98092

Highline College
Des Moines, Washington
www.highline.edu

CB code: 4348

▶ Public 2-year community college
▶ Commuter campus in small city

General. Founded in 1961. Regionally accredited. More than 60% students of color; representing the diversity of the community. More than 50 countries represented with well over 100 languages spoken among students. **Enrollment:** 6,489 undergraduates. **Degrees:** 1,115 associate awarded. **ROTC:** Army, Air Force. **Location:** 18 miles from Seattle. **Calendar:** Quarter, limited summer session. **Full-time faculty:** 150 total. **Part-time faculty:** 185 total. **Special facilities:** Sleep study laboratory, respiratory care patient care simulator, marine and science technology center.

Basis for selection. Open admission, but selective for some programs. School achievement record considered for health programs. College and work experience also considered for nursing.

High school preparation. Health occupation programs require chemistry and algebra.

2015-2016 Annual costs. Tuition/fees: $4,034; $9,437 out-of-state. Per-credit charge: $85 in-state; $206 out-of-state. Personal expenses: $1,960.

Financial aid. Need-based: Need-based aid available for part-time students. Work-study available nights, weekends and for part-time students.

Application procedures. Admission: No deadline. $24 fee. Admission notification on a rolling basis. **Financial aid:** Priority date 6/1; no closing date. FAFSA required. Applicants notified on a rolling basis starting 6/1.

Academics. Special study options: Accelerated study, cooperative education, cross-registration, distance learning, double major, dual enrollment of high school students, ESL, honors, independent study, internships, student-designed major. Bachelor's degree programs available on campus. **Credit/placement by examination:** AP, CLEP, institutional tests. **Support services:** GED preparation and test center, learning center, pre-admission summer program, reduced course load, remedial instruction, tutoring.

Majors. Business: General, accounting, administrative services, business admin, fashion, hospitality/recreation, international, office/clerical, sales/distribution, tourism/travel. **Communications:** Communications/speech/rhetoric, journalism. **Computer sciences:** General. **Education:** General, teacher assistance. **Engineering:** General. **English:** English lit. **Foreign languages:** General, French, German, linguistics. **Health services:** Dental assistant, health care admin, medical assistant, medical transcription, nursing (RN), respiratory therapy technology. **History:** General. **Liberal arts:** Arts/sciences, library assistant. **Math:** General. **Parks/recreation:** Health/fitness. **Physical sciences:** Astronomy, geology. **Psychology:** General. **Social sciences:** General, anthropology, economics, geography, sociology. **Visual/performing arts:** General, art, commercial/advertising art, dramatic, multimedia, music. **Work/family studies:** General, child care management, food/nutrition.

Most popular majors. Business/marketing 16%, health sciences 20%, liberal arts 53%.

Technology on campus. 100 workstations in library, computer center, student center.

Student life. Activities: Bands, choral groups, drama, literary magazine, music ensembles, student government, student newspaper, TV station, Indian and international student clubs, political forum, paralegal and arts societies, respiratory care club, academic honor society, campus crusade for Christ.

Athletics. NJCAA. **Intercollegiate:** Basketball, cross-country, soccer, softball W, track and field, volleyball W, wrestling M. **Team name:** Thunderbirds.

Student services. Adult student services, career counseling, student employment services, health services, minority student services, on-campus daycare, personal counseling, placement for graduates, veterans' counselor, women's services. **Physically disabled:** Services for visually, speech, hearing impaired. **Transfer:** Transfer adviser, college fairs on campus for students transferring to 4-year colleges.

Contact. E-mail: mkuwasaki@highline.edu
Phone: (206) 878-3710 ext. 3181 Fax: (206) 870-3782
Michelle Kuwasaki, Director of Admissions, Highline College, 2400 South 240th Street, Des Moines, WA 98198-9800

Lake Washington Institute of Technology
Kirkland, Washington
www.lwtech.edu
CB code: 1453

- Public 2-year technical college
- Commuter campus in large town

General. Founded in 1949. Regionally accredited. **Enrollment:** 1,651 degree-seeking undergraduates; 2,739 non-degree-seeking students. **Degrees:** 14 bachelor's, 568 associate awarded. **Location:** 10 miles from Seattle. **Calendar:** Quarter, extensive summer session. **Full-time faculty:** 78 total; 9% have terminal degrees, 23% minority, 51% women. **Part-time faculty:** 176 total; 11% have terminal degrees, 12% minority, 68% women.

Student profile. Among degree-seeking undergraduates, 15% enrolled in a transfer program, 83% enrolled in a vocational program, 19% already have a bachelor's degree or higher, 335 enrolled as first-time, first-year students, 623 transferred in from other institutions.

Part-time:	35%	Women:	54%
Out-of-state:	1%	25 or older:	29%

Transfer out. Colleges most students transferred to 2015: University of Washington, City University.

Basis for selection. Open admission, but selective for some programs. Limited admissions to nursing, dental hygiene, physical therapist assistant, Bachelor of Technology in Applied Design, Bachelor of Applied Science in Public Health, Bachelor of Applied Science in Transportation and Logistics Management.

2015-2016 Annual costs. Tuition/fees: $4,461; $9,864 out-of-state. Per-credit charge: $85 in-state; $206 out-of-state. Books/supplies: $1,281. Personal expenses: $1,710.

Financial aid. Need-based: Need-based aid available for part-time students. Work-study available nights, weekends and for part-time students.

Application procedures. Admission: No application fee. Admission notification on a rolling basis. **Financial aid:** Closing date 3/15. FAFSA, institutional form required. Applicants notified on a rolling basis starting 5/1.

Academics. Special study options: Accelerated study, cooperative education, distance learning, double major, dual enrollment of high school students, ESL, internships, liberal arts/career combination, weekend college. Bachelor's degree programs available on campus. License preparation in dental hygiene, nursing, occupational therapy, physical therapy. **Credit/placement by examination:** AP, CLEP, IB, institutional tests. **Support services:** GED preparation and test center, learning center, reduced course load, remedial instruction, study skills assistance, tutoring, writing center.

Majors. Business: General, accounting technology, administrative services, construction management. **Communications technology:** Animation/special effects. **Computer sciences:** Data entry, data processing, networking. **Education:** Early childhood. **Health services:** Dental assistant, dental hygiene, insurance coding, licensed practical nurse, massage therapy, medical assistant, nursing (RN), occupational therapy assistant, physical therapy assistant, pre-nursing. **Parks/recreation:** Sports admin. **Visual/performing arts:** Design.

Most popular majors. Computer/information sciences 11%, engineering/engineering technologies 8%, health sciences 40%, personal/culinary services 6%, trade and industry 13%.

Technology on campus. 1,200 workstations in library, computer center. Online course registration, online library, helpline, wireless network available.

Student life. Freshman orientation: Available. Preregistration for classes offered. **Activities:** Literary magazine, student government.

Student services. Adult student services, career counseling, services for economically disadvantaged, student employment services, financial aid counseling, on-campus daycare, personal counseling, placement for graduates, veterans' counselor. **Physically disabled:** Services for visually, speech, hearing impaired. **Transfer:** Pre-admission transcript evaluation for new students. Transfer adviser, college fairs on campus for students transferring to 4-year colleges.

Contact. E-mail: admissions@lwtech.edu
Phone: (425) 739-8104 Fax: (425) 739-8110
Ruby Hayden, Vice President of Student Services, Lake Washington Institute of Technology, West Building, W201, Kirkland, WA 98034

Lower Columbia College
Longview, Washington
www.lowercolumbia.edu
CB code: 4402

- Public 2-year community college
- Commuter campus in small city

General. Founded in 1934. Regionally accredited. **Enrollment:** 1,411 degree-seeking undergraduates; 1,797 non-degree-seeking students. **Degrees:** 574 associate awarded. **Location:** 50 miles from Portland, Oregon, 120 miles from Seattle. **Calendar:** Quarter, limited summer session. **Full-time faculty:** 67 total. **Part-time faculty:** 129 total. **Special facilities:** Fine and performing arts center, gym and fitness center.

Student profile. Among degree-seeking undergraduates, 315 enrolled as first-time, first-year students.

Part-time:	40%	25 or older: 45%
Women:	64%	

Transfer out. Colleges most students transferred to 2015: Washington State University, University of Washington, Central Washington University, Eastern Washington University, Western Washington University.

Basis for selection. Open admission, but selective for some programs. Special requirements for nursing program and medical assistant program.

2015-2016 Annual costs. Tuition/fees: $4,212; $9,615 out-of-state. Per-credit charge: $85 in-state; $205 out-of-state. Books/supplies: $1,155. Personal expenses: $1,848.

Financial aid. Need-based: Need-based aid available for part-time students. Work-study available nights, weekends and for part-time students.

Application procedures. Admission: No deadline. No application fee. Admission notification on a rolling basis. **Financial aid:** Priority date 5/26; no closing date. FAFSA, institutional form required. Applicants notified on a rolling basis starting 4/8; must reply within 2 week(s) of notification.

Academics. Special study options: Cooperative education, cross-registration, distance learning, dual enrollment of high school students, ESL, independent study, internships, liberal arts/career combination, student-designed major, teacher certification program. Bachelor's degree programs available on campus. License preparation in nursing. **Credit/placement by examination:** AP, CLEP, institutional tests. **Support services:** GED preparation and test center, learning center, reduced course load, remedial instruction, study skills assistance, tutoring, writing center. Comprehensive tutoring and other support services available in LCC's Learning Commons.

Majors. Business: Accounting, accounting technology, administrative services, business admin, office technology, office/clerical. **Computer sciences:** General, computer science, data entry, data processing, networking, programming. **Education:** Elementary, teacher assistance. **Engineering:** General. **English:** English lit. **Health services:** Licensed practical nurse, medical assistant, medical secretary, nursing (RN), nursing assistant, substance abuse counseling. **Liberal arts:** Arts/sciences. **Protective services:** Law enforcement admin. **Work/family studies:** Child development.

Technology on campus. 450 workstations in library, computer center, student center. Online course registration, online library, wireless network available.

Student life. Freshman orientation: Mandatory. Preregistration for classes offered. **Housing:** Apartments normally available in local community. **Activities:** Bands, choral groups, dance, drama, international student organizations, literary magazine, music ensembles, musical theater, student government, theater club, student nurses organization, welding, campus entertainment, diesel mechanics club, Phi Theta Kappa.

Athletics. NJCAA. **Intercollegiate:** Baseball M, basketball, soccer W, softball W, volleyball W. **Team name:** Red Devils.

Student services. Adult student services, career counseling, services for economically disadvantaged, student employment services, financial aid counseling, on-campus daycare, personal counseling, placement for graduates, veterans' counselor. **Physically disabled:** Services for visually, speech, hearing impaired. **Transfer:** Re-entry adviser, pre-admission transcript evaluation for new students. Transfer center, transfer adviser, college fairs on campus for students transferring to 4-year colleges.

Contact. E-mail: entry@lowercolumbia.edu
Phone: (360) 442-2311 Toll-free number: (866) 900-2311
Fax: (360) 442-2379
Nichole Seroshek, Registrar, Lower Columbia College, 1600 Maple Street, Longview, WA 98632-0310

North Seattle College
Seattle, Washington
www.northseattle.edu   CB code: 4554

▶ Public 2-year community college
▶ Commuter campus in very large city

General. Founded in 1970. Regionally accredited. Associate degree and certificate programs available via e-learning; college is committed to sustainability and environmentally responsible practices. **Enrollment:** 2,356 degree-seeking undergraduates; 3,534 non-degree-seeking students. **Degrees:** 4 bachelor's, 699 associate awarded. **Location:** 8 miles from downtown. **Calendar:** Quarter, limited summer session. **Full-time faculty:** 90 total; 31% minority, 60% women. **Part-time faculty:** 248 total; 18% minority, 66% women. **Class size:** 43% < 20, 56% 20-39, less than 1% 40-49, less than 1% 50-99. **Special facilities:** Wetlands, wellness center, observatory. **Partnerships:** Formal partnerships with Rolex Watch USA, Comcast, Lennox / HVAC, Northwest Hospital, City of Seattle Municipal Court.

Student profile. Among degree-seeking undergraduates, 657 enrolled as first-time, first-year students.

Part-time:	55%	Women:	52%
Out-of-state:	2%	25 or older:	63%

Transfer out. Colleges most students transferred to 2015: University of Washington, Seattle University, Seattle Pacific University, Washington State University, Western Washington University.

Basis for selection. Open admission. Applicants with deficient English or Math skills are required to take remedial courses to qualify for college level work.

2015-2016 Annual costs. Tuition/fees: $4,019; $9,422 out-of-state. Per-credit charge: $85 in-state; $206 out-of-state. Books/supplies: $1,026. Personal expenses: $1,570.

2014-2015 Financial aid. Need-based: 87% of total undergraduate aid awarded as scholarships/grants, 13% as loans/jobs. Need-based aid available for part-time students. Work-study available nights, weekends and for part-time students.

Application procedures. Admission: No deadline. No application fee. Admission notification on a rolling basis. **Financial aid:** Priority date 3/15, closing date 6/30. FAFSA required. Applicants notified on a rolling basis starting 6/1; must reply by 9/15.

Academics. Special study options: Cooperative education, cross-registration, distance learning, dual enrollment of high school students, ESL, independent study, internships, liberal arts/career combination, study abroad. Bachelor's degree programs available on campus. License preparation in nursing, paramedic, real estate. **Credit/placement by examination:** AP, CLEP, IB, institutional tests. 45 credit hours maximum toward associate degree. **Support services:** GED preparation and test center, learning center, reduced course load, remedial instruction, study skills assistance, tutoring, writing center.

Majors. Business: General, accounting technology, administrative services, office management, office technology, office/clerical, real estate. **Communications technology:** General. **Computer sciences:** Networking. **Education:** General, early childhood. **Health services:** Licensed practical nurse, medical assistant, nursing (RN), office assistant, pharmacy assistant. **Visual/performing arts:** General, art, dramatic, music, studio arts.

Most popular majors. Engineering/engineering technologies 7%, health sciences 14%, liberal arts 73%.

Technology on campus. 2,000 workstations in library, computer center, student center. Commuter students can connect to campus network. Online course registration, online library, helpline, student web hosting, wireless network available.

Student life. Freshman orientation: Available. Preregistration for classes offered. Students can select from in-person or on-line orientations. **Activities:** Bands, choral groups, drama, international student organizations, literary magazine, music ensembles, radio station, student government, symphony orchestra, TV station, Phi Theta Kappa, Black student union, Indonesian community club, Vietnamese student association, art group, student leadership council, Muslim student association, bio-med club, golf club, investment club.

Student services. Adult student services, career counseling, services for economically disadvantaged, student employment services, financial aid counseling, minority student services, on-campus daycare, personal counseling, placement for graduates, veterans' counselor, women's services. **Physically disabled:** Services for visually, speech, hearing impaired. **Transfer:** Transfer adviser, college fairs on campus for students transferring to 4-year colleges.

Contact. E-mail: ARRC@sattlecolleges.edu
Phone: (206) 934-3663 Fax: (206) 934-3671
Kathy Rhodes, Registrar / Dean of Enrollment Services, North Seattle College, 9600 College Way North, Seattle, WA 98103-3599

Northwest Indian College
Bellingham, Washington
www.nwic.edu   CB code: 3973

- Public 2-year tribal college
- Commuter campus in small town

General. Regionally accredited. **Enrollment:** 616 degree-seeking undergraduates. **Degrees:** 32 bachelor's, 64 associate awarded. **Location:** 8 miles from Bellingham. **Calendar:** Quarter, limited summer session. **Full-time faculty:** 24 total. **Part-time faculty:** 97 total.

Transfer out. Colleges most students transferred to 2015: Western Washington University, University of Washington, Lewis-Clark State College.

Basis for selection. Open admission. **Adult students:** SAT/ACT scores not required.

2015-2016 Annual costs. Tuition/fees: $4,455; $11,079 out-of-state. Per-credit charge: $105 in-state; $289 out-of-state. Room/board: $4,950. Books/supplies: $1,032. Personal expenses: $2,040.

Financial aid. Need-based: Need-based aid available for part-time students. Work-study available nights, weekends and for part-time students. **Non-need-based:** Scholarships awarded for academics.

Application procedures. Admission: Priority date 5/1; no deadline. $10 fee. Application must be submitted on paper. Admission notification on a rolling basis. **Financial aid:** No deadline. FAFSA, institutional form required. Applicants notified on a rolling basis.

Academics. Special study options: Cooperative education, distance learning, dual enrollment of high school students, independent study, internships, student-designed major. Bachelor's degree programs available on campus. **Credit/placement by examination:** AP, CLEP, institutional tests. **Support services:** GED preparation and test center, learning center, reduced course load, remedial instruction, study skills assistance, tutoring, writing center.

Majors. Area/ethnic studies: Native American. **Business:** Business admin. **Computer sciences:** Information technology. **Education:** Early childhood, Native American. **Health services:** Substance abuse counseling. **Physical sciences:** General.

Most popular majors. Area/ethnic studies 25%, health sciences 10%, liberal arts 65%.

Technology on campus. 90 workstations in dormitories, library, computer center, student center. Dormitories wired for high-speed internet access and linked to campus network. Online course registration, helpline, repair service, wireless network available.

Student life. Freshman orientation: Available. Preregistration for classes offered. First days of fall quarter. **Housing:** Guaranteed on-campus for all undergraduates. Coed dorms, wellness housing available. $200 fully refundable deposit. Family housing available. **Activities:** Drama, student government, student newspaper, service learning center, culture club.

Athletics. Intercollegiate: Basketball. **Intramural:** Basketball. **Team name:** Eagles.

Student services. Adult student services, alcohol/substance abuse counseling, career counseling, services for economically disadvantaged, student employment services, financial aid counseling, minority student services, on-campus daycare. **Transfer:** Pre-admission transcript evaluation for new students. Transfer adviser, college fairs on campus for students transferring to 4-year colleges.

Contact. E-mail: admissions@nwic.edu
Phone: (360) 676-2772 ext. 4269
Toll-free number: (866) 676-2772 ext. 4269 Fax: (360) 392-4333
Crystal Bagby, Associate Dean of Student Services, Northwest Indian College, 2522 Kwina Road, Bellingham, WA 98226-9217

Northwest School of Wooden Boatbuilding
Port Hadlock, Washington
www.nwswb.edu   CB code: 3116

- Private 1-year technical and maritime college
- Commuter campus in small town
- Application essay required

General. Accredited by ACCSC. **Enrollment:** 62 degree-seeking undergraduates. **Degrees:** 33 associate awarded. **Location:** 60 miles from Seattle. **Calendar:** Quarter, limited summer session. **Full-time faculty:** 6 total. **Class size:** 33% < 20, 67% 20-39. **Special facilities:** Lumber-milling room, two boatshops, sail loft, 2,000 square foot boat building shop.

Student profile.

Out-of-state:	55%	**25 or older:**	84%
Women:	15%		

Basis for selection. Open admission, but selective for some programs. Students must have a high school diploma or GED equivalency prior to the first day of school. **Home schooled:** State high school equivalency certificate required. **Learning Disabled:** Accommodations are carefully planned for students with special learning needs in collaboration with the Admissions Coordinator and the Boat Building Instructors. Institution highly recommends that prospective students visit the Boat School campus to meet directly with the Admissions Coordinator and to ensure that the school is a match for the students' personal and professional goals and aspirations.

2016-2017 Annual costs. Tuition/fees: $14,650. Per-credit charge: $225. Books/supplies: $1,500. **Additional information:** Tuition information is for 9-month diploma program. 12-month degree program: $19,400.

Financial aid. All financial aid based on need. Work-study available nights, weekends and for part-time students.

Application procedures. Admission: No deadline. $100 fee. Admission notification on a rolling basis. **Financial aid:** No deadline. FAFSA, institutional form required.

Academics. Traditional and contemporary wooden and composite boatbuilding, including woodworking, drafting, lofting, repair and restoration, and yacht interiors. Supplemental non-credit, non-clock hour workshops are available in sailmaking, rigging, boat design, carving, welding, and diesel systems. **Special study options:** Accelerated study. **Credit/placement by examination:** AP, CLEP, IB. The Student Services Coordinator can help students connect with academic advising resources.

Technology on campus. 2 workstations in library. Wireless network available.

Student life. Freshman orientation: Mandatory. Preregistration for classes offered.

Student services. Career counseling, student employment services, financial aid counseling, veterans' counselor. **Transfer:** Re-entry adviser, pre-admission transcript evaluation for new students.

Contact. E-mail: info@nwswb.edu
Phone: (360) 385-4948 Fax: (360) 385-5089
Betsy Davis, Executive Director, Northwest School of Wooden Boatbuilding, 42 North Water Street, Port Hadlock, WA 98339

Olympic College
Bremerton, Washington   CB member
www.olympic.edu   CB code: 4583

- Public 2-year community and liberal arts college
- Commuter campus in large town

General. Founded in 1946. Regionally accredited. College sites at Bremerton, Shelton and Poulsbo. Classes also offered off-campus at West Sound Technical Center. **Enrollment:** 7,881 undergraduates. **Degrees:** 29 bachelor's, 1,243 associate awarded. **Location:** 30 miles from Seattle by ferry, 35 miles from Tacoma by highway. **Calendar:** Quarter, extensive summer session. **Full-time faculty:** 129 total. **Part-time faculty:** 364 total. **Partnerships:** Formal partnerships with Puget Sound Naval Shipyard, WestSound Technical, US Navy, and the Navy College Program Distance Learning Partnership.

Student profile. 60% enrolled in a transfer program, 40% enrolled in a vocational program.

25 or older:	48%	**Live on campus:**	1%

Transfer out. Colleges most students transferred to 2015: University of Washington, Central Washington University, Washington State University, Western Washington University.

Basis for selection. Open admission, but selective for some programs. Admission to nursing, physical therapy assistant, medical office assistant and Bachelor's degree programs based on several requirements which may include: completion of prerequisite courses, course grade or cumulative academic GPA, test scores, special certifications. English and Math placement assessment administered to degree/certificate-seeking applicants or for those who wish to enroll in English or Math classes. Specific programs require students to attend a pre-application orientation, letter of recommendation, essay and/or resume. **Adult students:** SAT/ACT scores not required. All students, including international students, must complete an English and mathematics skills level test upon arrival for placement at the appropriate level. **Home schooled:** Transcript of courses and grades required. Applicants may submit a letter of recommendation instead of a high school transcript. **Learning Disabled:** Students with learning disabilities may self-identify and access services such as special testing, note-taking, counseling, course selection, sign language interpreters, materials in alternate format, specialized equipment and adaptive technology and other similar accommodations.

2015-2016 Annual costs. Tuition/fees: $4,521; $9,924 out-of-state. Per-credit charge: $85 in-state; $206 out-of-state. Room only: $4,500. Books/supplies: $1,026. Personal expenses: $1,752.

Financial aid. Need-based: Need-based aid available for part-time students. Work-study available nights, weekends and for part-time students. **Non-need-based:** Scholarships awarded for academics, state residency. **Additional information:** Waivers available for select groups including Fallen Veterans, Children of Deceased or Disabled Law Enforcement Officers, and others.

Application procedures. Admission: No deadline. No application fee. Admission notification on a rolling basis. **Financial aid:** Priority date 3/1; no closing date. FAFSA, institutional form required. Applicants notified on a rolling basis starting 6/1; must reply within 2 week(s) of notification.

Academics. Special study options: Cooperative education, cross-registration, distance learning, dual enrollment of high school students, ESL, external degree, independent study, internships, liberal arts/career combination, student-designed major. 2+2 program with Washington State University and Western Washington University to complete Bachelors' program on the Olympic College campus. Bachelor's degree programs available on campus. License preparation in nursing, physical therapy. **Credit/placement by examination:** AP, CLEP, IB, institutional tests. Credit awarded by exam, Co-op Education, or CLEP varies by degree program. **Support services:** GED preparation and test center, learning center, reduced course load, remedial instruction, study skills assistance, tutoring, writing center. Education planning, course selection, orientation, counseling and testing services.

Majors. Business: Accounting technology, administrative services, business admin, organizational leadership. **Communications technology:** Photo/film/video. **Computer sciences:** Networking. **Education:** Early childhood. **Health services:** Medical assistant, nursing (RN), physical therapy assistant, substance abuse counseling.

Technology on campus. 1,300 workstations in library, computer center, student center. Dormitories wired for high-speed internet access and linked to campus network. Commuter students can connect to campus network. Online course registration, online library, helpline, student web hosting, wireless network available.

Student life. Freshman orientation: Mandatory. Preregistration for classes offered. In-person or online. In-person orientation takes place before advising. **Policies:** Student code of conduct. **Housing:** Coed dorms available. Apartments available for out-of-region students. International students may choose Homestay. One dorm room meets ADA requirements. **Activities:** Bands, choral groups, drama, international student organizations, music ensembles, musical theater, opera, student government, student newspaper, symphony orchestra, American Sign Language Club, Photo, African-American Caribbean Heritage, Computer Programming 2.0, Engineering Club, International students club, Gay/Straight Alliance, gaming, outdoor/wildlife and Phi Theta Kappa, Clay club.

Athletics. Intercollegiate: Baseball M, basketball, cross-country, golf, softball W, track and field, volleyball W. **Intramural:** Basketball, table tennis. **Team name:** Rangers.

Student services. Adult student services, career counseling, services for economically disadvantaged, student employment services, financial aid counseling, minority student services, on-campus daycare, personal counseling, placement for graduates, veterans' counselor. **Physically disabled:** Services for visually, speech, hearing impaired. **Transfer:** Re-entry adviser, pre-admission transcript evaluation for new students. Transfer adviser, college fairs on campus for students transferring to 4-year colleges.

Contact. E-mail: prospect@olympic.edu
Phone: (360) 475-7479 Toll-free number: (800) 259-6718 ext. 7479
Fax: (360) 475-7202
Jennifer Glasier, Dean, Enrollment Services, Olympic College, 1600 Chester Avenue, Bremerton, WA 98337-1699

Peninsula College
Port Angeles, Washington
www.pencol.edu   **CB code: 4615**

◗ Public 2-year community college
◗ Commuter campus in large town

General. Founded in 1961. Regionally accredited. **Enrollment:** 1,386 degree-seeking undergraduates. **Degrees:** 22 bachelor's, 400 associate awarded. **Location:** 75 miles from Seattle. **Calendar:** Quarter, limited summer session. **Full-time faculty:** 50 total. **Part-time faculty:** 106 total. **Class size:** 82% < 20, 17% 20-39, less than 1% 40-49, less than 1% 50-99. **Special facilities:** Marine laboratory, dam removal project.

Student profile.

Out-of-state: 1%   **25 or older:**   41%

Basis for selection. Open admission, but selective for some programs. Special requirements for Nursing program and Medical Assistance program. COMPASS/ASSET required for full-time applicants for placement only. Bachelor of Applied Science program has special admission requirements including possession of an associate's degree. Admission to college does not guarantee admission to all courses or vocational education programs. Additional applications may be necessary. **Adult students:** SAT/ACT scores not required.

2015-2016 Annual costs. Tuition/fees: $4,344; $9,747 out-of-state. Per-credit charge: $85 in-state; $206 out-of-state. Books/supplies: $972. Personal expenses: $1,679.

Financial aid. Need-based: Need-based aid available for part-time students. Work-study available nights, weekends and for part-time students. **Non-need-based:** Scholarships awarded for academics, athletics, job skills.

Application procedures. Admission: No deadline. No application fee. Admission notification on a rolling basis. **Financial aid:** Closing date 4/1. FAFSA, institutional form required. Applicants notified on a rolling basis starting 6/1; must reply within 2 week(s) of notification.

Academics. Special study options: Distance learning, double major, dual enrollment of high school students, ESL, honors, internships, liberal arts/career combination, study abroad. Bachelor's degree programs available on campus. License preparation in nursing. **Credit/placement by examination:** AP, CLEP, institutional tests. 10 credit hours maximum toward associate degree. Must complete minimum 30 quarter hours of credit in residency with 2.75 GPA. **Support services:** GED preparation and test center, learning center, reduced course load, remedial instruction, study skills assistance, tutoring, writing center.

Honors college/program. Students accepted into the Honors program will possess two attributes necessary for success: excitement to be a part of the learning process and a desire to be actively involved in a unique honors experience, readiness or completion of college-level English and math.

Majors. Business: Accounting, accounting technology, administrative services, business admin, marketing, office management. **Communications:** Journalism. **Computer sciences:** General, applications programming, data processing, networking, vendor certification, web page design. **Conservation:** Fisheries. **Education:** Early childhood. **Health services:** Home attendant, medical assistant, medical secretary, nursing (RN), substance abuse counseling. **Liberal arts:** Arts/sciences. **Protective services:** Corrections, law enforcement admin. **Work/family studies:** Child care management, child care service.

Most popular majors. Health sciences 17%, liberal arts 64%, natural resources/environmental science 7%.

Technology on campus. 79 workstations in library, computer center, student center. Online course registration, online library, wireless network available.

Student life. Freshman orientation: Available. Preregistration for classes offered. **Activities:** Jazz band, choral groups, dance, drama, literary magazine, music ensembles, student government, student newspaper, Christian collegiate fellowship, communications careers club, Native American Nations, Phi Theta Kappa, Phi Beta Lambda, IT club, basketball club, German club.

Athletics. Intercollegiate: Basketball, soccer. **Intramural:** Basketball, soccer, tennis, volleyball. **Team name:** Pirates.

Student services. Adult student services, career counseling, services for economically disadvantaged, student employment services, financial aid counseling, on-campus daycare, personal counseling, placement for graduates, veterans' counselor. **Physically disabled:** Services for visually, hearing impaired. **Transfer:** Pre-admission transcript evaluation for new students.

Transfer adviser, college fairs on campus for students transferring to 4-year colleges.

Contact. E-mail: admissions@pencol.edu
Phone: (360) 452-9277 Toll-free number: (877) 452-9277
Fax: (360) 417-6581
Krista Francis, Enrollment Service Manager, Peninsula College, 1502 East Lauridsen Boulevard, Port Angeles, WA 98362

Pierce College
Lakewood, Washington
www.pierce.ctc.edu

CB code: 4103

◆ Public 2-year community college
◆ Commuter campus in small city

General. Founded in 1967. Regionally accredited. Colleges in Puyallup and Lakewood. Education centers at Jointbase Lewis McChord (JBLM), McNeil Island, Cedar Creek, Western State Hospital and Rainier School. **Enrollment:** 6,805 degree-seeking undergraduates. **Degrees:** 1,164 associate awarded. **ROTC:** Army. **Location:** 10 miles from downtown. **Calendar:** Quarter, limited summer session. **Full-time faculty:** 75 total. **Part-time faculty:** 38 total. **Special facilities:** Bird refuge, international house (video conferencing center for international/cross-cultural communications).

Transfer out. Colleges most students transferred to 2015: University of Washington, Evergreen State College, Central Washington University, St. Martin's University, Western Washington University.

Basis for selection. Open admission, but selective for some programs. Admissions to dental hygiene and veterinary technology programs based on college course work, high school GPA, and/or related work experience. Running Start students must test at college level in English prior to admission. Students required to take ASSET or COMPASS placement tests to register for math, English, or reading courses. **Adult students:** SAT/ACT scores not required. Placement testing required for English and Quantitative courses. **Learning Disabled:** Accommodations for placement testing.

High school preparation. Algebra, biology, and chemistry required of veterinary technology applicants. Dental hygiene applicants have special mathematics/science requirements.

2015-2016 Annual costs. Tuition/fees: $4,187; $9,590 out-of-state. Per-credit charge: $85 in-state; $206 out-of-state. Books/supplies: $1,000.

Financial aid. Need-based: Need-based aid available for part-time students. Work-study available nights, weekends and for part-time students. **Non-need-based:** Scholarships awarded for academics, athletics, music/drama.

Application procedures. Admission: No deadline. $25 fee. Admission notification on a rolling basis. March 1 closing date for veterinary technology applications, February 1 for dental hygiene. High school students admitted early through Running Start Program. Must test at college level prior to admission. **Financial aid:** Closing date 5/1. FAFSA, institutional form required. Applicants notified on a rolling basis starting 4/15.

Academics. Special study options: Cooperative education, cross-registration, distance learning, double major, dual enrollment of high school students, ESL, independent study, internships, student-designed major, study abroad, weekend college. License preparation in dental hygiene, nursing. **Credit/placement by examination:** AP, CLEP, institutional tests. 25 credit hours maximum toward associate degree. Credit by exam does not count toward degree residency requirement. **Support services:** GED preparation and test center, learning center, pre-admission summer program, reduced course load, remedial instruction, study skills assistance, tutoring, writing center.

Majors. Biology: General. **Business:** General, accounting technology, administrative services, business admin, office management, office/clerical. **Computer sciences:** Computer graphics, networking, support specialist. **Education:** Business, early childhood, elementary, teacher assistance. **Foreign languages:** Translation. **General:** Maintenance, site management. **Health services:** Dental hygiene, medical secretary, mental health services, nursing (RN), substance abuse counseling, veterinary technology/assistant. **Liberal arts:** Arts/sciences. **Parks/recreation:** Sports admin. **Physical sciences:** General. **Protective services:** Disaster management, fire services admin, law enforcement admin.

Technology on campus. Online course registration, online library, helpline, wireless network available.

Student life. Freshman orientation: Mandatory. Preregistration for classes offered. Orientation offered quarterly and throughout summer. **Activities:** Bands, choral groups, drama, literary magazine, music ensembles, musical theater, student government, student newspaper, ethnic and foreign student associations, religious organizations, special interest clubs, Phi Theta Kappa.

Athletics. Intercollegiate: Baseball M, basketball, soccer M, softball W, volleyball W. **Intramural:** Cheerleading. **Team name:** Raiders.

Student services. Adult student services, career counseling, services for economically disadvantaged, student employment services, financial aid counseling, minority student services, on-campus daycare, personal counseling, veterans' counselor, women's services. **Physically disabled:** Services for visually, speech, hearing impaired. **Transfer:** Transfer center, transfer adviser, college fairs on campus for students transferring to 4-year colleges.

Contact. E-mail: admiss1@pierce.ctc.edu
Phone: (253) 964-6501 Fax: (253) 964-6427
Maggie Segesser, Director of Admissions, Pierce College, 9401 Farwest Drive SW, Lakewood, WA 98498-1999

Renton Technical College
Renton, Washington
www.RTC.edu

CB code: 0790

◆ Public 2-year technical college
◆ Commuter campus in large town

General. Founded in 1942. Regionally accredited. **Enrollment:** 3,359 undergraduates. **Degrees:** 298 associate awarded. **Location:** 10 miles from Seattle. **Calendar:** Quarter, extensive summer session. **Full-time faculty:** 68 total. **Part-time faculty:** 190 total.

Basis for selection. Open admission, but selective for some programs. Lottery system is used for Nursing admissions. Selective admissions are used for BAS Application Development. **Adult students:** Must complete on-campus assessment.

2015-2016 Annual costs. Tuition/fees: $4,161; $9,564 out-of-state. Per-credit charge: $85 in-state; $206 out-of-state. Books/supplies: $1,030. Personal expenses: $1,640.

Financial aid. All financial aid based on need. Need-based aid available for part-time students. Work-study available nights, weekends and for part-time students.

Application procedures. Admission: No deadline. $30 fee. Application must be submitted on paper. Admission notification on a rolling basis. **Financial aid:** Priority date 5/1, closing date 7/1. FAFSA, institutional form required. Applicants notified on a rolling basis.

Academics. Many programs have co-op component. **Special study options:** Cooperative education, distance learning, dual enrollment of high school students, ESL, external degree, internships, liberal arts/career combination, student-designed major. Bachelor's degree programs available on campus. License preparation in nursing, real estate. **Credit/placement by examination:** AP, CLEP, institutional tests. Up to 75% of a program requirements may be fulfilled. **Support services:** GED preparation and test center, learning center, remedial instruction, study skills assistance, tutoring.

Majors. Business: Accounting technology, administrative services, office management, office technology. **Computer sciences:** Applications programming, computer science, networking, programming. **Education:** Business, early childhood, elementary, teacher assistance, voc/tech. **Engineering:** Electrical. **General:** Maintenance. **Health services:** Anesthesiologist assistant, dental assistant, health information management, insurance coding, licensed practical nurse, massage therapy, medical assistant, ophthalmic technology, pharmacy assistant, surgical technology. **Work/family studies:** Child care management.

Most popular majors. Business/marketing 16%, computer/information sciences 18%, education 9%, health sciences 32%, trade and industry 17%.

Technology on campus. 150 workstations in library, computer center, student center. Online library available.

Student life. Freshman orientation: Mandatory. Preregistration for classes offered. **Activities:** Student government.

Student services. Adult student services, career counseling, student employment services, financial aid counseling, minority student services, on-campus daycare, personal counseling, placement for graduates, veterans' counselor. **Physically disabled:** Services for visually, speech, hearing impaired. **Transfer:** Pre-admission transcript evaluation for new students. Transfer adviser for students transferring to 4-year colleges.

Contact. E-mail: pbrown@rtc.edu
Phone: (425) 235-5840 Fax: (425) 235-7832
Patrick Brown, Registrar, Renton Technical College, 3000 NE Fourth Street, Renton, WA 98056-4195

Seattle Central College
Seattle, Washington
www.seattlecentral.edu   CB code: 4033

- Public 2-year community and technical college
- Commuter campus in very large city

General. Founded in 1966. Regionally accredited. **Enrollment:** 8,154 undergraduates. **Degrees:** 25 bachelor's, 1,020 associate awarded. **Calendar:** Quarter, limited summer session. **Full-time faculty:** 169 total; 24% minority. **Part-time faculty:** 446 total; 30% minority.

Basis for selection. Open admission, but selective for some programs. Limited admission to health sciences and vocational programs. SAT and ACT may be assessed in lieu of placement exam. Portfolio required for Graphic Design, Commercial Photography. **Adult students:** SAT/ACT scores not required. **Home schooled:** Transcript of courses and grades required. **Learning Disabled:** Must check in with Disability Support Services to receive accommodations.

2015-2016 Annual costs. Tuition/fees: $3,712; $9,115 out-of-state. Per-credit charge: $78 in-state; $198 out-of-state. Books/supplies: $924. Personal expenses: $1,896.

Financial aid. All financial aid based on need. Need-based aid available for part-time students. Work-study available nights, weekends and for part-time students. **Additional information:** Currently enrolled international students can apply for institutional scholarship in second year of study.

Application procedures. Admission: No deadline. No application fee. Admission notification on a rolling basis. **Financial aid:** Closing date 7/27. FAFSA, institutional form required. Applicants notified on a rolling basis; must reply within 2 week(s) of notification.

Academics. Special study options: Cooperative education, distance learning, dual enrollment of high school students, ESL, exchange student, independent study, internships, study abroad. Bachelor's degree programs available on campus. **Credit/placement by examination:** AP, CLEP, IB, institutional tests. **Support services:** GED preparation and test center, learning center, remedial instruction, study skills assistance, tutoring, writing center.

Majors. Business: Business admin, fashion. **Communications:** Advertising, communications/speech/rhetoric. **Communications technology:** Graphic/printing, graphics, photo/film/video, printing management. **Computer sciences:** General, applications programming, information technology, programming. **Education:** General. **Foreign languages:** Sign language interpretation. **General:** Carpentry. **Health services:** Preop/surgical nursing, respiratory therapy technology. **Liberal arts:** Arts/sciences. **Visual/performing arts:** Commercial photography. **Work/family studies:** Textile manufacture.

Most popular majors. Health sciences 14%, liberal arts 63%, personal/culinary services 6%.

Technology on campus. 190 workstations in library, computer center, student center. Online library, wireless network available.

Student life. Freshman orientation: Mandatory. Preregistration for classes offered. **Activities:** Jazz band, choral groups, dance, drama, international student organizations, student government, student newspaper, numerous ethnic/minority, socio-political, cultural clubs available.

Student services. Career counseling, services for economically disadvantaged, student employment services, financial aid counseling, minority student services, personal counseling, veterans' counselor, women's services. **Physically disabled:** Services for visually, speech, hearing impaired. **Transfer:** Transfer adviser, college fairs on campus for students transferring to 4-year colleges.

Contact. E-mail: admissionis.central@seattlecolleges.edu
Phone: (206) 934-5450 Fax: (206) 934-6321
Diane Coleman, Dean of Enrollment Services/Registrar, Seattle Central College, 1701 Broadway, Seattle, WA 98122

Shoreline Community College
Shoreline, Washington
www.shoreline.edu   CB code: 4738

- Public 2-year community college
- Commuter campus in small city

General. Founded in 1964. Regionally accredited. **Enrollment:** 2,990 degree-seeking undergraduates. **Degrees:** 920 associate awarded. **Location:** 10 miles from Seattle. **Calendar:** Quarter, limited summer session. **Full-time faculty:** 114 total. **Part-time faculty:** 262 total.

Student profile.

Out-of-state: 1%   25 or older: 47%

Transfer out. Colleges most students transferred to 2015: University of Washington, Western Washington University.

Basis for selection. Open admission, but selective for some programs. SAT, ACT, or ASSET required for English and math placement unless student has taken college-level English or math with grades of C or better. Nursing and dental hygiene programs use competitive admissions process. Out-of-state students only from certain states are admitted to Shoreline's Virtual College for online instruction. Please contact admissions office for details.

2015-2016 Annual costs. Tuition/fees: $4,208; $9,611 out-of-state. Per-credit charge: $84 in-state; $205 out-of-state. Books/supplies: $924. Personal expenses: $3,516.

Financial aid. Need-based: Work-study available nights, weekends and for part-time students. **Additional information:** Tuition and/or fee waiver for students with need on space-available basis.

Application procedures. Admission: No deadline. No application fee. Admission notification on a rolling basis. **Financial aid:** Closing date 3/31. FAFSA, institutional form required. Applicants notified on a rolling basis starting 8/1; must reply within 3 week(s) of notification.

Academics. Special study options: Cooperative education, cross-registration, distance learning, dual enrollment of high school students, ESL, independent study, internships, study abroad. Senior College for senior citizens. **Credit/placement by examination:** AP, CLEP, IB. **Support services:** GED preparation and test center, learning center, remedial instruction, tutoring.

Majors. Biology: Biotechnology. **Business:** Accounting technology, business admin, fashion, international, logistics, marketing, sales/distribution, small business admin. **Communications:** Broadcast journalism. **Communications technology:** Graphic/printing. **Computer sciences:** General, data processing, database management, networking, web page design. **Education:** Early childhood, special ed, teacher assistance. **Engineering:** General, civil, mechanical. **Health services:** Clinical lab assistant, dental hygiene, dietetics, health information technology, nursing (RN). **Liberal arts:** Arts/sciences. **Physical sciences:** General, oceanography. **Protective services:** Law enforcement admin. **Visual/performing arts:** Cinematography, commercial/advertising art, design, music management, music performance, photography, theater design. **Work/family studies:** Food/nutrition.

Technology on campus. 450 workstations in library, computer center. Commuter students can connect to campus network. Online library, helpline, wireless network available.

Student life. Freshman orientation: Mandatory. Preregistration for classes offered. Two to three hours, prior to each quarter. **Activities:** Bands, choral groups, drama, international student organizations, literary magazine, music ensembles, musical theater, opera, student government, student newspaper, black student union, arts and entertainment board, women's club, Cambodian club, Vietnamese club, DEC, Phi Theta Kappa.

Athletics. NJCAA. **Intercollegiate:** Baseball M, basketball, soccer, softball W, tennis, volleyball W. **Intramural:** Archery, basketball, bowling, diving, fencing, golf, racquetball, skiing, soccer, softball W, swimming, tennis, volleyball. **Team name:** Dolphins.

Student services. Adult student services, career counseling, student employment services, financial aid counseling, health services, minority student services, on-campus daycare, personal counseling, placement for graduates, veterans' counselor, women's services. **Physically disabled:** Services for visually, hearing impaired. **Transfer:** Transfer adviser, college fairs on campus for students transferring to 4-year colleges.

Contact. E-mail: sccadmis@ctc.edu
Phone: (206) 546-4621 Fax: (206) 546-5835
Chris Melton, Registrar, Shoreline Community College, 16101 Greenwood Avenue North, Seattle, WA 98133

Skagit Valley College
Mount Vernon, Washington
www.skagit.edu
CB code: 4699

◆ Public 2-year community college
◆ Commuter campus in large town

General. Founded in 1926. Regionally accredited. 2 campuses, 2 centers: Mount Vernon (main campus) and Oak Harbor on Whidbey Island. Two centers located at South Whidbey and San Juan Island. **Enrollment:** 5,977 undergraduates. **Degrees:** 632 associate awarded. **Location:** 60 miles from Seattle, 90 miles from Vancouver, British Columbia. **Calendar:** Quarter, extensive summer session. **Full-time faculty:** 103 total. **Part-time faculty:** 157 total. **Partnerships:** Contract programs with Washington businesses, Tech Prep, College in the High School.

Transfer out. Colleges most students transferred to 2015: Everett Community College, Whatcom Community College, Western Washington University, Edmonds Community College, University of Washington.

Basis for selection. Open admission, but selective for some programs. Open Admissions except Nursing. High school diploma required for some programs.

2015-2016 Annual costs. Tuition/fees: $4,448; $9,851 out-of-state. Per-credit charge: $85 in-state; $205 out-of-state. Books/supplies: $900. Personal expenses: $1,650.

Financial aid. All financial aid based on need. Need-based aid available for part-time students. Work-study available nights, weekends and for part-time students.

Application procedures. Admission: No deadline. No application fee. Admission notification on a rolling basis. **Financial aid:** Priority date 5/1; no closing date. FAFSA, institutional form required. Applicants notified on a rolling basis starting 7/1; must reply within 2 week(s) of notification.

Academics. Special study options: Cooperative education, cross-registration, distance learning, dual enrollment of high school students, ESL, external degree, honors, independent study, internships. License preparation in nursing. **Credit/placement by examination:** AP, CLEP, IB, institutional tests. 15 credit hours maximum toward associate degree. **Support services:** GED preparation and test center, learning center, pre-admission summer program, reduced course load, remedial instruction, study skills assistance, tutoring, writing center.

Majors. Business: Accounting, administrative services, business admin, hospitality/recreation. **Communications:** Communications/speech/rhetoric. **Computer sciences:** General, applications programming, information systems, programming. **Conservation:** Environmental science. **Education:** Early childhood. **Health services:** Licensed practical nurse, nursing (RN), prenursing. **Liberal arts:** Arts/sciences. **Protective services:** Firefighting, law enforcement admin. **Visual/performing arts:** Commercial/advertising art.

Technology on campus. 250 workstations in library, computer center. Commuter students can connect to campus network. Online course registration, helpline, repair service, student web hosting available.

Student life. Freshman orientation: Available. Preregistration for classes offered. Orientation/registration/testing before start of each quarter. Evening and day orientation at beginning of each quarter. **Housing:** Apartments available. $180 deposit. **Activities:** Bands, choral groups, dance, drama, literary magazine, music ensembles, musical theater, radio station, student government, student newspaper, symphony orchestra, Calling All Color, nurses club, firefighters club, Campus Christian Fellowship, sailing club, Delta Epsilon Chi, ski club, horticultural club, Phi Theta Kappa, international club.

Athletics. Intercollegiate: Baseball M, basketball, golf, soccer, softball W, tennis, volleyball W. **Intramural:** Badminton, baseball M, basketball, bowling, golf, sailing, soccer, softball, tennis, volleyball. **Team name:** Cardinals.

Student services. Adult student services, career counseling, services for economically disadvantaged, student employment services, financial aid counseling, health services, minority student services, on-campus daycare, personal counseling, placement for graduates, veterans' counselor, women's services. **Physically disabled:** Services for visually, speech, hearing impaired. **Transfer:** Re-entry adviser, pre-admission transcript evaluation for new students. Transfer center, transfer adviser, college fairs on campus for students transferring to 4-year colleges.

Contact. E-mail: admissions@skagit.edu
Phone: (360) 416-7697 Toll-free number: (877) 385-5360
Fax: (360) 416-7890
Skagit Valley College, 2405 East College Way, Mount Vernon, WA 98273

South Puget Sound Community College
Olympia, Washington
CB member
www.spscc.ctc.edu
CB code: 4578

◆ Public 2-year community and junior college
◆ Commuter campus in small city

General. Founded in 1962. Regionally accredited. **Enrollment:** 3,585 degree-seeking undergraduates. **Degrees:** 1,035 associate awarded. **ROTC:** Air Force. **Location:** 60 miles from Seattle. **Calendar:** Quarter, limited summer session. **Full-time faculty:** 93 total; 10% minority, 53% women. **Part-time faculty:** 220 total; 6% minority, 58% women. **Class size:** 65% < 20, 35% 20-39, less than 1% 40-49.

Transfer out. Colleges most students transferred to 2015: Evergreen State College, St. Martin University, University of Washington, Washington State University, Western Washington State University.

Basis for selection. Open admission, but selective for some programs. Special requirements for nursing, dental assisting, fire protection. **Adult students:** CASAS required for Adult Basic Education.

High school preparation. College-preparatory program recommended.

2015-2016 Annual costs. Tuition/fees: $4,068; $9,471 out-of-state. Per-credit charge: $85 in-state; $206 out-of-state. Books/supplies: $1,030. Personal expenses: $1,640.

Financial aid. Need-based: Need-based aid available for part-time students. Work-study available nights, weekends and for part-time students. **Non-need-based:** Scholarships awarded for academics, athletics.

Application procedures. Admission: Closing date 9/5. No application fee. Admission notification on a rolling basis beginning on or about 12/1. Early applicants register in mid-July for fall quarter. **Financial aid:** Priority date 5/1, closing date 6/27. FAFSA, institutional form required. Applicants notified on a rolling basis starting 7/10; must reply within 2 week(s) of notification.

Academics. Special study options: Cooperative education, cross-registration, distance learning, dual enrollment of high school students, ESL, honors, independent study, internships, study abroad, weekend college. License preparation in dental hygiene, nursing. **Credit/placement by examination:** AP, CLEP, IB, institutional tests. 45 credit hours maximum toward associate degree. **Support services:** GED preparation and test center, learning center, remedial instruction, study skills assistance, tutoring, writing center.

Majors. Business: General, accounting, administrative services, hospitality admin, office/clerical. **Computer sciences:** Applications programming, data processing, information systems. **Education:** Early childhood. **Health services:** Dental assistant, licensed practical nurse, medical assistant, medical secretary, nursing assistant. **Liberal arts:** Arts/sciences. **Protective services:** Firefighting.

Most popular majors. Business/marketing 8%, health sciences 12%, liberal arts 54%, science technologies 6%.

Technology on campus. 117 workstations in library, computer center, student center. Commuter students can connect to campus network. Online course registration, online library, wireless network available.

Student life. Freshman orientation: Available. Preregistration for classes offered. **Activities:** Jazz band, choral groups, drama, international student organizations, literary magazine, music ensembles, musical theater, student government, student newspaper.

Athletics. Intercollegiate: Baseball W, basketball, soccer M, softball W. **Team name:** Clippers.

Student services. Adult student services, career counseling, services for economically disadvantaged, student employment services, financial aid counseling, minority student services, on-campus daycare, personal counseling, placement for graduates, veterans' counselor. **Physically disabled:** Services for visually, speech, hearing impaired. **Transfer:** Transfer adviser, college fairs on campus for students transferring to 4-year colleges.

Contact. E-mail: enrollmentservices@spscc.ctc.edu
Phone: (360) 754-7711 ext. 5241 Fax: (360) 596-5907
Heidi Dearborn, Director of Admissions and Registration, South Puget Sound Community College, 2011 Mottman Road, SW, Olympia, WA 98512-6218

South Seattle College
Seattle, Washington
www.southseattle.edu   CB code: 4759

▶ Public 2-year community college
▶ Commuter campus in very large city

General. Founded in 1969. Regionally accredited. **Enrollment:** 3,592 degree-seeking undergraduates. **Degrees:** 41 bachelor's, 476 associate awarded. **Location:** 5 miles from downtown Seattle. **Calendar:** Quarter, limited summer session. **Full-time faculty:** 108 total; 33% minority, 44% women. **Part-time faculty:** 304 total; 17% minority, 55% women. **Special facilities:** College operated bakery and restaurants, arboretum, Seattle Chinese garden.

Transfer out. Colleges most students transferred to 2015: University of Washington.

Basis for selection. Open admission, but selective for some programs. COMPASS, ESL COMPASS tests used for placement and counseling. **Learning Disabled:** Referred to Educational Support Services Office.

High school preparation. College-preparatory program required.

2015-2016 Annual costs. Tuition/fees: $3,901; $9,304 out-of-state. Per-credit charge: $87 in-state; $207 out-of-state. Books/supplies: $1,050. Personal expenses: $1,980.

2014-2015 Financial aid. Need-based: 92% of total undergraduate aid awarded as scholarships/grants, 8% as loans/jobs. Need-based aid available for part-time students. Work-study available nights, weekends and for part-time students. **Non-need-based:** Scholarships awarded for academics, state residency.

Application procedures. Admission: No deadline. No application fee. Admission notification on a rolling basis. **Financial aid:** Priority date 3/15, closing date 5/9. FAFSA, institutional form required. Applicants notified on a rolling basis starting 7/1.

Academics. Special study options: Cross-registration, distance learning, dual enrollment of high school students, ESL, independent study, internships, study abroad. Concurrent enrollment agreements with other colleges. Bachelor's degree programs available on campus. License preparation in aviation, nursing. **Credit/placement by examination:** AP, CLEP, IB, institutional tests. South will allow CLEP to count in certain areas of distribution. **Support services:** GED preparation and test center, learning center, reduced course load, remedial instruction, study skills assistance, tutoring, writing center.

Majors. Biology: General. **Business:** General, accounting, hospitality admin, office management, office technology, restaurant/food services. **Computer sciences:** LAN/WAN management, system admin. **Engineering:** General, software. **General:** Electrician. **Health services:** Licensed practical nurse, premedicine, prenursing, prepharmacy. **Liberal arts:** Arts/sciences. **Physical sciences:** Chemistry.

Technology on campus. 855 workstations in library, computer center, student center. Commuter students can connect to campus network. Online course registration, online library, wireless network available.

Student life. Freshman orientation: Mandatory. Preregistration for classes offered. **Policies:** Enrollment in 5 or more credits and 2.5 cumulative GPA required to serve as student government representative. **Activities:** Choral groups, international student organizations, literary magazine, student government, Vietnamese Student Association, Black Student Union, Phi Theta Kappa, Students for Sustainability, engineering club, international student club, Muslim Student Association, business club, Christian club, MECHA, Multiculture Alliance, veterans club.

Athletics. Intramural: Football (non-tackle), soccer, table tennis, ultimate frisbee, volleyball.

Student services. Adult student services, alcohol/substance abuse counseling, career counseling, services for economically disadvantaged, student employment services, financial aid counseling, minority student services, on-campus daycare, personal counseling, placement for graduates, veterans' counselor, women's services. **Physically disabled:** Services for visually, speech, hearing impaired. **Transfer:** Re-entry adviser, pre-admission transcript evaluation for new students. Transfer center, transfer adviser, college fairs on campus for students transferring to 4-year colleges.

Contact. E-mail: SOAR@seattlecolleges.edu
Phone: (206) 934-7943
Vanessa Calonzo, Director of Student Outreach, Admissions and Recruitment, South Seattle College, 6000 16th Avenue, SW, Seattle, WA 98106-1499

Spokane Community College
Spokane, Washington
www.scc.spokane.edu   CB code: 4739

▶ Public 2-year community college
▶ Commuter campus in small city

General. Founded in 1963. Regionally accredited. **Enrollment:** 6,960 undergraduates. **Degrees:** 1,156 associate awarded. **ROTC:** Army, Naval, Air Force. **Location:** 2 miles from downtown. **Calendar:** Quarter, limited summer session. **Full-time faculty:** 181 total. **Part-time faculty:** 102 total. **Special facilities:** Nursery, floral shop, automotive repair service center, cosmetology center.

Student profile.

Out-of-state:	4%	25 or older:	54%

Transfer out. Colleges most students transferred to 2015: Eastern Washington University, Washington State University.

Basis for selection. Open admission, but selective for some programs. Admission to college does not guarantee acceptance into every program. ASSET used for placement. Admissions deadline is three weeks prior to the start of a quarter. **Home schooled:** If under 18, must be deemed able to benefit from curricular offerings of college. Required to take ASSET or COMPASS tests and must place at college level.

2015-2016 Annual costs. Tuition/fees: $4,146; $9,549 out-of-state. Per-credit charge: $85 in-state; $206 out-of-state. Books/supplies: $1,002. Personal expenses: $2,352.

Financial aid. Need-based: Work-study available nights, weekends and for part-time students. **Non-need-based:** Scholarships awarded for athletics.

Application procedures. Admission: Closing date 8/31. $25 fee, may be waived for applicants with need. Admission notification on a rolling basis beginning on or about 1/1. **Financial aid:** Priority date 5/13; no closing date. FAFSA, institutional form required. Applicants notified on a rolling basis; must reply within 2 week(s) of notification.

Academics. Special study options: Cooperative education, cross-registration, distance learning, dual enrollment of high school students, ESL, independent study, internships, student-designed major, study abroad. License preparation in nursing, paramedic. **Credit/placement by examination:** AP, CLEP, institutional tests. 60 credit hours maximum toward associate degree. **Support services:** Learning center, reduced course load, remedial instruction, study skills assistance, tutoring, writing center.

Majors. Business: General, accounting, administrative services, banking/financial services, business admin, management information systems, marketing, office management, office technology, office/clerical, selling, vehicle parts marketing. **Computer sciences:** Applications programming, data processing, information systems. **Conservation:** Forest resources, forestry, water/wetlands/marine, wildlife/wilderness. **General:** Carpentry, power transmission. **Health services:** Cardiovascular technology, clinical lab technology, dental assistant, EMT paramedic, medical secretary, optician, pharmacy assistant, recreational therapy, respiratory therapy technology, surgical technology, ward clerk. **Liberal arts:** Arts/sciences. **Parks/recreation:** Facilities management. **Protective services:** Corrections, fire services admin, law enforcement admin, police science, security services.

Technology on campus. 913 workstations in library, computer center, student center. Online course registration available.

Student life. Freshman orientation: Available. Preregistration for classes offered. **Activities:** Drama, literary magazine, student government, student newspaper.

Athletics. Intercollegiate: Baseball M, basketball, cross-country, golf, soccer, softball W, tennis, track and field, volleyball W. **Team name:** Big Foot.

Student services. Adult student services, career counseling, services for economically disadvantaged, student employment services, financial aid counseling, minority student services, on-campus daycare, personal counseling, placement for graduates, veterans' counselor. **Physically disabled:** Services for visually, speech, hearing impaired. **Transfer:** College fairs on campus for students transferring to 4-year colleges.

Contact. E-mail: SCCInfo@scc.spokane.edu
Phone: (509) 533-8860 Toll-free number: (800) 248-5644 ext. 8006
Fax: (509) 533-8181
Sherry Carroll, Manager, Admissions/Student Entry & Success, Spokane Community College, 1810 North Greene Street, Spokane, WA 99217-5399

Spokane Falls Community College
Spokane, Washington
www.spokanefalls.edu   CB code: 4752

- Public 2-year community college
- Commuter campus in small city
- Interview required

General. Founded in 1967. Regionally accredited. **Enrollment:** 8,530 undergraduates. **Degrees:** 1,120 associate awarded. **ROTC:** Army. **Location:** 4 miles from downtown. **Calendar:** Quarter, limited summer session. **Full-time faculty:** 173 total. **Part-time faculty:** 151 total. **Special facilities:** Theater, performing arts center, 60-foot Foucault pendulum.

Transfer out. **Colleges most students transferred to 2015:** Spokane Community Colleges, Big Bend Community College.

Basis for selection. Open admission, but selective for some programs. Admission to college does not guarantee acceptance to every program. ASSET test required for placement. Our admissions deadline is now three weeks prior to the start of a quarter.

2015-2016 Annual costs. Tuition/fees: $4,535; $9,938 out-of-state. Per-credit charge: $85 in-state; $206 out-of-state. Books/supplies: $1,134. Personal expenses: $3,110.

Financial aid. All financial aid based on need. Need-based aid available for part-time students. Work-study available nights, weekends and for part-time students.

Application procedures. Admission: Closing date 8/31. $25 fee. Admission notification on a rolling basis. **Financial aid:** Priority date 5/13; no closing date. FAFSA, institutional form required. Applicants notified on a rolling basis starting 5/15; must reply within 2 week(s) of notification.

Academics. Special study options: Cooperative education, cross-registration, distance learning, dual enrollment of high school students, ESL, honors, independent study, internships, study abroad, weekend college. License preparation in physical therapy, real estate. **Credit/placement by examination:** AP, CLEP, institutional tests. 60 credit hours maximum toward associate degree. **Support services:** GED preparation and test center, learning center, remedial instruction, study skills assistance, tutoring, writing center.

Majors. Business: General, business admin, fashion, management information systems, marketing, office management, office/clerical. **Communications technology:** Recording arts. **Computer sciences:** General, support specialist, web page design, word processing. **Education:** Early childhood, elementary, mathematics, physics, teacher assistance. **Engineering:** Chemical, electrical, mechanical. **Foreign languages:** Sign language interpretation. **Health services:** Athletic training, clinical lab technology, health information technology, medical assistant, nursing (RN), occupational therapy assistant, orthotics/prosthetics, physical therapy assistant, prenursing, substance abuse counseling, vocational rehab counseling. **Liberal arts:** Arts/sciences, library assistant. **Parks/recreation:** Sports admin. **Physical sciences:** General. **Visual/performing arts:** Commercial photography, commercial/advertising art, interior design.

Technology on campus. 400 workstations in library, computer center.

Student life. Freshman orientation: Mandatory. Preregistration for classes offered. **Policies:** Student conduct code. **Activities:** Bands, choral groups, drama, literary magazine, music ensembles, opera, student government, student newspaper, symphony orchestra.

Athletics. Intercollegiate: Baseball M, basketball, cross-country, golf, soccer, softball W, tennis, track and field. **Intramural:** Basketball, soccer, table tennis, tennis, volleyball.

Student services. Adult student services, career counseling, services for economically disadvantaged, student employment services, financial aid counseling, health services, minority student services, on-campus daycare, personal counseling, placement for graduates, veterans' counselor, women's services. **Physically disabled:** Services for visually, hearing impaired. **Transfer:** Transfer adviser, college fairs on campus for students transferring to 4-year colleges.

Contact. E-mail: sfccinfo@spokanefalls.edu
Phone: (509) 533-3305 Toll-free number: (888) 509-7944
Fax: (509) 533-3237
Steve Bays, Dean of Enrollment Services and Student Development, Spokane Falls Community College, 3410 West Fort George Wright Drive, Spokane, WA 99224

Tacoma Community College
Tacoma, Washington   CB member
www.tacomacc.edu   CB code: 4826

- Public 2-year community college
- Commuter campus in small city

General. Founded in 1965. Regionally accredited. Programs offered at Tacoma Campus and Gig Harbor Center. **Enrollment:** 7,384 undergraduates. **Degrees:** 1,217 associate awarded. **Location:** 30 miles from Seattle, 30 miles from Olympia. **Calendar:** Quarter, limited summer session. **Full-time faculty:** 123 total. **Part-time faculty:** 331 total.

Student profile.

Out-of-state: 1% **25 or older:**   50%

Transfer out. Colleges most students transferred to 2015: University of Washington.

Basis for selection. Open admission, but selective for some programs. **Adult students:** Accuplacer assessment required for students intending to enroll in 6 or more credits; students taking math or English; students enrolling in a degree or certificate program. **Learning Disabled:** Students who wish to receive accommodations need to present documentation to the college.

High school preparation. College-preparatory program recommended. 23 units recommended. Recommended units include English 4, mathematics 3, social studies 4, history 3, science 3 (laboratory 1), foreign language 2, computer science 1, visual/performing arts 1 and academic electives 1.

2015-2016 Annual costs. Tuition/fees: $4,251; $9,654 out-of-state. Per-credit charge: $85 in-state; $206 out-of-state. Books/supplies: $1,026.

Financial aid. All financial aid based on need. Need-based aid available for part-time students. Work-study available nights, weekends and for part-time students.

Application procedures. Admission: No deadline. No application fee. Admission notification on a rolling basis. **Financial aid:** Priority date 3/26; no closing date. FAFSA, institutional form required. Applicants notified on a rolling basis starting 7/20; must reply within 4 week(s) of notification.

Academics. Special study options: Distance learning, dual enrollment of high school students, ESL, internships, study abroad. Concurrent enrollment with nearby community colleges. Bachelor's degree programs available on campus. License preparation in nursing, paramedic, radiology. **Credit/placement by examination:** AP, CLEP, IB, institutional tests. 45 credit hours maximum toward associate degree. **Support services:** GED preparation and test center, learning center, reduced course load, remedial instruction, study skills assistance, tutoring, writing center.

Majors. Biology: General. **Business:** General, accounting technology, business admin. **Computer sciences:** Networking. **Education:** Elementary, teacher assistance. **Engineering:** Electrical, mechanical. **Health services:** EMT paramedic, health information technology, medical radiologic technology/radiation therapy, medical secretary, nursing (RN), respiratory therapy assistant, sonography. **Liberal arts:** Arts/sciences. **Physical sciences:** General. **Protective services:** Law enforcement admin.

Most popular majors. Business/marketing 14%, health sciences 26%, liberal arts 49%.

Technology on campus. 185 workstations in library, computer center, student center. Commuter students can connect to campus network. Online course registration, online library, helpline, wireless network available.

Student life. Freshman orientation: Mandatory. Preregistration for classes offered. **Housing:** Homestay Program available for international students. **Activities:** Jazz band, choral groups, international student organizations, literary magazine, music ensembles, student government, student newspaper.

Athletics. Intercollegiate: Baseball M, basketball, soccer, volleyball W. **Team name:** Titans.

Student services. Adult student services, career counseling, services for economically disadvantaged, student employment services, financial aid counseling, minority student services, on-campus daycare, personal counseling, veterans' counselor. **Physically disabled:** Services for visually, speech, hearing impaired. **Transfer:** Pre-admission transcript evaluation for new students. Transfer adviser, college fairs on campus for students transferring to 4-year colleges.

Contact. E-mail: admit@tacomacc.edu
Phone: (253) 566-5001 Fax: (253) 566-6011
Steve Ashpole, Director of Enrollment Services/Registrar, Tacoma Community College, 6501 South 19th Street, Tacoma, WA 98466-9971

Walla Walla Community College
Walla Walla, Washington
www.wwcc.edu   **CB code: 4963**

- Public 2-year community and technical college
- Commuter campus in large town

General. Founded in 1967. Regionally accredited. Academic and vocational courses offered at educational center at Clarkston, WA, and Department of Corrections at the Washington State Penitentiary and Coyote Ridge Corrections Center. **Enrollment:** 6,572 undergraduates. **Degrees:** 721 associate awarded. **Location:** 158 miles from Spokane, 262 miles from Seattle. **Calendar:** Quarter, limited summer session. **Full-time faculty:** 124 total. **Part-time faculty:** 214 total. **Class size:** 78% < 20, 19% 20-39, less than 1% 40-49, 2% 50-99. **Special facilities:** Enology (winemaking), viticulture, culinary, Water Environmental Center and John Deere facilities. **Partnerships:** Formal partnerships with John Deere & Company training center, Cisco Corporation.

Student profile. 45% enrolled in a transfer program, 65% enrolled in a vocational program.

Out-of-state:	20%	25 or older:	45%

Transfer out. Colleges most students transferred to 2015: Washington State University, Lewis & Clark College, Walla Walla University, Eastern Washington University, University of Idaho.

Basis for selection. Open admission, but selective for some programs. Special requirements for health science and vocational programs. COMPASS or ASSET placement tests used for English, reading, math. **Learning Disabled:** Flexible procedures; early registration.

High school preparation. Recommended units include English 4, mathematics 4 and science 3.

2015-2016 Annual costs. Tuition/fees: $4,203; $9,606 out-of-state. Per-credit charge: $85 in-state; $206 out-of-state. Books/supplies: $1,000. Personal expenses: $1,800.

Financial aid. Need-based: Need-based aid available for part-time students. Work-study available nights, weekends and for part-time students. **Non-need-based:** Scholarships awarded for academics, athletics, leadership, music/drama.

Application procedures. Admission: No deadline. No application fee. Admission notification on a rolling basis. **Financial aid:** Priority date 3/1; no closing date. FAFSA, institutional form required. Applicants notified on a rolling basis starting 6/1; must reply within 2 week(s) of notification.

Academics. Special study options: Cooperative education, distance learning, dual enrollment of high school students, ESL, external degree, honors, independent study, internships, liberal arts/career combination. License preparation in nursing, paramedic. **Credit/placement by examination:** AP, CLEP, IB, institutional tests. 23 credit hours maximum toward associate degree. **Support services:** GED preparation and test center, learning center, pre-admission summer program, reduced course load, remedial instruction, study skills assistance, tutoring, writing center.

Majors. Business: Accounting technology, banking/financial services, business admin, executive assistant, office management, retailing. **Communications technology:** Desktop publishing. **Computer sciences:** Data entry, data processing, information systems, networking, web page design, webmaster. **Education:** Early childhood, teacher assistance. **General:** Carpentry. **Health services:** Medical secretary, nursing (RN). **Liberal arts:** Arts/sciences. **Parks/recreation:** Facilities management. **Protective services:** Corrections, criminal justice, firefighting.

Most popular majors. Agriculture 10%, business/marketing 6%, health sciences 22%, liberal arts 39%, trade and industry 10%.

Technology on campus. 716 workstations in library, computer center, student center. Commuter students can connect to campus network. Online course registration, online library, helpline, repair service, student web hosting, wireless network available.

Student life. Freshman orientation: Mandatory. Preregistration for classes offered. **Activities:** Jazz band, choral groups, dance, drama, music ensembles, musical theater, student government, student newspaper.

Athletics. NAIA. **Intercollegiate:** Baseball M, basketball, golf, rodeo, soccer, softball W, volleyball W. **Intramural:** Basketball, softball, volleyball. **Team name:** Warriors.

Student services. Adult student services, career counseling, services for economically disadvantaged, student employment services, financial aid counseling, on-campus daycare, personal counseling, placement for graduates, veterans' counselor, women's services. **Physically disabled:** Services for visually, speech, hearing impaired. **Transfer:** Re-entry adviser, pre-admission transcript evaluation for new students. Transfer center, transfer adviser, college fairs on campus for students transferring to 4-year colleges.

Contact. E-mail: admissions@wwcc.edu
Phone: (509) 527-4283 Toll-free number: (877) 992-9922
Fax: (509) 527-3661
Carlos Delgadillo, Director of Admissions/Registrar, Walla Walla Community College, 500 Tausick Way, Walla Walla, WA 99362-9972

Wenatchee Valley College
Wenatchee, Washington
www.wvc.edu   **CB code: 4942**

- Public 2-year community college
- Commuter campus in large town

General. Founded in 1939. Regionally accredited. Central Washington University has branch facilities on campus. **Enrollment:** 2,465 degree-seeking undergraduates. **Degrees:** 1,739 associate awarded. **Location:** 145 miles from Seattle, 170 miles from Spokane. **Calendar:** Quarter, limited summer session. **Full-time faculty:** 73 total. **Part-time faculty:** 183 total. **Class size:** 55% < 20, 43% 20-39, 1% 40-49, less than 1% 50-99, less than 1% >100.

Student profile.

Out-of-state:	3%	Live on campus:	2%
25 or older:	51%		

Transfer out. Colleges most students transferred to 2015: Central Washington University, Washington State University, Eastern Washington University, University of Washington, Western Washington University.

Basis for selection. Open admission, but selective for some programs. Allied health applicants must submit supplemental application form that details work completed in specific program prerequisites. **Home schooled:** Applicants must be affiliated with their local school district. **Learning Disabled:** Students are encouraged to meet with Special Populations Coordinator.

2015-2016 Annual costs. Tuition/fees: $3,951; $9,354 out-of-state. Per-credit charge: $85 in-state; $206 out-of-state. Room only: $3,975. Books/supplies: $972.

Financial aid. Need-based: Need-based aid available for part-time students. Work-study available nights, weekends and for part-time students. **Non-need-based:** Scholarships awarded for academics, athletics.

Application procedures. Admission: No deadline. No application fee. Admission notification on a rolling basis. **Financial aid:** Closing date 3/1. FAFSA required. Applicants notified by 7/2; must reply within 3 week(s) of notification.

Academics. Special study options: Accelerated study, cooperative education, cross-registration, distance learning, double major, dual enrollment of high school students, ESL, independent study, internships, liberal arts/career combination, student-designed major. Bachelor's degree programs available on campus. License preparation in nursing, paramedic, radiology. **Credit/placement by examination:** AP, CLEP, institutional tests. 15 credit hours maximum toward associate degree. At least 15 credits must be completed in residence before credits earned by examination will be applied. **Support services:** GED preparation and test center, remedial instruction, study skills assistance, tutoring, writing center.

Majors. Business: Accounting technology, business admin, office management. **Computer sciences:** Networking. **Conservation:** General. **Education:** Early childhood. **Health services:** Clinical lab assistant, nursing (RN), radiologic technology/medical imaging, sonography, substance abuse counseling. **Liberal arts:** Arts/sciences. **Protective services:** Police science.

Most popular majors. Health sciences 20%, liberal arts 70%.

Technology on campus. 75 workstations in library, computer center, student center. Dormitories wired for high-speed internet access. Online course registration, online library, helpline, student web hosting, wireless network available.

Student life. Freshman orientation: Available. Preregistration for classes offered. **Housing:** Coed dorms available. Housing available nearby. **Activities:** Jazz band, choral groups, dance, drama, music ensembles, student government, professional associations, Inter-Varsity Fellowship.

Athletics. NJCAA. **Intercollegiate:** Baseball M, basketball, soccer, softball W, volleyball W. **Intramural:** Basketball. **Team name:** Knights.

Student services. Adult student services, career counseling, services for economically disadvantaged, student employment services, financial aid counseling, minority student services, on-campus daycare, personal counseling, veterans' counselor. **Physically disabled:** Services for visually, speech, hearing impaired. **Transfer:** Pre-admission transcript evaluation for new students. College fairs on campus for students transferring to 4-year colleges.

Contact. Phone: (509) 682-6806 Toll-free number: (877) 982-4698 Fax: (509) 682-6801
William Maxwell, Registrar, Wenatchee Valley College, 1300 Fifth Street, Wenatchee, WA 98801-1799

Whatcom Community College
Bellingham, Washington   **CB member**
www.whatcom.ctc.edu   **CB code: 1275**

◆ Public 2-year community college
◆ Commuter campus in small city

General. Founded in 1970. Regionally accredited. Whatcom Community College is an accredited, comprehensive two-year college serving 11,000 students annually. On its 72-acre campus in Bellingham, WA, and through online courses, Whatcom offers transfer degrees, professional and technical training programs, as well as basic education, job skills, and Community & Continuing Education classes. Established in 1967, Whatcom has been accredited by the Northwest Commission on Colleges and Universities since 1976. **Enrollment:** 4,020 full-time, degree-seeking students. **Degrees:** 969 associate awarded. **Location:** 90 miles from Seattle, 60 miles from Vancouver, Canada. **Calendar:** Quarter, limited summer session. **Full-time faculty:** 78 total. **Part-time faculty:** 232 total. **Class size:** 28% < 20, 70% 20-39, 2% 40-49.

Transfer out. Colleges most students transferred to 2015: Western Washington University, University of Washington, Washington State University, Central Washington University, Eastern Washington University.

Basis for selection. Open admission, but selective for some programs. All applicants apply online for general admissions to the college. Applicants wishing to apply to the following selective entry programs must also submit a separate application: Visual Communications and Allied Health Programs.

High school preparation. College-preparatory program recommended. Recommended units include English 4, mathematics 4, social studies 3, science 2 (laboratory 1), foreign language 3, visual/performing arts 1 and academic electives 1.

2015-2016 Annual costs. Tuition/fees: $4,400; $9,803 out-of-state. Per-credit charge: $85 in-state; $206 out-of-state. Books/supplies: $1,080. Personal expenses: $2,238.

Financial aid. Need-based: Need-based aid available for part-time students. Work-study available nights, weekends and for part-time students. **Non-need-based:** Scholarships awarded for academics, athletics, state residency.

Application procedures. Admission: Priority date 6/23; no deadline. No application fee. Admission notification on a rolling basis. **Financial aid:** Closing date 4/1. FAFSA, institutional form required. Applicants notified on a rolling basis starting 7/1; must reply within 3 week(s) of notification.

Academics. Special study options: Accelerated study, cooperative education, distance learning, dual enrollment of high school students, ESL, honors, independent study, internships, student-designed major, study abroad. License preparation in nursing. **Credit/placement by examination:** AP, CLEP, IB, institutional tests. 15 credit hours maximum toward associate degree. **Support services:** GED preparation and test center, learning center, reduced course load, remedial instruction, study skills assistance, tutoring, writing center.

Majors. Business: General, accounting. **Computer sciences:** Computer science, data processing, systems analysis. **Education:** General, early childhood, teacher assistance. **Health services:** Massage therapy, medical assistant, nursing (RN), physical therapy assistant. **Liberal arts:** Arts/sciences. **Protective services:** Police science. **Visual/performing arts:** Commercial/advertising art.

Most popular majors. Health sciences 13%, liberal arts 79%.

Technology on campus. 294 workstations in library, computer center, student center. Online course registration, online library, wireless network available.

Student life. Freshman orientation: Available. Preregistration for classes offered. Prior to fall, winter and spring quarters, new student orientation sessions held for students along with a separate parent track. Students take campus tour, attend workshops, meet faculty. **Activities:** Jazz band, choral groups, drama, film society, international student organizations, student government, student newspaper, Phi Theta Kappa, Japanese Anime, Deaf Students Fellowship, health and wellness club, international friendship club, snow club, Gay-Straight Alliance, multicultural club.

Athletics. Intercollegiate: Basketball, soccer, volleyball W. **Intramural:** Badminton, basketball, soccer, tennis, volleyball. **Team name:** Orcas.

Student services. Adult student services, alcohol/substance abuse counseling, career counseling, student employment services, financial aid counseling, on-campus daycare, personal counseling, veterans' counselor. **Physically disabled:** Services for visually, speech, hearing impaired. **Transfer:** Re-entry adviser for new students. Transfer center, transfer adviser, college fairs on campus for students transferring to 4-year colleges.

Contact. E-mail: admit@whatcom.ctc.edu
Phone: (360) 383-3030 Fax: (360) 383-3031
Michael Singletary, Registrar, Whatcom Community College, 237 West Kellogg Road, Bellingham, WA 98226

Yakima Valley Community College
Yakima, Washington
www.yvcc.edu   **CB code: 4993**

◆ Public 2-year community college
◆ Commuter campus in small city

General. Founded in 1928. Regionally accredited. Additional campus in Grandview and dormitories (Student Residence Center) available on Yakima campus. **Enrollment:** 4,105 undergraduates. **Degrees:** 760 associate awarded. **Location:** 150 miles from Seattle. **Calendar:** Quarter, extensive summer session. **Full-time faculty:** 111 total. **Part-time faculty:** 171 total. **Special facilities:** College-operated winery, dental clinic, community library; automotive technology lab.

Transfer out. Colleges most students transferred to 2015: Central Washington University, Washington State University.

Basis for selection. Open admission, but selective for some programs. Special requirements for nursing, radiology, dental hygiene, allied health, and veterinary technology programs. COMPASS required for placement and advising of degree-seeking students and for math/English placement. Previous college/university transcripts showing successful completion of English and math courses may replace COMPASS. Essay required for radiologic technology.

High school preparation. College-preparatory program recommended.

2015-2016 Annual costs. Tuition/fees: $4,319; $9,722 out-of-state. Per-credit charge: $85 in-state; $206 out-of-state. Books/supplies: $1,026. Personal expenses: $1,614.

Financial aid. Need-based: Need-based aid available for part-time students. Work-study available nights, weekends and for part-time students. **Non-need-based:** Scholarships awarded for athletics.

Application procedures. Admission: Closing date 8/14 (receipt date). $20 fee. Admission notification on a rolling basis. **Financial aid:** Closing date 4/15. FAFSA required. Applicants notified on a rolling basis starting 8/1; must reply within 2 week(s) of notification.

Academics. Special study options: Cooperative education, distance learning, dual enrollment of high school students, ESL, honors, independent study, internships, liberal arts/career combination, weekend college. Bachelor's degree programs available on campus. License preparation in dental hygiene, nursing, radiology. **Credit/placement by examination:** AP, CLEP, IB, institutional tests. 45 credit hours maximum toward associate degree. **Support services:** GED preparation and test center, learning center, remedial instruction, study skills assistance, tutoring, writing center. Math center.

Majors. Business: General, accounting technology, business admin, entrepreneurial studies, marketing, office management. **Communications technology:** Radio/TV, recording arts. **Computer sciences:** Data processing, support specialist, web page design. **Education:** Early childhood, teacher assistance. **Engineering:** General. **General:** Electrician. **Health services:**

Dental hygiene, insurance coding, medical assistant, medical radiologic technology/radiation therapy, medical secretary, nursing (RN), substance abuse counseling, surgical technology, veterinary technology/assistant. **Liberal arts:** Arts/sciences. **Physical sciences:** General. **Protective services:** Law enforcement admin. **Visual/performing arts:** Design.

Most popular majors. Business/marketing 10%, health sciences 24%, liberal arts 52%.

Technology on campus. 323 workstations in dormitories, library, computer center, student center. Dormitories wired for high-speed internet access. Commuter students can connect to campus network. Online course registration, online library, helpline, wireless network available.

Student life. Freshman orientation: Mandatory. Preregistration for classes offered. Held three weeks prior to the beginning of each quarter. **Housing:** Single-sex dorms, wellness housing available. $250 partly refundable deposit. **Activities:** Bands, choral groups, drama, international student organizations, music ensembles, musical theater, student government, student newspaper, Mecha, Veterans, Tiin Ma, International Club, Phi Theta Kappa, Action, Auto, allied health clubs.

Athletics. NJCAA. **Intercollegiate:** Baseball M, basketball, soccer W, softball W, volleyball W. **Intramural:** Basketball. **Team name:** Yaks.

Student services. Adult student services, career counseling, services for economically disadvantaged, financial aid counseling, on-campus daycare, personal counseling, veterans' counselor. **Physically disabled:** Services for visually, speech, hearing impaired. **Transfer:** Pre-admission transcript evaluation for new students. Transfer adviser, college fairs on campus for students transferring to 4-year colleges.

Contact. E-mail: admis@yvcc.edu
Phone: (509) 574-4712 Fax: (509) 574-4649
Luis Gutierrez, Registrar and Director for Enrollment Services, Yakima Valley Community College, PO Box 22520, Yakima, WA 98907-2520

West Virginia

Contact. E-mail: tharris@national-college.edu
Phone: (304) 431-1600
Tonya Elmore, Director of Admissions, American National University:
Princeton, 421 Hilltop Drive, Princeton, WV 24739

American National University: Parkersburg
Parkersburg, West Virginia
www.an.edu

♦ For-profit 2-year career college
♦ Small city

General. Accredited by ACICS. **Enrollment:** 52 degree-seeking undergraduates. **Degrees:** 1 bachelor's, 22 associate awarded. **Calendar:** Quarter. **Full-time faculty:** 2 total. **Part-time faculty:** 10 total.

Basis for selection. Open admission.

2016-2017 Annual costs. Tuition/fees: $14,460. Per-credit charge: $317.

Financial aid. Need-based: Work-study available nights, weekends and for part-time students.

Application procedures. Admission: $50 fee.

Academics. Credit/placement by examination: AP, CLEP.

Majors. Business: Business admin. **Computer sciences:** Information systems. **Health services:** EMT paramedic, health care admin, medical assistant, office assistant, surgical technology.

Contact. Phone: (304) 699-3005
Larry Steele, Regional Director of Admissions, American National
University: Parkersburg, 110 Park Center Drive, Parkersburg, WV 26101

American National University: Princeton
Princeton, West Virginia
www.an.edu   **CB code: 3246**

♦ For-profit 2-year business college
♦ Commuter campus in small city

General. Accredited by ACICS. **Enrollment:** 104 degree-seeking undergraduates. **Degrees:** 26 associate awarded. **Calendar:** Quarter. **Full-time faculty:** 1 total. **Part-time faculty:** 13 total.

Basis for selection. Open admission. Interview recommended.

2016-2017 Annual costs. Tuition/fees: $14,460. Per-credit charge: $317. Books/supplies: $1,200.

Financial aid. All financial aid based on need. Need-based aid available for part-time students. Work-study available nights, weekends and for part-time students.

Application procedures. Admission: No deadline. $50 fee, may be waived for applicants with need. Admission notification on a rolling basis. **Financial aid:** No deadline. FAFSA required. Applicants notified on a rolling basis starting 9/1.

Academics. Special study options: Double major, internships, liberal arts/career combination. **Credit/placement by examination:** AP, CLEP, institutional tests. **Support services:** Tutoring.

Majors. Business: Accounting, administrative services, business admin, office management. **Computer sciences:** Computer science. **Health services:** Medical assistant.

Technology on campus. 35 workstations in computer center.

Student life. Freshman orientation: Mandatory. Preregistration for classes offered.

Student services. Career counseling, personal counseling.

Blue Ridge Community and Technical College
Martinsburg, West Virginia   **CB member**
www.blueridgectc.edu   **CB code: 4892**

♦ Public 2-year community and technical college
♦ Commuter campus in small city

General. Regionally accredited. **Enrollment:** 2,016 degree-seeking undergraduates; 3,536 non-degree-seeking students. **Degrees:** 471 associate awarded. **Location:** Downtown. **Calendar:** Semester, limited summer session. **Full-time faculty:** 61 total; 13% have terminal degrees, 69% women. **Part-time faculty:** 121 total; 9% have terminal degrees, 60% women. **Class size:** 55% < 20, 41% 20-39, 2% 40-49, 2% 50-99, less than 1% >100.

Student profile. Among degree-seeking undergraduates, 388 enrolled as first-time, first-year students.

Part-time:	47%	Asian American:	1%
Out-of-state:	4%	Hispanic/Latino:	4%
Women:	65%	Multi-racial, non-Hispanic:	3%
African American:	9%	25 or older:	65%

Transfer out. Colleges most students transferred to 2015: Shepherd University.

Basis for selection. Open admission. **Adult students:** Students without ACT/SAT may take the ACCUPLACER in-house. **Home schooled:** Transcript of courses and grades, state high school equivalency certificate required.

High school preparation. Recommended units include English 4, mathematics 4, social studies 2, history 1, science 3 (laboratory 3), foreign language 2 and visual/performing arts 1.

2015-2016 Annual costs. Tuition/fees: $3,696; $6,456 out-of-state. Per-credit charge: $144 in-state; $278 out-of-state. Books/supplies: $1,270. Personal expenses: $2,000.

Financial aid. Need-based: Need-based aid available for part-time students. Work-study available nights, weekends and for part-time students.

Application procedures. Admission: No deadline. $25 fee, may be waived for applicants with need. Application must be submitted on paper. Admission notification on a rolling basis. **Financial aid:** No deadline. FAFSA required. Applicants notified on a rolling basis; must reply within 2 week(s) of notification.

Academics. Special study options: Dual enrollment of high school students, ESL, independent study, internships, liberal arts/career combination. License preparation in dental hygiene, nursing, paramedic, physical therapy, real estate. **Credit/placement by examination:** AP, CLEP, institutional tests. **Support services:** Learning center, reduced course load, remedial instruction, tutoring, writing center.

Majors. Business: General, accounting, business admin, entrepreneurial studies, office technology. **Computer sciences:** Information systems. **Health services:** Clinical lab technology, EMT paramedic, medical assistant, nursing (RN), physical therapy assistant, surgical technology. **Liberal arts:** Arts/sciences. **Protective services:** Criminal justice, fire safety technology, firefighting.

Most popular majors. Business/marketing 8%, computer/information sciences 14%, health sciences 19%, liberal arts 43%.

Technology on campus. 135 workstations in library, computer center, student center. Online course registration, online library, helpline, student web hosting, wireless network available.

Student life. Freshman orientation: Available. Preregistration for classes offered.

Athletics. Team name: Bruins.

Student services. Adult student services, career counseling, student employment services, financial aid counseling, placement for graduates, veterans' counselor. **Physically disabled:** Services for visually, speech, hearing impaired. **Transfer:** Pre admission transcript evaluation for new students. College fairs on campus for students transferring to 4-year colleges.

Contact. E-mail: bneal@blueridgectc.edu
Phone: (304) 260-4380 ext. 2109 Fax: (304) 260-4376
Brenda Neal, Director of Access, Blue Ridge Community and Technical
College, 13650 Apple Harvest Drive, Martinsburg, WV 25403

BridgeValley Community and Technical College
Montgomery, West Virginia
www.bridgevalley.edu   CB code: 5786

- Public 2-year community and technical college
- Commuter campus in small town

General. Regionally accredited. **Enrollment:** 1,000 undergraduates.
Degrees: 405 associate awarded. **Location:** 25 miles from Charleston. **Calendar:** Semester, limited summer session. **Full-time faculty:** 38 total. **Part-time faculty:** 34 total. **Special facilities:** Advanced technology building.
Partnerships: Formal partnership with Toyota for work/study program in
electrical/mechanical instrumentation.

Basis for selection. Open admission, but selective for some programs.
Selective admissions to dental hygiene, respiratory therapy, veterinarian technology, and blasting technology programs. **Adult students:** If adults have
not taken the SAT or ACT, they may take the compass or accuplacer test.
Home schooled: Transcript of courses and grades required.

2015-2016 Annual costs. Books/supplies: $1,292. Personal expenses:
$946.

Financial aid. Need-based: Work-study available nights, weekends and
for part-time students.

Application procedures. Admission: No deadline. No application fee.
Admission notification on a rolling basis.

Academics. Special study options: Accelerated study, dual enrollment of
high school students. License preparation in dental hygiene. **Credit/placement by examination:** AP, CLEP, institutional tests. **Support services:**
GED preparation, learning center, remedial instruction, study skills assistance, tutoring.

Majors. Business: Accounting, business admin, executive assistant, hospitality admin, hospitality/recreation, office management. **Computer sciences:**
General. **General:** Blasting, building construction. **Health services:** Dental
hygiene, facilities admin, health information management, medical assistant,
medical secretary, office admin, office assistant, receptionist, respiratory
therapy assistant, respiratory therapy technology, veterinary technology/
assistant.

Technology on campus. Dormitories wired for high-speed internet
access and linked to campus network. Commuter students can connect to
campus network. Wireless network available.

Student life. Freshman orientation: Mandatory. Preregistration for
classes offered. Held the weekend before the beginning of the fall semester.
Housing: Coed dorms, single-sex dorms available. **Activities:** Student government, student newspaper.

Student services. Student employment services, financial aid counseling,
placement for graduates, veterans' counselor. **Physically disabled:** Services
for hearing impaired. **Transfer:** Pre-admission transcript evaluation for
new students.

Contact. E-mail: admissions@bridgemont.edu
Phone: (304) 734-6604 Fax: (304) 734-6698
Joyce Surbaugh, Director of Enrollment Management, BridgeValley
Community and Technical College, 619 Second Avenue, Montgomery,
WV 25136

Eastern West Virginia Community and Technical College
Moorefield, West Virginia
www.easternwv.edu   CB code: 3837

- Public 2-year community and technical college
- Commuter campus in rural community

General. Regionally accredited. **Enrollment:** 526 degree-seeking undergraduates. **Degrees:** 93 associate awarded. **Location:** 55 miles from Winchester, VA. **Calendar:** Semester, limited summer session. **Part-time faculty:**
36 total.

Transfer out. Colleges most students transferred to 2015: Shepherd
College, West Virginia University, Potomac State College.

Basis for selection. Open admission. Degree-seeking students required
to take ACCUPLACER. **Home schooled:** Transcript of courses and grades
required. Applicants advised to take GED.

Financial aid. Need-based: Need-based aid available for part-time students. Work-study available nights, weekends and for part-time students.

Application procedures. Admission: No deadline. No application fee.
Admission notification on a rolling basis. **Financial aid:** Priority date 6/1;
no closing date. FAFSA, institutional form required. Applicants notified on
a rolling basis; must reply within 2 week(s) of notification.

Academics. Special study options: Distance learning, double major, dual
enrollment of high school students, external degree, internships, student-designed major. License preparation in nursing, paramedic. **Credit/placement by examination:** AP, CLEP, institutional tests. **Support services:**
GED preparation and test center, reduced course load, remedial instruction,
study skills assistance, tutoring.

Majors. Business: Administrative services, business admin. **Computer sciences:** Information systems. **Liberal arts:** Arts/sciences. **Work/family studies:** Child care service.

Technology on campus. Online course registration, online library, wireless network available.

Student life. Freshman orientation: Mandatory. Preregistration for
classes offered. General orientation program is 3 hours long. Second program
required for students taking online courses. **Activities:** Student government.

Student services. Adult student services, services for economically disadvantaged, financial aid counseling, veterans' counselor. **Physically disabled:**
Services for visually, hearing impaired. **Transfer:** Pre-admission transcript
evaluation for new students. College fairs on campus for students transferring
to 4-year colleges.

Contact. E-mail: askeast@eastern.wvnet.edu
Phone: (304) 434-8000 Toll-free number: (877) 982-2322
Fax: (304) 434-7004
Robert Eagle, Dean of Academics and Learner Support Services, Eastern
West Virginia Community and Technical College, 316 Eastern Drive,
Moorefield, WV 26836

Huntington Junior College
Huntington, West Virginia
www.huntingtonjuniorcollege.edu   CB code: 7310

- For-profit 2-year junior college
- Commuter campus in small city

General. Founded in 1936. Regionally accredited. **Enrollment:** 685 undergraduates. **Degrees:** 148 associate awarded. **Location:** 45 miles from Charleston. **Calendar:** Quarter, extensive summer session. **Full-time faculty:** 21
total. **Part-time faculty:** 20 total.

Basis for selection. Open admission. Interview recommended.

2015-2016 Annual costs. Personal expenses: $1,500.

Financial aid. Need-based: Work-study available nights, weekends and
for part-time students.

Application procedures. Admission: No deadline. No application fee.
Admission notification on a rolling basis. **Financial aid:** No deadline. Applicants notified on a rolling basis.

Academics. Special study options: Distance learning, honors, internships.
Credit/placement by examination: AP, CLEP, institutional tests. **Support
services:** Learning center, reduced course load, remedial instruction, study
skills assistance, tutoring.

Majors. Business: General, accounting, administrative services. **Computer
sciences:** General, database management, programming, web page design.
Foreign languages: Classics. **Health services:** Dental assistant, insurance
coding, medical assistant.

Technology on campus. 117 workstations in library, computer center.
Online course registration, online library, helpline available.

Student life. Freshman orientation: Mandatory. Preregistration for
classes offered. 3 hour program held during the first day of class.

Student services. Career counseling, student employment services, financial aid counseling, personal counseling, placement for graduates, veterans' counselor. **Physically disabled:** Services for visually, hearing impaired. **Transfer:** Pre-admission transcript evaluation for new students. Transfer center for students transferring to 4-year colleges.

Contact. E-mail: admissions@huntingtonjuniorcollege.edu
Phone: (304) 697-7550 Toll-free number: (800) 344-4522
Fax: (304) 697-7554
James Garrett, Director of Marketing and Education Services, Huntington Junior College, 900 Fifth Avenue, Huntington, WV 25701

Kanawha Valley Community and Technical College
South Charleston, West Virginia
www.kvctc.edu

- Public 2-year community and technical college
- Commuter campus in small town

General. Regionally accredited. **Location:** 10 miles from Charleston. **Calendar:** Semester.

Annual costs/financial aid. Books/supplies: $1,292. Personal expenses: $5,444.

Contact. Phone: (304) 205-6600
Director of Admissions, 2001 Union Carbide Drive, South Charleston, WV 25303

Mountain State College
Parkersburg, West Virginia
www.msc.edu   CB code: 2389

- For-profit 2-year junior and career college
- Commuter campus in large town
- Interview required

General. Founded in 1888. Accredited by ACICS. All programs can be taken online. **Enrollment:** 189 degree-seeking undergraduates. **Degrees:** 27 associate awarded. **Location:** 81 miles from Charleston. **Calendar:** Quarter. **Full-time faculty:** 7 total. **Part-time faculty:** 6 total. **Special facilities:** Legal resource center, dependency resource center.

Basis for selection. Open admission. CPAT required for placement. **Home schooled:** Interview required.

2015-2016 Annual costs. Books/supplies: $2,500.

Financial aid. **Need-based:** Work-study available nights, weekends and for part-time students.

Application procedures. **Admission:** No deadline. $115 fee. Admission notification on a rolling basis. **Financial aid:** No deadline. FAFSA required. Applicants notified on a rolling basis.

Academics. **Special study options:** Accelerated study, cooperative education, distance learning, double major, internships. **Credit/placement by examination:** AP, CLEP. **Support services:** Study skills assistance, tutoring.

Majors. Business: Accounting, administrative services, hospitality/recreation, tourism promotion, tourism/travel. **Computer sciences:** General, applications programming. **Health services:** Medical assistant, medical transcription, mental health services, substance abuse counseling.

Most popular majors. Computer/information sciences 10%, health sciences 90%.

Technology on campus. 47 workstations in library, computer center. Commuter students can connect to campus network. Online library, helpline, wireless network available.

Student life. Freshman orientation: Mandatory. Preregistration for classes offered. Held the week prior to beginning of quarter. **Activities:** Student government, student newspaper.

Student services. Career counseling, student employment services, financial aid counseling, personal counseling, placement for graduates.

Contact. E-mail: adm@msc.edu
Phone: (304) 485-5487 Toll-free number: (800) 841-0201
Fax: (304) 485-3524
Gary Dailey, Director of Career Services, Mountain State College, 1508 Spring Street, Parkersburg, WV 26101-3993

New River Community and Technical College
Beckley, West Virginia
www.newriver.edu   CB code: 5943

- Public 2-year community and technical college
- Commuter campus in large town

General. Regionally accredited. **Enrollment:** 2,900 undergraduates. **Degrees:** 232 associate awarded. **Calendar:** Semester, limited summer session. **Full-time faculty:** 59 total. **Part-time faculty:** 120 total.

Student profile.

Out-of-state:	1%	25 or older:	50%

Basis for selection. Open admission. **Adult students:** COMPASS required for placement.

2015-2016 Annual costs. Tuition/fees: $3,706; $4,834 out-of-state. Books/supplies: $600.

Financial aid. **Need-based:** Work-study available nights, weekends and for part-time students.

Application procedures. **Admission:** No deadline. No application fee.

Academics. **Special study options:** Accelerated study, distance learning, double major, dual enrollment of high school students, internships, weekend college. License preparation in nursing, paramedic, physical therapy. **Credit/placement by examination:** AP, CLEP, institutional tests. **Support services:** Remedial instruction, tutoring.

Majors. Business: General, accounting, banking/financial services, hospitality admin, marketing, tourism/travel. **Communications technology:** General. **Computer sciences:** General, information technology, LAN/WAN management. **Conservation:** Environmental science. **Education:** General, teacher assistance. **Health services:** Medical assistant. **Protective services:** Corrections, law enforcement admin.

Most popular majors. Business/marketing 22%, education 14%, health sciences 11%, legal studies 14%, liberal arts 32%.

Technology on campus. 200 workstations in computer center, student center. Wireless network available.

Student life. Freshman orientation: Mandatory, $50 fee. Preregistration for classes offered. **Activities:** Model UN, student government, student newspaper, social services club.

Student services. Career counseling, student employment services, financial aid counseling, placement for graduates, veterans' counselor. **Physically disabled:** Services for visually, speech, hearing impaired.

Contact. E-mail: admissions@newriver.edu
Phone: (866) 349-3739 Fax: (304) 929-5484
Tracy Evans, Director of Enrollment Services, New River Community and Technical College, 167 Dye Drive, Beckley, WV 25801

Pierpont Community and Technical College
Fairmont, West Virginia
www.pierpont.edu   CB code: 6455

- Public 2-year community and technical college
- Large town

General. Regionally accredited. **Enrollment:** 2,700 degree-seeking undergraduates. **Degrees:** 350 associate awarded. **Calendar:** Semester. **Full-time faculty:** 56 total. **Part-time faculty:** 178 total.

Basis for selection. Open admission.

2015-2016 Annual costs. Tuition/fees: $4,560; $10,632 out-of-state. Room/board: $7,750. Books/supplies: $1,000. Personal expenses: $1,500.

Financial aid. **Need-based:** Work study available nights, weekends and for part-time students.

Application procedures. Admission: No deadline. No application fee. **Financial aid:** No deadline.

Academics. Credit/placement by examination: AP.

Majors. Business: Office technology, restaurant/food services. **Education:** Early childhood. **Health services:** Prephysical therapy, preveterinary, radiologic technology/medical imaging, respiratory therapy assistant. **Liberal arts:** Arts/sciences. **Protective services:** Police science.

Athletics. Team name: Pride.

Contact. E-mail: admit@pierpont.edu
Phone: (304) 333-3684 Toll-free number: (800) 297-0999
Jennifer Weist, Associate Vice President for Student Services, Pierpont Community and Technical College, 1201 Locust Avenue, Fairmont, WV 26554

Potomac State College of West Virginia University
Keyser, West Virginia
www.potomacstatecollege.edu   CB code: 5539

▶ Public 2-year branch campus and junior college
▶ Commuter campus in small town

General. Founded in 1901. Regionally accredited. **Enrollment:** 1,224 degree-seeking undergraduates; 251 non-degree-seeking students. **Degrees:** 24 bachelor's, 335 associate awarded. **Location:** 80 miles from Morgantown, 150 miles from Baltimore. **Calendar:** Semester, limited summer session. **Full-time faculty:** 45 total; 29% have terminal degrees, 4% minority, 53% women. **Part-time faculty:** 40 total; 2% have terminal degrees, 2% minority, 55% women. **Class size:** 48% < 20, 45% 20-39, 4% 40-49, 2% 50-99. **Special facilities:** 2 fully operational farms, indoor riding arena to support agriculture and forestry programs, demonstration kitchen for hospitality program.

Student profile. Among degree-seeking undergraduates, 588 enrolled as first-time, first-year students, 45 transferred in from other institutions.

Part-time:	6%	Multi-racial, non-Hispanic:	4%
Out-of-state:	37%	International:	1%
Women:	52%	25 or older:	11%
African American:	21%	Live on campus:	51%
Hispanic/Latino:	3%		

Transfer out. Colleges most students transferred to 2015: West Virginia University, Fairmont State College, Frostburg State University.

Basis for selection. Open admission, but selective for out-of-state students.

2015-2016 Annual costs. Tuition/fees: $3,864; $10,080 out-of-state. Room/board: $8,476. Books/supplies: $1,050. **Additional information:** Tuition for students residing in border counties is $6,240.

Financial aid. Need-based: Need-based aid available for part-time students. Work-study available nights, weekends and for part-time students. **Non-need-based:** Scholarships awarded for academics, athletics.

Application procedures. Admission: No deadline. No application fee. Admission notification on a rolling basis beginning on or about 9/15. English ACT used in conjunction with high school GPA to place students in either college-level or remedial composition courses. Scores also used for math placement. **Financial aid:** Priority date 3/1; no closing date. FAFSA required. Applicants notified on a rolling basis starting 3/15; must reply within 2 week(s) of notification.

Academics. Special study options: Distance learning, double major, dual enrollment of high school students, honors, internships, study abroad. Bachelor's degree programs available on campus. **Credit/placement by examination:** AP, CLEP, IB, institutional tests. **Support services:** Learning center, reduced course load, remedial instruction, tutoring.

Majors. Biology: General. **Business:** Administrative services, business admin, hospitality admin, office technology. **Communications:** Journalism. **Computer sciences:** Information technology. **Conservation:** Environmental studies, forest management, wildlife/wilderness, wood science. **Education:** Early childhood, elementary, environmental, physical, secondary. **Engineering:** Civil, electrical, mechanical. **English:** English lit. **Foreign languages:** General. **Health services:** Athletic training, clinical lab technology, predental, premedicine, prenursing, preoccupational therapy, prepharmacy, prephysical therapy, preveterinary. **History:** General. **Human services:** Social work. **Math:** General. **Parks/recreation:** Facilities management, sports admin.

Physical sciences: Chemistry, geology, physics. **Protective services:** Criminal justice, law enforcement admin. **Psychology:** General. **Social sciences:** Economics, political science, sociology.

Most popular majors. Agriculture 7%, business/marketing 13%, education 11%, health sciences 8%, liberal arts 31%, security/protective services 8%.

Technology on campus. 50 workstations in dormitories, library, student center. Dormitories wired for high-speed internet access. Online library, helpline, repair service, student web hosting, wireless network available.

Student life. Freshman orientation: Mandatory, $50 fee. Preregistration for classes offered. **Housing:** Guaranteed on-campus for freshmen. Coed dorms, single-sex dorms, special housing for disabled available. $200 fully refundable deposit, deadline 8/15. Dorm for agriculture and agricultural-related majors available. **Activities:** Bands, campus ministries, choral groups, drama, music ensembles, musical theater, student government, student newspaper, agriculture and forestry club, Circle K, equestrian club, criminal justice club, engineering club, peer advocates, life sciences club, campus and community ministry, black student alliance, Relay for Life.

Athletics. NJCAA. **Intercollegiate:** Baseball M, basketball, cross-country, lacrosse, soccer, softball W, volleyball W. **Intramural:** Basketball. **Team name:** Catamounts.

Student services. Alcohol/substance abuse counseling, career counseling, services for economically disadvantaged, student employment services, financial aid counseling, health services, on-campus daycare, personal counseling, placement for graduates, veterans' counselor. **Physically disabled:** Services for visually, hearing impaired. **Transfer:** Pre-admission transcript evaluation for new students.

Contact. E-mail: go2psc@mail.wvu.edu
Phone: (304) 788-6820 Toll-free number: (800) 262-7332
Fax: (304) 788-6939
Beth Little, Director of Enrollment Services, Potomac State College of West Virginia University, 75 Arnold Street, Keyser, WV 26726

Southern West Virginia Community and Technical College
Mount Gay, West Virginia
www.southernwv.edu
CB member
CB code: 0770

▶ Public 2-year community and technical college
▶ Commuter campus in small town

General. Founded in 1971. Regionally accredited. Additional campuses in Williamson, Saulsville, and Foster. **Enrollment:** 2,002 degree-seeking undergraduates. **Degrees:** 217 associate awarded. **Location:** 60 miles from Charleston. **Calendar:** Trimester, limited summer session. **Full-time faculty:** 72 total. **Part-time faculty:** 35 total. **Special facilities:** Allied health and technology building.

Transfer out. Colleges most students transferred to 2015: Marshall University, West Virginia University, West Virginia State University, Mountain State University, Concord University.

Basis for selection. Open admission, but selective for some programs. Limited admissions to nursing, medical laboratory, radiologic technology, dental hygiene, respiratory technology, and surgical technology programs. Application and criteria are posted on web page by 10/1 and deadline to submit application is 1/31. **Adult students:** Adult students may take ACCUPLACER to determine placement in English and math. **Home schooled:** Transcript of courses and grades required. **Learning Disabled:** Meeting with disability counselor recommended.

2015-2016 Annual costs. Tuition/fees: $3,582; $5,298 out-of-state. Per-credit charge: $133 in-state; $202 out-of-state. Books/supplies: $1,200. Personal expenses: $900.

Financial aid. Need-based: Need-based aid available for part-time students. Work-study available nights, weekends and for part-time students.

Application procedures. Admission: No deadline. No application fee. Admission notification on a rolling basis. **Financial aid:** No deadline. FAFSA required. Applicants notified on a rolling basis.

Academics. Special study options: Distance learning, dual enrollment of high school students, independent study, teacher certification program. Fast Track courses. Bachelor's degree programs available on campus. License preparation in dental hygiene, nursing, paramedic, radiology. **Credit/placement by examination:** AP, CLEP, institutional tests. 24 credit hours maximum toward associate degree. **Support services:** GED preparation, learning center, reduced course load, remedial instruction, tutoring.

Majors. Business: Accounting, business admin, executive assistant. **Computer sciences:** Information technology. **Health services:** Clinical lab technology, dental hygiene, EMT paramedic, health aide, medical radiologic technology/radiation therapy, nursing (RN), respiratory therapy technology, surgical technology. **Liberal arts:** Arts/sciences. **Protective services:** Criminal justice. **Work/family studies:** Child care management.

Most popular majors. Business/marketing 17%, health sciences 50%, liberal arts 22%.

Technology on campus. Online course registration, online library, helpline, wireless network available.

Student life. Freshman orientation: Available. Preregistration for classes offered. Offered to first-time freshman, or students with less than 30 credit hours. **Activities:** Drama, musical theater, student government, special interest clubs.

Student services. Adult student services, career counseling, student employment services, financial aid counseling, on-campus daycare, personal counseling, placement for graduates, veterans' counselor. **Physically disabled:** Services for visually, speech, hearing impaired. **Transfer:** Transfer adviser, college fairs on campus for students transferring to 4-year colleges.

Contact. Phone: (304) 896-7443 Toll-free number: (866) 798-2821 Fax: (304) 792-7056
Teri Wells, Registrar, Southern West Virginia Community and Technical College, PO Box 2900, Mount Gay, WV 25637

Valley College
Martinsburg, West Virginia
www.valley.edu   CB code: 3176

◗ For-profit 2-year career college
◗ Commuter campus in large town
◗ Interview required

General. Accredited by ACICS. Additional campuses in Princeton and Beckley. Business Administration A.A.S. degree and Health Services Administration A.A.S. degree are available online at sister campus (Valley College, Beckley). **Enrollment:** 140 undergraduates. **Location:** 20 miles from Winchester, VA; 20 miles from Hagerstown, MD. **Calendar:** Differs by program, extensive summer session. **Full-time faculty:** 4 total; 75% women.

Basis for selection. Open admission. **Home schooled:** Transcript of courses and grades, state high school equivalency certificate required.

2015-2016 Annual costs. Books/supplies: $1,750. Personal expenses: $4,923.

Financial aid. Need-based: Need-based aid available for part-time students. Work-study available nights, weekends and for part-time students.

Application procedures. Admission: No deadline. No application fee. Admission notification on a rolling basis. Institutional placement test administered for students without ACT or SAT. **Financial aid:** No deadline. FAFSA, institutional form required. Applicants notified on a rolling basis.

Academics. Credit/placement by examination: AP, CLEP. **Support services:** Remedial instruction, study skills assistance.

Technology on campus. 42 workstations in computer center. Online library, wireless network available.

Student life. Freshman orientation: Mandatory. Preregistration for classes offered. Orientation held during first week of classes.

Student services. Career counseling, student employment services, financial aid counseling, placement for graduates. **Transfer:** Pre-admission transcript evaluation for new students.

Contact. E-mail: martinsburg@valley.edu
Phone: (304) 263-0979 Fax: (304) 263-2413
Matthew Jenkins, Corporate Director of Operations, Valley College, 287 Aikens Center, Martinsburg, WV 25404

West Virginia Business College: Nutter Fort
Benwood, West Virginia
www.wvbc.edu   CB code: 2546

◗ For-profit 2-year business college
◗ Commuter campus in small city

General. Accredited by ACICS. **Location:** 35 miles from Morgantown. **Calendar:** Quarter.

Annual costs/financial aid. Diploma programs: $10,000-$12,000. Associate programs: $19,000. Additional fees may apply. Need-based financial aid available to full-time and part-time students.

Contact. Phone: (304) 232-0361
Director, 1052 Main Street, Wheeling, WV 26003

West Virginia Business College: Wheeling
Wheeling, West Virginia
www.wvbc.edu

◗ For-profit 2-year business and career college
◗ Commuter campus in small city
◗ Interview required

General. Accredited by ACICS. **Enrollment:** 147 undergraduates. **Degrees:** 37 associate awarded. **Location:** 50 miles from Pittsburgh. **Calendar:** Quarter, extensive summer session. **Part-time faculty:** 20 total. **Class size:** 97% < 20, 3% 20-39.

Basis for selection. Open admission. **Home schooled:** State high school equivalency certificate required.

2015-2016 Annual costs. Books/supplies: $1,800. **Additional information:** Diploma programs: $10,000-$12,000. Associate programs: $19,000. Additional fees may apply.

Financial aid. Need-based: Work-study available nights, weekends and for part-time students.

Application procedures. Admission: No deadline. $50 fee. Application must be submitted on paper. Admission notification on a rolling basis.

Academics. Credit/placement by examination: AP, CLEP. 8 credit hours maximum toward associate degree. **Support services:** Study skills assistance, tutoring.

Majors. Business: Administrative services, business admin. **Computer sciences:** General, support specialist, word processing. **Health services:** Clinical lab technology, health aide, health care admin, health information technology, home attendant, insurance coding, insurance specialist, medical assistant, medical transcription, office admin, office assistant, receptionist, sterile processing technology, surgical technology.

Most popular majors. Business/marketing 25%, computer/information sciences 13%, health sciences 25%, legal studies 13%.

Technology on campus. Online library, wireless network available.

Student life. Activities: Student government, student newspaper.

Student services. Career counseling, financial aid counseling, placement for graduates.

Contact. E-mail: jweir@wvbc.edu
Phone: (304) 232-0631 ext. 13 Fax: (304) 232-0363
Brandy Kuri, Director of Admissions, West Virginia Business College: Wheeling, 1052 Main Street, Wheeling, WV 26003

West Virginia Junior College
Morgantown, West Virginia
www.wvjc.edu   CB code: 3179

◗ For-profit 2-year junior college
◗ Large town

General. Accredited by ACICS. **Enrollment:** 291 undergraduates. **Degrees:** 136 associate awarded. **Calendar:** Quarter. **Full-time faculty:** 1 total. **Part-time faculty:** 7 total.

Basis for selection. Open admission.

2015-2016 Annual costs. Books/supplies: $210. Personal expenses: $4,111. **Additional information:** Associate programs: $25,250, books and supplies $420.

Financial aid. Need-based: Need-based aid available for part-time students. Work-study available nights, weekends and for part-time students.

Application procedures. Admission: No deadline. $25 fee. Admission notification on a rolling basis. Prospective students meet with admissions counselor as part of application process. **Financial aid:** No deadline. FAFSA required. Applicants notified on a rolling basis.

Academics. Credit/placement by examination: AP, CLEP.

Majors. Business: Business admin, office technology. **Computer sciences:** Information systems, information technology. **Health services:** Insurance coding, medical assistant.

Contact. E-mail: info@wvjc.edu
Phone: (304) 296-8282
Leann Cardozo, Academic Director, West Virginia Junior College, 148 Willey Street, Morgantown, WV 26505

West Virginia Junior College: Bridgeport
Bridgeport, West Virginia
www.wvjc.edu

- For-profit 2-year health science and junior college
- Commuter campus in large town
- Interview required

General. Accredited by ACICS. **Enrollment:** 188 undergraduates. **Degrees:** 95 associate awarded. **Location:** 40 miles from Morgantown. **Calendar:** Quarter, extensive summer session. **Full-time faculty:** 8 total. **Part-time faculty:** 7 total.

Basis for selection. Open admission, but selective for some programs. Applicants are required to meet with an Admissions Representative. Specific programs have additional admissions requirements. Medical programs must have on file evidence of student liability insurance and Hepatitis B immunization prior to performing externships. **Adult students:** SAT/ACT scores not required. **Home schooled:** State high school equivalency certificate required.

2015-2016 Annual costs. Books/supplies: $210. Personal expenses: $3,991. **Additional information:** Diploma programs: $16,850-$20,282, books and supplies $280. Associate programs: $25,250, books and supplies $420.

Financial aid. Need-based: Need-based aid available for part-time students. Work-study available nights, weekends and for part-time students.

Application procedures. Admission: No deadline. $25 fee. Application must be submitted on paper. Admission notification on a rolling basis. **Financial aid:** No deadline. FAFSA required.

Academics. Special study options: Distance learning, internships. **Credit/placement by examination:** AP, CLEP. **Support services:** Study skills assistance, tutoring.

Majors. Business: Business admin. **Computer sciences:** Information technology. **Health services:** Dental assistant, medical assistant, medical secretary.

Technology on campus. 100 workstations in library, computer center. Commuter students can connect to campus network. Online course registration, online library, repair service, wireless network available.

Student life. Freshman orientation: Mandatory. Preregistration for classes offered. One day session held on the Friday before start of classes.

Student services. Adult student services, career counseling, student employment services, financial aid counseling, placement for graduates, veterans' counselor. **Physically disabled:** Services for visually, speech, hearing impaired. **Transfer:** Pre-admission transcript evaluation for new students.

Contact. E-mail: admissions@wvjcinfo.net
Phone: (304) 842-4007 ext. 110
Toll-free number: (800) 470-5627 ext. 110 Fax: (304) 842-8191
Sharron Stephens, Executive Director, West Virginia Junior College: Bridgeport, 176 Thompson Drive, Bridgeport, WV 26330

West Virginia Junior College: Charleston
Charleston, West Virginia
www.wvjc.edu   CB code: 3180

- For-profit 2-year junior and career college
- Commuter campus in small city
- Interview required

General. Accredited by ACICS. **Enrollment:** 213 degree-seeking undergraduates. **Degrees:** 72 associate awarded. **Calendar:** Quarter, extensive summer session. **Full-time faculty:** 8 total. **Part-time faculty:** 9 total.

Basis for selection. Open admission.

2015-2016 Annual costs. Books/supplies: $210. Personal expenses: $2,946. **Additional information:** Diploma programs: $16,850-$20,282, books and supplies $280. Associate programs: $25,250, books and supplies $420.

Financial aid. Need-based: Need-based aid available for part-time students. Work-study available nights, weekends and for part-time students.

Application procedures. Admission: No deadline. $25 fee. Application must be submitted on paper. Admission notification on a rolling basis. **Financial aid:** No deadline. FAFSA required. Applicants notified on a rolling basis.

Academics. Special study options: Distance learning. **Credit/placement by examination:** AP, CLEP, institutional tests. **Support services:** Tutoring.

Majors. Business: Business admin. **Computer sciences:** General. **Health services:** Medical secretary, office assistant.

Most popular majors. Business/marketing 10%, computer/information sciences 12%, health sciences 61%, legal studies 13%.

Technology on campus. 130 workstations in library, computer center. Online library available.

Student life. Freshman orientation: Mandatory. Preregistration for classes offered.

Student services. Adult student services, alcohol/substance abuse counseling, career counseling, financial aid counseling, placement for graduates. **Transfer:** Pre-admission transcript evaluation for new students.

Contact. Phone: (304) 345-2820
Darren Webster, Director of Admissions, West Virginia Junior College: Charleston, 1000 Virginia Street East, Charleston, WV 25301

West Virginia Northern Community College
Wheeling, West Virginia
www.wvncc.edu   CB code: 0674

- Public 2-year community and technical college
- Commuter campus in large town

General. Founded in 1972. Regionally accredited. **Enrollment:** 1,429 degree-seeking undergraduates; 584 non-degree-seeking students. **Degrees:** 309 associate awarded. **Location:** 45 miles from Pittsburgh. **Calendar:** Semester, limited summer session. **Full-time faculty:** 59 total; 8% have terminal degrees, 5% minority, 66% women. **Part-time faculty:** 111 total; 5% have terminal degrees, 55% women.

Student profile. Among degree-seeking undergraduates, 349 enrolled as first-time, first-year students.

Part-time:	43%	Women:	68%
Out-of-state:	23%		

Transfer out. Colleges most students transferred to 2015: West Liberty State College, Wheeling Jesuit University, West Virginia University, Bethany College, Ohio Eastern University.

Basis for selection. Open admission, but selective for some programs. Applicants to health science programs must meet all general admission criteria for the college, complete a separate Health Science application (including application fee), and provide official copies of their high school transcript and any prior college transcripts. Selection of applicants is a continuous process. Early application is recommended. **Home schooled:** May be required to submit written verification of subject mastery.

High school preparation. Strong science and math background recommended for health science applicants.

Two-Year Colleges

2015-2016 Annual costs. Tuition/fees: $3,275; $9,875 out-of-state.

Financial aid. Need-based: Need-based aid available for part-time students. Work-study available nights, weekends and for part-time students.

Application procedures. Admission: No deadline. No application fee. Admission notification on a rolling basis. **Financial aid:** Priority date 3/15; no closing date. FAFSA, institutional form required. Applicants notified on a rolling basis starting 3/10.

Academics. Special study options: Accelerated study, distance learning, dual enrollment of high school students, independent study, internships, liberal arts/career combination. 2+2 Programs in Business Administration, Criminal Justice, Pre-Psychology with Social Work, Elementary Education, Pre-Teacher Education, and Pre Secondary Teacher Education with West Liberty University. 2+2 Programs in Accounting/Business Administration, Mental Health and Human Services, Social Work with Franciscan University of Steubenville. 2+2 Program in Computer Information Tech with Wheeling Jesuit University. 2+2 Program in Social Work with WVU. License preparation in nursing. **Credit/placement by examination:** AP, CLEP, institutional tests. 45 credit hours maximum toward associate degree. **Support services:** Learning center, remedial instruction, study skills assistance, tutoring.

Majors. Business: General, administrative services. **Computer sciences:** Programming. **Engineering:** Robotics. **Health services:** Health information technology, medical assistant, medical radiologic technology/radiation therapy, nursing (RN), respiratory therapy technology, surgical technology. **Human services:** Social work. **Liberal arts:** Arts/sciences. **Protective services:** Police science.

Most popular majors. Business/marketing 21%, computer/information sciences 15%, engineering/engineering technologies 27%, legal studies 8%, liberal arts 78%, personal/culinary services 7%, public administration/social services 11%, security/protective services 9%, trade and industry 9%.

Technology on campus. 405 workstations in library, computer center, student center. Commuter students can connect to campus network. Online course registration, online library, wireless network available.

Student life. Freshman orientation: Available. Preregistration for classes offered. **Activities:** Student government, student newspaper, Community Outreach Opportunity Program (COOP).

Athletics. Intramural: Basketball, bowling, football (non-tackle), golf, soccer, softball, volleyball. **Team name:** Thundering Chickens.

Student services. Adult student services, career counseling, student employment services, financial aid counseling, placement for graduates, veterans' counselor. **Physically disabled:** Services for visually, speech, hearing impaired. **Transfer:** Transfer adviser, college fairs on campus for students transferring to 4-year colleges.

Contact. E-mail: admissions@mail.wvncc.edu
Phone: (304) 233-5900 ext. 8838 Fax: (304) 232-8187
Janet Fike, Vice President of Student Services/Director of Financial Aid, West Virginia Northern Community College, 1704 Market Street, Wheeling, WV 26003

West Virginia University at Parkersburg
Parkersburg, West Virginia   **CB member**
www.wvup.edu   **CB code: 5932**

❧ Public 2-year community college
❧ Commuter campus in large town

General. Founded in 1971. Regionally accredited. **Enrollment:** 3,800 degree-seeking undergraduates. **Degrees:** 261 bachelor's, 414 associate awarded. **Location:** 80 miles from Charleston; 110 miles from Columbus, Ohio. **Calendar:** Semester, limited summer session. **Full-time faculty:** 95 total. **Part-time faculty:** 185 total. **Class size:** 56% < 20, 40% 20-39, 2% 40-49, 1% 50-99.

Student profile.

Out-of-state: 3%   **25 or older:**   44%

Basis for selection. Open admission, but selective for some programs. Special requirements for nursing, surgical technology, paramedic science and bachelor's degree programs. SAT or ACT (ACT preferred) required but not used in admission decisions. Interview required for nursing program.

High school preparation. 16 units recommended. Recommended units include English 4, mathematics 3, social studies 4, science 3 (laboratory 2). Social studies recommendations may be fulfilled with history units.

2015-2016 Annual costs. Tuition/fees: $3,660; $13,020 out-of-state. Books/supplies: $1,000. Personal expenses: $1,400.

Financial aid. Need-based: Need-based aid available for part-time students. Work-study available nights, weekends and for part-time students. **Non-need-based:** Scholarships awarded for academics, leadership, state residency.

Application procedures. Admission: No deadline. No application fee. Admission notification on a rolling basis. **Financial aid:** Priority date 3/1; no closing date. FAFSA required. Applicants notified on a rolling basis; must reply within 2 week(s) of notification.

Academics. Special study options: Cooperative education, cross-registration, distance learning, dual enrollment of high school students, ESL, external degree, honors, independent study, internships, teacher certification program, weekend college. License preparation in nursing, paramedic. **Credit/placement by examination:** AP, CLEP, IB, institutional tests. **Support services:** Learning center, reduced course load, remedial instruction, study skills assistance, tutoring.

Majors. Business: Executive assistant, management information systems. **Communications:** Journalism. **Computer sciences:** Information systems. **Education:** Elementary, teacher assistance. **Health services:** Nursing (RN). **Liberal arts:** Arts/sciences. **Protective services:** Criminal justice.

Most popular majors. Business/marketing 20%, health sciences 16%, liberal arts 41%, security/protective services 6%.

Technology on campus. 435 workstations in library, computer center. Online course registration, online library, helpline, wireless network available.

Student life. Freshman orientation: Mandatory. Preregistration for classes offered. **Activities:** Choral groups, drama, literary magazine, music ensembles, musical theater, student government, student newspaper, reading association, environmental action group, multicultural awareness coalition, psychology club, Campus Christian Fellowship, criminal justice organization, Spark (community volunteers), student nursing association, American Welding Society.

Athletics. Intramural: Basketball, bowling, golf, softball, table tennis, volleyball. **Team name:** Riverhawks.

Student services. Adult student services, career counseling, services for economically disadvantaged, student employment services, financial aid counseling, on-campus daycare, personal counseling, placement for graduates, veterans' counselor. **Physically disabled:** Services for visually, speech, hearing impaired. **Transfer:** Pre-admission transcript evaluation for new students. Transfer adviser, college fairs on campus for students transferring to 4-year colleges.

Contact. E-mail: info@mail.wvup.edu
Phone: (304) 424-8220 Fax: (304) 424-8332
Christine Post, Assistant Dean for Enrollment Management, West Virginia University at Parkersburg, 300 Campus Drive, Parkersburg, WV 26104-8647

Wisconsin

Blackhawk Technical College
Janesville, Wisconsin
www.blackhawk.edu　　CB code: 7319

▶ Public 2-year technical college
▶ Commuter campus in small city

General. Founded in 1912. Regionally accredited. **Enrollment:** 2,249 degree-seeking undergraduates. **Degrees:** 278 associate awarded. **Location:** 75 miles from Milwaukee and Chicago. **Calendar:** Semester, limited summer session. **Full-time faculty:** 96 total; 6% have terminal degrees, 3% minority, 53% women. **Part-time faculty:** 271 total; less than 1% have terminal degrees, 5% minority, 45% women. **Class size:** 81% < 20, 19% 20-39.

Student profile. Among degree-seeking undergraduates, 100% enrolled in a vocational program, 3% already have a bachelor's degree or higher, 361 enrolled as first-time, first-year students.

Part-time: 58%　Women: 58%
Out-of-state: 1%

Basis for selection. Open admission, but selective for some programs. Applicants to nursing, radiography, sonography, and physical therapist assistant programs must meet additional testing and course requirements.

2015-2016 Annual costs. Tuition/fees: $4,045; $5,971 out-of-state. Per-credit charge: $128 in-state; $193 out-of-state. Books/supplies: $1,665. Personal expenses: $2,289. **Additional information:** Material fees vary by program: Minimum $4.50 per course. $10 per credit for online courses.

2014-2015 Financial aid. Need-based: 54% of total undergraduate aid awarded as scholarships/grants, 46% as loans/jobs. Need-based aid available for part-time students. Work-study available nights, weekends and for part-time students.

Application procedures. Admission: Priority date 9/1; no deadline. $30 fee. Admission notification on a rolling basis beginning on or about 10/1. **Financial aid:** Closing date 4/30. FAFSA required. Applicants notified on a rolling basis starting 3/15.

Academics. Special study options: Accelerated study, distance learning, dual enrollment of high school students, ESL, independent study, internships, student-designed major. License preparation in nursing, physical therapy, radiology. **Credit/placement by examination:** AP, CLEP. 30 credit hours maximum toward associate degree. **Support services:** GED preparation and test center, learning center, pre-admission summer program, reduced course load, remedial instruction, study skills assistance, tutoring, writing center.

Majors. Business: Accounting, administrative services, business admin, human resources, marketing. **Computer sciences:** Networking, web page design. **Education:** Early childhood. **Health services:** Clinical lab technology, medical secretary, nursing (RN), physical therapy assistant, radiologist assistant, sonography. **Protective services:** Firefighting, police science.

Most popular majors. Business/marketing 22%, computer/information sciences 7%, education 10%, engineering/engineering technologies 7%, health sciences 25%, personal/culinary services 7%, security/protective services 15%.

Technology on campus. 75 workstations in library, computer center, student center. Online course registration, helpline, wireless network available.

Student life. Freshman orientation: Available. Preregistration for classes offered. **Activities:** Campus ministries, student government.

Student services. Alcohol/substance abuse counseling, career counseling, services for economically disadvantaged, student employment services, financial aid counseling, minority student services, placement for graduates, veterans' counselor. **Physically disabled:** Services for visually, speech, hearing impaired.

Contact. Phone: (608) 757-7665 Fax: (608) 743-4407
Edward Robinson, Vice President Student Services, Blackhawk Technical College, PO Box 5009, Janesville, WI 53547-5009

Bryant & Stratton College: Milwaukee
Milwaukee, Wisconsin
www.bryantstratton.edu　　CB code: 3617

▶ For-profit 2-year business and junior college
▶ Commuter campus in very large city
▶ Application essay, interview required

General. Founded in 1854. Regionally accredited. **Enrollment:** 1,266 degree-seeking undergraduates. **Degrees:** 16 bachelor's, 71 associate awarded. **Location:** 75 miles from Chicago. **Calendar:** Trimester, extensive summer session. **Full-time faculty:** 53 total. **Part-time faculty:** 155 total. **Class size:** 75% < 20, 25% 20-39.

Basis for selection. School achievement record, test scores, interview important. SAT/ACT scores can take place of school's entrance exam.

2015-2016 Annual costs. Tuition/fees: $17,190. Per-credit charge: $573. Books/supplies: $750. **Additional information:** Tuition and fees may vary by program.

Financial aid. All financial aid based on need. Work-study available nights, weekends and for part-time students.

Application procedures. Admission: Closing date 9/22. $35 fee. Admission notification on a rolling basis. **Financial aid:** Closing date 9/22. FAFSA required. Applicants notified on a rolling basis; must reply within 2 week(s) of notification.

Academics. Special study options: Distance learning, double major, internships. License preparation on campus provided for Medical Coding and Certified Secretary, and Medical Assisting (exam given on campus). Bachelor's degree programs available on campus. **Credit/placement by examination:** AP, CLEP, institutional tests. 30 credit hours maximum toward associate degree. **Support services:** Reduced course load, remedial instruction, study skills assistance, tutoring.

Majors. Business: General, accounting, administrative services. **Computer sciences:** Information systems, information technology, systems analysis. **Health services:** Medical assistant, medical secretary, nursing (RN). **Protective services:** Law enforcement admin. **Visual/performing arts:** Graphic design.

Most popular majors. Business/marketing 45%, computer/information sciences 31%, health sciences 22%.

Technology on campus. 100 workstations in library, computer center.

Student life. Freshman orientation: Mandatory. Preregistration for classes offered. **Housing:** Nearby dormitories available through St. Catherine's Residence for Women. **Activities:** Student government, student newspaper, Association for Information Technology Professionals, Collegiate Secretaries International, Allied Health Association, Phi Beta Lambda, student board.

Athletics. Team name: Bobcats.

Student services. Career counseling, student employment services, financial aid counseling, personal counseling, placement for graduates, veterans' counselor. **Transfer:** Re-entry adviser, pre-admission transcript evaluation for new students. Transfer adviser for students transferring to 4-year colleges.

Contact. Phone: (414) 276-5200 Fax: (414) 276-3930
Rick Hubbard, Director of Admissions, Bryant & Stratton College: Milwaukee, 310 West Wisconsin Avenue, Suite 500, Milwaukee, WI 53203

Chippewa Valley Technical College
Eau Claire, Wisconsin
www.cvtc.edu　　CB code: 0786

▶ Public 2-year technical college
▶ Commuter campus in small city

General. Founded in 1912. Regionally accredited. **Enrollment:** 4,197 degree-seeking undergraduates; 1,820 non-degree-seeking students. **Degrees:** 948 associate awarded. **Location:** 90 miles from Minneapolis-St. Paul. **Calendar:** Semester, limited summer session. **Special facilities:** Health education center, NanoRite center, energy education center. **Partnerships:** Formal partnerships with University of Wisconsin Family Medicine Clinic, University of Wisconsin-Marquette, University of Wisconsin-Stout, University of Wisconsin Eau Claire, UW-SysNet, Wisconsin Indianhead Technical College, Lakeland College, and many other companies and agencies.

Student profile. Among degree-seeking undergraduates, 11% enrolled in a transfer program, 878 enrolled as first-time, first-year students, 727 transferred in from other institutions.

Part-time:	53%	25 or older:	41%
Women:	59%		

Transfer out. Colleges most students transferred to 2015: University of Wisconsin Eau Claire, University of Wisconsin Stout, University of Wisconsin River Falls.

Basis for selection. Open admission, but selective for some programs. Additional testing, course, and GPA requirements for applicants to nursing, dental hygiene, radiography, surgical technologist, medical assistant, physical therapist assistant, pharmacy technician, renal dialysis technician, architectural structural design, manufacturing engineering technologist, nano engineering technology, electro-mechanical technology, paramedic, firemedic. **Adult students:** SAT/ACT scores not required.

High school preparation. Algebra and science requirements for some degree programs.

2015-2016 Annual costs. Tuition/fees: $4,102; $6,028 out-of-state. Per-credit charge: $128 in-state; $193 out-of-state.

2014-2015 Financial aid. Need-based: Need-based aid available for part-time students. Work-study available nights, weekends and for part-time students.

Application procedures. Admission: No deadline. $30 fee, may be waived for applicants with need. Admission notification on a rolling basis. **Financial aid:** Priority date 3/15; no closing date. FAFSA required. Applicants notified on a rolling basis starting 4/30; must reply within 2 week(s) of notification.

Academics. Special study options: Distance learning, double major, dual enrollment of high school students, ESL, external degree, independent study, internships, liberal arts/career combination, student-designed major. License preparation in dental hygiene, nursing, paramedic, physical therapy, radiology. **Credit/placement by examination:** AP, CLEP, institutional tests. 34 credit hours maximum toward associate degree. 50% of semester hours needed for degree may be earned as credit by examination. **Support services:** GED preparation and test center, learning center, reduced course load, remedial instruction, study skills assistance, tutoring. Supplemental instruction.

Majors. Business: Accounting, administrative services, business admin, human resources, marketing, operations. **Computer sciences:** Networking, programming. **Education:** Early childhood. **Health services:** Clinical lab technology, dental hygiene, EMT paramedic, health information technology, medical radiologic technology/radiation therapy, nursing (RN), physical therapy assistant, respiratory therapy technology, sonography, substance abuse counseling. **Liberal arts:** Arts/sciences. **Protective services:** Police science.

Most popular majors. Business/marketing 27%, computer/information sciences 8%, engineering/engineering technologies 9%, health sciences 40%, security/protective services 8%.

Technology on campus. 1,750 workstations in library, computer center, student center. Commuter students can connect to campus network. Online course registration, online library, helpline, repair service, wireless network available.

Student life. Freshman orientation: Mandatory. Preregistration for classes offered. **Activities:** Student government, student newspaper, Student Impact, Diversity Student Organization, Pride Alliance.

Student services. Career counseling, services for economically disadvantaged, student employment services, financial aid counseling, health services, minority student services, personal counseling, placement for graduates, veterans' counselor. **Physically disabled:** Services for visually, speech, hearing impaired. **Transfer:** Pre-admission transcript evaluation for new students. Transfer center, college fairs on campus for students transferring to 4-year colleges.

Contact. E-mail: infocenter@cvtc.edu
Phone: (715) 833-6200 Toll-free number: (800) 547-2882
Fax: (715) 833-6470
Paige Wegner, Director of Enrollment Services, Chippewa Valley Technical College, 620 West Clairemont Avenue, Eau Claire, WI 54701-6162

College of Menominee Nation
Keshena, Wisconsin
www.menominee.edu   CB code: 3974

▸ Private 2-year community college
▸ Commuter campus in rural community

General. Regionally accredited. **Enrollment:** 661 undergraduates. **Degrees:** 11 bachelor's, 37 associate awarded. **Location:** 150 miles from Madison, 35 miles from Green Bay. **Calendar:** Semester, limited summer session. **Full-time faculty:** 31 total. **Part-time faculty:** 22 total. **Class size:** 77% < 20, 23% 20-39.

Transfer out. Colleges most students transferred to 2015: University of Wisconsin-Green Bay, University of Wisconsin-Oshkosh, Silver Lake College.

Basis for selection. Open admission, but selective for some programs. ACCUPLACER required of all students for placement. **Home schooled:** Must present state certification of completion of requirements. **Learning Disabled:** Students should meet with disability adviser upon registration.

2015-2016 Annual costs. Tuition/fees: $7,600. Room/board: $6,800. Books/supplies: $846.

Financial aid. All financial aid based on need. Need-based aid available for part-time students. Work-study available nights, weekends and for part-time students.

Application procedures. Admission: Closing date 8/30 (receipt date). No application fee. Admission notification on a rolling basis. **Financial aid:** Priority date 4/15; no closing date. FAFSA required. Applicants notified on a rolling basis.

Academics. Some courses are offered off-site via broadcasting. **Special study options:** Double major, independent study, internships, liberal arts/career combination, teacher certification program, weekend college. Bachelor's degree programs available on campus. **Credit/placement by examination:** AP, CLEP, institutional tests. **Support services:** Learning center, reduced course load, remedial instruction, study skills assistance, tutoring, writing center.

Majors. Biology: General. **Business:** Accounting, administrative services, business admin, office/clerical. **Computer sciences:** General. **Conservation:** General. **Education:** Early childhood, kindergarten/preschool. **Health services:** Nursing (RN), prenursing, substance abuse counseling. **Human services:** General. **Liberal arts:** Arts/sciences. **Math:** General. **Social sciences:** General.

Most popular majors. Business/marketing 20%, education 19%, health sciences 19%, liberal arts 26%.

Technology on campus. 65 workstations in library, computer center. Commuter students can connect to campus network. Online library, wireless network available.

Student life. Freshman orientation: Mandatory. Preregistration for classes offered. Held for 3 hours approximately 1 week prior to classes. **Activities:** Student government, Circle K, Young Democrats.

Student services. Adult student services, alcohol/substance abuse counseling, career counseling, services for economically disadvantaged, financial aid counseling, minority student services, personal counseling, veterans' counselor. **Physically disabled:** Services for visually, speech, hearing impaired. **Transfer:** Pre-admission transcript evaluation for new students. College fairs on campus for students transferring to 4-year colleges.

Contact. E-mail: tjames@menominee.edu
Phone: (715) 799-5600 ext. 3053
Toll-free number: (800) 567-2344 ext. 3053 Fax: (715) 799-4392
Tessa James, Admissions and Enrollment Manager, College of Menominee Nation, N 172 State Highway 47/55, Keshena, WI 54135-1179

Fox Valley Technical College
Appleton, Wisconsin   CB member
www.fvtc.edu   CB code: 0747

▸ Public 2-year technical college
▸ Commuter campus in small city

General. Founded in 1967. Regionally accredited. **Enrollment:** 6,621 degree-seeking undergraduates; 4,190 non-degree-seeking students. **Degrees:**

1,089 associate awarded. **Location:** 100 miles from Milwaukee. **Calendar:** Semester, limited summer session. **Full-time faculty:** 319 total; 42% women. **Part-time faculty:** 770 total; 47% women. **Special facilities:** Public safety training center.

Student profile. Among degree-seeking undergraduates, 983 enrolled as first-time, first-year students.

Part-time:	63%	Hispanic/Latino:	4%
Women:	50%	Native American:	1%
African American:	3%	Multi-racial, non-Hispanic:	1%
Asian American:	5%	25 or older:	41%

Transfer out. Colleges most students transferred to 2015: University of Wisconsin Oshkosh.

Basis for selection. Open admission, but selective for some programs.

2015-2016 Annual costs. Tuition/fees: $4,373; $6,299 out-of-state. Per-credit charge: $128 in-state; $193 out-of-state. Books/supplies: $1,742. Personal expenses: $1,918.

2014-2015 Financial aid. All financial aid based on need. 44% of total undergraduate aid awarded as scholarships/grants, 56% as loans/jobs. Need-based aid available for part-time students. Work-study available nights, weekends and for part-time students.

Application procedures. **Admission:** Closing date 8/15 (receipt date). $30 fee, may be waived for applicants with need. Admission notification on a rolling basis. **Financial aid:** Priority date 4/15; no closing date. FAFSA required. Applicants notified on a rolling basis.

Academics. **Special study options:** Accelerated study, distance learning, double major, dual enrollment of high school students, ESL, internships, student-designed major, study abroad. License preparation in aviation, dental hygiene, nursing, occupational therapy, paramedic, physical therapy. **Credit/placement by examination:** AP, CLEP, institutional tests. 45 credit hours maximum toward associate degree. **Support services:** GED preparation and test center, learning center, reduced course load, remedial instruction, study skills assistance, tutoring, writing center.

Majors. **Business:** Accounting, administrative services, banking/financial services, business admin, event planning, hospitality admin, human resources, logistics, marketing, office management. **Communications:** Radio/TV. **Communications technology:** Graphics. **Computer sciences:** Networking, programming, support specialist, webmaster. **Conservation:** General. **Education:** Early childhood. **English:** Technical writing. **General:** Site management. **Health services:** Dental hygiene, EMT paramedic, health information technology, nursing (RN), occupational therapy assistant, office admin, substance abuse counseling. **Protective services:** Firefighting, forensics, forest/wildland firefighting, police science. **Visual/performing arts:** Interior design.

Technology on campus. 250 workstations in library, computer center, student center. Commuter students can connect to campus network. Online course registration, online library, helpline, repair service, wireless network available.

Student life. **Freshman orientation:** Mandatory. Preregistration for classes offered. Held on various dates 2 months prior to beginning of semester. **Activities:** Student government, student newspaper, over 40 curriculum-related clubs.

Athletics. NJCAA. **Intercollegiate:** Basketball, volleyball W. **Intramural:** Basketball, football (non-tackle), soccer, softball, table tennis, volleyball. **Team name:** Foxes.

Student services. Adult student services, alcohol/substance abuse counseling, career counseling, services for economically disadvantaged, student employment services, financial aid counseling, health services, minority student services, on-campus daycare, personal counseling, placement for graduates, veterans' counselor, women's services. **Physically disabled:** Services for visually, speech, hearing impaired.

Contact. E-mail: admissions@fvtc.edu
Phone: (920) 735-5645 Toll-free number: (800) 735-3882
Fax: (920) 735-2484
Lisa Schmid, Director Enrollment Management, Fox Valley Technical College, 1825 North Bluemound Drive, Appleton, WI 54912-2277

Gateway Technical College
Kenosha, Wisconsin
www.gtc.edu

CB member
CB code: 0761

- Public 2-year technical college
- Commuter campus in small city

General. Founded in 1911. Regionally accredited. Campuses in Elkhorn, Kenosha and Racine. **Enrollment:** 6,291 degree-seeking undergraduates. **Degrees:** 644 associate awarded. **Location:** 30 miles from Milwaukee, 60 miles from Chicago. **Calendar:** Semester, limited summer session. **Full-time faculty:** 300 total. **Part-time faculty:** 100 total.

Basis for selection. Open admission, but selective for some programs. **Home schooled:** Letter from student confirming completion of the equivalent of 12th grade through a home-schooling program.

High school preparation. Chemistry and biology required for nursing and other health-care program applicants.

2015-2016 Annual costs. Tuition/fees: $4,176; $6,102 out-of-state. Per-credit charge: $128 in-state; $193 out-of-state. Books/supplies: $910. Personal expenses: $1,461.

Financial aid. **Need-based:** Need-based aid available for part-time students. Work-study available nights, weekends and for part-time students. **Non-need-based:** Scholarships awarded for state residency.

Application procedures. **Admission:** No deadline. $30 fee. Admission notification on a rolling basis. **Financial aid:** Priority date 7/1; no closing date. FAFSA, institutional form required. Applicants notified on a rolling basis starting 5/1; must reply within 2 week(s) of notification.

Academics. **Special study options:** Accelerated study, cooperative education, cross-registration, distance learning, double major, dual enrollment of high school students, ESL, honors, independent study, internships, student-designed major. License preparation in aviation, nursing, paramedic, physical therapy, radiology. **Credit/placement by examination:** AP, CLEP, institutional tests. 48 credit hours maximum toward associate degree. Institutional biology and chemistry test required for nursing applicants. **Support services:** GED preparation and test center, learning center, remedial instruction, tutoring.

Majors. **Business:** Accounting, administrative services, hotel/motel admin, marketing, operations. **Communications technology:** Radio/TV. **Computer sciences:** Networking, programming, support specialist, webmaster. **Education:** Early childhood, teacher assistance. **English:** Technical writing. **Health services:** Clinical lab technology, health information technology, medical radiologic technology/radiation therapy, nursing (RN), physical therapy assistant, surgical technology. **Protective services:** Firefighting, police science. **Visual/performing arts:** Graphic design, interior design. **Work/family studies:** Child care management.

Technology on campus. 270 workstations in library, computer center, student center. Online course registration, helpline, wireless network available.

Student life. **Freshman orientation:** Available. Preregistration for classes offered. **Activities:** Radio station, student government, student newspaper, A wide variety of occupationally-oriented and community-related organizations.

Student services. Adult student services, alcohol/substance abuse counseling, career counseling, services for economically disadvantaged, student employment services, financial aid counseling, minority student services, personal counseling, placement for graduates, veterans' counselor. **Physically disabled:** Services for visually, speech, hearing impaired. **Transfer:** Transfer adviser, college fairs on campus for students transferring to 4-year colleges.

Contact. E-mail: admissionsgroup@gtc.edu
Phone: (262) 741-8168 Toll-free number: (800) 247-7122
Fax: (262) 741-8115
Susan Roberts, Director of Admissions, Gateway Technical College, 400 County Road H, Elkhorn, WI 53121

Globe University: Appleton
Grand Chute, Wisconsin
www.globeuniversity.edu

- For-profit 2-year career college
- Commuter campus in small city
- Interview required

General. Regionally accredited; also accredited by ACICS. **Enrollment:** 203 undergraduates. **Degrees:** 2 bachelor's, 50 associate awarded. **Location:** 3 miles from downtown. **Calendar:** Quarter, extensive summer session. **Full-time faculty:** 4 total. **Part-time faculty:** 4 total. **Partnerships:** Formal partnership with Microsoft Developers Network Academic Alliance (MSDNAA).

Basis for selection. Open admission. **Adult students:** SAT/ACT scores not required.

2015-2016 Annual costs. Tuition/fees: $18,702. Books/supplies: $1,260.

Financial aid. Need-based: Need-based aid available for part-time students. Work-study available nights, weekends and for part-time students.

Application procedures. Admission: No deadline. $50 fee. Admission notification on a rolling basis. **Financial aid:** No deadline. FAFSA, institutional form required. Applicants notified on a rolling basis starting 7/1; must reply within 2 week(s) of notification.

Academics. Special study options: Distance learning, independent study, internships, liberal arts/career combination. **Credit/placement by examination:** AP, CLEP. **Support services:** Remedial instruction, study skills assistance, tutoring, writing center.

Majors. Business: Accounting, business admin. **Health services:** Massage therapy, medical assistant, medical secretary, veterinary technology/assistant. **Protective services:** Law enforcement admin.

Most popular majors. Business/marketing 7%, health sciences 84%.

Technology on campus. 60 workstations in library, computer center, student center. Commuter students can connect to campus network. Online library, helpline, student web hosting, wireless network available.

Student life. Freshman orientation: Mandatory. Preregistration for classes offered. Day and evening sessions held the week prior to classes starting. **Activities:** Literary magazine.

Student services. Career counseling, student employment services, financial aid counseling, placement for graduates. **Transfer:** Re-entry adviser for new students.

Contact. Phone: (920) 364-1100 Toll-free number: (877) 440-1110 Gina Havlovick, Director of Admissions, Globe University: Appleton, 5045 West Grande Market Drive, Grand Chute, WI 54913

Globe University: Eau Claire
Eau Claire, Wisconsin
www.globeuniversity.edu

- For-profit 2-year career college
- Commuter campus in small city
- Interview required

General. Regionally accredited; also accredited by ACICS. **Enrollment:** 153 undergraduates. **Degrees:** 11 bachelor's, 44 associate awarded. **Location:** 2 miles from downtown. **Calendar:** Quarter, extensive summer session. **Partnerships:** Formal partnerships with Microsoft Developers Network Academic Alliance (MSDNAA).

Basis for selection. Open admission. **Adult students:** SAT/ACT scores not required.

2015-2016 Annual costs. Tuition/fees: $18,702. Books/supplies: $1,260.

Financial aid. Need-based: Need-based aid available for part-time students. Work-study available nights, weekends and for part-time students.

Application procedures. Admission: No deadline. $50 fee. Admission notification on a rolling basis. **Financial aid:** No deadline. FAFSA, institutional form required. Applicants notified on a rolling basis starting 7/1; must reply within 2 week(s) of notification.

Academics. Special study options: Distance learning, independent study, internships, liberal arts/career combination. **Credit/placement by examination:** AP, CLEP. **Support services:** Remedial instruction, study skills assistance, tutoring, writing center.

Majors. Business: Accounting, business admin, marketing. **Computer sciences:** Networking. **Health services:** Massage therapy, medical assistant, medical secretary, veterinary technology/assistant. **Protective services:** Law enforcement admin.

Most popular majors. Business/marketing 14%, health sciences 68%, legal studies 8%, security/protective services 12%.

Technology on campus. 60 workstations in library, computer center, student center. Commuter students can connect to campus network. Online library, helpline, student web hosting, wireless network available.

Student life. Freshman orientation: Mandatory. Preregistration for classes offered. Day and evening sessions held the week prior to classes starting. **Activities:** Literary magazine.

Student services. Career counseling, student employment services, financial aid counseling, placement for graduates. **Transfer:** Re-entry adviser for new students.

Contact. Phone: (715) 855-6600 Toll-free number: (877) 530-8080 Wesley Escondo, Campus Director, Globe University: Eau Claire, 4955 Bullis Farm Road, Eau Claire, WI 54701

Globe University: La Crosse
Onalaska, Wisconsin
www.globeuniversity.edu

- For-profit 2-year career college
- Commuter campus in large town
- Interview required

General. Regionally accredited; also accredited by ACICS. **Enrollment:** 178 undergraduates. **Degrees:** 16 bachelor's, 60 associate awarded. **Calendar:** Quarter, extensive summer session. **Partnerships:** Formal partnerships with Microsoft Developers Network Academic Alliance (MSDNAA).

Basis for selection. Open admission. **Adult students:** SAT/ACT scores not required.

2015-2016 Annual costs. Tuition/fees: $18,702. Books/supplies: $1,260.

Financial aid. Need-based: Need-based aid available for part-time students. Work-study available nights, weekends and for part-time students.

Application procedures. Admission: No deadline. $50 fee. Admission notification on a rolling basis. **Financial aid:** No deadline. FAFSA, institutional form required. Applicants notified on a rolling basis starting 7/1; must reply within 2 week(s) of notification.

Academics. Special study options: Distance learning, independent study, internships, liberal arts/career combination. **Credit/placement by examination:** AP, CLEP. **Support services:** Remedial instruction, study skills assistance, tutoring, writing center.

Majors. Business: Accounting, business admin, marketing. **Computer sciences:** Networking. **Health services:** Massage therapy, medical assistant, medical secretary, veterinary technology/assistant. **Protective services:** Law enforcement admin.

Most popular majors. Business/marketing 10%, computer/information sciences 9%, health sciences 69%, legal studies 7%.

Technology on campus. 60 workstations in library, computer center, student center. Commuter students can connect to campus network. Online library, helpline, student web hosting, wireless network available.

Student life. Freshman orientation: Mandatory. Preregistration for classes offered. Day and evening sessions held the week prior to classes starting. **Activities:** Literary magazine.

Student services. Career counseling, student employment services, financial aid counseling, placement for graduates. **Transfer:** Re-entry adviser for new students.

Contact. E-mail: rkrueger@globeuniversity.edu
Phone: (608) 779-2600 Toll-free number: (877) 540-8777 Rachel Simonson, Director of Admissions, Globe University: La Crosse, 2651 Midwest Drive, Onalaska, WI 54650

Globe University: Madison East
Madison, Wisconsin
www.globeuniversity.edu

- For-profit 2-year career college
- Commuter campus in small city
- Interview required

General. Accredited by ACICS. **Enrollment:** 217 undergraduates. **Degrees:** 15 bachelor's, 65 associate awarded. **Calendar:** Quarter, extensive summer session. **Partnerships:** Formal partnerships with Microsoft Developers Network Academic Alliance (MSDNAA).

Basis for selection. Open admission. **Adult students:** SAT/ACT scores not required.

2015-2016 Annual costs. Tuition/fees: $18,702. Books/supplies: $1,260.

Financial aid. Need-based: Need-based aid available for part-time students. Work-study available nights, weekends and for part-time students.

Application procedures. Admission: No deadline. $50 fee. Admission notification on a rolling basis. **Financial aid:** No deadline. FAFSA, institutional form required. Applicants notified on a rolling basis starting 7/1; must reply within 2 week(s) of notification.

Academics. Special study options: Distance learning, independent study, internships, liberal arts/career combination. **Credit/placement by examination:** AP, CLEP. **Support services:** Remedial instruction, study skills assistance, tutoring, writing center.

Majors. Business: Accounting, business admin. **Computer sciences:** Networking. **Health services:** Massage therapy, medical assistant, medical secretary, veterinary technology/assistant. **Protective services:** Law enforcement admin. **Visual/performing arts:** Graphic design, music management.

Most popular majors. Business/marketing 11%, health sciences 59%, security/protective services 6%, visual/performing arts 17%.

Technology on campus. 60 workstations in library, computer center, student center. Commuter students can connect to campus network. Online library, helpline, student web hosting, wireless network available.

Student life. Freshman orientation: Mandatory. Preregistration for classes offered. Day and evening sessions available the week prior to classes starting. **Activities:** Literary magazine.

Student services. Career counseling, student employment services, financial aid counseling, placement for graduates. **Transfer:** Re-entry adviser for new students.

Contact. E-mail: kgross@globeuniversity.edu
Phone: (608) 216-9400 Toll-free number: (877) 790-9494
Kristina Gross, Director of Admissions, Globe University: Madison East, 4901 Eastpark Boulevard, Madison, WI 53718

Globe University: Middleton
Middleton, Wisconsin
www.globeuniversity.edu

▸ For-profit 2-year career college
▸ Commuter campus in large town
▸ Interview required

General. Regionally accredited; also accredited by ACICS. **Enrollment:** 182 undergraduates. **Degrees:** 11 bachelor's, 61 associate awarded. **Location:** 8 miles from downtown. **Calendar:** Quarter, extensive summer session. **Partnerships:** Formal partnerships with Microsoft Developers Network Academic Alliance (MSDNAA).

Basis for selection. Open admission. **Adult students:** SAT/ACT scores not required.

2015-2016 Annual costs. Tuition/fees: $18,702; $26,352 out-of-state. Books/supplies: $1,260.

Financial aid. Need-based: Need-based aid available for part-time students. Work-study available nights, weekends and for part-time students.

Application procedures. Admission: No deadline. $50 fee. Admission notification on a rolling basis. **Financial aid:** No deadline. FAFSA, institutional form required. Applicants notified on a rolling basis starting 7/1; must reply within 2 week(s) of notification.

Academics. Special study options: Distance learning, independent study, internships, liberal arts/career combination. **Credit/placement by examination:** AP, CLEP. **Support services:** Remedial instruction, study skills assistance, tutoring, writing center.

Majors. Business: Accounting, business admin, marketing. **Computer sciences:** Networking. **Health services:** Massage therapy, medical assistant, medical secretary, veterinary technology/assistant. **Parks/recreation:** Physical fitness technician. **Protective services:** Law enforcement admin.

Most popular majors. Business/marketing 19%, health sciences 59%, legal studies 6%, security/protective services 9%.

Technology on campus. 60 workstations in library, computer center, student center. Commuter students can connect to campus network. Online library, helpline, student web hosting, wireless network available.

Student life. Freshman orientation: Mandatory. Preregistration for classes offered. Day and evening sessions held the week prior to classes starting. **Activities:** Literary magazine.

Student services. Career counseling, student employment services, financial aid counseling, placement for graduates. **Transfer:** Re-entry adviser for new students.

Contact. Phone: (877) 830-6999
Laurie Anne Caamal, Director of Admissions, Globe University: Middleton, 1345 Deming Way, Middleton, WI 53562

Globe University: Wausau
Rothschild, Wisconsin
www.globeuniversity.edu

▸ For-profit 2-year career college
▸ Commuter campus in small town
▸ Interview required

General. Regionally accredited; also accredited by ACICS. **Enrollment:** 122 undergraduates. **Degrees:** 8 bachelor's, 43 associate awarded. **Calendar:** Quarter, extensive summer session. **Partnerships:** Formal partnerships with Microsoft Developers Network Academic Alliance (MSDNAA).

Basis for selection. Open admission. **Adult students:** SAT/ACT scores not required.

2015-2016 Annual costs. Tuition/fees: $18,702. Books/supplies: $1,260.

Financial aid. Need-based: Need-based aid available for part-time students. Work-study available nights, weekends and for part-time students.

Application procedures. Admission: No deadline. $50 fee. Admission notification on a rolling basis. **Financial aid:** No deadline. FAFSA, institutional form required. Applicants notified on a rolling basis starting 7/1; must reply within 2 week(s) of notification.

Academics. Special study options: Distance learning, independent study, internships, liberal arts/career combination. **Credit/placement by examination:** AP, CLEP. **Support services:** Remedial instruction, study skills assistance, tutoring, writing center.

Majors. Business: Accounting, business admin, marketing. **Computer sciences:** Networking. **Health services:** Massage therapy, medical assistant, medical secretary, veterinary technology/assistant. **Protective services:** Law enforcement admin.

Most popular majors. Business/marketing 19%, health sciences 66%, security/protective services 10%.

Technology on campus. 60 workstations in library, computer center, student center. Commuter students can connect to campus network. Online library, helpline, student web hosting, wireless network available.

Student life. Freshman orientation: Mandatory. Preregistration for classes offered. Day and evening sessions held the week prior to classes starting. **Activities:** Literary magazine.

Student services. Career counseling, student employment services, financial aid counseling, placement for graduates. **Transfer:** Re-entry adviser for new students.

Contact. Phone: (715) 301-1300 Toll-free number: (877) 323-1313
Andrea Palas, Director of Admissions, Globe University: Wausau, 1480 Country Road XX, Rothschild, WI 54474

Lac Courte Oreilles Ojibwa Community College
Hayward, Wisconsin
www.lco.edu   **CB code: 7351**

▸ Public 2-year community college
▸ Commuter campus in small town

General. Regionally accredited. Located on the Lac Courte Oreilles Reservation. **Enrollment:** 309 degree-seeking undergraduates; 62 non-degree-seeking students. **Degrees:** 61 associate awarded. **Calendar:** Semester, limited summer session. **Full-time faculty:** 17 total. **Part-time faculty:** 34 total.

Student profile. Among degree-seeking undergraduates, 54 enrolled as first-time, first-year students, 13 transferred in from other institutions.

Part-time:	51%	Native American:	80%
Women:	66%	Multi-racial, non-Hispanic:	1%
African American:	2%	25 or older:	60%

Transfer out. 2% of students enrolled in the transfer program go on to 4-year colleges.

Basis for selection. Open admission. **Home schooled:** State high school equivalency certificate required.

2015-2016 Annual costs. Tuition/fees: $5,700. Per-credit charge: $190. Books/supplies: $300.

Financial aid. Need-based: Work-study available nights, weekends and for part-time students.

Application procedures. Admission: No deadline. $10 fee, may be waived for applicants with need. Application must be submitted on paper. Admission notification on a rolling basis. **Financial aid:** No deadline. FAFSA required. Applicants notified on a rolling basis.

Academics. Special study options: Cooperative education, distance learning, double major, independent study, liberal arts/career combination. **Credit/placement by examination:** AP, CLEP. 6 credit hours maximum toward associate degree. **Support services:** GED preparation and test center, remedial instruction, study skills assistance, tutoring.

Majors. Area/ethnic studies: Native American. **Business:** Accounting, business admin, logistics, office management, sales/distribution, small business admin. **Education:** Early childhood. **Health services:** Medical assistant, nursing (RN), office admin. **Human services:** Social work. **Liberal arts:** Arts/sciences. **Work/family studies:** Food/nutrition.

Most popular majors. Business/marketing 11%, health sciences 8%, liberal arts 8%, natural resources/environmental science 8%.

Technology on campus. Wireless network available.

Student life. Freshman orientation: Mandatory. Preregistration for classes offered. **Activities:** Drama, student government.

Student services. Career counseling, financial aid counseling. **Transfer:** Transfer center, college fairs on campus for students transferring to 4-year colleges.

Contact. Phone: (715) 634-4790 ext. 104 Fax: (715) 634-5049
Annette Wiggins, Registrar, Lac Courte Oreilles Ojibwa Community College, 13466 West Trepania Road, Hayward, WI 54843

Lakeshore Technical College
Cleveland, Wisconsin — CB member
www.gotoltc.edu — CB code: 0618

- Public 2-year technical college
- Commuter campus in rural community

General. Founded in 1912. Regionally accredited. **Enrollment:** 2,138 degree-seeking undergraduates. **Degrees:** 354 associate awarded. **Location:** 15 miles from Sheboygan, 65 miles from Milwaukee. **Calendar:** Continuous, limited summer session. **Full-time faculty:** 111 total. **Part-time faculty:** 277 total. **Special facilities:** Five wind turbines, rescue tower, emergency vehicle obstacle driving course, culinary facilities, environmental campus. **Partnerships:** Formal partnerships with all public schools and employers in Manitowoc and Sheboygan counties for Career Prep, such as Snap-On tool.

Student profile.

| Out-of-state: | 1% | 25 or older: | 75% |

Transfer out. Colleges most students transferred to 2015: Silver Lake College, Lakeland College, Marian College.

Basis for selection. Open admission, but selective for some programs. All health-related, public safety and child care programs require background checks and physical examinations. **Home schooled:** State high school equivalency certificate required.

2015-2016 Annual costs. Tuition/fees: $4,064; $5,990 out-of-state. Per-credit charge: $128 in-state; $193 out-of-state. Books/supplies: $1,742. Personal expenses: $2,002.

2014-2015 Financial aid. All financial aid based on need. 64% of total undergraduate aid awarded as scholarships/grants, 36% as loans/jobs. Need-based aid available for part-time students. Work-study available nights, weekends and for part-time students.

Application procedures. Admission: No deadline. $30 fee, may be waived for applicants with need. Admission notification on a rolling basis. **Financial aid:** Priority date 6/1; no closing date. FAFSA, institutional form required. Applicants notified on a rolling basis starting 6/1; must reply within 3 week(s)' of notification.

Academics. Special study options: Accelerated study, cooperative education, cross-registration, distance learning, double major, dual enrollment of high school students, ESL, exchange student, honors, independent study, internships, student-designed major. License preparation in nursing, paramedic, real estate. **Credit/placement by examination:** AP, CLEP, institutional tests. **Support services:** GED preparation and test center, learning center, pre-admission summer program, reduced course load, remedial instruction, study skills assistance, tutoring.

Majors. Business: Accounting, administrative services, business admin, hotel/motel admin, human resources, logistics, marketing, operations. **Computer sciences:** Computer graphics, networking, support specialist, web page design. **Education:** Early childhood. **Health services:** Clinical lab technology, dental hygiene, EMT paramedic, medical radiologic technology/radiation therapy, nursing (RN), pharmacy assistant, radiologic technology/medical imaging. **Parks/recreation:** Golf management. **Protective services:** Firefighting, police science.

Most popular majors. Business/marketing 16%, computer/information sciences 7%, health sciences 9%.

Technology on campus. 950 workstations in library, computer center, student center. Online course registration, online library, helpline, wireless network available.

Student life. Freshman orientation: Available. Preregistration for classes offered. **Activities:** Student government, student newspaper.

Student services. Adult student services, alcohol/substance abuse counseling, career counseling, services for economically disadvantaged, student employment services, financial aid counseling, health services, minority student services, on-campus daycare, personal counseling, placement for graduates, veterans' counselor. **Physically disabled:** Services for visually, speech, hearing impaired. **Transfer:** Re-entry adviser, pre-admission transcript evaluation for new students. Transfer adviser, college fairs on campus for students transferring to 4-year colleges.

Contact. E-mail: admissions@gotoltc.edu
Phone: (920) 693-1109 Toll-free number: (888) 468-6582
Fax: (920) 693-3561
Don Geiger, Director, Student Services, Lakeshore Technical College, 1290 North Avenue, Cleveland, WI 53015-9761

Madison Area Technical College
Madison, Wisconsin
www.madisoncollege.edu — CB code: 1536

- Public 2-year community and technical college
- Commuter campus in small city

General. Founded in 1912. Regionally accredited. 5 Madison locations and campuses in in Fort Atkinson, Portage, Reedsburg, and Watertown. **Enrollment:** 11,232 degree-seeking undergraduates. **Degrees:** 1,369 associate awarded. **Location:** 68 miles from Milwaukee. **Calendar:** Semester, limited summer session. **Full-time faculty:** 468 total. **Part-time faculty:** 1,224 total. **Special facilities:** Ingenuity Center, telepresence classrooms, satellite downlink.

Student profile.

| Out-of-state: | 2% | 25 or older: | 10% |

Transfer out. Colleges most students transferred to 2015: University of Wisconsin-Madison.

Basis for selection. Open admission, but selective for some programs. School achievement record, class rank, test scores considered for all health occupation programs.

High school preparation. High school academic subject requirements for health and technical programs.

2015-2016 Annual costs. Tuition/fees: $4,216; $6,104 out-of-state. Per-credit charge: $128 in-state; $193 out-of-state. Books/supplies: $760. Personal expenses: $1,340.

Financial aid. Need-based: Work-study available nights, weekends and for part-time students.

Application procedures. Admission: No deadline. $35 fee, may be waived for applicants with need. Admission notification on a rolling basis. Early application recommended for programs with limited enrollment. **Financial aid:** Closing date 4/15. FAFSA required. Applicants notified on a rolling basis starting 4/15.

Academics. College transfer program, advanced technical certificates, apprenticeships available. **Special study options:** Accelerated study, cross-registration, distance learning, dual enrollment of high school students, ESL, external degree, internships. Bachelor's degree programs available on campus. License preparation in nursing. **Credit/placement by examination:** AP, CLEP, institutional tests. 32 credit hours maximum toward associate degree. **Support services:** GED preparation, learning center, reduced course load, remedial instruction, study skills assistance, tutoring.

Majors. Business: Accounting, administrative services, business admin, communications, fashion, finance, hospitality admin, hospitality/recreation, human resources, insurance, office management, real estate, tourism/travel. **Communications technology:** Graphic/printing. **Computer sciences:** General, programming. **Health services:** Clinical lab technology, dental hygiene, EMT paramedic, health information management, medical assistant, medical radiologic technology/radiation therapy, medical secretary, mental health services, nursing (RN), occupational therapy assistant, respiratory therapy technology, veterinary technology/assistant. **Liberal arts:** Arts/sciences. **Protective services:** Police science. **Visual/performing arts:** Commercial photography, commercial/advertising art, design, interior design. **Work/family studies:** Child care management, food/nutrition.

Most popular majors. Business/marketing 28%, computer/information sciences 7%, family/consumer sciences 6%, health sciences 19%, trade and industry 12%, visual/performing arts 7%.

Technology on campus. 470 workstations in library, computer center.

Student life. Freshman orientation: Available. Preregistration for classes offered. **Policies:** Student life department promotes a variety of cultural diversity and activities and plays an active role in student government activities. **Activities:** Jazz band, choral groups, drama, music ensembles, student government, student newspaper.

Athletics. NJCAA. **Intercollegiate:** Baseball M, basketball, bowling, cross-country M, golf M, softball W, volleyball W, wrestling M. **Intramural:** Basketball, racquetball, soccer, swimming, table tennis, tennis, volleyball. **Team name:** Wolf Pack.

Student services. Career counseling, student employment services, health services, on-campus daycare, personal counseling, placement for graduates, veterans' counselor. **Physically disabled:** Services for visually, speech, hearing impaired. **Transfer:** Transfer adviser for students transferring to 4-year colleges.

Contact. Phone: (608) 246-6100 Toll-free number: (800) 322-6282 Fax: (608) 258-2329
Stephanie Dean, Admissions Administrator, Madison Area Technical College, 1701 Wright Street, Madison, WI 53704-2599

Madison Media Institute
Madison, Wisconsin
www.mediainstitute.edu   **CB member**

▸ For-profit 2-year visual arts and music college
▸ Large city
▸ Application essay, interview required

General. Accredited by ACCSC. **Enrollment:** 372 undergraduates. **Degrees:** 23 bachelor's, 131 associate awarded. **Calendar:** Trimester, extensive summer session. **Full-time faculty:** 25 total. **Part-time faculty:** 25 total.

Basis for selection. Open admission.

2015-2016 Annual costs. Books/supplies: $420.

Financial aid. Need-based: Work-study available nights, weekends and for part-time students.

Application procedures. Admission: No deadline. $30 fee. Admission notification on a rolling basis. **Financial aid:** No deadline.

Academics. Special study options: Accelerated study, internships. **Credit/placement by examination:** AP, CLEP. **Support services:** Tutoring.

Majors. Communications: Digital media. **Communications technology:** General, animation/special effects, photo/film/video, recording arts.

Technology on campus. 150 workstations in computer center.

Student life. Freshman orientation: Available. Preregistration for classes offered.

Student services. Transfer: Re-entry adviser, pre-admission transcript evaluation for new students. Transfer adviser for students transferring to 4-year colleges.

Contact. E-mail: mmi@madisonmedia.com
Toll-free number: (800) 236-4997
Steve Hutchings, Director of Admissions, Madison Media Institute, 2702 Agriculture Drive, Madison, WI 53718

Mid-State Technical College
Wisconsin Rapids, Wisconsin   **CB member**
www.mstc.edu   **CB code: 0635**

▸ Public 2-year technical college
▸ Commuter campus in large town

General. Founded in 1967. Regionally accredited. Branch campuses in Marshfield and Stevens Point, outreach center in Adams Friendship. **Enrollment:** 3,100 degree-seeking undergraduates. **Degrees:** 398 associate awarded. **Location:** 20 miles from Stevens Point, 115 miles from Madison. **Calendar:** Semester, limited summer session. **Full-time faculty:** 91 total; 10% have terminal degrees, 1% minority, 56% women. **Part-time faculty:** 131 total; 3% have terminal degrees, 2% minority, 53% women.

Student profile.

Out-of-state:	1%	25 or older: 50%

Basis for selection. Open admission, but selective for some programs. Students must take ACCUPLACER entrance exam for placement. Certain programs have additional admission requirements. **Home schooled:** Transcript of courses and grades required. Proof of completion of 12th grade required.

High school preparation. College-preparatory program recommended. Recommended units include English 4, mathematics 4, science 4 and computer science 1. Biology, anatomy, physiology, chemistry, medical terminology recommended for health programs. Information processing, general business, business law, economics, accounting recommended for business programs. Geometry, drafting, chemistry, advanced math recommended for technical and industrial programs.

2015-2016 Annual costs. Tuition/fees: $4,044; $5,970 out-of-state. Per-credit charge: $128 in-state; $193 out-of-state. Books/supplies: $1,036. Personal expenses: $1,774.

Financial aid. Need-based: Need-based aid available for part-time students. Work-study available nights, weekends and for part-time students. **Non-need-based:** Scholarships awarded for academics, leadership.

Application procedures. Admission: No deadline. $30 fee, may be waived for applicants with need. Admission notification on a rolling basis. **Financial aid:** Priority date 4/15; no closing date. FAFSA required. Applicants notified on a rolling basis starting 5/30; must reply within 2 week(s) of notification.

Academics. Special study options: Accelerated study, distance learning, double major, dual enrollment of high school students, ESL, independent study, internships, student-designed major. Online programs. License preparation in nursing, paramedic. **Credit/placement by examination:** AP, CLEP, institutional tests. **Support services:** GED preparation and test center, learning center, reduced course load, remedial instruction, study skills assistance, tutoring.

Majors. Biology: Bioinformatics. **Business:** Accounting, administrative services, business admin, human resources, marketing, operations. **Computer sciences:** Networking, programming. **Conservation:** Urban forestry. **Education:** Early childhood. **Engineering:** Transportation. **Health services:** Clinical research coordinator, EMT paramedic, nursing (RN), respiratory therapy technology. **Physical sciences:** Atmospheric science. **Protective services:** Corrections, police science.

Most popular majors. Business/marketing 31%, computer/information sciences 11%, engineering/engineering technologies 8%, health sciences 22%, security/protective services 11%, trade and industry 11%.

Technology on campus. 600 workstations in library, computer center, student center. Online course registration, online library, helpline, wireless network available.

Student life. Freshman orientation: Available. Preregistration for classes offered. **Activities:** Student government, Association for Information Technology Professionals, automotive & diesel tech club, Campus Crusade for Christ, civil technology club, criminal justice-corrections club, cosmetology and barbering club, early childhood education club, electronics club, law enforcement organization, Mid-State Renewable Energy Society.

Student services. Adult student services, alcohol/substance abuse counseling, career counseling, services for economically disadvantaged, student employment services, financial aid counseling, minority student services, personal counseling, placement for graduates, veterans' counselor, women's services. **Physically disabled:** Services for visually, speech, hearing impaired. **Transfer:** Pre-admission transcript evaluation for new students. Transfer adviser, college fairs on campus for students transferring to 4-year colleges.

Contact. E-mail: enrollment@mstc.edu
Phone: (715) 422-5596 Toll-free number: (888) 575-6782
Fax: (715) 422-5440
Amanda Lang, Director of Enrollment Management, Mid-State Technical College, 500 32nd Street North, Wisconsin Rapids, WI 54494

Milwaukee Area Technical College
Milwaukee, Wisconsin
www.matc.edu   CB code: 1475

- Public 2-year junior and technical college
- Commuter campus in very large city

General. Founded in 1912. Regionally accredited. Campuses in Milwaukee, Oak Creek, Mequon, and West Allis. **Enrollment:** 14,574 degree-seeking undergraduates; 5,964 non-degree-seeking students. **Degrees:** 1,516 associate awarded. **Location:** 85 miles from Chicago. **Calendar:** Semester, limited summer session. **Full-time faculty:** 528 total; 38% minority, 53% women. **Part-time faculty:** 750 total; 22% minority, 50% women. **Class size:** 65% < 20, 35% 20-39, less than 1% 40-49, less than 1% 50-99. **Special facilities:** Restaurant (by culinary students), on site day care (by early childhood education students), dental hygiene clinic (by students under the supervision of local dentists), optical dispensary and bakery (by students).

Student profile. Among degree-seeking undergraduates, 14% enrolled in a transfer program, 86% enrolled in a vocational program, 3% already have a bachelor's degree or higher, 1,363 enrolled as first-time, first-year students, 612 transferred in from other institutions.

Part-time:	71%	Hispanic/Latino:	13%
Out-of-state:	1%	Native American:	1%
Women:	56%	Multi-racial, non-Hispanic:	3%
African American:	30%	25 or older:	55%
Asian American:	5%		

Transfer out. Colleges most students transferred to 2015: University of Wisconsin-Milwaukee, Waukesha County Technical College, Cardinal Stritch University, Gateway Technical College, Alverno College.

Basis for selection. Open admission, but selective for some programs. Special requirements for health programs. **Adult students:** SAT/ACT scores not required. All students take ACCUPLACER unless they have 12 college credits from a transferring institution. **Home schooled:** Must complete ACCUPLACER testing.

High school preparation. Specific subject requirements for some programs.

2015-2016 Annual costs. Tuition/fees: $4,794; $6,720 out-of-state. Per-credit charge: $145 in-state; $209 out-of-state. Books/supplies: $1,700. Personal expenses: $2,100.

2014-2015 Financial aid. Need-based: 52% of total undergraduate aid awarded as scholarships/grants, 48% as loans/jobs. Need-based aid available for part-time students. Work-study available nights, weekends and for part-time students. **Non-need-based:** Scholarships awarded for academics.

Application procedures. Admission: Closing date 7/29 (postmark date). $30 fee. Admission notification on a rolling basis. Youth apprentice option program available for high school students to take courses for college credit in their high school or on campus in certain subject areas. These are formal partnerships set up with local high schools. **Financial aid:** Priority date 3/15;

---

no closing date. FAFSA required. Applicants notified on a rolling basis starting 4/15.

Academics. Special study options: Accelerated study, combined bachelor's/graduate degree, cooperative education, distance learning, double major, dual enrollment of high school students, ESL, honors, independent study, internships, liberal arts/career combination, student-designed major, study abroad, teacher certification program, weekend college. Teacher education program with guaranteed admission to University of Wisconsin-Milwaukee. License preparation in aviation, dental hygiene, nursing, radiology. **Credit/placement by examination:** AP, CLEP, IB, institutional tests. Credit awarded to students completing CLEP exams through UW-Milwaukee in variety of general education subjects. Challenge exams offered on-campus for selected math courses. No limit on credit by exam. **Support services:** GED preparation and test center, learning center, reduced course load, remedial instruction, study skills assistance, tutoring, writing center. Student accommodations.

Majors. Architecture: Technology. **Business:** Accounting, administrative services, banking/financial services, business admin, fashion, hotel/motel admin, logistics, marketing, operations, real estate, tourism/travel. **Communications technology:** Graphic/printing, graphics, radio/TV. **Computer sciences:** Computer graphics, networking, programming, support specialist, webmaster. **Education:** Early childhood. **Foreign languages:** Sign language interpretation. **Health services:** Anesthesiologist assistant, cardiovascular technology, clinical lab technology, dental hygiene, dental lab technology, dietetic technician, electroencephalograph technology, medical radiologic technology/radiation therapy, medical secretary, occupational therapy, occupational therapy assistant, office admin, physical therapy assistant, respiratory therapy assistant, respiratory therapy technology, surgical technology. **Liberal arts:** Arts/sciences. **Protective services:** Firefighting, police science. **Visual/performing arts:** Commercial photography, game design, graphic design, interior design, music technology.

Most popular majors. Business/marketing 21%, computer/information sciences 7%, engineering/engineering technologies 6%, health sciences 29%, liberal arts 7%, security/protective services 8%.

Technology on campus. 500 workstations in library, computer center, student center. Commuter students can connect to campus network. Online course registration, online library, helpline, wireless network available.

Student life. Freshman orientation: Mandatory. Preregistration for classes offered. Online orientation required. In-person orientation offered several times before the semester begins. **Housing:** Certified housing available at nearby colleges and other facilities. **Activities:** Jazz band, literary magazine, music ensembles, student government, student newspaper, TV station, student senate, student life committee, African American student club, American Culinary Federation, architectural technology club, Association of Information Technology Professionals, campus Bible fellowship, criminal justice student organization, environmental club, Phi Theta Kappa Honor Society, paralegal association.

Athletics. NJCAA. **Intercollegiate:** Baseball M, basketball M, volleyball W. **Intramural:** Baseball M, basketball, soccer, softball W, volleyball W. **Team name:** Stormers.

Student services. Adult student services, alcohol/substance abuse counseling, career counseling, services for economically disadvantaged, student employment services, financial aid counseling, health services, legal services, minority student services, on-campus daycare, personal counseling, placement for graduates, veterans' counselor, women's services. **Physically disabled:** Services for visually, speech, hearing impaired. **Transfer:** Re-entry adviser, pre-admission transcript evaluation for new students. Transfer center, transfer adviser, college fairs on campus for students transferring to 4-year colleges.

Contact. E-mail: adamss4@matc.edu
Phone: (414) 297-6542 Fax: (414) 297-7800
Trevor Kubatzke, Vice President, Student Services, Milwaukee Area Technical College, 700 West State Street, Milwaukee, WI 53233-1443

Moraine Park Technical College
Fond du Lac, Wisconsin   CB member
www.morainepark.edu   CB code: 0667

- Public 2-year technical college
- Commuter campus in large town

General. Founded in 1967. Regionally accredited. Campus locations in Beaver Dam and West Bend. **Enrollment:** 3,143 degree-seeking undergraduates. **Degrees:** 466 associate awarded. **Location:** 60 miles from Milwaukee. **Calendar:** Semester, limited summer session. **Full-time faculty:** 146 total. **Part-time faculty:** 129 total.

Basis for selection. Open admission, but selective for some programs. Students without high school diploma may be admitted to certain limited job-entry preparation programs. **Learning Disabled:** Accommodations are provided as requested; students need to notify disability resources.

High school preparation. 16 units recommended. Recommended units include English 3, mathematics 2, social studies 2 and science 2.

2015-2016 Annual costs. Tuition/fees: $4,252; $6,178 out-of-state. Per-credit charge: $128 in-state; $193 out-of-state. Books/supplies: $1,665.

Financial aid. **Need-based:** Need-based aid available for part-time students. Work-study available nights, weekends and for part-time students. **Non-need-based:** Scholarships awarded for academics, job skills, leadership, minority status, state residency.

Application procedures. **Admission:** No deadline. $30 fee, may be waived for applicants with need. Admission notification on a rolling basis. **Financial aid:** Priority date 5/1; no closing date. FAFSA, institutional form required. Applicants notified on a rolling basis starting 5/15; must reply within 2 week(s) of notification.

Academics. **Special study options:** Accelerated study, distance learning, double major, dual enrollment of high school students, ESL, independent study, internships, student-designed major, weekend college. License preparation in real estate. **Credit/placement by examination:** AP, CLEP, institutional tests. 30 credit hours maximum toward associate degree. **Support services:** GED preparation and test center, learning center, pre-admission summer program, reduced course load, remedial instruction, tutoring.

Majors. **Business:** Accounting, administrative services, marketing, office management, office technology, sales/distribution. **Communications technology:** Graphic/printing. **Computer sciences:** Applications programming, data processing. **Health services:** EMT paramedic, health information technology, medical secretary, nursing (RN), substance abuse counseling. **Protective services:** Corrections, fire safety technology, police science. **Work/family studies:** Child care management, family studies.

Most popular majors. Business/marketing 20%, computer/information sciences 10%, engineering/engineering technologies 9%, health sciences 35%, security/protective services 6%, trade and industry 8%.

Technology on campus. Commuter students can connect to campus network. Online library, helpline, wireless network available.

Student life. **Freshman orientation:** Mandatory. Preregistration for classes offered. **Activities:** Student government.

Student services. Career counseling, student employment services, health services, on-campus daycare, personal counseling, placement for graduates, veterans' counselor. **Physically disabled:** Services for visually, hearing impaired. **Transfer:** College fairs on campus for students transferring to 4-year colleges.

Contact. Phone: (920) 924-3408 Toll-free number: (800) 472-4554
Fax: (920) 924-3421
Bonita Bauer, Dean of Admissions and Retention, Moraine Park Technical College, 235 North National Avenue, Fond du Lac, WI 54935-1940

Nicolet Area Technical College
Rhinelander, Wisconsin
www.nicoletcollege.edu   **CB code: 0713**

- Public 2-year community and technical college
- Commuter campus in small town

General. Founded in 1967. Regionally accredited. **Enrollment:** 1,139 undergraduates. **Degrees:** 179 associate awarded. **Location:** 225 miles from Milwaukee, 200 miles from Madison. **Calendar:** Semester, limited summer session. **Full-time faculty:** 52 total. **Part-time faculty:** 39 total. **Class size:** 74% < 20, 26% 20-39. **Special facilities:** Theater; sustainable energy initiative including wind turbine, solar powered day care center, alternative energy demonstration sites; walking trail; canoe/kayak rental.

Student profile.

Out-of-state:	1%	25 or older:	52%

Transfer out. Colleges most students transferred to 2015: University of Wisconsin-Stevens Point, University of Wisconsin-Eau Claire, University of Wisconsin-Madison, University of Wisconsin-Oshkosh.

Basis for selection. Open admission, but selective for some programs. ACCUPLACER required for placement. ACT and high school grades used

---

in some cases. **Home schooled:** Federal ability to benefit criteria used for admissions.

High school preparation. Recommended units include English 4, mathematics 3, social studies 3 and science 3.

2015-2016 Annual costs. Tuition/fees: $4,046; $5,972 out-of-state. Per-credit charge: $128 in-state; $193 out-of-state. Books/supplies: $1,352. Personal expenses: $1,700.

Financial aid. **Need-based:** Work-study available nights, weekends and for part-time students.

Application procedures. **Admission:** Priority date 8/1; no deadline. $30 fee, may be waived for applicants with need. Admission notification on a rolling basis beginning on or about 9/1. **Financial aid:** Priority date 4/1; no closing date. FAFSA, institutional form required. Applicants notified on a rolling basis starting 6/1; must reply within 2 week(s) of notification.

Academics. **Special study options:** Accelerated study, distance learning, double major, dual enrollment of high school students, ESL, independent study, internships, liberal arts/career combination, student-designed major. Bachelor's degree programs available on campus. License preparation in nursing, radiology, real estate. **Credit/placement by examination:** AP, CLEP, ACT, institutional tests. 44 credit hours maximum toward associate degree. **Support services:** GED preparation and test center, learning center, reduced course load, remedial instruction, study skills assistance, tutoring.

Majors. **Business:** Accounting, administrative services, business admin. **Communications technology:** Graphics. **Computer sciences:** General, computer graphics, computer science, data processing, information technology, LAN/WAN management, networking, programming, web page design, webmaster. **Education:** Early childhood. **Health services:** Nursing (RN), radiologic technology/medical imaging, surgical technology. **Liberal arts:** Arts/sciences. **Protective services:** Police science. **Visual/performing arts:** Graphic design. **Work/family studies:** Child care management.

Most popular majors. Business/marketing 28%, computer/information sciences 15%, education 8%, engineering/engineering technologies 7%, health sciences 14%, liberal arts 12%, security/protective services 9%.

Technology on campus. 80 workstations in library, computer center. Commuter students can connect to campus network. Online course registration, online library, helpline, wireless network available.

Student life. **Freshman orientation:** Mandatory. Preregistration for classes offered. Half-day session held 2 days before start of classes. Optional evening session available. **Activities:** Drama, musical theater, student government, Business Professionals of America, Phi Theta Kappa, peace coalition, Campus Crusade for Christ, Junior Chapter of American Culinary Federation, SAGED.

Student services. Adult student services, alcohol/substance abuse counseling, career counseling, services for economically disadvantaged, student employment services, financial aid counseling, minority student services, on-campus daycare, personal counseling, placement for graduates, veterans' counselor, women's services. **Physically disabled:** Services for visually, speech, hearing impaired. **Transfer:** Pre-admission transcript evaluation for new students. Transfer center, transfer adviser, college fairs on campus for students transferring to 4-year colleges.

Contact. E-mail: inquire@nicoletcollege.edu
Phone: (715) 365-4451 Toll-free number: (800) 544-3039 ext. 4451
Fax: (715) 365-4901
Susan Kordula, Director of Admissions/PK-16 Pathways, Nicolet Area Technical College, Box 518, Rhinelander, WI 54501

Northcentral Technical College
Wausau, Wisconsin   **CB member**
www.ntc.edu   **CB code: 0735**

- Public 2-year community and technical college
- Commuter campus in small city

General. Founded in 1911. Regionally accredited. Regional campuses located in Antigo, Medford, Merrill, Phillips, Spencer and Wittenberg. **Enrollment:** 3,710 degree-seeking undergraduates; 803 non-degree-seeking students. **Degrees:** 514 associate awarded. **Location:** 200 miles from Milwaukee and Minneapolis-St. Paul, 150 miles from Madison. **Calendar:** Semester, limited summer session. **Full-time faculty:** 133 total. **Part-time faculty:** 1 total. **Special facilities:** Agriculture center of excellence, dairy farm, wood technology center of excellence, advanced manufacturing and engineering center of excellence, public safety center of excellence, center for geriatric education.

Student profile. Among degree-seeking undergraduates, 772 enrolled as first-time, first-year students.

Part-time:	61%	Asian American:	7%
Women:	60%	Native American:	2%
African American:	1%		

Basis for selection. Open admission, but selective for some programs. Special requirements for health programs including application portfolio. ACCUPLACER or ACT required for placement. **Home schooled:** State high school equivalency certificate required.

2015-2016 Annual costs. Tuition/fees: $4,308; $6,234 out-of-state. Per-credit charge: $128 in-state; $193 out-of-state. Books/supplies: $1,200.

2015-2016 Financial aid. Need-based: 59% of total undergraduate aid awarded as scholarships/grants, 41% as loans/jobs. Need-based aid available for part-time students. Work-study available nights, weekends and for part-time students.

Application procedures. Admission: No deadline. $30 fee. Admission notification on a rolling basis. **Financial aid:** No deadline. FAFSA required. Applicants notified on a rolling basis.

Academics. Special study options: Accelerated study, distance learning, double major, dual enrollment of high school students, ESL, honors, independent study, internships, student-designed major, weekend college. Bachelor's degree programs available on campus. License preparation in dental hygiene, nursing, paramedic, radiology. **Credit/placement by examination:** AP, CLEP, IB, institutional tests. 24 credit hours maximum toward associate degree. **Support services:** GED preparation and test center, learning center, pre-admission summer program, reduced course load, remedial instruction, study skills assistance, tutoring, writing center.

Majors. Architecture: Technology. **Business:** Accounting, accounting/business management, accounting/finance, administrative services, business admin, insurance, marketing, small business admin. **Communications technology:** Graphic/printing. **Computer sciences:** Data entry, networking, programming, support specialist, web page design, webmaster. **Education:** Early childhood. **Engineering:** Electrical, engineering mechanics. **Foreign languages:** Sign language interpretation. **Health services:** Clinical lab assistant, clinical lab technology, dental hygiene, EMT paramedic, nursing (RN), radiologic technology/medical imaging, substance abuse counseling. **Protective services:** Firefighting, police science. **Work/family studies:** Child care service.

Technology on campus. Commuter students can connect to campus network. Online course registration, online library, helpline, wireless network available.

Student life. Freshman orientation: Available. Preregistration for classes offered. **Activities:** International student organizations, student government, student newspaper.

Athletics. Intramural: Basketball, football (non-tackle), softball, volleyball. **Team name:** Timberwolves.

Student services. Adult student services, career counseling, services for economically disadvantaged, student employment services, financial aid counseling, health services, minority student services, on-campus daycare, personal counseling, placement for graduates. **Physically disabled:** Services for visually, speech, hearing impaired. **Transfer:** Pre-admission transcript evaluation for new students. Transfer center, transfer adviser, college fairs on campus for students transferring to 4-year colleges.

Contact. E-mail: admissions@ntc.edu
Phone: (715) 675-3331 Toll-free number: (888) 682-7144
Sarah Dillon, Dean of College Enrollment, Northcentral Technical College, 1000 West Campus Drive, Wausau, WI 54401

Northeast Wisconsin Technical College
Green Bay, Wisconsin   CB member
www.nwtc.edu   CB code: 4190

- Public 2-year community and technical college
- Commuter campus in small city
- Application essay required

General. Founded in 1913. Regionally accredited. **Enrollment:** 8,526 degree-seeking undergraduates. **Degrees:** 1,138 associate awarded. **Location:** 129 miles from Milwaukee, 150 miles from Madison. **Calendar:** Semester, limited summer session. **Full-time faculty:** 272 total; 4% minority, 48% women. **Part-time faculty:** 1,158 total; 5% minority, 54% women. **Special**

---

facilities: Horticultural Learning Center. **Partnerships:** Formal partnership with Snap-on Incorporated.

Transfer out. Colleges most students transferred to 2015: University of Wisconsin-Green Bay, University of Wisconsin-Oshkosh.

Basis for selection. Open admission, but selective for some programs. Special requirements for health programs. **Home schooled:** State high school equivalency certificate required.

High school preparation. College-preparatory program required.

2015-2016 Annual costs. Tuition/fees: $4,274; $6,200 out-of-state. Per-credit charge: $128 in-state; $192 out-of-state. Books/supplies: $1,472. Personal expenses: $1,920.

Financial aid. Need-based: Need-based aid available for part-time students. Work-study available nights, weekends and for part-time students.

Application procedures. Admission: Closing date 9/5 (receipt date). $30 fee, may be waived for applicants with need. Admission notification on a rolling basis beginning on or about 9/15. **Financial aid:** Priority date 4/15; no closing date. FAFSA required. Applicants notified on a rolling basis starting 6/1; must reply within 2 week(s) of notification.

Academics. Special study options: Accelerated study, distance learning, double major, dual enrollment of high school students, ESL, honors, independent study, internships, liberal arts/career combination, study abroad, weekend college. License preparation in dental hygiene, nursing, paramedic, physical therapy, radiology, real estate. **Credit/placement by examination:** AP, CLEP, institutional tests. 48 credit hours maximum toward associate degree. **Support services:** GED preparation and test center, learning center, reduced course load, remedial instruction, study skills assistance, tutoring, writing center.

Majors. Architecture: Technology. **Business:** Accounting, administrative services, business admin, hospitality/recreation, logistics, sales/distribution. **Computer sciences:** General, networking. **Education:** Early childhood. **Health services:** Dental hygiene, geriatric nursing, health care admin, health information management, medical secretary, nursing (RN), physical therapy assistant, respiratory therapy technology. **Protective services:** Fire safety technology, police science. **Work/family studies:** Child care management.

Technology on campus. Online course registration, online library, helpline, wireless network available.

Student life. Freshman orientation: Available. Preregistration for classes offered. 2-hour program in conjunction with registration. **Activities:** International student organizations, student government, Asian American student association, African American student association, Native American student association, Hispanic student association, Students Taking Responsibility in Drug Education, Phi Theta Kappa International Honor Society.

Athletics. Intramural: Basketball, football (non-tackle), volleyball.

Student services. Adult student services, alcohol/substance abuse counseling, career counseling, services for economically disadvantaged, student employment services, financial aid counseling, health services, minority student services, personal counseling, placement for graduates, veterans' counselor. **Physically disabled:** Services for visually, speech, hearing impaired. **Transfer:** Re-entry adviser for new students. Transfer adviser, college fairs on campus for students transferring to 4-year colleges.

Contact. Phone: (920) 498-5444
Toll-free number: (800) 422-6982 ext. 5444 Fax: (920) 498-6882
Erin DeGrand, Program Enrollment Supervisor, Northeast Wisconsin Technical College, 2740 West Mason Street, Green Bay, WI 54307-9042

Rasmussen College: Green Bay
Green Bay, Wisconsin
www.rasmussen.edu

- For-profit 2-year career college
- Small city

General. Regionally accredited. **Enrollment:** 441 degree-seeking undergraduates. **Degrees:** 26 bachelor's, 123 associate awarded. **Calendar:** Quarter. **Full-time faculty:** 14 total. **Part-time faculty:** 42 total.

Basis for selection. Open admission, but selective for some programs. **Adult students:** SAT/ACT scores not required.

2016-2017 Annual costs. Tuition/fees (projected): $13,455. Per-credit charge: $299. Personal expenses: $2,214.

Financial aid. Need-based: Need-based aid available for part-time students. Work-study available nights, weekends and for part-time students.

Application procedures. Admission: No deadline. No application fee. Admission notification on. a rolling basis. **Financial aid:** No deadline. FAFSA, institutional form required. Applicants notified on a rolling basis.

Academics. Credit/placement by examination: AP, CLEP.

Majors. Business: Accounting, business admin, human resources, management information systems, marketing. **Computer sciences:** Support specialist, web page design. **Education:** Early childhood, teacher assistance. **Engineering:** Software. **Health services:** Clinical lab technology, health information technology, medical assistant, medical secretary, nursing (RN), pharmacy assistant. **Protective services:** Criminal justice. **Visual/performing arts:** Game design.

Contact. Phone: (920) 593-8400
Susan Hammerstrom, Director of Admissions, Rasmussen College: Green Bay, 904 South Taylor Street, Suite 100, Green Bay, WI 54303-2349

Rasmussen College: Wausau
Wausau, Wisconsin
www.rasmussen.edu

- For-profit 2-year career college
- Large town

General. Regionally accredited. **Enrollment:** 346 degree-seeking undergraduates. **Degrees:** 42 bachelor's, 137 associate awarded. **Calendar:** Quarter. **Full-time faculty:** 10 total. **Part-time faculty:** 43 total.

Basis for selection. Open admission, but selective for some programs.

2016-2017 Annual costs. Tuition/fees (projected): $13,455. Per-credit charge: $299.

Financial aid. Need-based: Need-based aid available for part-time students. Work-study available nights, weekends and for part-time students.

Application procedures. Admission: No deadline. No application fee. Admission notification on a rolling basis. **Financial aid:** No deadline. FAFSA, institutional form required. Applicants notified on a rolling basis.

Academics. Credit/placement by examination: AP, CLEP.

Majors. Business: Accounting, business admin, human resources, management information systems, marketing. **Computer sciences:** Support specialist, web page design. **Education:** Teacher assistance. **Engineering:** Software. **Health services:** Health information technology, medical assistant, medical secretary, nursing (RN), pharmacy assistant. **Protective services:** Criminal justice. **Visual/performing arts:** Game design.

Contact. E-mail: susan.hammerstrom@rasmussen.edu
Phone: (715) 841-8000
Susan Hammerstrom, Director of Admissions, Rasmussen College: Wausau, 1101 Westwood Drive, Wausau, WI 54401

Southwest Wisconsin Technical College
Fennimore, Wisconsin
www.swtc.edu   **CB code: 0900**

- Public 2-year technical college
- Commuter campus in rural community
- Interview required

General. Founded in 1967. Regionally accredited. **Enrollment:** 1,356 degree-seeking undergraduates. **Degrees:** 197 associate awarded. **Location:** 75 miles from Madison. **Calendar:** Semester, limited summer session. **Full-time faculty:** 92 total. **Part-time faculty:** 19 total. **Special facilities:** Disc golf course.

Student profile.

Out-of-state:	6%	**Live on campus:**	8%
25 or older:	38%		

Basis for selection. Open admission, but selective for some programs. Some health care programs require a background check as well as completion of certain coursework prior to program admission. SAT, ACT or COMPASS test scores are utilized for course placement purposes. Psychological Services

Bureau Test required for nursing RN applicants, C-NET test required for LPN applicants. **Adult students:** SAT/ACT scores not required.

2015-2016 Annual costs. Tuition/fees: $4,114; $6,040 out-of-state. Per-credit charge: $128 in-state; $193 out-of-state. Books/supplies: $1,744. Personal expenses: $1,916.

Financial aid. Need-based: Work-study available nights, weekends and for part-time students.

Application procedures. Admission: No deadline. $30 fee. Admission notification on a rolling basis beginning on or about 9/1. Students notified of admission before 7/1 must pay tuition deposit of $100; students applying after that date must pay deposit as part of application process. **Financial aid:** Priority date 4/15; no closing date. FAFSA, institutional form required. Applicants notified on a rolling basis starting 5/15; must reply within 4 week(s) of notification.

Academics. Special study options: Accelerated study, distance learning, double major, dual enrollment of high school students, ESL, independent study, internships, liberal arts/career combination, student-designed major. License preparation in nursing, real estate. **Credit/placement by examination:** AP, CLEP, institutional tests. **Support services:** GED preparation and test center, learning center, pre-admission summer program, reduced course load, remedial instruction, study skills assistance, tutoring, writing center.

Majors. Business: Accounting, administrative services, business admin, office management. **Computer sciences:** Networking, programming, web page design. **Education:** Early childhood. **Health services:** Clinical lab technology, cytotechnology, health information technology, mental health services, midwifery, nursing (RN), physical therapy assistant. **Liberal arts:** Arts/sciences. **Parks/recreation:** Golf management. **Protective services:** Police science.

Most popular majors. Agriculture 10%, business/marketing 17%, computer/information sciences 10%, education 7%, engineering/engineering technologies 7%, health sciences 33%.

Technology on campus. 250 workstations in library, computer center, student center. Dormitories wired for high-speed internet access. Online course registration, online library, helpline, wireless network available.

Student life. Freshman orientation: Mandatory. Preregistration for classes offered. One-half day session held one day prior to beginning of classes. **Housing:** Special housing for disabled, apartments, wellness housing available. $300 fully refundable deposit, deadline 5/1. Coed apartment style housing available on-campus. **Activities:** Student government, student newspaper, Business Professionals of America, National Student Nursing Association, Post-Secondary Agricultural Students, Phi Theta Kappa, Blue Line Organization, Skills U.S.A., Southwest Accounting Team, Human Services Associate Club, Graphic Innovation Group, Student Senate.

Athletics. NJCAA. **Intercollegiate:** Golf. **Intramural:** Basketball, softball, volleyball. **Team name:** Chargers.

Student services. Alcohol/substance abuse counseling, career counseling, services for economically disadvantaged, student employment services, financial aid counseling, health services, minority student services, on-campus daycare, personal counseling, placement for graduates, veterans' counselor, women's services. **Physically disabled:** Services for visually, hearing impaired. **Transfer:** Transfer adviser for students transferring to 4-year colleges.

Contact. E-mail: studentservices@swtc.edu
Phone: (608) 822-3262 ext. 2354
Toll-free number: (800) 362-3322 ext. 2354 Fax: (608) 822-6019
Holly Miller, Dean of Students, Southwest Wisconsin Technical College, 1800 Bronson Boulevard, Fennimore, WI 53809

University of Wisconsin-Baraboo/Sauk County
Baraboo, Wisconsin
www.baraboo.uwc.edu   **CB code: 1996**

- Public 2-year branch campus and liberal arts college
- Commuter campus in large town
- SAT or ACT (ACT writing optional) required

General. Founded in 1968. Regionally accredited. **Enrollment:** 600 degree-seeking undergraduates. **Degrees:** 120 associate awarded. **Location:** 40 miles from Madison. **Calendar:** Semester, limited summer session. **Full-time faculty:** 18 total. **Part-time faculty:** 18 total. **Class size:** 57% < 20, 42% 20-39, less than 1% 40-49.

Student profile.

Out-of-state: 1% 25 or older: 17%

Transfer out. Colleges most students transferred to 2015: University of Wisconsin-Madison, University of Wisconsin-LaCrosse, University of Wisconsin-Stevens Point, University of Wisconsin-Whitewater, University of Wisconsin-Platteville.

Basis for selection. High school courses, rank in upper 75% of class, ACT or SAT most important. Students in bottom 25% may be admitted based on individual record and circumstances. Students not admitted may be deferred and admitted the following semester. Special attention given to returning adult, homeschooled, learning disabled, and minority students. ACT or SAT used for advisory purposes only for most students. Interview required for those with borderline academic records and class rank. **Adult students:** SAT/ACT scores not required if applicant over 21. Placement test required of students without college credit English and/or math courses. **Home schooled:** Transcript of courses and grades, interview required. Interview, portfolio of curriculum, method of assessment, work samples and experiences recommended. **Learning Disabled:** Interview recommended; recent professional testing required to create program accommodations.

High school preparation. 17 units required. Required and recommended units include English 4, mathematics 3-4, social studies 3, science 3-4 (laboratory 3-4), foreign language 2 and academic electives 4. Math must be college preparatory.

2015-2016 Annual costs. Tuition/fees: $5,178; $12,162 out-of-state. Per-credit charge: $198 in-state; $489 out-of-state. Books/supplies: $680. Personal expenses: $1,690.

Financial aid. All financial aid based on need. Need-based aid available for part-time students. Work-study available nights, weekends and for part-time students.

Application procedures. Admission: Priority date 6/1; deadline 8/31 (receipt date). $45 fee, may be waived for applicants with need. Admission notification on a rolling basis beginning on or about 9/15. **Financial aid:** Priority date 4/15; no closing date. FAFSA, institutional form required. Applicants notified on a rolling basis starting 4/15; must reply within 3 week(s) of notification.

Academics. Required courses for associate degree available evenings over 4-year period. Bachelor's degree available on campus through University of Wisconsin Milwaukee. **Special study options:** Cross-registration, distance learning, dual enrollment of high school students, external degree, honors, independent study, internships, liberal arts/career combination, study abroad. Bachelor's degree programs available on campus. **Credit/placement by examination:** AP, CLEP, IB, institutional tests. **Support services:** Learning center, reduced course load, remedial instruction, study skills assistance, tutoring, writing center.

Majors. Liberal arts: Arts/sciences.

Technology on campus. 60 workstations in library, computer center, student center. Commuter students can connect to campus network. Online course registration, online library, wireless network available.

Student life. Freshman orientation: Mandatory, $200 fee. Preregistration for classes offered. Orientation in 3 parts over summer. **Policies:** Students participate actively in campus governance and committee work with faculty and staff. **Housing:** Privately owned apartments adjacent to campus available. **Activities:** Bands, choral groups, drama, literary magazine, music ensembles, student government, student newspaper, Campus Crusade for Christ, Phi Theta Kappa, Wellness Alliance, business club, Native American club, cine club, UWB Ambassadors, green club, art club, Future Educators.

Athletics. NJCAA. **Intercollegiate:** Basketball M, soccer, tennis, volleyball W. **Intramural:** Basketball, cross-country, racquetball, softball, volleyball. **Team name:** Fighting Spirits.

Student services. Adult student services, alcohol/substance abuse counseling, career counseling, financial aid counseling, minority student services, personal counseling, veterans' counselor. **Physically disabled:** Services for visually, speech, hearing impaired. **Transfer:** Pre-admission transcript evaluation for new students. Transfer adviser, college fairs on campus for students transferring to 4-year colleges.

Contact. E-mail: apply@wisconsin.edu
Phone: (608) 355-5230 Fax: (608) 355-5289
Ruth Joyce, Assistant Dean for Student Services, University of Wisconsin-Baraboo/Sauk County, 1006 Connie Road, Baraboo, WI 53913-1098

University of Wisconsin-Barron County
Rice Lake, Wisconsin
www.barron.uwc.edu CB code: 1772

- Public 2-year branch campus and junior college
- Commuter campus in small town
- SAT or ACT (ACT writing optional) required

General. Founded in 1966. Regionally accredited. **Enrollment:** 422 degree-seeking undergraduates. **Degrees:** 75 associate awarded. **Location:** 80 miles from Minneapolis-St. Paul, 50 miles from Eau Claire. **Calendar:** Semester, limited summer session. **Full-time faculty:** 26 total. **Part-time faculty:** 19 total. **Special facilities:** Observatory, amphitheater.

Student profile.

Out-of-state: 2% 25 or older: 21%

Basis for selection. Rank in upper 75% of class ensures admission. Students in bottom 25% or those submitting GED scores evaluated on individual basis. ACT preferred. **Adult students:** SAT/ACT scores not required if applicant over 21.

High school preparation. 16 units required. Required units include English 4, mathematics 3, social studies 3 and science 2.

2015-2016 Annual costs. Tuition/fees: $5,184; $12,168 out-of-state. Per-credit charge: $198 in-state; $489 out-of-state. Books/supplies: $780. Personal expenses: $1,750.

Financial aid. Need-based: Need-based aid available for part-time students. Work-study available nights, weekends and for part-time students.

Application procedures. Admission: Priority date 7/1; no deadline. $44 fee, may be waived for applicants with need. Admission notification on a rolling basis. **Financial aid:** Priority date 4/15; no closing date. FAFSA required. Applicants notified on a rolling basis starting 6/1.

Academics. Special study options: Cross-registration, dual enrollment of high school students, internships. **Credit/placement by examination:** AP, CLEP, institutional tests. **Support services:** Learning center, pre-admission summer program, reduced course load, remedial instruction, tutoring.

Majors. Liberal arts: Arts/sciences.

Technology on campus. 24 workstations in library, computer center.

Student life. Freshman orientation: Available, $50 fee. Preregistration for classes offered. **Activities:** Bands, choral groups, drama, music ensembles, musical theater, student government, student newspaper, Phi Theta Kappa.

Athletics. NJCAA. **Intercollegiate:** Baseball M, basketball, golf, soccer, volleyball W. **Intramural:** Basketball, table tennis, volleyball. **Team name:** Chargers.

Student services. Adult student services, career counseling, student employment services, health services, personal counseling, veterans' counselor. **Physically disabled:** Services for visually, speech, hearing impaired. **Transfer:** Transfer adviser, college fairs on campus for students transferring to 4-year colleges.

Contact. Phone: (715) 234-8176 Fax: (715) 234-8024
Dale Fenton, Director of Student Services, University of Wisconsin-Barron County, 1800 College Drive, Rice Lake, WI 54868

University of Wisconsin-Fond du Lac
Fond du Lac, Wisconsin
www.fdl.uwc.edu CB code: 1942

- Public 2-year liberal arts college
- Commuter campus in large town
- SAT or ACT (ACT writing optional) required

General. Founded in 1968. Regionally accredited. **Enrollment:** 626 undergraduates. **Degrees:** 125 associate awarded. **Location:** 70 miles from Milwaukee. **Calendar:** Semester, limited summer session. **Full-time faculty:** 20 total. **Part-time faculty:** 20 total. **Class size:** 31% < 20, 65% 20-39, 5% 40-49. **Special facilities:** Nature preserve, arboretum.

Student profile.

Out-of-state: 1% 25 or older: 28%

Transfer out. Colleges most students transferred to 2015: University of Wisconsin-Oshkosh, University of Wisconsin-Milwaukee, University of Wisconsin-Madison, University of Wisconsin-Stevens Point, University of Wisconsin-Green Bay.

Basis for selection. Rank in upper 75% of class ensures admission. Students in bottom 25% will be considered. Applicants with Wisconsin GED score of 250 or higher ensured admission. Applicants admitted who rank in bottom 25% of class may have course credit restrictions during first semester or may be required to participate in summer school classes as condition of continued enrollment. ACT preferred. **Adult students:** SAT/ACT scores not required if applicant over 21. **Home schooled:** Transcript of courses and grades required.

High school preparation. College-preparatory program recommended. 17 units required. Required units include English 4, mathematics 3, social studies 3, science 3 and academic electives 4.

2015-2016 Annual costs. Tuition/fees: $5,209; $12,193 out-of-state. Per-credit charge: $198 in-state; $489 out-of-state. Books/supplies: $950.

Financial aid. Need-based: Need-based aid available for part-time students. Work-study available nights, weekends and for part-time students. **Non-need-based:** Scholarships awarded for academics, leadership, music/drama.

Application procedures. Admission: Priority date 8/15; no deadline. $44 fee, may be waived for applicants with need. Admission notification on a rolling basis beginning on or about 9/15. **Financial aid:** Priority date 4/15; no closing date. FAFSA required. Applicants notified on a rolling basis starting 6/1; must reply within 2 week(s) of notification.

Academics. Special study options: Accelerated study, cross-registration, distance learning, dual enrollment of high school students, independent study, liberal arts/career combination, study abroad. Bachelor's degree programs available on campus. **Credit/placement by examination:** AP, CLEP, IB, institutional tests. 18 credit hours maximum toward associate degree. **Support services:** Learning center, pre-admission summer program, reduced course load, remedial instruction, study skills assistance, tutoring.

Majors. Liberal arts: Arts/sciences.

Technology on campus. 60 workstations in library, computer center. Commuter students can connect to campus network. Online course registration, online library, wireless network available.

Student life. Freshman orientation: Mandatory, $85 fee. Preregistration for classes offered. **Housing:** Student housing available at nearby Marian College. **Activities:** Bands, choral groups, drama, literary magazine, music ensembles, musical theater, student government, student newspaper, symphony orchestra.

Athletics. NJCAA. **Intercollegiate:** Basketball, golf, soccer, tennis, volleyball W. **Intramural:** Basketball M, bowling, volleyball. **Team name:** Falcons.

Student services. Career counseling, financial aid counseling, personal counseling, veterans' counselor. **Physically disabled:** Services for visually, speech, hearing impaired. **Transfer:** Transfer adviser for students transferring to 4-year colleges.

Contact. E-mail: fdl-info@uwc.edu
Phone: (920) 929-1122 Fax: (920) 929-3605
Joyce Atkins, Admissions Director, University of Wisconsin-Fond du Lac, 400 University Drive, Fond du Lac, WI 54935-2950

University of Wisconsin-Fox Valley
Menasha, Wisconsin
www.uwfox.uwc.edu   CB code: 1889

▶ Public 2-year liberal arts college
▶ Commuter campus in small city
▶ SAT or ACT (ACT writing optional) required

General. Founded in 1933. Regionally accredited. **Enrollment:** 1,549 undergraduates. **Degrees:** 185 associate awarded. **Location:** 90 miles from Milwaukee. **Calendar:** Semester, limited summer session. **Full-time faculty:** 41 total. **Part-time faculty:** 28 total. **Class size:** 100% < 20. **Special facilities:** Planetarium, earth science museum, communication arts center.

Student profile. 99 transferred in from other institutions.

Basis for selection. Rank in upper 75% of class ensures admission. Students in bottom 25% may be placed on waiting list and SAT/ACT may be

considered. Course unit requirements must be met. **Adult students:** SAT/ACT scores not required if applicant over 22. **Home schooled:** Transcript of courses and grades required.

High school preparation. College-preparatory program recommended. 17 units required. Required and recommended units include English 4, mathematics 3, social studies 3, science 3, foreign language 2 and academic electives 4. Math units must be in algebra, geometry, and higher level.

2015-2016 Annual costs. Tuition/fees: $5,294; $12,278 out-of-state. Books/supplies: $500. Personal expenses: $900.

Financial aid. Need-based: Need-based aid available for part-time students. Work-study available nights, weekends and for part-time students. **Non-need-based:** Scholarships awarded for academics, leadership.

Application procedures. Admission: Priority date 8/1; no deadline. $44 fee, may be waived for applicants with need. Admission notification on a rolling basis. **Financial aid:** Priority date 4/15; no closing date. FAFSA required. Applicants notified on a rolling basis starting 6/1; must reply within 3 week(s) of notification.

Academics. Enrollment includes admissions to all University of Wisconsin Colleges campuses. **Special study options:** Accelerated study, distance learning, dual enrollment of high school students, honors, independent study, internships. Bachelor's degree programs available on campus. **Credit/placement by examination:** AP, CLEP, institutional tests. **Support services:** Learning center, reduced course load, remedial instruction, study skills assistance, tutoring, writing center.

Majors. Liberal arts: Arts/sciences.

Technology on campus. 100 workstations in library, computer center. Commuter students can connect to campus network. Online course registration, online library, student web hosting, wireless network available.

Student life. Freshman orientation: Mandatory, $140 fee. Preregistration for classes offered. Day-long program. **Housing:** Apartments available. **Activities:** Bands, choral groups, dance, drama, film society, international student organizations, literary magazine, music ensembles, musical theater, radio station, student government, student newspaper, symphony orchestra, TV station.

Athletics. NJCAA. **Intercollegiate:** Basketball, soccer, tennis, volleyball. **Intramural:** Baseball M. **Team name:** Cyclones.

Student services. Adult student services, alcohol/substance abuse counseling, career counseling, services for economically disadvantaged, financial aid counseling, minority student services, on-campus daycare, personal counseling, veterans' counselor. **Physically disabled:** Services for visually, speech, hearing impaired. **Transfer:** Transfer adviser, college fairs on campus for students transferring to 4-year colleges.

Contact. Phone: (920) 832-2620 Fax: (920) 832-2850
Carla Rabe, Associate Dean of Student Affairs and enrollment management Northeast region, University of Wisconsin-Fox Valley, 1478 Midway Road, Menasha, WI 54952-2850

University of Wisconsin-Manitowoc
Manitowoc, Wisconsin
www.manitowoc.uwc.edu   CB code: 1890

▶ Public 2-year branch campus and liberal arts college
▶ Commuter campus in large town
▶ SAT or ACT required

General. Founded in 1933. Regionally accredited. **Enrollment:** 508 degree-seeking undergraduates. **Degrees:** 90 associate awarded. **Location:** 45 miles from Green Bay. **Calendar:** Semester, limited summer session. **Full-time faculty:** 20 total; 5% minority. **Part-time faculty:** 20 total.

Student profile.

Out-of-state:	1%	25 or older: 25%

Transfer out. Colleges most students transferred to 2015: University of Wisconsin-Green Bay, University of Wisconsin-Oshkosh, University of Wisconsin-Madison, University of Wisconsin-Milwaukee, University of Wisconsin-Stevens Point.

Basis for selection. Rank in top 75% of high school class and 19 ACT ensures admission. Students in bottom 25% or ACT below 19 will be considered but may be admitted in the high risk category. Interview may be required for applicants in bottom quarter of class. **Adult students:** SAT/ACT scores

Two-Year Colleges

not required if applicant over 21. **Home schooled:** Transcript of courses and grades required. **Learning Disabled:** Students must meet with campus coordinator for students with disabilities for information about support programs.

High school preparation. College-preparatory program recommended. 17 units required. Required units include English 4, mathematics 3, social studies 3, science 3 and academic electives 4.

2015-2016 Annual costs. Tuition/fees: $5,108; $12,092 out-of-state. Per-credit charge: $198 in-state; $489 out-of-state. Books/supplies: $1,020. Personal expenses: $1,730.

Financial aid. All financial aid based on need. Need-based aid available for part-time students. Work-study available nights, weekends and for part-time students.

Application procedures. Admission: Priority date 7/1; no deadline. $44 fee, may be waived for applicants with need. Admission notification on a rolling basis beginning on or about 9/1. **Financial aid:** Priority date 3/1; no closing date. FAFSA required. Applicants notified on a rolling basis starting 5/1; must reply within 2 week(s) of notification.

Academics. Special study options: Cross-registration, dual enrollment of high school students, honors, independent study. Bachelor's degree programs available on campus. **Credit/placement by examination:** AP, CLEP, IB, institutional tests. 18 credit hours maximum toward associate degree. **Support services:** Learning center, reduced course load, remedial instruction, tutoring, writing center.

Majors. Liberal arts: Arts/sciences.

Technology on campus. 60 workstations in library, computer center. Commuter students can connect to campus network. Online course registration, online library, helpline, wireless network available.

Student life. Freshman orientation: Mandatory, $100 fee. Preregistration for classes offered. One-day program. **Activities:** Bands, choral groups, drama, literary magazine, music ensembles, student government, symphony orchestra.

Athletics. NAIA, NJCAA. **Intercollegiate:** Basketball, tennis, volleyball W. **Intramural:** Basketball, football (non-tackle), volleyball. **Team name:** Blue Devils.

Student services. Adult student services, career counseling, financial aid counseling, personal counseling, veterans' counselor. **Physically disabled:** Services for visually, speech, hearing impaired. **Transfer:** Re-entry adviser for new students. Transfer adviser for students transferring to 4-year colleges.

Contact. E-mail: manadmit@uwc.edu
Phone: (920) 683-4707 Fax: (920) 683-4776
George Henze, Assistant Campus Dean for Student Affairs, University of Wisconsin-Manitowoc, 705 Viebahn Street, Manitowoc, WI 54220-6699

University of Wisconsin-Marathon County
Wausau, Wisconsin
www.uwmc.uwc.edu   CB code: 1995

- Public 2-year liberal arts college
- Commuter campus in small city
- SAT or ACT (ACT writing optional) required

General. Founded in 1933. Regionally accredited. Guaranteed transfer program to University of Wisconsin 4-year schools. **Enrollment:** 1,138 degree-seeking undergraduates. **Degrees:** 90 associate awarded. **Location:** 180 miles from Milwaukee, 180 miles from Minneapolis-St. Paul. **Calendar:** Semester, limited summer session. **Full-time faculty:** 30 total. **Part-time faculty:** 48 total. **Special facilities:** Planetarium, hiking and cross-country ski trails, indoor skating and curling rinks.

Student profile.

Out-of-state:	3%	Live on campus:	12%
25 or older:	28%		

Basis for selection. Rank in upper 75% of class ensures admission. Students in bottom 25% and those with GED admitted on basis of interview. **Adult students:** SAT/ACT scores not required if applicant over 21. **Learning Disabled:** Must provide official documentation for review of accommodations 90 days in advance.

High school preparation. 17 units required. Required and recommended units include English 4, mathematics 3-4, social studies 3-4, science 3-4 and

foreign language 4. Math units must be algebra, geometry or other courses leading to calculus.

2015-2016 Annual costs. Tuition/fees: $5,132; $12,116 out-of-state. Per-credit charge: $198 in-district; $489 out-of-district. Room/board: $4,924. Books/supplies: $700. Personal expenses: $900.

Financial aid. All financial aid based on need. Need-based aid available for part-time students. Work-study available nights, weekends and for part-time students.

Application procedures. Admission: Priority date 8/15; no deadline. $44 fee, may be waived for applicants with need. Admission notification on a rolling basis. **Financial aid:** Priority date 4/15; no closing date. FAFSA, institutional form required. Applicants notified on a rolling basis starting 6/1; must reply within 3 week(s) of notification.

Academics. Special study options: Cross-registration, dual enrollment of high school students, honors, independent study, internships, liberal arts/career combination, study abroad. Bachelor's degree programs available on campus. **Credit/placement by examination:** AP, CLEP, IB, institutional tests. 18 credit hours maximum toward associate degree. **Support services:** Learning center, pre-admission summer program, reduced course load, remedial instruction, study skills assistance, tutoring, writing center.

Majors. Liberal arts: Arts/sciences.

Technology on campus. 92 workstations in dormitories, library, computer center. Dormitories wired for high-speed internet access and linked to campus network. Online library, helpline available.

Student life. Freshman orientation: Available, $100 fee. Preregistration for classes offered. One-day program held week before start of fall classes. **Policies:** Zero tolerance alcohol and drug policy in residence hall. **Housing:** Coed dorms available. $100 deposit. **Activities:** Bands, choral groups, drama, literary magazine, music ensembles, musical theater, student government, student newspaper, symphony orchestra, Christian Fellowship, business club, computer club, drama club, international relations club, biology club, gay/lesbian/bisexual student association.

Athletics. NJCAA. **Intercollegiate:** Basketball, golf, soccer, tennis, volleyball W. **Intramural:** Archery, badminton, basketball, bowling, fencing, golf, handball, racquetball, skiing, skin diving, softball, swimming, table tennis, tennis, volleyball. **Team name:** Huskies.

Student services. Adult student services, career counseling, student employment services, personal counseling, veterans' counselor. **Physically disabled:** Services for visually, hearing impaired. **Transfer:** Transfer adviser, college fairs on campus for students transferring to 4-year colleges.

Contact. E-mail: uwmc@uwe.edu
Phone: (715) 261-6241 Toll-free number: (888) 367-8962
Fax: (715) 261-6331
Franklyn Taylor, Admissions Director, University of Wisconsin-Marathon County, 518 South Seventh Avenue, Wausau, WI 54401-5396

University of Wisconsin-Marinette
Marinette, Wisconsin
www.marinette.uwc.edu   CB code: 1891

- Public 2-year branch campus and liberal arts college
- Commuter campus in large town
- SAT or ACT (ACT writing optional), application essay required

General. Founded in 1946. Regionally accredited. **Enrollment:** 350 degree-seeking undergraduates. **Degrees:** 52 associate awarded. **Location:** 50 miles from Green Bay, 170 miles from Milwaukee. **Calendar:** Semester, limited summer session. **Full-time faculty:** 15 total. **Part-time faculty:** 15 total.

Student profile.

Out-of-state:	20%	25 or older:	23%

Transfer out. Colleges most students transferred to 2015: University of Wisconsin-Green Bay, University of Wisconsin-Oshkosh, University of Wisconsin-Stevens Point, University of Wisconsin-Madison, Northern Michigan University.

Basis for selection. Class rank, GPA, courses, ACT scores, and involvement important. Applicants not meeting minimum standards may be accepted but required to take reduced course load and/or noncredit courses to remedy deficiencies. **Adult students:** SAT/ACT scores not required if applicant over 21. **Home schooled:** Transcript of courses and grades required.

High school preparation. 17 units required. Required units include English 4, mathematics 3, social studies 3 and science 3. 4 electives of computer science, business, foreign language and/or fine arts required.

2015-2016 Annual costs. Tuition/fees: $5,105; $12,089 out-of-state. Per-credit charge: $198 in-state; $489 out-of-state. Books/supplies: $860. Personal expenses: $1,690.

Financial aid. All financial aid based on need. Need-based aid available for part-time students. Work-study available nights, weekends and for part-time students.

Application procedures. Admission: Priority date 7/1; no deadline. $44 fee, may be waived for applicants with need. Admission notification on a rolling basis. Students may be conditionally admitted prior to receipt of ACT scores, but may not register for classes until scores are received. **Financial aid:** Priority date 4/15; no closing date. FAFSA required. Applicants notified on a rolling basis.

Academics. Special study options: Accelerated study, cross-registration, distance learning, dual enrollment of high school students, ESL, independent study, study abroad. Bachelor's degree programs available on campus. **Credit/placement by examination:** AP, CLEP, institutional tests. **Support services:** Reduced course load, remedial instruction, study skills assistance, tutoring, writing center.

Majors. Area/ethnic studies: Women's. **Liberal arts:** Arts/sciences.

Technology on campus. 80 workstations in library, computer center, student center. Online course registration, online library, helpline, wireless network available.

Student life. Freshman orientation: Mandatory, $100 fee. Preregistration for classes offered. **Activities:** Bands, choral groups, drama, international student organizations, literary magazine, music ensembles, musical theater, student government, student newspaper, Phi Theta Kappa.

Athletics. NJCAA. **Intercollegiate:** Basketball, volleyball W. **Intramural:** Basketball, bowling, football (non-tackle), skiing, table tennis, volleyball. **Team name:** Buccaneers.

Student services. Adult student services, career counseling, services for economically disadvantaged, student employment services, financial aid counseling, minority student services, personal counseling, veterans' counselor. **Physically disabled:** Services for visually, speech, hearing impaired. **Transfer:** Transfer adviser, college fairs on campus for students transferring to 4-year colleges.

Contact. E-mail: ssinfo@uwc.edu
Phone: (715) 735-4301 Fax: (715) 735-4304
Cynthia Bailey, Assistant Campus Dean for Student Services, University of Wisconsin-Marinette, 750 West Bay Shore Street, Marinette, WI 54143

University of Wisconsin-Marshfield/Wood County
Marshfield, Wisconsin
www.marshfield.uwc.edu   **CB code: 1997**

▶ Public 2-year branch campus college
▶ Commuter campus in small city
▶ SAT or ACT (ACT writing optional) required

General. Founded in 1964. Regionally accredited. Two-year transfer program prepares students for any four-year program in Wisconsin system. Students can also enroll in the Bachelor of Applied Arts and Science Degree. **Enrollment:** 650 degree-seeking undergraduates. **Degrees:** 91 associate awarded. **Location:** 138 miles from Madison. **Calendar:** Semester, limited summer session. **Full-time faculty:** 19 total. **Part-time faculty:** 20 total. **Class size:** 30% < 20, 67% 20-39, 1% 40-49, 2% 50-99.

Student profile.

Out-of-state:	1% **25 or older:**	28%

Transfer out. Colleges most students transferred to 2015: University of Wisconsin-Steven's Point, University of Wisconsin-Eau Claire, University of Wisconsin-Madison.

Basis for selection. Rank in top 75% of class and 17 specified high school academic units ensures admission. Students in bottom 25% of their class and/or with missing credits or low scores may be asked to submit additional paperwork or letters of recommendation. Students not admitted may be admitted to a following semester. Placement tests required in math and English. **Adult students:** SAT/ACT scores not required if applicant over

---

21 or out of high school 3 years or more. **Home schooled:** Transcript of courses and grades required.

High school preparation. 17 units required. Required and recommended units include English 4, mathematics 3-4, social studies 3, science 3-4 and academic electives 4.

2015-2016 Annual costs. Tuition/fees: $5,288; $12,272 out-of-state. Per-credit charge: $198 in-state; $489 out-of-state. Room only: $4,800. Books/supplies: $500.

Financial aid. Need-based: Need-based aid available for part-time students. Work-study available nights, weekends and for part-time students. **Non-need-based:** Scholarships awarded for academics.

Application procedures. Admission: No deadline. $44 fee, may be waived for applicants with need. Admission notification on a rolling basis. **Financial aid:** Closing date 4/15. FAFSA required. Applicants notified on a rolling basis starting 4/1.

Academics. Special study options: Accelerated study, cross-registration, distance learning, dual enrollment of high school students, independent study, internships, study abroad. Bachelor's degree programs available on campus. **Credit/placement by examination:** AP, CLEP, institutional tests. **Support services:** Learning center, pre-admission summer program, reduced course load, remedial instruction, study skills assistance, tutoring, writing center.

Majors. Liberal arts: Arts/sciences.

Technology on campus. 40 workstations in library, computer center, student center. Dormitories wired for high-speed internet access. Commuter students can connect to campus network. Online course registration, online library, helpline, wireless network available.

Student life. Freshman orientation: Mandatory, $55 fee. Preregistration for classes offered. 1-day session held in late August. **Housing:** Apartments available. **Activities:** Bands, choral groups, drama, literary magazine, music ensembles, musical theater, student government, student newspaper, symphony orchestra, Inter-Varsity Christian Fellowship, business club, nursing association, program board, honor fraternity, student education association.

Athletics. NJCAA. **Intercollegiate:** Basketball, golf, tennis, volleyball W. **Intramural:** Basketball, bowling, football (tackle) M, soccer, softball, tennis, volleyball. **Team name:** Marauders.

Student services. Adult student services, alcohol/substance abuse counseling, career counseling, student employment services, financial aid counseling, personal counseling, veterans' counselor. **Physically disabled:** Services for visually, speech, hearing impaired. **Transfer:** Transfer adviser, college fairs on campus for students transferring to 4-year colleges.

Contact. E-mail: msfadmit@uwc.edu
Phone: (715) 389-6500 Fax: (715) 384-1718
Brittany Lueth, Assistant Campus Dean for Student Affairs, University of Wisconsin-Marshfield/Wood County, 2000 West Fifth Street, Marshfield, WI 54449

University of Wisconsin-Richland
Richland Center, Wisconsin
www.richland.uwc.edu   **CB code: 1662**

▶ Public 2-year liberal arts college
▶ Commuter campus in small town

General. Founded in 1967. Regionally accredited. **Enrollment:** 320 degree-seeking undergraduates. **Degrees:** 84 associate awarded. **Location:** 60 miles from Madison, 60 miles from LaCrosse. **Calendar:** Semester, limited summer session. **Full-time faculty:** 21 total; 14% minority. **Part-time faculty:** 11 total. **Class size:** 63% < 20, 37% 20-39.

Student profile.

Out-of-state:	1%	**Live on campus:**	43%
25 or older:	13%		

Transfer out. Colleges most students transferred to 2015: University of Wisconsin-LaCrosse, University of Wisconsin-Stevens Point, University of Wisconsin-Platteville, University of Wisconsin-Madison, University of Wisconsin-Eau Claire,.

Basis for selection. Open admission, but selective for some programs. Rank in upper 75% of class ensures admission. Students in bottom 25% may be admitted on discretionary category basis. Qualified students denied admission will be admitted at later date. Interview may be required for applicants in bottom 25% of class. **Adult students:** SAT/ACT scores not required if applicant over 21. **Home schooled:** Transcript of courses and grades required.

High school preparation. 17 units required. Required units include English 4, mathematics 3, social studies 3, science 3 and academic electives 4. 4 of the required units may be in foreign language, fine arts, computer science or other academic areas.

2015-2016 Annual costs. Tuition/fees: $5,330; $12,314 out-of-state. Per-credit charge: $198 in-state; $489 out-of-state. Books/supplies: $1,020. Personal expenses: $1,730.

Financial aid. All financial aid based on need. Need-based aid available for part-time students. Work-study available nights, weekends and for part-time students.

Application procedures. Admission: No deadline. $44 fee, may be waived for applicants with need. Admission notification on a rolling basis. **Financial aid:** Priority date 4/1; no closing date. FAFSA required. Applicants notified on a rolling basis starting 5/15; must reply within 3 week(s) of notification.

Academics. Associate of arts and science degree accepted throughout University of Wisconsin System as transfer tool; satisfies general education requirements of any system campus. Online writing lab available to students at all times. **Special study options:** Cross-registration, distance learning, dual enrollment of high school students, independent study, internships. Bachelor's degree programs available on campus. **Credit/placement by examination:** AP, CLEP, institutional tests. **Support services:** Learning center, reduced course load, remedial instruction, study skills assistance, tutoring, writing center.

Majors. Liberal arts: Arts/sciences.

Technology on campus. 64 workstations in dormitories, library, computer center, student center. Dormitories wired for high-speed internet access and linked to campus network. Commuter students can connect to campus network. Online course registration, online library, helpline, repair service, wireless network available.

Student life. Freshman orientation: Mandatory, $120 fee. Preregistration for classes offered. Held during the first week of fall classes. **Housing:** Coed dorms, apartments available. $200 deposit. Suites are available. **Activities:** Concert band, choral groups, drama, international student organizations, music ensembles, student government, International club, Diminuendos (A Capella club), Gay-Straight Alliance, Campus Democrats, College Republicans, InterVarsity Christian Fellowship, Earth club, Collegiate 4-H , Richland Nurses (RN) club, Paranormal Researchers.

Athletics. Intercollegiate: Basketball, volleyball W. **Intramural:** Basketball, football (non-tackle), softball, volleyball. **Team name:** Roadrunners.

Student services. Adult student services, alcohol/substance abuse counseling, career counseling, student employment services, financial aid counseling, personal counseling, veterans' counselor. **Physically disabled:** Services for visually impaired. **Transfer:** Pre-admission transcript evaluation for new students. Transfer adviser, college fairs on campus for students transferring to 4-year colleges.

Contact. E-mail: rlninfo@uwc.edu
Phone: (608) 647-6186 ext. 3 Fax: (608) 647-2275
Annette Hackbarth-Onson, Assistant Campus Dean Student Affairs, University of Wisconsin-Richland, 1200 Highway 14 West, Richland Center, WI 53581

University of Wisconsin-Rock County
Janesville, Wisconsin
www.rock.uwc.edu   CB code: 1998

▶ Public 2-year branch campus and liberal arts college
▶ Commuter campus in small city
▶ SAT or ACT (ACT writing optional) required

General. Founded in 1966. Regionally accredited. **Enrollment:** 1,220 degree-seeking undergraduates. **Degrees:** 180 associate awarded. **Location:** 40 miles from Madison. **Calendar:** Semester, limited summer session. **Full-time faculty:** 33 total. **Part-time faculty:** 23 total. **Class size:** 51% < 20, 46% 20-39, 2% 40-49, less than 1% 50-99.

Student profile.

Out-of-state:	1%	25 or older:	25%

Transfer out. Colleges most students transferred to 2015: University of Wisconsin-Whitewater, University of Wisconsin-Madison.

Basis for selection. Rank in upper 75% of class ensures admission. Students in bottom 25% and those with GED admitted under special conditions. SAT or ACT scores used for students with GED or in bottom 25% of class. Essays considered. **Adult students:** SAT/ACT scores not required if applicant over 21. **Home schooled:** Transcript of courses and grades required.

High school preparation. 17 units recommended. Recommended units include English 4, mathematics 3, social studies 3, science 3 and academic electives 4.

2015-2016 Annual costs. Tuition/fees: $5,118; $12,102 out-of-state. Per-credit charge: $198 in-state; $489 out-of-state. Books/supplies: $500. Personal expenses: $810.

Financial aid. All financial aid based on need. Need-based aid available for part-time students. Work-study available nights, weekends and for part-time students.

Application procedures. Admission: No deadline. $44 fee. Admission notification on a rolling basis. **Financial aid:** Closing date 3/15. FAFSA, institutional form required. Applicants notified on a rolling basis starting 6/1; must reply within 3 week(s) of notification.

Academics. Special study options: Cross-registration, distance learning, dual enrollment of high school students, independent study, study abroad. Bachelor's degree programs available on campus. **Credit/placement by examination:** AP, CLEP, institutional tests. **Support services:** Learning center, reduced course load, remedial instruction, study skills assistance, tutoring, writing center.

Majors. Liberal arts: Arts/sciences.

Technology on campus. 50 workstations in library, computer center. Commuter students can connect to campus network.

Student life. Freshman orientation: Mandatory, $95 fee. Preregistration for classes offered. 3-hour sessions held in May, June, July, and August. **Activities:** Bands, choral groups, dance, drama, literary magazine, music ensembles, student government, student newspaper, symphony orchestra, Future Educators, adult student organization.

Athletics. NJCAA. **Intercollegiate:** Soccer, tennis, volleyball W. **Intramural:** Badminton, basketball, soccer, softball, tennis, volleyball. **Team name:** Rattlers.

Student services. Adult student services, alcohol/substance abuse counseling, career counseling, services for economically disadvantaged, student employment services, financial aid counseling, minority student services, personal counseling, veterans' counselor. **Physically disabled:** Services for visually, hearing impaired. **Transfer:** Re-entry adviser for new students. Transfer adviser, college fairs on campus for students transferring to 4-year colleges.

Contact. E-mail: rckinfo@uwc.edu
Phone: (608) 758-6523 Fax: (608) 758-6579
Kristin Fillhouer, Assistant Campus Dean for Student Services, University of Wisconsin-Rock County, 2909 Kellogg Avenue, Janesville, WI 53546-5699

University of Wisconsin-Sheboygan
Sheboygan, Wisconsin
www.sheboygan.uwc.edu   CB code: 1994

▶ Public 2-year community and liberal arts college
▶ Commuter campus in small city
▶ SAT or ACT (ACT writing optional), application essay required

General. Founded in 1933. Regionally accredited. **Enrollment:** 769 undergraduates. **Degrees:** 108 associate awarded. **Location:** 60 miles from Milwaukee, 50 miles from Green Bay. **Calendar:** Semester, limited summer session. **Full-time faculty:** 22 total. **Part-time faculty:** 25 total. **Special facilities:** Aquaponics lab.

Student profile.

Out-of-state:	1%	25 or older:	31%

Transfer out. Colleges most students transferred to 2015: University of Wisconsin-Milwaukee, University of Wisconsin-Green Bay, University of Wisconsin-Oshkosh, University of Wisconsin-Madison, University of Wisconsin-Stevens Point.

Basis for selection. Open admission. Personal statement required for application. **Adult students:** SAT/ACT scores not required if applicant over 21.

High school preparation. 17 units required. Required units include English 4, mathematics 3, social studies 3 and science 3. Additional 4 units required from English, social science, math, natural science, foreign language, fine arts, or computer science.

2015-2016 Annual costs. Tuition/fees: $5,136; $12,120 out-of-state. Books/supplies: $500. Personal expenses: $1,690.

Financial aid. Need-based: Need-based aid available for part-time students. Work-study available nights, weekends and for part-time students. **Non-need-based:** Scholarships awarded for academics, art, leadership, music/drama.

Application procedures. Admission: Priority date 6/30; no deadline. $44 fee, may be waived for applicants with need. Application must be submitted online. Admission notification on a rolling basis. **Financial aid:** Priority date 4/15; no closing date. FAFSA, institutional form required. Applicants notified on a rolling basis starting 6/1; must reply within 2 week(s) of notification.

Academics. Special study options: Distance learning, dual enrollment of high school students, exchange student, honors, independent study, internships, study abroad. Bachelor's degree programs available on campus. **Credit/placement by examination:** AP, CLEP, IB, ACT, institutional tests. **Support services:** Learning center, reduced course load, remedial instruction, study skills assistance, tutoring, writing center.

Majors. Liberal arts: Arts/sciences.

Technology on campus. 80 workstations in library, computer center, student center. Commuter students can connect to campus network. Online course registration, online library, helpline, wireless network available.

Student life. Freshman orientation: Mandatory. Preregistration for classes offered. **Activities:** Bands, choral groups, drama, literary magazine, music ensembles, musical theater, student government, student newspaper, TV station, Intervarsity Christian Fellowship, Circle K, Southeat Asian Club, Latin American Student Organization.

Athletics. NJCAA. **Intercollegiate:** Basketball M, golf, soccer, tennis, volleyball W. **Intramural:** Basketball, football (non-tackle), ultimate frisbee, volleyball. **Team name:** Wombats.

Student services. Adult student services, alcohol/substance abuse counseling, career counseling, financial aid counseling, personal counseling, veterans' counselor. **Physically disabled:** Services for visually, speech, hearing impaired. **Transfer:** Pre-admission transcript evaluation for new students. Transfer center, transfer adviser, college fairs on campus for students transferring to 4-year colleges.

Contact. E-mail: uwshb@uwc.edu
Phone: (920) 459-6633 Fax: (920) 459-6602
Bryan Bain, Assistant Campus Dean for Student Affairs & Enrollment Management, University of Wisconsin-Sheboygan, One University Drive, Sheboygan, WI 53081

University of Wisconsin-Washington County
West Bend, Wisconsin
www.washington.uwc.edu   CB code: 1993

▶ Public 2-year branch campus and liberal arts college
▶ Commuter campus in large town
▶ SAT or ACT (ACT writing optional) required

General. Founded in 1968. Regionally accredited. **Enrollment:** 810 undergraduates. **Degrees:** 165 associate awarded. **Location:** 70 miles from Madison, 35 miles from Milwaukee. **Calendar:** Semester, limited summer session. **Full-time faculty:** 26 total. **Part-time faculty:** 32 total. **Special facilities:** Observatory.

Student profile.

Out-of-state: 2%   25 or older: 17%

Transfer out. Colleges most students transferred to 2015: University of Wisconsin-Milwaukee, University of Wisconsin-Oshkosh, University of Wisconsin-Whitewater, University of Wisconsin-Madison.

Basis for selection. Rank in top 75% of class ensures admission. Students in bottom 25% placed in discretionary category. Qualified students not admitted for specific semester applied for will be admitted at later date. ACT

---

preferred. Interview required for applicants with GED or those ranking in bottom 25% of high school class. **Adult students:** SAT/ACT scores not required if applicant over 21. **Home schooled:** Transcript of courses and grades required.

High school preparation. 17 units required. Required units include English 4, mathematics 3, social studies 3, science 3 and academic electives 4.

2015-2016 Annual costs. Tuition/fees: $5,094; $12,078 out-of-state. Per-credit charge: $198 in-state; $489 out-of-state. Books/supplies: $1,020. Personal expenses: $1,730.

Financial aid. Need-based: Need-based aid available for part-time students. Work-study available nights, weekends and for part-time students. **Non-need-based:** Scholarships awarded for academics.

Application procedures. Admission: Priority date 8/1; no deadline. $44 fee, may be waived for applicants with need. Admission notification on a rolling basis beginning on or about 11/1. **Financial aid:** Priority date 4/15; no closing date. FAFSA required. Applicants notified on a rolling basis starting 4/30; must reply within 3 week(s) of notification.

Academics. Special study options: Cross-registration, distance learning, dual enrollment of high school students, honors, independent study, internships, study abroad. Collaborative B.A. degree programs in organizational administration, information resources, communications, BSN in nursing, all in cooperation with University of Wisconsin-Milwaukee. Bachelor's degree programs available on campus. **Credit/placement by examination:** AP, CLEP, IB, institutional tests. **Support services:** Learning center, pre-admission summer program, reduced course load, remedial instruction, study skills assistance, tutoring, writing center.

Majors. Liberal arts: Arts/sciences.

Technology on campus. 78 workstations in library, computer center. Commuter students can connect to campus network. Wireless network available.

Student life. Freshman orientation: Mandatory, $75 fee. Preregistration for classes offered. **Activities:** Bands, choral groups, dance, drama, literary magazine, music ensembles, musical theater, student government, student newspaper, symphony orchestra, Phi Theta Kappa honorary society, Literary Guild, business club, Student Impact.

Athletics. NAIA. **Intercollegiate:** Basketball, golf, soccer, tennis, volleyball W. **Intramural:** Basketball, softball, volleyball. **Team name:** Wildcats.

Student services. Adult student services, career counseling, financial aid counseling, personal counseling, veterans' counselor. **Physically disabled:** Services for hearing impaired. **Transfer:** Pre-admission transcript evaluation for new students. Transfer center, transfer adviser, college fairs on campus for students transferring to 4-year colleges.

Contact. Phone: (262) 335-5201 Fax: (262) 335-5274
Maria Graciano, Admissions Specialist, University of Wisconsin-Washington County, 400 University Drive, West Bend, WI 53095

University of Wisconsin-Waukesha
Waukesha, Wisconsin
www.waukesha.uwc.edu   CB code: 1999

▶ Public 2-year branch campus and junior college
▶ Commuter campus in small city
▶ SAT or ACT (ACT writing optional) required

General. Founded in 1966. Regionally accredited. **Enrollment:** 1,929 degree-seeking undergraduates. **Degrees:** 258 associate awarded. **Location:** 17 miles from Milwaukee. **Calendar:** Semester, limited summer session. **Full-time faculty:** 64 total; 95% have terminal degrees, 16% minority, 44% women. **Part-time faculty:** 29 total; 86% have terminal degrees, 7% minority, 34% women. **Special facilities:** 98-acre environmental studies field station.

Student profile.

Out-of-state: 1%   25 or older: 24%

Transfer out. Colleges most students transferred to 2015: University of Wisconsin-Milwaukee, University of Wisconsin-Whitewater, University of Wisconsin-Madison, Univeristy of Wisconsin-Oshkosh, Univeristy of Wisconsin-Parkside.

Basis for selection. Rank in top 75% of class, 19 ACT. CGPA of 2.0 or better ensures admission. Students who do not meet these standards may be admitted conditionally or with an admission interview. **Adult students:** SAT/ACT scores not required if applicant over 21.

High school preparation. 17 units required. Required and recommended units include English 4, mathematics 3, social studies 3, science 3, foreign language 2 and academic electives 4.

2015-2016 Annual costs. Tuition/fees: $5,102; $12,086 out-of-state. Per-credit charge: $198 in-state; $489 out-of-state. Books/supplies: $980. Personal expenses: $1,690.

Financial aid. Need-based: Need-based aid available for part-time students. Work-study available nights, weekends and for part-time students. **Non-need-based:** Scholarships awarded for academics, alumni affiliation, art, leadership, minority status, music/drama, state residency.

Application procedures. Admission: Priority date 4/1; no deadline. $44 fee, may be waived for applicants with need. Admission notification on a rolling basis beginning on or about 9/15. **Financial aid:** Priority date 4/1; no closing date. FAFSA required. Applicants notified on a rolling basis starting 4/1; must reply within 3 week(s) of notification.

Academics. Special study options: Accelerated study, cross-registration, distance learning, dual enrollment of high school students, honors, independent study, internships, study abroad. Bachelor's degree programs available on campus. **Credit/placement by examination:** AP, CLEP, IB, institutional tests. CLEP general exams must be taken before 16 degree credits completed. **Support services:** Learning center, pre-admission summer program, reduced course load, remedial instruction, study skills assistance, tutoring, writing center.

Majors. Liberal arts: Arts/sciences.

Technology on campus. 90 workstations in library, computer center, student center. Commuter students can connect to campus network. Online course registration, wireless network available.

Student life. Freshman orientation: Mandatory, $230 fee. Preregistration for classes offered. Sessions held periodically throughout summer. **Activities:** Bands, choral groups, dance, drama, literary magazine, music ensembles, musical theater, student government, student newspaper, Diversity club, Phi Theta Kappa honor society, Campus Crusade for Christ, College Democrats, College Republicans, Circle K, African American Union, Organization of Latin American Leaders.

Athletics. NJCAA. Intercollegiate: Basketball, cheerleading W, cross-country, golf, soccer, tennis, volleyball W. **Team name:** Cougars.

Student services. Adult student services, career counseling, financial aid counseling, on-campus daycare, personal counseling, veterans' counselor. **Physically disabled:** Services for visually, speech, hearing impaired. **Transfer:** Transfer adviser, college fairs on campus for students transferring to 4-year colleges.

Contact. E-mail: wakadmit@uwc.edu
Phone: (262) 521-5041 Fax: (262) 521-5530
Deb Kusick, Senior Admission Specialist, University of Wisconsin-Waukesha, 1500 North University Drive, Waukesha, WI 53188

Waukesha County Technical College
Pewaukee, Wisconsin
www.wctc.edu   **CB code: 0724**

▶ Public 2-year technical college
▶ Commuter campus in large town

General. Founded in 1923. Regionally accredited. **Enrollment:** 4,889 degree-seeking undergraduates; 3,039 non-degree-seeking students. **Degrees:** 723 associate awarded. **Location:** 15 miles from Milwaukee. **Calendar:** Semester, limited summer session. **Full-time faculty:** 196 total. **Part-time faculty:** 668 total. **Special facilities:** Green energy training facilities, wind turbine, green roofs.

Student profile. Among degree-seeking undergraduates, 100% enrolled in a vocational program, 9% already have a bachelor's degree or higher, 564 enrolled as first-time, first-year students.

Part-time:	68%	Hispanic/Latino:	8%
Women:	47%	Native American:	1%
African American:	8%	Multi-racial, non-Hispanic:	2%
Asian American:	2%	25 or older:	54%

Transfer out. Colleges most students transferred to 2015: University of Wisconsin - Milwaukee, Carroll University, Cardinal Stritch University.

Basis for selection. Open admission, but selective for some programs. Individual programs may have additional requirements or prerequisites, and some programs may have wait lists. Some health occupations programs may require interviews and a general college preparatory background of prerequisites. **Adult students:** SAT/ACT scores not required. **Home schooled:** Transcript of courses and grades required.

2015-2016 Annual costs. Tuition/fees: $4,083; $6,009 out-of-state. Per-credit charge: $128 in-state; $193 out-of-state. Books/supplies: $1,750. Personal expenses: $2,000. **Additional information:** Materials fees vary by program; minimum $5 per course. $10 per credit fee for online courses.

2014-2015 Financial aid. Need-based: 34% of total undergraduate aid awarded as scholarships/grants, 66% as loans/jobs. Work-study available nights, weekends and for part-time students. **Non-need-based:** Scholarships awarded for academics.

Application procedures. Admission: No deadline. $30 fee, may be waived for applicants with need. Admission notification on a rolling basis. **Financial aid:** Priority date 4/1; no closing date. FAFSA required. Applicants notified on a rolling basis starting 4/30.

Academics. Special study options: Accelerated study, cooperative education, distance learning, double major, dual enrollment of high school students, ESL, independent study, internships, student-designed major, study abroad. License preparation in dental hygiene, nursing, paramedic, real estate. **Credit/placement by examination:** AP, CLEP, institutional tests. **Support services:** GED preparation and test center, learning center, remedial instruction, study skills assistance, tutoring, writing center.

Majors. Business: Accounting, administrative services, business admin, hotel/motel/restaurant management, human resources, international marketing, marketing, office management, real estate. **Communications technology:** Graphics. **Computer sciences:** Networking, programming, support specialist. **Education:** Early childhood, teacher assistance. **Health services:** Clinical lab technology, dental hygiene, EMT paramedic, health information technology, medical radiologic technology/radiation therapy, mental health services, nursing (RN), physical therapy assistant, surgical technology. **Protective services:** Firefighting, police science. **Visual/performing arts:** Digital arts, graphic design, interior design.

Most popular majors. Business/marketing 28%, computer/information sciences 11%, engineering/engineering technologies 11%, health sciences 20%, security/protective services 12%, visual/performing arts 6%.

Technology on campus. Commuter students can connect to campus network. Online course registration, online library, helpline, wireless network available.

Student life. Freshman orientation: Mandatory, $10 fee. Preregistration for classes offered. Six-hour orientation. **Activities:** Student government, Campus Crusade for Christ, diversity club, Gay/Straight Alliance (G.L.O.W.-Gay Lesbian or Whatever), veterans club.

Student services. Adult student services, career counseling, services for economically disadvantaged, student employment services, financial aid counseling, minority student services, on-campus daycare, personal counseling, placement for graduates, veterans' counselor. **Physically disabled:** Services for visually, speech, hearing impaired. **Transfer:** Pre-admission transcript evaluation for new students. College fairs on campus for students transferring to 4-year colleges.

Contact. E-mail: info@wctc.edu
Phone: (262) 691-5200 Fax: (262) 691-5123
Kathleen Kazda, Manager, Advising/Admissions/Assessment, Waukesha County Technical College, Office of Admissions, C-019, Pewaukee, WI 53072

Western Technical College
La Crosse, Wisconsin
www.westerntc.edu   **CB code: 1087**

▶ Public 2-year community and technical college
▶ Commuter campus in small city

General. Founded in 1912. Regionally accredited. **Enrollment:** 4,525 degree-seeking undergraduates. **Degrees:** 564 associate awarded. **Location:** 200 miles from Milwaukee, 150 miles from Minneapolis-St. Paul. **Calendar:** Semester, limited summer session. **Full-time faculty:** 209 total. **Part-time faculty:** 519 total.

Student profile.

Out-of-state:	9%	25 or older:	36%

Basis for selection. Open admission, but selective for some programs. Standardized test scores required for admission into selected programs. COMPASS required for placement if ACT scores not available. Interviews recommended for placement, portfolios recommended for commercial art applicants for placement.

High school preparation. Recommended units include English 3, mathematics 2, social studies 3 and science 2.

2015-2016 Annual costs. Tuition/fees: $4,164; $6,090 out-of-state. Per-credit charge: $126 in-state; $189 out-of-state. Books/supplies: $1,400. Personal expenses: $1,774.

Financial aid. Need-based: Need-based aid available for part-time students. Work-study available nights, weekends and for part-time students.

Application procedures. Admission: No deadline. $30 fee, may be waived for applicants with need. Admission notification on a rolling basis. **Financial aid:** Priority date 3/1; no closing date. FAFSA, institutional form required. Applicants notified on a rolling basis starting 4/1.

Academics. Special study options: Accelerated study, cooperative education, distance learning, double major, dual enrollment of high school students, ESL, honors, independent study, internships, student-designed major. License preparation in nursing, occupational therapy, paramedic, physical therapy, radiology, real estate. **Credit/placement by examination:** AP, CLEP, institutional tests. 45 credit hours maximum toward associate degree. **Support services:** GED preparation and test center, learning center, reduced course load, remedial instruction, study skills assistance, tutoring, writing center.

Majors. Business: Accounting, administrative services, business admin, finance, human resources, marketing, operations. **Computer sciences:** Networking, support specialist, web page design. **Education:** Early childhood, teacher assistance. **Health services:** Clinical lab technology, EMT paramedic, health information technology, nursing (RN), occupational therapy assistant, office admin, physical therapy assistant, radiologic technology/medical imaging, respiratory therapy technology, surgical technology. **Liberal arts:** Arts/sciences. **Protective services:** Fire safety technology, police science. **Visual/performing arts:** Design, graphic design, interior design. **Work/family studies:** Child care management.

Most popular majors. Business/marketing 33%, computer/information sciences 6%, engineering/engineering technologies 10%, health sciences 31%, security/protective services 8%.

Technology on campus. 145 workstations in dormitories, library, computer center. Dormitories wired for high-speed internet access and linked to campus network. Commuter students can connect to campus network. Online course registration, online library, helpline, repair service, wireless network available.

Student life. Freshman orientation: Mandatory. Preregistration for classes offered. General school orientation held in August. **Housing:** Coed dorms available. **Activities:** Student government, multicultural club, Campus Crusade for Christ.

Athletics. NJCAA. **Intercollegiate:** Baseball M, basketball, volleyball W. **Intramural:** Badminton, basketball, bowling, volleyball. **Team name:** Cavaliers.

Student services. Adult student services, alcohol/substance abuse counseling, career counseling, services for economically disadvantaged, student employment services, financial aid counseling, health services, minority student services, on-campus daycare, personal counseling, placement for graduates, veterans' counselor, women's services. **Physically disabled:** Services for visually, speech, hearing impaired. **Transfer:** Pre-admission transcript evaluation for new students.

Contact. E-mail: EnrollServices@westerntc.edu
Phone: (608) 785-9476 Toll-free number: (800) 322-9982
Fax: (608) 785-9148
Sandra Peterson, Admissions, Registration and Records, Western Technical College, 400 Seventh St N, La Crosse, WI 54601

Wisconsin Indianhead Technical College

Shell Lake, Wisconsin **CB member**
www.witc.edu **CB code: 1580**

♦ Public 2-year technical college
♦ Commuter campus in small town
♦ Interview required

General. Founded in 1972. Regionally accredited. 4 campuses and 2 outreach centers covering 11 county area. **Enrollment:** 2,558 degree-seeking

undergraduates; 336 non-degree-seeking students. **Degrees:** 411 associate awarded. **Calendar:** Semester, limited summer session. **Full-time faculty:** 151 total. **Part-time faculty:** 112 total. **Partnerships:** Formal partnerships with CISCO Network Academy, CompTIA, Microsoft and VMware.

Student profile. Among degree-seeking undergraduates, 99% enrolled in a vocational program, 4% already have a bachelor's degree or higher, 532 enrolled as first-time, first-year students.

Part-time:	56%	Native American:	2%
Out-of-state:	8%	Multi-racial, non-Hispanic:	2%
Women:	60%	25 or older:	49%
African American:	1%		

Transfer out. Colleges most students transferred to 2015: University of Wisconsin.

Basis for selection. Open admission, but selective for some programs. ACCUPLACER used for skills assessment and placement. Developmental coursework required if scores below established range. **Home schooled:** Statement describing home school structure and mission, transcript of courses and grades required. Must pass ability to benefit assessment.

High school preparation. College-preparatory program recommended.

2015-2016 Annual costs. Tuition/fees: $4,655; $6,575 out-of-state. Per-credit charge: $126 in-state; $189 out-of-state. Books/supplies: $1,664. Personal expenses: $1,822.

2014-2015 Financial aid. All financial aid based on need. 55% of total undergraduate aid awarded as scholarships/grants, 45% as loans/jobs. Need-based aid available for part-time students. Work-study available nights, weekends and for part-time students.

Application procedures. Admission: No deadline. $30 fee. Admission notification on a rolling basis. **Financial aid:** Priority date 4/15; no closing date. FAFSA required. Applicants notified on a rolling basis starting 4/15; must reply by 9/1 or within 4 week(s) of notification.

Academics. Special study options: Accelerated study, cooperative education, cross-registration, distance learning, double major, dual enrollment of high school students, ESL, external degree, independent study, internships, liberal arts/career combination, student-designed major, study abroad. License preparation in dental hygiene, nursing, occupational therapy, paramedic, real estate. **Credit/placement by examination:** AP, CLEP, institutional tests. **Support services:** GED preparation and test center, learning center, pre-admission summer program, reduced course load, remedial instruction, study skills assistance, tutoring, writing center.

Majors. Business: Accounting, administrative services, business admin, finance, human resources, marketing, office management. **Computer sciences:** Networking, programming, support specialist, web page design. **Education:** Early childhood. **Engineering:** Materials. **Health services:** EMT paramedic, health information technology, medical secretary, mental health services, nursing (RN), occupational therapy assistant. **Protective services:** Corrections, police science.

Most popular majors. Business/marketing 32%, computer/information sciences 12%, family/consumer sciences 15%, health sciences 29%, security/protective services 9%.

Technology on campus. 780 workstations in library, computer center, student center. Commuter students can connect to campus network. Online course registration, online library, helpline, repair service, wireless network available.

Student life. Freshman orientation: Available. Preregistration for classes offered. **Housing:** Apartments available. **Activities:** Student government, student newspaper, technical student organizations, vocational student organizations.

Student services. Adult student services, career counseling, services for economically disadvantaged, student employment services, financial aid counseling, health services, minority student services, personal counseling, placement for graduates, veterans' counselor. **Physically disabled:** Services for visually, speech, hearing impaired. **Transfer:** College fairs on campus for students transferring to 4-year colleges.

Contact. E-mail: laura.sullivan@witc.edu
Phone: (715) 468-2815 ext. 2280
Toll-free number: (800) 243-9482 ext. 2280 Fax: (715) 468-2819
Laura Sullivan, Director of Enrollment, Wisconsin Indianhead Technical College, 505 Pine Ridge Drive, Shell Lake, WI 54871

Wyoming

Casper College
Casper, Wyoming
www.caspercollege.edu

CB code: 4043

- Public 2-year community college
- Commuter campus in small city

General. Founded in 1945. Regionally accredited. **Enrollment:** 2,429 degree-seeking undergraduates; 1,433 non-degree-seeking students. **Degrees:** 565 associate awarded. **Location:** 280 miles from Denver. **Calendar:** Semester, limited summer session. **Full-time faculty:** 148 total; 32% have terminal degrees, 3% minority, 43% women. **Part-time faculty:** 110 total; 11% have terminal degrees, 6% minority, 51% women. **Class size:** 74% < 20, 25% 20-39, less than 1% 40-49, less than 1% 50-99. **Special facilities:** Wildlife museum, geological museum, family resource center, fitness center, Western history center.

Student profile. Among degree-seeking undergraduates, 72% enrolled in a transfer program, 27% enrolled in a vocational program, 658 enrolled as first-time, first-year students, 219 transferred in from other institutions.

Part-time:	31%	Native American:	1%
Women:	61%	Multi-racial, non-Hispanic:	2%
African American:	1%	International:	1%
Asian American:	1%	25 or older:	33%
Hispanic/Latino:	6%	Live on campus:	17%

Transfer out. Colleges most students transferred to 2015: University of Wyoming, Colorado State University, Chadron State College, Valley City State Universtiy, Colorado Mesa University.

Basis for selection. Open admission, but selective for some programs and for out-of-state students. 2.0 GPA required for out-of-state applicants. Selective admission for nursing, respiratory therapy, radiology; requirements vary by program. Audition recommended for music, theater, athletics and forensics; portfolio recommended for art. **Home schooled:** Program must be accredited and recognized by state department of education as being equivalent to high school diploma.

High school preparation. College-preparatory program recommended. Recommended units include English 4, mathematics 4, social studies 3, science 4 and foreign language 2.

2015-2016 Annual costs. Tuition/fees: $2,640; $6,624 out-of-state. Per-credit charge: $83 in-state; $249 out-of-state. Room/board: $6,294. Books/supplies: $1,200. Personal expenses: $2,610. **Additional information:** Western Undergraduate Exchange (WUE) students qualify for reduced rates.

Financial aid. Need-based: Need-based aid available for part-time students. Work-study available nights, weekends and for part-time students. **Non-need-based:** Scholarships awarded for academics, art, athletics, leadership, music/drama, state residency.

Application procedures. Admission: Priority date 8/1; deadline 8/15 (postmark date). No application fee. Admission notification on a rolling basis beginning on or about 2/1. **Financial aid:** Priority date 3/15; no closing date. FAFSA required. Applicants notified on a rolling basis starting 4/1.

Academics. Special study options: Cooperative education, cross-registration, distance learning, dual enrollment of high school students, honors, independent study, internships. Bachelor's degree programs available on campus. License preparation in nursing, paramedic, radiology. **Credit/placement by examination:** AP, CLEP, IB, institutional tests. 30 credit hours maximum toward associate degree. **Support services:** GED preparation and test center, learning center, remedial instruction, study skills assistance, tutoring, writing center.

Majors. Area/ethnic studies: Women's. **Biology:** General. **Business:** Accounting, accounting technology, administrative services, business admin, construction management, entrepreneurial studies, hospitality admin, marketing, office technology, retailing. **Communications:** Communications/speech/rhetoric, journalism, media studies. **Computer sciences:** Programming, security, web page design, webmaster. **Conservation:** Environmental science, wildlife/wilderness. **Education:** Art, elementary, kindergarten/preschool, music, physical, social studies, technology/industrial arts. **Engineering:** General. **English:** English lit. **Foreign languages:** General. **Health services:** Athletic training, clinical lab technology, EMT paramedic, nursing (RN), occupational therapy assistant, pharmacy assistant, predental, premedicine, preoccupational therapy, preoptometry, prepharmacy, prephysical therapy, preveterinary, radiologic technology/medical imaging, respiratory therapy technology, substance abuse counseling. **History:** General. **Human services:** Social work. **Liberal arts:** Arts/sciences. **Math:** General. **Physical sciences:** Chemistry, geology, physics. **Protective services:** Criminal justice, disaster management, firefighting, forensics. **Psychology:** General. **Social sciences:** Anthropology, economics, GIS/cartography, international relations, political science, sociology. **Visual/performing arts:** Acting, art, dance, graphic design, music, music performance, musical theater, photography, studio arts, theater design.

Most popular majors. Agriculture 8%, education 7%, health sciences 28%, liberal arts 15%.

Technology on campus. 120 workstations in library, computer center. Dormitories wired for high-speed internet access and linked to campus network. Commuter students can connect to campus network. Helpline, wireless network available.

Student life. Freshman orientation: Mandatory. Preregistration for classes offered. One-day new student orientation held the week before classes begin. **Housing:** Coed dorms, apartments, wellness housing available. $200 fully refundable deposit. **Activities:** Bands, campus ministries, choral groups, dance, drama, literary magazine, music ensembles, musical theater, student government, student newspaper, symphony orchestra, Latter-Day Saints student association, Baptist student union, Phi Theta Kappa, Phi Rho Pi, student nurses association, Students in Free Enterprise, AG club, student activities board, Bakkai.

Athletics. NJCAA. **Intercollegiate:** Basketball, rodeo, volleyball W. **Intramural:** Basketball, bowling, football (non-tackle), soccer, softball, tennis, volleyball. **Team name:** Thunderbirds.

Student services. Adult student services, alcohol/substance abuse counseling, career counseling, student employment services, financial aid counseling, health services, legal services, on-campus daycare, personal counseling, placement for graduates, veterans' counselor. **Physically disabled:** Services for visually, speech, hearing impaired. **Transfer:** College fairs on campus for students transferring to 4-year colleges.

Contact. E-mail: kfoltz@caspercollege.edu
Phone: (307) 268-2458 Toll-free number: (800) 442-2963
Fax: (307) 268-2611
Kyla Foltz, Director of Admissions, Casper College, 125 College Drive, Casper, WY 82601

Central Wyoming College
Riverton, Wyoming
www.cwc.edu

CB code: 4115

- Public 2-year community college
- Commuter campus in large town

General. Founded in 1966. Regionally accredited. Partnership with the National Outdoor Leadership School (NOLS). **Enrollment:** 1,045 degree-seeking undergraduates; 1,141 non-degree-seeking students. **Degrees:** 206 associate awarded. **Location:** 120 miles from Casper; 240 miles from Billings, MT. **Calendar:** Semester, limited summer session. **Full-time faculty:** 58 total; 78% have terminal degrees, 5% minority, 55% women. **Part-time faculty:** 140 total; 24% have terminal degrees, 5% minority, 47% women. **Class size:** 76% < 20, 20% 20-39, 2% 40-49, 1% 50-99, less than 1% >100. **Special facilities:** Rodeo arena, fine arts center, Microsoft training laboratory, Cisco training laboratory, Native American artifacts, canyon center, Wyoming PBS station. **Partnerships:** Formal partnerships with Microsoft, Cisco (training labs, software), National Outdoor Leadership School (NOLS).

Student profile. Among degree-seeking undergraduates, 66% enrolled in a transfer program, 34% enrolled in a vocational program, 271 enrolled as first-time, first-year students, 98 transferred in from other institutions.

Part-time:	43%	Hispanic/Latino:	10%
Out-of-state:	13%	Native American:	11%
Women:	60%	Multi-racial, non-Hispanic:	4%
African American:	2%	25 or older:	34%
Asian American:	1%	Live on campus:	10%

Transfer out. Colleges most students transferred to 2015: University of Wyoming, Valley City State University, Brigham Young University, Utah State University, University of Wisconsin-Oshkosh.

Basis for selection. Open admission, but selective for some programs. Special admission to nursing program; minimum GPA and test scores required. Certain music courses require audition.

2015-2016 Annual costs. Tuition/fees: $2,892; $6,876 out-of-state. Per-credit charge: $83 in-state; $249 out-of-state. Room/board: $5,130. Books/supplies: $1,200. Personal expenses: $1,500. **Additional information:** Western Undergraduate Exchange (WUE) students qualify for reduced rates.

2015-2016 Financial aid. Need-based: 144 full-time freshmen applied for aid; 105 deemed to have need; 105 received aid. 83% of total undergraduate aid awarded as scholarships/grants, 17% as loans/jobs. Need-based aid available for part-time students. Work-study available nights, weekends and for part-time students. **Non-need-based:** Awarded to 238 full-time undergraduates, including 93 freshmen. Scholarships awarded for academics, alumni affiliation, art, athletics, leadership, minority status, music/drama, state residency.

Application procedures. Admission: No deadline. No application fee. Admission notification on a rolling basis beginning on or about 1/1. **Financial aid:** Priority date 4/15; no closing date. FAFSA, institutional form required. Applicants notified on a rolling basis starting 5/1; must reply within 2 week(s) of notification.

Academics. Special study options: Cooperative education, cross-registration, distance learning, double major, dual enrollment of high school students, external degree, honors, independent study, student-designed major, teacher certification program. Bachelor's degree programs available on campus. License preparation in dental hygiene, nursing, paramedic. **Credit/placement by examination:** AP, CLEP, institutional tests. 32 credit hours maximum toward associate degree. Some DANTES and APE exams accepted. **Support services:** GED preparation and test center, learning center, reduced course load, remedial instruction, study skills assistance, tutoring, writing center.

Majors. Area/ethnic studies: Native American. **Biology:** General. **Business:** General, accounting, accounting technology, administrative services, business admin, customer service support, entrepreneurial studies, hotel/motel admin. **Communications:** Radio/TV. **Computer sciences:** Computer science. **Conservation:** Environmental science. **Education:** Early childhood, elementary, secondary, teacher assistance. **Engineering:** General, environmental. **English:** English lit. **General:** Carpentry, maintenance. **Health services:** Athletic training, nursing (RN), office assistant. **Liberal arts:** Arts/sciences. **Math:** General. **Parks/recreation:** General, facilities management. **Physical sciences:** General, geology. **Protective services:** Firefighting, homeland security, law enforcement admin. **Psychology:** General. **Social sciences:** General, GIS/cartography. **Visual/performing arts:** General, acting, art, commercial photography, dramatic, graphic design, music, theater design. **Work/family studies:** Child care management.

Most popular majors. Business/marketing 6%, health sciences 19%, liberal arts 26%, security/protective services 8%, visual/performing arts 6%.

Technology on campus. 450 workstations in dormitories, library, computer center, student center. Dormitories wired for high-speed internet access and linked to campus network. Commuter students can connect to campus network. Online course registration, online library, wireless network available.

Student life. Freshman orientation: Mandatory. Preregistration for classes offered. **Housing:** Coed dorms, apartments available. $225 partly refundable deposit, deadline 5/1. **Activities:** Bands, choral groups, dance, drama, music ensembles, musical theater, radio station, student government, student newspaper, TV station, American Indian club, multicultural club, social science club, veterans club, Hispanic club, law and justice club, science club, Phi Theta Kappa, American Indian science and engineering society.

Athletics. NJCAA. **Intercollegiate:** Basketball, cross-country M, golf, rodeo, volleyball W. **Intramural:** Badminton, basketball, cross-country M, golf, skiing, soccer, softball, swimming, table tennis, tennis, volleyball, weight lifting. **Team name:** Rustlers.

Student services. Adult student services, alcohol/substance abuse counseling, career counseling, services for economically disadvantaged, student employment services, financial aid counseling, personal counseling, placement for graduates, veterans' counselor. **Physically disabled:** Services for visually, hearing impaired. **Transfer:** College fairs on campus for students transferring to 4-year colleges.

Contact. E-mail: admit@cwc.edu
Phone: (307) 855-2119 Toll-free number: (800) 865-0193
Fax: (307) 855-2065
Deborah Lively, Student Recruiter, Central Wyoming College, 2660 Peck Avenue, Riverton, WY 82501

Eastern Wyoming College
Torrington, Wyoming
www.ewc.wy.edu　　　　　　　　　CB code: 4700

- Public 2-year community college
- Commuter campus in small town

General. Founded in 1948. Regionally accredited. **Enrollment:** 611 degree-seeking undergraduates; 1,104 non-degree-seeking students. **Degrees:** 171 associate awarded. **Location:** 190 miles from Denver. **Calendar:** Semester, limited summer session. **Full-time faculty:** 44 total. **Part-time faculty:** 44 total. **Special facilities:** Veterinarian technology facility, cosmetology services.

Student profile. Among degree-seeking undergraduates, 64% enrolled in a transfer program, 36% enrolled in a vocational program, 205 enrolled as first-time, first-year students.

Part-time:	34%	Native American:	1%
Women:	61%	Multi-racial, non-Hispanic:	1%
African American:	1%	International:	2%
Hispanic/Latino:	8%		

Transfer out. Colleges most students transferred to 2015: University of Wyoming, Chadron State College, Black Hills State.

Basis for selection. Open admission. **Home schooled:** Transcript of courses and grades required. ACT recommended. Signed statement that student was homeschooled required for financial aid.

2015-2016 Annual costs. Tuition/fees: $2,712; $6,696 out-of-state. Room/board: $6,136. Books/supplies: $1,300. Personal expenses: $1,500. **Additional information:** Western Undergraduate Exchange (WUE) students qualify for reduced rates.

Financial aid. Need-based: Need-based aid available for part-time students. Work-study available nights, weekends and for part-time students. **Non-need-based:** Scholarships awarded for academics, alumni affiliation, art, athletics, leadership, music/drama. **Additional information:** Installment payment plan on room and board contracts offered.

Application procedures. Admission: No deadline. No application fee. Admission notification on a rolling basis. **Financial aid:** Priority date 3/15; no closing date. FAFSA, institutional form required. Applicants notified on a rolling basis starting 1/1.

Academics. Special study options: Cross-registration, distance learning, dual enrollment of high school students, ESL, independent study, internships. License preparation on campus for welding and joining, veterinary technology, and cosmetology. Bachelor's degree programs available on campus. **Credit/placement by examination:** AP, CLEP, IB, institutional tests. 15 credit hours maximum toward associate degree. **Support services:** GED preparation and test center, learning center, pre-admission summer program, reduced course load, remedial instruction, study skills assistance, tutoring, writing center.

Majors. Biology: General. **Business:** Accounting, administrative services, business admin, office management. **Communications:** Communications/speech/rhetoric. **Conservation:** Wildlife/wilderness. **Education:** Agricultural, business, early childhood, elementary, mathematics, music, physical, secondary. **English:** English lit. **Foreign languages:** General. **Health services:** Predental, premedicine, prepharmacy, preveterinary, veterinary technology/assistant. **Liberal arts:** Arts/sciences. **Math:** General, statistics. **Protective services:** Correctional facilities, criminal justice, police science. **Social sciences:** General, economics. **Visual/performing arts:** Art, music.

Technology on campus. 120 workstations in dormitories, library, student center. Dormitories wired for high-speed internet access. Online course registration, online library, helpline available.

Student life. Freshman orientation: Available. Preregistration for classes offered. Held in fall 1 day prior to first day of classes. **Housing:** Coed dorms, wellness housing available. $150 fully refundable deposit. **Activities:** Concert band, campus ministries, choral groups, musical theater, student government.

Athletics. NJCAA. **Intercollegiate:** Basketball, golf M, rodeo, volleyball W. **Intramural:** Basketball, volleyball. **Team name:** Lancers.

Student services. Adult student services, alcohol/substance abuse counseling, career counseling, student employment services, financial aid counseling, personal counseling, placement for graduates, veterans' counselor. **Physically disabled:** Services for visually, speech, hearing impaired. **Transfer:** Transfer adviser, college fairs on campus for students transferring to 4-year colleges.

Contact. E-mail: rex.cogdill@ewc.wy.edu
Phone: (307) 532-8230 Toll-free number: (800) 658-3195
Fax: (307) 532-8222
Rex Cogdill, Vice President for Student Services, Eastern Wyoming
College, 3200 West C Street, Torrington, WY 82240

Laramie County Community College
Cheyenne, Wyoming
www.lccc.wy.edu
CB code: 0360

- Public 2-year community college
- Commuter campus in small city

General. Founded in 1968. Regionally accredited. Additional campus in
Laramie, outreach centers in Pine Bluffs and FE Warren AFB. **Enrollment:**
3,021 degree-seeking undergraduates; 1,127 non-degree-seeking students.
Degrees: 640 associate awarded. **ROTC:** Army, Air Force. **Location:** 4
miles from downtown, 100 miles from Denver. **Calendar:** Semester, limited
summer session. **Full-time faculty:** 120 total; 22% have terminal degrees,
7% minority, 53% women. **Part-time faculty:** 175 total; 10% minority, 62%
women. **Class size:** 74% < 20, 25% 20-39, less than 1% 40-49. **Special
facilities:** Bureau of Land Management park, indoor arena.

Student profile. Among degree-seeking undergraduates, 524 enrolled as
first-time, first-year students.

Part-time:	41%	Hispanic/Latino:	12%
Out-of-state:	15%	Native American:	1%
Women:	61%	International:	1%
African American:	3%	25 or older:	40%
Asian American:	1%	Live on campus:	13%

Transfer out. Colleges most students transferred to 2015: University
of Wyoming.

Basis for selection. Open admission, but selective for some programs.
Special requirements for dental hygiene, diagnostic medical sonography,
equine studies, nursing, physical therapist assistant, radiography, surgical
technology, and wind energy programs. Interview required for equine studies.
Home schooled: Students must complete institutional home schooler form
and attach to transcript. **Learning Disabled:** Interview with Disability
Resource Center coordinator to arrange accommodations.

2015-2016 Annual costs. Tuition/fees: $3,144; $7,128 out-of-state.
Room/board: $7,200. Books/supplies: $1,320. Personal expenses: $900.
Additional information: Western Undergraduate Exchange (WUE) students
qualify for reduced tuition and fees $4,128.

2014-2015 Financial aid. Need-based: 266 full-time freshmen applied
for aid; 200 deemed to have need; 193 received aid. Average need met was
71%. Average scholarship/grant was $1,694; average loan $2,796. 1% of
total undergraduate aid awarded as scholarships/grants, 99% as loans/jobs.
Need-based aid available for part-time students. Work-study available nights,
weekends and for part-time students. **Non-need-based:** Awarded to 1,551
full-time undergraduates, including 359 freshmen. Scholarships awarded for
academics, alumni affiliation, art, athletics, job skills, leadership, minority
status, music/drama, religious affiliation, state residency.

Application procedures. Admission: No application fee. Admission
notification on a rolling basis. Preferrably turned in with application, must be
submitted no later than move-in-day. Nursing, radiology, and dental hygiene
applications due 2/1; diagnostic medical sonography due 3/1; wind energy
technology due 7/31. Housing deposit due at time of housing application;
refundable in full until 5/1, in part 5/2-7/1, non-refundable after 7/1. **Financial
aid:** Priority date 4/1; no closing date. FAFSA, institutional form required.
Applicants notified on a rolling basis starting 4/1; must reply within 2 week(s)
of notification.

Academics. Special study options: Cooperative education, distance learning, double major, dual enrollment of high school students, ESL, independent
study, internships. License preparation in dental hygiene, nursing, paramedic,
radiology. **Credit/placement by examination:** AP, CLEP, IB, ACT, institutional tests. 15 credit hours maximum toward associate degree. **Support
services:** GED preparation and test center, learning center, remedial instruction, study skills assistance, tutoring, writing center.

Majors. Biology: General. **Business:** General, accounting, business admin,
entrepreneurial studies. **Communications:** Communications/speech/rhetoric,
digital media, media studies. **Computer sciences:** Computer science, programming. **Conservation:** Wildlife/wilderness. **Education:** General, early
childhood, physical. **Engineering:** General. **English:** English lit. **Foreign
languages:** Spanish. **Health services:** Dental hygiene, EMT paramedic, nursing (RN), physical therapy assistant, prepharmacy, radiologic technology/
medical imaging, sonography, surgical technology. **History:** General.

Human services: General. **Liberal arts:** Humanities. **Math:** General. **Philos-
ophy/religion:** Religion. **Physical sciences:** Chemistry. **Protective services:**
Corrections, firefighting, law enforcement admin. **Psychology:** General.
Social sciences: General, anthropology, economics, political science, sociology. **Visual/performing arts:** Art, music.

Most popular majors. Business/marketing 9%, education 9%, health sciences 24%, liberal arts 19%.

Technology on campus. 1,090 workstations in dormitories, library, computer center, student center. Dormitories wired for high-speed internet access
and linked to campus network. Commuter students can connect to campus
network. Online course registration, online library, helpline, repair service,
student web hosting, wireless network available.

Student life. Freshman orientation: Available. Preregistration for classes
offered. **Housing:** Coed dorms, wellness housing available. $100 fully refund-
able deposit. **Activities:** Bands, choral groups, drama, international student
organizations, literary magazine, music ensembles, musical theater, student
government, student newspaper.

Athletics. NJCAA. **Intercollegiate:** Basketball M, equestrian, rodeo, soccer, volleyball W. **Team name:** Golden Eagles.

Student services. Adult student services, alcohol/substance abuse counseling, career counseling, services for economically disadvantaged, student
employment services, financial aid counseling, health services, on-campus
daycare, personal counseling, placement for graduates, veterans' counselor.
Physically disabled: Services for visually, speech, hearing impaired. **Transfer:** College fairs on campus for students transferring to 4-year colleges.

Contact. E-mail: learnmore@lccc.wy.edu
Phone: (307) 778-1357 Toll-free number: (800) 522-2993 ext. 1357
Fax: (307) 778-1350
Holly Bruegman, Director of Admissions, Laramie County Community
College, 1400 East College Drive, Cheyenne, WY 82007-3299

Northwest College
Powell, Wyoming
www.nwc.edu
CB code: 4542

- Public 2-year community and junior college
- Residential campus in small town

General. Founded in 1946. Regionally accredited. **Enrollment:** 1,425
degree-seeking undergraduates; 272 non-degree-seeking students. **Degrees:**
311 associate awarded. **Location:** 90 miles from Billings, MT. **Calendar:**
Semester, limited summer session. **Full-time faculty:** 77 total; 35% have
terminal degrees. **Part-time faculty:** 69 total. **Special facilities:** Field station, observatory.

Student profile. Among degree-seeking undergraduates, 320 enrolled as
first-time, first-year students.

Part-time:	35%	Native American:	1%
Out-of-state:	21%	Multi-racial, non-Hispanic:	2%
Women:	58%	International:	4%
African American:	1%	25 or older:	23%
Hispanic/Latino:	8%		

Transfer out. Colleges most students transferred to 2015: University of
Wyoming, Montana State University-Billings, Montana State University,
Brigham Young University-Idaho, Utah State University.

Basis for selection. Open admission, but selective for some programs
and for out-of-state students. Admissions for out-of-state applicants based
on GPA (2.0 and above) and placement test scores. Nursing and Equine
Riding and Training programs require extra applications and qualifications.
Placement tests in math and English required for all first-time freshmen.
Adult students: Accuplacer placement test on-campus can substitute for
SAT/ACT for English and math placement. **Home schooled:** Applicants
must also submit the Home School Transcript Evaluation Form. **Learning
Disabled:** Individuals must identify needs in order to procure services.

High school preparation. College-preparatory program recommended.
17 units recommended. Recommended units include English 4, mathematics
4, social studies 3, science 4 (laboratory 3) and foreign language 2.

2015-2016 Annual costs. Tuition/fees: $2,779; $6,763 out-of-state. Per-
credit charge: $83 in-state; $249 out-of-state. Room/board: $5,198. Books/
supplies: $1,000. Personal expenses: $1,684. **Additional information:** The
WUE (Western Undergraduate Exchange) program provides discounted tuition rates for residents of the following states: AK, AZ, CA, CNMI, CO,
HI, ID, MT, NV, NM, ND, OR, SD, UT, & WA. Nebraska residents also
qualify for this reduced rate.

Financial aid. Need-based: Need-based aid available for part-time students. Work-study available nights, weekends and for part-time students. **Non-need-based:** Scholarships awarded for academics, alumni affiliation, art, athletics, leadership, music/drama, state residency.

Application procedures. Admission: No deadline. No application fee. Admission notification on a rolling basis. **Financial aid:** Priority date 3/1; no closing date. FAFSA, institutional form required. Applicants notified on a rolling basis; must reply within 2 week(s) of notification.

Academics. Free peer tutoring available in evenings and weekends. **Special study options:** Cooperative education, distance learning, double major, dual enrollment of high school students, ESL, independent study, internships, liberal arts/career combination, study abroad. License preparation in aviation, nursing. **Credit/placement by examination:** AP, CLEP, institutional tests. **Support services:** GED preparation and test center, learning center, reduced course load, remedial instruction, study skills assistance, tutoring, writing center. TRIO (Student Support Services) program.

Majors. Biology: General. **Business:** General, accounting, administrative services, business admin. **Communications:** Broadcast journalism, communications/speech/rhetoric, journalism. **Communications technology:** Desktop publishing, graphic/printing, radio/TV. **Conservation:** Management/policy. **Education:** Agricultural, elementary, kindergarten/preschool, secondary. **Engineering:** General. **English:** English lit. **Foreign languages:** Spanish. **Health services:** Athletic training, nursing (RN), predental, premedicine, preoccupational therapy, preoptometry, prepharmacy, prephysical therapy, preveterinary, veterinary technology/assistant. **History:** General. **Liberal arts:** Arts/sciences. **Math:** General. **Parks/recreation:** General, health/fitness. **Physical sciences:** Chemistry, physics. **Protective services:** Law enforcement admin. **Psychology:** General. **Social sciences:** General, anthropology, archaeology, international relations, political science, sociology. **Visual/performing arts:** Art, cinematography, commercial photography, commercial/advertising art, music, play/screenwriting.

Most popular majors. Agriculture 11%, business/marketing 6%, education 6%, engineering/engineering technologies 7%, health sciences 16%, liberal arts 14%, visual/performing arts 12%.

Technology on campus. 500 workstations in dormitories, library, computer center, student center. Dormitories wired for high-speed internet access and linked to campus network. Commuter students can connect to campus network. Online library, helpline, repair service, wireless network available.

Student life. Freshman orientation: Available, $30 fee. Preregistration for classes offered. Held the weekend prior to start of fall semester. **Housing:** Guaranteed on-campus for freshmen. Coed dorms, single-sex dorms, apartments, themed housing available. $125 partly refundable deposit. **Activities:** Bands, campus ministries, choral groups, drama, film society, international student organizations, literary magazine, music ensembles, Model UN, musical theater, opera, radio station, student government, student newspaper, symphony orchestra, TV station.

Athletics. NJCAA. **Intercollegiate:** Basketball, rodeo, soccer, volleyball W, wrestling M. **Intramural:** Basketball, football (non-tackle), golf, softball, ultimate frisbee, volleyball. **Team name:** Trappers.

Student services. Adult student services, alcohol/substance abuse counseling, career counseling, services for economically disadvantaged, financial aid counseling, health services, minority student services, on-campus daycare, personal counseling, veterans' counselor. **Physically disabled:** Services for visually, speech, hearing impaired. **Transfer:** Pre-admission transcript evaluation for new students. Transfer center, transfer adviser, college fairs on campus for students transferring to 4-year colleges.

Contact. E-mail: west.hernandez@nwc.edu
Phone: (307) 754-6101 Toll-free number: (800) 560-4692
Fax: (307) 754-6249
West Hernandez, Admissions Manager, Northwest College, Orendorff Building, Powell, WY 82435-1898

Sheridan College
Sheridan, Wyoming
www.sheridan.edu

CB code: 4536

▸ Public 2-year community college
▸ Commuter campus in large town

General. Founded in 1948. Regionally accredited. **Enrollment:** 1,941 degree-seeking undergraduates; 701 non-degree-seeking students. **Degrees:** 514 associate awarded. **Location:** 150 miles from Casper; 130 miles from Billings, MT. **Calendar:** Semester, limited summer session. **Full-time faculty:** 99 total; 19% have terminal degrees, 1% minority, 46% women. **Part-time faculty:** 118 total; 10% have terminal degrees, 58% women. **Special**

facilities: Geological museum, federal depository for government publications, observatory, Caesar the Allosaurus replica, indoor and outdoor arena and stabling for horses.

Student profile. Among degree-seeking undergraduates, 64% enrolled in a transfer program, 36% enrolled in a vocational program, 561 enrolled as first-time, first-year students, 102 transferred in from other institutions.

Part-time:	35%	Native American:	2%
Out-of-state:	16%	Multi-racial, non-Hispanic:	3%
Women:	57%	International:	2%
African American:	1%	25 or older:	40%
Asian American:	1%	Live on campus:	15%
Hispanic/Latino:	7%		

Transfer out. 17% of students enrolled in the transfer program go on to 4-year colleges. **Colleges most students transferred to 2015:** University of Wyoming, Chadron State, Black Hills State University, Montana State University, South Dakota School of Mines.

Basis for selection. Open admission, but selective for some programs. Special admissions for nursing, dental hygiene, massage therapy, diesel technology, and welding; requirements vary by program.

High school preparation. One chemistry required of dental hygiene applicants.

2015-2016 Annual costs. Tuition/fees: $2,952; $6,936 out-of-state. Per-credit charge: $83 in-state; $249 out-of-state. Room/board: $6,170. Books/supplies: $1,367. Personal expenses: $1,200. **Additional information:** Western Undergraduate Exchange (WUE) students qualify for reduced rates.

Financial aid. Need-based: Need-based aid available for part-time students. Work-study available nights, weekends and for part-time students. **Non-need-based:** Scholarships awarded for academics, art, athletics, leadership, music/drama, state residency.

Application procedures. Admission: No deadline. No application fee. Admission notification on a rolling basis. **Financial aid:** Priority date 3/1; no closing date. FAFSA, institutional form required. Applicants notified on a rolling basis; must reply within 3 week(s) of notification.

Academics. Special study options: Cooperative education, distance learning, double major, dual enrollment of high school students, ESL, independent study, internships, liberal arts/career combination. Bachelor's degree programs available on campus. License preparation in dental hygiene, nursing. **Credit/placement by examination:** AP, CLEP, institutional tests. 18 credit hours maximum toward associate degree. **Support services:** GED preparation and test center, learning center, reduced course load, remedial instruction, study skills assistance, tutoring, writing center.

Majors. Biology: General. **Business:** General, hospitality admin. **Computer sciences:** General, information systems, security, webmaster. **Education:** Early childhood, elementary, secondary. **Engineering:** General. **English:** English lit. **General:** Building construction. **Health services:** Dental hygiene, massage therapy, nursing (RN). **History:** General. **Human services:** Community org/advocacy. **Math:** General. **Parks/recreation:** Exercise sciences, health/fitness. **Protective services:** Criminal justice, law enforcement admin. **Psychology:** General. **Social sciences:** General. **Visual/performing arts:** Art, dramatic, music.

Most popular majors. Business/marketing 6%, education 7%, health sciences 17%, liberal arts 31%, trade and industry 10%.

Technology on campus. 930 workstations in dormitories, library, computer center, student center. Dormitories wired for high-speed internet access and linked to campus network. Commuter students can connect to campus network. Online library, helpline, wireless network available.

Student life. Freshman orientation: Mandatory. Preregistration for classes offered. A three hour session during the summer, plus 8 online modules that need to be passed with 80% or greater. **Policies:** Non-smoking campus. **Housing:** Coed dorms, single-sex dorms, special housing for disabled, apartments, gender-neutral housing, themed housing available. $125 fully refundable deposit. **Activities:** Bands, campus ministries, choral groups, drama, international student organizations, music ensembles, musical theater, student government, student newspaper, Nursing club, Dental Auxiliary, veterans club, Baptist Collegiate Ministries, Newman club, international students, construction club, student senate.

Athletics. NJCAA. **Intercollegiate:** Basketball, cross-country, rodeo, soccer, volleyball W. **Intramural:** Basketball, bowling, football (non-tackle), lacrosse, sand volleyball, soccer, softball, ultimate frisbee, volleyball. **Team name:** Generals.

Student services. Adult student services, alcohol/substance abuse counseling, career counseling, services for economically disadvantaged, student

employment services, financial aid counseling, personal counseling, placement for graduates, veterans' counselor. **Physically disabled:** Services for visually, speech, hearing impaired. **Transfer:** Pre-admission transcript evaluation for new students. Transfer adviser, college fairs on campus for students transferring to 4-year colleges.

Contact. E-mail: admissions@sheridan.edu
Phone: (307) 674-6446 ext. 2002
Toll-free number: (800) 913-9139 ext. 2002 Fax: (307) 674-3373
Joseph Mueller, Executive Director of Admissions, Sheridan College, PO Box 1500, Sheridan, WY 82801-1500

Western Wyoming Community College
Rock Springs, Wyoming
www.westernwyoming.edu   CB code: 4957

- Public 2-year community college
- Commuter campus in large town

General. Founded in 1959. Regionally accredited. **Enrollment:** 1,797 degree-seeking undergraduates; 1,478 non-degree-seeking students. **Degrees:** 416 associate awarded. **Location:** 180 miles from Salt Lake City. **Calendar:** Semester, limited summer session. **Full-time faculty:** 79 total. **Part-time faculty:** 224 total. **Class size:** 83% < 20, 17% 20-39. **Special facilities:** Dinosaur museum, natural history museum, wildlife exhibit, fully functioning closed-loop well site simulator, exercise science and wellness building, compression technology building, high desert outdoor walking path, aquatic center.

Student profile. Among degree-seeking undergraduates, 205 enrolled as first-time, first-year students.

Part-time:	39%	25 or older:	52%
Out-of-state:	55%	Live on campus:	10%
Women:	60%		

Transfer out. Colleges most students transferred to 2015: University of Wyoming, Utah State University, Idaho State University.

Basis for selection. Open admission, but selective for some programs. Admissions to nursing program based on academic performance, pre-entrance exam and prerequisite course completion. **Home schooled:** State high school equivalency certificate required. If home school is not through an accredited institution, student needs to obtain GED.

High school preparation. Recommended units include English 4, mathematics 3, social studies 2, science 3 (laboratory 1) and foreign language 2.

2015-2016 Annual costs. Tuition/fees: $2,400; $6,384 out-of-state. Per-credit charge: $101 in-state; $267 out-of-state. Room/board: $4,472. Books/supplies: $1,500. Personal expenses: $1,200. **Additional information:** Western Undergraduate Exchange (WUE) students qualify for reduced rates.

2014-2015 Financial aid. Need-based: 54% of total undergraduate aid awarded as scholarships/grants, 46% as loans/jobs. Need-based aid available for part-time students. Work-study available nights, weekends and for part-time students. **Non-need-based:** Scholarships awarded for academics, art, athletics, music/drama, state residency.

Application procedures. Admission: No deadline. No application fee. Application must be submitted online. Admission notification on a rolling basis. **Financial aid:** Priority date 4/1; no closing date. FAFSA required. Applicants notified on a rolling basis starting 2/15; must reply within 2 week(s) of notification.

Academics. Special study options: Cooperative education, distance learning, dual enrollment of high school students, ESL, external degree, honors, independent study, internships. Online tutoring provided through Smart Thinking at no charge to students. Bachelor's degree programs available on campus. License preparation in nursing. **Credit/placement by examination:** AP, CLEP, IB, institutional tests. 40 credit hours maximum toward associate degree. **Support services:** GED preparation and test center, learning center, remedial instruction, study skills assistance, tutoring.

Honors college/program. Competitive program, open to 20 students a year. Students participate in challenging courses and travel to cultural and educational events at expense of institution.

Majors. Biology: General, ecology, wildlife. **Business:** Accounting, administrative services, business admin, marketing, office technology. **Communications:** Communications/speech/rhetoric, journalism. **Computer sciences:** General, computer science, data processing, information systems. **Conservation:** General, environmental studies, water/wetlands/marine, wildlife/wilderness. **Education:** General, elementary, multi-level teacher, secondary. **Engineering:** General. **English:** English lit. **Foreign languages:** Spanish. **Health**

services: Licensed practical nurse, medical assistant, medical secretary, predental, premedicine, prenursing, prepharmacy, preveterinary. **History:** General. **Human services:** Social work. **Math:** General. **Parks/recreation:** Exercise sciences. **Physical sciences:** Chemistry, geology. **Protective services:** Law enforcement admin. **Psychology:** General. **Social sciences:** General, anthropology, archaeology, criminology, international relations, political science, sociology. **Visual/performing arts:** General, art, ceramics, dance, dramatic, music, studio arts, theater design.

Most popular majors. Business/marketing 9%, education 9%, health sciences 14%, liberal arts 19%, psychology 6%, trade and industry 12%.

Technology on campus. 250 workstations in dormitories, library, computer center, student center. Dormitories wired for high-speed internet access and linked to campus network. Commuter students can connect to campus network. Online course registration, online library, helpline, wireless network available.

Student life. Freshman orientation: Mandatory. Preregistration for classes offered. Program for students and parents. Students must also complete an online orientation component. **Housing:** Coed dorms, special housing for disabled, apartments available. $150 partly refundable deposit. **Activities:** Bands, campus ministries, choral groups, dance, drama, international student organizations, music ensembles, musical theater, radio station, student government, student newspaper, Phi Theta Kappa, outdoor club, ambassadors, Students Without Borders.

Athletics. NJCAA. **Intercollegiate:** Basketball, cheerleading, soccer, volleyball W, wrestling M. **Intramural:** Basketball, football (non-tackle), softball, table tennis, tennis, volleyball. **Team name:** Mustangs.

Student services. Adult student services, alcohol/substance abuse counseling, career counseling, student employment services, financial aid counseling, on-campus daycare, personal counseling, placement for graduates, veterans' counselor. **Physically disabled:** Services for visually, hearing impaired. **Transfer:** Pre-admission transcript evaluation for new students. Transfer adviser, college fairs on campus for students transferring to 4-year colleges.

Contact. E-mail: admissions@wwcc.wy.edu
Phone: (307) 382-1648 Toll-free number: (800) 226-1181
Fax: (307) 382-1636
Erin Grey, Director of Admissions, Western Wyoming Community College, Box 428, Rock Springs, WY 82902-0428

American Samoa

American Samoa Community College
Pago Pago, American Samoa
www.amsamoa.edu   CB code: 0020

▶ Public 2-year community college
▶ Commuter campus in large town

General. Founded in 1970. Regionally accredited. Only institution of higher education in American Samoa and only land grant institution in the South Pacific. Students seeking 4-year degrees often transfer to colleges in Hawaii or mainland United States. **Enrollment:** 1,285 degree-seeking undergraduates. **Degrees:** 8 bachelor's, 260 associate awarded. **ROTC:** Army. **Location:** 9 miles from downtown. **Calendar:** Semester, limited summer session. **Full-time faculty:** 61 total; 8% have terminal degrees, 92% minority, 48% women. **Part-time faculty:** 19 total; 5% have terminal degrees, 90% minority, 58% women.

Student profile. Among degree-seeking undergraduates, 385 enrolled as first-time, first-year students, 3 transferred in from other institutions.

Part-time:	45%	Native Hawaiian/Pacific islander:	90%
Women:	67%	International:	9%
Asian American:	1%	25 or older:	16%

Transfer out. Colleges most students transferred to 2015: University of Hawaii, Manoa; University of Hawaii, Hilo; Chaminade University of Honolulu; Hawaii Pacific University.

Basis for selection. Open admission. Institutional placement exam may be required for applicants without SAT/ACT scores.

2015-2016 Annual costs. Tuition/fees: $3,550. Books/supplies: $2,340.

2015-2016 Financial aid. All financial aid based on need. 164 full-time freshmen applied for aid; 164 deemed to have need; 164 received aid. Average need met was 29%. Average scholarship/grant was $2,842. 99% of total undergraduate aid awarded as scholarships/grants, 1% as loans/jobs. Need-based aid available for part-time students. Work-study available nights, weekends and for part-time students.

Application procedures. Admission: No deadline. No application fee. **Financial aid:** No deadline. FAFSA required. Applicants notified on a rolling basis; must reply by 9/25 or within 3 week(s) of notification.

Academics. Special study options: Cross-registration, double major, independent study, liberal arts/career combination, teacher certification program. Bachelor's degree programs available on campus. License preparation in nursing. **Credit/placement by examination:** AP, CLEP, SAT, ACT, institutional tests. Credit by examination for course credit may be taken only once. "E" grades for credit by examination will not be counted toward overall grade point average and cumulative grade point average. Credits earned by examination are not covered under federal financial aid. **Support services:** GED preparation, learning center, reduced course load, remedial instruction, study skills assistance, tutoring.

Majors. Business: Accounting, business admin. **Conservation:** Management/policy. **Education:** General, elementary, multi-level teacher. **General:** Maintenance. **Health services:** Nursing assistant. **Liberal arts:** Arts/sciences. **Protective services:** Criminal justice, forensics. **Social sciences:** Political science. **Visual/performing arts:** Art, music. **Work/family studies:** General.

Most popular majors. Business/marketing 12%, education 7%, health sciences 7%, liberal arts 57%, security/protective services 7%.

Technology on campus. 104 workstations in library, computer center. Helpline, repair service available.

Student life. Freshman orientation: Mandatory. Preregistration for classes offered. **Activities:** Bands, choral groups, drama, international student organizations, music ensembles, student government, student newspaper, Phi Theta Kappa, Polynesian club, Christian club, You Are Not Alone Coalition (emotional support for young people).

Athletics. Intramural: Basketball, golf, tennis, volleyball, weight lifting. **Team name:** Chiefs.

Student services. Alcohol/substance abuse counseling, career counseling, services for economically disadvantaged, student employment services, financial aid counseling, health services, personal counseling, veterans' counselor. **Transfer:** Pre-admission transcript evaluation for new students. Transfer adviser for students transferring to 4-year colleges.

Contact. E-mail: admissions@amsamoa.edu
Phone: (684) 699-9155 ext. 334 Fax: (684) 699-1083
Elisapeta Leuma, Admissions Officer, American Samoa Community College, PO Box 2609, Pago Pago, AS 96799-2609

Guam

Guam Community College
Barrigada, Guam
www.guamcc.edu   CB code: 2302

▶ Public 2-year community and technical college
▶ Commuter campus in small city

General. Founded in 1977. Regionally accredited. **Enrollment:** 1,979 degree-seeking undergraduates. **Degrees:** 217 associate awarded. **ROTC:** Army. **Calendar:** Semester, limited summer session. **Full-time faculty:** 115 total; 6% have terminal degrees. **Part-time faculty:** 94 total; 1% have terminal degrees. **Class size:** 11% < 20, 87% 20-39, 2% 40-49.

Basis for selection. Open admission.

High school preparation. Recommended units include English 4, mathematics 3, social studies 3, science 2 and academic electives 9.

2016-2017 Annual costs. Tuition/fees (projected): $4,194; $4,944 out-of-state. Per-credit charge: $130 in-state; $155 out-of-state. Books/supplies: $1,200. Personal expenses: $2,650.

Financial aid. Need-based: Work-study available nights, weekends and for part-time students.

Academics. Special study options: Cooperative education, cross-registration, double major, dual enrollment of high school students, independent study, internships. **Credit/placement by examination:** AP, CLEP, institutional tests. 48 credit hours maximum toward associate degree. **Support services:** GED preparation and test center, learning center, remedial instruction, study skills assistance, tutoring.

Majors. Business: Accounting, office management, office technology, sales/distribution, tourism/travel. **Computer sciences:** Computer science. **Education:** Early childhood, teacher assistance. **Health services:** Medical assistant. **Liberal arts:** Arts/sciences. **Protective services:** Law enforcement admin. **Visual/performing arts:** Graphic design. **Work/family studies:** Institutional food production.

Most popular majors. Business/marketing 7%, computer/information sciences 14%, education 19%, legal studies 13%, personal/culinary services 15%, security/protective services 21%.

Technology on campus. 79 workstations in library, computer center, student center. Commuter students can connect to campus network. Online course registration, online library, wireless network available.

Student life. Freshman orientation: Available. Preregistration for classes offered. **Activities:** Student government.

Student services. Adult student services, alcohol/substance abuse counseling, career counseling, services for economically disadvantaged, student employment services, financial aid counseling, health services, personal counseling, placement for graduates, veterans' counselor. **Physically disabled:** Services for visually, speech, hearing impaired. **Transfer:** Re-entry adviser for new students.

Contact. E-mail: patrick.clymer@guamcc.edu
Phone: (671) 735-5531 Fax: (671) 734-5238
Patrick Clymer, Coordinator of Admissions and Registration, Guam Community College, PO Box 23069 GMF, Barrigada, GU 96921

Bermuda

Bermuda College
Paget, Bermuda
www.bercol.bm

CB member
CB code: 2581

- Public 2-year community college
- Commuter campus in small city

General. **Enrollment:** 842 degree-seeking undergraduates. **Degrees:** 54 associate awarded. **Calendar:** Semester, limited summer session. **Full-time faculty:** 70 total.

Basis for selection. Open admission, but selective for some programs.

2015-2016 Annual costs. Tuition/fees: $3,460.

Financial aid. **Need-based:** Work-study available nights, weekends and for part-time students.

Application procedures. **Admission:** Closing date 5/1. $50 fee. **Financial aid:** Closing date 6/5.

Academics. **Special study options:** Bachelor's degree programs available on campus. **Credit/placement by examination:** AP, CLEP, institutional tests. **Support services:** Study skills assistance, tutoring.

Majors. **Business:** Business admin, hospitality admin, office management. **Computer sciences:** General. **Education:** General. **General:** Carpentry, plumbing.

Technology on campus. 70 workstations in library, computer center. Wireless network available.

Student life. **Freshman orientation:** Available. Preregistration for classes offered. **Activities:** Dance, drama, literary magazine, music ensembles, student government.

Student services. Career counseling. **Transfer:** College fairs on campus for students transferring to 4-year colleges.

Contact. E-mail: admissions@college.bm
Phone: (441) 239-4048 Fax: (441) 239-4051
Carleen Place, Admissions Director, Bermuda College, PO Box PG 297, Paget, BM

Two-Year Colleges

Early Decision and Early Action table

The following table lists early decision and early action policies at 508 colleges, which are listed alphabetically by state or country. Colleges were asked to supply the deadline for student applications and the date by which the college will notify the applicant of a decision to admit, deny admission, or defer the application to the regular admission cycle. If a college offers two early decision cycles, both sets of dates are listed.

Some colleges support both a binding early decision plan and a nonbinding early action plan and report dates for both. Colleges with binding early decision plans were asked to give the number of students who applied for early decision and the number of those applicants admitted to the fall 2015 freshman class.

Institution	Early Applicants		Early Decision		Early Action	
	Number Applied	Number admitted	Apply by	Notified by	Apply by	Notified by
Alabama						
Birmingham-Southern College					11/15	12/15
Arizona						
Arizona Christian University					11/1	11/5
Prescott College	7	3	12/1	12/15		
Arkansas						
Hendrix College	955	843			11/15	12/15
Lyon College					10/31	11/15
University of Arkansas	10778	9310			11/1	12/15
California						
Azusa Pacific University					11/15	1/15
Biola University	2798	2218	11/15 1/15	1/15 2/15	11/15	1/15
California Baptist University					12/15	1/31
California Institute of Technology					11/1	12/15
California Lutheran University	2563	1882			11/1	1/15
California Maritime Academy					10/31	12/15
California Polytechnic State University: San Luis Obispo	4081	1103	10/31	12/15		
California State University: Sacramento					11/30	
Chapman University					11/1	1/10
Claremont McKenna College	675	185	11/1 1/1	12/15 2/15		
Concordia University Irvine					12/1	12/15
Design Institute of San Diego						
Harvey Mudd College	436	77	11/15 1/5	12/15 2/15		
Laguna College of Art and Design			2/2	2/2		
Loyola Marymount University	3697	2404			11/1	12/20
Menlo College					11/15	1/15

Institution	Early Applicants		Early Decision		Early Action	
	Number Applied	Number admitted	Apply by	Notified by	Apply by	Notified by
Mills College	202	165			11/15	12/1
Mount Saint Mary's University					12/1	1/30
Notre Dame de Namur University					12/1	12/15
Occidental College	255	105	11/15 1/1	12/15 2/1		
Pitzer College	405	118	11/15 1/1	12/18 12/2		
Point Loma Nazarene University					11/15	12/21
Pomona College			11/1 1/1	12/15 2/15		
Santa Clara University	5400	3468	11/1	12/15	11/1	12/23
Scripps College	219	102	11/15 1/1	12/15 2/15		
Simpson University					8/31	12/1
Soka University of America	75	29			11/1	12/1
St. Mary's College of California					11/15	1/15
Stanford University	7297	741			11/1	12/15
The Master's College	261	249			11/15	12/22
University of Redlands					11/15	1/15
University of San Francisco	4079	3115	11/15	12/31	11/15	12/31
University of the Pacific					11/15	1/15
Westmont College					11/15	1/5
Whittier College	1296	972			11/15	12/30

Colorado

Institution	Number Applied	Number admitted	Apply by	Notified by	Apply by	Notified by
Colorado College	4019	1055	11/15 1/1	12/15 2/10	11/15	12/18
Colorado State University	7545	7536			12/1	2/1
Fort Lewis College					1/15	3/15
University of Colorado Boulder	15129	14047			11/15	2/1
University of Denver	11600	10740			11/1	1/15

Connecticut

Institution	Number Applied	Number admitted	Apply by	Notified by	Apply by	Notified by
Connecticut College	347	243	11/15 1/1	12/15 2/15		
Fairfield University	5815	3934	11/15 1/15	12/15 2/15	11/1	12/20
Mitchell College			11/15	12/1		
Quinnipiac University	433	267	11/1	12/1		
Sacred Heart University	5459	942	12/1	12/15	12/15	1/31
Trinity College			11/15 1/1	12/15 2/15		
United States Coast Guard Academy	648	157			11/15	2/1
University of Hartford					11/15	12/1
University of New Haven	168	100	12/1	12/15	12/15	1/15
Wesleyan University	960	370	11/15 1/1	12/15 2/15		
Yale University					11/1	12/15

Delaware

Institution	Number Applied	Number admitted	Apply by	Notified by	Apply by	Notified by
Delaware College of Art and Design					12/1	12/21

District of Columbia

Institution	Number Applied	Number admitted	Apply by	Notified by	Apply by	Notified by
American University	805	702	11/15 1/15	12/31 2/15		
Catholic University of America			11/15	12/20	11/1	12/20
George Washington University			11/10 1/10	12/15 2/1		
Georgetown University	6857	1353			11/1	12/15
Howard University	3942	2528			11/1	12/20

Institution	Early Applicants		Early Decision		Early Action	
	Number Applied	Number admitted	Apply by	Notified by	Apply by	Notified by
Trinity Washington University					12/1	1/1
Florida						
Adventist University of Health Sciences	75	38			5/1	
Eckerd College					11/15	12/15
Flagler College	532	283	11/1	12/15		
Florida Southern College	173	71	12/1	12/15		
Lynn University	803	736			11/15	12/15
Palm Beach Atlantic University	22	22			3/31	4/15
Ringling College of Art and Design					11/1	12/15
Rollins College			11/15 1/15	12/15 2/1		
University of Miami	15268	7369	11/1 1/1	12/20 2/15	11/1	1/20
University of South Florida: Saint Petersburg					11/15	12/1
University of Tampa	12594	7381			11/15	12/15
Georgia						
Abraham Baldwin Agricultural College			3/1			
Agnes Scott College	29	29	11/1	12/1	11/15	12/15
Brewton-Parker College					6/1	
Emory University	2437	723	11/1 1/1	12/15 2/15		
Georgia College and State University	1636	827			11/1	1/7
Georgia Institute of Technology	11702	5823			10/15	1/10
Georgia Southwestern State University			12/15	1/15		
Georgia State University					11/15	1/30
Mercer University					11/1	11/15
Morehouse College			11/1	12/15	11/1	12/15
Oglethorpe University					11/15	12/5
Oxford College of Emory University	1074	275	11/1 1/1	12/15 2/15		
Spelman College	1674	1169	11/1	12/15	11/15	12/31
University of Georgia					10/15	12/1
University of North Georgia					11/15	
Wesleyan College			11/15 1/15	12/15 2/15		
Hawaii						
Hawaii Pacific University					11/15	11/15
Idaho						
College of Idaho					11/16	12/21
New Saint Andrews College	37	37			12/11	1/1
Northwest Nazarene University					2/15	12/15
Illinois						
Augustana College			11/1	11/15	11/1	12/1
DePaul University					11/15	1/15
Governors State University			11/15	12/15	11/15	12/15
Illinois College					12/15	12/23
Illinois Institute of Technology					12/1	
Illinois Wesleyan University					11/15	1/15
Knox College	1765	1064			12/1	12/31
Lake Forest College	1087	861	11/15		11/15	
Lakeview College of Nursing						
Moody Bible Institute			12/1	1/15		
Northwestern University	2667	1012	11/1	12/15		

Institution	Early Applicants		Early Decision		Early Action	
	Number Applied	Number admitted	Apply by	Notified by	Apply by	Notified by
School of the Art Institute of Chicago					12/1	2/15
St. Francis Medical Center College of Nursing			9/12	10/12		
Trinity College of Nursing & Health Sciences				12/20		
University of Chicago					11/1	
University of Illinois at Chicago					11/1	12/1
Wheaton College	1041	711			11/1	12/31

Indiana

Institution	Number Applied	Number admitted	Apply by	Notified by	Apply by	Notified by
Butler University					11/1	12/20
DePauw University	69	52	11/1	12/1	12/1	1/15
Earlham College	10	10	11/1	12/1	12/1	2/1
Grace College					12/1	12/20
Hanover College	2215	1559			12/1	12/20
Purdue University					11/1	12/12
Rose-Hulman Institute of Technology	2277	1873			11/1	12/15
Saint Mary's College	82	68	11/15	12/15		
Taylor University					12/1	12/20
University of Evansville	2965	1830			12/1	12/15
University of Notre Dame	3606	1403			11/1	12/21
Wabash College	941	628	11/15	12/1	12/1	12/19

Iowa

Institution	Number Applied	Number admitted	Apply by	Notified by	Apply by	Notified by
Coe College					12/10	1/20
Cornell College	766	622	11/1 2/1	12/15 3/1	12/1	2/1
Grinnell College	316	169	11/15 1/1	12/15 2/1		
Wartburg College					12/1	

Kentucky

Institution	Number Applied	Number admitted	Apply by	Notified by	Apply by	Notified by
Bellarmine University					11/1	11/15
Centre College	1503	1252	11/15	12/15	12/1	1/15
Transylvania University					12/1	12/20

Louisiana

Institution	Number Applied	Number admitted	Apply by	Notified by	Apply by	Notified by
Centenary College of Louisiana					12/1	1/15
Dillard University					12/1	12/30
Tulane University	17670	6828			11/15	12/15

Maine

Institution	Number Applied	Number admitted	Apply by	Notified by	Apply by	Notified by
Bates College	679	273	11/15 1/1	12/20 2/15		
Bowdoin College	950	243	11/15 1/1	12/15 2/15		
Colby College	576	249	11/15 1/1	12/15 2/15		
College of the Atlantic	36	28	12/1 1/15	12/15 1/30		
Maine College of Art	88	88			12/1	1/1
Maine Maritime Academy			11/30	2/1	11/30	2/1
Saint Joseph's College of Maine					11/15	12/17
Thomas College					12/15	12/31
Unity College					12/15	1/15
University of Maine					12/15	1/31
University of Maine at Farmington	208	208			11/15	12/15
University of Maine at Machias					12/15	
University of New England	1896	1592			12/1	12/31

Institution	Early Applicants		Early Decision		Early Action	
	Number Applied	Number admitted	Apply by	Notified by	Apply by	Notified by
Maryland						
Goucher College	1731	1478	11/15	12/15	12/1	2/1
Johns Hopkins University	1866	540	11/1	12/15		
Loyola University Maryland					11/1	1/15
Maryland Institute College of Art			11/15	12/15		
McDaniel College			1/15	2/1	12/1	12/22
Morgan State University					11/15	2/15
Mount St. Mary's University	529	434			12/1	12/25
Salisbury University	3943	2733	11/15	12/15	12/1	1/15
St. John's College	93	87			11/15	12/15
St. Mary's College of Maryland					11/1	12/20
University of Maryland: Baltimore County					11/1	12/15
University of Maryland: College Park					11/1	1/31
Washington College	111	64	11/15 12/15	12/15 1/15	12/1	1/15
Massachusetts						
Amherst College	483	173	11/15	12/15		
Assumption College	2398	2156			11/1	12/15
Babson College			11/1	12/15	11/1	1/1
Bay Path University					12/15	1/2
Becker College			11/15	12/15	11/15	12/15
Bentley University	158	104	11/15	12/22		
Berklee College of Music					11/1	1/31
Boston College	5558	2288			11/1	12/25
Boston University	1643	708	11/1 1/4	12/15 1/3		
Brandeis University			11/1 1/1	12/15 2/1		
Bridgewater State University	2135	1938			11/15	12/15
Clark University	2305	1811	11/1	12/15	11/1	12/15
College of the Holy Cross	442	331	12/15	1/15		
Curry College	2770	1533			12/1	12/15
Dean College	304	299			12/20	1/15
Emerson College	2936	1897			11/1	12/15
Emmanuel College	3069	2555			11/1	12/15
Framingham State University					11/15	12/15
Gordon College	1252	1187	10/15	11/1	10/15	11/1
Hampshire College			11/15 1/1	12/15 2/1	12/1	2/15
Harvard College	5918	976			11/1	12/16
Lasell College					11/15	12/1
Lesley University					12/1	12/23
Massachusetts College of Art and Design	235	197			12/1	1/5
Massachusetts College of Liberal Arts	505	452			12/1	12/15
Massachusetts Institute of Technology	6519	625			11/1	12/20
Massachusetts Maritime Academy					11/1	12/31
Merrimack College	2874	2722	11/15	12/20	11/15	12/20
Montserrat College of Art					12/1	12/15
Mount Holyoke College	321	161	11/15 1/1	1/1 2/1		
Nichols College	690	421			12/1	12/5
Northeastern University	773	239	11/1	12/15	11/1	12/31
Regis College					12/1	12/20
Salem State University					11/15	12/1

Institution	Early Applicants		Early Decision		Early Action	
	Number Applied	Number admitted	Apply by	Notified by	Apply by	Notified by
Simmons College	2677	1703			12/1	1/15
Smith College			11/15 1/1	12/15 1/31		
Springfield College			12/1	2/1		
Stonehill College	2589	2112	12/1	12/31	11/1	12/31
Suffolk University	2230	1841			11/15	12/15
Tufts University	1839	721	11/1 1/1	12/15 2/15		
University of Massachusetts Amherst	15868	11030			11/1	12/30
University of Massachusetts Boston					12/1	1/31
University of Massachusetts Dartmouth	1263	1226			11/15	12/15
University of Massachusetts Lowell	3812	2807			11/1	12/15
Wellesley College			11/1	12/15		
Wheaton College	1446	1097	11/15 1/15	12/15 2/15	11/15	1/15
Wheelock College					12/1	12/20
Williams College	593	244	11/15	12/15		
Worcester Polytechnic Institute	5667	3495			11/1	12/20
Worcester State University					11/15	12/15

Michigan

Institution	Early Applicants		Early Decision		Early Action	
Albion College	1043	947	12/1	10/15		
Central Michigan University					5/1	5/8
College for Creative Studies					12/1	12/15
Hillsdale College	168	101	11/1	12/1		
Kalamazoo College			11/15 2/15	12/1 3/1	11/15	12/20
Kettering University					11/15	12/15
Madonna University					11/1	
Michigan State University					10/17	11/20
University of Michigan					11/1	12/24

Minnesota

Institution	Early Applicants		Early Decision		Early Action	
Carleton College	689	211	11/15 1/15	12/15 2/15		
College of St. Benedict	1332	1100			11/15	12/15
Gustavus Adolphus College					11/1	11/15
Hamline University	33	33	11/1	11/15	12/1	
Macalester College	227	121	11/15 1/1	12/15 2/7		
McNally Smith College of Music	456	126	2/1 2/1		2/1	
Minneapolis College of Art and Design			12/1	12/14	12/1	12/15
St. John's University	1069	882			11/15	12/15
St. Olaf College	245	180	1/15 1/8	12/15 2/1		

Mississippi

Institution	Early Applicants		Early Decision		Early Action	
Millsaps College					11/15	1/15
Mississippi College			12/1	12/15		

Missouri

Institution	Early Applicants		Early Decision		Early Action	
Cox College			11/1	12/1		
Fontbonne University						
Stephens College			11/15	12/1	1/1	1/15
Washington University in St. Louis	1652	615	11/15	12/15		

Montana

Institution	Early Applicants		Early Decision		Early Action	
Carroll College					12/1	1/1

Institution	Early Applicants		Early Decision		Early Action	
	Number Applied	Number admitted	Apply by	Notified by	Apply by	Notified by
Nebraska						
Nebraska Wesleyan University			12/1			
New Hampshire						
Colby-Sawyer College					12/1	
Dartmouth College	1856	482	11/1	12/15		
New Hampshire Institute of Art	125	122			12/7	12/24
Rivier University					11/15	12/1
Saint Anselm College	2442	1856			11/15	1/15
Southern New Hampshire University					11/15	12/15
University of New Hampshire	9855	6375			11/15	12/1
New Jersey						
Bloomfield College	672	511			12/1	12/23
Caldwell University					12/1	1/1
Drew University	63	50	11/15 2/1	12/15 2/21		
Felician University					11/15	12/23
Georgian Court University	434	425			11/15	12/30
Kean University					12/1	
Montclair State University					11/15	12/15
Princeton University	3848	766			11/1	12/15
Ramapo College of New Jersey			11/1	12/5		
Rider University	2814	1934			11/15	12/15
Rutgers, The State University of New Jersey: New Brunswick/Piscataway Campus					11/1	1/31
Saint Peter's University					12/1	1/31
Seton Hall University					11/15	12/30
Stevens Institute of Technology	798	444	11/15 1/15	12/15 2/15		
The College of New Jersey	600	412	11/15	12/15		
William Paterson University of New Jersey					12/1	1/15
New Mexico						
St. John's College	111	104			11/15	12/15
New York						
Adelphi University	2969	2563			12/1	12/31
Albany College of Pharmacy and Health Sciences	89	62	11/1 12/1	11/15 12/15		
Alfred University			12/1	12/15		
Bard College	1599	967	11/1		11/1	1/1
Barnard College	748	321	11/1	12/15		
Canisius College					11/1	12/1
Clarkson University	180	146	12/1	1/1		
Colgate University	829	387	11/15 1/15	12/15		
College of Mount St. Vincent					11/15	12/1
College of Saint Rose	2971	2496			12/1	12/15
Columbia University	3337	632	11/1	12/15		
Columbia University: School of General Studies					3/1	5/1
Concordia College					11/15	12/15
Cooper Union for the Advancement of Science and Art	228	68	12/1			
Cornell University	4560	1196	11/1			
Eugene Lang College The New School for Liberal Arts					11/1	12/20

Institution	Early Applicants		Early Decision		Early Action	
	Number Applied	Number admitted	Apply by	Notified by	Apply by	Notified by
Five Towns College			10/15 12/1	11/1 12/15		
Fordham University	18322	9133	11/1	12/20	11/1	12/20
Hamilton College	616	236	11/15 1/1	12/15 2/15		
Hartwick College	17	13	11/1	12/1		
Hobart and William Smith Colleges	389	319	11/15 1/15	12/15 2/1		
Hofstra University	14989	8772			11/15	12/15
Iona College					12/1	12/19
Ithaca College	6603	5547	11/1	12/15	12/1	2/1
Jewish Theological Seminary of America	22	17	11/15 1/15	12/15 2/15		
LIM College					11/15	12/15
LIU Brooklyn					12/1	12/31
LIU Post					12/1	12/31
Le Moyne College	2520	1963			11/15	12/15
Manhattan College	73	68	11/15	12/15		
Manhattanville College					12/1	12/20
Mannes College The New School for Music					11/1	12/20
Maria College			12/1	1/15		
Marist College			11/15 2/1	12/15 2/15	11/15	1/30
Mercy College					12/1	1/2
Molloy College	349	286			12/1	12/15
Monroe College						
Nazareth College	275	238	11/15 1/15	12/15 2/1		
New York Institute of Technology	1450	1274			11/1	12/1
New York University			11/1 1/1	12/15 2/15		
North Country Community College			11/15	12/15		
Pace University	5853	5279			12/1	1/1
Pace University: Pleasantville/Briarcliff	1631	1382			12/1	1/1
Parsons The New School for Design					11/1	12/20
Pratt Institute					11/1	12/22
Rensselaer Polytechnic Institute	554	358	11/1 12/15	12/12 1/16		
Rochester Institute of Technology	1329	857	12/1	1/15		
SUNY College at Cortland					11/15	1/1
SUNY College at Fredonia	57	48	11/1	11/15		
SUNY College at Geneseo	238	215	11/15	12/15		
SUNY College at New Paltz					11/15	12/15
SUNY College at Old Westbury			11/1	12/15		
SUNY College at Oneonta					11/15	12/1
SUNY College at Oswego	310	139	11/30	12/15		
SUNY College at Purchase					11/15	12/15
SUNY College of Environmental Science and Forestry	147	96	12/1	1/15		
SUNY Maritime College	134	69	11/1	12/15		
SUNY Polytechnic Institute					11/15	12/15
SUNY University at Albany					11/15	11/15
SUNY University at Binghamton	10295	4935			11/15	1/15
SUNY University at Buffalo	384	353	11/15	1/15	11/15	
Sarah Lawrence College	155	99	11/1 1/1	12/15 2/15		
Siena College	4745	3342	12/1	1/1	12/1	1/1

Institution	Early Applicants		Early Decision		Early Action	
	Number Applied	Number admitted	Apply by	Notified by	Apply by	Notified by
Skidmore College	415	279	11/15 1/15	12/15 2/15		
St. John Fisher College	111	71	12/1	1/15		
St. Lawrence University	251	227	11/1 2/1			
Syracuse University	1839	1190	11/15			
The King's College					11/30	12/15
The Sage Colleges	486	372			12/1	12/15
Union College	399	239	11/15 1/15	12/15 2/1		
University of Rochester	801	332	11/1	12/15		
Utica College	661	619	11/15 11/15	12/15 12/15		
Vassar College	692	269	11/15 1/1	12/15 2/1		
Wagner College			12/1	1/2	12/1	1/5
Webb Institute	27	8	10/15	12/15		
Wells College	112	93	12/15	1/15	12/15	2/1
Yeshiva University			11/1	12/15		

North Carolina

Institution	Number Applied	Number admitted	Apply by	Notified by	Apply by	Notified by
Davidson College	638	309	11/15 1/2	12/15 2/1		
Duke University	3048	817	11/1	12/15		
Elon University	7041	3628	11/1	12/1	11/10	12/20
Greensboro College					12/15	1/15
Guilford College			11/1	11/15	12/1	1/1
High Point University	7392	6191	11/2	11/23	11/16	12/18
Lenoir-Rhyne University					11/7	11/21
Meredith College	71	71	10/30	11/15		
North Carolina State University					10/15	1/30
Piedmont International University			11/1	12/1	11/1	12/1
Queens University of Charlotte					12/1	12/15
University of North Carolina at Asheville					11/15	12/15
University of North Carolina at Chapel Hill	17158	6707			10/15	1/31
University of North Carolina at Charlotte	7468	5977			11/1	1/30
University of North Carolina at Wilmington					11/1	1/20
Wake Forest University			11/15			
Warren Wilson College			11/15	12/1	11/15	12/15
Western Carolina University					11/15	12/15
William Peace University					11/15	12/15

Ohio

Institution	Number Applied	Number admitted	Apply by	Notified by	Apply by	Notified by
Case Western Reserve University	10309	4999	11/1 1/15	12/15 2/1	11/1	12/15
Cincinnati College of Mortuary Science			7/25 7/25	7/25 7/25		
Cleveland Institute of Art	324	106			12/1	12/15
College of Wooster	3082	2083	11/1 1/15	11/15 2/1	11/15	12/31
Columbus College of Art and Design	292	177			12/1	12/20
Denison University			11/15 1/15	12/1 2/1		
John Carroll University					12/1	12/15
Kenyon College	428	250	11/15 1/15	12/15 2/1		

Institution	Early Applicants		Early Decision		Early Action	
	Number Applied	Number admitted	Apply by	Notified by	Apply by	Notified by
Miami University: Oxford			11/15	12/15	12/1	2/1
Oberlin College	520	281	11/15 1/2	12/15 2/1		
Ohio State University: Columbus Campus	20500	13553			11/1	1/15
Ohio Wesleyan University	78	44	11/15	11/30	1/15	1/30
University of Akron	7930	6377			11/1	12/31
University of Cincinnati					12/1	
University of Dayton					12/15	2/1
Wittenberg University	3896	3200	11/15	12/1	12/1	1/1

Oklahoma

Institution	Early Applicants		Early Decision		Early Action	
University of Tulsa	1066	981			11/1	12/15

Oregon

Institution	Early Applicants		Early Decision		Early Action	
George Fox University					11/15	12/23
Lewis & Clark College	2075	1747	11/1	12/15	11/1	12/31
Linfield College	790	778			11/15	1/15
Oregon State University					11/1	12/20
Reed College			11/15 12/20	12/15 2/1		
University of Oregon					11/1	12/15
Willamette University					11/15	12/31

Pennsylvania

Institution	Early Applicants		Early Decision		Early Action	
Allegheny College	188	113	11/15 1/15	12/15 2/1		
Bryn Mawr College	279	140	11/15 1/1	12/15 2/1		
Bucknell University	830	437	11/15 1/15	12/15 2/15		
Carnegie Mellon University	1143	326	11/1	12/15		
Community College of Allegheny County						
Dickinson College	3264	1747	11/15 1/15	12/15 2/15	12/1	2/1
Drexel University					11/1	
Duquesne University	1925	1100	11/1	11/15	12/1	1/15
Franklin & Marshall College	555	340	11/15 1/15	12/15 2/15		
Gettysburg College	444	301	11/15 1/15	12/15 2/15		
Grove City College	1024	849	11/15	12/15		
Haverford College	323	150	11/15	12/15		
Juniata College	111	97	11/15 2/15	12/23		
La Salle University	2632	2206			11/15	12/15
Lafayette College	704	342	11/15 2/1	12/15 2/15		
Lebanon Valley College	118	98	11/1	12/1		
Lehigh University	999	582	11/15 1/1	12/15 2/15		
Lycoming College			11/15	12/1	12/1	12/15
Muhlenberg College	354	288	2/15			
Pennsylvania Academy of the Fine Arts	70	64	12/1		12/1	12/15
Saint Joseph's University					11/15	12/25
Susquehanna University	2386	2058	11/15 2/15	12/1 3/1	11/1	12/1
Swarthmore College	567	202	11/15 1/1	12/15 2/15		

Institution	Early Applicants		Early Decision		Early Action	
	Number Applied	Number admitted	Apply by	Notified by	Apply by	Notified by
Temple University	6546	4933			11/1	1/10
University of Pennsylvania	5488	1316	11/1	12/15		
University of Scranton	5906	4600			11/15	12/15
Ursinus College			2/1	2/15	1/1	2/1
Villanova University	8627	3897			11/1	12/20
Washington & Jefferson College	3447	1734	12/1	12/15	1/15	2/15
Westminster College					11/15	12/1

Puerto Rico

Institution	Number Applied	Number admitted	Apply by	Notified by	Apply by	Notified by
University of Puerto Rico: Aguadilla					1/15	1/30
University of Puerto Rico: Arecibo			3/31	3/31		
University of Puerto Rico: Mayaguez					1/30	2/15

Rhode Island

Institution	Number Applied	Number admitted	Apply by	Notified by	Apply by	Notified by
Brown University	3043	617	11/1	12/15		
Bryant University	3327	2570	11/17 1/15	12/15 2/15	12/1	1/15
Providence College	196	171	12/1	1/1	11/15	1/1
Rhode Island School of Design	127	85	11/1	12/7		
Roger Williams University	5143	4529			12/1	12/1
Salve Regina University	2096	1519			11/1	12/25
University of Rhode Island	13302	10769			12/1	1/31

South Carolina

Institution	Number Applied	Number admitted	Apply by	Notified by	Apply by	Notified by
College of Charleston	7160	5730			11/1	1/1
Erskine College					11/1	11/15
Furman University	2968	2193	11/1	11/15	11/1	12/20
Medical University of South Carolina						
Presbyterian College	1087	819	11/1	12/1	11/15	12/15
Southern Wesleyan University						
University of South Carolina: Columbia					10/15	12/20
Wofford College	1849	1541	11/1	12/1	11/15	2/1

Tennessee

Institution	Number Applied	Number admitted	Apply by	Notified by	Apply by	Notified by
Fisk University					12/1	12/31
Rhodes College	188	143	11/1 1/1	12/1 2/1	11/15	1/15
Sewanee: The University of the South	2970	1547	11/15 1/15	12/15 2/15	12/1	2/15
Vanderbilt University	3582	815	11/1 1/1	12/15 2/15		

Texas

Institution	Number Applied	Number admitted	Apply by	Notified by	Apply by	Notified by
Abilene Christian University	6090	2969			11/1	12/1
Austin College			11/1	12/4	12/1	1/15
Baylor University					11/1	1/15
Our Lady of the Lake University of San Antonio				12/31	11/14	12/31
Rice University	1389	283	11/1	12/15		
Southern Methodist University	687	209	11/1 1/15	12/31 4/1	11/1	12/31
Southwestern University					11/15	2/15
Tarleton State University					3/1	
Texas Christian University	8364	5548	11/1	12/5	11/1	12/15
Texas Lutheran University			12/15 2/1			
Texas Southern University						
Trinity University	71	54	11/1 1/1	12/15 2/15	11/1	12/15

Institution	Early Applicants		Early Decision		Early Action	
	Number Applied	Number admitted	Apply by	Notified by	Apply by	Notified by
University of Dallas					12/1	1/15
University of St. Thomas					12/1	12/15
Utah						
Neumont University	302	256			11/2	11/23
University of Utah					12/1	1/15
Vermont						
Bennington College	405	293	11/15 1/3	12/20 2/1	12/1	2/1
Champlain College	478	380	11/15 1/15	12/15 2/15		
Green Mountain College					11/1	12/14
Lyndon State College					11/1	12/15
Marlboro College			11/15	12/1	1/15	2/1
Middlebury College	961	313	11/1 1/1	12/15 2/15		
Saint Michael's College	3250	2535			11/1	12/21
Sterling College	68	50	11/15	12/1	12/15	1/15
University of Vermont	6254	4763			11/1	12/15
Virginia						
Christendom College					12/1	12/15
Christopher Newport University	4136	3070	11/15	12/15	12/1	1/15
College of William and Mary	1070	540	11/1	12/1		
Emory & Henry College					12/1	1/1
George Mason University	10275	7896			11/1	12/15
Hampden-Sydney College	188	76	11/1	12/1	1/15	2/15
Hampton University					11/1	12/15
Hollins University	876	638	10/15	11/1	11/15	12/1
James Madison University					11/1	1/15
Longwood University	2860	1676			12/1	1/15
Lynchburg College			11/15	12/15		
Old Dominion University	3997	3471			12/1	1/15
Patrick Henry College					11/1	12/1
Radford University	4215	3727			12/1	1/15
Randolph College					11/15	1/1
Randolph-Macon College					11/15	1/1
Roanoke College	51	45	11/10	11/26		
Sweet Briar College					11/1	12/19
University of Mary Washington	2390	2199	11/1	12/7	11/15	1/31
University of Richmond	791	331	11/15 1/15	12/15 2/15		
University of Virginia	16081	4851			11/1	1/31
University of Virginia's College at Wise	798	625			12/1	12/15
Virginia Military Institute	396	235	11/15	12/15		
Virginia Polytechnic Institute and State University	2169	1245	11/1	12/15		
Washington and Lee University	577	225	11/1 1/1	12/22 2/1		
Washington						
Cornish College of the Arts					12/1	
Gonzaga University					11/15	1/15
Northwest University					11/15	12/15
Seattle Pacific University					11/15	1/5
Seattle University					11/15	12/23

Institution	Early Applicants		Early Decision		Early Action	
	Number Applied	Number admitted	Apply by	Notified by	Apply by	Notified by
University of Puget Sound	122	114	11/15 1/1	12/15 2/15		
Whitman College	166	126	11/15 1/1	12/20 2/1		
Whitworth University					11/30	12/20
West Virginia						
Shepherd University	699	297			11/15	12/15
Wisconsin						
Beloit College			11/1	11/30	11/1	12/15
Lawrence University					12/15	1/25
Milwaukee Institute of Art & Design					12/1	12/15
Canada						
Simon Fraser University					2/28	4/15
Egypt						
American University in Cairo					5/1	
Germany						
University of Karlsruhe	30	15	4/15	5/15		
Italy						
American University of Rome					1/1	1/15
John Cabot University					11/15	12/15
Lebanon						
American University of Beirut	467	467			11/30	1/30
Lebanese American University	2362	1380			1/31	3/1
Mexico						
Universidad Anahuac						
Morocco						
Al Akhawayn University			3/31	5/15		
Switzerland						
Ecole Hoteliere de L'ausanne					12/1	2/15
Franklin University Switzerland					12/1	1/15
Les Roches International School of Hotel Management						
United Kingdom						
University of Chichester						

Wait list table

Students who are wait listed have met a college's admission requirements, but will only be offered a place in the freshman class if space becomes available. The table that follows shows wait list outcomes for students who applied for admission to the freshman class of 2015-2016 at 276 colleges, which are listed alphabetically by state.

Institution	Total applied	Number placed on wait list	Number accepting place on wait list	Number on wait list admitted
Alabama				
Samford University	3196	197	129	60
Arkansas				
Hendrix College	1714	0		
University of Arkansas	20542	160	147	125
California				
California Institute of Technology	6507	615	429	0
California Lutheran University	6573	292	102	68
California Maritime Academy	1206	154	62	6
Charles Drew University of Medicine and Science		0		
Claremont McKenna College	7156	919	453	75
Harvey Mudd College	4119	534	354	11
Loyola Marymount University	13288	2037	501	174
Mills College	839	46	9	2
Occidental College	5911	705	359	26
Pitzer College	4149	1021	895	23
San Diego State University	58970	2474	1037	27
Santa Clara University	14899	2203	1112	278
Scripps College	2613	641	284	0
Soka University of America	451	42	42	21
Southern California Institute of Architecture	214	28	18	15
St. Mary's College of California	4852	318	104	14
Stanford University	24797	1256	927	0
Thomas Aquinas College	189	37	37	21
University of California: Berkeley	77660	3760	2445	1340
University of California: Davis	64510	9033	2733	2030
University of California: Irvine	71768	7361	4035	131
University of California: Riverside	38505	6231	3737	2770
University of Redlands	4790	131	53	47
University of San Diego	13675	1133	530	341
University of San Francisco	15462	1	0	
University of the Pacific	14449	367	143	45
Westmont College	2077	42	35	29
Yeshiva Ohr Elchonon Chabad/West Coast Talmudical Seminary	94	15	15	0
Colorado				
Colorado College	8060	1119	232	24
Colorado School of Mines	11752	1654	236	6

Institution	Total applied	Number placed on wait list	Number accepting place on wait list	Number on wait list admitted
University of Colorado Boulder	31291	2110	363	0
University of Denver	15036	2442	452	36

Connecticut

Institution	Total applied	Number placed on wait list	Number accepting place on wait list	Number on wait list admitted
Central Connecticut State University	8686	140	140	129
Connecticut College	5182	1306	637	61
Fairfield University	10767	2573	875	94
Quinnipiac University	22745	1570	860	75
United States Coast Guard Academy	2214	148	148	36
University of Connecticut	34978	5808	3110	697
Wesleyan University	9822	1877	884	12

Delaware

Institution	Total applied	Number placed on wait list	Number accepting place on wait list	Number on wait list admitted
University of Delaware	24881	2138	851	0

District of Columbia

Institution	Total applied	Number placed on wait list	Number accepting place on wait list	Number on wait list admitted
American University	16735	2778	269	8
George Washington University	19837	3827	1354	62
Georgetown University	19478	2184	1249	149

Florida

Institution	Total applied	Number placed on wait list	Number accepting place on wait list	Number on wait list admitted
Flagler College	5260	48	20	20
New College of Florida	1655	178	51	30
Rollins College	4922	102	33	10
Stetson University	11216	522	497	192
Trinity College of Florida	64	6	3	2
University of Central Florida	35572	3928	2267	305
University of Miami	33415	5563	1295	73

Georgia

Institution	Total applied	Number placed on wait list	Number accepting place on wait list	Number on wait list admitted
Agnes Scott College	1461	0		
Berry College	4347	20	6	1
Emory University	20492	3809	1910	45
Georgia Institute of Technology	27277	3397	2031	38
Morehouse College	2288	178	122	112
Oxford College of Emory University	9734	5124	1051	101
Spelman College	5051	333	250	19
University of Georgia	21945	954	585	34

Idaho

Institution	Total applied	Number placed on wait list	Number accepting place on wait list	Number on wait list admitted
New Saint Andrews College	63	0		

Illinois

Institution	Total applied	Number placed on wait list	Number accepting place on wait list	Number on wait list admitted
Bradley University	9186	0	0	0
Illinois Wesleyan University	3744	193	40	21
Knox College	3445	123	23	3
Northwestern University	32122	2614	1452	43
Robert Morris University: Chicago	2945	0	0	0
Trinity College of Nursing & Health Sciences	5	36	36	8
University of Illinois at Urbana-Champaign	34277	2074	1601	0
Wheaton College	1971	409	117	32

Indiana

Institution	Total applied	Number placed on wait list	Number accepting place on wait list	Number on wait list admitted
Hanover College	3355	0		
Rose-Hulman Institute of Technology	4331	326	149	37
St. Mary-of-the-Woods College	283	0		
University of Indianapolis	7216	60	60	39
Wabash College	1247	32	31	5

Institution	Total applied	Number placed on wait list	Number accepting place on wait list	Number on wait list admitted
Iowa				
Cornell College	1936	13	2	2
Grinnell College	6414	1224	474	18
Northeast Iowa Community College	1107	77	77	55
St. Luke's College	15	5	5	2
Kentucky				
Centre College	2716	183	42	19
Louisiana				
Tulane University	26257	3413	921	0
Maine				
Bates College	5651	1536	672	11
Colby College	7593	1497	634	42
Maryland				
Goucher College	3577	61	44	7
Johns Hopkins University	24716	2752	1747	187
Loyola University Maryland	13867	2347	424	150
McDaniel College	2864	72	14	6
Mount St. Mary's University	6113	0		
United States Naval Academy	16101	187	143	4
University of Maryland: Baltimore County	10629	404	404	280
Washington College	6847	384	363	2
Massachusetts				
Amherst College	8568	1398	643	33
Assumption College	4769	289	110	17
Bentley University	8346	1898	575	92
Berklee College of Music	7682	232	187	23
Boston College	29486	7072	3897	351
Boston Conservatory	1216	30	30	1
Boston University	54781	4381	2214	4
Brandeis University	10528	1553	595	25
College of the Holy Cross	6595	1307	494	8
Emerson College	8618	1569	949	44
Endicott College	4009	44	44	0
Gordon College	1832	7	0	0
Hampshire College	2071	128	47	5
Massachusetts College of Art and Design	1273	15	15	7
Massachusetts Institute of Technology	18306	652	575	52
Merrimack College	7751	969	827	207
New England Conservatory of Music	1170	114	85	21
Smith College	5006	773	398	132
Stonehill College	5892	390	98	24
University of Massachusetts Amherst	40010	5450	1278	26
University of Massachusetts Dartmouth	7591	37	37	0
University of Massachusetts Lowell	10638	973	340	32
Wellesley College	4555	1404	843	30
Wheaton College	4322	404	104	29
Williams College	6883	1603	573	53
Worcester Polytechnic Institute	10172	2472	1373	41
Michigan				
Hillsdale College	1859	79	15	6
Kalamazoo College	2455	228	102	102
University of Michigan	51761	14960	4512	90

Institution	Total applied	Number placed on wait list	Number accepting place on wait list	Number on wait list admitted
Minnesota				
Carleton College	6722	1350	442	16
Dunwoody College of Technology	428	11	11	11
Macalester College	6030	350	177	0
St. Olaf College	7571	729	150	113
Missouri				
College of the Ozarks	3122	865	856	4
Metro Business College: Jefferson City	19	20	18	10
Saint Louis University	13216	164	164	107
Nebraska				
College of Saint Mary	314	0		
New Hampshire				
Dartmouth College	20507	1852	963	129
Saint Anselm College	3955	472	173	27
New Jersey				
Bloomfield College	3027	0		
Princeton University	27290	1207	818	39
Ramapo College of New Jersey	7106	946	336	244
Rider University	9851	58	58	26
Stevens Institute of Technology	6540	1047	358	187
Stockton University	5482	600	600	250
The College of New Jersey	11290	1837	541	96
New Mexico				
St. John's College	177	0		
New York				
Bard College	7044	200	167	18
Barnard College	6655	1195	130	6
Clarkson University	6906	56	10	6
Colgate University	8724	1896	913	49
Cooper Union for the Advancement of Science and Art	3258	315	305	11
Cornell University	41900	3583	2231	81
Eastman School of Music of the University of Rochester	932	106	84	32
Finger Lakes Community College	3017	100	100	10
Fordham University	42811	8184	2607	14
Hamilton College	5434	958	365	47
Hobart and William Smith Colleges	4488	622	178	21
Hofstra University	27991	612	193	120
Ithaca College	16519	1286	180	33
Juilliard School	2551	47	44	14
Keuka College	2290	88	88	88
LIM College	1242	18	15	15
Le Moyne College	6877	198	24	1
Manhattan College	8313	423	117	86
Marist College	9213	3645	1188	108
Nazareth College	3677	60	1	0
Pratt Institute	4819	935	450	23
Rensselaer Polytechnic Institute	17752	4087	2203	57
SUNY College at Geneseo	9118	542	180	49
SUNY College at New Paltz	14655	783	673	113
SUNY College at Plattsburgh	8261	93	34	1
SUNY College of Environmental Science and Forestry	1619	236	56	24

Institution	Total applied	Number placed on wait list	Number accepting place on wait list	Number on wait list admitted
SUNY College of Technology at Alfred	4912	115	115	53
SUNY College of Technology at Canton	2853	88	88	25
SUNY Maritime College	1342	89	87	0
SUNY University at Buffalo	23629	1657	558	181
Sarah Lawrence College	2814	1025	636	99
Siena College	8919	564	564	11
Skidmore College	8508	1742	378	13
St. Elizabeth College of Nursing	21	27	25	15
St. John's University	36086	1624	0	1142
St. Lawrence University	5835	73	13	0
Syracuse University	33254	5592	1578	659
Union College	5996	1167	626	64
Vassar College	7556	1017	485	10
Wagner College	2803	112	95	20

North Carolina

Institution	Total applied	Number placed on wait list	Number accepting place on wait list	Number on wait list admitted
Elon University	10256	2718	1031	26
High Point University	10910	883	883	282
North Carolina State University	21099	2433	1010	19
University of North Carolina School of the Arts	887	109	78	30
University of North Carolina at Chapel Hill	31953	3144	1513	78
University of North Carolina at Wilmington	11444	132	78	78

Ohio

Institution	Total applied	Number placed on wait list	Number accepting place on wait list	Number on wait list admitted
Case Western Reserve University	22807	9446	5119	518
College of Wooster	5748	726	68	10
Denison University	6110	515	439	21
Kenyon College	7076	2876	998	17
Miami University: Oxford	27454	3269	899	
Oberlin College	7815	1126	310	78
Ohio State University: Columbus Campus	40249	1556	304	304
Xavier University	10661	98	17	8

Oklahoma

Institution	Total applied	Number placed on wait list	Number accepting place on wait list	Number on wait list admitted
University of Oklahoma	12002	1322	1322	209

Oregon

Institution	Total applied	Number placed on wait list	Number accepting place on wait list	Number on wait list admitted
Lewis & Clark College	7368	775	225	1
University of Oregon	22000	1186	481	31
University of Portland	11202	2862	713	33
Willamette University	6332	433	168	53

Pennsylvania

Institution	Total applied	Number placed on wait list	Number accepting place on wait list	Number on wait list admitted
Allegheny College	4324	239	239	17
Bloomsburg University of Pennsylvania	9795	49	49	22
Bryn Mawr College	2890	872	427	0
Bucknell University	10967	2427	922	59
Carlow University	945	0		
Carnegie Mellon University	20547	5526	2835	4
Dickinson College	6031	848	261	0
Elizabethtown College	3453	33	27	6
Gannon University	4213	139	61	39
Grove City College	1541	160	149	55
Haverford College	3467	883	354	12
Lafayette College	7465	1532	428	3
Lehigh University	12843	4232	1847	0
Lycoming College	1845	76	52	20
Messiah College	2469	0		

Institution	Total applied	Number placed on wait list	Number accepting place on wait list	Number on wait list admitted
Millersville University of Pennsylvania	6053	292	292	88
Muhlenberg College	5015	1690	314	41
Neumann University	2253	0		
Penn State University Park	53472	1473	1473	1445
Robert Morris University	6579	184	184	18
St. Vincent College	1908	0		
Susquehanna University	5304	0		
Temple University	28886	1852	568	161
University of Pennsylvania	37268	2474	1438	90
University of Pittsburgh	30626	2382	559	170
University of Scranton	10049	1525	533	205
Washington & Jefferson College	6835	29	9	3
West Chester University of Pennsylvania	12624	1571	277	0
Widener University	5421	74	20	0

Puerto Rico

Institution	Total applied	Number placed on wait list	Number accepting place on wait list	Number on wait list admitted
EDP University of Puerto Rico: Hato Rey	331	182	116	96

Rhode Island

Institution	Total applied	Number placed on wait list	Number accepting place on wait list	Number on wait list admitted
Bryant University	6705	391	117	2
Providence College	10215	2430	604	158
Rhode Island School of Design	2516	275	275	18
Roger Williams University	9597	450	135	49
University of Rhode Island	21261	1262	394	20

South Carolina

Institution	Total applied	Number placed on wait list	Number accepting place on wait list	Number on wait list admitted
Clemson University	22396	2249	790	783
Furman University	5043	208	51	14
Presbyterian College	2072	0		
Wofford College	2795	174	67	16

Tennessee

Institution	Total applied	Number placed on wait list	Number accepting place on wait list	Number on wait list admitted
Rhodes College	4666	1290	277	45
Sewanee: The University of the South	4509	1039	202	21

Texas

Institution	Total applied	Number placed on wait list	Number accepting place on wait list	Number on wait list admitted
Our Lady of the Lake University of San Antonio	3113	478	478	73
Rice University	17951	2237	1659	127
Southern Methodist University	12992	1757	572	122
Southwestern University	3736	42	10	1
Texas Christian University	18423	1644	556	28
Trinity University	5563	257	110	37
University of Texas at Austin	43592	769	213	18

Vermont

Institution	Total applied	Number placed on wait list	Number accepting place on wait list	Number on wait list admitted
Bennington College	1106	17	16	5
Champlain College	5587	146	14	4
Middlebury College	8891	1304	530	33
Saint Michael's College	4767	243	58	7
Sterling College	101	0		
University of Vermont	25274	3759	866	0

Virginia

Institution	Total applied	Number placed on wait list	Number accepting place on wait list	Number on wait list admitted
Bridgewater College	7187	72	17	10
Christopher Newport University	7366	1566	547	232
College of William and Mary	14952	3552	1676	187
George Mason University	21981	1884	940	350
James Madison University	21439	2500	1200	500
Old Dominion University	9510	685	685	222

Institution	Total applied	Number placed on wait list	Number accepting place on wait list	Number on wait list admitted
Radford University	7617	939	301	290
Randolph-Macon College	2968	219	58	13
University of Mary Washington	5549	341	63	11
University of Richmond	9977	4070	1547	151
University of Virginia	30840	3547	2081	402
Virginia Commonwealth University	16293	447	446	13
Virginia Military Institute	1779	362	166	42
Virginia Polytechnic Institute and State University	22280	2118	1544	0
Washington and Lee University	5377	1983	764	193

Washington

Gonzaga University	6729	332	128	0
Seattle Pacific University	5227	794	794	135
Seattle University	7806	691	292	61
University of Puget Sound	5827	480	227	21
Western Washington University	9933	596	286	136
Whitman College	3790	872	370	67

Wisconsin

Beloit College	3552	81	32	3
Lawrence University	3014	249	70	7
Marquette University	20486	3681	1137	1055

Mexico

Instituto Tecnologico y de Estudios Superiores de Occidente	3203	133	133	116

Tables and Indexes

Indexes

College type

Liberal arts colleges

Four-year

Alabama

Athens State University
Birmingham-Southern College
Concordia College
Faulkner University
Huntingdon College
Judson College
Miles College
Oakwood University
Spring Hill College
Stillman College
Talladega College
University of Mobile
University of Montevallo

Alaska

Alaska Pacific University
University of Alaska
　Southeast

Arizona

Arizona Christian University
Prescott College

Arkansas

Arkansas Baptist College
Arkansas Tech University
Ecclesia College
Henderson State University
Hendrix College
John Brown University
Lyon College
Ouachita Baptist University
Philander Smith College
University of the Ozarks
Williams Baptist College

California

American Jewish University
Antioch University
　Los Angeles
　Santa Barbara
California Lutheran University
California State University
　Bakersfield
　Chico
　Monterey Bay
　San Bernardino
　Stanislaus
Chapman University
Claremont McKenna College
Concordia University Irvine
Fresno Pacific University
Harvey Mudd College
Hope International University
Horizon University
Humboldt State University
Humphreys College
La Sierra University

Marymount California
　University
The Master's College
Menlo College
Mills College
Mount Saint Mary's University
New Charter University
NewSchool of Architecture &
　Design
Notre Dame de Namur
　University
Occidental College
Pacific Union College
Patten University
Pepperdine University
Pitzer College
Point Loma Nazarene University
Pomona College
Providence Christian College
St. Mary's College of California
San Diego Christian College
San Jose State University
Scripps College
Soka University of America
Sonoma State University
Stanford University
Thomas Aquinas College
University of Redlands
University of the West
Vanguard University of
　Southern California
Westmont College
Whittier College
William Jessup University

Colorado

Adams State University
Colorado Christian University
Colorado College
Colorado Heights University
Colorado Mesa University
Fort Lewis College
Metropolitan State University of
　Denver
Naropa University
Regis University
United States Air Force
　Academy
Western State Colorado
　University

Connecticut

Albertus Magnus College
Connecticut College
Eastern Connecticut State
　University
Holy Apostles College and
　Seminary
Mitchell College
Trinity College
University of Saint Joseph
Wesleyan University

Delaware

Wesley College
Wilmington University

District of Columbia

Gallaudet University
Trinity Washington University

University of the District of
　Columbia

Florida

Ave Maria University
Beacon College
Bethune-Cookman University
Eckerd College
Edward Waters College
Flagler College
Florida College
Florida Memorial University
Florida Southern College
Jacksonville University
New College of Florida
Palm Beach Atlantic University
Rollins College
St. John Vianney College
　Seminary
Southeastern University
University of Tampa
Warner University

Georgia

Agnes Scott College
Berry College
Brenau University
Brewton-Parker College
Carver College
College of Coastal Georgia
Columbus State University
Covenant College
Dalton State College
Emmanuel College
Fort Valley State University
Georgia College and State
　University
Georgia Gwinnett College
Georgia Southwestern State
　University
LaGrange College
Middle Georgia State College
Morehouse College
Oglethorpe University
Paine College
Piedmont College
Point University
Reinhardt University
Savannah State University
Shorter University
South Georgia State College
Spelman College
Thomas University
Toccoa Falls College
Truett-McConnell College
University of North Georgia
Wesleyan College
Young Harris College

Hawaii

Brigham Young University-
　Hawaii
Hawaii Pacific University
University of Hawaii
　Hilo
　West Oahu

Idaho

College of Idaho
Lewis-Clark State College
New Saint Andrews College

Illinois

Augustana College
Benedictine University
Blackburn College
Columbia College Chicago
Concordia University Chicago
Dominican University
Elmhurst College
Eureka College
Greenville College
Hebrew Theological College
Illinois College
Illinois Wesleyan University
Judson University
Knox College
Lake Forest College

MacMurray College
McKendree University
Monmouth College
North Central College
North Park University
Olivet Nazarene University
Principia College
Quincy University
Rockford University
St. Augustine College
Shimer College
Trinity Christian College
Trinity International University
University of Chicago
University of Illinois
　Springfield
University of St. Francis
Wheaton College

Indiana

Anderson University
Bethel College
Calumet College of St. Joseph
DePauw University
Earlham College
Franklin College
Goshen College
Grace College
Hanover College
Holy Cross College
Huntington University
Indiana Wesleyan University
Manchester University
Marian University
Martin University
Oakland City University
Saint Joseph's College
Saint Mary's College
St. Mary-of-the-Woods College
Taylor University
University of Evansville
University of Indianapolis
University of Saint Francis
University of Southern Indiana
Wabash College

Iowa

Briar Cliff University
Buena Vista University
Central College
Clarke University
Coe College
Cornell College
Divine Word College
Dordt College
Graceland University
Grand View University
Grinnell College
Iowa Wesleyan College
Loras College
Luther College
Maharishi University of
　Management
Morningside College
Mount Mercy University
Northwestern College
Simpson College
Upper Iowa University
Waldorf University
Wartburg College
William Penn University

Kansas

Baker University
Benedictine College
Bethany College
Bethel College
Central Christian College of
　Kansas
Friends University
Kansas Wesleyan University
McPherson College
MidAmerica Nazarene
　University
Newman University
Ottawa University
Southwestern College

Sterling College
Tabor College

Kentucky

Alice Lloyd College
Asbury University
Bellarmine University
Berea College
Brescia University
Centre College
Georgetown College
Kentucky State University
Kentucky Wesleyan College
Lindsey Wilson College
Midway College
St. Catharine College
Thomas More College
Transylvania University
Union College
University of Pikeville
University of the Cumberlands

Louisiana

Centenary College of Louisiana
Dillard University
Louisiana College
Loyola University New Orleans
St. Joseph Seminary College
University of Holy Cross

Maine

Bates College
Bowdoin College
Colby College
College of the Atlantic
Saint Joseph's College of Maine
Thomas College
Unity College
University of Maine
　Farmington
　Machias

Maryland

Coppin State University
Goucher College
Hood College
McDaniel College
Mount St. Mary's University
Notre Dame of Maryland
　University
St. John's College
St. Mary's College of Maryland
Salisbury University
University of Baltimore
Washington Adventist
　University
Washington College

Massachusetts

American International College
Amherst College
Anna Maria College
Assumption College
Bard College at Simon's Rock
Bay Path University
Becker College
Cambridge College
Clark University
College of the Holy Cross
Curry College
Eastern Nazarene College
Elms College
Emmanuel College
Endicott College
Fisher College
Fitchburg State University
Gordon College
Hampshire College
Harvard College
Hellenic College/Holy Cross
Lasell College
Lesley University
Massachusetts College of
　Liberal Arts
Merrimack College
Mount Holyoke College
Mount Ida College
Newbury College

Nichols College
Pine Manor College
Regis College
Simmons College
Smith College
Springfield College
Stonehill College
Wellesley College
Wheaton College
Wheelock College
Williams College
Worcester State University

Michigan

Adrian College
Albion College
Alma College
Aquinas College
Calvin College
Concordia University
Cornerstone University
Finlandia University
Grace Bible College
Hillsdale College
Hope College
Kalamazoo College
Kuyper College
Madonna University
Marygrove College
Michigan Jewish Institute
Olivet College
Robert B. Miller College
Rochester College
Siena Heights University
Spring Arbor University

Minnesota

Augsburg College
Bethany Lutheran College
Bethel University
Carleton College
College of St. Benedict
College of St. Scholastica
Concordia College: Moorhead
Crown College
Gustavus Adolphus College
Hamline University
Macalester College
St. Catherine University
St. John's University
St. Olaf College
Southwest Minnesota State
 University
University of Minnesota
 Morris
University of Northwestern - St.
 Paul

Mississippi

Belhaven University
Blue Mountain College
Millsaps College
Mississippi University for
 Women
Mississippi Valley State
 University
Rust College
Tougaloo College
William Carey University

Missouri

Avila University
Central Methodist University
College of the Ozarks
Columbia College
Culver-Stockton College
Drury University
Evangel University
Fontbonne University
Hannibal-LaGrange University
Lincoln University
Lindenwood University
Missouri Baptist University
Missouri Southern State
 University
Missouri Valley College
Missouri Western State
 University

Rockhurst University
Stephens College
Truman State University
Westminster College
William Jewell College

Montana

Carroll College
Rocky Mountain College
Salish Kootenai College
University of Great Falls
University of Montana
University of Montana: Western

Nebraska

Chadron State College
College of Saint Mary
Doane College
Hastings College
Midland University
Nebraska Wesleyan University
Peru State College
Union College
Wayne State College
York College

Nevada

Nevada State College
Sierra Nevada College

New Hampshire

Colby-Sawyer College
Dartmouth College
Franklin Pierce University
Granite State College
Keene State College
New England College
Northeast Catholic College
Saint Anselm College
Thomas More College of
 Liberal Arts
University of New Hampshire at
 Manchester

New Jersey

Bloomfield College
Caldwell University
Centenary College
The College of New Jersey
College of St. Elizabeth
Drew University
Felician University
Georgian Court University
Kean University
Pillar College
Ramapo College of New Jersey
Stockton University
William Paterson University of
 New Jersey

New Mexico

Institute of American Indian
 Arts
New Mexico Institute of Mining
 and Technology
St. John's College
Santa Fe University of Art and
 Design
University of the Southwest

New York

Bard College
Barnard College
Boricua College
Canisius College
Cazenovia College
City University of New York
 Baruch College
 Brooklyn College
 City College
 College of Staten Island
 Hunter College
 John Jay College of
  Criminal Justice
 Lehman College
 Medgar Evers College
 Queens College
 York College
Colgate University

College of Mount St. Vincent
College of New Rochelle
College of Saint Rose
Columbia University
 School of General Studies
Concordia College
D'Youville College
Daemen College
Dominican College of Blauvelt
Dowling College
Elmira College
Eugene Lang College The New
 School for Liberal Arts
Excelsior College
Hamilton College
Hartwick College
Hilbert College
Hobart and William Smith
 Colleges
Houghton College
Iona College
Ithaca College
Jewish Theological Seminary of
 America
Keuka College
The King's College
Le Moyne College
Long Island University
 LIU Brooklyn
 LIU Post
Manhattan College
Manhattanville College
Marist College
Marymount Manhattan College
Medaille College
Medaille College: Rochester
Mercy College
Metropolitan College of New
 York
Molloy College
Mount Saint Mary College
Nazareth College
Nyack College
Paul Smith's College
Roberts Wesleyan College
St. Francis College
St. John Fisher College
St. Joseph's College New York:
 Suffolk Campus
St. Joseph's College, New York
St. Lawrence University
St. Thomas Aquinas College
Sarah Lawrence College
Siena College
Skidmore College
SUNY
 College at Brockport
 College at Buffalo
 College at Cortland
 College at Fredonia
 College at Geneseo
 College at New Paltz
 College at Old Westbury
 College at Oneonta
 College at Plattsburgh
 College at Potsdam
 College at Purchase
 College of Environmental
  Science and Forestry
 Empire State College
Touro College
Union College
Utica College
Vassar College
Wagner College
Wells College

North Carolina

Barton College
Belmont Abbey College
Bennett College for Women
Brevard College
Campbell University
Catawba College
Chowan University
Davidson College
Elizabeth City State University

Elon University
Gardner-Webb University
Greensboro College
Guilford College
High Point University
Johnson C. Smith University
Lees-McRae College
Lenoir-Rhyne University
Livingstone College
Mars Hill University
Meredith College
Methodist University
Montreat College
North Carolina Wesleyan
 College
Pfeiffer University
St. Andrews University
Saint Augustine's University
Salem College
Shaw University
University of North Carolina
 Asheville
 Pembroke
Warren Wilson College
William Peace University

North Dakota

Minot State University
University of Jamestown
Valley City State University

Ohio

Ashland University
Bluffton University
Cedarville University
Central State University
College of Wooster
Defiance College
Denison University
Heidelberg University
Hiram College
Kenyon College
Lake Erie College
Marietta College
Mount St. Joseph University
Muskingum University
Notre Dame College
Oberlin College
Ohio Dominican University
Ohio Wesleyan University
Otterbein University
Pontifical College Josephinum
Tiffin University
University of Rio Grande
Ursuline College
Walsh University
Wilberforce University
Wilmington College
Wittenberg University

Oklahoma

Bacone College
Hillsdale Free Will Baptist
 College
Langston University
Mid-America Christian
 University
Oklahoma Baptist University
Oklahoma City University
Oklahoma Panhandle State
 University
Oklahoma Wesleyan University
Oral Roberts University
St. Gregory's University
Southeastern Oklahoma State
 University
Southern Nazarene University
Southwestern Christian
 University
University of Science and Arts
 of Oklahoma

Oregon

Art Institute of Portland
Concordia University
Corban University
Eastern Oregon University
Gutenberg College

Lewis & Clark College
Linfield College
Marylhurst University
Reed College
Southern Oregon University
Warner Pacific College
Western Oregon University
Willamette University

Pennsylvania

Albright College
Allegheny College
Alvernia University
Bryn Athyn College
Bryn Mawr College
Cabrini College
Cedar Crest College
Chatham University
Chestnut Hill College
Dickinson College
Elizabethtown College
Franklin & Marshall College
Geneva College
Gettysburg College
Gratz College
Grove City College
Gwynedd Mercy University
Haverford College
Immaculata University
Juniata College
Keystone College
King's College
La Roche College
La Salle University
Lafayette College
Lebanon Valley College
Lincoln University
Lock Haven University of
 Pennsylvania
Lycoming College
Mercyhurst University
Messiah College
Millersville University of
 Pennsylvania
Misericordia University
Moravian College
Mount Aloysius College
Muhlenberg College
Rosemont College
St. Francis University
St. Vincent College
Seton Hill University
Susquehanna University
Swarthmore College
Thiel College
University of Pittsburgh
 Greensburg
 Johnstown
University of Scranton
University of Valley Forge
Ursinus College
Washington & Jefferson College
Waynesburg University
Westminster College
Wilson College
York College of Pennsylvania

Puerto Rico

Atlantic University College
Inter American University of
 Puerto Rico
 Aguadilla Campus
 Arecibo Campus
Universidad Adventista de las
 Antillas
Universidad Metropolitana
University of Puerto Rico
 Aguadilla
 Arecibo
 Cayey University College
 Humacao
University of the Sacred Heart

Rhode Island

Brown University
Bryant University
Providence College

Rhode Island College
Salve Regina University

South Carolina

Allen University
Benedict College
Bob Jones University
Charleston Southern University
Claflin University
Coker College
College of Charleston
Columbia College
Converse College
Erskine College
Francis Marion University
Furman University
Lander University
Limestone College
Morris College
Newberry College
North Greenville University
Presbyterian College
Southern Wesleyan University
University of South Carolina
   Aiken
   Beaufort
Voorhees College
Wofford College

South Dakota

Dakota Wesleyan University
Mount Marty College
Northern State University
Oglala Lakota College
Sinte Gleska University
University of Sioux Falls

Tennessee

American Baptist College
Aquinas College
Austin Peay State University
Bethel University
Bryan College
   Dayton
Carson-Newman University
Cumberland University
Fisk University
Freed-Hardeman University
King University
Lane College
Lee University
LeMoyne-Owen College
Lincoln Memorial University
Lipscomb University
Martin Methodist College
Maryville College
Milligan College
Rhodes College
Sewanee: The University of the
   South
Southern Adventist University
Tennessee Wesleyan College
Trevecca Nazarene University
Tusculum College
Union University
Williamson College

Texas

Austin College
Concordia University Texas
East Texas Baptist University
Houston Baptist University
Howard Payne University
Huston-Tillotson University
Jarvis Christian College
Lubbock Christian University
McMurry University
Midwestern State University
Paul Quinn College
St. Edward's University
St. Mary's University
Schreiner University
Southwestern Adventist
   University
Southwestern Christian College
Southwestern University
Texas College
Texas Lutheran University

University of Dallas
University of St. Thomas
Wayland Baptist University
Wiley College

Utah

Stevens-Henager College
   Ogden
Westminster College

Vermont

Bennington College
Burlington College
Castleton State College
Champlain College
College of St. Joseph in
   Vermont
Goddard College
Green Mountain College
Johnson State College
Lyndon State College
Marlboro College
Middlebury College
Saint Michael's College
Southern Vermont College
Sterling College

Virginia

Averett University
Bluefield College
Bridgewater College
Christendom College
Christopher Newport University
Eastern Mennonite University
Emory & Henry College
Ferrum College
Hampden-Sydney College
Hollins University
Lynchburg College
Mary Baldwin College
Patrick Henry College
Randolph College
Randolph-Macon College
Roanoke College
Southern Virginia University
Sweet Briar College
University of Richmond
University of Virginia's College
   at Wise
Virginia Military Institute
Virginia Union University
Virginia University of
   Lynchburg
Virginia Wesleyan College
Washington and Lee University

Washington

Antioch University
   Seattle
Evergreen State College
Gonzaga University
Heritage University
Northwest University
Trinity Lutheran College
University of Puget Sound
Walla Walla University
Whitman College
Whitworth University

West Virginia

Alderson-Broaddus University
Bethany College
Bluefield State College
Concord University
Davis and Elkins College
Glenville State College
Ohio Valley University
Salem International University
West Virginia State University
West Virginia University
   Institute of Technology
West Virginia Wesleyan College
Wheeling Jesuit University

Wisconsin

Alverno College
Beloit College
Carroll University
Carthage College

Concordia University Wisconsin
Edgewood College
Lakeland College
Lawrence University
Maranathan Baptist University
   Maranatha Baptist
    University
Marian University
Mount Mary University
Northland College
Ripon College
St. Norbert College
Silver Lake College of the Holy
   Family
University of Wisconsin
   Green Bay
   River Falls
   Superior
Wisconsin Lutheran College

Austria

Webster Vienna Private
   University

Belgium

Vesalius College

France

American University of Paris

Greece

Deree College, The American
   College of Greece

Italy

American University of Rome
John Cabot University

Kuwait

American University of Kuwait

Lebanon

Notre Dame University: Louaize

Morocco

Al Akhawayn University

Netherlands

Webster University the
   Netherlands

Pakistan

Forman Christian College

Switzerland

Franklin University Switzerland

United Kingdom

Richmond, The American
   International University in
   London

Two-year

Arkansas

Arkansas State University
   Newport
Crowley's Ridge College
National Park College

California

Antelope Valley College
Deep Springs College
Feather River College
Fresno City College

Colorado

Colorado Mountain College

Florida

Florida SouthWestern State
   College

Georgia

Andrew College
Georgia Highlands College
Georgia Perimeter College
Gordon State College
Oxford College of Emory
   University

Hawaii

Hawaii Tokai International
   College

Illinois

Lincoln College

Indiana

Ancilla College

Iowa

Kaplan University
   Cedar Rapids

Kansas

Donnelly College
Hesston College

Maine

Kennebec Valley Community
   College

Massachusetts

Dean College
Marian Court College

Michigan

Montcalm Community College

Missouri

Cottey College
Crowder College
Missouri State University: West
   Plains
Stevens Institute of Business &
   Arts

New Jersey

Assumption College for Sisters
Rowan College at Gloucester

New Mexico

Luna Community College

New York

Maria College
SUNY
   College of Technology at
    Alfred
   College of Technology at
    Delhi

Ohio

Chatfield College

Pennsylvania

University of Pittsburgh
   Titusville

Puerto Rico

Colegio de Cinematografía,
   Artes y Televisión

South Carolina

Clinton College
Spartanburg Methodist College
University of South Carolina
   Union

Tennessee

Hiwassee College

Texas

Alvin Community College
Eastfield College
Jacksonville College
Lamar State College at Orange
North Lake College

Vermont

Community College of Vermont
Landmark College

Virginia

Richard Bland College

Washington

Olympic College

Wisconsin

University of Wisconsin
   Baraboo/Sauk County
   Fond du Lac
   Fox Valley
   Manitowoc
   Marathon County
   Marinette
   Richland
   Rock County
   Sheboygan
   Washington County

Upper-division colleges

Alabama

Athens State University
United States Sports Academy

Arizona

Northcentral University

California

Antioch University
   Los Angeles
   Santa Barbara
California Institute of Integral
   Studies
John F. Kennedy University
Pacific Oaks College
Samuel Merritt University

Illinois

Lakeview College of Nursing
Resurrection University
Rush University
Saint Anthony College of
   Nursing
St. Francis Medical Center
   College of Nursing
St. John's College

Kansas

University of Kansas Medical
   Center

Louisiana

Louisiana State University
   Health Sciences Center

Maryland

University of Maryland
   Baltimore

Michigan

Walsh College of Accountancy
   and Business Administration

Minnesota

Northwestern Health Sciences
   University

Mississippi

University of Mississippi
   Medical Center

Missouri

Goldfarb School of Nursing at
   Barnes-Jewish College
Midwest University
St. Luke's College

Nebraska

University of Nebraska
   Medical Center

Nevada

Roseman University of Health
   Sciences

New York

SUNY
Downstate Medical Center
Upstate Medical University

Puerto Rico

Carlos Albizu University: San
Juan

South Carolina

Medical University of South
Carolina

Texas

Austin Graduate School of
Theology
Texas A&M University
Baylor College of Dentistry
Texarkana
Texas Tech University Health
Sciences Center
University of Texas
Health Science Center at
Houston
Medical Branch at
Galveston

Virginia

Catholic Distance University

Washington

Antioch University
Seattle
Bastyr University

Agricultural colleges

Four-year

Alabama Agricultural and
Mechanical University, AL
Alcorn State University, MS
Louisiana State University and
Agricultural and Mechanical
College, LA
Mississippi State University,
MS
SUNY
College of Agriculture and
Technology at
Morrisville, NY
University of Puerto Rico
Mayaguez, PR
Utuado, PR
Wilmington College, OH

Two-year

Abraham Baldwin Agricultural
College, GA
Bainbridge State College, GA
Nebraska College of Technical
Agriculture, NE
Ohio State University
Agricultural Technical
Institute, OH
SUNY
College of Agriculture and
Technology at Cobleskill,
NY

Arts/music colleges

Four-year

Academy of Art University, CA
American Academy of Art, IL
Art Academy of Cincinnati, OH
Art Center College of Design,
CA
Art Institute of Atlanta, GA

Art Institute of California
Hollywood, CA
Inland Empire, CA
Orange County, CA
Sacramento, CA
San Diego, CA
San Francisco, CA
Art Institute of Dallas, TX
Art Institute of Fort Lauderdale,
FL
Art Institute of Houston, TX
Art Institute of Las Vegas, NV
Art Institute of Michigan, MI
Art Institute of Philadelphia, PA
Art Institute of Phoenix, AZ
Art Institute of Pittsburgh, PA
Art Institute of Portland, OR
Art Institute of Seattle, WA
Art Institute of Tucson, AZ
Art Institute of Washington, VA
Art Institutes International
Minnesota, MN
Berklee College of Music, MA
Boston Conservatory, MA
Brooks Institute, CA
California College of the Arts,
CA
California Institute of the Arts,
CA
Cleveland Institute of Art, OH
Cleveland Institute of Music,
OH
College for Creative Studies, MI
Columbia College
Hollywood, CA
Columbia College Chicago, IL
Columbus College of Art and
Design, OH
Conservatory of Music of
Puerto Rico, PR
Cooper Union for the
Advancement of Science and
Art, NY
Cornish College of the Arts,
WA
Creative Center, NE
Curtis Institute of Music, PA
DePauw University, IN
DigiPen Institute of Technology,
WA
Digital Media Arts College, FL
Eastman School of Music of the
University of Rochester, NY
Escuela de Artes Plasticas de
Puerto Rico, PR
Ex'pression College, CA
Fashion Institute of Technology,
NY
Five Towns College, NY
Full Sail University, FL
Illinois Institute of Art
Chicago, IL
Schaumburg, IL
Institute of American Indian
Arts, NM
Interior Designers Institute, CA
International Academy of
Design and Technology
Chicago, IL
Detroit, MI
Henderson, NV
International Academy of
Design and Technology:
Tampa, FL
Johns Hopkins University:
Peabody Conservatory of
Music, MD
Juilliard School, NY
Kansas City Art Institute, MO
Laguna College of Art and
Design, CA
Lawrence University, WI
Lyme Academy College of Fine
Arts, CT
Maine College of Art, ME
Manhattan School of Music, NY

Mannes College The New
School for Music, NY
Maryland Institute College of
Art, MD
Marymount Manhattan College,
NY
Massachusetts College of Art
and Design, MA
McNally Smith College of
Music, MN
Memphis College of Art, TN
Miami International University
of Art and Design, FL
Milwaukee Institute of Art &
Design, WI
Minneapolis College of Art and
Design, MN
Montserrat College of Art, MA
Moore College of Art and
Design, PA
Mt. Sierra College, CA
New England Conservatory of
Music, MA
New Hampshire Institute of Art,
NH
New York School of Interior
Design, NY
NewSchool of Architecture &
Design, CA
Northwest College of Art &
Design, WA
O'More College of Design, TN
Oberlin College, OH
Oregon College of Art & Craft,
OR
Otis College of Art and Design,
CA
Pacific Northwest College of
Art, OR
Paier College of Art, CT
Paris College of Art, FR
Parsons The New School for
Design, NY
Pennsylvania Academy of the
Fine Arts, PA
Pennsylvania College of Art and
Design, PA
Platt College
San Diego, CA
Pratt Institute, NY
Rhode Island School of Design,
RI
Ringling College of Art and
Design, FL
Rocky Mountain College of
Art & Design, CO
San Francisco Art Institute, CA
San Francisco Conservatory of
Music, CA
Santa Fe University of Art and
Design, NM
Savannah College of Art and
Design, GA
School of the Art Institute of
Chicago, IL
School of the Museum of Fine
Arts, MA
School of Visual Arts, NY
Southern California Institute of
Architecture, CA
Southwest University of Visual
Arts, NM
Southwest University of Visual
Arts, AZ
Southwestern University, TX
University of North Carolina
School of the Arts, NC
University of the Arts, PA
VanderCook College of Music,
IL
Visible Music College, TN
Watkins College of Art,
Design & Film, TN

Two-year

American Academy of Dramatic
Arts, NY

American Academy of Dramatic
Arts: West, CA
Antonelli College
Cincinnati, OH
Antonelli Institute of Art and
Photography, PA
Art Institute of California
Los Angeles, CA
Art Institute of Cincinnati, OH
Broadview University
Broadview Entertainment
Arts University, UT
Dean College, MA
Delaware College of Art and
Design, DE
Delta College of Arts &
Technology, LA
Douglas Education Center, PA
Fashion Institute of Design and
Merchandising
Los Angeles, CA
San Diego, CA
San Francisco, CA
Hussian College, School of Art,
PA
ITT Technical Institute
Plymouth Meeting, PA
Madison Media Institute, WI
Nossi College of Art, TN
Platt College
Los Angeles, CA
Sessions College for
Professional Design, AZ
Sullivan College of Technology
and Design, KY
Villa Maria College of Buffalo,
NY
Virginia Marti College of Art
and Design, OH

Bible colleges

Four-year

Alaska Bible College, AK
Allegheny Wesleyan College,
OH
American Baptist College, TN
American Indian College of the
Assemblies of God, AZ
Apex School of Theology, NC
Appalachian Bible College, WV
Arizona Christian University,
AZ
Arlington Baptist College, TX
Austin Graduate School of
Theology, TX
Baptist Bible College, MO
Baptist College of Florida, FL
Baptist Missionary Association
Theological Seminary, TX
Baptist University of the
Americas, TX
Barclay College, KS
Beulah Heights University, GA
Biola University, CA
Bob Jones University, SC
Boise Bible College, ID
Boston Baptist College, MA
Cairn University, PA
California Christian College,
CA
Calvary Bible College and
Theological Seminary, MO
Carolina Christian College, NC
Carver College, GA
Central Baptist College, AR
Central Christian College of the
Bible, MO
Clear Creek Baptist Bible
College, KY
College of Biblical Studies-
Houston, TX
Columbia International
University, SC

Criswell College, TX
Crossroads Bible College, IN
Crossroads College, MN
Dallas Christian College, TX
Davis College, NY
Ecclesia College, AR
Emmaus Bible College, IA
Faith Baptist Bible College and
Theological Seminary, IA
Faith Evangelical College &
Seminary, WA
Family of Faith College, OK
Global University, MO
God's Bible School and College,
OH
Grace Bible College, MI
Grace University, NE
Great Lakes Christian College,
MI
Heritage Christian University,
AL
Hobe Sound Bible College, FL
Horizon University, CA
Huntsville Bible College, AL
International Baptist College,
AZ
Johnson University, TN
Johnson University: Florida, FL
Kentucky Christian University,
KY
Kentucky Mountain Bible
College, KY
The King's University, TX
Kuyper College, MI
La Sierra University, CA
Lancaster Bible College, PA
Laurel University, NC
Life Pacific College, CA
Lincoln Christian University, IL
Luther Rice University, GA
Manhattan Christian College,
KS
Maranathan Baptist University
Maranatha Baptist
University, WI
Mid-Atlantic Christian
University, NC
Montana Bible College, MT
Moody Bible Institute, IL
Nazarene Bible College, CO
Nebraska Christian College, NE
New Hope Christian College,
OR
New Orleans Baptist
Theological Seminary, LA
Northpoint Bible College, MA
Oak Hills Christian College,
MN
Ohio Christian University, OH
Ozark Christian College, MO
Pillar College, NJ
Point University, GA
St. Louis Christian College, MO
Shasta Bible College and
Graduate School, CA
Shiloh University, IA
Southeastern Baptist College,
MS
Southeastern Baptist Theological
Seminary, NC
Southeastern Bible College, AL
Southern Baptist Theological
Seminary, KY
Southern California Seminary,
CA
Southwestern Assemblies of
God University, TX
Southwestern Baptist
Theological Seminary, TX
Southwestern Christian College,
TX
SUM Bible College &
Theological Seminary, CA
Summit University, PA
Theological University of the
Caribbean, PR
Toccoa Falls College, GA

Tri-State Bible College, OH
Trinity Baptist College, FL
Trinity Bible College, ND
Trinity College of Florida, FL
Universidad Pentecostal Mizpa,
PR
Virginia Baptist College, VA
W.L. Bonner Bible College, SC
Welch College, TN
William Jessup University, CA
World Mission University, CA

Two-year

Epic Bible College, CA
Rosedale Bible College, OH

Business colleges

Four-year

American National University
Salem, VA
American University of Puerto
Rico, PR
Babson College, MA
Baker College
of Allen Park, MI
of Auburn Hills, MI
of Cadillac, MI
of Clinton Township, MI
of Flint, MI
of Muskegon, MI
of Owosso, MI
of Port Huron, MI
Bellevue University, NE
Bentley University, MA
Berkeley College, NY
Berkeley College, NJ
Berkeley College of New York
City, NY
Beulah Heights University, GA
Briarcliffe College, NY
Bryant & Stratton College
Eastlake, OH
Bryant University, RI
California College San Diego,
CA
California Miramar University,
CA
California State University
Stanislaus, CA
California University of
Management and Sciences,
CA
Capitol Technology University,
MD
Chadron State College, NE
City College
Fort Lauderdale, FL
City University of New York
Baruch College, NY
Clarion University of
Pennsylvania, PA
Cleary University, MI
Cogswell Polytechnical College,
CA
Colorado Heights University,
CO
Daniel Webster College, NH
Davenport University, MI
Deree College, The American
College of Greece, GR
DeVry College of New York
Midtown Campus, NY
Dowling College, NY
Ecole Hoteliere de Lausanne,
CH
Everest University
Orange Park, FL
Fashion Institute of Technology,
NY
Fisher College, MA
Five Towns College, NY
Fort Lewis College, CO
Franklin University, OH

Globe Institute of Technology,
NY
Goldey-Beacom College, DE
Herzing University
Atlanta, GA
Birmingham, AL
Brookfield, WI
Kenosha, WI
Madison, WI
Toledo, OH
Hickey College, MO
Humphreys College, CA
Husson University, ME
Huston-Tillotson University, TX
Independence University, UT
Indiana Institute of Technology,
IN
Instituto Tecnologico Autonomo
de Mexico, MX
Instituto Tecnologico y de
Estudios Superiores de
Occidente, MX
International Business College,
IN
Iona College, NY
ITT Technical Institute
Owings Mills, MD
Tulsa, OK
Jones College, FL
Keystone College, PA
King's College, PA
Lasell College, MA
LIM College, NY
Lincoln University, CA
Mayville State University, ND
Menlo College, CA
Merrimack College, MA
Metropolitan College of New
York, NY
Midstate College, IL
Millsaps College, MS
Monroe College, NY
Mount Ida College, MA
Mount Washington College, NH
Mt. Sierra College, CA
National American University
Albuquerque, NM
Bloomington, MN
Rapid City, SD
Newbury College, MA
Nichols College, MA
Northern New Mexico College,
NM
Northwestern Polytechnic
University, CA
Northwood University
Michigan, MI
Texas, TX
Peirce College, PA
Post University, CT
Presentation College, SD
Restaurant School at Walnut
Hill College, PA
Rockhurst University, MO
St. Ambrose University, IA
Savannah State University, GA
Silicon Valley University, CA
Southeastern Baptist College,
MS
Southern California Institute of
Technology, CA
Stevens-Henager College
Murray, UT
SUNY
College at Old Westbury,
NY
SUNY Polytechnic Institute, NY
Thomas College, ME
Touro University Worldwide,
CA
Universidad Anahuac, MX
University of Greenwich, GB
University of the Potomac, VA
University of the Potomac, DC
University of the Southwest,
NM
University of the West, CA

Virginia College
Huntsville, AL
Walsh College of Accountancy
and Business Administration,
MI
Webber International University,
FL
Webster Vienna Private
University, AT
Western International
University, AZ

Two-year

American National University
Charlottesville, VA
Danville, VA
Harrisonburg, VA
Lynchburg, VA
Martinsville, VA
Princeton, WV
Berks Technical Institute, PA
Bidwell Training Center, PA
Bradford School, OH
Brown Mackie College
Akron, OH
Atlanta, GA
Cincinnati, OH
Findlay, OH
Fort Wayne, IN
Hopkinsville, KY
Merrillville, IN
Miami, FL
North Kentucky, KY
Bryant & Stratton College
Albany, NY
Amherst, NY
Buffalo, NY
Henrietta, NY
Milwaukee, WI
Rochester, NY
Southtowns, NY
Syracuse, NY
Virginia Beach, VA
Business Informatics Center,
NY
Cambria-Rowe Business
College, PA
Cambria-Rowe Business
College: Indiana, PA
City College
Gainesville, FL
College of Court Reporting, IN
College of Westchester, NY
Columbia Central University
Yauco, PR
Concorde Career College
Kansas City, MO
Daymar College
Chillicothe, OH
Louisville, KY
Owensboro, KY
Daymar Institute
Clarksville, TN
Delta School of Business &
Technology, LA
Douglas Education Center, PA
DuBois Business College, PA
Huntingdon, PA
Oil City, PA
Duluth Business University, MN
Eagle Gate College: Murray,
UT
Elmira Business Institute, NY
Elmira Business Institute:
Vestal, NY
Empire College, CA
Fashion Institute of Design and
Merchandising
Los Angeles, CA
San Diego, CA
San Francisco, CA
Florida Career College
Miami, FL
Pembroke Pines, FL
Florida Technical College
Lakeland, FL
Forrest Junior College, SC

Fortis College
Orange Park, FL
Ravenna, OH
Gallipolis Career College, OH
Hallmark University, TX
Harrison College
Grove City, OH
Indianapolis, IN
Herzing University
Winter Park, FL
Humacao Community College,
PR
ICPR Junior College, PR
International Business College:
Indianapolis, IN
ITT Technical Institute
Canton, MI
Hilliard, OH
Kansas City, MO
Kennesaw, GA
Newburgh, IN
Jamestown Business College,
NY
Kaplan Career Institute
Pittsburgh, PA
Kaplan College
Hammond, IN
San Diego, CA
Kaplan University
Hagerstown, MD
South Portland, ME
Key College, FL
LDS Business College, UT
Lincoln College of New
England, CT
Lincoln College of Technology
Dayton, OH
Long Island Business Institute,
NY
Marian Court College, MA
McCann School of Business and
Technology
Dickson City, PA
Hazleton, PA
Metro Business College
Rolla, MO
Miami-Jacobs Career College
Sharonville, OH
Miller-Motte Technical College
Clarksville, TN
Minneapolis Business College,
MN
MTI College, CA
National College
Bristol, TN
Danville, KY
Florence, KY
Kettering, OH
Knoxville, TN
Lexington, KY
Louisville, KY
Nashville, TN
Pikeville, KY
Richmond, KY
New England College of
Business and Finance, MA
Ohio Business College
Hilliard, OH
Sandusky, OH
Sheffield, OH
Penn Commercial Business and
Technical School, PA
Pennsylvania Institute of Health
and Technology, PA
Pioneer Pacific College:
Springfield, OR
Plaza College, NY
Remington College
Memphis, TN
South Coast College, CA
South Hills School of
Business & Technology, PA
Southeastern College
Greenacres, FL
Miami Lakes, FL
Stenotype Institute: Jacksonville,
FL

Stevens Institute of Business &
Arts, MO
Taylor Business Institute, IL
Trumbull Business College, OH
University of Northwestern
Ohio, OH
Utica School of Commerce, NY
Virginia College
Austin, TX
Biloxi, MS
Greenville, SC
Pensacola, FL
School of Business and
Health in Chattanooga,
TN
Virginia Marti College of Art
and Design, OH
Wade College, TX
West Virginia Business College
Nutter Fort, WV
Wheeling, WV

Culinary schools

Four-year

Art Institute of Atlanta, GA
Art Institute of California
Hollywood, CA
Inland Empire, CA
Orange County, CA
Sacramento, CA
San Francisco, CA
Art Institute of Houston, TX
Art Institute of Las Vegas, NV
Art Institute of Phoenix, AZ
Art Institute of Pittsburgh, PA
Art Institute of Seattle, WA
Art Institute of Tucson, AZ
Art Institute of Washington, VA
Art Institutes International
Minnesota, MN
Culinary Institute of America,
NY
Kendall College, IL
Paul Smith's College, NY
Restaurant School at Walnut
Hill College, PA
Southern New Hampshire
University, NH

Two-year

Atlantic Cape Community
College, NJ
Chef's Academy, NC
Culinary Institute LeNotre, TX
Institute of Technology: Clovis,
CA
Keystone Technical Institute,
PA
L'Ecole Culinaire, MO
Le Cordon Bleu College of
Culinary Arts
Austin, TX
Chicago, IL
Los Angeles, CA
Miami, FL
Minneapolis-St. Paul, MN
Orlando, FL
Portland, OR
San Francisco, CA
Scottsdale, AZ
Lincoln College of New
England, CT
New England Culinary Institute,
VT
Platt College
Moore, OK
Tulsa, OK
Schoolcraft College, MI
Southwestern Oregon
Community College, OR
Virginia College
Richmond, VA
Savannah, GA

Tables and Indexes

Louisiana State University
Eunice, LA
Maine College of Health
Professions, ME
Maria College, NY
Metro Business College
Jefferson City, MO
Miller-Motte Technical College
Clarksville, TN
Conway, SC
Myotherapy Institute, NE
Ohio Business College
Hilliard, OH
Ohio College of Massotherapy,
OH
Pacific College of Oriental
Medicine: San Diego, CA
Phillips Beth Israel School of
Nursing, NY
Pioneer Pacific College:
Springfield, OR
Platt College
Moore, OK
Tulsa, OK
Plaza College, NY
Ponce Paramedical College, PR
Remington College
Greenspoint Campus, TX
St. Elizabeth College of
Nursing, NY
St. Joseph's College of Nursing,
NY
St. Luke's College, IA
St. Vincent's College, CT
South College, NC
Southeast Missouri Hospital
College of Nursing and
Health Sciences, MO
Southeastern College
Greenacres, FL
Miami Lakes, FL
State College of Florida,
Manatee-Sarasota, FL
Swedish Institute, NY
Texas County Technical
College, MO
Trocaire College, NY
Universal Technology College
of Puerto Rico, PR
Vatterott College
Des Moines, IA
Vet Tech Institute, PA
Virginia College
Augusta, GA
Austin, TX
Baton Rouge, LA
Biloxi, MS
Charleston, SC
Columbia, SC
Columbus, GA
Macon, GA
Montgomery, AL
Pensacola, FL
Tulsa, OK
Wallace State Community
College at Hanceville, AL
West Virginia Junior College
Bridgeport, WV

Schools of mortuary science

Two-year

American Academy McAllister
Institute of Funeral Service,
NY
Cincinnati College of Mortuary
Science, OH
Commonwealth Institute of
Funeral Service, TX
Dallas Institute of Funeral
Service, TX
Eastwick College
Hackensack, NJ

John A. Gupton College, TN
Mid-America College of Funeral
Service, IN

Seminary/rabbinical colleges

Four-year

Austin Graduate School of
Theology, TX
Baptist Bible College, MO
Baptist Missionary Association
Theological Seminary, TX
Beis Medrash Heichal Dovid,
NY
Beth Hamedrash Shaarei Yosher
Institute, NY
Beth Hatalmud Rabbinical
College, NY
Beth Medrash Govoha, NJ
Beulah Heights University, GA
Bob Jones University, SC
Calvary Bible College and
Theological Seminary, MO
Central Yeshiva Tomchei
Tmimim-Lubavitch, NY
Charlotte Christian College and
Theological Seminary, NC
Conception Seminary College,
MO
Criswell College, TX
Divine Word College, IA
Earlham College, IN
Erskine College, SC
Faith Baptist Bible College and
Theological Seminary, IA
Faith Evangelical College &
Seminary, WA
George Fox University, OR
Global University, MO
Hebrew Theological College, IL
Hellenic College/Holy Cross,
MA
Holy Apostles College and
Seminary, CT
Holy Trinity Orthodox
Seminary, NY
International Baptist College,
AZ
Kehilath Yakov Rabbinical
Seminary, NY
The King's University, TX
Luther Rice University, GA
Machzikei Hadath Rabbinical
College, NY
Manthano Christian College, MI
The Master's College, CA
Mesivta Torah Vodaath
Seminary, NY
Midwest University, MO
Mirrer Yeshiva Central Institute,
NY
Moody Bible Institute, IL
Moravian College, PA
Mount Angel Seminary, OR
Multnomah University, OR
Ner Israel Rabbinical College,
MD
New Orleans Baptist
Theological Seminary, LA
Nyack College, NY
Ohr Somayach Tanenbaum
Education Center, NY
Piedmont International
University, NC
Pontifical College Josephinum,
OH
Rabbi Jacob Joseph School, NJ
Rabbinical Academy Mesivta
Rabbi Chaim Berlin, NY
Rabbinical College Beth Shraga,
NY
Rabbinical College Bobover
Yeshiva B'nei Zion, NY

Rabbinical College Ch'san Sofer
of New York, NY
Rabbinical College of America,
NJ
Rabbinical College of Long
Island, NY
Rabbinical College of Ohr
Shimon Yisroel, NY
Rabbinical College of Telshe,
OH
Rabbinical Seminary of
America, NY
Sacred Heart Major Seminary,
MI
St. Charles Borromeo Seminary
- Overbrook, PA
St. John Vianney College
Seminary, FL
St. Joseph Seminary College,
LA
Shasta Bible College and
Graduate School, CA
Shor Yoshuv Rabbinical
College, NY
Southeastern Baptist Theological
Seminary, NC
Southern Baptist Theological
Seminary, KY
Southern California Seminary,
CA
Southwestern Baptist
Theological Seminary, TX
SUM Bible College &
Theological Seminary, CA
Talmudic University, FL
Talmudical Academy of New
Jersey, NJ
Talmudical Institute of Upstate
New York, NY
Talmudical Seminary Oholei
Torah, NY
Talmudical Yeshiva of
Philadelphia, PA
Telshe Yeshiva-Chicago, IL
Theological University of the
Caribbean, PR
Torah Temimah Talmudical
Seminary, NY
U.T.A. Mesivta-Kiryas Joel, NY
United Talmudical Seminary,
NY
University of Dubuque, IA
Virginia University of
Lynchburg, VA
World Mission University, CA
Yeshiva and Kolel Bais
Medrash Elyon, NY
Yeshiva and Kollel Harbotzas
Torah, NY
Yeshiva Beth Yehuda-Yeshiva
Gedolah of Greater Detroit,
MI
Yeshiva College of the Nations
Capital, MD
Yeshiva D'Monsey Rabbinical
College, NY
Yeshiva Derech Chaim, NY
Yeshiva Gedolah Imrei Yosef
D'Spinka, NY
Yeshiva Gedolah Rabbinical
College, FL
Yeshiva Gedolah Zichron
Moshe, NY
Yeshiva Karlin Stolin, NY
Yeshiva of Nitra, NY
Yeshiva of the Telshe Alumni,
NY
Yeshiva Ohr Elchonon Chabad/
West Coast Talmudical
Seminary, CA
Yeshiva Shaar Hatorah, NY
Yeshiva Shaarei Torah of
Rockland, NY
Yeshivas Novominsk, NY
Yeshivat Mikdash Melech, NY
Yeshivath Beth Moshe, PA
Yeshivath Viznitz, NY

Two-year

Salvation Army College for
Officer Training at
Crestmont, CA

Teacher's colleges

Four-year

American Indian College of the
Assemblies of God, AZ
Arlington Baptist College, TX
Athens State University, AL
Austin College, TX
Baker University, KS
Baptist College of Florida, FL
Bluefield College, VA
California State University
Monterey Bay, CA
Cambridge College, MA
Canisius College, NY
Clarion University of
Pennsylvania, PA
College of St. Joseph in
Vermont, VT
Concordia University, OR
Concordia University, MI
Dalton State College, GA
Dowling College, NY
Elmira College, NY
Emmanuel College, GA
Fitchburg State University, MA
Fort Valley State University,
GA
Frostburg State University, MD
Glenville State College, WV
Great Basin College, NV
Heritage University, WA
Humphreys College, CA
Johnson University: Florida, FL
Kendall College, IL
Lander University, SC
Lesley University, MA
Louisiana State University
Shreveport, LA
Lyndon State College, VT
Manhattanville College, NY
Mayville State University, ND
National-Louis University, IL
Nevada State College, NV
New England College, NH
Northwestern Oklahoma State
University, OK
Oglala Lakota College, SD
Pacific Oaks College, CA
Peru State College, NE
Piedmont College, GA
Plymouth State University, NH
Rabbinical College of Long
Island, NY
Rabbinical College of Telshe,
OH
Reinhardt University, GA
Rhode Island College, RI
Rust College, MS
St. Joseph's College New York:
Suffolk Campus, NY
St. Joseph's College, New York,
NY
Savannah State University, GA
Southeastern Oklahoma State
University, OK
Southeastern University, FL
SUNY
College at Buffalo, NY
College at Cortland, NY
College at Geneseo, NY
College at Plattsburgh, NY
College at Potsdam, NY
Tennessee Wesleyan College,
TN
Thomas College, ME
Trinity Baptist College, FL
Union College, KY

University of Hawaii
West Oahu, HI
University of Maine
Farmington, ME
University of Montana:
Western, MT
University of the Southwest,
NM
Valley City State University,
ND
VanderCook College of Music,
IL
Wayne State College, NE
Welch College, TN
West Virginia State University,
WV
Western Oregon University, OR
Wheelock College, MA
William Woods University, MO
Worcester State University, MA
York College, NE

Technical and career colleges

Four-year

Art Institute of Fort Lauderdale,
FL
Baker College
of Auburn Hills, MI
of Clinton Township, MI
of Flint, MI
of Muskegon, MI
of Owosso, MI
of Port Huron, MI
Bluefield State College, WV
Central Penn College, PA
Charter College, AK
City College
Fort Lauderdale, FL
City University of New York
New York City College of
Technology, NY
Coleman University, CA
CollegeAmerica
Fort Collins, CO
Colorado Technical University,
CO
DeVry College of New York
Midtown Campus, NY
Ex'pression College, CA
Florida Career College
Boynton Beach, FL
Jacksonville, FL
Lauderdale Lakes, FL
Riverview, FL
Hamilton Technical College, IA
Herzing University
Atlanta, GA
Birmingham, AL
Brookfield, WI
Kenner, LA
Kenosha, WI
Toledo, OH
Hickey College, MO
International Academy of
Design and Technology
Chicago, IL
Detroit, MI
Henderson, NV
Sacramento, CA
International Academy of
Design and Technology:
Tampa, FL

Lake Area Technical Institute, SD
Lake Region State College, ND
Lake Superior College, MN
Lake Washington Institute of Technology, WA
Lakeland Community College, OH
Lakes Region Community College, NH
Lakeshore Technical College, WI
Lamar Institute of Technology, TX
Lamar State College at Port Arthur, TX
Laurel Business Institute, PA
Laurel Technical Institute, PA
Le Cordon Bleu College of Culinary Arts
   Atlanta, GA
   Scottsdale, AZ
Lincoln College of Technology
   Denver, CO
   Grand Prairie, TX
   Indianapolis, IN
   Nashville, TN
   West Palm Beach, FL
Lincoln Technical Institute
   Allentown, PA
   Northeast Philadelphia, PA
   Philadelphia, PA
Los Angeles Trade and Technical College, CA
Madison Area Technical College, WI
Manchester Community College, NH
Manhattan Area Technical College, KS
Marion Technical College, OH
Martin Community College, NC
Maysville Community and Technical College, KY
McCann School of Business and Technology
   Dickson City, PA
   Hazleton, PA
   Pottsville, PA
   Sunbury, PA
McDowell Technical Community College, NC
Mesabi Range College, MN
Mesalands Community College, NM
Metropolitan Career Center Computer Technology Institute, PA
Metropolitan Community College, NE
Mid-Plains Community College, NE
Mid-State Technical College, WI
Midlands Technical College, SC
Miller-Motte College
   Cary, NC
   Fayetteville, NC
Miller-Motte Technical College, SC
   Chattanooga, TN
   Lynchburg, VA
Milwaukee Area Technical College, WI
Minneapolis Business College, MN
Minneapolis Community and Technical College, MN
Minnesota State College - Southeast Technical, MN
Minnesota State Community and Technical College, MN
Minnesota West Community and Technical College, MN
Missouri College, MO
Mitchell Technical Institute, SD

Moraine Park Technical College, WI
Morrison Institute of Technology, IL
MTI College, CA
Nash Community College, NC
Nashua Community College, NH
Nashville State Community College, TN
National College
   Kettering, OH
   Knoxville, TN
   Nashville, TN
National Park College, AR
Naugatuck Valley Community College, CT
New Castle School of Trades, PA
New Mexico Junior College, NM
New River Community and Technical College, WV
NHTI-Concord's Community College, NH
Nicolet Area Technical College, WI
North Arkansas College, AR
North Central Kansas Technical College, KS
North Central State College, OH
North Dakota State College of Science, ND
North Georgia Technical College, GA
Northcentral Technical College, WI
Northeast State Community College, TN
Northeast Wisconsin Technical College, WI
Northeastern Technical College, SC
Northern Maine Community College, ME
Northland Community & Technical College, MN
Northland Pioneer College, AZ
Northwest Florida State College, FL
Northwest Kansas Technical College, KS
Northwest School of Wooden Boatbuilding, WA
Northwest State Community College, OH
Northwest Technical College, MN
Northwest-Shoals Community College, AL
Northwestern College, IL
Northwestern Connecticut Community College, CT
Nossi College of Art, TN
Nunez Community College, LA
Ohio Technical College, OH
Ohio Valley College of Technology, OH
Oklahoma City Community College, OK
Oklahoma State University Institute of Technology:
   Okmulgee, OK
   Oklahoma City, OK
Orangeburg-Calhoun Technical College, SC
Orleans Technical Institute, PA
Owensboro Community and Technical College, KY
Ozarka College, AR
Ozarks Technical Community College, MO
Pellissippi State Community College, TN
Penn Commercial Business and Technical School, PA
Pennco Tech, PA

Pennsylvania Institute of Technology, PA
Piedmont Technical College, SC
Pierpont Community and Technical College, WV
Pima Community College, AZ
Pine Technical & Community College, MN
Pinnacle Career Institute:
   Kansas City, MO
Pitt Community College, NC
Pittsburgh Institute of Aeronautics, PA
Pittsburgh Institute of Mortuary Science, PA
Platt College
   Los Angeles, CA
PowerSport Institute, OH
Pratt Community College, KS
Prince Institute of Professional Studies, AL
Pulaski Technical College, AR
Quinebaug Valley Community College, CT
Rainy River Community College, MN
Randolph Community College, NC
Ranken Technical College, MO
Redstone College, CO
Refrigeration School, AZ
Remington College
   Baton Rouge, LA
   Cleveland, OH
   Dallas, TX
   Fort Worth, TX
   Greenspoint Campus, TX
   Little Rock, AR
   Memphis, TN
   Nashville, TN
   Shreveport, LA
   Westchase Campus, TX
Renton Technical College, WA
Ridgewater College, MN
Riverland Community College, MN
Rochester Community and Technical College, MN
Rosedale Technical Institute, PA
Rowan-Cabarrus Community College, NC
Sage College, CA
St. Cloud Technical and Community College, MN
St. Paul College, MN
Salt Lake Community College, UT
Sampson Community College, NC
San Jacinto College, TX
San Juan College, NM
Santa Barbara Business College, CA
   Bakersfield, CA
   Rancho Mirage, CA
   Santa Maria, CA
   Ventura, CA
Savannah Technical College, GA
Seattle Central College, WA
Seward County Community College, KS
Shelton State Community College, AL
Sisseton Wahpeton College, SD
Somerset Community College, KY
South Central College, MN
South Florida State College, FL
South Hills School of Business & Technology, PA
South Texas College, TX
Southeast Kentucky Community and Technical College, KY
Southeast Technical Institute, SD

Southeastern Technical College, GA
Southern Arkansas University Tech, AR
Southern Crescent Technical College, GA
Southern Maine Community College, ME
Southern Regional Technical College, GA
Southern Union State Community College, AL
Southern West Virginia Community and Technical College, WV
Southwest Wisconsin Technical College, WI
Southwestern Indian Polytechnic Institute, NM
Spartanburg Community College, SC
Springfield Technical Community College, MA
State Technical College of Missouri, MO
Stautzenberger College, OH
Stevens-Henager College
   Boise, ID
Sullivan College of Technology and Design, KY
SUNY
   College of Agriculture and Technology at Cobleskill, NY
   College of Technology at Alfred, NY
   College of Technology at Canton, NY
   College of Technology at Delhi, NY
Technical Career Institutes, NY
Technical College of the Lowcountry, SC
Terra State Community College, OH
TESST College of Technology
   Baltimore, MD
   Beltsville, MD
   Towson, MD
Texas County Technical College, MO
Texas State Technical College, TX
   Harlingen, TX
   Marshall, TX
   West Texas, TX
Thaddeus Stevens College of Technology, PA
Three Rivers Community College, CT
Tri-County Technical College, SC
Triangle Tech
   Bethlehem, PA
   DuBois, PA
   Erie, PA
   Greensburg, PA
   Pittsburgh, PA
   Sunbury, PA
Trident Technical College, SC
Truckee Meadows Community College, NV
Tulsa Welding School, OK
United Tribes Technical College, ND
Universal Technical Institute, AZ
University of Arkansas Community College at Hope, AR
University of Hawaii Honolulu Community College, HI
University of Northwestern Ohio, OH
University of Southernmost Florida, FL

Vatterott College
   Berkeley, MO
   Cleveland, OH
   Des Moines, IA
   Joplin, MO
   Kansas City, MO
   Memphis, TN
   O'Fallon, MO
   Oklahoma City, OK
   Quincy, IL
   St. Joseph, MO
   Spring Valley, NE
   Springfield, MO
   Sunset Hills, MO
   Tulsa, OK
Vermilion Community College, MN
Vet Tech Institute, PA
Vet Tech Institute of Houston, TX
Virginia College
   Jacksonville, FL
   Mobile, AL
   Spartanburg, SC
Wake Technical Community College, NC
Walla Walla Community College, WA
Washington County Community College, ME
Waukesha County Technical College, WI
West Georgia Technical College, GA
West Kentucky Community and Technical College, KY
West Virginia Northern Community College, WV
Western Dakota Technical Institute, SD
Western Piedmont Community College, NC
Western Technical College, TX
Western Technical College, WI
Western Technical College:
   Diana Drive, TX
Wichita Area Technical College, KS
Williamsburg Technical College, SC
Williamson College of the Trades, PA
Wiregrass Georgia Technical College, GA
Wisconsin Indianhead Technical College, WI
York County Community College, ME
York Technical College, SC
YTI Career Institute
   Altoona, PA
   Lancaster, PA
   York, PA
Zane State College, OH

Special characteristics

Colleges for men

Four-year

Beis Medrash Heichal Dovid, NY
Beth Hamedrash Shaarei Yosher Institute, NY
Beth Hatalmud Rabbinical College, NY
Beth Medrash Govoha, NJ
Central Yeshiva Tomchei Tmimim-Lubavitch, NY
Conception Seminary College, MO
Hampden-Sydney College, VA
Holy Trinity Orthodox Seminary, NY
Kehilath Yakov Rabbinical Seminary, NY
Machzikei Hadath Rabbinical College, NY
Mesivta Torah Vodaath Seminary, NY
Mirrer Yeshiva Central Institute, NY
Morehouse College, GA
Mount Angel Seminary, OR
Ner Israel Rabbinical College, MD
Ohr Somayach Tanenbaum Education Center, NY
Pontifical College Josephinum, OH
Rabbinical Academy Mesivta Rabbi Chaim Berlin, NY
Rabbinical College Beth Shraga, NY
Rabbinical College Bobover Yeshiva B'nei Zion, NY
Rabbinical College Ch'san Sofer of New York, NY
Rabbinical College of America, NJ
Rabbinical College of Long Island, NY
Rabbinical College of Ohr Shimon Yisroel, NY
Rabbinical College of Telshe, OH
Rabbinical Seminary of America, NY
St. Charles Borromeo Seminary - Overbrook, PA
St. John Vianney College Seminary, FL
St. Joseph Seminary College, LA
Shor Yoshuv Rabbinical College, NY
Talmudic University, FL
Talmudical Academy of New Jersey, NJ
Talmudical Institute of Upstate New York, NY
Talmudical Seminary Oholei Torah, NY
Talmudical Yeshiva of Philadelphia, PA
Telshe Yeshiva-Chicago, IL
Torah Temimah Talmudical Seminary, NY
U.T.A. Mesivta-Kiryas Joel, NY
United Talmudical Seminary, NY
Wabash College, IN
Yeshiva and Kolel Bais Medrash Elyon, NY

Yeshiva and Kollel Harbotzas Torah, NY
Yeshiva Beth Yehuda-Yeshiva Gedolah of Greater Detroit, MI
Yeshiva College of the Nations Capital, MD
Yeshiva D'Monsey Rabbinical College, NY
Yeshiva Derech Chaim, NY
Yeshiva Gedolah Imrei Yosef D'Spinka, NY
Yeshiva Gedolah Rabbinical College, FL
Yeshiva Gedolah Zichron Moshe, NY
Yeshiva Karlin Stolin, NY
Yeshiva of Nitra, NY
Yeshiva of the Telshe Alumni, NY
Yeshiva Ohr Elchonon Chabad/ West Coast Talmudical Seminary, CA
Yeshiva Shaar Hatorah, NY
Yeshiva Shaarei Torah of Rockland, NY
Yeshivas Novominsk, NY
Yeshivat Mikdash Melech, NY
Yeshivath Beth Moshe, PA
Yeshivath Viznitz, NY

Two-year

Deep Springs College, CA
Williamson College of the Trades, PA

Colleges for women

Four-year

Agnes Scott College, GA
Alverno College, WI
Barnard College, NY
Bay Path University, MA
Bennett College for Women, NC
Brenau University, GA
Bryn Mawr College, PA
Cedar Crest College, PA
College of St. Elizabeth, NJ
College of Saint Mary, NE
Columbia College, SC
Converse College, SC
Hollins University, VA
Judson College, AL
Mary Baldwin College, VA
Meredith College, NC
Midway College, KY
Mills College, CA
Moore College of Art and Design, PA
Mount Holyoke College, MA
Mount Mary University, WI
Mount Saint Mary's University, CA
Notre Dame of Maryland University, MD
St. Catherine University, MN
Saint Mary's College, IN
Salem College, NC
Scripps College, CA
Simmons College, MA
Smith College, MA
Spelman College, GA
Stephens College, MO
Sweet Briar College, VA
University of Saint Joseph, CT
Ursuline College, OH
Wellesley College, MA
Wesleyan College, GA

Two-year

Assumption College for Sisters, NJ
Cottey College, MO

Affiliated with a religion

African Methodist Episcopal Church

Four-year

Allen University, SC
Edward Waters College, FL
Paul Quinn College, TX
Wilberforce University, OH

African Methodist Episcopal Zion Church

Four-year

Livingstone College, NC

American Baptist Churches in the USA

Four-year

Alderson-Broaddus University, WV
Arkansas Baptist College, AR
Bacone College, OK
Benedict College, SC
Eastern University, PA
Florida Memorial University, FL
Franklin College, IN
Judson University, IL
Keuka College, NY
Linfield College, OR
Ottawa University, KS
University of Sioux Falls, SD

Assemblies of God

Four-year

American Indian College of the Assemblies of God, AZ
Evangel University, MO
North Central University, MN
Northpoint Bible College, MA
Northwest University, WA
Southeastern University, FL
Southwestern Assemblies of God University, TX
SUM Bible College & Theological Seminary, CA
Trinity Bible College, ND
University of Valley Forge, PA
Vanguard University of Southern California, CA

Baptist faith

Four-year

American Baptist College, TN
Arlington Baptist College, TX
Averett University, VA
Baptist Bible College, MO
Baptist College of Health Sciences, TN
Baptist Missionary Association Theological Seminary, TX
Baptist University of the Americas, TX
Baylor University, TX
Bluefield College, VA
Boston Baptist College, MA
Campbell University, NC
Campbellsville University, KY
Cedarville University, OH
Central Baptist College, AR
Corban University, OR
Dallas Baptist University, TX
East Texas Baptist University, TX
Georgetown College, KY
Hardin-Simmons University, TX
Houston Baptist University, TX
Howard Payne University, TX
International Baptist College, AZ

Judson College, AL
LeMoyne-Owen College, TN
Luther Rice University, GA
Maranathan Baptist University Maranatha Baptist University, WI
Mars Hill University, NC
Missouri Baptist University, MO
Morris College, SC
Ouachita Baptist University, AR
Piedmont International University, NC
Samford University, AL
Selma University, AL
Shasta Bible College and Graduate School, CA
Shaw University, NC
Southeastern Baptist College, MS
Summit University, PA
University of Mary Hardin-Baylor, TX
University of Mobile, AL
University of the Cumberlands, KY
Virginia Baptist College, VA
Virginia Union University, VA
William Carey University, MS

Two-year

Jacksonville College, TX

Baptist General Conference

Four-year

Bethel University, MN
Oakland City University, IN

Brethren Church

Four-year

Ashland University, OH
Elizabethtown College, PA
Emmaus Bible College, IA
Grace College, IN

Christian and Missionary Alliance

Four-year

Crown College, MN
Nyack College, NY
Simpson University, CA
Toccoa Falls College, GA

Christian Church

Four-year

Belmont University, TN
Bethesda University of California, CA
Bryn Athyn College, PA
Cairn University, PA
Central Christian College of the Bible, MO
Cincinnati Christian University, OH
Crossroads College, MN
Grace Bible College, MI
Great Lakes Christian College, MI
Hillsdale College, MI
Hope International University, CA
Johnson University, TN
Johnson University: Florida, FL
Liberty University, VA
Life Pacific College, CA
Manhattan Christian College, KS
Milligan College, TN
Nebraska Christian College, NE
New Saint Andrews College, ID
Piedmont College, GA
Pillar College, NJ
Point University, GA

St. Louis Christian College, MO
Shiloh University, IA
Southwestern Baptist Theological Seminary, TX
Visible Music College, TN

Two-year

Salvation Army College for Officer Training at Crestmont, CA

Christian Church (Disciples of Christ)

Four-year

Barton College, NC
Bethany College, WV
Chapman University, CA
Columbia College, MO
Culver-Stockton College, MO
Eureka College, IL
Hiram College, OH
Jarvis Christian College, TX
Lynchburg College, VA
Midway College, KY
Northwest Christian University, OR
Texas Christian University, TX
Transylvania University, KY
William Woods University, MO

Christian Methodist Episcopal Church

Four-year

Lane College, TN
Miles College, AL
Paine College, GA
Texas College, TX

Christian Reformed Church

Four-year

Calvin College, MI
Dordt College, IA
Kuyper College, MI

Church of Christ

Four-year

Abilene Christian University, TX
Amridge University, AL
Austin Graduate School of Theology, TX
Faulkner University, AL
Freed-Hardeman University, TN
Harding University, AR
Heritage Christian University, AL
Lincoln Christian University, IL
Lipscomb University, TN
Lubbock Christian University, TX
Mid-Atlantic Christian University, NC
Ohio Christian University, OH
Ohio Valley University, WV
Oklahoma Christian University, OK
Pepperdine University, CA
Rochester College, MI
Southwestern Christian College, TX
York College, NE

Two-year

Crowley's Ridge College, AR

Church of God

Four-year

Anderson University, IN
Lee University, TN
Mid-America Christian University, OK

Theological University of the
Caribbean, PR
University of Findlay, OH
Warner Pacific College, OR
Warner University, FL

Church of Jesus Christ of Latter-day Saints

Four-year

Brigham Young University, UT
Brigham Young University-
Hawaii, HI
Brigham Young University-
Idaho, ID
Southern Virginia University,
VA

Two-year

LDS Business College, UT

Church of the Brethren

Four-year

Bridgewater College, VA
Manchester University, IN
McPherson College, KS

Church of the Nazarene

Four-year

Eastern Nazarene College, MA
MidAmerica Nazarene
University, KS
Mount Vernon Nazarene
University, OH
Nazarene Bible College, CO
Northwest Nazarene University,
ID
Olivet Nazarene University, IL
Point Loma Nazarene
University, CA
Southern Nazarene University,
OK
Trevecca Nazarene University,
TN

Cumberland Presbyterian Church

Four-year

Bethel University, TN

Episcopal Church

Four-year

Bard College, NY
Clarkson College, NE
St. Augustine College, IL
Saint Augustine's University,
NC
St. Luke's College, MO
Sewanee: The University of the
South, TN
Voorhees College, SC

Evangelical Covenant Church of America

Four-year

North Park University, IL

Evangelical Free Church of America

Four-year

Trinity International University,
IL

Evangelical Lutheran Church in America

Four-year

Augsburg College, MN
Augusta University
Augustana University, SD
Augustana College, IL
Bethany College, KS

California Lutheran University,
CA
Capital University, OH
Carthage College, WI
Concordia College: Moorhead,
MN
Finlandia University, MI
Gettysburg College, PA
Grand View University, IA
Gustavus Adolphus College,
MN
Lenoir-Rhyne University, NC
Luther College, IA
Midland University, NE
Muhlenberg College, PA
Newberry College, SC
Pacific Lutheran University,
WA
Roanoke College, VA
St. Olaf College, MN
Susquehanna University, PA
Texas Lutheran University, TX
Thiel College, PA
Waldorf University, IA
Wartburg College, IA
Wittenberg University, OH

Evangelical Lutheran Synod

Four-year

Bethany Lutheran College, MN

Free Methodist Church of North America

Four-year

Central Christian College of
Kansas, KS
Greenville College, IL
Roberts Wesleyan College, NY
Seattle Pacific University, WA
Spring Arbor University, MI

Free Will Baptists

Four-year

California Christian College,
CA
University of Mount Olive, NC
Welch College, TN

General Association of Regular Baptist Churches

Four-year

Faith Baptist Bible College and
Theological Seminary, IA

interdenominational tradition

Four-year

Asbury University, KY
Azusa Pacific University, CA
Biola University, CA
Bryan College
Dayton, TN
College of the Ozarks, MO
Columbia International
University, SC
Cornerstone University, MI
Ecclesia College, AR
Faith Evangelical College &
Seminary, WA
God's Bible School and College,
OH
Grace University, NE
Heritage University, WA
Hobe Sound Bible College, FL
John Brown University, AR
Laurel University, NC
Messiah College, PA
Moody Bible Institute, IL
Multnomah University, OR

Oak Hills Christian College,
MN
Palm Beach Atlantic University,
FL
Patten University, CA
Regent University, VA
Taylor University, IN
Trinity College of Florida, FL
Williamson College, TN

Jewish faith

Four-year

American Jewish University,
CA
Beis Medrash Heichal Dovid,
NY
Beth Hamedrash Shaarei Yosher
Institute, NY
Beth Hatalmud Rabbinical
College, NY
Beth Medrash Govoha, NJ
Central Yeshiva Tomchei
Tmimim-Lubavitch, NY
Gratz College, PA
Hebrew Theological College, IL
Jewish Theological Seminary of
America, NY
Kehilath Yakov Rabbinical
Seminary, NY
Machzikei Hadath Rabbinical
College, NY
Mesivta Torah Vodaath
Seminary, NY
Michigan Jewish Institute, MI
Mirrer Yeshiva Central Institute,
NY
Ner Israel Rabbinical College,
MD
Ohr Somayach Tanenbaum
Education Center, NY
Rabbinical Academy Mesivta
Rabbi Chaim Berlin, NY
Rabbinical College Beth Shraga,
NY
Rabbinical College Bobover
Yeshiva B'nei Zion, NY
Rabbinical College Ch'san Sofer
of New York, NY
Rabbinical College of America,
NJ
Rabbinical College of Long
Island, NY
Rabbinical College of Telshe,
OH
Rabbinical Seminary of
America, NY
Shor Yoshuv Rabbinical
College, NY
Talmudic University, FL
Talmudical Academy of New
Jersey, NJ
Talmudical Institute of Upstate
New York, NY
Talmudical Seminary Oholei
Torah, NY
Talmudical Yeshiva of
Philadelphia, PA
Telshe Yeshiva-Chicago, IL
Torah Temimah Talmudical
Seminary, NY
U.T.A. Mesivta-Kiryas Joel, NY
United Talmudical Seminary,
NY
Yeshiva and Kolel Bais
Medrash Elyon, NY
Yeshiva and Kollel Harbotzas
Torah, NY
Yeshiva Beth Yehuda-Yeshiva
Gedolah of Greater Detroit,
MI
Yeshiva College of the Nations
Capital, MD
Yeshiva D'Monsey Rabbinical
College, NY
Yeshiva Derech Chaim, NY

Yeshiva Gedolah Imrei Yosef
D'Spinka, NY
Yeshiva Gedolah Rabbinical
College, FL
Yeshiva Gedolah Zichron
Moshe, NY
Yeshiva Karlin Stolin, NY
Yeshiva of Nitra, NY
Yeshiva of the Telshe Alumni,
NY
Yeshiva Ohr Elchonon Chabad/
West Coast Talmudical
Seminary, CA
Yeshiva Shaar Hatorah, NY
Yeshiva Shaarei Torah of
Rockland, NY
Yeshivas Novominsk, NY
Yeshivat Mikdash Melech, NY
Yeshivath Beth Moshe, PA

Two-year

Bramson ORT College, NY

Lutheran Church

Four-year

Trinity Lutheran College, WA
Valparaiso University, IN

Lutheran Church - Missouri Synod

Four-year

Concordia College, NY
Concordia College, AL
Concordia University, OR
Concordia University, MI
Concordia University, NE
Concordia University Chicago,
IL
Concordia University Irvine, CA
Concordia University St. Paul,
MN
Concordia University Texas, TX
Concordia University
Wisconsin, WI

Lutheran Church in America

Four-year

Wagner College, NY

Mennonite Brethren Church

Four-year

Fresno Pacific University, CA
Tabor College, KS

Mennonite Church

Four-year

Bethel College, KS
Bluffton University, OH
Eastern Mennonite University,
VA
Goshen College, IN

Two-year

Hesston College, KS
Rosedale Bible College, OH

Missionary Church

Four-year

Bethel College, IN

Moravian Church in America

Four-year

Moravian College, PA
Salem College, NC

nondenominational tradition

Four-year

Alaska Bible College, AK
Amberton University, TX
Appalachian Bible College, WV
Arizona Christian University,
AZ
Beulah Heights University, GA
Bob Jones University, SC
Boise Bible College, ID
Calvary Bible College and
Theological Seminary, MO
Carolina Christian College, NC
Colorado Christian University,
CO
Dallas Christian College, TX
Davis College, NY
Friends University, KS
Gordon College, MA
Grove City College, PA
Horizon University, CA
Kenyon College, OH
The King's College, NY
The King's University, TX
Lancaster Bible College, PA
LeTourneau University, TX
Limestone College, SC
The Master's College, CA
New Hope Christian College,
OR
Occidental College, CA
Oral Roberts University, OK
Ozark Christian College, MO
Patrick Henry College, VA
Providence Christian College,
CA
San Diego Christian College,
CA
Southeastern Bible College, AL
University of Northwestern - St.
Paul, MN
University of the Southwest,
NM
Westmont College, CA
Wheaton College, IL
William Jessup University, CA
World Mission University, CA

Two-year

Williamson College of the
Trades, PA

Pentecostal Holiness Church

Four-year

Emmanuel College, GA
Southwestern Christian
University, OK
Universidad Pentecostal Mizpa,
PR

Presbyterian Church (USA)

Four-year

Agnes Scott College, GA
Alma College, MI
Arcadia University, PA
Austin College, TX
Belhaven University, MS
Blackburn College, IL
Bloomfield College, NJ
Buena Vista University, IA
Carroll University, WI
Centre College, KY
Coe College, IA
Davidson College, NC
Davis and Elkins College, WV
Eckerd College, FL
Forman Christian College, PK
Hampden-Sydney College, VA
Hanover College, IN
Hastings College, NE
Illinois College, IL

King University, TN
Lees-McRae College, NC
Lindenwood University, MO
Lyon College, AR
Macalester College, MN
Mary Baldwin College, VA
Maryville College, TN
Millikin University, IL
Missouri Valley College, MO
Monmouth College, IL
Muskingum University, OH
Presbyterian College, SC
Queens University of Charlotte, NC
Rhodes College, TN
St. Andrews University, NC
Schreiner University, TX
Stillman College, AL
Trinity University, TX
Tusculum College, TN
University of Dubuque, IA
University of Jamestown, ND
University of Pikeville, KY
University of the Ozarks, AR
University of Tulsa, OK
Waynesburg University, PA
Westminster College, MO
Westminster College, PA
Whitworth University, WA
William Peace University, NC
Wilson College, PA

Reformed Church in America

Four-year

Central College, IA
Hope College, MI
Northwestern College, IA

Reformed Presbyterian Church of North America

Four-year

Geneva College, PA

Roman Catholic Church

Four-year

Albertus Magnus College, CT
Alvernia University, PA
Alverno College, WI
Anna Maria College, MA
Aquinas College, MI
Aquinas College, TN
Assumption College, MA
Ave Maria University, FL
Avila University, MO
Barry University, FL
Bayamon Central University, PR
Bellarmine University, KY
Belmont Abbey College, NC
Benedictine College, KS
Benedictine University, IL
Boston College, MA
Brescia University, KY
Briar Cliff University, IA
Cabrini College, PA
Caldwell University, NJ
Calumet College of St. Joseph, IN
Canisius College, NY
Cardinal Stritch University, WI
Carlow University, PA
Carroll College, MT
Catholic Distance University, VA
Catholic University of America, DC
Chaminade University of Honolulu, HI
Chestnut Hill College, PA
Christendom College, VA
Christian Brothers University, TN

Clarke University, IA
College of Mount St. Vincent, NY
College of New Rochelle, NY
College of St. Benedict, MN
College of St. Elizabeth, NJ
College of St. Joseph in Vermont, VT
College of Saint Mary, NE
College of St. Scholastica, MN
College of the Holy Cross, MA
Conception Seminary College, MO
Creighton University, NE
DePaul University, IL
DeSales University, PA
Divine Word College, IA
Dominican University, IL
Duquesne University, PA
Edgewood College, WI
Elms College, MA
Emmanuel College, MA
Fairfield University, CT
Felician University, NJ
Fontbonne University, MO
Fordham University, NY
Franciscan University of Steubenville, OH
Gannon University, PA
Georgetown University, DC
Georgian Court University, NJ
Gonzaga University, WA
Gwynedd Mercy University, PA
Hilbert College, NY
Holy Apostles College and Seminary, CT
Holy Cross College, IN
Holy Family University, PA
Holy Names University, CA
Immaculata University, PA
Instituto Tecnologico y de Estudios Superiores de Occidente, MX
Iona College, NY
John Carroll University, OH
John Paul the Great Catholic University, CA
King's College, PA
La Roche College, PA
La Salle University, PA
Le Moyne College, NY
Lewis University, IL
Loras College, IA
Lourdes University, OH
Loyola Marymount University, CA
Loyola University Chicago, IL
Loyola University Maryland, MD
Loyola University New Orleans, LA
Madonna University, MI
Manhattan College, NY
Marian University, IN
Marian University, WI
Marquette University, WI
Marygrove College, MI
Marylhurst University, OR
Marymount California University, CA
Marymount University, VA
Marywood University, PA
Mercy College of Health Sciences, IA
Mercy College of Ohio, OH
Mercyhurst University, PA
Merrimack College, MA
Misericordia University, PA
Molloy College, NY
Mount Aloysius College, PA
Mount Angel Seminary, OR
Mount Carmel College of Nursing, OH
Mount Marty College, SD
Mount Mary University, WI
Mount Mercy University, IA

Mount St. Joseph University, OH
Mount Saint Mary College, NY
Mount Saint Mary's University, CA
Mount St. Mary's University, MD
Neumann University, PA
Newman University, KS
Niagara University, NY
Northeast Catholic College, NH
Notre Dame College, OH
Notre Dame de Namur University, CA
Notre Dame of Maryland University, MD
Notre Dame University: Louaize, LB
Ohio Dominican University, OH
Our Lady of the Lake College, LA
Our Lady of the Lake University of San Antonio, TX
Pontifical Catholic University of Puerto Rico, PR
Pontifical College Josephinum, OH
Presentation College, SD
Providence College, RI
Quincy University, IL
Regis College, MA
Regis University, CO
Resurrection University, IL
Rivier University, NH
Rockhurst University, MO
Rosemont College, PA
Sacred Heart Major Seminary, MI
Sacred Heart University, CT
St. Ambrose University, IA
Saint Anselm College, NH
Saint Anthony College of Nursing, IL
Saint Bonaventure University, NY
St. Catharine College, KY
St. Catherine University, MN
St. Charles Borromeo Seminary - Overbrook, PA
St. Edward's University, TX
St. Francis College, NY
St. Francis Medical Center College of Nursing, IL
St. Francis University, PA
St. Gregory's University, OK
St. John Fisher College, NY
St. John Vianney College Seminary, FL
St. John's College, IL
St. John's University, NY
St. John's University, MN
St. Joseph Seminary College, LA
Saint Joseph's College, IN
Saint Joseph's College of Maine, ME
Saint Joseph's University, PA
Saint Leo University, FL
Saint Louis University, MO
Saint Louis University: Madrid, ES
Saint Martin's University, WA
Saint Mary's College, IN
St. Mary's College of California, CA
St. Mary's University, TX
St. Mary's University of Minnesota, MN
St. Mary-of-the-Woods College, IN
Saint Michael's College, VT
St. Norbert College, WI
Saint Peter's University, NJ
Saint Thomas University, FL
St. Vincent College, PA
Saint Xavier University, IL

Salve Regina University, RI
Santa Clara University, CA
Seattle University, WA
Seton Hall University, NJ
Seton Hill University, PA
Siena College, NY
Siena Heights University, MI
Silver Lake College of the Holy Family, WI
Spalding University, KY
Spring Hill College, AL
Stonehill College, MA
Thomas Aquinas College, CA
Thomas More College, KY
Thomas More College of Liberal Arts, NH
Trinity Washington University, DC
Universidad Anahuac, MX
University of Dallas, TX
University of Dayton, OH
University of Detroit Mercy, MI
University of Great Falls, MT
University of Holy Cross, LA
University of Mary, ND
University of Notre Dame, IN
University of Portland, OR
University of Saint Francis, IN
University of St. Francis, IL
University of Saint Joseph, CT
University of St. Mary, KS
University of St. Thomas, TX
University of St. Thomas, MN
University of San Diego, CA
University of San Francisco, CA
University of Scranton, PA
University of the Incarnate Word, TX
University of the Sacred Heart, PR
Ursuline College, OH
Villanova University, PA
Viterbo University, WI
Walsh University, OH
Wheeling Jesuit University, WV
Xavier University, OH
Xavier University of Louisiana, LA

Two-year

Ancilla College, IN
Assumption College for Sisters, NJ
Benedictine University at Springfield, IL
Chatfield College, OH
Donnelly College, KS
Good Samaritan College of Nursing and Health Science, OH
Laboure College, MA
St. Elizabeth College of Nursing, NY
St. Joseph's College of Nursing, NY
St. Vincent's College, CT
Trocaire College, NY
Villa Maria College of Buffalo, NY

Seventh-day Adventists

Four-year

Adventist University of Health Sciences, FL
Andrews University, MI
Kettering College, OH
La Sierra University, CA
Loma Linda University, CA
Oakwood University, AL
Pacific Union College, CA
Southern Adventist University, TN
Southwestern Adventist University, TX
Union College, NE

Universidad Adventista de las Antillas, PR
Walla Walla University, WA
Washington Adventist University, MD

Society of Friends (Quaker)

Four-year

Barclay College, KS
Earlham College, IN
George Fox University, OR
Guilford College, NC
William Penn University, IA
Wilmington College, OH

Southern Baptist Convention

Four-year

Anderson University, SC
Baptist College of Florida, FL
Blue Mountain College, MS
Brewton-Parker College, GA
California Baptist University, CA
Carson-Newman University, TN
Charleston Southern University, SC
Chowan University, NC
Clear Creek Baptist Bible College, KY
Criswell College, TX
Gardner-Webb University, NC
Hannibal-LaGrange University, MO
Louisiana College, LA
Mississippi College, MS
New Orleans Baptist Theological Seminary, LA
North Greenville University, SC
Oklahoma Baptist University, OK
Shorter University, GA
Southeastern Baptist Theological Seminary, NC
Southern Baptist Theological Seminary, KY
Southwest Baptist University, MO
Truett-McConnell College, GA
Union University, TN
Wayland Baptist University, TX
Williams Baptist College, AR

Ukrainian Catholic Church

Two-year

Manor College, PA

United Brethren in Christ

Four-year

Huntington University, IN

United Church of Christ

Four-year

Catawba College, NC
Defiance College, OH
Dillard University, LA
Doane College, NE
Drury University, MO
Elmhurst College, IL
Heidelberg University, OH
Lakeland College, WI
Northland College, WI
Olivet College, MI
Pacific University, OR
Rocky Mountain College, MT
Talladega College, AL
Tougaloo College, MS

United Methodist Church

Four-year

Adrian College, MI
Alaska Pacific University, AK
Albion College, MI
Albright College, PA
Allegheny College, PA
American University, DC
Baker University, KS
Baldwin Wallace University, OH
Bennett College for Women, NC
Bethune-Cookman University, FL
Birmingham-Southern College, AL
Brevard College, NC
BryanLGH College of Health Sciences, NE
Centenary College, NJ
Centenary College of Louisiana, LA
Central Methodist University, MO
Claflin University, SC
Clark Atlanta University, GA
Columbia College, SC
Cornell College, IA
Dakota Wesleyan University, SD
DePauw University, IN
Drew University, NJ
Emory & Henry College, VA
Emory University, GA
Ferrum College, VA
Florida Southern College, FL
Green Mountain College, VT
Greensboro College, NC
Hamline University, MN
Hendrix College, AR
High Point University, NC
Huntingdon College, AL
Huston-Tillotson University, TX
Iowa Wesleyan College, IA
Kansas Wesleyan University, KS
Kentucky Wesleyan College, KY
LaGrange College, GA
Lebanon Valley College, PA
Lindsey Wilson College, KY
Lycoming College, PA
MacMurray College, IL
Martin Methodist College, TN
McKendree University, IL
McMurry University, TX
Methodist University, NC
Millsaps College, MS
Morningside College, IA
Nebraska Methodist College of Nursing and Allied Health, NE
Nebraska Wesleyan University, NE
North Carolina Wesleyan College, NC
North Central College, IL
Ohio Northern University, OH
Ohio Wesleyan University, OH
Oklahoma City University, OK
Otterbein University, OH
Pfeiffer University, NC
Philander Smith College, AR
Randolph College, VA
Randolph-Macon College, VA
Reinhardt University, GA
Rust College, MS
Shenandoah University, VA
Simpson College, IA
Southern Methodist University, TX
Southwestern College, KS
Southwestern University, TX

Tennessee Wesleyan College, TN
Texas Wesleyan University, TX
Union College, KY
University of Evansville, IN
University of Indianapolis, IN
University of Mount Union, OH
Virginia Wesleyan College, VA
Wesley College, DE
Wesleyan College, GA
West Virginia Wesleyan College, WV
Wiley College, TX
Willamette University, OR
Wofford College, SC
Young Harris College, GA

Two-year

Andrew College, GA
Hiwassee College, TN
Louisburg College, NC
Oxford College of Emory University, GA
Spartanburg Methodist College, SC

Wesleyan Church

Four-year

Houghton College, NY
Indiana Wesleyan University, IN
Oklahoma Wesleyan University, OK
Southern Wesleyan University, SC

Wisconsin Evangelical Lutheran Synod

Four-year

Martin Luther College, MN
Wisconsin Lutheran College, WI

Historically Black colleges

Four-year

Alabama Agricultural and Mechanical University, AL
Alabama State University, AL
Albany State University, GA
Alcorn State University, MS
Allen University, SC
Arkansas Baptist College, AR
Benedict College, SC
Bennett College for Women, NC
Bethune-Cookman University, FL
Bluefield State College, WV
Bowie State University, MD
Central State University, OH
Cheyney University of Pennsylvania, PA
Claflin University, SC
Clark Atlanta University, GA
Concordia College, AL
Coppin State University, MD
Delaware State University, DE
Dillard University, LA
Edward Waters College, FL
Elizabeth City State University, NC
Fayetteville State University, NC
Fisk University, TN
Florida Agricultural and Mechanical University, FL
Florida Memorial University, FL
Fort Valley State University, GA
Grambling State University, LA

Hampton University, VA
Harris-Stowe State University, MO
Howard University, DC
Huston-Tillotson University, TX
Jackson State University, MS
Jarvis Christian College, TX
Johnson C. Smith University, NC
Kentucky State University, KY
Lane College, TN
Langston University, OK
LeMoyne-Owen College, TN
Lincoln University, MO
Lincoln University, PA
Livingstone College, NC
Miles College, AL
Mississippi Valley State University, MS
Morehouse College, GA
Morgan State University, MD
Morris College, SC
Norfolk State University, VA
North Carolina Agricultural and Technical State University, NC
North Carolina Central University, NC
Oakwood University, AL
Paine College, GA
Paul Quinn College, TX
Philander Smith College, AR
Prairie View A&M University, TX
Rust College, MS
Saint Augustine's University, NC
Savannah State University, GA
Selma University, AL
Shaw University, NC
South Carolina State University, SC
Southern University New Orleans, LA
Southern University and Agricultural and Mechanical College, LA
Southwestern Christian College, TX
Spelman College, GA
Stillman College, AL
Talladega College, AL
Tennessee State University, TN
Texas College, TX
Texas Southern University, TX
Tougaloo College, MS
Tuskegee University, AL
University of Arkansas Pine Bluff, AR
University of Maryland Eastern Shore, MD
University of the District of Columbia, DC
University of the Virgin Islands, VI
Virginia State University, VA
Virginia Union University, VA
Virginia University of Lynchburg, VA
Voorhees College, SC
West Virginia State University, WV
Wilberforce University, OH
Wiley College, TX
Winston-Salem State University, NC
Xavier University of Louisiana, LA

Two-year

Bishop State Community College, AL
Clinton College, SC
Coahoma Community College, MS
Denmark Technical College, SC

Gadsden State Community College, AL
Hinds Community College, MS
Lawson State Community College, AL
St. Philip's College, TX
Shelton State Community College, AL
Southern University Shreveport, LA

Hispanic serving colleges

Four-year

Adams State University, CO
American University of Puerto Rico, PR
Angelo State University, TX
Antioch University Santa Barbara, CA
Atlantic University College, PR
Baptist University of the Americas, TX
Bayamon Central University, PR
Boricua College, NY
California Christian College, CA
California State Polytechnic University: Pomona, CA
California State University
  Bakersfield, CA
  Dominguez Hills, CA
  Fresno, CA
  Fullerton, CA
  Long Beach, CA
  Los Angeles, CA
  Monterey Bay, CA
  Northridge, CA
  San Bernardino, CA
  San Marcos, CA
  Stanislaus, CA
Calumet College of St. Joseph, IN
Caribbean University, PR
Carlos Albizu University, FL
Carlos Albizu University: San Juan, PR
City University of New York
  City College, NY
  John Jay College of Criminal Justice, NY
  Lehman College, NY
  New York City College of Technology, NY
College of Biblical Studies-Houston, TX
College of Mount St. Vincent, NY
Colorado Heights University, CO
Conservatory of Music of Puerto Rico, PR
Dominican University, IL
Eastern New Mexico University, NM
EDP University of Puerto Rico: Hato Rey, PR
EDP University of Puerto Rico: San Sebastian, PR
Escuela de Artes Plasticas de Puerto Rico, PR
Florida International University, FL
Fresno Pacific University, CA
Heritage University, WA
Hodges University, FL
Houston Baptist University, TX
Humphreys College, CA

Inter American University of Puerto Rico
  Aguadilla Campus, PR
  Arecibo Campus, PR
  Barranquitas Campus, PR
  Bayamon Campus, PR
  Fajardo Campus, PR
  Guayama Campus, PR
  Metropolitan Campus, PR
  Ponce Campus, PR
  San German Campus, PR
La Sierra University, CA
Mercy College, NY
Mount Angel Seminary, OR
Mount Saint Mary's University, CA
New Jersey City University, NJ
New Mexico Highlands University, NM
New Mexico Institute of Mining and Technology, NM
New Mexico State University, NM
Northeastern Illinois University, IL
Northern New Mexico College, NM
Northwood University Texas, TX
Notre Dame de Namur University, CA
Nova Southeastern University, FL
Our Lady of the Lake University of San Antonio, TX
Pacific Oaks College, CA
Pontifical Catholic University of Puerto Rico, PR
St. Augustine College, IL
St. Edward's University, TX
St. John Vianney College Seminary, FL
St. Mary's University, TX
Saint Peter's University, NJ
Saint Thomas University, FL
San Diego State University, CA
Sul Ross State University, TX
Texas A&M International University, TX
Texas A&M University
  Corpus Christi, TX
  Kingsville, TX
Texas State University, TX
Turabo University, PR
Universidad Adventista de las Antillas, PR
Universidad Central del Caribe, PR
Universidad del Este, PR
Universidad Metropolitana, PR
Universidad Pentecostal Mizpa, PR
Universidad Politecnica de Puerto Rico, PR
University College of San Juan, PR
University of California
  Merced, CA
  Riverside, CA
University of Houston, TX
  Clear Lake, TX
  Downtown, TX
  Victoria, TX
University of La Verne, CA
University of New Mexico, NM
University of Puerto Rico
  Aguadilla, PR
  Arecibo, PR
  Bayamon University College, PR
  Carolina Regional College, PR
  Cayey University College, PR
  Mayaguez, PR
  Medical Sciences, PR
  Ponce, PR
  Rio Piedras, PR
  Utuado, PR

University of St. Thomas, TX
University of Texas
   Brownsville, TX
   El Paso, TX
   Pan American, TX
   San Antonio, TX
   of the Permian Basin, TX
University of the Incarnate
   Word, TX
University of the Sacred Heart,
   PR
University of the Southwest,
   NM
Vaughn College of Aeronautics
   and Technology, NY
Western New Mexico
   University, NM
Whittier College, CA
Woodbury University, CA

Two-year

Allan Hancock College, CA
Amarillo College, TX
Antelope Valley College, CA
Arizona Western College, AZ
Bakersfield College, CA
Barstow Community College,
   CA
Bergen Community College, NJ
Big Bend Community College,
   WA
Brazosport College, TX
Brookhaven College, TX
Broward College, FL
Cabrillo College, CA
Canada College, CA
Capital Community College, CT
Central Arizona College, AZ
Central New Mexico
   Community College, NM
Centro de Estudios
   Multidisciplinarios, PR
Cerritos College, CA
Chabot College, CA
Chaffey College, CA
Citrus College, CA
City College
   Altamonte Springs, FL
   Miami, FL
City Colleges of Chicago
   Harold Washington College,
     IL
   Harry S. Truman College,
     IL
   Malcolm X College, IL
   Richard J. Daley College,
     IL
   Wilbur Wright College, IL
City University of New York
   Borough of Manhattan
     Community College, NY
   Bronx Community College,
     NY
   Hostos Community College,
     NY
   LaGuardia Community
     College, NY
   Queensborough Community
     College, NY
Clarendon College, TX
Clovis Community College, NM
Coastal Bend College, TX
Cochise College, AZ
College of the Canyons, CA
College of the Desert, CA
College of the Sequoias, CA
Contra Costa College, CA
Crafton Hills College, CA
Cuyamaca College, CA
Cypress College, CA
Del Mar College, TX
Dodge City Community
   College, KS
Dona Ana Community College
   of New Mexico State
   University, NM
Donnelly College, KS

East Los Angeles College, CA
Eastern New Mexico University:
   Roswell, NM
Eastfield College, TX
El Camino College, CA
El Centro College, TX
El Paso Community College,
   TX
Elgin Community College, IL
Estrella Mountain Community
   College, AZ
Evergreen Valley College, CA
Fresno City College, CA
Fullerton College, CA
Galveston College, TX
Garden City Community
   College, KS
GateWay Community College,
   AZ
Gavilan College, CA
Hartnell College, CA
Houston Community College
   System, TX
Howard College, TX
Hudson County Community
   College, NJ
Humacao Community College,
   PR
Imperial Valley College, CA
Laredo Community College, TX
Lee College, TX
Lone Star College System, TX
Long Beach City College, CA
Los Angeles City College, CA
Los Angeles County College of
   Nursing and Allied Health,
   CA
Los Angeles Harbor College,
   CA
Los Angeles Mission College,
   CA
Los Angeles Pierce College, CA
Los Angeles Trade and
   Technical College, CA
Los Angeles Valley College,
   CA
Los Medanos College, CA
Luna Community College, NM
Merced College, CA
Mesalands Community College,
   NM
Miami Dade College, FL
Midland College, TX
Modesto Junior College, CA
Monterey Peninsula College,
   CA
Morton College, IL
Mount San Antonio College,
   CA
Mount San Jacinto College, CA
Mountain View College, TX
Napa Valley College, CA
New Mexico Junior College,
   NM
New Mexico State University
   Alamogordo, NM
   Carlsbad, NM
   Grants, NM
North Lake College, TX
Northern Essex Community
   College, MA
Northwest Vista College, TX
Norwalk Community College,
   CT
Odessa College, TX
Otero Junior College, CO
Oxnard College, CA
Palo Alto College, TX
Palo Verde College, CA
Palomar College, CA
Pasadena City College, CA
Passaic County Community
   College, NJ
Phoenix College, AZ
Pima Community College, AZ
Porterville College, CA
Pueblo Community College, CO

Reedley College, CA
Rio Hondo College, CA
Riverside City College, CA
St. Philip's College, TX
San Antonio College, TX
San Bernardino Valley College,
   CA
San Diego City College, CA
San Diego Mesa College, CA
San Jacinto College, TX
San Joaquin Delta College, CA
San Jose City College, CA
Santa Ana College, CA
Santa Barbara City College, CA
Santa Fe Community College,
   NM
Santa Monica College, CA
Santiago Canyon College, CA
Seward County Community
   College, KS
South Mountain Community
   College, AZ
South Plains College, TX
South Texas College, TX
Southwest Texas Junior College,
   TX
Southwestern College, CA
Taft College, CA
Texas State Technical College
   Harlingen, TX
Trinidad State Junior College,
   CO
Triton College, IL
Union County College, NJ
Universal Technology College
   of Puerto Rico, PR
Urban College of Boston, MA
Valencia College, FL
Ventura College, CA
Victor Valley College, CA
Victoria College, TX
Waubonsee Community
   College, IL
West Hills College: Coalinga,
   CA
West Hills College: Lemoore,
   CA
West Los Angeles College, CA
Western Texas College, TX
Wharton County Junior College,
   TX
Woodland Community College,
   CA
Yakima Valley Community
   College, WA

Tribal colleges

Four-year

Haskell Indian Nations
   University, KS
Institute of American Indian
   Arts, NM
Oglala Lakota College, SD
Salish Kootenai College, MT
Sinte Gleska University, SD

Two-year

Aaniiih Nakoda College, MT
Bay Mills Community College,
   MI
Blackfeet Community College,
   MT
Cankdeska Cikana Community
   College, ND
Chief Dull Knife College, MT
College of Menominee Nation,
   WI
Dine College, AZ
Fond du Lac Tribal and
   Community College, MN
Fort Berthold Community
   College, ND

Fort Peck Community College,
   MT
Lac Courte Oreilles Ojibwa
   Community College, WI
Little Big Horn College, MT
Little Priest Tribal College, NE
Nebraska Indian Community
   College, NE
Sisseton Wahpeton College, SD
Sitting Bull College, ND
Southwestern Indian Polytechnic
   Institute, NM
Stone Child College, MT
Turtle Mountain Community
   College, ND
United Tribes Technical
   College, ND

Undergraduate enrollment size

Four-year

Alabama

Amridge University
Concordia College
Heritage Christian University
Herzing University
 Birmingham
Huntsville Bible College
ITT Technical Institute
 Birmingham
Judson College
Selma University
Southeastern Bible College
United States Sports Academy
University of Phoenix
 Birmingham
Virginia College
 Huntsville

Alaska

Alaska Bible College
Alaska Pacific University

Arizona

American Indian College of the
 Assemblies of God
Arizona Christian University
Art Institute of Tucson
Brown Mackie College
 Tucson
Chamberlain College of Nursing
 Phoenix
DeVry University
 Phoenix
Dunlap-Stone University
Harrison Middleton University
International Baptist College
ITT Technical Institute
 Tempe
 Tucson
Northcentral University
Prescott College
Southwest University of Visual
 Arts

Arkansas

Ecclesia College
ITT Technical Institute
 Little Rock
Lyon College
Philander Smith College
University of Phoenix
 Little Rock
 Northwest Arkansas
University of the Ozarks
Williams Baptist College

California

Academy of Couture Art
American Jewish University
Antioch University
 Santa Barbara
Argosy University
 Inland Empire
 Los Angeles
 Orange County
 San Diego
 San Francisco Bay Area
Bergin University of Canine
 Studies
Bethesda University of
 California
Brooks Institute
California Christian College

California Institute of Integral
 Studies
California Miramar University
California National University
 for Advanced Studies
California University of
 Management and Sciences
Charles Drew University of
 Medicine and Science
Cogswell Polytechnical College
Coleman University
Columbia College
 Hollywood
Design Institute of San Diego
Ex'pression College
Golden Gate University
Holy Names University
Horizon University
Humphreys College
Interior Designers Institute
International Academy of
 Design and Technology
 Sacramento
ITT Technical Institute
 Lathrop
 Oxnard
 Rancho Cordova
 San Bernardino
 Sylmar
 Torrance
John F. Kennedy University
John Paul the Great Catholic
 University
Laguna College of Art and
 Design
Life Pacific College
Lincoln University
Mt. Sierra College
NewSchool of Architecture &
 Design
Northwestern Polytechnic
 University
Pacific Oaks College
Pacific States University
Platt College
 Ontario
 San Diego
Providence Christian College
Samuel Merritt University
San Francisco Art Institute
San Francisco Conservatory of
 Music
Shasta Bible College and
 Graduate School
Silicon Valley University
Soka University of America
Southern California Institute of
 Architecture
Southern California Institute of
 Technology
Southern California Seminary
SUM Bible College &
 Theological Seminary
Thomas Aquinas College
Touro University Worldwide
University of the West
World Mission University
Yeshiva Ohr Elchonon Chabad/
 West Coast Talmudical
 Seminary

Colorado

Argosy University
 Denver
Aspen University
CollegeAmerica
 Colorado Springs
 Fort Collins
Colorado Heights University
DeVry University
 Westminster
ITT Technical Institute
 Westminster
Naropa University
National American University
 Denver

Platt College
 Aurora
University of Phoenix
 Southern Colorado
Westwood College
 Aurora
 Online

Connecticut

Holy Apostles College and
 Seminary
Lyme Academy College of Fine
 Arts
Mitchell College
Paier College of Art
Post University

Delaware

Goldey-Beacom College
Wesley College

District of Columbia

University of Phoenix
 Washington DC
University of the Potomac

Florida

Argosy University
 Sarasota
 Tampa
Baptist College of Florida
Beacon College
Carlos Albizu University
Chamberlain College of Nursing
 Jacksonville
 Miramar
City College
 Fort Lauderdale
DeVry University
 Miramar
Digital Media Arts College
Everest University
 Orange Park
Everglades University
 Boca Raton
 Orlando
Florida College
Hobe Sound Bible College
International Academy of
 Design and Technology
 Orlando
International Academy of
 Design and Technology:
 Tampa
ITT Technical Institute
 Ft. Lauderdale
 Jacksonville
 Lake Mary
 Miami
 Tampa
Johnson University: Florida
Jones College
Jose Maria Vargas University
Remington College
 Tampa
 of Nursing
St. John Vianney College
 Seminary
Talmudic University
Trinity Baptist College
Trinity College of Florida
Webber International University
Yeshiva Gedolah Rabbinical
 College

Georgia

Beulah Heights University
Brewton-Parker College
Carver College
Herzing University
 Atlanta
ITT Technical Institute
 Duluth
Life University
Luther Rice University
Paine College
Wesleyan College

Hawaii

Argosy University
 Hawaii

Idaho

Boise Bible College
ITT Technical Institute
 Boise
New Saint Andrews College
University of Phoenix
 Idaho

Illinois

American Academy of Art
Argosy University
 Chicago
 Schaumburg
Blackburn College
Blessing-Rieman College of
 Nursing
East-West University
Eureka College
Hebrew Theological College
International Academy of
 Design and Technology
 Chicago
ITT Technical Institute
 Arlington Heights
Lakeview College of Nursing
Lincoln Christian University
MacMurray College
Methodist College
Midstate College
National University of Health
 Sciences
Principia College
Resurrection University
Rush University
Saint Anthony College of
 Nursing
St. Francis Medical Center
 College of Nursing
St. John's College
Shimer College
Telshe Yeshiva-Chicago
Trinity College of Nursing &
 Health Sciences
VanderCook College of Music
Westwood College
 Chicago Loop
 DuPage
 River Oaks

Indiana

Chamberlain College of Nursing
 Indianapolis
Crossroads Bible College
Holy Cross College
International Business College
ITT Technical Institute
 Fort Wayne
Martin University
Oakland City University
St. Mary-of-the-Woods College
University of Phoenix
 Indianapolis

Iowa

Allen College
Divine Word College
Emmaus Bible College
Faith Baptist Bible College and
 Theological Seminary
Hamilton Technical College
Iowa Wesleyan College
Kaplan University
 Cedar Falls
 Mason City
Maharishi University of
 Management
Shiloh University
University of Phoenix
 Des Moines

Kansas

Barclay College
Bethany College
Bethel College

Kansas Wesleyan University
Manhattan Christian College
McPherson College
Ottawa University
Sterling College
Tabor College
University of Kansas Medical
 Center

Kentucky

Alice Lloyd College
Clear Creek Baptist Bible
 College
ITT Technical Institute
 Louisville
Kentucky Christian University
Kentucky Mountain Bible
 College
Kentucky Wesleyan College
St. Catharine College
University of Phoenix
 Louisville

Louisiana

Centenary College of Louisiana
Herzing University
 Kenner
ITT Technical Institute
 St. Rose
St. Joseph Seminary College
University of Phoenix
 Louisiana
 Shreveport

Maine

College of the Atlantic
Maine College of Art
Unity College
University of Maine
 Machias

Maryland

Capitol Technology University
ITT Technical Institute
 Owings Mills
Johns Hopkins University:
 Peabody Conservatory of
 Music
Ner Israel Rabbinical College
St. John's College
University of Phoenix
 Maryland
Yeshiva College of the Nations
 Capital

Massachusetts

Bard College at Simon's Rock
Boston Architectural College
Boston Baptist College
Boston Conservatory
Franklin W. Olin College of
 Engineering
Hellenic College/Holy Cross
Montserrat College of Art
New England Conservatory of
 Music
Northpoint Bible College
Pine Manor College
School of the Museum of Fine
 Arts
University of Phoenix
 Boston

Michigan

Cleary University
Concordia University
Finlandia University
Grace Bible College
Great Lakes Christian College
International Academy of
 Design and Technology
 Detroit
Kuyper College
Marygrove College
Robert B. Miller College
Sacred Heart Major Seminary
University of Phoenix
 West Michigan

Yeshiva Beth Yehuda-Yeshiva
Gedolah of Greater Detroit

Minnesota

Bethany Lutheran College
Brown College
  Brooklyn Center
  Mendota Heights
Crossroads College
Globe University
  Minneapolis
  Moorhead
  Woodbury
Martin Luther College
McNally Smith College of
  Music
Minneapolis College of Art and
  Design
Minnesota School of Business
  Blaine
  Elk River
  Lakeville
  Plymouth
  Richfield
  Rochester
  St. Cloud
  Shakopee
National American University
  Bloomington
  Roseville
Northwestern Health Sciences
  University
Oak Hills Christian College
University of Minnesota
  Rochester
University of Phoenix
  Minneapolis-St. Paul

Mississippi

Blue Mountain College
Southeastern Baptist College
University of Mississippi
  Medical Center
University of Phoenix
  Jackson

Missouri

Baptist Bible College
Calvary Bible College and
  Theological Seminary
Central Christian College of the
  Bible
Chamberlain College of Nursing
  St. Louis
Conception Seminary College
DeVry University
  Kansas City
Goldfarb School of Nursing at
  Barnes-Jewish College
Hickey College
ITT Technical Institute
  Arnold
  Earth City
Kansas City Art Institute
Logan University
Missouri Tech
National American University
  Kansas City
  Lee's Summit
Research College of Nursing
St. Louis Christian College
St. Luke's College
Stephens College

Montana

Montana Bible College

Nebraska

College of Saint Mary
Creative Center
ITT Technical Institute
  Omaha
Nebraska Christian College
York College

Nevada

International Academy of
  Design and Technology
  Henderson

ITT Technical Institute
  Henderson
Roseman University of Health
  Sciences
Sierra Nevada College
University of Phoenix
  Northern Nevada

New Hampshire

Daniel Webster College
New Hampshire Institute of Art
Northeast Catholic College
Thomas More College of
  Liberal Arts
University of New Hampshire at
  Manchester

New Jersey

Pillar College
Rabbi Jacob Joseph School
Rabbinical College of America
Talmudical Academy of New
  Jersey
University of Phoenix
  Jersey City

New Mexico

Institute of American Indian
  Arts
ITT Technical Institute
  Albuquerque
National American University
  Albuquerque
St. John's College
Southwest University of Visual
  Arts
University of the Southwest

New York

Beis Medrash Heichal Dovid
Berkeley College
Beth Hamedrash Shaarei Yosher
  Institute
Beth Hatalmud Rabbinical
  College
Central Yeshiva Tomchei
  Tmimim-Lubavitch
College of New Rochelle
Davis College
Eastman School of Music of the
  University of Rochester
Five Towns College
Globe Institute of Technology
Holy Trinity Orthodox Seminary
Jewish Theological Seminary of
  America
Juilliard School
Kehilath Yakov Rabbinical
  Seminary
The King's College
Machzikei Hadath Rabbinical
  College
Manhattan School of Music
Mannes College The New
  School for Music
Medaille College: Rochester
Mesivta Torah Vodaath
  Seminary
Mirrer Yeshiva Central Institute
New York School of Interior
  Design
Ohr Somayach Tanenbaum
  Education Center
Rabbinical Academy Mesivta
  Rabbi Chaim Berlin
Rabbinical College Beth Shraga
Rabbinical College Bobover
  Yeshiva B'nei Zion
Rabbinical College Ch'san Sofer
  of New York
Rabbinical College of Long
  Island
Rabbinical College of Ohr
  Shimon Yisroel
Rabbinical Seminary of America
Shor Yoshuv Rabbinical College

SUNY
  Downstate Medical Center
  Upstate Medical University
Talmudical Institute of Upstate
  New York
Talmudical Seminary Oholei
  Torah
Torah Temimah Talmudical
  Seminary
Webb Institute
Wells College
Yeshiva and Kolel Bais
  Medrash Elyon
Yeshiva and Kollel Harbotzas
  Torah
Yeshiva D'Monsey Rabbinical
  College
Yeshiva Derech Chaim
Yeshiva Gedolah Imrei Yosef
  D'Spinka
Yeshiva Gedolah Zichron
  Moshe
Yeshiva Karlin Stolin
Yeshiva of Nitra
Yeshiva of the Telshe Alumni
Yeshiva Shaar Hatorah
Yeshiva Shaarei Torah of
  Rockland
Yeshivas Novominsk
Yeshivat Mikdash Melech
Yeshivath Viznitz

North Carolina

Apex School of Theology
Bennett College for Women
Brevard College
Cabarrus College of Health
  Sciences
Carolina Christian College
Laurel University
Mid-Atlantic Christian
  University
Montreat College
Piedmont International
  University
St. Andrews University
Southeastern Baptist
  Theological Seminary
University of Phoenix
  Charlotte
  Raleigh
Warren Wilson College

North Dakota

Trinity Bible College

Ohio

Allegheny Wesleyan College
Antioch University
  Midwest
Art Academy of Cincinnati
Bryant & Stratton College
  Eastlake
  Parma
Chamberlain College of Nursing
  Columbus
Chamberlain College Of
  Nursing
  Chamberlain College of
    Nursing: Cleveland
Cincinnati Christian University
Cleveland Institute of Art
Cleveland Institute of Music
Defiance College
God's Bible School and College
Herzing University
  Toledo
Kettering College
Pontifical College Josephinum
Rabbinical College of Telshe
Tri-State Bible College
University of Phoenix
  Cleveland
Ursuline College
Wilberforce University

Oklahoma

Family of Faith College
Hillsdale Free Will Baptist
  College
ITT Technical Institute
  Tulsa
St. Gregory's University
Southwestern Christian
  University
University of Phoenix
  Oklahoma City
  Tulsa

Oregon

Gutenberg College
ITT Technical Institute
  Portland
Marylhurst University
Mount Angel Seminary
Multnomah University
New Hope Christian College
Northwest Christian University
Oregon College of Art & Craft
Pacific Northwest College of
  Art
University of Phoenix
  Oregon
Warner Pacific College

Pennsylvania

Bryn Athyn College
Chatham University
Cheyney University of
  Pennsylvania
DeVry University
  Fort Washington
Gratz College
Harrisburg University of
  Science and Technology
Moore College of Art and
  Design
Penn State
  Beaver
  DuBois
  Fayette, The Eberly Campus
  Greater Allegheny
  New Kensington
  Schuylkill
  Shenango
  Wilkes-Barre
Pennsylvania Academy of the
  Fine Arts
Pennsylvania College of Art and
  Design
Restaurant School at Walnut
  Hill College
Rosemont College
Summit University
Talmudical Yeshiva of
  Philadelphia
University of Phoenix
  Harrisburg
  Philadelphia
  Pittsburgh
Wilson College
Yeshivath Beth Moshe

Puerto Rico

Bayamon Central University
Carlos Albizu University: San
  Juan
Conservatory of Music of
  Puerto Rico
Escuela de Artes Plasticas de
  Puerto Rico
Theological University of the
  Caribbean
Universidad Central del Caribe
Universidad Pentecostal Mizpa
University of Phoenix
  Puerto Rico
University of Puerto Rico
  Medical Sciences

South Carolina

Allen University
Columbia International
  University

Erskine College
ITT Technical Institute
  Greenville
Medical University of South
  Carolina
University of Phoenix
  Columbia
Voorhees College
W.L. Bonner Bible College

South Dakota

Mount Marty College
Presentation College
Sinte Gleska University

Tennessee

Aquinas College
Argosy University
  Nashville
ITT Technical Institute
  Knoxville
  Memphis
  Nashville
Memphis College of Art
O'More College of Design
University of Phoenix
  Knoxville
Virginia College
  School of Business and
    Health in Knoxville
Visible Music College
Watkins College of Art,
  Design & Film
Welch College
Williamson College

Texas

Amberton University
Argosy University
  Dallas
Arlington Baptist College
Austin Graduate School of
  Theology
Baptist Missionary Association
  Theological Seminary
Baptist University of the
  Americas
Chamberlain College of Nursing
  Houston
College of Biblical Studies-
  Houston
Criswell College
Dallas Christian College
DeVry University
  Houston
  Irving
The King's University
National American University
  Austin
Northwood University
  Texas
Paul Quinn College
Southwestern Adventist
  University
Southwestern Baptist
  Theological Seminary
Southwestern Christian College
Texas A&M University
  Baylor College of Dentistry
University of Phoenix
  Austin
University of Texas
  Health Science Center at
    Houston
  Medical Branch at
    Galveston
West Coast University: Dallas

Utah

Argosy University
  Salt Lake City
Broadview University
  Orem
ITT Technical Institute
  Murray
Neumont University

Mississippi

Antonelli College
  Hattiesburg
  Jackson
Blue Cliff College
  Gulfport
Virginia College
  Biloxi
  Jackson

Missouri

Bolivar Technical College
Brown Mackie College
  St. Louis
Cottey College
ITT Technical Institute
  Kansas City
L'Ecole Culinaire
Metro Business College
  Jefferson City
  Rolla
Missouri College
Southeast Missouri Hospital
  College of Nursing and
  Health Sciences
Stevens Institute of Business &
  Arts
Texas County Technical College
Vatterott College
  Joplin
  Kansas City
  O'Fallon
  St. Joseph
  Springfield
  Sunset Hills

Montana

Aaniiih Nakoda College
Blackfeet Community College
Chief Dull Knife College
Dawson Community College
Fort Peck Community College
Little Big Horn College
Miles Community College
Stone Child College

Nebraska

Kaplan University
  Lincoln
  Omaha
Little Priest Tribal College
Myotherapy Institute
Nebraska College of Technical
  Agriculture
Nebraska Indian Community
  College
Vatterott College
  Spring Valley
Wright Career College
  Omaha

Nevada

Career College of Northern
  Nevada
Carrington College
  Las Vegas
  Reno

New Jersey

Assumption College for Sisters
Eastern International College
Eastwick College
  Hackensack

New Mexico

Brookline College
  Albuquerque
Carrington College
  Albuquerque
New Mexico Military Institute
Southwestern Indian Polytechnic
  Institute

New York

American Academy McAllister
  Institute of Funeral Service
American Academy of Dramatic
  Arts

Bramson ORT College
City University of New York
  Guttman Community
  College
Cochran School of Nursing
Elmira Business Institute
Elmira Business Institute: Vestal
Helene Fuld College of Nursing
Institute of Design and
  Construction
Island Drafting and Technical
  Institute
ITT Technical Institute
  Albany
  Getzville
  Liverpool
Jamestown Business College
Mildred Elley
  Albany
  New York City
New York Career Institute
Phillips Beth Israel School of
  Nursing
St. Elizabeth College of Nursing
St. Joseph's College of Nursing
Utica School of Commerce
Villa Maria College of Buffalo
Wood Tobe-Coburn School

North Carolina

Carolinas College of Health
  Sciences
Chef's Academy
King's College
Louisburg College
Miller-Motte College
  Cary
  Fayetteville
Pamlico Community College
South College
Virginia College in Greensboro

North Dakota

Cankdeska Cikana Community
  College
Dakota College at Bottineau
Fort Berthold Community
  College
Lake Region State College
Turtle Mountain Community
  College
United Tribes Technical College
Williston State College

Ohio

Antonelli College
  Cincinnati
Art Institute of Cincinnati
ATS Institute of Technology
Aultman College of Nursing and
  Health Sciences
Bradford School
Brown Mackie College
  Akron
  Findlay
  North Canton
Bryant & Stratton College
  Cleveland
Chatfield College
Cincinnati College of Mortuary
  Science
Davis College
Daymar College
  Chillicothe
ETI Technical College of Niles
Fortis College
  Cuyahoga
  Ravenna
Gallipolis Career College
Good Samaritan College of
  Nursing and Health Science
Harrison College
  Grove City
Herzing University
International College of
  Broadcasting

ITT Technical Institute
  Dayton
  Hilliard
  Norwood
  Strongsville
  Youngstown
Kaplan College
  Dayton
Lincoln College of Technology
  Dayton
Miami-Jacobs Career College
  Columbus
  Dayton
  Sharonville
Ohio Business College
  Hilliard
  Sandusky
  Sheffield
Ohio College of Massotherapy
Ohio State University
  Agricultural Technical
  Institute
Ohio Valley College of
  Technology
PowerSport Institute
School of Advertising Art
Stautzenberger College
Stautzenberger College:
  Brecksville
Vatterott College
  Cleveland
Virginia Marti College of Art
  and Design

Oklahoma

College of the Muscogee Nation
Platt College
  Moore
  Oklahoma City Central
  Tulsa
Vatterott College
  Oklahoma City
  Tulsa
Virginia College
  Tulsa
Wright Career College
  Oklahoma City
  Tulsa

Oregon

Le Cordon Bleu College of
  Culinary Arts
  Portland
Tillamook Bay Community
  College

Pennsylvania

Antonelli Institute of Art and
  Photography
Bidwell Training Center
Bradford School: Pittsburgh
Cambria-Rowe Business College
Career Training Academy
Career Training Academy:
  Monroeville
Career Training Academy:
  Pittsburgh
Commonwealth Technical
  Institute
Consolidated School of Business
  Lancaster
  York
Dean Institute of Technology
Douglas Education Center
DuBois Business College
  Huntingdon
  Oil City
Erie Institute of Technology
Fortis Institute
  Erie
  Forty Fort
Hussian College, School of Art
ITT Technical Institute
  Pittsburgh
  Plymouth Meeting
JNA Institute of Culinary Arts
Johnson College

Kaplan Career Institute
  Franklin Mills
  Harrisburg
  Pittsburgh
Keystone Technical Institute
Lansdale School of Business
Laurel Business Institute
Laurel Technical Institute
Lincoln Technical Institute
  Allentown
  Northeast Philadelphia
  Philadelphia
Manor College
McCann School of Business and
  Technology
  Hazleton
  Pottsville
Metropolitan Career Center
  Computer Technology
  Institute
Orleans Technical Institute
Penn Commercial Business and
  Technical School
Pennco Tech
Pennsylvania Institute of Health
  and Technology
Pennsylvania Institute of
  Technology
Pittsburgh Institute of
  Aeronautics
Pittsburgh Institute of Mortuary
  Science
Rosedale Technical Institute
South Hills School of
  Business & Technology
Triangle Tech
  Bethlehem
  DuBois
  Erie
  Greensburg
  Pittsburgh
  Sunbury
University of Pittsburgh
  Titusville
Valley Forge Military College
Vet Tech Institute
Williamson College of the
  Trades
YTI Career Institute
  Altoona
  Lancaster
  York

Puerto Rico

Colegio de Cinematografía,
  Artes y Televisión
Columbia Central University
  Yauco
Humacao Community College

South Carolina

Clinton College
Forrest Junior College
Golf Academy of America
  Myrtle Beach
Miller-Motte Technical College
  Conway
University of South Carolina
  Union
Virginia College
  Charleston
  Columbia
  Florence
  Greenville
  Spartanburg
Williamsburg Technical College

South Dakota

Globe University
  Sioux Falls
Kilian Community College
Sisseton Wahpeton College

Tennessee

Chattanooga College
Daymar Institute
  Clarksville
  Murfreesboro
  Nashville

Fountainhead College of
  Technology
Hiwassee College
Miller-Motte Technical College
  Chattanooga
  Clarksville
Nossi College of Art
Remington College
  Nashville
Virginia College
  School of Business and
  Health in Chattanooga
West Tennessee Business
  College

Texas

Commonwealth Institute of
  Funeral Service
Court Reporting Institute of
  Dallas
Culinary Institute LeNotre
Dallas Institute of Funeral
  Service
Golf Academy of America
  Dallas
Hallmark University
International Academy of
  Design and Technology
  San Antonio
ITT Technical Institute
  Arlington
  Austin
  Houston North
  Houston West
  Richardson
  San Antonio
  Webster
Jacksonville College
Le Cordon Bleu College of
  Culinary Arts
  Austin
Remington College
  Fort Worth
  Webster Campus
  Westchase Campus
Virginia College
  Austin
Wade College
Western Technical College:
  Diana Drive

Utah

Broadview University
  Broadview Entertainment
  Arts University
  Layton
  West Jordan
Careers Unlimited
Eagle Gate College: Layton
Eagle Gate College: Murray
Provo College
Vista College: Online

Vermont

Landmark College
New England Culinary Institute

Virginia

Advanced Technology Institute
Eastern Shore Community
  College
Miller-Motte Technical College
  Lynchburg
Virginia College
  Richmond

Washington

Carrington College
  Spokane
Northwest Indian College
Northwest School of Wooden
  Boatbuilding

West Virginia

Huntington Junior College
Valley College
West Virginia Business College
  Wheeling

West Virginia Junior College
  Bridgeport
  Charleston

Wisconsin

College of Menominee Nation
Globe University
  Appleton
  Eau Claire
  La Crosse
  Madison East
  Middleton
  Wausau
Lac Courte Oreilles Ojibwa
  Community College
Madison Media Institute
University of Wisconsin
  Barron County
  Fond du Lac
  Marshfield/Wood County
  Richland

Wyoming

Eastern Wyoming College

Small (750-1,999)

Four-year

Alabama

Birmingham-Southern College
Huntingdon College
Miles College
Oakwood University
Spring Hill College
Stillman College
Talladega College
University of Mobile
University of West Alabama

Arizona

Art Institute of Phoenix
National Paralegal College
University of Advancing
  Technology
Western International University

Arkansas

Arkansas Baptist College
Central Baptist College
Hendrix College
John Brown University
Ouachita Baptist University
University of Arkansas
  for Medical Sciences

California

Alliant International University
Antioch University
  Los Angeles
Art Center College of Design
Art Institute of California
  Hollywood
  Orange County
  Sacramento
  San Diego
  San Francisco
California College of the Arts
California College San Diego
California Institute of
  Technology
California Institute of the Arts
California Maritime Academy
Claremont McKenna College
Concordia University Irvine
DeVry University
  Pomona
Dominican University of
  California
Harvey Mudd College
Hope International University
ITT Technical Institute
  National City
Loma Linda University
Marymount California
  University

The Master's College
Menlo College
Mills College
Notre Dame de Namur
  University
Otis College of Art and Design
Pacific Union College
Patten University
Pitzer College
Pomona College
San Diego Christian College
Scripps College
Simpson University
Stanbridge College
University of Phoenix
  Bay Area
Vanguard University of
  Southern California
West Coast University
  Los Angeles
West Coast University: Ontario
West Coast University: Orange
  County
Westmont College
Westwood College
  Anaheim
  Inland Empire
  South Bay
Whittier College
William Jessup University
Woodbury University

Colorado

American Sentinel University
Colorado Technical University
Johnson & Wales University
  Denver
Nazarene Bible College
Rocky Mountain College of
  Art & Design
University of Phoenix
  Denver
Western State Colorado
  University
Westwood College
  Denver North

Connecticut

Albertus Magnus College
Charter Oak State College
Connecticut College
United States Coast Guard
  Academy
University of Saint Joseph

District of Columbia

Gallaudet University
Strayer University

Florida

Adventist University of Health
  Sciences
Art Institute of Fort Lauderdale
Ave Maria University
DeVry University
  Orlando
Eckerd College
Edward Waters College
Florida Memorial University
Hodges University
Johnson & Wales University
  North Miami
Lynn University
New College of Florida
Ringling College of Art and
  Design
Rollins College
Saint Thomas University
University of Phoenix
  North Florida
  South Florida
  West Florida
University of South Florida
  Sarasota-Manatee
Warner University

Georgia

Agnes Scott College
Bauder College
Brenau University
Chamberlain College of Nursing
  Atlanta
Covenant College
DeVry University
  Decatur
Emmanuel College
LaGrange College
Oglethorpe University
Piedmont College
Point University
Reinhardt University
Shorter University
South University
  Savannah
Thomas University
Toccoa Falls College
Truett-McConnell College
University of Phoenix
  Augusta
Westwood College
  Atlanta Midtown
  Northlake
Young Harris College

Hawaii

Chaminade University of
  Honolulu
University of Phoenix
  Hawaii

Idaho

College of Idaho
Northwest Nazarene University

Illinois

Chamberlain College of Nursing
  Chicago
Concordia University Chicago
DeVry University
  Chicago
Greenville College
Illinois College
Illinois Institute of Art
  Chicago
  Schaumburg
Illinois Wesleyan University
Judson University
Kendall College
Knox College
Lake Forest College
Monmouth College
National-Louis University
Quincy University
Rockford University
Trinity Christian College
Trinity International University
University of Phoenix
  Chicago
University of St. Francis
Westwood College
  O'Hare Airport

Indiana

Anderson University
Bethel College
Calumet College of St. Joseph
Earlham College
Franklin College
Goshen College
Grace College
Hanover College
Huntington University
Manchester University
Marian University
Saint Joseph's College
Saint Mary's College
Taylor University
Trine University
University of Saint Francis
Wabash College

Iowa

Briar Cliff University
Buena Vista University

Central College
Clarke University
Coe College
Cornell College
Dordt College
Graceland University
Grand View University
Grinnell College
Kaplan University
  Des Moines
Loras College
Mercy College of Health
  Sciences
Morningside College
Mount Mercy University
Northwestern College
Simpson College
University of Dubuque
Waldorf University
Wartburg College
William Penn University

Kansas

Baker University
Benedictine College
Central Christian College of
  Kansas
Friends University
Haskell Indian Nations
  University
MidAmerica Nazarene
  University
Newman University
Southwestern College
University of St. Mary

Kentucky

Asbury University
Beckfield College
Berea College
Brescia University
Centre College
Georgetown College
Kentucky State University
Midway College
Southern Baptist Theological
  Seminary
Spalding University
Thomas More College
Transylvania University
Union College
University of Pikeville
University of the Cumberlands

Louisiana

Dillard University
Louisiana College
Louisiana State University
  Health Sciences Center
Our Lady of the Lake College
University of Holy Cross
University of Phoenix
  Baton Rouge

Maine

Bates College
Bowdoin College
Colby College
Maine Maritime Academy
Saint Joseph's College of Maine
Thomas College
University of Maine
  Farmington
  Fort Kent
  Presque Isle

Maryland

Goucher College
Hood College
Maryland Institute College of
  Art
McDaniel College
Mount St. Mary's University
Notre Dame of Maryland
  University
St. Mary's College of Maryland
University of Maryland
  Baltimore

Washington Adventist
  University
Washington College

Massachusetts

American International College
Amherst College
Anna Maria College
Assumption College
Bay Path University
Cambridge College
Eastern Nazarene College
Elms College
Emmanuel College
Fisher College
Gordon College
Hampshire College
Lasell College
Lesley University
Massachusetts College of Art
  and Design
Massachusetts College of
  Liberal Arts
Massachusetts Maritime
  Academy
Mount Ida College
Nichols College
Regis College
Simmons College
Wheaton College
Wheelock College

Michigan

Adrian College
Albion College
Alma College
Andrews University
Aquinas College
Art Institute of Michigan
Baker College
  of Cadillac
  of Port Huron
College for Creative Studies
Cornerstone University
Hillsdale College
Kalamazoo College
Kettering University
Lawrence Technological
  University
Northwood University
  Michigan
Olivet College
Rochester College
University of Phoenix
  Metro Detroit
Walsh College of Accountancy
  and Business Administration

Minnesota

Argosy University
  Twin Cities
Art Institutes International
  Minnesota
Carleton College
College of St. Benedict
Crown College
North Central University
St. John's University
St. Mary's University of
  Minnesota
University of Minnesota
  Crookston
  Morris
University of Northwestern - St.
  Paul

Mississippi

Millsaps College
Mississippi Valley State
  University
Rust College
Tougaloo College

Missouri

Avila University
Central Methodist University
College of the Ozarks
Columbia College

Cox College
Culver-Stockton College
Drury University
Evangel University
Fontbonne University
Hannibal-LaGrange University
Harris-Stowe State University
Missouri Baptist University
Missouri Valley College
Ozark Christian College
Rockhurst University
University of Phoenix
  St. Louis
Westminster College
William Jewell College
William Woods University

Montana

Carroll College
Montana State University
  Northern
Rocky Mountain College
Salish Kootenai College
University of Great Falls
University of Montana: Western

Nebraska

Clarkson College
Concordia University
Doane College
Hastings College
Midland University
Nebraska Methodist College of
  Nursing and Allied Health
Nebraska Wesleyan University
Peru State College
Union College
University of Nebraska
  Medical Center

Nevada

Art Institute of Las Vegas

New Hampshire

Colby-Sawyer College
Franklin Pierce University
Granite State College
Mount Washington College
New England College
Rivier University
Saint Anselm College

New Jersey

Bloomfield College
Caldwell University
Centenary College
College of St. Elizabeth
DeVry University
  North Brunswick
Drew University
Felician University
Georgian Court University

New Mexico

New Mexico Institute of Mining
  and Technology
Northern New Mexico College
Santa Fe University of Art and
  Design
University of Phoenix
  New Mexico
Western New Mexico
  University

New York

Albany College of Pharmacy
  and Health Sciences
Alfred University
Bard College
Boricua College
Briarcliffe College
Cazenovia College
City University of New York
  CUNY Online
College of Mount St. Vincent
Concordia College
Cooper Union for the
  Advancement of Science and
  Art

D'Youville College
Daemen College
DeVry College of New York
  Midtown Campus
Dominican College of Blauvelt
Dowling College
Elmira College
Eugene Lang College The New
  School for Liberal Arts
Hamilton College
Hartwick College
Hilbert College
Houghton College
Keuka College
LIM College
Manhattanville College
Marymount Manhattan College
Metropolitan College of New
  York
Nyack College
Paul Smith's College
Roberts Wesleyan College
The Sage Colleges
Saint Bonaventure University
St. Joseph's College, New York
St. Thomas Aquinas College
Sarah Lawrence College
SUNY
  College of Environmental
    Science and Forestry
  Maritime College
SUNY Polytechnic Institute
U.T.A. Mesivta-Kiryas Joel
United States Merchant Marine
  Academy
United Talmudical Seminary
Vaughn College of Aeronautics
  and Technology
Wagner College

North Carolina

Barton College
Belmont Abbey College
Catawba College
Chowan University
Davidson College
Greensboro College
Guilford College
Johnson C. Smith University
Lees-McRae College
Lenoir-Rhyne University
Livingstone College
Mars Hill University
Meredith College
Pfeiffer University
Queens University of Charlotte
Saint Augustine's University
Salem College
Shaw University
University of North Carolina
  School of the Arts
William Peace University

North Dakota

Dickinson State University
Mayville State University
University of Jamestown
Valley City State University

Ohio

Bluffton University
Central State University
Columbus College of Art and
  Design
DeVry University
  Columbus
Heidelberg University
Hiram College
Kenyon College
Lake Erie College
Lourdes University
Malone University
Marietta College
Mercy College of Ohio
Mount Carmel College of
  Nursing
Mount St. Joseph University

Mount Vernon Nazarene
  University
Muskingum University
Notre Dame College
Ohio Dominican University
Ohio Northern University
Ohio State University
  Lima Campus
  Mansfield Campus
  Marion Campus
Ohio Wesleyan University
Union Institute & University
University of Rio Grande
Urbana University
Wilmington College
Wittenberg University

Oklahoma

Bacone College
Northwestern Oklahoma State
  University
Oklahoma Baptist University
Oklahoma Christian University
Oklahoma City University
Oklahoma Panhandle State
  University
Oklahoma Wesleyan University
Southern Nazarene University
Spartan College of Aeronautics
  and Technology
University of Science and Arts
  of Oklahoma

Oregon

Art Institute of Portland
Concordia University
Corban University
Linfield College
Oregon Health & Science
  University
Pacific University
Reed College
Willamette University

Pennsylvania

Allegheny College
Art Institute of Philadelphia
Art Institute of Pittsburgh
Bryn Mawr College
Cabrini College
Cairn University
Carlow University
Cedar Crest College
Central Penn College
Chestnut Hill College
Delaware Valley University
Elizabethtown College
Geneva College
Gwynedd Mercy University
Haverford College
Holy Family University
Immaculata University
Juniata College
Keystone College
King's College
La Roche College
Lancaster Bible College
Lebanon Valley College
Lincoln University
Lycoming College
Marywood University
Moravian College
Mount Aloysius College
Peirce College
Penn State
  Brandywine
  Hazleton
  Lehigh Valley
  Mont Alto
  Worthington Scranton
  York
Pennsylvania College of Health
  Sciences
St. Francis University
St. Vincent College
Seton Hill University
Swarthmore College
Thiel College

Thomas Jefferson University
University of Pittsburgh
  Bradford
  Greensburg
University of the Arts
University of Valley Forge
Ursinus College
Washington & Jefferson College
Waynesburg University
Westminster College

Puerto Rico

American University of Puerto
  Rico
Atlantic University College
EDP University of Puerto Rico:
  San Sebastian
Inter American University of
  Puerto Rico
  Guayama Campus
National University College
  Arecibo
  Ponce
  Rio Grande
Universidad Adventista de las
  Antillas
University College of San Juan
University of Puerto Rico
  Utuado

South Carolina

Claflin University
Coker College
Columbia College
Converse College
Limestone College
Morris College
Newberry College
Presbyterian College
Southern Wesleyan University
University of South Carolina
  Beaufort
Wofford College

South Dakota

Augusta University
  Augustana University
Dakota State University
Dakota Wesleyan University
National American University
  Rapid City
Oglala Lakota College
University of Sioux Falls

Tennessee

Baptist College of Health
  Sciences
Bryan College
  Dayton
Carson-Newman University
Christian Brothers University
Fisk University
Freed-Hardeman University
Johnson University
Lane College
LeMoyne-Owen College
Lincoln Memorial University
Martin Methodist College
Maryville College
Milligan College
Sewanee: The University of the
  South
South College
Tennessee Wesleyan College
Trevecca Nazarene University
Tusculum College
University of Phoenix
  Memphis

Texas

Art Institute of Dallas
Art Institute of Houston
Austin College
Concordia University Texas
East Texas Baptist University
Hardin-Simmons University
Howard Payne University
Huston-Tillotson University

Jarvis Christian College
LeTourneau University
Lubbock Christian University
McMurry University
Our Lady of the Lake
  University of San Antonio
Schreiner University
Southwestern Assemblies of
  God University
Southwestern University
Sul Ross State University
Texas A&M University
  Texarkana
Texas College
Texas Lutheran University
Texas Tech University Health
  Sciences Center
Texas Wesleyan University
University of Dallas
University of Phoenix
  Dallas Fort Worth
  San Antonio
University of St. Thomas
Wiley College

Utah

Independence University
University of Phoenix
  Utah

Vermont

Castleton State College
Johnson State College
Lyndon State College
Saint Michael's College
Vermont Technical College

Virginia

Art Institute of Washington
Averett University
Bluefield College
Bridgewater College
Eastern Mennonite University
Emory & Henry College
Ferrum College
Hampden-Sydney College
ITT Technical Institute
  Springfield
Jefferson College of Health
  Sciences
Mary Baldwin College
Randolph-Macon College
Roanoke College
Shenandoah University
University of Management and
  Technology
University of Phoenix
  Northern Virginia
  Richmond
University of Virginia's College
  at Wise
Virginia Military Institute
Virginia Union University
Virginia Wesleyan College
Washington and Lee University
Westwood College
  Annandale
  Arlington Ballston

Washington

Art Institute of Seattle
City University of Seattle
DigiPen Institute of Technology
Heritage University
Northwest University
Saint Martin's University
Walla Walla University
Whitman College

West Virginia

Alderson-Broaddus University
Bluefield State College
Davis and Elkins College
Glenville State College
University of Charleston
West Virginia University
  Institute of Technology

West Virginia Wesleyan College
Wheeling Jesuit University

Wisconsin

Alverno College
Beloit College
Cardinal Stritch University
Edgewood College
Lawrence University
Marian University
Mount Mary University
Ripon College
Wisconsin Lutheran College

Virgin Islands

University of the Virgin Islands

Bulgaria

American University in Bulgaria

Italy

John Cabot University

Morocco

Al Akhawayn University

Switzerland

Les Roches International School
of Hotel Management

United Kingdom

Richmond, The American
International University in
London

Two-year

Alabama

Alabama Southern Community
College
Central Alabama Community
College
Chattahoochee Valley
Community College
Enterprise State Community
College
George C. Wallace State
Community College at Selma
Jefferson Davis Community
College
Lurleen B. Wallace Community
College
Remington College
Mobile

Arizona

Brookline College
Phoenix
Bryan University
Dine College
Le Cordon Bleu College of
Culinary Arts
Scottsdale
Refrigeration School

Arkansas

Arkansas State University
Mid-South
Mountain Home
Black River Technical College
College of the Ouachitas
Cossatot Community College
of the University of
Arkansas
East Arkansas Community
College
Phillips Community College of
the University of Arkansas
South Arkansas Community
College
Southeast Arkansas College
University of Arkansas
Community College at
Hope
Community College at
Morrilton

California

Art Institute of California
Los Angeles

Barstow Community College
Carrington College
Sacramento
San Jose
Concorde Career College
Garden Grove
San Diego
Copper Mountain College
Feather River College
Institute of Technology: Clovis
Kaplan College
San Diego
Vista
Le Cordon Bleu College of
Culinary Arts
Los Angeles
MTI College
San Joaquin Valley College

Colorado

Colorado Northwestern
Community College
Concorde Career College
Aurora
IBMC College
Fort Collins
IntelliTec College
Lincoln College of Technology
Denver
Morgan Community College
Northeastern Junior College
Otero Junior College
Trinidad State Junior College

Connecticut

Asnuntuck Community College
Northwestern Connecticut
Community College
Quinebaug Valley Community
College

Florida

Brown Mackie College
Miami
Chipola College
Florida Gateway College
Florida Keys Community
College
Le Cordon Bleu College of
Culinary Arts
Miami
Orlando
North Florida Community
College
Southeastern College
Greenacres

Georgia

Brown Mackie College
Atlanta
Le Cordon Bleu College of
Culinary Arts
Atlanta
Oxford College of Emory
University
Southeastern Technical College
Virginia College
Augusta

Hawaii

Remington College
Honolulu
University of Hawaii
Kauai Community College

Illinois

Benedictine University at
Springfield
Danville Area Community
College
Highland Community College
Illinois Eastern Community
Colleges
Olney Central College
Le Cordon Bleu College of
Culinary Arts
Chicago
Lincoln College
Northwestern College

Rend Lake College
Sauk Valley Community
College
Shawnee Community College
Southeastern Illinois College
Spoon River College

Indiana

Lincoln College of Technology
Indianapolis

Iowa

Clinton Community College
Ellsworth Community College
Iowa Lakes Community College
Muscatine Community College
Northwest Iowa Community
College
Southeastern Community
College
Southwestern Community
College

Kansas

Cloud County Community
College
Coffeyville Community College
Colby Community College
Dodge City Community College
Fort Scott Community College
Highland Community College
Labette Community College
Pratt Community College
Seward County Community
College

Kentucky

Brown Mackie College
Louisville

Louisiana

Blue Cliff College
Metairie
Nunez Community College

Maine

Kaplan University
South Portland
York County Community
College

Maryland

Chesapeake College
Kaplan University
Hagerstown

Massachusetts

Bay State College
Berkshire Community College
Dean College
Laboure College
Urban College of Boston

Michigan

Bay College
Glen Oaks Community College
Gogebic Community College
Kirtland Community College
Montcalm Community College
Southwestern Michigan College
West Shore Community College

Minnesota

Dunwoody College of
Technology
Fond du Lac Tribal and
Community College
Hibbing Community College
Itasca Community College
Mesabi Range College
Minnesota State College -
Southeast Technical
Pine Technical & Community
College

Mississippi

Southwest Mississippi
Community College

Missouri

Concorde Career College
Kansas City
Missouri State University: West
Plains
North Central Missouri College
Pinnacle Career Institute:
Kansas City
Ranken Technical College
State Technical College of
Missouri
Vatterott College
Berkeley

Montana

Helena College University of
Montana
Montana State University
Great Falls College

Nebraska

Mid-Plains Community College
Western Nebraska Community
College

Nevada

Kaplan College
Las Vegas

New Hampshire

Lakes Region Community
College
River Valley Community
College
White Mountains Community
College

New Jersey

Eastwick College
Salem Community College
Warren County Community
College

New Mexico

Clovis Community College
Luna Community College
Navajo Technical University
New Mexico State University
Alamogordo
Grants

New York

Clinton Community College
College of Westchester
Columbia-Greene Community
College
Long Island Business Institute
Maria College
Plaza College
Sullivan County Community
College
Swedish Institute
Trocaire College
Ulster County Community
College

North Carolina

Beaufort County Community
College
Bladen Community College
Brunswick Community College
Carteret Community College
College of the Albemarle
Halifax Community College
Haywood Community College
James Sprunt Community
College
Lenoir Community College
Martin Community College
Mayland Community College
McDowell Technical
Community College
Montgomery Community
College
Nash Community College
Piedmont Community College
Roanoke-Chowan Community
College

Rockingham Community
College

Southeastern Community
College
Southwestern Community
College
Tri-County Community College
Wilson Community College

Ohio

Belmont College
Bowling Green State University:
Firelands College
Brown Mackie College
Cincinnati
Cleveland Institute of
Electronics
Edison State Community
College
Fortis College
Centerville
Hondros College
Kent State University
East Liverpool
Salem
Tuscarawas
Marion Technical College
North Central State College
Northwest State Community
College
Ohio Technical College
Remington College
Cleveland
Washington State Community
College
Wright State University: Lake
Campus

Oklahoma

Eastern Oklahoma State College
Seminole State College
Tulsa Welding School

Oregon

Blue Mountain Community
College
Clatsop Community College
Klamath Community College
Pioneer Pacific College
Treasure Valley Community
College
Umpqua Community College

Pennsylvania

Berks Technical Institute
Harcum College
Lackawanna College
New Castle School of Trades
Pennsylvania Highlands
Community College
Thaddeus Stevens College of
Technology

Puerto Rico

Centro de Estudios
Multidisciplinarios
EDIC College
Huertas College
Universal Technology College
of Puerto Rico

South Carolina

Denmark Technical College
Northeastern Technical College
Spartanburg Methodist College
University of South Carolina
Lancaster
Salkehatchie
Sumter

South Dakota

Lake Area Technical Institute
Mitchell Technical Institute
Southeast Technical Institute
Western Dakota Technical
Institute

Tables and Indexes

Tennessee

Dyersburg State Community
  College
Lincoln College of Technology
  Nashville
Remington College
  Memphis
Vatterott College
  Memphis

Texas

Clarendon College
Frank Phillips College
Galveston College
Lamar State College at Port
  Arthur
Lincoln College of Technology
  Grand Prairie
Remington College
  Dallas
  Greenspoint Campus
Texas State Technical College
  Marshall
  West Texas
Western Technical College

Virginia

Dabney S. Lancaster
  Community College
Paul D. Camp Community
  College
Richard Bland College

Washington

Big Bend Community College
Grays Harbor College
Lake Washington Institute of
  Technology
Lower Columbia College
Peninsula College

West Virginia

BridgeValley Community and
  Technical College
Eastern West Virginia
  Community and Technical
  College
Potomac State College of West
  Virginia University
West Virginia Northern
  Community College

Wisconsin

Nicolet Area Technical College
Southwest Wisconsin Technical
  College
University of Wisconsin
  Fox Valley
  Rock County
  Sheboygan
  Washington County

Wyoming

Central Wyoming College
Northwest College
Sheridan College
Western Wyoming Community
  College

American Samoa

American Samoa Community
  College

**Medium to large
(2,000-7,499)**

Four-year

Alabama

Alabama Agricultural and
  Mechanical University
Alabama State University
Athens State University
Auburn University at
  Montgomery
Faulkner University

Jacksonville State University
Samford University
Tuskegee University
University of Alabama
  Huntsville
University of Montevallo
University of North Alabama
Virginia College
  Birmingham

Alaska

Charter College
University of Alaska
  Fairbanks
  Southeast

Arizona

Embry-Riddle Aeronautical
  University
  Prescott Campus

Arkansas

Harding University
Henderson State University
Southern Arkansas University
University of Arkansas
  Fort Smith
  Monticello
  Pine Bluff

California

Art Institute of California
  Inland Empire
Azusa Pacific University
Biola University
Brandman University
California Baptist University
California Coast University
California Lutheran University
California State University
  Channel Islands
  Monterey Bay
Chapman University
Fresno Pacific University
La Sierra University
Loyola Marymount University
Mount Saint Mary's University
Occidental College
Pepperdine University
Point Loma Nazarene University
St. Mary's College of California
Santa Clara University
Stanford University
Trident University International
University of California
  Merced
University of La Verne
University of Phoenix
  Central Valley
  Sacramento Valley
  San Diego
University of Redlands
University of San Diego
University of San Francisco
University of the Pacific

Colorado

Adams State University
Colorado Christian University
Colorado College
Colorado School of Mines
Colorado State University
  Pueblo
Fort Lewis College
Regis University
United States Air Force
  Academy
University of Denver

Connecticut

Eastern Connecticut State
  University
Fairfield University
Quinnipiac University
Sacred Heart University
Trinity College
University of Bridgeport
University of Hartford
University of New Haven

Wesleyan University
Western Connecticut State
  University
Yale University

Delaware

Delaware State University

District of Columbia

American University
Catholic University of America
Georgetown University
Howard University
Trinity Washington University
University of the District of
  Columbia

Florida

Barry University
Bethune-Cookman University
Embry-Riddle Aeronautical
  University
Flagler College
Florida Institute of Technology
Florida Southern College
Jacksonville University
Miami International University
  of Art and Design
Nova Southeastern University
Palm Beach Atlantic University
Saint Leo University
Southeastern University
Stetson University
University of Phoenix
  Central Florida
University of South Florida
  Saint Petersburg
University of Tampa

Georgia

Albany State University
Armstrong State University
Art Institute of Atlanta
Augusta University
Berry College
Clark Atlanta University
Clayton State University
College of Coastal Georgia
Columbus State University
Dalton State College
Emory University
Fort Valley State University
Georgia College and State
  University
Georgia Southwestern State
  University
Mercer University
Morehouse College
Savannah State University
South Georgia State College
Spelman College
University of Phoenix
  Atlanta

Hawaii

Brigham Young University-
  Hawaii
Hawaii Pacific University
University of Hawaii
  Hilo
  West Oahu

Idaho

Lewis-Clark State College

Illinois

Augustana College
Aurora University
Benedictine University
Bradley University
Chicago State University
Dominican University
Eastern Illinois University
Elmhurst College
Governors State University
Illinois Institute of Technology
Lewis University
McKendree University
Millikin University

North Central College
North Park University
Olivet Nazarene University
Robert Morris University:
  Chicago
Roosevelt University
Saint Xavier University
School of the Art Institute of
  Chicago
University of Chicago
University of Illinois
  Springfield
Wheaton College

Indiana

Butler University
DePauw University
Indiana Institute of Technology
Indiana University
  East
  Kokomo
  Northwest
  South Bend
  Southeast
Indiana Wesleyan University
ITT Technical Institute
  Indianapolis
Purdue University
  North Central
Rose-Hulman Institute of
  Technology
University of Evansville
University of Indianapolis
Valparaiso University

Iowa

Drake University
Luther College
St. Ambrose University
Upper Iowa University

Kansas

Emporia State University
Pittsburg State University
Washburn University

Kentucky

Bellarmine University
Campbellsville University
Lindsey Wilson College
Morehead State University
Sullivan University

Louisiana

Grambling State University
Louisiana State University
  Alexandria
  Shreveport
Loyola University New Orleans
McNeese State University
Nicholls State University
Northwestern State University
Southern University and
  Agricultural and Mechanical
  College
University of Louisiana at
  Monroe
University of New Orleans
Xavier University of Louisiana

Maine

Husson University
University of Maine
  Augusta
University of New England
University of Southern Maine

Maryland

Bowie State University
Coppin State University
Frostburg State University
Johns Hopkins University
Loyola University Maryland
Morgan State University
Stevenson University
United States Naval Academy
University of Baltimore
University of Maryland
  Eastern Shore

Massachusetts

Babson College
Becker College
Bentley University
Berklee College of Music
Brandeis University
Clark University
College of the Holy Cross
Curry College
Emerson College
Endicott College
Fitchburg State University
Framingham State University
Harvard College
Massachusetts Institute of
  Technology
MCPHS University
Merrimack College
Mount Holyoke College
Smith College
Springfield College
Stonehill College
Suffolk University
Tufts University
University of Massachusetts
  Dartmouth
Wellesley College
Wentworth Institute of
  Technology
Western New England
  University
Westfield State University
Williams College
Worcester Polytechnic Institute
Worcester State University

Michigan

Baker College
  of Allen Park
  of Auburn Hills
  of Clinton Township
  of Flint
  of Jackson
  of Muskegon
  of Owosso
Calvin College
Davenport University
Hope College
Lake Superior State University
Madonna University
Michigan Jewish Institute
Michigan Technological
  University
Siena Heights University
Spring Arbor University
University of Detroit Mercy
University of Michigan
  Dearborn
  Flint

Minnesota

Augsburg College
Bemidji State University
Bethel University
College of St. Scholastica
Concordia College: Moorhead
Concordia University St. Paul
Gustavus Adolphus College
Hamline University
Macalester College
Metropolitan State University
Minnesota State University
  Moorhead
St. Catherine University
St. Olaf College
Southwest Minnesota State
  University
University of St. Thomas

Mississippi

Alcorn State University
Belhaven University
Delta State University
Jackson State University
Mississippi College

Mississippi University for
Women
William Carey University

Missouri

Lincoln University
Maryville University of Saint
Louis
Missouri Southern State
University
Missouri University of Science
and Technology
Missouri Western State
University
Northwest Missouri State
University
Southwest Baptist University
Truman State University
Washington University in St.
Louis
Webster University

Montana

Montana State University
Billings
Montana Tech of the University
of Montana

Nebraska

Bellevue University
Chadron State College
Creighton University
University of Nebraska
Kearney
Wayne State College

Nevada

Great Basin College
Nevada State College

New Hampshire

Dartmouth College
Keene State College
Plymouth State University
Southern New Hampshire
University

New Jersey

Berkeley College
Beth Medrash Govoha
The College of New Jersey
Fairleigh Dickinson University
College at Florham
Metropolitan Campus
Monmouth University
New Jersey City University
New Jersey Institute of
Technology
Princeton University
Ramapo College of New Jersey
Rider University
Rutgers, The State University of
New Jersey
Camden Campus
Newark Campus
Saint Peter's University
Seton Hall University
Stevens Institute of Technology

New Mexico

Eastern New Mexico University
New Mexico Highlands
University

New York

Adelphi University
Barnard College
Berkeley College of New York
City
Canisius College
City University of New York
Medgar Evers College
York College
Clarkson University
Colgate University
College of Saint Rose
Columbia University
School of General Studies
Culinary Institute of America

Hobart and William Smith
Colleges
Hofstra University
Iona College
Ithaca College
Le Moyne College
Long Island University
LIU Brooklyn
LIU Post
Manhattan College
Marist College
Medaille College
Mercy College
Molloy College
Monroe College
Mount Saint Mary College
Nazareth College
New York Institute of
Technology
Niagara University
Pace University
Pace University: Pleasantville/
Briarcliff
Parsons The New School for
Design
Pratt Institute
Rensselaer Polytechnic Institute
St. Francis College
St. John Fisher College
St. Joseph's College New York:
Suffolk Campus
St. Lawrence University
School of Visual Arts
Siena College
Skidmore College
SUNY
College at Brockport
College at Cortland
College at Fredonia
College at Geneseo
College at New Paltz
College at Old Westbury
College at Oneonta
College at Oswego
College at Plattsburgh
College at Potsdam
College at Purchase
College of Agriculture and
Technology at Morrisville
Touro College
Union College
United States Military Academy
University of Rochester
Utica College
Vassar College
Yeshiva University

North Carolina

Campbell University
Duke University
Elizabeth City State University
Elon University
Fayetteville State University
Gardner-Webb University
High Point University
Johnson and Wales University
Charlotte
Methodist University
Miller-Motte College
Wilmington
North Carolina Central
University
North Carolina Wesleyan
College
University of Mount Olive
University of North Carolina
Asheville
Pembroke
Wake Forest University
Wingate University
Winston-Salem State University

North Dakota

Minot State University
University of Mary

Ohio

Ashland University
Baldwin Wallace University
Capital University
Case Western Reserve
University
Cedarville University
College of Wooster
Denison University
Franciscan University of
Steubenville
Franklin University
John Carroll University
Oberlin College
Ohio Christian University
Ohio State University
Newark Campus
Ohio University
Chillicothe Campus
Southern Campus at Ironton
Zanesville Campus
Otterbein University
Shawnee State University
Tiffin University
University of Findlay
University of Mount Union
Walsh University
Xavier University

Oklahoma

Cameron University
East Central University
Langston University
Mid-America Christian
University
Northeastern State University
Oral Roberts University
Rogers State University
Southeastern Oklahoma State
University
Southwestern Oklahoma State
University
University of Tulsa

Oregon

Eastern Oregon University
George Fox University
Lewis & Clark College
Oregon Institute of Technology
Southern Oregon University
University of Portland
Western Oregon University

Pennsylvania

Albright College
Alvernia University
Arcadia University
Bucknell University
California University of
Pennsylvania
Carnegie Mellon University
Clarion University of
Pennsylvania
DeSales University
Dickinson College
Duquesne University
East Stroudsburg University of
Pennsylvania
Eastern University
Edinboro University
of Pennsylvania
Franklin & Marshall College
Gannon University
Gettysburg College
Grove City College
La Salle University
Lafayette College
Lehigh University
Lock Haven University of
Pennsylvania
Mansfield University of
Pennsylvania
Mercyhurst University
Messiah College
Millersville University of
Pennsylvania
Misericordia University

Muhlenberg College
Neumann University
Penn State
Abington
Altoona
Berks
Erie, The Behrend College
Harrisburg
Pennsylvania College of
Technology
Philadelphia University
Point Park University
Robert Morris University
Saint Joseph's University
Shippensburg University of
Pennsylvania
Slippery Rock University of
Pennsylvania
Susquehanna University
University of Pittsburgh
Johnstown
University of Scranton
University of the Sciences
Villanova University
Widener University
Wilkes University
York College of Pennsylvania

Puerto Rico

Caribbean University
Columbia Central University
Caguas
EDP University of Puerto Rico:
Hato Rey
Inter American University of
Puerto Rico
Aguadilla Campus
Arecibo Campus
Barranquitas Campus
Bayamon Campus
Fajardo Campus
Metropolitan Campus
Ponce Campus
San German Campus
National University College
Bayamon
Pontifical Catholic University of
Puerto Rico
Universidad Politecnica de
Puerto Rico
University of Puerto Rico
Aguadilla
Arecibo
Bayamon University
College
Carolina Regional College
Cayey University College
Humacao
Ponce
University of the Sacred Heart

Rhode Island

Brown University
Bryant University
New England Institute of
Technology
Providence College
Rhode Island College
Rhode Island School of Design
Roger Williams University
Salve Regina University

South Carolina

Anderson University
Benedict College
Bob Jones University
Charleston Southern University
The Citadel
Francis Marion University
Furman University
Lander University
North Greenville University
South Carolina State University
University of South Carolina
Aiken
Upstate
Winthrop University

South Dakota

Black Hills State University
Northern State University
South Dakota School of Mines
and Technology

Tennessee

Belmont University
Bethel University
King University
Lee University
Lipscomb University
Rhodes College
Southern Adventist University
Tennessee State University
Union University
University of Phoenix
Nashville
University of Tennessee
Martin
Vanderbilt University

Texas

Abilene Christian University
Angelo State University
Dallas Baptist University
Houston Baptist University
Midwestern State University
Prairie View A&M University
Rice University
St. Edward's University
St. Mary's University
Southern Methodist University
Texas A&M International
University
Texas A&M University
Galveston
Kingsville
Texas Southern University
Trinity University
University of Houston
Clear Lake
Victoria
University of Mary Hardin-
Baylor
University of Phoenix
Houston Westside
University of Texas
Brownsville
Tyler
of the Permian Basin
University of the Incarnate
Word
Wayland Baptist University
West Texas A&M University

Utah

Dixie State University
Southern Utah University
Stevens-Henager College
Murray
Westminster College

Vermont

Champlain College
Middlebury College
Norwich University

Virginia

Christopher Newport University
College of William and Mary
Hampton University
Longwood University
Lynchburg College
Marymount University
Norfolk State University
Regent University
University of Mary Washington
University of Richmond
Virginia State University

Washington

Evergreen State College
Gonzaga University
Pacific Lutheran University
Seattle Pacific University
Seattle University
University of Puget Sound

Tables and Indexes

University of Washington
Bothell
University of Washington
Tacoma
Whitworth University

West Virginia

Concord University
Fairmont State University
Shepherd University
West Liberty University
West Virginia State University

Wisconsin

Carthage College
Concordia University Wisconsin
Herzing University
Madison
Lakeland College
Milwaukee School of
Engineering
St. Norbert College
University of Wisconsin
Green Bay
Parkside
River Falls
Superior
Viterbo University

Egypt

American University in Cairo

France

Institut d'Etudes Politiques de
Paris

Greece

Deree College, The American
College of Greece

Kuwait

American University of Kuwait

Lebanon

American University of Beirut
Notre Dame University: Louaize

Pakistan

Forman Christian College

Turkey

Koc University

United Arab Emirates

American University in Dubai

Two-year

Alabama

Bevill State Community College
Bishop State Community
College
Faulkner State Community
College
Gadsden State Community
College
George C. Wallace Community
College at Dothan
Lawson State Community
College
Northeast Alabama Community
College
Northwest-Shoals Community
College
Shelton State Community
College
Snead State Community College
Southern Union State
Community College
Wallace State Community
College at Hanceville

Arizona

Arizona Western College
Central Arizona College
Cochise College
Coconino County Community
College
Eastern Arizona College
GateWay Community College

Mohave Community College
Northland Pioneer College
South Mountain Community
College
Universal Technical Institute

Arkansas

Arkansas State University
Beebe
Newport
National Park College
North Arkansas College

California

Berkeley City College
Canada College
Cerro Coso Community College
College of Alameda
College of Marin
College of the Redwoods
College of the Siskiyous
Columbia College
Contra Costa College
Crafton Hills College
Fashion Institute of Design and
Merchandising
Los Angeles
Gavilan College
Lake Tahoe Community College
Lassen Community College
Mendocino College
Merritt College
Napa Valley College
Ohlone College
Oxnard College
Palo Verde College
Porterville College
Taft College
Victor Valley College
West Hills College: Coalinga
West Hills College: Lemoore
Westwood College
Los Angeles
Woodland Community College
Yuba College

Colorado

Aims Community College
Colorado Mountain College
Community College of Aurora
Pueblo Community College

Connecticut

Capital Community College
Goodwin College
Housatonic Community College
Manchester Community College
Middlesex Community College
Naugatuck Valley Community
College
Norwalk Community College
Three Rivers Community
College
Tunxis Community College

Delaware

Delaware Technical Community
College
Jack F. Owens Campus
Stanton/Wilmington
Campus
Terry Campus

Florida

College of Central Florida
Florida Career College
Miami
Florida National University
Florida Technical College
Orlando
Gulf Coast State College
Lake-Sumter State College
Northwest Florida State College
Saint Johns River State College
South Florida State College

Georgia

Abraham Baldwin Agricultural
College

Ashworth College
Athens Technical College
Atlanta Metropolitan College
Atlanta Technical College
Bainbridge State College
Coastal Pines Technical College
Darton College
East Georgia State College
Georgia Highlands College
Georgia Northwestern Technical
College
Georgia Piedmont Technical
College
Gordon State College
North Georgia Technical
College
Savannah Technical College
Southern Crescent Technical
College
West Georgia Technical College
Wiregrass Georgia Technical
College

Hawaii

University of Hawaii
Hawaii Community College
Honolulu Community
College
Maui College
Windward Community
College

Idaho

North Idaho College

Illinois

Black Hawk College
Carl Sandburg College
Heartland Community College
Illinois Central College
Illinois Valley Community
College
John Wood Community College
Kankakee Community College
Kaskaskia College
Kishwaukee College
Lake Land College
Lewis and Clark Community
College
Lincoln Land Community
College
McHenry County College
Morton College
Prairie State College
Richland Community College
South Suburban College of
Cook County

Indiana

Harrison College
Indianapolis
Ivy Tech Community College
Bloomington
Columbus
East Central
Kokomo
Lafayette
North Central
Richmond
South Central
Southeast
Southwest
Wabash Valley

Iowa

Hawkeye Community College
Iowa Central Community
College
Iowa Western Community
College
Marshalltown Community
College
North Iowa Area Community
College
Northeast Iowa Community
College
Scott Community College

Western Iowa Tech Community
College

Kansas

Allen County Community
College
Cowley County Community
College
Garden City Community
College
Hutchinson Community College
Kansas City Kansas Community
College
Wichita Area Technical College

Kentucky

Big Sandy Community and
Technical College
Elizabethtown Community and
Technical College
Gateway Community and
Technical College
Hazard Community and
Technical College
Hopkinsville Community
College
Madisonville Community
College
Maysville Community and
Technical College
Owensboro Community and
Technical College
Somerset Community College
Southeast Kentucky Community
and Technical College
West Kentucky Community and
Technical College

Louisiana

Bossier Parish Community
College
Louisiana State University
Eunice
River Parishes Community
College
South Louisiana Community
College
Southern University
Shreveport

Maine

Central Maine Community
College
Eastern Maine Community
College
Kennebec Valley Community
College
Southern Maine Community
College

Maryland

Allegany College of Maryland
Baltimore City Community
College
Carroll Community College
Cecil College
Frederick Community College
Hagerstown Community College
Harford Community College
Wor-Wic Community College

Massachusetts

Cape Cod Community College
Greenfield Community College
Holyoke Community College
Massachusetts Bay Community
College
Massasoit Community College
Mount Wachusett Community
College
North Shore Community
College
Northern Essex Community
College
Quincy College
Quinsigamond Community
College
Roxbury Community College

Springfield Technical
Community College

Michigan

Alpena Community College
Jackson College
Kalamazoo Valley Community
College
Kellogg Community College
Lake Michigan College
Mid Michigan Community
College
Monroe County Community
College
Muskegon Community College
North Central Michigan College
Northwestern Michigan College
St. Clair County Community
College

Minnesota

Alexandria Technical and
Community College
Anoka Technical College
Central Lakes College
Dakota County Technical
College
Hennepin Technical College
Inver Hills Community College
Lake Superior College
Minnesota State Community and
Technical College
Minnesota West Community
and Technical College
North Hennepin Community
College
Northland Community &
Technical College
Ridgewater College
Riverland Community College
Rochester Community and
Technical College
St. Cloud Technical and
Community College
St. Paul College
South Central College

Mississippi

Coahoma Community College
Copiah-Lincoln Community
College
East Central Community
College
East Mississippi Community
College
Itawamba Community College
Jones County Junior College
Meridian Community College
Mississippi Delta Community
College
Northeast Mississippi
Community College

Missouri

Crowder College
East Central College
Jefferson College
Mineral Area College
Moberly Area Community
College
St. Charles Community College
State Fair Community College

Montana

Flathead Valley Community
College

Nebraska

Central Community College
Northeast Community College

Nevada

Western Nevada College

New Hampshire

Great Bay Community College
Manchester Community College
Nashua Community College

NHTI-Concord's Community
College

New Jersey

Atlantic Cape Community
College
Cumberland County College
Mercer County Community
College
Raritan Valley Community
College
Rowan College at Gloucester
Sussex County Community
College

New Mexico

Eastern New Mexico
University: Roswell
New Mexico Junior College
San Juan College
Santa Fe Community College

New York

Adirondack Community College
ASA College
Broome Community College
Cayuga Community College
City University of New York
Hostos Community College
Corning Community College
Dutchess Community College
Finger Lakes Community
College
Fulton-Montgomery Community
College
Genesee Community College
Herkimer County Community
College
Jamestown Community College
Jefferson Community College
Mohawk Valley Community
College
Niagara County Community
College
North Country Community
College
Orange County Community
College
Rockland Community College
Schenectady County
Community College
SUNY
College of Agriculture and
Technology at Cobleskill
College of Technology at
Alfred
College of Technology at
Canton
College of Technology at
Delhi
Technical Career Institutes
Tompkins Cortland Community
College

North Carolina

Alamance Community College
Asheville-Buncombe Technical
Community College
Blue Ridge Community College
Catawba Valley Community
College
Central Carolina Community
College
Cleveland Community College
Coastal Carolina Community
College
Craven Community College
Davidson County Community
College
Edgecombe Community College
Forsyth Technical Community
College
Gaston College
Isothermal Community College
Johnston Community College
Mitchell Community College
Richmond Community College
Robeson Community College

Rowan-Cabarrus Community
College
Sandhills Community College
South Piedmont Community
College
Stanly Community College
Surry Community College
Wayne Community College
Western Piedmont Community
College
Wilkes Community College

North Dakota

Bismarck State College
North Dakota State College of
Science

Ohio

Central Ohio Technical College
Clark State Community College
Eastern Gateway Community
College
Hocking College
James A. Rhodes State College
Kent State University
Ashtabula
Geauga
Stark
Trumbull
Miami University
Hamilton
Middletown
Southern State Community
College
Terra State Community College
University of Akron: Wayne
College
University of Cincinnati
Blue Ash College
Clermont College
University of Northwestern
Ohio
Zane State College

Oklahoma

Carl Albert State College
Connors State College
Murray State College
Northeastern Oklahoma
Agricultural and Mechanical
College
Oklahoma State University
Institute of Technology:
Okmulgee
Oklahoma City
Redlands Community College
Rose State College

Oregon

Central Oregon Community
College
Clackamas Community College
Linn-Benton Community
College
Rogue Community College
Southwestern Oregon
Community College

Pennsylvania

Butler County Community
College
Community College of Beaver
County
Lehigh Carbon Community
College
Luzerne County Community
College
Reading Area Community
College
Westmoreland County
Community College

Puerto Rico

ICPR Junior College
Ponce Paramedical College

South Carolina

Aiken Technical College
Florence-Darlington Technical
College
Horry-Georgetown Technical
College
Orangeburg-Calhoun Technical
College
Piedmont Technical College
Spartanburg Community College
Technical College of the
Lowcountry
Tri-County Technical College
York Technical College

Tennessee

Cleveland State Community
College
Columbia State Community
College
Jackson State Community
College
Motlow State Community
College
Northeast State Community
College
Roane State Community College
Volunteer State Community
College
Walters State Community
College

Texas

Alvin Community College
Angelina College
Brazosport College
Cedar Valley College
Cisco College
Coastal Bend College
College of the Mainland
Grayson College
Hill College
Howard College
Kilgore College
Lamar Institute of Technology
Lamar State College at Orange
Midland College
Mountain View College
Northeast Texas Community
College
Odessa College
Panola College
Paris Junior College
Ranger College
Southwest Texas Junior College
Temple College
Texarkana College
Texas State Technical College
Harlingen
Trinity Valley Community
College
Vernon College
Victoria College
Weatherford College
Western Texas College
Wharton County Junior College

Utah

LDS Business College
Snow College

Vermont

Community College of Vermont

Virginia

Blue Ridge Community College
Central Virginia Community
College
Danville Community College
Germanna Community College
John Tyler Community College
Lord Fairfax Community
College
Mountain Empire Community
College
New River Community College
Patrick Henry Community
College

Piedmont Virginia Community
College
Rappahannock Community
College
Southside Virginia Community
College
Southwest Virginia Community
College
Virginia Highlands Community
College
Virginia Western Community
College
Wytheville Community College

Washington

Bates Technical College
Bellingham Technical College
Cascadia College
Centralia College
Clover Park Technical College
Columbia Basin College
Everett Community College
Highline College
North Seattle College
Renton Technical College
Shoreline Community College
Skagit Valley College
South Puget Sound Community
College
Spokane Community College
Tacoma Community College
Walla Walla Community
College
Wenatchee Valley College
Whatcom Community College
Yakima Valley Community
College

West Virginia

Blue Ridge Community and
Technical College
New River Community and
Technical College
Pierpont Community and
Technical College
West Virginia University at
Parkersburg

Wisconsin

Blackhawk Technical College
Bryant & Stratton College
Milwaukee
Chippewa Valley Technical
College
Fox Valley Technical College
Lakeshore Technical College
Northcentral Technical College
University of Wisconsin
Waukesha
Waukesha County Technical
College
Western Technical College
Wisconsin Indianhead Technical
College

Wyoming

Casper College
Laramie County Community
College

Guam

Guam Community College

Large (7,500-14,499)

Four-year

Alabama

Troy University
University of Alabama
Birmingham
University of South Alabama

Alaska

University of Alaska
Anchorage

Arizona

Argosy University
Online

Arkansas

Arkansas State University
Arkansas Tech University
University of Arkansas
Little Rock
University of Central Arkansas

California

Academy of Art University
California State University
Bakersfield
Dominguez Hills
East Bay
San Marcos
Stanislaus
Humboldt State University
National University
Sonoma State University

Colorado

Colorado Mesa University
University of Colorado
Colorado Springs
Denver
University of Northern Colorado

Connecticut

Central Connecticut State
University
Southern Connecticut State
University

Delaware

Wilmington University

District of Columbia

George Washington University

Florida

Embry-Riddle Aeronautical
University
Worldwide Campus
Florida Agricultural and
Mechanical University
Florida Gulf Coast University
University of Miami
University of North Florida
University of West Florida

Georgia

Georgia Gwinnett College
Georgia Institute of Technology
Savannah College of Art and
Design
University of West Georgia
Valdosta State University

Hawaii

University of Hawaii
Manoa

Idaho

Idaho State University
University of Idaho

Illinois

Chamberlain College of Nursing
Addison
Columbia College Chicago
DeVry University
Online
Loyola University Chicago
Northeastern Illinois University
Northern Illinois University
Northwestern University
Southern Illinois University
Carbondale
Southern Illinois University
Edwardsville
Western Illinois University

Indiana

Indiana State University
Indiana University
Purdue University Fort
Wayne

Purdue University
Calumet
University of Notre Dame
University of Southern Indiana

Iowa

University of Northern Iowa

Kansas

Fort Hays State University
Grantham University
Wichita State University

Kentucky

Eastern Kentucky University
Murray State University
Northern Kentucky University
University of Louisville

Louisiana

Louisiana Tech University
Southeastern Louisiana
University
Tulane University

Maine

University of Maine

Maryland

Salisbury University
University of Maryland
Baltimore County

Massachusetts

Boston College
Bridgewater State University
Salem State University
University of Massachusetts
Boston
Lowell

Michigan

Ferris State University
Northern Michigan University
Saginaw Valley State University

Minnesota

Capella University
Minnesota State University
Mankato
Saint Cloud State University
University of Minnesota
Duluth
Walden University
Winona State University

Mississippi

University of Southern
Mississippi

Missouri

Lindenwood University
Saint Louis University
Southeast Missouri State
University
University of Central Missouri
University of Missouri
Kansas City
St. Louis

Montana

Montana State University
University of Montana

Nebraska

University of Nebraska
Omaha

New Hampshire

University of New Hampshire

New Jersey

Kean University
Rowan University
Stockton University
William Paterson University of
New Jersey

New Mexico

New Mexico State University

New York

City University of New York
Baruch College
Brooklyn College
City College
College of Staten Island
John Jay College of
Criminal Justice
Lehman College
Cornell University
Fashion Institute of Technology
Fordham University
Rochester Institute of
Technology
St. John's University
SUNY
College at Buffalo
Empire State College
Farmingdale State College
University at Albany
University at Binghamton
Syracuse University

North Carolina

North Carolina Agricultural and
Technical State University
University of North Carolina
Wilmington
Western Carolina University

North Dakota

North Dakota State University
University of North Dakota

Ohio

Bowling Green State University
Cleveland State University
University of Dayton
University of Toledo
Wright State University
Youngstown State University

Oklahoma

University of Central Oklahoma

Pennsylvania

Bloomsburg University of
Pennsylvania
Indiana University of
Pennsylvania
Kutztown University of
Pennsylvania
University of Pennsylvania
West Chester University of
Pennsylvania

Puerto Rico

Turabo University
Universidad del Este
Universidad Metropolitana
University of Puerto Rico
Mayaguez
Rio Piedras

Rhode Island

Johnson & Wales University
Providence
University of Rhode Island

South Carolina

Coastal Carolina University
College of Charleston

South Dakota

South Dakota State University
University of South Dakota

Tennessee

Austin Peay State University
East Tennessee State University
Tennessee Technological
University
University of Tennessee
Chattanooga

Texas

Baylor University
Lamar University
Stephen F. Austin State
University
Tarleton State University
Texas A&M University
Commerce
Corpus Christi
Texas Christian University
Texas Woman's University
University of Houston
Downtown

Vermont

University of Vermont

Virginia

ECPI University
Liberty University
Radford University

Washington

Central Washington University
Eastern Washington University
Western Washington University

West Virginia

Marshall University

Wisconsin

Marquette University
University of Wisconsin
Eau Claire
La Crosse
Oshkosh
Platteville
Stevens Point
Stout
Whitewater

Wyoming

University of Wyoming

Lebanon

Lebanese American University

New Zealand

University of Canterbury

United Kingdom

King's College London
University of Sussex

Two-year

Alabama

Calhoun Community College
Jefferson State Community
College

Arizona

Chandler-Gilbert Community
College
Estrella Mountain Community
College
Paradise Valley Community
College
Phoenix College
Scottsdale Community College
Yavapai College

Arkansas

Northwest Arkansas Community
College
Pulaski Technical College

California

Allan Hancock College
Antelope Valley College
Butte College
Cabrillo College
Chabot College
Coastline Community College
College of San Mateo
College of the Canyons
College of the Desert
College of the Sequoias
Cosumnes River College
Cuesta College

Cuyamaca College
Cypress College
Evergreen Valley College
Folsom Lake College
Foothill College
Fullerton College
Golden West College
Hartnell College
Imperial Valley College
Irvine Valley College
Laney College
Las Positas College
Los Angeles Harbor College
Los Angeles Mission College
Los Angeles Southwest College
Los Angeles Trade and
Technical College
Los Medanos College
Merced College
MiraCosta College
Mission College
Monterey Peninsula College
Moorpark College
Moreno Valley College
Norco College
Reedley College
Saddleback College
San Bernardino Valley College
San Deigo Miramar College
San Diego Miramar College
San Joaquin Delta College
San Jose City College
Shasta College
Skyline College
Solano Community College
Ventura College
West Los Angeles College
West Valley College

Colorado

Arapahoe Community College
Community College of Denver
Pikes Peak Community College
Red Rocks Community College

Connecticut

Gateway Community College

Florida

Daytona State College
Florida SouthWestern State
College
Indian River State College
Pasco-Hernando State College
Pensacola State College
Polk State College
State College of Florida,
Manatee-Sarasota
Tallahassee Community College

Georgia

Central Georgia Technical
College
Georgia Military College

Hawaii

University of Hawaii
Kapiolani Community
College

Idaho

College of Southern Idaho
College of Western Idaho

Illinois

Elgin Community College
Harper College
Joliet Junior College
Moraine Valley Community
College
Oakton Community College
Rock Valley College
Southwestern Illinois College
Triton College
Waubonsee Community College

Indiana

Ivy Tech Community College
Northeast
Northwest
Vincennes University

Iowa

Des Moines Area Community
College
Kirkwood Community College

Kansas

Butler Community College

Kentucky

Bluegrass Community and
Technical College
Jefferson Community and
Technical College

Louisiana

Baton Rouge Community
College

Maryland

Anne Arundel Community
College
College of Southern Maryland
Howard Community College
Prince George's Community
College

Massachusetts

Bristol Community College
Bunker Hill Community College
Middlesex Community College

Michigan

Delta College
Grand Rapids Community
College
Henry Ford Community College
Lansing Community College
Mott Community College
Schoolcraft College
Washtenaw Community College
Wayne County Community
College

Minnesota

Anoka-Ramsey Community
College
Century College
Minneapolis Community and
Technical College
Normandale Community
College

Mississippi

Hinds Community College
Mississippi Gulf Coast
Community College
Northwest Mississippi
Community College

Missouri

Ozarks Technical Community
College
St. Louis Community College

Nebraska

Metropolitan Community
College
Southeast Community College

Nevada

Truckee Meadows Community
College

New Jersey

Bergen Community College
Brookdale Community College
Camden County College
County College of Morris
Essex County College
Hudson County Community
College
Middlesex County College
Ocean County College

Passaic County Community College
Rowan College at Burlington County
Union County College

New Mexico
Dona Ana Community College of New Mexico State University

New York
City University of New York
  Bronx Community College
  Queensborough Community College
Erie Community College
Hudson Valley Community College
Monroe Community College
Onondaga Community College
Westchester Community College

North Carolina
Cape Fear Community College
Fayetteville Technical Community College
Guilford Technical Community College
Pitt Community College

Ohio
Cincinnati State Technical and Community College
Columbus State Community College
Lakeland Community College
Lorain County Community College
Owens Community College
Stark State College

Oklahoma
Oklahoma City Community College
Tulsa Community College

Oregon
Chemeketa Community College
Lane Community College
Mt. Hood Community College

Pennsylvania
Bucks County Community College
Delaware County Community College
Harrisburg Area Community College
Montgomery County Community College
Northampton Community College

South Carolina
Greenville Technical College
Midlands Technical College

Tennessee
Chattanooga State Community College
Nashville State Community College
Pellissippi State Community College
Southwest Tennessee Community College

Texas
Amarillo College
Brookhaven College
Central Texas College
Del Mar College
Eastfield College
El Centro College
Laredo Community College
McLennan Community College
Navarro College
North Central Texas College
North Lake College
Northwest Vista College
Palo Alto College
Richland College
St. Philip's College
South Plains College
Texas State Technical College
Tyler Junior College

Virginia
J. Sargeant Reynolds Community College
Thomas Nelson Community College

Washington
Bellevue College
Clark College
Edmonds Community College
Green River Community College
Olympic College
Pierce College
Seattle Central College
South Seattle College
Spokane Falls Community College

Wisconsin
Gateway Technical College
Milwaukee Area Technical College

Very large (15,000 or more)

Four-year

Alabama
Auburn University
Columbia Southern University
University of Alabama

Arizona
Arizona State University
Grand Canyon University
Northern Arizona University
University of Arizona
University of Phoenix Phoenix-Hohokam

Arkansas
University of Arkansas

California
Ashford University
California Polytechnic State University: San Luis Obispo
California State Polytechnic University: Pomona
California State University
  Chico
  Fresno
  Fullerton
  Long Beach
  Los Angeles
  Northridge
  Sacramento
  San Bernardino
San Diego State University
San Francisco State University
San Jose State University
University of California
  Berkeley
  Davis
  Irvine
  Los Angeles
  Riverside
  San Diego
  Santa Barbara
  Santa Cruz
University of Phoenix Southern California
University of Southern California

Colorado
Colorado State University
Metropolitan State University of Denver
University of Colorado Boulder

Connecticut
University of Connecticut

Delaware
University of Delaware

Florida
Florida Atlantic University
Florida International University
Florida State University
Full Sail University
Keiser University
University of Central Florida
University of Florida
University of South Florida

Georgia
Georgia Southern University
Georgia State University
Kennesaw State University
University of Georgia
University of North Georgia

Idaho
Boise State University
Brigham Young University-Idaho

Illinois
DePaul University
Illinois State University
University of Illinois
  Chicago
  Urbana-Champaign

Indiana
Ball State University
Indiana University
  Bloomington
  Purdue University Indianapolis
Purdue University

Iowa
Iowa State University
Kaplan University Davenport
University of Iowa

Kansas
Kansas State University
University of Kansas

Kentucky
University of Kentucky
Western Kentucky University

Louisiana
Louisiana State University and Agricultural and Mechanical College
University of Louisiana at Lafayette

Maryland
Towson University
University of Maryland
  College Park
  University College

Massachusetts
Boston University
Northeastern University
University of Massachusetts Amherst

Michigan
Central Michigan University
Eastern Michigan University
Grand Valley State University
Michigan State University
Oakland University
University of Michigan

Wayne State University
Western Michigan University

Minnesota
University of Minnesota Twin Cities

Mississippi
Mississippi State University
University of Mississippi

Missouri
Missouri State University
Park University
University of Missouri Columbia

Nebraska
University of Nebraska Lincoln

Nevada
University of Nevada
  Las Vegas
  Reno

New Jersey
Montclair State University
Rutgers, The State University of New Jersey
  New Brunswick/Piscataway Campus
Thomas Edison State University

New Mexico
University of New Mexico

New York
City University of New York
  Hunter College
  New York City College of Technology
  Queens College
Excelsior College
New York University
SUNY
  University at Buffalo
  University at Stony Brook

North Carolina
Appalachian State University
East Carolina University
North Carolina State University
University of North Carolina
  Chapel Hill
  Charlotte
  Greensboro

Ohio
Kent State University
Miami University Oxford
Ohio State University Columbus Campus
Ohio University
University of Akron
University of Cincinnati

Oklahoma
Oklahoma State University
University of Oklahoma

Oregon
Oregon State University
Portland State University
University of Oregon

Pennsylvania
Drexel University
Penn State University Park
Temple University
University of Pittsburgh

South Carolina
Clemson University
University of South Carolina Columbia

Tennessee
Middle Tennessee State University
University of Memphis
University of Tennessee Knoxville

Texas
Sam Houston State University
Texas A&M University
Texas State University
Texas Tech University
University of Houston
University of North Texas
University of Texas
  Arlington
  Austin
  Dallas
  El Paso
  Pan American
  San Antonio
University Of Texas Rio Grande Valley

Utah
Brigham Young University
University of Utah
Utah State University
Utah Valley University
Weber State University
Western Governors University

Virginia
George Mason University
James Madison University
Old Dominion University
University of Virginia
Virginia Commonwealth University
Virginia Polytechnic Institute and State University

Washington
University of Washington
Washington State University

West Virginia
American Public University System
West Virginia University

Wisconsin
University of Wisconsin Madison Milwaukee

Canada
McGill University
Memorial University of Newfoundland
Simon Fraser University
University of Alberta
University of British Columbia
University of Manitoba
University of Toronto
University of Waterloo

Mexico
Universidad Autonoma de Coahuila

New Zealand
University of Auckland

United Kingdom
University of Greenwich

Two-year

Alabama
Community College of the Air Force

Arizona
Mesa Community College
Penn Foster College
Pima Community College
Rio Salado College

Tables and Indexes

California

American River College
Bakersfield College
Cerritos College
Chaffey College
Citrus College
City College of San Francisco
De Anza College
Diablo Valley College
East Los Angeles College
Fresno City College
Glendale Community College
Grossmont College
Long Beach City College
Los Angeles City College
Los Angeles Pierce College
Los Angeles Valley College
Modesto Junior College
Mount San Antonio College
Mount San Jacinto College
Orange Coast College
Palomar College
Pasadena City College
Rio Hondo College
Riverside City College
Sacramento City College
San Diego City College
San Diego Mesa College
Santa Ana College
Santa Barbara City College
Santa Monica College
Santa Rosa Junior College
Santiago Canyon College
Sierra College
Southwestern College

Colorado

Front Range Community
College

Florida

Broward College
Eastern Florida State College
Florida State College at
Jacksonville
Hillsborough Community
College
Miami Dade College
Palm Beach State College
St. Petersburg College
Santa Fe College
Seminole State College of
Florida
Southern Technical College
Valencia College

Georgia

Georgia Perimeter College

Illinois

College of DuPage
College of Lake County

Indiana

Ivy Tech Community College
Central Indiana

Kansas

Barton County Community
College
Johnson County Community
College

Louisiana

Delgado Community College

Maryland

Community College of
Baltimore County
Montgomery College

Michigan

Macomb Community College
Oakland Community College

Missouri

Metropolitan Community
College - Kansas City

Nevada

College of Southern Nevada

New Mexico

Central New Mexico
Community College

New York

City University of New York
Borough of Manhattan
Community College
Kingsborough Community
College
LaGuardia Community
College
Nassau Community College
Suffolk County Community
College

North Carolina

Central Piedmont Community
College
Wake Technical Community
College

Ohio

Cuyahoga Community College
Sinclair Community College

Oregon

Portland Community College

Pennsylvania

Community College of
Allegheny County
Community College of
Philadelphia

Rhode Island

Community College of Rhode
Island

South Carolina

Trident Technical College

Texas

Austin Community College
Blinn College
Collin County Community
College District
El Paso Community College
Houston Community College
System
Lone Star College System
San Antonio College
San Jacinto College
South Texas College
Tarrant County College

Utah

Salt Lake Community College

Virginia

Northern Virginia Community
College
Tidewater Community College

Wisconsin

Madison Area Technical
College

Admission selectivity

Admit under 50% of applicants

Four-year

Alabama
Alabama State University
Oakwood University
Spring Hill College

Alaska
Alaska Pacific University

Arkansas
University of Arkansas
Pine Bluff

California
California Institute of Technology
California Institute of the Arts
California Polytechnic State University: San Luis Obispo
California State Polytechnic University: Pomona
California State University
Fullerton
Long Beach
Monterey Bay
Northridge
Chapman University
Claremont McKenna College
Harvey Mudd College
Holy Names University
Hope International University
La Sierra University
Laguna College of Art and Design
Menlo College
Occidental College
Pacific Union College
Pepperdine University
Pitzer College
San Diego State University
San Francisco Conservatory of Music
Santa Clara University
Scripps College
Soka University of America
Stanford University
University of California
Berkeley
Davis
Irvine
Los Angeles
Santa Barbara
University of La Verne
University of Southern California

Colorado
Colorado College
Colorado School of Mines
United States Air Force Academy

Connecticut
Connecticut College
Post University
Trinity College
United States Coast Guard Academy
Wesleyan University
Yale University

District of Columbia
American University
George Washington University
Georgetown University

Howard University
University of the District of Columbia

Florida
Ave Maria University
Florida International University
Florida Southern College
Saint Thomas University
Southeastern University
University of Central Florida
University of Florida
University of Miami
University of South Florida
University of South Florida
Saint Petersburg
Sarasota-Manatee
University of West Florida

Georgia
Clayton State University
Emmanuel College
Emory University
Georgia Institute of Technology
Paine College
Point University
Savannah State University
Spelman College
Toccoa Falls College
Wesleyan College

Illinois
Augustana College
North Park University
Northwestern University
Robert Morris University: Chicago
University of Chicago

Indiana
Calumet College of St. Joseph
University of Notre Dame

Iowa
Allen College
Emmaus Bible College
Graceland University
Grinnell College
Maharishi University of Management

Kansas
McPherson College
Sterling College
University of St. Mary

Kentucky
Alice Lloyd College
Berea College
Brescia University
Kentucky State University

Louisiana
Tulane University

Maine
Bates College
Bowdoin College
Colby College

Maryland
Johns Hopkins University
Johns Hopkins University: Peabody Conservatory of Music
Maryland Institute College of Art
United States Naval Academy
University of Maryland
College Park
Eastern Shore

Massachusetts
Amherst College
Babson College
Bentley University
Berklee College of Music
Boston College
Boston Conservatory
Boston University

Brandeis University
College of the Holy Cross
Emerson College
Franklin W. Olin College of Engineering
Harvard College
Massachusetts Institute of Technology
New England Conservatory of Music
Northeastern University
Smith College
Tufts University
Wellesley College
Williams College
Worcester Polytechnic Institute

Michigan
Andrews University
University of Michigan

Minnesota
Carleton College
Macalester College
McNally Smith College of Music
St. Olaf College
University of Minnesota
Rochester
Twin Cities

Mississippi
Blue Mountain College
Tougaloo College

Missouri
College of the Ozarks
Missouri Valley College
Park University
St. Louis Christian College
Washington University in St. Louis

New Hampshire
Dartmouth College
Northeast Catholic College

New Jersey
The College of New Jersey
Princeton University
Stevens Institute of Technology

New Mexico
Eastern New Mexico University
New Mexico Institute of Mining and Technology

New York
Bard College
Barnard College
City University of New York
Baruch College
Brooklyn College
City College
Hunter College
Lehman College
Queens College
Colgate University
College of New Rochelle
Columbia University
School of General Studies
Cooper Union for the Advancement of Science and Art
Cornell University
Daemen College
Eastman School of Music of the University of Rochester
Fashion Institute of Technology
Fordham University
Hamilton College
Juilliard School
The King's College
Marist College
New York School of Interior Design
Rensselaer Polytechnic Institute
St. Lawrence University
Skidmore College

SUNY
College at New Paltz
College at Oneonta
College at Plattsburgh
College at Purchase
Farmingdale State College
University at Binghamton
University at Stony Brook
Syracuse University
Touro College
Union College
United States Military Academy
University of Rochester
Vassar College
Webb Institute

North Carolina
Barton College
Catawba College
Davidson College
Duke University
Johnson C. Smith University
Mid-Atlantic Christian University
Pfeiffer University
University of Mount Olive
University of North Carolina
Chapel Hill
School of the Arts
Wake Forest University

Ohio
Case Western Reserve University
Central State University
Columbus College of Art and Design
Denison University
Kenyon College
Oberlin College
Ohio State University
Columbus Campus
Wilberforce University

Oklahoma
Oral Roberts University
Southern Nazarene University
University of Tulsa

Oregon
Corban University
Reed College

Pennsylvania
Albright College
Bryn Mawr College
Bucknell University
Carnegie Mellon University
Cheyney University of Pennsylvania
Dickinson College
Franklin & Marshall College
Gettysburg College
Haverford College
Lafayette College
Lehigh University
Muhlenberg College
Pennsylvania College of Art and Design
Swarthmore College
University of Pennsylvania
Villanova University
Washington & Jefferson College
York College of Pennsylvania

Puerto Rico
Inter American University of Puerto Rico
Guayama Campus
Metropolitan Campus
University of Puerto Rico
Aguadilla
Carolina Regional College
Humacao
Rio Piedras
Utuado

Rhode Island
Brown University
Rhode Island School of Design

South Carolina
Coker College
Columbia International University

Tennessee
Bryan College
Dayton
Christian Brothers University
Memphis College of Art
Rhodes College
Sewanee: The University of the South
Vanderbilt University
Watkins College of Art, Design & Film

Texas
Abilene Christian University
Baylor University
Dallas Baptist University
Houston Baptist University
Huston-Tillotson University
LeTourneau University
Rice University
Southern Methodist University
Southwestern Adventist University
Southwestern University
Texas A&M International University
Texas A&M University Commerce
Texas Christian University
Texas Wesleyan University
Trinity University
University of Texas
Austin

Vermont
Middlebury College

Virginia
Bridgewater College
College of William and Mary
Liberty University
University of Richmond
University of Virginia
Virginia Union University
Washington and Lee University

Washington
DigiPen Institute of Technology
Whitman College

West Virginia
Ohio Valley University

Wisconsin
University of Wisconsin
Madison

Egypt
American University in Cairo

Germany
University of Karlsruhe

Mexico
Universidad Autonoma de Coahuila

Pakistan
Forman Christian College

Spain
Saint Louis University: Madrid

Turkey
Koc University

United Kingdom
King's College London

Two-year

California
Fashion Institute of Design and Merchandising
Los Angeles
San Francisco

Georgia

East Georgia State College
Oxford College of Emory
    University

New York

Maria College

Pennsylvania

Valley Forge Military College

Admit 50 to 75% of applicants

Four-year

Alabama

Birmingham-Southern College
Faulkner University
Huntingdon College
Jacksonville State University
Judson College
Tuskegee University
University of Alabama
University of Mobile
University of Montevallo
University of North Alabama
University of West Alabama

Arizona

Arizona Christian University
Prescott College

Arkansas

Arkansas State University
Ecclesia College
Henderson State University
John Brown University
Lyon College
Ouachita Baptist University
Southern Arkansas University
University of Arkansas
Williams Baptist College

California

Biola University
Brandman University
California Baptist University
California Lutheran University
California State University
    Chico
    Dominguez Hills
    East Bay
    Fresno
    Los Angeles
    Sacramento
    San Bernardino
    San Marcos
    Stanislaus
Cogswell Polytechnical College
Concordia University Irvine
Loyola Marymount University
Marymount California
    University
Point Loma Nazarene University
San Diego Christian College
San Francisco Art Institute
San Francisco State University
San Jose State University
Simpson University
Southern California Institute of
    Architecture
University of California
    Merced
    Riverside
    Santa Cruz
University of Redlands
University of San Diego
University of San Francisco
University of the Pacific
Whittier College
Woodbury University
Yeshiva Ohr Elchonon Chabad/
    West Coast Talmudical
    Seminary

Colorado

Regis University
University of Colorado
    Denver
University of Denver

Connecticut

Central Connecticut State
    University
Eastern Connecticut State
    University
Fairfield University
Quinnipiac University
Sacred Heart University
Southern Connecticut State
    University
University of Bridgeport
University of Connecticut
University of Hartford
Western Connecticut State
    University

Delaware

University of Delaware

District of Columbia

Gallaudet University

Florida

Adventist University of Health
    Sciences
Baptist College of Florida
Barry University
Beacon College
Bethune-Cookman University
Eckerd College
Embry-Riddle Aeronautical
    University
        Worldwide Campus
Flagler College
Florida Agricultural and
    Mechanical University
Florida Atlantic University
Florida Gulf Coast University
Florida Institute of Technology
Florida State University
Jacksonville University
Keiser University
New College of Florida
Nova Southeastern University
Rollins College
Saint Leo University
Stetson University
University of North Florida
University of Tampa

Georgia

Agnes Scott College
Albany State University
Armstrong State University
Augusta University
Berry College
Brenau University
Clark Atlanta University
College of Coastal Georgia
Columbus State University
Georgia Southern University
Georgia Southwestern State
    University
Georgia State University
Kennesaw State University
LaGrange College
Life University
Mercer University
Piedmont College
Savannah College of Art and
    Design
South Georgia State College
University of Georgia
University of North Georgia
University of West Georgia
Valdosta State University

Hawaii

University of Hawaii
    Hilo
    West Oahu

Idaho

Northwest Nazarene University
University of Idaho

Illinois

Blackburn College
Blessing-Rieman College of
    Nursing
Bradley University
DePaul University
Dominican University
Eastern Illinois University
Elmhurst College
Greenville College
Illinois College
Illinois Institute of Technology
Illinois Wesleyan University
Knox College
Lake Forest College
Lewis University
Lincoln Christian University
Loyola University Chicago
MacMurray College
McKendree University
Millikin University
Monmouth College
North Central College
Northeastern Illinois University
Northern Illinois University
Quincy University
School of the Art Institute of
    Chicago
Trinity College of Nursing &
    Health Sciences
University of Illinois
    Springfield
    Urbana-Champaign
University of St. Francis
Western Illinois University
Wheaton College

Indiana

Anderson University
Ball State University
Bethel College
Butler University
DePauw University
Earlham College
Franklin College
Goshen College
Hanover College
Indiana Institute of Technology
Indiana State University
Indiana University
    East
    Kokomo
    Purdue University
        Indianapolis
Manchester University
Marian University
Oakland City University
Purdue University
Purdue University
    Calumet
Rose-Hulman Institute of
    Technology
Saint Joseph's College
St. Mary-of-the-Woods College
University of Evansville
University of Indianapolis
University of Southern Indiana
Wabash College

Iowa

Briar Cliff University
Buena Vista University
Central College
Clarke University
Coe College
Cornell College
Dordt College
Drake University
Faith Baptist Bible College and
    Theological Seminary
Luther College
Morningside College
Mount Mercy University

Northwestern College
St. Ambrose University
Upper Iowa University
Waldorf University
Wartburg College
William Penn University

Kansas

Barclay College
Bethel College
Central Christian College of
    Kansas
Haskell Indian Nations
    University
Kansas Wesleyan University
Newman University
Tabor College

Kentucky

Asbury University
Centre College
Eastern Kentucky University
Georgetown College
Kentucky Mountain Bible
    College
Spalding University
Union College
University of Louisville
University of the Cumberlands

Louisiana

Centenary College of Louisiana
Louisiana College
Northwestern State University
University of Louisiana at
    Lafayette
University of New Orleans
Xavier University of Louisiana

Maryland

Bowie State University
Frostburg State University
Loyola University Maryland
Morgan State University
Mount St. Mary's University
Salisbury University
Stevenson University
Towson University
University of Baltimore
University of Maryland
    Baltimore County
Washington College

Massachusetts

American International College
Becker College
Clark University
Eastern Nazarene College
Elms College
Emmanuel College
Endicott College
Fisher College
Fitchburg State University
Framingham State University
Hampshire College
Massachusetts College of Art
    and Design
Massachusetts College of
    Liberal Arts
Massachusetts Maritime
    Academy
Mount Holyoke College
Pine Manor College
Simmons College
University of Massachusetts
    Amherst
    Boston
    Lowell
Wentworth Institute of
    Technology
Wheaton College
Worcester State University

Michigan

Adrian College
Alma College
Aquinas College
Calvin College
Central Michigan University

Eastern Michigan University
Grace Bible College
Hillsdale College
Hope College
Kalamazoo College
Kettering University
Kuyper College
Lawrence Technological
    University
Madonna University
Marygrove College
Michigan State University
Northwood University
    Michigan
Oakland University
Olivet College
Spring Arbor University
University of Detroit Mercy
University of Michigan
    Dearborn
    Flint

Minnesota

Augsburg College
College of St. Benedict
College of St. Scholastica
Concordia University St. Paul
Gustavus Adolphus College
Hamline University
Minneapolis College of Art and
    Design
St. Catherine University
St. John's University
Southwest Minnesota State
    University
University of Minnesota
    Morris
Winona State University

Mississippi

Belhaven University
Jackson State University
Millsaps College
Mississippi State University
University of Southern
    Mississippi

Missouri

Avila University
Central Methodist University
Columbia College
Culver-Stockton College
Drury University
Evangel University
Hannibal-LaGrange University
Kansas City Art Institute
Lindenwood University
Maryville University of Saint
    Louis
Missouri Baptist University
Northwest Missouri State
    University
Rockhurst University
Saint Louis University
Stephens College
University of Missouri
    Kansas City
Webster University
Westminster College
William Jewell College

Montana

Carroll College
Rocky Mountain College

Nebraska

College of Saint Mary
Creighton University
Union College
York College

Nevada

Nevada State College

New Hampshire

Colby-Sawyer College
Daniel Webster College
New Hampshire Institute of Art
Plymouth State University

Rivier University
Saint Anselm College

New Jersey

Bloomfield College
Caldwell University
College of St. Elizabeth
Drew University
Kean University
Montclair State University
New Jersey Institute of
Technology
Ramapo College of New Jersey
Rider University
Rowan University
Rutgers, The State University of
New Jersey
Camden Campus
New Brunswick/Piscataway
Campus
Newark Campus
Saint Peter's University
Stockton University
William Paterson University of
New Jersey

New Mexico

New Mexico State University
University of New Mexico

New York

Adelphi University
Albany College of Pharmacy
and Health Sciences
Alfred University
City University of New York
John Jay College of
Criminal Justice
Clarkson University
D'Youville College
Dominican College of Blauvelt
Dowling College
Eugene Lang College The New
School for Liberal Arts
Five Towns College
Hobart and William Smith
Colleges
Hofstra University
Ithaca College
Jewish Theological Seminary of
America
Le Moyne College
Manhattan College
Manhattanville College
Mannes College The New
School for Music
Medaille College: Rochester
Mercy College
Metropolitan College of New
York
New York Institute of
Technology
Niagara University
Parsons The New School for
Design
Pratt Institute
Rochester Institute of
Technology
The Sage Colleges
Saint Bonaventure University
St. John Fisher College
St. John's University
St. Joseph's College New York:
Suffolk Campus
St. Joseph's College, New York
Sarah Lawrence College
School of Visual Arts
Siena College

SUNY
College at Brockport
College at Buffalo
College at Cortland
College at Fredonia
College at Geneseo
College at Old Westbury
College at Oswego
College at Potsdam
College of Agriculture and
Technology at Morrisville
College of Environmental
Science and Forestry
Maritime College
University at Albany
University at Buffalo
SUNY Polytechnic Institute
Vaughn College of Aeronautics
and Technology
Wagner College
Wells College

North Carolina

Appalachian State University
Belmont Abbey College
Chowan University
East Carolina University
Elon University
Fayetteville State University
Guilford College
High Point University
Johnson and Wales University
Charlotte
Lees-McRae College
Livingstone College
Mars Hill University
Meredith College
Montreat College
North Carolina Agricultural and
Technical State University
North Carolina Central
University
North Carolina State University
North Carolina Wesleyan
College
Saint Augustine's University
Shaw University
University of North Carolina
Charlotte
Greensboro
Pembroke
Wilmington
William Peace University
Wingate University
Winston-Salem State University

North Dakota

Minot State University
University of Jamestown

Ohio

Baldwin Wallace University
Bluffton University
Capital University
Cedarville University
Cleveland Institute of Art
College of Wooster
Defiance College
Hiram College
Lake Erie College
Malone University
Marietta College
Mercy College of Ohio
Miami University
Oxford
Muskingum University
Ohio Christian University
Ohio Northern University
Ohio University
Ohio Wesleyan University
Otterbein University
University of Dayton
Xavier University
Youngstown State University

Oklahoma

Hillsdale Free Will Baptist
College

Langston University
Northwestern Oklahoma State
University
Oklahoma Christian University
Oklahoma City University
Oklahoma Wesleyan University
St. Gregory's University
Southeastern Oklahoma State
University
University of Central Oklahoma

Oregon

Concordia University
Lewis & Clark College
Multnomah University
Northwest Christian University
University of Oregon
University of Portland
Warner Pacific College

Pennsylvania

Allegheny College
Alvernia University
Cabrini College
Cedar Crest College
Delaware Valley University
Drexel University
Eastern University
Elizabethtown College
Geneva College
Holy Family University
King's College
La Salle University
Lebanon Valley College
Lycoming College
Marywood University
Millersville University of
Pennsylvania
Misericordia University
Moore College of Art and
Design
Moravian College
Penn State
Schuylkill
Shenango
University Park
Pennsylvania College of Health
Sciences
Philadelphia University
Point Park University
Rosemont College
St. Francis University
St. Vincent College
Slippery Rock University of
Pennsylvania
Temple University
Thiel College
University of Pittsburgh
University of Pittsburgh
Bradford
Greensburg
University of Scranton
University of the Arts
University of the Sciences
West Chester University of
Pennsylvania
Widener University

Puerto Rico

Bayamon Central University
Conservatory of Music of
Puerto Rico
Inter American University of
Puerto Rico
Aguadilla Campus
Bayamon Campus
Ponce Campus
San German Campus
Turabo University
Universidad Metropolitana
University College of San Juan
University of Puerto Rico
Ponce

Rhode Island

Bryant University
Providence College
Rhode Island College

Salve Regina University
University of Rhode Island

South Carolina

Anderson University
Charleston Southern University
Clemson University
Coastal Carolina University
Converse College
Francis Marion University
Furman University
Limestone College
Newberry College
North Greenville University
Presbyterian College
University of South Carolina
Aiken
Beaufort
Columbia
Winthrop University
Wofford College

South Dakota

Augusta University
Augustana University
Mount Marty College

Tennessee

Carson-Newman University
Lane College
Lipscomb University
Maryville College
Middle Tennessee State
University
Milligan College
Southern Adventist University
Tennessee State University
Tennessee Wesleyan College
Trevecca Nazarene University
Tusculum College
University of Tennessee
Martin

Texas

Austin College
East Texas Baptist University
Hardin-Simmons University
McMurry University
Our Lady of the Lake
University of San Antonio
St. Mary's University
Sam Houston State University
Stephen F. Austin State
University
Tarleton State University
Texas A&M University
Texas Lutheran University
Texas Southern University
Texas State University
Texas Tech University
Texas Woman's University
University of Houston
Clear Lake
University of North Texas
University of Texas
Dallas
Tyler
West Texas A&M University

Utah

Southern Utah University

Vermont

Bennington College
Champlain College
Green Mountain College
Norwich University
Southern Vermont College
Sterling College
University of Vermont
Vermont Technical College

Virginia

Averett University
Christopher Newport University
Eastern Mennonite University
George Mason University
Hampden-Sydney College
Hampton University

Hollins University
James Madison University
Lynchburg College
Randolph-Macon College
Roanoke College
Virginia Commonwealth
University
Virginia Military Institute
Virginia Polytechnic Institute
and State University

Washington

Cornish College of the Arts
Gonzaga University
Seattle University
University of Washington
Whitworth University

West Virginia

Alderson-Broaddus University
Bethany College
Fairmont State University
Glenville State College
University of Charleston
West Liberty University
West Virginia University
Institute of Technology

Wisconsin

Alverno College
Beloit College
Carthage College
Concordia University Wisconsin
Lawrence University
Maranathan Baptist University
Maranatha Baptist
University
Marquette University
Milwaukee Institute of Art &
Design
Milwaukee School of
Engineering
Mount Mary University
Northland College
Ripon College
University of Wisconsin
Milwaukee
Oshkosh
Superior
Whitewater

Belgium

Vesalius College

Bulgaria

American University in Bulgaria

Canada

McGill University
Simon Fraser University
University of British Columbia

Greece

Deree College, The American
College of Greece

Italy

John Cabot University

Lebanon

American University of Beirut

United Arab Emirates

American University in Dubai

United Kingdom

University of Chichester

Two-year

Alabama

Marion Military Institute

Arkansas

University of Arkansas
Community College at
Morrilton

Tables and Indexes

California

Fashion Institute of Design and
  Merchandising
    San Diego

Connecticut

St. Vincent's College

Delaware

Delaware College of Art and
  Design

Georgia

Andrew College
Georgia Perimeter College
Gordon State College

Massachusetts

Dean College
Laboure College

New York

St. Elizabeth College of Nursing
SUNY
  College of Technology at
    Alfred
  College of Technology at
    Delhi

Pennsylvania

Manor College

South Carolina

Spartanburg Methodist College

South Dakota

Mitchell Technical Institute

**Admit over 75% of
applicants**

Four-year

Alabama

Auburn University
Auburn University at
  Montgomery
Samford University
Southeastern Bible College
Troy University
University of Alabama
  Huntsville
University of South Alabama

Arizona

Arizona State University
Embry-Riddle Aeronautical
  University
    Prescott Campus
Northern Arizona University
University of Arizona

Arkansas

Arkansas Tech University
Harding University
Hendrix College
University of Central Arkansas
University of the Ozarks

California

Art Center College of Design
Azusa Pacific University
California College of the Arts
California Maritime Academy
California State University
  Bakersfield
Dominican University of
  California
Humboldt State University
John Paul the Great Catholic
  University
The Master's College
Mills College
Mount Saint Mary's University
St. Mary's College of California
Thomas Aquinas College

Westmont College
William Jessup University

Colorado

Colorado Mesa University
Colorado State University
Fort Lewis College
Johnson & Wales University
  Denver
Naropa University
University of Colorado
  Boulder
  Colorado Springs
Western State Colorado
  University

Connecticut

Albertus Magnus College
Holy Apostles College and
  Seminary
Paier College of Art
University of New Haven
University of Saint Joseph

District of Columbia

Catholic University of America

Florida

Everglades University
  Boca Raton
  Orlando
Florida College
Johnson & Wales University
  North Miami
Lynn University
Palm Beach Atlantic University
Ringling College of Art and
  Design
Trinity College of Florida

Georgia

Covenant College
Georgia College and State
  University
Georgia Gwinnett College
Morehouse College
Oglethorpe University
Reinhardt University
Truett-McConnell College

Hawaii

Chaminade University of
  Honolulu
Hawaii Pacific University
University of Hawaii
  Manoa

Idaho

Boise State University
College of Idaho
Idaho State University
Lewis-Clark State College
New Saint Andrews College

Illinois

Aurora University
Hebrew Theological College
Illinois State University
Olivet Nazarene University
Principia College
Rasmussen College
  Mokena/Tinley Park
Southern Illinois University
  Carbondale
Southern Illinois University
  Edwardsville
University of Illinois
  Chicago
VanderCook College of Music

Indiana

Grace College
Holy Cross College
Huntington University
Indiana University
  Bloomington
  Northwest
  South Bend
  Southeast

Indiana Wesleyan University
Saint Mary's College
Taylor University
Trine University
University of Saint Francis
Valparaiso University

Iowa

Grand View University
Iowa State University
Loras College
Shiloh University
Simpson College
University of Dubuque
University of Iowa
University of Northern Iowa

Kansas

Baker University
Benedictine College
Bethany College
Emporia State University
Fort Hays State University
Kansas State University
Pittsburg State University
Southwestern College
University of Kansas
Wichita State University

Kentucky

Bellarmine University
Campbellsville University
Morehead State University
Murray State University
Northern Kentucky University
Thomas More College
Transylvania University
Western Kentucky University

Louisiana

Louisiana State University
  Shreveport
Louisiana State University and
  Agricultural and Mechanical
  College
Loyola University New Orleans
McNeese State University
Nicholls State University
Southeastern Louisiana
  University
University of Louisiana at
  Monroe

Maine

College of the Atlantic
Husson University
Maine College of Art
Thomas College
Unity College
University of Maine
University of Maine
  Farmington
  Fort Kent
  Presque Isle
University of New England
University of Southern Maine

Maryland

Goucher College
Hood College
McDaniel College
St. John's College
St. Mary's College of Maryland

Massachusetts

Anna Maria College
Assumption College
Bard College at Simon's Rock
Bay Path University
Bridgewater State University
Curry College
Gordon College
Lasell College
MCPHS University
Merrimack College
Newbury College
Nichols College
Regis College

School of the Museum of Fine
  Arts
Stonehill College
Suffolk University
University of Massachusetts
  Dartmouth
Western New England
  University
Westfield State University
Wheelock College

Michigan

Albion College
Davenport University
Ferris State University
Grand Valley State University
Lake Superior State University
Michigan Technological
  University
Saginaw Valley State University
Wayne State University
Western Michigan University

Minnesota

Bemidji State University
Bethany Lutheran College
Bethel University
Concordia College: Moorhead
Martin Luther College
Minnesota State University
  Moorhead
Saint Cloud State University
St. Mary's University of
  Minnesota
University of Minnesota
  Crookston
  Duluth
University of St. Thomas

Mississippi

Alcorn State University
Mississippi University for
  Women
University of Mississippi

Missouri

Calvary Bible College and
  Theological Seminary
Conception Seminary College
Fontbonne University
Missouri Southern State
  University
Missouri State University
Missouri University of Science
  and Technology
Research College of Nursing
Southeast Missouri State
  University
Truman State University
University of Central Missouri
University of Missouri
  Columbia
  St. Louis
William Woods University

Montana

Montana Bible College
Montana State University
  Billings
Montana Tech of the University
  of Montana
University of Great Falls
University of Montana

Nebraska

Concordia University
Creative Center
Doane College
Nebraska Wesleyan University
University of Nebraska
  Kearney
  Lincoln
  Omaha

Nevada

University of Nevada
  Las Vegas
  Reno

New Hampshire

Franklin Pierce University
Keene State College
New England College
Southern New Hampshire
  University
University of New Hampshire

New Jersey

Berkeley College
Centenary College
Fairleigh Dickinson University
  College at Florham
    Metropolitan Campus
Felician University
Georgian Court University
Monmouth University
New Jersey City University

New Mexico

St. John's College

New York

Canisius College
Cazenovia College
City University of New York
  College of Staten Island
College of Mount St. Vincent
College of Saint Rose
Culinary Institute of America
Elmira College
Hartwick College
Hilbert College
Houghton College
Iona College
Keuka College
LIM College
Long Island University
  LIU Brooklyn
  LIU Post
Marymount Manhattan College
Molloy College
Mount Saint Mary College
Nazareth College
Nyack College
Pace University
Pace University: Pleasantville/
  Briarcliff
St. Francis College
St. Thomas Aquinas College
SUNY
  Empire State College
Utica College
Yeshiva University

North Carolina

Cabarrus College of Health
  Sciences
Greensboro College
Lenoir-Rhyne University
Queens University of Charlotte
University of North Carolina
  Asheville
Warren Wilson College

North Dakota

North Dakota State University
University of North Dakota
Valley City State University

Ohio

Ashland University
Bowling Green State University
Cincinnati Christian University
Cleveland State University
Franciscan University of
  Steubenville
Heidelberg University
John Carroll University
Kent State University
Mount Carmel College of
  Nursing
Mount St. Joseph University
Mount Vernon Nazarene
  University
Ohio Dominican University
Tiffin University
University of Akron

University of Cincinnati
University of Findlay
University of Mount Union
Ursuline College
Walsh University
Wittenberg University
Wright State University

Oklahoma

Cameron University
Northeastern State University
Oklahoma Baptist University
Oklahoma State University
Rogers State University
University of Oklahoma

Oregon

Eastern Oregon University
George Fox University
Linfield College
Marylhurst University
Mount Angel Seminary
Oregon State University
Pacific Northwest College of
 Art
Pacific University
Portland State University
Southern Oregon University
Western Oregon University
Willamette University

Pennsylvania

Bloomsburg University of
 Pennsylvania
Bryn Athyn College
Cairn University
California University of
 Pennsylvania
Carlow University
Chatham University
Chestnut Hill College
DeSales University
Duquesne University
Edinboro University
 of Pennsylvania
Gannon University
Grove City College
Gwynedd Mercy University
Immaculata University
Indiana University of
 Pennsylvania
Juniata College
Keystone College
Kutztown University of
 Pennsylvania
La Roche College
Lincoln University
Lock Haven University of
 Pennsylvania
Mansfield University of
 Pennsylvania
Mercyhurst University
Messiah College
Neumann University
Penn State
 Abington
 Altoona
 Beaver
 Berks
 Brandywine
 DuBois
 Erie, The Behrend College
 Fayette, The Eberly Campus
 Greater Allegheny
 Harrisburg
 Hazleton
 Lehigh Valley
 Mont Alto
 New Kensington
 Wilkes-Barre
 Worthington Scranton
 York
Robert Morris University
Saint Joseph's University
Seton Hill University
Shippensburg University of
 Pennsylvania
Susquehanna University

Talmudical Yeshiva of
 Philadelphia
University of Pittsburgh
 Johnstown
University of Valley Forge
Ursinus College
Waynesburg University
Westminster College
Wilkes University

Puerto Rico

EDP University of Puerto Rico:
 Hato Rey
EDP University of Puerto Rico:
 San Sebastian
Escuela de Artes Plasticas de
 Puerto Rico
Theological University of the
 Caribbean
Universidad Politecnica de
 Puerto Rico
University of Puerto Rico
 Arecibo
 Mayaguez

Rhode Island

Johnson & Wales University
 Providence
Roger Williams University

South Carolina

Benedict College
Bob Jones University
The Citadel
College of Charleston
Columbia College
Morris College
South Carolina State University
Voorhees College

South Dakota

Dakota State University
South Dakota School of Mines
 and Technology
South Dakota State University

Tennessee

Austin Peay State University
Belmont University
Bethel University
East Tennessee State University
Fisk University
Freed-Hardeman University
University of Memphis
University of Tennessee
 Chattanooga
 Knoxville

Texas

Angelo State University
Howard Payne University
Lamar University
Lubbock Christian University
Midwestern State University
Prairie View A&M University
St. Edward's University
Schreiner University
Sul Ross State University
Texas A&M University
 Corpus Christi
 Kingsville
University of Dallas
University of Houston
 Downtown
University of Mary Hardin-
 Baylor
University of St. Thomas
University of Texas
 San Antonio
 of the Permian Basin
University Of Texas Rio Grande
 Valley
University of the Incarnate
 Word
Wayland Baptist University

Utah

Neumont University
University of Utah
Westminster College

Vermont

Saint Michael's College

Virginia

Bluefield College
Christendom College
Emory & Henry College
Longwood University
Mary Baldwin College
Marymount University
Old Dominion University
Patrick Henry College
Radford University
Randolph College
Regent University
Shenandoah University
Sweet Briar College
University of Mary Washington
University of Virginia's College
 at Wise
Virginia State University
Virginia Wesleyan College

Washington

Central Washington University
Eastern Washington University
Evergreen State College
Northwest University
Pacific Lutheran University
Saint Martin's University
Seattle Pacific University
University of Puget Sound
University of Washington
 Bothell
University of Washington
 Tacoma
Washington State University
Western Washington University

West Virginia

Bluefield State College
Marshall University
Shepherd University
West Virginia State University
West Virginia University
West Virginia Wesleyan College

Wisconsin

Bellin College
Cardinal Stritch University
Edgewood College
Marian University
St. Norbert College
University of Wisconsin
 Eau Claire
 Green Bay
 La Crosse
 Parkside
 Platteville
 River Falls
 Stout

Wyoming

University of Wyoming

Virgin Islands

University of the Virgin Islands

Canada

University of Toronto

France

American University of Paris

Kuwait

American University of Kuwait

Lebanon

Lebanese American University

Two-year

Alabama

George C. Wallace Community
 College at Dothan

Iowa

St. Luke's College

Massachusetts

Bay State College

Minnesota

Duluth Business University
Dunwoody College of
 Technology

New Jersey

Assumption College for Sisters

New York

American Academy McAllister
 Institute of Funeral Service
College of Westchester
Jamestown Business College
Long Island Business Institute
SUNY
 College of Agriculture and
  Technology at Cobleskill
 College of Technology at
  Canton
Villa Maria College of Buffalo

North Carolina

Louisburg College

Ohio

Art Institute of Cincinnati
Aultman College of Nursing and
 Health Sciences

Pennsylvania

University of Pittsburgh
 Titusville

Texas

Hallmark University

Wisconsin

University of Wisconsin
 Fox Valley

Open admission

Four-year

Alabama

Amridge University
Columbia Southern University
Concordia College
Huntsville Bible College
Miles College
Selma University
Talladega College
United States Sports Academy
University of Phoenix
 Birmingham
Virginia College
 Birmingham
 Huntsville

Alaska

Alaska Bible College
Charter College
University of Alaska
 Anchorage
 Fairbanks

Arizona

Argosy University
 Online
 Phoenix
Brown Mackie College
 Tucson
Dunlap-Stone University
Harrison Middleton University
International Baptist College
National Paralegal College
University of Phoenix
 Phoenix-Hohokam
 Southern Arizona
Western International University

Arkansas

Arkansas Baptist College
University of Arkansas
 Fort Smith
 Monticello
University of Phoenix
 Little Rock
 Northwest Arkansas

California

Academy of Art University
Academy of Couture Art
Alliant International University
Antioch University
 Los Angeles
Argosy University
 Inland Empire
 Los Angeles
 Orange County
 San Diego
 San Francisco Bay Area
Ashford University
Bergin University of Canine
 Studies
California Christian College
California Coast University
California College San Diego
California Miramar University
Coleman University
Columbia College
 Hollywood
Horizon University
Interior Designers Institute
International Academy of
 Design and Technology
 Sacramento
John F. Kennedy University
National University
Pacific States University
Patten University
Platt College
 San Diego
Southern California Institute of
 Technology
Southern California Seminary
Stanbridge College
SUM Bible College &
 Theological Seminary
Trident University International
University of Phoenix
 Bay Area
 Central Valley
 Sacramento Valley
 San Diego
 Southern California
West Coast University: Ontario
West Coast University: Orange
 County

Colorado

American Sentinel University
Argosy University
 Denver
Aspen University
CollegeAmerica
 Colorado Springs
 Fort Collins
Colorado Technical University
National American University
 Denver
Nazarene Bible College
Platt College
 Aurora
Rocky Mountain College of
 Art & Design
University of Phoenix
 Denver
 Southern Colorado

Delaware

Wilmington University

District of Columbia

University of Phoenix
 Washington DC
University of the Potomac

Heritage University
University of Phoenix
    Western Washington
Walla Walla University

West Virginia

American Public University
    System

Wisconsin

Globe University
    Green Bay
Herzing University
    Madison
Rasmussen College
    Appleton
University of Phoenix
    Milwaukee

Canada

Memorial University of
    Newfoundland
University of Manitoba

Guatemala

Universidad del Valle de
    Guatemala

Lebanon

Notre Dame University: Louaize

Mexico

Instituto Tecnologico y de
    Estudios Superiores de
    Occidente

Poland

Warsaw University of
    Technology

Two-year

Alabama

Alabama Southern Community
    College
Bevill State Community College
Bishop State Community
    College
Calhoun Community College
Central Alabama Community
    College
Chattahoochee Valley
    Community College
Enterprise State Community
    College
Faulkner State Community
    College
Gadsden State Community
    College
George C. Wallace State
    Community College at Selma
Jefferson Davis Community
    College
Jefferson State Community
    College
Lawson State Community
    College
Lurleen B. Wallace Community
    College
Northeast Alabama Community
    College
Northwest-Shoals Community
    College
Remington College
    Mobile
Shelton State Community
    College
Snead State Community College
Southern Union State
    Community College
Virginia College
    Mobile
Wallace State Community
    College at Hanceville

Alaska

Ilisagvik College

Arizona

Arizona Western College
Brookline College
    Phoenix
    Tempe
    Tucson
Bryan University
Carrington College
    Mesa
    Phoenix
    Phoenix Westside
    Tucson
Central Arizona College
Chandler-Gilbert Community
    College
Cochise College
Coconino County Community
    College
Dine College
Eastern Arizona College
Estrella Mountain Community
    College
GateWay Community College
Le Cordon Bleu College of
    Culinary Arts
    Scottsdale
Mesa Community College
Mohave Community College
Northland Pioneer College
Paradise Valley Community
    College
Penn Foster College
Phoenix College
Pima Community College
Refrigeration School
Rio Salado College
Scottsdale Community College
Sessions College for
    Professional Design
South Mountain Community
    College
Tohono O'odham Community
    College
Universal Technical Institute
Yavapai College

Arkansas

Arkansas Northeastern College
Arkansas State University
    Beebe
    Mid-South
    Mountain Home
Black River Technical College
Bryan University
    Rogers
College of the Ouachitas
Cossatot Community College
    of the University of
    Arkansas
Crowley's Ridge College
East Arkansas Community
    College
National Park College
North Arkansas College
Northwest Arkansas Community
    College
Ozarka College
Phillips Community College of
    the University of Arkansas
Pulaski Technical College
Remington College
    Little Rock
Rich Mountain Community
    College
South Arkansas Community
    College
Southeast Arkansas College
Southern Arkansas University
    Tech
University of Arkansas
    Community College at
    Batesville
    Community College at
    Hope

California

Allan Hancock College
American River College
Antelope Valley College
Bakersfield College
Barstow Community College
Berkeley City College
Bryan College: Sacramento
Butte College
Cabrillo College
Canada College
Cerritos College
Cerro Coso Community College
Chabot College
Chaffey College
Citrus College
City College of San Francisco
Coastline Community College
College of Alameda
College of Marin
College of San Mateo
College of the Canyons
College of the Desert
College of the Redwoods
College of the Sequoias
College of the Siskiyous
Columbia College
Concorde Career College
    Garden Grove
    San Diego
Contra Costa College
Copper Mountain College
Cosumnes River College
Crafton Hills College
Cuesta College
Cuyamaca College
Cypress College
De Anza College
Diablo Valley College
East Los Angeles College
El Camino College
Empire College
Evergreen Valley College
Feather River College
Folsom Lake College
Foothill College
Fremont College
Fresno City College
Fullerton College
Gavilan College
Glendale Community College
Golden West College
Golf Academy of America
    San Diego
Grossmont College
Hartnell College
Imperial Valley College
Irvine Valley College
Kaplan College
    Palm Springs
    Riverside
    Sacramento
    Salida
    San Diego
    Vista
Lake Tahoe Community College
Laney College
Las Positas College
Lassen Community College
Le Cordon Bleu College of
    Culinary Arts
    Los Angeles
Long Beach City College
Los Angeles City College
Los Angeles Harbor College
Los Angeles Mission College
Los Angeles Pierce College
Los Angeles Southwest College
Los Angeles Trade and
    Technical College
Los Angeles Valley College
Los Medanos College
Mendocino College
Merced College
Merritt College
MiraCosta College
Mission College

Modesto Junior College
Monterey Peninsula College
Moorpark College
Moreno Valley College
Mount San Antonio College
Mount San Jacinto College
Napa Valley College
Norco College
Ohlone College
Orange Coast College
Oxnard College
Palo Verde College
Palomar College
Pasadena City College
Porterville College
Reedley College
Rio Hondo College
Riverside City College
Sacramento City College
Saddleback College
Sage College
Salvation Army College for
    Officer Training at Crestmont
San Bernardino Valley College
San Deigo Miramar College
    San Diego Miramar College
San Diego City College
San Diego Mesa College
San Joaquin Delta College
San Joaquin Valley College
San Jose City College
Santa Ana College
Santa Barbara Business College
    Rancho Mirage
    Santa Maria
Santa Barbara City College
Santa Monica College
Santa Rosa Junior College
Santiago Canyon College
Shasta College
Sierra College
Skyline College
Solano Community College
South Coast College
Southwestern College
Taft College
Ventura College
Victor Valley College
West Hills College: Coalinga
West Hills College: Lemoore
West Los Angeles College
West Valley College
Woodland Community College
Yuba College

Colorado

Aims Community College
Arapahoe Community College
CollegeAmerica
    Denver
Colorado Mountain College
Colorado Northwestern
    Community College
Colorado School of Healing
    Arts
Colorado School of Trades
Community College of Aurora
Community College of Denver
Ecotech Institute
Front Range Community
    College
IBMC College
    Fort Collins
IntelliTec College
IntelliTec College: Grand
    Junction
Lamar Community College
Lincoln College of Technology
    Denver
Morgan Community College
Northeastern Junior College
Otero Junior College
Pikes Peak Community College
Pueblo Community College
Red Rocks Community College
Redstone College
Trinidad State Junior College

Connecticut

Asnuntuck Community College
Capital Community College
Gateway Community College
Goodwin College
Housatonic Community College
Lincoln College of New
    England
Manchester Community College
Middlesex Community College
Naugatuck Valley Community
    College
Northwestern Connecticut
    Community College
Norwalk Community College
Quinebaug Valley Community
    College
Three Rivers Community
    College
Tunxis Community College

Delaware

Delaware Technical Community
    College
    Jack F. Owens Campus
    Stanton/Wilmington
    Campus
    Terry Campus

Florida

Broward College
Brown Mackie College
    Miami
Chipola College
City College
    Altamonte Springs
    Gainesville
College of Business and
    Technology
    Cutler Bay
    Flagler
    Hialeah
    Kendall
    Miami Gardens
College of Central Florida
Daytona State College
Eastern Florida State College
Florida Career College
    Miami
Florida College of Natural
    Health
    Bradenton
    Miami
    Pompano Beach
Florida Gateway College
Florida Keys Community
    College
Florida National University
Florida SouthWestern State
    College
Florida State College at
    Jacksonville
Florida Technical College
    Orlando
Fortis College
    Orange Park
    Winter Park
Golf Academy of America
    Orlando
Gulf Coast State College
Herzing University
    Winter Park
Hillsborough Community
    College
Indian River State College
Lake-Sumter State College
Le Cordon Bleu College of
    Culinary Arts
    Orlando
Lincoln College of Technology
    West Palm Beach
Miami Dade College
North Florida Community
    College
Northwest Florida State College
Palm Beach State College
Pasco-Hernando State College

Pensacola State College
Polk State College
Rasmussen College
   Pasco/Land O'Lakes
Saint Johns River State College
St. Petersburg College
Santa Fe College
Seminole State College of
   Florida
South Florida State College
Southern Technical College
Southwest Florida College
   Tampa
State College of Florida,
   Manatee-Sarasota
Tallahassee Community College
Valencia College
Virginia College
   Jacksonville
   Pensacola

Georgia

Albany Technical College
Ashworth College
Athens Technical College
Atlanta Technical College
Augusta Technical College
Brown Mackie College
   Atlanta
Central Georgia Technical
   College
Chattahoochee Technical
   College
Coastal Pines Technical College
Columbus Technical College
Darton College
Georgia Military College
Georgia Northwestern Technical
   College
Georgia Piedmont Technical
   College
Gupton Jones College of
   Funeral Service
Gwinnett College
Gwinnett Technical College
Le Cordon Bleu College of
   Culinary Arts
   Atlanta
North Georgia Technical
   College
Savannah Technical College
Southeastern Technical College
Southern Crescent Technical
   College
Southern Regional Technical
   College
Virginia College
   Augusta
   Columbus
   Macon
   Savannah
West Georgia Technical College
Wiregrass Georgia Technical
   College

Hawaii

University of Hawaii
   Hawaii Community College
   Honolulu Community
      College
   Kapiolani Community
      College
   Kauai Community College
   Leeward Community
      College
   Maui College
   Windward Community
      College

Idaho

Broadview University
   Boise
College of Southern Idaho
College of Western Idaho
Eastern Idaho Technical College
Stevens-Henager College
   Boise

Illinois

Black Hawk College
Carl Sandburg College
City Colleges of Chicago
   Harold Washington College
   Harry S. Truman College
   Kennedy-King College
   Malcolm X College
   Olive-Harvey College
   Richard J. Daley College
   Wilbur Wright College
College of DuPage
College of Lake County
Coyne College
Danville Area Community
   College
Elgin Community College
Fox College
Harper College
Heartland Community College
Highland Community College
Illinois Central College
Illinois Eastern Community
   Colleges
   Frontier Community
      College
   Lincoln Trail College
   Olney Central College
   Wabash Valley College
Illinois Valley Community
   College
John A. Logan College
John Wood Community College
Joliet Junior College
Kankakee Community College
Kaskaskia College
Kishwaukee College
Lake Land College
Le Cordon Bleu College of
   Culinary Arts
   Chicago
Lewis and Clark Community
   College
Lincoln Land Community
   College
McHenry County College
Moraine Valley Community
   College
Morrison Institute of
   Technology
Morton College
Northwestern College
Oakton Community College
Parkland College
Prairie State College
Rasmussen College
   Aurora
   Rockford
   Romeoville/Joliet
Rend Lake College
Richland Community College
Rock Valley College
Rockford Career College
Sauk Valley Community
   College
Shawnee Community College
South Suburban College of
   Cook County
Southeastern Illinois College
Southwestern Illinois College
Spoon River College
Triton College
Vatterott College
   Quincy
Waubonsee Community College

Indiana

American National University
   Fort Wayne
   Indianapolis
   South Bend
Ancilla College
Brown Mackie College
   Fort Wayne
   Michigan City
   South Bend
College of Court Reporting

Fortis College
   Indianapolis
Harrison College
   Indianapolis
Ivy Tech Community College
   Bloomington
   Central Indiana
   Columbus
   East Central
   Kokomo
   Lafayette
   North Central
   Northeast
   Northwest
   Richmond
   South Central
   Southeast
   Southwest
   Wabash Valley
Kaplan College
   Indianapolis
Lincoln College of Technology
   Indianapolis
Mid-America College of
   Funeral Service
Vincennes University

Iowa

Clinton Community College
Des Moines Area Community
   College
Ellsworth Community College
Hawkeye Community College
Iowa Central Community
   College
Iowa Lakes Community College
Iowa Western Community
   College
Kaplan University
   Cedar Rapids
Kirkwood Community College
Marshalltown Community
   College
Muscatine Community College
North Iowa Area Community
   College
Northeast Iowa Community
   College
Northwest Iowa Community
   College
Scott Community College
Southeastern Community
   College
Southwestern Community
   College
Vatterott College
   Des Moines
Western Iowa Tech Community
   College

Kansas

Allen County Community
   College
Barton County Community
   College
Brown Mackie College
   Salina
Butler Community College
Cloud County Community
   College
Coffeyville Community College
Colby Community College
Cowley County Community
   College
Dodge City Community College
Donnelly College
Fort Scott Community College
Garden City Community
   College
Hesston College
Highland Community College
Hutchinson Community College
Independence Community
   College
Johnson County Community
   College
Kansas City Kansas Community
   College

Labette Community College
Manhattan Area Technical
   College
Neosho County Community
   College
North Central Kansas Technical
   College
Northwest Kansas Technical
   College
Pratt Community College
Seward County Community
   College
Wichita Area Technical College
Wright Career College
   Overland Park
   Wichita

Kentucky

Ashland Community and
   Technical College
Big Sandy Community and
   Technical College
Bluegrass Community and
   Technical College
Brown Mackie College
   Hopkinsville
   Louisville
   North Kentucky
Daymar College
   Bowling Green
   Louisville
   Owensboro
   Paducah
Elizabethtown Community and
   Technical College
Gateway Community and
   Technical College
Hazard Community and
   Technical College
Henderson Community College
Hopkinsville Community
   College
Jefferson Community and
   Technical College
Lincoln College of Technology
   Florence
Madisonville Community
   College
Maysville Community and
   Technical College
National College
   Danville
   Florence
   Lexington
   Louisville
   Pikeville
   Richmond
Owensboro Community and
   Technical College
Somerset Community College
Southeast Kentucky Community
   and Technical College
Spencerian College
Spencerian College: Lexington
West Kentucky Community and
   Technical College

Louisiana

Baton Rouge Community
   College
Baton Rouge School of
   Computers
Blue Cliff College
   Metairie
   Shreveport
Bossier Parish Community
   College
Delgado Community College
Delta College of Arts &
   Technology
Delta School of Business &
   Technology
ITI Technical College
Louisiana State University
   Eunice
Nunez Community College

Remington College
   Baton Rouge
   Lafayette
   Shreveport
River Parishes Community
   College
South Louisiana Community
   College
Southern University
   Shreveport
Virginia College
   Baton Rouge
   Shreveport

Maine

Beal College
Central Maine Community
   College
Eastern Maine Community
   College
Kaplan University
   South Portland
Kennebec Valley Community
   College
Landing School of Boatbuilding
   and Design
Southern Maine Community
   College
Washington County Community
   College
York County Community
   College

Maryland

Allegany College of Maryland
Anne Arundel Community
   College
Baltimore City Community
   College
Carroll Community College
Cecil College
Chesapeake College
College of Southern Maryland
Community College of
   Baltimore County
Frederick Community College
Garrett College
Hagerstown Community College
Harford Community College
Howard Community College
Kaplan University
   Hagerstown
Montgomery College
Prince George's Community
   College
TESST College of Technology
   Baltimore
   Beltsville
   Towson
Wor-Wic Community College

Massachusetts

Berkshire Community College
Bristol Community College
Bunker Hill Community College
Cape Cod Community College
Greenfield Community College
Holyoke Community College
Massachusetts Bay Community
   College
Massasoit Community College
Middlesex Community College
Mount Wachusett Community
   College
New England College of
   Business and Finance
North Shore Community
   College
Northern Essex Community
   College
Quincy College
Quinsigamond Community
   College
Roxbury Community College
Springfield Technical
   Community College
Urban College of Boston

Michigan

Alpena Community College
Bay College
Bay Mills Community College
Delta College
Glen Oaks Community College
Gogebic Community College
Grand Rapids Community
   College
Henry Ford Community College
Jackson College
Kalamazoo Valley Community
   College
Kellogg Community College
Kirtland Community College
Lake Michigan College
Lansing Community College
Macomb Community College
Mid Michigan Community
   College
Monroe County Community
   College
Montcalm Community College
Mott Community College
Muskegon Community College
North Central Michigan College
Northwestern Michigan College
Oakland Community College
Saginaw Chippewa Tribal
   College
St. Clair County Community
   College
Schoolcraft College
Southwestern Michigan College
Washtenaw Community College
Wayne County Community
   College
West Shore Community College

Minnesota

Academy College
Alexandria Technical and
   Community College
Anoka Technical College
Anoka-Ramsey Community
   College
Central Lakes College
Century College
Dakota County Technical
   College
Fond du Lac Tribal and
   Community College
Hennepin Technical College
Herzing University
   Minneapolis
Hibbing Community College
Institute of Production and
   Recording
Inver Hills Community College
Itasca Community College
Lake Superior College
Le Cordon Bleu College of
   Culinary Arts
   Minneapolis-St. Paul
Leech Lake Tribal College
Mesabi Range College
Minneapolis Business College
Minneapolis Community and
   Technical College
Minnesota School of Business
   Brooklyn Center
Minnesota State College -
   Southeast Technical
Minnesota State Community and
   Technical College
Minnesota West Community
   and Technical College
Normandale Community
   College
North Hennepin Community
   College
Northland Community &
   Technical College
Northwest Technical College
Pine Technical & Community
   College

Rainy River Community
   College
Rasmussen College
   Bloomington
   Brooklyn Park
   Eagan
   Mankato
   St. Cloud
Ridgewater College
Riverland Community College
Rochester Community and
   Technical College
St. Cloud Technical and
   Community College
St. Paul College
South Central College
Vermilion Community College
White Earth Tribal and
   Community College

Mississippi

Antonelli College
   Hattiesburg
   Jackson
Coahoma Community College
Copiah-Lincoln Community
   College
East Central Community
   College
East Mississippi Community
   College
Hinds Community College
Holmes Community College
Itawamba Community College
Jones County Junior College
Meridian Community College
Mississippi Delta Community
   College
Mississippi Gulf Coast
   Community College
Northeast Mississippi
   Community College
Northwest Mississippi
   Community College
Pearl River Community College
Southwest Mississippi
   Community College

Missouri

Bolivar Technical College
Brown Mackie College
   St. Louis
Concorde Career College
   Kansas City
Crowder College
East Central College
Jefferson College
L'Ecole Culinaire
Metro Business College
   Jefferson City
   Rolla
Metropolitan Community
   College - Kansas City
Mineral Area College
Missouri College
Missouri State University: West
   Plains
Moberly Area Community
   College
North Central Missouri College
Ozarks Technical Community
   College
Pinnacle Career Institute:
   Kansas City
Ranken Technical College
St. Charles Community College
St. Louis Community College
Southeast Missouri Hospital
   College of Nursing and
   Health Sciences
State Fair Community College
State Technical College of
   Missouri
Stevens Institute of Business &
   Arts
Texas County Technical College
Three Rivers Community
   College

Vatterott College
   Berkeley
   Joplin
   Kansas City
   O'Fallon
   St. Joseph
   Springfield
   Sunset Hills
Wentworth Military Junior
   College

Montana

Aaniiih Nakoda College
Blackfeet Community College
Chief Dull Knife College
Dawson Community College
Flathead Valley Community
   College
Fort Peck Community College
Helena College University of
   Montana
Little Big Horn College
Miles Community College
Montana State University
   Great Falls College
Stone Child College

Nebraska

Central Community College
Kaplan University
   Lincoln
   Omaha
Little Priest Tribal College
Metropolitan Community
   College
Mid-Plains Community College
Myotherapy Institute
Nebraska College of Technical
   Agriculture
Nebraska Indian Community
   College
Northeast Community College
Southeast Community College
Western Nebraska Community
   College
Wright Career College
   Omaha

Nevada

Career College of Northern
   Nevada
College of Southern Nevada
Kaplan College
   Las Vegas
Truckee Meadows Community
   College
Western Nevada College

New Hampshire

Great Bay Community College
Lakes Region Community
   College
Manchester Community College
Nashua Community College
NHTI-Concord's Community
   College
River Valley Community
   College
White Mountains Community
   College

New Jersey

Atlantic Cape Community
   College
Bergen Community College
Brookdale Community College
Camden County College
County College of Morris
Cumberland County College
Eastern International College
Eastwick College
Essex County College
Hudson County Community
   College
Mercer County Community
   College
Middlesex County College
Ocean County College

Passaic County Community
   College
Raritan Valley Community
   College
Rowan College at Burlington
   County
Rowan College at Gloucester
Salem Community College
Sussex County Community
   College
Union County College
Warren County Community
   College

New Mexico

Brookline College
   Albuquerque
Central New Mexico
   Community College
Clovis Community College
Dona Ana Community College
   of New Mexico State
   University
Eastern New Mexico
   University: Roswell
Luna Community College
Mesalands Community College
Navajo Technical University
New Mexico Junior College
New Mexico State University
   Alamogordo
   Carlsbad
   Grants
San Juan College
Santa Fe Community College
Southwestern Indian Polytechnic
   Institute

New York

Adirondack Community College
ASA College
Broome Community College
Bryant & Stratton College
   Buffalo
   Southtowns
   Syracuse
Business Informatics Center
Cayuga Community College
City University of New York
   Borough of Manhattan
      Community College
   Bronx Community College
   Hostos Community College
   Kingsborough Community
      College
   LaGuardia Community
      College
   Queensborough Community
      College
Clinton Community College
Corning Community College
Dutchess Community College
Elmira Business Institute
Elmira Business Institute: Vestal
Erie Community College
Finger Lakes Community
   College
Fulton-Montgomery Community
   College
Genesee Community College
Herkimer County Community
   College
Hudson Valley Community
   College
Institute of Design and
   Construction
Island Drafting and Technical
   Institute
Jamestown Community College
Jefferson Community College
Mildred Elley
   Albany
   New York City
Mohawk Valley Community
   College
Monroe Community College
Nassau Community College
New York Career Institute

Niagara County Community
   College
North Country Community
   College
Onondaga Community College
Orange County Community
   College
Rockland Community College
Schenectady County
   Community College
Suffolk County Community
   College
Sullivan County Community
   College
Technical Career Institutes
Tompkins Cortland Community
   College
Trocaire College
Ulster County Community
   College
Utica School of Commerce
Westchester Community College

North Carolina

Alamance Community College
Asheville-Buncombe Technical
   Community College
Beaufort County Community
   College
Bladen Community College
Blue Ridge Community College
Brunswick Community College
Caldwell Community College
   and Technical Institute
Cape Fear Community College
Carolinas College of Health
   Sciences
Carteret Community College
Catawba Valley Community
   College
Central Carolina Community
   College
Central Piedmont Community
   College
Chef's Academy
Cleveland Community College
Coastal Carolina Community
   College
College of the Albemarle
Craven Community College
Davidson County Community
   College
Durham Technical Community
   College
Edgecombe Community College
Fayetteville Technical
   Community College
Forsyth Technical Community
   College
Gaston College
Guilford Technical Community
   College
Halifax Community College
Haywood Community College
Isothermal Community College
James Sprunt Community
   College
Johnston Community College
Lenoir Community College
Martin Community College
Mayland Community College
McDowell Technical
   Community College
Miller-Motte College
   Cary
Mitchell Community College
Montgomery Community
   College
Nash Community College
Pamlico Community College
Piedmont Community College
Pitt Community College
Randolph Community College
Richmond Community College
Roanoke-Chowan Community
   College
Robeson Community College

Rockingham Community
College
Rowan-Cabarrus Community
College
Sampson Community College
Sandhills Community College
South College
South Piedmont Community
College
Southeastern Community
College
Southwestern Community
College
Stanly Community College
Surry Community College
Tri-County Community College
Vance-Granville Community
College
Virginia College in Greensboro
Wake Technical Community
College
Wayne Community College
Western Piedmont Community
College
Wilkes Community College
Wilson Community College

North Dakota

Bismarck State College
Cankdeska Cikana Community
College
Dakota College at Bottineau
Fort Berthold Community
College
Lake Region State College
North Dakota State College of
Science
Rasmussen College
Bismarck
Sitting Bull College
Turtle Mountain Community
College
United Tribes Technical College
Williston State College

Ohio

ATS Institute of Technology
Belmont College
Bowling Green State University:
Firelands College
Bradford School
Brown Mackie College
Akron
Cincinnati
Findlay
North Canton
Bryant & Stratton College
Cleveland
Central Ohio Technical College
Chatfield College
Cincinnati State Technical and
Community College
Clark State Community College
Cleveland Institute of
Electronics
Columbus State Community
College
Cuyahoga Community College
Daymar College
Chillicothe
Eastern Gateway Community
College
Edison State Community
College
ETI Technical College of Niles
Fortis College
Centerville
Cuyahoga
Gallipolis Career College
Harrison College
Grove City
Hocking College
International College of
Broadcasting
James A. Rhodes State College
Kaplan College
Dayton

Kent State University
Ashtabula
East Liverpool
Geauga
Salem
Stark
Trumbull
Tuscarawas
Lakeland Community College
Lincoln College of Technology
Dayton
Lorain County Community
College
Marion Technical College
Miami University
Hamilton
Middletown
Miami-Jacobs Career College
Sharonville
National College
Canton
Cincinnati
Columbus
Kettering
Stow
Willoughby Hills
Youngstown
North Central State College
Northwest State Community
College
Ohio Business College
Hilliard
Sandusky
Sheffield
Ohio College of Massotherapy
Ohio State University
Agricultural Technical
Institute
Ohio Technical College
Owens Community College
PowerSport Institute
Rosedale Bible College
Sinclair Community College
Southern State Community
College
Stark State College
Stautzenberger College
Stautzenberger College:
Brecksville
Terra State Community College
Trumbull Business College
University of Akron: Wayne
College
University of Cincinnati
Blue Ash College
Clermont College
Vatterott College
Cleveland
Washington State Community
College
Wright State University: Lake
Campus
Zane State College

Oklahoma

Carl Albert State College
College of the Muscogee Nation
Connors State College
Eastern Oklahoma State College
Murray State College
Northeastern Oklahoma
Agricultural and Mechanical
College
Northern Oklahoma College
Oklahoma City Community
College
Oklahoma State University
Institute of Technology:
Okmulgee
Oklahoma City
Platt College
Moore
Oklahoma City Central
Tulsa
Redlands Community College
Rose State College
Seminole State College

Tulsa Community College
Tulsa Welding School
Vatterott College
Oklahoma City
Virginia College
Tulsa
Western Oklahoma State
College
Wright Career College
Oklahoma City
Tulsa

Oregon

Blue Mountain Community
College
Central Oregon Community
College
Chemeketa Community College
Clackamas Community College
Clatsop Community College
Klamath Community College
Lane Community College
Le Cordon Bleu College of
Culinary Arts
Portland
Linn-Benton Community
College
Mt. Hood Community College
Pioneer Pacific College
Portland Community College
Rogue Community College
Southwestern Oregon
Community College
Tillamook Bay Community
College
Treasure Valley Community
College
Umpqua Community College

Pennsylvania

Bucks County Community
College
Butler County Community
College
Cambria-Rowe Business College
Career Training Academy
Career Training Academy:
Monroeville
Career Training Academy:
Pittsburgh
Commonwealth Technical
Institute
Community College of
Allegheny County
Community College of Beaver
County
Community College of
Philadelphia
Consolidated School of Business
Lancaster
York
Dean Institute of Technology
Delaware County Community
College
Douglas Education Center
DuBois Business College
Huntingdon
Oil City
Erie Institute of Technology
Fortis Institute
Erie
Harrisburg Area Community
College
JNA Institute of Culinary Arts
Kaplan Career Institute
Broomall
Franklin Mills
Harrisburg
Keystone Technical Institute
Lackawanna College
Lansdale School of Business
Lehigh Carbon Community
College
Lincoln Technical Institute
Allentown
Northeast Philadelphia
Philadelphia

Luzerne County Community
College
McCann School of Business and
Technology
Hazleton
Pottsville
Montgomery County
Community College
Northampton Community
College
Penn Commercial Business and
Technical School
Pennco Tech
Pennsylvania Highlands
Community College
Pennsylvania Institute of Health
and Technology
Pennsylvania Institute of
Technology
Pittsburgh Institute of
Aeronautics
Reading Area Community
College
Rosedale Technical Institute
South Hills School of
Business & Technology
Triangle Tech
Bethlehem
DuBois
Erie
Greensburg
Pittsburgh
Sunbury
Westmoreland County
Community College
YTI Career Institute
Altoona
Lancaster
York

Puerto Rico

Centro de Estudios
Multidisciplinarios
Colegio de Cinematografía,
Artes y Televisión
Columbia Central University
Yauco
EDIC College
Huertas College
Humacao Community College
ICPR Junior College
Ponce Paramedical College
Universal Technology College
of Puerto Rico

Rhode Island

Community College of Rhode
Island

South Carolina

Aiken Technical College
Central Carolina Technical
College
Clinton College
Denmark Technical College
Florence-Darlington Technical
College
Forrest Junior College
Golf Academy of America
Myrtle Beach
Greenville Technical College
Horry-Georgetown Technical
College
Midlands Technical College
Miller-Motte Technical College
Conway
Northeastern Technical College
Orangeburg-Calhoun Technical
College
Piedmont Technical College
Spartanburg Community College
Technical College of the
Lowcountry
Tri-County Technical College
Trident Technical College
University of South Carolina
Lancaster

Virginia College
Charleston
Columbia
Florence
Greenville
Spartanburg
Williamsburg Technical College
York Technical College

South Dakota

Globe University
Sioux Falls
Kilian Community College
Lake Area Technical Institute
Sisseton Wahpeton College
Southeast Technical Institute
Western Dakota Technical
Institute

Tennessee

Chattanooga State Community
College
Cleveland State Community
College
Columbia State Community
College
Daymar Institute
Clarksville
Murfreesboro
Nashville
Dyersburg State Community
College
Fountainhead College of
Technology
Jackson State Community
College
John A. Gupton College
Miller-Motte Technical College
Chattanooga
Clarksville
Motlow State Community
College
Nashville State Community
College
National College
Bartlett
Bristol
Knoxville
Madison
Memphis
Nashville
Northeast State Community
College
Pellissippi State Community
College
Remington College
Nashville
Roane State Community College
Southwest Tennessee
Community College
Vatterott College
Memphis
Virginia College
School of Business and
Health in Chattanooga
Volunteer State Community
College
Walters State Community
College

Texas

Alvin Community College
Amarillo College
Angelina College
Austin Community College
Blinn College
Brazosport College
Brookhaven College
Cedar Valley College
Central Texas College
Cisco College
Clarendon College
Coastal Bend College
College of the Mainland
Collin County Community
College District
Court Reporting Institute of
Dallas

Culinary Institute LeNotre
Dallas Institute of Funeral
  Service
Del Mar College
Eastfield College
El Centro College
El Paso Community College
Frank Phillips College
Galveston College
Golf Academy of America
  Dallas
Grayson College
Hill College
Houston Community College
  System
Howard College
International Academy of
  Design and Technology
  San Antonio
Jacksonville College
Kilgore College
Lamar Institute of Technology
Lamar State College at Orange
Lamar State College at Port
  Arthur
Laredo Community College
Le Cordon Bleu College of
  Culinary Arts
  Austin
Lee College
Lincoln College of Technology
  Grand Prairie
Lone Star College System
McLennan Community College
Midland College
Mountain View College
Navarro College
North Central Texas College
North Lake College
Northeast Texas Community
  College
Northwest Vista College
Odessa College
Palo Alto College
Panola College
Paris Junior College
Ranger College
Remington College
  Dallas
  Fort Worth
  Greenspoint Campus
  Webster Campus
  Westchase Campus
Richland College
St. Philip's College
San Antonio College
San Jacinto College
South Plains College
South Texas College
Southwest Texas Junior College
Tarrant County College
Temple College
Texarkana College
Texas State Technical College
  Harlingen
  Marshall
  West Texas
Trinity Valley Community
  College
Tyler Junior College
Vernon College
Victoria College
Virginia College
  Austin
Wade College
Weatherford College
Western Technical College
Western Technical College:
  Diana Drive
Western Texas College
Wharton County Junior College

Utah

Broadview University
  Broadview Entertainment
  Arts University
  Layton
  West Jordan

Eagle Gate College: Layton
Eagle Gate College: Murray
LDS Business College
Provo College
Salt Lake Community College
Snow College
Vista College: Online

Vermont

Community College of Vermont

Virginia

American National University
  Charlottesville
  Danville
  Harrisonburg
  Lynchburg
  Martinsville
Blue Ridge Community College
Bryant & Stratton College
  Richmond
  Virginia Beach
Central Virginia Community
  College
Dabney S. Lancaster
  Community College
Danville Community College
Eastern Shore Community
  College
Germanna Community College
J. Sargeant Reynolds
  Community College
John Tyler Community College
Lord Fairfax Community
  College
Miller-Motte Technical College
  Lynchburg
Mountain Empire Community
  College
New River Community College
Northern Virginia Community
  College
Patrick Henry Community
  College
Paul D. Camp Community
  College
Piedmont Virginia Community
  College
Rappahannock Community
  College
Southside Virginia Community
  College
Southwest Virginia Community
  College
Thomas Nelson Community
  College
Tidewater Community College
Virginia College
  Richmond
Virginia Highlands Community
  College
Virginia Western Community
  College
Wytheville Community College

Washington

Bates Technical College
Bellevue College
Bellingham Technical College
Big Bend Community College
Cascadia College
Centralia College
Clark College
Clover Park Technical College
Columbia Basin College
Edmonds Community College
Everett Community College
Grays Harbor College
Green River Community
  College
Highline College
Lake Washington Institute of
  Technology
Lower Columbia College
North Seattle College
Northwest Indian College
Northwest School of Wooden
  Boatbuilding

Olympic College
Peninsula College
Pierce College
Renton Technical College
Seattle Central College
Shoreline Community College
Skagit Valley College
South Puget Sound Community
  College
South Seattle College
Spokane Community College
Spokane Falls Community
  College
Tacoma Community College
Walla Walla Community
  College
Wenatchee Valley College
Whatcom Community College
Yakima Valley Community
  College

West Virginia

American National University
  Parkersburg
  Princeton
Blue Ridge Community and
  Technical College
BridgeValley Community and
  Technical College
Eastern West Virginia
  Community and Technical
  College
Huntington Junior College
Mountain State College
New River Community and
  Technical College
Pierpont Community and
  Technical College
Potomac State College of West
  Virginia University
Southern West Virginia
  Community and Technical
  College
Valley College
West Virginia Business College
  Wheeling
West Virginia Junior College
  Bridgeport
  Charleston
West Virginia Northern
  Community College
West Virginia University at
  Parkersburg

Wisconsin

Blackhawk Technical College
Chippewa Valley Technical
  College
College of Menominee Nation
Fox Valley Technical College
Gateway Technical College
Globe University
  Appleton
  Eau Claire
  La Crosse
  Madison East
  Middleton
  Wausau
Lac Courte Oreilles Ojibwa
  Community College
Lakeshore Technical College
Madison Area Technical
  College
Madison Media Institute
Mid-State Technical College
Milwaukee Area Technical
  College
Moraine Park Technical College
Nicolet Area Technical College
Northcentral Technical College
Northeast Wisconsin Technical
  College
Rasmussen College
  Green Bay
  Wausau
Southwest Wisconsin Technical
  College

University of Wisconsin
  Richland
  Sheboygan
Waukesha County Technical
  College
Western Technical College
Wisconsin Indianhead Technical
  College

Wyoming

Casper College
Central Wyoming College
Eastern Wyoming College
Laramie County Community
  College
Northwest College
Sheridan College
Western Wyoming Community
  College

American Samoa

American Samoa Community
  College

Guam

Guam Community College

Bermuda

Bermuda College

Admission/ placement policies

Tables and Indexes

No closing date

Four-year

Alabama

Amridge University
Athens State University
Birmingham-Southern College
Columbia Southern University
Faulkner University
Herzing University
　Birmingham
Huntingdon College
ITT Technical Institute
　Birmingham
Jacksonville State University
Judson College
Oakwood University
Selma University
Southeastern Bible College
Stillman College
Talladega College
Troy University
United States Sports Academy
University of Alabama
University of Alabama
　Birmingham
University of Mobile
University of North Alabama
University of Phoenix
　Birmingham
University of West Alabama
Virginia College
　Birmingham
　Huntsville

Alaska

Charter College

Arizona

American Indian College of the
　Assemblies of God
Art Institute of Tucson
Brown Mackie College
　Tucson
Chamberlain College of Nursing
　Phoenix
DeVry University
　Phoenix
Dunlap-Stone University
Embry-Riddle Aeronautical
　University
　Prescott Campus
Grand Canyon University
Harrison Middleton University
International Baptist College
ITT Technical Institute
　Tempe
　Tucson
Northcentral University
Northern Arizona University
Prescott College
Southwest University of Visual
　Arts
University of Advancing
　Technology
University of Phoenix
　Phoenix-Hohokam
　Southern Arizona
Western International University

Arkansas

Arkansas Baptist College
Arkansas Tech University
Harding University

ITT Technical Institute
　Little Rock
John Brown University
Ouachita Baptist University
University of Arkansas
　Fort Smith
　Monticello
　Pine Bluff
University of Central Arkansas
University of Phoenix
　Little Rock
　Northwest Arkansas
University of the Ozarks
Williams Baptist College

California

Academy of Art University
Alliant International University
American Jewish University
Antioch University
　Santa Barbara
Art Center College of Design
Art Institute of California
　Hollywood
　Orange County
　Sacramento
　San Diego
　San Francisco
Ashford University
Brandman University
Brooks Institute
California Baptist University
California Christian College
California Coast University
California College of the Arts
California College San Diego
California National University
　for Advanced Studies
California State University
　Dominguez Hills
　San Bernardino
Cogswell Polytechnical College
Coleman University
Concordia University Irvine
Design Institute of San Diego
DeVry University
　Pomona
Dominican University of
　California
Ex'pression College
Golden Gate University
Humphreys College
Interior Designers Institute
International Academy of
　Design and Technology
　Sacramento
ITT Technical Institute
　Lathrop
　National City
　Oxnard
　Rancho Cordova
　San Bernardino
　Sylmar
　Torrance
John F. Kennedy University
John Paul the Great Catholic
　University
Lincoln University
Loma Linda University
Marymount California
　University
The Master's College
Mills College
Mt. Sierra College
National University
NewSchool of Architecture &
　Design
Notre Dame de Namur
　University
Otis College of Art and Design
Pacific Oaks College
Pacific States University
Pacific Union College
Platt College
　Ontario
　San Diego
Providence Christian College

Samuel Merritt University
San Diego Christian College
San Francisco Art Institute
Shasta Bible College and
　Graduate School
Simpson University
Southern California Institute of
　Technology
Southern California Seminary
Thomas Aquinas College
Trident University International
University of La Verne
University of Phoenix
　Bay Area
　Central Valley
　Sacramento Valley
　San Diego
　Southern California
University of San Francisco
West Coast University
　Los Angeles
West Coast University: Ontario
West Coast University: Orange
　County
Westmont College
Westwood College
　Anaheim
　Inland Empire
　South Bay
Whittier College
Woodbury University
World Mission University
Yeshiva Ohr Elchonon Chabad/
　West Coast Talmudical
　Seminary

Colorado

Adams State University
American Sentinel University
Aspen University
CollegeAmerica
　Colorado Springs
　Fort Collins
Colorado Heights University
Colorado Mesa University
Colorado Technical University
DeVry University
　Westminster
ITT Technical Institute
　Westminster
Johnson & Wales University
　Denver
Naropa University
National American University
　Denver
Nazarene Bible College
Platt College
　Aurora
Rocky Mountain College of
　Art & Design
University of Colorado
　Colorado Springs
　Denver
University of Phoenix
　Denver
　Southern Colorado
Western State Colorado
　University
Westwood College
　Aurora
　Denver North
　Online

Connecticut

Albertus Magnus College
Charter Oak State College
Eastern Connecticut State
　University
Holy Apostles College and
　Seminary
Lyme Academy College of Fine
　Arts
Mitchell College
Paier College of Art
Post University
Sacred Heart University
Southern Connecticut State
　University

University of Bridgeport
University of Hartford
University of New Haven
University of Saint Joseph
Western Connecticut State
　University

Delaware

Delaware State University
Goldey-Beacom College
Wesley College
Wilmington University

District of Columbia

Strayer University
University of Phoenix
　Washington DC
University of the Potomac

Florida

Art Institute of Fort Lauderdale
Ave Maria University
Barry University
Beacon College
Bethune-Cookman University
Carlos Albizu University
Chamberlain College of Nursing
　Jacksonville
　Miramar
City College
　Fort Lauderdale
DeVry University
　Miramar
　Orlando
Digital Media Arts College
Eckerd College
Edward Waters College
Embry-Riddle Aeronautical
　University
　Worldwide Campus
Everest University
　Orange Park
Everglades University
　Boca Raton
　Orlando
Florida Institute of Technology
Florida Memorial University
Florida Southern College
Full Sail University
Hodges University
International Academy of
　Design and Technology
　Orlando
International Academy of
　Design and Technology:
　Tampa
ITT Technical Institute
　Ft. Lauderdale
　Jacksonville
　Miami
　Tampa
Johnson & Wales University
　North Miami
Jones College
Jose Maria Vargas University
Keiser University
Miami International University
　of Art and Design
Palm Beach Atlantic University
Rasmussen College
　Fort Myers
　New Port Richey
　Ocala
　Tampa/Brandon
Remington College
　Tampa
Ringling College of Art and
　Design
Saint Leo University
Saint Thomas University
Schiller International University
Stetson University
Talmudic University
University of North Florida

University of Phoenix
　Central Florida
　North Florida
　South Florida
　West Florida
University of Tampa
Warner University

Georgia

Art Institute of Atlanta
Bauder College
Brenau University
Carver College
Chamberlain College of Nursing
　Atlanta
Clayton State University
College of Coastal Georgia
DeVry University
　Decatur
Georgia College and State
　University
Herzing University
　Atlanta
Luther Rice University
Reinhardt University
Savannah College of Art and
　Design
Shorter University
South Georgia State College
South University
　Savannah
Thomas University
University of Phoenix
　Atlanta
　Augusta
　Columbus
　Savannah
Westwood College
　Atlanta Midtown
　Northlake
Young Harris College

Hawaii

Chaminade University of
　Honolulu
University of Phoenix
　Hawaii

Idaho

Idaho State University
ITT Technical Institute
　Boise
University of Phoenix
　Idaho

Illinois

American Academy of Art
American InterContinental
　University
Argosy University
　Schaumburg
Augustana College
Aurora University
Benedictine University
Blackburn College
Blessing-Rieman College of
　Nursing
Bradley University
Chamberlain College of Nursing
　Addison
　Chicago
Chicago State University
Columbia College Chicago
DeVry University
　Chicago
　Online
Dominican University
East-West University
Elmhurst College
Greenville College
Hebrew Theological College
Illinois College
Illinois Institute of Art
　Chicago
　Schaumburg
Illinois Wesleyan University

International Academy of
Design and Technology
Chicago
ITT Technical Institute
Arlington Heights
Judson University
Kendall College
Lake Forest College
Lewis University
Lincoln Christian University
Loyola University Chicago
MacMurray College
McKendree University
Midstate College
Millikin University
Monmouth College
National-Louis University
North Central College
Principia College
Quincy University
Rasmussen College
Mokena/Tinley Park
Robert Morris University:
Chicago
Roosevelt University
Rush University
St. Augustine College
Saint Xavier University
Shimer College
Telshe Yeshiva-Chicago
Trinity Christian College
Trinity College of Nursing &
Health Sciences
Trinity International University
University of Illinois
Springfield
University of Phoenix
Chicago
VanderCook College of Music
Western Illinois University
Westwood College
DuPage
O'Hare Airport
River Oaks

Indiana

Calumet College of St. Joseph
Chamberlain College of Nursing
Indianapolis
Crossroads Bible College
Franklin College
Hanover College
Indiana Institute of Technology
Indiana University
Bloomington
East
Kokomo
Northwest
South Bend
Southeast
Indiana Wesleyan University
International Business College
ITT Technical Institute
Fort Wayne
Indianapolis
Manchester University
Martin University
Oakland City University
Purdue University
Purdue University
North Central
Saint Joseph's College
Saint Mary's College
St. Mary-of-the-Woods College
Taylor University
University of Evansville
University of Indianapolis
University of Phoenix
Indianapolis
University of Saint Francis
Valparaiso University
Wabash College

Iowa

Briar Cliff University
Buena Vista University
Clarke University
Cornell College

Drake University
Emmaus Bible College
Graceland University
Hamilton Technical College
Iowa State University
Iowa Wesleyan College
Kaplan University
Cedar Falls
Davenport
Des Moines
Mason City
Loras College
Luther College
Maharishi University of
Management
Morningside College
Northwestern College
St. Ambrose University
Simpson College
University of Dubuque
University of Phoenix
Des Moines
Upper Iowa University
Waldorf University
Wartburg College
William Penn University

Kansas

Baker University
Benedictine College
Bethany College
Central Christian College of
Kansas
Emporia State University
Fort Hays State University
Friends University
Grantham University
Kansas State University
Kansas Wesleyan University
Manhattan Christian College
McPherson College
Newman University
Ottawa University
Pittsburg State University
Sterling College
Tabor College
University of Kansas
University of Kansas Medical
Center
University of St. Mary
Wichita State University

Kentucky

Alice Lloyd College
Asbury University
Beckfield College
Brescia University
Campbellsville University
Clear Creek Baptist Bible
College
ITT Technical Institute
Louisville
Kentucky Mountain Bible
College
Kentucky Wesleyan College
Lindsey Wilson College
Midway College
Morehead State University
St. Catharine College
Southern Baptist Theological
Seminary
Spalding University
Sullivan University
Transylvania University
Union College
University of Kentucky
University of Phoenix
Louisville

Louisiana

Herzing University
Kenner
ITT Technical Institute
St. Rose
Louisiana State University
Alexandria
Shreveport
Loyola University New Orleans

New Orleans Baptist
Theological Seminary
Nicholls State University
Northwestern State University
St. Joseph Seminary College
Southern University
New Orleans
Southwest University
University of Holy Cross
University of Louisiana at
Lafayette
University of Louisiana at
Monroe
University of Phoenix
Baton Rouge
Louisiana
Shreveport

Maine

Maine College of Art
Saint Joseph's College of Maine
University of Maine
University of Maine
Farmington
Presque Isle
University of Southern Maine

Maryland

Bowie State University
Capitol Technology University
Frostburg State University
Hood College
McDaniel College
Ner Israel Rabbinical College
Notre Dame of Maryland
University
St. John's College
Stevenson University
University of Maryland
University College
University of Phoenix
Maryland

Massachusetts

American International College
Anna Maria College
Becker College
Boston Architectural College
Bridgewater State University
Cambridge College
Curry College
Eastern Nazarene College
Elms College
Fisher College
Fitchburg State University
Framingham State University
Lasell College
Lesley University
Massachusetts College of Art
and Design
Massachusetts College of
Liberal Arts
Massachusetts Maritime
Academy
MCPHS University
Montserrat College of Art
Mount Ida College
Newbury College
Nichols College
Northpoint Bible College
School of the Museum of Fine
Arts
University of Massachusetts
Dartmouth
University of Phoenix
Boston
Wentworth Institute of
Technology
Western New England
University

Michigan

Albion College
Alma College
Andrews University
Aquinas College

Baker College
of Allen Park
of Auburn Hills
of Cadillac
of Clinton Township
of Flint
of Jackson
of Muskegon
of Owosso
of Port Huron
Concordia University
Cornerstone University
Davenport University
Eastern Michigan University
Hope College
International Academy of
Design and Technology
Detroit
Kettering University
Lawrence Technological
University
Madonna University
Manthano Christian College
Michigan Jewish Institute
Michigan State University
Michigan Technological
University
Northern Michigan University
Northwood University
Michigan
Robert B. Miller College
Rochester College
Saginaw Valley State University
University of Michigan
Dearborn
University of Phoenix
Metro Detroit
West Michigan
Walsh College of Accountancy
and Business Administration
Western Michigan University
Yeshiva Beth Yehuda-Yeshiva
Gedolah of Greater Detroit

Minnesota

Art Institutes International
Minnesota
Bemidji State University
Bethel University
Brown College
Mendota Heights
Capella University
College of St. Benedict
College of St. Scholastica
Concordia College: Moorhead
Crown College
Globe University
Minneapolis
Moorhead
Woodbury
Hamline University
Martin Luther College
McNally Smith College of
Music
Minnesota School of Business
Blaine
Elk River
Lakeville
Plymouth
Richfield
Rochester
St. Cloud
Shakopee
Minnesota State University
Mankato
National American University
Bloomington
Northwestern Health Sciences
University
Oak Hills Christian College
Rasmussen College
Blaine
Lake Elmo/Woodbury
Moorhead
St. Catherine University
St. John's University

Southwest Minnesota State
University
University of Minnesota
Crookston
Rochester
Twin Cities
University of Phoenix
Minneapolis-St. Paul
University of St. Thomas
Walden University

Mississippi

Alcorn State University
Belhaven University
Blue Mountain College
Delta State University
Mississippi College
Mississippi State University
Mississippi University for
Women
Rust College
Tougaloo College
University of Mississippi
Medical Center
University of Phoenix
Jackson
University of Southern
Mississippi
William Carey University

Missouri

Avila University
Baptist Bible College
Calvary Bible College and
Theological Seminary
Central Christian College of the
Bible
Central Methodist University
Chamberlain College of Nursing
St. Louis
College of the Ozarks
Columbia College
DeVry University
Kansas City
Evangel University
Goldfarb School of Nursing at
Barnes-Jewish College
Hannibal-LaGrange University
Harris-Stowe State University
Hickey College
ITT Technical Institute
Arnold
Earth City
Lincoln University
Lindenwood University
Logan University
Missouri Baptist University
Missouri Southern State
University
Missouri Tech
Missouri Valley College
Missouri Western State
University
National American University
Kansas City
Northwest Missouri State
University
Research College of Nursing
Rockhurst University
Southwest Baptist University
Stephens College
Truman State University
University of Central Missouri
University of Missouri
Columbia
University of Phoenix
Kansas City
St. Louis
Westminster College
William Woods University

Montana

Montana Bible College
Montana State University
Billings
Northern
Montana Tech of the University
of Montana

Rocky Mountain College
Salish Kootenai College
University of Montana
University of Montana: Western

Nebraska

Bellevue University
Chadron State College
Clarkson College
College of Saint Mary
Creative Center
Doane College
Grace University
Hastings College
Herzing University
Omaha School of Massage
Therapy and Healthcare
ITT Technical Institute
Omaha
Midland University
Nebraska Christian College
Nebraska Methodist College of
Nursing and Allied Health
Peru State College

Nevada

Art Institute of Las Vegas
Great Basin College
International Academy of
Design and Technology
Henderson
ITT Technical Institute
Henderson
University of Phoenix
Las Vegas
Northern Nevada

New Hampshire

Colby-Sawyer College
Daniel Webster College
Franklin Pierce University
Granite State College
Mount Washington College
New England College
New Hampshire Institute of Art
Northeast Catholic College
Plymouth State University
Rivier University
Southern New Hampshire
University
Thomas More College of
Liberal Arts

New Jersey

Berkeley College
Caldwell University
Centenary College
College of St. Elizabeth
DeVry University
North Brunswick
Fairleigh Dickinson University
College at Florham
Metropolitan Campus
Felician University
Rider University
Seton Hall University
Talmudical Academy of New
Jersey
Thomas Edison State University
University of Phoenix
Jersey City

New Mexico

Eastern New Mexico University
ITT Technical Institute
Albuquerque
National American University
Albuquerque
New Mexico Highlands
University
New Mexico State University
St. John's College
Santa Fe University of Art and
Design
Southwest University of Visual
Arts
University of New Mexico

University of Phoenix
New Mexico
University of the Southwest

New York

Adelphi University
Beis Medrash Heichal Dovid
Berkeley College
Berkeley College of New York
City
Beth Hamedrash Shaarei Yosher
Institute
Boricua College
Briarcliffe College
Cazenovia College
Central Yeshiva Tomchei
Tmimim-Lubavitch
City University of New York
Brooklyn College
College of Staten Island
Medgar Evers College
College of Mount St. Vincent
College of New Rochelle
Concordia College
Culinary Institute of America
D'Youville College
Daemen College
Davis College
DeVry College of New York
Midtown Campus
Dominican College of Blauvelt
Dowling College
Elmira College
Excelsior College
Five Towns College
Globe Institute of Technology
Hartwick College
Hofstra University
Houghton College
Kehilath Yakov Rabbinical
Seminary
Keuka College
The King's College
Le Moyne College
LIM College
Long Island University
LIU Brooklyn
LIU Post
Manhattan College
Manhattanville College
Marymount Manhattan College
Medaille College
Medaille College: Rochester
Mercy College
Mesivta Torah Vodaath
Seminary
Metropolitan College of New
York
Mirrer Yeshiva Central Institute
Molloy College
Monroe College
New York Institute of
Technology
New York School of Interior
Design
Nyack College
Ohr Somayach Tanenbaum
Education Center
Pace University
Pace University: Pleasantville/
Briarcliff
Paul Smith's College
Rabbinical Academy Mesivta
Rabbi Chaim Berlin
Rabbinical College Beth Shraga
Rabbinical College Bobover
Yeshiva B'nei Zion
Rabbinical College of Long
Island
Rabbinical College of Ohr
Shimon Yisroel
Rochester Institute of
Technology
The Sage Colleges
St. Francis College
St. John Fisher College
St. John's University

St. Joseph's College New York:
Suffolk Campus
St. Joseph's College, New York
St. Thomas Aquinas College
School of Visual Arts
Shor Yoshuv Rabbinical College
SUNY
College at Buffalo
College at Cortland
College at Fredonia
College at Old Westbury
College at Oneonta
College at Oswego
College at Potsdam
College of Environmental
Science and Forestry
Empire State College
University at Binghamton
University at Buffalo
Upstate Medical University
Talmudical Seminary Oholei
Torah
Torah Temimah Talmudical
Seminary
Touro College
U.T.A. Mesivta-Kiryas Joel
United Talmudical Seminary
Utica College
Vaughn College of Aeronautics
and Technology
Yeshiva and Kolel Bais
Medrash Elyon
Yeshiva and Kollel Harbotzas
Torah
Yeshiva D'Monsey Rabbinical
College
Yeshiva Derech Chaim
Yeshiva Gedolah Zichron
Moshe
Yeshiva Karlin Stolin
Yeshiva of Nitra
Yeshiva of the Telshe Alumni
Yeshiva Shaar Hatorah
Yeshiva Shaarei Torah of
Rockland
Yeshivas Novominsk
Yeshivat Mikdash Melech
Yeshivath Viznitz

North Carolina

Apex School of Theology
Barton College
Bennett College for Women
Brevard College
Cabarrus College of Health
Sciences
Campbell University
Carolina Christian College
Catawba College
Charlotte Christian College and
Theological Seminary
Chowan University
Gardner-Webb University
Greensboro College
Guilford College
Johnson and Wales University
Charlotte
Johnson C. Smith University
Lees-McRae College
Lenoir-Rhyne University
Livingstone College
Mars Hill University
Meredith College
Methodist University
Mid-Atlantic Christian
University
Miller-Motte College
Wilmington
Montreat College
North Carolina Wesleyan
College
Pfeiffer University
Piedmont International
University
St. Andrews University
Saint Augustine's University
Salem College

University of Mount Olive
University of Phoenix
Charlotte
Raleigh
Warren Wilson College
William Peace University
Wingate University

North Dakota

Mayville State University
Minot State University
Rasmussen College
Fargo
Trinity Bible College
University of Jamestown
University of Mary
University of North Dakota
Valley City State University

Ohio

Ashland University
Baldwin Wallace University
Central State University
Chamberlain College Of
Nursing
Chamberlain College of
Nursing: Cleveland
Chamberlain College of Nursing
Columbus
Cleveland Institute of Art
Defiance College
DeVry University
Columbus
Franciscan University of
Steubenville
Franklin University
God's Bible School and College
Hiram College
John Carroll University
Kettering College
Lourdes University
Malone University
Mercy College of Ohio
Notre Dame College
Ohio Christian University
Ohio Dominican University
Ohio University
Chillicothe Campus
Eastern Campus
Lancaster Campus
Southern Campus at Ironton
Zanesville Campus
Otterbein University
Pontifical College Josephinum
Shawnee State University
Tiffin University
Tri-State Bible College
Union Institute & University
University of Findlay
University of Mount Union
University of Phoenix
Cleveland
University of Rio Grande
University of Toledo
Urbana University
Ursuline College
Wittenberg University
Wright State University
Xavier University

Oklahoma

Bacone College
Cameron University
East Central University
Hillsdale Free Will Baptist
College
ITT Technical Institute
Tulsa
Mid-America Christian
University
Northeastern State University
Northwestern Oklahoma State
University
Oklahoma Christian University
Oklahoma Panhandle State
University
Oklahoma State University
Oklahoma Wesleyan University

Oral Roberts University
Rogers State University
St. Gregory's University
Southeastern Oklahoma State
University
Southwestern Christian
University
Southwestern Oklahoma State
University
Spartan College of Aeronautics
and Technology
University of Central Oklahoma
University of Phoenix
Oklahoma City
Tulsa
University of Tulsa

Oregon

Art Institute of Portland
George Fox University
ITT Technical Institute
Portland
Linfield College
Marylhurst University
Multnomah University
Northwest Christian University
Oregon College of Art & Craft
Pacific Northwest College of
Art
Portland State University
Southern Oregon University
University of Phoenix
Oregon
Warner Pacific College
Western Oregon University
Willamette University

Pennsylvania

Albright College
Alvernia University
Art Institute of Philadelphia
Bloomsburg University of
Pennsylvania
Bryn Athyn College
Cabrini College
Cairn University
Carlow University
Cedar Crest College
Central Penn College
Chestnut Hill College
Cheyney University of
Pennsylvania
DeVry University
Fort Washington
Eastern University
Edinboro University
of Pennsylvania
Elizabethtown College
Gannon University
Geneva College
Gratz College
Harrisburg University of
Science and Technology
Holy Family University
Immaculata University
Indiana University of
Pennsylvania
King's College
Kutztown University of
Pennsylvania
La Roche College
La Salle University
Lancaster Bible College
Lebanon Valley College
Lincoln University
Lock Haven University of
Pennsylvania
Mansfield University of
Pennsylvania
Marywood University
Mercyhurst University
Messiah College
Millersville University of
Pennsylvania
Misericordia University
Mount Aloysius College
Neumann University
Peirce College

Penn State
Abington
Altoona
Beaver
Berks
Brandywine
DuBois
Erie, The Behrend College
Fayette, The Eberly Campus
Greater Allegheny
Harrisburg
Hazleton
Lehigh Valley
Mont Alto
New Kensington
Schuylkill
Shenango
University Park
Wilkes-Barre
Worthington Scranton
York
Pennsylvania Academy of the
Fine Arts
Pennsylvania College of Art and
Design
Philadelphia University
Point Park University
Restaurant School at Walnut
Hill College
Robert Morris University
Rosemont College
Saint Joseph's University
Shippensburg University of
Pennsylvania
Slippery Rock University of
Pennsylvania
Susquehanna University
Talmudical Yeshiva of
Philadelphia
Thiel College
Thomas Jefferson University
University of Phoenix
Harrisburg
Philadelphia
Pittsburgh
University of Pittsburgh
University of Pittsburgh
Bradford
Greensburg
University of the Arts
Ursinus College
Waynesburg University
West Chester University of
Pennsylvania
Widener University
Wilkes University
Yeshivath Beth Moshe
York College of Pennsylvania

Puerto Rico

American University of Puerto
Rico
Atlantic University College
Bayamon Central University
Columbia Central University
Caguas
EDP University of Puerto Rico:
Hato Rey
EDP University of Puerto Rico:
San Sebastian
Inter American University of
Puerto Rico
Arecibo Campus
Barranquitas Campus
Guayama Campus
Theological University of the
Caribbean
Turabo University
Universidad Adventista de las
Antillas
Universidad del Este
Universidad Politecnica de
Puerto Rico
University of Phoenix
Puerto Rico

Rhode Island

Johnson & Wales University
Providence
New England Institute of
Technology
Salve Regina University

South Carolina

Benedict College
Charleston Southern University
The Citadel
Columbia College
Converse College
ITT Technical Institute
Greenville
Lander University
Morris College
Newberry College
University of Phoenix
Columbia
University of South Carolina
Upstate
Voorhees College
W.L. Bonner Bible College
Winthrop University

South Dakota

Augusta University
Augustana University
Dakota State University
National American University
Rapid City
Northern State University
Oglala Lakota College
Sinte Gleska University
South Dakota School of Mines
and Technology
University of South Dakota

Tennessee

Aquinas College
Bethel University
Bryan College
Dayton
Carson-Newman University
Christian Brothers University
Cumberland University
Fisk University
Freed-Hardeman University
ITT Technical Institute
Knoxville
Nashville
King University
Lee University
Lincoln Memorial University
Lipscomb University
Maryville College
Memphis College of Art
Middle Tennessee State
University
Milligan College
South College
Southern Adventist University
Tusculum College
University of Phoenix
Knoxville
Memphis
Nashville
University of Tennessee
Martin
Welch College
Williamson College

Texas

Amberton University
Arlington Baptist College
Art Institute of Dallas
Art Institute of Houston
Austin Graduate School of
Theology
Baptist University of the
Americas
Chamberlain College of Nursing
Houston
College of Biblical Studies-
Houston
Criswell College
Dallas Baptist University

DeVry University
Houston
Irving
Hardin-Simmons University
Houston Baptist University
Howard Payne University
Jarvis Christian College
The King's University
LeTourneau University
National American University
Austin
Paul Quinn College
St. Mary's University
Southwestern Assemblies of
God University
Southwestern Baptist
Theological Seminary
Southwestern University
Stephen F. Austin State
University
Sul Ross State University
Texas A&M University
Texarkana
Texas College
Texas Wesleyan University
University of Mary Hardin-
Baylor
University of Phoenix
Austin
Dallas Fort Worth
Houston Westside
San Antonio
University of Texas
Arlington
University of the Incarnate
Word
Wayland Baptist University
West Coast University: Dallas
West Texas A&M University
Wiley College

Utah

Broadview University
Orem
Independence University
ITT Technical Institute
Murray
Neumont University
Stevens-Henager College
Logan
Murray
Ogden
Orem
University of Phoenix
Utah
Utah State University
Western Governors University

Vermont

Castleton State College
College of St. Joseph in
Vermont
Green Mountain College
Johnson State College
Lyndon State College
Marlboro College
Norwich University
Southern Vermont College
Vermont Technical College

Virginia

Art Institute of Washington
Averett University
Catholic Distance University
Chamberlain College of Nursing
Arlington
Christendom College
DeVry University
Arlington
Eastern Mennonite University
ECPI University
Emory & Henry College
Ferrum College
Hollins University
ITT Technical Institute
Chantilly
Norfolk
Richmond

Jefferson College of Health
Sciences
Liberty University
Longwood University
Lynchburg College
Mary Baldwin College
Marymount University
Radford University
Shenandoah University
Stratford University: Falls
Church
Stratford University:
Woodbridge
University of Management and
Technology
University of Mary Washington
University of Phoenix
Northern Virginia
Richmond
University of the Potomac
Virginia Baptist College
Virginia University of
Lynchburg
Virginia Wesleyan College
Westwood College
Annandale
Arlington Ballston

Washington

Art Institute of Seattle
Central Washington University
City University of Seattle
Cornish College of the Arts
DeVry University
Federal Way
DigiPen Institute of Technology
Evergreen State College
Faith Evangelical College &
Seminary
Heritage University
International Academy of
Design and Technology
Seattle
ITT Technical Institute
Seattle
Spokane
Northwest College of Art &
Design
Pacific Lutheran University
Seattle University
Trinity Lutheran College
University of Phoenix
Western Washington
University of Washington
Bothell
Walla Walla University
Washington State University

West Virginia

Alderson-Broaddus University
American Public University
System
Appalachian Bible College
Bethany College
Concord University
Davis and Elkins College
Glenville State College
Marshall University
Salem International University
Shepherd University
University of Charleston
West Liberty University
West Virginia University
Institute of Technology
Wheeling Jesuit University

Wisconsin

Alverno College
Bellin College
Beloit College
Cardinal Stritch University
Carroll University
Carthage College
Globe University
Green Bay
Herzing University
Madison
Lakeland College

Maranathan Baptist University
Maranatha Baptist
University
Marian University
Milwaukee School of
Engineering
Mount Mary University
Northland College
Rasmussen College
Appleton
Ripon College
St. Norbert College
Silver Lake College of the Holy
Family
University of Phoenix
Milwaukee
University of Wisconsin
Green Bay
La Crosse
Milwaukee
Oshkosh
Platteville
River Falls
Stevens Point
Stout
Wisconsin Lutheran College

Belgium

Vesalius College

France

American University of Paris

Greece

Deree College, The American
College of Greece

Italy

American University of Rome

Mexico

Instituto Tecnologico Autonomo
de Mexico

New Zealand

University of Auckland

Spain

Saint Louis University: Madrid

Switzerland

Franklin University Switzerland

United Arab Emirates

American University in Dubai

United Kingdom

Richmond, The American
International University in
London
University of Chichester

Two-year

Alabama

Alabama Southern Community
College
Bevill State Community College
Bishop State Community
College
Calhoun Community College
Central Alabama Community
College
Chattahoochee Valley
Community College
Community College of the Air
Force
Enterprise State Community
College
Faulkner State Community
College
Gadsden State Community
College
George C. Wallace Community
College at Dothan
George C. Wallace State
Community College at Selma
Jefferson Davis Community
College

Jefferson State Community
College
Lawson State Community
College
Lurleen B. Wallace Community
College
Northeast Alabama Community
College
Northwest-Shoals Community
College
Remington College
Mobile
Shelton State Community
College
Southern Union State
Community College
Virginia College
Mobile
Wallace State Community
College at Hanceville

Arizona

Arizona Western College
Brookline College
Phoenix
Tempe
Tucson
Bryan University
Carrington College
Mesa
Phoenix
Phoenix Westside
Tucson
Central Arizona College
Chandler-Gilbert Community
College
Cochise College
Coconino County Community
College
Dine College
Eastern Arizona College
Estrella Mountain Community
College
GateWay Community College
Le Cordon Bleu College of
Culinary Arts
Scottsdale
Mesa Community College
Mohave Community College
Northland Pioneer College
Paradise Valley Community
College
Penn Foster College
Phoenix College
Pima Community College
Refrigeration School
Rio Salado College
Scottsdale Community College
South Mountain Community
College
Tohono O'odham Community
College
Universal Technical Institute
Yavapai College

Arkansas

Arkansas Northeastern College
Arkansas State University
Beebe
Mid-South
Newport
Black River Technical College
Bryan University
Rogers
College of the Ouachitas
Cossatot Community College
of the University of
Arkansas
East Arkansas Community
College
National Park College
North Arkansas College
Northwest Arkansas Community
College
Ozarka College
Phillips Community College of
the University of Arkansas
Pulaski Technical College

Remington College
Little Rock
Rich Mountain Community
College
South Arkansas Community
College
Southeast Arkansas College
University of Arkansas
Community College at
Batesville
Community College at
Hope
Community College at
Morrilton

California

Allan Hancock College
American River College
Antelope Valley College
Art Institute of California
Los Angeles
Bakersfield College
Barstow Community College
Berkeley City College
Bryan College: Sacramento
Butte College
Cabrillo College
Canada College
Carrington College
Citrus Heights
Pleasant Hill
Sacramento
San Jose
San Leandro
Stockton
Cerritos College
Cerro Coso Community College
Chaffey College
Citrus College
City College of San Francisco
Coastline Community College
College of Alameda
College of Marin
College of San Mateo
College of the Canyons
College of the Redwoods
College of the Sequoias
College of the Siskiyous
Columbia College
Concorde Career College
Garden Grove
North Hollywood
San Diego
Contra Costa College
Copper Mountain College
Cosumnes River College
Crafton Hills College
Cuesta College
Cuyamaca College
Cypress College
De Anza College
Diablo Valley College
East Los Angeles College
El Camino College
Empire College
Evergreen Valley College
Fashion Institute of Design and
Merchandising
Los Angeles
San Diego
San Francisco
Feather River College
Folsom Lake College
Foothill College
Fremont College
Fresno City College
Fullerton College
Gavilan College
Glendale Community College
Golden West College
Golf Academy of America
San Diego
Grossmont College
Hartnell College
Imperial Valley College
Irvine Valley College

Kaplan College
Riverside
Sacramento
Salida
Vista
Lake Tahoe Community College
Laney College
Las Positas College
Lassen Community College
Le Cordon Bleu College of
Culinary Arts
Los Angeles
San Francisco
Long Beach City College
Los Angeles Mission College
Los Angeles Southwest College
Los Angeles Valley College
Los Medanos College
Mendocino College
Merced College
Merritt College
MiraCosta College
Mission College
Modesto Junior College
Monterey Peninsula College
Moorpark College
Moreno Valley College
Mount San Antonio College
MTI College
Napa Valley College
Norco College
Ohlone College
Orange Coast College
Oxnard College
Palomar College
Platt College
Los Angeles
Porterville College
Professional Golfers Career
College
Reedley College
Rio Hondo College
Riverside City College
Sacramento City College
Saddleback College
Sage College
Salvation Army College for
Officer Training at Crestmont
San Bernardino Valley College
San Deigo Miramar College
San Diego Miramar College
San Diego City College
San Diego Mesa College
San Joaquin Delta College
San Joaquin Valley College
San Jose City College
Santa Ana College
Santa Barbara Business College
Bakersfield
Rancho Mirage
Santa Maria
Ventura
Santa Monica College
Santa Rosa Junior College
Shasta College
Sierra College
Skyline College
Solano Community College
Southwestern College
Taft College
Ventura College
Victor Valley College
West Hills College: Coalinga
West Hills College: Lemoore
West Los Angeles College
West Valley College
Westwood College
Los Angeles
Woodland Community College
Yuba College

Colorado

Aims Community College
Arapahoe Community College
Bel-Rea Institute of Animal
Technology

CollegeAmerica
Denver
Colorado Mountain College
Colorado Northwestern
Community College
Colorado School of Healing
Arts
Colorado School of Trades
Community College of Aurora
Community College of Denver
Concorde Career College
Aurora
Front Range Community
College
IBMC College
Fort Collins
IntelliTec College
IntelliTec College: Grand
Junction
Lamar Community College
Lincoln College of Technology
Denver
Morgan Community College
Northeastern Junior College
Pikes Peak Community College
Red Rocks Community College
Redstone College

Connecticut

Asnuntuck Community College
Capital Community College
Goodwin College
Housatonic Community College
Lincoln College of New
England
Manchester Community College
Naugatuck Valley Community
College
Northwestern Connecticut
Community College
Norwalk Community College
Quinebaug Valley Community
College
St. Vincent's College
Three Rivers Community
College
Tunxis Community College

Delaware

Delaware College of Art and
Design
Delaware Technical Community
College
Jack F. Owens Campus
Stanton/Wilmington
Campus
Terry Campus

Florida

Broward College
Brown Mackie College
Miami
Chipola College
City College
Altamonte Springs
Gainesville
Miami
College of Business and
Technology
Cutler Bay
Flagler
Hialeah
Kendall
Miami Gardens
Daytona State College
Eastern Florida State College
Florida Career College
Miami
Florida College of Natural
Health
Bradenton
Maitland
Miami
Pompano Beach
Florida Keys Community
College
Florida National University

Florida State College at
Jacksonville
Florida Technical College
Orlando
Fortis College
Orange Park
Winter Park
Golf Academy of America
Orlando
Gulf Coast State College
Herzing University
Winter Park
Indian River State College
Key College
Le Cordon Bleu College of
Culinary Arts
Miami
Orlando
Lincoln College of Technology
West Palm Beach
Miami Dade College
North Florida Community
College
Northwest Florida State College
Pasco-Hernando State College
Pensacola State College
Polk State College
Rasmussen College
Pasco/Land O'Lakes
Saint Johns River State College
St. Petersburg College
Santa Fe College
South Florida State College
Southeastern College
Greenacres
Southern Technical College
Southwest Florida College
Tampa
State College of Florida,
Manatee-Sarasota
Tallahassee Community College
University of Southernmost
Florida

Georgia

Albany Technical College
Ashworth College
Athens Technical College
Atlanta Metropolitan College
Augusta Technical College
Brown Mackie College
Atlanta
Central Georgia Technical
College
Coastal Pines Technical College
Columbus Technical College
Darton College
East Georgia State College
Georgia Military College
Georgia Northwestern Technical
College
Gordon State College
Gupton Jones College of
Funeral Service
Gwinnett College
Le Cordon Bleu College of
Culinary Arts
Atlanta
Savannah Technical College
Southeastern Technical College
Southern Crescent Technical
College
Southern Regional Technical
College
Virginia College
Augusta
Macon
West Georgia Technical College
Wiregrass Georgia Technical
College

Hawaii

Remington College
Honolulu

University of Hawaii
  Honolulu Community
    College
  Kauai Community College
  Maui College
  Windward Community
    College

Idaho

Broadview University
  Boise
Carrington College
  Boise
College of Southern Idaho
College of Western Idaho
Eastern Idaho Technical College
North Idaho College
Stevens-Henager College
  Boise

Illinois

Benedictine University at
  Springfield
Black Hawk College
Carl Sandburg College
City Colleges of Chicago
  Harold Washington College
  Harry S. Truman College
  Kennedy-King College
  Malcolm X College
  Olive-Harvey College
  Richard J. Daley College
  Wilbur Wright College
College of DuPage
College of Lake County
Danville Area Community
  College
Elgin Community College
Fox College
Harper College
Heartland Community College
Highland Community College
Illinois Central College
Illinois Eastern Community
  Colleges
  Frontier Community
    College
  Lincoln Trail College
  Olney Central College
  Wabash Valley College
Illinois Valley Community
  College
John A. Logan College
John Wood Community College
Joliet Junior College
Kankakee Community College
Kaskaskia College
Kishwaukee College
Lake Land College
Le Cordon Bleu College of
  Culinary Arts
  Chicago
Lewis and Clark Community
  College
Lincoln College
Lincoln Land Community
  College
MacCormac College
McHenry County College
Moraine Valley Community
  College
Morrison Institute of
  Technology
Morton College
Northwestern College
Oakton Community College
Parkland College
Prairie State College
Rasmussen College
  Aurora
  Rockford
  Romeoville/Joliet
Rend Lake College
Richland Community College
Rock Valley College
Rockford Career College
Sauk Valley Community
  College

Shawnee Community College
South Suburban College of
  Cook County
Southeastern Illinois College
Southwestern Illinois College
Spoon River College
Taylor Business Institute
Triton College
Vatterott College
  Quincy
Waubonsee Community College

Indiana

American National University
  Fort Wayne
  Indianapolis
  South Bend
Ancilla College
Brown Mackie College
  Fort Wayne
  Merrillville
  Michigan City
  South Bend
Fortis College
  Indianapolis
Harrison College
  Indianapolis
International Business College:
  Indianapolis
Ivy Tech Community College
  Bloomington
  Central Indiana
  Columbus
  East Central
  Kokomo
  Lafayette
  North Central
  Northeast
  Northwest
  Richmond
  South Central
  Southeast
  Southwest
  Wabash Valley
Kaplan College
  Hammond
  Indianapolis
Lincoln College of Technology
  Indianapolis
Mid-America College of
  Funeral Service
Vincennes University

Iowa

Clinton Community College
Des Moines Area Community
  College
Ellsworth Community College
Hawkeye Community College
Iowa Central Community
  College
Iowa Lakes Community College
Iowa Western Community
  College
Kaplan University
  Cedar Rapids
Kirkwood Community College
Marshalltown Community
  College
Muscatine Community College
North Iowa Area Community
  College
Northeast Iowa Community
  College
Northwest Iowa Community
  College
St. Luke's College
Scott Community College
Southeastern Community
  College
Southwestern Community
  College
Vatterott College
  Des Moines
Western Iowa Tech Community
  College

Kansas

Allen County Community
  College
Barton County Community
  College
Brown Mackie College
  Salina
Butler Community College
Cloud County Community
  College
Coffeyville Community College
Colby Community College
Cowley County Community
  College
Dodge City Community College
Donnelly College
Fort Scott Community College
Garden City Community
  College
Hesston College
Highland Community College
Hutchinson Community College
Independence Community
  College
Johnson County Community
  College
Kansas City Kansas Community
  College
Labette Community College
Manhattan Area Technical
  College
Neosho County Community
  College
North Central Kansas Technical
  College
Northwest Kansas Technical
  College
Pratt Community College
Seward County Community
  College
Wichita Area Technical College
Wright Career College
  Overland Park

Kentucky

Big Sandy Community and
  Technical College
Brown Mackie College
  Hopkinsville
  Louisville
  North Kentucky
Daymar College
  Bowling Green
  Louisville
  Owensboro
  Paducah
Elizabethtown Community and
  Technical College
Gateway Community and
  Technical College
Hazard Community and
  Technical College
Hopkinsville Community
  College
Jefferson Community and
  Technical College
Lincoln College of Technology
  Florence
Maysville Community and
  Technical College
National College
  Danville
  Florence
  Lexington
  Louisville
  Pikeville
  Richmond
Somerset Community College
Southeast Kentucky Community
  and Technical College
Spencerian College: Lexington
Sullivan College of Technology
  and Design
West Kentucky Community and
  Technical College

Louisiana

Baton Rouge School of
  Computers
Blue Cliff College
  Metairie
  Shreveport
Delgado Community College
Delta College of Arts &
  Technology
Delta School of Business &
  Technology
ITI Technical College
Nunez Community College
Remington College
  Baton Rouge
  Lafayette
  Shreveport
South Louisiana Community
  College
Southern University
  Shreveport
Virginia College
  Baton Rouge

Maine

Beal College
Central Maine Community
  College
Eastern Maine Community
  College
Kaplan University
  South Portland
Kennebec Valley Community
  College
Landing School of Boatbuilding
  and Design
Northern Maine Community
  College
Southern Maine Community
  College
York County Community
  College

Maryland

Allegany College of Maryland
Anne Arundel Community
  College
Carroll Community College
Cecil College
Chesapeake College
College of Southern Maryland
Community College of
  Baltimore County
Frederick Community College
Garrett College
Hagerstown Community College
Harford Community College
Howard Community College
Kaplan University
  Hagerstown
Montgomery College
Prince George's Community
  College
TESST College of Technology
  Baltimore
  Beltsville
  Towson
Wor-Wic Community College

Massachusetts

Bay State College
Benjamin Franklin Institute of
  Technology
Berkshire Community College
Bristol Community College
Bunker Hill Community College
Cape Cod Community College
Greenfield Community College
Holyoke Community College
ITT Technical Institute
  Norwood
  Wilmington
Laboure College
Massachusetts Bay Community
  College
Massasoit Community College
Middlesex Community College

Mount Wachusett Community
  College
New England College of
  Business and Finance
North Shore Community
  College
Northern Essex Community
  College
Quincy College
Quinsigamond Community
  College
Roxbury Community College
Springfield Technical
  Community College
Urban College of Boston

Michigan

Alpena Community College
Delta College
Glen Oaks Community College
Grand Rapids Community
  College
Henry Ford Community College
ITT Technical Institute
  Troy
Jackson College
Kalamazoo Valley Community
  College
Kellogg Community College
Kirtland Community College
Lake Michigan College
Macomb Community College
Mid Michigan Community
  College
Monroe County Community
  College
Montcalm Community College
Mott Community College
Muskegon Community College
North Central Michigan College
Northwestern Michigan College
Oakland Community College
Saginaw Chippewa Tribal
  College
St. Clair County Community
  College
Schoolcraft College
Southwestern Michigan College
Washtenaw Community College
Wayne County Community
  College
West Shore Community College

Minnesota

Academy College
Alexandria Technical and
  Community College
Anoka Technical College
Anoka-Ramsey Community
  College
Central Lakes College
Century College
Dakota County Technical
  College
Duluth Business University
Dunwoody College of
  Technology
Fond du Lac Tribal and
  Community College
Hennepin Technical College
Herzing University
  Minneapolis
Hibbing Community College
Institute of Production and
  Recording
Lake Superior College
Le Cordon Bleu College of
  Culinary Arts
  Minneapolis-St. Paul
Mesabi Range College
Minneapolis Business College
Minneapolis Community and
  Technical College
Minnesota School of Business
  Brooklyn Center
Minnesota State College -
  Southeast Technical

Minnesota West Community
and Technical College
North Hennepin Community
College
Northland Community &
Technical College
Northwest Technical College
Pine Technical & Community
College
Rainy River Community
College
Rasmussen College
Bloomington
Brooklyn Park
Eagan
Mankato
St. Cloud
Ridgewater College
Riverland Community College
St. Paul College
South Central College
Vermilion Community College

Mississippi

Antonelli College
Hattiesburg
Jackson
Blue Cliff College
Gulfport
Coahoma Community College
Copiah-Lincoln Community
College
East Central Community
College
East Mississippi Community
College
Hinds Community College
Holmes Community College
Itawamba Community College
Jones County Junior College
Meridian Community College
Mississippi Gulf Coast
Community College
Northeast Mississippi
Community College
Northwest Mississippi
Community College
Pearl River Community College
Southwest Mississippi
Community College
Virginia College
Biloxi
Jackson

Missouri

Bolivar Technical College
Cottey College
Crowder College
East Central College
Jefferson College
Metro Business College
Jefferson City
Rolla
Metropolitan Community
College - Kansas City
Mineral Area College
Missouri College
Moberly Area Community
College
Ozarks Technical Community
College
Pinnacle Career Institute:
Kansas City
Ranken Technical College
St. Charles Community College
St. Louis Community College
Southeast Missouri Hospital
College of Nursing and
Health Sciences
State Fair Community College
State Technical College of
Missouri
Stevens Institute of Business &
Arts
Texas County Technical College
Three Rivers Community
College

Vatterott College
Berkeley
St. Joseph
Springfield
Sunset Hills

Montana

Aaniiih Nakoda College
Blackfeet Community College
Chief Dull Knife College
Dawson Community College
Flathead Valley Community
College
Fort Peck Community College
Helena College University of
Montana
Little Big Horn College
Miles Community College
Montana State University
Great Falls College
Stone Child College

Nebraska

Central Community College
Kaplan University
Lincoln
Omaha
Metropolitan Community
College
Mid-Plains Community College
Nebraska College of Technical
Agriculture
Nebraska Indian Community
College
Northeast Community College
Southeast Community College
Western Nebraska Community
College

Nevada

Career College of Northern
Nevada
Carrington College
Las Vegas
Reno
College of Southern Nevada
Kaplan College
Las Vegas
Truckee Meadows Community
College
Western Nevada College

New Hampshire

Great Bay Community College
Lakes Region Community
College
Manchester Community College
Nashua Community College
NHTI-Concord's Community
College
River Valley Community
College
White Mountains Community
College

New Jersey

Assumption College for Sisters
Atlantic Cape Community
College
Bergen Community College
Brookdale Community College
Camden County College
County College of Morris
Cumberland County College
Eastern International College
Eastwick College
Eastwick College
Hackensack
Essex County College
Hudson County Community
College
Mercer County Community
College
Middlesex County College
Ocean County College
Passaic County Community
College

Raritan Valley Community
College
Rowan College at Burlington
County
Rowan College at Gloucester
Salem Community College
Sussex County Community
College
Union County College
Warren County Community
College

New Mexico

Brookline College
Albuquerque
Central New Mexico
Community College
Clovis Community College
Dona Ana Community College
of New Mexico State
University
Eastern New Mexico
University: Roswell
Luna Community College
Mesalands Community College
New Mexico Junior College
New Mexico Military Institute
New Mexico State University
Alamogordo
Carlsbad
San Juan College
Santa Fe Community College

New York

Adirondack Community College
American Academy McAllister
Institute of Funeral Service
American Academy of Dramatic
Arts
ASA College
Bramson ORT College
Broome Community College
Business Informatics Center
Cayuga Community College
City University of New York
Borough of Manhattan
Community College
College of Westchester
Columbia-Greene Community
College
Corning Community College
Dutchess Community College
Elmira Business Institute
Elmira Business Institute: Vestal
Erie Community College
Fulton-Montgomery Community
College
Genesee Community College
Helene Fuld College of Nursing
Hudson Valley Community
College
Institute of Design and
Construction
Island Drafting and Technical
Institute
ITT Technical Institute
Albany
Getzville
Liverpool
Jamestown Business College
Jamestown Community College
Jefferson Community College
Long Island Business Institute
Mildred Elley
Albany
New York City
Mohawk Valley Community
College
New York Career Institute
North Country Community
College
Plaza College
Rockland Community College
Schenectady County
Community College
Suffolk County Community
College

Sullivan County Community
College
SUNY
College of Agriculture and
Technology at Cobleskill
College of Technology at
Alfred
College of Technology at
Canton
College of Technology at
Delhi
Swedish Institute
Technical Career Institutes
Tompkins Cortland Community
College
Trocaire College
Ulster County Community
College
Utica School of Commerce
Villa Maria College of Buffalo
Westchester Community College
Wood Tobe-Coburn School

North Carolina

Alamance Community College
Asheville-Buncombe Technical
Community College
Beaufort County Community
College
Bladen Community College
Blue Ridge Community College
Brunswick Community College
Caldwell Community College
and Technical Institute
Cape Fear Community College
Carteret Community College
Catawba Valley Community
College
Central Carolina Community
College
Central Piedmont Community
College
Chef's Academy
Cleveland Community College
Coastal Carolina Community
College
College of the Albemarle
Craven Community College
Davidson County Community
College
Edgecombe Community College
Fayetteville Technical
Community College
Forsyth Technical Community
College
Gaston College
Guilford Technical Community
College
Halifax Community College
Haywood Community College
Isothermal Community College
James Sprunt Community
College
Johnston Community College
King's College
Lenoir Community College
Martin Community College
Mayland Community College
McDowell Technical
Community College
Miller-Motte College
Cary
Mitchell Community College
Montgomery Community
College
Nash Community College
Pamlico Community College
Piedmont Community College
Pitt Community College
Randolph Community College
Richmond Community College
Roanoke-Chowan Community
College
Rockingham Community
College
Rowan-Cabarrus Community
College

Sampson Community College
Sandhills Community College
South College
South Piedmont Community
College
Southeastern Community
College
Southwestern Community
College
Stanly Community College
Surry Community College
Tri-County Community College
Vance-Granville Community
College
Wake Technical Community
College
Wayne Community College
Western Piedmont Community
College
Wilkes Community College
Wilson Community College

North Dakota

Bismarck State College
Cankdeska Cikana Community
College
Dakota College at Bottineau
Fort Berthold Community
College
Lake Region State College
North Dakota State College of
Science
Rasmussen College
Bismarck
Sitting Bull College
Turtle Mountain Community
College
United Tribes Technical College
Williston State College

Ohio

Antonelli College
Cincinnati
Art Institute of Cincinnati
ATS Institute of Technology
Belmont College
Bradford School
Brown Mackie College
Akron
Cincinnati
Findlay
North Canton
Central Ohio Technical College
Chatfield College
Cincinnati State Technical and
Community College
Clark State Community College
Cleveland Institute of
Electronics
Cuyahoga Community College
Eastern Gateway Community
College
Edison State Community
College
ETI Technical College of Niles
Fortis College
Centerville
Cuyahoga
Ravenna
Gallipolis Career College
Good Samaritan College of
Nursing and Health Science
Harrison College
Grove City
Herzing University
Hocking College
Hondros College
International College of
Broadcasting
ITT Technical Institute
Dayton
Norwood
Strongsville
Youngstown
James A. Rhodes State College
Kaplan College
Dayton

Vermont

Community College of Vermont
Landmark College
New England Culinary Institute

Virginia

Advanced Technology Institute
American National University
    Charlottesville
    Danville
    Harrisonburg
    Lynchburg
    Martinsville
Blue Ridge Community College
Bryant & Stratton College
    Richmond
    Virginia Beach
Central Virginia Community
    College
Dabney S. Lancaster
    Community College
Danville Community College
Eastern Shore Community
    College
Germanna Community College
J. Sargeant Reynolds
    Community College
John Tyler Community College
Lord Fairfax Community
    College
Miller-Motte Technical College
    Lynchburg
Mountain Empire Community
    College
New River Community College
Northern Virginia Community
    College
Patrick Henry Community
    College
Paul D. Camp Community
    College
Piedmont Virginia Community
    College
Rappahannock Community
    College
Richard Bland College
Southside Virginia Community
    College
Southwest Virginia Community
    College
Thomas Nelson Community
    College
Tidewater Community College
Virginia Highlands Community
    College
Virginia Western Community
    College
Wytheville Community College

Washington

Bates Technical College
Bellevue College
Bellingham Technical College
Big Bend Community College
Carrington College
    Spokane
Cascadia College
Centralia College
Clover Park Technical College
Edmonds Community College
Everett Community College
Grays Harbor College
Green River Community
    College
Highline College
Lower Columbia College
North Seattle College
Northwest Indian College
Northwest School of Wooden
    Boatbuilding
Olympic College
Peninsula College
Pierce College
Renton Technical College
Seattle Central College
Shoreline Community College
Skagit Valley College

South Seattle College
Tacoma Community College
Walla Walla Community
    College
Wenatchee Valley College
Whatcom Community College

West Virginia

American National University
    Princeton
Blue Ridge Community and
    Technical College
BridgeValley Community and
    Technical College
Eastern West Virginia
    Community and Technical
    College
Huntington Junior College
Mountain State College
New River Community and
    Technical College
Pierpont Community and
    Technical College
Potomac State College of West
    Virginia University
Southern West Virginia
    Community and Technical
    College
Valley College
West Virginia Business College
    Wheeling
West Virginia Junior College
    Bridgeport
    Charleston
West Virginia Northern
    Community College
West Virginia University at
    Parkersburg

Wisconsin

Blackhawk Technical College
Chippewa Valley Technical
    College
Gateway Technical College
Globe University
    Appleton
    Eau Claire
    La Crosse
    Madison East
    Middleton
    Wausau
Lac Courte Oreilles Ojibwa
    Community College
Lakeshore Technical College
Madison Area Technical
    College
Madison Media Institute
Mid-State Technical College
Moraine Park Technical College
Nicolet Area Technical College
Northcentral Technical College
Rasmussen College
    Green Bay
    Wausau
Southwest Wisconsin Technical
    College
University of Wisconsin
    Barron County
    Fond du Lac
    Fox Valley
    Manitowoc
    Marathon County
    Marinette
    Marshfield/Wood County
    Richland
    Rock County
    Sheboygan
    Washington County
    Waukesha
Waukesha County Technical
    College
Western Technical College
Wisconsin Indianhead Technical
    College

Wyoming

Central Wyoming College
Eastern Wyoming College

Northwest College
Sheridan College
Western Wyoming Community
    College

American Samoa

American Samoa Community
    College

SAT Subject Tests required for admission

Four-year

Arkansas

Lyon College*

California

Fresno Pacific University*
Harvey Mudd College
Pomona College*

Maryland

Morgan State University*

Massachusetts

Amherst College*
Harvard College
Massachusetts Institute of
    Technology
Tufts University*
Wellesley College*
Williams College

New Hampshire

Dartmouth College*

New York

Barnard College*
Hamilton College*
New York University*
SUNY*
    College at Buffalo
Vassar College*
Webb Institute

North Carolina

Duke University*

Pennsylvania

Haverford College*

Puerto Rico

University of Puerto Rico
    Mayaguez

Rhode Island

Brown University*

Texas

Rice University*

Vermont

Middlebury College*

West Virginia

Alderson-Broaddus University*

Canada

University of Toronto

United Kingdom

King's College London

SAT Subject Tests recommended for admission

Four-year

California

California Baptist University*
Chapman University
Mills College
Occidental College*

Simpson University*
Stanford University
University of California
    Berkeley
    Irvine
    Santa Barbara
University of the Pacific*

Connecticut

Yale University

Delaware

University of Delaware

District of Columbia

Georgetown University
Howard University

Florida

University of South Florida
    Sarasota-Manatee

Georgia

Morehouse College*

Illinois

Columbia College Chicago*

Indiana

Indiana University
    Bloomington
University of Saint Francis*

Iowa

Shiloh University*

Kansas

Friends University*

Maine

University of Maine*
    Fort Kent

Maryland

Johns Hopkins University*

Massachusetts

Massachusetts Maritime
    Academy

Michigan

Hillsdale College

Minnesota

Carleton College

Montana

University of Great Falls*

New Jersey

Felician University*
Princeton University

New York

City University of New York
    Queens College
Clarkson University
SUNY
    College at Old Westbury
University of Rochester
Vaughn College of Aeronautics
    and Technology*

North Carolina

Davidson College*
North Carolina Central
    University*

Oregon

Reed College

Pennsylvania

Lafayette College
Lehigh University
St. Francis University
University of Pennsylvania

Virginia

Hampden-Sydney College
University of Virginia
Washington and Lee University

Canada

University of Alberta

France

Institut d'Etudes Politiques de
    Paris*

Switzerland

Franklin University Switzerland

Two-year

Florida

Pasco-Hernando State College

Georgia

Gordon State College

New York

St. Elizabeth College of Nursing

* ACT accepted as an alternative to SAT Subject Tests

Tables and Indexes

Colleges that offer ROTC

Air Force ROTC

Four-year

Alabama

Alabama State University
Auburn University
Auburn University at
   Montgomery
Birmingham-Southern College
Faulkner University
Huntingdon College
Miles College
Samford University
Spring Hill College
Stillman College
Troy University
Tuskegee University
University of Alabama
University of Alabama
   Birmingham
University of Mobile
University of Montevallo
University of South Alabama
University of West Alabama

Alaska

Alaska Pacific University
University of Alaska
   Anchorage

Arizona

Arizona Christian University
Arizona State University
DeVry University
   Phoenix
Embry-Riddle Aeronautical
   University
   Prescott Campus
Northern Arizona University
University of Arizona

Arkansas

John Brown University
University of Arkansas
   Fort Smith

California

Azusa Pacific University
Biola University
California Baptist University
California Institute of
   Technology
California Lutheran University
California Maritime Academy
California State University
   Dominguez Hills
   Fresno
   Los Angeles
   Northridge
   Sacramento
   San Bernardino
   San Marcos
Chapman University
Claremont McKenna College
Dominican University of
   California
Harvey Mudd College
Holy Names University
Loyola Marymount University
The Master's College
Menlo College
National University
Notre Dame de Namur
   University
Occidental College
Pepperdine University
Pitzer College

Point Loma Nazarene University
Pomona College
St. Mary's College of California
Samuel Merritt University
San Diego Christian College
San Diego State University
San Francisco State University
San Jose State University
Santa Clara University
Scripps College
Sonoma State University
Stanford University
University of California
   Berkeley
   Davis
   Irvine
   Los Angeles
   Riverside
   Santa Barbara
   Santa Cruz
University of Redlands
University of San Diego
University of San Francisco
University of Southern
   California
University of the Pacific
Vanguard University of
   Southern California
West Coast University: Orange
   County
Westmont College
William Jessup University

Colorado

Colorado Christian University
Colorado School of Mines
Colorado State University
Metropolitan State University of
   Denver
Regis University
University of Colorado
   Boulder
   Denver
University of Denver
University of Northern Colorado

Connecticut

Central Connecticut State
   University
Eastern Connecticut State
   University
Fairfield University
Quinnipiac University
Sacred Heart University
Southern Connecticut State
   University
University of Connecticut
University of Hartford
University of New Haven
Wesleyan University
Western Connecticut State
   University
Yale University

Delaware

Delaware State University
University of Delaware
Wilmington University

District of Columbia

American University
Catholic University of America
George Washington University
Georgetown University
Howard University
Trinity Washington University
University of the District of
   Columbia

Florida

Barry University
Bethune-Cookman University
Eckerd College
Embry-Riddle Aeronautical
   University
Florida Agricultural and
   Mechanical University
Florida Atlantic University

Florida College
Florida International University
Florida Southern College
Florida State University
Lynn University
Saint Leo University
University of Central Florida
University of Florida
University of Miami
University of South Florida
University of Tampa
University of West Florida

Georgia

Agnes Scott College
Clayton State University
Emory University
Georgia Institute of Technology
Georgia State University
Kennesaw State University
Morehouse College
Oglethorpe University
Spelman College
University of Georgia
University of West Georgia
Valdosta State University

Hawaii

Brigham Young University-
   Hawaii
Chaminade University of
   Honolulu
Hawaii Pacific University
University of Hawaii
   Manoa
   West Oahu

Idaho

Lewis-Clark State College
University of Idaho

Illinois

Elmhurst College
Illinois Institute of Technology
Lewis University
Loyola University Chicago
McKendree University
North Central College
North Park University
Northeastern Illinois University
Northwestern University
Saint Xavier University
Shimer College
Southern Illinois University
   Carbondale
Southern Illinois University
   Edwardsville
University of Chicago
University of Illinois
   Chicago
   Urbana-Champaign
Wheaton College

Indiana

Bethel College
Butler University
DePauw University
Holy Cross College
Indiana State University
Indiana University
   Bloomington
   Purdue University
      Indianapolis
   South Bend
   Southeast
Purdue University
Rose-Hulman Institute of
   Technology
Saint Mary's College
St. Mary-of-the-Woods College
Trine University
University of Notre Dame
Valparaiso University

Iowa

Coe College
Drake University
Grand View University

Iowa State University
University of Iowa

Kansas

Baker University
Kansas State University
Manhattan Christian College
MidAmerica Nazarene
   University
University of Kansas
University of St. Mary
Washburn University

Kentucky

Asbury University
Bellarmine University
Centre College
Georgetown College
Kentucky State University
Midway College
Northern Kentucky University
Spalding University
Thomas More College
Transylvania University
University of Kentucky
University of Louisville
Western Kentucky University

Louisiana

Dillard University
Grambling State University
Louisiana State University and
   Agricultural and Mechanical
   College
Louisiana Tech University
Loyola University New Orleans
Our Lady of the Lake College
Southern University
   New Orleans
Southern University and
   Agricultural and Mechanical
   College
Tulane University
University of Holy Cross
University of New Orleans
Xavier University of Louisiana

Maine

University of Maine
   Augusta
University of Southern Maine

Maryland

Bowie State University
Goucher College
Johns Hopkins University
Loyola University Maryland
Salisbury University
Stevenson University
Towson University
University of Maryland
   Baltimore County
   College Park

Massachusetts

American International College
Amherst College
Anna Maria College
Assumption College
Bay Path University
Becker College
Bentley University
Boston College
Boston University
Brandeis University
Bridgewater State University
Clark University
College of the Holy Cross
Eastern Nazarene College
Elms College
Emmanuel College
Harvard College
Massachusetts Institute of
   Technology
MCPHS University
Merrimack College
Mount Holyoke College
Nichols College
Northeastern University

Pine Manor College
Salem State University
Smith College
Springfield College
Tufts University
University of Massachusetts
   Amherst
   Boston
   Lowell
Wellesley College
Wentworth Institute of
   Technology
Western New England
   University
Westfield State University
Williams College
Worcester Polytechnic Institute
Worcester State University

Michigan

Central Michigan University
Concordia University
Eastern Michigan University
Finlandia University
Lawrence Technological
   University
Michigan State University
Michigan Technological
   University
Oakland University
Olivet College
Spring Arbor University
University of Michigan
University of Michigan
   Dearborn
Wayne State University

Minnesota

Augsburg College
Bethel University
College of St. Scholastica
Concordia College: Moorhead
Concordia University St. Paul
Hamline University
Macalester College
Minnesota State University
   Moorhead
North Central University
St. Catherine University
University of Minnesota
   Crookston
   Duluth
   Twin Cities
University of Northwestern - St.
   Paul
University of St. Thomas

Mississippi

Belhaven University
Jackson State University
Millsaps College
Mississippi College
Mississippi State University
Mississippi University for
   Women
University of Mississippi
University of Southern
   Mississippi
William Carey University

Missouri

Central Methodist University
Columbia College
Fontbonne University
Harris-Stowe State University
Lincoln University
Lindenwood University
Missouri University of Science
   and Technology
Saint Louis University
Southeast Missouri State
   University
Stephens College
University of Central Missouri
University of Missouri
   Columbia
   St. Louis

Washington·University in St.
Louis
Webster University
Westminster College

Montana

Montana State University

Nebraska

Bellevue University
Clarkson College
College of Saint Mary
Concordia University
Creighton University
Doane College
Grace University
Nebraska Methodist College of
Nursing and Allied Health
Nebraska Wesleyan University
University of Nebraska
Lincoln
Medical Center
Omaha
York College

Nevada

Nevada State College
University of Nevada
Las Vegas

New Hampshire

Colby-Sawyer College
Daniel Webster College
Franklin Pierce University
Granite State College
Keene State College
New England College
Plymouth State University
Rivier University
University of New Hampshire

New Jersey

The College of New Jersey
Fairleigh Dickinson University
College at Florham
Metropolitan Campus
Felician University
Kean University
Monmouth University
New Jersey City University
New Jersey Institute of
Technology
Princeton University
Ramapo College of New Jersey
Rutgers, The State University of
New Jersey
Camden Campus
New Brunswick/Piscataway
Campus
Newark Campus
Saint Peter's University
Stevens Institute of Technology
William Paterson University of
New Jersey

New Mexico

National American University
Albuquerque
New Mexico State University
University of New Mexico

New York

Adelphi University
Barnard College
Cazenovia College
City University of New York
Queens College
Clarkson University
College of Mount St. Vincent
College of Saint Rose
Columbia University
School of General Studies
Cornell University
Dowling College
Elmira College
Fordham University
Hamilton College
Hobart and William Smith
Colleges

Iona College
Ithaca College
Le Moyne College
Manhattan College
Mercy College
Mesivta Torah Vodaath
Seminary
Nazareth College
New York Institute of
Technology
New York University
Pace University
Rensselaer Polytechnic Institute
Roberts Wesleyan College
Rochester Institute of
Technology
The Sage Colleges
St. Francis College
St. John Fisher College
St. Lawrence University
St. Thomas Aquinas College
Siena College
Skidmore College
SUNY
College at Brockport
College at Cortland
College at Geneseo
College at Old Westbury
College at Oswego
College at Potsdam
College of Agriculture and
Technology at Morrisville
College of Environmental
Science and Forestry
Farmingdale State College
University at Albany
University at Binghamton
University at Stony Brook
SUNY Polytechnic Institute
Syracuse University
Union College
United States Merchant Marine
Academy
University of Rochester
Utica College
Vaughn College of Aeronautics
and Technology

North Carolina

Belmont Abbey College
Bennett College for Women
Catawba College
Davidson College
Duke University
East Carolina University
Elon University
Fayetteville State University
Gardner-Webb University
Greensboro College
High Point University
Meredith College
Methodist University
North Carolina Agricultural and
Technical State University
North Carolina Central
University
North Carolina State University
University of Mount Olive
University of North Carolina
Chapel Hill
Charlotte
Greensboro
Pembroke
William Peace University
Wingate University

North Dakota

Mayville State University
North Dakota State University
University of North Dakota

Ohio

Ashland University
Baldwin Wallace University
Bowling Green State University
Capital University
Case Western Reserve
University

Cedarville University
Central State University
Cleveland Institute of Art
Cleveland State University
Franciscan University of
Steubenville
Heidelberg University
Hiram College
John Carroll University
Kent State University
Lourdes University
Miami University
Oxford
Mount Carmel College of
Nursing
Mount St. Joseph University
Ohio Christian University
Ohio Northern University
Ohio State University
Columbus Campus
Lima Campus
Mansfield Campus
Marion Campus
Newark Campus
Ohio University
Ohio University
Lancaster Campus
Ohio Wesleyan University
Otterbein University
Tiffin University
University of Akron
University of Cincinnati
University of Dayton
University of Findlay
University of Mount Union
University of Toledo
Wilberforce University
Wittenberg University
Wright State University
Xavier University
Youngstown State University

Oklahoma

Langston University
Oklahoma Baptist University
Oklahoma Christian University
Oklahoma City University
Oklahoma State University
Oral Roberts University
St. Gregory's University
Southern Nazarene University
University of Oklahoma
University of Tulsa

Oregon

Concordia University
Corban University
George Fox University
Linfield College
Oregon State University
Pacific University
Portland State University
University of Oregon
University of Portland
Warner Pacific College
Western Oregon University
Willamette University

Pennsylvania

Bloomsburg University of
Pennsylvania
Bryn Athyn College
Bryn Mawr College
Cabrini College
Cairn University
Carlow University
Carnegie Mellon University
Chatham University
Drexel University
Duquesne University
East Stroudsburg University of
Pennsylvania
Eastern University
Keystone College
King's College
La Roche College
La Salle University
Lincoln University

Marywood University
Misericordia University
Neumann University
Penn State
Abington
Altoona
Brandywine
Hazleton
New Kensington
University Park
Wilkes-Barre
Worthington Scranton
Point Park University
Robert Morris University
Rosemont College
Saint Joseph's University
St. Vincent College
Swarthmore College
Temple University
Thomas Jefferson University
University of Pennsylvania
University of Pittsburgh
University of Pittsburgh
Greensburg
University of Scranton
University of the Sciences
Villanova University
Washington & Jefferson College
West Chester University of
Pennsylvania
Widener University
Wilkes University

Puerto Rico

Bayamon Central University
Inter American University of
Puerto Rico
Aguadilla Campus
Bayamon Campus
Fajardo Campus
Metropolitan Campus
San German Campus
Pontifical Catholic University of
Puerto Rico
Turabo University
Universidad Metropolitana
Universidad Politecnica de
Puerto Rico
University of Puerto Rico
Mayaguez
Rio Piedras

Rhode Island

Brown University

South Carolina

Anderson University
Benedict College
Charleston Southern University
The Citadel
Claflin University
Clemson University
College of Charleston
Southern Wesleyan University
University of South Carolina
Columbia
Winthrop University

South Dakota

Augusta University
Augustana University
Dakota State University
South Dakota State University
University of Sioux Falls

Tennessee

Austin Peay State University
Belmont University
Christian Brothers University
LeMoyne-Owen College
Lipscomb University
Middle Tennessee State
University
Rhodes College
Tennessee State University
Tennessee Technological
University
Tennessee Wesleyan College

University of Memphis
University of Tennessee
Knoxville
Vanderbilt University
Welch College

Texas

Angelo State University
Baylor University
Concordia University Texas
Dallas Baptist University
Houston Baptist University
Huston-Tillotson University
Lamar University
Lubbock Christian University
Midwestern State University
Prairie View A&M University
Rice University
St. Edward's University
St. Mary's University
Southern Methodist University
Texas A&M University
Commerce
Texas Christian University
Texas Lutheran University
Texas State University
Texas Tech University
Texas Wesleyan University
Texas Woman's University
Trinity University
University of Dallas
University of Houston
Downtown
Victoria
University of Mary Hardin-
Baylor
University of North Texas
University of St. Thomas
University of Texas
Arlington
Austin
Dallas
San Antonio
University of the Incarnate
Word
Wayland Baptist University

Utah

Brigham Young University
University of Utah
Utah State University
Utah Valley University
Weber State University
Westminster College

Vermont

Lyndon State College
Norwich University
Saint Michael's College

Virginia

George Mason University
James Madison University
Liberty University
Mary Baldwin College
University of Virginia
Virginia Military Institute
Virginia Polytechnic Institute
and State University

Washington

Central Washington University
Saint Martin's University
Seattle Pacific University
Seattle University
University of Washington
University of Washington
Bothell
University of Washington
Tacoma
Washington State University

West Virginia

Fairmont State University
Shepherd University
West Virginia University

Wisconsin

Alverno College
Carroll University
Carthage College
Edgewood College
Maranathan Baptist University
  Maranatha Baptist
  University
Marquette University
Milwaukee School of
  Engineering
University of Wisconsin
  Madison
  Milwaukee
  Stout
  Superior
  Whitewater
Wisconsin Lutheran College

Wyoming

University of Wyoming

Two-year

Alabama

Bishop State Community
  College
Jefferson State Community
  College
Marion Military Institute
Shelton State Community
  College

Arizona

Coconino County Community
  College
Estrella Mountain Community
  College
GateWay Community College
Mesa Community College
Phoenix College
Pima Community College
Yavapai College

Arkansas

Northwest Arkansas Community
  College

California

Canada College
Chabot College
College of the Sequoias
Cuyamaca College
De Anza College
Foothill College
Fresno City College
Irvine Valley College
Los Angeles Mission College
Mission College
Mount San Antonio College
Ohlone College
Riverside City College
Sacramento City College
San Diego City College
Solano Community College
West Valley College

Colorado

Arapahoe Community College
Red Rocks Community College

Connecticut

Capital Community College
Tunxis Community College

Florida

Broward College
Daytona State College
Eastern Florida State College
Miami Dade College
Santa Fe College
Tallahassee Community College
Valencia College

Georgia

Oxford College of Emory
  University

Hawaii

University of Hawaii
  Honolulu Community
  College

Illinois

John A. Logan College
Lincoln Land Community
  College
Parkland College
Shawnee Community College
Southwestern Illinois College

Indiana

Vincennes University

Iowa

Hawkeye Community College
Iowa Western Community
  College

Maryland

Anne Arundel Community
  College
Prince George's Community
  College

Massachusetts

Holyoke Community College
Middlesex Community College
Quinsigamond Community
  College

Michigan

Lansing Community College

Minnesota

Anoka-Ramsey Community
  College
Century College
Inver Hills Community College
North Hennepin Community
  College

Mississippi

East Mississippi Community
  College
Northwest Mississippi
  Community College

New Jersey

Brookdale Community College
Raritan Valley Community
  College
Union County College

New Mexico

Central New Mexico
  Community College
Dona Ana Community College
  of New Mexico State
  University
New Mexico State University
  Alamogordo

New York

Hudson Valley Community
  College
Maria College
Mohawk Valley Community
  College
Monroe Community College
Onondaga Community College
Schenectady County
  Community College
SUNY
  College of Technology at
  Canton

North Carolina

Catawba Valley Community
  College
Randolph Community College

Ohio

Columbus State Community
  College
Cuyahoga Community College
Hocking College

Kent State University
  East Liverpool
  Salem
  Stark
  Trumbull
  Tuscarawas
Miami University
  Hamilton
  Middletown
Ohio State University
  Agricultural Technical
  Institute
Sinclair Community College
University of Akron: Wayne
  College
University of Cincinnati
  Blue Ash College

Oklahoma

Northeastern Oklahoma
  Agricultural and Mechanical
  College
Rose State College

Oregon

Linn-Benton Community
  College

Pennsylvania

Valley Forge Military College

South Carolina

Tri-County Technical College
University of South Carolina
  Salkehatchie

Tennessee

Southwest Tennessee
  Community College

Texas

Alvin Community College
Austin Community College
College of the Mainland
Collin County Community
  College District
Houston Community College
  System
Lone Star College System
McLennan Community College
North Central Texas College
San Antonio College
San Jacinto College
Tarrant County College
Weatherford College

Utah

LDS Business College
Salt Lake Community College

Virginia

Piedmont Virginia Community
  College

Washington

Clark College
Highline College
South Puget Sound Community
  College
Spokane Community College

Wyoming

Laramie County Community
  College

Four-year

Alabama

Alabama Agricultural and
  Mechanical University
Alabama State University
Auburn University
Auburn University at
  Montgomery
Birmingham-Southern College

Faulkner University
Huntingdon College
Jacksonville State University
Judson College
Miles College
Samford University
Spring Hill College
Stillman College
Talladega College
Troy University
Tuskegee University
University of Alabama
University of Alabama
  Birmingham
  Huntsville
University of Mobile
University of Montevallo
University of North Alabama
University of South Alabama

Alaska

University of Alaska
  Anchorage
  Fairbanks

Arizona

Arizona State University
Embry-Riddle Aeronautical
  University
  Prescott Campus
Grand Canyon University
Northern Arizona University
Southwest University of Visual
  Arts
University of Arizona

Arkansas

Arkansas State University
Arkansas Tech University
Central Baptist College
Henderson State University
Hendrix College
John Brown University
Ouachita Baptist University
University of Arkansas
  Fort Smith
  Little Rock
  Monticello
  Pine Bluff
University of Central Arkansas
Williams Baptist College

California

Azusa Pacific University
Biola University
California Baptist University
California Institute of
  Technology
California Lutheran University
California Polytechnic State
  University: San Luis Obispo
California State Polytechnic
  University: Pomona
California State University
  Dominguez Hills
  Fresno
  Fullerton
  Long Beach
  Los Angeles
  Northridge
  Sacramento
  San Bernardino
  San Marcos
Chapman University
Claremont McKenna College
Harvey Mudd College
Holy Names University
Hope International University
Loyola Marymount University
The Master's College
Mills College
National University
Occidental College
Pepperdine University
Pitzer College
Point Loma Nazarene University
Pomona College
St. Mary's College of California

Samuel Merritt University
San Diego Christian College
San Diego State University
San Francisco State University
San Jose State University
Santa Clara University
Scripps College
Sonoma State University
Stanford University
University of California
  Berkeley
  Davis
  Irvine
  Los Angeles
  Riverside
  Santa Barbara
  Santa Cruz
University of La Verne
University of Redlands
University of San Diego
University of San Francisco
University of Southern
  California
Vanguard University of
  Southern California
Westmont College
Whittier College

Colorado

Colorado Christian University
Colorado College
Colorado School of Mines
Colorado State University
Colorado State University
  Pueblo
Colorado Technical University
Johnson & Wales University
  Denver
Metropolitan State University of
  Denver
Regis University
University of Colorado
  Boulder
  Colorado Springs
  Denver
University of Denver
University of Northern Colorado

Connecticut

Central Connecticut State
  University
Eastern Connecticut State
  University
Fairfield University
Quinnipiac University
Southern Connecticut State
  University
Trinity College
University of Bridgeport
University of Connecticut
University of Hartford
University of New Haven
Western Connecticut State
  University
Yale University

Delaware

Delaware State University
University of Delaware
Wesley College
Wilmington University

District of Columbia

American University
Catholic University of America
George Washington University
Georgetown University
Howard University
Trinity Washington University
University of the District of
  Columbia

Florida

Barry University
Bethune-Cookman University
Eckerd College
Embry-Riddle Aeronautical
  University

Florida Agricultural and
Mechanical University
Florida Atlantic University
Florida College
Florida Institute of Technology
Florida International University
Florida Memorial University
Florida Southern College
Florida State University
Jacksonville University
Palm Beach Atlantic University
Saint Leo University
Southeastern University
Stetson University
University of Central Florida
University of Florida
University of Miami
University of North Florida
University of South Florida
University of South Florida
Saint Petersburg
University of Tampa
University of West Florida

Georgia

Agnes Scott College
Albany State University
Armstrong State University
Augusta University
Clark Atlanta University
Clayton State University
Columbus State University
Covenant College
Emory University
Fort Valley State University
Georgia College and State
University
Georgia Gwinnett College
Georgia Institute of Technology
Georgia Southern University
Georgia State University
Kennesaw State University
Mercer University
Middle Georgia State College
Morehouse College
Oglethorpe University
Paine College
Savannah State University
Spelman College
University of Georgia
University of North Georgia
Wesleyan College

Hawaii

Brigham Young University-
Hawaii
Chaminade University of
Honolulu
Hawaii Pacific University
University of Hawaii
Hilo
Manoa
West Oahu

Idaho

Boise State University
Brigham Young University-
Idaho
College of Idaho
Idaho State University
Lewis-Clark State College
Northwest Nazarene University
University of Idaho

Illinois

Aurora University
Benedictine University
Bradley University
Chicago State University
DePaul University
Eastern Illinois University
Elmhurst College
Illinois Institute of Technology
Illinois State University
Illinois Wesleyan University
Judson University
Lewis University
Loyola University Chicago

McKendree University
Monmouth College
North Central College
North Park University
Northeastern Illinois University
Northern Illinois University
Northwestern University
Olivet Nazarene University
Robert Morris University:
Chicago
Shimer College
Southern Illinois University
Carbondale
Southern Illinois University
Edwardsville
University of Chicago
University of Illinois
Chicago
Urbana-Champaign
University of St. Francis
Western Illinois University
Wheaton College

Indiana

Ball State University
Bethel College
Butler University
DePauw University
Franklin College
Holy Cross College
Indiana Institute of Technology
Indiana State University
Indiana University
Bloomington
Kokomo
Northwest
Purdue University Fort
Wayne
Purdue University
Indianapolis
South Bend
Southeast
Indiana Wesleyan University
Marian University
Purdue University
Purdue University
Calumet
Rose-Hulman Institute of
Technology
Saint Mary's College
St. Mary-of-the-Woods College
University of Evansville
University of Indianapolis
University of Notre Dame
University of Southern Indiana
Valparaiso University

Iowa

Allen College
Briar Cliff University
Buena Vista University
Clarke University
Coe College
Drake University
Grand View University
Iowa State University
Loras College
Morningside College
University of Dubuque
University of Iowa
University of Northern Iowa

Kansas

Baker University
Benedictine College
Haskell Indian Nations
University
Kansas State University
Manhattan Christian College
MidAmerica Nazarene
University
Pittsburg State University
University of Kansas
University of St. Mary
Washburn University

Kentucky

Asbury University
Bellarmine University
Campbellsville University
Centre College
Eastern Kentucky University
Georgetown College
Kentucky State University
Kentucky Wesleyan College
Midway College
Morehead State University
Murray State University
Northern Kentucky University
Spalding University
Thomas More College
Transylvania University
University of Kentucky
University of Louisville
Western Kentucky University

Louisiana

Dillard University
Grambling State University
Louisiana College
Louisiana State University
Alexandria
Shreveport
Louisiana State University and
Agricultural and Mechanical
College
Louisiana Tech University
Loyola University New Orleans
Northwestern State University
Our Lady of the Lake College
Southeastern Louisiana
University
Southern University
New Orleans
Southern University and
Agricultural and Mechanical
College
Tulane University
University of Holy Cross
University of Louisiana at
Lafayette
University of Louisiana at
Monroe
University of New Orleans
Xavier University of Louisiana

Maine

Colby College
Husson University
Maine Maritime Academy
Saint Joseph's College of Maine
University of Maine
University of Maine
Augusta
University of New England
University of Southern Maine

Maryland

Bowie State University
Capitol Technology University
Coppin State University
Goucher College
Hood College
Johns Hopkins University
Loyola University Maryland
Maryland Institute College of
Art
McDaniel College
Morgan State University
Mount St. Mary's University
Notre Dame of Maryland
University
Salisbury University
Stevenson University
Towson University
University of Baltimore
University of Maryland
Baltimore County
College Park

Massachusetts

American International College
Amherst College
Assumption College

Babson College
Bay Path University
Becker College
Bentley University
Boston College
Boston University
Brandeis University
Bridgewater State University
Clark University
College of the Holy Cross
Curry College
Eastern Nazarene College
Elms College
Emmanuel College
Endicott College
Fisher College
Fitchburg State University
Gordon College
Hampshire College
Harvard College
Massachusetts Institute of
Technology
Massachusetts Maritime
Academy
MCPHS University
Mount Holyoke College
Nichols College
Northeastern University
Pine Manor College
Regis College
Salem State University
Simmons College
Smith College
Springfield College
Stonehill College
Suffolk University
Tufts University
University of Massachusetts
Amherst
Boston
Dartmouth
Lowell
Wellesley College
Wentworth Institute of
Technology
Western New England
University
Westfield State University
Wheaton College
Worcester Polytechnic Institute
Worcester State University

Michigan

Adrian College
Alma College
Aquinas College
Baker College
of Jackson
Calvin College
Central Michigan University
Concordia University
Cornerstone University
Davenport University
Eastern Michigan University
Ferris State University
Finlandia University
Grace Bible College
Hope College
Kalamazoo College
Kuyper College
Madonna University
Michigan State University
Michigan Technological
University
Northern Michigan University
Olivet College
Spring Arbor University
University of Michigan
University of Michigan
Dearborn
Flint
Wayne State University
Western Michigan University

Minnesota

Augsburg College
Bethany Lutheran College
Bethel University

College of St. Benedict
Concordia College: Moorhead
Concordia University St. Paul
Crown College
Gustavus Adolphus College
Hamline University
Macalester College
Minnesota State University
Mankato
Moorhead
North Central University
St. Catherine University
Saint Cloud State University
St. John's University
St. Mary's University of
Minnesota
University of Minnesota
Twin Cities
University of Northwestern - St.
Paul
University of St. Thomas
Winona State University

Mississippi

Alcorn State University
Belhaven University
Delta State University
Jackson State University
Millsaps College
Mississippi College
Mississippi State University
Mississippi University for
Women
Mississippi Valley State
University
Tougaloo College
University of Mississippi
University of Southern
Mississippi
William Carey University

Missouri

Avila University
Calvary Bible College and
Theological Seminary
Central Methodist University
College of the Ozarks
Columbia College
Drury University
Evangel University
Fontbonne University
Harris-Stowe State University
Lincoln University
Lindenwood University
Maryville University of Saint
Louis
Missouri Baptist University
Missouri Southern State
University
Missouri State University
Missouri University of Science
and Technology
Missouri Valley College
Missouri Western State
University
Northwest Missouri State
University
Park University
Research College of Nursing
Rockhurst University
Saint Louis University
Southwest Baptist University
Stephens College
Truman State University
University of Central Missouri
University of Missouri
Columbia
Kansas City
St. Louis
Washington University in St.
Louis
Webster University
Westminster College
William Jewell College
William Woods University

Montana

Carroll College
Montana State University
    Billings
Rocky Mountain College
University of Montana

Nebraska

Bellevue University
BryanLGH College of Health
    Sciences
Chadron State College
Clarkson College
College of Saint Mary
Concordia University
Creighton University
Doane College
Nebraska Wesleyan University
University of Nebraska
    Kearney
    Lincoln
    Medical Center
    Omaha
Wayne State College
York College

Nevada

University of Nevada
    Las Vegas
    Reno

New Hampshire

Colby-Sawyer College
Daniel Webster College
Dartmouth College
Franklin Pierce University
Granite State College
Keene State College
New England College
Plymouth State University
Rivier University
Saint Anselm College
Southern New Hampshire
    University
University of New Hampshire

New Jersey

Berkeley College
Bloomfield College
Caldwell University
The College of New Jersey
Fairleigh Dickinson University
    College at Florham
    Metropolitan Campus
Felician University
Kean University
Monmouth University
New Jersey City University
New Jersey Institute of
    Technology
Princeton University
Ramapo College of New Jersey
Rider University
Rowan University
Rutgers, The State University of
    New Jersey
    Camden Campus
    New Brunswick/Piscataway
        Campus
    Newark Campus
Saint Peter's University
Seton Hall University
Stevens Institute of Technology

New Mexico

New Mexico State University
Southwest University of Visual
    Arts
University of New Mexico

New York

Adelphi University
Alfred University
Barnard College
Canisius College
Cazenovia College

City University of New York
    Baruch College
    City College
    Lehman College
    Queens College
    York College
Clarkson University
Colgate University
College of Mount St. Vincent
College of New Rochelle
College of Saint Rose
Columbia University
    School of General Studies
Cooper Union for the
    Advancement of Science and
    Art
Cornell University
D'Youville College
Daemen College
Dowling College
Elmira College
Fordham University
Hamilton College
Hilbert College
Hobart and William Smith
    Colleges
Hofstra University
Houghton College
Iona College
Ithaca College
The King's College
Le Moyne College
Long Island University
    LIU Brooklyn
    LIU Post
Manhattan College
Manhattanville College
Marist College
Medaille College
Mercy College
Molloy College
Monroe College
Mount Saint Mary College
Nazareth College
New York Institute of
    Technology
New York University
Niagara University
Pace University
Pratt Institute
Rensselaer Polytechnic Institute
Roberts Wesleyan College
Rochester Institute of
    Technology
The Sage Colleges
Saint Bonaventure University
St. Francis College
St. John Fisher College
St. John's University
St. Lawrence University
Siena College
Skidmore College
SUNY
    College at Brockport
    College at Buffalo
    College at Cortland
    College at Fredonia
    College at Geneseo
    College at Old Westbury
    College at Oswego
    College at Plattsburgh
    College at Potsdam
    College of Agriculture and
        Technology at Morrisville
    College of Environmental
        Science and Forestry
    Farmingdale State College
    Maritime College
    University at Albany
    University at Binghamton
    University at Buffalo
    University at Stony Brook
    Upstate Medical University
SUNY Polytechnic Institute
Syracuse University
Talmudical Seminary Oholei
    Torah

Union College
United States Merchant Marine
    Academy
University of Rochester
Utica College
Vaughn College of Aeronautics
    and Technology
Wagner College

North Carolina

Appalachian State University
Belmont Abbey College
Bennett College for Women
Campbell University
Catawba College
Davidson College
Duke University
East Carolina University
Elizabeth City State University
Elon University
Fayetteville State University
Gardner-Webb University
Greensboro College
High Point University
Johnson and Wales University
    Charlotte
Livingstone College
Meredith College
Methodist University
Mid-Atlantic Christian
    University
North Carolina Agricultural and
    Technical State University
North Carolina Central
    University
North Carolina State University
North Carolina Wesleyan
    College
Pfeiffer University
Saint Augustine's University
Salem College
Shaw University
University of North Carolina
    Chapel Hill
    Charlotte
    Greensboro
    Pembroke
Wake Forest University
William Peace University
Wingate University
Winston-Salem State University

North Dakota

Mayville State University
North Dakota State University
University of North Dakota

Ohio

Ashland University
Baldwin Wallace University
Bowling Green State University
Capital University
Case Western Reserve
    University
Cedarville University
Central State University
Cleveland Institute of Art
Cleveland State University
Denison University
DeVry University
    Columbus
Franciscan University of
    Steubenville
Franklin University
Heidelberg University
Hiram College
John Carroll University
Kent State University
Lourdes University
Miami University
    Oxford
Mount Carmel College of
    Nursing
Mount St. Joseph University
Notre Dame College
Ohio Dominican University
Ohio Northern University

Ohio State University
    Columbus Campus
    Lima Campus
    Mansfield Campus
    Marion Campus
    Newark Campus
Ohio University
Ohio University
    Lancaster Campus
Ohio Wesleyan University
Otterbein University
Tiffin University
University of Akron
University of Cincinnati
University of Dayton
University of Findlay
University of Mount Union
University of Toledo
Urbana University
Ursuline College
Wilberforce University
Wittenberg University
Wright State University
Xavier University
Youngstown State University

Oklahoma

Cameron University
Langston University
Northeastern State University
Oklahoma Christian University
Oklahoma City University
Oklahoma State University
Southern Nazarene University
University of Central Oklahoma
University of Oklahoma

Oregon

Corban University
Eastern Oregon University
Lewis & Clark College
Oregon State University
Pacific University
Portland State University
Southern Oregon University
University of Oregon
University of Portland
Western Oregon University
Willamette University

Pennsylvania

Albright College
Alvernia University
Arcadia University
Bloomsburg University of
    Pennsylvania
Bryn Athyn College
Bucknell University
Cabrini College
California University of
    Pennsylvania
Carlow University
Carnegie Mellon University
Chatham University
Cheyney University of
    Pennsylvania
Clarion University of
    Pennsylvania
DeSales University
Dickinson College
Drexel University
Duquesne University
East Stroudsburg University of
    Pennsylvania
Eastern University
Edinboro University
    of Pennsylvania
Gannon University
Geneva College
Gettysburg College
Holy Family University
Immaculata University
Indiana University of
    Pennsylvania
Keystone College
King's College
Kutztown University of
    Pennsylvania

La Roche College
La Salle University
Lafayette College
Lehigh University
Lincoln University
Lock Haven University of
    Pennsylvania
Lycoming College
Mansfield University of
    Pennsylvania
Marywood University
Mercyhurst University
Millersville University of
    Pennsylvania
Misericordia University
Moravian College
Muhlenberg College
Neumann University
Penn State
    Abington
    Altoona
    Berks
    Brandywine
    Erie, The Behrend College
    Harrisburg
    Lehigh Valley
    Mont Alto
    University Park
    Wilkes-Barre
    Worthington Scranton
Pennsylvania College of
    Technology
Point Park University
Robert Morris University
Rosemont College
St. Francis University
Saint Joseph's University
St. Vincent College
Seton Hill University
Shippensburg University of
    Pennsylvania
Slippery Rock University of
    Pennsylvania
Summit University
Susquehanna University
Swarthmore College
Temple University
University of Pennsylvania
University of Pittsburgh
University of Pittsburgh
    Bradford
    Greensburg
    Johnstown
University of Scranton
University of the Sciences
Villanova University
Washington & Jefferson College
Waynesburg University
West Chester University of
    Pennsylvania
Westminster College
Widener University
Wilkes University
Wilson College

Puerto Rico

American University of Puerto
    Rico
Bayamon Central University
Caribbean University
EDP University of Puerto Rico:
    Hato Rey
Inter American University of
    Puerto Rico
    Aguadilla Campus
    Arecibo Campus
    Bayamon Campus
    Guayama Campus
    Metropolitan Campus
    San German Campus
Pontifical Catholic University of
    Puerto Rico
Turabo University
Universidad del Este
Universidad Metropolitana
Universidad Politecnica de
    Puerto Rico

University of Puerto Rico
  Aguadilla
  Arecibo
  Bayamon University
    College
  Cayey University College
  Mayaguez
  Ponce
  Rio Piedras
  Utuado

Rhode Island

Brown University
Bryant University
Johnson & Wales University
  Providence
Providence College
Rhode Island College
Rhode Island School of Design
Roger Williams University
Salve Regina University
University of Rhode Island

South Carolina

Allen University
Benedict College
Charleston Southern University
The Citadel
Claflin University
Clemson University
Coastal Carolina University
Columbia College
Converse College
Francis Marion University
Furman University
Lander University
Limestone College
Morris College
Newberry College
North Greenville University
Presbyterian College
South Carolina State University
Southern Wesleyan University
University of South Carolina
  Columbia
  Upstate
Voorhees College
Winthrop University
Wofford College

South Dakota

Augusta University
  Augustana University
Black Hills State University
Dakota State University
Dakota Wesleyan University
Mount Marty College
National American University
  Rapid City
South Dakota School of Mines
  and Technology
South Dakota State University
University of South Dakota

Tennessee

Austin Peay State University
Belmont University
Carson-Newman University
Christian Brothers University
Cumberland University
East Tennessee State University
Fisk University
Lane College
LeMoyne-Owen College
Lincoln Memorial University
Lipscomb University
Middle Tennessee State
  University
Rhodes College
Tennessee Technological
  University
Tennessee Wesleyan College
Trevecca Nazarene University
Union University
University of Memphis

University of Tennessee
  Chattanooga
  Knoxville
  Martin
Vanderbilt University
Welch College

Texas

Baylor University
Concordia University Texas
Dallas Baptist University
Houston Baptist University
Huston-Tillotson University
Lubbock Christian University
Our Lady of the Lake
  University of San Antonio
Prairie View A&M University
Rice University
St. Edward's University
St. Mary's University
Sam Houston State University
Southern Methodist University
Southwestern Assemblies of
  God University
Stephen F. Austin State
  University
Tarleton State University
Texas A&M International
  University
Texas A&M University
  Corpus Christi
  Kingsville
Texas Christian University
Texas Lutheran University
Texas Southern University
Texas State University
Texas Tech University
Texas Wesleyan University
Texas Woman's University
Trinity University
University of Dallas
University of Houston
  Downtown
University of Mary Hardin-
  Baylor
University of North Texas
University of St. Thomas
University of Texas
  Arlington
  Austin
  Brownsville
  Dallas
  Pan American
  San Antonio
University Of Texas Rio Grande
  Valley
University of the Incarnate
  Word
Wayland Baptist University

Utah

Brigham Young University
Dixie State University
Southern Utah University
University of Utah
Utah State University
Utah Valley University
Weber State University
Westminster College

Vermont

Castleton State College
Champlain College
Johnson State College
Lyndon State College
Middlebury College
Norwich University
Saint Michael's College
University of Vermont
Vermont Technical College

Virginia

Christopher Newport University
College of William and Mary
George Mason University
Hampden-Sydney College
Hampton University
James Madison University

Liberty University
Longwood University
Mary Baldwin College
Marymount University
Norfolk State University
Old Dominion University
Radford University
Randolph-Macon College
Regent University
Southern Virginia University
University of Mary Washington
University of Richmond
University of Virginia
University of Virginia's College
  at Wise
Virginia Commonwealth
  University
Virginia Military Institute
Virginia Polytechnic Institute
  and State University
Virginia State University
Virginia Union University
Virginia Wesleyan College
Washington and Lee University

Washington

Central Washington University
DeVry University
  Federal Way
Eastern Washington University
Gonzaga University
Northwest University
Pacific Lutheran University
Saint Martin's University
Seattle Pacific University
Seattle University
University of Puget Sound
University of Washington
University of Washington
  Bothell
University of Washington
  Tacoma
Walla Walla University
Washington State University
Whitworth University

West Virginia

Fairmont State University
Glenville State College
Marshall University
West Virginia State University
West Virginia University
West Virginia University
  Institute of Technology

Wisconsin

Alverno College
Bellin College
Carroll University
Edgewood College
Maranathan Baptist University
  Maranatha Baptist
    University
Marian University
Marquette University
Milwaukee School of
  Engineering
Ripon College
St. Norbert College
University of Wisconsin
  Eau Claire
  Green Bay
  La Crosse
  Madison
  Milwaukee
  Oshkosh
  Parkside
  Platteville
  River Falls
  Stevens Point
  Stout
  Whitewater
Viterbo University

Wyoming

University of Wyoming

Virgin Islands

University of the Virgin Islands

Korea

Yonsei University

Two-year

Alabama

Bishop State Community
  College
Gadsden State Community
  College
Jefferson State Community
  College
Marion Military Institute
Shelton State Community
  College
Southern Union State
  Community College

Arizona

Coconino County Community
  College
GateWay Community College
Mesa Community College
Paradise Valley Community
  College
Phoenix College
Pima Community College
Yavapai College

Arkansas

Arkansas State University
  Beebe
College of the Ouachitas
Northwest Arkansas Community
  College

California

Canada College
Chabot College
City College of San Francisco
De Anza College
Diablo Valley College
Foothill College
Fresno City College
Los Angeles Mission College
Riverside City College
Sacramento City College
San Diego City College
West Valley College

Colorado

Arapahoe Community College
Community College of Denver
Red Rocks Community College

Connecticut

Capital Community College
Tunxis Community College

Florida

Broward College
Daytona State College
Eastern Florida State College
Florida State College at
  Jacksonville
Hillsborough Community
  College
Miami Dade College
Northwest Florida State College
Pasco-Hernando State College
Pensacola State College
Polk State College
Santa Fe College
Seminole State College of
  Florida
Tallahassee Community College
Valencia College

Georgia

East Georgia State College
Georgia Military College
Oxford College of Emory
  University

Hawaii

University of Hawaii
  Honolulu Community
    College
  Windward Community
    College

Idaho

North Idaho College

Illinois

Carl Sandburg College
John A. Logan College
Kankakee Community College
Kaskaskia College
Kishwaukee College
Lewis and Clark Community
  College
Lincoln Land Community
  College
Parkland College
Shawnee Community College
Southwestern Illinois College
Spoon River College
Waubonsee Community College

Indiana

Vincennes University

Iowa

Hawkeye Community College
Iowa Western Community
  College

Kentucky

Elizabethtown Community and
  Technical College
Jefferson Community and
  Technical College
Owensboro Community and
  Technical College

Maine

Eastern Maine Community
  College

Maryland

Allegany College of Maryland
Anne Arundel Community
  College
Prince George's Community
  College

Massachusetts

Holyoke Community College
Middlesex Community College
Mount Wachusett Community
  College
Quinsigamond Community
  College
Roxbury Community College

Michigan

Lansing Community College
Washtenaw Community College

Minnesota

Anoka-Ramsey Community
  College
Inver Hills Community College
North Hennepin Community
  College

Mississippi

East Mississippi Community
  College
Hinds Community College
Jones County Junior College
Northeast Mississippi
  Community College

Missouri

Metropolitan Community
  College - Kansas City
State Fair Community College
Wentworth Military Junior
  College

Nevada

College of Southern Nevada
Truckee Meadows Community
College

New Jersey

Brookdale Community College
Middlesex County College
Raritan Valley Community
College

New Mexico

Central New Mexico
Community College
Dona Ana Community College
of New Mexico State
University
New Mexico Military Institute

New York

Erie Community College
Genesee Community College
Herkimer County Community
College
Hudson Valley Community
College
Maria College
Mohawk Valley Community
College
Monroe Community College
Niagara County Community
College
Onondaga Community College
SUNY
College of Technology at
Alfred
College of Technology at
Canton

North Carolina

Pitt Community College
Wake Technical Community
College

Ohio

Cincinnati State Technical and
Community College
Columbus State Community
College
Hocking College
Kent State University
East Liverpool
Salem
Stark
Trumbull
Tuscarawas
Ohio State University
Agricultural Technical
Institute
Sinclair Community College
University of Akron: Wayne
College
University of Cincinnati
Blue Ash College
Clermont College
University of Northwestern
Ohio

Oregon

Central Oregon Community
College
Linn-Benton Community
College

Pennsylvania

Community College of
Philadelphia
Harrisburg Area Community
College
Lackawanna College
Lehigh Carbon Community
College
Valley Forge Military College

Rhode Island

Community College of Rhode
Island

South Carolina

Greenville Technical College
Orangeburg-Calhoun Technical
College
Spartanburg Methodist College
Tri-County Technical College
University of South Carolina
Lancaster
Salkehatchie
Sumter

Tennessee

Jackson State Community
College
Pellissippi State Community
College
Southwest Tennessee
Community College
Walters State Community
College

Texas

Angelina College
Austin Community College
Central Texas College
Del Mar College
El Centro College
El Paso Community College
Houston Community College
System
Laredo Community College
Lone Star College System
Northwest Vista College
Palo Alto College
St. Philip's College
San Antonio College
San Jacinto College
Tarrant County College

Utah

LDS Business College
Salt Lake Community College

Virginia

John Tyler Community College
Piedmont Virginia Community
College
Richard Bland College
Southside Virginia Community
College
Tidewater Community College

Washington

Clark College
Highline College
Pierce College
Spokane Community College
Spokane Falls Community
College

Wyoming

Laramie County Community
College

American Samoa

American Samoa Community
College

Guam

Guam Community College

Naval ROTC

Four-year

Alabama

Auburn University
Stillman College
Tuskegee University

Arizona

Arizona State University
University of Arizona

California

California Maritime Academy
California State University
San Marcos
Loyola Marymount University
National University
Point Loma Nazarene University
Samuel Merritt University
San Diego State University
Sonoma State University
Stanford University
University of California
Berkeley
Davis
Los Angeles
Santa Cruz
University of Redlands
University of San Diego
University of Southern
California

Colorado

Regis University
University of Colorado
Boulder

Connecticut

Yale University

District of Columbia

Catholic University of America
George Washington University
Georgetown University
University of the District of
Columbia

Florida

Embry-Riddle Aeronautical
University
Florida Agricultural and
Mechanical University
Florida State University
Jacksonville University
University of Florida
University of North Florida
University of South Florida
University of Tampa

Georgia

Armstrong State University
Clark Atlanta University
Clayton State University
Emory University
Georgia Institute of Technology
Georgia State University
Morehouse College
Oglethorpe University
Savannah State University
Spelman College

Hawaii

Brigham Young University-
Hawaii

Idaho

Lewis-Clark State College
University of Idaho

Illinois

Illinois Institute of Technology
Loyola University Chicago
Northwestern University
Shimer College
University of Illinois
Chicago
Urbana-Champaign

Indiana

Indiana University
South Bend
Purdue University
Saint Mary's College
University of Notre Dame

Iowa

Iowa State University

Kansas

University of Kansas
Washburn University

Louisiana

Dillard University
Louisiana State University and
Agricultural and Mechanical
College
Loyola University New Orleans
Southern University
New Orleans
Southern University and
Agricultural and Mechanical
College
Tulane University
University of Holy Cross
University of New Orleans
Xavier University of Louisiana

Maine

Husson University
Maine Maritime Academy
University of Maine
University of Maine
Augusta

Maryland

University of Maryland
Baltimore County
College Park

Massachusetts

Boston College
Boston University
College of the Holy Cross
Harvard College
Massachusetts Institute of
Technology
Massachusetts Maritime
Academy
MCPHS University
Northeastern University
Tufts University
University of Massachusetts
Boston
Worcester Polytechnic Institute
Worcester State University

Michigan

Eastern Michigan University
Finlandia University
University of Michigan
University of Michigan
Dearborn

Minnesota

Augsburg College
Macalester College
University of Minnesota
Twin Cities
University of St. Thomas

Mississippi

Tougaloo College
University of Mississippi

Missouri

Columbia College
Lincoln University
Stephens College
University of Missouri
Columbia

Nebraska

BryanLGH College of Health
Sciences
Nebraska Wesleyan University
University of Nebraska
Lincoln
York College

New Hampshire

Daniel Webster College
Rivier University

New Jersey

Princeton University
Rutgers, The State University of
New Jersey
New Brunswick/Piscataway
Campus
Newark Campus

New Mexico

National American University
Albuquerque
University of New Mexico

New York

Barnard College
College of New Rochelle
College of Saint Rose
Columbia University
School of General Studies
Cornell University
Eastman School of Music of the
University of Rochester
Fordham University
Mesivta Torah Vodaath
Seminary
Molloy College
Rensselaer Polytechnic Institute
Rochester Institute of
Technology
The Sage Colleges
St. John Fisher College
SUNY
College at Brockport
Farmingdale State College
Maritime College
Talmudical Seminary Oholei
Torah
Union College
United States Merchant Marine
Academy
University of Rochester

North Carolina

Duke University
North Carolina State University
University of North Carolina
Chapel Hill

Ohio

Cleveland Institute of Art
Miami University
Oxford
Mount Carmel College of
Nursing
Ohio State University
Columbus Campus
Lima Campus
Mansfield Campus
Marion Campus
Newark Campus
Ohio University
Lancaster Campus

Oklahoma

University of Oklahoma

Oregon

Oregon State University
Western Oregon University

Pennsylvania

Carlow University
Carnegie Mellon University
Chatham University
Drexel University
Duquesne University
Penn State
University Park
Robert Morris University
Saint Joseph's University
Swarthmore College
Temple University
Thomas Jefferson University
University of Pennsylvania
University of Pittsburgh
Villanova University
Widener University

Puerto Rico

Inter American University of
Puerto Rico
Bayamon Campus
Ponce Campus
Universidad Metropolitana

Rhode Island

Brown University

South Carolina

Allen University
The Citadel
University of South Carolina
    Columbia

Tennessee

Belmont University
Christian Brothers University
Fisk University
Tennessee Wesleyan College
University of Memphis
Vanderbilt University

Texas

Houston Baptist University
Huston-Tillotson University
Prairie View A&M University
Rice University
Texas A&M University
    Galveston
University of Houston
University of Texas
    Arlington
    Austin

Utah

University of Utah
Weber State University
Westminster College

Vermont

Norwich University

Virginia

Hampton University
Mary Baldwin College
Norfolk State University
Old Dominion University
Regent University
University of Virginia
Virginia Military Institute
Virginia Polytechnic Institute
    and State University

Washington

Seattle Pacific University
Seattle University
University of Washington
University of Washington
    Bothell
University of Washington
    Tacoma
Washington State University

Wisconsin

Edgewood College
Marquette University
Milwaukee School of
    Engineering
University of Wisconsin
    Madison
    Milwaukee

Two-year

Arizona

GateWay Community College
Mesa Community College
Pima Community College

California

Contra Costa College
Diablo Valley College
Foothill College
Mission College
Riverside City College
Sacramento City College

Connecticut

Capital Community College
Tunxis Community College

Florida

Florida State College at
    Jacksonville

Pasco-Hernando State College
Tallahassee Community College

Georgia

Oxford College of Emory
    University

Illinois

Lincoln Land Community
    College
Parkland College
Shawnee Community College

Iowa

Hawkeye Community College

Minnesota

Anoka-Ramsey Community
    College
North Hennepin Community
    College

New Mexico

Central New Mexico
    Community College

New York

Maria College
Monroe Community College

Ohio

Cuyahoga Community College
Miami University
    Hamilton
    Middletown
Ohio State University
    Agricultural Technical
        Institute
University of Cincinnati
    Blue Ash College

Oregon

Linn-Benton Community
    College

South Carolina

University of South Carolina
    Salkehatchie

Virginia

Tidewater Community College

Washington

Spokane Community College

Colleges with NCAA sports

Baseball Division I

Alabama

Alabama Agricultural and
Mechanical University M
Alabama State University M
Auburn University M
Jacksonville State University M
Samford University M
Troy University M
University of Alabama M
University of Alabama
Birmingham M
University of South Alabama M

Arizona

Arizona State University M
University of Arizona M

Arkansas

Arkansas State University M
University of Arkansas
Pine Bluff M
University of Central Arkansas
M

California

California Polytechnic State
University: San Luis Obispo
M
California State University
Bakersfield M
Fresno M
Fullerton M
Long Beach M
Northridge M
Sacramento M
Loyola Marymount University
M
Pepperdine University M
St. Mary's College of California
M
San Diego State University M
San Jose State University M
Santa Clara University M
Stanford University M
University of California
Berkeley M
Davis M
Irvine M
Los Angeles M
Riverside M
Santa Barbara M
University of San Diego M
University of San Francisco M
University of Southern
California M
University of the Pacific M

Colorado

United States Air Force
Academy M
University of Northern Colorado
M

Connecticut

Central Connecticut State
University M
Fairfield University M
Quinnipiac University M
Sacred Heart University M
University of Connecticut M
University of Hartford M
Yale University M

Delaware

Delaware State University M
University of Delaware M

District of Columbia

George Washington University
M
Georgetown University M

Florida

Bethune-Cookman University M
Florida Agricultural and
Mechanical University M
Florida Atlantic University M
Florida Gulf Coast University M
Florida International University
M
Florida State University M
Jacksonville University M
Stetson University M
University of Central Florida M
University of Florida M
University of Miami M
University of North Florida M
University of South Florida M

Georgia

Georgia Institute of Technology
M
Georgia Southern University M
Georgia State University M
Kennesaw State University M
Mercer University M
Savannah State University M
University of Georgia M

Hawaii

University of Hawaii
Manoa M

Illinois

Bradley University M
Chicago State University M
Eastern Illinois University M
Illinois State University M
Northern Illinois University M
Northwestern University M
Southern Illinois University
Carbondale M
Southern Illinois University
Edwardsville M
University of Illinois
Chicago M
Western Illinois University M

Indiana

Ball State University M
Butler University M
Indiana State University M
Indiana University
Bloomington M
Purdue University Fort
Wayne M
Purdue University M
University of Evansville M
University of Notre Dame M
Valparaiso University M

Iowa

University of Iowa M

Kansas

Kansas State University M
University of Kansas M
Wichita State University M

Kentucky

Eastern Kentucky University M
Morehead State University M
Murray State University M
University of Kentucky M
University of Louisville M
Western Kentucky University M

Louisiana

Grambling State University M
Louisiana State University and
Agricultural and Mechanical
College M
Louisiana Tech University M
McNeese State University M
Nicholls State University M

Northwestern State University
M
Southeastern Louisiana
University M
Southern University and
Agricultural and Mechanical
College M
Tulane University M
University of Louisiana at
Lafayette M
University of Louisiana at
Monroe M
University of New Orleans M

Maine

University of Maine M

Maryland

Coppin State University M
Mount St. Mary's University M
Towson University M
United States Naval Academy
M
University of Maryland
Baltimore County M
College Park M
Eastern Shore M

Massachusetts

Boston College M
College of the Holy Cross M
Harvard College M
Northeastern University M
University of Massachusetts
Amherst M

Michigan

Central Michigan University M
Eastern Michigan University M
Michigan State University M
Oakland University M
University of Michigan M
Western Michigan University M

Minnesota

University of Minnesota
Twin Cities M

Mississippi

Alcorn State University M
Jackson State University M
Mississippi State University M
Mississippi Valley State
University M
University of Mississippi M

Missouri

Missouri State University M
Saint Louis University M
Southeast Missouri State
University M
University of Missouri
Columbia M

Nebraska

Creighton University M
University of Nebraska
Lincoln M
Omaha M

Nevada

University of Nevada
Las Vegas M

New Hampshire

Dartmouth College M

New Jersey

Fairleigh Dickinson University
Metropolitan Campus M
Monmouth University M
New Jersey Institute of
Technology M
Princeton University M
Rider University M
Seton Hall University M

New Mexico

New Mexico State University M
University of New Mexico M

New York

Barnard College M
Canisius College M
Columbia University M
Cornell University M
Fordham University M
Hofstra University M
Iona College M
Long Island University
LIU Brooklyn M
Manhattan College M
Marist College M
New York Institute of
Technology M
Niagara University M
Saint Bonaventure University M
St. John's University M
Siena College M
SUNY
University at Albany M
University at Binghamton
M
University at Buffalo M
University at Stony Brook
M
United States Military Academy
M
Wagner College M

North Carolina

Appalachian State University M
Campbell University M
Davidson College M
Duke University M
East Carolina University M
Elon University M
Gardner-Webb University M
High Point University M
North Carolina Agricultural and
Technical State University M
North Carolina Central
University M
North Carolina State University
M
University of North Carolina
Asheville M
Chapel Hill M
Wake Forest University M
Western Carolina University M

North Dakota

North Dakota State University
M
University of North Dakota M

Ohio

Bowling Green State University
M
Kent State University M
Miami University
Oxford M
Ohio State University
Columbus Campus M
Ohio University M
University of Cincinnati M
University of Dayton M
University of Toledo M
Wright State University M
Xavier University M
Youngstown State University M

Oklahoma

Oklahoma State University M
Oral Roberts University M
University of Oklahoma M

Oregon

Oregon State University M
University of Oregon M
University of Portland M

Pennsylvania

Bucknell University M
La Salle University M
Lafayette College M
Lehigh University M
Penn State
University Park M

Saint Joseph's University M
University of Pennsylvania M
University of Pittsburgh M
Villanova University M

Rhode Island

Brown University M
Bryant University M
University of Rhode Island M

South Carolina

Charleston Southern University
M
The Citadel M
Clemson University M
Coastal Carolina University M
College of Charleston M
Furman University M
Presbyterian College M
University of South Carolina
Columbia M
Upstate M
Winthrop University M
Wofford College M

South Dakota

South Dakota State University
M

Tennessee

Austin Peay State University M
Belmont University M
East Tennessee State University
M
Lipscomb University M
Middle Tennessee State
University M
Tennessee Technological
University M
University of Memphis M
University of Tennessee
Knoxville M
Martin M
Vanderbilt University M

Texas

Baylor University M
Dallas Baptist University M
Houston Baptist University M
Lamar University M
Prairie View A&M University
M
Rice University M
Sam Houston State University
M
Stephen F. Austin State
University M
Texas A&M University M
Corpus Christi M
Texas Christian University M
Texas Southern University M
Texas Tech University M
University of Houston M
University of Texas
Arlington M
Austin M
San Antonio M

Utah

Brigham Young University M
University of Utah M
Utah Valley University M

Virginia

College of William and Mary M
George Mason University M
James Madison University M
Liberty University M
Longwood University M
Norfolk State University M
Old Dominion University M
Radford University M
University of Richmond M
University of Virginia M
Virginia Commonwealth
University M
Virginia Military Institute M

Washington

Gonzaga University M
Seattle University M
University of Washington M
Washington State University M

West Virginia

Marshall University M
West Virginia University M

Wisconsin

University of Wisconsin
Milwaukee M

Baseball Division II

Alabama

Auburn University at
Montgomery M
Miles College M
Spring Hill College M
Stillman College M
Tuskegee University M
University of Alabama
Huntsville M
University of Montevallo M
University of North Alabama M
University of West Alabama M

Arizona

Grand Canyon University M

Arkansas

Arkansas Tech University M
Harding University M
Henderson State University M
Ouachita Baptist University M
Southern Arkansas University M
University of Arkansas
Fort Smith M
Monticello M

California

Academy of Art University M
Azusa Pacific University M
California Baptist University M
California State Polytechnic
University: Pomona M
California State University
Chico M
Dominguez Hills M
East Bay M
Los Angeles M
Monterey Bay M
San Bernardino M
Stanislaus M
Fresno Pacific University M
Holy Names University M
Point Loma Nazarene
University M
San Francisco State University
M
Sonoma State University M
University of California
San Diego M

Colorado

Adams State University M
Colorado Christian University
M
Colorado Mesa University M
Colorado School of Mines M
Colorado State University
Pueblo M
Metropolitan State University of
Denver M
Regis University M

Connecticut

Post University M
Southern Connecticut State
University M
University of Bridgeport M
University of New Haven M

Delaware

Wilmington University M.

Florida

Barry University M
Eckerd College M
Flagler College M
Florida Institute of Technology
M
Florida Southern College M
Lynn University M
Nova Southeastern University M
Palm Beach Atlantic University
M
Rollins College M
Saint Leo University M
University of Tampa M
University of West Florida M

Georgia

Albany State University M
Clark Atlanta University M
Columbus State University M
Emmanuel College M
Georgia Southwestern State
University M
Morehouse College M
Paine College M
Shorter University M
University of North Georgia M
University of West Georgia M
Valdosta State University M
Young Harris College M

Hawaii

Hawaii Pacific University M
University of Hawaii
Hilo M

Idaho

Northwest Nazarene University
M

Illinois

Lewis University M
McKendree University M
Quincy University M
University of Illinois
Springfield M

Indiana

Oakland City University M
Saint Joseph's College M
University of Indianapolis M
University of Southern Indiana
M

Iowa

Upper Iowa University M

Kansas

Emporia State University M
Fort Hays State University M
Newman University M
Pittsburg State University M
Washburn University M

Kentucky

Bellarmine University M
Kentucky State University M
Kentucky Wesleyan College M
Northern Kentucky University
M

Massachusetts

American International College
M
Assumption College M
Bentley University M
Merrimack College M
Stonehill College M

Michigan

Grand Valley State University
M
Hillsdale College M
Northwood University
Michigan M

Saginaw Valley State University
M
Wayne State University M

Minnesota

Bemidji State University M
Concordia University St. Paul
M
Minnesota State University
Mankato M
Saint Cloud State University M
Southwest Minnesota State
University M
University of Minnesota
Crookston M
Duluth M
Winona State University M

Mississippi

Delta State University M
Mississippi College M

Missouri

Drury University M
Lincoln University M
Lindenwood University M
Maryville University of Saint
Louis M
Missouri Southern State
University M
Missouri University of Science
and Technology M
Missouri Western State
University M
Northwest Missouri State
University M
Rockhurst University M
Southwest Baptist University M.
Truman State University M
University of Central Missouri
M
William Jewell College M

Montana

Montana State University
Billings M

Nebraska

University of Nebraska
Kearney M
Wayne State College M

New Hampshire

Franklin Pierce University M
Saint Anselm College M
Southern New Hampshire
University M

New Jersey

Bloomfield College M

New Mexico

Eastern New Mexico University
M
New Mexico Highlands
University M

New York

Adelphi University M
City University of New York
Queens College M
College of Saint Rose M
Concordia College M
Dominican College of Blauvelt
M
Dowling College M
Le Moyne College M
Long Island University
LIU Post M
Mercy College M
Molloy College M
Nyack College M
Pace University M
St. Thomas Aquinas College M

North Carolina

Barton College M
Belmont Abbey College M
Brevard College M
Catawba College M

Chowan University M
Lenoir-Rhyne University M
Mars Hill University M
Pfeiffer University M
Saint Augustine's University M
University of Mount Olive M
University of North Carolina
Pembroke M
Wingate University M
Winston-Salem State University
M

North Dakota

Minot State University M
University of Mary M

Ohio

Ashland University M
Cedarville University M
Lake Erie College M
Malone University M
Notre Dame College M
Ohio Dominican University M
Tiffin University M
University of Findlay M
Urbana University M
Walsh University M

Oklahoma

Cameron University M
East Central University M
Northeastern State University M
Northwestern Oklahoma State
University M
Oklahoma Baptist University M
Oklahoma Christian University
M
Oklahoma Panhandle State
University M
Rogers State University M
Southeastern Oklahoma State
University M
Southern Nazarene University
M
Southwestern Oklahoma State
University M
University of Central Oklahoma
M

Oregon

Western Oregon University M

Pennsylvania

Bloomsburg University of
Pennsylvania M
California University of
Pennsylvania M
Chestnut Hill College M
Clarion University of
Pennsylvania M
East Stroudsburg University of
Pennsylvania M
Gannon University M
Indiana University of
Pennsylvania M
Kutztown University of
Pennsylvania M
Lincoln University M
Lock Haven University of
Pennsylvania M
Mansfield University of
Pennsylvania M
Mercyhurst University M
Millersville University of
Pennsylvania M
Philadelphia University M
Seton Hill University M
Shippensburg University of
Pennsylvania M
Slippery Rock University of
Pennsylvania M
University of Pittsburgh
Johnstown M
West Chester University of
Pennsylvania M

South Carolina

Anderson University M
Benedict College M

Claflin University M
Coker College M
Erskine College M
Francis Marion University M
Lander University M
Limestone College M
Newberry College M
North Greenville University M
Southern Wesleyan University
M
University of South Carolina
Aiken M

South Dakota

Northern State University M
University of Sioux Falls M

Tennessee

Carson-Newman University M
Christian Brothers University M
King University M
Lane College M
Lee University M
LeMoyne-Owen College M
Lincoln Memorial University M
Trevecca Nazarene University
M
Tusculum College M
Union University M

Texas

Abilene Christian University M
Angelo State University M
Lubbock Christian University M
St. Edward's University M
St. Mary's University M
Tarleton State University M
Texas A&M International
University M
Texas A&M University
Kingsville M
University of Texas
of the Permian Basin M
University of the Incarnate
Word M
West Texas A&M University M

Utah

Dixie State University M

Vermont

Saint Michael's College M

Virginia

University of Virginia's College
at Wise M
Virginia State University M

Washington

Central Washington University
M
Saint Martin's University M

West Virginia

Alderson-Broaddus University
M
Bluefield State College M
Concord University M
Davis and Elkins College M
Fairmont State University M
Glenville State College M
Ohio Valley University M
Salem International University
M
Shepherd University M
University of Charleston M
West Liberty University M
West Virginia State University
M
West Virginia Wesleyan
College M
Wheeling Jesuit University M

Wisconsin

University of Wisconsin
Parkside M

Baseball Division III

Alabama

Birmingham-Southern College M
Huntingdon College M

Arkansas

Hendrix College M
University of the Ozarks M

California

California Institute of Technology M
California Lutheran University M
Chapman University M
Claremont McKenna College M
Harvey Mudd College M
Occidental College M
Pitzer College M
Pomona College M
Scripps College M
University of La Verne M
University of Redlands M
Whittier College M

Connecticut

Albertus Magnus College M
Eastern Connecticut State University M
Mitchell College M
Trinity College M
United States Coast Guard Academy M
Wesleyan University M
Western Connecticut State University M

Delaware

Wesley College M

District of Columbia

Catholic University of America M
Gallaudet University M

Georgia

Berry College M
Covenant College M
Emory University M
Oglethorpe University M
Piedmont College M

Illinois

Augustana College M
Aurora University M
Benedictine University at Springfield M
Blackburn College M
Concordia University Chicago M
Dominican University M
Elmhurst College M
Eureka College M
Greenville College M
Illinois College M
Illinois Institute of Technology M
Illinois Wesleyan University M
Knox College M
MacMurray College M
Millikin University M
Monmouth College M
North Central College M
North Park University M
Principia College M
Rockford University M
University of Chicago M
Wheaton College M

Indiana

Anderson University M
DePauw University M
Earlham College M
Franklin College M
Hanover College M
Manchester University M

Rose-Hulman Institute of Technology M
Trine University M
Wabash College M

Iowa

Buena Vista University M
Central College M
Coe College M
Cornell College M
Grinnell College M
Loras College M
Luther College M
Simpson College M
University of Dubuque M
Wartburg College M

Kentucky

Berea College M
Centre College M
Spalding University M
Thomas More College M
Transylvania University M

Louisiana

Centenary College of Louisiana M
Louisiana College M

Maine

Bates College M
Bowdoin College M
Colby College M
Husson University M
Saint Joseph's College of Maine M
Thomas College M
University of Maine Farmington M
Presque Isle M
University of Southern Maine M

Maryland

Frostburg State University M
Hood College M
Johns Hopkins University M
McDaniel College M
St. Mary's College of Maryland M
Salisbury University M
Stevenson University M
Washington College M

Massachusetts

Amherst College M
Anna Maria College M
Babson College M
Becker College M
Brandeis University M
Bridgewater State University M
Clark University M
Curry College M
Eastern Nazarene College M
Elms College M
Emerson College M
Endicott College M
Fitchburg State University M
Framingham State University M
Gordon College M
Lasell College M
Lesley University M
Massachusetts College of Liberal Arts M
Massachusetts Institute of Technology M
Massachusetts Maritime Academy M
Newbury College M
Nichols College M
Salem State University M
Springfield College M
Suffolk University M
Tufts University M
University of Massachusetts Dartmouth M
Wentworth Institute of Technology M
Western New England University M

Westfield State University M
Wheaton College M
Williams College M
Worcester Polytechnic Institute M
Worcester State University M

Michigan

Adrian College M
Albion College M
Alma College M
Calvin College M
Finlandia University M
Hope College M
Kalamazoo College M
Olivet College M

Minnesota

Augsburg College M
Bethany Lutheran College M
Bethel University M
Carleton College M
College of St. Scholastica M
Concordia College: Moorhead M
Gustavus Adolphus College M
Hamline University M
Macalester College M
Martin Luther College M
North Central University M
St. John's University M
St. Mary's University of Minnesota M
St. Olaf College M
University of Minnesota Morris M
University of Northwestern - St. Paul M
University of St. Thomas M

Mississippi

Belhaven University M
Millsaps College M
Rust College M

Missouri

Fontbonne University M
Webster University M
Westminster College M

Nebraska

Nebraska Wesleyan University M

New Hampshire

Colby-Sawyer College M
Daniel Webster College M
Keene State College M
New England College M
Plymouth State University M
Rivier University M

New Jersey

Centenary College M
The College of New Jersey M
Drew University M
Fairleigh Dickinson University College at Florham M
Kean University M
Montclair State University M
New Jersey City University M
Ramapo College of New Jersey M
Rowan University M
Rutgers, The State University of New Jersey Camden Campus M
Newark Campus M
Stevens Institute of Technology M
William Paterson University of New Jersey M

New York

Bard College M
Cazenovia College M

City University of New York Baruch College M
City College M
College of Staten Island M
John Jay College of Criminal Justice M
Clarkson University M
College of Mount St. Vincent M
D'Youville College M
Elmira College M
Hamilton College M
Hilbert College M
Houghton College M
Ithaca College M
Keuka College M
Manhattanville College M
Medaille College M
Mount Saint Mary College M
New York University M
Rensselaer Polytechnic Institute M
Rochester Institute of Technology M
St. John Fisher College M
St. Joseph's College New York: Suffolk Campus M
St. Joseph's College, New York M
St. Lawrence University M
Skidmore College M
SUNY
College at Brockport M
College at Cortland M
College at New Paltz M
College at Old Westbury M
College at Oneonta M
College at Oswego M
College at Plattsburgh M
College at Purchase M
College of Technology at Alfred M
College of Technology at Canton M
Maritime College M
Union College M
United States Merchant Marine Academy M
University of Rochester M
Utica College M
Vassar College M
Yeshiva University M

North Carolina

Greensboro College M
Guilford College M
Methodist University M
North Carolina Wesleyan College M
William Peace University M

Ohio

Baldwin Wallace University M
Bluffton University M
Capital University M
Case Western Reserve University M
College of Wooster M
Defiance College M
Denison University M
Heidelberg University M
Hiram College M
John Carroll University M
Kenyon College M
Marietta College M
Muskingum University M
Oberlin College M
Ohio Northern University M
Ohio Wesleyan University M
Otterbein University M
University of Mount Union M
Wilmington College M
Wittenberg University M

Oregon

George Fox University M
Lewis & Clark College M
Linfield College M

Pacific University M
Willamette University M

Pennsylvania

Albright College M
Allegheny College M
Alvernia University M
Arcadia University M
Cairn University M
Chatham University M
DeSales University M
Dickinson College M
Eastern University M
Elizabethtown College M
Franklin & Marshall College M
Geneva College M
Gettysburg College M
Grove City College M
Gwynedd Mercy University M
Haverford College M
Immaculata University M
Juniata College M
Keystone College M
King's College M
La Roche College M
Lancaster Bible College M
Lebanon Valley College M
Marywood University M
Messiah College M
Misericordia University M
Moravian College M
Mount Aloysius College M
Muhlenberg College M
Neumann University M
Penn State
Abington M
Altoona M
Berks M
Erie, The Behrend College M
Harrisburg M
Pennsylvania College of Technology M
St. Vincent College M
Susquehanna University M
Swarthmore College M
Thiel College M
University of Pittsburgh Bradford M
Greensburg M
University of Scranton M
Ursinus College M
Washington & Jefferson College M
Waynesburg University M
Westminster College M
Widener University M
Wilkes University M
York College of Pennsylvania M

Rhode Island

Rhode Island College M
Roger Williams University M
Salve Regina University M

Tennessee

Maryville College M
Rhodes College M
Sewanee: The University of the South M

Texas

Austin College M
Concordia University Texas M
East Texas Baptist University M
Hardin-Simmons University M
Howard Payne University M
LeTourneau University M
McMurry University M
Schreiner University M
Southwestern University M
Sul Ross State University M
Texas Lutheran University M
Trinity University M
University of Dallas M
University of Mary Hardin-Baylor M

University of Texas
  Dallas M
  Tyler M

Vermont

Lyndon State College M
Middlebury College M
Norwich University M
Southern Vermont College M

Virginia

Averett University M
Bridgewater College M
Christopher Newport University M
Eastern Mennonite University M
Emory & Henry College M
Ferrum College M
Hampden-Sydney College M
Lynchburg College M
Marymount University M
Randolph-Macon College M
Roanoke College M
Shenandoah University M
Southern Virginia University M
University of Mary Washington M
Virginia Wesleyan College M
Washington and Lee University M

Washington

Pacific Lutheran University M
University of Puget Sound M
Whitman College M
Whitworth University M

West Virginia

Bethany College M

Wisconsin

Beloit College M
Carroll University M
Carthage College M
Edgewood College M
Lakeland College M
Lawrence University M
Maranathan Baptist University
  Maranatha Baptist University M
Marian University M
Milwaukee School of
  Engineering M
Northland College M
Ripon College M
St. Norbert College M
University of Wisconsin
  La Crosse M
  Platteville M
  Stevens Point M
  Superior M
Wisconsin Lutheran College M

Arkansas

Arkansas State University
University of Arkansas
  Pine Bluff
University of Central Arkansas

California

California Polytechnic State
  University: San Luis Obispo
California State University
  Bakersfield
  Fresno
  Fullerton
  Long Beach
  Northridge
  Sacramento
Loyola Marymount University
Pepperdine University
St. Mary's College of California
San Diego State University
San Jose State University
Santa Clara University
Stanford University
University of California
  Berkeley
  Davis
  Irvine
  Los Angeles
  Riverside
  Santa Barbara
University of San Diego
University of San Francisco
University of Southern
  California
University of the Pacific

Colorado

Colorado State University
United States Air Force
  Academy
University of Colorado
  Boulder
University of Denver
University of Northern Colorado

Connecticut

Central Connecticut State
  University
Fairfield University
Quinnipiac University
Sacred Heart University
University of Connecticut
University of Hartford
Yale University

Delaware

Delaware State University
University of Delaware

District of Columbia

American University
George Washington University
Georgetown University
Howard University

Florida

Bethune-Cookman University
Florida Agricultural and
  Mechanical University
Florida Atlantic University
Florida Gulf Coast University
Florida International University
Florida State University
Jacksonville University
Stetson University
University of Central Florida
University of Florida
University of Miami
University of North Florida
University of South Florida

Georgia

Georgia Institute of Technology
Georgia Southern University
Georgia State University
Kennesaw State University
Mercer University

Savannah State University
University of Georgia

Hawaii

University of Hawaii
  Manoa

Idaho

Boise State University
Idaho State University
University of Idaho

Illinois

Bradley University
Chicago State University
DePaul University
Eastern Illinois University
Illinois State University
Loyola University Chicago
Northern Illinois University
Northwestern University
Southern Illinois University
  Carbondale
Southern Illinois University
  Edwardsville
University of Illinois
  Chicago
Western Illinois University

Indiana

Ball State University
Butler University
Indiana State University
Indiana University
  Bloomington
  Purdue University Fort
    Wayne
  Purdue University
    Indianapolis
Purdue University
University of Evansville
University of Notre Dame
Valparaiso University

Iowa

Drake University
Iowa State University
University of Iowa
University of Northern Iowa

Kansas

Kansas State University
University of Kansas
Wichita State University

Kentucky

Eastern Kentucky University
Morehead State University
Murray State University
University of Kentucky
University of Louisville
Western Kentucky University

Louisiana

Grambling State University
Louisiana State University and
  Agricultural and Mechanical
  College
Louisiana Tech University
McNeese State University
Nicholls State University
Northwestern State University
Southeastern Louisiana
  University
Southern University and
  Agricultural and Mechanical
  College
Tulane University
University of Louisiana at
  Lafayette
University of Louisiana at
  Monroe
University of New Orleans

Maine

University of Maine

Maryland

Coppin State University
Loyola University Maryland

Morgan State University
Mount St. Mary's University
Towson University
United States Naval Academy
University of Maryland
  Baltimore County
  College Park
  Eastern Shore

Massachusetts

Boston College
Boston University
College of the Holy Cross
Harvard College
Northeastern University
University of Massachusetts
  Amherst

Michigan

Central Michigan University
Eastern Michigan University
Michigan State University
Oakland University
University of Detroit Mercy
University of Michigan
Western Michigan University

Minnesota

University of Minnesota
  Twin Cities

Mississippi

Alcorn State University
Jackson State University
Mississippi State University
Mississippi Valley State
  University
University of Mississippi

Missouri

Missouri State University
Saint Louis University
Southeast Missouri State
  University
University of Missouri
  Columbia
  Kansas City

Montana

Montana State University
University of Montana

Nebraska

Creighton University
University of Nebraska
  Lincoln
  Omaha

Nevada

University of Nevada
  Las Vegas

New Hampshire

Dartmouth College
University of New Hampshire

New Jersey

Fairleigh Dickinson University
  Metropolitan Campus
Monmouth University
New Jersey Institute of
  Technology
Princeton University
Rider University
Seton Hall University

New Mexico

New Mexico State University
University of New Mexico

New York

Barnard College
Canisius College
Colgate University
Columbia University
Cornell University
Fordham University
Hofstra University
Iona College

Long Island University
  LIU Brooklyn
Manhattan College
Marist College
Niagara University
Saint Bonaventure University
St. Francis College
St. John's University
Siena College
SUNY
  University at Albany
  University at Binghamton
  University at Buffalo
  University at Stony Brook
Syracuse University
United States Military Academy
Wagner College

North Carolina

Appalachian State University
Campbell University
Davidson College
Duke University
East Carolina University
Elon University
Gardner-Webb University
High Point University
North Carolina Agricultural and
  Technical State University
North Carolina Central
  University
North Carolina State University
University of North Carolina
  Asheville
  Chapel Hill
Wake Forest University
Western Carolina University

North Dakota

North Dakota State University
University of North Dakota

Ohio

Bowling Green State University
Cleveland State University
Kent State University
Miami University
  Oxford
Ohio State University
  Columbus Campus
Ohio University
University of Akron
University of Cincinnati
University of Dayton
University of Toledo
Wright State University
Xavier University
Youngstown State University

Oklahoma

Oklahoma State University
Oral Roberts University
University of Oklahoma

Oregon

Oregon State University
Portland State University
University of Oregon
University of Portland

Pennsylvania

Bucknell University
Drexel University
Duquesne University
La Salle University
Lafayette College
Lehigh University
Penn State
  University Park
Robert Morris University
St. Francis University
Saint Joseph's University
Temple University
University of Pennsylvania
University of Pittsburgh
Villanova University

Basketball Division I

Alabama

Alabama Agricultural and
  Mechanical University
Alabama State University
Auburn University
Jacksonville State University
Samford University
Troy University
University of Alabama
University of Alabama
  Birmingham
University of South Alabama

Arizona

Arizona State University
Northern Arizona University
University of Arizona

Rhode Island

Brown University
Bryant University
Providence College
University of Rhode Island

South Carolina

Charleston Southern University
The Citadel M
Clemson University
Coastal Carolina University
College of Charleston
Furman University
Presbyterian College
South Carolina State University
University of South Carolina
    Columbia
    Upstate
Winthrop University
Wofford College

South Dakota

South Dakota State University
University of South Dakota

Tennessee

Austin Peay State University
Belmont University
East Tennessee State University
Lipscomb University
Middle Tennessee State
    University
Tennessee State University
Tennessee Technological
    University
University of Memphis
University of Tennessee
    Chattanooga
    Knoxville
    Martin
Vanderbilt University

Texas

Baylor University
Houston Baptist University
Lamar University
Prairie View A&M University
Rice University
Sam Houston State University
Southern Methodist University
Stephen F. Austin State
    University
Texas A&M University
    Corpus Christi
Texas Christian University
Texas Southern University
Texas Tech University
University of Houston
University of North Texas
University of Texas
    Arlington
    Austin
    El Paso
    San Antonio

Utah

Brigham Young University
Southern Utah University
University of Utah
Utah State University
Utah Valley University
Weber State University

Vermont

University of Vermont

Virginia

College of William and Mary
George Mason University
Hampton University
James Madison University
Liberty University
Longwood University
Norfolk State University
Old Dominion University
Radford University
University of Richmond
University of Virginia

Virginia Commonwealth
    University
Virginia Military Institute M

Washington

Eastern Washington University
Gonzaga University
Seattle University
University of Washington
Washington State University

West Virginia

Marshall University
West Virginia University

Wisconsin

Marquette University
University of Wisconsin
    Green Bay
    Madison
    Milwaukee

Wyoming

University of Wyoming

Basketball Division II

Alabama

Auburn University at
    Montgomery
Miles College
Spring Hill College
Stillman College
Tuskegee University
University of Alabama
    Huntsville
University of Montevallo
University of North Alabama
University of West Alabama

Alaska

University of Alaska
    Anchorage
    Fairbanks

Arizona

Grand Canyon University

Arkansas

Arkansas Tech University
Harding University
Henderson State University
Ouachita Baptist University
Southern Arkansas University
University of Arkansas
    Fort Smith
    Monticello

California

Academy of Art University
Azusa Pacific University
California Baptist University
California State Polytechnic
    University: Pomona
California State University
    Chico
    Dominguez Hills
    East Bay
    Los Angeles
    Monterey Bay
    San Bernardino
    Stanislaus
Dominican University of
    California
Fresno Pacific University
Holy Names University
Humboldt State University
Notre Dame de Namur
    University
Point Loma Nazarene University
San Francisco State University
Sonoma State University
University of California
    San Diego

Colorado

Adams State University
Colorado Christian University
Colorado Mesa University
Colorado School of Mines
Colorado State University
    Pueblo
Fort Lewis College
Metropolitan State University of
    Denver
Regis University
University of Colorado
    Colorado Springs
Western State Colorado
    University

Connecticut

Post University
Southern Connecticut State
    University
University of Bridgeport
University of New Haven

Delaware

Goldey-Beacom College
Wilmington University

District of Columbia

University of the District of
    Columbia

Florida

Barry University
Eckerd College
Flagler College
Florida Institute of Technology
Florida Southern College
Lynn University
Nova Southeastern University
Palm Beach Atlantic University
Rollins College
Saint Leo University
University of Tampa
University of West Florida

Georgia

Albany State University
Clark Atlanta University
Clayton State University
Columbus State University
Emmanuel College
Fort Valley State University
Georgia Southwestern State
    University
Morehouse College M
Paine College
Shorter University
University of North Georgia
University of West Georgia
Valdosta State University
Young Harris College

Hawaii

Brigham Young University-
    Hawaii
Chaminade University of
    Honolulu
Hawaii Pacific University
University of Hawaii
    Hilo

Idaho

Northwest Nazarene University

Illinois

Lewis University
McKendree University
Quincy University
University of Illinois
    Springfield

Indiana

Oakland City University
Saint Joseph's College
University of Indianapolis
University of Southern Indiana

Iowa

Upper Iowa University

Kansas

Emporia State University
Fort Hays State University
Newman University
Pittsburg State University
Washburn University

Kentucky

Bellarmine University
Kentucky State University
Kentucky Wesleyan College
Northern Kentucky University

Maryland

Bowie State University

Massachusetts

American International College
Assumption College
Bentley University
Merrimack College
Stonehill College

Michigan

Ferris State University
Grand Valley State University
Hillsdale College
Lake Superior State University
Michigan Technological
    University
Northern Michigan University
Northwood University
    Michigan
Saginaw Valley State University
Wayne State University

Minnesota

Bemidji State University
Concordia University St. Paul
Minnesota State University
    Mankato
    Moorhead
Saint Cloud State University
Southwest Minnesota State
    University
University of Minnesota
    Crookston
    Duluth
Winona State University

Mississippi

Delta State University
Mississippi College

Missouri

Drury University
Lincoln University
Lindenwood University
Maryville University of Saint
    Louis
Missouri Southern State
    University
Missouri University of Science
    and Technology
Missouri Western State
    University
Northwest Missouri State
    University
Rockhurst University
Southwest Baptist University
Truman State University
University of Central Missouri
William Jewell College

Montana

Montana State University
    Billings

Nebraska

Chadron State College
University of Nebraska
    Kearney
Wayne State College

New Hampshire

Franklin Pierce University
Saint Anselm College
Southern New Hampshire
    University

New Jersey

Bloomfield College
Georgian Court University

New Mexico

Eastern New Mexico University
New Mexico Highlands
    University
Western New Mexico
    University

New York

Adelphi University
City University of New York
    Queens College
College of Saint Rose
Concordia College
Daemen College
Dominican College of Blauvelt
Dowling College
Le Moyne College
Long Island University
    LIU Post
Mercy College
Molloy College
New York Institute of
    Technology
Nyack College
Pace University
Roberts Wesleyan College
St. Thomas Aquinas College

North Carolina

Barton College
Belmont Abbey College
Brevard College
Catawba College
Chowan University
Elizabeth City State University
Fayetteville State University
Johnson C. Smith University
Lees-McRae College
Lenoir-Rhyne University
Livingstone College
Mars Hill University
Pfeiffer University
Queens University of Charlotte
Saint Augustine's University
Shaw University
University of Mount Olive
University of North Carolina
    Pembroke
Wingate University
Winston-Salem State University

North Dakota

Minot State University
University of Mary

Ohio

Ashland University
Cedarville University
Central State University
Lake Erie College
Malone University
Notre Dame College
Ohio Dominican University
Tiffin University
University of Findlay
Urbana University
Ursuline College F
Walsh University

Oklahoma

Cameron University
East Central University
Northeastern State University
Northwestern Oklahoma State
    University
Oklahoma Baptist University
Oklahoma Christian University

Oklahoma Panhandle State
University
Rogers State University
Southeastern Oklahoma State
University
Southern Nazarene University
Southwestern Oklahoma State
University
University of Central Oklahoma

Oregon

Western Oregon University

Pennsylvania

Bloomsburg University of
Pennsylvania
California University of
Pennsylvania
Chestnut Hill College
Cheyney University of
Pennsylvania
Clarion University of
Pennsylvania
East Stroudsburg University of
Pennsylvania
Edinboro University
of Pennsylvania
Gannon University
Holy Family University
Indiana University of
Pennsylvania
Kutztown University of
Pennsylvania
Lincoln University
Lock Haven University of
Pennsylvania
Mansfield University of
Pennsylvania
Mercyhurst University
Millersville University of
Pennsylvania
Philadelphia University
Seton Hill University
Shippensburg University of
Pennsylvania
Slippery Rock University of
Pennsylvania
University of Pittsburgh
Johnstown
West Chester University of
Pennsylvania

Puerto Rico

University of Puerto Rico
Bayamon University
College
Rio Piedras

South Carolina

Anderson University
Benedict College
Claflin University
Coker College
Converse College F
Erskine College
Francis Marion University
Lander University
Limestone College
Newberry College
North Greenville University
Southern Wesleyan University
University of South Carolina
Aiken

South Dakota

Black Hills State University
Northern State University
South Dakota School of Mines
and Technology
University of Sioux Falls

Tennessee

Carson-Newman University
Christian Brothers University
King University
Lane College
Lee University
LeMoyne-Owen College
Lincoln Memorial University

Trevecca Nazarene University
Tusculum College
Union University

Texas

Abilene Christian University
Angelo State University
Dallas Baptist University M
Lubbock Christian University
Midwestern State University
St. Edward's University
St. Mary's University
Tarleton State University
Texas A&M International
University
Texas A&M University
Commerce
Kingsville
Texas Woman's University F
University of Texas
of the Permian Basin
University of the Incarnate
Word
West Texas A&M University

Utah

Dixie State University

Vermont

Saint Michael's College

Virginia

University of Virginia's College
at Wise
Virginia State University
Virginia Union University

Washington

Central Washington University
Saint Martin's University
Seattle Pacific University
Western Washington University

West Virginia

Alderson-Broaddus University
Bluefield State College
Concord University
Davis and Elkins College
Fairmont State University
Glenville State College
Ohio Valley University
Salem International University
Shepherd University
University of Charleston
West Liberty University
West Virginia State University
West Virginia Wesleyan College
Wheeling Jesuit University

Wisconsin

University of Wisconsin
Parkside

Canada

Simon Fraser University

Basketball Division III

Alabama

Birmingham-Southern College
Huntingdon College

Arkansas

Hendrix College
University of the Ozarks

California

California Institute of
Technology
California Lutheran University
Chapman University
Claremont McKenna College
Harvey Mudd College
Occidental College
Pitzer College
Pomona College
Scripps College

University of California
Santa Cruz
University of La Verne
University of Redlands
Whittier College

Colorado

Colorado College

Connecticut

Albertus Magnus College
Connecticut College
Eastern Connecticut State
University
Mitchell College
Trinity College
United States Coast Guard
Academy
University of Saint Joseph F
Wesleyan University
Western Connecticut State
University

Delaware

Wesley College

District of Columbia

Catholic University of America
Gallaudet University
Trinity Washington University F

Georgia

Agnes Scott College F
Berry College
Covenant College
Emory University
Oglethorpe University
Piedmont College
Wesleyan College F

Illinois

Augustana College
Aurora University
Benedictine University at
Springfield
Blackburn College
Concordia University Chicago
Dominican University
Elmhurst College
Eureka College
Greenville College
Illinois College
Illinois Institute of Technology
Illinois Wesleyan University
Knox College
Lake Forest College
MacMurray College
Millikin University
Monmouth College
North Central College
North Park University
Principia College
Rockford University
University of Chicago
Wheaton College

Indiana

Anderson University
DePauw University
Earlham College
Franklin College
Hanover College
Manchester University
Rose-Hulman Institute of
Technology
Saint Mary's College F
Trine University
Wabash College M

Iowa

Buena Vista University
Central College
Coe College
Cornell College
Grinnell College
Loras College
Luther College
Simpson College

University of Dubuque
Wartburg College

Kentucky

Berea College
Centre College
Spalding University
Thomas More College
Transylvania University

Louisiana

Centenary College of Louisiana
Louisiana College

Maine

Bates College
Bowdoin College
Colby College
Husson University
Maine Maritime Academy
Saint Joseph's College of Maine
Thomas College
University of Maine
Farmington
Presque Isle
University of New England
University of Southern Maine

Maryland

Frostburg State University
Goucher College
Hood College
Johns Hopkins University
McDaniel College
Notre Dame of Maryland
University F
St. Mary's College of Maryland
Salisbury University
Stevenson University
Washington College

Massachusetts

Amherst College
Anna Maria College
Babson College
Becker College
Brandeis University
Bridgewater State University
Clark University
Curry College
Eastern Nazarene College
Elms College
Emerson College
Emmanuel College
Endicott College
Fitchburg State University
Framingham State University
Gordon College
Lasell College
Lesley University
Massachusetts College of
Liberal Arts
Massachusetts Institute of
Technology
Mount Holyoke College F
Mount Ida College
Newbury College
Nichols College
Pine Manor College
Regis College
Salem State University
Simmons College F
Smith College F
Springfield College
Suffolk University
Tufts University
University of Massachusetts
Dartmouth
Wellesley College F
Wentworth Institute of
Technology
Western New England
University
Westfield State University
Wheaton College
Wheelock College
Williams College

Worcester Polytechnic Institute
Worcester State University

Michigan

Adrian College
Albion College
Alma College
Calvin College
Finlandia University
Hope College
Kalamazoo College
Olivet College

Minnesota

Augsburg College
Bethany Lutheran College
Bethel University
Carleton College
College of St. Benedict F
College of St. Scholastica
Concordia College: Moorhead
Gustavus Adolphus College
Hamline University
Macalester College
Martin Luther College
North Central University
St. Catherine University F
St. John's University M
St. Mary's University of
Minnesota
St. Olaf College
University of Minnesota
Morris
University of Northwestern - St.
Paul
University of St. Thomas

Mississippi

Belhaven University
Millsaps College
Rust College

Missouri

Fontbonne University
Webster University
Westminster College

Nebraska

Nebraska Wesleyan University

New Hampshire

Colby-Sawyer College
Daniel Webster College
Keene State College
New England College
Plymouth State University
Rivier University

New Jersey

Centenary College
The College of New Jersey
College of St. Elizabeth F
Drew University
Fairleigh Dickinson University
College at Florham
Kean University
Montclair State University
New Jersey City University
Ramapo College of New Jersey
Rowan University
Rutgers, The State University of
New Jersey
Camden Campus
Newark Campus
Stevens Institute of Technology
William Paterson University of
New Jersey

New York

Alfred University
Bard College
Cazenovia College

City University of New York
  Baruch College
  Brooklyn College
  City College
  College of Staten Island
  Hunter College
  John Jay College of
    Criminal Justice
  Medgar Evers College
  York College
Clarkson University
College of Mount St. Vincent
College of New Rochelle F
D'Youville College
Elmira College
Hamilton College
Hartwick College
Hilbert College
Houghton College
Ithaca College
Keuka College
Manhattanville College
Medaille College
Mount Saint Mary College
Nazareth College
New York University
Rensselaer Polytechnic Institute
Rochester Institute of
  Technology
The Sage Colleges
St. John Fisher College
St. Joseph's College New York:
  Suffolk Campus
St. Joseph's College, New York
St. Lawrence University
Sarah Lawrence College M
Skidmore College
SUNY
  College at Brockport
  College at Buffalo
  College at Cortland
  College at Geneseo
  College at New Paltz
  College at Old Westbury
  College at Oneonta
  College at Oswego
  College at Plattsburgh
  College at Potsdam
  College at Purchase
  College of Agriculture and
    Technology at Cobleskill
  College of Agriculture and
    Technology at Morrisville
  College of Technology at
    Alfred
  College of Technology at
    Canton
  Maritime College M
Union College
United States Merchant Marine
  Academy
University of Rochester
Utica College
Vassar College
Wells College
Yeshiva University

North Carolina

Greensboro College
Guilford College
Meredith College F
Methodist University
North Carolina Wesleyan
  College
Salem College F
William Peace University

Ohio

Baldwin Wallace University
Bluffton University
Capital University
Case Western Reserve
  University
College of Wooster
Defiance College
Denison University
Franciscan University of
  Steubenville

Heidelberg University
Hiram College
John Carroll University
Kenyon College
Marietta College
Muskingum University
Oberlin College
Ohio Northern University
Ohio Wesleyan University
Otterbein University
University of Mount Union
Wilmington College
Wittenberg University

Oregon

George Fox University
Lewis & Clark College
Linfield College
Pacific University
Willamette University

Pennsylvania

Albright College
Allegheny College
Alvernia University
Arcadia University
Bryn Athyn College
Bryn Mawr College F
Cabrini College
Cairn University
Carnegie Mellon University
Cedar Crest College F
Chatham University
DeSales University
Dickinson College
Eastern University
Elizabethtown College
Franklin & Marshall College
Geneva College
Gettysburg College
Grove City College
Gwynedd Mercy University
Haverford College
Immaculata University
Juniata College
Keystone College
King's College
La Roche College
Lancaster Bible College
Lebanon Valley College
Lycoming College
Marywood University
Messiah College
Misericordia University
Moravian College
Mount Aloysius College
Muhlenberg College
Neumann University
Penn State
  Abington
  Altoona
  Berks
  Erie, The Behrend College
  Harrisburg
Pennsylvania College of
  Technology
Rosemont College
St. Vincent College
Susquehanna University
Swarthmore College
Thiel College
University of Pittsburgh
  Bradford
  Greensburg
University of Scranton
Ursinus College
Washington & Jefferson College
Waynesburg University
Westminster College
Widener University
Wilkes University
Wilson College
York College of Pennsylvania

Rhode Island

Rhode Island College
Roger Williams University
Salve Regina University

Tennessee

Maryville College
Rhodes College
Sewanee: The University of the
  South

Texas

Austin College
Concordia University Texas
East Texas Baptist University
Hardin-Simmons University
Howard Payne University
LeTourneau University
McMurry University
Schreiner University
Southwestern University
Sul Ross State University
Texas Lutheran University
Trinity University
University of Dallas
University of Mary Hardin-
  Baylor
University of Texas
  Dallas
  Tyler

Vermont

Green Mountain College
Johnson State College
Lyndon State College
Middlebury College
Norwich University
Southern Vermont College

Virginia

Averett University
Bridgewater College
Christopher Newport University
Eastern Mennonite University
Emory & Henry College
Ferrum College
Hampden-Sydney College M
Hollins University F
Lynchburg College
Mary Baldwin College F
Marymount University
Randolph College
Randolph-Macon College
Roanoke College
Shenandoah University
Southern Virginia University
University of Mary Washington
Virginia Wesleyan College
Washington and Lee University

Washington

Pacific Lutheran University
University of Puget Sound
Whitman College
Whitworth University

West Virginia

Bethany College

Wisconsin

Alverno College F
Beloit College
Carroll University
Carthage College
Edgewood College
Lakeland College
Lawrence University
Maranathan Baptist University
  Maranatha Baptist
    University
Marian University
Milwaukee School of
  Engineering
Mount Mary University F
Northland College
Ripon College
St. Norbert College
University of Wisconsin
  Eau Claire
  La Crosse
  Platteville
  Stevens Point
  Superior
Wisconsin Lutheran College

Bowling Division I

Alabama

Alabama Agricultural and
  Mechanical University F
Alabama State University F
University of Alabama
  Birmingham F

Arkansas

Arkansas State University F

Connecticut

Sacred Heart University F

Delaware

Delaware State University F

District of Columbia

Howard University F

Florida

Bethune-Cookman University F
Florida Agricultural and
  Mechanical University F

Indiana

Valparaiso University F

Louisiana

Grambling State University F
Louisiana Tech University F
Southern University and
  Agricultural and Mechanical
  College F
Tulane University F

Maryland

Coppin State University F
Morgan State University F
University of Maryland
  Eastern Shore F

Mississippi

Jackson State University F

Nebraska

University of Nebraska
  Lincoln F

New Jersey

Fairleigh Dickinson University
  Metropolitan Campus F
Monmouth University F

New York

Long Island University
  LIU Brooklyn F
St. Francis College F

North Carolina

North Carolina Agricultural and
  Technical State University F

Pennsylvania

St. Francis University F

Tennessee

Vanderbilt University F

Texas

Prairie View A&M University F
Sam Houston State University F
Stephen F. Austin State
  University F
Texas Southern University F

Virginia

Hampton University F
Norfolk State University F

Bowling Division II

Connecticut

Post University F

Illinois

McKendree University F

Maryland

Bowie State University F

Missouri

Lincoln University F
Maryville University of Saint
  Louis F
University of Central Missouri F

New Hampshire

Franklin Pierce University F

New York

Adelphi University F
Daemen College F
Molloy College F

North Carolina

Chowan University F
Elizabeth City State University
  F
Fayetteville State University F
Johnson C. Smith University F
Livingstone College F
Saint Augustine's University F
Shaw University F

Ohio

Ursuline College F

Pennsylvania

Chestnut Hill College F
Cheyney University of
  Pennsylvania F
Kutztown University of
  Pennsylvania F

Virginia

Virginia State University F
Virginia Union University F

West Virginia

Salem International University F

Bowling Division III

Illinois

Aurora University F
Elmhurst College F

Kentucky

Spalding University F
Thomas More College F

Michigan

Adrian College F

New Jersey

New Jersey City University F

New York

Medaille College F

Pennsylvania

Mount Aloysius College F
Penn State
  Altoona F
Thiel College F
University of Pittsburgh
  Bradford F

Cross-country Division I

Alabama

Alabama Agricultural and
  Mechanical University F
Alabama State University

Tables and Indexes

Auburn University
Jacksonville State University
Samford University
Troy University
University of Alabama
University of Alabama
 Birmingham F
University of South Alabama

Arizona

Arizona State University
Northern Arizona University
University of Arizona

Arkansas

Arkansas State University
University of Arkansas
 Pine Bluff
University of Central Arkansas

California

California Polytechnic State
 University: San Luis Obispo
California State University
 Bakersfield F
 Fresno
 Fullerton
 Long Beach
 Northridge
 Sacramento
Loyola Marymount University
Pepperdine University
St. Mary's College of California
San Diego State University F
San Jose State University
Santa Clara University
Stanford University
University of California
 Berkeley
 Davis
 Irvine
 Los Angeles
 Riverside
 Santa Barbara
University of San Diego
University of San Francisco
University of Southern
 California F
University of the Pacific F

Colorado

Colorado State University
United States Air Force
 Academy
University of Colorado
 Boulder
University of Northern Colorado

Connecticut

Central Connecticut State
 University
Fairfield University
Quinnipiac University
Sacred Heart University
University of Connecticut
University of Hartford
Yale University

Delaware

Delaware State University
University of Delaware F

District of Columbia

American University
George Washington University
Georgetown University
Howard University

Florida

Bethune-Cookman University
Florida Agricultural and
 Mechanical University
Florida Atlantic University
Florida Gulf Coast University
Florida International University
Florida State University
Jacksonville University
Stetson University
University of Central Florida F

University of Florida
University of Miami
University of North Florida
University of South Florida

Georgia

Georgia Institute of Technology
Georgia Southern University F
Georgia State University F
Kennesaw State University
Mercer University
Savannah State University
University of Georgia

Hawaii

University of Hawaii
 Manoa F

Idaho

Boise State University
Idaho State University
University of Idaho

Illinois

Bradley University
Chicago State University
DePaul University
Eastern Illinois University
Illinois State University
Loyola University Chicago
Northern Illinois University F
Northwestern University F
Southern Illinois University
 Carbondale
Southern Illinois University
 Edwardsville
University of Illinois
 Chicago
Western Illinois University

Indiana

Ball State University F
Butler University
Indiana State University
Indiana University
 Bloomington
 Purdue University Fort
 Wayne
 Purdue University
 Indianapolis
Purdue University
University of Evansville
University of Notre Dame
Valparaiso University

Iowa

Drake University
Iowa State University
University of Iowa
University of Northern Iowa

Kansas

Kansas State University
University of Kansas
Wichita State University

Kentucky

Eastern Kentucky University
Morehead State University
Murray State University
University of Kentucky
University of Louisville
Western Kentucky University

Louisiana

Grambling State University
Louisiana State University and
 Agricultural and Mechanical
 College
Louisiana Tech University
McNeese State University
Nicholls State University
Northwestern State University
Southeastern Louisiana
 University
Southern University and
 Agricultural and Mechanical
 College
Tulane University

University of Louisiana at
 Lafayette
University of Louisiana at
 Monroe
University of New Orleans

Maine

University of Maine

Maryland

Coppin State University
Loyola University Maryland
Morgan State University
Mount St. Mary's University
Towson University F
United States Naval Academy
University of Maryland
 Baltimore County
 College Park F
 Eastern Shore

Massachusetts

Boston College
Boston University
College of the Holy Cross
Harvard College
Northeastern University
University of Massachusetts
 Amherst

Michigan

Central Michigan University
Eastern Michigan University
Michigan State University
Oakland University
University of Detroit Mercy
University of Michigan
Western Michigan University F

Minnesota

University of Minnesota
 Twin Cities

Mississippi

Alcorn State University
Jackson State University
Mississippi State University
Mississippi Valley State
 University
University of Mississippi

Missouri

Missouri State University F
Saint Louis University
Southeast Missouri State
 University
University of Missouri
 Columbia
 Kansas City

Montana

Montana State University
University of Montana

Nebraska

Creighton University
University of Nebraska
 Lincoln
 Omaha F

Nevada

University of Nevada
 Las Vegas F

New Hampshire

Dartmouth College
University of New Hampshire

New Jersey

Fairleigh Dickinson University
 Metropolitan Campus
Monmouth University
New Jersey Institute of
 Technology
Princeton University
Rider University
Seton Hall University

New Mexico

New Mexico State University
University of New Mexico

New York

Barnard College
Canisius College
Colgate University
Columbia University
Cornell University
Fordham University
Hofstra University
Iona College
Long Island University
 LIU Brooklyn F
Manhattan College
Marist College
Niagara University
Saint Bonaventure University
St. Francis College
St. John's University F
Siena College
SUNY
 University at Albany
 University at Binghamton
 University at Buffalo
 University at Stony Brook
Syracuse University
United States Military Academy
Wagner College

North Carolina

Appalachian State University
Campbell University
Davidson College
Duke University
East Carolina University
Elon University
Gardner-Webb University
High Point University
North Carolina Agricultural and
 Technical State University
North Carolina Central
 University
North Carolina State University
University of North Carolina
 Asheville
 Chapel Hill
Wake Forest University
Western Carolina University

North Dakota

North Dakota State University
University of North Dakota

Ohio

Bowling Green State University
Cleveland State University F
Kent State University
Miami University
 Oxford
Ohio State University
 Columbus Campus
Ohio University
University of Akron
University of Cincinnati
University of Dayton
University of Toledo
Wright State University
Xavier University
Youngstown State University

Oklahoma

Oklahoma State University
Oral Roberts University
University of Oklahoma

Oregon

Oregon State University F
Portland State University
University of Oregon
University of Portland

Pennsylvania

Bucknell University
Duquesne University
La Salle University
Lafayette College

Lehigh University
Penn State
 University Park
Robert Morris University F
St. Francis University
Saint Joseph's University
Temple University
University of Pennsylvania
University of Pittsburgh
Villanova University

Rhode Island

Brown University
Bryant University
Providence College
University of Rhode Island

South Carolina

Charleston Southern University
The Citadel
Clemson University
Coastal Carolina University
College of Charleston
Furman University
Presbyterian College
South Carolina State University
University of South Carolina
 Columbia F
 Upstate
Winthrop University
Wofford College

South Dakota

South Dakota State University
University of South Dakota

Tennessee

Austin Peay State University
Belmont University
East Tennessee State University
Lipscomb University
Middle Tennessee State
 University
Tennessee State University
Tennessee Technological
 University
University of Memphis
University of Tennessee
 Chattanooga
 Knoxville
 Martin
Vanderbilt University

Texas

Baylor University
Houston Baptist University
Lamar University
Prairie View A&M University
Rice University
Sam Houston State University
Southern Methodist University F
Stephen F. Austin State
 University
Texas A&M University
 Corpus Christi
Texas Christian University
Texas Southern University
Texas Tech University
University of Houston
University of North Texas
University of Texas
 Arlington
 Austin
 El Paso
 San Antonio

Utah

Brigham Young University
Southern Utah University
University of Utah F
Utah State University
Utah Valley University
Weber State University

Vermont

University of Vermont

Virginia

College of William and Mary
George Mason University

Hampton University
James Madison University F
Liberty University
Longwood University
Norfolk State University
Radford University
University of Richmond
University of Virginia
Virginia Commonwealth
University
Virginia Military Institute

Washington

Eastern Washington University
Gonzaga University
Seattle University
University of Washington
Washington State University

West Virginia

Marshall University
West Virginia University F

Wisconsin

Marquette University
University of Wisconsin
Green Bay
Madison
Milwaukee

Wyoming

University of Wyoming

Cross-country Division II

Alabama

Auburn University at
Montgomery
Miles College
Spring Hill College
Stillman College
Tuskegee University
University of Alabama
Huntsville
University of Montevallo
University of North Alabama
University of West Alabama

Alaska

University of Alaska
Anchorage
Fairbanks

Arizona

Grand Canyon University

Arkansas

Arkansas Tech University F
Harding University
Henderson State University F
Ouachita Baptist University F
Southern Arkansas University
University of Arkansas
Fort Smith
Monticello

California

Academy of Art University
Azusa Pacific University
California Baptist University
California State Polytechnic
University: Pomona
California State University
Chico
East Bay
Los Angeles F
Monterey Bay
San Bernardino F
Stanislaus
Dominican University of
California
Fresno Pacific University
Holy Names University
Humboldt State University
Notre Dame de Namur
University

Point Loma Nazarene
University F
San Francisco State University
Sonoma State University F
University of California
San Diego

Colorado

Adams State University
Colorado Christian University
Colorado Mesa University
Colorado School of Mines
Colorado State University
Pueblo
Fort Lewis College
Metropolitan State University of
Denver
Regis University
University of Colorado
Colorado Springs
Western State Colorado
University

Connecticut

Post University
Southern Connecticut State
University
University of Bridgeport
University of New Haven

Delaware

Goldey-Beacom College
Wilmington University

District of Columbia

University of the District of
Columbia F

Florida

Flagler College
Florida Institute of Technology
Florida Southern College
Lynn University F
Nova Southeastern University
Palm Beach Atlantic University
F
Rollins College
Saint Leo University
University of Tampa
University of West Florida

Georgia

Albany State University
Clark Atlanta University
Clayton State University
Columbus State University
Emmanuel College
Fort Valley State University
Georgia Southwestern State
University F
Morehouse College M
Paine College
Shorter University
University of North Georgia F
University of West Georgia
Valdosta State University
Young Harris College

Hawaii

Brigham Young University-
Hawaii
Chaminade University of
Honolulu
Hawaii Pacific University
University of Hawaii
Hilo F

Idaho

Northwest Nazarene University

Illinois

Lewis University
McKendree University
Quincy University
University of Illinois
Springfield

Indiana

Oakland City University
Saint Joseph's College

University of Indianapolis
University of Southern Indiana

Iowa

Upper Iowa University F

Kansas

Emporia State University
Fort Hays State University
Newman University
Pittsburg State University

Kentucky

Bellarmine University
Kentucky State University
Kentucky Wesleyan College
Northern Kentucky University

Maryland

Bowie State University

Massachusetts

American International College
Assumption College
Bentley University
Merrimack College
Stonehill College

Michigan

Ferris State University
Grand Valley State University
Hillsdale College
Lake Superior State University
Michigan Technological
University
Northern Michigan University F
Northwood University
Michigan
Saginaw Valley State University
Wayne State University

Minnesota

Bemidji State University F
Concordia University St. Paul
Minnesota State University
Mankato
Moorhead
Saint Cloud State University
Southwest Minnesota State
University
University of Minnesota
Duluth
Winona State University

Mississippi

Delta State University F
Mississippi College

Missouri

Drury University
Lincoln University F
Lindenwood University
Maryville University of Saint
Louis
Missouri Southern State
University
Missouri University of Science
and Technology
Northwest Missouri State
University
Rockhurst University F
Southwest Baptist University
Truman State University
University of Central Missouri
William Jewell College

Montana

Montana State University
Billings

Nebraska

Chadron State College
University of Nebraska
Kearney
Wayne State College

New Hampshire

Franklin Pierce University
Saint Anselm College

Southern New Hampshire
University

New Jersey

Bloomfield College
Georgian Court University

New Mexico

Eastern New Mexico University
New Mexico Highlands
University
Western New Mexico
University

New York

Adelphi University
City University of New York
Queens College
College of Saint Rose
Concordia College
Daemen College
Dominican College of Blauvelt
Dowling College
Le Moyne College
Long Island University
LIU Post
Molloy College
New York Institute of
Technology
Nyack College
Pace University
Roberts Wesleyan College
St. Thomas Aquinas College

North Carolina

Barton College
Belmont Abbey College
Brevard College
Catawba College
Chowan University
Elizabeth City State University
Fayetteville State University
Johnson C. Smith University
Lees-McRae College
Lenoir-Rhyne University
Livingstone College
Mars Hill University
Pfeiffer University
Queens University of Charlotte
Saint Augustine's University
Shaw University
University of Mount Olive
University of North Carolina
Pembroke
Wingate University
Winston-Salem State University

North Dakota

Minot State University
University of Mary

Ohio

Ashland University
Cedarville University
Central State University
Lake Erie College
Malone University
Notre Dame College
Ohio Dominican University
Tiffin University
University of Findlay
Urbana University
Ursuline College F
Walsh University

Oklahoma

Cameron University M
East Central University
Northwestern Oklahoma State
University
Oklahoma Baptist University
Oklahoma Christian University
Oklahoma Panhandle State
University
Rogers State University
Southeastern Oklahoma State
University F
Southern Nazarene University

Southwestern Oklahoma State
University F
University of Central Oklahoma
F

Oregon

Western Oregon University

Pennsylvania

Bloomsburg University of
Pennsylvania
California University of
Pennsylvania
Chestnut Hill College
Cheyney University of
Pennsylvania
Clarion University of
Pennsylvania F
East Stroudsburg University of
Pennsylvania
Edinboro University
of Pennsylvania
Gannon University
Holy Family University
Indiana University of
Pennsylvania
Kutztown University of
Pennsylvania
Lincoln University
Lock Haven University of
Pennsylvania
Mansfield University of
Pennsylvania
Mercyhurst University
Millersville University of
Pennsylvania F
Philadelphia University
Seton Hill University
Shippensburg University of
Pennsylvania
Slippery Rock University of
Pennsylvania
University of Pittsburgh
Johnstown
West Chester University of
Pennsylvania

Puerto Rico

University of Puerto Rico
Bayamon University
College
Rio Piedras

South Carolina

Anderson University
Benedict College
Claflin University
Coker College
Converse College F
Erskine College
Francis Marion University
Limestone College
Newberry College
North Greenville University
Southern Wesleyan University
University of South Carolina
Aiken F

South Dakota

Black Hills State University
Northern State University
South Dakota School of Mines
and Technology
University of Sioux Falls

Tennessee

Carson-Newman University
Christian Brothers University
King University
Lane College
Lee University
LeMoyne-Owen College
Lincoln Memorial University
Trevecca Nazarene University
Tusculum College
Union University

Texas

Abilene Christian University
Angelo State University
Dallas Baptist University
Lubbock Christian University
Midwestern State University F
St. Edward's University
Tarleton State University
Texas A&M International
University
Texas A&M University
Commerce
Kingsville
University of Texas
of the Permian Basin
University of the Incarnate
Word
West Texas A&M University

Utah

Dixie State University

Vermont

Saint Michael's College

Virginia

University of Virginia's College
at Wise
Virginia State University
Virginia Union University

Washington

Central Washington University
Saint Martin's University
Seattle Pacific University
Western Washington University

West Virginia

Alderson-Broaddus University
Bluefield State College
Concord University
Davis and Elkins College
Fairmont State University
Glenville State College
Ohio Valley University
Salem International University
University of Charleston
West Liberty University
West Virginia State University
F
West Virginia Wesleyan College
Wheeling Jesuit University

Wisconsin

University of Wisconsin
Parkside

Canada

Simon Fraser University

Cross-country Division III

Alabama

Birmingham-Southern College

Arkansas

Hendrix College
University of the Ozarks

California

California Institute of
Technology
California Lutheran University
Chapman University
Claremont McKenna College
Harvey Mudd College
Mills College F
Occidental College
Pitzer College
Pomona College
Scripps College
University of California
Santa Cruz
University of La Verne
University of Redlands
Whittier College

Colorado

Colorado College

Connecticut

Connecticut College
Eastern Connecticut State
University
Mitchell College
Trinity College
United States Coast Guard
Academy
University of Saint Joseph F
Wesleyan University

Delaware

Wesley College

District of Columbia

Catholic University of America
Gallaudet University

Georgia

Agnes Scott College F
Berry College
Covenant College
Emory University
Oglethorpe University
Piedmont College

Illinois

Augustana College
Aurora University
Benedictine University at
Springfield
Blackburn College
Concordia University Chicago
Dominican University
Elmhurst College
Eureka College
Greenville College
Illinois College
Illinois Institute of Technology
Illinois Wesleyan University
Knox College
Lake Forest College
Millikin University
Monmouth College
North Central College
North Park University
Principia College
Rockford University
University of Chicago
Wheaton College

Indiana

Anderson University
DePauw University
Earlham College
Franklin College
Hanover College
Manchester University
Rose-Hulman Institute of
Technology
Saint Mary's College F
Trine University
Wabash College M

Iowa

Buena Vista University
Central College
Coe College
Cornell College
Grinnell College
Loras College
Luther College
Simpson College
University of Dubuque
Wartburg College

Kentucky

Berea College
Centre College
Spalding University
Thomas More College
Transylvania University

Louisiana

Centenary College of Louisiana
Louisiana College

Maine

Bates College
Bowdoin College
Colby College
Husson University
Maine Maritime Academy
Saint Joseph's College of Maine
Thomas College
University of Maine
Farmington
Presque Isle
University of New England
University of Southern Maine

Maryland

Frostburg State University
Goucher College
Hood College
Johns Hopkins University
McDaniel College
St. Mary's College of Maryland
Salisbury University
Stevenson University

Massachusetts

Amherst College
Anna Maria College
Babson College
Brandeis University
Bridgewater State University
Clark University
Curry College F
Eastern Nazarene College
Elms College
Emerson College
Emmanuel College
Endicott College
Fitchburg State University
Framingham State University
Gordon College
Lasell College
Lesley University
Massachusetts College of
Liberal Arts
Massachusetts Institute of
Technology
Massachusetts Maritime
Academy
Mount Holyoke College F
Mount Ida College
Newbury College
Nichols College
Pine Manor College
Regis College
Simmons College F
Smith College F
Springfield College
Suffolk University
Tufts University
University of Massachusetts
Dartmouth
Wellesley College F
Wentworth Institute of
Technology M
Western New England
University
Westfield State University
Wheaton College
Wheelock College
Williams College
Worcester Polytechnic Institute
Worcester State University

Michigan

Adrian College
Albion College
Alma College
Calvin College
Hope College
Kalamazoo College
Olivet College

Minnesota

Augsburg College
Bethany Lutheran College
Bethel University
Carleton College
College of St. Benedict F

College of St. Scholastica
Concordia College: Moorhead
Gustavus Adolphus College
Hamline University
Macalester College
Martin Luther College
North Central University
St. Catherine University F
St. John's University M
St. Mary's University of
Minnesota
St. Olaf College
University of Minnesota
Morris
University of Northwestern - St.
Paul
University of St. Thomas

Mississippi

Belhaven University
Millsaps College
Rust College

Missouri

Fontbonne University
Webster University
Westminster College

Nebraska

Nebraska Wesleyan University

New Hampshire

Colby-Sawyer College
Daniel Webster College
Keene State College
New England College
Plymouth State University
Rivier University

New Jersey

Centenary College
The College of New Jersey
Drew University
Fairleigh Dickinson University
College at Florham
Montclair State University F
New Jersey City University
Ramapo College of New Jersey
Rowan University
Rutgers, The State University of
New Jersey
Camden Campus
Newark Campus
Stevens Institute of Technology

New York

Alfred University
Bard College
Cazenovia College
City University of New York
Baruch College
Brooklyn College
City College
College of Staten Island
Hunter College
John Jay College of
Criminal Justice
Medgar Evers College
York College
Clarkson University
College of Mount St. Vincent
College of New Rochelle F
D'Youville College
Elmira College
Hamilton College
Hartwick College
Hilbert College
Houghton College
Ithaca College
Keuka College
Manhattanville College
Medaille College
Mount Saint Mary College
Nazareth College
New York University
Rensselaer Polytechnic Institute
Rochester Institute of
Technology
The Sage Colleges

St. John Fisher College
St. Joseph's College New York:
Suffolk Campus
St. Joseph's College, New York
St. Lawrence University
Sarah Lawrence College
SUNY
College at Brockport
College at Buffalo
College at Cortland
College at Geneseo
College at New Paltz
College at Old Westbury
College at Oneonta
College at Oswego
College at Plattsburgh
College at Potsdam
College at Purchase
College of Agriculture and
Technology at Cobleskill
College of Agriculture and
Technology at Morrisville
College of Technology at
Alfred
College of Technology at
Canton
Maritime College
Union College
United States Merchant Marine
Academy
University of Rochester
Utica College
Vassar College
Wells College
Yeshiva University

North Carolina

Guilford College
Meredith College F
Methodist University
North Carolina Wesleyan
College F
Salem College F
William Peace University

Ohio

Baldwin Wallace University
Bluffton University
Capital University
Case Western Reserve
University
College of Wooster
Defiance College
Denison University
Franciscan University of
Steubenville
Heidelberg University
John Carroll University
Kenyon College
Marietta College
Muskingum University
Oberlin College
Ohio Northern University
Ohio Wesleyan University
Otterbein University
University of Mount Union
Wilmington College
Wittenberg University

Oregon

George Fox University
Lewis & Clark College
Linfield College
Pacific University
Willamette University

Pennsylvania

Albright College
Allegheny College
Alvernia University
Arcadia University
Bryn Athyn College
Bryn Mawr College F
Cabrini College
Cairn University
Carnegie Mellon University
Cedar Crest College F
Chatham University

DeSales University
Dickinson College
Eastern University
Elizabethtown College
Franklin & Marshall College
Geneva College
Gettysburg College
Grove City College
Gwynedd Mercy University
Haverford College
Immaculata University
Juniata College
Keystone College
King's College
La Roche College
Lancaster Bible College
Lebanon Valley College
Lycoming College
Marywood University
Messiah College
Misericordia University
Moravian College
Mount Aloysius College
Muhlenberg College
Neumann University
Penn State
    Abington
    Altoona
    Berks
    Erie, The Behrend College
    Harrisburg
Pennsylvania College of
    Technology
Rosemont College
St. Vincent College
Susquehanna University
Swarthmore College
Thiel College
University of Pittsburgh
    Bradford
    Greensburg
University of Scranton
Ursinus College
Washington & Jefferson College
Waynesburg University
Westminster College
Widener University
Wilkes University
Wilson College
York College of Pennsylvania

Rhode Island

Rhode Island College
Roger Williams University
Salve Regina University

Tennessee

Maryville College
Rhodes College
Sewanee: The University of the
    South

Texas

Austin College
Concordia University Texas
East Texas Baptist University
Hardin-Simmons University
LeTourneau University
McMurry University
Schreiner University
Southwestern University
Sul Ross State University
Texas Lutheran University
Trinity University
University of Dallas
University of Texas
    Dallas
    Tyler

Vermont

Green Mountain College
Johnson State College
Lyndon State College
Middlebury College
Norwich University
Southern Vermont College

Virginia

Averett University
Bridgewater College
Christopher Newport University
Eastern Mennonite University
Emory & Henry College
Ferrum College
Hampden-Sydney College M
Lynchburg College
Mary Baldwin College F
Marymount University
Randolph College
Roanoke College
Shenandoah University
Southern Virginia University
University of Mary Washington
Virginia Wesleyan College
Washington and Lee University

Washington

Pacific Lutheran University
University of Puget Sound
Whitman College
Whitworth University

West Virginia

Bethany College

Wisconsin

Alverno College F
Beloit College
Carroll University
Carthage College
Edgewood College
Lakeland College
Lawrence University
Maranathan Baptist University
    Maranatha Baptist
        University
Marian University
Milwaukee School of
    Engineering
Mount Mary University F
Northland College
Ripon College
St. Norbert College
University of Wisconsin
    Eau Claire
    La Crosse
    Platteville
    Stevens Point
    Superior
Wisconsin Lutheran College

Fencing Division I

California

Stanford University

Colorado

United States Air Force
    Academy

Connecticut

Sacred Heart University
Yale University

Illinois

Northwestern University F

Indiana

University of Notre Dame

Massachusetts

Boston College
Harvard College

Michigan

University of Detroit Mercy

New Jersey

Fairleigh Dickinson University
    Metropolitan Campus F
New Jersey Institute of
    Technology
Princeton University

New York

Barnard College
Columbia University
Cornell University F
St. John's University

North Carolina

Duke University
University of North Carolina
    Chapel Hill

Ohio

Cleveland State University
Ohio State University
    Columbus Campus

Pennsylvania

Lafayette College
Penn State
    University Park
Temple University F
University of Pennsylvania

Rhode Island

Brown University

Texas

University of the Incarnate
    Word

Fencing Division II

California

University of California
    San Diego

Michigan

Wayne State University

New York

City University of New York
    Queens College F
Long Island University
    LIU Post F

Fencing Division III

California

California Institute of
    Technology

Maryland

Johns Hopkins University

Massachusetts

Brandeis University
Massachusetts Institute of
    Technology
Tufts University F
Wellesley College F

New Jersey

Drew University
Stevens Institute of Technology

New York

City University of New York
    City College F
    Hunter College
New York University
Vassar College
Yeshiva University

Pennsylvania

Haverford College

Wisconsin

Lawrence University

Field hockey Division I

California

Stanford University F
University of California
    Berkeley F
    Davis F
University of the Pacific F

Connecticut

Fairfield University F
Quinnipiac University F
Sacred Heart University F
University of Connecticut F
Yale University F

Delaware

University of Delaware F

District of Columbia

American University F
Georgetown University F

Illinois

Northwestern University F

Indiana

Ball State University F
Indiana University
    Bloomington F

Iowa

University of Iowa F

Kentucky

University of Louisville F

Maine

University of Maine F

Maryland

Towson University F
University of Maryland
    College Park F

Massachusetts

Boston College F
Boston University F
College of the Holy Cross F
Harvard College F
Northeastern University F
University of Massachusetts
    Amherst F

Michigan

Central Michigan University F
Michigan State University F
University of Michigan F

Missouri

Missouri State University F
Saint Louis University F

New Hampshire

Dartmouth College F
University of New Hampshire F

New Jersey

Monmouth University F
Princeton University F
Rider University F

New York

Barnard College F
Colgate University F
Columbia University F
Cornell University F
Hofstra University F
Siena College F
SUNY
    University at Albany F
Syracuse University F

North Carolina

Appalachian State University F
Davidson College F
Duke University F
University of North Carolina
    Chapel Hill F
Wake Forest University F

Ohio

Kent State University F
Miami University
    Oxford F
Ohio State University
    Columbus Campus F
Ohio University F

Pennsylvania

Bucknell University F
Drexel University F
La Salle University F
Lafayette College F
Lehigh University F
Lock Haven University of
    Pennsylvania F
Penn State
    University Park F
St. Francis University F
Saint Joseph's University F
Temple University F
University of Pennsylvania F
Villanova University F

Rhode Island

Brown University F
Bryant University F
Providence College F

Vermont

University of Vermont F

Virginia

College of William and Mary F
James Madison University F
Liberty University F
Longwood University F
Old Dominion University F
University of Richmond F
University of Virginia F
Virginia Commonwealth
    University F

Field hockey Division II

Connecticut

Southern Connecticut State
    University F

Kentucky

Bellarmine University F

Massachusetts

American International College
    F
Assumption College F
Bentley University F
Merrimack College F
Stonehill College F

Missouri

Lindenwood University F

New Hampshire

Franklin Pierce University F
Saint Anselm College F
Southern New Hampshire
    University F

New York

Adelphi University F
Dowling College F
Long Island University
    LIU Post F
Mercy College F
Pace University F
St. Thomas Aquinas College F

Pennsylvania

Bloomsburg University of
    Pennsylvania F
East Stroudsburg University of
    Pennsylvania F
Indiana University of
    Pennsylvania F
Kutztown University of
    Pennsylvania F
Mansfield University of
    Pennsylvania F
Mercyhurst University F
Millersville University of
    Pennsylvania F
Seton Hill University F

Tables and Indexes

Field hockey
Division II

Shippensburg University of
Pennsylvania F
Slippery Rock University of
Pennsylvania F
West Chester University of
Pennsylvania F

South Carolina

Limestone College F
Newberry College F

Vermont

Saint Michael's College F

Field hockey Division III

Arkansas

Hendrix College F

Connecticut

Connecticut College F
Eastern Connecticut State
University F
Trinity College F
Wesleyan University F
Western Connecticut State
University F

Delaware

Wesley College F

District of Columbia

Catholic University of America
F

Indiana

DePauw University F
Earlham College F

Kentucky

Centre College F
Transylvania University F

Maine

Bates College F
Bowdoin College F
Colby College F
Husson University F
Saint Joseph's College of Maine
F
Thomas College F
University of Maine
Farmington F
University of New England F
University of Southern Maine F

Maryland

Frostburg State University F
Goucher College F
Hood College F
Johns Hopkins University F
McDaniel College F
Notre Dame of Maryland
University F
St. Mary's College of Maryland
F
Salisbury University F
Stevenson University F
Washington College F

Massachusetts

Amherst College F
Anna Maria College F
Babson College F
Becker College F
Bridgewater State University F
Clark University F
Elms College F
Endicott College F
Fitchburg State University F
Framingham State University F
Gordon College F
Lasell College F
Massachusetts Institute of
Technology F
Mount Holyoke College F

Mount Ida College F
Nichols College F
Regis College F
Salem State University F
Simmons College F
Smith College F
Springfield College F
Tufts University F
University of Massachusetts
Dartmouth F
Wellesley College F
Western New England
University F
Westfield State University F
Wheaton College F
Wheelock College F
Williams College F
Worcester Polytechnic Institute
F
Worcester State University F

New Hampshire

Colby-Sawyer College F
Daniel Webster College F
Keene State College F
New England College F
Plymouth State University F
Rivier University F

New Jersey

The College of New Jersey F
Drew University F
Fairleigh Dickinson University
College at Florham F
Kean University F
Montclair State University F
Ramapo College of New Jersey
F
Rowan University F
Stevens Institute of Technology
F
William Paterson University of
New Jersey F

New York

Elmira College F
Hamilton College F
Hartwick College F
Houghton College F
Ithaca College F
Keuka College F
Manhattanville College F
Nazareth College F
Rensselaer Polytechnic Institute
F
St. John Fisher College F
St. Lawrence University F
Skidmore College F
SUNY
College at Brockport F
College at Cortland F
College at Geneseo F
College at New Paltz F
College at Oneonta F
College at Oswego F
College of Agriculture and
Technology at Morrisville
F
Union College F
University of Rochester F
Utica College F
Vassar College F
Wells College F

Ohio

College of Wooster F
Denison University F
Kenyon College F
Oberlin College F
Ohio Wesleyan University F
Wittenberg University F

Pennsylvania

Albright College F
Alvernia University F
Arcadia University F
Bryn Mawr College F
Cabrini College F

Cedar Crest College F
DeSales University F
Dickinson College F
Eastern University F
Elizabethtown College F
Franklin & Marshall College F
Gettysburg College F
Gwynedd Mercy University F
Haverford College F
Immaculata University F
Juniata College F
Keystone College F
King's College F
Lebanon Valley College F
Marywood University F
Messiah College F
Misericordia University F
Moravian College F
Muhlenberg College F
Neumann University F
Susquehanna University F
Swarthmore College F
University of Scranton F
Ursinus College F
Washington & Jefferson College
F
Widener University F
Wilkes University F
Wilson College F
York College of Pennsylvania F

Rhode Island

Roger Williams University F
Salve Regina University F

Tennessee

Rhodes College F
Sewanee: The University of the
South F

Vermont

Middlebury College F

Virginia

Bridgewater College F
Christopher Newport University
F
Eastern Mennonite University F
Ferrum College F
Lynchburg College F
Randolph-Macon College F
Roanoke College F
Shenandoah University F
Sweet Briar College F
University of Mary Washington
F
Virginia Wesleyan College F
Washington and Lee University
F

West Virginia

Bethany College F

Football (tackle) Division IA

Alabama

Auburn University M
Troy University M
University of Alabama M
University of Alabama
Birmingham M
University of South Alabama M

Arizona

Arizona State University M
University of Arizona M

Arkansas

Arkansas State University M
University of Arkansas M

California

California State University
Fresno M
San Diego State University M
San Jose State University M

Stanford University M
University of California
Berkeley M
Los Angeles M
University of Southern
California M

Colorado

Colorado State University M
United States Air Force
Academy M
University of Colorado
Boulder M

Connecticut

University of Connecticut M

Florida

Florida Atlantic University M
Florida International University
M
Florida State University M
University of Central Florida M
University of Florida M
University of Miami M
University of South Florida M

Georgia

Georgia Institute of Technology
M
Georgia Southern University M
Georgia State University M
University of Georgia M

Hawaii

University of Hawaii
Manoa M

Idaho

Boise State University M
University of Idaho M

Illinois

Northern Illinois University M
Northwestern University M

Indiana

Ball State University M
Indiana University
Bloomington M
Purdue University M
University of Notre Dame M

Iowa

Iowa State University M
University of Iowa M

Kansas

Kansas State University M
University of Kansas M

Kentucky

University of Kentucky M
University of Louisville M
Western Kentucky University M

Louisiana

Louisiana State University and
Agricultural and Mechanical
College M
Louisiana Tech University M
Tulane University M
University of Louisiana at
Lafayette M
University of Louisiana at
Monroe M

Maryland

United States Naval Academy
M
University of Maryland
College Park M

Massachusetts

Boston College M
University of Massachusetts
Amherst M

Michigan

Central Michigan University M
Eastern Michigan University M

Michigan State University M
University of Michigan M
Western Michigan University M

Minnesota

University of Minnesota
Twin Cities M

Mississippi

Mississippi State University M
University of Mississippi M

Missouri

University of Missouri
Columbia M

Nebraska

University of Nebraska
Lincoln M

Nevada

University of Nevada
Las Vegas M

New Mexico

New Mexico State University M
University of New Mexico M

New York

SUNY
University at Buffalo M
Syracuse University M
United States Military Academy
M

North Carolina

Appalachian State University M
Duke University M
East Carolina University M
North Carolina State University
M
University of North Carolina
Chapel Hill M
Wake Forest University M

Ohio

Bowling Green State University
M
Kent State University M
Miami University
Oxford M
Ohio State University
Columbus Campus M
Ohio University M
University of Akron M
University of Cincinnati M
University of Toledo M

Oklahoma

Oklahoma State University M
University of Oklahoma M

Oregon

Oregon State University M
University of Oregon M

Pennsylvania

Penn State
University Park M
Temple University M
University of Pittsburgh M

South Carolina

Clemson University M
University of South Carolina
Columbia M

Tennessee

Middle Tennessee State
University M
University of Memphis M
University of Tennessee
Knoxville M
Vanderbilt University M

Texas

Baylor University M
Rice University M
Southern Methodist University
M
Texas A&M University M

Texas Christian University M
Texas Tech University M
University of Houston M
University of North Texas M
University of Texas
    Austin M
    El Paso M
    San Antonio M

Utah

Brigham Young University M
University of Utah M
Utah State University M

Virginia

Old Dominion University M
University of Virginia M

Washington

University of Washington M
Washington State University M

West Virginia

Marshall University M
West Virginia University M

Wisconsin

University of Wisconsin
    Madison M

Wyoming

University of Wyoming M

Football (tackle) Division IAA

Alabama

Alabama Agricultural and
    Mechanical University M
Alabama State University M
Jacksonville State University M
Samford University M

Arizona

Northern Arizona University M

Arkansas

University of Arkansas
    Pine Bluff M
University of Central Arkansas
    M

California

California Polytechnic State
    University: San Luis Obispo
    M
California State University
    Sacramento M
University of California
    Davis M
University of San Diego M

Colorado

University of Northern Colorado
    M

Connecticut

Central Connecticut State
    University M
Sacred Heart University M
Yale University M

Delaware

Delaware State University M
University of Delaware M

District of Columbia

Georgetown University M
Howard University M

Florida

Bethune-Cookman University M
Florida Agricultural and
    Mechanical University M
Jacksonville University M
Stetson University M

Georgia

Kennesaw State University M
Mercer University M
Savannah State University M

Idaho

Idaho State University M

Illinois

Eastern Illinois University M
Illinois State University M
Southern Illinois University
    Carbondale M
Western Illinois University M

Indiana

Butler University M
Indiana State University M
Valparaiso University M

Iowa

Drake University M
University of Northern Iowa M

Kentucky

Eastern Kentucky University M
Morehead State University M
Murray State University M

Louisiana

Grambling State University M
McNeese State University M
Nicholls State University M
Northwestern State University
    M
Southeastern Louisiana
    University M
Southern University and
    Agricultural and Mechanical
    College M

Maine

University of Maine M

Maryland

Morgan State University M
Towson University M

Massachusetts

College of the Holy Cross M
Harvard College M

Mississippi

Alcorn State University M
Jackson State University M
Mississippi Valley State
    University M

Missouri

Missouri State University M
Southeast Missouri State
    University M

Montana

Montana State University M
University of Montana M

New Hampshire

Dartmouth College M
University of New Hampshire
    M

New Jersey

Monmouth University M
Princeton University M

New York

Barnard College M
Colgate University M
Columbia University M
Cornell University M
Fordham University M
Marist College M
SUNY
    University at Albany M
    University at Stony Brook
    M
Wagner College M

North Carolina

Campbell University M
Davidson College M
Elon University M
Gardner-Webb University M
North Carolina Agricultural and
    Technical State University M
North Carolina Central
    University M
Western Carolina University M

North Dakota

North Dakota State University
    M
University of North Dakota M

Ohio

University of Dayton M
Youngstown State University M

Oregon

Portland State University M

Pennsylvania

Bucknell University M
Duquesne University M
Lafayette College M
Lehigh University M
Robert Morris University M
St. Francis University M
University of Pennsylvania M
Villanova University M

Rhode Island

Brown University M
Bryant University M
University of Rhode Island M

South Carolina

Charleston Southern University
    M
The Citadel M
Coastal Carolina University M
Furman University M
Presbyterian College M
South Carolina State University
    M
Wofford College M

South Dakota

South Dakota State University
    M
University of South Dakota M

Tennessee

Austin Peay State University M
East Tennessee State University
    M
Tennessee State University M
Tennessee Technological
    University M
University of Tennessee
    Chattanooga M
    Martin M

Texas

Houston Baptist University M
Lamar University M
Prairie View A&M University
    M
Sam Houston State University
    M
Stephen F. Austin State
    University M
Texas Southern University M

Utah

Southern Utah University M
Weber State University M

Virginia

College of William and Mary M
Hampton University M
James Madison University M
Liberty University M
Norfolk State University M
University of Richmond M
Virginia Military Institute M

Washington

Eastern Washington University
    M

Football (tackle) Division II

Alabama

Miles College M
Stillman College M
Tuskegee University M
University of North Alabama M
University of West Alabama M

Arkansas

Arkansas Tech University M
Harding University M
Henderson State University M
Ouachita Baptist University M
Southern Arkansas University M
University of Arkansas
    Monticello M

California

Azusa Pacific University M
Humboldt State University M

Colorado

Adams State University M
Colorado Mesa University M
Colorado School of Mines M
Colorado State University
    Pueblo M
Fort Lewis College M
Western State Colorado
    University M

Connecticut

Southern Connecticut State
    University M
University of New Haven M

Florida

Florida Institute of Technology
    M
University of West Florida M

Georgia

Albany State University M
Clark Atlanta University M
Fort Valley State University M
Morehouse College M
Shorter University M
University of West Georgia M
Valdosta State University M

Illinois

McKendree University M
Quincy University M

Indiana

Saint Joseph's College M
University of Indianapolis M

Iowa

Upper Iowa University M

Kansas

Emporia State University M
Fort Hays State University M
Pittsburg State University M
Washburn University M

Kentucky

Kentucky State University M
Kentucky Wesleyan College M

Maryland

Bowie State University M

Massachusetts

American International College
    M
Assumption College M
Bentley University M
Merrimack College M
Stonehill College M

Michigan

Ferris State University M
Grand Valley State University
    M
Hillsdale College M
Michigan Technological
    University M
Northern Michigan University
    M
Northwood University
    Michigan M
Saginaw Valley State University
    M
Wayne State University M

Minnesota

Bemidji State University M
Concordia University St. Paul
    M
Minnesota State University
    Mankato M
    Moorhead M
Saint Cloud State University M
Southwest Minnesota State
    University M
University of Minnesota
    Crookston M
    Duluth M
Winona State University M

Mississippi

Delta State University M
Mississippi College M

Missouri

Lincoln University M
Lindenwood University M
Missouri Southern State
    University M
Missouri University of Science
    and Technology M
Missouri Western State
    University M
Northwest Missouri State
    University M
Southwest Baptist University M
Truman State University M
University of Central Missouri
    M
William Jewell College M

Nebraska

Chadron State College M
University of Nebraska
    Kearney M
Wayne State College M

New Hampshire

Saint Anselm College M

New Mexico

Eastern New Mexico University
    M
New Mexico Highlands
    University M
Western New Mexico
    University M

New York

Long Island University
    LIU Post M
Pace University M

North Carolina

Brevard College M
Catawba College M
Chowan University M
Elizabeth City State University
    M
Fayetteville State University M
Johnson C. Smith University M
Lenoir-Rhyne University M
Livingstone College M
Mars Hill University M
Saint Augustine's University M
Shaw University M
University of North Carolina
    Pembroke M
Wingate University M

Winston-Salem State University M

North Dakota

Minot State University M
University of Mary M

Ohio

Ashland University M
Central State University M
Lake Erie College M
Malone University M
Notre Dame College M
Ohio Dominican University M
Tiffin University M
University of Findlay M
Urbana University M
Walsh University M

Oklahoma

East Central University M
Northeastern State University M
Northwestern Oklahoma State
   University M
Oklahoma Baptist University M
Oklahoma Panhandle State
   University M
Southeastern Oklahoma State
   University M
Southern Nazarene University
   M
Southwestern Oklahoma State
   University M
University of Central Oklahoma
   M

Oregon

Western Oregon University M

Pennsylvania

Bloomsburg University of
   Pennsylvania M
California University of
   Pennsylvania M
Cheyney University of
   Pennsylvania M
Clarion University of
   Pennsylvania M
East Stroudsburg University of
   Pennsylvania M
Edinboro University
   of Pennsylvania M
Gannon University M
Indiana University of
   Pennsylvania M
Kutztown University of
   Pennsylvania M
Lincoln University M
Lock Haven University of
   Pennsylvania M
Mercyhurst University M
Millersville University of
   Pennsylvania M
Seton Hill University M
Shippensburg University of
   Pennsylvania M
Slippery Rock University of
   Pennsylvania M
West Chester University of
   Pennsylvania M

South Carolina

Benedict College M
Limestone College M
Newberry College M
North Greenville University M

South Dakota

Black Hills State University M
Northern State University M
South Dakota School of Mines
   and Technology M
University of Sioux Falls M

Tennessee

Carson-Newman University M
Lane College M
Tusculum College M

Texas

Abilene Christian University M
Angelo State University M
Midwestern State University M
Tarleton State University M
Texas A&M University
   Commerce M
   Kingsville M
University of Texas
   of the Permian Basin M
University of the Incarnate
   Word M
West Texas A&M University M

Utah

Dixie State University M

Virginia

University of Virginia's College
   at Wise M
Virginia State University M
Virginia Union University M

Washington

Central Washington University
   M

West Virginia

Alderson-Broaddus University
   M
Concord University M
Fairmont State University M
Glenville State College M
Shepherd University M
University of Charleston M
West Liberty University M
West Virginia State University
   M
West Virginia Wesleyan
   College M

Canada

Simon Fraser University M

**Football (tackle)
Division III**

Alabama

Birmingham-Southern College
   M
Huntingdon College M

Arkansas

Hendrix College M

California

California Lutheran University
   M
Chapman University M
Claremont McKenna College M
Harvey Mudd College M
Occidental College M
Pitzer College M
Pomona College M
Scripps College M
University of La Verne M
University of Redlands M
Whittier College M

Connecticut

Trinity College M
United States Coast Guard
   Academy M
Wesleyan University M
Western Connecticut State
   University M

Delaware

Wesley College M

District of Columbia

Catholic University of America
   M
Gallaudet University M

Georgia

Berry College M

Illinois

Augustana College M
Aurora University M
Benedictine University at
   Springfield M
Concordia University Chicago
   M
Elmhurst College M
Eureka College M
Greenville College M
Illinois College M
Illinois Wesleyan University M
Knox College M
Lake Forest College M
MacMurray College M
Millikin University M
Monmouth College M
North Central College M
North Park University M
Rockford University M
University of Chicago M
Wheaton College M

Indiana

Anderson University M
DePauw University M
Earlham College M
Franklin College M
Hanover College M
Manchester University M
Rose-Hulman Institute of
   Technology M
Trine University M
Wabash College M

Iowa

Buena Vista University M
Central College M
Coe College M
Cornell College M
Grinnell College M
Loras College M
Luther College M
Simpson College M
University of Dubuque M
Wartburg College M

Kentucky

Centre College M
Thomas More College M

Louisiana

Louisiana College M

Maine

Bates College M
Bowdoin College M
Colby College M
Husson University M
Maine Maritime Academy M

Maryland

Frostburg State University M
Johns Hopkins University M
McDaniel College M
Salisbury University M
Stevenson University M

Massachusetts

Amherst College M
Anna Maria College M
Becker College M
Bridgewater State University M
Curry College M
Endicott College M
Fitchburg State University M
Framingham State University M
Massachusetts Institute of
   Technology M
Massachusetts Maritime
   Academy M
Mount Ida College M
Nichols College M
Springfield College M
Tufts University M

University of Massachusetts
   Dartmouth M
Western New England
   University M
Westfield State University M
Williams College M
Worcester Polytechnic Institute
   M
Worcester State University M

Michigan

Adrian College M
Albion College M
Alma College M
Finlandia University M
Hope College M
Kalamazoo College M
Olivet College M

Minnesota

Augsburg College M
Bethel University M
Carleton College M
College of St. Scholastica M
Concordia College: Moorhead
   M
Gustavus Adolphus College M
Hamline University M
Macalester College M
Martin Luther College M
St. John's University M
St. Olaf College M
University of Minnesota
   Morris M
University of Northwestern - St.
   Paul M
University of St. Thomas M

Mississippi

Belhaven University M
Millsaps College M

Missouri

Westminster College M

Nebraska

Nebraska Wesleyan University
   M

New Hampshire

Plymouth State University M

New Jersey

The College of New Jersey M
Fairleigh Dickinson University
   College at Florham M
Kean University M
Montclair State University M
Rowan University M
William Paterson University of
   New Jersey M

New York

Alfred University M
Hamilton College M
Hartwick College M
Ithaca College M
Rensselaer Polytechnic Institute
   M
St. John Fisher College M
St. Lawrence University M
SUNY
   College at Brockport M
   College at Buffalo M
   College at Cortland M
   College of Agriculture and
      Technology at Morrisville
      M
   College of Technology at
      Alfred M
   Maritime College M
Union College M
United States Merchant Marine
   Academy M
University of Rochester M
Utica College M

North Carolina

Greensboro College M
Guilford College M
Methodist University M
North Carolina Wesleyan
   College M

Ohio

Baldwin Wallace University M
Bluffton University M
Capital University M
Case Western Reserve
   University M
College of Wooster M
Defiance College M
Denison University M
Heidelberg University M
Hiram College M
John Carroll University M
Kenyon College M
Marietta College M
Muskingum University M
Oberlin College M
Ohio Northern University M
Ohio Wesleyan University M
Otterbein University M
University of Mount Union M
Wilmington College M
Wittenberg University M

Oregon

George Fox University M
Lewis & Clark College M
Linfield College M
Pacific University M
Willamette University M

Pennsylvania

Albright College M
Allegheny College M
Carnegie Mellon University M
Dickinson College M
Franklin & Marshall College M
Geneva College M
Gettysburg College M
Grove City College M
Juniata College M
King's College M
Lebanon Valley College M
Lycoming College M
Misericordia University M
Moravian College M
Muhlenberg College M
St. Vincent College M
Susquehanna University M
Thiel College M
Ursinus College M
Washington & Jefferson College
   M
Waynesburg University M
Westminster College M
Widener University M
Wilkes University M

Rhode Island

Salve Regina University M

Tennessee

Maryville College M
Rhodes College M
Sewanee: The University of the
   South M

Texas

Austin College M
East Texas Baptist University M
Hardin-Simmons University M
Howard Payne University M
McMurry University M
Southwestern University M
Sul Ross State University M
Texas Lutheran University M
Trinity University M
University of Mary Hardin-
   Baylor M

Vermont

Middlebury College M
Norwich University M

Virginia

Averett University M
Bridgewater College M
Christopher Newport University M
Emory & Henry College M
Ferrum College M
Hampden-Sydney College M
Randolph-Macon College M
Shenandoah University M
Southern Virginia University M
Washington and Lee University M

Washington

Pacific Lutheran University M
University of Puget Sound M
Whitworth University M

West Virginia

Bethany College M

Wisconsin

Beloit College M
Carroll University M
Carthage College M
Lakeland College M
Lawrence University M
Maranathan Baptist University
    Maranatha Baptist
    University M
Ripon College M
St. Norbert College M
University of Wisconsin
    Eau Claire M
    La Crosse M
    Platteville M
    Stevens Point M
Wisconsin Lutheran College M

Golf Division I

Alabama

Alabama Agricultural and
    Mechanical University M
Alabama State University
Auburn University
Jacksonville State University
Samford University
Troy University
University of Alabama
University of Alabama
    Birmingham
University of South Alabama

Arizona

Arizona State University
Northern Arizona University F
University of Arizona

Arkansas

Arkansas State University
University of Arkansas
    Pine Bluff M
University of Central Arkansas

California

California Polytechnic State
    University: San Luis Obispo
California State University
    Bakersfield
    Fresno
    Fullerton
    Long Beach
    Northridge
    Sacramento
Loyola Marymount University M
Pepperdine University
St. Mary's College of California M
San Diego State University

San Jose State University
Santa Clara University
Stanford University
University of California
    Berkeley
    Davis
    Irvine
    Los Angeles
    Riverside
    Santa Barbara M
University of San Diego M
University of San Francisco
University of Southern
    California
University of the Pacific M

Colorado

Colorado State University
United States Air Force
    Academy M
University of Colorado
    Boulder
University of Denver
University of Northern Colorado

Connecticut

Central Connecticut State
    University
Fairfield University
Quinnipiac University F
Sacred Heart University
University of Connecticut M
University of Hartford
Yale University

Delaware

Delaware State University F
University of Delaware

District of Columbia

George Washington University M
Georgetown University

Florida

Bethune-Cookman University
Florida Agricultural and
    Mechanical University M
Florida Atlantic University
Florida Gulf Coast University
Florida International University F
Florida State University
Jacksonville University
Stetson University
University of Central Florida
University of Florida
University of Miami F
University of North Florida
University of South Florida

Georgia

Georgia Institute of Technology M
Georgia Southern University
Georgia State University
Kennesaw State University
Mercer University
Savannah State University
University of Georgia

Hawaii

University of Hawaii
    Manoa

Idaho

Boise State University
Idaho State University F
University of Idaho

Illinois

Bradley University
Chicago State University
DePaul University M
Eastern Illinois University
Illinois State University
Loyola University Chicago
Northern Illinois University
Northwestern University

Southern Illinois University
    Carbondale
Southern Illinois University
    Edwardsville
University of Illinois
    Chicago F
Western Illinois University

Indiana

Ball State University
Butler University
Indiana State University F
Indiana University
    Bloomington
    Purdue University Fort
    Wayne
    Purdue University
    Indianapolis
Purdue University
University of Evansville
University of Notre Dame
Valparaiso University

Iowa

Drake University
Iowa State University
University of Iowa
University of Northern Iowa

Kansas

Kansas State University
University of Kansas
Wichita State University

Kentucky

Eastern Kentucky University
Morehead State University
Murray State University
University of Kentucky
University of Louisville
Western Kentucky University

Louisiana

Louisiana State University and
    Agricultural and Mechanical
    College
Louisiana Tech University M
McNeese State University
Nicholls State University M
Southeastern Louisiana
    University M
Tulane University F
University of Louisiana at
    Lafayette M
University of Louisiana at
    Monroe
University of New Orleans M

Maryland

Loyola University Maryland M
Towson University
United States Naval Academy
University of Maryland
    College Park
    Eastern Shore M

Massachusetts

Boston College
Boston University F
College of the Holy Cross
Harvard College

Michigan

Central Michigan University F
Eastern Michigan University
Michigan State University
Oakland University
University of Detroit Mercy
University of Michigan
Western Michigan University F

Minnesota

University of Minnesota
    Twin Cities

Mississippi

Alcorn State University
Jackson State University
Mississippi State University

Mississippi Valley State
    University
University of Mississippi

Missouri

Missouri State University
University of Missouri
    Columbia
    Kansas City

Montana

Montana State University F
University of Montana F

Nebraska

Creighton University
University of Nebraska
    Lincoln
    Omaha

Nevada

University of Nevada
    Las Vegas

New Hampshire

Dartmouth College

New Jersey

Fairleigh Dickinson University
    Metropolitan Campus
Monmouth University
Princeton University
Rider University M
Seton Hall University

New Mexico

New Mexico State University
University of New Mexico

New York

Barnard College
Canisius College M
Colgate University M
Columbia University
Cornell University M
Fordham University M
Hofstra University
Iona College M
Long Island University
    LIU Brooklyn
Manhattan College M
Niagara University
Saint Bonaventure University M
St. Francis College
St. John's University
Siena College
SUNY
    University at Albany F
    University at Binghamton M
United States Military Academy M
Wagner College

North Carolina

Appalachian State University
Campbell University
Davidson College M
Duke University
East Carolina University
Elon University
Gardner-Webb University
High Point University
North Carolina Central
    University M
North Carolina State University
University of North Carolina
    Chapel Hill
Wake Forest University
Western Carolina University

North Dakota

North Dakota State University
University of North Dakota

Ohio

Bowling Green State University
Cleveland State University
Kent State University

Miami University
    Oxford M
Ohio State University
    Columbus Campus
Ohio University
University of Akron
University of Cincinnati
University of Dayton
University of Toledo
Wright State University M
Xavier University
Youngstown State University

Oklahoma

Oklahoma State University
Oral Roberts University
University of Oklahoma

Oregon

Oregon State University
Portland State University F
University of Oregon

Pennsylvania

Bucknell University
Drexel University M
La Salle University M
Lafayette College M
Lehigh University
Penn State
    University Park
Robert Morris University M
St. Francis University
Saint Joseph's University M
Temple University M
University of Pennsylvania
Villanova University M

Rhode Island

Brown University
Bryant University M
University of Rhode Island M

South Carolina

Charleston Southern University
The Citadel F
Clemson University
Coastal Carolina University
College of Charleston
Francis Marion University M
Furman University
Presbyterian College
University of South Carolina
    Columbia
    Upstate
Winthrop University
Wofford College

South Dakota

South Dakota State University
University of South Dakota

Tennessee

Austin Peay State University
Belmont University
East Tennessee State University
Lipscomb University
Middle Tennessee State
    University
Tennessee State University
Tennessee Technological
    University
University of Memphis
University of Tennessee
    Chattanooga
    Knoxville
    Martin M
Vanderbilt University

Texas

Baylor University
Houston Baptist University
Lamar University
Prairie View A&M University
Rice University M
Sam Houston State University
Southern Methodist University
Stephen F. Austin State
    University

Texas A&M University
  Corpus Christi F
Texas Christian University
Texas Southern University
Texas Tech University
University of Houston
University of North Texas
University of Texas
  Arlington M
  Austin
  El Paso
  San Antonio

Utah

Brigham Young University
Southern Utah University
University of Utah M
Utah State University M
Utah Valley University
Weber State University

Virginia

College of William and Mary
George Mason University M
Hampton University
James Madison University
Liberty University M
Longwood University
Old Dominion University
Radford University
University of Richmond
University of Virginia
Virginia Commonwealth
  University M

Washington

Eastern Washington University
  F
Gonzaga University
Seattle University
University of Washington
Washington State University

West Virginia

Marshall University
West Virginia University M

Wisconsin

Marquette University M
University of Wisconsin
  Green Bay
  Madison

Wyoming

University of Wyoming

Golf Division II

Alabama

Miles College M
Spring Hill College
University of Montevallo
University of North Alabama M
University of West Alabama

Arizona

Grand Canyon University

Arkansas

Arkansas Tech University
Harding University
Henderson State University
Southern Arkansas University
University of Arkansas
  Fort Smith
  Monticello

California

Academy of Art University
California Baptist University
California State University
  Chico
  Dominguez Hills M
  East Bay
  Monterey Bay
  San Bernardino M
  Stanislaus M

Dominican University of
  California
Holy Names University
Notre Dame de Namur
  University M
Point Loma Nazarene
  University F
Sonoma State University
University of California
  San Diego M

Colorado

Adams State University
Colorado Christian University
Colorado Mesa University
Colorado School of Mines M
Colorado State University
  Pueblo
Fort Lewis College
Metropolitan State University of
  Denver F
Regis University
University of Colorado
  Colorado Springs

Connecticut

Post University

Delaware

Goldey-Beacom College M
Wilmington University M

Florida

Barry University
Eckerd College
Flagler College
Florida Institute of Technology
Florida Southern College
Lynn University
Nova Southeastern University
Palm Beach Atlantic University
Rollins College
Saint Leo University
University of Tampa
University of West Florida

Georgia

Clayton State University M
Columbus State University
Emmanuel College
Georgia Southwestern State
  University M
Morehouse College M
Paine College M
Shorter University
University of North Georgia
University of West Georgia
Valdosta State University M
Young Harris College

Hawaii

Brigham Young University-
  Hawaii M
Chaminade University of
  Honolulu M
Hawaii Pacific University
University of Hawaii
  Hilo

Idaho

Northwest Nazarene University

Illinois

Lewis University
McKendree University
Quincy University
University of Illinois
  Springfield

Iowa

Upper Iowa University

Kansas

Fort Hays State University
Newman University
Washburn University M

Kentucky

Bellarmine University
Kentucky State University M
Kentucky Wesleyan College
Northern Kentucky University

Massachusetts

American International College
  M
Assumption College
Bentley University M
Merrimack College F

Michigan

Ferris State University
Grand Valley State University
Hillsdale College M
Lake Superior State University
Northern Michigan University
Northwood University
  Michigan
Saginaw Valley State University
  M
Wayne State University

Minnesota

Bemidji State University
Concordia University St. Paul
Minnesota State University
  Mankato
  Moorhead F
Saint Cloud State University
Southwest Minnesota State
  University F
University of Minnesota
  Crookston
Winona State University

Mississippi

Delta State University M
Mississippi College M

Missouri

Drury University
Lincoln University
Lindenwood University
Maryville University of Saint
  Louis
Missouri Southern State
  University M
Missouri Western State
  University
Northwest Missouri State
  University F
Rockhurst University
Southwest Baptist University
Truman State University F
University of Central Missouri
William Jewell College

Montana

Montana State University
  Billings

Nebraska

Chadron State College F
University of Nebraska
  Kearney

New Hampshire

Franklin Pierce University
Saint Anselm College M
Southern New Hampshire
  University

New Mexico

Western New Mexico
  University

New York

Adelphi University
College of Saint Rose
Concordia College M
Daemen College M
Dominican College of Blauvelt
  M
Dowling College M
Le Moyne College

Long Island University
  LIU Post F
Nyack College M
Roberts Wesleyan College M
St. Thomas Aquinas College M

North Carolina

Barton College
Belmont Abbey College
Brevard College
Catawba College
Chowan University
Elizabeth City State University
  M
Fayetteville State University M
Johnson C. Smith University M
Lenoir-Rhyne University
Livingstone College M
Mars Hill University
Pfeiffer University
Queens University of Charlotte
Saint Augustine's University M
University of Mount Olive
University of North Carolina
  Pembroke F
Wingate University

North Dakota

Minot State University

Ohio

Ashland University
Cedarville University M
Lake Erie College
Malone University
Notre Dame College
Ohio Dominican University
Tiffin University
University of Findlay
Urbana University
Ursuline College F
Walsh University

Oklahoma

Cameron University
East Central University
Northeastern State University
Northwestern Oklahoma State
  University
Oklahoma Baptist University
Oklahoma Christian University
Oklahoma Panhandle State
  University
Rogers State University
Southeastern Oklahoma State
  University M
Southern Nazarene University
Southwestern Oklahoma State
  University
University of Central Oklahoma

Pennsylvania

California University of
  Pennsylvania
Chestnut Hill College M
Clarion University of
  Pennsylvania
East Stroudsburg University of
  Pennsylvania F
Gannon University
Indiana University of
  Pennsylvania M
Kutztown University of
  Pennsylvania F
Mercyhurst University
Millersville University of
  Pennsylvania
Philadelphia University M
Seton Hill University F
University of Pittsburgh
  Johnstown M
West Chester University of
  Pennsylvania

South Carolina

Anderson University
Benedict College M
Coker College
Converse College F

Erskine College
Lander University
Limestone College
Newberry College
North Greenville University
Southern Wesleyan University
University of South Carolina
  Aiken M

South Dakota

Black Hills State University F
South Dakota School of Mines
  and Technology
University of Sioux Falls

Tennessee

Carson-Newman University
Christian Brothers University
King University
Lee University
LeMoyne-Owen College M
Lincoln Memorial University
Trevecca Nazarene University
Tusculum College
Union University

Texas

Abilene Christian University M
Angelo State University F
Dallas Baptist University
Lubbock Christian University
Midwestern State University
St. Edward's University
St. Mary's University
Tarleton State University F
Texas A&M International
  University
Texas A&M University
  Commerce
  Kingsville F
University of the Incarnate
  Word
West Texas A&M University

Utah

Dixie State University

Vermont

Saint Michael's College M

Virginia

University of Virginia's College
  at Wise
Virginia State University M
Virginia Union University M

Washington

Saint Martin's University
Western Washington University

West Virginia

Alderson-Broaddus University
Bluefield State College M
Concord University
Davis and Elkins College M
Fairmont State University
Glenville State College
Ohio Valley University
Salem International University
Shepherd University M
University of Charleston
West Liberty University
West Virginia State University
  M
West Virginia Wesleyan College
Wheeling Jesuit University

Wisconsin

University of Wisconsin
  Parkside M

Canada

Simon Fraser University

Golf Division III

Alabama

Birmingham-Southern College
Huntingdon College

Arkansas

Hendrix College

California

California Lutheran University
Chapman University M
Claremont McKenna College
Harvey Mudd College
Occidental College
Pitzer College
Pomona College
Scripps College
University of California
    Santa Cruz F
University of La Verne
University of Redlands
Whittier College

Connecticut

Albertus Magnus College M
Mitchell College M
Trinity College M
Wesleyan University M

Delaware

Wesley College M

Georgia

Berry College
Covenant College
Emory University M
Oglethorpe University
Piedmont College

Illinois

Augustana College
Aurora University
Benedictine University at
    Springfield
Blackburn College M
Dominican University M
Elmhurst College
Eureka College M
Illinois College
Illinois Wesleyan University
Knox College
Lake Forest College
MacMurray College
Millikin University
Monmouth College
North Central College
North Park University
Rockford University M
Wheaton College

Indiana

Anderson University
DePauw University
Franklin College
Hanover College
Manchester University
Rose-Hulman Institute of
    Technology
Saint Mary's College F
Trine University
Wabash College M

Iowa

Buena Vista University
Central College
Coe College
Grinnell College
Loras College
Luther College
Simpson College
University of Dubuque
Wartburg College

Kentucky

Berea College M
Centre College
Spalding University
Thomas More College
Transylvania University

Louisiana

Centenary College of Louisiana
Louisiana College

Maine

Bates College
Bowdoin College
Husson University M
Maine Maritime Academy M
Saint Joseph's College of Maine
    M
University of Maine
    Farmington M
    Presque Isle M
University of New England M

Maryland

Hood College M
McDaniel College
Stevenson University

Massachusetts

Amherst College
Babson College M
Becker College M
Eastern Nazarene College M
Elms College M
Emmanuel College M
Endicott College M
Massachusetts College of
    Liberal Arts M
Mount Holyoke College F
Newbury College M
Nichols College M
Salem State University M
Springfield College M
Suffolk University M
Tufts University M
University of Massachusetts
    Dartmouth M
Wellesley College F
Wentworth Institute of
    Technology M
Western New England
    University M
Westfield State University
Williams College
Worcester State University M

Michigan

Adrian College
Albion College
Alma College
Calvin College
Finlandia University M
Hope College
Kalamazoo College
Olivet College

Minnesota

Augsburg College
Bethany Lutheran College
Bethel University
Carleton College
College of St. Benedict F
College of St. Scholastica
Concordia College: Moorhead
Gustavus Adolphus College
Macalester College
Martin Luther College
North Central University
St. Catherine University F
St. John's University M
St. Mary's University of
    Minnesota
St. Olaf College
University of Minnesota
    Morris
University of Northwestern - St.
    Paul
University of St. Thomas

Mississippi

Belhaven University M
Millsaps College

Missouri

Fontbonne University
Webster University M
Westminster College

Nebraska

Nebraska Wesleyan University

New Hampshire

Daniel Webster College M

New Jersey

Centenary College M
Fairleigh Dickinson University
    College at Florham
New Jersey City University M
Rutgers, The State University of
    New Jersey
    Camden Campus M
Stevens Institute of Technology
    M
William Paterson University of
    New Jersey M

New York

Clarkson University M
D'Youville College M
Elmira College
Hamilton College
Ithaca College F
Keuka College
Manhattanville College
Medaille College M
Mount Saint Mary College M
Nazareth College
New York University
Rensselaer Polytechnic Institute
    M
The Sage Colleges M
St. John Fisher College
St. Joseph's College New York:
    Suffolk Campus M
St. Lawrence University
Skidmore College M
SUNY
    College at Cortland F
    College at Old Westbury M
    College at Oswego M
    College at Potsdam M
    College at Purchase M
    College of Agriculture and
        Technology at Cobleskill
    College of Agriculture and
        Technology at Morrisville
        M
    College of Technology at
        Canton M
Union College F
University of Rochester M
Utica College M
Vassar College F
Yeshiva University M

North Carolina

Greensboro College
Guilford College M
Methodist University
North Carolina Wesleyan
    College M
William Peace University M

Ohio

Baldwin Wallace University
Capital University
College of Wooster
Defiance College
Denison University
Heidelberg University
Hiram College
John Carroll University
Kenyon College M
Muskingum University
Ohio Northern University
Ohio Wesleyan University
Otterbein University
University of Mount Union
Wittenberg University

Oregon

George Fox University
Lewis & Clark College
Linfield College

Pacific University
Willamette University

Pennsylvania

Albright College
Allegheny College
Alvernia University
Arcadia University
Bryn Athyn College M
Cabrini College M
Cairn University M
Carnegie Mellon University
DeSales University M
Dickinson College
Eastern University
Elizabethtown College M
Franklin & Marshall College
Gettysburg College
Grove City College
Immaculata University M
Keystone College M
King's College M
La Roche College M
Lebanon Valley College
Lycoming College M
Marywood University
Messiah College M
Misericordia University
Moravian College M
Mount Aloysius College
Muhlenberg College
Neumann University
Penn State
    Abington M
    Altoona M
    Berks M
    Erie, The Behrend College
    Harrisburg M
Pennsylvania College of
    Technology M
Rosemont College M
St. Vincent College
Susquehanna University
Swarthmore College M
Thiel College
University of Pittsburgh
    Bradford M
    Greensburg M
University of Scranton M
Ursinus College
Washington & Jefferson College
Waynesburg University
Westminster College
Widener University M
Wilkes University
Wilson College M
York College of Pennsylvania
    M

Rhode Island

Rhode Island College
Roger Williams University M

Tennessee

Maryville College M
Rhodes College
Sewanee: The University of the
    South

Texas

Concordia University Texas
Hardin-Simmons University
Howard Payne University
LeTourneau University
McMurry University
Schreiner University
Southwestern University
Texas Lutheran University
Trinity University
University of Dallas
University of Mary Hardin-
    Baylor
University of Texas
    Dallas
    Tyler

Vermont

Green Mountain College M
Johnson State College M
Middlebury College

Virginia

Averett University M
Bridgewater College
Christopher Newport University
    M
Eastern Mennonite University
Ferrum College M
Hampden-Sydney College M
Hollins University F
Lynchburg College M
Marymount University
Randolph-Macon College
Roanoke College M
Shenandoah University
Virginia Wesleyan College M
Washington and Lee University

Washington

Pacific Lutheran University
University of Puget Sound
Whitman College
Whitworth University

West Virginia

Bethany College

Wisconsin

Alverno College F
Carroll University
Carthage College
Edgewood College
Lakeland College
Lawrence University M
Marian University
Milwaukee School of
    Engineering M
Mount Mary University F
Northland College
St. Norbert College
University of Wisconsin
    Eau Claire
    Platteville F
    Stevens Point F
    Superior
Wisconsin Lutheran College

Gymnastics Division I

Alabama

Auburn University F
University of Alabama F

Alaska

University of Alaska
    Anchorage F

Arizona

Arizona State University F
University of Arizona F

Arkansas

University of Arkansas F

California

California State University
    Sacramento F
San Jose State University F
Stanford University
University of California
    Berkeley
    Davis F
    Los Angeles F

Colorado

United States Air Force
    Academy
University of Denver F

Connecticut

Yale University F

District of Columbia

George Washington University
F

Florida

University of Florida F

Georgia

University of Georgia F

Idaho

Boise State University F

Illinois

Illinois State University F
Northern Illinois University F
University of Illinois
Chicago

Indiana

Ball State University F

Iowa

Iowa State University F
University of Iowa

Kentucky

University of Kentucky F

Louisiana

Louisiana State University and
Agricultural and Mechanical
College F

Maryland

Towson University F
United States Naval Academy
M
University of Maryland
College Park F

Michigan

Central Michigan University F
Eastern Michigan University F
Michigan State University F
University of Michigan F
Western Michigan University F

Minnesota

University of Minnesota
Twin Cities

Missouri

Southeast Missouri State
University F
University of Missouri
Columbia F

Nebraska

University of Nebraska
Lincoln

New Hampshire

University of New Hampshire F

New York

Cornell University F
United States Military Academy
M

North Carolina

North Carolina State University
F
University of North Carolina
Chapel Hill F

Ohio

Bowling Green State University
F
Kent State University F
Ohio State University
Columbus Campus

Oklahoma

University of Oklahoma

Oregon

Oregon State University F

Pennsylvania

Penn State
University Park

Temple University F
University of Pennsylvania F
University of Pittsburgh F

Rhode Island

Brown University F

Utah

Brigham Young University F
Southern Utah University F
University of Utah F
Utah State University F

Virginia

College of William and Mary

Washington

University of Washington F

West Virginia

West Virginia University F

Gymnastics Division II

Connecticut

Southern Connecticut State
University F
University of Bridgeport F

Missouri

Lindenwood University F

Pennsylvania

West Chester University of
Pennsylvania F

Texas

Texas Woman's University F

Washington

Seattle Pacific University F

Gymnastics Division III

Louisiana

Centenary College of Louisiana
F

Massachusetts

Springfield College

Minnesota

Gustavus Adolphus College F
Hamline University F
Winona State University F

New York

Ithaca College F
SUNY
College at Brockport F
College at Cortland F

Pennsylvania

Ursinus College F

Rhode Island

Rhode Island College F

Wisconsin

University of Wisconsin
Eau Claire F
La Crosse F

Ice Hockey Division I

Alabama

University of Alabama
Huntsville M

Alaska

University of Alaska
Anchorage M
Fairbanks M

Colorado

Colorado College M
United States Air Force
Academy M
University of Denver M

Connecticut

Quinnipiac University
Sacred Heart University
University of Connecticut
Yale University

Indiana

University of Notre Dame M

Maine

University of Maine

Massachusetts

American International College
M
Bentley University M
Boston College
Boston University
College of the Holy Cross
Harvard College
Merrimack College
Northeastern University
University of Massachusetts
Amherst M

Michigan

Ferris State University M
Lake Superior State University
M
Michigan State University M
Michigan Technological
University M
Northern Michigan University
M
University of Michigan M
Western Michigan University M

Minnesota

Bemidji State University
Minnesota State University
Mankato
Saint Cloud State University
University of Minnesota
Duluth
Twin Cities

Nebraska

University of Nebraska
Omaha M

New Hampshire

Dartmouth College
University of New Hampshire

New Jersey

Princeton University

New York

Canisius College M
Clarkson University
Colgate University
Cornell University
Niagara University M
Rensselaer Polytechnic Institute
Rochester Institute of
Technology
St. Lawrence University
Syracuse University F
Union College
United States Military Academy
M

North Dakota

University of North Dakota

Ohio

Bowling Green State University
M

Miami University
Oxford M
Ohio State University
Columbus Campus

Pennsylvania

Mercyhurst University
Penn State
University Park
Robert Morris University

Rhode Island

Brown University
Providence College

Vermont

University of Vermont

Wisconsin

University of Wisconsin
Madison

Ice Hockey Division II

Connecticut

Post University

Massachusetts

Assumption College M
Stonehill College M

Missouri

Lindenwood University F

New Hampshire

Franklin Pierce University
Saint Anselm College
Southern New Hampshire
University M

Vermont

Saint Michael's College

Ice Hockey Division III

Connecticut

Connecticut College
Trinity College
Wesleyan University

Illinois

Aurora University M
Lake Forest College

Maine

Bowdoin College
Colby College
University of New England
University of Southern Maine

Maryland

Stevenson University F

Massachusetts

Amherst College
Babson College M
Becker College
Curry College M
Endicott College
Fitchburg State University M
Framingham State University M
Nichols College
Salem State University
Suffolk University M
Tufts University M
University of Massachusetts
Dartmouth M
Wentworth Institute of
Technology M
Western New England
University M
Westfield State University M
Williams College
Worcester State University M

Michigan

Adrian College
Finlandia University

Minnesota

Augsburg College
Bethel University
College of St. Benedict F
College of St. Scholastica
Concordia College: Moorhead
Gustavus Adolphus College
Hamline University
St. Catherine University F
St. John's University M
St. Mary's University of
Minnesota
St. Olaf College
University of St. Thomas

New Hampshire

Daniel Webster College
New England College
Plymouth State University

New York

Elmira College
Hamilton College
Manhattanville College
Nazareth College M
Skidmore College M
SUNY
College at Brockport M
College at Buffalo
College at Cortland
College at Geneseo M
College at Oswego
College at Plattsburgh
College at Potsdam
College of Agriculture and
Technology at Morrisville
College of Technology at
Canton
Utica College

Pennsylvania

Chatham University F
Neumann University

Rhode Island

Salve Regina University

Vermont

Middlebury College
Norwich University

Wisconsin

Lawrence University M
Marian University
Milwaukee School of
Engineering M
Northland College M
St. Norbert College
University of Wisconsin
Eau Claire
Stevens Point
Superior

Lacrosse Division I

California

California State University
Fresno F
St. Mary's College of California
F
San Diego State University F
Stanford University F
University of California
Berkeley F
Davis F
University of Southern
California F

Colorado

United States Air Force
Academy M

University of Colorado
  Boulder F
University of Denver

Connecticut

Central Connecticut State
  University F
Fairfield University
Quinnipiac University
Sacred Heart University
University of Connecticut F
University of Hartford M
Yale University

Delaware

Delaware State University F
University of Delaware

District of Columbia

American University F
George Washington University
  F
Georgetown University
Howard University F

Florida

Jacksonville University
Stetson University F
University of Florida F

Georgia

Kennesaw State University F
Mercer University

Illinois

Northwestern University F

Indiana

University of Notre Dame

Kentucky

Bellarmine University M
University of Louisville F

Maryland

Johns Hopkins University
Loyola University Maryland
Mount St. Mary's University
Towson University
United States Naval Academy
University of Maryland
  Baltimore County
  College Park

Massachusetts

Boston College F
Boston University
College of the Holy Cross
Harvard College
University of Massachusetts
  Amherst

Michigan

Central Michigan University F
University of Detroit Mercy
University of Michigan

New Hampshire

Dartmouth College
University of New Hampshire F

New Jersey

Monmouth University
New Jersey Institute of
  Technology M
Princeton University

New York

Barnard College F
Canisius College
Colgate University
Columbia University F
Cornell University
Hofstra University
Iona College F
Long Island University
  LIU Brooklyn F
Manhattan College
Marist College
Niagara University F
Saint Bonaventure University F

St. John's University M
Siena College
SUNY
  University at Albany
  University at Binghamton
  University at Stony Brook
Syracuse University
United States Military Academy
Wagner College

North Carolina

Campbell University F
Davidson College F
Duke University
Elon University F
Gardner-Webb University F
High Point University
University of North Carolina
  Chapel Hill

Ohio

Ohio State University
  Columbus Campus
University of Cincinnati F

Oregon

University of Oregon F

Pennsylvania

Bucknell University
Drexel University
Duquesne University F
La Salle University F
Lafayette College
Lehigh University
Penn State
  University Park
Robert Morris University
St. Francis University F
Saint Joseph's University
Temple University F
University of Pennsylvania
Villanova University

Rhode Island

Brown University
Bryant University
Providence College M

South Carolina

Coastal Carolina University F
Furman University
Presbyterian College F
Winthrop University F

Tennessee

Vanderbilt University F

Vermont

University of Vermont

Virginia

College of William and Mary F
George Mason University F
Hampton University M
James Madison University F
Liberty University F
Longwood University F
Old Dominion University F
Radford University F
University of Richmond
University of Virginia
Virginia Commonwealth
  University F
Virginia Military Institute M

Wisconsin

Marquette University

Lacrosse Division II

Alabama

University of Alabama
  Huntsville
University of Montevallo F

California

Notre Dame de Namur
  University M

Colorado

Adams State University
Colorado Mesa University
Colorado State University
  Pueblo
Fort Lewis College F
Regis University F

Connecticut

Post University
Southern Connecticut State
  University F
University of Bridgeport F
University of New Haven F

Delaware

Wilmington University F

District of Columbia

University of the District of
  Columbia

Florida

Florida Institute of Technology
Florida Southern College
Lynn University M
Rollins College
Saint Leo University
University of Tampa

Georgia

Emmanuel College
Shorter University
Young Harris College

Illinois

McKendree University F

Indiana

University of Indianapolis

Massachusetts

American International College
Assumption College
Bentley University
Merrimack College
Stonehill College F

Michigan

Grand Valley State University F

Missouri

Lindenwood University
Rockhurst University

New Hampshire

Franklin Pierce University
Saint Anselm College
Southern New Hampshire
  University

New Jersey

Georgian Court University

New York

Adelphi University
City University of New York
  Queens College F
College of Saint Rose M
Dominican College of Blauvelt
Dowling College
Le Moyne College
Long Island University
  LIU Post
Mercy College
Molloy College
New York Institute of
  Technology M
Nyack College F
Pace University
Roberts Wesleyan College
St. Thomas Aquinas College

North Carolina

Belmont Abbey College
Brevard College

Catawba College
Chowan University F
Lees-McRae College
Lenoir-Rhyne University
Mars Hill University M
Pfeiffer University
Queens University of Charlotte
University of Mount Olive
Wingate University

Ohio

Lake Erie College
Notre Dame College F
Tiffin University F
University of Findlay F
Urbana University F
Ursuline College F
Walsh University

Oklahoma

Oklahoma Baptist University F

Pennsylvania

Bloomsburg University of
  Pennsylvania F
Chestnut Hill College
East Stroudsburg University of
  Pennsylvania F
Edinboro University
  of Pennsylvania F
Gannon University F
Holy Family University F
Indiana University of
  Pennsylvania F
Kutztown University of
  Pennsylvania F
Lock Haven University of
  Pennsylvania F
Mercyhurst University
Millersville University of
  Pennsylvania F
Philadelphia University F
Seton Hill University
Shippensburg University of
  Pennsylvania F
Slippery Rock University of
  Pennsylvania F
West Chester University of
  Pennsylvania F

South Carolina

Coker College
Converse College F
Erskine College F
Limestone College
Newberry College F
North Greenville University

Tennessee

Lincoln Memorial University
Tusculum College

Vermont

Saint Michael's College

Virginia

University of Virginia's College
  at Wise F

West Virginia

Alderson-Broaddus University
Davis and Elkins College
Ohio Valley University M
Shepherd University F
University of Charleston F
West Virginia Wesleyan
  College F
Wheeling Jesuit University

Lacrosse Division III

Alabama

Birmingham-Southern College
Huntingdon College

Arkansas

Hendrix College

California

Chapman University F
Claremont McKenna College F
Harvey Mudd College F
Occidental College F
Pitzer College F
Pomona College F
Scripps College F
University of Redlands F
Whittier College

Colorado

Colorado College

Connecticut

Albertus Magnus College
Connecticut College
Eastern Connecticut State
  University
Mitchell College
Trinity College
United States Coast Guard
  Academy
University of Saint Joseph F
Wesleyan University
Western Connecticut State
  University

Delaware

Wesley College

District of Columbia

Catholic University of America

Georgia

Berry College
Oglethorpe University
Piedmont College

Illinois

Augustana College
Aurora University
Benedictine University at
  Springfield
Concordia University Chicago
Elmhurst College
Illinois Institute of Technology
  F
Illinois Wesleyan University
North Central College F

Indiana

DePauw University
Franklin College F
Hanover College
Saint Mary's College F
Trine University
Wabash College M

Iowa

Cornell College
Loras College F
University of Dubuque
Wartburg College F

Kentucky

Centre College
Thomas More College F
Transylvania University

Louisiana

Centenary College of Louisiana
  M

Maine

Bates College
Bowdoin College
Colby College
Husson University
Maine Maritime Academy
Saint Joseph's College of Maine
Thomas College
University of Maine
  Farmington
University of New England
University of Southern Maine

Maryland

Frostburg State University
Goucher College
Hood College
McDaniel College
Notre Dame of Maryland
  University F
St. Mary's College of Maryland
Salisbury University
Stevenson University
Washington College

Massachusetts

Amherst College
Anna Maria College M
Babson College
Becker College
Bridgewater State University F
Clark University M
Curry College
Elms College F
Emerson College
Emmanuel College
Endicott College
Fitchburg State University F
Framingham State University F
Gordon College
Lasell College
Massachusetts College of
  Liberal Arts F
Massachusetts Institute of
  Technology
Massachusetts Maritime
  Academy
Mount Holyoke College F
Mount Ida College
Nichols College
Regis College
Salem State University
Simmons College F
Smith College F
Springfield College
Tufts University
University of Massachusetts
  Dartmouth
Wellesley College F
Wentworth Institute of
  Technology
Western New England
  University
Westfield State University F
Wheaton College
Wheelock College
Williams College
Worcester State University F

Michigan

Adrian College
Albion College
Alma College
Calvin College
Hope College
Kalamazoo College
Olivet College

Minnesota

Augsburg College F
University of Northwestern - St.
  Paul F

Mississippi

Millsaps College

Missouri

Fontbonne University M

New Hampshire

Colby-Sawyer College F
Daniel Webster College
Keene State College
New England College
Plymouth State University
Rivier University

New Jersey

Centenary College
The College of New Jersey F
College of St. Elizabeth F

Drew University
Fairleigh Dickinson University
  College at Florham
Kean University
Montclair State University
Ramapo College of New Jersey
  F
Rowan University F
Rutgers, The State University of
  New Jersey
    Camden Campus F
Stevens Institute of Technology

New York

Alfred University
Bard College
Cazenovia College
Clarkson University
College of Mount St. Vincent
Elmira College
Hamilton College
Hartwick College
Hilbert College
Houghton College
Ithaca College
Keuka College
Manhattanville College
Medaille College
Mount Saint Mary College
Nazareth College
Rensselaer Polytechnic Institute
Rochester Institute of
  Technology
The Sage Colleges F
St. John Fisher College
St. Joseph's College New York:
  Suffolk Campus F
St. Lawrence University
Skidmore College
SUNY
    College at Brockport
    College at Buffalo F
    College at Cortland
    College at Geneseo
    College at New Paltz F
    College at Old Westbury F
    College at Oneonta
    College at Oswego
    College at Plattsburgh M
    College at Potsdam
    College at Purchase
    College of Agriculture and
      Technology at Cobleskill
      M
    College of Agriculture and
      Technology at Morrisville
    College of Technology at
      Alfred M
    College of Technology at
      Canton
    Maritime College
Union College
United States Merchant Marine
  Academy
University of Rochester F
Utica College
Vassar College
Wells College

North Carolina

Greensboro College
Guilford College
Meredith College F
Methodist University

Ohio

Baldwin Wallace University
Capital University
College of Wooster
Defiance College M
Denison University
Franciscan University of
  Steubenville
Hiram College
John Carroll University
Kenyon College
Muskingum University
Oberlin College

Ohio Northern University
Ohio Wesleyan University
Otterbein University
University of Mount Union
Wilmington College
Wittenberg University

Oregon

George Fox University F
Linfield College F
Pacific University F

Pennsylvania

Albright College
Allegheny College F
Alvernia University
Arcadia University
Bryn Athyn College
Bryn Mawr College F
Cabrini College
Cedar Crest College F
DeSales University M
Dickinson College
Eastern University
Elizabethtown College
Franklin & Marshall College
Gettysburg College
Gwynedd Mercy University
Haverford College
Immaculata University
Keystone College
King's College
La Roche College M
Lancaster Bible College F
Lebanon Valley College
Lycoming College
Marywood University
Messiah College
Misericordia University
Moravian College
Muhlenberg College
Neumann University
Penn State
  Abington F
Rosemont College
St. Vincent College
Susquehanna University
Swarthmore College
Thiel College
University of Scranton
Ursinus College
Washington & Jefferson College
Waynesburg University F
Westminster College M
Widener University
Wilkes University
York College of Pennsylvania

Rhode Island

Rhode Island College F
Roger Williams University
Salve Regina University

Tennessee

Rhodes College
Sewanee: The University of the
  South

Texas

Southwestern University
University of Dallas

Vermont

Green Mountain College
Johnson State College
Lyndon State College M
Middlebury College
Norwich University
Southern Vermont College F

Virginia

Bridgewater College
Christopher Newport University
Ferrum College
Hampden-Sydney College M
Hollins University F
Lynchburg College
Marymount University
Randolph College

Randolph-Macon College
Roanoke College
Shenandoah University
Southern Virginia University
Sweet Briar College F
University of Mary Washington
Virginia Wesleyan College
Washington and Lee University

Washington

University of Puget Sound F
Whitman College F

West Virginia

Bethany College M

Wisconsin

Beloit College
Carroll University
Carthage College
Milwaukee School of
  Engineering M

Rifle Division I

Alabama

Jacksonville State University
University of Alabama
  Birmingham

Colorado

United States Air Force
  Academy

Georgia

Georgia Southern University F

Kentucky

Morehead State University
Murray State University
University of Kentucky

Maryland

United States Naval Academy

Mississippi

University of Mississippi F

Nebraska

University of Nebraska
  Lincoln F

New York

United States Military Academy

North Carolina

North Carolina State University

Ohio

Ohio State University
  Columbus Campus
University of Akron

South Carolina

The Citadel
Wofford College

Tennessee

University of Memphis
University of Tennessee
  Martin

Texas

Texas Christian University F
University of Texas
  El Paso F

Virginia

Virginia Military Institute

West Virginia

West Virginia University

Rifle Division II

Alaska

University of Alaska
  Fairbanks

Georgia

University of North Georgia

Rifle Division III

Connecticut

United States Coast Guard
  Academy

Massachusetts

Massachusetts Institute of
  Technology

New York

City University of New York
  John Jay College of
    Criminal Justice

Rowing (crew) Division I

Alabama

University of Alabama F

California

California State University
  Sacramento F
Loyola Marymount University F
St. Mary's College of California
  F
San Diego State University F
Santa Clara University F
Stanford University F
University of California
  Berkeley F
  Los Angeles F
University of San Diego F
University of Southern
  California F

Connecticut

Fairfield University F
Sacred Heart University F
University of Connecticut F
Yale University F

Delaware

University of Delaware F

District of Columbia

George Washington University
  F
Georgetown University F

Florida

Jacksonville University F
Stetson University F
University of Central Florida F
University of Miami F

Indiana

Indiana University
  Bloomington F
University of Notre Dame F

Iowa

Drake University F
University of Iowa F

Kansas

Kansas State University F
University of Kansas F

Kentucky

University of Louisville F

Maryland

Loyola University Maryland F
United States Naval Academy F

Massachusetts

Boston College F
Boston University F
College of the Holy Cross F
Harvard College F

Massachusetts Institute of
Technology F
Northeastern University F
University of Massachusetts
Amherst F

Michigan

Eastern Michigan University F
Michigan State University F
University of Michigan F

Minnesota

University of Minnesota
Twin Cities F

Nebraska

Creighton University F

New Hampshire

Dartmouth College F

New Jersey

Princeton University F

New York

Barnard College F
Canisius College F
Colgate University F
Columbia University F
Cornell University F
Fordham University F
Iona College F
Marist College F
SUNY
University at Buffalo F
Syracuse University F

North Carolina

Duke University F
University of North Carolina
Chapel Hill F

Ohio

Ohio State University
Columbus Campus F
University of Dayton F

Oklahoma

University of Oklahoma F

Oregon

Oregon State University F
University of Portland F

Pennsylvania

Bucknell University F
Drexel University F
Duquesne University F
La Salle University F
Lehigh University F
Robert Morris University F
Saint Joseph's University F
Temple University F
University of Pennsylvania F
Villanova University F

Rhode Island

Brown University F
University of Rhode Island F

South Carolina

Clemson University F

Tennessee

University of Tennessee
Knoxville F

Texas

Southern Methodist University F
University of Texas
Austin F

Virginia

George Mason University F
Old Dominion University F
University of Virginia F

Washington

Gonzaga University F
Seattle University F

University of Washington F
Washington State University F

West Virginia

West Virginia University F

Wisconsin

University of Wisconsin
Madison F

**Rowing (crew)
Division II**

California

Humboldt State University F
University of California
San Diego F

Florida

Barry University F
Florida Institute of Technology
F
Nova Southeastern University F
Rollins College F
University of Tampa F

Massachusetts

Assumption College F
Merrimack College F

New Hampshire

Franklin Pierce University F

Oklahoma

University of Central Oklahoma
F

Pennsylvania

Mercyhurst University F
Philadelphia University F

Washington

Seattle Pacific University F
Western Washington University
F

West Virginia

University of Charleston F

**Rowing (crew)
Division III**

California

Mills College F

Connecticut

Connecticut College F
Trinity College F
United States Coast Guard
Academy F
Wesleyan University F

Illinois

North Park University F

Maine

Bates College F
Colby College F

Maryland

Washington College F

Massachusetts

Clark University F
Massachusetts Maritime
Academy F
Mount Holyoke College F
Simmons College F
Smith College F
Tufts University F
Wellesley College F
Williams College F
Worcester Polytechnic Institute
F

New Jersey

Rutgers, The State University of
New Jersey
Camden Campus F

New York

D'Youville College F
Hamilton College F
Ithaca College F
Rochester Institute of
Technology F
St. John Fisher College F
St. Lawrence University F
Sarah Lawrence College F
Skidmore College F
SUNY
Maritime College F
Union College F
University of Rochester F

Ohio

Marietta College F

Oregon

Lewis & Clark College F
Pacific University F
Willamette University F

Pennsylvania

Bryn Mawr College F
Franklin & Marshall College F

Washington

Pacific Lutheran University F
University of Puget Sound F

Skiing Division I

Colorado

University of Colorado
Boulder
University of Denver

Massachusetts

Boston College
Harvard College

Montana

Montana State University

New Hampshire

Dartmouth College
University of New Hampshire

New Mexico

University of New Mexico

Rhode Island

Brown University F

Utah

University of Utah

Vermont

University of Vermont

Wisconsin

University of Wisconsin
Green Bay

Skiing Division II

Alaska

University of Alaska
Anchorage
Fairbanks

Michigan

Michigan Technological
University
Northern Michigan University

Minnesota

Saint Cloud State University F

Vermont

Saint Michael's College

Skiing Division III

Maine

Bates College
Bowdoin College
Colby College
University of Maine
Presque Isle

Massachusetts

Babson College
Williams College

Minnesota

College of St. Scholastica
St. Olaf College

New Hampshire

Colby-Sawyer College
New England College
Plymouth State University

New York

Clarkson University
St. Lawrence University

Vermont

Middlebury College

Soccer Division I

Alabama

Alabama Agricultural and
Mechanical University F
Alabama State University F
Auburn University F
Jacksonville State University F
Samford University F
Troy University F
University of Alabama F
University of Alabama
Birmingham
University of South Alabama F

Arizona

Arizona State University F
Northern Arizona University F
University of Arizona F

Arkansas

Arkansas State University F
University of Arkansas F
Pine Bluff F
University of Central Arkansas

California

California Polytechnic State
University: San Luis Obispo
California State University
Bakersfield
Fresno F
Fullerton
Long Beach F
Northridge
Sacramento
Loyola Marymount University
Pepperdine University F
St. Mary's College of California
San Diego State University
San Jose State University
Santa Clara University
Stanford University
University of California
Berkeley
Davis
Irvine
Los Angeles
Riverside
Santa Barbara

University of San Diego
University of San Francisco
University of Southern
California F
University of the Pacific

Colorado

Colorado College F
Colorado State University F
United States Air Force
Academy
University of Colorado
Boulder F
University of Denver
University of Northern Colorado
F

Connecticut

Central Connecticut State
University
Fairfield University
Quinnipiac University
Sacred Heart University
University of Connecticut
University of Hartford
Yale University

Delaware

Delaware State University F
University of Delaware

District of Columbia

American University
George Washington University
Georgetown University
Howard University

Florida

Florida Atlantic University
Florida Gulf Coast University
Florida International University
Florida State University F
Jacksonville University
Stetson University
University of Central Florida
University of Florida F
University of Miami F
University of North Florida
University of South Florida

Georgia

Georgia Southern University
Georgia State University
Kennesaw State University F
Mercer University
University of Georgia F

Hawaii

University of Hawaii
Manoa F

Idaho

Boise State University F
Idaho State University F
University of Idaho F

Illinois

Bradley University M
Chicago State University F
DePaul University
Eastern Illinois University
Illinois State University F
Loyola University Chicago
Northern Illinois University
Northwestern University
Southern Illinois University
Edwardsville
University of Illinois
Chicago
Western Illinois University

Indiana

Ball State University F
Butler University
Indiana State University F
Indiana University
Bloomington
Purdue University Fort
Wayne
Purdue University
Indianapolis

Purdue University F
University of Evansville
University of Notre Dame
Valparaiso University

Iowa

Drake University
Iowa State University F
University of Iowa F
University of Northern Iowa F

Kansas

University of Kansas F

Kentucky

Eastern Kentucky University F
Morehead State University F
Murray State University F
University of Kentucky
University of Louisville
Western Kentucky University F

Louisiana

Grambling State University F
Louisiana State University and
Agricultural and Mechanical
College F
Louisiana Tech University F
McNeese State University F
Nicholls State University F
Northwestern State University F
Southeastern Louisiana
University F
Southern University and
Agricultural and Mechanical
College F
University of Louisiana at
Lafayette F
University of Louisiana at
Monroe F

Maine

University of Maine F

Maryland

Loyola University Maryland
Mount St. Mary's University F
Towson University F
United States Naval Academy
University of Maryland
Baltimore County
College Park

Massachusetts

Boston College
Boston University
College of the Holy Cross
Harvard College
Northeastern University
University of Massachusetts
Amherst

Michigan

Central Michigan University F
Eastern Michigan University F
Michigan State University
Oakland University
University of Detroit Mercy
University of Michigan
Western Michigan University

Minnesota

University of Minnesota
Twin Cities F

Mississippi

Alcorn State University F
Jackson State University F
Mississippi State University F
Mississippi Valley State
University F
University of Mississippi F

Missouri

Missouri State University
Saint Louis University
Southeast Missouri State
University F

University of Missouri
Columbia F
Kansas City

Montana

University of Montana F

Nebraska

Creighton University
University of Nebraska
Lincoln F
Omaha

Nevada

University of Nevada
Las Vegas

New Hampshire

Dartmouth College
University of New Hampshire

New Jersey

Fairleigh Dickinson University
Metropolitan Campus
Monmouth University
New Jersey Institute of
Technology
Princeton University
Rider University
Seton Hall University

New Mexico

New Mexico State University F
University of New Mexico

New York

Barnard College
Canisius College
Colgate University
Columbia University
Cornell University
Fordham University
Hartwick College M
Hofstra University
Iona College
Long Island University
LIU Brooklyn
Manhattan College
Marist College
Niagara University
Saint Bonaventure University
St. Francis College M
St. John's University
Siena College
SUNY
University at Albany
University at Binghamton
University at Buffalo
University at Stony Brook
Syracuse University
United States Military Academy
Wagner College F

North Carolina

Appalachian State University
Campbell University
Davidson College
Duke University
East Carolina University F
Elon University
Gardner-Webb University
High Point University
North Carolina State University
University of North Carolina
Asheville
Chapel Hill
Wake Forest University
Western Carolina University F

North Dakota

North Dakota State University F
University of North Dakota F

Ohio

Bowling Green State University
Cleveland State University
Kent State University F
Miami University
Oxford F

Ohio State University
Columbus Campus
Ohio University F
University of Akron
University of Cincinnati
University of Dayton
University of Toledo F
Wright State University
Xavier University
Youngstown State University F

Oklahoma

Oklahoma State University F
Oral Roberts University
University of Oklahoma F

Oregon

Oregon State University
Portland State University F
University of Oregon F
University of Portland

Pennsylvania

Bucknell University
Drexel University
Duquesne University
La Salle University
Lafayette College
Lehigh University
Penn State
University Park
Robert Morris University
St. Francis University
Saint Joseph's University
Temple University
University of Pennsylvania
University of Pittsburgh
Villanova University

Rhode Island

Brown University
Bryant University
Providence College
University of Rhode Island

South Carolina

Charleston Southern University
F
The Citadel F
Clemson University
Coastal Carolina University
College of Charleston
Francis Marion University F
Furman University
Presbyterian College
South Carolina State University
F
University of South Carolina
Columbia
Upstate
Winthrop University
Wofford College

South Dakota

South Dakota State University F
University of South Dakota F

Tennessee

Austin Peay State University F
Belmont University
East Tennessee State University
Lipscomb University
Middle Tennessee State
University F
Tennessee Technological
University F
University of Memphis
University of Tennessee
Chattanooga F
Knoxville F
Martin F
Vanderbilt University F

Texas

Baylor University F
Houston Baptist University
Lamar University F
Prairie View A&M University F
Rice University F

Sam Houston State University F
Southern Methodist University
Stephen F. Austin State
University F
Texas A&M University F
Corpus Christi F
Texas Christian University F
Texas Southern University F
Texas Tech University F
University of Houston F
University of North Texas F
University of Texas
Austin F
El Paso F
San Antonio F

Utah

Brigham Young University F
Southern Utah University F
University of Utah F
Utah State University F
Utah Valley University
Weber State University F

Vermont

University of Vermont

Virginia

College of William and Mary
George Mason University
Hampton University F
James Madison University
Liberty University
Longwood University
Old Dominion University
Radford University
University of Richmond F
University of Virginia
Virginia Commonwealth
University
Virginia Military Institute

Washington

Eastern Washington University
F
Gonzaga University
Seattle University
University of Washington
Washington State University F

West Virginia

Marshall University
West Virginia University

Wisconsin

Marquette University
University of Wisconsin
Green Bay
Madison
Milwaukee

Wyoming

University of Wyoming F

Alabama

Auburn University at
Montgomery
Spring Hill College
University of Alabama
Huntsville
University of Montevallo
University of North Alabama F
University of West Alabama

Arizona

Grand Canyon University

Arkansas

Harding University
Ouachita Baptist University

California

Academy of Art University
Azusa Pacific University
California Baptist University

California State Polytechnic
University: Pomona
California State University
Chico
Dominguez Hills
East Bay
Los Angeles
Monterey Bay
San Bernardino
Stanislaus
Dominican University of
California
Fresno Pacific University
Holy Names University
Humboldt State University
Notre Dame de Namur
University
Point Loma Nazarene University
San Francisco State University
Sonoma State University
University of California
San Diego

Colorado

Adams State University
Colorado Christian University
Colorado Mesa University
Colorado School of Mines
Colorado State University
Pueblo
Fort Lewis College
Metropolitan State University of
Denver
Regis University
University of Colorado
Colorado Springs
Western State Colorado
University F

Connecticut

Post University
Southern Connecticut State
University
University of Bridgeport
University of New Haven

Delaware

Goldey-Beacom College
Wilmington University

District of Columbia

University of the District of
Columbia M

Florida

Barry University
Eckerd College
Flagler College
Florida Institute of Technology
Florida Southern College
Lynn University
Nova Southeastern University
Palm Beach Atlantic University
Rollins College
Saint Leo University
University of Tampa
University of West Florida

Georgia

Clayton State University
Columbus State University F
Emmanuel College
Georgia Southwestern State
University
Shorter University
University of North Georgia
University of West Georgia F
Valdosta State University F
Young Harris College

Hawaii

Brigham Young University-
Hawaii
Chaminade University of
Honolulu
Hawaii Pacific University
University of Hawaii
Hilo

Idaho

Northwest Nazarene University

Illinois

Lewis University
McKendree University
Quincy University
University of Illinois
    Springfield

Indiana

Oakland City University
Saint Joseph's College
University of Indianapolis
University of Southern Indiana

Iowa

Upper Iowa University

Kansas

Emporia State University F
Fort Hays State University
Newman University
Washburn University F

Kentucky

Bellarmine University
Kentucky Wesleyan College
Northern Kentucky University

Massachusetts

American International College
Assumption College
Bentley University
Merrimack College
Stonehill College

Michigan

Ferris State University F
Grand Valley State University F
Michigan Technological
    University F
Northern Michigan University F
Northwood University
    Michigan
Saginaw Valley State University

Minnesota

Bemidji State University F
Concordia University St. Paul F
Minnesota State University
    Mankato F
    Moorhead F
Saint Cloud State University F
Southwest Minnesota State
    University F
University of Minnesota
    Crookston F
    Duluth F
Winona State University F

Mississippi

Delta State University
Mississippi College

Missouri

Drury University
Lindenwood University
Maryville University of Saint
    Louis
Missouri Southern State
    University F
Missouri University of Science
    and Technology
Missouri Western State
    University F
Northwest Missouri State
    University F
Rockhurst University
Southwest Baptist University
Truman State University
University of Central Missouri F
William Jewell College

Montana

Montana State University
    Billings

Nebraska

University of Nebraska
    Kearney F
Wayne State College F

New Hampshire

Franklin Pierce University
Saint Anselm College
Southern New Hampshire
    University

New Jersey

Bloomfield College
Georgian Court University

New Mexico

Eastern New Mexico University
New Mexico Highlands
    University F

New York

Adelphi University
City University of New York
    Queens College
College of Saint Rose
Concordia College
Daemen College
Dominican College of Blauvelt
Dowling College
Le Moyne College
Long Island University
    LIU Post
Mercy College
Molloy College
New York Institute of
    Technology
Nyack College
Pace University F
Roberts Wesleyan College
St. Thomas Aquinas College

North Carolina

Barton College
Belmont Abbey College
Brevard College
Catawba College
Chowan University
Lees-McRae College
Lenoir-Rhyne University
Mars Hill University
Pfeiffer University
Queens University of Charlotte
University of Mount Olive
University of North Carolina
    Pembroke
Wingate University

North Dakota

Minot State University F
University of Mary

Ohio

Ashland University F
Cedarville University
Lake Erie College
Malone University
Notre Dame College
Ohio Dominican University
Tiffin University
University of Findlay
Urbana University
Ursuline College F
Walsh University

Oklahoma

East Central University F
Northeastern State University
Northwestern Oklahoma State
    University F
Oklahoma Baptist University
Oklahoma Christian University
Rogers State University
Southern Nazarene University
Southwestern Oklahoma State
    University F
University of Central Oklahoma
    F

Oregon

Western Oregon University F

Pennsylvania

Bloomsburg University of
    Pennsylvania
California University of
    Pennsylvania
Chestnut Hill College
Clarion University of
    Pennsylvania F
East Stroudsburg University of
    Pennsylvania
Edinboro University
    of Pennsylvania F
Gannon University
Holy Family University
Indiana University of
    Pennsylvania F
Kutztown University of
    Pennsylvania F
Lincoln University F
Lock Haven University of
    Pennsylvania
Mansfield University of
    Pennsylvania F
Mercyhurst University
Millersville University of
    Pennsylvania
Philadelphia University
Seton Hill University
Shippensburg University of
    Pennsylvania
Slippery Rock University of
    Pennsylvania
University of Pittsburgh
    Johnstown
West Chester University of
    Pennsylvania

South Carolina

Anderson University
Coker College
Converse College F
Erskine College
Francis Marion University M
Lander University
Limestone College
Newberry College
North Greenville University
Southern Wesleyan University
University of South Carolina
    Aiken

South Dakota

Northern State University F
South Dakota School of Mines
    and Technology M
University of Sioux Falls F

Tennessee

Carson-Newman University
Christian Brothers University
King University
Lee University
Lincoln Memorial University
Trevecca Nazarene University
Tusculum College
Union University

Texas

Abilene Christian University F
Angelo State University F
Dallas Baptist University
Lubbock Christian University
Midwestern State University
St. Edward's University
St. Mary's University
Texas A&M International
    University
Texas A&M University
    Commerce F
Texas Woman's University F
University of Texas
    of the Permian Basin
University of the Incarnate
    Word
West Texas A&M University

Utah

Dixie State University

Vermont

Saint Michael's College

Washington

Central Washington University
    F
Saint Martin's University
Seattle Pacific University
Western Washington University

West Virginia

Alderson-Broaddus University
Concord University
Davis and Elkins College
Fairmont State University F
Ohio Valley University
Salem International University
Shepherd University
University of Charleston
West Liberty University F
West Virginia Wesleyan College
Wheeling Jesuit University

Wisconsin

University of Wisconsin
    Parkside

Canada

Simon Fraser University

Soccer Division III

Alabama

Birmingham-Southern College
Huntingdon College

Arkansas

Hendrix College
University of the Ozarks

California

California Institute of
    Technology M
California Lutheran University
Chapman University
Claremont McKenna College
Harvey Mudd College
Mills College F
Occidental College
Pitzer College
Pomona College
Scripps College
University of California
    Santa Cruz
University of La Verne
University of Redlands
Whittier College

Colorado

Colorado College M

Connecticut

Albertus Magnus College
Connecticut College
Eastern Connecticut State
    University
Mitchell College
Trinity College
United States Coast Guard
    Academy
University of Saint Joseph F
Wesleyan University
Western Connecticut State
    University

Delaware

Wesley College

District of Columbia

Catholic University of America
Gallaudet University
Trinity Washington University F

Georgia

Agnes Scott College F
Berry College
Covenant College
Emory University
Oglethorpe University
Piedmont College
Wesleyan College F

Illinois

Augustana College
Aurora University
Benedictine University at
    Springfield
Blackburn College
Concordia University Chicago
Dominican University
Elmhurst College
Eureka College
Greenville College
Illinois College
Illinois Institute of Technology
Illinois Wesleyan University
Knox College
Lake Forest College
MacMurray College
Millikin University
Monmouth College
North Central College
North Park University
Principia College
Rockford University
University of Chicago
Wheaton College

Indiana

Anderson University
DePauw University
Earlham College
Franklin College
Hanover College
Manchester University
Rose-Hulman Institute of
    Technology
Saint Mary's College F
Trine University
Wabash College M

Iowa

Buena Vista University
Central College
Coe College
Cornell College
Grinnell College
Loras College
Luther College
Simpson College
University of Dubuque
Wartburg College

Kentucky

Berea College
Centre College
Spalding University
Thomas More College
Transylvania University

Louisiana

Centenary College of Louisiana
Louisiana College

Maine

Bates College
Bowdoin College
Colby College
Husson University
Maine Maritime Academy
Saint Joseph's College of Maine
Thomas College
University of Maine
    Farmington
    Presque Isle
University of New England
University of Southern Maine

Maryland

Frostburg State University
Goucher College

Hood College
Johns Hopkins University
McDaniel College
Notre Dame of Maryland University F
St. Mary's College of Maryland
Salisbury University
Stevenson University
Washington College

Massachusetts

Amherst College
Anna Maria College
Babson College
Becker College
Brandeis University
Bridgewater State University
Clark University
Curry College
Eastern Nazarene College
Elms College
Emerson College
Emmanuel College
Endicott College
Fitchburg State University
Framingham State University
Gordon College
Lasell College
Lesley University
Massachusetts College of Liberal Arts
Massachusetts Institute of Technology
Massachusetts Maritime Academy
Mount Holyoke College F
Mount Ida College
Newbury College
Nichols College
Pine Manor College
Regis College
Salem State University
Simmons College F
Smith College F
Springfield College
Suffolk University
Tufts University
University of Massachusetts Dartmouth
Wellesley College F
Wentworth Institute of Technology
Western New England University
Westfield State University
Wheaton College
Wheelock College
Williams College
Worcester Polytechnic Institute
Worcester State University

Michigan

Adrian College
Albion College
Alma College
Calvin College
Finlandia University
Hope College
Kalamazoo College
Olivet College

Minnesota

Augsburg College
Bethany Lutheran College
Bethel University
Carleton College
College of St. Benedict F
College of St. Scholastica
Concordia College: Moorhead
Gustavus Adolphus College
Hamline University
Macalester College
Martin Luther College
North Central University
St. Catherine University F
St. John's University M
St. Mary's University of Minnesota

St. Olaf College
University of Minnesota Morris
University of Northwestern - St. Paul
University of St. Thomas

Mississippi

Belhaven University
Millsaps College

Missouri

Fontbonne University
Webster University
Westminster College

Nebraska

Nebraska Wesleyan University

New Hampshire

Colby-Sawyer College
Daniel Webster College
Keene State College
New England College
Plymouth State University
Rivier University

New Jersey

Centenary College
The College of New Jersey
College of St. Elizabeth F
Drew University
Fairleigh Dickinson University College at Florham
Kean University
Montclair State University
New Jersey City University
Ramapo College of New Jersey
Rowan University
Rutgers, The State University of New Jersey
  Camden Campus
  Newark Campus
Stevens Institute of Technology
William Paterson University of New Jersey

New York

Alfred University
Bard College
Cazenovia College
City University of New York
  Baruch College M
  Brooklyn College
  City College
  College of Staten Island
  Hunter College M
  John Jay College of Criminal Justice
  Medgar Evers College
  York College
Clarkson University
College of Mount St. Vincent
D'Youville College
Elmira College
Hamilton College
Hartwick College F
Hilbert College
Houghton College
Ithaca College
Keuka College
Manhattanville College
Medaille College
Mount Saint Mary College
Nazareth College
New York University
Rensselaer Polytechnic Institute
Rochester Institute of Technology
The Sage Colleges
St. John Fisher College
St. Joseph's College New York: Suffolk Campus
St. Joseph's College, New York
St. Lawrence University
Sarah Lawrence College
Skidmore College

SUNY
  College at Brockport
  College at Buffalo
  College at Cortland
  College at Geneseo
  College at New Paltz
  College at Old Westbury
  College at Oneonta
  College at Oswego
  College at Plattsburgh
  College at Potsdam
  College at Purchase
  College of Agriculture and Technology at Cobleskill
  College of Agriculture and Technology at Morrisville
  College of Technology at Alfred
  College of Technology at Canton
  Maritime College
Union College
United States Merchant Marine Academy M
University of Rochester
Utica College
Vassar College
Wells College
Yeshiva University

North Carolina

Greensboro College
Guilford College
Meredith College F
Methodist University
North Carolina Wesleyan College
Salem College F
William Peace University

Ohio

Baldwin Wallace University
Bluffton University
Capital University
Case Western Reserve University
College of Wooster
Defiance College
Denison University
Franciscan University of Steubenville
Heidelberg University
Hiram College
John Carroll University
Kenyon College
Marietta College
Muskingum University
Oberlin College
Ohio Northern University
Ohio Wesleyan University
Otterbein University
University of Mount Union
Wilmington College
Wittenberg University

Oregon

George Fox University
Lewis & Clark College F
Linfield College
Pacific University
Willamette University

Pennsylvania

Albright College
Allegheny College
Alvernia University
Arcadia University
Bryn Athyn College M
Bryn Mawr College F
Cabrini College
Cairn University
Carnegie Mellon University
Cedar Crest College F
Chatham University F
DeSales University
Dickinson College
Eastern University
Elizabethtown College

Franklin & Marshall College
Geneva College
Gettysburg College
Grove City College
Gwynedd Mercy University
Haverford College
Immaculata University
Juniata College
Keystone College
King's College
La Roche College
Lancaster Bible College
Lebanon Valley College
Lycoming College
Marywood University
Messiah College
Misericordia University
Moravian College
Mount Aloysius College
Muhlenberg College
Neumann University
Penn State
  Abington
  Altoona
  Berks
  Erie, The Behrend College
  Harrisburg
Pennsylvania College of Technology
Rosemont College
St. Vincent College
Susquehanna University
Swarthmore College
Thiel College
University of Pittsburgh
  Bradford
  Greensburg
University of Scranton
Ursinus College
Washington & Jefferson College
Waynesburg University
Westminster College
Widener University
Wilkes University
Wilson College
York College of Pennsylvania

Rhode Island

Rhode Island College
Roger Williams University
Salve Regina University

Tennessee

Maryville College
Rhodes College
Sewanee: The University of the South

Texas

Austin College
Concordia University Texas
East Texas Baptist University
Hardin-Simmons University
Howard Payne University
LeTourneau University
McMurry University
Schreiner University
Southwestern University
Sul Ross State University F
Texas Lutheran University
Trinity University
University of Dallas
University of Mary Hardin-Baylor
University of Texas
  Dallas
  Tyler

Vermont

Green Mountain College
Johnson State College
Lyndon State College
Middlebury College
Norwich University
Southern Vermont College

Virginia

Averett University
Bridgewater College
Christopher Newport University
Eastern Mennonite University
Emory & Henry College
Ferrum College
Hampden-Sydney College M
Hollins University F
Lynchburg College
Mary Baldwin College F
Marymount University
Randolph College
Randolph-Macon College
Roanoke College
Shenandoah University
Southern Virginia University
Sweet Briar College F
University of Mary Washington
Virginia Wesleyan College
Washington and Lee University

Washington

Pacific Lutheran University
University of Puget Sound
Whitman College
Whitworth University

West Virginia

Bethany College

Wisconsin

Alverno College F
Beloit College
Carroll University
Carthage College
Edgewood College
Lakeland College
Lawrence University
Maranathan Baptist University
  Maranatha Baptist University
Marian University
Milwaukee School of Engineering
Mount Mary University F
Northland College
Ripon College
St. Norbert College
University of Wisconsin
  Eau Claire F
  La Crosse F
  Platteville
  Stevens Point F
  Superior
Wisconsin Lutheran College

Softball Division I

Alabama

Alabama Agricultural and Mechanical University F
Alabama State University F
Auburn University F
Jacksonville State University F
Samford University F
Troy University F
University of Alabama F
University of Alabama Birmingham F
University of South Alabama F

Arizona

Arizona State University F
University of Arizona F

Arkansas

University of Arkansas F
  Pine Bluff F
University of Central Arkansas F

California

California Polytechnic State University: San Luis Obispo F

California State University
Bakersfield F
Fresno F
Fullerton F
Long Beach F
Northridge F
Sacramento F
Loyola Marymount University F
St. Mary's College of California F
San Diego State University F
San Jose State University F
Santa Clara University F
Stanford University F
University of California
Berkeley F
Davis F
Los Angeles F
Riverside F
Santa Barbara F
University of San Diego F
University of the Pacific F

Colorado

Colorado State University F
University of Northern Colorado F

Connecticut

Central Connecticut State University F
Fairfield University F
Quinnipiac University F
Sacred Heart University F
University of Connecticut F
University of Hartford F
Yale University F

Delaware

Delaware State University F
University of Delaware F

District of Columbia

George Washington University F
Georgetown University F
Howard University F

Florida

Bethune-Cookman University F
Florida Agricultural and Mechanical University F
Florida Atlantic University F
Florida Gulf Coast University F
Florida International University F
Florida State University F
Jacksonville University F
Stetson University F
University of Central Florida F
University of Florida F
University of North Florida F
University of South Florida F

Georgia

Georgia Institute of Technology F
Georgia Southern University F
Georgia State University F
Kennesaw State University F
Mercer University F
Savannah State University F
University of Georgia F

Hawaii

University of Hawaii
Manoa F

Idaho

Boise State University F
Idaho State University F

Illinois

Bradley University F
DePaul University F
Eastern Illinois University F
Illinois State University F
Loyola University Chicago F
Northern Illinois University F

Northwestern University F
Southern Illinois University
Carbondale F
Southern Illinois University
Edwardsville F
University of Illinois
Chicago F
Western Illinois University F

Indiana

Ball State University F
Butler University F
Indiana State University F
Indiana University
Bloomington F
Purdue University Fort
Wayne F
Purdue University
Indianapolis F
Purdue University F
University of Evansville F
University of Notre Dame F
Valparaiso University F

Iowa

Drake University F
Iowa State University F
University of Iowa F
University of Northern Iowa F

Kansas

University of Kansas F
Wichita State University F

Kentucky

Eastern Kentucky University F
Morehead State University F
Murray State University F
University of Kentucky F
University of Louisville F
Western Kentucky University F

Louisiana

Grambling State University F
Louisiana State University and
Agricultural and Mechanical
College F
Louisiana Tech University F
McNeese State University F
Nicholls State University F
Northwestern State University F
Southeastern Louisiana
University F
Southern University and
Agricultural and Mechanical
College F
University of Louisiana at
Lafayette F
University of Louisiana at
Monroe F

Maine

University of Maine F

Maryland

Coppin State University F
Morgan State University F
Mount St. Mary's University F
Towson University F
University of Maryland
Baltimore County F
College Park F
Eastern Shore F

Massachusetts

Boston College F
Boston University F
College of the Holy Cross F
Harvard College F
University of Massachusetts
Amherst F

Michigan

Central Michigan University F
Eastern Michigan University F
Michigan State University F
Oakland University F
University of Detroit Mercy F

University of Michigan F
Western Michigan University F

Minnesota

University of Minnesota
Twin Cities F

Mississippi

Alcorn State University F
Jackson State University F
Mississippi State University F
Mississippi Valley State
University F
University of Mississippi F

Missouri

Missouri State University F
Saint Louis University F
Southeast Missouri State
University F
University of Missouri
Columbia F
Kansas City F

Montana

University of Montana F

Nebraska

Creighton University F
University of Nebraska
Lincoln F
Omaha F

Nevada

University of Nevada
Las Vegas F

New Hampshire

Dartmouth College F

New Jersey

Fairleigh Dickinson University
Metropolitan Campus F
Monmouth University F
Princeton University F
Rider University F
Seton Hall University F

New Mexico

New Mexico State University F
University of New Mexico F

New York

Barnard College F
Canisius College F
Colgate University F
Columbia University F
Cornell University F
Fordham University F
Hofstra University F
Iona College F
Long Island University
LIU Brooklyn F
Manhattan College F
Marist College F
Niagara University F
Saint Bonaventure University F
St. John's University F
Siena College F
SUNY
University at Albany F
University at Binghamton F
University at Buffalo F
University at Stony Brook F
Syracuse University F
United States Military Academy F
Wagner College F

North Carolina

Appalachian State University F
Campbell University F
East Carolina University F
Elon University F
Gardner-Webb University F
North Carolina Agricultural and
Technical State University F
North Carolina Central
University F

North Carolina State University F
University of North Carolina
Chapel Hill F
Western Carolina University F

North Dakota

North Dakota State University F
University of North Dakota F

Ohio

Bowling Green State University F
Cleveland State University F
Kent State University F
Miami University
Oxford F
Ohio State University
Columbus Campus F
Ohio University F
University of Akron F
University of Dayton F
University of Toledo F
Wright State University F
Youngstown State University F

Oklahoma

Oklahoma State University F
University of Oklahoma F

Oregon

Oregon State University F
Portland State University F
University of Oregon F

Pennsylvania

Bucknell University F
Drexel University F
La Salle University F
Lafayette College F
Lehigh University F
Penn State
University Park F
Robert Morris University F
St. Francis University F
Saint Joseph's University F
University of Pennsylvania F
University of Pittsburgh F
Villanova University F

Rhode Island

Brown University F
Bryant University F
Providence College F
University of Rhode Island F

South Carolina

Charleston Southern University F
Coastal Carolina University F
College of Charleston F
Furman University F
Presbyterian College F
South Carolina State University F
University of South Carolina
Columbia F
Upstate F
Winthrop University F

South Dakota

South Dakota State University F
University of South Dakota F

Tennessee

Austin Peay State University F
Belmont University F
East Tennessee State University F
Lipscomb University F
Middle Tennessee State
University F
Tennessee State University F
Tennessee Technological
University F
University of Memphis F

University of Tennessee
Chattanooga F
Knoxville F
Martin F

Texas

Baylor University F
Houston Baptist University F
Lamar University F
Prairie View A&M University F
Sam Houston State University F
Stephen F. Austin State
University F
Texas A&M University
Corpus Christi F
Texas Southern University F
Texas Tech University F
University of Houston F
University of North Texas F
University of Texas
Arlington F
Austin F
El Paso F
San Antonio F

Utah

Brigham Young University F
Southern Utah University F
University of Utah F
Utah State University F
Utah Valley University F
Weber State University F

Virginia

George Mason University F
Hampton University F
James Madison University F
Liberty University F
Longwood University F
Norfolk State University F
Radford University F
University of Virginia F

Washington

Seattle University F
University of Washington F

West Virginia

Marshall University F

Wisconsin

University of Wisconsin
Green Bay F
Madison F

Softball Division II

Alabama

Auburn University at
Montgomery F
Miles College F
Spring Hill College F
Stillman College F
Tuskegee University F
University of Alabama
Huntsville F
University of Montevallo F
University of North Alabama F
University of West Alabama F

Arizona

Grand Canyon University F

Arkansas

Arkansas Tech University F
Harding University F
Henderson State University F
Ouachita Baptist University F
Southern Arkansas University F
University of Arkansas
Monticello F

California

Academy of Art University F
Azusa Pacific University F
California Baptist University F

California State University
Chico F
Dominguez Hills F
East Bay F
Monterey Bay F
San Bernardino F
Stanislaus F
Dominican University of
California F
Holy Names University F
Humboldt State University F
Notre Dame de Namur
University F
San Francisco State University
F
Sonoma State University F
University of California
San Diego F

Colorado

Adams State University F
Colorado Christian University F
Colorado Mesa University F
Colorado School of Mines F
Colorado State University
Pueblo F
Fort Lewis College F
Metropolitan State University of
Denver F
Regis University F
University of Colorado
Colorado Springs F

Connecticut

Post University F
Southern Connecticut State
University F
University of Bridgeport F
University of New Haven F

Delaware

Goldey-Beacom College F
Wilmington University F

Florida

Barry University F
Eckerd College F
Flagler College F
Florida Institute of Technology
F
Florida Southern College F
Lynn University F
Nova Southeastern University F
Palm Beach Atlantic University
F
Rollins College F
Saint Leo University F
University of Tampa F
University of West Florida F

Georgia

Albany State University F
Clark Atlanta University F
Columbus State University F
Emmanuel College F
Fort Valley State University F
Georgia Southwestern State
University F
Paine College F
Shorter University F
University of North Georgia F
University of West Georgia F
Valdosta State University F
Young Harris College F

Hawaii

Brigham Young University-
Hawaii F
Chaminade University of
Honolulu F
Hawaii Pacific University F
University of Hawaii
Hilo F

Idaho

Northwest Nazarene University
F

Illinois

Lewis University F
McKendree University F
Quincy University F
University of Illinois
Springfield F

Indiana

Oakland City University F
Saint Joseph's College F
University of Indianapolis F
University of Southern Indiana
F

Iowa

Upper Iowa University F

Kansas

Emporia State University F
Fort Hays State University F
Newman University F
Pittsburg State University F
Washburn University F

Kentucky

Bellarmine University F
Kentucky State University F
Kentucky Wesleyan College F
Northern Kentucky University F

Maryland

Bowie State University F

Massachusetts

American International College
F
Assumption College F
Bentley University F
Merrimack College F
Stonehill College F

Michigan

Ferris State University F
Grand Valley State University F
Hillsdale College F
Lake Superior State University
F
Northwood University
Michigan F
Saginaw Valley State University
F
Wayne State University F

Minnesota

Bemidji State University F
Concordia University St. Paul F
Minnesota State University
Mankato F
Moorhead F
Saint Cloud State University F
Southwest Minnesota State
University F
University of Minnesota
Crookston F
Duluth F
Winona State University F

Mississippi

Delta State University F
Mississippi College F

Missouri

Drury University F
Lincoln University F
Lindenwood University F
Maryville University of Saint
Louis F
Missouri Southern State
University F
Missouri University of Science
and Technology F
Missouri Western State
University F
Northwest Missouri State
University F
Rockhurst University F
Southwest Baptist University F
Truman State University F

University of Central Missouri F
William Jewell College F

Montana

Montana State University
Billings F

Nebraska

Chadron State College F
University of Nebraska
Kearney F
Wayne State College F

New Hampshire

Franklin Pierce University F
Saint Anselm College F
Southern New Hampshire
University F

New Jersey

Bloomfield College F
Georgian Court University F

New Mexico

Eastern New Mexico University
F
New Mexico Highlands
University F
Western New Mexico
University F

New York

Adelphi University F
City University of New York
Queens College F
College of Saint Rose F
Concordia College F
Dominican College of Blauvelt
F
Dowling College F
Le Moyne College F
Long Island University
LIU Post F
Mercy College F
Molloy College F
New York Institute of
Technology F
Nyack College F
Pace University F
St. Thomas Aquinas College F

North Carolina

Barton College F
Belmont Abbey College F
Brevard College F
Catawba College F
Chowan University F
Elizabeth City State University
F
Fayetteville State University F
Johnson C. Smith University F
Lees-McRae College F
Lenoir-Rhyne University F
Livingstone College F
Mars Hill University F
Pfeiffer University F
Queens University of Charlotte
F
Saint Augustine's University F
Shaw University F
University of Mount Olive F
University of North Carolina
Pembroke F
Wingate University F
Winston-Salem State University
F

North Dakota

Minot State University F
University of Mary F

Ohio

Ashland University F
Cedarville University F
Lake Erie College F
Malone University F
Notre Dame College F
Ohio Dominican University F
Tiffin University F

University of Findlay F
Urbana University F
Ursuline College F
Walsh University F

Oklahoma

Cameron University F
East Central University F
Northeastern State University F
Northwestern Oklahoma State
University F
Oklahoma Baptist University F
Oklahoma Christian University
F
Oklahoma Panhandle State
University F
Rogers State University F
Southeastern Oklahoma State
University F
Southern Nazarene University F
Southwestern Oklahoma State
University F
University of Central Oklahoma
F

Oregon

Western Oregon University F

Pennsylvania

Bloomsburg University of
Pennsylvania F
California University of
Pennsylvania F
Chestnut Hill College F
Clarion University of
Pennsylvania F
East Stroudsburg University of
Pennsylvania F
Edinboro University
of Pennsylvania F
Gannon University F
Holy Family University F
Indiana University of
Pennsylvania F
Kutztown University of
Pennsylvania F
Lincoln University F
Lock Haven University of
Pennsylvania F
Mansfield University of
Pennsylvania F
Mercyhurst University F
Millersville University of
Pennsylvania F
Philadelphia University F
Seton Hill University F
Shippensburg University of
Pennsylvania F
Slippery Rock University of
Pennsylvania F
University of Pittsburgh
Johnstown F
West Chester University of
Pennsylvania F

South Carolina

Anderson University F
Benedict College F
Claflin University F
Coker College F
Converse College F
Erskine College F
Francis Marion University F
Lander University F
Limestone College F
Newberry College F
North Greenville University F
Southern Wesleyan University F
University of South Carolina
Aiken F

South Dakota

Black Hills State University F
Northern State University F
University of Sioux Falls F

Tennessee

Carson-Newman University F
Christian Brothers University F

King University F
Lane College F
Lee University F
LeMoyne-Owen College F
Lincoln Memorial University F
Trevecca Nazarene University F
Tusculum College F
Union University F

Texas

Abilene Christian University F
Angelo State University F
Lubbock Christian University F
Midwestern State University F
St. Edward's University F
St. Mary's University F
Tarleton State University F
Texas A&M International
University F
Texas A&M University
Commerce F
Kingsville F
Texas Woman's University F
University of Texas
of the Permian Basin F
University of the Incarnate
Word F
West Texas A&M University F

Utah

Dixie State University F

Vermont

Saint Michael's College F

Virginia

University of Virginia's College
at Wise F
Virginia State University F
Virginia Union University F

Washington

Central Washington University
F
Saint Martin's University F
Western Washington University
F

West Virginia

Alderson-Broaddus University F
Bluefield State College F
Concord University F
Davis and Elkins College F
Fairmont State University F
Glenville State College F
Ohio Valley University F
Salem International University F
Shepherd University F
University of Charleston F
West Liberty University F
West Virginia State University
F
West Virginia Wesleyan
College F
Wheeling Jesuit University F

Wisconsin

University of Wisconsin
Parkside F

Canada

Simon Fraser University F

Softball Division III

Alabama

Birmingham-Southern College F
Huntingdon College F

Arkansas

Hendrix College F
University of the Ozarks F

California

California Lutheran University F
Chapman University F
Claremont McKenna College F

Harvey Mudd College F
Occidental College F
Pitzer College F
Pomona College F
Scripps College F
University of La Verne F
University of Redlands F
Whittier College F

Connecticut

Albertus Magnus College F
Eastern Connecticut State
    University F
Mitchell College F
Trinity College F
United States Coast Guard
    Academy F
University of Saint Joseph F
Wesleyan University F
Western Connecticut State
    University F

Delaware

Wesley College F

District of Columbia

Catholic University of America
    F
Gallaudet University F
Trinity Washington University F

Georgia

Agnes Scott College F
Berry College F
Covenant College F
Emory University F
Piedmont College F
Wesleyan College F

Illinois

Augustana College F
Aurora University F
Benedictine University at
    Springfield F
Blackburn College F
Concordia University Chicago F
Dominican University F
Elmhurst College F
Eureka College F
Greenville College F
Illinois College F
Illinois Wesleyan University F
Knox College F
Lake Forest College F
MacMurray College F
Millikin University F
Monmouth College F
North Central College F
North Park University F
Principia College F
Rockford University F
University of Chicago F
Wheaton College F

Indiana

Anderson University F
DePauw University F
Franklin College F
Hanover College F
Manchester University F
Rose-Hulman Institute of
    Technology F
Saint Mary's College F
Trine University F

Iowa

Buena Vista University F
Central College F
Coe College F
Cornell College F
Grinnell College F
Loras College F
Luther College F
Simpson College F
University of Dubuque F
Wartburg College F

Kentucky

Berea College F
Centre College F
Spalding University F
Thomas More College F
Transylvania University F

Louisiana

Centenary College of Louisiana
    F
Louisiana College F

Maine

Bates College F
Bowdoin College F
Colby College F
Husson University F
Saint Joseph's College of Maine
    F
Thomas College F
University of Maine
    Farmington F
    Presque Isle F
University of New England F
University of Southern Maine F

Maryland

Frostburg State University F
Hood College F
McDaniel College F
Notre Dame of Maryland
    University F
Salisbury University F
Stevenson University F
Washington College F

Massachusetts

Amherst College F
Anna Maria College F
Babson College F
Becker College F
Brandeis University F
Bridgewater State University F
Clark University F
Curry College F
Eastern Nazarene College F
Elms College F
Emerson College F
Emmanuel College F
Endicott College F
Fitchburg State University F
Framingham State University F
Gordon College F
Lasell College F
Lesley University F
Massachusetts College of
    Liberal Arts F
Massachusetts Institute of
    Technology F
Massachusetts Maritime
    Academy F
Mount Ida College F
Newbury College F
Nichols College F
Pine Manor College F
Regis College F
Salem State University F
Simmons College F
Smith College F
Springfield College F
Suffolk University F
Tufts University F
University of Massachusetts
    Dartmouth F
Wellesley College F
Wentworth Institute of
    Technology F
Western New England
    University F
Westfield State University F
Wheaton College F
Wheelock College F
Williams College F
Worcester Polytechnic Institute
    F
Worcester State University F

Michigan

Adrian College F
Albion College F
Alma College F
Calvin College F
Finlandia University F
Hope College F
Kalamazoo College F
Olivet College F

Minnesota

Augsburg College F
Bethany Lutheran College F
Bethel University F
Carleton College F
College of St. Benedict F
College of St. Scholastica F
Concordia College: Moorhead F
Gustavus Adolphus College F
Hamline University F
Macalester College F
Martin Luther College F
North Central University F
St. Catherine University F
St. Mary's University of
    Minnesota F
St. Olaf College F
University of Minnesota
    Morris F
University of Northwestern - St.
    Paul F
University of St. Thomas F

Mississippi

Belhaven University F
Millsaps College F
Rust College F

Missouri

Fontbonne University F
Webster University F
Westminster College F

Nebraska

Nebraska Wesleyan University
    F

New Hampshire

Daniel Webster College F
Keene State College F
New England College F
Plymouth State University F
Rivier University F

New Jersey

Centenary College F
The College of New Jersey F
College of St. Elizabeth F
Drew University F
Fairleigh Dickinson University
    College at Florham F
Kean University F
Montclair State University F
New Jersey City University F
Ramapo College of New Jersey
    F
Rowan University F
Rutgers, The State University of
    New Jersey
    Camden Campus F
    Newark Campus F
Stevens Institute of Technology
    F
William Paterson University of
    New Jersey F

New York

Alfred University F
Cazenovia College F
City University of New York
    Baruch College F
    Brooklyn College F
    College of Staten Island F
    Hunter College F
    John Jay College of
        Criminal Justice F
    York College F
Clarkson University F

College of Mount St. Vincent F
College of New Rochelle F
D'Youville College F
Elmira College F
Hamilton College F
Hilbert College F
Houghton College F
Ithaca College F
Keuka College F
Manhattanville College F
Medaille College F
Mount Saint Mary College F
Nazareth College F
New York University F
Rensselaer Polytechnic Institute
    F
Rochester Institute of
    Technology F
The Sage Colleges F
St. John Fisher College F
St. Joseph's College New York:
    Suffolk Campus F
St. Joseph's College, New York
    F
St. Lawrence University F
Sarah Lawrence College F
Skidmore College F
SUNY
    College at Brockport F
    College at Buffalo F
    College at Cortland F
    College at Geneseo F
    College at New Paltz F
    College at Old Westbury F
    College at Oneonta F
    College at Oswego F
    College at Plattsburgh F
    College at Potsdam F
    College at Purchase F
    College of Agriculture and
        Technology at Cobleskill
        F
    College of Agriculture and
        Technology at Morrisville
        F
    College of Technology at
        Alfred F
    College of Technology at
        Canton F
Union College F
University of Rochester F
Utica College F
Yeshiva University F

North Carolina

Greensboro College F
Guilford College F
Meredith College F
Methodist University F
North Carolina Wesleyan
    College F
Salem College F
William Peace University F

Ohio

Baldwin Wallace University F
Bluffton University F
Capital University F
Case Western Reserve
    University F
College of Wooster F
Defiance College F
Denison University F
Franciscan University of
    Steubenville F
Heidelberg University F
Hiram College F
John Carroll University F
Kenyon College F
Marietta College F
Muskingum University F
Oberlin College F
Ohio Northern University F
Ohio Wesleyan University F
Otterbein University F
University of Mount Union F
Wilmington College F
Wittenberg University F

Oregon

George Fox University F
Lewis & Clark College F
Linfield College F
Pacific University F
Willamette University F

Pennsylvania

Albright College F
Allegheny College F
Alvernia University F
Arcadia University F
Cabrini College F
Cairn University F
Cedar Crest College F
Chatham University F
DeSales University F
Dickinson College F
Eastern University F
Elizabethtown College F
Franklin & Marshall College F
Geneva College F
Gettysburg College F
Grove City College F
Gwynedd Mercy University F
Haverford College F
Immaculata University F
Juniata College F
Keystone College F
King's College F
La Roche College F
Lancaster Bible College F
Lebanon Valley College F
Lycoming College F
Marywood University F
Messiah College F
Misericordia University F
Moravian College F
Mount Aloysius College F
Muhlenberg College F
Neumann University F
Penn State
    Abington F
    Altoona F
    Berks F
    Erie, The Behrend College
        F
    Harrisburg F
Pennsylvania College of
    Technology F
Rosemont College F
St. Vincent College F
Susquehanna University F
Swarthmore College F
Thiel College F
University of Pittsburgh
    Bradford F
    Greensburg F
University of Scranton F
Ursinus College F
Washington & Jefferson College
    F
Waynesburg University F
Westminster College F
Widener University F
Wilkes University F
Wilson College F
York College of Pennsylvania F

Rhode Island

Rhode Island College F
Roger Williams University F
Salve Regina University F

Tennessee

Maryville College F
Rhodes College F
Sewanee: The University of the
    South F

Texas

Austin College F
Concordia University Texas F
East Texas Baptist University F
Hardin-Simmons University F
Howard Payne University F
LeTourneau University F
Schreiner University F

Tables and Indexes

Southwestern University F
Sul Ross State University F
Texas Lutheran University F
Trinity University F
University of Dallas F
University of Mary Hardin-
Baylor F
University of Texas
Dallas F
Tyler F

Vermont

Johnson State College F
Lyndon State College F
Middlebury College F
Norwich University F
Southern Vermont College F

Virginia

Averett University F
Bridgewater College F
Christopher Newport University
F
Eastern Mennonite University F
Emory & Henry College F
Ferrum College F
Lynchburg College F
Mary Baldwin College F
Randolph College F
Randolph-Macon College F
Roanoke College F
Shenandoah University F
Southern Virginia University F
Sweet Briar College F
University of Mary Washington
F
Virginia Wesleyan College F

Washington

Pacific Lutheran University F
University of Puget Sound F
Whitworth University F

West Virginia

Bethany College F

Wisconsin

Alverno College F
Beloit College F
Carroll University F
Carthage College F
Edgewood College F
Lakeland College F
Lawrence University F
Maranathan Baptist University
Maranatha Baptist
University F
Marian University F
Milwaukee School of
Engineering F
Mount Mary University F
Northland College F
Ripon College F
St. Norbert College F
University of Wisconsin
Eau Claire F
La Crosse F
Platteville F
Stevens Point F
Superior F
Wisconsin Lutheran College F

**Swimming and diving
Division I**

Alabama

Auburn University
University of Alabama

Arizona

Arizona State University
Northern Arizona University F
University of Arizona

Arkansas

University of Arkansas F

California

California Polytechnic State
University: San Luis Obispo
California State University
Bakersfield
Fresno F
Loyola Marymount University F
Pepperdine University F
San Diego State University F
San Jose State University F
Stanford University
University of California
Berkeley
Davis F
Los Angeles F
Santa Barbara
University of San Diego F
University of Southern
California
University of the Pacific

Colorado

Colorado State University F
United States Air Force
Academy
University of Denver
University of Northern Colorado
F

Connecticut

Central Connecticut State
University F
Fairfield University
Sacred Heart University F
University of Connecticut
Yale University

Delaware

University of Delaware

District of Columbia

American University
George Washington University
Georgetown University
Howard University

Florida

Florida Atlantic University
Florida Gulf Coast University F
Florida International University
F
Florida State University
University of Florida
University of Miami
University of North Florida F

Georgia

Georgia Institute of Technology
Georgia Southern University F
University of Georgia

Hawaii

University of Hawaii
Manoa

Idaho

Boise State University F
University of Idaho F

Illinois

Eastern Illinois University
Illinois State University F
Northwestern University
Southern Illinois University
Carbondale
University of Illinois
Chicago
Western Illinois University

Indiana

Ball State University
Butler University F
Indiana University
Bloomington
Purdue University
Indianapolis

Purdue University
University of Evansville
University of Notre Dame
Valparaiso University

Iowa

Iowa State University F
University of Iowa
University of Northern Iowa F

Kansas

University of Kansas F

Kentucky

University of Kentucky
University of Louisville

Louisiana

Louisiana State University and
Agricultural and Mechanical
College
Tulane University F

Maine

University of Maine

Maryland

Loyola University Maryland
Mount St. Mary's University F
Towson University
United States Naval Academy
University of Maryland
Baltimore County

Massachusetts

Boston College
Boston University
College of the Holy Cross
Harvard College
Northeastern University F
University of Massachusetts
Amherst

Michigan

Eastern Michigan University
Michigan State University
Oakland University
University of Michigan

Minnesota

University of Minnesota
Twin Cities

Missouri

Missouri State University
Saint Louis University
University of Missouri
Columbia

Nebraska

University of Nebraska
Lincoln F
Omaha F

Nevada

University of Nevada
Las Vegas

New Hampshire

Dartmouth College
University of New Hampshire F

New Jersey

Monmouth University
New Jersey Institute of
Technology M
Princeton University
Rider University
Seton Hall University

New Mexico

New Mexico State University F
University of New Mexico F

New York

Barnard College
Canisius College
Colgate University
Columbia University
Cornell University
Fordham University

Iona College
Long Island University
LIU Brooklyn F
Manhattan College
Marist College
Niagara University
Saint Bonaventure University
St. Francis College
Siena College F
SUNY
University at Binghamton
University at Buffalo
United States Military Academy
Wagner College F

North Carolina

Campbell University F
Davidson College
Duke University
East Carolina University
Gardner-Webb University
North Carolina Agricultural and
Technical State University F
North Carolina State University
University of North Carolina
Asheville F
Chapel Hill

North Dakota

University of North Dakota

Ohio

Bowling Green State University
F
Cleveland State University
Miami University
Oxford
Ohio State University
Columbus Campus
Ohio University F
University of Akron F
University of Cincinnati
University of Toledo F
Wright State University
Xavier University
Youngstown State University F

Oregon

Oregon State University F

Pennsylvania

Bucknell University
Drexel University
Duquesne University F
La Salle University
Lafayette College
Lehigh University
Penn State
University Park
St. Francis University F
University of Pennsylvania
University of Pittsburgh
Villanova University

Rhode Island

Brown University
Bryant University
Providence College
University of Rhode Island F

South Carolina

Clemson University F
University of South Carolina
Columbia

South Dakota

South Dakota State University
University of South Dakota

Tennessee

University of Tennessee
Knoxville
Vanderbilt University F

Texas

Rice University F
Southern Methodist University
Texas A&M University
Texas Christian University
University of Houston F

University of North Texas F
University of Texas
Austin

Utah

Brigham Young University
University of Utah

Vermont

University of Vermont F

Virginia

College of William and Mary
George Mason University
James Madison University F
Liberty University F
Old Dominion University
University of Richmond F
University of Virginia
Virginia Military Institute

Washington

Seattle University
Washington State University F

West Virginia

Marshall University F
West Virginia University

Wisconsin

University of Wisconsin
Green Bay
Madison
Milwaukee

Wyoming

University of Wyoming

**Swimming and diving
Division II**

Alaska

University of Alaska
Fairbanks F

Arizona

Grand Canyon University

Arkansas

Henderson State University
Ouachita Baptist University

California

Azusa Pacific University F
California Baptist University
California State University
East Bay F
Fresno Pacific University
University of California
San Diego

Colorado

Adams State University
Colorado Mesa University
Colorado School of Mines
Colorado State University
Pueblo F
Western State Colorado
University F

Connecticut

Southern Connecticut State
University
University of Bridgeport

Florida

Florida Institute of Technology
Florida Southern College
Lynn University F
Nova Southeastern University
Rollins College
Saint Leo University
University of Tampa
University of West Florida F

Georgia

Emmanuel College

Illinois

Lewis University
Quincy University F

Indiana

University of Indianapolis

Kentucky

Bellarmine University

Massachusetts

Assumption College F
Bentley University
Merrimack College F

Michigan

Grand Valley State University
Hillsdale College F
Northern Michigan University
Saginaw Valley State University
Wayne State University

Minnesota

Minnesota State University
    Mankato F
    Moorhead F
Saint Cloud State University

Mississippi

Delta State University

Missouri

Drury University
Lindenwood University
Maryville University of Saint
    Louis
Missouri University of Science
    and Technology M
Truman State University
William Jewell College

Nebraska

University of Nebraska
    Kearney F

New York

Adelphi University
City University of New York
    Queens College
College of Saint Rose
Le Moyne College
Long Island University
    LIU Post F
Pace University

North Carolina

Catawba College
Lenoir-Rhyne University
Mars Hill University
Queens University of Charlotte
Wingate University

Ohio

Ashland University
Malone University
Notre Dame College
Tiffin University
University of Findlay
Urbana University
Ursuline College F

Oklahoma

Oklahoma Baptist University

Pennsylvania

Bloomsburg University of
    Pennsylvania
California University of
    Pennsylvania F
Clarion University of
    Pennsylvania
East Stroudsburg University of
    Pennsylvania F
Edinboro University
    of Pennsylvania
Gannon University

Indiana University of
    Pennsylvania
Kutztown University of
    Pennsylvania F
Lock Haven University of
    Pennsylvania F
Millersville University of
    Pennsylvania F
Shippensburg University of
    Pennsylvania
West Chester University of
    Pennsylvania

South Carolina

Converse College F
Limestone College

South Dakota

Northern State University F

Tennessee

Carson-Newman University
King University

Texas

University of Texas
    of the Permian Basin
University of the Incarnate
    Word

Vermont

Saint Michael's College

West Virginia

Alderson-Broaddus University
Davis and Elkins College
Fairmont State University
West Virginia Wesleyan College
Wheeling Jesuit University

Canada

Simon Fraser University

Swimming and diving Division III

Alabama

Birmingham-Southern College

Arkansas

Hendrix College

California

California Institute of
    Technology
California Lutheran University
Chapman University
Claremont McKenna College
Harvey Mudd College
Mills College F
Occidental College
Pitzer College
Pomona College
Scripps College
University of California
    Santa Cruz
University of La Verne
University of Redlands
Whittier College

Colorado

Colorado College

Connecticut

Connecticut College
Eastern Connecticut State
    University F
Trinity College
United States Coast Guard
    Academy
University of Saint Joseph F
Wesleyan University
Western Connecticut State
    University F

District of Columbia

Catholic University of America
Gallaudet University

Georgia

Berry College
Emory University

Illinois

Augustana College
Eureka College
Illinois College
Illinois Institute of Technology
Illinois Wesleyan University
Knox College
Lake Forest College
Millikin University
Monmouth College
North Central College
Principia College
University of Chicago
Wheaton College

Indiana

DePauw University
Franklin College
Manchester University
Rose-Hulman Institute of
    Technology
Wabash College M

Iowa

Coe College
Grinnell College
Loras College
Luther College
Simpson College

Kentucky

Centre College
Transylvania University

Louisiana

Centenary College of Louisiana

Maine

Bates College
Bowdoin College
Colby College
Husson University
Saint Joseph's College of Maine
University of New England F

Maryland

Frostburg State University
Goucher College
Hood College
Johns Hopkins University
McDaniel College
Notre Dame of Maryland
    University F
St. Mary's College of Maryland
Salisbury University
Stevenson University
Washington College

Massachusetts

Amherst College
Babson College
Brandeis University
Bridgewater State University
Clark University
Elms College
Gordon College
Massachusetts Institute of
    Technology
Mount Holyoke College F
Regis College
Simmons College F
Smith College F
Springfield College
Tufts University
University of Massachusetts
    Dartmouth
Wellesley College F
Western New England
    University F
Westfield State University F
Wheaton College
Williams College
Worcester Polytechnic Institute

Michigan

Albion College
Alma College
Calvin College
Hope College
Kalamazoo College
Olivet College

Minnesota

Augsburg College F
Carleton College
College of St. Benedict F
Concordia College: Moorhead F
Gustavus Adolphus College
Hamline University
Macalester College
St. Catherine University F
St. John's University M
St. Mary's University of
    Minnesota
St. Olaf College
University of Minnesota
    Morris F
University of St. Thomas

Nebraska

Nebraska Wesleyan University

New Hampshire

Colby-Sawyer College
Keene State College
Plymouth State University F

New Jersey

The College of New Jersey
Drew University
Fairleigh Dickinson University
    College at Florham
Montclair State University
Ramapo College of New Jersey
Rowan University
Stevens Institute of Technology
William Paterson University of
    New Jersey

New York

Alfred University
Bard College
Cazenovia College
City University of New York
    Baruch College
    Brooklyn College
    College of Staten Island
    Hunter College F
    John Jay College of
        Criminal Justice F
    York College
Clarkson University
College of Mount St. Vincent
College of New Rochelle F
Hamilton College
Hartwick College
Ithaca College
Mount Saint Mary College
Nazareth College
New York University
Rensselaer Polytechnic Institute
Rochester Institute of
    Technology
St. Joseph's College New York:
    Suffolk Campus F
St. Joseph's College, New York
    F
St. Lawrence University
Sarah Lawrence College
Skidmore College
SUNY
    College at Brockport
    College at Buffalo
    College at Cortland
    College at Geneseo
    College at New Paltz
    College at Old Westbury
    College at Oneonta
    College at Oswego
    College at Potsdam
    College at Purchase
    College of Agriculture and
        Technology at Cobleskill
    College of Technology at
        Alfred
    Maritime College

Union College
United States Merchant Marine
    Academy
University of Rochester
Utica College
Vassar College
Wells College

North Carolina

Greensboro College
Guilford College F

Ohio

Baldwin Wallace University
Case Western Reserve
    University
College of Wooster
Denison University
Franciscan University of
    Steubenville F
Hiram College
John Carroll University
Kenyon College
Oberlin College
Ohio Northern University
Ohio Wesleyan University
University of Mount Union
Wilmington College
Wittenberg University

Oregon

Lewis & Clark College
Linfield College
Pacific University
Willamette University

Pennsylvania

Albright College
Allegheny College
Arcadia University
Bryn Mawr College F
Cabrini College
Carnegie Mellon University
Cedar Crest College F
Chatham University
Dickinson College
Elizabethtown College
Franklin & Marshall College
Gettysburg College
Grove City College
Juniata College F
King's College
Lebanon Valley College
Lycoming College
Marywood University
Messiah College
Misericordia University
Penn State
    Altoona
    Erie, The Behrend College
St. Vincent College
Susquehanna University
Swarthmore College
University of Pittsburgh
    Bradford
University of Scranton
Ursinus College
Washington & Jefferson College
Westminster College
Widener University
Wilkes University
York College of Pennsylvania

Rhode Island

Rhode Island College F
Roger Williams University

Tennessee

Rhodes College
Sewanee: The University of the
    South

Texas

Austin College
McMurry University
Southwestern University
Trinity University

Vermont

Middlebury College
Norwich University

Virginia

Bridgewater College F
Emory & Henry College F
Ferrum College
Hampden-Sydney College M
Hollins University F
Marymount University
Randolph-Macon College
Sweet Briar College F
University of Mary Washington
Washington and Lee University

Washington

Pacific Lutheran University
University of Puget Sound
Whitman College
Whitworth University

West Virginia

Bethany College

Wisconsin

Beloit College
Carroll University
Carthage College
Lawrence University
Ripon College
University of Wisconsin
  Eau Claire
  La Crosse
  Stevens Point

Tennis Division I

Alabama

Alabama Agricultural and
  Mechanical University
Alabama State University
Auburn University
Jacksonville State University
Samford University
Troy University
University of Alabama
University of Alabama
  Birmingham
University of South Alabama

Arizona

Arizona State University F
Northern Arizona University
University of Arizona

Arkansas

Arkansas State University F
University of Arkansas
  Pine Bluff
University of Central Arkansas
  F

California

California Polytechnic State
  University: San Luis Obispo
California State University
  Fresno
  Fullerton F
  Long Beach F
  Northridge F
  Sacramento
Loyola Marymount University
Pepperdine University
St. Mary's College of California
San Diego State University
San Jose State University F
Santa Clara University
Stanford University
University of California
  Berkeley
  Davis
  Irvine
  Los Angeles
  Riverside
  Santa Barbara

University of San Diego
University of San Francisco
University of Southern
  California
University of the Pacific

Colorado

Colorado State University F
United States Air Force
  Academy
University of Colorado
  Boulder F
University of Denver
University of Northern Colorado

Connecticut

Fairfield University
Quinnipiac University
Sacred Heart University
University of Connecticut
University of Hartford
Yale University

Delaware

Delaware State University F
University of Delaware

District of Columbia

George Washington University
Georgetown University
Howard University

Florida

Bethune-Cookman University
Florida Agricultural and
  Mechanical University
Florida Atlantic University
Florida Gulf Coast University
Florida International University
  F
Florida State University
Stetson University
University of Central Florida
University of Florida
University of Miami
University of North Florida
University of South Florida

Georgia

Georgia Institute of Technology
Georgia Southern University
Georgia State University
Kennesaw State University
Mercer University
Savannah State University F
University of Georgia

Hawaii

University of Hawaii
  Manoa

Idaho

Boise State University
Idaho State University
University of Idaho

Illinois

Bradley University F
Chicago State University
DePaul University
Eastern Illinois University
Illinois State University
Northern Illinois University
Northwestern University
Southern Illinois University
  Carbondale
Southern Illinois University
  Edwardsville
University of Illinois
  Chicago
Western Illinois University

Indiana

Ball State University
Butler University
Indiana University
  Bloomington
  Purdue University
  Indianapolis
Purdue University

University of Evansville F
University of Notre Dame
Valparaiso University

Iowa

Drake University
Iowa State University F
University of Iowa
University of Northern Iowa F

Kansas

Kansas State University F
University of Kansas F
Wichita State University

Kentucky

Eastern Kentucky University
Morehead State University
Murray State University
University of Kentucky
University of Louisville
Western Kentucky University F

Louisiana

Grambling State University F
Louisiana State University and
  Agricultural and Mechanical
  College
Louisiana Tech University F
McNeese State University F
Nicholls State University
Northwestern State University F
Southeastern Louisiana
  University F
Southern University and
  Agricultural and Mechanical
  College F
Tulane University
University of Louisiana at
  Lafayette
University of Louisiana at
  Monroe F
University of New Orleans

Maryland

Coppin State University
Loyola University Maryland
Morgan State University
Mount St. Mary's University
Towson University F
United States Naval Academy
University of Maryland
  Baltimore County
  College Park F
  Eastern Shore

Massachusetts

Boston College
Boston University
College of the Holy Cross
Harvard College
University of Massachusetts
  Amherst F

Michigan

Eastern Michigan University F
Michigan State University
Oakland University F
University of Detroit Mercy
University of Michigan
Western Michigan University

Minnesota

University of Minnesota
  Twin Cities

Mississippi

Alcorn State University
Jackson State University
Mississippi State University
University of Mississippi

Missouri

Missouri State University F
Saint Louis University
Southeast Missouri State
  University F
University of Missouri
  Columbia F
  Kansas City

Montana

Montana State University
University of Montana

Nebraska

Creighton University
University of Nebraska
  Lincoln
  Omaha

Nevada

University of Nevada
  Las Vegas

New Hampshire

Dartmouth College

New Jersey

Fairleigh Dickinson University
  Metropolitan Campus
Monmouth University
New Jersey Institute of
  Technology
Princeton University
Rider University
Seton Hall University F

New Mexico

New Mexico State University
University of New Mexico

New York

Barnard College
Colgate University
Columbia University
Cornell University
Fordham University
Hofstra University
Long Island University
  LIU Brooklyn F
Marist College
Niagara University
Saint Bonaventure University
St. Francis College
St. John's University
Siena College
SUNY
  University at Albany F
  University at Binghamton
  University at Buffalo
  University at Stony Brook
Syracuse University F
United States Military Academy
Wagner College

North Carolina

Appalachian State University
Campbell University
Davidson College
Duke University
East Carolina University
Elon University
Gardner-Webb University
North Carolina Agricultural and
  Technical State University
North Carolina Central
  University
North Carolina State University
University of North Carolina
  Asheville
  Chapel Hill
Wake Forest University
Western Carolina University F

North Dakota

University of North Dakota

Ohio

Bowling Green State University
  F
Cleveland State University
Miami University
  Oxford F
Ohio State University
  Columbus Campus
University of Akron F
University of Cincinnati F
University of Dayton
University of Toledo

Wright State University
Xavier University
Youngstown State University

Oklahoma

Oklahoma State University
Oral Roberts University
University of Oklahoma

Oregon

Portland State University
University of Oregon
University of Portland

Pennsylvania

Bucknell University
Drexel University
Duquesne University
La Salle University
Lafayette College
Lehigh University
Penn State
  University Park
St. Francis University
Saint Joseph's University
Temple University
University of Pennsylvania
University of Pittsburgh F
Villanova University

Rhode Island

Brown University
Bryant University
Providence College F
University of Rhode Island F

South Carolina

Charleston Southern University
  F
The Citadel M
Clemson University
Coastal Carolina University
College of Charleston
Furman University
Presbyterian College
South Carolina State University
University of South Carolina
  Columbia
  Upstate
Winthrop University
Wofford College

South Dakota

South Dakota State University
University of South Dakota F

Tennessee

Austin Peay State University
Belmont University
East Tennessee State University
Lipscomb University
Middle Tennessee State
  University
Tennessee State University
Tennessee Technological
  University M
University of Memphis
University of Tennessee
  Chattanooga
  Knoxville
  Martin F
Vanderbilt University

Texas

Baylor University
Lamar University
Prairie View A&M University
Rice University
Sam Houston State University F
Southern Methodist University
Stephen F. Austin State
  University F
Texas A&M University
  Corpus Christi
Texas Christian University
Texas Tech University
University of Houston F
University of North Texas F

University of Texas
Arlington
Austin
El Paso F
San Antonio

Utah

Brigham Young University
Southern Utah University
University of Utah
Utah State University
Weber State University

Virginia

College of William and Mary
George Mason University
Hampton University
James Madison University
Liberty University
Longwood University
Norfolk State University
Old Dominion University
Radford University
University of Richmond
University of Virginia
Virginia Commonwealth
University

Washington

Eastern Washington University
Gonzaga University
Seattle University
University of Washington
Washington State University F

West Virginia

Marshall University F
West Virginia University F

Wisconsin

Marquette University
University of Wisconsin
Green Bay
Madison
Milwaukee F

Wyoming

University of Wyoming F

Tennis Division II

Alabama

Auburn University at
Montgomery
Spring Hill College
Stillman College
Tuskegee University
University of Alabama
Huntsville
University of Montevallo F
University of North Alabama
University of West Alabama

Arizona

Grand Canyon University

Arkansas

Arkansas Tech University F
Harding University
Henderson State University F
Ouachita Baptist University
University of Arkansas
Fort Smith

California

Academy of Art University F
Azusa Pacific University
California State University
Los Angeles F
Stanislaus F
Dominican University of
California F
Holy Names University
Notre Dame de Namur
University F
Point Loma Nazarene University
Sonoma State University

University of California
San Diego

Colorado

Colorado Christian University
Colorado Mesa University
Colorado State University
Pueblo
Metropolitan State University of
Denver

Connecticut

Post University
University of New Haven F

Delaware

Goldey-Beacom College F

District of Columbia

University of the District of
Columbia

Florida

Barry University
Eckerd College
Flagler College
Florida Institute of Technology
Florida Southern College
Lynn University
Nova Southeastern University F
Palm Beach Atlantic University
Rollins College
Saint Leo University
University of Tampa F
University of West Florida

Georgia

Albany State University F
Clark Atlanta University F
Clayton State University F
Columbus State University
Emmanuel College
Fort Valley State University
Georgia Southwestern State
University
Morehouse College M
Shorter University
University of North Georgia
University of West Georgia F
Valdosta State University
Young Harris College

Hawaii

Brigham Young University-
Hawaii
Chaminade University of
Honolulu F
Hawaii Pacific University
University of Hawaii
Hilo

Illinois

Lewis University
McKendree University
Quincy University
University of Illinois
Springfield

Indiana

Oakland City University
Saint Joseph's College
University of Indianapolis
University of Southern Indiana

Iowa

Upper Iowa University F

Kansas

Emporia State University
Fort Hays State University F
Newman University
Washburn University

Kentucky

Bellarmine University
Kentucky Wesleyan College F
Northern Kentucky University

Maryland

Bowie State University F

Massachusetts

American International College
Assumption College
Bentley University
Merrimack College
Stonehill College

Michigan

Ferris State University
Grand Valley State University
Hillsdale College
Lake Superior State University
Michigan Technological
University
Northwood University
Michigan
Saginaw Valley State University
F
Wayne State University

Minnesota

Bemidji State University F
Minnesota State University
Mankato F
Moorhead F
Saint Cloud State University
Southwest Minnesota State
University F
University of Minnesota
Crookston F
Duluth F
Winona State University F

Mississippi

Delta State University
Mississippi College

Missouri

Drury University
Lincoln University F
Lindenwood University
Maryville University of Saint
Louis F
Missouri Western State
University F
Northwest Missouri State
University
Rockhurst University
Southwest Baptist University
Truman State University
William Jewell College

Nebraska

University of Nebraska
Kearney

New Hampshire

Franklin Pierce University
Saint Anselm College
Southern New Hampshire
University

New Jersey

Bloomfield College M

New Mexico

Western New Mexico
University

New York

Adelphi University
City University of New York
Queens College
College of Saint Rose F
Concordia College
Daemen College
Le Moyne College
Long Island University
LIU Post F
Molloy College F
New York Institute of
Technology
Roberts Wesleyan College
St. Thomas Aquinas College

North Carolina

Barton College
Belmont Abbey College
Brevard College
Catawba College
Chowan University
Elizabeth City State University
F
Fayetteville State University F
Johnson C. Smith University
Lees-McRae College
Lenoir-Rhyne University
Livingstone College F
Mars Hill University
Pfeiffer University
Queens University of Charlotte
Shaw University
University of Mount Olive
Wingate University
Winston-Salem State University
F

North Dakota

University of Mary F

Ohio

Ashland University F
Cedarville University
Tiffin University
University of Findlay
Ursuline College F
Walsh University

Oklahoma

Cameron University
East Central University
Northeastern State University F
Oklahoma Baptist University
Southeastern Oklahoma State
University
Southern Nazarene University F
University of Central Oklahoma
F

Pennsylvania

Bloomsburg University of
Pennsylvania
California University of
Pennsylvania F
Chestnut Hill College
Cheyney University of
Pennsylvania F
Clarion University of
Pennsylvania F
East Stroudsburg University of
Pennsylvania F
Edinboro University
of Pennsylvania
Holy Family University F
Indiana University of
Pennsylvania F
Kutztown University of
Pennsylvania
Mercyhurst University
Millersville University of
Pennsylvania
Philadelphia University
Seton Hill University F
Shippensburg University of
Pennsylvania F
Slippery Rock University of
Pennsylvania F
West Chester University of
Pennsylvania

Puerto Rico

University of Puerto Rico
Bayamon University
College
Rio Piedras

South Carolina

Anderson University
Benedict College
Coker College
Converse College F
Erskine College
Francis Marion University

Lander University
Limestone College
Newberry College
North Greenville University
Southern Wesleyan University
University of South Carolina
Aiken

South Dakota

University of Sioux Falls F

Tennessee

Carson-Newman University
Christian Brothers University
King University
Lane College
Lee University
LeMoyne-Owen College
Lincoln Memorial University
Tusculum College

Texas

Abilene Christian University
Dallas Baptist University
Midwestern State University
St. Edward's University
St. Mary's University
Tarleton State University F
Texas A&M University
Kingsville F
University of Texas
of the Permian Basin
University of the Incarnate
Word

Utah

Dixie State University F

Vermont

Saint Michael's College

Virginia

University of Virginia's College
at Wise
Virginia State University
Virginia Union University

West Virginia

Alderson-Broaddus University F
Bluefield State College
Concord University
Davis and Elkins College
Fairmont State University
Salem International University
Shepherd University
University of Charleston
West Liberty University
West Virginia State University
West Virginia Wesleyan College

Tennis Division III

Alabama

Birmingham-Southern College
Huntingdon College

Arkansas

Hendrix College
University of the Ozarks

California

California Institute of
Technology
California Lutheran University
Chapman University
Claremont McKenna College
Harvey Mudd College
Mills College F
Occidental College
Pitzer College
Pomona College
Scripps College
University of California
Santa Cruz
University of La Verne F
University of Redlands
Whittier College

Colorado

Colorado College

Connecticut

Albertus Magnus College
Connecticut College
Mitchell College
Trinity College
United States Coast Guard
Academy M
University of Saint Joseph F
Wesleyan University
Western Connecticut State
University

District of Columbia

Catholic University of America
Trinity Washington University F

Georgia

Agnes Scott College F
Berry College
Covenant College
Emory University
Oglethorpe University
Piedmont College
Wesleyan College F

Illinois

Augustana College
Aurora University
Benedictine University at
Springfield F
Blackburn College F
Concordia University Chicago
Dominican University
Elmhurst College
Greenville College
Illinois College
Illinois Wesleyan University
Knox College
Lake Forest College
Millikin University
Monmouth College
North Central College
North Park University F
Principia College
University of Chicago
Wheaton College

Indiana

Anderson University
DePauw University
Earlham College
Franklin College
Hanover College
Manchester University
Rose-Hulman Institute of
Technology
Saint Mary's College F
Trine University
Wabash College M

Iowa

Buena Vista University
Central College
Coe College
Cornell College
Grinnell College
Loras College
Luther College
Simpson College
University of Dubuque
Wartburg College

Kentucky

Berea College
Centre College
Thomas More College
Transylvania University

Louisiana

Centenary College of Louisiana
Louisiana College

Maine

Bates College
Bowdoin College
Colby College

Husson University F
Thomas College
University of Southern Maine

Maryland

Frostburg State University
Goucher College
Hood College
Johns Hopkins University
McDaniel College
Notre Dame of Maryland
University F
St. Mary's College of Maryland
Salisbury University
Stevenson University
Washington College

Massachusetts

Amherst College
Anna Maria College F
Babson College
Becker College
Brandeis University
Bridgewater State University
Clark University
Curry College
Eastern Nazarene College
Emerson College
Endicott College
Gordon College
Lesley University
Massachusetts College of
Liberal Arts
Massachusetts Institute of
Technology
Mount Holyoke College F
Mount Ida College F
Newbury College
Nichols College
Regis College
Salem State University
Simmons College F
Smith College F
Springfield College
Suffolk University
Tufts University
University of Massachusetts
Dartmouth
Wellesley College F
Wentworth Institute of
Technology
Western New England
University
Wheaton College
Wheelock College M
Williams College
Worcester State University F

Michigan

Adrian College
Albion College
Alma College
Calvin College
Hope College
Kalamazoo College
Olivet College

Minnesota

Bethany Lutheran College
Bethel University
Carleton College
College of St. Benedict F
College of St. Scholastica
Concordia College: Moorhead
Gustavus Adolphus College
Hamline University
Macalester College
Martin Luther College
North Central University
St. Catherine University F
St. John's University M
St. Mary's University of
Minnesota
St. Olaf College
University of Minnesota
Morris

University of Northwestern - St.
Paul
University of St. Thomas

Mississippi

Belhaven University
Millsaps College
Rust College

Missouri

Fontbonne University
Webster University
Westminster College

Nebraska

Nebraska Wesleyan University

New Hampshire

Colby-Sawyer College
Plymouth State University F

New Jersey

The College of New Jersey
College of St. Elizabeth F
Drew University
Fairleigh Dickinson University
College at Florham
Kean University F
Ramapo College of New Jersey
Rutgers, The State University of
New Jersey
Camden Campus
Newark Campus
Stevens Institute of Technology
William Paterson University of
New Jersey F

New York

Alfred University
Bard College
City University of New York
Baruch College
Brooklyn College
City College
College of Staten Island
Hunter College
John Jay College of
Criminal Justice
York College M
College of New Rochelle F
D'Youville College
Elmira College
Hamilton College
Hartwick College
Houghton College
Ithaca College
Keuka College
Medaille College F
Mount Saint Mary College
Nazareth College
New York University
Rensselaer Polytechnic Institute
Rochester Institute of
Technology
The Sage Colleges
St. John Fisher College
St. Joseph's College New York:
Suffolk Campus
St. Joseph's College, New York
St. Lawrence University
Sarah Lawrence College
Skidmore College
SUNY
College at Brockport F
College at Cortland F
College at Geneseo F
College at New Paltz F
College at Oneonta
College at Oswego
College at Plattsburgh F
College at Purchase
Union College
United States Merchant Marine
Academy M
University of Rochester
Utica College
Vassar College
Wells College F
Yeshiva University

North Carolina

Greensboro College
Guilford College
Meredith College F
Methodist University
North Carolina Wesleyan
College
Salem College F
William Peace University

Ohio

Baldwin Wallace University
Capital University
Case Western Reserve
University
College of Wooster
Defiance College
Denison University
Franciscan University of
Steubenville
Heidelberg University
John Carroll University
Kenyon College
Marietta College
Muskingum University
Oberlin College
Ohio Northern University
Ohio Wesleyan University
Otterbein University
University of Mount Union
Wittenberg University

Oregon

George Fox University
Lewis & Clark College
Linfield College
Pacific University
Willamette University

Pennsylvania

Albright College
Allegheny College
Alvernia University
Arcadia University
Bryn Athyn College
Bryn Mawr College F
Cabrini College
Cairn University F
Carnegie Mellon University
Cedar Crest College F
Dickinson College
Eastern University
Elizabethtown College
Franklin & Marshall College
Geneva College F
Gettysburg College
Grove City College
Gwynedd Mercy University
Haverford College
Immaculata University
Juniata College
Keystone College
King's College
La Roche College F
Lancaster Bible College
Lebanon Valley College
Lycoming College
Marywood University
Messiah College
Misericordia University
Moravian College
Mount Aloysius College
Muhlenberg College
Neumann University
Penn State
Abington
Altoona
Berks
Erie, The Behrend College
Harrisburg
Pennsylvania College of
Technology
Rosemont College
St. Vincent College
Susquehanna University
Swarthmore College
Thiel College

University of Pittsburgh
Bradford
Greensburg
University of Scranton
Ursinus College
Washington & Jefferson College
Waynesburg University
Westminster College
Wilkes University
York College of Pennsylvania

Rhode Island

Rhode Island College
Roger Williams University
Salve Regina University

Tennessee

Maryville College
Rhodes College
Sewanee: The University of the
South

Texas

Austin College
Concordia University Texas
East Texas Baptist University
Hardin-Simmons University
Howard Payne University
LeTourneau University
McMurry University
Schreiner University
Southwestern University
Sul Ross State University
Texas Lutheran University
Trinity University
University of Mary Hardin-
Baylor
University of Texas
Dallas
Tyler

Vermont

Green Mountain College
Johnson State College
Lyndon State College
Middlebury College
Norwich University M

Virginia

Averett University
Bridgewater College
Christopher Newport University
Emory & Henry College
Ferrum College
Hampden-Sydney College M
Hollins University F
Lynchburg College
Mary Baldwin College F
Randolph College
Randolph-Macon College
Roanoke College
Shenandoah University
Southern Virginia University
Sweet Briar College F
University of Mary Washington
Virginia Wesleyan College
Washington and Lee University

Washington

Pacific Lutheran University
University of Puget Sound
Whitman College
Whitworth University

West Virginia

Bethany College

Wisconsin

Alverno College F
Beloit College F
Carroll University
Carthage College
Edgewood College
Lakeland College
Lawrence University
Marian University
Milwaukee School of
Engineering
Mount Mary University F

Ripon College
St. Norbert College
University of Wisconsin
  Eau Claire
  La Crosse
  Stevens Point F
Wisconsin Lutheran College

Track, indoor Division I

Alabama

Alabama Agricultural and
  Mechanical University
Alabama State University
Auburn University
Jacksonville State University F
Samford University
Troy University F
University of Alabama
University of Alabama
  Birmingham F
University of South Alabama

Arizona

Arizona State University
Northern Arizona University
University of Arizona

Arkansas

Arkansas State University
University of Arkansas
  Pine Bluff
University of Central Arkansas

California

California Polytechnic State
  University: San Luis Obispo
  F
California State University
  Bakersfield F
  Fresno F
  Fullerton F
  Long Beach
  Northridge
  Sacramento
San Diego State University F
San Jose State University F
Stanford University
University of California
  Berkeley
  Davis F
  Irvine F
  Los Angeles
  Riverside
  Santa Barbara F
University of San Francisco
University of Southern
  California

Colorado

Colorado State University
United States Air Force
  Academy
University of Colorado
  Boulder
University of Northern Colorado

Connecticut

Central Connecticut State
  University
Quinnipiac University F
Sacred Heart University
University of Connecticut
University of Hartford
Yale University

Delaware

Delaware State University
University of Delaware F

District of Columbia

American University
George Washington University
Georgetown University
Howard University

Florida

Bethune-Cookman University
Florida Agricultural and
  Mechanical University
Florida Atlantic University F
Florida Gulf Coast University F
Florida International University
Florida State University
Jacksonville University F
University of Central Florida F
University of Florida
University of Miami
University of North Florida
University of South Florida

Georgia

Georgia Institute of Technology
Georgia Southern University F
Georgia State University F
Kennesaw State University
Savannah State University
University of Georgia

Hawaii

University of Hawaii
  Manoa F

Idaho

Boise State University
Idaho State University
University of Idaho

Illinois

Bradley University
Chicago State University
DePaul University
Eastern Illinois University
Illinois State University
Loyola University Chicago
Northern Illinois University F
Northwestern University F
Southern Illinois University
  Carbondale
Southern Illinois University
  Edwardsville
University of Illinois
  Chicago
Western Illinois University

Indiana

Ball State University F
Butler University
Indiana State University
Indiana University
  Bloomington
  Purdue University Fort
    Wayne F
  Purdue University
    Indianapolis
Purdue University
University of Notre Dame
Valparaiso University

Iowa

Drake University
Iowa State University
University of Iowa
University of Northern Iowa

Kansas

Kansas State University
University of Kansas
Wichita State University

Kentucky

Eastern Kentucky University
Murray State University F
University of Kentucky
University of Louisville
Western Kentucky University

Louisiana

Grambling State University
Louisiana State University and
  Agricultural and Mechanical
  College
Louisiana Tech University
McNeese State University
Nicholls State University F

Northwestern State University
Southeastern Louisiana
  University
Southern University and
  Agricultural and Mechanical
  College
Tulane University F
University of Louisiana at
  Lafayette
University of Louisiana at
  Monroe
University of New Orleans

Maine

University of Maine

Maryland

Coppin State University
Loyola University Maryland F
Morgan State University
Mount St. Mary's University
Towson University F
United States Naval Academy
University of Maryland
  Baltimore County
  College Park F
  Eastern Shore

Massachusetts

Boston College
Boston University
College of the Holy Cross
Harvard College
Northeastern University
University of Massachusetts
  Amherst

Michigan

Central Michigan University
Eastern Michigan University
Michigan State University
Oakland University
University of Detroit Mercy
University of Michigan
Western Michigan University F

Minnesota

University of Minnesota
  Twin Cities

Mississippi

Alcorn State University
Jackson State University
Mississippi State University
Mississippi Valley State
  University
University of Mississippi

Missouri

Missouri State University F
Saint Louis University
Southeast Missouri State
  University
University of Missouri
  Columbia
  Kansas City

Montana

Montana State University
University of Montana

Nebraska

University of Nebraska
  Lincoln
  Omaha F

Nevada

University of Nevada
  Las Vegas F

New Hampshire

Dartmouth College
University of New Hampshire

New Jersey

Fairleigh Dickinson University
  Metropolitan Campus
Monmouth University
New Jersey Institute of
  Technology

Princeton University
Rider University

New Mexico

New Mexico State University F
University of New Mexico

New York

Barnard College
Canisius College
Colgate University
Columbia University
Cornell University
Fordham University
Iona College
Long Island University
  LIU Brooklyn
Manhattan College
Marist College
St. Francis College
St. John's University F
Siena College
SUNY
  University at Albany
  University at Binghamton
  University at Buffalo
  University at Stony Brook
Syracuse University
United States Military Academy
Wagner College

North Carolina

Appalachian State University
Campbell University
Davidson College
Duke University
East Carolina University
Elon University F
Gardner-Webb University
High Point University
North Carolina Agricultural and
  Technical State University
North Carolina Central
  University
North Carolina State University
University of North Carolina
  Asheville
  Chapel Hill
Wake Forest University
Western Carolina University

North Dakota

North Dakota State University
University of North Dakota

Ohio

Bowling Green State University
  F
Cleveland State University F
Kent State University
Miami University
  Oxford F
Ohio State University
  Columbus Campus
Ohio University F
University of Akron
University of Cincinnati
University of Dayton F
University of Toledo F
Wright State University F
Xavier University
Youngstown State University

Oklahoma

Oklahoma State University
Oral Roberts University
University of Oklahoma

Oregon

Oregon State University
Portland State University
University of Oregon
University of Portland

Pennsylvania

Bucknell University
Duquesne University F
La Salle University
Lafayette College

Lehigh University
Penn State
  University Park
Robert Morris University F
St. Francis University
Saint Joseph's University
Temple University F
University of Pennsylvania
University of Pittsburgh
Villanova University

Rhode Island

Brown University
Bryant University
Providence College
University of Rhode Island

South Carolina

Charleston Southern University
The Citadel
Clemson University
Coastal Carolina University F
College of Charleston F
Furman University
South Carolina State University
University of South Carolina
  Columbia
  Upstate
Winthrop University
Wofford College

South Dakota

South Dakota State University
University of South Dakota

Tennessee

Austin Peay State University F
Belmont University
East Tennessee State University
Lipscomb University
Middle Tennessee State
  University
Tennessee State University
Tennessee Technological
  University F
University of Memphis
University of Tennessee
  Chattanooga F
  Knoxville
Vanderbilt University F

Texas

Baylor University
Houston Baptist University
Lamar University
Prairie View A&M University
Rice University
Sam Houston State University
Southern Methodist University F
Stephen F. Austin State
  University
Texas A&M University
  Corpus Christi
Texas Christian University
Texas Southern University
Texas Tech University
University of Houston
University of North Texas
University of Texas
  Arlington
  Austin
  El Paso
  San Antonio

Utah

Brigham Young University
Southern Utah University
University of Utah F
Utah State University
Utah Valley University
Weber State University

Vermont

University of Vermont

Virginia

College of William and Mary
George Mason University
Hampton University

James Madison University F
Liberty University
Norfolk State University
Radford University F
University of Richmond F
University of Virginia
Virginia Commonwealth
University
Virginia Military Institute

Washington

Eastern Washington University
Gonzaga University
Seattle University
University of Washington
Washington State University

West Virginia

Marshall University F
West Virginia University F

Wisconsin

Marquette University
University of Wisconsin
Madison
Milwaukee

Wyoming

University of Wyoming

Track, indoor Division II

Alabama

University of Alabama
Huntsville
University of Montevallo
University of North Alabama F

Alaska

University of Alaska
Anchorage

Arizona

Grand Canyon University

Arkansas

Harding University

California

Academy of Art University
Azusa Pacific University
California State University
Dominguez Hills F
Los Angeles F
Stanislaus F
San Francisco State University
F

Colorado

Adams State University
Colorado Mesa University
Colorado School of Mines
Colorado State University
Pueblo
Fort Lewis College F
Metropolitan State University of
Denver
University of Colorado
Colorado Springs
Western State Colorado
University

Connecticut

Southern Connecticut State
University
University of New Haven

District of Columbia

University of the District of
Columbia F

Florida

Flagler College

Georgia

Clayton State University
Emmanuel College
Shorter University

Idaho

Northwest Nazarene University

Illinois

Lewis University
McKendree University
Quincy University
University of Illinois
Springfield F

Indiana

Saint Joseph's College
University of Indianapolis
University of Southern Indiana

Iowa

Upper Iowa University F

Kansas

Emporia State University
Fort Hays State University
Pittsburg State University

Kentucky

Bellarmine University
Kentucky State University
Kentucky Wesleyan College
Northern Kentucky University

Maryland

Bowie State University

Massachusetts

American International College
Assumption College
Bentley University
Merrimack College
Stonehill College

Michigan

Ferris State University
Grand Valley State University
Hillsdale College
Lake Superior State University
Northern Michigan University F
Northwood University
Michigan
Saginaw Valley State University
Wayne State University F

Minnesota

Bemidji State University F
Concordia University St. Paul
Minnesota State University
Mankato
Moorhead
Saint Cloud State University
Southwest Minnesota State
University
University of Minnesota
Duluth
Winona State University F

Mississippi

Mississippi College

Missouri

Drury University
Lincoln University
Lindenwood University
Maryville University of Saint
Louis
Missouri Southern State
University
Missouri University of Science
and Technology
Northwest Missouri State
University
Southwest Baptist University
Truman State University
University of Central Missouri
William Jewell College

Montana

Montana State University
Billings

Nebraska

Chadron State College
University of Nebraska
Kearney
Wayne State College

New Hampshire

Franklin Pierce University

New Jersey

Georgian Court University

New Mexico

Eastern New Mexico University
New Mexico Highlands
University F

New York

Adelphi University
City University of New York
Queens College
College of Saint Rose
Daemen College
Le Moyne College
Long Island University
LIU Post
Molloy College
Roberts Wesleyan College
St. Thomas Aquinas College

North Carolina

Barton College
Belmont Abbey College
Johnson C. Smith University
Lees-McRae College
Lenoir-Rhyne University
Livingstone College
Mars Hill University
Pfeiffer University
Queens University of Charlotte
Saint Augustine's University
University of Mount Olive
University of North Carolina
Pembroke
Wingate University
Winston-Salem State University
F

North Dakota

Minot State University
University of Mary

Ohio

Ashland University
Cedarville University
Central State University
Lake Erie College
Malone University
Notre Dame College
Ohio Dominican University
Tiffin University
University of Findlay
Ursuline College F
Walsh University

Oklahoma

Oklahoma Baptist University
Oklahoma Christian University
Southern Nazarene University
University of Central Oklahoma
F

Oregon

Western Oregon University

Pennsylvania

Bloomsburg University of
Pennsylvania
California University of
Pennsylvania
Chestnut Hill College
Cheyney University of
Pennsylvania
Clarion University of
Pennsylvania F
East Stroudsburg University of
Pennsylvania
Edinboro University
of Pennsylvania F

Holy Family University
Indiana University of
Pennsylvania
Kutztown University of
Pennsylvania
Lincoln University
Lock Haven University of
Pennsylvania
Mansfield University of
Pennsylvania
Millersville University of
Pennsylvania F
Seton Hill University
Shippensburg University of
Pennsylvania
Slippery Rock University of
Pennsylvania
University of Pittsburgh
Johnstown
West Chester University of
Pennsylvania

South Carolina

Anderson University
Benedict College
Claflin University
Coker College
Converse College F
Limestone College
North Greenville University
Southern Wesleyan University

South Dakota

Black Hills State University
Northern State University
South Dakota School of Mines
and Technology
University of Sioux Falls

Tennessee

Carson-Newman University
King University
Lee University
Trevecca Nazarene University

Texas

Abilene Christian University
Angelo State University F
Dallas Baptist University
Midwestern State University F
Tarleton State University
Texas A&M University
Commerce
Kingsville
University of the Incarnate
Word
West Texas A&M University

Virginia

Virginia State University
Virginia Union University

Washington

Central Washington University
Saint Martin's University
Seattle Pacific University
Western Washington University

West Virginia

Alderson-Broaddus University
Concord University
University of Charleston
West Liberty University
West Virginia Wesleyan College
Wheeling Jesuit University

Wisconsin

University of Wisconsin
Parkside

Canada

Simon Fraser University

Track, indoor Division III

Alabama

Birmingham-Southern College

Arkansas

Hendrix College
University of the Ozarks

California

California Institute of
Technology
Claremont McKenna College
Harvey Mudd College
Occidental College
Scripps College
University of La Verne
University of Redlands

Colorado

Colorado College F

Connecticut

Connecticut College
Eastern Connecticut State
University
Trinity College
United States Coast Guard
Academy
Wesleyan University

Delaware

Wesley College

District of Columbia

Catholic University of America

Georgia

Berry College
Emory University
Oglethorpe University

Illinois

Augustana College
Aurora University
Benedictine University at
Springfield
Concordia University Chicago
Elmhurst College
Greenville College
Illinois College
Illinois Institute of Technology
Illinois Wesleyan University
Knox College
Millikin University
Monmouth College
North Central College
North Park University
Principia College
Rockford University
University of Chicago
Wheaton College

Indiana

Anderson University
DePauw University
Earlham College
Franklin College
Hanover College
Manchester University
Rose-Hulman Institute of
Technology
Trine University
Wabash College M

Iowa

Buena Vista University
Central College
Coe College
Cornell College
Grinnell College
Loras College
Luther College
Simpson College
University of Dubuque
Wartburg College

Kentucky

Berea College
Centre College
Spalding University
Thomas More College
Transylvania University

Maine

Bates College
Bowdoin College
Colby College

Husson University F
Saint Joseph's College of Maine
University of Southern Maine

Maryland

Frostburg State University
Goucher College
Hood College
Johns Hopkins University
McDaniel College
Salisbury University
Stevenson University

Massachusetts

Amherst College
Brandeis University
Bridgewater State University
Emmanuel College
Fitchburg State University
Lasell College
Lesley University
Massachusetts Institute of
    Technology
Mount Holyoke College F
Regis College
Smith College F
Springfield College
Tufts University
University of Massachusetts
    Dartmouth
Wellesley College F
Westfield State University
Wheaton College
Williams College
Worcester Polytechnic Institute
Worcester State University

Michigan

Adrian College
Albion College
Alma College
Calvin College
Olivet College

Minnesota

Augsburg College
Bethany Lutheran College
Bethel University
Carleton College
College of St. Benedict F
College of St. Scholastica
Concordia College: Moorhead
Gustavus Adolphus College
Hamline University
Macalester College
North Central University
St. Catherine University F
St. John's University M
St. Mary's University of
    Minnesota
St. Olaf College
University of Minnesota
    Morris
University of Northwestern - St.
    Paul
University of St. Thomas

Mississippi

Belhaven University

Missouri

Fontbonne University
Webster University
Westminster College

Nebraska

Nebraska Wesleyan University

New Hampshire

Colby-Sawyer College
Keene State College
New England College
Plymouth State University

New Jersey

The College of New Jersey
Montclair State University
Ramapo College of New Jersey
Rowan University

Rutgers, The State University of
    New Jersey
    Camden Campus
    Newark Campus
Stevens Institute of Technology

New York

Alfred University
City University of New York
    City College
    Hunter College
    Medgar Evers College
    York College
Hamilton College
Houghton College
Ithaca College
Manhattanville College
Mount Saint Mary College
Nazareth College
New York University
Rensselaer Polytechnic Institute
Rochester Institute of
    Technology
St. John Fisher College
St. Joseph's College New York:
    Suffolk Campus
St. Lawrence University
SUNY
    College at Brockport
    College at Buffalo
    College at Cortland
    College at Geneseo
    College at Oneonta
    College at Oswego
    College at Plattsburgh
    College of Agriculture and
        Technology at Cobleskill
    College of Technology at
        Alfred
Union College
United States Merchant Marine
    Academy
University of Rochester
Utica College

North Carolina

Guilford College
Methodist University

Ohio

Baldwin Wallace University
Bluffton University
Capital University
Case Western Reserve
    University
College of Wooster
Defiance College
Denison University
Heidelberg University
John Carroll University
Kenyon College
Marietta College
Muskingum University
Oberlin College
Ohio Northern University
Ohio Wesleyan University
Otterbein University
University of Mount Union
Wilmington College
Wittenberg University

Oregon

George Fox University
Lewis & Clark College
Linfield College
Pacific University
Willamette University

Pennsylvania

Albright College
Allegheny College
Alvernia University
Bryn Mawr College F
Carnegie Mellon University
Chatham University
DeSales University
Dickinson College
Eastern University

Elizabethtown College
Franklin & Marshall College
Geneva College
Gettysburg College
Grove City College
Gwynedd Mercy University
Haverford College
Immaculata University
Juniata College
Keystone College
King's College
Lebanon Valley College
Messiah College
Misericordia University
Moravian College
Muhlenberg College
Neumann University
Penn State
    Erie, The Behrend College
    Harrisburg
St. Vincent College
Susquehanna University
Swarthmore College
Thiel College
Ursinus College
Washington & Jefferson College
Waynesburg University
Westminster College
Widener University
York College of Pennsylvania

Rhode Island

Rhode Island College

Tennessee

Rhodes College
Sewanee: The University of the
    South

Texas

Hardin-Simmons University
McMurry University
Texas Lutheran University
Trinity University
University of Dallas
University of Texas
    Tyler

Vermont

Middlebury College

Virginia

Bridgewater College
Christopher Newport University
Eastern Mennonite University
Lynchburg College
Randolph College
Roanoke College
Shenandoah University
University of Mary Washington
Virginia Wesleyan College
Washington and Lee University

Washington

University of Puget Sound
Whitworth University

West Virginia

Bethany College

Wisconsin

Beloit College
Carroll University
Carthage College
Edgewood College
Lakeland College
Lawrence University
Marian University
Milwaukee School of
    Engineering
Ripon College
St. Norbert College
University of Wisconsin
    Eau Claire
    La Crosse
    Platteville
    Stevens Point
    Superior
Wisconsin Lutheran College

Track, outdoor Division I

Alabama

Alabama Agricultural and
    Mechanical University
Alabama State University
Auburn University
Jacksonville State University F
Samford University
Troy University
University of Alabama
University of Alabama
    Birmingham F
University of South Alabama

Arizona

Arizona State University
Northern Arizona University
University of Arizona

Arkansas

Arkansas State University
University of Arkansas
    Pine Bluff
University of Central Arkansas

California

California Polytechnic State
    University: San Luis Obispo
California State University
    Bakersfield
    Fresno
    Fullerton
    Long Beach
    Northridge
    Sacramento
Loyola Marymount University
Pepperdine University
St. Mary's College of California
San Diego State University F
San Jose State University F
Santa Clara University
Stanford University
University of California
    Berkeley
    Davis
    Irvine
    Los Angeles
    Riverside
    Santa Barbara
University of San Diego F
University of San Francisco
University of Southern
    California
University of the Pacific F

Colorado

Colorado State University
United States Air Force
    Academy
University of Colorado
    Boulder
University of Northern Colorado

Connecticut

Central Connecticut State
    University
Quinnipiac University F
Sacred Heart University
University of Connecticut
University of Hartford
Yale University

Delaware

Delaware State University
University of Delaware F

District of Columbia

American University
George Washington University
Georgetown University
Howard University

Florida

Bethune-Cookman University
Florida Agricultural and
    Mechanical University

Florida Atlantic University F
Florida Gulf Coast University M
Florida International University
Florida State University
Jacksonville University F
University of Central Florida F
University of Florida
University of Miami
University of North Florida
University of South Florida

Georgia

Georgia Institute of Technology
Georgia Southern University F
Georgia State University F
Kennesaw State University
Mercer University F
Savannah State University
University of Georgia

Hawaii

University of Hawaii
    Manoa F

Idaho

Boise State University
Idaho State University
University of Idaho

Illinois

Bradley University
Chicago State University
DePaul University
Eastern Illinois University
Illinois State University
Loyola University Chicago
Northern Illinois University F
Northwestern University F
Southern Illinois University
    Carbondale
Southern Illinois University
    Edwardsville
University of Illinois
    Chicago
Western Illinois University

Indiana

Ball State University F
Butler University
Indiana State University
Indiana University
    Bloomington
    Purdue University Fort
        Wayne F
    Purdue University
        Indianapolis
Purdue University
University of Notre Dame
Valparaiso University

Iowa

Drake University
Iowa State University
University of Iowa
University of Northern Iowa

Kansas

Kansas State University
University of Kansas
Wichita State University

Kentucky

Eastern Kentucky University
Morehead State University
Murray State University F
University of Kentucky
University of Louisville
Western Kentucky University

Louisiana

Grambling State University
Louisiana State University and
    Agricultural and Mechanical
    College
Louisiana Tech University
McNeese State University
Nicholls State University F
Northwestern State University

Southeastern Louisiana
University
Southern University and
Agricultural and Mechanical
College
Tulane University
University of Louisiana at
Lafayette
University of Louisiana at
Monroe
University of New Orleans

Maine

University of Maine

Maryland

Coppin State University
Loyola University Maryland F
Morgan State University
Mount St. Mary's University
Towson University F
United States Naval Academy
University of Maryland
Baltimore County
College Park
Eastern Shore

Massachusetts

Boston College
Boston University
College of the Holy Cross
Harvard College
Northeastern University
University of Massachusetts
Amherst

Michigan

Central Michigan University
Eastern Michigan University
Michigan State University
Oakland University
University of Detroit Mercy
University of Michigan
Western Michigan University F

Minnesota

University of Minnesota
Twin Cities

Mississippi

Alcorn State University
Jackson State University
Mississippi State University
Mississippi Valley State
University
University of Mississippi

Missouri

Missouri State University F
Saint Louis University
Southeast Missouri State
University
University of Missouri
Columbia
Kansas City

Montana

Montana State University
University of Montana

Nebraska

University of Nebraska
Lincoln
Omaha F

Nevada

University of Nevada
Las Vegas F

New Hampshire

Dartmouth College
University of New Hampshire

New Jersey

Fairleigh Dickinson University
Metropolitan Campus
Monmouth University
New Jersey Institute of
Technology

Princeton University
Rider University

New Mexico

New Mexico State University F
University of New Mexico

New York

Barnard College
Canisius College
Colgate University
Columbia University
Cornell University
Fordham University
Iona College
Long Island University
LIU Brooklyn
Manhattan College
Marist College
Niagara University F
St. Francis College
St. John's University F
Siena College
SUNY
University at Albany
University at Binghamton
University at Buffalo
University at Stony Brook
Syracuse University
United States Military Academy
Wagner College

North Carolina

Appalachian State University
Campbell University
Davidson College
Duke University
East Carolina University
Elon University F
Gardner-Webb University
High Point University
North Carolina Agricultural and
Technical State University
North Carolina Central
University
North Carolina State University
University of North Carolina
Asheville
Chapel Hill
Wake Forest University
Western Carolina University

North Dakota

North Dakota State University
University of North Dakota

Ohio

Bowling Green State University
F
Cleveland State University F
Kent State University
Miami University
Oxford
Ohio State University
Columbus Campus
Ohio University F
University of Akron
University of Cincinnati
University of Dayton F
University of Toledo F
Wright State University F
Xavier University
Youngstown State University

Oklahoma

Oklahoma State University
Oral Roberts University
University of Oklahoma

Oregon

Oregon State University
Portland State University
University of Oregon
University of Portland

Pennsylvania

Bucknell University
Duquesne University
La Salle University

Lafayette College
Lehigh University
Penn State
University Park
Robert Morris University F
St. Francis University
Saint Joseph's University
Temple University F
University of Pennsylvania
University of Pittsburgh
Villanova University

Rhode Island

Brown University
Bryant University
Providence College
University of Rhode Island

South Carolina

Charleston Southern University
The Citadel
Clemson University
Coastal Carolina University
College of Charleston F
Furman University
South Carolina State University
University of South Carolina
Columbia
Upstate
Winthrop University
Wofford College

South Dakota

South Dakota State University
University of South Dakota

Tennessee

Austin Peay State University F
Belmont University
East Tennessee State University
Lipscomb University
Middle Tennessee State
University
Tennessee State University
Tennessee Technological
University
University of Memphis
University of Tennessee
Chattanooga F
Knoxville
Vanderbilt University F

Texas

Baylor University
Houston Baptist University
Lamar University
Prairie View A&M University
Rice University
Sam Houston State University
Southern Methodist University F
Stephen F. Austin State
University
Texas A&M University
Corpus Christi
Texas Christian University
Texas Southern University
Texas Tech University
University of Houston
University of North Texas
University of Texas
Arlington
Austin
El Paso
San Antonio

Utah

Brigham Young University
Southern Utah University
University of Utah F
Utah State University
Utah Valley University
Weber State University

Vermont

University of Vermont

Virginia

College of William and Mary
George Mason University

Hampton University
James Madison University F
Liberty University
Norfolk State University
Radford University F
University of Richmond F
University of Virginia
Virginia Commonwealth
University
Virginia Military Institute

Washington

Eastern Washington University
Gonzaga University
Seattle University
University of Washington
Washington State University

West Virginia

Marshall University F
West Virginia University F

Wisconsin

Marquette University
University of Wisconsin
Madison
Milwaukee

Wyoming

University of Wyoming

Alabama

Miles College F
Spring Hill College
Stillman College
Tuskegee University
University of Alabama
Huntsville
University of Montevallo
University of North Alabama F
University of West Alabama

Alaska

University of Alaska
Anchorage

Arizona

Grand Canyon University

Arkansas

Harding University
Southern Arkansas University

California

Academy of Art University
Azusa Pacific University
California Baptist University
California State Polytechnic
University: Pomona
California State University
Chico
Dominguez Hills F
East Bay
Los Angeles
Monterey Bay F
San Bernardino F
Stanislaus
Fresno Pacific University
Humboldt State University
Point Loma Nazarene
University F
San Francisco State University
F
Sonoma State University F
University of California
San Diego

Colorado

Adams State University
Colorado Christian University
Colorado Mesa University
Colorado School of Mines
Colorado State University
Pueblo

Fort Lewis College F
Metropolitan State University of
Denver
University of Colorado
Colorado Springs
Western State Colorado
University

Connecticut

Post University
Southern Connecticut State
University
University of New Haven

District of Columbia

University of the District of
Columbia F

Florida

Florida Institute of Technology
Florida Southern College
Nova Southeastern University
Saint Leo University
University of Tampa

Georgia

Albany State University
Clark Atlanta University
Clayton State University
Columbus State University
Emmanuel College
Fort Valley State University
Morehouse College M
Paine College
Shorter University
University of West Georgia F

Idaho

Northwest Nazarene University

Illinois

Lewis University
McKendree University
Quincy University

Indiana

Saint Joseph's College
University of Indianapolis
University of Southern Indiana

Iowa

Upper Iowa University F

Kansas

Emporia State University
Fort Hays State University
Pittsburg State University

Kentucky

Bellarmine University
Kentucky State University
Kentucky Wesleyan College
Northern Kentucky University

Maryland

Bowie State University

Massachusetts

American International College
Assumption College
Bentley University
Merrimack College
Stonehill College

Michigan

Ferris State University
Grand Valley State University
Hillsdale College
Lake Superior State University
Michigan Technological
University
Northern Michigan University F
Northwood University
Michigan
Saginaw Valley State University
Wayne State University F

Minnesota

Bemidji State University F
Concordia University St. Paul

Minnesota State University
Mankato
Moorhead
Saint Cloud State University
Southwest Minnesota State
University
University of Minnesota
Duluth
Winona State University F

Mississippi

Mississippi College

Missouri

Drury University
Lincoln University
Lindenwood University
Maryville University of Saint
Louis
Missouri Southern State
University
Missouri University of Science
and Technology
Northwest Missouri State
University
Southwest Baptist University
Truman State University
University of Central Missouri
William Jewell College

Montana

Montana State University
Billings

Nebraska

Chadron State College
University of Nebraska
Kearney
Wayne State College

New Hampshire

Franklin Pierce University
Southern New Hampshire
University F

New Jersey

Bloomfield College
Georgian Court University

New Mexico

Eastern New Mexico University
New Mexico Highlands
University F

New York

Adelphi University
City University of New York
Queens College
College of Saint Rose
Daemen College
Dominican College of Blauvelt
Le Moyne College
Long Island University
LIU Post
Molloy College
Roberts Wesleyan College
St. Thomas Aquinas College

North Carolina

Barton College
Belmont Abbey College
Brevard College
Johnson C. Smith University
Lees-McRae College
Lenoir-Rhyne University
Livingstone College
Mars Hill University
Pfeiffer University
Queens University of Charlotte
Saint Augustine's University
Shaw University F
University of Mount Olive
University of North Carolina
Pembroke
Wingate University
Winston-Salem State University
F

North Dakota

Minot State University
University of Mary

Ohio

Ashland University
Cedarville University
Central State University
Lake Erie College
Malone University
Notre Dame College
Ohio Dominican University
Tiffin University
University of Findlay
Ursuline College F
Walsh University

Oklahoma

East Central University
Oklahoma Baptist University
Oklahoma Christian University
Rogers State University
Southern Nazarene University
University of Central Oklahoma
F

Oregon

Western Oregon University

Pennsylvania

Bloomsburg University of
Pennsylvania
California University of
Pennsylvania
Chestnut Hill College
Cheyney University of
Pennsylvania
Clarion University of
Pennsylvania F
East Stroudsburg University of
Pennsylvania
Edinboro University
of Pennsylvania
Holy Family University
Indiana University of
Pennsylvania
Kutztown University of
Pennsylvania
Lincoln University
Lock Haven University of
Pennsylvania
Mansfield University of
Pennsylvania
Millersville University of
Pennsylvania F
Philadelphia University
Seton Hill University
Shippensburg University of
Pennsylvania
Slippery Rock University of
Pennsylvania
University of Pittsburgh
Johnstown
West Chester University of
Pennsylvania

Puerto Rico

University of Puerto Rico
Bayamon University
College
Rio Piedras

South Carolina

Anderson University
Benedict College
Claflin University
Coker College
Converse College F
Francis Marion University
Limestone College
North Greenville University
Southern Wesleyan University

South Dakota

Black Hills State University
Northern State University

South Dakota School of Mines
and Technology
University of Sioux Falls

Tennessee

Carson-Newman University
Christian Brothers University
King University
Lane College
Lee University
Lincoln Memorial University
Trevecca Nazarene University

Texas

Abilene Christian University
Angelo State University
Dallas Baptist University
Midwestern State University F
Tarleton State University
Texas A&M University
Commerce
Kingsville
University of the Incarnate
Word
West Texas A&M University

Virginia

Virginia State University
Virginia Union University

Washington

Central Washington University
Saint Martin's University
Seattle Pacific University
Western Washington University

West Virginia

Alderson-Broaddus University
Concord University
Glenville State College
Salem International University
University of Charleston
West Liberty University
West Virginia Wesleyan College
Wheeling Jesuit University

Wisconsin

University of Wisconsin
Parkside

Canada

Simon Fraser University

**Track, outdoor
Division III**

Alabama

Birmingham-Southern College

Arkansas

Hendrix College
University of the Ozarks

California

California Institute of
Technology
California Lutheran University
Chapman University
Claremont McKenna College
Harvey Mudd College
Occidental College
Pitzer College
Pomona College
Scripps College
University of California
Santa Cruz
University of La Verne
University of Redlands
Whittier College

Colorado

Colorado College

Connecticut

Connecticut College
Eastern Connecticut State
University

Trinity College
United States Coast Guard
Academy
Wesleyan University

Delaware

Wesley College

District of Columbia

Catholic University of America
Gallaudet University

Georgia

Berry College
Emory University
Oglethorpe University
Piedmont College

Illinois

Augustana College
Aurora University
Benedictine University at
Springfield
Concordia University Chicago
Elmhurst College
Eureka College
Greenville College
Illinois College
Illinois Institute of Technology
Illinois Wesleyan University
Knox College
Millikin University
Monmouth College
North Central College
North Park University
Principia College
Rockford University
University of Chicago
Wheaton College

Indiana

Anderson University
DePauw University
Earlham College
Franklin College
Hanover College
Manchester University
Rose-Hulman Institute of
Technology
Trine University
Wabash College M

Iowa

Buena Vista University
Central College
Coe College
Cornell College
Grinnell College
Loras College
Luther College
Simpson College
University of Dubuque
Wartburg College

Kentucky

Berea College
Centre College
Spalding University
Thomas More College
Transylvania University

Maine

Bates College
Bowdoin College
Colby College
Husson University F
Saint Joseph's College of Maine
University of Maine
Farmington
University of Southern Maine

Maryland

Frostburg State University
Goucher College
Hood College
Johns Hopkins University
McDaniel College
Salisbury University
Stevenson University

Massachusetts

Amherst College
Babson College
Brandeis University
Bridgewater State University
Emmanuel College
Fitchburg State University
Gordon College
Lasell College
Lesley University
Massachusetts Institute of
Technology
Mount Holyoke College F
Nichols College
Regis College
Smith College F
Springfield College
Tufts University
University of Massachusetts
Dartmouth
Wellesley College F
Westfield State University
Wheaton College
Williams College
Worcester Polytechnic Institute
Worcester State University

Michigan

Adrian College
Albion College
Alma College
Calvin College
Hope College
Olivet College

Minnesota

Augsburg College
Bethany Lutheran College
Bethel University
Carleton College
College of St. Benedict F
College of St. Scholastica
Concordia College: Moorhead
Gustavus Adolphus College
Hamline University
Macalester College
Martin Luther College
North Central University
St. Catherine University F
St. John's University M
St. Mary's University of
Minnesota
St. Olaf College
University of Minnesota
Morris
University of Northwestern - St.
Paul
University of St. Thomas

Mississippi

Belhaven University
Millsaps College
Rust College

Missouri

Fontbonne University
Webster University
Westminster College

Nebraska

Nebraska Wesleyan University

New Hampshire

Colby-Sawyer College
Keene State College
New England College
Plymouth State University

New Jersey

The College of New Jersey
Montclair State University
Ramapo College of New Jersey
Rowan University
Rutgers, The State University of
New Jersey
Camden Campus
Newark Campus
Stevens Institute of Technology

New York

Alfred University
Bard College
City University of New York
  City College
  Hunter College
  Medgar Evers College
  York College
Hamilton College
Houghton College
Ithaca College
Manhattanville College
Mount Saint Mary College
Nazareth College
New York University
Rensselaer Polytechnic Institute
Rochester Institute of
  Technology
St. John Fisher College
St. Joseph's College New York:
  Suffolk Campus
St. Lawrence University
SUNY
  College at Brockport
  College at Buffalo
  College at Cortland
  College at Geneseo
  College at Oneonta
  College at Oswego
  College at Plattsburgh
  College of Agriculture and
    Technology at Cobleskill
  College of Technology at
    Alfred
Union College
United States Merchant Marine
  Academy
University of Rochester
Utica College
Vassar College

North Carolina

Guilford College
Meredith College F
Methodist University

Ohio

Baldwin Wallace University
Bluffton University
Capital University
Case Western Reserve
  University
College of Wooster
Defiance College
Denison University
Franciscan University of
  Steubenville
Heidelberg University
John Carroll University
Kenyon College
Marietta College
Muskingum University
Oberlin College
Ohio Northern University
Ohio Wesleyan University
Otterbein University
University of Mount Union
Wilmington College
Wittenberg University

Oregon

George Fox University
Lewis & Clark College
Linfield College
Pacific University
Willamette University

Pennsylvania

Albright College
Allegheny College
Alvernia University
Bryn Mawr College F
Carnegie Mellon University
Chatham University
DeSales University
Dickinson College
Eastern University
Elizabethtown College

Franklin & Marshall College
Geneva College
Gettysburg College
Grove City College
Gwynedd Mercy University
Haverford College
Immaculata University
Juniata College
Keystone College
King's College
Lebanon Valley College
Marywood University
Messiah College
Misericordia University
Moravian College
Muhlenberg College
Neumann University
Penn State
  Erie, The Behrend College
  Harrisburg
St. Vincent College
Susquehanna University
Swarthmore College
Thiel College
Ursinus College
Washington & Jefferson College
Waynesburg University
Westminster College
Widener University
York College of Pennsylvania

Rhode Island

Rhode Island College
Roger Williams University
Salve Regina University F

Tennessee

Rhodes College
Sewanee: The University of the
  South

Texas

Austin College
Concordia University Texas
East Texas Baptist University
Hardin-Simmons University
McMurry University
Southwestern University
Sul Ross State University
Texas Lutheran University
Trinity University
University of Dallas
University of Texas
  Tyler

Vermont

Green Mountain College
Johnson State College
Middlebury College

Virginia

Bridgewater College
Christopher Newport University
Eastern Mennonite University
Lynchburg College
Randolph College
Roanoke College
Shenandoah University
University of Mary Washington
Virginia Wesleyan College
Washington and Lee University

Washington

Pacific Lutheran University
University of Puget Sound
Whitworth University

West Virginia

Bethany College

Wisconsin

Beloit College
Carroll University
Carthage College
Edgewood College
Lakeland College
Lawrence University
Marian University

Milwaukee School of
  Engineering
Ripon College
St. Norbert College
University of Wisconsin
  Eau Claire
  La Crosse
  Platteville
  Stevens Point
  Superior
Wisconsin Lutheran College

Volleyball Division I

Alabama

Alabama Agricultural and
  Mechanical University F
Alabama State University F
Auburn University F
Jacksonville State University F
Samford University F
Troy University F
University of Alabama F
University of Alabama
  Birmingham F
University of South Alabama F

Arizona

Arizona State University F
Northern Arizona University F
University of Arizona F

Arkansas

Arkansas State University F
University of Arkansas F
  Pine Bluff F
University of Central Arkansas
  F

California

California Polytechnic State
  University: San Luis Obispo
  F
California State University
  Bakersfield F
  Fresno F
  Fullerton F
  Long Beach F
  Northridge F
  Sacramento F
Loyola Marymount University F
Pepperdine University F
St. Mary's College of California
  F
San Diego State University F
San Jose State University F
Santa Clara University F
Stanford University F
University of California
  Berkeley F
  Davis F
  Irvine F
  Los Angeles F
  Riverside F
  Santa Barbara F
University of San Diego F
University of San Francisco F
University of Southern
  California F
University of the Pacific F

Colorado

Colorado State University F
United States Air Force
  Academy F
University of Colorado
  Boulder F
University of Denver F
University of Northern Colorado
  F

Connecticut

Central Connecticut State
  University F
Fairfield University F
Quinnipiac University F

Sacred Heart University F
University of Connecticut F
University of Hartford F
Yale University F

Delaware

Delaware State University F
University of Delaware F

District of Columbia

American University F
George Washington University
  F
Georgetown University F
Howard University F

Florida

Bethune-Cookman University F
Florida Agricultural and
  Mechanical University F
Florida Atlantic University F
Florida Gulf Coast University F
Florida International University
  F
Florida State University F
Jacksonville University F
Stetson University F
University of Central Florida F
University of Florida F
University of Miami F
University of North Florida F
University of South Florida F

Georgia

Georgia Institute of Technology
  F
Georgia Southern University F
Georgia State University F
Kennesaw State University F
Mercer University F
Savannah State University F
University of Georgia F

Hawaii

University of Hawaii
  Manoa F

Idaho

Boise State University F
Idaho State University F
University of Idaho F

Illinois

Bradley University F
Chicago State University F
DePaul University F
Eastern Illinois University F
Illinois State University F
Loyola University Chicago F
Northern Illinois University F
Northwestern University F
Southern Illinois University
  Carbondale F
Southern Illinois University
  Edwardsville F
University of Illinois
  Chicago F
Western Illinois University F

Indiana

Ball State University F
Butler University F
Indiana State University F
Indiana University
  Bloomington F
  Purdue University Fort
    Wayne F
  Purdue University
    Indianapolis F
Purdue University F
University of Evansville F
University of Notre Dame F
Valparaiso University F

Iowa

Drake University F
Iowa State University F
University of Iowa F
University of Northern Iowa F

Kansas

Kansas State University F
University of Kansas F
Wichita State University F

Kentucky

Eastern Kentucky University F
Morehead State University F
Murray State University F
University of Kentucky F
University of Louisville F
Western Kentucky University F

Louisiana

Grambling State University F
Louisiana State University and
  Agricultural and Mechanical
  College F
Louisiana Tech University F
McNeese State University F
Nicholls State University F
Northwestern State University F
Southeastern Louisiana
  University F
Southern University and
  Agricultural and Mechanical
  College F
Tulane University F
University of Louisiana at
  Lafayette F
University of Louisiana at
  Monroe F
University of New Orleans F

Maryland

Coppin State University F
Loyola University Maryland F
Morgan State University F
Towson University F
United States Naval Academy F
University of Maryland
  Baltimore County F
  College Park F
  Eastern Shore F

Massachusetts

Boston College F
College of the Holy Cross F
Harvard College F
Northeastern University F

Michigan

Central Michigan University F
Eastern Michigan University F
Michigan State University F
Oakland University F
University of Michigan F
Western Michigan University F

Minnesota

University of Minnesota
  Twin Cities F

Mississippi

Alcorn State University F
Jackson State University F
Mississippi State University F
Mississippi Valley State
  University F
University of Mississippi F

Missouri

Missouri State University F
Saint Louis University F
Southeast Missouri State
  University F
University of Missouri
  Columbia F
  Kansas City F

Montana

Montana State University F
University of Montana F

Nebraska

Creighton University F
University of Nebraska
  Lincoln F
  Omaha F

Nevada

University of Nevada
Las Vegas F

New Hampshire

Dartmouth College F
University of New Hampshire F

New Jersey

Fairleigh Dickinson University
Metropolitan Campus F
New Jersey Institute of
Technology F
Princeton University F
Rider University F
Seton Hall University F

New Mexico

New Mexico State University F
University of New Mexico F

New York

Barnard College F
Canisius College F
Colgate University F
Columbia University F
Cornell University F
Fordham University F
Hofstra University F
Iona College F
Long Island University
LIU Brooklyn F
Manhattan College F
Marist College F
Niagara University F
St. Francis College F
St. John's University F
Siena College F
SUNY
University at Albany F
University at Binghamton F
University at Buffalo F
University at Stony Brook F
Syracuse University F
United States Military Academy
F

North Carolina

Appalachian State University F
Campbell University F
Davidson College F
Duke University F
East Carolina University F
Elon University F
Gardner-Webb University F
High Point University F
North Carolina Agricultural and
Technical State University F
North Carolina Central
University F
North Carolina State University
F
University of North Carolina
Asheville F
Chapel Hill F
Wake Forest University F
Western Carolina University F

North Dakota

North Dakota State University F
University of North Dakota F

Ohio

Bowling Green State University
F
Cleveland State University F
Kent State University F
Miami University
Oxford F
Ohio State University
Columbus Campus F
Ohio University F
University of Akron F
University of Cincinnati F
University of Dayton F
University of Toledo F
Wright State University F

Xavier University F
Youngstown State University F

Oklahoma

Oral Roberts University F
University of Oklahoma F

Oregon

Oregon State University F
Portland State University F
University of Oregon F
University of Portland F

Pennsylvania

Bucknell University F
Duquesne University F
La Salle University F
Lafayette College F
Lehigh University F
Penn State
University Park F
Robert Morris University F
St. Francis University F
Temple University F
University of Pennsylvania F
University of Pittsburgh F
Villanova University F

Rhode Island

Brown University F
Bryant University F
Providence College F
University of Rhode Island F

South Carolina

Charleston Southern University
F
The Citadel F
Clemson University F
Coastal Carolina University F
College of Charleston F
Furman University F
Presbyterian College F
South Carolina State University
F
University of South Carolina
Columbia F
Upstate F
Winthrop University F
Wofford College F

South Dakota

South Dakota State University F
University of South Dakota F

Tennessee

Austin Peay State University F
Belmont University F
East Tennessee State University
F
Lipscomb University F
Middle Tennessee State
University F
Tennessee State University F
Tennessee Technological
University F
University of Memphis F
University of Tennessee
Chattanooga F
Knoxville F
Martin F

Texas

Baylor University F
Houston Baptist University F
Lamar University F
Prairie View A&M University F
Rice University F
Sam Houston State University F
Southern Methodist University F
Stephen F. Austin State
University F
Texas A&M University
Corpus Christi F
Texas Christian University F
Texas Southern University F
Texas Tech University F
University of Houston F
University of North Texas F

University of Texas
Arlington F
Austin F
El Paso F
San Antonio F

Utah

Brigham Young University F
Southern Utah University F
University of Utah F
Utah State University F
Utah Valley University F
Weber State University F

Virginia

College of William and Mary F
George Mason University F
Hampton University F
James Madison University F
Liberty University F
Norfolk State University F
Radford University F
University of Virginia F
Virginia Commonwealth
University F

Washington

Eastern Washington University
F
Gonzaga University F
Seattle University F
University of Washington F
Washington State University F

West Virginia

Marshall University F
West Virginia University F

Wisconsin

Marquette University F
University of Wisconsin
Green Bay F
Madison F
Milwaukee F

Wyoming

University of Wyoming F

Volleyball Division II

Alabama

Miles College F
Spring Hill College F
Stillman College F
Tuskegee University F
University of Alabama
Huntsville F
University of Montevallo F
University of North Alabama F
University of West Alabama F

Alaska

University of Alaska
Anchorage F
Fairbanks F

Arizona

Grand Canyon University F

Arkansas

Arkansas Tech University F
Harding University F
Henderson State University F
Ouachita Baptist University F
Southern Arkansas University F
University of Arkansas
Fort Smith F
Monticello F

California

Academy of Art University F
Azusa Pacific University F
California Baptist University F
California State Polytechnic
University: Pomona F

California State University
Chico F
Dominguez Hills F
East Bay F
Los Angeles F
Monterey Bay F
San Bernardino F
Stanislaus F
Dominican University of
California F
Fresno Pacific University F
Holy Names University F
Humboldt State University F
Notre Dame de Namur
University F
Point Loma Nazarene
University F
San Francisco State University
F
Sonoma State University F
University of California
San Diego F

Colorado

Adams State University F
Colorado Christian University F
Colorado Mesa University F
Colorado School of Mines F
Colorado State University
Pueblo F
Fort Lewis College F
Metropolitan State University of
Denver F
Regis University F
University of Colorado
Colorado Springs F
Western State Colorado
University F

Connecticut

Post University F
Southern Connecticut State
University F
University of Bridgeport F
University of New Haven F

Delaware

Goldey-Beacom College F
Wilmington University F

Florida

Barry University F
Eckerd College F
Flagler College F
Florida Institute of Technology
F
Florida Southern College F
Lynn University F
Nova Southeastern University F
Palm Beach Atlantic University
F
Rollins College F
Saint Leo University F
University of Tampa F
University of West Florida F

Georgia

Albany State University F
Clark Atlanta University F
Columbus State University F
Emmanuel College F
Fort Valley State University F
Paine College F
Shorter University F
University of West Georgia F
Valdosta State University F

Hawaii

Brigham Young University-
Hawaii F
Chaminade University of
Honolulu F
Hawaii Pacific University F
University of Hawaii
Hilo F

Idaho

Northwest Nazarene University
F

Illinois

Lewis University F
McKendree University F
Quincy University F
University of Illinois
Springfield F

Indiana

Oakland City University F
Saint Joseph's College F
University of Indianapolis F
University of Southern Indiana
F

Iowa

Upper Iowa University F

Kansas

Emporia State University F
Fort Hays State University F
Newman University F
Pittsburg State University F
Washburn University F

Kentucky

Bellarmine University F
Kentucky State University F
Kentucky Wesleyan College F
Northern Kentucky University F

Maryland

Bowie State University F

Massachusetts

American International College
F
Assumption College F
Bentley University F
Merrimack College F
Stonehill College F

Michigan

Ferris State University F
Grand Valley State University F
Hillsdale College F
Lake Superior State University
F
Michigan Technological
University F
Northern Michigan University F
Northwood University
Michigan F
Saginaw Valley State University
F
Wayne State University F

Minnesota

Bemidji State University F
Concordia University St. Paul F
Minnesota State University
Mankato F
Moorhead F
Saint Cloud State University F
Southwest Minnesota State
University F
University of Minnesota
Crookston F
Duluth F
Winona State University F

Mississippi

Mississippi College F

Missouri

Drury University F
Lindenwood University F
Maryville University of Saint
Louis F
Missouri Southern State
University F
Missouri University of Science
and Technology F
Missouri Western State
University F
Northwest Missouri State
University F
Rockhurst University F
Southwest Baptist University F
Truman State University F

University of Central Missouri F
William Jewell College F

Montana

Montana State University
Billings F

Nebraska

Chadron State College F
University of Nebraska
Kearney F
Wayne State College F

New Hampshire

Franklin Pierce University F
Saint Anselm College F
Southern New Hampshire
University F

New Jersey

Bloomfield College F
Georgian Court University F

New Mexico

Eastern New Mexico University
F
New Mexico Highlands
University F
Western New Mexico
University F

New York

Adelphi University F
City University of New York
Queens College F
College of Saint Rose F
Concordia College F
Daemen College F
Dominican College of Blauvelt
F
Dowling College F
Le Moyne College F
Long Island University
LIU Post F
Mercy College F
Molloy College F
New York Institute of
Technology F
Nyack College F
Pace University F
Roberts Wesleyan College F

North Carolina

Barton College F
Belmont Abbey College F
Brevard College F
Catawba College F
Chowan University F
Elizabeth City State University
F
Fayetteville State University F
Johnson C. Smith University F
Lees-McRae College F
Lenoir-Rhyne University F
Livingstone College F
Mars Hill University F
Pfeiffer University F
Queens University of Charlotte
F
Saint Augustine's University F
Shaw University F
University of Mount Olive F
University of North Carolina
Pembroke F
Wingate University F
Winston-Salem State University
F

North Dakota

Minot State University F
University of Mary F

Ohio

Ashland University F
Cedarville University F
Central State University F
Lake Erie College F
Malone University F
Notre Dame College F

Ohio Dominican University F
Tiffin University F
University of Findlay F
Urbana University F
Ursuline College F
Walsh University F

Oklahoma

Cameron University F
East Central University F
Northwestern Oklahoma State
University F
Oklahoma Baptist University F
Oklahoma Panhandle State
University F
Southeastern Oklahoma State
University F
Southern Nazarene University F
Southwestern Oklahoma State
University F
University of Central Oklahoma
F

Oregon

Western Oregon University F

Pennsylvania

California University of
Pennsylvania F
Chestnut Hill College F
Cheyney University of
Pennsylvania F
Clarion University of
Pennsylvania F
East Stroudsburg University of
Pennsylvania F
Edinboro University
of Pennsylvania F
Gannon University F
Holy Family University F
Indiana University of
Pennsylvania F
Kutztown University of
Pennsylvania F
Lincoln University F
Lock Haven University of
Pennsylvania F
Mercyhurst University F
Millersville University of
Pennsylvania F
Philadelphia University F
Seton Hill University F
Shippensburg University of
Pennsylvania F
Slippery Rock University of
Pennsylvania F
University of Pittsburgh
Johnstown F
West Chester University of
Pennsylvania F

Puerto Rico

University of Puerto Rico
Bayamon University
College F
Rio Piedras F

South Carolina

Anderson University F
Benedict College F
Claflin University F
Coker College F
Converse College F
Erskine College F
Francis Marion University F
Lander University F
Limestone College F
Newberry College F
North Greenville University F
Southern Wesleyan University F
University of South Carolina
Aiken F

South Dakota

Black Hills State University F
Northern State University F
South Dakota School of Mines
and Technology F
University of Sioux Falls F

Tennessee

Carson-Newman University F
Christian Brothers University F
King University F
Lane College F
Lee University F
LeMoyne-Owen College F
Lincoln Memorial University F
Trevecca Nazarene University F
Tusculum College F
Union University F

Texas

Abilene Christian University F
Angelo State University F
Dallas Baptist University F
Lubbock Christian University F
Midwestern State University F
St. Edward's University F
St. Mary's University F
Tarleton State University F
Texas A&M International
University F
Texas A&M University
Commerce F
Kingsville F
Texas Woman's University F
University of Texas
of the Permian Basin F
University of the Incarnate
Word F
West Texas A&M University F

Utah

Dixie State University F

Vermont

Saint Michael's College F

Virginia

University of Virginia's College
at Wise F
Virginia State University F
Virginia Union University F

Washington

Central Washington University
F
Saint Martin's University F
Seattle Pacific University F
Western Washington University
F

West Virginia

Alderson-Broaddus University F
Bluefield State College F
Concord University F
Davis and Elkins College F
Fairmont State University F
Glenville State College F
Ohio Valley University F
Salem International University F
Shepherd University F
University of Charleston F
West Liberty University F
West Virginia State University
F
West Virginia Wesleyan
College F
Wheeling Jesuit University F

Wisconsin

University of Wisconsin
Parkside F

Canada

Simon Fraser University F

Volleyball Division III

Alabama

Birmingham-Southern College F
Huntingdon College F

Arkansas

Hendrix College F

California

California Institute of
Technology F
California Lutheran University F
Chapman University F
Claremont McKenna College F
Harvey Mudd College F
Mills College F
Occidental College F
Pitzer College F
Pomona College F
Scripps College F
University of California
Santa Cruz F
University of La Verne F
University of Redlands F
Whittier College F

Colorado

Colorado College F

Connecticut

Albertus Magnus College F
Connecticut College F
Eastern Connecticut State
University F
Mitchell College F
Trinity College F
United States Coast Guard
Academy F
University of Saint Joseph F
Wesleyan University F
Western Connecticut State
University F

Delaware

Wesley College F

District of Columbia

Catholic University of America
F
Gallaudet University F
Trinity Washington University F

Georgia

Agnes Scott College F
Berry College F
Covenant College F
Emory University F
Oglethorpe University F
Piedmont College F
Wesleyan College F

Illinois

Augustana College F
Aurora University F
Benedictine University at
Springfield F
Blackburn College F
Concordia University Chicago F
Dominican University F
Elmhurst College F
Eureka College F
Greenville College F
Illinois College F
Illinois Institute of Technology
F
Illinois Wesleyan University F
Knox College F
Lake Forest College F
MacMurray College F
Millikin University F
Monmouth College F
North Central College F
North Park University F
Principia College F
Rockford University F
University of Chicago F
Wheaton College F

Indiana

Anderson University F
DePauw University F
Earlham College F
Franklin College F
Hanover College F

Manchester University F
Rose-Hulman Institute of
Technology F
Saint Mary's College F
Trine University F

Iowa

Buena Vista University F
Central College F
Coe College F
Cornell College F
Grinnell College F
Loras College F
Luther College F
Simpson College F
University of Dubuque F
Wartburg College F

Kentucky

Berea College F
Centre College F
Spalding University F
Thomas More College F
Transylvania University F

Louisiana

Centenary College of Louisiana
F

Maine

Bates College F
Bowdoin College F
Colby College F
Husson University F
Maine Maritime Academy F
Saint Joseph's College of Maine
F
University of Maine
Presque Isle F
University of New England F
University of Southern Maine F

Maryland

Frostburg State University F
Goucher College F
Hood College F
Johns Hopkins University F
McDaniel College F
Notre Dame of Maryland
University F
St. Mary's College of Maryland
F
Salisbury University F
Stevenson University F
Washington College F

Massachusetts

Amherst College F
Anna Maria College F
Babson College F
Becker College F
Brandeis University F
Bridgewater State University F
Clark University F
Curry College F
Eastern Nazarene College F
Elms College F
Emerson College F
Emmanuel College F
Endicott College F
Framingham State University F
Gordon College F
Lasell College F
Lesley University F
Massachusetts College of
Liberal Arts F
Massachusetts Institute of
Technology F
Massachusetts Maritime
Academy F
Mount Holyoke College F
Mount Ida College F
Newbury College F
Pine Manor College F
Regis College F
Salem State University F
Simmons College F
Smith College F
Springfield College F

Suffolk University F
Tufts University F
University of Massachusetts Dartmouth F
Wellesley College F
Wentworth Institute of Technology F
Western New England University F
Westfield State University F
Wheaton College F
Williams College F
Worcester Polytechnic Institute F
Worcester State University F

Michigan
Adrian College F
Albion College F
Alma College F
Calvin College F
Finlandia University F
Hope College F
Kalamazoo College F
Olivet College F

Minnesota
Augsburg College F
Bethany Lutheran College F
Bethel University F
Carleton College F
College of St. Benedict F
College of St. Scholastica F
Concordia College: Moorhead F
Gustavus Adolphus College F
Hamline University F
Macalester College F
Martin Luther College F
North Central University F
St. Catherine University F
St. Mary's University of Minnesota F
St. Olaf College F
University of Minnesota Morris F
University of Northwestern - St. Paul F
University of St. Thomas F

Mississippi
Belhaven University F
Millsaps College F
Rust College F

Missouri
Fontbonne University F
Webster University F
Westminster College F

Nebraska
Nebraska Wesleyan University F

New Hampshire
Colby-Sawyer College F
Daniel Webster College F
Keene State College F
Plymouth State University F
Rivier University F

New Jersey
Centenary College F
College of St. Elizabeth F
Fairleigh Dickinson University College at Florham F
Kean University F
Montclair State University F
New Jersey City University F
Ramapo College of New Jersey F
Rowan University F
Rutgers, The State University of New Jersey
Camden Campus F
Newark Campus F
Stevens Institute of Technology F
William Paterson University of New Jersey F

New York
Alfred University F
Bard College F
Cazenovia College F
City University of New York
Baruch College F
Brooklyn College F
City College F
College of Staten Island F
Hunter College F
John Jay College of Criminal Justice F
Medgar Evers College F
York College F
Clarkson University F
College of Mount St. Vincent F
College of New Rochelle F
D'Youville College F
Elmira College F
Hamilton College F
Hartwick College F
Hilbert College F
Houghton College F
Ithaca College F
Keuka College F
Manhattanville College F
Medaille College F
Mount Saint Mary College F
Nazareth College F
New York University F
Rochester Institute of Technology F
The Sage Colleges F
St. John Fisher College F
St. Joseph's College New York: Suffolk Campus F
St. Joseph's College, New York F
St. Lawrence University F
Sarah Lawrence College F
Skidmore College F
SUNY
College at Brockport F
College at Buffalo F
College at Cortland F
College at Geneseo F
College at New Paltz F
College at Old Westbury F
College at Oneonta F
College at Oswego F
College at Plattsburgh F
College at Potsdam F
College at Purchase F
College of Agriculture and Technology at Cobleskill F
College of Agriculture and Technology at Morrisville F
College of Technology at Alfred F
College of Technology at Canton F
Maritime College F
Union College F
United States Merchant Marine Academy F
University of Rochester F
Utica College F
Vassar College F
Wells College F
Yeshiva University F

North Carolina
Greensboro College F
Guilford College F
Meredith College F
Methodist University F
North Carolina Wesleyan College F
Salem College F
William Peace University F

Ohio
Baldwin Wallace University F
Bluffton University F
Capital University F

Case Western Reserve University F
College of Wooster F
Defiance College F
Denison University F
Franciscan University of Steubenville F
Heidelberg University F
Hiram College F
John Carroll University F
Kenyon College F
Marietta College F
Muskingum University F
Oberlin College F
Ohio Northern University F
Ohio Wesleyan University F
Otterbein University F
University of Mount Union F
Wilmington College F
Wittenberg University F

Oregon
George Fox University F
Lewis & Clark College F
Linfield College F
Pacific University F
Willamette University F

Pennsylvania
Albright College F
Allegheny College F
Alvernia University F
Arcadia University F
Bryn Athyn College F
Bryn Mawr College F
Cabrini College F
Cairn University F
Carnegie Mellon University F
Cedar Crest College F
Chatham University F
DeSales University F
Dickinson College F
Eastern University F
Elizabethtown College F
Franklin & Marshall College F
Geneva College F
Gettysburg College F
Grove City College F
Gwynedd Mercy University F
Haverford College F
Immaculata University F
Juniata College F
Keystone College F
King's College F
La Roche College F
Lancaster Bible College F
Lebanon Valley College F
Lycoming College F
Marywood University F
Messiah College F
Misericordia University F
Moravian College F
Mount Aloysius College F
Muhlenberg College F
Neumann University F
Penn State
Abington F
Altoona F
Berks F
Erie, The Behrend College F
Harrisburg F
Pennsylvania College of Technology F
Rosemont College F
St. Vincent College F
Susquehanna University F
Swarthmore College F
Thiel College F
University of Pittsburgh
Bradford F
Greensburg F
University of Scranton F
Ursinus College F
Washington & Jefferson College F
Waynesburg University F
Westminster College F

Widener University F
Wilkes University F
York College of Pennsylvania F

Rhode Island
Rhode Island College F
Roger Williams University F
Salve Regina University F

Tennessee
Maryville College F
Rhodes College F
Sewanee: The University of the South F

Texas
Austin College F
Concordia University Texas F
East Texas Baptist University F
Hardin-Simmons University F
Howard Payne University F
LeTourneau University F
McMurry University F
Schreiner University F
Southwestern University F
Sul Ross State University F
Texas Lutheran University F
Trinity University F
University of Dallas F
University of Mary Hardin-Baylor F
University of Texas
Dallas F
Tyler F

Vermont
Green Mountain College F
Johnson State College F
Lyndon State College F
Middlebury College F
Norwich University F
Southern Vermont College F

Virginia
Averett University F
Bridgewater College F
Christopher Newport University F
Eastern Mennonite University F
Emory & Henry College F
Ferrum College F
Hollins University F
Lynchburg College F
Mary Baldwin College F
Marymount University F
Randolph College F
Randolph-Macon College F
Roanoke College F
Shenandoah University F
Southern Virginia University F
University of Mary Washington F
Virginia Wesleyan College F
Washington and Lee University F

Washington
Pacific Lutheran University F
University of Puget Sound F
Whitman College F
Whitworth University F

West Virginia
Bethany College F

Wisconsin
Alverno College F
Beloit College F
Carroll University F
Carthage College F
Edgewood College F
Lakeland College F
Lawrence University F
Maranathan Baptist University
Maranatha Baptist University F
Marian University F
Milwaukee School of Engineering F

Mount Mary University F
Northland College F
Ripon College F
St. Norbert College F
University of Wisconsin
Eau Claire F
La Crosse F
Platteville F
Stevens Point F
Superior F
Wisconsin Lutheran College F

Water polo Division I

California
California State University Long Beach M
Loyola Marymount University M
Pepperdine University M
San Jose State University M
Santa Clara University M
Stanford University M
University of California
Berkeley M
Davis M
Irvine M
Los Angeles M
Santa Barbara M
University of Southern California M
University of the Pacific M

Colorado
United States Air Force Academy M

District of Columbia
George Washington University M

Maryland
United States Naval Academy M

Massachusetts
Harvard College M

New Jersey
Princeton University M

New York
Fordham University M
Iona College M
St. Francis College M

Pennsylvania
Bucknell University M

Rhode Island
Brown University M

Water polo Division II

California
California Baptist University M
Fresno Pacific University M
University of California San Diego M

Pennsylvania
Gannon University M
Mercyhurst University M

West Virginia
Salem International University M

Water polo Division III

California
California Institute of Technology M

Tables and Indexes

California Lutheran University M
Chapman University M
Claremont McKenna College M
Harvey Mudd College M
Occidental College M
Pitzer College M
Pomona College M
Scripps College M
University of La Verne M
University of Redlands M
Whittier College M

Connecticut
Connecticut College M

Illinois
Monmouth College M

Maryland
Johns Hopkins University M

Massachusetts
Massachusetts Institute of
Technology M

Pennsylvania
Penn State
Erie, The Behrend College
M
Washington & Jefferson College
M

Wrestling Division I

Arizona
Arizona State University M

California
California Polytechnic State
University: San Luis Obispo
M
California State University
Bakersfield M
Stanford University M

Colorado
United States Air Force
Academy M
University of Northern Colorado
M

Connecticut
Sacred Heart University M

District of Columbia
American University M

Idaho
Boise State University M

Illinois
Northern Illinois University M
Northwestern University M
Southern Illinois University
Edwardsville M

Indiana
Indiana University
Bloomington M
Purdue University M

Iowa
Iowa State University M
University of Iowa M
University of Northern Iowa M

Maryland
United States Naval Academy
M
University of Maryland
College Park M

Massachusetts
Harvard College M

Michigan
Central Michigan University M
Eastern Michigan University M

Michigan State University M
University of Michigan M

Minnesota
University of Minnesota
Twin Cities M

Missouri
University of Missouri
Columbia M

Nebraska
University of Nebraska
Lincoln M

New Jersey
Princeton University M
Rider University M

New York
Barnard College M
Columbia University M
Cornell University M
Hofstra University M
SUNY
University at Binghamton
M
University at Buffalo M
United States Military Academy
M

North Carolina
Appalachian State University M
Campbell University M
Davidson College M
Duke University M
Gardner-Webb University M
North Carolina State University
M
University of North Carolina
Chapel Hill M

North Dakota
North Dakota State University
M

Ohio
Cleveland State University M
Kent State University M
Ohio State University
Columbus Campus M
Ohio University M

Oklahoma
Oklahoma State University M
University of Oklahoma M

Oregon
Oregon State University M

Pennsylvania
Bloomsburg University of
Pennsylvania M
Bucknell University M
Clarion University of
Pennsylvania M
Drexel University M
Edinboro University
of Pennsylvania M
Franklin & Marshall College M
Lehigh University M
Lock Haven University of
Pennsylvania M
Penn State
University Park M
University of Pennsylvania M
University of Pittsburgh M

Rhode Island
Brown University M

South Carolina
The Citadel M

South Dakota
South Dakota State University
M

Tennessee
University of Tennessee
Chattanooga M

Utah
Utah Valley University M

Virginia
George Mason University M
Old Dominion University M
University of Virginia M
Virginia Military Institute M

West Virginia
West Virginia University M

Wisconsin
University of Wisconsin
Madison M

Wyoming
University of Wyoming M

Wrestling Division II

Arizona
Grand Canyon University M

Arkansas
Ouachita Baptist University M

California
California Baptist University M
San Francisco State University
M

Colorado
Adams State University M
Colorado Mesa University M
Colorado School of Mines M
Colorado State University
Pueblo M
Western State Colorado
University M

Georgia
Emmanuel College M
Shorter University M

Illinois
McKendree University M

Indiana
University of Indianapolis M

Iowa
Upper Iowa University M

Kansas
Fort Hays State University M
Newman University M

Massachusetts
American International College
M

Minnesota
Minnesota State University
Mankato M
Moorhead M
Saint Cloud State University M
Southwest Minnesota State
University M

Missouri
Lindenwood University M
Maryville University of Saint
Louis M
Truman State University M
University of Central Missouri
M

Nebraska
Chadron State College M
University of Nebraska
Kearney M

New Mexico
New Mexico Highlands
University M

New York
Long Island University
LIU Post M

North Carolina
Belmont Abbey College M
University of North Carolina
Pembroke M

North Dakota
Minot State University M
University of Mary M

Ohio
Ashland University M
Lake Erie College M
Notre Dame College M
Tiffin University M
University of Findlay M

Oklahoma
University of Central Oklahoma
M

Pennsylvania
East Stroudsburg University of
Pennsylvania M
Gannon University M
Kutztown University of
Pennsylvania M
Mercyhurst University M
Millersville University of
Pennsylvania M
Seton Hill University M
Shippensburg University of
Pennsylvania M
University of Pittsburgh
Johnstown M

South Carolina
Anderson University M
Coker College M
Limestone College M
Newberry College M

South Dakota
Northern State University M

Tennessee
King University M

West Virginia
Alderson-Broaddus University
M
Ohio Valley University M
West Liberty University M
Wheeling Jesuit University M

Wisconsin
University of Wisconsin
Parkside M

Canada
Simon Fraser University M

Wrestling Division III

Alabama
Huntingdon College M

Arkansas
University of the Ozarks M

Connecticut
Trinity College M
United States Coast Guard
Academy M
Wesleyan University M

Illinois
Augustana College M
Elmhurst College M
Millikin University M
North Central College M
University of Chicago M
Wheaton College M

Indiana
Manchester University M
Trine University M
Wabash College M

Iowa
Buena Vista University M
Central College M
Coe College M
Cornell College M
Loras College M
Luther College M
Simpson College M
University of Dubuque M
Wartburg College M

Maine
University of Southern Maine M

Maryland
Johns Hopkins University M
McDaniel College M

Massachusetts
Bridgewater State University M
Springfield College M
Western New England
University M
Williams College M
Worcester Polytechnic Institute
M

Michigan
Adrian College M
Alma College M
Olivet College M

Minnesota
Augsburg College M
Concordia College: Moorhead
M
St. John's University M
St. Olaf College M

New Hampshire
Daniel Webster College M
Plymouth State University M

New Jersey
Centenary College M
The College of New Jersey M
Stevens Institute of Technology
M

New York
City University of New York
Hunter College M
College of Mount St. Vincent M
Ithaca College M
New York University M
Rochester Institute of
Technology M
SUNY
College at Brockport M
College at Cortland M
College at Oneonta M
College at Oswego M
College of Technology at
Alfred M
United States Merchant Marine
Academy M

North Carolina
Greensboro College M

Ohio
Baldwin Wallace University M
Case Western Reserve
University M
Heidelberg University M
John Carroll University M
Muskingum University M
Ohio Northern University M
University of Mount Union M

Oregon
Pacific University M

Pennsylvania
Elizabethtown College M
Gettysburg College M

King's College M
Lycoming College M
Messiah College M
Muhlenberg College M
Pennsylvania College of
   Technology M
Thiel College M
University of Scranton M
Ursinus College M
Washington & Jefferson College
   M
Waynesburg University M
Wilkes University M
York College of Pennsylvania
   M

Rhode Island

Rhode Island College M
Roger Williams University M

Vermont

Norwich University M

Virginia

Ferrum College M
Hampden-Sydney College M
Southern Virginia University M
Washington and Lee University
   M

Wisconsin

Lakeland College M
Milwaukee School of
   Engineering M
University of Wisconsin
   Eau Claire M
   La Crosse M
   Platteville M
   Stevens Point M

Alphabetical index of colleges

Tables and Indexes

Tables and Indexes

Tables and Indexes